2002

THE COMPLETE
ENCYCLOPEDIA OF
WORLD AIRCRAFT

THE COMPLETE ENCYCLOPEDIA OF
WORLD AIRCRAFT

GENERAL EDITORS: PAUL EDEN AND SOPH MOENG

BARNES
&NOBLE
BOOKS
NEW YORK

This edition published by Barnes & Noble Inc.,
by arrangement with Amber Books Ltd
2002 Barnes & Noble Books

10 9 8 7 6 5 4 3 2 1

ISBN 0-7607-3432-1

Library of Congress Cataloging-in-Publication Data
available upon request.

Production and jacket design by:
Amber Books Ltd
Bradley's Close
74–77 White Lion Street
London N1 9PF

This material was previously published as part of the reference set *World Aircraft Information Files*

Printed in Italy

Introduction

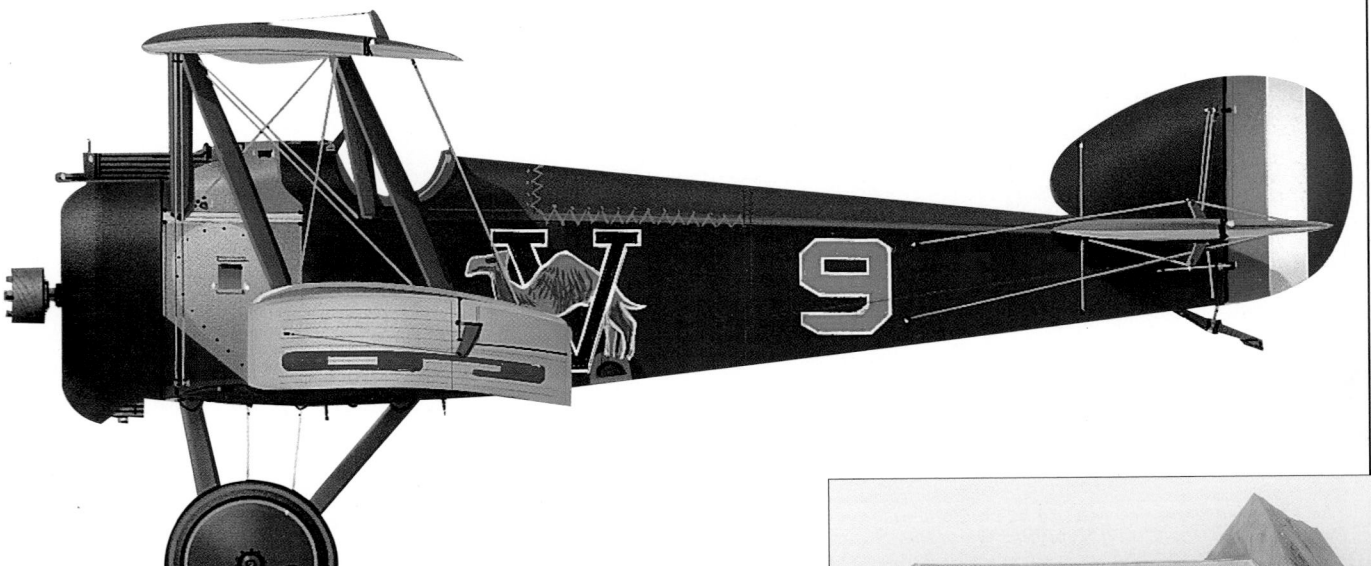

The Sopwith Camel was regarded as the finest British fighter of World War I.

When Wilbur Wright completed the first controlled flight of a powered aircraft on 17 December 1903, the flying machine was viewed as little more than a novelty. A century later, mankind has harnessed the potential of this flimsy machine to create a spectacular variety of aircraft for every task. Huge, economical and safe airliners have vastly increased the frequency and ease of trans-continen-

latest high-tech super-fighter.

After the pioneer aviators had established the basic principles of aeronautics in the early years of the twentieth century, aircraft such as the Blériot XI quickly accomplished some headline-grabbing flights, but it was World War I which drove the first great strides in aircraft development. The handful of flying machines that had served the military prior to the

history of these early fighting machines, including key types such as the Albatros D-series scouts, Bristol Fighter, Fokker's Dr I Triplane and E I Eindecker, RAF S.E.5a, SPAD and Sopwith Camel.

With the coming of peace came a renewed interest in aviation as a means of transport to rival the ship or train. Many of the earliest commercial flights were undertaken by military-surplus aircraft such as the Airco DH.4s that were used on the first regular London-Paris service. Nevertheless, some of the more forward-thinking manufacturers soon began producing airliners and full details of aircraft such as the Blériot-SPAD S.33, de Havilland DH.34, Fokker F.II and Handley Page W.8 can be found in The Encyclopedia of World Aircraft. A number of monumentally important manufacturers also emerged during the 1920s, especially in America, and the rise of makers such as Boeing, Douglas and Lockheed can be traced through the history of their aircraft. Types of particular importance during this time were relatively few, but Boeing's P-26 Peashooter monoplane fighter and Model 247 airliner stand out among them. As storm clouds began to gather in the mid 1930s, the new generation of modern monoplane fighters, epitomised by the Hawker Hurricane, Messerschmitt Bf 109 and Supermarine

The all-wood construction de Havilland Mosquito possessed outstanding performance as a bomber, night-fighter and in the photo-reconnaissance role.

Spitfire, were first taking flight. A quantum leap in airliner design had also occurred in the wake of the Model 247, with the Boeing Stratoliner, Douglas DC-3 and Lockheed Super Electra and Ventura all finding military roles as transports or spawning bomber derivatives.

From the Stratoliner was derived one of the greatest bombers of World War II, the B-17 Flying Fortress, while the DC-3 became as important as the Jeep in the Allied war effort, known as the C-47 Skytrain with US forces and the Dakota with the RAF. the Lockheed Hudson and Ventura series of bombers and maritime aircraft were

touched by the design genius of 'Kelly' Johnson, whose further work (including the P-80 Shooting Star, F-104 Starfighter, SR-71 Blackbird and U-2) features strongly in the Lockheed section. All of the major combat aircraft of World War II – Avro Lancaster, de Havilland Mosquito, Messerschmitt Bf 109, Mitsubishi A6M Zero, North American P-51 Mustang – are detailed in the book, as well as many of the support and training aircraft and lesser combat designs.

Perhaps the most striking result of World War II in terms of aerospace technology was the increased performance of those machines produced in 1945

The Douglas C-47 Dakota provided the Allies with an unparalleled transport capability, and the type remained in service for decades after World War II.

tal travel, making the world a much smaller place, while military aviation has undoubtedly been the single greatest influence on modern warfare.

This comprehensive encyclopedia charts the development and evolution of a century of aerospace technology,detailing aircraft ranging from the most primitive machine to the

conflict was soon joined by new aircraft primarily designed for the reconnaissance and artillery-spotting roles. From Germany came the Albatros B.I and C.I and from the UK the Royal Aircraft Factory B.E.2, all three types establishing their manufacturers as key players in the major air war that was about to unfold. This book reveals the full

The North American X-15 was designed for high speed at high altitude, reaching a maximum of 4,534 mph (7297 km/h), a record which it holds to this day.

5

The Mikoyan-Gurevich MiG-29 has been a success on the export market, with Russia supplying the aircraft to countries, including Poland, Cuba, the Czech Republic, Germany, Hungary, Iran, Iraq, North Korea, Peru, Romania, Yemen and the former Yugoslavia.

Air France and Lufthansa were the first airlines to place the Airbus A340 into service. The aircraft is now in widespread use on long-range routes.

The Bell AH-1 Huey Cobra proved very useful to US forces in the close support and attack roles during the Vietnam War.

compared to those of 1939. Both Britain and Germany had fielded operational jets in the last two years of the war (the Gloster Meteor and Messerschmitt's Me 262 respectively). Hence came perhaps the greatest revolution of them all – the use of jet engines and swept wings.

This new technology, much of it based on German research, along with the added urgency of the Cold War, spurred aircraft design to new levels of achievement. In 1947 'Chuck' Yeager took the Bell X-1 through the 'sound barrier'. As described later in the book, the X-1 led to a series of experimental X-planes, including the North American X-15, the fastest piloted aircraft yet built. A new breed of swept wing fighters began with the North American F-86 Sabre and MiG-15, two aircraft thrown into combat together over the skies of Korea. As the Cold War escalated the East and West confronted each other with evermore sophisti-cated aircraft including the Avro Vulcan, Boeing B-52 Stratofortress, English Electric Lightning, General Dynamics F-111 Aardvark, McDonnell Douglas F-4 Phantom II, MiG-21 'Fishbed' and Tupolev Tu-95 'Bear'.

At the beginning of the 21st century the US fields fleets of McDonnell Douglas and Boeing F-15 Eagles, Lockheed Martin F-16 Fighting Falcons and Boeing F/A-18 Hornets, while modern Russia continues to produce the outstanding MiG-29 'Fulcrum' and Sukhoi Su-27 'Flanker'. For many air forces the future is just around the corner with fourth generation fighters like the Dassault Rafale, Eurofighter Typhoon and Lockheed Martin F-22 Raptor being readied for service.

Post-war development in the world of civil aviation can also be traced through this book's pages, with the broad scope of airliners including the superlative Aérospatiale/BAC Concorde and Boeing 747 featuring strongly. Neither have the business and general avia-tion communities been forgotten, with the classic designs of Beech, Cessna and Piper featuring as strongly as those from Gulfstream and Learjet.

This information-packed encyclopedia is profusely illustrated with full-colour artwork, detailed technical drawings and photographs, many from rare archive sources, to provide an indispensable source of reference to the world's civil and military fixed-wing aircraft and helicopters. Each entry is provided with a detailed development history and, where appro-priate, a complete table of variant and specification data. For the casual enthu-siast it represents the ideal single-reference work, while for the more-serious enthusiast and aviation professional it represents a concise source of detailed information. Laid out in an easy-to-follow A-to-Z format by manufacturer, allowing the desired information to be reached quickly and effi-ciently, this book also acts as a guide to the world's aircraft manufacturers, whose histories can be charted through the text of the highly-detailed individ-ual aircraft entries.

AAMSA A9B-M Quail

As the result of an agreement between Industrias Unidas SA of Mexico and Rockwell International Corporation of the USA, the company known as Aeronautica Agricola Mexicana SA (AAMSA) was formed in 1971 to take over from Rockwell's Commercial Products Group manufacture of two crop-dusting agricultural aircraft, the Aero Commander Quail Commander and Sparrow Commander agricultural aircraft. They had identical airframes and differed primarily in terms of engine fit. The Sparrow

Commander was powered by a 235-hp (175-kW) Lycoming O-540-B2B5 engine, while the Quail was fitted with a more powerful IO-540 engine. Production of both types ended in the USA in 1970.

Construction of the Sparrow Commander continued in Mexico, as the AAMSA Sparrow. Only very small numbers had been built by 1975, when production was terminated. Manufacture then switched to the Quail Commander, designated **A9B-M Quail**.

The Quail was a braced low-wing monoplane of

composite construction. Its wings were based on wooden spars, with metal leading-edge skins and the remainder of the structure fabric-covered; fuselage and tail unit were steel-tube structures with fabric covering. The non-retracting tailwheel landing gear had robust spring shock-absorption for rough-field operation. The engine had a fixed-pitch or optional variable-pitch propeller.

The Quail had standard features for an agricultural aircraft, namely an enclosed cabin for the pilot, with a robust steel-tube overturn structure for his protection; cable-cutters on the landing gear and windscreen; a cable deflector

between the pilot's canopy and the tail fin, and provisions for communications avionics and night-flying equipment. A 22.5-cu ft (0.64-m³) glass-fibre/polyester chemical hopper was fitted as standard with a capacity of 170 US gal (643 litres) of liquid, or 1,200 lb (545 kg) of dry

powder chemicals.

The Quail was manufactured in component form at the Industrias Unidas industrial complex at Pasteje in Mexico for assembly and marketing by its associated Aircraft Parts and Development Corporation in Laredo, Texas. By 1978 43 Quails had been built.

AAMSA A9B-M Quail

SPECIFICATION

AAMSA A9B-M Quail
Type: single-seat crop dusting/ agricultural aircraft
Powerplant: one 300-hp (224-kW) Avco Lycoming IO-540-K1A5 flat-six piston engine
Performance: maximum level speed 120 mph (193 km/h) at sea level; normal operating speed 90-100 mph (145-161 km/h); service

ceiling 16,000 ft (4875 m); range 300 miles (1483 km)
Weights: empty 1,800 lb (816 kg); maximum take-off 3,800 lb (1724 kg); payload 1,200 lb (545 kg) of dry chemicals
Dimensions: wing span 34 ft 9 in (15.76 m); length 24 ft (10.89 m); height 7 ft 8 in (3.48 m); wing area 182 sq ft (16.91 m²)

The A9M-B Quail crop-spraying and agricultural aircraft was a version of the Rockwell Quail Commander produced under licence in Mexico. AAMSA built around 45 examples.

AASI Jetcruzer

Aerodynamics & Structures Inc. (ASI), set up by former airline pilot Darius Sharifzadeh, was succeeded by Advanced Aerodynamics and Structures Inc. (AASI) to develop the **Jetcruzer** range of business aircraft. The design of the **AASI Jetcruzer 450** was initiated in March 1983, with prototype construction beginning five years later. Exhibited at the NBAA show in October 1988, it flew for the first time on 11 January 1989, powered by a 420-shp (313-kW) Allison 250-C20S engine. The pre-production prototype flew three months later.

Built of lightweight graphite composite to reduce weight, the Jetcruzer is of pusher canard configuration, reminiscent of a scaled-down Beech Starship. As a six-seat turboprop business and utility transport, the aircraft is in the

same class as the SOCATA TBM 700 and light twins such as the Piper Seneca IV. The Jetcruzer 450 is no longer manufactured.

AASI is concentrating instead on the **Jetcruzer 500** model. This is a pressurised version of the 450 which differs in having smaller windows, a 6-ft (1.83-m) increase in fuselage length and an 850-shp (634-kW) PT6A-66A powerplant; the earlier aircraft had the 650-shp (485-kW) PT6A-27 in intended production form. Currently offered in corporate, executive, air ambulance and freight models, the aircraft had chalked up 77 firm orders and 32 options by early 1996. A prototype Jetcruzer 500 was flown for the first time on 22 August 1997.

A larger version of the 500, the **Jetcruzer 650**, was designed as a

The Jetcruzer range of business aircraft couples a novel canard configuration with advanced construction techniques to produce a high-performance, low-cost business aircraft. The six-seat Jetcruzer 500 is the definitive production version, and further advanced derivatives are planned.

10/13-seat turboprop commuter and utility transport. Construction of a prototype and the first production machine began in December 1992. Work on another design, the 10/13-seat pressurised twin-turbofan **Stratocruzer 1250-ER**, began in September 1991 as a logical development of the Jetcruzer. Important features were intercontinental range at high speed, and low cost of purchase and maintenance. During 1995 AASI sought a financial partner before development of the aircraft could proceed.

AASI also builds unmanned air vehicles (UAVs) and plans to offer the Jetcruzer 500 (in **ML-1** form) as a UAV as well as in piloted form (as the **ML-2**) to military buyers. The military utility version

of the Jetcruzer 650 is termed the **ML-4**, while the larger Stratocruzer is envisaged for surveillance missions as the **ML-5**.

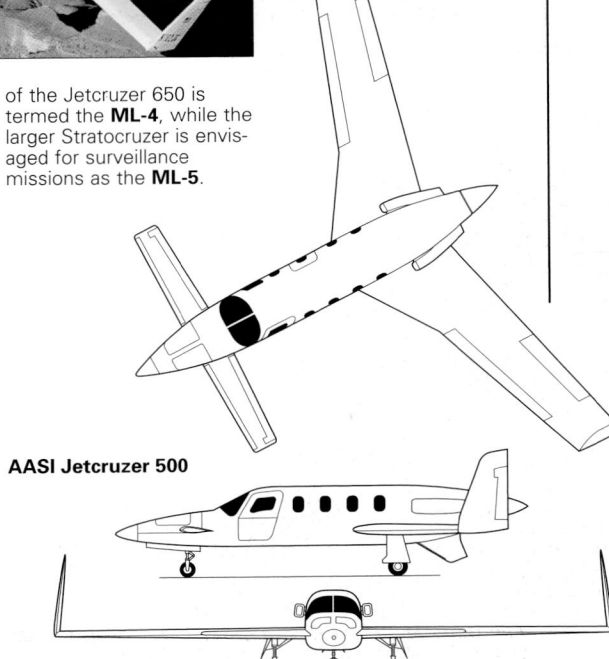
AASI Jetcruzer 500

SPECIFICATION

AASI Jetcruzer 500
Type: six-seat, single-engined business transport
Powerplant: one 850-shp (634-kW) Pratt & Whitney Canada PT6A-66 turboprop
Performance: maximum operating speed and maximum cruising speed 345 mph (556 km/h) at 22,000 ft (6700 m); service ceiling 30,000 ft (9140 m); take-off distance to 50 ft (15 m) 1,530 ft (530 m); landing distance from 50 ft (15 m) 1,430 ft

(436 m); maximum range 1,818 miles (2926 km) at economical cruising speed at 10,000 ft (3050 m)
Weights: empty 2,950 lb (1338 kg); maximum take-off 5,500 lb (2495 kg)
Dimensions: wing span 42 ft 2 in (12.85 m); foreplane span 18 ft 9 in (5.71 m); length 28 ft 2 in (8.59 m); height 10 ft 5 in (3.17 m); wing area 193.2 sq ft (17.94 m²); foreplane area 39.90 sq ft (3.71 m²)

A.C.A.Z. C.2

The **A.C.A.Z. C.2** was an all-metal two-seat fighter reconnaissance biplane. Built by Ateliers de Construction Aéronautique de Zeebrugge, or ZACCO (Zeebrugge Aeronautical Construction Company), the machine was constructed entirely from Duralumin sheet. An interesting feature was that all four wings were identical and interchangeable.

The pilot and observer were accommodated in tandem. Armament consisted of one 0.303-in (7.7-mm) Vickers machine-gun fitted to fire through the propeller hub, and twin Lewis guns on a movable mounting over the gunner's seat. Provision for the installation of photographic equipment was also made.

The C.2 was evaluated by the Aéronautique Militaire Belge in early 1926. On 9 March 1928, an attempt was made to fly it to the Belgian Congo with a crew of three: Thieffry, Lang and Guersin. Unfortunately, the aircraft was forced to land in France due to overloading. It was repaired and was later written off on 25 January 1933.

The C.2 fighter biplane was designed and built in Belgium. The prototype was evaluated by the Belgian military but the design was not put into production.

SPECIFICATION	
A.C.A.Z. C.2	
Type: two-seat fighter/ reconnaissance biplane	**Weights:** empty 2,778 lb (1260 kg); maximum take-off 4,563 lb (2070 kg)
Powerplant: one 450-hp (336-kW) Hispano-Suiza I2.Ga piston engine	**Dimensions:** wing span 41 ft 0⅛ in (12.50 m); length 27 ft 0⅞ in (8.25 m); height 11 ft 2 in (3.40 m); wing area 436.58 sq ft (40.56 m²)
Performance: maximum level speed 155 mph (250 km/h); climb to 19,685 ft (6000 m) in 35 minutes; service ceiling 24,606 ft (7500 m); endurance 3½ hours	**Armament:** one 0.303-in (7.7-mm) Vickers machine-gun firing through propeller hub and twin 0.303-in (7.7-mm) Lewis guns

A.D. Flying-Boat

esigned in the autumn of 1915 by the Air Department of the British Admiralty – which accounts for the designation – the **A.D. Flying-Boat** was intended to serve in patrol and reconnaissance roles. The aircraft was a two-seat, single-engined, unequal-span braced biplane. Its wings could be folded forward for shipboard stowage, and the braced biplane tail unit incorporated twin fins and rudders. The construction of two prototypes began in late 1915, with May, Harden & May of Southampton responsible for building the first hull. This monocoque wooden structure was of unusually smooth surface finish, and was one of the first hulls to be designed by Lieutenant Linton Hope, then a member of the Air Department's design team. He later became well known for his specialised knowledge of flying-boat design and construction.

Completion of the first prototype was carried out at Southampton by Pemberton-Billing Ltd (later the Supermarine Aviation Works Ltd), and it was this company which built the second prototype and the 27 production aircraft that followed. The original order had comprised 85 aircraft, but the remaining contracts were cancelled in March 1918. The first prototype was powered initially by a 200-hp (149-kW) Hispano Suiza engine driving a four-bladed pusher propeller. Early testing showed that the Flying-Boat porpoised badly on the water, but once airborne its flying characteristics improved. The aircraft was used by the Royal Naval Air Service on patrol duties, armed with one forward-firing 0.303-in (7.7-mm) Lewis machine-gun and with provision for carrying light bombs. Like many World War I aircraft, the Flying-Boat's performance was limited by the powerplants available. Although its on-water behaviour improved subsequently, the type saw no significant service before all 27 production aircraft were declared obsolete in late 1918.

Nineteen of these Flying-Boats were repurchased by Supermarine soon after the war. They were converted for civil use under the designation **Supermarine Channel I** with 160-hp (119-kW) Beardmore engines installed, or **Channel II** when powered by the 240-hp (179-kW) Siddeley Puma engine. The reconfigured Flying-Boats provided accommodation for a pilot and three passengers in three open cockpits and saw considerable use in the United Kingdom and abroad. Foreign examples were operated in Bermuda, Chile, Cuba, Japan, New Zealand, Norway and Trinidad.

SPECIFICATION	
A.D. Flying-Boat	
Type: two-seat patrol/ reconnaissance flying-boat	
Powerplant: one 200-hp (149-kW) Hispano Suiza inline piston engine	
Performance: maximum level speed 100 mph (161 km/h) at 2,000 ft (610 m), cruising speed 90 mph (145 km/h) at 10,000 ft (3050 m); service ceiling 11,000 ft (3355 m); endurance 4 hours 30 minutes	
Weights: empty 2,508 lb (1138 kg); maximum take-off 3,567 lb (1618 kg)	
Dimensions: wing span, upper 50 ft 4 in (15.34 m), lower 39 ft 7¼ in (12.07 m); length 30 ft 7 in (9.32 m); height 13 ft 1 in (3.99 m); wing area 479 sq ft (44.50 m²)	
Armament: one 0.303-in (7.7-mm) Lewis gun on mounting in bow cockpit	

The Flying-Boat was based on an excellent Linton Hope hull, but was built only in small numbers before the end of World War I relegated it to civil operations.

A.D. Navyplane

Two examples of the **A.D. Navyplane** two-seat pusher floatplane were ordered in January 1916 for the Royal Naval Air Service (RNAS). The aircraft was designed by Harold Bolas of the Air Department in collaboration with Messrs R.J. Mitchell and Richardson of Supermarine Aviation Works Ltd, which developed the aircraft. Perhaps the most remarkable feature of the Navyplane's structure was its monocoque nacelle which weighed no more than 80 lb (36 kg).

Serial numbers were allocated for seven Navyplanes, (9095-'96, N.1070-'74) but just one prototype (9095) was completed. It was originally fitted with an American Smith Static ten-cylinder single-row engine, and flight tested in August 1916 by Lieutenant-Commander John Seddon. This powerplant was later replaced by the AR.1 rotary engine (later re-designated BR.1 for Bentley Rotary 1) and retested in May 1917. However, even without a military load and observer, the Navyplane's performance proved to be too poor and it was officially deleted on 27 August 1917.

SPECIFICATION	
A.D. Navyplane	
Type: two-seat pusher armed reconnaissance floatplane	empty 2100 lb (952 kg); maximum take-off 3,102 lb (1157 kg)
Powerplant: one 150-hp (112-kW) Smith Static radial engine; (later) one 150-hp (112-kW) Admiralty Rotary 1 rotary piston engine	**Dimensions:** wing span 36 ft (10.97 m); wing chord 1.52 m (5 ft); gap between wings 6 ft 6 in (1.98 m); tailplane span 15 ft 6 in (4.72 m); airscrew diameter 8 ft 10 in (2.69 m); length 27 ft 9 in (8.46 m); height 12 ft 9 in (3.89 m); total wing area 364.00 sq ft (33.80 m²)
Performance: maximum level speed 64 mph (104 km/h); climb to 2,000 ft (907 m) in 30 minutes; service ceiling 1,300 ft (396 m); endurance 6 hours	**Armament:** one 0.303-in (7.7-mm) Lewis machine-gun on movable mounting for observer
Weights: (applicable for aircraft fitted with Smith Static engine)	

The Navyplane's intended missions were bombing and reconnaissance, for which roles it was equipped with a wireless. Armament consisted of just a single Lewis gun for the observer.

A.D. Scout (Sparrow)

The **A.D. Scout** was an anti-airship fighter designed by Harris Booth of the Air Department at the Admiralty. Later known unofficially as the **'Sparrow'**, the Scout was an extraordinary biplane with single-bay staggered wings.

Made of wood with fabric-covered surfaces, the Scout's unusual appearance resulted primarily from the large mainplane gap being below, rather than above,

the high-mounted nacelle which housed the armament, pilot and engine. The rudders and large outsize tailplane were carried by four parallel tailbooms. The aircraft had a very narrow track main undercarriage, and the lower booms, set approximately 11 ft (3.35 m) apart, provided an additional measure of stability during taxiing.

The Scout was armed with a single Lewis

machine-gun. Its intended armament was the much heavier-calibre Davis recoilless gun, but in view of the fragility of the Scout's construction, this weapon was never fitted.

Four prototypes were ordered in 1915 and two each were built by Hewlett & Blondeau and by Black-

Developed during the early days of World War I as a counter to the German airship threat, the A.D. Scout was a single-seat fighter of extraordinary design. No. 1536 was one of two Scouts built by Blackburn and is seen at Chingford, Essex, in 1915.

burn Aeroplane and Motor Company. The Scout was flown by pilots of the Royal Naval Air Service who found it to be seriously overweight

and difficult to handle. No further development was therefore attempted, and all four Scouts were subsequently scrapped.

SPECIFICATION	
A.D. Scout	**Dimensions:** wing span 33 ft 5 in
Type: single-seat anti-airship biplane fighter	(10.18 m); length 22 ft 9 in (6.93 m); height 10 ft 3 in (3.12 m)
Powerplant: one 100-hp (75-kW) Gnome Monosoupape rotary piston engine	**Armament:** one 0.303-in (7.7-mm) Lewis machine-gun mounted on nacelle floor; one
Performance: maximum level speed 84 mph (135 km/h); endurance 2½ hours	Davis recoilless gun firing 2-lb (1-kg) shells (intended armament, not fitted)

A.D. Seaplane Type 1000

One of the first aircraft designed for the torpedo bomber role, the **Air Department Seaplane Type 1000** (so designated after its serial number) was designed in 1914 by Harris Booth. At the time of its first flight this was the largest aeroplane yet built in the UK. It was a floatplane of typical wire-braced/fabric-covered wooden construction, with provision for drop loads under the lower

wing's centre section.

The Type 1000 was an unequal-span biplane with a glazed and ungainly central control nacelle ending at its rear in an engine and pusher propeller. Outboard on either side of the nacelle was a boom with massively cowled engines and four-bladed tractor propellers at its front and the empennage at its rear. Two pontoon main floats were mounted under the

lower wing in line with the booms, with two smaller rear floats. The dihedralled outer panels of the wing were separated on each side by two sets of interplane struts, while overhanging ailerons supported by kingposts and cables, were fitted to the outboard trailing edges of the upper wing.

Some seven machines were ordered from J. Samuel White, but only one was completed. Trials were highly disappointing, since the machine was found to be too heavy and its alighting gear decidedly flimsy by comparison.

The Seaplane was to have been armed with torpedoes (probably of

The AD Seaplane Type 1000 had the distinction of being the largest aeroplane yet flown in Britain when it appeared at the beginning of World War I. Like many designs typical of the period, it was overweight and development was halted after just one example had been built.

810-lb/367-kg weight and 14 in/356-mm diameter), light bombs and a fixed heavy gun, but its excess weight precluded their installation. Further devel-

opment was abandoned, but the sole example is known to have survived until 1916, probably at the Royal Naval Air Service's Felixstowe base.

SPECIFICATION	
A.D. Type 1000 Seaplane	**Dimensions:** wing span 115 ft 0 in (35.05 m)
Type: five-seat torpedo and bomber floatplane	**Armament:** (proposed) one or two
Powerplant: three 310-hp (231-kW) Sunbeam Vee piston engines	torpedoes (probably 14-in/356-mm diameter) or bombs and one 12-pdr (5.4-kg) gun

ADA Light Combat Aircraft

By late-1997, India had yet to fly its LCA, despite assistance from American, French and Israeli manufacturers. The aircraft represents an ambitious attempt to develop and produce a next-generation combat aircraft by an industry more familiar with the licenced production of foreign designs.

Faced with Pakistan and China as potentially dangerous enemies on its north-western and northern borders respectively, India maintains a large and effective air force. Since the

time of India's defeat in skirmishes with Chinese forces in 1962, the Indian Air Force (IAF) has relied heavily on the USSR as its major supplier of warplanes and ground equipment. By

the early-1980s the most important of the Soviet-supplied warplanes, constituting more than 50 per cent of the IAF's strength, was the Mikoyan-Gurevich MiG-21 'Fishbed' in both Soviet-supplied and Indian licence-manufactured forms. This type was already obsolescent, however, and from 1981, in the face of Pakistani and Chinese efforts to modernise their air forces, the Indian defence ministry planned to start the process of acquiring a successor to the MiG-21.

The course selected was based on the desire to exploit the country's developing aircraft design and production capabilities by creating an Indian solution to the IAF's needs. An indigenous design would also ensure full role optimisation and reduce the flow

of Indian financial resources out of the country. At the same time, India's dependence on imports from the increasingly troubled USSR would be diminished.

Project clearance was given in 1983 and in June 1984 the **Aeronautical Development Agency (ADA)** was established in Bangalore to undertake project design and supervision. The ADA grouping combines the Indian Gas Turbine Research Establishment and Hindustan Aeronautics Ltd., which were respectively allocated the tasks of developing an indigenous engine (the GTX-35VS Kaveri turbofan designed with the aid of the French company SNECMA) and of undertaking production of the new aircraft.

A feasibility study completed in 1985 envisaged the primary tasks of the **Light Combat Aircraft (LCA)** to be air superiority,

with close support and interdiction as important secondary roles. The French aircraft manufacturer Dassault was brought in to serve as consultant during the project definition phase, which extended from spring-1987 to late-1988.

This allowed the completion of the basic design by 1990, when the LCA was revealed as a lightweight single-seat all-weather multi-role fighter of control-configured (negative stability) configuration, powered by a single after-burning turbofan. The aircraft has been optimised for key features such as agility, rapid acceleration, good field performance and the carriage of a weapons load more than double that of the MiG-21.

In configuration, the LCA's airframe is based on an oval-section fuselage with a shoulder-set delta wing. This has compound sweep on its leading

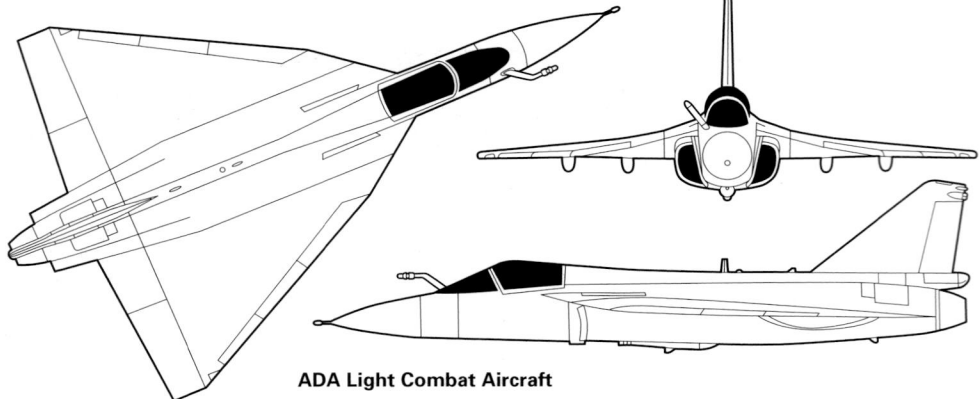

ADA Light Combat Aircraft

edges, which exhibit considerable twist between their inboard and outboard ends. The moving surfaces comprise three-segment flaps on the leading edge and two-section trailing-edge elevons.

All control surfaces are operated via a full quadruplex digital fly-by-wire control system, designed jointly by Lockheed Martin Electronics and the Indian Aeronautical Development Establishment.

The cockpit is equipped with HOTAS (Hands On Throttle And Stick) controls, a HUD (Head Up Display)

and two Sextant Avionique colour multi-function CRTs (Cathode Ray Tubes) compatible with the use of night vision goggles for the presentation of flight information and data from the LCA's sensors. These avionics are integrated with other elements of the electronic suite such as the Otherton Honeywell INS (Inertial Navigation System) via a central computer and three MIL-1553B databuses.

The LCA's sensors include a HAL/Electronics Research & Development Establishment multi-mode pulse-Doppler radar and a

FLIR (Forward-Looking Infra-Red). The radar warning receiver provides data for the in-built defensive system, which is based on an electronic jammer and chaff/flare dispenser. The LCA's radar has suffered from a troubled development and was the subject of an Indian request for assistance from Israeli radar firms in March 1995. The LCA has a Utility Systems Management System to monitor the 'health' of each system and optimise its performance.

Composite materials and advanced alloys such as aluminium-lithium alloys are used extensively throughout the LCA's airframe, keeping weight to a minimum and therefore allowing the establishment of a 28,660 lb (13000 kg) maximum take-off weight with more than 8,818 lb (4000 kg) of external stores. Composite materials amount to over 30 per cent of the structure weight, and extensive use is made of CFRPs (Carbon-Fibre Reinforced Plastics) in the wings, control surfaces and vertical tail. Aluminium-lithium alloy is used in the rest of the airframe with the exception of hot areas near the engine, where titanium alloy is employed.

Fixed armament planned for the LCA comprises a Russian-sourced 23-mm GSh-23L twin-barreled cannon, mounted internally and supplied with 220 rounds of ammunition. Up to 8818 lb (4000 kg) of stores may be carried on seven external hardpoints, one under the fuselage and three under each wing. Primary air-to-air armament comprises two beyond-visual-range weapons of unspecified type, and two short-range missiles, also of unspecified type, but probably the highly-manoeuvrable Vympel R-73 (AA-11 'Archer') from Russia.

The LCA is to be powered by a single indigenously developed Kaveri turbofan operated via a British-supplied Dowty/Smiths full-authority digital engine control system. The Kaveri programme has suffered considerable delay, however, and 11 General Electric F404-GE-F2J3 turbofans have therefore had to be purchased from the United States for installation in the prototypes and development aircraft. The engine is installed in the rear fuselage and is fed by two air intakes under the wing leading edges. The fixed geometry of the inlets restricts maximum speed

of the LCA to about Mach 1.6, but avoids extra design complexity. Splitter plates draw off boundary-layer air from the forward fuselage. Landing field performance is improved by a brake parachute housed in a fairing beneath the rudder.

An internal fuel capacity of 660 gal (3000 litres) can be augmented by means of a fixed inflight-refuelling probe fitted on the starboard side of the forward fuselage. The centreline hardpoint and two inner hardpoints under each wing are 'plumbed' for the carriage of external fuel tanks. The LCA can carry up to five 176-gal (800-litre) drop tanks to augment its internal fuel.

In November 1996 the first LCA prototype was rolled out, but up to the time of writing in late 1997, the type has yet to fly as a result of development problems. India has therefore requested Israeli aid in completing the LCA to flight-test status and in the implementation of the flight test programme, whose start was initially pushed back to 1997 and then to 1998 at the earliest. The IAF has a requirement for some 200 such aircraft, but it now seems highly unlikely that the planned in-service date of 2002 can be attained since development is well behind schedule and it is currently impossible for the Indian authorities to grant authorisation, due in 1997, for the production of the LCA.

Further development of the LCA is planned, including a two-seat model for operational conversion, weapons and continuation training roles. A maritime strike variant is also planned for use by the Indian naval air arm, where the type is likely to deploy the proven BAe Sea Eagle anti-ship missile.

SPECIFICATION

ADA Light Combat Aircraft
Type: single-seat multi-role fighter
Powerplant: (prototype) one General Electric F404-GE-F2J3 turbofan rated at 18,097-lb (80.50-kN) thrust with afterburning; production aircraft are to be fitted with one Kaveri GTX-35VS turbofan rated at 11,533-lb (51.30-kN) thrust dry and 18,030-lb (80.20-kN) thrust with afterburning
Performance: maximum speed 1,056 mph (1700 km/h) or Mach 1.6 at high altitude; initial climb rate 39,370 ft (12000 m) per minute; service ceiling more than 50,035 ft (15250 m)
Weights: empty about 12,125 lb (5500 kg); normal take-off

18,739 lb (8500 kg); maximum take-off 28,660 lb (13000 kg)
Dimensions: span 26 ft 10¾ in (8.20 m); length 43 ft 3¾ in (13.20 m); height 14 ft 5¼ in (4.40 m); wing area about 403.66 sq ft (37.50 m²)
Armament: one 23-mm Gryazev-Shipunov GSh-23L fixed forward-firing twin-barreled cannon, and more than 8,818 lb (4000 kg) of stores on seven hardpoints, including short- and medium-range AAMs, ASMs, anti-ship missiles, bombs of various types, rocket launchers and ECM pods; likely weapons include R-73 (NATO AA-11 'Archer') short-range AAMs and British Aerospace Sea Eagle anti-ship missiles

---

Adamoli-Cattani fighter

In 1918, Signori Adamoli and Cattani designed the smallest practicable single-seat fighter around the most powerful rotary

engine of the time, the 200-hp (149-kW) Le Rhône. Of wooden construction with fabric skinning, the fighter was an unequal-

span unstaggered biplane with Warren truss-type interplane bracing. Unusually, conventional ailerons were replaced by

interlinked and hinged wing leading edges which varied the wing's camber to provide lateral control. Rigid tubes rather than cables were used to actuate the movable tail surfaces.

Construction of the prototype **Adamoli-Cattani fighter** was begun at the Farina works in Turin, but was then transferred to the

Officine Moncenisio in Condove for completion. Initial static testing revealed that the engine only developed 160 hp (119 kW) and the fighter was thus seriously underpowered. These limited trials took place at the end of World War I and further development of the fighter was abandoned after the Armistice.

The sound aeronautical design philosophy of fitting a powerful engine into the small airframe of the Adamoli-Cattani fighter was undermined, when the engine was found to be underpowered.

SPECIFICATION

Adamoli-Cattani fighter
(estimated for fully-rated engine)
Type: single-seat biplane fighter
Powerplant: one 200-hp (149-kW) Le Rhône rotary piston engine
Performance: maximum level speed 186 mph (300 km/h);

endurance 2½ hours
Weights: empty 1,036 lb (470 kg); loaded 1488 lb (675 kg)
Dimensions: wing span 28 ft 2½ in (8.60 m); length 20 ft 0⅛ in (6.10 m)
Armament: two 0.303-in (7.7-mm) machine-guns

AEG 'B' series

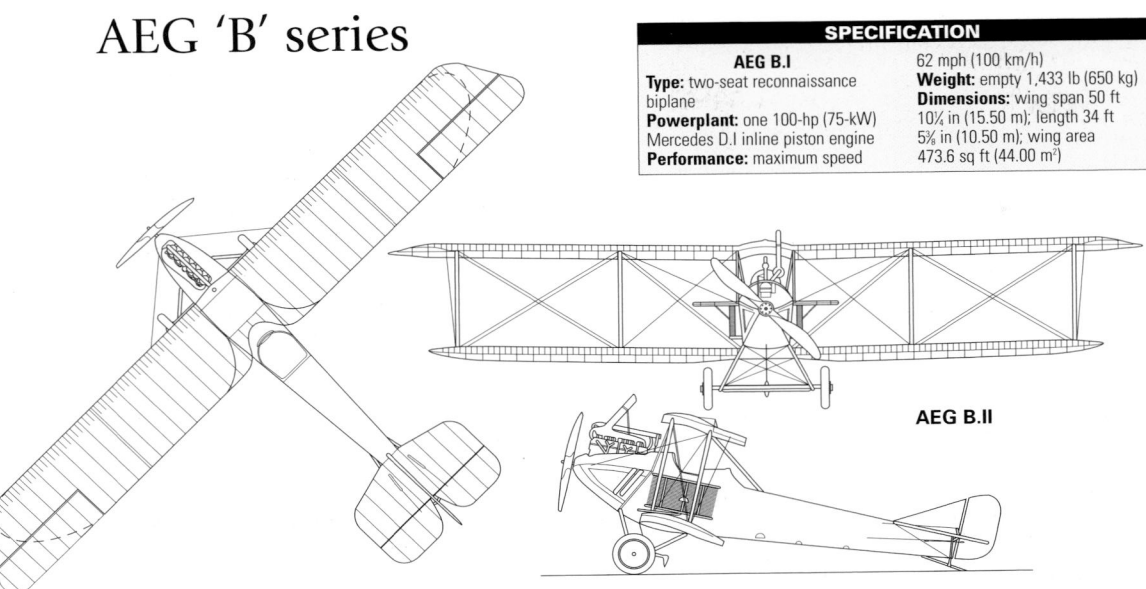

AEG B.II

SPECIFICATION

AEG B.I

Type: two-seat reconnaissance biplane
Powerplant: one 100-hp (75-kW) Mercedes D.I inline piston engine
Performance: maximum speed

62 mph (100 km/h)
Weight: empty 1,433 lb (650 kg)
Dimensions: wing span 50 ft 10¼ in (15.50 m); length 34 ft 5⅜ in (10.50 m); wing area 473.6 sq ft (44.00 m²)

At an early date Allgemeine Elektrizitäts Gesellschaft (AEG), the major German electrical company, formed an aviation division that designed and built its first aircraft in 1910: this **Z.1** biplane was followed by a monoplane, a flying-boat and a floatplane. By the start of World War I, AEG had become well established as an aircraft manufacturer, and was soon called upon to provide military aircraft for the German air service.

As a start, small numbers of an unarmed two-seat reconnaissance aircraft were acquired for service in 1914. These **Z.6** three-bay biplanes of unequal span became the company's first mass-production type and, served with the military designation **B.I**.

The machine introduced what was to become a standard form of construction for AEG's aircraft: almost the entire structure was of welded steel tube, the wings each having two tubular steel spars with wooden ribs to provide the required aerofoil contours, under a covering of fabric. The tailskid landing gear included an unusual feature, namely a nosewheel unit mounted beneath the engine to protect the propeller from damage if the aircraft nosed-over during landing. The engine installation was almost unbelievably untidy, for most of the 100-hp (75-kW) Mercedes D.I inline engine was exposed above the streamlined nose cowling. Large cooling radiators for the engine were mounted on each side of the fuselage.

The **B.II** which followed later in 1914 represented an attempt to tidy up the basic design. This **Z.9** type was a two-bay biplane of reduced span, and introduced the more powerful 120-hp (89-kW) Mercedes D.II engine, but no attempt had been made to improve the powerplant/radiator installation, which was of the characteristic pointed AEG type with louvred side panels and a 'rhino horn' vertical exhaust.

The B.II was followed in 1915 by the generally similar **B.III** that retained the same powerplant but incorporated some detail improvements, including a rounded fin-and-rudder assembly, as the result of experience gained through service use of the B.I and B.II. The B.III was built only in small numbers as the last of AEG's unarmed reconnaissance types, for little time had been lost by the combatants in the introduction of weapons that could be used to attack and destroy an adversary's aircraft. This resulted in the replacement of the unarmed 'B' category aircraft in German service by armed 'C' category machines.

AEG 'C' series

Little development of AEG 'B' series biplanes was necessary for the evolution of the **KZ.9** that was introduced in March 1915 as the **AEG C.I**. The first armed two-seater from AEG was little more than a B.II, the best of the 'B' series types, fitted with a 150-hp (112-kW) Benz Bz.III inline engine. The observer was relocated to the rear cockpit, which was fitted with a Schneider Drehring gun mounting for a 0.312-in (7.92-mm) MG 14 Parabellum trainable machine-gun, for defence against attack from the rear and flanks.

As 1915 progressed, the emphasis in two-seat reconnaissance aircraft changed gradually from a stable reconnaissance platform towards a more manoeuvrable machine that could evade enemy scouts and fight back. The **C.II** of October 1915 was thus a refined version of the C.I and, more importantly, its dimensions were reduced to improve agility.

An experimental **C.III** soon followed the C.II. This introduced a deep fuselage that completely filled the gap between the biplane wings, the object being to provide the crew with an unobstructed forward view over the upper wing. By seating the pilot aft, it was now possible for the observer to fire the machine-gun forward, clear of the propeller disc. There must have been shortcomings, however, for despite the ingenuity of the idea, no production examples of the C.III were built.

The most extensively built member of the 'C' series was the **C.IV**. Its development by Georg König, designer of the earlier 'B' and 'C' types, was spurred by the German army air service's appreciation of the growing significance that should be attached to aerial reconnaissance. Generally similar in configuration to the C.II but a little larger than this machine, the C.IV introduced a more powerful Mercedes D.III engine, a fixed forward-firing machine-gun for the pilot, and a three-position variable-incidence tailplane, adjustable on the ground to ease the trimming of the type. The C.IV was built entirely of steel tube of varying diameter and gauge, except for its wooden wing ribs. Production figures for the C.IV are not known precisely, but are estimated at more than 400 including a number of **C.IVa** versions with a 180-hp (134-kW) Argus inline engine. C.IVs

AEG produced a total of 658 'C' types, the majority being the C.IV which gave useful service with German front-line combat units. The experimental C.VII was fitted with a Mercedes D.III engine.

were also built by the Fokker factory at Schwerin.

The 'C' series ended with experimental versions including one **C.IV-N** night bomber, generally similar to the C.IV except for increased-span three-bay wings and a 150-hp (112-kW) Benz Bz.III engine for the carriage of six 110-lb (50-kg) bombs; a **C.V** two-seat reconnaissance prototype similar to the basic C.IV but with a 220-hp (164-kW) Mercedes engine; two **C.VII** aircraft with single-bay wings and the Mercedes D.III engine; one improved single-bay **C.VIII** machine with the same powerplant; and the **C.VIII Dr** (*Dreidecker* or triplane) version of the C.VIII.

SPECIFICATION

AEG C.IV

Type: two-seat armed reconnaissance biplane
Powerplant: one 160-hp (119-kW) Mercedes D.III six-cylinder, water-cooled inline piston engine
Performance: maximum speed 98 mph (158 km/h); climb to 3,280 ft (1000 m) in 6 minutes; service ceiling 16,405 ft (5000 m); endurance four hours
Weights: empty 1,764 lb

(800 kg); maximum take-off 2,469 lb (1120 kg)
Dimensions: wing span 44 ft 1½ in (13.45 m); length 23 ft 5½ in (7.15 m); height 10 ft 11¾ in (3.35 m); wing area 419.81 sq ft (39.00 m²)
Armament: one 0.312-in (7.92-mm) LMG 08/15 fixed forward-firing machine-gun, and one 0.312-in (7.92-mm) LMG 14 Parabellum trainable rearward-firing machine-gun

AEG C.IV two-seat armed reconnaissance biplane of Fliegerabteilung (A) 224 based at Château Bellingkamps in the spring of 1917.

AEG 'D' series

AEG's first fighter design was the **D.I**, a stocky single-bay biplane of mainly steel tube construction under a fabric covering. A notable feature of the D.I was the use of single-spar wings. Three prototypes were built, and the first of these appeared in May 1917. Type testing took place later in August and September

after the fuselage had been lengthened by 1 ft 3¾ in (0.4 m). The second and third prototypes (D 4401/17 and D 5002/17 respectively) differed by having cheek-type radiators, those of the **D.III** being longer than those of the **D.II**.

The D.I proved difficult to fly, and one of the prototypes crashed during testing.

Britain's successful Sopwith Triplane led AEG to develop the Dr.I in October 1917. Poor performance and handling precluded its further development.

Nevertheless, 20 pre-series examples of the D.I were ordered for front-line evaluation with the standard fighter armament of two 0.312-in (7.92 mm) LMG 08/15 fixed forward-firing machine-guns with a synchronisation system to allow them to fire through the disc swept by the two-bladed propeller. The contract was cancelled, however, after the loss of a second prototype in a crash on 5 September 1917.

After one of the most agile and fast-climbing of British fighters, the Sopwith Triplane, had been captured intact, the Germans launched a wide-ranging programme of triplane design and development. One machine that reached the prototype stage was the AEG version of the concept, which was the **Dr.I** that was in essence a *Dreidecker* (triplane) variant of the D.I. This mated a triplane wing arrangement to the D.I's

fuselage, tail surfaces, engine and armament. Flight testing revealed that the type possessed poor

performance and handling characteristics, and further development of the Dr.I was swiftly abandoned.

AEG's first effort to produce a fighter resulted in the stocky D.I which appeared in May 1917. The D.III, or third version, featured 'ear'-type radiators.

SPECIFICATION	
AEG D.I	(685 kg); maximum take-off
Type: single-seat biplane fighter	2,072 lb (940 kg)
Powerplant: one 160-hp (119-kW) Daimler D.IIIa inline piston engine	**Dimensions:** wing span 27 ft 10⅝ in (8.50 m); length 20 ft 0⅛ in (6.10 m); height 8 ft 8⅜ in (2.65 m); wing area 173.73 sq ft (16.14 m²)
Performance: maximum speed 137 mph (220 km/h); climb to 3,280 ft (1000 m) in 2 minutes 30 seconds	
Weights: empty 1,510 lb	**Armament:** two 0.312-in (7.92-mm) LMG 08/15 fixed forward-firing machine-guns

AEG 'G' series

The introduction of bomber squadrons to the Western Front after the start of World War I was not long delayed: Germany introduced *Kampfstaffel* (battle squadron) units early in 1915. The aircraft that equipped them were used primarily as multi-gun fighter platforms when first put into service, but soon their potential for tactical and strategic bombing was appreciated. It was in 1915 that the first of AEG's twin-engined biplane bombers appeared. Powered by two 100-hp (75-kW) Mercedes D.I engines, the **AEG G.I** was essentially an enlarged

version of the C.IV that was 75 per cent heavier and yet had only about 24 per cent more power. Only a single example was built.

First seen in mid-1915, the **G.II** was a slightly larger version of the G.I with the uprated power-plant of two 150-hp (112-kW) Benz Bz.III engines and, at various stages, single or triple vertical tail surfaces. Defensive armament consisted of two or three 0.312-in (7.92-mm) machine-guns and, with a crew of three, the G.II could carry 441 lb (200 kg) of bombs. About 15 G.IIs were built before the type

was supplanted by the **G.III**, which was also produced only in limited numbers. This carried a bombload of 661 lb (300 kg) and was powered by two 220-hp (1164-kW) Mercedes D.IV inline engines driving opposite-turning propellers.

It was not until the end of 1916 that the definitive **G.IV** variant entered service. Like its predecessors, this was of welded steel tube construction covered with fabric except on the plywood-skinned nose section. More powerful Mercedes engines were installed, and a maximum of four crew could be accommodated. All the cockpits were interconnected, enabling the crew to change positions in flight if circumstances dictated. Although demonstrating the best performance of any of the company's 'G' series aircraft, the G.IV was hampered by limited range when carrying a crew of three, and the maximum bombload of 882 lb (400 kg). As a result, it was used largely on short-range tactical operations behind Allied lines on the Western Front. Without a bombload, it was

used on occasions for long-distance aerial photography and reconnaissance.

Production of the AEG 'G' series bombers totalled 542 aircraft, of which about 500 were of the G.IV variant. Around 50 of these bombers served until as late as August 1918. Small numbers of experimental G.IVs were built for assessment by the *Schlstas* at the Front. These included the **G.IVb** with a three-bay

wing cellule of increased span; and the **G.IVK** with a 20-mm Becker cannon in the nose. Intended for long-range missions, the **G.V** was the largest AEG bomber design of all but appeared too late to see service in World War I. Limited numbers served as transports during 1919 with the German airline Deutsche Luftreederei. One flew from Berlin to Eskjö in Sweden in 4 hr 7 minutes.

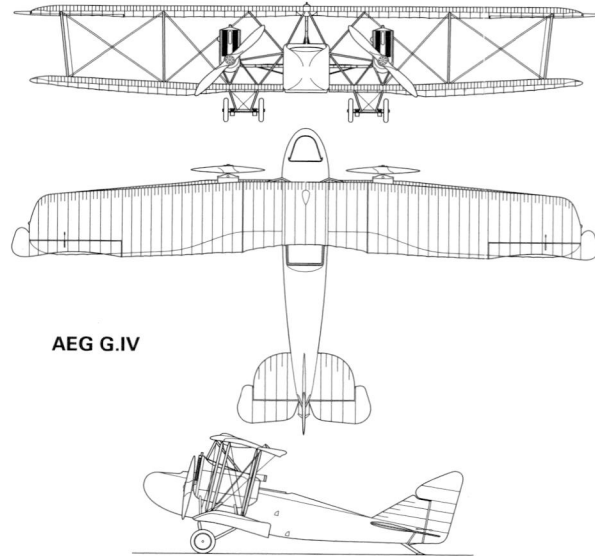

AEG G.IV

Early German twin-engined bombers were known as K types. The AEG G.I (initially known as K.1) and G.III (foreground) were both unsuccessful designs and were only built in small numbers.

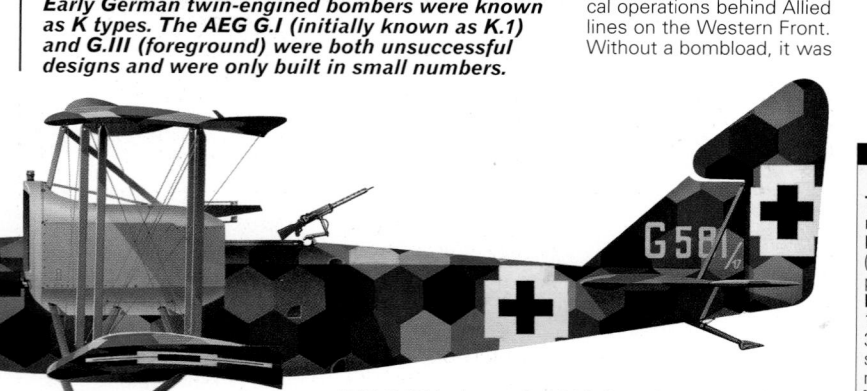

AEG G.IV twin-engined biplane bomber of Bogohl 4, Staffel 19 based at Bazuel, summer 1918.

SPECIFICATION	
AEG G.IV	8,003 lb (3630 kg)
Type: three/four-seat bomber and reconnaissance aircraft	**Dimensions:** wing span 60 ft 4½ in (18.40 m); length 31 ft 9¾ in (9.70 m); height 12 ft 9½ in (3.90 m); wing area 721.21 sq ft (67.00 m²)
Powerplant: two 260-hp (194-kW) Mercedes D.IVa inline piston engines	
Performance: maximum speed 103 mph (165 km/h); climb to 3,280 ft (1000 m) in 5 minutes; service ceiling 14,765 ft (4500 m); maximum endurance five hours	**Armament:** two 0.312-in (7.92-mm) LMG 14 Parabellum trainable machine-guns, one on ring mounting in forward cockpit and one on rail mounting in the rear cockpit; maximum bombload 882 lb (400 kg)
Weights: empty 5,291 lb (2400 kg); maximum take-off	

AEG 'J' series

Late in 1915 the German army air service introduced *Fliegerabteilung-Infanterie* (infantry contact patrol) units of the type that would today be regarded as close support squadrons. Proving to be valuable when used on a small scale during the Battle of Verdun early in 1916, such units were soon the subject of a high-priority programme of expansion and re-equipment. The **AEG J.I** was developed hurriedly to meet this

Removal of the J.II's armour plating gave a useful payload capacity for civilian applications. After the Armistice, a number of J.IIs were used as transports by Deutsche Luft-Reederei.

requirement until more suitable purpose-designed infantry contact patrol aircraft, such as the Junkers J.I, became available.

The AEG J.I was essentially a C.IV fitted with the uprated 200-hp (149-kW) Benz Bz.IV inline engine. However, the 40-hp (30-kW) increase in power over the C.IV's D.III engine was used to offset the 860-lb (390-kg) gain in weight due to armour plate protection for the J.I's crew

The AEG J.I was developed to meet a need for an aircraft to support infantry units in the field. Heavily armoured, it was fitted with two downward-firing guns, for strafing ground targets.

and engine. This sheet steel protection extended from the nose to the rear cockpit and was 2 in (51 mm) thick. Primary armament comprised two LMG 08/15 guns mounted in the floor of the rear cockpit. Pointing forward and downward at an angle of about 45°, they could be used for strafing enemy trenches or columns of infantry. In addition, the observer had a trainable LMG 14 gun on a ring mounting. The J.I's increased weight caused ailerons to be added to the C.IV's lower wing to improve lateral control. The **J.II** of 1918 was similar, but introduced an improved control system and horn-balanced control surfaces.

Fin area was also increased to improve directional stability. These modifications caused an increase in weight of 55 lb (25 kg).

AEG built more than 600 J.Is and J.IIs. A number of J.IIs saw service with civil operators after the end of World War I.

SPECIFICATION	
AEG J.I	3,836 lb (1740 kg)
Type: two-seat infantry contact patrol aircraft	**Dimensions:** wing span 44 ft 2 in (13.46 m); length 23 ft 7½ in (7.20 m); height 10 ft 11¾ in (3.35 m); wing area 357.16 sq ft (33.18 m²)
Powerplant: maximum speed 94 mph (150 km/h); climb to 3,280 ft (1000 m) in 6 minutes; service ceiling 14,765 ft (4500 m); endurance 2 hours 30 minutes	
Performance: maximum speed 62 mph (100 km/h)	**Armament:** two 0.312-in (7.92-mm) MG 08/15 fixed forward-/downward-firing machine-guns and one 0.312-in (7.92-mm) LMG 14 Parabellum trainable rearward-firing machine-gun
Weight: empty 3,208 lb (1455 kg); maximum take-off	

AEG PE/DJ.I series

The **AEG PE** (*Panzer-Einsitzer*) was a single-seat armoured ground-attack fighter and proved to be unique among aircraft designed for this task in that it was of triplane configuration. The PE featured an armoured fuselage of light alloy construction, and fabric-covered flying surfaces with dural tubular wing spars. Taking to the air for the first time in March 1918, the machine proved easy to fly but was found to have poor stability. It was considered by the Idflieg (Inspektion

der Fliegertruppe) to possess inadequate performance for fighter-versus-fighter combat. German military ideology considered the idea of a dedicated single-seat, ground-attack aircraft to be unacceptable.

However, the concept was continued in another design; even before flight testing of the PE had taken place, AEG had begun development of an advanced Panzer-Einsitzer biplane, known as the **DJ.I**. It was an equal-span biplane whose two-bay

Similar in concept to the British Sopwith Salamander, the AEG PE triplane was a dedicated ground-attack fighter. Its performance was deemed inadequate for aerial combat.

The DJ.I was one of the most promising German designs to emerge during World War I, but further development was curtailed by the Armistice.

wing cellule dispensed with flying and landing wires, and instead used I-section aerofoil-section interplane struts of broad chord so that incidence-bracing wires could be deleted. The fabric-covered wings had dural spars. The fuselage had aluminium sheet skinning and embodied some

armour protection for the engine, fuel tank and pilot. Three DJ.I prototypes were built, the first making the type's maiden flight in July 1918. The first two aircraft were fitted with the 195-hp (145-kW) Benz Bz.IIIb Vee-8

engine driving a four-bladed airscrew, while the third had the more powerful 240-hp (179-kW) Maybach Mb.IVa powerplant. Flight testing of the DJ.I was still under way as World War I ended in November 1918.

SPECIFICATION	
AEG DJ.I	(1182 kg); maximum take-off 3,031 lb (1375 kg)
Type: single-seat armoured attack fighter	**Dimensions:** span 32 ft 9¾ in (10.00 m); length 21 ft 11⅜ in (6.69 m); height 9 ft 10 in (3.00 m)
Powerplant: one 195-hp (145-kW) Benz Bz.IIIb inline piston engine	
Performance: maximum speed 112 mph (180 km/h); climb to 3,280 ft (1000 m) in 4 minutes	**Armament:** (planned) two 0.312-in (7.92-mm) LMG 08/15 fixed forward-firing machine-guns and provision for four light anti-personnel bombs
Weight: empty 2,606 lb	

AEG R.I series

During 1916, AEG received an order for two **R.I 'Giant'** four-engined heavy bombers. Unusually, all four engines were grouped together inside the fuselage and drove the four-bladed

airscrews at 750 rpm via a system of transmission shafts and gear boxes. Two-bladed airscrews were later substituted. One machine (R.I 21/16) was completed, and made its

first flight in 1916. The aircraft later crashed with the loss of all seven crew during a trial flight on 3 September. The cause of the crash was later traced to insufficient hardening of the wood glue in one of the airscrews, causing it to delaminate. A second

machine, R.I 22/16, was still incomplete at the end

of World War I and was eventually scrapped.

SPECIFICATION	
AEG R.I	**Weights:** empty 19,845 lb (9000 kg); loaded 28,003 lb (12500 kg)
Type: heavy bomber	**Dimensions:** wing span 118 ft 1½ in (36.00 m); length 63 ft 11½ in (19.5 m)
Powerplant: four Mercedes D.IVa inline piston engines each rated at 260 hp (194 kW)	

Aeritalia (Fiat) G91R

Designed by Giuseppe Gabrielli of Fiat (later Aeritalia and now Alenia), the **G91** was developed to meet a NATO requirement issued to the European aircraft industry early in 1954. NMBR/1 called for a light attack/close support type able to attack targets no more than 170 miles (275 km) from a poorly prepared forward base. It was intended that the winning design should become standard equipment in NATO's European air forces. However, this was not to be the case, even though the G91 was built in substantial numbers in Italy and under licence in West Germany, and eventually became an important type with three air forces.

Resembling a scaled-down version of the North American F-86K Sabre in configuration, the first of four G91 prototypes made its maiden flight on 9 August 1956. During its evaluation trials at Brétigny in France during 1957, the G91 met all of the demands of the specification, especially with regard to its ability to operate with and without external loads from semi-prepared grass airstrips.

The initial G91 production version was a ground-attack fighter, for which the primary armament consisted of four 0.50-in (12.7-mm) Colt-Browning machine-guns. Delivery of 26 essentially pre-production aircraft began early in 1958 (a 27th was finished to the **G91A** STOL experimental standard). The G91 began operational evaluation with 103º Gruppo Caccia Tattico Leggero of the Italian air force during February 1959. At the same time, the new West German air force had also decided to adopt the G91, and a licence-production agreement between Fiat and Flugzeug Union Süd (Messerschmitt, Dornier and Heinkel) was

signed on 11 March 1959. The G91's primary role was expanded from light attack to include high-speed armed reconnaissance. This led to the development of a more specialised variant of the basic G91 as the first true production variant.

First flown in 1959, the **G91R/1** differed from the basic G91 by having a shorter nose which carried three 70-mm focal length Vinten cameras for forward and oblique photography at low altitude, with vertical photography possible at higher altitude. The **G91R/1A** (25 built) was similar except for its improved navigational aids (as fitted to the **G91R/3** variant to make it independent of ground installations). The **G91R/1B** (50 built) featured a strengthened structure, higher-capacity wheel brakes, tubeless tyres and some equipment changes. Two G91R/1s were evaluated by the US Air Force during 1961-62.

In Italian service the three G91R/1 variants were operated mainly by the three *gruppi* of the 2º and 32º Stormi based, respectively, at San Angelo and Brindisi. The Italian air force began to retire its G91Rs in the late-1980s as increasing numbers of the AMX International AMX became available; the last G91Rs were withdrawn from service in April 1992.

The G91R/3 was based on the G91R/1B but was built to a West German specification. It was armed with two 30-mm DEFA cannon instead of four machine-guns, and featured Doppler navigation and a Position and Homing Indicator. The G91R/3 was the first subject of the licence-production agreement between Fiat and FUS in Germany: of the total of 344 West German aircraft, 74 were built by Fiat (with 12 assembled by

Dornier) and the remaining 270 in Germany as the first jet warplane produced in that country since 1945. The first Dornier-built G91R/3 flew on 20 July 1965 and the last in May 1966.

The G91R/3 became operational in West Germany in May 1962, and served initially at Husum and Pferdsfeld with, respectively, JBG 41 and 42. These units later became LKG 41 and 42 in the light attack and close support roles, and were complemented by LKG 43 and 44 at Oldenburg and Leipheim, respectively, with AKG 53 and 54 operating in the reconnaissance role from Erding and Oldenburg. The G91R/3 was also operated by a number of lesser Luftwaffe operational and training units.

Two G91R/3s were thoroughly evaluated by the US Army during 1961 although no production order followed. USAF insistence that the Army should not operate its own fixed-wing aircraft had prevailed.

The G91R was retired from West German front-line operational service from the mid-1970s as it was progressively replaced by the Dassault/Dornier Alpha Jet A and McDonnell Douglas F-4F Phantom II. The last aircraft left service in the mid-1980s.

The final G91R variant was the **G91R/4**, which was basically the G91R/3 with G91R/1 armament and some equipment changes. Some 50 were ordered with US financing for delivery to Greece and Turkey under the terms of the Mutual Aid

Program, but the aircraft were then diverted to the West German air force, thus beginning the final chapter in the G91R's operational history.

Later, the Luftwaffe's remaining 40 G91R/4s were transferred to the Portuguese air force, and were supplemented by some 40 G91R/3s which subsequently became surplus to Luftwaffe requirements. The Portuguese aircraft saw considerable operational use in the country's wars of the late 1960s and early 1970s, fighting independence movements in its colonies of Angola and Mozambique in southern Africa, as well as Guinea-Bissau in western Africa. The last Portuguese G91Rs were not retired until 1993.

Receiving almost 400 aircraft, with over 200 of them produced under licence, the Luftwaffe was the largest operator of the G91. Nicknamed 'Gina', the G91 served in the light attack and weapons training roles.

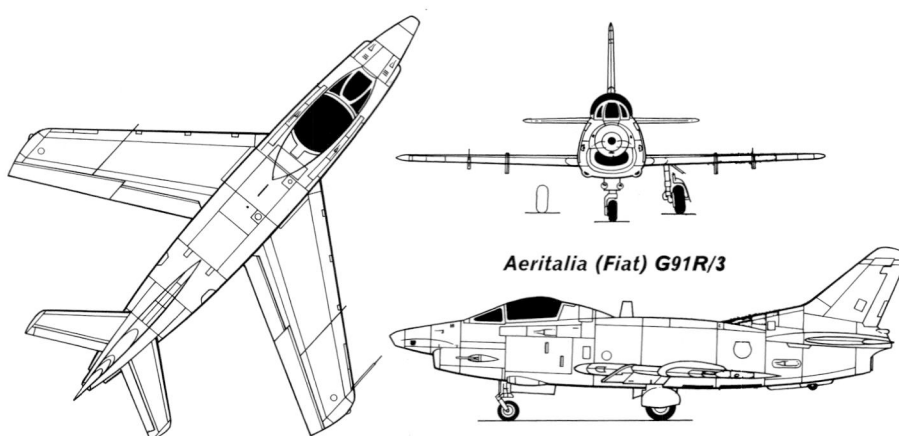

Aeritalia (Fiat) G91R/3

SPECIFICATION

Aeritalia (Fiat) G91R/1

Type: single-seat tactical attack and reconnaissance fighter

Powerplant: one 5,000-lb st (22.24-kN) Fiat-built Bristol Siddeley BOr.3 Orpheus Mk 803-2 turbojet

Performance: maximum speed at sea level 668 mph (1075 km/h) and 675 mph (1086 km/h) at 5,000 ft (1525 m); economical cruising speed 403 mph (650 km/h); initial climb rate 6,003 ft (1830 m) per minute; service ceiling 42,978 ft (13100 m); ferry range 1,150 miles (1850 km) with drop tanks; combat radius 200 miles (320 km) with standard fuel and maximum warload

Weight: empty 6,834 lb (3100 kg); normal take-off 11,993 lb (5440 kg); maximum

take-off 12,125 lb (5500 kg)

Dimensions: span 28 ft 1 in (8.56 m); length 33 ft 9¼ in (10.30 m); height 13 ft 1¼ in (4.00 m); wing area 176.75 sq ft (16.42 m²)

Armament: four 0.5-in (12.7-mm) Colt-Browning machine-guns with 300 rounds per gun and up to 1,500 lb (680 kg) of disposable stores carried on four underwing hardpoints, and generally comprising two 500-lb (227-kg) and two 250-lb (113-kg) bombs, multiple launchers for 2-, 2.75- or 3.2-in (50-, 70- or 81-mm) unguided rockets, pods each containing one 0.5-in (12.7-mm) machine-gun and 150 rounds, AS.20 or AS.30 wire-guided air-to-surface missiles, and tactical nuclear weapons

---

The Aeronautica Militare Italiana (Italian air force) was a major operator of the G91R/1 variant of the 'Gina'. Illustrated is a G91R/1A of 51ª Aerobrigata, 14º Stormo.

Portugal's G91R/3s and R/4s saw extensive combat service in Africa during the late-1960s and into the 1970s. They subsequently received a two-tone green/brown wrap-round camouflage.

Aeritalia (Fiat) G91T

The **G91T** two-seat version of the G91 ground-attack fighter evolved during 1958 as a transonic trainer for the flying and weapons training role. It was designed as a minimum-change development of the G91R to yield an aircraft suitable for both training and secondary combat tasks. The airframe was similar to that of the basic G91R except for a slight lengthening of the fuselage that allowed the incorporation of the new cockpit. Pupil and instructor were seated in tandem on Martin-Baker Mk W4 ejection seats, as used in the Aeritalia G91R.

Flying for the first time on 31 May 1960, the G91T was powered by an Orpheus Mk 803-2 turbojet. A total of 76 **G91T/1** aircraft was delivered to the Italian air force, whose main operator of the Aeritalia type was the Scuola Volo Basico Avanzato Aviogetti, home-based at Amendola.

Differing only in equipment changes, a total of 66 **G91T/3** aircraft was built for the West German air force, comprising 44 Italian- and 22 German-built machines. The last Dornier-built G91/3 was delivered to the Luftwaffe on 19 October 1972. A

Considerable numbers of G91Ts served with the West German air force. The aircraft was a useful performer in the advanced and weapons training roles for pilots going on to the G91R and F-104G Starfighter.

G91T/4 version, based on the G91T/1 but having the avionics of the Lockheed F-104G Starfighter, was never built.

The G91T remained in service with the West

German air force into the late 1980s (24 served with the civilian-operated Condor Flugdienst at Husum up to 1992 to provide target facilities for the military), and until late 1993 with the Portuguese air force, which flew at least 10 second-hand German aircraft. The

Portuguese air force latterly equipped its G91R and G91T aircraft with AIM-9L Sidewinder AAMs for the secondary air defence role. Some 50 aircraft remained in service with the Italian air force into the mid-1990s, before retirement in favour of the AMX(T).

Like the majority of Italian G91Ts, SA-23 was based at Amendola (Foggia) with the Scuola Volo Avanzato Aviogetti. It is shown as it appeared during 1966, with large patches of high-conspicuity Dayglo orange paint.

SPECIFICATION	
Aeritalia (Fiat) G91T/1 generally similar to the **G91R/1** except for the following: **Performance:** maximum level speed 640 mph (1030 km/h) at 5,000 ft (1525 m), service ceiling 40,000 ft (12190 m) **Weights:** basic operating 8,520 lb (3865 kg), normal take-off	12,125 lb (5500 kg), maximum take-off 13,338 lb (6050 kg) **Dimensions:** length 38 ft 3½ in (11.67 m), height 14 ft 7¼ in (4.45 m) **Armament:** two 0.5-in (12.7-mm) machine-guns and two underwing hardpoints for light bombs, rocket pods, or drop tanks

Aeritalia (Fiat/Alenia) G91Y

Whereas the original G91R fighter-bomber and tactical reconnaissance aircraft was designed as a single-engined warplane to a NATO specification, the **G91Y** (or 'Yankee' as it is unofficially known) was developed by Fiat (which became Aeritalia in November 1969 and Alenia in December 1990) to meet an Italian air force requirement of 1965.

The aircraft was to be an improved version of the G91R offering greater warload, performance and operational survivability. Compared with the G91R, the 'Yankee' differed fundamentally in being twin-engined. Its power-plants were two J85 afterburning turbojets located side-by-side in a revised rear fuselage, which gave 63 per cent more thrust than the single-

engined arrangement of the G91R for only an 18 per cent increase in weight. This offered a significant boost to performance and warload-carrying capability. In order to increase combat radius, one engine could be shut down during the cruise phase of a mission. Fuel capacity of the fuselage and inner wing tanks was 704 Imp gal (3200 litres) compared to the G91R's figure of 354 Imp gal (1610 litres), and drop tanks could be carried on two wing pylons.

The G91Y retained the G91R's three-camera nose. It also had the later G91R variants' armament of two fixed forward-firing 30-mm DEFA cannon, but was capable of carrying an increased disposable warload. This included bombs of up to 1,000-lb (454-kg), napalm tanks, or

Four G91Ys of 32° Stormo photographed over Brindisi show the machine's obvious likeness to the older and less-capable G91R. Some of the Stormo's anti-shipping aircraft wore fearsome sharkmouths.

four rocket pods (seven- and 28-tube units for 2-in/50-mm rockets, or four-tube pods for 5-in/127-mm rockets). The avionics fit was also more comprehensive than that of

the G91R, and included a position and homing indicator, twin-axis gyro platform, Doppler navigation, air-data computer, radar altimeter and, as a considerable boost to the pilot's tactical

awareness, a HUD as an integral part of the nav/attack system.

Given the emphasis placed on the G91Y's STOL performance, provision was made for RATO (Rocket-Assisted Take-Off) units which could halve the take-off run, and an airfield arrester hook for use with SATS (Short Airfield for Tactical Support) installations. Operating from a semi-prepared surface, the G91Y could lift off in just 3,000 ft (915 m) without RATO units and land from 50 ft (15 m) in only 1,970 ft (600 m) without the hook.

With the obvious exception of the engine compartment, the G91Y's airframe was based on that of the G91T two-seat

Unlike its more widely used predecessor, the G91R, the G91Y was operated by only one country. The aircraft constituted a potent light-attack and reconnaissance force within the Aeronautica Militare Italiana, and this machine of 8° Stormo shows a typical underwing load of tanks and rocket pods.

trainer, although accommodation was provided for only a pilot in an armoured, air-conditioned, pressurised cockpit fitted with a Martin-Baker zero/zero ejection seat. The wing had a sweep of 38°, and full-span slats and electrically actuated slotted flaps were fitted on its leading and trailing edges, respectively. Two airbrakes were hinged beneath the centre fuselage, and the entire rear fuselage (together with the variable-incidence trimming tailplane) was removed for engine access.

The first of two prototypes made its maiden flight on 27 December 1966 at Caselle. An order for 20 pre-production aircraft, of which the first flew in July 1968, was followed by contracts for another 53 production aircraft. In the event, production ended after the delivery of 67 of the originally planned total of 75 aircraft. A projected **G91YT** two-seat advanced trainer was not developed, and the sole **G91YS** was demonstrated to the Swiss air arm without gaining an order. Deliveries to the Italian air force's 8° Stormo at Cervia began in May 1970 for a single oversized squadron (101° Gruppo), while the 13° Gruppo of the 32° Stormo at Brindisi re-equipped from August 1973, assigning some of its aircraft the anti-ship role and decorating them with sharkmouth markings. It was originally envisaged that the G91Y would be gradually replaced by the AMX from 1987, but delays with the service introduction of the latter meant that the above units were still operational on the G91Y early in 1994, with service scheduled to last into 1998. However, they were retired in 1996.

Aeritalia (Fiat) G91Y

SPECIFICATION

Aeritalia (Fiat/Alenia) G91Y
Type: single-seat tactical attack and reconnaissance fighter
Powerplant: two 4,080-lb st (18.15-kN) with afterburning General Electric J85-GE-13A turbojets
Performance: maximum speed 645 mph (1038 km/h) at 30,000 ft (9145 m) and 691 mph (1111 km/h) at sea level; cruising speed 497 mph (800 km/h) at 35,000 ft (10670 m); initial climb rate 17,000 ft (5180 m) per minute with afterburning; climb to 42,000 ft (12200 m) in 4 minutes 30 seconds with afterburning; service ceiling 41,000 ft (12500 m); ferry range 2,175 miles (3500 km) with drop tanks; typical combat radius 373 miles (600 km) on a lo-lo-lo attack mission with a 2,910-lb (1320-kg) warload
Weights: empty equipped 8,598 lb (3900 kg); normal take-off 17,196 lb (7800 kg); maximum take-off 19,180 lb (8700 kg)
Dimensions: span 29 ft 6½ in (9.01 m); length 38 ft 3½ in (11.67 m); height 14 ft 6 in (4.43 m); wing area 195.16 sq ft (18.13 m²)
Armament: two 30-mm DEFA cannon with 125 rounds per gun, and up to 4,000 lb (1914 kg) of disposable stores

Aer Lualdi L.55, L.57 and L.59

Aer Lualdi & C. S.p.A. was founded in 1953 for the design, development and production of Italian helicopters designed by Carlo Lualdi but based on the Rotor-Matic type of main rotor patented in the USA by Hiller Aircraft Corp. Aer Lualdi soon became the Italian licensee for this rotor system. The first Italian helicopter with this type of rotor was the 85-hp (63.4-kW) Continental-powered **Lualdi-Tassotti ES 53**, whose rotor was improved by a Lualdi gyroscopic system that was claimed to provide smoother flight and easier handling characteristics.

Experience with this machine allowed Lualdi to progress to the design of the **L.55**, which introduced a fully streamlined fuselage structure and was powered by a 180-hp (134-kW) Lycoming O-360 flat-four piston engine. Lualdi then developed the two-seat L.55 into the more capable **L.57** with a larger-diameter main rotor, a tail rotor of glass-reinforced plastic construction, and a number of operational improvements including the provision of an autopilot.

Lualdi next moved forward into the production stage of his helicopter programme with the **L.59**. It was in essence a four-seat development of the L.57 with an uprated powerplant and front and rear sets of paired seats in an extensively glazed cabin accessed by a car-type door on each side. The helicopter was of light alloy construction with a monocoque boom, and in configuration was of the pod-and-boom type with a two-bladed main rotor of light alloy construction and a two-bladed tail rotor of glass-reinforced plastic construction. The landing gear comprised a pair of tubular metal skids with upturned forward ends and, for ground handling, wheels that were otherwise carried under the boom just forward of the guard below the tail rotor.

The 260-hp (194-kW) IO-470-D engine was installed in the nose and discharged its spent gases via a substantial central exhaust under the fuselage between the skids. Fuel was drawn from a pair of streamlined tanks mounted side-by-side on short pylons above the cabin and to either side of the main rotor pylon. Provision was also made for the carriage of two litters, and for the addition of a rescue hoist. Two L.59 prototypes were manufactured by Macchi at Varese, with technical assistance from Sud-Aviation. A moderately successful test programme was flown from 1960, but, although early plans had been made for the construction of an initial batch of 50 production helicopters, the L.59 programme was terminated as considerably more capable light helicopters became available. The first prototype was bought by the Italian army's air corps for evaluation in the observation role and was later transferred to a museum.

Aer Lualdi ceased trading in the period 1963-64.

SPECIFICATION

Aer Lualdi L.59
Type: four-seat light general-purpose helicopter
Powerplant: one 260-hp (194-kW) Continental IO-470-D flat-six piston engine
Performance: maximum speed 99 mph (160 km/h) at optimum altitude; cruising speed 86 mph (139 km/h); initial climb rate 820 ft (250 m) per minute; absolute ceiling 19,355 ft (5900 m); hovering ceiling 9,515 ft (2900 m) in ground effect and 5,575 ft (1700 m) out of ground effect; endurance 3 hours 30 minutes
Weights: empty 1,631 lb (740 kg); maximum take-off 2,646 lb (1200 kg)
Dimensions: main rotor diameter 34 ft 9½ in (10.60 m); fuselage length 29 ft 9½ in (9.08 m); height 9 ft 10 in (3.00 m); main rotor disc area 949.92 sq ft (88.25 m²)

Aermacchi (Lockheed) AL.60

Under the name Conestoga, 10 AL.60 C-5s were supplied to the Central African Republic from 1971. The aircraft proved ideal for bush flying.

All the design work on this aircraft was carried out in the United States by Lockheed, which first flew the prototype in 1959. Financial considerations persuaded the company to offer the type for licensed construction abroad. Lockheed-Azcarte in Mexico built 18 as the **LASA-60** in 1960, for the Fuerza Aérea Mexicana, but the chief licensee was Italy's Aermacchi. With room for six people in the cabin, and good rough-field performance, the **AL.60** was also suitable for the casevac role. The original aircraft was improved to become the **AL.60C** by uprating the engine and adding a parachute door. It was this version, with its associated tailwheel undercarriage, which was eventually sold, as the **AL.60C-5 Conestoga**, to the Central African Republic (two remained late in 1997) and Mauretania (one remained in late 1997). A second version, the **AL.60F-5 Trojan** with tricycle undercarriage, was sold to the Rhodesian air force.

SPECIFICATION

Aermacchi (Lockheed) AL.60F-5 Conestoga/Trojan
Type: eight-seat utility aircraft
Powerplant: one Textron Lycoming IO-720-A1A rated at 400 hp (298 kW)
Performance: maximum level speed 'clean' at sea level 135 kt (156 mph; 251 km/h); maximum cruising speed at 10,000 ft (3050 m) 125 kt (144 mph; 232 km/h); economical cruising speed at 5,000 ft (1525 m) 94 kt (108 mph; 174 km/h); maximum rate of climb at sea level 1,085 ft (331 m) per minute; service ceiling 13,615 ft (4150 m); take-off run 645 ft (196 m) at maximum take-off weight; take-off distance to 50 ft (15 m) 1,100 ft (335 m) at maximum take-off weight; landing distance from 50 ft (15 m) 845 ft (258 m) at normal landing weight
Range: 560 nm (645 miles; 1037 km)
Fuel and load: internal fuel 75.9 Imp gal (345 litres); external fuel none; maximum payload 1,440 lb (653 kg)
Weights: empty 2,394 lb (1086 kg); operating empty 2,731 lb (1239 kg); maximum take-off 4,500 lb (2041 kg)
Dimensions: wing span 39 ft 4 in (11.99 m); aspect ratio 7.35; wing area 210.44 sq ft (19.55 m²); length 28 ft 10½ in (8.80 m); height 10 ft 10 in (3.30 m)

Aermacchi AM.3

Intended to replace ageing Cessna L-19 Bird Dogs then serving with the Italian army, the **AM.3** high-wing observation/liaison aircraft was a joint venture by Aerfer (later Aeritalia) and Aermacchi. Forming the basis of its design were the wings and tailplane of the Aermacchi AL.60, allied to a revised fin and a new narrower, low-drag fuselage built by Aerfer.

Two AM.3 prototypes (I-AEAN and I-RAIC) were built; allocated the designation **MB-335A**, the first (assembled by Aermacchi) made its initial flight on 12 May 1967, and was followed by the Aerfer-built second prototype on 12 August 1968. The AM.3 was evaluated extensively by the Italian army but as no production order was as yet forthcoming, Aefer and Aermacchi began develop-

ment of an improved AM.3.

The prototypes were powered by the 340-hp (254-kW) Continental GTSIO-520-C flat-six engine, but were later fitted with the Piaggio-built Lycoming GSO-480B1B6. This was fitted to production standard aircraft, resulting in the redesignation **AM.3C**.

The prototype AM.3C (I-TAAA) was rolled out almost exactly five years after the initial flight of the first AM.3 prototype and incorporated a number of significant modifications. The outer wing panels were lengthened by a total of 3 ft 2½ in (0.98 m), raising gross wing area by 14.21 sq ft (1.32 m²); the nose was lengthened and refined aerodynamically; new fairings were added under the fuselage to provide attachment points

for the wing struts and mainwheel legs.

The AM.3C's cabin was optimised to offer good visibility at all times. The Plexiglass windows were bulged laterally and extended very low on the cockpit sides. The nose sloped sharply to give good forward view even when taxiing. The cabin normally accommodated a pilot and co-pilot in tandem with dual controls. A third seat at the rear could be removed to accommodate a stretcher or freight, with access via three doors in the sides of the cabin.

The AM.3C's roles were envisaged as forward air control (FAC), armed patrol, helicopter escort, liaison and light transport, photo reconnaissance, battlefield illumination and casualty evacuation.

The anticipated Italian army order did not materialize as the SIAI-Marchetti SM.1019 was selected in preference to the AM.3C. Provision of a single NATO M-4A stores attachment rack under each wing made the AM.3 suitable as a light tactical ground support aircraft. This feature was almost certainly responsible for sales to two export customers. The South African Air Force purchased 40 AM.3Cs, the aircraft being delivered between May 1972 and December 1974, while a further three were delivered to Rwanda.

In SAAF service the aircraft was known as the **Bosbok**. Operated by No. 41 Sqn at Johannesburg

One of the prototype AM.3s was briefly evaluated by the USAF, Army and USM, as part of their Pave-COIN requirement for a FA aircraft.

and by No. 42 Sqn at Potcheftsroom in the army co-operation and FAC roles, Bosboks were used extensively during 'externals' – South African anti-guerilla operations in Namibia and Angola – in the early to mid-1980s. They were especially valuable in Namibia where there was relatively little threat from ground fire. SAAF defence

cuts during the early 1990s forced the retirement of the Bosbok by September 1992. Two examples were preserved while the remainder were sold to civil operators. The 1994 civil war in Rwanda saw the destruction of much of that air force's equipment and it is highly unlikely that any AM.3Cs remain operational in Rwandan service.

SPECIFICATION

Aermacchi AM.3C

Type: two-seat light tactical support/observation aircraft
Powerplant: one 340-hp (254-kW) Piaggio-Lycoming GSO-480B1B6 six-cylinder horizontally-opposed air-cooled piston engine with mechanical supercharger
Performance: maximum speed at 8,005 ft (2440 m) 173 mph (278 km/h); cruising speed at 75 per cent power at 8,005 ft (2440 m) 153 mph (246 km/h); stalling speed 48 mph (77 km/h) (flaps extended, reduced power); climb to 9,850 ft (3302 m) in 7 minutes 30 seconds; service ceiling 27,560 ft (8400 m); take-off run 279 ft (85 m); landing run 217 ft (66 m); maximum range at cruising speed (with 30-min reserves) 615 miles (990 km)

Weights: empty 2,381 lb (1080 kg); maximum take-off (with underwing weapons) 3,748 lb (1700 kg)
Dimensions: wing span 41 ft 5⅝ in (12.64 m); length 28 ft 7¾ in (8.73 m); height 8 ft 11 in (2.72 m); wing area 219.2 sq ft (20.26 m²)
Armament: total weapons load of 750 lb (340 kg) carried on two underwing hardpoints; stores include MATRA twin 0.3-in (7.62-mm) machine-gun pods, General Electric 0.3-in (7.62-mm) Minigun pods; MATRA rocket launchers with 6 x 2.75-in (70-mm) or 7 x 2-in (50-mm) FFAR rockets, light cluster bombs; Nord AS.11 or AS.12 wire-guided ASMs; 250 lb (113-kg) general-purpose bombs; target identification and marking bombs

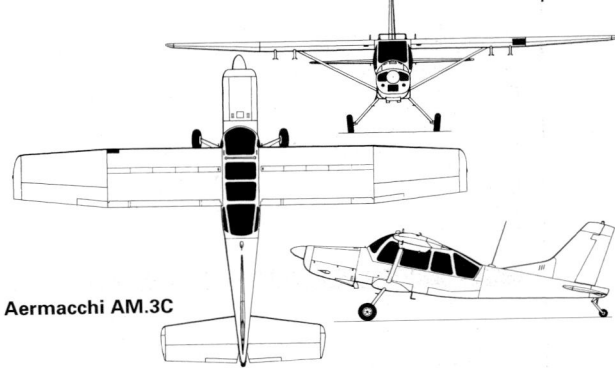

Aermacchi AM.3C

Aermacchi MB-326

The Ghana Air Force was one of the earliest foreign MB-326 operators, receiving nine MB-326Fs from mid-1965 for service with the training school at Tamale. The five survivors have been placed in storage.

In an unbroken history dating back to the period before World War I, Aeronautica Macchi has produced more than 7,000 aircraft of its own design; approximately ten per cent of that total have been examples of the **MB-326** family of jet trainers and light attack aircraft which, along with the Hunting (BAC) Jet Provost and Aérospatiale (Fouga) Magister, is one of the classics of its type and remained in production for two decades.

Dr Ing. Ermanno Bazzocchi, Aermacchi's technical director and chief engineer, began design work on the MB-326 as a two-seat basic trainer during 1954, and the first of two prototypes flew on 10 December 1957. This aircraft was powered by one 1,750-lb st (7.78-kN) Bristol Siddeley (later Rolls-Royce) Viper 8 turbojet, but the second prototype and

the 15 pre-production aircraft ordered for the Aeronautica Militare Italiana (AMI, or Italian air force) were each powered by the first standard engine, the Viper ASV.11 turbojet rated at 2,500 lb st (11.12 kN).

Following its acceptance of these aircraft, the AMI began to receive 85 production trainers during February 1962. Intended for all stages of flying training, the MB-326 is based on an airframe that is simple and robust. Instructor and student pilot sit in tandem in a pressurised cabin on lightweight ejection seats, the instructor's seat to the rear being slightly higher than the student in the front seat.

The MB-326 has been built in many variants, and from the beginning of the programme was seen as possessing potential for development with a light attack capability. This was

first offered in the proposed **MB-326A** variant with six underwing hardpoints for a variety of external stores, but the AMI at that time had no requirement for such a type. However, orders for similar aircraft were received from Ghana and Tunisia for nine **MB-326F** and eight **MB-326B** aircraft respectively; four unarmed **MB-326D** trainers were built as pilot trainers for Alitalia, the Italian state airline. The **MB-326H** with full armament capability was assembled or licence-

built in Australia by CAC (Commonwealth Aircraft Corporation) as the **CA-30** for the Royal Australian Air Force and Navy (87 and 10 aircraft respectively). The last of the early versions were 135 of a total of 151 **MB-326M** aircraft assembled or licence-built in the Transvaal by the Atlas Aircraft Corporation for the South African Air Force, by which the type is known as the **Impala Mk 1**. Some 16 complete aircraft were delivered by Macchi from June 1966, and the first 40 of the Atlas-assembled

aircraft contained Italian components.

The more powerful Viper ASV.20 engine was introduced early in 1967 to create the **MB-326G**: in combination with a strengthened airframe, the uprated powerplant allowed the carriage of a warload of 4,000 lb (1814 kg), twice the weight of that possible in the earlier variants. The MB-326G was built as the **MB-326GB** for the Argentine navy (eight) and the air forces of Zaire (17) and Zambia (22), while EMBRAER in Brazil licence-

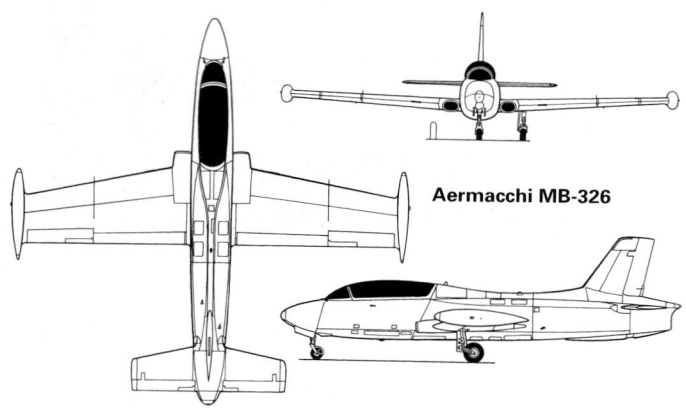

Aermacchi MB-326

The RAN's surviving 'Macchis' were transferred to the RAAF. Now replaced on advanced training units, Australia's remaining MB-326Hs are used for fighter support, including attack lead-in training.

built 182 similar **MB-326GC** aircraft for the air forces of Brazil (167 **AT-26 Xavante**), Paraguay (nine) and Togo (six). Eleven ex-Brazilian EMB-326GBs were later transferred to the Argentine navy air arm in 1983 to help offset its losses in the Falklands war of 1982.

Aermacchi delivered to the AMI six **MB-326E**s with the basic airframe of the MB-326GB but the lower-rated Viper 11 of the MB-326, and also converted six earlier MB-326s to the same configuration. The final two-seat version was the **MB-326L** advanced trainer that was based upon the single-seat MB-326K (see below): two were supplied to Dubai and

four to the Tunisian air force.

The delivery of the final EMB-326 in February 1983 completed MB-326 production at the 761st aircraft.

By early-1998 the MB-326 was becoming obsolescent and had been withdrawn from service by Ghana and Italy. It remains in service with the Argentine navy (16), Brazil (50 EMB-326), Paraguay (nine including two transferred from Brazil), Togo (four), Tunisia (seven), Republic of Congo, latterly Zaire (nine, estimated) and Zambia (10, estimated).

The eight survivors of the Australian navy's

CA-30s were transferred to the RAAF in mid-1983. By 1985, a total of 82 'Macchis' had been cycled through a life-extension programme which added new components to the wing and fuselage structures, as well as including cockpit and avionics upgrades.

The discovery of structural problems has served to hasten further the departure of the type from RAAF service so that only 28 examples currently remain operational. In South Africa, the once-prominent Impala Mk 1 force has been reduced from 115 in 1994 to just 37 in early-1998.

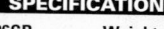

SPECIFICATION

Aermacchi MB-326GB
Type: two-seat basic/advanced trainer and light attack aircraft
Powerplant: one Rolls-Royce (Bristol Siddeley) Viper 20 Mk 540 turbojet rated at 3,410-lb st (15.17-kN)
Performance: maximum level speed 'clean' at optimum altitude 468 kt (539 mph; 867 km/h); cruising speed at optimum altitude 430 kt (495 mph; 797 km/h); maximum rate of climb at sea level 3,100 ft (945 m) per minute at maximum take-off weight; service ceiling 39,000 ft (11890 m) at 10,500 lb (4763 kg); combat radius 350 nm (403 miles; 648 km) on a hi-lo-hi attack mission with a 1,695-lb (769-kg) warload

Weights: basic operating 5,640 lb (2558 kg); normal take-off 9,805 lb (4447 kg); maximum take-off 11,500 lb (5216 kg)
Dimensions: wing span 33 ft 3½ in (10.15 m) without tip tanks and 35 ft 7 in (10.85 m) with tip tanks; wing aspect ratio 6.08; overall length 35 ft ¼ in (10.67 m); height 12 ft 2 in (3.72 m); wing area 208.29 sq ft (19.35 m²)
Armament: provision for 4,000 lb (1814 kg) of weapons on six underwing hardpoints, including AS.11 or AS.12 ASMs; 500-lb (227-kg) GP bombs; MATRA SA-10 30-mm ADEN cannon pods; 0.5-in (12.7-mm) and 0.3-in (7.62-mm) gun pods; 1.46-in (37-mm), 2.75-in (70-mm), 3.15-in (80-mm) and 5-in (127-mm) rocket pods

Aermacchi MB-326K

Early use of the MB-326 had revealed that it was an excellent and stable weapons platform, as was later proved by the success of its dedicated light-attack variants. However, it was not until 22 August 1970 that Aermacchi flew the first prototype of its single-seat development intended for the ground attack and close air support roles. Originally to have been designated **MB-336** as a result of its changes from MB-326 two-seaters, this

retained the same Viper ASV.20 Mk 540 as late-production MB-326s.

It had been intended to provide even more power in the full-production variant, so the second prototype introduced the Viper Mk 632-43 turbojet. Increased power allowed the incorporation of more potent fixed forward-firing armament in the form of two 30-mm DEFA cannon installed in the lower part of the forward fuselage. The increased fuselage volume

gained by elimination of the second seat provided space for the ammunition magazines for the cannon, extra fuel tankage, and the avionics formerly located in the nose. In most other respects the airframe of what was finally designated as the **MB-326K** was similar to that of the MB-326GB. Some additional localised structural reinforcement was introduced to compensate for the increased stress of low-level manoeuvres, for which hydraulically servo-powered ailerons were also provided.

Six underwing pylons were provided for carriage of up to 4,000 lb (1814 kg) of a variety of external stores.

Although the test and development programme proceeded without major problems, there was a gap of almost two years before the first order was finalised for three MB-326K aircraft to provide Dubai with a counter-insurgency flight. Later deliveries included three more aircraft for Dubai, with others for Ghana (six), Tunisia (eight) and Zaire (six).

Following previous experience with manufacture of MB-326M trainers, South Africa subsequently acquired a licence in 1974 to produce the MB-326K, commencing with assembly of seven Italian-built kits and progressing to almost

90 per cent manufacture in South Africa, where the type is known as the **Atlas Impala Mk 2**. The aircraft was used extensively during South Africa's anti-guerilla conflicts in Angola and Namibia.

In the first half of 1998 the MB-326K remained in service with Dubai (three), Ghana (four), Republic of Congo, latterly Zaire (six), South Africa (37) and Tunisia (two).

The attack version of Aermacchi's jet trainer did not prove as successful in export terms. Dubai was the major operator with six aircraft procured.

SPECIFICATION

Aermacchi MB-326K
Type: single-seat close air support and tactical reconnaissance aircraft
Powerplant: one Piaggio-built Rolls-Royce (Bristol Siddeley) Viper Mk 632-43 turbojet rated at 4,000 lb st (17.79 kN)
Performance: maximum level speed 480 kt (553 mph; 890 km/h) at 5,000 ft (1525 m); maximum rate of climb at sea level 6,500 ft (1980 m) per minute; service ceiling 47,000 ft (14325 m); range more than 1,149 nm (1,323 miles; 2130 km) with two drop tanks; combat radius 145 nm (167 miles; 268 km) on a lo-lo-lo attack mission with a 2,822-lb (1280-kg) warload
Weights: empty equipped 6,885 lb (3123 kg); normal take-off 10,240 lb (4645 kg); maximum take-off 13,000 lb (5897 kg)

Dimensions: span 35 ft 7 in (10.85 m) over tip tanks; length 35 ft 0¼ in (10.67 m); height 12 ft 2 in (3.72 m); wing area 208.29 sq ft (19.35 m²)
Armament: two 30-mm DEFA 553 cannon with 125 rounds per gun, and up to 4,000 lb (1814 kg) of external stores on six underwing hardpoints; stores include 500-lb (227-kg), 750-lb (340-kg) and 1,000-lb (454-kg) general-purpose bombs; napalm containers; 0.3-in (7.62-mm) Minigun pods; AS.11 or AS.12 ASMs; MATRA R550 Magic short-range AAMs for limited point interception capability; various launchers for 37-mm, 68-mm (2.68-in), 100-mm (3.94-in), 2.75-in (70-mm) or 5-in (127-mm) unguided rockets or, on the innermost port hardpoint, a four-camera reconnaissance pod

Aermacchi MB-339A

From experience gained in manufacturing more than 750 examples of the highly-successful MB-326 jet trainer, Aermacchi developed a successor version which differed mainly by having a new and deeper forward fuselage section. This rectified the MB-326's limited visibility from the rear seat by raising it.

In 1972 Aermacchi received a study contract from the Aeronautica Militare Italiana (AMI, or Italian air force) for a second-generation jet trainer to succeed the MB-326 and Aeritalia G91T. No fewer than nine separate design studies were undertaken. Seven were **MB-338** versions which featured numerous engine variations of single or twin Rolls-Royce Viper, SNECMA Larzac, Rolls-Royce/SNECMA Adour, Rolls-Royce RB.401 and Garrett TFE731 turbojets or turbofans. Most of the designs offered little advance in performance over late model MB-326s or offered a marked increase in performance but only at a considerably higher initial cost. The most encouraging studies considered by the AMI were the two proposed models of the **MB-339**, powered by either a single Larzac turbofan (**MB-339L**) or a single Viper Mk 600 series turbojet (**MB-339V**). Moreover, the MB-339's airframe shared much in common with that of the MB-326K, as the only major changes at this stage were the new forward fuselage

Survivors of the AMI's 107 MB-339As operate mainly with the 212º and 213º Gruppi of the 61ª Brigata Aerea at Lecce Galatina. Most have now received an overall light grey camouflage scheme.

(with its raised rear seat, modified cockpit and much superior all-round view), enlarged vertical tail surfaces and two outward-canted ventral strakes.

In February 1975, the AMI decided to adopt the version powered by a single Viper 632-43 turbojet developed jointly by Rolls-Royce and Fiat Aviazione, to meet its requirements.

The first of two **MB-339X** prototypes (MM588) made its maiden flight on 12 August 1976. The second prototype (MM589) took to the air on 20 May 1977 with minor detail modifications. Compared to the MB-326, the MB-339 has a more comprehensive avionics fit, including TACAN navigation computer, blind landing instrumentation, IFF, and both VHF and UHF radio. Fuselage and permanent wingtip tanks provide a total 2,425 lb (1100 kg) of internal fuel, and the middle pylon under each wing can carry one 71.5-Imp gal (325-litre) drop tank.

The MB-339A can carry up to 4,497 lb (2040 kg) of external stores for weapons training and secondary light ground-attack missions.

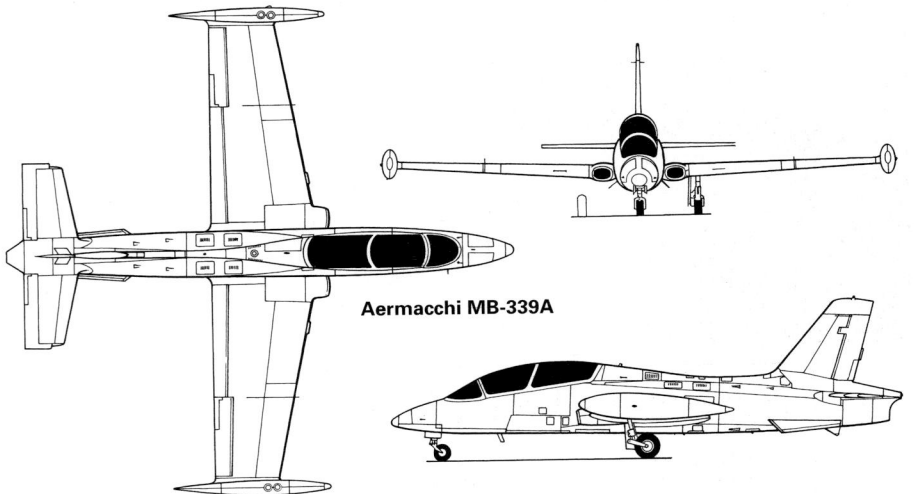

Aermacchi MB-339A

SPECIFICATION

Aermacchi MB-339A

Type: two-seat basic and advanced flying trainer with weapons training and light attack capabilities

Powerplant: one Piaggio-built Rolls-Royce (Bristol Siddeley) Viper Mk 632-43 turbojet rated at 4,000 lb st (17.79 kN)

Performance: maximum level speed 441 kt (508 mph; 817 km/h) at 30,000 ft (9145 m) and 485 kt (558 mph; 898 km/h) at sea level; range 950 nm (1,094 miles; 1760 km) with internal fuel; combat radius 320 nm (368 miles; 593 km) on a hi-lo-hi attack mission with four Mk 82 bombs and two drop tanks; maximum rate of climb at sea level 6,595 ft (2010 m) per minute; climb to 30,000 ft (9145 m) in 7 minutes

6 seconds; service ceiling 48,000 ft (14630 m)

Weights: empty equipped 6,889 lb (3125 kg); normal take-off 9,700 lb (4400 kg); maximum take-off 12,996 lb (5895 kg)

Dimensions: span 35 ft 7½ in (10.86 m) over tip tanks; length 36 ft (10.97 m); height 13 ft 1¾ in (3.99 m); wing area 207.74 sq ft (19.30 m²)

Armament: up to 4,500 lb (2040 kg) of external stores carried on six underwing hardpoints; stores include Mk 80 series GP bombs up to 1,000-lb (454-kg), 30-mm DEFA cannon or 12.7-mm gun pods, 7.62-mm Minigun pods, pods containing rockets of various calibre, BAP-100 anti-runway bombs, MATRA R550 Magic 2 or AIM-9L/P AAMs

Flight testing of the two prototypes preceded the delivery of an initial 100 **MB-339A** production aircraft (and one prototype raised to production standard) to the AMI, with which the type entered service in August 1979 at the Scuola Volo Basico Iniziale su Aviogetti at Lecce. Nineteen MB-339As were delivered in **MB-339PAN** form, with their tip tanks removed and smoke-generating equipment added, for service from 1982 with the 313º Gruppo Pattuglia Aerobatica Nazionale, better known as the 'Frecce Tricolori', the Italian national aerobatic team. A further five MB-339As were subsequently converted to this

configuration to offset attrition. Another AMI special version is the **MB-339RM** (*Radiomisure*, or radio calibration) aircraft, four of which (converted from AMI MB-339As) were operated with the 8ª Squadriglia of the 14º Stormo RM, the radio aids and electronic warfare wing based at Pratica di Mare. They were withdrawn in the late 1980s and have been reroled as standard trainers.

Deliveries of the main batch of MB-339As ended in 1987, and were followed by a further final batch of six aircraft as attrition replacements in 1994.

The MB-339A has not achieved the same level of success as its predecessor

but has still managed respectable export sales to the Argentine navy (10), Dubai air wing (seven), and the air forces of Ghana (four), Malaysia (13), Nigeria (12) and Peru (16).

The MB-339's sole combat use to date came during the 1982 Falklands conflict when six of 10 **MB-339AA**s delivered to the Argentine navy were pressed into service as light attack aircraft.

In co-operation with Lockheed and Hughes, Aermacchi proposed a modified version of the MB-339 to meet the USAF and USN's requirement for a Joint Primary Aircraft Training System (JPATS). A former MB-339AA was converted to serve as the **T-Bird II** demonstrator (I-RAIB). Fitted with a 4,000-lb st (17.79-kN) Viper 680-582 engine, it made its initial flight on 8 April 1992. In June 1995 it was announced that the JPATS competition had been won by the Raytheon Beech Mk II, an improved and 'Americanised' version of the Pilatus PC-9. Further development of the T-Bird II was abandoned.

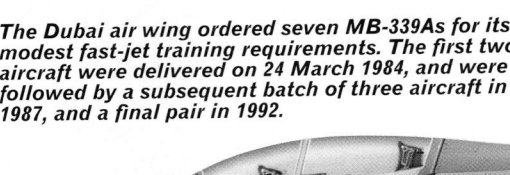

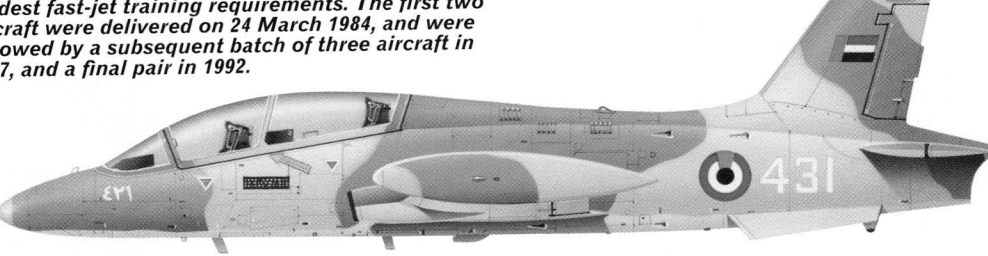

The Dubai air wing ordered seven MB-339As for its modest fast-jet training requirements. The first two aircraft were delivered on 24 March 1984, and were followed by a subsequent batch of three aircraft in 1987, and a final pair in 1992.

Aermacchi MB-339B/C

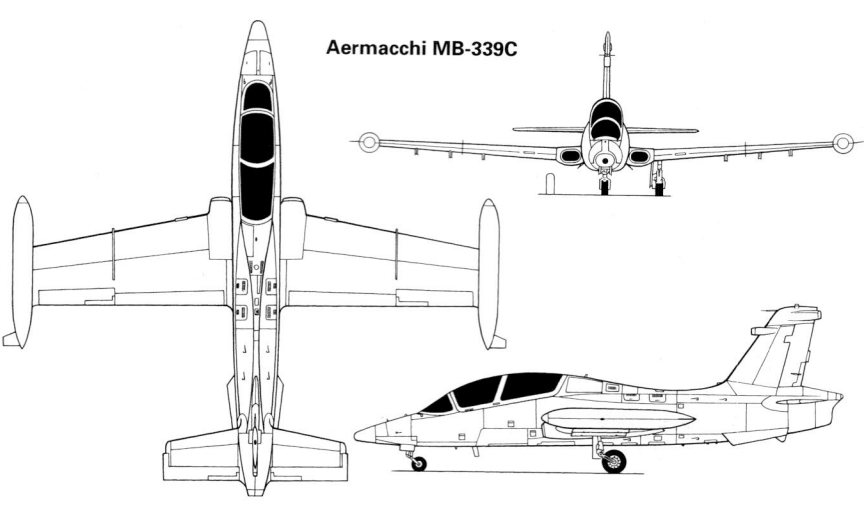

Aermacchi MB-339C

Further development of the MB-339A began in the early 1980s and initially led to the **MB-339B**. It was intended as an advanced trainer with enhanced light ground-attack capabilities. Aermacchi produced a demonstrator (I-GROW) which was first flown in 1984 with an uprated 4,400-lb st (19.57-kN) Viper 680-43 engine and enlarged tip tanks.

Further development of the MB-339B was curtailed in favour of an even more advanced MB-339, designed as a low-cost lead-in fighter trainer and light attack aircraft with advanced navigation/attack avionics. Development of this version was initiated at the request of the AMI, which was examining the possibility of supplementing its Tornado IDS fleet with simpler aircraft for the lower-cost

maintenance of combat proficiency. Aermacchi initially proposed an upgraded MB-339 designated **MB-340**, but the resulting modifications led to a variant with the designation **MB-339C**. It retains the MB-339B's uprated Viper powerplant and enlarged tip tanks but introduces a substantially upgraded avionics fit.

This includes a Litton LR80 twin-gyro inertial platform, GEC Avionics 620K tactical area navigation system, GEC AD-660 Doppler velocity sensor, Kaiser Sabre HUD/WAC (Head-Up Display/Weapons Aiming Computer), a stores management system, a FIAR/Ericsson P.0702 laser rangefinder, Aeritalia multi-function CRT (Cathode Ray Tube) display compatible with the AGM-65 Maverick TV-guided air-to-surface

missile, Elettronica ELT-156 radar warning receiver and Honeywell radar altimeter. The MB-339C also features revised nose contours, plus provision for a detachable refuelling probe.

As well as the AGM-65 weapon, the MB-339C is also equipped to launch stand-off anti-ship missiles such as the Marte 2 and AS.34 Kormoran, and laser-guided bombs.

The MB-339C prototype (I-AMDA) made its initial flight on 17 December 1985. The AMI was originally reported in early 1989 to be the launch customer with a requirement for 20 aircraft to serve in the operational and continuation training roles. The first production MB-339C (I-TRON) made its initial flight on 8 November 1989, but the sole customer to date for the type has been the Royal New Zealand Air Force. This service ordered 18 **MB-339CB**s in May 1990 to replace the BAC Strikemasters of No. 14 Squadron based at Ohakea. Initial deliveries began on

13 March 1991, followed by the remainder in 1992-93.

In 1986 the Italian government awarded Aermacchi a contract to integrate the OTO Melara Marte 2A anti-ship missile with the MB-339 to give AMI MB-339As a secondary wartime role. This was envisaged as the destruction of fast attack craft on the basis of target co-ordinates and launch data transmitted by Dassault Atlantic 1 maritime reconnaissance aircraft. Trials with this weapon began on a prototype **MB-339AM** (converted from an AMI MB-339A) on 24 April 1991. The MB-339AM is broadly equivalent to the MB-339C. Following successful Marte launches at the Salto di Quirra NATO firing range in Sardinia, the MB-339AM was qualified for an additional operational capability in early 1995. However, the AMI opted not to upgrade its MB-339As to this standard and instead chose to purchase new-build examples of the **MB-339CD (C Digital)** for advanced/lead-

in fighter training. This development of the MB-339C is powered by the lower-rated Viper Mk 632-43 turbojet and features even more advanced avionics, based on a MIL 1553B digital databus. They include a single central mission computer, a ring-laser gyro INS (inertial navigation system) with GPS update, and an EFIS (Electronic Flight Instrumentation System) cockpit with HOTAS (Hands On Throttle and Stick) controls, a wide-angle HUD, and three liquid-crystal cockpit MFDs (Multi-Function Displays).

Converted from an AMI MB-339A, the first pre-production MB-339CD was rolled out on 12 April 1996 and made its first flight 12 days later. Full AMI operational clearance is expected in early 1998 and deliveries of 15 MB-339CDs are scheduled to follow to the 61° Stormo at Lecce.

The sole export customer for the MB-339CD to date has been the Eritrean air force, which ordered six **MB-339CE**s, non-digital MB-339C variants fitted with the uprated Viper 680 engine. The first Eritrean aircraft were delivered in 1996. The **MB-339FD (Full Digital)** is the export equivalent of the MB-339CD which also has the uprated engine. It was offered to the Royal Australian Air Force as a replacement for its MB-326s but lost to the British Aerospace Hawk.

Total deliveries of two-seat MB-339s currently comprise 208 production aircraft, two prototypes and three demonstrator aircraft.

Known unofficially as 'Macchis', the RNZAF's MB-339CBs are used for jet conversion and lead-in fighter training. They can be armed with gun pods and Maverick ASMs for their secondary combat role.

SPECIFICATION

Aermacchi MB-339C
(generally similar to the MB-339A except in the following particulars)
Powerplant: one Piaggio-built Rolls-Royce (Bristol Siddeley) Viper Mk 680-43 turbojet rated at 4,400-lb st (19.57 kN)
Performance: range 1,060 nm (1,221 miles; 1965 km) with internal fuel; combat radius 270 nm (311 miles; 500 km) on a hi-lo-hi attack mission with four Mk 82 bombs and two drop tanks; maximum rate of climb at sea level 7,085 ft (2160 m) per minute; climb to 30,000 ft (9145 m) in 6 minutes 42 seconds; service ceiling 46,700 ft (14235 m)
Weights: empty equipped 7,562 lb (3430 kg); normal take-off 10,983 lb (4982 kg); maximum take-off 14,000 lb (6350 kg)
Dimensions: span 36 ft 9¾ in (11.22 m) over tip tanks; overall length 36 ft 10½ in (11.24 m); wing area 207.74 sq ft (19.30 m²)
Armament: up to 4,000 lb

(1814 kg) of external stores carried on six underwing hardpoints; typical weapons include two MATRA R550 Magic or AIM-9 Sidewinder AAMs, two AGM-65 Maverick ASMs, two Marte 2A or AS.34 Kormoran anti-ship missiles, two laser-guided bombs up to 1,000 lb (454 kg), six multiple launchers for 1.97-in (50-mm), 2.68-in (68-mm), 2.75-in (70-mm) and 3.20-in (81-mm) rockets, four multiple launchers for 3.94-in (100-mm) and 5-in (127-mm) rockets, four 1,000-lb (454-kg) free-fall or retarded bombs, six 750-, 500- or 250-lb (340-, 227- or 113-kg) free-fall or retarded bombs, cluster bombs of various types up to 1,000 lb (454 kg), and two Macchi pods each containing one 30-mm DEFA 553 cannon with 120 rounds or one 0.5-in (12.7-mm) M3 machine-gun with 350 rounds; provision for one reconnaissance pod with four 70-mm Vinten cameras

Aermacchi MB-339K Veltro 2

In April 1983 the maiden flight took place of a development MB-339 (I-GROW) fitted with an uprated Viper Mk 680-43. This engine offered an additional 450 lb st (2.00 kN) as a result of compressor modifications and had already been evaluated after retrofit in the second MB-339X prototype. I-GROW was intended as the starting point for the MB-339B trainer and the **MB-339K** single-seat light ground attack and close air support fighter. The latter was proposed as the MB-339 series' counterpart to the MB-326 series' MB-326K variant. The MB-339K was initially called **Veltro 2**, thus perpetuating the name given to the Macchi MC.205V Veltro (greyhound), which is generally regarded as the best Italian fighter of World War II; however, the name was dropped in 1989.

The MB-339K retained the MB-339A's airframe, except for a new forward fuselage whose increased volume provided room for avionics stowage, an auxiliary fuel tank and the installation of two internally mounted DEFA cannon. Avionics were also greatly enhanced, and included an ECM jammer pod, plus head-up and/or TV displays. The prototype MB-339K (I-BITE) was built as a private venture with the standard Viper Mk 632-43 turbojet as its powerplant.

Aermacchi subsequently developed an upgraded MB-339K incorporating a more powerful Viper Mk 680-43 turbojet, an integrated nav/attack system, stores management system, weapon-aiming computer and HUD.

Developed as a private venture, the MB-339K was a single-seat ground-attack derivative of the MB-339A trainer. It failed to achieve any sales and further development was halted in the early 1990s.

Despite intensive marketing, however, Aermacchi has received no orders for either MB-339K version, probably resulting from a view among potential customers that there was insufficient improvement in overall capability and performance relative to the two-seat MB-339A and its MB-339C derivative.

SPECIFICATION

Aermacchi MB-339K
Type: single-seat light ground-attack aircraft
Powerplant: one Rolls-Royce Viper Mk 680-43 turbojet rated at 4,400 lb st (19.57 kN)
Dimensions: wing span 36 ft 9¾ in (11.22 m) over tip tanks; length 35 ft 7 in (10.85 m); height 13 ft 1¼ in (3.99 m); wing area 207.75 sq ft (19.30 m²)
Weights: empty equipped 7,154 lb (3245 kg); normal take-off 11,133 lb (5050 kg); maximum take-off 13,999 lb (6350 kg)
Performance: never-exceed speed 500 kt (575 mph; 927 km/h); maximum level speed 'clean' at sea level 486 kt (560 mph; 900 km/h); maximum rate of climb at sea level 7,875 ft (2400 m) per minute; service ceiling 46,000 ft (14020 m); combat radius 340 nm (391 miles; 630 km) on a hi-lo-hi attack mission with a 2,400-lb (1088-kg) warload, or 205 nm (236 miles; 380 km) on a lo-lo-lo attack mision with a 2,400-lb (1088-kg) warload
Armament: two 30-mm DEFA cannon in wingroots, each with 150 rounds, plus maximum weapons load of 4,266 lb (1935 kg) carried on six underwing stations; weapons include 500-lb (227-kg) bombs, rockets of 1.97-in (50-mm), 2.68-in (68-mm) (SNIA) and 3.19-in (81-mm) (SNORA), 3.94-in (100-mm) (Thomson-Brandt), 2.75-in (70-mm) and 5-in (127-mm) calibre, Elettronica ELT555 deception jamming and warning pod

The MB-339K was first flown on 30 May 1980 and subsequently displayed at the SBAC air show at Farnborough in September. It was registered I-BITE, following Aermacchi's trend of giving appropriate civilian registrations to its demonstrator aircraft.

Aero 2

Designed by Boris Cijan and Dorde Petkovic, the **Aero 2** was developed at the outbreak of World War II and a prototype was produced at the Ikarus factory as early as 1940. However, the subsequent German occupation of Yugoslavia led to the destruction of the nation's aircraft manufacturing plants, and further development was not begun until after the end of the war. In 1946 a government factory was established to begin the manufacture of aircraft of indigenous design. A range of competing designs was offered and the Aero 2 was subsequently selected to become the first product from this source.

The Aero 2 was of largely wooden construction with plywood stressed skins; the fuselage and tail unit were of similar construction, except for wooden-frame fabric-covered rudder and elevators. Tandem seating gave accommodation for a pilot and pupil/passenger, with dual controls as standard. The non-retractable landing gear had wheel brakes and a steerable tail-wheel. The first pre-production example made its maiden flight on 19 October 1946, and over 380 examples were manufactured until 1950 for service with the Yugoslav air force, and for civil use. A number of ex-air force Aero 2s were transferred to the Yugoslav Aero Club for use as sporting aircraft.

Among the variants were the **Aero 2B/2C/2F** with open cockpits, and the **Aero 2BE/2D/2E** with enclosed cockpits.

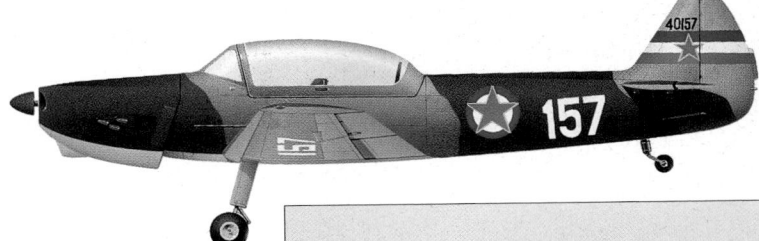

The Aero 2H was the twin-floatplane development of Aero's neat trainer design.

SPECIFICATION

Aero 2
Type: two-seat primary trainer
Powerplant: (2B/2BE) one 145-hp (108-kW) de Havilland Gipsy Major 10, or (2C/D/E/F/H) one 160-hp (119-kW) Walter Minor 6-III inline piston engine
Performance: maximum level speed 129 mph (208 km/h);
cruising speed 99 mph (160 km/h); service ceiling 14,765 ft (4500 m); range 423 miles (680 km)
Weight: maximum take-off 2,196 lb (996 kg)
Dimensions: span 34 ft 5¼ in (10.50 m); length 27 ft 8¾ in (8.45 m); height 8 ft 10¼ in (2.80 m); wing area 167.49 sq ft (15.56 m²)

Aero 3

First flown in 1956, the **Aero 3** entered production in 1957. It was designed to meet a Yugoslav air force specification for use in the primary training and army co-operation roles. Approximately equivalent to the DHC Chipmunk, the Aero 3 was entirely of wooden construction, unlike the Canadian all-metal aircraft. It succeeded the earlier Aero 2 in service from 1958, and had full dual controls and blind-flying equipment. The single-piece canopy could be jettisoned, if necessary. A few Aero 3s remained in service until the late 1970s, when they were replaced by the UTVA-75. A small number of Aero 3s remain airworthy with private individuals.

Above: The Aero 3 was the standard trainer of the Yugoslav air force during the 1960s.

Right: After retirement from Yugoslav military service, a number of Aero 3s found their way into private hands, such as this French example.

SPECIFICATION

Aero 3
Type: two-seat primary trainer
Powerplant: one 190-hp (142-kW) Lycoming O-435-A piston engine
Performance: maximum speed 143 mph (230 km/h); cruising speed 112 mph (180 km/h); range at cruising speed 422 miles (680 km); ceiling 14,100 ft (4300 m)
Weights: loaded 2,646 lb (1198 kg)
Dimensions: wing span 34 ft 5 in (10.50 m); length 28 ft 1 in (8.58 m); height 8 ft 10 in (2.70m)

Aero 45 series

Among the early post-World War II products of the Czech aircraft industry was the **Aero 45** light twin, the '45' portion of the designation implying that it was of 4/5-seat capacity.

The all-metal Aero 45 had a range of interesting design features. Its two-spar wing comprised three sections, of which the centre part carried the engine nacelles, mounted at the leading edge, and two 105-hp (78-kW) Walter Minor 4-III engines. The fin was built integrally with the semi-monocoque fuselage. The Aero 45 was of largely metal construction, with fabric-covered control surfaces. The high standard of finish and extensive use of flush-riveted skinning both contributed to the aircraft's lively performance.

The cabin accommodated a pilot and passenger in front in two adjustable seats, with single or full dual controls. Two or three passengers sat on the rear bench, behind which was the baggage

Above: The Aero 145 was the ultimate version of this series. Its uprated Avia M332 supercharged engines gave a marked increase in performance, particularly on take-off and in the event of an inflight engine-failure.

Above: Approximately 130 were sold to the USSR where they were used by Aeroflot as trainers.

compartment. Capacity could be usefully increased if the rear bench was removed, and, thus modified, Aero 45s were frequently used as short-range transports carrying cargo and mail.

Provision was made for full instrumentation, navigation and radio equipment, and the Aero 45 was fully equipped for night flying. The retractable wheeled undercarriage could be replaced with floats or skis. The prototype Aero 45 made its maiden flight in July 1947. The type made its first public appearance in the UK in 1949 when an early production model won the Norton-Griffiths Trophy in the National Air Races at Coventry at a speed of 163 mph (262 km/h). The type's performance and pleasant handling characteristics were such that it was built in considerable numbers and exported widely. Approximately 700 Aero 45s were built, of which all but 80 were exported.

The design was refined progressively with the following **Super Aero 45**, which featured a range of minor improvements such as optional two-bladed metal airscrews (replacing the previous wooden items) and modified engine cowlings for improved cooling. The Super Aero 45 was offered as a four-seat cabin monoplane for sports and touring, flight instruction, air taxi and light transport.

The final version was the **Let Aero 145**. Developed by Let, this version introduced further refinements and substantially increased power. The Walter Minors were replaced with 140-hp (104-kW) Avia M332 supercharged engines.

Production of all aircraft of the Aero 45 series ended in 1963.

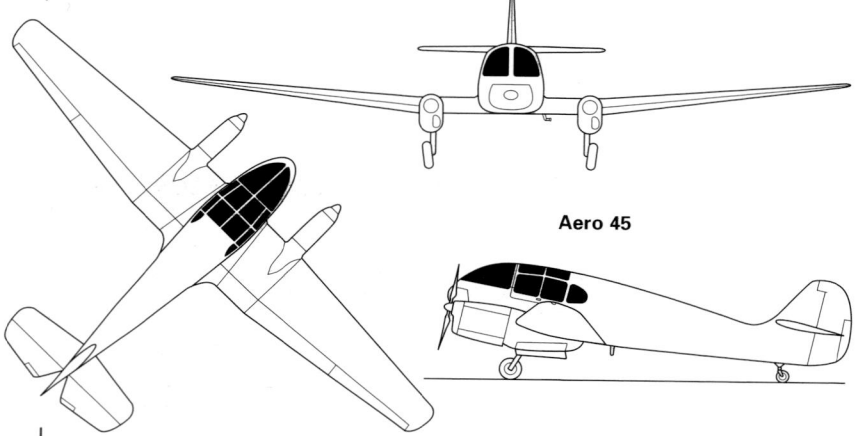

Aero 45

SPECIFICATION	
Aero Super Aero 45 **Type:** four-five-seat twin-engined light cabin monoplane **Powerplant:** two Walter Minor 4-III piston engines each rated at maximum of 105 hp (78 kW) for take-off and 80 hp (60-kW) for cruise **Performance:** maximum speed 168 mph (270 km/h); normal cruising speed (75 per cent power) 143 mph (230 km/h); economical cruising speed 112 mph (180 km/h); landing speed (55° flap) 62 mph (100 km/h); maximum rate of climb 826 ft (252 m) per minute; service ceiling 16,568 ft (5050 m); absolute single-engined ceiling 4,429 ft (1350 m); range with four passengers and full fuel load 870 miles (1400 km) at normal	cruising speed, maximum range 994 miles (1600 km); take-off run (15° flap) 722 ft (220 m); landing run (full flap and brakes) 902 ft (275 m); endurance 6 hr 40 min at normal cruising speed **Fuel capacity:** total 71 Imp gal (324 litres), comprising two 19-Imp gal (87-litre) centre-wing main tanks and two 16-Imp gal (75-litre) auxiliary tanks in outer wings **Weights:** empty (including equipment) 2,112 lb (960 kg); normal loaded 3,322 lb (1510 kg); maximum permissible weight 3,527 lb (1600 kg); total payload 1,411 lb (640 kg) **Dimensions:** wing span 40 ft 4¼ in (12.30 m); length 24 ft 8½ in (7.54 m); height 7 ft 6½ in (2.30 m); wing area 184 sq ft (17.09 m²)

Aero A.10

Aero Tovarna Letadel Dr Kabes was formed in Prague during 1919, initially to manufacture accessories for the aircraft industry. In a very short time, however, the company began to build copies of the biplanes developed by Phönix Flugzeugwerft in Austria. These Phönix designs were themselves derived from the Hansa-Brandenburg series, originated by that company's talented chief designer, Ernst Heinkel. From the construction of these airplanes of foreign origin, it was a comparatively short step to the design and manufacture of aircraft originated by Aero.

One of the first designs was the **Aero A.10** which had the distinction of being

Czechoslovakia's first commercial aircraft, the Aero A.10, served with the national airline CSA in the mid-1920s. Five passengers sat in the cabin while the pilot braved the elements in an open cockpit above the baggage compartment.

the first commercial aircraft to be built in Czechoslovakia. Primarily of wooden construction with fabric covering, the A.10's deep fuselage provided cabin accommodation for five passengers, with a baggage compartment behind the cabin, and the pilot in an open cockpit above the baggage compartment. The powerplant consisted of a Maybach six-cylinder inline engine, many of these being abandoned in Czechoslovakia by the Germans when World War I ended.

Construction of the prototype began during 1921, and this aircraft flew successfully in 1922. Four production A.10s followed, entering service with the Czech national airline Ceskoslovenské Aerolinie (CSA) in 1924 for use on the Prague-Bratislava route.

SPECIFICATION	
Aero A.10 **Type:** six-seat commercial transport **Powerplant:** one 240-hp (179-kW) Maybach Mb IVa inline piston engine **Performance:** maximum speed 99 mph (160 km/h); cruising speed 81 mph (130 km/h); service ceiling	19,030 ft (5800 m); range 323 miles (520 km) **Weights:** empty 2,860 lb (1297 kg); maximum take-off 4,510 lb (2046 kg) **Dimensions:** wing span 46 ft 7 in (14.20 m); length 33 ft 3¼ in (10.14 m); wing area 548.98 sq ft (51.00 m²)

Aero A.11

The **Aero A.11** was a highly successful inter-war design which was developed from the generally similar **A.12** (due to an oddity in the allocation of designations, the latter actually preceded the A.11). Designed by Antonín Husník, the A.11 was an unequal-span, single-bay biplane of wooden construction and fabric covering. Horn-balanced ailerons were provided only on the upper wing. The fuselage and braced tail unit had a basic structure of welded steel tube which was covered in fabric. The main wheels were mounted on a braced through-axle, with shock absorption provided by rubber bungee.

Two open cockpits accommodated the pilot and observer/gunner. The pilot sat level with the trailing-edge of the upper wing, which incorporated a large cut-out to enhance visibility. With the lessons of World War I still in mind, the reconnaissance A.11 was armed with a forward-firing Vickers machine-gun, with twin Lewis guns in the rear cockpit. Equipment included a camera installation and radio.

A key feature of the A.11's design was the provision for any of several types of powerplant without major structural changes, and this was instrumental in its long-term success. There were no fewer than 22 sub-variants, including a number that proceeded no further than the prototype stage.

The prototype and initial production A.11s were powered by a Walter W-IV (licensed BMW IV) Vee piston engine rated at 240 hp (179 kW) and cooled by a frontal radiator.

The A.11 was manoeuvrable, rugged and reliable. These qualities meant that the type was extensively built, with over 440 exam-

Fitted with a Hispano-Suiza 8Fb engine, the A.11 was sold to the Finnish air force, which operated it successfully during the late 1920s under the designation A.11H-S.

In 1926 an Ab.11 crewed by Stanovsky (pilot) and Simke (mechanic) completed a 9,320-mile (15000-km) publicity tour of 23 countries in Europe, North Africa and Asia Minor. They are shown on their return to the Aero plant at Kbely airport in Prague.

ples of all variants being produced.

The A.11 established a variety of records including: a Czech duration record of 13 hours 15 minutes, established by Captain Vicherek on 13 September 1925; in the same year, Aero A.11s took the first three places in the President's Prize Race; in 1927, one of several A.11s built for Finland, and flown by Aero's chief pilot, Novak, accomplished 225 loops in a few seconds under 45 minutes.

The designations **A.21**, **A.25** and **A.125** were used for three important derivatives of the basic A.11. The A.21 was the night training variant, and differed mainly in its role-dedicated equipment and 180-hp (134-kW) Breitfeld & Danek Perun I powerplant. The A.25 was the day training counterpart of the A.21, powered by a 185-hp (138-kW) BMW IIIa inline piston engine. The A.125 was essentially an A.11 powered by a Perun I.

Giving highly valuable service in spite of their relatively small numbers, these three variants saw extensive and effective service with the Czechoslovak Army Air Force through the late 1920s and early 1930s.

Aero A.11 variants

A.11H-S: reconnaissance and trainer version as supplied to Finland, generally similar to standard A.11, but incorporating some structural changes to allow for installation of the more powerful 300-hp (224-kW) Hispano Suiza 8Fb engine
A.11N: night reconnaissance version of the A.11, differing only in installed equipment
Ab.11: light bomber version of the A.11 (also available in **Ab.11d** (day) and **Ab.11n** (night) versions which differed in equipment) powered by a 240-hp (179-kW) Breitfeld & Danek Perun II engine
A.21: night trainer version, generally similar to the A.11 except for changed powerplant of one 180-hp (134-kW) Breitfeld & Danek Perun I engine
A.22: light civil transport version of the A.11, powered by a 240-hp (179-kW) Maybach Mb IVA engine; all military equipment removed and rear cockpit modified to provide seats for two passengers
A.25: day trainer version of the A.11, powered by one 185-hp (138-kW) BMW IIIa engine
A.29: designation of a twin floatplane version of the A.11; at least nine operated as target tugs by the Czech army air service; powerplant of one 240-hp (179-kW) Breitfeld & Danek Perun II engine; length 29 ft 6¼ in (9.00 m) and maximum level speed 122 mph (196 km/h) at 16,400 ft (5,000 m)
A.125: day trainer version of the A.11, differing from the A.25 by having one Breitfeld & Danek Perun I engine

SPECIFICATION	
Aero A.11	
Type: two-seat multi-purpose biplane	range 466 miles (750 km) **Weights:** empty 2,271 lb (1030 kg); maximum take-off 3,389 lb (1537 kg)
Powerplant: one 240-hp (179-kW) Walter W-IV inline piston engine	**Dimensions:** span (upper) 41 ft 11 in (12.78 m), (lower) 35 ft 5¼ in (10.80 m); length 26 ft 10¾ in
Performance: maximum level speed 133 mph (214 km/h); cruising speed 112 mph (180 km/h); service ceiling 24,935 ft (7600 m);	(8.20 m); height 10 ft 2 in (3.10 m); wing area (total) 393.00 sq ft (36.51 m²)

Aero A.12

Aero's **A.12** reconnaissance biplane was a highly influential design which led to the successful A.11 multi-purpose aircraft. The A.12 was an early example of the impressive capabilities of the fledgling aircraft industry in Czechoslovakia. The country had come into being only in October 1918, securing independence from the collapsing Austro-Hungarian empire at the end of World War I.

The A.12 was easily identified by cooling radiators mounted on each side of the engine cowling, instead of in front of the engine. It was powered by either a 220-hp (164-kW) Walter or a 240-hp (179-kW) Maybach Mb.IVA inline piston engine. The A.12 had a wing span of 41 ft 11¼ in (12.78 m), a length of 27 ft 2¾ in (8.30 m), and a maximum level speed of 125 mph (201 km/h).

Developed as a two-seat reconnaissance biplane, the Aero A.12 served in quantity with the Czech army air service.

Aero A.14

During World War I, the Hansa-Brandenburg C.I was operated by the Imperial Austro-Hungarian army air service in a variety of roles, including reconnaissance, artillery-spotting and light bombing.

From 1922, additional C.Is were built in Czechoslovakia by Aero under the designation **A.14**. Fitted with the 230-hp (172-kW) Breitfeld & Danek Hiero N engine, they were operated by both the Czech army air service and the fledgling national airline Ceskoslovenské Státni Aerolinie (CSA). As commercial transports, the A.14s carried up to two passengers.

Prior to the establishment of scheduled services, A.14s carried out route-proving flights from Prague to Bratislava. The first such flight was made by Major D. Skála on 1 March 1923 as part of a special test organised by the Czech army air service.

CSA was formally established on 19 July and, on 29 October, an A.14 piloted by K. Brabenec made Czechoslovakia's first regular domestic flight from Prague to Bratislava.

The establishment of scheduled services by Farman and DH.50 transports in October 1923 was preceded by route-proving flights by CSA A.14s.

Aero A.18

The Czechoslovak Army Air Force's requirement for a new single-seat fighter resulted in Aero's development of a new biplane which drew heavily from the successful A.11. It also built on Aero's previous efforts into developing a single-seat fighter – the Ae.02 and Ae.04.

The resulting **Aero A.18**

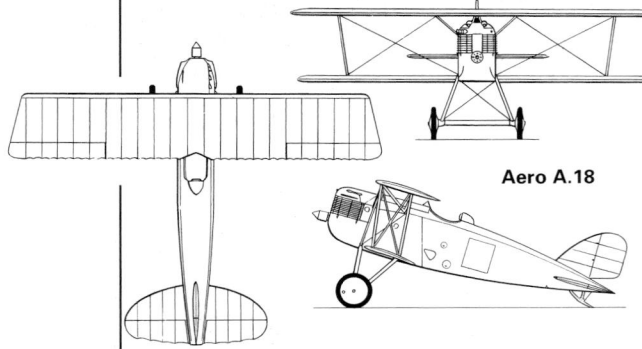

Aero A.18

was a single-bay biplane of unequal span which was of similar construction to the A.11, although only a single cockpit was provided. The ailerons, mounted on the upper wing, were without horn balances.

The initial A.18 version was powered by a 185-hp (138-kW) BMW IIIa engine. The armament comprised two Vickers machine-guns, synchronised to fire forward through the disc of

the two-bladed wooden propeller.

In the early 1920s, the Czech Aero Club organised a national aircraft race and Aero entered a specially prepared version of its fighter in the first event, flown in 1923. Designated **A.18B**, it differed from the standard air force version by having the wing span reduced to 18 ft 8½ in (5.70 m), giving a wing area of 105.92 sq ft (9.84 m²). Although the A.18B won the race, the achievement was something of an anti-climax, as the two contending aircraft both crashed during the event.

Anticipating stronger opposition in 1924, Aero used a similar airframe to that of the 1923 winner, but

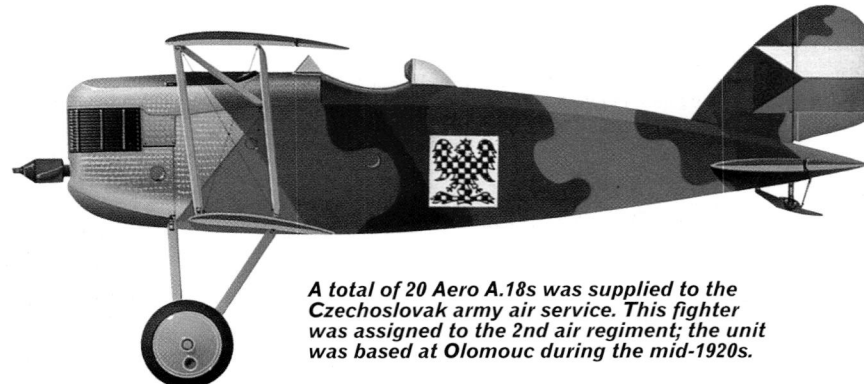

After some largely unsuccessful attempts at fighter design, Aero achieved a measure of success with its A.18. Relatively few examples were built for military use, but specially prepared A.18s won several air races, thus gaining valuable experience for Aero.

installed a version of the Walter W-IV engine with a high compression ratio that enabled it to develop 300 hp (224 kW). Designated **A.18C**, this demonstrated a top

speed of 171 mph (275 km/h), a performance good enough to win the 1924 race at an average of 162 mph (261 km/h).

SPECIFICATION

Aero A.18
Type: single-seat biplane fighter
Powerplant: (standard A.18) one 185-hp (138-kW) BMW IIIa inline piston engine
Performance: maximum level speed 142 mph (229 km/h); cruising speed 121 mph (195 km/h); service ceiling 29,530 ft (9000 m); range

249 miles (400 km)
Weights: empty 1,404 lb (637 kg); maximum take-off 1,900 lb (862 kg)
Dimensions: wing span 24 ft 11¼ in (7.60 m); length 19 ft 4¼ in (5.90 m); wing area 171.15 sq ft (15.90 m²)
Armament: two 0.303-in (7.7-mm) fixed forward-firing synchronised Vickers machine-guns

A total of 20 Aero A.18s was supplied to the Czechoslovak army air service. This fighter was assigned to the 2nd air regiment; the unit was based at Olomouc during the mid-1920s.

Aero A.20

First flown in 1923, the **Aero A.20** was a biplane fighter that did not progress past the prototype stage.

Design and construction of the A.20 ran in parallel with those of the A.18. It was similar to the A.18 in overall

configuration and construction, but was slightly larger, and was fitted with a more powerful Hispano-Suiza 8Fb Vee inline piston engine.

This powerplant was installed in the tapered nose with its two cylinder banks left exposed, and was cooled by a pair of lateral radiators on the lower sides of the fuselage below the cylinder banks. Despite its purposeful appearance, the A.20 offered only a modest increase in performance over the A.18 and further development was soon abandoned.

SPECIFICATION

Aero A.20
Type: single-seat biplane fighter
Powerplant: one Skoda (Hispano-Suiza) 8Fb Vee piston engine rated at 300 hp (224 kW)
Performance: maximum level speed 140 mph (225 km/h) at optimum altitude; cruising speed 118 mph (190 km/h) at optimum

altitude; climb to 16,405 ft (5000 m) in 14 minutes 10 seconds
Weights: empty 1,728 lb (784 kg); maximum take-off 2,381 lb (1080 kg)
Dimensions: span 31 ft 9⅞ in (9.70 m); length 21 ft 7¾ in (6.60 m); wing area 250.81 sq ft (23.30 m²)
Armament: two 0.303-in (7.7-mm) Vickers fixed forward-firing guns

The A.20 was developed in parallel with the A.18 but offered little improvement in performance.

Aero A.23

Originating in 1925, the **Aero A.23** eight/nine-seat civil transport represented a considerable improvement over the A.10 of five years earlier. The family relationship was still apparent but, like the more-developed military aircraft of Aero design, the A.23 lacked the large horn-balanced ailerons on the upper wing. The

fuselage was of similar slab-sided configuration to that of the A.10, but this ended in a conventional braced tail unit that included a fin. The enclosed cabin provided accommodation for six or seven passengers and included a toilet at the rear. The pilot, and a co-pilot or passenger, were seated in a large open cockpit above the baggage compartment at the rear of the cabin. The first of seven A.23s for

Ceskoslovenské Státni Aerolinie (CSA) entered service in 1926, and these aircraft were used on the

airline's Prague-Marienbad and Prague-Uzhorod routes. Some of these remained in service until the late 1930s.

The A.23 offered a useful increase in passenger carrying capability over the earlier A.10.

SPECIFICATION

Aero A.23
Type: eight/nine-seat civil transport
Powerplant: one 450-hp (336-kW) Walter-built Bristol Jupiter IV radial piston engine
Performance: maximum level speed 115 mph (185 km/h);

cruising speed 99 mph (160 km/h); service ceiling 18,045 ft (5500 m)
Weights: empty 4,100 lb (1860 kg); maximum take-off 6,945 lb (3150 kg)
Dimensions: wing span 54 ft 9½ in (16.70 m); length 41 ft 4 in (12.60 m); wing area 721.21 sq ft (67.00 m²)

Aero A.24

In the mid-1920s, a number of Europe's major aircraft manufacturers were developing large bomber aircraft. Following this trend, Aero designed the **Aero A.24**, a large biplane bomber with equal-span wings. The lower wing was mounted at the base of the deep slab-sided fuselage, with the upper wing carried well above it by interplane and centre-section struts. This gave ample room for the two engines to be mounted from the lower wing, some distance outboard from the fuselage, directly above the twin-wheeled main landing gear units. The fuselage incorporated open cockpits for a crew of three or four. Flight testing showed that the big A.24 was considerably underpowered, taking more than 36 minutes to climb to 9,840 ft (3000 m). A more powerful version was projected, with two Bristol Jupiter engines, each developing 400 hp (298 kW). This was to have been designated A.27, but was never built.

The twin-engined A.24 was an unsuccessful attempt by Aero to develop a large bomber.

SPECIFICATION	
Aero A.24	**Weights:** empty 6,526 lb
Type: twin-engined night bomber	(2960 kg); maximum take-off
Powerplant: two 240-hp (179-kW)	9,945 lb (4511 kg)
Maybach Mb IV inline piston	**Dimensions:** wing span 72 ft 10 in
engines	(22.20 m); length 44 ft 11¼ in
Performance: maximum level	(13.70 m); wing area 1,141.01 sq ft
speed 96 mph (155 km/h); cruising	(106.00 m²)
speed 68 mph (110 km/h); service	**Armament:** maximum bomb load
ceiling 11,810 ft (3600 m); range	of 2,205 lb (1000 kg), no self-
373 miles (600 km)	defence armament carried

Aero A.29

The **Aero A.29** was the first seaplane of any type to be designed and built in Czechoslovakia. The A.29 was a twin-float development of the A.11 reconnaissance biplane. The fixed tailskid landing gear of the A.11 was replaced on the A.29 by a wire-braced arrangement of two single-step wooden floats. These increased the overall length to 29 ft 6¼ in (9.00 m). The A.29 was powered by a Breitfeld & Danek Perun II piston engine rated at 240 hp (179 kW) which gave a top speed of 122 mph (196 km/h) at 16,400 ft (5,000 m).

Making its first appearance in 1926, the unarmed A.29 was intended for use mainly in the target-towing role, and at least nine examples were operated by the Czech Army Air Service. The floatplanes were based at the establishment created at a site leased from Yugoslavia on the coast of the Adriatic Sea, and were generally operated for the training of anti-aircraft gunners.

Aero A.30 series

Efforts to produce an even more potent version of the A.11 had been attempted in 1925. This involved the installation of a 450-hp (336-kW) Lorraine-Dietrich engine, but early testing showed that this would over-stress the aircraft's

The A.230 was the production version of the A.30. The rampant lion badge identifies this A.230 as an example from the 3rd Air Regiment of the Czech Army Air Service.

structure. Accordingly, design began in 1926 of a larger version and, because this differed quite considerably from the earlier A.11, it was allocated the new designation, **A.30**.

The A.30 was somewhat larger in overall dimensions than its predecessor, and had an upper wing considerably greater in span than the lower wing.

Early testing of the A.30 revealed that it had a number of shortcomings, but in 1927, after considerable development and refinement of the design, Aero received initial orders for supply of the A.30 to the Czech Army Air Service.

One of these A.30s held the world speed record for a 2,205-lb (1000-kg)

Yet another development of the ubiquitous A.11 design, the A.30 boasted almost double the power of the earlier machine. It was only after considerable refinement that the type was finally accepted for military service.

A.30 variants

A.130: designation of a prototype powered by a Walter-built Bristol Jupiter VI of 500 hp (373-kW)
A.230: production version with divided main landing gear units, otherwise generally similar to A.30; powerplant of one 490-hp (365-kW) Lorraine-Dietrich inline piston engine
A.330: version of A.30 powered by one 650-hp (485-kW) Praga (formerly Breitfeld Danek) ESV engine
A.430: designation of projected version of A.30 of which only a single prototype was built, powered by a 650-hp (485-kW) Avia Vr-36 engine

SPECIFICATION	
Aero A.30	**Weights:** empty 3,219 lb
Type: two-seat long-range	(1460 kg); maximum take-off
reconnaissance/light bomber	5,975 lb (2710 kg)
aircraft	**Dimensions:** wing span 50 ft 2¼ in
Powerplant: one 500-hp (373-kW)	(15.30 m); length 32 ft 9¾ in
Skoda L inline piston engine	(10.00 m); height 10 ft 9¾ in
Performance: maximum level	(3.30 m); wing area 553.28 sq ft
speed 151 mph (243 km/h),	(51.40 m²)
cruising speed 121 mph	**Armament:** one fixed forward-
(195 km/h); service ceiling	firing Vickers machine-gun, two
21,325 ft (6500 m); endurance	Lewis guns on a flexible mounting
5 hours 30 minutes; range	in the aft cockpit, and maximum
621 miles (1000 km)	bombload of 1,102 lb (500 kg)

payload carried over a 310.7-mile (500-km) closed-circuit. Gained in August 1927, at an average speed of 132.7 mph (213.56 km/h) it was held for a period of just two months.

Aero A.32 series

The experimental installation of a Walter-built Bristol Jupiter engine in an A.11 led to an order from the Czech Ministry of Defence for 31 production aircraft under the designation **A.11J**. By the time that this version had been developed to production status, to serve with the Czech Army Air Service in an army co-operation role, so many modifications had been incorporated that it was given the new designation, **Aero A.32**.

Of similar overall size to the A.11, it differed by having equal-span biplane wings, the upper-wing ailerons being mass-balanced instead of horn-balanced, and the tail unit dispensed with horn-balanced elevators. The A.32 used a similar method of construction to the A.11, but was powered by a Walter-built Bristol Jupiter IV radial engine. The initial production A.32s began to enter the Army Air Service in 1928.

Aero also developed several successful versions of the basic A.32 design. The **A.321F** was an attack version produced for the Finnish air force, of which just one example was delivered in 1929. It was powered by a 450-hp (336-kW) Isotta Fraschini Asso Cassia inline piston engine. The Finnish air force eventually procured the definitive **A.32GR** attack version, powered by a 450-hp (336-kW) Bristol Jupiter radial engine built under licence by Gnome-Rhône. A total of 15 A.32GRs was delivered in 1929; most of these served for many years as trainers

SPECIFICATION	
Aero A.32	**Weights:** empty 2,306 lb
Type: two-seat army co-operation	(1046 kg); maximum take-off
aircraft	4,226 lb (1917 kg)
Powerplant: one 450-hp (336-kW)	**Dimensions:** span 40 ft 8 in
Walter-built Bristol Jupiter IV	(12.40 m); length 26 ft 10¾ in
radial piston engine	(8.20 m); height 10 ft 2 in (3.10 m);
Performance: maximum level	wing area 392.90 sq ft (36.50 m²)
speed 140 mph (226 km/h);	**Armament:** two fixed forward-
cruising speed 119 mph	firing Vickers machine-guns, two
(192 km/h); service ceiling	Lewis guns on flexible mount in
18,045 ft (5500 m); endurance	rear cockpit, and up to eight
4 hours; range 497 miles	22-lb (10-kg) anti-personnel bombs
(800 km)	on underwing racks

after only short service in the attack role.

The designations **Ap.32** and **Apb.32** were applied to improved versions of the A.32 for service with the Czech forces. These differed by having divided-type main landing gear units, which also incorporated streamlined fairings over the shock-absorbers, plus detail refinements. These versions retained the powerplants of the original A.32, but the improvements which had been made gave them a maxi-

mum level speed of 146 mph (235 km/h), cruising speed of 124 mph (200 km/h), service ceiling of 21,980 ft (6700 m), and range of 559 miles (900 km).

When production of all A.32s ended in 1932, a total of 116 examples of differing versions had been built by Aero.

Developed for Czech forces, the Ap.32 was a version of the A.32 with detailed improvements which gave a slight increase in performance.

Aero A.34

Following the lead set by the de Havilland Moth in 1925, Aero developed a small two-seat sporting biplane in 1929 under the designation **A.34**.

Like de Havilland's pacesetting Moth, the A.34 was an equal-span single-bay biplane whose wings could be folded. This simplified the problems of storage,

and of towing to and from an airfield.

The A.34's basic wing structure was all-wood, except for the metal-frame ailerons mounted on the lower wing, and all wings were fabric covered. Metal tube skids were mounted beneath the wingtips of the lower wing to protect the structure in a wing-down landing. The fuselage was of wood, the braced tail unit of

steel tube, and both of these structures were fabric-covered.

Two open cockpits in tandem accommodated a pilot and passenger/pupil. Dual controls and an access door to the forward cockpit were standard.

Aero developed two variants of the A.34. The **A.34W** was a generally similar version, powered by a 105-hp (78-kW) Walter Junior inverted inline piston

engine. The performance was virtually unchanged, but the uprated powerplant allowed an 80-lb (36-kg) increase in payload. The

A.134 was also similar, with only one prototype being built. It was powered by a 130-hp (97-kW) Walter NZ radial piston engine

SPECIFICATION	
Aero A.34	199 miles (320 km)
Type: two-seat sporting biplane	**Weights:** empty 882 lb (400 kg);
Powerplant: one 85-hp (63-kW)	maximum take-off 1,411 lb
Walter Vega radial piston engine	(640 kg)
Performance: maximum level	**Dimensions:** wing span 28 ft
speed 99 mph (160 km/h), cruising	10½ in (8.80 m); length 22 ft 2¾ in
speed 87 mph (140 km/h); service	(6.80 m); wing area 229.28 sq ft
ceiling 9,840 ft (3000 m); range	(21.30 m²)

Aero A.35

With the **A.35** transport of 1928, Aero came very close to providing ideal accommodation for the pilot, seating him high on the fuselage just forward of the wing leading-edge in a roomy cockpit. The words 'very

close' are used advisedly, because the pilot had not quite gained the luxury of an enclosed flight deck: there was a windscreen and a transparent roof, but a lack of side windows ensured that he received the full benefits of the fresh air to prevent him dropping off to sleep. For the fifth passen-

ger who shared the pilot's cockpit in a side-by-side seating arrangement, it must have seemed far from ideal.

In other respects, the A.35 was quite advanced, introducing a braced high-wing monoplane configuration, and a separate enclosed cabin seating four passengers, in two

pairs, with ample baggage space at the rear of the cabin. The wings were of wood with fabric covering, while the fuselage and braced tail unit were constructed of steel tube, and were also covered in fabric. Divided-type main landing gear units with single wheels, and a tail-

skid, completed the airframe structure. Powerplant of the prototype was a 220-hp (164-kW) Wright Whirlwind radial engine, but production aircraft had a Walter Castor radial engine, mounted uncowled.

Aero built a total of eight production A.35s. Six of these were delivered to the Czech national airline, CSA, the remaining two being supplied to an industrial company. These two aircraft were probably among the earliest used for business purposes.

The A.35 had a relatively advanced design, but was archaic in one major respect: the pilot still had to brave the elements from an unenclosed cockpit.

SPECIFICATION	
Aero A.35	range 410 miles (660 km)
Type: five-seat monoplane transport	**Weights:** empty 2,469 lb
Powerplant: one 240-hp (179-kW)	(1120 kg); maximum take-off
Walter Castor radial piston engine	4,189 lb (1900 kg)
Performance: maximum level	**Dimensions:** wing span 47 ft
speed 122 mph (197 km/h),	6¾ in (14.50 m); length 31 ft 9¾ in
cruising speed 103 mph (165 km/h);	(9.70 m); height 8 ft 6¼ in (2.60 m);
service ceiling 15,750 ft (4800 m);	wing area 308.93 sq ft (28.70 m²)

Aero A.38

Introduced in 1929, the **Aero A.38** civil transport combined features of two earlier types to provide accommodation for a pilot and up to nine passengers. The wings and tail unit of the A.23 were married to

the landing gear and a longer fuselage developed from that of the A.35.

The pilot's accommodation was identical to that of the A.35, which meant that, if necessary, a ninth passenger could be seated beside him. The enclosed cabin, which had doors on each side, seated eight passen-

gers in pairs, and had a toilet and baggage space at the rear. Only five A.38s were built, comprising three for CSA being identified as **A.38-1**: these each had a Walter-built Bristol Jupiter IV engine. The remaining two

examples of the **A.38-2** each had a French-built Gnome-Rhône Jupiter 9A2 radial engine of similar power, and were produced for the French Compagnie Internationale de Navigation Aérienne.

Aero reverted to biplane configuration with its A.38 transport design of 1929. This combined the biplane wings of the A.23 of 1925 with a fuselage developed from that of the A.35 of 1928.

SPECIFICATION	
Aero A.38-1	15,750 ft (4800 m); range 354 miles
Type: nine-seat biplane transport	(570 km)
Powerplant: one 450-hp (336-kW)	**Weights:** empty 3,836 lb (1740 kg);
Walter-built Bristol Jupiter IV	maximum take-off 6,945 lb (3150 kg)
radial piston engine	**Dimensions:** span 54 ft 9½ in
Performance: maximum level	(16.70 m); length 42 ft 0 in
speed 118 mph (190 km/h),	(12.80 m); height 14 ft 9¼ in
cruising speed 103 mph	(4.50 m); wing area 721.21 sq ft
(165 km/h); service ceiling	(67.00 m²)

Aero A.42

Many bombers developed in Europe during the late 1920s were cumbersome biplane designs. One of the exceptions was the elegant **A.42** which was developed by Aero's designers Rabes and Husník in 1929 as a day/night bomber. Two protoypes (the **A.42.1** and **A.42.2**) were built, and flight testing began in 1930. The A.42 was a high-wing monoplane with fixed tailwheel undercarriage.

The A.42's performance was such that, suitably stripped of all military equipment, the prototypes were used on several high-profile flights.

On 20 September 1930, an A.42 piloted by Vojteck Svozil set three new international records around a 621-mile (1,000-km) closed circuit, carrying respectively, no payload, and payloads of 1,102-lb (500-kg) and 2,205-lb

(1000-kg). The average speed was 157 mph (252 km/h).

In military service, it was envisaged that the A.42 would have a crew of three. The pilot and observer were to be seated side-by-side so that the latter could move between the seats and, while lying prone on the fuselage floor, act as bombardier, or fire a ventral machine-gun. Light bombs were carried externally on racks under the fuselage. The third crew man was the radio operator who also served as the rear gunner, firing a machine-gun on a flexible mounting in a dorsal fairing.

Despite its performance, the A.42's military application proved less than perfect. Among several problems were cramped accommodation for the three crew, and poor field performance, the type's

take-off and landing distances being deemed excessive. Several of these faults were rectified, but the Czech air force took the opportunity to demand a major modification: replacement of the A.42's wooden wings with metal ones. Aero's A.100 design seemed more promising and further development of the A.42 was abandoned.

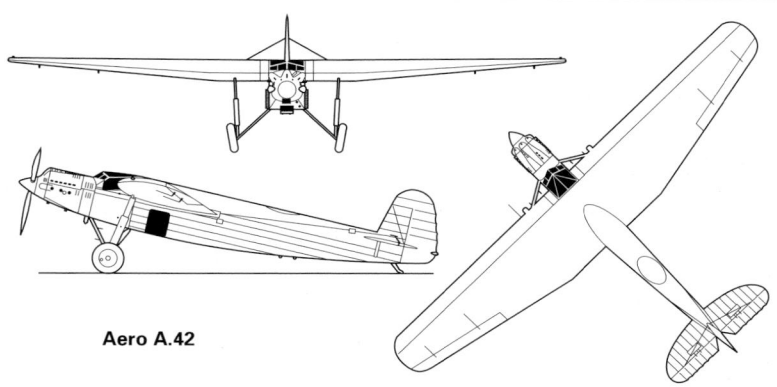

Aero A.42

SPECIFICATION	
Aero A.42	22,966 ft (7000 m); range 621 miles (1000 km)
Type: three-seat day/night bomber	**Weights:** empty 6,481 lb (2940 kg); maximum take-off 10,450 lb (4740 kg)
Powerplant: one 800-hp (597-kW) Praga-built Isotta Fraschini Asso-1000 18-cylinder double-banked inline piston engine	**Dimensions:** wing span 68 ft 3½ in (20.82 m); length 45 ft 3¼ in (13.80 m); height 11 ft 1¾ in (3.40 m); wing area 635 sq ft (59.13 m²)
Performance: maximum level speed 168 mph (270 km/h); cruising speed 155 mph (250 km/h); time to climb to 16,404 ft (5000 m) 50 minutes; service ceiling	**Armament:** one ventral 7.9-mm machine-gun and one rear-firing 7.9-mm machine-gun in dorsal turret

Aero A.100

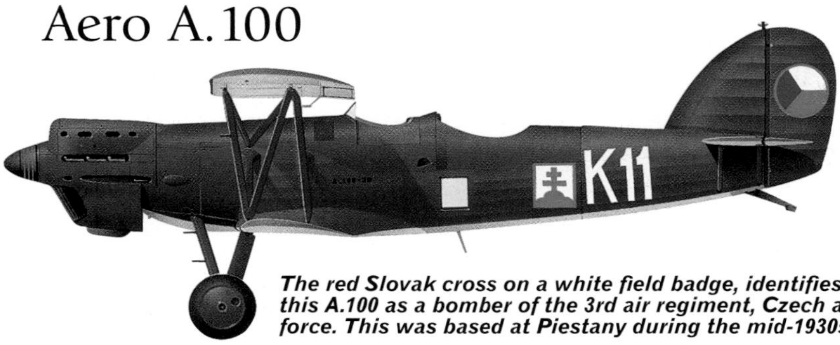

The red Slovak cross on a white field badge, identifies this A.100 as a bomber of the 3rd air regiment, Czech air force. This was based at Piestany during the mid-1930s.

The A.430 prototype was built as a variant of the A.30 production reconnaissance/bomber aircraft. It was eventually developed and refined to the point where it offered considerably better performance than the original A.30.

Redesignating the A.430 as the **Aero A.100**, the company offered it to the Czech Ministry of Defence which, in 1933, initiated a design competition for aircraft of a similar specification. The A.100 was eventually declared the winner of this competition and, over the next two years, a total of 44 was built for service with the Czech air force.

The A.100 was generally similar in configuration to the A.30, and shared the same composite basic structure (wooden wings and metal fuselage), with fabric covering. However, the A.100 introduced oleo-pneumatic shock-struts for the main landing gear units.

Aero developed two major variants of the A.100. The **A.101** was a bomber version that was scaled up by around 10 per cent. As well as having larger overall dimensions, it also differed

by having an 800-hp (597-kW) Praga-built Isotta Fraschini Asso-1000 engine, an enlarged rear cockpit, and a rudder of increased area. It had a wing span of 55 ft 9¼ in (17.00 m), a length of 39 ft 8 in (12.09 m), and a wing area of 614.64 sq ft (57.10 m²). The uprated engine allowed the A.101 to operate with a payload increased by 1,294 lb (587 kg) but, with a top speed of only 159 mph (256 km/h), the overall performance of this version was slightly inferior to that of the A.100. Aero built a total of 29 A.101s and these machines served with the Slovak air force during World War II.

Further development of the A.101 resulted in the **Ab.101**, a slightly larger

bomber version that was produced from 1936 as a stop-gap measure to strengthen the nation's defences. There was a prone camera or bombing position for the observer, and provision was made within the forward fuselage for bombs to be carried internally.

The Ab.101's powerplant comprised one 750-hp (559-kW) Praga-built Hispano-Suiza 12Ydrs engine. Given its higher weight, the slight decrease in power caused a considerable reduction in performance. A total of 64 Ab.101s was supplied to the Czech air force, or for export. These machines saw operational combat use during the Spanish Civil War. Aero built a total of 137 A.100s, A.101s and Ab.101s.

SPECIFICATION	
Aero A.100	**Weights:** empty 4,497 lb (2040 kg); maximum take-off 7,099 lb (3220 kg)
Type: two-seat long-range reconnaissance aircraft	**Dimensions:** wing span 48 ft 2¾ in (14.70 m); length 34 ft 9¼ in (10.60 m); height 11 ft 5¾ in (3.50 m); wing area 476.86 sq ft (44.30 m²)
Powerplant: one 650-hp (485-kW) Avia-built Hispano-Suiza Vr-36 12-cylinder inline piston engine	
Performance: maximum level speed 168 mph (270 km/h); cruising speed 143 mph (230 km/h); service ceiling 21,325 ft (6500 m); endurance 4 hours; range 590 miles (950 km)	**Armament:** two fixed forward-firing 0.31-in (7.92-mm) machine-guns in fuselage sides, twin Lewis guns on flexible mount in rear cockpit, plus maximum bombload of 1,322 lb (600 kg)

Aero A.100 operational history

The major combat use of the A.100 came during the Spanish Civil War, where it served on both sides. In early 1937, the Czechoslovak government authorised the shipment of a batch of A.101s to the Spanish Republican forces, but these never reached their intended destination. On 15 April, the Nationalist cruiser *Admiral Cervera* intercepted the Panamanian cargo vessel, *Hordena*, en route from Gdynia to Santander. Among the cargo that was seized were 22 A.100s. These aircraft were re-assembled and, two months later, were formed into a unit designated Grupo 17 of the Nationalist Air Force (and assigned serials 17-1 to 17-22). Used initially as bombers during August 1937 in the area of Brunete, they mainly flew army co-operation and reconnaissance missions. At the end of the war, they were relegated to training duties at the Observers' School at Malaga. A second batch of A.100s did reach the Spanish Republican forces and were used operationally, but some 16 surviving aircraft were later operated by the Nationalists when the Republicans surrendered the airfield at Madrid/Bajaras at the cessation of hostilies.

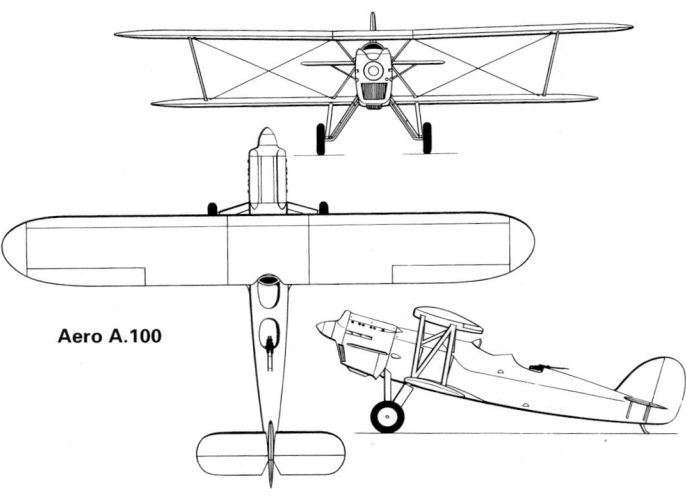

Aero A.100

Aero A.102

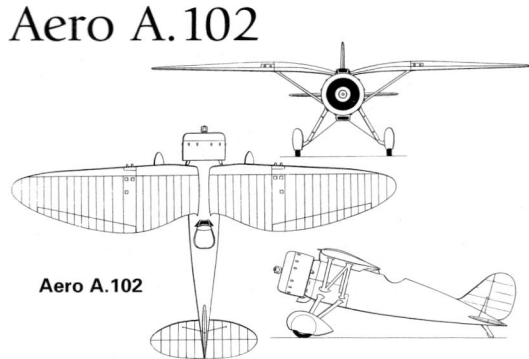

Aero A.102

Avia's domination as supplier of fighters to the Czech air force was not challenged seriously until the early 1930s when several companies proposed designs for a new fighter. Aero's elegant but abortive **A.102** biplane design of 1932 was followed in 1933 by the **A.102D** semi-cantilever, low-wing monoplane design, but this too was rejected.

The A.102 design was revised yet further as a high-wing monoplane and, in this form, a prototype was first flown in July 1934. The aircraft was heavily influenced by the contemporary Polish PZL P.11 and P.24 fighters. The elliptical plan gull wings were braced by N-struts and tapered sharply. Two machine-guns were mounted at the widest part of each wing half.

The A.102 was of mainly all-metal construction with fabric covering, but at several places (especially in the front of the fuselage), duralumin sheet was used as covering.

Flight testing revealed that the A.102 had a good rate of climb and manoeuvrability. The take-off run was a remarkable 443 ft (135 m), but the type's landing characteristics were not good. The high landing speed meant that any pilots used to biplanes would have needed great skill to cope. The A.102 suffered two accidents, in 1934 and 1936. Each time, the aircraft was repaired and the flight trials continued. However, the Czech Ministry of Defence was not interested in the type. Avia's B.35 fighter spelled the A.102's demise and development was abandoned.

SPECIFICATION	
Aero A.102	
Type: single-seat fighter	endurance 1 hour 40 minutes
Powerplant: one 930-hp (694-kW) Walter-built Gnome-Rhône Mistral Major 14Krsd radial piston engine	**Weight:** maximum take-off 4,489 lb (2036 kg)
Performance: maximum level speed 270 mph (434 km/h); service ceiling 10,000 ft (3050 m);	**Dimensions:** span 36 ft 3 in (11.05 m); length 23 ft 11½ in (7.30 m)
	Armament: four machine-guns of unspecified calibre and type

The A.102 had no flaps and the relatively small wing was highly loaded. This gave a very high touchdown speed of 87 mph (140 km/h).

Aero A.200

The A.200 successfully competed in a 1934 contest for touring and sports aircraft.

SPECIFICATION	
Aero A.200	
Type: four-seat cabin monoplane	service ceiling 16,405 ft (5000 m); range 497 miles (800 km)
Powerplant: one 200-hp (149-kW) Walter Bora radial piston engine	**Weights:** empty 1,235 lb (560 kg); maximum take-off 2,094 lb (950 kg)
Performance: maximum level speed 158 mph (255 km/h); cruising speed 137 mph (220 km/h);	**Dimensions:** span 36 ft 5 in (11.10 m); length 25 ft 7 in (7.80 m); wing area 178.69 sq ft (16.60 m²)

Under the designation **A.200**, Aero prepared a sporting aircraft to compete in the 1934 Challenge de Tourisme Internationale, a contest for sports and touring aircraft. The A.200 emerged as a neat four-seat cabin monoplane with braced wings. It was designed to have good short field performance, and its fabric-covered wings incorporated wide-span trailing-edge flaps. The wings were also foldable for easy storage or transport.

Aero built two A.200s (OK-AMA and OK-AMB) for the competition and these proved highly successful, winning the first Team Prize of Nations in the contest. To mark this success, OK-AMB was preserved and is now exhibited at the Czech air force museum at Kbely near Prague.

Aero A.200

Aero A.204/A.300/A.304

In 1936, Aero designed a new light transport which, it was thought, would appeal to the Czech national airline, CSA. Aerodynamically, the **A.204** represented a large step forward with NACA-cowled engines and a clean, low-mounted wing. The wing structure was of wood with plywood stressed skins, while the fuselage and tail unit structure were of welded steel tube with fabric covering. Another innovation for Aero was the retractable landing gear, although the tailwheel was non-retracting and was provided with a speed fairing.

Accommodation was provided for a crew of two, and eight passengers. The cabin was sufficiently advanced to be heated and ventilated. It had individual, adjustable seats with reading lights and a hand luggage rack above each, fore and aft main baggage compartments, and a toilet.

Testing proved successful, and it came as a shock to Aero to discover that, instead of buying the indigenous product, CSA had decided to equip with British Airspeed Envoys of similar performance. As a result, only the prototype A.204 was built. However, a number of variants of the A.204 met with more success.

The growing international tension in Europe at the beginning of 1938 made it essential for Czechoslovakia to adopt urgent measures to strengthen its armed forces. Minimal changes to the A.204 design created the **A.304** interim light bomber, which was similar in appearance to the Avro Anson. The Walter Pollux IIR engines were replaced by 430-hp (321-kW) Walter Super Castor 1-MRs. The A.304 carried a crew of three, and was armed with two machine-guns (one in the nose and one in a dorsal turret). It could carry up to 661 lb (300 kg) of bombs. A total of 15 A.304s was supplied to the Czech air force.

Further development of the A.204/A.304 led to a more purposeful bomber, in the form of the **A.300**. The major change was the installation of two 830-hp (619-kW) Bristol Mercury IX radial piston engines, this requiring wing strengthening and the provision of a new tail unit with twin vertical surfaces. Other changes included accommodation for a crew of four, and provision for a 2,205-lb (1000-kg) bombload. Maximum speed was estimated at 292 mph (470 km/h), service ceiling at 20,670 ft (6300 m) and range at 746 miles (1200 km).

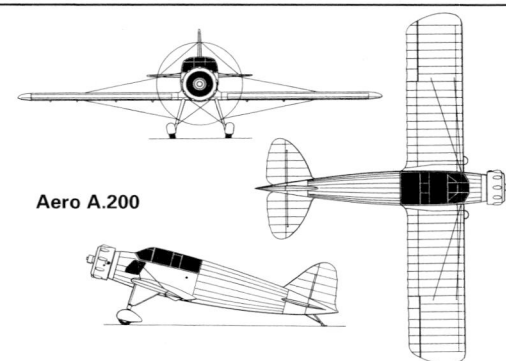

Following the German invasion of Czechoslovakia in early 1939, the Czech air force's Aero A.304 bombers were taken over and impressed into the service of German and Bulgarian forces.

SPECIFICATION	
Aero A.204	
Type: 10-seat light transport	service ceiling 19,030 ft (5800 m); range 559 miles (900 km)
Powerplant: two 360-hp (268-kW) Walter Pollux IIR radial piston engines	**Weights:** empty 6,283 lb (2850 kg); maximum take-off 9,480 lb (4300 kg)
Performance: maximum level speed 199 mph (320 km/h); cruising speed 178 mph (286 km/h);	**Dimensions:** span 63 ft (19.20 m); length 43 ft 3¾ in (13.20 m); height 11 ft 1¾ in (3.40 m); wing area 495.16 sq ft (46.00 m²)

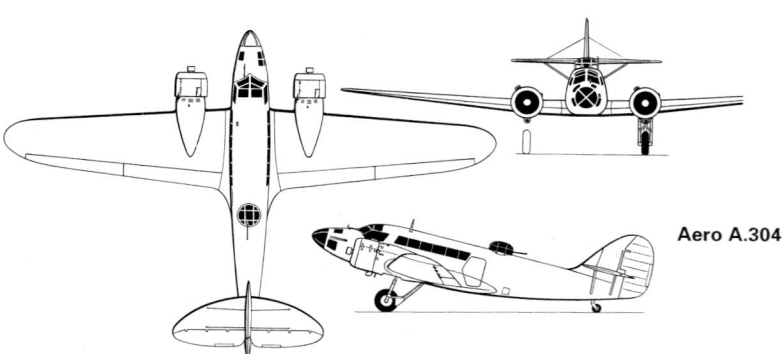

Aero A.304

Aero Ae 02 and Ae 04

Czechoslovakia was the first independent state to be formed after the break-up of the Austro-Hungarian empire at the end of World War I. The new republic contained the ex-Hungarian regions of Slovakia and Carpathian Ruthenia. The most western of these territories were highly industrialised and provided Czechoslovakia with the potential for the development and maintenance of the major military forces it would need to survive in the turbulence of central Europe after World War I.

The air arm of the Czech-oslovak army soon came into existence on the basis of the air units of the Czech Legions that had fought in France and Russia in World War I, and its equipment was initially a miscellany of obsolescent types inherited from the Austro-Hungarian forces and supplemented by a number of French types. Thoughts soon turned to the creation of an indigenous design and manufacturing capability, however, and an early leader in this field was the Aero Tovarna Letadel, whose chief designers were A. Husník and A. Vlasak.

The first fighter designed by this team was the **Aero Ae 02**, which was also the first fighter of Czechoslovak origin to fly, an event that took place in 1920. The Ae 02 was a wire-braced biplane of mixed construction covered largely with fabric. The fuselage was built of welded steel tube. The single-bay wing cellule was based on a flat upper wing that was carried above the fuselage by two outward-canted sets of N-type cabane struts with the centre supported by an inverted-Vee strut. It featured large aerodynamically balanced ailerons on the outboard ends of its trailing edge. The slightly smaller lower wing had dihedral and was separated from the upper wing on each side by a single I-type interplane strut.

A notable feature was the location of the fuel tank, not in the fuselage but in an aerodynamically shaped fairing for the mainwheel axle in the fashion pioneered by the Fokker D.VII fighter. At that time, efforts were being made to keep the fuel as far away as possible from the engine, in case it

was holed and set on fire. The sole Ae 02 prototype was powered by an imported Hispano-Suiza 8 Vee piston engine located in the forward fuselage, driving a two-bladed wooden propeller. The engine was cooled by a frontal radiator, and discharged its spent gases via short exhausts.

The Ae 02 took part in the 1921 air meetings. Piloted by Josef Novak, chief pilot of the Aerovka factory, it won the silver cup of the Czech Aeroclub for the best overall performance at the First International Flying Meeting, first prize for aerobatics, and second prize on two speed tests when it achieved a maximum speed of 137 mph (220 km/h).

Although it handled well, the Ae 02 was not put into production. It was clear that greater things could be expected of the **Ae 04**, and further development of the Ae 02 was therefore discontinued.

In addition to the Ae 02, Aero was also working on the development of other designs. One of these was the **Ae 03**, a single-seat biplane designed by Karl Rosner. This was a portly high-altitude reconnaissance aircraft of wooden construction and was fitted with cameras and armed with a single machine-gun. Power came from a Hispano-Suiza G Aa engine fitted with an early Rateau turbo-compressor. However, with the combined weight of the engine and this device, the Ae 03 was too heavy to meet the initial requirements of the test

In the early 1920s, Aero developed two fighter designs which, despite some noteworthy flying achievements, did not reach production status. The Ae 02 (above) was the first Czech fighter to fly, and gave rise to the generally similar Ae 04 (below).

programme and it was not completed.

The second fighter designed by A. Husník and A. Vlasak, the **Ae 04** was a logical development of the previous Ae 02 design, with the same basic configuration. The Ae 04 was of mixed construction with a fuselage frame of dural tube, and wooden wings. The wheel axle was faired as a small lifting surface. During the course of its trials and development, the Ae 04 prototype underwent a fair measure of modification, the most notable

feature being the replacement of the frontal radiator by a lower-drag chin radiator. This allowed the nose contours to be made cleaner with a neat fairing covering the otherwise protruding cylinder bank.

The Ae 04 was the main exhibit at the Second International Aircraft Exhibition in 1921, just before which it was flown by Rudolf Polanski to set a new Czechoslovak national altitude record of 20,869 ft (6361 m). Like the Ae 02, the Ae 04 was not put into production.

SPECIFICATION

Aero Ae 04

Type: single-seat fighter prototype
Powerplant: one BMW IIIa inline piston engine rated at 185 hp (138 kW)
Performance: maximum level speed 140 mph (225 km/h) at sea level; climb to 16,405 ft (5000 m) in 14 minutes

Weights: empty 1,477 lb (670 kg); maximum take-off weight 1,984 lb (900 kg)
Dimensions: span 25 ft 3⅛ in (7.70 m); length 18 ft 4½ in (5.60 m); wing area 157.15 sq ft (14.60 m²)
Armament: two 0.303-in (7.7-mm) Vickers machine-guns

Aero Ae 50

A Czech defence ministry requirement for an artillery observation aircraft was met by two designs, the Praga E-55 and the lighter **Aero Ae 50** (also designated **LB-50**). The Ae 50's highly unusual configuration was designed to give good low-speed controlled flight for orbiting battlefields, as well as a high standard of all-round visibility and short field performance. The two crew comprised a pilot and observer, who were seated in tandem in an extensively glazed cockpit.

The braced high-mounted wing was fitted with full-

span leading edge slats. To increase wing camber even further, a slot spanning almost half of each wing was mounted on the outer portion of the slats. The cockpit glazing even extended to the centre section of the wing, with minimal obstruction from the carry-through structures of the wing and tailboom. The Ae 50 was of essentially all-metal construction, with canvas covering the wing and all the control surfaces. Unusually, it was fitted with a fixed reverse tricycle undercarriage.

A further unusual feature of the Ae 50 was its potential for a double tow. It could tow a glider or, with

its engine stopped, could itself be towed by another powered aircraft. This capability was useful in the event of an overall flight longer than the flying range of the Ae 50. Furthermore, its wings could be folded so that the aircraft could be towed by car, or transported on the load platform of a lorry.

The prototype Ae 50 was first flown on 14 April 1949 and was then returned to the factory to repair a range of faults discovered during the brief flight testing. Insufficient directional stability was corrected by substantially increasing the size of the Ae 50's tail fin, while malfunctioning of the automatic slot on the leading edge of the wing was corrected by setting the slot permanently in the open position. Other minor faults were gradually rectified. However, the most serious problem – that of excessive weight – remained, and further development of the interesting Ae 50 was halted.

SPECIFICATION

Aero Ae 50

Type: two-seat artillery observation aircraft
Powerplant: one 105-hp (78-kW) Walter Minor 4-III four-cylinder air-cooled inline piston engine
Performance: maximum speed 109 mph (176 km/h); service ceiling 14,337 ft (4370 m); climb to

6,562 ft (2000 m) in 14 minutes 40 seconds; range 298 miles (480 km)
Weights: empty 1,043 lb (473 kg); maximum take-off 1,609 lb (730 kg)
Dimensions: wing span 34 ft 4½ in (10.48 m); length 23 ft 3½ in (7.10 m); height 8 ft 0⅞ in (2.46 m); wing area 162.00 sq ft (15.10 m²)

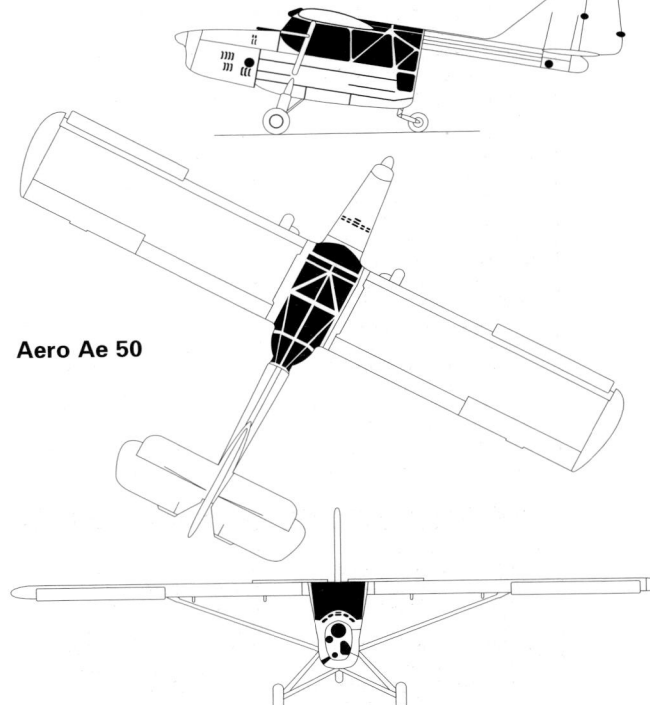

Aero Ae 50

Aero Ae 270 Ibis

With the break-up of the Soviet Union, Aero faced the prospect of reduced sales to a more difficult as well as diminishing military market and, in the late 1980s, decided to add a civil type to its product list.

Announced in the spring of 1990, the **Aero Ae 270 Ibis** (initially known as the **L-270**) emerged with a similar configuration to two rival types, the Pilatus PC-12 and the SOCATA TBM 700. All three aircraft are designed as utility and executive transports but, whereas the French and Swiss aircraft are aimed at the upper ends of their markets, with full pressurisation, the Czech aircraft is targeted at a

broader spectrum of potential operators. The type was initially proposed in two forms: the **Ae 270 U** unpressurised utility transport has fixed landing gear, optional deicing and a Walter (originally) Motorlet M 601F turboprop; while the **Ae 270 MP** pressurised transport has retractable landing gear, deicing and a Pratt & Whitney Canada PT6A-42 turboprop.

Further assessment of the private market then resulted in planning for a total of four sub-variants, two of them with wheeled landing gear, and the other two with wheeled twin-float alighting gear for full amphibious capability. The unpressurised landplane model is the **Ae 270 W** with landing gear, optional deicing, Czech avionics, no autopilot and an M 601F

turboprop driving an Avia propeller. The **Ae 270 P** is the pressurised landplane model with retractable landing gear, deicing, Western avionics (by Bendix/King), an autopilot and a PT6A-42 turboprop driving a Hamilton Standard propeller. The other two sub-variants are the **Ae 270 FW** and **Ae 270 PW**, which are the amphibious floatplane versions of the Ae 270 W and Ae 270 P respectively.

Accommodation on all variants is provided for one or two pilots, and a maximum of nine passengers or 2,646 lb (1200 kg) of freight. Alternative cabin layouts, each with a lavatory, are available for six/seven-seat business or four-seat club variants. High lift aerodynamic devices comprise mechanically operated outboard ailerons and upper-wing spoilers as well as hydraulically operated inboard Fowler flaps. The wing also carries integral tankage for some 250 Imp gal (1135 litres) of fuel. In the floatplane models, a small ventral fin and two auxiliary fins toward the outboard ends of the tailplane are added to the otherwise conventional tail unit to counteract the directionally destabilising effect of the floats.

The high cost of further development of the Ae 270 led Aero to search for a suitable partner to provide

investment funds and, in 1995, Aero signed a joint-venture manufacturing agreement with AIDC of Taiwan through the creation of Ibis Aerospace. However, the programme was then delayed by a dispute about ownership of the project in which each partner holds 50 per cent, with Aero supplying the design rights

and AIDC some US$44 million of capital. This would have been used to set up a production line designed to deliver some 850 aircraft for sale in Asia and Europe in the period up to 2010. On 15 March 1997, an agreement was eventually signed with the Taiwanese government for co-production of the Ae 270 in Taiwan.

Aero Ae 270 Ibis

The Ae 270 utility transport is an attempt by Aero to diversify its products away from military aircraft. Potential customers are being offered a range of sub-versions, which differ in key features such as engines, avionics, undercarriage and pressurisation.

Aero HC-2, Z-35 and HC-4

During the 1950s and 1960s, Aero Group built a number of small helicopters which met with limited degrees of success. Their development was due in particular to J. Slechta who designed the first prototype, designated **XE-II**, as early as 1950. This was followed by the **HC-2 Heli-Baby** light

general-purpose machine, which became the most successful Czech helicopter.

In the late 1950s, it was officially announced that 200 HC-2s were being built for domestic and military use and for export. Although they served in small numbers with the Czech air force, this figure has not

been confirmed, and the actual number built is probably much smaller.

A similar type to the HC-2 was built at Aero's Moravan works at Otrokovice as the **Z-35 Heli-Trener**. Designed by Jan Mikula, this was first flown in **XZ-35** prototype form in 1960. The Z-35 was constructed almost entirely of aluminium and was powered by a 140-hp (104-kW) Walter M 332 engine which drove a similar rotor system to the HC-2. Unusually, the Z-35's engine was mounted in front of the pilot in the lower forward fuselage. The Z-35 could carry a payload of 397 lb (180 kg), and had an all-up weight of just over 1,102 lb (500 kg), a maximum speed of 98 mph (157 km/h) and a range of 155 miles (250 km).

From experience with the HC-2, Slechta's efforts culminated in the larger **HC-3** 4/5-seat general-purpose helicopter which made its first flight in May 1960. This was intended for a variety of duties in addition to passenger transport, including air ambulance, crop-spraying, search and rescue, and training. Power

was initially provided by a Walter M 108DHK 240-hp (179-kW) engine but, in 1962, a version was flown with an uprated M 360 engine. The HC-3 had a maximum speed of

100 mph (161 km/h) and a maximum take-off weight of 3,137 lb (1423 kg). The main rotor was 38 ft (11.58 m) in diameter while the fuselage length was 32 ft 9½ in (10.00 m).

Below: The Z-35 Heli-Trener was intended for diverse missions such as aerial photography, aeromedical transport, crop spraying, geological survey support and power-line patrol.

Below: The HC-3 resembled a scaled-up version of the HC-2, but introduced an enclosed cabin and non-retractable four-wheeled undercarriage.

The HC-2 light helicopter was Czechoslovakia's most successful rotary-wing aircraft. The two crew sat side-by-side in a cabin which had no doors.

Aero L-29 Delfin

Even for a type designed for service mainly with the air forces of the Warsaw Pact, which operated vast numbers of aircraft and consequently issued large production orders, a manufacturing total of more than 3,500 examples of a single type indicates a particularly successful design. Such was the case with the **Aero L-29 Delfin** (dolphin), later allocated the NATO ASCC reporting name **'Maya'**.

The type was evolved to supersede the piston-engined trainers then in service with the Czechoslovak air force for both the basic and advanced flying training roles, essentially taking the pupil right through to the operational training phase.

Under the leadership of Zdenek Rublic and K. Tomas, Aero's designers developed a trainer which was robust, easy to maintain and simple to fly. The L-29's docile and forgiving handling characteristics meant that it could withstand even gross mishandling from student pilots.

The aircraft that emerged was straightforward with a relatively thick-section unswept wing, which had only moderate taper and dihedral on the outer panels. Interestingly, the L-29 achieved a top speed of Mach 0.75 despite the lack of a swept wing. The flat inboard sections of the wing were distinctly tapered in thickness and chord, the front portions of these sections forming the air intakes. There were no high-lift devices on the leading edges, and the trailing edges were occupied by outboard ailerons and inboard flaps. These gave the L-29 a low landing speed of 83 mph (135 km/h), as well as good field performance.

Under separate canopy sections, the pupil and instructor sat in tandem on Aero-designed synchronised ejection seats, with the instructor slightly higher than the pupil. They were equipped with manual controls which had no servo assistance.

The L-29 had two main fuel tanks, one annular and the other cylindrical, in the centre section of the fuselage near the wings. These tanks were located near the aircraft's centre of gravity to minimise fuel travel and therefore trim changes due to fuel consumption. Power was provided by a Motorlet M 701 turbojet, which could be removed in one and a half hours. The rear fuselage was fixed by eight quick-release couplings and could be detached in 13 minutes by three mechanics.

The L-29's wide-track undercarriage and low-pressure tyres allowed it to be operated from grass, sand or waterlogged strips. Ground handling was facilitated by entry steps built in to the fuselage. Operational equipment included a gun camera for gunnery training, while two underwing racks could carry up to 441 lb (200 kg) of stores for weapons training.

The **XL-29** prototype, powered by a Bristol Siddeley Viper turbojet, made its maiden flight on 5 April 1959. Following the flight trials of a second prototype which was powered by the Czechoslovak-designed

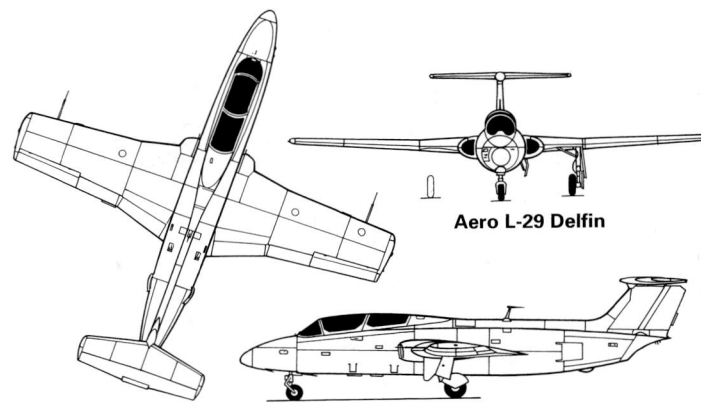
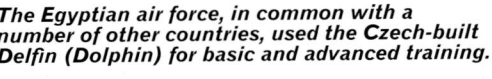

Aero L-29 Delfin

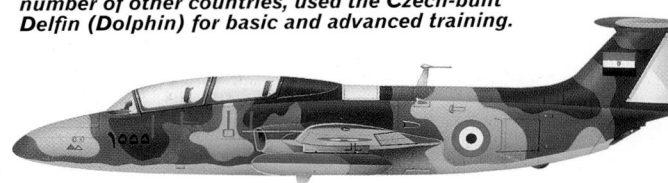

The Egyptian air force, in common with a number of other countries, used the Czech-built Delfin (Dolphin) for basic and advanced training.

By the late 1970s, the L-29 was the most successful Czech-built aircraft. It has been in service around the world, especially in ex-Warsaw Pact countries, and has seen combat in a number of conflicts.

L-29 Delfin operational history

Able to carry only a relatively small weapons load, the L-29 has been only occasionally used in an operational role. The most significant use came during the bloody Biafran conflict from 1967-1970. To combat secessionist Biafran forces, the Nigerian air force (NAF) had a pressing requirement for 10-15 jet trainers for use in the light attack role. After the West refused assistance, the federal Nigerian forces turned to the Eastern Bloc for help. With Soviet backing, the Czech government organised an arms airlift and, on 13 August 1967, Soviet air force An-12 transports (wearing Aeroflot markings) airfreighted L-29s and MiG-17 fighters (plus technicians and pilots) to Kano airport. Although figures differ, the number of airfreighted L-29s is generally put at six. A further pair of Delfins was ferried to Nigeria by Czech pilots, and four more L-29s arrived by sea aboard a Polish vessel.

When the L-29s were eventually re-assembled, it appears that they were generally flown by mercenary pilots (British, Rhodesian and South African) with Nigerian air force aircrew in the back seats as observers/navigators. At least one L-29 was destroyed by Biafran ground fire early in the war, but the majority of the 20 or so NAF jets (both L-29s and MiG-17s) written off were lost in accidents due to the tropical weather and lack of aircrew experience. Towards the end of the conflict, many NAF L-29s became unserviceable through lack of spare parts, although four reportedly remained operational. Among the final missions of the war, rocket-armed L-29s operated by the NAF were used to interdict the night air bridge to re-supply Biafran forces.

L-29s were also used during the October 1973 Yom Kippur War to supplement MiG-17 and Su-7 ground-attack aircraft and to provide close support for Egyptian ground forces. With its small silhouette, the aircraft apparently acquitted itself extremely well in combat, delivering its bombs and rockets with great accuracy.

Motorlet M 701 turbojet (this latter powerplant was selected for production aircraft from mid-1960), a small pre-production batch of L-29 aircraft was built for competitive service evaluation. This took place during 1961 against Polish and Soviet types, namely the PZL-Mielec TS-11 Iskra and Yakovlev Yak-30 respectively.

The XL-29's excellent all-round performance resulted in the type's selection as the L-29 to serve as the standard trainer of all the Warsaw Pact air arms with the exception of the Polish air force, which opted instead for the TS-11. There were just two sub-variants of the basic type. The first was the single-seat **L-29A Delfin Akrobat** that was built only in small numbers for aerobatic use, with the second being the **L-29R** dedicated attack version that appeared only in prototype form.

The standard L-29 trainer entered service in 1963, and became Czechoslovakia's first operational jet aircraft of indigenous design. Large-scale orders for the USSR, Eastern European Warsaw Pact members and for export resulted in the production of some 3,600 L-29s. Of this total, the majority was delivered to the USSR, Bulgaria, Czechoslovakia, East Germany, Hungary and Romania, of which around 2,000 L-29s were delivered to the Soviet air force and the DOSAAF paramilitary flying training organisation. The remainder of the production was allocated for export to several Soviet client states including Afghanistan, Egypt, Guinea, Indonesia, Iraq, Mali, Nigeria, Syria and Uganda. In addition to its normal training role, the L-29 was also used by operational units for secondary tasks such as instrument flying practice.

In early 1998 it is likely that the L-29 is still on the inventory of many of the above air forces either operationally or in storage. Many L-29s are now being sold as warbirds in the UK and the USA.

SPECIFICATION

Aero L-29 Delfin 'Maya'
Type: two-seat basic and advanced flying trainer with limited armament training capability
Powerplant: one Motorlet (Walter) M 701c 500 turbojet rated at 1,962 lb st (8.73 kN)
Performance: maximum speed 407 mph (655 km/h) at 16,405 ft (5000 m), and 385 mph (620 km/h) at sea level; cruising speed 339 mph (545 km/h) at 16,405 ft (5000 m); initial climb rate 2,756 ft (840 m) per minute; climb to 16,405 ft (5000 m) in 8 minutes; service ceiling 36,090 ft (11000 m); absolute ceiling 39,370 ft (12000 m); ferry range 555 miles (894 km) with two drop tanks, and typical range 397 miles (640 km) with standard fuel; endurance 2 hours 30 minutes with drop tanks or 2 hours with standard fuel
Weights: empty 5,212 lb (2364 kg); normal take-off 7,231 lb (3280 kg); maximum take-off 7,804 lb (3540 kg)
Dimensions: wing span 33 ft 9 in (10.29 m); length 35 ft 5 in (10.81 m); height 10 ft 3 in (3.13 m); wing area 213.67 sq ft (19.85 m²)
Armament: up to 441 lb (200 kg) of stores carried on two underwing hardpoints; weapons generally comprised of two pods each carrying one 0.3-in (7.62-mm) machine-gun, or two 220- or 110-lb (100- or 50-kg) bombs, or two multiple launchers for 2.17-in (55-mm) unguided rockets

Aero L-39C, L-39Z, L-139 Albatros

Vast experience with the L-29 in diverse climates and operating conditions was accrued by Warsaw Pact and Soviet client air forces. This experience highlighted several faults, including the type's low power and the tendency of the engine to fail on take-off from wet or slushy runways due to the low air intake position.

Despite its shortcomings, the overall success of the L-29 meant that no design competition was initiated to develop a successor, and Aero was solely allocated the task of designing the new trainer, a process which began three years after the L-29 entered service.

The new aircraft was developed primarily to meet a Soviet air force requirement, and the design team led by Dipl. Ing. Jan Vlcek developed the configuration using wind tunnels at TsAGi (Central Hydrodynamic Research Institute) in Moscow.

The resulting **Aero L-39 Albatros** introduced a conventional rather than T-tail but, like the L-29, it has a straight low-mounted wing for better handling at lower airspeeds. Although the unswept wing limits flight performance, the L-39's maximum speed is a useful Mach 0.83 by comparison with the L-29's Mach 0.75.

The L-39's modular structure comprises three major sub-assemblies – main fuselage, rear fuselage/tail unit and wing. The entire wing is a one-piece structure including the permanent tip tanks. Unusually, the swept fin is constructed integrally with the rear fuselage, which is removable to provide easy access to the engine for servicing. Including detachable items such as the nosecone, control surfaces, landing gear and canopies, the entire airframe of the L-39 consists of little more than a couple of dozen basic components. This enables any unit to be replaced quickly and easily.

The L-39 introduced a much enhanced overall performance, due primarily to the adoption of a more powerful engine; the Soviet ZMDB Progress AI-25 TL turbofan, known as the Walter Titan. The twin-spool AI-25 offers practically double the power output of the L-29's Motorlet M 701 turbojet, but with significantly reduced fuel consumption. The engine is an uprated, fully aerobatic derivative of the unit used on the three-engined Yakovlev Yak-40 regional airliner.

The L-39's cockpit was designed to be as similar as possible to that of the Soviet MiG-21 and the layout follows the fighter's general panel arrangement, using the same gunsight and many of the same instruments. The pupil and instructor are seated on Aero VS-1-BRI zero/93-mph (150-km/h) ejection seats. The greater vertical staggering of the seats improves all-round visibility, particularly from the rear seat.

A Safir 5 turbine auxiliary power unit supplies compressed air for starting, and makes the aircraft independent of ground power sources for engine starting, fuel flow or other services. Low-pressure tyres and a robust undercarriage enable the L-39 to operate from rough unprepared or grass airstrips.

By the end of 1970, five flying and two ground testing prototypes had been completed. Preliminary flight tests resulted in the introduction of slightly larger and longer air intake trunks. A pre-production batch of 10 aircraft joined the flight test programme in 1971 and series production began the following year. In late 1972, the L-39 was officially selected to replace the L-29 by Czechoslovakia, the USSR and East Germany. Service acceptance trials in Czechoslovakia and the USSR were successfully undertaken during 1973, and the L-39 began to enter service, initially with the Czech air force, in the spring of 1974.

The Albatros made its first appearance in the West at the 1977 Paris Air Show, by which time approximately 1,000 examples had been ordered, with 400-500 already in service. Since then, the L-39 has emulated much of the success of its forebear, the L-29, and, to date, more than 2,800 L-39 aircraft have been produced.

These Czech L-39ZAs demonstrate the capability of this armed variant to carry underfuselage cannon and underwing weapons.

L-39 operators

Total production of the L-39 (excluding L-39MS) currently stands at 2,849 examples, comprising 2,247 L-39Cs, 8 L-39Vs, 347 L-39ZOs and 247 L-39ZAs. Of this total, nearly three-quarters, consisting of some 2,094 L-39Cs, was supplied to the USSR. It is therefore unsurprising that large numbers of L-39s remain in service in Russia and other republics of the former USSR such as Belarus and the Ukraine. Other operators include Afghanistan (24 L-39Cs), Algeria (32 L-39Cs), Bulgaria (36 L-39ZAs), Cuba (25 L-39Cs), Czech Republic (40 L-39C, L-39V and L-39ZA machines out of an original 80 Czechoslovak aircraft), Egypt (10 L-39ZOs transferred from Libya), Ethiopia (20 L-39Cs), Hungary (19 L-39ZOs), Iraq (30 out of an original 81 L-39ZOs), Libya (about 150 out of an original 181 L-39ZOs), Nicaragua (an unknown number of L-39C and L-39ZO aircraft transferred from other countries), Nigeria (24 L-39ZAs), North Korea (12 or more aircraft), Romania (32 L-39 ZAs), Syria (90 aircraft out of an original 55 L-39ZO and 44 L-39ZA machines), Slovak Republic (14 L-39C, L-39ZA and L-39V machines out of an original 80 Czechoslovak aircraft), Thailand (36 L-39ZA/ARTs) and Vietnam (24 L-39Cs). East Germany's aircraft (including 52 L-39ZO and a few L-39V machines) were retired on German reunification and several have now been sold.

L-39 variants

L-39C: (C for *Cvicny* or training), standard basic and advanced trainer
L-39V: related target tug variant of L-39C, only eight were built for Czechoslovakia and East Germany
L-39ZO: (Z for *Zbrojni* or armed), weapons trainer variant; first flight on 25 August 1975; features reinforced wings and four underwing weapon stations; flown from the front seat only; rear seat removed to provide space for avionics or an additional fuel tank
L-39ZA: ground-attack/reconnaissance development of L-39ZO, first flight 29 September 1976; features reinforced landing gear, and a semi-recessed pod under the forward fuselage housing a 23-mm GSh-23L two-barrel cannon with 150 rounds of ammunition; gun/rocket firing and weapons release controls include an electrically-controlled ASP-3 NMU-39 Z gyroscopic gunsight and an FKP-2-2 gun camera in the front cockpit only
L-39ZA/MP: (MP for Multi-Purpose), variants of L-39ZA with more sophisticated avionics for the lead-in fighter training role; intended for export, only flown in demonstrator form; features Western electronics including a HUD, and an integrated digital nav/attack system (mission computer, an AlliedSignal Bendix/King avionics and other navigation equipment)
L-39ZA/ART: similar variant to L-39ZA sold to the Thai air force with Elbit electronics
L-39MS (L-59): further developed version of the basic L-39
L-139 Albatros 2000: L-39 version offered for US Air Force/US Navy JPATS competition to find a new primary and basic flying trainer; co-development agreement signed with AlliedSignal in June 1991; L-139 powered by 4,080-lb st (18.15-kN) AlliedSignal (Garrett) TFE731-4-1T turbofan; features VS-2A zero/zero ejection seats, a Flight Visions HUD and AlliedSignal Bendix/King avionics; first flight 8 May 1993, but aircraft did not win the JPATS competition, losing out to the Beech T-6 Texan II, and there has been no further interest.

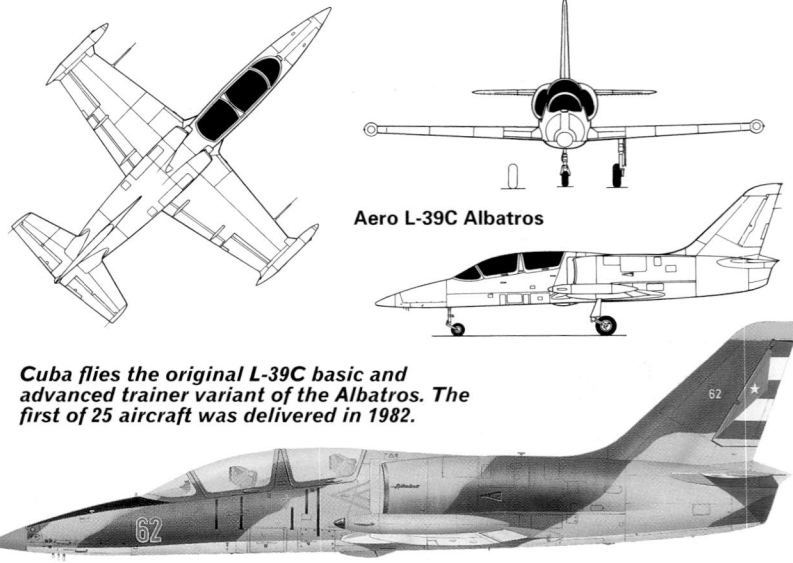

Aero L-39C Albatros

Cuba flies the original L-39C basic and advanced trainer variant of the Albatros. The first of 25 aircraft was delivered in 1982.

Aero L-59 (L-39MS) and L-159 Albatros

Development of the **Aero L-39MS Albatros** commenced in the early 1980s with the intention of creating a variant that remedied the original L-39C's perceived lack of thrust. The first of three prototypes made its maiden flight on 30 September 1986, and the improvements resulting from the alterations were sufficiently impressive for the L-39MS to be readied for production with the revised designation, **L-59**.

Compared with the standard L-39, the L-59 is a much more capable aircraft, featuring a strengthened airframe, new avionics

(including a HUD) and a new, more powerful engine. Developed jointly by Lotarev in the USSR and ZVL in Czechoslovakia, the DV-2 is a turbofan rated at 4,850 lb st (21.57 kN), which can be retrofitted into existing L-39s. Other changes incorporated in the L-59 include new lightweight flaps, untabbed ailerons, fully powered elevators, and revised landing gear with new brakes. Externally, the L-59 is identifiable from the L-39 series by its more pointed nose-cone and reshaped fin-tip.

The first L-59 off the production line flew on 1 October 1989 as part of

the manufacturing effort to meet Egyptian and Tunisian orders, and six early L-59 aircraft serve with the air force of the Slovak Republic. Egypt ordered 48 **L-59E** aircraft, equipped with US avionics by AlliedSignal Bendix/King, for a reported $200 million, and delivery of these aircraft was completed between 29 January 1993 and early in 1994. Twelve similar aircraft were ordered by Tunisia.

Further development of the L-59 began in 1994 to meet a Czech air force requirement for a lead-in fighter trainer/light-attack aircraft; the service eventually placed an order for 72 **L-159**s, a single-seat light fighter/attack derivative of the L-59. A two-seat L-59 was converted to serve as an interim L-159 prototype and was rolled out on 12 June 1997, with the type's maiden flight following in September. In production form, the L-159 has provision for a 5,159-lb (2340-kg) weapon load carried on seven hardpoints (one under the fuselage and six under the wings).

A range of engines was considered to power the L-159, and Aero selected the AlliedSignal (Garrett)/ITEC F124-GA-100 turbofan rated at 6,300 lb st

(28.02 kN) to power production L-159s for the Czech air force. This engine gave the L-159 an increase of 30 to 100 per cent in most performance parameters compared to the basic L-39. As examples, the L-159 has Mach 0.85 capability, and a sea level climb rate of 9,250 ft (2819 m) per minute, significant increases over the basic L-39's figures. Rolls-Royce Adour and CDV-2 turbofans are being offered as alternative powerplants for export L-159s.

Other changes incorporated in the L-159 include an extra fuel tank fitted into the space formerly occupied by the rear cockpit, giving an additional 655 lb (297 kg) of fuel, and

a wider rear fuselage. The single-seat cockpit has a zero-zero ejection seat, is protected by composite and ceramic armour, and has a radically revised avionics suite. This was integrated by Rockwell Collins (winner over Elbit and Sextant Avionique) and is based around a MIL 1553B digital databus. New systems include HOTAS controls, a Flight Visions FV-3000 HUD, Honeywell H-764G strap-down ring laser INS with GPS input, AlliedSignal Bendix/King liquid crystal colour multi-function head-down displays, and compatibility with night vision goggles. The comprehensively upgraded defensive suite includes GEC-Marconi Sky Guardian 200 RWR and Vinten Vicon 78 Series 455 ECM.

SPECIFICATION

Aero L-59E Albatros
Type: two-seat basic and advanced flying trainer with secondary weapons training and light attack capabilities
Powerplant: one ZMDB Progress (Lotarev/ZVL) DV-2 turbofan rated at 4,850 lb st (21.57 kN)
Performance: maximum speed 537 mph (864 km/h) at 16,405 ft (5000 m); initial climb rate 5,512 ft (1680 m) per minute; service ceiling 38,715 ft (11800 m); range 1,243 miles (2000 km) with two drop tanks
Weights: empty 8,885 lb (4030 kg) with ventral cannon pack; normal take-off 11,883 lb (5390 kg); maximum take-off 15,432 lb (7000 kg)

Dimensions: wing span 31 ft 3½ in (9.54 m) including tip tanks; length 40 ft ¼ in (12.20 m); height 15 ft 7 in (4.77 m); wing area 202.37 sq ft (18.80 m²)
Armament: one 23-mm Gryazev-Shipunov GSh-23L fixed forward-firing cannon on the fuselage centreline hardpoint, and up to 2,844 lb (1290 kg) of stores on four underwing hardpoints, generally comprising R-60 (AA-8 'Aphid') short-range AAMs, 1,102-, 551- and 220-lb (500-, 250- and 100-kg) free-fall or retarded bombs, 130-mm (5.12-in) S-130 unguided rockets, and UV-16-57 multiple launchers, each carrying 16 55-mm (2.17-in) S-5 unguided rockets

The L-39MS/-59 represents an attempt to breathe life back into the Albatros design. A more powerful and economical turbofan is central to the effort.

Aero L-60 Brigadyr

A Czech defence ministry requirement for a light utility/ battlefield observation aircraft was met in the early 1950s by the two-seat Aero Ae 50, which was not put into production. Aero's next attempt to produce a type to fulfil similar missions was the **XL-60** and this met with greater success. Built at Chocen, the XL-60 was larger than the Ae 50, and had a more conventional layout. It shared some resemblance to the Mraz Cap (almost 150 examples of which were built as licence-built variants of Germany's Fiesler Fi 156 Storch).

To provide good short field performance and the

necessary control at the low operational speeds envisaged for the type, the XL-60's braced, high-mounted wing had full-span leading-edge slats and large double-slotted flaps. Like the Ae 50, the XL-60 also had an extensively glazed cockpit which gave excellent all-round vision for the crew. Accommodation was provided for a pilot and two or three observers.

The XL-60 was initially powered by an Argus 10C engine and made its first flight on 24 December 1953, subsequently being fitted with a Walter M-208B engine rated at 240 hp (179 kW). Flight testing of the prototype resulted in extensive modifications to produce a second prototype, OK-JEA. The definitive version of the type, known as the **L-60 Brigadyr**, featured an enlarged passenger cabin to provide an optional

fourth seat, a modified rear fuselage and an extended dorsal fin. Power was provided by a modified version of the M-208B engine, known as the Praga Doris B and rated at 220 hp (164 kW).

A batch of around 50 **L-60A**s (also designated **K-60**) entered operational service with the Czech air force. Others went to flying clubs for general use and for glider towing as the **L-60D** and **L-60F**. A specialised crop spraying version was developed as the **L-60B** with a hopper for dry chemicals in the rear

SPECIFICATION

Aero (Let) L-60 Brigadyr
Type: light utility/battlefield observation aircraft
Powerplant: one Praga Doris B piston engine rated at 220 hp (164 kW)
Performance: max speed 120 mph (193 km/h); cruising speed 109 mph (175 km/h); service

ceiling 14,764 ft (4500 m); climb to 3,281 ft (1000 m) in 4 minutes 36 seconds; range 447 miles (720 km)
Weights: empty 1,896 lb (860 kg); maximum take-off 3,020 lb (1370 kg)
Dimensions: wing span 45 ft 9½ in (13.96 m); length 28 ft (8.54 m); wing area 261.56 sq ft (24.30 m²)

cabin and a large duster unit under the fuselage or underwing spray bars, while an ambulance version was designated **L-60E**.

The Praga Doris engine proved troublesome and many production Brigadyrs were subsequently re-engined by Aerotechnik with Polish-built 260-hp Ivchenko AI-14RA radial engines (**L-60S**) or with the M-462RF radial engine (**L-60SF**).

A total of 273 Brigadyrs was produced between 1958 and 1968, with a significant number being exported.

The L-60 Brigadyr with its superb short-field performance, proved to be a useful type in a wide range of civilian and military applications.

Aero Boero 95/115/150/180 Series F

Aircraft production in the Argentine Republic is centred on Cordoba and the factories of both Aero Boero and Fabrica Militar de Aviones are situated there. The former

company has concentrated on the single-engine high-wing monoplane formula and has built a number of such machines.

The **Aero Boero 95** was flown in prototype form on

12 March 1959 and initial production models from 1961 had a 95-hp (71-kW) Continental C90 engine. The model 95 was a three-seater suitable for private flying or, in a modified

form, for agricultural work. All-metal construction was used with fabric covering.

Other variants flown included the model **95A de Lujo** with a 100-hp (75-kW) Continental 0-200-A engine;

the model **95A Fumigador** with the same engine but equipped with crop-dusting or spraying equipment which included a 55-Imp gallon (250-litre) capacity chemical tank; and the model **95B**, construction of which began in 1953 and which had an unspecified

150-hp (112-kW) engine.

By mid-1965, Aero Boero was producing a second series of 10 model 95s and was planning to offer licence production to Peru and Uruguay but it is not known whether this plan came to fruition.

Further development led to the **Aero Boero 115**, with a 115-hp (186-kw) Avco Lycoming O-235 engine and a number of cosmetic improvements to the airframe, including wheel fairings. Reinforced plastics and aluminium alloy were introduced respectively for the engine cowling, flaps and ailerons and this variant made its first flight in March 1969, receiving its certificate of airworthiness in May 1969; production began two months later.

By early 1972, 45 of the model 95/115 series had been built and production ended in January 1973. The

following month, a modified version, the **Aero Boero 115BS**, was flown. This featured greater wing span, a swept fin and rudder, and greater fuel capacity – about 25 were built before production ended.

Using the same basic airframe as the 95/115 series, the **Aero Boero 180** was a little larger and accommodated four people. Its 180-hp (134-kW) Avco Lycoming O-360-A1A gave improved performance and extended its ceiling to 23,000 ft (7010 m) a particularly useful feature in the mountainous areas of South America. However, this version was rapidly succeeded in production by a three-seater bearing the same designation and using the same engine, and further descriptions of the model 180 refer to this model.

The first standard production aircraft were designated

model **180RV,** and deliveries began at the end of 1969. A number of variants were available and those with the 180-hp (134-kW) Avco Lycoming engine included the model **180RVR** (glider-tug) and model **180Ag** (agricultural aircraft). For customers who wanted the economy of a smaller engine, the models **150RV** and **150Ag** were available, powered by a 150-hp (112-kW) Avco Lycoming O-320-A2B engine, but in other respects were similar to the model 180s.

Production of the model 180/150 series is nearing the 100 mark, and an unorthodox development is the model **180SP**, basically a model 180Ag with the addition of shortspan (19 ft 8-in/6.00-m) lower wings to make it a biplane. While retaining the 115-mph (185-km/h) maximum cruising speed of the 180Ag, the

Early in 1998, in excess of 400 Aero Boero 115 had been built. The majority of these were part of a Brazilian government order for 450 aircraft.

biplane can offer a stalling speed of only 35 mph (56 km/h) against 55 mph (89 km/h) and greatly reduced take-off and landing runs. The agricultural tanks on the model 180SP are carried in the lower wings, instead of beneath the fuselage as was the case with the model 180Ag. Both versions are, of course, operated as single-seaters

in the agricultural role.

A high-altitude version of the model 180, known as the **Condor**, was flown in June 1971. This was a two-seater with modified wing tips, and a turbocharger for the engine was optional. At least four were built.

SPECIFICATION	
Aero Boero 180	at sea level; service ceiling 21,980 ft
Type: three-seat general purpose monoplane	(6100 m); range 733 miles (1180 km)
Powerplant: one 180-hp (134-kW) Avco Lycoming O-360-A1A flat-four piston engine	**Weights:** empty 1,212 lb (550 kg); maximum take-off 1,861 lb (844 kg) **Dimensions:** span 35 ft 2 in (10.72 m); length 23 ft 10¼ in
Performance: maximum speed 152 mph (245 km/h) at sea level; cruising speed 131 mph (211 km/h)	(7.27 m); height 6 ft 10 ¾ in (2.10 m); wing area 177.3 sq ft (16.47 m²)

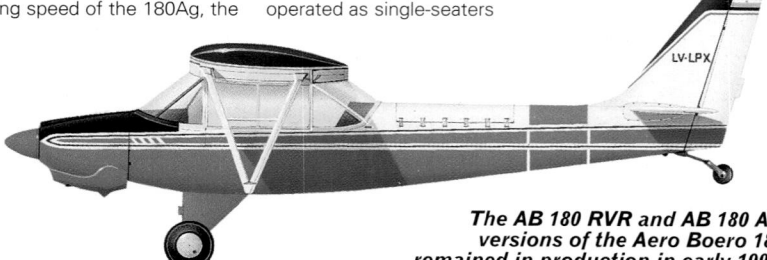

The AB 180 RVR and AB 180 AG versions of the Aero Boero 180 remained in production in early 1997.

Aero Boero 210 and 260

First flown in prototype form on 22 April 1971, the **Aero Boero 210** had been designed from 1968 as a

four-seat high-wing cabin lightplane of mixed metal and wood construction, with a Ceconite covering.

Some 35.2 Imp gal (160 litres) of fuel were supplied from two tanks in the wing to the air-cooled engine, which initially comprised one Continental IO-360 flat-six piston engine rated at 210 hp

The four-seat AB 210 utilised composite construction in an effort to save weights and achieve high performance. Only one example was flown.

SPECIFICATION	
Aero Boero 210	service ceiling 19,685 ft (6000 m);
Type: four-seat lightplane	range 497 miles (800 km)
Powerplant: one Continental IO-360 flat-six piston engine rated at 210 hp (157 kW)	**Weights:** empty 1,477 lb (670 kg); maximum take-off 2,425 lb (1100 kg)
Performance: maximum cruising speed 140 mph (225 km/h) at 5,905 ft (1800 m); initial climb rate 1,181 ft (360 m) per minute;	**Dimensions:** wing span 34 ft 2¼ in (10.42 m); length 24 ft 3⅛ in (7.40 m); height 8 ft 10¼ in (2.70 m); wing area 176.53 sq ft (16.40 m²)

(157 kW) and drove a two-bladed constant-speed propeller. The sole Aero Boero 210 prototype was then upgraded to **Aero Boero 260** standard by the replacement of this engine with a Lycoming O-540 flat-

six piston engine rated at 260 hp (194 kW).

Although plans were laid for production of this aircraft, construction was, in fact, limited to only two prototypes, one of them reserved for static testing.

Aero Boero 260AG

In mid-1971, Aero Boero designed the **AG.235/260**, a braced low-wing monoplane that was intended for the dedicated agricultural role. The AG.235/260 was of steel and light alloy construction under a covering of Ceconite. The welded steel tube fuselage was of basically rectangu-

lar section with rounded upper and lower deckings. This carried the nose-mounted engine, the payload tank, the high-set heated and ventilated cockpit that was accessed by a jettisonable starboard-side door, a port-side utility compartment, and the tail unit which was a wire-

braced unit of welded steel tube construction.

Some 35.2 Imp gal (160 litres) of fuel were supplied from wing tanks to the powerplant, which was a Lycoming O-540 air-cooled flat-six piston engine rated at 260 hp (194 kW) and driving a two-blade McCauley propeller.

For its crop-spraying role, the aircraft was to have good low-speed and low-level handling. A glassfibre tank ahead of the cockpit held 110 Imp gal (500 litres) of liquid or 1,102 lb (500 kg) of dry chemical for delivery by hopper or spraying equipment under the wing.

The AG.235/260 was first flown in prototype form on 23 December 1973. It was anticipated that the aircraft, later redesignated the

Although a promising design the AB 260 AG was still awaiting financing for production go ahead during 1997.

AG.260, would be certificated in 1983 with delivery of production aircraft following this. In the event, however, certification was not achieved and the programme was suspended.

In the early 1990s, the programme was revived as Aero Boero began a heavy marketing campaign for what had now become the

Aero Boero 260AG with modifications. Dimensions were altered by the enlargement of the wing tips and a decrease in overall length. Fuel capacity was increased to 52.8 Imp gal (240 litres), and the centrally mounted hopper enlarged to carry 121 Imp gal (550 litres) of insecticide.

SPECIFICATION	
AG.235/260	at optimum altitude; initial climb
Type: single-seat agricultural aeroplane	rate 984 ft (300 m) per minute **Weights:** empty 1,521 lb
Powerplant: one Textron Lycoming O-540-H2B5D flat-six piston engine rated at 260 hp (194 kW)	(690 kg); maximum take-off 2,976 lb (1350 kg) **Dimensions:** wing span 35 ft
Performance: maximum speed 155 mph (250 km/h) at sea level; cruising speed 137 mph (220 km/h)	9⅜ in (10.90 m); length 23 ft 11½ in (7.30 m); height 6 ft 5½ in (1.97 m); wing area 186.00 sq ft (17.28 m²)

Aerocar Aerocar

Based at Longview, in Washington State, Moulton B. Taylor had long dreamed of developing a 'roadable aircraft', a vehicle that could be used as a family car and, when a journey by air was more practical, could be given rapidly-attached wings, tail unit and propeller. The idea was not entirely new for, as early as 1921, Rene Tampier had exhibited an aeroplane of this type at the Paris Salon.

Taylor established a company in February 1948 to begin the task of making his dream into a reality. By October 1949, the proto-type of his Aerocar had been completed and, powered by a Lycoming O-290 engine, made its first flight soon after.

It was followed by the improved pre-production **Aerocar I** which was awarded FAA certification on 13 December 1956 after lengthy testing. Four additional Model Is were built, for demonstration purposes and for sale, and these six vehicles accumulated more than 200,000 miles (321890 km) of road travel, and over 5,000 flight hours. One Aerocar I also gained FAA certification fitted with an uprated O-360 engine.

The Aerocar I was claimed to perform like any other light aircraft of similar size and horsepower. Its attributes included good

stability and handling.

The car's frame and running gear were made of high-strength aluminium and welded steel, covered by a fibreglass skin, while the wings, tail unit and control surfaces were all-metal. The driver/pilot used the same steering wheel for driving or flying. The wings could be folded and towed as a trailer.

It is unclear whether Aerocar actually built any production versions of its unique design, and the company subsequently developed a non-roadable version of the Aerocar I as the **Aerocar Aero-Plane**. This used the Lycoming engine and folding wings of the Aerocar I, while the elimination of automotive components saved sufficient weight to allow the carriage of two extra passengers. The Aero-Plane made its first flight from Longview in February 1960 and, like its forebear, did not enter quantity production.

The final version was the much improved two-seat **Aerocar III**, which was converted from an earlier Aerocar I, and was based on a fairly conventional front-wheel drive motor car. Major differences over the Aerocar I included a new streamlined body, greater capacity fuel tank, and a new three-position landing gear, with partial electric retraction.

Power was provided by

Above: Small wheels, sited at the outboard leading edges of the Aerocar I's wings, acted as trailer wheels when the aircraft was functioning as an automobile. The engine was situated in the rear of the passenger cabin.

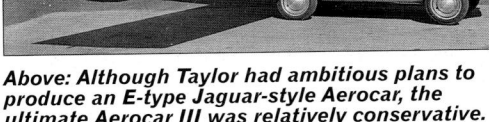

Above: Although Taylor had ambitious plans to produce an E-type Jaguar-style Aerocar, the ultimate Aerocar III was relatively conservative.

an Avco Lycoming O-320 engine, de-rated to give 143 hp (107 kW) for flight and 40 hp (30 kW) for road use. The engine drove the road wheels or, alternatively, a two-bladed Hartzell pusher propeller via an extended drive shaft within the detachable tail boom. The latter also mounted a tail unit of Y-configuration. The Aerocar III's 24-US gal (91-litre) fuel tank gave a cruising flight range of over 300 miles (483 km).

Braced monoplane wings could be attached in a high-wing configuration at the rear of the car and, unless the safety locks for wings and tailboom were all correctly engaged, it was not possible to start the engine for flight in the aero-plane mode.

Conversion from air to road use could be accomplished by one person in about five minutes. On arrival at an airfield, the wings and tail assembly could be detached and towed behind the car,

mounted on retractable wheels set in the leading-edge of the wing roots.

The prototype Aerocar III was first flown in June 1968. Hopes were high for greater commercial success for this version, but the type suffered the same fate as its predecessor and did not enter quantity production. Moulton Taylor's dream was finally shattered by changing legislation for American automobiles. To meet the new requirements of the 1970s the

Autocar would have to become too heavy and expensive to be a practical proposition.

In Italy, Aerauto SA explored the roadable aircraft concept with a vehicle designated **PL.5C**. However, this relied upon the use of a rear-mounted engine and pusher propeller for both air and ground propulsion, and consequently would have had only limited application for road use if its development had been pursued.

Above: The wings, rear fuselage and tail of the Aerocar Model II Aero-Plane were identical to those of the Aerocar I.

SPECIFICATION	
Aerocar Aerocar III **Type:** two-seat roadable aircraft **Powerplant:** one 143-hp (107-kW) derated Avco Lycoming O-320-A1A flat-four piston engine **Performance:** (A: aircraft; B: car) cruising speed A 125 mph (201 km/h) at 5,000 ft (1525 m), B 70 mph (113 km/h); service ceiling 12,000 ft (3660 m); range A 500 miles (805 km);	B 300 miles (483 km) **Weights:** empty A 1,500 lb (680 kg), B 1,100 lb (499 kg); maximum take-off 2,100 lb (953 kg) **Dimensions:** wing span 34 ft (10.36 m); length A 23 ft (7.01 m), B 11 ft (3.35 m), B towing wings/tail assembly 26 ft 6 in (8.08 m); height A 7 ft (2.13 m), B with trailer 8 ft (2.44 m); wing area 190.00 sq ft (17.65 m²)

Aerocar Coot

Although best remembered as perhaps the single most important exponent of the convertible car/aeroplane concept, Moulton B. Taylor had a number of other aeronautical enthusiasms including the amphibian flying boat. A basic design developed in the later 1960s was the **Aerocar Coot**, two separate forms of which later appeared as the **Sooper Coot Model A** and the **Coot Model B**, both intended for private builders as well as company construction.

The basic variant, the first of which was completed in June 1969, was the Coot Model B, distinguished by its pair of

light alloy booms extending to the rear from the outer ends of the wing centre section's trailing edge, and carrying two swept vertical tail surfaces with a flat horizontal surface between them. The Sooper Coot Model A first flew in February 1971 and differed from the Coot Model B in having a more conventional rear fuselage carrying a swept vertical tail and a strut-braced horizontal surface. This rear fuselage and empennage could be of fabric-covered steel tube, wooden monocoque, or all-metal construction.

The rest of the airframe was of wooden construction, with the exception of

the fabric-covered metal ailerons, and fibreglass engine nacelle, foredeck and, in the Model A, fuselage/hull shell. The design was of the 'float/wing' type, in which lateral stabil-

ity was provided by the centre section of the mid-set wing, whose dihedraled outer panels could be manually folded to the rear. The 'float/wing' design obviated the need for

underwing stabilising floats, as the two halves of the centre section served as sponsons, and the proximity of the wing to the water also created a 'pressure wedge' that provided low

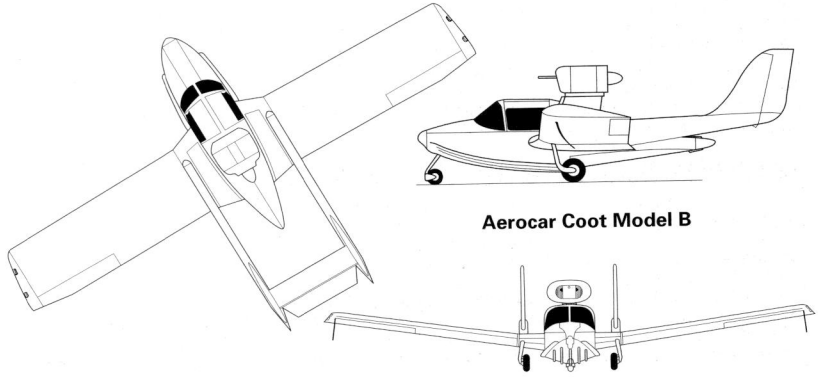

Aerocar Coot Model B

SPECIFICATION

Aerocar Sooper Coot Model A
Type: two-seat amphibian flying boat
Powerplant: typically one Franklin 335 flat-six piston engine rated at 180 hp (134 kW), or one Continental C-125 flat-four piston engine rated at 125 hp (93 kW) in Model B
Performance: (Model B) maximum cruising speed 130 mph (209 km/h) at optimum altitude; economical cruising speed at

50 per cent power 110 mph (177 km/h) at optimum altitude; maximum rate of climb 1,250 ft (381 m) per minute, take-off run (land) 200 ft (60 m)
Weights: empty 1,100 lb (499 kg); maximum take-off 1,950 lb (862 kg)
Dimensions: wing span 36 ft (10.97 m), or 37 ft (11.28 m) for Model B; length 20-22 ft (6.10-6.71 m); height 8 ft (2.44 m); wing area 180.00 sq ft (16.72 m²)

take-off and landing speeds without any recourse to flaps or other high-lift devices. The three single-wheel units of the landing gear were manually retractable (with provision for powered operation), the nose unit retracting into the underside of the bow and the main units into the underside of the wing.

The core of the structure was the forward

fuselage/hull, which was based on seven bulkheads, and was of basically flat-sided section with a Vee bottom carrying one or two steps in the Model B and Model A, respectively. The upper hull carried the extensively glazed raised cabin for two persons. At its rear, the cabin incorporated the leading edge of the pylon that supported the engine, which was

encased in a trim nacelle and drove a two-bladed, constant-speed metal propeller of the pusher type. Both Coots were designed for air-cooled engines in the power rating of 100-150 hp (75-112 kW), but some units with ratings up to 220 hp (164 kW) were used when flying from higher altitudes in Alaska or the Andes, for example.

Aero Commander 100 and 200

The Aero Commander line of single-engined aircraft began on 12 July 1965 when Rockwell-Standard Corporation acquired both Volaircraft Inc. and Meyers Aircraft Company. Several existing Volaircraft and Meyers designs remained in production at Aero Commander's factory in Albany, Georgia, giving Rockwell a comprehensive model line-up with which to challenge similar designs from light aircraft manufacturers such as Cessna, Beechcraft and Piper.

The **Volaire Model 1050** and **Volaire Model 10** became the **Aero Commander 100** and **Aero Commander 100A** respec-

tively. The Aero Commander 100 was a four-seat braced high-wing monoplane with fixed tricycle landing gear, powered by a 150-hp (112-kW) Avco Lycoming O-320-A2B flat-four engine.

In 1968, some improvements were incorporated in the Aero Commander 100's front and rear windshields to produce the **Darter Commander**. Production of this version ended in 1969, after a total of 335 examples had been produced.

Rockwell obtained certification of an improved version of the Darter in September 1967. It was hoped that the increased performance offered by this version, known as the **Model 100-180 Lark Commander**, would appeal to a far wider range of users than sporting and weekend private pilots.

The Lark Commander was generally similar in configuration to the Cessna Model 150, but differed mainly by having a more powerful engine – a 180-hp (134-kW) Lycoming O-360-A2F. It also had a swept fin and rudder which replaced the Darter's angular tail, a larger, more aerodynamically refined

engine cowling, a much improved cabin interior, and new wheel fairings. Production began in 1968 and ended after 213 examples had been built.

Production of the **Meyers 200C** by Aero Commander led to its redesignation as the **Aero Commander 200**. This was a high-performance four-seat cantilever low-wing monoplane with retractable landing gear, powered by a 285-hp (213-kW) Continental IO-520-A flat-six engine. For a short period, this aircraft was known as the **Aero Commander Spark**.

Rockwell's development of its own series of single-engined light aircraft (detailed separately under **Rockwell Commander 100 series**) and the failure of the Model 200 to gain a secure foothold in its partic-

The Darter Commander's (illustrated) most obvious feature was its forward-raked vertical fin. The aircraft was a little-modified variant of the Commander 100.

ular sector of the market led to the termination of Aero Commander 200 production in mid-1967 after 88 examples had been built. The penultimate Model 200 airframe served as the basis of the **T200E** experimental light twin-engined design.

The Aero Commander 200 did achieve a brief moment of international fame on 28 September 1965 when, flown by

Mrs Gerry Mock, the type established an international speed record for its class of 206.73 mph (332.71 km/h) over a 310.7-mile (500-km) closed circuit.

Rockwell subsequently sold type certificates and production rights of both Meyers and Volaircraft designs to other small US light aircraft manufacturers, which had little success in either developing or relaunching production of the Aero Commander 100 and Aero Commander 200 designs. Interceptor Corporation acquired rights to produce the latter, and built two prototypes with Garrett TPE-331 turboprops, the first of which flew on 27 June 1969. No further development work was undertaken.

Known briefly as the Aero Commander Spark, the Aero Commander 200 was a stylish four seater. The aircraft found a disappointingly small number of buyers.

SPECIFICATION

Aero Commander 200
Type: four-seat light cabin monoplane
Powerplant: one 285-hp (213-kW) Continental IO-520-A flat-six piston engine
Performance: maximum speed 215 mph (346 km/h); cruising speed 210 mph (338 km/h); service

ceiling 18,500 ft (5640 m); range 900 miles (1448 km)
Weights: empty 1,940 lb (880 kg); maximum take-off 3,000 lb (1361 kg)
Dimensions: wing span 30 ft 6 in (9.30 m); length 24 ft 4 in (7.42 m); height 7 ft 4 in (2.24 m); wing area 161.5 sq ft (15.00 m²)

Aero Commander 520

In 1944, Ted R. Smith was a project engineer with Douglas, where he had worked on designs such as the A-20 and A-26 Invader light bombers. With the

end of World War II in sight, he left Douglas in December of that year and set up the Aero Design and Engineering Company to develop and manufacture

his own aircraft. The company's first design was the **Aero Commander L.3805** five/seven-seat light twin aircraft which first flew in April 1948. Power came from two 190-hp (142-kW) Lycoming GO-435C engines, which gave a maximum sea level speed of 181 mph (291 km/h), and a cruising range of up to 850 miles (1368 km) at 10,000 ft (3048 m) cruise altitude. To prove the type's performance, the L.3805 made a 1,160-mile (1867-km) non-

stop demonstration flight from Oklahoma City to Washington DC, taking off and flying on one engine, with the other propeller stowed in the baggage compartment.

The sole L.3805 (N1946) prototype served as the basis for a production version known as the **Aero Commander 520**, which was built at a new factory in Bethany, near Oklahoma City. The production Aero Commander 520 differed by having an enlarged cabin, more powerful 260-hp (194-kW) Lycoming GO-435-C2B flat-six engines, and greatly increased fuel capacity. The first production machine (N4001B) was rolled out in late August 1951 and was delivered to its first customer, the publisher of the *Chicago Tribune* newspaper, on 5 February 1952.

The Aero Commander

twins proved popular with many business customers primarily on account of their excellent short-field performance, good handling characteristics and ease of operation. Excellent visibility was provided from the large cabin which gave a big, roomy feel for both pilot and passengers. The Aero Commander 520 gave rise to a long and successful range of derivatives which were of generally similar configuration, with a high-mounted wing and a tricycle undercarriage. This gave minimal clearance between the undersurface of the fuselage and the ground to provide easy passenger access.

A total of 150 Aero Commander 520s was built for both civilian and military customers. Three were evaluated by the US Army under the designation **YL-26** (later **YU-9A**).

Above: A single example of the L.3805 prototype was manufactured. It completed its maiden flight in April 1948.

Right: Considerable refinement of the L.3805 produced the Aero Commander 520.

Aero Commander 560 and 500 Shrike Commander series

The Commander 520 gave rise to a successful range of derivatives which differed mainly in their choice of powerplants. Initially, these engines gave rise to the designation of each variant, the model number being related to the combined horsepower of the two engines.

Thus the Aero Commander 520 was superseded in production in

standard accommodation for five, and moderately more powerful Lycoming GO-480-D1A engines. These were housed in larger, aerodynamically refined nacelles. Each nacelle was moved 2½ in (6 cm) outboard, with an accompanying decrease in cabin noise level. Optional long-range tanks could also be fitted in the outer wings to increase maximum

Aero Commander 500U

1954 by the improved **Aero Commander 560** (80 built) which had 280-hp (209-kW) GO-480-B engines with three-bladed airscrews, a strengthened structure to allow a 500-lb (227-kg) increase in take-off weight, and a new, slightly swept fin for greater stability. The USAF evaluated a single example under the designation **YL-26A**.

The 560 was followed by the **Aero Commander 560A** (99 built) which had a redesigned and simplified main landing gear, a 10-in (25-cm) cabin stretch forward of the wing to give

range to over 1,650 miles (2655 km). The Aero Commander 560A was also offered with Lycoming GO-480-C1B-6 high-compression piston engines, giving 295 hp (220 kW) at take-off rating.

In military service, 15 Commander 560As were delivered to the USAF for use as VIP transports. Designated **L-26A** (later **U-4A**), one served as the personal transport of President Eisenhower, being used to fly him on the 80-mile (129-km) route between Washington, DC and his farm in Gettysburg.

The US Army also acquired a single **L-26B** (later **U-9B**).

The 560A was followed by the **Commander 560E** (93 built) which was most readily identified by its increased span wing, a 30-in (76-cm) extension being fitted to each wingtip. This enabled the 560E's payload to be increased by 400 lb (181 kg), and required the installation of heavier brakes and wheels. The increased aerodynamic efficiency was augmented by fitting the 560A's optional high-compression engines. These features increased maximum speed to 222 mph (357 km/h), and Aero even managed to reduce the price of this model by US$1,100.

The next model offered by Aero was an attempt to challenge the lighter twin market dominated by types such as the Cessna 310 and Piper Apache. The **Aero Commander 360** was essentially a lighter version of the 560E, with two 180-hp (134-kW) engines. This model was unsuccessful and development was halted after the prototype had been built.

Growing interest in a lighter, more economical variant of the Commander twin series saw the introduction in 1958 of the **Aero Commander 500**. This retained the cabin, baggage compartment and structure of the 560E (rated for 8,000-lb/3629-kg take-off weight), but featured lower-rated 250-hp (186-kW) Lycoming GO-540-A engines, and a take-off weight reduced to 6,000 lb (2722 kg). The model met with greater success than the Aero Commander 360, with 101 examples built.

In 1960, the Aero Design and Engineering Company became a division of Rockwell-Standard Corporation and its name

was changed to Aero Commander.

Further development of the 500 series resulted in the **Aero Commander 500A** (99 built) with fuel-injected Continental IO-470-M engines, and the **Aero Commander 500B** (217 built), a version of the 560E with fuel injected Lycoming IO-540s. These engines were fitted in new slimmer, pointed engine nacelles with exhaust gases routed over the wing to reduce cabin noise. The nacelles required a new type of main undercarriage, the wheels of which turned through 90° on retraction so that they were stowed horizontally in the rear of the nacelles. The 500B received FAA type certification on 21 April 1961.

By 1964, all four piston-engined Commander twins in production were replaced by a single type. This was the **Aero Commander 500U** (56 built), which was known after 1967 as the **Shrike Commander**. The 'U' suffix was intended to indicate that the Model 500 satisfied the FAA's Part 3 Utility Category Requirements.

The 500U was essentially a 500B with a squared-off fin and a

pointed nose, and could carry an average useful load of 2,230 lb (1012 kg). Standard seating was provided for four passengers, the two forward seats for pilot and co-pilot/passenger having dual controls. Alternative seating arrangements could provide for a maximum of seven passengers and a pilot in high-density configuration, or all but the pilot's seat could be removed to enable a useful volume of cargo to be carried. In cases where cargo was frequently transported, a strengthened floor could be provided, and it was possible to have quick-change interiors to carry passengers and/or freight. There was ample space for the installation of a wide range of avionics and equipment, including survey cameras, and the utility value of the aircraft appealed to several air forces.

In 1967, North American and Rockwell-Standard Corporation merged to become the North American Rockwell Corporation, and Rockwell's General Aviation Division continued with the development of the Shrike Commander. These developments are therefore described separately under Rockwell Commander.

The Commander 560F was generally similar to the 680F, but featured unsupercharged IGO-540 engines and a consequent reduction in take-off weight.

SPECIFICATION

Aero Commander 500U

Type: four/seven-seat light business transport

Powerplant: two 290-hp (216-kW) Avco Lycoming IO-540-E1B5 flat-six piston engines

Performance: maximum level speed at sea level 215 mph (346 km/h); maximum cruising speed at 9,000 ft (2745 m) 203 mph (326 km/h); maximum rate of climb at sea level 1,340 ft

(408 m) per minute; service ceiling 19,400 ft (5915 m); take-off run to 50 ft (15 m) 1,915 ft (584 m); range with maximum fuel and 45-minute reserves 1,078 miles (1735 km)

Weights: empty equipped 4,635 lb (2102 kg); maximum take-off 6,750 lb (3062 kg)

Dimensions: span 49 ft ½ in (14.95 m); length 36 ft 9¾ in (11.22 m); height 14 ft 6 in (4.42 m); wing area 255 sq ft (23.69 m²)

Argentina received the first of its Shrike Commanders in 1968 and retains the type in service.

T-137

Military Commander 500 twins

Commander twins have entered military service mainly in the liaison and aerial survey roles. In 1968, the Argentinian armed forces took delivery of 15 500U Shrike Commanders configured as six-seaters. Over 30 years later, the eight survivors remain in service with the Argentinian air force, flying liaison duties in support of regional commands and HQs. The Mexican air force uses the Model 500S for light transport and photographic reconnaissance. Other Commander twin users include the Ejército de Colombiana (Colombian army), and the armed forces of Benin which fly the 500B.

Aero Commander 680 series

Development of the Aero Commander 560A followed two distinct paths: via the Aero Commander 560E and the **Aero Commander 680 Super** which resembled the Commander 560A

but differed primarily by having much increased power. Its two 340-hp (254-kW) GSO-480-A1A-6 supercharged engines could maintain full power up to 10,000 ft (3048 m)

and had increased fuel capacity. The prototype first flew on 14 May 1960, and a total of 254 examples was built for both civil and military use. The USAF procured two as presiden-

tial transports (**L-26C**, later **U-4B**). The US Army operated four similar machines as light utility transports (later designated **U-9C**). The US Army also acquired two with SLAR (side-looking airborne radar) as **RL-26D** (later **RU-9D**) and a single **NL-26D** (later

NU-9D) with special electronics equipment. Following service with the US Army, an example of the RU-9D served with the US Navy's test and evaluation squadron VX-5 at China Lake, supporting air-to-surface weapons and tactics development.

After 1967, production of the Grand Commander continued as the Courser Commander (illustrated).

The **Aero Commander 680E** (100 built) was essentially a lighter version of the 560E with a 560A-type undercarriage, while the **Aero Commander 680F** (126 built) was a 680E with new undercarriage and 380-hp (283-kW) fuel-injected Lycoming IGSO-540-B1A super-charged engines in refined 'speed-line' nacelles.

A major innovation for the Commander twins arrived in the form of cabin pressurisation. This enabled the aircraft to operate at high altitudes and so fly faster and more economically. This feature was introduced on a version of the Aero Commander 680 Super designated **Aero Commander 720 AltiCruiser**. Although this was general aviation's first new-production pressurised aircraft, it attracted little interest, with only 13 examples built when production ceased in 1960.

Slightly greater success met a pressurised version of the 680E, designated **Aero Commander 680FP**. This made its first flight in July 1961, and a total of 26 examples was built. Further development of the 680F resulted in the enlarged **Aero Commander 680FL Grand Commander**. Making its first flight on 29 December 1962, this featured a fuselage stretched by 6 ft 2 in (1.88 m), with larger cabin windows. The tailplane was increased in both span and area. The flight deck was segregated from the cabin, and the stretched fuselage enabled from four to nine passengers to be carried, according to cabin layout. FAA certification was received in May 1963 and deliveries ended after 157 examples had been built. A pressurised version, the **Aero Commander 680FL(P) Pressurized Grand Commander** (37 built), made its first flight in April 1963, and became available in production form after August 1964; thereafter all Commander twins had pressurised cabins.

In 1965, there was further expansion of the line with the introduction of turbine power on the **Aero Commander 680T Turbo Commander** (56 built). Making its first flight on the last day of 1964, this was a version of the 680FL(P) powered by two 575-shp (429-kW) Garrett AiResearch TPE331-43 turboprops which greatly increased overall performance. Other differences included a 5-ft (1.54-m) reduction in wing span. Production deliveries began in May 1966.

The **680V Turbo Commander** was essentially a similar version with minor modifications and a slightly increased take-off weight, while the **680W Turbo II Commander** (46 built) was a 680V with revised cabin windows (a large aft panoramic window replacing two smaller windows), a squared-off fin and a pointed nose to provide an aerodynamically cleaner installation for the weather radar. The engines were upgraded to 605-shp (451-kW) AiResearch TPE331-43BL turboprops.

In 1966, a modified version of the Turbo Commander, known as the **EMA-Commander** (for **Expanded Mission Aircraft**), was proposed to the USAF and US Army as a back-up counter-insurgency aircraft for a variety of uses including: photographic reconnaissance, logistic support, airborne command post and even light attack. A revised cabin interior was offered, giving a useable cargo space of 302 cu ft (8.55 m³), and allowing the carriage of 12 paratroops over 315 nm (363 miles; 584 km). This version was not developed further, however.

Production of the basic Commander 680 ended in 1965 and further changes came in 1967, after which the Grand Commander was marketed as the **Courser Commander**.

North American Rockwell Corporation (formed by the merger of Rockwell-Standard Corporation and North American Aviation in 1967) was subsequently renamed Rockwell International Corporation in 1973. Further developments of the Commander 680 series of twin-engined aircraft are therefore described separately under the Rockwell Commander twin series.

Relatively small numbers of the Commander 680 series entered military service. In 1998, a handful of aircraft remain operational with the Colombian navy, Greek army, Indonesian army, Pakistani air force and the US Army. The aircraft are typically employed in communications, general transport and photographic survey roles.

SPECIFICATION	
Aero Commander 680W Turbo II Commander	2,025 ft (617 m) per minute; service ceiling 25,000 ft (7620 m); range with maximum fuel and 45-minute reserves 1,094 miles (1760 km)
Type: eight/ten-seat light business transport	
Powerplant: two 605-shp (451-kW) Garret AiResearch TPE331-43BL turboprops	**Weights:** empty equipped 5,783 lb (2614 kg); maximum take-off 9,400 lb (4264 kg)
Performance: maximum level speed at sea level 290 mph (467 km/h); maximum cruising speed 280 mph (451 km/h); maximum rate of climb at sea level	**Dimensions:** span 44 ft (13.41 m); length 43 ft 1¼ in (13.14 m); height 14 ft 6 in (4.42 m); wing area 242.5 sq ft (22.53 m²)

Aero Commander 1121 Jet Commander

The conservative design of the Jet Commander is shown to great effect by the first prototype. The machine nevertheless offered fine performance.

By the late 1950s, US companies were rapidly expanding, with sites dispersed all over the continental USA. Demand grew for higher-speed business transports and Aero Commander set about developing a business jet to meet this need. In 1961, design was initiated of the **Aero Commander Model 1121 Jet Commander** high-speed business jet.

The aircraft was of mid-wing configuration with all-swept tail surfaces. Pod-mounted on each side of the rear fuselage, the two engines comprised General Electric CJ610-1 turbojets which conferred a respectable cruising speed of around 500 mph (805 km/h) at an altitude of 41,000 ft (12497 m). Standard accommodation was provided for a pilot and up to eight passengers in a pressurised cabin ahead of the wing. Advanced avionics were fitted for navigation, communications and bad weather flying.

The prototype Jet Commander (N610J) made the type's maiden flight on 27 January 1963 from Aero Commander's research and development facility at Norman, Oklahoma. Initial flight testing revealed its exceptional low-speed performance and ability to operate from relatively short runways.

However, the demand for additional payload resulted in the prototype's modification. It emerged as a considerably larger and heavier aircraft, with a 30-in (76-cm) fuselage stretch forward of the wing, relocation of the baggage and electronics areas inside the pressure vessel of the cabin, and relocated fuselage tanks. The Jet Commander's payload was thus increased by 1,500 lb (680 kg), giving a greater choice in cabin configurations. A standard executive layout with a buffet and lavatory provided accommodation for four passengers and two pilots. A pair of eyebrow windows above the cockpit windshield was also added to improve visibility in turns.

Built to full production configuration, the second prototype (N612J) made its first flight on 14 April 1964; a third airframe was produced for structural testing. The first production Jet Commander was flown on 5 October 1964 and FAA Type approval was given on 4 November 1964. The Jet Commander became the first business jet to be certificated for landings in conditions of 100-ft (30-m) cloud base and ¼-mile (400-m) forward visibility. The first delivery was made to the Timken Roller Bearing Company on 11 January 1965.

By January 1967, over 125 Jet Commanders had been ordered, of which 70 had been delivered. With the proposed merger between Rockwell-Standard and North American, the future of the Jet Commander was placed in doubt. US Department of Justice anti-trust legislations blocked such a merger as the new corporation would have two business jets: the Jet Commander and Rockwell's Sabreliner.

Rockwell's Aero Commander division therefore put the rights to produce the Jet Commander up for sale. Israel Aircraft Industries (IAI) stepped in with US$25 million to acquire all tooling and production rights for the aircraft, thus clearing the way for the establishment of the North American Rockwell Corporation.

Production of the Jet Commander was continued to fulfil outstanding orders, before its termination in 1968. Further development and production of the aircraft was undertaken by IAI under the designation **Commodore Jet**.

SPECIFICATION	
Aero Commander Model 1121 Jet Commander	minute; operational ceiling 45,000 ft (13716 m); range with maximum fuel and maximum payload at economical cruising speed with no reserves 1,840 miles (2961 km)
Type: high-speed twin-jet light business aircraft	
Powerplant: two General Electric CJ610-1 turbojets each rated at 2,850 lb (12.68 kN) of thrust	**Weights:** basic operating weight 10,075 lb (4570 kg); maximum take-off 16,800 lb (7620 kg)
Performance: maximum speed at 25,000 ft (7620 m) 525 mph (845 km/h); maximum cruising speed at 35,000 ft (10668 m) 500 mph (805 km/h); rate of climb at sea level 5,000 ft (1524 m) per	**Dimensions:** wing span 43 ft 7¾ in (13.20 m); length 50 ft 5 in (15.37 m); height 15 ft 9½ in (4.81 m); wing area 303.3 sq ft (28.18 m²)

Aero-Flight Streak series

Aero-Flight Aircraft Corporation was established at Long Beach, California in the late 1940s. Its first design was the **AFA-1 Streak-85** two-seat light cabin monoplane. Powered by an 85-hp (63-kW)

Continental C85-12J engine, this sleek all-metal low-wing design incorporated such features as slotted trailing-edge flaps and hydraulically-retractable tricycle landing gear. Subsequent developments

included the **AFA-2 Streak-125** with a 125-hp (93-kW) Continental C-125 engine and the **AFA-3 Streak-165**. Although only modestly powered, the clean lines of these aircraft ensured excellent performance.

SPECIFICATION	
Aero-Flight Streak-165	(338 km/h); service ceiling
Type: two-seat cabin monoplane	25,500 ft (7770 m); range
Powerplant: one 165-hp (123-kW)	1,000 miles (1609 km)
Franklin 6V4-165-B32 flat-six piston	**Weights:** empty 1,045 lb (474 kg);
engine	maximum take-off 1,695 lb (769 kg)
Performance: maximum level	**Dimensions:** span 25 ft 3 in
speed 219 mph (352 km/h);	(7.70 m); length 22 ft 4 in (6.81 m);
cruising speed 210 mph	height 8 ft 3 in (2.51 m)

Aeromarine 39

The Aeromarine Plane and Motor Company was established at Keyport, New Jersey before the beginning of World War I. In 1917, the company received what was then the largest order placed by the US Navy for naval aircraft. This comprised 50 of the company's Model **39-A** and 150 of the very similar Model **39-B** unequal-span biplanes.

Both of these types were two-seat trainers, and both were built with wheel or float landing gear. Both versions could have fixed tailskid landing gear or alternative floats and this latter installation was a major distinguishing feature of the two types. The Model 39-A had twin wooden floats and was powered by a 100-hp

(75-kW) Hall-Scott A-7A four-cylinder inline piston engine. The Model 39-B was around 300 lb (136 kg) heavier and was powered by a similarly-rated Curtiss OXX-6 eight-cylinder powerplant of Vee layout. The float landing gear of this version was also very different, incorporating a long central float and underwing stabilising floats, and this configuration became standard for all future US Navy floatplanes.

All of these aircraft were completed and delivered for service with the US Navy, a number of them remaining in use for some years after the war had ended. Two were used after World War I for early deck landing trials, equipped with experimental arrester gear of different

Quick to realise the importance of a sound basic training syllabus for its fledgling pilots, the US Navy ordered 50 Model 39-As. The aircraft were used to train the pilots who were to fly from the USN's first aircraft-carrier.

designs. After initial testing using a simulated carrier deck at Langley Field, Virginia, Lt Cdr Geoffrey DeChevalier – flying a Model 39-B on 26 October 1922 – recorded the first

deck landing on the US Navy's first aircraft carrier, the USS *Langley*. Arrester gear on this aircraft included what would now be considered a conventional arrester hook plus

hooks mounted on the landing gear and designed to engage with fore-and-aft wires on the carrier's deck. These wires were intended to keep the aircraft running straight along the deck.

In addition to being an excellent basic trainer, the Aeromarine-39B introduced the float configuration that was to become standard for US Navy floatplanes. The aircraft could also operate on wheeled or ski undercarriage (illustrated).

SPECIFICATION	
Aeromarine 39-A	(2285 m); endurance 4 hours
Type: two-seat land- or water-	35 minutes
based trainer	**Weights:** empty 1,650 lb (748 kg);
Powerplant: one 100-hp (75-kW)	maximum take-off 2,220 lb (1007 kg)
Hall-Scott A-7A inline piston	**Dimensions:** wing span, upper
engine	47 ft (14.33 m), lower 36 ft
Performance: maximum speed	(10.97 m); length 26 ft 3 in
73 mph (117 km/h) at sea level;	(8.00 m); height 12 ft 8¾ in
climb to 5,000 ft (1525 m) in	(3.88 m); wing area 494 sq ft
27 minutes; service ceiling 7,500 ft	(45.89 m²)

Aeromarine 40F

Under the designation **Model 40F**, the US Navy ordered 200 flying boat trainers from Aeromarine in early 1918 but, with the cancellation of contracts that followed the end of World War I, only 50 of these were completed and delivered. The Aeromarine

40F was an unequal-span two-bay biplane. The lower wing was mounted on the upper surface of the hull and carried a strut-braced balancer float beneath each wingtip. Directly above this wing, the Curtiss OXX-6 engine – which drove a two-bladed pusher propeller

– was strut-mounted to be positioned just below the upper wing. The hull was of plywood construction with side-by-side seating for the instructor and student pilot in an open bow cockpit. The conventional braced tail unit had large control surfaces. Unusually, these light flying-boats could be operated if required from ice or snow-covered surfaces, with optional skis mounted beneath the hull and balancer floats. Few of the 50 aircraft delivered to the US Navy were received before the end of the war, with the result that very few were used in the training role for which they had been produced.

A promising career for the Aeromarine 40F as the US Navy's basic flying boat trainer was curtailed by the end of World War I, which brought widespread contract cancellations. Only 50 of an order for 200 were actually delivered, carrying the serial numbers A5040 to A5089.

SPECIFICATION	
Aeromarine 40F	to 2,100 ft (640 m)
Type: two-seat flying boat trainer	**Weights:** empty 1,925 lb (873 kg);
Powerplant: one 100-hp (75-kW)	maximum take-off 2,485 lb
Curtiss OXX-6 Vee piston engine	(1127 kg)
Performance: maximum level	**Dimensions:** wing span upper
speed 70 mph (113 km/h) at sea	48 ft 4 in (14.73 m), lower 37 ft 4 in
level; landing speed 38 mph	(11.38 m); length 28 ft 11 in (8.81 m);
(61 km/h); rate of climb 10 minutes	wing area 504 sq ft (46.82 m²)

Aeromarine 75

In the years immediately after World War I, Aeromarine designed and initiated modification of the **Model 75** 12-passenger commercial flying boat

forecasting, like many other manufacturers in Europe and the USA, a considerable demand for civil air services. They were to discover, as did all other

manufacturers with similarly ambitious ideas, that they had anticipated such a requirement by a number of years.

Aeromarine's design for this early commercial flying boat was a conversion of the **Curtiss F-5L**, and

SPECIFICATION	
Aeromarine 75	**Weight:** maximum take-off
Type. commercial flying boat	14,348 lb (6508 kg)
Powerplant: two 350-hp (261-kW)	**Dimensions:** span upper 103 ft
Liberty 12 Vee piston engines	9 in (31.62 m), lower 78 ft (23.77 m);
Performance: cruising speed	length 49 ft 4 in (15.04 m); height
75 mph (121 km/h); range	18 ft 9¾ in (5.72 m); wing area
830 miles (1335 km)	1,397 sq ft (129.78 m²)

accommodated its 12 passengers in two cabins forward and aft of the unequal span biplane wing, with the crew of two in an open cockpit in the hull directly beneath the upper wing. Constructed of plywood, the hull incorporated very clean lines; the wings and braced tail unit were of fabric-covered wooden structure, with balancer floats mounted beneath the wingtips of the lower wing. Powerplant comprised two Liberty engines, each strut-mounted from the lower

wing some distance outboard of the hull and each driving a two-bladed tractor propeller.

Two Aeromarine Model 75s were used by Aeromarine Airways Inc. on a Key West-Havana air service until 1923.

The Aeromarine 75 flying cruiser Mendoza arrived in New York from Key West, having carried 27 people, the largest number ever carried by a commercial flying boat in America at the time.

Aeromarine 700

During 1917, the US Navy ordered from Aeromarine four seaplanes which had the company designation **Model 700**. Only two of these large three-bay biplanes (serialled A142 and

A143) were accepted for service and one was used in the very first experiments carried out by this service to determine the ability of an aircraft to fly in the torpedo-launching role.

Powerplant consisted of a 90-hp (67-kW) Aeromarine six-cylinder inline piston engine. This was mounted in the nose in a very cleanly-cowled installation. The landing gear comprised two floats that were long enough to eliminate the need for an additional

balancing float at the tail. Mounted as individual structures beneath the lower wing, these floats were spaced wide apart not only to ensure good water stability but also to allow adequate room for a torpedo to be carried beneath the fuselage.

Unfortunately, the Model 700 was severely under-powered and its very limited payload of 700 lb (318 kg) led to tests being conducted with a lightweight dummy torpedo. As a result of this, the trials were short-lived and somewhat inconclusive.

Aeromarine AS-1 and AS-2

US Navy interest in the seaplane scout type of aircraft, which had been operated by German forces

during World War I, resulted in the construction by Aeromarine of three aircraft in this class: a

single **AS-1** and two of an improved version, the **AS-2**. All three entered service with the US Navy, being used for evaluation during the 1920s, but the AS-1 was clearly little more than the prototype of Aeromarine's design to meet this requirement. An unequal-span biplane with well-staggered wings, the AS-1 had a slab-sided fuselage strut mounted on two large floats. The most

unusual feature of the design was the provision of a tailplane and elevators mounted in line with the upper surface of the fuselage, with the fin and rudder beneath. This layout was adopted to provide the gunner, accommodated in the rearmost of the two open cockpits, with a completely unobstructed horizontal and upward field of fire through an arc of 180°. The Wright-built Hispano-Suiza engine was mounted in the nose of the fuselage, but left

uncowled.

The AS-2s were of essentially the same configuration, but had equal-span biplane wings, and incorporated design refinements which enclosed a similar engine in cowlings, and introduced a modified tail unit. This had increased fin and rudder areas, both of these surfaces projecting slightly above the level of the fuselage upper surface and, by comparison with the AS-1, reducing to some small extent the gunner's field of fire to the rear.

SPECIFICATION	
Aeromarine AS-1	rate of climb 10 minutes to 5,000 ft
Type: two-seat seaplane scout aircraft	(1525 m); range 200 miles (322 km)
Powerplant: one 300-hp (224-kW) Wright-built Hispano-Suiza E Vee piston engine	**Weights:** empty 1,743 lb (791 kg); maximum take-off 2,730 lb (1238 kg)
Performance: maximum level speed 110 mph (177 km/h); cruising speed 52 mph (84 km/h);	**Dimensions:** wing span, upper 37 ft 6 in (11.43 m), lower 36 ft 6 in (11.13 m); length 30 ft (9.14 m); height 11 ft (3.35 m); wing area 391 sq ft (36.32 m²)

Aeromarine PG-1

Considerable US interest went into the creation of armoured attack aircraft such as the GA-1, designed by the US Army Air Service's Engineering Division at McCook Field, Ohio, but built by Boeing as its Model 10. A large triplane with considerable armour protection and armament that included

one 37-mm cannon as well as eight 0.3-in (7.62-mm) machine-guns, the GA-1 had very poor performance and handling and only 10 aircraft were built.

The development of this and other types did indicate the importance that armoured ground-attack aircraft might exercise in future wars, however, and

in May 1921, the USAAS therefore contracted the Aeromarine Plane and Motor Company to manufacture three prototype examples of a fighter capable of downing such attack aircraft and also of operating in the ground-attack role. Under the leadership of Isaac M. 'Mac' Laddon, the design team arrived at the resulting **Aeromarine PG-1**. This single-seat sesquiplane had a larger-chord flat upper wing with horn-balanced ailerons at the outer ends of its trailing edges. The smaller-chord lower wing

extended in two dihedralled halves from the lower longerons of a fuselage with a notably deep central section. The pilot theoretically had excellent upward and forward fields of vision, and he was also protected by armour, which extended forwards to cover the engine.

The core of the PG-1's planned operational capability was the heavy nature of its fixed forward-firing armament. This comprised one 37-mm Baldwin cannon in a moteur-canon installation between the two cylinder banks of the engine and firing through the propeller hub, plus one 0.5-in (12.7-mm) Browning machine-gun. The latter could be used to register

the target before the slow-firing 37-mm cannon was brought into action.

Making its maiden flight on 22 August 1922, the first PG-1 was powered by one Packard 1A-1116 Vee piston engine rated at 346 hp (258 kW), as the proposed powerplant, the Wright K-2 engine, had not yet been cleared for flight. The second aircraft joined the test programme slightly later and the third machine was not completed. Evaluation was carried out with two types of Packard engine and with the K-2, but the PG-1 proved to have dismal fields of vision for the pilot, poor performance and high levels of vibration, so further development was abandoned.

Aeromarine's PG-1 was an unusual attempt to create a pursuit (P) and ground-attack (G) aircraft. Severe vibration, possibly caused by the PG-1's armour, contributed greatly to the type's demise.

SPECIFICATION	
Aeromarine PG-1	**Weights:** empty 3,030 lb
Type: single-seat destroyer and ground-attack fighter	(1374 kg); maximum take-off 3,918 lb (1777 kg)
Powerplant: one Wright K-2 Vee piston engine rated at 330 hp (246 kW)	**Dimensions:** wing span 40 ft (12.19 m); length 24 ft 6 in (7.47 m); height 8 ft (2.44 m); wing area 389 sq ft (36.14 m²)
Performance: maximum speed 130 mph (209 km/h) at sea level; climb to 6,500 ft (1980 m) in 9 minutes 30 seconds; range 195 miles (314 km)	**Armament:** one 37-mm Baldwin fixed forward-firing cannon, and one 0.5-in (12.7-mm) Browning fixed forward-firing machine-gun

Aeromere F.8.L America

The resurgence of Italy's aviation industry after World War II saw the foundation of several new companies specialising in the design and production of lightplanes for the European general aviation market. One of these companies was Aviamilano Costruzioni Aeronautiche, established at Milan in the early 1950s. Its chief designer was Stelio Frati, who developed a high-performance two-seat cabin monoplane designated **Falco F.8.L**. This first flew in prototype form on 15 June 1955, powered by a 90-hp (67-kW) Continental flat-four engine. Due to its clean lines and excellent finish, exceptional performance was achieved from the beginning by the initial production **F.8.L Series I** aircraft on the quite modest power of a 135-hp (101-kW) Avco Lycoming O-290-D2 flat-four engine. The introduction of a 150-hp (112-kW) Avco Lycoming O-320 engine on the second production batch resulted in the changed designation of **Falco F.8.L Series II**.

In the mid-1950s, Aeromere Societá per Azioni was established at Gardolo Airport, Tento and, in the belief that the F.8.L would prove to be a marketable proposition in the USA, the company negotiated with Aviamilano for licence construction rights. The resulting version, built by Aeromere, had the designation **F.8.L America**, and was generally similar to Aviamilano's Series II aircraft, being powered by the O-320 engine. It differed in construction, however, to satisfy the US CAR (Civil Airworthiness Regulations) Part 3 requirements, and had an ultimate load factor of 8.7 with full load.

Of cantilever low-wing monoplane configuration, the airframe was basically of wood with plywood skins. The wing incorporated electrically-actuated split flaps, and all control surfaces were of metal construction. Retractable tricycle landing gear and a well streamlined transparent canopy complemented the clean airframe contours. The two-seat accommodation was heated and ventilated, and included dual controls as standard.

In 1964, Aeromere was taken over by Dr Laverda, the company being renamed Laverda Societá per Azioni and continuing to produce under licence a version with a 160-hp (119-kW) Avco Lycoming O-340 flat-four engine under the designation of **Super Falco**.

In 1979, the Super Falco was placed back in production by the Sequoia Aircraft Corporation in the USA.

SPECIFICATION

Aeromere F.8.L America
Type: two-seat touring/training aircraft
Powerplant: one 150-hp (112-kW) Avco Lycoming O-320 flat-four piston engine
Performance: maximum level speed 202 mph (325 km/h) at sea level; maximum cruising speed 190 mph (305 km/h) at 4,920 ft (1500 m); service ceiling 19,030 ft (5800 m); maximum range with 30-minute reserves 715 miles (1150 km)
Weights: empty 1,146 lb (520 kg); maximum take-off 1,720 lb (780 kg)
Dimensions: span 26 ft 3 in (8.00 m), length 21 ft 4 in (6.50 m); height 7 ft 5¼ in (2.27 m); wing area 107.64 sq ft (10.00 m²)

Aeromot Ximango series

Aeromot Indústria Mecanico-Metalurgica Ltda is one of the constituent elements of the important Aeromot industrial group that came into existence in Brazil during 1967 with the establishment of Aeromot Aeronaves e Motores S.A. Aeromot Indústria began its life as the designer and manufacturer of seats for EMBRAER aircraft, and later designed and made other components for these aircraft as well as seats for Airbus, Boeing, Fokker and McDonnell Douglas transport aircraft. A move in a related direction was indicated in July 1985 by the company's purchase of the assets of the Aérostructure (Fournier) motor glider manufacturer's factory in France, together with all manufacturing rights to the **RF-10** motor glider. The Brazilian company then adapted and improved the motor glider for production in three forms – for sporting, pilot training and paramilitary use.

The first of these developments is the Aeromot **AMT-100 Ximango**, which is a minimum-change version of the RF-10, and received Brazilian certification in June 1986. The Ximango is a cantilever low-wing monoplane of GFRP (glass-fibre reinforced plastic) construction except for the carbon-fibre main spar and light alloy airbrakes on the upper surfaces of the wing. Side-by-side seats accommodate a pilot and co-pilot/passenger under a single-piece canopy that hinges up and back at the rear for access. The outer wing panels can be folded upward and inward to reduce overall width to 33 ft 3½ in (10.15 m) on the ground. The landing gear comprises a fixed but steerable tailwheel, and main units that retract inward into the wing roots.

The Ximango is powered by an 80-hp (60-kW) Limbach L 2000 EO1 flat-four piston engine driving a two-bladed Hoffman variable-pitch propeller, and is offered in its basic form as well as two sub-variants for more specialised use. These are the **AMT-100P Ximango**, intended for military and police use, and **AMT-100R Ximango** general reconnaissance variant. Both types have two side windows below the canopy, as well as provision for a ventral pod for 220 lb (100 kg) of weapons and/or reconnaissance equipment. Sales of these models have been made to the Brazilian military police and other law enforcement agencies.

A Brazilian development of the RF-10, the **AMT-200 Super Ximango** first flew in July 1992 and was certificated in February 1993. This is essentially a development of the AMT-100 with a revised powerplant of one Rotax 912A flat-four piston engine rated at 80 hp (60 kW) but driving a larger-diameter propeller for improved performance. By the middle of 1995, Aeromot had delivered about 150 Ximangos (100 AMT-100 and 50 AMT-200 aircraft) to customers in nine countries.

The **AMT-300 Turbo Ximango** is a development of the AMT-200 with a number of aerodynamic improvements, plus a Rotax 914F turbocharged engine driving a constant-speed propeller. The aircraft had been scheduled to make its first flight in December 1997.

With production currently running at three per month, the Super Ximango has been sold in countries such as Argentina, Germany and the USA.

SPECIFICATION

Aeromot AMT-100 Ximango and AMT-200 Super Ximango
Type: two-seat training and sporting motor glider
Powerplant: (AMT-100) one Limbach L 2000 EO1 flat-four piston engine rated at 80 hp (60 kW), or (AMT-200) one Rotax 912A flat-four piston engine rated at 80 hp (60 kW)
Performance: (AMT-100) cruising speed, maximum 118 mph (190 km/h) at optimum altitude and economical 112 mph (180 km/h) at optimum altitude; initial climb rate 433 ft (132 m) per minute; service ceiling 16,405 ft (5000 m); range 857 miles (1380 km); endurance 7 hours
Performance: (AMT-200) cruising speed, maximum 127 mph (205 km/h) at optimum altitude; initial climb rate 590 ft (180 m) per minute; service ceiling 16,405 ft (5000 m); range 777 miles (1250 km); endurance 6 hours 30 minutes
Weights: (AMT-100) empty 1,323 lb (600 kg); maximum take-off 1,764 lb (800 kg)
Weights: (AMT-200) empty 1,334 lb (605 kg); maximum take-off 1,874 lb (850 kg)
Dimensions: wing span 57 ft 3¾ in (17.47 m); length 25 ft 10½ in (7.89 m) for AMT-100 and 26 ft 5 in (8.05 m) for AMT-200; height 6 ft 4 in (1.93 m); wing area 201.29 sq ft (18.70 m²)

Aeronautica Umbra AUT.18

The company known as Aeronautica Umbra S.A. Costruzioni Aeronautiche e Meccaniche was created in 1935 at Foligno, and initially concentrated its efforts on sub-contract work for other companies. Umbra gradually moved into the design of its own aircraft, however, after the establishment of a design office under the supervision of Ing. Felice Trojani. When the Italian air ministry issued its 1936 requirement for the first generation of Italian monoplane fighters, Umbra decided to offer its own design despite more experienced opposition from Fiat, Macchi, Meridionali

and Reggiane in the form of, respectively, the G.50 Freccia, C.200 Saetta, Ro.51 and Re.2000 Falco.

Like its competitors, the **AUT.18** (**Aeronautica Umbra Trojani 18** – the last referring to the wing area originally planned) was hampered by the availability only of air-cooled radial piston engines of modest power at a time when virtually every European fighter designer was able to use a higher-powered engine, generally of the liquid-cooled Vee type.

The AUT.18 was a wholly conventional monoplane of light alloy stressed-skin construction.

The low-set dihedralled cantilever wing extended from stubs built integral to the fuselage. The design featured a completely retractable tailwheel undercarriage with main units that retracted inward and upward into the wing roots and undersurface of the fuselage.

The AUT.18's powerplant was a Fiat A.80 RC.41 radial piston engine installed inside a NACA cowling although, in April 1940, a closer-fitting cowling, with movable cooling gills on its trailing edge, was introduced. The engine was rated at 1,030 hp (768 kW) for take-off and drove a

three-bladed variable-pitch metal propeller. Armament comprised just two 0.5-in (12.7-mm) machine-guns installed, somewhat unusually for a contemporary Italian fighter, in the wing outside the propeller disc.

Just one AUT.18 was ordered for competitive evaluation against the other

prototypes and this was first flown on 22 April 1939. By November 1940, flight trials had revealed indifferent performance and handling at a time when the G.50 and C.200 were already in production, so all further work on the AUT.18 was terminated in favour of other better designs.

SPECIFICATION	
Aeronautica Umbra AUT.18	497 miles (800 km)
Type: single-seat fighter prototype	**Weights:** empty 5,115 lb
Powerplant: one Fiat A.80 RC.41	(2320 kg); maximum take-off
radial piston engine rated at	6,559 lb (2975 kg)
1,030 hp (768 kW)	**Dimensions:** wing span 37 ft
Performance: maximum speed	8¾ in (11.50 m); length 28 ft ⅞ in
298 mph (480 km/h) at optimum	(8.56 m); height 9 ft 5½ in (2.88 m);
altitude; cruising speed 278 mph	wing area 201.29 sq ft (18.70 m²)
(447 km/h) at optimum altitude;	**Armament:** two 0.5-in (12.7-mm)
climb to 19,685 ft (6000 m) in	Breda-SAFAT fixed forward-firing
8 minutes 12 seconds; range	machine-guns

Aeronca 'C' series

In November 1928, the Aeronautical Corporation of America was incorporated to design and construct light aircraft for the general aviation market, and had the distinction of being the first aviation manufacturer in America to build a true light aeroplane for sale to the general public. From the above company title

the name Aeronca was derived, the renamed Aeronca Aircraft Corporation coming into existence in 1941.
The basic design of what was to become the **Aeronca C-2** stemmed from a prototype lightplane designed by Jean A. Roche, an engineer in the US Air Service. Aeronca set out to

improve upon this design, and also designed and developed a small two-cylinder horizontally-opposed engine to power it. When introduced in February 1930, the C-2's ungainly appearance resulted in a somewhat lighthearted reception. It was only when the capability of this single-seater had been appreciated, with economic operation that gave a range of 240 miles (386 km) on

8 US gallons (30 litres) of petrol, that humour gave place to interest.
When C-2s began to establish class records, and achieve a number of headline-gaining flights in the USA, interest turned to enthusiasm, and the embryo company was involved in building C-2s as fast as it could.
Of wire-braced high-wing monoplane configuration, the Aeronca C-2 had a wing

of composite wood and metal construction with fabric covering. The fabric-covered fuselage and braced tail unit had basic structures of welded steel tube. Fixed tailskid landing gear, an open cockpit beneath the wing, and powerplant in the fuselage nose, completed the simple C-2. Well over 100 were built before the introduction of the C-3 two-seat version reduced sales, and then superseded the C-2 which had established Aeronca as a manufacturer of light aircraft.

A design totally redolent of the late 1920s and early 1930s, the Aeronca 'C' series was produced in quite substantial numbers. Several examples have survived into the 1990s. Illustrated is the two-seat C-3 model introduced in 1931 and built in a number of engine types.

SPECIFICATION	
Aeronca C-2	km/h); service ceiling 16,000 ft
Type: single-seat, light high-wing	(4875 m); range 240 miles
sporting aircraft	(386 km)
Powerplant: one 26-hp (19-kW)	**Weights:** empty 398 lb (181 kg);
Aeronca E-107A flat-two piston	maximum take-off 672 lb (305 kg)
engine	**Dimensions:** wing span 36 ft
Performance: maximum level	(10.97 m); length 20 ft (6.10 m);
speed 80 mph (129 km/h),	height 7 ft 6 in (2.29 m); wing area
cruising speed 65 mph (105	142.00 sq ft (13.19 m²)

Aeronca 'C' series variants

C-1 Cadet: high-performance version of the C-2, incorporating a strengthened fuselage, reduced wing span, the more powerful 36-hp (27-kW) Aeronca E-113 flat-two engine, and some design refinements; only about three built; maximum level speed 95 mph (153 km/h), cruising speed 80 mph (129 km/h), service ceiling 12,500 ft (3810 m), empty weight 426 lb (193 kg), maximum take-off weight 700 lb (318 kg), span 29 ft (8.84 m) and wing area 115 sq ft (10.68 m²)
C-2 Deluxe: version of the C-2 which incorporated a wider fuselage and a number of design refinements; empty weight 426 lb (193 kg) and maximum take-off weight 700 lb (318 kg)
C-2N Scout: de-luxe sport version of the C-2, of which about four were built, incorporated the refinements of the C-2 Deluxe, plus a 36-hp (27-kW) Aeronca E-113 or E-113A engine
PC-2: seaplane version of the C-2 with twin APC float installation; empty weight 470 lb (213 kg) and maximum take-off weight 694 lb (315 kg)
PC-2 Deluxe: seaplane version of the C-2 Deluxe; empty weight 498 lb (226 kg) and maximum take-off weight 722 lb (327 kg)
C-3 Duplex: two-seat version of the C-2, introduced in 1931, and of which something in excess of 400 were built before production ended in 1937; side-by-side seating arrangement, with dual controls optional, or standard in trainer version known as Collegian; progressive introduction of improvements during six-year production run; powered by 36-hp (27-kW) Aeronca E-113, E113A or E-113B, or 40-hp (30-kW) E-113C; late versions had a maximum level speed of 90 mph (145 km/h), cruising speed of 75 mph (121 km/h), service ceiling of 12,000 ft (3660 m) range of 190 miles (306 km), empty weight of 569 lb (258 kg) and maximum take-off weight of 1,006 lb (456 kg): built under licence in the UK as the Aeronca 100 with the 36-hp (27-kW) JAP J.99 engine
PC-3: seaplane version of the C-3 with EDO or Warner floats; empty weight of late versions 658 lb (298 kg) and maximum take-off weight 1,069 lb (485 kg)

Viewed as an improvement to the tiny single-seat C-2, the later C-3 was a two-seat high-wing cabin monoplane powered by a 40-hp (30-kW) engine.

Aeronca 'K' Scout series

Aeronca achieved notable early success with its 'C' series of lightplanes but, by 1936, it had become evident that the type had reached the limit of its potential and the company initiated development of a successor in August 1935.

The new aircraft was to use the company's reliable single-ignition two-cylinder E-113 engine although, under chief designer Roger E. Schlemmer, Aeronca took the opportunity to give the new two-seater a far more modern appearance than the 'C' series.

The wing was virtually identical, both in construction and in its high-wing mounting, but the 'C' series' wire bracing was replaced by Vee stream-lined-section lift struts. Fixed tailskid landing gear included stalky main units that were cleanly faired, concealing the oleo-pneumatic shock-absorbers. The majority of owners appear to have elected for the optional tailwheel. The cabin was completely enclosed, and provided

side-by-side accommodation for two on a bench seat. A major change in the cabin was the installation of control wheels in place of a single stick held by both pilots.

The far more sophisticated design was reflected by options that included cabin and carburettor box-heating, a propeller spinner, and wheel brakes. In addition to the standard E-113CB powerplant, the Model K was offered with 45-hp (34-kW) E-113CD or E-113CDB engines. A further option was a second cabin door (to port), which became obligatory on all versions equipped with floats.

Development of the resulting **Aeronca 'K'** series encountered several major problems which delayed production of the type. These problems included poor take-off characteristics, a high-drag landing gear, and the dual-wheel control system, the first on an American lightplane. These problems took time to fix and so the

company concentrated its efforts instead on the low-wing **Aeronca 'L'** series (described below). Consequently, this model preceded the 'K' series into production by over a year. Work on the Model K was restarted in October 1936, but it was not until January 1937 that the prototype model (X17440) was unveiled publicly.

However, hopes for sales of the 'K' series were dashed when disaster struck the Aeronca factory on 21 January 1937. Located at Lunken Airport, Cincinnati, the plant was inundated by 30 ft (10 m) of flood water from the Ohio River. When the waters had receded, production of the 'L' series was terminated, and Aeronca thereafter concentrated its efforts on the 'K' series. The first production Model K (the name **Scout** was apparently little used) was finished in April 1937 and was followed by a further 296 examples by the end of the year.

The Model K Scout was the first of a line. More significantly, it established a basic configuration that, with only minor alterations, was to serve not only for a prolific range of pre-war versions, but also for most of the subsequent Aeronca aircraft marketed under a variety of names. The aircraft was relatively easy to fly, manoeuvrable, reliable, and had generally docile handling characteristics for the novice pilot.

A classic high-wing monoplane of the late 1930s, the Aeronca K Scout was built on a relatively wide scale, and laid the foundations for Aeronca's successful range of post-war light aircraft.

Aeronca 'K' Scout series variants

Aeronca K Scout: basic high-wing cabin monoplane; total of 363 built (comprising prototype and 297 production examples in 1937, and 65 in 1938)
Aeronca KS Sea Scout: seaplane version of Model 'K' with Edo Model 1070 twin-float landing gear; 14 built
Aeronca KC Scout: introduced May 1938; improved version of the Model K with split-axle type main landing gear units and a 40-hp (30-kW) Continental A-40-4 air-cooled flat-four piston engine as standard; 35 built
Aeronca KC (CF) Scout: version of the KC Scout with the Continental A-40 replaced by a 40-hp (30-kW) Franklin 4AC-150 Series 40 flat-four engine, plus split-axle landing gear; about six built
Aeronca KF: generally similar to the Model KC Scout, but powered by a 50-hp (37-kW) Franklin 4AC-150 Series 50 flat-four engine; six built
Aeronca KL: version generally similar to the Model KC Scout, but powered instead by a 50-hp (37-kW) Lycoming O-145A engine; five built
Aeronca KM: version generally similar to the model KC Scout, but powered instead by a 50-hp (37-kW) Menasco M-50 Pirate flat-four engine; the Menasco engine was quickly dropped as single-ignition engines were made illegal for new light aircraft designs, and all other engines offered were dual-ignition models; nine built
Aeronca KCA: improved version of Model K with detail refinements, powered by 50-hp (37-kW) Continental A-50-1 flat-four engine; 65 built

---

SPECIFICATION

Aeronca K Scout
Type: two-seat cabin monoplane
Powerplant: one 42-hp (31-kW) Aeronca E-113CB flat-two piston engine
Performance: maximum level speed 93 mph (150 km/h) at sea level; cruising speed 85 mph (137 km/h); initial climb rate 450 ft (137 m) per minute; service ceiling 12,000 ft (3660 m); range 255 miles (410 km)
Weights: empty 590 lb (268 kg); maximum take-off 1,040 lb (472 kg)
Dimensions: wing span 36 ft (10.97 m); length 20 ft 7 in (6.27 m); height 6 ft 7 in (2.01 m); wing area 146.35 sq ft (16.60 m²)

Aeronca 'L' series

Aeronca's chief designer, Roger Schlemmer, had been heavily influenced by the five-seat Fairchild F-45 of 1934 and adopted a similar low-wing layout for the **Aeronca 'L'** series. Design was initiated within one month of the high-wing Model K, and the two prototypes were built side-by-side on Aeronca's factory floor.

Schlemmer's efforts resulted in a neat cabin monoplane, which incorporated elements from the design of the Model K, such as the vertical tail surfaces. Following Aeronca's established method, the wing was of composite wood and light alloy construction, with fabric covering. Basic struc-

ture of the fuselage and the wire-braced tail unit was welded steel tube, which was fabric-covered. Landing gear was of the fixed tailwheel type, the main units covered by large streamlined 'trousers' that were faired into the under-surface of the wings.

The prototype Model L was fitted with Aeronca's reliable E-113C engine, and it made its first flight in November 1935, following which it was evident that the aircraft was pitifully underpowered.

However, it appeared to have good sales potential and plans were made immediately to introduce a more powerful engine. With a 70-hp (52-kW) Le Blond five-cylinder radial air-cooled

engine installed in the prototype, it was clear that the Model L had great potential. Minor modifications were made to prepare the type for production. Features included the widening of the cabin, the offsetting of a fin to correct for torque, and an improved braking system. Aeronca offered three major variants of the Model L, each with successively greater power. Deliveries of the initial version, the **LA**, began in early 1936.

Accommodation for two, side-by-side, was provided in a cabin which was large enough to have baggage space behind the seats. Optional items included an electrical system (with storage battery), powered by a wind-driven generator, an engine starter, and landing and navigation lights. Dual controls, additional instrumentation, cabin heating and radio could also be provided to the individual customer's requirements.

The **Aeronca LB** was generally similar to the LA, but was fitted with an 85-hp (63-kW) Le Blond 5DF engine which increased top speed to 120 mph (193 km/h). This version

proved the most popular of the 'L' series, with 27 examples built. The **Aeronca LC** was also generally similar to the LA, but was powered by a 90-hp (67-kW) Warner Scarab Junior five-cylinder radial engine which gave a maximum level speed of 123 mph (198 km/h). The engine, which required a different mounting, was tailored to the needs of individual customers The LC was the final production version, of which about 25 were built before being superseded by the Model K in 1937. The **Aeronca LCS** was a seaplane version of the LC, equipped with Edo

floats. Just one example was built (NC16289), and this was later converted to a standard landplane configuration.

Unfortunately, Aeronca had produced a light aircraft far ahead of its time, and sales of the type proved disappointing. During 1936, the company actually produced twice as many C-3s as 'L's. Its fate was sealed by the flooding of the Aeronca factory in January 1937. Following this disaster, the Aeronca board decided to terminate production of the type and concentrate its efforts on the high-wing Model K.

SPECIFICATION

Aeronca LA
Type: two-seat low-wing cabin monoplane
Powerplant: one 70-hp (52-kW) Le Blond 5DE radial piston engine
Performance: maximum level speed 115 mph (185 km/h) at sea level; cruising speed 100 mph (161 km/h); service ceiling 12,000 ft (3660 m); range 500 miles (805 km)
Weights: empty 1,036 lb (470 kg); maximum take-off 1,680 lb (762 kg)
Dimensions: span 36 ft (10.97 m); length 22 ft 6 in (6.86 m); height 7 ft (2.13 m); wing area 150 sq ft (13.94 m²)

The Aeronca L was conceptually ahead of its time. It proved popular, but not to the same extent as the more successful 'C' series, despite its superior performance and comfort.

Aeronca Model 7 Champion/L-16 series

The L-16 was a military version of the civil Model 7 Champion, and served briefly as a liaison/artillery spotter aircraft during the Korean War.

Shortly after World War II, aircraft manufacturers began gearing up for civil production. Aeronca designed a new model that combined the features of the pre-war Model 50-T/ Model 65-Ts and the Defender. Designed by Ray Hermes, the Model **7AC Champion** was the first US lightplane to be certificated after World War II.

The type shared the same general high-wing configuration and construction as its predecessors, but featured a slightly reduced wingspan. The main change concerned the accommodation, the two occupants being seated in tandem, and

with dual controls provided as standard. This layout provided the Champion with a significant sales advantage over the directly competing Piper J-3 Cub, as it could be flown solo from the front seat.

The Champion actually first flew in mid-1944, but was not officially revealed until November 1945. Immediately after World War II, the US lightplane market experienced a boom and Aeronca's Champion proved extremely successful. Demand was so high that Aeronca built no fewer than 7,200 Champions between 1946 and 1948. The type became

known popularly as the 'Champ' or the 'Airknocker'. The **'Farm Wagon'** was a version developed for agricultural use, with the rear seat being replaced by a 200-lb (91-kg) cargo bin for farm supplies or grain.

The demand for better performance was met by installing the 85-hp Continental C-85-8F or -12F engine to produce the Model **7DC Champion**.

Prior to this, the military had become interested once more in lightplanes for liaison purposes and ordered 509 of the 85-hp (63-kW) **7BCM** models in 1947 as the **L-16A**; 376 were produced originally for the Air National Guard. These were structurally identical to the civil Champions except for the addition of O-58A/L-3 style cockpit transparencies. Aeronca also produced the **L-16B**s (Model **7CCM**) with 90-hp (67-kW) Continental C-90-12F engines and minor changes. The US Army had never intended to operate the L-16 in the liaison/ observation role, but this changed with the outbreak of the Korean War in 1950. Many L-16As were impressed into front-line military service, while the L-16Bs were used as training aircraft in the USA. The

L-16 was not a great success in either role, and both were quickly replaced by more capable types. After US Army service, the L-16s were operated by the Civil Air Patrol from 1952-54, and virtually all had been retired two years later.

Aeronca matched the L-16B with the civil model **7EC** of 1950 which shared the same features. Unfortunately, the lightplane

boom collapsed in 1948 and the Champion soon went out of production after Aeronca had produced some 10,000 examples. Aeronca ended production of complete aircraft in 1950.

Production of the Model 7 Champion resumed in June 1954 when Champion Aircraft Corp. acquired manufacturing rights to the type. Remarkably, production of the Champion was again re-instated in 1977 after Champion merged with Bellanca.

SPECIFICATION	
Aeronca 7AC Champion	initial climb rate 500 ft (152 m) per
Type: two-seat high-wing cabin monoplane	minute; service ceiling 12,600 ft (3840 m); range 270 miles (435 km)
Powerplant: one 65-hp (48-kW) Continental A-65-8 or A-65-8F flat-four piston engine	**Weights:** empty 730 lb (331 kg); maximum take-off 1,240 lb (562 kg)
Performance: maximum level speed 100 mph (161 km/h); cruising speed 90 mph (145 km/h);	**Dimensions:** wing span 35 ft 2 in (10.72 m); length 21 ft 6 in (6.55 m); height 7 ft (2.13 m); wing area 170 sq ft (15.79 m²)

Aeronca Model 7 Champion variants

Aeronca 7AC Champion: basic tandem high-wing lightplane

Aeronca 7ACS Champion: seaplane variant, generally similar to landplane version, except for the provision of Edo twin float landing gear; empty weight 810 lb (367 kg) and maximum take-off weight 1,320 lb (599 kg)

Aeronca 7BCM (L-16A): version supplied to the US Army as **L-16A**, powered by 85-hp (63-kW) Continental O-190-1 (C-85) engine; 509 built

Aeronca 7CCM (L-16B): version supplied to US Army as **L-16B**, powered by 90-hp (67-kW) Continental O-205-1 (C-90) engine, also featured enlarged fin and auxiliary tanks; maximum level speed 110 mph (177 km/h), cruising speed 100 mph (161 km/h), service ceiling 14,500 ft (4420 m), range 350 miles (563 km), maximum take-off weight 1,450 lb (658 kg); 226 built

Aeronca 7DC Champion: increased gross weight civil version of L-16B, powered by an 85-hp (63-kW) Continental engine, seaplane variant known as Model **7DCS**; 184 built

Aeronca 7EC Champion: final production version built by Aeronca before the manufacturing rights were acquired by Champion Aircraft Corp. in June 1954; increased gross weight version of model 7CCM, powered by a 90-hp (67-kW) Continental C90-12 engine, and incorporating a 12-volt electrical system; 773 built

The Aeronca 7 Champion series proved to be the company's most extensively-built aircraft, with a figure in excess of 10,000 being manufactured between 1946 and 1951. In August 1946, the Aeronca factory was turning out 43 Champions per day.

Aeronca Model 11 Chief/Super Chief

At the end of World War II, Aeronca updated its pre-war Chief line of side-by-side seating lightplanes to produce the Model **11 Chief**. Designed by Ray Hermes, this was essentially a side-by-side development of the Model

7DC Champion. The two types shared an 80 per cent commonality of parts including the wing, tail, landing gear and engine installation. The Chief was powered by an 65-hp (48-kW) Continental A-65-8F engine, which was installed in a

revised cowling to improve the forward field of view.

The first Model **11AC Chief** was flown in mid-1945, but was not officially introduced until November 1946. The Model **11BC Chief** appeared the following year and was powered by an 85-hp (63-kW) Continental C-85-8F engine. Both versions were available as seaplanes (**11ACS** and **11BCS**, respectively).

In late 1947, Aeronca developed the **Aeronca 11CC Super Chief** which was readily identifiable by

its curved dorsal fin extension to meet the new trim requirements called for by the US CAR Section 03. The Model 11CC also had a wider forward fuselage, provision for auxiliary fuel, and it generally had a more luxurious standard of equipment.

The Model 11 proved popular, but did not achieve the huge production total of

the Champion series of lightplanes. Aeronca built a total of 2,418 Model 11s, comprising 1,867 Model 11AC Chiefs, 93 Model 11ACS Chief seaplanes and 181 Model 11BC Chiefs and 11BCS seaplanes. By the time the Model 11CC appeared, the US post-war lightplane boom was waning and Aeronca lowered its price to stimulate sales. Reportedly, Aeronca sold only 277 Model 11CCs between 1948 and 1951.

The Model 11CC Super Chief was the ultimate example of Aeronca's side-by-side series of lightplanes and was also offered as a seaplane.

SPECIFICATION	
Aeronca 11CC Super Chief	rate 650 ft (198 m) per minute;
Type: two-seat lightplane	service ceiling 14,500 ft (4420 m); range 370 miles (563 km)
Powerplant: one 85-hp (63-kW) Continental C-85-8F flat-four piston engine	**Weights:** empty 820 lb (372 kg); maximum take-off 1,350 lb (612 kg)
Performance: maximum speed 110 mph (177 km/h) at sea level; cruising speed 97 mph (156 km/h) at optimum altitude; initial climb	**Dimensions:** wing span 36 ft 1 in (10.99 m); length 20 ft 5 in (6.22 m); height 6 ft 7 in (2.01 m); wing area 175 sq ft (16.23 m²)

Aeronca Model 15AC Sedan

While generally similar in appearance to production examples of the Model 7 Champion family, the Model **15A Sedan** was very different from any other product of the Aeronca company, primarily because of its four-seat layout. Its design included a new single-spar braced wing, of all-metal construction except for fabric covering of the ailerons; a lengthened fuselage to provide accommodation for four, seated in pairs; and a tail unit. Powerplant was usually a 145-hp (108-kW) Continental C-145-2 engine, but a few examples had a 165-hp (123-kW) Franklin 6A40-165-B3. Standard features and equipment included hydraulic wheel brakes, a fully castoring tailwheel, dual controls, folding front seats to simplify access to the rear seats, an aft cabin baggage compartment of 120-lb (54-kg) capacity, cabin heating and ventilation, and a full electrical system.

The Model 15AC first appeared in 1947 and went into production the following year, at a time when the US post-war lightplane boom was waning. The sturdy Sedan proved itself suited to utility operations and was also offered with floatplane (as the Model **S15AC Sedan**) and ski undercarriages.

Aeronca subsequently sold the manufacturing rights to the Model 15 Sedan to E.J. Trytek of Syracuse, which did not build the aircraft itself. The type was built under licence in India as the **HAL Pushpak**, and later formed the basis of the **HAL HAOP-27 Krishak** army co-operation aircraft.

Aeronca built an estimated 400 examples of its sturdy Model 15AC Sedan four-seater.

SPECIFICATION

Aeronca Model 15AC Sedan
Type: four-seat cabin monoplane
Powerplant: one 145-hp (108-kW) Continental C-145-2 flat-six piston engine
Performance: maximum speed 129 mph (208 km/h); cruising speed 114 mph (183 km/h) at optimum altitude; service ceiling 12,400 ft (3780 m); range 450 miles (724 km)
Weights: empty 1,150 lb (522 kg); maximum take-off 2,050 lb (930 kg)
Dimensions: wing span 37 ft 6 in (11.43 m); length 25 ft 3 in (7.70 m); height 7 ft (2.13 m); wing area 200 sq ft (18.58 m²)

Aeronca Model 50 Chief and Model 65 Super Chief

The initial K Scout series sold well during 1937 and, the following year, Aeronca introduced a number of powerplant options. The K model naming system was also discarded and variants were named thereafter by their powerplants. In 1938, the updated K became the Model **50 Chief**, and was offered with 50-hp (37-kW) Continental, Franklin, Lycoming or Menasco engines. These engines were also available on late variants of the preceding Model K series. The Model 50 was slightly bigger and heavier than the Model K, and featured an 8-in (2-cm) increase in chord to give a 15 per cent increase in wing area, a tailwheel undercarriage, and refined nose contours. The fuselage was also widened to give more comfortable seating in the side-by-side layout.

Undoubtedly the Chief's most remarkable achievement took place on 29 November 1938 when Johnny Jones, a DC-3 pilot with American Airlines, flew a **50-C Chief** non-stop from Los Angeles to New York in 30 hours and 47 minutes. After covering a total distance of 2,785 miles (4482 km), smashing previous records in its category, the Chief was reported still to have had enough fuel for a further five hours of flight. The aircraft had been fitted with three additional fuel tanks which gave it a total capacity of 146 US gal (553 litres).

Continental managed to squeeze extra power out of the basic A-50 engine to produce 65 hp (48 kW) and, when fitted to the Aeronca lightplane, this became the Model **65 Super Chief**.

A brand-new Model **65-C** was flown non-stop from New York to New Orleans, a distance of 1,180 miles (1899 km).

Both the Chief and Super Chief proved popular lightplanes, and were sold in respectable numbers to flying schools, clubs and weekend sportsmen. The Super Chief remained in production until the USA entered the war following the Japanese attack on Pearl Harbor, after which manufacture was halted. Aeronca delivered two examples of the Model **65-LB Chief** to the US Army Air Corps for evaluation as the **L-3G** (described separately). Production of the Super Chief was resumed in 1946, but this version was renamed Model **11AC Chief** (described separately).

The Aeronca 50-C was the first of the lightplanes to have a fully-cowled Continental engine. The aircraft was evaluated by the US Army Air Corps.

Aeronca Model 50 Chief and Model 65 Super Chief variants

Aeronca KCA: improved version of the Model K with some design refinements, powered by a 50-hp (37-kW) Continental A-50-1 flat-four engine; 65 built
Aeronca 50-C Chief: improved version of Model KCA with wing chord increased by 8 in (20 cm), wider and lengthened fuselage; about 200 built
Aeronca 50-F Chief: version of the Model 50-C with a 50-hp (37-kW) Franklin 4AC flat-four engine; 31 built
Aeronca 50-L Chief: version of the Model 50-C Chief with a 50-hp (37-kW) Lycoming O-145 flat-four engine, introduced late 1938
Aeronca 50-LA Chief: version of the Model 50-L Chief with various improvements and fully-cowled engine; versions with 65-hp (48-kW) Lycoming engine known as Model **65-LA Chief** (O-145-1 engine), and the military-specification Model **65-LB Chief** (O-145-1)
Aeronca 50-M Chief: version of the Model 50-C Chief with a 50-hp (37-kW) Menasco M-50 Pirate flat-four engine; one built
Aeronca 65-C Super Chief: version of the Model 50-C Chief powered by a 65-hp (48-kW) Continental A-65 flat-four engine
Aeronca 65-CA Super Chief: version of the Model 65-C Super Chief, incorporating as standard entry door on each side of cabin, second door optional on Model 65-C

SPECIFICATION

Aeronca 65-CA Super Chief
Type: two-seat cabin monoplane
Powerplant: one 65-hp (48-kW) Continental A-65 flat-four engine
Performance: maximum level speed 105 mph (169 km/h) at sea level; cruising speed 95 mph (153 km/h); initial climb rate 550 ft (168 m) per minute; service ceiling 14,000 ft (4267 m); range 260 miles (418 km)
Weights: empty 590 lb (268 kg); maximum take-off 1,040 lb (472 kg)
Dimensions: wing span 36 ft (10.97 m); length 20 ft 7 in (6.27 m); height 6 ft 7 in (2.01 m); wing area 146.35 sq ft (16.60 m²)

Aeronca Model 50-T/65-T Tandem Trainer series

With war clouds looming in Europe, America was gearing up for hostilities and, foreseeing the need for a much greater number of trained pilots, the US government initiated the Civilian Pilot Training Program (CPTP).

Aeronca's Chief series had been offered for the CPTP with only moderate success as the type was hampered by its side-by-side seating. Aeronca therefore drew up plans to develop a brand new lightplane with tandem seating specifically for the CPTP.

Designed by James A. Weagle, the configuration and structure of the **Aeronca Tandem Trainer** were thoroughly conventional, with the occupants at dual stick controls and all instruments on a single panel ahead of the front seat. In order to improve visibility for the instructor, the rear seat was placed some 5 in (13 cm) higher than the front seat. The welded steel tube fuselage had four longerons in the cabin area but, like the preceding C and K models, also had three longerons aft.

The resulting aircraft was announced in March 1940, with deliveries beginning two months later. Aeronca initially offered the Model

SPECIFICATION

Aeronca 65-TC Tandem Trainer
Type: two-seat cabin monoplane
Powerplant: one 65-hp (48-kW) Continental A-65-7 flat-four piston engine
Performance: maximum level speed 94 mph (151 km/h) at sea level; cruising speed 80 mph (129 km/h); initial climb rate 600 ft (183 m) per minute; service ceiling 15,000 ft (4572 m); range 230 miles (370 km)
Weights: empty 727 lb (330 kg); maximum take-off 1,150 lb (522 kg)
Dimensions: wing span 36 ft (10.97 m); length 22 ft 4 in (6.81 m); height 7 ft 2 in (2.18 m); wing area 169 sq ft (15.70 m²)

A few Tandem Trainers saw service with civilian operators, but the majority were used on the CPTP. When the USA entered the war, the Tandem Trainer was patriotically renamed **Defender**, which was based on the Model 65-TA series. A few Tandems were built at Aeronca's factory at Lunken Airport, Cincinnati, but the majority were manufactured at the company's new plant at Middletown, Ohio. In April 1941, the company changed its name to the Aeronca Aircraft Corp.

Over 800 examples of the Model 50-T and Model 65-T series were built for the CPTP, and their successful operation led to evaluation of the type by the US Army Air Corps, and subsequent military service as the widely-produced **O-58** and, later, **L-3** Grasshopper (described separately) series of observation and liaison aircraft.

50 TC, Model **50 TL** and Model **50 TF** with 50-hp (37-kW) engines from, respectively, Continental, Lycoming and Franklin. However, the company soon followed the example of other manufacturers who were fitting 65-hp (48-kW) engines, and produced the Model **65-TC/65-TF/65-TL** series. The Lycoming-powered models seemed to have been the most popular. The improved Model **65-TA** series (Model **65-TAC** etc) had its fuselage width increased by 4 in (10 cm), a higher gross weight of 1,250 lb (567 kg), and suffered marginally inferior performance.

Aeronca Tandem Trainer variants

Model 50-TC: tandem two-seat trainer powered by 50-hp (37-kW) Continental A-50-7 engine; 16 built
Model 50-TF/Model 50-TL: versions of Model 50-TC powered by 50-hp (37-kW) Franklin 4AC-150 and Lycoming O-145-A1 engines, respectively; offered but not built
Model 65-TC: version of Model 50-TC fitted with 65-hp (48-kW) Continental A-65-7 engine (125 built); improved version known as **Model 65-TAC** (138 built)
Model 65-TF: version of Model 65-TC powered by 65-hp (48-kW) Franklin 4AC-176-B2 engine (113 built); improved version known as **Model 65-TAF** (103 built)
Model 65-TL: version of Model 65-TC powered by 65-hp (48-kW) Lycoming O-145-B1 engine (232 built); improved version known as **Model 65-TAL** (99 built)

Aeronca O-58/L-3 Grasshopper/TG-5

The L-3 Grasshopper was widely used by the US Army during World War II for spotting and liaison duties. Its short-field performance allowed it to fly from any patch of ground close to the army's position.

Aeronca's Model 65-TC series of tandem two-seat lightplanes had been operated successfully as pilot trainers. With US participation in World War II approaching, the US Army developed an interest in lightplanes for observation and liaison purposes, and briefly evaluated these at manoeuvres in the southern USA. Following the initial success of these trials, which led to the formation of a 'Grasshopper squadron', the service bought four Model 65-TCs from Aeronca under the pre-production designation **YO-58**, plus four each from competitors Piper and Taylorcraft for more formal service tests.

These aircraft underwent a full field evaluation during the US Army's annual manoeuvres, and proved highly successful. It took very little time for the service to appreciate that these lightweight airplanes had a great deal to offer, both in terms of communications and in support of armed forces in the field.

The YO-58s did so well that the US Army ordered 50 production versions designated **O-58A**. These featured extensive changes: the fuselage was made 4 in (10 cm) wider, construction was changed to four longerons for the full length (previous Aeronca lightplanes having three longerons aft), and extensive glasswork was added around and behind the cabin to increase the observer's field of view.

A corresponding civil version without extensive cockpit glazing was developed late in 1941 as the **Defender**.

Civil production ended early in 1942, but the US Army models kept going. The 20 O-58As eventually built were followed by 335 **O-58B**s, which featured increased window area and additional military equipment as standard (such as two-way radios), and a gross weight increased to 1,850 lb (839 kg).

On 2 April 1942, the US Army Air Force dropped the O-for-Observation designation for lightplanes and introduced the L-for-Liaison classification; future YO-58s and O-58s became **L-3**s, and O-58As became **L-3A**s. Existing O-58s changed their identity to L-3Bs, and further orders took total production of this version to 875. Aeronca also produced 490 **L-3C**s with revised radios and other improved military equipment.

In 1942, the US Army acquired 48 various Aeronca lightplanes, including Defenders and Super Chiefs, from private owners, assigning them the designations **L-3D** through **L-3J**. These were pressed into military service when the United States became involved in World War II.

Most of the US Army Air Force's L-3s did not see active combat service and were used instead for training duties in the USA. A number of crated L-3Cs were shipped to North Africa, and some saw service in the Mediterranean theatre of operations with the US Army's II Corps Air Observation Post School, after which they were handed over to the Free French Army. However, it is reported that, in September 1943, at least one L-3C was in use with the II Corps Artillery Air Section in Sicily. The L-3's limited combat role came to an end after a review of all army liaison flying. Conducted by the US Army Air Force's Operations, Commitments and Requirements Division, its report (published the following month) declared the L-3 operationally obsolete.

To fulfil the requirement for a trainer suitable for glider pilots, Aeronca developed an unpowered version of the Model 65-TC. This retained the wings, tail unit and aft fuselage of the L-3, but introduced a new front fuselage which provided a third seat forward for an instructor, the original tandem seats being used by two pupils; all three occupants had similar flying controls and instruments. A total of 250 of these training gliders was supplied to the USAAF under the designation **TG-5**, and three supplied to the US Navy for evaluation were identified as **LNR**.

Above: Large numbers of Aeronca lightplanes remain airworthy some 60 years after they were built. This O-58B flies with the Confederate Air Force in the United States.

Above: The TG-5 was an unusual three-seat glider variant of the L-3, with a new section grafted onto the nose. Many TG-5s were converted back to powered configuration after the end of World War II.

SPECIFICATION

Aeronca L-3C Grasshopper
Type: two-seat light liaison and observation monoplane
Powerplant: one 65-hp (48-kW) Continental O-170-3 (A-65-8) flat-four piston engine
Performance: maximum speed 87 mph (140 km/h); cruising speed 46 mph (74 km/h); initial climb rate 400 ft (122 m per minute); service ceiling 7,750 ft (2362 m); range 190 miles (306 km)
Weights: empty 865 lb (392 kg); maximum take-off 1,800 lb (816 kg), (L-3) 1,300 lb (590 kg), (L-3B) 1,850 lb (839 kg)
Dimensions: span 35 ft (10.67 m); length 21 ft (6.40 m); height 7 ft 8 in (2.34 m); wing area 158 sq ft (14.68 m²)

Aeroprogress/ROKS-Aero T-101 & T-106 Grach

ROKS-Aeroprogress was established after the effective collapse of the USSR during 1990 but is now known as the Aeroprogress Corporation with ROKS-Aero as its design bureau. This organisation was created in Moscow to design, develop and manufacture a wide range of aircraft. These include utility, commuter, amphibian floatplane, aerobatic, agricultural, training, firefighting and attack aircraft, as well as WIG (Wing-In-Ground effect) vehicles, replicas and other machines.

In September 1991, the design bureau began work on its first type, the **T-101 Grach** (rook). Developed as a successor to the classic Antonov An-2 utility biplane, in order to keep purchase and operating costs low, it does not have features such as advanced avionics and pressurisation. 'Modern' features include a high-wing monoplane layout, and turboprop power. The rectangular section fuselage incorporates a cabin 14 ft 9 in (4.50 m) long, 5 ft 3 in (1.60 m) wide and 6 ft ⅞ in (1.85 m) high. This cabin is accessed by a large upward-opening freight door on the port side to the rear of the wing and incorporating a smaller inward-opening passenger door. The cabin can seat nine passengers or carry 3,086 lb (1400 kg) of freight.

The straight braced wing has moderate dihedral. To ensure good field performance, high-lift devices comprise full span automatic leading-edge slats and electrically-actuated slotted trailing-edge flaps inboard of the ailerons. All primary control surfaces are manually operated.

The Grach is a modern turboprop-powered replacement for the venerable An-2 biplane. This mock-up of the amphibious T-101V variant was exhibited at the MosAeroshow in 1995.

The prototype made its maiden flight on 7 December 1994, powered by a Mars (Omsk) TVD-10B turboprop rated at 947 shp (706 kW) and driving a three-bladed constant-speed propeller. Six wing tanks store a total of 264 Imp gal (1200 litres) of fuel.

Aeroprogress has developed several variants of the basic Grach design although these have yet to proceed beyond the model stage.

The most radical evolution under development is the twin-engined **T-106**. Powered by two TVD-10B or PT6A turboprops, this also features a long nose fairing for radar and/or baggage, shorter and cleaner main landing gear units, and a cantilever tailplane. The lower-fuselage sponsons are moved further aft to support forward- rather than rearward-sloping wing struts.

The T-106 is much larger overall than the T-101, with increases of 5 ft (1.70 m) in wingspan, and 5 ft 1½ in (1.56 m) in height. Maximum payload is increased to 4,409 lb (2000 kg). Development of the T-106 has reached the full mock-up stage. A first flight was planned for 1998 but this has now slipped.

The T-106 is essentially a twin-engined, longer-nosed development of the T-101 Grach. This is the full scale mock-up, as the type has yet to proceed to the prototype stage.

T-101 Grach variants

T-101E: intended for Western markets, with more comprehensive Bendix/King avionics, powered by 1,230-shp (917-kW) Pratt & Whitney Canada PT6A-65AR turboprop, or 1,000-shp (746-kW) AlliedSignal TPE331-14 turboprop, rated to carry a 4,409-lb (2000-kg) payload after take-off at a maximum weight of 12,500 lb (5670 kg)
T-101V: amphibious variant with twin-float landing gear, increasing overall length to 49 ft 11½ in (15.23 m) and maximum take-off weight to 12,600 lb (5715 kg), with a maximum payload of 3,307 lb (1500 kg)
T-101P: firefighting model with specialised equipment
T-101L: model equipped with ski landing gear
T-101Skh: agricultural model with revised low-set wing carrying spray bars
T-101S: military variant with swept winglets, four hardpoints under the wing, wing-tip hardpoints for gun pods or similar stores, and larger sponsons, each fitted with one hardpoint
T-102, T-103, T-104: designations reserved for future development variants with tricycle landing gear, a wing of greater area, and more powerful engines

SPECIFICATION

Aeroprogress/ROKS-Aero T-101 Grach
Type: light utility transport
Powerplant: one Mars (Omsk) TVD-10B turboprop rated at 947 shp (706 kW)
Performance: maximum speed 186 mph (300 km/h) at 9,845 ft (3000 m); cruising speed 155 mph (250 km/h) at 9,845 ft (3000 m); service ceiling 13,125 ft (4000 m); range 434 miles (700 km) with maximum payload, and 789 miles (1270 km) with maximum fuel
Weights: empty 7,342 lb (3330 kg); maximum take-off 11,574 lb (5250 kg)
Dimensions: wing span 59 ft 8½ in (18.20 m); length 49 ft 5 in (15.06 m); height 15 ft 11⅓ in (4.86 m); wing area 469.64 sq ft (43.63 m²)

Aeroprogress/ROKS-Aero T-407 Skvorets

ROKS-Aero began design of the **T-407 Skvorets** (starling) light utility aircraft in early 1993. The type is intended to fulfil a wide variety of utility roles and this is reflected in its basic design. The single-engined aircraft has a simple high-wing configuration with fixed undercarriage and a rectangular section fuselage. The cabin seats up to two crew and a maximum of five passengers. For alternative freight-carrying roles, the T-407 is fitted with a large, horizontally-split door to port at the rear of the cabin. The T-407's intended powerplant is the proven M-14P radial piston engine, although Teledyne Continental pistons and Allison turboprops are also being offered as alternatives.

Such was the speed of development that a full scale mock-up of the T-407 (registered 'RA-93407') was exhibited at the MosAeroshow air show in August 1993. However, like many other Russian aircraft manufacturers, the Aeroprogress/ROKS-Aero concern lacks funding for further development of its designs. Construction of a prototype T-407 was undertaken by the Krunichev plant (affiliated to Aeroprogress) during 1995 but, since then, no news of its further development has emerged.

The T-407 is another promising single-engined light utility design to emerge from ROKS-Aero. However, the type has yet to progress beyond mock-up stage.

SPECIFICATION

Aeroprogress/ROKS-Aero T-407 Skvorets
Type: single-engined light utility aircraft
Powerplant: one Vedeneyev (VOKBM) M-14P nine-cylinder air-cooled radial piston engine rated at 355 hp (265 kW)
Performance: maximum cruising speed 133 mph (215 km/h) at 6,560 ft (2000 m); range 472 miles (760 km) with maximum payload and 45-minute reserves
Weights: empty 2,755 lb (1250 kg); maximum take-off 4,585 lb (2080 kg)
Dimensions: wingspan 39 ft 9¼ in (12.12 m); length 32 ft 9¾ in (10.00 m); height 14 ft 5¼ in (4.40 m); wing area 270.6 sq ft (25.14 m²)

Aeroprogress/ROKS-Aero T-411 Aist-2

Among the broad range of types developed by Aeroprogress is the **T-411 Aist-2** (stork-2). This is intended as a multi-role utility transport with short take-off and landing (STOL) capability. The Aist-2 is a high-wing four-seat cabin monoplane built largely of aluminium alloy and steel with light alloy and synthetic fabric covering.

Alternative layouts allow for the carriage of a pilot and one litter plus one medical attendant, or a mixed passenger/freight payload up to a maximum weight of 800 lb (363 kg), or a pupil in the flying training role. The T-411 can also be configured for the glider towing, patrol, agricultural and aerial photography roles.

To provide the required STOL performance, the Aist-2's wing carries fixed slats across the full span of its leading edge and slotted flaps on the trailing edge inboard of the flaps. The fixed tailwheel landing gear features faired main units with spatted wheels that can be replaced by skis for winter operation.

The powerplant is the reliable Vedeneyev M-14P air-cooled radial piston engine which drives a two-bladed variable-pitch propeller. Fuel is supplied from two wing root tanks.

Design of the Aist-2 was begun in November 1992 and the type made its first flight on 10 November 1993. Series production of the Aist-2 began in December 1994.

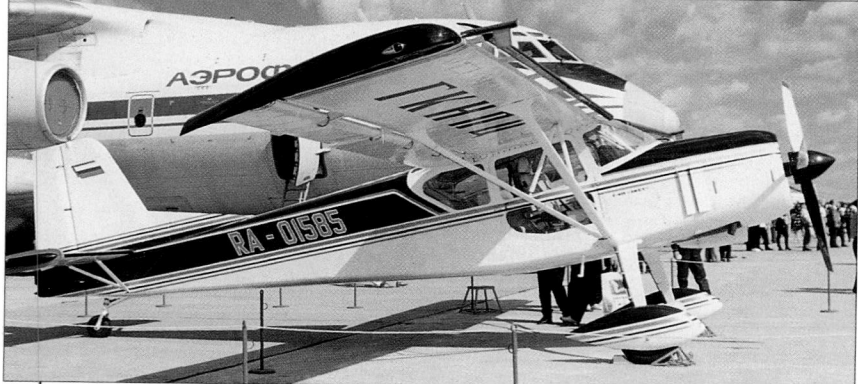

Manufactured at the Krunichev plant, the Aist-2 is one of the few ROKS-Aero programmes in series production.

SPECIFICATION

Aeroprogress/ROKS-Aero T-411 Aist-2
Type: four-seat light utility STOL aircraft
Powerplant: one VOKBM M-14P (Vedeneyev) nine-cylinder air-cooled radial piston engine rated at 355 hp (265 kW)
Performance: maximum speed 121 mph (190 km/h) at 1,640 ft (500 m); economical cruising speed 82 mph (132 km/h) at 1,640 ft (500 m); initial rate of climb 985 ft (300 m) per minute; service ceiling 9,842 ft (3000 m); range 311 miles (500 km) with maximum payload
Weights: empty 2,425 lb (1100 kg); maximum take-off 3,527 lb (1600 kg)
Dimensions: wingspan 41 ft 4 in (12.60 m); length 30 ft 8½ in (9.36 m); height 8 ft 4¾ in (2.56 m); wing area 258.9 sq ft (24.05 m²)

Aeroprogress/ROKS-Aero miscellaneous projects

Aeroprogress is currently in the same position as every other Russian aircraft manufacturer. Capital is short for design and development, while potential purchasers in the CIS lack the resources to order significant numbers of new aircraft, even when these offer considerable operational advantages.

Although some of ROKS-Aero's designs are entirely new, several are yet further multi-role iterations of the basic T-101 Grach. As well as civil and military utility transport, these can also be configured for medevac with litter mountings, SAR with specialised equipment, forest surveillance and firefighting roles.

One such type is the **T-130 Fregat** (frigate) which is essentially an amphibian counterpart to the T-106. The Fregat features a two-step boat hull (with trailing water rudder) which incorporates wide lateral sponsons, thus removing the need for stabilising floats. Powerplant is altered to a tandem push/pull pair of Walter M 601E or Pratt & Whitney PT6A turboprops housed in a nacelle above the upper fuselage. The cabin can carry up to 15 passengers, or alternatively a freight load of up to 3,307 lb (1500 kg).

Another derivative of the basic T-101 design is the **T-201 Aist**. This is proposed to fulfil the above tasks, as well as agricultural spraying and aerial photography. Slightly larger overall than T-101, the T-201 features more sophisticated avionics, which can include weather radar and a wing optimised for improved STOL performance with a higher-lift aerofoil section and double-slotted trailing-edge flaps. The T-201 can carry up to 12 passengers, or a maximum payload of 4,409 lb (2000 kg).

ROKS-Aero has also proposed a specialised variant of the T-201 as a heavyweight agricultural aircraft. The single-seat **T-203 Pchel** (bee) has a low-set wing with automatic full span leading-edge slats to meet the necessary high-lift requirements when the T-203 is at its normal spraying speed of 94-124 mph (150-200 km/h). Spray bars to release agricultural chemicals are fitted under the rear part of the wing, and these are supplied from a 484-Imp gal (2200-litre) chemical agent tank in the cabin. The cabin can also carry a limited freight load when the tank is empty, the maximum payload weight being 5,071 lb (2300 kg).

A further iteration of the T-101 Grach is the **T-610 Voyage** which is intended to fulfil similar roles. Its cabin can carry two crew and up to 10 passengers. Construction of full-scale mock-ups and even of prototypes has been undertaken on most of these T-101 derivatives. Several had been scheduled to make their maiden flights between 1995 and 1996, but these dates have subsequently been delayed.

A completely new design is the **T-274 Titan** which is planned as a STOL medium airlifter for the civil and military markets. The T-274 is intended to bridge the payload/range gap between two obsolescent types, the smaller Antonov An-26 'Curl' and larger Antonov An-12 'Cub', and has a typical airlifter configuration. The hold can accommodate a payload of up to 28,660 lb (13000 kg) of freight or fully-equipped troops including paratroops. The large ventral ramp/door is split laterally: the bottom part of this hinges downwards to serve as a ramp or slides forward under the hold to allow direct loading at truckbed height. Projected powerplant of the T-274 comprises four Klimov TV7-117 turboprops,

Another type with little hope of entering production, the T-602 Oryol (Eagle) business transport exists only in model form.

driving six-bladed propellers of composite construction.

Another completely new design is the **T-433 Flamingo**. This light multi-role amphibian flying boat features side-by-side seating for a pilot and passenger, and up to three more passengers on a rear bench seat. This can be removed to permit the carriage of light freight and/or other items required for the alternative roles. The T-433 has a shoulder-mounted wing and is powered by an M-14P radial piston engine, installed in a nacelle above the upper fuselage. It has been offered with an alternative powerplant, the Allison 250 turboprop, which offers higher power and greater fuel economy.

Similar in concept to the four-seat American Lake LA-4 Buccaneer, the two-seat T-433 Flamingo is a light single-engined amphibian intended primarily for civil use; alternative roles include patrol, SAR and survey. Like many other ROKS-Aero designs, its development is being hampered by lack of funds.

Aero Resources J-2

While working with the McCulloch Aircraft Corporation, D. K. Jovanovich designed a two-seat light autogyro which was first flown in June 1962. This was subsequently put into production by McCulloch as the **J-2**, following FAA certification, gained on 6 May 1970. In 1974, Aero Resources Inc., established at Gardena, California, accepted responsibility for continued production of the J-2, but a limited demand for aircraft of this category saw production terminated after about 18 months.

The Aero Resources J-2's rotor had three all-metal blades attached to a steel rotor hub, carried on a mast structure integrating with those of the fuselage and the engine mounting. The fuselage pod, of light alloy tube basic structure with a glass-fibre shell, included an enclosed two-seat cabin and a bay for the aft-mounted engine driving a two-bladed pusher propeller. Short-span mid-set cantilever stub wings served to mount the twin tail booms, each with fin and rudder, and united at the base of the fins by a fixed horizontal surface. The main units of the non-retractable tricycle landing gear were mounted beneath the stub wings.

The **Super J-2** was basically similar to the J-2, but was powered by a 200-hp (149-kW) Avco Lycoming IO-360 flat-four engine. This increased empty weight to 1,090 lb (494 kg) and maximum take-off weight to 1,600 lb (726 kg) but gave a corresponding increase in range to 220 miles (354 km) with maximum payload.

SPECIFICATION	
Aero Resources J-2 **Type:** two-seat light autogyro **Powerplant:** one 180-hp (134-kW) Avco Lycoming O-360-A2D flat-four piston engine **Performance:** maximum level speed 110 mph (177 km/h); service ceiling 10,000 ft (3050 m); range	with maximum payload 200 miles (322 km) **Weights:** empty 1,000 lb (454 kg); maximum take-off 1,500 lb (680 kg) **Dimensions:** rotor diameter 26 ft (7.92 m); length 16 ft (4.88 m); height 8 ft 6 in (2.59 m); rotor disc area 533 sq ft (49.52 m²)

Aerospace General Mini-Copter

Gilbert Magill's interest in the design and development of ultra-light helicopters for use in the military pilot rescue role led to an unusual type of aircraft. Magill's first interest in such a type had been embodied in the Rotor-Craft RH-1 Pinwheel helicopter, and the same basic concept was retained for the **Aerospace General Mini-Copter**. This was intended to be dropped to a downed pilot so that he could fly himself to safety or to a location from where he could be picked up by a more conventional fixed-wing aircraft or helicopter. As such, the design could be folded for ease of transportation and paradropping.

The basis of the design comprised a very simple welded steel tube A-frame fuselage and a two-bladed rotor. Torqueless power was provided by a pair of rocket motors faired into the tips of the rotor blades. Weighing less than 8 oz (0.227 kg), each rocket provided 42 lb st (0.187 kN) by the passage of 90 per cent hydrogen peroxide in liquid form through a silver-plated catalyst bed. Oxygen and water were thus created which, at the motor's temperature of 1,340°F (727°C), created a reaction jet of superheated steam. The rotor was controlled by a hanging arm, and the basic layout was completed by a tubular steel tail boom carrying a Vee tail for stability and a single-blade counterbalanced rotor for directional control purposes.

The helicopter was developed in three forms: the basic **Mini-Copter Configuration 1**, with the rotor/control unit and two 5.8-Imp gal (26.5-litre) fuel tanks strapped to the pilot; the more comfortable **Mini-Copter Configuration 2**, with the A-frame core carrying a pilot's seat, the fuel tanks and twin-skid landing gear; and the longer-range **Mini-Copter Configuration 3**, with the A-frame adapted to mount a McCulloch flat-four piston engine driving a pusher propeller. In Configuration 3, the lateral tanks were increased to a total capacity of 16.6 Imp gal (75.7 litres) of fuel for the piston engine, and a tank for 3.33 Imp gal (15.1 litres) of hydrogen peroxide was added at the top of the A-frame. This provided sufficient fuel for six take-offs in helicopter mode and, after transition to forward flight at 30 mph (48 km/h), the tip motors were switched off and the machine then operated as

The Mini-Copter was conceived as a means of rescuing US airmen shot down over Vietnam. The idea failed to gain official backing and the project was eventually abandoned in 1980.

SPECIFICATION	
Aerospace General Mini-Copter (Configuration 3) **Type:** lightweight one-man helicopter **Powerplant:** two Aerospace General rocket motors, each rated at 42 lb st (0.187 kN), and one McCulloch flat-four piston engine rated at 90 hp (67.1 kW) **Performance (with rockets and petrol engine):** maximum speed 140 mph (225 km/h) at optimum	altitude; initial climb rate more than 2,500 ft (762 m) per minute; service ceiling more than 18,000 ft (5485 m); range 250 miles (402 km) **Weights:** empty 275 lb (125 kg); maximum take-off 650 lb (295 kg) **Dimensions:** main rotor diameter 18 ft (5.49 m); length 8 ft (2.44 m) without main rotor; height 7 ft (2.13 m) to top of rotor hub; main rotor disc area 254.50 sq ft (23.64 m²)

an autogyro, with the piston engine providing the power.

The design of the Mini-Copter commenced in 1972, and the first machine made its maiden flight on 31 March 1973. The type was then evaluated by the US Navy, which had ordered a total of three prototypes. On the completion of the naval trials, these machines were passed to the US Army, which also received another such helicopter for evaluation as the **MDV-1 (Mini-Copter Demonstration Vehicle-1)**. The civil **MC-8 Mini-Copter** variant was first flown in 1977, but the entire programme was discontinued in 1980, when no orders had materialised for either the civil or the military variant.

Aero Spacelines Guppy series

During the 1950s, large numbers of Boeing Stratocruisers were being retired from airline service following the introduction of turboprop and early jet airliners, and many of these were bought by Lee Mansdorf, an aircraft broker, and stored at Van Nuys, California. At the same time, NASA was encountering problems in transporting massive stage sections of rockets for its space programme from manufacturers in California to test sites in Louisiana and Mississippi, and to the launch complex at Cape Canaveral, Florida.

John M. 'Jack' Conroy, believed that a Stratocruiser could be modified to incorporate a large-diameter freight hold capable of carrying outsize cargo such as NASA's rockets. Conroy, a former USAAF bomber and transport pilot, was flying for a commercial airfreight company and was also serving with the Air National Guard, flying Boeing C-97 Stratofreighters, the military transport variant of the Stratocruiser airliner.

Conroy took his idea to Mansdorf, who agreed to supply the airframes. Conroy proposed a projected conversion, which he presented to NASA in 1960. NASA was sceptical of the idea, but Dr Werner von Braun offered the use of the Administration's wind tunnel facilities for detailed design studies, which led to the first **B377PG Pregnant Guppy**. This retained many of the airliner's major components, but featured a stretched fuselage with a new bulbous upper section to handle outsize cargo. The entire rear fuselage and tail section detached aft of the wing trailing edge for loading.

The prototype Pregnant Guppy was first flown on 19 September 1962. Despite the addition of some 5,000 lb (2272 kg) of structural weight, the pilots found that it handled little differently to a C-97 and was only 5 mph (8 km/h) slower. Feasibility studies had predicted that the additional drag of the 'bubble top' would reduce its cruise speed by at least 40 mph (64 km/h) and make

The first of the Guppy series was the Pregnant Guppy. Based on the Stratocruiser airliner, the B377PG's new upper fuselage section caused only a small increase in drag, and gave slightly superior flying characteristics.

handling difficult, particularly in the event of engine failure. However, Conroy successfully demonstrated controlled flight with two engines shut down.

Once certificated by the FAA, the Pregnant Guppy was quickly pressed into service by NASA in the summer of 1963. The US Department of Defense awarded Conroy's newly-created Aero Spacelines Corporation an exclusive operating contract to trans-

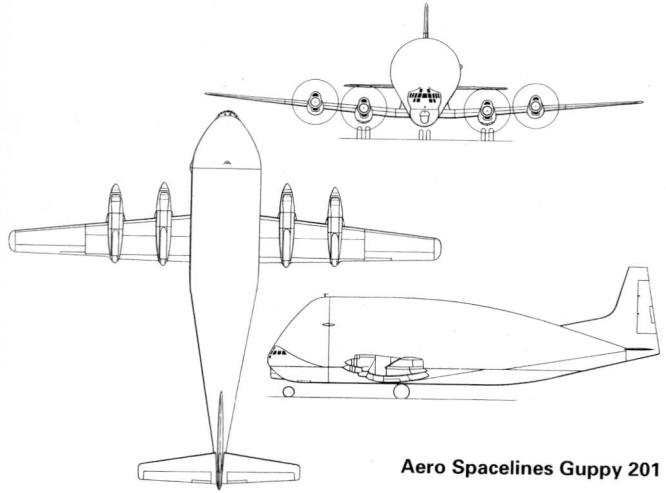

Aero Spacelines Guppy 201

Making its first flight in May 1967, N1037V was the sole piston-powered Mini Guppy. It featured an upper fuselage section of reduced diameter, but with a longer constant section.

port Saturn rocket sections, on the strength of which Conroy bought 25 surplus Stratocruisers and C-97s for cannibilisation.

It quickly became apparent that the Pregnant Guppy was not large enough to meet all of NASA's needs. A second aircraft was modified, using parts from four C-97 airframes. This was significantly larger than the first variant, and featured increases in fuselage length, wingspan and the diameter of the upper fuselage section. Fin area and rudder size were also increased to meet stability requirements. The R-4360 piston engines were

replaced by four 7,000-shp (5220-kW) Pratt & Whitney T34-P-7 turboprops which gave a massive increase in installed power. The **B377SG Super Guppy** made its first flight on 31 August 1965. With a 108 ft 10 in (33.17 m) long, 49,790 cu ft (1410 m³) capacity cargo hold, it was then the world's largest aircraft in terms of volume, and the only aircraft capable of carrying the massive third stage of the Saturn V launch vehicle. The left-hand side of the forward fuselage hinged so that the entire nose could be swung sideways for loading.

The Super Guppy

entered contract service with NASA in March 1966. Operating on special FAA permits, both Guppies carried around 85 per cent of the Saturn and Apollo programmes' hardware, flying 11 of the 13 Apollo launchers, and command, service and lunar modules. In 1979, NASA purchased the Super Guppy for logistical support duties on the Space Shuttle programme. A planned six-engined Guppy was never built, nor was the **'Colossal Guppy'** which would have been based on a Boeing B-52 Stratofortress bomber with a 40-ft (12.1-m) diameter cargo hold and total payload of 200,000 lb (90720 kg).

Following completion of the Super Guppy, Jack Conroy created the **B377MG Mini Guppy**. Based on a standard Stratocruiser, it featured the Super Guppy's extended span wing and a new section fuselage of reduced diameter, and first flew on 24 May 1967. Having logged just two flight hours, it flew the next

day to France to participate in the Paris air show.

The piston-powered Mini Guppy was followed by the **Guppy 101** which was broadly similar, but featured turboprop power in the form of Allison 501 engines. The sole example first flew on 13 March 1970 and was tragically lost two months later at Edwards AFB during its flight test programme.

The Mini Guppies were succeeded by the definitive Guppy variant, the **Guppy 201**. This was similar in dimensions to the piston-powered Super Guppy, but retained the Allison 501 turboprop powerplant of the Guppy 101. The first example was flown on 24 August 1970, and was followed by a second exactly a year later.

European interest in the Guppy had been kindled during the Mini Guppy's demonstration at Paris in 1967. The two Guppy 201s built by Aero Spacelines were purchased by Airbus Industrie at Toulouse in 1971 and 1972 for use in

support of the pan-European Airbus airliner programme. So successful were they in this role that Airbus Industrie acquired production rights and technical material, and commissioned UTA Industries at Le Bourget Airport, Paris, to manufacture two more Guppy 201s, which were delivered in 1982 and 1983.

The Guppy 201's swing-out nose section opened through 110° via a self-contained powered wheel, and outsize loads could be accommodated in the 25 ft 6 in (7.77 m) diameter hold.

The four Guppies of the Airbus Skylink programme were used extensively and made a significant contribution to the Airbus programmes. They were operated on behalf of Airbus Industrie by UTA subsidiary, Compagnie Aéromaritime d'Affretement SA until 1989, when Airbus Industrie took over the direct management of the aircraft. The final Guppy flight for Airbus took place in December 1997, and the aircraft's role is now performed by the SATIC Beluga.

Aero Spacelines Guppy variants

B377PG Pregnant Guppy: initial Guppy version retaining wings, Pratt & Whitney R-4360-B6 Wasp Major piston engines, tail surfaces and cockpit section of Boeing Model 377 Stratocruiser airliner; fuselage length increased by 16 ft 8 in (5.08 m), new bulbous upper section added above lower deck level, providing an internal diameter of 19 ft 9 in (6.02 m) and a total volume of 29,187 cu ft (826.5 m³); entire rear fuselage and tail section detached aft of the wing trailing edge for loading; one aircraft built (N1024V)

B377SG Super Guppy: second variant, using YC-97J engine testbed airframe (52-2693) as basis; fuselage length increased by 30 ft 10 in (9.4 m), wingspan by 15 ft (4.57 m), by means of a centre-section 'plug', and the internal cargo hold diameter increased to 25 ft 6 in (7.77 m); fin height increased by 6 ft 6 in (1.98 m), tailplane span increased to 50 ft (15.24 m); left-hand side of forward fuselage hinged so that entire nose could be swung sideways for loading; constant section 'figure of eight' fuselage; cargo hold length of 108 ft 10 in (33.17 m) and volume of 49,790 cu ft (1,410 m³); C-97 standard Pratt & Whitney R-4360-B6 piston engines replaced by four 7,000-shp (5220-kW) Pratt & Whitney T34-P-7 turboprop engines; one built (N1038V), sold to NASA in 1979

'Colossal Guppy': proposed version based on Boeing B-52 Stratofortress bomber, with a 40-ft (12.1-m) diameter cargo hold and total payload of 200,000 lb (90720 kg); not built

B377MG Mini Guppy: version based on Model 377 Stratocruiser but with Super Guppy's increased span wing and tailplane; overall length shortened to 132 ft 10 in (40.49 m); internal cargo hold diameter of 15 ft 5 in (4.70 m) with longer constant section; swing tail hinged to starboard for loading; one built (N1037V); first Guppy to achieve full FAA certification

Guppy 101: version similar to Mini Guppy, powered by 4,912-hp (3663-kW) Allison 501-D22C turboprops; fuselage length 135 ft 6 in (41.30 m); fuselage diameter same as that of B377 Mini Guppy; first Guppy version with powered nose; one built (N111AS)

Guppy 201: version similar in overall dimensions to the Super Guppy, with a 143 ft 10-in (43.84-m) long fuselage; tailplane span increased further to 57 ft 4 in (17.48 m); usable cargo hold volume 39,000 cu ft (1104.4 m³); powered by four 4,912-shp (3663-kW) Allison 501-D22C turboprops; two built for delivery to Airbus Industrie in 1971-72 (N211AS & N212AS, re-registered F-BGTV and F-BPPA, respectively), followed by further two (F-GDSG & F-GEAI) in 1982-83 built by UTA Industries at Le Bourget Airport, Paris

The four Guppies of the Airbus Skylink programme flew a round-the-clock service, shuttling completed components and sub-assemblies to the final assembly plants to Toulouse and Hamburg. One of the Guppy 201s remains in service in the US with NASA.

SPECIFICATION	
Aero Spacelines Guppy 201 **Type:** outsize cargo-carrying aircraft **Powerplant:** four Allison 501-D22C turboprops, each rated at 4,912 shp (3663 kW) **Performance:** cruising speed at 25,000 ft (7620 m) 253 mph (407 km/h); maximum cruising speed 288 mph (463 km/h); initial rate of climb 1,500 ft (457 m) per minute;	service ceiling 25,000 ft (7620 m); range with maximum payload with IFR reserves 505 miles (813 km) **Weights:** empty 100,000 lb (45359 kg); maximum take-off 170,000 lb (77110 kg); maximum payload 54,000 lb (24494 kg) **Dimensions:** wing span 156 ft 3 in (47.62 m); length 143 ft 6 in (43.84 m); height 48 ft 6 in (14.78 m); wing area 1,965 sq ft (182.52 m²)

Aérospatiale SA 315B Lama

The **Aérospatiale SA 315B Lama** evolved to meet an Indian armed forces requirement of 1968 and was intended primarily for operations in 'hot-and-high' conditions. The basic design of the Lama combines the reinforced airframe of a Sud Alouette II with the dynamic components of an Aérospatiale SA 316B Alouette III, including its Artouste powerplant and rotor system. The SA 315 prototype was first flown on 17 March 1969, and received its French Certificate of Airworthiness on 30 September 1970. The name Lama was bestowed by its manufacturers in July 1971.

From the outset, the SA 315B excelled in load-to-altitude performance. During a series of demonstration flights in the Indian Himalayas in 1969, an SA 315B, carrying a crew of two and 308 lb (120 kg) of fuel, landed and took off at the highest altitude ever recorded: 24,605 ft (7500 m). On 21 June 1972, a Lama with only a pilot aboard established a helicopter absolute height record of 40,820 ft (12442 m). These achievements, and the strong reputation for reliability established by its close relations, the Alouette II and III, ensured a good reception on the market. By 1971, arrangements had already been completed for licence-production of the SA 315B by HAL at Bangalore in India. The first Indian-assembled Lama flew on 6 October 1972, with deliveries commencing in December 1973. The HAL-produced Lama was renamed **Cheetah**.

Like the Alouette series, the SA 315B Lama can be fitted out for various commercial roles, such as light passenger transport, or for agricultural tasks, while the military variants include conversions for liaison, observation, photography, ambulance (two stretchers and one medical attendant), and other duties. For air/sea rescue, a hoist with a capacity of 352 lb (160 kg) can be fitted.

The Lama's excellent alti- tude performance makes it particularly well suited to mountainous districts: the production Lama can transport underslung external loads of up to 2,205 lb (1000 kg) at an altitude of 8,200 ft (2500 m). Another important factor is its universal landing gear consisting of skids with removable wheels for ground handling, provision for floats for normal operations from water, and emergency flotation gear, inflatable in the air.

In 1978, agreement was reached between Aérospatiale and Helibras in Brazil for the assembly of SA 315B Lamas, leading to full licence-production. The resulting **HB 315B Gavião** version is operated by the Bolivian air force and the Brazilian navy.

French production of the SA 315B had ceased by 1991, with a total of 407 delivered. Production in India was initially for the Indian Air Force, equipping Nos 659-662 AOP/liaison squadrons. Since 1987, these units have been part of the Indian Army Air Corps. Current production of the Cheetah by HAL at Bangalore stands at 197 examples, including 20 assembled from French

Between them, the Chilean air force and army operate 16 SA 315B Lamas for observation duties. The outstanding altitude performance of these helicopters is well appreciated in this mountainous country.

components. Lamas continue to fly with the air arms of Angola, Argentina (air force and army), Cameroon, Chile (air force and army), Ecuador, El Salvador, Peru (army) and Togo.

While the Lama has found great favour with military operators, many civilian users have also come to appreciate its capabilities. The aircraft is especially useful for load-hauling at altitude in mountainous regions.

SPECIFICATION

Aérospatiale SA 315B Lama
Type: five-seat general-purpose helicopter
Powerplant: one 970-shp (649-kW) Turboméca Artouste IIIB turboshaft, derated to 550 shp (410 kW)
Performance: (at 5,070-lb/ 2300-kg take-off weight) maximum cruising speed 75 mph (120 km/h); maximum rate of climb at sea level 768 ft (234 m) per minute; service ceiling 9,840 ft (3000 m); hovering ceiling in ground effect 9,675 ft (2950 m); hovering ceiling out of ground effect 5,085 ft (1550 m); range 320 miles (515 km)
Weights: empty 2,251 lb (1021 kg); normal take-off 4,300 lb (1950 kg); maximum take-off with externally-slung cargo 5,070 lb (2300 kg)
Dimensions: main rotor diameter 36 ft 1 in (11.02 m); fuselage length 33 ft 8 in (10.26 m); height 10 ft 1 in (3.09 m); main rotor disc area 1,026.5 sq ft (95.38 m²)

Aérospatiale (Sud) SA 316/SA 319B Alouette III

The reliability and sales success of the Alouette II prompted Sud-Aviation to initiate development of an advanced version. Increased power from a more powerful turboshaft engine and improved aerodynamics were considered essential to give the new machine greater payload capability and enhanced performance and, at the same time, the opportunity was taken to introduce new equipment.

Initially designated **Sud SE 3160**, the prototype **Alouette III** incorporated a cabin that was both larger and more completely equipped than that of its predecessor, and this cabin was able to carry a pilot and six passengers with baggage holds for luggage and parcels, or a pilot and six equipped troops in the battlefield mobility role, or two litters and two sitting casualties or medical attendants in the casevac role, or freight if the passenger seating was removed; there was also provision for an external sling for loads weighing up to 1,653 lb (750 kg). Power was provided by a 550-shp (410-kW) Artouste III turboshaft with dynamic components (derived from those of the Alouette II) comprising an extended-diameter main rotor and three-bladed tail rotor. The centre section and tail boom were covered, and tricycle landing gear was fitted.

Registered F-ZWVQ, the prototype Alouette III made its maiden flight on 28 February 1959 and, in June 1960, the new aircraft reached 15,781 ft (4810 m) on Mont Blanc.

It immediately aroused the interest of the French forces, who needed a fast, well-armed machine for the war in Algeria. Military trials were carried out with various weapons fits, including wire-guided missiles and pivot-mounted guns. Able to fly at 113 kt (130 mph/ 210 km/h), the Alouette III was well suited to the armed forces' requirements, but the Algerian conflict ended before the type entered service.

The initial production version was the **SA 316A Alouette III** and initial deliv-

Aérospatiale (Sud) SA 319B Alouette III

SPECIFICATION

Aérospatiale SA 316B Alouette III
Type: general-purpose helicopter
Powerplant: one 870-shp (649-kW) Turboméca Artouste IIIB turboshaft, derated to 570 shp (425 kW)
Performance: (standard version, at maximum take-off weight) maximum speed at sea level 130 mph (210 km/h); maximum cruising speed at sea level 115 mph (185 km/h); initial climb rate 950 ft (260 m) per minute; service ceiling 10,500 ft (3200 m); hovering ceiling in ground effect 9,450 ft (2880 m); hovering ceiling out of ground effect 5,000 ft (1520 m); range with maximum fuel at sea level 298 miles (480 km); range at optimum altitude 335 miles (540 km)
Weights: empty 2,520 lb (1143 kg); maximum take-off 4,950 lb (2200 kg)
Dimensions: main rotor diameter 36 ft 1¾ in (11.02 m); length 42 ft 1½ in (12.84 m) with rotors turning and fuselage 32 ft 10¾ in (10.03 m); height 9 ft 10 in (3.00 m); main rotor disc area 1,026.68 sq ft (95.38 m²)

eries of this helicopter were made mainly to foreign customers, starting with three examples for the Burmese air force in 1961.

This was followed by others to the South African Air Force and the Rhodesian Air Force. The French ALAT (army aviation) and Aéronavale took only 11 such helicopters between them from the initial production batch, and other early military customers included Peru and the Danish navy.

The SA 316A was covered by an agreement in June 1962 between Sud and Hindustan Aeronautics Ltd for manufacture of the Alouette III at Bangalore in India as the **HAL Chetak**. This variant is described separately.

The SA 316A was only built in modest numbers in France before the introduction of the definitive model, the **SA 316B Alouette III**. This was fitted with an 870-shp (649-kW) Turboméca Artouste IIIB turboshaft derated to 570 shp (425 kW), driving strengthened main and tail rotor transmissions. The SA 316B first flew on 27 June 1968 and its uprated powerplant enabled the Alouette III to carry an increased payload.

Licensed production agreements for the SA 316B were signed with

Many Alouette IIIs are employed by civilian and paramilitary organisations in rescue and security roles.

ICA-Brasov in Romania, where some 230 of the type were built with the designation **ICA-Brasov IAR-316B**, and with FFA in Switzerland where 60 such helicopters were manufactured, while the HAL licence was also extended to this improved variant. Some IAR-316Bs were exported via Aérospatiale to Pakistan, Algeria and Angola.

The capability of the SA 316B soon led to the adoption of the type for military service in a two-seat form for use in a variety of roles with a range of weapon options that made them suitable for light attack (typically two multiple launchers for 2.68-in/68-mm unguided rockets, or four AS11 or AS12 wire-guided light ASMs) or the anti-submarine task (typically two Mk 44 or Mk 46 torpedoes, reduced to one torpedo when magnetic anomaly detection equipment was installed).

The SA 316B was followed by the **SA 316C** which entered production in 1970. Powered by an 870-shp (649-kW) Turboméca Artouste IIID engine derated to 600 shp (447 kW), this variant was built only in limited numbers.

As with the Alouette II, a version was then introduced with the Turboméca Astazou turboshaft, this upgraded development being the **SA 319B Alouette III Astazou**. Powered by an 870-shp (649-kW) Astazou XIV

The Irish Army Air Corps received the first of its eight Alouette IIIs in 1963. All remain in service, with the only major mishap occurring in 1995 when one aircraft was seriously damaged. The helicopters are tasked with SAR along Ireland's east coast.

For many years, the Alouette III in Dutch service was epitomised by the colourful machines of the Grasshoppers display team. The majority of the Alouette IIIs served in the more sombre colour scheme illustrated, however. Six aircraft remain in service, transporting members of the Dutch royal family.

turboshaft derated to 600 shp (447 kW), this version offered much higher performance and considerably improved fuel economy as a result of its greater thermal efficiency. The variant first flew in 1967, but full production was not begun until 1973.

A navalised version of the Alouette III was developed to deal with small surface craft such as fast torpedo-boats. This could be armed with an autostabilisation system, ORB 31 surveillance radar, APX-Bézu gyro-stabilised sight and two AS12 wire-guided missiles. For the ASW role, it could carry two Mk 44 homing torpedoes beneath the fuselage and MAD gear in a streamlined container which was towed aft of the helicopter on a 164-ft (50-m) cable. For the air-sea rescue role, a hoist with a capacity of 496 lb (225 kg) was mounted on the port side of the fuselage.

The Alouette III was a highly successful product and production of all Alouette III variants by Sud and Aérospatiale (created in 1970 by the merger of Sud and Nord) totalled 1,453 helicopters for no fewer than 74 countries, of which some 60 operated the type in military service.

The Alouette III has acquitted itself extremely well in many different operating environments on account of its reliability, ease of maintenance and adaptability. The type has fulfilled utility transport, liaison, light transport, fire support, anti-shipping, search and rescue, armed reconnaissance, close air

Alouette III in combat

The Alouette III was used extensively to support combat operations by both the SAAF and Rhodesian Air Force during the 'bush wars' of the late 1970s and throughout the 1980s. SAAF Alouette IIIs took the brunt of fighting during airborne assaults in South West Africa (Namibia) and Angola, and played a crucial role in every big cross-border 'external'. The Alouette III carried out a variety of roles including target-spotting, airborne control, search and rescue and fire support. The Rhodesian air force operated two specialised versions of the Alouette III in support of quick-reaction units to intercept terrorist forces. The G-Car four-troop transport was armed with two side-mounted Browning machine-guns, whereas the K-Car was a dedicated gunship variant with a single 20-mm Mauser cannon mounted in the cabin and firing to port. Alouette IIIs have also seen combat service with the Portuguese air force in support of Portugal's withdrawal from its African colonies during the 1970s (in Guinea-Bissau and Angola).

Alouette III operators

The Alouette III is currently operated by the air forces of Angola, Argentina (navy), Austria, Belgium (navy), Bophutatswana, Burkina Faso, Burundi, Cameroon, Chile (navy), Congo, Ecuador, El Salvador, Equatorial Guinea, France (all three air arms), Gabon, Ghana, Guinea, Guinea-Bissau, Indonesia, Iraq, Ireland, Lebanon, Libya (all three air arms), Malawi, Malaysia, Mexico (all three air arms), Mozambique, Myanmar, Netherlands, Nicaragua, Pakistan (all three air arms), Peru (army and navy), Portugal, Romania, Rwanda, Serbia, South Africa, Spain, Surinam, Switzerland, Tunisia, United Arab Emirates (Abu Dhabi), Venda, Venezuela, the Democratic Republic of Congo (formerly Zaïre) and Zimbabwe. Chetaks built by HAL in India are operated by Ethiopia, India (all three air arms), Nepal and the Seychelles.

support/counter-insurgency, anti-armour, anti-submarine, plane guard, observation and training roles. It has also been the mount for several national helicopter aerobatic teams. In civilian and paramilitary service it has also carried out mountain rescue and policing/internal security duties.

Further radical development of the Alouette III was undertaken in both Romania and South Africa during the early 1980s. ICA-Brasov used the dynamic components of the locally-manufactured Alouette III to produce a low-cost ground-attack heli-

copter as the **IAR-317 Airfox**, but development was cancelled by Romania's President Ceausescu before he was toppled from power. In South Africa, Atlas Aircraft Corporation developed the **XH-1 Alpha** light attack helicopter in great secrecy to fulfil a similar role. Again, development of the type was cancelled, but valuable lessons were learned and these were applied to other indigenous gunship helicopter projects.

Very low-scale production of the Alouette III is confined to India, where no more than five are built annually.

SPECIFICATION
Aérospatiale SA 319B Alouette III Astazou

Aérospatiale SA 319B Alouette III Astazou
(generally similar to SA 316B Alouette III except in the following parameters:)
Powerplant: one 870-shp (649-kW) Turboméca Astazou XIV turboshaft derated to 600 shp (447 kW)
Performance: maximum speed 136 mph (220 km/h) at sea level;

cruising speed 122 mph (197 km/h) at sea level; initial climb rate 885 ft (270 m) per minute; hovering ceiling 10,170 ft (3100 m) in ground effect and 5,575 ft (1700 m) out of ground effect; range 375 miles (605 km) with six passengers
Weights: empty 2,513 lb (1140 kg); maximum take-off 4,960 lb (2250 kg)
Armament: generally unarmed, but see main text

Aérospatiale SA 330 Puma

In the early 1960s, Sud-Aviation began the design and development of a twin turbine-powered helicopter that would not only meet a French army requirement for an all-weather tactical and logistic transport, but which would be suitable also for use by other armed forces. The Anglo-French helicopter agreement (concluded on 2 April 1968) gave Westland Helicopters in the UK joint production of these aircraft. Intended initially for service with the French army and the Royal Air Force, the latter required this helicopter for deployment as a tactical transport.

The resulting helicopter was designated **SA 330**, and named **Puma**. Eight prototypes were ordered in June 1963, the first taking to the air at Marignane on 15 April 1965, and the last going to the UK for evaluation. On 25 November 1970, just over two years after that delivery, the first of an initial batch of 40 for the RAF flew at Yeovil.

The Puma's fuselage is a conventional all-metal semi-monocoque structure, with the powerplant mounted externally on top of the fuselage shell and forward of the main rotor assembly. The rotor is driven via a main gearbox, with twin free-wheeling spur gears to combine the outputs of the two turboshaft engines to a single main drive shaft. In the event of an engine failure, the remaining engine continues to drive the rotor and, should both engines fail, the auto-rotating main rotor continues to drive the auxiliary take-offs for the shaft-driven tail rotor, alternator, dual hydraulic pumps, and ventilation fan. The tail boom carries the flapping-hinge five-bladed tail rotor on the starboard side and a horizontal stabiliser on the port side. Early main rotor blades were of light alloy construction, but those fitted since 1976 are composite units of glass-

fibre, carbon-fibre and honeycomb construction, with anti-abrasion leading-edges of stainless steel. The Puma has semi-retracting tricycle-type landing gear, with twin wheels on each unit, all of which are partly exposed when retracted.

The initial production versions were powered by two 1,320-shp (984-kW) Turboméca Turmo turboshafts, giving a maximum take-off weight of 14,109 lb (6400 kg) and limiting speed of 151 kt (174 mph/280 km/h). These early models comprised the **SA 330B** for French ALAT (Aviation Légère de l'Armée de Terre), **SA 330C** for military export, **SA 330E** as the RAF's **Puma HC.Mk 1**, and the civilian **SA 330F**. In 1974, availability of the 1,575-shp (1174-kW) Turmo IVC powerplant better equipped the Puma for 'hot-and-high' operations, increasing its take-off weight to 16,314 lb (7400 kg). Production in this guise concerned the civilian **SA 330G** and military **SA 330H**, although the French air force, which bought 37, used the misleading designation **SA 330Ba**.

Glass-fibre rotor blades became available in 1977, uprating the G and H to **SA 330J** and **SA 330L**, respectively. The new blades were retrofitted to some early aircraft, including those of the RAF and 40 per cent of ALAT's 132 SA 330Bs. The French army also bought 15 SA 330Ba versions and a few attrition replacement helicopters from the Romanian assembly line after Aérospatiale ceased production with the 686th Puma.

ICA (now IAR) at Brasov, Romania, obtained a licence for the SA 330L in 1977 and had built about 180 by the end of 1992, including nearly 70 exported. While Pumas normally carry 15 fully-equipped troops or a

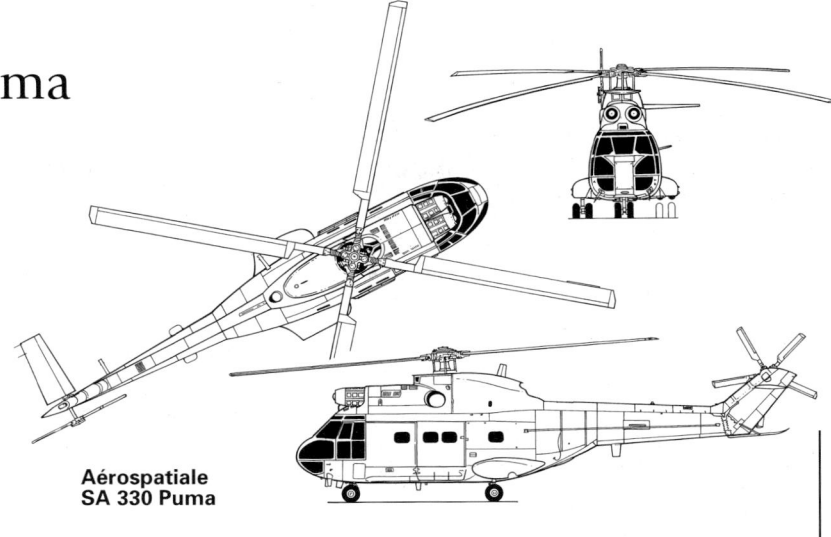

**Aérospatiale
SA 330 Puma**

maximum underslung payload of 7,055 lb (3200 kg), the Romanian variant additionally has a powerful armament option, typically comprising four rocket pods and four AT-3 'Sagger' anti-tank missiles on outrigger pylons, plus two machine-gun pods scabbed to the forward fuselage. British army and ALAT Pumas can carry a pintle-mounted machine-gun in the cabin door, some of the latter's machines additionally receiving a prominent nose-mounted OMERA ORB 37 radar. Five of Portugal's 10 Pumas have ORB 31 radar and flotation gear for their SAR task. All were converted locally by OGMA during the late 1980s to **SA 330S** standard, with SA 330L systems and rotors, plus Makila powerplants as in the **AS 332 Super Puma**. In Indonesia, IPTN assembled 11 SA 330Js from French kits, the last in 1983. South Africa, isolated by a UN arms embargo, pursued its own line of Puma development which culminated in the **Atlas XH-2/CSH-2 Rooivalk** tandem-seat attack helicopter. More recognisable as Pumas were the two **Atlas XTP-1** conversions of standard SA 330s, which undertook development work for the

SPECIFICATION

Aérospatiale (now Eurocopter France) SA 330L Puma
Powerplant: two Turboméca Turmo IVC turboshafts each rated at 1,575 shp (1175 kW)
Performance: never-exceed speed 182 mph (204 km/h); maximum cruising speed 'clean' at optimum altitude 168 mph (271 km/h); maximum rate of climb at sea level 1,810 ft (552 m) per minute; service ceiling 19,685 ft (6000 m); hovering ceiling 14,435 ft (4400 m) in ground effect and 13,940 ft (4250 m) out of ground effect;

range 355 miles (572 km)
Weights: empty 7,970 lb (3615 kg); maximum take-off 16,534 lb (7500 kg); maximum payload 7,055 lb (3200 kg)
Dimensions: main rotor diameter 49 ft 2½ in (15.00 m); length overall, rotors turning 59 ft 6½ in (18.15 m) and fuselage 46 ft 1½ in (14.06 m); height overall 16 ft 10½ in (5.14 m); main rotor disc area 1,902.20 sq ft (176.71 m²); tail rotor disc area 78.13 sq ft (7.26 m²)
Armament: generally unarmed, but see main text

Rooivalk. They also appear to have led to evaluation of a gunship Puma which was reportedly undergoing SAAF evaluation in the early 1990s following cancellation of official funding for the Rooivalk. Using Rooivalk systems and weapons pylons, the gunship would have Atlas Swift laser-guided anti-tank missiles and Atlas Darter or Viper AAMs. In parallel, South Africa has undertaken its own Makila re-engining programme, turning Pumas into what are locally called **Gemsboks** with the additional power necessary to replace SAAF SA 321 Super Frelons.

Some 35 military operators have acquired Pumas, most of which remain in service, while 135 helicopters were delivered to

civilian organisations, many for oil exploration support; some civilian-standard Pumas are used by heads of state.

Abu Dhabi, Chile (army), Kuwait, Morocco, Nigeria, Pakistan and Zaïre (now the Democratic Republic of Congo), plus countries already mentioned, received 10 or more Pumas for military purposes. Those of the RAF are particularly advanced in terms of operational aids, having acquired 'polyvalent' air intake filters, an ARI.18228 radar warning receiver, cockpit lighting compatible with night-vision goggles and, for the 1991 Gulf War, M130 chaff/flare dispensers and AN/AAR-47 missile approach warning systems. RAF Pumas in Northern Ireland additionally have an AN/ALQ-144 IR jammer to deflect heat-seeking missiles. Some of these RAF Pumas are believed to be equipped with the Ferranti/Barr and Stroud Type 221 thermal imager for surveillance duties, under the code-name Pleasant 3.

One ALAT Puma is a testbed for the underslung Orchidée/Horizon battlefield surveillance radar. For the future, in addition to any South African developments, Romania is offering a 'glass cockpit' version called **Puma 2000** which features a night-vision system and pilot's helmet-mounted head-up display.

RAF Pumas have equipment that reflects the often hazardous conditions in which they operate. Equipment ranges from IR jammers and thermal imaging devices for duties in Northern Ireland to chaff dispensers, night-vision goggles and missile warning receivers for operations in the Gulf.

Aérospatiale (Eurocopter) SA 341/SA 342 Gazelle

Successor to the ubiquitous Sud Alouette II, the **Gazelle** originated in a mid-1960s project by Sud Aviation. Despite using many of its predecessor's dynamic systems, the **X.300** design, soon redesignated **SA 341**, achieved increased speed and manoeuvrability through adoption of a more powerful turboshaft, an aerodynamically-shaped cabin and covered tailboom, and advanced rotor technology. Part of the last-mentioned came from a 1964 agreement with MBB of West Germany for joint development of a rigid main rotor head and fibreglass blades – normal today, but both advanced concepts for their time. Simplicity, strength and reduced maintenance demands are

(268-kW) Astazou II powerplant, following abandonment by Turboméca of the proposed 450-shp (336-kW) Oredon. A machine with more representative rotors followed on 12 April 1968, demonstrating control difficulties which resulted in the abovementioned compromises in the design philosophy. Revised as the SA 341, and named Gazelle in July 1969, the pre-production version had a longer cabin with two rear access doors, larger tail surfaces and a 590-shp (440-kW) Astazou III. Series manufacture began with a civil-registered demonstrator flying on 6 August 1971.

Seven versions were launched initially: **SA 341B**, the British army **Gazelle AH.Mk 1**; **SA 341C**, Royal

Great Britain is one of more than 20 countries that fly the Gazelle. What is more, all three British armed services operated the SA 341 in one form or another, with the army using its aircraft for scouting, casualty evacuation and anti-tank duties.

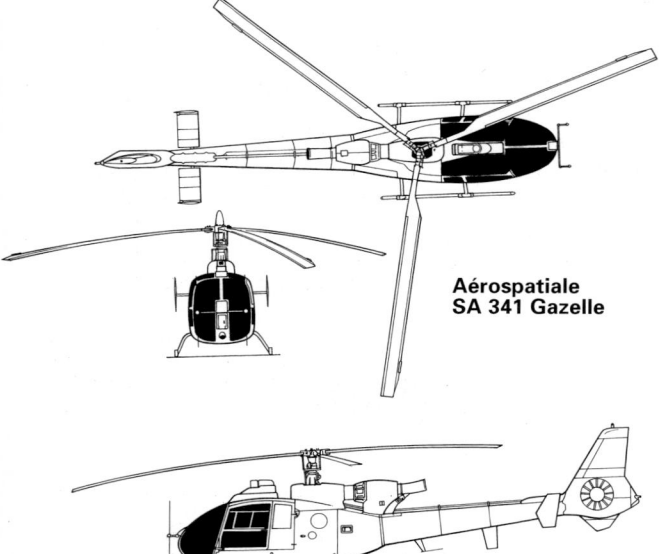

**Aérospatiale
SA 341 Gazelle**

achieved by a rigid head, but a compromise was made at the prototype stage, in which the Gazelle's main rotors had flap hinges without drag hinges. Additionally, the revolutionary fenestron was designed to be shielded from forward airflow.

UK requirements to expand its rotary-wing industry resulted in the Anglo-French helicopter agreement of 22 February 1967, in which the Gazelle, Puma and British-designed Lynx came under joint Westland-Sud (Aérospatiale after 1 January 1970) parentage. The **SA 340** prototype flew on 7 April 1967 with non-standard, conventional rotors and the Alouette II's 360-shp

Navy **HT.Mk 2** trainer; **SA 341D**, Royal Air Force **HT.Mk 3** trainer; **SA 341E**, Royal Air Force **HCC.Mk 4** VIP transport (all with Astazou IIIN); **SA 341F**, French army (ALAT) with Astazou IIIC; **SA 341G**, civilian; and **SA 341H**, military export. When the Westland line closed in 1984, it had built 294 Gazelles, including 282 for the UK forces, 212 of which were AH.Mk 1s. No HCC.Mk 4s were constructed as such. Generally unarmed, the AH.Mk 1 carried rockets during the 1982 Falklands War, while nearly 70 were fitted during the late 1980s with magnifying sights for target-finding on behalf of the missile-armed Westland Lynx. Of 170 SA 341Fs,

The SA 342L, with its improved fenestron, has replaced the K on the export market. France also operates some 30 aircraft that had been built originally for China.

ALAT (the French army) converted 40 to carry four Euromissile HOT anti-tank missiles, as **SA 341M**s, and 62 with a GIAT M621 20-mm cannon to starboard and SFOM 80 sight as the **SA 341F/Canon**. Others have acquired a SFIM M334 Athos scouting sight similar to that of the AS 532 Cougar.

Powered by an 858-shp (640-kW) Astazou XIVH, the **SA 342** flew in prototype form on 11 May 1973, replacing the SA 341 after 628 had been built in France and the UK. Foreign exports began with the civil **SA 342J** and military **SA 342K**, the latter soon replaced by the **SA 342L** with an improved fenestron. The ALAT equivalent is designated **SA 342M** and over 200 have been delivered since 1 February 1980, armed with four HOTs and an M397 sight – the latter was replaced by the nightcapable Viviane from the early 1990s. For the 1991 Gulf War, 30 were converted to **SA 342M/Celtic,** with a pair of MATRA Mistral airto-air missiles on the port side and a SFOM 80 sight. The definitive anti-helicopter model is the **SA 342M/ATAM** and this

designation is applied to 30 conversions, with four Mistrals and a T2000 sight. SA 342Ms have an Astazou XIVM turboshaft with automatic start-up and a maximum take-off weight of 4,188 lb (1900 kg), increased to 4,409 lb (2000 kg) in wartime. Its avionics include an autopilot as well as a Nadir self-contained navigation system.

Egypt, Iraq, Morocco and Syria, among others, have equivalents to the HOT- and cannon-armed Gazelles, but versions built in the former Yugoslavia by SOKO at Mostar (BosniaHerzegovina) have Russian armament options. Following 132 **SA 341H Partizans**, SOKO was well advanced with 170

SA 342Ls before civil war intervened in 1991. Versions comprise the **SA 341L HERA** scout and **SA 342L GAMA**, the latter armed with four AT-3 'Sagger' antitank missiles and two SA-7 'Grail' SAMs converted to AAMs, plus an M334 sight.

Gazelles serve with some 25 military operators. In addition to those already mentioned, Abu Dhabi, Ecuador, Kuwait and Qatar acquired 10 or more, while single-figure operators are Angola, Burundi, Cameroon, Chad, China, Cyprus, Gabon, Guinea Republic, Ireland, Kenya, Lebanon, Rwanda, Senegal and Trinidad. Civilian sales were about 170. NonYugoslav production was in excess of 1,260 by the time production ceased in the period 1995-96.

SPECIFICATION

Aérospatiale (now Eurocopter France) SA 341F Gazelle
Powerplant: one Turboméca Astazou IIIA turboshaft, rated at 590 shp (440 kW)
Performance: never-exceed speed at sea level 168 kt (193 mph; 310 km/h); maximum cruising speed at sea level 142 kt (164 mph; 264 km/h); maximum rate of climb at sea level 1,770 ft (540 m) per minute; service ceiling 16,405 ft (5000 m); hovering ceiling 9,350 ft

(2850 m) in ground effect and 6,560 ft (2000 m) out of ground effect; range 361 nm (416 miles; 670 km) with standard fuel
Weights: empty 2,028 lb (920 kg); maximum take-off 3,968 lb (1800 kg)
Dimensions: main rotor diameter 34 ft 5½ in (10.50 m); length overall, rotor turning 39 ft 3⅜ in (11.97 m) and fuselage 31 ft 3⅜ in (9.53 m); height overall 10 ft 5¼ in (3.18 m); main rotor disc area 932.08 sq ft (86.59 m²)

Aérospatiale SA 349 Gazelle

The prototype SA 340 Gazelle (F-ZWRF) was modified by Aérospatiale to investigate dynamic phenomena encountered during high-speed flight. The resulting **SA 349Z** had stub fixed wings with minimal taper fitted on either side of the cabin, and made its first flight in 1972. The SA 349Z conducted a long series of trials which led to the definitive second machine, the **SA 349-2** (F-ZWRN). This was fitted with an Astazou XIVH turboshaft, substantially modified rotor blades, and wing control surfaces that

were fitted to enable the helicopter to explore high manoeuvrability rather than high speed.

The wing was of a zero-lift aerodynamic profile which generated relatively little lift at high speed but, by offloading the rotor, it thus greatly increased manoeuvrability. Ailerons were fitted to increase the rate of roll, as well as spoilers/air brakes for rapid deceleration in case of engine failure.

The SA 349-2 first flew on 20 January 1977, and made the first of a series of test flights on 1 March

1977. During these trials, it demonstrated a maximum speed of 186 mph (300 km/h). However, Aérospatiale's engineers concluded that the drag due to the wings was too high and further development of the idea was halted. Nevertheless, both SA 349s contributed much useful data in the development of advanced rotor head designs.

The SA 349-2 clearly demonstrates the raised leading-edge airbrakes and drooped aileron of its experimental wing.

Aérospatiale AS 350 Ecureuil

Introduced in 1975, the **Aérospatiale AS 350 Ecureuil (Squirrel)** six-seat light multi-purpose helicopter was developed to succeed the long-established Alouette III.

Benefiting from experience gained on the Alouettes, as well as from the SA 360 Dauphin, the design effort concentrated on reducing operating costs and noise levels. This led to the development of a three-bladed main rotor with an advanced and entirely new rotor head made of composite material and dubbed Starflex by Aérospatiale. Conventional

With the addition of Conair's firefighting equipment, the versatile Ecureuil has added yet another role to its portfolio. Here the aircraft refills its tanks.

main rotor blade hinges were replaced by maintenance-free ball-joints, and linked to glassfibre blades (which are fatigueless) with stainless steel protection for the blade leading-edges.

The Ecureuil's airframe also made extensive use of advanced materials, including new polycarbonates and glassfibre composites. The Ecureuil's cabin was clearly optimised for business users, with extensive soundproofing to enable easy conversation at normal voice levels, and a high degree of comfort for both passengers and pilots. Three luggage holds were fitted to give a total volume of 46.97 cu ft (1.33 m³).

Aérospatiale identified North America as a crucial market and developed two versions of the Ecureuil, differing primarily in powerplant. Intended for other than North American

markets, the **AS 350B** was fitted with a Turboméca Arriel 1B single-shaft free-turbine turboshaft rated at 641-shp (478-kW). The **AS 350C** was aimed at the North American market. Dubbed **AStar**, this version was powered by a 616-shp (459-kW) Avco Lycoming LTS101-600A.2 turboshaft developed in the USA at about the same time as the Arriel was developed in France. The first Ecureuil to fly, on 27 June 1974, was a Lycoming-engined version (F-WVEH), followed by an Arriel-powered Ecureuil (F-WVKI) on 14 February 1975.

The Ecureuil's excellent manoeuvrability, comfort, performance and handling responses have led to steady sales to both civil and military customers and, by 1 January 1997, Eurocopter (formed by the merger of Aérospatiale and

The AS 350B series has found customers around the world. Asian operators include Asahi Helicopters of Japan.

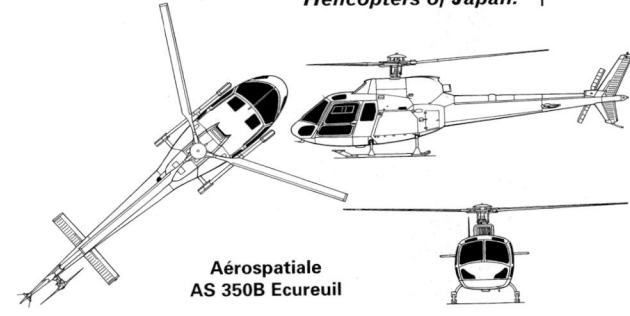

Aérospatiale AS 350B Ecureuil

SPECIFICATION

Aérospatiale AS 350B Ecureuil
Type: six-seat general-purpose helicopter
Powerplant: one Turboméca Arriel 1B turboshaft rated at 641 shp (478 kW) for take-off and 592 shp (441 kW) for continuous operation
Performance: (at take-off weight of 3,750 lb;1700 kg) never-exceed speed 169 mph (272 km/h); maximum cruising speed 144 mph (232 km/h); initial rate of climb 2,245 ft (684 m) per minute; hovering ceiling 14,270 ft (4350 m) in ground effect and 11,975 ft

(3650 m) out of ground effect; service ceiling above 20,000 ft (6100 m); range with maximum fuel at sea level, no reserves 441 miles (710 km)
Weights: empty 2,304 lb (1045 kg); maximum normal take-off 4,299 lb (1950 kg)
Dimensions: main rotor diameter 35 ft ¾ in (10.69 m); length, rotors turning 42 ft 8 in (13 m); fuselage length 35 ft 9½ in (10.91 m); height 10 ft 1¼ in (3.08 m); main rotor disc area 966.12 sq ft (89.75 m²)
Armament: see text for details

MBB in 1992) had received orders for 2,019 single-engined Ecureuils.

Aérospatiale developed a twin-engined version of the Ecureuil in 1978, and this is described separately under the heading **Eurocopter (Aérospatiale) AS 355 Ecureuil 2/AS 555 Fennec**.

Some of the technologies developed for this variant and its successors have been applied subsequently to the single-engined Ecureuils.

This led initially to the 'hot and high' **AS 350B1** which mated the enlarged chord main and tail rotor blades of the twin-engined Ecureuil with a new Turboméca Arriel 1D turboshaft rated at 684 shp (440 kW).

The new components allowed an increase in maximum take-off weight of 551 lb (250 kg). On 14 May 1985, the AS 350B1 demonstrated its performance by setting new world records in its class for time to climb, attaining 9,843 ft (3000 m) in 2 minutes 59 seconds and establishing new records for 19,685 ft (6000 m) and 29,528 ft (9000 m). First deliveries of the AS 350B1 took place in 1986. The improved payload capacity of the B1 led to the development of the **AS 350 Firefighter**. Initially for service with the

French Sécurité Civile, the Firefighter carries a Conair-developed streamlined tank with a capacity of 154 Imp gal (700 litres).

The generally similar **AS 350B2** succeeded the AS 350B1 in production during 1988/89 and is powered by the 724-shp (540-kW) Arriel 1D1. The North American market received the 615-shp (459-kW) AlliedSignal LTS101-600A3-powered **AS 350D AStar** as its equivalent to the B2.

Although the Ecureuil was aimed primarily at civil customers, military operators have adopted the type for a variety of roles. Aérospatiale developed a fully-armed version of the Ecureuil as the **AS 350L**, which is based on the civilian AS 350B1, and is thus fitted with some of the uprated components from

the twin-engined Ecureuil.
The AS 350L and related **AS 350L2** have a wide range of weapon options including a side-mounted 20-mm M621 cannon, door-mounted 0.3-in (7.62-mm) machine-gun, twin 0.3-in (7.62-mm) gun pods, and rocket pods of 2.7-in (68-mm) and 2-in (51-mm) calibre. An anti-tank version

was subsequently developed with a Saab/Emerson Electric Heli-TOW anti-tank system and armament of four Hughes TOW anti-tank guided missiles. Twelve of the latter ordered by Denmark were redesignated **AS 550C2 Fennec** in 1990 before delivery. Other military versions offered became **AS 550U2**

(unarmed, utility), **AS 550A2** (armed, cannon or rockets), **AS 550C2** (armed, anti-tank missiles), **AS 550M2** (unarmed, naval utility) and **AS 550S2** (armed, naval anti-shipping).
The Ecureuil has been assembled under licence in Brazil by Helibras and is similar to AS 350B standard. Versions are identified

as **HB 350B/B1** (unarmed) or **HB 350L1** (armed), with the name **Esquilo**. Deliveries comprised about 25 HB 350B/B1s for the Brazilian air force, under the designations **CH-50** and **TH-50** for communications and training, respectively, and nine for the Brazilian navy, with machine-gun and rocket pod armament. The

Brazilian army has 36 fully-armed HB 350L1s under the designation **HA-1**.
Military Ecureuils also fly with Abu Dhabi (UAE), Australia, Benin, Botswana, Central African Republic, Ecuador (army), France (navy and army), Gabon, Guinea Republic, Mali, Paraguay, Peru, Singapore and Tunisia.

Aérospatiale SA 360/SA 361/SA 365 Dauphin/Dauphin 2

Developed as a larger replacement for the highly successful Alouette III utility helicopter, the **Aérospatiale Dauphin** has itself proved a success in both civil and military applications, both at home and for export customers.
The first version, designated **SA 360C**, had a maximum take-off weight of 6,612 lb (3000 kg) and featured a four-bladed main rotor, a 13-bladed fenestron, tailwheel landing gear, and standard accommodation for a pilot and up to nine passengers, with alternative payloads of 3,130 lb (1420 kg) internally or 2,865 lb (1300 kg) slung externally.
The first of two SA 360 prototypes (F-WSQL) made its maiden flight on 2 June 1972. This was initially powered by a single 980-shp (730-kW) Astazou XVI turboshaft, but was later re-engined with the engine intended for production helicopters, the 1,050-shp (783-kW) Astazou XVIIIA.
Piloted by Roland Coffignot, this helicopter established three class

speed records in May 1973, with a maximum speed of 194 mph (312 km/h) over a 1.9-mile (3-km) closed circuit.
The first prototype was joined in flight testing by a second machine which flew on 29 January 1973, and French airworthiness certification was awarded in December 1975. The first delivery to customers took place in January 1976.
A military variant of the SA 360 was developed by Aérospatiale as a private venture and intended as a light assault helicopter. The resulting **SA 361H** was fitted with a Starflex rotor head (originally developed for the AS 350 Ecureuil) and an uprated 1,400-shp (1043-kW) Astazou XXB turboshaft. As an assault helicopter it could carry up to 13 fully-equipped troops and, in the combat role, it could be armed with eight Euromissile HOT anti-tank missiles. These were aimed by a SFIM APX M397 stabilised roof-mounted sight, complemented by a nose-mounted SFIM Vénus night-vision system. Following trials of this

machine, it was decided that the Dauphin's military potential lay in a twin-engined version, which offered a greater margin of safety. The sole SA 361H was taken on charge by the French army for trials and remains in use.
Development of the basic SA 360C with twin engines led to the **SA 365C Dauphin 2** which first flew in prototype form on 24 January 1975. It was powered by two 650-shp (485-kW) Turboméca Arriel turboshafts and was certificated for single-pilot operation in IFR conditions. Initial deliveries took place in February 1978.
The SA 365C was followed in 1979 by the **SA 365N Dauphin 2**, which introduced a retractable tricycle undercarriage, greater use of composites in the construction and a radar nose. With

With their tailwheel undercarriages and single engines (indicated by the single exhaust), the SA 360 (illustrated) and SA 361 are easily recognised.

a take-off weight of 8,818 lb (4000 kg), this model first flew on 31 March 1979. A production SA 365N set a new London-Paris helicopter speed record in February 1980, achieving an average speed of 199 mph (321 km/h).
US Coast Guard interest in the Dauphin as a rescue helicopter led to the **SA 366G/HH-65A Dolphin** which was followed in production by the **SA 365N1**. This introduced an 11-bladed fenestron and uprated 724-shp (540-kW) Arriel 1C1 engines. Initial deliveries of this variant were made in January 1987. Further improvements resulted in the **SA 365N2** with Arriel 1C2 engines and the option for an EFIS cockpit. In January 1990, Aérospatiale redesignated its helicopters, the Dauphin 2 becoming the **AS 365N**. This variant was manufactured under licence in China by HAMC as the **Harbin Z-9**.
Aérospatiale also developed two dedicated military variants, the **AS 365F** and

AS 365M, both of which are described under the heading **Eurocopter AS 565 Panther**.
Current military or government operators comprise Bophuthatswana 1 SA 365N1; Burkina Faso 2 SA 365N2s; Cameroon 1 SA 365N; Congo 1 SA 365C; Dominican Republic 1 SA 365C; Fiji 1 SA 365N; France 3 SA 365Ns (air force), 1 SA 361 (army); India 6 SA 365Ns; Ivory Coast 3 SA 365Cs; Malawi 1 SA 365N; Rwanda 1 SA 365N, and Sri Lanka 2 SA 365Cs. Many of these aircraft are operated on VIP transport duties. Surprisingly, relatively few Dauphins have found their way into French military service. Three SA 365Ns are operated by GLAM (Groupe de Liaison Aériennes Ministérielles), an air force unit based at Villacoublay which is tasked with ministerial and other VIP transport duties.
Early in 1998, Eurocopter flew the first prototype of its new AS 365N4 wide-bodied helicopter.

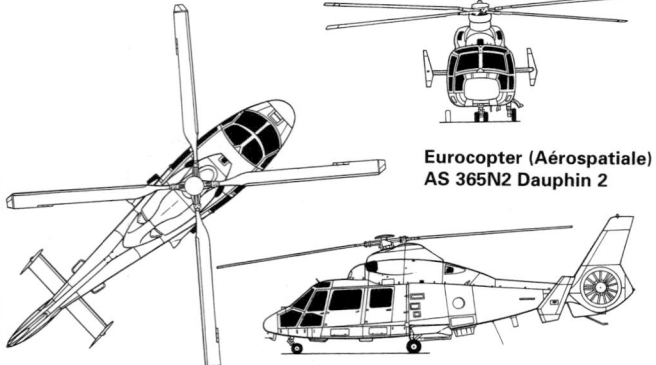

Eurocopter (Aérospatiale) AS 365N2 Dauphin 2

The Dauphin has achieved a degree of success as a business/VIP transport helicopter. This example is a Eurocopter AS 365N2 and wears the striking colours of Hankyu Airlines of Japan.

SPECIFICATION

Aérospatiale (now Eurocopter) AS 365N1 Dauphin 2
Powerplant: two Turboméca Arriel 1C1 turboshafts, each rated at 724 shp (540 kW) for take-off and 586 shp (437 kW) for continuous running
Performance: never-exceed speed at sea level 160 kt (184 mph; 296 km/h); maximum cruising speed at sea level 153 kt (176 mph; 283 km/h); maximum rate of climb at sea level 1,300 ft (396 m) per minute; service ceiling 11,810 ft (3600 m); hovering ceiling

6,890 ft (2100 m) in ground effect and 3,610 ft (1100 m) out of ground effect; range 460 nm (530 miles; 852 km) on standard fuel
Weights: empty equipped 4,764 lb (2161 kg); maximum take-off 9,039 lb (4100 kg)
Dimensions: main rotor diameter 39 ft 2 in (11.94 m); fenestron diameter 3 ft 7⅜ in (1.10 m); length overall, rotor turning 45 ft 6½ in (13.88 m) and fuselage 38 ft 2 in (11.63 m); height overall 13 ft ¾ in (3.98 m); main rotor disc area 1,205.26 sq ft (111.97 m²)

Aérospatiale SA 366/HH-65A Dolphin

Aérospatiale developed a variant of the Dauphin, under the designation **SA 366G1**, to meet a US Coast Guard requirement to replace its elderly Sikorsky HH-52 rescue helicopters. The resulting helicopter is designated **HH-65A Dolphin**, and is tasked with the SRR (short-range recovery) mission from both shore bases and Coast Guard vessels.

Several design features contribute to its improved operating safety, including the passive failure characteristics of the automatic flight control system, and the omnidirectional airspeed system which provides information while the HH-65 is hovering. Inflatable flotation bags enable waterborne operations up to sea state 5.

The Dolphin has a comprehensive communi-cations and navigation suite, which was the responsibility of prime contractor, Rockwell Collins. This includes sophisticated radio systems and a datalink for the trans-mission of parameters such as aircraft position to ship or shore base. A nose-mounted Northrop Sea Hawk FLIR sensor aids poor weather rescue opera-tions. The HH-65's all-weather rescue equip-ment includes a starboard-side rescue hoist and searchlight. The stan-dard crew of three comprises pilot, co-pilot and hoist operator.

The Dolphin has a basic internal fuel capacity of 300 US gal (1135 litres), but an additional 47.5 US gal (180 litres) of fuel can be carried in an optional baggage compart-ment tank. For ferry flights, an optional tank replacing the rear seats can raise capacity by a further 125.5 US gal (475 litres).

The first HH-65A flew in France on 23 July 1980, and was later shipped to an Aérospatiale division in Texas for installation of US equipment and certification. The Coast Guard procured a total of 96 HH-65As, and received the first of these on 1 February 1987. Two helicopters were loaned to the United States Navy Test Pilots' School at Patuxent River, while the others are distributed to Coast Guard air stations at Astoria, Borenquin, Brooklyn, Cape Cod, Cape May, Chicago, Corpus Christi, Detroit, Elizabeth City, Houston, Los Angeles, Miami, Mobile, New Orleans, North Bend, Port Angeles, Sacramento, San Diego and Savannah.

The Dolphin has been criticised for being under-powered, especially in recent times as ever more equipment has been added. A programme to re-engine with Allison/Garrett LHTEC T800s reached prototype trials stage, but has progressed no further.

In 1985, two United States Coast Guard trials aircraft were purchased for military use by Israel which, at one time, intended to buy a further 20 for service from its naval patrol boats. Known locally as the **Dolpheen**, the two HH-65As were augmented in 1996 by five AS 365 Dauphin 2s, known as the **Atalef (Bat)**.

Aérospatiale HH-65A Dolphin

Procured to replace the Sikorsky HH-52, the HH-65A Dolphin regularly operates with US Coast Guard patrol boats in the short-range SAR role.

SPECIFICATION	
Aérospatiale SA 366G1/HH-65A Dolphin **Type:** rescue helicopter **Powerplant:** two Textron Lycoming LTS101-750A-1 turboshafts, each rated at 680 shp (507 kW) **Performance:** never-exceed speed 175 kt (201 mph; 324 km/h); maximum cruising speed at optimum altitude 139 kt (160 mph; 257 km/h); hovering ceiling 7,510 ft (2290 m) in ground effect and 5,340 ft (1627 m) out-of-ground effect; range 410 nm (472 miles;	760 km) with maximum fuel or 216 nm (248 miles; 400 km) with maximum passenger payload; rescue range 166 nm (191 miles; 307 km); endurance 4 hours **Weights:** empty equipped 5,992 lb (2718 kg); maximum take-off 8,928 lb (4050 kg) **Dimensions:** main rotor diameter 39 ft 2 in (11.94 m); length overall, rotors turning 45 ft 6½ in (13.88 m) and fuselage 38 ft 1¾ in (11.63 m); height overall 13 ft ¾ in (3.98 m); rotor disc area 1,205.23 sq ft (111.97 m²)

Aérospatiale SN 601 Corvette

Aérospatiale was a late entrant into the business jet field. Development of such a type had begun in 1967, when a suitable small jet became available. Sud-Aviation and Nord-Aviation initially worked on separate designs, but pooled their efforts in December 1967 to create the **SN 600**. This was briefly known as the **Diplomate**, but was there-after called **Corvette**. The project was taken over by Aérospatiale in 1970 after the merger between the two firms, and thus became the company's first design.

The SN 600's spacious cabin allowed a wide range of layouts. Roles envisaged included third-level regional transport, air ambulance, executive transport, light freight transport or training. The cabin could seat up to 12 passengers in a high-density arrangement.

The Corvette emerged as an attractive low-wing aircraft with twin turbofan engines, pod-mounted on each side of the rear fuse-lage. The tailplane was mounted half way up the fin to keep it clear of efflux from the turbofan engines. Those initially considered included the Pratt & Whitney JT15D, derived from the PT6 turboprop, and the SNECMA/ Turboméca Larzac. The fuel efficiency of these engines was intended to reduce operat-ing costs and thus make the Corvette a viable alternative to twin turboprops.

Another strength was good short- and rough-field capability. The wings were fitted with double-slotted trailing-edge Fowler-type flaps, three-section spoil-ers, and hydraulically-actuated airbrakes above and below the wing surface. The landing gear was fitted with low-pres-sure tyres and an anti-skid braking system.

Construction of the SN 600 prototype (F-WRSN) began in December 1968 and this made its first flight on 16 July 1970, powered by 2,200-lb (9.79-kN) thrust JT15D-1 turbofans. Unfortunately, after completing more than 270 flight hours, this aircraft was destroyed during stall testing on 23 March 1971.

The test programme prompted a number of design changes. which led to the redesignation of Corvette as the **SN 601**. Major changes involved the stretching of the fuselage and the adoption of marginally more powerful JT15D-4 engines.

The lengthened fuselage allowed production aircraft to accommodate a maxi-mum of 14 passengers, seated in a pressurised and air-conditioned cabin. Enclosed in a separate flight

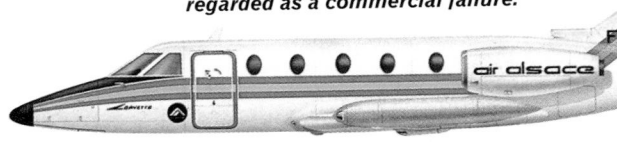

An Aérospatiale SN 601 Corvette of Air Alsace, based in France. Despite the aircraft's many attractive features, it was regarded as a commercial failure.

The Corvette was sold only in small numbers. Small regional operators, such as Touraine Air Transport, found that the type had insufficient capacity, while most business users found it too large to be used as an executive transport.

SPECIFICATION	
Aérospatiale SN 601 Corvette **Type:** light multi-purpose twin-engined jet transport **Powerplant:** two 2,500-lb (11.12-kN) thrust Pratt & Whitney Canada JT15D-4 turbofans **Performance:** maximum cruising speed 472 mph (760 km/h) at 30,000 ft (9145 m); economic cruising speed 352 mph (566 km/h); service ceiling 41,000 ft (12500 m); range with maximum fuel and 45-min reserves	1,588 miles (2555 km); range with 12 passengers and 45-min reserves 966 miles (1555 km) **Weights:** empty 7,738 lb (3510 kg); maximum take-off 14,551 lb (6600 kg) **Dimensions:** span 42 ft 2 in (12.87 m) and 45 ft 2 in (13.74 m) with optional tip tanks fitted; length 45 ft 4 in (13.83 m); height 13 ft 10 in (4.23 m); wing area 236.81 sq ft (22.00 m²)

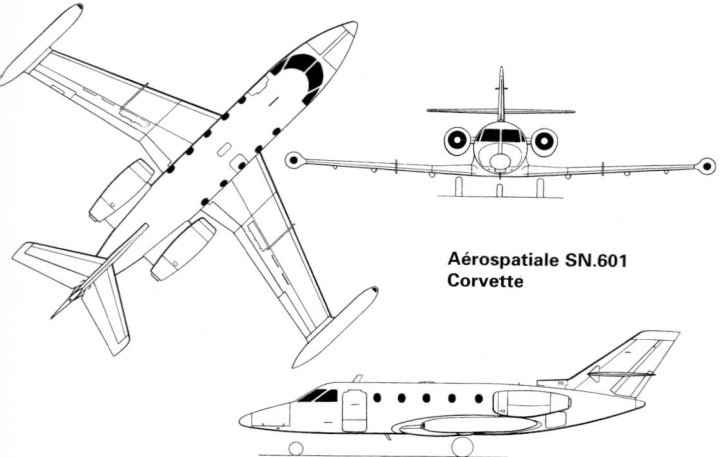

Aérospatiale SN.601 Corvette

deck, the crew of two had blind-flying instrumentation fitted as standard, but avionics equipment was installed to the customer's specification. As an executive transport, standard accommodation was provided for six passengers and one or two aircrew.

The prototype SN 601 Corvette made its maiden flight on 20 December 1972, and was followed by a second aircraft on 7 March 1973. Two airframes were built for static testing. Two further Corvettes joined the test programme in November 1973 and January 1974. French certification was awarded on 28 May 1974, followed by FAA FAR Part 25 certification in September of that year. In the same month, the first customer, Air Alpes, took delivery of the first production **Corvette 100**.

Sales were initially promising, with other deliveries to domestic French regional operators. However, Aérospatiale had only built 40 examples when production was terminated in 1978 due to a lack of orders, probably because of strong international competition from well-established rivals in this particular category of aircraft.

Aérospatiale proposed three variants of the Corvette, none of which was built. The **SN 602** was offered primarily to meet a French air force requirement for an off-the-shelf utility/liaison aircraft. It would have been powered by 2,756-lb (1250-kg) thrust SNECMA/Turboméca M49 Larzac 03 turbofans for commonality with the air force's Alpha Jet advanced trainers. With an overall length of 50 ft 2 in (15.80 m), the 18-seat **Corvette 200** would have been some 15 per cent larger overall than the Corvette 100, with a maximum take-off weight of 18,700 lb (8300 kg) – some two tonnes heavier than the Corvette 100. The **Corvette 300** was planned as a three-engined variant.

Aérospatiale SN 601 Corvette operators

Corvettes were operated as third-level regional aircraft by Africair (Senegal), Air Algérie, Air Alpes, Air Alsace, Air Languédoc, Air Inter Gabon, Air National (USA), Cogesat (France), JetStar Holland, Scan Fly (Sweden), SFACT (France), SotrAmat (Belgium), Sterling Airways, TAT, Uni-Air. In addition, they were used as VIP transports by the governments of Bangui and Benin. Several were also operated by French agencies including the Protection Civile and the Centre d'Essais en Vol (CEV). The last example was used by the CEV for general hack duties and was not retired until 1997.

Aérospatiale (SOCATA) TB 30B Epsilon

Based at Tarbes, SOCATA, Aérospatiale's light-aircraft subsidiary, began development in 1977 of a military basic trainer based on its TB 10 Tobago four/five-seat lightplane. Redesigned to meet a specification drawn up by the Armée de l'Air for a tandem trainer, the new design was proposed in **TB 30A** and **TB 30B** versions, with engines of 260 hp (194 kW) and 300 hp (224 kW), respectively.

The TB 30B gained a development contract in 1979, and the first prototype was flown on 22 December 1979. The second prototype, flown on 12 July 1980, introduced the increased span, rounded wingtips, redesigned rear fuselage and tail which had been finalised for production aircraft, which were given the name **Epsilon**. Following completion of

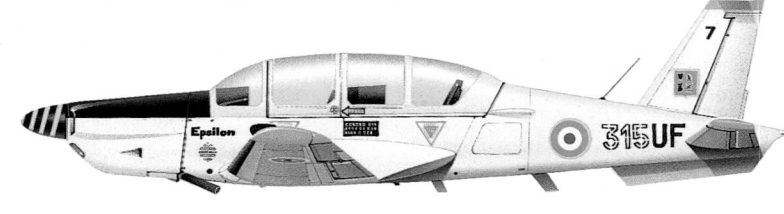

Serving in the training role since 1983, Epsilons allow direct-entry pilots to receive a 23-week (66 hours) elementary flight instruction course.

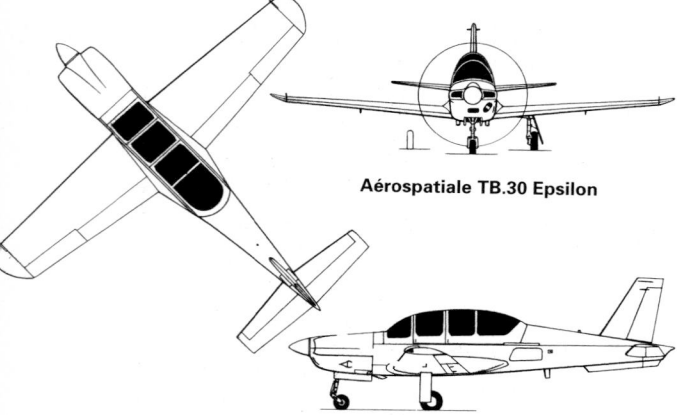

Aérospatiale TB.30 Epsilon

the development programme, the first production aircraft was flown on 29 June 1983.

Of all-metal construction, the Epsilon has retractable tricycle landing gear, a large aft-sliding canopy and a cockpit layout and flying characteristics that are intended to prepare pupils for the Armée de l'Air's advanced jet trainer, the Dassault-Breguet/Dornier Alpha Jet. Fully aerobatic and stressed for g limits of +6.7 and -3.35, the Epsilon has a Christen fuel system to permit up to two minutes of inverted flight.

On 6 January 1982, before the development programme was completed, the Armée de l'Air ordered 150, for delivery at the rate of 30 per year. Two initial production batches were approved in 1982, each covering 30 aircraft. The Epsilon duly entered service with the Centre d'Expériences Aériennes Militaires (CEAM) at Mont-de-Marsan on 29 July 1983, to establish the training syllabus. Epsilons began to equip

Groupement Ecole (GE) 315 at Cognac/Château-bernard in June 1984, this unit eventually receiving 150 Epsilons by late 1989. GE 315 is the Basic Flying School (Ecole de Formation Pilotage de Base) and receives direct-entry aircrew for a 23-week course involving 66½ hours. Four Flying Instruction Squadrons (EIV – Escadron d'Instruction en Vol) are partnered by the Instructors' School (Ecole des Moniteurs) to provide a 73-hour course.

Export orders for the Epsilon have been restricted to just two customers. The Portuguese air force took delivery from 1989 of 18 Epsilons, all apart from one being assembled locally by OGMA. These aircraft were operated initially by Esquadra 104 at Sintra. An armed version of the Epsilon was ordered by the Togolese air force in late 1984. This version is equipped with four under-wing hardpoints, carrying a total of 661 lb (300 kg) of stores with pilot only, or 441 lb (200 kg) with two crew. Three aircraft were delivered in 1986 and were followed by a single attrition replacement in 1987.

All bar one of Portugal's 18 Epsilons were assembled locally by OGMA. Operated initially by Esquadra 104 at Sintra, they are now flown from Beja in southern Portugal by Esquadra 101.

SPECIFICATION

Aérospatiale TB 30B Epsilon
Type: tandem primary trainer
Powerplant: one Textron Lycoming AEIO-540-L1B5D flat-six piston engine rated at 300 hp (224 kW)
Performance: never-exceed speed 323 mph (520 km/h); maximum level speed 'clean' at sea level 236 mph (378 km/h); cruising speed at 6,005 ft (1830 m) 222 mph (358 km/h); maximum rate of climb at sea level 1,850 ft (564 m) per minute; service ceiling 23,000 ft (7010 m); take-off run 1,345 ft (410 m) at maximum take-off weight; take-off distance to 50 ft (15 m) 2,100 ft (640 m) at maximum take-off weight; landing distance from 50 ft (15 m) 1,444 ft (440 m) at normal landing weight; landing run 820 ft (250 m) at normal landing weight; range 777 miles (1250 km); endurance 3 hours 45 minutes
Weights: empty equipped 2,055 lb (932 kg); maximum take-off 2,755 lb (1250 kg)
Dimensions: wingspan 25 ft 11¾ in (7.92 m); length 24 ft 10¾ in (7.59 m); height 8 ft 8¾ in (2.66 m); wing area 96.88 sq ft (9.00 m²)
Armament: four ALKAN hardpoints for up to 1056 lb (480 kg) of ordnance, including twin 0.3-in (7.62-mm) machine-gun pods; 110-lb (50-kg) or 265-lb (120-kg) SAMP bombs; pods containing six 68-mm MATRA F2D or Thomson-Brandt rockets; ALKAN 500 cartridge launchers containing 74-mm Lacroix grenades; flares and rescue equipment pods

Aérospatiale (SOCATA) TB 31 Omega

Following the success of the TB 30 Epsilon, SOCATA decided to capitalise on its experience with the design and manufacture of this type, and began development in 1983 of a turboprop version as a private venture. This was originally proposed under the designation **TB 30C**.

The company's primary objective was to produce a type to meet the Armée de l'Air's requirement to replace the Fouga Magister jet trainer.

The prototype Epsilon 01 was used at first as a flying testbed for the turboprop powerplant, a 450-shp (335-kW) Turboméca TP319 flat-rated to 350 shp (261 kW), which was housed in an extensively revised nose cowling with a chin intake. Initially fitted with a Ratier-Figeac three-blade composite propeller, this **Turbo Epsilon** made its first flight on 9 November 1985 but, after extensive engine development, underwent further modifications to emerge in 1989 as the **TB 31 Omega**.

This featured a fully developed 488-shp (364-kW) TP319-1A2 Arrius turboprop, derated to 360 shp (268 kW) and driving a Hartzell propeller, as well as a new two-piece moulded canopy for improved cockpit visibility. Optional equipment included two Martin-Baker Mk 15FC lightweight zero-height ejection seats able to operate at 60-kt (69 mph; 111 km/h) in a vertically stepped arrangement. The cockpit layout and handling characteristics were tailored to simulate as closely as possible those of a combat aircraft. Other changes were the introduction of EFIS instrumentation and a dorsal fin. A successful flight-test programme began on 30 April 1989 and confirmed the Omega's substantial increase in performance. However, the French government's preference for the more powerful EMBRAER Tucano has so far inhibited SOCATA from commencing production of the TB 31.

SPECIFICATION

Aérospatiale (SOCATA) TB 31 Omega
Type: basic flying trainer
Powerplant: one 488-shp (364-kW) Turboméca TP319 1A2 Arrius turboprop derated to 360 shp (268 kW)
Performance: maximum speed 322 mph (519 km/h) at 16,000 ft (4875 m); cruising speed, maximum 269 mph (434 km/h) at 10,000 ft (3050 m) and economical 220 mph (354 km/h) at optimum altitude; initial climb rate 2,100 ft (640 m) per minute; service ceiling 30,000 ft (9145 m); range 795 miles (1280 km) with 20-minute reserves
Weights: empty 1,896 lb (860 kg); maximum take-off 3,197 lb (1450 kg)
Dimensions: wingspan 25 ft 11¾ in (7.92 m); length 25 ft 7½ in (7.81 m); height 8 ft 9½ in (2.68 m); wing area 96.88 sq ft (9.00 m²)
Armament: up to 661 lb (300 kg) of stores carried on four ALKAN underwing hardpoints, and generally similar to those offered on TB 30B Epsilon

The Omega remains solely in prototype form due to the French government's preference for the more powerful EMBRAER Tucano.

Aérospatiale/British Aerospace (BAC) Concorde

In the late 1950s, both Bristol Aircraft Ltd in the UK and Sud Aviation in France were carrying out independent design studies for a practical supersonic transport. In 1960, Bristol became a wholly-owned subsidiary of, and was ultimately absorbed into, the British Aircraft Corporation, or BAC, and Sud Aviation was merged with Nord-Aviation and SEREB in 1970 to form the Société Nationale Industrielle Aérospatiale. Both companies decided that the design and construction of such an aircraft was feasible, but that the cost of its development would be completely beyond the capability of any individual company. Indeed, it soon became clear that development costs were likely to exceed a figure which could be faced by either the British or French government alone. There thus followed discussions which resulted in the signing of agreements on 29 November 1962 to bring about international collaboration for the realisation of what was seen then as a highly desirable and readily marketable commodity. The governments of the UK and France agreed to provide the cash to finance development, and the British Aircraft Corporation and Rolls-Royce finalised agreements with Sud Aviation and the Société Nationale d'Etude et de Construction de Moteurs d'Aviation (SNECMA) for collaboration in the design and manufacture of a joint supersonic transport (SST). This eventually became the appropriately named Concorde, symbolising the determination of the two nations' manufacturing companies to produce a safe, reliable, world-leadng aircraft.

Design and development of Concorde required the solution of many complex technological problems if the collaborating companies were to achieve their aim of manufacturing a safe and reliable SST. The first bridge to be crossed was a decision on maximum speed. If the intention was to cruise at a speed between Mach 2.5 and Mach 3.0, then problems would be faced from kinetic heating due to air friction. During extended periods of high-speed cruising flight, this would raise the temperature of certain areas of the aircraft's structure to such an extent that conventional light alloys would be unable to maintain their structural integrity. Manned research vehicles and a number of operational military aircraft have subsequently been developed to fly at sustained speeds of Mach 3 or over. Their structures, however, contain considerable amounts of heat-resistant metals such as titanium or stainless steel, but use of these materials on a fairly large scale for a Mach 2.5-3.0 Concorde would have increased its structural costs very considerably. Instead, it was decided to limit the airliner's speed to Mach 2.2.

Aérospatiale and BAC, shared the design development and construction, with the French partner responsible for wings and wing control surfaces, the rear cabin section, air-conditioning, hydraulics, navigation and radio systems, and flying controls. BAC was responsible for the three forward fuselage sections, rear fuselage, vertical tail surfaces, engine nacelles and ducting, engine installation, fire warning and extinguishing systems, electrical, fuel and oxygen systems, and noise and thermal insulation.

Concorde is of cantilever low-wing configuration with a large-area delta wing, and a long, narrow fuselage with a maximum internal width of 8 ft 7 in (2.63 m). The tail unit consists only of a vertical fin and rudder, for control in pitch and roll is provided by six elevons spaced across the trailing edge of the delta wing. The landing gear has twin wheels on the nose unit and a four-wheel bogie on each main unit. Standard accommodation provides for a crew of three on the flight deck, with provision for a fourth seat behind the pilot, and there is a variety of four-abreast seating layouts to suit the requirements of individual airlines. The maximum possible seating capacity allows for

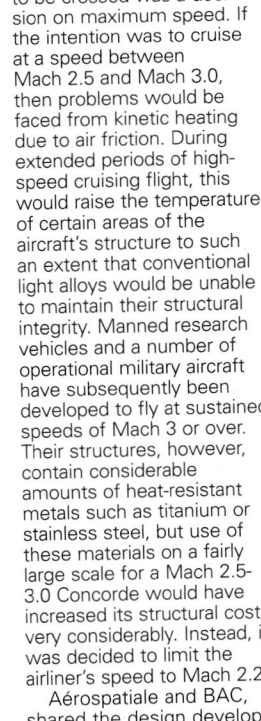

F-BVFA was the fifth production Concorde built. Flying first on 25 October 1975, it subsequently entered service with Air France on the Paris-Dakar-Rio de Janeiro route on 21 January 1976.

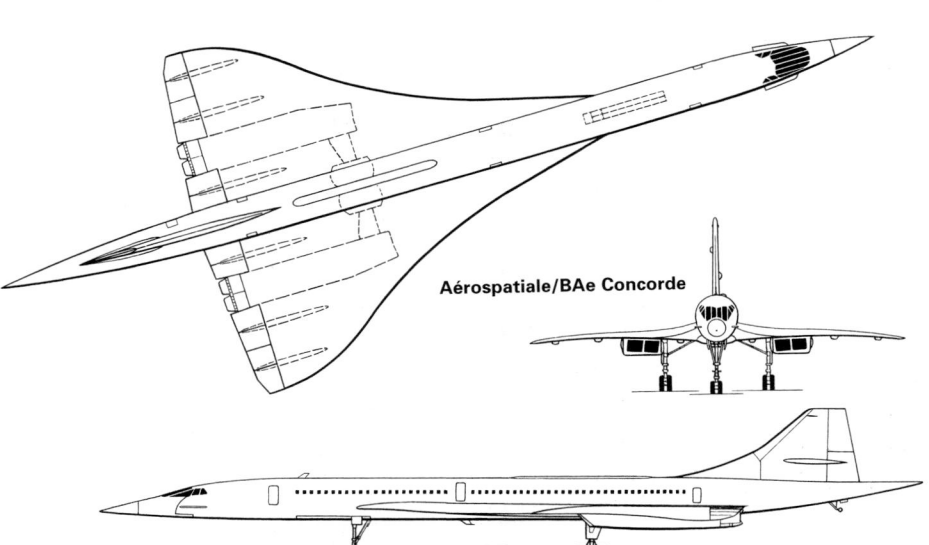

Aérospatiale/BAe Concorde

Seen taking to the air for the first time is the last production Concorde (G-BFKX). This aircraft was later re-registered G-BOAF and is still in operation with BA on transatlantic routes.

the carriage of up to 144 passengers. Powerplant consists of four Rolls-Royce/SNECMA Olympus 593 Mk 610 turbojet engines, this particular version of the Olympus

being developed specially to power Concorde.

Concorde has some particularly interesting design features which are the result of its configuration and usage. For example, the delta-wing planform requires that the aircraft is flown at a fairly steep angle of attack at low subsonic speeds, which means that its flight crew would have a more restricted view of the ground during take-off, initial climb, approach and landing unless some

special provision were made. This resulted in the design of a fuselage nose section which could be drooped to improve the forward view under the above conditions, and of a retractable visor, which is raised hydraulically, to fair in the windscreen during normal cruising flight.

Much of Concorde's total fuel capacity of 31,645 US gal (120000 litres) is contained within the wing but a percentage is held in four fuselage tanks. The fuel is used for two other tasks in addition to the primary role of fuelling the engines: firstly, the large volume of fuel within the wing structure acts as a heat sink to reduce the wing temperature in prolonged supersonic flight; and, secondly, fuel is transferred automatically throughout the network of storage tanks to maintain the aircraft's centre of gravity in cruising flight. In addition, a group of trim tanks maintains the correct

relationship between the aircraft's centre of gravity and its aerodynamic centre of pressure, fuel being moved aft during acceleration, and forward as the aircraft returns to a subsonic flight regime.

Much of the efficiency and reliability of the powerplant result from the computer-controlled variable-area air intakes, which ensure that the optimum air flow reaches each engine under all operating conditions. The Concorde's flight deck and cabin are air-conditioned and pressurised, and the advanced avionics include an automatic flight control system, and triplicated inertial navigation systems.

Construction of the first two Concorde prototypes began in February 1965, Concorde 001 being built by Aérospatiale at Toulouse, and 002 by BAC at Filton, Bristol. The first flight of 001 (F-WTSS) was made on 2 March 1969, and that of the British-assembled 002 (G-BSST) on 9 April 1969.

As early flight testing of these two aircraft revealed no fundamental problems, 001 was used for a sales and demonstration tour which began on 4 September 1971. More or less simultaneously, 002 was giving demonstration flights to interested airlines, politicians and the press, and it was not until 2 June 1972 that it, too, carried out a sales tour of the Middle and Far East, this including visits to Australia and Japan. Despite the inherent problems of Concorde, posed by the fact that it was an SST, and such drawbacks as engine noise, sonic boom, fuel consumption and cost, there was considerable interest in the aircraft and its earth-shrinking potential for business and VIP travel. Soon, more than 70 aircraft had been ordered, and the prospects for resounding commercial success then seemed quite possible. With such customers on the order book as Air Canada, Air

France, American Airlines, BOAC, Eastern Air Lines, Japan Air Lines, Lufthansa, Pan American, Qantas, SABENA, TWA and United Airlines, it was reasonable to assume that successful deployment by these companies would result in a new generation of airline orders.

By the time that full passenger-carrying certification had been awarded by the British and French authorities in late 1975, flight testing of prototype, pre-production and the first production Concordes totalled 5,335 hours. SST scheduled services were inaugurated simultaneously by Air France and British Airways on 21 January 1976 but, by then, the escalating cost of these aircraft and the activity of anti-Concorde environmentalists had reduced the order book to the 14 aircraft ordered by the above two airlines. There was, of course, a strong belief that the successful operation of these aircraft by Air France and British Airways would generate new orders, but this did not occur. A significant factor in this lack of sales has been the large increases in the cost of aviation fuel.

The Concorde fleets of Air France and British Airways have currently amassed thousands of hours at supersonic flight. All seven aircraft remain active with BA, while Air France has six in service and has placed one Concorde in storage. Scheduled services chiefly serve transatlantic routes, although due to the aircraft's cachet, specialist charter flights are also made. Concorde has probably generated more pride, plus more noise and environmental-pollution hatred, than any other civil airliner built to date. To whichever one of these groups an individual belongs, there are few who would not agree that Concorde, one of the first fruits of international collaboration, has proved a supreme technological aviation success.

SPECIFICATION

Aérospatiale/BAC Concorde
Type: supersonic commercial transport
Powerplant: four Rolls-Royce/SNECMA Olympus 593 Mk 610 turbojet engines, each rated at 38,050-lb (169.26-kN) thrust with 17 per cent afterburning
Performance: cruising speed for optimum range Mach 2.04 at 51,300 ft (15635 m), equivalent to 1,354 mph (2179 km/h); service ceiling 60,000 ft (18290 m); range

with maximum fuel 4,090 miles (6582 km) with FAR fuel reserves and payload of 19,500 lb (8845 kg); range with maximum payload at Mach 2.02 cruise 3,870 miles (6228 km) with FAR fuel reserves
Weights: operating empty 173,500 lb (78698 kg); maximum take-off 408,000 lb (185066 kg)
Dimensions: wingspan 83 ft 10 in (25.55 m); length 203 ft 9 in (62.10 m); height 37 ft 5 in (11.40 m); wing area 3,856 sq ft (358.22 m²)

Aerostar AG-6

Known as IAv Bacau until the general restructuring of Romanian industry following the overthrow of the communist regime, Aerostar is one of the most important aircraft manufacturing and maintenance organisations in Romania. In the latter stages of the communist regime, the organisation was tasked with the final development of a biplane designed by INCREST

(now INAv) in the early 1980s for the agricultural and forestry patrol roles.

The **AG-6** was a slightly unequal-span single-bay biplane constructed of welded steel tube and Dural under a covering of Dural and fabric. The central fuselage section around the centre of gravity was occupied by the tank for the 231 Imp gal (1050 litres) of chemical agent. This was sprayed

via bars under the lower wing in the case of a liquid or dispensed from a hopper under the fuselage in the case of a dust agent. To the rear of the tank was the enclosed pilot's cockpit.

The AG-6 was powered by a VOKBM (Vedeneyev) M-14P radial engine driving a two-bladed variable-pitch propeller, although a three-bladed unit was planned for production models. Work on the construction of the AG-6 prototype began in mid-1986 and it made its

maiden flight on 12 January 1989. Aerostar intended to put the type into full-scale production following the end of manufacture of the

Kamov Ka-126 helicopter at the IAR plant. In the event, this did not happen and further development of the AG-6 was halted.

SPECIFICATION

Aerostar AG-6
Type: single-seat agricultural biplane
Powerplant: one VOKBM (Vedeneyev) M-14P radial piston engine rated at 360 hp (268.5 kW)
Performance: maximum speed 118 mph (190 km/h) at optimum altitude; cruising speed 109 mph (175 km/h) at optimum altitude;

initial climb rate 689 ft (210 m) per minute; service ceiling 16,405 ft (5000 m); range 329 miles (530 km)
Weights: empty 2,021 lb (917 kg); maximum take-off 4,189 lb (1900 kg)
Dimensions: wingspan 34 ft 7¾ in (10.56 m); length 22 ft 10 in (6.96 m); height 10 ft 6 in (3.20 m); wing area 279.86 sq ft (26.00 m²)

Aerostar (Yakovlev) Yak-52

Together with its single-seat Yak-50 counterpart, the **Yakovlev Yak-52** was developed to provide the Soviet air force with a successor for the Yak-18 primary trainer. First flown in 1976 (after the first Yak-50), the Yak-52 proved a successful design and its production was assigned to the IAv factory at Bacau in Romania.

Manufacture began there in 1979, the first Yak-52 flying at Bacau early in 1980. Deliveries to the Soviet Union began later in 1980 and, by June 1992, IAv had completed 1,600 Yak-52s, virtually all for the former Soviet air force, with production set to continue through 1998.

The fully-aerobatic Yak-52 features tandem seating. All three wheels of the tricycle undercarriage remain fully exposed when retracted, to give a measure of protection in the event of wheels-up landings. The Yak-52 is powered by the 360-hp (268-kW) Vedeneyev M-14P radial engine, but Aerostar has also flown a developed prototype, known as the **Condor**, with a 300-hp (224-kW) Lycoming AEIO-540-L1B5D piston engine and redesigned tail unit.

The name of the

The Yak-52 was built in large numbers by IAv (later Aerostar) in Romania for the former Soviet paramilitary flying organisation, DOSAAF.

company responsible for the factory has now changed to Aerostar SA, and the designation is rendered as **Iak-52**. In addition to the former Soviet air forces, the type is in widespread use with the Romanian air force as a primary trainer. Twelve were also purchased by Hungary in 1994.

SPECIFICATION

Aerostar (Yakovlev) Yak-52
Type: two-seat basic trainer
Powerplant: one VMKB (Vedeneyev) M-14P nine-cylinder air-cooled radial piston engine rated at 360 hp (268 kW)
Performance: maximum level speed at sea level 177 mph (285 km/h); maximum climb rate at sea level 1,970 ft (600 m) per minute; service ceiling 13,125 ft (4000 m); range 270 nm (310 miles/ 500 km) at 1,640 ft (500 m) with maximum fuel and 20-minute reserves
Weights: empty 2,238 lb (1015 kg); maximum take-off 2,877 lb (1305 kg)
Dimensions: wing span 30 ft 6¼ in (9.30 m); length 25 ft 5 in (7.75 m); height 8 ft 10¼ in (2.70 m)

Aérostructure (Fournier) RF-10

First flown on 6 March 1981, the **RF-10** had been designed in France by René Fournier as the latest member of his series of motor-gliders and ultra-light aircraft based on classic sailplane design principles.

Generally similar to the RF-9, the RF-10 introduced an all-composite structure with a carbonfibre main spar and an uprated powerplant, the Limbach L 2000 EO1 flat-four engine rated at 80 hp (59.6 kW). After completing a second prototype, Fournier sold rights in the RF-10 to Aérostructure SARL, which put the type into production with a T-tail replacing the low-mounted tailplane of the prototypes.

The first production RF-10 flew on 10 May 1984 and about a dozen were built. Four were bought by the Portuguese air force to serve with No. 802 Squadron at the Air Force Academy, at Sintra. These enable career officers to go solo before embarking on their flying training course. The entire rights package for the RF–10 was subsequently

acquired by Aeromot of Porto Alegre in Brazil, where the type has been further developed and manufactured as the Aeromot Ximango series.

Three RF-10s, operated by Esquadra 802, provide initial flying experience for cadets of the Portuguese Air Force Academy.

SPECIFICATION

Aérostructure (Fournier) RF-10
Type: two-seat motor-glider and elementary flying trainer
Powerplant: one Limbach L 2000 EO1 flat-four piston engine rated at 80 hp (59.6 kW)
Performance: maximum cruising speed 124 mph (200 km/h) at optimum altitude; economical cruising speed 112 mph (180 km/h) at optimum altitude; maximum gliding speed 153 mph (245 km/h) in smooth air and 112 mph (180 km/h) in rough air; initial climb rate 492 ft (150 m) per minute
Weights: empty 1,323 lb (600 kg); maximum take-off 1,764 lb (800 kg)
Dimensions: wing span 57 ft 3¾ in (17.47 m); length 25 ft 10¼ in (7.89 m); height 6 ft 4 in (1.93 m); wing area 201.29 sq ft (18.70 m²)

Aerotec A-122 Uirapuru/T-23 and YT-17 Tangará/T-23B

Aerotec was a Brazilian aircraft company created during 1962 in São Paulo. One of its first efforts was the **A-122 Uirapuru** which began as a private venture design by two engineers who then proposed it to the company.

The A-122 was a low-wing monoplane of light alloy construction with side-by-side accommodation in an enclosed cockpit, and had fixed tricycle landing gear. Power was provided by a Lycoming O-235-C1 flat-four piston engine rated at 108 hp (80.5 kW). The prototype A-122 was flown on 2 June 1965, and was followed by a second example powered by an uprated O-320-A rated at 150 hp (112 kW).

The basic type was adopted by the Brazilian air force (FAB) to replace its Fokker S.11s and S.12s in the primary training role.

In October 1967 the service placed an order for 30 machines, and the prototypes were followed by two military pre-production examples, the first of which made its maiden flight on 23 January 1968. These were followed by 28 (later increased to 68) **A-122A** aircraft to production standard with 160-hp (119-kW) O-320-B2B engines. Designated **T-23 Uirapuru**, the type entered service with the Academia da Força Aérea (air force academy) at Pirasununga, São Paulo. The two pre-production aircraft were later upgraded to full production standard. The FAB eventually received a total 76 A-122As (serialled 0940-0999 and 1730-1745).

Further military Uirapurus were supplied to the Bolivian and Paraguayan air forces, which took 18 and eight respectively. Paraguay later supplemented its force with 12 ex-Brazilian machines. Of these some eight T-23s remain in service in Paraguay with the air force's academy at Campo Grande and 12 are operational with the

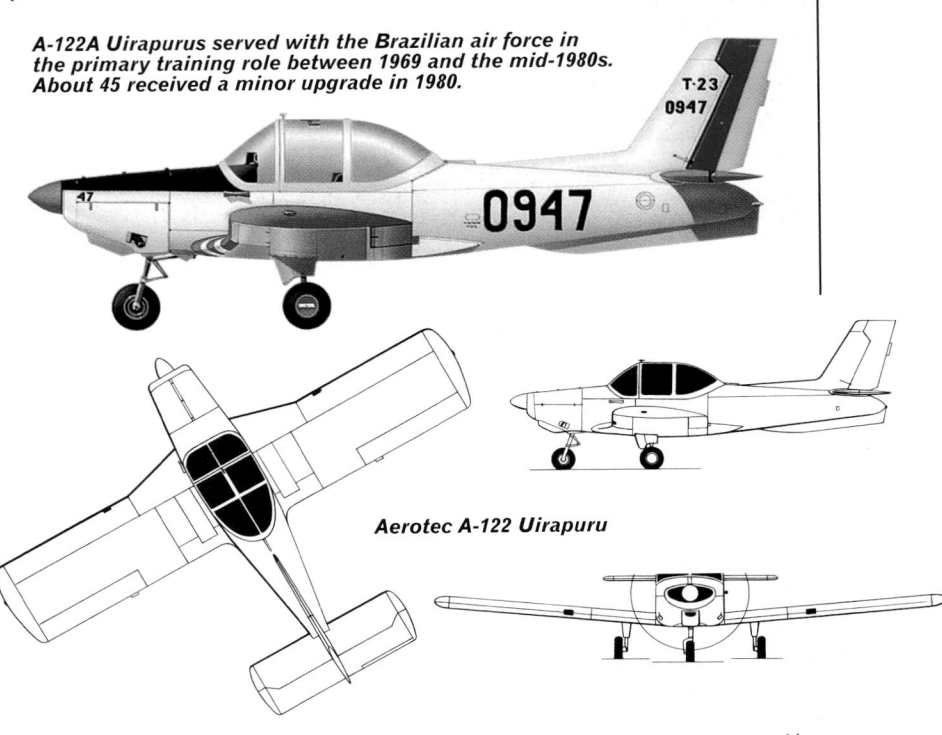

A-122A Uirapurus served with the Brazilian air force in the primary training role between 1969 and the mid-1980s. About 45 received a minor upgrade in 1980.

Aerotec A-122 Uirapuru

The YT-17 Tangará was an updated version of the Uirapuru which was evaluated by Brazil, and produced in limited numbers for Bolivia.

Bolivian air force's military aviation college at Santa Cruz. The Brazilian air force retired its surviving aircraft from trainer service in 1980, but retained a few for miscellaneous duties. Aerotec also built 20 civil examples, designated **A-122B**, which were supplied to Brazilian state-supported flying clubs. Production of the Uirapuru ended in 1977 with 155 examples of the two A-122 models having been built.

An update of the basic A-122 design resulted in the **A-132**. This is a fully-aerobatic version of the A-122 with a more powerful 200-hp (149-kW) Avco Lycoming IO-360-C1C6 flat-four piston engine. Other improvements include a wing span increased by 19¾ in (0.50 m), greater vertical tail surface area, an improved cockpit canopy and provision for wing tip tanks for greater endurance. The prototype A-132 made its maiden flight on 26 February 1981 and was originally designated **T-23B Uirapuru II**. This was later changed to **YT17 Tangará**.

Production of 100 aircraft was planned but in the event did not take place. However, some features of the A-132 were incorporated in 45 of the Brazilian air force's T-23s that were upgraded in 1979-80. Six Tangará trainers were finally completed in 1986 for sale to the Bolivian air force: these remain in service with the Bolivian air force's military aviation college at Santa Cruz, supplementing its T-23s.

SPECIFICATION	
Aerotec A-122A (T-23) Uirapuru **Type:** two-seat primary flying trainer **Powerplant:** one Textron Lycoming O-320-B2B flat-four piston engine rated at 160 hp (119 kW) **Performance:** maximum speed 140 mph (225 km/h) at sea level; maximum cruising speed 115 mph (185 km/h) at 4,920 ft (1500 m);	initial climb rate 787 ft (240 m) per minute; service ceiling 14,765 ft (4500 m); range 497 miles (800 km) **Weights:** empty 1,190 lb (540 kg); maximum take-off 1,852 lb (840 kg) **Dimensions:** wing span 27 ft 10¾ in (8.50 m); length 21 ft 8 in (6.60 m); height 8 ft 10 in (2.70 m); wing area 145.32 sq ft (13.50 m²)

Aerotechnik L-13 Vivat

The Aerotechnik company of the Czech Republic specialises in the development and production of motor gliders and hot-air balloons as well as the manufacture of light piston engines and their retrofit in aircraft such as the Zlin Z–226 and Z–336, and the Let L-40 Meta Sokol and Aero L-60 Brigadyr. The company's main product is the **L-13 Vivat** motor-glider, of which more than 150 have been delivered to customers in Europe, North America (both Canada and the USA) and South Africa.

The Vivat was developed as a powered version of the classic Blanik sailplane from which it inherited its slightly forward-swept wing planform. The L-13 has a standard motor-glider configuration with a mid-set cantilever wing of high aspect ratio. Side-by-side accommodation is provided for two in an enclosed cockpit under a Perspex canopy that lifts up and back on struts for access and egress. The landing gear comprises a fixed tail-wheel and main units enclosed in neat fairings and carrying spatted wheels.

The flying surfaces are of light alloy construction with fabric-covered control surfaces, and are fitted with slotted flaps. The wings can be removed and the two halves of the tailplane folded upward for ease of transportation. The oval-section fuselage is of welded metal tube construction with a glass-fibre skin while the rear fuselage is a semi-monocoque unit of light alloy.

The first model was the **L-13SW Vivat**. This was developed from mid-1976 as a general-purpose type optimised for training with clearance for stalling and unlimited spinning. The first of three prototypes made its maiden flight in May 1978. Some 83 production

The L-13SDM is currently one of the two models of Vivats being actively marketed within Europe. Private pilots have been quick to praise the docile handling characteristics of this motor glider.

examples of this variant were delivered. These were fitted with a mechanically semi-retractable monowheel unit complemented by retractable stabilising outrigger units in the wing-tip fairings. Power was provided by an Aerotechnik (Walter) Mikron III (S) A inline piston engine rated at 65 hp (48.5 kW) and driving an Aeron Brno or Hoffmann twin-bladed propeller. This gave a maximum gliding speed of 143 mph (230 km/h) in smooth air and, in powered mode with the Hoffmann propeller, a maximum cruising speed of 115 mph (185 km/h).

The two current variants of the Vivat are the **L-13SDM** and **L-13SDL**. These have a fixed main landing gear arrangement based on two cantilever legs but differ from each other in their powerplants: the SDM has a Mikron III AE inline engine rated at 65 hp (48.5 kW) and driving a Hoffmann two-bladed propeller, while the SDL has a Limbach L 2000 EO1 flat-four piston engine rated at 67 hp (50 kW) and driving a Mühlbauer two-bladed propeller.

The two models are basically similar in terms of size, weight and all aspects of performance except range. The Mikron-powered sub-variant has a range of 311 miles (600 km) and endurance of 3 hours by comparison with the Limbach-powered sub-variant's endurance of 3 hours 20 minutes.

SPECIFICATION	
Aerotechnik L-13SDL Vivat **Type:** two-seat motor-glider optimised for training **Powerplant:** one Limbach L 2000 EO1 flat-four piston engine rated at 67 hp (50 kW) for take-off **Performance:** maximum speed 109 mph (175 km/h) at optimum altitude; cruising speed, maximum 99 mph (160 km/h) at optimum	altitude; initial climb rate 492 ft (150 m) per minute; service ceiling not available; range 354 miles (570 km) **Weights:** empty 1,124 lb (510 kg); maximum take-off 1,587 lb (720 kg) **Dimensions:** wing span 55 ft 1⅞ in (16.80 m); length 27 ft 2¾ in (8.30 m); height 7 ft 6½ in (2.30 m); wing area 217.44 sq ft (20.20 m²)

Aerotécnica AC-11

The Spanish company, Aerotécnica SA entered into the field of rotary-wing flight by securing the services of a French designer, Jean Cantinieau, and the purchase of his first fully-developed design, the **Matra-Cantinieau MC-101**. This was an evolution of the pioneering **MC-100** which was built by Matra and which made its first flight in 1952.

The basic designation given to the resulting family of Spanish helicopters was AC, which denoted the collaboration between Aerotécnica and Cantinieau.

In Spain the MC-101 became the **AC-11**, and

The unusual Aerotécnica AC-11 remained only in prototype form, but was very useful in paving the way for a series of larger and more practical helicopter designs.

was notable for its extreme structural simplicity. The 'fuselage' was a sled-like unit that carried the powerplant (shielded only on its lower and front sections) at the extreme front and also the main rotor assembly (gearbox and three-bladed rotor), as well as supporting the triangular open boom that carried the tail rotor. Carried under this 'fuselage' was the rest of the simplified airframe, which comprised the cockpit and landing gear.

The cockpit provided side-by-side accommodation for a pilot and one passenger, who were seated behind a broad windscreen which had curved-back outer sections. The landing gear was a conventional side-by-side arrangement of two large tubular curved skids.

SPECIFICATION	
Aerotécnica AC-11 **Type:** two-seat light helicopter **Powerplant:** one Avco Lycoming O-290-D2 flat-four piston engine rated at 135 hp (101 kW) **Performance:** maximum speed 67 mph (108 km/h) at sea level; cruising speed 50 mph (80 km/h) at optimum altitude; initial climb rate	356 ft (109 m) per minute; service ceiling 8,200 ft (2500 m); endurance 2 hours **Weights:** empty 1,179 lb (535 kg); maximum take-off 1,687 lb (765 kg) **Dimensions:** main rotor diameter 27 ft 10¾ in (8.50 m); length 21 ft 11¾ in (6.70 m); rotor disc area 610.82 sq ft (56.75 m²)

Aerotécnica AC-12

Following its initial experience with the AC-11, Aerotécnica developed a much improved design known as the **AC-12** which retained the AC-11's unusual pod-and-boom configuration. The engine was located at the extreme forward end of the boom above the front of the cabin pod. The engine drove a three-bladed main rotor, via a reduction gear and gearbox designed and built by the ENHASA propeller company. The main and tail rotor blades were of composite construction with Dural spars, Dural ribs, and an interior filling of Klegecell plastic foamed resin under a glassfibre skin. The rest of the airframe was of light alloy construction. The cabin provided accommodation for two with dual controls as standard.

Built by AISA (Aeronautica Industrial SA), the prototype AC-12 made its first flight on 20 July 1956. About 12 production AC-12s, designated **EC-XJ-2**s were supplied to the Spanish air force for training duties.

SPECIFICATION	
Aerotécnica AC-12	hovering ceiling 7,875 ft (2400 m)
Type: two-seat light utility helicopter	in ground effect; range 199 miles (320 km)
Powerplant: one Avco Lycoming O-360-B2A flat-four piston engine rated at 168 hp (125 kW)	**Weights:** empty 1,058 lb (480 kg); normal take-off 1,587 lb (720 kg); maximum take-off 1,653 lb (750 kg)
Performance: maximum speed 87 mph (140 km/h) at sea level; cruising speed 71 mph (120 km/h) at optimum altitude; initial climb rate 985 ft (300 m) per minute; service ceiling 14,110 ft (4300 m);	**Dimensions:** main rotor diameter 27 ft 10½ in (8.50 m); length overall 27 ft 3 in (8.30 m); fuselage length 24 ft 9 in (7.55 m); height 9 ft ¼ in (2.75 m); main rotor disc area 610.82 sq ft (56.75 m²)

Aerotécnica AC-13

The **Aerotécnica AC-13A** was a three-seat development of the AC-12 with a wholly revised powerplant. The AC-12's Lycoming piston engine was replaced by a Turboméca Artouste I turboshaft. Another new feature was the elimination of the anti-torque rotor at the tail in favour of an exhaust-deflection system. This was used in conjunction with two movable vertical tail surfaces to give directional control. Although recognisably related to the earlier Aerotécnica designs in its pod-and-boom layout, the AC-13A introduced a more conventional pod-and-boom fuselage with an extensively glazed pod for the crew.

Two prototype AC-13s were built under licence by the SNCAN (Société Nationale des Constructions Aéronautiques du Nord) under the designation **Nord N.1750 Norelfe**. These were subsequently bought by the Spanish government once it had become clear that there was no French interest in the type.

SPECIFICATION	
Aerotécnica AC-13A	initial climb rate 902 ft (275 m) per
Type: three-seat light utility helicopter	minute; service ceiling 19,900 ft (6065 m); hovering ceiling 8,695 ft
Powerplant: one Turboméca Artouste I turboshaft engine rated at 260 shp (194 kW) for take-off	(2650 m) in ground effect; range 214 miles (345 km)
Performance: maximum speed 92 mph (148 km/h) at optimum altitude; cruising speed, maximum 87 mph (140 km/h) at optimum altitude and economical 78 mph (125 km/h) at optimum altitude;	**Weights:** empty 1,268 lb (575 kg); normal take-off 1,764 lb (800 kg); maximum take-off 1,940 lb (880 kg)
	Dimensions: main rotor diameter 29 ft 8 in (9.04 m); length 25 ft 7 in (7.80 m); height 9 ft ¼ in (2.75 m); rotor disc area 690.89 sq ft (64.18 m²)

Aerotécnica AC-14, AC-15 and AC-21

First flown on 16 July 1957, the **Aerotécnica AC-14** was an enlarged five-seat version of the AC-13A fitted with an uprated powerplant. This was the Artouste IIB turboshaft which drove a four- rather than three-bladed rotor directly from the engine's gearbox via a universal joint.

The AC-14 had the same pod-and-boom configuration as the AC-13A. Differences included a larger cabin pod with extensive soundproofing, a door on each side, and accommodation for the pilot in front, plus four passengers in two side-by-side pairs. A novel feature of the design was the provision for the exhaust-deflection system of torque control to be closed down once the helicopter had attained sufficient forward speed at which point the vertical tail surfaces could undertake this function. The engine's spent gases were then exhausted directly to the rear for additional thrust, resulting in a slight increase in the type's level speed.

Just 10 AC-14s were built, and these saw limited service with the Spanish air force with the military designation **EC-XZ-4**. The helicopters were used as liaison aircraft and as crop sprayers. For this latter role the main fuel tankage in the rear of the cabin pod was reduced from 53.5 Imp gal (244 litres) to 16.3 Imp gal (74 litres). There was also provision for the passenger seats to be replaced by litters so that the helicopter could perform casevac missions.

Aerotécnica's next two helicopter designs were the **AC-15**, powered by an Avco Lycoming O-435-V flat-six piston engine rated at between 245 and 260 hp (183 and 194 kW), and the **AC-21** which was a much enlarged development of the AC-14. Powered by two 550-shp (410-kW) Artouste III turboshafts, the AC-21 accommodated a crew of two and up to 14 passengers. The AC-21 could also act as a cargo transport, for which freight could be easily loaded and unloaded via clamshell rear doors.

SPECIFICATION	
Aerotécnica AC-14	985 ft (300 m) per minute; service
Type: five-seat utility light helicopter	ceiling 20,830 ft (6350 m); hovering ceiling 16,075 ft (4900 m) in ground effect; range 292 miles (470 km)
Powerplant: one Turboméca Artouste IIB turboshaft engine rated at 400 shp (298 kW)	**Weights:** empty 1,378 lb (625 kg); maximum take-off 2,646 lb (1200 kg)
Performance: maximum speed 112 mph (180 km/h) at sea level; cruising speed, maximum 99 mph (160 km/h) at optimum altitude and economical 75 mph (120 km/h) at optimum altitude; initial climb rate	**Dimensions:** main rotor diameter 31 ft 6 in (9.60 m); length overall, rotors turning 36 ft 10 in (11.22 m); fuselage length 26 ft 8 in (8.13 m); height 10 ft 2 in (3.10 m); main rotor disc area 779.14 sq ft (72.38 m²)

Aerotek NGT and Atlas ACE

The South African government's Council for Scientific and Industrial Research formed an Aeronautical Systems Technology Division which is informally known as Aerotek. In September 1985 this concern began development work on the **NGT (Next Generation Trainer)** within the context of **Project Ovid**. This aimed to establish a South African capability to design and construct aircraft based on composite materials.

Design of the type as a turboprop-powered trainer indicated that thought had already been given to its possible selection as the South African Air Force's next trainer, replacing elderly North American T-6G Texan/Harvard piston-engined trainers.

The NGT's structure made extensive use of Kevlar and glassfibre, the object being to create an airframe that was cheaper and easier to make and maintain than that of the Pilatus PC-7, while still offering about the same level of performance and overall capability.

The NGT was of standard trainer configuration, and had straight-tapered wings with considerable dihedral. The conventional tail unit had strakes ahead of the tailplane's roots and a substantial dorsal fillet ahead of the fin. The pupil and instructor sat in tandem on vertically staggered Martin-Baker Mk 16L zero/zero lightweight ejection seats under a long one-piece canopy hinged along its starboard side and incorporating a roll-over bar. The NGT was powered by a Pratt & Whitney Canada PT6A-25 turboprop engine rated at 750 shp (559 kW) and driving a three-bladed Hartzell constant-speed metal propeller.

The task of building the NGT prototype was entrusted to the Atlas Aircraft Corporation, a division of the Armscor Group until April 1992 when it became the Atlas Aviation (Pty) Ltd, a division of Denel (Pty) Ltd which was created out of Armscor.

Although intended primarily as a two-seat trainer, the ACE was capable of carrying gun packs, bombs and rockets on six underwing hardpoints.

The NGT prototype made its maiden flight on 29 April 1991 and trials confirmed that it was fully aerobatic and possessed no major handling problems.

Later in 1991 the type was proposed to the SAAF, which conducted an evaluation of several types, including the Aérospatiale

SPECIFICATION	
Atlas ACE 1	drop tanks
Type: two-seat intermediate trainer	**Weights:** empty 3,406 lb (1545 kg); normal take-off 4,850 lb (2200 kg); maximum take-off 7,054 lb (3200 kg)
Powerplant: one Pratt & Whitney Canada PT6A-25C turboprop engine rated at 750 shp (559 kW)	**Dimensions:** wing span 35 ft 5¼ in (10.80 m); length 35 ft 5¼ in (10.80 m); height 13 ft 5¼ in (4.10 m); wing area 193.75 sq ft (18.00 m²)
Performance: maximum speed 311 mph (500 km/h) at 5,000 ft (1525 m); economical cruising speed 230 mph (370 km/h) at 15,000 ft (4570 m); initial climb rate 2,750 ft (838 m) per minute; service ceiling 33,000 ft (10060 m); range 1,082 miles (1741 km) with	**Armament:** up to 2,205 lb (1000 kg) of stores carried on six underwing hardpoints, two of them plumbed for drop tanks

TB.31 Omega, EMBRAER EMB-312 Tucano and PZL-130 Turbo Orlik. The service eventually opted for the Pilatus PC-7 Mk II to replace its Harvards.

Atlas then decided in 1993 to offer the type on the export market as the **ACE (All-Composites Evaluator)**. The prototype ACE was badly damaged in a wheels-up landing during February 1995 after a fail-ure in the longitudinal control system, and a second prototype was soon ordered. The type has yet to achieve any sales, and is currently offered in two variants: the **ACE 1**, modelled closely on the NGT and intended for inter-mediate training, and the **ACE 2**, intended for advanced training. The latter remains at the project stage and features a strengthened and l engthened airframe, powered by a PT6A-68R turboprop engine rated at 1,200 shp (895 kW), or engines of up to 1,600 shp (1193 kW).

AFCO RL-3 Monsoon

The **RL-3 Monsoon** was a low-wing light aircraft which was designed and built in India during the late 1950s. The Monsoon was a prod-uct of young Italian engi-neer Renato Levi and AFCO, a ship-building concern, and was intended primarily for sports flying and training.

The RL-3 was intended to be manufactured easily and was thus simple in concept. The aircraft was constructed almost entirely of plywood with fabric covering, using indigenous timber and other materials for ease of maintenance and repair.

In order to prevent the airframe from degrading due to humidity and temperature, the wooden airframe was bonded with synthetic adhesives and . sealed with epoxy resin film prior to covering with fabric. The use of glass reinforced plastic was

The AFCO RL-3 Monsoon was an attractive two-seat light aircraft designed and built in India.

confined to components such as the nose cowl, spinner, and wing tips.

The simple main under-carriage legs consisted of tapered sprung steel rods thus dispensing with the need for shock absorbers.

SPECIFICATION	
AFCO RL-3 Monsoon	speed 50 mph (80 km/h); initial
Type: two-seat side-by-side training and sports light aircraft	climb rate 1,000 ft (305 m) per minute
Powerplant: one Continental C-85-8F flat-four piston engine rated at 85 hp (63 kW)	**Weights:** empty 660 lb (299 kg); maximum take-off 1,200 lb (544 kg)
Performance: maximum speed 130 mph (209 km/h); cruising speed 115 mph (185 km/h); landing	**Dimensions:** wing span 25 ft (7.62 m); length 19 ft 3 in (5.87 m); height 5 ft 4 in (1.63 m); wing area 111 sq ft (10.31 m²)

Ago Ao 192 Kurier

Ago Flugzeugwerke GmbH was established in 1934 at Oschersleben, and its initial work was to produce other companies' aircraft. Its first private venture was a seven-seat light transport intended for the Kurier (courier) multi-purpose role. This was developed follow-ing the great success of the Heinkel He 70 Blitz as a fast light transport.

Ago's design received the official designation **Ao 192**, and took shape as a clean twin-engined low-wing monoplane that incorporated a number of advanced features.

Like the Blitz, the type was optimised to have a high cruising speed, and considerable attention was therefore paid to drag reduction by careful aero-dynamic design and the use of flush rivetting for the light alloy skin. Accommodation in the main air-conditioned cabin was provided for five passengers, as well as mail, freight or baggage. Unusually, the flight deck was equipped with dual flying controls, thus making the Ao 192 also suitable for training.

The wing comprised a flat centre section fitted with a one-piece full-span flap, and sharply di-hedralled, tapered outer panels each fitted with full span ailerons.

A retractable under-carriage was fitted, with the main legs retracting outward to lie flat within the thin outer wing panels. Powerplant comprised a pair of Argus As 10 inverted-Vee piston engines installed in very small nacelles angled out from the centreline and each driving a twin-bladed propeller. Alternative powerplants were proposed for export customers and these included Hirth, Gipsy Six and Menasco Buccaneer engines.

Powered by Argus 10C engines and fitted with a low-set elliptical tailplane, the **Ao 192 V1** prototype (D-OAGO) made its maiden flight in the summer of 1935, and was soon followed by the **Ao 192 V2** second prototype (D-OCTB).

This received a shorter nose, as well as a larger strut-braced tailplane which was relocated to a position about one-third of the way up the fin to correct some instability and tail flutter problems encountered by the Ao 192 V1. The first prototype was revised to the same standard as the second machine, and in the course of a protracted development period the fuselage was redesigned to accommodate six passen-gers. At the same time As 10E engines were fitted, and the main landing gear units were revised to retract rearward into the undersides of the enlarged engine nacelles. The Ao 192 V2 took part in the Isle of Man air races of 4–7 June 1938 in which it finished seventh.

The **Ao 192 V3** produc-tion prototype (D-ODAF) incorporated all these changes and reached flight status in 1938. Conducted mainly by Luftwaffe test pilots at Rechlin, the flight test programme revealed that the Ao 192 had excel-lent flying characteristics, and the type duly entered what was planned as full-scale production. Ago planned several variants of the Ao 192 for both civil and military use, desig-nated **Ao 192B** and **Ao 192C** respectively.

However, the company's licence-manufacturing commitments were so extensive that only six Ao 192Bs were completed. These were all taken over by the German authorities for use as the personal transports of high-ranking officials. The Ago concern itself had been taken over by the giant Junkers firm in late 1936.

Proposed Ago Ao 192B/Ao 192C variants

Ao 192B: basic civil model planned in several variants, all unbuilt
Ao 192BV: touring/transport aircraft/mailplane; two crew plus six passengers, plus 60 cu ft (1.7 m³) of freight; seats removable for freight transport to give volume of 109 cu ft (3.1 m³)
Ao 192BL: aerial survey aircraft with electrically-driven wide-angle camera and dark room for onboard film-processing, one/two pilots plus observer and photographer
Ao 192BS: ambulance aircraft, accommodation for two litters and attendant
Ao 192DF: dual-control radio and instrument trainer; accommodation for a pilot, a radio instructor and three trainees
Ao 192DV: dual-control touring, passenger and freight aircraft
Ao 192E-1: four-seat personnel transport with more comfortable accommodation, additional baggage space, D/F radio and poor-visibility landing aid equipment
Ao 192C: designation reserved for military variants, all unbuilt
Ao 192CA: light reconnaissance aircraft with crew of two/three; armament of three 0.312-in (7.92-mm) MG 15 machine-guns (two fixed forward and one flexible upper rear), plus eight 26-lb (12-kg) bombs, and reconnaissance cameras
Ao 192CB: light bomber sub-variant of Ao 192CA, retaining three-gun armament but with provision for four 110-lb (50-kg) bombs
Ao 192CL: armed reconnaissance sub-variant of Ao 192CA retaining three-gun armament
Ao 192CN: smokescreen-laying aircraft
Ao 192CS: medical evacuation aircraft

SPECIFICATION	
Ago Ao 192B Kurier	(2000 m); climb to 3,280 ft (1000 m)
Type: light passenger transport	in 3 minutes 12 seconds; service
Powerplant: two Argus As 10E inverted-Vee piston engines each rated at 270 hp (201 kW)	ceiling 11,465 ft (5200 m); range 684 miles (1100 km)
Performance: maximum speed 208 mph (335 km/h) at 6,560 ft (2000 m); maximum cruising speed 179 mph (288 km/h) at 6,560 ft (2000 m); economical cruising speed 147 mph (238 km/h) at 6,560 ft	**Weights:** empty 3,616 lb (1640 kg); maximum take-off 6,504 lb (2950 kg) **Dimensions:** wing span 44 ft 5 in (13.54 m); length 36 ft ¼ in (10.98 m); height 11 ft 11⅜ in (3.64 m); wing area 269.54 sq ft (25.04 m²)

The Ao 192 was one of the most advanced twin-engined transport designs of the mid-1930s. Ago's commitments to other projects meant that the design was not developed further, however.

Ago C.I

The name Ago is derived from the initial letters of the company founded in 1911 by German car and aviation pioneer, Gustav Otto. Then named Aeroplanbau G. Otto und Alberti, the organisation was renamed Aerowerke Gustav Otto early in 1912 and, later in the same year it was renamed the Ago Flugzeugwerke GmbH.

In common with many other European manufacturers at the beginning of World War I, Ago's first designs were intended for the observation/communications role. Allocated the company designation **DH 6**, its first military aircraft was a two-seat biplane of unusual pod-and-boom configuration. Given the military designation **C.I**, much of its design was contributed by a Swiss engineer, August Haefeli, who had worked earlier for the Farman brothers in France. The C.I's three-bay biplane wing clearly owed much to the design of Farman wing structures, and was of wooden construction with fabric covering. The fuselage consisted of a central nacelle incorporating two open cockpits, with the pilot seated aft and the observer accommodated in the nose position. Driving a pusher propeller, the Benz Bz.III engine was mounted at the rear of the nacelle and was cooled by lateral radiators.

Outboard of the central nacelle, two streamlined booms of oval cross-section were located between the wings by unusual bifurcated interplane struts in the innermost position, and stretched aft to carry a balanced 'comma' rudder on each. The two booms were united by a tailplane, which mounted a conventional elevator.

The landing gear included a tailskid beneath the aft end of each boom, a single wheel on each main unit and, forward of these, two additional wheels beneath the nose to prevent the aircraft from nosing over on poor landing surfaces.

The C.I was produced in only comparatively small numbers, and saw service on the Western Front from the summer of 1915.

In its later production form, the C.I was powered by a 160-hp (119-kW) Mercedes D.III engine and cooled by lateral radiators moved further to the rear. Other changes included a four-bay wing with span increased to 49 ft 2⅖ in (15.00 m) and revised vertical tail surfaces in which small triangular fins carried plain rudders.

All C.I aircraft were armed with a single 0.312-in (7.92-mm) Parabellum trainable forward-firing machine-gun in the nose position. The size of the machine initially persuaded the Royal Flying Corps that the C.I had a crew of six and an armament of at least three trainable machine-guns.

The designation **C.I-W** was given to a development of the C.I as a seaplane, which had a side-by-side pair of single-step wooden floats. This was evaluated by the German navy, but no production ensued.

SPECIFICATION

Ago C.I (three-bay type)
Type: two-seat reconnaissance aircraft
Powerplant: one Benz Bz.III inline piston engine rated at 150 hp (112 kW)
Performance: maximum level speed 90 mph (145 km/h) at sea level; climb to 9,845 ft (3000 m) in 30 minutes; service ceiling 14,765 ft (4500 m); endurance about 4 hours
Weights: empty 1,764 lb (800 kg); maximum take-off 2,910 lb (1320 kg)
Dimensions: span 47 ft 7 in (14.50 m); length 32 ft 3⅖ in (9.84 m)
Armament: one 0.312-in (7.92-mm) Parabellum trainable machine-gun

Ago C.II

Designed with the company designation **DH 7**, the **Ago C.II** was a structurally-refined version of the C.I. These improvements increased the strength and also helped to reduce drag for the attainment of usefully higher performance. Compared to the C.I, the C.II featured an uprated powerplant, revised vertical tail surfaces for improved directional stability and control, and the replacement of the two radiator sections on the sides of the central nacelle by a single radiator under the centre section of the upper wing.

The C.II first appeared in late 1915 and entered service early in 1916, when it complemented rather than replaced the C.I. The three-bay C.II was also produced in limited numbers with a four-bay configuration. The wingspan was increased to 60 ft ½ in (18.30 m) for improved altitude capability.

Two such examples were evaluated by the German navy's air service under the designation **C.II-W**. Fitted with a side-by-side pair of single-step wooden floats, this had an overall length of 36 ft 10⅝ in (11.24 m). Of these two floatplanes, one was fitted with a standard two-bladed wooden propeller of the basic landplane, while the other was evaluated with a four-bladed wooden propeller.

SPECIFICATION

Ago C.II (three-bay model)
Type: two-seat reconnaissance aircraft
Powerplant: one Benz Bz.IV inline piston engine rated at 220 hp (164 kW)
Performance: maximum speed 85 mph (137 km/h) at sea level
Weights: empty 2,998 lb (1360 kg); maximum take-off 4,290 lb (1946 kg)
Dimensions: span 47 ft 6⅞ in (14.50 m); length 32 ft 3⅜ in (9.84 m); height 10 ft 5 in (3.18 m)
Armament: one 0.312-in (7.92-mm) Parabellum trainable machine-gun

The Ago C.II was essentially a structurally-refined version of the company's previous C.I observation and liaison biplane design. Two examples of the C.II-W floatplane (illustrated) were evaluated by the Imperial German navy, but no orders were placed.

Ago C.III

By 1916 it was clear that, although they possessed good handling and adequate firepower, the Ago C.I and C.II were hampered in terms of agility and outright performance by their size and resultant weight, which were both somewhat higher than those of Allied two-seat reconnaissance and observation aircraft with an equivalent powerplant. In 1916, therefore, the company undertook the design of the **Ago C.III** that was, in essence, a scaled-down version of the C.II.

This featured a simplified and lightened landing gear. The pair of skids under the rear sections of the booms were complemented by a wire-braced main unit of the spreader-bar type with the axle carried at the closed ends of two Vee struts extending downward and outward from the lower longerons. Somewhat surprisingly, the powerplant was also scaled down, and comprised a Mercedes D.III inline piston engine installed at the rear of the central nacelle to drive a pusher propeller turning in the gap between the two booms.

No details of the C.III's performance have survived, but from the fact that the type remained only a prototype and was not ordered into production, it is reasonable to assume that, although the C.III may have offered better manoeuvrability than the C.II, its performance was deemed inadequate. The C.III evolved at a time when the Allied powers were introducing advanced fighters with a forward-firing machine-gun armament synchronised to fire through the propeller disc.

SPECIFICATION

Ago C.III
Type: two-seat reconnaissance and observation aircraft
Powerplant: one Mercedes D.III inline piston engine rated at 160 hp (119 kW)
Dimensions: wingspan 36 ft 1⅛ in (7.00 m); length 22 ft 11⅝ in (7.00 m)
Armament: one 0.312-in (7.92-mm) Parabellum trainable machine-gun

Ago C.IV

It had become apparent by 1916 that the twin-boom layout used in the Ago C.I and C.II had been rendered obsolete by the advent of Allied fighters of the small tractor biplane or sesquiplane type over World War I's Western Front theatre. These fighters offered levels of agility and performance markedly superior to those of Germany's older two-seat warplanes. In response, Ago began development of a wholly new and more capable reconnaissance and observation aircraft, the **C.IV**.

This appeared in 1916 as a two-bay biplane with a fuselage of mixed construction (wooden longerons and steel tube spacers). Light alloy panels were used as covering between the nose and the front unit of the main landing gear unit, plywood between this point and the rear cockpit, and fabric aft of the latter point. The two crew sat in what was by now regarded as an obsolete layout, with the observer/gunner in the front cockpit, and pilot in the rear cockpit.

The equal-span wing was of fabric-covered wooden construction, with upper and lower wings of essentially similar planform. Both surfaces were flat and with moderate taper in both chord and thickness, and featured ailerons.

The fuselage was conventional and terminated in a braced tail unit that included a fin and rudder similar to those of the C.I.

The C.IV was powered by a Benz Bz.IV inline piston engine rated at 220 hp (164 kW). Unlike previous Ago types, this was mounted in the nose and drove a two-bladed wooden tractor propeller which

In its earliest form, the C.IV was devoid of fixed vertical tail surfaces. It entered service with a fixed fin, which improved directional stability.

incorporated a spinner. The engine was fitted with a prominent 'rhino horn' exhaust stack to starboard. An innovative feature was the radiator which was built into the root end of the starboard upper wing to reduce aerodynamic drag. The gravity-feed fuel tank was located in a matching position in the root end of the port wing. The water and fuel pipes were built into the cabane struts for reduced drag.

The C.IV was fitted with a fixed tailskid landing gear typical of the period. However, the axle carrying the main units had a measure of shock absorption by using bungee and steel spiral springs, and a wire-operated 'claw'-type brake was attached to the centreline of the main landing gear unit's spreader bar.

The C.IV proved more successful than previous Ago types and was ordered in large numbers. However, the final number built was much smaller, and only 70 C.IVs were produced by Ago and two sub-contractors: Flugzeugbau Schütte-Lanz and Waggonfabrik Jos Rathgeber.

This small total was probably a result of contract cancellations for, although reasonably fast, the C.IV was very unstable and unpopular with its crews.

Efforts were made to improve its handling by the addition of a strut-linked aileron on each outboard end of the lower wing's trailing edge, and the enlargement of the vertical tail surface by the addition of a small strut-braced fixed fin ahead of the balanced rudder, but no further production was undertaken.

SPECIFICATION

Ago C.IV
Type: two-seat reconnaissance biplane aircraft
Powerplant: one Benz Bz.IV inline piston engine rated at 200 hp (164 kW)
Performance: maximum speed 118 mph (190 km/h) at sea level; climb to 9,845 ft (3000 m) in 22 minutes; service ceiling 18,045 ft (5500 m); range 466 miles (750 km)
Weights: empty 1,984 lb (900 kg); maximum take-off 2,976 lb (1350 kg)
Dimensions: wingspan 39 ft ½ in (11.90 m); length 27 ft ⅜ in (8.25 m); height 11 ft 5⅝ in (3.50 m); wing area 403.66 sq ft (37.50 m²)
Armament: one 0.312-in (7.92-mm) LMG 08/15 fixed forward-firing machine-gun and one 0.312-in (7.92-mm) Parabellum trainable rearward-firing machine-gun

Ago miscellaneous types

None of the Ago aircraft was built in significant numbers, and those covered in separate entries were complemented by several types which only reached prototype stage.

The **Ago C.VII** combined the powerplant, fuselage and tail unit of the C.IV with a wholly new two-bay wing. This featured upper and lower wings of constant-chord, and its most unusual feature was the use of thin steel strip in place of the standard wires for the flying and landing control lines.

Powered by a 260-hp (194-kW) Mercedes D.IVa engine, the sole **C.VIII** prototype appears to have been a development of the C.VII with a revised rear fuselage terminating in a horizontal rather than vertical knife-edge and a modified tail unit.

Two prototype **S I** two-bay biplanes were under final construction as World War I ended. The type was designed for the low-level attack role, with an armament of two 0.312-in (7.92-mm) machine-guns and a 20-mm cannon. Given its intended role, the S I was probably fitted with armour protection for the crew, its 160-hp (194-kW) Basse und Selve BuS.III engine, and its fuel and oil systems. The most advanced feature of the airframe was the wide-track main landing gear which comprised a pair of single-wheel units.

Another type which only reached prototype stage was the **Ago DV 3** which appeared in 1915. This was a very workmanlike single-seat biplane powered by a 100-hp (74.6-kW) Oberursel Ur.I rotary piston engine. This was installed in a very neat cowling and drove a two-bladed wooden propeller fitted with a large spinner. The only performance data recorded for the DV 3 include a maximum speed of 93 mph (150 km/h) and a climb to 3,280 ft (1000 m) in eight minutes.

Agricopteros Scamp Model B

The Scamp B is an unorthodox light agricultural biplane.

Perhaps one of the most unusual agricultural aircraft developed was that produced by Agricopteros Ltda at Cali, in Colombia. Seeking an existing design that would be suitable for conversion to a light 'agplane', and one that would be cheap to acquire and operate, engineer Maximo Tedesco obtained from Aerosport Inc. in the USA two kits of its single-seat **Scamp Model A.** This had been designed as an easy-to-fly lightplane that could be built without too much difficulty by amateur constructors, either from plans or kits.

Tedesco decided that this little all-metal biplane had just the qualities that he needed for his project. In conjunction with Aerosport, he introduced several modifications to make the Scamp more suited to the demands of agricultural spraying, the most important being an increase in wingspan to give greater wing area. In addition, ailerons were added to the lower wings to enhance roll control, and a more powerful engine was installed. As a result, the agricultural **Agricopteros Scamp B** has a maximum take-off weight some 23 per cent greater than that of the US homebuilt version. Subsequently, Tedesco rounded off his project by designing for it a complete spray installation comprising a glassfibre chemical tank for under-fuselage mounting, a wind-driven pump, and a spraybar. Collectively, the entire system weighs only 38 lb (17 kg) in an empty state. An unusual feature of this installation is that the chemical hopper can alternatively be used as an auxiliary fuel tank. Production Scamp Bs are produced from kits supplied by Aerosport Inc., with the addition of the spray system.

SPECIFICATION

Agricopteros Scamp Model B
Type: light agricultural aircraft
Powerplant: one 100-hp (75-kW) Revmaster-modified Volkswagen motor car engine
Performance: maximum level speed 95 mph (153 km/h); cruising speed 87 mph (140 km/h); service ceiling 8,500 ft (2590 m); range at cruising speed 150 miles (241 km)
Weights: empty 572 lb (259 kg); maximum take-off 945 lb (429 kg)
Dimensions: wingspan 19 ft 6 in (5.94 m); length 14 ft 4 in (4.37 m); height 5 ft 8 in (1.73 m); wing area 116.5 sq ft (10.82 m²)

Agusta Model 115

Giovanni Agusta was one of Italy's aviation pioneers, building his first aircraft in 1907. His company, Costruzioni Aeronautiche Giovanni Agusta SpA, was established in 1923 and, like Westland Aircraft in Britain, was destined to become a major constructor of rotary-wing aircraft.

In 1961, the company announced development of a new general-purpose helicopter under the designation of **Agusta 115**. Agusta had been undertaking licence manufacture of the Bell 47 general-purpose helicopter since 1954, and its new four-seat design showed clearly its derivation from the Bell 47 line. The Model 115 retained the complete rotor system of the Model 47J-3, with the tail rotor carried on a typical Bell open-structure triangular-section tail boom. Completely new was the four-seat enclosed cabin, provided with a large door on each side to facilitate the helicopter's use in the utility role.

Provision was made for the installation of a hoist and flotation gear for the rescue role, and the transportation of a medical attendant and three litters (one in the cabin and two covered litters carried externally) for the air ambulance role.

The powerplant was also new, consisting of a Turboméca Astazou II turboshaft. This gave a significant improvement in the type's high-altitude performance, compared to the Bell 47's piston engine. The Astazou powerplant enabled the Agusta 115 to take-off and land at maximum gross weight without weight limitations up to an altitude of 13,800 ft (4206 m). No production examples were built.

Derived essentially from the Bell Model 47, which Agusta built under licence, the Model 115 was a clean design that failed to attract production orders.

SPECIFICATION

Agusta 115
Type: four-seat general-purpose light helicopter
Powerplant: one Turboméca Astazou II turboshaft rated at 480 shp (358 kW)
Performance: maximum level speed 106 mph (170 km/h); cruising speed 93 mph (150 km/h); service ceiling 15,585 ft (4750 m); hovering ceiling 13,800 ft (4206 m) in ground effect and 11,150 ft (3399 m) out of ground effect; range 162 miles (260 km) at cruising speeds with standard fuel
Weights: empty 1,609 lb (730 kg); maximum take-off 2,976 lb (1350 kg)
Dimensions: main rotor diameter 37 ft 2 in (11.33 m); overall length, rotors turning 43 ft 7⅝ in (13.30 m); fuselage length 32 ft 5¾ in (9.90 m); height 9 ft 7¾ in (2.94 m); main rotor disc area 1,085.25 sq ft (100.82 m²)

Agusta A 101G

Agusta began the design and construction in 1958 of an aircraft to meet an Italian air force requirement for a medium-sized multi-role helicopter. The programme was broadly equivalent to Sud-Aviation's Super Frelon and was initially designated **AZ 101G**. Under the direction of the company's chief designer, Filippo Zapatta, the design team at Cascina Costa originally devised a 16-seat helicopter which was ahead of its time both in terms of configuration and powerplant. At a time when most contemporary medium-haul transport helicopters were powered by piston engines, Agusta chose turbine power in the form of three 750-shp (559-kW) Turboméca Turmo 3 turboshafts for a significantly increased power-to-weight ratio and performance.

In 1959, the passenger capacity was revised to 35 passengers, and 1,000-shp (746-kW) Bristol Siddeley Gnome engines were specified, the machine now having a design maximum loaded weight of 24,910 lb (11299 kg).

The type was subsequently revised further and given the definitive Agusta designation **A 101G**. Few details on the type were released until mid-1961, when an ASW version was announced.

A prototype was built for evaluation by the Italian air force, and flew for the first time on 19 October 1964. Power was provided by three Bristol Siddeley Gnome H.1200 turboshaft engines, each developing 1,250 shp (932 kW), and driving a single five-bladed main rotor system via a collective main gearbox. The tailfin mounted a six-bladed anti-torque tail rotor and a large horizontal stabiliser to starboard.

In many respects, the Agusta A 101 G was ahead of its time, the concept behind the helicopter being slightly ahead of the structural capabilities of the period. MM80358 was the first of three prototypes and was revised to a later configuration. All saw limited use with the Italian air force.

The A 101G incorporated a large-capacity cabin with a sliding cabin door on each side, as well as a large rear-loading ramp for cargo or vehicles. The helicopter could be flown with the ramp open to help accommodate bulky freight loads or for rapid unloading. Typical cabin loads included 35 passengers and 770 lb (349 kg) of baggage, or the equivalent in weight of equipped troops, or up to 14,330 lb (6500 kg) of cargo or, if used in the ambulance role, 18 stretcher cases with up to five attendants. The A 101G was also proposed as a flying crane with loads of up to 11,023 lb (5000 kg) carried externally on a hook mounted in the middle of the cabin floor.

As flown originally, the A 101G prototype (serial MM 80358) had quadricycle landing gear, but this was changed subsequently by the deletion of the forward pair of wheel units, and their replacement by a twin-wheel castoring nose unit.

Only two additional prototypes were built, and these featured a number of revisions, including more powerful Gnome H.1400 engines, each rated at 1,400 shp (1044 kW), a small fuselage stretch incorporating a seventh cabin window, and aerodynamically-refined side sponsons. All three prototypes saw limited service with the AMI (Italian air force), principally for evaluation by the AMI's RSV at Pratica di Mare.

A projected civil transport version was developed by Agusta as the **A 101H**, which was to be powered by three 1,750-shp (1305-kW) Bristol Siddeley Gnome H.1800 turboshaft engines. Similarly rated General Electric T58-16 turboshafts were offered as alternative powerplants.

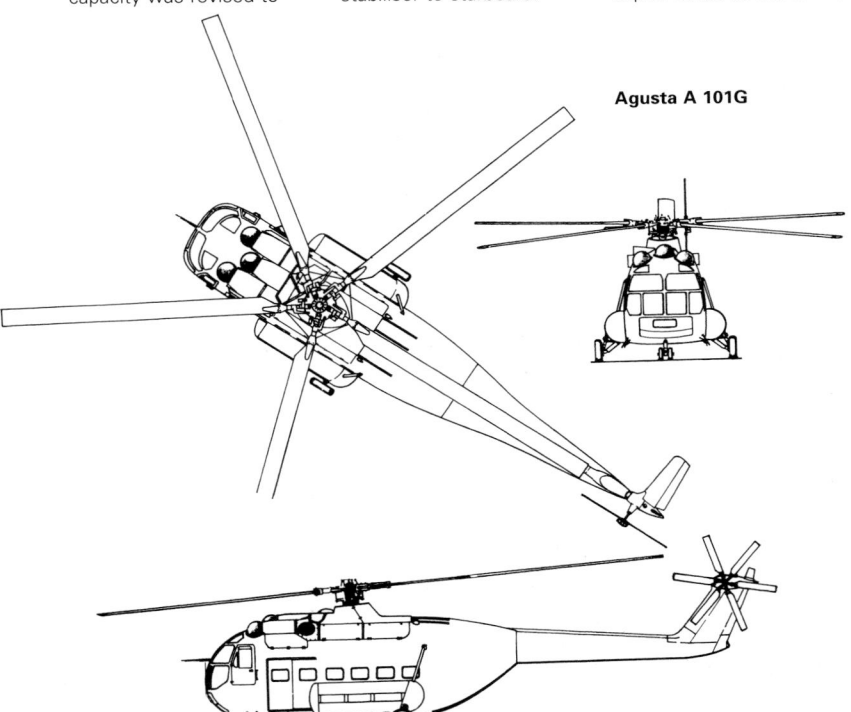

Agusta A 101G

SPECIFICATION

Agusta A 101G (definitive prototype configuration)
Type: medium-sized multi-role helicopter
Powerplant: three Bristol Siddeley Gnome H.1400 turboshafts, each rated at 1,400 shp (1044 kW) for continuous operation
Performance: maximum speed 143 mph (230 km/h); maximum cruising speed 114 mph (183 km/h); service ceiling 8,530 ft (2600 m); standard range 348 miles (560 km)
Weights: empty 14,110 lb (6400 kg); maximum take-off 28,440 lb (12900 kg)
Dimensions: main rotor diameter 65 ft 3 in (19.90 m); tail rotor diameter 10 ft 8 in (3.25 m); fuselage length 59 ft 1 in (18.01 m); height 16 ft 2 in (4.94 m); main rotor disc area 3,347.69 sq ft (311.00 m²)

Agusta A 103

Based on the licence-built Bell 47, the **Agusta A 103** was a single-seat light helicopter intended for general-purpose use. While retaining the Bell 47's two-bladed main rotor complete with stabiliser bar, the rest of the airframe featured improved and cleaner lines. In particular, the Bell-type open structure triangular-section tail boom was replaced by a neat enclosed boom of light alloy. Care had also been taken to refine the construction of the cabin and skid landing gear. The A 103 was first flown in prototype form in October 1953, but no production examples were built.

SPECIFICATION

Agusta A 103
Type: single-seat light helicopter
Powerplant: one 82-hp (61-kW) Agusta MV GA.70/V flat-four piston engine
Performance: maximum level speed 93 mph (150 km/h); hovering ceiling in ground effect 6,560 ft (2000 m); range 280 miles (450 km)
Weights: empty 617 lb (280 kg); maximum take-off 1,014 lb (460 kg)
Dimensions: main rotor diameter 24 ft 3¼ in (7.40 m); length 20 ft 1¼ in (6.13 m); height 7 ft 3¾ in (2.23 m); main rotor disc area 462.86 sq ft (43.00 m²)

The A 103 represented a stage in the transition from the licence-built Bell 47 towards an indigenous design.

Agusta A 104 Helicar

The **Agusta A 104 Helicar** two-seat helicopter was a development of the single-seat A 103, and was similarly intended for multi-role duties. The name Helicar ambitiously reflected the hope that, because it could be easily disassembled for stowage and re-assembled for flight by one person, some examples might be sold to private owners. The A 104 had a cabin with side-by-side seating, and dual controls as an optional feature. The other major change lay in the installation of a more powerful air-cooled engine but, despite the good performance of the A 104, only a single prototype was built, this flying for the first time in December 1960.

The A 104 was developed from the earlier A 103 design and was essentially a refined two-seat version of the Bell 47.

SPECIFICATION	
Agusta A 104 Helicar **Type:** two-seat light helicopter **Powerplant:** one 138-hp (103-kW) Agusta MV A.1401V flat-four piston engine, derated to 120 hp (89 kW) **Performance:** maximum level speed 103 mph (165 km/h); cruising speed 84 mph (135 km/h); hovering ceiling in ground effect	9,840 ft (3000 m); range 205 miles (330 km) **Weights:** empty 838 lb (380 kg); maximum take-off 1,411 lb (640 kg) **Dimensions:** main rotor diameter 26 ft 1 in (7.95 m); tail rotor diameter 4 ft ¼ in (1.24 m); fuselage length 20 ft 10 in (6.35 m); height 7 ft 8½ in; main rotor disc area 534.34 sq ft (49.64 m²)

Agusta A 105

Designed as what was hoped would be a practical expression of the concept embodied in the A 104, the **Agusta A 105** was intended as a two-seat utility helicopter suitable for a whole range of civil and military tasks. These included battlefield reconnaissance, liaison, supply, training, agricultural spraying and, with a platform on each side of the central fuselage, the transport of equipment or up to four troops over a range reduced to 62 miles (100 km).

Derived from the A 104, the A 105 was of typical light alloy construction with a pod-and-boom type of configuration. The boom extended rearward and slightly upward from the lower part of the pod's rear. The pod was extensively glazed with a door on each side, and carried a crew of two with dual controls. The turboshaft engine was installed behind the upper part of the pod. As Bell's Italian licensee, Agusta had extensive experience of Bell-type dynamic systems and the A 105 was therefore fitted with a two-bladed main rotor (complete with a Bell stabilising bar) and a two-bladed tail rotor. The airframe was completed by the landing gear, which comprised a side-by-side pair of tubular steel skids with upturned fronts and two retractable ground-handling wheels toward their rears.

Agusta planned to build three prototype A 105s, and the first of these flew on 1 November 1964, but no production followed as it was quickly appreciated that the type lacked the power and payload for effective commercial or tactical use. However, further development of the

In its A 105B form (illustrated), the A 105 represented a practical light helicopter. It was destined never to enter production, however.

A 105 led to the four-seat **A 105B** which was proposed for essentially the same roles as those of the A 105. The A 105B had a number of modifications compared to its predecessor: the dynamic system was enlarged slightly, with small increases in the diameters of both the main and tail rotors. The cleaner lines resulting from the enlarged cabin gave the A 105B a slightly improved performance. At similar take-off weights and with the same engine power, the A 105B had a maximum level speed of 130 mph (210 km/h). A prototype A 105B was first flown in spring 1965 but, like the A 105, the type did not succeed in achieving production status.

SPECIFICATION	
Agusta A 105 **Type:** two-seat utility light helicopter **Powerplant:** one Agusta (Turboméca) TAA.230 turboshaft engine rated at 270 shp (201 kW) for take-off and 240 shp (179 kW) for continuous running **Performance:** maximum speed 121 mph (195 km/h) at sea level; cruising speed 115 mph (185 km/h) at optimum altitude; initial climb rate 1,020 ft (312 m) per minute;	hovering ceiling 10,170 ft (3100 m) in ground effect and 6,560 ft (2000 m) out of ground effect; range 205 miles (330 km) **Weights:** empty 1,069 lb (485 kg); normal take-off 1,984 lb (900 kg); maximum take-off 2,205 lb (1000 kg) **Dimensions:** main rotor diameter 27 ft 6¹⁄₁₆ in (8.40 m); tail rotor diameter 4 ft 3 in (1.30 m); fuselage length 22 ft ½ in (6.72 m); height 7 ft 11½ in (2.42 m); main rotor disc area 596.53 sq ft (55.42 m²)

Agusta A 106

Among the helicopters planned by Agusta during the mid-1960s was a single-engined, seven-seat design intended for civil use under the designation A 109. This later evolved into the **A 109C Hirundo** which is described separately. Development of a single-seat military variant of the original A 109 was begun in July 1965 and led to the **Agusta A 106**. This took shape as a small high-performance helicopter whose primary role was

anti-submarine warfare, armed with two torpedoes.

The A 106 had a foldable two-bladed teetering main rotor and conventional tail rotor, both of aluminium alloy construction. Auxiliary flotation gear could be fitted to the skid framework, which had removable wheels for ground manoeuvring. Power was provided by a Turboméca-Agusta TAA.230 turboshaft with a maximum rating of 300 shp (224 kW) at take-off and derated to 260 shp (194 kW)

for continuous running.

The pilot sat in a fully-enclosed cabin which was fitted for operations in poor visibility with comprehensive instrumentation and avionics. Single-pilot operation was further aided by an electronic three-axis stability augmentation system developed by Ferranti, which provided a stable firing platform and damped out external disturbances. Mission equipment included Julie active acoustic echo ranging and two Mk 44 homing torpedoes carried externally under the fuselage. Alternative roles included casevac, for which two external litters could be carried, or light transport, for which an underfuselage hook could be fitted to carry under-slung loads.

Fuel capacity could be augmented by optional tanks which raised capacity

from a standard 44 Imp gal (200 litres) to 132 Imp gal (600 litres).

A prototype A 106 was first flown in November 1965, and thereafter the type endured a particularly protracted development. The Italian naval air arm vacillated over placing production orders and it was not until 1972 that the service ordered a small production batch for evaluation. Five A 106s were operated by the air arm of the Italian navy (Marinavia)

from 'Impavido'-class ships in the anti-submarine warfare role, supplementing larger naval ASW helicopters such as the SH-3D, AB 204AS and AB 212ASW. The A 106 was even proposed for army service in 1970; the torpedoes could be replaced by an alternative armament of machine-guns, rockets and a bomb dispenser.

A lack of forthcoming orders led to the cancellation of the A 106 programme in 1973.

The diminutive, single-seat A 106 was a promising design which nevertheless failed to enter full-scale service.

SPECIFICATION	
Agusta A 106 **Type:** shipboard single-seat anti-submarine helicopter **Powerplant:** one 300-shp (224-kW) Turboméca-Agusta TAA.230 turboshaft, derated to 260 shp (194 kW) **Performance** (at take-off weight with two torpedoes): maximum speed at sea level 109 mph (176 km/h); cruising speed 104 mph (167 km/h); initial climb rate 1,220 ft (372 m) per minute; hovering ceiling in ground effect 9,850 ft (3000 m); hovering ceiling out of ground effect 3,775 ft (1150 m); range with maximum	internal and external fuel 460 miles (740 km); endurance 2 hours **Weights:** empty 1,300 lb (590 kg); maximum take-off 3,086 lb (1400 kg) **Dimensions:** main rotor diameter 31 ft 2 in (9.50 m); length, rotors turning 36 ft (9.50 m); overall length, blades and tail boom folded 22 ft 8 in (10.97 m); height 8 ft 2 in (2.50 m); main rotor disc area 763 sq ft (70.88 m²) **Armament:** two Mk 44 homing torpedoes, or 10 depth charges, or (ground attack) two 0.3-in (7.62-mm) machine-guns and 10 3.15-in (80-mm) rockets

Agusta A 109 Hirundo

Having been involved in the licence-building of other manufacturers' helicopters, Agusta used its growing experience in helicopter design/construction to produce the **Agusta A 109**, the company's first own-design helicopter to enter large-scale production.

The A 109 was designed primarily for the civil market, but it has also been bought, to a lesser extent, by military operators. The A 109 helicopter features retractable landing gear, a fully articulated, four-bladed main rotor using blades of bonded aluminium alloy construction over a Nomex core, and a swept vertical tail surface with a two-bladed tail rotor to port.

The initial A 109 was powered by a single Turboméca Astazou XII turboshaft rated at 690 shp (515 kW), but was revised in 1967 to the uprated and considerably more reliable twin-engined powerplant of two Allison 250-C14s, each rated at 370 shp (276 kW). The **A 109B** was planned as a utility model for military use, but was abandoned in 1969. Agusta instead concentrated on the eight-seat civil **A 109C Hirundo** (swallow), the first of three prototypes flying on 4 August 1970. However, it was 1976 before deliveries began of the production version of the helicopter, by then redesignated the **A 109A**. This model soon proved a commercial success, being used not only as a light passenger transport, but also as an air ambulance, for freight carriage, and for search and rescue.

Several air arms procured the type in small numbers for liaison and utility transport. Of four bought by Argentina, two were captured by British forces during the Falklands War of 1982 and pressed into service with No. 7 Regiment, Army Air Corps, at Netheravon, and later augmented by two more. These are used primarily to support SAS special operations with No. 8 Flight, flying mostly from Hereford.

From September 1981, the basic civil model was redesignated the **A 109A Mk II** following modifications including an uprated transmission, a new tail rotor driveshaft, a structurally redesigned boom and detailed cockpit improvements. In 1989, a 'wide-body' A 109C version with uprated transmission was introduced, featuring a more roomy and comfortable cabin. One example was delivered to 31° Stormo of the AMI as a presidential transport.

By this time, it had been fully appreciated that as a result of its very good performance, the A 109 offered greater military potential than originally envisaged, and the type was therefore developed to fill a variety of military roles including the scout, casevac and attack tasks. The Italian army's Aviazione Leggera dell'Esercito procured 24 examples of the **A 109EOA** (Elicottero d'Osservazione Avanzata, or advanced observation helicopter), with the uprated powerplant of two Allison 250-C20Rs, each rated at 450 shp (335.5 kW). These were all delivered during 1988 to a standard that included sliding rather than hinged cabin doors for rapid access, a roof-mounted SFIM M334-25 daylight sight with boresighted CILAS laser rangefinder and a variety of armament options – the latter was carried on two outrigger pylons installed one on each side of the main cabin. Further militarisation resulted in fixed landing gear, ECM equipment and a crashworthy fuel system being fitted.

Agusta currently offers as its principal military model the **A 109CM**, which is based on the A 109EOA but has a wider range of options including different sights. The Belgian army is the only customer so far, with 46 such **A 109BA** machines comprising 18 configured as scouts and the remaining 28 configured for the anti-armour role, with the local designations **A 109HO** and **A 109HA**, respectively. The scouts feature a Saab Helios roof-mounted observation sight, while the anti-tank helicopters have a Saab/ESCO HeliTOW 2 sight and provision for eight Hughes TOW-2A anti-armour missiles. The A 109BA helicopters were assembled in Belgium by SABCA, and feature cable-cutters for enhanced low-level flight safety in a northern European operational environment littered with potentially lethal power and telephone cables.

Looking to African and Middle Eastern markets, more recent development has been concentrated on the multi-role **A 109K** for 'hot-and-high' applications, with new powerplant driving an uprated transmission, a lengthened nose to accommodate a more comprehensive array of avionics, and a number of detail improvements.

The first flight of an A 109K took place in April 1983, and current orders stand at 16 **A 109K2** rescue machines for the Swiss mountain rescue service and three similar helicopters for the Dubai police. Dedicated military versions are the **A 109KM** land-based version, with fixed landing gear and sliding cabin doors, and the similar **A 109KN** naval version, which adds ship-borne capability and maritime weapons.

Military A 109s can be armed with 0.3- or 0.5-in (7.62- or 12.7-mm) trainable machine-guns pintle-mounted in the cabin doorways, and also have four hardpoints extended from the sides of the lower fuselage on pylons for the carriage of many different stores, including 0.3- or 0.5-in (7.62- or 12.7-mm) machine-gun pods, 2.75- or 3.15-in (70- or 80-mm) rocket launchers, up to eight TOW anti-tank missiles and Stinger short-range air-to-air missiles. The A 109 can also carry light UAVs (unmanned air vehicles) and, in the maritime role, can launch anti-ship missiles.

The latest developments in the A 109 series have been the **A 109G** coastal patrol and law enforcement variant powered by Allison 250-C20Rs, and the **A 109 Power** with substantially uprated power in the form of two Pratt & Whitney PW206C turboshafts, each rated at 640 shp (477 kW).

Agusta has delivered over 500 A 109 helicopters of all versions to date.

First delivered in September 1981, the uprated A 109A Mk II featured improved avionics and structural details. From 1983, the major fuselage components were built in Greece.

Deliveries of the A 109 to Italy's military police force began in 1979. A total of 17 A 109As and 12 A 109A Mk IIs was originally received, but a joint total of just 25 remained in service in the late 1990s.

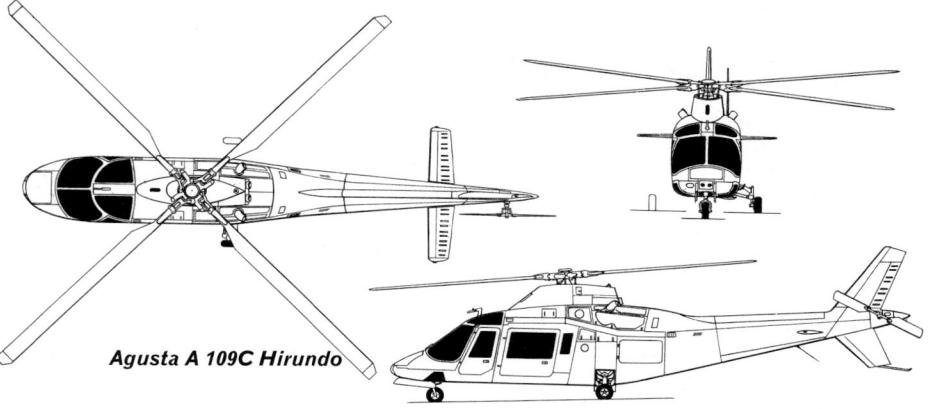

Agusta A 109C Hirundo

Agusta A 119 Koala

First flown early in 1995, the Agusta A 119 Koala is a light utility helicopter derived structurally and conceptually from the A 109 helicopter, although it differs most obviously in the use of fixed twin-skid landing gear in place of the earlier type's retractable tricycle landing gear. The fuselage is of aluminium alloy construction, and the dynamic system is of the classic light helicopter type, with the single turboshaft engine located above the rear part of the pod-and-boom fuselage's pod section, and immediately to the rear of the gearbox that translates the power to the rotor system. The latter comprises a four-bladed main rotor (with fully articulated composite blades attached to a titanium alloy hub), and a two-bladed tail rotor on its port side.

Agusta hopes that many operators will see the diminutive A 119 as the ideal replacement for older helicopters in the same class as Agusta's earlier AB 206 JetRanger, for example.

The prototype was built with the powerplant of one Turboméca Arriel I turboshaft, rated at 800 shp (596.5 kW), but the engine selected for the production version, after consideration of Allison and Pratt & Whitney Canada units, was the latter's PT6B-37/1. It is claimed that the Koala offers 30 per cent more cabin volume than any comparable single-engined light helicopter, and the incorporation of a single large sliding door on each side of the cabin provides easy access for six passengers (or two litters when used in the medevac role). A seventh passenger can be carried alongside the pilot if required.

Agusta A 129 Mangusta

Conceived in response to an Italian army requirement of the mid-1970s, the **Agusta A 129 Mangusta** (mongoose) was the first dedicated attack helicopter to be designed, built and deployed by a European country. It was also the first in the world to be built around an advanced MIL-STD 1553B digital databus, which allows a high degree of automation, considerably reducing the crew workload.

The first A 129 prototype made its official maiden flight on 15 September 1983, at Cascina Costa (though it had already taken to the air twice before on 11 and 13 September). Like all those that followed, this aircraft was powered by two Piaggio-built Rolls-Royce Gem 2-2 Mk 1004D

The 'Vega' regiment, based at Pordenone-Casarsa della Delizia in northern Italy, is the Italian army's premier A 129 unit. The black chequered design on the tailfin of these aircraft is a regimental marking.

turboshaft engines. Agusta built four development aircraft, which were later joined by a fifth example after one of the initial A 129s was written off. All of these aircraft had flown by 1985.

During 1986 and 1987, a smooth flight test and weapons test programme led to a December 1987 contract for the first batch of 15 aircraft for Italian Army Aviation – today known as Aviazione Esercito (AVES). The original Italian requirement had been for 100 Mangustas, in distinct anti-tank and scout versions. As the threat of all-out war in Europe receded, the final order was cut back to 60 A 129s.

The first five aircraft were delivered to the Army Aviation training centre at Viterbo, in October 1990, for operational trials and training. A total of 45 A 129s had been delivered to AVES when production was stopped in 1992. Funding problems, and changing operational needs, forced the Italian army to re-evaluate its

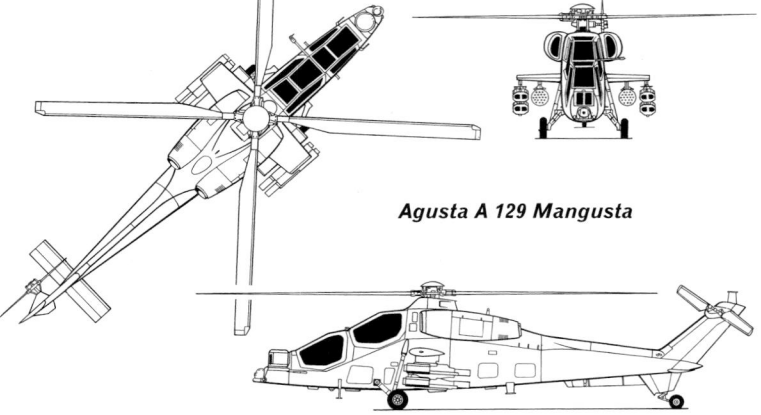

Agusta A 129 Mangusta

requirement for dedicated anti-tank helicopters. The need for a more multi-role helicopter was reinforced when Mangustas were deployed on UN peace-keeping duties to Somalia between 1992 and 1994.

The chief front-line AVES Mangusta unit is now 7° Regimento Elicotteri d'Attacco (7th attack helicopter regiment) 'Vega'. The standard armament of Italy's Mangustas, designed for a primary anti-tank role, comprises up to 2,646 lb (1200 kg) of external stores on four stub-wing pylons, including up to eight TOW-2A anti-tank missiles, 52 2.75-in (70-mm) rockets or larger 3.19-in (81-mm) SNIA-BPD Medusa rockets. Underwing 12.7-mm gun pods have also been qualified for carriage by Mangustas.

The pilot (rear cockpit) and co-pilot gunner each have a Honeywell IHADSS (Integrated Helmet And Display Sighting System) helmet-mounted sight. Above the nose, the Mangusta is fitted with a Saab HeliTOW sight for use with the TOW missiles. HeliTOW comprises a high-resolution optical sight, a FLIR, and laser rangefinder/designator. A smaller FLIR, known as

HIRNS (Helicopter Infra-Red Navigation System) is fitted below and in front of the HeliTOW system, for use by the pilot actually flying the aircraft.

Most systems on board the Mangusta – such as navigation, communication and weapons control – are routed through the fully-digital IMS (Integrated Multiplex System). Each crew member has an IMS screen and keyboard to control information, which negates the need for many control panels that would otherwise fill up the cockpit.

Italy will acquire its remaining 15 A 129s in an updated and rebuilt form, taking in many of the improvements developed by the A 129 International.

Agusta A 129 International

The **A 129 International** is a growth version of the proven Mangusta, but with true multi-role and multi-mission capability. It introduces two FADEC-equipped 1,362-shp (1016-kW) Allison/AlliedSignal (formerly Garrett) LHTEC CTS800-2 turboshafts, a five-bladed rotor and a nose-mounted gun. The International has a primary mission weight of 10,582 lb (4800 kg) and a maximum mission weight of 11,243 lb (5100 kg). Some 2,204 lb (1000 kg) of extra fuel has been squeezed into the airframe.

On 9 January 1995, Agusta flew the prototype of what was the (near) definitive A 129 International, fitted with the new five-bladed rotor and purpose-built gun system. The rotor head used Agusta's tried, tested (and patented), fully articulated design, with five Elastomeric bearings and all-composite blades. A TM167B 20-mm cannon was mounted in the nose. The first International development airframe, 902, flew with large cheek fair-ings to house new avionics and cannon ammunition. Late in 1996, 902's place was taken by a second aircraft, I-INTR/800. It was fitted with T800 engines from the beginning, and the new rotor system was added in early 1997. To reflect its status as the first 'true' International, its iden-tity was changed to 29800, although it is owned by Agusta and is on the Italian civil register.

In the International, the Italian army saw an opportu-nity to add new capabilities to its existing aircraft. The AVES has decided to acquire a version of the A 129 International that retains the existing Rolls-Royce engines, but incorporates the new rotors and armament. Neither will the International's all-new glass cockpit be fitted to the Italian army aircraft, at least under current plans. A total of 15 new-standard aircraft will be acquired to complete the ALE's original order for 60 A 129s. The so-called 'Batch Three' deliveries are commonly referred to as *multiruolo* (multi-role) aircraft, but are more

formally titled A 129 da Combattimento (combat).

Inside the International cockpit each crew station will be fitted with colour flat-panel displays, includ-ing a moving digital map system with overlaid displays. A new FLIR/targeting system will also be fitted to the International, which will be compatible with the AGM-114 Hellfire and will allow customers to oper-ate with a mix of four Hellfires and four TOWs on the same aircraft. Another new weapon to be added to the A 129 International is the Stinger air-to-air missile.

There are several ongo-ing attack helicopter competitions/requirements in which Agusta sees a future for the A 129 International. The company is concentrating its export activities on Turkey, Australia, Slovenia, Malaysia, Singapore, Spain

The Italian army will acquire a multiruolo (multirole) version of the A 129 International that retains the original Gem engines, but adds the new five-bladed rotor and 20-mm cannon.

and Sweden. Most of these countries have requirements in the short-term for small orders with an overriding need for multi-mission capability in a low-intensity conflict.

Agusta AZ-8L

Under the designation **AZ-8L**, Agusta's chief designer Dr Filippo Zappata schemed a four-engined short- to medium-range transport aircraft, the first such Italian aircraft to be designed after World War II. The AZ-8L seemed suffi-ciently promising for the Italian air ministry to award the company a contract for the construction of a proto-type, which first took to the air from Milan's Malpensa airport on 9 June 1958.

The resulting aircraft had a very clean external finish and was powered by four Alvis Leonides Mk 22 radial engines. Mounted in closely-cowled nacelles, these drove three-bladed de Havilland constant-speed feathering propellers each of 9-ft (2.74-m) diame-ter. The wing incorporated Frise-type ailerons, wide-span slotted trailing-edge flaps, and de-icing boots on the outer wing panels. Similar boots were applied to the leading edges of the fin and tailplane. The retractable tricycle landing gear had twin wheels on each main unit, and the air-conditioned cabin could accommodate 22-26 passengers in a tourist class configuration, or up to 6,170 lb (2800 kg) of freight as an alternative payload. Agusta also proposed a higher-capacity version of the AZ-8L. This was to have seated 30 passengers in a slightly longer, moder-ately pressurised cabin.

Although evaluated for

civil use, as well as by the Italian air force, no produc-tion examples were built. The AZ-8L prototype served as a 'hack' transport with the Italian air force's RSV experimental centre until the late 1960s.

The AZ-8L was Italy's first four-engined post-war transport. The promising design was not put into production and the sole prototype was used as a 'hack' by the Italian air force.

SPECIFICATION	
Agusta AZ-8L	
Type: short/medium-range transport	range with maximum payload 404 miles (650 km); range with 5,800-lb (2631-kg) payload 691 miles (1112 km)
Powerplant: four 540-hp (403-kW) Alvis Leonides Mk 22 radial piston engines	**Weights:** empty equipped 16,799 lb (7620 kg); maximum take-off 24,912 lb (11300 kg)
Performance: maximum speed at sea level 260 mph (418 km/h); cruising speed at 9,840 ft (3000 m) 230 mph (370 km/h); initial climb rate 1,854 ft (339 m) per minute; service ceiling 24,600 ft (7500 m);	**Dimensions:** wingspan 83 ft 8 in (25 m); length 63 ft 9¼ in (19.44 m); height 21 ft 7¾ in (6.60 m), wing area 719.05 sq ft (66.80 m²)

Agusta CP-110

In 1951, Agusta designed a four-seat cabin monoplane which the company hoped would prove to be attrac-tive for both civil and military use, and a prototype **CP-110** was constructed in the experimental work-shops of the Milan Technical School.

Basically of all-wood construction with plywood skins, the CP-110 was of conventional low-wing monoplane configuration, but incorporated retractable tricycle landing gear. A pilot and three passengers were accommodated in an enclosed cabin with individ-ual front seats, dual controls as standard, and a rear bench seat for two passen-gers. Powerplant consisted of an Alfa 110ter inverted inline air-cooled engine.

After an initial series of flight trials, the CP-110 was evaluated further by the Italian air force at its test centre at Guidonia.

The Agusta CP-110 was yet another European lightplane that could not break the dominance of American rivals.

SPECIFICATION	
Agusta CP-110	
Type: four-seat cabin monoplane	cruising speed 149 mph (240 km/h); range 621 miles (1000 km)
Powerplant: one 145-hp (108-kW) Alfa 110ter inverted inline air-cooled piston engine	**Weights:** empty 1,499 lb (680 kg); maximum take-off 2,425 lb (1100 kg)
Performance: maximum level speed 171 mph (275 km/h);	**Dimensions:** wingspan 34 ft 9¼ in (10.60 m); length 23 ft 11½ in (7.30 m)

Agusta CP-111

Designed by Ing. Ermenegildo Preti, and first flown in 1951, the **Agusta CP-111** was essentially a three-seat version of the CP-110 four-seat cabin touring aeroplane. The CP-111 was of plywood-covered wooden construction and differed from its predecessor mainly in its landing gear, which was of the fixed rather than retractable tailwheel type, and in its uprated Avco Lycoming O-435-1 powerplant.

Despite the introduction of the higher-rated engine, the performance of the CP-111 was inferior to that of the CP-110 at the same maximum take-off weight, largely as a result of the higher drag of the engine installation and fixed landing gear.

SPECIFICATION

Agusta CP-111
Type: three-seat basic trainer and communications aircraft
Powerplant: one Avco Lycoming O-435-1 flat-four piston engine rated at 185 hp (138 kW)
Performance: maximum speed 137 mph (220 km/h) at optimum altitude; cruising speed 118 mph (190 km/h) at optimum altitude; range 404 miles (650 km)
Weights: maximum take-off 2,425 lb (1100 kg)
Dimensions: wingspan 34 ft 9 in (10.60 m); length 24 ft 3⅜ in (7.40 m); height 9 ft ¼ in (2.75 m)

The CP-111 was a three-seat, more powerful derivative of the CP-110. Failing to attract military or civil orders, it remained only a prototype.

Agusta-Bell AB 102

Under the designation **Agusta-Bell AB 102**, Agusta designed a seven/nine-seat passenger transport helicopter which was intended for both civil and military applications. The type was essentially a redesign of Bell's unsuccessful Model 48, and used the dynamic components from Bell's HU-1A utility helicopter.

In other respects, the AB 102 was of conventional pod-and-boom configuration, the tail pylon mounting a two-bladed anti-torque rotor. Tubular skid landing gear was provided, and powerplant consisted of a Canadian-built Pratt & Whitney R-1340 radial engine mounted in the aft cabin.

The forward cabin was furnished to accommodate a pilot and seven/nine passengers, but alternative configurations included an ambulance layout with four stretchers and seating for a medical attendant, and a combined passenger/cargo interior. Up to 1,940 lb (880 kg) of freight could be carried internally in an all-cargo role. An electric hoist was also an option for use in SAR operations.

A prototype AB 102 was first flown in February 1959, and the type became the first Italian helicopter to be awarded US certification to Civil Air Regulations Part 6 requirements.

Despite its operational flexibility, the AB 102 failed to satisfy either civil or military requirements for such a machine and it was only produced in very limited numbers. This included two helicopters used for passenger services between Milan and Turin.

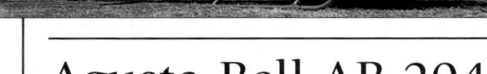

Designed to meet both civil and military needs, the AB 102 was in essence a redesign of Bell's unsuccessful Model 48, but proved only marginally more successful.

SPECIFICATION

Agusta-Bell AB 102
Type: general-purpose helicopter
Powerplant: one 600-hp (447-kW) Pratt & Whitney R-1340-S1H4 radial piston engine
Performance (at normal take-off weight): maximum level speed at sea level 110 mph (177 km/h); cruising speed at 6,000 ft (1830 m) 99 mph (160 km/h); service ceiling 12,795 ft (3900 m); hovering ceiling in ground effect 9,200 ft (2810 m); range with seven passengers and 250 lb (113 kg) of baggage 220 miles (350 km)
Weights: empty 3,990 lb (1810 kg); normal take-off 6,008 lb (2725 kg); maximum take-off 6,669 lb (3025 kg)
Dimensions: main rotor diameter 47 ft 6¾ in (14.50 m); length overall 58 ft 9½ in (17.92 m); fuselage length 41 ft 9 in (12.73 m); height 10 ft 7¼ in (3.23 m); main rotor disc area 1,777.50 sq ft (165.13 m²)

Agusta-Bell AB 204

Having forged links with the Bell company through licensed Italian production of the Bell Model 47 from 1954, Agusta then went on to produce several hundred examples of the **Bell Model 204B**, equivalent to the US Army's **UH-1B**. As the **Agusta-Bell AB 204**, this Italian-built utility helicopter was supplied for military and civil use with seating for up to 11 including the pilot, and provision for the carriage of freight (either internally or as a slung load) or litters.

Several different turboshaft powerplant options were offered: these were the Lycoming T53-L-11A rated at 1,100 shp (820 kW); the Rolls-Royce (originally Bristol Siddeley) Gnome H.1000 or H.1200 rated at 1,000 or 1,200 shp (746 or 895 kW) respectively; and the General Electric T58-GE-3 rated at 1,290 shp (962 kW). Greater operational versatility was provided by the availability of pontoons to replace the skids for water/swamp operations. The first **AB 204B** flew in May 1961, and the four main sub-variants of the baseline utility helicopter with the Gnome engine were the **AB 204B-11** with the H.1000 engine and a main rotor diameter of 44 ft (13.41 m); the **AB 204B-12** with the H.1000 engine and a main rotor diameter of 48 ft (14.63 m); the **AB 204B-21** with the H.1200 engine and a main rotor diameter of 44 ft (13.41 m); and the **AB 204B-22** with the H.1200 engine and a main rotor diameter of 48 ft (14.63 m).

Of some 26 AB 204Bs received by the Austrian air force since 1963, around 14 remain in service, although around six of these are held in storage.

Agusta also developed the **AB 204AS** for naval anti-submarine use, and this model had a main rotor increased in diameter by 4 ft (1.22 m) to permit a 990-lb (49-kg) increase in maximum take-off weight and a general improvement in performance. There was also provision for Ekco or APQ-195 radar, dunking sonar, long-range fuel, all-weather instrumentation, an autostabilisation system, and armament, the last in the form of two Mk 44/Mk 46 torpedoes or air-to-surface missiles.

Production of the AB 204 series lasted until 1974 and totalled 238 helicopters. About a dozen nations purchased the AB 204 for military use, but it now only remains in service in limited numbers.

The AB 204 serves with the Swedish army (as seen here) and air force, where it is known under the local designation Hkp 3.

Operators comprise No. 2 Squadron of Helicopter Wing III of the Austrian air force, the Turkish Gendarmerie, and the Yemen Arab Republic air force. By far the largest operators of the type are the Swedish air arms. The army operates AB 204s (under the local designation **Hkp 3C**) with two medium-lift helicopter squadrons. These are due to be retired in 2001. Similar **Hkp 3B**s are operated in the search and rescue role by Swedish air force units F16 at Uppsala and F10 Ängelhom. These AB 204s are due to be retired in 1999.

The AB 204AS has been retired by the Italian and Spanish navies, but a few remain in service with Turkish naval aviation.

SPECIFICATION

Agusta-Bell AB 204AS
Type: anti-submarine and anti-surface vessel helicopter
Powerplant: one General Electric T58-GE-3 turboshaft engine rated at 1,290 shp (962 kW)
Performance: maximum cruising speed 104 mph (167 km/h) at sea level; radius 69 miles (111 km) for a sonar patrol of 1 hour 40 minutes
Weights: empty 6,480 lb (2939 kg); maximum take-off 9,500 lb (4309 kg)
Dimensions: main rotor diameter 48 ft (14.63 m); length overall 57 ft (17.37 m) with rotors turning and fuselage 41 ft 7 in (12.67 m); height 12 ft 7½ in (3.84 m); main rotor disc area 1,809.56 sq ft (168.11 m²)
Armament: see main text

Agusta-Bell AB 205

The **Agusta-Bell AB 205** is a variant of the Bell Model 205 built under licence granted by Bell in 1966 to Costruzioni Aeronautiche Giovanni Agusta SpA in Italy. Like its US counterpart, the AB 205 differed from the AB 204 in having a longer cabin with increased cabin space to accommodate up to 14 troops plus a pilot, and was powered by an uprated T53 engine. This in turn necessitated uprating of the dynamic components, and the AB 205 was fitted as standard with a 48-ft 3½-in (14.63-m) diameter main rotor, replacing the AB 204's 44-ft (13.41-m) diameter unit.

In its basic military form,

the AB 205 corresponds to Bell UH-1D/UH-1H Iroquois series in service with the US forces and elsewhere. Like the UH-1D/H, the AB 205 has proved a very useful multi-purpose utility helicopter and has been widely exported.

It is equipped for night flying and can be employed for troop, passenger or equipment transport, casualty evacuation, rescue and other tasks, as well as tactical ground support. According to role, the basic airframe can be easily adapted to take floats, snow skids, rescue hoist and stretchers, or be fitted with armament. Stripped of all internal fittings, the cabin

Above: Twenty AB 205s serve with the Iranian army; this example is armed with the French-supplied Aérospatiale SS11 anti-tank missile.

has a clear volume of 220 cu ft (6.2 m³) for cargo-carrying.

Normally unarmed, the AB 205 could have a pintle-mounted machine-gun in the cabin, firing through the door, or air-to-surface missiles mounted externally each side of the cabin.

From 1969, production in Italy focused on the **AB 205A-1** version with a number of minor improvements as well as higher operating weights. Apart from being slightly longer, the Italian-built variant is powered by the same type of engine as the AB 205 military series (T53-L-13B) while the Bell 205A-1 has a different sub-type (T53-L-13A) of similar power rating. The AB 205A-1 is designed for rapid conversion to other tasks as an air freighter flying crane (capacity 5,000 lb (2268 kg)), ambulance (six stretchers and one/two medical attendants), rescue helicopter or VIP transport.

Agusta also built the prototypes of two twin-turboshaft variants, namely the **AB 205BG** with a pair of Rolls-Royce (originally Bristol Siddeley) Gnome

In civilian service, the AB 205 is operated in the light transport and passenger-carrying roles. Many civil Spanish examples have previously served with the military.

Agusta-Bell AB 205 operators

Substantial use of the AB 205 continues, although production ended in 1988. The largest single operator is Turkey, whose army and Gendarmerie have around 125 and 5 such helicopters, respectively. Although most Turkish AB 205s serve primarily as transports, for SAR and for training, several have been configured as gunships and have taken part in operations against PKK guerillas in western Turkey. The Italian army flies 80 AB 205A helicopters with the local designation **EM-2** and has provided detachments in support of UN peacekeeping operations in Lebanon, Namibia and Kurdistan, and for the EC Monitor Mission in the former Yugoslavia. Both the Greek army and Greek air force are substantial operators, the latter's No. 358 Mira providing flights for SAR and VIP flights at various bases. Other operators of the AB 205A for transport/utility tasks are the Iranian army and navy, the Moroccan air force, the Sultan of Oman's air force (No. 14 Squadron), the Royal Saudi air force (Nos 12 and 14 Squadrons), the Republic of Singapore air force (Nos 120 and 123 Squadrons), the Tanzanian People's Defence Force, the Republic of Tunisia air force (No. 31 Squadron), the Turkish army, the Ugandan army air force, the Zambian air force and Air Defence Command. In Spain, the air force's Esc 783/Ala 78 has a few remaining in secondary service for IFR training under the local designation **HE.10B**.

SPECIFICATION

Agusta-Bell AB 205
Type: 15-seat multi-purpose military/civil helicopter
Powerplant: one 1,400-shp (1044-kW) Avco Lycoming T53-L-13B turboshaft, derated to 1,250-shp (933 kW) for take-off and 1,100 shp (820 kW) for continuous running
Performance: (at normal take-off weight) maximum speed at sea level 138 mph (222 km/h); cruising speed 132 mph (212 km/h); initial climb rate 1,800 ft (548 m) per minute; service ceiling 15,000 ft (4570 m); hovering ceiling in ground effect 17,000 ft (5180 m) and 11,000 ft (3350 m) out of ground effect; maximum range with standard tanks and no

reserves 360 miles (580 km); maximum endurance with standard tanks and no reserves 3 hours 48 minutes
Weights: empty 4,800 lb (2177 kg) normal take-off 8,500 lb (3680 kg); maximum take-off 9,500 lb (4309 kg)
Dimensions: main rotor diameter 48 ft 3½ in (14.72 m); tail rotor diameter 8 ft 6 in (2.59 m); length overall 57 ft 2½ in (17.98 m) with rotors turning, fuselage length 41 ft 10¾ in (12.77 m), height 14 ft 8 in (4.48 m), main rotor disc area 1,831.6 sq ft (170.16 m²)
Armament: generally none, although pintle-mounted machine-guns can be mounted in the cabin doors

H.1200 engines and the **AB 205TA** with two Turbomeca Astazou engines, but neither of these achieved production.

Production of the AB 205 series ended in 1988 after the delivery of 490 helicopters, most of them to air arms.

Agusta-Bell AB 206 JetRanger

The long-established partnership between Bell and Agusta was continued by the granting of licence-production rights of the Bell Model 206 JetRanger light utility helicopter to Agusta SpA in 1966, and the first licence-built **Agusta-Bell AB 206A JetRanger** commercial helicopters were rolled off the production line late in 1967. Apart from very minor local modifications, these machines were similar to their American counterparts and were powered by 317-shp (236-kW) Allison 250-C18 turboshaft engines.

Production of the improved Bell Model 206B JetRanger II began in 1971 and was followed by the corresponding **Agusta-Bell AB 206B JetRanger II** in 1972. This new version combined the same airframe with an uprated Allison 250-C20 engine to give improved performance, particularly in 'hot and high' conditions for only a small weight penalty.

Agusta assigned the designations **AB 206A-1** and **AB 206B-1** to optimised military variants of this version that incorporated features of the US Army's OH-58A Kiowa,

including the high-skid landing gear option, main rotor diameter increased to 35 ft 4 in (10.77 m), local airframe strengthening, additional access doors, and provision for armament similar to the

options developed for the American version. This usually comprises a centrally-mounted flexible machine-gun.

The improved **AB 206B JetRanger III** followed in 1978, with the 400-shp (298-kW) Allison 250-C20B engine derated to 317 shp

(236 kW) and a number of detail improvements, including an enlarged and improved tail rotor mast. The JetRanger III has a higher hover ceiling and a generally improved performance at altitude. Production deliveries began early in 1978.

The Italian army purchased 150 AB 206s, in a basic civil configuration. This has allowed the AB 206 to be passed on to air units of the Italian police which uses the helicopter for observation duties.

Sweden operates 19 JetRangers for liaison, observation and spotting duties. Ten serve with the Swedish navy for anti-submarine duties, being suitably armed with a single torpedo or three depth charges.

Only small numbers of Italian-built JetRanger helicopters were sold to civil operators, and the majority of the sales were made to military users. The Italian army purchased 150 **AB 206** machines, starting with 16 in a basically civil configuration for training with the army designation **ERI-2**. The original Allison 250-C18 engines were subsequently replaced by the more powerful Allison 250-C20 model, helicopters with these engines continuing in service as AB 206A-2 machines. Operated with the service designation **ERI-3**, the remainder of the helicopters for the Italian army were of the AB 206A-1 variant, but these have also now been fitted with the Allison 250-C20 engine and features of the JetRanger III/OH-58C, with the revised designation **AB 206C-1**. They serve the Italian army's Aviazione Leggera in the Elicottero di Ricognizione (reconnaissance helicopter) role, distributed among 16 of the ERI squadrons at bases throughout Italy.

Austria's Luftstreitkräfte bought 12 AB 206A-1 helicopters for the training and SAR roles, in 2 Staffel of Hubschraubergeschwader 1 at Tulln, and the Royal Saudi air force has 20 for training use by Nos 12 and 14 Squadrons at Taif with another six reserved for the SAR task. Morocco retains in service some 20 of the

25 JetRangers acquired, which included 20 of the AB 206B version to supplement five AB 205A machines bought in 1975. Sweden operates the AB 206A under the local designation **Hkp 6A**. Fitted with extended skid landing gear and underfuselage weapon racks, 19 of the type are on army charge for liaison, observation and spotting duties, while 10 are used by the Swedish navy as part of the anti-submarine force with one torpedo or three depth charges as offensive capability.

The Iranian air force continues to be a major operator of the JetRanger, with more than 80 AB 206A/B helicopters used for liaison duties, while further examples are used in a similar role by the navy (10) and air force (two).

Smaller numbers of Italian-built JetRangers serve in Greece (two with the air force's No. 358

Mira Elikopteron for SAR and VIP flights, and over 15 with the army), Libya (five used by the army), Malta (one AB 206A for coastal duties and SAR), Oman (three AB 206B machines used by No. 14 Squadron at Seeb), the Amiri Guard air wing of Sharjah (three AB 206B helicopters), the Spanish army (four AB 206A-1 machines transferred from the air force as **HR.12A** helicopters at the Centro de Ensenanza de las FAMET for training), Tanzania (two AB 206B machines), Uganda (four operated by the police of which the three survivors were later transferred to

the army air force) and the Yemen Arab Republic (six).

Under the same general designation, AB 206, Agusta has also undertaken licence-production of the Bell Model 206L LongRanger. Evolved from the JetRanger II and powered by an uprated Allison 250-C20B engine, this has a longer fuselage, seating up to seven passengers. The generally similar Agusta licence-built variant is known as AB 206L LongRanger.

Of the total of more than 7,000 JetRangers of all versions built to date, about 1,000 are of Italian manufacture, contributed by Agusta.

SPECIFICATION

Agusta-Bell AB 206B JetRanger III
Type: five-seat utility light helicopter
Powerplant: one 400-shp (298-kW) Allison 250-C20 turboshaft engine derated to 317 shp (236 kW)
Performance: maximum speed 140 mph (226 km/h) at optimum altitude; cruising speed 133 mph (214 km/h) at optimum altitude; initial climb rate 1,360 ft (415 m) per minute; service ceiling more than 20,000 ft (6095 m); hovering ceiling 11,325 ft (3450 m) in ground effect and 5,800 ft (1770 m) out of ground effect; maximum range with standard fuel and no reserves 418 miles (673 km); maximum endurance with standard fuel and no reserves 4 hours
Weights: empty 1,504 lb (682 kg); normal take-off 3,200 lb (1452 kg) with an internal payload; maximum take-off 3,350 lb (1519 kg) with an external payload
Dimensions: main rotor diameter 33 ft 4 in (10.16 m); length overall 39 ft 2 in (11.94 m) with rotors turning and fuselage 31 ft 2 in (9.50 m); height 9 ft 6 in (2.91 m); main rotor disc area 872.66 sq ft (81.07 m²)
Armament: none

Agusta-Bell AB 212

Production of the Bell Model 212 in Italy followed quickly upon the development in the USA of this twin-engined derivative of the Bell 205, undertaken in the first instance to meet USAF and Canadian Forces requirements. In essence, the Bell 212 (and essentially similar **Agusta-Bell AB 212**) comprised the airframe of the Model 205 combined with the Pratt & Whitney Canada PT6T-3 Turbo Twin-Pac powerplant. The latter comprised paired PT6 turboshaft engines offering far greater operational reliability as either of the engines could sustain the helicopter in level flight. In its accommodation and equipment options, the AB 212 closely resembled the AB 205A-1 but offers enhanced performance as well as greater reliability.

Deliveries of the Italian-built version started in late autumn 1971.

The standard AB 212 carries a pilot and up to 14 passengers, but the cabin is easily adaptable for other roles, including VIP transport. Optional equipment includes a rescue hoist, external cargo hook, auxiliary fuel tanks, and float and snow landing gear, according to customer's requirements. The cabin can also be converted into an ambulance and has space for six stretchers and two medical attendants.

Following the precedent set with the AB 204AS, Agusta alone developed an anti-surface vessel/submarine warfare version of the AB 212 as the **AB 212ASV/ASW**. Designed to operate from small shipboard platforms,

the type features local strengthening, the addition of deck mooring points and increased airframe protection against salt-water corrosion.

The most notable external change is the addition of a dorsal radome for the antenna of the search radar (options of several types including Ferranti Seaspray). The main changes are internal and concern the outfitting of the cabin as a tactical centre manned by two

operators, with all-weather flight instrumentation and, perhaps most importantly, the introduction of an automatic flight-control system.

This last system combines inputs from the automatic stabilisation system, radar altimeter, Doppler navigation system and other sensors to provide automatic transition from cruise to sonar hover (and vice versa) under all weather conditions by day and night. The automatic navigation system also locates the helicopter's position on the radar's tactical display screen, which additionally shows target data provided by the Bendix AQS-18B/F variable-depth dunking sonar.

With its search radar and

The AB 212 provides helicopter crews with twin-engine reliability for commercial operations. Passenger variants are equipped with a furnished rear cabin.

The Turkish navy has an operational fleet of 10 AB 212ASWs. The aircraft are currently flown by 351 Filo.

target data transmission system the AB 212ASW can also be used as a passive guidance post for ship-launched surface-to-surface stand-off missiles.

To provide a SAR capability, a hydraulically-operated external hoist is fitted. The normal crew comprises three or four including the two-man tactical crew and two pilots, with provision for up to seven passengers, or four litters plus an attendant.

For other tasks, the AB 212ASW can be fitted with either a 5,000-lb (2270-kg) capacity external cargo hook, a 595-lb (270-kg) rescue hoist, inflatable emergency pontoons, and internal and external auxiliary fuel tanks.

Agusta began work on the AB 212ASW in 1971, and the Italian navy successfully evaluated the prototype in 1973.

Agusta-Bell AB 212 (continued)

Production examples of the AB 212ASV/ASW entered service in 1976 and, to date, the company has built more than 100 examples for seven operators, of which the largest is the Italian navy, with 60 such machines delivered.

Of these, the first 12 had MEL ARI.5955 radar and the remainder APS-705 radar matched to the AS12 light air-to-surface missile for the ASV mission. As the navy's standard shipboard helicopter aboard its destroyers and frigates, the AB 212ASV/ASW carries a pair of Mk 44, Mk 46 or MQ44 homing torpedoes in the anti-submarine role, or AS12 ASMs in the anti-ship role, although the helicopters surviving in Italian service were later upgraded with the Marte Mk II system (including SMA MM/APS-706 radar) for air-launched Sea Killer Mk 2 anti-ship missiles.

Greece received 14 AB 212ASV/ASW helicopters including three for ECM use and the others for deployment on two 'Elli'-class frigates, while the Peruvian navy's air arm has five of the type for reconnaissance. Spain's 10 AB 212ASV/ASW machines are armed with AS12s and machine-guns, and are used by Tercera Escuadrilla (Eslla 003) from the assault transport *Galicia* for close-support duties. The Turkish navy bought an initial 12 and then an additional four helicopters of this type with Seaspray radar and Sea Skua ASMs, and these operated at first from the service's 'Yavuz'-class frigates. Venezuela has six AB 212ASV/ASW helicopters with OTO-Melara Sea Killer armament for its Esc Aero Antisubmarino 3, based at Puerto Cabello, to operate from the service's 'Sucre'-class frigates.

A 1983 contract covered the sale of 10 helicopters to Iraq, but this contract was placed under embargo and discussions for their release were finally ended by the Iraqi invasion of Kuwait. Approximately 20 were ordered for the Iranian navy early in 1974, with provision for AS12 wire-guided missiles, and these light ASMs were used for attacks on shipping in the Persian Gulf during 1985-86. The Iranians have received few spare parts, so the helicopters suffer from poor serviceability and are now probably non-operational.

Substantial numbers of AB 212 helicopters serve in military roles. In Austria, the air force has 23 AB 212s split between Hubschraubergeschwader I and III at Tulln and Hörsching, respectively, for the utility and transport roles. The Italian air force has 35 such machines divided between 208° Gruppo, 72° Stormo at Frosinone for training, and 85° Gruppo, 15° Stormo at Ciampino for SAR, and several of the 600-series squadrons that provide communications for the operational units at base level. Some 14 examples of the AB 212 are operational with the Italian army as **EM-3** machines for service with two squadrons (Nos 520 and 530) fulfilling the transport role at Pontecagnano and Fontanarossa, respectively, with two on detachment to the Malta Helicopter Flight. For training and support missions, some 25 of 30 AB 212s originally obtained by Saudi Arabia serve with Nos 12 and 14 Squadrons at Taif. Other operators include Dubai with two, Lebanon (up to seven), Morocco (five), Spain (six in army service), Sudan (10), the Yemen Arab Republic (six) and Zambia (two).

The AB 212ASV/ASW has proved to be a very capable naval helicopter with navies worldwide.

SPECIFICATION

Agusta-Bell AB 212ASV/ASW
Type: medium anti-ship and anti-submarine helicopter with secondary utility capability
Powerplant: one Pratt & Whitney Canada PT6T-6 Turbo Twin Pac coupled turboshaft engine rated at 1,875 shp (1398 kW), derated to 1,290 shp (962 kW)
Performance: maximum speed 122 mph (196 km/h) at sea level; cruising speed 115 mph (185 km/h) at optimum altitude with armament; initial climb rate 1,300 ft (396 m) per minute; hovering ceiling 10,500 ft (3200 m) in ground effect and 1,300 ft (396 m) out of ground effect; range 414 miles (667 km) with auxiliary fuel and 382 miles (615 km) on an ASV mission with AS12 missiles; average search endurance with Mk 46 torpedoes 3 hours 12 minutes; maximum endurance with auxiliary tanks 5 hours
Weights: empty 7,540 lb (3420 kg); maximum take-off 11,177 lb (5070 kg) for the ASW mission with two Mk 46 torpedoes, or 10,961 lb (4973 kg) for the ASV mission with AS12 missiles, or 10,883 lb (4937 kg) for the SAR mission
Dimensions: main rotor diameter 48 ft (14.63 m); length overall 57 ft 1 in (17.40 m) with rotors turning and fuselage 42 ft 4¾ in (12.92 m); height 14 ft 10¼ in (4.53 m); main rotor disc area 1,808.52 sq ft (168.10 m²)
Armament: up to 1,080 lb (490 kg) of stores (see main text)

Agusta-Bell AB 412 Grifone

Collaborating closely with Bell, Agusta launched production of the Model 412 in civil guise during 1981 as the **Agusta-Bell 412** and began deliveries to customers in January 1983.

The Model 412 is essentially a Model 212 (AB 212) with a four-bladed main rotor. Agusta proceeded to develop a dedicated military variant, largely to meet the requirements of the Italian military and quasi-military services. This was first flown in August 1982, with the designation **AB 412 Grifone** (griffon).

The type was designed to cope with a wide variety of roles that could include direct fire support and area suppression with one or two side-mounted cannon; scouting and reconnaissance with rocket pods and cable cutters; air defence with AAMs or other weapons; assault transport carrying up to 14 combat-equipped troops; and battlefield support including the casevac role with the facility for carrying six litters plus two attendants. Subsequently, a maritime model was evolved for SAR, surveillance, mission monitoring etc., for which it was provided with a 360° search radar with its antenna in a radome above the roof of the cockpit, FLIR and TV sensors, four-axis autopilot, and a special navigation system.

Special features of the Grifone include strengthened landing gear to absorb higher landing impacts; energy-absorbing armour-protected seats, armour for selected airframe areas; cabin floor fittings to provide for a wide variety of attachments for seats, stretchers, internal hoist or other special equipment; crash-attenuating seats; plus provision for IR emission-reduction devices on the engine exhausts.

In Italy, the AB 412 is now used by no fewer than six military and government agencies, including the national forest service and national fire service. A major user is the Carabinieri, with 32, while the SNPC (national civilian protection service) has at least four. Under Italian navy control, the coastguard has a growing fleet, with a total of 24 likely to enter service.

A total of 23 out of an original 25 AB 412s remain in service with the Esercito Italiano (Italian army), under the designation **EM-4**, indicating the fourth type of Elicottero Multiruolo, or multi-role helicopter. Principal EM-4 units are the 511 and 512 Squadrons at Viterbo as part of 51° Gruppo Squadroni EM 'Leone' and one of the squadrons of the 49° GSEM 'Capricornon' at Casara.

Agusta has also sold five Grifones to the Uganda army air force, which uses them as gunships in an armed anti-guerrilla role, and 12 to the Air Force of Zimbabwe, including two equipped for VIP/ambulance missions. Other operators include the Finnish coast guard (two), the Dubai air wing (three), Lesotho (two) and the Venezuelan army (two). The AB 412 is also operated in the UK by the Defence Helicopter Training School as the **Griffon HT.Mk 1**.

The AB 412 has a wide variety of armament options. Provision is made for one or two 25-mm Oerlikon Contraves KBA-B fixed forward-firing cannon on the lower sides of the fuselage, or alternatively for one 0.5-in (12.7-mm) FN-Browning M3 machine-gun with 400 rounds in a Lucas Helicopter Gun Turret under the nose, and/or one or two 0.5-in (12.7-mm) M3 machine-guns or 0.3-in (7.62-mm) trainable lateral-firing machine-guns mounted in the cabin door(s). The more common disposable weaponload is carried on two hardpoints (one on each side of the fuselage), and generally comprises four or eight BGM-71 TOW anti-tank missiles, or four Sea Skua or similar light anti-ship missiles, or four short-range AAMs, or four anti-radar missiles, or two 0.5-in (12.7-mm) or 0.3-in (7.62-mm) machine-gun pods, or two multiple launchers, each carrying seven, 12 or 19 3.2-in (81-mm) Medusa or SNORA unguided rockets.

Some 23 Agusta AB 412s are employed by the Italian army in a multi-role capacity.

SPECIFICATION

Agusta-Bell AB 412 Grifone
Type: 16-seat medium utility helicopter
Powerplant: one 1,800-shp (1342-kW) Pratt & Whitney Canada PT6T-3B Turbo Twin Pac coupled turboshaft flat-rated at 1,400 shp (1044 kW) for take-off and 1,130 shp (843 kW) for continuous running
Performance: maximum speed 161 mph (259 km/h) at sea level; cruising speed 144 mph (232 km/h) at 4,920 ft (1500 m); initial climb rate 1,437 ft (438 m) per minute; service ceiling 17,000 ft (5180 m); hovering ceiling 4,100 ft (1250 m) in ground effect and 2,200 ft (670 m) out of ground effect; range 500 miles (805 km) with standard fuel; endurance 4 hours 12 minutes
Weights: empty 6,263 lb (2841 kg); maximum take-off 11,905 lb (5400 kg)
Dimensions: main rotor diameter 46 ft (14.02 m); length overall 56 ft (17.07 m) with rotors turning and fuselage 42 ft 4⅔ in (12.92 m); height 14 ft 2 in (4.32 m); main rotor disc area 1,661.90 sq ft (154.40 m²)

Agusta-Sikorsky AS-61

Under licence from Sikorsky, Agusta put the SH-3D upgraded version of the SH-3A Sea King anti-submarine helicopter into production in Italy in 1967 as the **Agusta-Sikorsky ASH-3D**. This differed from the American original in features such as airframe strengthening, a revised tailplane, an uprated power-plant and modified armament and avionics. The ASH-3D was armed with up to four 515-lb (234-kg) Mk 46 torpedoes or two large anti-ship missiles, and was equipped with SMA MM/APS-705 surveillance radar or SMA MM/APS-706 radar for compatibility with the Marte Mk II system for Sea Killer Mk 2 anti-ship missiles. Delivery to the Aviazione per la Marina Militare Italiana (AMMI – Italian naval aviation) began in 1969.

Production of up to 38 helicopters for the Italian navy included several variants with different equipment standards, such as the **ASH-3D/TS (Trasporto Speziale**, or special transport). Two of this subvariant were delivered to the Italian air force for VIP transport, and the type was also exported in limited numbers (with the designation **AS-61A-4**) for logistics transport as well as VIP use. Operators of this version have included Egypt (two), Iraq (six), Iran (two), Saudi Arabia (one for air force use) and Venezuela (four for army use).

The final batch of helicopters was to **ASH-3H** standard, equivalent to the US Navy's SH-3H multi-role version with role optimisation for ASW/ASV roles. Mission equipment comprises ASQ-13F or ASQ-18 dunking sonar as well as SMA MM/APS-707 surveillance radar with its antenna in a chin radome.

When configured as a transport, the ASH-3H can lift a load of 6,000 lb (2722 kg) carried internally,

Licensed production of the S-61 series in Italy resulted in a number of variants of this versatile design. These included the ASH-3D/TS for the Italian air force.

or 8,000 lb (3629 kg) carried externally as a slung load. Other roles include anti-ship missile defence, electronic warfare and tactical trooping.

The ASH-3H variant serves with the 1° and 3° Grupelicot of the AMMI. Agusta-built Sea Kings also serve in the ASW role with the naval air arms of Argentina (2), Brazil (3) and Peru (6).

The final variant of the AS-61 to be developed was a version equivalent to the US Coast Guard's HH-3F Pelican search and rescue helicopter. The resulting **AS-61R Pelican** was built to meet an Italian air force requirement for a combat rescue helicopter. The service initially acquired 20 and ordered 15 more in 1992.

The AS-61R has search radar (using an antenna in a nose radome offset to port), a watertight fuselage, and provision for 15 litters and six seated survivors. The AS-61R machines have been upgraded with new RWRs, chaff/flare dispensers and a dark-green camouflage colour scheme. Two armed AS-61Rs were deployed to Somalia in 1993 to aid the United Nations effort.

SPECIFICATION

Agusta-Sikorsky AS-61R Pelican
Type: medium-range search-and-rescue helicopter
Powerplant: two General Electric T58-GE-100 turboshaft engines each rated at 1,500 shp (1118 kW)
Performance: maximum speed 162 mph (261 km/h) at sea level; cruising speed, maximum 150 mph (241 km/h) at sea level and economical 86 mph (139 km/h) at sea level; initial climb rate 1,340 ft (408 m) per minute; service ceiling 11,100 ft (3385 m); hovering ceiling 7,200 ft (2195 m) in ground effect; radius 57 miles (92 km) on a SAR mission with a loiter of 5 hours; endurance 8 hours
Weights: empty 13,250 lb (6010 kg); normal take-off 21,240 lb (9634 kg); maximum take-off 22,050 lb (10002 kg)
Dimensions: main rotor diameter 62 ft (18.90 m); length overall 73 ft (22.25 m) and fuselage 57 ft 3 in (17.45 m); height 18 ft 1 in (5.51 m); main rotor disc area 3,019.07 sq ft (280.47 m²)

Ahrens AR 404

In the mid 1970s, the Ahrens Aircraft Corporation was formed to develop a four-engined turboprop utility transport to replace the ubiquitous Douglas DC-3. Designated **AR 404**, this was a rugged design with emphasis on simplicity and ease of maintenance.

The constant-section rectangular fuselage was unpressurised and the main cabin ended in an upswept ramp which could be lowered in flight to airdrop cargo or paratroops.

Construction of the prototype began in August 1975 and, remarkably, this aircraft (N404AR) made its first flight at Oxnard, California, on 1 December 1976. At the controls was the renowned former Lockheed test pilot, Herman 'Fish' Salmon.

The Ahrens Aircraft Corporation had been given favourable incentives to establish a production facility for the AR 404 in Puerto Rico, and the company relocated its main manufacturing plant to the former SAC air base at Ramey to the north-west of the island.

Flight testing resulted in a number of modifications to prepare the type for production. The fixed main landing gear units were replaced with sponsons, each housing a single retractable double-bogie gear unit. Other modifications included a fuselage stretch of 4 ft (1.22 m), an increase in fin area and incorporation of a fin fillet.

Two-crew operation was envisaged for the flight deck, with a maximum capacity of 30 passengers in '2 + 1' configuration with a central aisle. Baggage was to be carried in a 160-cu ft (4.53-m³) rear-loaded container. In the freight role, the AR 404 could also accommodate four standard LD-3 containers.

The first such production-standard aircraft to be built entirely in Puerto Rico flew on 26 October 1979, and this joined the prototype in the flight test programme.

This revealed that the type had generally excellent manoeuvrability and stability and, although no high-lift devices were fitted

N404AR was the first of the two AR 404s to be completed. The design showed great promise.

to the wing, the AR 404's field performance was comparable to that of purpose-designed STOL transports.

Ahrens had envisaged that 50 per cent of sales would be made to paramilitary customers and the type was offered as a 26-troop transport, with alternative roles such as SAR, ASW and maritime patrol.

The local Puerto Rican government had planned to fund both the certification process and production of an initial batch of 18 aircraft. A second aircraft built to the intended production standard, was first flown from Ramey on 23 September 1981.

Ahrens planned to produce 12 to 16 aircraft for delivery in 1982, followed by some 24 to 30 in 1983. More than 100 letters of intent to purchase were received by the company, and provisional delivery positions had been

All the classic features of post-war tactical transports were incorporated into the AR 404, including an upswept rear fuselage.

advised. More than half of the scheduled production was for operators in North America, the remainder being for an anticipated worldwide market.

The AR 404 was one of four designs submitted to the US Air Force to meet its requirement for a new European Distribution System Aircraft transport. The contract was eventually awarded to the Shorts C-23A Sherpa. At the same time, Ahrens was looking ahead, and was planning the **AR 402**, a twin-engined derivative of the AR 404, powered by two Garrett TPE331-11 turboprops.

However, Ahrens' ambitious plans were thwarted and neither type was produced. Lack of orders of the AR 404 led the Ahrens Aircraft Corporation to declare bankruptcy in 1982.

Two years later, the president, Peter Ahrens, subsequently relocated the aircraft development part of his business to his native Sweden. Based at Malmo Sturup regional airport, the Scandinavian Aircraft Construction Co. offered a new design which was clearly based on the AR 404. Designated **KM-180**, this was a 40-seat transport which was offered with the option of a pressurised fuselage. Further development of the type was halted in 1986.

SPECIFICATION

Ahrens AR 404
Type: 30-seat passenger/utility transport
Powerplant: four 420-shp (313-kW) Allison 250-B17B turboprops
Performance: maximum speed 219 mph (352 km/h) at 6,000 ft (1525 m); cruising speed 195 mph (314 km/h) at 5,000 ft (1525 m); service ceiling 18,040 ft (5500 m); range 1,388 miles (2234 km)
Weights: empty 9,500 lb (4309 kg); normal payload 5,125 lb (2342 kg); maximum payload 8,800 lb (3992 kg); maximum take-off 17,500 lb (7938 kg)
Dimensions: span 66 ft (20.12 m) length 52 ft 9 in (16.08 m); height 18 ft 6 in (5.64 m); wing area 422 sq ft (39.20 m²)

Aichi AB-4

In 1931, the Imperial Japanese Navy air arm instructed Aichi, by now becoming well established as the designer and manufacturer of seaplanes, to begin design of a reconnaissance flying boat, that could be catapult-launched from the navy's larger surface warships.

Had it been appreciated in the countries that were to fight against Japan, from a time 10 years in the future, the requirement was a sure indication of the nature of Japan's ambitions for far-ranging naval superiority in the Pacific Ocean. It demanded a flying boat capable of undertaking tasks as diverse as communications with long-range submarines, night-reconnaissance and nocturnal gunnery observation.

Designed by Morishige Mori, under the supervision of Tetsuo Miki and bearing more than a superficial similarity to the Heinkel HD 55, the three-seat **Aichi AB-4** flying boat was an equal-span single-bay biplane, of all-metal construction. The outer wing panels were designed to fold to the rear, to reduce the flying boat's shipboard hangarage requirements. The type was powered by a Gasuden Urakaze inverted inline piston engine cooled by an underset radiator and driving a two-bladed wooden pusher propeller.

The first AB-4 prototype was completed in May 1932, and during its trials received a number of modifications to its vertical tail surface. The results of the trials were generally favourable, although criticism was raised about the flying boat's take-off and landing performance, together with the poor crew accommodation in general and the pilot's inadequate fields of vision in particular.

The Imperial Japanese Navy nonetheless accepted the type as the **Experimental 6-Shi Night-Reconnaissance Flying Boat** and, in the period from 1932-34, another five prototypes were delivered for operational evaluation. By 1935, the AB-4 was deemed obsolescent for naval service, therefore no production was undertaken and eventually three machines were transferred to civil use, in the hands of the Nippon Koku Yuso Kenkyusho (Japan Air Transport Research Association).

In its civil form, the flying boat became the **AB-4 Transport Flying Boat**, and each was modified under the supervision of the NKYK's Seiji Nakamae. Wingspan was increased to 45 ft 11 in (14.00 m) while the hull was slightly shortened. The first civil AB-4 became a freighter, with payload in the forward part of the hull, after the removal of the bow gun position and all military equipment; the second machine became a five-seat transport, with the pilot relocated to the bow position and a cabin with small windows installed in the central part of the hull. The third AB-4 was similar to the second, but had seating capacity increased to six and larger cabin windows. All three of the flying boats saw considerable service in and around the waters of the Japanese home islands until 1937.

The first two AB-4 conversions retained the Urakaze inverted inline piston engine of the naval original, but the third machine had a 450-hp (335.5-kW) Napier Lion W-type piston engine. All three civil AB-4 flying boats were generally similar in overall dimensions and performance to the military variant.

Having proved a disappointment in military service, the AB-4 was modified to serve in a new role as a civil transport.

SPECIFICATION

Aichi AB-4 (Experimental 6-Shi Night-Reconnaissance Flying Boat)
Type: three-seat night-reconnaissance flying boat
Powerplant: one Gasuden Urakaze inverted inline piston engine rated at 330 hp (246 kW)
Performance: maximum speed 103 mph (165 km/h) at sea level; cruising speed 70 mph (113 km/h) at optimum altitude; climb to 9,185 ft (2800 m) in 60 minutes 30 seconds

Weights: empty 3,549 lb (1610 kg); normal take-off 5,180 lb (2350 kg); maximum take-off 5,732 lb (2600 kg) for a catapult launch
Dimensions: wingspan 44 ft 3¼ in (13.50 m); length 32 ft (9.75 m); height 12 ft 11 in (3.94 m); wing area 507 sq ft (47.10 m²)
Armament: one 0.303-in (7.7-mm) trainable forward-firing machine gun in the bow position, plus provision for flare bombs up to a weight of 74.5 lb (33.75 kg)

Aichi AB miscellaneous types

Aichi Tokei Denki K.K. (Aichi Watch and Electric Machinery Co. Ltd) began to produce aircraft in 1920 through the creation of an Aircraft Department and later became celebrated as the Aichi Kokuki K.K. (Aichi Aircraft Co. Ltd). This became a separate company in 1943 and was one of Japan's major aircraft manufacturers throughout World War II.

Aichi's efforts during the 1920s were mainly concerned with the production and adaptation of existing European designs for Japanese purposes. These achieved only limited success but, under the aegis of chief designer, Tetsuo Miko, the company achieved growing success during the 1930s with its own seaplane designs, the most notable being the **AB-4** (described above).

Among the first types schemed was the **AB-1** transport aircraft, which was developed in 1926 to meet a requirement for Japan's growing civil air transport network.

Aichi offered a design based on the Heinkel HD 25, which had entered limited production in Japan as the **Navy Type 2 Reconnaissance Seaplane**. The resulting **AB-1 Transport** was an enlarged version of the HD 25, with an enclosed four-seat cabin and powered by a licence-built Lorraine-Dietrich 12 W-type engine. Provision was made for either fixed tail-skid landing gear or twin-float alighting gear.

Built in 1928, the AB-1 was evaluated against two rival designs from Mitsubishi and Nakajima. All had uninspiring performance and were not chosen. Just one AB-1 was operated in landplane form during 1929 by the newly-formed Nihon Koku Yuso K.K. (Japan Air Transport Co. Ltd). The machine was passed to Tokyo Koku K.K., and was operated as a floatplane for many years on the route linking Tokyo and Shimoda.

In 1924, Aichi developed the **Experimental Type 15-Ko Reconnaissance Seaplane** to replace the Junkers W 33 seaplanes in service with the Japanese naval air arm. Aichi had built the W 33 as the **Type Hansa** and its Type 15 design was clearly inspired by the German aircraft, although changes included a new wing and float design. Four prototypes were built for evaluation between 1925-26. The Type 15 suffered from poor stability and the competition was won by a Nakajima type.

A slightly more successful design was the **Aichi Navy Type 90-1** (short designation **E3A1**) which was accepted for service in 1931. However, the E3A had poor performance and Aichi's chief designer developed the **AB-2** to meet the same requirement. This type enjoyed the distinction of being the first shipboard reconnaissance aircraft to be designed and built in Japan without foreign involvement.

Two AB-2 prototypes were built in 1930 for evaluation as the **Experimental Catapult-Launched Reconnaissance Seaplane**. Trials soon revealed that there were problems with the AB-2's engine, as well as the airframe. The whole programme was terminated after the loss of a prototype as a result of an inflight engine fire.

Aichi subsequently adapted its AB-2 design to meet a 1928 requirement from the Chinese government for a small single-seat reconnaissance floatplane. The **AB-3** had outer wing panels that were detachable for reduced shipboard hangarage requirements.

The sole prototype was completed in January 1932, and was evaluated as the **Experimental Single-Seat Reconnaissance Floatplane**. These trials revealed an all-round performance slightly better than specified, coupled with improved handling char-

Designed for the Chinese navy, the sole AB-3 was completed in January 1932 and initially tested in Japan.

SPECIFICATION

Aichi AB-3 (Experimental Single-Seat Reconnaissance Floatplane)
Type: single-seat reconnaissance floatplane
Powerplant: one Gasuden Jimpu radial piston engine rated at 150 hp (112 kW)
Performance: maximum speed 121 mph (195 km/h) at sea level; cruising speed 85 mph (137 km/h)

at 1,640 ft (500 m); climb to 9,845 ft (3000 m) in 15 minutes 40 seconds; service ceiling 14,110 ft (4300 m)
Weights: empty 1,267 lb (575 kg); maximum take-off 1,741 lb (790 kg)
Dimensions: wingspan 29 ft 6 in (9.00 m); length 21 ft 8 in (6.60 m); height 9 ft 5 in (2.88 m); area 209.90 sq ft (19.50 m²)
Armament: none

acteristics compared to those of the AB-2. The AB-3 was accepted, but was not put into even limited production, the Chinese preferring the indigenously designed Ning Hai.

In 1931, the Imperial Japanese Navy air arm placed a contract with Aichi to develop a high-performance reconnaissance floatplane. Despite the emergence of an indigenous Japanese aircraft design capability, at about this time, the navy and Aichi decided that the requirement could best be met by subcontracting the task to a foreign manufacturer, namely Heinkel. The

German company responded with its three-seat He 62 design that was in essence an updated version of the HD 28.

The He 62 prototype was completed in 1932 and, after initial flight trials, this was shipped to Japan. With the addition of a longer-span wing and Lorraine-Dietrich Courlis W-type powerplant, this became the **Aichi AB-5**.

The type was evaluated as the **Experimental Three-Seat Reconnaissance Seaplane**, but was not ordered into production, even though it offered performance considerably better than the types it had

been designed to replace.

However, elements of the AB-5 were retained for the following **AB-6**. This introduced greater power in the form of the 630-hp (470-kW) Type 91 W-type engine, as well as an enclosed cockpit for the three crew.

The AB-6 prototype was completed in February 1933 and the type was evaluated as the **Experimental 7-Shi Reconnaissance Seaplane**. It was found to handle well on water, but performance in the air was well below that estimated and required. The prototype was then extensively revised, among the modifi-

cations being a reduction in wingspan. These changes boosted the maximum speed without significant increase in landing speed but, although the AB-6 had good stability, handling and climb rate, it was deemed inferior to the rival Kawanishi design in overall performance and armament, and was therefore not ordered into production.

In 1932, the Imperial Japanese Navy air arm ordered prototypes from Mitsubishi and Nakajima to replace its Mitsubishi B2M (Navy Type 89 Carrier Attack Aeroplane). At the same time, two private-venture designs were submitted by Yokosuka

and Aichi. The latter's three-seat **AB-8** design was completed in September 1932 and was evaluated as the **Experimental 7-Shi Carrier Attack Aeroplane**.

The type was powered by a Courlis W-type engine driving a three-bladed metal fixed-pitch propeller. Armament comprised a single torpedo or bomb carried under the fuselage.

The competition was won by a Yokosuka design, and the sole AB-8 was then used as a company 'hack' and air test machine for a number of years, before being scrapped.

Aichi B7A Ryusei

The requirement for a large torpedo-/dive-bomber for operation from a new, larger class of aircraft-carrier caused the Imperial Japanese Navy to draw up, in 1941, the specification of an aircraft to replace the Nakajima B6N and Yokosuka D4Y.

The service's demanding specification called for an aircraft capable of 345 mph (555 km/h) at 19,680 ft (6000 m) and of carrying an

internal bombload of up to 1,102 lb (500 kg) or a 1,764-lb (800-kg) torpedo externally. A powerful engine was thus essential and the navy selected what was virtually an experimental powerplant for this task: the Nakajima Homare 11 twin-row radial, developing around 1,800 hp (1342 kW).

Aichi designed a large aircraft around this engine. The deep oval-section fuselage and tail unit were

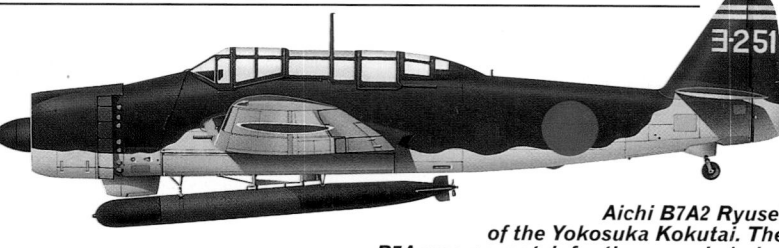

Aichi B7A2 Ryusei of the Yokosuka Kokutai. The B7A was no match for the overwhelming US air power in the Pacific.

conventional, the former providing enclosed accommodation for a crew of two. A novel feature was the mid-mounted wing which had an inverted gull-wing configuration. This layout was chosen so that the main units of the retractable tailwheel landing gear would be as short as possible. A section of each outer wing panel folded to ease carrier stowage.

The **AM-23** prototype was flown in mid-1942 and the type was evaluated under the designation **Navy Experimental 16-Shi Carrier Attack Bomber (Aichi B7A1)**. However, the combination of problems from the airframe, coupled with the teething troubles of the new engine, meant that it was almost two years before the type was ordered

into production in April 1944 as the **Navy Carrier Attack Bomber Ryusei** (Shooting Star), or **Aichi B7A2**. Production lines were established by both Aichi Kokuki K.K. and the Naval Air Arsenal at Omura.

The nine pre-production models of the B7A1 were powered by the Homare 11, but this engine was supplanted in production aircraft by the improved Homare 12, which developed 1,825 hp (1361 kW) for take-off and 1,670 hp (1245 kW) at 7,870 ft (3000 m).

The Ryusei emerged as an extremely manoeuvrable aircraft with excellent handling qualities and a good performance. However, it arrived too late to have any impact on the outcome of the war for the Japanese. By the time it entered service, when it was allocated the Allied codename 'Grace', the Japanese navy no longer had any carriers from which it could operate. The B7A saw only limited use from land bases, initially around Japanese coastal waters,

and latterly during the closing weeks of the war in the *kamikaze* role.

Further development of the B7A led to the **B7A2 Experimental**, a sole example of which was flown with a 2,000-hp (1491-kW) Nakajima Homare 23 engine.

This powerplant possessed many short-comings in general, proving unreliable and difficult to maintain. In order to overcome these difficulties, the **Ryusei-Kai** was developed with a 2,200-hp (1641-kW) Mitsubishi MK9A Kinsei engine and work on the prototype of this version was begun in January 1945, with production proposed as the **B7A3**.

However, the Aichi factory was destroyed when a serious earthquake struck the Tokai district in May 1945. This halted further development of the B7A3, as well as production of all Ryuseis, after approximately 80 had been built by Aichi, and a further 25 at Omura.

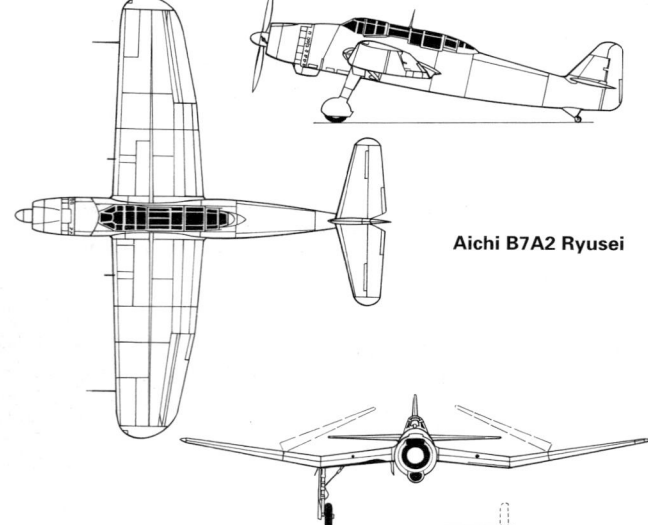

Aichi B7A2 Ryusei

The Ryusei, here illustrated in B7A1 form, was destined never to fly from an operational Imperial Japanese Navy aircraft-carrier, due to its late arrival in the war.

SPECIFICATION

Aichi B7A2 Ryusei
Type: carrier-based torpedo-/dive-bomber
Powerplant: one Nakajima NK9C Homare 12 radial piston engine rated at 1,825 hp (1361 kW) for take-off
Performance: maximum level speed at 21,490 ft (6550 m) 351 mph (565 km/h); climb to 13,125 ft (4000 m) in 6 minutes 55 seconds; service ceiling 36,910 ft (11250 m); maximum range 1,889 miles (3040 km)
Weights: empty 8,400 lb

(3810 kg); maximum take-off 12,401 lb (5625 kg); maximum overload 14,330 lb (6500 kg)
Dimensions: wing span 47 ft 3 in (14.40 m); length 37 ft 8½ in (11.49 m); height 13 ft 4¼ in (4.08 m); wing area 381.05 sq ft (35.40 m²)
Armament: (late production B7A2) two wing-mounted 20-mm Type 99 Model 2 cannon and one 0.51-in (13-mm) Type 2 machine-gun on flexible mount in aft position, plus one 1,764-lb (800-kg) torpedo, or one 1,102-lb (500-kg) bomb or two 551-lb (227-kg) bombs

Aichi D1A

In the early 1930s, the Imperial Japanese Navy air arm issued its 6- and 7-Shi requirements for a new two-seat carrierborne dive-bomber. After Nakajima and Yokosuka responded with unsuccessful prototypes, the service issued to Aichi and Nakajima an 8-Shi requirement for the same type of warplane.

Aichi decided that its best course of approach was to sub-contract the work to a foreign manufacturer and the Japanese company established a working relationship with Ernst Heinkel Flugzeugwerke in Germany, ordering a single example of its **He 66** design. This was the export version of the He 50 dive-bomber equipping German units at that time in one- and two-seat versions.

In terms of performance, the He 66 was obsolescent, largely as a result of the high drag generated by its interplane struts and bracing wires. However, the design offered adequate

structural strength, the ability to operate on both wheeled landing gear or float alighting gear, and viceless handling characteristics in diving flight.

The Heinkel-built prototype differed from the He 66 primarily in its use of a two- rather than four-bladed wooden propeller and the attachment of the main landing gear shock-absorber legs to the underside of the lower wing rather than the lower longerons. Another notable feature was an underfuselage crutch to swing the bomb well clear of the propeller disc before the bomb was released.

After it had reached Japan, the prototype was adapted to **Aichi AB-9** standard under the supervision of Tokuichiro Gomei and Yoshimichi Kobayashi. The original 715-hp (533-kW) Siemens SAM-22B radial piston engine was replaced by a 580-hp (432.5-kW) Nakajima Kotobuki 2-Kai-1 engine driving a two-bladed

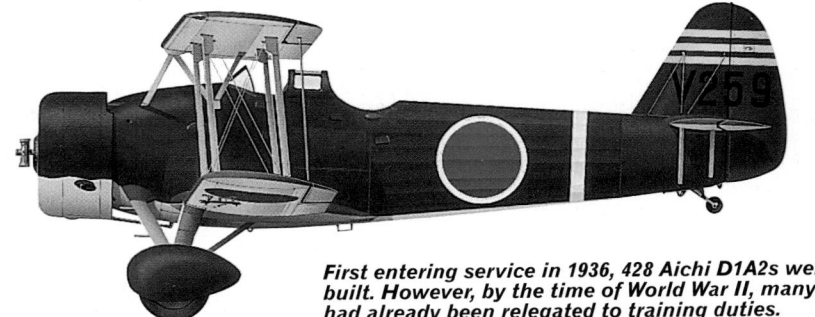

First entering service in 1936, 428 Aichi D1A2s were built. However, by the time of World War II, many had already been relegated to training duties.

metal propeller.

The navy air arm evaluated the prototype in this form as the **Experimental 8-Shi Special Bomber**, a non-standard designation adopted for security reasons to avoid all suggestion of dive-bombing capability. The Aichi type was deemed superior to the rival Nakajima design, and was ordered into production as the **Navy Type 94 Carrier Bomber**, with the short designation **D1A**.

Production examples, of which 162 were built, had the radial engine enclosed by a Townend ring. Other modifications included the introduction of slightly swept wings, and replacement of the tailskid by a non-castoring tailwheel. The last 44 had 580-hp (433-kW) Kotobuki 3 engines.

An improved **Aichi D1A2 (Navy Type 96 Carrier Bomber)** appeared in 1936-7, powered by a more powerful Nakajima Hikari 1 radial engine and this model also introduced a NACA engine cowling, wheel spats, and improved

Although it was a useful weapon in the Sino-Japanese war, the Aichi D1A dive-bomber series was obsolete by the time of Japan's attack on Pearl Harbor in December 1941.

windscreens. Production of this version totalled 428.

Both D1A versions were used in combat action during the second Sino-Japanese conflict in 1937. A D1A2 was responsible for sinking the river gunboat USS *Panay* in the Yangtze River on 12 December 1937, during

the evacuation of Nanking, so causing an international incident. Only a small number of D1A1s remained in use with training units at the time of Japan's attack on Pearl Harbor. About 70 D1A2s were then serving in second-line units, and these were allocated the Allied codename **'Susie'**.

SPECIFICATION

Aichi D1A2
Type: two-seat carrier-based dive-bomber
Powerplant: one Nakajima Hikari 1 radial piston engine rated at 730 hp (544 kW)
Performance: maximum level speed at 10,500 ft (3200 m) 193 mph (310 km/h); cruising speed at 3,280 ft (1000 m) 137 mph (220 km/h); climb to 9,845 ft (3000 m) in 7 minutes 50 seconds; service ceiling 22,965 ft (7000 m);

range 578 miles (930 km)
Weights: empty 3,342 lb (1516 kg); maximum take-off 5,754 lb (2610 kg)
Dimensions: wingspan 37 ft 4¾ in (11.40 m); length 30 ft 6 in (9.30 m); height 11 ft 2¼ in (3.41 m); wing area 373.52 sq ft (34.70 m²)
Armament: two fixed 0.303-in (7.7-mm) Type 92 machine-guns and one flexible 0.303-in (7.7-mm) Type 92 machine-gun, plus one 551-lb (250-kg) and two 66-lb (30-kg) bombs

Aichi D3A

The D1A was Aichi's first design to achieve mass production, and its success prompted the Imperial Japanese Navy to issue its 11-Shi requirement in 1936 for a replacement carrier dive-bomber. Known as the **Aichi D3A**, this warplane became far better known than its predecessor.

The type's wing planform owed much to the elliptical wings of the Heinkel He 70. The non-retractable tailwheel landing gear incorporated main units

with large speed fairings.

Powered by the 730-hp (544-kW) Hikari 1 radial engine that had also been fitted to D1A2s, the prototype made its first flight in January 1938, and subsequent testing showed that the aircraft was underpowered. It had a tendency to snap roll in tight turns, and had ineffective dive-brakes. The second prototype incorporated modifications to overcome these shortcomings, including an increased span wing, changed

Codenamed 'Val' by the Allies, the Aichi D3A was a devastating dive-bomber. Illustrated is a D3A2 of the Yokosuka Kokutai.

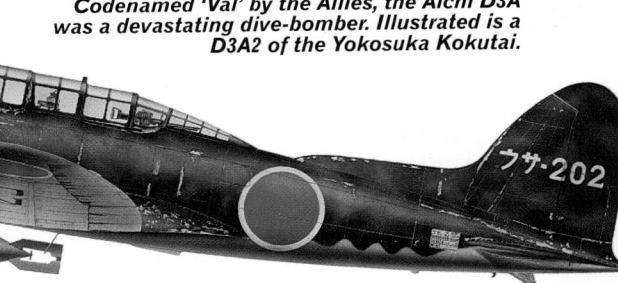

Aichi D3A variants

D3A1: initial production version designated Navy Type 99 Carrier Bomber Model 11 (476 built)
D3A2 Model 12: prototype of improved version with a 1,300-hp (969-kW) Mitsubishi Kinsei 54 engine, increased fuel tankage, modified rear canopy, and introducing a propeller spinner (one built)
D3A2 Model 22: production version of the above; maximum level speed of 267 mph (430 km/h) at 20,340 ft (6200 m); service ceiling 34,450 ft (10500 m); empty weight 5,666 lb (2570 kg), and maximum take-off weight 8,378 lb (3800 kg) (1,016 built)
D3A2-K: trainer version produced by conversions of existing D3A1/2s

outboard wing section leading edges to solve the roll problem, strengthened dive-brakes and an 840-hp (626-kW) Mitsubishi Kinsei 3 radial engine.

In this form, it proved superior to Nakajima's contender for this requirement and, in December 1939, was ordered into production under the designation **Navy Type 99 Carrier Bomber Model 11 (Aichi D3A1)**.

Production aircraft differed from the second prototype by having a small decrease in wing span, and

directional stability was improved by the addition of a long dorsal fin. Power was again increased, with the introduction of a 1,000-hp (746-kW) Mitsubishi Kinsei 43 engine on early production models.

The D3A1 completed carrier trials and saw operational service in late 1940 with the Imperial Japanese Navy in support of Japanese land forces in China and Indo-China. Despite this, the D3A came as a complete surprise to the Americans on 7 December 1941 when a

total of 129 of these dive-bombers was launched in two waves by six Japanese carriers attacking the US Navy base at Pearl Harbor. D3A1s were the first Japanese aircraft to drop bombs on moored American warships. A total of 15 D3A1s was lost during the great raid.

Identified by the Allies under the codename 'Val', the D3A was used in all major carrier actions during the first 10 months of the war in the Pacific theatre and sank more Allied vessels than any other

The Aichi D3A was Japan's principal carrier-based dive-bomber for the first two years of the Pacific War. The type's dive brakes are clearly visible under the wings of this D3A1.

HMS *Dorsetshire* on 5 April 1942.

The 'Val' also played a major role during the Battle of the Coral Sea in May 1942 and the Battle of Midway the following month. However, the type suffered particularly heavy losses to US Navy F4F Wildcat fighters during these encounters. The D3A was not fitted with any armour plating or self-sealing fuel tanks, and only carried a light defensive armament.

Despite the introduction of the improved **D3A2** version in 1942, the type was rapidly approaching obsolescence and was increasingly relegated to second-line duties.

Axis aircraft. Notable achievements included the sinking of the the British aircraft-carrier HMS *Hermes* (the first such type to be sunk by carrier-based warplanes) and the cruisers HMS *Cornwall* and

Nevertheless, the D3A remained in service until its retirement in late 1944. It even served in small numbers as a *kamikaze* aircraft and as a trainer as

its career drew to a close.

Almost 1,500 D3As of different versions were built, including about 201 by Showa before production ended.

SPECIFICATION	
Aichi D3A2 Model 22	maximum take-off 8,378 lb (3800 kg)
Type: two-seat carrier or land-based dive-bomber	**Dimensions:** wingspan 47 ft 1½ in (14.37 m); length 33 ft 5¼ in (10.20 m); height 12 ft 7½ in (3.85 m); wing area 375.67 sq ft (34.90 m²)
Powerplant: one Mitsubishi Kinsei 54 radial piston engine rated at 1,300 hp (970 kW)	
Performance: maximum level speed at 20,340 ft (6200 m) 267 mph (430 km/h); cruising speed at 9,840 ft (3000 m) 183 mph (295 km/h); climb to 9,845 ft (3000 m) in 5 minutes 48 seconds; service ceiling 34,450 ft (10500 m); range 840 miles (1352 km)	**Armament:** two 0.303-in (7.7-mm) fixed forward-firing Type 97 machine-guns with 791 rounds per gun and one 0.303-in (7.7-mm) Type 92 machine-gun on flexible mount in rear cockpit with 1,000 rounds, plus one 551-lb (250-kg) and two 132-lb (60-kg) bombs
Weights: empty 5,666 lb (2570 kg);	

Aichi E10A

Throughout the 1920s and 1930s, the Imperial Japanese Navy placed considerable emphasis on nocturnal surface warfare. The validity of this concept was well proven in several of the battles that took place between Japanese and US naval forces in the waters of the Solomon Islands in late 1942 and early 1943 in the Pacific theatre of World War II.

This form of warfare therefore gave rise to a requirement for a nocturnal

reconnaissance aircraft to shadow and to locate the enemy force. The Imperial Japanese Navy air arm decided that the optimum means was a shipborne flying-boat that could be launched by catapult from light cruisers (or alternatively take off from the sea after being crane-launched from a seaplane tender). It would then patrol at low altitude on long-endurance missions as it sought the enemy and reported its position by radio for attack by Japanese destroyers.

Following an initial protracted programme to

The Aichi E10A1 was a small three-seat flying-boat developed for the nocturnal reconnaissance role. Only 15 were built, and these were withdrawn from front-line service before the start of the Pacific War.

SPECIFICATION	
Aichi E10A1 (Navy Type 96 Reconnaissance Seaplane)	13,515 ft (4120 m); range 1,150 miles (1851 km)
Type: three-seat reconnaissance flying-boat	**Weights:** empty 4,629 lb (2100 kg); maximum take-off 7,275 lb (3300 kg)
Powerplant: one Aichi Type 91 W-type piston engine rated at 650 hp (485 kW)	**Dimensions:** wingspan 50 ft 10¼ in (15.50 m); length 36 ft 9½ in (11.22 m); height 14 ft 9 in (4.50 m); wing area 560.82 sq ft (52.10 m²)
Performance: maximum speed 128 mph (206 km/h) at sea level; cruising speed 66 mph (106 km/h) at 3,280 ft (1000 m); climb to 9,845 ft (3000 m) in 17 minutes 42 seconds; service ceiling	**Armament:** one 0.303-in (7.7-mm) trainable forward-firing machine-gun

find such an aircraft, the Imperial Japanese Navy air arm issued in 1934 to Aichi and Kawanishi a requirement for a night-reconnaissance seaplane. Aichi's response was the **AB-12** flying boat designed by a team under the supervision of Morishige Mori, who evolved a type which strongly resembled the Supermarine Seagull Mk V that had first flown in the preceding year.

The AB-12 was thus a two-bay biplane flying boat of light-alloy construction (skinned in stressed light-

alloy on the hull and fabric on the flying surfaces) with a single-step hull and two underwing stabilising floats. The enclosed cockpit had an open bow position for the single trainable machine-gun that formed the type's only armament. The wing panels were designed to fold rearward to facilitate shipboard storage.

The AB-12 prototype made its first flight in December 1934, and soon proved itself to possess considerably better stability in the air than the rival Kawanishi design, and was

accordingly ordered into production for service as the **Navy Type 96 Reconnaissance Seaplane**, to which the short designation **E10A1** was given.

Production began in August 1936, with service deliveries taking place the following year. Production of 15 such aircraft lasted to 1937, and these were phased out of first-line service late in 1941, although they remained operational in second-line roles, such as training, into 1943. The Aichi E10A1 received the Allied reporting name **'Hank'**.

Aichi E11A

The **Aichi E11A1** night-reconnaissance flying-boat, codenamed **'Laura'** by the Allies, first flew in prototype form in June 1937.

Competing against the Kawanishi E11K1, it proved to have superior performance, and was ordered into production as the **Navy Type 98 Night-Reconnaissance Seaplane**.

The E11A's two-step hull

carried a braced tail unit, with the tailplane and elevator mounted almost halfway up the fin. The E11A had a crew of three. The open bow position mounted a defensive machine-gun and could also be used during on-water manoeuvres, such as making fast to a buoy.

To enhance stability on the water, balancer floats were mounted beneath each lower wing, close to the wingtip. The Hiro Type 91 Model 22 inline engine was mounted at the centre-section of the upper wing, and drove a pusher propeller with spinner.

Production of E11A1s totalled 17 aircraft, and these saw limited use in their intended role during the early stages of the war in the Pacific theatre.

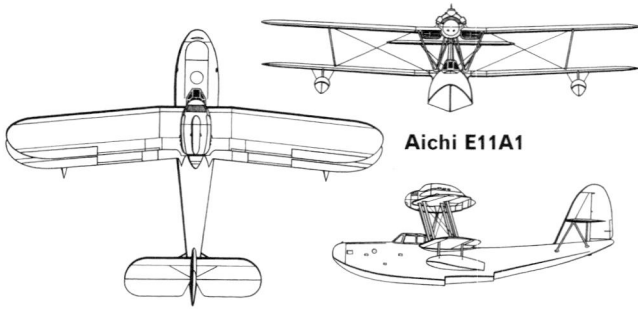

Aichi E11A1

SPECIFICATION	
Aichi E11A1	service ceiling 14,520 ft (4425 m); range 1,209 miles (1945 km)
Type: night-reconnaissance flying-boat	**Weights:** empty 4,248 lb (1927 kg); maximum take-off 7,275 lb (3300 kg)
Powerplant: one Hiro Type 91 Model 22 inline piston engine rated at 620 hp (462 kW)	**Dimensions:** wingspan 47 ft 6¾ in (14.50 m); length 35 ft 1¼ in (10.70 m); height 18 ft ½ in (5.50 m)
Performance: maximum level speed at 7,875 ft (2400 m) 134 mph (215 km/h); cruising speed 81 mph (130 km/h); climb to 9,845 ft (3000 m) in 18 minutes 30 seconds;	**Armament:** one 0.303-in (7.7-mm) Type 92 machine-gun on flexible mount in bow cockpit

Aichi E12A

In June 1937, the Imperial Japanese Navy air arm issued a requirement for an advanced two-seat reconnaissance floatplane capable of being launched by catapult from its major surface warships. Aichi's response was the E12A, which was designed under the supervision of Yoshishiro Matsuo with the assistance of Morishige Mori and Yasunori Ozawa.

The E12A was a cantilever low-wing monoplane of basically all-metal stressed-skin construction with the exception of its fabric-covered control surfaces. The wing had a semi-elliptical planform and its outer panels folded upwards to facilitate storage in the ships' hangars. The single-step metal floats were carried under the inner wing panels by pairs of struts supplemented by bracing wires. Powerplant consisted of a Mitsubishi Zuisei two-row radial piston engine enclosed in a long-chord cowling and driving a two-bladed constant-speed metal propeller.

Two **E12A1** prototypes were built in 1938, and one of these made the type's first flight in late 1938.

The E12A was evaluated with the designation **Experimental 12-Shi Two-seat Reconnaissance Seaplane**. Aichi had dropped out of the competition before this stage, so

the E12A1 was evaluated against the Nakajima E12N1 and, while it was found to have good performance, it was also discovered to be deficient in stability and handling. The type was therefore not ordered into production, although many of its features found their way into the **Aichi 12-Shi Three-seat Reconnaissance Seaplane** that

The E12A1 was an experimental reconnaissance seaplane, from which was developed the more successful E13A1 design.

was accepted for service as the **Navy Type 0 Three-seat Reconnaissance Seaplane (Aichi E13A1)**.

Aichi E13A

Developed from a two-seat reconnaissance seaplane design (E12A), the **Aichi E13A** was designed to meet a 1937 Imperial Japanese Navy requirement for a long-range reconnaissance floatplane to replace the Kawanishi E7K2. The prototype of this three-seat aircraft was completed in late 1938.

Powered by a Kinsei 43 radial engine, the E13A proved superior to the competing Kawanishi E13K1 during service tests, and was ordered into production as the Navy **Type 0 Reconnaissance Seaplane Model 11 (Aichi E13A1)**.

Aichi had built a total of 133 by 1942, when manufacture switched to the Watanabe (later Kyushu Hikoki KK) plant at Zasshonokuma. The production total of 1,418 aircraft included 50 built by the Hiro Naval Arsenal.

Identified by the Allies under the codename **'Jake'**, E13A1s were embarked aboard Japanese cruisers and seaplane

An Aichi E13A 'Jake' reconnaissance floatplane of the Imperial Japanese Navy.

tenders in 1941. Carrying a single 551-lb (250-kg) bomb apiece, E13A1s launched from the cruisers *Chiku-ma*, *Kinugasa* and *Tone*, flew a series of raids on the Hankow-Canton railway in support of Japanese forces in China. Soon afterwards, they accompanied the Japanese 8th Cruiser Division to conduct reconnaissance patrols during the strike against Pearl Harbor in December 1941.

In all, it is estimated that, by mid-1943, more than 250 E13A1s were at sea aboard Japanese ships, though their use was severely curtailed whenever American fighters were in evidence. Nevertheless, they continued to serve right up to the end of the war, many of them being ultimately used in *kamikaze* attacks in the closing stages of the war.

Aichi developed two variants of the basic design. Introduced in late 1944, the **E13A1a Model 11A** featured improved float bracing struts, a propeller spinner and more advanced radio equipment. The **E13A1b Model 11B** was based on the E13A1a, but was fitted with anti-surface vessel radar.

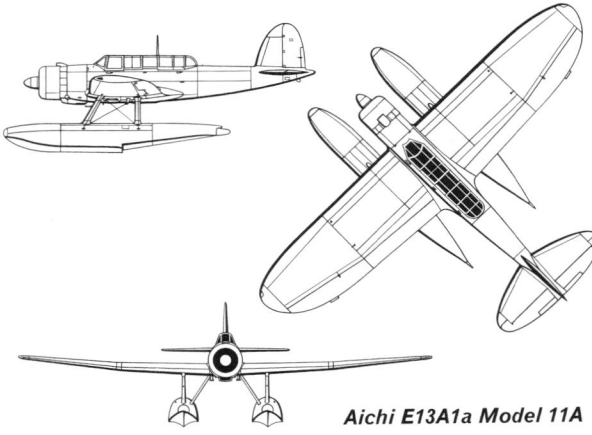

Aichi E13A1a Model 11A

The E13A was numerically the most important of all Japanese float seaplanes of World War II. The type had a remarkable range and endurance and could sustain a patrol for over 15 hours.

Aichi E13A1 'Jake' at Midway

Following the Japanese attack on Pearl Harbor, E13A1s were embarked on the battleships and cruisers of the *Kantais* (fleets), including the battleship *Haruna* and cruisers *Chiku-ma* and *Tone* of Vice Admiral Nagumo's Carrier Striking Force at the Battle of Midway. Because of mechanical problems with the ships' catapults, there were delays in launching one of the four E13A1s to search for the American carriers at dawn on the crucial 4 June 1942, thus depriving the Japanese of the vital initiative during the early stages of the assault on Midway. Furthermore the *Chiku-ma*'s E13A1 was forced to return early when it suffered engine trouble, further reducing the all-important search area. One of the other 'Jake' pilots, from the cruiser *Tone*, eventually sighted the American fleet, but at first failed to report the presence of carriers, causing a further 30-minute delay in arming the strike aircraft which were awaiting orders to launch from Japanese carriers. As it was, when the Americans launched their first strike, the pilots found the decks of the carriers *Akakgi*, *Kaga*, *Soryu* and *Hiryu* packed with aircraft which should have been attacking the American fleet.

Aichi E16A Zuiun

The design of a twin-float reconnaissance seaplane to supersede the E13A1 was begun by Aichi in October 1940. In early 1941, the Imperial Japanese Navy drew up a specification based upon the company's **AM-22** design.

The first of three prototypes was initially flown during May 1942, but the resolution of stability problems and buffeting from the dive-brakes occupied 15 months, the navy ordering the **Aichi E16A1** into production in August 1943 as the **Navy**

Reconnaissance Seaplane Model 11 Zuiun (Auspicious Cloud).

The single-step floats each included a controllable rudder to assist in on-water operation, and the forward mounting strut of the floats incorporated hydraulically-actuated dive-brakes to allow the E16A1 to operate also as a dive-bomber. Powerplant of the prototype and of early production aircraft consisted of a 1,300-hp (969-kW) Mitsubishi Kinsei 51 radial engine, driving a three-bladed propeller.

The E16A1 was an excellent design, but entered service at a time when the Allies had gained air superiority. As a result, these aircraft, allocated the Allied codename **'Paul'**, suffered very heavy losses, particularly in the Philippines, during 1944. The majority of the E16A1s which survived were used for *kamikaze* operations at Okinawa in March-July 1945.

Significant numbers of E16A1s were carried by the battleships *Hyuga* and *Ise*, which were each capable of accommodating up to 22 Zuiuns. The destruction of these warships became the main priority of the US 3rd Fleet during the months preceding the assault on Iwo Jima. They were eventually destroyed by American naval air attack on the port of Kure at the end of July 1945.

Production of the E16A totalled 193 by Aichi and 59 by Nippon. The design was further improved to produce the **E16A2**. This designation was given to a prototype fitted with a 1,560-hp (1163-kW) Mitsubishi MK8P Kinsei 62 radial piston engine. The aircraft was being flight-tested at the time of the Japanese surrender in 1945.

Designed to replace the successful E13A1, the Aichi E16A1 was an excellent reconnaissance floatplane. Unfortunately for the Japanese, it entered service only after the Allies had achieved total air superiority.

SPECIFICATION

Aichi E16A1 (late-production)
Type: two-seat long-range reconnaissance floatplane
Powerplant: one Mitsubishi MK8D Kinsei 54 radial piston engine rated at 1,300 hp (969 kW)
Performance: maximum level speed at 18,045 ft (5500 m) 273 mph (440 km/h); cruising speed at 16,405 ft (5000 m) 208 mph (335 km/h); climb to 9,845 ft (3000 m) in 4 minutes 40 seconds; service ceiling 32,810 ft (10000 m); maximum range 1,504 miles (2420 km)

Weights: empty 6,493 lb (2945 kg) maximum take-off 10,038 lb (4553 kg)
Dimensions: wingspan 42 ft ¼ in (12.81 m); length 35 ft 6½ in (10.83 m); height 15 ft 8½ in (4.79 m); wing area 301.40 sq ft (28.00 m²)
Armament: two 20-mm wing-mounted Type 99 Model 2 cannon and one 0.51-in (13-mm) Type 2 machine-gun on flexible mount in aft position, plus one 551-lb (250-kg) bomb on underfuselage mounting

Aichi E16A

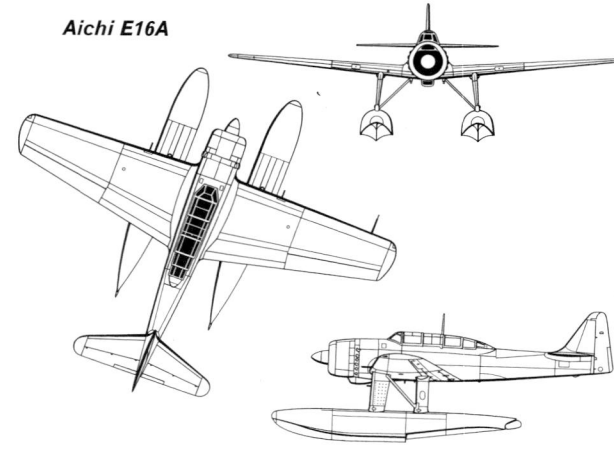

Aichi H9A

Development of the **Aichi H9A1** began in early 1940, its intended role being that of an advanced trainer for crews that would eventually operate the Kawanishi H8K1 high-performance flying-boat.

The H9A was a parasol-wing monoplane, with a two-step hull and tail unit very similar to that of the E11A1. Strut-mounted and wire-braced stabilising floats were mounted beneath each wing. The hull provided accommodation for a standard crew of five plus three trainees, and incorporated semi-retractable wheeled beaching gear.

Three H9A prototypes were built, the first being flown in September 1940. These were followed by a total of 27 production machines built by Aichi, and an additional four by Nippon Hikoki.

They were used primarily for training missions but, unknown to the Allies, they fulfilled this role in virtual total obscurity. During the closing stages of the war, the H9A was deployed on anti-submarine patrol duties, and then equipped to carry bombs or depth-charges on underwing racks.

The Aichi H9A was one of the few Japanese aircraft of which the Allies had no knowledge until almost the end of the Pacific war. The type was, consequently, not allocated a codename.

SPECIFICATION

Aichi H9A
Type: twin-engined training flying-boat
Powerplant: two Nakajima Kotobuki 41 radial piston engines each rated at 710 hp (529 kW)
Performance: maximum level speed at 9,845 ft (3000 m) 196 mph (315 km/h); cruising speed 137 mph (220 km/h); climb to 9,845 ft (3000 m) in 11 minutes 15 seconds; service ceiling 22,245 ft (6780 m); range 1,336 miles (2150 km)

Weights: empty 10,803 lb (4900 kg); maximum take-off 16,535 lb (7500 kg)
Dimensions: wingspan 78 ft 8¾ in (24.00 m); length 55 ft 7¼ in (16.95 m); height 17 ft 2¾ in (5.25 m); wing area 681.38 sq ft (63.30 m²)
Armament: two 0.303-in (7.7-mm) Type 92 fixed forward-firing machine-guns and one similar gun on flexible mount in aft cockpit, plus up to 683 lb (310 kg) of bombs or depth-charges

Aichi H9A1

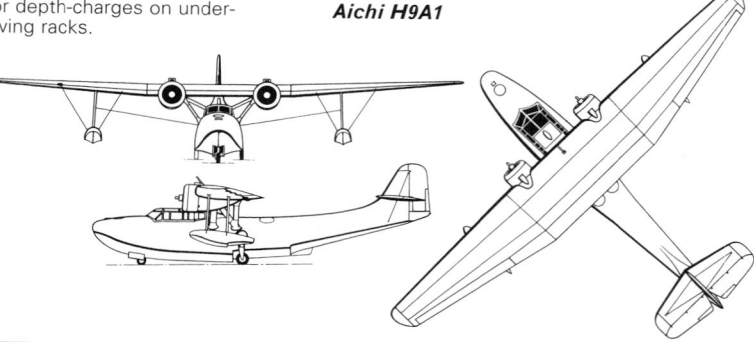

Aichi HD 23

An unusual and ultimately disappointing naval fighter, the **Aichi HD 23 (Experimental Type-H Carrier Fighter)** was designed to a 1926 Imperial Japanese Navy requirement for a new carrierborne fighter to replace its Mitsubishi Type 10 Carrier Fighter, for use aboard the carrier *Hosho*.

Considerable thought went into facilitating a safe escape for the pilot in the event of the aircraft ditching. A boat-like hull and jettisonable undercarriage were employed, along with a device which stopped the propeller in a horizontal position prior to ditching. The aircraft proved unmanoeuvrable, however, and was overweight and excessively nose-heavy. This, in combination with poor visibility for the pilot, led to the type being abandoned.

From the outset, the HD 23 showed little promise as a fighter.

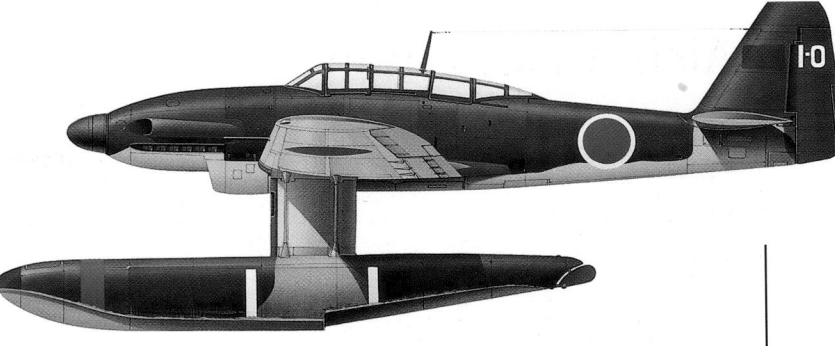

Aichi M6A Seiran

The **Aichi M6A Seiran** (mountain haze) was undoubtedly one of the most interesting aircraft to be developed by Japan during World War II. The spur for the design was the intention of the Imperial Japanese Navy, expressed in the 4th Reinforcement Programme, to procure no fewer than 18 'I-400'-class submarines. These giant vessels each had a submerged displacement of 6,500 tons and a cruising radius of 47,875 miles (77045 km). The submarines were intended for long-range operations against both merchant and naval shipping, and included in their design was a water-tight hangar capable of carrying two aircraft.

Procurement of the 'I-400' class was subsequently cut to five boats after it was decided that larger numbers of smaller attack submarines were more important to the Japanese war effort. However, each 'I-400' class was now to be fitted with a larger hangar permitting the carriage of three warplanes.

In 1942, Aichi was instructed to begin the design of the required aircraft, the original specification calling for a warplane capable of delivering a 1,874-lb (850-kg) weapon over a range of 700 miles (1130 km). This would be launched by catapult and, as the flight was intended as a one-way mission, the aircraft would therefore need no landing gear. This specification was later amended to include twin-float alighting gear that could be jettisoned if higher speed were needed in a combat situation.

The resulting **AM-24** design was prepared under the supervision of Norio Ozaki, Yasushiro Ozawa and Morishige Mori, and was developed with considerable speed. This was despite the complexities imposed by the need to build fold points into the airframe so that the complete machine could be stowed in the small hangar provided on the submarine. Otherwise, the

most notable features of the design, apart from its use of a liquid-cooled engine, were the two large single-step floats carried on cantilever legs under the wings, a highly advanced double-slotted wing flap system (which had been perfected on the E16A Zuiun) and the complex folding system employed for the wings and tail unit: the wings turned on their rear spars to lie flat along the sides of the fuselage, the tip of the vertical tail surface folded to starboard, and the horizontal tail surfaces folded downward. Such was the skill of the design team, however, that despite the apparent complexity of the system and the lack of space on board the launching submarine, the M6A could be readied for flight by a team of four men in only seven minutes.

The first of eight **M6A1** prototypes was completed in November 1942. This was powered by an Aichi AE1P Atsuta 30 inverted-Vee piston engine rated at 1,400 hp (1044 kW). The other seven prototypes differed only in small details, including the use of the identically-rated Atsuta 31 engine. Production aircraft (18 built) were fitted with the Atsuta 32 engine.

Designed at the same

Although several countries built aircraft for carriage and launching by submarine, the Aichi M6A Seiran was the sole type to have been developed as an attack aircraft, all the others having been planned for the reconnaissance and observation roles.

time as the Seiran, the **M6A-1K Nanzan** (southern mountain) was built only in prototype form during 1945. Two of these trainer aircraft were completed, with the omission of the Seiran's folding fin top and the addition of tailwheel landing gear with inward-retracting main units.

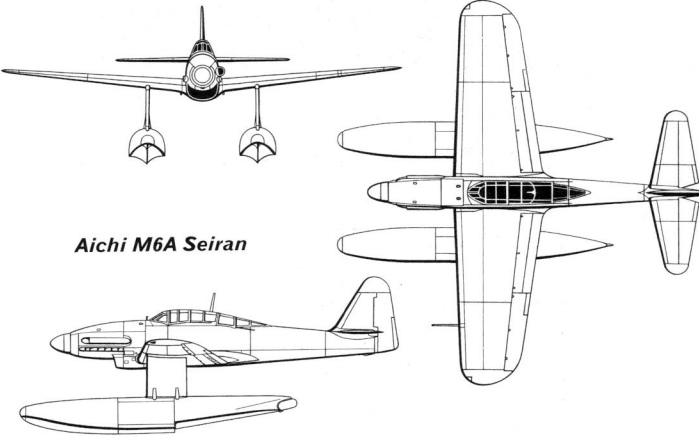

Aichi M6A Seiran

SPECIFICATION

Aichi M6A1 Seiran
Type: two-seat submarine-based attack aircraft
Powerplant: one Aichi AE1P Atsuta 32 inverted-Vee piston engine rated at 1,400 hp (1044 kW) for take-off and 1,250 hp (932 kW) at 5,580 ft (1700 m)
Performance: maximum speed 295 mph (475 km/h) at 17,060 ft (5200 m); cruising speed 184 mph (296 km/h) at 9,845 ft (3000 m); climb to 9,845 ft (3000 m) in 5 minutes 48 seconds; service ceiling 32,480 ft (9900 m); range

739 miles (1189 km)
Weights: empty 7,277 lb (3301 kg); normal take-off 8,907 lb (4040 kg); maximum take-off 9,800 lb (4445 kg)
Dimensions: wingspan 40 ft 2¾ in (12.62 m); length 38 ft 2¼ in (11.64 m); height 15 ft ⅓ in (4.58 m); wing area 290.62 sq ft (27.00 m²)
Armament: one 0.51-in (13-mm) trainable rearward-firing machine-gun, and up to 1,874 lb (800 kg) of bombs in the form of one 1,874-lb (800-kg) or two 551-lb (250-kg) weapons

Originally known as the M6A1-K Seiran Kai, the trainer derivative of the submarine-based Seiran was never to reach production status.

The Panama Canal bomber

The 18 production examples of the M6A1 Seiran were delivered to the Imperial Japanese Navy between October 1944 and July 1945. Ten aircraft put to sea in the 'I-400' and smaller 'I-13' class submarines of the 1st Submarine Flotilla in July 1945 with the intention of attacking the lock gates of the vital Panama Canal. Three M6A1s were each carried by the I-400 and I-401, with a further pair each carried by the I-13 and I-14. However, realising that their most worthwhile targets were already massed in the Pacific, the Japanese re-directed the flotilla against the huge US Navy base at Ulithi atoll, 300 miles (480 km) southwest of the Marianas. The flotilla was at sea when the atomic bombs dropped on Hiroshima and Nagasaki brought the war to an end. All ten Seirans were destroyed.

Aichi S1A Denko

The air arms of the Imperial Japanese Army and Navy were notably slow to appreciate the threat that might be posed to the home islands by American heavy bombing by night. When such a threat began to develop as Boeing B-29 Superfortress heavy bombers were deployed to China, the short-term expedient adopted was the adaptation of the Nakajima J1N Gekko long-range

escort fighter as the J1N1-S for the night-interception role with primitive radar. This type was operated only by the navy air arm, and was intended as an interim type pending the advent of a purpose-designed night-fighter. The official requirement issued late in 1943 called for a radar-equipped night-fighter armed with at least two 30-mm cannon and with a performance that included

a maximum speed of 426 mph (685 km/h) at 29,530 ft (9000 m), a climb to 19,685 ft (6000 m) in eight minutes, and an endurance of five hours.

Aichi responded with its **Denko** (bolt of light) design, an advanced twin-engined night-fighter of mid-wing configuration and all-metal construction with the exception of its fabric-covered control surfaces. The Denko had a number of advanced features including ailerons that drooped in concert with the flaps and

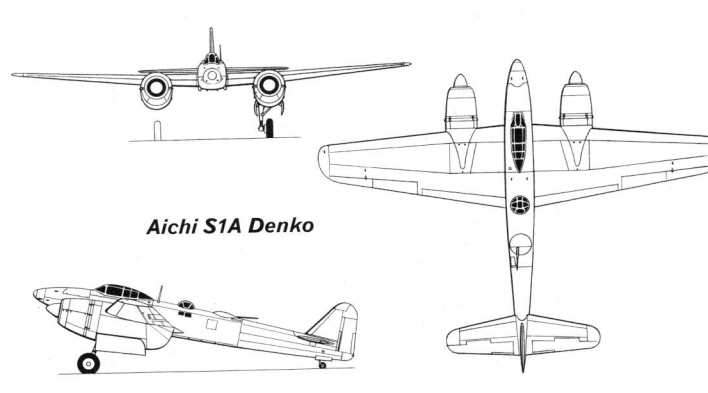

Aichi S1A Denko

The S1A Denko night fighter was developed to counter B-29 Superfortress bomber attacks on the Japanese mainland. Only two prototypes were built – both were destroyed by American bombing.

ment comprised two 30-mm and two 20-mm cannon. The pilot sat in a cockpit over the leading edge of the wing under a heavily-framed canopy. The radar operator/gunner sat in a separate enclosed cockpit over the trailing edge of the wing, and controlled the rearward firing armament of two 20-mm cannon which were fitted in a power-operated dorsal barbette.

The Denko was powered by two fan-cooled Nakajima NK9K-S Homare 22 two-row radial piston engines, which each drove a four-bladed constant-speed metal propeller. It was clear from an early stage of the programme that the navy air arm's insistence on the use of the Homare engine would result in performance being lower than required.

wing- and fuselage-mounted air brakes so that the aircraft could close rapidly in a stern chase and then decelerate quickly to avoid overtaking the target and thus maximise the time during which the target could be held under fire.

Fixed forward-firing arma-

Aichi hoped, however, that production aircraft could be fitted with a turbocharged powerplant of two NK9K-L Homare 24 radial engines to boost maximum speed to 423 mph (680 km/h) at high altitude.

The navy air arm ordered the construction of proto-

types with the designation **Experimental 18-Shi Night-Fighter Denko** (short designation **S1A**), but the first two prototypes were destroyed, somewhat ironically as a result of bombing, shortly before the end of World War II in August 1945.

SPECIFICATION

Aichi S1A Denko (estimated)
Type: two-seat night-fighter
Powerplant: two Nakajima NK9K-S Homare 22 radial piston engines each rated at 2,000 hp (1491 kW) for take-off and 1,620 hp (1208 kW) at 20,995 ft (6400 m)
Performance: maximum speed 367 mph (590 km/h) at 26,245 ft (8000 m); cruising speed 277 mph (445 km/h) at 13,125 ft (4000 m); climb to 29,530 ft (9000 m) in 14 minutes 45 seconds; service ceiling 39,370 ft (12000 m); standard range 1,053 miles (1695 km)

Weights: empty 16,138 lb (7320 kg); normal take-off 22,443 lb (10180 kg); maximum take-off 25,375 lb (11510 kg)
Dimensions: wingspan 57 ft 5 in (17.50 m); length 49 ft 6½ in (15.10 m); height 15 ft 1 in (4.61 m); area 505.90 sq ft (47.00 m²)
Armament: two 30-mm and two 20-mm fixed forward-firing cannon in the forward fuselage, two 20-mm trainable cannon in a power-operated dorsal barbette, and up to 551 lb (250 kg) of bombs

AIDC AT-3 Tsu Chung

The first of the two AT-3 basic trainer prototypes. The AT-3 replaced the Lockheed T-33 in RoCAF service.

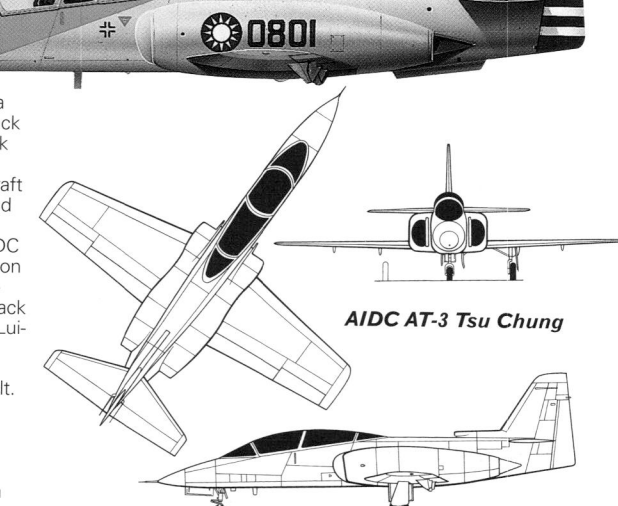

AIDC AT-3 Tsu Chung

Known to the Republic of China air force (RoCAF) as the **Tsu Chung**, the **AIDC AT-3** tandem two-seat basic trainer provides the initial 120-hour jet training course at the Air Force Academy, Kangshan air base.

The AT-3 was the first military jet aircraft developed in Taiwan to achieve series production. Development was begun in 1975 by the Aero Industry Development Centre (AIDC), and the first of two (**XAT-3**) prototypes entered flight testing on 16 September 1980. Contracts were subsequently placed on behalf of

the RoCAF for 60 production aircraft, the first of which was flown on 6 February 1984, with the last example being delivered by early 1990.

The AT-3 has a one-piece carry-through wing, which uses a multi-spar light alloy structure with heavy-plate machined skinning and the fuselage is a light alloy semi-monocoque. The two crew are accommodated on zero-zero ejection seats under individual manually-operated canopies. Fuel is carried in two rubber-impregnated nylon bladder fuselage tanks.

In the late 1980s, two

Above: Taiwan's camouflaged AT-3s have a close-support role.

Below: An AT-3B radar-equipped two-seater formates with one of the two A-3/AT-3A single-seat attack prototypes.

prototypes were built of a dedicated single-seat attack variant, featuring an attack radar and armed with an integral cannon. This aircraft was named **Lui-Meng** and designated either **A-3** or **AT-3A** (both appear in AIDC publicity material). A version which combined the two-seat airframe with the attack avionics and radar of the Lui-Meng was designated **AT-3B**, of which 18 are believed to have been built.

Taiwan's AT-3s chiefly operate with the Basic Training Group (approximately 40 aircraft) at the Air Academy. However, a number of AT-3s (approximately 12) wear green and brown camouflage, and are believed to have a distinct close-support/attack role. The AT-3Bs are believed to be flown by No. 35 Squadron.

Some, though not all, of these aircraft have been fitted with a Westinghouse AN/APG-66 radar and fire

control system, and are certain to have expanded weapons capability.

Development continued with the **AT-5A/B**, single- and two-seat variants of an upgraded aircraft with

new avionics and improved engines. Neither of these types reached fruition, and further development of all models of the AT-3 is believed to have been terminated.

SPECIFICATION

AIDC AT-3 Tsu Chung
Type: two-seat advanced trainer/light attack aircraft
Powerplant: two Garrett TFE731-2-2L turbofans each rated at 3,500 lb st (15.57 kN)
Performance: maximum level speed 'clean' at 36,000 ft (10975 m) 462 mph (743 km/h) and at sea level 558 mph (898 km/h); cruising speed at 36,000 ft (10975 m) 548 mph (882 km/h); maximum rate of climb at sea level 10,100 ft (3078 m) per minute; service ceiling 48,000 ft (14625 m); take-off run 1,500 ft (458 m) at maximum take-off weight; take-off distance to 50 ft (15 m) 2,200 ft (671 m) at maximum take-off weight; landing distance from 50 ft (15 m) 3,100 ft (945 m) at normal landing weight; landing run

2,200 ft (671 m) at normal landing weight; range 1,416 miles (2279 km) with standard fuel; endurance 3 hours 12 minutes
Weights: empty equipped 8,500 lb (3856 kg); normal take-off 11,500 lb (5216 kg); maximum take-off 17,500 lb (7938 kg)
Dimensions: wingspan 34 ft 3¾ in (10.46 m); tailplane span 15 ft 10¼ in (4.83 m); length including probe 42 ft 4 in (12.90 m); height 14 ft 3¾ in (4.36 m); wheel track 13 ft (3.96 m); wheel base 18 ft (5.49 m); wing area 236.06 sq ft (21.93 m²)
Armament: maximum ordnance 6,000 lb (2722 kg)
Fuel: internal fuel 2,800 lb (1270 kg); external fuel up to 1,950 lb (884 kg) in two 150-US gal (568-litre) drop tanks

AIDC Ching-Kuo

Also known as the Indigenous Defence Fighter, the Ching-Kuo is usually armed with weapons of Taiwanese manufacture. These include the Sky Sword I and underfuselage Sky Sword II, as illustrated.

Taiwan's ambitious programme to develop an advanced fighter to replace its fleet of F-5s and F-104s began in 1982, after the US government placed an embargo on the sale of the Northrop F-20 and any comparable fighter. The same restrictions were not placed on technical assistance, however, and US aerospace companies have collaborated closely with AIDC to develop an indigenous fighter and weapons system. The overall programme, codenamed An Hsiang (Safe Flight), has been managed through four subsidiary programmes for airframe, engines, avionics and armament systems.

The airframe was developed with assistance from General Dynamics in the Ying Yang (Soaring Eagle) programme and the prototypes and first 160 production aircraft were to be powered by two Allied-Signal/Garrett TFE-1042-70 (F125) turbofans. These are afterburning versions of the Garrett TFE731, developed under the Yun Han (Cloud Man) programme, which produce 6,060 lb st dry and 9,460 lb st with afterburning (26.80 and 42.08 kN). More powerful versions of the F125 or General Electric J101 were considered for later aircraft. Avionics were developed by a team led by Smiths Industries under a programme codenamed Tien Lei (Sky Thunder), and the primary missile armament has been developed

in the Tien Chien (Sky Sword) programme. The aircraft is equipped with a new Golden Dragon GD-53 multi-mode pulse-Doppler radar based on the GE AN/APG-67(V) developed for the F-20, but incorporating some technology from the Westinghouse AN/APG-66 (used by the F-16A). The aircraft also has a Honeywell H423 inertial navigation system, and Bendix/King multi-function and head-up displays.

Of conventional all-metal construction (although an increasing proportion of composites has been introduced on production aircraft), the **Ching-Kuo** is of conventional configuration, albeit with wing/fuselage blending. Elliptical intakes are located below long LERXes for good high-Alpha performance. The pilot sits on a Martin-Baker Mk 12 ejection seat, under a blown canopy, and behind a single-piece windscreen. The pressurised cockpit is fitted with a sidestick controller, a wide-angle HUD, and three multi-function look-down displays. The aircraft has an internal 20-mm M61A1 cannon beneath the port LERX, and has two underfuselage and two underwing hardpoints, in addition to its wingtip missile launch rails. Weapons include a variety of indigenous missiles, including the IR-homing Sky Sword I, the longer-range SARH Sky Sword II (two in tandem recesses under the fuselage only) or

three Hsiung Feng II (Male Bee II) anti-ship missiles.

The first of three single-seat prototypes made its maiden flight on 28 May 1989, but was seriously damaged when a tyre blew and the nosewheel collapsed during a take-off in front of the Taiwanese President on 29 October 1989. The second prototype flew on 27 September 1989, but was lost in a fatal crash caused by vibration during transonic acceleration on 12 July 1990. The third prototype, with modified engine intakes, made its maiden flight on 10 January 1990, and was followed by the fourth prototype, the first two-seater, on 10 July 1990.

There was originally a requirement for 256 aircraft, some of which would be two-seat trainers, and some of which could be configured for anti-shipping duties. The aircraft is named after a former President of Taiwan, Chiang Ching-Kuo.

Ching-Kuo weapon options

In addition to the internal M61A1 20-mm Vulcan cannon, weapons identified with the Ching-Kuo include the GBU-12 500-lb (227-kg) LGB, the CBU-87 Rockeye, the AGM-65B TV Maverick ASM, the AIM-9P Sidewinder IR-homing AAM and the indigenous Sky Sword I and Sky Sword II AAMs. The Sky Sword I closely resembles an AIM-9B or AIM-9D (though with wider span tailfins), while the Sky Sword II is similar to the AIM-7 Sparrow in appearance. For the anti-shipping role, the Ching-Kuo may be armed with three indigenous Hsiung Feng II sea-skimming anti-ship missiles. One of the two-seaters has been noted with an extra pair of underwing pylons accommodating a pair of F-5E-style 275-US gal (1040-litre) external fuel tanks.

The first of 10 pre-production aircraft was rolled out on 9 March 1992, and this introduced new enlarged engine intakes, a small ventral fin and tubular RWR fairings on the LERXes. Deliveries to the air force began earlier than the expected date of January 1994. On 10 February 1993, No. 7 'Seed' squadron publicly unveiled its aircraft, which included two production single-seaters and two production two-seaters, for

the first time. Also present, and apparently on charge, were the rebuilt first prototype and the fourth prototype. In March 1993, the country's legislature announced that procurement would be limited to only 130 aircraft, to equip two, instead of the planned four, wings.

Ching-Kuo represents a formidable addition to the RoCAF inventory, with genuine beyond visual range capability.

SPECIFICATION

AIDC Ching-Kuo
Type: single-seat multi-role fighter
Powerplant: two ITEC (Garrett/AIDC) TFE-1042-70 (F125) turbofans each rated at 6,060 lb st (26.80 kN) dry and 9,460 lb st (42.08 kN) with afterburning
Performance: maximum level speed 'clean' at 36,000 ft (10975 m) more than 792 mph (1275 km/h); maximum rate of climb at sea level 50,000 ft (15240 m) per minute;

service ceiling 55,000 ft (16760 m)
Weights: normal take-off 20,000 lb (9072 kg)
Dimensions: wingspan over wingtip missile rails 28 ft (8.53 m); length including probe 46 ft 7½ in (14.21 m); height 15 ft 3 in (4.65 m); wing area 261.1 sq ft (24.26 m²)
Fuel: internal fuel 4,650 lb (2198 kg)
g limits: +6.5

AIDC T-CH-1 Chung Tsing

Notable for a layout that bears more than a passing resemblance to that of the North American T-28, the **AIDC T-CH-1 Chung Tsing** tandem two-seat basic flying trainer was developed in the early 1970s to meet a requirement of the Republic of China air force. The first military aircraft of indigenous Taiwanese design to achieve production status, the T-CH-1 prototype was first flown on 23 November 1973, and production of 50 T-CH-1 trainers began in 1976,

with deliveries ending during 1981.

Powered by a T53-L-701 turboprop licence-manufactured in Taiwan, the T-CH-1 is a cantilever low-wing monoplane of light alloy stressed-skin construction with retractable tricycle landing gear and a substantial framed canopy (with sliding sections for access and egress) over the pupil and instructor. The T-CH-1 entered service at the RoCAF academy at Kang Shan in 1977, remaining the standard basic flying

trainer at this establishment until the introduction of a new training syllabus in

which part of the spectrum covered by the T-CH-1 was taken over by the Beech T-34C and the remainder by the locally designed AT-3.

Progressively phased out

of academy service from 1985, the T-CH-1 was adapted for the weapons training task, equipping No. 72 Squadron of the 1st Tactical Fighter Wing based

The similarity of the T-CH-1 to the T-28 Trojan is marked, although the Taiwanese machine is turboprop-powered, unlike the earlier American design.

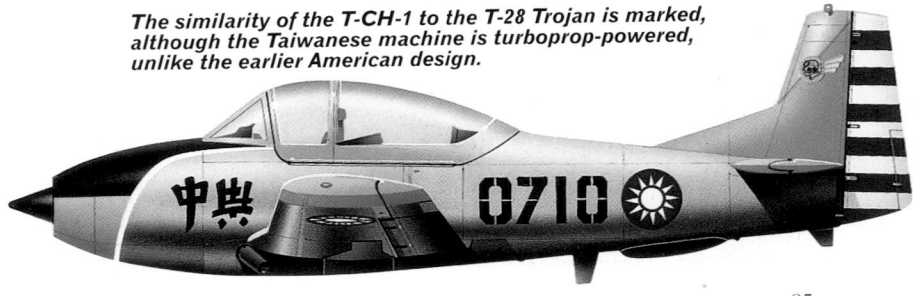

This camouflaged T-CH-1 demonstrates the good visibility afforded both the instructor and pupil by the aircraft's large canopy.

at Tainan, where some 15 examples now remain in service with the revised designation **A-CH-1**; although the T-CH-1 had not been fitted with armament during its period of service at the academy, all the aircraft had been built with underwing hardpoints and their adaptation to A-CH-1 weapons trainer standard was thus a comparatively simple matter. A few more aircraft have a reconnaissance

camera installed in the lower fuselage and operate

with the revised designation **R-CH-1**.

SPECIFICATION

AIDC T-CH-1 Chung Tsing
Type: two-seat basic flying trainer with armament training capability
Powerplant: one Textron Lycoming T53-L-701 turboprop rated at 1,450 ehp (1081 kW)
Performance: maximum level speed 'clean' at 15,000 ft (4570 m) 368 mph (592 km/h); maximum cruising speed at 15,000 ft (4570 m) 253 mph (407 km/h); maximum rate of climb at sea level 3,400 ft

(1036 m) per minute; service ceiling 32,000 ft (9755 m); range 1,249 miles (2010 km)
Weights: empty equipped 5,750 lb (2608 kg); normal take-off 7,500 lb (3402 kg); maximum take-off 11,150 lb (5057 kg)
Fuel: 255 US gal (963 litres)
Dimensions: wingspan 40 ft (12.19 m); length 33 ft 8 in (10.26 m); height 12 ft (3.66 m); wing area 271.00 sq ft (25.18 m²)

AIDC XC-2

In January 1973, the AIDC started work on its second type, the **XC-2** transport aircraft, that was designed to appeal to both civil and military operators through its possession of such features as a quick-change cabin and its ability to operate from short airfields with unprepared surfaces.

The aircraft that emerged from this process was of the classic airlifter layout, with a high-set wing, upswept rear fuselage with a rear ramp/loading door and retractable tricycle landing gear, with the single-wheel main units retracting into external sponsons that left the hold clear of obstructions for the payload.

The XC-2 was of standard stressed-skin construction in light alloy with a high-set flightdeck which provided accommodation for the flight crew of three. To the rear of this was a cabin 26 ft 6½ in (8.095 m) long, with a

width of 8 ft 5 in (2.57 m) and a height of 7 ft 3½ in (2.23 m); access was provided by one starboard- and two port-side doors.

The XC-2 prototype made its maiden flight on 26 February 1979, with the powerplant of two T53-L-701A turboprops driving three-bladed variable-pitch Hamilton Standard metal propellers. Limited test-flying was completed, but the programme was terminated without any commitment to a production model.

AIDC XC-2

SPECIFICATION

AIDC XC-2
Type: short/medium-range medium transport aircraft
Powerplant: two Avco Lycoming T53-L-701A turboprops each rated at 1,450 ehp (1081 kW) for take-off
Performance: maximum speed at sea level 244 mph (392 km/h); maximum cruising speed at 10,000 ft (3050 m) 230 mph (370 km/h); maximum rate of climb at sea level 1,500 ft (457 m) per minute; service ceiling 26,300 ft

(8015 m); range 1,032 miles (1661 km) with maximum fuel, or 298 miles (400 km) with maximum payload
Weights: empty 15,500 lb (7031 kg); maximum take-off 27,500 lb (12474 kg)
Dimensions: wingspan 81 ft 8⅓ in (24.90 m); length 65 ft 11⅓ in (20.10 m); height 25 ft 3⅓ in (7.72 m); area 703.98 sq ft (65.40 m²)
Payload: up to 38 passengers or 8,500 lb (3855 kg) of freight

Although a design of some promise, the XC-2 failed to make any impression on either its home market or the already cluttered export market.

Air Tractor Model AT-300 Air Tractor series

Leland Snow, president of Air Tractor Inc. located at Olney, Texas, established the Snow Aeronautical Company in 1965 to manufacture and develop an agricultural aircraft of his own design. He was, almost certainly, better equipped than most to create a new and efficient 'agplane', for several years of experience as an agpilot had provided an acute appreciation of some of the shortcomings of existing aircraft within this category. The **Snow S-2A** and **S-2B** received certification on 2 April 1959 and 29 July

1958, respectively, and were followed by the improved **S-2C** before the company was acquired by the Rockwell Standard Corporation in 1965.

Leland Snow then established Air Tractor Inc. to build the **Air Tractor Model AT-300 Air Tractor** series as a new agricultural aircraft derived from the **S-2R**. Construction of the prototype/pre-production aircraft began in August 1972 after the design had been started in January 1971, and this machine made its maiden flight in September 1973.

The AT-302 is basically an AT-301 fitted with an Avco Lycoming (now Textron Lycoming) turboprop engine.

A cantilever low-wing monoplane of all-metal (steel and light alloy) construction except for the fabric-covered control surfaces on the tail unit,

A single Pratt & Whitney R-1340 powers the AT-301 and the AT-301B, which features a larger chemical hopper.

the initial **Model AT-301** has a wing whose trailing edge incorporates large Fowler flaps to facilitate short-field operations, and extensive care was taken in the design process to ensure that the fuselage structure was adequately sealed to prevent the ingress of corrosive chemicals. Similarly, the pilot's

enclosed cabin was sealed with ventilation by uncontaminated fresh air. Agricultural provisions comprise a 320-US gal (266.5-Imp gal; 1211-litre) chemical hopper and, under the trailing edge of the wing, a 72-nozzle spraybar as standard, with a spreader for dry chemicals optional.

Air Tractor Model AT-300 Air Tractor series (continued)

Although it shares the basic airframe of the AT-301, the AT-302 is easily distinguished by means of its turboprop engine mounted in a streamlined nose and its three-bladed propeller.

plant, while the **Model AT-302**, that first flew in June 1977, introduced turbine power in the form of one 600-shp (447-kW) Avco Lycoming LTP 101-600A1A turboprop, and this altered the length to 29 ft 6 in (8.99 m). It also led to other changes such as a maximum speed of 170 mph (274 km/h), maximum cruising speed of 165 mph (266 km/h), range of 400 miles (644 km) with maximum fuel, empty weight of 3,250 lb (1474 kg) equipped with spray gear, and maximum take-off weight of 6,600 lb (2994 kg).

The Model AT-300 series was produced in two main variants, of which the second spawned a subvariant. The **Model AT-301** is the baseline variant, as described on Sheet 40, with a piston-engined power-

The **Model AT-302A** is generally similar to the Model AT-302, but incorporates a higher capacity 400-US gal (333-Imp gal; 1514-litre) chemical hopper to allow for the economic dispersal of dry chemicals at high application rates after take-off at a maximum weight of 7,200 lb (3266 kg).

SPECIFICATION

Air Tractor Model AT-301 Air Tractor
Type: single-seat agricultural aircraft
Powerplant: one Pratt & Whitney R-1340 Wasp radial piston engine rated at 600 hp (447 kW) for take-off
Performance: maximum speed at sea level 165 mph (266 km/h); maximum cruising speed at 6,000 ft (1830 m) 150 mph (241 km/h); maximum rate of climb at sea level 1,600 ft (488 m) per minute; range 350 miles (563 km) with maximum fuel
Weights: empty equipped 3,650 lb (1656 kg); maximum take-off 6,900 lb (3130 kg)
Dimensions: wingspan 45 ft (13.72 m); length 27 ft (8.23 m); height 8 ft 6 in (2.59 m); wing area 270.00 sq ft (25.08 m²)

Air Tractor Model AT-400 Air Tractor series

An improved development of the AT-300 series, the **Air Tractor Model AT-400 Turbo Air Tractor** featured a larger 400-US gal (333-Imp gal; 1514-litre) hopper with a 3 ft 2-in (0.97-m) wide gate for the high-rate dispersal of dry chemicals, high-flotation landing gear with larger wheels and low-pressure tyres, a number of system improvements, and the

powerplant of one Pratt & Whitney PT6A-15AG turboprop rated at 680 shp (507 kW) and driving a constant-speed three-bladed Hartzell metal reversible-pitch propeller.

The Model AT-400 was otherwise similar to the Model AT-301. The basic type was then taken in hand for further development in several forms as the **Model AT-401**, **Model AT-401A**,

Model AT-401B, **Model AT-402** and **Model AT-402B**.

The Model AT-401 was developed in 1986 as an improved version of the Model AT-301 with the powerplant of one 600-hp (447-kW) Pratt & Whitney R-1340 Wasp radial piston engine. The aircraft features the larger hopper of the Model AT-400 and an enlarged wing.

The Model AT-401A was a development of the Model AT-401, with the revised powerplant of one PZL-3S Series 2 radial piston engine, a Polish unit rated at 592 hp (441.5 kW). Production of this variant was abandoned after the completion of just one example. The Model AT-401B is the successor to the Model AT-401 with Hoerner downward-curved wingtips for a span of 51 ft 1¼ in (15.57 m), and is the current production variant

Depending on the operating environment and available funds, some customers prefer the piston-power of the AT-401.

of the Model AT-401 family.

The Model AT-402 is a development of the Model AT-400 with the larger wing of the Model AT-401, and first flew in August 1988.

The type was later improved with the Hoerner wingtips to become the Model AT-402B that is the current production version of the AT-400 series.

SPECIFICATION

Air Tractor Model AT-400 Turbo Air Tractor
Type: single-seat agricultural aircraft
Powerplant: one Pratt & Whitney Canada PT6A-15AG, -27 or -28 turboprop rated at 680 shp (507 kW) for take-off
Performance: maximum speed at sea level 200 mph (322 km/h) without spray equipment and 185 mph (298 km/h) with spray equipment; cruising speed, economical at 8,000 ft (2440 m)
165 mph (265 km/h) without spray equipment for ferrying; working speed at low level 130-145 mph (209-233 km/h); maximum rate of climb at sea level 1,500 ft (457 m) per minute
Weights: empty equipped 3,739 lb (1696 kg); maximum take-off 7,800 lb (3538 kg)
Dimensions: wingspan 45 ft 1¼ in (13.75 m); length 29 ft 6 in (8.99 m); height 8 ft 6 in (2.59 m); area 270.00 sq ft (25.08 m²)

Air Tractor Model AT-500 series

In the mid-1980s, the next step in the process of Air Tractor evolution was taken with the **Air Tractor Model AT-500** (now no longer named the Air Tractor) that was, in essence, an improved version of the Model AT-401 with the same powerplant, but with a number of structural improvements (longer and wider fuselage using increased-diameter steel tubing in its structure), and the payload hopper in the forward fuselage ahead of the cockpit increased in capacity to 418 Imp gal (1900 litres) to allow effective deployment with lower-density fertilisers.

The Model AT-500 spawned a number of variants including the **Model AT-501**, **Model AT-501A**, **Model AT-502**, **Model AT-502B**, **Model AT-503** and **Model AT-503A**. A

Representing little more than an improved AT-400, the AT-500 introduced a revised structure and increased chemical capacity.

generally similar **Model AT-602** has also been built. The Model AT-501 was certificated in June 1987 with provision for easy conversion to turboprop power in the field.

The Model AT-502 first flew in April 1987 as a development of the Model AT-503 and the first were delivered later that same year as turbine-powered 'agplanes' with one Pratt & Whitney Canada PT6A-15AG, -27 or -28 turboprop rated at 680 shp (507 kW) or PT6A-34 or -34AG turboprop rated at 750 shp (559 kW). A sub-variant of the AT-502, the Model AT-502B, has a wing of

thicker section and 2 ft (0.61 m) greater span, with Hoerner downward-curved tips. The longer wingspan has led to the 502B having an improved take-off and climb performance compared to the AT-502. A

further sub-variant of the Model AT-502 is the Model AT-502A, intended for operations in mountainous areas. It first flew in February 1992, with changes that included a larger vertical tail surface

and the revised powerplant of one 1,100-shp (820-kW) PT6A-45R turboprop driving a five-bladed Hartzell slow-turning propeller. It also shares with the AT-502B its increased wingspan.

Development of the

In addition to the AT-502 (illustrated), Air Tractor has developed the similar AT-602 to fill the gap in its range between the AT-502B and AT-802A.

SPECIFICATION

Air Tractor Model AT-502B Air Tractor
Type: single-seat agricultural aircraft
Powerplant: one Pratt & Whitney PT6A-15AG, -27 or -28 turboprop rated at 680 shp (507 kW), or one Pratt & Whitney Canada PT6A-34 or -34AG turboprop rated at 750 shp (559 kW) for take-off
Performance: (PT6A-34AG engine) maximum speed at sea level 180 mph (290 km/h); cruising speed

at 8,000 ft (2440 m) 157 mph (253 km/h); working speed 120-145 mph (193-233 km/h); maximum rate of climb at sea level 925 ft (282 m) per minute; range 500 miles (805 km)
Weights: empty equipped 4,300 lb (1950 kg); maximum take-off 9,500 lb (4309 kg)
Dimensions: wing span 52 ft (15.85 m); length 32 ft 6 in (9.91 m); height 9 ft 9½ in (2.99 m); area 312.00 sq ft (28.99 m²)

Model AT-503 was launched in September 1985 in response to a request from the Department of State for an aircraft to be used in the anti-narcotics effort and is, in essence, a development of the Model AT-400/401 with a fuselage lengthened by 1 ft 10 in (0.56 m) to allow the incorporation of a revised two-seat cockpit, allowing the type to be used as a trainer as well as for field operations. The sole Model AT-503 first flew on 25 April 1986 and was later sold to Spain for firefighting use, and the Model AT-503A production variant was similar, although based on the Model AT-502, with the empty weight increased to 4,480 lb (2032 kg). Three AT-503As were built, the last being delivered in 1991.

Air Tractor Model AT-800 series

By the late 1980s, the continued demand for 'agplanes', combined with the growing requirement for firefighting aircraft, persuaded Leland Snow that the time was ripe for the development of a new larger, more powerful aircraft than his company's current machines. The result was the **Air Tractor Model AT-800** series, the design of which was launched in July 1989, with the maiden flight of the first of two prototypes on 30 October 1990.

The greater size and weight of this new model required a higher-rated version of the PT6A turbo-prop that was the standard engine for the later aircraft of the turbine-engined series of Air Tractors, in this instance driving a constant-speed five-bladed and reversible-pitch Hartzell metal propeller, and the fuel capacity was increased to a standard figure of 250 US gal (208 Imp gal; 946 litres). Provision was also made for a payload of 810 US gal (674 Imp gal;

3066 litres) of agricultural chemical, firefighting retardant or water in two large fuselage tanks (installed between the cockpit and the engine) and one small tank in the ventral fairing that accommodated the gate box.

The three current variants of the Model AT-800 series are the **Model AT-802**, **Model AT-802A** and **Model AT-802AF**. Certificated in April 1993, the Model AT-802 is a two-seat agricultural and training version, while the Model AT-802A first flew on 6 July 1992 and is the single-seat counterpart of the Model AT-802, with the same powerplant and weight options. The Model AT-802AF is the firefighting counterpart of the Model AT-802A with single-seat accommodation.

The Model AT-802 provides accommodation for a second crewmember or for training purposes.

SPECIFICATION

Air Tractor Model AT-802AF
Type: single-seat firefighting aircraft
Powerplant: one Pratt & Whitney Canada PT6A-67AG or -67AF turboprop rated at 1,350 shp (1007 kW) for take-off
Performance: maximum speed at sea level 210 mph (338 km/h); maximum cruising speed at 5,500 ft (1675 m) 195 mph (314 km/h); maximum rate of climb

at sea level 800 ft (244 m) per minute; service ceiling 13,000 ft (3960 m); range 500 miles (805 km)
Weights: empty equipped 6,300 lb (2858 kg) as a sprayer or 6,670 lb (3025 kg) as a firefighter; maximum take-off 16,000 lb (7257 kg)
Dimensions: wingspan 58 ft (17.68 m); length 36 ft 4 in (11.07 m); height 11 ft (3.35 m); area 391.00 sq ft (36.33 m²)

Air & Space Model 18-A

Based at Muncie, Indiana, between 1962 and 1968, the Air & Space Manufacturing Inc. had as its sole product a modified version of the **Umbaugh Model 18-A** autogyro. The **Model 18-A** provided tandem two-seat accommodation in an enclosed cabin with dual controls and a large starboard-side door.

The three-bladed wood, metal and glassfibre rotor was carried at the top of a substantial pylon on the centre of gravity position. The powerplant was located at the rear of the fuselage pod to drive a constant-speed two-bladed Hartzell pusher propeller.

The Model 18-A was certificated early in 1965, and deliveries by the end of the same year amounted to a total of 110 machines, with others following before Air & Space went out of business.

SPECIFICATION

Air & Space Model 18-A
Type: two-seat autogyro
Powerplant: one Avco Lycoming O-360 flat-four piston engine rated at 180 hp (134 kW) for take-off
Performance: maximum speed at optimum altitude 110 mph (177 km/h); maximum cruising speed at optimum altitude 100 mph (161 km/h); maximum rate of climb at sea level 710 ft (216 m)

per minute; service ceiling 12,000 ft (3660 m); range 300 miles (483 km) with maximum payload
Weight: maximum take-off 1,800 lb (816 kg)
Dimensions: rotor diameter 35 ft (10.67 m); length overall 19 ft 10 in (6.05 m); height 9 ft 3 in (2.82 m); rotor disk area 962.11 sq ft (89.38 m²)

Having achieved some sales success in the 1960s, the Model 18-A was placed back into low-rate production by US-based Farrington Aircraft in 1991.

Airbus Industrie A300

During 1965-66, there were various alignments of European manufacturers making design proposals for a new short-range transport aircraft. Hawker Siddeley, Breguet and Nord came up with five separate proposals, and considerable interest was expressed in their first HBN-100 concept with a powerplant of what were then new-technology turbofan engines, and a seating capacity of 200-300 passengers. Sud came up with a very similar design, the 241/269-seat Galion, offered in conjunction with Dassault. These two proposals were then considered in detail and, even at this very early stage, there was no doubt that development costs would necessitate international co-operation. West Germany was therefore invited to join a consortium for the design, development and manufacture of a European 'airbus' which would be based on the HBN-100 design proposal. Arbeitsgemeinschaft Airbus was the initial title of the West German industrial representative on the consortium, this becoming Deutsche Airbus GmbH on 4 September 1967. Hawker Siddeley was selected as the British partner, with the French element provided not by Nord but by Sud, which had considerable collaborative experience with British companies as a result of the Aérospatiale/BAC Concorde project.

On 28 May 1969, France and West Germany decided to go ahead with development of the European 'airbus' as the **A300**, and construction of the first machine began in September 1969. Unfortunately, the lack of enthusiasm and orders for this project resulted in the British government refusing to become a member of the consortium. At great risk to itself, Hawker Siddeley therefore undertook to meet part of the development costs itself. Later, the Netherlands and Spain, represented by Fokker-VFW and Construcciones Aeronauticas SA (CASA) respectively, joined the manufacturing group.

In December 1970, Airbus Industrie was established to manage the A300 programme. Aérospatiale, of which Sud-Aviation had become a part, was responsible for the manufacture of the entire forward fuselage, lower centre fuselage and engine pylons, and also for final assembly. Deutsche Airbus was concerned with the major proportion of the fuselage structure (including the forward fuselage between the flight deck and wing box, upper centre fuselage and rear fuselage) and the vertical tail surfaces. Hawker Siddeley Aviation (now British Aerospace) designed the advanced wing, and worked in collaboration with Fokker-VFW (later Fokker) which was responsible for the manufacture of the wing's moving surfaces. CASA was responsible for the horizontal tail surfaces, fuselage main doors, and landing gear doors.

Twin General Electric CF6 turbofans were selected for the A300 and mounted in pods carried by forward-swept pylons beneath the wings. A licence agreement was signed for the assembly of the engine in France by the Société Nationale d'Etude et de Construction des Moteurs (SNECMA) using a large proportion of components made by SNECMA and Motoren- und Turbinen-Union (MTU).

After construction of the first development aircraft began in 1969, there was only one major change in the airframe design – an increase of 3 in (8 cm) in the diameter of the fuselage, in order to make the freight holds compatible with those of US-standard freight containers.

An advanced feature of the A300 is the Hawker Siddeley-designed wing. This has moderate quarter-chord sweep of 28° and a section which provides good distribution of lift across the entire wing chord. This has allowed the construction of a thicker and structurally more efficient wing, which enhances low-speed performance and also offers greater fuel capacity. The A300's all-speed ailerons droop automatically when the flaps are operated, and its Fowler flaps increase wing chord by 25 per cent when fully extended.

Accommodation varies according to role and the requirements of individual airlines, with a flight crew of three and cabin seating arrangements for between 220 and 336 according to layout (six-, seven-, eight- or nine-abreast with two aisles) and seat pitch.

The first **A300A1** made the type's maiden flight on 28 October 1972, the second similar aircraft following on 5 February 1973. The first two **A300B2** aircraft, representing the basic production version, flew on 28 June and 20 November 1973, respectively, and these four aircraft flew a combined total of almost 1,600 hours before French and West German certification was awarded on 15 March 1974. The US Federal Aviation Administration granted certification on 30 May 1974 and included clearance for automatic approach and landing in Category II weather conditions, upgraded to Category IIIa on 30 September 1974. The A300B2 entered service with Air France on 30 May 1974, operating on the route between Paris and London. Continuing operations proved that the claims of the marketing team had not been exaggerated, for the A300B was economical and reliable and, in addition, the ground crews found it easy to operate and maintain.

Nevertheless, orders were slow to materialise, and it seemed that, once again, a European airliner, despite its excellence, had failed to break into a market dominated by the US aircraft industry.

However, there was a major change of fortune in 1978, starting on 6 April when Eastern Air Lines bought four **A300B4** machines which it had been operating on an evaluation basis for six months, and then followed with an order for 25 more aircraft with another nine on option. In fact, during 1978, a total of 70 firm orders and 27 options was gained, more than doubling the order book. In 1978, Airbus' decision to proceed with A310 development led the British government to become a risk-sharing partner of the group.

By September 1997, sales of the A300 series amounted to 488 aircraft (including 248 of the original A300B series).

The current version, the

With the addition of a trim fuel tank in its tailplane, the long-range A300-600R achieves a maximum range of 4,775 miles (7685 km) with a load of 266 passengers and their baggage.

A300B/C variants

A300B1: initial version, two built
A300B2 (later **A300B2-200**): with CF6-50 turbofans, fuselage stretched by 8 ft 8 in (2.65 m)
A300B2K (later **A300B2-200**): with wing root leading-edge flaps for improved field performance
A300B2-220: with JT9D-59A turbofans
A300B2-320: as B2-220 but with higher empty and landing weights
A300B4 (later A300B4-100): long-range version
A300B4-120: B4-100 with JT9D turbofans
A300B4-200: higher-weight version
A300B4-200FF: with two-crew flight deck
A300C4: convertible passenger/freight version with reinforced cabin floor and other changes

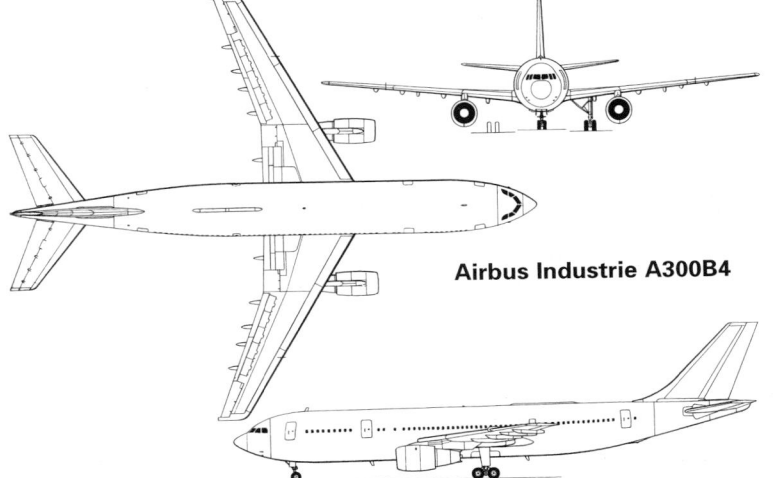

Airbus Industrie A300B4

SPECIFICATION

Airbus Industrie A300-600 (Improved Version)
Type: large-capacity short-/medium-range transport
Powerplant: two General Electric CF6-80C2A1 turbofans each rated at 59,000 lb st (262.45 kN)
Performance: maximum cruising speed 557 mph (897 km/h) at 30,000 ft (9145 m); economical cruise 543 mph (875 km/h) at 31,000 ft (9450 m); maximum operating altitude 40,000 ft (12190 m); range 4,297 miles (6852 km) with 266 passengers and baggage
Weights: empty operating 198,665 lb (90115 kg); maximum take-off 363,755 lb (165000 kg)
Dimensions: wingspan 147 ft 1 in (44.84 m); length 177 ft 5 in (54.08 m); height 54 ft 3 in (16.53 m); wing area 2,798.71 sq ft (260.00 m²)
Payload: between 266 and 375 passengers depending on layout and seat pitch, or up to 87,391 lb (39885 kg) of freight

Lufthansa was an early customer for the A300, initially ordering 11, including this A300B2-100.

A300-600, was developed from the A300B4-200 and first flown on 8 July 1983. This has greater passenger and freight capacity as a result of the introduction of the rear fuselage of the A310, with the pressure bulkhead moved farther aft to allow the incorporation of two more seat rows. Other changes to improve the type's payload/range characteristics include the use of simplified systems and composites in the secondary structure for reduced weight, a wing revised with simple Fowler flaps and greater trailing-edge camber, a two-man EFIS flight deck and new digital avionics.

The new model entered service with JT9D-7R4H1 turbofans, while an **Improved Version** followed in 1985 with CF6-80C2 or Pratt & Whitney PW4000 series turbofans, as well as carbon discs on the undercarriage brakes, wingtip fences, and a 'new world' flight deck. Later developments have included the **A300-600R** extended-range model that entered service in 1988 with a fuel trim tank in the tailplane; the **A300-600 Convertible**, analogous to the A300C4 with provision for up to 375 passengers, or 102,710 lb (46590 kg) of freight, or a mix of passengers and freight; and the **A300-600 Freighter** a dedicated cargo carrier with provision for up to 121,290 lb (55017 kg) of freight.

Airbus Industrie A310

With the A300 in service, a number of European operators expressed growing enthusiasm for a version of about 200-seat capacity, especially if such an airliner could offer fuel economy similar to that demonstrated by the A300B2/B4 already in service. Motivated by this growing interest, Airbus Industrie finalised the design of the smaller-capacity variant, now identified as the **A310** and, in July 1978, the decision was taken to proceed with its development. The manufacturing process made maximum exploitation of commonality of components (structure and systems) between the A300 and the A310, for the latter is basically a variant of the former with the fuselage shortened by 13 frames. Changes included new engine pylons, modification of the landing gear and tail unit, a new wing specially designed by British Aerospace, and a re-profiled rear fuselage allowing the seating to be extended farther aft. The wing was claimed to be aerodynamically more efficient throughout the entire flight regime than the earlier design and this combined with optimum use of the available cabin space to enable the A310 to demonstrate an exceptional 'fuel per seat' factor after it entered service in April 1983.

The A310 made its maiden flight on 3 April 1982 and the type received preliminary French and

Almost full-span trailing-edge flaps are a feature of both the A300 and A310, although the A310 has an entirely new wing design.

West German certification in March 1983, when initial deliveries were also made to Lufthansa and Swissair for service from the following month. Category IIIa and IIIb certifications followed from the European authority in September 1983 and November 1984 respectively, and US Federal Aviation Administration certification was awarded early in 1985.

The A310 had originally been planned in **A310-100** and **A310-200** forms for short- and medium-range operations, respectively, but the -100 was cancelled and the -200 was then developed from an original maximum take-off weight of 266,755 lb (121000 kg) to 305,555 lb (138600 kg) standard, and 313,050 lb (142000 kg) optional with increased fuel capacity. As launched, the A310-200 had the choice of two turbofan engine types, namely the General Electric CF6-80A3 rated at 50,000 lb st (222.41 kN) or the Pratt & Whitney JT9D-7R4D1 rated at 48,000 lb st (213.51 kN), in each case supplied from tankage for 12,098 Imp gal (14,530 US gal/55000 litres) of fuel. Uprated engines that later became available included the CF6-80C2, PW4152 and PW4156A at ratings up to 59,000 lb st (262.45 kN).

Accommodation in the first production model comprised a standard two-man flight crew (with seats for another two), and between 210 and 280 passengers in a cabin that could be laid out with six-, seven-, eight- or nine-abreast seating with two aisles. The total payload was 72,443 lb (32860 kg) including freight or baggage in up to 13 LD3 standard containers carried in a hold under the passenger cabin.

Sub-variants of the A310-200 are the **A310-200C** convertible passenger/freight variant, of which the first was delivered in November 1984, and the **A310-200F** pure freighter version. Further development of the basic airliner resulted in the **A310-300**, which is an extended-range passenger variant that was certificated in, and delivered from, April 1986. The -300 introduced the small triangular wingtip fences that were also added to the A310-200 from this time. The basic maximum take-off weight was raised to 330,695 lb (150000 kg) to allow an increase in fuel capacity by the addition of tankage in the tailplane in a fashion that also permitted an improvement in fuel-burn efficiency by making possible precise in-flight trimming of the aircraft. Provision was also made for two additional fuel tanks in the centre section.

The A310-300 was additionally offered with three maximum take-off weight options higher than the standard figure. The first A310-300 flew on 8 July 1985, and deliveries began in December of the same year. By September 1997, Airbus Industrie had received orders for 260 such aircraft, including five delivered to the Canadian Armed Forces with the designation **CC-150 Polaris**.

From the time of its first flight, the A310 proved to be even more efficient than its designers had hoped. The aircraft remains in widespread airline service.

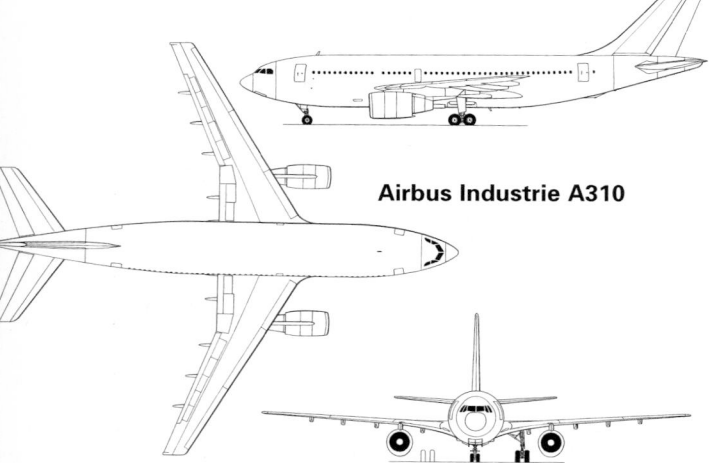

Airbus Industrie A310

SPECIFICATION	
Airbus Industrie A310-300	take-off weight of 361,560 lb
Type: large-capacity short-/	(164000 kg)
medium-range transport	**Weights:** empty operating
Powerplant: two Pratt & Whitney	between 177,130 lb and 178,135 lb
PW4156A turbofans each rated at	(80344 kg and 80801 kg); maximum
56,000 lb st (249.10 kN)	take-off between 330,675 lb and
Performance: economical cruising	361,560 lb (150000 kg and
speed 528 mph (850 km/h)	164000 kg)
between 31,000 ft and 41,000 ft	**Dimensions:** wingspan 144 ft
(9450 m and 12495 m); range	(43.89 m); length 153 ft 1 in
5,005 miles (8056 km), with	(46.66 m); height 51 ft 10 in
220 passengers and 230-mile	(15.80 m); wing area 2,357.37 sq ft
(370-km) diversion, or 5,523 miles	(219.00 m²)
(8889 km) with additional fuel and	**Payload:** see above within context
take-off weight of 346,125 lb	of a maximum payload between
(157000 kg), or 5,984 miles	70,805 lb and 70,896 lb (32117 kg
(9630 km) with additional fuel and	and 32158 kg)

Airbus Industrie A319

The technical and commercial success of its A320 airliner persuaded Airbus Industrie that there was scope for versions of this model with shorter and longer fuselages for lesser and greater passenger payloads, respectively. The **Airbus Industrie A319** short-fuselage model was the second of these to be launched, with the A319 sales effort beginning in May 1992 and the programme being officially launched in June 1993. The

major factor differentiating the A319 from the A320 is the fuselage, which is seven frames shorter in the A319, giving a typical two-class accommodation for 124 passengers. In overall terms, however, the two types are very closely related, and this has the added attraction that there is a common pilot rating for all three members of the A320 family.

Final assembly of the first A319-100 began in March 1996, and this aircraft made the type's

maiden flight in September 1996 to begin a certification programme that was successfully completed to allow the delivery of the first aircraft to Swissair in time to start revenue-earning services in May 1996. Unlike the earlier series of the Airbus Industrie family of airliners, which are assembled in France, the A319 is assembled in Germany by what is now known as Daimler-Benz Aerospace Airbus.

The basic **A319** has a maximum take-off weight of 141,095 lb (64000 kg), but the A319 is also

The first A319 was the 546th aircraft of the A319/A320/A321 family to be completed.

offered in increased fuel capacity options with maximum take-off weights of 149,910 lb, 154,320 lb and 166,445 lb (68000 kg, 70000 kg and 75500 kg),

The similarity of the A319 to the A320 is marked, although the shorter fuselage of the A319 is obvious.

respectively, and also as a corporate jet as the **A319CJ**, for delivery from 1999. Seven additional fuel tanks allow the A319CJ to carry 10 passengers in considerable luxury over a range of 7,208 miles (11600 km). By September 1997 Airbus had received orders for some 148 A319s.

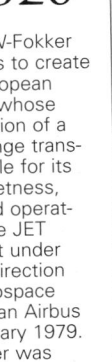

SPECIFICATION	
Airbus Industrie A319 **Type:** medium-capacity short-/medium-range transport **Powerplant:** two CFM International CFM56-5A4 or IAE V2522-A5 turbofans, each rated at 22,000 lb st (97.86 kN) dry; or alternatively two CFM International CFM56-5A5 or IAE V2524-5 turbofans, each rated at 23,500 lb st (105.53 kN) **Performance:** maximum cruising speed 561 mph (903 km/h) at 39,000 ft (11885 m); economical cruise 514 mph (827 km/h) at	39,000 ft (11885 m); range 2,186 miles (3518 km), with maximum payload and reserves for a 230-mile (370-km) diversion **Weights:** empty operating 88,535 lb (40160 kg); maximum take-off 141,095 lb (64000 kg) **Dimensions:** wingspan 111 ft 3 in (33.91 m); length 110 ft 11 in (33.80 m); height 38 ft 8½ in (11.80 m); wing area 1,317.55 sq ft (122.40 m²) **Payload:** see above within the context of a maximum payload of 37,125 lb (16840 kg)

Airbus Industrie A320

In June 1981, the Airbus Industrie consortium decided to launch a new short-/medium-range airliner in the 150-seat category. This decision followed about 10 years of preliminary design activity, directly or indirectly involving all the major European aircraft manufacturers, both separately and in a number of collaborative teams. In 1977, Aérospatiale linked with British Aerospace of the UK, MBB of West

Germany and VFW-Fokker of the Netherlands to create the JET (Joint European Transport) group, whose aim was the creation of a short-/medium-range transport aircraft notable for its 'new order of quietness, fuel efficiency and operating economy'. The JET work was brought under Airbus Industrie direction when British Aerospace formally became an Airbus partner on 1 January 1979.

The new airliner was

Such is the popularity of the A320 that the type has made considerable inroads into the sales of Boeing and, in the past, McDonnell Douglas, even in the US market which has traditionally been dominated by the latter manufacturers.

SPECIFICATION	
Airbus Industrie A320-200 (highest-weight option) **Type:** medium-capacity short-/medium-range transport **Powerplant:** two CFM International CFM56-5B4 turbofans each rated at 26,500 lb st (117.88 kN), or two IAE V2525-A5 turbofans each rated at 25,000 lb st (111.21 kN) **Performance:** maximum cruising speed 561 mph (903 km/h), at 39,000 ft (11885 m); economical cruise 518 mph (834 km/h) at 39,000 ft (11885 m); take-off run 8,795 ft (2680 m); range 3,395 miles (5463 km), with 150 passengers and provision for a	230-mile (370-km) diversion **Weights:** empty operating between 92,113 lb and 92,746 lb (41782 kg and 42069 kg); maximum take-off between 162,040 lb and 169,755 lb (73500 kg and 77000 kg) **Dimensions:** wingspan 113 ft 3 in (33.91 m); length 123 ft 3 in (37.57 m); height 38 ft 8½ in (11.80 m); wing area 1,317.55 sq ft (122.40 m²) **Payload:** between 150 and 179 passengers, plus baggage and freight up to a total of between 41,735 lb and 42,372 lb (18931 kg and 19220 kg), in the highest- and lowest-weight options respectively

generally described as a '150-seat' machine as this was currently the typical mixed-class capacity considered probable to meet the requirements of airlines in the closing stages of the 20th century. At the time of the marketing launch, there was still interest in a larger capacity, however, so the type was offered in **A320-100** and **A320-200** forms with different fuselage lengths offering 154- and 172-seat capacities. Air France was the first to

announce an intention to purchase the A320 in both these versions. However, in March 1984, Airbus decided to trim its plans to a single-length fuselage providing accommodation for 162 passengers, but in an aircraft offered at two weight options with different fuel capacities, and it was to these configurations that the A320-100 and A320-200 designations were now applied. Although it bears a very strong family relationship to

the preceding A300 and A310 in terms of its basic layout, the A320 was a completely new design that nonetheless made full use of the structural and aerodynamic ideas that had proved so successful in the A300 and A310. Much use is made of the latest materials (including composites, employed for elements of the primary structure for the first time in a commercial transport) and also of advanced-technology features in the aircraft's

Distinctive wingtip fences were introduced on the A320-200. These devices increase wing efficiency which, in turn, decreases fuel burn.

systems and equipment. The most important of these advanced-technology features include a quadruplex fly-by-wire control system, sidestick controllers for the two

pilots who make up the entire flight crew, computerised control functions, an electronic flight instrumentation system and electronic centralised aircraft monitor. The A320

is the world's first commercial transport aircraft with fly-by-wire and sidestick controller systems, in this instance the Thomson-CSF/SFENA digital system.

Development and

construction of the A320 is shared between the Airbus Industrie partners in the same way as for the A300 and A310, and the primary responsibilities are exercised by British Aerospace (24 per cent of the work share) for the wing, Aérospatiale (34 per cent) for the forward fuselage and nose, Deutsche Airbus (35 per cent) for the centre and rear fuselage, CASA (5 per cent) for the rear fuselage panels and tailplane, and Belairbus (2 per cent) for the leading edge of the wing.

The first A320 made the type's maiden flight on 22 February 1987, and European certification for the A320-100 was granted in February 1988, allowing deliveries to be made from March of the same year. Certification of the A320-200 followed in November 1988. Both variants were initially delivered with CFM56-5A1 turbofans each rated at 23,500 lb st

(104.53 kN). Aircraft with IAE V2500-A1 turbofans each rated at 25,000 lb st (111.21 kN) followed, after revised certification in April 1989. The important American certifications of the variants with the CFM and IAE engines were granted in December 1988 and July 1989, respectively. Production of the A320-100 totalled only 21 aircraft and, with the end of this run, the **A320-200** became just the **A320** as the standard model in the range. This model is otherwise differentiated from the A320-100 by the delta-shaped fences at its wingtips, tankage in the wing centre section for an additional 1,763 Imp gal (2,118 US gal/8016 litres) of fuel, and a higher maximum take-off weight. By September 1997, Airbus Industrie had received orders for 816 A320-200 (or A320) aircraft, the later examples with uprated engine options.

Airbus Industrie A321

The **A321** long-fuselage model was the first of the A320 derivatives to reach the market. The programme was announced in May 1989 and officially launched in November of that year. The A321 fuselage is lengthened by 22 ft 9 in (6.94 m) compared to that of the A320. This 'stretch' was created by the insertion of plugs fore and aft of the wing, these measuring 14 ft (4.67 m) and 8 ft 9 in (2.67 m), respectively, in length. This lengthening increased the typical accommodation to 200 passengers in a single class all-economy layout, or 185 in a dual first- and economy-class arrangement. Other less obvious changes were the replacement of the over-wing emergency exits by hatches in the new plugs, modification of the fuel system, a measure of structural reinforcement to the airframe and landing gear, and an extension of the wing's trailing edge

with double-slotted flaps for improved field performance. In overall terms, therefore, the A321 is still very closely related to the preceding A320 and following A319.

The development programme was undertaken with four aircraft, built at Daimler-Benz Aerospace Airbus company's new final assembly facility at Hamburg, Germany. The first of these new aircraft made the type's maiden flight on 11 March 1993 with two IAE V2530-A5 turbofans, each rated at 30,000 lb st (133.45 kN). The second followed in May 1993 with the alternative powerplant of two identically-rated CFM International CFM56-5B turbofans. The A321 received European certification with these different powerplants in December 1993 and February 1994 respectively, and the first delivery was made to Lufthansa during January

With its extended fuselage, the A321 offers accommodation which fits neatly between the maximum capacity of the Boeing 737-400 and the standard lowest-density seating arrangement of the Boeing 757. Thus, depending on operator requirements, the A321 is able to compete with both US types.

1994, revenue-earning services starting in March of the same year.

The baseline **A321-100** has a maximum take-off weight of 182,980 lb (83000 kg) with a fuel capacity of 5,213 Imp gal (23700 litres), and has since been complemented by an extended-range version, the **A321-200**. This model was launched in April 1995 with an order from Aero Lloyd and is

intended mainly for the holiday charter type of operation, as well as North American domestic services. Among the changes are a reinforced structure, higher-thrust versions of the same two basic engine alternatives, including the CFM International CFM56-5B2 turbofan rated at 31,000 lb st (137.89 kN), and additional tankage, adding 638 Imp gal (2900 litres) to the overall fuel capacity for a range boost of up to 460 miles

(740 km) despite an increase in the maximum take-off weight to 196,200 lb (88995 kg).

The first A321-200 was delivered to Airworld/International Lease Finance Corporation in March 1997, and Airbus has now offered developments of this model with weight increased to 205,025 lb (93000 kg), with still further enlargement of the fuel capacity for a range of up to 3,417 miles (5500 km). By September 1997 Airbus had received orders for 220 A321s.

With the A320 already in service, pre-certification trials of the A321 were relatively swift. Here the minimum 'un-stick' speed is being investigated.

SPECIFICATION
Airbus Industrie A321-100 **Type:** medium-capacity short-/medium-range transport **Powerplant:** two CFM International CFM56-5B1 or IAE V2530-A5 turbofans, each rated at 30,000 lb st (133.45 kN) **Performance:** maximum cruising speed 561 mph (903 km/h) at 39,000 ft (11885 m); economical cruise 522 mph (840 km/h) at 39,000 ft (11885 m); take-off run (with CFM56-5B1 engines) 7,515 ft (2290 m) range 2,646 miles	(4259 km) with maximum payload and reserves for a 230-mile (370-km) diversion **Weights:** empty operating 105,495 lb (47852 kg); maximum take-off 182,980 lb (83000 kg) **Dimensions:** wing span 111 ft 10 in (34.09 m); length 146 ft 10 in (44.51 m); height 38 ft 9 in (11.81 m); wing area 1,317.55 sq ft (122.40 m²) **Payload:** maximum payload of 47,725 lb (21648 kg); seating details in text

Airbus Industrie A330

On 5 June 1987, after the completion of a project study lasting several years, Airbus Industrie began a programme for the full development, marketing and production of the **Airbus Industrie A330** and A340 as a pair of advanced airliners able to compete in technical and cost terms with the latest American designs such as the Boeing Models 767 and 777. Both of the new Airbus aircraft were optimised for service with airlines operating long-distance routes with high passenger volumes, and were the first airliners 100 per cent created with the aid of a computer-aided design (CAD) system. The A330 and A340 share the same fuselage, tail unit, landing gear, flight deck and wing geometry. For the best combination of range and useful load capacity with low operating costs, the A330 was designed with a twin-engined power-plant for medium-/long-range routes, while the A340 was planned for very long range routes with a four-engined powerplant. The same basic wing is used by both types with the differences limited to

insignificant changes to the internal structure and leading-edge slats.

Both models profited considerably from the flight control technology developed for earlier Airbus aircraft, including their fly-by-wire control system with sidestick controllers, the advanced two-man 'glass' cockpit with an Electronic Flight Instrumentation System (EFIS) and an Electronic Centralised Aircraft Monitor (ECAM). The cross section of the circular fuselage matches that of the A300 and the A310, allowing the use of the same cabin equipment and reducing design and development costs.

As with all Airbus designs, the individual members of this European consortium are responsible for the development and manufacture of their respective parts of the A330 and A340. Aérospatiale makes the flight deck, engine pylons and part of the central fuselage and also undertakes final assembly at its facility located near Toulouse in south-western France; British Aerospace (supported by Textron

Aerospace of the USA as a sub-contractor) manufactures the wing; Daimler-Benz Aerospace Airbus fabricates most of the fuselage, fin and interior; CASA builds the tailplane; and Belairbus creates the leading-edge slats and the tracks on which they move.

Like other members of the Airbus family of wide- and narrow-body airliners, the key to the operating efficiency of the A330 is the wing, which is about 40 per cent larger in area than that of the A300-600, has a quarter-chord sweep of 30°, and is notable for the winglets extending upward, outward and rearward from its tips. These reduce cruising drag.

The first A330 made the type's maiden flight on 2 November 1992 with General Electric CF6-80E1A2 turbofans each rated at 67,500 lb st (300.25 kN), and of the two alternative powerplants the first to fly on the A330 was the higher thrust Rolls-Royce Trent 768/772 turbofan on 31 January 1994, followed by the Pratt & Whitney PW4164/4168 rated at 68,000 lb st (302.48 kN). European and American certification of the CF6-powered model was achieved in October 1993, allowing the start of deliveries to Air Inter in December of the same year for the launch of initial

revenue-earning services during the course of January 1994.

The A330 is currently offered in two variants, as the initial **A330-300** and, despite its lower designation number, the following **A330-200**. The A330-300 is the basic version with accommodation for between 335 and 440 passengers, and a power-plant of two CF6-80E1 turbofans, or two PW4164/4168 turbofans, or two Trent 768/772 turbofans of up to 71,100 lb st (316.27 kN). The A330-200 was first flown on 13 August 1997 for service from April 1998, initially with Canada 3000, and is essentially a version of the -300 offering reduced capacity, but a longer range, through the shortening of the fuselage by

17 ft 6 in (5.33 m) and the use of a strengthened wing derived from that of the A340-300. It can carry a maximum load of 380 passengers over a range of more than 6,215 miles (10000 km), or up to 253 passengers over a range of more than 7,455 miles (12000 km), after take-off at a maximum weight of 507,055 lb (230000 kg).

The **A330-400X** is a proposal for a stretched version of the A330-300, with similar weights and powerplant, for a two-class arrangement of 370 passengers, in a fuselage lengthened by 20 ft 10 in (6.35 m) and offering a full-load range of some 4,535 miles (7300 km).

By September 1997 Airbus Industrie had received 182 orders for A330 series aircraft.

Cathay Pacific opted for the Rolls-Royce Trent turbofan to power its fleet of A330s. The carrier also flies the longer-ranged A340.

SPECIFICATION

Airbus Industrie A330-300
Type: large-capacity medium-/long-range airliner
Powerplant: two General Electric CF6-80E1A2 turbofans, each rated at 67,500 lb st (300.25 kN); or two Pratt & Whitney PW4164/4168 turbofans, each rated at 68,000 lb st (302.48 kN); or two Rolls-Royce Trent 768/772 turbofans, each rated at up to 71,100 lb st (316.27 kN)
Performance: maximum cruising speed 576 mph (927 km/h) at 41,000 ft (12495 m); economical cruise 535 mph (862 km/h) at 39,000 ft (11885 m); service ceiling 41,000 ft (12495 m); range 5,178 miles (8334 km), with 335 passengers and reserves for a 230-mile (370-km) diversion
Weights: empty operating between 264,575 lb and 266,245 lb (120012 kg and 120851 kg); maximum take-off 467,375 lb (212000 kg)
Dimensions: wing span 197 ft 10 in (60.30 m); length 208 ft 10 in (63.65 m); height 54 ft 11 in (16.74 m); wing area 3,908.50 sq ft (363.10 m²)
Payload: maximum payload between 101,740 lb and 103,390 lb (46149 kg and 46988 kg)

The combination of range and payload capabilities offered by the A330 has allowed it to break into the highly competitive Far East market.

Airbus Industrie A340

The **Airbus Industrie A340** may be regarded as the ultra long-range counterpart of the A330, with a four- rather than two-engined powerplant. The two types were planned and developed in concert, and have basically the same airframe with the exception of the limited modifications to the wing structure and leading-edge slats required for the carriage of the A340's four turbofan engines.

The **A340-300**, the longer of the two four-engined models planned from the outset, made its

first flight at Toulouse on 25 October 1991. This machine was the first of six development aircraft, made up of four A340-300s and two shorter-fuselage **A340-200**s. The first A340-200 made its maiden flight on 1 April 1992.

Both types were granted their European certification in December 1992 and American certification in May 1993, some two months after both types had entered revenue-earning service, with Air France and Lufthansa respectively.

Four lower-powered engines give the A340 a greatly increased range on the same fuel capacity, when compared to the A330.

Air France and Lufthansa were the first airlines to place the A340 into service. The aircraft is now in widespread use and has found particular favour on extremely long-range routes, such as those to the Far East from Europe.

In a typical two-class layout the A340-300 accommodates 375 passengers as standard, or 440 passengers optional. Intended for longer-range operations, the A340-200 does not require the A340-300's two-wheel auxiliary main landing gear unit under the fuselage, and has its fuselage shortened by some two frames to 194 ft 10 in (59.39 m) for the carriage, in a typical three-class layout, of 263 passengers as standard, or 303 passengers as an option. Both versions were powered, in their initial production forms, by four CFM International CFM56-5C2 turbofans each rated at 31,200 lb st (138.78 kN), but later

options are the CFM56-5C3 rated at 32,500 lb st (144.57 kN), and the CFM56-5C4 rated at 34,000 lb st (151.24 kN). Fuel capacity for both A340 models is 30,488 Imp gal (138600 litres).

In April 1996 Singapore Airlines introduced the **A340-300 HGW** (High Gross Weight) variant originally known as the **A340-300X** and intended for longer-range services. This model has strengthened landing gear units, a beefed-up wing structure, the uprated powerplant of four CFM56-5C4 turbofans, and additional fuel capacity, increasing the range by 250 miles (400 km). At a maximum take-off weight

of 597,450 lb (271000 kg) it can carry a typical load of 295 passengers over a distance of 8,228 miles (13242 km).

The **A340-200 HGW** (otherwise **A340-8000**) features increased fuel capacity in the rear of the cargo hold, greater weights and the same powerplant as the A340-300 HGW, and is a very-long-range model with 232-seat accommodation for a range of some 9,195 miles (14800 km), after take-off at a maximum weight of 606,260 lb (275000 kg).

The **A340-300 Combi** is the combined passenger and freight version of the A340-300 with a large door to the main deck on the

left side of the rear fuselage. A typical load is four freight containers and 221 passengers in three classes.

There are a number of proposed variants. The **A340-500** is a longer-range version of the A340-300, with a wing enlarged by some 20 per cent for a span of 208 ft 8 in (63.6 m), carrying additional fuel for a capacity 48 per cent greater than that of the A340-300, a four rather than two-wheel auxiliary main landing gear unit on the centreline, and a powerplant of four Rolls-Royce Trent 500 turbofans each rated at 52,830 lb st (235 kN), for a range of 9,530 miles (15335 km) with 316 passengers, after take-off at a maximum weight of 784,830 lb (356000 kg). The **A340-600** is proposed as the high-capacity (up to 550 seats)

counterpart of the A340-500, with a fuel capacity 38 per cent greater than that of the A340-300, a fuselage lengthened by 24 ft 9 in (7.54 m), for the carriage of 372 passengers over a range of 8,675 miles (13960 km), after take-off at a maximum weight of 784,830 lb (356000 kg). The **A340M** is the projected military variant of the A340-300 basic version for various roles, such as personnel transport for up to 434 passengers, VIP passenger transport, pure freight flying, mixed transport for personnel and supplies (for example 295 persons and 20 tons of freight) with similar design to the A340-300 Combi, or for use as an inflight refuelling tanker.

By September 1997 Airbus had received 182 orders for the A340 series.

SPECIFICATION

Airbus A340-300
Type: large-capacity medium-/long-range transport
Powerplant: four CFM International CFM56-5C2 turbofans, each rated at 31,200 lb st (138.78 kN); or four CFM56-5C3 turbofans, each rated at 32,500 lb st (144.57 kN); or four CFM56-5C4 turbofans, each rated at 34,000 lb st (151.24 kN)
Performance: maximum cruising speed 569 mph (915 km/h) at 41,000 ft (12495 m); economical cruise 537 mph (864 km/h) at 39,000 ft (11885 m); range

7,710 miles (12416 km), with 295 passengers and reserves for a 230-mile (370-km) diversion
Weights: empty operating 279,700 lb (126873 kg); maximum take-off between 566,575 lb and 573,200 lb (257000 kg and 260000 kg)
Dimensions: wing span 197 ft 10 in (60.30 m); length 208 ft 10 in (63.65 m); height 54 ft 11 in (16.74 m); wing area 3,908.50 sq ft (363.10 m²)
Payload: maximum payload of 103,900 lb (47127 kg)

Airco (de Havilland) DH.1

The name Airco (an abbreviation for Aircraft Manufacturing Company) figured greatly in early British aviation history, the company being established by George Holt Thomas at Hendon during the early months of 1912. Holt Thomas had acquired rights for the manufacture in the UK of aircraft designed by the Farman brothers. After gaining experience in the

construction of these early aircraft, he decided to expand the company's field of endeavour by initiating indigenous design and, in June 1914, Holt Thomas engaged one of the country's most promising designers to head this department. This was Geoffrey (later Sir Geoffrey) de Havilland, who had already gained extensive experience at the Royal

Aircraft Factory, Farnborough.

The first design by de Havilland for Airco was the **Airco (de Havilland) DH.1**. The DH.1 was intended for use as a reconnaissance and interceptor type and, as a forward-firing machine-gun was considered essential for the latter role, a two-seat pusher layout was adopted. The DH.1 was a two-bay biplane with a

wire-braced wooden structure under a covering largely of fabric. The landing gear was of the fixed tailskid type and, in the prototype, first seen in January 1915, the main units incorporated coil spring and concealed oleo-struts for shock absorption. Another unusual feature of the prototype was the use of airbrakes, which were small aerofoil surfaces on each side of the fuselage nacelle which could be turned through 90° to present a flat surface to the airstream; these surfaces proved to be ineffective, however, and were

A combined total of 100 DH.1s and 1As was built. In spite of the apparent fragility of its open construction, the aircraft proved to be a useful combat machine for its time.

soon removed. Accommodation was provided for a pilot (aft) and an observer/gunner in the forward part of the fuselage nacelle, and at its rear was mounted a Renault inline engine driving a pusher propeller which rotated within the four tail booms.

The **DH.1A** was a derivative of the DH.1 with the originally intended powerplant of one Beardmore inline piston engine rated at 120 hp (89 kW). The use of this higher-rated engine resulted in a slightly improved performance and increased weights.

The DH.1 and DH.1A remained in service until early in 1917, the majority of the aircraft serving with training and Home Defence units, but a small number saw overseas service with the Middle East Brigade of the RFC.

SPECIFICATION

Airco (de Havilland) DH.1
Type: two-seat reconnaissance/interceptor aircraft
Powerplant: one Renault inline piston engine rated at 70 hp (52 kW)
Performance: maximum speed at 3,500 ft (1070 m) 80 mph (129 km/h); initial climb rate 350 ft (107 m) per minute; climb to 3,500 ft (1070 m) in 11 minutes

15 seconds
Weights: empty 1,356 lb (615 kg); maximum take-off 2,044 lb (927 kg)
Dimensions: span 41 ft (12.50 m); length 28 ft 11 in (8.83 m); height 11 ft 4 in (3.45 m); wing area 362.25 sq ft (33.65 m²)
Armament: one 0.303-in (7.7-mm) trainable forward-firing Lewis machine-gun on pillar mounting in forward cockpit

Airco (de Havilland) DH.2

Geoffrey de Havilland's second fighter design was the **Airco (de Havilland) DH.2** and this was, in essence, a scaled-down version of the DH.1, with single-seat accommodation and an air-cooled rotary piston engine in place of the DH.1's water-cooled inline piston engine. A mounting for a single Lewis gun was provided on each side of the central nacelle, and the pilot was expected to set up the gun on whichever of the mounts would provide the better opportunity for hitting his target. In moving the gun from side-to-side and changing its 47-round ammunition drums, the pilot was hard pressed to retain control of an aircraft that, until a fair amount of experience had been gained, was considered tricky to fly.

The 'tricky to fly' criti-cism resulted from sensi-tive controls but, in fact, this factor made the DH.2 a first-class fighter for its period after significant numbers of the new type had become operational early in 1916. When confronting the once-dreaded Fokker monoplanes, particularly during the 1st Battle of the Somme (summer 1916), the DH.2 was able to regain air superiority for the Royal Flying Corps and then retain this superiority until the pendulum swung once more in favour of the German air service late in 1916.

The difficulty of handling the Lewis gun was eventu-ally overcome, by mounting the gun centrally on the nacelle, the pilot then aiming the aircraft rather than the gun. By early in 1917, the DH.2 was outclassed on the Western Front, but continued to serve for some time in Macedonia and Palestine. However, none remained in RAF service by the autumn of 1918.

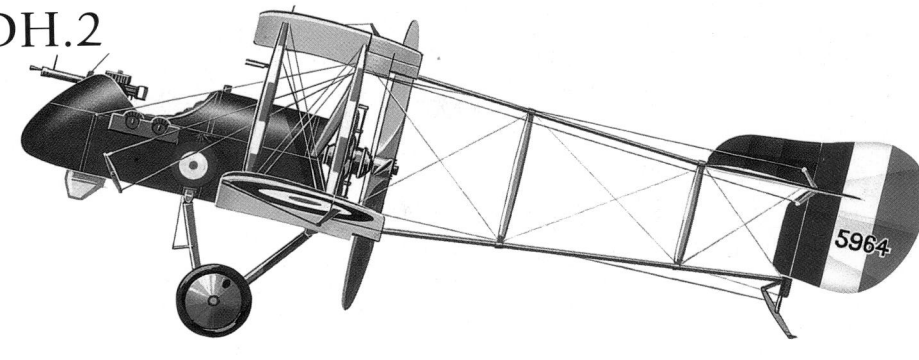

Major Lanoe G. Hawker used this aircraft to lead the first operational DH.2 unit, No. 24 Sqn, RFC.

SPECIFICATION

Airco (de Havilland) DH.2
Type: single-seat fighter
Powerplant: one Gnome Monosoupape rotary piston engine rated at 100 hp (74.6 kW), although some later aircraft had one Le Rhône rotary piston engine rated at 110 hp (82 kW)
Performance: (Gnome engine) maximum speed at sea level 93 mph (150 km/h); climb to 6,000 ft (1830 m) in 11 minutes; service ceiling 14,000 ft (4265 m); endurance 2 hours 45 minutes
Weights: empty 943 lb (428 kg); maximum take-off 1,441 lb (654 kg)
Dimensions: span 28 ft 3 in (8.61 m); length 25 ft 2½ in (7.68 m); height 9 ft 6½ in (2.91 m); wing area 249.00 sq ft (23.13 m²)
Armament: one 0.303-in (7.7-mm) forward-firing Lewis machine-gun

Airco (de Havilland) DH.3

Under the designation **Airco (de Havilland) DH.3**, Geoffrey de Havilland designed a large two-bay biplane for the bomber role. The wide-span wings were made to fold in order to save hangar space, and were carried above a slender fuselage that terminated in the curved rudder that was to become a feature of many sub-sequent de Havilland designs. The conventional tailskid landing gear was complemented by two wheels beneath the front of the fuselage, which extended well forward of the main wheels, to prevent the nose from bumping on the ground. The powerplant comprised two Beardmore engines mounted between the wings, with each driving a pusher propeller mounted on an extension shaft to ensure that it cleared the trailing edge of the wing.

Accommodation was provided for a crew of three: the pilot in an open cockpit just forward of the wing cellule, and the two gunners in individual cock-pits, one in the nose forward of the pilot and the other just to the rear of the wings.

A second prototype was built with more powerful Beardmore engines each rated at 160 hp (119 kW), and with cut-outs in the wing trailing edges in the area of the propellers so that the extended drive-shafts could be eliminated. This machine was desig-nated as the **DH.3A**, but neither type entered production. Both were reportedly burned on the Airco scrap heap on 7 July 1917, ironically during a Gotha raid on London.

SPECIFICATION

Airco (de Havilland) DH.3
Type: three-seat bomber
Powerplant: two Beardmore inline piston engines each rated at 120 hp (89 kW)
Performance: maximum speed at sea level 95 mph (153 km/h); climb to 6,500 ft (1980 m) in 23 minutes 30 seconds; endurance 8 hours
Weights: empty 3,980 lb (1805 kg); maximum take-off 5,810 lb (2635 kg)
Dimensions: span 60 ft 10 in (18.54 m); length 36 ft 10 in (11.23 m); height 14 ft 6 in (4.42 m); wing area 793.00 sq ft (73.67 m²)
Armament: two 0.303-in (7.7-mm) trainable Lewis machine-guns, plus an unknown bomb load

Believing that strategic bombing of Germany would not be necessary, Britain's War Office cancelled the DH.3 project in 1917 after only two prototypes had been built.

Airco (de Havilland) DH.4

Regarded generally as the best day bomber to see large-scale service during World War I, the **Airco (de Havilland) DH.4** was designed around an uprated version of the Beardmore inline piston engine. The DH.4, was a conventional two-bay biplane of wire-braced wooden construction covered largely with fabric except on the forward fuselage, where additional strength was provided by plywood skin-ning. The braced tail unit had an adjustable tailplane, which allowed the pilot to trim the aircraft in flight, and the landing gear was of the fixed tailskid type. The fuselage incorporated two open cockpits.

When considerable delays occurred in getting the Beardmore engine into production, an alternative engine, rated at 250 hp (186 kW), became available from Rolls-Royce. This engine was to become known as the Eagle, and the DH.4 was to use this powerplant as standard. When the 375-hp (280-kW) Eagle VIII became available, DH.4s fitted with this engine were superior in performance to most of the fighters of the period.

Initially equipping the Royal Flying Corps' No. 55 Squadron early in 1917, the DH.4 was operating with no fewer than nine Royal Air Force and 13 American squadrons by the late spring of 1918. The type also served with the Royal Naval Air Service for coastal patrol, and was also used to equip home defence squadrons.

However, a fundamental weakness in the D.H 4, which only emerged in service, resulted from the wide spacing of the two cockpits. This layout had been adopted to ensure that the pilot had good downward and forward fields of vision for bomb-aiming purposes, and the observer/gunner a maxi-

This Westland-built DH.4 illustrates the unusual spinner that was fitted to the four-bladed propeller of some aircraft. Also shown to advantage is the installation of the observer's Lewis gun.

mum field of fire for his Lewis gun(s). But lack of any effective means of communication between the two-man crew made the DH.4 extremely vulnerable when intercepted by enemy fighters and forced into combat.

The DH.4 was also manufactured under subcontract, and the combined total output reached 1,449 aircraft. The DH.4 also flew on active service with a variety of engines other than the Rolls-Royce III, IV and Eagle, these including the RAF 3a, Siddeley Puma and a Fiat unit. Increasing engine powers required larger-diameter propellers, steadily reducing clearance between the propeller tip and the ground, and resulted in the main landing gear units being extended to cater for future growth. Two examples of the DH.4 were modified to mount a

Coventry Ordnance Works (COW) quick-firing gun which fired a 1½-lb (0.68-kg) shell. Installed to fire almost vertically upward, this gun was intended for attacks on German Zeppelins but, by the time the aircraft were ready for service, Zeppelin raids on the UK had ended.

The DH.4 also has the distinction of being the only early British aircraft to have been built in large numbers in the USA, where the type was designated as the **DH-4** and was the only US-built aircraft of British origin to be flown operationally in France. By the end of World War I a total of 3,227 DH-4 aircraft with the Liberty Vee piston engine rated at 420 hp (313 kW), had been built. Of these, 1,885 were shipped across to France for use by the American Expeditionary Force, although only about one-third of these were used

Some 4,846 examples of the DH-4 were built. Post-war, the aircraft were used in a wide range of roles, including photographic survey.

operationally.

The career of the DH.4 was destined to continue long after the Armistice of November 1918, war surplus examples of British manufacture going to the Belgian, Greek, Japanese and Spanish air forces, and American-built machines continuing to serve with the US Army Air Service and with many Latin American countries. Large numbers of variants appeared in the USA during the early post-war years, many being conversions of ex-military aircraft, and many pioneering flights were made with them. Two DH-4B aircraft of the USAAC were used, for example, in the first successful experiments with inflight refuelling.

The DH.4 was not limited to military applications in these early years of peace, however. In the UK it was the earliest type to be used

as a civil transport by Holt Thomas' Aircraft Transport & Travel Ltd for the first cross-Channel service between London and Paris. It was also used by Handley Page Transport Ltd and the Belgian airline SNETA. In the USA, a number of

DH-4s were acquired by the US Post Office Department in 1919 and converted into mailplanes, remaining in use until 1927. Canada, which received 12 of the aircraft as an 'Imperial Gift' from the UK, used the type for spotting forest fires.

Variants

Variants worthy of note included the **DH.4A**, which was the designation applied after the war in the UK to civil conversions with an enclosed two-seat passenger cabin formed from the rear cockpit; the **DH-4A**, which was the US-built version with a revised and increased-capacity fuel system; the **DH-4B**, which was a much improved model with a plywood-covered fuselage and the positions of the pilot's cockpit and fuel tank reversed so that the two members of the crew were located closer together; and the **DH.4R** which was a single racing aircraft produced as a conversion with a clipped lower wing and the powerplant of one Napier Lion W-type piston engine rated at 450 hp (335.5 kW) for a maximum speed of 150 mph (241 km/h).

SPECIFICATION	
Airco (de Havilland) DH.4	4⅜ in (12.92 m); length 30 ft 8 in
Type: two-seat day bomber	(9.35 m); height 11 ft (3.35 m);
Powerplant: one Rolls-Royce	wing area 434.00 sq ft (40.32 m²)
Eagle VIII Vee piston engine rated	**Armament:** one (RFC) or two
at 375 hp (280 kW)	(RNAS) 0.303-in (7.7-mm) fixed
Performance: maximum speed at	forward-firing Vickers machine-
sea level 143 mph (230 km/h);	guns and one or two 0.303-in
maximum rate of climb at sea level	(7.7-mm) trainable rearward-firing
1,300 ft (396 m) per minute; climb	Lewis machine-guns in the rear
to 6,000 ft (1830 m) in 4 minutes	cockpit, plus up to 460 lb (209 kg)
50 seconds; service ceiling	of bombs carried on racks under
22,000 ft (6705 m); endurance	the fuselage and lower wing; the
3 hours 45 minutes	American-built DH-4 had two
Weights: empty equipped 2,387 lb	0.3-in (7.62-mm) fixed forward-
(1083 kg); maximum take-off	firing Marlin machine-guns, but its
3,472 lb (1575 kg)	armament was otherwise as in
Dimensions: wing span 42 ft	British production

Airco (de Havilland) DH.5

Whatever the shortcomings of the pioneering DH.1 and DH.2 fighters, their pusher configuration had ensured that the pilots of these aircraft had excellent fields of vision.

The **Airco (de Havilland)**

DH.5, designed in 1916, was created as a successor to the single-seat DH.2, and was the first 'scout', as fighters were then designated, of de Havilland design to introduce a Constantinesco interrupter

gear. The tractor configuration promised far better performance, but Geoffrey de Havilland was anxious to ensure that the pilot should not suffer by having a field of view much inferior to that offered by the DH.2.

This consideration was responsible for the unusual layout of the DH.5, with considerable backward stagger of the wings so that the pilot could be seated forward of the leading edge of the upper wing.

Apart from this feature, the DH.5 was of conventional construction and entered service with the Royal Flying Corps' Nos. 24 and 32 Squadrons in May 1917. When flown by experienced pilots, it soon proved itself to be a most useful weapon, but its handling characteristics and high-altitude performance, which were inferior to those of many contemporary Allied and enemy

aircraft, made it very vulnerable in inexperienced hands. After suffering fairly heavy losses in November 1917, the DH.5 was relegated to the ground-attack role until being replaced in first-line service by the Royal Aircraft Factory S.E.5a during January 1918. The DH.5 was then used as an advanced trainer, but only for a short period.

Production of the DH.5 totalled about 550 machines, 200 being delivered by Airco and the balance by sub-contractors. For experimental purposes a single example was powered by a Clerget rotary piston engine rated at 110 hp (82 kW).

With an airframe of considerable strength, the DH.5 was fully aerobatic, although its unusual layout caused some pilots to distrust it.

SPECIFICATION	
Airco (de Havilland) DH.5	(458 kg); maximum take-off
Type: single-seat fighter	1,492 lb (677 kg)
Powerplant: one Le Rhône rotary	**Dimensions:** span 25 ft 8 in
piston engine rated at 110 hp	(7.82 m); length 22 ft (6.71 m);
(82 kW)	height 9 ft 1½ in (2.78 m); wing
Performance: maximum speed at	area 212.10 sq ft (19.70 m²)
10,000 ft (3050 m) 102 mph	**Armament:** one 0.303-in (7.7 mm)
(164 km/h); maximum rate of climb	fixed forward-firing Vickers
at sea level 1,200 ft (366 m) per	machine-gun, plus four 25-lb
minute; climb to 6,500 ft (1980 m)	(11.3-kg) bombs carried on
in 6 minutes 55 seconds; service	underwing racks; one DH.5 was
ceiling 16,000 ft (4875 m);	flown with a Vickers machine-gun
endurance 2 hours 45 minutes	firing upward and forward at an
Weights: empty 1,010 lb	angle of about 45°

Airco (de Havilland) D.H.6

Designed in 1916 as a primary flying trainer, the Airco (de Havilland) **D.H.6** was of conventional biplane configuration, with tail surfaces that were fabric-covered over a structure of steel tube frames and wooden ribs. The landing gear was rugged in deference to the abuse it was likely to experience and included underwing skids to protect the wingtips in bad landings. A communal open cockpit for instructor and pupil made certain that there was no communication problem.

Early testing showed that the D.H.6 was a virtually viceless and unspinnable aircraft with innocuous stall characteristics: the type was so docile, in fact, that it was deliberately made unstable to prepare trainees for the less gentle aircraft to which they would be introduced at a later stage. Ordered into production early in 1917, almost 2,300 D.H.6s were built, and served with the Royal Flying Corps and Royal Air Force until the type was replaced by the Avro Type 504K. In addition

to those built by the parent company, the D.H.6 was produced by a number of sub-contractors.

The **D.H.6A** designation was accorded unofficially late in 1918 to aircraft having some changes in wing configuration reducing the area to 413.00 sq ft (38.37 m²), and has also been quoted for aircraft with the revised powerplant of one Curtiss OX-5 engine.

From March 1918, ex-RFC D.H.6 machines

entered service with the RNAS for anti-submarine patrol duties, and five flights of the aircraft were operated off the Irish coast by the US Navy air service. On such patrols the aircraft were flown as single-seaters with a bombload of up to 100 lb (45 kg).

When World War I ended, the RAF had just

over 1,000 D.H.6 aircraft still on charge, and many were acquired for civil use when they were auctioned as war surplus material. In addition to these military and civil aircraft, 60 were built under licence by Hispano-Suiza SA in Spain from 1921, these serving as trainers with the Spanish air force.

The D.H.6 was a conventional design which proved itself to be cheap and easy to build. During its service life it was given many names – most detrimental. These included 'clutching hand' due to the aircraft's low stalling speed characteristics, which new pilots found hard to master.

SPECIFICATION

Airco (de Havilland) D.H.6
Type: two-seat primary flying trainer
Powerplant: one RAF 1a inline piston engine rated at 90 hp (67 kW) was standard, but some production batches had a Renault inline engine rated at 80 hp (60 kW) or Curtiss OX-5 Vee engine rated at 90 hp (67 kW) when the RAF 1a was in short supply
Performance: (RAF 1a engine) maximum speed at sea level 70 mph (113 km/h); maximum rate

of climb at sea level 225 ft (69 m) per minute; climb to 6,500 ft (1980 m) in 29 minutes; endurance 2 hours 45 minutes
Weights: empty 1,460 lb (662 kg); maximum take-off 2,027 lb (919 kg)
Dimensions: wingspan 35 ft 11 in (10.95 m); length 27 ft 3½ in (8.32 m); height 10 ft 9½ in (3.29 m); wing area 436.30 sq ft (40.53 m²)
Armament: up to 100 lb (45 kg) of bombs carried under the lower wing for anti-submarine patrol

Airco (de Havilland) D.H.9

As a result of daylight attacks on London by German bombers, the British government decided in mid-1917 to increase the strength of the Royal Flying Corps. Consequently, the Air Board directed that a large proportion of the squadrons that would now be established should be equipped with bomber aircraft. Large numbers of the excellent D.H.4 were ordered, but it was appreciated that a new longer-range bomber would be needed. There was a reluctance to scrap the facilities that had been developed for large-scale production of the D.H.4, and efforts were therefore made to retain as much as possible of that aircraft's structure in Airco's new design.

The Airco (de Havilland) **D.H.9** prototype was produced by modification of a D.H.4. The D.H.9 thus retained the same wings and tail unit in concert with generally similar landing gear, but the fuselage was completely new and char-

acterised by features such as the much improved and more streamlined nose, and the location of the pilot's cockpit directly above the lower wing's trailing edge; the latter brought the pilot and observer/gunner closer so that communication presented no problem. The prototype was powered by one BHP inline piston engine rated at 230 hp (172 kW).

Early testing, which began in July 1917, proceeded so well that existing D.H.4 contracts held by sub-contractors were amended to cover production of the D.H.9. Early production aircraft had a Siddeley-built BHP engine, but a new lightweight version of this engine, known as the Puma and developed by Siddeley-Deasy, was selected as the major production engine. Rated at 300 hp (224 kW), this was expected to give the D.H.9 outstanding perfor-

mance. However, ensuing problems meant that its reliability could only be assured by de-rating output to 230 hp (172 kW), so the performance of the new bomber was inferior to that of the D.H.4 which it was intended to replace. Later, a 430-hp (320-kW) inline Napier Lion engine was installed, which at last gave the D.H.9 a worthwhile performance; but the latter engine arrived too late to see wartime service.

Despite this inadequacy, resulting in serious losses when the type was first introduced during April 1918 by the RFC in France, more than 3,200 aircraft were built in the UK by Airco and 12 sub-contractors. The higher-performance D.H.4 soldiered on, and was supplemented rather than supplanted by the D.H.9. In areas less active than the Western Front, the D.H.9 did rather better, notably in Macedonia and Palestine, and the type

was also used to strengthen British coastal defence and anti-Zeppelin patrols. With the end of World War I, the D.H.9 soon faded from the RFC (now RAF) scene, and was replaced by the D.H.9A. Surplus to British requirements, D.H.9s were widely exported and the type was built under licence by Hispano-Suiza for service with the Spanish air force. At least 25 were still in service when the Spanish Civil War started in July 1936.

Other aircraft were built by SABCA in Belgium. The Netherlands Army Aircraft Factory also assembled 10 new D.H.9 aircraft built by the de Havilland Aircraft Company in 1923 and, in 1934, these were each revised with a Wright Whirlwind radial piston engine rated at 465 hp (347 kW). Despite this sort of demand, England still had large numbers of surplus aircraft; in late 1930, these were scrapped and burned during the following year.

Fitted with the Napier Lion inline, the D.H.9 had acceptable performance, including a maximum speed of 144 mph (232 km/h).

Variants

The designation D.H.9B was used for aircraft converted to civil use with single passengers fore and aft of the pilot, D.H.9C for aircraft converted to civil use with a single passenger forward of the pilot and two passengers behind him, and D.H.9J for the SAAF's M'pala I and also for the D.H.9J aircraft modernised in the late 1920s for use by the de Havilland School of Flying.

SPECIFICATION

Airco D.H.9
Type: two-seat day bomber
Powerplant: one Siddeley Puma inline piston engine rated at 230 hp (172 kW)
Performance: maximum speed at 6,500 ft (1980 m) 110.5 mph (178 km/h); maximum rate of climb at sea level 625 ft (284 m) per minute; climb to 6,500 ft (1980 m) in 10 minutes 20 seconds; service ceiling 15,500 ft (4725 m); endurance 4 hours 30 minutes
Weights: empty 2,230 lb

(1012 kg); maximum take-off 3,325 lb (1508 kg)
Dimensions: wingspan 42 ft 4½ in (12.92 m); length 30 ft 5 in (9.27 m); height 11 ft 3½ in (3.44 m); wing area 434.00 sq ft (40.32 m²)
Armament: one 0.303-in (7.7-mm) Vickers fixed forward-firing Vickers machine-gun and one or two 0.303-in (7.7-mm) Lewis trainable rearward-firing guns on a Scarff ring in the rear cockpit, plus up to 460 lb (209 kg) of bombs

Airco (de Havilland) D.H.9A

The poor performance of the D.H.9 could clearly be overcome by the introduction of a more powerful and reliable engine. With Rolls-Royce already hard-pressed, it was decided that quantities of Liberty 12 engines would be ordered from the USA. Airco, which was deeply involved with the new D.H.9, requested that the Westland Aircraft Works at Yeovil, Somerset, redesign the D.H.9 to accept the Liberty engine. Westland, which had built large numbers of D.H.4 and D.H.9 aircraft under sub-contract, did better than that and combined the best features of both types with the American engine. At the same time, to ensure maximum benefit from the extra power, it strengthened the fuselage structure and introduced wings of increased span and chord. The Airco (de Havilland) D.H.9A proto-type made the type's maiden flight with an Eagle VIII, with the first Liberty-engined machine flying shortly after this. Initial deliveries were made to the Royal Air Force during June 1918.

Some 885 D.H.9A bombers were built by Westland and sub-contractors, and the type came to be regarded as the outstanding strategic bomber of World War I. Production of the D.H.9A continued in the post-war years, when the type served the RAF reliably during air policing operations in Iraq and on the northwest frontier of India. Westland was kept busy repairing and refurbishing these aircraft (nicknamed 'Nine-Ack', usually short-ened to 'Ninak') until they were finally withdrawn from RAF service in 1931. The RAF's D.H.9A warplanes also equipped eight UK-based day bomber squadrons and six auxiliary squadrons, maintained the Cairo-Baghdad desert air mail service, and served in Egypt and Palestine.

The D.H.9A spawned a number of subvariants, created either by de Havilland rather than Airco, which went out of business in the aftermath of World War I, or by foreign inter-ests. The **D.H.9AJ** Stag was a single prototype with improved main landing gear and the powerplant of one Bristol Jupiter VI radial piston engine rated at 465 hp (347 kW). The **D.H.9R** was a single racing machine with a sesquiplane wing layout and the power-plant of one Napier Lion II W-type piston engine rated at 465 hp (347 kW). The designation Engineering Division **USD-9A** was applied to nine generally similar US-built D.H.9A aircraft with the 0.3-in (7.62-mm) Browning fixed forward-firing machine-gun relocated from the port to the starboard side of the forward fuselage, and a modified rudder. The designation Engineering Division **USD-9B** was applied to a single USD-9A conversion fitted with the Liberty 12A engine rated at 420 hp (313 kW).

D.H.9As belonging to No. 39 Squadron are seen in close formation during a training flight in 1923.

Airco (de Havilland) D.H.10 Amiens

When Germany began to make daylight bombing raids on London in 1917, the immediate British reaction was to provide the Royal Flying Corps with retaliatory weapons, including the D.H.9 and D.H.9A. This basic type was suitable only as a stop-gap, however, so Geoffrey de Havilland began design of the Airco (de Havilland) **D.H.10**, which was to be named **Amiens**. The urgency of the situation was such that there was no time to origi-nate a completely new design, so the D.H.3 of 1916 formed the basis of the new bomber.

Generally similar in over-all configuration to the D.H.3, the D.H.10 was somewhat larger and of far more robust construction. The first of three proto-types was the **Amiens Mk I** that made the type's maiden flight on 4 March 1918 with the powerplant of two BHP inline piston engines, each rated at 230 hp (172 kW). These engines were mounted between the wings in a pusher layout, and the wing trailing edges incorporated cut-outs to provide clear-ance for the propellers. The other two prototypes had their engines installed in a tractor configuration, these machines being the **Amiens Mk II** with Rolls-Royce Eagle VIII Vee piston engines each rated at 360 hp (268 kW), and the **Amiens Mk III** with Liberty 12 Vee piston engines each rated at 400 hp (298 kW).

In all three of these aircraft the engines were mounted between the wings, the engine nacelles carried on short struts from the lower wing structure. A fourth prototype was flown with the engines mounted directly on the lower wing and, as this resulted in improved performance, it was the standard adopted for the production model, which was known to its manufacturer as the **D.H.10A** and to the Royal Air Force as the **Amiens Mk IIIA**.

Like the contemporary Vickers Vimy and Handley Page V/1500, the Amiens was destined not to see operational service with the RAF during World War I. A total of 1,295 had been ordered, but only eight had reached the RAF before the war ended. Production continued, and eventually totalled about 220 aircraft.

The designation **D.H.10B** was probably used for a single civil-registered D.H.10 used for air-mail operations, while the

D.H.10C Amiens Mk IIIC was the version (probably intended for mass produc-tion) with Eagle VIII engines, each rated at 375 hp (280 kW), which were mounted directly onto the lower wing.

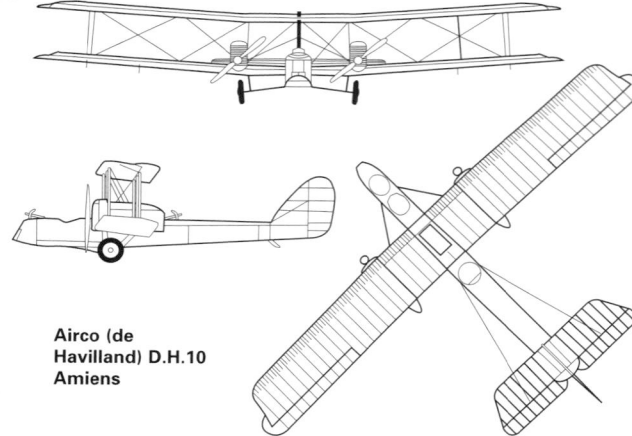

Airco (de Havilland) D.H.10 Amiens

Clearly visibly on this Amiens Mk II is the heavily glazed nose section for the bombardier.

Airspeed AS.4 Ferry

Airspeed Ltd was established at Portsmouth, in the British county of Hampshire, during 1934. One of the company's original directors was Sir Alan Cobham, who had set himself the task of making the British public interested in civil aviation. One method of achieving this was to make it easy and comparatively cheap for people to make a short flight – and thus to experience for themselves what air travel would be like. Alan Cobham's Air Display 'flying circuses', appearing around the UK during the summer months of the years 1932-36, proved to be a highly successful form of air education, its aircraft carrying nearly a million passengers during that period.

Requiring a small multi-engined airliner to carry such passengers, Cobham arranged for Airspeed to design and construct two suitable aircraft. Designated **Airspeed AS.4** – and later named **Ferry** – these were the first powered aircraft produced by Airspeed. They were of unusual biplane configuration, with a cranked lower wing; two of the three engines were installed in nacelles, located on the angle where the anhedralled inner panels met the dihedralled outer panels and the third engine was installed on the leading edge of the upper wing's centre section, rather than in the nose as was otherwise standard for three-engined aircraft of the day. Airspeed's arrangement gave the pilot a much better forward view. A rather ugly slab-sided fuselage with accommodation for 10 passengers, a conventional braced tail unit and wide-track tailskid landing gear with main-wheels, partially enclosed by wheel fairings, completed the airframe structure. This was primarily of wood, under a thin covering of plywood, on the fuselage and fabric on the flying surfaces. The three engines were of equal power output but while the unit on the upper wing was a de Havilland Gipsy III inverted inline piston engine, those on the lower wing, directly above the main wheels, were Gipsy II upright inline units.

First flown on 5 April 1932, the prototype was generally satisfactory and was followed soon after by the second machine. During the first year of their commercial operation, these two aircraft carried approximately 92,000 passengers. Only a further two examples were built, these being supplied initially to the fledgling Midland and Scottish Air Ferries.

A distinctive feature of Airspeed's AS.4 were the cranked lower wings which were attached to the upper fuselage.

SPECIFICATION	
Airspeed AS.4 Ferry	(3050 m) in 38 minutes; absolute
Type: 10-passenger airliner and air-experience transport	ceiling 13,000 ft (3960 m); range 320 miles (515 km)
Powerplant: three de Havilland Gipsy II/III inline piston engines, each rated at 120 hp (89 kW) for take-off	**Weights:** empty equipped 3,440 lb (1560 kg); maximum take-off 5,600 lb (2540 kg)
Performance: maximum speed at sea level 108 mph (174 km/h); cruising speed at 1,000 ft (305 m) 85 mph (137 km/h); maximum rate of climb at sea level 520 ft (158 m) per minute; climb to 10,000 ft	**Dimensions:** wingspan 55 ft (16.76 m); length 39 ft 8 in (12.09 m); height 14 ft 3 in (4.34 m); wing area 641.00 sq ft (59.55 m²)
	Payload: see above within the context of a maximum payload of 1,500 lb (680 kg)

Airspeed AS.5 Courier

The first Airspeed design to be built in a significant number was the **AS.5 Courier**, designed by one of the founding directors, A. Hessell Tiltman. The aircraft originated from a proposal which Tiltman made in 1931, but with the new company very short of capital, it was not until September 1932 that work began on construction of the prototype.

The conventional cantilever low-wing monoplane layout – and the mixed steel tube and wood construction – meant that the Courier introduced what was then a most advanced feature for British aircraft, namely tailwheel landing gear with retractable main units. Powered by an uncowled Armstrong Siddeley Lynx IVC radial piston engine, rated at 240 hp (179 kW), the prototype made its maiden flight on 11 April 1933. The engine installation was later revised, with the cylinder heads enclosed in a neat Townend ring cowling, and production versions for 'English' use received the designation **AS.5A**. The alternative 'Colonial' version had an Armstrong Siddeley Cheetah V radial piston engine, which was rated at 305 hp (227 kW), and was designated as the **AS.5B**.

In February 1934, the RAF acquired one five/six-seat AS.5A for use as a communications machine, returning it to Airspeed in 1935 for the incorporation of drag and high-lift devices for, once airborne, the Courier was reluctant to return to mother earth.

With its retractable landing gear, the Courier was capable of a remarkably high cruising speed. One example was used unsuccessfully by Sir Alan Cobham in an attempt to fly non-stop from England to India using inflight refuelling.

Production of the Courier totalled 16 aircraft and, of these, 10 served with the RAF for communications and transport during World War II. These comprised the original example procured for the RAF plus nine aircraft impressed from civil sources. Only one survived the war with the RAF, to be returned to civil service on 18 January 1946.

SPECIFICATION	
Airspeed AS.5B Courier	17,000 ft (5180 m); range
Type: five/six-seat light transport	640 miles (1030 km)
Powerplant: one Armstrong Siddeley Cheetah V radial piston engine rated at 305 hp (227 kW) for take-off	**Weights:** empty 2,328 lb (1056 kg); maximum take-off 4,000 lb (1814 kg)
Performance: maximum speed at sea level 165 mph (226 km/h); cruising speed at 1,000 ft (305 m) 145 mph (233 km/h); maximum rate of climb at sea level 940 ft (286 m) per minute; service ceiling	**Dimensions:** wingspan 47 ft (14.33 m); length 28 ft 6 in (8.69 m); wing area 250.00 sq ft (23.23 m²)
	Payload: see above within the context of a maximum payload of 900 lb (408 kg)

Airspeed AS.6 Envoy

The design of the aircraft that became the Airspeed **AS.6 Envoy** began late in 1933, and the intention behind its creation was the marketing of a larger, twin-engined development of the AS.5 Courier. The prototype made its maiden flight on 26 June 1934 and a total of 49 aircraft was built.

With standard accommodation for a pilot and up to eight passengers, the Envoy was of conventional all-wood construction under a covering of stressed plywood except on the fabric-covered control surfaces. A variable-incidence tailplane and tailwheel landing gear with retractable main units were features of the design which was built between 1934 and 1939 in three versions. The initial **AS.6 Envoy Series I** (17 examples built) had a plain wing without trailing-edge flaps; the **AS.6 Envoy Series II** (13 aircraft) introduced split flaps; and the **AS.6 Envoy Series III** (19 aircraft) was generally similar to the Series II but introduced a number of detail improvements. A wide range of

With exceptional visibility afforded to the pilot and an enlarged cabin for eight passengers, the Envoy was adopted for commercial operations by a host of countries including Britain, Japan, China and South Africa.

radial piston engines could be used in the Envoy's twin-engined powerplant.

Envoys were exported to China, Czechoslovakia, France, India and Japan. For military service they were used by the RAF, Royal Navy and South African Air Force, and a number was also operated in the Spanish Civil War. The first Envoy Series II to be supplied to the RAF was of historical signifi-

A small number of SAAF and RAF Envoys was converted to carry bombs, and mounted one forward-firing and one dorsal-turreted machine-gun.

cance as this machine was the founder member of The King's (later The Queen's) Flight. The RAF also acquired two Envoys for communications service in India, and five for home service in a similar role, and at least one of these was used throughout World War II by the Fleet Air Arm. In addition, three impressed Envoys served with the RAF during that war. South Africa acquired seven Envoys in 1936; three of these were used by the SAAF and had an armament comprising one 0.303-in (7.7-mm) fixed forward-firing machine-gun and one 0.303-in (7.7-mm) machine-gun in a dorsal turret. The four civil Envoys which made up the total, and which were built for South African Airways, were capable of quick conversion for use in a military role.

A special variant of the AS.6 was built as the AS.8 Viceroy, for participation in the 1934 MacRobertson air race.

SPECIFICATION	
Airspeed AS.6J Envoy	ceiling 22,500 ft (6860 m); typical range 650 miles (1046 km)
Type: nine-seat light transport	
Powerplant: two Armstrong Siddeley Cheetah IX radial piston engines, each rated at 350 hp (261 kW) for take-off	**Weights:** empty equipped 4,057 lb (1840 kg); maximum take-off 6,300 lb (2858 kg)
Performance: maximum speed at 7,300 ft (2225 m) 210 mph (338 km/h); cruising speed at 10,000 ft (3050 m) 180 mph (290 km/h); climb to 10,000 ft (3050 m) in 8 minutes; service	**Dimensions** wingspan 52 ft 4 in (10.52 m); length 34 ft 6 in (10.53 m); height 9 ft 6 in (2.90 m); wing area 339.00 sq ft (31.49 m²)
	Payload: maximum payload of 1,377 lb (625 kg)

Airspeed AS.10 Oxford

In 1936, Airspeed was given the opportunity of submitting a proposal to meet the Air Ministry's Specification T.23/36 for a twin-engined trainer. Airspeed's design for this was based on the successful AS.6 Envoy.

The **AS.10** prototype made its first flight on 19 June 1937 and token deliveries began in November of that year, with four of the first six going to the RAF's Central Flying School and the other two to No. 11 Flying Training School. The **Oxford** shared its predecessor's construction and tailwheel landing gear with retractable main units. The variations came in powerplant, internal layout and, in the **Oxford Mk I**, provision of an Armstrong Whitworth gun turret with one 0.303-in (7.7-mm) machine-gun for the training of air gunners.

The Oxford was built in very large numbers and used extensively for the Empire Air Training Scheme (EATS) after the start of World War II. The normal accommodation was for a crew of three at any one time, but in addition to seats for a pilot/pupil and co-pilot/instructor, there were positions for the training of an air gunner, bomb-aimer, camera operator, navigator and radio operator. Dual controls were standard, making the Oxford suitable for use as a twin-engined trainer. With the dual-control set removed from the co-pilot's position, a bomb-aimer could take up a prone position and drop smoke practice bombs carried in a centre-section well, or the seat could be moved back on rails and a chart table, hinged to the fuselage side, erected for

In RAF service Oxfords fulfilled a number of roles, most numerous of which was serving as navigational or radio-operational trainers. All were to receive the standard green/brown camouflage of the period.

use by a trainee navigator – and an aft-facing seat behind the co-pilot's position was available for a radio operator. A hood was also available so that the Oxford could be used for instrument training.

The Oxford Mk I was a general-purpose, bombing and gunnery trainer, the **Oxford Mk II** was a pilot, radio operator and navigator trainer: both these variants were powered by two 375-hp (280-kW) Armstrong Siddeley Cheetah X engines. The **Oxford Mk V** was equipped for the same role as the Oxford Mk II, but was powered by two 450-hp (335.5-kW) Pratt & Whitney R-985-AN-6 Wasp Juniors. The **Oxford Mk III**, of which only one was built, was powered by two 425-hp (318-kW) Cheetah XV radial engines. The **Oxford Mk IV** was projected as a pilot trainer version of the Oxford Mk III, but none was built. One example of an Oxford Mk II aircraft was fitted experimentally with two 250-hp (186-kW) de Havilland Gipsy Queen inline piston engines. Odd variants included an early Oxford Mk I equipped with special McLaren landing gear, the main units of which could be offset to cater for a reasonable degree of crosswind at both take-off and landing, and one with a tail unit which included twin endplate fins and rudders, especially installed for a series of spin recovery tests.

The outbreak of World War II created an enormous demand for these trainers, not only for use by the RAF, but by those nations involved in the EATS. Examples also went to the Free French air force and, under reverse Lend-Lease, a number were used by USAAF units in Europe. In addition to their use for training purposes, a number of the aircraft were equipped to serve as air ambulances and many more served with some 10 anti-aircraft co-operation squadrons. The Fleet Air Arm also equipped one training unit, No. 758 Instrument Flying Squadron, with the Oxford from June 1942.

Demand for the Oxford was well beyond Airspeed's production capacity, the company building a total of 4,961. Other construction by de Havilland (1,515), Percival Aircraft (1,360) and Standard Motors (750) gave a grand total of 8,586. Airspeed built its last example in July 1945 and the Oxford remained in service with the RAF's No. 10 Advanced Flying Training School at Pershore until 1954. Many were supplied after the war to the Dutch air force.

In accordance with their training role, bright yellow undersurfaces and large red codes were introduced to the Oxford fleet to aid conspicuity.

SPECIFICATION	
Airspeed AS.10 Oxford Mk V	climb to 10,000 ft (3050 m) in 6 minutes; service ceiling 21,000 ft (6400 m); range 700 miles (1127 km)
Type: three-seat general-purpose trainer	
Powerplant: two Pratt & Whitney R-985-AN-6 Wasp Junior radial piston engines, each rated at 450 hp (335.5 kW) for take-off	**Weights:** empty equipped 5,670 lb (2572 kg); maximum take-off 8,000 lb (3269 kg)
Performance: maximum speed at 4,100 ft (1250 m) 202 mph (325 km/h); maximum rate of climb at sea level 2,000 ft (610 m) per minute;	**Dimensions:** wingspan 53 ft 4 in (16.26 m); length 34 ft 6 in (10.52 m); height 11 ft 1 in (3.38 m); wing area 348.00 sq ft (32.33 m²)

Airspeed AS.30 and AS.50 Queen Wasp

K8888 was the second Queen Wasp built for the Royal Navy.

The Air Ministry's Specification Q.32/35 called for a pilotless target aircraft offering a higher speed and more effective control system than that of the de Havilland Queen Bee.

The **Airspeed AS.30** design gained an order in May 1936 for two prototypes. One of these was to have wheeled landing gear, for evaluation by the Royal Air Force, and the other twin-float alighting gear, for evaluation by the Royal Navy, for air-firing practice at sea.

A single-bay biplane with tapered wings, the AS.30 had only a single I-section streamline interplane strut on each side and a minimum of bracing wires. The enclosed cabin was equipped with a single seat for a pilot, so that the AS.30 could be flown independently of its radio control system for checking purposes and delivery flights. The powerplant was based on one Armstrong Siddeley Cheetah IX radial engine, in a cowling generally similar to that used for the AS.6J Envoy.

Named **Queen Wasp**, the landplane and float-plane prototypes flew for the first time on 11 June 1937 and 19 October 1937, respectively. Testing began shortly after and the second Royal Navy aircraft was successfully catapulted from HMS *Pegasus* in November of the same year. As had been the case with the single-engined Courier, however, the type's low-speed control handling characteristics were considered to be poor. This probably accounts for the fact that only three more examples were completed. The latter were built to **AS.50** standard as trainers, and delivered to the Royal Air Force.

It is interesting to note the fact that – despite the comparatively unsophisticated nature of contemporary radio equipment – the automatic flight central system of the Queen Wasp was most advanced. Not only were there many fail-safe devices, but a simple and functional autoland feature was provided.

SPECIFICATION

Airspeed AS.30 Queen Wasp
Type: pilotless target aircraft
Powerplant: one Armstrong Siddeley Cheetah IX radial piston engine rated at 350 hp (261 kW) for take-off
Performance: (landplane) maximum speed at 8,000 ft (2440 m) 172 mph (277 km/h); cruising speed at 10,000 ft (3050 m) 151 mph (243 km/h); service ceiling 20,000 ft (6095 m)
Weights: maximum take-off 3,500 lb (1588 kg) as a landplane and 3,800 lb (1724 kg) as a floatplane
Dimensions: wingspan 31 ft (9.45 m); length 24 ft 4 in (7.42 m) as a landplane and 29 ft 1 in (8.86 m) as a floatplane; height 10 ft 1 in (3.07 m) as a landplane and 13 ft (3.96 m) as a floatplane

Airspeed AS.39 Fleet Shadower

Calling for a carrier-based aircraft able to maintain contact with an enemy surface force by night, the S.23/37 requirement presented a number of major design problems – including the provision of excellent low-speed handling qualities and considerable endurance in a reliable aircraft, small enough to operate from the flight decks of current aircraft-carriers.

The unusual features to meet the designated role included a most complicated wing to make low-speed cruising flight possible over a period of several hours. Each wing mounted two engines, providing a broad slipstream to act on two-section flaps, that extended over the full span of the trailing edge and whose outer sections could be used differentially as ailerons. In addition, the wing incorporated automatic slots on the full span of its leading edge, was constructed to have airtight compartments for buoyancy in the event of a ditching, and could be folded to the rear for shipboard stowage. The fuselage provided accommodation for a crew of three: an observer in the nose with clear vision windows around him; the pilot in a cockpit high on the fuselage, forward of the wing; and a radio operator in the fuselage to the rear of the pilot. The pilot's elevated seating position made it desirable that take-offs and landings should be made with the fuselage almost parallel with the deck; this resulted in the adoption of a highly unorthodox fixed tailwheel landing gear arrangement.

The Fleet Shadower's unusual appearance resulted from the exacting requirements of its specification.

The **AS.39 Fleet Shadower** prototype first flew on 18 October 1940, but in subsequent flight tests proved to be disappointing. As a result, only one prototype was built.

SPECIFICATION

Airspeed AS.39 Fleet Shadower
Type: three-seat carrierborne night reconnaissance aircraft
Powerplant: four Pobjoy Niagara V radial piston engines, each rated at 130 hp (97 kW) for take-off
Performance: cruising speed at 5,000 ft (1525 m) 113 mph (182 km/h); maximum rate of climb at sea level 865 ft (264 m) per minute; climb to 10,000 ft (3050 m) in 18 minutes; service ceiling 14,700 ft (4480 m); endurance about six hours
Weights: empty equipped 4,592 lb (2083 kg); maximum take-off 6,935 lb (3146 kg)
Dimensions: wingspan 53 ft 4 in (16.26 m); length 40 ft (12.19 m); height 10 ft 6 in (3.20 m)

Airspeed AS.45 Cambridge

Designed to satisfy the Air Ministry's Specification T.34/39 for an advanced flying trainer, the **Airspeed AS.45** design was conventional in appearance and in the same general mould as the Miles Master, being of cantilever low-wing monoplane layout, with retractable tailwheel landing gear and an air-cooled radial piston engine. Following Air Ministry approval of the design, which was given the provisional name of **Cambridge**, two prototypes were ordered. The first completed its maiden flight on 19 February 1941.

The type had wings and a tail unit of wood covered with stressed plywood except for the fabric-covered control surfaces. The fuselage was of plywood-covered steel tube construction and built integrally with the centre section of the wing. This latter feature provided the pupil and instructor, who were seated in tandem under an extensively glazed framed canopy, with some protection in the event of an accident. Four doors were provided, two on each side, so that exit in an emergency could be made from either side. The main units of the Dowty landing gear retracted inwards, the wheels lying flush in the undersurface of the wing centre section. The powerplant was based on one Bristol Mercury VIII radial piston engine rated at 730 hp (544 kW) and driving a three-bladed constant-speed propeller.

Flight testing of the two prototypes revealed that the AS.45's low-speed flight characteristics were less than ideal and that its maximum speed was below that which had been estimated. Both aircraft were handed over to the Royal Air Force in July 1942, following a decision not to proceed with production.

Built to withstand the rigours of pilot training, the AS.45 featured 'crashworthy' accommodation for pilot and instructor.

SPECIFICATION

Airspeed AS.45 Cambridge
Type: two-seat advanced flying trainer
Powerplant: one Bristol Mercury VIII radial piston engine rated at 730 hp (544 kW) for take-off
Performance: maximum cruising speed at 16,000 ft (4875 m) 237 mph (381 km/h); economical cruising speed at 12,500 ft (3810 m) 228 mph (365 km/h); climb to 15,000 ft (4570 m) in 12 minutes 30 seconds; service ceiling 24,800 ft (7560 m); range 680 miles (1094 km)
Dimensions: wingspan 42 ft (12.80 m); length 36 ft 1 in (11.00 m); height 11 ft 6 in (3.51 m); wing area 280.00 sq ft (26.94 m²)

Airspeed AS.51 and AS.58 Horsa

In December 1940, Airspeed received the Air Ministry's Specification X.26/40 calling for a troop-carrying glider, and this was to have almost double the capacity of the US-built Waco CG-4A Hadrian. Following acceptance of the **Airspeed AS.51** design proposal, the Air Ministry ordered seven prototypes: two were assembled by Fairey as flight test aircraft, and the other five were assembled at Airspeed's factory at Portsmouth for use by the British Army for loading and unloading trials.

The AS.51 consisted of 30 separate assemblies built mainly by woodworking subcontractors such as furniture manufacturers. These were subsequently assembled and test flown at Royal Air Force MUs

(Maintenance Units), and some 3,000 of the gliders were eventually completed in this way. Only about 700 of all the AS.51 gliders were actually manufactured, assembled and test flown in one place, namely Airspeed's factory at Christchurch in Hampshire.

Produced simultaneously with the AS.51, which was designated the **Horsa Mk I** in service, was the **AS.58** with a hinged nose for the direct loading of vehicles and guns, and this variant was designated as the **Horsa Mk II** in service.

The Horsa was of almost entirely wooden construction, covered with a stressed plywood skin. The cantilever high-set wing was fitted with underwing dive-brakes. The fuselage was in three

sections, providing accommodation for two pilots and a maximum of 25 troops. The landing gear was of the fixed tricycle type, and there was provision for the main units to be jettisoned before a landing on rough ground, where the nosewheel and sprung landing skid on the underfuselage centreline had to suffice. The AS.58 had twin nosewheels.

Towed by an Armstrong Whitworth Whitley, the first AS.51 prototype made its maiden flight from Fairey's Great West Aerodrome on 12 September 1941 and, soon after, the Horsa began to enter regular service with the RAF.

The first significant operational use of the Horsa was on 10 July 1943 when 27 survivors of 30 air-towed from the UK to North Africa were deployed during the invasion of Sicily. The type later played an important part in the Normandy invasion of June 1944, operated by the RAF and the USAAF, and in the invasion of southern France in August 1944, at Arnhem in September 1944, and during the Rhine crossing in March 1945.

Likely production totals are the original seven prototypes; 470 Mk I and 225 Mk II gliders built by Airspeed; 300 Mk I and 65 Mk II gliders by the Austin

Wearing D-Day invasion stripes, a Horsa Mk I approaches to land. The underfuselage skid is clearly visible between the mainwheels.

Motor Company; and 1,461 Mk I and 1,271 Mk II gliders by subcontractors in the woodworking industry, of

which the most important was the furniture manufacturer, Harris Lebus. This amounts to a grand total of 3,799 machines.

DG597 was the prototype AS.51 Horsa. It was photographed in September 1941, around the time of its first flight, and is shown with its flaps down.

SPECIFICATION	
Airspeed AS.51 and AS.58 Horsa **Type:** troop and cargo assault transport glider **Performance:** maximum towing speed 150 mph (241 km/h); normal gliding speed 110 mph (161 km/h) **Weights:** empty 8,370 lb (3797 kg); maximum take-off 15,500 lb (7031 kg) for the Horsa Mk I and 15,750 lb (7144 kg) for	the Horsa Mk II **Dimensions:** wingspan 88 ft (26.82 m); length 67 ft (20.42 m) for the Horsa Mk I and 67 ft 11 in (20.70 m) for the Horsa Mk II; height 19 ft 6 in (5.94 m) for the Horsa Mk I and 20 ft 4 in (6.20 m) for the Horsa Mk II; wing area 1,104.00 sq ft (102.56 m²)

Airspeed AS.57 Ambassador

The Brabazon Committee, set up in World War II to establish guidelines for the post-war development of British commercial aviation, included in its report of early 1943 a recommendation for the design and construction of a short-/medium-range transport with a twin-engined powerplant and accommodation for about 30 passengers. This resulted in the **Airspeed AS.57 Ambassador**, designed by a team headed by Arthur

Hagg even as World War II was still continuing.

The AS.57 prototype made its maiden flight on 10 July 1947 and, just over a year later, the first (and also the only) order was received from British European Airways, which contracted for 20 aircraft. The Ambassador was a very attractive aircraft of cantilever high-wing mono-

Although it exhibited clean lines and the convenience of a low-set fuselage, the AS.57 could not compete with newer turbine-powered designs.

plane configuration and all-metal construction, and its fuselage was stressed for cabin pressurisation. The distinctive three-finned tail unit was carried high on an upswept rear fuselage, and the retractable tricycle landing gear incorporated twin wheels on each unit. Accommodation was provided for a crew of three on the flight deck,

with maximum seating for 47 passengers in the cabin. The powerplant was based on two powerful Bristol Centaurus sleeve-valve radial piston engines.

As a result of delays in development, it was not until 13 March 1952 that BEA was able to make its first scheduled service with the AS.57. So much time had been lost by then that the Ambassador had been overtaken technically by more advanced aircraft such as the Vickers Viscount turboprop-powered airliner, and no further sales interest was shown. Despite this fact, BEA's AS.57 airliners, which were operated as the 'Elizabethan' class,

proved a successful and well-liked interim type during their six years with the British airline. The aircraft subsequently saw service with operators who included BKS, Butler Air Transport (Australia), Dan-Air, Globe Air and Overseas Aviation.

The second prototype was later used for development testing of the Bristol Proteus 705, Rolls-Royce Tyne and Rolls-Royce Dart turboprops, and was still airworthy in 1969, more than 20 years after its first flight. The third prototype was used for testing of the Napier Eland turboprop, but was later converted to airline standards and sold to Dan-Air.

SPECIFICATION	
Airspeed AS.57 Ambassador **Type:** twin-engined short-/medium-range transport **Powerplant:** two Bristol Centaurus 661 two-row sleeve-valve radial piston engines each rated at 2,600 hp (1939 kW) for take-off **Performance:** maximum cruising speed at 20,000 ft (6095 m) 300 mph (483 km/h); economical cruising speed at optimum altitude 248 mph (399 km/h); maximum rate	of climb at 5,000 ft (1525 m) 1,520 ft (463 m) per minute; range with maximum payload 720 miles (1159 km) **Weights:** empty operating 35,884 lb (16277 kg); maximum take-off 52,500 lb (23814 kg) **Dimensions:** wingspan 115 ft (35.05 m); length 81 ft (24.69 m); height 18 ft 4 in (5.59 m); wing area 1,200.00 sq ft (111.48 m²) **Payload:** see above

Airspeed AS.65 Consul

Airspeed's directors had appreciated, even as World War II was continuing, that the company's AS.10 Oxford would prove easy to convert as a light civil transport in the immediate post-war years. As soon as the war ended the company began to buy Oxford trainers back from the British government, and the resulting aircraft, incorporating minor modifications, were subsequently remarketed under the designation **Airspeed AS.65 Consul**.

The modifications included the provision of two additional windows, a longer nose to accommodate a forward baggage compartment, the installation of a partition between the cabin and the crew position, and a change in tailplane incidence to move the centre of gravity forward. Accommodation could be provided for up to six passengers, and alternative layouts were available for the ambulance, freight, communications, and executive transport roles.

Approximately 160 such conversions were completed.

The Consul was little more than an Oxford modified for civil use.

SPECIFICATION	
Airspeed AS.65 Consul **Type:** twin-engined utility transport **Powerplant:** two Armstrong Siddeley Cheetah X radial piston engines each rated at 395 hp (295 kW) for take-off **Performance:** maximum speed at 4,800 ft (1465 m) 190 mph (306 km/h); economic cruising speed at 10,000 ft (3050 m) 145 mph (233 km/h); maximum rate of climb at sea level 1,230 ft	(375 m) per minute; climb to 10,000 ft (3050 m) in 10 minutes; range with maximum fuel 635 miles (1022 km) **Weights:** empty equipped 6,000 lb (2722 kg); maximum take-off 8,250 lb (3742 kg) **Dimensions:** wingspan 53 ft 4 in (16.26 m); length 35 ft 6 in (10.82 m) (tail down); height 10 ft 1 in (3.07 m) (tail down); wing area 348.00 sq ft (32.33 m²)

Airtech CN.235

The Spanish air force maintains a small fleet of CN.235s, which are flown as transports alongside C.212s and C-130 Hercules.

Following the success of their C.212 Aviocar utility light transport, CASA of Spain and IPTN (Industri Pesawat Terbang Nusantara) of Indonesia joined forces on a 50/50 basis to create Airtech (Aircraft Technology Industries) specifically for the design and development of a larger and more efficient pressurised transport for both civil and military use. Work on the resulting **CN.235** began in 1980, and prototypes were simultaneously constructed in the partner countries.

The Spanish prototype made its maiden flight on 11 November 1983, the Indonesian prototype following it into the air on 30 December of the same year. The CN.235 was certificated in June 1986, the first production aircraft made its maiden flight in August of the same year, and deliveries from the Indonesian and Spanish production lines began in December 1986 and February 1987 respectively. The CN.235 entered service with Merpati Nusantara Airlines in March 1988. In January 1990 a licence was signed with Tusas Aerospace Industries (TAI) for the assembly and then the construction of 50 aircraft in Turkey.

The main variants of the CN.235 series up to the middle of 1998 have been the **CN.235 Series 10** initial model with a powerplant of two General Electric CT7-7A turboprops each rated at 1,700 shp (1268 kW); the Spanish-built **CN.235 Series 100** and Indonesian-built **CN.235 Series 110** improved model with a powerplant of two CT7-9C turboprops, each flat-rated at 1,750 shp (1305 kW) for take-off, in new nacelles of composite construction; the **CN.235 Series 200** and **CN.235 Series 220** with structural strengthening for operation at higher weight, aerodynamic refinement of the rudder and the leading edges of the wing; the **CN.235 Series 330 Phoenix** Indonesian-developed variant intended to meet an Australian military requirement with more advanced avionics as well as provision for an ECM system; the **CN.235 M** military transport model; the Spanish-built **CN.235 MP Persuader** and the Indonesian-built **CN.235 MPA** maritime patrol types with advanced avionics, including provision for nose or ventral search radar, FLIR, ECM and dedicated mission systems, as well as anti-ship missiles or anti-submarine torpedoes carried on six hardpoints under the wing; and the **CN.235 QC** quick-change cargo/passenger transport.

The civil variants are typically fitted out for up to 44 passengers or 13,227 lb (6600 kg) of freight, while the CN.235 M military transport version is tailored to short-range cargo/trooping missions with its hold laid out for up to 48 troops, or 24 litters plus four attendants, or 13,227 lb (6600 kg) of freight.

Military sales have been brisk, and air forces in some 20 countries currently fly various versions of the aircraft.

CASA's CN.235 Persuader is a specialised maritime patrol version of the basic CN.235 transport.

Airtech CN.235

SPECIFICATION	
Airtech CN-235 M Series 100 **Type:** short-range medium utility transport **Powerplant:** two General Electric CT7-9C turboprops each flat-rated at 1,750 shp (1305 kW) without automatic power reserve or 1,870 shp (1394.5 kW) with automatic power reserve **Performance:** maximum speed 240 kt (276 mph; 445 km/h) at sea level; maximum cruising speed 248 kt (286 mph; 460 km/h) at 15,000 ft (4570 m); initial climb rate 1,900 ft (579 m) per minute; service	ceiling 26,600 ft (8110 m); range 2,350 nm (2,706 miles; 4355 km) with a payload of 7,936 lb (3600 kg) or 810 nm (932 miles; 1501 km) with max payload **Weights:** operating empty 19,400 lb (8800 kg); maximum take-off 36,376 lb (16500 kg) **Dimensions:** wing span 84 ft 8 in (25.81 m); length 70 ft 2½ in (21.35 m); height 26 ft 10 in (8.18 m); wing area 636.17 sq ft (59.10 m²) **Armament:** up to 7,716 lb (2500 kg) of anti-ship missiles or anti-submarine torpedoes

AISA Autogyro GN

AISA (Aeronáutica Industrial SA) was established in Madrid during 1923. The company was involved in the construction of some of the earliest of Juan de la Cierva's Autogiro machines in 1927, and from the early 1970s sought to revive its capabilities as a designer and manufacturer of light aircraft with the **AISA Autogyro GN**.

The GN was basically of light alloy construction and had enclosed accommodation for the pilot and three passengers in the extensively glazed forward section of the semi-monocoque central nacelle whose rear was occupied by the powerplant. The engine was located behind and below the tall pylon carrying the four-bladed rotor, which was of the fully-articulated type with provision for a 'jump-start' vertical take-off capability via a clutch system from the engine. The rest of the

The Autogyro GN was unlikely to have achieved many sales in the face of competition from conventional lightplanes and helicopters.

airframe comprised a short-span mid-set wing that carried the oval-section booms which themselves supported the main units of the fixed tricycle landing gear as well as the tail unit of two vertical surfaces and the single horizontal surface.

The design phase was protracted, and it was only in 1979 that AISA began construction of two prototypes. The first was completed and flown for

the first time in the autumn of 1981, but only the most limited trials were undertaken in the spring of 1982 before the programme was terminated.

SPECIFICATION	
AISA Autogyro GN	range 497 miles (800 km) with maximum fuel; endurance 6 hours with two passengers
Type: four-seat autogyro	
Powerplant: one Avco Lycoming IO-540-K1A5 flat-six piston engine rated at 300 hp (224 kW)	**Weights:** (estimated) empty 2,090 lb (948 kg); maximum take-off 3,086 lb (1400 kg)
Performance: (estimated) maximum speed 129.5 kt (149 mph; 240 km/h) at sea level; maximum cruising speed 114 kt (132 mph; 212 km/h) at sea level; initial climb rate 1,181 ft (360 m) per minute;	**Dimensions:** rotor diameter 38 ft 7 in (11.76 m); fuselage length 21 ft 4 in (6.50 m); height 10 ft 6 in (3.20 m); rotor disc area 1,169.21 sq ft (108.62 m²)

AISA I-11 Peque

Following their retirement from military service, many I-11B Peques entered the civil market for use as touring aircraft.

In the late 1940s Iberavia S.A. collaborated with Aeronáutica Industrial SA (AISA) in the design of a two-seat touring and training machine known as the **I-11**. AISA then took over Iberavia's aviation interests and continued development of the I-11 as its own project. The I-11 was intended as a lightplane able to undertake the touring and training roles, the latter with full aerobatic capability when flown by only one person. The resulting **AISA I-11** prototype made its maiden flight in 1950.

The tricycle landing gear of the all-wood I-11 was not attractive to potential Spanish customers, who expressed an interest in a tailwheel version. AISA

therefore evolved the **I-11B Peque** with a tailwheel undercarriage, the new aircraft first flying in prototype form on 16 October 1953. Production totalled 180 aircraft in two versions with either basic instrumentation (70 aircraft) or more sophisticated blind-flying instrumentation (110

aircraft), and 125 of the total entered Spanish air force service as training and liaison machines, with the service designation **L.8C**. Some 64 of the surviving machines were sold onto the civil market in 1967 and 1968 as the first stage of the type's retirement from military service.

SPECIFICATION	
AISA I-11B Peque	(200 m) per minute; service ceiling 15,420 ft (4700 m); range with maximum fuel 404 miles (650 km)
Type: two-seat primary and basic flying trainer	
Powerplant: (typically) one Continental C90-12F flat-four piston engine rated at 90 hp (67 kW) for take-off	**Weights:** empty equipped 982 lb (421 kg); maximum take-off in a semi-aerobatic configuration 1,474 lb (670 kg)
Performance: maximum speed 124 mph (200 km/h) at optimum altitude; maximum cruising speed 110 mph (177 km/h) at optimum altitude; initial climb rate 726 ft	**Dimensions:** wingspan 30 ft 7¾ in (9.34 m); length 21 ft 2¾ in (6.47 m); height 6 ft 2¾ in (1.90 m); wing area 144.24 sq ft (13.40 m²)

AISA I-115

During the mid- and late 1940s Iberavia S.A. and Aeronáutica Industrial SA (AISA) collaborated on the design of two training machines, the I-11 and the type that became known as the **AISA I-115**.

The resulting aircraft was intended for operation as a two-seater in the primary flying trainer role and as a

single-seater for aerobatic training. It was a cantilever low-wing monoplane of basically wooden construction, whose layout had clearly been strongly influenced by that of the de Havilland Canada DHC-1 Chipmunk.

The I-115 prototype made its maiden flight on 16 July 1952 and, following

the placement of significant orders for service with the Spanish air force, a production line was laid down. Full-scale production began in 1954, and deliveries amounted to 200 machines

Known in Spanish air force service as the E.6, the I-115 served well in the basic trainer role.

in all. A few of these aircraft remained in service up to the late 1970s, but by that time most of the

surviving aircraft had either been scrapped or handed over to various Spanish flying clubs.

SPECIFICATION	
AISA I-115	at optimum altitude; initial climb rate 738 ft (225 m) per minute; service ceiling 14,435 ft (4400 m); endurance 5 hours
Type: two-seat primary trainer or single-seat aerobatic trainer	
Powerplant: one ENMA (Elizalde) G-IVB Tigre inverted inline piston engine rated at 150 hp (112 kW) for take-off	**Weights:** empty 1,349 lb (612 kg); maximum take-off 1,984 lb (900 kg)
Performance: (in two-seat form) maximum speed 149 mph (240 km/h) at optimum altitude; cruising speed 127 mph (204 km/h)	**Dimensions:** wingspan 31 ft 3 in (9.54 m); length 24 ft 1 in (7.35 m); height 6 ft 10 in (2.10 m); wing area 150.70 sq ft (14.00 m²)

AJEP (Wittman) Tailwind

In 1953 Steve Wittman flew the prototype of the **Model W-8 Tailwind** as a monoplane that he could offer for home construction. Since that time, fairly large numbers of the Tailwind have been built in the period up to the mid-

1990s, the primary variants being the Model W-8, the basic type with the 90-hp (67.1-kW) Continental C90 engine (or similar) and tailwheel landing gear; the **Model W-9**, offered from 1958 with the 160-hp (119-kW) Lycoming

O-320-B1A engine and tricycle landing gear; and the **Model W-10**, offered from the late 1980s as a development of the Model W-8 with provision for 150-hp (112-kW)-class engines, including specially adapted car engines.

From the late 1970s, the Tailwind was marketed in the UK as a complete aircraft known under the designation **AJEP (Wittman) Tailwind**. These machines were offered with a choice of three engine types driving either a fixed- or variable-pitch propeller, and also in two forms as the **Tailwind Series 1** and the **Tailwind Series 2** with fixed tailwheel and tricycle landing gear, respectively. The AJEP version of the

Some 14 Tailwinds remained on the UK register in 1998, including this O-200A-powered W-8.

Tailwind featured a number of differences to the baseline American aircraft, but in basic layout was a braced high-wing monoplane of mixed construction under a covering of plywood and fabric.

The first AJEP-built Tailwind was completed in March 1976, and a remotely-controlled drone version of the Tailwind Series 1 was developed by BAC (Guided Weapons), a division of BAe.

Albatros L.1, L.2 and L.5 (B.I, B.II and B.III)

The first notable aircraft to be produced by this German manufacturer was the **Albatros L.1**. The type first flew in 1913 and entered production in 1914 for civil, as well as military use, the latter with the designation **B.I**.

The L.1 was largely of wooden construction and in configuration was an unequal-span biplane, with a tractor powerplant and fixed tailskid landing gear.

The powerplant was based on a Mercedes D.I or D.II inline piston engine, installed with most of its cylinder bank exposed, cooled by an overhead radiator, exhausted via a vertical 'ram's horn' exhaust stack on the star-

board side, and supplied with fuel from a gravity-feed tank.

The L.1 entered production in a revised form with adjustable lateral radiators as well as a taller and considerably more angular vertical tail surface, that now included a strut-braced fin. The aircraft was in limited military service on the outbreak of World War I, when it became the B.I as the first machine in the 'B' class of unarmed two-seaters. Further production was centred on a more standardised model with a three-bay wing cellule offering greater strength in the military role.

Shortly before the outbreak of war, Albatros

introduced a refined version of the L.1 as the **L.2**, with a two-bay wing cellule of shorter span and this was taken into military service as the **B.II**, with a powerplant of one Mercedes D.I or D.II inline piston engine, or sometimes one Benz Bz.II inline piston engine.

Large numbers of this type were in first-line service until the end of 1915, when the advent of modern Allied fighters meant the relegation of the B.II to second-line tasks, such as training and liaison. The success of the B.II as a trainer – in which it remained in service right up to the end of World War I (in November 1918) and indeed until after its end, and into 1919 with the Royal Swedish air

force – was reflected in production of the **B.IIa**, as a dedicated dual-control trainer.

The sole **W.1** was a development of the B.II with twin-float alighting gear for the unarmed coastal reconnaissance role, but was not ordered into production.

The **L.5 (B.III)** was an improved version of the

B.II, introduced in 1915. Built only in small numbers, since the advent of the 'C' category of armed two-seaters had made the type redundant, the B.III featured a revised tail unit of a type that became familiar on later Albatros warplanes. This had a tailplane with a curved leading edge and a fin of lower aspect ratio.

This B.III served with Fliegeresatzabteilung (FEA) 1 at Döberitz during the winter of 1916-17.

The sole W.1 was basically a float-equipped B.II with a three-bay wing.

Albatros L.6 and L.8 (C.I and C.II)

With the availability in 1915 of higher-powered engines, the new 'C' category of armed two-seater biplanes was introduced, to succeed the 'B' category unarmed two-seater types in the reconnaissance and artillery-spotting roles. The

armament was to comprise a single 0.312-in (7.92-mm) LMG 14 Parabellum trainable machine-gun.

Albatros responded to this need with its **L.6** design, that entered service as the **C.I** and was little more than an enlarged B.II, with provision

for any of the new engines. The positions of the observer and gunner were reversed. The observer now became an observer/gunner in the rear seat, a location which provided him with improved fields of fire with his new weapon. The C.I

proved popular with its crews for its armament, good performance and considerable strength and the type was built in moderately large numbers.

In an effort to create an aerodynamically cleaner version of the C.I with improved performance, the **C.Ia** was created by the replacement of the two

lateral radiators with a box-type radiator on the centreline of the upper-wing leading edge. It was delivered in only small numbers, as the improved Albatros C.III was on the verge of full production. A **C.Ib** dual-control trainer version was introduced in 1917.

The **L.8**, completed early in 1916 as the sole **C.II**, was

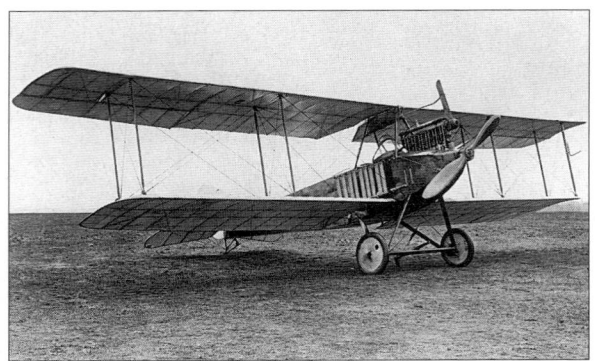

Both the tall exhaust pipe and fuselage-mounted radiators are clearly illustrated by this C.I.

an experimental type designed for evaluation of the pusher configuration for the 'C' category role. The type used the wing cellule and main landing gear arrangement of the C.I, with a Benz Bz.III inline piston engine rated at 150 hp (112 kW), located at the rear of the central nacelle.

SPECIFICATION

Albatros C.I
Type: two-seat reconnaissance and artillery-spotting aircraft
Powerplant: one Benz Bz.III inline piston engine rated at 150 hp (112 kW) for take-off, or one Mercedes D.III inline piston engine rated at 160 hp (119 kW) for take-off, or one Argus As.III inline piston engine rated at 180 hp (134 kW) for take-off
Performance: maximum speed 87 mph (140 km/h) at sea level; climb to 6,560 ft (2000 m) in 25 minutes; service ceiling 9,845 ft (3000 m); endurance 2 hours 30 minutes
Weights: empty equipped 1,929 lb (875 kg); maximum take-off 2,623 lb (1190 kg)
Dimensions: wingspan 42 ft 4 in (12.90 m); length 25 ft 9 in (7.85 m); height 10 ft 3⅜ in (3.14 m); wing area 434.88 sq ft (40.40 m²)
Armament: one 0.312-in (7.92-mm) LMG 14 Parabellum trainable rearward-firing machine-gun, and sometimes provision for the carriage of 154 lb (70 kg) of bombs

Albatros L.10 and L.16 (C.III and C.VI)

Successor to the C.I and the most prolific of all Albatros two-seater warplanes, the **Albatros L.10** was essentially a development of the B.III unarmed two-seater. The positions of the observer and pilot were reversed so that the former now occupied the rear seat and became an observer/gunner with a ring-mounted 0.312-in (7.92-mm) LMG 14

Parabellum trainable rearward-firing machine-gun, giving the aircraft a useful defensive capability. The aircraft's armament capability was further enhanced by the retrofit, when made feasible by the development of an effective synchronisation system, of a 0.312-in (7.92-mm) LMG 08/15 fixed forward-firing machine-gun.

The primary feature in

Leutnant Bruno Maass of Fliegerabteilung 14 flew this C.III on the Eastern Front during 1916.

which the **C.III**, as the type was designated in its service form, was distinguishable from the C.I was its completely different and considerably more curvaceous tail unit. The horizontal surface had a totally curved outline, and the vertical surface retained the low-aspect ratio fin of triangular shape, but in this instance carrying a plain rudder with a rounded trailing-edge shape. The new tail unit made the C.III significantly more sensitive to control inputs in the directional and longitudinal planes, with clear advan-

tages in the type of more agile air combat that was developing in the second half of 1915.

Such was the success of the type in initial service, from a time late in 1915, that large-scale production was begun. The C.III remained in German service right up until the end of World War I.

The sole **W.2** was a floatplane development of the C.III with a powerplant of one Mercedes D.III inline piston engine rated at 160 hp (119 kW), larger vertical tail surfaces, a modified upper-wing centre section, and a very clean

side-by-side installation of two floats. The machine was delivered to the Imperial German naval air service in June 1916, with armament restricted to the trainable machine-gun in the rear cockpit, and the type did not enter production after evaluation in the patrol role.

Known to the parent company as the **L.16**, the **C.VI** was built in small numbers as an improved C.III with slightly different dimensions, and its engine bearers strengthened to accept the Argus As.III inline piston engine rated at 180 hp (134 kW).

SPECIFICATION

Albatros C.III
Type: two-seat reconnaissance and artillery-spotting aircraft
Powerplant: one Benz Bz.III inline piston engine rated at 150 hp (112 kW) for take-off, or one Mercedes D.III inline piston engine rated at 160 hp (119 kW) for take-off
Performance: maximum speed 87 mph (140 km/h) at sea level; climb to 6,560 ft (2000 m) in 22 minutes; service ceiling 11,150 ft (3400 m); endurance 4 hours
Weights: empty equipped 1,876 lb (851 kg); maximum take-off 2,982 lb (1353 kg)
Dimensions: wingspan 38 ft 4 in (11.69 m); length 26 ft 3 in (8.00 m); height 10 ft 2 in (3.10 m) with D.III engine or 10 ft (3.07 m) with Bz.III engine; wing area 397.31 sq ft (36.91 m²)
Armament: one 0.312-in (7.92-mm) LMG 08/15 fixed forward-firing machine-gun in the upper starboard side of the fuselage with synchronisation equipment to fire through the propeller disc, and one 0.312-in (7.92-mm) LMG 14 Parabellum trainable rearward-firing machine-gun in the rear cockpit plus, in some aircraft, provision for the carriage between the cockpits of a vertical drum-shaped container for 198 lb (90 kg) of light bombs

Albatros L.11 and L.21 (G.II and G.III)

In 1916, the manufacturer flew the sole **Albatros L.11** prototype of its **G.II** medium bomber. This was of typical Albatros construction and was clearly intended to allow the carriage of the heaviest possible bombload. The design's interplane struts were rigid enough to remove the need for incidence bracing wires, and the powerplant of two Benz Bz.III inline piston engines, each rated at 150 hp (112

kW), was located in very neat nacelles above the lower wing to drive two-bladed pusher propellers fitted with spinners.

The same basic concept was adopted for the **L.21** that followed later in 1916 as the production version of the G.II, for service as the **G.III**. The fuselage had open positions for the crew of three (pilot and two gunners), and carried the flying surfaces. The latter comprised the wire-braced

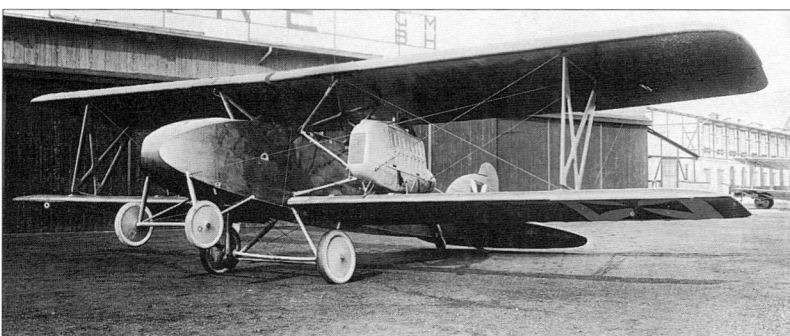

One G.II was built, with the developed G.III variant entering service. The clean installation of the Mercedes engines of the G.II is readily apparent.

tail unit of typical Albatros shaping, and the unequal-span biplane wing cellule, which was of the single-bay type and carried the two engines.

The nacelles for the two Benz Bz.IVa inline piston engines, each rated at 220 hp (164 kW) and driving a two-bladed wooden propeller with a spinner, were attached to the structure of the lower-wing

centre section and braced laterally by struts to the upper and lower longerons. The tail was supported by a skid but, unlike on the G.II, there was no supplementary nosewheel unit.

The production total and operational career of the G.III are uncertain, it being

known only that the type was used in limited numbers on the Macedonian front, where the maximum number of aircraft operational at any one time was about 10. It seems unlikely that any use was made of the G.III after the autumn of 1917.

SPECIFICATION

Albatros G.III
Type: three-seat medium bomber
Powerplant: two Benz Bz.IVa inline piston engines each rated at 220 hp (164 kW) for take-off
Performance: maximum speed 93 mph (150 km/h) at sea level; climb to 6,560 ft (2000 m) in 25 minutes; endurance 4 hours
Weights: empty equipped 4,550 lb (2064 kg); maximum take-off 6,944 lb (3150 kg)
Dimensions: wingspan 59 ft ⅔ in (18.00 m); length 39 ft ⅓ in (11.90 m); wing area 850.38 sq ft (79.00 m²)
Armament: single 0.312-in (7.92-mm) LMG 14 Parabellum trainable machine-guns in the nose and dorsal positions, and up to about 716 lb (325 kg) of bombs

Albatros L.14 (C.V)

Late in 1915, Mercedes started work on its more powerful D.IV engine and the promise of this persuaded Albatros to develop a successor to the C.III, which was now outmoded and also lacked the structural strength to handle the weight and power of the new engine.

The design team there-fore opted for a new **Albatros L.14** design that was nonetheless very similar to the early aircraft. Although the new engine was larger, its gearbox raised the thrust line and thereby made possible a cleaner nose section. This was further improved by the installation of the engine as a completely

enclosed unit with only the water header tank and star-board-side 'rhino horn' exhaust manifold exposed.

The aircraft that entered service as the **C.V** was a marginally unequal-span biplane based on a fuselage of wooden construction covered with plywood except on the area of the extreme nose and upper decking as far to the rear as the forward cockpit, which was skinned with light alloy.

The C.V entered service in the second half of 1916, and although its ground-crews were happy with the performance of their new warplane, its pilots were less than happy with the cumbersome nature of the aircraft in the air, where agility was hampered by the machine's size, weight, and unbalanced lateral and longitudinal control

This specially-decorated C.V was the 2,500th Albatros aircraft to be built. The Mercedes-engined machine was adorned during 1917 as a fitting tribute to the company's success.

surfaces. Albatros immediately set about the development of an improved version, where-upon the initial variant became the **C.V/16**.

An improved version of the C.V/16, the **C.V/17**, was introduced early in 1917. The C.V/17 proved a much better aircraft to

handle in the air. What Albatros could not address, however, was the unreliability of the engine, so only limited production was undertaken and the maximum number of C.V aircraft in service at any one time was 65, shortly before the type was withdrawn late in 1917.

SPECIFICATION

Albatros C.V/16

Type: two-seat reconnaissance and artillery-spotting aircraft
Powerplant: one Mercedes D.IV inline piston engine rated at 220 hp (164 kW) for take-off
Performance: maximum speed 106 mph (170 km/h) at sea level; climb to 9,845 ft (3000 m) in 16 minutes 30 seconds; service ceiling 17,060 ft (5200 m); endurance 3 hours 15 minutes
Weights: empty equipped 2,357 lb (1069 kg); maximum take-off

3,494 lb (1585 kg)
Dimensions: wingspan 41 ft 11 in (12.78 m); length 29 ft 4⅜ in (8.95 m); height 14 ft 9 in (4.50 m); wing area 467.17 sq ft (43.40 m²)
Armament: one synchronised 0.312-in (7.92-mm) LMG 08/15 fixed forward-firing machine-gun in the forward fuselage and one 0.312-in (7.92-mm) LMG 14 Parabellum trainable rearward-firing machine gun in the rear cockpit, and up to 397 lb (180 kg) of bombs

Albatros L.15 and L.17 (D.I and D.II)

Although the Germans had gained almost total air superiority over the Western Front in the winter of 1915-16, from the spring of 1916 this situation was reversed as the Allies introduced the Nieuport Nie.11 and Airco (de Havilland) DH.2 fighters.

A requirement was there-fore identified for a biplane fighter that was sturdy enough to withstand the stresses of combat flying without difficulty and could use one of the new water-cooled inline engines rated at 150 hp (112 kW) or more. Such power was needed to

make practical the use of a two-gun armament without the extra weight of the guns affecting performance.

Albatros's response was the **L.15** that first appeared in prototype form during August 1916 as an equal-span biplane based on the company's recent design experience in two-spar wing structures and all-wood fuselages. Either one Benz Bz.III or Mercedes D.III inline piston engine could be installed.

It was decided that heavy armament was more impor-tant than manoeuvrability

and the validity of this reasoning was fully confirmed when the L.15 entered service in September 1916 as the **D.I** with the first Jastas (Jagdstaffeln). It flew initially in mixed units that also operated the earlier Fokker and Halberstadt biplane fighters, until there were enough aircraft to allow the creation of homogeneously equipped units, of which the first was Jasta 2, commanded by Hauptmann Oswald Boelcke.

Probably fewer than 75 D.I fighters had been completed before the type was supplanted in produc-tion by an improved model during November 1916. The D.I's main operational limitation was the poor forward and upward fields of vision provided to its pilot, and this was reme-died in the **L.17**, which was produced for service as the **D.II** and powered by the Mercedes D.III engine. In this aircraft, the inter-plane gap was reduced so that the upper wing was more level with the pilot's line of sight. As a result of this simple change, the D.II was a better fighter than the D.I, and was then

Although the D.I was a generally competent fighter, pilots found that the position of its upper wing impaired visibility during combat.

further improved by the addition of revised radia-tors which created less drag.

The Imperial Austro-Hungarian army air service received 20 **D.II Series 53** fighters built by Oeffag. These featured the 185-hp (138-kW) Austro-Daimler inline piston engine and sometimes a revised arma-ment of two 0.315-in (8-mm) Schwarzlose machine-guns.

Replacement of the D.I and D.II by the more capa-ble D.III began in January 1917. In this month, the D.II

force reached a front-line peak of 214 aircraft and, by November of the same year, the D.I and D.II had virtually disappeared from first-line service. By 1918 most of the survivors were serving as advanced flying and fighter trainers.

After the end of World War I, Germany was banned from the production of mili-tary aircraft, and it is worth noting that it was at this time that Albatros intro-duced a new series of L-series designations which helped to conceal its contin-ued work on such aircraft.

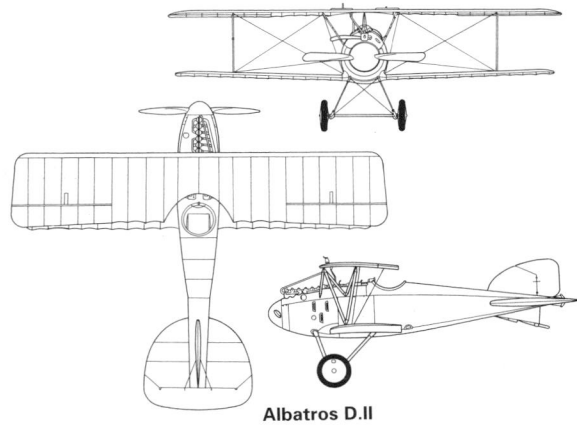

Albatros D.II

SPECIFICATION

Albatros D.I

Type: single-seat fighter
Powerplant: one Benz Bz.III inline piston engine rated at 150 hp (112 kW) for take-off, or one Mercedes D.III inline piston engine rated at 160 hp (119 kW) for take-off
Performance: maximum speed 109 mph (175 km/h) at sea level; climb to 6,560 ft (200 m) in 9 minutes 6 seconds; service ceiling 17,060 ft (5200 m);

endurance 1 hour 30 minutes
Weights: empty equipped 1,426 lb (647 kg); maximum take-off 1,980 lb (898 kg)
Dimensions: wingspan 27 ft 10⅜ in (8.50 m); length 24 ft 3⅓ in (7.40 m); height 9 ft 8⅛ in (2.95 m); wing area 246.50 sq ft (22.90 m²)
Armament: two synchronised 0.312-in (7.92-mm) LMG 08/15 fixed forward-firing machine-guns

Manfred von Richthofen, the 'Red Baron', scored his first confirmed victory while flying this D.II on 17 September 1916.

Albatros L.18 (C.VII)

As soon as it became clear that the service career of its C.V was likely to be affected adversely by the reliability problems of its Mercedes D.IV engine, Albatros started to plan a successor with a more reliable powerplant, for which the new 260-hp (194-kW) Mercedes D.IVa six-cylinder inline piston engine seemed an inevitable choice. This engine was not immediately available, however, so the company's design team started work on an interim type to replace the C.V, and this appeared late in 1916 as the **Albatros L.18**, which was ordered as the **C.VII**. This interim type made extensive use of C.V components and assemblies wherever possible.

Demonstrating the classic shape of the Albatros empennage, this C.VII also shows the shorter nose profile of the type when compared to the C.V.

The C.VII therefore had the appearance of a hybrid type combining C.V/16 and C.V/17 features, and the area in which the type was most readily distinguishable from the C.V was its forward fuselage, which was extensively revised for the accommodation of the shorter and lighter engine, much of whose cylinder block was exposed to the airstream.

The powerplant was one 200-hp (149-kW) Benz Bz.IV engine, exhausted via a vertical 'rhino horn' manifold on the starboard side of the cylinder bank.

The C.VII proved to be very successful, with good performance and excellent handling. By February 1917, 350 of the aircraft were operational and the type served until the end of World War I.

SPECIFICATION

Albatros C.VII
Type: two-seat reconnaissance and artillery-spotting aircraft
Powerplant: one Benz Bz.IV inline piston engine rated at 200 hp (149 kW) for take-off
Performance: maximum speed 106 mph (170 km/h) at sea level; climb to 6,560 ft (2000 m) in 17 minutes; service ceiling 16,405 ft (5000 m); endurance 3 hours 20 minutes
Weights: empty equipped 2,189 lb (989 kg); maximum take-off 3,417 lb (1550 kg)
Dimensions: wingspan 41 ft 11 in (12.78 m); length 28 ft 6 in (8.70 m); height 11 ft 9 in (3.60 m); wing area 467.17 sq ft (43.40 m²)
Armament: one synchronised 0.312-in (7.92-mm) LMG 08/15 fixed forward-firing machine-gun and one 0.312-in (7.92-mm) LMG 14 Parabellum trainable rearward-firing machine-gun in the rear cockpit

Albatros L.20 (D.III)

Even as his D.I and D.II fighters were entering production, Dipl.-Ing. Robert Thelen, the Albatros Werke's chief designer, was working on the creation of a more advanced type in which the D.II was adapted with features of the French-built Nieuport Nie.11.

The sesquiplane wing of the Nie.11 was of most interest, and such a wing cellule was therefore combined with the fuselage, tail unit, landing gear and powerplant of the D.II fighter to create the new **Albatros D.III**, which received the retrospective company designation **L.20**.

The powerplant of one Mercedes D.IIIa inline engine was cooled by a radiator of aerofoil shape. This was installed centrally in the first aircraft, but was subsequently offset to starboard so that combat damage would not result in the release of scalding water over the pilot.

The D.III offered considerable operational advantages over the D.II, and entered large-scale production from January 1917. Initially entering service with Jasta 11, by April of 1917, the D.III equipped all 37 first-line Jagdstaffeln on the Western Front. The type almost immediately gained the nickname 'Vee-strutter' with pilots of the Royal Flying Corps, who very soon accorded the aircraft a very high level of respect

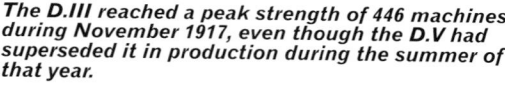

The D.III reached a peak strength of 446 machines during November 1917, even though the D.V had superseded it in production during the summer of that year.

for its undoubted combat capability. This was most fully revealed in the 'Bloody April' of 1917, when the pilots of the German fighter arm, and of the D.III in particular, inflicted a very heavy toll on British pilots.

The D.III had its faults, however. It was found to possess a measure of structural weakness in the lower wing, and manoeuvring flight and high-speed dives could lead to catastrophic wing failure.

By the summer of 1917, the D.III had been rendered obsolescent by the advent of more capable Allied fighters. From July 1917, therefore, the D.III was largely replaced by the improved Albatros D.V and was only in limited service at the end of World War I. The D.III reached its operational peak strength in November 1917, when there were some 446 of the type in service on the Western Front. Demand for the type exceeded Albatros's production capacity, so additional aircraft were built in Germany by the Ostdeutsche Albatros Werke, and in Austria-Hungary by Oeffag (Oesterreichische Flugzeugfabrik A.G.). This last produced three series of D.III fighters for the Austro-Hungarian army air service with the Austro-Daimler inline piston engine: the **D.III Series 53.2** had the 185-hp (148-kW) unit; the **D.III Series 153** had the 200-hp (149-kW) unit; and the **D.III Series 253** had the 225-hp (168-kW) unit.

After World War I, some D.IIIs were delivered to the army air service of the newly-independent Poland.

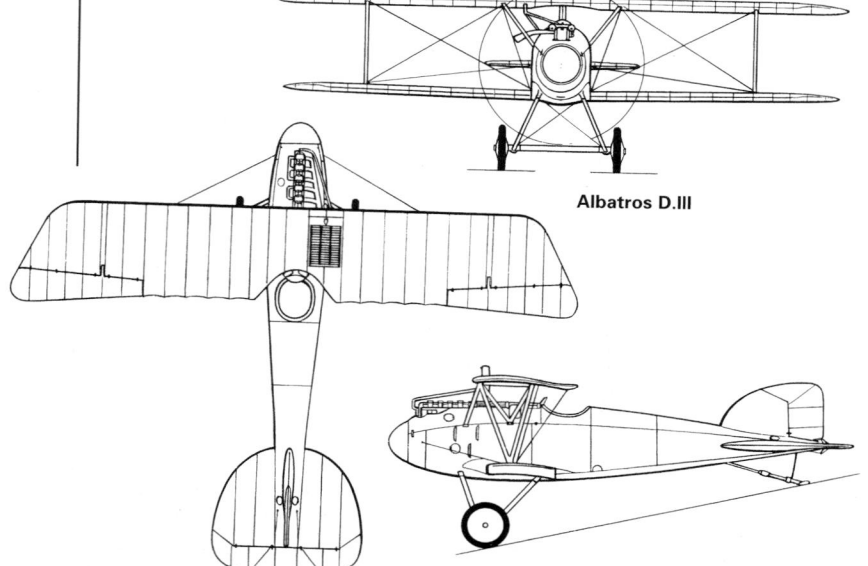

Albatros D.III

SPECIFICATION

Albatros D.III
Type: single-seat fighter
Powerplant: one Mercedes D.IIIa piston engine rated at 160 hp (119 kW) for take-off
Performance: maximum speed 109 mph (175 km/h) at 3,280 ft (1000 m); climb to 9,845 ft (3000 m) in 12 minutes 1 second; service ceiling 18,045 ft (5500 m); endurance 2 hours
Weights: empty equipped 1,457 lb (661 kg); maximum take-off 1,953 lb (886 kg)
Dimensions: wingspan 29 ft 8 in (9.05 m); length 24 ft 1⅛ in (7.33 m); height 9 ft 9 in (2.98 m); wing area 220.67 sq ft (20.50 m²)
Armament: two synchronised 0.312-in (7.92-mm) LMG 08/15 fixed forward-firing machine-guns on the upper part of the forward fuselage

Albatros L.22 (D.IV)

Uniting the D.Va fuselage with a wing based on that of the D.II failed to produce a viable fighter.

In the second half of 1916, Mercedes developed a geared version of its classic D.III piston engine; the reduction gearing reduced the engine's 1,400 revolutions per minute to the propeller's 900 revolutions per minute. Moreover, the raising of the propeller axis effectively lowered the engine, making possible an installation with the tops of the cylinder's banks fully contained in the forward fuselage, for a significant reduction of drag. In November 1916, the Imperial German army air service ordered three examples of the **Albatros D.IV** (with the retrospective designation **L.22**) with this engine type, as a possible successor to the D.III.

The D.IV was a result of the same type of evolutionary approach that had already witnessed the development of the D.III – from the D.I and D.II – through the introduction of Nieuport features. Thelen now decided that the best way to achieve useful improvements to the D.III was to improve the fighter with a biplane – rather than the sesquiplane – wing cellule based on that of the D.II, and to combine this with a D.Va fuselage.

The resulting D.IV offered a number of advantages over the D.III, but it is believed that only one aircraft was completed and flown due to problems with the engine. This machine survived until April 1918 and was test-flown with two-, three- and four-bladed propellers.

SPECIFICATION

Albatros L.22 (D.IV)
Type: single-seat fighter
Powerplant: one Mercedes D.III (geared version) inline piston engine rated at 160 hp (119 kW) for take-off
Performance: maximum speed 102.5 mph (165 km/h) at sea level; endurance 2 hours 12 minutes
Dimensions: wingspan 29 ft 8 in (9.04 m); length 24 ft ⅝ in (7.33 m); wing area 220.67 sq ft (20.50 m²)
Armament: (not fitted during tests) two synchronised fixed forward-firing 7.92-mm (0.312-in) LMG 08/15 machine-guns

Albatros L.23 (C.IX)

The **Albatros C.IX** (retrospective designation **L.23**) was built to the extent of just three aircraft in the course of 1917. It is thought that, after the type had been rejected for production, one machine may have been used as the personal transport of Rittmeister Manfred Freiherr von Richthofen.

The C.IX was of typical Albatros construction, although the upper and lower wings were separated on each side by a single set of interplane struts without incidence-bracing wires. Another unusual feature was a semi-'dogtooth' discontinuity in the leading edges of both the upper and lower wings.

A feature of the design was the excellent field of fire for the observer/gunner in the rear cockpit, which was built up into a 'pulpit' by upward- and inward-curved fuselage sides. The 'pulpit' also lessened the chances of the gunner hitting the fin of his own aircraft with gunfire.

SPECIFICATION

Albatros L.23 (C.IX)
Type: two-seat reconnaissance and artillery observation aircraft
Powerplant: one Mercedes D.III inline piston engine rated at 160 hp (119 kW) for take-off
Performance: maximum speed 96.5 mph (155 km/h) at sea level; climb to 13,125 ft (4000 m) in 30 minutes; endurance about 2 hours 30 minutes
Weights: empty 1,742 lb (790 kg); maximum take-off 2,535 lb (1150 kg)
Dimensions: wingspan 34 ft 1½ in (10.40 m); length 26 ft 11⅝ in (8.22 m); height 8 ft 11⅓ in (2.74 m)
Armament: one 0.312-in (7.92-mm) LMG 08/15 fixed forward-firing machine-gun and one 0.312-in (7.92-mm) LMG 14 Parabellum trainable rearward-firing machine-gun in the rear cockpit

The C.IX of 1917 boasted similar fuselage and tail construction to the Albatros 'D'-type fighters.

Albatros L.24 (D.V and D.Va)

By April 1917, the Imperial German army air service appreciated that the superiority of its D.III fighter was being eroded over the Western Front. Thelen had already planned the D.IV using a similar approach to that of the D.III, but without using the unproved geared version of the Mercedes D.III engine. Thelen therefore planned the **Albatros D.V** (retrospective designation **L.24**) as an aerodynamically refined and structurally lightened version of the D.III, with the fully oval-section fuselage of the D.IV and the powerplant of one high-compression Mercedes D.IIIa inline engine. The D.V was therefore a sesquiplane of basically wooden construction covered with plywood and fabric.

The D.V offered little improvement over the D.III and was not much more of a match for the latest, improved Allied fighters. Even so, the D.V was better able to hold its own in the hands of its more experienced pilots, the nature of the defensive air fighting now generally practised by the Germans and the ready availability of the D.V in large numbers.

Introduced in October 1917, the **D.Va** was a simple development of the D.V with the aileron-actuation system of the D.III, namely wires running

Albatros D.V

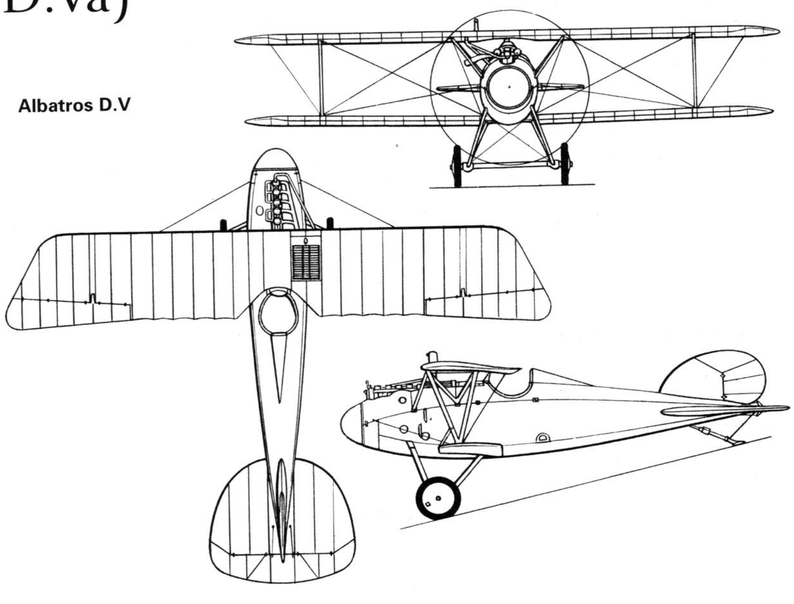

SPECIFICATION

Albatros L.24 (D.Va)
Type: single-seat fighter
Powerplant: one Mercedes D.IIIa piston engine rated at 180 hp (134 kW) for take-off
Performance: maximum speed 117 mph (188 km/h) at 3,280 ft (1000 m); climb to 9,845 ft (3000 m) in 17 minutes 8 seconds; service ceiling 18,700 ft (5700 m); endurance 2 hours
Weights: empty equipped 1,515 lb (687 kg); maximum take-off 2,066 lb (937 kg)
Dimensions: wingspan 29 ft 8 in (9.04 m); length 24 ft ⅝ in (7.33 m); height 8 ft 10¼ in (2.70 m); wing area 228.20 sq ft (21.20 m²)
Armament: two synchronised fixed forward-firing 0.312-in (7.92-mm) LMG 08/15 machine-guns

through the lower wing and thence upward to crank levers on the ailerons, which were fitted to the upper wing.

By the time that the D.Va entered service, it seems likely that around 900 D.V and 1,612 D.Va fighters had been ordered. Numerical peaks were reached on the Western Front by the D.V in November 1917 with 131 aircraft, and by the D.Va in March 1918 with 928 aircraft. Other D.V and D.Va fighters were operational on the Italian and Palestinian fronts, as well as with home-based training establishments, so a total of well in excess of 2,000 had been built before production ceased in 1918.

This D.Va wears the personal markings of Leutnant H. J. von Hippel of Jagdstaffel 5 in the spring of 1918.

Albatros L.25 (C.X)

Considerable care was taken to ensure that the C.X was as aerodynamically refined as possible.

The promise of the new 260-hp (194-kW) Mercedes D.IVa engine persuaded Albatros to design an advanced two-seater biplane for the reconnaissance and artillery observation roles, as a successor to the C.VII.

The **Albatros L.25** (**C.X**) introduced a wider, deeper and longer fuselage, whose additional volume allowed the incorporation of oxygen equipment for the pilot, substantial radio equipment for the observer/gunner, and a wing cellule that offered greatly increased performance and controllability thanks to its increased span and revised planform.

The C.X proved to have good performance and range, and was therefore generally used in the long-range reconnaissance role, for which there were some 300 of the type in service, with units operating over the Western Front by October 1917.

SPECIFICATION

Albatros L.25 (C.X)
Type: two-seat reconnaissance and artillery observation aircraft
Powerplant: one Mercedes D.IVa inline piston engine rated at 260 hp (194 kW) for take-off
Performance: maximum speed 109 mph (175 km/h) at sea level; climb to 6,560 ft (2000 m) in 6 minutes 30 seconds; service ceiling 16,405 ft (5000 m); endurance 3 hours 25 minutes
Weights: empty equipped 2,315 lb (1050 kg); maximum take-off 3,677 lb (1668 kg)
Dimensions: wingspan 47 ft ¼ in (14.36 m); length 30 ft (9.15 m); height 11 ft 1⅞ in (3.40 m); wing area 459.63 sq ft (42.70 m²)
Armament: one synchronised 0.312-in (7.92-mm) LMG 08/15 fixed forward-firing machine-gun on the starboard upper side of the forward fuselage and one 0.312-in (7.92-mm) LMG 14 Parabellum trainable rearward-firing machine gun in the rear cockpit, plus provision for light bombs

Albatros L.26 (C.XI) and L.27 (C.XII)

A finely streamlined fuselage and proven engine, ensured the C.XII success over the Western Front.

The **L.26** (**C.XI**) remained only a project, so the next Albatros two-seater model was the **Albatros L.27** (**C.XII**). This was in essence a development of the C.X, incorporating the lessons that the company had learned with its single-seat fighters of the 'D' category.

An immediately apparent difference between the C.X and C.XII was the latter's different exhaust manifold, which discharged to starboard and slightly downward instead of over the upper wing. The more subtle – and generally more important – changes included a fuselage of elliptical cross section with a finer rear section whose reduced keel area offered a reduction in drag, but demanded compensation in the form of a ventral fin, to which the tailskid was attached, for the maintenance of directional stability. The horizontal tail surface was also reduced in area to maintain the aircraft's longitudinal sensitivity, and this revised surface was now of more oval shape with a tailplane skinned in plywood.

The C.XII entered service in 1918 and remained operational right up to the end of World War I.

SPECIFICATION

Albatros L.27 (C.XII)
Type: two-seat reconnaissance and artillery observation aircraft
Powerplant: one Mercedes D.IVa inline piston engine rated at 260 hp (194 kW) for take-off
Performance: maximum speed 109 mph (175 km/h) at sea level; climb to 6,560 ft (2000 m) in 8 minutes; service ceiling 16,405 ft (5000 m); endurance 3 hours 15 minutes
Weights: empty equipped 2,251 lb (1021 kg); maximum take-off 3,613 lb (1639 kg)
Dimensions: wingspan 47 ft 1⅞ in (14.37 m); length 29 ft ⅜ in (8.85 m); height 10 ft 7⅞ in (3.25 m); wing area 459.63 sq ft (42.70 m²)
Armament: one synchronised 0.312-in (7.92-mm) LMG 08/15 fixed forward-firing machine gun on the starboard upper side of the forward fuselage and one 0.312-in (7.92-mm) LMG 14 Parabellum trainable rearward-firing machine gun in the rear cockpit, plus provision for light bombs

Albatros L.34 (D.VII)

Following the failure of its twin-boom **L.28** (**D.VI**) fighter, the **L.34** (**D.VII**) was another of the experimental fighters designed and built by Albatros at the end of World War I, in the hope that air superiority could be won from the British and French over the Western Front. The D.VII was modelled more closely on the traditional Albatros configuration than the D.VI (that, in fact, followed it into the air despite its lower designation number), although with a stockier and sturdier fuselage and a staggered single-bay wing cellule.

The D.VII was of wooden construction covered with wood veneer on the fuselage and fin, and with fabric on the wings, horizontal tail surface and rudder. The pilot was accommodated in an open cockpit under a cut-out on the trailing edge of the upper wing's centre section, and the landing gear was of the fixed tailskid type with a main unit of the conventional through-axle design.

The D.VII had the standard German fighter armament of the period, but the powerplant was slightly unusual in being based on the Vee type Benz Bz.IIIb engine, rather than on the inline type engine which was more common on German fighters with water-cooled powerplants. The use of this engine meant that a shorter, blunt nose could be adopted, with the heads of the two cylinder banks protruding through the upper part of the cowling.

Only limited flight trials were undertaken after initial test results indicated that the D.VII did not have the qualities required of a front-line warplane.

Just one prototype of the disappointing D.VII fighter was built.

SPECIFICATION

Albatros L.34 (D.VII)
Type: single-seat fighter prototype
Powerplant: one Benz Bz.IIIb Vee piston engine rated at 195 hp (145.5 kW) for take-off
Performance: maximum speed 127 mph (204 km/h) at sea level; climb to 6,560 ft (2000 m) in 7 minutes; endurance 2 hours
Weights: empty 1,389 lb (630 kg); maximum take-off 1,951 lb (885 kg)
Dimensions: wingspan 30 ft 6⅞ in (9.32 m); length 21 ft 8½ in (6.61 m)
Armament: two synchronised fixed forward-firing 0.312-in (7.92-mm) LMG 08/15 machine-guns

Albatros L.36 (Dr.I)

In the early part of 1917, the Imperial German army air service was spurred on by the success of the Sopwith Triplane fighter to order the design and prototype construction of several kinds of triplane fighter in an effort to create a type offering a rate of climb and a level of agility altogether superior to those of its standard biplane fighters. Albatros therefore created a triplane fighter prototype that was known as the **L.36** (**Dr.I**).

Flown in the summer of 1917 for comparative evaluation against the D.V biplane fighter, the Dr.I was little more than a D.V with one Daimler D.IIIa inline piston engine and an unstaggered single-bay triplane wing cellule.

The flight test programme clearly revealed the fact that the Dr.I offered no advantage over the D.V, and the triplane therefore progressed no further than the prototype stage.

SPECIFICATION

Albatros L.36 (Dr.I)
Type: single-seat triplane fighter prototype
Powerplant: one Daimler D.IIIa inline piston engine rated at 180 hp (134 kW) for take-off
Dimensions: wingspan 28 ft 6⅝ in (8.70 m); length 24 ft ⅝ in (7.33 m)
Armament: two fixed forward-firing 0.312-in (7.92-mm) LMG 08/15 machine-guns

The Dr.I's wings were of parallel chord, with an aileron at the trailing edge of each outer wing.

Albatros L.37 (D.IX)

Although it was based on the same type of veneer-covered wooden fuselage as its predecessors, the Albatros **L.37** (**D.IX**) fighter departed from the company's practice in that the fuselage was not of oval section, but of slab-sided section with a flat bottom and sides under a rounded upper decking.

The tail unit and wing cellule were similar to those of the D.VII. The two-bladed wooden propeller was not fitted with a spinner and the fuselage ended in a rounded shape just ahead of the engine.

In other respects, the D.IX was of typical German fighter standard, with its fixed tailskid landing gear (with a main unit of the through-axle type), and armament of two synchronised rifle-calibre machine-guns in the upper decking of the forward fuselage, firing through the propeller disc.

The sole D.IX prototype made its maiden flight early in 1918, but its performance can only be described only as disappointing and all further development was soon terminated.

SPECIFICATION

Albatros L.37 (D.IX)
Type: single-seat fighter prototype
Powerplant: one Daimler D.IIIa inline piston engine rated at 180 hp (134 kW) for take-off
Performance: maximum speed 96 mph (155 km/h) at sea level; climb to 3,280 ft (1000 m) in 4 minutes
Weights: empty 1,492 lb (677 kg); maximum take-off 1,977 lb (897 kg)
Dimensions: wingspan 34 ft 1½ in (10.40 m); length 21 ft 9⅞ in (6.65 m)
Armament: two 0.312-in (7.92-mm) LMG 08/15 fixed forward-firing machine-guns

The D.IX unsuccessfully united the wings of the D.VII with a new, slab-sided, fuselage.

Albatros L.38 (D.X)

The **Albatros L.38** (**D.X**) was designed and built in parallel with the D.IX and had the same type of slab-sided fuselage. Power came from one Benz Bz.IIIbo eight-cylinder Vee piston engine driving a two-bladed wooden propeller fitted with a large spinner that led to a more aerodynamically refined type of nose entry. The D.X's tail unit was of the same modified 'fishtail' type that had been introduced on the D.VII.

The D.X made its maiden flight early in 1918 and was one of the types evaluated competitively in the Imperial German army air service's second 'D' type fighter competition at Adlershof in June and July 1918. During the evaluation, the D.X distinguished itself neither in performance nor handling, and proceeded no further than the prototype stage.

SPECIFICATION

Albatros L.38 (D.X)
Type: single-seat fighter prototype
Powerplant: one Benz Bz.IIIbo Vee piston engine rated at 195 hp (145.5 kW) for take-off
Performance: maximum speed 96 mph (155 km/h) at sea level; climb to 16,405 ft (5000 m) in 22 minutes; endurance 1 hour 30 minutes
Weights: empty 1,468 lb (666 kg); maximum take-off 1,995 lb (905 kg)
Dimensions: wingspan 32 ft 3⅜ in (9.84 m); length 20 ft 3⅓ in (6.18 m); height 9 ft ⅜ in (2.75 m)
Armament: two 0.312-in (7.92-mm) LMG 08/15 fixed forward-firing machine guns

With its lacklustre performance, the D.X once took 35 minutes 36 seconds to reach 16,400 ft (5000 m).

Albatros L.39 (Dr.II)

Using the disappointing D.X as its basis, the Dr.II fighter prototype featured a staggered triplane wing.

The **Albatros L.39** (**Dr.II**) was produced in parallel with the D.X as a triplane version of the original biplane. The wing cellule was very heavily staggered, with the lower and central wings aligned with the bottom and upper lines of the fuselage and the upper wing above and ahead of them. The narrow chord of the upper wing made the aerofoil-shaped radiator of the D.X impractical, so the Dr.II had a pair of frontal-type radiators installed on each side of the centreline between the central and upper wings. There is no doubt that the high drag associated with this installation was responsible for a severe degradation of performance, and the type's inevitable failure as a fighter design.

Given its indifferent handling and poor performance, the Dr.II was submitted for only limited flight trials during the spring of 1918, and no production plans were ever contemplated.

SPECIFICATION

Albatros L.39 (Dr.II)
Type: single-seat triplane fighter prototype
Powerplant: one Benz Bz.IIIbo Vee piston engine rated at 195 hp (145.5 kW) for take-off
Weights: empty 1,490 lb (676 kg); maximum take-off 2,017 lb (915 kg)
Dimensions: wingspan 32 ft 9⅔ in (10.00 m); length 20 ft 3⅓ in (6.18 m); height 10 ft 11½ in (3.34 m); wing area 286.32 sq ft (26.60 m²)
Armament: two fixed forward-firing 0.312-in (7.92-mm) LMG 08/15 machine-guns

Albatros L.40 (J.I)

In 1916, Albatros developed a ground-attack aircraft under the designation **Albatros L.40 (J.I)**. An essential feature of the type was armour protection for the crew and for vital elements of the airframe and powerplant against the effects of ground fire. This required the design and building of a new type of fuselage of established Albatros construction, but of slab-sided rather than oval section to facilitate the

addition of the 1,078 lb (490 kg) of armour, which comprised 0.2-in (5-mm) chrome nickel steel plates bolted onto the sides and bottom of the fuselage around the cockpit area.

In an effort to speed up the development and production of this potentially decisive type, the J.I was completed with the wing cellule of the C.XII, with a small amount of sweep on the outer panels to compensate for the weight of the armour and to

Following World War I, some Albatros J.I attack aircraft were exported to Poland, as illustrated.

maintain the centre of gravity in the correct position.

Oddly enough, given the higher weight of the J.I, the powerplant was altered from the C.XII's 260-hp (194-kW) Mercedes D.IVa inline engine to the Benz Bz.IV rated at 200 hp (149 kW), and this inevitably meant a reduction in overall performance levels. The engine was cooled by a radiator mounted frontally ahead of the junction of the upper wing's two halves, and any puncture of the radiator would result in the crew being sprayed with scalding water.

The J.I first flew in the summer of 1916 and entered immediate production for service from the autumn of the same year. Despite failings such as poor performance and the centrally-mounted radiator, the J.I soon acquired a good reputation as a 'ground strafer', with its fixed armament of two 0.312-in (7.92-mm) LMG 08/15 machine guns aligned to fire obliquely forward and downward at an angle of 45°.

It was appreciated from the beginning of its programme that the J.I

ground-attack warplane was most limited in tactical terms by the vulnerability of its powerplant, which was not accorded the armoured protection provided for the two members of the crew. This deficiency was addressed in the **Albatros L.42 (J.II)**, four examples of which were built with armour protection for the engine and a number of other refinements. Initially flown with similar armament to the J.I, a pair of identical weapons in a conventional installation was subsequently fitted.

SPECIFICATION	
Albatros L.40 (J.I)	(1398 kg); maximum take-off
Type: two-seat close-support aircraft	3,986 lb (1808 kg)
Powerplant: one Benz Bz.IV inline piston engine rated at 200 hp (149 kW) for take-off	**Dimensions:** wingspan 46 ft 4¾ in (14.14 m); length 28 ft 11¾ in; height 11 ft ¾ in; wing area 460.93 sq ft (42.82 m²)
Performance: maximum speed 87 mph (140 km/h) at sea level; climb to 3,280 ft (1000 m) in 11 minutes 24 seconds; endurance 2 hours 30 minutes	**Armament:** two fixed forward/downward-firing 0.312-in (7.92-mm) LMG 08/15 machine-guns and one 0.312-in (7.92-mm) LMG 14 Parabellum trainable machine gun in the rear cockpit
Weights: empty 3,082 lb	

Albatros L.41 (D.XI)

Albatros L.41 (D.XI)

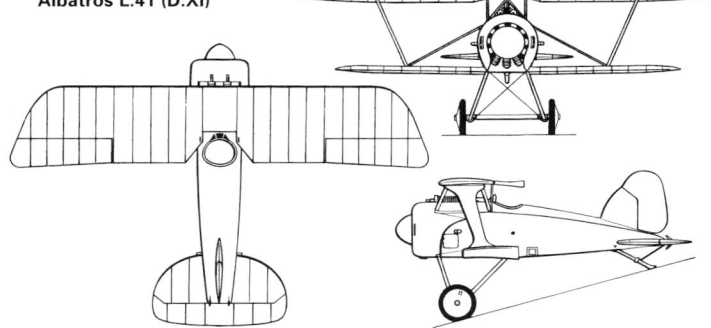

With the **L.41 (D.XI)**, Albatros used a rotary engine for the first time on one of its 'D' type aircraft. The Siemens-Halske Sh III was installed in a horseshoe cowling and, in the

initial aircraft, drove a four-bladed tractor propeller. The latter was changed to a two-bladed unit in the second aircraft, which also incorporated changes to the ailerons. Single inter-

Illustrated here in its second form, the D.XI exhibited excellent performance in tests.

plane struts, augmented by twin diagonal bracing struts, dispensed with the need for bracing wires between the wings.

Although the D.XIs demonstrated excellent climb performance during the second 'D' type competition, no production was undertaken.

SPECIFICATION	
Albatros L.41 (D.XI)	30 minutes
Type: single seat fighter	**Weights:** empty 1,087 lb (494 kg); loaded 1,516 lb (689 kg)
Powerplant: one 160-hp (215-kW) Siemens-Halske Sh III rotary piston engine	**Dimensions:** wingspan 26 ft 3 in; length 18 ft 3¾ in; height 9 ft 4⅝ in; wing area 199.8 sq ft (18.5 m²)
Performance: maximum speed 119 mph (190 km/h); climb to 16,400 ft (4998 m) in 15 minutes 6 seconds; endurance 1 hour	**Armament:** two fixed forward-firing 0.312-in (7.92-mm) Spandau machine-guns

Albatros L.43 (D.XII)

The last fighter type to be completed by the company before the end of World War I, the **Albatros L.43 (D.XII)** was in essence a derivative of the D.X fighter prototype with the same

type of fuselage, but a different powerplant and modified wings.

First flown in March 1918, the first of the two D.XII prototypes had horn-balanced ailerons on the

upper wing and the powerplant of one Daimler D.IIIa inline piston engine driving a two-bladed propeller without a spinner. The second machine first flew in the following month with changes that included unbalanced ailerons and the so-called Bohme type of main landing gear with a third strut on each side and compressed air rather than bungee rubber shock absorption. One of the prototypes was rated highly during the Imperial German army air service's second 'D' type fighter competition. The second prototype was subsequently revised with the powerplant of one BMW

Two D.XIIs were completed, the first (illustrated above) being powered by a Daimler D.IIIa engine.

IIIa inline piston engine rated at 185 hp (138 kW) for participation in the

third and final 'D' type fighter competition in October 1918.

SPECIFICATION	
Albatros L.43 (D.XII)	maximum take-off 1,675 lb (760 kg)
Type: single-seat fighter prototype	**Dimensions:** wing span 26 ft 10⅞ in (8.20 m); length 18 ft 11¾ in (5.78 m); height 9 ft 2¼ in (2.80 m); wing area 213.55 sq ft (19.84 m²)
Powerplant: one Daimler D.IIIa inline piston engine rated at 180 hp (134 kW) for take-off	**Armament:** two fixed forward-firing 0.312-in (7.92-mm) LMG 08/15 machine-guns
Performance: maximum speed 112 mph (180 km/h) at sea level; climb to 26,245 ft (8000 m) in 54 minutes; endurance 1 hour	
Weights: empty 1,279 lb (580 kg);	

Albatros L.59 and L.60

Designed and built in 1923, the **Albatros L.59** was a single-seat low-wing monoplane based on an essentially wooden structure. The thick-section cantilever wing was tapered in both chord and thickness, and the large 'trousered' main units of the fixed tailskid landing gear were mounted beneath, and braced to, the wing's centre section. A slab-sided fuselage provided accommodation for the pilot in an open cockpit, which was offset to port, and a conventional tail unit and tailskid were mounted at the aft end of the fuselage structure. Power was provided by a Siemens-Halske radial.

A generally similar two-seat variant was built at the same time under the designation **L.60**. This differed from the L.59 in having an uprated powerplant and provision for a passenger in a second open cockpit located to the rear of the pilot and offset to starboard.

SPECIFICATION

Albatros L.59
Type: single-seat touring monoplane
Powerplant: one Siemens-Halske radial piston engine rated at 55 hp (41 kW) for take-off
Performance: maximum speed 87 mph (140 km/h) at 3,280 ft (1000 m); climb to 3,280 ft (1000 m) in 9 minutes
Weights: empty 767 lb (348 kg); maximum take-off 1,058 lb (480 kg)

Designed specifically for touring, the L.59 provided open accommodation for the pilot. In its two-seat L.60 form, a second open cockpit was added.

Albatros L.65 (AFG Memel 1)

Following World War I, Germany was banned by the Allied powers from the construction or possession of military aircraft. A subterfuge most commonly adopted in the aircraft industry to avoid this ban was the establishment of subsidiary companies in neutral countries. Thus, Albatros-Flugzeugwerke created the Allgemeine Flug-Gesellschaft Memel company in Lithuania during 1925. The company's first product was the **AFG Memel 1**, or **Albatros L.65**, a neat fighter of unequal-span biplane layout.

The new fighter was of largely wooden construction covered with plywood except on the forward part of the fuselage, which was skinned with light alloy panels. The core of the structure was the fuselage, which was slab-sided with a flat bottom but a rounded upper decking. The upper and lower wings were separated on each side by a single wide-chord I-type interplane strut and the nature of the wing cellule obviated all need for incidence and the normal arrangement of flying and landing wires.

The powerplant was one Napier Lion W-type piston engine with the heads of its three cylinder banks enclosed in large external fairings and driving a two-bladed propeller. The **L.65-I** first prototype was powered by a Lion engine rated at 450 hp (335.5 kW), while the **L.65-II** second prototype first flew in 1926 with a Lion engine rated at 565 hp (421 kW). The second prototype offered somewhat better performance than the first machine, but although evaluated by Germany's clandestine army air service, the aircraft did not secure a production order.

SPECIFICATION

Albatros L.65-II (AFG Memel 1-II)
Type: single-seat fighter prototype
Powerplant: one Napier Lion W-type piston engine rated at 565 hp (421 kW) for take-off
Performance: maximum speed 155.5 mph (250 km/h) at sea level; service ceiling 26,245 ft (8000 m)
Dimensions: wingspan 33 ft 9⅔ in (10.30 m); length 20 ft 2⅛ in (6.15 m); height 9 ft 2⅛ in (2.80 m)
Armament: two fixed forward-firing 0.312-in (7.92-mm) machine-guns

Germany continued fighter development during the inter-war period, as proven by the L.65. Such testing paved the way for a rapid build-up of airpower during the 1930s.

Albatros L.68 Alauda

The Albatros Werke AG was dissolved as a company in early 1925 and then reformed as the Albatros-Flugzeugwerke GmbH, with this reorganisation also marking a change in the company's products. Typical of this new trend was the two-seat trainer designated as the **Albatros L.68c Alauda**. Of single-bay biplane configuration with N-type interplane struts, the L.68c had wings of wooden construction covered with plywood and fabric, while the fuselage and the braced tail unit were of welded steel-tube under a fabric covering.

Although the L.68 remained in service for many years, the only other important production variant of the aircraft was the **L.68e**, which was powered by one 200-hp (149-kW) Armstrong Siddeley Lynx radial piston engine. The new engine provided a maximum speed of 114.5 mph (184 km/h).

SPECIFICATION

Albatros L.68c Alauda
Type: two-seat training aircraft
Powerplant: one Siemens-Halske Sh.12 radial piston engine rated at 100 hp (74.6 kW) for take-off
Performance: maximum speed 84 mph (135 km/h) at sea level; climb to 6,560 ft (2000 m) in 24 minutes
Weights: empty 1,312 lb (595 kg); maximum take-off 1,929 lb (875 kg)
Dimensions: wingspan 33 ft 1⅕ in (10.10 m); length 21 ft 3 in (6.48 m); height 9 ft 5 in (2.87 m), wing area 269.11 sq ft (25.00 m^2)

While the two-seat L.68s were the most widespread, the single-seat L.68a (illustrated) also saw service.

Albatros L.72

The **Albatros L.72** was a transport aircraft designed to carry a pilot and four passengers, but could alternatively be used for the carriage of freight or newspapers. The L.72 had an unstaggered single-bay biplane wing cellule of fabric-covered metal construction, and both the fuselage and the braced tail unit were of fabric-covered welded steel tube construction. To the rear of the wing, the fuselage was of notably deep section and, at the rear, the upper surface carried only a small rectangular fin that was trailed by a high-aspect-ratio rudder hinged over most of its length to the vertical knife-edge in which the fuselage terminated. The landing gear was of typical Albatros tailskid type and, with only the top of its cylinder bank protruding in a vertical fairing, the BMW inline piston engine was very neatly cowled in the tapered nose.

The pilot was accommodated in an open cockpit immediately to the rear of the engine and below the upper wing, with the enclosed passenger cabin behind and below the cockpit. When the aircraft was used for the bulk delivery of newspapers, however, the cabin was provided with two folding seats and two vertically-arranged chutes which extended through the lower surface of the fuselage. These

A total of three L.72s was completed between 1926-7 and all three remained in service throughout the early 1930s.

chutes could carry up to 32 22-lb (10-kg) parcels of newspapers, which could be dropped individually or collectively by means of a control in the cockpit.

SPECIFICATION

Albatros L.72
Type: light transport aircraft
Powerplant: one BMW IV inline piston engine rated at 300 hp (224 kW) for take-off
Performance: maximum speed 99.5 mph (160 km/h) at sea level; cruising speed 92 mph (148 km/h) at optimum altitude; service ceiling 10,170 ft (3100 m)
Weights: empty 2,965 lb (1345 kg); maximum take-off 4,608 lb (2090 kg)
Dimensions: wingspan 42 ft 7¾ in (13.00 m); length 34 ft 5¼ in (10.50 m); height 11 ft 9¾ in (3.60 m); wing area 479.01 sq ft (44.50 m²)
Payload: four passengers or 705 lb (320 kg) of freight

Albatros L.73

Designed for service with Deutsche Lufthansa, the **Albatros L.73** was an impressive twin-engined civil transport intended specifically for night operations. A large two-bay biplane of basically all-metal construction, covered with fabric and light alloy panels, the L.73 had a conventional braced tail unit and fixed tailskid landing gear. Two BMW engines were mounted, one on each side of the fuselage, midway between the wings. The pilot and co-pilot were seated side-by-side in a covered compartment in the fuselage nose which was provided with a windscreen, but had open

SPECIFICATION

Albatros L.73
Type: night transport aircraft
Powerplant: two BMW IVa inline piston engines each rated at 240 hp (179 kW) for take-off
Performance: maximum speed 90 mph (145 km/h) at sea level; climb to 3,280 ft (1000 m) in 14 minutes; endurance 4 hours
Weights: empty 6,667 lb (3024 kg); maximum take-off 10,163 lb (4610 kg)
Dimensions: wing span 55 ft 9¼ in (17.00 m); length 47 ft 10¾ in (14.60 m); height 15 ft 5 in (4.70 m); wing area 990.31 sq ft (92.00 m²)
Payload: eight passengers

sides. The pilots had dual controls, radio equipment, and an early gyroscopic turn indicator. The enclosed passenger cabin was heated and ventilated, and had accommodation for eight passengers in comfortable seating, with a

Two L.73s were built, being named **Preussen** *and* **Brandenburg.** *They entered service with Lufthansa in 1926.*

toilet to the rear. Four of the seats could be converted into two sleeping bunks.

Both the aircraft entered

service with Lufthansa in 1926. They were used on night sectors of domestic and international routes up until 1930.

Albatros L.75A Esel

Of generally similar construction to its predecessor, the L.68 Alauda, the **Albatros L.75A Esel** (ass) was developed as an advanced trainer offering higher levels of overall performance. It introduced certain modifications such as a variable-incidence tailplane, a strengthened main landing gear unit, a steerable tailskid, more sophisticated accommodation (with provision for radio and photographic equipment), parachutes, full dual instrumentation to

SPECIFICATION

Albatros L.75A Esel
Type: two-seat advanced flying trainer
Powerplant: one BMW Va inline piston engine rated at 350 hp (261 kW) for take-off
Performance: maximum speed 135 mph (217 km/h) at sea level; cruising speed 110.5 mph (178 km/h) at optimum altitude;
service ceiling 21,325 ft (6500 m); range 994 miles (1600 km)
Weights: empty 2,392 lb (1085 kg); maximum take-off 3,935 lb (1785 kg)
Dimensions: wingspan 41 ft (12.50 m); length 32 ft 9¾ in (10.00 m); height 10 ft 8 in (3.25 m); wing area 398.28 sq ft (37.00 m²)

accompany its dual controls and a far more powerful BMW inline piston engine enclosed

Having supplanted the L.68 in production, the L.75A served widely with Germany's training organisations.

inside a neat cowling.

Like the L.68, the L.75A remained in service for a long period and was additionally operated by the Deutsche Verkehrsfliegerschule for the training of promising pilots selected from the youth organisations.

Albatros L.77v

Designed by Albatros as a derivative of its **L.76 Aeolus** two-seat reconnaissance and training aircraft of 1926, the **Albatros L.77v** was intended to meet an official but clandestine German requirement for a reconnaissance and fighter aircraft to be used for training purposes at its secret

The BMW engine of the L.77v drove a two-bladed wooden propeller. Long fairings covered the engine's protruding cylinder banks.

SPECIFICATION

Albatros L.77v
Type: two-seat fighter and reconnaissance aircraft
Powerplant: one BMW VI 5,5 Vee piston engine rated at 600 hp (447.5 kW) for take-off
Performance: maximum speed 137 mph (220 km/h) at 4,920 ft (1500 m); endurance 2 hours 12 minutes
Weights: empty 3,796 lb (1722 kg); maximum take-off 5,688 lb (2580 kg)
Dimensions: wingspan 41 ft 10½ in (12.76 m)
Armament: two fixed forward-firing 0.312-in (7.92-mm) machine-guns, and one 0.312-in (7.92-mm) trainable machine-gun in the rear cockpit

base at Lipezk in Russia. All four L.77vs were built under licence by Heinkel and completed late in 1928. The aircraft was a sesquiplane with a fabric-covered welded steel tube fuselage. Tandem open cockpits were provided for the pilot and observer/gunner. The staggered wings were of wood under a covering of plywood and fabric.

One of the L.77v aircraft was lost while being tested in March 1929, but the other three saw moderately extensive use at Lipezk for trials purposes including the evaluation of a 20-mm trainable cannon, before being relocated in December 1929 to the Rechlin test centre in Germany, where they survived to October 1931.

Albatros L.100

Under the designation **Albatros L.100**, the company designed a three-seat sporting aircraft which, as a considerable departure from previous Albatros practice, was largely of metal construction and monoplane configuration.

The low-set wing was of light alloy construction

Offering accommodation for three people, the L.100 lightplane never entered series production.

under a covering of fabric, was braced to the sides of the upper fuselage above the cabin on each side by an inverted-Vee strut, and could be folded for stor-

age. The fuselage and tail unit were based on welded steel tube structures under a covering of fabric. The landing gear was of the fixed tailskid type, the main units having

shock absorbers and wheel brakes.

The extensively glazed cabin was fully enclosed, and the accommodation comprised the pilot and co-pilot/passenger side-by-side

at the front of the cabin with full dual controls, and a single seat for another passenger at the rear of the cabin. It is thought that only one example of the L.100 was completed.

SPECIFICATION	
Albatros L.100	**Performance:** cruising speed 93 mph (150 km/h) at optimum altitude; service ceiling 16,405 ft (5000 m); range 497 miles (800 km)
Type: three-seat sporting aircraft	
Powerplant: one Argus As.8 inverted inline piston engine rated at 110 hp (82 kW) for take-off	

Albatros L.101

Appearing in 1930, the **L.101** was a two-seat touring and training aircraft. Of parasol-wing monoplane configuration, the L.101 featured an all-metal structure under a covering of fabric. The aircraft also featured a wing folding

mechanism, tail unit and undercarriage similar to that of the L.100.

Accommodation for the pilot and passenger/pupil was provided in tandem cockpits, and the landing gear was of the fixed tail-skid type.

SPECIFICATION	
Albatros L.101	altitude; service ceiling 16,405 ft (5000 m); range 466 miles (750 km)
Type: two-seat touring and training aircraft	**Weights:** empty 1,135 lb (515 kg); maximum take-off 1,830 lb (830 kg)
Powerplant: one Argus As.8a inverted inline piston engine rated at 110 hp (82 kW) for take-off	**Dimensions:** wingspan 41 ft (12.50 m); length 27 ft 10⅝ in (8.50 m)
Performance: cruising speed 99.5 mph (160 km/h) at optimum	

The L.101 exhibited a classic parasol wing configuration, with the wing strut-mounted above the fuselage.

Albatros W.3 (VT)

During the early part of World War I the Imperial German navy air service became interested in using torpedo-armed aircraft in the anti-ship role. The service therefore ordered

single examples, from a number of different manufacturers, of seaplane designs capable of carrying a standard torpedo over a tactically useful range. As initial experiments with LVG

and Albatros landplanes proved unsatisfactory, the Albatros company began the development of a new biplane type as its **VT (Versuchs-Torpedoflugzeug**, or experimental torpedoplane).

Later known as the **Albatros W.3**, the VT was a

SPECIFICATION	
Albatros W.3 (VT)	**Dimensions:** wingspan 74 ft 5⅝ in (22.70 m); length 42 ft 11⅞ in (13.10 m)
Type: two/three-seat torpedo bomber floatplane prototype	
Powerplant: two Mercedes D.III inline piston engines each rated at 160 hp (119 kW) for take-off	**Armament:** one air-launched torpedo, and two trainable 0.312-in (7.92-mm) LMG 14 Parabellum machine-guns
Performance: maximum speed 82.5 mph (133 km/h) at sea level	

Carrying the serial number 527, the W.3 proved successful in trials, but was abandoned in favour of the generally similar W.5.

twin-float seaplane powered by two Mercedes D.III inline piston engines located in nacelles on the upper surface of the lower wing to drive pusher propellers. The aircraft's main structure was of wood with plywood covering of the fuselage and fin, and with fabric on the rest of the flying surfaces. The alighting gear comprised a side-by-side pair of plywood-covered wooden floats.

Completed in July 1916, the single W.3 passed its official trials at the navy's Seeflugzeug-versuchskommando (SVK, or seaplane

experimental centre) located in Warnemünde and was then delivered to the Torpedo-versuchsanstalt (TVA, or torpedo experimental establishment) at Ackernförde for installation of its torpedo-carrying equipment, after which the W.3 was transferred back to the SVK for final trials. These proved generally satisfactory, but the design did not enter production as greater capabilities were expected from the similar but larger **W.5**. Five examples of the latter entered service in 1918.

Albatros W.4

Frequent attacks by British and, to a lesser extent, French flying boats and floatplanes on German air stations along the southern coast of the North Sea –

extensively used by the Imperial German naval air service for its seaplanes – persuaded the German admiralty to order the development of a float-

plane fighter. Since the requirement was urgent, manufacturers were to modify existing fighter aircraft to incorporate float alighting gear.

Albatros based its contender on the fuselage of its D.II with twin-float

alighting gear and new flying surfaces derived from those of the D.I. A range of different float configurations was tried during the lifetime of the aircraft. This is only part of the story, however for, as ordered in prototype form in June 1916, the

Albatros W.4 had larger dimensions as well as numerous detail changes. The most noticeable of these was the deletion of the landplane-type ventral fin and, in compensation, an increase in the area of the W.4's upper fin.

SPECIFICATION	
Albatros W.4	**Weights:** empty 1,742 lb (790 kg);
Type: single-seat fighter floatplane	maximum take-off 2,359 lb
Powerplant: one Mercedes D.III	(1070 kg)
inline piston engine rated at	**Dimensions:** span 31 ft 2 in
160 hp (119 kW) for take-off	(9.50 m); length 27 ft 10¾ in
Performance: maximum speed	(8.50 m); height 11 ft 11¾ in
99.5 mph (160 km/h) at sea level;	(3.65 m); wing area 340.15 sq ft
climb to 3,280 ft (1000 m) in	(31.60 m²)
6 minutes 30 seconds; service	**Armament:** one or two fixed
ceiling 9,845 ft (3000 m);	forward-firing 0.312-in (7.92-mm)
endurance 3 hours	LMG 08/15 machine-guns

The prototype made its maiden flight in September 1916 and revealed an excellent combination of handling qualities and performance. The type was therefore ordered into production for service from a time late in 1916, with production continuing into December 1917.

Replacement of the W.4 by the more effective purpose-designed Hansa-Brandenburg W.12 started in the last weeks of 1917. In June 1918, however, there were still 65 W.4s (out of a total production run of 118) in first-line service, with another 24 flying as operational trainers.

Undoubtedly the most successful of Albatros's waterborne aircraft, the W.4 was a most successful fighter. The aircraft featured two fuel tanks, each of 16-Imp gal (73-litre) capacity, to give an endurance of three hours.

Alcock A.1 Scout

Designed and built by Flight Lieutenant John W. Alcock, later to acquire fame as the partner of Arthur Whitten Brown (the pair constituting the crew of the Vickers Vimy that achieved the first non-stop flight across the Atlantic), the **Alcock A.1**

Scout was nicknamed the 'Sopwith Mouse'. This was because it was made almost completely from components and assemblies from crashed or otherwise written-off Sopwith Triplane, Pup and Camel fighters.

The fabric-covered wooden aircraft comprised the fuselage, main landing gear and much of the lower wing of a Triplane in combination with the outer panels of a Pup's upper wing and a Camel's horizontal tail surface. These were combined with new upper- and lower-wing centre sections. Another new feature in the wire-

SPECIFICATION	
Alcock A.1 Scout	24 ft 3 in (7.39 m); length about
Type: single-seat fighter	19 ft 1 in (5.82 m); height about
Powerplant: one Clerget 9Z rotary	7 ft 9 in (2.36 m)
piston engine rated at 110 hp	**Armament:** one fixed forward-
(82 kW) for take-off	firing 0.303-in (7.7-mm) Vickers
Dimensions: wingspan about	machine-gun

braced tail unit, which may have included a Sopwith rudder, was the vertical

surface with upper and lower triangular fins.

The A.1 was first flown in October 1917 under the power of one Gnome Monosoupape rotary piston engine rated at 100 hp (74.6 kW), although this engine was later replaced by a Clerget 9Z.

The machine was destroyed when it struck a DH.4 on the ground early in 1918, while serving operationally with the RNAS.

The sole A.1 was never flown by Alcock, but was on the strength of No. 2 Wing RNAS during 1917-18.

Alekseyev I-211

Semyon Mikhailovich Alekseyev first rose to prominence in the Lavochkin Experimental Design Bureau, in which he was primarily responsible for the detail design of the La-5 and La-7 fighters. At the end of World War II, Alekseyev moved from the Lavochkin bureau and, in September 1946, was authorised to create his own design bureau.

The first machine from the new bureau was the **Alekseyev I-211**, a prototype that made its maiden

flight in the autumn of 1947. A turbojet-powered fighter, the I-211 featured two Lyul'ka TR-1 turbojets each rated at 3,009 lb st (13.39 kN), rather than the engine for which it had been designed, the Lyul'ka AL-1 turbojet rated at 2,205 lb st (9.81 kN). The TR-1 was the first axial-flow turbojet of Soviet design to fly and, as used in the I-211, was both unreliable and considerably under-developed with a typical output of only some 70 per cent of the rated thrust.

The I-211 was a mid-wing monoplane of light alloy stressed-skin construction, with its engines in nacelles mounted centrally in its wing. Each unit of its tricycle landing gear carried two wheels. The planned armament was three 37-mm Nudel'man-Suranov NS-37 cannon or two 57-mm cannon, but the installation of this armament was

scheduled only for the second prototype with the uprated powerplant of two TR-1A engines each rated at 3,318 lb st (14.76 kN).

The I-211 was notable for the considerable volume of its circular-section fuselage, which made its feasible to provide a considerable internal fuel capacity for good endurance, as well as a significant quantity of

ammunition for the cannon armament, which was installed under the floor of the pressurised cockpit with a high-set clearview canopy. The problems with the TR-1 engine meant that a production commitment was out of the question, however, and all development of the I-211 was terminated in favour of the I-215 after the completion of only limited trials.

SPECIFICATION	
Alekseyev I-211 (estimated	(1550 km)
with fully-rated powerplant)	**Weights:** empty 9,612 lb
Type: single-seat fighter prototype	(4360 kg); maximum take-off
Powerplant: two Lyul'ka TR-1	16,424 lb (7450 kg)
turbojets each rated at 3,009 lb st	**Dimensions:** wingspan 40 ft 2½ in
(13.39 kN)	(12.25 m); length 37 ft 10⅓ in
Performance: maximum speed	(11.54 m); height 12 ft ⅞ in
581 mph (935 km/h) at sea level;	(3.68 m); wing area 269.11 sq ft
climb to 16,405 ft (5000 m) in	(25.00 m²)
3 minutes; range 963 miles	

With its high-set canopy providing exceptional visibility and its powerful armament, the I-211 was a promising fighter with an unreliable powerplant.

Alekseyev I-212

Despite its lower designation number in the USSR's official Istrebitel (fighter) sequence, the **Alekseyev I-212** was a later design than the I-215, of which it was basically a scaled-up version with a higher-rated powerplant. The spur for the development of the I-212 was the increasing level of vulnerability felt by the USSR toward the USA's vastly superior strategic bombing capability.

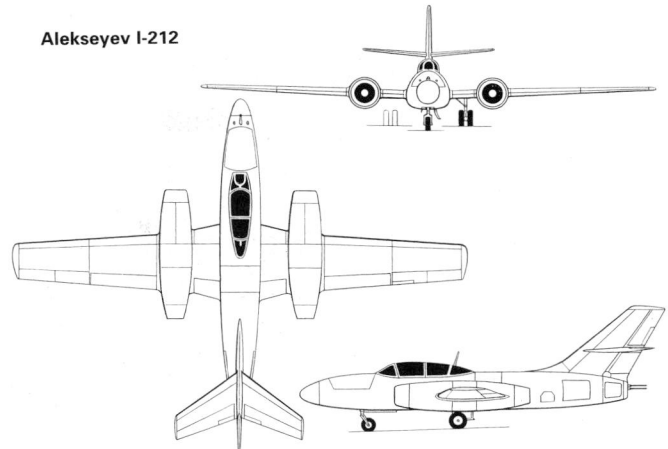

Alekseyev I-212

The official requirement was for a high-performance interceptor with search radar (and associated operator, who was free to swing his seat rearward for operation of a twin-gun barbette) and a fixed forward-firing armament of four 20-mm cannon.

In response to this, Alekseyev began taxitests with the I-212 prototype in 1948 and some reports suggest that the aircraft may not have flown before the I-212 programme was terminated. The radar was never fitted, and the nose-mounted fixed forward-firing armament in the event comprised one 37-mm cannon with 75 rounds and two 23-mm weapons. A planned reconnaissance variant was probably never built.

SPECIFICATION	
Alekseyev I-212 **Type:** two-seat interceptor prototype **Powerplant:** two Rolls-Royce Nene I turbojets each rated at 5,000 lb st (22.24 kN) **Performance:** maximum speed 621.5 mph (1000 km/h) at optimum altitude; service ceiling 48,555 ft (14800 m); range 1,926 miles (3100 km)	**Weights:** empty 11,310 lb (5130 kg); maximum take-off 20,392 lb (9250 kg) **Dimensions:** wingspan 53 ft 1¾ in (16.20 m); length 42 ft 7 in (12.98 m); wing area 355.22 sq ft (33.00 m²) **Armament:** one 37-mm NS-37 and two 23-mm NS-23 forward-firing cannon, plus two 20-mm cannon in rearward-facing B-20 barbette

Alekseyev I-215

Alekseyev felt that its I-211 design would achieve greater success under the power of two Rolls-Royce Derwent engines. The export of this British engine to the USSR had been actively encouraged and, as well as securing a number of these capable engines from the UK, the USSR also started to produce its own version of the Derwent V as the RD-500.

Two British-built engines were therefore installed in an incomplete I-211 prototype, which thereupon became the **Alekseyev I-215**. The task of revising the nacelles designed for the TR-1 to take the Derwent centrifugal-flow engine was simple, and other changes introduced at the same time were a provision in the nose for radar, the revision of the pressurised cockpit to accept a primitive ejection seat and the addition to the wing of air brakes.

The first I-215 prototype made its maiden flight on 31 December 1947, and the flight trials confirmed that the greater power and reliability of the Derwent powerplant transformed the flight performance. However, the increased power had not been planned into the structure from the start, and this resulted in the onset of fatigue-cracking in the wing's centre section. This could be cured by structural strengthening, but this in turn required the relocation of the twin-wheel main landing gear units from the wing to the fuselage. The result was the **I-215D Dubler** (double) second prototype with the reinforced centre section and the landing gear rearranged to a pair of twin-wheel units in tandem in a 'bicycle' arrangement under the fuselage. The two units retracted fore and aft of the main fuel tankage, and two stabilising outrigger units retracted into fairings under the engine nacelles.

The I-215D started its flight test programme in the spring of 1948, and the type displayed a level of performance that resulted in immediate recommendation for the start of series production. It had a fixed forward-firing armament of three 37-mm Nudel'man-Suranov NS-37 cannon, or two 57-mm NS-57 cannon, or two 37-mm 111P-57 cannon. It was at about this time, however, that Stalin received disparaging remarks about the I-212 ("another copy of the Me 262") from Aleksandr Yakovlev, and ordered the dissolution of the Alekseyev bureau.

Unlike the I-212 which followed it, the I-215 was apparently extensively flight-tested, albeit without radar or full operational equipment.

Alekseyev I-215

SPECIFICATION	
Alekseyev I-215 **Type:** single-seat fighter prototype **Powerplant:** two Rolls-Royce Derwent V turbojets each rated at 3,500 lb st (15.57 kN) **Performance:** maximum speed 603 mph (970 km/h) at sea level; climb to 16,405 ft (5000 m) in 2 minutes 48 seconds; range 1,429 miles (2300 km)	**Weights:** empty 8,840 lb (4010 kg); maximum take-off 15,190 lb (6890 kg) **Dimensions:** wingspan 40 ft 2½ in (12.25 m); length 37 ft 10¼ in (11.54 m); height 12 ft ⅞ in (3.68 m); wing area 269.11 sq ft (25.00 m²) **Armament:** see above

Alenia (Aeritalia/Lockheed) F-104ASA Starfighter

In 1981, the Aeronautica Militare Italiana started to plan an upgrade programme for 153 of its F-104S aircraft. With Aeritalia (amalgamated with Selenia late in 1990 to create the Alenia group) as prime contractor, the **Aggiornamento Sistema d'Arma (ASA**, or armament system modernisation) programme was designed to upgrade the F-104S's low-level interception capability and also to improve its air-to-ground performance.

The main changes included the replacement of the original fire-control radar and the addition of a moving target indicator, and the introduction of the Selenia Aspide Mk 1A AAM. These three factors conferred a look-down/shoot-down capability over a maximum range of around 22 miles (35 km).

The associated onboard guidance equipment for the Aspide was miniaturised so that the gun bay of the **F-104ASA** could again fulfil its function of housing the 20-mm M61A1 Vulcan six-barrel rotary cannon, and the F-104ASA's ground-attack capability was enhanced by the addition of the ALQ-70 or ALQ-73 ECM systems. Provision was also made for the all-aspect AIM-9L Sidewinder AAM.

Flight testing began in July 1983 and the first production-standard F-104ASA conversion was accepted on 19 November 1986. The last of the 147 aircraft was redelivered late in 1991.

Studies were made for

Limited funds have been made available to modestly upgrade some ASAs (illustrated) to ASAM standard.

further F-104ASA improvements through a proposed Operational Capacity Extension programme (including a completely new radar, a head-up display and an inflight refuelling probe) to extend the utility of the F-104ASA beyond the originally planned date of 2005 in the event of delays to the Eurofighter programme. However, with Eurofighter delays a reality and budgetary constraints making any further major F-104 upgrading an impossibility, these proposals were abandoned and Italy decided to lease 24 examples of the Panavia Tornado F.Mk 3 from the RAF pending the delayed delivery of the Eurofighter.

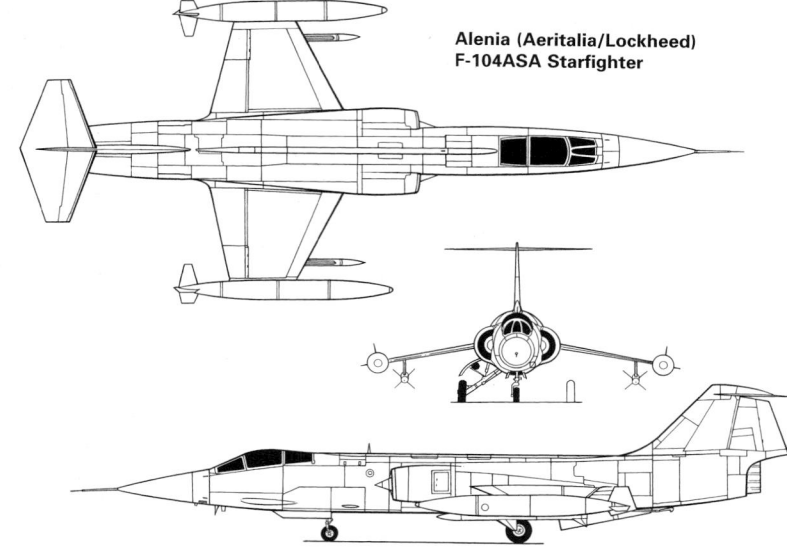

Alenia (Aeritalia/Lockheed) F-104ASA Starfighter

SPECIFICATION

Alenia (Aeritalia/Lockheed) F-104ASA Starfighter
Type: single-seat air-defence and ground-attack warplane
Powerplant: one General Electric J79-GE-19 turbojet rated at 11,870 lb st (52.80 kN) dry and 17,900 lb st (79.62 kN) with afterburning
Performance: maximum speed 1,450 mph (2333 km/h) or Mach 2.20 at 36,000 ft (10975 m); maximum cruising speed 610 mph (981 km/h) at 36,000 ft (12975 m); initial climb rate 55,000 ft (16764 m) per minute; service ceiling 58,000 ft (17680 m); combat radius 775 miles (1247 km) with maximum fuel
Weights: empty 14,903 lb (6760 kg); maximum take-off 30,996 lb (14060 kg)
Dimensions: wingspan 21 ft 11 in (6.68 m) without tip tanks; length 54 ft 9 in (16.69 m); height 13 ft 6 in (4.11 m); wing area 196.10 sq ft (18.22 m²)
Armament: one 20-mm M61A1 Vulcan cannon, and up to 7,496 lb (3400 kg) of external stores

Alenia (Aeritalia/Fiat) G222

The **Fiat G222** proposal was drawn up to meet the outlines of NATO's Basic Military Requirement Four (NBMR4) of 1962, which called for a practical V/STOL transport for service with NATO air forces. None of the proposals was adopted, but the Aeronautica Militare Italiana (AMI) believed that Fiat's proposal could form the basis of a useful transport if finalised as a more conventional design. Therefore, in 1968, the AMI signed a contract for two **G222TCM** prototypes and a static test airframe. The manufacture of these machines was delayed by two successive total redesigns, in the course of which Fiat was turned into Aeritalia by a November 1969 merger with IRI-

Libya received Tyne-engined G222Ts because of a US embargo on the export of T64 engines to the country.

Finmeccanica. Hence, it was not until 18 July 1970 that the first prototype made its maiden flight, the second prototype following it into the air on 22 July 1971.

These aircraft began operational evaluation with the AMI in December 1971. Highly successful tests resulted in a contract for 44 production examples of the **G222**, of which the first flew on 23 December 1975 as a twin-engined aircraft of typical modern airlifter configuration. The G222 remained in production in its first iteration into early 1989, and was built in a number of subvariants.

After the USAF's selection of the G222 to meet a requirement for a type to serve in Central America, production of the G222 was restarted by Alenia (as Aeritalia had become in December 1990 after its merger with Selenia) for the provision of basic airframes for completion in the USA by Chrysler as **C-27A Spartan** aircraft. Alenia is also working with Lockheed

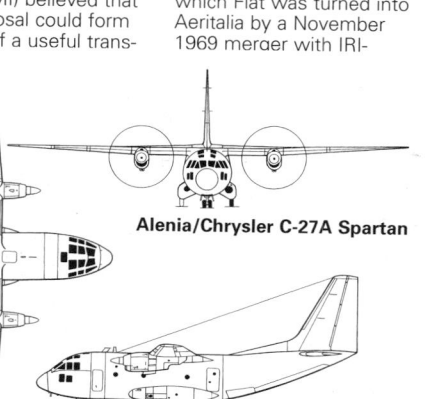

Alenia/Chrysler C-27A Spartan

Variants

G222: baseline military transport
G222R/M (Radio Misure): radio/radar calibration aircraft
G222SAA (Sistema Aeronautico Antincendio): firefighter with equipment to disperse water or fire retardants
G222T: powered by two 4,860-shp (3624-kW) Rolls-Royce Tyne RTy.20 Mk 801 turboprops for the Libyan air force. Known locally as the **G222L**
G222VS (Versione Speciale): electronic warfare aircraft, also known as the **G222GE (Guerra Elettronica)** and operated in the Sigint and Elint roles with an electronics suite that probably includes the Elettronica ELT/999 strategic Comint system

Martin on the **C-27J**, a derivative of the G222 which uses two Allison AE 2100 turboprops and six-bladed propellers as fitted to the C-130J, and also shares some of the latter's systems.

SPECIFICATION

Alenia (Aeritalia/Fiat) G222
Type: tactical medium transport
Powerplant: two Fiat (General Electric) T64-GEP4D turboprop engines each flat-rated at 3,400 shp (2535 kW)
Performance: maximum speed 336 mph (540 km/h) at 15,010 ft (4575 m); cruising speed 273 mph (439 km/h) at 19,685 ft (6000 m); initial climb rate 1,706 ft (520 m) per minute; service ceiling 25,000 ft (7620 m); typical range 852 miles (1371 km) with maximum payload or 1,555 miles (2502 km) with 36 litters plus four attendants
Weights: empty 34,612 lb (15700 kg); maximum take-off 61,728 lb (28000 kg)
Dimensions: wingspan 94 ft 2 in (28.70 m); length 74 ft 5½ in (22.70 m); height 32 ft 1¾ in (9.80 m); wing area 882.67 sq ft (82.00 m²)
Payload: up to 46 troops, or 40 paratroops, or 36 litters plus four attendants, or 21,164 lb (9600 kg) of freight

Two G222 groups and a single C-130H group form the basis of Italy's tactical airlift capability.

All American Model 10 Ensign

Immediately after the conclusion of World War II, All American Aircraft Inc., a company better known as a specialised subcontractor for aircraft manufacturers, started work on the design of a two-seat light sporting aircraft. The prototype of the **All American Model 10-A Ensign** made its maiden flight before the

end of 1945. The Ensign was an all-metal, cantilever low-wing monoplane with fixed tricycle landing gear and side-by-side accommodation for the pilot and

An attractive design, which offered excellent visibility, the Ensign could not penetrate an already crowded market.

passenger in a high-set cockpit under a large Plexiglas canopy.

It was planned that the production model should offer dual controls as an option, but with the light-plane market flooded by suitable war-surplus ex-military types, no variants of the Ensign were actually to enter production.

Allied LRA and Bristol LRQ

The US Navy had shown intermittent interest in the possible use of gliders from as early as 1920, but the German use of glider-borne assault troops at the beginning of May 1940 added a new sense of urgency. Among the US Navy's projects was a transport glider of the flying boat type with very clean lines, and two prototypes of this type were built by the Allied Aviation Corporation as the **XLRA-1**.

The design incorporated a large two-step flying-boat hull, and jettisonable wheeled landing gear was also provided to offer an amphibious capability. Unusually, the roots and inner sections of the low-

Had the XLRA-1 reached the production stage, it would most probably have been employed by US airborne troops in the Pacific theatre.

set cantilever monoplane wing rested on the water to provide stability, removing the need for drag-producing stabilising floats under the wings. Moreover, provision was made for the installation of a small engine to enable the craft to manoeuvre on the water.

Four additional proto-

types were ordered from the Bristol Aeronautical Corporation, only two of which were built with the designation **Bristol XLRQ-1**, but production

was cancelled in 1943 when the US Navy decided that its requirements could be satisfied much more effectively by using powered aircraft.

Ambrosini S.7

Sergio Stefanutti designed the sleek Ambrosini **S.A.I.7** two-seat touring aircraft between October 1938 and April 1939. The S.A.I.7 was a sleek cantilever low-wing monoplane of wooden construction with fully retractable tailwheel landing gear. The first two aircraft were intended to take part in the prestigious 4th Avio Raduno del Littorio contest for touring aircraft on 15 July 1939, and made their maiden flights within days of each other, just before the competition opened.

Although the S.A.I.7s did not win the contest, their performance impressed the Italian authorities, especially after one machine captured an international speed record over the 100-km (62.1-mile) closed circuit on 27 August 1939. Even so, little was heard of the S.A.I.7 during World

Variants

S.A.I.7: two racing monoplanes powered by one 280-hp (209-kW) Hirth HM.508D engine
S.A.I.7 Trainer: two-seat fighter trainer of which 10 were built in 1943 with a conventional cockpit enclosure and the powerplant of one 280-hp (209-kW) Isotta-Fraschini Beta RC.10 inverted inline piston engine
S.7: post-war version designed as a single- or two-seat training/touring aircraft
Super S.7 Supersette: a more powerful version of the S.7 that first appeared in 1952 and of which 10 were completed with the powerplant of one 350-hp (261-kW) de Havilland Gipsy Queen 70 inverted inline engine and other changes; one was flown with a cut-down rear fuselage and one 400-hp (298-kW) Alfa Romeo 121 RC engine, while another was fitted with a swept wing as part of the development programme for the Sagittario light jet fighter

War II, although the experimental **S.A.I.107**, **S.A.I.207** and **S.A.I.403** light fighters were developed from it during this period, and 10 of the S.A.I.7 militarised two-seat fighter trainer version appeared during 1943. In 1949, however, Ambrosini placed the type in full-scale production. This post-war **S.7** version introduced an Alfa Romeo powerplant, but there were few other major changes.

Most of the 145 examples of the S.7, some of them built in single-seat configuration, formed the equipment of various flight

Thanks to its fine streamlining, the S.7 achieved high performance on low engine power.

training centres attached to the AMI (Aeronautica Militare Italiana). Apart from its military service, which

terminated in 1956, the S.7 participated in numerous competitions and achieved considerable success.

Ambrosini S.1001 Grifo and S.1002 Trasimenus

Developed from the pre-war S.A.I.2S, the **Ambrosini S.1001 Grifo** was designed in two versions: as a four-seat tourer and as a two-seat military trainer. No produc-tion of the trainer version, with the powerplant of one 145-hp (108-kW) de Havilland Gipsy Major 10 inverted inline piston engine, was undertaken, but limited numbers of the

Offering accommodation for a pilot and three passengers, the S.1001 was a typically elegant Ambrosini design.

SPECIFICATION	
Ambrosini S.1001 Grifo	(210 km/h) at optimum altitude; range 528 miles (850 km)
Type: four-seat touring aircraft	
Powerplant: one Alfa Romeo 110ter (licence-built de Havilland Gipsy Major 10) inverted inline piston engine rated at 130 hp (96.9 kW)	**Weights:** empty 1,543 lb (700 kg); maximum take-off 2,337 lb (1060 kg)
	Dimensions: wingspan 32 ft 5¾ in (9.90 m); length 25 ft 7 in (7.80 m); height 9 ft ½ in (2.75 m); wing area 163.62 sq ft (15.20 m²)
Performance: maximum speed 149 mph (240 km/h) at optimum altitude; cruising speed 130.5 mph	

cabin tourer were built. Limited production was also undertaken of the two-seat **S.1002 Trasimenus** basic trainer development, which had a wing of increased dihedral for better lateral stability and increased span.

Ambrosini S.A.I.2S

The **S.A.I.2S** was a four-seat cabin tourer designed for participation in the 1937 Italian air racing season, and its general success paved the way for the production of relatively large numbers of the type.

A cantilever low-wing monoplane with an exten-sively glazed cabin which accommodated four people on side-by-side seats at the front and rear, the S.A.I.2S featured such advanced features as Handley Page automatic slots on the outboard ends of its wings, giving a land-ing speed of just 52 mph (84 km/h). The wide-track main undercarriage units each carried spatted wheels on their carefully trousered legs.

The powerplant installa-tion was totally different from the otherwise similar **S.A.I.2** of 1935, as it was based on an inverted inline piston engine driving a two-bladed propeller fitted with a spinner.

An S.A.I.2S makes a turn during a 621-mile (1000-km) race. The type achieved some success in competitions.

SPECIFICATION	
Ambrosini S.A.I.2S	service ceiling 19,685 ft (6000 m); range 603 miles (970 km)
Type: four-seat touring aircraft	
Powerplant: one Alfa Romeo 115-I inverted inline piston engine rated at 200 hp (149 kW)	**Weights:** empty 1,962 lb (890 kg); maximum take-off 3,119 lb (1415 kg)
Performance: maximum speed 155.5 mph (250 km/h) at optimum altitude; cruising speed 133.5 mph (215 km/h) at optimum altitude;	**Dimensions:** wingspan 34 ft 11⅓ in (10.65 m); length 25 ft 5 in (7.75 m); height 9 ft 2¼ in (2.80 m); wing area 192.68 sq ft (17.90 m²)

Ambrosini S.A.I.3

The **S.A.I.3** was a cantilever low-wing mono-plane with wings of elliptical planform, based on an oval-section fuselage with two open (or in some later aircraft enclosed) cockpits. Designed for training and touring, the S.A.I.3 had its looks marred somewhat by a clumsy, fixed undercarriage. The powerplant could be based

An aircraft of elegant basic design, the S.A.I.3 featured tandem seating for two, often beneath fully-glazed canopies.

on either of two engine types, namely the Fiat A.50 specified below, or the Alfa Romeo 110 inverted inline piston engine rated at 130 hp (96.9 kW).

The **S.A.I.3S** was a development of the basic type with the powerplant of one Bramo Sh.14A-4 radial piston engine rated at 160 hp (119 kW) and the wing reduced in chord. Predictably, the S.A.I.3S offered far superior perfor-mance to the S.A.I.3.

SPECIFICATION	
Ambrosini S.A.I.3	(170 km/h) at optimum altitude; service ceiling 13,125 ft (4000 m); range 385 miles (620 km)
Type: two-seat touring and training aircraft	
Powerplant: one Fiat A.50 radial piston engine rated at 85 hp (63.4 kW)	**Weights:** empty 1,213 lb (550 kg); maximum take-off 1,742 lb (790 kg)
Performance: maximum speed 124 mph (200 km/h) at optimum altitude; cruising speed 105.5 mph	**Dimensions:** wingspan 34 ft 3½ in (10.45 m); length 23 ft 1½ in (7.05 m); height 9 ft 2¼ in (2.80 m); wing area 150.70 sq ft (14.00 m²)

Ambrosini S.A.I.107 and S.A.I.207

The S.A.I.7's high speed/power ratio caught the imagination of the Italian air force which saw consid-erable possibilities in the concept of a lightweight interceptor of basically wooden construction that could be built in large numbers without drawing on the country's strategic stockpile of aluminium alloys. However, it was 1941 before work began on a fighter trainer derived from the S.A.I.7 with the original HM.508D engine replaced by an Isotta-Fraschini Beta RC.10 inverted-Vee piston engine in an airframe characterised by a longer fuselage, a wider-span wing, a modified cockpit enclosure and the original tailskid replaced by a fixed tailwheel.

By the time the first of 10 S.7 fighter trainers had flown, however, Italy's increasingly difficult military position led to renewed interest in the S.A.I.7's potential for development into a lightweight fighter, and in 1942 Ambrosini evolved the **Ambrosini S.A.I.107** as an experimen-tal fighter. The new type was essentially a single-seat derivative of the fighter trainer with a considerably more powerful engine in the form of the Isotta-Fraschini Gamma RC.35 IS inverted-Vee piston engine rated at 540 hp (403 kW). This prototype recorded a maxi-mum level speed of 348 mph (560 km/h) and confirmed that a viable interceptor was possible.

With its 540-hp (403-kW) engine, the S.A.I.107 had a maximum speed of 348 mph (560 km/h) and a maximum take-off weight of 2,025 lb (1000 kg).

Ambrosini S.A.I.107 and S.A.I.207 (continued)

Ambrosini then produced the **S.A.I.207** with full operational equipment, which also featured a more powerful engine driving a three-bladed propeller. Flight trials began in 1942, with the aircraft demonstrating excellent performance. Indeed, the first S.A.I.207 recording a dive speed of 596 mph (960 km/h) at 9,845 ft (3000 m), corresponding to Mach 0.86.

The Italian air ministry ordered Ambrosini to begin work on a pre-production batch of S.A.I.207 fighters and placed an order for 2,000 production aircraft. In the event only 13 of the pre-production aircraft were completed, three of them being used in operational trials during July 1943. Nevertheless, the S.A.I.207 was cancelled in favour of the S.A.I.403 Dardo.

Some 13 S.A.I.207s were allocated to the 3° Stormo Caccia Terrestre at Ciampino.

SPECIFICATION

Ambrosini S.A.I.207
Type: single-seat lightweight interceptor fighter
Powerplant: one Isotta-Fraschini Delta RC.40 inverted-Vee piston engine rated at 750 hp (560 kW)
Performance: maximum speed 398 mph (640 km/h) at 14,765 ft (4500 m); cruising speed 304 mph (490 km/h) at optimum altitude; climb to 19,685 ft (6000 m) in 7 minutes 34 seconds; service ceiling 39,370 ft (12000 m); range 528 miles (850 km)
Weights: empty 3,858 lb (1750 kg); maximum take-off 5,324 lb (2415 kg)
Dimensions: wingspan 29 ft 6¼ in (9.00 m); length 26 ft 3¼ in (8.02 m); height 7 ft 10½ in (2.40 m); wing area 149.62 sq ft (13.90 m²)
Armament: two 20-mm Mauser MG 151/20 fixed forward-firing cannon and two 0.5-in (12.7-mm) Breda-SAFAT fixed forward-firing machine-guns

Ambrosini S.A.I.403 Dardo

Intended as a lightweight fighter, with a cantilever low-wing configuration and a basically wooden structure under a stressed skinning of plywood, the **Ambrosini S.A.I.403 Dardo** (dart or arrow) was essentially a more sophisticated version of the S.A.I.207 with an upgraded powerplant in the form of the Isotta-Fraschini Delta RC.21/60 Serie I-IV inverted-Vee piston engine rated at 750 hp (560 kW) and driving a three-bladed constant-speed Piaggio propeller. It also featured fully retractable landing gear, a variable incidence tailplane and strengthened structure.

The first S.A.I.403 flew late in 1942 and revealed exceptional performance, which resulted in termination of S.A.I.207 production in favour of building 3,000 examples of the S.A.I.403. None of these fighters had been delivered before the Italian armistice with the Allies. The sole prototype was lost in a crash after its wings detached in flight.

Some testing of the Dardo was carried out in German markings. Both Heinkel and Mitsubishi wanted to build the type.

SPECIFICATION

Ambrosini S.A.I.403 Dardo
Type: single-seat lightweight interceptor fighter
Powerplant: one Isotta-Fraschini Delta RC.21/60 Serie I-IV inverted-Vee piston engine rated at 750 hp (560 kW)
Performance: maximum speed 404 mph (650 km/h) at 23,620 ft (7200 m); climb to 19,685 ft (6000 m) in 6 minutes 40 seconds; service ceiling 39,815 ft (12135 m); range 1,165 miles (1875 km) with drop tanks or 581 miles (935 km) with internal fuel
Weights: empty 4,372 lb (1893 kg); maximum take-off 5,820 lb (2640 kg)
Dimensions: wingspan 32 ft 1¾ in (9.80 m); length 26 ft 10¾ in (8.20 m); height 9 ft 6 in (2.90 m); wing area 155.65 sq ft (14.46 m²)
Armament: see **Variants**

Variants

Dardo-A: lightweight interceptor with two 0.5-in (12.7-mm) Breda-SAFAT machine-guns
Dardo-B: general-purpose fighter with two 20-mm MG 151/20 cannon and two 0.5-in (12.7-mm) machine-guns
Dardo-C: long-range version with the two 20-mm cannon and provision for two 33-Imp gal (150-litre) drop tanks. Internal fuel capacity increased from the 66 Imp gal (300 litres) of the Dardo-A/B to 90.2 Imp gal (410 litres)

Ambrosini SS.3 and SS.4

In 1938 Ambrosini's chief designer Sergio Stefanutti, designed a two-seat canard research aircraft, and this was built under the designation **SS.3** by the Stabilimento Construzioni Aeronautiche. Powered by a 38-hp (28.3-kW) CNA IIbis flat-two piston engine, the SS.3 featured a forward-mounted lifting surface and a rear-mounted wing with conventional ailerons and, at about mid-span on each half of the wing, a vertical tail surface combining a fin and a rudder. Trials of the SS.3 revealed poor performance, but good handling characteristics.

Stefanutti therefore decided to press ahead with the design of what would be the world's first interceptor fighter with the canard layout. The resulting **Ambrosini SS.4** had slightly smaller overall dimensions than the SS.3, a much more powerful engine, and retractable tricycle landing gear. The SS.4 prototype made its maiden flight on 7 March 1939, and gave every indication that the performance and handling would both be excellent. However, the sole example was lost in a crash following engine failure the following day, with the death of Ambrosini's test pilot Ambrogio Colombo. The SS.4 programme was subsequently cancelled despite its considerable promise, to allow Ambrosini to concentrate its efforts on the more conventional S.A.I.207.

SPECIFICATION

Ambrosini SS.4 (estimated)
Type: single-seat interceptor fighter
Powerplant: one Isotta-Fraschini Asso XI RC.40 Vee piston engine rated at 960 hp (716 kW)
Performance: maximum speed 335.5 mph (540 km/h) at 16,405 ft (5000 m)
Weights: empty 3,968 lb (1800 kg); maximum take-off 5,401 lb (2450 kg)
Dimensions: wingspan 40 ft 5 in (12.32 m); length 22 ft 1¼ in (6.74 m); height 8 ft 1½ in (2.48 m); wing area 188.37 sq ft (17.50 m²)
Armament: one 30-mm and two 20-mm fixed forward-firing cannon in the nose

Of distinctive canard layout, the SS.4 might have been a fine operational interceptor, had Ambrosini's design efforts not been directed to the S.A.I.207 following the unfortunate loss of the SS.4 prototype.

Ambrosini Sagittario and Ariete

After successful tests with a 45° sweptback wing fitted to an S.7, Stefanutti designed the **Ambrosini Sagittario** (archer) with the powerplant of one Turboméca Marboré turbojet rated at 882 lb st (3.92 kN). This prototype was intended principally for aerodynamic research into the nature and problems of compressibility at transonic speeds and was built largely of wood. The aircraft flew for the first time on 5 January 1953.

In the Sagittario, the new swept flying surfaces were combined with a development of the Super S.7's fuselage with the central section of its fuselage deepened to carry the turbojet. Air reached the engine via a circular inlet in the lengthened nose and a plain exhaust nozzle was fitted below the cockpit.

The **Sagittario 2** was then developed, making its maiden flight on 19 May 1956 under the power of one Rolls-Royce Derwent 9 turbojet rated at 3,600 lb st (16.01 kN). This more advanced machine was a virtually new design of all-metal construction but retained the Sagittario's basic layout.

Designed for the clear-weather interception and close support roles, the Sagittario 2 was the first aircraft of Italian design to exceed Mach 1 when it reached Mach 1.1 in a shallow dive on 4 December 1956. The Sagittario 2 possessed a limited measure of 'developability' as a warplane, but was abandoned in favour of the more promising **Aerfer Ariete** (Battering Ram) or simply **Ariete** (Ram).

Basically similar to the Sagittario II, the Ariete represented the next step toward the development of the finally abortive **Leone** (Lion) mixed-power light interceptor fighter, which was being worked upon with the financial support of the US government. The Ariete retained the flying surfaces of the Sagittario II in combination with a revised fuselage to accommodate a Rolls-Royce Soar auxiliary turbojet.

The Ariete prototype flew for the first time on 27 March 1958, and trials revealed that the use of the auxiliary turbojet offered much enhanced take-off, climb and combat performance. However, the auxiliary engine acted as dead weight during normal flight, severely reducing range, and with more advanced aircraft available the project was abandoned. A conversion trainer derivative was also cancelled.

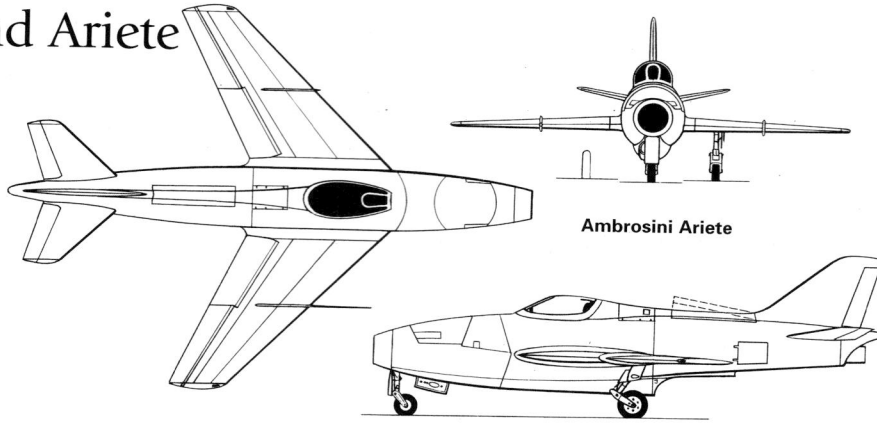

Ambrosini Ariete

Although capable of supersonic flight, the Sagittario 2 could not compete with rival designs.

An auxiliary door in the rear of the Ariete's spine allowed additional air to reach the engine.

Ames AD-1

During the mid-1970s, the National Aeronautics and Space Administration (NASA) decided to investigate the potential of the so-called 'slew wing', in which a single-piece wing is pivoted at its centre so that it can be slewed in flight at any angle up to 60° relative to the fuselage's longitudinal datum. NASA's aim was to investigate the capabilities of the wing in terms of drag reduction at high speeds with the wing slewed, without loss of the straight wing's better low-speed handling and superior take-off and landing performance with the wing moved into a conventional position.

Some 24 companies responded to NASA's call to tender, and early in 1978 NASA selected the Ames Industrial Corporation as the winner. The resulting **Ames AD-1** was built during 1978 on the basis largely of structural concepts and materials developed by Burt Rutan, who was retained as consultant. The AD-1's structure was based on a glassfibre bonded foam core, with varying layers of cloth (between three and 36) used to ensure the right strength in the required areas. The AD-1 was based on a long and very slender fuselage of oval section carried on the ground by fixed but very low tricycle landing gear of glassfibre construction and a combination of very narrow track but long base length. Power was provided by a pair of small turbojets in nacelles attached by short pylons to the fuselage under the trailing edge of the wing. The flying surfaces comprised a tail unit with single horizontal and vertical surfaces, and a high-aspect ratio wing that was tapered in thickness and chord to its rounded tips. The wing slewing system was based on two electric motors providing a slew rate of 3° per second.

The sole AD-1 was delivered to NASA's Dryden Flight Research Center at Edwards AFB, California, in May 1979, and there followed a test programme that revealed the basic soundness of the idea without suggesting any radical improvement over conventional wing arrangements.

NASA hoped that the 'slew-wing' system would generate all the benefits of the swing-wing configuration, without the latter's complexity.

Amiot 110

Between the two World Wars, the French aircraft manufacturing organisation, headed by Félix Amiot, was best known for its bombers. A departure from this practice occurred in 1928, however, when the company produced the **Amiot 110** single-seat fighter. This was its contender for the 'Jockey' competition designed to find a lightweight interceptor on which the air defence of France against strategic bombing attack could be based.

Two examples of the all-metal fuselage Amiot 110 were built with a fabric- and metal-covered wing in the case of the first and second prototypes respectively. Of parasol-wing monoplane configuration, the 110 featured a finely streamlined engine installation and had the appearance of a sesquiplane by the enclosure of its jettisonable fuel tank in a lower-fuselage installation resembling a stub wing.

The first Amiot 110 made its maiden flight in June 1928 and, just over one year later, on 1 July 1929, this machine was lost in an accident. No further development of the type was undertaken.

For engine cooling, a single radiator was installed between each of the V-struts of the 110's main landing gear.

SPECIFICATION

Amiot 110C.1
Type: single-seat fighter
Powerplant: one Hispano-Suiza 12Mb Vee piston engine rated at 500 hp (373 kW)
Performance: maximum speed 184 mph (296 km/h) at optimum altitude; climb to 13,125 ft (4000 m) in 6 minutes; range 311 miles (500 km)
Weights: empty 2,469 lb (1120 kg); maximum take-off 3,307 lb (1500 kg)
Dimensions: wingspan 34 ft 5⅓ in (10.50 m); length 21 ft 4 in (6.50 m); height 9 ft 2¼ in (2.83 m); wing area 226.05 sq ft (21.00 m²)
Armament: two fixed forward-firing 0.295-in (7.5-mm) Vickers machine-guns

Amiot 122

Amiot produced two related record-breaking versions of its **Amiot 120**: the **Amiot 121**, which was lost in a rough landing during June 1927; and the **Amiot 122S**, which completed a circuit of the Mediterranean as well as one of the Sahara.

As these record attempts were being made, Amiot completed the third example of the 120 as the **Amiot 122** prototype of a three-seat warplane intended for the bomber and bomber escort roles. This prototype first flew in 1928, and was extensively displayed to the air arms of friendly nations as well as to the French air force. A lack of lift, however, meant that when the aircraft entered service with the French air force as the **Amiot 122BP.3**, it had wings of increased span and area.

The Amiot 122 was of light alloy construction covered with fabric except over the engine and forward fuselage, which were skinned in light alloy. The biplane wing cellule was backward-staggered and virtually of the sesquiplane type as the lower wing was considerably smaller in area than the upper wing.

The French air force initially placed an order for 50 examples of the Amiot 122BP.3, and these entered service during 1930 with the 11ième Régiment based at Metz in eastern France. Brazil ordered five aircraft in 1931, and in 1934 the French air force received a final batch of 30 aircraft. Poland also considered an order for the type in its revised **Amiot 123** two-seat form, but lost interest after the loss of the prototype in the Azores during an attempt to make the first Polish flight across the Atlantic Ocean.

During 1932, three Amiot 122 aircraft were revised as testbeds for different engines as the **Amiot 124, 125** and **126**.

The Amiot 124 had a 1,000-hp (746-kW) Hispano-Suiza 18Sb W-type piston engine, the Amiot 125 a 900-hp (671-kW) Renault 18Jbr, and the Amiot 126 a 900-hp (671-kW) Lorraine-Dietrich 18Gad Orion. Although all of these engines offered improved performance, the 122 was conceptually obsolete and no production followed.

SPECIFICATION

Amiot 122BP.3
Type: three-seat day bomber and bomber escort
Powerplant: one Lorraine-Dietrich 18Kd W-type piston engine rated at 650 hp (484 kW)
Performance: maximum speed 127 mph (205 km/h) at optimum altitude; service ceiling 20,340 ft (6200 m); range 621 miles (1000 km)
Weights: empty 6,173 lb (2800 kg); maximum take-off 9,259 lb (4200 kg)
Dimensions: wingspan 70 ft 6½ in (21.50 m); length 45 ft ¼ in (13.72 m); height 16 ft 10¾ in (5.15 m); wing area 1,022.60 sq ft (95.00 m²)
Armament: two fixed forward-firing 0.295-in (7.5-mm) Vickers machine-guns, two trainable rearward-firing 0.295-in (7.5-mm) Lewis machine-guns in the dorsal position, and one trainable rearward-firing 0.295-in (7.5-mm) Lewis machine-gun in the ventral position, plus up to 1,764 lb (800 kg) of bombs

French Amiot 122BP.3 bombers flew with the 11ième Air Régiment of the French air force. The aircraft was nicknamed 'La Grosse Julie' ('Fat Julie').

Amiot 140 to 143

After its redesignation as the Société Anonyme des Avions Amiot, Félix Amiot's company was one of four French manufacturers that responded to a 1928 French air ministry requirement for a four-seat aircraft for use in the day and night bomber, long-range reconnaissance, and bomber escort roles.

The type was based on an all-metal structure centred on a slab-sided fuselage with a ventral gondola for the navigator/bombardier (forward), weapons bay (centre) and radio operator/ventral gunner (rear). The fuselage also supported the mid/shoulder-set cantilever wing whose airfoil section was thick enough to allow the inclusion of a crawlway, enabling a member of the crew to reach the engines' accessory bays and the fuel tanks in flight. The two engines were supplied by six fuel tanks, all of which could be jettisoned in the event of a fire although, from the 41st machine, the tanks were made non-jettisonable. The **Amiot 140** also featured a fixed tailwheel type landing gear.

The first of two Amiot 140 prototypes flew in April 1931 with a powerplant of two 650-hp (485-kW) Lorraine 12Fas W-type piston engines. An initial production order for 40 aircraft was placed during November 1933, while Amiot continued to develop alternative versions as the **Amiot 141**, the **Amiot 142** and the **Amiot 143**, all with different powerplants.

Early in 1934, the French air ministry decided to revise its order for the Amiot 140 to cover the Amiot 143 with Gnome-Rhône 14Kirs/Kjrs engines and a fully-enclosed cockpit. With a number of other refinements, this became the standard production configuration and the first of 138 aircraft entered service in July 1935. Initial aircraft were delivered in **Amiot 143M.4** configuration, but after the obsolescence of the multi-place de combat (multi-seat combat aircraft) concept had been recognised, the aircraft received the revised designation **Amiot 143Bn.4** in the Bombardement de nuit quatre-place (four-seat night bomber) category. Some late aircraft were delivered in **Amiot 143B.5** (Bombardement cinq-place, or five-seat bomber) day bomber configuration.

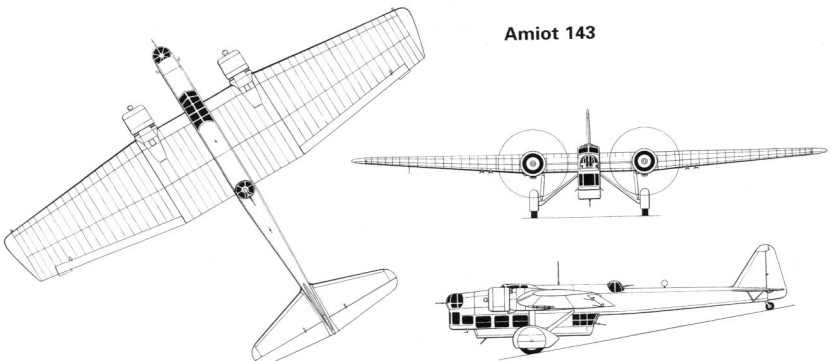

Amiot 143

SPECIFICATION

Amiot 143B.5
Type: five-seat day bomber and reconnaissance aircraft
Powerplant: two Gnome-Rhône 14Kirs/Kjrs Mistral-Major radial piston engines each rated at 870 hp (640 kW) at 10,550 ft (3215 m)
Performance: maximum speed 193 mph (310 km/h) at 13,125 ft (4000 m); maximum cruising speed 168 mph (270 km/h) at 13,125 ft (4000 m); climb to 13,125 ft (4000 m) in 14 minutes 20 seconds; service ceiling 25,920 ft (7900 m); typical range 746 miles (1200 km)
Weights: empty 13,448 lb (6100 kg); maximum take-off 21,385 lb (9700 kg)
Dimensions: wingspan 80 ft 4½ in (24.53 m); length 59 ft 11 in (18.26 m); height 18 ft 7½ in (5.68 m); wing area 1,076.39 sq ft (100.00 m²)
Armament: four trainable 0.295-in (7.5-mm) MAC 1934 machine-guns, one each in the nose turret, dorsal turret, forward-fuselage floor hatch and in the rear of the ventral gondola, plus up to 3,527 lb (1600 kg) of bombs

Amiot 143s were flown bravely in attempts to destroy bridges ahead of the German advance.

The Amiot 143 was wholly obsolete as a bomber when World War II broke out, but the French air force still had 91 of the type in service: of which six were in storage, 29 were operated by training units and 56 were front-line bombers. Nocturnal leaflet-dropping raids were flown over Germany in the first months of the war and four units were still equipped with the Amiot 143 when Germany invaded France. A number of aircraft were still operational when France capitulated, and the Vichy French air force continued to fly the 143 as a transport until February 1944.

Amiot 340 and 350 series

On 6 December 1937, the elegant **Amiot 340.01** prototype completed its maiden flight. The aircraft had originated as the sole prototype of the **Amiot 341** long-range mail transport, but before this had flown it was converted to a three-man bomber, powered by two Gnome-Rhône 14N-0/1 radial engines. In this revised Amiot 340.01 form, the prototype was flown for official acceptance trials at the end of March 1938.

As a result, a number of modifications were recommended, including the installation of Gnome-Rhône 14N-20/21 engines; a new ventral gun position for a fourth crew member; and the introduction of a new tail unit with a dihedralled tailplane and twin endplate fin-and-rudder assemblies. Redesignated as the **Amiot 351.01**, the aircraft undertook successful trials and a number of variants were proposed.

Reorganisation in the French aerospace industry meant that production examples of the very promising 351.01, which had first flown in December 1937, did not start to enter service in numbers until it was too late for it to combat the German invasion. The first two **Amiot 354s** did not reach an operational unit until 7 April 1940 and, of the total of about 62 which had been delivered before the fall of France, most

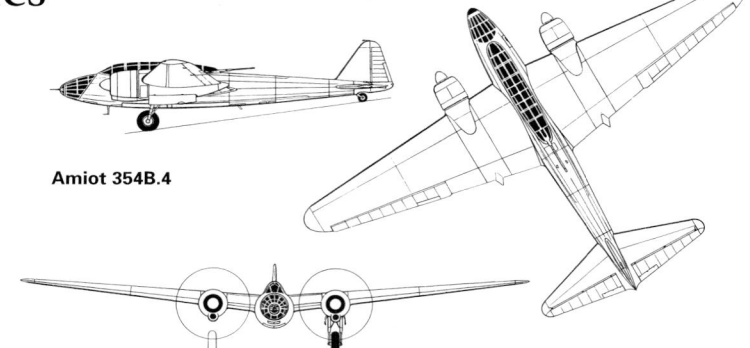

Amiot 354B.4

Clean lines and an elegant tail design distinguished the Amiot 351.01. About 24 Amiot 351 production aircraft were delivered.

were destroyed on the ground during air attacks. A number of the aircraft were overhauled at a later date and, with additional fuel tanks in the bomb bay, were used by Air France for services between Vichy France and overseas territories. Four were seized by the Germans and used by the Luftwaffe: one Amiot 354 was later abandoned by the hard-pressed Luftwaffe as German forces retreated into Germany and this survived to serve with the Groupe de Liaisons Aériennes Ministérielles from 1946.

Variants

Amiot 351: production variant with short-span wings, shorter fuselage and increased endplate area. Powered by two Gnome-Rhône 14N-38/39 radial engines each rated at 950 hp (708 kW) at 12,140 ft (3700 m)
Amiot 354: as 351, but with the single fin-and-rudder of the Amiot 340.01
Amiot 350: project to re-engine the 340.01 with two Hispano-Suiza 12Y-28/29 Vee engines
Amiot 353: project with two Rolls-Royce Merlin III Vee engines
Amiot 354B.4: production variant
Amiot 355.01: prototype with two 1,200-hp (895-kW) Gnome-Rhone 14R-2/3 radial engines with two-speed superchargers
Amiot 356.01: prototype with two 1,130-hp (843-kW) Rolls-Royce Merlin X Vee engines
Amiot 351: project for a high-altitude bomber with pressurised accommodation and two Hispano-Suiza 12Z turbocharged engines

SPECIFICATION

Amiot 354B.4
Type: four-seat medium bomber
Powerplant: two Gnome-Rhône 14N-48/49 radial piston engines each rated at 1,060 hp (790 kW)
Performance: maximum speed 298 mph (480 km/h) at 13,125 ft (4000 m); maximum cruising speed 249 mph (400 km/h) at 13,125 ft (4000 m); climb to 13,125 ft (4000 m) in 8 minutes 48 seconds; service ceiling 32,810 ft (10000 m); range 1,554 miles (2500 km) with a 1,764-lb (800-kg) bombload
Weights: empty 10,417 lb (4725 kg); maximum take-off 24,912 lb (11300 kg)
Dimensions: wingspan 74 ft 10¾ in (22.83 m); length 47 ft 6¾ in (14.50 m); height 13 ft 4½ in (4.08 m); wing area 721.18 sq ft (67.00 m²)
Armament: one trainable rearward-firing 20-mm Hispano-Suiza HS-404 cannon in the dorsal turret and two trainable 0.295-in (7.5-mm) MAC 1934 machine-guns (one each in nose and ventral positions), plus up to 2,646 lb (1200 kg) of bombs

AMX International AMX

In April 1978, Aeritalia and Aermacchi combined their resources to meet AMI requirements for an advanced multi-purpose strike/reconnaissance aircraft. The programme received extra impetus in 1980 when it was joined by Brazil. A common specification, including good short-field performance, high subsonic operating speeds and advanced nav/attack systems, allowed initial agreement in July 1981 for the joint procurement of 266 aircraft. These comprised 79 AMXs for Brazil and 187 for Italy, plus six prototypes, from Aeritalia, Aermacchi and EMBRAER production lines, as well as licensed-construction, in Italy, of the AMX's Rolls-Royce Spey Mk 807 turbofan.

The initial AMX flew at Aeritalia's flight-test centre in May 1984, and the first of two Brazil-assembled prototypes followed in October 1985. Tragically, the first Italian prototype crashed fatally on take-off after an engine problem on 1 June 1984, but development was then concluded by the four remaining prototypes.

Design features include HOTAS, INS, head-up and head-down displays, digital databus, active and passive ECM, and provision for air-to-air refuelling.

SPECIFICATION

AMX International AMX
Type: single-seat close air support and reconnaissance aircraft
Powerplant: one Fiat/Piaggio/Alfa Romeo Avio/CELMA-built Rolls-Royce Spey RB.168 Mk 807 turbofan rated at 11,030 lb st (49.06 kN)
Performance: maximum level speed 'clean' and maximum cruising speed at 36,000 ft (10975 m) 568 mph (914 km/h); maximum rate of climb at sea level 10,250 ft (3124 m) per minute; service ceiling 42,650 ft (13000 m); take-off run 3,220 ft (982 m) at maximum take-off weight; ferry range 2,073 miles (3336 km) with two 290-US gal (1100-litre) drop tanks; combat radius 345 miles (556 km) on a lo-lo-lo attack mission with a 2,000-lb (907-kg) warload, or 576 miles (926 km) on a hi-lo-hi attack mission with a 6,000-lb (2722-kg) warload
Weights: operating empty 14,771 lb (6700 kg); maximum take-off 28,660 lb (13000 kg)
Dimensions: wingspan 32 ft 9¾ in (10.00 m) over wingtip AAMs; length 44 ft 6½ in (13.58 m); height 15 ft ¼ in (4.576 m); wing area 226.05 sq ft (21.00 m²)
Armament: one internal 20-mm M61A1 cannon (or two internal 30-mm DEFA 554 cannon in Brazilian aircraft) plus a maximum ordnance load of 8,377 lb (3800 kg)

Five squadrons of the Italian air force fly the AMX, including one dedicated training unit which flies the AMX-T (illustrated).

AMX International AMX (continued)

By mid-1998, programme totals had increased to 332 aircraft, including 66 two-seat **AMX-Ts** (known in Brazil as **A-1Bs**). Retaining the same dimensions and combat capabilities as the single-seat AMX (**A-1** in Brazil), the trainer version replaces a fuel bay behind the original cockpit with a second Martin-Baker Mk 10L ejection seat, causing some reduction in range. The first of three AMX-T prototypes initially flew in Italy on 14 March 1990, although funding problems delayed first flight of the Brazilian two-seat prototype until 14 August 1991. Radar-equipped versions of the AMX-T have also been considered in Brazil and Italy for enhanced all-weather, ECR and maritime strike roles, and Italian trials with the Exocet anti-ship missile proved successful. In the reconnaissance role, the AMX can either carry external photo or IR pods, or can be equipped with any one of three sensor pallets for internal carriage in the forward fuselage.

AMI pilots began training on the AMX in 1988, with the first operational squadron receiving its first aircraft on 7 November 1989. The first Brazilian A-1 unit began to receive its aircraft on 17 October 1989. Venezuela announced its intention to purchase AMX in 1998.

This is Brazil's first production A-1. The AMX was initially plagued by problems, many relating to US unwillingness to supply high-tech avionics systems.

Anahuac Tauro

Fabrica de Aviones Anahuac S.A. was formed in Mexico in the mid-1960s to develop agricultural aircraft that would be suited to the country's specific need. Work on such a design began in January 1967, and the resulting **Anahuac Tauro** (bull) first flew in **Tauro 300** prototype form on 3 December 1968. Seven production examples of this version were produced, powered by one 300-hp (224-kW) Jacobs R-755-A2M1 radial engine. During 1972-73 an improved variant, designated **Tauro 350**, was introduced, with an uprated engine. The basic structure of the Tauro is of metal, with fabric-covered wings and tail surfaces. A 192-Imp gal (873-litre) chemical hopper is mounted within the fuselage, forward of the cockpit bulkhead.

Of typical agplane configuration, the Tauro family met with moderate sales success. Production ceased during the early 1980s.

SPECIFICATION	
Anahuac Tauro 350	service ceiling 19,000 ft (5790 m); range 233 miles (375 km) with maximum fuel
Type: single-seat agricultural aircraft	**Weights:** empty 2,112 lb (958 kg); maximum take-off 4,550 lb (2064 kg)
Powerplant: one 350-hp (261-kW) Jacobs R-755-SM radial piston engine	**Dimensions:** wing span 37 ft 6 in (11.44 m); length 26 ft 11 in (8.21 m); height 7 ft 8 in (2.34 m); wing area 217.87 sq ft (20.24 m²)
Performance: maximum speed 120 mph (193 km/h) at sea level; economic cruising speed 85 mph (137 km/h) at 5,000 ft (1525 m);	

Anatra D 'Anade' and 'Anakler' and DS 'Anasal'

Late in 1915 Anatra sought to repair its reputation, hard hit by the problems of the VI bomber, by introducing the two-seat **Anatra D** reconnaissance aircraft. Designed (as indicated by the designation) by the French engineer Elysée Alfred Descamps (known to the Russians as Dekan), the D was to be based on a captured Albatros two-seater. The D was otherwise known as the **'Anade'** and was a staggered, unequal-span biplane of fabric-covered wooden construction with fixed tailskid landing gear. The powerplant comprised one 100-hp (74.6-kW) Gnome-Rhône Monosoupape rotary piston engine, or in some later aircraft one 130-hp (97-kW) Clerget 9 rotary engine, with aircraft so engined receiving the designation **'Anakler'**.

The D made its maiden flight on 15 December 1915. In April 1916 an initial order was placed for 80 'Anade' aircraft, which entered service in time for participation in the great Russian summer offensive of 1916. A number of problems arose in service, however, including the D's nose heaviness in the glide, control difficulties, and loss of power resulting from engine overheating. The higher authorities were well pleased with the type, though, and in October 1916 and early 1917 placed orders for another 400 and 300, respectively.

The main problem with the D was the tendency of the wings to suffer catastrophic structural failure. This was the result of Russia's shortage of high-grade seasoned timber for aircraft production purposes, resulting in the use of wing spars that were scarfed from shorter lengths of timber with a glued and bound-linen joint. Even so, production of the 'Anade' and 'Anakler' continued up to the time of the Bolshevik revolution in November 1917, when production ceased after the delivery of some 205 aircraft.

Introduced in the summer of 1917, the **DS** or **'Anasal'** (Anatra Salmson) was an improved version of the D. It featured the addition of a fixed forward-firing machine-gun and the powerplant changed to one Salmson (Canton-Unnè) 9 water-cooled radial piston engine, with a large radiator under the junction of the upper-wing halves. Production of the DS had reached about 70 aircraft before it ended when the Soviet revolution began. A few of the aircraft later found their way into Czechoslovak hands.

A neat cowling disguised the Anatra D's rotary engine. The Albatros on which the D was based was powered by an inline unit.

SPECIFICATION	
Anatra DS	**Weights:** empty 1,800 lb (816 kg); maximum take-off 2,570 lb (1166 kg)
Type: two-seat reconnaissance and artillery spotting aircraft	**Dimensions:** wing span 37 ft 5 in (11.42 m); length 26 ft 6⅛ in (8.10 m); height 10 ft 5⅝ in (3.19 m); wing area 398.28 sq ft (37.00 m²)
Powerplant: one Salmson (Canton-Unnè) 9 radial piston engine rated at 150 hp (112 kW)	**Armament:** one 0.3-in (7.62-mm) fixed forward-firing machine-gun, and one 0.3-in (7.62-mm) trainable rearward-firing machine-gun
Performance: maximum speed 89 mph (143 km/h) at 6,500 ft (1980 m); climb to 6,500 ft (1980 m) in 13 minutes; service ceiling 14,100 ft (4300 m); endurance 3 hours 30 minutes	

Anatra VI

The Zavod A. A. Anatra (A. A. Anatra Works) was established in 1913 and, during World War I, was one of the five largest manufacturers of aircraft in Russia.

In 1915 Anatra was licence-building the Voisin Type 5 (otherwise **Type LAS**) bomber. Wishing to improve the type's performance, especially in terms of speed and climb rate, Anatra commissioned Lieutenant V. Ivanov to design an upgraded version, which materialised as the **VI** (**Voisin-Ivanov**). In fact, it was little altered from the original Type 5 except in details designed to reduce the French original's high level of drag.

The Anatra VI was therefore still a pusher aircraft of fabric-covered wooden construction, but in overall appearance differed from the French original in having a deeper nacelle, a rudder with a shortened lower portion and reduced aileron area as a result of the removal of ailerons on the lower wing. Through these changes, Ivanov succeeded in improving speed by 13 mph (21 km/h) and reducing the time needed to reach 6,560 ft (2000 m) by 5 minutes. Unfortunately, lateral control was now distinctly poor, the controls in general were not very effective and, as it had not been strengthened despite the aircraft's higher weight, the landing gear was prone to failure.

Anatra received an order for 139 examples of the VI to be delivered between March 1915 and March 1916, but the last of the aircraft was completed only in the middle of 1918. The type was notably unpopular with Russian aircrews, and this dislike continued even after 1917, when Ivanov introduced improvements

that cured most of the VI's major problems, with the exception of the inherent weakness of the landing gear.

A high accident rate, mostly connected with the VI's lack of lateral stability, led to Anatra being heavily criticised for poor design and workmanship.

SPECIFICATION

Anatra VI
Type: two-seat day bomber and reconnaissance aircraft
Powerplant: one Salmson (Canton-Unnè) 9 radial piston engine rated at 150 hp (112 kW)
Performance: maximum speed 78 mph (125 km/h) at sea level; climb to 9,515 ft (2900 m) in 38 minutes 30 seconds; service ceiling 11,485 ft (3500 m); endurance 3 hours 30 minutes
Weights: empty 1,878 lb (852 kg); maximum take-off 2,650 lb (1202 kg)
Dimensions: wing span 48 ft 2¾ in (14.70 m); length 31 ft 2 in (9.50 m); wing area 419.81 sq ft (39.00 m²)
Armament: one 0.3-in (7.62-mm) trainable forward-firing machine-gun in the nose

Anderson Greenwood AG-14

The Anderson Greenwood AG-14 was first flown on 1 October 1947. Of all-metal construction, the aircraft had a fuselage pod, a mid-set cantilever wing, and twin booms, each carrying a vertical surface and rudder, and joined at the rear by a single horizontal surface. The landing gear was of the fixed tricycle type, and the engine was mounted to drive a pusher propeller between the booms. An enclosed cabin seated two, side-by-side, with dual controls as standard. Only four production examples were built.

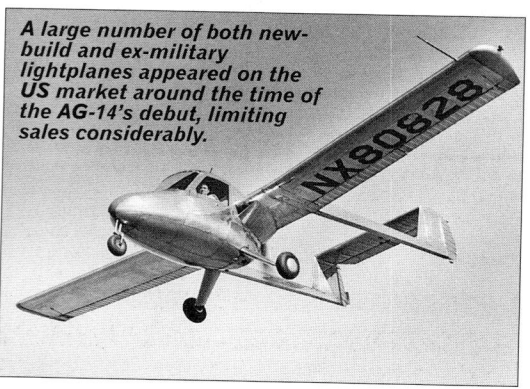

A large number of both new-build and ex-military lightplanes appeared on the US market around the time of the AG-14's debut, limiting sales considerably.

SPECIFICATION

Anderson Greenwood AG-14
Type: two-seat cabin monoplane
Powerplant: one Continental C90 flat-four piston engine rated at 90 hp (67 kW)
Performance: maximum speed 120 mph (193 km/h) at optimum altitude; cruising speed 110 mph (177 km/h) at optimum altitude; initial climb rate 700 ft (213 m) per minute; service ceiling 19,000 ft (5790 m)
Weights: empty 850 lb (386 kg); maximum take-off 1,400 lb (635 kg)
Dimensions: wing span 34 ft (10.36 m); length 22 ft 6 in (6.86 m); height 7 ft 6 in (2.29 m); wing area 120.00 sq ft (11.15 m²)

Anderson EA-1 Kingfisher

In 1960, amateur aircraft builder and pilot Earl Anderson (who later became a Boeing 747 pilot) began work on a two-seat amphibious light aircraft. Some nine years later, on 24 April 1969, the **Anderson EA-1 Kingfisher** completed its maiden flight.
The Kingfisher is based on the standard wing of a Piper Cub lightplane, which is mounted above, and braced to, the conventional single-step wood and fibre-glass hull. Amphibious capability was provided by the externally-mounted, manually retractable tail-wheel landing gear. The engine, which can be of virtually any type in the power rating between 100 and 150 hp (74.6 and 112 kW), is located in a nacelle mounted on struts above the wing.
Anderson began the sale of plans for his successful design to other home-builders. More than 100 Kingfishers were soon under construction around the world, and many were completed and flown.

SPECIFICATION

Anderson EA-1 Kingfisher
Type: two-seat light amphibian
Powerplant: typically one Continental O-200 flat-four piston engine rated at 100 hp (74.6 kW)
Performance: maximum speed 120 mph (193 km/h) at sea level; cruising speed 85 mph (137 km/h) at 1,000 ft (305 m); initial climb rate 500 ft (152 m) per minute; service ceiling 10,000 ft (3050 m); range 200 miles (322 km) with maximum fuel
Weights: empty 1,032 lb (468 kg); maximum take-off 1,500 lb (680 kg)
Dimensions: wing span 36 ft 1 in (11.00 m); length 23 ft 6 in (7.16 m); height 8 ft (2.44 m)

The Kingfisher's manually-retractable main landing gear units were accommodated externally, avoiding the complexity of providing internal bays.

Andreasson aircraft

Swedish-born Björn Andreasson is best remembered as the designer of the **BA-7**, which entered moderately large-scale production as the **Junior** by MFI in Sweden and Bölkow in West Germany. He was also a prolific designer of lightplanes, both in the USA and after his return to his home country. The most notable Andreasson aircraft other than the BA-7 were the **BA-4**, **BA-6** and **BA-11**, all of interest for their cleverly conceived designs and structures optimised for cleanliness, maximum strength/weight ratio, and full aerobatic capability on a low-powered engine.
The Andreasson BA-4 was designed in the USA shortly after the end of World War II as a small, single-bay biplane of fabric-covered wooden construction with fixed tail-wheel landing gear. Only a single example was built, but the design was modernised in the early 1960s to create the **BA-4B** of largely metal construction. It was built in prototype form in Sweden.
The BA-6 was another type designed in the USA, in this instance as a cantilever low-wing monoplane of plywood-covered wooden construction with an enclosed single-seat cockpit. First flown in 1955, the BA-6 was intended for construction by amateur groups and flying clubs, was fully aerobatic, and could be powered by flat-four piston engines in the power range between 65 and 85 hp (48.5 and 63.5 kW), most typically the Continental A65 or Continental A85 units, respectively.
The BA-11 was an extension of the same basic concept, being a single-bay biplane with fixed tailwheel landing gear including spring steel cantilever main units. The aircraft was of all-metal construction and offered accommodation for one or two persons in tandem under a long moulded canopy, although it was flown as a single-seater for aerobatic competition.

Despite its diminutive size, the BA-4B proved to be a useful aerobatic biplane. A handful remained on the British register in the late 1990s.

SPECIFICATION

Andreasson BA-4B
Type: single-seat aerobatic lightplane
Powerplant: one Rolls-Royce (Continental) O-200-A flat-four piston engine rated at 100 hp (74.6 kW)
Performance: maximum speed 140 mph (225 km/h) at optimum altitude; maximum cruising speed 120 mph (193 km/h) at optimum altitude; initial climb rate 2,000 ft (609 m) per minute; range 175 miles (280 km)
Weights: maximum take-off 827 lb (375 kg)
Dimensions: wing span 17 ft 7 in (5.34 m); length 15 ft (4.57 m); wing area 89.34 sq ft (8.30 m²)

ANF Les Mureaux 113, 114, 115 and 117

In 1930 Ateliers des Mureaux merged with Ateliers des Constructions du Nord de la France to create an organisation generally known as ANF Les Mureaux. This company continued to produce the series of parasol-wing monoplanes designed for Les Mureaux under the supervision of André Brunet. The first of these to enter service was the **ANF Les Mureaux 113**, which was in essence the production version of the two-seat **ANF Les Mureaux 110**, but revised in this application from the original tactical reconnaissance role of the 110 to the reconnaissance role to meet a 1928 requirement.

The ANF Les Mureaux 113 was a parasol-wing monoplane of basically all-metal construction. The crew of two was accommodated in a tandem arrangement of open cockpits with the observer/gunner in the rear cockpit protected from the elements by an oversize windscreen. Power was provided by the 650-hp (485-kW) Hispano-Suiza 12Ybrs Vee engine and some 49 examples of the **ANF Les Mureaux 113R.2** production variant were delivered in 1934.

There were three important developments from the 113. The first of these was the **ANF Les Mureaux 114**, of which two were built and others converted from ANF Les Mureaux 113 standard for service as **ANF Les Mureaux**

114CN.2 night-fighters with small underwing searchlights and an armament of four machine-guns. Some 115 examples of the **ANF Les Mureaux 115** were built (excluding the prototype that first flew in January 1935) to the **ANF Les Mureaux 115R.2B.2** reconnaissance bomber standard derived from the ANF Les Mureaux 113 with an uprated engine and provision for an external bombload. The final model was the **ANF Les Mureaux 117**, of which 16 were completed to the **ANF Les Mureaux 117R.2B.2** improved reconnaissance bomber standard with a useful bombload of up to 882 lb (400 kg).

By the outbreak of World War II, some 221 ANF Les Mureaux parasol-wing aircraft were in French service, final deliveries of the ANF Les Mureaux 115 taking place only in September 1939.

Operating over the German lines during the first weeks of war, the units equipped with ANF Les Mureaux aircraft suffered heavy losses as a result of their aircraft's obsolescence. Indeed, the first French aircraft to be

The 114CN.2 was modified for the night-fighting role, although the pilot's night-vision must have been affected by the unshrouded exhausts.

shot down by German forces was an ANF Les Mureaux 115 flying a reconnaissance mission on 8 September 1939. At the end of that month, all ANF Les Mureaux aircraft were restricted to missions in close proximity to the front line. French observation units still had 119 Mureaux aircraft in service when the German Blitzkrieg was launched on 10 May 1940, although most of these were restricted to training and liaison duties. At the time of the 25 June 1940 Armistice, all 53 ANF Les Mureaux parasol monoplanes left in the

unoccupied zone of France were reduced to scrap.

Two further variants were produced. The **ANF Les Mureaux 113GR** was powered by a supercharged Hispano-Suiza 12Ybrs engine and, in June 1934, the aircraft won the prized Coupe Bibesco, a 'point-to-point' air race between Romanian and French military aircraft. Lastly, a single **ANF Les Mureaux 200** prototype, with a glazed canopy over the crew accommodation, was tested in the three-seat tactical reconnaissance and observation role in January 1936.

SPECIFICATION

ANF Les Mureaux 115R.2B.2
Type: two-seat reconnaissance bomber
Powerplant: one Hispano-Suiza 12Ycrs Vee engine rated at 860 hp (641 kW)
Performance: maximum speed 211 mph (340 km/h) at 13,125 ft (4000 m); climb to 16,405 ft (4000 m) in 8 minutes 10 seconds; service ceiling 34,120 ft (10400 m); range 932 miles (1500 km)

Weights: maximum take-off 5,644 lb (2560 kg)
Dimensions: wingspan 50 ft 6⅓ in (15.40 m); length 32 ft 7¾ in (9.95 m); height 11 ft 9 in (3.58 m); wing area 375.67 sq ft (34.90 m²)
Armament: one 20-mm fixed forward-firing cannon and two 0.295-in (7.5-mm) trainable rearward-firing machine-guns, plus an external bombload of up to 661 lb (300 kg)

ANF Les Mureaux 120

In 1928 the French air force issued an RN.3 requirement for a three-seat night reconnaissance aircraft, and ANF Les Mureaux responded with its **ANF Les Mureaux 120** design, a cantilever high-wing monoplane of basically all-metal construction and fairly ungainly shaping.

The first of the two ANF Les Mureaux 120 prototypes flew in 1931 powered by two Lorraine 9Na radial engines, while the second machine followed in 1932 with identically rated Gnome-Rhône 7Kb Titan radial engines. Flight trials revealed engine cooling problems, and although these were soon solved through modifications to the engines' ring cowlings, official interest in the type soon waned and further development was abandoned.

Twin machine-gun installations in the nose and amidships positions provided self-defence for the ANF Les Mureaux 120. The project was abandoned even after initial problems had been overcome.

SPECIFICATION

ANF Les Mureaux 120RN.3
Type: three-seat night reconnaissance aircraft
Powerplant: two Lorraine 9Na or Gnome-Rhône 7Kb Titan radial engines each rated at 300 hp (224 kW)
Performance: maximum speed 142 mph (228 km/h) at optimum altitude; service ceiling 21,325 ft (6500 m)

Weights: maximum take-off 5,765 lb (2615 kg)
Dimensions: wingspan 55 ft 9½ in (17.00 m); length 36 ft 9 in (11.20 m); wing area 489.77 sq ft (45.50 m²)
Armament: four trainable 0.303-in (7.7-mm) machine-guns, one or two each in the nose position and in the dorsal position

ANF Les Mureaux 170

ANF Les Mureaux produced the **170** to meet a 1930 French air force requirement for a new C.1-class single-seat fighter with a supercharged engine to provide a speed of at least 218 mph (350 km/h). The all-metal aircraft featured a gull-type, shoulder-mounted wing and fixed tailskid landing gear. The wing was braced to the fuselage on either side

Large spats covered the strut-mounted main wheels of the aesthetically-pleasing ANF Mureaux 170C.1.

by twin parallel struts.

The first of two **ANF Les Mureaux 170.01** prototypes made its maiden flight in November 1932, and among its other notable features were the lightness of the fuselage (made possible by its thin but strong Dural skin), ailerons that could be lowered collectively to serve as flaps, a radiator installation in a ventral box

fairing under the fuselage centre section, and the location of the fixed armament in the leading edges of the wing. Considerable effort went into the development of the fighter, but although it possessed generally good performance, the type was rejected for production as a result of the pilot's poor fields of downward vision, which made landing extremely difficult and were also a disadvantage in combat.

SPECIFICATION

ANF Les Mureaux 170C.1
Type: single-seat fighter
Powerplant: one Hispano-Suiza 12Xbrs Vee piston engine rated at 690 hp (515 kW)
Performance: maximum speed 236 mph (380 km/h) at 14,765 ft (4500 m); climb to 32,810 ft (10000 m) in 23 minutes 25 seconds; service ceiling

34,120 ft (10400 m)
Weights: empty 2,643 lb (1199 kg); maximum take-off 3,682 lb (1670 kg)
Dimensions: wingspan 37 ft 4 in (11.38 m); length 25 ft 11 in (7.90 m); height 9 ft 10 in (3.00 m); wing area 210.55 sq ft (19.56 m²)
Armament: two 0.295-in (7.5-mm) fixed forward-firing machine-guns

ANF Les Mureaux 180

Flown for the first time on 10 February 1935, the **ANF Les Mureaux 180** was a fighter of the C.2 two-seat class. It was basically an enlarged and slightly modernised development of the ANF Les Mureaux 170 with the same engine in a different installation, which was characterised by a frontal radiator.

As first flown, the ANF Les Mureaux 180 was fitted with a 690-hp (515-kW) Hispano-Suiza 12Xbrs engine, but in April 1935 this engine was replaced by a Hispano-Suiza 12Xcrs engine with provision for a moteur-canon installation for one 20-mm cannon firing through the hollow propeller shaft. At much the same time, the tail unit was also revised to incorporate twin vertical surfaces that improved directional stability and control as well as providing the gunner with improved rearward fields of fire. The type's evaluation continued until 1936, when the revised design was abandoned as obsolete.

With the fixed main undercarriage and less than ideal wing installation of the ANF Les Mureaux 170, the 180 featured a fully enclosed cockpit as its one concession to modern fighter design.

SPECIFICATION

ANF Les Mureaux 180C.2 (final form)
Type: two-seat fighter
Powerplant: one Hispano-Suiza 12Xcrs Vee piston engine rated at 690 hp (515 kW)
Performance: maximum speed 235 mph (379 km/h) at 16,405 ft (5000 m); climb to 21,325 ft (6500 m) in 7 minutes 30 seconds; range 466 miles (750 km)
Weights: empty 2,791 lb (1266 kg); maximum take-off 4,306 lb (1953 kg)
Dimensions: wingspan 37 ft 4⅜ in (11.40 m); length 25 ft 8 in (7.83 m); height 10 ft 8⅜ in (3.26 m); wing area 210.54 sq ft (19.56 m²)
Armament: one 20-mm fixed forward-firing cannon, one 0.295-in (7.5-mm) fixed forward-firing machine-gun, and one 0.295-in (7.5-mm) trainable rearward-firing machine-gun in the rear of the cockpit

ANF Les Mureaux 190

During the mid-1930s many air forces wished to acquire 'modern' fighters, seeking the best aircraft that were technically possible within the constraints of peacetime budgets. Thus there emerged a vogue for lightweight fighters, many of them based on racing aircraft. A contender for the substantial French order anticipated for such a type was the all-metal **ANF Les Mureaux 190** that made its first flight in July 1936.

The unarmed **ANF Les Mureaux 190.01** prototype was of compact overall size with an enclosed cockpit and a low-set wing of semi-elliptical planform. The main units of its fixed tail-skid landing gear were carefully faired and spatted. During its trials the type revealed excellent manoeuvrability, and its fine lines made a considerable contribution to its good performance on only modest power. In 1937, however, it was decided to discontinue the whole programme as the selected engine, a 450-hp (336-kW) Salmson inverted-Vee unit of the air-cooled type, was causing so many problems that further development would clearly have been unprofitable.

A fine example of pre-World War II lightweight fighter design, the 190 failed due to incurable problems with its powerplant.

SPECIFICATION

ANF Les Mureaux 190C.1
Type: single-seat lightweight fighter
Powerplant: one Salmson 12Vars inverted-Vee engine rated at 450 hp (336 kW)
Performance: maximum speed 311 mph (500 km/h) at 13,125 ft (4000 m); service ceiling 32,810 ft (10000 m); endurance 2 hours 30 minutes
Weights: empty 1,874 lb (850 kg); maximum take-off 2,844 lb (1290 kg)
Dimensions: wingspan 27 ft 5 in (8.38 m); length 23 ft 7½ in (7.20 m); height 9 ft 10 in (3.00 m); wing area 107.64 sq ft (10.00 m²)
Armament: (proposed) one 20-mm fixed forward-firing cannon and two 0.295-in (7.5-mm) fixed forward-firing machine-guns

Ansaldo A.1 Balilla

The prototype of the **Ansaldo A.1 Balilla** (hunter) fighter flew for the first time in November 1917 as a biplane of wooden construction covered largely with fabric except on the fuselage. The A.1 retained the basic fuselage design of the Ansaldo SVA series, but had a wing braced by a pair of parallel vertical struts on each side rather than by W-form Warren-truss bracing. However, the SPAD S.VII was purchased by the Italian military instead of the A.1, which lacked manoeuvrability.

In March 1918 the A.1 was demonstrated with an increased gap between the wings, which were also increased in area. These modifications, plus the introduction of an SPA 6A engine, resulted in an overall improvement in performance and a production order then followed. Series manufacture of the A.1 totalled 166 aircraft, which were delivered before the end of World War I, but the A.1 saw only brief first-line service with the Italian air force in the home defence role.

After World War I, the air force of the newly created Poland bought 75 aircraft, and these served with the renowned Kosciuszko squadron during the Russo-Polish War of 1920.

Incredibly, in the following year Ansaldo delivered 30 examples of the A.1 to the USSR, and between 1921 and 1924, the Polish firm of Plage & Laskiewicz completed the licensed production of some 50 more A.1 fighters.

In the post-war years, the A.1 appeared in a number of aeronautical displays and competitions. A lightweight, reduced-span racing version finished third in the 1920 Pulitzer Trophy competition in the USA, but efforts to sell the type to the US Army Air Service were unsuccessful.

With its 400-hp (298-kW) Curtis K-12 engine driving a four-bladed propeller, the modified Balilla racer achieved some success in the US.

SPECIFICATION

Ansaldo A.1 Balilla
Type: single-seat fighter
Powerplant: one SPA 6A inline piston engine rated at 205 hp (153 kW) or, in higher-compression form, 220 hp (164 kW)
Performance: maximum speed 137 mph (220 km/h) at sea level; climb to 9,845 ft (3000 m) in 8 minutes 30 seconds; service ceiling 16,405 ft (5000 m); range 342 miles (550 km); endurance 2 hours 30 minutes
Weights: empty 1,411 lb (640 kg); maximum take-off 1,951 lb (885 kg)
Dimensions: wingspan 25 ft 2½ in (7.68 m); length 21 ft 3¾ in (6.50 m); height 9 ft 4 in (2.85 m); wing area 226.05 sq ft (21.00 m²)
Armament: two fixed forward-firing 0.303-in (7.7-mm) machine-guns

Ansaldo A.300

Drawing on experience with its SVA biplanes, the Ansaldo company began work in 1918 on a biplane of wood and metal construction, intended from the start as a two-seat reconnaissance aircraft and light bomber offering flight characteristics considerably superior to those of the SVA series. The result was the **Ansaldo A.300** that

first flew in prototype form early in 1919, and proved to be manoeuvrable and responsive. As a result, the test programme progressed rapidly and the A.300 was able to make a demonstration tour of several European countries.

The high performance of the A.300 was attractive to a number of new countries after World War I, and this

led to small orders for the **A.300/2** initial production version including some for Poland. The three-seat **A.300/3** followed at the end of 1920, with a number being exported to Spain, Belgium and Poland, the Poles using their aircraft in operations against the Soviets in the Russo-Polish War.

Ansaldo was still not wholly satisfied with the design, and therefore developed the **A.300/4** which introduced engine cooling by means of twin Lamblin radiators. Some 30 A.300/4 aircraft were purchased by Poland in 1924, these proving to be more reliable than the total of about 70 A.300/2 machines built under licence between 1921 and 1924, which were prone to structural failures. The newly constituted Regia Aeronautica (Italian air force) ordered large

Just one A.300C, with accommodation for two crew and four passengers, is likely to have been built.

numbers of the A.300/4 version, the final figure nearing 700, and the type played a prominent part in the lengthy Italian campaign in North Africa which finally ended in the conquest of Libya.

Later versions were the Lorraine-powered **A.300/5** and the passenger-carrying

A.300C and **A.300T**. The only other development to go into production, however, was the **A.300/6**, which featured detail design improvements compared with the A.300/4. An **A.400** prototype had a Lorraine engine and updated design, but did not enter production.

SPECIFICATION

Ansaldo A.300/4
Type: two-seat reconnaissance aircraft
Powerplant: one Fiat A.12bis inline engine rated at 230 hp (224 kW)
Performance: maximum speed 124 mph (200 km/h) at sea level; climb to 16,405 ft (5000 m) in 33 minutes 30 seconds; service ceiling 18,045 ft (5500 m); endurance 3 hours 30 minutes

Weights: empty 2,645 lb (1200 kg); maximum take-off 3,748 lb (1700 kg)
Dimensions: wing span 36 ft 10½ in (11.24 m); length 28 ft 8½ in (8.75 m); height 9 ft 9 in (2.97 m); wing area 425.19 sq ft (39.50 m²)
Armament: two fixed forward-firing 0.303-in (7.7-mm) machine-guns and one trainable rearward-firing 0.303-in (7.7-mm) machine-gun in the rear cockpit

Ansaldo AC.2 and AC.3

After Ansaldo's experience with licensed production of the Dewoitine D.1 as the **AC.2**, it applied the same basic practice to its next fighter, which was a derivative of the Dewoitine D.9 known as the **Ansaldo AC.3**. The AC.3 prototype made its maiden flight early in 1926, and differed from

the D.9 mainly in its slightly shortened fuselage and modestly enlarged wing. In terms of its construction and general configuration the AC.3 was basically similar to the AC.2 with the exception of its powerplant, in which the AC.2's water-cooled Vee engine was replaced by an air-cooled

radial engine installed in the nose inside a neat hemi-spherical cowling through which its cylinder heads protruded for improved engine cooling.

The fixed forward-firing armament of the AC.3 comprised two 0.303-in (7.7-mm) synchronised machine-guns in the upper part of the forward fuse-lage and two 0.303-in (7.7-mm) free-firing machine-guns in the leading edges of the wing, although these latter were sometimes replaced by a single gun fixed on the centre section to fire obliquely upward and forward.

Production of the AC.3 totalled 150 aircraft delivered between September

Armament of the AC.3 parasol-wing fighter, consisted of two Vickers machine-guns firing through the propeller arc and one or two Darne machine-guns in the wing.

1926 and April 1927. In the early 1930s it was recognised that the aircraft were obsolete in the fighter role, and the surviving machines

were therefore relegated to the increasingly important ground-attack role. The last aircraft were retired only in the summer of 1938.

SPECIFICATION

Ansaldo AC.3
Type: single-seat fighter
Powerplant: one 420-hp (313-kW) Gnome-Rhône (Bristol) Jupiter IV nine-cylinder single-row radial piston engine
Performance: maximum speed 153 mph (247 km/h) at sea level; climb to 9,845 ft (3000 m) in 6 minutes 12 seconds; service ceiling 31,170 ft (9500 m);

endurance 2 hours 50 minutes
Weights: empty 2,114 lb (959 kg); maximum take-off 2,981 lb (1352 kg)
Dimensions: wing span 41 ft 11¾ in (12.80 m); length 23 ft 10½ in (7.28 m); height 9 ft 7½ in (2.93 m); wing area 269.11 sq ft (25.00 m²)
Armament: four, sometimes three, fixed forward-firing 0.303-in (7.7-mm) machine-guns

Ansaldo SVA and ISVA

In the summer of 1916 Umberto Savoia and Rodolfo Verduzio, with the assistance of Celestino Rosatelli, began work on a project for a fighter biplane. It was the intention of the design team, which was part of the Italian technical directorate of military aviation, to create a warplane superior to any of its contemporaries of the

same basic type. That autumn the Italian ministry of war gave its backing to the project, and Giovanni Ansaldo & Co. was requested to build proto-types and obtain factory space for series production. Ansaldo created the Società Anonima Aeronautica Ansaldo for the purpose, and the new fighter thus became known

as the **Ansaldo SVA** with the designation reflecting the first letters of the two main designers' surnames and of the manufacturer.

The first prototype made its maiden flight on 19 March 1917 as an unequal-span biplane of wooden construction with a

Designed by the Italian military and adopted for construction by Ansaldo, the SVA proved itself to be an excellent reconnaissance aircraft.

plywood-covered fuselage and fabric-covered flying surfaces. The basic design included an open cockpit and fixed tailskid landing gear. Notable features were

the W-form Warren truss interplane bracing, which removed the need for flying and landing wires, and the long and comparatively narrow fuselage with a rear

SPECIFICATION

Ansaldo SVA-2
Type: single-seat reconnaissance fighter
Powerplant: one SPA 6A inline engine rated at 205 hp (153 kW)
Performance: maximum speed 137 mph (220 km/h) at sea level; climb to 9,845 ft (3000 m) in 11 minutes 20 seconds; endurance 3 hours

Weights: empty 1,477 lb (670 kg); maximum take-off 2,100 lb (952 kg)
Dimensions: wing span 29 ft 10¼ in (9.10 m); length 26 ft 6⅝ in (8.10 m); height 8 ft 8½ in (2.65 m); wing area 260.49 sq ft (24.20 m²)
Armament: two synchronised fixed forward-firing 0.303-in (7.7-mm) Vickers machine-guns

portion of inverted-triangular section that reduced weight and also improved the pilot's downward fields of vision to the rear.

The SVA had very good performance, but was inherently stable and therefore considered to lack the level of agility required to operate in the fighter-versus-fighter role. However, it was also recognised that the SVA's combination of stability and exceptional range made it suitable for the reconnaissance fighter role, and it was for this role that the type was then earmarked. Meanwhile the first production aircraft, designated **SVA-2**, were being delivered from the autumn of 1917, and these 65 machines were used mainly for the training task.

The only variant of the SVA in its initial form was the **ISVA**, the initial letter of the designation standing for Idro (water). This was a fighter floatplane derivative of the SVA-2 and was built in 1918 to the extent of 50 aircraft for the defence of Italian naval bases and for coastal reconnaissance. The sole appreciable difference between the SVA-2 and the ISVA was the latter's floatplane alighting gear. The ISVA was powered by the SPA 6A engine and armed with two 0.303-in (7.7-mm) Vickers fixed forward-firing machine-guns.

Built at La Spezia in 1918, the ISVA was a useful floatplane fighter, with a maximum speed of 112 mph (180 km/h) and an endurance of 3 hours.

Ansaldo SVA-3

The **Ansaldo SVA-3** was the counterpart of the SVA-4 built under licence by AER at Orbassano as a reconnaissance fighter, and differed in no significant details from the SVA-4.

In the spring of 1918, however, AER produced the **SVA-3 Ridotto** (reduced) as a fast-climbing interceptor derivative of the SVA-3 optimised for the protection of Italian localities deep behind the front line but nonetheless threatened by Austro-Hungarian and German bombing attacks, especially those by airships. Built only in small numbers, the SVA-3 Ridotto was distinguishable from the SVA-3 mainly by its higher-rated SPA 6A engine, and its wing cellule of smaller span and area.

The armament of the SVA-3 Ridotto was the standard pair of fixed forward-firing Vickers machine-guns, but these were sometimes supplemented by a third weapon arranged to fire obliquely forward and upward to engage potential targets from below.

An SPA 6A engine with a higher compression ratio gave the SVA-3 Ridotto extra power for its interceptor role.

SPECIFICATION

Ansaldo SVA-3 Ridotto
Type: single-seat point interceptor
Powerplant: one SPA 6A six-cylinder inline engine rated at 220 hp (164 kW)
Performance: maximum speed 149 mph (240 km/h) at optimum altitude; climb to 13,125 ft (4000 m) in 13 minutes; endurance 3 hours
Weights: empty 1,470 lb (667 kg); maximum take-off 1,965 lb (891 kg)
Dimensions: wing span 25 ft 5⅛ in (2.65 m); length 26 ft 6⅞ in (8.10 m); height 8 ft 8⅓ in (2.65 m); wing area 236.81 sq ft (22.00 m^2)
Armament: two or three fixed forward-firing 0.303-in (7.7-mm) Vickers machine-guns

Ansaldo SVA-4

The **Ansaldo SVA-4** was the first production model of the SVA series to be built in substantial numbers, entering production in the late autumn of 1917 and operational service in February 1918.

Although the type had initially been promoted as a fighter, Italian fighter pilots were slow to appreciate the speed and climb advantages of the comparatively large and heavy SVA-4, and still preferred their smaller, lighter and therefore more agile fighters of French design. The SVA-4 was thus used almost exclusively for the long-range reconnaissance fighter role. In this revised task the twin machine-gun armament was often reduced to the port-side Vickers gun only, and two cameras were installed in the bottom of the fuselage.

It was in this reconnaissance role that the SVA began to come into its own as a major operational type, for its long range allowed the SVA-4 to reach and photograph targets deep in the Austro-Hungarian rear areas without real fear of interception. The high speed and good climb performance allowed the pilot to enter combat and to break off from it almost completely at his own discretion, thereby removing all need for escort.

SPECIFICATION

Ansaldo SVA-4
Type: single-seat reconnaissance fighter
Powerplant: one SPA 6A six-cylinder inline engine rated at 205 hp (153 kW)
Performance: maximum speed 134 mph (216 km/h) at optimum altitude; climb to 9,845 ft (3000 m) in 12 minutes; endurance 3 hours 36 minutes
Weights: empty 1,545 lb (701 kg); maximum take-off 2,150 lb (949 kg)
Dimensions: wing span 29 ft 10¼ in (9.10 m); length 26 ft 6⅞ in (8.10 m); height 8 ft 8⅓ in (2.65 m); wing area 260.49 sq ft (24.20 m^2)
Armament: one or two fixed forward-firing 0.303-in (7.7-mm) Vickers machine-guns

Built by two Ansaldo factories located at Borzoli and Bolzaneto respectively, the SVA-4 carried two cameras aft of its fuselage fuel tank.

Ansaldo SVA-5 and SVA-9

The **Ansaldo SVA-5** was the definitive model of the SVA series in its original single-seat form, and was a long-range warplane notionally intended for the fighter role but almost exclusively operated in the reconnaissance and bomber roles, the latter with light bombs in special clips on the sides of the fuselage. The SVA-5 accounted for the majority of the 1,248 SVA series aircraft built in 1917-18.

Two subvariants of the SVA-5 were produced, one of them a reconnaissance and light bomber model, and the other a long-range escort fighter. The escort model lacked reconnaissance cameras but featured increased fuel capacity.

While the early aircraft were powered by the standard SPA 6A engine, later aircraft switched to the high-compression version of the same engine rated at 220 hp (164 kW). Production of the SVA series continued to 1928 and eventually totalled more than 2,000 aircraft, and a number of the SVA-5 aircraft completed after World War I were fitted with a 250-hp (187-kW) Isotta-Fraschini V6 engine for a maximum speed of 149 mph (240 km/h).

One of the most celebrated operators of the type was the 87ª Squadriglia, and it was at the suggestion of this unit's commanding officer, that a pair of two-seat developments of the SVA-5 was created as the totally unarmed **SVA-9** and the **SVA-10**. The SVA-9 featured wings of increased span and area, and its central fuselage was revised to accommodate a separate cockpit located between the engine and the pilot's cockpit. The task of this two-seater was to operate as a 'mothership' for formations of SVA-5s, and also to serve as a two-seat trainer for the single-seat model. The SVA-9 was not built in large numbers, but survived into the first half of the 1930s as a trainer.

This SVA-9 was discovered in 1956 and restored. The aircraft has its original engine, and is part of the Fyfield Collection at Washington, Connecticut.

SPECIFICATION

Ansaldo SVA-5
Type: single-seat reconnaissance fighter and light bomber
Powerplant: one SPA 6A six-cylinder inline engine rated at 205 hp (153 kW)
Performance: maximum speed 143 mph (230 km/h) at sea level; climb to 9,845 ft (3000 m) in 10 minutes; endurance 3 hours
Weights: empty 1,499 lb (680 kg); maximum take-off 2,315 lb (1050 kg)
Dimensions: wing span 29 ft 10¼ in (9.10 m); length 26 ft 6⅞ in (8.10 m); height 8 ft 8⅓ in (2.65 m); wing area 260.49 sq ft (24.20 m^2)
Armament: two fixed forward-firing 0.303-in (7.7-mm) Vickers machine-guns, plus a small bomb load or reconnaissance cameras on fuselage clips

Ansaldo SVA-10

It soon became clear that the SVA-9's performance was not high enough to offer a virtually complete immunity to interception, and Ansaldo therefore developed the **SVA-10** as the armed version of the SVA-9 with the positions of the pilot and second crewman reversed so that the latter now occupied the rear cockpit as an observer/gunner equipped with a rearward-firing machine-gun. The pilot was also provided with armament, although to save weight only one forward-firing machine-gun was installed; provision was also made for the carriage of a light bomb load in a similar manner to the SVA-5.

The SVA-10, which was introduced to squadron service in 1918 and remained in service into the second half of the 1920s, was delivered with two different types of engine,

namely the Isotta-Fraschini Semi-Asso inline unit as the **SVA-10/IF**, or the 220-hp (164-kW) SPA 6A inline unit as the slightly slower, but faster climbing **SVA-10/SPA**.

On one of the final Italian missions of World War I, an Italian soldier-poet, Gabriele d'Annunzio, was flown in an SVA-10 on a leaflet-dropping raid.

SPECIFICATION

Ansaldo SVA-10/IF
Type: two-seat day bomber and reconnaissance aircraft
Powerplant: one Isotta-Fraschini Semi-Asso six-cylinder inline engine rated at 250 hp (186 kW)
Performance: maximum speed 134 mph (215 km/h) at optimum altitude; climb to 13,125 ft (4000 m) in 14 minutes; service ceiling 16,405 ft (5000 m); endurance 5 hours
Weights: empty 1,609 lb (730 kg);

maximum take-off 2,337 lb (1060 kg)
Dimensions: wing span 30 ft 1⅗ in (9.18 m); length 29 ft 10¼ in (9.10 m); height 10 ft 2 in (3.10 m); wing area 289.56 sq ft (26.90 m²)
Armament: one 0.303-in (7.7-mm) fixed forward-firing machine-gun and one 0.303-in (7.7-mm) trainable rearward-firing machine gun in the rear cockpit, plus a light bomb load

Antoinette monoplanes

The Antoinette company's aircraft and engine designer, Leon Levavasseur, produced two experimental designs before the appearance of his first truly successful machine, the **Antoinette IV** that made its maiden flight on 9 October 1908. In definitive form, as first tested in the following February, the Antoinette IV was a high-wing monoplane with angular wings of considerable area, and a fuselage of small, triangular cross-section owing much to the designer's experience as a builder of racing motor boats. Wing-tip ailerons were fitted for lateral control, and the tail surfaces were of cruciform configuration.

On 19 February 1909 the Antoinette IV flew successfully from Mourmelon, covering 3.1 miles (5 km) before landing. By then an association had been formed between the Antoinette company and Hubert Latham, an English sportsman resident in France, which resulted in widespread fame for both parties.

Latham twice attempted to fly the English Channel: on 19 July 1909 he took off from Sangatte on the French coast in the Antoinette IV and covered some 7 miles (11.2 km) before coming down in the water with engine failure.

On 25 July 1909, Louis Blériot had made his successful crossing, but an undeterred Latham made a second attempt on 27 July 1909, flying the new **Antoinette VII**, which incorporated the then-conventional wing-warping controls in place of the Antoinette IV's ailerons. This time Latham had clear sight of the English shore, only about 1 mile (1.6 km) away, when again he had to come down in the sea. Undaunted, Latham took the duly repaired Antoinette VII to the Grande Semaine d'Aviation de la Champagne at Reims the following month, carrying off the height competition with an altitude of 509 ft (155 m) and coming second in the speed event at 42.8 mph (68.9 km/h).

During the next two years Antoinette monoplanes were well to the fore at numerous major aviation meetings, flown by Latham and various other pioneer pilots, but by 1912 Jane's *Aircraft* reported that 'the company has ceased to exist', and Leon Levavasseur's graceful designs soon vanished from the scene.

SPECIFICATION

Antoinette IV and Antoinette VII
Type: single-seat sporting monoplane
Powerplant: one Antoinette eight-cylinder Vee engine rated at 50 hp (37.3 kW) (Antoinette IV), or one Antoinette eight-cylinder Vee engine rated at 60 hp (44.7 kW) (Antoinette VII)

Performance: maximum speed 43.5 mph (70 km/h)
Weight: maximum take-off 1,301 lb (590 kg)
Dimensions: wing span 42 ft (12.80 m), length 37 ft 8¾ in (11.50 m): height 9 ft 10 in (3.00 m); wing area 538.21 sq ft (50.00 m²)

Leon Levavasseur named his Antoinette series after his daughter. This aircraft, which has suffered a landing mishap, clearly shows the twin-wheels used by the pilot to control the wing-warping system.

Variants

Antoinette I: Uncompleted project of 1907-8 for a canard monoplane with a pusher propeller
Gastambide-Mengin I: The precursor of the classic Antoinette monoplane series. Notable for its 50-hp (37-kW) Antoinette engine driving a tractor propeller and ungainly quadricycle landing gear. The machine achieved four hops in the hands of the mechanic Boyer between 8 and 14 February 1908, the best being of 164 yards (150 m)
Antoinette II (or Gastambide-Mengin II): Between February and August 1908 the Gastambide-Mengin I was rebuilt in this revised form with triangular wing-tip ailerons and other modifications. The machine achieved some three flights, the best on 21 August 1908 lasting 1 minute 36 seconds and including the first circle flown by a monoplane. On 20 August Robert Gastambide became the first passenger to be carried by a monoplane
Antoinette III: Alternative designation for the abortive **Ferber IX** after Capitaine Ferdinand Ferber had joined the Société Antoinette for a short time
Antoinette IV: The first truly successful Antoinette monoplane. Flown between October 1908 and August 1909, making 50 flights, including a best of 96.06 miles (154.6 km) in 2 hours 17 minutes 21 seconds, a world distance record on 26 August 1909
Antoinette V: Similar to the Antoinette IV but fitted with ailerons. Made some 20 flights between December 1908 and September 1909, the best lasting 15 minutes
Antoinette VI: Similar to the Antoinettes IV and V, but introduced wing-warping for lateral control. Made some 15 flights between April and July 1909, the best lasting 12 minutes
Antoinette VII: This aircraft was similar to the Antoinettes IV, V and VI but with wing-warping and was powered by an uprated Antoinette engine. The machine was flown in July and August 1909, its best flight covering 43.5 miles (70 km) in 1 hour 1 minute 52 seconds on 26 August 1909.
Antoinette VIII: Similar to the Antoinettes IV, V, VI and VII with wing-warping and a 50-hp (37.3-kW) Antoinette engine. Its best flight lasted 16 minutes
Antoinette (1909 general type): Production model of 1909-11 offered at a price of £1,000. The type had the 50-hp (37-kW) Antoinette eight-cylinder inline engine and maximum speed of 43.5 mph (70 km/h)
Military Monoplane: Built to an order placed by Latham and incorporating many of his ideas, the Military Monoplane was known alternatively as the **Antoinette-Latham** or **Monobloc**. The intention was that the aircraft should compete in the 1911 Concours Militaire at Reims with the hope of arousing the interest of the French war office and thus attracting orders. Unfortunately, the machine never flew but did contribute much to contemporary thinking on military aircraft design

Antonov A-7

Also known as the **RF-8** in the Red Front series of gliders for the Soviet air forces, the **Antonov A-7** was announced in a December 1940 design competition to find the best possible assault glider for the re-equipment of the Soviet airborne arm. The A-7 was of remarkably clean overall design and of wooden construction, with the exception of the fabric

A rather cleaner design than its contemporaries, the A-7 featured retractable landing gear.

on the control surfaces and the area of the wing to the rear of the main spar.

The core of the structure was the fuselage, which

was almost of the pod-and-boom type with an enclosed cockpit and accommodation for a maximum of nine troops in a virtually windowless passenger compartment. The latter was accessed by two pairs of double doors (one forward on the port side and the other aft on the starboard side). The tail-skid landing gear included manually retractable main units, stowed in wells in the lower fuselage sides.

Production totalled 400 machines, with deliveries commencing in May 1941, and these saw limited service behind enemy lines in World War II, when their standard tug was the Tupolev SB-2.

Antonov An-2, An-3 and An-4 'Colt'

With an interest in gliding that dated from his schooldays, Oleg Konstantinovich Antonov started his aeronautical career as a designer of gliders and sailplanes. During World War II, however, he was concerned primarily with the development and production of powered aircraft, and also worked as a designer in the Yakovlev design bureau. After the war Antonov was allowed to form his own bureau to design and develop a new 'do anything, go anywhere' aircraft, and this emerged as the **Antonov An-2** that later received the NATO reporting designation **'Colt'** but was initially designated as the **SKh-1 (Selsko-Khozyaistvennyi-1**, or agricultural-economic no.1) and flown in prototype form on 31 August 1947, before the Antonov designation was applied.

A single-bay sesquiplane, with a single I-type interplane strut on each side and bracing by dual

North Korea used the An-2 for covert operations into South Korea. The biplanes were able to fly low enough and slowly enough to avoid interception.

Pictured in September 1981, this An-2 belonged to a Czechoslovakian aeroclub and was decorated with local motifs. The versatility of the An-2 has assured its employment in a vast array of disparate roles.

flying and landing wires, the An-2 is of almost entirely all-metal construction. The exception is the fabric covering of the wings (to the rear of the front spar) and the tailplane. The large-capacity fuselage is a semi-monocoque structure, providing a heated and ventilated crew compartment to accommodate two. The tailplane is strut-braced, and the robust tailwheel landing gear can be provided with low-pressure tyres, floats or skis.

The powerplant of the prototype consisted of a 760-hp (567-kW) Shvetsov ASh-21 radial engine, but later production aircraft from Antonov had the 1,000-hp (746-kW) Shvetsov ASh-62IR engine.

Since 1960 main production of the An-2 series has been the responsibility of WSK-PZL in Poland with a Polish-made version of the ASh-62 engine, and the An-2 has also been built under licence in China as the **Shijiazhuang Y-5 (Yunshuji-5**, or transport aeroplane type 5). The combined production from these three sources is estimated at more than 18,500 examples, of which more than 11,950 aircraft have been manufactured in Poland.

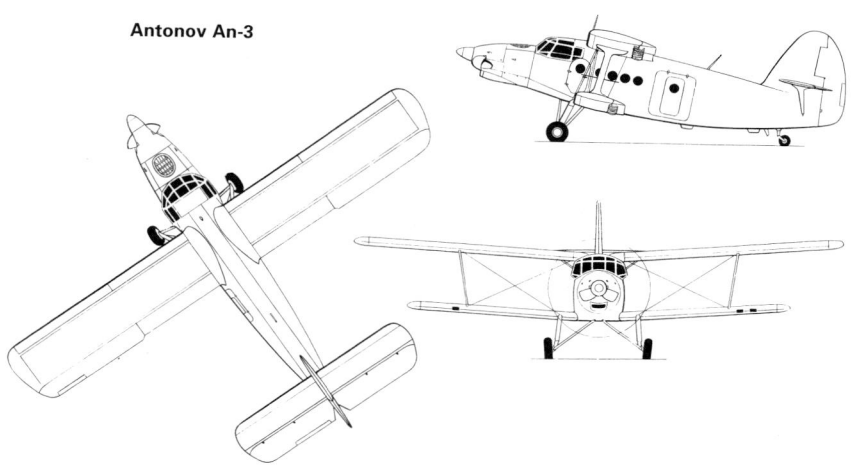

Very few An-2s remain in regular airline service, although passenger versions were widely exported.

Variants (Soviet-built)

An-2F: An experimental artillery observation model of 1948 with a glazed fuselage mid-section, dorsal machine-gun position, and twin vertical tail surfaces
An-2L: Fire-fighting model equipped for the carriage of chemicals in glass containers under the wings and fuselage
An-2P (Passazhirskii): Basic general-purpose model for up to 12 passengers or 2,733 lb (1210 kg) of freight
An-2P (Protivopozharnyi): Fire-fighting variant of the An-2V, developed in 1964 and able to uplift 273 Imp gal (1240 litres) of water in its floats
An-2S: Agricultural model of the An-2 Passazhirskii, with spray equipment and long-stroke main landing gear legs
An-2V: See An-4 (below)
An-2ZA: See An-6 (below)
An-3: First mention of the An-3 came in the early months of 1972, when it was reported that Antonov was developing a version of its An-2 intended specifically for agricultural operations. It was not until 1979 that confirmation was received that a prototype had been created as a conversion of a production An-2 with the nose revised to a longer and more slender configuration accommodating a 940-shp (701-kW) Glushyenkov TVD-10B turboprop engine driving a larger-diameter but slower-turning propeller intended to provide safe operation at low airspeeds. The aircraft was also outfitted for the carriage of a chemical payload 40 per cent greater than that of the An-2
An-4: Bureau designation of the variant that entered service as the An-2V, the letter suffix standing for **Vodyanoi** or 'water floatplane'. Fitted with twin light metal floats with rudders for water steering, the An-2V was built in some numbers
An-6: Bureau designation of the variant that entered service as the An-2ZA, a variant of the An-2 intended specially for the role of high-altitude meteorological research with a glazed position immediately in front of the fin for an observer. The ZA suffix stands for **Zondirovanie Atmosfery**, translatable as 'air sampling'. In the An-4 the ASh-62IR engine was boosted by a TK turbocharger mounted on the starboard side of the cowling in an arrangement that enabled the An-4 to maintain rated power up to an altitude of 32,810 ft (10000 m). The spinner of the An-2 standard model was deleted to aid engine cooling, and the original ailerons were replaced by an unslotted variety. Only a limited number of examples of this variant was completed

Antonov An-3

Antonov An-2, An-3 and An-4 'Colt' (continued)

An-2 aircraft are still in extensive use in a number of roles, both with civil and military operators. They have served widely in the passenger transport capacity (carrying up to 12 adults and two children) with Aeroflot and the airlines of the countries aligned with the former USSR, but very few now remain in scheduled service; those of Interflug were possibly the last to be listed in this role, but there is no doubt that many of these reliable aircraft are still used for passenger carrying, agricultural work and many other utility roles.

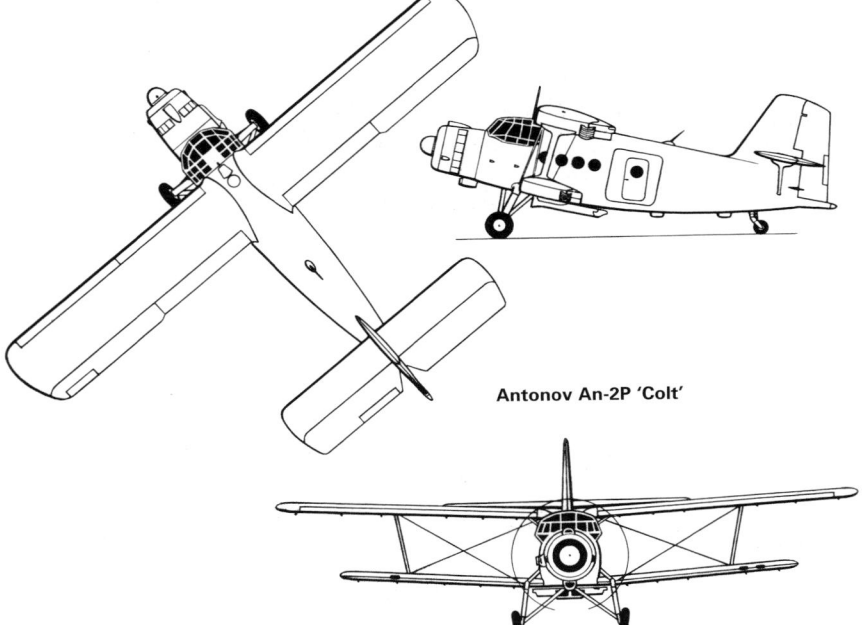

Antonov An-2P 'Colt'

Variants (Polish-built)

An-2 Geofiz: Geophysical survey model
An-2M: Twin-float version of the An-2T, and basically similar to the Soviet-built An-2V
An-2P: Passenger model with better soundproofing than the Soviet version, and fitted with an improved propeller
An-2PK: Five-seat executive transport model
An-2P Photo: Special model equipped for photogrammetric operations
An-2PR: Television relay model
An-2R: Specialised agricultural model introduced in 1961 with hermetic sealing of the cockpit, revised tail surfaces of greater area, a more advanced propeller, and a fibreglass container for 431 Imp gal (1960 litres) of chemicals or 2,976 lb (1350 kg) of fertiliser dust
An-2S: Ambulance model with provision for six litters plus medical attendants
An-2T: Basic general-purpose model
An-2TD: Paratroop model with tip-up seats for 12 soldiers
An-2TP: Passenger/freight model based on the An-2TD
Lala-1: Experimental model of 1972 with the rear fuselage and tail unit replaced by twin booms and a revised tail unit, which allowed installation of a turbofan in the stump fuselage as a step in the development of the PZL M-15 Belphegor agricultural aircraft

SPECIFICATION

Antonov (WSK-PZL Mielec) An-2P
Type: one/two-crew light general-purpose transport aircraft
Powerplant: one PZL Kalisz (Shvetsov) ASz-62IR nine-cylinder single-row radial engine rated at 1,000 hp (746 kW)
Performance: maximum speed 160 mph (258 km/h) at 5,740 ft (1750 m); cruising speed 115 mph (185 km/h) at optimum altitude; initial climb rate 689 ft (210 m) per minute; service ceiling 14,425 ft (4400 m); range 560 miles (900 km) with a 1,102-lb (500-kg) payload
Weights: Empty 7,605 lb (3450 kg); maximum take-off 12,125 lb (5500 kg)
Dimensions: wing span 59 ft 7¾ in (18.18 m); length 41 ft 9½ in (12.74 m) with the tail up; height 20 ft (6.10 m) with the tail up; wing area 769.86 sq ft (71.52 m²)
Payload: 12 adults and two children, or freight

Antonov An-8 'Camp'

With the **Antonov An-8** (NATO reporting designation **'Camp'**), Antonov initiated a continuing series of high-wing monoplane designs in the large-capacity turboprop transport category suitable for operations from sub-standard airfields. The first An-8 prototype made its debut at the 1956 Soviet Aviation Day display, and the five prototypes were then followed by some 100 production examples before manufacture of the An-8 gave way to that of the four-engined **An-10**.

The all-metal An-8 was powered by two wing-mounted Kuznetsov turboprop engines and had tricycle landing gear with four-wheel main bogies, these retracting into blisters on each side of the fuselage. This feature, combined with the upswept rear fuselage, allowed the creation of a large and unobstructed hold, with access provided by an arrangement of rear doors and a ramp. Accommodation was provided for 40 fully equipped troops or 48 civilian passengers plus the crew of six, and the An-8 had a glazed navigator's nose section, in common with most Soviet transport aircraft of the period. In its original configuration, moreover, the An-8 was provided with a tail barbette, complete with one 23-mm NR-23 cannon, for rear defence, but this position was later faired over in service. A handful of An-8s remain in service with civil operators.

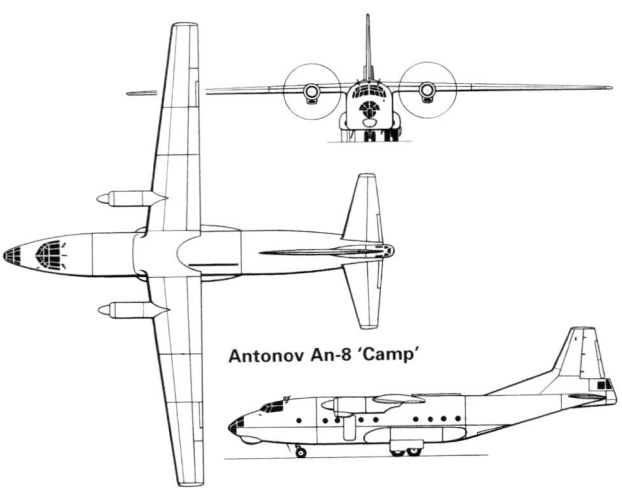

Antonov An-8 'Camp'

In service the An-8 was nicknamed 'Keet' (whale). The An-8 featured a highly efficient wing, but was initially plagued by engine problems.

SPECIFICATION

Antonov An-8 'Camp'
Type: six-crew general-purpose transport
Powerplant: two Kuznetsov NK-6-TV2 turboprop engines each rated at 5,097 eshp (3800 ekW)
Performance: maximum cruising speed 373 mph (600 km/h) at optimum altitude; service ceiling 31,495 ft (9600 m); range 2,175 miles (3500 km) with maximum fuel and 1,417 miles (2280 km) with maximum payload
Weights: empty 46,847 lb (21250 kg); maximum take-off, 83,776 lb (38000 kg)
Dimensions: wing span 121 ft 4¾ in (37.00 m); length 100 ft 10¼ in (30.74 m) without armament; height 31 ft 10 in (9.70 m); wing area 1,261.57 sq ft (117.20 m²)
Armament: one trainable rearward-firing 23-mm NR-23 cannon in tail barbette

Antonov An-10 Ukraina 'Cat'

The **Antonov An-10** (NATO designation **'Cat'**) was developed from the An-8 as a more capable four-engined heavy transport to meet a requirement from Aeroflot for a larger medium-haul transport able to carry 75 passengers into and out of poorly equipped airfields and even semi-prepared airstrips.

The prototype flew for the first time on 7 March 1957, and differed from the An-8 in having a new circular-section monocoque, pressurised fuselage and a lower-set tail unit including a ventral fin. The latter failed to prevent a number of lateral stability problems and was in due course supplemented by two small endplate fins. The An-10 retained the dorsal fin of

Both the single dorsal fin and twin ventral fins of the An-10A are shown to advantage. The aircraft retained the glazed nose so typical of Soviet transport designs of the period.

the An-8 and had a similar wing, but with considerable anhedral on the outer sections. Pre-production aircraft were powered by four 3,996-eshp (2980-ekW) Kuznetsov NK-4 turboprop engines, but the production aircraft entering Aeroflot service during the summer of 1959 had the revised powerplant of four Ivchyenko AI-20 turbo-props. The normal crew was five, and there was provision for up to 85 passengers.

The enlarged **An-10A** flew its first scheduled Aeroflot service in February 1960. It had a 6-ft 6¾-in (2.00-m) 'plug' inserted in the fuselage to allow the incorporation of two more seat rows, thereby boosting passenger capacity to 100. Most An-10A aircraft had the single ventral fin and the An-10's endplate surfaces replaced by twin splayed-out ventral fins.

Production of the An-10 and An-10A totalled some 200 aircraft and ended in the early 1960s. The An-10A was used for the establishment of several international payload-over-distance records in 1960 and 1961. At their peak the An-10 and An-10A provided the backbone of many Aeroflot passenger services, but the type was withdrawn from Aeroflot service from 1972 as a result of a number of accidents caused by structural failures. Both types bore the name **Ukraina** in honour of Kiev, the capital of the Ukraine, where the Antonov OKB (experimental design bureau) is still located.

An experimental high-density version of the An-10A, known as the **An-10V** (design bureau designation **An-16**), was revealed in 1958 and first flew in 1963 with provision for 132 passengers in a fuselage stretched by a further 9 ft 10 in (3.00 m), but it is believed that only a single prototype was built. However, a version of the standard An-10A, with a high-density seating arrangement for 110 passengers, was used on Moldavian and Ukrainian routes from 1968.

SPECIFICATION

Antonov An-10A Ukraina 'Cat'
Type: medium-haul commercial transport
Powerplant: four Ivchyenko AI-20 turboprop engines each rated at 3,996 eshp (2980 ekW)
Performance: Maximum cruising speed 423 mph (680 km/h) at optimum altitude; service ceiling 39,370 ft (12000 m); range 2,532 miles (4075 km) with maximum fuel and 746 miles (1200 km) with maximum payload
Weights: empty 65,697 lb (29800 kg); maximum take-off 121,473 lb (55100 kg)
Dimensions: wing span 124 ft 8 in (38.00 m); length 111 ft 6½ in (34.00 m); height 30 ft 3 in (9.83 m); wing area 1,286.33 sq ft (119.50 m²)
Payload: 100 passengers or 31,966 lb (14500 kg) of freight

Antonov An-12 'Cub'

The **An-12** prototype made its maiden flight during 1958. It is estimated that more than 900 aircraft of the series were built at Kiev before production ceased during 1973, and more of the same basic type have been produced in China under the designation **Shaanxi Y-8**.

Developed from the An-10 passenger transport, the An-12 was designed from the start as a military transport and civil freighter, with a rear-loading ramp like that of the An-8 and a partially pressurised 14-seat compartment forward of the main portion of the freight compartment. Most of the production aircraft lacked the integral ramp however, and therefore possessed an upswept rear fuselage characterised by a pair of longitudinally split

In standard military transport form, the An-12 is more or less an equivalent to the West's C-130 Hercules. The anhedraled outer wing panels inherited from the An-10 are clearly visible in this view, as are the extensive flaps.

Having been built as a transport, the 'Cub' soon evolved into a number of other roles. This An-12PS 'Cub-B' is typical of the special variants that were produced by conversion. The PS was a dedicated search and rescue/Elint platform.

Principal An-12BK variants

An-12BKB: bomber (inspired by India's extemporised use of the An-12BP in this role during the 1971 war with Pakistan) with the external bomb racks that were standard on the An-12 supplemented by internal stowage
An-12BK-VKP Zebra: aerial command post
An-12BKSh: flying classroom
An-12BK-IS: replacement for the An-12B-I
An-12PP 'Cub-C': dedicated ECM platform with palletised electrical generators and control equipment, and possibly chaff cutters and dispensers in the cabin. Externally identifiable by the array of antennas on its underside, the cooling scoops and heat exchanger outlets fore and aft of the wing, and the bulged, ogival tailcone which replaces the normal gun turret
An-12BK-PPS 'Cub-D': ECM platform with a different equipment fit and characterised by huge external pods on the lower 'corners' of the forward fuselage and on each side of the fin's base
An-12BKT: tanker for the refuelling of aircraft on the ground
An-12BKK: VIP transport
An-12BKTs Tsyklon: meteorological research aircraft

inward-opening doors and a third upward-opening door to their rear.

Entering service in 1959, the An-12 was produced in several versions of which the standard transport subvariants all enjoy the basic **'Cub-A'** reporting designation. The core model from which all subsequent development stretched was the An-12 that introduced nosewheel steering, and subvariant conversions of this were the **An-12P** introduced in 1963 with additional fuel in underfloor tanks, the **An-12T** optimised for the carriage of liquids, and the **An-12UD** with provision for two 880-Imp gal (4000-litre) tanks to be installed inside the hold.

Built from 1961, the **An-12A** introduced the 3,997-eshp (2980-ekW) AI-20A turboprop engines and had its fuel capacity enlarged to 4,227 US gal (3,520 Imp gal; 16000 litres) by the addition of four cells in the wing. Subvariants of this model included the **An-12AP** conversions with the same additional fuel tankage as the An-12P, and the **An-12PL**, of which two examples were completed in 'winterised' form for Arctic operations.

Built from 1963 as the most important of the variants, the **An-12B** introduced an APU in the port landing gear fairing to provide independence from ground services, and a further enlargement in the standard fuel capacity to 4,290 Imp gallons (19500 litres) by the addition of outer-wing tanks.

The final production variant of the An-12 series was the **An-12BK** that entered manufacture in 1967 as a comprehensively modernised An-12B.

Although replacement of the USSR's An-12 force by the Ilyushin Il-76 'Candid' began in 1974, large numbers currently remain in service with the Russian air force and Aeroflot's fleet of An-12 aircraft could also be commandeered if extra lifting capacity were required.

SPECIFICATION

Antonov An-12BK 'Cub-A'
Type: six-crew medium transport
Powerplant: four ZMDB Progress (Ivchyenko) AI-20M turboprop engines each rated at 4,252 eshp (3170 ekW)
Performance: maximum speed 482 mph (777 km/h) at optimum altitude; cruising speed 373 mph (600 km/h) at optimum altitude; service ceiling 34,450 ft (10500 m); range 4,225 miles (6800 km) with maximum fuel and 2,236 miles (3600 km) with maximum payload
Weights: empty 78,263 lb (35500 kg); maximum take-off 134,480 lb (61000 kg)
Dimensions: wing span 124 ft 8 in (38.00 m); length 108 ft 7¼ in (33.10 m); height 34 ft 6½ in (10.53 m); wing area 1,310.01 sq ft (121.70 m²)
Armament: two 23-mm trainable rearward-firing cannon in the tail position
Payload: 100 paratroops or 44,092 lb (20000 kg) of freight

Antonov An-12 'Cub' (continued)

The An-12's main future role lies in the many 'special duties' conversions. In India, replacement by the Il-76 has been completed and all surviving An-12 machines have been withdrawn and advertised for sale. Polish aircraft have also been retired. Surviving operators include the Czech Republic, Egypt, Ethiopia, Ukraine and Yemen, while some aircraft may still be active in Iraq and Sudan.

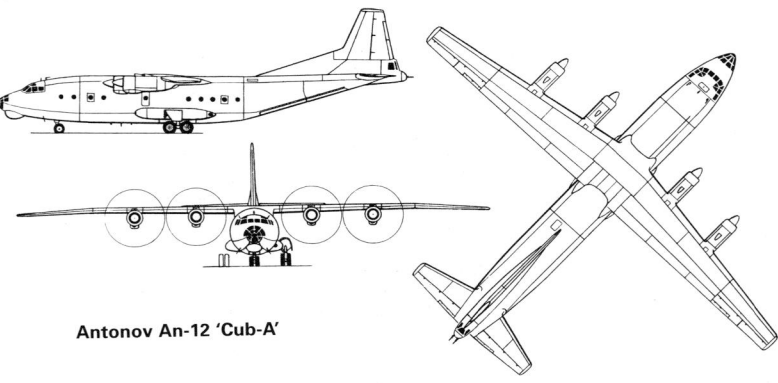

Antonov An-12 'Cub-A'

An-12B variants

An-12MGA: civil transport and **An-12BP** standard military transport, with underfloor tankage as well as increased wing tankage
An-12BM: single conversion for trials with the Molniya 1 communications satellite
An-12PS 'Cub-B': conversions and new-build aircraft delivered from 1969 and characterised by two prominent ventral radomes and a host of blade antennas
An-12B-I: conversions delivered from 1964 to an interim ECM standard
An-12BSh: conversions for the navigation training role
An-12BL: one conversion for examination of the feasibility of fitting transport aircraft with anti-radar missiles to improve their survivability over hostile territory
An-12B Kubrik: one conversion for the testing of IR sensors
An-12B-VKP Zebra: conversions delivered from 1970 for the aerial command post role
An-12RKR: conversions designed for environmental sampling to detect nuclear, chemical and biological agents

Antonov An-14 Pchelka 'Clod'

The **Antonov An-14 Pchelka** (Little Bee) (NATO reporting designation **'Clod'**) was designed in 1957 as a STOL freighter and feederliner, which could be flown by inexperienced pilots. With its high-aspect-ratio braced wing, and tail unit with endplate vertical surfaces, the type shows signs of inspiration from the French Hurel-Dubois transports of the early 1950s.

Other features of the An-14 are a pod-and-boom fuselage, and fixed tricycle landing gear including main units attached to the ends of the low-set stub wing whose tips also support the lower ends of the I-type wing-bracing struts. The first An-14 flew on 15 March 1958, and there followed a lengthy development period before the new light transport entered service in 1965. Production

Built to an Aeroflot specification, the An-14 was designed to offer smaller capacity than the An-2 but with a similarly rugged structure.

versions feature a very different tail design from the prototype, and the planform of the wing and the arrangement of the high-lift devices is also modified. The nose was slightly lengthened, and clamshell doors were fitted to the rear fuselage to provide straight-in access to the cabin.
Production lasted to 1975 and is thought to have totalled about 300 aircraft.

Like the less capable Yak-12 which it replaced in Aeroflot service, the An-14 could operate from wheel, float or ski landing gear.

SPECIFICATION

Antonov An-14 Pchelka 'Clod'
Type: one/two-crew light general-purpose STOL transport
Powerplant: two ZMDB Progress (Ivchyenko) AI-14RF nine-cylinder single-row radial engines each rated at 300 hp (224 kW)
Performance: maximum speed 138 mph (222 km/h) at 3,280 ft (1000 m); cruising speed 112 mph (180 km/h) at 6,560 ft (2000 m); initial climb rate 1,004 ft (306 m) per minute; service ceiling 14,765 ft (4500 m); range 497 miles (800 km) with maximum fuel and 404 miles (650 km) with maximum payload

Weights: empty 5,732 lb (2600 kg); maximum take-off 7,209 lb (3270 kg)
Dimensions: wing span 72 ft 3 in (21.99 m); length 37 ft 3 in (11.36 m); height 15 ft 2½ in (4.63 m); wing area 427.56 sq ft (39.72 m²)
Payload: up to nine passengers, or six litters, 1,587 lb (720 kg) of freight, or 220 Imp gal (1000 litres) of chemicals dispensed via spraybars along the trailing edges of the stub wing, bracing struts and outer wing panels

Antonov An-22 Antei 'Cock'

When the prototype of the **Antonov An-22 Antei**, known to NATO as the **'Cock'**, appeared at the 1965 Paris air show, only months after its maiden flight on 27 February 1965, it generated a storm of interest as it was then the largest aircraft in the world. The An-22 had the astonishingly high maximum take-off weight of 542,328 lb (246000 kg), but nonetheless possessed relatively good take-off performance. This capability was achieved by the use of a potent powerplant and an arrangement of powerful high-lift devices.
In many respects the An-22 is little more than a scaled-up An-12, with a new tail unit with twin

vertical surfaces to provide better control characteristics in asymmetric flight, and to avoid the creation of excessive height. Like the An-12, the An-22 has a pressurised forward compartment (including the flightdeck and a compartment for 28 or 29 passengers) and an unpressurised main cargo hold. Unlike the An-12, though, it does have an integral rear loading ramp, plus four travelling gantries and two winches for the handling of heavy cargo. The landing gear, which consists of twin nosewheels and three twin-wheel levered suspension units per side, is designed to allow off-runway operation, and the main units retract into

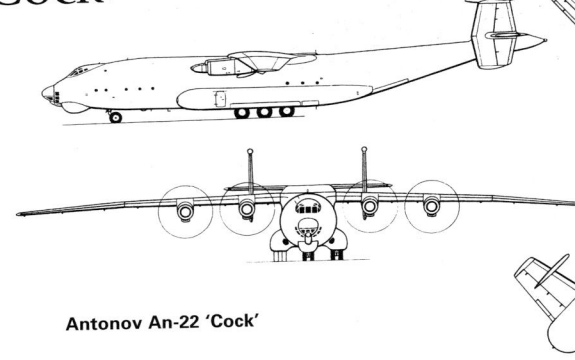

Antonov An-22 'Cock'

lateral blisters that leave the fuselage unobstructed for the carriage of payload in the large hold. The pressures of the tyres can be adjusted from the cockpit

to optimise the landing gear for landing weight and runway surface. Three separate nose radars allow all-weather operation and accurate navigation over

huge distances.
Until the introduction of the An-124, the An-22 was the only Soviet transport capable of carrying main battle tanks, and the 45

Illustrated in Military Transport Organisation (VT-A) colours, the An-22 was the result of a joint VT-A and Aeroflot requirement. The aircraft was cleared for production as the An-22M in 1971.

SPECIFICATION

Antonov An-22M Antei 'Cock'
Type: five-crew heavy logistics transport
Powerplant: four KKBM (Kuznetsov) NK-12MA turboprop engines each rated at 15,000 shp (11185 kW)
Performance: maximum speed 460 mph (740 km/h) at optimum altitude; cruising speed 323 mph (520 km/h) at optimum altitude; service ceiling 24,605 ft (7500 m); range 6,804 miles (10950 km) with

a 99,206-lb (45000-kg) payload and maximum fuel or 3,197 miles (5000 km) with maximum payload
Weights: empty 251,323 lb (114000 kg); maximum take-off 551,146 lb (250000 kg)
Dimensions: wing span 211 ft 4 in (64.40 m); length about 190 ft (57.92 m); height 41 ft 1½ in (12.53 m); wing area 3,713.67 sq ft (345.00 m²)
Payload: up to 176,367 lb (80000 kg) of freight

aircraft left in service in the late 1990s (out of perhaps 100 produced) are kept extremely busy.

A handful of An-22 aircraft are used for the external carriage of outsized cargos (mainly An-124 wings). Most of the aircraft wear airline colours, but a few machines seem to be permanently attached to the Russian air force's transport command. The notionally civil aircraft are also available for military use whenever needed.

The An-22 was named Antei (Antheus) after the giant son of Poseidon and Gaia.

Antonov An-24 'Coke'

Known in the West by its NATO reporting designation **'Coke'**, the **Antonov An-24** was created in response to an official requirement for a turbine-engined short-range civil transport to succeed the piston-engined Ilyushin Il-14 'Crate' in service with Aeroflot. Starting work late in 1957, Antonov therefore created the design for a short/medium-range, 32/40-seat aircraft. Among the requirements for the new type were the ability to operate from small unpaved airfields, and a combination of flight and powerplant characteristics that would permit the aircraft to operate between locations with considerable variations in altitude and/or ambient temperature. On 27 December 1959, the first of two prototypes made its maiden flight, the somewhat lengthy interval between the origination of the design and the first flight resulting from a change in specification to 44-seat accommodation.

Of typically 'Antonov configuration' in its overall layout, the An-24 has a high-set wing incorporating wide-span trailing-edge flaps of the Fowler type.

Six An-24RVs were delivered to the Czechoslovak air force (illustrated). Four survivors were divided between the Czech and Slovak air forces when the country divided, each force gaining two.

The tail unit is conventional, with the addition of a fairly large ventral fin on production aircraft, and the fuselage is a semi-monocoque structure introducing bonded/welded construction. The hydraulically retractable tricycle landing gear has twin wheels on each unit, a steerable and fully castoring nose unit, and includes the means of adjusting tyre pressures both in flight and on the ground to permit operation from a variety of different runway surfaces.

Production aircraft entered service with Aeroflot in July 1962 for crew training and proving flights as well as freight services, but it was not until December 1963 that the An-24 entered passenger service. The initial model with accommodation for 44 passengers was soon complemented by a number of variants and production of the An-24 series for civil and military operators lasted to 1978 and totalled some 1,100 aircraft.

An-24s have served mostly as airliners, as typified by this aircraft belonging to CAAC. An-24s are built under licence in China as the Xian Y-7.

SPECIFICATION

Antonov An-24T 'Coke'
Type: two/three-crew short-range transport
Powerplant: two ZMDB Progress (Ivchyenko) AI-24A turboprop engines each rated at 2,250 eshp (1670 ekW)
Performance: maximum cruising speed 280 mph (450 km/h) at 19,685 ft (6000 m); initial climb rate about 1,509 ft (460 m) per minute; service ceiling 27,560 ft

(8400 m); range 1,864 miles (3000 km) with a 3,554-lb (1612-kg) payload and 397 miles (640 km) with maximum payload
Weights: empty 30,996 lb (14060 kg); maximum take-off 43,651 lb (19800 kg)
Dimensions: wing span 95 ft 9½ in (29.20 m); length 77 ft 2½ in (23.53 m); height 27 ft 3½ in (8.32 m); wing area 779.98 sq ft (72.46 m²)

Variants

An-24V: lengthened cabin for the carriage of 50 passengers, powerplant of two AI-24V engines with water injection for boosted power and a TG-16 APU in the starboard engine nacelle
An-24V Series II: standard 50-passenger accommodation, with alternative mixed passenger/freight, convertible cargo/passenger, all-freight, or executive interiors
An-24RV: with provision for the TG-16 APU to be replaced by a 1,984-lb (8.83-kN) Tumanskii RU-19-300 booster turbojet serving as an APU for start-up and then supplying all electrical power as well as 480 lb st (2.14 kN) of thrust for take-off and climb
An-24T: specialised freighter with the standard passenger door in the rear of the cabin deleted and replaced by an upward-opening ventral freight door; twin ventral fins outboard of the freight door replace the single ventral fin, and a roof-mounted cargo hoist and floor-mounted conveyor system are fitted
An-24RT: An-24T with the auxiliary turbojet
An-24P: evaluated with equipment for airdropping parachute-equipped firefighters for rapid reaction to newly reported forest fires

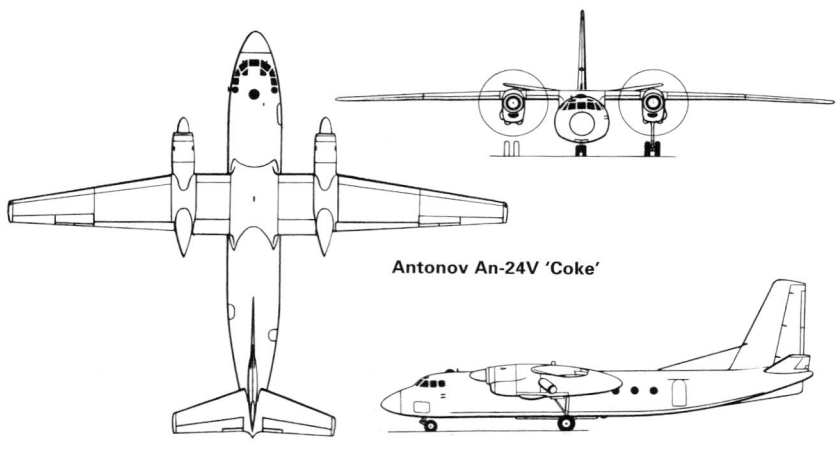

Antonov An-24V 'Coke'

Antonov An-26 'Curl'

The Force Aérienne de la République du Mali received three An-24s and two An-26s (illustrated). Of these, just two of the former and a single example of the latter remain in service into the late 1990s.

Although derived from the An-24, the **Antonov An-26** (NATO reporting designation **'Curl'**) was created as a new design with a host of improved features and additions. The most obvious of these changes is a new rear loading ramp, which forms the underside of the upswept rear fuselage when closed, but which can be slid forward along tracks on each side of the underside of the fuselage to lie directly under the cabin, clear of the open hatch. This is especially useful when loading directly from a truck or for air-dropping. The actuators for the ramp-sliding mechanism are enclosed in prominent fibreglass fairings on each side of the rear fuselage, directly ahead of deep ventral strakes which 'enclose' the more sharply swept rear fuselage.

First seen in 1969, the **An-26 'Curl-A'** is fitted with a Tumanskii RU-19A-300 booster turbojet in the rear of the starboard engine nacelle. As well as acting as an APU, this can be used as a take-off booster and for generally increasing performance. Many An-26s are also fitted with a large observation 'bubble' on the port side of the forward fuselage, replacing the normal navigator's window,

for use in conjunction with an OPB-1R optical sight for the accurate delivery of air-dropped cargo loads or paratroops.

Less obvious is the fact that the An-26 has a fully pressurised cargo hold (the first Soviet military transport aircraft so equipped), or that on all but the earliest aircraft the belly has been toughened to withstand the erosion and abrasion inherent in rough field operation: a sheet of Bimetal (a bonded ply of Dural with an outer face of titanium) protects the undersurfaces from debris. Other improvements adopted at the same time included more powerful AI-24T engines driving propellers of enlarged diameter, although since 1980 many engines have been upgraded to the AI-24VT standard.

Internally the An-26 features an electrically or manually operated conveyor flush with the cabin floor, while the **An-26B** introduced in 1981 has roller gangs (panels fitted with rollers) which can be swung up against the cabin walls when not in use. An electrically powered mobile winch of 4,409 lb (2000-kg) capacity runs along rails on the cabin ceiling. In all An-26 versions, the interior can be

reconfigured within 30 minutes as a transport with tip-up seats along the cabin sides to seat 38-40 passengers, or for casevac with 24 litters in the **An-26M** variant. Parachute static line points are also fitted as standard.

Modest numbers of An-26 aircraft have been converted as **An-26RTR** Elint/Sigint/EW platforms. These bear the NATO reporting name **'Curl-B'**, and have a profusion of swept blade antennas above and below the cabin. Painted as standard transports and often operating from the same bases, these aircraft remain in use with the Russian air force. Former East German 'special duties' An-26 aircraft were designated **An-26ST** (sometimes reported as **An-26SM** for calibration and **An-26M** for Elint). Similarly modified An-26 aircraft are also in Czech service.

An unusually active combat role has been

undertaken by An-26s in Angola and Mozambique, where bomb racks have been fitted to turn the aircraft into extemporised counter-insurgency warplanes. These bomb racks are fitted on the fuselage, below the trailing edge of the wing roots. Some An-26 aircraft, most notably those used in Afghanistan, also carry pylon-mounted chaff/flare dispensers. A fire-fighting version of the An-26 has also been developed as the **An-26P** with tanks along the fuselage under the wing. Two other special-purpose types produced as conversions are the

An-26BRL for research into the nature of pack ice, and the **An-26L** navaid calibration type.

Antonov An-26 production ended in 1985 after about 1,410 aircraft had been built, most of them for military operators in countries which include Afghanistan, Angola, Bulgaria, China, the Czech Republic, Germany, Hungary, Iraq, Libya, Poland, Romania, Russia, Serbia, Slovakia, Ukraine, Vietnam, Yemen and Zambia. Some 425 of the aircraft were delivered to civil operators round the world, 200 of these being allocated to Aeroflot.

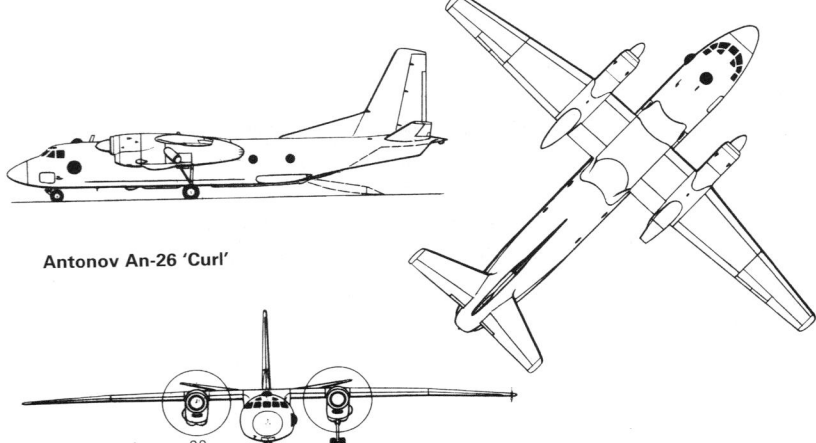

Antonov An-26 'Curl'

Hungary's No. 1 'Camel' Transport Squadron maintains a fleet of nine An-26 freighters.

SPECIFICATION

Antonov An-26B 'Curl-A'
Type: five-crew short-haul light transport
Powerplant: two ZMDB Progress (Ivchyenko) AI-24VT turboprop engines each rated at 2,820 ehp (2103 kW) and one Soyuz (Tumanskii) RU-19A-300 turbojet engine rated at 1,765 lb st (7.85 kN)
Performance: maximum speed 336 mph (540 km/h) at 16,405 ft (5000 m); cruising speed 273 mph (440 km/h) at 19,685 ft (6000 m); initial climb rate 1,575 ft (480 m)

per minute; service ceiling 24,605 ft (7500 m); range 1,585 miles (2550 km) with maximum fuel and 683 miles (1100 km) with maximum payload
Weights: empty 33,950 lb (15400 kg); maximum take-off 53,790 lb (24400 kg)
Dimensions: wing span 95 ft 9½ (29.20 m); length 78 ft 1 in (23.80 m); height 28 ft 1½ in (8.58 m); wing area 807.10 sq ft (74.98 m²)
Payload: up to 40 passengers or 12,125 lb (5500 kg) of freight

Antonov An-28 'Cash'

The **Antonov An-28** (NATO reporting designation **'Cash'**) was designed in the USSR (in what is now the Ukraine) as a turboprop-powered successor to the An-2 'Colt' for short-range routes requiring semi-STOL capability and the ability to operate from indifferent airfields. The type was originally conceived in the early 1960s as the **An-14A**, an enlarged and turboprop-powered development of

the An-14, but the design process was extremely slow and the **An-14M** prototype finally flew only in September 1969 with retractable tricycle landing gear and a powerplant of two 850-shp (634-kW) Klimov (Isotov) TVD-850 turboprops.

The An-14M completed its flight trials in 1972, but during 1973 its designation was altered to **An-28** to reflect a major revision of

the basic design to reduce cost and weight, and in 1975 it was decided to revise the type still further with a powerplant of two OMKB Mars (Glushenkov) TVD-10B turboprops.

As part of a Soviet/Polish production agreement, it was decided in 1978 that the type should be built in Poland by WSK-PZL Mielec with a licensed version of the Soviet engine, and the first Polish-built machine flew in July 1984.

Accessed by an upward/downward-opening double

PZL-Mielec's An-28 B1T prototype was converted from a standard An-28 in 1992 and later redesignated as the An-28 Bryza 1TD. The sliding rear door is clearly seen here beneath the fuselage.

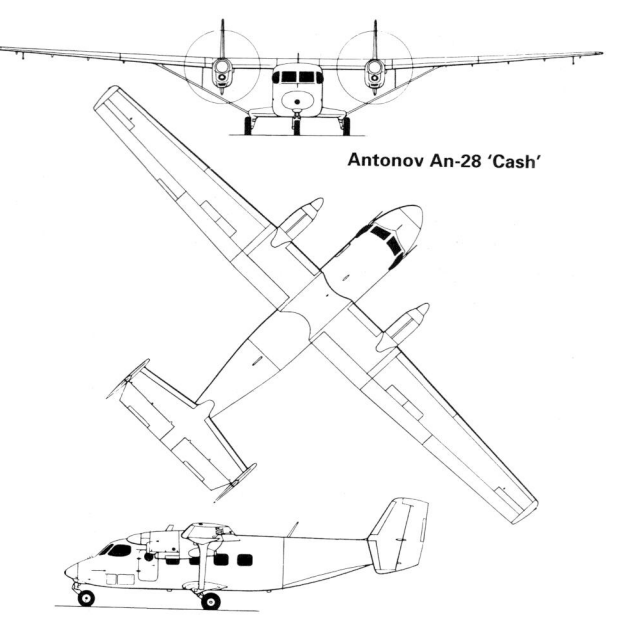

Antonov An-28 'Cash'

clamshell door arrangement below the upswept tail unit, the cabin of the An-28 can be configured for the all-passenger, all-freight and mixed passenger/freight roles, and the handling of freight is facilitated by the provision over the forward part of the cabin of a hoist rated at 1,102 lb (500 kg). Small numbers of the type have entered service with the Polish air force as communications and liaison aircraft.

The **An-28RM Bryza 1RM** is a specialised SAR and medevac version with upgraded avionics (including a search radar with its antenna in a ventral radome, Doppler navigation and a GPS receiver) as well as provision for the release of a life raft and a cabin reconfigured for the carriage of litters. Three of the type have been deliv-

ered to the Polish air force, which has a requirement for an eventual eight machines and may also take the **An-28TD Bryza 1TD** transport optimised for airdrop operations with the clamshell rear doors replaced by a single door arranged to slide forward under the fuselage.

PZL Mielec has also flown an **M-28 Skytruck** westernised development of the basic An-28, fitted with US-sourced Bendix/King avionics and powered by 1,100-shp (820-kW) Pratt & Whitney Canada PT6A-65B turboprops driving Hartzell five-bladed propellers.

SPECIFICATION

Antonov An-28 'Cash'
Type: two-crew short-range utility light transport
Powerplant: two PZL Rzeszow (OMKB Mars [Glushenkov]) TWD-10B turboprop engines each rated at 960 shp (716 kW)
Performance: maximum cruising speed 217 mph (350 km/h) at 9,845 ft (3000 m); initial climb rate 1,640 ft (500 m) per minute; service ceiling more than 19,685 ft (6000 m); range 848 miles (1365 km) with a 2,205-lb (1000-kg) payload and maximum fuel, or

348 miles (560 km) with maximum payload
Weights: empty 8,598 lb (3900 kg); maximum take-off 14,330 lb (6500 kg)
Dimensions: wing span 72 ft 4½ in (22.06 m); length 42 ft 11⅚ in (13.10 m); height 16 ft 1 in (4.90 m); wing area 427.56 sq ft (39.72 m²)
Payload: up to 17 passengers, or six litters, or five seated casualties plus one medical attendant, or six paratroops, or 4,409 lb (2000 kg) of freight

Antonov An-30 'Clank'

Based on the airframe of the An-24RT freighter and first flown in 1974, the **Antonov An-30** (NATO reporting designation **'Clank'**) is a dedicated photographic and survey platform, with appropriate role equipment and a completely redesigned forward fuselage. A considerably raised cockpit gives access to the new glazed nose which accommodates the relocated navigator's compartment. There are few other structural changes (although some cabin windows are deleted) and the machine could theoretically be reconfigured for passenger or cargo duties by removing survey equipment and by fitting cover plates over the camera apertures, which are normally closed by remotely controlled doors.

The An-30 is spacious, and a toilet, buffet and crew rest area with armchairs and couches are provided for the crew of seven (pilot, co-pilot, navigator, engineer, radio operator and two photographers), together with a darkroom and film storage area. The last two facilities account for the removal of the cabin windows.

The An-30 can carry a variety of mapping and

survey equipment, including magnetometers for mineral surveys and microwave radiometers for surveying ice build-up, snow cover, flooding, soil type or seasonal changes in vegetation. More commonly, the An-30 can carry a variety of optical cameras (both vertical and oblique) in fixed or gyro-stabilised mountings. An extremely accurate navigation computer maintains the pre-programmed course, altitude and speed.

A cloud-seeding version, the **An-30M 'Sky Cleaner'**, has been developed to disperse granular carbon dioxide and to fire meteorological cartridges into clouds, inducing rain or snowfall for agricultural of firefighting purposes.

Production of the An-30 was limited to 132 aircraft and only a handful serve on in the air forces of Bulgaria, the Czech Republic, Hungary, Romania, Russia and, perhaps, the Ukraine and Vietnam.

In addition to its extended, glazed nose, the An-30 also features a flightdeck raised by 3 ft 3 in (1 m) and an increased fuel capacity of 1,364 Imp gal (6200 litres).

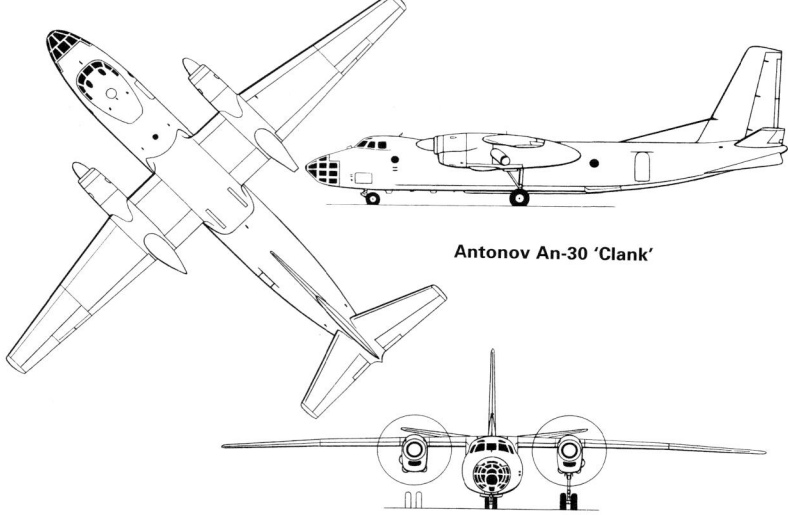

Antonov An-30 'Clank'

After the break-up of the USSR, Aeroflot lost its small fleet of An-30s. A proposal by Antonov to wet-lease examples of the highly-specialised An-30 to foreign operators eventually came to nothing.

SPECIFICATION

Antonov An-30 'Clank'
Type: seven-crew aerial survey aircraft
Powerplant: two ZMDB Progress (Ivchyenko) AI-24VT turboprop engines each rated at 2,820 eshp (2103 ekW) and one Soyuz (Tumanskii) RU-19A-300 turbojet rated at 1,764 lb st (7.85 kN)
Performance: maximum speed 336 mph (540 km/h) at optimum altitude; cruising speed 267 mph (430 km/h) at 19,685 ft (6000 m);

service ceiling 23,950 ft (7300 m) without APU and 27,230 ft (8300 m) with APU; range 1,634 miles (2630 km)
Weights: empty 34,369 lb (15590 kg); maximum take-off 50,705 lb (23000 kg)
Dimensions: wing span 95 ft 9½ in (29.20 m); length 79 ft 7 in (24.26 m); height 27 ft 3½ in (8.32 m); wing area 807.10 sq ft (74.98 m²)

Antonov An-32 'Cline'

In Indian air force service, the An-32 replaced the Fairchild C-82 Packet and Douglas DC-3. The superb high-altitude performance and rough-field capabilities of the 'Cline' are greatly appreciated.

Known to NATO by the reporting designation **'Cline'**, the **Antonov An-32** replaced the An-26 in production. The An-32 was created as a development of the An-26, offering improved take-off performance, ceiling and payload, especially under 'hot-and-high' conditions. The An-32 retains the superb cargo ramp of its predecessor, and its loading and internal cargo-handling capabilities are enhanced by the provision of an electrically powered winch rated at 6,614 lb (3000 kg) and removable roller conveyors, the latter also being useful for air-dropping freight, or the extraction of loads by drag-parachute. As an alternative to freight, up to 50 passengers, 42 paratroops, or 24 stretcher patients plus three attendants can be accommodated in the spacious cabin.

Although the An-32 was originally offered with a choice of powerplant, all production aircraft are fitted with the 5,043-ehp (3760-kW) Ivchyenko AI-20D Series 5 turboprop engine, which is similar to, but more powerful than, the engine used by the An-12 and Ilyushin Il-18. These engines are mounted above the wing to give greater clearance for the increased-diameter propellers, reduce the danger of debris ingestion, and decrease noise levels in the cabin. The overwing position results in very deep nacelles because the bulk of the An-26's original nacelle has been retained to accommodate the improved main landing gear units when retracted. The overwing portion of the nacelle extended back only to about mid-chord on the An-32 prototype that was first revealed at the 1977 Paris Air Show, but extends back almost to the trailing edge of the original underwing nacelle on production aircraft. The 'turbojet APU' of the An-26 and some An-24 versions has been replaced by a simple TG-1GM APU in the starboard landing gear fairing.

Besides these aerodynamic refinements, the landing gear extension/retraction mechanism, and the de-icing, air conditioning, electrical and engine starting systems have all been improved. The improvements to the An-32 have been extremely successful, producing an aircraft which can operate from airfields with elevations of up to 14,765 ft (4500 m) above sea level, and which has set a host of world records for payload-to-height and sustained altitude operations.

In 1993 the first **An-32B** was seen, with an uprated powerplant for increased maximum payload. At the Paris Air Show of the same year, Antonov demonstrated the **An-32P** (Protivopozharny) water-bomber version of the type under the name **Firekiller**. Like the similar An-26 conversion, the An-32P features side-mounted tanks with a total capacity of 17,637 lb (8000 kg), although on the An-32 these tanks are substantially larger and faired into the fuselage. Flares are carried to induce precipitation over fires. However, the tanks have to be refilled on the ground, necessitating specialised pumping equipment, and the radius of action is quoted at a mere 93 miles (150 km). The increased maximum take-off weight of this version is 65,476 lb (29700 kg).

The An-32 has attracted a number of military customers, including the USSR and its successors, Afghanistan, Bangladesh, Cuba, India, Mongolia, Peru and Tanzania. India's order for 95 aircraft, with the local name **Sutlej**, was to have been met by licensed production but this plan fell through and India's aircraft are imported, albeit with a high content of indigenous equipment and avionics.

In addition to the basic transport version of the An-32, firefighting, fishery protection, air ambulance and agricultural versions have been offered for sale, while Peru's 15 An-32 aircraft have two bomb racks on each side of the fuselage below the wing.

Antonov An-32 'Cline'

In addition to its more obvious differences from the An-26, the An-32 features ventral fins of greater area, an enlarged tailplane and complex high-lift devices on the wing.

SPECIFICATION

Antonov An-32 'Cline'
Type: three-/four-crew short/medium range transport
Powerplant: two ZMKB Progress (Ivchyenko) AI-20D Series 5 turboprop engines each rated at 5,042 ehp (3760 kW)
Performance: maximum cruising speed 329 mph (530 km/h) at 26,245 ft (8000 m); service ceiling 30,840 ft (9400 m); range 1,566 miles (2520 km) with maximum fuel and 746 miles (1200 km) with maximum payload
Weights: empty 38,158 lb (17308 kg); maximum take-off 59,524 lb (27000 kg)
Dimensions: wing span 95 ft 9½ in (29.20 m); length 78 ft ¼ in (23.78 m); height 28 ft 8½ in (8.75 m); wing area 807.10 sq ft (74.98 m²)
Payload: see above, or up to 14,771 lb (6700 kg) of freight

Antonov An-70

The **Antonov An-70** is the result of a programme initiated in 1975 to create a successor to the Antonov An-12. In overall layout the An-70 resembles its predecessor in being a high-wing monoplane of typical airlifter layout with the main landing gear (a tandem arrangement of three twin-wheel units on each side) retracting into external fairings, and an upswept rear fuselage and tail unit allowing the incorporation of a ventral ramp/door arrangement providing easy access to the large hold. The hold has an inbuilt cargo-handling system, is pressurised, and can be outfitted with seats for 300 troops or racks for 206 litters as alternatives to freight and/or vehicles or paratroops. The hold's sill height can be varied to facilitate the loading and unloading of freight to and from vehicles of different truckbed heights.

The An-70 is slightly larger than the proposed European FLA (for which competition the An-70 has been recommended by Germany) but considerably smaller than the Boeing (McDonnell Douglas) C-17 Globemaster III. Some 28 per cent of the airframe is made of composite materials, and other advanced features are a fly-by-wire control system with three digital and six analog channels, a fly-by-hydraulics back-up system, and an anhedralled wing with a supercritical section and, on each side, two-section double-slotted flaps whose outer elements are preceded by a three-section spoiler.

The An-70 was the first

Each of the An-70's propfan blades is electrically de-iced and of composite construction. An export variant with a radical change to CFM56-5A1 turbofan engines has been proposed.

Antonov's second An-70 prototype demonstrates the type's extensive high-lift devices.

aircraft to fly anywhere in the world with an all-propfan powerplant. This comprises four D-27 units each driving a contra-rotating assembly of 14 scimitar-type blades (eight and six in the front and rear propellers respectively). The An-70 prototype

made its first flight on 16 December 1994, but was lost on 10 February of the following year following an in-flight collision with its Antonov An-72 chaseplane. This machine was then replaced by a second prototype that made its maiden flight on 24 April 1997 and was delivered for official trials in mid-1998.

Relatively large-scale orders are expected, and the variants under active consideration include the baseline An-70 military transport, the **An-70-100** military STOL transport with a two- rather than three-crew cockpit, the **An-70T** civil transport, the **An-70T-100** civil transport with the revised powerplant of two unspecified propfan

engines, the **An-70TK** convertible passenger/freight transport for the civil market with accommodation for 150 passengers or 66,138 lb (30000 kg) of freight, and the **An-77** military STOL transport based on the

An-70-100 for the export market but with a two- or three-man cockpit.

Other possibilities under longer-term consideration are tanker, AEW, SAR, maritime patrol, firefighting, ecological monitoring, and medevac variants.

SPECIFICATION	
Antonov An-70	103,615-lb (47000-kg) payload after a conventional take-off, or 901 miles (1450 km) with a 77,161-lb (25000-kg) payload after a short take-off
Type: four-crew STOL medium transport	
Powerplant: four ZMKB Progress (Ivchyenko) D-27 propfan engines each rated at 13,800 shp (10290 kW)	**Weights:** maximum take-off 286,596 lb (130000 kg)
Performance: (estimated) cruising speed 466 mph (750 km/h) at between 29,520 and 39,380 ft (9000 and 12000 m); range 838 miles (1350 km) with a	**Dimensions:** wing span 144 ft 6 in (44.06 m); length 133 ft 7 in (40.73 m); height 53 ft 9 in (16.38 m) **Payload:** maximum payload 103,615 lb (47000 kg)

Antonov An-72, An-74 'Coaler' and An-71 'Madcap'

The **Antonov An-72** (NATO reporting designation **'Coaler'**), was developed as a turbofan-powered STOL transport to replace the turboprop-engined An-26. The first of the two prototypes made its maiden flight on 22 December 1977 and the prototypes, together with eight pre-production machines, received the reporting designation **'Coaler-A'**. Production was initiated at Kharkov of a slightly modified aircraft with extended outer wing panels, a lengthened fuselage, no ventral fins and other detail changes. This initial production version

was designated **An-72A**, and received the reporting designation **'Coaler-C'** because it appeared after the West had seen the long-span wing and lengthened fuselage on the **An-74**, which was allocated the reporting designation **'Coaler-B'**.

Because its new type flew for the first time only 17 months after the superficially similar Boeing YC-14, Antonov was unfairly accused of directly copying the US machine. There were certainly similarities between the two types in their configurations, including a high-set wing, a T-tail, and high-

mounted turbofan engines which discharged over the upper surface of the wing, using the Coanda effect in which jet exhaust is entrained by the extended flaps to increase lift dramatically. The high-set wing gives an unobstructed freight hold and eases production, while the high-set engines allow upper-surface blowing, as described above, but also minimise FOD ingestion problems.

The An-72's cargo ramp is little changed from that fitted to the An-32. However, telescopic struts fold down from the rear of each fairing for the main landing gear units to support the rear fuselage when the ramp is swung forward under the belly for direct loading. The landing gear itself is similarly novel, and optimised for operation from semi-prepared strips with low-pressure tyres, twin nosewheels and main units which consist of two tandem trailing arms, each with a single mainwheel.

The An-72 has been built in several versions. The **An-72AT** is a dedicated freighter equipped to handle standard international containers. The **An-72S** is an executive transport which can be reconfigured as a freighter, or as a 38-seat transport with tip-up seats along the cabin sides, or as an air ambulance with eight litters and an attendant.

The latest version of the aircraft is the **An-72P** dedicated maritime surveillance platform. Operational An-72Ps wear three-tone camouflage, and are armed with a 23-mm GSh-23L cannon in the starboard main landing gear fairing as well as underwing rocket pods. A novel system of bombs carried on an internal hoist has been displayed, and the An-72P

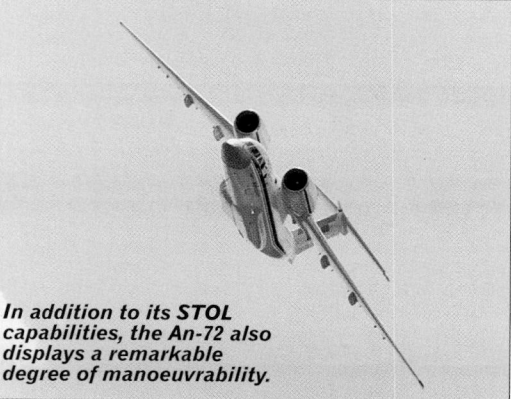

In addition to its STOL capabilities, the An-72 also displays a remarkable degree of manoeuvrability.

is currently being offered with a range of anti-ship missiles, torpedoes and depth charges. The aircraft features an advanced inertial navigation system, linked to on-board cameras which allow it to photograph target ships and record their exact position with great accuracy, and prominent bulged 'eyeball' windows aft of the flight deck give a better field of view. Linked to the auto-pilot, the navigation system can also automatically fly a wide variety of search patterns, and can be used to calculate the speed and course of targets. The An-72P has an endurance in excess of five hours. Antonov has now entered into a partnership with several Israeli firms under the leadership of IAI, for an An-72P derivative with much improved systems including an Elta-supplied surveillance radar, an Elisra ESM system, and El-Op stabilised, large-aperture, high-resolution all-weather sensor fit. The An-72P's current sensor fit includes A-86P lateral and oblique cameras for daytime use, UA-47 vertical night cameras, and a TV system beneath the port main landing gear fairing. The cameras are housed under

the tail, alongside the photo-flash ejection system.

The An-72P retains the pressurised fuselage of the transport version and can accommodate up to 40 folding passenger seats. Alternatively, 22 fully equipped paratroops can be carried. A typical eight-hour maritime mission can survey an area of 6,485 sq miles (16800 km²). Three Antonov An-72Ps (of a total of eight ordered) entered service with a Russian border guard unit based on the Pacific coast during July 1992, and the Ukrainian navy air arm had up to five similar aircraft.

The original **An-74** is a dedicated exploration support version optimised for operation in polar regions and designed to replace the ageing Ilyushin Il-14 transport aircraft then in use for supporting Arctic scientific stations, Antarctic expeditions, and for observing and monitoring ice floes and ice build-up. Because it was the first version noted in the West after the original prototypes and pre-production aircraft, it received the reporting designation 'Coaler-B', and it was only later revealed as a development of the initial An-72A version.

Antonov designed the An-74 with polar missions in mind. As such, the aircraft are often seen in a high-conspicuity red and white Aeroflot colour scheme, rather than the usual blue and white.

An-74 'Coaler-B' variants

An-74-200: freighter with D-36 Series 3A engines, loading winch and roller conveyors in the cabin floor. Maximum payload 22,046 lb (10000 kg)

An-74T-200: development of An-74-200 with cargo winch and roller conveyors in the cabin floor.

An-74T-100: version of the An-74T-200 with a navigator included in the flight crew

An-74TK-200: basic convertible passenger/freighter with a flight crew of two and provision for 52 passengers or 22,046 lb (10000 kg) of freight

An-74TK-100: derivative of the An-74TK-200 with a navigator included in the flight crew

An-74 Salon: executive transport with provision for the carriage of a car

Antonov An-72, An-74 'Coaler' and An-71 'Madcap' (cont)

The An-74 has the same basic airframe as the An-72A, although there are no blister observation windows aft of the flight deck and at the front of the cabin on the port side. It also has a larger radome, which gives a pronounced 'droop' to the nose. Fuel capacity is significantly increased, there is a system to de-ice the wing, tail unit and engine inlets, and provision is made for a wheel/ski landing gear to be fitted for operations

from snow. The An-74 has spawned a family of variants, only some of which have the prominent nose radome of the basic aircraft, but most seem to have the observation blisters.

Production of the Antonov An-72 and An-74 series continues at the rate of about 20 aircraft per year (from lines at Kharkov and Omsk), and by mid-1996 about 250 aircraft had been completed. Further improved variants are likely

to appear, and there are plans to re-engine the An-72 and An-74 with more powerful ZMKB Progress (Lotarev) D-436K turbofan engines each rated at 16,534 lb st (73.55 kN).

A further, more radical version of the An-72 is the **Antonov An-71** (NATO reporting designation **'Madcap'**), which was designed as a carrierborne AEW type. The aircraft was first observed by Western analysts in the mid-1980s, when its radically revised tail unit was seen in the background of a photograph of President Gorbachev visiting the headquarters of the Antonov design bureau.

The An-71 features a rear fuselage both shortened and revised in shape to compensate for the larger area of the completely different vertical tail surface, which is larger than that of the An-72 and swept forward to carry the rotodome supporting the

antenna for the radar of its integrated AEW system. The highly automated AEW suite is controlled by three operators at stations in the modified hold. Target data are transmitted to a surface station or other aircraft by means of jam-resistant communications channels, but the onboard operators can undertake air traffic control in addition to airborne early warning.

The aircraft was designed for operations away from base for a

period of up to 30 days without the need for special servicing or maintenance. The first Antonov An-71 made its maiden flight on 12 July 1985, but in 1990 the whole programme then fell prey to the stringent financial cuts that followed the economic and political collapse of the USSR into the CIS. It is worth noting, however, that Antonov is still promoting the An-71 on the export market as a land-based AEW platform.

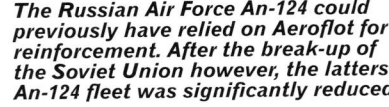

Antonov An-71 'Madcap'

Antonov An-124 Ruslan 'Condor'

The Russian Air Force An-124 could previously have relied on Aeroflot for reinforcement. After the break-up of the Soviet Union however, the latters An-124 fleet was significantly reduced.

Only a small number of the 54 **Antonov An-124 Ruslan** aircraft delivered by late 1995 are assigned directly to the air transport arm of the Russian air forces, but there is provision for most if not all civil-registered aircraft to be called into military service. Named after Pushkin's legendary giant, the An-124 is in many respects comparable to the slightly smaller Lockheed Martin C-5 Galaxy, which has a very similar configuration. The An-124 remains the world's largest production aircraft, only the one-off An-225 being bigger, and has set a series of world records, most notably exceeding by 53 per cent the C-5's payload to an altitude of 6,560 ft (2000 m).

Designed to meet a requirement of Aeroflot and the Soviet air forces for a

long-range heavy transport to replace the Antonov An-22 Antei, the An-124 first flew on 26 December 1982. The type entered service with Aeroflot in January 1986 and with the Soviet air forces in 1987.

The aircraft has an upward-hinging 'visor-type' nose (with a folding nose ramp) and an enormous set of rear loading doors (with a three-part folding ramp), a combination which allows simultaneous loading or unloading from both ends, or allows vehicles to be 'driven through'.

The vast cargo hold has a titanium floor with roller gangs and retractable cargo tie-down points. It is only lightly pressurised, although there is a fully pressurised upper passenger deck for up to 88 people. For ease of loading the aircraft can be made to

'kneel' in a nose-down position by retracting the nosewheels and supporting the nose on retractable feet.

Equipped with fly-by-wire controls, An-124 has a supercritical wing, and makes extensive use of composite materials for weight saving. It is capable of carrying virtually any load including all Soviet main battle tanks, helicopters and other military cargo.

The An-124 is the transport model, and derivatives of this baseline variant include the **An-124-100** commercial transport with

a maximum take-off weight of 864,198 lb (392000 kg), the **An-124-100M** version of the An-124-100 with Western avionics, and the **An-124-102**, which has an EFIS flight deck allowing the crew to be reduced to three (two pilots and a flight engineer). The

An-124-130 is a projected development of the basic type with four General Electric CF6-80 turbofan engines, and the type has also been considered in a convertible transport/firebombing version able to lift 200 tonnes of water in the firebombing role.

Antonov's Ruslan received the NATO codename 'Condor'.

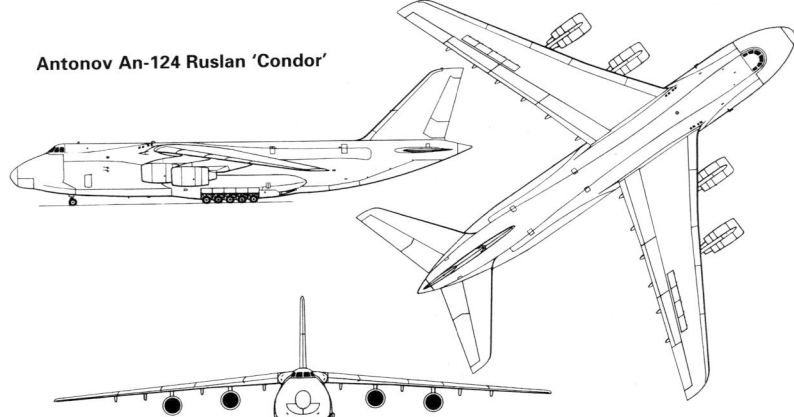

Antonov An-124 Ruslan 'Condor'

Antonov An-225 Mriya 'Cossack'

Despite high-profile appearances at a number of international air shows and a headline-grabbing series of 106 world records, the **Antonov An-225 Mriya** (dream) (NATO reporting name **'Cossack'**) remains something of an enigma. It was seemingly developed as successor to the two Myasischchev VM-T Atlant (converted M-4 'Bison') aircraft in use for the carriage of outsize loads, particularly those

associated with the Soviet space programme's Energiya rockets.

The sole An-225 made its maiden flight on 21 December 1988, and flew with the Buran space shuttle on its back on 13 May 1989, visiting the Paris air show in the same year. Until recently, however, when reports suggested that it might fly again, the aircraft languished in storage, losing engines and other components to active An-124 transports. The pair of VM-T aircraft remains active, and reports suggest that more VM-T machines may be produced through conversion of surplus 'Bison' aircraft. Ambitious plans for the An-225 – including a production run and leasing deal, as a launcher for the UK's now-defunct HOTOL recoverable spacecraft – seem to have fallen through, despite the huge

potential of this exceptional machine.

The first aircraft to fly with a gross weight in excess of 1,000,000 lb (453600 kg), the An-225 is an ingenious derivative of the An-124 designed to offer a 50 per cent improvement in payload and maximum take-off weight. This goal was achieved by the provision of a stretched fuselage, a powerplant with six rather than four engines, and a main landing gear arrangement with seven rather than five pairs of wheels on each side, together with redesign of the tail unit with a dihedralled horizontal surface and twin endplate vertical surfaces (allowing over-the-fuselage carriage of the space shuttle), deletion of the rear ramp/door arrangement, and enlargement of the wing's span and area. The last-mentioned improved lifting capability as well as reliev-

Not only did the 'Cossack'/Buran combination perform in the 1989 Paris flying display, but it was also taxied across the airfield's sodden grass.

ing airflow problems when external loads are carried.

A second aircraft began to take shape alongside

standard An-124 transports in the early 1990s, but remains unfinished and apparently unwanted.

Mountings for outsize loads are located over the aircraft's mid-section.

SPECIFICATION	
Antonov An-225 Mriya 'Cossack'	maximum payload or 9,570 miles (15400 km) with maximum fuel
Type: six-crew super-heavy transport	**Weights:** maximum take-off 1,322,275 lb (600000 kg)
Powerplant: six ZMKB Progress (Lotarev) D-18T turbofan engines each rated at 51,587 lb st (229.47 kN)	**Dimensions:** wingspan 290 ft (88.40 m); length 275 ft 7 in (84.00 m); height 59 ft 8½ in (18.20 m); wing area 9,741.66 sq ft (905.00 m²)
Performance: maximum cruising speed 528 mph (850 km/h) at optimum altitude; range 2,796 miles (4500 km) with	**Payload:** up to 551,146 lb (250000 kg) of freight

Antonov KT

The **Antonov KT** was an extremely imaginative if not altogether practical design for a flying tank (**Kr'lya Tanka**) and was developed in 1940 after Oleg Konstantinovich Antonov had revealed his skill in the creation of weight-carrying gliders with the excellent A-7. The object of the exercise was to assess the viability of the notion of supplying partisan forces,

operating in the area behind an enemy's front line, with light armoured vehicles as a means of improving their capability against the enemy's lines of communication.

A T-60 light tank was used as the 'fuselage' of the KT and its unlocked tracks served as the 'landing gear'. To this were added an unstaggered biplane wing cellule

of plywood- and fabric-covered wooden construction and a pair of booms carrying a tail unit with twin vertical surfaces and a high-set single horizontal surface. The aerodynamic controls were designed for operation by the tank driver from his standard position, and a single lever was provided for the complete set of flying surfaces to be jettisoned as soon as the KT (also known as the **A-40** and **A-T**) had come to a halt after landing.

The towing aircraft was a heavy bomber such as the Petlyakov Pe-8 or Tupolev TB-3. Although Western sources claim that the KT never managed even a take-off, Soviet

This illustration shows how the KT may have looked in flight. The aircraft allegedly made at least one flight, with the tank surviving the landing.

sources averred that a single successful flight was, in fact, achieved in 1941 or 1942. The whole

programme secured only the most limited official support, and was cancelled soon after this.

SPECIFICATION	
Antonov KT	12,787-lb (5800-kg) light tank
Type: single-crew light tank delivery system	**Dimensions:** wingspan 59 ft ¾ in (18.00 m); length of air portion 39 ft 6¾ in (12.06 m); wing area 923.57 sq ft (85.80 m²)
Weights: maximum take-off 17,205 lb (7804 kg) including the	

Arado Ar 64

On the basis of his SD II and SD III fighters, which had been developed in parallel, Ing. Walter Rethel evolved the **Arado Ar 64** in response to a 1929 requirement of the German war

ministry for a successor to the Fokker D.XIII fighter currently equipping the Germans' clandestine flying training school at Lipezk in the USSR. The Ar 64 was of mixed construction, with

a welded steel tube fuselage and a wooden wing cellule under a covering of fabric. The **Ar 64a** first prototype that first flew in the spring of 1930 was powered by a 530-hp (395-kW) Bristol Jupiter VI radial engine built under licence by Siemens and driving a four-bladed wooden propeller. In the following year there appeared two **Ar 64b** prototypes with the 640-hp (477-kW) BMW VI 6,3 Vee engine; the sole **Ar 64c** prototype was based on the Ar 64a with some

structural alterations.

The two production models, of which 20 were delivered as the first fighters to be built in 'quantity' in Germany since the end of World War I, were the **Ar 64D** and **Ar 64E**. The Ar 64D introduced a revised main landing gear unit and an enlarged vertical tail surface, and was powered by a geared Jupiter VI engine driving a four-bladed propeller. The Ar 64E was basically similar except for its powerplant,

which was based on a direct-drive Jupiter VI engine with a two-bladed propeller. Deliveries of these aircraft started in the summer of 1932, and after the first 19 had served initially at the Jagdfliegerschule (fighter training school) at Schleissheim, the survivors were later reallocated to the fighter units of the Fliegergruppen Döberitz and Damm, in which they complemented Arado Ar 65 biplane fighters.

Both the Ar 64a and generally similar Ar 64c (illustrated) featured four-bladed propellers, which were later used on the Ar 64D. The Ar 64c introduced a metal propeller.

SPECIFICATION	
Arado Ar 64D/E	**Weights:** empty 2,667 lb (1210 kg); maximum take-off 3,704 lb (1680 kg)
Type: single-seat fighter	**Dimensions:** wingspan 32 ft 5¾ in (9.90 m); length 27 ft 8 in (8.43 m)
Powerplant: one Siemens (Bristol) Jupiter VI radial engine rated at 530 hp (395 kW)	**Armament:** two 0.312-in (7.92-mm) fixed forward-firing machine-guns
Performance: maximum speed 156 mph (250 km/h) at 16,405 ft (5000 m)	

Arado Ar 65

Arado planned the **Ar 65** as a successor to the Ar 64, and the first of three prototypes flew in the summer of 1931. These three machines were the **Ar 65a**, **Ar 65b** and **Ar 65c**, which differed from each other only in minor details of equipment and structure but differed from the Ar 64 mainly in their powerplant of one BMW VI 7,3 Vee engine. Early test-flying of these prototypes indicated the need for fairly extensive development before the basic type could be deemed adequate for production and service. This led to the evolution of the **Ar 65d** that first flew in 1932 as a development of the Ar 65a, with the engine thrust line and forward fuselage contours lowered, the rear fuselage deepened, and extra interplane struts added. Despite a significant increase in maximum take-off weight, performance and handling were somewhat improved.

The Ar 65d paved the way for the main production variants of the Ar 65 series, which were built from 1933 as the **Ar 65E** and **Ar 65F**, of which the latter had a slightly superior equipment standard, increasing its maximum take-off weight by 88 lb (40 kg). The primary feature distinguishing these two variants from the Ar 65d, however, was the deletion of the earlier model's internal fuselage stowage for six 22-lb (10-kg) bombs. Production of the Ar 65E and Ar 65F lasted until early 1936 and amounted to 85 aircraft, and these machines served alongside the Ar 64 in the fighter units of the Fliegergruppen Döberitz and Damm. After only a few months of service, however, the Ar 65E and Ar 65F were supplemented and then replaced by the Heinkel He 51, and from 1935 the Arado machines were used in the fighter training role and to equip the Luftwaffe's first dive-bomber unit. In 1937, Germany presented the Bulgarian air force with 12 of the aircraft.

This Arado Ar 65F was used as an advanced trainer by a flying school in the Luftkreis III (Dresden) area.

SPECIFICATION

Arado Ar 65E
Type: single-seat fighter
Powerplant: one BMW VI 7,3 Vee engine rated at 750 hp (559 kW)
Performance: maximum speed 187 mph (300 km/h) at 5,415 ft (1650 m); cruising speed 152 mph (245 km/h) at optimum altitude; climb to 3,280 ft (1000 m) in 1 minute 30 seconds; service ceiling 24,935 ft (7600 m)
Weights: empty 3,329 lb (1510 kg); maximum take-off 4,255 lb (1930 kg)
Dimensions: wingspan 36 ft 9 in (11.20 m); length 27 ft 6¾ in (8.40 m); height 11 ft 2¾ in (3.42 m); wing area 322.92 sq ft (23.00 m²)
Armament: two 0.312-in (7.92-mm) fixed forward-firing machine-guns

Arado Ar 66

The last design completed for Arado by Ing. Walter Rethel before his transfer to the Messerschmitt organisation, the **Arado Ar 66** was a single-bay biplane trainer of mixed construction. Characteristic features were the swept-back wing panels, long-chord ailerons on both the upper and lower wings, and the slightly anachronistic tail unit with the strut-braced tailplane mounted on a raised rear fuselage fairing ahead of the vertical tail surface, which comprised only a substantial rudder without any fixed fin.

The **Ar 66a** prototype first flew in 1932 as a landplane, while the **Ar 66b** second prototype was completed to a seaplane standard with alighting gear based on a side-by-side pair of wooden floats, and the rudder was enlarged by an extension below the bottom of the sternpost with a ventral fin ahead of it. Ten production-standard **Ar 66B** floatplanes were subsequently built.

The Ar 66 entered series production as the **Ar 66C** that was delivered to the Luftwaffe from 1933. The Ar 66C remained in Luftwaffe service after the start of World War II. Indeed, as late as 1943, the type was pressed into service, alongside the Gotha Go 145 trainer, by the night ground-attack Störkampfstaffeln (harassing squadrons) on the Eastern Front.

Above: Built as a trainer, the Ar 66 mounted offensive operations with 4.4- and 8.8-lb (2- and 4-kg) anti-personnel fragmentation bomblets.

Left: A complex arrangement of struts was employed to support the wooden floats of the Ar 66B. Although ten production examples were built, the type failed to see operational service.

SPECIFICATION

Arado Ar 66C
Type: two-seat primary and basic flying trainer
Powerplant: one Argus As 10C inverted-Vee engine rated at 240 hp (179 kW)
Performance: maximum speed 131 mph (210 km/h) at sea level; cruising speed 109 mph (175 km/h) at optimum altitude; initial climb rate 853 ft (260 m) per minute; service ceiling 14,765 ft (4500 m); range 444 miles (715 km)
Weights: empty 1,996 lb (905 kg); maximum take-off 2,933 lb (1330 kg)
Dimensions: wingspan 32 ft 9¾ in (10.00 m); length 27 ft 2¾ in (8.30 m); height 9 ft 7½ in (2.93 m); wing area 318.95 sq ft (29.63 m²)

Arado Ar 67

In the closing months of 1933, Arado flew what proved to be the sole example of the **Arado Ar 67**, which was somewhat smaller and lighter than the Arado Ar 65. The aircraft was of mixed construction and based on an oval-section fuselage of welded steel tube construction covered with fabric aft and light alloy panels forward. Offering only moderately good performance and handling, the Ar 67 was discontinued in favour of the superior **Arado Ar 68**.

Provision was made for the Ar 67 to carry 1,000 rounds of ammunition for its two machine-guns which, in the event, were not fitted.

SPECIFICATION

Arado Ar 67
Type: single-seat fighter
Powerplant: one Rolls-Royce Kestrel VI Vee engine rated at 640 hp (477 kW)
Performance: maximum speed 211 mph (340 km/h) at 12,370 ft (3770 m); initial climb rate 1,575 ft (480 m) per minute; climb to 3,280 ft (1000 m) in 1 minute 30 seconds
Weights: empty 2,800 lb (1270 kg); maximum take-off 3,660 lb (1660 kg)
Dimensions: wingspan 31 ft 9 in (9.68 m); length 25 ft 11 in (7.90 m); height 10 ft 2 in (3.10 m); wing area 269.74 sq ft (25.06 m²)
Armament: (proposed) two 0.312-in (7.92 mm) fixed forward-firing machine-guns

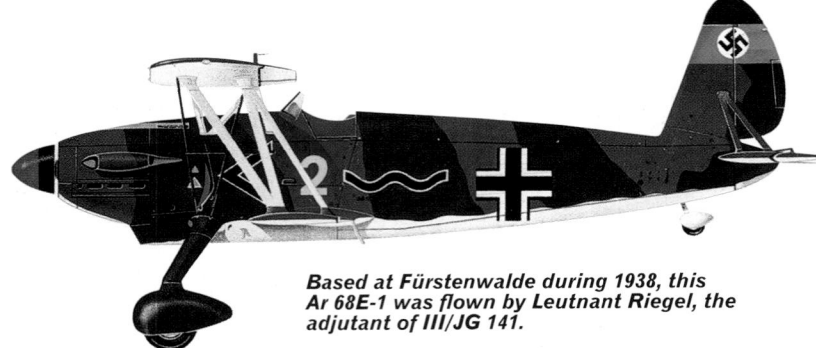

Arado Ar 68

The **Arado Ar 68** was the last biplane fighter to enter front-line service with the Luftwaffe. Reaching contemporary standards of aerodynamic efficiency, the aircraft had an oval-section fuselage of steel tube construction with light alloy panels covering the rear decking and forward sections, while the rest of the fuselage was covered with fabric. The single-bay wings were of wooden construction under a covering of plywood and fabric. The distinctive shaping of the vertical tail surface, which was to be used almost without exception on subsequent single-engined designs from the Arado stable, was introduced on the Ar 68.

The **Ar 68a** prototype flew for the first time in the summer of 1934 with the 550-hp (410-kW) BMW VId

Vee engine, and in this form the aircraft was deemed to have disappointing performance. This deficiency was partially overcome in the **Ar 68b** second prototype, which was powered by the 610-hp (455-kW) Junkers Jumo 210 inverted-Vee engine. This engine provided not only greater power and therefore performance, but also improved the forward field of vision from the cockpit. Even so, the drag of the Jumo 210's chin radiator depressed the performance potential, and a redesigned unit was therefore installed in the **Ar 68c** third prototype. First flown in the summer of 1935, the Ar 68c was also the first of the aircraft to be fitted with the intended armament of two fixed forward-firing machine-guns. The **Ar 68d** and

Ar 68e fourth and fifth prototypes were powered by the BMW VI and Jumo 210 engines respectively, and were regarded as being the pre-production prototypes for the two production variants, which were the Jumo-engined **Ar 68E-1** and BMW-engined **Ar 68F-1**.

It had been planned that the Jumo 210 engine should be standard in the production version of the Ar 68, but delays in its manufacture meant that the Ar 68F-1 was introduced in the spring and summer of 1936 as an interim model with the 750-hp (559-kW) BMW VI 7,3Z engine. Later in 1936, supplies of the Jumo 210Da (subsequently replaced by the identically-rated Jumo 210Ea) engine had reached the point at which manufacture and delivery of the Ar 68E-1

A Jumo 210Da engine, complete with two-stage supercharger, powered the Ar 68e.

became feasible, and the type entered service in the spring of 1937, two of these aircraft later undergoing operational evaluation in 1938 during the Spanish Civil War. By the outbreak of World War II, the Ar 68 series had been largely supplanted by the Messerschmitt Bf 109 in first-line units, the surviving machines being allocated mainly to the Jagdfliegerschulen (fighter pilot schools), but a small number remained operational as an interim night-fighter.

The **Ar 68G** designation was reserved for an abortive model with a supercharged BMW engine, and the sole **Ar 68H** was a prototype with the 850-hp (634-kW) BMW 132 radial engine for an increase of 41 mph (65 km/h) in maximum speed. The Ar 68H also had an enclosed cockpit with a rearward-sliding canopy and its firepower was enhanced by the addition of two 0.312-in (7.92-mm) fixed forward-firing machine guns in the leading edge of the upper wing.

Based at Fürstenwalde during 1938, this Ar 68E-1 was flown by Leutnant Riegel, the adjutant of III/JG 141.

SPECIFICATION	
Arado Ar 68E-1	**Weights:** empty 4,057 lb
Type: single-seat fighter	(1840 kg); maximum take-off
Powerplant: one Junkers Jumo	5,457 lb (2475 kg)
210Da inverted-Vee engine rated	**Dimensions:** wingspan 36 ft 1 in
at 690 hp (515 kW)	(11.00 m); length 31 ft 2 in
Performance: maximum speed	(9.50 m); height 10 ft 9 in (3.28 m);
208 mph (335 km/h) at 8,695 ft	wing area 293.86 sq ft (27.30 m²)
(2650 m); initial climb rate 2,480 ft	**Armament:** two 0.312-in
(756 m) per minute; climb to	(7.92-mm) fixed forward-firing
19,685 ft (6000 m) in 10 minutes;	machine-guns, plus provision under
service ceiling 26,575 ft (8100 m);	the fuselage for six 22-lb (10-kg)
range 258 miles (415 km)	bombs

Arado Ar 76

Intended as a single-seat advanced trainer which could double as a lightweight fighter in the emergency home-defence role, the **Arado Ar 76** initially flew, in the form of the **Ar 76a** first prototype,

during 1934, followed in the course of 1935 by the **Ar 76 V2** and **Ar 76 V3,** the second and third prototypes. The Ar 76 was a parasol-wing monoplane with fixed tailwheel landing gear. The basic structure of

the fuselage and wing was of welded steel tubing and wood respectively and, with the exception of the forward fuselage which was covered with light alloy panels, the whole airframe was covered with fabric.

Although impressive, the Ar 76 suffered some setbacks during its test programme. The first prototype was lost in a crash at an early date. Modification of the tail unit, which was of characteristic Arado type, overcame all of the

Some changes to the tail assembly were incorporated into the Ar 76 V2 prototype.

problems, but the rival Focke-Wulf Fw 56 Stösser was preferred by the German air ministry. Even so, a small batch of

Ar 76A-1 production aircraft was built, and the type served for some time with distinction at Luftwaffe flying schools.

SPECIFICATION	
Arado Ar 76A-1	**Weights:** empty 1,653 lb (750 kg);
Type: single-seat advanced flying	maximum take-off 2,359 lb
trainer and lightweight fighter	(1070 kg)
Powerplant: one Argus As 10C	**Dimensions:** wingspan 31 ft 2 in
inverted-Vee engine rated at	(9.50 m); length 23 ft 7½ in
240 hp (179 kW)	(7.20 m); height 8 ft 4⅜ in (2.55 m);
Performance: maximum speed	wing area 143.16 sq ft (13.30 m²)
166 mph (267 km/h) at sea level;	**Armament:** (trainer) one fixed
cruising speed 137 mph (220 km/h)	forward-firing 0.312-in (7.92-mm)
at optimum altitude; initial climb	machine-gun or (fighter) two fixed
rate 1,417 ft (432 m) per minute;	forward-firing 0.312-in (7.92-mm)
climb to 16,405 ft (5000 m) in	machine-guns, plus provision for
21 minutes; service ceiling 20,995 ft	three 22-lb (10-kg) bombs on
(6400 m); range 292 miles (470 km)	underfuselage racks

Arado Ar 77

After it had issued its 1934 requirement for a multi-role aircraft to serve in the crew training, light transport and communications roles, the German air ministry

ordered prototypes of the twin-engined **Arado Ar 77** and Focke-Wulf Fw 58 Weihe designs for a competitive evaluation. This lead to the selection of a

single type for series production. The Arado design team laid out the Ar 77 as a cantilever low-wing monoplane with fully enclosed accommodation in an oval-section fuselage and featuring a high-aspect-ratio wing.

The Ar 77 prototypes were produced in two forms as the **Ar 77A** and **Ar 77B**, these being differentiated largely by their

A spatted and trousered undercarriage added to the streamlined look of the Ar 77.

structures as the Ar 77A was of mixed wood and Dural construction, whereas the Ar 77B was of wooden construction. The

Ar 77 was deemed to offer adequate performance and handling, but the Fw 58 was preferred for the production order.

SPECIFICATION	
Arado Ar 77A	3,280 ft (1000 m) in 3 minutes
Type: four-seat multi-role training,	30 seconds; service ceiling 16,405 ft
light transport and communications	(5000 m); range 292 miles (470 km)
aircraft	**Weights:** empty 4,255 lb
Powerplant: two Argus As 10C	(1930 kg); maximum take-off
inverted-Vee piston engines each	6,481 lb (2940 kg)
rated at 240 hp (179 kW)	**Dimensions:** wingspan 62 ft
Performance: maximum speed	11⅞ in (19.20 m); length 41 ft ⅛ in
149 mph (240 km/h) at sea level;	(12.50 m); height 10 ft 6 in
cruising speed 124 mph (200 km/h)	(3.20 m); wing area 543.60 sq ft
at optimum altitude; climb to	(50.50 m²)

Arado Ar 79

Designed as an aerobatic two-seat training and touring aircraft intended for the civil market, the **Arado Ar 79** was the manufacturer's first 'modern' monoplane type with enclosed accommodation, cantilever flying surfaces and retractable main landing gear units. The type first appeared in prototype form during 1938 with the powerplant of one Hirth

Offering side-by-side accommodation for two in a fully enclosed cabin, the Ar 79 was a useful touring cabin monoplane.

HM 504A-2 inverted inline engine. The forward fuselage was of welded steel-tube construction under a covering of light alloy panels, and provided side-by-side accommodation under a rearward-sliding canopy. The rear fuselage was of light alloy semi-monocoque construction, and the wing was of single-spar wooden construction with plywood and fabric covering.

The Ar 79 set a number of international class speed

records during 1938, and later in the same year an Ar 79 was prepared for an attempt on the long-distance record. A jettisonable 23.3-Imp gal (106-litre) fuel tank was fitted under the fuselage and a fixed 114.4-Imp gal (520-litre) tank at the rear of the cabin. The aircraft was ferried from Brandenberg to Benghazi in Libya, the starting point for the 3,916.5-mile (6303-km) non-stop flight to Gaya in India. The flight, from 29 to 31 December, was made at an average speed of 99.5 mph (160 km/h).

SPECIFICATION

Arado Ar 79	climb to 3,280 ft (1000 m) in
Type: two-seat training and touring aircraft	3 minutes 48 seconds; service ceiling 18,040 ft (5500 m); range
Powerplant: one Hirth HM 504A-2 inverted inline engine rated at 105 hp (78 kW)	636 miles (1025 km) **Weights:** empty 1,014 lb (460 kg); maximum take-off 1,675 lb (760 kg)
Performance: maximum speed 143 mph (230 km/h) at sea level; cruising speed 127 mph (205 km/h) at optimum altitude; initial climb rate 787 ft (240 m) per minute;	**Dimensions:** wingspan 32 ft 9¾ in (10.00 m); length 24 ft 11¼ in (7.60 m); height 6 ft 10⅔ in (2.10 m); wing area 150.70 sq ft (14.00 m²)

Arado Ar 80

The **Ar 80** was Arado's first monoplane fighter, and was one of four types selected for prototype construction by the German air ministry in February 1934. The other three were the Focke-Wulf Fw 159, Heinkel He 112 and Messerschmitt Bf 109.

Ordered to the extent of several prototypes, like the other contenders, the Ar 80 was of all-metal construction. Its configuration of clean low-wing monoplane with a wing of inverted-gull layout allowed the use of short and therefore comparatively light main landing gear legs, which were neatly faired and carried spatted wheels. The tail unit was of the characteristic Arado type and in overall terms the design revealed the devotion of considerable attention to aerodynamic cleanliness.

The **Ar 80 V1** first prototype had an open cockpit and was powered by one 812-hp (605.5-kW) Rolls-Royce Kestrel V Vee engine, but was soon lost in a landing accident. The **Ar 80 V2** second prototype initially flew with the same type of engine but was then revised with the 695-hp (518-kW) Junkers Jumo 210Ca inverted-Vee engine. The Jumo 210 powerplant was retained for the **Ar 80 V3** third prototype. It was the first aircraft completed with armament in the form of one 20-mm cannon in a moteur-canon installation and two 0.312-in (7.92-mm) machine-guns in the upper part of the forward fuselage. This aircraft was later modified with a straight wing and a second seat for an observer.

The fourth and fifth prototypes were the **Ar 80 V4** and **Ar 80 V5**. These were basically similar to each other, and differed from their predecessors in having an enclosed cockpit and the powerplant of one Jumo 210Ga engine with a fuel-injection system rather than a conventional carburation system. The Ar 80 V4 and Ar 80 V5 underwent extensive tests before being returned to the manufacturer for use by the defensive flight operated by the company

Ar 80 V3, D-IPBN, was modified with a second seat for an observer to monitor the behaviour of Fowler flaps fitted to the aircraft in a test installation.

test pilots for the protection of the Arado factory at Warnemunde.

A development of the last two prototypes with the Jumo 210Ea engine and retractable main landing gear units was proposed as a production model, but all work on this variant was terminated upon the selection of the Bf 109 to meet the Luftwaffe's needs for a monoplane fighter.

SPECIFICATION

Arado Ar 80 V3 (initial form)	(1645 kg); maximum take-off 4,630 lb (2100 kg)
Type: single-seat fighter	**Dimensions:** wingspan 38 ft 8½ in
Powerplant: one Junkers Jumo 210Ca inverted-Vee engine rated at 695 hp (518 kW)	(11.80 m); length 33 ft 1½ in (10.10 m); height 9 ft 8⅛ in (2.95 m); wing area 226.05 sq ft
Performance: maximum speed 264 mph (425 km/h) at 13,125 ft (4000 m); climb to 13,125 ft (4000 m) in 5 minutes 48 seconds; service ceiling 32,810 ft (10000 m); range 373 miles (600 km)	(21.00 m²) **Armament:** one 20-mm fixed forward-firing cannon and two 0.312-in (7.92-mm) fixed forward-firing machine-guns
Weights: empty 3,626 lb	

Arado Ar 81

Arado was one of three companies invited to respond to the German air ministry's January 1935 requirement for a Sturzkampfflugzeug (dive-bomber). The requirement stipulated a two-man crew and performance not radically inferior to that of current fighters, and while Heinkel and Junkers responded with the He 118 and Ju 87 monoplanes, the **Arado Ar 81** was a single-bay biplane with fixed landing gear.

Of all-metal construction, the Ar 81 had an oval-section fuselage of almost pod-and-boom type, and an equal-span single-bay wing cellule with slightly swept-back outer panels. A crew of two sat in tandem, the pilot and gunner in enclosed and semi-enclosed accommodation, respectively. The tail unit included a dihedral tailplane carrying endplate vertical surfaces. Cantilever main landing gear units and an underfuselage crutch arrangement were designed to swing the 551-lb (250-kg) bomb clear of the propeller disc before it was released.

The **Ar 81 V1** first prototype made its maiden flight late in 1935 with a Junkers Jumo 210C engine driving a three-bladed propeller. Flight trials indicated a measure of instability, and the **Ar 81 V2** was therefore completed with a flat and strut-braced tailplane raised slightly above the rear fuselage on a long-chord pylon. Trials of the Ar 81 V2 revealed that the instability had been mitigated but not entirely removed, so the **Ar 81 V3** was completed with a rear fuselage of greater section carrying a more orthodox tail unit of characteristic Arado shaping with single horizontal and vertical surfaces, and a revised powerplant driving a two-bladed variable-pitch propeller.

The Ar 81 V3 joined the flight test programme late in the spring of 1936, and tests revealed that the machine was strong, stable in level flight and in the dive, manoeuvrable, and in most performance respects superior to the Ju 87. The biplane configuration was deemed obsolescent if not actually obsolete, however, and the Junkers Ju 87 had already received the production order.

SPECIFICATION

Arado Ar 81 V3	6,768 lb (3070 kg)
Type: two-seat dive-bomber	**Dimensions:** wingspan 36 ft 1 in (11.00 m); length 37 ft 8¾ in
Powerplant: one Junkers Jumo 210Ca inverted-Vee engine rated at 640 hp (477 kW)	(11.50 m); height 11 ft 10 in (3.60 m); wing area 383.21 sq ft (35.60 m²)
Performance: maximum speed 215 mph (345 km/h) at 13,125 ft (4000 m); climb to 13,125 ft (4000 m) in 11 minutes; service ceiling 26,255 ft (8000 m); range 429 miles (690 km)	**Armament:** (proposed) one 0.312-in (7.92-mm) fixed forward-firing machine-gun, and one 0.312-in (7.92-mm) trainable rearward-firing machine gun, plus one 551-lb (250-kg) bomb carried under the fuselage
Weights: empty 4,244 lb (1925 kg); maximum take-off	

Having no dihedral on its tailplane, the Arado Ar 81 V2 also featured additional tailplane bracing struts when compared to the Ar 81 V1 machine.

Arado Ar 95

The **Arado Ar 95** was designed during 1935 as a two-seat floatplane for the coastal patrol, reconnaissance and light attack roles. The aircraft was of all-metal construction covered largely with fabric except on the forward part of the fuselage, which was skinned with light alloy. In configuration, it was a single-bay biplane with parallel-chord outer wing panels which were attached to upper and lower centre-sections of inverse taper and chord. This unusual feature was intended to provide easier access to the cockpits from the lower wingroot, which was thicker and of wider chord, and improved

upward visibility resulted from the thinner and narrower upper-wing centre-section. The side-by-side single-step floats were strut-braced to the fuselage and lower-wing centre-section. The twin cockpits were enclosed by a sliding canopy, the rear of the cockpit being left open to permit the use of a trainable machine-gun. The latter was complemented by a fixed forward-firing weapon of the same calibre in the upper part of the forward fuselage.

The **Ar 95 V1** first prototype made its maiden flight in 1937 with the 880-hp (656-kW) BMW 132De radial engine, while the **Ar 95 V2** second prototype

This is one of the Arado Ar 95A-1s which served with 3./SAGr (Seeaufklärungsgruppe) 125 in the Baltic Sea during the summer of 1941.

Official German interest in the Ar 95 was limited, since it was considered that it would be obsolete by the time Germany could commission the first of its aircraft-carriers. In the event, no carriers were completed and the Ar 95 found use as a trainer.

was powered by the 690-hp (515-kW) Junkers Jumo 210 inverted-Vee engine. Both of these prototypes were evaluated competitively against the two prototypes of the Focke-Wulf Fw 62 single-float seaplane. The BMW-powered version was judged worthy of further development, and a batch of six prototype and pre-production aircraft served a trial period with the Condor Legion during

the Spanish Civil War. However, the Ar 95 was not immediately adopted for German military use.

Undaunted, Arado offered the design for export as the **Ar 95W** float-plane, ordered by Turkey in 1938, and as the **Ar 95L** landplane with fixed, spatted landing gear it was subject to an order from Chile. The latter was

fulfilled before the start of World War II but, much to the chagrin of their intended recipients, the Turkish aircraft were instead diverted to the Luftwaffe under the designation **Ar 95A-1**, seeing wartime service as trainers with the Seeaufklärungsgruppen (coastal reconnaissance wings).

SPECIFICATION	
Arado Ar 95A-1	(2450 kg); maximum take-off
Type: two-seat coastal patrol and light attack floatplane	7,870 lb (3560 kg)
Powerplant: one BMW 132De radial engine rated at 880 hp (656 kW)	**Dimensions:** wingspan 41 ft ⅛ in (12.50 m); length 36 ft 5 in (11.10 m); height 11 ft 9¾ in (3.60 m); wing area 488.70 sq ft (45.40 m²)
Performance: maximum speed 191 mph (308 km/h) at 9,845 ft (3000 m); cruising speed 159 mph (255 km/h) at 3,935 ft (1200 m); initial climb rate 1,280 ft (390 m) per minute; service ceiling 23,945 ft (7300 m); range 684 miles (1100 km)	**Armament:** one 0.312-in (7.92-mm) fixed forward-firing machine-gun and one 0.312-in (7.92-mm) trainable rearward-firing machine-gun, plus either one 1,764-lb (800-kg) torpedo or one 1,102-lb (500-kg) bomb on a rack under the fuselage
Weights: empty 5,402 lb	

Arado Ar 96

With a total production run of more than 11,500 aircraft by the end of World War II, the **Arado Ar 96** was the Luftwaffe's standard advanced flying trainer, and was a cantilever low-wing monoplane of the stressed-skin type with fully enclosed tandem accommodation for the pupil and instructor. Designed by Dipl. Ing. Walter Blume, the Ar 96 made its maiden flight during 1938 in the form of the **Ar 96 V1** prototype, which was powered by the 240-hp (179-kW) Argus As 10C inverted-Vee engine. It initially had outward-retracting main landing gear legs, soon replaced by inward-retracting units for greater wheel track and therefore improved stability on the ground.

The aircraft successfully completed its German air ministry trials, paving the way for an order for a modest number of **Ar 96A-1** initial production aircraft that were delivered in 1939 with the As 10C

engine. By this time it was clear that the basic design could profitably handle a considerably higher-rated engine, so the main production model – the **Ar 96B** – was ordered in 1940 with the 465-hp (347-kW) Argus As 410A-1 inverted-Vee engine driving a two-bladed propeller. Its lengthened fuselage allowed an increase in the fuel tankage. It is thought that there were several sub-variants of the Ar 96B model, known types being the **Ar 96B-1** unarmed pilot trainer, **Ar 96B-2** with a fixed forward-firing machine-gun, **Ar 96B-5** pilot gunnery trainer, and **Ar 96B-7** with provision for the external carriage of bombs in the ground-attack and dive-bomber training roles. There was also a gunner training model, probably produced in small numbers by conversion, with a trainable rearward-firing machine-gun in the modified rear of the two-seat cockpit.

Arado itself built only a few Ar 96B aircraft, the

Shown here in prototype form, the Arado Ar 96 proved to be an exceptionally versatile trainer in service.

majority being completed by a Junkers subsidiary, Ago Flugzeugwerke and, from mid-1941, by the Czech company Avia which was joined in the programme by the Prague-based Letov organisation in 1944. Czech production continued until 1948, aircraft being supplied to the Czech air force under the designation **Avia C.2B-1**.

SPECIFICATION	
Arado Ar 96B-2	range 615 miles (990 km)
Type: two-seat advanced flying trainer	**Weights:** empty 2,854 lb (1295 kg); maximum take-off 3,748 lb (1700 kg)
Powerplant: one Argus As 410A-1 inverted-Vee engine rated at 465 hp (347 kW)	**Dimensions:** wingspan 36 ft 1 in (11.00 m); length 29 ft 10¼ in (9.10 m); height 8 ft 6½ in (2.60 m); wing area 184.07 sq ft (17.10 m²)
Performance: maximum speed 205 mph (330 km/h) at sea level; cruising speed 183 mph (295 km/h) at optimum altitude; initial climb rate 1,000 ft (305 m) per minute; service ceiling 23,295 ft (7100 m);	**Armament:** one 0.312-in (7.92-mm) fixed forward-firing machine-gun

Arado Ar 96 (cont.)

The **Ar 96C**, of which just one pre-production batch was built, was a development of the Ar 96B. It had the 480-hp (358-kW) Argus As 410C engine and a small transparency in the lower fuselage so that the type could be used in the bomber training role. A development of the Ar 96 that failed to reach fruition

(the Ar 396 being preferred) was the **Ar 296**, with the 600-hp (447.5-kW) Argus As 411 inverted-Vee engine.

Built to the extent of 11,546 examples, the Ar 96 represented the backbone of Luftwaffe pilot training throughout World War II.

Arado Ar 195

Arado built three prototypes of the **Arado Ar 195** navalised version of the Ar 95, and the first of these machines, the **Ar 195 V1**, made its maiden flight in 1937. The type was being considered as part of the air group to be embarked on the aircraft carrier *Graf Zeppelin*. The aircraft was ordered in prototype form for competitive evaluation against the Fieseler Fi 167 as a carrierborne multi-role type with a folding wing cellule, the strength to undertake diving attacks at speeds of up to 373 mph (600 km/h), flotation gear, and provision for main landing gear units that could be jettisoned prior to an emergency ditching.

The other main changes effected in the process of turning the Ar 95 into the Ar 195 were a measure of airframe strengthening, the addition of an arrester hook and catapult spools, a wing cellule with straight rather than swept-back outer panels and, in order to improve the forward field of vision for deck landing, a cockpit moved considerably farther forward (so that the pilot sat under the upper wing's leading edge), and a canopy of increased height.

Trials of the Ar 195 V1, **Ar 195 V2** and **Ar 195 V3** indicated wholly inadequate performance as a result of the revised airframe's greater drag and increased weight. The Fi 167, on the other hand, exceeded the official requirement in every respect as well as offering phenomenal STOL capability and, as a result, all further development of the Ar 195 was terminated.

Three examples of the disappointing Ar 195 were completed (the Ar 195 V1 is illustrated). The type was proposed to equip the aircraft-carrier Graf Zeppelin, the keel of which was laid on 28 December 1936.

SPECIFICATION	
Arado Ar 195 V3	(1940 kg); maximum take-off
Type: two-seat carrierborne torpedo bomber and reconnaissance aircraft	8,091 lb (3670 kg)
	Dimensions: wingspan 41 ft (12.50 m); length 34 ft 5⅓ in (10.50 m); height 11 ft 9¾ in (3.60 m); wing area 495.14 sq ft (46.00 m²)
Powerplant: one BMW 132M radial engine rated at 830 hp (619 kW)	
Performance: maximum speed 180 mph (290 km/h) at 6,560 ft (2000 m); cruising speed 156 mph (250 km/h) at optimum altitude; climb to 13,125 ft (4000 m) in 14 minutes; service ceiling 19,685 ft (6000 m); range 404 miles (650 km)	**Armament:** one 0.312-in (7.92-mm) fixed forward-firing machine-gun, and one 0.312-in (7.92-mm) trainable rearward-firing machine-gun, plus one 1,543-lb (700-kg) torpedo or one 551-lb (250-kg) and four 110-lb (50-kg) bombs carried under the fuselage and lower wing
Weights: empty 4,277 lb	

Arado Ar 196

In the autumn of 1936 the technical department of the German air ministry issued a requirement for a catapult-launched floatplane to replace the Heinkel He 60. The requirement was for a two-seat aircraft with single- or twin-float alighting gear, and powered by an engine rated at between 800 and 900 hp (597 and 671 kW). Of the competing proposals, the Focke-Wulf Fw 62 biplane and **Arado Ar 196** monoplane were selected for initial construction and development.

The Ar 196 was of all-metal construction, its rectangular-section steel tube fuselage frame being faired to an oval section by the use of formers and stringers, with metal skinning forward and fabric covering aft. The wings were metal-skinned two-spar structures, hinged at the trailing edge to fold back along the fuselage sides once the outboard wing-to-float struts had been detached at the float end. Each of the twin floats housed a fuel tank.

Evaluation of the first and second prototypes, **Ar 196 V1** and **Ar 196 V2**, was undertaken in the summer of 1937 at much the same time as the initial evaluation of the Fw 62 prototypes, but the clear superiority of the more advanced Arado machine quickly eliminated the Focke-Wulf contender. Powered by an 880-hp (656-kW) BMW 132De radial engine, the Ar 196 had initially been ordered to the extent of four prototypes, the first two being completed to **Ar 196A** standard with twin floats and the other two (**Ar 196 V3** and **Ar 196 V4**) to the **Ar 196B** standard with a single, larger main float and two small stabilising floats under the outer wing.

The fourth prototype was the first to be fitted with weapons in the form of two wing-mounted 20-mm fixed forward-firing cannon in the leading edges of the wing and one 0.312-in (7.92-mm) fixed forward-firing machine-gun in the starboard side of the forward fuselage. A fifth prototype, the **Ar 196 V5** (completed to Ar 196B standard) was fitted with the more powerful 960-hp (716-kW) BMW 132K radial engine driving a

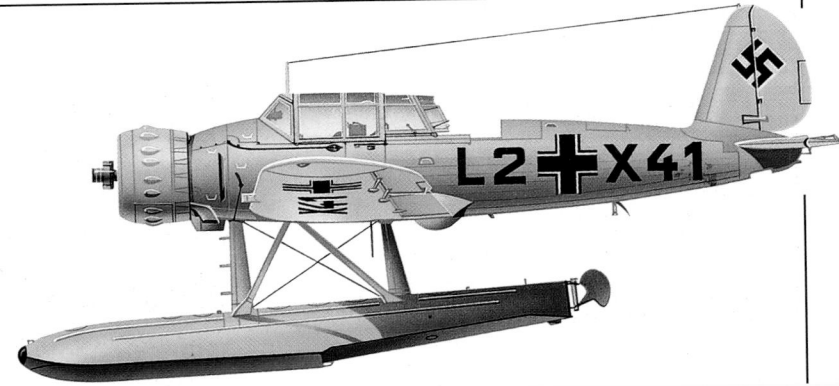

The Ar 196 in all its variants proved to be an outstanding success with the Luftwaffe, serving throughout World War II.

three-bladed variable-pitch propeller, and with revised accommodation.

Although comparative evaluation of the hydrodynamic qualities of the alternative float configurations showed that no distinct advantage could be discerned for either layout, the twin-float version was preferred and 10 pre-production floatplanes were subsequently ordered.

Total production of the Ar 196A was well in excess of 500 aircraft, including those

Variants

Ar 196A-0: pre-production batch of 10 aircraft, fitted with bomb racks and rear cockpit-mounted 0.312-in (7.92-mm) machine-gun only

Ar 196A-1: 20 aircraft with minor changes, built in 1939 and operated from major German warships. An example from the Hipper's flight was captured in Norway and later evaluated at the Marine Aircraft Experimental Establishment, Helensburgh in 1940

Ar 196A-2: for coastal patrol duties, with the armament increased by the addition of two 20-mm cannon in the wing and one 0.312-in (7.92-mm) machine-gun in the fuselage

Ar 196A-3: structurally-strengthened version with additional radio equipment and new three-bladed variable-pitch propeller; also built by SNCA and Fokker

Ar 196A-4: catapult version of the Ar 196A-3, 24 being ordered to replace A-1 machines with Bordfliegerstaffeln

Ar 196A-5: final production version with improved radio equipment and rearward defensive armament boosted to a pair of 0.312-in (7.92-mm) machine-guns; last of 91 aircraft built by Fokker in August 1944

Ar 196B-0: pre-production batch of version with single main float and two stabilising floats, delivered for service evaluation in 1940-1

Ar 196C: project for an aerodynamically refined version cancelled in 1941

built in 1942-3 in France, and between April and August 1943 by Fokker in the Netherlands. The first ship to take its Ar 196 to sea was the pocket battleship KMS *Admiral Graf Spee.*

The Ar 196 was also used widely for coastal patrol, and a spectacular early success was the capture of the crippled British submarine HMS *Seal* by two Ar 196A float-planes of 1./Küstenflieger-gruppe 706 based at Aalborg in Denmark. The Ar 196 served in most major battle zones and also with the Bulgarian and Romanian air forces.

In November 1939, deliveries of the Ar 196A-2 began. It was the first production variant to be fitted with the powerful fixed forward-firing armament which gave the Ar 196 such formidable firepower.

Arado Ar 197

Developed with carrier operations in mind, the **Arado Ar 197** was developed in parallel with the

Ar 68H which it closely resembled, and was intended as a single-seat biplane fighter and light bomber. The **Ar 197 V1** first prototype was powered by a 900-hp (671-kW) Daimler-Benz DB 600A inverted-Vee engine, while the **Ar 197 V2** second prototype had the 815-hp (608-kW) BMW 132J radial engine. The latter machine was completed with catapult

The Ar 197 V3 was considered to be a production prototype. The type was cancelled, however, when it was realised that a German aircraft-carrier was at least two years away from completion.

spools and arrester hook. Both aircraft flew in the spring of 1937, followed closely by the **Ar 197 V3** third prototype that was basically an improved version of the Ar 197 V2 with the uprated power-

plant of one 880-hp (656-kW) BMW 132De engine as well as provision under the fuselage for a drop tank. Limited evaluation of the three aircraft was not followed by any production order.

Arado Ar 199

Designed to meet a requirement for a floatplane trainer, the **Arado Ar 199** was a technical success, but then fell victim to a change in official policy and was not ordered into production. The aircraft was of modern design and construction, being a cantilever low-wing monoplane of light alloy stressed-skin construction. Accommodation was provided for three persons (pupil and instructor side-by-side at the front with provision for a trainee navigator or radio operator behind them) in a substantial cockpit covered by a framed canopy with a sliding section for access and egress. The trainer had a tail unit of typical Arado design, alighting gear in the form of

Photographed after its entry into Luftwaffe service, this Ar 199 has the vaned-spinner. It also shows a typical Arado arrangement of bracing struts and wires for the twin float alighting gear.

a side-by-side pair of metal floats carried under the inner parts of the wing by a neat arrangement of wire-braced struts, and a neatly cowled engine driving a two-bladed propeller. The entire airframe was stressed for the rigours of repeated catapult launches.

The first and second prototypes, **Ar 199 V1** and **Ar 199 V2**, were officially evaluated in 1939, with the design having been

begun in 1938. One of the aircraft was at one time fitted with the vaned spinner associated with the Argus pitch-change mechanism for the propeller. After it had been decided not to order the type into production as the **Ar 199A**, these two machines were taken into Luftwaffe service for use as trainers.

Arado Ar 231

The German navy's successful use of the U-boat against Allied shipping would be enhanced, it was argued, by giving the submarines an improved tactical intelligence-gathering capability in the form of a small reconnaissance

aircraft that could be carried aboard the boat on patrol. The main requirements were that the aircraft should be storable in a container 6 ft 6¾ in (2.00 m) in diameter and that dismantling or re-erecting the airframe should

take just a minute or two in order to minimise the time during which the U-boat was at risk on the surface. The complete launching or recovery procedure, including the use of a crane to lift the machine into or out of the water, was planned to take no more than six minutes under operational conditions.

Arado Ar 231 (cont)

Arado's response to the specification was the **Arado Ar 231**, featuring one of the earliest fin-mounted tailplanes. The vertical tail surface was of very low aspect ratio, thereby reducing the overall height but also contributing to the poor handling qualities that became evident during the flight test programme. The side-by-side pair of floats could be raised to rest

alongside the fuselage, chined bottoms outward, and the centre-section of the parasol wing was transversely angled so that the port wing was mounted higher than the starboard wing, allowing these two outer panels to be folded back on top of one another. The outer wing panels were of constant thickness and chord, swept back, and each braced by a single strut.

During 1941 the **Ar 231 V1** to **Ar 231 V6** prototypes were completed, each powered by the Hirth HM 501 engine driving a two-bladed propeller. The Ar 231 programme was cancelled early in 1942 in favour of the Focke-Achgelis Fa 330 Bachstelze single-seat rotor kite.

The unique configuration of the Ar 231 arose from the need to fold the aircraft for stowage in the tight confines of a submarine.

Arado Ar 232

Early in 1940, work began on the design of a transport aircraft that could initially supplement and then supplant the venerable and ubiquitous Junkers Ju 52/3m tri-motor transport. The types that emerged as contenders in this difficult role were the twin-engined **Arado Ar 232**, three-engined Junkers Ju 252 and Ju 352, and six-engined Messerschmitt Me 323A. It is arguable that the most radical and far-sighted of these designs was the Ar 232, which featured a pod-and-boom fuselage

allowing the incorporation of a hydraulically operated rear loading door, and a novel arrangement of 11 pairs of small wheels to support the fuselage during loading and unloading operations after the main units of the tricycle landing gear arrangement had been partially raised by means of two hydraulic rams. Other features of the design were a high-set wing and a tail unit with the single horizontal surface carrying two endplate vertical surfaces.

The first two prototypes, flown in 1941, were the **Ar 232 V1** and **Ar 232 V2**,

each powered by two 1,600-hp (1193-kW) BMW 801MA radial engines, but the insatiable demands of the Focke-Wulf Fw 190 production lines necessitated a change of engine for subsequent aircraft. The

selection of the lower-powered BMW-Bramo 323B-2 meant that four engines were needed, and the **Ar 232 V3** third prototype therefore introduced a 5-ft 7-in (1.70-m) increase in wing centre-section span to accommodate them. This was the first of 20 **Ar 232B-0** models, some of which saw service with Luftwaffe units, initially on the Eastern Front, and later

in the war with Kampfgeschwader 200, the Luftwaffe's special missions unit.

Although major airframe sections were built, no examples were completed of the **Ar 432**, which was planned as a development of the Ar 232 with wood and steel in place of the strategically important and increasingly scarce light alloys used in the Ar 232.

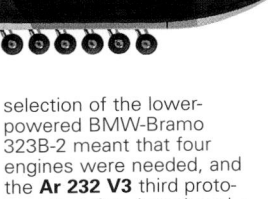

This pre-production standard Ar 232A-0 is seen as it appeared when on the strength of Transportfliegerstaffel 5 in late 1944, employed on special transport duties.

In service, the Ar 232, represented here by the Ar 232 V2, was nicknamed 'Tausendfüssler' (millipede) due to its multi-unit undercarriage.

SPECIFICATION	
Arado Ar 232B-0 **Type:** four-crew medium transport **Powerplant:** four BMW-Bramo 323R-2 radial engines each rated at 1,200 hp (895 kW) **Performance:** maximum speed 211 mph (340 km/h) at 15,090 ft (4600 m); cruising speed 180 mph (290 km/h) at 6,560 ft (2000 m); service ceiling 26,245 ft (8000 m); range 658 miles (1060 km) **Weights:** empty 28,224 lb (12802 kg); maximum take-off 46,595 lb (21135 kg)	**Dimensions:** wing span 109 ft 10¾ in (33.50 m); length 77 ft 2 in (23.52 m); height 18 ft 8 in (5.69 m); wing area 1,534.98 sq ft (142.60 m²) **Armament:** one 0.51-in (13-mm) trainable forward-firing machine-gun in the nose, one or two 0.51-in (13-mm) trainable rearward-firing machine-gun pods at the rear of the fuselage pod and one 20-mm trainable cannon in a power-operated dorsal turret **Payload:** up to 9,921 lb (4500 kg)

Arado Ar 234

Arado's Ar 234 was the first turbojet-powered bomber, despite the fact that it was originally designed in response to a requirement of the German air ministry for a fast reconnaissance aircraft. Work on the Ar 234 began late in 1940 and, early in the following year, the Arado design team completed a project study designated **E.370**. This was the start of a design process that resulted in the emergence in prototype form of the Ar 234 early in 1943. A shoulder-wing monoplane with its engines in nacelles attached to the undersur-

face of the wing, the Ar 234 featured a fuselage whose cross section was so small that it could not incorporate conventional retractable landing gear, a problem initially solved by the adoption of a jettisonable take-off trolley for take-off and extendible skids for landing.

Delays in the development of the Junkers turbojet engines meant that the first shipset of Jumo 004B-0 engines was not delivered until February 1943. The waiting prototype airframe was then fitted with these engines so that taxiing trials could begin in

March. By May, two flight-cleared engines had been installed and the maiden flight took place on 15 June. The original take-off technique was to jettison the trolley upon reaching a height of 195 ft (60 m), five recovery parachutes being deployed to return the

equipment safely to the ground for re-use. The parachute system proved troublesome, however, and after the first two trolleys had been destroyed it was decided that the wheels would be released immediately upon take-off.

The trolley-equipped

version was designated as the **Ar 234A**. The third prototype, which first flew on 22 August 1943, was equipped with RATO

Originally a prototype for the B-series, Ar 234 V13 was rebuilt for C-series trials.

Variants

Ar 234B-0: 20 pre-production aircraft, the majority of which were used for intensive development; without ejection seats or cabin pressurisation

Ar 234B-1: reconnaissance version

Ar 234B-2: bomber version with maximum 4,409-lb (2000-kg) bombload

Ar 234C: production four-engined version with BMW 003A-1 engines; 19th prototype was to this standard and first flown on 30 September 1944

Ar 234C-1: four-engined equivalent of B-1 but with full cabin pressurisation and armed with two 20-mm rearward-firing cannon

Ar 234C-2: four-engined equivalent of B-2

Ar 234C-3: multi-purpose version; 21st to 25th prototypes completed with raised and redesigned cockpits; armed as C-1 but with two additional 20-mm cannon beneath the nose; variable bombload on three ETC 504 racks

Ar 234C-3/N: proposed two-seat night-fighter with two 30-mm and two 20-mm forward-firing cannon as well as FuG 218 Neptun V radar

Ar 234C-4: armed reconnaissance version with two cameras and four 20-mm cannon

Ar 234C-5: 28th prototype was completed with side-by-side seating for pilot and bomb-aimer as development aircraft for this proposed version

Ar 234C-6: proposed two-seat reconnaissance type as pioneered by 29th prototype

Ar 234C-7: night-fighter similar to C-3/N, but with side-by-side crew and enhanced FuG 245 Bremen centimetric radar

Ar 234C-8: proposed single-seat bomber with two 2,381-lb st (10.59-kN) Jumo 004D engines

Ar 234D: 31st to 40th prototypes, under construction at the war's end, were to have been representatives of this version with a powerplant of two 2,866-lb st (12.75-kN) Heinkel-Hirth HeS 011A engines

Ar 234D-1: proposed Heinkel-Hirth HeS 011A-powered reconnaissance type

Ar 234D-2: proposed Heinkel-Hirth HeS 011A-powered bomber

Ar 234P: projected night-fighter series

Ar 234P-1: two-seater with four BMW 003A-1 engines and an armament of one 30-mm and one 20-mm cannon

Ar 234P-2: two-seater with redesigned cockpit protected by 0.51-in (13-mm) armour plate

Ar 234P-3: HeS 011A-powered equivalent of P-2 but with two 30-mm and two 20-mm cannon

Ar 234P-4: as P-3 but with Jumo 004D engines

Ar 234P-5: three-seat version with HeS 011A engines as well as four 30-mm and one 20-mm cannon

An early Ar 234B-1 of Sonderkommando Sperling flying from Rheine in late 1944, this aircraft carries Walter HWK 500A-1 Rauchgeräte RATO (rocket assisted take-off) gear underwing.

units for rocket-assisted take-off, and the pressurised cockpit boasted an ejection seat. The fourth and fifth prototypes flew on 15 September and 20 December 1943, respectively. The next to fly was the eighth prototype, fitted with four 1,764-lb (7.85-kN) BMW 003A-1 engines arranged in pairs; the same powerplant, this time in four separate nacelles, powered the sixth prototype that first flew on 8 April 1944. By then the Junkers 004B engines had been uprated from 1,852 lb (8.24 kN) to 1,962 lb (8.73 kN), and two such engines were installed in the seventh and last of the A-series prototypes.

The inability of the Ar 234 to be moved easily before the wheeled trolley had been fitted was clearly unacceptable in an operational environment, so the B-series (named **Blitz** – lightning) was evolved with a slightly widened fuselage to allow the incorporation of conventional tricycle landing gear, albeit with main units of relatively narrow track. The eighth prototype was

the first of the new model, and first flew on 10 March 1944. It was followed on 2 April by the 10th machine, which lacked cabin pressurisation and an ejection seat, but was fitted with bomb racks beneath the engine nacelles and used to test the BZA bomb-aiming computer. Of the remaining B-series prototypes, the most important was the 13th with two pairs of BMW 003A-1 engines, and the 15th and 17th each with two BMW engines, and used as testbeds to hasten the solving of the turbojet's thrust control problems.

Despite their lack of mobility on the ground, the fifth and seventh proto-

types were subjected during July 1944 to operational evaluation in the reconnaissance role. Fitted with Walter RATO units, these aircraft defied interception during numerous sorties over Allied territory from their base at Reims, France and were later joined by a number of **Ar 234B-1** models which, in small numbers, equipped experimental reconnaissance units. Two units were still operational at the war's end.

The bomber version first became operational with KG 76 and the Ar 234 was also flown by Kommando Bonow, an experimental night-fighter unit.

SPECIFICATION

Arado Ar 234B-2 Blitz
Type: single-seat multi-role warplane
Powerplant: two Junkers Jumo 004B turbojet engines each rated at 1,962 lb st (8.73 kN)
Performance: maximum speed 460 mph (740 km/h) at 19,685 ft (6000 m); climb to 19,685 ft (6000 m) in 17 minutes 30 seconds with 3,307-lb (1500-kg) bombload;

service ceiling 32,810 ft (10000 m); range 1,013 miles (1630 km)
Weights: empty 11,464 lb (5200 kg); maximum take-off 21,715 lb (9850 kg)
Dimensions: wing span 46 ft 3½ in (14.10 m); length 41 ft 5½ in (12.64 m); height 14 ft 1½ in (4.30 m); wing area 284.18 sq ft (26.40 m²)

Arado Ar 240 and Ar 440

In 1938 the German air ministry requested proposals for a fast twin-engined warplane fitted with two FA 13 armament system (a periscopic sighting system and guns in remotely controlled barbettes) installations. The contenders were the Ago Ao 225 and the **E.240** designed by Hans Rebeski and redesignated as the **Arado Ar 240** when awarded a contract. As a result of development problems the barbettes were not fitted to the first two prototypes, which were mid-wing monoplanes powered by two 1,075-hp

(802-kW) Daimler-Benz DB 601A inverted-Vee engines. The second aircraft was armed, but only with two 20-mm forward-firing cannon in the nose and two 0.312-in (7.92-mm) forward-firing machine-guns in the wingroots.

As a result of instability problems with the first two Ar 240 prototypes, the third appeared after major redesign incorporating a 4-ft 1½-in (1.25-m) fuselage 'stretch'. At the same time, the pressurised cockpit was moved forward and a new tailcone, with small fins, replaced the original

tail-mounted dive-brake. First flown in the spring of 1941, this was the first Ar 240 with the FA 13 barbettes: installed one above and the other below the fuselage, both to the rear of the cockpit; each barbette carried two 0.312-in (7.92-mm) machine-guns. The barbettes were removed during the summer of

1941, when two cameras were fitted for a period of operational evaluation with a reconnaissance unit, the 3./Aufklarungsgruppe Oberbefehlshaber der Luftwaffe. The fourth prototype was fitted with two 1,750-hp (1305-kW) DB 603A engines.

A number of pre-production machines were completed and some were flown by Luftwaffe units for operational trials. The Ago factory at Oschersleben

was tasked with the manufacture of 40 production examples of the Ar 240. In December 1942, however, the programme was discontinued as a result of continued teething problems with this ambitious project.

A number of major airframe changes, and the FA 13 system, were incorporated in the marginally improved Ar 240 V3 prototype.

SPECIFICATION

Arado Ar 240A
Type: two-seat multi-role warplane
Powerplant: two Daimler-Benz DB 601E inverted-Vee engines each rated at 1175 hp (877 kW)
Performance: maximum speed 385 mph (620 km/h) at 19,685 ft (6000 m); cruising speed 345 mph (555 km/h) at 19,685 ft (6000 m); climb to 19,685 ft (6000 m) in 11 minutes; service ceiling 34,450 ft (10500 m); range 1,243 miles (2000 km)

Weights: empty 13,669 lb (6200 kg); maximum take-off 20,833 lb (9450 kg)
Dimensions: span 43 ft 9 in (13.33 m); length 42 ft (12.80 m); height 12 ft 11½ in (3.95 m); wing area 336.92 sq ft (31.30 m²)
Armament: two 0.312-in (7.92-mm) fixed forward-firing machine-guns in the wingroots and two FA 13 barbettes each with two 0.312-in (7.92-mm) trainable machine-guns in the ventral and dorsal positions

Arado Ar 240 and Ar 440 (cont.)

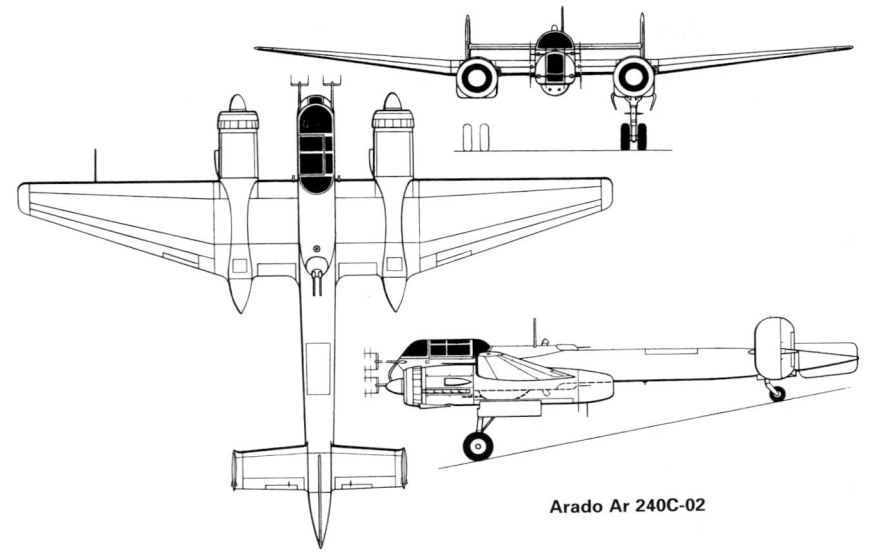

Arado Ar 240C-02

Variants

Ar 240A: five pre-production aircraft, the first two being armed reconnaissance aircraft which appeared in October 1942; the third machine had its DB 601E engines replaced by two 1,880-hp (1402-kW) BMW 801TJ radial engines, and the last two, which were unarmed, had two 1,750-hp (1305-kW) DB 603A engines
Ar 240B: two pre-production examples, flown in October and December 1942, and powered by two 1,475-hp (1100-kW) DB 605A engines with water-methanol injection
Ar 240C: incorporating a new wing of increased span and improved profile; four pre-production examples of this heavy fighter-bomber were flown in 1943, all of them with 1,750-hp (1305-kW) DB 603A-2 engines; the last two had a power boost system which involved the injection of nitrous oxide into the supercharger, and which increased the maximum level speed by 35 mph (56 km/h); the first carried four 20-mm forward-firing cannon and two 0.51-in (13-mm) machine-guns in each of the two barbettes; two additional 20-mm forward-firing cannon were fitted in a ventral housing on the second machine, a night-fighter version; proposed production models, to be powered by 1,900-hp (1417-kW) DB 603G engines, were the **Ar 240C-1** heavy fighter, **Ar 240C-2** night-fighter, **Ar 240C-3** light bomber and **Ar 240C-4** high-altitude reconnaissance aircraft; development was then abandoned in favour of the Ar 440
Ar 440: further development with lengthened fuselage; four prototypes were completed and flown in the summer and autumn of 1942, the first being a rebuild of the third prototype Ar 240, with 1,900-hp (1417-kW) DB 603G engines; production Ar 440 warplanes would have been powered by two 2,000-hp (1491-kW) DB 627A/B engines, but the whole programme was suspended in 1943

Arado Ar 396

The Arado Ar 96 trainer was to have been developed further as the Ar 296 with the higher-rated Argus As 411 engine, but shortages of strategic materials led instead to the introduction of the **Arado Ar 396** with an airframe revised with the minimum amount of metal. At the same time, the aircraft's systems were simplified in features such as manually- rather than power-operated flaps and main landing gear units that

A tandem two-seat basic trainer, the Ar 396 was developed in France.

were only semi-retractable. Development of this cheaper variant was entrusted to the Société Industrielle pour l'Aéronautique (SIPA) in occupied France, and the first of three prototypes flew on 29 December 1944, after France's liberation. Letov in Czechoslovakia was also to

have built the Ar 396, but none reached the Luftwaffe before the cessation of hostilities. SIPA subsequently built more

than 200 examples for the French armed forces in **S.10**, **S.11** and **S.12** variants, the last of them with an all-metal structure.

Variants

Ar 396A-1: advanced flying trainer also operated in the single-seat gunnery trainer role
Ar 396A-2: unarmed instrument flying trainer

SPECIFICATION

Arado Ar 396A-1
Type: two-seat advanced flying trainer
Powerplant: one Argus As 411MA inverted-Vee engine rated at 580 hp (433 kW)
Performance: maximum speed 220 mph (355 km/h) at 7,870 ft (2400 m); cruising speed 171 mph (275 km/h) at sea level; climb to 13,125 ft (4000 m) in 10 minutes 18 seconds; service ceiling 22,960 ft (6900 m); range 373 miles (600 km)
Weights: empty 3,623 lb (1643 kg); maximum take-off 4,541 lb (2060 kg)
Dimensions: wingspan 36 ft 1 in (11.00 m); length 30 ft 5¾ in (9.30 m); height 8 ft ½ in (2.45 m); wing area 196.99 sq ft (18.30 m²)
Armament: one 0.312-in (7.92-mm) fixed forward-firing machine-gun, plus two 110-lb (50-kg) bombs carried on underwing racks

Arado L I

Designed by Dipl. Ing. Hoffmann, the single **Arado L I** parasol-wing monoplane was registered to the Mecklenberg aero club in July 1929, and was an open-cockpit two-seater powered by a Salmson radial engine. Construction was of wood throughout, with plywood and fabric covering. Flown by its designer, the L I was destroyed in a fatal crash at Orly on 5 August 1929, during that year's Europa Rundflug.

Designed for sporting use, the L I accommodated its two occupants in tandem open cockpits.

SPECIFICATION

Arado L I
Type: two-seat sporting aircraft
Powerplant: one 40-hp (30-kW) Salmson 9AD radial engine rated at 40 hp (29.8 kW)
Performance: maximum speed 87 mph (140 km/h) at sea level
Weights: empty 595 lb (270 kg); maximum take-off 1,102 lb (500 kg)
Dimensions: wingspan 32 ft 9¾ in (10.00 m); length 19 ft 8 in (6.00 m); height 7 ft 6¾ in (2.30 m); wing area 156.10 sq ft (14.50 m²)

Arado L II

Registered officially in February 1930, the **Arado L II** designed by Walter Rethel was a two-seat cabin monoplane of mixed construction that included a fabric-covered welded steel tube fuselage and wooden wings. Power was provided by an Argus As 8 four-cylinder inline engine.

The **L IIa** was a development with folding wings and modified landing gear, and four of these aircraft took part in the 1930 Europa Rundflug. The L IIa differed from the L II in details such as its empty weight of 915 lb (415 kg), maximum take-off weight of 1,543 lb (700 kg), wingspan of 36 ft 1 in (11.00 m) and wing area of 182.99 sq ft (17.00 m²).

A revised undercarriage and space-saving folding wings were two features differentiating the L IIa (illustrated) from the L II.

SPECIFICATION

Arado L II
Type: two-seat cabin monoplane
Powerplant: one Argus As 8 inverted inline piston engine rated at 80 hp (59.6 kW)
Performance: maximum speed 99.5 mph (160 km/h) at 3,280 ft (1000 m)
Weights: empty 893 lb (405 kg); maximum take-off 1,477 lb (670 kg)
Dimensions: wingspan 34 ft 5¾ in (10.50 m); length 22 ft ½ in (6.72 m); height 7 ft 5¾ in (2.28 m); wing area 171.15 sq ft (15.90 m²)

Arado S I and S III

The Arado Handelsgesellschaft GmbH was founded in 1925, taking over the factory established at Warnemunde on the German coast by Flugzeugbau Friedrichshafen GmbH in 1917. The company's first product, which appeared in the year of its foundation, was the **Arado S I** sporting aircraft, a two-seater of sesquiplane configuration with open accommodation and power provided by a 100-hp (74.6-kW) Bristol Lucifer radial engine. Only one example was built, together with two **S Ia** aircraft that differed from the S I only in their powerplant of one 110-hp (82-kW) Siemens-Halske Sh.12 radial engine. This engine type was also used for the very similar **S III**, an aircraft that differed only in detail from the S Ia standard.

Arado's S Ia was a re-engined, but otherwise similar, version of the S I.

Left: A number of detail changes led to the redesignated Arado S III. All three models were built in very limited numbers.

SPECIFICATION

Arado S I
Type: two-seat sporting aircraft
Powerplant: one Bristol Lucifer radial engine rated at 100 hp (74.6 kW)
Performance: maximum speed 91 mph (147 km/h) at sea level
Weights: empty 1,323 lb (600 kg); maximum take-off 2,017 lb (915 kg)
Dimensions: wingspan 37 ft 8¾ in (11.50 m); length 24 ft 1⅜ in (7.35 m); height 8 ft 8⅓ in (2.65 m); wing area 283.10 sq ft (26.30 m²)

Arado SC I and SC II

An improved and strengthened version of the S I with a somewhat more powerful engine to make it more capable in the flying training role, the **Arado SC I** appeared in 1926 and was of similar construction to its predecessor. The type was evaluated for use at the clandestine German flying school at Lipezk in the USSR, but in the event the aircraft of the small production batch that followed the prototype were delivered to the Deutsche Verkehrsfliegerschule (DVS) located outside Berlin. The school was officially engaged in the training of civil pilots, but many of these were, of course, destined for Germany' secret air force. The very similar **SC II** was introduced in 1928 with a further increase in available power through the installation of the 320-hp (239-kW) BMW Va engine. The SC II appeared at the 1928 Berlin and Paris shows and, like the SC I, was adopted as a trainer at the DVS.

SPECIFICATION

Arado SC I
Type: two-seat training aircraft
Powerplant: one BMW IV inline piston engine rated at 230 hp (172 kW)
Performance: maximum speed 114 mph (183 km/h) at sea level; service ceiling 17,060 ft (5200 m)
Weights: empty 2,205 lb (1000 kg); maximum take-off 3,307 lb (1500 kg)
Dimensions: wingspan 42 ft 4⅔ in (12.92 m); length 31 ft 9⅞ in (9.70 m); height 10 ft 2 in (3.10 m); wing area 315.39 sq ft (29.30 m²)

Structural strengthening, more power and revised cockpits created the SC I out of the S I.

Arado SD I

A potent-looking fighter design, the SD I was denied a production order in favour of the improved SD II.

The Arado company's first fighter design was the **Arado SD I**, which was the work of Ing. Walter Rethel after he had joined the company from the Fokker works at Schwerin. As a result, the SD I revealed a measure of Fokker influence in its overall configuration and construction. The latter included a fuselage of welded steel tube covered with light alloy forward of the single-seat cockpit and fabric to the rear of this line, a wire-braced tail unit of fabric-covered welded steel tube, and a wing cellule of wooden construction covered with plywood and fabric. This highly staggered wing cellule was of the sesquiplane type with an upper wing that was considerably larger than the lower wing, although both surfaces were similar in shape as they were tapered in thickness and chord to their rounded tips. The upper and lower wings were separated on each side by a single set of N-type interplane struts angled out from bottom to top, lacked flying and landing wires, and had long-span ailerons only on the outer panels of the upper wing. The fixed tailskid landing gear included a main unit of the through-axle type with a shock absorber in each forward unit of the Vee struts.

Designed and constructed as the first fighter ordered by the German war ministry for the clandestine German air force, the SD I was destined to be built only in prototype form. The first of the two SD I prototypes made its maiden flight on 27 October 1927, and trials revealed generally adequate performance and handling except at the low-speed end of the flight envelope. The latter, combined with official distrust of the aircraft's structural integrity, was sufficient for the ministry to order a termination of the development programme in favour of the completely new Arado SD II design.

SPECIFICATION

Arado SD I
Type: single-seat fighter
Powerplant: one Gnome-Rhóne (Bristol) Jupiter radial engine rated at 425 hp (317 kW)
Performance: maximum speed 171 mph (275 km/h) at 16,405 ft (5000 m)
Weights: empty 1,874 lb (850 kg); maximum take-off 2,712 lb (1230 kg)
Dimensions: wingspan 27 ft 6¾ in (8.40 m); length 22 ft 1¾ in (6.75 m)
Armament: two 0.312-in (7.92-mm) fixed forward-firing machine-guns

Arado SD II

Although of similar construction to the SD I, with a welded steel tube fuselage and empennage and wooden wing cellule, all under a covering of light alloy and fabric on the fuselage, fabric on the empennage, and plywood and fabric on the wing cellule, the **Arado SD II** was a single-seat fighter designed by Ing. Walter Rethel was both larger and considerably heavier than its predecessor. Other significant changes from the SD I were a strut-braced tailplane, a wing cellule with panels of constant thickness and chord, as well as N-type interplane struts and conventional flying and landing wires. In addition, the main landing gear was revised, with each wheel carried by a Vee strut extending from the fuselage centreline and braced by a shock-absorber strut rising to the relevant lower longeron, and a three- rather than two-bladed slow-turning propeller to absorb the power of the geared radial engine that was installed in a lower-drag nose installation than the engine of the SD I.

The SD II was designed for competitive evaluation against the Heinkel HD 37, and the sole example of this machine flew in 1929. The prototype revealed distinctly tricky handling characteristics, and its development was soon terminated.

SPECIFICATION

Arado SD II
Type: single-seat fighter
Powerplant: one Bristol Jupiter VI radial engine rated at 530 hp (395 kW)
Performance: maximum speed 146 mph (235 km/h) at 16,405 ft (5000 m)
Weights: empty 3,186 lb (1445 kg); maximum take-off 3,902 lb (1770 kg)
Dimensions: wingspan 32 ft 5¾ in (9.90 m); length 24 ft 4¼ in (7.40 m); wing area 247.58 sq ft (23.00 m²)
Armament: two 0.312-in (7.92-mm) fixed forward-firing machine-guns

Unusual for its period in being driven by a three-bladed propeller, the SD II was unsuccessful due to poor handling characteristics. The propeller was of wooden construction, as clearly illustrated.

Arado SD III

The **Arado SD III** was based on essentially the same airframe as the SD II. It differed from this type, with which it was built in parallel, only in its powerplant (a direct-drive Jupiter VI engine manufactured under licence in Germany by Siemens und Halske and driving a two- rather than three-bladed propeller) and in details of the airframe. The latter, dictated by the nature of the powerplant installation, included a shorter and more angular forward fuselage, and a shorter main landing gear arrangement (of greater forward rake), made possible by the smaller diameter of the propeller.

Flown for the first time in 1929, the SD III was not ordered into massed production, but it and its close relation, the SD II, were of importance as the direct ancestors of the Ar 64. This did enter limited production as the precursor of the more extensively-built Ar 65.

SPECIFICATION

Arado SD III
Type: single-seat fighter
Powerplant: one Siemens-Halske (Bristol) Jupiter VI radial engine rated at 510 hp (380 kW)
Performance: maximum speed 140 mph (225 km/h) at 13,125 ft (4000 m)
Dimensions: wingspan 32 ft 5¾ in (9.90 m); length 25 ft 5⅛ in (7.75 m); wing area 247.58 sq ft (23.00 m²)
Armament: two 0.312-in (7.92-mm) fixed forward-firing machine-guns

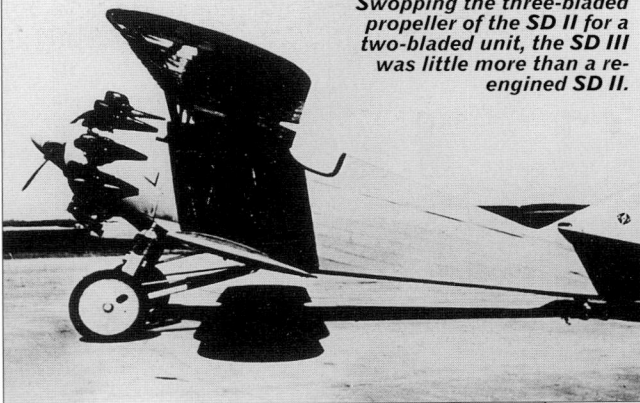

Swopping the three-bladed propeller of the SD II for a two-bladed unit, the SD III was little more than a re-engined SD II.

Arado SSD I

The introduction of efficient aircraft-launching catapults, which made it feasible for floatplanes to be operated effectively from ships at sea, encouraged Ing. Walter Rethel to design the **Arado SSD I** single-seat fighter floatplane. As with Rethel's landplane fighters, this type's very existence and role were kept a close secret in view of the restrictions placed by the Allied powers on Germany after World War I.

The SSD I bore no design commonality with the SD series of landplane fighter prototypes. In overall terms, it was an unequal-span staggered biplane (the halves of the upper wing very slightly gulled into the outer edges of the fuselage's upper surface just forward of the cockpit and the halves of the lower wing extended from the lower corners on the tunnel-type ventral radiator installation below the fuselage). The alighting gear was based on a single main float carried by wire-braced N-type struts and complemented by a pair of small stabilising floats strut-mounted under the outboard ends of the lower wing.

The fuselage was of welded steel tube construction covered with light alloy panels and fabric, while the empennage was of welded steel tube construction covered with fabric and included a strut-braced tailplane. The wings were of plywood-covered wooden construction with N-type interplane struts, normal flying and landing wires and, for the first time on an Arado fighter, ailerons on the lower as well as the upper wing.

The sole prototype, registered D-1905, was evaluated in 1930 at Travemunde in floatplane configuration, and was then revised with simple wheeled landing gear for further trials at Germany's secret training base at Lipezk in the USSR. The small production order was then given over to the rival Heinkel HD 38, and the SSD I was allocated to the Deutsche Verkehrsflieger-schule outside Berlin as a trainer in 1932.

SPECIFICATION

Arado SSD I
Type: single-seat fighter floatplane
Powerplant: one BMW VI 6,3 Vee engine rated at 650 hp (485 kW)
Performance: maximum speed 174 mph (280 km/h) at optimum altitude; service ceiling 21,325 ft (6500 m)
Weights: empty 3,587 lb (1627 kg); maximum take-off 4,475 lb (2030 kg)
Dimensions: wingspan 32 ft 9¾ in (10.00 m); length 27 ft 10⅞ in (8.50 m); wing area 333.69 sq ft (31.00 m²)
Armament: two 0.312-in (7.92-mm) fixed forward-firing machine-guns

With an airframe specially strengthened to withstand the stresses of repeated catapult launches, just one example of the SSD I was built, undergoing initial tests in 1929. No production orders for this attractive fighter were placed.

Arado W II

Two **Arado W II** twin-float seaplane trainers were built and registered to the Deutsche Verkehrsflieger-schule in June and December 1928. The W II was a low-wing monoplane and in constructional detail had a fabric-covered steel tube fuselage with a tandem arrangement of open cockpits and an engine nacelle that was an unusual forward extension of the lower nose. The wing was a two-spar wooden structure with fabric covering and the simple empennage included single horizontal and vertical surfaces (the fin braced from the

tailplane by a single strut on each side) with balanced control surfaces. A side-by-side pair of wooden floats was carried under the inboard ends of the wing by a wire-braced arrange-ment of steel struts.

The W II was a valuable floatplane trainer for Germany's emerging Luftwaffe.

SPECIFICATION	
Arado W II	**Weights:** empty 3,704 lb
Type: two-seat seaplane trainer	(1680 kg); maximum take-off
Powerplant: one Siemens-Halske	4,398 lb (1995 kg)
Sh.12 radial engine rated at 112 hp	**Dimensions:** wingspan 57 ft 1 in
(83.5 kW)	(17.40 m); length 41 ft 2 in
Performance: maximum speed	(12.55 m); height 10 ft 6 in
90 mph (145 km/h) at sea level;	(3.20 m); wing area 578.04 sq ft
service ceiling 6,760 ft (2060 m)	(53.70 m²)

Arctic Aircraft S1B2 Arctic Tern

The Interstate S-1B Cadet was one of a number of two-seat high-wing light aircraft ordered by the US Army for observation and liaison work early in World War II; others included the Piper Cub as well as designs by Aeronca, Taylorcraft and Stinson. The Cadet went to war under the US Army designation L-6, and 250 such aircraft were delivered. A fair number of these aircraft survived to pass into civil hands after the end of the war, but these soon dwin-dled to a mere handful of highly cherished aircraft.

The design was resur-rected, however, as the **Arctic Aircraft S1B2 Arctic Tern**, of which a small number was built by a company located at Anchorage, Alaska. Whereas the original Cadet had been based on the 102-hp (76-kW) Franklin flat-four engine, the Tern had a 150-hp (112-kW) Avco Lycoming O-320 engine. The introduction of improved constructional techniques and modern materials resulted in a 40-lb (18-kg) reduction in empty weight by compari-son with the 1940 standard. Optional fittings were floats and skis (essential for Alaskan oper-

An interesting rejuvenation of an existing design, the Arctic Tern used the basic airframe of the Interstate S-1 to produce an attractive utility aircraft which could be flown from wheel, ski or – as illustrated – float landing gear.

ations) as alternatives to the standard wheels, and another option was a ventrally-mounted auxiliary fuel tank or freight container. The Arctic Tern's rear seat was removable to give additional space for cargo, and the front seat could be folded to facilitate loading and unloading oper-ations. The two-place cabin was soundproofed and carpeted.

SPECIFICATION	
Arctic Aircraft S1B2 Arctic Tern	19,000 ft (5790 m); range 652 miles
Type: two-seat general utility	(1049 km)
aircraft	**Weights:** empty 1,073 lb
Powerplant: one Avco Lycoming	(4487 kg); maximum take-off
O-320 flat-four engine rated at	1,900 lb (862 kg)
150 hp (112 kW)	**Dimensions:** wingspan 36 ft
Performance: maximum speed	(10.97 m); length 24 ft (7.32 m);
175 mph (282 km/h) at sea level;	height 7 ft (2.13 m); wing area
cruising speed 117 mph (188 km/h)	186.00 sq ft (17.28 m²)
at sea level; service ceiling	

Armstrong Whitworth F.K.3

The Dutch designer Frederick Koolhoven joined Armstrong Whitworth in 1914 as the head of its new air department, and was responsible for a series of aircraft which bore his initials in their designations. The first two of these were the **F.K.1** biplane, of which only a single example was built, and the **F.K.2** simplified version of the RAF B.E.2c, of which seven were completed. Considerably greater success attended Koolhoven's next design, which was the **Armstrong Whitworth F.K.3**. This was another attempt to improve upon the B.E.2c, which Armstrong Whitworth was preparing to build for the Royal Flying Corps. When, in September 1915, the RFC in France advised against further production of the F.K.2, the order for the outstanding balance of 93 F.K.2 aircraft was trans-ferred to the F.K.3.

The F.K.3 was, in effect, the B.E.2c with a completely new tail unit incorporating a horn-balanced rudder and a tapered horizontal surface including an adjustable tailplane. In addition, the crew positions were reversed to locate the pilot in the front cockpit, the decking between the two cockpits was removed, and two sliding mountings for a Lewis gun were added in the rear cockpit.

The prototype had a 70-hp (52-kW) Renault engine, but production models used the RAF 1a engine rated at 90 hp (67.1 kW) or, in a few early aircraft, a Beardmore inline engine rated at 120 hp (89.5 kW); in each case, the engine drove a four-bladed propeller. Comparative trials at Upavon in May 1916 proved the slight superiority of the F.K.3 to the B.E.2c in performance terms, and this allowed the implemen-tation of the order placed in the previous year with Armstrong Whitworth. Further orders for a total of 400 aircraft were placed, the bulk coming from Luton-based Hewlett & Blondeau, and the remain-der from Armstrong Whitworth, but it is not certain that all of these aircraft were completed.

The Royal Flying Corps' No. 47 Squadron at Salonika was the only overseas-based unit to receive the Armstrong Whitworth F.K.3, which it operated for a vari-ety of operational duties. The great majority of these aircraft were retained in the UK, however, for use mainly in the training role, a task for which they proved very suitable until replaced by Avro Type 504 machines. Four war-surplus aircraft were used by civil opera-tors, but were short-lived.

This F.K.3 is one of a likely total of 300 built by Hewlett & Blondeau. The type's close similarity to the B.E.2c includes the centrally-mounted skid.

SPECIFICATION	
Armstrong Whitworth F.K.3	endurance 3 hours
Type: two-seat general-purpose	**Weights:** empty 1,386 lb (629 kg);
and training aircraft	maximum take-off 2,056 lb (983 kg)
Powerplant: one RAF 1a Vee	**Dimensions:** wingspan 40 ft ⅝ in
engine rated at 90 hp (67.1 kW)	(12.21 m); length 29 ft (8.84 m);
Performance: maximum speed	height 11 ft 10¾ in (3.63 m); wing
89 mph (143 km/h) at sea level;	area 442.00 sq ft (41.06 m²)
climb to 6,500 ft (1980 m) in	**Armament:** one or occasionally
26 minutes 30 seconds; service	two 0.303-in (7.7-mm) trainable
ceiling 12,000 ft (3660 m);	machine-guns in the rear cockpit

Armstrong Whitworth F.K.5 and F.K.6

There exists a measure of confusion about the exact nature of the three designs by Frederick Koolhoven for Armstrong Whitworth after the F.K.3. It seems probable, however, that the **F.K.4** was an airship car design based on the fuselage of the F.K.3, and that the **Armstrong Whitworth F.K.5** and **F.K.6** were two variants of a large triplane machine. The basic design of the triplane probably resulted from the considerable enthusiasm evident in British aeronautical thinking early in World War I for the so-called 'flying battleship' or 'aerial destroyer', which would be a substantial warplane possessing considerable endurance and heavy firepower. The latter took the form of multiple gun positions disposed for maximum fields of fire. It was felt that such an aircraft, which was in effect a heavy fighter, would provide its operators with a platform for the destruction of all aerial opponents. No thought had been given, however, to the practical matters of how such aerial behemoths, wholly defi-

cient in performance and agility, could bring an enemy to action if that enemy chose not to seek an engagement.

Multi-seat fighter designs were prepared by Armstrong Whitworth, Sopwith and Vickers, although it was the former's F.K.5 that was without doubt the most bizarre. The need to carry several gunners required a large airframe and thus a powerful engine, and for this task the new 250-hp (186-kW) Rolls-Royce Vee engine, later named the Eagle, was selected. The F.K.5 then began to mature as a large machine with a single-bay triplane wing cellule in which the central wing was of considerably greater span than the upper and lower wings. This central wing was braced by wires to the upper and lower wings, carried the ailerons on the outboard ends of its trailing edges, and supported on its upper surface, mid-way between the centreline and the interplane struts, two nacelles for gunners. These were located as far forward as

possible, ahead of the four-bladed propeller located at the front of a fuselage extending only marginally ahead of the central wing's leading edge. This fuselage extended to the rear to carry the pilot's cockpit (in a location to the rear of the wing cellule where he had very poor fields of vision) and the wire-braced tail unit. The tailskid landing gear was based on a central shock-absorber leg carrying a side-by-side pair of closely spaced wheels, and ground stability was provided by a single small wheel under each tip of the lower wing.

The F.K.5 was completed but never flown, which is perhaps fortunate for its crew as the aircraft's structure appeared extremely flimsy. However, the

concept was then taken farther by the F.K.6 that resulted from a British army requirement for a multi-seat escort fighter and airship destroyer. The F.K.6 was a larger triplane of more practical appearance, with a sturdier fuselage of increased size, which filled the gap between the lower and central wing as well as projecting some distance ahead of the wings' leading edges. The two-bay wing cellule featured less disparity between the span of the central wing and that of the upper and lower wings, while the gunner's nacelles were located under the

leading edge of the central wing in line with the inboard sets of interplane struts. A main landing gear arrangement, with two closely-spaced sets of wheels carried by a cross-axle supported at the bottom of two short but sturdy legs, was fitted.

Only one of the four F.K.6 prototypes ordered in March 1916 was completed and was sometimes erroneously known by the **F.K.12** designation. This aircraft undertook only perfunctory flight trials before the programme was terminated, it having become clear some time before that the unwieldy triplane 'aerial destroyer' concept was a technical and tactical dead end.

Two large box-like structures, mounted on the middle wing and protruding some way ahead of its leading edge, represented the accommodation provided for the F.K.5's two machine-gunners.

SPECIFICATION

Armstrong Whitworth F.K.6
Type: three-seat escort and anti-airship fighter
Powerplant: one Rolls-Royce Eagle Vee engine rated at 250 hp (186 kW)

Dimensions: wingspan 62 ft (18.90 m); length 37 ft (11.28 m); height 17 ft (5.18 m)
Armament: not fitted, but planned as two 2- or 6-lb (0.91- or 2.72-kg) trainable Davis recoilless guns

Armstrong Whitworth F.K.7 and F.K.8

Completed in prototype form during the summer of 1916, the **Armstrong Whitworth F.K.7** was designed by Frederick Koolhoven as a two-seat warplane embodying all the lessons that had been learned about the needs of general-purpose aircraft in the first part of World War I. The aircraft was therefore based on the smallest feasible airframe and the most powerful practical engine for a high power/weight ratio and thus good performance in combination with adequate manoeuvrability. In overall terms, the type was of typi-

cal wire-braced wooden construction under a covering of fabric except around the engine, where light alloy panels were used.

In configuration, the F.K.7 was a two-bay biplane with fixed tailskid landing gear including a main unit with oleo shock absorbers. Closely-spaced cockpits for the pilot and observer/gunner were provided, and armament took the form of one Vickers fixed forward-firing machine-gun and one Lewis trainable machine-gun on a Scarff ring mounting over the rear cockpit. The powerful control surfaces included a

horn-balanced rudder.

At this time, the Royal Flying Corps had just ordered the RAF R.E.8 as its new battlefield reconnaissance and observation type, but decided to order a batch of 50 Armstrong Whitworth aircraft as an insurance against unforeseen problems with the R.E.8. The first of these aircraft were completed very rapidly by August 1916 with the revised designation **F.K.8**. The type entered service with No. 35

Squadron, which moved to France in January 1917, and in France the new type found general favour except for its landing gear (replaced by that of the Bristol F.2 Fighter), horn-balanced rudder (altered to a pattern less susceptible to jamming as a result of combat damage), inverted-

Vee radiator installation (modified with larger-diameter tubes to prevent 'furring' and later replaced by a pair of lateral radiators), and Armstrong Whitworth synchronising gear for the fixed forward-firing gun (replaced by the Constantinesco gear).

These and other changes made the F.K.8 into a good type that soon gained the nickname 'Big Ack-W' to

This view of an early-production F.K.8 demonstrates the original undercarriage installation. A somewhat unorthodox structure, and with a single main strut, the undercarriage proved susceptible to failure.

SPECIFICATION

Armstrong Whitworth F.K.8
Type: two-seat general-purpose aircraft
Powerplant: one Beardmore inline engine rated at 160 hp (119 kW)
Performance: maximum speed 99 mph (159 km/h) at sea level; climb to 5,000 ft (1525 m) in 11 minutes; service ceiling 13,000 ft (3960 m); endurance 3 hours
Weights: empty 1,916 lb (869 kg);

normal take-off 2,811 lb (1285 kg); maximum take-off 3,011 lb (1366 kg)
Dimensions: wingspan 43 ft 6 in (13.26 m); length 31 ft (9.45 m); height 11 ft (3.35 m); wing area 540.00 sq ft (50.17 m²)
Armament: one 0.303-in (7.7-mm) fixed forward-firing machine-gun and one 0.303-in (7.7-mm) trainable rearward-firing machine-gun, plus up to 200 lb (91 kg) of bombs carried externally

Angus Sanderson & Co was awarded a contract for 200 F.K.8s, including the aircraft illustrated, on 5 July 1918.

differentiate it from the F.K.3 or 'Little Ack-W'. The success of the type was reflected in a steady expansion of orders placed with Armstrong Whitworth and Angus Sanderson, and total production is thought to have been in the order of 1,650 aircraft. The F.K.8 served operationally in France, Macedonia and Palestine (six, two and one squadrons, respectively) as well as in the UK (15 home defence, training and work-ing-up squadrons in addition to a number of specialised training schools).

Eight F.K.8 aircraft passed onto the civil register after World War I, the two most noteworthy examples being those operated in Australia by the Queensland and Northern Territory Aerial Services Ltd (later QANTAS) as charter machines. The remainder had all been written off by the end of 1920.

Armstrong Whitworth F.K.9 and F.K.10

The success of the Sopwith Triplane (imitated by a number of German triplane fighters) and earlier experience with a pair of altogether larger and wholly unsuccessful triplane 'aerial destroyer' fighters (the F.K.5 and F.K.6), combined to persuade Frederick Koolhoven that it was worth investigating the quadruplane layout in an attempt to create a highly agile fighter. The type was to derive its agility from the combination of the maximum lifting area within the minimum overall dimensions. Koolhoven's first quadruplane is believed to have been designated as the **Armstrong Whitworth F.K.9**. It was a two-seat fighter of typical design and construction for its period with the exception of its

highly staggered cellule of four basically identical wings, each with an aileron on the outboard ends of its trailing edge. The top and bottom wings each had a centre section, that of the latter carried under the fuselage by lower extensions of the parallel cabane struts. The latter carried the centre section of the upper wing at their tops and the inboard ends of the two middle wings on each side of their vertical centrepoints.

The F.K.9 was powered by one 110-hp (82-kW) Clerget rotary engine and its performance, when the aircraft was tested at the Central Flying School near Upavon in Wiltshire, was found to be disappointing. The F.K.9's other data included a maximum speed of 100 mph

(161 km/h) at sea level, the ability to climb to 6,000 ft (1830 m) in 12 minutes 30 seconds, service ceiling of 13,000 ft (3960 m), endurance of 3 hours, empty weight of 1,226 lb (556 kg), maximum take-off weight of 2,038 lb (924 kg), wingspan of 27 ft 9 in (8.46 m), length of 25 ft 10 in (7.87 m), height of 11 ft 4 in (3.45 m) and wing area of 355.00 sq ft (32.98 m²).

The F.K.9's lack of success led to the completion of a second aircraft, the **F.K.10**, with a number

of modifications. These included the installation of an uprated powerplant of one 130-hp (96.9-kW) Clerget rotary piston engine, although the 110-hp (82-kW) Clerget and Le Rhône rotary engines were also installed from time to time.

There was little improvement in performance, and the F.K.10 was not destined for a long career.

A few aircraft were built by Armstrong Whitworth (2), Angus Sanderson (5) and Phoenix Dynamo (2), but it is not clear why the limited production run of only 60 machines was not contracted to a single company. At least three of the aircraft were for the Royal Naval Air Service, where they were considered to be unsafe and these, along with the RFC aircraft, were withdrawn by mid-1917 and used as ground targets.

Two examples of the F.K.10, including this aircraft, were completed by the Phoenix Dynamo company. Koolhoven was not deterred by the failure of the F.K.10. He went on to design, but not build, the 15-wing F.K.11.

SPECIFICATION

Armstrong Whitworth F.K.10
Type: two-seat fighter and reconnaissance aircraft
Powerplant: one Clerget rotary piston engine rated at 130 hp (96.9 kW)
Performance: maximum speed 95 mph (153 km/h) at 3,000 ft (915 m); climb to 6,500 ft (1980 m) in 15 minutes 50 seconds; climb to 10,000 ft (3050 m) in 37 minutes 12 seconds; service ceiling 10,000 ft (3050 m); endurance

2 hours 30 minutes
Weights: empty 1,236 lb (561 kg); maximum take-off 2,019 lb (916 kg)
Dimensions: wingspan 27 ft 10 in (8.48 m); length 22 ft 3 in (6.78 m); height 11 ft 6 in (3.51 m); wing area 390.40 sq ft (36.27 m²)
Armament: one 0.303-in (7.7-mm) fixed forward-firing machine-gun and one 0.303-in (7.7-mm) trainable rearward-firing machine-gun

Armstrong Whitworth A.W.XIV Starling

Designed by John Lloyd to meet an official requirement of 1926, the **Armstrong Whitworth A.W.XIV Starling** was a single-seat fighter of typical design and construction for its period. In configuration, the aircraft was a single-bay biplane with a staggered unequal-span wing cellule (including a flat upper wing with ailerons and a dihedralled lower wing without ailerons) of fabric-covered mixed steel and wood construction, a fabric-covered steel tube fuselage, a neat tail unit with an adjustable tailplane and horn-balanced rudder. Its fixed tailskid landing gear included a main unit of

the spreader-bar type with oleo-pneumatic shock-absorbers in the forward units of the two Vee struts.

The Air Ministry ordered two A.W.XIV prototypes, and the first of these flew on 19 May 1927 with the powerplant of one 385-hp (287-kW) Armstrong Siddeley Jaguar VII radial engine in an exposed installation at the front of the fuselage to drive a two-bladed propeller fitted with a spinner. The engine was later altered to a Jaguar IV supercharged unit rated at 410 hp (307 kW) at 9,000 ft (2745 m) and installed with its cylinder heads enclosed in a narrow-chord Townend ring cowling.

The other details of the Starling with the Jaguar VII engine included a maximum speed of 177.5 mph (286 km/h) at 15,000 ft

(4570 m), the ability to climb to 10,000 ft (3050 m) in 7 minutes, service ceiling of 27,600 ft (8410 m), empty weight of 2,060 lb

(934 kg), maximum take-off weight of 3,095 lb (1404 kg), wingspan of 31 ft 4 in (9.55 m), length of 25 ft 2 in (7.67 m), height of 10 ft 6 in (3.20 m), and wing area of 264.40 sq ft (22.89 m²).

Starling Mk II A-2 featured narrow-chord wings. One or possibly two other Starlings were built with broad-chord wings.

Armstrong Whitworth A.W.XIV Starling (cont.)

The Starling's lack of success in its initial form meant that the second prototype was not completed and a new fighter was designed as the Starling Mk II, whereupon the first machine became the Starling Mk I. The new prototype was conceptually and structurally akin to the Starling

Mk I, but was in fact a completely new machine. Up to three **Starling Mk II** prototypes were completed and evaluated in 1930, one of them ordered to meet the original 1926 requirement for a land-based fighter, and the other two as private-venture machines with a wing cellule of increased area in

an effort to satisfy a fleet fighter requirement of 1926. Apart from the difference in their wing areas, the main alteration between the two subvariants was the Townend ring cowling installed over the engines of the fleet fighter prototypes. Neither subvariant gained any production orders.

SPECIFICATION	
Armstrong Whitworth A.W.XIV Starling Mk II	(3050 m) in 6 minutes 30 seconds
Type: single-seat interceptor fighter	**Weights:** maximum take-off 3,225 lb (1463 kg)
Powerplant: one Armstrong Siddeley Panther IIIA radial engine rated at 540 hp (403 kW)	**Dimensions:** wingspan 34 ft 3 in (10.44 m); length 24 ft 8½ in (7.53 m); height 11 ft 10 in (3.64 m); wing area 258.50 sq ft (24.01 m²)
Performance: maximum speed 184 mph (295 km/h) at 5,000 ft (1525 m); climb to 10,000 ft	**Armament:** two 0.303-in (7.7-mm) fixed forward-firing machine-guns

Armstrong Whitworth A.W.XV Atalanta

The Armstrong Whitworth Argosy biplane airliner did not differ appreciably in appearance from the other air transports that appeared soon after World War I, but the next few years witnessed a remarkable transformation to conceptually more advanced airliners. One of the first of this new generation of British monoplane airliners was the **Armstrong Whitworth A.W.XV Atalanta**. Ordered by Imperial Airways for its services in South Africa and between Karachi and Singapore, the A.W.XV was developed in response to a requirement calling for the ability to carry a 3,000-lb (1361-kg) payload, maintain 9,000 ft (2745 m) with one of its four engines stopped, and cruise at 115 mph (185 km/h). An obvious necessity with these routes was the ability to use small airfields at high altitudes in hot countries, and a range of 400 to 600 miles (645 to 966 km) was required.

The first Atalanta flew on 6 June 1932, and appeared at the first Society of British Aircraft Constructors display at Hendon on 27 June, going to Martlesham Heath for tests on 11 July and receiving its certificate of airworthiness in August. The remarkable speed with which this was achieved reflects the soundness of the basic design, and all eight Atalanta aircraft for Imperial Airways had been certificated by April 1933.

The first service was flown from Croydon, to Brussels and Cologne on 26 September 1932, and other routes followed. The first machine was severely damaged in a forced landing at Coventry on 20 October 1932 while in the manufacturer's charge for modifications, and the aircraft's individual name of *Atalanta* was transferred to the fourth aircraft, which had a sufficiently similar registration to avoid press

questions! The accident was caused by fuel starvation, but the aircraft was repaired and re-appeared with the name *Arethusa*.

The first aircraft left Croydon on 5 January 1933 for its proving flight to Cape Town, arriving on 14 February. Three more Atalanta aircraft joined it at the Germiston base in South Africa, for service between Cape Town and Kisumu in Kenya. Originally to replace de Havilland D.H.66 aircraft, they were too small for the traffic and therefore complemented rather than supplanted the older aircraft. A proving

flight to Australia in June 1933 attracted considerable interest but no order, QANTAS choosing instead the de Havilland D.H.86. On 1 July 1933, however, the first Atalanta inaugurated the direct air mail service between London and Karachi where, upon arrival, the mail was delivered to Indian Trans-Continental Airways. A second aircraft for Indian registry arrived soon afterwards and these two machines, plus two British-registered Atalanta aircraft, operated a Karachi-Calcutta service, later extended to Rangoon and Singapore.

Three Atalanta transports were lost before World War II, while the remaining five were taken over by the British Overseas Airways Corporation and in March 1941 were impressed into RAF service, based in India. They were later handed over to the Indian Air Force's No. 101 (GR) Squadron at Madras and used for coastal reconnaissance work, being armed with a single machine-gun operated by the navigator. One Atalanta was destroyed in a crash landing, and the last patrol was flown on 30 August 1942, after which the four survivors were withdrawn from service.

SPECIFICATION	
Armstrong Whitworth A.W.XV Atalanta	in 21 minutes 30 seconds; service ceiling 14,200 ft (4330 m); range 640 miles (1030 km)
Type: three-crew medium transport aircraft	**Weights:** empty 13,940 lb (6323 kg); maximum take-off 21,000 lb (9525 kg)
Powerplant: four Armstrong Siddeley Serval III radial engines each rated at 340 hp (254 kW)	**Dimensions:** wingspan 90 ft (27.43 m); length 71 ft 6 in (21.79 m); height 15 ft (4.57 m); wing area 1,285.00 sq ft (119.38 m²)
Performance: maximum speed 156 mph (251 km/h) at 3,000 ft (915 m); maximum cruising speed 130 mph (209 km/h) at 9,000 ft (2745 m); climb to 9,000 ft (2745 m)	**Payload:** between nine and 17 passengers plus freight

The Atalanta originally carried just nine passengers and a crew of three, with a considerable amount of payload space being allocated to mail. Later in its career, the A.W.XV's seating was increased to accommodate 17 passengers.

Armstrong Whitworth A.W.XVI

Designed in response to 1926 requirements issued by the Air Ministry for a naval fighter and a land fighter, the

Armstrong Whitworth A.W.XVI was initially built to the extent of two prototypes that made their first flights in

1931. The first of these machines was completed as the prototype of the proposed naval version, while the second was a landplane, and both machines were initially powered by the 540-hp (403-kW) Armstrong Siddeley Panther IIIA radial engine, a geared and super-

SPECIFICATION	
Armstrong Whitworth A.W.XVI	(8735 m); endurance 2 hours
Type: single-seat fighter	**Weights:** empty 2,795 lb (1268 kg); maximum take-off 4,067 lb (1845 kg)
Powerplant: one Armstrong Siddeley Panther IIIA rated at 540 hp (403 kW)	**Dimensions:** wingspan 33 ft (10.06 m); length 25 ft 6 in (7.77 m); height 11 ft 10 in (3.61 m); wing area 261.35 sq ft (24.28 m²)
Performance: maximum speed 203 mph (327 km/h) at 10,000 ft (3050 m); climb to 15,000 ft (4570 m) in 12 minutes 36 seconds; climb to 20,000 ft (6096 m) in 17 minutes 30 seconds; service ceiling 28,650 ft	**Armament (proposed):** two 0.303-in (7.7-mm) fixed forward-firing machine-guns

Easy to fly and land, the unarmed A.W.XVI was considered a pleasant aircraft to fly, and was highly manoeuvrable in the air.

charged unit driving a two-bladed propeller of considerable diameter. During 1933, the second prototype was revised with the 565-hp (421-kW) Panther VII engine in the course of extended

trials at the Aircraft and Armament Experimental Establishment at Martlesham Heath in Suffolk.

Late in 1931 Armstrong Whitworth built 18 production examples of the

A.W.XVI fighter. Seventeen of these aircraft were delivered to the Kwangsi air force in China. The other was used as an engine testbed before being sold to Sir Alan Cobham for use in

his air display tour of South Africa, where it attracted considerable interest but no orders.

In the UK the A.W.XVI land fighter had been planned as successor to the

Armstrong Whitworth Siskin and Gloster Gamecock, but was narrowly beaten for the production order by the Bristol Bulldog, largely on account of the unreliability of its Panther engine.

Armstrong Whitworth A.W.17 Aries

First flown on 3 May 1930, the **Armstrong Whitworth A.W.17 Aries** was an attempt by the manufacturer to improve upon its Atlas two-seater that was currently in well-established service with the Royal Air Force around the world. Assessment had revealed that the basic performance and handling of the Atlas were still adequate for the RAF's purposes so the Aries, which was slightly

larger than the Atlas, was designed not for better performance, but rather for ease of maintenance, something highly desirable at far-flung bases. For this reason, therefore, the Atlas's combination of single sets of outward-canted interplane struts and conventional flying and landing wires was replaced by struts of the Warren truss type that obviated all need for flying and landing wires. Moreover, the

fuselage was covered as far to the rear as the pilot's cockpit with easily detached light alloy panels that provided easy access to all internal equipment.

The Aries offered attractions over the Atlas, but the latter's adequate capabilities in secondary regions such as the Middle East meant that the RAF saw no advantage in the Aries and therefore did not procure any. Because of this, only two were built.

SPECIFICATION	
Armstrong Whitworth A.W.17 Aries	(8.64 m); height 10 ft 11 in (3.33 m); wing area 399.40 sq ft (37.10 m²)
Type: two-seat general-purpose and army co-operation warplane	**Armament:** one 0.303-in (7.7-mm) fixed forward-firing machine-gun,
Powerplant: one Armstrong Siddeley Jaguar IVC radial engine rated at 400 hp (298 kW)	and one 0.303-in (7.7-mm) trainable rearward-firing machine-gun, plus 480 lb (218 kg) of bombs
Dimensions: wingspan 42 ft (12.80 m); length 28 ft 4 in	carried on underwing racks

Armstrong Whitworth A.W.19

In 1931, the Air Ministry decided that the time was ripe for the start of the process to find a replacement for the Westland Wapiti two-seater in the general-purpose role. In July of that year, it therefore

released a requirement for a two-/three-seat warplane able to operate in the army co-operation, reconnaissance, day and night bombing, and dive-bombing roles, with a torpedo-bombing capability added later in

the same year. The task of designing an aircraft with adequate capabilities in all these tasks was daunting, but for manufacturers offered the very useful promise of a large production order. As a result, no fewer than 30 designs were offered by 12 companies and, of these companies, three received prototype contracts and another five decided to persevere with their offerings on a private-venture basis.

One of the latter offerings was the **Armstrong Whitworth A.W.19**, which was a substantial equal-span biplane of fabric-covered steel and light alloy construction. Its fuselage completely filled the gap between the staggered upper and lower wings, the fixed tailwheel landing gear had divided main units to facilitate the loading and release of large stores such as a bomb or torpedo, and

SPECIFICATION	
Armstrong Whitworth A.W.19	**Weights:** empty 4,298 lb
Type: three-crew general-purpose warplane	(1950 kg); maximum take-off 8,750 lb (3969 kg)
Powerplant: one Armstrong Siddeley Tiger VI radial piston engine rated at 810 hp (604 kW)	**Dimensions:** wingspan 49 ft 8 in (15.14 m); length 42 ft 2 in (12.85 m); height 13 ft (3.96 m);
Performance: maximum speed 163 mph (262 km/h) at 6,000 ft (1830 m) or 152 mph (245 km/h) at 15,000 ft (4572 m); climb to 10,000 ft (3050 m) in 8 minutes 48 seconds; climb to 20,000 ft (3050 m) in 16 minutes 36 seconds; service ceiling 21,000 ft (6400 m)	wing area 654.00 sq ft (60.76 m²)
	Armament: one 0.303-in (7.7-mm) fixed forward-firing machine-gun, and one 0.303-in (7.7-mm) trainable rearward-firing machine-gun, plus 2,000 lb (907 kg) of bombs or one torpedo carried externally

After failing to be procured by the RAF, the A.W.19 was then used as a testbed for engines such as the Tiger VI and VII up to June 1940, when the aircraft was scrapped.

the pilot's open cockpit was located ahead of the upper wing's leading edge in a position that offered excellent forward and downward fields of vision for improved capability in the dive-bombing and torpedo roles. The observer/gunner was located in a semi-enclosed position to the rear of the upper wing's trailing edge, while the navigator was in an enclosed cabin.

The A.W.19 prototype made its maiden flight on 26 February 1934, and was later bought by the Air

Ministry for official trials, which began at Martlesham Heath in Suffolk during April 1934. Trials revealed good performance and handling for an aircraft of the A.W.19's size and weight, but the aircraft suffered persistent engine overheating problems. All the biplane contenders for the original 1931 requirement had meanwhile been rendered obsolete by the monoplane prototype that had been developed by Vickers as a private venture and which led to the Wellesley.

Armstrong Whitworth A.W.23

In 1931 the Air Ministry released a requirement for a dual-role aircraft that could operate in the bomber and transport roles, and this resulted

One of the many uses for the A.W.23 was as a tanker aircraft. It took part in a number of trials with Imperial Airways aircraft during experimental Atlantic crossings.

in a three-cornered competition between the **Armstrong Siddeley A.W.23**, Bristol Type 138 and Handley Page H.P.51. The A.W.23 ultimately lost to the Type 138, which was ordered as the Bombay, but the former was of consider-

able importance in the sequence of Armstrong Whitworth aircraft as the precursor of the A.W.38 Whitley bomber. It was also the company's first twin-engined design since the Awana, its initial aircraft with retractable main landing gear units, and also the first with a new type of structure since the introduction of the Siskin Mk III with its steel structure in 1923.

Armstrong Whitworth A.W.23 (continued)

The A.W.23 had a basically rectangular-section fuselage of fabric-covered steel tube construction, a fabric-covered tail unit with a single strut-braced horizontal surface and twin strut-braced vertical surfaces, and a low-set cantilever wing. The wing was of largely light alloy construction covered with unstressed light alloy as far to the rear as the main spar and with fabric to the rear of this line. The powerplant

was based on two Armstrong Siddeley Tiger VI radial engines in nacelles on the leading edge of the wing. These engines drove four-bladed propellers that were initially of the fixed-pitch type, but later of the two-position variable-pitch type. Another innovative feature was the installation in the nose and tail of Armstrong Siddeley manually-operated turrets, each carrying one 0.303-in (7.7-mm) machine-gun.

Provision was also made for the internal carriage of bombs as an alternative to the standard load of freight or troops.

The A.W.23 prototype first flew on 4 June 1935, and was later used as an experimental inflight-refuelling tanker by Flight Refuelling Limited. It was placed in storage at Ford airfield in Sussex, where it was subsequently destroyed in an air raid during August 1940.

SPECIFICATION	
Armstrong Whitworth A.W.23 **Type:** four-/five-crew bomber and transport **Powerplant:** two Armstrong Siddeley Tiger VI radial engines each rated at 810 hp (604 kW) **Performance:** maximum speed 175 mph (282 km/h) at 6,000 ft (1830 m); climb to 10,000 ft (3050 m) in 19 minutes; service ceiling 20,000 ft (6095 m); range 900 miles (1448 km) **Weights:** maximum take-off 24,100 lb (10932 kg)	**Dimensions:** wingspan 88 ft (26.82 m); length 80 ft 9 in (24.61 m); height 19 ft 6 in (5.94 m); wing area 1,308.00 sq ft (121.51 m²) **Armament:** one 0.303-in (7.7-mm) trainable forward-firing machine-gun in the nose turret, and one 0.303-in (7.7-mm) trainable rearward-firing machine-gun in the tail turret, plus 5,000 lb (2268 kg) of bombs carried internally

Armstrong Whitworth A.W.27 Ensign

In 1934 the British government decided that all first-class mail for the Empire would in future be sent by air, and as a result Imperial Airways found itself in need of larger aircraft to service its routes. Although most of the requirements were to be met by Short flying boats, a new four-engined landplane was needed, in particular for European and Eastern routes.

In May 1934 the airline issued the relevant specification to Armstrong Whitworth and the result was the **Armstrong Whitworth A.W.27 Ensign**, the first of which was ordered in September 1934 at a price of £70,000. The contract stipulated delivery within two years, and in May 1935 the airline ordered another 11 aircraft at £37,000 each, most design, development and tooling costs having been taken into account in the price of the first machine. The airline contracted for a final two aircraft in January 1937, raising overall Ensign production to 14 aircraft.

As Armstrong Whitworth was busy with Whitley bomber production at its Coventry factory, the airliners were assembled in the Air Service Training workshops at Hamble. Imperial Airways constantly demanded detail changes to the design and construction and, as a result, the first Ensign was almost two years late, making its first flight from Hamble on 24 January 1938 – its powerplant consisted of four 800-hp (597-kW) Armstrong Siddeley Tiger IX radial engines. Subsequent tests at Martlesham Heath in June 1938 showed that the type was somewhat

underpowered and a number of minor problems also occurred, but a certificate of airworthiness was nevertheless issued.

In July 1938 the first aircraft flew a trip from Croydon to Paris, but proper services did not begin on the route until October. Just before Christmas 1938, three more aircraft had joined the first and left the UK as relief aircraft, carrying Christmas mail to Australia. All three became unserviceable, one at Athens, one at Karachi and another in India. The type was subsequently withdrawn and returned to the manufacturers for performance and reliability upgrading. A modest increase in performance was achieved by fitting more powerful Armstrong Siddeley Tiger IXC engines to the sixth aircraft and, in spite of problems, the Ensign fleet served the airline's European routes.

Some 11 aircraft had been delivered by the outbreak of World War II in 1939, and these aircraft were operated in two configurations. Four machines (named *Eddystone, Ettrick, Empyrean* and *Elysian*) were the European type, with seats for 40 passengers. The other seven (*Ensign, Egeria, Elsinore, Euterpe, Explorer, Euryalus* and *Echo*) were intended for Empire routes and were therefore outfitted for the carriage of 27 day passengers in three cabins or, alternatively, 20 night passengers in sleeping berths. The twelfth A.W.27 (*Endymion*) received its certificate of airworthiness in October 1939, and the fleet was evacuated to

Bristol's Whitchurch airport along with a number of other airliners. Camouflage was hastily applied, and the A.W.27 transports operated a twice-daily service between Heston and Paris (Le Bourget).

When the British Overseas Airways Corporation was formed in November 1939 by the merger of British Airways and Imperial Airways, ownership of the A.W.27 fleet passed to the new company. Wartime service soon began to take its toll, and *Elysian* was destroyed on the ground at Merville on 23 May 1940. Others followed, *Ettrick* being abandoned at Le Bourget (it was subsequently repaired and used by the Germans with Daimler-Benz engines) and *Endymion* being destroyed during an air raid on Whitchurch in November 1940.

The final two A.W.27 aircraft, whose construction had been halted on the outbreak of war, were completed in 1941. Named *Everest* and *Enterprise*, they were fitted with 950-hp (708-kW) Wright GR-1820 Cyclone radial engines for a total increase of 400 hp (298 kW) compared with the earlier Tigers, and in this form the type was designated **Ensign Mk II**. The remaining eight examples of what now became the **Ensign Mk I** were also re-engined, and with the extra power were considered more suitable for operation in hot climates. Used between West and East Africa and Egypt, the A.W.27 transports were hard pushed and, as the aircraft were out of production, the American-built Wright engines proved difficult to maintain.

G-ADSR was the first Ensign to join Imperial Airways' fleet. In addition to day-passenger and mail configurations, the type could also be configured as a 20-berth sleeper.

In the face of mounting problems it was decided to bring the survivors home, and seven (*Egeria, Elsinore, Explorer, Eddystone, Empyrean, Echo* and *Everest*) were scrapped at Hamble in 1947. *Enterprise*, which had been abandoned in West Africa during 1942, was salvaged by the Vichy French and, like *Ettrick*, was eventually

re-engined and flown by the Germans. The original *Ensign* had been damaged at Lagos in 1943 and was scrapped in 1945, while *Euterpe* and *Euryalus*, damaged at Almaza and Lympne respectively, were cannibalised for spares. *Eddystone* was the last flying A.W.27, making the long trek back from Cairo to Hurn in June 1946.

Variants

Ensign Mk I: retrospective designation of the initial 12 aircraft fitted with Armstrong Siddeley Tiger radials
Ensign Mk II: designation of the last two aircraft, built with four 950-hp (708-kW) Wright GR-1820-G102A Cyclone radial piston engines; eight Mk I aircraft were subsequently upgraded to Mk II standard; maximum speed 210 mph (338 km/h), cruising speed 180 mph (290 km/h), service ceiling 24,000 ft (7315 m), range 1,370 miles (2205 km), empty weight 36,586 lb (16595 kg) and maximum take-off weight 55,500 lb (25174 kg)

SPECIFICATION	
Armstrong Whitworth A.W.27 **Ensign Mk I** **Type:** five-crew medium transport **Powerplant:** four Armstrong Siddeley Tiger IXC radial engines each rated at 850 hp (634 kW) **Performance:** maximum speed 205 mph (330 km/h) at 7,000 ft (2135 m); maximum cruising speed 170 mph (274 km/h) at 7,000 ft (2135 m); climb to 3,000 ft (915 m) in 3 minutes 12 seconds; service ceiling	18,000 ft (5485 m); range 860 miles (1384 km) **Weights:** empty 32,920 lb (14932 kg); maximum take-off 49,000 lb (2226 kg) **Dimensions:** wingspan 123 ft (37.49 m); length 114 ft (34.75 m); height 23 ft (7.01 m); wing area 2,450 sq ft (227.62 m²) **Payload:** 40 passengers in 'Western' layout or 27 passengers in 'Eastern' layout

Armstrong Whitworth A.W.29

Designed to meet a 1932 requirement which was issued in April 1933, the **Armstrong Whitworth**

A.W.29 was planned as a two-seat day bomber but its programme suffered from the fact that the company's

design and prototyping capabilities were already overpressed by the A.W.27 Ensign airliner and A.W.38

Whitley bomber efforts. The type's main rival was the Fairey Battle and, by the time the single A.W.29 prototype made its maiden flight on 6 December 1936, the Battle had already been

in the air for nine months and had in fact been selected to satisfy the RAF's requirement.

The requirement called for the delivery of a 1,000-lb (454-kg) bombload

For Armstrong Whitworth, the A.W.29 was something of a technical breakthrough, since it employed structural and aerodynamic features that were new to the company.

able rearward-firing machine-gun in a manually-operated Armstrong Whitworth dorsal turret located some 12 ft (3.66 m) to the rear of the cockpit. It was operated by a gunner who also acted as radio operator, observer and bomb-aimer, the last with the aid of a flat transparency

in the lower surface of the fuselage.

Only a few test flights had been completed before the A.W.29 made a wheels-up landing. The damage caused to the aircraft, combined with the type's lack of orders, was enough to make the company decide not to repair it.

over a range of 1,000 miles (1909 km) at a speed of 200 mph (322 km/h), and the company's design team felt that an aircraft to meet this requirement could also be developed as a high-speed mailplane. In fact, nothing came of this commercial project, which would have carried mail in a compartment over the wing and the pilot in an open

cockpit in the rear fuselage.

The A.W.29 was a low-wing cantilever monoplane of basically all-metal construction with stalky main landing gear units designed to retract rearward into wells in the underside of the specially thickened wing roots. It was also notable for having a rear fuselage that was the first semi-monocoque structure

of this type developed by Armstrong Whitworth. The bombload was carried in wells in the thick inboard sections of the wing above spring-loaded doors that were pushed open by the weight of the bombs as they were released. The rest of the armament comprised one fixed forward-firing machine-gun for the pilot and one train-

SPECIFICATION	
Armstrong Whitworth A.W.29	9,000 lb (4082 kg)
Type: two-seat light day bomber	**Dimensions:** wingspan 49 ft
Powerplant: one Armstrong	(14.94 m); length 43 ft 10 in
Siddeley Tiger VIII radial engine	(13.36 m); height 13 ft 3 in (4.04 m);
rated at 920 hp (686 kW)	wing area 458.00 sq ft (42.55 m²)
Performance: maximum speed	**Armament:** one 0.303-in (7.7-mm)
225 mph (362 km/h) at 14,700 ft	fixed forward-firing machine-gun,
(4480 m); climb to 15,000 ft	and one 0.303-in (7.7-mm)
(4570 m) in 16 minutes 48 seconds;	trainable rearward-firing machine
service ceiling 21,000 ft (6400 m);	guns in the dorsal turret, plus
range 685 miles (1102 km)	1,000 lb (454 kg) of bombs carried
Weights: maximum take-off	internally

Armstrong Whitworth A.W.35 Scimitar

The **Armstrong Whitworth A.W.35 Scimitar** was a development of the A.W.XVI with a number of aerodynamic and structural refinements. It was also fitted with the revised powerplant of one Armstrong Siddeley Panther VII radial engine rated at 565 hp (421 kW) at 12,000 ft (3660 m) and installed under a long-chord ring cowling. Two A.W.35 prototypes were built and first flown in 1933 for competitive evaluation against the Gloster

Gladiator, Hawker High-Speed Fury and Vickers Jockey, eventually losing to the Gladiator.

The only order for the A.W.35 was placed by the Norwegian army air service, which contracted for just four examples of the fighter in a form revised with the Panther XIA engine rated at 730 hp (544 kW). These machines were delivered early in 1936 and remained in use as trainers until 1939. With the lack of other overseas interest, and Armstrong

Whitworth's involvement with the Whitley bomber programme, the Scimitar made no further progress. The last survivor was one of the prototypes used by

the manufacturer as a company demonstrator. It was stored during World War II and survived intact until it was scrapped in October 1958.

Some reports suggest that the Scimitar could have been a better fighter than the Gladiator, but for its unreliable engine.

SPECIFICATION	
Armstrong Whitworth A.W.35 Scimitar	**Weights:** empty 2,956 lb (1341 kg); maximum take-off
Type: single-seat fighter	4,100 lb (1860 kg)
Powerplant: one Armstrong	**Dimensions:** wingspan 33 ft
Siddeley Panther VII radial engine	(10.06 m); length 25 ft (7.62 m);
rated at 565 hp (421 kW)	height 12 ft (3.66 m); wing area
Performance: maximum speed	261.35 sq ft (24.28 m²)
221 mph (356 km/h) at 14,000 ft	**Armament:** two 0.303-in (7.7-mm)
(4265 m); climb to 10,000 ft	fixed forward-firing machine-guns,
(3050 m) in 5 minutes 15 seconds;	plus 80 lb (36 kg) of bombs carried
service ceiling 31,600 ft (9630 m);	on an underwing rack
endurance 2 hours 30 minutes	

Armstrong Whitworth A.W.38 Whitley

Designed to meet an Air Ministry bomber requirement circulated in July 1934, the **Armstrong Whitworth A.W.38 Whitley** was the most extensively built of the company's designs, production reaching a total of 1,814 aircraft. It also marked a departure from Armstrong Whitworth's traditional steel tube construction, the Whitley's fuselage being a light alloy monocoque structure.

Production was authorised while the aircraft was

still in the design stage, an order for 80 aircraft being placed in August 1935. The prototype took to the air on its maiden flight at Whitley Abbey on 17 March 1936, the machine's two Armstrong Siddeley Tiger IX engines turning the then-new type of three-bladed variable-pitch de Havilland propeller. A second prototype built to a 1935 specification had more powerful Tiger XI engines and successfully completed its first flight on 24 February 1937.

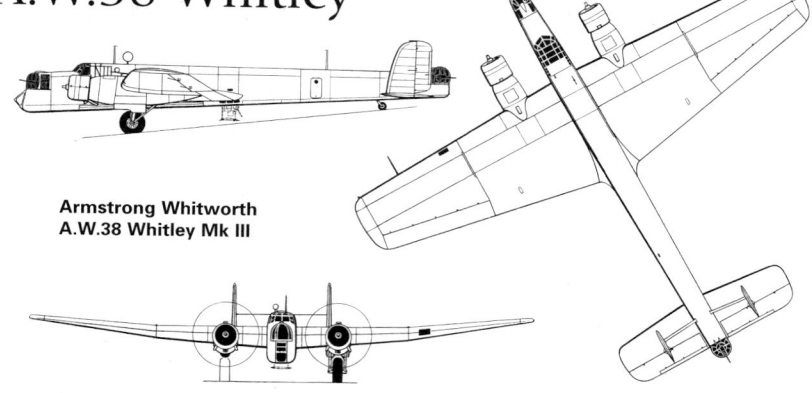

Armstrong Whitworth A.W.38 Whitley Mk III

Armstrong Whitworth A.W.38 Whitley (continued)

Trials at the Aircraft and Armament Experimental Establishment at Martlesham Heath were undertaken in the autumn of 1936. The first production **Whitley Mk I** bombers were delivered early in 1937, including the second aircraft which was flown to RAF Dishforth on 9 March for No. 10 Squadron. Thirty-four Mk I bombers were built with 795-hp (593-kW) Tiger IX engines before the **Whitley Mk II** was introduced. This mark had 845-hp (630-kW) Tiger VIII engines with two-speed superchargers, the first fitted to an RAF type; 46 Whitley Mk II bombers completed the initial order for 80 aircraft.

The Whitley Mks I and II had manually-operated Armstrong Whitworth nose and tail turrets, each carrying one 0.303-in (7.7-mm) Vickers machine-gun. In the **Whitley Mk III** the nose turret was replaced by a power-operated Nash & Thompson turret, and a retractable ventral turret with two 0.303-in (7.7-mm) Browning machine-guns was added. The 80 Whitley Mk III aircraft also had modified bomb bays to accommodate larger bombs.

By far the most numerous of the Whitley variants were those with Rolls-Royce Merlin Vee engines. A Whitley Mk I was fitted with Merlin IIs and test flown at Hucknall on 11 February 1938, although engine failure prematurely concluded the second flight. The programme was quickly resumed, however, and during April and May the aircraft carried out trials at Martlesham Heath. Merlin IV engines of 1,030 hp (768 kW) were installed in production **Whitley Mk IV** bombers, the first of which flew on 5 April 1939. Other changes incorporated in this version included a power-operated Nash & Thompson tail turret with four 0.303-in (7.7-mm) Browning guns. A transparent panel was added in the lower nose to improve the view for the bomb-aimer, and two additional wing tanks were fitted to increase the fuel capacity. Production totalled

33 aircraft together with seven **Whitley Mk IVA** machines which had 1,145-hp (854-kW) Merlin X engines.

The same engines were retained for the **Whitley Mk V**, which incorporated a number of improvements. The most noticeable of these were modified fins with straight leading edges and an extension of 1 ft 3 in (0.38 m) to the rear fuselage to provide a wider field of fire for the rear gunner. Rubber de-icer boots were fitted to the wing leading edges, and fuel capacity was further increased by enlargement of the standard tankage and the incorporation of provision for extra tanks carried in the bomb bay. Production reached a total of 1,466 aircraft.

The **Whitley Mk VI** was a version projected with Pratt & Whitney engines, studied as an insurance against short supply of Merlins. It was not built, however, and the ultimate production variant was thus the **Whitley Mk VII** which was essentially a Mk V with auxiliary fuel tanks in the bomb bay and in the rear fuselage to increase the range to 2,300 miles (2701 km) for the new variant's revised primary role, namely maritime reconnaissance. Externally, the Mk VII aircraft could be distinguished by the dorsal radar aerials of their ASV.Mk II air-to-surface radar. Production reached 146, and some Mk V aircraft were converted to this later standard.

As noted above, No. 10 Squadron at RAF Dishforth was the first to equip with the Whitley, which replaced the Handley Page Heyford in March 1937. Nos 51 and 58 Squadrons at RAF Leconfield soon followed and, during the night of 3 September 1939, 10

Whitley Mk III bombers from these two squadrons flew a leaflet raid over Bremen, Hamburg and the Ruhr. Just under a month later, during the night of 1 October, No. 10 Squadron flew a similar mission over Berlin. The first bombs were dropped on Berlin during the night of 25 August 1940, the attacking squadrons including Nos 51 and 78 with Whitley bombers. To mark the entry of Italy into the war, 36 Whitleys drawn from Nos 10, 51, 58, 77 and 102 Squadrons were tasked to raid Genoa and Turin during the night of 11 June 1940, although only 13 reached their targets due to a combination of poor weather and engine problems.

The Whitley was retired from Bomber Command in April 1942, the last operation being flown against Ostend during the night of 29 April, although some aircraft from operational training units were flown in the '1,000 Bomber' raid on Köln on the night of 30 May 1942.

Coastal Command's association with the Whitley began in September 1939 when No. 58 Squadron was transferred to Boscombe Down to operate anti-submarine patrols over the English Channel. This task lasted until February 1940, when the unit returned to Bomber Command, but during 1942 it took up patrol duties once again, flying over the Western Approaches from St Eval and Stornoway. Other units similarly occupied at that time included Nos 51 and 77 Squadrons, the latter operating in the Bay of Biscay area.

Whitley Mk Vs replaced the Avro Ansons of No. 502 Squadron at RAF Aldergrove in the autumn

At the beginning of World War II, the Whitley was the RAF's primary long-range bomber. This Mk V of No. 78 Sqn carries an array of mission symbols.

SPECIFICATION

Armstrong Whitworth Whitley Mk V

Type: five-crew long-range night bomber

Powerplant: two Rolls-Royce Merlin X Vee engines each rated at 1,145 hp (854 kW)

Performance: maximum speed 230 mph (370 km/h) at 16,400 ft (5000 m); cruising speed 210 mph (338 km/h) at 15,000 ft (4570 m); climb to 15,000 ft (4570 m) in 16 minutes; service ceiling 26,000 ft (7925 m); range 1,500 miles (2414 km)

Weights: empty 19,350 lb (8777 kg); maximum take-off 33,500 lb (15195 kg)

Dimensions: wingspan 84 ft (25.60 m); length 70 ft 6 in (21.49 m); height 15 ft (4.57 m); wing area 1,137.00 sq ft (105.63 m²)

Armament: one 0.303-in (7.7-mm) trainable forward-firing machine gun in the nose turret, four 0.303-in (7.7-mm) trainable rearward-firing machine-guns in the tail turret, plus 7,000 lb (3175 kg) of bombs

of 1940, and a second Coastal Command Whitley unit, No. 612 Squadron, formed in May 1941. The Whitley Mk V aircraft were replaced by the radar-equipped Whitley Mk VII, and such a machine of No. 502 Squadron sank the type's first German submarine when it attacked *U-205* in the Bay of Biscay on 30 November 1941.

Whitleys were also used by No. 1 Parachute Training School and were adapted for use as glider tugs, becoming attached to No. 21 Glider Conversion Unit at Brize Norton for the training of tug pilots. The paratroop raid on the German radar site at

Bruneval used Whitley aircraft of No. 51 Squadron. Moreover, the aircraft of 'special duty' units at RAF Tempsford (Nos 138 and 161 Squadrons) flew numerous sorties, dropping agents into occupied territory and supplying Resistance groups with arms and equipment. Fifteen Whitley Mk V aircraft were also handed over to the British Overseas Airways Corporation in May 1942 and, stripped of armament but with additional fuel tanks in the bomb bays, flew regularly from Gibraltar to Malta carrying supplies for the beleaguered island.

Based at RAF Dishforth, UK with No. 10 Squadron in 1937, this Whitley Mk I was typical of the early-production machines.

Armstrong Whitworth A.W.41 Albemarle

The **Albemarle** originated as the **Bristol Type 155** design to meet an Air Ministry requirement of 1938 for a twin-engined bomber, being allocated the company identification Type 155. With a change in the official specification, however, design responsi-

bility was transferred to Armstrong Whitworth, where a design team under the supervision of John Lloyd was set the difficult task of taking over another company's creation and adapting it to meet a requirement for a reconnaissance bomber. This

revised type began to take shape as the **Armstrong Whitworth A.W.41 Albemarle**, which was very different from the original Bristol concept in detail and construction.

Designed for mixed composite steel and wood construction, the prototype

flew in 1939 but was destroyed in a crash before the flight of the second prototype on 20 March 1940. The Albemarle's structure enabled the wide use of sub-contracting, even to small companies outside the aircraft industry (one source mentions

almost 1,000 sub-contractors), and an additional bonus came from the conservation of strategically important light alloys; the tricycle landing gear was of Lockheed design.

The first 32 aircraft were built as bombers, although they were not used as such, and there was considerable delay in establishing production lines. The first three Albemarle machines off the production line were completed in December 1941, by which time the decision had been made to adapt the type (which was heavy and lacked the performance for effective use in the reconnaissance bomber task) as a glider tug and airborne forces transport.

Deliveries to the Royal Air Force began in January 1943 when No. 295 Squadron received its first aircraft, and the type was blooded by Nos 296 and 297 Squadrons, part of No. 38 Wing operating from North Africa, in the invasion of Sicily in July 1943. On D-Day (6 June 1944) six of No. 295 Squadron's Albemarle aircraft, operating from Harwell, served as pathfinders for the 6th Airborne Division, dropping paratroops over Normandy. In the glider-tug role, four squadrons of Albemarle aircraft were used to tow Airspeed Horsa gliders to France in support of ground operations, while in September 1944 two of No. 38 Group's squadrons

Adorned with D-Day stripes, this No. 297 Sqn Albemarle GT.Mk V demonstrates the glider-towing apparatus seen trailing behind the aircraft. A flight of Albemarles from No. 295 Sqn acted as pathfinders during the initial stages of the D-Day landings.

participated in the Arnhem operation, towing gliders carrying troops of the 1st Airborne Division.

Production of the Albemarle, apart from the prototypes, was undertaken by A.W. Hawksley Ltd, part of the Hawker Siddeley Group, and came to an end in December 1944 after the completion of 602 aircraft. Original orders had covered 1,080 machines, but 478 from the second production batch were cancelled. Deliveries to the RAF consisted of 310 transport aircraft (78 **Albemarle ST.Mk I**, 99 **Albemarle ST.Mk II** and 133 **Albemarle ST.Mk VI** machines) and 246 glider tugs (80 **Albemarle GT.Mk I**, one **Albemarle GT.Mk II**, 49 **Albemarle GT.Mk V** and 117 **Albemarle Mk VI** machines). In addition to these were the original 32 bombers which were later converted to transport standard, and 10 Albemarle aircraft which were delivered to the Soviet air force from RAF stocks and were used as transports.

All Albemarle production aircraft used the Bristol Hercules XI engine, there also being a sole **Albemarle Mk IV** prototype with Wright Double Cyclone radial engines, and differences in the marks were primarily in equipment. The original bomber versions were fitted with a four-gun Boulton Paul dorsal turret, but weight considerations dictated the removal of this in the transports and glider tugs which, instead, mounted two Vickers 'K' hand-operated machine-guns.

While the Albemarle was not a particularly significant type, it did perform a useful role and therefore released other types for more vital tasks. In addition, because of its method of construction and the materials used, production did not unduly disturb the flow of more important types at a time when these were vital to the UK's survival.

Armstrong Whitworth A.W.41 Albemarle

SPECIFICATION

Armstrong Whitworth A.W.41 Albemarle Mk II
Type: four-crew transport and glider tug
Powerplant: two Bristol Hercules XI radial engines each rated at 1,590 hp (1186 kW)
Performance: (glider tug) maximum speed 265 mph (426 km/h) at 10,500 ft (3200 m); cruising speed 170 mph (274 km/h) at optimum altitude; initial climb rate 980 ft (299 m) per minute; service ceiling 18,000 ft (5485 m); range 1,300 miles (2092 km)
Weights: maximum take-off 36,500 lb (16556 kg)
Dimensions: wingspan 77 ft (23.47 m); length 59 ft 11 in (18.26 m); height 15 ft 7 in (4.75 m); wing area 803.50 sq ft (74.65 m²)
Armament: two 0.303-in (7.7-mm) trainable rearward-firing machine-guns in the dorsal position
Payload: one glider or paratroops

Armstrong Whitworth A.W.52

From the early days of flight there has been interest in the flying wing, or so-called tailless design. The concept of the **Armstrong Whitworth A.W.52** dates back to 1942 when the company's designer, John Lloyd, was asked by the Ministry of Supply to design a wing section for testing of laminar-flow drag by the National Physical Laboratory. The resulting tests indicated to Lloyd the possibility of designing a jet airliner along these lines, and he began work on such a type as the **A.W.50**, but then dropped it in favour of the A.W.52 twin-jet design.

In 1943 work began on a half-scale glider version, the **A.W.52G**, which was built mainly of wood, and this made its first flight on 2 March 1945 after being towed into the air by a Whitley tug. The A.W.52G was a tandem two-seater with fixed tricycle landing gear, and employed boundary layer control over the outer wing sections. With the shape of the concept proven, the Ministry of Supply ordered two experimental A.W.52 jet-powered aircraft to meet a requirement first enunciated late in 1944.

The first A.W.52 made its maiden flight at Boscombe Down on 13 November 1947 with the powerplant of two 5,000-lb st (22.24-kN) Rolls-Royce Nene turbojet engines, and was followed by the second machine with 3,500-lb (15.57-kN) Rolls-Royce Derwent turbojet engines on 1 September 1948. Of all-metal construction, the A.W.52 had an exceptionally smooth laminar-flow wing in which surface variations were less than one-five hundredth of an inch. Thermal wing de-icing was achieved by using hot gases from the engines, mixed with cold air from an external scoop.

Tests with the aircraft showed that the required laminar-flow performance could not be achieved with the swept wing, and further development was dropped. The first prototype was lost on 30 May 1949, following a severe asymmetric wingtip flutter problem. As test pilot J. O. Lancaster left the aircraft, he became the first person in the UK to use the Martin-Baker ejection seat in an emergency. The second A.W.52 was used by the Royal Aircraft Establishment at Farnborough until its disposal in June 1954.

In order to maintain the most efficient laminar flow possible, the A.W.52 featured exceptionally smooth wing skins with surface variations of less than 1/500 in (0.05 mm).

SPECIFICATION

Armstrong Whitworth A.W.52
Type: single-seat experimental flying wing
Powerplant: two Rolls-Royce Nene turbojet engines each rated at 5,000 lb st (22.24 kN)
Performance: maximum speed 500 mph (805 km/h) at sea level; initial climb rate 4,800 ft (1463 m) per minute; range 1,500 miles (2414 km)
Weights: empty 19,660 lb (8918 kg); maximum take-off 34,150 lb (15490 kg)
Dimensions: wing span 90 ft (27.43 m); length 37 ft 4 in (11.38 m); height 14 ft 5 in (4.39 m); wing area 1,314.00 sq ft (122.07 m²)

Armstrong Whitworth A.W.55 Apollo

Among the recommendations of the Brabazon Committee was the Type II short/medium-haul transport with accommodation for up to 24 passengers and intended for services within Europe. The Committee suggested that the Type II requirement should be investigated in two forms as piston- and turboprop-engined types, and in the latter category the Ministry of Supply received design tenders to

its 1946 requirement from Armstrong Whitworth and Vickers. The latter eventually emerged victorious with the classic Viscount.

The other design tender, the **Armstrong Whitworth A.W.55 Apollo** – ordered to the extent of two prototypes – was a low-wing cantilever monoplane of all-metal construction and elegant appearance. It featured a circular-section fuselage, a relatively high-aspect-ratio

wing, retractable tricycle landing gear with twin wheels on each unit, and a powerplant of four Armstrong Siddeley Mamba turboprops. The Mamba was based on an axial-flow compressor and was therefore slimmer than the rival Rolls-Royce Dart which employed a centrifugal-flow compressor.

The choice of an engine from a sister company was unfortunate for Armstrong Whitworth, for the axial-flow type of engine was less well developed than the centrifugal-flow type, and the problems of the Mamba contributed signally to the failure of the Apollo at a time when the success of the Dart was a key element in the greatness of the Viscount.

The A.W.55 made its maiden flight on 10 April 1949, but the flight test programme was seriously hampered by the Mamba's

Armstrong Whitworth originally flew the Apollo with three-bladed propellers, but later settled on four-bladed units. The aircraft was plagued by problems with its Mamba powerplant.

underdeveloped state. Improvements to the Mamba were made, but the type never rivalled the Dart for reliability and the Apollo was not ordered into production. The two proto-

types were then used for experimental purposes, the first machine being written off for flight purposes after a landing accident in April 1953, and the second being retired in December 1954.

SPECIFICATION

Armstrong Whitworth A.W.55 Apollo
Type: two/three-crew short/medium-haul transport
Powerplant: four Armstrong Siddeley Mamba Mk 504 turboprop engines each rated at 1,010 shp (753 kW)
Performance: maximum speed 330 mph (531 km/h) at optimum altitude; cruising speed 276 mph (444 km/h) at optimum altitude; initial climb rate 1,500 ft (457 m)

per minute; service ceiling 28,000 ft (8535 m); range 940 miles (1513 km)
Weights: empty 30,800 lb (13971 kg); maximum take-off 45,000 lb (20412 kg)
Dimensions: wingspan 92 ft (28.04 m); length 71 ft 6 in (21.79 m); height 26 ft (7.93 m); wing area 986.00 sq ft (91.60 m²)
Payload: up to 31 passengers; maximum payload 7,500-lb (3402-kg)

Armstrong Whitworth A.W.650 and A.W.660 Argosy

A British specification, issued in 1955 by the Air Ministry and calling for a medium-range freighter possessing civil and military applications, was the first step towards the creation of the **Armstrong Whitworth A.W.650 Argosy**. In the same year Armstrong Whitworth began work on the closely-related **A.W.65** civil and **A.W.66** military design projects with twin booms and a powerplant of two turboprop engines. By 1956 the poor chances of receiving military orders dictated that emphasis should be placed on a civil version.

In September, the company decided to proceed with a revised design as a private venture. Designated as the **A.W.650**, the new type still had a twin-boom layout but now in combination with a four-turboprop layout, and was initially named **Freightliner** although this was changed to **Argosy** in July 1958. The designation also became **HS.650**, reflecting Armstrong

Whitworth's membership of the new Hawker Siddeley Group.

The first Argosy made its maiden flight on 8 January 1959, less than two years after the drawings had been issued, and before the end of 1959 a further five aircraft had flown. The first four aircraft participated in the certification programme and a restricted certificate of airworthiness was issued in May 1959, full British and US certification being achieved in December 1960. The fourth aircraft was the first to appear in public, in this instance at the 1959 Paris Air Show.

European demonstration tours in October 1959, as a combined passenger/freighter priced fairly at £460,000, attracted interest but no orders. Riddle Airlines of Miami was the first customer, ordering four (later increased to seven) Argosies in February 1959 to be used on bulky freight-carrying contracts for the US Air Force. On expiration of this contract,

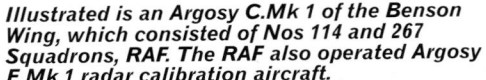

Illustrated is an Argosy C.Mk 1 of the Benson Wing, which consisted of Nos 114 and 267 Squadrons, RAF. The RAF also operated Argosy E.Mk 1 radar calibration aircraft.

the seven Argosies were operated in the US by Capitol Airlines and Zantop Air Transport.

British European Airways took delivery of the first of three **Argosy 102** aircraft in 1961 and operated its initial freight services in December of that year with the Argosies replacing Douglas DC-3s and Avro Yorks. Ten **Argosy Series 100s** were built and all except the third machine, eventually found their way to the USA for operation by the companies mentioned above. At least four later found their way back to UK operators.

A batch of 56 **A.W.660** aircraft, based on the civil Argosy Series 100 but with rear-loading ramp, was built for the Royal Air Force, which designated the type as the **Argosy C.Mk 1**. The final Argosy variant was the **Argosy Series 200**, whose sole model was the **Argosy 222** that first flew in March 1964. An enlarged

freight hold and wider doors permitted the carriage of six 108-in (2.74-m) cargo pallets, the standard size then in use on international jet transports. A redesigned wing saved 400 lb (181 kg) in weight and range was increased. These improvements persuaded BEA to trade in its Argosy 102 machines in part exchange for five Argosy 222s. The loss of one aircraft at Milan, in July 1965, caused BEA to buy the last of seven production aircraft (the first remained with the manufacturer until being withdrawn from use in

November 1965), but when another Argosy was burnt out on the ground in December 1967, no further replacement was ordered.

BEA's Argosy operations always lost money, and the corporation flew its last service with the type in April 1970. All four were subsequently sold to Transair. Two of these aircraft later went to Australian freight operator IPEC, while the other two were sold to Safe Air in New Zealand. A few of the RAF aircraft eventually found their way to civil operators which were already using the Argosy, but one went to Philippine Air Lines.

The Argosy was Armstrong Whitworth's last civil aircraft and also the last to bear the manufacturer's name.

SPECIFICATION

Armstrong Whitworth A.W.650 Argosy Series 100
Type: three/four-crew transport
Powerplant: four Rolls-Royce Dart Mk 526 turboprop engines each rated at 2,020 shp (1506 kW)
Performance: average cruising speed 280 mph (451 km/h) at optimum altitude; service ceiling 20,000 ft (6100 m); range 2,000 miles (3219 km)

Weights: empty 46,000 lb (20865 kg); maximum take-off 88,000 lb (39916 kg)
Dimensions: wingspan 115 ft (35.05 m); length 86 ft 9 in (26.44 m); height 29 ft 3 in (8.92 m); wing area 1,458.00 sq ft (135.14 m²)
Payload: up to 28,000 lb (12701 kg) of freight or 89 passengers

Armstrong Whitworth Ajax

First flown in or shortly before July 1925, the **Armstrong Whitworth Ajax** prototype differed so little from the near-contemporary Atlas that it is hard to understand why the manufacturer did not regarded this as merely a variant of the Atlas. The main difference between the two types was the provision on the Ajax of a gun ring over the observer/gunner's cockpit. This suggests that the type was initially regarded as a fighter and general-purpose aircraft, perhaps as a two-seat complement to the Armstrong Whitworth Siskin single-seat fighter. This was suggested by the use of cantilever tail surfaces to allow the omission of bracing wires and struts and thus improve the gunner's rearward fields of fire.

There followed another three examples of the Ajax, the last two of them in what was regarded at the time as a day-bomber configuration, and all four aircraft were delivered to the Royal Air Force. The Ajax was a single-bay biplane with fixed tailskid landing gear, and was of mixed construction with a fabric-covered steel tube fuselage and fabric-covered wooden wings.

The Ajax was slightly predated by the Atlas and such is the confusion surrounding the types that one Ajax may have been civil registered as an Atlas.

SPECIFICATION	
Armstrong Whitworth Ajax	**Weights:** empty 2,240 lb (1016 kg); maximum take-off 3,700 lb (1678 kg)
Type: two-seat general-purpose warplane	
Powerplant: one Armstrong Siddeley Jaguar radial engine rated at 385 hp (287 kW)	**Dimensions:** wingspan 39 ft 6 in (12.04 m); length 28 ft 3 in (8.61 m); wing area 392.00 sq ft (36.42 m²)
Performance: maximum speed 140 mph (225 km/h) at sea level; climb to 15,000 ft (4570 m) in 21 minutes 30 seconds; service ceiling 19,700 ft (6005 m); endurance 3 hours 15 minutes	**Armament:** one 0.303-in (7.7-mm) fixed forward-firing machine-gun, and one 0.303-in (7.7-mm) trainable rearward-firing machine-gun

Armstrong Whitworth Ara

The **Armstrong Whitworth Ara** was a two-bay biplane fighter designed in 1918 to exploit the capabilities of a new and promising engine, the ABC Dragonfly radial unit rated at 320 hp (238.5 kW). Three prototypes of the Ara, which was of typical fabric-covered wooden construction with an open cockpit and fixed tailskid landing gear, were ordered. However, problems with the development of the Dragonfly engine resulted in an October 1918 decision that all plans for the production of Dragonfly-engined fighters should be terminated.

In an effort to recoup something out of what had been a considerable industrial effort by the standards of the day, each of the companies that had received a contract for Dragonfly-engined fighter prototypes was allocated one example of the engine so that a single prototype of each type could be completed and test flown for comparative purposes. Armstrong Whitworth completed and flew the first Ara in the early part of 1919, with severe engine problems not deterring the construction of a second aircraft before deciding late in 1919 to close its air department. The department was revived in 1921 after the Siddeley Deasy Car Co. Ltd. bought the name of the Sir W. G. Armstrong, Whitworth & Co. Ltd.

On the second Ara (illustrated), the interplane gap was increased by mounting the lower wing beneath the fuselage.

SPECIFICATION	
Armstrong Whitworth Ara	endurance 3 hours 15 minutes
Type: single-seat fighter	**Weights:** empty 1,320 lb (599 kg); maximum take-off 1,930 lb (875 kg)
Powerplant: one ABC Dragonfly radial engine rated at 320 hp (239 kW)	**Dimensions:** wingspan 27 ft 5 in (8.35 m); length 20 ft 3 in (6.17 m); height 7 ft 10 in (2.39 m); wing area 257.00 sq ft (23.87 m²)
Performance: maximum speed 150 mph (241 km/h) at sea level; climb to 10,000 ft (3050 m) in 4 minutes 30 seconds; service ceiling 28,000 ft (8535 m);	**Armament:** two 0.303-in (7.7-mm) fixed forward-firing machine-guns

Armstrong Whitworth Argosy

When, in 1925, the newly created Imperial Airways adopted a new policy of using only multi-engined aircraft, the **Armstrong Whitworth Argosy** was one of the three new types it ordered. Armstrong Whitworth produced the Argosy, a large biplane with fixed tailskid landing gear and the company's first airliner, to a 1922 specification for a three-engined aircraft with a range of 500 miles (805 km). The first example flew in March 1926, following receipt of the Imperial Airways order. The second Argosy flew three months later, and was the first of the aircraft to be delivered to the airline, which received it the following month.

Imperial Airways lost no time in introducing its new airliner into service, the airline's first machine making its initial revenue flight between Croydon and Paris on 16 July 1926. On 1 May 1927 the airline inaugurated the luxury 'Silver Wing' service on this route; for standard services, the Argosy carried 20 passengers in the cabin, with the captain and first officer in an open cockpit just behind the nose-mounted engine. To allow the carriage of a steward, who served the gourmet meals for which the 'Silver Wing' service was famous, it was necessary to remove two passenger seats.

Imperial Airways soon ordered a further three (later increased to four) aircraft that entered service from 1929. The aircraft of this second batch were designated **Argosy Mk II** and had Armstrong Siddeley Jaguar IVA engines in place of the original Jaguar III units to permit a 1,200-lb (544-kg) increase in the maximum take-off weight. After delivery of the Argosy Mk IIs, the original three **Argosy Mk I** machines were re-engined with Jaguar IVA engines.

City of Glasgow *was the first Argosy Mk I delivered to Imperial Airways. It is illustrated wearing its original blue colour scheme.*

Variants

Argosy Mk I: designation of original batch, at first with 385-hp (287-kW) Jaguar IIIA direct-drive radials but later re-engined with Jaguar IVA radials; data as for Mk II except range of 330 miles (531 km), empty weight of 12,000 lb (5443 kg), maximum take-off weight of 18,000 lb (8165 kg), wingspan of 90 ft 8 in (27.64 m), length of 65 ft 10 in (20.07 m), height of 19 ft 10 in (6.05 m) and wing area 1,886.00 sq ft (175.22 m²)
Argosy Mk II: designation of second batch with three Jaguar IVA radials; this variant also featured some slight refinements in control by the use of servo tabs on the lower wing

SPECIFICATION	
Armstrong Whitworth Argosy Mk II	at optimum altitude; climb to 3,000 ft (915 m) in 4 minutes 30 seconds; range 520 miles (837 km)
Type: two/three-crew medium transport	
Powerplant: three Armstrong Siddeley Jaguar IVA geared radial piston engines each rated at 420 hp (313 kW)	**Weights:** empty 12,090 lb (5484 kg); maximum take-off 19,200 lb (8709 kg)
Performance: maximum speed 110 mph (177 km/h) at optimum altitude; cruising speed between 90 and 95 mph (145 and 153 km/h)	**Dimensions:** wingspan 90 ft 4 in (27.53 m); length 67 ft 20.42 m); height 20 ft (6.10 m); wing area 1,873.00 sq ft (174.01 m²)
	Payload: up to 20 passengers

Armstrong Whitworth Argosy (continued)

The Argosy opened the first Empire air mail link with India on 30 March 1929, carrying the mail to Basle, where it was transferred by train to Genoa and then by air, via various stops, to Karachi. The Argosy fleet was gradually whittled down by accidents: in April 1931 an Argosy burned out in a crash at Croydon during a crew training flight, and two months later another Argosy was lost in a forced landing near Aswan: fortunately no-one was injured in either incident. However, an unexplained fire in the air over Belgium, in March 1933, resulted in a crash in which the crew of three and all 12 passengers were killed. With H.P.42s entering service, the last Argosies were retired. The final machine, an Argosy Mk II named *City of Manchester*, was purchased by United Airways in July 1935 and used for joy-riding at Blackpool during the summer of 1936. It was subsequently taken over by British Airways and was retired in December 1936.

Armstrong Whitworth Awana

The **Armstrong Whitworth Awana** troop transport competed with the Vickers Victoria to meet a 1920 requirement, and the Air Ministry ordered two prototypes of each type. The Awana could carry 25 troops and was a substantial biplane with fixed tailskid landing gear. It featured a mixed structure that combined a steel tube fuselage, wire-braced and fabric-covered, with long-span fabric-covered wooden wings which could be folded.

The prototype made its maiden flight on 28 June 1923 and then went to Martlesham Heath for tests. The aircraft's performance was reasonable, but there were some problems with the landing gear when taxiing, and control during landing was said to be poor. Other criticisms levelled at the Awana were that its steel tube fuselage was too flexible and should have been of heavier construction; that it was difficult and time-consuming to fill the fuel tanks under the top wing by hand pump; that in several other respects the type's flimsiness would cause maintenance problems in service and that the cabin floor was weak.

A few improvements were incorporated in the second prototype, but the Awana lost out to the Victoria for the RAF's order.

SPECIFICATION

Armstrong Whitworth Awana
Type: two-crew troop transport aircraft
Powerplant: two Napier Lion W-type piston engines each rated at 450 hp (335.5 kW)
Performance: maximum speed 97 mph (156 km/h) at 3,000 ft (915 m); maximum cruising speed 86 mph (137 km/h) at optimum altitude; climb to 5,000 ft (1525 m) in 19 minutes 42 seconds; service ceiling 8,000 ft (2440 m); range 360 miles (579 km)
Weights: empty 10,000 lb (4536 kg); maximum take-off 18,450 lb (8369 kg)
Dimensions: wingspan 105 ft 6 in (32.16 m); length 68 ft (20.73 m); height 20 ft (6.10 m); wing area 2,300.00 sq ft (213.67 m²)
Payload: up to 20 troops

Among the many faults of the Awana was that its propeller tips passed too close to the fuselage, causing the windows to crack.

Armstrong Whitworth Atlas

First flown on 10 May 1925, the **Armstrong Whitworth Atlas** was the Royal Air Force's first aircraft specifically developed for the army co-operation role. Designed to a 1926 requirement, the Atlas was ordered in substantial quantities, a total of 446 aircraft (including 175 examples of the **Atlas Trainer** variant to a 1931 requirement) being built for the RAF.

Initially developed as a private venture, the civil prototype of the Atlas was converted to meet military standards and given a military serial, as were two other demonstrator aircraft. One of the latter appeared at the Paris air display of December 1926, and was subsequently shipped to South America for various demonstrations.

The Atlas was selected in preference to the Bristol Type 93 Boarhound, de Havilland DH.56 Hyena and Vickers Type 113 Vespa, and as a result of tests at Martlesham Heath, various modifications were made to improve certain performance aspects. There followed service trials at Andover in 1927, and No. 26 Squadron at Catterick in Yorkshire was the first to receive the Atlas in October 1927. Overseas deliveries began early in 1930 when the type began to replace No. 208 Squadron's Bristol F.2B Fighters in Egypt.

The Atlas proved versatile in service, and in addition to its army co-operation role it was used by a number of RAF stations for communications duties. The School of Photography at Farnborough also used the type. As a dual-control trainer, the Atlas became standard equipment in RAF flying training schools from 1931 until the time that Hawker Hart Trainers began to replace it two years later. Four civil aircraft were used by the Armstrong Whitworth flying school from 1931, when the school moved from Whitley to Hamble and became Air Service Training Ltd.

A number of foreign orders were placed for the military Atlas, the customers being Canada (16), Greece (2), China (14) and Japan (1). The Canadian deliveries covered six new aircraft, supplied between December 1927 and October 1929 and, in November 1934, a total of 10 ex-RAF aircraft. One of the Canadian aircraft was configured as a trainer, and the RCAF's Atlas aircraft withstood the tough Canadian environment well, the last of the type being retired only in 1942. One other ex-RAF aircraft was sold to Egypt. Including foreign sales, production of civil and military Atlases totalled 478 aircraft.

In the RAF the Hawker Audax began to replace the Atlas in its primary army co-operation role during February 1932, while the trainer Atlases began to give way to Hart Trainers in August 1933.

A message hook beneath the fuselage, forward-firing Vickers machine-gun and Scarff ring around the rear cockpit were features of all army co-op Atlases.

Variants

Atlas Mk I: production model to meet civil and military orders
Atlas Mk II: 14 aircraft for China with redesigned fuselage and larger fin to suit the type as a fighter and day bomber; other minor improvements and a powerplant comprising one 535-hp (399-kW) Armstrong Siddeley Panther IIA radial engine; maximum take-off weight 4,950 lb (2245 kg) and maximum speed 152 mph (245 km/h) at sea level; three civil examples of the Atlas Mk II were also built

SPECIFICATION

Armstrong Whitworth Atlas Mk I
Type: two-seat army co-operation and training aircraft
Powerplant: one Armstrong Siddeley Jaguar IVC radial engine rated at 400 hp (298 kW)
Performance: maximum speed 142 mph (229 km/h) at sea level; climb to 5,000 ft (1525 m) in 5 minutes 30 seconds; service ceiling 16,800 ft (5120 m); endurance 3 hours 15 minutes
Weights: empty 2,550 lb (1157 kg); maximum take-off 4,020 lb (1823 kg)
Dimensions: wingspan 39 ft 7 in (12.06 m); length 28 ft 7 in (8.71 m); height 10 ft 6 in (3.20 m); wing area 391.00 sq ft (36.32 m²)
Armament: one 0.303-in (7.7-mm) fixed forward-firing machine-gun and one 0.303-in (7.7-mm) trainable rearward-firing machine-gun, plus 480 lb (218 kg) of bombs carried on underwing racks

Armstrong Whitworth Siskin

Originating in the **Siddeley Deasy S.R.2 Siskin**, produced by Armstrong Whitworth's parent company in 1919, the **Armstrong Whitworth Siskin** in its developed form became the mainstay of the Royal Air Force's fighter force from the mid-1920s. The S.R.2 was designed for a 300-hp (224-kW) radial engine then being developed at Farnborough as the Royal Aircraft Factory 8. Further development of the engine was passed to Siddeley Deasy, but because of that company's involvement with the Puma engine, the RAF 8 was put to one side and the S.R.2 first flew with the 320-hp (239-kW) ABC Dragonfly radial engine. Although the aircraft's performance was good, the engine was a failure and the design was therefore modified for use with the 325-hp (242-kW) Armstrong Siddeley Jaguar radial engine. The first of three Siskin prototypes, now known as Armstrong Siddeley aircraft, flew in March 1921.

The Air Ministry's new policy of ordering only all-metal aircraft forced Armstrong Siddeley to redesign the Siskin, and after several composite wood and metal aircraft had been built, the first all-metal **Siskin Mk III**, ordered for the RAF in 1920, flew in May 1923. There followed an order for a pre-production batch of three aircraft, of which the first flew 10 months later.

Sales tours in Europe resulted in an order for 65 aircraft from Romania, the first being flown in October 1924, with six others following by the end of the year. However, the order was cancelled following the crash of a Romanian Siskin in which the pilot was fatally injured.

The first Siskin Mk III fighters for the RAF went to No. 41 Squadron at Northolt in May 1924, while No. 111 Squadron replaced its Sopwith Snipes with Siskins in the following month. Total Siskin Mk III production reached 465, including some two-seaters. Estonia, the Royal Canadian Air Force and Armstrong Whitworth's flying school each had two two-seat versions of the type, and the RAF also had some supplied new as two-seaters, while others were later converted to a similar standard.

Most prolific of the series was the **Siskin Mk IIIA**, the prototype of which was a conversion of the first Siskin Mk III and flew in October 1925. An Armstrong Siddeley Jaguar IV supercharged engine gave considerably superior performance, and 387 Siskin Mk IIIA fighters were subsequently built for the RAF, the total including 47 dual-control trainers. All but 135 were built under subcontract in the form of 84, 74, 52 and 42 machines delivered by Bristol, Gloster, Vickers and Blackburn respectively.

The first unit to be re-equipped with the new variant was No. 111 Squadron in September 1926, and 10 other squadrons used the Siskin Mk IIIA until No. 56 Squadron's aircraft were replaced by Bristol Bulldog fighters in October 1932. As a result of its evaluation of two Siskin Mk III fighters, the RCAF ordered 12 Siskin Mk IIIA machines, which were delivered between 1926 and 1931 in the form of some new and some ex-RAF aircraft. The Siskins of No. 1 (Fighter) Squadron, RCAF, were replaced by Hawker Hurricanes in 1939, and struck off charge from storage in 1947.

Variants

S.R.2 Siskin: original three aircraft built by the Siddeley Deasy Motor Car Co.
Siskin Mk II: civil prototype of 1923 flown in single- and two-seat configurations
Siskin Mk III: all-metal production version (64 aircraft all for the RAF) with the powerplant of one 325-hp (242-kW) Armstrong Siddeley Jaguar III radial piston engine, maximum speed of 134 mph (216 km/h) at 6,500 ft (1980 m), climb to 6,500 ft (1980 m) in 5 minutes, service ceiling of 20,500 ft (6250 m), endurance of 3 hours, empty weight of 1,830 lb (830 kg), maximum take-off weight of 2,735 lb (1241 kg), wingspan of 33 ft 1 in (10.08 m), length of 23 ft (7.01 m), height of 9 ft 9 in (2.95 m) and wing area of 293.00 sq ft (27.22 m²)
Siskin Mk IIIA: main production variant (340 and 12 aircraft for RAF and RCAF respectively)
Siskin Mk IIIB: single prototype with supercharged Jaguar VIII engine with reduction gear for a climb to 15,000 ft (4570 m) in 11 minutes 30 seconds, some 2 minutes better than could be managed by the Siskin Mk IIIA; at this altitude the Siskin Mk IIIB was some 20 mph (32 km/h) faster than the Siskin Mk IIIA despite a maximum take-off weight increased by 230 lb (104 kg); however, Martlesham Heath pilots criticised the Siskin Mk IIIB's handling, and the full-throttle endurance of only 1 hour was wholly inadequate
Siskin Mk IIIDC: two-seat dual-control trainer derivative that served with the Central Flying School, the RAF College, Cranwell and Nos 3 and 5 Flying Training Schools; other examples were used by most Siskin fighter squadrons (total 53 aircraft, in the form of 47 for the RAF, two for the RCAF, two for the AST and two for Estonia)
Siskin Mk IV: single civil aircraft developed for participation in the 1925 King's Cup Race; based on the Siskin Mk V but with a shorter-span wing cellule
Siskin Mk V: civil type developed for Romania but only two examples used for racing after cancellation of the Romanian order; metal and wood construction, with a two-spar lower wing; F. L. Barnard won the 1925 King's Cup Race in a Siskin Mk V at a speed of more than 151 mph (243 km/h)

Armstrong Whitworth developed the more powerful Siskin IIIB as a successor to the RAF's Siskin IIIAs. No production followed.

SPECIFICATION

Armstrong Whitworth Siskin Mk IIIA
Type: single-seat fighter
Powerplant: one Armstrong Siddeley Jaguar IV radial engine rated at between 420 and 450 hp (313 and 336 kW)
Performance: maximum speed 156 mph (251 km/h) at sea level; climb to 15,000 ft (4570 m) in 10 minutes 30 seconds; service ceiling 27,000 ft (8230 m); endurance 1 hour 12 minutes at full throttle
Weights: empty 2,061 lb (935 kg); maximum take-off 3,012 lb (1366 kg)
Dimensions: wingspan 33 ft 2 in (10.11 m); length 25 ft 4 in (7.72 m); height 10 ft 2 in (3.10 m); wing area 293.00 sq ft (27.22 m²)
Armament: two 0.303-in (7.7-mm) fixed forward-firing machine-guns, plus up to 80 lb (36 kg) of bombs carried on an underwing rack

Armstrong Whitworth Wolf

Designed originally as a two-seat reconnaissance aircraft, the **Armstrong Whitworth Wolf** had its fuselage, like that of the Bristol F.2 Fighter, mounted between the upper and lower wings, to which it was joined by a series of clumsy struts. Armstrong Whitworth received an order for three aircraft, and the first of these flew on 19 January 1923 with a mixed structure that combined a steel tube fuselage with wooden wings. No production order was forthcoming, and the Wolf aircraft seem to have been used at the Royal Aircraft Establishment, Farnborough, for experimental flying, including the testing of automatic controls.

Seeing the possibility of using the type as a trainer, Armstrong Whitworth built three civil examples of the

Designed as a two-seat reconnaissance aircraft, the Wolf was rejected by the RAF and a total of just six was built.

Wolf for the RAF Reserve Flying School at Whitley, which the company operated. The first two of these were delivered in February and August 1923, the last following, rather surprisingly, six years later. The aircraft gave good service and were popular with pilots, although the landing gear and rigging gave maintenance problems. The machines were withdrawn from service in 1931 and scrapped, the newest aircraft going to Hamble as an instructional airframe.

SPECIFICATION

Armstrong Whitworth Wolf
Type: two-seat reconnaissance and training aircraft
Powerplant: one Armstrong Siddeley Jaguar III radial engine rated at 350 hp (261 kW)
Performance: maximum speed 110 mph (177 km/h) at 10,000 ft (3050 m); climb to 5,000 ft (1525 m) in 6 minutes 30 seconds; service ceiling 15,150 ft (4620 m); endurance 3 hours 15 minutes
Weights: empty 2,690 lb (1220 kg); maximum take-off 4,090 lb (1855 kg)
Dimensions: wingspan 39 ft 10 in (12.14 m); length 31 ft (9.45 m); height 13 ft (3.96 m); wing area 488.00 sq ft (45.34 m²)
Armament: one 0.303-in (7.7-mm) fixed forward-firing machine-gun and one 0.303-in (7.7-mm) trainable rearward-firing machine-gun

Arrow Active

Arrow Aircraft Ltd, established in Leeds, Yorkshire, was primarily a manufacturer of aircraft components, but in 1931 built one example of a single-seat aerobatic biplane designed largely by A. C. Thornton. Of conventional biplane configuration with an all-metal structure under a covering largely of fabric, a cut-out in the centre of the upper wing's

trailing edge and I-section interplane struts, this **Arrow Active I** had tailskid landing gear with a main landing gear arrangement of the divided-axle type. Its powerplant comprised a Cirrus Hermes IIB inverted inline engine. Although the manufacturer had hopes that there might be some military interest in the aircraft, this failed to materialise. The Active was used as a

sporting type until destroyed in an accident late in 1935.

The **Active II** designation was used for one aircraft generally similar to the above except for its introduction of centre-section struts, and the installation of a 120-hp (89-kW) de Havilland Gipsy III engine. Rebuilt in 1951, the aircraft was given a 145-hp (108-kW) de Havilland Gipsy Major engine, and in late 1998 was still on the British register, some 47 years after its rebuild.

A seemingly promising design, the original Active failed to gain production orders. The survival of the single Active II (illustrated) proves the type's sound basic design.

SPECIFICATION

Arrow Active I	
Type: single-seat aerobatic aircraft	altitude; cruising speed 125 mph (210 km/h) at optimum altitude
Powerplant: one Cirrus Hermes IIB inverted inline engine rated at 115 hp (86 kW)	**Weights:** empty 853 lb (387 kg); maximum take-off 1,210 lb (549 kg)
Performance: maximum speed 140 mph (225 km/h) at optimum	**Dimensions:** wingspan 24 ft (7.32 m); length 18 ft 7 in (5.66 m)

Arsenal 0.101

The sole **Arsenal 0.101** was an interesting aircraft designed as a flying testbed for aerofoil sections and control surfaces. Its basic configuration was that of a fairly conventional mid-wing monoplane. It was unusual only in the

position of the enclosed cockpits (for a pilot and observer in tandem) well aft on the fuselage. The wing and tail unit were all-wooden structures, but the fuselage was a composite of metal and wood. The landing gear was of the

fixed tailwheel type, and power was provided by a Renault 12S inverted-Vee piston engine.

Because of the research nature of the aircraft, it was equipped for the very accurate recording of data such as lift and drag loads, pressure distribution, and a variety of other factors. Of particular interest was the fact that the dimensions of the 0.101 had been chosen to ensure that the aircraft could be tested in the wind tunnel at Chalais-Meudon without the need for disassembly, so permitting the cross-checking of wind tunnel and flight test figures using the complete aircraft.

Designed and flown in the late 1940s, the 0.101 was an ingenious research platform. The observer was denied any view forwards, but was able to look across the wings from small fuselage windows.

SPECIFICATION

Arsenal 0.101	
Type: two-seat lightweight research aircraft	(2500 m); service ceiling 26,245 ft (8000 m)
Powerplant: one Renault 12S inverted-Vee engine rated at 495 hp (369 kW)	**Weight:** maximum take-off 3,814 lb (1730 kg)
Performance: maximum speed 280 mph (450 km/h) at 8,200 ft	**Dimensions:** wingspan 27 ft ¾ in (8.25 m); length 24 ft 11¼ in (7.60 m); height 10 ft 6 in (3.20 m); wing area 94.73 sq ft (8.80 m²)

Arsenal VG.30, VG.33 and VB.10

The Arsenal de l'Aéronautique, generally abbreviated to just Arsenal, was established as a national design authority for military aircraft, together with a limited production capability, at the time of the wholesale nationalisation of the French aircraft industry in 1936. One of the first designs from the new authority was the **Arsenal VG.30** single-seat fighter created, as indicated by the prefix of its designation, by Ingénieur-Général Vernisse (director of the authority) and Jean Galtier. The type was designed in competition with the Caudron

C.713 to meet a French air force requirement for a lightweight fighter, and was of 'modern' monoplane fighter design except for its wooden structure, which was of the stressed-skin variety. The intended powerplant was the Potez 12Dc flat-12 engine, an air-cooled unit rated at 610 hp (455 kW) at 3,280 ft (1000 m). It drove a reduction gearbox that allowed the incorporation of a 20-mm Hispano-Suiza HS-404 cannon in an engine-mounted installation to fire through the hollow propeller shaft.

Manufacture of the

prototype was seriously delayed by problems with the Potez engine, and the **VG.30.01** prototype finally made its maiden flight on 1 October 1938, with the revised powerplant of one Hispano-Suiza 12Xcrs Vee engine rated at 690 hp (515 kW). This was installed in a forward fuselage that had to be considerably altered from the intended configuration, not only because of the new engine's different layout, but also due to the fact that it was a liquid-cooled unit.

The VG.30 offered better performance than the Morane-Saulnier MS.406 that had been selected as the French air force's first 'modern' monoplane fighter, but further development was discontinued in favour of more advanced derivatives. The first two of these did not fly. The **VG.31** was to have been powered by the 860-hp (642-kW) Hispano-Suiza 12Y-31 engine (cooled by a radiator moved farther to the rear),

Flown for the first time in 1939, the VG.33 was an elegant and aerodynamically very clean design. Its lines were marred, however, by a substantial underfuselage radiator installation.

with a wing reduced in area to 129.17 sq ft (12.00 m²) from the VG.30's figure of 150.70 sq ft (14.00 m²), but it was not built. The **VG.32** had the original wing but the powerplant of one 1,040-hp (776-kW) Allison V-1710-C15 Vee engine, and its sole prototype was captured by the Germans just weeks before the type was scheduled to make its first flight.

The first VG.30 derivative

to fly was therefore the **VG.33**, which was in effect the production version of the VG.30 and produced as a rival to the Dewoitine D.520, Morane-Saulnier MS.450 and Ouest CAO.200, as a possible successor to the MS.406. The first example made its maiden flight on 24 May 1939, and orders were placed for an initial 220 aircraft that were to have been complemented by

SPECIFICATION

Arsenal VG.33	
Type: single-seat fighter	6,393 lb (2900 kg)
Powerplant: one Hispano-Suiza 12Y-31 Vee piston engine rated at 860 hp (642 kW)	**Dimensions:** wingspan 35 ft 5¼ in (10.80 m); length 28 ft ⅔ in (8.55 m); height 10 ft 10⅓ in (3.31 m) with the tail up; wing area 150.70 sq ft (14.00 m²)
Performance: maximum speed 367 mph (590 km/h) at sea level; service ceiling 36,090 ft (11000 m); range 746 miles (1200 km)	**Armament:** one 20-mm fixed forward-firing cannon and four 0.295-in (7.5-mm) fixed forward-firing machine-guns
Weights: empty 4,519 lb (2050 kg); maximum take-off	

another 1,000 machines. Another three prototypes were built, but only 19 of the production aircraft had been completed by the Chantiers Aéro-Maritimes de la Seine before Germany defeated France in June 1940.

Development of the same basic design concept resulted in the **VB.10** heavy fighter and fighter-bomber that was ordered in May 1940. Designed by Vernisse and M. Badie, the

VB.10 was of all-metal construction and designed around a twin-engined powerplant, with single units fore and aft of the single-seat cockpit, driving a contra-rotating assembly of two three-bladed propellers. Work on the VB.10 continued at a slow pace under the Vichy regime which ruled the rump of France up to its occupation by the Germans in November 1942. The first prototype

finally made its maiden flight on 7 July 1945 with the powerplant of two 860-hp (641-kW) Hispano-Suiza 12Y-31 engines that were replaced in the second prototype by two 1,150-hp (858-kW) Hispano-Suiza 12Z-12/13 engines. The fixed forward-firing armament consisted of four 20-mm cannon and six 0.5-in (12.7-mm) machine-guns.

An order was placed for 200 (later trimmed to 50)

production aircraft with the revised powerplant of two 1,150-hp (858-kW) Hispano-Suiza 12Zars-15/16 engines and the reduced armament of four 20-mm cannon. The first of these aircraft was completed in November 1947, and the production contract for what was by now an obsolete type was cancelled in September 1948 after the manufacture of a mere four aircraft. The other data for the VB.10 included a maximum level

speed of 435 mph (700 km/h) at 24,605 ft (7500 m), initial climb rate of 2,008 ft (612 m) per minute; service ceiling of 36,120 ft (11010 m), range of 1,056 miles (1700 km), empty weight of 13,735 lb (6230 kg), normal take-off weight of 19,533 lb (8860 kg), wingspan of 50 ft 9⅞ in (15.49 m), length of 42 ft 7 in (12.98 m), height of 17 ft ¾ in (5.20 m) and wing area of 382.12 sq ft (35.50 m²).

Arsenal VG.34, VG.35 and VG.36

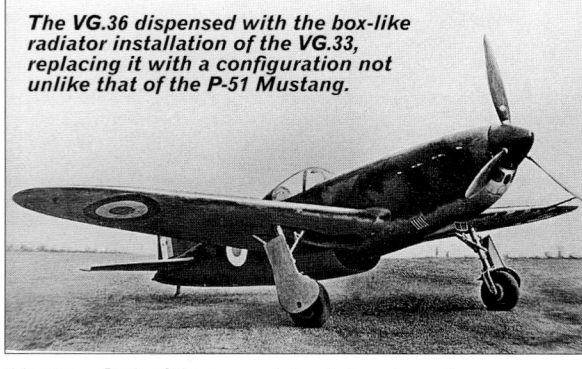

The VG.36 dispensed with the box-like radiator installation of the VG.33, replacing it with a configuration not unlike that of the P-51 Mustang.

The VG.33 had a radiator bath under the fuselage in line with the cockpit for the cooling of its Hispano-Suiza 12Y engine, and the same basic configuration was retained in the two next developments of the VG.30 series, namely the **Arsenal VG.34** and **VG.35**. These

were little more than the airframe (complete with fixed forward-firing armament) of the VG.33 with different engines. The VG.34 first flew on 20 January 1940 with the 910-hp (679-kW) Hispano-Suiza 12Y-45. It attained a maximum level speed of

357 mph (575 km/h) at 20,340 ft (620 m), while the VG.35 made its maiden flight on 25 February 1940 with the 1,000-hp (746-kW) Hispano-Suiza 12Y-51 inline piston engine.

Slight changes were effected in the **VG.36** that first flew on 14 May 1940: the rear fuselage was revised so that its undersurface was a faired extension of the radiator bath, which was modified in cross section with greater width but reduced depth.

Only single examples of each of these developments were completed and flown, but the **VG.37** and **VG.38** failed to reach even

this stage. Both of these types remained unrealised projects, the former being planned with a 1,000-hp (746-kW) Hispano-Suiza Vee engine that ultimately did not materialise, and the

latter being planned as a high-altitude fighter with the powerplant of one Hispano-Suiza 77 Vee engine boosted by a pair of exhaust-driven Brown-Boveri turbochargers.

SPECIFICATION	
Arsenal VG.36	**Dimensions:** wingspan 35 ft 5¼ in (10.80 m); length 26 ft 6⅝ in (8.10 m); height 10 ft 10½ in (3.31 m); wing area 150.70 sq ft (14.00 m²)
Type: single-seat fighter	
Powerplant: one Hispano-Suiza 12Y-51 Vee engine rated at 1,000 hp (746 kW)	
Performance: maximum speed 367 mph (590 km/h) at 22,965 ft (7000 m); range 684 miles (1100 km)	**Armament:** one 20-mm fixed forward-firing cannon and four 0.295-in (7.5-mm) fixed forward-firing machine-guns

Arsenal VG.70

Designed by a team under the supervision of Jean Galtier, the Arsenal VG.70 was a research aircraft intended to investigate the use of a turbojet powerplant in a fighter-type airframe. Of cantilever shoulder-wing monoplane configuration, the VG.70 incorporated an enclosed pilot's cockpit, swept tail surfaces and retractable tricycle landing gear. The Junkers Jumo

004B-2 turbojet powerplant was mounted within the fuselage and was aspirated by means of a virtually

semi-circular inlet under the fuselage in line with the cockpit. The engine exhausted through a plain nozzle. The VG.70 began flight testing soon after the end of World War II.

Of unusual configuration, the VG.70 combined a German turbojet with a French airframe to provide data on jet propulsion. The underfuselage intake must have rendered the engine vulnerable to FOD.

SPECIFICATION	
Arsenal VG.70	(900 km/h) at optimum altitude
Type: single-seat research aircraft	**Weights:** maximum take-off 6,614 lb (3000 kg)
Powerplant: one Junkers Jumo 004B-2 turbojet engine rated at 1,896 lb st (8.43 kN)	**Dimensions:** wingspan 27 ft 10¾ in (8.50 m); length 31 ft 9¾ in (9.70 m); height 7 ft 6½ in (2.30 m); wing area 161.46 sq ft (15.00 m²)
Performance: (estimated) maximum speed 559 mph	

Arsenal-Delanne 10

In 1936 the designer Maurice Delanne first proposed the use of the Nédanovich biplane (tandem monoplane) layout for a military aircraft. The concept was thought to require validation, and as a result the Société Anonyme Française de Recherches Aéronautiques

(SAFRA) produced a light two-seat monoplane of this tandem-wing configuration as the **Delanne 20** with the powerplant of one 180-hp (134-kW) Régnier R6 engine. Although this machine was lost during its first test flight on 10 August 1938, a second machine was manufactured and successfully flown from March 1939.

With the technical and aerodynamic feasibility of the tandem-wing monoplane configuration now proved, SAFRA was ordered by the French air ministry to pass its data on

the tandem-wing layout to the Arsenal de l'Aéronautique, which then began work on the **Arsenal-Delanne 10** as a C.2 (two-seat fighter) aircraft of this radical layout. Apart from the slots on the leading edge of the front wing, the fighter closely followed the layout of the Delanne 20 and was of stressed-skin light alloy construction. An unusual feature of the design was the closing of the wheel well doors once the mainwheels had been extended in order to offer an undisturbed airflow over the lower fuselage. The enclosed cockpit was located to the rear of the fuel tank; the pilot in the front seat and the gunner in the rear seat had excellent fields of fire in the hemisphere immediately

behind the aircraft. The strut-braced front wing was of the inverted gull type, while the rear wing was a cantilever unit with swept leading edges and endplate vertical surfaces.

The Arsenal-Delanne 10 prototype had only just been completed when the invading German forces seized Villacoublay in June 1940, and the German air

ministry was sufficiently impressed to order continued work on the type. After extensive delays, the Arsenal-Delanne 10 achieved its maiden flight during October 1941. With initial trials completed, the fighter was ferried to a German experimental centre for continued evaluation, but its subsequent history remains unknown.

The ultimate fate of the unusually configured Arsenal-Delanne 10 fighter is unknown.

SPECIFICATION	
	(2880 kg)
Arsenal-Delanne 10	**Dimensions:** wingspan 33 ft 2 in (10.11 m); length 24 ft ½ in (7.33 m); height 10 ft ½ in (3.06 m); wing area 242.19 sq ft (22.50 m²)
Type: two-seat multi-role fighter	
Powerplant: one Hispano-Suiza 12Ycrs Vee engine rated at 860 hp (641 kW)	
Performance: maximum speed 342 mph (550 km/h) at 14,765 ft (4500 m); climb to 16,405 ft (5000 m) in 6 minutes 30 seconds; service ceiling 32,810 ft (10000 m); endurance 1 hour 30 minutes	**Armament:** (proposed) one 20-mm fixed forward-firing cannon and two 0.295-in (7.5-mm) fixed forward-firing machine-guns, plus two 0.295-in (7.5-mm) trainable rearward-firing machine-guns
Weight: normal take-off 6,349 lb	

ASTA (GAF) Nomad Missionmaster and Searchmaster

The Government Aircraft Factories (GAF) organisation, which was reconstituted in 1986 as the AeroSpace Technologies of Australia Pty Ltd (ASTA) and sold to the Rockwell Corporation of the USA during 1995, was the main producer of aircraft in Australia. As there were only limited military aircraft requirements, it was decided to develop a small turboprop-powered STOL machine suitable for both military and civil use.

Development began in the late 1960s, and the first of two GAF N2 Nomad prototypes made its initial flight on 23 July 1971. Of braced high-wing monoplane configuration, the Nomad has STOL performance as a result of its full-span double-slotted flaps and drooping ailerons. The powerplant consists of two Allison turboprop engines each driving a constant-speed reversible-pitch propeller.

The first versions of the Nomad were the **N22** intended for the civil market with accommodation for up to 12 passengers, and the **N24** utility model intended for military as well as civil use, with its fuselage lengthened by 3 ft 9 in (1.14 m) for the accommodation of 17 passengers. Later production versions included the higher-weight **N22B** for 14 passengers, and the improved **N24A**. A twin-float **N22F**, subsequently named **Floatmaster**, was certificated in the USA during 1979, and an amphibious version gained certification during 1980. The Nomad failed to secure the sales that had been expected of the type, and production ended in 1984 after the completion of 170 aircraft of the Nomad family. About half of these were delivered in **Nomad Missionmaster** form (four underwing hardpoints and load-bearing drop-doors in the cabin floor) to military operators in Australia, Indonesia, Papua New Guinea, the Philippines and Thailand. The 25 Australian aircraft were retained to 1995, when the survivors were grounded as a result of their poor safety record and structural problems which prevented the use of full-flap deflection and thus made STOL operations impossible. The last 20

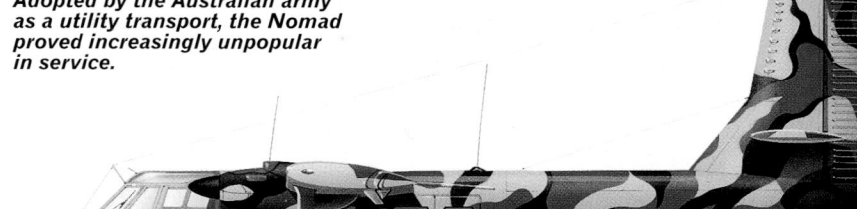

Adopted by the Australian army as a utility transport, the Nomad proved increasingly unpopular in service.

aircraft were then sold to the Indonesian navy.

The **ASTA (GAF) Nomad Searchmaster** is the dedicated maritime patrol and surveillance counterpart of the Missionmaster. The two primary variants are the **Nomad N22 Searchmaster B** coastal patrol model and the **Nomad N22 Searchmaster L** improved version of the Searchmaster B, with its larger radar antenna in an undernose 'guppy' radome.

Two subvariants of the Searchmaster L were available as the **Searchmaster L I** with baseline APS-504(V)2 radar and the **Searchmaster L II** with upgraded APS-504(V)5 radar supplemented by an underbelly FLIR sensor.

Searchmasters were sold to Indonesia, Marshall Islands, Papua New Guinea, the Philippines and Thailand.

Each of the Nomad's main undercarriage units is mounted within a sponson at the tip of a short stub wing. This keeps the cabin clear of obstruction and also provides a mounting point for the wing struts.

With its undernose radar antenna, the Searchmaster is able to provide 360° radar coverage. The aircraft has proven useful in the fisheries protection role.

SPECIFICATION	
ASTA (GAF) N22B Nomad **Type:** one/two-crew STOL utility aircraft **Powerplant:** two Allison 250-B17C turboprop engines each rated at 420 shp (313 kW) **Performance:** normal cruising speed 193 mph (311 km/h) at optimum altitude; initial climb rate 1,460 ft (445 m) per minute; service ceiling 21,000 ft (6400 m); range 840 miles (1352 km) **Weights:** empty 4,740 lb (2150 kg); maximum take-off	8,500 lb (3856 kg) **Dimensions:** wingspan 54 ft 2⅓ in (16.52 m); length 41 ft 2⅔ in (12.56 m); height 18 ft 1½ in (5.52 m); wing area 324.00 sq ft (30.10 m²) **Armament:** generally none, although provision was made on military aircraft for up to 2,000 lb (907 kg) of disposable stores carried on four underwing hardpoints **Payload:** 14 passengers or 3,600 lb (1633 kg) of freight

Atlas C4M Kudu

The Atlas Aircraft Corporation was absorbed into Armscor in 1969 and from 1992 was known as the Atlas Aviation (Pty) Ltd division of Denel (Pty) Ltd. However, since November 1996, Atlas Aviation (Pty) Ltd has been known as Denel Aviation.

Atlas' first wholly indigenous product was the **C4M Kudu** which Atlas insisted was developed entirely in South Africa, although there is a clear design connection with the Aeritalia/Aermacchi AM.3C. In addition, the Kudu's Avco Lycoming engine was licence-built in Italy.

The Kudu, as the military

SPECIFICATION	
Atlas C4M Kudu **Type:** one/two-crew STOL utility light transport **Powerplant:** one Avco Lycoming GSO-480-B1B3 flat-six engine rated at 340 hp (254 kW) **Performance:** maximum speed 161 mph (259 km/h) at 8,000 ft (2440 m); maximum cruising speed 145 mph (233 km/h) at 10,000 ft (3050 m); initial climb rate 800 ft (244 m) per minute; service ceiling 14,000 ft (4270 m); range 806 miles	(1297 km) with maximum fuel or 460 miles (740 km) with an 882-lb (400-kg) payload **Weights:** empty 2,711 lb (1230 kg); maximum take-off 4,497 lb (2040 kg) **Dimensions:** wingspan 42 ft 10¾ in (13.075 m); length 30 ft 6½ in (9.31 m); height 12 ft (3.66 m); wing area 225.73 sq ft (20.97 m²) **Payload:** see above

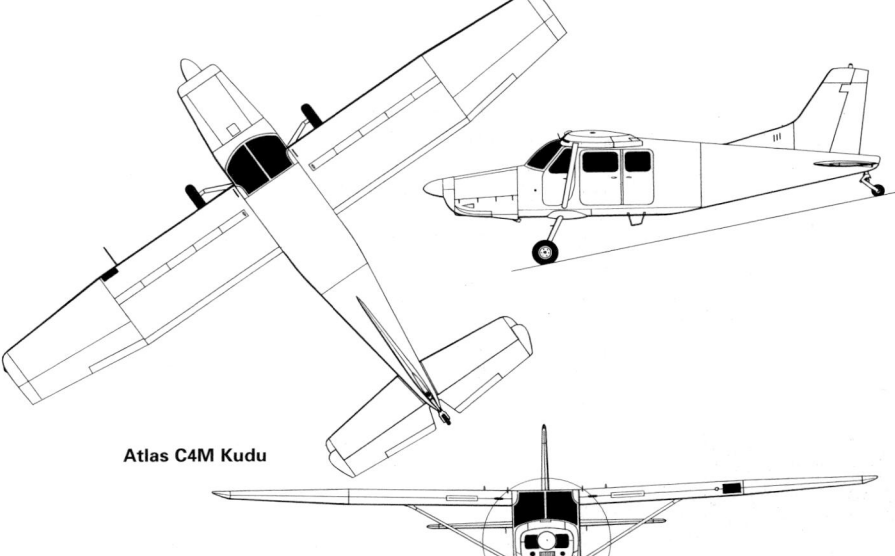

Atlas C4M Kudu

Although it features less cabin glazing than the Aermacchi AM.3C, the Kudu clearly owes much to the Italian design. At least one SAAF aircraft was modified for use in the casevac role.

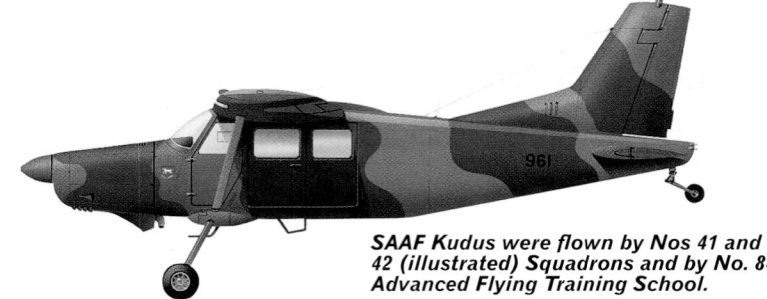

SAAF Kudus were flown by Nos 41 and 42 (illustrated) Squadrons and by No. 84 Advanced Flying Training School.

C4M was known, was intended primarily as a general-purpose transport. Accommodation was provided for a crew of two as well as four to six soldiers in the cabin, or 1,235 lb (560 kg) of freight. Loading was effected via a double door on the port side, and there was a slid-ing door for parachute-jumping on the starboard side. Other military applica-tions included supply dropping and aerial survey, there being a trap-door in the fuselage floor for use as a camera opening or for air-dropping; and the Kudu could also be operated in the casevac role.

The first prototype of the C4M was a civil aircraft that made its initial flight on 16 February 1974, followed by a military Kudu proto-type on 18 June 1975. It seems probable that more than 40 Kudus had been built by the end of 1979. The last were retired in the early 1990s.

Atlas Cheetah

A November 1977 United Nations embargo on the delivery of weapons to South Africa forced the South African Air Force (SAAF) to place a high priority on a mid-life upgrade of the aircraft surviving from the 74 Dassault Mirage III fighters and related types received during 1963-70. The upgrade was revealed on 16 July 1986 with the unveiling of a two-seat Mirage IIID2Z converted to the new **Atlas Cheetah** standard that benefited from Israeli technology (a fact that was officially denied) and closely resem-bled the IAI Kfir.

Aerodynamic modifica-tions include Kfir-type small nose side-strakes to prevent yaw departure at high angles of attack, dog-toothed outboard leading-edge extensions, short fences replacing lead-ing-edge slots, canard foreplanes on the upper parts of the engine air inlets, and fixed droop on the lead-ing edges of the wing. The converted two-seat aircraft also have curved strakes below the cockpit along the lower fuselage.

Structural modifications aimed at increasing the minimum life of the wing main spar have progressed through several (proposed) progressive stages of modi-fication with a view to reducing fatigue problems

to providing a life extension of up to 1,250 hours for a complete refurbishment with a newly manufactured main spar.

The conversions from two-seat and R2Z standards are powered by a SNECMA Atar 9K50 turbojet engine, for which Atlas had a manu-facturing licence. Other conversions retain the origi-nal Atar 9C or 9D turbojets. Another improvement was the addition of an inflight-refuelling probe, which permits take-off with a lower fuel load and a corre-spondingly higher warload.

Performance improve-ments include reductions in specific fuel consumption, take-off distance, minimum speed and climb, increased specific excess power, sustained load factor and sustained turn rate. The canard surfaces permit the maximum take-off weight to be increased by 1,543 lb (700 kg) for a penalty of under 5 per cent in level acceleration time and maxi-mum level speed.

The avionics upgrade is probably based on the Elbit System 81 (or possibly the upgraded System 82) weapons delivery and navi-gation system fitted to the Kfir-C2 (or C7). The HUD, computer terminal unit and armament control and display panel function via a MIL-1553B databus, and allow for pre-flight program-ming and HOTAS pilot

Starting life as a Mirage IIID2Z, 845 was the first aircraft to be modified to Cheetah D standard.

operation. The nav/attack system includes an inertial system and options include a helmet-mounted sight (of indigenous or Israeli origin) and a radar altimeter. The Kfir-type drooped nose houses an Elta ELM-2001B radar ranging unit. Like the Kfir, the Cheetah features a fuselage plug ahead of the windscreen to accommo-date the extra avionics. Self-protection systems include an SPS-2000 RWR system with antennae in the nose and in the trailing edge of the fin and possibly a jammer system in the former rocket motor fairing.

The **Cheetah DZ** differs primarily from the **Cheetah EZ** by having a longer nose, like that of the Kfir-T, with more pronounced droop and accommodating avion-ics displaced from the spine. An undernose fairing directly to the rear of the pitot boom contains two radar warning antennae and a large cooling intake.

The Cheetah's fixed armament comprises two 30-mm DEFA cannon, and all of its other weapons have officially been stated to be of South African manufacture. These include the V3B Kukri/V3C

Darter dogfight missiles (plus the possibility of newly developed medium- and long-range AAMs). Also included are air-to-surface items such as the AS30 ASM (which also forms the basis of a reported smart weapon used with an indigenous designator pod), cluster bombs, rockets and combined fuel/rocket pods. These loads are carried on the hardpoints inherited from the Mirage III supple-mented by two hardpoints (like those of the Kfir-C7) fitted directly ahead of the wing/engine inlet trunking.

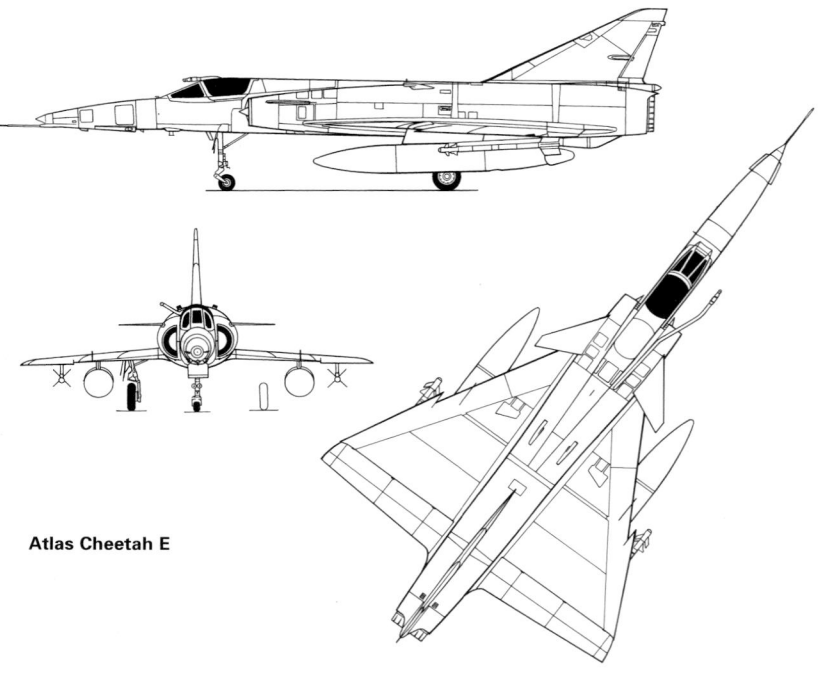

Atlas Cheetah E

SPECIFICATION

Atlas Cheetah C
Type: single-seat multi-role fighter
Powerplant: one SNECMA Atar 9C turbojet engine rated at 9,436 lb st (41.97 kN) dry and 13,668 lb st (60.80 kN) with afterburning or, more probably, one Atar 9K50 turbojet engine rated at 11,923 lb st (49.03 kN) dry and 15,873 lb st (70.82 kN) with afterburning
Performance: maximum speed 1,453 mph (2338 km/h) or Mach

2.20 at 39,370 ft (12000 m); maximum cruising speed 594 mph (956 km/h) at 36,090 ft (11000 m); service ceiling 55,775 ft (17000 m)
Dimensions: wingspan 26 ft 11⅜ in (8.22 m); length 51 ft 4¼ in (15.65 m) including probe; height 14 ft 11¼ in (4.55 m); wing area 374.60 sq ft (34.80 m²)
Armament: two 30-mm fixed forward-firing cannon and up to 8,818 lb (400 kg) of disposable stores carried externally

Atlas Cheetah (continued)

The first Cheetah conversions comprised eight Mirage IIID2Z trainers adapted to two-seat Cheetah DZ standard. These were declared operational in 1987 as trainers with a possible first-line role as pathfinders for Cheetah EZ single-seat warplanes. The SAAF had a total of 16 Mirage IIIDZ and D2Z two-seaters available for conversion after retirement from service in the first part of the 1990s, but at least another four aircraft have been produced as conversions from two-seat Mirage III aircraft secured

from an undisclosed source, but possibly from Israeli stocks.

The Cheetah EZ is the single-seat version of the family, and more than 26 such aircraft have been produced as conversions from 21 SAAF aircraft (14 Mirage IIIEZ, four Mirage IIIRZ and three Mirage IIIR2Z machines) as well as at least five Mirage III aircraft secured from an undisclosed source. The aircraft apparently retain their original engines, and the Mirage IIIRZ and Mirage IIIR2Z conversions retain their original photo-

reconnaissance nose configurations.

The **Cheetah R2** further upgraded model was revealed in April 1992 as a development of the Cheetah concept. Its ACW (Advanced Combat Wing) incorporates fixed and drooped leading edges for reduced supersonic drag, it has a 14 per cent improvement in sustained turn rate, increased internal fuel capacity and wing-tip rails for two short-range AAMs all at a weight penalty of 1,323 lb (600 kg) by comparison with the Cheetah EZ.

To mark the 75th anniversary of the SAAF in 1995, No. 2 Squadron applied this extravagant colour scheme to one of its Cheetah Cs. The aircraft soon earned the nickname 'Spotty'.

Atlas Impala

In the mid-1960s South Africa finalised a contract to build the Aermacchi MB-326M variant of the MB-326GB, suitable for the advanced training and counter-insurgency roles. An initial 16 kits were supplied by Aermacchi, these being assembled by Atlas for a first flight on 11 May 1966. The next 30 kits were less complete, requiring Atlas to fabricate a percentage of the structure before assembly. After this, an additional 105 were built almost wholly by Atlas, the last of these aircraft being completed in

1974. These machines entered service with the South African Air Force under the designation **Atlas Impala Mk 1**, being initially received by the Flying Training School at Langebaanweg, where the aircraft were flown by No. 83 Jet Flying School for the streaming of jet- and transport-assigned pilots. The two-seat trainer is also the mount of the *Silver Falcons*, the five-ship aerobatic display team of the South African Air Force.

South Africa also acquired a licence for the MB-326KM subvariant of

A replacement for the Impala Mk 2 is being sought. Meanwhile, the aircraft continues to fly with No. 85 Combat Flying School and as a light-attack platform with No. 8 Squadron.

Aermacchi's single-seat MB-326. Atlas production began yet again with the assembly of Italian-supplied kits, in this instance for seven aircraft, and progressed to almost 90 per cent manufacture in South Africa of a further 93 aircraft. The first of the aircraft entered service

with the SAAF on 22 April 1974 under the designation **Impala Mk 2**, and this type differs from the MB-326KM in minor details, primarily by retaining the same powerplant as the Impala Mk 1 instead of the more powerful version of the Viper turbojet engine used in the MB-326K.

A mixture of Impala

Mks 1 and 2 serve in the COIN/advanced training role, and Impala Mk 2s are also used in the streaming of future Cheetah pilots. The aircraft were also used extensively in South Africa's bush wars in Angola and Namibia, where the main tasks were ground-attack/close-support and aerial reconnaissance.

Although the two-seat Impala Mk 1 continues to fly with the Silver Falcons, the aircraft is gradually being replaced by the PC-7 Mk II Astra, which was originally ordered to replace the Harvard.

SPECIFICATION

Atlas Impala Mk 2
Type: single-seat light attack warplane with operational and armament training capabilities
Powerplant: one Rolls-Royce (Bristol Siddeley) Viper 20 Mk 540 turbojet engine rated at 3,410 lb st (15.17 kN)
Performance: maximum speed 553 mph (890 km/h) at 5,000 ft (1525 m); initial climb rate 6,500 ft (1981 m) per minute; climb to 36,000 ft (10975 m) in 9 minutes 30 seconds; service ceiling 47,000 ft (14325 m); range more than 1,323 miles (2130 km) with drop tanks; radius 167 miles

(268 km) on a lo-lo-lo attack mission with a warload of 2,822 lb (1280 kg)
Weights: empty 6,534 lb (2964 kg); maximum take-off 13,000 lb (5897 kg)
Dimensions: wingspan 33 ft 3⅜ in (10.15 m) without tip tanks and 35 ft 7 in (10.85 m) with tip tanks; length 35 ft ¼ in (10.67 m); height 12 ft 2 in (3.72 m); wing area 208.29 sq ft (19.35 m²)
Armament: two 30-mm fixed forward-firing cannon, and up to 4,000 lb (1814 kg) of disposable stores carried on six underwing hardpoints

Atlas XH-1 Alpha, XH-2 and Denel CSH-2 Rooivalk

The **Atlas** (now **Denel**) **Rooivalk** (red kestrel) programme continues despite defence cuts which once threatened the SAAF's requirement for this helicopter. The aircraft is the first operational result of a development programme launched in 1981 for an indigenous attack helicopter. The programme initially involved the **XH-1 Alpha** and **XTP-2**

Beta as concept-proving and systems test-beds. The XH-1 was a one-off systems test-bed based on the airframe and dynamic system of the Aérospatiale Alouette III light helicopter. Ordered from Atlas in March 1981, the XH-1 first flew on 27 February 1986 with a narrow pod-and-boom fuselage carrying the pilot and gunner in a stepped arrangement of

tandem cockpits. The gunner controlled a 20-mm trainable cannon under the nose by means of a helmet-mounted sight system. The tail unit and fixed tailwheel landing gear were completely new.

The definitive Rooivalk prototype, originally designated **XH-2 (Experimental Helicopter No. 2)**, made its maiden flight on 11 February 1990. The type

was later redesignated **CSH-2 (Combat Support Helicopter No. 2)** and, later still, **XDM (Experimental Development Model)**. A second prototype, the **ADM (Advanced Development Model)** flew soon after this and was tasked with avionics and weapons development. Externally, this second machine differed from the first prototype in having a

cropped fin, although the first prototype was later modified to a similar external configuration.

Although it looks like an entirely new machine, the Rooivalk is based on a degree of reverse engineering of the Aérospatiale Puma using the same Turboméca Turmo IV engines (albeit in slightly uprated form) and the same main rotor. The fuse-

South Africa is currently the only confirmed Rooivalk customer. The long-term SAAF requirement potentially covers 36 aircraft.

lage is entirely new, incorporating some composite structural components, with stepped tandem cockpits for the pilot and co-pilot/gunner (rear and front respectively). These crew positions were reversed in the second prototype, which retained full dual controls as well as the same three CRT displays and a HUD in each cockpit. The cockpits are covered by canopies formed from flat-plate or single curvature sheets to minimise glint. The engines are mounted on the sides of the fuselage, farther to the rear than on the Puma,

to give the pilot a better field of view, and this dictated a redesign of the transmission system.

A gyro-stabilised turret at the nose contains an automatic target detection and tracking system which incorporates a laser rangefinder, FLIR and TV camera, and the two crewmen each have a helmet-mounted sight system. The cockpit is NVG-compatible, and night/all-weather capability is improved by twin redundant mission computers, twin weapon-aiming computers and a Doppler-based navigation system

with moving map displays.

The Rooivalk is heavily armed, with an indigenous 20-mm Armscor GA-1 Rattler cannon turret-mounted under the nose. An alternative turret, containing a 30-mm DEFA 553 cannon, is also said to be a possibility. The cannon is backed up by weapons carried on the four underwing pylons. These can accommodate an 18-round launcher for 2.68-in (68-mm) rockets, or four-round launchers for the Atlas Swift laser-guided anti-tank missile. Air-to-air missiles can be carried at the wingtips.

Provision is made for IR jammers and other ECM equipment, and the airframe is well protected by armour. If the helicopter takes a catastrophic hit, the crewmen's energy-absorbing seats have a high degree of crashworthiness.

The full production stan-

dard Rooivalk, of which the SAAF has ordered an initial 16 examples as four operational evaluation and 12 operational helicopters, will differ from the prototypes in a number of important respects. These include the location of the pilot behind the weapon system operator, improved IR exhaust suppressors (pointing directly up into the rotor disc), and enlarged sponson cheeks housing avionics and ammunition. A pair of external seats can be fitted to these cheeks,

allowing a Rooivalk to pick up the crew of a downed helicopter, or to transport special forces soldiers.

The Rooivalk has secured considerable interest from possible export customers, but as of September 1998 this interest had not yielded any concrete orders.

No. 16 Squadron SAAF will probably become the first regular Rooivalk unit, with Malaysia likely to become the type's second operator.

Showing little resemblance to the Alouette III from which it was derived, the XH-1 proved a number of Rooivalk systems.

SPECIFICATION	
Atlas CSH-2 Rooivalk	**Weights:** empty 13,029 lb
Type: two-seat attack helicopter	(5910 kg); maximum take-off
Powerplant: two Atlas Topaz	19,290 lb (8750 kg)
(locally-upgraded Turboméca	**Dimensions:** main rotor diameter
Makila 1A2) turboshaft engines	51 ft 1½ in (15.58 m); length overall
each rated at 2,000 shp (1491 kW)	61 ft 5½ in (18.73 m) with rotors
Performance: maximum cruising	turning; height 17 ft ¼ in (5.19 m);
speed 172 mph (278 km/h) at	main rotor disc area 2,052.15 sq ft
optimum altitude; initial climb rate	(190.64 m²)
2,200 ft (671 m) per minute;	**Armament:** one 20-mm trainable
service ceiling 20,000 ft (6095 m);	forward-firing cannon, and up to
hovering ceiling 18,200 ft (5545 m)	3,446 lb (2032 kg) of disposable
in ground effect and 16,500 ft	stores carried on four underwing
(5030 m) out of ground effect;	and two wingtip hardpoints
range 584 miles (940 km)	

Aubert PA-20 Cigale, Cigale-Major and Super Cigale series

In 1936 Paul Aubert designed the **Aubert PA-20 Cigale** (cicada) as a lightweight two-seat trainer. The prototype completed its trials successfully after a first flight in 1938, but was destroyed during World War II.

After the end of the war, Aubert updated the design of his pre-war prototype to

create the **PA-201 Cigale** that was powered by the 140-hp (104-kW) Renault 4Pei inverted inline engine and which possessed sufficient agility to win several competitions. This paved the way for the design of a more developed **PA-204 Cigale-Major**, which flew for the first time on 21 April 1947. Of all-wood construction,

the PA-204 was of high-wing cantilever monoplane configuration, with a conventional tail unit and fixed tailwheel landing gear. Power was provided by the 140-hp (104-kW) SNECMA-built Renault 4Pei engine, and an enclosed cabin offered accommodation for four.

In its ultimate form as the PA-204 Super Cigale, the design was further refined. Flown originally in June 1955 as the **PA-204S** conversion of the second PA-204 prototype with the 170-hp (127-kW) SNECMA-built Régnier 4LO-2 inverted inline engine, the type became available in production form as the **PA-204L** with Avco Lycoming engines in the power range of 135-180 hp

(101-134 kW). The type was first flown with a Lycoming engine on 27 July 1955, and several Super Cigales were then acquired by the Aéro-Club Air France.

The cantilever wing of the PA-20 series allowed it to dispense with bracing struts, as illustrated by the first PA-204 Cigale-Major.

SPECIFICATION	
Aubert PA-204L Super Cigale	service ceiling 14,765 ft (4500 m);
Type: four-seat touring and	range 1,168 miles (1880 km)
sporting aircraft	**Weights:** empty 1,411 lb (640 kg);
Powerplant: one Avco Lycoming	maximum take-off 2,756 lb
O-320 flat-four engine rated at	(1250 kg)
150 hp (112 kW)	**Dimensions:** wingspan 32 ft
Performance: maximum speed	9¾ in (10.00 m); length 24 ft 7¼ in
158 mph (255 km/h) at optimum	(7.50 m); height 7 ft 10½ in
altitude; cruising speed 143 mph	(2.40 m); wing area 138.86 sq ft
(230 km/h) at optimum altitude;	(12.90 m²)

Auster AOP.Mk 9

A successor to the Auster AOP.Mk 6 was required in the mid-1950s, and Auster developed a completely

new design as the **Auster Model B.5** that was ordered as the **Auster AOP.Mk 9**. Of the same

braced high-wing configuration as its predecessor, the Auster AOP.Mk 9 was of slightly lower loaded weight but had a considerably more powerful engine, that combined with a larger

wing, carrying split flaps and drooping ailerons, to provide greatly improved take-off and landing performance. The type also possessed excellent rough-field capabilities and could

operate from ploughed fields and muddy surfaces, thanks to its robust landing gear with large low-pressure tyres. It could fly as a light transport in addition to its primary AOP tasking.

Auster AOP.Mk 9 (continued)

The rear cockpit floor was removable and could easily be replaced by a new floor, bringing within its scope such tasks as casualty evacuation, photographic work and cable-laying.

Variants

Auster 9: five surplus AOP.Mk 9 aircraft converted for civil use
Auster 9M: surplus army aircraft bought by Captain M. Somerton-Rayner in 1967 and later fitted with a 180-hp (134-kW) Avco Lycoming O-360-A1D engine
Auster AOP.Mk 11: three-seat STOL development of the AOP.Mk 9 by Beagle aircraft with the 260-hp (194-kW) Rolls-Royce (Continental) IO-470-D engine; one example only, also known as the **Beagle A.115** or **E.3**

The Auster AOP.Mk 9 prototype flew for the first time on 19 March 1954, and deliveries began in February 1955. The new aircraft was soon in action overseas, initially against terrorists in Malaya with No. 656 Squadron.

With No. 653 Squadron in Aden, engine problems began to be a serious impediment to sustained operations, for the Cirrus Bombardier unit suffered from a loss of power when operating from strips at a height of 4,000-7,000 ft (1220-2135 m). The reduced power resulted in a poor climb rate, which was dangerous in view of the possibility of hostile armed tribesmen lurking near such airfields. By this time the army was thinking seriously of helicopters for AOP work, however, and funds were not available for Auster improvements. A total of 145 such aircraft was built, and some were supplied to the Indian army as well as to the Indian and South African air forces.

All of the Auster AOP.Mk 9's standard fuel capacity was contained in a starboard wingroot bag tank.

Developed as a replacement for the British Taylorcraft Auster AOP.Mk 6, the Auster AOP.Mk 9 offered increased performance. A number of examples have been preserved.

SPECIFICATION

Auster AOP.Mk 9
Type: two/three-seat air observation post and general-purpose aircraft
Powerplant: one Blackburn Cirrus Bombardier 203 inverted inline engine rated at 180 hp (134 kW)
Performance: maximum speed 127 mph (204 km/h) at optimum altitude; cruising speed 110 mph (177 km/h) at optimum altitude; initial climb rate 930 ft (285 m) per minute; take-off run 325 ft (99 m), take-off run to clear 50 ft (15 m) 630 ft (192 m), landing run 180 ft (55 m), landing distance from 50 ft (15 m) 450 ft (137 m); service ceiling 19,500 ft (5945 m); range 242 miles (389 km)
Weights: empty 1,590 lb (721 kg); maximum take-off 2,330 lb (1057 kg)
Dimensions: wingspan 36 ft 5 in (11.10 m); length 23 ft 8½ in (7.23 m); height 8 ft 11 in (2.72 m); wing area 197.50 sq ft (18.35 m²)

Auster Model B.4

First flown on 7 September 1951, the four-seat **Auster Model B.4** was designed and built as a freighter and air ambulance. The machine was based on a pod-and-boom fuselage whose payload-carrying pod section was laid out for the carriage of the pilot and up to three passengers, or freight, or litters. Straight-in access to the payload section was provided by clamshell rear doors that could be removed entirely. In overall configuration the Model B.4 was a high-wing monoplane with a strut-braced wing, a tail unit with single horizontal and vertical surfaces, and fixed quadricycle landing gear in which the divided main units were complemented by two small tailwheels on the sides of the pod.

After initial trials the aircraft was taken in hand for a number of modifications, of which the most noticeable was the enlargement of the vertical tail surface. The single prototype was evaluated by the British army, but no orders were placed for either the proposed civil or military production models.

SPECIFICATION

Auster Model B.4
Type: four-seat utility transport optimised for the freight and air ambulance roles
Powerplant: one Blackburn Cirrus Bombardier 702 inverted inline engine rated at 180 hp (134 kW)
Performance: maximum speed 121 mph (195 km/h) at 1,000 ft (305 m); cruising speed 103 mph (166 km/h) at optimum altitude; initial climb rate 670 ft (204 m) per minute; range 280 miles (451 km)
Weights: empty 1,730 lb (785 kg); maximum take-off 2,700 lb (823 kg)
Dimensions: wingspan 24 ft 8 in (7.52 m); length 37 ft (11.28 m); height 8 ft 4½ in (2.55 m)

The B.4 featured a range of optional floors, each carrying different fittings and enabling the aircraft to be optimised for a range of roles.

Auster B.8 Agricola

After touring New Zealand in 1954 to assess the type of agricultural aircraft needed in farming country of this type, Auster's chief designer R. E. Bird laid out the draft plans for two agricultural aircraft. These were the **Model B.6** high-wing monoplane with a Blackburn Cirrus Bombardier inverted inline engine and the **Auster Model B.8 Agricola** (Latin for farmer) low-wing monoplane. Only the Model B.8 was built, as its low-wing configuration was thought to offer the pilot better fields of vision in low-level operations and to provide better dispersal of sprayed insecticide or dumped fertiliser through the supplementary effect of the wing downwash.

The Model B.8 was of Auster's well established welded metal construction (carefully protected against corrosion) under a largely fabric covering, and features of the utilitarian design were a basically rectangular-section fuselage with a flattened nose, and sharply dihedralled outer wing panels for good stability. Adequate field performance and a sturdy fixed tailwheel landing gear was provided and the high-set pilot's cockpit was sealed against toxic payloads. Provision was made in a small port-holed compartment behind the cockpit for two passengers, and under the cockpit was space for either a tank holding 144 Imp gal (655 litres) of liquid insecticide or a hopper carrying 1,680 lb (762 kg) of dry fertiliser.

The first Agricola made its maiden flight on 8 December 1955, but sales were disappointing and only eight aircraft were built by Auster, a ninth later being completed in New Zealand from spares.

SPECIFICATION

Auster Model B.8 Agricola
Type: one/three-seat agricultural aircraft
Powerplant: one Continental O-470-B flat-six engine rated at 240 hp (179 kW)
Performance: maximum speed 127 mph (205 km/h) at optimum altitude; cruising speed 101 mph (163 km/h) at optimum altitude; initial climb rate 610 ft (186 m) per minute; range 220 miles (354 km)
Weights: empty 1,920 lb (871 kg); maximum take-off 3,840 lb (1742 kg)
Dimensions: wingspan 42 ft (12.80 m); length 28 ft 1 in (8.56 m); height 8 ft 4 in (2.54 m); wing area 254.70 sq ft (23.66 m²)
Payload: see above

A single Agricola, ZK-BXO, built from spares in New Zealand, survived into late 1998 with its New Zealand owner. In October the aircraft was offered for sale in an airworthy condition.

Auster J-1 Autocrat, Aiglet and Workmaster

During the closing stages of World War II, the British Taylorcraft company began to consider its post-war sales prospects and, after careful consideration of the most likely markets, decided to proceed with the development of a more economical version of the Auster Mk V. For test and development purposes a single example of the Auster Mk V was modified with the 100-hp (75-kW) Blackburn Cirrus Minor 2 inverted inline engine. The company at the same time started on the construction of a prototype out of the airframe of the crashed Model Plus D prototype, and this duly flew with a designation almost as long as the aircraft: the **Taylorcraft Auster Mk V Series J-1 Autocrat**. Soon after this, on 7 March 1946, the company changed its name to Auster Aircraft Ltd, whereupon the new aircraft became the **Auster J-1 Autocrat**.

By that time (December 1945), first production aircraft had been delivered, differing from the prototype by having a mass- instead of horn-balanced rudder. The Autocrat proved to be one of the most successful light aircraft built in the UK after World War II, more than 400 such aircraft being produced and paving the way for the development of many well-known Auster types. Despite these numbers, there were only a few designation changes.

First was the **J-1A**, of which a small number were provided with a fourth seat but the aircraft later reverted to the standard three-seat cabin layout. Installing a 120-hp (89-kW) de Havilland Gipsy Major I inverted inline engine produced the **J-1N Alpha**, and one aircraft with a 140-hp (108-kW) Gipsy Major 10 Mk 2-2 engine was designated **J-1S**.

In an attempt to provide more power for a crop-dusting variant of its Autocrat, Auster took a standard airframe in 1950 and installed a 130-hp (97-kW) de Havilland Gipsy Major 1 engine, a change that also required an increase in the area of the vertical tail surface. In this revised form the aircraft became the **J-1B Aiglet**. Fourteen J-1B aircraft were registered in the UK and 72 were exported, the majority to Australia and New Zealand. Australasian aircraft were assembled, fitted with engines, and distributed by Kingsford Smith Aviation Services.

Following its experience with the J-1B, Auster designed a bigger and more powerful successor as the **J-1U Workmaster**, intended mainly for operations in the Sudan and Central Africa as well as the UK. Based on the standard J-1N airframe in a strengthened form, fitted with a larger vertical tail surface incorporating a dorsal fin fillet, and using main landing gear units with low-pressure tyres and hydraulic brakes, the first J-1U flew on 22 February 1958, powered by the 180-hp (134-kW) Avco Lycoming O-360-A1A flat-six engine. Eight British-register entered the British-register and two further J-1Us were built for export.

The J-1 seated two people in the forward cockpit (with dual controls) and one passenger behind, sitting on the starboard side facing to port, or two passengers facing forwards at the rear of the cabin.

SPECIFICATION

Auster J-1B Aiglet
Type: one-/three-seat agricultural aircraft
Powerplant: one de Havilland Gipsy Major 1 inverted inline engine rated at 130 hp (97 kW)
Performance: maximum speed 126 mph (203 km/h) at optimum altitude; cruising speed 105 mph (169 km/h) at optimum altitude; initial climb rate 900 ft (274 m) per minute; service ceiling 18,000 ft (5485 m); range 220 miles (354 km)
Weights: empty 1,223 lb (555 kg); maximum take-off 2,000 lb (907 kg)
Dimensions: wingspan 36 ft (10.97 m); length 23 ft 8¼ in (7.22 m); height 6 ft 6 in (1.98 m); wing area 185.00 sq ft (17.19 m²)

Auster J-2 Arrow, J-3 Atom and J-4 Archer

In 1945 the British Taylorcraft company built the prototype of a braced high-wing monoplane that had no official designation but was intended as the precursor of a series to succeed the Model Plus C. With side-by-side accommodation for two in a small cabin, the new aircraft was powered by a 65-hp (49-kW) Avco Lycoming O-145-B3 flat-four engine and, although it did not itself enter production, it paved the way for the improved **Auster J-2 Arrow** that first flew in the summer of 1946 with the powerplant of one Continental C-75-12 engine.

The use of an American engine was forced on the company due to the lack of a British unit of the right power. However, this meant that sales were necessarily curtailed in the UK at a time when severe restrictions were imposed on the import of non-essential items from countries outside the British Empire and Commonwealth as the UK sought to recover from the financial cost of World War II. Thus only 15 J-2 aircraft were registered in the UK, seven of them to Auster itself, and another 26 were exported, mostly to Australia.

Auster was still interested in the creation of a lower-powered type that would be cheaper to buy and operate and, in an effort to create and exploit such a niche in the market, produced the **J-3 Atom** as the airframe of the J-2 with a horn- rather than mass-balanced rudder and the powerplant of one 65-hp (49-kW) Continental C-65-12 flat-four engine. The prototype first flew in 1946, but the type did not enter production.

The **J-4 Archer** was a further development of the J-2, in this instance with a British engine in an effort to avoid the import restrictions placed on American engines. The selected unit was the 90-hp (67-kW) Blackburn Cirrus Minor 1 inverted inline engine, and it was with this more powerful but heavier and less fuel-efficient engine that the first J-4 undertook its maiden flight toward the end of 1946. There was little British interest in a two-seat lightplane, however, and production amounted to only 29 aircraft, all of which were initially registered in the UK but which soon emulated the J-2 by generally being sold to overseas buyers.

Originally G-AJPV on the UK civil register, J-2 Arrow VH-KAE was transferred to Australia in May 1950. The type proved unpopular in the UK and the majority were exported.

Using the basic airframe of the J-1, the Arrow, Atom and Archer met with little sales success. The J-4 (illustrated) was a more powerful development of the J-2.

SPECIFICATION

Auster J-2 Arrow
Type: two-seat touring and sporting aircraft
Powerplant: one Continental C-75-12 flat-four engine rated at 75 hp (56 kW)
Performance: maximum speed 98 mph (158 km/h) at optimum altitude; cruising speed 87 mph (140 km/h) at optimum altitude; initial climb rate 430 ft (131 m) per minute; range 320 miles (515 km)
Weights: empty 872 lb (396 kg); maximum take-off 1,450 lb (658 kg)
Dimensions: wingspan 36 ft (10.97 m); length 22 ft 9 in (6.93 m); height 6 ft 6 in (1.98 m); wing area 185.00 sq ft (17.19 m²)

Auster J-5 Autocar

The need for a four-seat tourer to supplement the three-seat J-1 Autocrat led, via the abortive **Model P Avis** (four-seat civil **Avis Mk 1** and military **Avis Mk 2** air ambulance) of 1947, to the development of the **Auster J-5B Autocar** that first flew in August 1949. Powered by a Gipsy Major 1 engine, just 15 were registered in the UK, although a total of 65 machines were sold overseas in 16 countries.

The demand for more power for the maintenance of performance under 'hot and high' conditions then led in 1950 to the development, on an experimental basis, of the sole **J-5E** with the 155-hp (116-kW) Blackburn Cirrus Major 3 engine. This was in effect the prototype for the identically-powered **J-5G** that first flew in July 1951. The great majority of the 90 J-5G production aircraft were exported since they had been built specifically for use in hot climates, but five British-registered examples were used in the Sudan on crop-spraying operations. Temporarily wearing military markings, another went to Malaya as a sprayer operating for the Colonial Insecticides Research Unit. The most unusual J-5G was one used by Saunders-Roe for its experimental hydro-ski landing gear tests in the Solent during 1958.

In addition, Auster developed the **J-5** and **J-8 Aiglet Trainer** and **Alpine**. Sharing only its name with the J-1B Aiglet, the Auster **J-5F Aiglet Trainer** was based on the airframe of the J-5 with a new shorter-span wing and, stressed for aerobatics, the prototype first flew on 2 June 1951.

There followed 27 production aircraft regis-tered in the UK, and 40 more machines were sold overseas, including 17 for the Pakistan air force. British buyers included Tom Hayhow, who set up 28 point-to-point class records within Europe before he died in April 1953 after being forced down in the Austrian Alps while attempting a London-Belgrade record.

H. B. Showell flew a J-5F from Cambridge to Australia and back between October 1953 and January 1954.

Production of the Aiglet Trainer ended in 1958 after the type had been built in a number of variants.

Very few J-5G Autocars remained in the UK. The aircraft had a more powerful engine and was especially suited to crop spraying in hot climates.

SPECIFICATION	
Auster J-5B Autocar **Type:** four-seat touring aircraft **Powerplant:** one de Havilland Gipsy Major 1 inverted inline engine rated at 130 hp (97 kW) **Performance:** maximum speed 117 mph (188 km/h) at optimum altitude; cruising speed 106 mph (171 km/h) at optimum altitude; initial climb rate 525 ft (160 m) per	minute; service ceiling 11,000 ft (3355 m); range 260 miles (418 km) **Weights:** empty 1,334 lb (605 kg); maximum take-off 2,400 lb (1089 kg) **Dimensions:** wingspan 36 ft (10.97 m); length 23 ft 4 in (7.11 m); height 6 ft 6 in (1.98 m); wing area 185.00 sq ft (17.19 m²)

Autocar variants

J-5G Autocar: export version with one 155-hp (116-kW) Blackburn Cirrus Major 3 inverted inline engine
J-5GL Autocar: sole example of a J-5G rebuilt with an Avco Lycoming engine
J-5H Autocar: sole example of a J-5B revised with the 145-hp (108-kW) Blackburn Cirrus Major 2 inverted inline engine
J-5P Autocar: designation of some 20 aircraft with the 145-hp (108-kW) de Havilland Gipsy Major 10 inverted inline engine
J-5V Autocar: development by Beagle Aircraft with the 160-hp (119-kW) Avco Lycoming O-320-B2B flat-four engine; acted as the development prototype for the D series

Aiglet Trainer and Alpine variants

J-5K Aiglet Trainer: designation of one aircraft with the 155-hp (116-kW) Blackburn Cirrus Major 3 inverted inline engine
J-5L Aiglet Trainer: designation of 10 aircraft powered by the 145-hp (108-kW) de Havilland Gipsy Major 10 Mk 21 inverted inline engine
J-5R Alpine: designation of six hybrid aircraft with the fuselage of the Aiglet Trainer, but the wings of the J-1 Autocrat fitted with the ailerons of the Aiglet Trainer; the prototype was converted from a J-5L using the same powerplant
J-5Q Alpine: lower-powered variant of the J-5R with one 130-hp (97-kW) de Havilland Gipsy Major 1 inverted inline engine; four were built
J-8L Aiglet Trainer: designation of the J-5K after being re-engined with the powerplant of the J-5L

Austin fighters

Albert Ball, one of the great air aces of World War I, started work as an apprentice with the Austin Motor Company before joining the British army at the outbreak of war. He transferred to the Royal Flying Corps in January 1916, and while serving in France as a second lieutenant drew up a specification embodying his ideas for the ideal fighter aircraft.

After some judicious string-pulling, Austin was given an order covering the construction of two prototypes of the **Austin-Ball A.F.B.1** in which the detail design was undertaken by C. H. Brooks. The A.F.B.1 was of typical construction for its period, being based on a wire-braced wooden structure covered largely with fabric. Its design features included an unusually deep fuselage with its upper line only slightly under the lower surface of the upper wing, giving the pilot good upward and forward fields of vision, and a fixed armament of two 0.303-in (7.7-mm) Lewis machine-guns.

The A.F.B.1's Hispano-Suiza 8 engine gave it a very good performance, but since the RAF S.E.5a and the Sopwith Camel were both in quantity production, there was no place for the A.F.B.1 in the RFC's plans.

Designed and built as a private venture to compete with the Sopwith Snipe, the **Austin A.F.T.3 Osprey** was a triplane of ungainly appearance and, like its competitor, was fitted with a 230-hp (172-kW) Bentley B.R.2 rotary piston engine. First flown in February 1918, the Osprey prototype revealed a performance somewhat worse than that of the Snipe, and the construction of the planned second and third proto-types was immediately cancelled.

Another Austin fighter that failed to progress further than the prototype stage was the **Greyhound**, a tandem two-seat type designed by John Kenworthy and intended for the fighter-reconnaissance role as a possible successor to the Bristol F.2 Fighter. The Greyhound was one of many poten-tially useful fighters whose chances were slighted by the 320-hp (239-kW) ABC Dragonfly I radial engine. The flight tests of the Greyhound's three proto-types began in May 1919, but no development or production were seriously considered.

Of simple construction, the Osprey was built for ease of maintenance. Its layout owed much to the Sopwith Triplane.

SPECIFICATION	
Austin-Ball A.F.B.1 **Type:** single-seat fighter **Powerplant:** one Hispano-Suiza 8 Vee engine rated at 200 hp (149 kW) **Performance:** maximum speed 138 mph (222 km/h) at sea level; climb to 10,000 ft in 8 minutes 55 seconds; service ceiling 22,000 ft (6705 m); endurance	2 hours 15 minutes **Weights:** empty 1,525 lb (692 kg); maximum take-off 2,077 lb (942 kg) **Dimensions:** wingspan 30 ft (9.14 m); length 21 ft 6 in (6.55 m); height 9 ft 3 in (2.82 m); wing area 290.00 sq ft (26.94 m²) **Armament:** two 0.303-in (7.7-mm) forward-firing machine-guns

Avia B.34

With the departure of chief designers Paul Beneš and Miroslav Hajn, Ing. František Novotný took over as the head of Avia's military aircraft design department and introduced a completely new family of related and evolutionary fighter designs. His first design to be built was the **Avia B.34**, a single-seat fighter biplane of all-metal construction with fabric-covered surfaces.

Initial testing took place in 1932 and, following reports from the test pilot, the prototype was taken in hand for considerable modi-fication including the redesign of the vertical tail surface and provision for a new cowling for the 740-hp (552-kW) Hispano-Suiza 12Nbr engine. The revised machine was known as the B.34/1, and successful trials paved the way for 12 production aircraft with a larger vertical tail surface, narrower-chord interplane struts, unspatted wheels and the powerplant of a licence-built version of the Hispano-Suiza 12Nbr engine, the Avia Vr 30 Vee engine. The aircraft formed part of the equipment of the Czechoslovak 3rd Air Regiment for several years from 1934.

A second prototype, the **B.34/2**, began a chain of development which led eventually to the B.534. This B.34/2 was at first

powered by a 600-hp (447-kW) Avia Rr 29 radial engine, but was never flown in this form. When fitted with an inline engine it was redesignated as the **B.534/1**. The radial-engined prototype was offered to the Czech authorities as the **B.234**, and versions

with Gnome-Rhône Mistral and Armstrong Siddeley Panther radial engines were designated as the **B.334** and **B.444** respectively, but neither of these was built.

SPECIFICATION

Avia B.34/1
Type: single-seat fighter
Powerplant: one Avia Vr 30 Vee engine rated at 760 hp (567 kW)
Performance: maximum level speed 196 mph (315 km/h) at sea level; cruising speed 174 mph (280 km/h) at optimum altitude; initial climb rate 2,362 ft (720 m) per minute; service ceiling 22,965 ft

(7000 m); range 373 miles (600 km)
Weights: empty 2,877 lb (1305 kg); maximum take-off 3,814 lb (1730 kg)
Dimensions: wingspan 30 ft 10 in (9.40 m); length 23 ft 9½ in (7.25 m); wing area 257.26 sq ft (23.90 m²)
Armament: two 0.303-in (7.7-mm) fixed forward-firing machine-guns

In its initial prototype form, the B.34 featured large wheel spats over the undercarriage main wheels.

Avia B.35

Test-flown for the first time on 28 September 1938, the **Avia B.35/1** was the prototype of a low-wing monoplane fighter designed by František Novotny in response to a 1935 Czechoslovak requirement for a successor to the Avia B.534 biplane fighter. The **B.35** was of moderately advanced concept, but with apparently anachronistic fixed tailwheel landing gear. The designer opted for this on the grounds that it would reduce development time and cost and, through its lighter weight and clean design, would have little effect on performance in overall terms. The wing was of elliptical planform and of wooden construc-

tion covered with a bonded plywood and Dural material, while the fuselage was of steel-tube construction covered with light alloy panels and fabric fore and aft of the cockpit respectively.

The **B.35/1** was initially flown with the Hispano-Suiza 12Ydrs Vee engine rated at 860 hp (641 kW) at 13,125 ft (4000 m). This engine was later replaced by an identically-rated Hispano-Suiza 12Ycrs unit with provision between the cylinder banks for a 20-mm cannon firing through the hollow propeller shaft. The B.35/1 was very impressive in its trials, in which it recorded excellent performance especially in speed, but crashed in November 1938. The **B.35/2** second prototype, with revised ailerons and flaps as well as

a fuselage of slightly increased cross section, was already nearing completion and began its flight test programme in February 1939, a month before the German occupation of unhappy Czechoslovakia.

Development continued under German control, and resulted in the **B.35/3** third prototype that first flew in August 1939. This featured retractable main landing gear units that hinged outward to lie flat in wells in the undersurface of the wing. The aircraft also had non-elliptical leading edges, and was the first of the prototypes to fly with the initially proposed armament of one 20-mm Oerlikon engine-mounted cannon and two 0.312-in (7.92-mm) fixed forward-firing machine-guns in the forward fuselage.

This elegant monoplane fighter was hindered by its use of fixed landing gear, albeit neatly trousered and spatted. The aircraft is illustrated in B.35/2 form with revised ailerons.

SPECIFICATION

Avia B.35/1
Type: single-seat fighter
Powerplant: one Avia (Hispano-Suiza) 12Ycrs Vee engine rated at 860 hp (641 kW)
Performance: maximum speed 308 mph (495 km/h) at 13,125 ft (4000 m); cruising speed 270 mph (435 km/h) at optimum altitude;

initial climb rate 2,559 ft (780 m) per minute; range 311 miles (500 km)
Weights: empty 3,726 lb (1690 kg); maximum take-off 4,850 lb (2200kg)
Dimensions: wingspan 33 ft 7½ in (10.25 m); length 27 ft 10⅔ in (8.50 m); height 8 ft 6½ in (2.60 m); wing area 185.47 sq ft (17.23 m²)

Avia B.122

One of the finest aerobatic aircraft of the 1930s, the **Avia B.122** was a new machine in almost every respect even though it was in fact a development of the BH-22. An equal-span biplane, it had a rectangular fuselage of welded steel tube, with detachable metal

panels forward and fabric covering aft. The wings were of wooden construction covered with fabric.

The first prototype flew early in 1934, and was soon followed by a second prototype with a redesigned vertical tail surface of increased area, and a Townend ring around its 260-hp (194-kW) Walter Castor II radial engine.

The B.122 proved very successful in European aerobatic competitions and a team of three outstanding pilots took second and third places at the contest staged in conjunction with the 1936 Berlin Olympic Games.

A total of 35 **Ba.122** aircraft was ordered for the Czechoslovak air arm as aerobatic fighter trainers, and 15 more were exported to the USSR. Then 45 examples of the Castor-engined **Bs.122** version were delivered to Czechoslovak training units. After the German occupation of Czechoslovakia 12 aircraft, comprising Ba.122 and Bs.122 machines, were handed over to the puppet Slovak government, and 12 Bs.122 machines were sold to Bulgaria.

Variants

B.222: version with a NACA close-cowled Rk 17 engine, wheel spats and pilot's headrest
B.322: experimental version with enclosed cockpit and Townend-ringed Rk 17 engine
Ba.422: final development (two aircraft) with the upper wing gulled into the fuselage and the powerplant of one Avia Rk 17 engine; **Ba.422.2** gave a brilliant exhibition at the aerobatic display held at St Germain-en-Laye in France during July 1938

Of classic aerobatic biplane layout, the B.122 was a single-seater of exceptional performance. The aircraft illustrated lacks an engine cowling.

SPECIFICATION

Avia Ba.122
Type: single-seat aerobatic aircraft
Powerplant: one Avia Rk 17 radial engine rated at 355 hp (265 kW)
Performance: maximum speed 168 mph (270 km/h) at optimum altitude; cruising speed 143 mph (230 km/h) at optimum altitude;

service ceiling 22,965 ft (7000 m); range 286 miles (460 km)
Weights: empty 1,898 lb (861 kg); maximum take-off 2,383 lb (1081 kg)
Dimensions: wing span 29 ft ½ in (8.85 m); length 22 ft 3¾ in (6.80 m); height 9 ft 6¼ in (2.90 m); wing area 231.97 sq ft (21.55 m²)

Avia B.135

SPECIFICATION

Avia B.135
Type: single-seat fighter
Powerplant: one Avia (Hispano-Suiza) 12Ycrs Vee engine rated at 860 hp (641 kW)
Performance: maximum speed 332 mph (535 km/h) at 13,125 ft (4000 m); cruising speed 286 mph (460 km/h) at optimum altitude; initial climb rate 2,657 ft (810 m) per minute; service ceiling 27,890 ft (8500 m); range 342 miles (550 km)

Weights: empty 4,548 lb (2063 kg); maximum take-off 5,615 lb (2547 kg)
Dimensions: wingspan 35 ft 7⅛ in (10.85 m); length 27 ft 10⅔ in (8.50 m); height 8 ft 6½ in (2.60 m); wing area 182.99 sq ft (17.00 m²)
Armament: one 20-mm fixed forward-firing cannon and two 0.312-in (7.92-mm) fixed forward-firing machine-guns

Following their occupation of Czechoslovakia in March 1939, the Germans ordered the continued development of the Avia B.35/3 single-seat fighter prototype. A new all-metal wing was added to create a new fighter that received the designation **Avia B.135**, and this began its flight test programme in 1940.

The new type aroused the interest of a visiting Bulgarian military mission.

As a result, an order for 12 examples of the B.135 was placed as a lead-in to Bulgarian licensed manufacture of 50 examples of the type as the **DAR 11 Ljastuvka** (swallow) at Lovech. The 12 B.135 fighters were built in the summer of 1942 and

entered service with the Bulgarian air force's fighter pilot school, although they also went on to see some operational service in 1944 and flew for many years.

The B.135 offered a combination of good armament and adequate performance.

Avia B.158

Projected by Robert Nebesář in 1935, the **Avia B.58** medium bomber was to have been powered by two 420-hp (313-kW) Avia Rk 17 air-cooled radial engines. The following year it was decided to employ Hispano-Suiza 12Ydrs liquid-cooled Vee engines giving twice the power, and a revised design, known as the **Avia B.158**, was created for the version with this powerplant. This incorporated other changes including the replacement of the original single centre-line vertical tail surface with twin endplate vertical tail surfaces, and the fixed spatted landing gear with a more modern type in which the main legs retracted into the engine nacelles.

The B.158 had an inverted-gull wing, and was completed in prototype form during the summer of 1938. Test flights were still being carried out when the whole of Czechoslovakia was occupied by the Germans in March 1939. Bearing German insignia the sole prototype contin-ued its test programme in the summer of 1939, but testing appears to have been halted and the aircraft appears to have been scrapped soon after.

A potentially useful bomber design, the B.158 was overtaken by invading German forces and test-flown in Luftwaffe markings.

SPECIFICATION

Avia B-158
Type: medium bomber
Powerplant: two Avia (Hispano-Suiza) 12Ydrs Vee engines each rated at 860 hp (641 kW)
Performance: maximum speed 270 mph (435 km/h) at optimum altitude; service ceiling 27,885 ft (8500 m); range 684 miles (1100 km)
Weights: empty 9,480 lb (4300 kg); maximum take-off 16,005 lb (7260 kg)
Dimensions: wingspan 52 ft 6 in (16.00 m); length 39 ft 4½ in (12.00 m); wing area 462.86 sq ft (43.00 m²)
Armament: (proposed) one 0.303-in (7.7-mm) trainable machine-gun in each of the nose, dorsal and ventral positions, plus up to 2,205 lb (1000 kg) of bombs carried internally

Avia B.534

The **Avia B.534** was the most important Czechoslovak aircraft of the period between the two world wars, with production reaching 566 machines, a total greater than that of any other Czechoslovak type. The B.534 was a classic single-seat biplane-fighter and the origins of the type can be found in the B.34 fighter.

The second B.34 prototype was completed as the B.34/2 with one Avia Rr 29 radial engine, but the failure of this engine led to the revision of the airframe with the Avia (Hispano-Suiza) 12Ybrs Vee engine. The B.34/2 first flew in this form during August 1933 and at the completion of its trials was redesignated as the **B.534/1**. A **B.534/2** second prototype was then built with an enclosed cockpit, an enlarged rudder and revised landing gear with faired main wheels.

Further development was delayed when both prototypes were damaged in crash landings during 1934, but the decision had already been made to order the B.534 for the Czechoslovak air arm, with five main production variants eventually evolving.

By the time of the Munich crisis in September 1938, the B.534 fighters formed the equipment of 21 first-line Czechoslovak fighter squadrons. After the occupation of the country, the puppet Slovak government used some B.534 fighters in the brief border war with Hungary. Three Slovak squadrons subsequently took part in the 1941 invasion of the USSR, operating on the Ukrainian sector of the front, but by mid-1942 all three units had been re-equipped and the B.534 had been relegated to training.

During the winter of 1939-40, Bulgaria received 78 B.534 fighters, which later flew combat sorties against US B-24 Liberator bombers returning from the disastrous raid on the Ploesti oilfields in Romania on 1 August 1943. The Luftwaffe used other B.534 and **Bk.534** aircraft as advanced trainers and tugs for training gliders. Some were fitted with canopies providing all-round vision and others, with arrester hooks, were used for deck landing trials and training for the aircraft carrier *Graf Zeppelin*.

Finally, three B.534 fighters were used by the insurgents at Tri Duby airfield during the Slovak National Rising in the late summer of 1944. Two were lost on the ground during Luftwaffe raids and the third was burned to prevent it from being captured by the Germans.

Captured from the Slovak air force and pressed into service with the Hungarian air arm, this B.534-IV is seen in a later guise, wearing Hungarian civil markings while flying as a glider tug in 1942-43.

A pair of Slovak air force Bk.534 cannon-armed fighters. The B.534 was one of the final mass-produced biplane fighters and joined the likes of the Fiat CR.42 and Gloster Gladiator as the ultimate expression of this design philosophy.

SPECIFICATION

Avia B-534-IV
Type: single-seat fighter
Powerplant: one Avia (Hispano-Suiza) 12Ydrs Vee engine rated at 850 hp (634 kW)
Performance: maximum speed 245 mph (394 km/h) at 14,435 ft (4400 m); cruising speed 214 mph (345 km/h) at optimum altitude; initial climb rate 2,953 ft (900 m) per minute; service ceiling 34,775 ft (10600 m); range 360 miles (580 km)
Weights: empty 3,219 lb (1460 kg); maximum take-off 4,674 lb (2120 kg)
Dimensions: span 30 ft 10 in (9.40 m); length 26 ft 10⅞ in (8.20 m); height 10 ft 2 in (3.10 m); wing area 253.61 sq ft (23.56 m²)
Armament: four 0.303-in (7.7-mm) fixed forward-firing machine-guns, plus up to six 44-lb (20-kg) bombs on underwing hardpoints

Production variants

B.534-I: first production version; similar to the second prototype except for its wood rather than metal propeller, open cockpit, and unspatted main wheels. Production totalled 46 aircraft with the fixed forward-firing armament of four 0.303-in (7.7-mm) machine-guns installed as two in the fuselage and the other two in fairings on the lower wing
B.534-II: all four machine-guns mounted in the sides of the fuselage, requiring the introduction of enlarged fuselage side blister fairings to house them. Underwing racks for light bombs were fitted; 100 built
B.534-III: featured spatted main wheels and had the carburettor air inlet moved forward under the nose. Six of this version were exported to Greece and 14 to Yugoslavia. Total of 46 built
B.534-IV: featured a rearward-sliding cockpit canopy and also a raised aft fuselage decking. Total Czechoslovak orders for this version were 253
Bk.534: a cannon-armed development of the B-534-IV. It was intended that its Hispano-Suiza 12Ycrs engine would have a 20-mm Oerlikon cannon mounted in the Vee of the engine cylinders to fire through the hollow propeller shaft, but cannon shortages forced many Bk.534 fighters to fly with three machine-guns, two mounted in the fuselage sides and one in place of the engine cannon. Some B.534-IV and Bk.534 fighters had the standard tail skid replaced by a castoring tailwheel

Avia BH-3 and BH-4

The Avia company (Avia ack. spolecnost pro prumysl letecky) was founded as a manufacturer of aircraft in the Czechoslovak Republic during 1919. Design was placed in the hands of Pavel Beneš and Miroslav Hajn, and their first aircraft was the **BH-Exprevit** that first flew in 1920 as a single-seat sporting type. The machine was a strut-braced low-wing monoplane of wooden construction, and powered by a 30-hp (22-kW) Daimler motorcycle engine. Interest in the type led to its development into the **BH-1**. This retained the same slab-sided plywood-covered fuselage, and a tail unit including a rectangular rudder without a fin. The two-seat **BH-1bis** was powered by a 48-hp (36-kW) Gnome Omega engine, and aroused patriotic enthusiasm at various aviation meetings during 1921. The **BH-2** was an ultra-light monoplane, but it is not certain whether or not it was flown.

The design of the **Avia BH-3** showed considerable courage as it was a strut-braced low-wing monoplane fighter. The BH-3 was derived conceptually from the BH-1 sporting type, but was

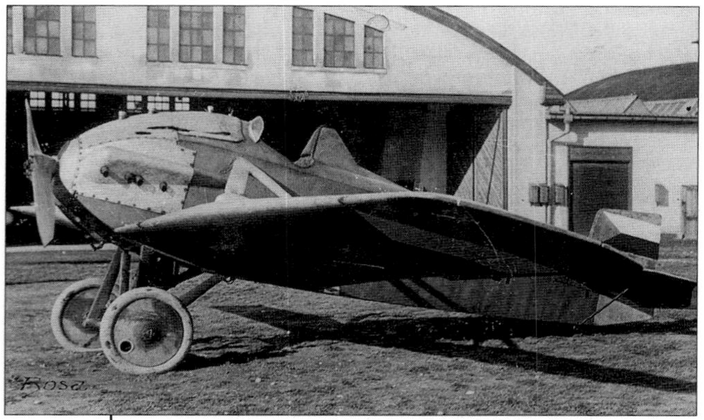

A derivation of the BH-3, the BH-4 fighter prototype featured a deeper forward fuselage to accommodate its Hispano-Suiza engine.

greatly refined and considerably more strongly built. The prototype flew in 1921 and revealed excellent flight characteristics, so there followed 10 production examples with the service designation **B.3**. The standard engine was the BMW IIIa inline engine with a retractable radiator beneath the fuselage, but the fourth machine was fitted experimentally with a 240-hp (179-kW) Walter W-IV inline engine cooled by a radiator attached to the main legs of the landing gear.

Avia also developed the **BH-4**, which featured a modified main landing gear unit with larger wheels, a measure of structural strengthening, a taller pylon to protect the pilot in the event of a turn-over accident on landing, and a deeper and more streamlined forward fuselage carrying the more powerful Hispano-Suiza 8Ba Vee engine. Performance in overall terms showed no improvement over that of the BH-3, and no production was undertaken.

The B.3 remained in service until 1927.

SPECIFICATION

Avia BH-3
Type: single-seat fighter
Powerplant: one BMW IIIa inline engine rated at 185 hp (138 kW)
Performance: maximum speed 140 mph (225 km/h) at optimum altitude; cruising speed 118 mph (190 km/h) at optimum altitude; climb to 16,405 ft (5000 m) in 10 minutes 30 seconds; service ceiling 25,590 ft (7800 m); range 311 miles (500 km)
Weights: empty 1,753 lb (795 kg); maximum take-off 2,308 lb (1047kg)
Dimensions: wing span 33 ft 7⅛ in (10.24 m); length 22 ft 11¼ in (6.99 m); height 9 ft 2 in (2.79 m); wing area 169.64 sq ft (15.76 m²)
Armament: two 0.303-in (7.7-mm) fixed forward-firing machine-guns

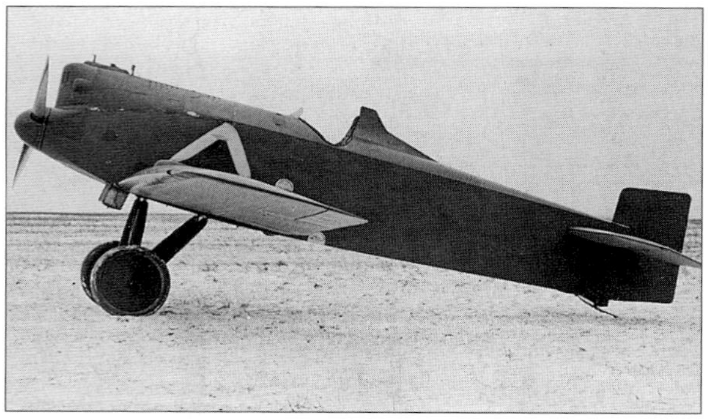

The smaller roll-over pylon of the BH-3 (illustrated) compared to the BH-4 is evident. The square-tipped rudder and lack of fixed vertical tail surfaces was common to both types, while the retractable radiator of the BH-3 may also be seen.

Avia BH-6

The **Avia BH-6** single-seat fighter prototype was flight tested in 1923 after being designed as a biplane in parallel with the BH-7 monoplane to use a Hispano-Suiza 8Fb Vee engine built under licence in Czechoslovakia by Skoda. The two aircraft used essentially the same slim fuselage, tail unit and landing gear, and were of wooden construction under a covering largely of fabric. The BH-6 was the biplane half-brother of this small family, and its wing cellule was somewhat unusual in that the flat upper wing, supported over the fuselage by a faired single strut, was of smaller span than the lower wing, which was dihedralled and separated from the upper wing on each side by single interplane struts angled inward from bottom to top. The sole machine was lost in an accident shortly after beginning its flight trials.

SPECIFICATION

Avia BH-6
Type: single-seat fighter
Powerplant: one Skoda (Hispano-Suiza) 8Fb Vee engine rated at 310 hp (231 kW)
Performance: maximum speed 137 mph (220 km/h) at optimum altitude; cruising speed 124 mph (200 km/h) at optimum altitude
Weights: empty 1,936 lb (878 kg); maximum take-off 2,601 lb (1180 kg)
Dimensions: wingspan 32 ft 8⅞ in (9.98 m); length 21 ft 2¾ in (6.47 m); height 9 ft 5⅜ in (2.88 m); wing area 243.26 sq ft (22.60 m²)
Armament: two 0.303-in (7.7-mm) fixed forward-firing machine-guns

Using a wing cellule of highly unusual layout, the BH-6 was an attractive but flawed design. Cooling for the Skoda-built engine was provided by a radiator attached to each of the mainwheel strut units.

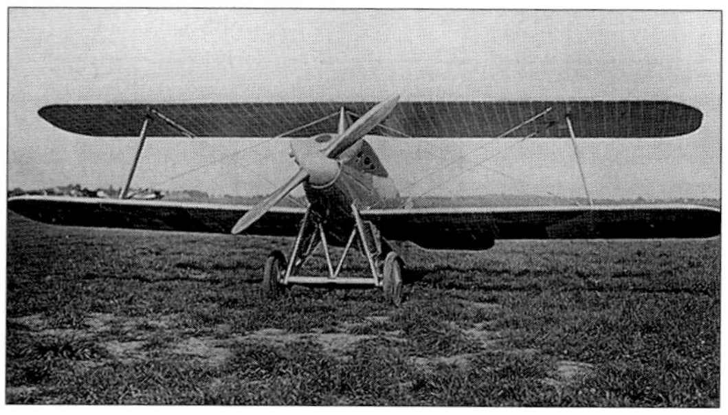

Avia BH-7

First flown in the spring of 1923, the **Avia BH-7A** single-seat fighter was in effect the monoplane counterpart of the BH-6 biplane fighter prototype. It used the same basic powerplant and fuselage, combined with a parasol wing. The BH-7A main landing gear arrangement differed little from that of the BH-6 and it also retained the twin engine-coolant radiators of the biplane. The similarity to the BH-6 was continued into the type's flight test programme, which was prematurely curtailed after the machine had been involved in two accidents.

The **BH-7B** was developed from the BH-7A as a racer, the main change being effected to the wing, which was reduced in span and area, and also faired directly into the upper fuselage. The racer was powered by a supercharged version of the Hispano-Suiza 8Fb engine and, like the fighter, was unsuccessful.

SPECIFICATION

Avia BH-7A
Type: single-seat fighter
Powerplant: one Skoda (Hispano-Suiza) 8Fb Vee engine rated at 310 hp (231 kW)
Performance: maximum speed 149 mph (240 km/h) at optimum altitude; cruising speed 127 mph (205 km/h) at optimum altitude; climb to 16,405 ft (5000 m) in 12 minutes 30 seconds; service ceiling 26,245 ft (8000 m); range 298 miles (480 km)
Weights: empty 1,885 lb (855 kg); maximum take-off 2,537 lb (1150 kg)
Dimensions: wing span 34 ft 1⅜ in (10.40 m); length 22 ft 5¼ in (6.84 m); height 9 ft 3⅜ in (2.83 m); wing area 195.37 sq ft (18.15 m²)
Armament: (proposed) two 0.303-in (7.7-mm) fixed forward-firing machine-guns

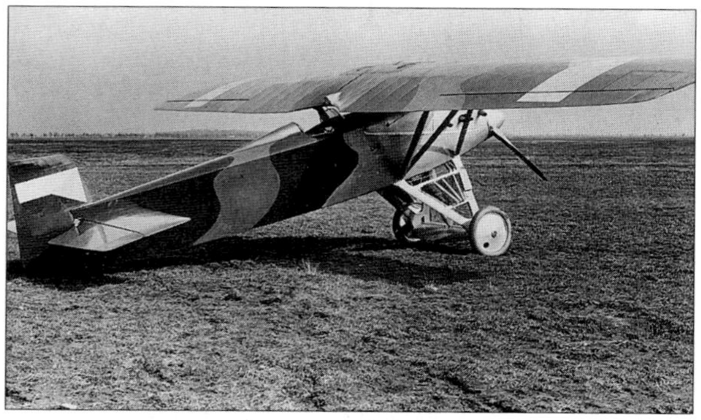

Forward visibility for the BH-7 pilot would have been appaling, especially during landing, and would hardly have suited the type to a combat role. In the event, both the BH-7 and BH-6 proved to be design dead ends.

Avia BH-8

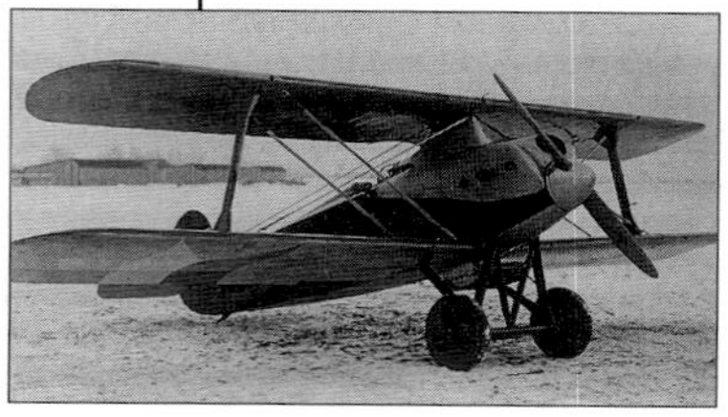

The **Avia BH-8** single-seat fighter biplane was an interim experimental design between the BH-6 and BH-17. Similar in general configuration to the BH-6 with a biplane wing cellule in which the flat upper wing was of smaller span than the dihedralled lower wing, the BH-8 had a faired pyramid structure carrying the upper wing above the fuselage instead of the more familiar strutting. The BH-8 was test-flown in the latter half of 1923, but its development was then abandoned in favour of the more promising BH-17.

An improvement on the BH-6, the BH-8 was abandoned in favour of the BH-17.

SPECIFICATION

Avia BH-8
Type: single-seat fighter
Powerplant: one Skoda (Hispano-Suiza) 8Fb Vee engine rated at 310 hp (231 kW)
Performance: maximum speed 138 mph (222 km/h) at optimum altitude; climb to 16,405 ft (5000 m) in 14 minutes 40 seconds
Weights: empty 1,858 lb (843 kg); maximum take-off 2,520 lb (1143 kg)
Dimensions: wing span 31 ft 1¼ in (9.48 m); length 21 ft 3½ in (6.49 m); height 9 ft 1 in (2.77 m); wing area 238.00 sq ft (22.11 m²)
Armament: (proposed) two 0.303-in (7.7-mm) fixed forward-firing machine-guns

Avia BH-9, BH-10, BH-11 and BH-12

The **Avia BH-9** was a strut-braced low-wing touring and sporting monoplane and was derived directly from the BH-5. Powered by a 60-hp (45-kW) Walter NZ radial engine, the BH-9 flew in prototype form during 1923. Czechoslovak army interest led to an order for 10 examples for the liaison and primary training tasks, and these aircraft had the military designation **B.9**. The **BH-10** was a single-seat aerobatic derivative of the BH-9. The first example

appeared in 1924, and at least 20 of the aircraft were built, 10 of them as **B.10** machines for the Czechoslovak air arm.

The **BH-11** was a 1923 two-seater very similar to the BH-9. Deliveries amounted to 15 aircraft delivered to the Czechoslovak air arm under the designation **B.11**. In 1929 there appeared the **BH-11B Antelope** as a sporting version for the civil market. Produced only in small numbers, the BH-11B

was somewhat larger and heavier than the BH-11, while the **BH-11C** had the same engine as the BH-11 and increased span.

The **BH-12** was another two-seat development of the BH-9, and was generally similar to the earlier type except for its slightly modified wing profile. The machine appeared in 1924 in response to the need for a sporting aircraft, and a notable feature was the provision for the wings to be folded for transport or stowage; the wing halves pivoted around the front spar and were then secured to the fuselage sides. Thus folded, the BH-12 could be towed by a car or moved by hand.

Featuring a distinctive anti-roll pylon behind the cockpit, the BH-10 was an aerobatic version of the BH-9.

Closely based on the BH-9, the BH-11 could achieve a maximum speed of 109 mph (176 km/h) and boasted a range of 435 miles (700 km).

SPECIFICATION	
Avia BH-9	service ceiling 14,765 ft (4500 m);
Type: two-seat sporting and primary training aircraft	range 292 miles (470 km)
Powerplant: one Walter NZ radial engine rated at 60 hp (45 kW)	**Weights:** empty 761 lb (345 kg); maximum take-off 1,213 lb (550 kg)
Performance: maximum speed 98 mph (158 km/h) at optimum altitude; cruising speed 78 mph (125 km/h) at optimum altitude;	**Dimensions:** wingspan 31 ft 10½ in (9.72 m); length 21 ft 9½ in (6.64 m); height 8 ft 3½ in (2.53 m); wing area 146.39 sq ft (13.60 m²)

Avia BH-17

Developed from the BH-6 via the BH-8, which it closely resembled, the

Avia BH-17 single-seat biplane fighter was accepted for production in

1924, and deliveries to the Czechoslovak air arm totalled 24 such machines for service with the designation **B.17**. By comparison with the BH-8, the BH-17 was lighter and had a wing

cellule of reduced span and area. The B.17 revealed in service that it had generally better handling characteris-

tics than its predecessor, but proved unreliable and was soon withdrawn from first-line duties.

A substantial cabane structure connected the upper wing of the BH-17 to its upper fuselage. The structure neatly contained both the oil and water tanks, but allowed the pilot only a limited view forwards.

SPECIFICATION	
Avia BH-17	26,245 ft (8000 m); range 311 miles (500 km)
Type: single-seat fighter	
Powerplant: one Skoda (Hispano-Suiza) 8Fb Vee engine rated at 310 hp (231 kW)	**Weights:** empty 1,680 lb (762 kg); maximum take-off 2,546 lb (1155 kg)
Performance: maximum speed 146 mph (235 km/h) at optimum altitude; cruising speed 128 mph (206 km/h) at optimum altitude; climb to 16,405 ft (5000 m) in 14 minutes; service ceiling	**Dimensions:** wingspan 29 ft ⅞ in (8.86 m); length 22 ft 6 in (46.86 m); wing area 229.28 sq ft (21.30 m²) **Armament:** two 0.303-in (7.7-mm) fixed forward-firing machine-guns

Avia BH-19

In 1924, the year in which the **Avia BH-19** low-wing monoplane fighter made its appearance, Avia was taken over by the Miloš Bondy a Spol company, which was

itself taken over by the Skoda organisation in 1926. From that year, the name Avia was restored.

Designed by Paul Beneš and Miroslav Hajn, who

were convinced that the monoplane configuration offered significant advantages over the biplane layout for the single-seat fighter, the BH-19 seemed to offer the probability of excellent performance, and trials of the first prototype in fact confirmed this initial estimate. However, the trials programme also revealed that the BH-19 had a number of control deficiencies as well as an undesirable tendency towards aileron flutter.

The Czechoslovak air arm was nevertheless

impressed by the BH-19's performance, and informed Avia that it would order the type if the problems could be solved. Despite the fact that the first prototype crashed during a speed run, the company completed a second prototype. The trials

of this new machine showed that the design team had failed to rectify the design's handling problems, and the Czechoslovak war ministry then requested the company to discontinue its efforts to create a monoplane fighter.

The BH-19 was cancelled as a result of control problems.

SPECIFICATION	
Avia BH-19	ceiling 26,245 ft (8000 m); range 323 miles (520 km)
Type: single-seat fighter	
Powerplant: one Skoda (Hispano-Suiza) 8Fb Vee engine rated at 310 hp (231 kW)	**Weights:** empty 1,746 lb (792 kg); maximum take-off 2,546 lb (1155 kg)
Performance: maximum level speed 152 mph (245 km/h) at optimum altitude; cruising speed 133 mph (215 km/h) at optimum altitude; climb to 16,405 ft (5000 m) in 15 minutes; service	**Dimensions:** wingspan 35 ft 5¼ in (10.80 m); length 24 ft 2⅛ in (7.37 m); wing area 196.99 sq ft (18.30 m²) **Armament:** two 0.303-in (7.7-mm) fixed forward-firing machine-guns

Avia BH-21

First flown in January 1925, the **Avia BH-21** was the result of a process of evolution by Beneš and Hajn in their attempt to overcome problems encountered in service with the BH-17 single-seat fighter. One such problem was the obstruction of the

pilot's view caused by the faired pyramid supporting the upper wing's centre section above the fuselage – in the BH-21 this was replaced by conventional cabane struts.

Adopted by the Czechoslovak air arm as the **B.21**, the new fighter

proved robust and gave a good performance. Some 137 were acquired for Czechoslovak service, and the type was successful in a competition held by the Belgian authorities in June 1925. This led to the purchase of one Czech-built machine and the licensed manufacture of 44 more.

The B.21 saw widespread use in the Czechoslovak

Variants

BH-21J: standard BH-21 experimentally fitted with a Bristol Jupiter radial engine; the type proved successful and led to the development of the BH-33

BH-21R: clipped-wing racing development of the BH-21 fighter, first flown in early 1925 with its wing area trimmed and its powerplant altered to the more potent Hispano-Suiza 8Fb engine rated at 400 hp (298 kW) and driving a specially-developed propeller; the BH-21R won the Czechoslovak national air races held in September 1925, covering the 124.3-mile (200-km) course at an average speed of 186.78 mph (300.59 km/h)

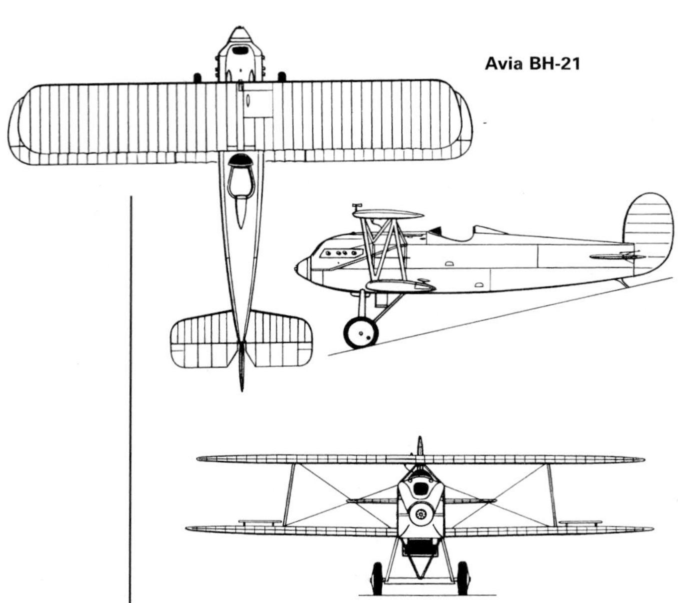

Avia BH-21

fighter squadrons until replaced by the Avia BH-33 in the early 1930s. At air shows the BH-21's capabilities as an aerobatic mount were excellently demonstrated, and this quality combined with the BH-21's excellent turn of speed to pave the way for various further developments.

SPECIFICATION

Avia BH-21
Type: single-seat fighter
Powerplant: one Avia (Hispano-Suiza) 8Fb Vee engine rated at 310 hp (231 kW)
Performance: maximum speed 152 mph (245 km/h) at 9,845 ft (3000 m); climb to 16,405 ft (5000 m) in 13 minutes; service ceiling 18,045 ft (5500 m); range 342 miles (550 km)
Weights: empty 1,587 lb (720 kg); maximum take-off 2,390 lb (1084 kg)
Dimensions: wingspan 29 ft 2⅞ in (8.90 m); length 22 ft 6½ in (6.87 m); height 8 ft 11¾ in (2.74 m); wing area 236.38 sq ft (21.96 m^2)
Armament: two 0.303-in (7.7-mm) fixed forward-firing machine-guns

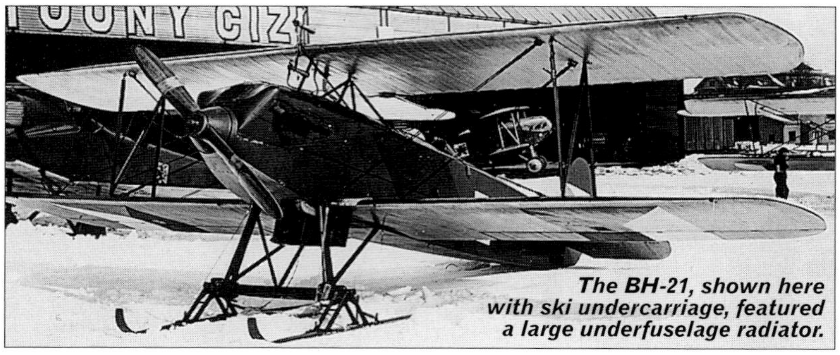

The BH-21, shown here with ski undercarriage, featured a large underfuselage radiator.

Avia BH-22 and BH-23

The Czechoslovak authorities recognised the excellent manoeuvrability of the BH-21 in giving Avia a production order for 30 examples of the **Avia BH-22**, a lighter-weight unarmed version for the aerobatic training role. The BH-22 had the 180-hp (134-kW) Hispano-Suiza 8Aa engine, reduced wing stagger and a generally strengthened structure for aerobatics. After long service at air force pilot training schools, several were sold to aero clubs.

Evolved from the BH-22 with the initial designation **Avia BH-22N**, the type then known as the **BH-23** reversed the process that had created the BH-22 trainer out of the BH-21 fighter by adding armament and night-flying equipment to the BH-22 in an effort to produce a night fighter. The two prototypes were completed and test-flown in 1926 with specialised equipment that included small searchlights. No production aircraft followed.

SPECIFICATION

Avia BH-23
Type: single-seat night fighter
Powerplant: one Skoda (Hispano-Suiza) 8Aa Vee engine rated at 180 hp (134 kW)
Performance: maximum speed 130 mph (210 km/h) at optimum altitude; cruising speed 118 mph (190 km/h) at optimum altitude
Weights: empty 1,554 lb (705 kg); maximum take-off 1,938 lb (879 kg)
Dimensions: wingspan 29 ft 2⅞ in (8.90 m); length 22 ft 6½ in (6.87 m); height 8 ft 11¾ in (2.74 m); wing area 236.38 sq ft (21.96 m^2)
Armament: two 0.303-in (7.7-mm) fixed forward-firing machine-guns

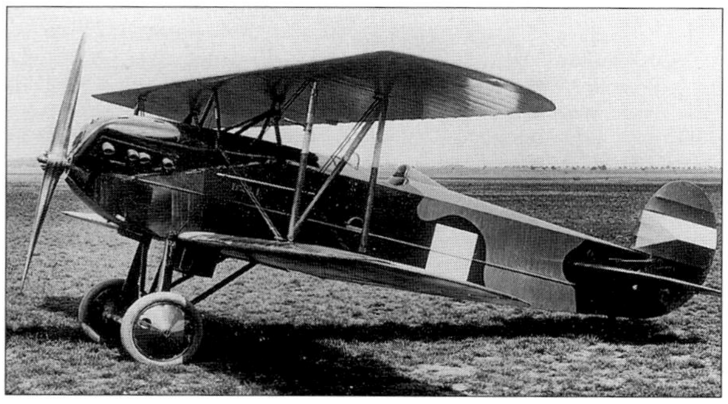

A single-seat fully aerobatic trainer, the BH-22 carried a camera gun for use in advanced fighter tactics training.

Avia BH-26

The **Avia BH-26** was a reconnaissance fighter which first flew in prototype form during 1927, and represented Avia's initial attempt to create a two-seat fighter. Like previous designs by Beneš and Hajn, the BH-26 had a balanced rudder but no fixed fin ahead of it. Experience showed the need for a fin and rudder assembly however, and this duly appeared as a typically Avia angular design on production aircraft.

Each lower wing featured a long-span aileron, aerodynamically balanced by means of a small auxiliary aerofoil surface attached to the aileron by three struts. It is believed that some eight series machines were built for the Czechoslovak air arm. Designated **B.26**, it is likely that these aircraft saw little first-line service.

SPECIFICATION

Avia BH-26
Type: two-seat reconnaissance fighter
Powerplant: one Walter (Bristol) Jupiter IV radial engine rated at 450 hp (336 kW)
Performance maximum speed 150 mph (242 km/h) at optimum altitude; normal cruising speed 137 mph (220 km/h) at optimum altitude; climb to 16,405 ft (5000 m) in 13 minutes 20 seconds; service ceiling 27,885 ft (8500 m); range 329 miles (530 km)
Weights: empty 2,271 lb (1030 kg); maximum take-off 3,594 lb (1630 kg)
Dimensions: wingspan 35 ft 5⅛ in (10.80 m); length 29 ft ⅜ in (8.85 m); height 10 ft 11⅞ in (3.35 m); wing area 333.69 sq ft (31.00 m^2)
Armament: two 0.303-in (7.7-mm) fixed forward-firing machine-guns, and two 0.303-in (7.7-mm) trainable rearward-firing machine-guns

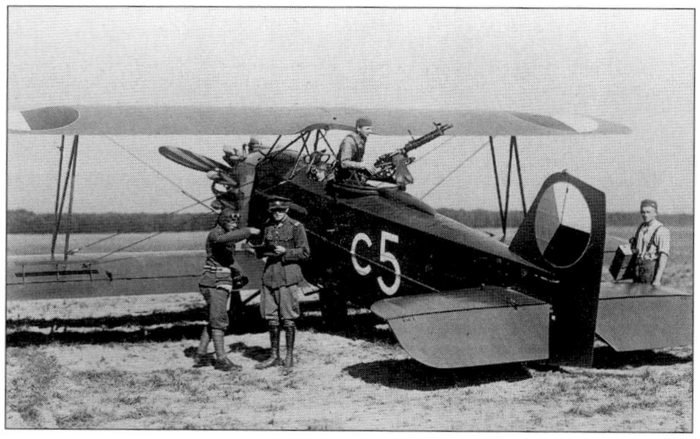

Although a fighter-reconnaissance type, this B.26 was photographed in the service of the Czech Central Flying School in 1930. The observer's machine-gun and its mounting ring, along with the aircraft's revised fin and rudder, are worthy of note.

Avia BH-33

The **Avia BH-33** was the last design by Beneš and Hajn to be built by Avia. It was, in essence, a development of the experimental Jupiter-engined BH-21J. Unlike other BH types, the BH-33, which first appeared in prototype form during 1927, was designed with a fin and rudder assembly from the outset. As with all Avia biplane fighters, the BH-33 had an upper wing of shorter span than the lower. It also featured aerodynamically-balanced ailerons on the trailing edges of the lower wings.

A small number of the production version, incorporating several refinements, including a modified tail design and improved landing gear, was ordered for the Czechoslovak air arm. In 1928 Poland acquired a manufacturing licence and, after PZL had produced 10 pre-production aircraft, the PWS company manufactured from 1930 a total of 50 full-production machines under the designation **PWS 'A'**. Three BH-33 aircraft were also sold to Belgium.

SPECIFICATION

Avia BH-33
Type: single-seat fighter
Powerplant: one Walter (Bristol) Jupiter VI radial engine rated at 543 hp (405 kW)
Performance: maximum speed 177 mph (285 km/h) at optimum altitude; cruising speed 148 mph (238 km/h) at optimum altitude; initial climb rate 2,067 ft (630 m) per minute; service ceiling 31,170 ft (9500 m); range 280 miles (450 km)
Weights: empty 1,830 lb (830 kg); maximum take-off 2,762 lb (1253 kg)
Dimensions: wingspan 29 ft 2⅞ in (8.90 m); length 23 ft 1⅛ in (7.04 m); height 9 ft 1⅞ in (2.79 m); wing area 238.97 sq ft (22.20 m^2)
Armament: two synchronised 0.303-in (7.7-mm) fixed forward-firing machine-guns

Avia BH-33 (continued)

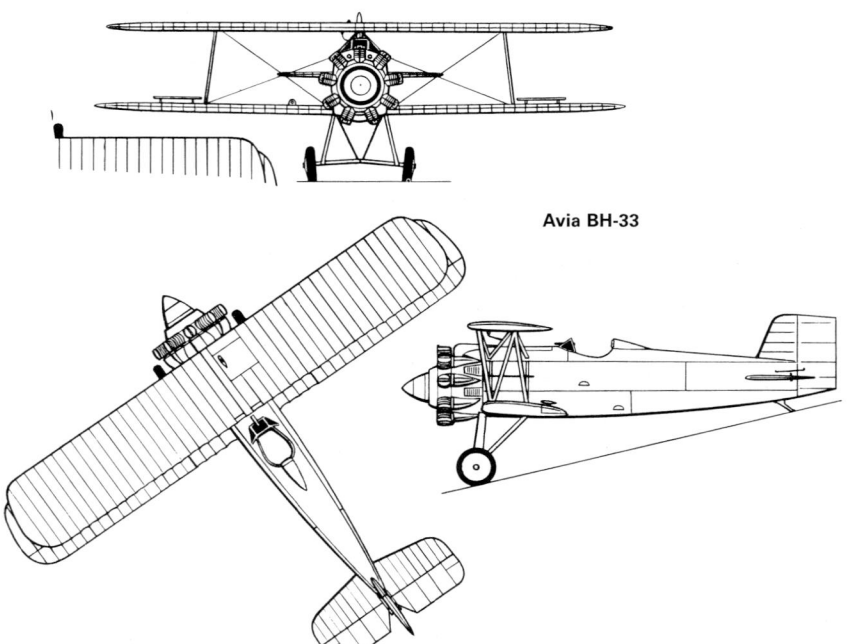

Avia BH-33

Variants

BH-33E: the 1929 result of a radical redesign of the basic BH-33, the BH-33E was in structural respects almost a new aircraft. The traditional Avia slab-sided wooden fuselage was replaced by an elliptical-section design of welded steel tube. A small number of BH-33Es were supplied to the Czechoslovak air arm under the designation **B.33**, three each were exported to the USSR and to Belgium, and 20 were sold to Yugoslavia, where another 24 were subsequently built under licence

BH-33L: this was an improved development of the BH-33E with wings of greater span and a Skoda L W-type engine with frontal radiator; first flown late in 1929, the BH-33L proved an admirable aircraft well suited for Czechoslovak military service under the designation **Ba.33**. Some 80 examples were built and served as standard equipment of several air regiments until the late 1930s

BH-133: single 1930 experimental development of the BH-33E with the 525-hp (391-kW) BMW-built Pratt & Whitney Hornet radial engine

A fine 1930s' fighter, the BH-33L was built in considerable numbers for the Czech air arm.

Avia S.99 and S.199

In the later stages of World War II the Avia factory at Prague-Cakovice was allocated the task of assembling Messerschmitt Bf 109G-6 and Bf 109G-14 single-seat fighters and also Bf 109G-12 two-seat conversion trainers from components made in Germany. At the time of Germany's surrender large quantities of components remained intact at the factory, and a small batch of Bf 109G aircraft was completed under the designation **Avia S.99**, 20 of these being assigned to the National Air Guard.

The subsequent destruction of all surviving stocks of Daimler-Benz DB 605 engines in a fire made it necessary for a different engine to be introduced. The type most readily available in adequate numbers was the Junkers Jumo 211F engine, and work was soon started on the adaptation of the basic Bf 109G airframe to accept this somewhat different engine, which was fitted with a paddle-bladed VS 11 propeller. The combination of the S.99 airframe and the Jumo 211F engine resulted in the model known as the **S.199**, of which the first example flew on 25 March 1947. Initial trials revealed that the S.199 possessed very poor handling characteristics, resulting in the nickname 'Mezek' (mule), but for lack of any alternative the S.199 was ordered into full production for the Czechoslovak air force, which received its first aircraft in February 1948.

This S.199 was one of those converted from S.99 standard by Avia. The aircraft retained the machine-gun fairings of the S.99, but did not have the earlier model's engine cannon installation.

Production up to 1951 totalled 551 aircraft including a small number of two-seat **CS.199** conversion trainers. Of the overall total, 129 were assembled by Letov and the balance by Avia. Desperate for fighters in the face of a UN embargo, Israel purchased twenty-five S.199s in 1948, and on 29 May that year, the first Israeli S.199 combat mission was flown.

SPECIFICATION

Avia S 199
Type: single-seat fighter
Powerplant: one Junkers Jumo 211F Vee engine rated at 1,350 hp (1007 kW)
Performance: maximum speed 371 mph (598 km/h) at 19,685 ft (6000 m); cruising speed 287 mph (462 km/h) at optimum altitude; initial climb rate 2,697 ft (822 m) per minute; service ceiling 31,170 ft (9500 m); range 534 miles (860 km)

Weights: empty 6,305 lb (2860 kg); maximum take-off 8,236 lb (3736 kg)
Dimensions: wingspan 32 ft 6½ in (9.92 m); length 29 ft 4 in (8.94 m); height 8 ft 6 in (2.59 m); wing area 177.61 sq ft (16.50 m²)
Armament: two 20-mm fixed forward-firing cannon and two 0.51-in (13-mm) fixed forward-firing machine-guns

AVIA F.L.3

In the late 1930s Francis Lombardi designed for the Italian company AVIA (Azionaria Vercelles Industrie Aeronautiche) a two-seat cabin monoplane that it designated as the **AVIA F.L.3**, and this flew for the first time during 1939. A cantilever low-wing monoplane with fixed tail-wheel landing gear and powered by a Continental flat-four engine, the F.L.3 offered side-by-side seating for the pilot and passenger. Production was initiated before World War II, and during the course of the conflict some 400 examples were impressed for service with the Italian and German air forces. Some of the aircraft were stripped of their propellers but not their CNA D.4 flat-four engines, which were required to maintain the centre of gravity in the correct position, for use as training gliders.

After an initial cessation in 1943, production resumed after the end of

F.L.3s were popular with flying clubs after World War II. This example belonged to the Venice flying club and features an enclosed cockpit. The aircraft was also available with open accommodation.

SPECIFICATION

AVIA F.L.3
Type: two-seat cabin aircraft
Powerplant: one CNA D.4 flat-four piston engine rated at 80 hp (60 kW)
Performance: maximum speed 121 mph (195 km/h) at optimum altitude; cruising speed 93 mph (150 km/h) at optimum altitude; initial climb rate 607 ft (185 m) per

minute; service ceiling 16,405 ft (5000 m); range 509 miles (820 km)
Weights: empty 661 lb (300 kg); maximum take-off 1,135 lb (515 kg)
Dimensions: wing span 32 ft 3¾ in (9.85 m); length 20 ft 10¾ in (6.37 m); height 5 ft 7⅛ in (1.71 m); wing area 154.47 sq ft (14.35 m²)
Accommodation: pilot and passenger

the war in 1945 with the 85-hp (63-kW) Continental C-85 flat-four engine and

the aircraft continued as an AVIA product until 1947 and the absorption of that

company into the Lombardi organisation. Lombardi continued to build the

popular F.L.3, and when production ended in late 1948 a combined total of

about 700 of these aircraft had been manufactured by the two companies.

Aviamilano (Laverda) F.8.L Falco and Aeromere F.8.L America

Aviamilano Costruzioni Aeronautiche was established at Milan in the early 1950s and developed a high-performance two-seat cabin monoplane designated as the **Aviamilano F.8.L Falco**. The Falco flew for the first time in prototype form on 15 June 1955

with the powerplant of one 90-hp (68-kW) Continental flat-four engine. Of advanced design, the Falco demonstrated exceptional performance which, because of its clean lines and excellent finish, was achieved by the initial production **F.8.L Series I**

aircraft on the quite modest power of a 135-hp (101-kW) Avco Lycoming O-290-D2 flat-four engine. The introduction of a 150-hp (112-kW) Avco Lycoming O-320 engine on the second production batch resulted in the changed designation **F.8.L Series II**.

In the mid-1950s the Aeromere Societé per Azioni was established, and in the belief that the F.8.L would prove to be a marketable proposition in the USA, negotiated with Aviamilano for licence construction rights. The resulting version built by Aeromere had the designa-

Modified to meet more demanding US regulations, the Aeromere F.8.L Super Falco was stressed to withstand 8.7 g when fully loaded.

tion **F.8.L Series III America**, and was generally similar to Aviamilano's Series II aircraft, being powered by the O-320 engine, but differed in construction to satisfy the US CAR Part 3 requirements.

Of low-wing cantilever monoplane configuration, the F.8.L had an airframe of basically wooden construction covered with plywood skins. The clean lines of the airframe were comple-

mented by retractable tricycle landing gear and a well streamlined canopy covering a two-seat cockpit with dual controls as standard.

In 1964 Aeromere was taken over by Dr Giovanni Battista Laverda, the company being renamed Laverda Societé per Azioni and continuing the licensed production of an **F.8.L Series IV Super Falco** version with a 160-hp (119-kW) Avco Lycoming O-320 flat-four engine.

SPECIFICATION	
Laverda F.8.L Series IV Super Falco	initial climb rate 984 ft (300 m) per minute; service ceiling 19,685 ft (6000 m); range 870 miles (1400 km)
Type: two-seat touring and training aircraft	**Weights:** empty 1,212 lb (550 kg); maximum take-off 1,808 lb (820 kg)
Powerplant: one Avco Lycoming O-320-B3B flat-four engine rated at 160 hp (119 kW)	**Dimensions:** wing span 26 ft 3 in (8.00 m); length 21 ft 4 in (6.50 m); height 7 ft 6 in (2.27 m); wing area 107.64 sq ft (10.00 m²)
Performance: maximum speed 202 mph (325 km/h) at sea level; maximum cruising speed 180 mph (290 km/h) at 4,920 ft (1500 m);	

Aviamilano P.19 Scricciolo

A side-by-side two-seater, the **Aviamilano P.19 Scricciolo** ('Wren') was designed by Professor Ing. Ermenogildo Preti to meet the requirements of the Italian Aero Club. The prototype flew for the first time on 13 December 1959

and received type approval in the following April. After successful evaluation an initial series of 25 aircraft had all been delivered by mid-1963.

Three versions of the Scricciolo were offered. The second production

batch, designated P.19 and delivered from 1965, had a Continental flat-four engine with a two-bladed fixed-pitch wooden propeller. Some were fitted and others retrofitted with fixed tricycle landing gear in place of the normal tailwheel layout, and in this form were designated **P.19 trs**. A requirement for a glider tug led, in 1964, to the introduction of the **P.19R** with the more powerful 150-hp (112-kW) Lycoming O-320-A1A flat-four engine, which could use either a fixed-pitch or constant-speed propeller.

A total of 50 P.19s of all variants was produced. The type proved popular both as a trainer and glider tug.

All versions of the Scricciolo had a welded steel-tube fuselage with fabric covering, and wings

and tail unit of wooden construction, with the wing leading edges being of glassfibre-reinforced plastic.

SPECIFICATION	
Aviamilano P.19 Scricciolo	rate 550 ft (168 m) per minute; service ceiling 10,170 ft (3100 m); range 400 miles (644 km)
Type: two-seat light aircraft	
Powerplant: one Continental O-200-A flat-four engine rated at 100-hp (75 kW)	**Weights:** empty 1,157 lb (525 kg); maximum take-off 1,731 lb (785 kg)
Performance: maximum speed 130 mph (210 km/h) at sea level; cruising speed 115 mph (185 km/h) at optimum altitude; initial climb	**Dimensions:** wing span 33 ft 7¼ in (10.24 m); length 23 ft ¾ in (7.03 m); height 6 ft 7 in (2.02 m); wing area 150.70 sq ft (14.0 m²)

Avian Model 2/180 Gyroplane

Avian Aircraft Ltd. was created in February 1959 in Ontario, Canada, for the express purpose of designing, building and marketing the **Avian Model 2/180 Gyroplane**. This was a wingless machine with propulsion by means of a ducted fan unit (including a

rudder) at the rear of the fuselage. The type was of mixed construction under a skin of glassfibre; the fuselage had a steel primary and alloy secondary structure and the three blades of the rotor had steel spars in a wooden core.

The fuselage had a basi-

cally oval-section design and carried two or three persons in tandem under a long canopy at the front with the fuel tank, rotor pylon and engine in the rear. The airframe was completed by the fixed tricycle landing gear.

The first **Model 2/180B** prototype made its maiden flight in the spring of 1960 with a clutched mechanical linkage between the engine and the rotor for pre-flight 'spin up' to a speed of 300 rpm (by comparison with the normal windmilling speed of 263 rpm). This machine was damaged in an accident and replaced by a generally similar second prototype, which first flew

An ambitious attempt at making the autogyro concept popular among civil buyers, the Gyroplane failed to find a market niche. The heated cabin was fitted with two or three glassfibre seats.

on 16 February 1961. There followed three pre-production machines, but in the early 1970s plans for the proposed **Model 2/180A**

production model (initially schemed with compressed-air nozzles at the rotor tips for a 'jump start' capability) fell into abeyance.

SPECIFICATION	
Avian Model 2/180 Gyroplane	minute; service ceiling 14,000 ft (4275 m); range 400 miles (644 km)
Type: two/three-seat autogyro	
Powerplant: one Avco Lycoming IO-360 flat-four engine rated at 200 hp (149 kW)	**Weights:** empty 1,400 lb (635 kg); maximum take-off 2,000 lb (907 kg)
Performance: maximum speed 120 mph (193 km/h) at optimum altitude; cruising speed 110 mph (177 km/h) at optimum altitude; initial climb rate 870 ft (265 m) per	**Dimensions:** rotor diameter 37 ft (11.28 m); length, fuselage 16 ft (4.88 m); height 7 ft 4 in (2.24 m); rotor disc area 1,075.21 sq ft (99.89 m²)

Aviatik B I and B II (Germany)

Germany-based Automobil und Aviatik AG began the design and construction of aircraft in 1910, gradually developing its capabilities to the point at which, in 1913, it created the highly successful series of **Pfeil** (arrow) aircraft that were copied in Italy and Russia.

The company's **Aviatik P.15**, designed by Robert Wild as a general-purpose two-seater, was adopted by the Imperial German army air service as the **B I** and saw service on both the Eastern and Western Fronts. It was an unstaggered two-bay unequal span biplane of typical fabric-covered wooden construction with fixed tailskid landing gear. In the

later **P.15A** variant that still carried the service designation B I, the struts supporting the overhanging portions of the upper wing were removed, and a triangular fin was added in front of the 'comma' type rudder.

Appearing in 1915 for service as the **B II**, the **P.15B** was an improved version of the P.15A. Its powerplant was uprated to one 120-hp (90-kW) Mercedes D.II inline engine located in a cleaner nose installation and exhausting over the upper wing via a starboard-side 'rhino horn' stack. The type was produced in a number of variants with a two- or three-bay wing cellule possessing either dihedral

or sweep, and either with or without the diagonal auxiliary struts that braced the overhanging portions of the upper wing. With the retirement of the 'B' category unarmed two-seaters from first-line service between the end of 1915 and the first part of 1916, the surviving Aviatik aircraft were relegated to second-line tasks such as training and liaison.

Following Wild's move from Germany to Italy in 1914, the Italian army air service decided to adopt a licence-built development of the Aviatik B I as one of its standard craft with an assortment of engine types, and production between 1915 and 1918 totalled 568 aircraft.

The first three variants to be produced in Italy were the **SAML A.1** with a powerplant of one 100-hp (75-kW) Fiat A.10 inline engine, the **A.2** with a powerplant of one 120-hp (90-kW) Le Rhône rotary engine and the **A.3** with the powerplant of one 110-hp (82-kW) Colombo rotary engine. With the

As with the majority of early 'B'-type aircraft, the Aviatik B I seated its observer forwards and pilot to the rear. While this arrangement was less than ideal in combat, the type was built in considerable numbers both in Germany and Italy.

exception of their powerplants and the fact that a 0.26-in (6.5-mm) Revelli trainable machine-gun could be installed, the aircraft were basically similar to the German original.

Production of the A.1, A.2 and A.3 totalled 63 aircraft, and it was mainly these types that were used for the reconnaissance and artillery-spotting roles during 1915 and 1916. Most of the Italian aircraft (505 of the 568 machines) were completed to the

SAML Aviatik standard, although with an uprated powerplant, and were generally used in the training role up to 1930 after becoming obsolete in the operational role. The powerplant mostly comprised either one Salmson (Canton-Unné) radial engine rated at 140 hp (104 kW) or one Isotta-Fraschini V-4B inline engine rated at 160 hp (119 kW).

SPECIFICATION	
Aviatik B I	
Type: two-seat reconnaissance and artillery-spotting aircraft	**Weights:** empty 1,466 lb (665 kg); maximum take-off 2,403 lb (1090 kg)
Powerplant: one Mercedes D.I inline engine rated at 100 hp (75 kW)	**Dimensions:** wingspan 45 ft 9 in (13.95 m); length 26 ft 3 in (8.00 m); height 10 ft 10 in (3.30 m)
Performance: maximum speed 62 mph (100 km/h) at sea level; climb to 3,280 ft (1000 m) in 15 minutes; endurance 4 hours	**Armament:** generally none, but the observer sometimes carried a carbine or pistol

Aviatik C I (Austria-Hungary)

The Austro-Hungarian aero industry produced few world-class warplanes in World War I, but the **Aviatik C I** was one of them. Designed by Dipl.-Ing. Julius von Berg and often known as the **Berg C I**, the C I was a half-brother to the D I fighter with slightly increased dimensions and,

in its initial form, a slightly lower-rated engine. In the case of both warplanes speed was very high, but this capability was achieved only at the expense of a reduction in structural weight and therefore, most unfortunately, in strength.

The C I was a trim two-seater with fixed tailskid

landing gear and was a staggered single-bay biplane of the equal-span type. It was of mixed steel and wood construction covered with fabric on the flying surfaces and plywood on the fuselage, and the powerplant was based on one Austro-Daimler inline engine driving a two-bladed propeller. The armament comprised two Schwarzlose machine-guns, one fixed and the other trainable.

The C I had excellent performance, especially in speed, range, climb rate and service ceiling, therefore, despite its lack of strength and its inability to operate into and out of small airfields, the type was ordered into large-

The aerodynamically refined lines of the Aviatik C III mask the fact that the type was little changed from the basic C I. A spinner and revised engine/exhaust installation defined the C III.

scale production by Ungarische Lloyd Flugzeug und Motorenfabrik (**C I Serie 47**), Jakob Lohner (**C I Serie 114**), MAG (**C I Serie 91**) and Wiener Karosserie und Flugzeugfabrik (**C I Serie 83**) in addition to the

parent company (**C I Serie 37**) with the 185-hp (138-kW) engine. The type was also produced with the 200-hp (149-kW) version of the same engine by Aviatik (**C I Serie 137**), Lohner (**C I Serie 214**) and WKF (**C I Serie 183**).

SPECIFICATION	
Aviatik C I	3 hours 30 minutes
Type: two-seat reconnaissance and artillery-spotting warplane	**Weights:** empty 1,411 lb (640 kg); maximum take-off 1,896 lb (860 kg)
Powerplant: one Austro-Daimler inline engine rated at 185 hp (138 kW)	**Dimensions:** wingspan 27 ft 6¾ in (8.40 m); length 25 ft 2 in (7.67 m); height 9 ft 9 in (2.97 m)
Performance: maximum speed 116 mph (187 km/h) at sea level; climb to 16,405 ft (5000 m) in 28 minutes; service ceiling 20,995 ft (6400 m); endurance	**Armament:** one 0.315-in (8-mm) fixed forward-firing machine-gun, and one 0.315-in (8-mm) trainable rearward-firing machine-gun

Aviatik 'C' category aircraft (Germany)

First appearing early in 1915 after design as the **Aviatik P.25**, the **C I** was in essence a development of the B II concept with a higher-rated powerplant, a number of structural and aerodynamic refinements, and provision for the observer in the front cockpit to be armed with a single 0.312-in (7.92-mm) Parabellum machine-gun; in this feature the C I was the only 'C' category armed two-seater to have its

observer/gunner in the front cockpit.

The C I was an unstaggered two-bay biplane of the unequal-span type with fixed tailskid landing gear and a tail unit whose vertical surface comprised only a balanced rudder of the 'comma' type. The type was of typical fabric-covered wooden construction.

The C I entered production on a scale that was comparatively large for the

period. However, operational service soon revealed that the forward location of the observer/gunner and his weapon was a serious tactical problem, especially as the gun's fields of fire were highly limited and as it took some time for the observer/gunner to unship his machine-gun and relocate it to the other side of the cockpit. As an immediate semi-solution, single Parabellum machine-guns

were carried on the cockpit side-rails, but the additional weight and drag of the second machine-gun degraded performance to an appreciable degree. The final solution that was belatedly adopted was the revision of some aircraft to **C Ia** standard with the positions of the pilot and observer/gunner reversed so that the latter occupied the rear cockpit that was now fitted with a ring mounting for more effec-

tive use of a single rearward-firing machine-gun.

The **C II** was developed from the C I concept, with a powerplant of one 200-hp (149-kW) Benz Bz.IV inline piston engine, no fin, and the observer/gunner still located ahead of the pilot, whose position was improved by the adoption of a headrest. The type did not enter production.

Although the C I was moderately successful, it was clear that refinement could also pay handsome dividends in terms of

Among Aviatik's range of 'C' type aircraft was the successful C VI. The aircraft was not, in fact, an Aviatik design, being little more than a licence-built D. F. W. C V.

improved performance, and this resulted in the evolution of the **C III**. A general cleaning-up of the exhaust and radiator systems produced an 11.25-mph (18-km/h) improvement in the maximum speed with the same engine. Other aerodynamic and fuel system changes were also introduced at this time.

Oddly enough, the C III was initially delivered with the same type of armament installation as the

C I, but numbers of the aircraft were revised to **C IIIa** standard with the positions of the pilot and observer/gunner reversed in the manner pioneered in the C Ia. The C IIIa was a much improved warplane, and its high performance meant that the type was often used as an escort for slower 'C' category single-engined aircraft and even, on occasion, for 'G' category twin-engined bombers.

Later 'C' category biplanes of Aviatik design were comparatively numerous, but none of them entered production. Only a single prototype of the **C V** was built, with a deeper fuselage than the C III and the lower wing of the biplane wing cellule at the base of the fuselage. The upper wing was of the gull-wing configuration with its roots attached high on the fuselage, and provided both pilot and observer with an excellent forward view. The tail unit and landing gear were similar to those of the C III, but the depth of the fuselage made it possible to install a 180-hp (134-kW) Argus As III inline engine completely within neat cowlings. The armament comprised one 0.312-in (7.92-mm) LMG 08/15 fixed forward-firing machine-gun and one flexible 0.312-in (7.92-mm) LMG 14 Parabellum trainable machine-gun.

Very few details were recorded about the **C VIII**, of which only a single prototype appears to have been built. It was a very clean single-bay biplane, incorporating a cut-out in the trailing edge of the upper wing to improve the pilot's field of vision. The 160-hp (119-kW) Mercedes D.II engine in the nose had most of its cylinders exposed, but the nose entry was enhanced by the inclusion of a large propeller spinner. The tail unit and landing gear were

similar to those of Aviatik's earlier aircraft, but as the C VIII was of 1917 vintage, the two-seat accommodation was arranged with the pilot seated ahead of the observer/gunner.

Built to the extent of three prototypes, the **C IX** appears to have been a development of the C VIII but with a wing cellule which, being of two-bay configuration, was probably of increased span. Two of these aircraft had ailerons on both wings, while one had them only on the upper wing, and there were variations in the contours of the tail units.

SPECIFICATION	
Aviatik C I	
Type: two-seat reconnaissance and artillery-spotting warplane	(450 km); endurance 3 hours
Powerplant: one Mercedes D.III inline engine rated at 160 hp (119 kW)	**Weights:** empty 1,653 lb (750 kg); maximum take-off 2,738 lb (1242 kg)
Performance: maximum speed 88 mph (142 km/h) at sea level; climb to 6,560 ft (2000 m) in 21 minutes; service ceiling 11,485 ft (3500 m); range 280 miles	**Dimensions:** wingspan 40 ft ⅛ in (12.50 m); length 26 ft (7.93 m); height 9 ft 8¾ in (2.95 m); wing area 462.86 sq ft (43.00 m²)
	Armament: one 0.312-in (7.92-mm) trainable lateral-firing machine-gun

Aviatik D II

The first fighter to bear the Aviatik name was the **D I**, which was in fact the Halberstadt D II built under licence and later redesignated more informatively as the **Halberstadt D II(Av)**. Thus the first fighter of Aviatik design as well as manufacture was the

Aviatik D II, which was designed and built in prototype form during the later part of 1916. The D II was of moderately advanced concept and construction for its period and, in common with contemporary German fighters, was armed with two 0.312-in (7.92-mm)

MG 08/15 synchronised machine-guns in the upper part of the forward fuselage.

In configuration the aircraft was an unequal-span biplane of wood and fabric construction, with an oval section fuselage of steel-tube construction forwards and wood aft, a staggered single-bay wing cellule, an open pilot's cockpit, and fixed tailskid landing gear. The tail unit was slightly unusual in that the vertical surface comprised a balanced rudder of the 'comma' type complemented by a ventral fin.

The D II failed to find official favour during trials, and only the one machine was built.

Showing signs of considerable structural and aerodynamic refinement, the Aviatik D II had a fuselage skinned mostly in plywood. This feature was typical of Albatros fighter designs, which also employed similar propeller spinners.

SPECIFICATION	
Aviatik D II	
Type: single-seat fighter	7 minutes 12 seconds
Powerplant: one Mercedes D.III inline engine rated at 160 hp (119 kW)	**Dimensions:** wingspan 29 ft (8.84 m); length 22 ft 4½ in (6.82 m); height 9 ft 5 in (2.87 m)
Performance: maximum speed 93 mph (150 km/h) at sea level; climb to 3,280 ft (1000 m) in	**Armament:** two 0.312-in (7.92-mm) fixed forward-firing machine-guns

Aviatik D III

Making its maiden flight in the course of November 1917, the first prototype of the **Aviatik D III** was fitted with one Benz Bz IIIbo Vee engine, a direct-drive Vee unit rated at 195 hp (146 kW). The machine was an unequal-span biplane of mixed construction with steel-tube and wood forward and rear fuselage sections under a plywood skinning, and fabric-covered wood for the heavily staggered single-bay wing cellule. The tail unit was orthodox and the armament was the standard German fighter installation of a pair of synchronised machine-guns in the upper part of the forward fuselage.

The D III was type-tested at Adlershof near Berlin during 9-12 February 1918 and, after modification by the manufacturer, was returned to Adlershof in April for further evaluation. For this stage of the programme the initial prototype was complemented by a second prototype with a revised powerplant, namely one Bz IIIbm inline engine with a reduction gear.

An unusual design feature of the Aviatik D III was its underfuselage keel structure. The lower wing was mounted to the keel, thus increasing the interplane gap.

Aviatik D III (continued)

By this time a small batch of D III machines with the Bz IIIbo engine was being manufactured for a full service test and evaluation, as the Aviatik fighter was generally seen as offering performance superior to that of the Albatros D.V. In spite of this excellent performance no further production was undertaken however. Virtually no realistic flight data have survived other than those derived from the climb tests carried out by the first prototype in March 1918.

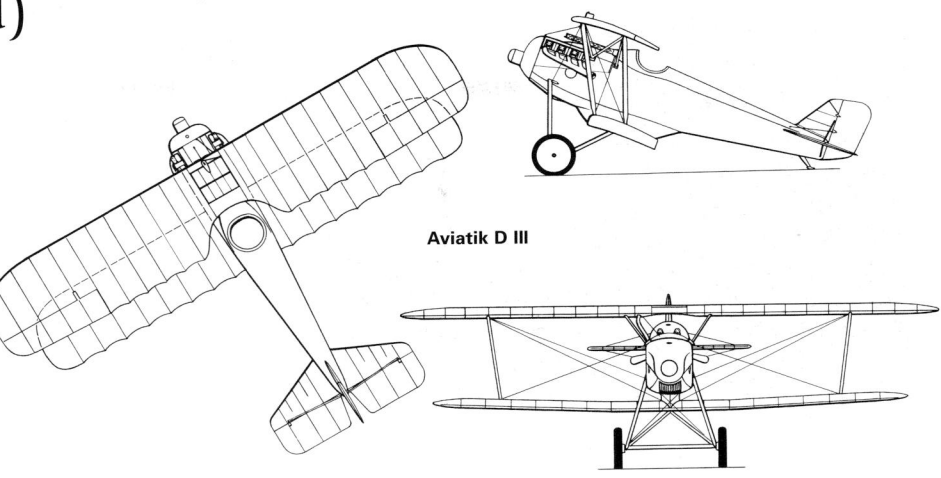

Aviatik D III

SPECIFICATION

Aviatik D III
Type: single-seat fighter
Powerplant: one Benz Bz IIIbo Vee engine rated at 195 hp (146 kW)
Performance: climb to 9,845 ft (3000 m) in 11 minutes
Weights: maximum take-off 1,905 lb (864 kg)
Dimensions: wingspan 29 ft 6¾ in (9.00 m); wing area 226.05 sq ft (21.00 m²)
Armament: two 0.312-in (7.92-mm) fixed forward-firing machine-guns

Aviatik D IV, D V, D VI and D VII

Prototypes of both the **D IV** and **D V** appeared in the spring and early summer of 1918, but both were delayed by engine teething problems and there is no direct evidence that either type flew.

The **Aviatik D VI**, whose single prototype made its maiden flight during August 1918, bore little except the most basic conceptual relationship to its single-seat fighter predecessors from the Aviatik stable, and was a staggered two-bay biplane of wooden construction with a plywood-covered fuselage and fabric-covered wings and tail surfaces. A notable feature was the incorporation of rounded tips on the

Of wholly conventional construction, the **D VI** *was unusual for the time in its use of a four-bladed propeller.*

slightly dihedralled lower wing, and of raked tips on the flat upper wing, the outboard ends of whose trailing edges carried large horn-balanced ailerons.

It had been planned that the D VI would take part in the second 'D' category competition held at Adlershof in June 1918 but, as a result of problems with the Bz.IIIbm engine's reduction gearbox, the type was too late for this contest. By the time testing had revealed the type's excellent flight characteris-

tics, the D VI had already been overtaken by the Fokker D.VII.

For the third 'D' category competition to be held in October 1918, Aviatik proposed the **D VII**. Basically similar to the D VI except for its new tail unit, only one prototype was completed before the end of World War I.

SPECIFICATION

Aviatik D VI
Type: single-seat fighter
Powerplant: one Benz Bz.IIIbm Vee engine rated at 195 hp (146 kW)
Performance: maximum speed 117 mph (188 km/h) at optimum altitude; climb to 16,405 ft (5000 m) in 17 minutes 48 seconds
Weights: empty 1,653 lb (750 kg); maximum take-off 2,072 lb (9401 kg)
Dimensions: wingspan 31 ft 8⅔ in (9.66m); length, 20 ft ⅛ in (6.10 m); height 8 ft 2½ in (2.50 m)
Armament: two 0.312-in (7.92-mm) fixed forward-firing machine-guns

Aviatik 30.24

Appearing in May 1917, following the mid-1916 appearance of the Sopwith Triplane, the **Aviatik 30.24** was in essence a triplane development of the D I

biplane fighter. The agility of the new type was good, but the additional drag of the modified wing cellule meant a slight reduction in performance compared to that of the similarly engined D I biplane, though the triple had a four- rather than two-bladed propeller. Only the single prototype was built.

One of several German machines designed in response to the Sopwith Triplane, the 30.24 met with little success.

SPECIFICATION

Aviatik 30.24
Type: single-seat fighter
Powerplant: one Austro-Daimler inline engine rated at 200 hp (149 kW)
Performance: maximum speed 108 mph (174 km/h) at sea level; climb to 6,560 ft (2000 m) in 4 minutes 9 seconds
Weights: empty 1,367 lb (620 kg); maximum take-off 1,900 lb (862 kg)
Dimensions: wingspan 23 ft 8¼ in (7.22 m); length 22 ft 6 in (6.86 m); height 9 ft (2.75 m); wing area 242.19 sq ft (22.50 m²)
Armament: two 0.315-in (8-mm) fixed forward-firing machine-guns

Aviatik 30.27 and 30.29

Appearing for the first time early in 1918, the Aviatik 30.27 and generally similar Aviatik 30.29 prototypes marked something of a departure from Aviatik's previous practice as they were powered by the 160-hp (119-kW) Steyr copy of the Le Rhône 11 rotary engine. Biplanes with a single-bay unstaggered wing cellule, the two

Attractive fighters of adequate performance, the 30.27 (illustrated) and 30.29 suffered from a lack of structural integrity. No production aircraft stemmed from either type.

SPECIFICATION

Aviation 30.27 (definitive form)
Type: single-seat fighter
Powerplant: one Steyr (Le Rhône) rotary engine rated at 160 hp (119 kW)
Performance: maximum speed 115 mph (185 km/h) at 2,625 ft (800 m); climb to 6,560 ft (2000 m) in 3 minutes 45 seconds
Weights: empty 851 lb (386 kg); maximum take-off 1,336 lb (606 kg)
Dimensions: wingspan 22 ft 4½ in (6.82 m); length 16 ft 4¾ in (5.00 m); height 8 ft 6¾ in (2.61 m)
Armament: two 0.315-in (8-mm) fixed forward-firing machine-guns

types were of wooden construction under a covering of plywood on the fuselage (except for a forward section covered with light alloy panels) and of fabric on the flying surfaces, and each carried the standard armament of two machine-guns.

Each of the two aircraft was initially evaluated with a two-bladed propeller, but this was later replaced by a four-bladed unit and at the same time the original engine cowling, of the horseshoe type, was replaced by a full ring cowling with slots round its lower half.

Both prototypes took part in the Austro-Hungarian 'D' category competition of July 1918, the 30.29 crashing when the leading edge of its upper wing collapsed as its pilot entered a loop. No production ensued.

Aviatik (Berg) D I

With the company at a low ebb, Aviatik was reorganised and new management, including the German Dipl.-Ing. Julius von Berg as chief engineer, was brought in.

Berg soon started work on the design of aircraft that would transform Aviatik's fortunes for the better, although his first two designs were rejected out of hand when submitted in June 1916 to the Fliegerarsenal (aviation arsenal), which wanted Aviatik to concentrate on the C II programme. These designs were eventually to mature, however, as the C I armed two-seater and D I single-seat fighter.

Some information about the two Berg-designed aircraft finally reached Oberst Emil Uzelac, commanding the Imperial Austro-Hungarian army air service, and in the course of August 1916 he demanded the highest possible priority for the two new designs. The D I was a single-seat machine with fixed tailskid landing gear and a staggered single-bay

biplane wing cellule of the equal-span type. The type was of wood and metal construction covered with fabric on the flying surfaces and plywood on the fuselage. Its powerplant was based on one Austro-Daimler inline engine driving a two-bladed propeller, and this engine was installed high in the forward fuselage.

In September 1916 Aviatik received an order for 100 D Is, of which three prototypes and four (later increased to seven) preproduction aircraft were being built with the powerplant of one 185-hp (138-kW) Austro-Daimler engine. The Aviatik 30.19, the first of the prototypes, made the type's maiden flight on 24 January 1917, and the pilot's report was highly enthusiastic about the fighter's rate of climb and agility. Technical experts were less happy with the machine's strength as the wing cellule of the second prototype failed during static tests. However, adequate if not exceptional strength was

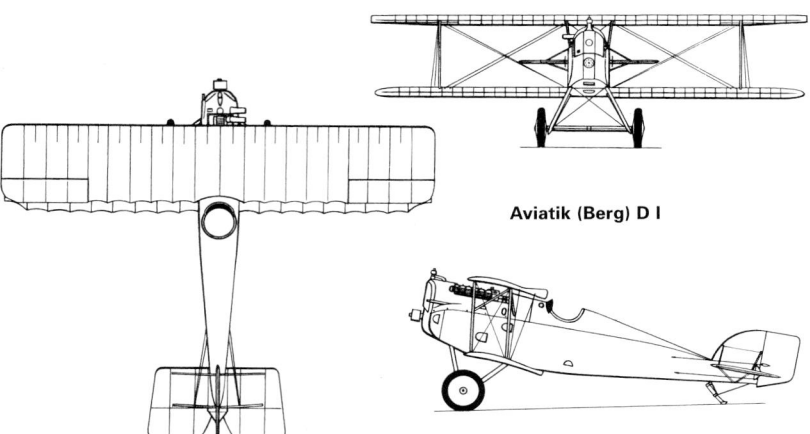

Aviatik (Berg) D I

Three styles of radiator installation were used on the D I: a nose-mounted unit (illustrated), an upper wing leading-edge unit or two 'ear' type radiators on the forward fuselage sides.

finally secured by building the upper wing as a single-piece structure and reinforcing the spars of the lower wing. The last prototype completed successful trials up to March 1917, and was then revised as the first experimental Aviatik D II with wing cellule devoid of bracing.

Pre-production D I fighters entered limited service in the middle of May 1917, but the service debut of production aircraft was further delayed to August of the same year by the belated decision to incorporate further strengthening of the airframe along the lines pioneered in the structurally-similar Aviatik C I. It was during August and September 1917 that the D I finally entered full service. Contrary to Aviatik's assurance to the Fliegerarsenal, in the **D I Serie 38** and **D I Serie 138** initial batches, the armament still comprised only one unsynchronised Schwarzlose machine-gun, but from January 1918 aircraft were delivered with the synchronised arma-

ment of two similar machine-guns.

The D I remained in production by Aviatik right through to the end of World War I, and comprised aircraft in four series that were produced in parallel according to the availability of the engine relevant to each series. These four models were the D I Serie 38, the D I Serie 138, the **D I Serie 238** and the **D I Serie 338**. Had production continued to the end of December 1918 as planned, some 990 aircraft would have been completed.

Licence-built variants included the **D I Series 115**, the **D I Serie 315**, **D I Serie 48**, **D I Serie 248**,

D I Serie 348, **D I Serie 92**, **D I Serie 101**, **D I Serie 201**, **D I Serie 84**, **D I Serie 184**, **D I Serie 284** and the **D I Serie 384**. Apart from being produced by different manufacturers, the primary differences were in terms of engine installation.

With the defeat of Austria-Hungary in November 1918, the D I disappeared from service with the exception of a number of D I Serie 348 and D I Serie 92 fighters. These saw operational service with the Red Air Corps of the Hungarian communist party during 1919 in the turbulence that followed the dissolution of the Austro-Hungarian Empire.

SPECIFICATION	
Aviatik D I Serie 138 **Type:** single-seat fighter **Powerplant:** one Austro-Daimler inline engine rated at 200 hp (149 kW) **Performance:** maximum speed 121 mph (195 km/h) at sea level; climb to 16,405 ft (5000 m) in 19 minutes 57 seconds; service ceiling 19,685 ft (6000 m);	endurance 2 hours 30 minutes **Weights:** empty 1,345 lb (610 kg); maximum take-off 2,063 lb (936 kg) **Dimensions:** wingspan 26 ft 3 in (8.00 m); length 22 ft 6 in (6.86 m); height 8 ft 2 in (2.48 m); wing area 234.66 sq ft (21.80 m²) **Armament:** two 0.315-in (8-mm) fixed forward-firing machine-guns

Aviatik (Berg) D II

With a fuselage virtually identical to that of the D I fighter, the **Aviatik D II** prototype made its maiden flight in the summer of 1917. This **Aviatik 30.22** used much of the D I's Aviatik 30.21 third prototype, and was most notably characterised by a short-span cantilever lower wing. The prototype was followed by 19 aircraft manufactured for front-line evaluation, and these were powered by either the 200- or 225-hp (149- or 168-kW) versions of the Austro-Daimler inline

engine in the **D II Serie 39** or **D II Serie 339** variants, of which the latter had a maximum speed of 137 mph (220 km/h). Both models had a four-bladed propeller, and the armament that had by now become standard for Austro-Hungarian fighters, namely two 0.315-in (8-mm) Schwarzlose machine-guns.

The D II's unusual empennage design featured a small fixed dorsal surface and a tall broad-chord rudder.

Aviatik (Berg) DII (continued)

The first three production aircraft were flight-tested during November 1917, and seven were then evaluated at the front. However, it was subsequently decided that Aviatik should undertake licensed manufacture of the rival Fokker D.VII biplane fighter and this decision ended all plans to build the D II in quantity. One D II airframe was experimentally fitted with a 200-hp (149-kW) Hiero inline engine as the Aviatik 30.38, and this machine took part in the 'D' category fighter competition of July 1918.

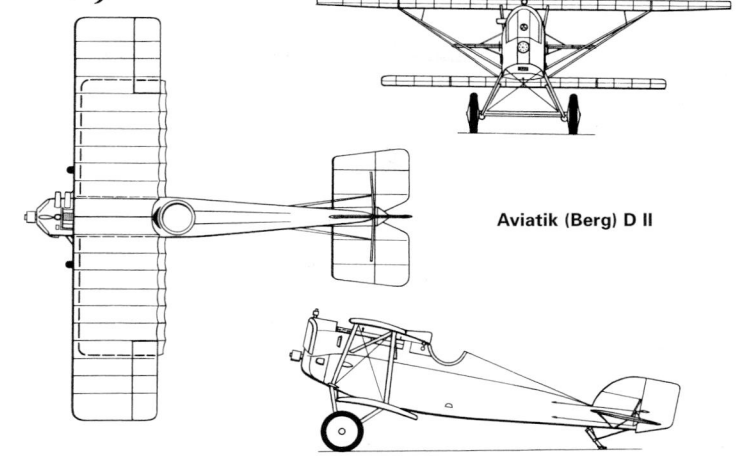

Aviatik (Berg) D II

SPECIFICATION

Aviatik D II Serie 39
Type: single-seat fighter
Powerplant: one Austro-Daimler inline engine rated at 200 hp (149 kW)
Performance: maximum speed 130 mph (210 km/h) at sea level; climb to 6,560 ft (2000 m) in 6 minutes 36 seconds

Weights: empty 1,294 lb (587 kg); maximum take-off 1,786 lb (810 kg)
Dimensions: wingspan 24 ft 7¼ in (7.50m); length 22 ft 10¾ in (6.98 m)
Armament: two 0.315-in (8-mm) fixed forward-firing machine-guns

Aviation Scotland ARV-1 Super2

The type generally known as the **Aviation Scotland ARV-1 Super2** began life as a product of Island Aircraft (originally ARV Aviation) but was then bought late in 1991 by Aviation Scotland Ltd. In June 1993 Aviation Scotland and the Swedish company, Uvan Invest AB, created ASL Hagfors Aero AB and in 1994 production of the Super2 was transferred entirely to Sweden for continued manufacture as the **ASL Opus 280**.

The type is a simple two-seat cabin monoplane with side-by-side accommodation and a high-set wing braced on each side by a single strut, and notable for the slight forward sweep of its dihedralled halves. The Super2 was planned as a type that would appeal largely through its low purchase, maintenance and operating costs, and as a

An ambitious attempt to produce a cheap light aircraft, the Super2 was initially plagued by engine problems, which caused the collapse of ARV Aviation.

result was schemed on the basis of a structure making extensive use of superplastically formed aluminium alloy pressings under an aluminium alloy skin.

The first of three prototype and demonstrator aircraft flew on 11 March 1985, and the type received British certification in July 1986. The type entered production with the Hewland Engineering (later Mid-West Aero-Engines) AE 75 three-cylinder inline engine rated at 77-hp (57-kW) and driving a two-bladed propeller

of the fixed-pitch type. The two versions available in the late 1990s were the Opus 280 built in Sweden with the Rotax 912A engine and the **ARV-K1 Super2** kit version of the standard Super2 with the

MWAE 75D engine. Also under development is a version with an uprated powerplant in the form of the MWAE 100R twin-rotor rotary engine rated at 95-hp (71-kW).

SPECIFICATION

ASL Opus 280
Type: two-seat light sporting and touring aircraft
Powerplant: one Rotax 912A flat-four engine rated at 80 hp (60 kW)
Performance: maximum speed 120 mph (193 km/h) at optimum altitude; cruising speed 109 mph (176 km/h) at optimum altitude;

initial climb rate 650 ft (198 m) per minute; range 471 miles (759 km)
Weights: empty 728 lb (330 kg); maximum take-off 1,168 lb (530 kg)
Dimensions: wing span 28 ft 6 in (8.69 m); length 18 ft (5.49 m); height 7 ft 7 in (2.31 m); wing area 92.50 sq ft (8.59 m²)

Aviation Traders ATL.90 Accountant

In the early 1950s a number of companies explored the possibility of building a Douglas DC-3 replacement. The **Aviation Traders ATL.90 Accountant**, a twin-engined light transport with accommodation for 28 passengers, was a brave attempt to fill this gap, particularly since Aviation Traders was not an aircraft manufacturing company. The choice of powerplant for the Accountant was dictated by the success of the Rolls-Royce Dart turbo-prop in the Vickers Viscount, and the Accountant made its first flight on the power of two Darts from the manufacturer's home airfield at Southend on 9 July 1957.

Early in January 1958 Airwork acquired the Aviation Traders group of companies, which was headed by Freddie Laker, and since there were no immediate orders in

prospect, development of the Accountant was abandoned. The first of a planned three prototypes was therefore the only example completed, and this was later cocooned at Southend, where it was eventually broken up for scrap in February 1960. A further variant, the **Accountant Mk II** derivative with its fuselage lengthened for the carriage of 40 passengers, was proposed but never built.

Aviation Traders had gained experience of aircraft construction techniques by carrying out aircraft maintenance and modification. The ATL.90 was nevertheless a fine achievement.

SPECIFICATION

Aviation Traders ATL.90 Accountant
Type: medium-range airliner
Powerplant: two Rolls-Royce Dart R.Da.6 Mk 512 turboprop engines each rated at 1,740 ehp (1298 ekW)
Performance: maximum speed 295 mph (475 km/h) at 25,000 ft (7620 m); maximum cruising speed 292 mph (470 km/h) at 15,000 ft (4570 m); initial climb rate 1,500 ft (457 m) per minute; climb to

25,000 ft (7620 m) in 27 minutes 36 seconds; range 2,090 miles (3364 km)
Weights: empty 16,961 lb (7693 kg); maximum take-off 28,500 lb (12928 kg)
Dimensions: wingspan 82 ft 6 in (25.15 m); length 62 ft 1 in (18.93 m); height 25 ft 3½ in (7.70 m); wing area 632.00 sq ft (58.71 m²)
Accommodation: 28 passengers

Aviation Traders ATL.98 Carvair

The need to supplement, and eventually replace, the Bristol Freighter Mk 32 on car-carrying services across the English Channel led to the development of the **Aviation Traders ATL.98 Carvair**, the name being a contraction of Car via air. Increased range and capacity were required, and

Aviation Traders concluded that the conversion of an existing aircraft would prove more economic than the development of a completely new design. The type chosen as the basis of the conversion was the Douglas DC-4, which was robust and reliable, comparatively cheap

In addition to the bulbous nose section and revised flightdeck position, Aviation Traders also added a taller fin to the DC-4 airframe to restore directional stability.

to acquire from larger airlines that were updating their fleets, and had a considerable spares backing. The conversion, planned with technical assistance from Douglas, consisted basically of a new and longer forward fuselage, with the flightdeck high above the new front hold, which had a side-hinged nose door through which vehicles could be loaded. The standard layout could accommodate five cars forward and 22 passengers in the rear cabin, but an alternative all-passenger layout could carry a maximum of 65 passengers. In addition to the fuselage conversion, a new vertical tail surface of increased height and area was provided. First flown on

21 June 1961, the Carvair entered service, initially with British United Air Ferries, in March 1962. Some 21 conversions were completed, serving with Aer Lingus, Aviaco, Ansett-

ANA, British United Air Ferries, and Interocean Airways. The aircraft subsequently changed hands several times, and only a small number remained in service into the mid-1980s.

A hinged nose door granted access to the main hold of the Carvair. A special loading ramp was used to lift cargo and cars up to the cabin floor. Many aircraft found employment as standard freighters, as well as car ferries.

SPECIFICATION	
Aviation Traders ATL.98 Carvair **Type:** two/three-crew air ferry transport **Powerplant:** four Pratt & Whitney R-2000-7M2 Twin Wasp radial engines each rated at 1,450 hp (1081 kW) **Performance:** maximum speed 250 mph (402 km/h) at optimum altitude; maximum cruising speed 213 mph (343 km/h) at optimum altitude; initial climb rate 650 ft (198 m) per minute; service ceiling	18,700 ft (5700 m); range 2,300 miles (3701 km) with maximum payload **Weights:** empty 41,885 lb (18999 kg); maximum take-off 73,800 lb (33475 kg) **Dimensions:** wingspan 117 ft 6 in (35.81 m); length 102 ft 7 in (31.27 m); height 29 ft 10 in (9.09m); wing area 1,462.00 sq ft (135.82 m²) **Payload:** 19,335 lb (8770 kg) of cars and passengers

Avioane IAR-99 Soim

The **IAR-99 Soim (Hawk)** was designed in the early 1980s in the Institutul de Aviatie at Bucharest and was put into production at Craiova by Intreprinderea de Avioane (IAv). In the reorganisation of the state aircraft industry following the collapse of the Ceausescu regime, the Craiova factory became a part of the Avioane subsidiary of the IAROM holding company.

A conventional design for a straight-wing single-jet aircraft, the Soim was conceived as a basic/advanced trainer with secondary ground-attack/close-support capability. Tandem seating in zero-zero ejection seats was arranged in a pressurised cockpit with the rear seat raised for improved forward view. Following the first flight on 21 December 1985, the IAR-99 entered service with

Although a competent trainer, the IAR-99 (illustrated in prototype form) has been dogged by political upheaval and funding problems.

the Romanian Air Force (AMR) in 1988 and in excess of 21 have since been delivered.

An upgraded version for sale outside Romania was first announced in 1991. It was planned to incorporate major systems and completely updated avionics of Western origin, including a HUD and modern gunsight, with possible modification of the Viper engine to increase thrust. In the event, this **New IAR-99** was displayed at the 1997 Paris Air Show, having been produced by a team consisting of Elbit (Israel) and Avioane. No orders have yet been forthcoming. A further upgraded

version, designated **IAR-109 Swift**, appears to have been abandoned.

At the 1998 Farnborough International Air Show, Avioane flew an example of the Soim modified as a lead-in trainer for the Romanian Air Force's upgraded MiG-21 Lancers. This is apparently the only Soim upgrade to have received production funding; some US$21 million has been granted to modify up to 24 aircraft.

SPECIFICATION	
IAR-99 Soim (standard version for Romanian Air Force) **Type:** advanced jet trainer and light attack aircraft **Powerplant:** one Turbomecanica Romanian-built Rolls-Royce Viper Mk 632-41M turbojet rated at 4,000 lb st (17.79 kN) **Performance:** maximum level speed at sea level 537 mph (865 km/h) maximum climb rate at sea level 6,890 ft (2100 m) per minute; service ceiling 42,325 ft (12,900 m); maximum range with	internal fuel 683 miles (1100 km); lo-lo-hi 217 miles (350 km) **Weights:** empty equipped 7,055 lb (3200 kg); maximum take-off 9,700 lb (4400 kg) **Dimensions:** wingspan 32 ft 3¾ in (9.85 m); length 36 ft 1½ in (11.01 m); height 12 ft 9½ in (3.90 m); wing area 201.4 sq ft (18.71 m²) **Armament:** 23-mm GSh-23 ventral gun pod, plus bombs, rocket launchers, or IR-guided AAMs up to a total of 2,204 lb (1000 kg)

Avions de Transport Régional ATR 42 and ATR 72

The organisation known as Avions de Transport Régional was established in February 1982 to produce a regional airliner known as the **Avions de Transport Régional ATR 42**. This type had been launched three months earlier as a collaborative venture between Aérospatiale of France and Aeritalia of Italy, and the aircraft was derived

from preliminary designs by both companies. Seating capacity was fixed at 42 passengers, but from the start of development there was some pressure to increase the seating capacity, and the stretched **ATR 72** was launched four years after the go-ahead for the ATR 42 had been given.

The division of the programme between the

two partner companies allocated the wing to Aérospatiale and the fuselage and tail unit to Aeritalia, which became part of the Alenia group in December 1990. The flightdeck and cabin, the powerplant and the electrical and flight-control systems are also French responsibilities, while the hydraulic, air-conditioning

and pressurisation systems are Italian responsibilities. Assembly and flight-testing of the civil version of the ATR 42 are undertaken at Toulouse in south-west France, while any major production of the **ATR 42F** paramilitary freighter, or the **ATM 42** proposed military freighter, or any civil freighter development with a ventral ramp/door

arrangement would be undertaken at Naples in southern Italy.

The first of two ATR 42 prototypes made its maiden flight on 16 August 1984 and the first production-standard ATR 42 flew on 30 April 1985. Following French and Italian certification on 25 October 1985, revenue-earning services began in December 1985.

Avions de Transport Régional ATR 42 and ATR 72 (cont.)

The **ATR 42-100** and **ATR 42-200** designations were initially used for planned versions with maximum take-off weights of 32,848 lb (14900 kg) and 34,722 lb (15750 kg) respectively, the latter with a redesigned cabin permitting an increase in seating capacity to 50. By the time deliveries were being made however, the ATR 42-200 had become the basis of the initial production model, which was the **ATR 42-300** with still higher weights and delivered in two subvariants as the **ATR 42-310** with 2,000-shp (1491-kW) Pratt & Whitney Canada PW120 engines and the **ATR 42-320** with 2,100-shp (1567-kW) PW121 engines.

By the middle of 1998 ATR had secured orders for some 340 examples of the ATR 42 and delivered 335 of these.

The stretched ATR 72 was launched in January 1986, and had been schemed as a higher-capacity development of the ATR 42 with an uprated powerplant, larger fuel capacity and increased overall dimensions for an increase in passenger capacity to between 64 and 74 passengers according to the seating pitch.

The first of three prototypes made the type's maiden flight on 27 October 1988 and the first deliveries were made in October 1989. By the middle of 1998 ATR had secured orders for some 220 examples of the ATR 72 and delivered 210.

Planned variants include the **ATR 52C** freighter model with a ventral ramp/door arrangement for the civil as well as military markets, and the **ATR 82** stretched version of the ATR 72 with accommodation for up to 80 passengers. A development on the most recent examples of the ATR 72 and indeed ATR 42 families is a carbonfibre composite tail to reduce weight.

The longer fuselage of the ATR 72 is immediately apparent. While airliner versions can carry a maximum of 74 passengers, the freighters can accommodate up to 13 small cargo containers.

ATR 42 Variants

ATR 42-400: first flown on 12 July 1995 with PW121A engines driving six- rather than four-bladed propellers
ATR 42-500: first flown on 16 September 1994 with 2,400-shp (1789-kW) Pratt & Whitney Canada PW127E engines and a new-look cabin
ATR 42 Cargo: quick-change development with provision for the carriage of up to 8,818 lb (4000 kg) of freight in nine containers
ATR 42L: freighter development proposed with a lateral door
ATR 42 Calibration: navaid-calibration model

ATR 72 Variants

ATR 72-200: initial production model
ATR 72-210: delivered from December 1992 and developed from the ATR 72-200 for better 'hot-and-high' performance derived from the installation of an uprated powerplant of two Pratt & Whitney Canada PW127 turboprop engines each rated at 2,480 shp (1849 kW) and driving improved propellers with composite blades on steel hubs
ATR 72-210A: certificated in January 1997 and later redesignated as the ATR 72-500, this is a development of the ATR 72-210 with six- rather than four-bladed propellers, higher weights and a new-look cabin

A number of ATR 42s are flown in Air France colours by smaller airlines such as Air Littoral and Brit Air. The type continues to prove popular in a highly competitive marketplace.

SPECIFICATION	
Avions de Transport Régional ATR 42-310	46 passengers
Type: two/three-crew regional transport aircraft	**Weights:** empty 22,674 lb (10285 kg); maximum take-off 36,817 lb (16700 kg)
Powerplant: two Pratt & Whitney Canada PW120 turboprop engines each rated at 2,000 shp (1491 kW)	**Dimensions:** wing span 80 ft 7½ in (24.57 m); length 74 ft 4½ in (22.67 m); height 24 ft 10¾ in (7.59 m); wing area 586.65 sq ft (54.50 m²)
Performance: maximum cruising speed 305 mph (490 km/h) at 17,000 ft (5180 m); initial climb rate 2,100 ft (640 m) per minute; service ceiling 25,000 ft (7620 m); range 1,208 miles (1944 km) with	**Payload:** up to 10,835 lb (4915 kg) including between 42 and 50 passengers depending on seat pitch

Avro Biplane and Triplane

After experiments with models, Alliott Verdon Roe built his first full-size aircraft, a tail-first biplane, in 1907. Modelled on the Wright configuration, it was built in stables at Putney, London. In September 1907 the aircraft was taken to Brooklands, Surrey, for use in an attempt to win a £2,500 prize for the first aircraft to fly round the motor racing track before the end of the year. The 9-hp (6.7-kW) JAP engine proved inadequate to coax the **Avro Biplane** (otherwise the **Roe I Biplane**) into the air, however. The pioneer then borrowed a 24-hp (17.9-kW) Antoinette engine and, after some modifications to the twin propellers following blade failures, the aircraft made

several unannounced hops before being damaged beyond repair when it was dropped by racetrack attendants while being lifted over a fence.

Following the demise of the Roe I, Roe turned to the triplane configuration. In partnership with J. A. Prestwick, designer of the JAP engine, Roe began work on a new aircraft to this general layout, but the design soon foundered together with the partnership. With little money but an abundance of enthusiasm, Roe pressed ahead with the design of another triplane, at first to be powered by a 6-hp (4.5-kW) JAP engine but later by a 9-hp (6.7-kW) JAP unit. The result was the **Avro Triplane No.1 (Roe I**

Triplane), an ungainly and fragile machine with triplane wings and horizontal tail surfaces. The triangular-section fuselage was uncovered, and the outer 5 ft (1.52 m) of the wings folded to facilitate storage and transport.

Erected on the Lea Marshes in Essex, the Triplane No.1 was named *The Blues* after the braces made by Roe's brother's company which had provided financial support. It made a number of short hops, the first of them on 5 June 1909. As Roe's piloting skills developed, these hops were gradually extended, and on 23 July Roe achieved a flight of 900 ft (274 m). The machine was now re-engined with a 24-hp (18-kW) Antoinette engine and in this form made several short flights at the Blackpool Meeting that October. After this Roe transferred his operations to Wembley, where the Triplane No.1 crashed lightly on 24 December. Three more of these 20-ft

Once airborne, the fragility of even the most advanced of Roe's triplanes, the Triplane No.4, was obvious. The series served to advance both Roe's design and piloting skills, however.

(6.10-m) triplanes were produced with 9-, 20- and 35-hp (6.7-, 15- and 26-kW) JAP engines.

Roe's next venture was the larger **Triplane No.2 (Roe II)** powered by a 35-hp (27-kW) JAP engine. Despite its greater power, however, the Triplane No.2 achieved a best flight of only 600 ft (183 m).

Roe now created a more ambitious machine, but again of triplane configuration. This was the **Mercury**, a two-seater with

a plywood-covered fuselage, powered by a 35-hp (26-kW) Green engine driving a two-bladed tractor propeller (the earlier machines had featured four-bladed propellers).

By this time Roe's ideas had been refined to accord with what was fast becoming the aerodynamic norm. The result was the **Triplane No.3 (Roe III)**, of which six were built in Manchester. Like the Mercury, the Triplane No.3 was a two-seater. While the triplane

SPECIFICATION	
Avro Triplane No.3 (Roe III)	(249 kg)
Type: two-seat triplane	**Dimensions:** span, upper and centre 31 ft (9.45 m), and lower 20 ft (6.10 m); length 23 ft (7.01 m); height 9 ft (2.74 m); wing area 362.00 sq ft (33.63 m²)
Powerplant: one Green inline engine rated at 35 hp (26 kW)	
Performance: maximum speed 40 mph (64 km/h) at sea level	
Weight: maximum take-off 550 lb	

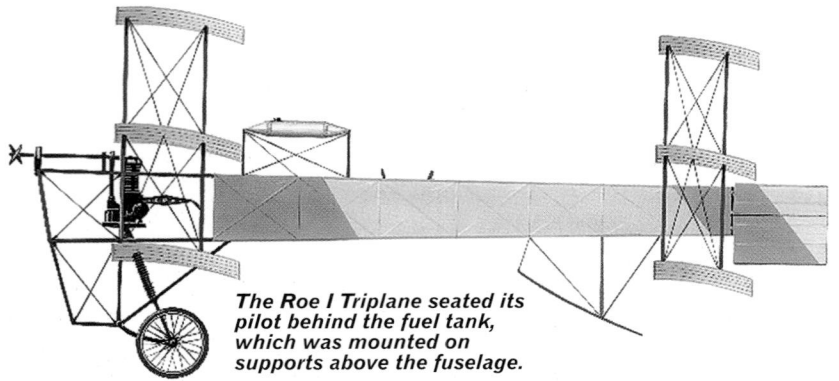

The Roe I Triplane seated its pilot behind the fuel tank, which was mounted on supports above the fuselage.

second and third Triplanes No.3, powered respectively by Green and JAP engines, suffered an unusual fate: they were to have been used by Roe during the Blackpool Meeting of July and August 1910, but were both burned out when set on fire by sparks from the engine of the train on which they were being transported. Roe thus used the fourth example at Blackpool: this had been hurriedly built from spares in Manchester.

The final triplane of the series was the **Triplane No.4 (Roe IV)**, which was also a product of 1910. This

machine was a large single-seater powered by a 35-hp (26-kW) Green engine. The wings spanned 42 ft (12.80 m), and lateral control was effected by differential warping of the upper two wings. The fuselage was 30 ft (9.14 m) long and terminated in a large single tailplane with substantial elevators. Weighing some 650 lb (295 kg) loaded, the Triplane No.4 was used for instructional purposes at Brooklands, Surrey. The triangular-section fuselage was retained, but the forward portion was clad in thin aluminium sheet.

layout for the wings and horizontal tail was retained, the Triplane No.3 was more strongly built than its

predecessors, ailerons replaced wing-warping for lateral control, and longitudinal control was allocated

to conventional elevators rather than to the variable-incidence wing system of the earlier triplanes. The

Avro Type D

The **Avro Type D** biplane marked A. V. Roe's break from the triplane configuration, and although only some six Type D aircraft were built, all of them were different. The first, flown on 1 April 1911 at Brooklands, was powered by a 35-hp (26-kW) Green engine and proved, according to various pilots, to be 'stable, vice-less and easy to fly'. Its first few weeks

C. Howard Pixton flew the first Type D on its maiden flight in 1911. Later he used the same machine for a flight with Mrs Roe.

proved very busy with attempts on endurance records, involvement in a race, demonstrations for the Parliamentary Aerial Defence Committee, and

so on. Bought for trials with the naval airship tender *Hermione*, the Type D was tested with floats and made the first British take-off from water on 18 November 1911.

A modified Type D, built

to compete in the Daily Mail Circuit of Britain Race, had a 60-hp (45-kW) ENV engine but crashed before the race began. The other aircraft, an unconfirmed total of four, were powered by the engines mentioned

above as well as the 45-hp (34-kW) Green, 35-hp (26-kW) Viale and 50-hp (37-kW) Isaacson unit. Three of the aircraft survived until withdrawn from use at Shoreham in May 1914.

SPECIFICATION	
Avro Type D	
Type: two-seat biplane	**Weight:** maximum take-off 500 lb (227 kg)
Powerplant: one Green inline engine rated at 35 hp (26 kW)	**Dimensions:** wing span 31 ft (9.45 m); length 28 ft (8.53 m); height 9 ft 2 in (2.79 m); wing area 310.00 sq ft (28.80 m²)
Performance: maximum speed 46 mph (78 km/h) at sea level	

Avro Type E (Type 500)

Designed to meet a War Office specification of 1911, the **Avro Type E** prototype was designed and built within the nine months demanded by the specification. Basically an improved version of its predecessor, the **Avro Duigan Biplane** (a single example of which was built), the Type E was a biplane with an unstaggered two-bay wing cellule, fixed landing gear, a structure of wire-braced wood under a covering of fabric, and the powerplant of one 60-hp (45-kW) ENV engine.

The type made its first flight on 3 March 1912. Although this was successful, the machine was destroyed in a fatal crash on 29 June 1913 while being flown by a student pilot at the Avro School.

A second Type E with a Gnome rotary engine had flown on 3 May 1912, and its improved performance secured a War Office order for three aircraft, these subsequently being described by Avro as its **Type 500**. The Type 500s were used as dual-control trainers and further orders

for four two-seat and five single-seat machines were soon received.

The Admiralty had by now taken an interest in the Type 500, and in 1913 its Air Department ordered six examples, the last of which was delivered in the following year. One Type 500 was bought by public subscription and presented to the Portuguese govern-

ment in October 1912, another was used by Avro as a company demonstrator, and a third was used extensively by its owner, J. Laurence Hall, before being commandeered by the War Office in 1914.

Service use of the Type 500 inevitably led to alterations among them the modification of the underwing skids, ailerons to

In service, the loop-like skids beneath the outer wings of the Type 500 were sometimes replaced with braced bamboo rods.

replace wing warping, and the adoption of a new rudder shape. One machine was re-engined with a 100-hp (75-kW) Gnome rotary engine.

SPECIFICATION	
Avro Type 500	minutes
Type: two-seat basic flying trainer	**Weights:** empty 900 lb (408 kg); maximum take-off 1,360 lb (617 kg)
Powerplant: one Gnome rotary engine rated at 50 hp (37 kW)	**Dimensions:** wingspan 36 ft (10. 97 m); length 29 ft (8.84 m); height 9 ft 9 in (2.97 m); wing area 330.00 sq ft (30.66 m2)
Performance: maximum speed 61 mph (98 km/h) at sea level; initial climb rate 440 ft (134 m) per minute; endurance 2 hours 30	

Avro Type F

Possessing the distinction of being the world's first aircraft with a completely

enclosed cabin, glazed by a series of celluloid windows, the **Avro Type F**

made its maiden flight on 1 May 1912 as a wire-braced mid-wing monoplane of wooden construction under a covering of fabric. The

streamline-section fuselage featured internal piano wire bracing and was only 2 ft (0.61 m) in width at its widest point, making it a fairly tight fit for the single

occupant. The fuel tankage was located in the fuselage, and the pilot entered the aircraft through an aluminium trapdoor in the roof of the cabin.

Avro Type F (cont.)

An uncowled 35-hp (26-kW) Viale radial engine from a Type D was used in the Type F, and the landing gear was of the fixed tail-skid type.

Although some test flying was undertaken from Brooklands, the Type F did not progress beyond the prototype stage. Following a minor landing accident on 25 May 1912 in which the aircraft turned over on landing, and a second, more serious landing mishap on 13 September 1912, the Type F did not fly again.

Offering cramped and uncomfortable accommodation for its single occupant, the Type F could be dismantled for storage. Large circular portholes were provided in the fuselage sides, through which the pilot was to thrust his head when flying in poor visibility.

SPECIFICATION	
Avro Type F	**Weights:** empty 550 lb (249 kg);
Type: single-seat cabin monoplane	maximum take-off 800 lb (363 kg)
Powerplant: one Viale radial	**Dimensions:** wingspan 29 ft
engine rated at 35 hp (26 kW)	(8.84 m); length 23 ft (7.01 m);
Performance: maximum speed	height about 7 ft 6 in (2.29 m);
65 mph (105 km/h) at sea level	wing area 158.00 sq ft (14.68 m²)

Avro Type G

Following soon after the Type F, the **Avro Type G** was the first biplane to sport a cabin. The two-seat Type G was designed for the British Military Aeroplane Trials held in August 1912.

Using the same wing cellule, tail unit and landing gear as the Type 500, two Type G aircraft were begun, one with a 60-hp (45-kW) Green engine and the other with a similarly rated ABC eight-cylinder unit, but the latter engine was not available in time and its aircraft was not completed.

Damaged in a down-wind landing during the trials, the Type G was repaired and resumed its tests, eventually winning the assembly tests in only 14½ minutes and coming first in fuel consumption tests, but did not win a major award because of its poor rate of climb.

On 24 October 1912, flown by F. P. Raynham, the Type G established a British duration record of 7 hours 31 minutes 30 seconds at Brooklands,

beaten just one hour later by Harry Hawker in the Sopwith Wright biplane with 8 hours 23 minutes. Nothing was heard of the Type G after 1913.

Using much of the experience gained on the Type F, the Type G used a very narrow cabin to accommodate two people.

SPECIFICATION	
Avro Type G	minute; range 345 miles (555 km)
Type: two-seat military biplane	**Weights:** empty 1,191 lb (540 kg);
Powerplant: one Green inline	maximum take-off 1,792 lb (813 kg)
engine rated at 60 hp (45 kW)	**Dimensions:** wingspan 35 ft 3 in
Performance: maximum speed	(10.74 m); length 28 ft 6 in
62 mph (100 km/h) at sea level;	(8.69 m); height 9 ft 9 in (2.97 m);
initial climb rate 105 ft (32 m) per	wing area 335.00 sq ft (31.12 m²)

Avro Type 501 and Type 503 (Type H)

As a development of the layout adopted in the Type 500, Avro ventured into seaplane design with the **Avro Type H** (later **Type 501**), tested on Lake Windermere in January 1913. Flown originally as an amphibian, the aircraft utilised a single wide main float which incorporated wheels in its underside. Mounted beneath the fuselage, this float was augmented by two stabilising floats under the tips of the lower wing. Modified to twin float configuration and powered by a Gnome rotary engine, the Type 501 was delivered to the Admiralty. The floats proved to be too heavy, however, and the machine was subsequently modified to landplane configuration.

Only one Type 501 was built before an enlarged version, the similarly powered **Type 503**, flew from Avro's new facility at Shoreham on 28 May 1913. A demonstration flight for the Inspector of Naval Aircraft helped to secure an order for three Type 503s for the RNAS. The prototype was bought by the German government, and became the first aircraft to fly the almost 40 miles (64 km) across the North Sea from Wilhelmshaven on the north German coast to the island of Heligoland.

At least one Type 503 was flown in landplane configuration (illustrated). During RNAS trials in August 1913, it achieved 65.1 mph (104.8 km/h).

SPECIFICATION	
Avro Type 501	**Weights:** empty 1,740 lb (789 kg);
Type: two-seat floatplane	maximum take-off 2,700 lb
Powerplant: one Gnome rotary	(1225 kg)
engine rated at 100 hp (75 kW)	**Dimensions:** wingspan 47 ft 6 in
Performance: maximum speed	(14.48 m); length 33 ft (10.06 m);
55 mph (89 km/h) at a floatplane	height 12 ft 6 in (3.81 m); wing
and 65 mph (105 km/h) as a	area 478.00 sq ft (44.41 m²)
landplane	

Avro Type 504

The **Type 504**'s origins lay in the Type 500, and the first Type 504 flew at Brooklands in July 1913 as a biplane with a staggered two-bay wing cellule, fixed tailskid landing gear including a central skid on the main unit, and the powerplant of one 80-hp (60-kW) Gnome rotary engine. In the summer of 1913 the War Office placed a contract for 12 such aircraft for the Royal Flying Corps. Several other Type 504 aircraft were ordered by individuals, some with floats and other modifications, but it was in military service use that the Type 504 was to achieve fame.

It was a Type 504 that gained the dubious distinction of being the first British aircraft to be brought down by the enemy, when a machine of No. 5 Squadron was hit by infantry fire over Belgium on 22 August 1914.

The Admiralty had also ordered the Type 504, and its first four aircraft took part in the Royal Naval Air Service's famous raid on the Zeppelin sheds at Friedrichshafen on 21 November 1914 with the loss of one of their number. The Type 504 did not see much active service, however, before it was relegated to training, a task which it performed admirably.

Modifications to the basic design began with the **Type 504A**, which had smaller ailerons and broader struts, and the production of 63 basic Type 504 machines was followed by that of 50 Type 504A aircraft. By the end of the war in 1918 production of the Type 504

Built for the Oxford University Arctic Expedition, the Type 504Q was based on the Type 504N and developed via the abortive Type 504P. It featured a widened fuselage and enclosed cabin.

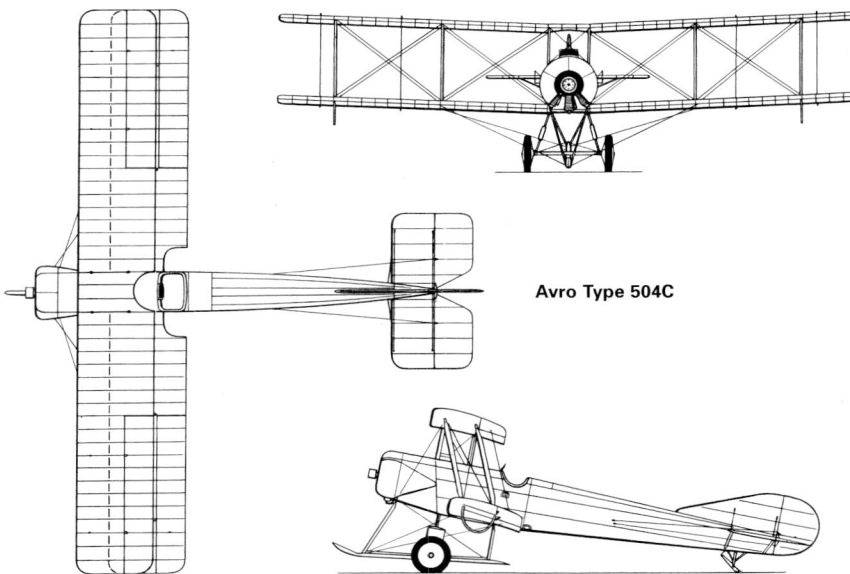

Avro Type 504C

SPECIFICATION	
Avro Type 504N	service ceiling 14,600 ft (4450 m); range 250 miles (402 km)
Type: two-seat basic trainer	
Powerplant: one Armstrong Siddeley Lynx IVC radial engine rated at 180 hp (134 kW)	**Weights:** empty 1,584 lb (718 kg); maximum take-off 2,240 lb (1016 kg)
Performance: maximum speed 100 mph (161 km/h) at sea level; cruising speed 85 mph (137 km/h) at optimum altitude; initial climb rate 770 ft (4900 m) per minute;	**Dimensions:** wingspan 36 ft (10.97 m); length 28 ft 6 in (8.69 m); height 10 ft 11 in (3.33 m); wing area 320.00 sq ft (29.73 m²)

series had reached more than 8,000 aircraft.

Early production examples of the Type 504 had used the 80-hp (60-kW) Gnome Monosoupape rotary engine in place of the prototype's Gnome. Following the Type 504A came the **Type 504B** for the RNAS with a larger fin and modified tailskid; the **Type 504C** single-seat model for the RNAS in the anti-Zeppelin role; and a similar single-seat development, the **Type 504D**, for the RFC. All of these variants were somewhat underpowered with the 80-hp (60-kW) Gnome rotary engine.

A strengthened and modified Type 504C was used for trials with a catapult, and in this form was designated as the **Type 504H**. Earlier, an Avro 504B had been tested with arrester gear.

In an attempt to upgrade performance, the company produced the **Type 504E** for the RNAS, using the 100-hp (75-kW) Gnome Monosoupape engine. A number of other changes were made, including a reduction of the wing stagger, and production amounted to 10 aircraft.

The Type 504 really came into its own as a trainer with the advent in 1916 of the **Type 504J**

with the same engine as the Type 504E. Production Type 504Js were delivered from 1917.

Because of the Type 504's early replacement as a front-line aircraft, orders for its Monosoupape engines had been allowed to run down, and engine manufacture was now not keeping up with airframe production. To alleviate the situation, surplus rotary engines were recalled and fitted into the new airframes, so the Type 504J machines were delivered with 130-hp (97-kW) Clerget and 110-hp (82-kW) or 80-hp (60-kW) Le Rhône engines. The necessary modifications to adapt the airframe for the variety of engines that could be installed were carried out by Avro, resulting in the designation **Type 504K** for subsequent aircraft, regardless of engine type.

After World War I the Type 504 continued in service as the standard RAF trainer until replaced by the **Type 504N**.

With the end of World War I, surplus Type 504s proved particularly suitable for civilian use and more than 300 were registered in the UK between 1919 and 1930. In addition, many Type 504Ks were sold abroad and licensed production was undertaken

in Australia, Belgium and Canada. After Britain gave some 30 504Ks to the Japanese in 1921 Nakajima built 280 land- and float-plane trainers based on the design and known locally as the **Type 504L** and **Type 504S** respectively. Yokosuka also designed a version of the 504K, known as the **K1Y**, of which some 104 were built by various Japanese companies.

Two more comparatively early variants of the Type 504 deserve mention. The **Type 504L** was the first post-war variant, and was a floatplane of which six were built as three-seat aircraft with the powerplant of one 150-hp (112-kW) Bentley B.R.1 rotary engine. Additionally, some Type 504K aircraft were revised with the 130-hp (97-kW) Clerget engine and float alighting gear.

The **Type 504M** was an attempt to provide the market with a two-seat cabin biplane, and was based on the standard Type 504K fuselage built up and fitted with a plywood roof with portholes added. Only one was built.

Such was the usefulness of the Type 504 as a trainer in the period following World War I, that the type was modified to accept one of the new radial engines. The result was the

Type 504N whose most noticeable differences from its predecessors were its redesigned landing gear without the central skid, and tapered ailerons. The first Type 504N aircraft were two ordered by the Air Ministry in 1925; these employed airframes built in 1918 that had never been used. One had the 100-hp (75-kW) Bristol Lucifer radial engine and the other the 180-hp (134-kW) Armstrong Siddeley Lynx radial engine: the latter engine was chosen for production aircraft, of which 598 were completed between 1925 and 1932.

Often known as the **Lynx-Avro**, the Type 504N replaced the Type 504K in the RAF's flying training schools and also served as communications aircraft with Auxiliary Air Force and

South Africa. Licensed manufacture was undertaken in Denmark and Belgium. In Canada, some Type 504K aircraft of the Royal Canadian Air Force were converted to Type 504N standard by Canadian Vickers, which also produced other Type 504N aircraft, including a single-float seaplane.

The single Type 504N supplied in January 1927 to Japan paved the way for the **Yokosuka K2Y** introduced in 1928 as the **K2Y1** with the 130-hp (97-kW) Mitsubishi-manufactured Armstrong Siddeley Mongoose radial engine and then improved in 1929 as the **K2Y2** with the 160-hp (119-kW) Gasuden Jimpu 2 radial engine. Some 360 K2Y aircraft were built by various companies until 1940.

A pair of Avro 504Ns cavorts at low level. This superb trainer allowed the Type 504 to remain in RAF service into the early 1930s and it paved the way for Avro to build the Tutor as its replacement.

university air squadrons.

The first RAF instrument flying course began in September 1931 at Wittering, when six Type 504N aircraft were introduced with blind-flying hoods, turn indicators and a 1° reduction in dihedral to reduce inherent instability.

Early production aircraft had a wooden fuselage and tapered ailerons, but later examples had a welded steel tube fuselage and rectangular ailerons. Almost 80 early Type 504K aircraft were converted to Type 504N standard as an economy measure.

Export customers of the Type 504N included Belgium, Brazil, Chile, Denmark, Greece, Japan, Sweden, Thailand and

In 1932 the RAF selected the Avro Tutor as replacement for the Type 504N, and by the following year the latter had been declared obsolete. A number came on to the civil market and became well known throughout the UK. A surprising extension of the Type 504N's military service came in 1940, when seven civilian aircraft were impressed into RAF service. Two were destroyed in a hangar fire before they could be used, and two others were scrapped. The remaining three served with a Special Duty Flight and were used to tow wooden gliders out to sea so that trainee radar operators could attempt to track them.

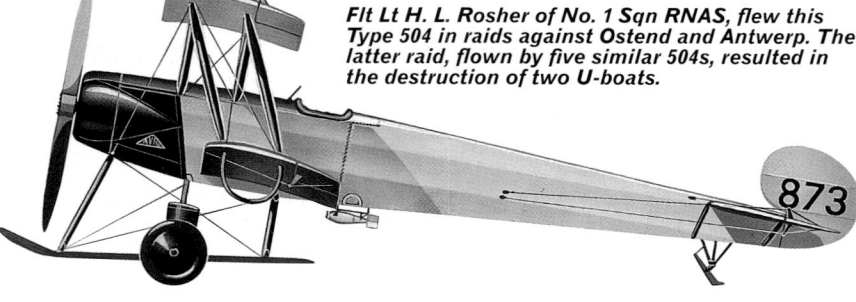

Flt Lt H. L. Rosher of No. 1 Sqn RNAS, flew this Type 504 in raids against Ostend and Antwerp. The latter raid, flown by five similar 504s, resulted in the destruction of two U-boats.

873

Avro Type 523 Pike

Designed by Roy Chadwick, the **Avro Type 523 Pike** was the first of the company's aircraft to be named. The Type 523 was intended to provide the Admiralty with an aircraft suitable for the long-range escort and reconnaissance roles but, in the course of the machine's development, the company incorporated internal bomb stowage so that the type would be suitable for general-purpose duties, including short-range bombing. A large three-bay biplane of wooden construction with fabric covering, the Pike accommodated a crew of three in open cockpits, the pilot just forward of the wing and the two gunners in bow and rear positions. First flown in May 1916, the Pike was subsequently tested by the Admiralty, but failed to win a production order. A second prototype was built with a different powerplant, namely two 150-hp (112-kW) Green

inline engines, and this had the designation **Type 523A Pike**. Both of these aircraft were used by the company for experimental work through the remaining years of World War I.

The Type 523 featured pusher engines, while the engines of the 523A drove tractor propellers. More powerful Types 523B and 523C were planned, but not built.

SPECIFICATION	
Avro Type 523 Pike	(1814 kg); maximum take-off
Type: three-seat general-purpose military aircraft	6,064 lb (2751 kg)
Powerplant: two Sunbeam Vee engines each rated at 160 hp (119 kW)	**Dimensions:** wingspan 60 ft (18.29 m); length 39 ft 1 in (11.91 m); height 11 ft 8 in (3.56 m); wing area 815.00 sq ft (75.71 m²)
Performance: maximum speed 97 mph (156 km/h) at sea level; climb to 10,000 ft (3050 m) in 27 minutes; endurance 7 hours	**Armament:** one 0.303-in (7.7-mm) trainable machine-gun in each of the nose and dorsal positions, plus bombs carried internally
Weights: empty 4,000 lb	

Avro Type 529

While the Admiralty had placed no order for production of the Avro Type 523 Pike, in 1916 it ordered for evaluation in the long-range bombing role two prototype aircraft that were, in effect, slightly larger versions of the Pike. Apart from dimensional changes, the wing cellule was designed to fold from points just outboard of the engines, the tail unit was revised, and the powerplant of the first of the aircraft to be completed, under the designation

Fully-cowled engines mounted on the lower wing were introduced by the Type 529A.

Avro Type 529, comprised two Falcon Vee engines, mounted between the wings and driving counter-rotating tractor propellers.

The second prototype, designated **Type 529A**, was generally similar except for its powerplant, which comprised two 230-hp (172-kW) Galloway-built BHP inline engines mounted on the lower wing, revised fuel system, revised wing cellule and increased maximum take-off weight. Forward-looking features of the design provided the rear gunner with dual controls and the front gunner/bomb-aimer with Gosport tube commu-

nication with the pilot for guidance over the target during a bombing attack.

Trials revealed that the aircraft had good performance and the only major criticism was poor control in the longitudinal plane. No production order was placed and only the two prototypes were built.

SPECIFICATION	
Avro Type 529	**Weights:** empty 4,736 lb
Type: three-seat long-range bomber	(2148 kg); maximum take-off 6,309 lb (2862 kg)
Powerplant: two Rolls-Royce Falcon Vee engines each rated at 190 hp (142 kW)	**Dimensions:** span 63 ft (19.20 m); length 39 ft 8 in (12.09 m); height 13 ft (3.96 m); wing area 922.50 sq ft (85.70 m²)
Performance: maximum speed 95 mph (153 km/h) at 8,000 ft (2440 m); climb to 6,500 ft (1980 m) in 11 minutes 25 seconds; service ceiling 13,500 ft (4115 m); endurance 5 hours	**Armament:** one 0.303-in (7.7-mm) trainable machine-gun in each of the nose and dorsal positions, plus (Type 529A) up to 20 50-lb (23-kg) bombs carried internally

Avro Type 531 Spider

Ailerons were fitted only to the Spider's upper wing. Reports from a number of pilots confirmed the type's exceptional handling.

With an eye to securing an Air Ministry order for a new single-seat fighter, Avro produced the **Type 531 Spider** as a private venture. This prototype made its maiden flight in April 1918 as a sesquiplane biplane of fabric-covered wooden construction with the Warren truss type of interplane strutting. The use of a large number of Type 504K components helped to introduce the possibility of rapid and economic manufacture. Extensive testing revealed that the Type 531 was very manoeuvrable and that the pilot had excellent fields of view in the upper hemi-

sphere as the cockpit was located under a circular cut-out in the centreline of the low-set upper wing so that the pilot's head was above the wing.

Unfortunately for Avro, the Sopwith Snipe had already been selected as the service's next fighter, and the single Spider prototype ended its days in the experimental role. A modified version, the **Type 531A**, appears not to have been completed.

Variant

Type 538: possibly built from parts earmarked for the Type 531A, the Type 538 was a considerably modified development, with an equal-span wing cellule, normal two-bay interplane strutting and a larger upper wing/fuselage gap; intended as a racing machine, the Type 538 was never used as such because of a defective main spar; powered by a 150-hp (112-kW) Bentley B.R.2 rotary engine, it was instead employed by the Avro Transport Co. as a communications machine

SPECIFICATION	
Avro Type 531	250 miles (402 km)
Type: single-seat fighter	**Weights:** empty 963 lb (437 kg);
Powerplant: one Clerget rotary engine rated at 130 hp (97 kW)	maximum take-off 1,517 lb (688 kg)
Performance: maximum speed 120 mph (193 km/h) at sea level; climb to 5,000 ft (1525 m) in 4 minutes; service ceiling 19,000 ft (5970 m); range about	**Dimensions:** wingspan 28 ft 6 in (8.69 m); length 20 ft 6 in (6.25 m); height 7 ft 10 in (2.39 m); wing area 189.00 sq ft (17.56 m²)
	Armament: one 0.303-in (7.7-mm) fixed forward-firing machine-gun

Avro Type 533 Manchester

First flown in December 1918, the **Avro Type 533 Manchester** represented a final development of the thinking first expressed in the Types 523 and 529. Generally similar to the Type 529A, with its engines mounted on the lower wing, the design incorporated some refinements including a deeper fuselage, balanced ailerons, and an improved tail unit. Like a number of British warplanes designed late in the war, the Type 533 was designed around the ABC Dragonfly radial engine, a type that suffered considerable development problems and was therefore replaced in the Type 533 by the 300-hp (224-kW) Siddeley Puma inline engine. This created the **Type 533 Mk II**, which flew long

SPECIFICATION	
Avro Type 533 Manchester Mk I	**Weights:** empty 4,887 lb (2217 kg);
Type: three-seat bomber and reconnaissance warplane	maximum take-off 7,390 lb (3352 kg)
Powerplant: two ABC Dragonfly I radial engines each rated at 320 hp (239 kW)	**Dimensions:** wingspan 60 ft (18.29 m); length 37 ft (11.28 m); height 12 ft 6 in (3.81 m); wing area 817.00 sq ft (75.90 m²)
Performance: maximum speed 115 mph (185 km/h) at optimum altitude; climb to 10,000 ft (3050 m) in 14 minutes 20 seconds; service ceiling 19,000 ft (5790 m)	**Armament:** one 0.303-in (7.7-mm) trainable machine-gun in each of the nose and dorsal positions, plus up to 880 lb (399 kg) of bombs carried internally

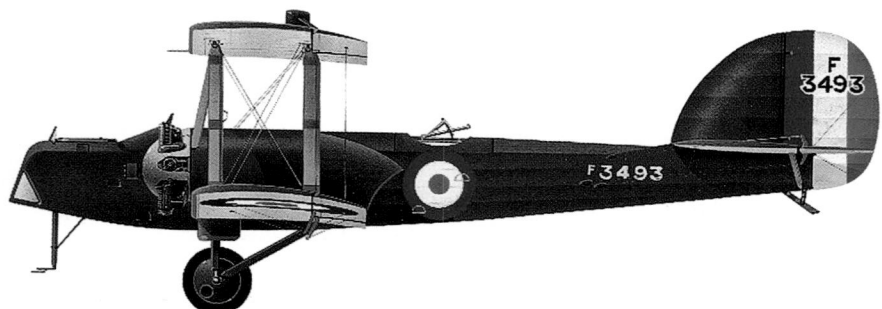

F3493 was the second Type 533 and was known as the Manchester Mk I.

before the Dragonfly-engined **Type 533 Mk I**. The latter was delivered by air after company tests, to the RAE at Martlesham Heath in October 1919.

Both versions performed quite well in official tests, proving that they could be looped and spun, but with no requirement for them following termination of the war, neither was ordered into production. A **Type 533 Mk III** version had been planned with the powerplant of two 400-hp (298-kW) Liberty engines, but although the airframe was completed the engines were never installed.

Avro Type 539

With the UK staging the first post-World War I Schneider Trophy contest in 1919, Avro decided to build and enter a contender, the **Avro Type 539**. In order to reduce weight and drag and thus achieve the highest possible speed, the Type 539 was the smallest practical single-seat machine that could be designed around the

selected engine, a Siddeley Puma inline unit. An unequal-span biplane with ailerons on both sets of wings, the Type 539 was of quite conventional construction, with two single-step floats that were long enough to eliminate the need for a third float beneath the tail. First flown on 29 August 1919, only 12 days before the day of the

This is Avro's Type 539A, pictured on 10 September 1919. A horn-balanced rudder, revised fin shape and civil registration mark had been added.

race, the Type 539 was considered to be generally satisfactory in terms of performance. However, when the machine was taking off to take part in the contest's seaworthiness trials, one of the floats was seriously damaged by floating debris. Avro was given five days in which to effect a repair, and used this time also to modify the tail unit.

When the little floatplane appeared again, it had been redesignated as the **Type 539A**. Testing of

the Type 539A revealed a performance too poor to warrant the floatplane's selection as part of the British team for the main event, with the result that it was delegated as the reserve machine. The

aircraft was subsequently converted to landplane configuration, then extensively modified and fitted with a 450-hp (336-kW) Napier Lion W-type engine. Redesignated as the **Type 539B**, it crashed in 1921.

SPECIFICATION

Avro Type 539	
Type: single-seat racing floatplane	maximum take-off 2,119 lb (961 kg) **Dimensions:** wingspan 25 ft 6 in (7.77 m); length 21 ft 4 in (6.50 m); height 9 ft 9 in (2.97 m); wing area 195.00 sq ft (18.12 m²)
Powerplant: one Siddeley Puma inline engine rated at 240 hp (179 kW)	
Weights: empty 1,670 lb (757 kg);	

Avro Type 547

Remembering his early success with the triplane formula, A. V. Roe decided to reiterate the configuration with a commercial transport, and the resulting

Avro Type 547 first flew early in 1920. The accommodation for the passengers and crew placed the pilot in an open cockpit above and behind

the four-seat enclosed cabin. Much of the machine consisted of surplus Type 504K parts, keeping costs low.

Interest in the UK proved non-existent. Surprisingly, however, QANTAS bought the Type 547 in November 1920, but it proved to be unsuitable for commercial flying and was withdrawn from use and dismantled in 1921.

The **Type 547A** was a modified version powered by a 240-hp (179-kW) Siddeley Puma engine, and built for the Air Ministry Small Commercial Aeroplane Competition of August 1920. Its perfor-

mance did not justify an award, and on 30 October 1920 the sole Type 547A was returned to the manufacturer and broken up after August 1921.

Like the Spider, the Type 547 used 504K components in an effort to reduce costs. A third Type 547 fuselage was built, but not used.

SPECIFICATION

Avro Type 547	
Type: five-seat commercial transport	15 minutes; range 230 miles (370 km) **Weights:** empty 2,077 lb (942 kg); maximum take-off 3,000 lb (1361 kg) **Dimensions:** wingspan 37 ft 3 in (11.35 m); length 29 ft 10 in (9.09 m); height 14 ft 5 in (4.39 m); wing area 498.00 sq ft (46.26 m²) **Payload:** four passengers
Powerplant: one Beardmore inline engine rated at 160 hp (119 kW)	
Performance: maximum speed 96 mph (154 km/h) at optimum altitude; cruising speed 83 mph (134 km/h) at optimum altitude; climb to 5,000 ft (1525 m) in	

Avro Type 549 Aldershot

Designed to Specification 2/20, the **Type 549 Aldershot** was the first new military aircraft from Avro after World War I, and also the first built by the company to have a metal fuselage.

Designed by Roy Chadwick and competing with the de Havilland Derby, the **Aldershot Mk I** won an order for two prototypes, which flew in 1922. Testing revealed the need for the fuselage to

be increased in length by some 6 ft (1.83 m), and in this form the first prototype was shown at the Hendon RAF Display in June of the same year. The machine was subsequently modified to accept, in place of its original Rolls-Royce Condor engine, a massive 16-cylinder Napier Cub X-type engine. Because this was a much heavier unit, new engine mountings, a four-wheel main landing gear arrangement and airframe strengthening were required, and in this form the type became the **Aldershot Mk II**, subsequently being used for engine research.

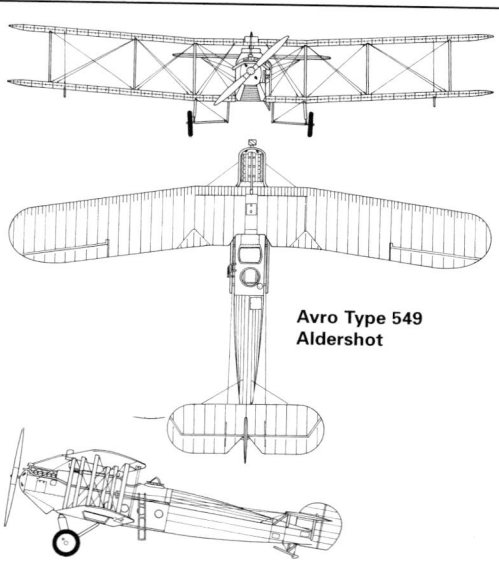

Avro Type 549 Aldershot

SPECIFICATION

Avro Type 549 Aldershot Mk III	
Type: three-seat heavy bomber	**Weights:** empty 6,310 lb (2862 kg); maximum take-off 10,950 lb (4967 kg) **Dimensions:** wingspan 68 ft (20.73 m); length 45 ft (13.72 m); height 15 ft 3 in (4.65 m); wing area 1,064.00 sq ft (98.85 m²) **Armament:** one 0.303-in (7.7-mm) trainable rearward-firing machine-gun, plus up to 2,000 lb (907 kg) of bombs carried internally
Powerplant: one Rolls-Royce Condor III Vee engine rated at 650 hp (485 kW)	
Performance: maximum speed 110 mph (177 km/h) at sea level; cruising speed 92 mph (148 km/h) at optimum altitude; service ceiling 14,500 ft (4420 m); range 625 miles (1006 km)	

Avro Type 549 Aldershot

In 1923 the Air Ministry ordered 15 examples of the Condor-powered type under the designation **Aldershot Mk III**. Being very stable, the Aldershot Mk III bombers were used extensively for night-flying during the two years of their service career. By 1925 the Air Ministry had decided that its bombers must be multi-engined, however, and the Aldershot bombers were replaced by the Hyderabad.

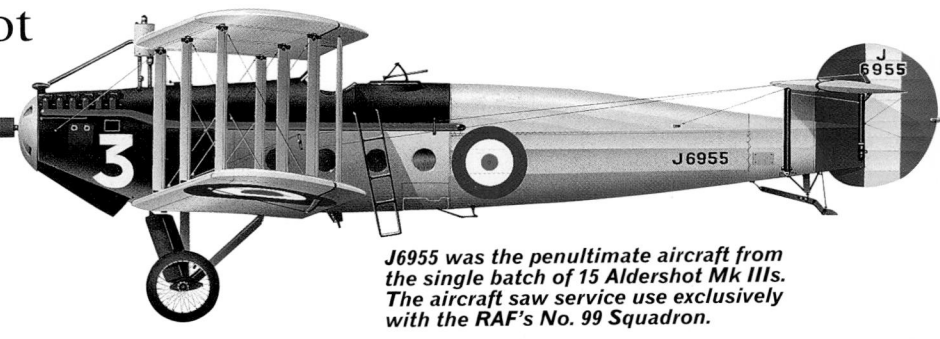

J6955 was the penultimate aircraft from the single batch of 15 Aldershot Mk IIIs. The aircraft saw service use exclusively with the RAF's No. 99 Squadron.

In its ultimate form as the Aldershot Mk IV (illustrated), the Type 549 employed a Typhoon I engine. A further, one-off, variant was produced when steel wings were fitted to an Aldershot Mk III as the Avro Type 549M.

Variants

Aldershot Mk I: two prototypes
Aldershot Mk II: one example powered by the 1,000-hp (746-kW) Napier Cub engine
Aldershot Mk III: production version
Aldershot Mk IV: as Aldershot Mk II, but re-engined with an 850-hp (634-kW) Beardmore Typhoon I engine under the company designation Type 549C

Avro Type 552

A need had been identified for a more powerful training and touring model to improve on the performance of the Type 504L. With a large number of Wolseley Viper engines available from war-surplus SE.5a fighters, it seemed only logical to try this out on a Type 504K airframe. The designation **Avro Type 551** was applied to the trials machine, but a number of modifications was needed to provide greater fuel capacity and more effective controls. The production models thus received the designations **Type 552** for the floatplane and **Type 552A** for the landplane.

An early customer for the Type 552 was the Argentine Ministry of Marine, whose naval aviation division ordered a batch for its newly established school of naval aviation. Work on these aircraft began in October 1921. Canadian users included the RCAF, which bought six single-seat long-range Type 552As in 1923. Licensed manufacture of five single-seaters and nine two-seaters was undertaken by Canadian Vickers at Montreal in 1924, these being used mainly for forest fire patrols.

Three civil Type 552A machines were assembled from spare parts by C. B. Field in Surrey in 1932. These were for Inca Aviation, a banner-towing company which also operated the prototype. The latter had appeared in

No record remains of the number of Type 552s delivered to Argentina, but the aircraft were all handed over during 1921-22. They retained the standard twin-float alighting gear.

several forms, including conversion to Autogiro configuration as the **Type 586** (Cierva C.8V) in 1927 and conversion back to Type 552A standard in 1930. The last known active Type 552A was the first Field conversion, which survived until September 1937.

The **Type 552B** designation was used for one single-float experimental version completed at Montreal in 1924.

SPECIFICATION

Avro Type 552	105 mph (169 km/h) at sea level
Type: two-seat advanced flying trainer	**Weights:** maximum take-off 2,260 lb (1025 kg)
Powerplant: one Wolseley Viper Vee engine rated at 180 hp (134 kW)	**Dimensions:** wingspan 36 ft (10.97 m); length 28 ft (8.53 m); height 10 ft 5 in (3.17 m); wing area 330.0 sq ft (30.66 m²)
Performance: maximum speed	

Avro Type 555 Bison

Avro entered carrier aviation with the **Avro Type 555 Bison**, a design to Specification 3/21 for a carrier-based fleet spotter and reconnaissance aircraft. Making its maiden flight in 1921, the first **Bison Mk I** prototype was soon joined by a second machine built to the revised Specification 33/22 and embodying a number of modifications, of which the most important was the removal of the upper wing from its joint with the fuselage and raising it on struts some 1 ft 3 in (0.38 m) above the fuselage. A third prototype appeared in 1923, and was followed by a production batch of 12 similar aircraft.

The production aircraft, to Specification 16/23, were based on the second prototype and in service had the designation **Bison Mk IA**. This batch was followed by multiple orders for a total of 35 more aircraft. All of these **Type 555A** aircraft served with the designation **Bison**

Mk II, and production was completed in April 1927.

In spite of the fact that it was basically a naval type, the Bison Mk IA was initially delivered in 1922 to the RAF's No. 3 Squadron, in whose service the type replaced the Westland Walrus on coastal reconnaissance work. No. 423 Fleet Spotter Flight was the first naval unit to receive the Bison, and these aircraft subsequently embarked on HMS *Eagle* for a Mediterranean cruise. Several other flights on the same carrier and on HMS *Furious* were similarly equipped, and No. 448 Flight at Hal Far, Malta, served ashore with Bison aircraft. All units subsequently received Fairey IIIFs in 1929 and the Bisons were retired.

An early production Bison was fitted with a central main and two subsidiary underwing floats plus retractable wheels as the **Type 555B**, but tests showed this arrangement to be unsatisfactory.

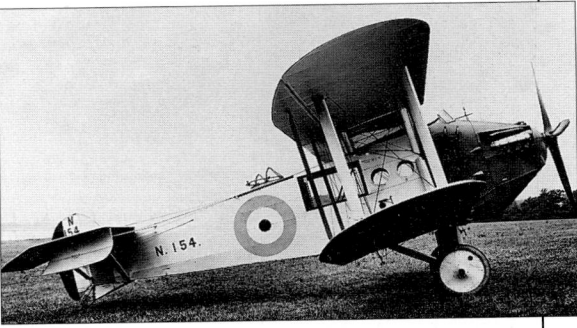

Centre-section struts raised the upper wing of the second Bison prototype by a height of 1 ft 3 in (0.38 m) above the fuselage.

Avro Bison Mk IA

SPECIFICATION

Avro Type 555 Bison Mk IA	(4270 m); range 340 miles (547 km)
Type: three-/four-seat fleet spotter aircraft	**Weights:** empty 4,160 lb (1887 kg); maximum take-off 5,800 lb (2631 kg)
Powerplant: one Napier Lion II W-type engine rated at 450 hp (336 kW)	**Dimensions:** wingspan 46 ft (14.02 m); length 36 ft (10.97 m); height 13 ft 10 in (4.22 m); wing area 630.00 sq ft (58.53 m²)
Performance: maximum speed 110 mph (177 km/h) at optimum altitude; cruising speed 90 mph (145 km/h) at optimum altitude; initial climb rate 600 ft (183 m) per minute; service ceiling 14,000 ft	**Armament:** one 0.303-in (7.7-mm) trainable machine-gun in the rear cockpit

Avro Type 557 Ava

Under the designation **Type 556**, Avro drew up the design of a single-engined aircraft to meet Specification 16/22, which detailed the requirement for a three-seat coastal defence torpedo bomber. This aircraft was not built, however, but in 1924 the company began construction of the prototype of a derived twin-engined machine whose size was dictated by the need to carry a 21-in (533-mm) Whitehead torpedo. Designed by Roy Chadwick, the resulting **Avro Type 557 Ava Mk I** was a three-bay foldable-wing biplane of wooden construction covered with fabric. The deep fuselage terminated in a biplane tail unit incorporating twin fins and rudders, the fixed tail-skid landing gear had twin-wheel main units, and the powerplant comprised two uncowled Rolls-Royce Condor engines strut-mounted between the wings. Side-by-side accommodation for two pilots was provided in an open cockpit, and gunners were located in the nose, dorsal, and ventral positions, the last being lowered for action. The torpedo was carried between the undercarriage legs.

An **Ava Mk II** second prototype was built, being of all-metal construction, with square rather than rounded wingtips, and of slightly reduced wingspan. A change in Admiralty policy, however, which resulted in the standardisation of an 18-in (457-mm) torpedo in place of the 21-in (533-mm) weapon, meant that aircraft of this size were not needed, and no further examples of the Ava were built.

Although it was completed in 1924, the Ava did not appear in public until the 1926 RAF display at Hendon.

SPECIFICATION

Avro Type 557 Ava Mk I
Type: five-seat coastal patrol warplane, torpedo bomber and night bomber
Powerplant: two Rolls-Royce Condor Vee engines each rated at 650 hp (485 kW)
Weights: empty 12,760 lb (5788 kg); maximum take-off 19,920 lb (9036 kg)
Dimensions: wingspan 96 ft 10 in (29.51 m); length 61 ft 9 in (18.82 m); height 19 ft 7¾ in (5.99 m); wing area 2,163.00 sq ft (200.94 m²)
Armament: one 0.303-in (7.7-mm) trainable machine-gun in each of the nose, dorsal and ventral positions, plus one 21-in (533-mm) torpedo carried externally or up to 2,000 lb (907 kg) of bombs carried internally

Avro Type 561 Andover

In June 1921 RAF de Havilland DH.10s opened an air-mail route across the Middle Eastern deserts, but the RAF was already seeking a replacement for the type and placed an order for the **Avro Type 561**, later named **Andover**. This was a large aircraft to be powered by a single engine, with an empty weight about 25 per cent greater than that of the DH.10. When Imperial Airways took over the route, the RAF requirement disappeared, and the military order was cut to just three aircraft, which served at RAF Halton in the air ambulance role.

Using the wings, landing gear and tail unit of the Type 549 Aldershot, the Andover had a new fuselage to accommodate 12 passengers or six stretcher cases. The pilot was in an open cockpit while the navigator, who was seated beside the pilot, had access to the cabin.

The Air Ministry ordered a fourth Andover to the **Type 563** standard in 1925, and this was configured as a 12-passenger airliner. Some cross-Channel proving flights were undertaken when the Type 563 was loaned to Imperial Airways and operated under civil markings, but it subsequently reverted to its service serial number, and joined the other three Andover aircraft.

The civil Type 563 featured 12 passenger seats arranged either side of a central aisle, along with luggage stowage facilities and a toilet.

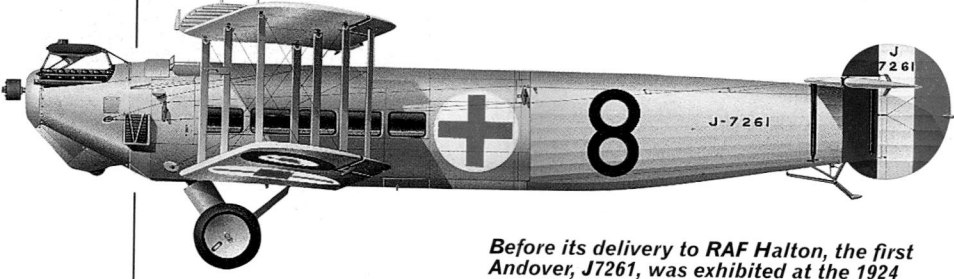

Before its delivery to RAF Halton, the first Andover, J7261, was exhibited at the 1924 Hendon air display. Up to six stretchers could be accommodated.

SPECIFICATION

Avro Type 561 Andover
Type: two-crew ambulance and transport
Powerplant: one Rolls-Royce Condor III Vee engine rated at 650 hp (485 kW)
Performance: maximum speed 110 mph (177 km/h) at optimum altitude; service ceiling 13,500 ft (4115 m); range 460 miles (740 km)
Weights: empty 6,980 lb (3166 kg); maximum take-off 11,500 lb (5216 kg)
Dimensions: wingspan 68 ft (20.72 m) length 51 ft 7 in (15.72 m); height 16 ft 1½ in (4.91 m); wing area 1,062.00 sq ft (98.66 m²)
Payload: 12 passengers or six litters

Avro Type 566 and Type 567 Avenger

On 26 June 1926 the company flew the private-venture prototype of the **Avro Type 566 Avenger** (later **Avenger Mk I**) single-seat fighter. Designed by Roy Chadwick, the Type 566 was an extremely clean unequal-span biplane. The wings were of wooden construction with fabric covering, but the fuselage was an oval-section monocoque structure of wood with mahogany planking, finally covered by fabric. Power was provided by a direct-drive Napier Lion VIII 12-cylinder engine.

Despite very good performance, the Avenger failed to attract interest sufficient for a production commitment, and was then modified as the **Type 567 Avenger Mk II** sporting machine with a revised equal-span wing cellule with ailerons on both the upper and lower wings for improved roll rate; other changes included I-type rather than parallel interplane struts, revised landing gear, and the installation of a more powerful 553-hp (412-kW) Napier Lion IX engine.

In September 1928, the Avenger Mk II was demonstrated to the Romanian government as a fighter, but no orders resulted.

Having gained some racing success, the aircraft was finally dismantled in 1931 for use as an instructional airframe.

SPECIFICATION

Avro Type 566 Avenger Mk I
Type: single-seat fighter
Powerplant: one Napier Lion VIII W-type engine rated at 525 hp (391 kW)
Performance: maximum speed 180 mph (290 km/h) at optimum altitude; cruising speed 130 mph (209 km/h) at optimum altitude; initial climb rate 2,100 ft (640 m) per minute; service ceiling 22,000 ft (6705 m)
Weights: empty 2,368 lb (1074 m); maximum take-off 3,220 lb (1461 kg)
Dimensions: wingspan 32 ft (9.75 m); length 25 ft 6 in (7.77 m); height 10 ft 3 in (3.12 m)
Armament: two 0.303-in (7.7-mm) fixed forward-firing machine-gun

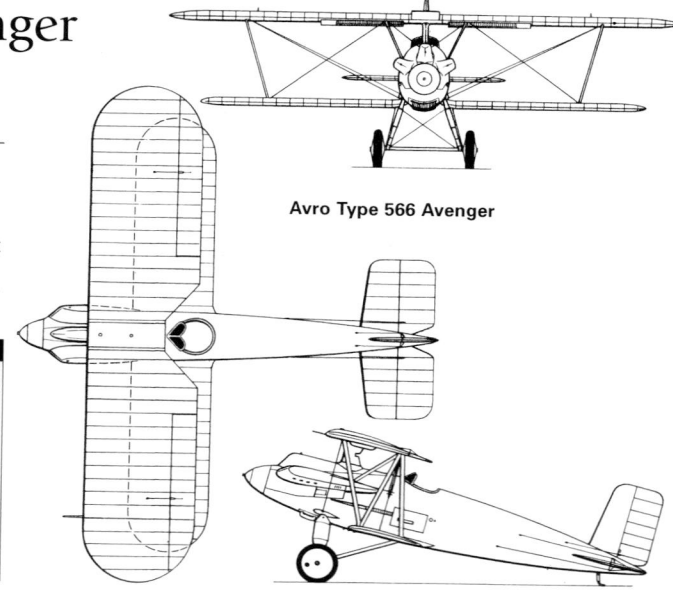

Avro Type 566 Avenger

Avro Type 571 and Type 572 Buffalo

The **Avro Type 571 Buffalo** was designed as a private venture to meet Specification 21/23, which detailed requirements for a two-seat ship-based torpedo-carrier for service with the Fleet Air Arm. It was a single-bay biplane with a folding wing cellule, and this cellule incorporated much of the structure developed for the company's earlier Bison Mk II. The tail unit was also

from the same source, but the fixed tailskid landing gear was quite different. The fuselage was completely new and, in view of the aircraft's intended usage which was primarily maritime, the rear fuselage contained flotation bags; provision was also made for the fuel to be jettisoned so that the main fuselage fuel tank would provide buoyancy in the event of a ditching.

Accommodation was provided for a crew of two – the pilot with an excellent high vantage point for carrier operations, and the second crew member, who also operated twin Lewis guns, with access to the radio compartment as well as to a prone bombing/camera position in the lower fuselage.

During evaluation of the Type 571 in 1927, Avro appreciated that in its existing form the Buffalo had little chance of winning a production contract in competition against the Blackburn Ripon and Handley Page H.P.31 Harrow. It was therefore taken back to the Hamble factory for the installation of all-metal rectangular wings which incorporated four Frise-type ailerons, and controllable Handley Page slots on the wing leading edges; at the same time, a more powerful Napier Lion

XIA engine was installed. Designated as the **Type 572 Buffalo Mk II** after these modifications had been carried out (the original form then being known retrospectively as the **Buffalo Mk I**), the machine

still failed to win a production contract. However, the prototype was acquired by the Air Ministry, and converted subsequently for operation as a floatplane. A bomber version, designated **Type 597**, was not built.

Illustrated here in Buffalo Mk I form, G-EBNW was later modified to Buffalo Mk II standard. In July 1928, the aircraft was passed, in Buffalo Mk II form, to the Air Ministry with the military serial N239.

SPECIFICATION	
Avro Type 572 Buffalo Mk II **Type:** two-seat carrierborne torpedo-bomber **Powerplant:** one Napier Lion XIA W-type engine rated at 530 hp (395 kW) **Performance:** maximum speed 135 mph (217 km/h) at optimum altitude; cruising speed 105 mph (169 km/h) at optimum altitude; initial climb rate 770 ft (235 m) per minute; service ceiling 11,000 ft (3355 m); range 400 miles (644 km)	**Weights:** empty 4,233 lb (1920 kg); maximum take-off 7,430 lb (3370 kg) **Dimensions:** wingspan 46 ft (14.02 m); length 37 ft 3 in (11.35 m); height 14 ft (4.27 m); wing area 684.00 sq ft (63.54 m²) **Armament:** one 0.303-in (7.7-mm) fixed forward-firing machine-gun and two 0.303-in (7.7-mm) trainable rearward-firing machine-guns, plus one 18-in (457-mm) torpedo carried externally

Avro Type 584 Avocet

In mid-1926 Avro began the design of a single-seat carrierborne fighter to the Air Ministry's Specification 17/25. Designed by Roy Chadwick, the resulting **Type 584 Avocet** was the company's first all-metal

biplane, and incorporated a highly-streamlined circular-section fuselage of small cross section. The tailplane could be folded upward for shipboard stowage, but the wings were not intended to fold, being designed

instead to be easily dismantled. To this end, the unequal-span biplane wing cellule had no wire bracing, but only heavy diagonal interplane struts.

Two prototypes were built, both having fixed tailskid landing gear as standard for operation from carriers. Provision was made, however, for the installation of floats which, together with standard catapult attachment, pilot's headrest and crane pick-up point, gave the type an alternative capability for operation from catapult-equipped cruisers. Service evaluation of the prototypes for the Fleet Air Arm did not lead to any production contract, but one of

the aircraft was later equipped with float landing gear and placed on the strength of the Royal Air Force's High Speed Flight, for use by pilots training for the Schneider Trophy races.

The Avocet flew with two tail configurations, the triangular fin and smaller rudder (illustrated), and with a smaller fin and oversized rudder.

SPECIFICATION	
Avro Type 584 Avocet **Type:** single-seat carrierborne fighter **Powerplant:** one Armstrong Siddeley Lynx IV radial engine rated at 180 hp (134 kW) **Performance:** maximum speed 133 mph (214 km/h) at optimum altitude **Weights:** empty 1,621 lb (735 kg);	maximum take-off 2,495 lb (1132 kg) **Dimensions:** wingspan 29 ft (8.84 m); length 24 ft 6 in (7.47 m); wing area 308.00 sq ft (28.61 m²) **Armament:** two 0.303-in (7.7-mm) fixed forward-firing machine-guns, plus four 20-lb (9-kg) bombs carried externally

Avro Type 594 and Type 616 Avian

The **Avro Type 594 Avian** was a contemporary of the de Havilland DH.60 Moth, although the Moth prototype first flew in February 1925, more than a year before the Avian. The latter was built for the *Daily Mail* two-seat light aircraft trials at Lympne in September 1926. That vital lead was to have far-reaching effects, putting de Havilland at the forefront of European light aircraft design.

The Avian prototype was the **Type 581**, and this had a 75-hp (56-kW) Armstrong Siddeley Genet radial engine. Modified as the **Type 581A**, the prototype flew with an 80-hp (60-kW) ADC Cirrus inline engine and achieved some fame in racing and long-distance events, culminating in a 15-day flight from Croydon

ZK-ACM was a Type 616 Sports Avian built by A. V. Roe Ltd in the UK and exported to New Zealand. The aircraft survived in an airworthy condition into the 1960s.

to Darwin in northern Australia after the machine had been adapted to **Type 581E** standard.

Two pre-production **Type 594 Avian Mk I**s were followed by nine production **Avian Mk II**s, six of them with the same Cirrus engine but some differences in the landing gear, and the other three for Australia with the 75-hp (56-kW) Genet II engine.

The first example of the **Avian Mk III**, with the 85-hp (63-kW) ADC Cirrus II engine, flew in mid-1927, and otherwise differed

from the Mk II only in having slimmer tubular steel interplane and centre-section struts. A total of 33 Avian Mk IIIs was built, including one for the RAF, before the introduction of the **Avian Mk IIIA**. This variant had its origins in the

revision of three earlier Avians with the 90-hp (67-kW) Cirrus III engine to compete in the 1928 King's Cup Race, and the Avian Mk IIIA production model, of which 58 were built, was also strengthened internally. At least two were

operated on floats.

The final development of the wooden version was the **Avian Mk IV** with modifications to the ailerons and landing gear. The standard engine was again the Cirrus III. Most of the Mk IV aircraft were sold

Variants

There were large numbers of sub-variants within each mark, so the list below can only describe the main variants:

Type 581 Avian: single prototype, subsequently modified as the Type 581A and Type 581E

Type 594 Avian Mk I: two pre-production aircraft with a lower engine mounting and split-axle landing gear

Type 594 Avian Mk II: nine initial production aircraft

Type 594 Avian Mk III: 33 aircraft to a standard essentially similar to that of the Avian Mk II except for its tubular steel interplane and cabane struts

Type 594 Avian Mk IIIA: 58 of a locally-strengthened production version

Type 594 Avian Mk IV: 90 of an improved development of the Avian Mk IIIA with revised ailerons and landing gear

Type 605 Avian: two floatplane conversions from Avian Mk IIIA standard

Type 616 Avian Mk IVM: about 190 of a developed version with a steel tube fuselage structure

Type 616 Sports Avian: version largely for racing, with cut-down rear decking, through-axle landing gear and low-drag windscreens

Type 616 Avian Mk IVA: single modified machine for Sir Charles Kingsford-Smith with a 120-hp (90-kW) de Havilland Gipsy inline and extra fuel, giving a range of 1,700 miles (2736 km)

Type 616 Avian Mk V: single special version for Sir Charles Kingsford-Smith as a long-range single-seater

Type 625 Avian Monoplane: two examples of a braced low-wing monoplane development with faired main landing gear legs

on the export market.

At the outbreak of World War II, most of the surviving Avians were impressed as instructional airframes, but four survived to be restored to the British civil register and two escaped military service.

Alongside the Avians of wooden construction, the **Type 616 Avian Mk IVM** with a steel tube fuselage was produced in some numbers, following 1929 tests with the prototype powered by a 90-hp (67-kW) Cirrus III. The heavier weight of the structure dictated the use of a more potent engine, and early production Mk IVM machines had either the 105-hp (78-kW) Cirrus Hermes I or 100-hp (75-kW) Genet Major engine. The type was also built in Canada, where 18 were completed for the RCAF with the 135-hp (101-kW)

Genet Major engine. At least five were built in the USA under licence by the Avian's US importer.

A small batch of **Type 616 Sports Avian** aircraft was built, some with 105-hp (78-kW) Hermes engines, and others with de Havilland Gipsy engines of 100-120 hp (75 kW-90 kW). Among the more unusual of this type were a pair of **Type 625 Avian Monoplane** machines, one with a Genet Major and the other with a Hermes. Both aircraft had been

scrapped by the end of World War II.

One **Avian Mk IVA**, named *Southern Cross Minor*, was built as a long-range single-seater for Sir Charles Kingsford-Smith, who later passed on a similar **Avian Mk V** to W. N. Lancaster for an attempt on the England-Cape Town record, which began in April 1933. No further news of Lancaster was heard until the remains of his aircraft were found in the Sahara in March 1962.

Avro Type 604 Antelope

The company's contender for the production order likely to result from Air Ministry Specification 12/26, the **Avro Type 604 Antelope** found itself in contention with such aircraft as the Fairey Fox Mk IIM and Hawker Hart. Given the excellence of the two rival types, it is not surprising that the somewhat pedestrian Avro design failed to progress past the prototype stage.

The prototype Antelope was flying by mid-summer 1928 and, in accordance with the specification, was an all-metal biplane. The fuselage provided accommodation for the crew of two including a gunner/bomb-aimer in the rear cockpit with access to a prone position for aiming and release of the bombs.

Following evaluation when it was found that the machine was able to exceed most performance requirements, the prototype went for service trials, after it was placed third behind the Fox IIM. After being returned to the factory for installation of dual controls, the machine was delivered to the Royal Aircraft Establishment, where it was used for experimental purposes.

After service evaluation in the UK with the RAF's No. 100 Sqn at Bicester, Buckinghamshire, the Antelope passed to the RAE at Farnborough where it was used exclusively as a propeller testbed. In the latter role, it was re-engined twice.

Avro Types 618 Ten, 619 Five, 624 Six and 642 Eighteen

The **Avro Type 618 Ten** resulted from a 1928 agreement for licensed British production of the highly successful Fokker F.VIIB-3m tri-motor airliner. Avro's agreement with Fokker gave the British company freedom to sell its aircraft throughout the countries of the British Commonwealth with the exception of Canada, and the name Ten was adopted to indicate the machine's standard accommodation for two crew and eight passengers.

British airworthiness requirements led to minor airframe changes, and the first Ten appeared at the 1929 Olympia Aero Show, subsequently being the first of five sold to Australian National Airways. Two other Tens were bought by the Brisbane-based Queensland Air Navigation Co. Ltd, while the last surviving Ten in Australia evacuated many people from New Guinea in 1941. Having performed so heroically, this aircraft escaped the Japanese only to be abandoned and fall into disrepair.

Five Type 618 Tens were delivered to British customers, two each to Imperial Airways and

G-AAYR was the prototype for Avro's Type 624 Six. A more radical variation on the F.VIIB-3m theme than the Ten, the Six originally flew with its wing engines mounted beneath the wing leading edge. They were later strut-mounted beneath the wing.

Variants

Type 619 Five: scaled-down version of Type 618 Ten, for a pilot and four passengers, with the powerplant of three 105-hp (78-kW) Armstrong Siddeley Genet Major I radial engines

Type 624 Six: this six-seater was slightly larger than the Type 619, but had the same powerplant and introduced side-by-side seating for two pilots; some changes were made as a result of flight-testing, and the first two Type 624 aircraft were later modified to Type 619 standard with the exception of their six-seat accommodation

Type 642 Eighteen: hardly recognisable as being a derivative of the original Fokker F.VIIB-3m, the Type 642 (only called Eighteen at the beginning of its career) combined the wing of the Type 618 with a new fuselage

Airwork and one to Midland & Scottish Air Ferries.

The last production Ten was delivered to the RAE's

Wireless and Equipment Flight in July 1936, and was later fitted with a Monospar wing.

Avro Type 618 Ten, 619 Five, 624 Six and 642 Eighteen (cont.)

SPECIFICATION

Avro Type 618 Ten

Type: two-crew commercial transport
Powerplant: three Armstrong Siddeley Lynx IVC radial engines each rated at 240 hp (179 kW)
Performance: maximum speed 115 mph (185 km/h) at optimum altitude; cruising speed 100 mph (161 km/h) at optimum altitude; initial climb rate 675 ft (206 m) per minute; service ceiling 16,000 ft (4875 m); range 400 miles (655 km)
Weights: empty 6,020 lb (2731 kg); maximum take-off 10,600 lb (4808 kg)
Dimensions: wingspan 71 ft 3 in (21.72 m); length 47 ft 6 in (14.48 m); height 12 ft 9 in (3.89 m); wing area 772.00 sq ft (71.72 m²)
Payload: eight passengers

Avro's Type 642 flew in at least three distinct forms. As the Type 642-2m it flew with both semi-circular and conventional (illustrated) nose profiles. It also flew as the four-engined Type 642-4m.

Avro Types 621 Tutor, 646 Sea Tutor and 626 Prefect

In the early 1930s it became necessary to replace the Avro Type 504N as the RAF's basic flying trainer, and the logical choice as its successor was the **Avro Type 621**, later named as the **Tutor**. Designed by Roy Chadwick in 1929, the Type 621 was of welded steel tube construction covered with fabric, and in configuration was an equal-span biplane of the single-bay type with fixed tailskid landing gear and two-seat accommodation in a tandem arrangement of open cockpits. The civil-registered prototype, powered by a 155-hp (116-kW) Armstrong Siddeley Mongoose IIIA radial engine, went to the Aircraft and Armament Experimental Establishment for comparative trials in December 1929.

Following evaluation against other aircraft, the Type 621 was selected by the RAF in 1930 and a trial batch of 21 aircraft was ordered to Specification 3/30, retaining the five-cylinder Mongoose engine in an uncowled installation. Virtually all the following production aircraft had the 240-hp (179-kW) Armstrong Siddeley Lynx IVC seven-cylinder radial engine under a narrow-chord Townend ring cowling. A number of Type 621 aircraft was built for the civil market, and yet more for foreign air forces, including three for the Irish air corps, RCAF and Chinese air force.

The RAF received 394 of the 795 aircraft built by the end of Tutor production in May 1936. The majority of these aircraft were built to Specification 18/31, but a number of **Type 646 Sea Tutor** twin-float seaplanes was completed against Specification 26/34 and delivered between 1934 and 1936. Sea Tutors had been withdrawn from service by April 1938. Deliveries of the standard Tutor began in 1933, and the Tutor soon became standard Flying Training School equipment. Many were also delivered to university air squadrons and station flights of the Auxiliary Air Force. In the UK, re-equipment with monoplane warplanes during the late 1930s persuaded the RAF to switch to monoplane trainers and the Tutor was phased out, being replaced in the elementary flying trainer role by the Miles Magister.

Following the signing of a licensed production agreement, 57 examples of the Tutor were manufactured in South Africa.

Following the success of its Type 621 Tutor, in 1930 Avro produced a redesign of the basic airframe specifically for foreign air forces. The new machine was the **Avro Type 626**, later named **Prefect**, and

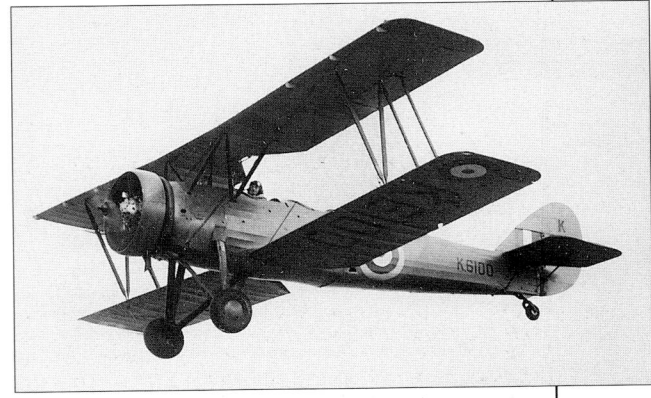

This Type 621 Tutor was part of the penultimate Tutor batch delivered to the RAF. One Tutor was rebuilt in 1948 and used by Avro's manager at Bracebridge Heath as a personal transport.

Type 621 variants

Type 621 Tutor Mk II: single example with modified wing strut arrangement
PWS 18: designation of 40 Tutor trainers built under licence by PWS in Poland

featured special conversion kits enabling the aircraft to be used for a wide variety of training roles. These included, in addition to the basic *ab initio* role, blind-flying, bombing, gunnery, navigation, night flying, photographic, seaplane and wireless instruction. The Type 626 was basically a two-seater, but had provision for a gunner's position behind the rear cockpit.

The Type 626 entered production with an impressive order book and by 1939, when construction ceased, 178 had been built to military orders. The RAF and Royal New Zealand Air Force aircraft were known by the name Prefect, the RAF machines being delivered between January and July 1935, and the RNZAF aircraft in July of that year. The former were specialised navigation trainers to replace the Mongoose-engined Type 621 Tutor in service with the School of Air Navigation at Andover. The Type 626 aircraft were delivered either with the 240-hp (179-kW) Armstrong Siddeley Lynx IVC or 260-hp (194-kW) Armstrong Siddeley Cheetah V radial engine. At least three Type 626 machines survived World War II to fly under civil markings.

The designation **Type 637** was applied to eight aircraft modified for the light armed patrol task in China and fitted with extra fuel tankage.

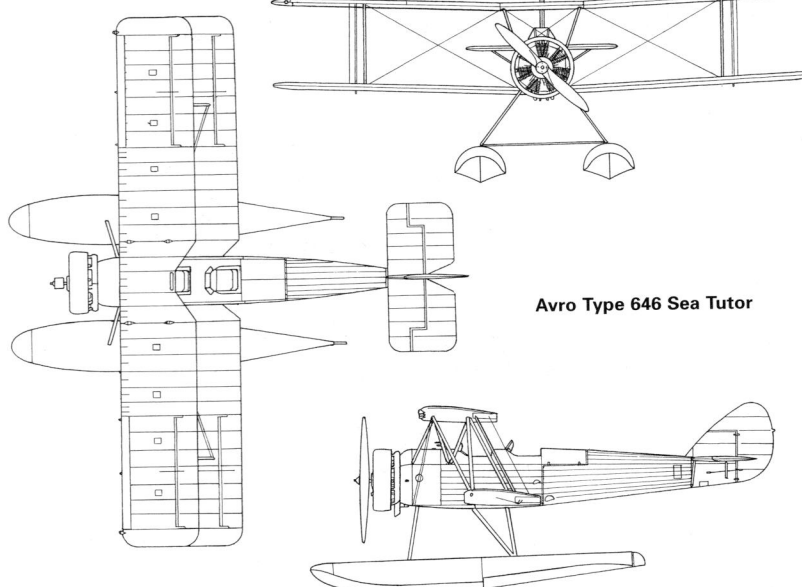

Avro Type 646 Sea Tutor

SPECIFICATION

Avro Type 621 Tutor

Type: two-seat elementary flying trainer
Powerplant: one Armstrong Siddeley Lynx IVC radial engine rated at 240 hp (179 kW)
Performance: maximum speed 122 mph (196 km/h) at optimum altitude; cruising speed 105 mph (169 km/h) at 1,000 ft (305 m); initial climb rate 1,000 ft (305 m) per minute; service ceiling 16,200 ft (4940 m); range 250 miles (402 km)
Weights: empty 1,844 lb (839 kg); maximum take-off 2,458 lb (1115 kg)
Dimensions: wingspan 34 ft (10.36 m); length 26 ft 6 in (8.08 m); height 9 ft 7 in (2.92 m); wing area 301.00 sq ft (27.96 m²)

Avro Type 627 Mailplane

During 1930, Canadian Airways issued a requirement for a mailplane for use on its newly introduced Prairie Air Mail service. To meet this requirement, Avro decided to adapt an existing airframe, the second example of the Type 604 Antelope that had not been completed. It had been intended to use this as the basis for the **Type 608 Hawk** fighter, but this project was not finished, and the provisional designation **Type 622** was allocated to the newly modified airframe.

Avro now decided that the specification could be met by comparatively little change to the Type 622, with the wing cellule, tail unit, and landing gear of the earlier Type 604 combined with a fuselage modified with removable fabric-covered panels in place of light alloy skinning. The main landing gear units were given speed fairings, and provision was made for operation in Canada with float or ski installations. The pilot's cockpit was moved well aft, giving ample room for the introduction of a fire-/waterproof mail hold in the forward fuselage. Cockpit heating and night-flying equipment were also installed.

Tested and demonstrated in this form, the **Avro Type 627 Mailplane** was shipped to Canada, but by the time of the machine's arrival the company had no finance to complete the purchase and the Type 627 was returned to the UK. After taking part in the King's Cup Race in 1932, the Type 627 was used during the following year as a testbed for a 700-hp (522-kW) Armstrong Siddeley Tiger IV radial engine, under the revised designation **Type 654**, before being dismantled during 1934.

SPECIFICATION	
Avro Type 627 Mailplane **Type:** single-seat mailplane **Powerplant:** one Armstrong Siddeley Panther IIA radial engine rated at 525 hp (391 kW) **Performance:** maximum speed 170 mph (274 km/h) at optimum altitude; cruising speed 147 mph (237 km/h) at optimum altitude; initial climb rate 1,200 ft (366 m)	per minute; service ceiling 19,000 ft (5790 m); range 560 miles (901 km) **Weights:** empty 3,077 lb (1396 kg); maximum take-off 5,150 lb (2336 kg) **Dimensions:** wingspan 36 ft (10.97 m); length 30 ft 10 in (9.40 m); height 10 ft 10 in (3.30 m); wing area 381.00 sq ft (35.39 m²)

In the King's Cup Air Race of 1932, the Mailplane achieved 176 mph (283 km/h) – the fastest speed in the race up to that time.

Avro Type 631 and Type 643 Cadet

Development of the **Cadet**, a slightly smaller version of the Tutor, began in 1931 with the **Avro Type 631 Cadet**, of which 35 were built for a number of private customers and the Irish Army Air Corps.

The Type 631 was followed by eight examples of the **Type 643 Cadet** introduced in 1934. Like the

This Type 643 Cadet operated from 1935 until it was scrapped in 1961.

Type 631, the Type 643 was powered by the Genet Major I engine, but had a slightly rounder fuselage with a raised rear seat. Four **Mk II Cadets** were built for private customers, 20 for Air Service Training and 34 for the Royal Australian Air Force, these last being delivered between November 1935 and February 1939 with revised rigging and fuel systems. It says much for the strength of these aircraft that 16 Australian machines survived World War II to be sold on the civil market. One ex-RAAF machine was converted as a single-seat crop-spraying machine with the revised powerplant of one 220-hp (164-kW) Jacobs R-755 radial engine.

The Air Service Training aircraft were camouflaged but retained their civil markings, and those that survived were pensioned off as instructional airframes after the war.

SPECIFICATION	
Avro Type 643 Mk II Cadet **Type:** two-seat primary flying trainer **Powerplant:** one Armstrong Siddeley Genet Major IA radial engine rated at 150 hp (112 kW) **Performance:** maximum speed 116 mph (187 km/h) at optimum altitude; cruising speed 100 mph (161 km/h) at optimum altitude;	initial climb rate 700 ft (213 m) per minute; service ceiling 12,000 ft (3660 m); range 325 miles (523 km) **Weights:** empty 1,286 lb (583 kg); maximum take-off 2,000 lb (907 kg) **Dimensions:** wing span 30 ft 2 in (9.20 m); length 24 ft 9 in (7.54 m); height 8 ft 10 in (2.69 m); wing area 262.00 sq ft (24.34 m²)

Avro Type 638, Type 639 and Type 640 Club Cadet series

In 1933 Avro introduced a version of its **Type 631 Cadet** for use by flying clubs and private owners. To this end, the **Avro Type 638 Club Cadet** differed from the Type 631 mainly in the reduction of its biplane wing cellule's stagger so that wing folding could be introduced to simplify the problems of storage. In its original form, as first flown in May 1933,

Club Cadet G-ACHP was used as a communications aircraft by Saunders-Roe during World War II.

the Club Cadet was powered by an Armstrong Siddeley Genet Major I radial engine, but five of the aircraft operated by the Airwork Flying Club were later re-engined with the 130-hp (97-kW) de Havilland Gipsy Major I inline engine. A single **Club Cadet Special** was built to a particular customer's order with the 140-hp (104-kW) Cirrus Hermes IVA inline engine.

Variants

Type 639 Cabin Cadet: a single example with an enclosed three-seat cabin with the pilot at the front and two passengers aft; cabin formed by enclosing the space between the fuselage and upper wing

Type 640 Cadet: three-seat version with open cockpits for the pilot (aft) and two passengers side-by-side in a wider forward fuselage; nine such aircraft were built, four of them with the 140-hp (104-kW) Hermes IV engine and the other five with the standard Genet Major engine

SPECIFICATION	
Avro Type 638 Club Cadet **Type:** two-seat sporting and training aircraft **Powerplant:** one Armstrong Siddeley Genet Major I radial engine rated at 135 hp (101 kW) **Performance:** maximum speed 115 mph (185 km/h) at optimum altitude; cruising speed 100 mph	(161 km/h) at optimum altitude; range 325 miles (523 km) **Weights:** empty 1,244 lb (564 kg); maximum take-off 2,000 lb (907 kg) **Dimensions:** wingspan 30 ft 2 in (9.19 m); length 24 ft 9 in (7.54 m); height 8 ft 9 in (2.67 m); wing area 262.00 sq ft (24.34 m²)

Avro Type 641 Commodore

In the early 1930s the cabin biplane tourer was beginning to develop as a major element of the American civil aviation scene, and this doubtless inspired Avro to develop the theme with the **Avro Type 641 Commodore**. An earlier venture along these lines had been the Type 639, a cabin version of the Club Cadet, which appeared in prototype form only during 1933. The Commodore was a much cleaner design, of metal construction, with a neat spatted landing gear and accommodation for up to five people.

G-ACNT, the first prototype Commodore, was dismantled in October 1939. It was finally scrapped in 1950.

The prototype was delivered to a customer in May 1934 and was followed by five production aircraft.

Avro Type 641 Commodore (cont.)

Unfortunately, the time was not yet ripe for such aircraft in the UK and no further orders followed.
The first and second production Commodores eventually served with the Egyptian army air force, after having initially been delivered to owners in the UK. Both aircraft were maintained from Egypt's stockpile of Type 626 parts. The third and fourth were impressed for military service in the UK after the outbreak of World War II. Of these two latter aircraft, one was damaged beyond repair in a crash at White Waltham in August 1941, while the other lasted just a year longer before being struck off charge.

Avro Type 652 Anson

The **Avro Type 652 Anson** enjoyed one of the longest production runs of any British aircraft, this status being maintained from 1934 until 15 May 1952 when the last **Anson T.Mk 21** completed its acceptance trials. The origins of the machine lay in an Imperial Airways requirement, sent to Avro in April 1933, for a commercial transport able to carry four passengers over a range of 420 miles (676 km) at a cruising speed of more than 130 mph (209 km/h); other elements of the requirement were a stalling speed of less than 60 mph (97 km/h) and the ability to maintain an altitude of 2,000 ft (610 m) on only one engine.

In August 1933 a design team headed by Roy Chadwick produced a study, bearing the designation **Type 652**, for a low-wing monoplane with retractable landing gear, a powerplant of two Armstrong Siddeley Cheetah V radial engines, and a maximum take-off weight of 6,500 lb (2948 kg), although a change in the airline's requirement raised the maximum weight to 7,650 lb (3470 kg).

An order for two Type 652s was placed in April 1934, and the first of these machines flew on 7 January 1935. Type certification was awarded in March, and the two aircraft were delivered to Imperial Airways on 11 March.

On 7 May 1934 the Air Ministry notified Avro of a requirement for a new twin-engined landplane for use in the coastal reconnaissance role, and requested information as to the possibility of adapting existing designs. A new design study, based on the Imperial Airways machine, received the designation **Type 652A**. This satisfied the specification of the Air Ministry, which then contracted for the delivery of a prototype in March 1935. This gave the company less than six months to complete detail design and build the prototype for the military version of an aircraft which had not then flown in civil form. External changes included rectangular rather than the Type 652's round windows, and the addition of an Armstrong Whitworth dorsal turret armed with a single 0.303-in (7.7-mm) Lewis gun.

The prototype made its maiden flight on 24 March 1935 and, after minor modifications to the tailplane, the machine was transferred to the Coastal Defence Development Unit for a competitive fly-off against the de Havilland DH.89M biplane. A fleet exercise provided a practical test of the two contenders' capabilities, and the superior range and endurance of the Type 652A enabled it to win the competition.

Specification 18/35 was written to cover the initial production variant, the **Anson GR.Mk I**, of which the first example flew on 31 December 1935. On 6 March 1936 No. 48 Squadron at Manston became the RAF's first operational unit with the Anson, and it also proved to be the last to use the type in front-line service, converting to the Lockheed Hudson in January 1942. Twenty-one Coastal Command squadrons used the Anson for the general reconnaissance and search-and-rescue roles. Further RAF orders followed, together with export contracts which included aircraft for Australia, Egypt, Estonia, Finland, Greece and Ireland, and almost

Anson T.Mk 20 VS504 was part of a batch of 48 such machines. Note the transparent nosecone of this bomb aimer/navigator trainer.

1,000 Ansons had been manufactured by the outbreak of World War II in September 1939. Some of these were training aircraft, and it was in this role that the Anson in fact made its greatest contribution to the Allied war effort.

Although Avro had proposed a trainer version as early as November 1936, there was some delay before the first **Anson Trainer** aircraft, with dual controls and trailing-edge flaps, made their appearance for service with operational training units, pilots' advanced flying units, schools of air navigation and army co-operation, air observer and air gunnery schools, the last using Ansons with Bristol B1 Mk VI power-operated turrets. Production of the **Anson Mk I** totalled some 6,742 aircraft.

On 18 December 1939 the British Commonwealth Air Training Plan was instituted, and the Anson was selected as one of the standard training aircraft for this plan. The production contract was placed in the UK, engineless airframes being shipped from the UK to Canada, where they were fitted with either Jacobs L-6MB or Wright R-975-E3 Whirlwind radial engines to become **Anson Mk III**s and **Anson Mk IV**s, respectively. The Mk IIIs

were later modified to incorporate Dowty hydraulically-actuated flaps and landing gear. British airframes delivered with turrets retained them, although most Ansons used in Canada did not have this equipment.

As the war situation in the UK deteriorated, and after the delivery of 223 airframes, production was launched in Canada. The first version produced entirely in Canada was the **Anson Mk II** with Jacobs engines, a moulded plywood nose, and hydraulically-actuated flaps and landing gear. The first of these aircraft flew on 21 August 1941, and production eventually totalled 1,832 machines, of which 50 were supplied to the US Army Air Forces as **AT-20** crew trainers.

The use of moulded plywood in the Anson Mk II led to the adoption of this material for the entire fuselage, in which the familiar 'glasshouse' or square windows gave way to circular portholes. With standard Mk II components fitted to this new fuselage, the aircraft became the **Anson Mk V**, and generally similar **Mk VI**, with the powerplant of two 450-hp

(336-kW) Pratt & Whitney R-985-AN-12B Wasp Junior radial engines and accommodation for five trainee crew members instead of three as in earlier versions. The Mk V navigation trainer was built to the extent of 1,050 aircraft, and a single example of a gunner training version, with a Bristol B1 Mk VI dorsal turret, was produced in 1943. The designations **Anson Mks VII, VIII** and **IX** were allocated to unbuilt Canadian versions.

Subsequent marks were developed and manufactured in the UK, beginning with the **Anson Mk X**, a Mk I development with a strengthened cabin floor for freight/passenger use, and this model saw service with the Air Transport Auxiliary as a communications type for ferry pilots. It retained the 350-hp (261-kW) Cheetah IX engines of the later Mk I aircraft as well as the manually operated landing gear, but the fluted cowlings were replaced by smooth cowlings as used on the two Type 652 machines. The maximum take-off weight was increased to 9,450 lb (4286 kg), and 103 of this version were built.

The raising of the roof line, to provide more headroom in the cabin for passengers, led to the introduction of the **Anson**

This Anson Mk I clearly demonstrates the type's fluted cowlings and dorsal turret. The expansive 'greenhouse' glazing is also prominent.

Mk XI and **Anson Mk XII**, which had hydraulically-operated flaps and landing gear as well as three large square windows on each side of the fuselage. The Anson Mk XI was powered by 395-hp (295-kW) Cheetah XIX engines driving Fairey-Reed fixed-pitch metal propellers, and the Anson Mk XII by 420-hp (313-kW) Cheetah XV engines with Rotol variable-pitch propellers. Later Mk XII aircraft were designated as **Anson Mk XII Series 2** machines to denote the provision of an all-metal wing in place of the previously standard wooden assembly. Ambulance versions of both marks were produced and production totalled 91 **Mk XI** and 254 **Mk XII** aircraft.

The **Anson Mks XIII** and **XIV** were to have been gunnery trainers but, like the **Anson Mks XV** and **XVI** which were to have been navigation and bombing trainers, these were not produced. The **Anson Mk XVII** designation was not allocated.

Early in 1945, with the end of the war in sight, the company produced a Mk XI airframe with five oval windows on each side of the fuselage and a furnished interior, meeting the requirements of the Brabazon Committee's civil transport Specification 19, as the **Nineteen**. It was operated over British internal routes and then put into production as a civil feederliner. Developed from the Nineteen were 12 **Eighteen** aircraft, which were specially equipped for police patrol, communications and aerial survey duties with the Royal Afghan air force. In addition, 13 **Eighteen-C** machines with Cheetah 15 engines were ordered by the Indian government for civil aircrew training.

The same aircraft in RAF service became the **Anson C.Mk 19**, and 264 of these were built between 1945 and 1947. Twenty were converted Mk XIIs, and 158 were **Anson C.Mk 19 Series 2** aircraft with metal wings and tailplanes. The **Anson T.Mk 20** was developed from the Anson C.Mk 19 Series 2 to Specification T.24/46 for service as a bombing and navigation trainer in Southern Rhodesia. This model was fitted with a transparent nose for the bomb aimer and with racks for 16 practice bombs under the fuselage and wings. The prototype flew on 5 August 1947 and was followed by 59 production aircraft. Specification T.25/46 covered the **Anson T.Mk 21** navigation trainer, which lacked the transparent nose and bomb racks of the T.Mk 20, but was otherwise similar. The Anson T.Mk 21 prototype made its maiden flight on 6 February 1948, and was followed by 252 production aircraft for Flying Training Command, the last finally closing the production line in May 1952. The T.Mk 21 was not the last production variant, however, that distinction falling to the **Anson T.Mk 22** which was developed to Specification T.26/46. Fifty-four of these radio trainers were built, the prototype having completed its maiden flight on 21 June 1948.

The Anson's long service career, spanning 32 years, ended officially on 28 June 1968 when six aircraft of the Southern Communications Squadron carried out a formation fly-past at their Bovington, Hampshire base.

SPECIFICATION

Avro Type 652A Anson GR.Mk I
Type: three-seat coastal reconnaissance aircraft
Powerplant: two Armstrong Siddeley Cheetah IX radial engines each rated at 350 hp (261 kW)
Performance: maximum speed 188 mph (303 km/h) at 7,000 ft (2135 m); cruising speed 158 mph (254 km/h) at optimum altitude; initial climb rate 960 ft (293 m) per minute; service ceiling 19,000 ft (5790 m); range 790 miles (1271 km)
Weights: empty 5,375 lb (2438 kg); maximum take-off 8,000 lb (3629 kg)
Dimensions: wingspan 56 ft 5 in (17.20 m); length 42 ft 3 in (12.88 m); height 13 ft 1 in (3.99 m); wing area 410.00 sq ft (38.09 m²)
Armament: one 0.303-in (7.7-mm) fixed forward-firing machine-gun and one 0.303-in (7.7-mm) trainable machine-gun in the dorsal turret, plus up to 360 lb (163 kg) of bombs carried internally

Avro Type 679 Manchester

Designed to specification P.13/36 as a twin-engined medium bomber with the new Rolls-Royce Vulture X-type engine, the **Manchester** was to have competed with the Handley Page HP.56 for a production order. The HP.56 was abandoned in 1937, leaving a clear field for the Avro-designed bomber.

The two Manchester prototypes first flew on 25 July 1939 and 26 May 1940. A production contract had already been placed for 200 aircraft in July 1937, and this total was later increased to 400.

Following flight trials, the wingspan was increased by 10 ft (3.05 m) and a central fin was added to supplement the pair of comparatively small endplate fin-and-rudder units. Later, after a number of aircraft had been delivered in this **Manchester Mk I** form, the central fin was deleted and the twin fins increased in area to create the **Manchester Mk IA**. The first prototype and first two production aircraft were delivered to the A&AEE at Boscombe Down for tests, while the second prototype went to the RAE at Farnborough.

The first deliveries were made to No. 207 Squadron, which reformed at Waddington on 1 November 1940, and six Manchester bombers of the 18 on squadron strength carried out their first operational flight, to Brest, on the night of 24/25 February 1941. As deliveries built up, further squadrons became equipped with the new bomber, but the Manchester quickly proved a failure mainly because of the unreliability of the Vulture engine and also due to the inability of this unit

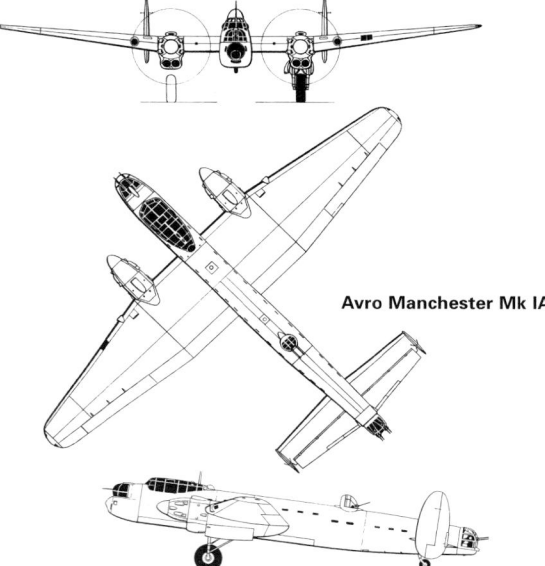

Avro Manchester Mk IA

SPECIFICATION

Avro Type 679 Manchester Mk I
Type: seven-seat medium bomber
Powerplant: two Rolls-Royce Vulture I X-type engines each rated at 1,760 hp (1312 kW)
Performance: maximum speed 265 mph (426 km/h) at 17,000 ft (5180 m); cruising speed 185 mph (298 km/h) at 15,000 ft (4570 m); service ceiling 19,200 ft (5850 m); range 1,630 miles (2623 km) with 8,100-lb (3674-kg) bombload
Weights: empty 29,432 lb (13350 kg); maximum take-off 50,000 lb (22680 kg)
Dimensions: wingspan 90 ft 1 in (27.46 m); length 68 ft 10 in (20.98 m); height 19 ft 6 in (5.94 m); wing area 1,131.00 sq ft (105.07 m²)
Armament: eight 0.303-in (7.7-mm) trainable machine-guns as two each in the nose and dorsal turrets and four in the tail turret, plus up to 10,350 lb (4695 kg) of bombs carried internally

to deliver its designed power. There were also a number of airframe defects, and it was with great relief that the squadrons began to relinquish their Manchesters from mid-1942 as Lancasters began to replace them. The last operation by Manchester aircraft of Bomber Command took place on 25/26 June 1942 against Bremen, and in the final tally it was found that the type had flown 1,269 sorties, dropping 1,826 tons (1885 tonnes) of HE (high explosive) plus incendiaries. Some 202 aircraft had been built, of which about 40 per cent were lost on operations and 55 written off in crashes. On the credit side of the balance, however, the Manchester paved the way for the Lancaster, and without the earlier type one must conjecture whether or not the RAF's finest bomber would ever have seen the light of day.

The short-span wings of the Manchester prototype are obvious in this view. Less apparent are the aircraft's short endplates and central fin.

Avro Type 683 Lancaster

While the **Lancaster** owed much to the Manchester, it was much more than a four-engined Manchester. A four-engined installation in the basic airframe had been proposed as the Manchester Mk III before deliveries of the Manchester began, and the prototype Lancaster was, in fact, a converted Manchester airframe with an enlarged wing centre section and four 1,145-hp (854-kW) Rolls-Royce Merlin X Vee engines. This prototype initially retained the Manchester's triple vertical tail surfaces, but was later modified with the larger tail unit with twin endplate vertical surfaces that became standard on the production version of the Lancaster.

Avro Type 683 Lancaster (continued)

The prototype flew on 9 January 1941 and later that month went to the A&AEE at Boscombe Down. The second prototype, with some modifications and Merlin XX engines, flew on 13 May 1941 while, by September of that year, the first prototype had been delivered to No. 44 Squadron at Waddington for crew training and evaluation. The new bomber was an immediate success, and large production orders were placed. Such was the speed of development in wartime that the first production Lancaster was flown in October 1941, a number of partially completed Manchester airframes being converted on the line to emerge with the designation **Lancaster Mk I** that was altered in 1942 to **Lancaster B.Mk I**.

Avro's first contract was for 1,070 Lancaster bombers, but other orders soon followed, and other companies soon took on the task of building complete aircraft.

The Lancaster soon began to replace the Manchester, and such was the impetus of production that a shortage of Merlin engines threatened. This was offset by licensed Merlin production by Packard in the USA. An additional insurance against Merlin shortages was provided by the adoption of a different engine, the 1,735-hp (1294-kW) Bristol Hercules VI or XVI radial unit, to create the **Lancaster Mk II** (later **Lancaster B.Mk II**). A

prototype was flown on 26 November 1941, and flight test results were sufficiently encouraging to warrant this version going into production by Armstrong Whitworth at Coventry. The first two Hercules-powered Lancaster bombers were completed in September 1942 and went to the A&AEE, where they were later joined by a third. Other Lancaster Mk II aircraft from this first production batch were delivered to No. 61 Squadron at Syerston, Nottingham, the service trials unit for this version and a former Lancaster Mk I squadron.

Gradually, the Lancaster B.Mk II began to re-equip other squadrons, but the Mk II never achieved the success of the Merlin-engined Lancaster; it was slightly slower, possessed a poorer ceiling, and had a bombload 4,000 lb (1814 kg) less than the other marks. Production ceased after 301 had been built, and the Armstrong Whitworth factory changed over to Lancaster B.Mk I bombers.

Meanwhile, the Merlin-engined Lancaster was going from strength to strength. The prototype's engines gave way to 1,280-hp (954-kW) Merlin XX and 22 units, or 1,620-hp (1208-kW) Merlin 24 units in production aircraft. Early thoughts of fitting a ventral turret were soon discarded, and the Lancaster B.Mk I had three Frazer-Nash hydraulically-operated turrets with a

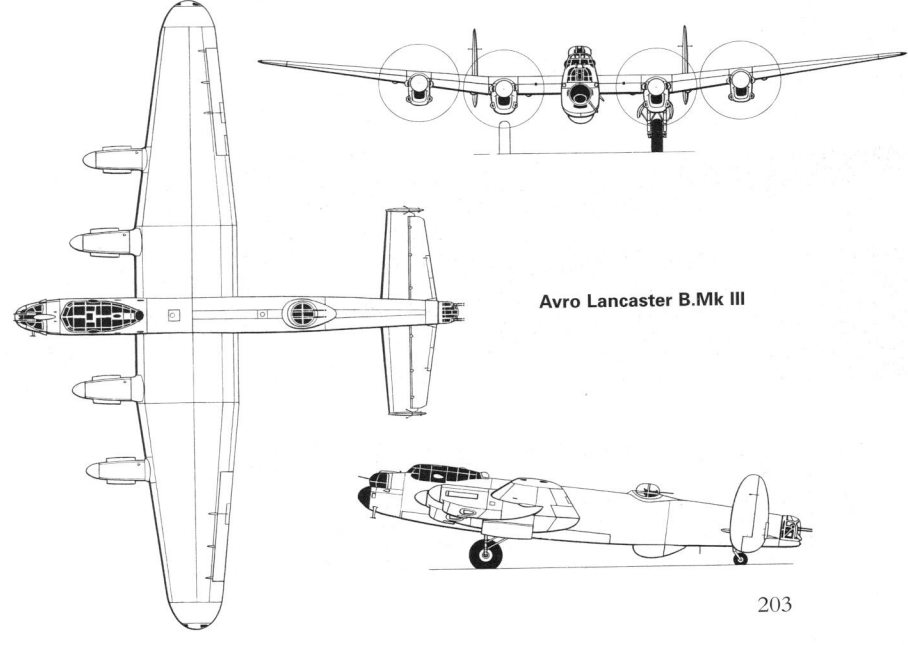

The Lancaster B.Mk X was built in Canada and powered by Packard-built Merlins. This example flew with the RCAF's No. 431 Sqn at Croft Spar, UK.

total of eight 0.303-in (7.7-mm) Browning machine-guns: two guns in each of the nose and dorsal turrets and four guns in the tail turret. The bomb bay, designed originally to carry 4,000 lb (1814 kg) of bombs, was enlarged progressively to carry larger and heavier bombs: initially up to 8,000 lb and 12,000 lb (3629 kg and 5443 kg) and eventually, in the **Lancaster B.Mk I (Special)**, to the enormous 12,000-lb (5443-kg) 'Tallboy' and 22,000-lb (9979-kg) 'Grand Slam', the latter the heaviest bomb carried by any aircraft in World War II.

As Packard-built Merlin engines became available, so the **Lancaster B.Mk III** appeared with these engines, although the B.Mk I remained in production alongside it. Externally, the B.Mk III was distinguishable by an enlarged bomb aimer's 'bubble' in the nose, but there were few other differences apart from minor equipment changes.

To swell the output over that possible from British production lines, Victory Aircraft in Canada was chosen in 1942 to build the Lancaster under the **Lancaster B.Mk X** designation. Powered by Packard-built Merlins, the Canadian-built Lancaster aircraft were delivered by air across the Atlantic and had their armament fitted

on arrival in the UK. The first B.Mk X was handed over on 6 August 1943, and 430 were built before production was completed.

Mention must be made of the **Lancaster B.Mk VI**, production of which was proposed with 1,635-hp (1219-kW) Merlin 85 or 87 engines. Nine airframes were converted by Rolls-Royce for comparative tests. No. 635 Squadron used several operationally on pathfinder work with the nose and dorsal turrets removed, and fitted with an improved H₂S radar bombing aid and early electronic countermeasures equipment. However, although performance was superior to that of the earlier marks, no production aircraft were built. The final production version of the Lancaster was the **Lancaster B.Mk VIII**, which had an American Martin dorsal turret with two 0.50-in (12.7-mm) guns in place of the normal Frazer-Nash turret; the new turret was also located farther forward.

Despite the other variants built from time to time, the Lancaster B.Mk I (**Lancaster B.Mk 1** from 1945) remained in production throughout World War II, and the last was delivered by Armstrong Whitworth on 2 February 1946. Production had encompassed two Mk I

prototypes as well as 3,425 Mk I, 301 Mk II, 3,039 Mk III, 180 Mk VII and 430 Mk X aircraft, for a grand total of 7,377 machines. These were built by Avro (3,673), Armstrong Whitworth (1,329), Austin Motors (330), Metropolitan Vickers (1,080), Vickers Armstrong (535) and Victory Aircraft (430). Some conversions between different mark numbers took place. Statistics show that at least 59 Bomber Command squadrons operated the Lancaster, which flew more than 156,000 sorties and dropped, in addition to 608,612 tons (618350 tonnes) of high-explosive bombs, more than 51 million incendiaries.

As the war in Europe was drawing to its close, plans were being made to modify a number of Lancaster bombers for operations in the Far East as part of Bomber Command's contribution to 'Tiger Force', but Japan surrendered before this could take place. A number of Lancasters was used to bring home prisoners of war from Europe, and various aircraft were modified for test-flying in the UK and other European countries. Some were supplied to the French navy and others were converted for temporary use as civil transports, with faired-in nose and tail areas, under the name **Avro Lancastrian**.

New engine cowlings were required by the Bristol Hercules radials of the Lancaster Mk II. The airframe was otherwise similar to that of the Mk I.

SPECIFICATION

0Avro Type 683 Lancaster Mk I
Type: seven-seat heavy bomber
Powerplant: four Rolls-Royce Merlin XX or 22 Vee engines each rated at 1,280 hp (954 kW) or four Merlin 24 engines each rated at 1,620 hp (1208 kW)
Performance: maximum speed 287 mph (462 km/h) at 11,500 ft (3505 m); cruising speed 210 mph (338 km/h) at 20,000 ft (6100 m); initial climb rate 250 ft (76 m) per minute; service ceiling 24,500 ft (7468 m); range 2,530 miles (4072 km) with a 7,000-lb (3175-kg)

bombload
Weights: empty 36,900 lb (16738 kg); maximum take-off 70,000 lb (31751 kg)
Dimensions: wingspan 102 ft (31.09 m); length 69 ft 6 in (21.18 m); height 20 ft (6.10 m); wing area 1,297.00 sq ft (120.49 m²)
Armament: eight 0.303-in (7.7-mm) trainable machine-guns as two each in the nose and dorsal turrets, and four in the tail turret, plus up to 14,000 lb (6350 kg) of bombs carried internally

Avro Lancaster B.Mk III

Avro Type 685 York

In February 1942 designer Roy Chadwick and his team completed the drawings for the **Avro Type 685 York** as a four-engined long-range transport. This design united the wings, tail assembly, landing gear and powerplant of the Lancaster bomber with a new square-section fuse-lage optimised for the transport role.

Shortly before the proto-type first flew on 5 July 1942, an official order was placed for four aircraft, the first two to have Rolls-

Royce Merlin XX Vee engines and the second pair Bristol Hercules VI radial engines. All four were in fact ultimately flown with Merlin engines, the sole Hercules-powered aircraft being the prototype which was re-engined with Hercules XVI units late in 1943 to become the **York C.Mk II**. To compensate for the additional side area forward of the centre of gravity, a central third fin was added from the third aircraft which, named *Ascalon*, was delivered to

Two VIP Yorks, MW100 *Ascalon (illustrated)* and MW101, both of No. 24 Sqn, RAF, covered in excess of 500,000 miles (804650 km) transporting the Prime Minister and other high-ranking officials.

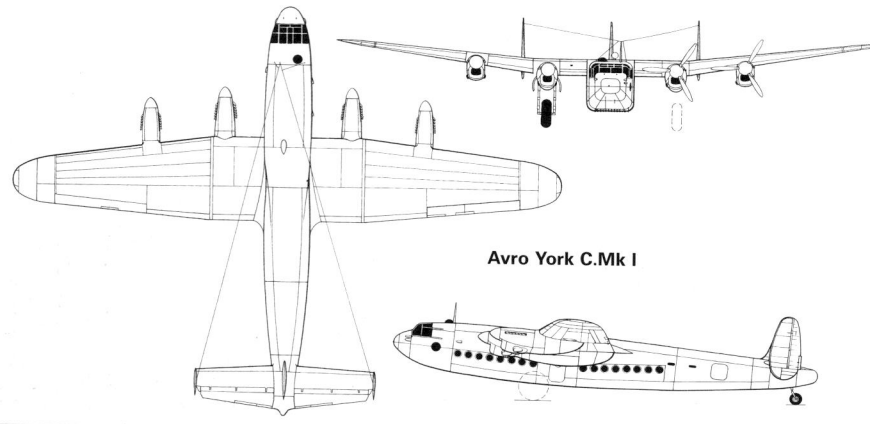

No. 24 Squadron at Northolt in March 1943. Equipped as a flying conference room princi-pally for the use of Prime Minister Winston Churchill, it carried Churchill to Algiers in May and, just a few days later, it carried George VI for his visit to troops in North Africa.

Production of the **York C.Mk I** built up slowly, and other VIP-configured York transports included those allocated to Lord Louis Mountbatten, Field Marshal Jan Smuts and the Duke of

Gloucester. Five early aircraft were delivered to BOAC for service from April 1944, and a further 25 machines were delivered from August 1945 for joint operation with Transport Command.

During 1945 No. 511 Squadron at Lyneham became the first unit to receive a full complement of Yorks and eventually 10 squadrons flew the aircraft in RAF service. Seven of these squadrons were equipped in time to perform 29,000 sorties in

the Berlin Airlift from 1 July 1948. Production ceased with the delivery of the 257th York on 29 April 1948. Total production comprised four prototypes, 208 aircraft for the RAF and 45 civil aircraft. The latter, with 1,620-hp (1208-kW) Merlin 502 engines, consisted of 25 machines for BOAC, 12 for British South American Airways Corporation, five for FAMA of Argentina, and two for UK-based Skyways Ltd. One York was built in Canada.

G-AGJA was the first of five Yorks in 'combi' freight/passenger configuration used by BOAC. Cargo was carried forwards, with 12 passengers aft.

SPECIFICATION

Avro Type 685 York C.Mk I
Type: three/four-crew long-range passenger and cargo transport
Powerplant: four Rolls-Royce Merlin T.24 Vee engines each rated at 1,620 hp (1208 kW)
Performance: maximum speed 298 mph (480 km/h) at 21,000 ft (6400 m); cruising speed 210 mph (338 km/h) at 10,000 ft (3050 m); initial climb rate 1,500 ft (457 m) per minute; service ceiling

23,000 ft (7010 m); range 2,700 miles (4345 km)
Weights: empty 42,040 lb (19069 kg); maximum take-off 68,597 lb (31115 kg)
Dimensions: wingspan 102 ft (31.09 m); length 78 ft 6 in (23.93 m); height 17 ft 10 in (5.44 m); wing area 1,297.00 sq ft (120.49 m²)
Payload: up to 24 passengers or 10,000 lb (4536 kg) of freight

Avro York C.Mk I

Avro Type 688 Tudor

Avro began design work in June 1944 on a four-engined aircraft under the designation **Avro Type 688 Tudor**. The Tudor was the first British pressurised transport to enter produc-tion and, in hindsight, the provision of seats for a mere 12 passengers seems ridiculous for an aircraft larger than the Avro York, occasionally fitted with 24 seats but normally carrying 18.

The prototype first flew on 14 June 1945, and production of an initial 14

(later increased to 20) **Tudor 1** airliners was inau-gurated, although in the event only 12 aircraft were completed. Trials revealed stability problems and land-ing gear deficiencies, but these were cured by redesign of the vertical tail surface and shortening of the landing gear units.

BOAC, for which the Tudor had been ordered, had continually requested modifications and in March 1946 a further 343 changes were demanded. A naming ceremony on 21 January

1947, when the fourth aircraft was christened *Elizabeth of England* as the flagship of the Tudor fleet, proved to be a hollow gesture, since BOAC rejected the type on 11 April 1947 as being inca-pable of transatlantic operation. When the newly formed British South American Airways required a replacement for the Avro Lancastrian, Avro 'stretched' the Tudor's fuselage by 6 ft (1.83 m), decreased the seat pitch and removed the flight engineer's station, enabling 32 passengers to be carried. The designation **Tudor 4** was applied to this configuration, while the **Tudor 4B** designation was used for a similar aircraft retaining the flight engi-neer, but having only 28 passenger seats. Three Tudor 1 aircraft were converted to Tudor 4/4B standard, and another 11 were built as such and, of these 14 machines, seven were supplied to BSAA. Services were operated satisfactorily until one of the aircraft disappeared northeast of Bermuda at the end of January 1948.

Almost a year later a second was lost in a similar way, after which the service was abandoned, the aircraft being stripped of pressurisation and furnishings for use on freight work.

The Tudor was back in service during the 1948 Berlin Airlift, when three were used by BOAC as **Tudor Freighter I** machines. The aircraft returned to store at Woodford near Manchester in August 1949, and all the aircraft stored here, as well

as some new Tudor aircraft in the Avro factory, were then sold as scrap.

Surprisingly, this was not the end of the Tudor story: 11 aircraft were in store at Tarrant Rushton and Ringway, and in September 1953 they were bought, together with components of another three, by Aviation Traders. The company flew the aircraft to Southend and completely refurbished them as replacements for the York on long-range charter work.

BSAA became the major Tudor operator. Two crashes afflicted the company's fleet. Both may have been attributable to faulty elevator servos, which could cause the elevators to break away in flight.

SPECIFICATION

Avro Type 688 Tudor 1
Type: three/four-crew commercial transport
Powerplant: four Rolls-Royce Merlin 621 Vee engines each rated at 1,760 hp (1312 kW)
Performance: maximum speed 260 mph (418 km/h) at optimum altitude; cruising speed 210 mph (338 km/h) at optimum altitude; initial climb rate 700 ft (213 m) per minute; service ceiling 26,000 ft

(7925 m); range 3,630 miles (5842 km)
Weights: empty 47,960 lb (21754 kg); maximum take-off 71,000 lb (32205 kg)
Dimensions: wingspan 120 ft (36.58 m); length 79 ft 6 in (24.23 m); height 20 ft 11 in (6.38 m); wing area 1,421.00 sq ft (132.01 m²)
Payload: up to 12 passengers

Variant

Type 688 Tudor 3: two VIP transports equipped for the carriage of nine passengers; otherwise basically similar to the Tudor 1

Avro Type 688 Tudor (continued)

The first aircraft was fitted with 1,760-hp (1312-kW) Merlin 623 engines, Shackleton-type wheels, seats for 42 passengers in an unpressurised fuselage, and other modifications, and received its certificate of airworthiness in February 1954, being followed by three more in the next year. Five Tudor 4Bs had large freight doors installed and became **Super Trader 4B** machines for use on long-distance charter flights, a task for which they proved admirably suited. They were finally withdrawn in 1959 after two aircraft had been lost in crashes.

Mention should be made of the **Tudor 8**, a conversion of the second Tudor prototype, via Tudor 4 standard, with four 5,000-lb st (22.24-kN) Rolls-Royce Nene turbojet engines in paired mountings beneath the wings. First flown on 6 September 1948, this machine was tested at Boscombe Down and provided useful data for the Avro Ashton which was to follow. The Tudor 8 was finally broken up at the Royal Aircraft Establishment at Farnborough in 1951.

Avro Type 689 Tudor

In its initial design form, the **Avro Type 689 Tudor** was a straightforward 'stretched' version of the Tudor 1 with a fuselage that was 25 ft (7.62 m) longer and 1 ft (0.30 m) greater in diameter than that of the earlier aircraft.

The type was planned with accommodation for 60 passengers for BOAC's short-stage Empire Air Routes, and a projected version for BEA was the **Avro 699**. BOAC placed an order for 30 and, following agreement with QANTAS and South African Airways on standardising the type on the Commonwealth routes, the order was increased to 79 in November 1944 while the aircraft was still on the drawing board. Like its stablemate, the larger Tudor suffered similar hold-ups because of changes demanded by the airlines, but on 10 March 1946 the first **Tudor 2** prototype made its initial flight.

Modifications were required as a result of problems similar to those encountered by the Tudor 1, but an increase in maximum weight and other changes had degraded the performance to an unacceptable level, resulting in cancellation of the QANTAS and SAA orders and bringing the total, all for BOAC, to 50. Despite the loss of the prototype in a crash that took the life of the designer Roy Chadwick among others, development continued.

The first production Tudor 2 had meanwhile been fitted with 1,750-hp (1305-kW) Bristol Hercules 120 radial engines in an attempt to improve the performance. Flown on 17 April 1946, the new version became the **Tudor 7**, and the sole example demonstrated no performance improvement.

Following the second production Tudor 2's tropical trials and their unsatisfactory outcome, orders were cut to 18 aircraft. These comprised the two Tudor 2 machines, 10 **Type 711A Trader** machines with tricycle landing gear, and six **Tudor 5** machines for British South American Airways. These last were fitted with the slightly uprated power-plant of four 1,770-hp (1320-kW) Merlin 621 engines and could accommodate 44 passengers, but never entered BSAA service. Instead, the interiors were stripped out and the aircraft were used in the Berlin Airlift as tankers alongside a Tudor 2, clocking up well over 3,160 sorties. When the operation was complete, the Tudors were refurbished for passenger work, but the loss of one with 80 fatalities in March 1950 marked the beginning of the end.

A few charter flights were operated and one Tudor 5 was used in Canada for a time, but all were gradually withdrawn and scrapped. None of the Type 711As were completed, nor were six **Tudor 6** machines for an Argentine airline, so the total for the Tudor 2, 5 and 7 aircraft reached only 11.

The lengthened and widened fuselage of the Type 689 compared to the Type 688 is clearly evident. Proposed as a 60-seat airliner, the Type 689 met with less success than its predecessor. Tudor 2, G-AGRY, flew during the Berlin Airlift.

SPECIFICATION

Avro Type 689 Tudor 5
Type: three/four-crew commercial transport
Powerplant: four Rolls-Royce Merlin 621 Vee engines each rated at 1,770 hp (1320 kW)
Performance: maximum speed 295 mph (475 km/h) at optimum altitude; cruising speed 235 mph (378 km/h) at optimum altitude; initial climb rate 740 ft (226 m) per minute; service ceiling 25,550 ft (7790 m); range 2,330 miles (3750 km)
Weights: empty 46,300 lb (21001 kg); maximum take-off 80,000 lb (36287 kg)
Dimensions: wingspan 120 ft (36.58 m); length 105 ft 7 in (32.18 m); height 24 ft 3 in (7.39 m); wing area 1,421.00 sq ft (132.01 m²)
Payload: up to 60 passengers

Avro Type 691 Lancastrian

The **Avro Type 691 Lancastrian** originated in Canada when, in 1942, a British-built Lancaster B.Mk III was stripped of its turrets and camouflage by Victory Aircraft of Toronto, which fitted it with pointed nose and tail fairings, plus three extra windows. Trans Canada Airlines evaluated the machine for freight services and found the performance and load-carrying capabilities satisfactory. Such was the current requirement for high-speed transports that the Lancaster was returned to Avro in the UK for more permanent conversion which involved, among other things, the provision of 10 passenger seats and the installation of extra fuel tanks to increase the range to 4,000 miles (6437 km). In its new form the aircraft inaugurated the Canadian government's transatlantic air service (operated by TCA) on 22 July 1943, with four tons of forces' mail.

The British certificate of airworthiness was granted on 1 September 1943, and TCA initiated conversion of two (later increased to seven) Canadian-built Lancaster B.Mk X aircraft. One was lost over the Atlantic in December 1944, and the original conversion was destroyed by fire while engaged in engine trials in June 1945; but the remaining Lancastrian continued to operate the route, which was extended from Prestwick to London in September 1946, as a scheduled passenger service. In this form the aircraft proved uneconomical, and were replaced the following year by Lockheed Constellations, after making 1,900 crossings of the Atlantic.

Problems with BOAC's Tudors encouraged Avro to undertake conversion of 20 Lancasters from the end of its production line. This involved a more detailed conversion than the Canadian aircraft, and the designation Avro Type 691 Lancastrian was adopted. With 500-Imp gal (2273-litre) fuel tanks in the bomb bay, the Lancastrian had a range of well over 4,000 miles (6437 km), and the first aircraft to be handed over early in 1945 established a record between the UK and New Zealand of 3.5 days. Operations were undertaken jointly on the Commonwealth routes with QANTAS, although the aircraft were flown initially in RAF markings with the designation **Lancastrian C.Mk 1**. One Lancastrian was lost in March 1946, and although the type was uneconomical to operate, prestige demanded the retention of this fast route.

Following proving trials with a BOAC **Lancastrian 1** on the South Atlantic route, an order was placed for six **Lancastrian 3** aircraft for the new BSAA, to begin operations in 1946. These had better accommodation for 13 passengers.

With the basic type proved on civil routes, Avro received an order for the **Lancastrian C.Mk 2** for the RAF. Basically similar to the civil Lancastrian 1 but with nine seats, the Lancastrian C.Mk 2 entered service in October 1945. Some 33 such aircraft were supplied, followed by 18 examples of the 10/13-seat **Lancastrian C.Mk 4** equivalent to the civil Lancastrian 3.

In all respects, the BSAA operation to South America proved unfortunate: of the six Lancastrians bought, four crashed between August 1946 and November 1947, and the other two were sold to Flight Refuelling, while two of the

As the first British-built Lancastrian, VB873 was delivered to BOAC in 1945. The aircraft was a more refined design than the Canadian-built Lancaster B.Mk X conversion which preceded it.

Although costly to operate, the Lancastrian was a vital long-range transport and airliner in the immediate post-war era. Some 33 Lancastrian C.Mk 2s (illustrated) were ordered by the RAF.

Tudors which replaced the Lancastrians disappeared en route. BSAA was subsequently absorbed by BOAC, and a further 12 Lancastrian 3s which had been ordered were delivered to other customers.

The independent operators made considerable use of Lancastrians, particularly during the Berlin Airlift, when they were used as petrol and Diesel oil tankers, with a capacity of 2,500 Imp gal (11365 litres).

Most of the surviving RAF Lancastrians later found their way on to the civil market, but a number served as engine testbeds. The first of these, converted by Rolls-Royce in 1946, was used with two 5,000-lb st (22.24-kN) Nene turbojets in the outboard engine positions, and it became the first commercial type in the world to fly solely on jet power when the inner piston engines were

stopped. Flying on only the Nene units, the Lancastrian covered the route from London to Paris in just 50 minutes during November 1946. Another Nene testbed followed, plus five machines as two for the de Havilland Ghost, two for the Rolls-Royce Avon and one for the Armstrong

Siddeley Sapphire. Two more were converted for piston engine test work with Rolls-Royce Griffon 57 units inboard and Merlin T.24/4 units outboard.

A total of 82 Lancastrians was built in the UK, plus the original three, supplemented by another six, in Canada.

SPECIFICATION

Avro Type 691 Lancastrian C.Mk 2
Type: three/four-crew transport
Powerplant: four Rolls-Royce Merlin T.24/2 Vee engines each rated at 1,635 hp (1219 kW)
Performance: maximum speed 310 mph (499 km/h) at 12,000 ft (3660 m); cruising speed 230 mph (370 km/h) at 17,500 ft (5335 m); initial climb rate 750 ft (229 m) per

minute; service ceiling 30,000 ft (9145 m); range 4,150 miles (6679 km)
Weights: empty 30,426 lb (13801 kg); maximum take-off 65,000 lb (29484 kg)
Dimensions: wingspan 102 ft (31.09 m); length 76 ft 10 in (23.42 m); height 19 ft 6 in (5.94 m); wing area 1,297.00 sq ft (120.49 m²)
Payload: up to nine passengers

Avro Type 694 Lincoln

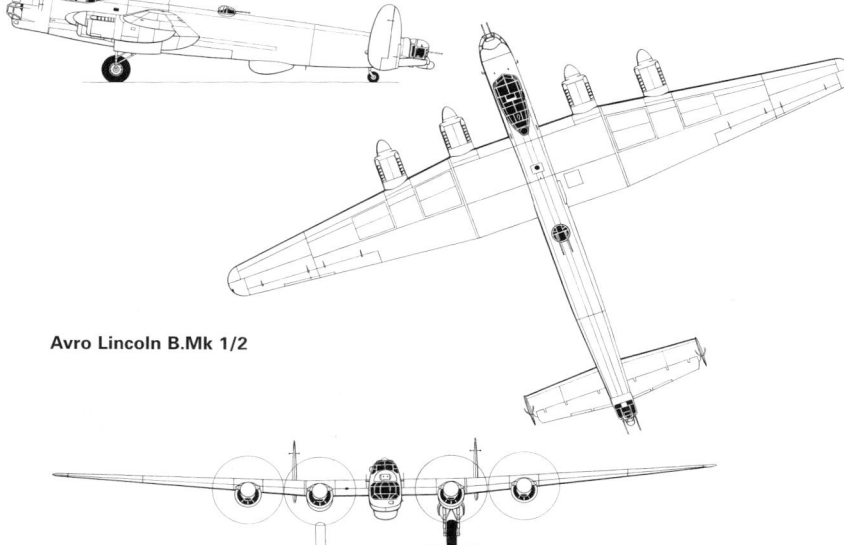

Avro Lincoln B.Mk 1/2

Although the Avro Lancaster was still the highly capable spearhead of Bomber Command's offensive power in 1943, the Air Ministry drew up Specification B.14/43 to cover its replacement. Known originally as the **Lancaster Mk IV**, Avro's design was for a long-range high-altitude development of the earlier aircraft with the power-plant of four Rolls-Royce Merlin 85 engines. A number of Lancaster components were used, but the extent of the changes was such that the machine was then redesignated as the **Avro Type 694 Lincoln**. A new wing of increased span and higher aspect ratio was mated with a longer fuselage, heavier defensive armament was fitted and, as the maximum weight rose, stronger landing gear units were required.

The unarmed first prototype made its maiden flight on 9 June 1944 and four days later was delivered to Boscombe Down for service trials. The second prototype was flown on 13 November 1944 and plans were made to produce a total of 2,254 aircraft. In the event, however, the end of World

War II meant that British production totalled only three prototype, 72 **Lincoln B.Mk I** (later **Lincoln B.Mk 1**) and 465 **Lincoln B.Mk II** (later **Lincoln B.Mk 2**) aircraft: these two variants had versions of the Merlin engine made by Rolls-Royce and Packard respectively. The last of the 168 Avro-built Lincoln bombers was delivered in the spring of 1946 and the last of 299 from Armstrong Whitworth's line on 5 April 1951. In 1947, 30 Mk II bombers were supplied to the Argentine air force. One **Lincoln Mk XV** was completed by Victory Aircraft in Canada, and the Government Aircraft Factory in Australia produced 43 **Lincoln Mk 30** and 30 **Lincoln Mk 30A** aircraft. In 1951, 20 of the Australian aircraft were fitted with a 6-ft 6-in (1.98-m) nose extension to house two radar operators and their equipment for the maritime reconnaissance role, resulting in the revised designation **Lincoln MR.Mk 31**.

The major operator of the Lincoln was the RAF, which received Lincoln B.Mk I bombers off the production line from February 1945. By VE-Day in May 1945 about 50 had

been test-flown and delivered to maintenance units or to specialist organisations for trials. The Bomber Development Unit at Feltwell received its first Lincoln on 21 May 1945, and the first RAF operational unit, No. 57 Squadron at East Kirby, received an initial allocation of three Lincoln B.Mk IIs for its Lincoln Trials Flight in August 1945. The B.Mk II was powered by Merlin 66

or 68 engines and was fitted with the Bristol B17 dorsal turret, Boulton Paul 'D' rear turret, and H₂S Mk IIIG bombing radar. The surrender of Japan and the disbandment of the 'Tiger Force' destined for the Pacific, coupled with delays in getting the Lincoln into service, meant that the

type was not used operationally during World War II. However, it was to see the RAF into the jet era, when it was replaced by the English Electric Canberra, and saw service in the Malayan and Kenyan Emergencies of the 1950s before finally being withdrawn in March 1963.

This Lincoln B.Mk 2 demonstrates the white over black colour scheme adopted for operations in hot climates. The type's Lancaster origins are obvious.

SPECIFICATION

Avro Type 694 Lincoln B.Mk I
Type: seven-seat long-range bomber
Powerplant: four Rolls-Royce Merlin 85 Vee engines each rated at 1,750 hp (1305 kW)
Performance: maximum speed 295 mph (475 km/h) at 15,000 ft (4750 m); cruising speed 215 mph (346 km/h) at 20,000 ft (6100 m); initial climb rate 800 ft (244 m) per minute; service ceiling 30,500 ft (9295 m); range 1,470 miles (2366 km) with maximum bombload

Weights: empty 43,400 lb (19686 kg); maximum take-off 75,000 lb (34019 kg)
Dimensions: wingspan 120 ft (36.58 m); length 78 ft 3½ in (23.86 m); height 17 ft 3½ in (5.27 m); wing area 1,421.00 sq ft (132.01 m²)
Armament: two 0.50-in (12.7-mm) trainable machine-guns in each of the nose, dorsal and tail turrets, plus up to 14,000 lb (6350 kg) of bombs carried internally

Avro Type 696 Shackleton

When the UK had a requirement for a new long-range maritime reconnaissance aircraft, discussions held during 1946 led to the proposal to develop a Lincoln Mk 3 to fulfil this role. Avro's extensive redesign of the Lincoln to fulfil this requirement then suggested a new designation for this long-range oceanic patroller, which thus became the **Avro Type 696 Shackleton**. The Shackleton retained the wing and landing gear of the Lincoln, but joined to a completely new fuselage

each side of the nose), two more 20-mm cannon in a dorsal turret, and two 0.50-in (12.7-mm) machine-guns in the tail, plus bombs or depth charges carried in a large bomb bay.

The first **Shackleton GR.Mk 1** (later **Shackleton MR.Mk 1**) made its maiden flight on 9 March 1949, the first production example flew on 24 October 1950, and the type entered service with No.120 Squadron and No. 236 OCU at Kinloss in February 1951. After working up, the aircraft began to replace

Distinguished by its wing tip tanks and clear-view cockpit canopy this MR. Mk 3 belonged to No. 206 Squadron and, wears the unit's octopus badge on its tail.

that was shorter and of increased cross-section for greater internal volume. The tail unit was moved from a low- to a high-set position, and the characteristic endplate fins of the Lancaster and Lincoln became rounder and more portly in appearance. Merlin engines gave place to Rolls-Royce Griffon engines each driving a pair of three-bladed contra-rotating propellers. The new fuselage provided accommodation for a crew of 10 and an armament of two 20-mm cannon (one on

the Lancaster MR.Mk 3 in service with Coastal Command squadrons.

The powerplant of the MR.Mk 1 consisted of Griffon 57A and Griffon 57 engines in the inboard and outboard positions respectively. The Shackletons of the second production batch were powered by four Griffon 57A engines, resulting in wider outboard nacelles and the changed designation Shackleton MR.Mk 1A. The Shackleton MR.Mk 2 was developed to overcome shortcomings revealed by

operational use of the MR.Mks 1 and 1A, notably the limited capability of the radar and the ineffectiveness of the nose and tail armament. A completely new streamlined nose was designed for the forward fuselage, carrying two 20-mm cannon above a bomb-aimer's position. The radar was relocated from a chin radome to a semi-retractable 'dustbin' radome, to the rear of the bomb bay, which provided 360° scan. Other changes included the replacement of the tail gun position by a transparent tail cone, and the replacement of the single fixed tailwheel by a retractable twin-wheel unit.

The last production version was the **Shackleton MR.Mk 3**, which was developed as the **Type 716** to provide greater overall capability. The type therefore incorporated a wing of changed planform with improved ailerons and wingtip fuel tanks. The MR.Mk 3 also gained a clear-view canopy and soundproofed ward room to accommodate a relief crew on extended patrols. The need to take-off at a somewhat higher weight was reflected in the replacement of the tail-wheel landing gear by tricycle landing gear with twin wheels on each unit. Deletion of the dorsal turret was the other readily noticeable external change, but provision of underwing hardpoints meant that a

variety of stores, including rocket projectiles, could be carried. Eight of the production run of 42 MR.Mk 3 aircraft were supplied to the South African Air Force. After production had ended, further expansion of the Shackleton's capability came in the mid-1960s, when a measure of structural strengthening was introduced to permit the incorporation of additional fuel capacity and the installation of two small 2,500-lb st (11.12-kN) Rolls-Royce Viper Mk 203 turbojet engines. Mounted in the outer nacelle on each wing, the Viper units provided additional power for take-off and climb under heavy load conditions.

Early versions of the Shackleton were superseded in service by the BAe Nimrod MR.Mks 1 and 2, but the last variant of this

veteran aircraft was the **AEW.Mk 2**. This was developed in 1971, to provide an alternative to the Fairey Gannet AEW.Mk 3. Some 12 AEW.Mk 2 aircraft were created as conversions from MR.Mk 2 standard, whose semi-retractable 'dustbin' radome was replaced by a fixed 'guppy' radome just forward of the bomb bay for the APS-20 surveillance radar removed from the Gannets. Other external changes provided a variety of aerials and antennas, but the major modifications were internal, to accommodate the essential equipment and the consoles for three on-duty radar operators. The AEW.Mk 2 aircraft served with the RAF's No. 8 Squadron, providing AEW support of maritime surface forces until July 1991.

SPECIFICATION

Avro Type 716 Shackleton MR. Mk 3 (Phase 3)
Type: maritime reconnaissance and anti-submarine aircraft
Powerplant: four Rolls-Royce Griffon 57A Vee engines each rated at 2,455 hp (1831 kW) and two Rolls-Royce Viper Mk 203 turbojet engines each rated at 2,500 lb st (11.12 kN)
Performance: maximum speed 302 mph (486 km/h) at optimum altitude; cruising speed 200 mph (322 km/h) at optimum altitude; initial climb rate 850 ft (259 m) per

minute; service ceiling 19,200 ft (5850 m); range 3,660 miles (5890 km)
Weights: empty 57,800 lb (26218 kg); maximum take-off 98,000 lb (44452 kg)
Dimensions: wing span 119 ft 10 in (36.52 m); length 92 ft 6 in (28.19 m); height 23 ft 4 in (7.11 m); wing area 1,421.00 sq ft (132.01 m²)
Armament: two 20-mm trainable forward-firing cannon, plus up to 10,000 lb (4536 kg) of weapons carried internally

Variants

Shackleton MR.Mk 1: one or possibly more aircraft equipped for experimental purposes with MAD (magnetic anomaly detection) equipment for the location of deep-diving submarines
Shackleton MR.Mk 2C: designation allocated to a number of MR.Mk 2 aircraft with the navigation and offensive equipment of the MR.Mk 3 for No. 205 Squadron at Singapore
Shackleton MR.Mk 4: designation of a projected but unbuilt version to be powered by four Napier Nomad E.145 compound gas turbine/Diesel engines
Shackleton T.Mk 4: designation of Mk 1 aircraft converted for use as trainers by the School of Maritime Reconnaissance (later MOTU)

The last operational Avro Shackletons were the AEW.Mk 2s of No. 8 Squadron, based at RAF Lossiemouth. All of these AEW conversions were given unofficial names from the 'Magic Roundabout' TV series.

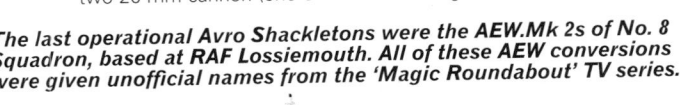

Avro Type 698 Vulcan

In the aftermath of World War II it was imperative that Britain could provide a deterrent against the threat of nuclear attack. Such a need initiated Specification B.14/46 for an aircraft that could be based anywhere

in the world, be able to attack a target some 1,700 miles (2,735 km) distant carrying a 10,000-lb (4536-kg) 'special bomb', have a full-load range of some 4,000 miles (6437 km), and possess the ability to cruise

at high speed at 40,000 ft (12190 m) and to make bombing attacks from heights up to 45,000 ft (13715 m). This requirement was finalised in Specification B.35/ 46, leading to design and development of Bomber Command's so-called 'V-bombers', namely the

Vickers Valiant, Avro Vulcan, and Handley Page Victor.

Each of these manufacturers had a different approach to the difficult technical problems involved. The Avro Type 698 Vulcan, second of the trio to enter service, had a wing of delta planform.

This offered excellent structural integrity, allied with great volume within the deep-section wing roots, plus a number of aerodynamic features that it was believed would prove to be desirable. The word 'believed' is used advisedly, for the design represented a step into a region of aero-

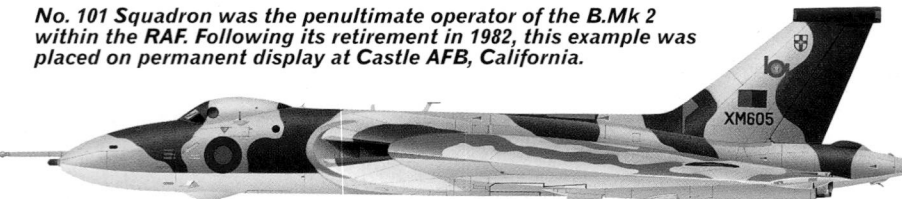

No. 101 Squadron was the penultimate operator of the B.Mk 2 within the RAF. Following its retirement in 1982, this example was placed on permanent display at Castle AFB, California.

dynamics about which little reliable information was currently available. To provide that essential data, the company built the Type 707 series of one-third scale research aircraft.

The first of two Vulcan prototypes made its maiden flight on 30 August 1952 with the powerplant of four 6,500-lb st (28.91-kN) Rolls-Royce Avon RA.3 turbojets, although these were later replaced by 8,000-lb st (35.59-kN) Armstrong Siddeley Sapphire turbojets and then 15,000-lb st (66.72-kN) Rolls-Royce Conway R.Co.7 turbofans before being lost in an accident on 14 September 1958. The second prototype was flown on 3 September 1953, and the first production **Vulcan B.Mk 1** took to the air on 4 February 1955. Official trials at Boscombe Down revealed that application of high 'g' at altitude could induce buffeting that could in turn lead to fatigue fail-

ure of the wing. Before the type entered service, therefore, the wing was modified by a reduction of the wing sweep from root to semi-span, producing a kinked, rather than straight leading edge. When flown in this form on 5 October 1955, the Vulcan was found to be entirely satisfactory, and the other Mk 1 aircraft already completed were modified to this standard. The circular-section fuselage was blended into the delta wing; the retractable tricycle landing gear had a nose unit with twin wheels and two main units each with an eight-wheel bogie; the tail unit consisted only of a fin and rudder as the elevators were incorporated in the trailing edge of the wing inboard of the ailerons. Accommodation was provided for a crew of five in a pressurised cabin, with the pilot and co-pilot side-by-side on ejection seats, but the electronics officer, navigator and radar operator also side-by-side

on aft-facing fixed seats. No defensive armament was carried, but a total of 21 1,000-lb (454-kg) bombs or mines could be carried in the internal bomb bay as conventional alternatives to the 'special weapon'. The powerplant varied, initial B.Mk 1 aircraft having 11,000-lb st (48.93-kN) Bristol Siddeley Olympus Mk 101 turbojets but later machines having Olympus Mk 102 or 104 engines each rated at 12,000 lb st (53.38 kN) or 13,500 lb st (60.05 kN) respectively.

During 1961 all in-service Mk 1 bombers were given a modified tailcone housing ECM equipment, resulting in the revised designation **Vulcan B.Mk 1A**.

The second prototype made its initial flight on 31 August 1957 in a new configuration to offer enhanced capability. This standard had more powerful engines and a considerably modified wing of greater area with a cranked and cambered leading edge as well as elevons in place of the B.Mk 1's combination of ailerons and elevators. Other changes added an APU and inflight-refuelling capability. The **Vulcan**

B.Mk 2 production version entered service during 1960, but when development of the Skybolt was abandoned in 1963, the Blue Steel became the variant's primary weapon. However, with the adoption of the submarine- launched Polaris missile, the Vulcan was adapted for a conventional long-range low-level attack role, equipped with advanced ECM equipment to help in the penetration of enemy airspace. During 1962-4 all in-service B.Mk 2s were re-engined with 20,000-lb st (88.96-kN) Olympus 301 engines.

The definitive standard, to which most B. Mk 2 aircraft were revised or delivered, was the **Vulcan B.Mk 2A** with Blue Steel capability, terrain-following radar for the low-level penetration role that had become the Vulcan's primary tasking in 1966, and an advanced ECM capability. By the time the last **Vulcan B.Mk 2/2A** had been delivered, most of the Vulcan B.Mk 1/1A bombers had disappeared from service. In 1973 some aircraft were revised to **Vulcan B.Mk 2MRR** standard for the maritime strategic reconnaissance role, with classified electronic, optical and other sensors as well, it is supposed, as additional fuel in the bomb bay.

In the early 1980s it was decided that the cost of

extending the fatigue live of the surviving aircraft was too high to be acceptable, this was mainly due to sealed for life components which were found to have passed their fatigue life. It was decided to withdraw all Vulcan aircraft between June 1981 and June 1982. This process was half complete when Argentine forces invaded the Falkland Islands in April 1982, and several aircraft were pooled from three squadrons to constitute composite force that could attack the Falkland Islands from a base on Ascension Island. Another six aircraft were revised to **Vulcan K.Mk 2** inflight-refuelling tanker standard with hose-and-drogue unit in the rear ECM bay and extra fuel in the redundant bomb bay. These aircraft were the last Vulcans to remain in service, and were retired in March 1984.

Production of the Vulcan totalled 134 aircraft in the form of 45 B.Mk 1 and 89 B.Mk 2 machines. It should be also be recorded that two B.Mk 1 aircraft were used for the development of new engines. One completed 1,000 hours of flight with the Rolls-Royce Olympus 593 turbofan and was used during Concorde development . Another, XA894 was fitted with an Olympus 22R in its weapons bay for the development of the TSR.2.

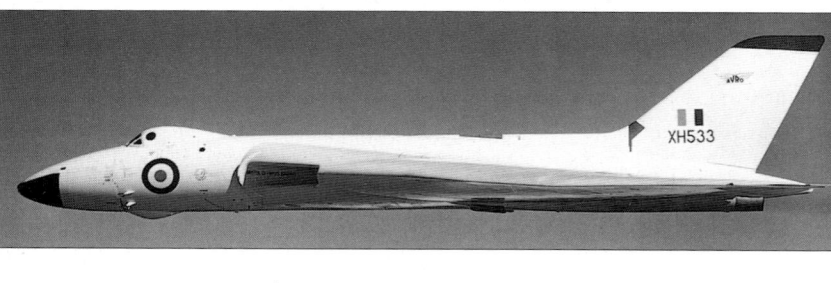

XH533 was the first of 89 B.Mk 2 airframes built by Avro, first flying on 19 August 1958. The first 11 aircraft were used for service acceptance trials.

The giant wing of the Vulcan is shown to great effect by this B.Mk 2MRR at low level. In the early 1970s matt camouflage upper surfaces were introduced along with Type B roundels.

SPECIFICATION

Avro Type 698 Vulcan B.Mk 2
Type: five-seat bomber
Powerplant: four Rolls-Royce Olympus 301 turbojet engines each rated at 20,000 lb st (88.96 kN)
Performance: maximum speed 645 mph (1038 km/h) at 40,000 ft (12190 m); cruising speed 625 mph (1006 km/h) at 40,000 ft (12190 m); service ceiling 55,000 ft (16765 m);

range about 4,600 miles (7403 km) with normal bomb load
Weights: maximum take-off about 250,000 lb (113398 kg)
Dimensions: wing span 111 ft (33.83 m); length 99 ft 11 in (30.45 m); height 27 ft 2 in (8.28 m); wing area 3,964.00 sq ft (368.26 m2)
Armament: up to 21,000 lb (9526 kg) of bombs carried internally

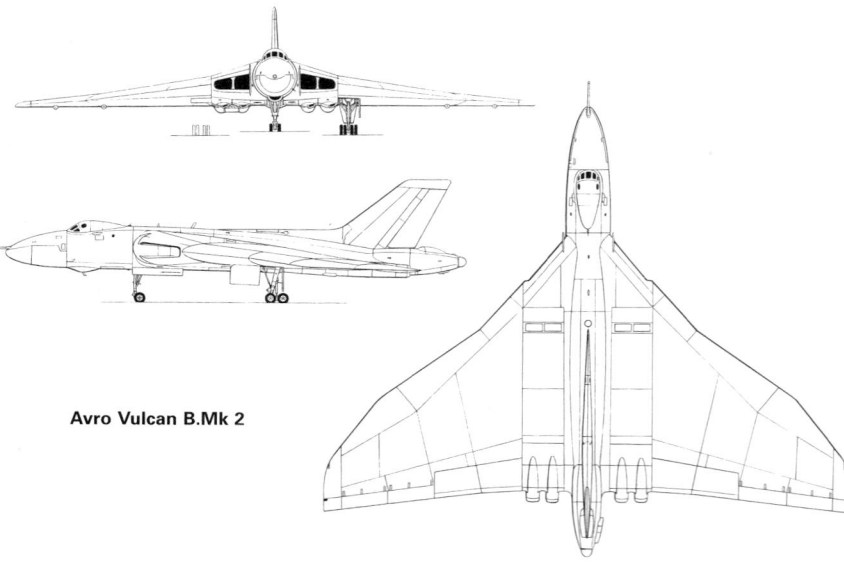

Avro Vulcan B.Mk 2

Avro Type 701 Athena

Air Ministry Specification T.7/45 called for a three-seat advanced trainer with a turboprop engine, and attracted entries in the form of the Boulton Paul P.108 and **Avro Type 701 Athena**. Three prototypes of the Athena were built,

two of them with the Armstrong Siddeley Mamba engine and one with the Rolls-Royce Dart. The first Mamba-powered **Athena T.Mk 1** made its maiden flight on 12 June 1948, but by this time the Air Ministry had decided,

in view of changing requirements in the Royal Air Force's training programme and difficulty in obtaining turboprop engines of sufficient reliability, to issue a new Specification T.14/47, which called for the installation of the Rolls-Royce Merlin 35 piston engine. Large stocks of these engines were available, and the Avro design was thereupon modified to accept the Merlin as the **Athena T.Mk 2**.

The first of four Merlin-engined prototypes flew on 1 August 1948 and in October 1949 the Central

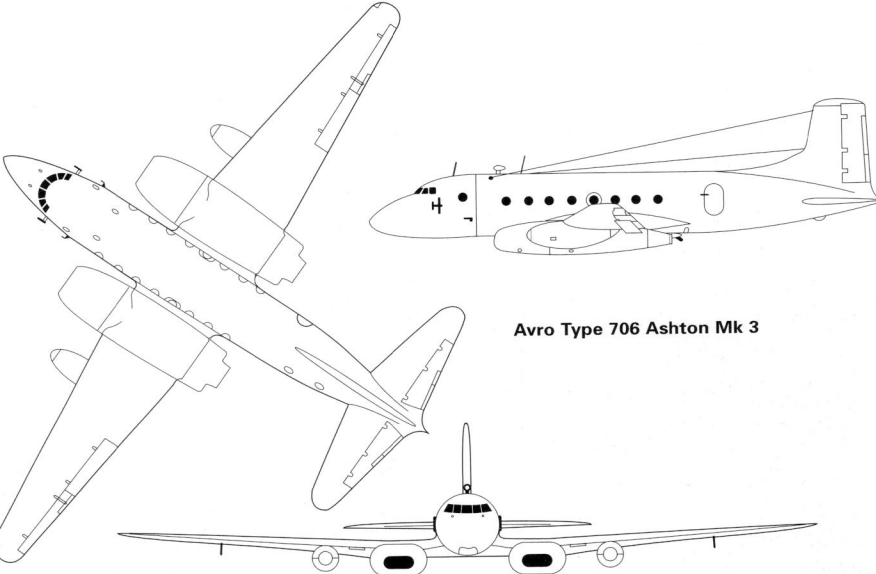

In Athena T.Mk 1 form, the Type 701 featured a finely streamlined nose and the original canopy style. The latter covered its three-seat cockpit.

Flying Establishment received the first two production Athena T.Mk 2s. These had a revised vertical surface incorporating a smaller fin and larger rudder, and a shortened canopy made feasible by the removal of the third seat,

which had become surplus to RAF requirement.

Only 15 production examples of the Athena were built, and these served with the RAF Flying College at Manby, replacing North American Harvard armament trainers.

SPECIFICATION	
Avro Type 701 Athena T.Mk 2 **Type:** two-seat advanced flying and armament trainer **Powerplant:** one Rolls-Royce Merlin 35 Vee engine rated at 1,280 hp (954 kW) **Performance:** maximum speed 293 mph (472 km/h) at 20,000 ft (6100 m); cruising speed 223 mph (359 km/h) at optimum altitude; initial climb rate 1,830 ft (558 m) per minute; service ceiling 29,000 ft (8840 m); range 550 miles	(885 km) **Weights:** empty 6,540 lb (2966 kg); maximum take-off 9,383 lb (4256 kg) **Dimensions:** wingspan 40 ft (12.19 m); length 37 ft 3½ in (11.37 m); height 12 ft 11 in (3.94 m); wing area 270.00 sq ft (25.08 m²) **Armament:** up to four 60-lb (27-kg) rocket projectiles under the wing

Avro Type 706 Ashton

Although a version of the jet-powered Tudor 8 with tricycle landing gear did not materialise, jet research aircraft were nevertheless required. The Ministry of Supply therefore ordered six examples of the **Avro Type 706 Ashton** based on a shortened Tudor 2 airframe with thicker skins. The aircraft had detail differences, and were used for a wide variety of tasks. The only **Ashton Mk 1** first flew on 1 September 1950, and eventually went to Boscombe Down for high-altitude jet research. The **Ashton Mk 2** second aircraft first flew in August 1951 and was flown initially by the RAE, but was later passed to the National Gas Turbine Establishment as a universal engine testbed. In this form, it flew successively with Rolls-Royce

Avon and Conway and Armstrong Siddeley Sapphire test installations.

The third machine, which was the first of three **Ashton Mk 3** aircraft, initially flew in July 1951 and served with the Radar Research Establishment for research into radar bombing. Number four, also a Mk 3, flew in December 1951 and was used by the RAE, before undertaking Bristol Olympus and Orpheus testing. Number five, the only **Ashton Mk 4**, first flew in November 1952 and was operated for visual bombing research and later for de-icing trials with the Sapphire engine. The final Ashton was another Mk 3, flown in April 1952, which undertook bomb ballistic research before undertaking Avon inlet icing trials.

Avro Type 706 Ashton Mk 3

SPECIFICATION	
Avro Type 706 Ashton **Type:** five-crew research aircraft **Powerplant:** four Rolls-Royce Nene 5 or 6 turbojet engines, each rated at 5,000 lb st (22.24 kN) **Performance:** maximum speed 439 mph (707 km/h) at optimum altitude; cruising speed 406 mph (653 km/h) at optimum altitude;	service ceiling 40,500 ft (12345 m); range 1,725 miles (2776 km) **Weights:** maximum take-off 82,000 lb (37195 kg) **Dimensions:** wingspan 120 ft (36.58 m); length 89 ft 6½ in (27.29 m); height 31 ft 3 in (9.53 m); wing area 1,421.00 sq ft (132.01 m²)

For Conway testing, the Ashton Mk 2 carried the experimental engine in a ventral nacelle. The aircraft appeared in this configuration at the 1955 Farnborough Air Show.

Avro Type 707

When Avro began design work on its Vulcan bomber, the largest delta-wing aircraft conceived up to that time, the aerodynamic and

control uncertainties of the pure-delta wing planform persuaded the company and the British authorities that it would be sensible to

Initially used as a familiarisation aircraft for the Type 707 series, the Type 707C survived on test duties at Farnborough into 1963.

build a small series of single-seat scale models to investigate various aspects of delta-wing performance and controllability.

The first **Avro Type 707** flew at Boscombe Down on 4 September 1949, and this machine was flown to Farnborough two days later

SPECIFICATION	
Avro Type 707B **Type:** single-seat delta-wing research aircraft **Powerplant:** one Rolls-Royce Derwent turbojet engine rated at 3,600 lb st (16.01 kN)	**Weights:** maximum take-off 9,500 lb (4309 kg) **Dimensions:** wingspan 33 ft (10.06 m); length 42 ft 4 in (12.90 m); height 11 ft 9 in

to be displayed statically at the SBAC exhibition before being destroyed in a fatal crash near Farnborough at the end of that month. The second aircraft was the **Type 707B** that first flew on 6 September 1950 and differed in detail from its

VX784, the first Type 707, had only the briefest of careers. It utilised a Meteor canopy.

predecessor, mainly in the degree of sweep on the wings' leading edges, and was used for low-speed research. At the other end of the scale came the third aircraft, a **Type 707A** that first flew at Boscombe Down in June 1951. This was designed for trials at high subsonic speeds and for the testing of power-operated controls, and was the first of the aircraft with

wingroot air inlets in place of the earlier machines' dorsal/lateral inlets. A further Type 707A flew in February 1953, and the fifth machine was a departure from the previous designs in being the **Type 707C** with side-by-side two-seat accommodation for pilot familiarisation purposes. All five Type 707 aircraft were powered by the Derwent turbojet engine.

Avro Canada C-102 Jetliner

In December 1945 A. V. Roe Ltd bought Victory Aircraft Ltd and its factory at Malton, Ontario, at which Canadian production of the Avro Lancaster bomber had been undertaken in World War II. This created A. V. Roe Canada Ltd (from 1954 Avro Aircraft Ltd), that was generally known as Avro Canada. One of the new company's first tasks was the origination in 1946 of the design for a medium-range civil transport with pressurised accommodation for 50 passengers. Similar in size and configuration to the British Avro

Tudor, this **Avro Canada C-102 Jetliner** differed primarily in having tricycle landing gear, a revised tail unit, and a turbojet powerplant. The prototype made its maiden flight on 10 August 1949, but only six days later was badly damaged as the result of a landing gear failure. The Jetliner was repaired and flying again within a few weeks, and its four Derwent 5 engines were replaced by two Derwent 8 units (starboard outer and port inner positions) and two Derwent 9 units for evaluation purposes. Despite active demonstra-

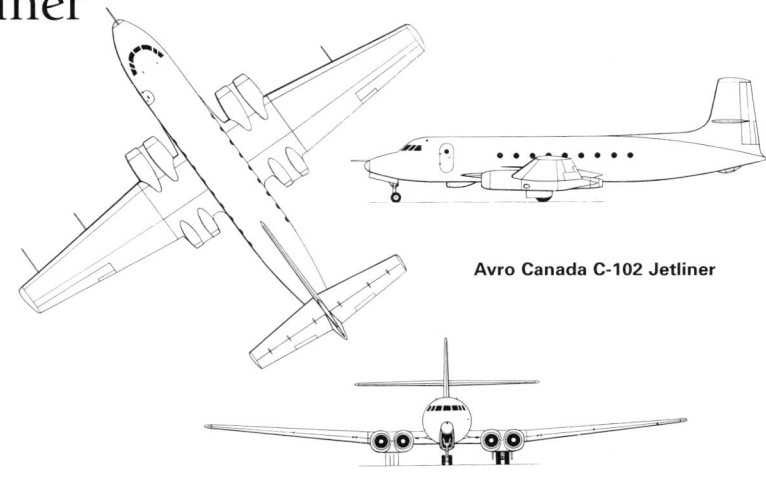

Avro Canada C-102 Jetliner

tions by the company, no orders were received and further development was abandoned. The following details apply to the prototype as originally flown.

With Derwent 8s and 9s, the C-102 completed high-speed Toronto-Ottawa and Toronto-New York flights.

SPECIFICATION	
Avro Canada C-102 Jetliner **Type:** three/four-crew medium-range civil transport **Powerplant:** four Rolls-Royce Derwent 5 turbojet engines each rated at 3,600 lb st (16.01 kN) **Performance:** maximum speed 458 mph (737 km/h) at 30,000 ft (9145 m); cruising speed 403 mph (649 km/h) at 30,000 ft (9145 m); initial climb rate 1,840 ft (561 m)	per minute; service ceiling 40,300 ft (12285 m); range 1,250 miles (2012 km) **Weights:** empty 37,000 lb (16738 kg); maximum take-off 65,000 lb (29484 kg) **Dimensions:** wingspan 98 ft 1 in (29.90 m); length 82 ft 5 in (25.12 m); height 26 ft 5 in (8.06 m); wing area 1,157.00 sq ft (107.49 m²) **Accommodation:** 50 passengers

Avro Canada CF-100 Canuck

No. 410 Squadron, RCAF flew this Canuck Mk 5. On its flank, the aircraft carried a large depiction of the Cougar from the squadron badge.

One of Avro Canada's most important products was the two-seat **Avro Canada CF-100** long-range fighter. This was intended for service with the Royal Canadian Air Force, mainly for the protection of Canada's northern reaches in all weather conditions against the threat of bomber attack. Design of

this aircraft was initiated in October 1946, and the first of two **CF-100 Mk 1** prototypes, powered by two Rolls-Royce Avon RA.3 turbojet engines each rated at 6,500 lb st (28.91 kN) dry, made the type's maiden flight on 19 January 1950. In overall configuration, the CF-100 was a cantilever low-wing

monoplane of all metal construction with a tail unit whose horizontal surface was located mid-way up the vertical surface. The retractable tricycle landing gear had twin wheels on each unit, and accommodation for two, in tandem, was provided in a pressurised cockpit under a long canopy.

Successful testing of the prototypes led to five **CF-100 Mk 2** unarmed pre-production aircraft, these being the first examples to be powered by the Orenda 1 or 2 turbojet built by the engine division of Avro Canada and rated at 6,000 lb st (26.69 kN) dry. When the first of these CF-100 Mk 2 aircraft made

its maiden flight on 20 June 1951 it was the first jet aircraft completely designed and built in Canada. Two of this pre-production batch were equipped as dual-control trainers with the revised designation **CF-100 Mk 2T**, and another example from this batch was the first to enter service with the RCAF, on 17 October 1951.

Orders followed for the **CF-100 Mk 3** production variant, which was named **Canuck** by the RCAF, and the first of these machines entered service soon after a first flight in early September 1952. The CF-100 Mk 3 was produced in two subvariants as the **CF-100 Mk 3A** with Orenda

2 engines each rated at 6,000 lb st (26.69 kN) dry, and the **CF-100 Mk 3B** with identically-rated Orenda 8 engines. Features of the Mks 3A and 3B included an armament of eight 0.50-in (12.7-mm) Colt-Browning machine-guns in a ventral pack, and nose-mounted APG-33 radar used in conjunction with the E-1 fire-control system. Orders totalled 66 aircraft in the form of 21 Mk 3A and 45 Mk 3B machines, and one Mk 3A was later converted as the sole **CF-100 Mk 3CT** (later **CF-100 Mk 3D**) dual-control trainer. There were also four new-build **CF-100 Mk 3T** dual-control trainers with Orenda 2 engines.

Variants

CF-100 Mk 2P: proposed photographic reconnaissance model
CF-100 Mk 4X: proposed development of the Mk 4B with an afterburning powerplant and a wing of reduced thickness/chord ratio
CF-100 Mk 5D: designation of a small number of Mk 5 aircraft converted for ECM (electronics countermeasures) duties
CF-100 Mk 5M: designation of seven Mk 5 aircraft modified for firing trials with four Sparrow II medium-range air-to-air missiles and the revised MG-2C fire-control system
CF-100 Mk 6: projected high-altitude version with Orenda 11R afterburning engines, four Sparrow II missiles and the MG-2D fire-control system
CF-100 Mk 7: projected high-altitude version with the E-9A fire-control system
CF-100 Mk 8: projected high-altitude version with Armstrong Siddeley Sapphire 7 engines

Avro Canada CF-100 Canuck (continued)

Production of the Mk 3 was followed by that of the **CF-100 Mk 4**, of which a single example had been flown on 11 October 1952 with Orenda 11 engines each rated at 7,300 lb st (32.47 kN) dry. This introduced a measure of structural redesign, a single-piece blown canopy, electrical de-icing of the wing and tail unit, reprofiled engine nacelles, and improved APG-40 radar

with the MG-2 fire-control system. A major weapon change was the addition of wingtip pods each containing 29 2¾-in (70-mm) unguided rockets. These could be complemented by 48 similar weapons in a ventral pack (although this never entered production) that could be interchanged with one containing eight machine-guns. The CF-100 Mk 4 pre-production machine was followed by

278 production aircraft delivered in two subvariants as 137 and 141 examples respectively of the **CF-100 Mk 4A** and **CF-100 Mk 4B** with two Orenda 9 or Orenda 11 engines, the latter each rated at 7,275 lb st (32.36 kN) dry.

The Mk 4 was followed by the major production version, which was the **CF-100 Mk 5** that first flew in production form on 24 October 1955. The type was powered by Orenda 11 or identically-rated Orenda 14 engines, but was intended for the high-altitude role and was therefore fitted with a wing increased in basic span from 52 ft (15.85 m) to 57 ft 2⅜ in (17.44 m), and it also had a larger tailplane. Production totalled 332 aircraft with armament limited to the rockets in the wingtip pods, which were used in conjunction with the

Wingtip fuel tanks could be installed for extended endurance or ferry flights. Although the tanks replaced the standard rocket packs, the Canuck Mk 4 and 5 still possessed eight machine-guns.

APG-40 radar and the MG-2 fire-control system. Some 53 of the aircraft were supplied to the Belgian air force's 1st All-Weather Interceptor Wing based at Beauvechain. In addition to the true

production Mk 5 fighters, 50 Mk 4B machines were converted to Mk 5 standard. The last CF-100 Canuck fighters were withdrawn from Canadian service only in the second half of 1981.

SPECIFICATION

Avro Canada CF-100 Mk 5 Canuck

Type: two-seat long-range all-weather fighter
Powerplant: two Orenda 11 or 14 turbojet engines each rated at 7,275 lb st (32.36 kN) dry
Performance: maximum speed 650 mph (1046 km/h) at 10,000 ft (3050 m); cruising speed 472 mph (760 km/h) at 38,000 ft (11580 m); initial climb rate 8,750 ft (2667 m) per minute; service ceiling 54,000 ft (16460 m); maximum range

2,000 miles (3220 km); typical radius (clean) 650 miles (1046 km)
Weights: empty 23,100 lb (10478 kg); maximum take-off 37,000 lb (16783 kg)
Dimensions: wingspan 64 ft 9⅝ in (19.75 m) over tip tanks or 60 ft 10 in (18.55 m) over tip pods; length 54 ft 1 in (16.50 m); height 14 ft 6⅝ in (4.43 m); wing area 591.00 sq ft (54.90 m²)
Armament: 58 2¾-in (70-mm) unguided air-to-air rockets in two wingtip pods

Avro Canada CF-105 Arrow

For the Canadian aviation industry, and for Avro Canada in particular, the traumatic story of the **Avro Canada CF-105 Arrow** was paralleled by that of the contemporary British Aircraft Corporation TSR.2 in the UK. Both of these formidable warplane types were destroyed, even before entering production, by inflexible policies formulated by politicians who, in 1957, were convinced that missile technology had advanced to a stage where manned interceptor aircraft would no longer be needed.

The first stages of development of a new two-seat all-weather fighter to supplant the CF-100 Canuck in service with the Royal Canadian Air force in the long-range interception role began in early 1953, at the time that the RCAF was forming its first CF-100 squadron. The requirement for the new supersonic interceptor was in no way a reflection of dissatisfaction

with the CF-100's capability, but showed an appreciation of the fact that something like a decade was needed to develop a new high-performance interceptor and associated weapons system and introduce them into squadron service. Avro Canada's design team tackled the new and demanding task with great enthusiasm, with the result that by April 1954 the company was involved in the manufacture of the first five **Arrow Mk 1** prototypes. The name derived from the new type's delta wing, which was set high on the fuselage. The latter had a sharp needle nose, widening just aft of the cockpit, where inlets on each side of the fuselage fed air to two turbojet engines mounted side by side within the fuselage. The Arrow Mk 1 aircraft were each powered by two Pratt & Whitney J75 engines, but it was intended that the following **Arrow Mk 2** aircraft would have engines of indigenous

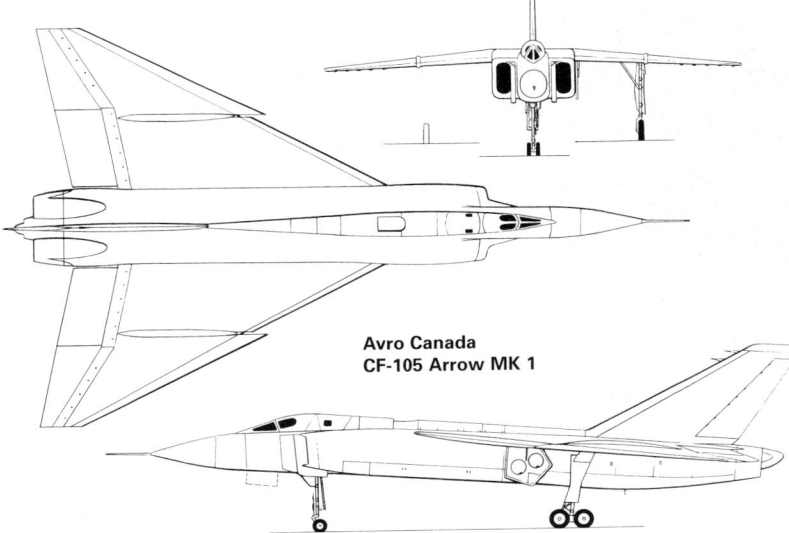

Avro Canada CF-105 Arrow MK 1

design and manufacture. These would be in the form of PS-13 Iroquois turbojet units developed by Avro Canada's Orenda engine division and rated at 19,250 lb st (85.63 kN) dry and 26,000 lb st (115.65 kN) with afterburning.

The first of the Arrow Mk 1 prototypes made its maiden flight on 25 March 1958, and all five of this version were being used for development and testing when the entire programme was cancelled on 20 February 1959. A final bitter edict was to ensure the destruction of the five Arrow Mk 1, one unflown Arrow Mk 2 and four almost complete Arrow Mk 2 aircraft. The armament envisaged for

the latter version was to have comprised eight Sparrow II medium-range AAMs carried in an internal weapons bay, in addition to an external fuel tank.

In spite of its potentially enormous firepower and performance, the CF-105 was cancelled. The first aircraft (illustrated) made just 25 flights.

SPECIFICATION

Avro Canada CF-105 Arrow Mk 1

Type: two-seat all-weather long-range interceptor
Powerplant: two Pratt & Whitney J75-P-3 or -5 turbojet engines each rated at 12,500 lb st (55.60 kN) dry and 18,500 lb st (82.29 kN) with afterburning
Performance: maximum speed 1,307 mph (2104 km/h) or Mach 1.98 at 50,000 ft (15240 m); cruising speed 607 mph (977 km/h) at 36,000 ft (10975 m); initial climb rate 39,000 ft (11887 m) per minute

with afterburning; service ceiling 50,000 ft (15240 m); typical radius 410 miles (660 km)
Weights: empty 49,040 lb (22244 kg); maximum take-off 68,602 lb (31118 kg)
Dimensions: wingspan 50 ft (15.24 m); length 77 ft 9¾ in (23.72 m) in the first three aircraft and 76 ft 9⅔ in (23.41 m) in the last two aircraft, in each case excluding the probe; height 21 ft 3 in (6.48 m); wing area 1,225.00 sq ft (113.80 m²)
Armament: none

Avro International RJ Avroliner

The civil transport currently known as the **Avro International RJ Avroliner** has undergone a chequered career so far as it name has been concerned, for the type was originally schemed as the **Hawker Siddeley HS.146** and then initially built as the **British Aerospace 146**. It was on 29 August 1973 that Hawker Siddeley Aviation announced that it was to receive support from the British government for the development of a new short-range transport as the HS.146. In its initial **HS.146 Series 100** version this was intended to provide accommodation for 71-88 passengers, to be capable of operation from short semi-prepared airstrips, and also to offer the benefits of comparatively low operating costs. The maiden flight of the first HS.146 Series 100 pre-production machine was then scheduled for December 1975.

This was not to be for, in the autumn of 1974, a worldwide recession resulted from the oil crisis of 1973-4, and in October Hawker Siddeley decided to suspend this HS.146 programme. As it was a suspension rather than a termination, minimal funds were allocated each year to keep the project alive, with design and research continuing on a restricted basis. Then, on 29 April 1977, Hawker Siddeley was absorbed into the newly-formed British Aerospace, and it was under the aegis of this new parent that full-scale design and development was then resumed. This followed intensive research into potential markets and following government approval on 10 July 1978 work was carried out at several factories of what became known as the British Aerospace Aircraft Group and then the British Aerospace Regional Aircraft element of British Aerospace (Commercial Aircraft) Ltd.

The HS.146 had originally evolved through a series of designs embracing both high- and low-wing configurations, and a variety of powerplant configurations. As the BAe 146, the basic design was finalised as a cantilever high-wing monoplane of light alloy construction, with features which included: a T-tail; tricycle landing gear with main units retracting into lateral blister fairings on the lower sides of the fuselage; and a basically circular-section fuselage of 11-ft 8-in (3.56-m) diameter to provide comfortable five-abreast seating for up to 71 passengers in a pressurised, air-conditioned environment – there was also an alternative six-abreast seating arrangement allowing accommodation of up to 94 passengers. BAe soon decided that the Series 100 should be partnered by a **BAe 146 Series 200**, with its fuselage lengthened by 7 ft 10 in (2.39 m) to provide seating for a maximum of 112 passengers.

The evaluation of suitable engines was extensive, but the final choice was the Avco Lycoming ALF 502R-3 high-bypass-ratio turbofan, four of these being mounted in underwing pods. Designed for operation from surfaces which can include short semi-prepared airstrips, the landing gear has twin wheels on each unit, and the combination of heavy-duty brakes, anti-skid units, lift-dumpers and airbrakes was schemed as the best way to provide the BAe 146 with exceptional short-field landing performance.

Risk-sharing partners brought into the programme included the Avco Corporation in the USA (providing powerplant and wing boxes) and Saab-Scania in Sweden (providing the tailplane and control surfaces). Short Brothers in the UK is a subcontractor, manufacturing the pylon-mounted engine nacelles.

The BAe 146 Series 100 prototype made its maiden flight on 3 September 1981, followed by a second machine on 25 January 1982, and it was on 4 February 1983 that this initial model gained its type certification. The first BAe 146 Series 200 flew on 1 August 1982 and received its type certification on the same data as the BAe 146 Series 100. There followed the **BAe 146 Series 300**, which was a development of the BAe 146 Series 100 with accommodation for between 103 and 128 passengers in a fuselage lengthened by the incorporation of two plugs, one 8 ft 1 in (2.46 m) and the other 7 ft 8 in (2.34 m) long ahead of and behind the wing. The first BAe 146 Series 300 flew in June 1988, and the type was certificated in September 1988.

Production of the BAe 146 series ended in 1993 after the completion of 219 aircraft, and by this time work was already well advanced on the **RJ (Regional Jetliner)** series as a successor type. Announced in August 1990, the RJ is in essence an updated version of the BAe 146 with features such as the more powerful AlliedSignal LF 507 turbofan rated at 7,000 lb st (31.14 kN) dry, structural strengthening of the wing, fuselage and landing gear for operation at higher weights, and all-digital avionics including a Honeywell Category IIIa flight-guidance system with an integrated windshear detection system. The effect of these changes was improved payload/range performance.

The RJ is offered in a number of variants with fuselages of different lengths and basic passenger capacity indicated by the numerical suffix in the designation. The first of the new series flew on 23 March 1992 and secured certification on 1 October 1993. By August 1998 BAe had secured orders for 147 examples of the RJ series.

Avro developed the RJ100 as a direct replacement for the BAe 146-300. The RJ range has proved just as popular as its predecessor, although a healthy second-hand BAe 146 market continues to flourish. SAM Colombia flies an all-RJ100 fleet, consisting of some nine aircraft.

Variants

BAe 146 Series 100: initial model with accommodation for between 92 and 94 passengers at a maximum take-off weight of 84,000 lb (38102 kg), increased to 97,000 lb (43999 kg) in the **'New Generation'** subvariant with a strengthened fuselage and provision for auxiliary fuel in fillet tanks

BAe 146 Series 200: second model with accommodation for between 82 and 112 passengers in a fuselage lengthened by 7 ft 10 in (2.39 m) and possessing a maximum take-off weight of 93,000 lb (42185 kg), increased to 97,000 lb (43999 kg) in the 'New Generation' subvariant

BAe 146 Series 300: third model with accommodation for between 103 and 128 passengers in a fuselage lengthened by 15 ft 9 in (4.80 m) and possessing a maximum take-off weight of 97,500 lb (44226 kg), increased to 101,500 lb (46040 kg) in the 'New Generation' subvariant

BAe 146-QT Quiet Trader: freighter model of any of the three original models

BAe 146-QC Convertible: convertible passenger/freight model of the BAe 146 Series 200 and 300

BAe 146 Statesman: executive transport version of any of the three original models; the Royal Air Force evaluated two leased aircraft with the designation **BAe 146 CC.Mk 1** before buying three **BAe 146 CC.Mk 2** aircraft for royal and VIP use

BAe 146M: proposed military transport version with rear-loading capability

BAe 146STA: proposed military transport derivative of the BAe 146-QT with side-loading capability

RJ 70: first subvariant of the updated series with accommodation for between 70 and 94 passengers in a fuselage 85 ft 11 in (26.20 m) long, and possessing a maximum take-off weight of 95,000 lb (43092 kg)

RJ 85: second subvariant of the updated series with accommodation for between 85 and 112 passengers in a fuselage lengthened by 93 ft 10 in (28.60 m), and possessing a maximum take-off weight of 97,000 lb (43999 kg)

RJ 100: third subvariant of the updated series with accommodation for between 100 and 125 passengers in a fuselage further lengthened to 101 ft 8 in (30.99 m), and possessing a maximum take-off weight of 101,500 lb (46040 kg)

RJ 115: derivative of the RJ 100 with additional emergency exits and other changes to permit carriage of between 116 and 128 passengers in a six-abreast arrangement

RJX: this designation is used for a possible further upgrade of the RJ for service in the 21st century with 15 per cent lower direct operating costs and 20 per cent lower maintenance costs; changes could include reduced structure weight through the use of composite materials, simplified electrical and hydraulic systems, higher cruising speed, liquid crystal displays and a powerplant of four AlliedSignal AS907 or Pratt & Whitney Canada PW308 turbofan engines

SPECIFICATION	
BAe 146 Series 100 **Type:** two-crew short-range commercial transport **Powerplant:** four 6,700-lb (3039-kg) thrust Avco Lycoming ALF 502R-3 or -5 turbofan engines each rated respectively at 6,700 lb st (29.80 kN) or 6,970 lb st (31.00 kN) **Performance:** maximum cruising speed 477 mph (767 km/h) at 29,000 ft (8840 m), economical cruising speed 416 mph (669 km/h) at 29,000 ft (8840 m); range 1,013 miles (1631 km) with	maximum payload or 1,865 miles (3002 km) with standard fuel **Weights:** empty 51,447 lb (23336 kg); maximum take-off 84,000 lb (38102 kg) **Dimensions:** wingspan 86 ft (26.21 m); length 85 ft 11 in (26.20 m); height 28 ft 3 in (8.61 m); wing area 832.00 sq ft (77.29 m²) **Payload:** see above, up to a maximum payload of 17,053 lb (7735 kg)

Avtek Model 400

The Avtek Corporation was established in Camarillo, California, during 1982 to develop the **Avtek Model 400**. The aircraft was designed initially by Al W. Mooney as a radical twin-turboprop executive transport with an essentially all-composite structure consisting mainly of Kevlar and Nomex (72 per cent) and graphite/carbonfibre (16 per cent). The machine is based on an oval-section fuselage carrying a pressurised cabin for the pilot and up to nine passengers. This is supported and controlled in the air by three sets of flying surfaces: from front to rear these are a straight, flat canard foreplane located above the pilot's seat and fitted with elevators; a swept, anhedralled wing carrying two-section ailerons (the inboard pair serving also as pitch-trim surfaces) on the less swept sections outboard of the engines – the more acutely swept inboard panels are sharply tapered in thickness and chord; and a tail unit comprising a vertical surface with a rudder. The powerplant comprises a pair of Pratt & Whitney Canada PT6A turboprops in nacelles, located on the junction of the inner and outer wing panels, and driving four-bladed pusher propellers. The airframe is completed by the tricycle landing gear with a single wheel on each unit.

A **Model N400AV** proof-of-concept prototype made its first flight on 17 September 1984, and was extensively modified in the spring of 1985. The changes included a fuselage lengthened by 3 ft 2 in (0.97 m); a wider cabin; greater fuel capacity in the leading-edge root extensions; new outer wing panels; a foreplane of greater span but reduced chord; a pair of outward-canted ventral fins added to the tail; and relocation of the main landing gear units.

This paved the way for the planned two initial production models, namely the **Model 400A** executive transport and the 12,499-lb (5669-kg) **Model 419**

SPECIFICATION

Avtek Model 400A
Type: one-crew executive transport
Powerplant: two Pratt & Whitney PT6A-3L/R turboprop engines each flat-rated at 680 shp (507 kW)
Performance: (estimated) maximum cruising speed 419 mph (675 km/h) at 22,000 ft (6705 m); initial climb rate 4,630 ft (1411 m) per minute; service ceiling 42,500 ft (12955 m); range 2,621 miles (4218 km)
Weights: empty 3,799 lb (1714 kg); maximum take-off 6,500 lb (2948 kg)
Dimensions: wingspan 35 ft (10.67 m); length 39 ft 4 in (11.99 m); height 11 ft 4 in (3.47 m); wing area 192.90 sq ft (17.92 m²) including canard foreplane
Payload: up to nine passengers

Express commuterliner derivative with accommodation for 19 passengers in a fuselage lengthened to 54 ft 5 in (16.62 m) and powered by two PT6A-45 turboprops each rated at 1,173 shp (875 kW). Another possibility is the **Explorer** derivative of the Model 400A for the maritime surveillance and ESM roles. This would have greater fuel capacity, a maximum take-off weight of 7,500 lb (3402 kg) and equipment to suit customer requirements.

Having flown its first prototype Avtek 400 in 1984, Avtek Corporation was scheduled to fly a second machine in 1997 for FAA certification in 1998. This appears not to have happened in spite of an impressive list of investors.

Ayres LM200 Loadmaster

Feeling that the growing volume of packages carried by air from the early 1990s would warrant the creation of a dedicated transport aircraft to supplement the cargo versions and conversions of airliners used for this task by most package-delivery services, Ayres started work on a dedicated utility transport in 1996. In November of the same year Ayres secured its initial, and indeed launch, customer for the **Ayres LM200 Loadmaster** in the form of Federal Express, which contracted for an initial 50 aircraft with options on 200 more.

The driving force behind the design was utility, and for this reason the LM200 is an unpressurised shoulder-wing cantilever monoplane of all-metal construction. It has comparatively small flying surfaces mated to an extremely capacious fuselage supported on the ground by fixed tricycle landing gear with a single wheel on each unit. The fuselage is of generally ungainly line but considerable volume, with the flightdeck (accessed by a port-side door) above the forward part of the hold, which is 23 ft (7.01 m) long with a maximum width and height of 8 ft (2.44 m) and 7 ft 1 in (2.17 m) respectively. The hold is accessed by a large port-side door at its rear, where there is also a baggage-loading door, and can carry three LD3 containers. The LM200 is powered by one LHTEC (AlliedSignal/Allison) CTP800-4T Twin Barrel turboprop engine, which comprises two T800 turboshafts driving a four-bladed Hamilton Standard propeller by means of a GKN Westland combining gearbox.

In 1998 Ayres completed its purchase of the Czech manufacturer, Let Kunovice, which will produce about half of the LM200 airframe by value (most notably the wing, tail unit and rear fuselage), assemblies and components being delivered to Albany, Georgia, for final assembly of the LM200. A number of existing Let components have been worked into the design to reduce design and development costs.

The first version of the LM200 is the freighter with a windowless hold, but Ayres has planned a number of developments including an amphibious freighter with twin floats, an airliner with a windowed cabin for up to 34 passengers, and a combi version with a windowed cabin for freight and up to 19 passengers. The company is also planning a more powerful military **LM250**. This will have the CTP800-50 turboprop, based on two T801 turboshafts as developed for the Sikorsky/Boeing RAH-66 Comanche helicopter, and will offer a combined rating of 3,080 shp (2296 kW).

The first LM200 is scheduled to fly in the first three months of 1999, with deliveries to Federal Express following in October of the same year.

SPECIFICATION

Ayres LM200 Loadmaster
Type: two-crew utility transport
Powerplant: one LHTEC CTP800-4T Twin Barrel turboprop rated at 2,700 shp (2013 kW)
Performance: (estimated) maximum cruising speed 196 mph (315 km/h) at optimum altitude; initial climb rate 1,861 ft (567 m) per minute; service ceiling 10,000 ft (3050 m); range 288 miles (463 km) with maximum payload or 1,841 miles (2963 km) with maximum fuel
Weights: empty 9,000 lb (4082 lb); maximum take-off 19,000 lb (6818 kg)
Dimensions: wingspan 64 ft (19.51 m); length 69 ft (21.03 m); height 22 ft 6 in (6.86 m); wing area 458.00 sq ft (42.55 m²)
Payload: up to 7,500 lb (3402 kg) of freight. See text for other payload options

Of highly unusual appearance, the LM200 has been tailored closely to customer requirements. The military LM250 version offers improved 'hot-and-high' performance.

Ayres Thrush

The association of the Rockwell-Standard Corporation with agricultural aircraft began in 1965, when it acquired the Snow Aeronautical Corporation. The latter had been established by Leland Snow in 1955 to manufacture an agricultural aircraft of his own design – a single-seat low-wing cantilever monoplane with fixed tailwheel landing gear. In its original production form as the **Snow S-2B**, this was powered by a Pratt & Whitney R-985 Wasp Junior radial engine rated at 450 hp (336 kW), and the first aircraft were delivered soon after the type's certification in 1958. There followed the lower-powered **S-2A** with the Continental W-670 radial engine rated at 220 hp (164 kW), the improved **450 S-2C** with the R-985 engine, and then the **650 S-2C** which introduced the Pratt & Whitney R-1340 Wasp radial engine rated at 600 hp (447 kW). By the end of 1965, Snow had built 250 S-2 aircraft of all versions.

Rockwell-Standard's Aero Commander Division initially concentrated its production activities on a generally similar but refined version of the S-2C. This was designated as the **Rockwell 600 S-2D Snow Commander**, renamed as the **Ag Commander S-2D** during the following year. By then, Rockwell-Commander had acquired rights to the **CallAir A-9** and slightly larger **B-1** agricultural aircraft. It built the A-9 (Avco Lycoming O-540-B2B5 engine rated at 235 hp/175 kW) as the **Ag Commander A-9**, a more powerful version as the **Ag Commander A-9 Super** with the IO-540 engine rated at 290 hp (216 kW), and the B-1 as the **Ag Commander B-1** with the Avco Lycoming IO-720-A1A engine rated at 400 hp (298 kW).

In 1967 the Ag Commander S-2D was replaced by a development designated as the **Thrush Commander**, which retained the same Pratt & Whitney R-1340-AN-1 engine rated at 600 hp (447 kW). In 1974 this was joined by the more powerful but otherwise similar **Thrush Commander S-2R** with the Wright R-1300-1B Cyclone radial engine rated at 800 hp (597 kW). In 1976 these two aircraft were renamed as the **Thrush Commander-600** and **Thrush Commander-800**, respectively.

In 1977 Rockwell sold the rights to the two Thrush Commander variants to the Ayres Corporation of Albany, Georgia. Ayres then expanded the line and, by 1984, was marketing a range that included the **Thrush S2R-R1340** with the R-1340 engine rated at 600 hp (447 kW); the **Pezetel Thrush S2R-R3S** with the Pezetel PZL-3S engine rated at 600 hp (447 kW); the **Bull Thrush S2R-1820** with the Wright R-1820 Cyclone radial engine rated at 1,200 hp (895 kW), with which the Bull Thrush was claimed to be the world's most powerfully-engined agricultural aircraft; and three turboprop-engined developments of the original piston-engined series under the designations **Turbo-Thrush S2R-T34**, **Turbo-Thrush S2R-T15** and **Turbo-Thrush SZR-T11** with respectively the Pratt & Whitney Canada PT6A-34AG engine rated at 750 shp (559 kW), the PT6A-15AG engine rated at 680 shp (507 kW), and the PT6A-11AG engine rated at 500 shp (373 kW).

In the mid-1990s Ayres discontinued production of its last two radial-engined models, the **Thrush S2R-R1340** and **Bull Thrush S2R-R1820** (by then known as the **600**

SPECIFICATION

Ayres Turbo-Thrush S2R-G10
Type: one/two-crew agricultural aircraft
Powerplant: one AlliedSignal (Garrett) TPE331-10 turboprop engine rated at 940 shp (701 kW)
Performance: maximum speed 159 mph (256 km/h) at sea level; cruising speed 150 mph (241 km/h) at optimum altitude; working speed 90-150 mph (145-241 km/h) at sea level; initial climb rate 2,500 ft (762 m) per minute; service ceiling 12,000 ft (3660 m); range 575 miles (926 km)
Weights: empty 4,500 lb (2041 kg); maximum take-off 9,000 lb (4082 kg)
Dimensions: wingspan 44 ft 5 in (13.54 m); length 33 ft (10.06 m); height 9 ft 2 in (2.79 m); wing area 326.60 sq ft (30.34 m²)
Payload: 333 Imp gal (400 US gal; 1514 litres) of liquid chemical or 3,280 lb (1487 kg) of dry chemical

Thrush S2R-R1340 and **600 Thrush S2R-R1820/510** respectively) to concentrate on two main turboprop-powered variants, the **Turbo-Thrush S2R** and the **700 Turbo-Thrush**. The former is available in its original **T11**, **T15** and **T34** subvariants, and also in five newer subvariants. These are the **Turbo-Thrush S2R-T65 NEDS (Narcotics Eradication Delivery System)**, with the PT6A-65AG turboprop rated at 1,376 shp (1026 kW) and driving a five-bladed propeller, for use in 'hot and high' conditions for the deployment of a large load of herbicide to destroy the plants used for the production of prohibited narcotics; the **Turbo-Thrush S2R-G1** with the AlliedSignal (Garrett) TPE331-1 turboprop rated at 665 shp (496 kW); the **Turbo-Thrush S2R-G6** with the

TPE331-6 turboprop rated at 750 shp (559 kW); the **Turbo-Thrush S2R-G10** with the TPE331-10 turboprop rated at 940 shp (701 kW); and the somewhat revised **V-1-A Vigilante** derivative of the Turbo-Thrush S2R-T65 NEDS, with the TPE331-14-GR turboprop, for the surveillance and close air support roles with equipment that can include a loudspeaker and up to 2,000 lb (907 kg) of disposable stores such as bombs, cannon and machine-gun pods, and multiple rocket-launchers on four underwing hardpoints.

The 700 Turbo-Thrush was developed as a derivative of the Turbo-Thrush S2R for the fire-fighting and special operations roles. It differs from the Turbo-Thrush in details such as its powerplant of one Soloy Dual Pac 785-1000 turboprop (paired and coupled Allison 250-C30S turbo-props) rated at 1,700 shp (1268 kW) and driving a four-bladed propeller, a wing increased in span to 54 ft (16.46 m), maximum take-off weight of 12,500 lb (5670 kg), and cruising speed of 150 mph (241 km/h) with a payload of 583 Imp gal (700 US gal; 2650 litres).

Ayres built the S2R-1340 as an equivalent to the Rockwell-built S-2R. The type was later redesignated S2R-600, in which form it is illustrated.

At first known as the Ayres Model S2R-T65/400 NEDS Turbo-Thrush (illustrated), the S2R-T65 NEDS flies hazardous anti-narcotics missions. The aircraft are armoured, but not armed.

Baade VL-DDR 152

The prototype of the **Baade VL-DDR 152**, designed by Professor Dipl.-Ing. Baade, and built in the Dresden factory of the East German state-owned Vereinigung

Volkseigener Betriese Flugzeugbau, was an all-metal civil transport aircraft of high-wing monoplane configuration. The wing incorporated considerable anhedral, had two

aerodynamic fences on the upper surface of each half, and carried fuel tanks at its tips. The conventional tail unit had swept surfaces, and the landing gear comprised a tandem arrangement of main units under the fuselage with small stabilising units under the outer panels of the wing. In the planned production variant, however, this would have been replaced by a retractable tricycle arrangement with four-wheel bogie main units and a twin-wheel steerable nose unit. The powerplant comprised four Type 014 turbojets pylon-mounted in side-by-side pairs beneath the wing.

After World War II, the Junkers EF 150 bomber design was completed by a Russian team under Baade. Flown but subsequently cancelled, the bomber formed the basis of the VL-DDR 152.

Each was rated at about 6,944 lb st (30.89 kN) dry, the engines being developed in the state engine factory at Chemnitz and, reportedly, derived from the Junkers 012 turbojet. Pressurised accommodation was provided for a

crew of four or five, and the cabin was intended to seat between 48 and 72 passengers in single- or mixed-class layouts respectively. So far as is known, only the single prototype was built and flown during the 1950s.

BAC One-Eleven

The airliner known as the **BAC One-Eleven** began life in 1956 in the project by Hunting Aircraft for a 32-seat transport with turbojet propulsion. Identified as the **Hunting H.107**, this initial concept was planned with a powerplant of two rear-mounted Bristol Orpheus 12B turbojets, but after evaluation in a wind tunnel, the design was amended to incorporate turbofan engines, then in the development stage. This led to a delay of four years, by which time Hunting Aircraft

had been acquired by the British Aircraft Corporation, and it was decided to resurrect the H.107 for further market research and development by the combined design teams of Hunting and Vickers. There was little commercial enthusiasm for what had by then become the **BAC.107** in its final Hunting configuration, with accommodation for 59 passengers, but there was sufficient interest for a version offering some 80 seats to warrant the

construction of a prototype and static test airframes. Designated as the **BAC.111** (and later named **One-Eleven**), the finally revised aircraft was of all-metal construction and incorporated a circular-section pressurised fuselage, a low-set swept monoplane wing incorporating Fowler-type flaps on its trailing edges and airbrakes/spoilers on its upper surface forward of the flaps, a T-tail including a variable-incidence tailplane, and hydraulically-retractable tricycle landing gear with two wheels on each unit. Accommodation was provided for a maximum of 79 passengers in five-abreast high-density seating and, in addition to a conventionally placed passenger door at the forward end of the cabin on the port side, the BAC One-Eleven also had a ventral airstair below the tail unit, giving access to or from the aft end of the cabin. The powerplant of the prototype **One-Eleven Series 200**, which was intended as the basic production version and made the type's first flight on 20 August 1963, consisted of two Rolls-Royce Spey Mk 506 turbofans each rated at 10,410 lb st (46.31 kN) dry. Two months later, on 22 October, this aircraft was lost during the flight development programme, together with a highly experienced crew of seven. Investigation showed the cause to be a deep stall,

resulting from the combination of a T-tail and rear-mounted engines, and remedial action included the installation of powered elevators, a stick-pusher, and modification of the wing leading edges. These changes were adequate to prevent the aircraft from assuming an inadvertent and dangerous angle of attack, a condition peculiar to this configuration, in which the wing loses lift and the horizontal tail surfaces are unable to restore longitudinal stability. Although responsible for a considerable extension of the One-Eleven's test and development programme, pushing the award of the type's certification to 5 April 1965, the detailed investigation of the cause and remedy of the deep-stall phenomenon proved to be of considerable value to aircraft designers and manufacturers worldwide.

Long before certification, in May 1963, BAC announced it intended to develop two other versions in addition to the basic Series 200. These were an increased payload/range **One-Eleven Series 300** with Spey Mk 511 turbofans each rated at 11,400 lb st (50.71 kN) dry, and a generally similar **One-Eleven Series 400** incorporating modifications to meet US requirements. As well as introducing more powerful engines, the Series 300 had increased fuel capacity as well as a strengthening of the wing and landing gear to cater

for an 8,500-lb (3856-kg) increase in gross weight.

Interest in the One-Eleven was growing after the placement of an initial order for 10 Series 200 aircraft by British United Airways, and the new airliner's market potential within the USA was demonstrated by an early order for six aircraft from Braniff International. When this was followed by orders from other US carriers, including American Airlines, the prospect for fairly large US sales seemed very good. However, by the time the One-Eleven received its FAA type approval on 16 April 1965, there was a growing number of aircraft competing within the same payload/range category, and total sales to US carriers failed to reach the figures that had at one time seemed possible.

The first One-Eleven services were flown by BUA between Gatwick and Genoa on 9 April 1965, with domestic routes following in January 1966, while in the USA Braniff's first revenue-earning flight with the One-Eleven took place on 25 April of the same year between Corpus Christi, Texas and Minneapolis, Minnesota. Production of the three initial versions of the One-Eleven totalled 134 aircraft: 56 examples of the Series 200, nine examples of the Series 300, and 69 examples of the Series 400.

The steadily increasing number of air travellers

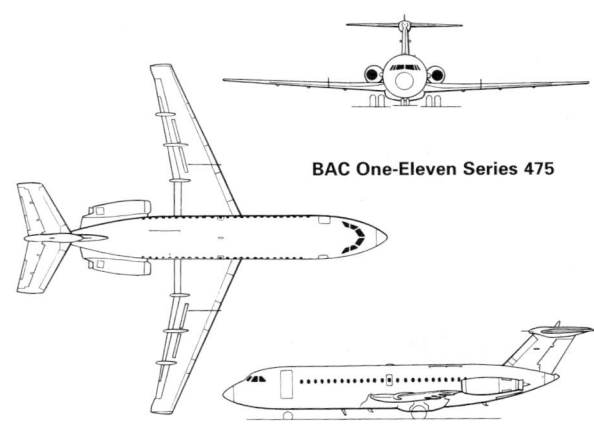

BAC One-Eleven Series 475

Reacting to changes in the marketplace, BAC produced the stretched One-Eleven Series 500. Philippine Airlines received 12 of the type.

meant that, within most categories of aircraft, carriers were looking for greater accommodation/payload capacity. 'Stretched', or increased-capacity, versions of the One-Eleven had been under consideration by BAC at much the same time as the original Series 200, 300 and 400 variants had been announced, but it was not until British European Airways began to show interest in an enlarged One-Eleven that the design of what was to become the **One-Eleven Series 500** was finalised. With a fuselage lengthened by 8 ft 4 in (2.54 m) forward, and 5 ft 2 in (1.57 m) aft, of the wing, the Series 500 could accommodate a maximum of 119 passengers. More

powerful engines were introduced, the wingspan increased by 5 ft (1.52 m), and the structure of both the wing and landing gear was strengthened to make possible a significant increase in gross weight. This was originally 91,000 lb (41277 kg) for take-off, but was later raised to a maximum of 104,500 lb (47400 kg). The prototype for the Series 500 was produced by conversion of the Series 400 development aircraft, and this flew for the first time in its new configuration on 30 June 1967. British certification was awarded on 15 August 1968, and BEA's first revenue-earning flight with the new model was flown on 17 November 1968.

The final variant was the **One-Eleven Series 475** intended for operation to and from smaller airports, or in 'hot-and-high' conditions. This model retained the standard fuselage and accommodation of the Series 400 in combination with the wing and powerplant of the Series 500 as well as modified landing gear to permit operation from lower-grade surfaces.

Total sales of the One-Eleven had reached a figure of 230 in the autumn of 1980, and in addition British Aerospace (successor to BAC) concluded arrangements under which the type was to be built under licence in Romania, as the **Rombac One-Eleven** (later **Romaero One-Eleven**) for both the domestic and

export markets. Three complete airframes were supplied to kick-start the programme in 1981-2, and the intention was then for Romania to receive components for a further 22 aircraft, leading to full Romanian production.

The Romanian programme fell far short of expectations, however, and effectively ended in the mid-1990s after the completion of 19 aircraft in the form of 10 **One-Eleven Series 495** and nine **One-Eleven Series 560** aircraft. The latter featured the fuselage of the Series 300 and 400 lengthened by 13 ft 6 in (4.12 m) and a wing extended in span by 5 ft (1.52 m), while the former combined the fuselage of the Series 400 with

the wing of the Series 560. Production was to have switched to the **Romaero Airstar 2500** development of the Series 560 with the powerplant of two Rolls-Royce Tay Mk 650 turbofans each rated at 15,100 lb st (67.17 kN) dry, but this programme seems to have fallen into abeyance.

In addition to Series 475 and 500 aircraft produced in standard airliner configuration, BAe also built two special variants. These comprised executive and freighter aircraft. The freighter conversion included the installation of a 10-ft x 6 ft 1-in (3.05-m x 1.85-m) cargo door in the port forward fuselage, and a quick-conversion freight-handling system.

BAC TSR.2

The oddly designated **BAC TSR.2** shares with the Anglo-French Concorde supersonic airliner a nerve-wracking and politically-dominated gestation, plus development costs that made a king's ransom pale into insignificance. In their time, however, each type was a brilliant achievement for the UK's aerospace industry, and much of the research and development carried out for the TSR.2, and for the turbojet engines intended to power it, proved of great value in making the Concorde the technological success it proved to be.

In the early 1950s there had been numerous attempts to define the requirements of an aircraft to replace the English Electric Canberra in service with the Royal Air Force. By the end of 1955 it was belatedly realised that the growing importance of a successor meant that the matter could no longer be deferred, and after discussion and investigation had occupied much of 1956 and 1957, General Operational Requirement 339 was issued toward the end of 1957 to provide overall details of the aircraft needed by the RAF. The response to this requirement, from the combined team of English Electric at Preston in Lancashire and Vickers-Armstrong at Weybridge in Surrey, was promising enough for the announcement, on 1 January 1959, that a decision had been reached to proceed with development of the TSR.2. Soon after this, Operational Requirement 343 was issued to define the overall weapon system, one that would be capable of all-weather operation at very high speed, at high or low

level, in the tactical strike and reconnaissance (TSR) role. In fact, the payload/range capability of a fully developed TSR.2 would also have given it an important strategic role.

In 1963 English Electric and Vickers-Armstrong were united as divisions of the British Aircraft Corporation, with a joint project team working on the complexities of an aircraft that represented a quantum leap in airframe, avionics, engine, and equipment technology. Materials used in its construction included aluminium-copper alloys for lower-temperature portions of the airframe, aluminium-lithium alloys for areas subjected to high-temperature kinetic heating, titanium alloys for structures in close proximity to the engines, and ultra-high-tensile steel for landing gear members. The TSR.2's configuration was that of a high-wing monoplane, chosen to minimise airflow complexities over a unique and important tail unit. For the same reason the wing, which was of delta planform with a 60° sweep on the leading

BAC TSR.2

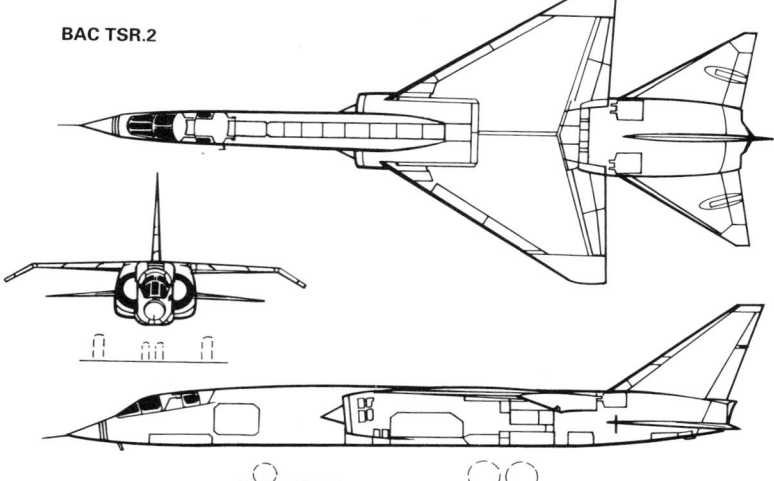

edges, was flat, with lateral stability provided by turned-down wingtips that extended beyond the span of the tailplane. The wing was also devoid of ailerons, fences, slats and slots, having only wide-span blown trailing-edge flaps to provide an almost unbelievable short-field take-off performance. The fuselage accommodated the pilot and navigator in tandem on Martin-Baker ejection seats, incorporated

airbrakes on each side of the fuselage between wing and tail unit, and housed the powerplant, comprising two Bristol Siddeley Olympus Mk 320 turbojets. The specially developed avionics would have given the TSR.2 unprecedented operational capability, with an onboard computer combining information received from an air data system, an inertial platform, and forward- and side-looking radar. Thus constantly

updated, the computer fed position and steering information to a pilot's head-up display, the navigator's instrument display, the autopilot, and the weapon arming and release systems. The radar and its associated equipment provided highly-accurate, multi-redundant terrain-following capability and, in the unlikely event of total system failure, would have automatically put the aircraft into a climb.

SPECIFICATION

BAC TSR.2
Type: two-seat strike, attack and reconnaissance aircraft
Powerplant: two Bristol Siddeley Olympus Mk 320 turbojet engines each rated at 30,610 lb st (136.16 kN) with afterburning
Performance: (specified in November 1962) maximum speed 1,485 mph (2390 km/h) or Mach 2.25 at high altitude; maximum cruising speed 836 mph (1345 km/h) or Mach 1.1 at 200 ft (61 m) and 1,355 mph (2181 km/h) or Mach 2.05 above 36,000 ft (1095 m); initial climb rate more than 50,000 ft (15240 m) per minute; operating ceiling 54,000 ft (16460 m); combat radius 1,150 miles (1851 km) on a hi-hi-hi

mission with 2,000-lb (907-kg) bombload or 800 miles (1287 km) on a lo-lo-lo mission; ferry range 4,250 miles (6840 km)
Weights: average mission take-off 80,000 lb (36287 kg); approximate maximum take-off 96,000 lb (43545 kg)
Dimensions: wingspan 37 ft (27.13 m) length 89 ft (27.13 m); height 24 ft (7.32 m); wing area 700.00 sq ft (65.03 m²)
Armament: (planned) up to 6,000 lb (2722 kg) of conventional or nuclear weapons carried in an internal weapons bay, plus up to 4,000 lb (1814 kg) of bombs, rocket pods or drop tanks carried on four underwing hardpoints

Short-sighted politicians cancelled the phenomenal TSR.2 which would have given Britain a massive lead in attack aircraft technology. A batch of F-111s, as the F-111K, was ordered and subsequently cancelled in the wake of the TSR.2 fiasco.

BAC TSR.2 (continued)

The TSR.2's first prototype made a successful 14-minute maiden flight from the Aeroplane and Armament Experimental Establishment at Boscombe Down on 27 September 1964. It was the only one of four completed aircraft to fly, however, and accumulated a total of 13 hours 9 minutes of flight before (just over six months later) the Labour government announced on 6 April 1965 the cancellation of the entire TSR.2 programme, then involving a total of 49 aircraft. This was not the result of technological failure, although the TSR.2's development was proving difficult as a result of the type's complexity and the novelty of many of its systems, but rather of a mix of rising costs and political ambitions, which thus proved more potent than enemy SAMs. As with Concorde, the TSR.2 had its protagonists and antagonists. Roland Beamont, one of the test pilots, knew it better than most and had begun to appreciate the capability of its superb terrain-following radar system, able to provide tree-top low-level flight at unprecedented speed, with 'rock-steady security'. He believed the TSR.2 to be 'one of the most remarkable designs in aviation history' and, like so many others associated with the procurement and development of this remarkable aircraft, regarded its demise as a very great loss to the RAF.

Bachem Ba 349 Natter

A trolley was used to transport the Ba 349 to the launch ramp. One of the solid-fuel booster rockets is visible beside this Ba 349A.

The Luftwaffe's urgent need for a weapon with which to combat Allied bomber streams more effectively led, early in 1944, to the German air ministry's issue of a requirement to Heinkel, Junkers, Messerschmitt and Bachem for what was, in effect, a cheap and semi-expendable piloted missile. The **Bachem BP 20 Natter** (Adder) project was selected for development and given the official designation **Ba 349**. Bachem's design office, headed by Dipl.-Ing. Erich Bachem and Herr H. Bethbeder, evolved a comparatively crude airframe in which emphasis was placed on ease of manufacture by unskilled woodworkers, without the use of complex jigs. The short stubby wings had no ailerons, lateral control being exercised by differential use of the elevators. The fuselage, with its small cockpit, housed a Walter 109-509A-2 sustainer rocket capable of producing 3,748 lb st (16.67 kN) for 70 seconds at full power, but also able to run at outputs as low as 331 lb st (1.47 kN) for increased endurance. The aircraft was to be launched vertically, and lift-off power was provided by four Schmidding 109-533 solid-fuel rocket motors, two on each side of the fuselage, and each producing 2,646 lb st (11.77 kN) for 10 seconds before being jettisoned.

The first of 15 Natter machines for the test programme became available in October 1944 and was used for unpowered handling trials after being towed aloft behind a Heinkel He 111. Following further piloted gliding tests, in December 1944, the programme switched to unmanned flights using the booster rockets only. The first vertical launch with booster and sustainer rockets firing, still without a pilot, took place on 23 February 1945. Just a few days later, test pilot Lothar Siebert was killed when, in making the first and almost certainly the only piloted vertical launch, the cockpit cover became detached in flight and the aircraft dived into the ground from about 5,000 ft (1525 m).

The operational tactics evolved for the Natter would have involved a vertical launch on autopilot, the pilot assuming manual control when positioned above the approaching bombers. Placed in a shallow dive, the Natter would then have been armed by jettisoning the nose cone to expose the battery of 24 Henschel Hs 217 Föhn 2.87-in (73-mm) or 33 R4M 2.17-in (55-mm) unguided rocket projectiles. After firing these rockets, the aircraft was to have been flown clear of the battle zone, and the pilot would then prepare to bale out. After the pilot had released his straps, the entire nose section would have been jettisoned by uncoupling the control column, moving it forward to release the safety catches, and then releasing mechanical catches to separate the nose from the rest of the fuselage. With the forward fuselage removed by the airflow, the pilot would have been effectively ejected by the deceleration of the rear section as it streamed a braking and recovery parachute, leaving him to descend on his own parachute. The rear fuselage was to have been salvaged to facilitate re-use of the Walter rocket motor.

SPECIFICATION

Bachem Ba 349A Natter
Type: single-seat point interceptor
Powerplant: one Walter 109-509A-2 sustainer rocket motor rated at 3,748 lb st (16.67 kN) and four Schmidding 109-533 booster rocket motors each rated at 2,646 lb st (11.77 kN)
Performance: (estimated) maximum speed 497 mph (800 km/h) at sea level; initial climb rate 36,415 ft (11100 m) per minute; service ceiling 45,920 ft (14000 m); radius of action at 39,360 ft (12000 m) 24.8 miles (40 km)
Weights: maximum take-off 4,850 lb (2200 kg)
Dimensions: wingspan 11 ft 9½ in (3.60 m); length 20 ft (6.10 m); wing area 29.60 sq ft (2.75 m²)
Armament: 24 2.87-in (73-mm) unguided Föhn rockets or 33 2.17-in (55-mm) unguided R4M rockets

Variants

Ba 349A: initial production version of which 200 were ordered (50 and 150 for the Luftwaffe and SS respectively); approximately 20 completed but not used operationally
Ba 349B: proposed improved version with increased wing and tail unit areas, the more powerful Walter 109-509C rocket motor providing 4,409 lb st (19.61 kN) and more effective throttle control down to 441 lb st (1.96 kN), enlarged fuel capacity, and armament boosted by the incorporation of two 30-mm cannon

BAJ Type IV

Having built two successful aircraft in 1913-14, Audenis and Jacob joined Boncourt to build the Type IV.

The **BAJ Type IV** was a C.2 category (two-seat fighter) biplane designed by Charles Audenis and built at Bron by the Boncourt-Audenis-Jacob organisation. The machine was powered by a fully cowled Hispano-Suiza 8Fb engine rated at 300 hp (224 kW), and its only marginally staggered equal-span two-bay wing cellule was braced by single faired I-type struts. The pilot and gunner were seated close together in tandem in an oval-section fuselage. The armament comprised one 0.303-in (7.7-mm) Vickers fixed forward-firing synchronised machine-gun and two 0.303-in (7.7-mm) Lewis trainable rearward-firing machine-guns on a TO.3 ring mounting.

The official order for **BAJ Type IVC.2** prototypes was placed in May 1918, and the first of these machines was moved to Villacoublay for flight tests in the following November. Last-minute alterations were made at the Hanriot company's workshops, and the aircraft reappeared at the end of January 1919. Flight testing proceeded successfully at Villacoublay, until the machine was returned to Bron for repairs during the summer. By that time a second prototype had been completed, and this was used to continue the flight tests. A fire in the Bron workshops led to all development being abandoned later in 1919.

SPECIFICATION

BAJ Type IVC.2
Type: two-seat fighter
Powerplant: one Hispano-Suiza 8Fb Vee engine rated at 300 hp (224 kW)
Armament: one 0.303-in (7.7-mm) Vickers fixed forward-firing machine-gun and two 0.303-in (7.7-mm) Lewis trainable rearward-firing machine-guns

Ball-Bartoe JW-1 Jetwing

Early in 1973 the Ball-Bartoe Aircraft Corporation of Boulder, Colorado, began the design of a turbofan-powered research aircraft which carried the designation **Ball-Bartoe JW-1 Jetwing**, the name pinpointing the area of research in which the company was interested, namely the evaluation of a new aerofoil design within the category known as a blown wing. In short, this involves a specialised wing structure permitting high-velocity air to be discharged over the wing's upper surface. This increases the energy of the boundary layer of air hugging the wing skin, and helps to delay the moment when the boundary layer begins to break away from the

Thanks to its unusual wing design, the JW-1 Jetwing could be controlled in the air at speeds as low as 40 mph (64.5 km/h). The airframe was of welded steel tube, skinned with light alloy and titanium panels.

wing surface, causing the turbulence that reduces the efficiency of the aerofoil.

In overall configuration the JW-1 was a single-seat mid-wing cantilever monoplane of all-metal construction. The tailwheel landing gear incorporated retractable main wheel units, and power was provided by a Pratt & Whitney Canada JT15D-1 turbofan. The moderately swept wing was the research feature of this design, incorporating a slot in its upper surface extending over approximately

70 per cent of the span and, through this, cool bleed air (ducted from the engine's fan stage) could be discharged over the wing. Directly above each slot was a narrow-chord auxiliary aerofoil surface, known as an augmentor,

which helped to control the airflow over the wing.

First flown on 11 July 1977, following initial testing of the aircraft in a large-diameter wind tunnel, the Jetwing completed a large number of evaluation flights during 1978.

SPECIFICATION

Ball-Bartoe JW-1 Jetwing
Type: single-seat research aircraft
Powerplant: one Pratt & Whitney Canada JT15D-1 turbofan engine rated at 2,200 lb st (9.79 kN)
Performance: maximum speed about 400 mph (644 km/h)

Weights: empty 2,500 lb (1134 kg); maximum take-off 3,336 lb (1513 kg)
Dimensions: wingspan 21 ft 9 in (6.63 m); length 29 ft (8.84 m); height 6 ft 1 in (1.85 m); wing area 105.00 sq ft (9.75 m²)

Barkley-Grow Model T8P-1

The Barkley-Grow Aircraft Corporation was established in 1935 to develop and manufacture the **Barkley-Grow Model T8P-1** as a two-crew civil transport with accommodation for six passengers. A feature of the machine's design was the multi-spar

wing construction created by Archibald S. Barkley to eliminate all need for ribs or bulkheads in the wing structure. Of low-wing cantilever monoplane configuration, the Model T8P-1 was of all-metal construction, the tail unit incorporating twin fins and

rudders and the landing gear being of the tailwheel type with fixed and spatted main units that could be replaced by floats. The powerplant comprised two Pratt & Whitney Wasp Junior radial engines, each in a nacelle mounted on the leading edge of the wing, directly over the main landing gear units.

The Model T8P-1 made its maiden flight in April 1937 and received its US certification in October of the same year, but proved only a modest commercial success. Potential American purchasers were generally unhappy about the apparent obsolescence of the fixed landing gear, but it helped sales in Canada as it facilitated the

To a certain extent, the sales potential of the T8P-1 was limited by its fixed undercarriage since aircraft of a similar capacity, such as the Lockheed 10 Electra, were already available with retractable landing gear. The T8P-1 was nevertheless ideally suited to the installation of ski or float undercarriage.

installation of the alternative floats and skis that made it a useful medium-lift 'bush plane'. Only 11 Model T8P-1 aircraft were

completed, and it seems probable that further development and production were terminated on the outbreak of World War II.

SPECIFICATION

Barkley-Grow Model T8P-1
Type: two-crew commercial transport
Powerplant: two Pratt & Whitney Wasp Junior SB radial engines each rated at 450 hp (336 kW)
Performance: maximum speed 224 mph (360 km/h) at 5,000 ft (1523 m); cruising speed 216 mph (348 km/h) at 9,600 ft (2925 m); initial climb rate 1,420 ft (433 m) per minute; service ceiling

27,000 ft (8230 m); range 470 miles (756 km)
Weights: empty 5,750 lb (2608 kg); maximum take-off 8,250 lb (3742 kg)
Dimensions: wingspan 50 ft 8 in (15.44 m); length 36 ft 2 in (11.02 m); height 9 ft 8 in (2.95 m); wing area 354.00 sq ft (32.89 m²)
Payload: up to six passengers or a maximum payload of 1,397 lb (634 kg)

Barling NBL

Although the US Army Air Service, like the air arms of most other nations, was desperately short of funds in the years that followed the end of World War I, some attempts were made to improve significant deficiencies. Senior officers appreciated that a strategic bombing capability was needed, and this led to the construction of the **XNBL-1** (**Experimental Night Bomber Long-range no.1**). This had been designed by Walter Barling of the Army Air Services' Engineering Division at McCook Field, Ohio, and was now built by the Witteman-Lewis Aircraft Corporation of Newark, New Jersey.

When first flown, on 22 August 1923, the XNBL-1 was the world's largest aircraft, with a triplane wing cellule spanning 120 ft (36.58 m), the middle wing being of reduced span and chord. The massive fuselage carried at its rear a biplane tail incorporating four fin-and-rudder units, the fins serving also as the interplane struts of the biplane horizontal tail structure. The incidence of these horizontal surfaces could be adjusted in flight, the entire tail unit being moved by a control in the pilot's cockpit. The tailskid landing gear was also of unusual design, the main units each having four wheels, plus a two-wheel

unit mounted beneath the nose of the fuselage to prevent the aircraft from nosing over during a rough-field landing. The forward pair of wheels on each main unit could be extended slightly during the approach, the touchdown being made on these four wheels and then, as speed fell off, the aircraft settling also on to the rear main wheels and the tail skid. Two pilots were accommodated side-by-side in an open cockpit, where they were provided with dual controls. Five other positions made it possible to deploy seven machine-guns to offer a spirited defence against any potential attacker.

Short on ceiling, power, range and speed, the immense XNBL-1 would have been an easy target for enemy fighters and was abandoned.

The weak point in the XNBL-1's design proved to be the powerplant, which comprised six Liberty engines. These were mounted between the lower and middle wings, the inboard installation comprising back-to-back pairs driving tractor and pusher propellers, with an outboard engine/tractor propeller unit on each side. The combined output of this powerplant was completely inadequate for the total weight involved, and the performance of the bomber was reported to be disappointing in terms of

speed, load, and endurance. So disappointing was the performance, in fact, that the 'Barling Bomber' was unable to cross the Appalachian Mountains during a flight from Dayton to Washington. With no funds available, further development of the bomber was abandoned in 1925, and the planned design and development of an improved **XNBL-2** were not funded. The XNBL-1 proved to be the one and only 'giant' aeroplane to be flown by the US Army's air arm for many years.

SPECIFICATION

Barling XNBL-1
Type: seven-seat experimental long-range bomber
Powerplant: six Liberty 12A Vee engines each rated at 420 hp (313 kW)
Performance: maximum speed 96 mph (154 km/h) at optimum altitude; cruising speed 61 mph (98 km/h); service ceiling 7,725 ft (2355 m); range 170 miles (274 km)

with a 5,000-lb (2268-kg) bombload
Weights: empty 27,703 lb (12566 kg); maximum take-off 42,569 lb (19309 kg)
Dimensions: wingspan 120 ft (36.58 m); length 65 ft (19.81 m); height 27 ft (8.23 m); wing area 4,200.00 sq ft (390.18 m²)
Armament: seven 0.3-in (7.62-mm) trainable machine-guns, plus up to 5,000 lb (2268 kg) of bombs

BAT F.K.22 and F.K.23 Bantam

When Frederick Koolhoven left Armstrong Whitworth in 1917 he joined the British Aerial Transport Co. Ltd, generally known as BAT. Koolhoven's first design for his new employer, was the **BAT F.K.22 Bantam** single-seat fighter. A two-bay biplane of wooden construction with a semi-monocoque fuselage, the F.K.22 was powered by the 120-hp (89-kW) ABC Mosquito radial engine, and the private-venture prototype with this engine first flew in September 1917. The prototype's performance was sufficiently encouraging for the placement of an order for six development aircraft. However, the failure of this Mosquito engine led to the installation of the somewhat more powerful

ABC Wasp I radial engine, rated at 170 hp (127 kW), in the first and third of the development aircraft, designated **F.K.22/1**. The second machine, powered by a Gnome Monosoupape rotary engine rated at 100 hp (75 kW) that was later replaced by a Le Rhône 9J rotary engine rated at 110 hp (82 kW), was the sole **F.K.22/2 Bantam Mk II**. In December 1917 it became the first of the development aircraft to fly, then undertaking the new type's initial development and evaluation trials at Martlesham Heath in January 1918.

The other three aircraft ordered under the original development contract were completed as **F.K.23 Bantam Mk I** machines.

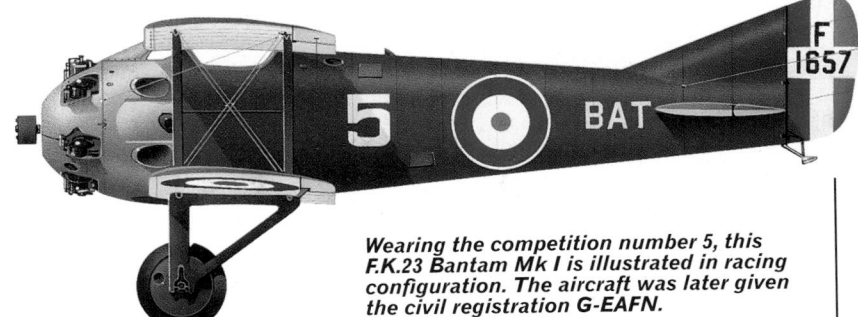

Wearing the competition number 5, this F.K.23 Bantam Mk I is illustrated in racing configuration. The aircraft was later given the civil registration G-EAFN.

The Bantam Mk I prototype retained the basic wooden structure but was of smaller size, the wingspan being reduced to 25 ft (7.62 m) and the length from 20 ft 8 in (6.30 m) to 18 ft 5 in (5.61 m). The Wasp engine was selected to power the Bantam Mk I, and flight tests began in May 1918. The other two prototypes, of a slightly larger and modified design, were also completed and were followed by at least nine of an additional development batch of 12 pre-production aircraft. The first of these was flown to the RAE at Farnborough on 26 July 1918. Two aircraft were sent overseas for evaluation, one to Villacoublay in France and one to Wright Field in the United States. The latter

was given the US project number **P.167**, and was eventually placed in storage on 30 September 1922.

The pre-production examples of the Bantam incorporated a number of design changes, mainly to overcome the unsatisfactory spin characteristics of the prototypes. The wingspan was increased, an enlarged horizontal tail surface was fitted, and the vertical tail surface was revised with a smaller fin and a larger rudder. Continuing engine problems and the post-war contraction of the RAF were among the factors which affected the future of the Bantam, although an attempt was made to over-

come the first of these by re-engining the last production example with a Wasp II engine rated at 200 hp (149 kW). Following the closure of BAT, Koolhoven purchased this machine and took it to the Netherlands, where it was again re-engined, this time with a 200-hp (149-kW) Armstrong Siddeley Lynx radial unit. Several examples of the Bantam later appeared on the British civil register, including one raced by BAT test pilot Major Christopher Draper at Hendon on 21 June 1919. This featured a lower wing clipped to half its original length, with the upper wing being supported by slanting struts.

SPECIFICATION

BAT F.K.23 Bantam Mk I
Type: single-seat fighter
Powerplant: one ABC Wasp I radial engine rated at 170 hp (127 kW)
Performance: maximum speed 128 mph (206 km/h) at 6,500 ft (1980 m); initial climb rate 1,250 ft (381 m) per minute; climb to 6,500 ft (1980 m) in 5 minutes 10 seconds; service ceiling 20,000 ft (6100 m); range 250 miles (402 km); endurance 2 hours 30 minutes
Weights: empty 833 lb (378 kg); maximum take-off 1,321 lb (599 kg)
Dimensions: wingspan 25 ft (7.62 m); length 18 ft 5 in (5.61 m); height 6 ft 9 in (2.06 m); wing area 185.00 sq ft (17.19 m²)
Armament: two 0.303-in (7.7-mm) Vickers fixed forward-firing machine-guns

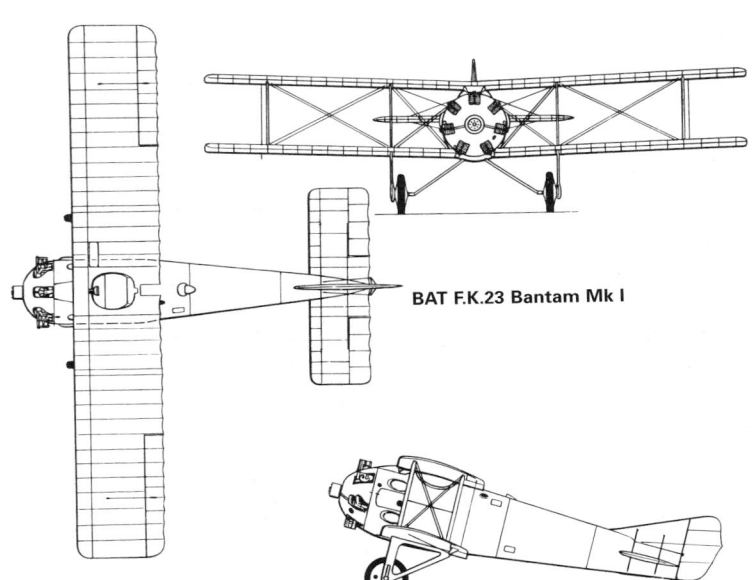

BAT F.K.23 Bantam Mk I

Generally similar to the F.K.23 Bantam Mk I, the F.K.22 Bantam Mk II (illustrated) was a slightly larger machine. The pilot's head protruded through a cut-out in the upper wing.

Variant

F.K.27: built in 1919 and test flown just once in 1920, the F.K.27 was a civil racing and aerobatic development of the Bantam series with a sesquiplane wing cellule and side-by-side accommodation for two; the type's data included the powerplant of one ABC Wasp II radial engine rated at 200 hp (149 kW), maximum speed of 142 mph (229 km/h), initial climb rate of 2,500 ft (762 m) per minute, wingspan of 26 ft (7.92 m), length of 20 ft 7 in (6.27 m), height of 7 ft 10 in (2.39 m) and wing area of 200.00 sq ft (18.58 m²)

BAT F.K.24 Baboon

Designed as a rugged but simple basic training aircraft, the Baboon was originally taken on by the RAF, before being raced.

Drawing on experience gained with the Bantam, the BAT design team, headed by Frederick Koolhoven with Robert Noorduyn as his chief assistant, created an elementary flying trainer

as a two-bay biplane known as the **BAT F.K.24 Baboon**. Gone were the sleek, rounded lines of the

Bantam, the Baboon instead having a simple flat-sided fuselage for ease of manufacture.

SPECIFICATION

BAT F.K.24 Baboon
Type: two-seat elementary flying trainer
Powerplant: one ABC Wasp I radial engine rated at 170 hp (127 kW)
Performance: maximum speed 90 mph (145 km/h) at sea level; climb to 10,000 ft (3050 m) in 12 minutes; endurance 2 hours
Weights: empty 950 lb (431 kg); maximum take-off 1,350 lb (612 kg)
Dimensions: wingspan 25 ft (7.62 m); length 22 ft 8 in (6.91 m); height 8 ft 10 in (2.69 m); wing area 259.00 sq ft (24.06 m²)

No attempt was made to fair or cowl the ABC Wasp radial engine, which was simply bolted to the fire-wall. Maintenance and repair costs were also to be minimised by the use of interchangeable upper and lower wing panels, ailerons, elevators and rudder.

A total of six aircraft was planned but, in fact, only one appears to have been completed in July 1918. Civil-registered to the British Aerial Transport Co. Ltd in May 1919, the Baboon scored its only sporting success on 26 July 1919 when, in the hands of Major Christopher Draper, it won the Hendon Trophy Race over a 20-mile (32-km) course which ran from Hendon to Bittacy Hill and back. It was eventually scrapped at Hendon during 1920.

BAT F.K.25 Basilisk

The last single-seat fighter designed for the British Aerial Transport Co. Ltd by Frederick Koolhoven, the **BAT F.K.25 Basilisk** was an altogether more potent machine than its predecessors, the closely related F.K.22 and F.K.23 Bantam, as it was created around the ABC Dragonfly, a radial unit schemed at ratings of more than 300 hp (224 kW). The Basilisk was derived conceptually from the Bantam, however, inasmuch as it was of typical wooden construction with a semi-monocoque fuselage, a two-bay unstaggered wing cellule of the equal-span type. It also had tailskid land-ing gear in which the main wheels were carried by half-axles extending downward and outward from the lower fuselage with their ends moving in slots at the closed ends of two Vee struts extending vertically below the wing in line with the inner pairs of parallel inter-plane struts. A notable difference was the hood-like fairing on the upper part of the forward fuselage; this covered the guns and provided a measure of protection for the pilot.

Three prototypes of the Basilisk were ordered, and the first of these made the type's maiden flight in the summer of 1918. The

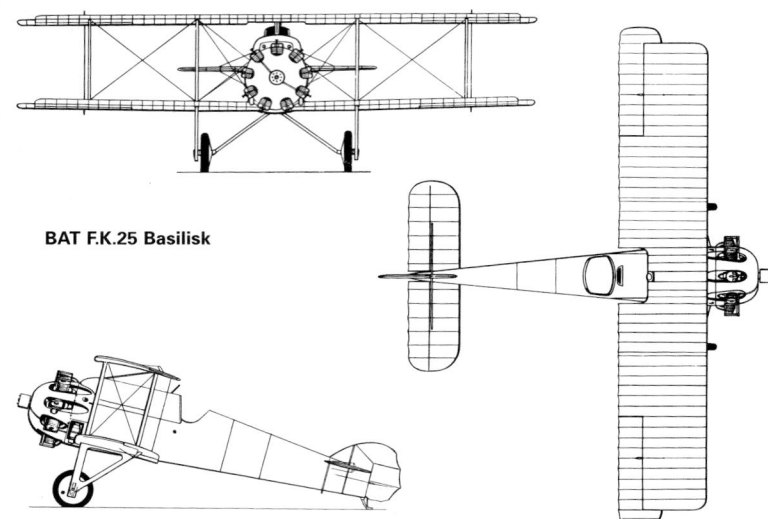

BAT F.K.25 Basilisk

second prototype was completed and flown in 1919 and differed from the first machine in its deeper hood element and its horn-balanced rather than plain ailerons. Along with the third prototype, the second aircraft continued to fly on

F2906, the unfortunate first prototype Basilisk, was lost during an attempt on the world altitude record in May 1919, due to an engine fire.

trials work at Martlesham Heath between July 1919 and September 1920. Development was finally terminated when the aircraft were grounded due to the gross unreliability of their Dragonfly engines.

SPECIFICATION	
BAT F.K.25 Basilisk	endurance 3 hours 15 minutes
Type: single-seat fighter	**Weights:** empty 1,454 lb (659 kg);
Powerplant: one ABC Dragonfly I	maximum take-off 2,182 lb (990 kg)
radial engine rated at 320 hp	**Dimensions:** wingspan 25 ft 4 in
(239 kW)	(7.72 m); length 20 ft 5 in (6.22 m);
Performance: maximum speed	height 8 ft 2 in (2.49 m); wing area
142 mph (228 km/h) at 6,500 ft	212.00 sq ft (19.69 m²)
(1980 m); climb to 10,000 ft	**Armament:** two 0.303-in (7.7-mm)
(3050 m) in 8 minutes 24 seconds;	Vickers fixed forward-firing
service ceiling 22,500 ft (6860 m);	machine-guns

BAT F.K.26

As World War I drew to a close, the thoughts of many manufacturers turned to the development of aircraft for civil transport duties, and the **BAT F.K.26** (designed by Frederick Koolhoven) could lay claim to being the first post-war machine specifically designed for the role. The airframe was of wooden construction covered with fabric, and its capacious fuselage provided accom-modation for four passengers in a cabin 8-ft (2.44-m) long, above and behind which sat the pilot in an open cockpit.

Built at BAT's Willesden, London factory, the proto-type made its first flight at Hendon in April 1919, closely followed by a second aircraft which appeared at the First Air Traffic Exhibition, held in Amsterdam in July of that year. The third machine, which adopted the desig-nation **BAT Commercial Mk 1**, was shown at the Olympia Aero Show in July 1920 and the fourth, manufactured in November 1919, had the distinction of being the last aircraft completed before BAT closed its doors, later serving with the Instone Air Line on services to Paris.

SPECIFICATION	
BAT F.K.26	per minute; service ceiling 8,000 ft
Type: one-crew civil transport	(2440 m); range 600 miles (966 km)
Powerplant: one Rolls-Royce	**Weights:** maximum take-off
Eagle VII Vee engine rated at	4,500 lb (2041 kg)
350 hp (261 kW)	**Dimensions:** wingspan 46 ft
Performance: maximum speed	(14.02 m); length 34 ft 8 in
122 mph (196 km/h) at sea level;	(10.57 m); height 11 ft 3 in (3.43 m)
initial climb rate 1,000 ft (305 m)	**Payload:** up to four passengers

Contemporary reports suggest that Koolhoven positioned the pilot above and behind the passenger cabin in order to increase his chances of survival in a crash, since he would be the only person on board capable of giving an accurate account of the event.

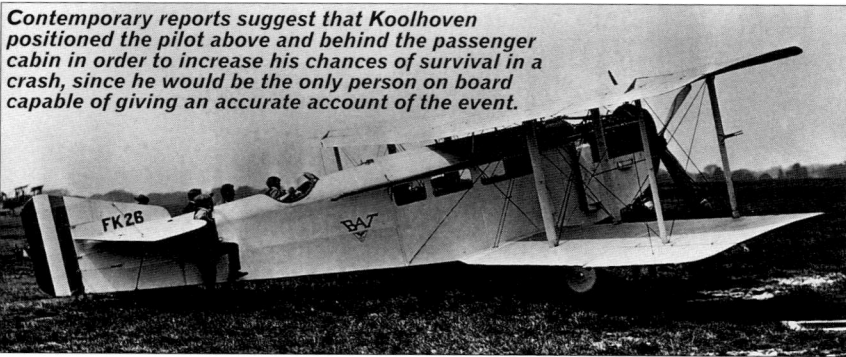

Baumann B-250 and Baumann B-290 Brigadier

Produced in modest numbers during the 1950s, the **Baumann B-290 Brigadier** light transport was a product of the Baumann Aircraft Corporation. The origin of the type can be found in the **B-250** prototype that first flew in June 1947 as a mid/shoulder-wing cantilever monoplane of light alloy construction with a semi-monocoque fuse-lage, plain tail unit, retractable tricycle landing gear, and a powerplant of two Continental C125 hori-zontally-opposed engines, each rated at 125 hp (93 kW). The engines were installed in wing-mounted nacelles and drove two-bladed pusher propellers with prominent spinners.

The B-250 handled adequately but was clearly somewhat underpowered, so the B-290 that entered limited production in 1952 switched to a higher-rated powerplant for improved performance. Even so, the type failed to attract major interest despite its radical appearance and compara-tively spacious accommodation in the large cabin located ahead of the wing's leading edge.

Baumann B-250 and Baumann B-290 Brigadier (cont.)

The configuration of the Brigadier may have been too radical for the 1950s US market, since the aircraft proved to be a commercial disaster.

SPECIFICATION	
Baumann B-290 Brigadier **Type:** light civil transport **Powerplant:** two Continental C145 flat-four engines each rated at 145 hp (108 kW) **Performance:** maximum speed 190 mph (306 km/h) at optimum altitude; cruising speed 165 mph (266 km/h) at optimum altitude; initial climb rate 1,200 ft (366 m)	per minute **Weights:** empty 2,150 lb (975 kg); maximum take-off 3,500 lb (1588 kg) **Dimensions:** wingspan 41 ft (12.50 m); length 27 ft 5 in (8.36 m); height 10 ft 4 in (31.5 m); wing area 207.00 sq ft (19.23 m²) **Accommodation:** four passengers

Beagle A.109 Airedale

On 16 April 1961, after Auster Aircraft had become Beagle-Auster Aircraft, the first flight of the **Beagle A.109 Airedale** took place. Clearly modelled on the unflown **Auster C.4**

Atlantic, the Airedale differed mainly in having a swept tail fin. Being based on earlier Auster models, however, the Airedale inherited their faults as well as their virtues, and was

thus characterised by a high structure weight, an enormous external exhaust system, multiple struts and fabric covering. As a result, the machine was no match for the contemporary Cessna Model 172 and Model 175s, to name only two of its rivals.

Just 43 Airedales were built, with the standard powerplant of one Avco Lycoming O-360-A1A horizontally-opposed engine. At the time of the prototype's first flight, aircraft with an engine or major items of equipment from the USA could not participate in the SBAC Display at

Farnborough. This was considered by Beagle to be of such importance that the prototype was re-engined with a Rolls-Royce (Continental) GO-300 engine, rated at 175 hp (130 kW), so that it could fly at Farnborough, and in this form the aircraft was the sole **A.111**.

SPECIFICATION	
Beagle A.109 Airedale **Type:** four-seat touring and sporting aircraft **Powerplant:** one Avco Lycoming O-360-A1A flat-four engine rated at 180 hp (134 kW) **Performance:** maximum speed 148 mph (233 km/h) at sea level; cruising speed 141 mph (227 km/h) at 5,000 ft (1525 m); initial climb	rate 650 ft (198 m) per minute; service ceiling 14,000 ft (4540 m); range 650 miles (1040 km) **Weights:** empty 1,630 lb (739 kg); maximum take-off 2,650 lb (1202 kg) **Dimensions:** wingspan 36 ft 4 in (11.07 m); length 26 ft 4 in (8.03 m); height 10 ft (3.05 m); wing area 185.00 sq ft (17.19 m²)

A somewhat overweight design, in production form the Airedale benefited from modifications to its furnishings and other equipment to reduce weight. Just 43 aircraft were completed.

Beagle A.113 Husky

The **Beagle A.113 Husky** was introduced in May 1963 as a rugged multipurpose version of the Auster D.5/180. Although named Husky by Beagle,

the aircraft was more often known as the **Beagle D.5/180** by virtue of its powerplant of one 180-hp (134-kW) Avco Lycoming O-360-A2A engine.

The first Husky was lost during ski demonstrations to the Swiss army in October 1963, but was followed by 14 production aircraft. Before the appearance of the definitive Husky, OGMA in Portugal had completed five of its D.5/160 aircraft (part of a large licensed production batch) to D.5/180 standard with the Avco Lycoming engine for use in agricultural work.

Huskies were used in Ghana and the UK for glider-towing, and one was presented to the Air Training Corps for air experience flights as XW635 *Spirit of Butlins*.

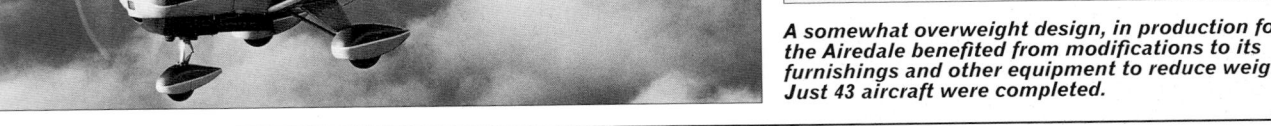

Only two Huskies were officially known as D.5/180 Huskies by the manufacturer, including the company demonstrator, G-ASBV. The other was an aircraft supplied to a Portuguese customer.

SPECIFICATION	
Beagle A.113 Husky **Type:** three-seat general-purpose aircraft **Powerplant:** one Avco Lycoming O-360-A2A flat-four engine rated at 180 hp (134 kW) **Performance:** maximum speed 125 mph (201 km/h) at sea level; cruising speed 95 mph (153 km/h) at optimum altitude; initial climb	rate 800 ft (244 m) per minute; service ceiling 14,500 ft (4420 m); range 580 miles (933 km) **Weights:** empty 1,416 lb (642 kg); maximum take-off 2,400 lb (1089 kg) **Dimensions:** wingspan 36 ft (10.97 m); length 23 ft 2 in (7.06 m); height 8 ft 8 in (2.64 m); wing area 185.00 sq ft (17.19 m²)

Beagle B.206 Basset

Beagle's first completely original design was the attractive **Beagle B.206**. The type made its maiden flight on 15 August 1961 as the **B.206X** prototype with five-seat accommodation and the powerplant of two 260-hp (194-kW) Continental engines. Of all-metal construction, the aircraft made its public debut at the Farnborough

Air Show during the following month, but Beagle then had second thoughts about the accommodation and enlarged the design to create the **B.206Y** that first flew on 12 August 1962 with seven-seat accommodation. The wingspan was increased and the powerplant altered to geared rather than direct-drive

Continental engines.

The first order was for the **B.206R** military version (designated B.206Z in prototype form), of which a total of 20 were delivered to the RAF from May 1965 for service with the designation **Basset CC.Mk 1**.

The first production example of the civil **B.206 Series 1** flew on 17 July 1964 with two 310-hp (231-kW) Rolls-Royce (Continental) IO-470-D flat-

XS766 was the second production Basset CC.Mk 1. In addition to standard communications duties, the Bassets were also tasked with the transport of V-bomber crews to dispersed bases.

six engines, and the first delivery was made to Rolls-Royce on 13 May 1965. Eleven Series 1 aircraft were built and, of these, two were later converted to **B.206 Series 2** standard.

Production of the B.206 Series 2 amounted to 47 aircraft. Two aircraft were delivered to the Royal Flying Doctor Service in Sydney, Australia, each being outfitted for the carriage of two stretcher cases, a doctor and an attendant. The main difference between the B.206 Series 1 and Series 2 (in prototype form **B.206S**) was the latter's uprated powerplant of two Rolls-

Royce (Continental) supercharged engines, although other refinements included extra windows and a freight door.

Other B.206 aircraft were found to be suitable for instrument flying training. Three **B.206 Series 3**

machines had a deeper rear fuselage and accommodation for 10 people, but this version was not developed further. Production of the B.206 came to an end in 1969 after the completion of 85 aircraft.

With the B.206, Beagle managed to combine a streamlined fuselage with a roomy cabin. The aircraft's instrument panel was wider than that of a Viscount airliner! G-ATYX was a B.206 Series 2.

SPECIFICATION

Beagle B.206 Series 2	per minute; service ceiling
Type: five/eight-seat light transport	27,100 ft (8260 m); range 1,600 miles (2575 km)
Powerplant: two Rolls-Royce (Continental) GTSIO-520-C flat-six engines each rated at 340 hp (254 kW)	**Weights:** empty 4,800 lb (2177 kg); maximum take-off 7,499 lb (3401 kg)
Performance: maximum speed 258 mph (415 km/h) at 16,000 ft (4875 m); cruising speed 218 mph (351 km/h) at 8,000 ft (2440 m); initial climb rate 1,340 ft (408 m)	**Dimensions:** wingspan 45 ft 9½ in (13.96 m); length 33 ft 8 in (10.26 m); height 11 ft 4 in (3.45 m); wing area 214.00 sq ft (19.88 m²)

Beardmore Inflexible

Having acquired a licence for the use of the Rohrbach principles of stressed-skin construction, in 1925 William Beardmore & Co. Ltd received an order for two large flying-boats and a larger landplane. The flying-boats, each powered by two Napier Lion engines,

were built by Rohrbach Metal Aeroplane Co. A/S in Copenhagen and delivered to Felixstowe for evaluation. They were given the type name **Beardmore Inverness**.

In the UK, Beardmore's W. S. 'Bill' Shackleton was given the design responsi-

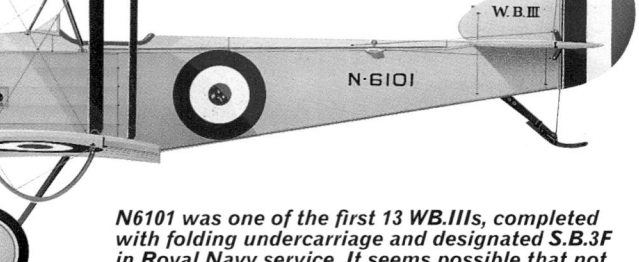

bility for the then-massive **Beardmore Inflexible** landplane. The components for the Inflexible were moved by road to the A&AEE at Martlesham Heath for erection and, on 5 March 1928, the machine completed its maiden flight. This confirmed that the

Constructed under the civil registration G-EBNG, the Inflexible ended its days as a testbed for the investigation of corrosion.

Inflexible was far too heavy for its powerplant of three Rolls-Royce Condor engines.

The machine appeared in the RAF Display at Hendon

on 30 June 1928 and was finally dismantled at Martlesham during 1930, ending its days as a test airframe for the investigation of corrosion.

SPECIFICATION

Beardmore Inflexible	altitude
Type: heavy transport aircraft	**Weights:** maximum take-off 37,000 lb (16783 kg)
Powerplant: three Rolls-Royce Condor II Vee engines each rated at 650 hp (485 kW)	**Dimensions:** wingspan 157 ft 6 in (48.01 m); length 75 ft 6 in (23.01 m)
Performance: maximum speed 109 mph (175 km/h) at optimum	

Beardmore WB.III

Beardmore was building the Sopwith Pup under licence when the RNAS decided to order a development of the type for shipboard use. In order to reduce the hangar space requirement, the company developed a version of the Pup with an unstaggered wing cellule that incorporated folding outer panels

under the designation **Beardmore WB.III**. The prototype was the last of a batch of Pups manufactured at Beardmore's Dalmuir factory, and its other changes from Pup standard included a lengthened fuselage modified to carry emergency flotation gear, a main landing gear unit designed to fold into

N6101 was one of the first 13 WB.IIIs, completed with folding undercarriage and designated S.B.3F in Royal Navy service. It seems possible that not all of the WB.IIIs ordered were actually built.

Variants

S.B.3F: designation of the first 13 production aircraft with a tripod-mounted 0.303-in (7.7-mm) Lewis machine-gun arranged to fire upward through a cut-out in the upper-wing centre section
S.B.3D: designation of the aircraft from the 14th machine onward with a jettisonable main landing gear unit, deletion of the wing-root interplane struts and introduction of conventional cable-operated ailerons without connecting struts; a 0.303-in (7.7-mm) Lewis forward-firing machine-gun was mounted above the upper-wing centre section

the bottom of the fuselage and modified bracing struts.

The prototype was officially accepted on 7 February 1917, and 100 production aircraft were ordered under the designation **Beardmore S.B.3** for service that included deployment on the aircraft carriers HMS *Furious*, *Nairana* and *Pegasus*.

SPECIFICATION

Beardmore WB.III	endurance 2 hours 45 minutes
Type: single-seat shipboard fighter	**Weights:** empty 890 lb (404 kg); maximum take-off 1,289 lb (585 kg)
Powerplant: one Le Rhône 9C or Clerget rotary engine rated at 80 hp (60 kW)	**Dimensions:** wingspan 25 ft (7.62 m); length 20 ft 2½ in (6.16 m); height 8 ft 1¼ in (2.47 m); wing area 243.00 sq ft (22.57 m²)
Performance: maximum speed 103 mph (166 km/h) at sea level; climb to 6,500 ft (1980 m) in 12 minutes 10 seconds; service ceiling 12,400 ft (3780 m);	**Armament:** one 0.303-in (7.7-mm) Lewis fixed forward-firing machine-gun

Bede aircraft

After just over two years as a performance engineer with North American Aviation James R. Bede, together with his father

James A. Bede, established Bede Aviation Corporation in 1960. Jim Bede (the younger) planned to design aircraft that

would bring aviation to a growing number of enthusiasts who wanted to build and fly their own aircraft. He also patented his own

method of Panel-Rib wing construction.

The result of this, together with other ideas that made construction very undemanding, led to a 17-year success story. Sadly the company, by then

called Bede Aviation Inc., collapsed in 1977 as a result of financial problems. During the intervening years Jim Bede produced a succession of brilliant designs, and brief details of these are given below.

Bede aircraft (continued)

Bede aircraft

BD-1: An all-metal two-seat sporting aircraft. The prototype was flown for the first time on 11 July 1963, and design rights were later acquired by American Aviation Corporation for development as a successful family of aircraft known as the **Yankee**, **Trainer** and **Traveler**. This company later became a subsidiary of the Grumman Corporation and was named Grumman American Corporation; it continued to produce the Trainer and Traveler

BD-2: Designed on the basis of the airframe of the Schweizer SGS 2-32 two-seat high-performance sailplane, the BD-2 was intended to be used for an unrefuelled round-the-world flight attempt. Carrying 470.5 Imp gal (565 US gal; 2139 litres) of fuel, the BD-2 was powered by a specially-modified Continental IO-360-C flat-six engine that could provide 225 hp (168 kW) for take-off, and as little as 30 hp (22.4 kW) in cruising flight at 20,000 ft (6095 m). A long-distance trial was made between 7 and 10 November 1969, during which a distance of 8,974 miles (14442 km) was covered in a non-stop flight time of 70 hours 15 minutes. The flight was terminated by a total electrical failure, and pressure of events prevented Jim Bede from making further progress with this remarkable aircraft

HB-1 Super Demoiselle: So named because of the similarity of its configuration to that of the Demoiselle built by aviation pioneer Alberto Santos-Dumont, the HB-1 was the first of Jim Bede's designs to introduce his Panel-Rib wing construction

BD-4: A two/four-seat all-metal sporting/utility aircraft, with Panel-Rib wing construction. Equipped with non-retractable tricycle landing gear and a roomy enclosed cabin. Well over 2,000 sets of plans had been sold when the company ceased trading

BD-6: A smaller, single-seat lightweight development of the BD-4

BD-7: A two/four-seat version of the BD-5, flown in prototype form in December 1976 with a pusher propeller. The BD-6, BD-7 and projected **BD-8** single-seat aerobatic machine did not advance any further because of the company's involvement with the BD-5 programme

BD-10: In the early 1990s Jim Bede created the Bede Jet Corporation to market plans and kits for the BD-4, and then moved forward to the design of the BD-10 as the world's first home-built type capable of supersonic speed. This resembled the F-15 Eagle in basic configuration although with a straight wing spanning 21 ft 6 in (6.55 m), and was a single-seat machine with pressurised accommodation. Power was provided by one General Electric CJ-610 turbojet engine rated at 2,950 lb st (13.12 kN), for an anticipated maximum speed of Mach 1.4. The prototype crashed in December 1994 as a result of tailplane flutter, in the process killing Jim Bede, and further attempts to certificate and market the type in both kit- and factory-built forms as the **Peregrine PJ-2 Falcon** have since failed. Bede Jet retains the rights for military developments of the BD-10 design, and is still seeking to secure orders for the **Monitor Jet MJ-7** that would be built in Canada for the training and unmanned target roles

BD-12: While continuing in its efforts to secure an initial order for the Monitor Jet MJ-7, Bede Jet has developed the BD-12 as a low-wing monoplane of extremely sleek lines with single-seat accommodation, fixed tricycle landing gear and the powerplant of one 150-hp (112-kW) Textron Lycoming O-320-E2D flat-four engine driving a pusher propeller. This engine creates the **BD-12C** subvariant, and other models offered are the **BD-12A** with an 80-hp (60-kW) engine and the **BD-12B** with a 100-hp (75-kW) engine

BD-14: A planned development of the BD-12 with a somewhat higher-rated powerplant

BD-5 Micro variants

BD-5 Micro: A revolutionary single-seat high-performance lightplane, over 5,000 orders were received for plans and kits of the Micro. It was this aircraft, and the proliferation of models and their associated problems, that brought financial disaster to Bede

BD-5A: prototype with low-set monoplane wing, butterfly tail unit, and 40-hp (30-kW) engine. First flown on 12 September 1971

BD-5B: originally an alternative to the BD-5A with a wing of greater span, but from 1974 revised with the butterfly tail replaced by a conventional unit, and a 70-hp (52-kW) engine

BD-5C: improved fully aerobatic version of BD-5B with reduced wingspan

BD-5D: factory-built production version of BD-5C

BD-5S: increased-span sailplane prototype flown in 1975

BD-5J: piston engine replaced by a small turbojet

BD-5JP: factory-built version of BD-5J which did not enter production

An aircraft of outstanding design and performance, the BD-10 has stumbled not only over the problems associated with private owners acquiring a Mach 1-plus capable aircraft, but also over the difficulties inherent in such an aircraft being home-built by amateur constructors.

SPECIFICATION	
Bede BD-5J	25,000 ft (7620 m); range 585 miles
Type: single-seat sporting aircraft	(941 km)
Powerplant: one Microturbo TRS 18 turbojet engine rated at 203 lb st (0.90 kN)	**Weights:** empty 450 lb (204 kg); maximum take-off 960 lb (435 kg)
Performance: maximum speed 276 mph (444 km/h) at sea level; initial climb rate 1,550 ft (472 m) per minute; service ceiling	**Dimensions:** wingspan 17 ft (5.18 m); length 12 ft 4¾ in (3.78 m); height 6 ft (1.83 m); wing area 37.80 sq ft (3.50 m²)

A functional if somewhat angular design, the BD-4 proved exceptionally popular with home builders. The aircraft utilised the Panel-Rib method of construction, which employed a tubular wing spar of light alloy over which were slid preformed glassfibre panel ribs that were then secured in position by epoxy resin and special tube clamps.

Beech Model 17 'Staggerwing'

Together with his wife Olive, Walter Beech established the Beech Aircraft Corporation during 1932. Late in 1950 Beech died, but was succeeded as chairman by Mrs Olive Beech who continued in this position into the early 1990s. By this time, the company had been fully absorbed into Raytheon, which had owned it since 1980.

A key to the company's early success was the **Beech Model 17**, although the high performance of the initial **Model 17R**, of which only two examples were built, meant that it was a machine for experienced pilots, and unsuitable for the far wider market that was sought. First flown during November 1932, the Model 17R was able to demonstrate a remarkable speed range of 60-200 mph (97-322 km/h). The most conspicuous feature of its configuration was the backward stagger of its biplane wing cellule. This layout had been selected to provide the pilot with a good field of view, to help structural integration, and because wind tunnel tests had shown that this particular layout offered a good combination of speed and stability. The basic structure was of welded steel tube, covered largely with fabric. The narrow-track tailwheel landing gear was unusual in that the main units were enclosed within large streamlined fairings, with provision for the wheels to be retracted in flight so that they were completely within the fairings. Enclosed cabin accommodation was provided for a pilot and three or four passengers, and the 420-hp (313-kW) Wright R-975-E2 Whirlwind radial engine was mounted within a

This beautifully restored Model 17 was pictured in 1985 wearing a Canadian registration. The aircraft is resplendent in Beech house colours.

tunnel-type cowling.

The excellent performance of the 'Staggerwing', as the type became popularly known, meant that the company's efforts were now concentrated upon making it easier to handle, especially on the ground, which led to a number of improvements including wider-track main landing gear units. However, the real turning point to wider market acceptance came with the **Model B17L**, first flown in late February 1934. This introduced a new lower wing of deeper aerofoil section, providing sufficient volume for the main landing gear units to be retracted fully into it. This, coupled with a 225-hp (168-kW) Jacobs L-4 radial engine, gave much more docile handling characteristics, while retaining a speed range of 45-175 mph (72-282 km/h). With just a little more power, provided by the 285-hp (213-kW) Jacobs L-5, the Model 17 allowed Beech to establish itself as a major aircraft manufacturer.

From that time a wide variety of 'Staggerwings' were built for both civil and military use in a steadily improved series of variants with a number of different engines. The civil versions included the **Model B17**, **Model C17**, **Model D17**, **Model E17** and **Model F17** variants before World War II, which were followed in the early post-war years by a much improved **Model G17S**, of which only 20 were built.

When, in 1939, the US Army Air Corps needed a small communications aircraft, the excellent performance of the Model 17 resulted in the procurement of three Model D17 machines for evaluation under the designation **YC-43**. However, it was not until the expansion of the USAAF began during 1941-2 that an initial production order for 27 was placed. This led to a total procurement of 207 Beech 17 aircraft under the designation **UC-43** with the powerplant of one 450-hp (336-kW) Pratt & Whitney

R-985-AN-1 engine. After the USA became involved in World War II, an additional 118 civil Model 17 aircraft were impressed for military service, these impressments comprising **Model D17R, D17S, F17D, E17B, C17R, D17A, C17B, B17R, C17L,** and **D17W** variants under the designations **UC-43A, UC-43B, UC-43C, UC-43D, UC-43E, UC-43F, UC-43G, UC-43H, UC-43J** and **UC-43K,** respectively.

The US Navy had acquired a single example of the 'Staggerwing' as early as 1939, this being a civil Model C17R which was designated as the **JB-1**. The designation **GB-1** was applied to 10 more aircraft (equivalent to the civil Model D17) acquired in 1939 and, later, to eight civil Model D17 machines impressed for military service. Wartime procurement totalled 342 **GB-2** aircraft, of which 105 were supplied to the UK under Lend-Lease, used primarily by the Royal Navy which named them **Traveller**, a name adopted also by the US Navy.

SPECIFICATION

Beech Model G17S
Type: four/five-seat light transport
Powerplant: one Pratt & Whitney R-985-AN-4 Wasp Junior radial engine rated at 450 hp (336 kW)
Performance: maximum speed 212 mph (341 km/h) at optimum altitude; cruising speed 185 mph (298 km/h) at 9,500 ft (2895 m); initial climb rate 1,250 ft (381 m) per minute; climb to 15,000 ft (4570 m) in just over 15 minutes; service ceiling 20,000 ft (6095 m); range about 1,000 miles (1609 km)
Weights: empty 2,800 lb (1270 kg); maximum take-off 4,250 lb (1928 kg)
Dimensions: wingspan 32 ft (9.75 m); length 26 ft 9 in (8.15 m); height 8 ft (2.44 m); wing area 296.50 sq ft (27.54 m²)

Beech Model 18

In 1935 Beech began the development of a six/eight-seat commercial transport identified as the **Beech Model 18**. The aircraft was to be a low-wing cantilever monoplane of all-metal construction with a semi-monocoque fuselage, a cantilever tail unit incorporating twin endplate vertical surfaces, and electrically retractable tailwheel landing gear. Float or ski landing gear were later added as options. Standard accommodation was provided for two crew and six passengers, and the initial powerplant installation comprised two 320-hp (239-kW) Wright R-760-E2 Whirlwind radial engines mounted in wing leading-edge nacelles. The initial **Model 18A** flew for the first time on 15 January 1937 and the type would remain in production for a record 32 years. Later, it proved a popular choice for conversion by a number of American companies, with

modifications intended to provide improved performance or greater capacity.

Like the Model 18A, however, the improved **Model 18B** with lower-powered engines sold in only small numbers, and the first sign that the company was on the right track came with the **Model 18D** of 1939. This had 330-hp (246-kW) Jacobs L-6 engines for improved performance, and had much the same economy of operation as the Model 18B. Only about 30 of these were sold in 1940, but the wartime demand for these aircraft then totalled more than 4,000 machines.

The first USAAC order, placed during 1940, was for the supply of 11 aircraft, similar to the civil **Model B18S**, for service as **C-45** staff transports. Subsequent procurement covered 20 **C-45A** machines for use in the utility transport role, and several interior and equip-

Beech introduced the civil D18S during 1947 as a six/nine-seat executive transport. Buyers paid $63,000 for a standard aircraft.

ment changes were made in the 223 **C-45B** machines that followed. Some of these aircraft were supplied to the UK under Lend-Lease, being designated **Expediter Mk I** in RAF service. The USAAF designations **C-45C, C-45D** and **C-45E** were applied respectively to two impressed Model B18S civil aircraft, two **AT-7** machines completed for transport duties, and six **AT-7B** machines similarly modified. The final, and indeed major, production version for the USAAF was the seven-seat **C-45F** with a slightly longer nose: no fewer than 1,137 of these were built. Lend-Lease deliveries from this procurement served with the Royal Navy and RAF as **Expediter Mk II** aircraft, and with the RCAF as **Expediter Mk III** aircraft. All of the foregoing C-45

designations were changed to the new **UC-45** category in January 1943.

In 1941 two dedicated trainer versions appeared as the **AT-7 Navigator** navigation trainer, of which 577 were built, and the **AT-11 Kansan** air gunnery and bombing trainer, production of which reached 1,582 examples. The last of the USAAF's versions of the Model 18 in World War II were photographic reconnaissance **F-2** machines: 14 civil Model B18S aircraft were purchased and converted with cabin-mounted mapping cameras and oxygen equipment. They were supplemented later by 13 **F-2A** conversions from C-45A standard with four cameras, and by 42

F-2B conversions from UC-45F standard (these had additional camera ports in both sides of the fuselage). In June 1948, under a general revision of the USAF designation system, all of the surviving F-2 photo/reconnaissance aircraft received the revised designation **RC-45A**. At the same time, a small number of drone directors – converted from UC-45F standard and given the designation **CQ-3** – became **DC-45F** machines.

The US Navy and US Marine Corps also used more than 1,500 examples of the Model 18. Initial procurement related to a version similar to the US Army's F-2, this being designated **JRB-1**, and followed by a **JRB-2** transport, and **JRB-3** and **JRB-4** aircraft equivalent to the USAAF/USAF C-45B and UC-45F, respectively.

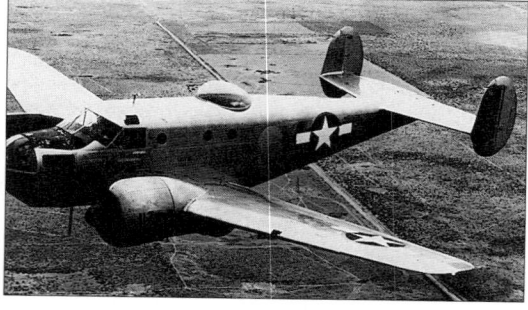

A specialised bomb-aimer trainer, the AT-11 featured a glazed nose. The type was unofficially named Kansan.

Beech Model 18 Continued

The US Navy ambulance and photographic versions of the Model 18 were the **SNB-2H** and **SNB-2P** respectively, while the **SNB-3Q** was configured as an electronic countermeasures trainer.

During 1951-52 all UC-45, AT-7 and AT-11 aircraft remaining in service with the USAF were remanufactured to zero-time condition and modernised, emerging with the new designations **C-45G** and **C-45H**. The former variant was fitted with an autopilot and R-985-AN-3 engines, and the latter with no autopilot and R-985-AN-14B engines. At the same time, US Navy SNB-2, SNB-2C and SNB-2P aircraft were remanufactured under the designations **SNB-5** and **SNB-5P**. Later, with the introduction of the tri-service unified designation scheme in 1962, in-service SNB aircraft were redesignated **TC-45J** and **RC-45J** respectively in the training and photographic roles.

With a return to peace, Beech resumed manufacture of the civil Model 18,

and in 1953 introduced a new larger and improved version of the D18S as the **Model E18S**, known as the **Super 18**. The prototype, with a number of structural improvements, was flown for the first time on 10 December 1953. Progressive improvement continued throughout the production of 754 Super 18 aircraft, the last examples of the final **Model H18** version being built during 1969.

In September 1963 Beech introduced optional retractable tricycle landing gear developed by Volpar Inc. of Los Angeles, California. This company also offered conversions of standard Beech 18s to **Volpar Turbo 18** standard with tricycle landing gear and Garrett TPE331 turboprops, and also the lengthened turboprop-powered 15-passenger **Volpar Turboliner**. Conversions offered by other manufacturers have included the nine-passenger **Dumod I** and 15-passenger **Dumod Liner** from the Dumod Corporation; and Pacific

Airmotive Corporation's 10-passenger **PAC Tradewind** and turboprop-powered **PAC Turbo Tradewind**. Available from Hamilton Aviation in the early 1980s were the **Hamilton Westwind II STD** and **Westwind III** turboprop-powered conversions, with accommodation for 17 and eight passengers, respectively.

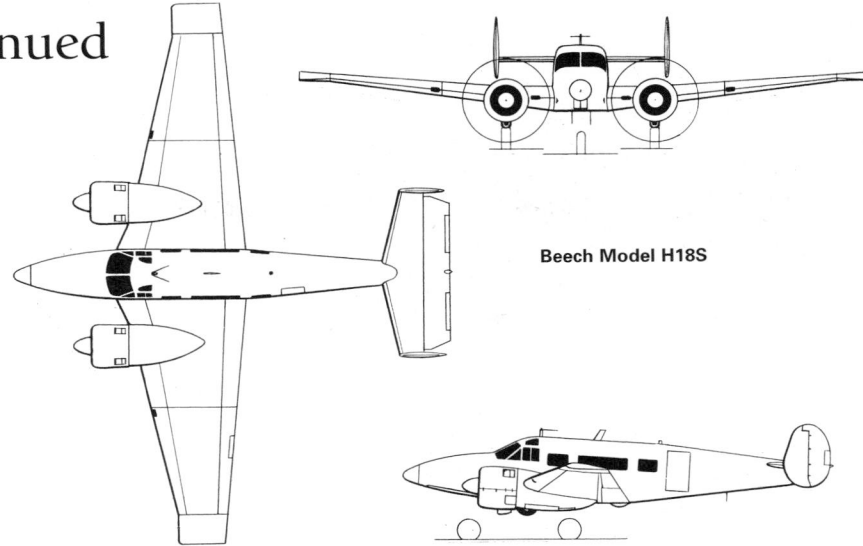

Beech Model H18S

Beech Model 23 Musketeer Sierra, Sport and Sundowner

On 23 October 1961 the prototype of a low-cost all-metal light business transport type to be known as the **Beech Model 23 Musketeer** was flown for the first time. The machine was of low-wing cantilever monoplane configuration with a fuselage providing enclosed cabin accommodation for a pilot and three passengers. It featured fixed tricycle landing gear, and the powerplant of the first production version – which was delivered from the autumn of 1962 – consisted of a single

160-hp (119-kW) Avco Lycoming O-320-D2B flat-four piston engine.

The early popularity of the type resulted in three Musketeer variants being marketed from late 1965. Identified as the **Musketeer Custom**, the two-seat (optional four-seat) **Musketeer Sport** and **Musketeer Super**, these differed mainly in their powerplant of one Avco Lycoming engine rated at 180, 150 and 200 hp (134, 112 and 149 kW) respectively. Optional aerobatic kits were also available for

the Musketeer Custom and Musketeer Sport when flown as two-seaters. A fourth version was introduced in late 1969 as the **Musketeer Super R**, which was a Musketeer Super with retractable tricycle landing gear.

A further change in marketing policy in 1971 resulted in the disappearance of the name Musketeer and, at the same time, production of the Musketeer Super was discontinued. The three remaining aircraft became known instead as the **Sundowner C23** (formerly Custom), **Sport R19** (Sport) and **Sierra A24R** (Super R). The designations were changed once more in 1974 to indicate engine horsepower, the three types becoming respectively **Sundowner 180**, **Sport 150** and **Sierra 200**. Manufacture of the Sport ended in 1978, but the Sundowner 180 and Sierra 200 remained in production into the mid-1980s, by which time well over 5,000 Musketeers of all types had been built.

Generally similar to the Model A23A Musketeer Custom III, the Model A23-24 Musketeer Super III (illustrated) was powered by a 200-hp (149-kW) IO-360-A2B engine.

Although primarily a four-seat tourer, the Sundowner can be flown as a two-seat aerobatic machine. In the latter role, the aircraft is cleared for Immelmann turns, loops, spins and a range of other manoeuvres.

Beech Model 26

The rapid expansion of US training facilities in 1941 created an urgent requirement for large numbers of trainer aircraft at a time when it seemed likely that

raw materials, notably aluminium and magnesium alloys, might have to be conserved for first-line types. Beech then created the **Model 26** as the first

all-wood trainer to be accepted by the USAAF, in this instance for service with the designation **AT-10 Wichita**. The design was optimised for sub-contraction to wood-working firms that were not specialists in the creation of aircraft

assemblies: 85 per cent of the airframe was manufactured on this basis, with final assembly by Beech at its Wichita factory.

For operation as a multi-engine conversion trainer, the Wichita was equipped with dual controls and an

autopilot, and entry to the cockpit was effected by means of rearward-sliding side windows. The AT-10 was powered by two Lycoming R-680 radial engines, and by 1943 Beech had completed four contracts for a total

Access to the AT-10's cockpit was gained via rearward- sliding windows. Around 50 per cent of the USAAF's multi-engined aircraft pilots received instruction on the type.

of 1,771 aircraft completed at Wichita. The last of these was delivered on 15 September 1943, and Beech then supplied engineering and production data to the Globe Aircraft Corporation of Dallas, Texas, so that a further 600 could be manufactured.

SPECIFICATION

Beech AT-10 Wichita
Type: two-seat multi-engined advanced flying trainer
Powerplant: two Lycoming R-680 radial engines each rated at 295 hp (220 kW)
Performance: maximum speed 198 mph (319 km/h) at optimum altitude; climb to 10,000 ft (3050 m) in 12 minutes 42 seconds; service ceiling 16,900 ft (5150 m); range 770 miles (1239 km)
Weights: empty 4,750 lb (2155 kg); maximum take-off 6,130 lb (2781 kg)
Dimensions: wingspan 44 ft (13.41 m); length 34 ft 4 in (10.46 m); wing area 298.00 sq ft (27.68 m²)

Beech Model 28 Destroyer

Two prototypes of this twin-engined attack aircraft were ordered from Beech in 1943 under the designation **XA-38**. Later named **Grizzly**, the **Model 28 Destroyer** was a large low-wing monoplane, with a fuselage accommodating a crew of three. Power was provided by two Wright R-3350 radial engines and, in addition to defensive armament, the Destroyer carried a 2.95-in (75-mm) gun for its attack role. Only the two prototypes were built, being delivered for evaluation in 1945, but no production order followed.

SPECIFICATION

Beech XA-38 Grizzly
Type: three-seat attack aircraft
Powerplant: two Wright R-3350-43 radial engines each rated at 2,300 hp (1715 kW)
Performance: maximum speed 370 mph (596 km/h) at 17,000 ft (5180 m); cruising speed 350 mph (563 km/h) at 16,000 ft (4875 m); initial climb rate 2,600 ft (793 m) per minute; service ceiling 29,000 ft (8840 m); range 1,625 miles (2615 km)
Weights: empty 22,480 lb (10197 kg); maximum take-off 35,265 lb (15996 kg)
Dimensions: wingspan 67 ft 4 in (20.52 m); length 51 ft 9 in (15.77 m); height 15 ft 6 in (4.72 m); wing area 626.00 sq ft (58.16 m²)
Armament: One 2.95-in (75-mm) T15E1 fixed forward-firing gun and two 0.5-in (12.7-mm) Browning fixed forward-firing machine-guns in the nose, two 0.5-in (12.7-mm) Browning trainable rearward/ lateral-firing machine-guns in the power-operated dorsal barbette, and two 0.5-in (12.7-mm) Browning trainable rearward/ lateral-firing machine-guns in the power-operated ventral barbette, plus up to 4,000 lb (1814 kg) of bombs carried on four underwing pylons

During an XA-38 test flight, a brand new P-51B Mustang was unable to match the Grizzly's speed. The latter was able on one occasion to demonstrate a maximum speed of 376.5 mph (604 km/h) at just 3,100 ft (945 m).

Beech Models 33, 35 and 36 Bonanza and Debonair

The **Beech Model 35 Bonanza** was the founder member of a remarkable family of aircraft, not only for the fact that production of Bonanzas of all types amounted to more than 15,000 by late 1981, but also because, at the beginning of that year, the V-tail Bonanza entered its 35th year of production, and continues to be produced in the late 1990s.

Flown for the first time on 22 December 1945, the Model 35 Bonanza prototype, which was notable for its Vee (or butterfly) tail, got off to an encouraging start. When the company announced that full-scale production was to begin in March 1947, it already had a backlog of around 1,500 orders. It was a moment for the benefits of wartime experience to pay off, for about 1,000 deliveries had been made by the end of that year.

The general configuration of the Model 35 has remained virtually unchanged throughout the aircraft's history. A low-wing cantilever monoplane of all-metal construction, including the distinctive tail unit, the Model 35 has an enclosed cabin providing seating for a pilot and three or four passengers. From the outset the Model 35 has had retractable tricycle landing gear and an optional feature throughout the years has been a landing gear safety system of Beech design. Named 'Magic Hand', this ensures that the wheels cannot be retracted accidentally on the ground, or a landing made with the wheels up. As first flown, the Model 35 was powered by a 185-hp (138-kW) Continental E-185-1 flat-six engine, but a variety of standard and optional powerplants have been installed during the long production run. They have included turbocharged units for the **Model V35 TC** and **Model V35B TC**.

Despite the large demand for the Vee-tailed Model 35, there were many potential buyers who considered this tail unit to be something of a gimmick, one that might present problems. To meet the needs of such people, Beech introduced the **Model 33 Debonair**, which first flew on 14 September 1959. With a conventional tail unit and a slightly lower-powered engine, the Debonair accommodated a pilot and three passengers. It represented a lower-cost version of the Bonanza, and was built and marketed in parallel until production of the Debonair, as such, ended in 1966, when almost 1,200 had been built. It was replaced in 1967 by the **Model E33 Bonanza**, a four/five-seat version that was virtually identical to the Vee-tailed Model 35 except for the provision of a conventional tail unit with a swept vertical surface. This version, in **Model F33A** standard and **Model F33C** aerobatic/utility versions, remains available in the late 1990s, by which time production of Model 33 Debonair and Bonanza aircraft was approaching an impressive total of some 4,500.

A third member of the Bonanza family was introduced in 1968 as the **Model 36 Bonanza** six-seat utility aircraft. It is basically a lengthened version of the Model V35B which combines the tail unit of the Model 33 with the strengthened landing gear developed for the Beech Baron. It also has double doors on the starboard side of the fuselage, making it easier to load or unload cargo when used in a utility role. These cargo doors are available optionally for the Model 33 and Model 35 aircraft. A turbocharged version of the Model 36 has been available since 1979 under the designation **Model A36 TC Turbo Bonanza**. Production of Model 36 Bonanzas totalled more than 3,350 aircraft by the late 1990s.

Since the introduction of each of these models, there has been steady improvement of the product, and a wide range of optional avionics and equipment is available for in-production versions.

Variant

Allison Prop-Jet Bonanza: produced by Allison in conjunction with Soloy Conversions Ltd, the Prop-Jet Bonanza was a conversion of the Model A36 Bonanza with the revised powerplant of one 420-hp (313-kW) Allison 250-B17 turboprop installed at the lengthened and strengthened forward section of the fuselage and supplied with fuel from a revised system incorporating finned tip tanks; a modest number of conversions was completed during the late 1970s and early 1980s

Introduced in 1970, the V35B introduced minor improvements over previous models. The Bonanza's V-tail arrangement was originally tested on a converted AT-10.

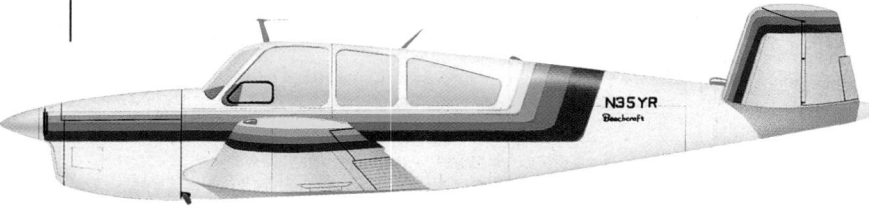

Beech, under the ownership of Raytheon, continued to produce the F33A Bonanza up until 1996. More than 3,300 aircraft were completed.

Beech Models 33, 35 and 36 Bonanza and Debonair (cont.)

Brief mention must be made of two military versions of the Model A36 Bonanza. Under the designation **QU-22B** (company designation **Model PD.1079**), some 27 aircraft were provided with special avionics equipment under the USAF's Pave Eagle programme for deployment in Vietnam to pick up and relay to a ground station the data transmitted from ground-based acoustic sensors. To meet the requirements of the USAF's Pave Coin competition, Beech developed a two-seat close-support armed version of the A36. Built as the Model **PD.249**, this prototype was evaluated as the **YAU-22A** with a wide variety of weapons carried on underwing racks that could accommodate loads of up to 1,180 lb (535 kg), but no production examples were built.

Available from 1981, the Model B36TC Bonanza offered an increase in fuel capacity and long-span wings. The type remains in production in 1998, with as many as 14 units per year being produced.

SPECIFICATION	
Beech Model B36TC Turbo Bonanza	per minute; service ceiling more than 25,000 ft (7620 m); range 1,256 miles (2022 km)
Type: four/six-seat light transport	**Weights:** empty 2,433 lb (1104 kg); maximum take-off 3,850 lb (1746 kg)
Powerplant: one Teledyne Continental TSIO-520-UB flat-six engine rated at 300 hp (224 kW)	**Dimensions:** wingspan 37 ft 10 in (11.53 m); length 27 ft 6 in (8.38 m); height 8 ft 7 in (2.62 m); wing area 188.10 sq ft (17.47 m²)
Performance: maximum speed 245 mph (394 km/h) at 22,000 ft (6705 m); cruising speed 230 mph (370 km/h) at 25,000 ft (7620 m); initial climb rate 1,053 ft (321 m)	

Beech Model 34 Twin-Quad

In 1949-50 Beech completed the prototype of probably the largest and most atypical aircraft built by the company. The machine was a passenger/cargo aircraft providing accommodation for a maximum of 20 passengers plus their baggage, and up to 1,000 lb (454 kg) of cargo or mail. Designated as the **Beech Model 34 Twin-Quad**, the new aircraft was of high-wing monoplane configuration, had a deep and basically rectangular fuselage, an enormous Vee (or butterfly) tail, and retractable tricycle landing gear. Power was provided by four war-surplus Avco Lycoming flat-eight engines, mounted in pairs within the wings, with the output of each pair combined by a special gearbox/automatic clutch to drive one Hamilton Standard, feathering propeller. In addition to the prototype, a second airframe was built for static testing, but no production aircraft resulted.

Among the unusual features of the Twin-Quad was its fuselage keel. This structure was designed to withstand the impact of a wheels-up landing and proved its ability to do so during such an incident.

SPECIFICATION	
Beech Model 34 Twin-Quad	23,000 ft (7010 m); range 1,450 miles (2335 km)
Type: two-crew short-range passenger/cargo transport	**Weights:** maximum take-off about 19,500 lb (8845 kg)
Powerplant: four Avco Lycoming GSO-580 flat-eight engines each rated at 375 hp (280 kW)	**Dimensions:** wingspan 70 ft (21.34 m); length 53 ft (16.15 m); height 17 ft (5.18 m)
Performance: (estimated) maximum speed 230 mph (370 km/h) at 8,000 ft (2440 m); cruising speed 180 mph (290 km/h) at 8,000 ft (2440 m); service ceiling	**Payload:** up to 20 passengers and 1,000 lb (454 kg) of freight and/or mail

Beech Model 45 Mentor

In 1948 Beech built, entirely as a private venture, a two-seat trainer evolved from the Vee-tail civil Bonanza. It differed primarily by having tandem seating for pupil and instructor and by the replacement of the Vee tail by a conventional tail unit. This **Beech Model 45 Mentor** flew for the first time on 2 December 1948.

At about this time the USAF, in common with many other air forces, was trying to make up its mind about the future trend of primary training. The problem facing all these services was whether or not initial training should be carried out on jet-powered aircraft. USAF planners chose the use of a piston-engined basic trainer as the more prudent course at that time, and among the various types evaluated for the service's next primary trainer were three **YT-34** examples of the Model 45, two of them with the 205-hp (153-kW) Continental E-185-8 engine and one with the 225-hp (168-kW) Continental E-225-8 engine. These three aircraft made their first flights in May, June and July 1950, and were tested extensively during the competition period, being flown not only by evaluation pilots, but also in the primary training role with pupils and instructors.

Almost three years later, on 4 March 1953, the USAF selected the Model 45 as its new primary trainer, under the designation **T-34A Mentor**, and ultimately 450 such aircraft were built for that service, 350 by Beech and 100 by the Canadian Car & Foundry Company. USN evaluation of the Model 45 began soon after the USAF had placed its initial contract and, on 17 June 1954, the navy ordered 290 of these trainers under the designation **T-34B** with the identically rated O-470-4 engine. A total of 423 such aircraft was eventually acquired by the US Navy.

In July 1951 one of the original prototypes was modified with two 0.3-in (7.62-mm) fixed forward-firing machine-guns in the wings together with provision for underwing racks capable of accepting six rockets or two 150-lb (68-kg) bombs. This derivative was evaluated by the USAF as a potential light close-support aircraft, but no orders materialised.

Canadian Car & Foundry also manufactured 25 Mentor trainers for the RCAF (24 of these subsequently being transferred

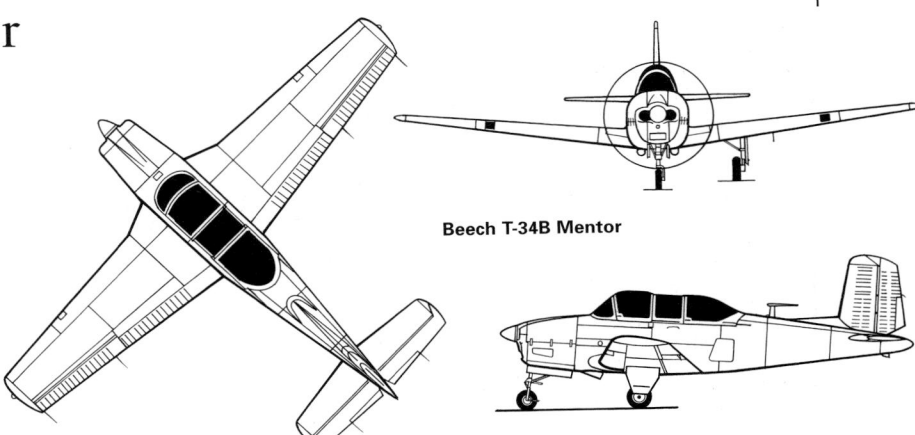

Beech T-34B Mentor

SPECIFICATION	
Beech T-34A Mentor	rate 1,210 ft (369 m) per minute; service ceiling 21,200 ft (6465 m); range 770 miles (1238 km)
Type: two-seat primary flying trainer	**Weights:** empty 2,055 lb (932 kg); maximum take-off 2,900 lb (1315 kg)
Powerplant: one Continental O-470-13 flat-six engine rated at 225 hp (168 kW)	**Dimensions:** wingspan 32 ft 10 in (10.01 m); length 25 ft 10 in (7.87 m); height 9 ft 7 in (2.92 m); wing area 177.60 sq ft (16.50 m²)
Performance: maximum speed 189 mph (304 km/h) at sea level; cruising speed 173 mph (278 km/h) at 10,000 ft (3050 m); initial climb	

to Turkey), and 75 were assembled by the FMA at Córdoba for the Argentine air force (which also received 15 from the parent company), while Fuji in Japan built 124 under licence for the Japanese Air Self-Defence Force and 36 for the Philippine air force. In addition, Beech widely exported T-34s. The US government also supplied T-34 machines through the Military Assistance Program to Spain and Saudi Arabia.

The Mentor became redundant in USAF service in 1960 with the introduction of all-through jet training while, in the USN, the Mentors were progressively phased out in favour of the Beech T-34C Turbo Mentor.

Beech beat off rival proposals from Temco and Ryan to win a USN order for the T-34B. The last was delivered in 1957 and the type served into the late 1970s.

Beech Model 45T Turbo Mentor

Not surprisingly, as the jet age began to mature, most piston-engined basic trainers were gradually phased out of service in favour of purpose-built jet-powered aircraft. It was within this context that the US Navy decided in 1973 to investigate the possibility of retaining the T-34 Mentor in service with its piston engine replaced by a turbine powerplant. Such a scheme offered a continuity of experience with the tough Mentor airframe and its excellent handling characteristics, and would provide the pupil pilot with an unbroken sequence of turbine-engine handling experience throughout his training. To evaluate this proposal, the navy instructed Beech to convert

two T-34Bs to turbine power as a type known to the manufacturer as the **Beech Model 45T Turbo Mentor** and to the service as the **YT-34C**.

The powerplant chosen by Beech was a Pratt & Whitney Canada PT6A-25 turboprop, provided with a torque limiter that restricted power output to some 56 per cent of maximum to ensure constant performance over a wide range of altitude and temperature conditions, and also offers extended engine life. The first YT-34C was flown on 21 September 1973 and, following a satisfactory evaluation of the two aircraft, Beech received initial contracts for the construction of 184 new machines, later increased to

a total of 352, all of which had been delivered by April 1990. In addition to the installation of the new engine, the production aircraft were also given structural strengthening to ensure an airframe fatigue life of some 16,000 hours. The first T-34C Turbo Mentor entered service with Training Air Wing 5 of the US Navy's Naval Air Training Command at NAS Whiting Field, Florida in November 1977, and

student training with the type began during the following January.

Beech subsequently developed a **T-34C-1** version for armament training, and this model is equipped with four underwing hardpoints having a total rating of 1,200 lb (544 kg). In addition to the armament training role, the T-34C-1 is also suitable for forward air control and

tactical attack training missions. The 129 examples of this version were delivered to the navies of Argentina, Ecuador, Peru and Uruguay, and to the air forces of Ecuador, Gabon, Indonesia, Morocco and Taiwan. An export civil version, known as the **Turbine Mentor 34C**, has also been delivered for use in Algeria's national pilot training school.

Beech initially built 184 production T-34Cs against an $89.5 million contract. In addition to its turboprop engine, increased fuel capacity and other modifications, the aircraft also featured the armament system of the Pave Coin Bonanza.

SPECIFICATION

Beech T-34C Turbo Mentor
Type: two-seat primary flying trainer
Powerplant: one 715-shp (533-kW) Pratt & Whitney Canada PT6A-25 turboprop engine torque-limited to a maximum output of 400 shp (298 kW)
Performance: maximum cruising speed 246 mph (396 km/h) at 17,000 ft (5180 m); initial climb

rate 1,480 ft (451 m) per minute; service ceiling more than 30,000 ft (9145 m); range 814 miles (1311 km)
Weights: empty 2,960 lb (1342 kg); maximum take-off 4,300 lb (1950 kg)
Dimensions: wingspan 33 ft 4 in (10.16 m); length 28 ft 8½ in (8.75 m); height 9 ft 7 in (2.92 m); wing area 179.60 sq ft (16.68 m²)

Beech Model 50 Twin Bonanza

The prototype of the **Beech Model 50 Twin Bonanza** first flew on 15 November 1949. Long before civil certification was received, the aircraft toured USAF bases for service appraisal, since Beech was anxious to secure military contracts

for the new model. The Twin Bonanza was the first post-war US type designed as a twin-engined light-plane with accommodation for a pilot and up to five passengers. The Model 50 was a low-wing cantilever monoplane of all-metal

construction, incorporating such features as slotted trailing-edge flaps, a conventional tail unit, retractable tricycle landing gear, and two 260-hp (194-kW) Avco Lycoming GO-435-C2 flat-six engines. Just before the end of the production run in 1963, the company was marketing the **Model D50E Twin Bonanza** which had benefited from 12 years of

improvement: the seating had been increased to provide accommodation for five or six passengers, and the powerplant comprised two 340-hp (254-kW) GO-480-G2F6 engines. Produced in parallel from 1960 was the **Model J50 Twin Bonanza**, which differed in its powerplant of two 340-hp (254-kW) IGSO-480-A1B6 supercharged engines.

In 1951 the US Army was looking for a light transport aircraft suitable for worldwide deployment. For economic reasons it was desirable that it should be a current production aircraft and, after careful consideration, four Twin Bonanza machines were procured for evaluation under the designation **YL-23**, the first being delivered on 30 January 1952.

Supercharged, fuel-injected Lycoming engines gave the 1961 Model J50 increased speed, range, load and altitude performance. It featured a longer, more pointed nose compared to earlier models.

SPECIFICATION

Beech L-23D
Type: six-seat staff transport
Powerplant: two Avco Lycoming O-480-1 flat-six engines each rated at 340 hp (254 kW)
Performance: maximum speed 233 mph (375 km/h) at optimum altitude; cruising speed 203 mph (327 km/h) at optimum altitude; initial climb rate 1,560 ft (475 m)

per minute; service ceiling 26,300 ft (8015 m); range 1,355 miles (2181 km)
Weights: empty 4,974 lb (2256 kg); maximum take-off 7,000 lb (3175 kg)
Dimensions: wingspan 45 ft 3½ in (13.80 m); length 31 ft 6½ in (9.61 m); height 11 ft 4 in (3.45 m); wing area 277.00 sq ft (25.73 m²)

Beech Model 50 Twin Bonanza (continued)

Tests having proved satisfactory, Beech received a contract to produce 55 generally similar aircraft under the designation **L-23A**, with power provided by 260-hp (194-kW) Avco Lycoming O-435-17 engines. The 40 **L-23B** machines which followed differed only in having metal rather than wooden propellers. The sole **XL-23C** was an evaluation model for the USAF. In November 1956 the US Army received the first of 83 **L-23D** aircraft developed from the then current **Model E50** (later **Model J50**) civil variant with supercharged engines, and 93 surviving L-23As and L-23Bs were later reworked to L-23D standard. During 1958-60 the US Army also received 20 **RL-23D** reconnaissance aircraft that were basically identical to the L-23D except for the addition of SLAR. The final military variant of the Twin Bonanza was the **L-23E**, a designation applied to six aircraft equivalent to the commercial Model E50. In the new tri-service designation system of 1962, the L-23D, RL-23D and L-23E were redesignated respectively as the **U-8D**, **RU-8D** and **U-8E**, and also given the name **Seminole**.

Beech Models 55, 56 and 58 Baron

The **Beech Model 95-55 Baron**, first flown on 29 February 1960, was developed from the earlier Model 95 Travel Air, from which it differed primarily in having the uprated powerplant of two 260-hp (194-kW) Continental IO-470-L flat-six engines, a swept fin and improved all-weather capability. Deliveries began in November 1960, while the **Model A55** was delivered from January 1962 with five-seat accommodation. The **Model B55** introduced in 1963 had four-seat and optional five/six-seat accommodation, and in 1965 the **Model C55** became available with more powerful Continental IO-520-C engines. The Model C55 incorporated a number of other improvements, including a tailplane of increased span and an extended nose baggage compartment, and was developed later as a separate Baron variant distinct from the Model B55.

The US Army chose the Model B55 for service as an instrument trainer and ordered an initial 55 under the designation **T-42A Cochise**. Ten more were procured for US Army service and then, in 1971, five for delivery to the Turkish army under the Military Assistance Program. By mid-1981, production of civil and military Model B55 Baron aircraft had passed 2,400 units, and about 1,200 examples of the **Model E55** (formerly **Model C/D55**) had been delivered.

In September 1967 deliveries began of a new **Model 56TC Baron**. This introduced the turbocharged powerplant of two 380-hp (283-kW) Avco Lycoming TIO-541-E1B4W engines. Air-conditioning was available as an option, Beech claiming this to be the first time that such a system had been offered on a lightweight twin. However, the higher cost of this version of the Baron meant that only 93 sales were achieved, and production was terminated in December 1971.

Before that date, the range had been extended when, in late 1969, Beech introduced the larger **Model 58 Baron**. First flown in June of that year with the same powerplant as the Model E55, namely two Continental IO-520-C flat-six engines each rated at 285 hp (213 kW), this new development had a lengthened fuselage. Double doors on the starboard side gave easy access to baggage/cargo space behind the rear seats. Delivery figures for this improved Baron which averaged about two per week for more than 12 years, paved the way for the introduction of a pressurised **Model 58P**, with first deliveries in late 1975. This was based on something of a composite airframe that combined the Model B55 wing, Model 58 tail unit, strengthened Model 58 fuselage to cater for pressurisation, and Model 60 Duke main landing gear units. The powerplant was two Continental turbocharged engines, currently TSIO-520-WE units.

The last addition to the range came with initial deliveries in June 1976 of the **Model 58TC** which, apart from being unpressurised, was generally similar to its immediate predecessor and retained its turbocharged powerplant. The Model 58 remained in production in the late 1990s, sales having passed 2,483 aircraft in 1998.

The Baron has proved to be a popular type, and by the end of 1981 sales of the series had exceeded 5,500 aircraft. In addition to these Beech production Barons, at least two turbo-prop conversions have been developed by other constructors. These include the **SFERMA Marquis**, produced in small numbers in France as the combination of the Beech-built Baron airframe with the powerplant of two 440-shp (328-kW) Turboméca Astazou engines; and the **American Jet Industries Turbo Star Baron** with the powerplant of two 400-shp (298-kW) Allison 250-B17 engines.

SPECIFICATION

Beech Model 58 Baron
Type: four/six-seat light transport
Powerplant: two Teledyne Continental IO-520-C flat-six piston engines each rated at 285 hp (213 kW)
Performance: maximum speed 239 mph (386 km/h) at sea level; cruising speed 234 mph (376 km/h) at 5,000 ft (1525 m); initial climb rate 1,735 ft (529 m) per minute; service ceiling 20,670 ft (6300 m); range 1,812 miles (2917 km)
Weights: empty 3,570 lb (1619 kg); maximum take-off 5,500 lb (2495 kg)
Dimensions: wingspan 37 ft 10 in (11.53 m); length 29 ft 10 in (9.09 m); height 9 ft 9 in (2.97 m); wing area 199.20 sq ft (18.51 m²)

When the Model 58P became available in late 1974, its pressurisation system maintained a cabin altitude equivalent to 8,000 ft (2440 m) at an altitude of 18,000 ft (5500 m).

Variants

Model 38P Lightning: first flown on 14 June 1982 as an experimental development of the Model 58P with one nose-mounted 865-shp (645-kW) Garrett TPE331-9 turboprop. It was intended as the basis for a projected production type with the Pratt & Whitney Canada PT6A-40 or -130 turboprop
SFERMA 60A Marquis: developed via the **Turbo-Travel Air** conversion of a single Model 95 Travel Air that first flew on 12 July 1960 with the wholly revised powerplant of two Turboméca Astazou turboprop engines

Beech Model 60 Duke

Beech entered the field of pressurised light aircraft for the general aviation market following a first flight of the **Beech Model 60 Duke** on 29 December 1966. The Duke was intended as a luxury four/six-seater and was provided with an extensive range of equipment.

The overall configuration was similar to that of the other Beech twins, but because it was intended for operation at higher weights it had strengthened landing gear, and a much more potent powerplant. The pressurisation system installed in later production aircraft had an advanced controller which allowed the selection of cabin altitude before take-off or landing.

Only two revised versions of the Model 60 appeared before the end of its production career in the early 1980s, namely the **Model A60** and **Model B60** introduced in 1971 and 1974, respectively. The first provided a 50-lb (23-kg) increase in maximum take-off weight, improved superchargers and upgraded trim, while the second offered a slightly larger cabin, increased fuel capacity and a new pressurisation system. Aircraft of this type are not cheap and, by American standards, the Duke was therefore built in comparatively small numbers, to a total of 593 aircraft.

SPECIFICATION

Beech Model B60 Duke
Type: four/six-seat light transport
Powerplant: two Avco Lycoming TIO-541-E1C4 flat-six engines each rated at 380 hp (283 kW)
Performance: maximum speed 283 mph (455 km/h) at 23,000 ft (7010 m); cruising speed 250 mph (402 km/h) at 25,000 ft (7620 m); initial climb rate 1,601 ft (488 m) per minute; service ceiling 30,000 ft (9145 m); range 1,344 miles (2165 km)
Weights: empty 4,423 lb (2006 kg); maximum take-off 6,775 lb (3073 kg)
Dimensions: wingspan 39 ft 3¾ in (11.97 m); length 33 ft 10 in (10.31 m); height 12 ft 4 in (3.76 m); wing area 212.90 sq ft (19.78 m²)

As the final Duke variant, the B60 was built to the extent of 350 examples before production ceased in 1982. The previous Models A60 and 60 had fallen out of production in 1973 and 1970 respectively, after totals of 121 and 122 had been built.

Beech Models 65, 70, 80 and 88 Queen Air

On 28 August 1958 Beech flew the prototype of the **Model 65 Queen Air** business aircraft. This seven/ nine-seat low-wing monoplane had retractable tricycle landing gear and the powerplant of two Avco Lycoming IGSO-480-A1B6 flat-six engines. Full IFR instrumentation was standard, and optional equipment such as an autopilot and navigation/ weather-avoidance radar could provide the Queen Air with the capability of a contemporary airliner.

In the following January Beech flew the first of three Model 65 aircraft for US Army evaluation. This resulted in orders totalling 71 machines for service with the designation **L-23F Seminole**. The Model 65 was generally similar to the earlier Model 50 Twin Bonanza which was already in service as the L-23 series; the Model 65 differed from the Model 50 primarily in its deeper-section fuselage and more powerful engines. In 1962 the L-23F was redesig-

nated as the **U-8F**, and some modified at a later date with improved accommodation became **U-8G** machines. Several commercial Queen Airs were acquired by the Japanese Maritime Self-Defence Force for use in the navigation training and transport roles, and others went to the air forces of Uruguay and Venezuela. An improved **Model A65** then introduced a swept vertical tail surface and greater fuel capacity, and a derivative of this with a high-density seating arrangement – for a crew of one or two plus 10 or nine passengers respectively – was known as the **Queen Airliner**. Mention should also be made of a Model 65 with two 500-shp (373-kW) Pratt & Whitney Canada PT6A-6 turboprop engines. Identified initially by the company as the **Model 65-90T**, this was evaluated by the US Army from 17 March 1964 as the **NU-8F**, and was basically the prototype of the Model 90 King Air.

Expansion of the Queen

Air line came on 22 June 1961 with the first flight of the more powerful **Model 80**, while the **Model A80**, introduced in January 1964, had increased wingspan that allowed for operation at higher weights. The final version was the **Model B80**, and its US Army equivalent the **Beech U-21A Ute,** incorporating a number of design and equipment improvements, and 11-seat Queen Airliner variants were available for each of these basic versions.

August 1965 witnessed the introduction of a pressurised version of the Model B80 with circular cabin windows. Identified

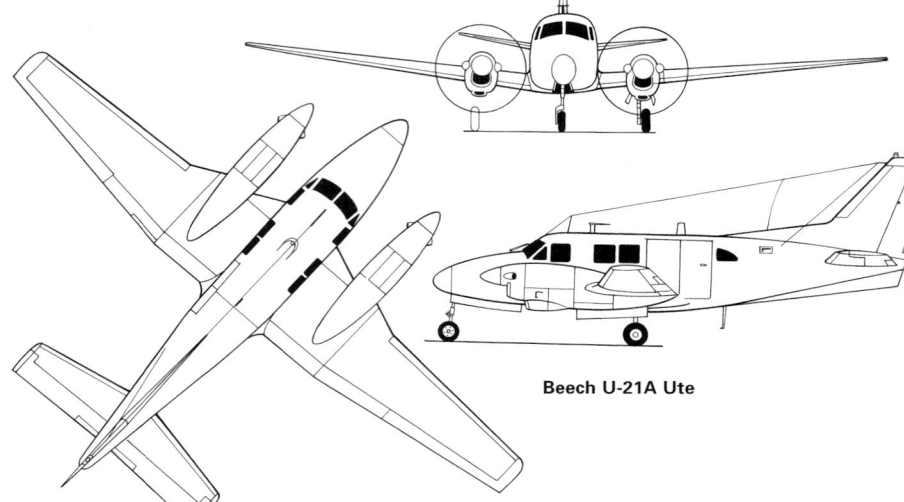

Beech U-21A Ute

as the **Model 88**, this was taken out of production during 1969 after only 45 aircraft had been built.

A third member of the Queen Air family was introduced in 1968. Known as the **Model 70**, this was basically the Model A65 with the increased-span wing of the Model B80. A Queen Airliner version was also available, and these aircraft had the operating

economy of the A65 plus improved load-carrying capability. Manufacture of the Models 65 and 70 was terminated at the end of 1971, at which time production figures totalled 404 and 42 aircraft respectively, the former figure including the U-8F. Production of the Model 80 continued until the end of 1978, by which time approximately 510 had been built.

This Philippines- registered Model B80 Queen Air demonstrates the variant's increased wingspan.

SPECIFICATION	
Beech Model A65 Queen Air	per minute; service ceiling
Type: seven/nine-seat business,	31,300 ft (9540 m); range
commuter and utility transport	1,660 miles (2671 km)
Powerplant: two Avco Lycoming	**Weights:** empty 4,960 lb
IGSO-540-A1E6 flat-six engines	(2449 kg); maximum take-off
each rated at 340 hp (254 kW)	7,700 lb (3493 kg)
Performance: maximum speed	**Dimensions:** wingspan 45 ft
239 mph (385 mph) at 12,000 ft	10½ in (13.98 m); length 35 ft 6 in
(3660 m); cruising speed 214 mph	(10.82 m); height 14 ft 2½ in
(344 km/h) at 15,000 ft (4570 m);	(4.33 m); wing area 288.06 sq ft
initial climb rate 1,300 ft (396 m)	(25.72 m²)

Beech Model 73 Jet Mentor

By the early 1950s the US Air Force had overcome its initial reluctance to make a decision about the use of turbojet-powered primary flying trainers, and as a result Beech began the private-venture development of a low-cost turbojet-powered trainer. Although it would appear that only a single prototype of the resulting **Beech Model 73 Jet Mentor** was built, it is worth brief mention as the USA's first lightweight trainer with the

powerplant of one turbojet.

In order to keep costs to the absolute minimum, extensive use was made of standard Model 45 Mentor components. Thus, the cantilever wing was basically the same as that of the Model 45, although changes had to be made at the roots to allow for the incorporation of air inlets for the turbojet engine. Power was provided by a prototype engine, the Continental YJ69, which was the licence-built

version of the French Turboméca Marboré.

First flown on 18 December 1955, the Jet Mentor failed to win a production order. The Canadian Car Company of Montreal, which had built T-34A Mentors for the USAF, then acquired production rights to meet a potential RCAF requirement, but although the Model 73 prototype was evaluated by that service, no production examples were ordered.

SPECIFICATION	
Beech Model 73 Jet Mentor	service ceiling 26,600 ft (8110 m);
Type: two-seat lightweight jet	range 500 miles (805 km)
trainer	**Weights:** empty 2,854 lb
Powerplant: one Continental	(1295 kg); maximum take-off
YT69-T-9 turbojet engine rated at	4,450 lb (2018 kg)
920 lb st (4.09 kN)	**Dimensions:** wingspan 32 ft 9 in
Performance: maximum speed	(9.98 m); length 30 ft (9.14 m);
288 mph (463 km/h) at optimum	height 9 ft 9½ in (2.98 m); wing
altitude; cruising speed 245 mph	area 177.60 sq ft (16.50 m²)
(394 km/h) at optimum altitude;	

The Model 73 provided accommodation for an instructor and pupil in tandem beneath a large power-actuated and jettisonable canopy. It was intended that dual instrumentation, air-conditioning, and ejection seats would be customer options.

Beech Model 76 Duchess

Late in 1974 Beech was flight testing a new four-seat light aircraft with a twin-engined powerplant. This was identified as the **PD 289**, but it was not until almost four years later that a production aircraft based on the PD 289 was available for delivery with the designation **Beech Model 76 Duchess**. The Duchess has a T-tail with a swept vertical tail surface, hydraulically retractable tricycle landing gear, and the powerplant of two counter-rotating Avco

Some 437 Model 76s were completed. Just one model was available, but customers could specify one of three trim levels.

Lycoming flat-four engines. An extensive range of factory-installed optional equipment and/or avionics was available to individual requirements.

The Duchess was developed with the training requirements of the Beech Aero Centers very much in mind, these requirements placing emphasis on good low-speed/single-engine flight handling characteristics. Consequently, the aircraft is ideal for the personal light twin market, but suited also for both light charter and multi-engine trainer use. Total deliveries in late 1981 were approaching the 400 mark, but in common with many other American light aircraft caught up in the downturn in the general aviation market during the mid-1980s, the Duchess went out of production in the middle of the decade.

SPECIFICATION	
Beech Model 76 Duchess	per minute; service ceiling 19,650 ft (5990 m); range 898 miles (1445 km)
Type: four-seat light transport and training aircraft	**Weights:** empty 2,466 lb (1119 kg); maximum take-off 3,900 lb (1769 kg)
Powerplant: two Avco Lycoming O-360-A1G6D flat-four engines each rated at 180 hp (134 kW)	**Dimensions:** wingspan 38 ft (11.58 m); length 29 ft ½ in (8.86 m); height 9 ft 6 in (2.90 m); wing area 181.00 sq ft (16.81 m²)
Performance: maximum speed 197 mph (317 km/h) at optimum altitude; cruising speed 191 mph (308 km/h) at 6,000 ft (1830 m); initial climb rate 1,248 ft (380 m)	

Beech Model 77 Skipper

Seating two side-by-side, the Skipper was built to the extent of 312 examples. The aircraft features a two-bladed Sensenich propeller and a total fuel capacity of 29 US gal (110 litres).

The design of the **PD 285** prototype, first flown on 6 February 1975, reflected the Beech Aero Centers' need for a modern single-engined trainer. At the time of its first flight, the PD 285 had a conventional tail unit, with a low-set tailplane and elevators, but by the time that production **Beech Model 77 Skipper** aircraft appeared in May 1979 the type had acquired a T-tail. This latter change was made in order to improve low-speed controllability and provide better spin-recovery characteristics.

Intended as a primary trainer with low initial and operating costs, the Model 77 was designed for ease of maintenance. The low-set monoplane wing of the Skipper incorporated a high-lift aerofoil section developed by NASA. The landing gear was of the fixed tricycle type with a steerable nosewheel unit, and power was provided by an Avco Lycoming piston engine.

By early 1981 well over 200 Skippers had been delivered, but in July of that year Beech announced that production had been suspended as a result of adverse market conditions.

SPECIFICATION	
Beech Model 77 Skipper	at 4,500 ft (1370 m); service ceiling 12,900 ft (3930 m); range 475 miles (765 km)
Type: two-seat trainer	**Weights:** empty 1,103 lb (501 kg); maximum take-off 1,675 lb (760 kg)
Powerplant: one Avco Lycoming O-235-L2C flat-four engine rated at 115 hp (86 kW)	**Dimensions:** wingspan 30 ft (9.14 m); length 24 ft (7.32 m); height 7 ft 10¾ in (2.41 m)
Performance: maximum speed 122 mph (196 km/h) at sea level; cruising speed 101 mph (163 km/h)	

Beech Model 90 King Air

Early in 1963 Beech started the flight tests of an aircraft, then identified as the **Beech Model 65-80 Queen Air**. The type had been developed mainly to satisfy a US Army requirement for a staff and utility transport and it was soon appreciated that the original designation was a little confusing, so the type became known temporarily as the **Model 65-90T** (T standing for turboprop). In due course, the turboprop-powered version of the Queen Air was renamed as the **King Air**. In effect, the Model 65-90T became the prototype for the **Model 90 King Air** series, but more specifically became the prototype of the unpressurised variant of the King Air for military service. Following the first flight of the Model 65-90T, a civil equivalent was produced in parallel with pressurised accommodation, and the first production prototype of this aircraft made its maiden flight on 20 January 1964 as the Model 90 King Air.

After US Army testing of the Model 65-90T, under the military designation **NU-8F**, an initial order was placed for 48 aircraft to serve with the designation and name **U-21A Ute**. Beech distinguished the military King Airs from civil versions with the designation **Model 65-A90-1**, and began modification of the civil aircraft to provide a utility interior. This accommodated a crew of two and up to 10 troops or up to 3,000 lb (1361 kg) of cargo.

Delivery of the U-21A began on 16 May 1967, and subsequent contracts resulted in the completion of more than 160 aircraft. These included U-21A and **RU-21A/RU-21D** variants with 550-shp (410-kW) Pratt & Whitney Canada PT6A-20 turboprops, and **RU-21B/RU-21C/RU-21E** variants with 620-shp (462-kW) PT6A-29 turboprops. The RU-21 was developed specially for operation in the electronic reconnaissance role in Southeast Asia and the RU-21B and RU-21C had the Beech designations **Model 65-A90-2** and **Model 65-A90-3** respec-

Beech Model T-44A

tively. The designation **U-21G** was applied to 17 aircraft for the USAF that were similar to the U-21A.

Late in 1964 Beech began deliveries of the civil Model 90 King Air, this having cabin pressurisation and accommodating a maximum of 10 persons including the pilot. The initial variant was superseded in early 1966 by the **Model A90** with more powerful PT6A-20 engines, and one of these aircraft was supplied for military service under the designation **VC-6A**.

The Model A90 was followed by a **Model B90** with detail improvements, and then in September 1970 by the **Model C90** with a more advanced cabin pressurisation and heating system. The Model C90 remains in production in the late 1990s, although development via the **Model**

Variant

Jetcrafters Taurus: Jetcrafters Inc. was established by 'Ed' Swearingen to develop a modification programme to improve the performance and operating economics of the Model 90 King Air; the original engines are replaced by two Pratt & Whitney Canada PT6A-135 turboprops each flat-rated at 700 shp (522 kW) and installed in nacelles of smaller cross-section

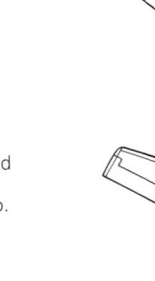

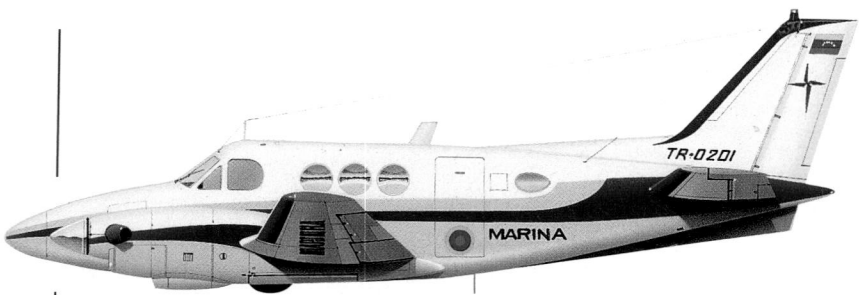

A single Model E90 King Air was delivered to the Venezuelan navy in 1978. The aircraft remains in service in the communications role.

C90-1, **Model C90A** and **Model C90B** has produced the current **Model C90C** and the $1.747 million (1995) **Model C90SE (Special Edition)**. Production of the civil Model 90 passed the 1,400 mark in 1995, and one Model C90 also entered USAF service as the sole **VC-6B**. Ten examples of the Model C90 serve with the Spanish air force and civil aviation school.

A first extension to the Model 90 range came in the early summer of 1972 with the introduction of the **Model E90**. This differed from its predecessor mainly in its adoption of more powerful PT6A-28 turboprops each flat-rated to 550 ehp (410 ekW). In 1976 Beech received a contract from the USN for an advanced pilot training aircraft that combined features of the Model C90 and Model E90, and 61 of this **T-44A** variant had been delivered by mid-1980.

The latest model of the King Air family, in terms of its core designation, is the **Model F90 Super King Air**, of which deliveries began in mid-1979. This combines the pressurised accommodation of the Model 90 with the wing and tail unit of the Models 100 King Air and Model 200 Super King Air respectively. Power is provided by two 750-shp (559-kW) PT6A-135 engines, driving slow-turning four-bladed propellers for a much quieter cabin environment.

A distinguishing feature of the Model F90 is its Model 200-style T-tail. The aircraft also features an advanced electrical system.

SPECIFICATION	
Beech Model C90B King Air	range 1,542 miles (2482 km)
Type: two-crew business aircraft	**Weights:** empty 6,675 lb
Powerplant: two Pratt & Whitney	(3028 kg); maximum take-off
Canada PT6A-21 turboprop engines	10,100 lb (4581 kg)
each rated at 550 shp (410 kW)	**Dimensions:** wingspan 50 ft 3 in
Performance: maximum cruising	(15.32 m); length 35 ft 6 in
speed 284 mph (457 km/h) at	(10.82 m); height 17 ft 3 in (5.26 m);
16,000 ft (4875 m); initial climb	wing area 293.94 sq ft (27.31 m²)
rate 2,003 ft (620 m) per minute;	**Payload:** up to eight passengers
service ceiling 28,900 ft (8810 m);	

Beech Model 95 Travel Air

The prototype of the **Beech Model 95 Travel Air** made its maiden flight on 6 August 1956. This four-seat twin-engined aircraft was originally named **Badger** but, learning that NATO had allocated this as the reporting name for the Tupolev Tu-16, the company used instead the name Travel Air. The Model 95 was a low-wing cantilever monoplane of all-metal construction, and among its features were

In its original form (illustrated), the Model 95 was produced throughout 1958-59 to a total of 301 units. The Model B95 was produced from 1960 with a price of $51,500.

retractable tricycle landing gear and the powerplant of two Avco Lycoming O-360-A1A engines. The new type was certificated on 18 June 1957, and initial deliveries to customers were made soon after.

Travel Air development started at the **Model B95** with a longer cabin and a tailplane of greater span, continued via the more powerful **Model B95A** introduced in 1961 and the longer-nosed **Model D95A** of 1962, and ended with the **Model E95**, whose production ended in 1967. By this time more than 700 Model 95s of all versions had been built. The **Model 95-55 Baron** was developed from the Model 95 during 1959.

SPECIFICATION	
Beech Model E95 Travel Air	service ceiling 18,700 ft (5700 m);
Type: four/five-seat light transport	range 1,170 miles (1883 km)
Powerplant: two Avco Lycoming	**Weights:** empty 2,650 lb
IO-360-B1B flat-four engines each	(1202 kg); maximum take-off
rated at 180 hp (134 kW)	4,200 lb (1905 m)
Performance: maximum speed	**Dimensions:** wingspan 37 ft 10 in
210 mph (338 km/h) at sea level;	(11.53 m); length 25 ft 11 in
cruising speed 200 mph (322 km/h)	(7.90 m); height 9 ft 6 in (2.90 m);
at 7,500 ft (2285 m); initial climb	wing area 199.20 sq ft (18.51 m²)
rate 1,300 ft (396 m) per minute;	

Beech Model 99 Airliner

During the early 1960s, the growing importance of American commuter airlines prompted Beech to design an aircraft specifically intended to capture a major share of this market. In 1965, therefore, the company began the development of what was then its largest production aircraft, the prototype flying for the first time in July 1966. Identified as the **Beech Model 99 Airliner**, the new type had a general configuration similar to that of the contemporary Queen Air, but its longer fuselage accommodated a crew of two and up to 15 passengers. Power was provided by two 550-shp (410-kW) Pratt & Whitney Canada PT6A-20 turboprops and options included a cargo door as well as a movable bulkhead that provided for various combinations of passengers and freight. The first production example was delivered on 2 May 1968, by which time an alternative **Model 99 Executive** version was available. Generally similar to the standard Model 99 Airliner, the Executive offered a variety of optional seating layouts and corporate interiors.

Improved **Model A99** and **Model B99** production versions followed, both available in the optional Executive variant, and these were powered by 680-shp (507-kW) PT6A-27 engines. By late 1976 demand for the Model 99 was falling, however, and production was terminated towards the end of 1977 after 164 aircraft had been delivered to 64 operators, most of them in the USA.

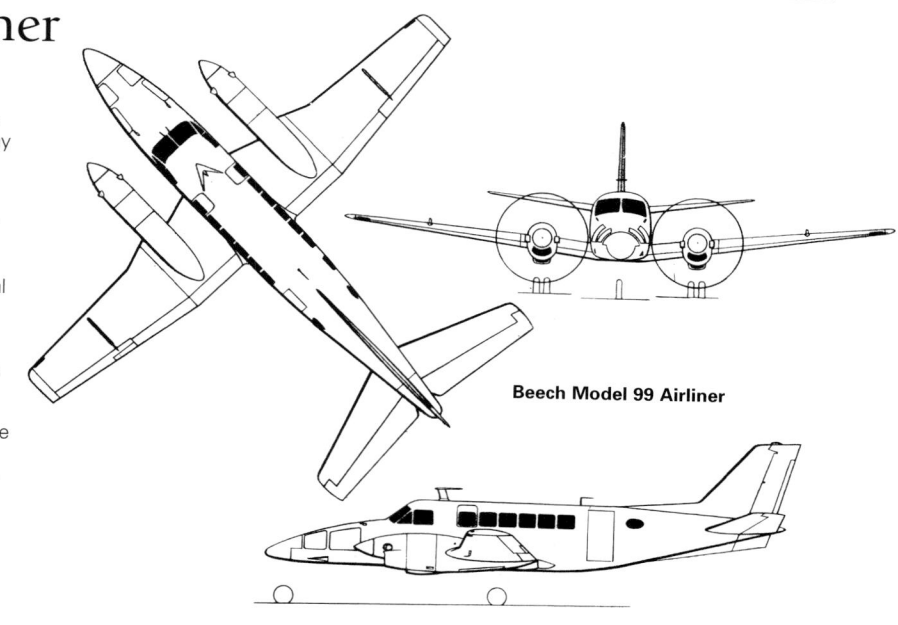

Beech Model 99 Airliner

Beech Model 99 Airliner (continued)

On May 1979 Beech announced its intention to re-enter the commuter airliner market. To speed the certification programme, an earlier production Model B99 machine was completely refurbished before being given the new powerplant of two PT6A-36 engines. Designated **Model C99**, this was flown for the first time on 20 June 1980, and the manufacture of production aircraft began in September 1980. Certification of the Model C99 was gained in July 1981, with initial deliveries following within two or three days. This type differs from the Model B99 primarily in having more powerful engines, but also incorporates a number of detail improvements. Production of the Model C99 ended in 1986, after the delivery of 76 aircraft.

In addition, Beech modified one Model 99 for stability experiments as the **PD 280** during 1975.

N4199C was built as a Model 99. Beech subsequently bought the aircraft back from Allegheny Airlines and modified it to serve as the Model C99 prototype.

SPECIFICATION	
Beech Model C99 Commuter **Type:** two-crew commuter and cargo transport **Powerplant:** two Pratt & Whitney Canada PT6A-36 turboprop engines each flat-rated to 715 shp (533 kW) **Performance:** maximum speed 308 mph (496 km/h) at 8,000 ft (2440 m); cruising speed 287 mph (462 km/h) at 8,000 ft (2440 m); initial climb rate 2,221 ft (677 m) per minute; service ceiling 28,080 ft (8560 m); range	1,048 miles (1687 km) **Weights:** empty 6,494 lb (2946 kg); maximum take-off 11,300 lb (5126 kg) **Dimensions:** wingspan 45 ft 10½ in (13.98 m); length 44 ft 6¾ in (13.58 m); height 14 ft 4¼ in (4.37 m); wing area 279.70 sq ft (25.98 m²) **Payload:** up to 15 passengers and/or freight for a maximum 3,250-lb (1474-kg) payload

Beech Model 100 King Air

Initial deliveries of the **Beech Model 100 King Air** were made in August 1969. The new variant differed from the earlier King Air types in several respects, including a new wing of reduced span and generally similar to that of the Model 99 Airliner, a fuselage lengthened to provide accommodation for a maximum of 15 persons, elevators and a rudder of increased area, twin-wheel main landing gear units, and the uprated powerplant of two 680-shp (507-kW) Pratt & Whitney Canada PT6A-28 turboprops.

In October 1971, with Model 100 production halted, Beech began deliveries of the improved **Model A100** with a number of detail improvements, and the first five of these aircraft were supplied to the US Army under the designation **U-21F**. The Model A100 remained in limited production to 1981; the production total was 241 aircraft, including examples procured by the Spanish air force and the **Universal Aircraft Com/Nav Evaluation (UNACE)** version. The latter was optimised for the rapid inspection and calibration of air navigation systems. Beech also built specially-modified camera-equipped versions of the Model A100 for aerial survey.

In parallel with Model A100 production from late 1975, Beech produced a complementary **Model**

Beech U-21F

B100 offering higher performance through the introduction of an uprated powerplant. Some 137 examples of the Model B100 had been completed by the time production ended in 1983.

The Model B100 (illustrated) combined the additional fuel tankage and four-bladed propellers of the Model A100 with uprated Garrett turboprops.

SPECIFICATION	
Beech Model B100 King Air **Type:** two-crew light executive/freight/passenger transport **Powerplant:** two Garrett TPE331-6-252B turboprop engines each rated at 715 shp (533 kW) **Performance:** maximum cruising speed 307 mph (495 km/h) at 12,000 ft (3660 m); initial climb rate 2,139 ft (652 m) per minute;	service ceiling 28,140 ft (8575 m); range 1,525 miles (2456 km) **Weights:** empty 7,082 lb (3212 kg); maximum take-off 11,800 lb (5352 kg) **Dimensions:** wingspan 45 ft 11 in (14.00 m); length 39 ft 11 in (12.17 m); height 15 ft 5 in (4.70 m) **Payload:** up to 13 passengers or freight

Beech Model 200 Super King Air

On 27 October 1972 Beech flew the prototype of a new and improved member of the King Air family which has become known as the **Beech Model 200 Super King Air**. This differs from the Model 100 King Air by having a wing of increased span, the conventional tail unit replaced by a T-tail, and increased fuel capacity for more powerful Pratt & Whitney PT6A-41 turboprop engines, for operations at higher weights.

From March 1981 the basic Model 200 was replaced by the **Model B200** that differs in having better cruise and altitude performance through the introduction of PT6A-42 turboprops and a higher cabin pressurisation differential. The Model B200 is still in production in the late 1990s. Sub-variants include the **Model B200C** with a cargo door on the port side of the rear cabin; the **Model B200SE (Special Edition)**, priced at $2.995 million (1996), with a Collins EFIS avionics package and autopilot; **Model B200T** with provision for removable fuel tanks at the tips of a wing, which is increased in span to 55 ft 5 in (16.92 m); and **Model B200CT** with cargo door and tips tanks.

In 1995 sales of the Super King Air series passed the 1,500 mark, and although most of these were aircraft for the civil market, almost 350 had been delivered to the US and foreign armed forces. Some of the latter fly the type in specialised roles; for example, in 1997 the Argentine naval air arm received the first of three **Cormoran** (cormorant) conversions for the coastal patrol task with Bendix RDR-1500 search radar.

Since 1981 when the Model B200 was first introduced, the type has undergone a series of improvements. The model remains in production and in 1996 was listed at a basic price of $3.699 million.

SPECIFICATION

Beech Model B200 Super King Air
Type: one/two-crew executive/passenger light transport
Powerplant: two Pratt & Whitney Canada PT6A-42 turboprops each rated at 850 shp (634 kW)
Performance: maximum speed 339 mph (545 km/h) at 25,000 ft (7620 m); cruising speed 333 mph (536 km/h) at 25,000 ft (7620 m); initial climb rate 2,450 ft (747 m) per minute; service ceiling more than 35,000 ft (10670 m); range 2,272 miles (3656 km)
Weights: empty 8,102 lb (3675 kg); maximum take-off 12,500 lb (5670 kg)
Dimensions: wingspan 54 ft 6 in (16.61 m); length 43 ft 9 in (13.34 m); height 15 ft (4.57 m); wing area 303.00 sq ft (28.15 m²)
Payload: up to 14 passengers

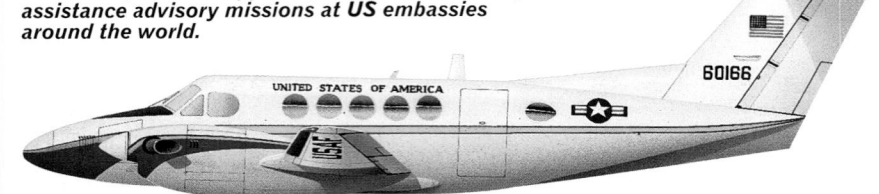

A number of C-12As were supplied to the US Air Force and flown in support of attaché and military assistance advisory missions at US embassies around the world.

Variants

Model B200T: two specially-equipped aircraft for the French Institut Géographique National for high-altitude photographic and weather observation duties

Maritime Patrol Model 200T: maritime patrol/multi-mission aircraft with wingtip fuel tanks, strengthened landing gear, hatch for dropping survival equipment, bubble observation window in aft cabin, and search radar with underfuselage radome

Model 1300 Commuter: produced in small numbers during the early 1980s as a commuterliner development of the Model B200 with accommodation for 13 passengers and a number of airframe and equipment changes including a pair of ventral fins and provision for a detachable ventral cargo pod

PD 290: in mid-1975 Beech was reported to be flying a prototype development of the Model 200 powered by two Pratt & Whitney JT15D turbofans

RU-21J Huron: three 'off the shelf' Model 200 aircraft bought by the US Army in 1971 for conversion to the special-mission role as RU-21J machines in the U-21 rather than C-12 sequence; the RU-21J was used for the battlefield Elint role within the Cefly Lancer programme, and carried a mass of electronic equipment similar to (but not as advanced as) that of the RC-12D

C-12A Huron: utility transport for the US Army and USAF (the latter without the name Huron) designated **Model A200** by Beech, with two 750-shp (559-kW) PT6A-38 turboprops and a payload of more than 2,300 lb (1043 kg). Entered service in July 1975. Has accommodation for two pilots and up to eight passengers. Later revised with PT6A-41 turboprops for full commonality with the improved C-12C

UC-12B: version for the USN and USMC designated **Model A200C** by Beech, procured at the same time as the C-12A. Has two PT6A-41 turboprops, high-flotation landing gear, and a cargo door

C-12C Huron: upgraded C-12A for the US Army, delivered with PT6A-41 turboprops. In 1996 the US Army was allocated most of the USAF's complement of C-12F aircraft, allowing it to retire its C-12Cs, most of the aircraft being passed to local government and law enforcement agencies in the USA, including the Air Interdiction Division of the US Customs Service, which took 16 aircraft

C-12D Huron: similar to the C-12C, with a cargo door, high-flotation landing gear and provision for tip tanks, Beech designation **Model A200CT**; deliveries were made to the US Army and USAF, with six of the Army aircraft being allocated the designation **UC-12D Huron** when delivered to the Army National Guard, and all of the USAF aircraft being deployed overseas in support of US embassies

RC-12D: initially 18 C-12Ds converted before delivery (13 and five to the US Army and Israeli air force, respectively) for use in the special-

mission role; in May 1983 the US Army contracted for an additional six aircraft of the same basic type, which were intended for the battlefield Sigint role in the South Korean and European theatres

C-12E: when reassigned to the support of various US embassies, 29 USAF C-12A machines were redesignated thus after retrofit with two PT6A-42 turboprops

C-12F Huron: delivered from May 1984, this is the OSA (Operational Support Airlift) version, designated **Model B200C** by Beech, with a side cargo door and provision for various payloads; initial deliveries comprised 46 aircraft for the USAF, followed by six for the US ANG and 44 for the US Army. In 1986 the USAF passed most of its aircraft to the US Army. The USN sub-variant is the **UC-12F**, and these 12 aircraft are to a standard generally similar to that of the UC-12B except for their maximum payload of more than 2,300 lb (1043 kg) and two PT6A-42 turboprops

RC-12F: two UC-12Fs converted to serve as range surveillance aircraft for use by the Pacific Missile Range Facilities

RC-12G Huron: an RC-12D variant for the US Army with systems integrated by Sanders and maximum take-off weight increased to 15,000 lb (6804 kg)

RC-12H Huron: an RC-12D variant for the US Army with systems integrated by ESL and maximum take-off weight increased to 15,000 lb (6804 kg); the variant's primary system is the ESL USD-9(V)2 Improved Guardrail V mission suite now integrated with the Advanced Quick Look Elint system to create the Guardrail Common Sensor system; the aircraft were delivered in 1985 and have also been retrofitted with the Dalmo-Victor APR-39(XE-2) RWR, Northrop ALQ-162 radar jammer, and Sanders ALQ-156 radar-homing missile detection and countermeasures implementation system

RC-12K Huron: highly classified RC-12D electronic warfare derivative for the US Army (34 aircraft, of which two were later transferred to Israel) delivered from the spring of 1988 with two PT6A-67 turboprops each flat-rated at 1,100 shp (820 kW), the Carousel IV-E INS integrated with the ASN-149 GPS receiver for extremely accurate navigation, and the Guardrail Common Sensor advanced electronic suite that allows the variant to be operated in the Comint role of the RC-12D in combination with the Elint mission of the Grumman RV-1D Mohawk

C-12L Huron: designation applied to the first three RU-21J aircraft stripped of their Guardrail electronic systems for use in the utility transport role

UC-12M: designation of the common standard to which the USN's UC-12B and UC-12F were adapted in 1987, when two were converted as **RC-12M** machines for use in the range surveillance role by the Pacific Missile Test Center

RC-12N Huron: derivative of the RC-12K with a 'glass' cockpit and the ASE/ACS (Aircraft Survivability Equipment/Avionics Control System) package

RC-12P Huron: designation applied to 12 RC-12N aircraft upgraded for the US Army with improved electronic systems (including datalink capability), optical fibre cabling, smaller wing pods, and maximum take-off weight increased to 16,500 lb (7484 kg)

RC-12Q Huron: designation applied to three RC-12P aircraft adapted with direct air satellite relay capability

C-12R Huron: Model B200C for the US Army Reserve and National Guard with EFIS cockpit

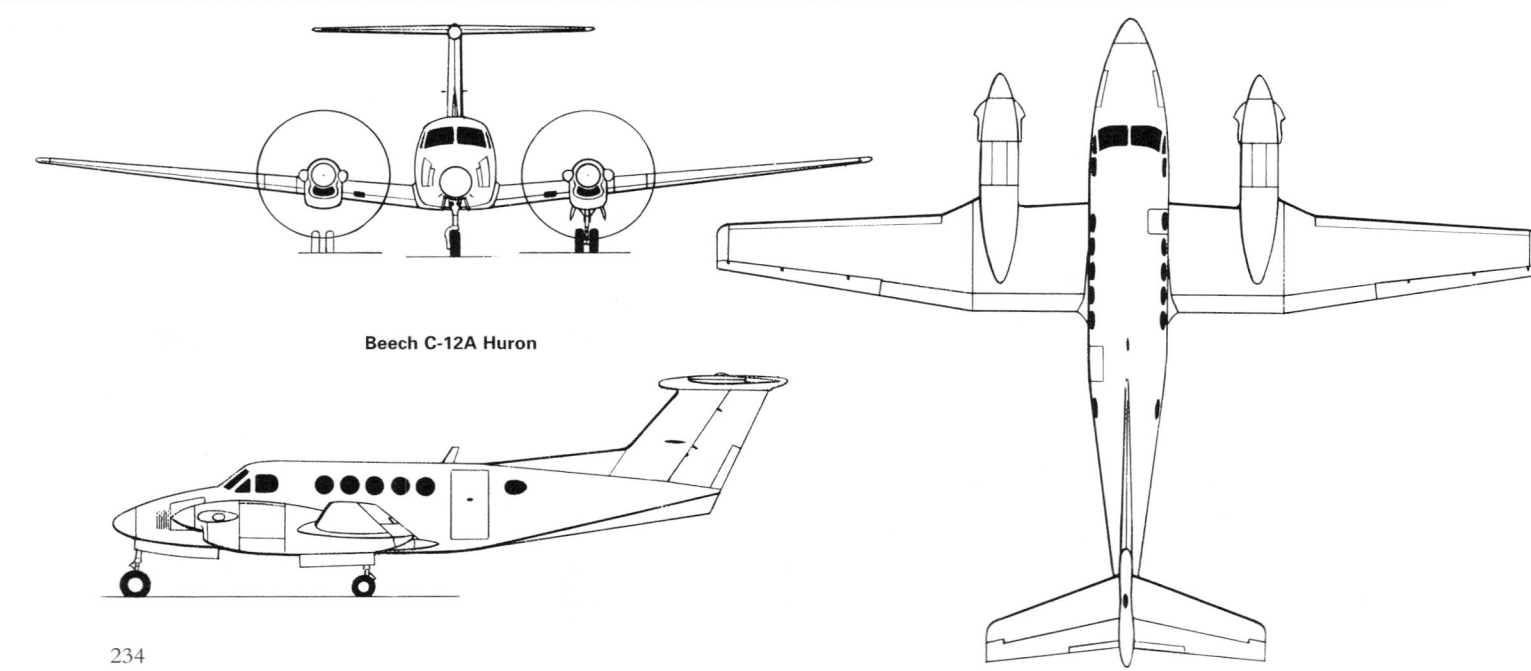

Beech C-12A Huron

Beech Model 300 and Model 350 Super King Air

Developed as an improved version of the Model 200 Super King Air, the **Model 300 Super King Air** was designed from August 1980, first flew in October 1981 as a Model 200 conversion, and was delivered from the spring of 1984. The Model 300 introduced a number of detail refinements, including a forward extension of the inboard section of the wing leading edge, forward movement of the propellers, aerodynamically faired exhausts, and revised reduced-area inlets for the uprated powerplant of two PT6A-60A turboprop engines.

The Model 300 was complemented from the late 1980s by the **Model 300LW Super King Air**, a lightweight variant with its maximum take-off weight restricted to 12,500 lb (5670 kg). This became the sole production model in October 1991.

The only military sale has been of a single **Model 300LW** to Morocco as a VIP transport. Raytheon Beechcraft continues to offer this latest development of the Super King Air series in both its Model 300LW and **Model 350**

forms, the latter having a longer fuselage and a wing of increased span with drag-reducing winglets. Accommodation is for a standard of 10 but maximum of 16 passengers. The Model 350 first flew in September 1988, with first deliveries made in March 1990, and from October 1991 replaced the standard Model 300 when the latter's production certification expired.

In addition to its 2 ft 10-in (0.86-m) fuselage extension and 1 ft 6-in (0.61-m) increase in wingspan, the Model 350 can also be distinguished from the Model 300 by the two extra cabin windows on either side of its cabin.

SPECIFICATION

Beech Model 300 Super King Air
Type: two-crew executive and commuter transport
Powerplant: two Pratt & Whitney Canada PT6A-60A turboprops each rated at 1,050 shp (783 kW)
Performance: maximum speed 365 mph (587 km/h) at high altitude; cruising speed 363 mph (583 km/h) at high altitude; initial climb rate 2,844 ft (867 m) per minute; service ceiling 35,000 ft (10670 m); range 2,256 miles (3630 km)
Weights: empty 8,490 lb (3851 kg); maximum take-off 14,000 lb (6350 kg)
Dimensions: wingspan 54 ft 6 in (16.61 m); length 43 ft 10 in (13.36 m); height 14 ft 4 in (4.37 m); wing area 303.00 sq ft (28.15 m²)
Payload: up to 13 passengers

Variants

Model 300AT Super King Air: airline pilot training derivative of the Model 300. Two ordered in June 1989 by Finnair
Model 350C Super King Air: derivative of the Model 350 with a freight door, complete with an inbuilt airstair
Model 350 Special Missions: overall designation for a variant that can be completed for tasks such as navaid calibration and aerial survey
RC-350 Guardian: Sigint and Elint derivative of the Model 350

Beech Model 400 Beechjet

In December 1985 Beech acquired all design and manufacturing rights to the **Mitsubishi MU-300 Diamond II** biz-jet. In May 1986 Beech flew the first of its **Model 400 Beechjet** derivation, which was superseded from November 1990, after the completion of 64 aircraft, by the improved **Model 400A**. The latter had a certificated ceiling raised to 45,000 ft (13715 m), a larger and more comfortable cabin and Collins EFIS. Some 200 Model 400A aircraft had been delivered by the closing stages of 1998. The standard accommodation of the Model 400 and Model 400A in their civil forms is two pilots and up to eight passengers.

The **T-1A Jayhawk** is a military development of the

Model 400A known to the manufacturer as the **Model 400T**, and provides the USAF with advanced training for the TTTS (Tanker Transport Training System) role. It is the first aircraft type to be delivered for the USAF's SUPT (Specialized Undergraduate Pilot Training) system.

The T-1A features increased fuel capacity, strengthened leading edges and windscreen for low-level birdstrike protection and increased air-conditioning capability. The Jayhawk also features six fewer cabin windows, plus a strengthened wing carry-through structure and engine attachment points to meet low-level flight stresses. For the SUPT role the aircraft carries instructor (right) and student (left)

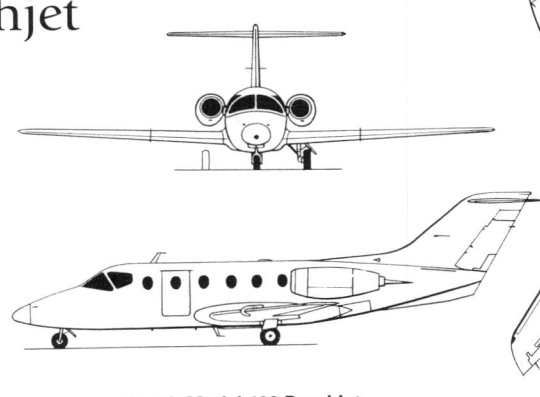

Beech Model 400 Beechjet

pilots, with a third observer/second student seat immediately behind. The cabin has four seats for passenger carriage or for additional students awaiting instruction.

The first production T-1A took to the air at Wichita, Kansas on 5 July 1991, and the first was formally handed over to the USAF on 17 January 1992. The first student courses began in September 1992. All 180 aircraft had been delivered

As part of a $755 million programme, the T-1A Jayhawk replaced the T-39B Sabreliner in USAF service.

by the middle of 1997.

In a somewhat ironic move, in January 1994 the JASDF received the first of nine **Model 400T T-400** aircraft, generally similar to the T-1A, for its Kawasaki

C-1 pilot training role. The Model 400T T-400 features thrust reversers, extra fuel, long-range inertial navigation and direction-finding systems, and regeared trim to simulate a heavier aircraft.

SPECIFICATION

Beech T-1A Jayhawk
Type: two-crew multi-engined transport and tanker crew trainer
Powerplant: two Pratt & Whitney Canada JT15D-5B turbofan engines each rated at 2,900 lb st (12.90 kN)
Performance: maximum speed 531 mph (854 km/h) at 29,000 ft (8840 m); cruising speed 515 mph (828 km/h) at 39,000 ft (11890 m); service ceiling 41,000 ft (12495 m); range 2,222 miles (3575 km) with
four passengers
Weights: empty 10,115 lb (4588 kg); maximum take-off 15,780 lb (7157 kg)
Dimensions: wingspan 43 ft 6 in (13.25 m); length 48 ft 5 in (14.75 m); height 13 ft 9 in (4.19 m); wing area 241.40 sq ft (22.43 m²)
Payload: up to four passengers or trainees for a 2,400-lb (1089-kg) payload

Beech Model 1900 Airliner

The **Beech Model 1900 Airliner** resulted from Beech's realisation that, with the end of Model 99 Airliner production, it had cut itself off from the rapidly growing regional and commuter airliner market of the late 1970s. In 1979, therefore, the company announced its intention of re-entering the market with one or more new types. The company was already at work on an aircraft with 30/40-seat accommodation and, if built, this would have been the largest Beech aircraft yet constructed. In an effort to secure a more immediate niche Beech started to plan a number of Model 200 Super King Air derivatives; the two types to emerge were the **Model 1300** with 13-passenger accommodation, and the Model 1900 with a lengthened fuselage for the carriage of 19 passengers.

In 1981 Beech began work on the construction of three Model 1900 prototypes. The first made the new type's maiden flight on 3 September 1982 with the powerplant of two Pratt & Whitney Canada PT6A-65B turboprops (flat-rated at 1,100 shp/820 kW for good performance under 'hot-

and-high' conditions) and a fuselage derived from that of the Model 200 but with the constant-section part of its fuselage lengthened by 14 ft (4.27 m). Many other parts of the airframe, most notably the wing centre-section and the tail unit, were derived from those of the Model 200 but strengthened for the higher weights of the Model 1900. A distinguishing feature of the design in its definitive form was the pair of small auxiliary fixed tail surfaces or 'stabilons' on the side of the rear fuselage, and the pair of small auxiliary fins or 'taillets' under the outer ends of the tailplane. A major innovation of later aircraft (the **Model 1900C-1** sub-variant) was the use of integral rather than bladder tanks in the wing for a 60 per cent increase in fuel capacity.

The new type was certificated in November 1983 and entered service in February 1984, but only three aircraft were delivered before the production standard shifted to the **Model 1900C** with an upward-opening cargo door in the port rear side of the cabin, which was outfitted for the carriage of 19 passengers. In July

1985 the Airliner was joined in service by the Model 1900C (and wet-wing Model 1900C-1 **Executive** or **ExecLiner** (originally to have been designated as the **Model 1200**) with the original type of small passenger door and a cabin more comfortably outfitted for between 12 and 18 executive passengers.

Production of the Model 1900C ended in 1991 after the delivery of some 225 aircraft, when the manufacturer switched to the improved **Model 1900D** standard with the height of

the cabin increased to provide genuine standing headroom and increased cabin volume, an increased cabin pressurisation differential, larger cabin windows and door, winglets at the tips of the wing for improved 'hot-and-high' performance, a pair of ventral strakes under the rear fuselage to improve directional stability, and the uprated powerplant of two PT6A-67D turboprops. The Model 1900 is one of the few 19-passenger airliners to remain in production during the late 1990s, and is also available in executive and all-cargo variants. Sales of the Model 1900 series had reached some 580 aircraft by August 1998 and the basic cost of the aircraft is quoted at \$4.775 million (1996).The Model 1900C-1 was the first to

receive military orders, a contract being placed in March 1986 by the USAF for six examples.

Delivered from September 1987 as the **C-12J**, the type replaced the last Convair C-131 aircraft serving with the ANG as mission support aircraft. Between January 1988 and late 1989, 12 Model 1900C-1s were delivered to the Republic of China air force for VIP use. Eight aircraft were ordered by the Egyptian air force for delivery from 1989, and of these machines six were delivered with electronic surveillance equipment and the remaining two, intended for maritime surveillance, with Litton search radar and Motorola SLAMMR (Side-Looking Airborne Multi-Mode Radar) and Singer ESM systems.

With its cabin roof raised by 1 ft 2 in (0.36 m), the Model 1900D's passengers acquired considerably increased headroom, while the aircraft itself took on a distinctly 'humpbacked' appearance.

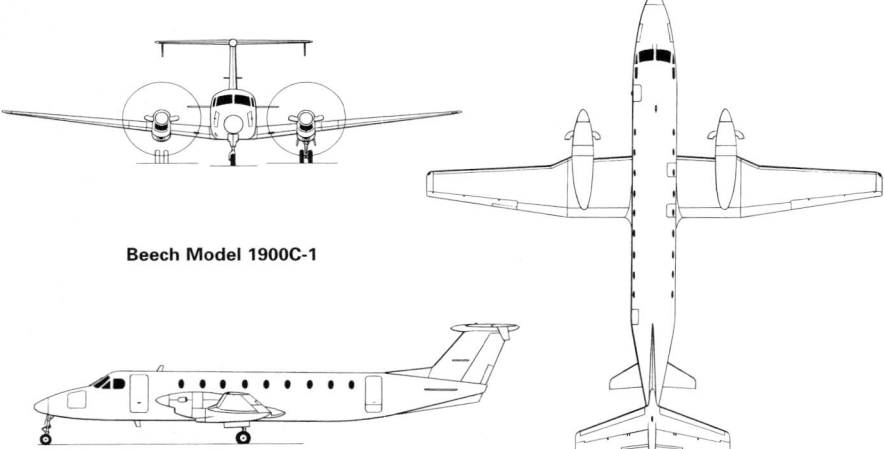

Beech Model 1900C-1

SPECIFICATION	
Beech Model 1900D Airliner **Type:** one/two-crew regional airliner, commuterliner and executive transport **Powerplant:** two Pratt & Whitney PT6A-67D turboprop engines each flat-rated at 1,279 shp (954 kW) **Performance:** maximum cruising speed 331 mph (533 km/h) at 16,000 ft (4875 m); initial climb rate 2,625 ft (800 m) per minute; service ceiling 33,000 ft (10060 m); range 1,726 miles (2778 km) with	10 passengers **Weights:** empty 10,615 lb (4815 kg); maximum take-off 16,950 lb (7688 kg) **Dimensions:** wingspan 57 ft 11½ in (17.67 m) over winglets; length 57 ft 10 in (17.63 m); height 15 ft 6 in (4.72 m); wing area 310.00 sq ft (28.80 m²) **Payload:** up to 19 passengers or freight within the context of a 5,300-lb (2404-kg) payload

Beech Model 2000 Starship 1

Preceded by an 85 per cent scale model constructed under the supervision of Burt Rutan, the **Beech Model 2000 Starship 1** was an extremely ambitious and unusual attempt to break the mould of business aircraft convention by adopting a radical canard configuration. The powerplant of two turboprops is mounted on the trailing edge of the wing, each engine driving a five-bladed pusher propeller. The engines were mounted as

close together as possible to reduce asymmetric thrust problems in the event of a single engine failure, and for the same reason they also had slightly toed-in thrust lines.

The core of the structure, which is largely of Nomex honeycomb and graphite/epoxy composite materials, is the nearly circular-section fuselage. The cabin and cockpit are located ahead of the powerplant as a means of reducing noise levels. The rear-mounted wing is

swept and of high aspect ratio with large leading-edge root extensions. It is a single-piece structure from tip to tip, where the two swept vertical surfaces (or 'tipsails' in Beech nomenclature) are installed. Located ahead of the cockpit are the two halves of the canard fore-plane: these are swept back at 30° in the cruising regime, but for take-off and landing are moved to a 4° forward-swept position as the aircraft's centre of lift moves with the deploy-

SPECIFICATION	
Beech Model 2000A Starship 1 **Type:** two-crew executive transport **Powerplant:** two Pratt & Whitney Canada PT6A-67A turboprop engines each fat-rated at 1,200 shp (895 kW) **Performance:** maximum cruising speed 385 mph (620 km/h) at 25,000 ft (7620 m); initial climb rate 2,748 ft (838 m) per minute; service ceiling 35,800 ft (10910 m);	range 1,742 miles (2804 km) **Weights:** empty 10,120 lb (4590 kg); maximum take-off 14,900 lb (6758 kg) **Dimensions:** wingspan 54 ft 4¾ in (16.60 m); length 46 ft 1 in (14.05 m); height 12 ft 11 in (3.94 m); wing area 280.90 sq ft (26.09 m²) **Payload:** up to six passengers up to a maximum payload of 2,480-lb (1125-kg)

ment of the area-increasing Fowler flaps on the trailing edges of the wing. The Model 2000 is controlled in

flight by canard elevators and the elevons in pitch, the rudders in yaw and the elevons alone in roll.

Beech Model 2000 Starship 1 (continued)

The first of six pre-production Starship 1 aircraft made its maiden flight on 15 February 1986 with two PT6A-65A-4 engines, and the type received full American two- and one-pilot certifications in December 1989 and May 1990 respectively. The first full-production Starship 1 flew on 25 April 1989, but production ended early in 1995 after the completion of only 53 aircraft, not all of which were sold as a result of considerable customer scepticism about so radical a design.

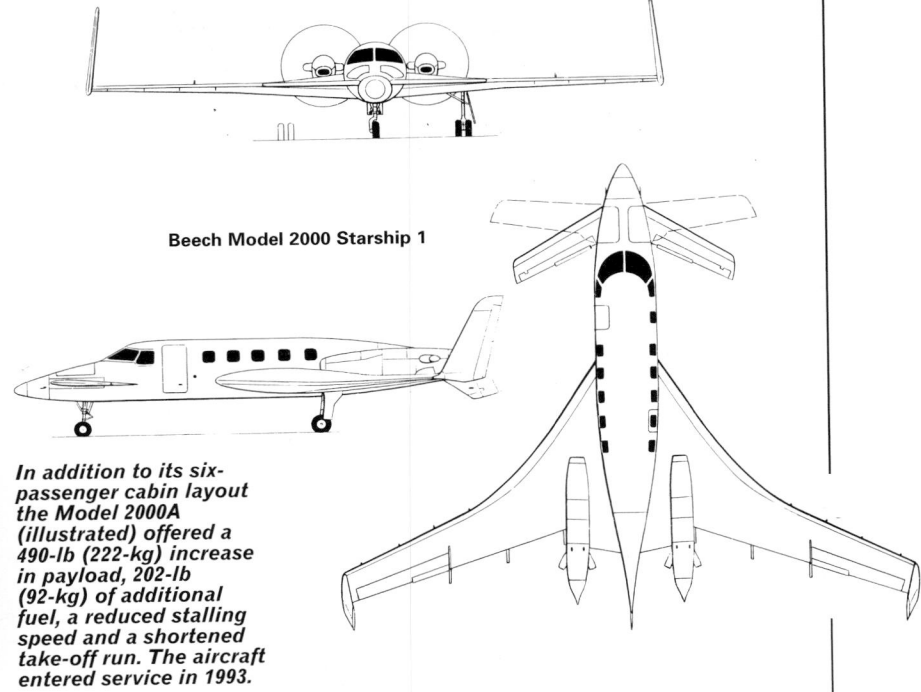

Beech Model 2000 Starship 1

Variants

Model 2000 Starship 1: designation of the first 20 aircraft with accommodation for between eight and 11 passengers
Model 2000A Starship 1: designation of the last 33 aircraft with accommodation for six passengers in a revised interior offering greater passenger and baggage volume as well as a larger lavatory at the rear of the cabin

In addition to its six-passenger cabin layout the Model 2000A (illustrated) offered a 490-lb (222-kg) increase in payload, 202-lb (92-kg) of additional fuel, a reduced stalling speed and a shortened take-off run. The aircraft entered service in 1993.

Bell D-2127 (X-22)

The **Bell D-2127** was developed to a 1962 US Navy contract for research into flight using a tilting arrangement of ducted propellers. The fuselage had rear-mounted stub wings, each having a duct unit built onto the leading edge of its outer section with an elevon in the slipstream from the three-bladed propeller. The 'foreplanes', mounted on each side of the fuselage just aft of the flightdeck, comprised a pair of similar duct/elevon combinations. Power was provided by four General Electric T58 turboshaft engines, mounted in pairs at the root of each of the stub wings, and employing cross-shafting to ensure that, in the event of an engine failure, all four ducts were still powered.

With the service designation **X-22A**, the first D-2127 flew on 17 March 1966, achieving four vertical take-offs. STOL take-offs were also made, but hydraulic failure resulted in a heavy landing on 8 August 1966, the aircraft then being assessed as beyond economical repair. The second prototype flew for the first time on 26 January 1967, and successfully continued the programme to its end, the flight test effort including the first successful transition to forward flight with the ducts rotated to their forward-facing positions, being achieved on 3 March 1967. The machine was handed over for continued use in tri-service, Federal Aviation Administration (FAA) and NASA V/STOL research projects on 19 May 1969 and was finally retired in the autumn of 1984.

While the Bell X-22A was built with retracting landing-gear, persistent problems eventually led to the latter being permanently locked in the extended position, as illustrated here by the second prototype, BuNo 151521.

SPECIFICATION	
Bell D-2127 (X-22A)	**Weights:** empty 11,458 lb
Type: two-crew tilting-duct V/STOL research aircraft	(5190 kg); maximum take-off 18,016 lb (8172 kg)
Powerplant: four General Electric YT58-GE-8D turboshaft engines each rated at 1,250 shp (932 kW)	**Dimensions:** wingspan 39 ft 3 in (11.96 m); foreplane span 23 ft (7.01 m); length 39 ft 7 in
Performance: maximum speed 316 mph (509 km/h) at sea level; cruising speed 213 mph (343 km/h) at 11,000 ft (3355 m); absolute ceiling 27,800 ft (8475 m); range 445 miles (716 km)	(12.06 m); height 19 ft 8 in (5.99 m); wing area area 286.00 sq ft (26.57 m²) equivalent for rear duct units and 139.00 sq ft (12.91 m²) equivalent for forward duct units

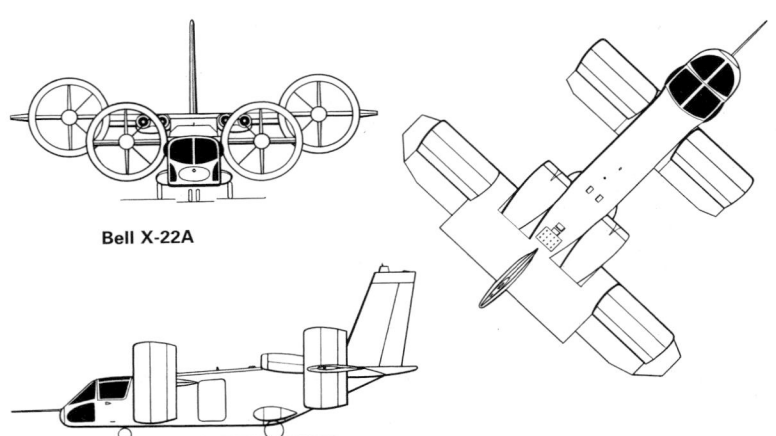

Bell X-22A

Variants

X-22A-1: proposed armed development
X-22B: proposed general-purpose development with T58-GE-5 turboshaft engines
X-22C: proposed cargo development with a rear ramp/door and Textron Lycoming T55-L-7 turboshaft engines

Bell FM Airacuda

Established in 1935 by Lawrence D. Bell, the Bell Aircraft Corporation began its operations by carrying out sub-contract work. The company's first aircraft design was for a long-range escort fighter, or destroyer, in a category similar to that of the Messerschmitt Bf 110. The Bell design was for a large twin-engined monoplane with retractable tailwheel landing gear. Its powerplant comprised two 1,150-hp (858-kW) Allison V-1710-13 Vee engines mounted centrally in long overwing nacelles and driving a three-bladed pusher propeller via an extension shaft. The forward end of each nacelle extended well ahead of the wing leading edge, providing accommodation for a gunner and a 37-mm T9 trainable cannon. Crawlways were provided in the wing so

that the gunners could transit between the fuselage and the gun positions. The **Bell XFM-1** prototype flew for the first time on 1 September 1937 and, after undertaking a successful evaluation of the type, the USAAC ordered 12 **YFM-1** service test aircraft that were the first to receive the name **Airacuda**. These aircraft were completed and delivered to the US Army in three subvariants: six YFM-1s similar to the prototype but with V-1710-23 engines; three **YFM-1A** machines with tricycle landing gear; and three **YFM-1B** aircraft with V-1710-41 engines. All had been delivered by late 1940, but no production contract ensued for several reasons, including the fact that the YFMs were slower than the bombers they were designed to escort.

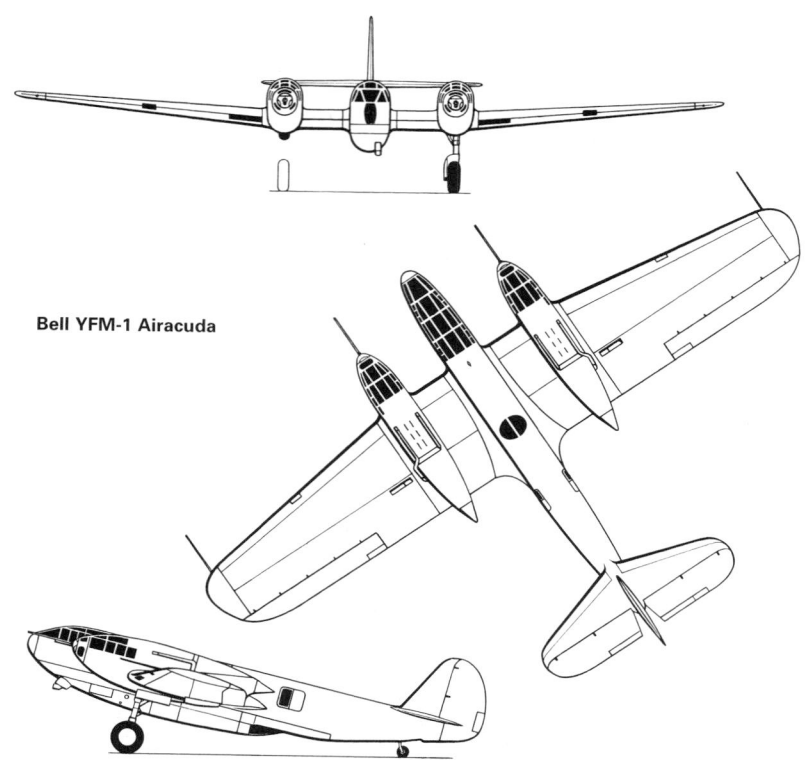

Bell YFM-1 Airacuda

SPECIFICATION

Bell YFM-1B Airacuda
Type: five-seat long-range escort fighter/destroyer
Powerplant: two Allison V-1710-41 Vee engines each rated at 1,090 hp (813 kW)
Performance: maximum speed 268 mph (431 km/h) at 12,600 ft (3840 m); cruising speed 200 mph (322 km/h) at 12,000 ft (3660 m); initial climb rate 1,500 ft (457 m) per minute; service ceiling 29,900 ft (9110 m); range 1,670 miles (2688 km)
Weights: empty 13,674 lb (6202 kg); maximum take-off 21,625 lb (9809 kg)

Dimensions: wingspan 70 ft (21.34 m); length 45 ft 11⅜ in (14.00 m); height 19 ft 6 in (5.94 m); wing area 685.70 sq ft (63.70 m²)
Armament: two 37-mm T9 trainable forward-firing cannon in the wing nacelles, one 0.3-in (7.62-mm) Browning trainable machine-gun in each of the dorsal and ventral positions, and one 0.5-in (12.7-mm) Browning trainable machine-gun in each of the two beam positions, plus up to 20 30-lb (13.6-kg) bombs carried internally

As well as the unusual configuration of the YFM-1, this view also shows the type's undernose periscope. The latter was installed to provide warning of attack from below.

Bell Model 5 (FL Airabonita)

When the US Navy issued a January 1938 specification for a lightweight, high-performance fighter, Bell responded with its **Model 5 Airabonita**, which was derived conceptually from the Model 11

Airacobra. The US Navy ordered a single **XFL-1** prototype in November 1938. In overall terms the Model 5 was closely related to the Model 11, but differed in having an airframe strengthened for

the rigours of carrierborne operation, an arrester hook and a number of other airframe alterations.

The XFL-1 prototype made its maiden flight on 13 May 1940, but the subsequent flight trials were hindered and delayed by problems with the engine and a measure of tail heaviness. The Bell

design team proposed to cure the latter by adding ballast in the nose, but the US Navy refused to allow this. As a result the XFL-1 was delivered to the US Navy somewhat later than anticipated, and the new fighter's official trials began only in July 1940. An immediate problem at this stage was the prototype's failure to secure carrier qualification as a result of landing gear difficulties.

The prototype was returned to Bell for modification in December 1940, and by February 1941 the US Navy had decided that the rival Vought design, which was developed into the F4U Corsair, clearly possessed far greater potential. In February 1942 the XFL-1 was used for anti-aircraft tests, in which it was destroyed, the wreckage of the aircraft surviving into the 1960s.

SPECIFICATION

Bell XFL-1 Airabonita
Type: single-seat carrierborne fighter
Powerplant: one Allison V-1710-6 Vee engine rated at 1,150 hp (858 kW)
Performance: maximum speed 336 mph (540 km/h) at 10,000 ft (3050 m); cruising speed 322 mph (518 km/h) at 20,000 ft (6095 m); initial climb rate 2,630 ft (802 m) per minute; climb to 20,000 ft (6095 m) in 9 minutes 12 seconds; service ceiling 30,900 ft (9420 m); range 1,072 miles (1725 km)

Weights: empty 5,161 lb (2341 kg); maximum take-off 7,212 lb (3271 kg)
Dimensions: wingspan 35 ft (10.67 m); length 29 ft 9⅜ in (9.07 m); height 12 ft 9⅜ in (3.90 m); wing area 232.00 sq ft (21.55 m²)
Armament: planned as one 37-mm T9 fixed forward-firing cannon or 0.5-in (12.7-mm) Browning machine-gun, and two 0.3-in (7.62-mm) Browning fixed forward-firing machine-guns

In addition to its tailwheel undercarriage, the XFL-1 also differed externally from the P-39 in having underwing radiators and larger flaps. The latter reduced stalling speed for easier carrier landings.

Bell Model 11 (P-39 Airacobra)

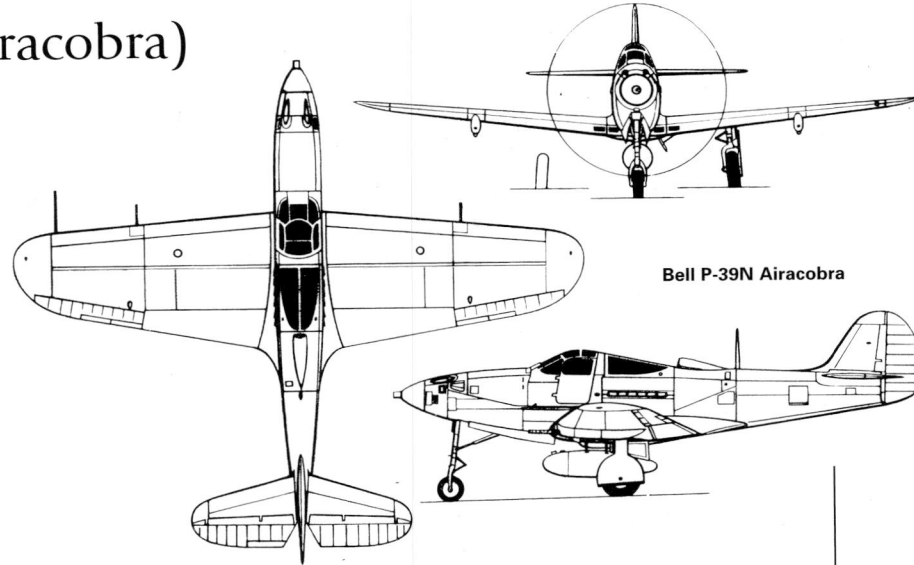

Bell P-39N Airacobra

The **Bell Model 11** fighter that served as the **P-39 Airacobra** and its P-63 successor were unique among US Army fighters of World War II in their power-plant installation. The Airacobra was also the US Army's first operational single-seat fighter with tricycle landing gear.

Early in 1935, Bell executives had been present at a demonstration of the T9 37-mm cannon. Impressed by what they had seen, they instigated the design of a fighter aircraft which would include a T9 cannon firing through the propeller hub, as well as two 0.5-in (12.7-mm) machine-guns mounted in the fuselage nose and synchronised to fire between the blades of the turning propeller. The decision to locate the cannon to fire through the propeller hub meant that the engine had to be mounted within the fuse-lage, directly above the rear half of the monoplane wing, with the propeller driven by an extension shaft which passed beneath the cockpit floor. In turn, this engine posi-tion, virtually over the aircraft's centre of gravity, highlighted the desirability of introducing a tricycle-type landing gear.

The concept was suffi-ciently attractive for the USAAC to place an October 1937 order for a single **XP-39** (Model 11) proto-type, and this flew for the first time on 6 April 1938. Twelve months later, following extensive evalua-tion by the US Army, 12 of the **YP-39** (**Model 12**) service test version were ordered, together with a single **YP-39A** with a supercharger rather than a turbocharger for the Allison V-1710 engine. Following service evaluation of the XP-39, the National Advisory Committee for Aeronautics (NACA) carried out a study of this proto-type, recommending a number of detail changes including deletion of the turbocharger. The original prototype, modified to this new configuration under the designation **XP-39B**, was test-flown and demon-strated improved performance. As a result, the turbocharger was omit-ted from all future aircraft; the 13 service test aircraft were completed to a stan-dard basically similar to that of the XP-39B with two additional 0.3-in (7.62-mm) machine-guns in the nose.

The new fighter was ordered into production in August 1939 with the initial designation **P-45**, which had reverted to P-39 before the first of the order for 80 aircraft was delivered. The first 20 of these aircraft, completed to an improved XP-39B standard, were designated **P-39C** (**Model 13**), but the remaining 60 were of the **P-39D** (**Model 15**) variant with two more 0.3-in (7.62-mm) machine-guns (all four weapons mounted in the wing), self-sealing fuel tanks, and provision for a 500-lb (227-kg) bomb or a drop tank carried on a fuselage centreline hardpoint.

The first large order, for a further 369 examples of the P-39D, was placed in September 1940. Initial deliveries of these began about seven months later, the first export **Airacobra** fighters ordered by a British Purchasing Commission beginning to come off the production line at about the same time. British orders totalled 675 **Model 14** aircraft similar to the P-39D except for the replacement of the 37-mm cannon by a 20-mm cannon, and the two 0.5-in (12.7-mm) and four 0.3-in (7.62-mm) machine-guns replaced by an equal number of 0.303-in (7.7-mm) weapons. The Airacobra began to reach the UK in July 1941. As soon as these machines entered service, however, the full implication of the decision to delete the turbocharger was appreci-ated for the first time, the Airacobra revealing a combi-nation of climb rate and high-altitude performance totally unacceptable for a fighter deployed in the European theatre. Thus only about 80 of the total order entered service with the RAF. More than 250 of the **Model 14A** were supplied to the Soviet air force under a British aid scheme; about 200 in the UK were trans-ferred to the 8th Army Air Force in late 1942, and about 200 were repos-sessed by the USAAF in the continental USA after the USA's entry into the war during December 1941. These ex-British Airacobra fighters received the non-standard designation **P-400** in USAAF service.

Construction of the Airacobra eventually reached 9,558 aircraft, but there were no major design changes in the several vari-ants which followed. The **P-39F** (**Model 15B**), of which 229 were built, succeeded the P-39D in production and differed from its predecessor only in having a hydraulically-operated Aeroproducts constant-speed propeller instead of the electrically-operated Curtiss type of the earlier models. The **P-39J**, of which 25 were built, had a different version of the Allison V-1710 engine, while the **P-39K** (217 **Model 26A** aircraft) and **P-39L** (261 **Model 26B** aircraft), both ordered initially under the designation **P-39G** (**Model 26**), differed in detail equip-ment and by installation of the more powerful V-1710-63 engine: the two variants had an Aeroproducts or Curtiss propeller respectively. The **P-39M** (248 **Model 26D** aircraft) had the lower-power V-1710-83 engine and a propeller of increased diameter. The final two production versions, the **P-39N** and **P-39Q** (**Model 26C/F** and **Model 26E** respectively), were built in large numbers for supply to the Soviet air force under Lend-Lease. As a means of boosting performance, the P-39N (2,547 aircraft) carried less fuel and armour, and the P-39Q (5,078 aircraft) could be identified by its two under-wing fairings, each housing a 0.5-in (12.7-mm) machine-gun in place of the four wing-mounted 0.3-in (7.62-mm) guns.

Of the total of 9,558 aircraft, no fewer than 4,773 (primarily P-39D/N/Q variants) were supplied to the USSR. Variants included three **XP-39E** experimental aircraft with laminar-flow wings, produced as prototypes for the abortive **P-76** powered by the Continental IV-1430-1 engine, and small numbers of **TP-39F** and **RP-39Q** two-seat trainers. Seven P-39 fighters were supplied to the USN for use as target drones under the designation **F2L**. A radio-controlled target version was proposed under the designation **A-7**, but was not developed to the hardware stage.

Although deletion of the turbocharger had limited the Airacobra's potential as a pure fighter, the type was used most success-fully in North Africa in late 1942 in the ground-attack role, and was deployed widely in the Pacific theatre by the USAAF. Until 1944, when more potent fighters began to enter service, the P-39 and basically contempo-rary Curtiss P-40 represented the main first-line equipment of the USAAF's fighter squadrons. A few P-39 fighters were used by the Portuguese air force, acquired after these aircraft had force-landed in Portugal, about 150 were supplied to Free French forces in the latter stages of the war, and a similar number went to the Italian co-belligerent air force.

With Curtiss Electric propellers in short supply, some P-39s were delivered without propellers. The situation was remedied by the development of the P-39F (illustrated) with an Aeroproducts unit.

SPECIFICATION

Bell P-39N Airacobra
Type: single-seat fighter and fighter-bomber
Powerplant: one Allison V-1710-85 Vee engine rated at 1,200 hp (895 kW)
Performance: maximum speed 376 mph (605 km/h) at 15,000 ft (4570 m); cruising speed 200 mph (322 km/h) at optimum altitude; climb to 15,000 ft (4570 m) in 6 minutes 6 seconds; service ceiling 38,270 ft (11665 m); range 975 miles (1569 km)

Weights: empty 6,400 lb (2903 kg); maximum take-off 8,800 lb (3992 kg)
Dimensions: wingspan 34 ft (10.36 m); length 30 ft 2 in (9.19 m); height 12 ft 5 in (3.75 m); wing area 213.00 sq ft (19.79 m²)
Armament: one 37-mm T9 fixed forward-firing cannon, two 0.5-in (12.7-mm) fixed forward-firing machine-guns and four 0.3-in (7.62-mm) fixed forward-firing machine-guns, plus one 500-lb (227-kg) bomb carried externally

Bell Model 27 (P-59 Airacomet)

In the USA the General Electric Company, which had wide experience of the design, development and construction of industrial turbines, was chosen initially to proceed with the development of US gas turbines based on pioneering British engine technology. Because of its geographical location close to the General Electric plant, Bell was chosen to design and build a fighter powered by the first American-built gas turbine. Realising that early engines would develop only limited thrust, the company elected for a twin-engined installation in its **Bell Model 27 Airacomet**, with one engine in the angle under the wing and fuselage on each side.

The overall configuration selected for the new type was that of a mid-wing monoplane with tricycle landing gear, with care taken to ensure a fairly high tailplane position so that it would be clear of the efflux from the turbojets.

The first **XP-59A** prototype, powered by two General Electric Type I-A turbojets each rated at 1,250 lb st (5.56 kN), was flown for the first time from Muroc Dry Lake on 1 October 1942. Two more XP-59As were built, followed by a batch of 13 **YP-59A** service test aircraft delivered in 1944, the majority of them with the powerplant of two General Electric I-16 (J31) turbojets each rated at 1,650 lb st (7.34 kN). There followed 20 **P-59A** and 30 **P-59B** Airacomet fighters with the further revised powerplant of two 1,650 lb st (7.34 kN) J31-GE-3 or J31-GE-5 engines, with the P-59B machines also having increased fuel capacity.

Flown for test and evaluation by the USAAF's 412th Fighter Group, a specially formed trials unit, the P-59 was found to have inadequate performance and also proved to be an indifferent gun platform. As a result, no further examples were built.

In common with the Meteor and Me 262, the Airacomet was initially plagued by engine problems. The XP-59A (illustrated) reached an altitude of just 25 ft (7.62 m) on its first flight.

SPECIFICATION	
Bell P-59B Airacomet	range 520 miles (837 km)
Type: single-seat fighter	**Weights:** empty 7,950 lb
Powerplant: two General Electric	(3606 kg); maximum take-off
J31-GE-5 turbojet engines each	13,000 lb (5902 kg)
rated at 2,000 lb st (8.90 kN)	**Dimensions:** wingspan 45 ft 6 in
Performance: maximum speed	(13.87 m); length 38 ft 1½ in
409 mph (658 km/h) at 35,000 ft	(11.62 m); height 12 ft (3.66 m);
(10670 m); cruising speed 375 mph	wing area 385.80 sq ft (35.84 m²)
(604 km/h) at optimum altitude;	**Armament:** one 37-mm M4 fixed
initial climb rate 3,200 ft (975 m)	forward-firing cannon and three
per minute; climb to 20,000 ft	0.5-in (12.7-mm) Browning fixed
(6095 m) in 7 minutes 24 seconds;	forward-firing machine-guns
service ceiling 46,200 ft (14080 m);	

Bell Model 30

While World War II was still in progress, Bell designed and built three examples of an experimental helicopter, the **Bell Model 30**. The first of these pioneering helicopters made its first free flight on 26 June 1943 after undertaking a small number of tethered flights between 29 December 1942 and January 1943, when it was damaged in an accident. The helicopter consisted of an enclosed fuselage, mounted on fixed tailwheel landing gear, with an open cockpit in the nose, and the powerplant mounted within the fuselage to the rear of the cockpit. The two-bladed main rotor incorporated the stabilising bar that was to become a feature of Bell helicopter design, and the two-bladed anti-torque tail rotor was carried on a slender tube extending from the tail.

The second Model 30 incorporated a number of improvements, including a semi-monocoque fuselage a revised anti-torque rotor mounting. The most conspicuous of the changes was the provision of two- rather than single-seat accommodation in an enclosed cabin with car-type doors. The third Model 30, which first flew on 25 April 1945, had quadricycle landing gear, a tubular tail boom, open single-seat accommodation (later improved by the installation of a Plexiglas bubble canopy to improve the pilot's comfort levels) and more advanced instrumentation. It was from these early experimental helicopters that the very extensively built Bell Model 47 production helicopter was developed.

As the second Model 30, NX41868 featured a fully-enclosed cockpit. As part of Bell's Model 30 demonstration programme, the aircraft was flown indoors on at least two occasions.

SPECIFICATION	
Bell Model 30	**Dimensions:** main rotor diameter
Type: experimental helicopter	33 ft (10.06 m); main rotor disc area
Powerplant: one Franklin 6AC flat-six engine rated at 160 hp (119 kW)	855.30 sq ft (79.46 m²)

Bell Model 32 (P-77)

In World War II the use of ever-growing fleets of bombers and fighters brought a real fear that there might be an acute shortage of the light alloys from which most were built. Based on a configuration originally considered by Bell as an alternative to the P-39, the **Tri-4**, as the type was originally known, was one of several projects intended to produce a fighter of so-called non-strategic materials. Designed under the leadership of Bob Woods, the aircraft had a basic structure of wood and was a low-wing cantilever monoplane with retractable tricycle landing gear and an enclosed cockpit located above the trailing edge of the wing.

After some changes, the definitive **Model 32** proposal won an order for six **XP-77** prototypes, of which the first was to be delivered in a mere six months. As a result of delays and rising costs, however, this commitment was reduced to two machines, and the first of these made its maiden flight only on 1 April 1944. Testing revealed a number of problems and seriously inadequate performance. Subsequently, in December 1944, after the second prototype had been destroyed in an accident two months earlier, the programme was halted.

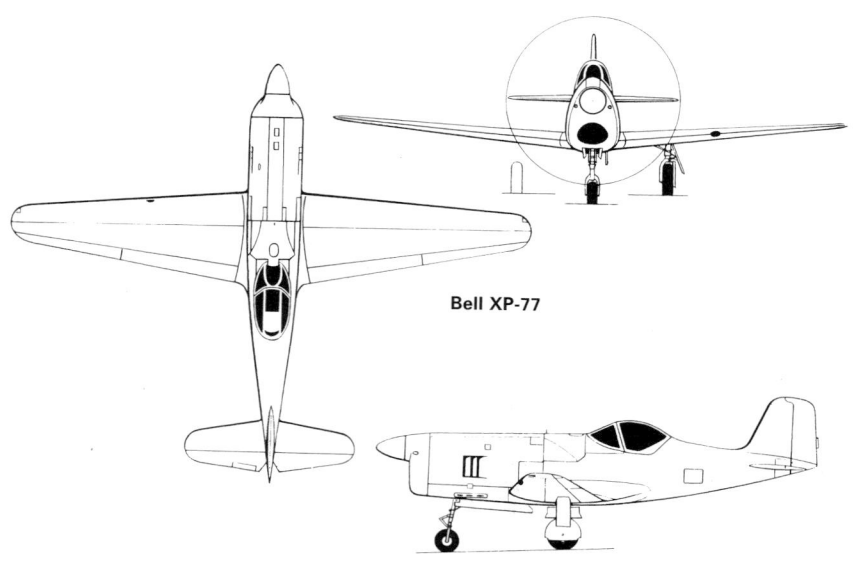

Bell XP-77

Bell Model 32 (P-77) (continued)

SPECIFICATION

Bell XP-77

Type: single-seat lightweight fighter and fighter-bomber

Powerplant: one Ranger XV-770-7 inverted-Vee engine rated at 520 hp (388 kW)

Performance: maximum speed 330 mph (531 km/h) at 4,000 ft (1220 m); initial climb rate 3,600 ft (1097 m) per minute; climb to 9,000 ft (2745 m) in 3 minutes 42 seconds; service ceiling 30,100 ft (9175 m); range 550 miles (885 km)

Weights: empty 2,855 lb (1295 kg); maximum take-off 4,028 lb (1827 kg)

Dimensions: wingspan 27 ft 6 in (8.38 m); length 22 ft 10½ in (6.97 m); height 8 ft 2¼ in (2.50 m); wing area 100.00 sq ft (9.29 m²)

Armament: two 0.5-in (12.7-mm) fixed forward-firing machine-guns, plus one 300-lb (136-kg) bomb carried externally

On 2 October 1944, the pilot of the second XP-77 (illustrated) was forced to abandon the aircraft when it entered an inverted spin. The XP-77 proved to have insufficient performance for an interceptor.

Bell Model 33 (P-63 Kingcobra)

At a fairly early stage in the development of its P-39 Airacobra fighter, Bell had undertaken a measure of work in an effort to enhance its performance by the introduction of aerodynamic improvements. Three experimental aircraft were built, each utilising the basic fuselage of the P-39D, to which was added a new laminar-flow wing with square tips and a revised tail unit. In fact, each of these three XP-39E aircraft had a different tail unit. It was originally planned to power these prototypes with the Continental IV-1430 12-cylinder inverted-Vee engine, which had demonstrated a power output in excess of 2,000 hp (1491 kW). In the event, however, the Allison V-1710 engine of little more than half of that power output was installed, presumably because of the Continental engine's lack of reliability. Testing of the XP-39E machines began in February 1942 and, proving satisfactory, the type was ordered into production under the designation P-76. Some 4,000 aircraft were to be built at Bell's facility at Marietta, Ohio, but were cancelled only three months later.

It was decided instead to build a larger and more powerful version as a fighter-bomber for the increasingly important close-support role, and the research and design development for the XP-39E was used in finalising the design of the **Bell Model 33**, which was ordered as the **P-63 Kingcobra**. In its layout the Kingcobra was generally similar to the P-39, but was somewhat larger, powered by a variant of the V-1710 engine more powerful than those installed in all but the P-39K and P-39L production aircraft, and optimised for the close-support role.

Two prototypes were ordered by the USAAC in June 1941 under the designation **XP-63**, and these made their first flights on 7 December 1942 and 5 February 1943, both powered by the 1,325-hp (988-kW) V-1710-47 engine. Both aircraft were lost early in testing, resulting in the construction of a third prototype, the **XP-63A**, that first flew on 26 April 1943 with the powerplant of one V-1710-93 engine possessing a war emergency rating of 1,500 hp (1119 kW).

Initial deliveries of the **P-63A** began in October 1943 and, by the time production ended in 1945, some 3,213 Kingcobras had been built in several versions. By far the majority of these aircraft, something in excess of 2,400 machines, was supplied to the USSR under Lend-Lease, and about 300 went to the Free French Armée de l'Air. Very few P-63s were delivered to the USAAF and, so far as is known, no Kingcobra aircraft were used operationally by that service.

The equipment of production batches varied considerably, resulting in many subvariants. The first production **P-63A-1** aircraft had the V-1710-93 engine, one 37-mm M4 cannon in the nose and two 0.5-in (12.7-mm) machine-guns in underwing fairings; other sub-types had two additional 0.5-in (12.7-mm) guns mounted in the fuselage nose. The P-63A-1 and **P-63A-5** could carry a 62.5-Imp gal (284-litre) or 146-Imp gal (663-litre) drop tank, or a 522-lb (237-kg) bomb beneath the fuselage, while the **P-63A-6** had underwing racks for two similar bombs or additional drop tanks. The **P-63A-10** could carry three air-to-surface unguided rockets beneath each wing. The weight of defensive armour, intended primarily to give protection from ground-fired weapons, increased progressively from 87.7 lb (39.8 kg) on the P-63A-1 to 236.3 lb (107.2 kg) on the P-63A-10.

The P-63A, whose production totalled 1,725 aircraft, was succeeded on the production line by the **P-63C** with the V-1710-117 engine, which offered an emergency war rating of 1,800 hp (1342 kW) with water injection. A distinctive identification feature of the P-63C, of which 1,227

Standard internal armament could be augmented by additional machine-guns in underwing fairings, as seen on this P-63A. Key distinguishing features between the P-39 and P-63 were the latter's four-bladed propeller and revised rudder shape.

examples were completed, was the small ventral fin. Other variants included a single **P-63D** with the V-1710-109 engine, a bubble canopy, and a wing of increased span; 13 of an ordered total of 2,943 **P-63E (Model 41)** warplanes to a standard that differed from that of the P-63D in its reversion to the standard cockpit canopy; and two **P-63F** warplanes differing from the P-63E only in their V-1710-135 engine and modified tail surfaces.

One other unusual version of the Kingcobra was built extensively (in excess of 300 aircraft) for use by the USAAF in a training programme involving the use of live ammunition. Developed from the P-63A, this **RP-63** model had all its armour and armament removed, and the external surface of its wing, fuselage and tail unit protected by the addition of a Dural skin covering weighing some 1,500 lb (680 kg). Other protection included bulletproof glass in windscreen and cockpit side and upper windows, the provision of a steel grille over the engine air inlet and steel guards for the exhaust stacks, and the

SPECIFICATION

Bell P-63A Kingcobra

Type: single-seat close-support fighter-bomber

Powerplant: one Allison V-1710-93 Vee engine rated at 1,325 hp (988 kW)

Performance: maximum speed 410 mph (660 km/h) at 25,000 ft (7620 m); cruising speed 378 mph (608 km/h) at optimum altitude; climb to 25,000 ft (7620 m) in 7 minutes 18 seconds; service ceiling 43,000 ft (13110 m); range 450 miles (724 km) with maximum weaponload; ferry range 2,200 miles (3541 km)

Weights: empty 6,375 lb (2892 kg); maximum take-off 10,500 lb (4763 kg)

Dimensions: wingspan 38 ft 4 in (11.68 m); length 32 ft 8 in (9.96 m); height 12 ft 7 in (3.84 m); wing area 248.00 sq ft (23.04 m²)

Armament: one 37-mm M4 fixed forward-firing cannon and four 0.5-in (12.7-mm) Browning fixed forward-firing machine-guns, plus up to three 522-lb (237-kg) bombs carried externally

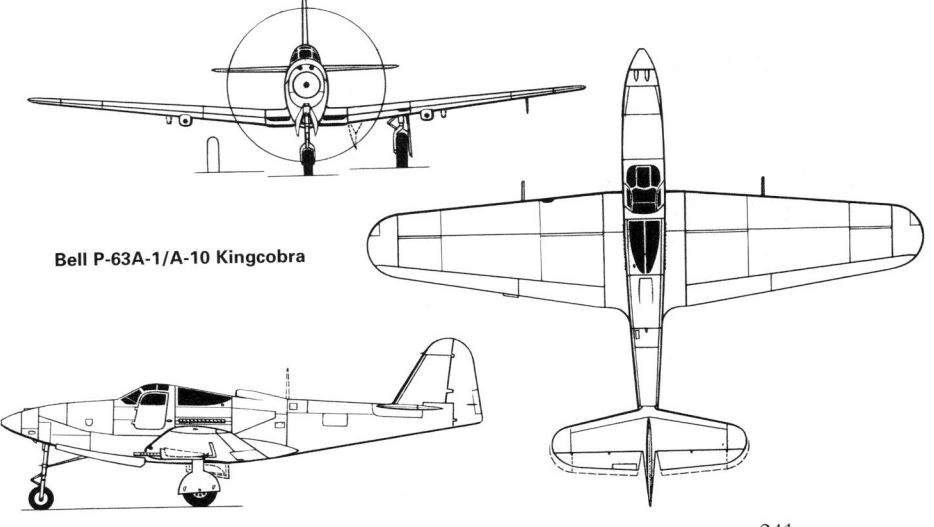

Bell P-63A-1/A-10 Kingcobra

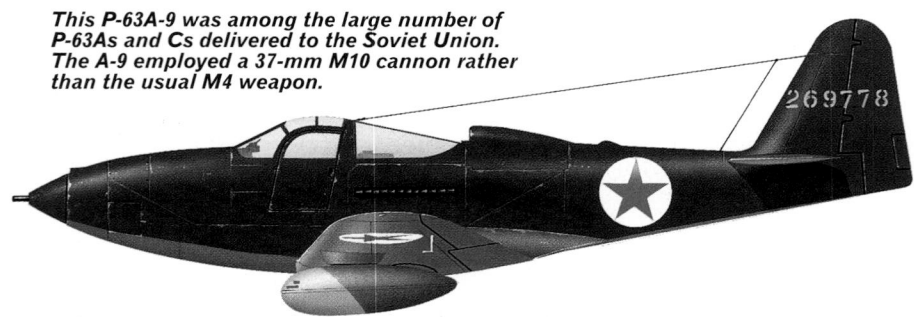

This P-63A-9 was among the large number of P-63As and Cs delivered to the Soviet Union. The A-9 employed a 37-mm M10 cannon rather than the usual M4 weapon.

use of a propeller with thick-walled hollow blades. All of these precautions were to make it possible for the aircraft to be flown as a target that could withstand, without significant damage, the impact of frangible bullets. When a hit was made by an attacking aircraft a red light blinked to confirm the accuracy of the attack. The first of these target aircraft were designated **RP-63A-11**; the

RP-63A-12 machines which followed had increased fuel tankage; the next production version, with the V-1710-117 engine, was the **RP-63C** and the final version was the **RP-63G** with the V-1710-135 engine. Although never flown as pilotless drones, the designations of these three versions were changed to **QF-63A**, **QF-63C** and **QF-63G** respectively.

Bell Model 42

After a survey had revealed the potential market for a civil helicopter larger than the Model 47, Lawrence 'Larry' Bell instructed Bell's helicopter design team to develop such a machine. The result was the **Bell Model 42**, which was an extremely far-sighted helicopter for its time and designed with very elegant streamlining for the maximum possible performance, which was to include a range of 450 miles (724 km) at a cruising speed of 130 mph (209 km). The helicopter was of all-metal construction with accommodation for five persons in the form of the pilot and co-pilot side-by-side at the front of the cockpit on separate seats, and three passengers behind them on a bench seat; access to the cabin was provided by two car-type doors.

The selected engine was the Pratt & Whitney R-985 Wasp Junior radial unit, and this was installed horizontally in the rear part of the pod-and-boom fuselage's pod section. The wooden main rotor was of typical Bell design and construction for the period and a three-bladed wooden anti-torque rotor was located on the starboard side of the semi-monocoque tail boom at the top of a backward-sloped pylon.

Unfortunately, the Model 42, from the time of its first flight in 1946, suffered from a large number of teething problems. Bell therefore transferred responsibility for the Model

42 from the main design team to the specialised helicopter unit. Total production was only three prototypes, however, for the expected civil market did not materialise.

Mechanical over-complexity and a non-existent market killed the Model 42 design. The first of three aircraft is illustrated during testing in 1949.

SPECIFICATION	
Bell Model 42	
Type: five-seat utility helicopter	at optimum altitude; service ceiling 13,000 ft (3965 m); range 300 miles (483 km)
Powerplant: one Pratt & Whitney R-985 Wasp Junior radial engine rated at 450 hp (336 kW)	**Weights:** maximum take-off 5,100 lb (2313 kg)
Performance: maximum speed 125 mph (201 km/h) at sea level; cruising speed 100 mph (161 km/h)	**Dimensions:** main rotor diameter 47 ft 6 in (14.48 m); main rotor disc area 1,772.05 sq ft (164.62 m²)

Bell Model 44 and Model 58 (X-1)

The advent of the rocket motor and the turbojet engine as practical propulsion units in World War II enabled designers to contemplate the development of aircraft capable of flying at speeds greater than that of sound. They then had to contend with the so-called 'heat barrier', which necessitated the development of new materials capable of withstanding the friction-generated (kinetic) heat encountered during supersonic flight.

In February 1945 the USAAF and NACA jointly promoted and financed the development of a series of research aircraft to investigate the problems of flight at supersonic speeds. A contract for these aircraft was duly awarded to Bell. The bullet-shaped **Bell Model 44** prototype, ordered with the service designation **XS-1** (later **X-1**), was first air-launched for an unpowered flight on 19 January 1946, when it was released from a specially modified Boeing B-29. The second prototype made the first powered flight on 9 December of the same year and, on 14 October 1947, Captain

With an enlarged fuselage to allow extra fuel capacity, the X-1A was one of three aircraft built in the wake of the original X-1. The X-1A was eventually destroyed after it was jettisoned from its B-29 mother ship.

Charles 'Chuck' Yeager piloted the aircraft through the 'sound barrier' for the first time, achieving 670 mph (1078 km/h) at 42,000 ft (12800 m), or

Mach 1.05. Just a few days later this machine set an altitude record of 70,119 ft (21372 m). A third X-1 was built but was later destroyed in an accident.

Variants

X-1A: first of three further X-1 airframes ordered in 1948 and manufactured with the company designation **Model 58**, this machine featured a bulged cockpit in place of the almost flat canopy of the XS-1, a lengthened fuselage for increased fuel capacity and turbo-driven fuel pumps in substitution for the original pressurised nitrogen-driven units; on 12 December 1953 Yeager flew the X-1A at Mach 2.35, and in June 1954 reached an altitude of more than 90,000 ft (27430 m)
X-1B: the second machine of the second batch, used for thermal research
X-1D: the third machine of the second batch, this aircraft was destroyed in August 1951 when jettisoned from its parent B-50 after an explosion
X-1E: reworked second prototype X-1, fitted with a new wing manufactured by Stanley Aviation with a 4 per cent thickness/chord ratio and decreased span, and with a redesigned cockpit canopy

SPECIFICATION	
Bell X-1A	
Type: rocket-propelled transonic and supersonic research aircraft	(22680 m); powered endurance 4 minutes 45 seconds
Powerplant: one Reaction Motors XLR11-RM-3 rocket motor rated at 6,000 lb st (26.69 kN)	**Weights:** empty 6,850 lb (3107 kg); maximum launch 14,750 lb (6691 kg)
Performance: maximum speed 1,450 mph (2333 km/h) or Mach 2.24 at high altitude; absolute ceiling 75,000 ft	**Dimensions:** wingspan 22 ft 10 in (6.96 m); length 30 ft 11 in (9.42 m); height 10 ft 10 in (3.30 m); wing area 115.00 sq ft (10.68 m²)

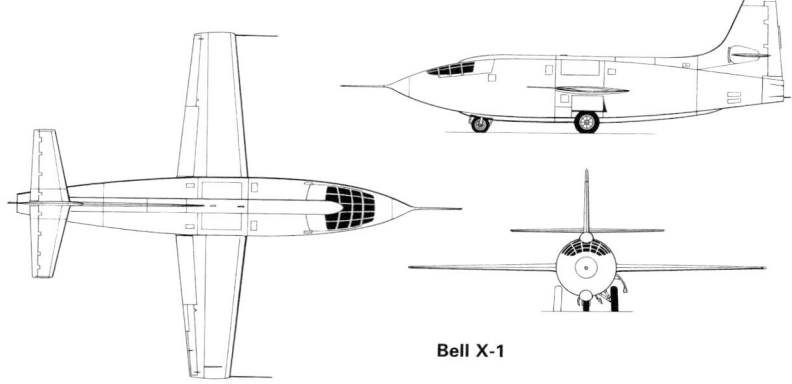

Bell X-1

Bell Model 47 (H-13, HTL and HUL)

It was on 8 December 1945 that the prototype of the **Bell Model 47** made its first flight as a development of the third example of the Model 30, and on 8 March 1946 this new type was awarded the first full certification for a civil helicopter anywhere in the world. The type remained in continuous production by Bell into 1973, and was also built under licence by Agusta, Kawasaki and Westland.

In 1947 the USAAF procured 28 of the improved **Model 47A**, powered by the 157-hp (117-kW) Franklin O-335-1 flat-six engine, for service evaluation: 15 of the helicopters received the designation **YR-13**, three more were **YR-13A** winterised machines for cold-weather trials in Alaska, and the balance of 10 machines went to the USN for evaluation as **HTL-1** trainers. Little time was lost by either service in deciding that the Model 47 was an excellent machine, and large-scale orders began.

The US Army's first order was issued in 1948, 65 being accepted under the designation **H-13B**, and all US Army versions of the Model 47 were later named **Sioux**. Fifteen of these were converted in 1952 for the external carriage of two litters with the revised designation **H-13C**. Two-seat **H-13D** helicopters with twin-skid rather than quadricycle-wheeled landing gear, litter-carrying capability and O-335-5 engines followed, and generally similar three-seat **H-13E** machines for the dual-control trainer role. The **H-13G** differed by

An early Bell Model 47B (foreground), seen in company with a Sikorsky S-51. Both manufacturers would soon become major players in the helicopter market. The Model 47B was the first production helicopter in the Model 47 family and featured car-like doors and windscreen.

introducing a small elevator, and the **H-13H** introduced the 250-hp (186-kW) Avco Lycoming VO-435 flat-six engine. Some of the H-13Hs were also used by the USAF, as were two examples of the **H-13J** with the VO-435 engine, rated at 240 hp (179 kW), for the use of the US president. Two H-13Hs converted for trial purposes, with a larger-diameter main rotor and the 225-hp (168-kW) Franklin 6VS-335 flat-six engine, were designated **H-13K**. In 1962 US Army H-13E, G, H and K helicopters were redesignated with the prefix letter O, for observation. USAF H-13H and H-13J helicopters were given the U prefix as utility helicopters. Later acquisitions were the three-seat **OH-13S** to supersede the **OH-13H**, and the **TH-1ST** two-seat instrument trainer.

USN procurement began with 12 and nine examples of the **HTL-2** and **HTL-3** respectively, but the first major version was the **HTL-4**, followed by the **HTL-5** with the O-335-5 engine and the **HTL-6** trainer with the small movable elevator. The **HUL-1** was acquired for service on board icebreaking ships, and the final **HTL-7** version for the USN was a two-seat dual-control instrument trainer with all-weather instrumentation. In 1962 the HTL-4, HTL-6, HTL-7 and HUL-1 were redesignated as the **TH-13L, TH-13M, TH-13N** and **UH-13P** respectively.

The Model 47 has also served with the armed forces of 39 other countries for a variety of tasks. There were also a number of experimental versions, of

Westland built the Model 47 extensively under licence. This Westland-built Model 47G-3B-1 shows the classic open-structure tail boom of many of the Model 47 variants. The Model 47G-3B-1 was chosen by the British Army to replace its Saro Skeeters.

which the two most important were probably the **Model 201** (service designation **XH-13F**) and the **Model 207 Sioux Scout**. The Model 201 was powered by one Continental XT51-T-3 turboshaft, a licence-built version of a French unit, rated at 280 shp (209 kW).

In parallel with production of military helicopters by both Bell and its licensees, there were civil versions for a wide variety of purposes. The earliest of these were the **Model 47B**, equivalent to the military YR-13 and HTL-1, with the 6ALV-335 engine rated at 175 hp (131 kW) and a two-seat enclosed cabin, and the agricultural/utility **Model 47B-3** with open crew positions. The following **Model 47D** with the 178-hp (133-kW) Franklin 6V4-178-B32 flat-six engine was the first variant to appear with a moulded 'goldfish bowl' canopy, and the **Model 47D-1** of 1949 introduced an open-work tail boom as on the H-13C.

A first important change came with the introduction of the **Model 47G**, which combined the three-seat capacity of the Model 47D-1 with the 200-hp

(149-kW) Franklin 6V4-200-C32AB flat-six engine. Substitution of the identically-rated Avco Lycoming VO-435-A1B engine resulted in the **Model 47G-2**, basically similar to the H-13H. A change to the 240-hp (179-kW) VO-435 engine brought the changed designation **Model 47G-2A**, followed in 1963 by the **Model 47G-2A-1** with a wider cabin, improved rotor blades and increased fuel capacity. Other engine installations included the Franklin 6VS-335-A supercharged engine in the **Model 47G-3**, the Avco Lycoming TVO-435 engine in the **Model 47G-3B**, the TVO-435-B1A turbocharged engine in the **Model 47G-3B-1**, the TVO-435-G1A turbocharged engine in the **Model 47G-3B-2**, the Avco Lycoming VO-540-B1B3 engine in the three-seat **Model 47G-4A**, and the VO-435-B1A engine in the three-seat **Model 47G-5** and **5A**. A two-seat agricultural version of the Model 47G-5 was known as the **Ag-5**, de luxe developments of the Model 47G introduced in 1955 were the **Model 47H** and **H-1 Bellairus** with a sound-proofed cabin for the pilot and two passengers, and a

civil version of the USAF's H-13J VIP transport was marketed as the **Model 47J Ranger** that was built in **J-1, J-2, J-2A, J-3 SuperRanger** and **J-3B-1** subvariants.

When Bell's production of the Model 47 came to an end, examples of the Model 47G-5 were the last to be built. Agusta and Kawasaki both produced helicopters comparable to some of Bell's civil Model 47 helicopters, and added variants of their own, most notably the **Agusta A 115**, the **Kawasaki KH-4** four-seat development of the Model 47G-3B, and the **Kawasaki KHR-1** that was a single KH-4 conversion used for the testing of a three-bladed rigid main rotor. In addition there have been specialised conversions by at least three US companies, including the high-performance **Carson Super C-4**, the **Continental Copters El Tomcat** single-seat agricultural helicopter (variants between the **Tomcat Mk I** and **Mk V**), and the **Texas Helicopters M-74 Wasp** and **M-79T Hornet** single-seat agricultural helicopters with the Allison 250-C20B turboshaft. Turboshaft conversions of several models have also been produced by Soloy.

SPECIFICATION

Bell Model 47G-5
Type: two/three-seat general utility helicopter
Powerplant: one Avco Lycoming VO-435-B1A flat-six engine rated at 265 hp (198 kW)
Performance: maximum speed 105 mph (196 km/h) at sea level; cruising speed 85 mph (137 km/h) at 5,000 ft (1525 m); initial climb rate 860 ft (262 m) per minute; service ceiling 10,500 ft (3200 m); hovering ceiling 5,900 ft (1800 m)

in ground effect and 1,350 ft (410 m) out of ground effect; range 256 miles (412 km)
Weights: empty 732 lb (786 kg); maximum take-off 2,850 lb (1293 kg)
Dimensions: main rotor diameter 37 ft 1½ in (11.32 m); length overall 43 ft 2½ in (13.17 m) and fuselage 32 ft 6 in (9.90 m); height 9 ft 3 in (2.82 m); main rotor disc area 1,082.49 sq ft (100.56 m²)

Bell Model 48 (H-12)

During 1946 Bell began the development of a new military helicopter that was basically an enlarged version of the Model 47. Identified as the **Bell Model 48** and derived from the unsuccessful Model 42 intended for the civil market, this was ordered by the USAAF to the extent of two **XR-12** prototypes with five-seat accommodation and the

powerplant of one 540-hp (403-kW) Pratt & Whitney R-1340-AN-1 radial engine. There was also a somewhat larger **XR-12B** (**Model 48A**) prototype with 12-seat accommodation and a more powerful variant of the Wasp. With the 1948 service type identification change from the R (rotary) to H (helicopter) designation for helicopters, the XR-12 and XR-12B

SPECIFICATION	
Bell YR-12B	
Type: 12-seat utility helicopter	(3900 m); hovering ceiling 4,350 ft (1325 m) in ground effect; range 300 miles (483 km)
Powerplant: one Pratt & Whitney R-1340-55 radial engine rated at 600 hp (447 kW)	**Weights:** maximum take-off 6,286 lb (2851 kg)
Performance: maximum speed 105 mph (169 km/h) at optimum altitude; cruising speed 90 mph (145 km/h) at optimum altitude; initial climb rate 450 ft (137 m) per minute; service ceiling 12,800 ft	**Dimensions:** main rotor diameter 47 ft 6 in (14.48 m); length overall 56 ft 9 in (17.30 m); height 11 ft 3¼ in (3.43 m); main rotor disc area 1,772.05 sq ft (164.62 m²)

became the **XH-12** and **XH-12B** respectively.

There were considerable development problems with the XR-12, and as a result the order for 34 production examples of the **R-12A** was cancelled in 1947. The single XR-12B was followed

by 10 examples of the **YR-12B** (later **YH-12B**) for service trials with the more powerful R-1340-55 radial engine. The continued development difficulties of the type meant that no order for an **H-12B** production variant was placed.

In its YH-12B version the Model 48 was somewhat revised with a wider cabin and quadricycle undercarriage. The project was effectively killed by problems with the main rotor.

Bell Model 52 (X-2)

Bearing a superficial resemblance to the earlier X-1 series of research prototypes apart from the obvious difference of swept flying surfaces, the **Bell Model 52**, ordered as the **X-2**, was designed to permit the investigation of flight at high speed (up to Mach 3) and at high altitude. Employing stainless steel for the wing and other areas likely to encounter high temperatures as a result of kinetic heating, the airframe was instrumented for the gathering of information about the effect of heating on structural materials. Powered by a Curtiss Wright XLR25-CW-1 throttlable rocket motor, the X-2 was fitted with a conventional nosewheel, but the

main landing gear unit comprised an extendable skid, complemented by auxiliary stabilising skids under the wing at midspan. A ground-handling trolley was used to manoeuvre the X-2 into position beneath its launch aircraft, a specially-adapted Boeing B-50, which was itself raised on hydraulic jacks to facilitate loading.

The test programme began on 27 June 1952 with unpowered flights and, while undergoing tests on the pressure and rocket fuel systems in preparation for a powered flight, the prototype was blown from the B-50 by an explosion. Bell's chief test pilot was killed in the blast, and the aircraft fell 30,000 ft (9145 m) into Lake Ontario.

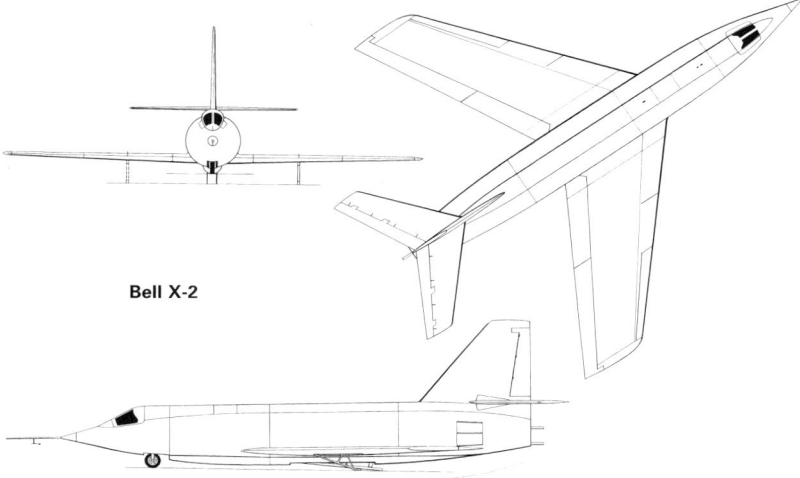

Bell X-2

The second X-2 made the type's first powered flight on 18 November 1955, and on 7 September 1956 it achieved an altitude of slightly more than 126,000 ft (38405 m).

Both X-2s were lost in accidents, 46-674 being the only one to actually undertake flight tests. Captain Milburn Apt lost his life in the aircraft when he jettisoned, but was unable to extricate himself from the X-2's escape capsule.

During a sortie on 27 September 1956, the second X-2 achieved a speed of Mach 3.196 which was not bettered until 1961. However, the mission ended in disaster

as the aircraft entered an undemanded left bank. Application of right rudder failed to correct the motion and the aircraft entered a Mach 3 flat spin and crashed fatally.

SPECIFICATION	
Bell X-2	
Type: single-seat research aircraft	(38465 m); powered endurance 10 minutes 55 seconds
Powerplant: one Curtiss Wright XLR25-CW-1 rocket motor rated at 15,000 lb st (66.72 kN)	**Weights:** empty 12,375 lb (5606 kg); maximum take-off 24,910 lb (11284 kg)
Performance: maximum speed 2,094 mph (3369 km/h) or Mach 3.196 at high altitude; absolute ceiling 126,200 ft	**Dimensions:** wingspan 32 ft 3 in (9.83 m); length 45 ft 5 in (13.84 m); height 11 ft 9 in (3.58 m); wing area 260.40 sq ft (24.19 m²)

Bell Model 54 (H-15)

In February 1946 the US Army issued a requirement for a two-seat light helicopter suitable for the observation task. The G & A Aircraft Company (Firestone) of Willow Grove, Pennsylvania, was deemed to have created

the most capable design and was therefore awarded a contract for three XR-14 light helicopter prototypes based on the powerplant of one 100-hp (75-kW) Continental A100 engine, but these were not built. Bell was placed second in

the design competition with its **Bell Model 54** proposal, and in May 1946 the company was instructed to start work on three **XR-15** prototypes which, in 1948, received the revised designation **XH-15**.

SPECIFICATION	
Bell XR-15	
Type: two/four-seat light utility observation and liaison helicopter	(322 km)
Powerplant: One Continental XO-470-5 flat-six engine rated at 275 hp (205 kW)	**Weights:** maximum take-off 2,800 lb (1268 kg)
Performance: maximum speed 105 mph (169 km/h) at sea level; absolute ceiling 20,000 ft (6095 m); range 200 miles	**Performance:** main rotor diameter 37 ft 4 in (11.38 m); length overall 44 ft 9 in (13.64 m) and fuselage 29 ft 4 in (8.94 m); height 8 ft 10½ in (2.71 m); main rotor disc area 1,094.66 sq ft (101.69 m²)

Bell Model 54 (H-15) (continued)

The XR-15 was a four-seat helicopter of basically all-metal construction and based conceptually on the well-proved dynamic system of earlier Bell helicopters, namely a main rotor with two built-up wooden blades and a stabilising bar at right angles to the blades. The landing gear was of the fixed quadricycle type with a single wheel on each unit, and a tail bumper was installed under the rear of the boom. The powerplant was based on one Continental O-470 engine, and this was installed in the rear part of the fuselage pod in a compartment with large lateral louvres.

Trials of the three prototypes revealed no major problems, but no production order was placed and all development of the XH-15 ended late in 1950.

Based on the dynamic systems of the Model 47, the Model 54 was little more than a strengthened version of the earlier machine for military use. Here, reinforcing ribs are evident on the tail boom of the first XR-15.

Bell Model 60 (X-5)

When US forces occupied the German town of Oberammergau in April 1945, they discovered an experimental facility whose contents included the almost complete prototype of the Messerschmitt P.1101, a single-seat jet research aircraft with ground adjustable wings. The leader of the investigating US team was Bell's chief designer, Robert J. Woods, and in the autumn of 1948, after the P.1101 had been assessed at Wright Field, Woods had it transferred to Bell as a test vehicle for his variable-sweep wing mechanism.

Unfortunately the P.1101 was damaged in transit, but in February 1949 Bell proposed the construction of two **Bell Model 60** variable-geometry prototypes. This was accepted by the USAAF, which ordered two such machines for evaluation with the designation **X-5**. Bearing a clear resemblance to the Messerschmitt design, the first X-5 carried out taxiing trials before being transferred to Edwards Air Force Base, where Jean 'Skip' Ziegler flew it for the first time on 20 June 1951. The first sweep variation was attempted for the fifth flight, on 27 July 1951. The aircraft could operate at three possible angles of sweep, from a minimum of 20° to a maximum of 60°.

The first prototype completed its variable-sweep programme and was then retained at Edwards AFB for use as a chaseplane, but the second was destroyed in a crash on 13 October 1953, after failing to recover from a spin, killing test pilot Major Raymond Popson.

Bell X-5

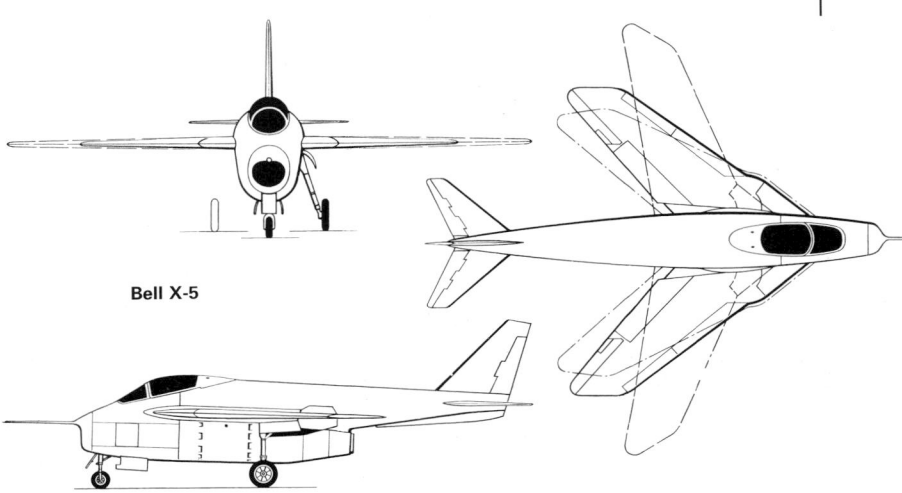

The first of the X-5s, 50-1838, was delivered one year late. In addition to much useful data, the flying characteristics bestowed on the X-5 by its swing wings made it an ideal chase platform.

SPECIFICATION	
Bell X-5	750 miles (1207 km)
Type: single-seat variable-geometry research aircraft	**Weights:** empty 6,350 lb (2880 kg); maximum take-off 9,875 lb (4479 kg)
Powerplant: one Allison J35-A-17 turbojet engine rated at 4,900 lb st (21.80 kN)	**Dimensions:** wingspan 33 ft 6 in (10.21 m) unswept and 20 ft 9 in (6.32 m) swept; length 33 ft 4 in (10.16 m); height 12 ft (3.66 m); wing area 175.00 sq ft (16.26 m²)
Performance: maximum speed about 705 mph (1135 km/h) at high altitude; absolute ceiling about 42,000 ft (12800 m); range about	

Although based on the principles of the P.1101, the X-5 was an altogether more advanced and complicated aircraft. Two machines were ordered at a cost of $2.4 million and the first was due to be delivered within one year of the contract being placed.

Bell Model 61 (HSL)

On 4 March 1953 Bell flew the prototype of its **Model 61** twin-rotor helicopter that had been designed in response to a USN requirement for a new anti-submarine weapon. Announced as the winner of the USN's competition in June 1950, resulting in an order for three **XHSL-1** prototype helicopters, the Model 61 was the first helicopter designed for the complete anti-submarine hunter/killer role, and is also unique among Bell designs in being, so far, the company's only tandem-rotor helicopter.

With a fuselage of basically rectangular section, the Model 61 had fixed quadricycle landing gear and two counter-rotating rotors with blades that could be folded manually. Two pilots and two sonar operators were carried. Weapons included bombs, depth charges, and AUM-N-8 Petrel air-to-underwater homing missiles.

The flight of the prototype was followed by a production order for 78 examples of the **HSL-1**, 18 of these being intended for supply to the UK under the terms of the Mutual Defense Assistance Program. The first of these helicopters entered service with the USN's HU-1 squadron in January 1957, but because of the aircraft's considerable shortcomings, none was supplied for the Royal Navy, and production for the USN was cut back so that only 50 were built. The fact that the type had only limited performance when carrying both hunting and killing equipment meant that the HSL-1 remained in front-line service for only a short period.

SPECIFICATION

Bell HSL-1
Type: four-seat carrierborne ASW helicopter
Powerplant: one Pratt & Whitney R-2800-50 Double Wasp radial piston engine rated at 1,900 hp (1417 kW)
Performance: maximum speed 115 mph (185 km/h) at sea level; cruising speed 95 mph (153 km/h)

at optimum altitude; range 350 miles (563 km)
Weights: maximum take-off 26,500 lb (12020 kg)
Dimensions: rotor diameter, each 51 ft 6 in (15.70 m); fuselage length 39 ft 2¾ in (11.96 m); height 14 ft 6 in (4.42 m); rotor disc area, total 4,166.14 sq ft (387.03 m²)
Armament: see above

Even with its rotors folded, the HSL-1 was too large for aircraft-carrier elevators. In addition, the aircraft's excessive noise signature made sonar operations next to impossible. Two further military variants, the D-216 and D-238, and a civil version, D-116, remained as unbuilt projects.

Bell Model 65 ATV

In 1952 a Bell concept for a jet-powered fighter gained a feasibility study contract, but the company opted as a private venture to proceed with a simple and therefore cheap proof-of-concept vehicle.

This was the **Bell Model 65 Air Test Vehicle (ATV)** which, in order to keep down costs and allow rapid design and construction, was based on an assembly using as many existing components as possible: the wing was that of a Cessna Model 170 with its outermost sections removed, the fuselage was that of a Schweizer glider, and the fixed twin-skid

landing gear was from a Bell Model 47. These elements formed the basis of a parasol-wing mono-plane that was completed by a T-tail and the power-plant of two small Fairchild J44 turbojets. These engines were attached to the sides of the fuselage on the centre of gravity position on a mounting that allowed their thrust line to be swivelled through 90° between the vertical for direct lift and the horizontal for direct thrust. In the fuselage, between and to the rear of the two J44 units, was a Turboméca Palouste gas generator that was used to supply

SPECIFICATION

Bell Model 65 ATV
Type: single-seat VTOL research aircraft
Powerplant: two Fairchild J44 turbojet engines each rated at

1,000 lb st (4.45 kN)
Weights: maximum take-off about 2,000 lb (907 kg)
Dimensions: wingspan 26 ft (7.93 m); length 21ft (6.40 m)

compressed air to the attitude-control system, which utilised nozzles at the wingtips and tail.

Built in a mere eight months, the Model 65 was completed in December 1953, and made its first hovering flight in January of the following year. Only one month later, however,

Evident in this view of the sole ATV are the nozzles for control in hovering flight. A single nozzle is visible at the wingtip, while a long pipe carries a second unit at the rear of the fuselage.

an engine failure damaged fuel lines and the resulting fire badly damaged the ATV. However, it was repaired and once more embarked on its trials

programme, which ended in the spring of 1955. None of its flights involved transition from jet-lifted hovering flight to wingborne horizontal flight.

Bell Model 68 (X-14)

Ordered by the USAF to the extent of one **X-14** for experimental purposes, the **Model 68** was intended only as a low-speed test vehicle and, in an effort to reduce development time and cost, extensive use was made of components from other aircraft: the wing, ailerons and parts of the fixed tricycle landing gear were those of the Beech Model 33 Bonanza, and the tail unit was derived from that of a Beech Model 45 Mentor. These were combined with a new fuselage, and two fixed external fuel tanks, pylon-mounted under the inboard section of the wing on each side of the fuselage.

The X-14 was powered by two 1,560-lb st (6.94-kN) Armstrong Siddeley ASV.8 Viper turbojets. These engines were installed as a side-by-side pair in the extreme nose of the machine. Their normal jetpipes were replaced by a pair of thrust diverters that allowed the efflux to be directed straight down for a vertical take-off and then diverted steadily to the rear to accelerate the machine forward into wingborne flight; the process was reversed for a vertical landing. In lift-borne flight, the aircraft was controlled by compressed-air reaction-control nozzles (using air tapped from the engine's

compressors) located at the wingtips and tail.

The X-14 made its first hovering flight on 17 February 1957, and on 24 May 1958 completed its first full translation to and from forward flight. The USAF accepted the X-14 soon after this and later allocated the machine to NASA. NASA decided that the X-14 was underpowered, and ordered the conversion of the X-14 into the **X-14A** with two 2,680-lb st (11.92-kN) General Electric J85-GE-5

turbojets. The conversion was completed in 1961, and the machine returned to research work before being adapted in 1971 as the **X-14B** with two J85-GE-19s. At the same time the machine was fitted with a programmable computer that allowed the duplication of the handling characteristics typical of the increasing number of VTOL

aircraft then becoming available. The X-14B continued in this role until it was badly damaged in a landing accident on 29 May 1981 and, was deemed not worthy of repair.

Developments that proceeded no further than the project stages were the **X-14C** with an enclosed cockpit, and the **X-14T** VTOL trainer.

Wearing USAF titles and in its original X-14 form, the Model 68 demonstrates its simple airframe design. Later in its career the aircraft would wear both NASA and US Army titles.

SPECIFICATION

Bell X-14B
Type: single-seat VTOL research and training aircraft
Powerplant: two General Electric J85-GE-19 turbojet engines each rated at 3,015 lb st (13.41 kN)
Performance: maximum speed 172 mph (277 km/h) at sea level; service

ceiling 18,000 ft (5485 m); range 300 miles (483 km)
Weights: empty 3,173 lb (1439 kg); maximum take-off 4,269 lb (1936 kg)
Dimensions: wingspan 33 ft 9½ in (10.30 m); length 26 ft (7.92 m); height 8 ft 9½ in (2.68 m); wing area 179.52 sq ft (16.68 m²)

Bell Model 200 (XV-3)

As early as 1943 Bell had appreciated the fact that the helicopter could never rival fixed-wing aircraft in terms of outright performance, especially in terms of payload/range capability over longer distances. It was this realisation that prompted the company's strong interest in the convertiplane.

The **Model 200** programme was initiated in 1950 in response to a joint US Army and USAF initiative to investigate the convertiplane concept for possible US Army use. The three most impressive

designs to emerge from this initiative were the Bell Model 200, the McDonnell Model 82 and the Sikorsky S-57, which received the initial service designations XH-33, XH-35 and possibly XH-36. The Sikorsky design, later redesignated as the XV-2, did not reach the hardware stage, but two prototypes were ordered of each of the Bell and McDonnell types, which were later redesignated as the **XV-3** and XV-1 respectively.

Powered by a Pratt & Whitney R-985 radial engine mounted in the rear

fuselage behind the extensively glazed cabin, the XV-3 had fixed twin-skid landing gear, a conventional tail unit and a mid/shoulder-mounted cantilever wing carrying at its tips two three-bladed articulated proprotors driven from the engine by means of transmission shafts and gearboxes. The proprotors were designed to act as conventional lifting rotors for vertical take-off and then to be tilted progressively forward for the achievement of forward flight, with the fixed wing then providing the necessary lift.

The first XV-3 achieved its maiden vertical take-off on 23 August 1955, and a number of successful partial transitions had been achieved before the prototype was damaged in an accident on 25 October 1956. The second machine, fitted with two-bladed semi-rigid proprotors in 1957, continued the

Both the first XV-3 and the second (illustrated) suffered from a number of complex technical problems. Nevertheless, they proved the practicality of the convertiplane concept.

programme and made the first full transition on 18 December 1958. During investigation of the flight envelope, speeds ranged from 15 mph (24 km/h) rearward to more than 180 mph (290 km/h) in forward flight, at heights up to 12,000 ft (3660 m). In the course of more than 250 flights, the XV-3 completed 100 full translations before being

grounded in 1962 after the discovery of a proprotor/pylon instability problem. The implementation of the necessary changes was completed in 1965, and the XV-3 was then used for 25 more 'flights' in the full-scale wind tunnel as NASA's Ames Research Center in California before suffering further damage and being discarded for further research.

SPECIFICATION	
Bell XV-3	
Type: four-seat convertiplane research aircraft	**Weights:** empty 3,600 lb (1633 kg); maximum take-off 4,800 lb (2177 kg)
Powerplant: one Pratt & Whitney R-985 Wasp radial engine rated at 450 hp (336 kW)	**Dimensions:** wing span 31 ft 3½ in (9.54 m); proprotor diameter, each 33 ft (10.06 m); length 30 ft 3½ in (9.23 m); height 13 ft 6 in (4.11 m); proprotor disc area, total 1,710.60 sq ft (158.91 m²); wing area 120.00 sq ft (11.15 m²)
Performance: maximum speed 180 mph (290 km/h) at 12,000 ft (3660 m); initial climb rate 1,400 ft (427 m) per minute	

Bell Model 204 (UH-1A/B/C/E/F/K/L/M/P Iroquois)

In 1954 the US Army initiated a design competition to speed the procurement of a new helicopter for service in the casualty evacuation, instrument training, and general utility roles, and in February 1955 selected the **Bell Model 204** proposal as winner. The new helicopter was known initially to the US Army as the **H-40**, changed to **HU-1** when it entered service, and given the official name **Iroquois**. This, however, never gained the popularity of the nickname **'Huey'**, which resulted from the HU-1 designation, which itself was altered to **UH-1** under the tri-service rationalisation scheme of 1962.

The US Army's first order was for three prototypes for testing and evaluation under the designation **XH-40**. The first of these prototypes made its maiden flight on

20 October 1956 with the powerplant of one 700-shp (522-kW) Avco Lycoming XT53-L-1 turboshaft and provision for the carriage of five troops internally and more in external pods. Just before the first flight, six examples of the **YH-40** service test model were ordered, all of them being delivered by August 1958 with a number of changes from XH-40 standard including the uprated powerplant of one 860-shp (641-kW) T53-L-1A turboshaft and the lengthening of the fuselage by 1 ft (0.305 m) for greater cabin volume. With the adoption of the US Army's own designation system in 1956, the first two variants became the **XHU-1** and **YHU-1** respec-

tively. By this time the US Army had ordered production of the type, and the first nine pre-production helicopters were delivered from June 1959 with the designation HU-1.

There followed 182 examples of the initial production variant, which was the **HU-1A** (**UH-1A** from 1962) that was built from the spring of 1959 with the T53-L-1A turboshaft de-rated to 770 shp (574 kW), and included 14 helicopters completed to **TH-1A** standard for instrument training with dual controls and blind-flying instrumentation. A single example of the HU-1A was later converted to **XH-1A** standard for trials with a 40-mm grenade

launcher in a nose turret.

The first major deployment of the UH-1A overseas was with the 55th Aviation Company in Korea, and HU-1A helicopters were among the first US Army aircraft to operate in South

Vietnam in the early 1960s.

The HU-1A was of light alloy construction with a semi-monocoque fuselage of pod-and-boom type, and fixed landing gear comprising a pair of skids. The machine employed a typical

A small number of TH-1Fs was delivered to the USAF for rescue and instrument training duties. This aircraft is pictured on the strength of the 37th Air Rescue and Recovery Squadron during Exercise Global Shield in 1979.

Civil and licence-built variants

Model 204B: built in small numbers for civil use and military export. Generally similar to the UH-1B with a 10-seat capacity, the larger-diameter rotor of the UH-1F, and the T5311A engine

Model 533: in 1959 the US Army's Transportation Research Command launched a programme to optimise rotor systems and consider methods of reducing drag in helicopters, and as a result the first YH-40 was modified to Model 533 standard with a cambered vertical tail surface to offload the anti-torque rotor, a streamlined fairing round the rotor mast, flush air inlets for the engine, lower-drag hinged doors and landing skids, and a modified main rotor without the stabilising bar; trials after the helicopter's first flight on 10 August 1962 with the T53-L-13 engine revealed a significant increase in speed; later additions included two Continental 1,700-lb st (7.56-kN) T69-T-9 turbojets in nacelles attached to the sides of the fuselage for a speed of 210 mph (338 km/h), and then a small swept wing to offload the main rotor and allow a maximum speed of 222 mph (357 km/h) or, with J69-T-29 turbojets, 236 mph (380 km/h); the final evolution was a pair of 3,300-lb st (14.68-kN) Pratt & Whitney JT12A-3 turbojets in nacelles at the tips of the stub wing for a maximum speed of 316 mph (508.5 km/h) in May 1969

HueyTug: special development of the UH-1C with a 2,650-shp (1976-kW) Avco Lycoming T55-L-7 turboshaft driving an improved 50-ft (15.24-m) diameter main rotor. As an experimental flying crane the HueyTug was thus capable of lifting a 6,000-lb (2722-kg) external load such as the M101 105-mm howitzer; the HueyTug did not enter production, but was important in the development of later Bell helicopters offering increased lifting capability

Fuji-Bell Model 204B and UH-1B: produced under licence by Fuji in Japan, under sub-licence from Mitsui, Bell's Japanese licensee, with the Kawasaki-assembled KT5311A civil and T53-K-13A military engines

Fuji-Bell Model 204B-2: differs from the Model 204B by having a tractor tail rotor and the 1,400-shp (1044-kW) KT5313B engine

Fuji XMH: made its maiden flight on 11 February 1970 as a research type with a wing spanning 22 ft 3 in (6.78 m)

Agusta-Bell AB 204: built in large numbers for both civil and military use

Military variants

UH-1E: T53-L-11-powered USMC variant based on the UH-1B, featuring a side-mounted personnel/rescue hoist, rotor brake, special avionics and, from October 1965, the Model 540 rotor. First flown in July 1963 with production totalling 212 helicopters including 20 examples of the **TH-1E** crew training version
UH-1F: USAF variant originally designated **H-48** and generally similar to the UH-1B but with the 1,290-shp (962-kW) General Electric T58-GE-3 turboshaft, a main rotor increased in diameter to 48 ft (14.63 m), accommodation for a pilot and up to 10 passengers or 4,000 lb (1814 kg) of freight. First flown in February 1964, with production totalling 146 helicopters including 26 of the **TH-1F** instrument and hoist training subvariant
HH-1K: 27 air/sea rescue derivatives of the UH-1E for the USN, with the T53-L-13 turboshaft
TH-1L and **UH-1L:** training and utility versions of the UH-1E with the T53-L-13 engine. 90 received by the USN
UH-1P: 20 UH-1F conversions for the psychological warfare role. Served with the USAF's 1st Special Operations Squadron

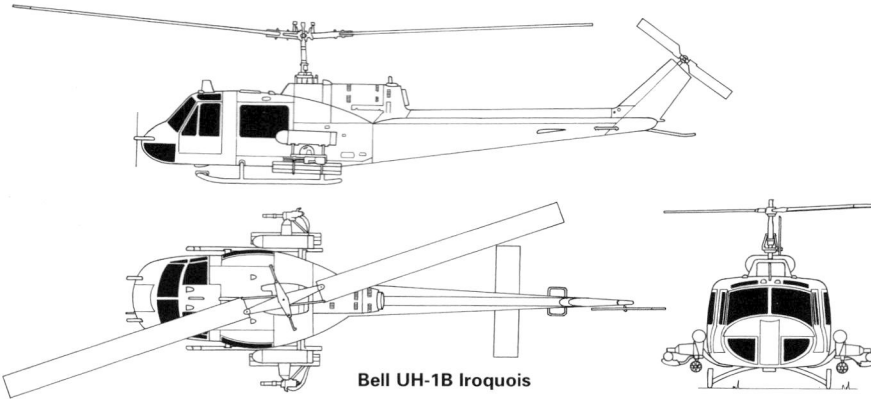

Bell UH-1B Iroquois

Bell main rotor and provided accommodation for a crew of two and six passengers or two litters.

The HU-1A was followed into service by the improved **HU-1B** (**UH-1B**), of which 1,010 were built excluding four **YUH-1B** service test machines. Early production examples had the 960-shp (716-kW) T53-L-5 engine, but later machines switched to the 1,100-shp (820-kW) T53-L-9, 9A and 11 engines. Other improvements in the HU-1B, which

was a far more capable tactical helicopter than the HU-1A, included a main rotor with wider-chord blades on a mast increased in height by 1 ft 1 in (0.33 m), and an enlarged cabin to accommodate a crew of two as well as up to seven passengers, or three litters or 3,000 lb (1361 kg) of freight.

Delivery of the HU-1B was completed between March 1961 and 1965, and the type had provision for armament in the form of two 0.3-in (7.62-mm) elec-

trically controlled machine-guns and packs of 24 2.75-in (70-mm) air-to-surface unguided rockets on each side of the fuse-lage. There were also a number of experimental armament installations including a nose-mounted turret carrying one 40-mm M5 grenade launcher and the XM30 armament system with two side-mounted 30-mm cannon.

In September 1965 the UH-1B was superseded by the **UH-1C**, which had an improved Model 540 'door-

hinge' rotor with still wider-chord blades. Driven by the T53-L-11 engine, this new main rotor conferred some increase in speed as well as improved manoeuvrabil-ity. Other changes were a fin of greater chord and a camber that generated a side force that helped to offload the tail rotor, improved elevators, and increased fuel capacity. The UH-1C had the same basic armament capability as the UH-1B, and production totalled 749 helicopters.

A few UH-1Cs were later

revised with the 1,400-shp (1044-kW) T53-L-13 engine to become **UH-1M** heli-copters. These were also fitted with launchers for up to six AGM-22A wire-guided ASMs, as the French AS11 was designated in US service. Some of these heli-copters were also used for trials of the Hughes INFANT (Iroquois Night Fighter And Night Tracker) system with low-light-level TV and searchlights used in conjunction with the M21 side-mounted armament system.

The first of the USN's TH-1L fleet was delivered in 1969 after an initial contract had been placed on 16 May 1968.

SPECIFICATION	
Fuji-Bell Model 204B-2	(383 km)
Type: one-crew utility helicopter	**Weights:** empty 4,800 lb
Powerplant: one Kawasaki	(2177 kg); maximum take-off
KT5313B turboshaft engine rated	8,500 lb (3856 kg)
at 1,400 shp (1044 kW)	**Dimensions:** main rotor diameter
Performance: maximum level and	48 ft (14.63 m); length overall 44 ft
maximum cruising speed 127 mph	8 in (13.61 m) and fuselage 40 ft
(204 km/h) at optimum altitude;	4¾ in (12.31 m); height 12 ft 4½ in
initial climb rate 1,930 ft (588 m)	(3.77 m) to top of main rotor head;
per minute; service ceiling	main rotor disc area 1,809.50 sq ft
19,000 ft (5790 m); hovering ceiling	(168.10 m²)
15,200 ft (4635 m) in ground effect	**Payload:** up to nine passengers,
and 10,500 ft (3200 m) out of	or litters or freight
ground effect; range 238 miles	

Bell Model 205 (UH-1D/H/U/V/X Iroquois)

Early in 1960 Bell proposed an improved version of the Model 204 as the **Model 205** with a lengthened fuselage to provide accom-modation for a pilot plus 12/14 troops, or six litters, or up to 4,000 lb (1814 kg) of freight in a cabin accessed on each side by larger doors. Bell also addressed the 'hot and high' limitations of the Model 204 by opting for the 1,100-shp (820-kW)

Avco Lycoming T53-L-11 turboshaft driving a main rotor with a diameter of 48 ft (14.63 m).

In July 1960 the US Army awarded Bell a contract for the supply of seven of these new heli-copters for service test under the designation **YUH-1D**, and the first of these made the new vari-ant's maiden flight on 16 August 1961. Following successful flight trials, the

type was ordered into production and the first **UH-1D** was delivered on 9 August 1963. Large-scale production followed for the US Army (2,008 heli-copters, of which 30 were later converted to **HH-1D** rescue standard) as well as for export, and another 348 generally similar helicopters were built under licence by Dornier in Germany for the West German army and air force.

The UH-1D still lacked adequate performance under 'hot and high' condi-tions, however, and was therefore replaced in production during 1967 by the more or less identical **UH-1H** with the 1,400-shp (1044-kW) T53-L-13 turboshaft. Delivery of the UH-1H began in September 1967, and this variant proved to be the final production version, with manufacture ending in December 1980 but then being resumed to satisfy a 55-helicopter order for Turkey, which received its last machine in 1986. The UH-1H was built exten-sively for the US Army (3,573 helicopters), and another 1,317 were built for export military orders.

Under the terms of licensed production agree-ments, the UH-1H was also built in Italy by Agusta, in Japan by Fuji and in Taiwan

by AIDC, of which the last delivered 118 helicopters for the Taiwanese forces between 1969 and 1976.

Variants of the UH-1H have included the **CH-118** (originally **CUH-1H**) built by Bell for the CAF's Mobile Command, which received the first of 10 examples in March 1968, and 30 **HH-1H** base rescue helicopters for service with the USAF.

The UH-1D and -1H were employed extensively on duties in South Asia, up to the end of US involvement. They were regarded as the workhorse helicopters par excellence of the Vietnam War. The type played a major role in special warfare operations in Laos, Cambodia, and in remote areas of South Vietnam, and USAF historians have noted that, in this latter theatre, nearly all battlefield casualties were evacuated by UH-1s.

Around 40 of El Salvador's original fleet of 76 UH-1Hs survives into the late 1990s. The first aircraft were delivered in 1976.

Bell Model 205 (UH-1D/H/U/V/X Iroquois) (continued)

After that time three UH-1H helicopters were converted for the Elint and electronic countermeasures role under the designation **EH-1H**, and examples with the relevant advanced Quick Fix I system were delivered from 1981. Under the US Army's SOTAS (Stand-Off Target Acquisition System) programme, four UH-1H helicopters already forming part of the service's force of **JUH-1H** special test conversions were modified for evaluation in the role of obtaining and relaying radar data about battlefield movements. Some 220 UH-1H helicopters were converted as **UH-1V** hoist-equipped rescue and casevac machines, and one UH-1H was converted as the three-seat **EH-1X** electronic warfare helicopter with the EH-1H's airframe and systems combined with the powerplant and IR jammer of the AH-1 HueyCobra.

The US Army and National Guard, the latter the major operator of the 'Huey' in the last years of the 20th century, intend to retain the basic UH-1H in large-scale service until well into the 21st century in roles that include command and control, electronic warfare, medical evacuation, minefield emplacement, resupply and troop transport. In order to make this plan possible, the existing fleet of UH-1H helicopters was cycled through a major product improvement programme to add advanced avionics and other life-extending equipment. Other improvements have been introduced in the form of new composite main rotor blades, Doppler navigation, and an improved cockpit.

The US Army's requirement for 491 LUHs (Light Utility Helicopters) is not likely to secure the required funding, so there is considerable pressure for the

ANG to take over the role with upgraded UH-1 helicopters. The ANG might therefore receive additional UH-1H helicopters for upgrading beside the 200 helicopters it already desires either to replace or, failing this, to rebuild. Many overseas operators of 'Huey' series helicopters are also interested in an upgrade for their ageing helicopters.

Three companies have proposed significant UH-1 upgrades, all of them based on the introduction of a modern engine and an upgrade of the helicopter's dynamic system although other elements include avionics improvements within a price varying between $750,000 and $1,000,000 per helicopter.

Bell Helicopters itself offers the **UH-1HP Huey II** with an overhaul-level upgrade of the current T53-L-13B engine, increasing power to 400 shp (298 kW) and bringing it to T53-L-703 standard. All of the related enhancements make use of existing Model 212 and UH-1N components and the Huey II prototype made its maiden flight in August 1992.

The fact that Bell has entered the lists for a 'Huey' upgrade has not deterred other companies from offering their own concepts for this potentially lucrative market. The two most interesting of Bell's opponents in this field are Global Helicopter Technology and US Helicopter. The offering from Global Helicopter is the **Huey 800**, in which the T53 turboshaft engine is replaced by the 1,399-shp (1043-kW) LHTEC T800-LHT-800 turboshaft which is significantly lighter and considerably more fuel-efficient. A major increase in range is therefore achieved and the first Huey 800 made its maiden flight in June 1992.

The US Helicopter upgrade is designated as

the **UH-1/T700 Ultra Huey**, and this is based on the same basic package of airframe and dynamic system improvements as the Huey II, but in this instance in combination with a 1,900-shp (1417-kW) General Electric T700-GE-701C turboshaft. The improvements derived from this package are essentially identical to those of the Huey II except that fuel consumption is not reduced.

Bell also produced a civil version of the UH-1H under the designation **Model 205A-1** with the T5313B

turboshaft de-rated to 1,250 shp (932 kW). Special attention was given to interior design to permit quick conversion for air freight, ambulance, executive, flying crane and search roles. Maximum accommodation is for a pilot and 14 passengers or 5,000 lb (2268 kg) of freight carried externally.

The Model 205 was also built in Japan under the terms of the same licensing and sub-licensing agreements as the Model 204. This **Fuji-Bell Model 205** was produced as the

Fuji-Bell HU-1H military variant with the Kawasaki T53-K-13B turboshaft, glassfibre main rotor blades, and a tractor rather than pusher tail rotor. The first HU-1H flew in July 1973, and military production totalled 107, of which the survivors are being upgraded with the designation **UH-1J**. The civil counterpart of the HU-1H is the **Fuji-Bell Model 205A-1** which is essentially similar to the American-built Model 205A-1 except for its Kawasaki KT5313B turboshaft engine.

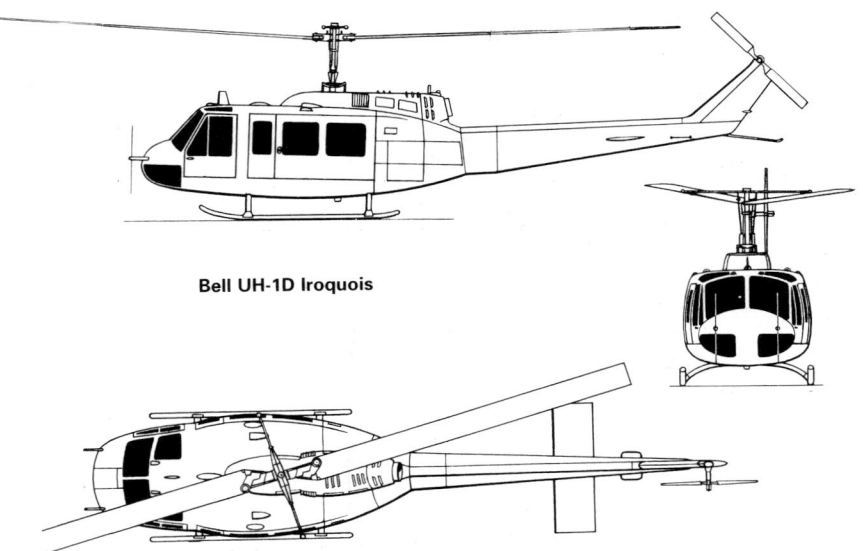

Bell UH-1D Iroquois

New Zealand received fifteen UH-1Ds from 1966, of which NZ3801 was the first. The aircraft wears the short-lived silver fern-adorned roundel.

SPECIFICATION	
Bell UH-1H Iroquois	effect; range 318 miles (511 km)
Type: one-crew utility helicopter	**Weights:** empty 5,210 lb (2363 kg); maximum take-off 9,500 lb (4309 kg)
Powerplant: one Textron Lycoming T53-L-13 turboshaft engine rated at 1,400 shp (1044 kW)	**Dimensions:** main rotor diameter 48 ft (14.63 m); length overall 57 ft 9¾ in (17.62 m) and fuselage 41 ft 10¼ in (12.77 m); height 14 ft 5½ in (4.41 m); main rotor disc area 1,809.56 sq ft (168.11 m²)
Performance: maximum level and maximum cruising speed 127 mph (204 km/h) at 5,700 ft (1735 m); initial climb rate 1,600 ft (488 m) per minute; service ceiling 12,600 ft (3840 m); hovering ceiling 13,600 ft (4145 m) in ground effect and 4,000 ft (1220 m) out of ground	**Payload:** up to 14 passengers, or six litters plus one medical attendant, or 4,000 lb (1814 kg) of freight

The UH-1D/H has come to epitomise the battlefield utility helicopter and the type will be an important component of the US armed forces into the 21st Century. This aircraft is fitted with cable-cutters above and below the forward fuselage and shows the larger cabin doors compared to the Model 204.

Bell Model 206A JetRanger (H-57 SeaRanger, H-58 Kiowa)

In 1960 the US Army launched a Light Observation Helicopter (LOH) design competition. The LOH was required to fulfil the casualty evacuation, close support, observation, photo-reconnaissance and transport roles previously undertaken by the Bell H-13, Cessna L-19 and Hiller H-23. The specification called for four-seat accommodation and a cruising speed of 120 mph (193 km/h) with a 400-lb (181-kg) payload. Design proposals were put forward by 12 US helicopter manufacturers, from whom Bell, Hiller and Hughes were each contracted to build five prototypes for competitive evaluation. From the tests which followed, the Hughes HO-6 (later OH-6) was selected for production as the US Army's LOH. Bell did not share the Army's doubts about its **Model 206** submission which was prototyped as the **YHO-4A** (from 1962 **YOH-4A**) and first flew on 8 December 1962.

After losing the LOH competition Bell therefore built a new prototype as the **Model 206A JetRanger**, which first flew on 10 January 1966 with a wider and considerably more streamlined fuselage and a stepped nose. The Model 206A received its civil certification in October 1966 and entered production, initially in the USA during 1966 and then later in Italy by Agusta, for delivery, from January 1957, to civil customers as well as a growing number of foreign military operators. The type was powered by the 317-shp (236-kW) Allison 250-C18A turboshaft and seated five people.

The US Army had

expected to procure some 4,000 OH-6As, but became somewhat disenchanted with Hughes for a combination of steeply rising unit cost and declining production rate. As a result, in 1967, the Army decided to curtail procurement of the OH-6A and re-open the LOH competition. On 8 March 1968 the Model 206A was announced as the winner, and production of the **OH-58 Kiowa** military version of the Model 206A started without delay to make possible the delivery of 2,200 examples by the end of 1973.

The **OH-58A** differed from the Model 206A in having a main rotor with a diameter of 35 ft 4 in (10.77 m) rather than 33 ft 4 in (10.16 m), the 317-shp (236-kW) T63-A-700 turboshaft, detail changes in internal layout for the carriage of a crew of two at the front and freight at the rear, and the provision of military avionics. Initial deliveries to the US Army began on 23 May 1969, and the Kiowa was soon deployed operationally in war-torn Vietnam.

Of the original 2,200 OH-58As ordered for the US Army, 74 were withdrawn from the production line for delivery to the CAF from December 1971 under the designation **COH-58A** (subsequently changed to **CH-136**). An additional US Army contract for 74 aircraft was issued in January 1973 to replace the helicopters diverted to Canada. The designation **OH-58B** was applied to 12 helicopters delivered to Austria during 1976 in a standard basically similar to that of the OH-58A.

Under a US Army development contract Bell

adapted one OH-58A in 1976 with an improved flat glass canopy for reduced 'glint' as well as the uprated powerplant of one 420-shp (313-kW) T63-A-720 turboshaft, a 'Black Hole' exhaust and a hot metal shroud for IR suppression. These changes created the **OH-58C**, and subsequently two additional conversions were carried out before production modification of 425 OH-58As to the definitive OH-58C configuration began in March 1978. A

further 150 aircraft were upgraded to the same standard by IAI for the US Army in West Germany.

US Navy acquisition of the Model 206A began with 40 **TH-57A SeaRanger** helicopters. Ordered in January 1968, the TH-57A is a dual-control trainer for the primary flying trainer role with the NATC and is basically a civil Model 206A with US Navy avionics. Further USN procurement resulted in the **TH-57B SeaRanger** and **TH-57C SeaRanger**, of

which 51 and 89 examples respectively were purchased. The TH-57Bs had all been delivered by late in 1985 and are to a Model 206B JetRanger III standard with the uprated Allison 250-C20 turboshaft flat-rated at 317 shp (236 kW). The TH-57C was ordered in January 1982 and delivered at much the same time as the TH-57B, and is a Model 206B derivative optimised for the advanced instrument training role with full IFR instrumentation.

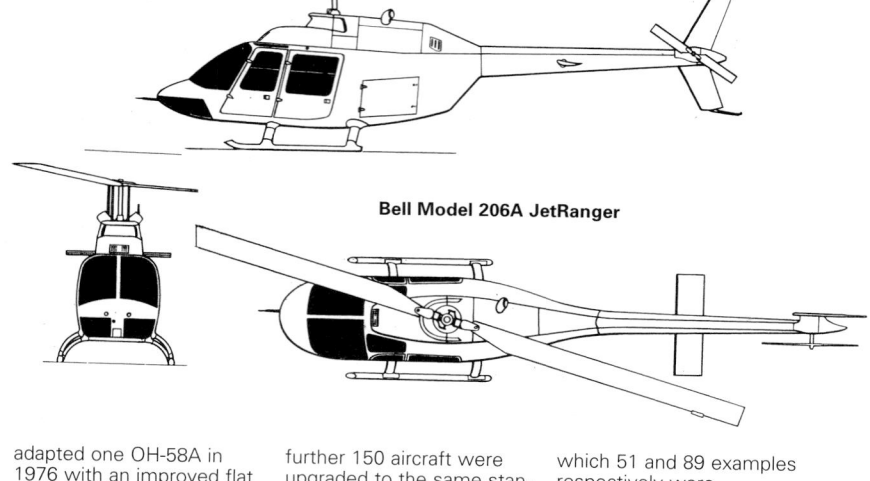

Bell Model 206A JetRanger

Above: At the end of the 20th century, Canada has only just withdrawn the last of its CH-136 fleet. Much of the aircraft's former role has been assumed by the Bell CH-146 Griffon. A number of CH-136s have appeared on the civil market.

Below: Apart from their bright paint scheme, little distinguished the TH-57As from their civilian Model 206A counterparts. This aircraft is a civilian-registered TH-57A on a pre-delivery flight.

SPECIFICATION

Bell OH-58A Kiowa
Type: two-seat observation and utility helicopter
Powerplant: one Allison T63-A-700 turboshaft engine rated at 317 shp (236 kW)
Performance: maximum cruising speed 122 mph (196 mph) at sea level; initial climb rate 1,780 ft (543 m) per minute; service ceiling 19,000 ft (5790 m); hovering ceiling 13,750 ft (4190 m) in ground effect and 9,000 ft (2745 m) out of ground effect; range 299 miles (481 km)
Weights: empty 1,583 lb (718 kg); maximum take-off 3,000 lb (1361 kg)

Dimensions: main rotor diameter 35 ft 4 in (10.77 m); length overall 40 ft 11¾ in (12.49 m) and fuselage 32 ft 3½ in (9.84 m); height 9 ft 6½ in (2.91 m); main rotor disc area 980.52 sq ft (91.09 m²)
Armament: generally none, although provision is made for one McDonnell Douglas M27 armament kit centred on one 7.62-mm General Electric M134 Minigun rotary six-barrel machine-gun with 2,000 rounds in an elevating mount on the port side of the fuselage
Payload: up to 1,534 lb (696 kg) of freight

Bell Model 206B JetRanger family

Early in 1971 Bell began delivery of the improved **Bell Model 206B JetRanger II**, which subsequently replaced the Model 206A as the main production variant of the civil helicopter. The Model 206B differed from its predecessor in its uprated powerplant of one 400-shp (298-kW) Allison 250-C20 turboshaft. The installation of this engine involved only minor airframe modification, so that it was also possible to provide kits for the upgrade of Model 206As to Model 206B standard. The Australian armed forces acquired this version under the designation **Model 206B-1 Kiowa**, 12 being supplied by Bell and 44 produced under a co-production agreement, with the Commonwealth Aircraft Corporation in Australia responsible for final assembly. Production of the JetRanger II ended in the summer of 1977, when it was replaced by the **Model 206B JetRanger III**. This introduced a more powerful

version of the standard turboshaft engine, the 420-shp (313-kW) Allison 250-C20B de-rated to 317 shp (236 kW), for further improved performance. This engine was also made available as an installation kit to upgrade JetRanger IIs to JetRanger III standard, and in its current **Model 206B-3** form with the Allison 250-C20J engine the JetRanger III was still the standard civil helicopter of the series in the late 1990s.

The Model 206B series has sold very well on the civil market, and has also entered military service with the air arms of numerous counties. Among these aircraft are more specialised variants such as the torpedo-armed **Model 206AS** anti-submarine model for the Chilean navy. In March 1993 the US Army selected the type to meet its NTH (New Training Helicopter) requirement, ordering the **Model TH-206** variant as the **TH-67A Creek** to replace the UH-1s

Bell's Model 206L LongRanger offers greater capacity than the JetRanger and has found a ready market among emergency medical service (EMS) and law enforcement agencies.

used in the pilot and instrument training roles. An initial quantity of 102 was ordered with the Allison 250-C20JN turboshaft in the IFR role. An order for 35 VFR helicopters followed, and in the late 1990s the US Army held options for a further 20 machines.

Since 1986 deliveries of the Model 206 series and subsequent civil helicopters from the Bell stable have been made from Bell Helicopter Textron Canada, which was established in October 1983 as a means of creating a helicopter industry in Canada and also offering Bell reduced production costs.

The capability and reliability of the JetRanger family resulted in Bell developing a medium-lift version under the designation **Model 206L-1 LongRanger**. This had the powerplant of the JetRanger III as well as a fuselage lengthened by 2 ft 1 in (0.63 m) to accommodate five passengers and two pilots. A double door was incorporated in the port side of the fuselage and other improvements included an advanced main rotor system.

Deliveries of the LongRanger began in October 1975, but this variant was superseded by the current production **Model 206L-2 LongRanger II** in mid-1978. The LongRanger II differs in having the more powerful Allison 250-C28B turboshaft with a maximum continuous rating of 489 shp (365 kW), a higher-rated transmission, and detail improvements. During 1981 the company was developing improved **Model L-3 LongRanger III** and **Model 206L-4 LongRanger IV** versions, the former introduced in 1983 with the 650-shp (485-kW) Allison 250-C30P turboshaft and detail improvements, while the latter was introduced in 1992 with seven-seat accommodation and an uprated transmission system, and was still the production standard in the late 1990s.

Two derivatives of the LongRanger are the **Model 206LT TwinRanger** delivered from January 1994 with two 450-shp (336-kW)

Allison 250-C20Rs and the **Tridair/Soloy Gemini ST** twin-engined rebuild of the LongRanger to the same standard as the TwinRanger. Like the JetRanger, the LongRanger has secured a number of military sales.

In 1980 Bell initiated development of a multi-role military variant under the designation **Model 206L TexasRanger** with one 500-shp (373-kW) Allison 250-C28B turboshaft, but this development proceeded no further than one demonstration helicopter. The same basic capability was offered by a Chilean development, the **Cardoen CB 206L-3** based on the LongRanger III, but this too eventually came to nothing.

By the late 1990s production of the Model 206 JetRanger by Bell and its licensees had passed an incredible 7,700 helicopters including 4,400 Model 206Bs and 2,2000 military variants, and that of the LongRanger had exceeded 1,650 machines.

The fixed skid landing gear of the JetRanger may be swapped for a float arrangement. In 1997, the price of a new Allison C20J-powered Model 206B-3 JetRanger III was $695,000.

SPECIFICATION

Bell Model 206B-3 JetRanger III
Type: one-crew general-purpose light helicopter
Powerplant: one 420-shp (313-kW) Allison 250-C20B turboshaft engine flat-rated to 317 shp (236 kW)
Performance: maximum cruising speed 133 mph (214 km/h) at sea level; initial climb rate 1,280 ft (390 m) per minute; service ceiling 13,500 ft (4115 m); hovering ceiling 12,800 ft (3900 m) in ground effect and 8,800 ft (2680 m) out of ground

effect; range 455 miles (732 km)
Weights: empty 1,677 lb (760 kg); maximum take-off 3,350 lb (1519 kg)
Dimensions: main rotor diameter 33 ft 4 in (10.16 m); length overall 38 ft 9½ in (11.82 m) and fuselage 31 ft 2 in (9.50 m); height 10 ft 4¼ in (3.17 m) with optional tall skids; main rotor disc area 872.67 sq ft (81.07 m²)
Payload: up to four passengers or 1,400 lb (635 kg) of freight carried internally, or 1,500 lb (680 kg) of freight carried externally

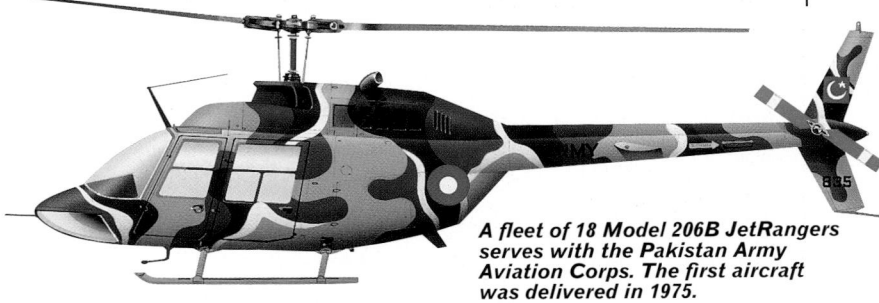

A fleet of 18 Model 206B JetRangers serves with the Pakistan Army Aviation Corps. The first aircraft was delivered in 1975.

Bell Model 207 Sioux Scout

When US involvement in South Vietnam was at an early stage, Bell decided to develop a lightweight close-support helicopter as a private venture. Based on

the US Army's OH-13S Sioux, the resulting Bell **Model 207 Sioux Scout** made its maiden flight on 27 June 1963.

The Sioux Scout retained

the dynamic system and 260-hp (194-kW) Avco Lycoming TVO-435 engine of the OH-13, was of generally similar dimensions, and also had skid

type landing gear. In most other respects the new helicopter differed considerably from its antecedent, having a completely redesigned enclosed and streamlined fuselage, providing accommodation for two in tandem. It also

introduced small horizontal and vertical tail surfaces, but otherwise the tail rotor and ventral fin arrangement were similar to those of the OH-13S. Short-span stub wings were introduced, set high on the fuselage immediately to the rear of the

251

main rotor pylon. The wing surfaces served not only to offload the main rotor in forward flight, to improve manoeuvrability and to

A number of classic gunship features were established by the Model 207, including the tandem seating arrangement with the gunner seated forwards.

provide carriage for auxiliary fuel tanks, but were also intended to incorporate underwing hardpoints for the carriage of various weapons. A traversing undernose chin turret housed two 0.3-in (7.62-mm) M60 elevating machine-guns, controlled by a gunner accommodated in the nose with his seat on a lower level than

that of the pilot, thus ensuring that both men had the best possible forward fields of vision.

The Model 207 remained only a prototype, but many of the new ideas incorporated in the Model 207 were very soon wedded to the utility UH-1B to produce the highly successful Bell Model 209 HueyCobra family.

Bell Model 209 (AH-1 HueyCobra)

First flown on 7 September 1965 as the private-venture **Model 209** powered by one 1,100-shp (820-kW) Avco Lycoming T53-L-11 turboshaft, this important helicopter was evolved from the company's **D-255 Iroquois Warrior** design concept. This was proposed to meet an urgent US Army demand for a helicopter gunship able to undertake three primary roles in Vietnam: the escort of troop-carrying UH-1s, the suppression of enemy defences around an LZ and the provision of fire support for the troops landed from these tactical transport machines.

The Iroquois Warrior concept had been based on the **D-245** design with small swept auxiliary wings and a slender fuselage. The vertically stepped arrangement of tandem cockpits located the co-pilot/gunner below and forward of the pilot, and the design included retractable skid landing gear, stub wings and the dynamic system of the Model 204. The US Army examined the Iroquois Warrior mock-up in June 1962, but with the proposed establishment of Air Cavalry Combat Brigades, Bell decided to evolve an attack helicopter tailored specifically to the needs of the new type of unit. A first step was the production of the Model 207 Sioux Scout prototype,

and concepts from the Model 207 were then embodied in the larger, turbine-powered **D-262**, which was in essence a scaled-down version of the D-255 to compete with the Lockheed CL-840 (later Model 87) and Sikorsky S-66 in the Advanced Aerial Fire-Support System (AAFSS) competition.

The D-262 was the first casualty of the competition, which was won by the Lockheed design that was ordered in the form of 10 YAH-56A Cheyenne service test helicopters. The AAFSS requirement had called for a highly sophisticated helicopter, but the order for the complicated Cheyenne was finally cancelled because of intractable technical and financial problems. By this time Bell had concluded that the development phase of the AAFSS programme would be so long that an interim type would be needed, and in December 1964 the company decided to proceed with the private-venture development of the **Model 209 Cobra** on the basis of the D-262. Work on the new helicopter started in March 1965, and key elements in the design were a fuselage with a width of only 3 ft 2 in (0.97 m), the boom and tail unit (complete with anti-torque rotor but a longer-span tailplane) of the

After a long programme of upgrading, the US Army arrived at the ultimate AH-1F. This aircraft offered full TOW capability with no affect on performance, along with advanced IR suppression features.

This early production AH-1G was one of the few aircraft completed with its tailrotor mounted to port. The machine's GAU-2B/A Minigun has been covered over.

UH-1C, small stub wings and retractable twin-skid landing gear. The narrow fuselage gave the Model 209 a small frontal cross section, with obvious advantages in reducing conspicuity and thus vulnerability. This armament comprised a fixed Emerson Electric chin turret carrying one 7.62-mm GAU-2B/A Minigun and various stores carried on four hardpoints under the stub wing.

Construction of the prototype was already well advanced when the US Army announced a requirement for an interim gunship helicopter for service in South Vietnam within 24 months. Bell offered its Model 209 in August 1965, it was evaluated against its two rivals (variants of the Kaman H-2 Seasprite and Sikorsky H-3 Sea King) and declared winner of the competition in March 1966. The US Army's procurement of the resulting **AH-1 HueyCobra** began with

just two pre-production helicopters based on the Model 209 but modified with fixed twin-skid landing gear and other changes. The first **AH-1G** was completed in May 1967 to permit deliveries from June 1967 with a powerplant of one 1,400-shp (1044-kW) T53-L-13 turboshaft engine derated to 1,100 shp (820 kW) and, in all but the first helicopters, the anti-torque rotor relocated from the port to the starboard side of the tail pylon.

The turret was initially the TAT-102A, although this was later supplanted by the TAT-141 turret carrying two Miniguns with 4,000 rounds per gun, or two 40-mm M129 grenade launchers with 300 rounds per weapon, or one example of each weapon. The turret was generally fired by the co-pilot/gunner and the disposable armament was usually controlled by the pilot.

The AH-1G proved very useful for the close support and attack roles in the Vietnamese fighting, and additional orders raised AH-1G production total to an eventual 1,126 units. Some 38 machines were transferred in February 1969 to the USMC and a few other examples were converted into **TH-1G** dual-control trainers.

In the early 1970s the ICAP (Improved Cobra Armament Program) resulted in the creation of the **AH-1Q** as an interim

anti-tank helicopter to fill the operational gap left by the cancellation of the AH-56 Cheyenne. The AH-1Q was therefore the AH-1G revised for carriage of the BGM-71 TOW heavyweight anti-tank missile. The US Army placed its ICAP contract in March 1972, and this specified the conversion of eight AH-1G helicopters to the improved **YAH-1Q** standard with TOW missiles and the HDFCS (Helmet-Directed Fire-Control Subsystem). The first conversion was delivered in February 1973, and successful trials paved the way for the January 1974 contract ordering an initial 101 AH-1Q 'production' conversions, followed by a further 189 ordered in December 1974.

Early operational service revealed that the AH-1Q was underpowered, and in the event only 92 such conversions were completed. The other 198 helicopters did not receive the conversion because the weight and drag of the TOW system seriously degraded manoeuvrability and performance with the existing powerplant.

As a result the US Army contracted with Bell for the ICAM (Improved Cobra Agility and Maneuverability) programme that was the first stage in a four-stage sequence of improvements that would finally yield a common standard, to be known as the **AH-1S HueyCobra**.

Bell Model 209 (AH-1 HueyCobra) (continued)

Financial constraints curtailed this effort, and the US Army eventually ended up with helicopters to four different standards, a fact later recognised in the replacement of the AH-1S designation by four other designations.

The core of Bell's response to the ICAM requirement was the 1,800-shp (1342-kW) T53-L-703 turboshaft, together with a revised transmission and the tail rotor of the Model 212. The first of two prototypes was the **YAH-1R** conversion of an AH-1G, while the second was the **YAH-1S** conversion of an AH-1Q with full TOW capability. The YAH-1R and YAH-1S were evaluated from December 1974, and such was their performance that in June 1975 the AH-1Q program was terminated. Existing AH-1Qs were converted to this first stage of the improved standard with the uprated dynamic system as well as fibre-glass main rotor blades, a primary offensive arma-ment of eight TOW anti-tank missiles, better defensive capabilities, and improved fire-control subsystems.

The designation **AH-1S (Modified) HueyCobra** was initially allocated, but in 1987 the revised designation AH-1S HueyCobra was decreed. Some 15 aircraft were later converted to **TH-1S (Modified) Night Stalker** standard for use by the Army National Guard as PNVS (Pilot's Night Vision Sensor) and IHADSS (Integrated Helmet And Display Sighting System) trainers for the AH-64A Apache, and in 1987 these helicopters were redesig-nated as **TH-1S**.

In 1975 the US Army undertook the PASS (Priority Aircraft Subsystem Suitability) programme to further improve the HueyCobra's capabilities. The aim was to improve the helicopter's capabilities against the new generation of Soviet anti-aircraft weapons. As a result of the review, Bell received orders for 305 (later reduced to 297) HueyCobra helicopters in three steadily improved versions. The first of these was the **AH-1S (Production) HueyCobra** with a flat-plate canopy, revised cockpit, an RWR, and (from the 67th heli-copter) Kaman K-747 composite-structure rotor

Bell AH-1F HueyCobra

blades with tapered tips. These 100 helicopters were redelivered between the summer of 1977 and August 1978, and from 1987 the variant received the revised designation **AH-1P HueyCobra**.

Sometimes known by the **Up-gun AH-1S HueyCobra** designation, the second version of the PASS improvement resulted in 98 new-build helicopters identi-cal to the AH-1S (Production) apart from their provision with the ECAS (Enhanced Cobra Armament System). The helicopters were redelivered between September 1978 and October 1979, and in 1987 the surviving examples of this variant received the revised designation **AH-1E HueyCobra**.

The third and definitive production version of the HueyCobra resulting from the PASS review was the **AH-1S (MC)**, the letter suffix standing for **Modernized Cobra**. This has all the features of the AH-1S (Production) and

AH-1S (ECAS) variants plus Doppler navigation, an IR jammer, a secure communi-cations system, and a new fire-control system. The initial 99 helicopters of this subvariant were delivered between November 1979 and April 1981, a supple-mentary batch of 50 was delivered from April 1981, and finally 337 AH-1Gs were rebuilt to the same standard between November 1979 and June 1982. In 1987 the variant received the revised designation **AH-1F**.

In-service aircraft are being further modernised with the C-NITE system (50 helicopters only) for noctur-nal and adverse-weather target detection, acquisition and engagement, provision for FIM-92A Stinger AAMs, a laser illumination warning system, and the C-Flex (Cobra Fleet Life Extension) upgrade. Israeli helicopters are being fitted with the IAI Cobra Laser Night Attack System to allow the firing of AGM-114A Hellfire missiles, cockpit and navigation improvements, a lengthened

tail boom and a four-bladed main rotor.

Bell and Textron Lycoming offer export customers an extensive upgrade package including the 2,000-shp (1491-kW) T53-L-70X turboshaft, the four-bladed main rotor, a lengthened tail boom, a digi-tal three-axis stability-augmentation system, and a combination of various reliability and maintainability improve-ments.

The **TAH-1F** is a dual-control trainer version of the AH-1F, and deliveries totalled 41 helicopters delivered as AH-1G conversions with the original designation **TAH-1S**. Finally, the **Fuji-Bell AH-1S** is the Japanese license-built version of the AH-1F with the 1,800-shp (1342-kW) Kawasaki (Textron Lycoming) T53-K-703 turboshaft.

Other than the USA, oper-ators of the HueyCobra have included Bahrain, Israel, Japan, Jordan, Pakistan, South Korea, Spain, Thailand and Turkey.

Bell Model 209 (AH-1 SeaCobra, SuperCobra, and AH-68)

In the autumn of 1967 the USMC received an initial batch of 38 AH-1Gs converted with naval avion-ics, a 20-mm M197 cannon in the chin turret, and a rotor brake. These heli-copters provided marine aviators with an interim close support capability for their ground forces in the northern part of South Vietnam and also generated useful experience in the operation of attack heli-copters. The USMC rightly felt that it needed a more specialised variant with the operational and flight safety advantages of a twin-engined powerplant, as well as a combination of avionics and weapons opti-mised for the USMC's particular role. The result

was the **AH-1J** that was first ordered in May 1968 to the extent of 69 heli-copters. The type made its maiden flight in October 1969, and was completely delivered to the USMC by February 1975.

The AH-1J was a deriva-tive of the AH-1G with the powerplant of the UH-1N, namely the 1,800-shp (1342-kW) Pratt & Whitney Canada T400-CP-400 coupled turboshaft engine flat-rated at 1,250 shp (932 kW). Further produc-tion was undertaken for Iran, which procured 202 examples of the **AH-1J International** derivative with a number of Model 309 KingCobra features and a powerplant of one 1,970-shp (1469-kW)

T400-WV-402 coupled turboshaft. The first 140 helicopters were otherwise similar to the standard AH-1J, but the remaining 62 were of the more capa-ble **AH-1J (TOW) International** anti-tank standard with an armament of eight TOW missiles. South Korea also took eight

of this version.

In a programme that in many ways paralleled the US Army's development of the AH-1G, the **AH-1T Improved SeaCobra** was

No AH-1T SeaCobras (illustrated) remain in the USMC inventory. This aircraft is loaded with pods for 2.75-in (70-mm) and 5-in (127-mm) rockets.

developed with features of the Model 309 KingCobra and Model 214 including a 48-ft (14.63-m) diameter main rotor and a higher-rated power train able to

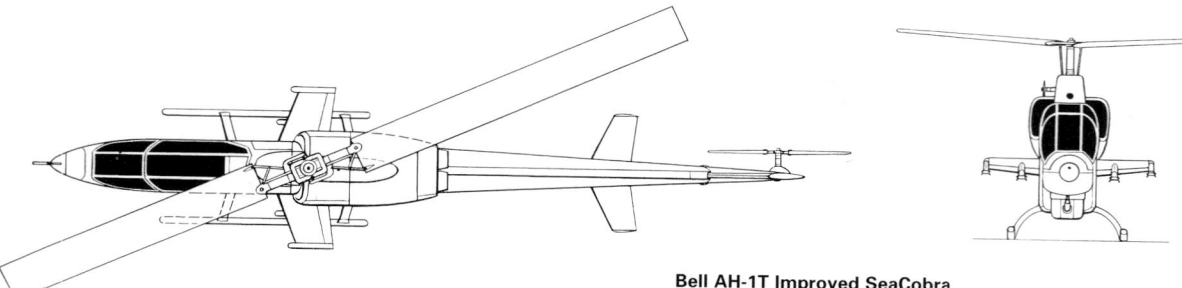

Bell AH-1T Improved SeaCobra

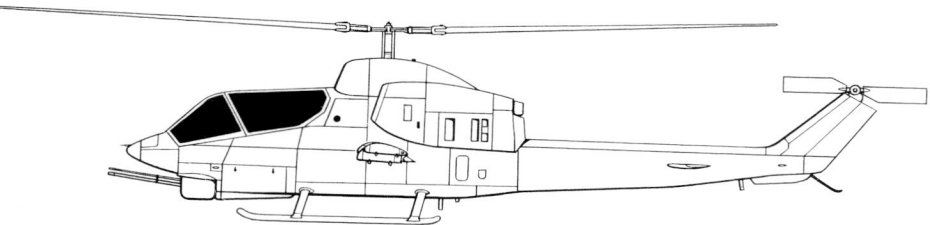

handle the full 1,970 hp (1469 kW) delivered by the Pratt & Whitney Canada T400-WV-402 coupled-turboshaft engine. The first of two AH-1J prototype conversions flew in May 1976, and the armament capability of this important variant, of which 57 were delivered from October 1977, includes BGM-71 TOW or AGM-114 Hellfire anti-tank missiles on the outboard underwing hardpoints. About 50 of the helicopters have been upgraded to further improved **AH-1W** standard.

Developed as the **AH-1T+** to remedy the performance shortfalls of the AH-1T under 'hot and high' conditions, the **AH-1W SuperCobra** was initially conceived to meet an Iranian requirement and first flew in April 1980 as an AH-1T adapted for the uprated powerplant of two

General Electric T700 turboshaft engines. Development of this prototype conversion eventually resulted in a helicopter so much more capable than the AH-1T that the USMC ordered the type as the AH-1W for service from 1987. The primary armament comprises eight BGM-71 TOW or AGM-114 Hellfire ATMs, supported by a pair of AIM-9L Sidewinder short-range AAMs and AGM-122 SideARM anti-radar missiles for battlefield self-defence. The 222 aircraft were delivered from March 1986. The **TAH-1W** designation is applied to one dual-control trainer based on the AH-1W.

Desiring to operate its AH-1 force to a date in the region of 2020, the USMC has contracted with Bell for the conversion of 180 existing AH-1W helicopters to the considerably more

capable **AH-1Z** standard characterised by some 30 per cent more power and an internal capacity increased by 30 per cent. In addition, the aircraft will incorporate a more advanced bearingless main rotor based on that of the Model 430 helicopter with four composite-construction blades, folding main rotor blades to facilitate hangarage on board ships and a four- rather than two-bladed tail rotor. The latter is based technically on the main rotor but with the blades not at 90° to each other, as a means of reducing noise. A new transmission system less susceptible to salt water corrosion and offering a rating of 2,625 shp (1957 kW) will also be fitted and a heavier weapons load and a new Litton Integrated Avionics System will be installed.

The IAS is based on identical cockpits for the gunner/co-pilot and pilot with side-mounted cyclic and collective controllers as well as two liquid-crystal multi-function displays. The installation of identical cockpits is made possible by the adoption of an improved Elbit-developed version of the Tamam/Kollsman Night Targeting System. Other elements of the IAS are a laser rangefinder, pilot's FLIR with its image presented on either the display element of the advanced GEC-Marconi helmet or a multi-function display, INS with GPS update, digital map system, digital data-link system, and digital data-loading system.

These elements are combined with an essentially new fuselage some 1 ft 8⅞ in (0.53 m) longer than the original to the rear of the pilot's doors to keep the centre of gravity in the right position, and with the additional volume used for additional avionics accommodation. The fuselage

retains only the nose, roof and doors of the original, and in combination with the powerplant of two uprated General Electric T700 turboshaft engines, this will result in a maximum take-off weight of 18,500 lb (8392 kg) including the heavier weapons load comprising mainly Hellfire ATMs, 2.75-in (70-mm) Hydra 70 air-to-surface unguided rockets and AIM-9 Sidewinders in addition to the 20-mm trainable cannon under the nose.

The first of three AH-1W prototype conversions is scheduled to fly in 2000 for the AH-1Z's service debut in 2005 (first five 'production' conversions) and completion of the whole programme by 2013. It is worth noting that the majority of the update programme is also being applied to the USMC's 100-strong UH-1N fleet to create the UH-1Y upgraded general-purpose helicopter within the context of a 275-strong AH-1Z and UH-1Y fleet.

The **AH-1(4B)W Viper** is the latest SeaCobra version offered by Bell as a private-venture development of the AH-1W SuperCobra, was the Model 680 four-blade bearingless main rotor, uprated transmission, an expanded manoeuvring envelope and greater agility, digital flight-control system, Doppler navigation, and night-targeting sights. In other respects, the AH-1(4B)W differs from the AH-1W in details such as its cranked stub wing with six hardpoints including overwing launchers for two SideARMs, and a total weaponload of 3,184 lb (1444 kg).

Operators of the SeaCobra and its derivatives have included, other than the USA, Iran, Iraq (machines captured from Iran), South Korea, Taiwan and Turkey.

In 1999, the AH-1W represents the spearhead of USMC attack helicopter operations. Faced with funds too limited to allow the acquisition of a navalised Apache, the USMC has opted to upgrade its AH-1Ws for service well into the 21st century.

SPECIFICATION
Bell AH-1W SuperCobra **Type:** two-seat close support, attack and anti-tank helicopter **Powerplant:** two 1,625-shp (1212-kW) General Electric T700-GE-401 turboshaft engines, transmission-limited to a total of 2,032 shp (1515 kW) **Performance:** maximum speed 175 mph (282 km/h) at sea level; initial climb rate 800 ft (244 m) per minute on one engine; service ceiling more than 12,000 ft (3660 m); hovering ceiling 14,750 ft (4495 m) in ground effect and 3,000 ft (915 m) out of ground effect; range 395 miles (635 km) **Weights:** empty 10,200 lb (4627 kg); maximum take-off 14,750 lb (6691 kg)	**Dimensions:** main rotor diameter 48 ft (14.63 m); length overall 58 ft (17.68 m); height 13 ft 6 in (4.11 m) to top of rotor head; main rotor disc area 1,809.56 sq ft (168.11 m²) **Armament:** one 20-mm M197 three-barrel cannon, plus up to 2,466 lb (1119 kg) of disposable stores such as BGM-71 or AGM-114 anti-tank missiles, AGM-65 Maverick air-to-surface missiles, AGM-122 SideARM anti-radar missiles, AIM-9 Sidewinder air-to-air missiles, multiple launchers for 2.75- and 5-in (70-and 127-mm) air-to-surface unguided rockets, and cluster bombs and fuel/air explosive weapons

Bell Model 212 Twin Two-Twelve (UH-1N)

On 1 May 1968 Bell announced that, following negotiations with the Canadian government and Pratt & Whitney Canada, an agreement had been reached for Bell to proceed with the development of a new helicopter based upon the airframe of the UH-1H Iroquois in service with the CAF under the designation CUH-1H. The CAF considered that a twin-turboshaft powerplant would provide a number of benefits and this paved the way for the development of the **Bell Model 212** and the Pratt & Whitney Canada PT6T coupled turboshaft powerplant. The programme had clearly been inspired, at least at the technical level, by the **Model 208 Twin Delta** prototype that had first flown in April 1965, and was now launched as a joint venture with financial backing from Bell, P&WC and

the Canadian government. The revolutionary feature of this new helicopter was the PT6T Twin Pac engine, which comprised two turboshaft engines mounted side-by-side and driving, via a combining gearbox, a single output shaft.

As installed in the Model 212 the PT6T-3 was limited to an output of 1,290 shp (962 kW) for take-off. However, in the event of the failure of either one of the two turbines, sensing torquemeters in the combining gearbox would signal the remaining turbine to develop a power output ranging between 1,025 and 800 shp (764 and 596 kW) for emergency and continuous operation respectively. This therefore permitted continued flight on only the one engine.

Initial deliveries of the Model 212's military version

Three batches of UH-1Ns were delivered to the USAF for a total of 79 aircraft. This machine boasts a cabin-mounted machine-gun in addition to side-mounted rocket pods.

were made to the USAF in 1970 for service under the designation **UH-1N**. The UH-1N began to reach the USN and USMC during 1971, and the first **CUH-1N** (later redesignated as the **CH-135**) for the CAF was handed over on 3 May 1971. There followed examples of the Model 212 being delivered to the air arms of at least 29 other countries.

A 14-passenger commercial version known as the **Twin Two-Twelve** was developed more or less simultaneously, this differing from the military model primarily in its cabin furnishing and avionics. The

Twin Two-Twelve gained US civil certification in June 1971 and in June 1977 the Twin Two-Twelve became the first helicopter to be certificated by the Federal Aviation Administration for single-pilot IFR operation with fixed floats.

The enhanced safety offered by the Turbo Twin Pac engine led to many sales to operators providing support for offshore gas/oil prospecting and production companies, as well as to air taxi organisa-

tions. By the late 1990s more than 900 examples of the Model 212 had been sold, current examples with the uprated PT6T-3B engine. Eight of the helicopters were delivered to the Civil Air Authority of China during 1979, and as such were the first helicopters supplied to the People's Republic of China by a US manufacturer.

The Model 212 was also built under licence by Agusta as the AB 212.

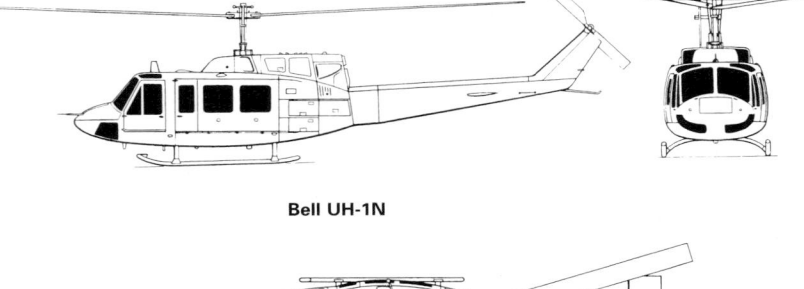

Bell UH-1N

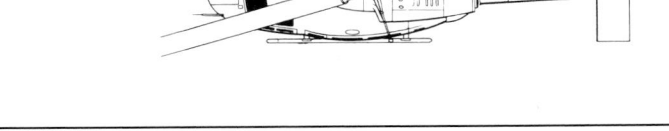

SPECIFICATION	
Bell Model 212 Twin Two-Twelve **Type:** one-crew utility helicopter **Powerplant:** one Pratt & Whitney Canada PT6T-3B Turbo Twin Pac coupled turboshaft flat-rated at 1,800 shp (1342 kW) for take-off and 1,600 shp (1193 kW) for continuous running **Performance:** maximum cruising speed 115 mph (185 km/h) at sea level; initial climb rate 1,320 ft (402 m) per minute; service ceiling 13,000 ft (3960 m); hovering ceiling 4,750 ft (1450 m) in ground effect and 8,600 ft (2620 m) at a weight	of 10,000 lb (4536 kg); range 272 miles (437 km) **Weights:** empty 6,183 lb (2805 kg); maximum take-off 11,200 lb (5080 kg) **Dimensions:** main rotor diameter; 48 2¼ ft (14.69 m); length overall 57 ft 3¼ in (17.46 m) and fuselage 42 ft 4¾ in (12.92 m); height 12 ft 6¾ in (3.83 m) to top of rotor head; main rotor disc area 1,871.91 sq ft (173.9 m²) **Payload:** up to 14 passengers or freight carried internally, or up to 5,000 lb (2268 kg) of freight carried externally

Bell Model 214B BigLifter

The success of the military Model 214A and Model 214C, developed exclusively for Iran, convinced Bell that there could be a significant market for a civil variant, for it would have a lifting capability better than any contemporary machine in the medium helicopter category. The company therefore announced early in 1974 its intention to develop such an aircraft under the designation **Bell Model 214B BigLifter**.

Generally similar in configuration to the

Designed to provide operators with a helicopter of exceptional lifting capacity, the Model 214B BigLifter failed to establish a niche for itself. A number remained in service in early 1999.

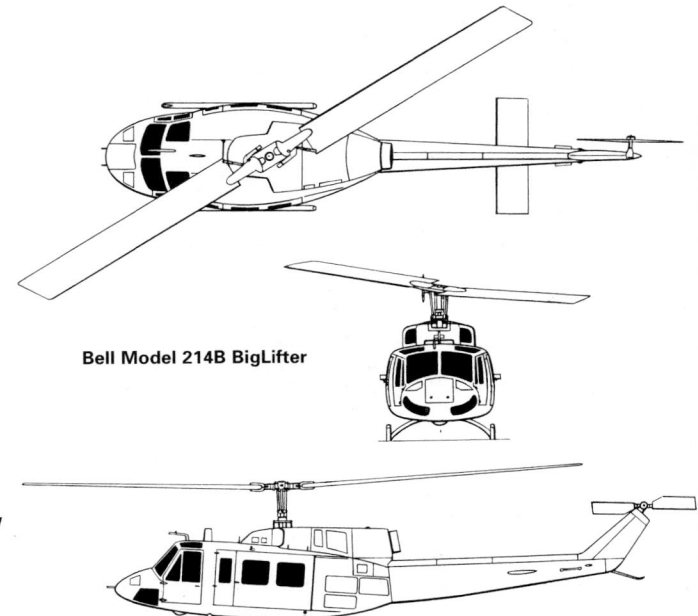

Bell Model 214B BigLifter

military helicopter, the BigLifter retains the same airframe, rotor/transmission systems, and powerplant, but differs by having emergency escape windows in the cargo doors, an engine fire-extinguishing system, and avionics suited to purely civil rather than military operation.

Two versions of the BigLifter were offered. The standard Model 214B was available in subvariants such as a 14-passenger transport with a crew of two, a cargo type with an external cargo hook, an agricultural type and a firefighting type able to drop fire retardant carried in cabin and underfuselage tanks. The alternative **Model 214B-1** was certificated to different standards in an alternative weight category.

The Model 214B was certificated on 27 January 1976, but the type secured only modest sales and was taken out of production in the early 1980s. Around 70 Model 214B/B-1 BigLifters were completed.

SPECIFICATION

Bell Model 214B BigLifter
Type: one-crew utility helicopter
Powerplant: one 2,930-shp (2185-kW) Avco Lycoming T5508D turboshaft engine flat-rated at 2,250 shp (1678 kW) for take-off
Performance: cruising speed 161 mph (259 km/h) at optimum altitude
Weights: maximum take-off 13,800 lb (6260 kg) for the Model 214B with an internal load or 16,000 lb (7257 kg) for the Model 214B and 214B-1 with an external load
Dimensions: main rotor diameter 50 ft (15.24 m); length overall 60 ft 9 in (18.52 m) and fuselage 49 ft 3 in (15.01 m); height 15 ft (4.57 m); main rotor disc area 1,963.50 sq ft (182.41 m²)
Payload: up to 14 passengers or freight carried internally, or 8,000 lb (3629 kg) of freight carried externally

Bell Model 214ST

Late in 1970 Bell completed the construction of a prototype identified as the **Model 214 HueyPlus**. This was, in effect, an improved version of the well-tried and proven UH-1H with the same basic airframe in combination with a more powerful 1,900-shp (1417-kW) Avco Lycoming T53-L-702 turboshaft. Other advanced features included the large two-bladed main rotor of the Model 309 KingCobra, and a measure of structural strengthening to permit operation at higher weights. In 1972 Iran approached Bell for a development of the UH-1 with better performance under 'hot and high' conditions. Bell responded with a development of the HueyPlus prototype known in its prototype form (three helicopters) as the **Model 214** and powered by one 2,050-shp (1529-kW) Avco Lycoming T55-L-7C turboshaft. Successful evaluation of these three prototypes led to a December 1972 order for 287 production helicopters.

All three of the Model 214STs delivered to the Venezuelan air force remain in service in 1999.

Preceded by another three prototypes, of which the first flew on 13 March 1974, the production variant was the **Model 214A**, which was designed as a 16-seat utility helicopter with one 2,930-shp (2185-kW) Avco Lycoming LTC4B-8D turboshaft. The Imperial Iranian army air service accepted the first production Model 214A in April 1975, and the last machine was completed in December of the same year. There followed 39 examples of the **Model 214C** for the Imperial Iranian air force in the SAR role with specialised equipment, and then six more model 214A helicopters delivered by late 1978. During the early part of this period the Iranian government had begun negotiations with European and US helicopter manufacturers with the intention of establishing an indigenous aircraft industry.

As a result, the country concluded an agreement with Bell during 1975 for the joint creation of facilities for this purpose in Iran, with 400 helicopters (Model 214A and the new **Model 214ST**) as its initial project. However, the Islamic fundamentalist revolution of early 1979 brought an end to this plan.

Bell decided to continue with independent development of the Model 214ST, originally schemed for Iranian operation with a higher capacity resulting from its stretched fuselage, as a commercial transport with multi-mission capability. The programme was foreshadowed by a Model 214A conversion that first flew during February 1977 with the powerplant of two General Electric T700-T1C turboshafts. The first of three full pre-production

This Model 214A is typical of those delivered to the Imperial Iranian army. It is likely that a large fleet of these helicopters remains in service.

prototypes of the Model 214ST, whose letter suffix initially stood for **Stretched Twin** but later **Super Transport**, made its maiden flight on 21 July 1979. All three helicopters were used in the development programme leading to FAA certification in 1982. A variant with wheel rather than skid landing gear was certificated in March 1983. Production of the Model 214ST began in 1981 and continued into 1988.

Another major change in the Model 214ST, by comparison with the Model 214A, was the replacement of the single Lycoming turboshaft by two General Electric turboshafts which, driving the rotor through a combining gearbox, provided true single-engined flight capability. Multi-mission capability was provided by the provision of easily removable passenger seating, full IFR avionics and instrumentation, emergency flotation gear, an external cargo suspension system, and an internally-mounted rescue hoist.

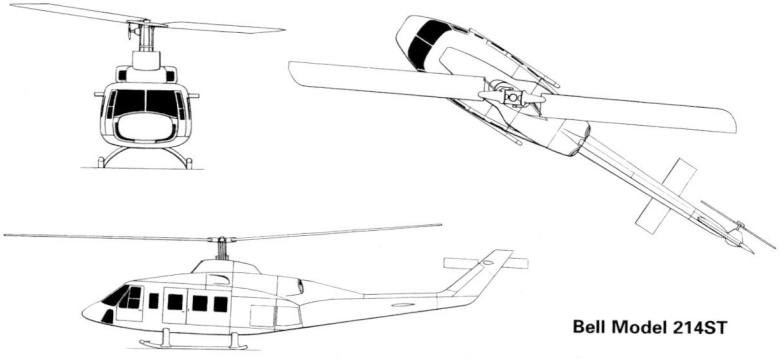

British Caledonian Helicopters was one of the first commercial Model 214ST operators. Two aircraft were received for work over the North Sea and from the People's Republic of China.

SPECIFICATION

Bell Model 214ST
Type: one/two-crew utility helicopter
Powerplant: two General Electric CT7-2A turboshaft engines each rated at 1,625 shp (1212 kW)
Performance: maximum cruising speed 161 mph (259 km/h) at sea level; initial climb rate 1,780 ft (543 m) per minute; service ceiling 7,000 ft (2135 m) on one engine; hovering ceiling 10,400 ft (3170 m) in ground effect; range 501 miles (807 km)
Weights: maximum take-off 17,200 lb (7802 kg)
Dimensions: main rotor diameter 52 ft (15.85 m); length overall 62 ft 2¼ in (18.95 m) and fuselage 49 ft 3½ in (15.02 m); height 15 ft 10½ in (4.84 m); main rotor disc area 2,123.37 sq ft (197.29 m²)
Payload: up to 18 passengers, or freight carried internally or externally

Bell Model 214ST

Bell Model 222

It was in April 1974 that Bell announced its intention to develop a new commercial helicopter which would be the first light twin-turbine commercial helicopter to be built in the USA. The first of five prototypes subsequently flew on 13 August 1976.

These **Bell Model 222** prototypes were used to complete the development and certification programme as quickly as possible, with FAA certification in VFR and IFR configurations gained in December 1979 and May 1980 respectively. The Model 222 benefits from new-technology features developed at an earlier date for both civil and military helicopters, and includes the vibration-reducing nodal suspension system of the Model 214ST, a no-lubricant elastomeric bearing main rotor hub, and glassfibre/stainless steel main rotor blades.

The airframe structure is primarily of light alloy, the fuselage having a short-span cantilever sponson

mounted on each side. Of aerofoil section, these sponsons provide some lift in forward flight and thus supplement the main rotor, and in addition provide accommodation for the main units of the retractable tricycle landing gear. The empennage has both upper and lower sweptback fins and a tailplane with endplates. The maximum high-density seating capacity is 10

One of the five Model 222 prototypes, N222AX demonstrates the revised tail configuration that was adopted by all Model 222 production aircraft. Only the first three prototypes flew with the original T-tail design.

persons in the form of one or two crew and nine or eight passengers respectively. In its production form the Model 222 was offered in three subvariants, namely the basic Model 222 with a standard seating configuration for a pilot and seven passengers; the **Model 222 Executive** fully equipped for IFR flight with a crew of one or two and luxury accommodation for six or five passengers respectively; and the **Model 222 Offshore**. The latter was equipped for IFR operation with a crew of two and with an emergency flotation system and auxiliary fuel tanks as standard.

A Model 222 delivered in January 1981 was notable as the 25,000th helicopter built by Bell. Production of the Model 222 series ended in the late 1980s.

Just two Bell Model 222s have entered military service, both Model 222UTs which were delivered to Uruguay.

SPECIFICATION

Bell Model 222A
Type: one/two-crew light helicopter
Powerplant: two Avco Lycoming LTS101-650C-3 turboshaft engines each rated at 620 shp (462 kW)
Performance: economical cruising speed 153 mph (246 km/h) at 4,000 ft (1220 m); initial climb rate 1,600 ft (487 m) per minute; service ceiling 20,000 ft (6095 m); hovering ceiling 4,200 ft (1280 m) in ground effect and 4,600 ft (1400 m) out of ground effect; range 325 miles (523 km)
Weights: empty 4,860 lb (2204 kg); maximum take-off 8,100 lb (3674 kg)
Dimensions: main rotor diameter 42 ft (12.80 m); length, fuselage 36 ft ¾ in (10.98 m); height 11 ft 6 in (3.51 m); main rotor disc area 1,385.44 sq ft (128.71 m²)
Payload: up to seven passengers or freight carried internally, or freight carried externally

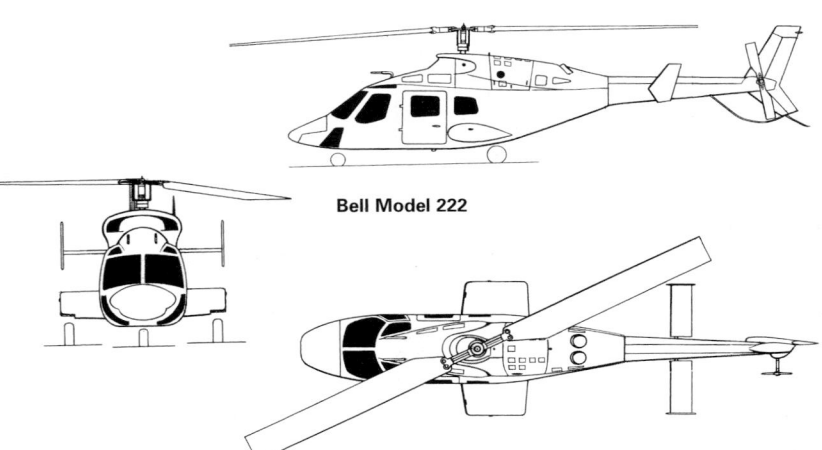

Bell Model 222

Variants

Model 222A: a simple development of the Model 222 with a main rotor increased in diameter
Model 222B: the second main production version, offered in the same subvariants as the Model 222 and Model 222A, was notable for changes such as seven/nine-seat accommodation, a taller rotor mast, the Model 222A's increased-diameter main rotor, an enlarged tail rotor, a lengthened tail boom, and the powerplant of two 684-shp (510-kW) LTS101-750C-1 turboshafts
Model 222UT: Utility Transport delivered from September 1983 as a derivative of the Model 222B with fixed twin-skid landing gear, accommodation for up to eight passengers, enlarged fuel capacity, and provision for a fuselage-mounted flotation system

Bell Model 230

Announced at the National Business Aircraft Association convention in 1989, the **Bell Model 230** was developed as successor to the Model 222 with basically the same airframe, but the powerplant of two Allison 250-C30G2 turboshaft engines in place of the Model 222's pair of AlliedSignal LTS101 turboshaft engines. The initial pair of Model 230 helicopters were Model 222 conversions, and the first of these made the type's maiden flight on 12 August 1991.

The Model 230 was certificated in March 1992 and the first production helicopter was delivered in November of the same year. The Model 230 is outfitted for the carriage of a maximum 10 persons in the form of two or one pilots plus up to eight or nine passengers respectively, although more common configurations are the six- and eight-seat executive layouts. The three main models are the **Model 230 Executive** with

Bell leased its Model 230 demonstrator to the Chilean navy for six months during 1993-4. No order for production aircraft resulted.

SPECIFICATION

Bell Model 230
Type: 10-seat multi-purpose light helicopter
Powerplant: two Allison 250-C30G2 turboshaft engines each rated at 700 shp (522 kW)
Performance: maximum cruising speed 162 mph (261 km/h) with retracted tricycle landing gear at sea level or 158 mph (254 km/h) with skid landing gear at sea level; service ceiling 15,500 ft (4725 m); hovering ceiling 12,400 ft (3780 m) in ground effect and 7,300 ft (2225 m) out of ground effect; range 346 miles (558 km) with retracted tricycle landing gear and 443 miles (713 km) with skid landing gear
Weights: empty 5,097 lb (2312 kg) with wheeled landing gear and 5,000 lb (2268 kg) with skid landing gear; maximum take-off 8,400 lb (3810 kg)
Dimensions: main rotor diameter 42 ft (12.80 m); length overall 50 ft 2 in (15.29 m) with wheeled landing gear and 49 ft 11½ in (15.23 m) with skid landing gear; height 11 ft 1½ in (3.39 m) over fin with wheeled landing gear and 10 ft 11 in (3.33 m) over fin with skid landing gear; main rotor disc area 1,385.44 sq ft (128.71 m²)
Payload: up to nine passengers or freight carried in the cabin, or up to 2,800 lb (1270 kg) of freight carried as a slung load

retractable tricycle landing gear, the **Model 230 Utility** with fixed twin-skid landing gear, and the **Model 230 EMS**

(Emergency Medical Service) medevac type. The latter accommodates one pilot plus one or two litters and four or three

attendants and/or seated casualties respectively.

In the early-1990s the Chilean navy evaluated one of the prototype

conversions for the shipboard role with an upgraded navigation system, improved avionics, a deck recovery

system, a rescue hoist, Bendix/King RDR 1500B search radar, a searchlight and a turret-mounted thermal imaging system.

Bell Model 301 (XV-15)

Given its very considerable experience with rotary-wing aircraft in general and with tilt-rotor aircraft in particular, it was hardly surprising that in 1973 Bell was selected as prime contractor for the research programme to prove the operational practicality of the tilt-rotor concept. The programme was launched jointly by the US Army's Air Mobility Research and Development Laboratory and NASA.

Bell naturally drew on its experience with the Model

200 in its evolution of the **Bell Model 301** design, and the programme was then extended by the receipt of USN funding in the later 1970s that permitted the ordering of two **XV-15** prototypes. The Model 301 looked like a small but conventional fixed-wing transport in its streamlined fuselage (with retractable tricycle landing gear), upswept tail unit carrying endplate vertical surfaces, and high-set cantilever wing. However, the Model 301 also employed

advanced proprotors located at the wingtips in swivelling nacelles that also accommodated individual turboshaft engines. Transverse cross-shafting ensured that either of the turboprop engines could drive both rotors in the event of a single engine failure, and the location of the engines in the tip-mounted nacelles meant that the fuselage was left free for payload. The design provided for vertical take-off, then a 12-second translation to wingborne

forward flight as the proprotors' rotational axes were swivelled through 90° to the horizontal plane so that the vertical proprotor discs provided forward thrust.

The first of the two XV-15 prototypes flew on 3 May 1977 and, after initial trials in VTOL mode, was used for comprehensive wind-tunnel tests. The second prototype made its first flight in April 1979, and it was this machine that

accomplished the XV-15's first free translation between vertical and horizontal flight three months later in July 1979. The XV-15 programme was a major success, and paved the way for the joint Bell/Boeing programme to develop the V-22 Osprey. It also contributed greatly to the Augusta Bell Model AB609 civil tiltrotor, which is scheduled to make its first flight late in 1999.

The first XV-15 prototype (illustrated) was used in a number of tests. These included measurements for the calculation of its radar signature and shipboard operations from the amphibious assault ship USS Tripoli during 1982.

SPECIFICATION	
Bell XV-15	
Type: two-crew experimental VTOL tilt-rotor research aircraft	**Weights:** empty 9,600 lb (4355 kg); maximum take-off 13,000 lb (5897 kg) for VTO or
Powerplant: two Avco Lycoming LTC1K-4K turboshaft engines each rated at 1,550 shp (1156 kW)	15,000 lb (6804 kg) for STO **Dimensions:** width overall 57 ft 2 in (17.42 m); span 35 ft 2 in
Performance: maximum speed 382 mph (615 km/h) at 17,000 ft (5180 m); cruising speed 349 mph (561 km/h) at 16,300 ft (4970 m); initial climb rate 3,150 ft (960 m) per minute; service ceiling 29,000 ft (8840 m); hovering ceiling 10,500 ft (3200 m) in ground effect and 8,650 ft (2635 m) out of ground effect; range 512 miles (825 km)	(10.72 m) including nacelles; proprotor diameter, each 25 ft (7.62 m); length 42 ft 1 in (12.83 m); height 15 ft 4 in (4.67 m); wing area 169.00 sq ft (15.70 m²); proprotor disc area, total 981.75 sq ft (91.20 m²) **Payload:** up to nine passengers or freight carried in the cabin

Bell Model 309 KingCobra

Late in 1969, with US forces beginning a slow withdrawal from Vietnam, the US Army began to express a growing concern with the balance of forces in Central Europe, where any communist aggression would be spearheaded by large numbers of Soviet armoured fighting vehicles, including very significant

quantities of battle tanks. The acquisition of an attack helicopter with tank-killing capability thus became a matter of the highest priority. The Lockheed AH-56A Cheyenne, developed to meet the US Army's Advanced Aerial Fire Support System requirement, seemed destined for cancellation.

Bell decided that the optimum weapon system to meet the needs of the US Army seemed to be the addition of the Hughes BGM-71 TOW heavyweight anti-tank missile to the type of airframe pioneered in the AH-1. It therefore determined to build two private-venture **Bell Model 309 KingCobra** prototypes, one of them with a single-engine and the other with twin engines. Construction of the prototypes began in January 1971 and the Model 309 was, in essence, a scaled-up version of the AH-1G/J. However, the fuselage was lengthened and stiffened, the tail unit redesigned for greater longitudinal stability, the nose considerably modified, a stub wing of greater span was installed, the fuel capacity enlarged and elements of the Model 211 HueyTug's dynamic

system were incorporated. These components took the form of the latter type's transmission, drive train and two-bladed main rotor.

The single-engined prototype retained the Model 211's 2,850-shp (2125-kW) Avco Lycoming T55-L-7C turboshaft engine flat-rated at 2,050 shp (1529 kW), but the twin-engined prototype switched to the 1,800-shp (1342-kW) Pratt & Whitney Canada T400-CP-400 coupled-turboshaft. Other features of the KingCobra were new avionics and systems for the primary anti-tank role, and its armament capability included up to 16 TOW missiles and a 20-mm General Electric three-barrel cannon in a trainable chin turret.

The first of the prototypes to fly was the twin-engined machine, which recorded its maiden flight on 10 September 1971, and the single-engined prototype

followed in January of the following year. The single-engined KingCobra suffered major damage in an accident during April 1972 and, in an effort to have a prototype available in the single-engined configuration likely to be required by the US Army, Bell then converted the surviving Model 309 to single-engined form.

In August 1972 the US Army cancelled the Cheyenne programme and later solicited proposals from Bell and Sikorsky for less sophisticated helicopters, which emerged as the Model 309 and S-67 respectively. Tests and demonstrations were successfully conducted with both types, but the US Army then revised its requirement in the new AAH (Advanced Attack Helicopter) programme. This resulted in the selection of the Hughes Model 77 design which was ordered as the AH-64 Apache.

Tested successfully alongside Sikorsky's S-67, the KingCobra was to lose out due to a change in US Army requirements. The surviving aircraft is preserved at the US Army Aviation Museum.

Bell Model 400 TwinRanger

In February 1983 the company announced the **Bell Model 400 TwinRanger** as the first helicopter of a new series intended for both the

commercial and military markets in single- and twin-engined forms with seven-seat accommodation. Although clearly based on the concept of the

Model 206 JetRanger series, the Model 400 was powered by two 250-C20R turboshaft engines and among its other features were a four-bladed main

rotor of the 'soft-in-plane' type and an advanced 'run dry' transmission/drive system, both similar to those of the Model 406.

The Model 400 was developed from 1983, and among the elements used in the development

process were a specially modified Model 206LM LongRanger that first flew in March 1983 with the four-bladed main rotor of the OH-58D, a strengthened tail boom, a tail rotor enclosed in a guard ring and increased fuel capacity.

Bell Model 400 TwinRanger (continued)

The Model 400's first proto-type made its maiden flight on 30 June 1984, and there followed three pre-production helicopters, of which the last introduced a revised tail unit with larger vertical surfaces and better-faired legs for the twin-skid landing gear. Plans were laid for production to be undertaken, with certification scheduled for August 1986. In the event major orders were not forthcoming and the programme was suspended.

Variants

Model 400A: proposed variant of the Model 400 with the powerplant of one 1,000-shp (746-kW) Pratt & Whitney Canada PW209T turboshaft
Model 440: proposed variant incorporating major components of composite construction

SPECIFICATION

Bell Model 400 TwinRanger
Type: seven-seat general-purpose light helicopter
Powerplant: two Allison 250-C20R turboshaft engines each rated at 443 shp (330 kW)
Performance: maximum speed 172 mph (278 km/h) at optimum altitude; cruising speed 152 mph (244 km/h) at 5,000 ft (1525 m); initial climb rate 1,521 ft (464 m) per minute; service ceiling 20,000 ft (6095 m); hovering ceiling 14,300 ft (4360 m) in ground effect and 10,200 ft (3110 m) out of ground effect; range 518 miles (834 km)
Weights: empty 3,146 lb (1427 kg); maximum take-off 5,500 lb (2495 kg)
Dimensions: main rotor diameter 37 ft 1 in (11.30 m); length overall 43 ft 11 in (13.39 m); height 11 ft 8 in (3.56 m); main rotor disc area 1,080.06 sq ft (100.34 m²)

N3185K was the first Model 400 prototype. It was joined in the air by three pre-production machines, the last flying in 1985. The first pre-production helicopter was later used as a ground test airframe.

Bell Model 406 (OH-58D Kiowa and Kiowa Warrior)

In September 1981 the **Bell Model 406** proposal won the US Army's AHIP (Army Helicopter Improvement Program) to develop a near-term scout helicopter capable of intelligence-gathering and surveillance duties, in addition to the support of attack helicopters and the direction of artillery fire. Bell was then awarded a development contract, and the first of five **OH-58D** prototypes made its maiden flight on 6 October 1983.

The Model 406 introduced a mast-mounted sight, specialised avionics, and a cockpit control and display subsystem. In addition, a four-bladed 'soft-in-plane' rotor with composite blades, a main rotor head yoke and elastomeric bearings were installed.

Initial plans envisaged the upgrading of 592 of the US Army's OH-58A helicopters to OH-58D standard, but were progressively trimmed to 477 and finally 207 examples, before rising to a currently planned total of 398 including 12 Gulf War attrition replacements. Deliveries began with the handing over of two OH-58Ds in December 1985, and the first deliveries to a Europe-based unit took place in June 1987. Under Operation Prime Chance, 15 OH-58Ds were modified from September 1987 for operations against Iranian fast patrol boats in the Persian Gulf: provision was made for Stinger air-to-air and Hellfire air-to-surface missiles in addition to 0.5-in (12.7-mm) machine-gun pods and rocket launchers.

The armament options of the Prime Chance OH-58D have been retained for an armed version of the OH-58D, designated as the **OH-58D(I) Kiowa Warrior**, to which standard all OH-58D helicopters are to be upgraded. The major modifications include an integrated weapons pylon on each side of the fuselage, uprated engine and transmission, increased maximum weight, RWR, IR jammer, laser warning receiver, tilted vertical fin, integrated avionics and a lightened structure. Newly-converted Kiowa Warriors were delivered from the 208th helicopter in May 1991 and 18 were temporarily flown with a 'stealthy' chisel nose.

An initial 81, and ultimately all, Kiowa Warriors are being further modified to the MPLH (Multi-Purpose Light Helicopter) standard with squatting landing gear, quick-fold rotor blades, horizontal stabiliser and tilted fin for transportation in C-130 freighters and speedy deployment for use by US Army rapid reaction forces. Further envisaged modifications include provision for a cargo hook and fittings for the external carriage of up to four litters or six troop seats.

A further Kiowa Warrior upgrade was also offered by Bell with new avionics including a FLIR, Honeywell helmet-mounted displays, and an upgraded navigation system. The company also offered an **OH-58X LUV (Light Utility Variant)** with lengthened nose and special 'stealth' coated windscreen.

The only export order for the full-standard OH-58D was placed in February 1992 by Taiwan for 12 such helicopters plus 14 options that were later exercised; the helicopters were delivered from July 1993 as the only new-build OH-58Ds.

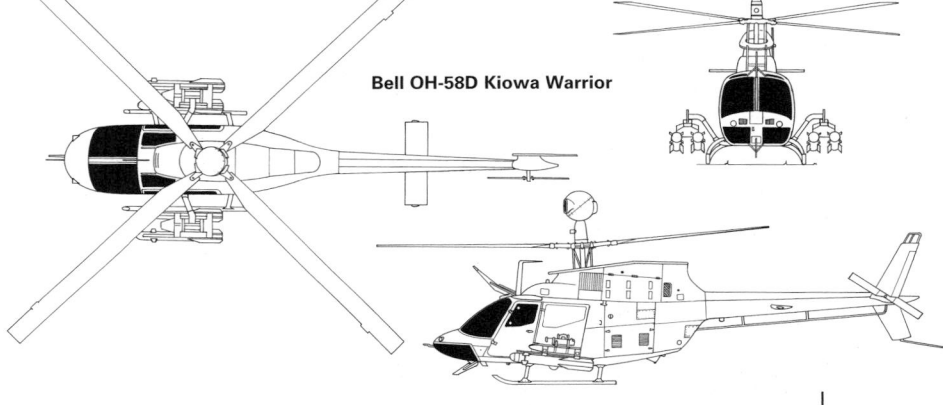

Bell OH-58D Kiowa Warrior

SPECIFICATION

Bell OH-58D(I) Kiowa Warrior
Type: two-seat scout and attack light helicopter
Powerplant: one Allison T703-AD-700 turboshaft engine rated at 650 shp (410 kW)
Performance: maximum speed 147 mph (247 km/h) at 4,000 ft (1220 m); cruising speed 131 mph (211 km/h) at optimum altitude; initial climb rate 1,540 ft (469 m) per minute; service ceiling 15,000 ft (4570 m); hovering ceiling 10,000 ft (3050 m) in ground effect and 6,900 ft (2105 m) out of ground effect; range 257 miles (413 km)
Weights: empty 3,289 lb (1492 kg); maximum take-off 5,500 lb (2495 kg)
Dimensions: main rotor diameter 35 ft (10.67 m); length overall 41 ft 2½ in (12.58 m) and fuselage 34 ft 3 in (10.44 m); height 12 ft 10½ in (3.93 m); main rotor disc area 962.11 sq ft (89.38 m²)
Armament: four FIM-92 Stinger or AGM-114 Hellfire missiles, or two seven-tube launchers for 2.75-in (70-mm) Hydra 70 air-to-surface unguided rockets, or one 0.5-in (12.7-mm) machine-gun pod, or a mix of these weapons

A television camera offering 12x magnification, IR thermal imager and laser rangefinder/designator are contained in the OH-58D's MMS.

Bell Model 406CS Combat Scout

A lighter, simplified export derivative of the OH-58D, the **Model 406CS Combat Scout** commenced flight-testing in June 1984, and in the same year entered a fly-off competition in Saudi Arabia. Retaining the main rotor, tail rotor and transmission of the OH-58D as well as a similar power-plant, the Model 406CS was nevertheless a down-graded version of the OH-58D, as export of the mast-mounted sight, Hellfire missile and special-ist cockpit electronics was then prohibited. Armament choices later included two 20-mm GIAT cannon pods, a quartet of TOW 2 or Hellfire anti-tank missiles, or combinations of Stinger air-to-air missiles, launchers for 2.75-in (70-mm) rockets, or 0.3- or 0.5-in (7.62- or 12.7-mm) machine-gun pods.

The Model 406CS is

Finished in desert camouflage, Bell's Model 406CS demonstrator is seen armed with a 0.3-in (7.62-mm) gun pod to port and 2.75-in (70-mm) rocket pod to starboard.

equipped with a hybrid cockpit with conventional instrumentation and elec-tronic displays for TOW missiles and communica-tions control. Other features include a roof-mounted Saab-Emerson HeliTOW sight with a fold-ing overhead direct-view optics tube, folding rotor blades and tailplane, and a squatting landing gear arrangement to facilitate rapid loading and redeploy-ment from C-130 transports. The type can also be upgraded with a laser rangefinder and desig-nator, an uprated transmission, and a 500-lb (227-kg) increase in maxi-mum take-off weight.

During the autumn of 1988 an order was placed on behalf of the Royal Saudi Land Forces' Army Aviation Command for 15 examples of the Model 406CS, and these heli-copters were delivered from June 1990 after the first flight of a production standard helicopter on 2 February. These heli-copters have frequently been mentioned with the designation MH-58D, but this is inaccurate in terms of the Saudi Arabian machines and does not correspond to any US Army machine.

SPECIFICATION

Bell Model 406CS Combat Scout
Type: two-seat scout and attack light helicopter
Powerplant: one Allison 250-C30U turboshaft engine rated at 650 shp (410 kW)
Performance: maximum speed 144 mph (242 km/h) at optimum altitude; cruising speed 138 mph (222 km/h) at optimum altitude; hovering ceiling 20,500 ft (6250 m) in ground effect and 14,500 ft (4420 m) out of ground effect; range 251 miles (404 km)
Weights: empty 2,271 lb (1030 kg); maximum take-off 5,000 lb (2268 kg)
Dimensions: main rotor diameter 35 ft (10.67 m); length overall 42 ft 2 in (12.85 m) and fuselage 34 ft 4¾ in (10.48 m); height 12 ft 10⅝ in (3.93 m); main rotor disc area 962.11 sq ft (89.38 m²)
Armament: see above

Bell Model 430

The **Bell Model 430** is basically a development of the Model 230 with a longer fuselage and a four-bladed main rotor. Design of the type began in 1991 and the first of two proto-type conversions from Model 230 standard made its maiden flight on 25 October 1994. The first aircraft featured retractable tricycle landing gear, while the second was completed with fixed twin-skid landing gear and first flew on 19 December 1994. Deliveries of the Model 430 began in June 1995.

The Model 430 remained in production into 1999, with a basic price tag of US$3.75 million (1997) for a VFR-equipped helicopter.

SPECIFICATION

Bell Model 430
Type: one/two-crew utility light helicopter
Powerplant: two Allison 250-C40B turboshaft engines each rated at 808 shp (603 kW)
Performance: maximum speed 159 mph (256 km/h) at optimum altitude with retracted wheel landing gear; cruising speed 151 mph (243 km/h) at optimum altitude with retracted wheel landing gear; service ceiling 18,340 ft (5590 m); hovering ceiling 11,350 ft (3460 m) in ground effect and 8,750 ft (2665 m) out of ground effect; range 313 miles (503 km)
with retracted wheel landing gear
Weights: empty 5,305 lb (2406 kg) with wheel landing gear; maximum take-off 9,000 lb (4082 kg) with wheel landing gear
Dimensions: main rotor diameter 42 ft (12.80 m); length overall 50 ft 2½ in (15.30 m) and fuselage 44 ft 1¼ in (13.44 m); height 12 ft 2½ in (3.72 m) to top of rotor head with wheel landing gear; main rotor disc area 1,385.44 sq ft (128.71 m²)
Payload: up to nine passengers or freight carried internally, or up to 3,500 lb (1587 kg) of freight carried externally

Bell P-83

In 1944 Bell began work on a longer-range fighter retain-ing the general configura-tion of the P-59. On 31 July 1944 the company's proposal won a USAAF contract for two **Bell XP-83** prototypes, and the first of these made its maiden flight on 25 February 1945. The fuselage of the XP-83 was deeper and wider than that of the P-59 to provide greater internal fuel capac-ity, which could be augmented by two under-wing drop tanks. Testing showed performance to be unsatisfactory and the project was abandoned.

SPECIFICATION

Bell XP-83
Type: single-seat long-range fighter
Powerplant: two General Electric J33-GE-5 turbojet engines each rated at 4,000 lb st (17.79 kN)
Performance: maximum speed 522 mph (840 km/h) at 15,660 ft (4775 m); initial climb rate 5,650 ft (1722 m) per minute; service ceiling 45,000 ft (13715 m); range 1,730 miles (2784 km)
Weights: empty 14,105 lb (6398 kg); maximum take-off 24,090 lb (10927 kg)
Dimensions: wingspan 53 ft (16.15 m); length 44 ft 10 in (13.66 m); height 15 ft 3 in (4.65 m); wing area 431.00 sq ft (40.04 m²)
Armament: six 0.5-in (12.7-mm) fixed forward-firing machine-guns in the nose and up to 2,000 lb (907 kg) of bombs

In view of the excessive fuel consumption of early jet engines, the XP-83 had increased internal fuel capacity.

Bell Boeing Model 901 (V-22 Osprey)

Bell and Boeing Vertol joined forces in the early 1980s to use the XV-15 as the basis of a machine to satisfy the Joint Services Advanced Vertical Lift Aircraft (formerly JVX) programme. Combining the vertical lift capabilities of a helicopter with the fast-cruise efficiencies of a fixed-wing turboprop aircraft, the resulting **Bell Boeing Model 901** was given the military designa-tion **V-22 Osprey**. It was designed around two Allison T406-AD-500 turboshaft engines located in nacelles at the tips of the slightly forward-swept wing, and driving three-bladed prop-rotors which could be swivelled through a total of 97.5°. The potential of the design was recognised in the June 1985 award of a US Navy-managed full-scale development contract.

The contract specified the manufacture of six prototypes as well as several static test airframes, with Bell respon-sible for the design and construction of the wing, nacelles, transmissions, proprotor and hub assem-blies and integration of the government-furnished engines. Boeing took responsibility for the fuse-lage, tail unit, overwing fairings and avionics inte-gration. Composite materials accounted for 59 per cent of the Model 901's airframe weight.

Bell Boeing Model 901 (V-22 Osprey) (cont.)

Initial joint service requirements were for 913 V-22s, comprising 552 **MV-22A** assault machines, each carrying up to 24 fully-armed troops, as CH-46 replacements for the USMC; 231 similar machines for the US Army; 80 **CV-22A** machines for the USAF in the role of long-range transport of special forces personnel; and 50 **HV-22A** machines for the USN's combat SAR, special warfare and fleet logistic support roles, with a 20,000-lb (9072-kg) payload. The USN also foresaw an additional need for up to 300 more V-22 aircraft optimised for the anti-submarine role. For shipboard stowage the wing of the V-22 was designed with a central pivot so that it could be turned through 90° into alignment with the top of the fuselage, the blades of the counter-rotating proprotors also folding in parallel.

Bell and Boeing were each responsible for the assembly and initial flight-testing of three of the prototypes, and Bell flew the first machine on 19 March 1989. On 14 September 1989 this V-22 achieved the first transition from helicopter to wingborne flight. The second and third machines followed from Bell on 9 August 1989 and 9 May 1990 respectively. Boeing flew the fourth and fifth aircraft on 21 December 1989 and 11 June 1991 respectively, and the sixth machine was not completed. The fifth machine was badly damaged in a non-fatal incident on its first flight, but the programme suffered a more serious setback on 21 July 1992 when the fourth machine crashed, killing all seven persons on board. The whole V-22 programme had already been under political and financial review since before the first flight, however, and attempts by the US Secretary of Defense to cancel the programme completely were blocked by Congress in 1992.

Flight-testing resumed in June 1993. Meanwhile, all except the USMC requirement had been deleted, and in mid-1992 this was reduced to a baseline figure of 300 aircraft, with optional increases to 600 or even 800 before settling at 425 as replacements for the CH-53 as well as the CH-46. The requirement was also thrown open to several competing helicopters through the USMC's Medium-Lift Replacement (MLR) helicopter programme of 1992, but the overall superiority of the V-22 was recognised in August 1993, when it was appreciated that only a tilt-rotor type could meet the demands of the USMC's final speed and range requirements.

Production of the V-22 was finally authorised in September 1994, the initial production model being the MV-22A scheduled for delivery to the USMC from mid-1999, with initial operational capability following in 2001. The other variants now to be procured include the HV-22A (48 aircraft), to be delivered to the USN from 2010, and the CV-22A (50 aircraft), to be delivered to the USAF from 2003.

Bell Boeing V-22 Osprey

Osprey Number 3 hints at the underslung load-carrying capabilities of the type. The ability to move heavy underslung loads in helicopter mode adds considerably to the versatility of the aircraft, further emphasising its unique nature.

SPECIFICATION

Bell Boeing MV-22A Osprey
Type: three/four-crew land-based and shipborne multi-mission tilt-rotor transport
Powerplant: two Allison T406-AD-400 turboshaft engines each rated at 6,150 shp (4586 kW)
Performance: (estimated) maximum cruising speed 115 mph (185 km/h) at sea level in helicopter mode and 361 mph (582 km/h) at optimum altitude in aircraft mode; initial climb rate 2,320 ft (707 m) per minute; service ceiling 26,000 ft (7925 m); hovering ceiling 14,200 ft (4330 m) out-of-ground effect; range 592 miles (935 km) in amphibious assault role and 2,418 miles (3892 km) in ferry mode after STO
Weights: (estimated) empty 33,140 lb (15032 kg); maximum take-off 47,500 lb (21546 kg) for VTO and 60,500 lb (27443 kg) for STO
Dimensions: width overall 83 ft 10 in (25.55 m); wingspan 46 ft (14.02 m) excluding nacelles; proprotor diameter, each 38 ft (11.58 m); length 57 ft 4 in (17.47 m) excluding probe; height 21 ft 9 in (6.63 m) with nacelles vertical; wing area 382.00 sq ft (35.49 m²); proprotor disc area, total 2,268.23 sq ft (210.72 m²)
Armament: probably one or two 0.5-in (12.7-mm) trainable multi-barrel rotary machine-guns
Payload: up to 24 troops, or 12 litters plus medical attendants or 20,000 lb (9072 kg) of freight carried internally, or 15,000 lb (6804 kg) of freight carried externally

Bellanca Model 14 and Model 17

In the late 1930s the Bellanca Aircraft Corporation decided to create a two/three-seat cabin lightplane. The result was a low-wing cantilever monoplane of mixed steel and wood construction covered with fabric and plywood. Among its advanced features were a fuselage of lifting section and, for the first time in a production-standard American lightplane, retractable main landing-gear. The **Bellanca Model 14 Junior** was initially flown during December 1937 in **Model 14-7** proto-type form with fixed landing gear and the powerplant of one 70-hp (52-kW) Le Blond 5E radial engine. During 1939 the **Model 14-9** was introduced as the initial production variant with the 90-hp (67-kW) Ken Royce (latterly Le Blond) 5F or 5G radial engine and retractable undercarriage.

Some 40 Model 14-9s were built, alongside small numbers of the **Model 14-9L Cruisair Junior** of 1941, the **Model 14-10** and the **Model 14-14**. All differed in powerplant details.

Bellanca then developed the Model 14 Junior into the **Model 14-12 Cruisair**, with the newly introduced horizontally-opposed type of engine.

The first major production model was the three/four-seat **Model 14-12-F3 Cruisair** that appeared in 1941, with the 120-hp (90-kW) Franklin 6AC-264-F3 flat-six engine.

Bellanca resumed production of the Model 14 after World War II as the

Model 14-13 Senior Cruisair, with the latest 150-hp (112-kW) Franklin 6A4-150-B3 engine.

Developments of the Model 14-13 were the **Model 14-13-2** introduced in 1948, the improved **Model 14-13-3** of 1949 and the **Model 14-13-3W** utility type.

In addition, the **Bellanca Viking** that was built into the mid-1980s was descended, through the products a number of differently named companies, from the Model 14-9 Junior, via the Model 14-13 Cruisair Senior and **Model 14-19 Cruisemaster**.

The Bellanca Aircraft Corporation sold full rights for the Model 14-19 to Northern Aircraft Inc., which became the Downer Aircraft Company Inc. in January 1959. More than 100 Cruisemasters were built before production changed to the **Downer Bellanca 260**, a modified version with tricycle landing-gear and a 260-hp (194-kW) Continental engine. Further changes resulted in manufacture being taken over by Inter-Air. By this time the designation had changed to **Model 14-19-3A** and the definitive configuration of the Viking had appeared.

By 1967 Inter-Air had become the Bellanca Sales Company and had further developed the aircraft into the **Bellanca 260C Model 14-19-3C**. At this time the **Viking 300** made its appearance as the combination of the 260C airframe and 300-hp (224-kW) Continental engine. The aircraft remained in production with Bellanca Aircraft Corporation up to 1980, by which time 1,670 Vikings had been built. Versions offered in 1980 were the Continental-engined **Model 17-30A Super Viking 300A**; the Avco Lycoming-engined **Model 17-31A Super Viking 300A** and the **Model 17-31ATC Turbo Viking 300A** with a turbocharged version of the Lycoming engine.

In 1982 Bellanca's surviving assets were bought by Viking Aviation, which built a small number of Vikings.

SPECIFICATION

Bellanca Model 17-31A Super Viking 300A
Type: four-seat touring and business lightplane
Powerplant: one Avco Lycoming IO-540-K1E5 flat-six engine rated at 300 hp (224 kW)
Performance: maximum speed 226 mph (364 km/h) at optimum altitude; maximum cruising speed 193 mph (311 km/h) at optimum altitude; initial climb rate 1,170 ft (356 m) per minute; service ceiling 18,200 ft (5180 m); range 833 miles (1340 km)
Weights: empty 2,236 lb (1014 kg); maximum take-off 3,325 lb (1508 kg)
Dimensions: wingspan 34 ft 2 in (10.41 m); length 26 ft 4 in (8.03 m); height 7 ft 4 in (2.24 m); wing area 161.50 sq ft (15.00 m²)

With its aerofoil-shaped fuselage, the Bellanca Cruisair became a classic lightplane. The aircraft illustrated is a post-war Model 14-13-3.

Bellanca Model 28

Given the fact that the pair of hyphen-separated numerals in the Bellanca designation system referred to the wing area and the installed horsepower respectively, it is hardly surprising that two different aircraft types were designated **Bellanca Model 28**.

The first of the two types was designed in the early 1930s as a high-performance two-seat monoplane for use in the 1934 MacRobertson air race from England to Australia. Powered by a 700-hp (522-kW) Pratt & Whitney Twin Wasp Junior radial engine and designated at that time as the **Model 28-70**, the machine was shipped to the UK but did not take part in the race. It was later used by British pilot James Mollison to make a New York-to-Croydon transatlantic crossing on 30 October 1936 in the record time of 13 hours 17 minutes.

Bellanca then began the development of a two-seat general-purpose military aircraft powered by a higher-rated engine. This **Model 28-90** was designed for the export market and provided accommodation in tandem cockpits enclosed by a long transparent canopy, and offensive weapons included three machine-guns, and underwing stores.

In 1937 France ordered a batch of 10 such aircraft for the mailplane role, but before delivery all were bought by the Republican government air force for use in the Spanish Civil War. The American government then embargoed the delivery of the Model 28-90s.

The final development of the original Model 28 was the **Model 28-110** designed to meet a Chinese requirement of 1938. The Model 28-110 was basically a development of the Model 28-90 with a higher-rated version of the R-1830 Twin Wasp engine, and it seems likely that considerable quantities of Model 28-90 components, already built for the Franco/Spanish order, were incorporated in the Chinese aircraft. The use and fate of the aircraft after their delivery to China remains unknown.

The second Model 28 was the altogether different **Model 28-92** monoplane built to special order for the Istres-Damascus-Paris air race of 1937 in particular. The machine was of low-wing cantilever monoplane configuration and had tail-wheel landing-gear with retractable main units. The machine's most unusual feature was its powerplant of three engines each fitted with a variable-pitch propeller, and comprising one 420-hp (313-kW) Ranger inverted inline engine in the nose and two 250-hp (186-kW) Menasco C-65 inverted inline engines, in the underwing nacelles, whose rear portions accommodated the main landing-gear units.

Accommodation for the pilot was provided in a cockpit behind the wing's trailing edge.

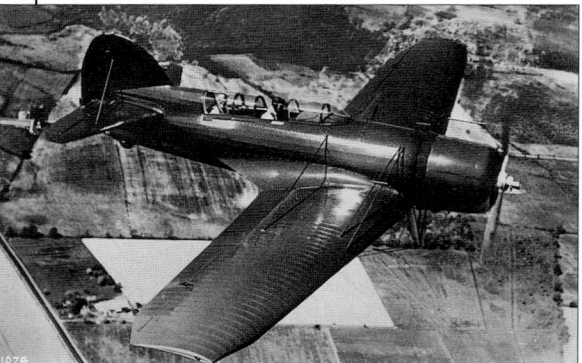

A military development of the Model 28-70, the Model 28-90 (illustrated) saw only limited service.

SPECIFICATION

Bellanca Model 28-110
Type: two-seat general-purpose military aircraft
Powerplant: one Pratt & Whitney R-1830-S3C3G Twin Wasp radial engine rated at 1,050 hp (729 kW)
Performance: maximum speed 290 mph (467 km/h) at optimum altitude; cruising speed 255 mph (410 km/h) at optimum altitude; initial climb rate 3,300 ft (1006 m) per minute; service ceiling 35,000 ft (10670 m); range 800 miles (1287 km)
Weights: empty 4,775 lb (2166 kg); maximum take-off 8,454 lb (3835 kg)
Dimensions: wingspan 46 ft 1¾ in (14.65 m); length 25 ft 11 in (7.90 m); height 8 ft 8 in (2.64 m); wing area 274.84 sq ft (25.53 m²)
Armament: four 0.3-in (7.62-mm) Browning fixed forward-firing machine-guns and one 0.3-in (7.62-mm) Browning trainable rearward-firing machine-gun, plus up to 1,600 lb (726 kg) of bombs carried under the wing

Bellanca Model 77 Bomber

Given the comparative success of its Model 66 Aircruiser, Bellanca decided to employ a similar configuration in a military type for the export market.

First flown in 1933, the **Model 77-140** was based on the Aircruiser, and its somewhat complex designation indicated that it had a wing area of 770.00 sq ft (71.53 m²) and a powerplant offering some 1,400 hp (1044 kW). The fuselage was of basically rectangular section and provided cabin accommodation for a crew of three or four, as well as provision for up to 15 passengers or freight. The fuselage was of metal construction, skinned with light alloy and fabric, and provision was made for the faired mainwheels to be replaced by a pair of floats to turn the Model 77-140 into a torpedo-bomber floatplane. Two were exported to Colombia for use in the landplane and floatplane forms.

The **Model 77-320 Bomber** was an uprated floatplane version, of which two examples were delivered to Colombia, with a powerplant of two Wright R-2600s.

Colombian pilots were reportedly 'afraid to fly' the four Model 77s delivered to the country.

SPECIFICATION

Bellanca Model 77-320 Bomber
Type: three/four-seat bomber and transport floatplane
Powerplant: two Wright R-2600 Cyclone 14 radial engines each rated at 1,600 hp (1193 kW)
Performance: maximum speed 225 mph (362 km/h) at 6,000 ft (1830 m); cruising speed 200 mph (322 km/h) at optimum altitude; service ceiling 28,000 ft (8535 m); range 900 miles (1448 km)
Weights: empty 11,500 lb (5216 kg); maximum take-off 19,700 lb (8936 kg)
Dimensions: wingspan 76 ft (23.16 m); length 45 ft 3 in (13.79 m); height 20 ft 6 in (6.25 m); wing area 770.00 sq ft (71.53 m²)
Armament: one 0.3-in (7.62-mm) Browning trainable machine-gun in each of the nose, dorsal, ventral 'tunnel' and two beam positions, plus up to 2,850 lb (1293 kg) of disposable stores (one torpedo or bombs) carried externally

Bellanca Model P Airbus and Aircruiser

In 1930 Bellanca flew the first example of the **Bellanca Model P-100 Airbus**, a 14-seat commercial monoplane with the powerplant of one 600-hp (448-kW) Curtiss Conqueror Vee engine. Developed from the 1928 **Model K**, the Model P in prototype form had good performance but suffered from the unreliability of its engine.

A unique feature of the Airbus was an extension of Bellanca's original concept of wing-bracing struts which helped to provide lift. On this larger model, and its subsequent developments, a large lifting surface acted as a combined strut and lower wing.

The design showed considerably more promise with the revised powerplant of one Wright Cyclone or Pratt & Whitney Hornet radial engine, each rated at 650 hp (485 kW), but commercial sales were few because of the Depression. The few examples that did appear were designated **Model P-200** and **Model P-300** with accommodation for 12 and 15 passengers respectively. At least one of the aircraft was operated in float-equipped form.

Bellanca was fortunate in securing an order for 14 aircraft from the USAAC. A batch of four aircraft designated **Y1C-27** and powered by 550-hp (410-kW) R-1860 Hornet engines was delivered for service tests, and there followed 10 **C-27A** aircraft with a 650-hp (485-kW) version of the same engine. An experimental but successful conversion of the second C-27A to **C-27B** standard with the 675-hp (503-kW) R-1820-17 Cyclone engine, resulted in the conversion of all the other C-27A aircraft to the improved **C-27C** standard with the 750-hp (559-kW) version of the same engine.

Further developments of the basic Airbus design

with an improved structure entered production as the **Aircruiser** in variants known as the **Model 66-70**, **Model 66-75** and **Model 66-76** with differently rated engines; these were all completed with 13-seat accommodation, and deliveries began in 1935. The type found considerable favour with Canadian operators, who appreciated its ability to operate with either wheeled landing gear or floats, and one was still flying in 1969. Production of the Airbus and Aircruiser amounted to 23 machines.

US Army C-27Cs offered accommodation for 12 passengers. Alternatively, they could be configured for the carriage of freight, with cargo loaded via a large door on the left rear fuselage.

SPECIFICATION

Bellanca Model P-200 Airbus
Type: one/two-crew utility transport
Powerplant: one Pratt & Whitney Hornet S3D1G radial engine rated at 650 hp (485 kW)
Performance: maximum speed 161 mph (259 km/h) at optimum altitude; cruising speed 141 mph (227 km/h) at optimum altitude; initial climb rate 650 ft (198 m) per minute; service ceiling 16,000 ft (4875 m); range 650 miles (1046 km)
Weights: empty 5,400 lb (2449 kg); maximum take-off 10,170 lb (4613 kg)
Dimensions: wingspan 65 ft (19.81 m); length 42 ft 9 in (13.03 m); height 11 ft 6½ in (3.52 m); wing area 652.00 sq ft (60.57 m²)
Payload: up to 12 passengers or 3,305 lb (1499 kg) of freight

Bellanca (Champion) Model 7/8 Champ, Citabria, Scout

In September 1970 Bellanca bought the assets of the Champion Aircraft Corporation, and with it the rights to that company's **Champion Model 7AC Champ**, a strut-braced high-set cabin monoplane of which more than 7,000 had been built. Bellanca decided to produce derivative versions, of which the most enduring were the **Model 7 Citabria** ('airbatic' reversed) and **Model 7 Scout**. Before the suspension of production in 1980, three versions of the former had been delivered.

The Citabria is based on welded steel tube basic structures, all covered with fabric. The landing gear is of the fixed tailwheel type, with speed fairings on the two more advanced **Citabria 150** versions. An enclosed cabin provides accommodation for two and, because of the type's aerobatic capability (with g limits of +5 and -2), the cabin door is jettisonable in an emergency.

The three versions available in 1979 were the **Model 7ECA Citabria Standard** with a 115-hp (88-kW) Avco Lycoming O-235-K2C flat-four engine, the more advanced **Model 7GCAA Citabria 150** with the 150-hp (112-kW) O-320-A2D engine, and the

Right: Aeronca built the Model 7 series up to 1954, when rights were passed to Champion. In 1970, Bellanca took over and achieved great success with aircraft such as this Citabria 150.

Optional float landing gear added to the usefulness of the Bellanca Model 8GCBC Scout. The Scout was built to a total of 360 examples.

SPECIFICATION

Bellanca Model 8GCBC Scout
Type: two-seat light aircraft
Powerplant: one Avco Lycoming O-360-C2E flat-four engine rated at 180 hp (134 kW)
Performance: maximum speed 135 mph (217 km/h) at sea level; cruising speed 122 mph (196 km/h) at optimum altitude; initial climb rate 1,080 ft (329 m) per minute; range 897 miles (1444 km)
Weights: empty 1,315 lb (597 kg); maximum take-off, normal 2,150 lb (975 kg) and agricultural 2,600 lb (1179 kg)
Dimensions: wingspan 36 ft 2 in (11.02 m); length 22 ft 9 in (6.93 m); height 8 ft 8 in (2.64 m); wing area 180.00 sq ft (16.72 m²)
Payload: up to 835 lb (379 kg) normal and 1,140 lb (517 kg) agricultural

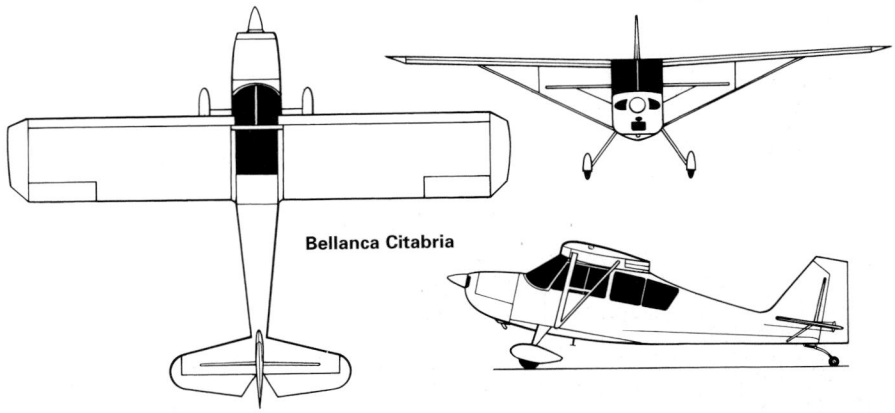

Bellanca Citabria

generally similar **Model 7GCBC Citabria 150S** with a wing increased in span and trailing-edge flaps. When production ended in 1980, more than

5,000 of these aircraft had been completed.

Bellanca also produced a utility version of the Citabria. This emerged as the **Model 7GCBC Scout**

at the beginning of 1971. It differed from the standard Citabria primarily by having an increased-span wing fitted with trailing-edge flaps. Float and ski landing

gear installations were optional, and this model could also be equipped for an agricultural role with spray-dispersal equipment.

When production ended

in 1980 more than 300 Scouts had been built, and a more powerful engine had been introduced on the final variant, which was the **Model 8GCBC Scout**.

Bellanca (Champion) Model 8 Decathlon

The **Champion Model 8KCAB Decathlon** was a derivation of both the Model 7 Champ and Model 8 Scout and was designed specifically as an aerobatic competition aircraft. The result was a machine generally similar in overall configuration to the Champ/Scout, with a wing of reduced span but wider chord and *g*-limits of -5 and +6. After its acquisition of Champion, Bellanca contin-

ued development and production of the Decathlon, and by 1979 three versions were available. These comprised the basic Decathlon, virtually the same as the original Model 8KCAB and powered by a 150-hp (112-kW) Avco Lycoming AEIO-320-E1B engine driving a fixed-pitch propeller, the **Decathlon CS** with a similar engine driving a constant-speed propeller

and the **Super Decathlon** derivative of the Decathlon CS with a more powerful engine driving a constant-

speed propeller. Production ended in 1980, after more than 550 Model 8s had been built.

Based closely on the Champ/Scout, the Decathlon series was optimised for aerobatics.

SPECIFICATION	
Bellanca Super Decathlon	initial climb rate 1,230 ft (375 m)
Type: two-seat aerobatic and sporting aircraft	per minute; service ceiling 16,000 ft (4875 m); maximum range
Powerplant: one Avco Lycoming AEIO-360-H1A flat-four engine rated at 180 hp (134 kW)	508 miles (818 km) **Weights:** empty 1,315 lb (596 kg); maximum take-off 1,800 lb (816 kg)
Performance: maximum speed 148 mph (238 km/h) at optimum altitude; cruising speed 143 mph (230 km/h) at optimum altitude;	**Dimensions:** wingspan 32 ft (9.75 m); length 22 ft 10¾ in (6.98 m); height 7 ft 9 in (2.36 m); wing area 169.10 sq ft (15.71 m²)

Beneš-Mráz Be.50 and Be.51 Beta Minor

Early in 1935 the company known as Beneš & Mráz Tovarna na Letadla was formed to design and manufacture a series of lightplanes. Ing. Paul Beneš had been responsible for the design and development of the Avia BH series.

The **Beneš-Mráz Be.50 Beta Minor** was a two-

seat lightplane intended for the sporting and training roles, and in configuration was a low-wing cantilever monoplane. The basic structure was of wood and accommodation comprised a tandem arrangement of two open cockpits.

The **Be.51 Beta Minor**

had slightly reduced wingspan and a fully-enclosed cabin. It proved a popular lightplane and, after its annexation of Czechoslovakia, Germany seized a number of the aircraft for use by the Luftwaffe in the communi-

cations and training roles. The **Beneš-Mráz Be.252 Beta-Scolar** was generally similar to the Be.50 and was designed as an advanced trainer with aerobatic capability, with a considerably strengthened structure.

In addition, the **Beneš-Mráz Be.550 Bibi** was developed from the Be.51. It featured side-by-side seating and lower structure weight.

An attractive design, similar to but predating the Miles Magister, the Be.50 achieved considerable success.

SPECIFICATION	
Beneš-Mráz Be.50 Beta Minor	ceiling 17,060 ft (5200 m); range
Type: two-seat training and touring aircraft	466 miles (750 km) **Weights:** empty 1,014 lb (460 kg);
Powerplant: one Walter Minor inverted inline engine rated at 95 hp (71 kW)	maximum take-off 1,609 lb (730 kg) **Dimensions:** wingspan 39 ft 10¾ in (12.16 m); length 25 ft 5½ in
Performance: maximum speed 121 mph (195 km/h); cruising speed 106 mph (170 km/h); service	(7.76 m); height 5 ft 10¾ in (1.80 m); wing area 175.45 sq ft (16.30 m²)

Bensen autogyros and helicopters

Dr Igor Bensen's first design was an unpowered rotor-kite which could be towed behind a motor car. Known in prototype form as

the **Bensen Model B-7 Gyro-Glider** and in 'production' form as the **Model B-8 Gyro-Glider**, this could be flown in the USA without a

pilot's licence and could be purchased either in kit form or as a complete aircraft.

The type remained available into the mid-1980s and was built in thousands over more than 25 years. An extensive range of other, often more advanced, products followed.

Bensen derived the float-equipped B-8MW Hydro-Copter (illustrated) from the B-8M Gyro-Copter. The latter was an autogyro derivative of the original, unpowered, B-8 Gyro-Glider.

SPECIFICATION	
Bensen Model B-8M Gyro-Copter (standard form)	service ceiling 12,500 ft (3810 m); range 100 miles (161 km)
Type: one/two-seat light autogyro	**Weights:** empty 247 lb (112 kg);
Powerplant: one McCulloch Model 4318GX or AX flat-four engine rated at 90 hp (67 kW) or 72 hp (54 kW) respectively	maximum take-off 500 lb (227 kg) **Dimensions:** rotor diameter 20 ft (6.10 m) or 22 ft (6.70 m); fuselage length 11 ft 4 in (3.45 m); height
Performance: maximum speed 85 mph (137 km/h) at sea level; cruising speed 60 mph (97 km/h) at optimum altitude; initial climb rate 1,000 ft (305 m) per minute;	11 ft 4 in (3.45 m); rotor disc area 314.16 sq ft (29.19 m²) or 380.13 sq ft (35.31 m²) depending on rotor diameter

Bensen autogyros and helicopters (continued)

Bensen aircraft

Model B-8HD: variant of the Model B-8 Super Bug later known as the **Super Gyro-Copter.** A hydraulic drive system turned the rotor and allowed short take-off runs and near-vertical landings
Model B-8W Hydro-Glider: twin-float seaplane version of the unpowered Gyro-Glider for towing behind a motor launch
Model B-8B Hydro-Boat: Model B-8W version with a boat hull
Model B-8M Gyro-Copter: autogyro version of the Gyro-Glider
Model B-8MH Hover-Gyro: advanced version, later known as the
Model B-18 Hover-Gyro, of the Model B-8M with hovering capability, plus backwards and sideways flight; achieved by the use of two co-axial rotors, the upper auto-rotating and the lower powered by a separate engine
Model B-8MJ Gyro-Copter: version of the Model B-8M with a 'Power Head' rotor spin-up system permitting a vertical (or jump) take-off

Model B-MW Hydro-Copter: version of the Model B-8M with float landing gear
Model B-8V Gyro-Copter: version of the Model B-8M with alternative powerplant
Model B-8 Super Bug: advanced version of the B-8M with a twin-engine installation, allowing the rotor to be spun-up prior to take-off to reduce take-off run
Model B-9 Little Zipster: helicopter evolution of the Model B-8 with a contra-rotating assembly of two co-axial rotors
Model B-10 Prop-Copter: one-man flying platform vehicle supported by two small powered rotors
Model B-80 Gyro-Copter: version of the Model B-8 series with reduced operating costs, and available in Model B-80 standard and
Model B-80D de-luxe variants
Mid-Jet: 100-lb (45-kg) ultra-lightweight helicopter powered by a pair of ramjets at the tips of its two-bladed rotor

Bereznyak-Isayev BI-1

The **Bereznyak-Isayev BI-1** was the world's first interceptor fighter designed specifically for liquid-fuel rocket propulsion. It had a fuselage of ovoid section and mostly wooden construction and a stubby wing of mixed construction with stressed skinning. The tail unit incorporated a dorsal and ventral centre-line vertical surface as well as circular endplate finlets and retractable tailwheel landing gear.

Five prototypes were built simultaneously in a high-priority programme, and the first prototype

(completed in a mere 35 days) made its initial flight on 10 September 1940 as a glider; the machine was used for aerodynamic and handling trials, and was towed to altitude by a Petlyakov Pe-2. These tests were successful, but because of the pressing need to evacuate the plant away from the threat of the advancing German forces, flight-testing of the first rocket-powered prototype was delayed. A short straight-line 'lift-off' was made in early May 1942, and on 15 May there followed the

first true test flight that lasted 3 minutes 9 seconds, the first in the world by a rocket-propelled fighter. Minor damage to the landing gear at the end of this flight slowed the development programme, but by then an initial series of 50 BI-1 fighters was under construction. Then, on 27 March 1943, the seventh BI-1 flight ended in a fatal crash.

Wind tunnel testing found no easy solution to the problem, diagnosed as a nose-down pitch at high

Powered by a volatile mixture of nitric acid and kerosene, the BI-1 was a brave attempt to produce a point interceptor of incredible performance.

speeds, and it was decided to suspend production while the seventh BI-1 was used in a further test programme. Progress was slow, for the BI-1 programme now had little priority. However, with a more powerful rocket motor installed, a revised BI-1 was flown early in 1945 but was badly damaged in a forced landing due to a problem with the ski landing gear. On 9 March the

repaired machine achieved a rate of climb of 16,340 ft (5465 m) per minute, but by that time the decision to end further development had been taken. At that time seven BI-1 aircraft (the BI-1 Nos 2, 3 and 7 were then redesignated as the **BI-2, BI-3** and **BI-7**) had been completed and 20 more were almost at final assembly stage. At least one aircraft was preserved.

SPECIFICATION

Bereznyak-Isayev BI-1 (third aircraft)
Type: point interceptor
Powerplant: one Dushkin/Shtokolov D-1A-1100 rocket motor rated at 2,425 lb st (10.78 kN)
Performance: (estimated) maximum speed 559 mph (900 km/h) at 16,405 ft (5000 m); initial climb rate 16,140 ft (4920 m) per minute; powered endurance

15 minutes
Weights: empty 1,775 lb (805 kg); maximum take-off 3,710 lb (1683 kg)
Dimensions: wingspan 21 ft 8 in (6.60 m); length 22 ft 9 in (6.94 m); height 6 ft 9 in (2.06 m)
Armament: two 20-mm ShVAK fixed forward-firing cannon in the nose

Beriev Be-2 (KOR-1)

Beriev responded to an urgent requirement for a shipboard reconnaissance aircraft for the Soviet navy with its 1934-5 development of a single-engined single-float biplane. The basic structure was of metal under a covering of fabric, except on the forward fuselage which had light alloy skins. Light alloy

was also used for the large centreline float and the two smaller stabilising floats strut-mounted beneath the outboard ends of the lower wing. The powerplant was based on a licence-built version of the Wright Cyclone.

Designated **Beriev KOR-1** and first flown in about April 1936, the new

floatplane made its service debut in 1937. Aircraft also equipped shore-based units for coastal reconnaissance

and the direction of fire from coastal gun batteries. Although considered obsolete by the time of

Germany's invasion of the USSR, all available KOR-1 (by then having the alternative designation **Be-2**)

SPECIFICATION

Beriev Be-2 (KOR-1)
Type: two-seat reconnaissance floatplane
Powerplant: one Mikulin M-25A radial engine rated at 700 hp (522 kW)
Performance: maximum speed 172 mph (245 km/h) at 6,560 ft (2000 m); climb to 3,280 ft (1000 m) in 3 minutes 12 seconds; service ceiling 21,655 ft (6600 m); range 621 miles (1000 km)
Weights: empty 3,968 lb (1800 kg); maximum take-off

5,922 lb (2686 kg)
Dimensions: wingspan 36 ft 1 in (11.00 m); length 28 ft 5½ in (8.67 m); height 12 ft 5½ in (3.80 m); wing area 315.39 sq ft (29.30 m²)
Armament: two 0.3-in (7.62-mm) ShKAS fixed forward-firing machine-guns above upper-wing centre section and one 0.3-in (7.62-mm) ShKAS trainable rearward-firing machine-gun in the rear cockpit, plus up to 220 lb (100 kg) of bombs underwing

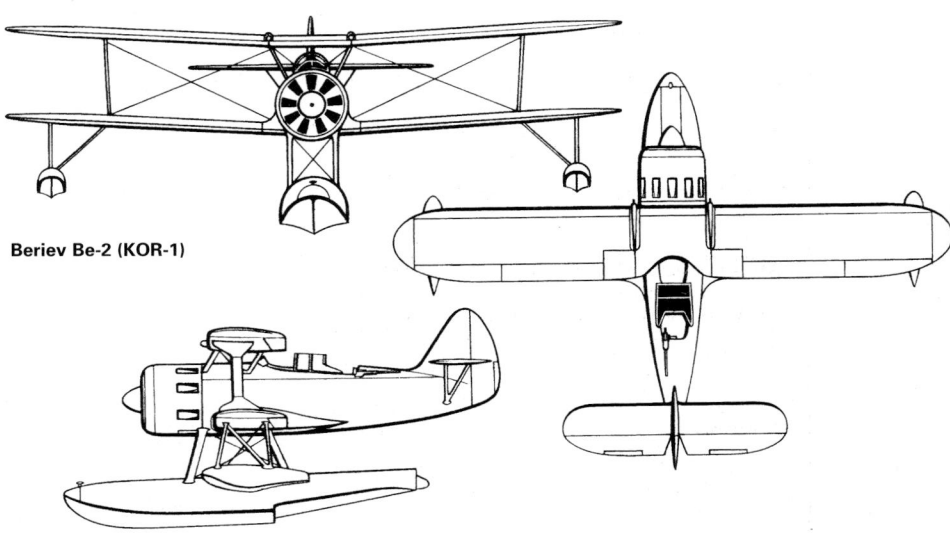

Beriev Be-2 (KOR-1)

aircraft were pressed into service, some being revised with wheeled landing gear for use in the close support role.

Production of the KOR-1 lasted until 1940 and amounted to some 300 aircraft, and it is worth noting that considerable problems with the airframe and engine limited the type's real usefulness.

As a floatplane, the KOR-1 never flew without some form of restriction. A number of new-build aircraft used wheeled landing gear.

Beriev Be-4 (KOR-2)

More or less in parallel with the construction and development of the KOR-1 floatplane, the Beriev bureau was working on the design of a small flying-boat. This was intended to fulfil the same requirement as the hastily developed KOR-1, but was expected to offer far superior performance.

First flown early in 1941, the **Beriev KOR-2** (later redesignated as the **Be-4**) was of all-metal construction with a wing-mounted engine nacelle. In configuration the

Representing a major advance over the KOR-1, the duties of the KOR-2 included flying as a catapult flying-boat from Soviet warships.

KOR-2 was a parasol-wing monoplane and an unusual feature was the selection of an inverted-gull wing.

Only a small number of these aircraft had been completed and delivered to the Soviet navy before their

factory was overrun in the autumn of 1941. Production of the Be-4 was resumed at the Krasnoyarsk factory in Central Asia during 1943 and an estimated 100 flying-boats were built before production ceased in 1945.

SPECIFICATION	
Beriev Be-4 (KOR-2)	6,085 lb (2760 kg)
Type: three-seat reconnaissance flying boat	**Dimensions:** wingspan 39 ft 4½ in (12.00 m); length 34 ft 5¼ in (10.50 m); height 13 ft 3 in (4.05 m); wing area 274.49 sq ft (25.50 m²)
Powerplant: one Shvetsov M-62 radial engine rated at 1,000 hp (746 kW)	
Performance: maximum speed 221 mph (356 km/h) at 15,420 ft (4700 m); climb to 16,405 ft (5000 m) in 12 minutes; service ceiling 26,575 ft (8100 m); range 716 miles (1150 km)	**Armament:** one 0.3-in (7.62-mm) ShKAS fixed forward-firing machine-gun in the bow and one 0.3-in (7.62-mm) ShKAS trainable rearward-firing machine-gun in the rear cockpit, plus up to 882 lb (400 kg) of bombs or depth charges carried on underwing racks
Weights: empty 4,590 lb (2082 kg); maximum take-off	

Beriev Be-6 'Madge'

A standard Soviet navy Be-6, with the MAD 'sting' and prominent water rudder clearly illustrated.

The Beriev design bureau began work on the design and development of a large maritime reconnaissance and bombing flying-boat in 1943, and the resulting **LL-143** prototype flew for the first time in 1945. The type revealed excellent capabilities and was developed into the **Be-6** for production to meet the Soviet naval air force's urgent requirement for a maritime reconnaissance and, increasingly, anti-submarine flying-boat.

The first Be-6 (NATO reporting designation **'Madge'**) flew initially in February 1949 and entered service in the following year. The type's most significant changes from LL-143 standard were an

uprated powerplant, modified wing structure, revised and lengthened bow allowing an increase in the crew from seven to eight, provision for a complete relief crew or for 40 assault troops, 'balconied' flight-deck glazing to provide better downward fields of

vision, bow-mounted spray fences to protect the propellers, more sophisticated equipment and a wholly revised armament fit. The equipment included a retractable radome aft of the second step. The armament comprised one 23-mm NR-23 cannon in the bow position and two 23-mm NR-23 cannon in each of the dorsal and tail positions, as well as 8,818 lb (4000 kg) of bombs/depth charges or two torpedoes on under-wing racks.

Prior to 1954, the majority of Be-6s were flying with an Ilyushin gun barbette in the tail. Later, this installation was replaced by the MAD boom.

More than 200 of these flying-boats were built for the Soviet naval air force as well as for limited utility service with Aeroflot. By 1954 the aircraft were in the throes of an upgrade programme that saw the replacement of the tail guns by the 'sting' sensor for a MAD (Magnetic Anomaly Detection)

system, and replacement of the nose guns by separate radomes for new surveillance and missile-guidance radars. A number of Be-6s was converted as dedicated transports. The Be-6 operated in front-line roles until the early 1970s, and a few remained in secondary roles into the late 1970s.

SPECIFICATION	
Beriev Be-6 'Madge'	ceiling 20,015 ft (6100 m); range 2,983 miles (4800 km)
Type: eight-crew maritime reconnaissance, bombing and anti-submarine flying boat	**Weights:** empty 41,506 lb (18827 kg); maximum take-off 63,933 lb (29000 kg)
Powerplant: two Shvetsov ASh-73TK radial engines each rated at 2,400 hp (1789 kW)	**Dimensions:** wingspan 108 ft 3½ in (33.00 m); length 77 ft 3¾ in (23.57 m); height 25 ft ¾ in (7.64 m); wing area 1,291.71 sq ft (120.00 m²)
Performance: maximum speed 257 mph (414 km/h) at 5,905 ft (1800 m); climb to 16,405 ft (5000 m) in 20 minutes; service	**Armament:** see above

Beriev KOR-4 (Be-8 'Mole')

It has been suggested that the **Beriev Be-8** (NATO reporting name **'Mole'**) was designed in World War II as a utility transport amphibian flying-boat, but work on the prototype was not started until the war had finished. The Be-8 prototype made its maiden flight in July 1947 and was an all-metal braced parasol-wing monoplane with a stepped hull.

Although probably schemed for a naval role, the type was considered more suitable for civil operations, although in the event only two 'production' examples of the Be-8 were completed for the use of Aeroflot. In the early 1950s one prototype was adapted for experiments, with the hydrofoils developed by the TsAGI (Central Aerodynamics and Hydrodynamics Institute).

Originally intended for use in the ambulance, photographic reconnaissance, training and communications roles, the Be-8 could taxi on land, but was not a true amphibian.

SPECIFICATION	
Beriev Be-8 'Mole'	range 749 miles (1205 km)
Type: two-crew utility amphibian flying-boat	**Weights:** empty 6,206 lb (2815 kg); normal take-off 7,989 lb (3624 kg)
Powerplant: one Shvetsov ASh-21 radial engine rated at 700 hp (522 kW)	**Dimensions:** wingspan 62 ft 4 in (19.00 m); length 42 ft 8 in (13.00 m); wing area 430.57 sq ft (40.00 m²)
Performance: maximum speed 165 mph (266 km/h) at 5,905 ft (1800 m); cruising speed 137 mph (220 km/h) at optimum altitude; service ceiling 18,045 ft (5500 m);	**Payload:** up to six passengers, or litters plus a medical attendant, or 882 lb (400 kg) of freight

Beriev Be-10 'Mallow'

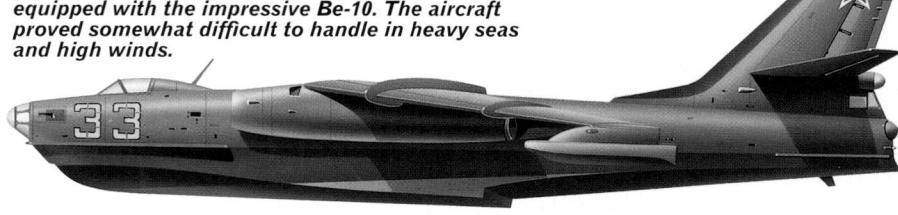

Two units of the Soviet Black Sea Fleet were equipped with the impressive Be-10. The aircraft proved somewhat difficult to handle in heavy seas and high winds.

The **Beriev Be-10** (NATO reporting name **'Mallow'**) possesses the distinction of having been the only turbojet-powered flying-boat to have attained true operational status. Developed from the R-1, the Be-10 was first revealed in public during the course of the 1961 Soviet Aviation Day display, when four of the type flew past in formation. During that summer, and under the designation **M-10**, the type established no fewer than 12 world-class records, of which the most outstanding were a speed of 912 km/h (566.7 mph) over a 15/25-km (9.3/15.5-mile) course, a speed of 875.86 km/h (544.24 mph) over a 1000-km (621-mile) closed circuit with a payload of 5000 kg (11,023 lb), and an altitude of 12733 m (41,775 ft) with a 10000-kg (22,046-lb) payload.

The Be-10 was of light alloy stressed-skin construction, and in configuration was a high-wing monoplane with a sharply swept wing. The wing had considerable anhedral, and incorporated two wing fences and a fixed wingtip stabilising float on each half. The aircraft was specifically designed to replace the Be-6, but it is thought that the type was built only in small numbers, largely as a result of its poor payload/range performance and the lack of any real need for the type's high outright flight performance. The Be-10 remained in service for a relatively short time.

SPECIFICATION	
Beriev Be-10 'Mallow'	take-off 102,515 lb (46500 kg)
Type: three-crew maritime patrol and reconnaissance flying-boat	**Dimensions:** (estimated) wingspan 82 ft (25.00 m); length 108 ft (33.00 m); wing area 1,399.35 sq ft (130.00 m²)
Powerplant: two Lyul'ka AL-7RV turbojet engines each rated at 14,330 lb st (63.74 kN)	**Armament:** possibly one 23-mm NR-23 fixed forward-firing cannon in the bow, and two 23-mm NR-23 or NS-23 trainable rearward-firing cannon in the tail position, plus up to 4,409 lb (2000 kg) of bombs or other weapons carried on racks under the wing
Performance: (estimated) maximum speed 567 mph (912 km/h) at optimum altitude; absolute ceiling 49,080 ft (14960 m); range 1,864 miles (3000 km)	
Weights: (estimated) empty 52,910 lb (24000 kg); maximum	

Large wing fences were added to the Be-10 during early testing. Considerable effort was also expended in ensuring that water could not enter the engine intakes.

Beriev Be-12 Chaika 'Mail'

The lessons learned in the design of the R-1 and Be-10 were incorporated in the design of a much improved flying-boat, based loosely on the Be-6 and originally identified by NATO as a re-engined version of the older type. In fact the **Beriev Be-12 Chaika** (seagull) (NATO reporting name **'Mail'**), designated **M-12** in AV-MF service, bears little more than a general resemblance to the Be-6, sharing with its predecessor only the gull-wing layout and a tail unit with endplate vertical surfaces. The greater power and lighter weight of a turboprop powerplant permitted a forward extension of the hull, with a new planing bottom similar to that of the Be-10. The prominent spray-suppressing strakes around the bow of the Be-10 were also utilised. The most significant change, however, was the addition of massive and sturdy retractable tailwheel landing gear, making the Be-12 amphibious and thus considerably more versatile than the earlier Beriev designs. The turreted gun armament of the Be-6 was deleted, the tail turret being replaced by MAD (Magnetic Anomaly Detection) gear in the tail above the tailwheel well, while the antenna for the search radar was installed in a long 'thimble' radome on the bow rather than in a retractable ventral dustbin radome, as on the Be-6. One of the drawbacks of the high-wing layout, namely the great height of the engines above the water/ground, was miti-gated by the design of engine cowling panels which dropped down to form strong working platforms for groundcrew.

The first Be-12 flew in around 1960 and the first of some 200 or more such aircraft entered service in 1964, with small numbers later transferred to the air forces of Syria and Vietnam. The considerable weight-lifting capability of the Be-12 was demon-strated in a series of class records for amphibians set up in 1964, 1968 and 1970, suggesting a normal weaponload as high as 11,023 lb (5000 kg).

The advent of 'Haze', 'Hormone and 'Helix' heli-copters and of the 'May'

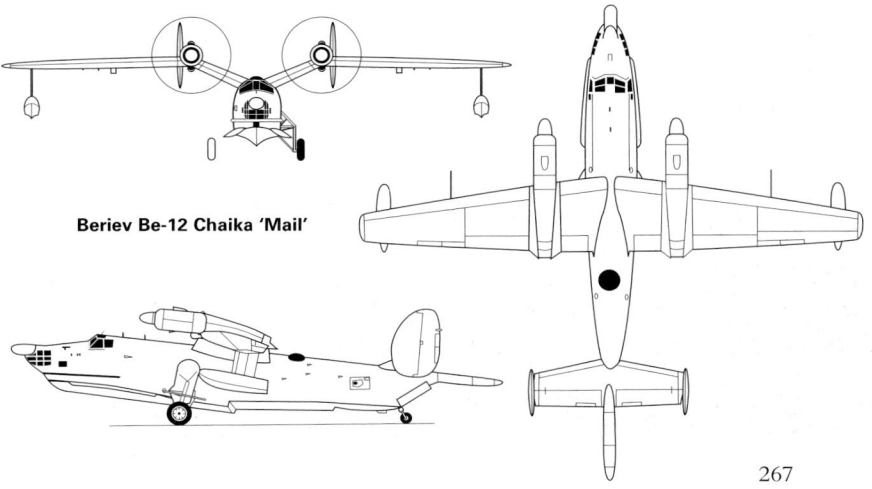

Beriev Be-12 Chaika 'Mail'

Both the nose-mounted radar and MAD installation are clearly evident on this Be-12. The Be-14 dispenses with the MAD gear and carries underwing equipment pods.

fixed-wing aircraft for the ASW role meant that there was a steadily diminishing ASW task for the Be-12, although the type is still in service in the late 1990s for the patrol, ASW and, in its **Be-14** form, high-speed search-and-rescue roles. The Be-12 has also been used for ecological reconnaissance (**Be-12EKO**), forest fire-fighting (**Be-12P**), scientific research (**Be-121**) and utility transport (**Be-12Nkh**).

SPECIFICATION

Beriev Be-12 Chaika 'Mail'
Type: six-crew maritime patrol, reconnaissance and ASW amphibian flying-boat
Powerplant: two ZMDB Progress (Ivchyenko) AI-20D turboprop engines each rated at 4,190 ehp (3124 ekW)
Performance: maximum speed 378 mph (608 km/h) at optimum altitude; patrol speed 199 mph (320 km/h) at optimum altitude; initial climb rate 2,990 ft (912 m) per minute; service ceiling 37,000 ft (11280 m); range

4,660 miles (7500 km)
Weights: empty 47,840 lb (21700 kg); maximum take-off 68,342 lb (31000 kg)
Dimensions: wingspan 97 ft 5¾ in (29.71 m); length 99 ft (30.17 m); height 22 ft 11½ in (7.00 m) with landing gear extended; wing area 1,130.25 sq ft (105.00 m²)
Armament: up to 11,023 lb (5000 kg) of disposable stores in the form of bombs, rockets or ASMs on underwing pylons, and depth charges and sonobuoys in fuselage bays

Beriev Be-30 'Cuff' and Be-32

The **Beriev Be-30** short-haul transport (NATO reporting name **'Cuff'**) was the first landplane to be designed and developed by the Beriev design bureau. Seen publicly for the first time in 1967, the Be-30 was reported to have flown initially on 3 March 1967. It is a high-wing monoplane of all-metal construction of and, because of the high-wing configuration, the main units of the tricycle landing gear incorporated very stalky legs which

retracted into the rear of the engine nacelles. The powerplant of the prototype consisted of two 740-hp (552-kW) ASh-21 radial engines, but two TVD-10 turboprops powered production aircraft. Accommodation was provided for up to 14 passengers.

It had been anticipated that the Be-30 would be built in large numbers for Aeroflot, which had issued the requirement for a type to succeed the Antonov

An-2, but only eight were produced, presumably because of a decision to use the Let L-410 as the standard short-haul type for service with Aeroflot.

In 1990, following the collapse of the USSR into the Commonwealth of Independent States, the Beriev experimental design bureau was renamed as the 'Taganrog Aviation Scientific-Technical Complex named after G. M. Beriev'. The CIS's

shortage of hard currency with which to continue purchase and support of the L-410 led to a renewed requirement for a Russian type, and in response Beriev resurrected a modestly updated and improved version of the Be-30 as the **Beriev Be-32**, which had originally flown in prototype form in 1976.

A widened fuselage characterises the new type

and the cabin can be configured in several forms to enable the Be-32 to carry out different tasks. The first Be-32 prototype was a Be-30 conversion that made its maiden flight in 1993 with the original TVD-10 engines, but the production model has more powerful, yet more economical, Pratt & Whitney Canada PT6A turboprop engines.

A design of little distinction, the Be-30 led directly to the improved Be-32. The first of these flew in 1976 and was subsequently abandoned. The programme was reborn in 1991.

SPECIFICATION

Beriev Be-32
Type: one/two-crew multi-purpose light transport
Powerplant: two Pratt & Whitney PT6A-65B turboprop engines each rated at 1,100 shp (820 kW)
Performance: (estimated) maximum cruising speed 298 mph (480 km/h) at 9,845 ft (3000 m); initial climb rate 1,476 ft (450 m) per minute; range 1,087 miles (1750 km)
Weights: empty 10,494 lb

(4760 kg); maximum take-off 16,093 lb (7300 kg)
Dimensions: wingspan 55 ft 9¼ in (17.00 m); length 51 ft 6 in (15.70 m); height 18 ft 1½ in (5.52 m); wing area 344.45 sq ft (32.00 m²)
Payload: up to 16 passengers or troops, or seven business-type passengers, or 15 paratroops, or six litters and 10 seated casualties plus one medical attendant, or 4,189 lb (1900 kg) of freight

Beriev Be-103

Designed from 1992, the **Beriev Be-103** is a general-purpose amphibian flying-boat. It is a mid/low-wing monoplane of all-metal construction with a two-step hull and provides accommodation for a pilot and up to five passengers.

Notable features of the design are its water-displacement wing that provides good lateral stability and thereby obviates the need for stabilising floats, and the powerplant of two piston engines carried in nacelles at the tips of pylons extending

from the sides of the rear fuselage. The position of the engines allows the propellers to be shielded from spray by the wing.

Prototype manufacture started in 1994, and the first prototype made its maiden on 15 July 1997, but crashed fatally in the following month. The importance of this machine for the continued development of Siberia and Russia's northern regions, where lakes and other suitable water bodies are widespread, is considerable and a second

prototype was manufactured in 1998. The originally planned powerplant was two 173-hp (129-kW) Balanov M-17

radial engines, but current thinking is centred on the use of US engines that will also provide greater export potential. A

cheaper version, with a single VOKBM M-14 radial engine in a nacelle above the rear fuselage, has also been considered.

SPECIFICATION

Beriev Be-103
Type: one/two-crew general-purpose amphibian flying-boat
Powerplant: two Teledyne Continental IO-360-ES4 flat-six engines each rated at 210 hp (157 kW)
Performance: (estimated) maximum speed 165 mph (265 km/h) at optimum altitude; cruising speed 149 mph (240 km/h) at optimum altitude; service ceiling

9,845 ft (3000 m); range 839 miles (1350 km)
Weights: maximum take-off 4,519 lb (2050 kg)
Dimensions: wingspan 41 ft 9 in (12.72 m); length 34 ft 3½ in (10.45 m); height 12 ft 9½ in (3.90 m); wing area 270.18 sq ft (25.10 m²)
Payload: up to five passengers or 882 lb (400 kg) of freight carried in the cabin

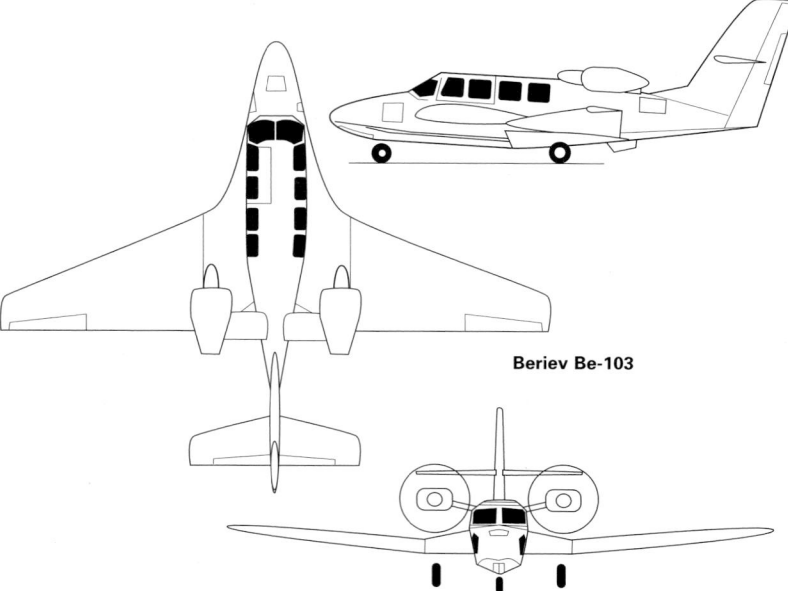

Beriev Be-103

Beriev Be-200

The **Beriev Be-200** is a multi-role amphibian flying-boat for civil tasks and is, in effect, a scaled-down and simplified version of the A-40 Albatross. Among the differences from the A-40 are the omission of all military electronics and provision for them, the relocation of the stabilising floats from the wingtips to points further inboard under the wing, the addition of winglets, the alteration of the main landing gear units

to twin-wheel units, the omission of the booster turbojets and the introduction of a Western avionics suite created by AlliedSignal.

The Be-200 is intended primarily as a forest fire-fighting machine with cabin provision for 30 fully-equipped smoke jumpers and tanks under the cabin floor for 26,456 lb (12000 kg) of water that can be scooped up from any suitable water body.

SPECIFICATION

Beriev Be-200
Type: two-crew multi-role amphibian flying boat
Powerplant: two ZMKB Progress (Ivchyenko) D-436T turbofan engines each rated at 16,534 lb st (73.55 kN)
Performance: (estimated) maximum speed 447 mph (720 km/h) at 22,965 ft (7000 m); cruising speed 435 mph (700 km/h) at 26,245 ft (8000 m); initial climb

rate 2,756 ft (840 m) per minute; service ceiling 36,090 ft (11000 m); range 2,486 miles (4000 km)
Weight: maximum take-off 79,365 lb (36000 kg)
Dimensions: wingspan 107 ft 3½ in (32.70 m); length 105 ft 1¾ in (32.05 m); height 29 ft 2½ in (8.90 m); wing area 1,264.16 sq ft (117.44 m²)
Payload: see above

Other roles envisaged for the type include passenger transport, with the cabin outfitted for 32 first-class or 68 tourist-class passengers, cargo-hauling with a range of 684 miles (1200 km) while carrying a 15,432-lb (7000-kg) payload; air ambulance and search and rescue. In 1998 it was reported that Beriev, now part of the Sukhoi industrial group, had suggested a militarised

version of the Be-200 to South Korea in the maritime reconnaissance role.

The maiden flight of the first of four Be-200 prototype and pre-production aircraft was planned for November 1995, but this

Severe delays in the financing of the powerplant package, and in the integration by the Russians of the AlliedSignal avionics into the aircraft's Aria 200 integrated avionics suite, have afflicted the Beriev Be-200 programme.

machine was completed only in September 1996 and the first flight was not until October 1998, after development delays. Orders for the Be-200 have been placed by three elements of the CIS's civil aviation organisation for an initial 109 aircraft.

Beriev A-40 and Be-42 Albatross 'Mermaid'

Design of the **Beriev A-40 Albatross** (NATO reporting name **'Mermaid'**) began during 1983 in an effort to create a successor to the Be-12 'Mail' and Ilyushin Il-38 'May' in the ASW, maritime patrol and minelaying roles, with search and rescue as a secondary capability. The prototype made its first flight during December 1986, and this new amphibian flying-boat became known to the West during 1987. In 1988 the director of US naval intelligence revealed that the provisional reporting name, **'TAG-D'** (the fourth new experimental aircraft spotted at Taganrog), had been allocated to a new amphibian photographed by a US satellite. On 20 August 1989 the prototype made a flypast at the Aviation Day display at Tushino, and articles about the new flying-boat began to appear in the Soviet press. The

second prototype made the type's Western debut at the 1991 Paris air show.

The A-40 is the largest amphibian ever built, and is of completely modern design, with its turbofan engines nacelle-mounted on pylons above the wing-roots. A turbojet take-off booster is fitted inside each pylon, with its nozzle usually covered by a vertically-split 'eyelid'. This powerplant location ensures that the inlets are protected from spray by the wing and small strakes on the sides of the bow. The single-step hull is of revolutionary design, described by its creators as the world's first 'variable-rise bottom', with unique double chines. This sets new standards of stability and controllability in the

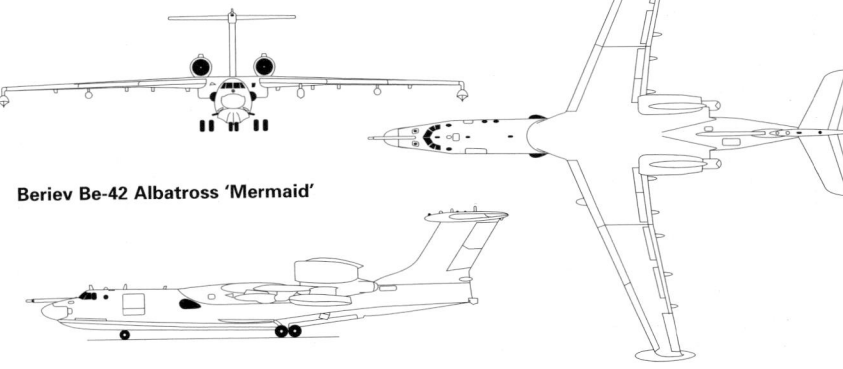

Beriev Be-42 Albatross 'Mermaid'

water and gives smaller *g* forces on take-off and landing. 'Unsticking' from the water is aided by the incorporation of small wedge-shaped boxes to the rear of the step.

Neither of the two A-40 prototypes has yet flown with a full mission avionics fit. The precarious state of the entire Albatross project must place the future of this incredible aircraft in doubt.

SPECIFICATION

Beriev A-40 Albatross 'Mermaid'
Type: eight-crew long-range ASW, maritime reconnaissance, minelaying and SAR amphibian flying-boat
Powerplant: two Aviadvigatel (Soloviev) D-30KPV turbofan engines each rated at 26,455 lb st (117.68 kN) and two RKBM RD-60K turbojet engines each rated at 5,511 lb st (24.52 kN)
Performance: maximum speed 472 mph (760 km/h) at 19,685 ft (6000 m); cruising speed 447 mph

(720 km/h) at 19,685 ft (6000 m); initial climb rate 5,906 ft (1800 m) with one engine inoperative; service ceiling 31,825 ft (9700 m); range 3,417 miles (5500 km)
Weight: maximum take-off 189,594 lb (86000 kg)
Dimensions: wingspan 136 ft 6½ in (41.62 m); length 143 ft 10 in (43.84 m) including probe; height 36 ft 3¾ in (11.07 m); wing area 2,152.85 sq ft (200.00 m²)
Armament: up to 14,330 lb (6500 kg) of bombs, depth charges, mines and torpedoes

Projected variants

Be-40P: transport with accommodation for 105 passengers
Be-40PT: mixed passenger and freight transport
Be-42: minimum-change SAR version, stripped of ASW equipment and without ESM wingtips. This variant would have a nine-man crew and would carry two liferafts, blood transfusion equipment, ECG machines and other surgical equipment. Up to 54 survivors could be accommodated, entering the aircraft via two side hatches which would each be equipped with mechanised ramps. Searchlights and IR sensors would be used for locating survivors. The first Be-42 was already under construction when the declining state of the CIS economy dictated a halt

The A-40 has a large surveillance, search and navigation radar with its antenna in a bow radome under the fixed inflight-refuelling probe as well as a large stores bay in the hull aft of the step. The large pods which form the wingroots accommodate electronic equipment as well as the retracted four-wheel main landing gear bogies. Slim ESM pods are carried on the wingtips.

It has been suggested that the basic A-40 ASW and patrol amphibian would have the service designation **Be-44**, which may have been the subject of an order by the Russian navy. The navy cannot afford the type, however, and the order has therefore been allowed to lapse. In the late 1990s, construction of the A-40 remains at just the two prototype aircraft.

Beriev MBR-2

Georgii Mikhailovich Beriev became one of the marine aircraft design team assembled under the leadership of the newly arrived expatriate French designer, Paul Aimé Richard, before moving to the marine aircraft section within the TsAGI (Central Aerodynamics and Hydrodynamics Institute) in Moscow. In was in this latter capacity that Beriev was posted to Taganrog on the Sea of Azov in 1930-1 to supervise the Soviet programme to improve and produce an Italian flying-boat, the Savoia-Marchetti S.62bis. In 1931 Beriev sought and received permission to design an improved flying-boat for service with the Soviet

Significantly revised in its MBR-2/AM-34 form (illustrated), the MBR-2 saw considerable operational service. The AM-34 engine drove a pusher-propeller.

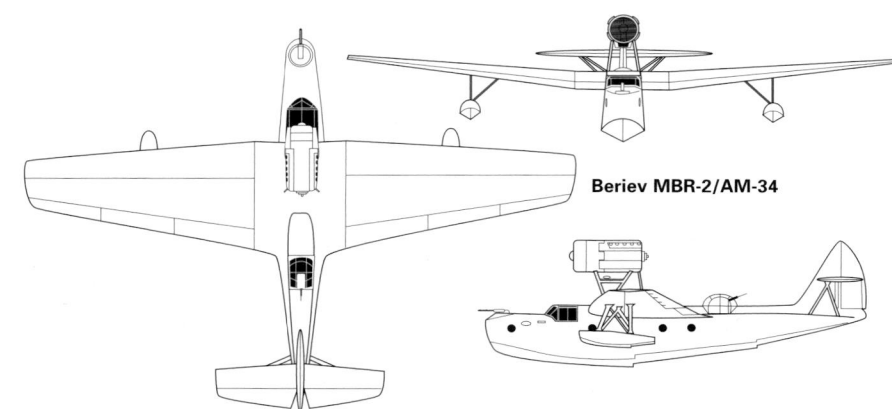

navy. In May 1931 work began on the type, originally designated as **Aircraft No. 25**, which was test-flown with the BMW VIF engine at about the time that Beriev received authorisation to create his own design bureau at Taganrog.

Successful trials of Aircraft No. 25 led to the decision to place the type in production as the **Beriev MBR-2 (Morskoi Blizhnii Razvyedchik-2**, or marine short-range reconnaissance no. 2). The aircraft was to

be Beriev's most successful, as 1,300 such flying-boats were built.

The primary change turning Aircraft No. 25 into the MBR-2 was the replacement of the original German engine by the M-17, which was a Soviet development of the BMW VI, in the form of its 730-hp (544-kW) M-17b variant. Deliveries of the **MBR-2/M-17** original model, intended for use in the short-range bombing and maritime reconnaissance roles, began in 1934. The flying-boat was a shoulder-wing cantilever monoplane of wooden

construction except for its tail unit and ailerons, which were of light alloy construction covered with fabric. Salient details of the MBR-2 included a two-step hull with plywood skinning over a wooden basic structure and an open pilot's cockpit.

Variants

MBR-2/AM-34: in 1935 Beriev carried out a radical redesign of the MBR-2 to provide a fully-enclosed cockpit for the pilot and a glazed cupola for the dorsal gunner, replace the M-17b engine with an 830-hp (619-kW) M-34NB (redesignated AM-34NB in 1937), introduce an entirely new curved fin and rudder and modern 0.3-in (7.62-mm) ShKAS machine-guns. The new version was soon placed in large-scale production, which continued to the completion of the MBR-2 production programme in 1942. The MBR-2/AM-34 served with all four main Soviet fleets and saw considerable operational service, first during the 'Winter War' with Finland, and then throughout the 'Great Patriotic War' of 1941-5. The type could be turned into an amphibian by the installation of fixed-wheel or ski landing gear, and after World War II served for nearly a decade on fishery patrol duties, latterly receiving the NATO reporting name **'Mote'**

MBR-2/M-103: in 1937 a standard MBR-2/AM-34 was modified to take the more powerful M-103, but no production was undertaken

MP-1: this **Morskoi Passazhirskii-1** (marine passenger no. 1) was a civil passenger version of the MBR-2/M-17 with accommodation for six passengers in an enclosed, soundproofed and thermally-insulated cabin. The type was used in some numbers

MP-1bis: a 1937 civil development of the MBR-2/AM-34, with similar capacity to that of the MP-1. One MP-1bis, piloted by Paulina Osipyenka, established a number of women's world records between 22 and 25 May 1937

MP-1T: freighter, basically similar to the MBR-2 except for its lack of armament

BU: five-seat naval variant optimised for co-operation with fast patrol boats and motor torpedo boats

SPECIFICATION	
Beriev MBR-2/M-17	(2475 kg); maximum take-off 9,039 lb (4100 kg)
Type: three-crew short-range reconnaissance and bombing flying-boat	**Dimensions:** wingspan 62 ft 4 in (19.00 m); length 44 ft 3¾ in (13.50 m); wing area 592.03 sq ft (55.00 m²)
Powerplant: one M-17b Vee engine rated at 730 hp (544 kW)	
Performance: maximum speed 126 mph (203 km/h) at sea level; cruising speed 99 mph (160 km/h) at optimum altitude; service ceiling 14,435 ft (4400 m); range 404 miles (650 km)	**Armament:** one 0.3-in (7.62-mm) PV-1 or ShKAS trainable machine-gun in each of the bow and dorsal positions, plus up to 1,102 lb (500 kg) of bombs or depth charges carried on underwing racks
Weights: empty 5,456 lb	

Beriev MBR-2/AM-34

Beriev MDR-5

The **Beriev MDR-5 (Morskoi Dalnii Razvyedchik-5**, or marine long-range reconnaissance no. 5) was a twin-engined flying-boat of high-wing cantilever monoplane configuration with provision for a crew of five, and embodied a two-step hull.

The first of two MDR-5 (alternative designation **MS-5** for **Morskoi Samolyet-5**, or marine aircraft no. 5) prototypes made its maiden flight in the spring of 1938 as a

pure flying-boat. The second prototype was completed with retractable amphibian landing gear, clearly inspired by that of the Sikorsky S-43, whose design influences were also readily apparent in the rest of the MDR-5. By the time the MDR-5 appeared, however, the competing Chyetverikov MDR-6 design had already been ordered into production, and the Beriev type proceeded no further than the prototype stage.

A crew of five flew the promising MDR-5, consisting of a bow gunner, navigator, observer, pilot and radio operator. The observer also acted as the rear gunner.

Beriev MDR-5 (continued)

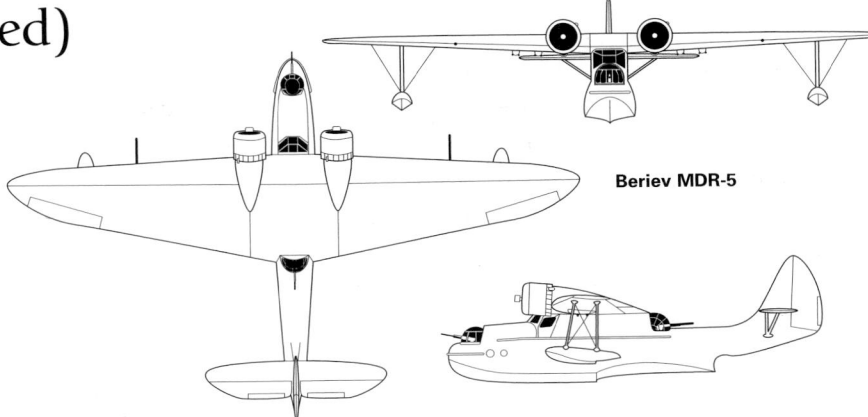

Beriev MDR-5

SPECIFICATION

Beriev MDR-5
Type: five-crew long-range maritime reconnaissance and bombing flying boat
Powerplant: two Tumanskii M-87A radial engines each rated at 950 hp (708 kW)
Performance: maximum speed 214 mph (345 km/h) at optimum altitude; climb to 16,405 ft (5000 m) in 21 minutes; service ceiling 26,740 ft (8150 m); range 1,500 miles (2415 km)
Weights: empty 13,410 lb (6083 kg); maximum take-off

20,282 lb (9200 kg)
Dimensions: wingspan 82 ft ½ in (25.00 m); length 52 ft 1¾ in (15.88 m); wing area 844.99 sq ft (78.50 m²)
Armament: one 0.3-in (7.62-mm) ShKAS trainable forward-firing machine-gun in the bow turret, one or two 0.3-in (7.62-mm) ShKAS trainable rearward-firing machine-guns in the dorsal turret, plus up to 2,205 lb (1000 kg) of bombs or depth charges carried on underwing racks

Beriev R-1

Work was started on the **Beriev R-1 (Reaktivnii-1**, or jet no. 1) in 1949 as the bureau's first turbojet-powered flying-boat. The bureau had first started to think of a flying-boat of this type as early as 1945, with a project for the LL-143 to be revised with two RD-45 turbojets. The R-1 was intended for research use and was somewhat smaller than the LL-143, but with the same shoulder-set gull-wing configuration. Other features of this all-metal type were a long single-step hull, a fighter-type pilot's cockpit offset to port, and stabilising floats that retracted in flight to form extensions of the tips of the straight wings.

The R-1 made its maiden flight on 30 May 1952 and was configured as a three-seat patrol bomber with full armament to allow a full exploration of the operational capabilities and limitations of a turbojet-powered flying-boat.

SPECIFICATION

Beriev R-1
Type: three-crew experimental reconnaissance and bombing flying-boat
Powerplant: two Klimov VK-1 turbojet engines each rated at 6,041 lb st (26.87 kN)
Performance: maximum speed 497 mph (800 km/h) at 22,965 ft (7000 m); service ceiling 37,730 ft (11500 m); range 1,243 miles (2000 km)
Weight: maximum take-off

37,479 lb (17000 kg)
Dimensions: wingspan 70 ft 2½ in (21.40 m); length 63 ft 9 in (19.43 m); wing area 624.33 sq ft (58.00 m²)
Armament: two 23-mm NR-23 fixed forward-firing cannon in the bow and two 23-mm NR-23 trainable rearward-firing cannon in the tail barbette, plus up to 2,205 lb (1000 kg) of bombs or depth charges carried on underwing hardpoints

Of similar general configuration to the LL-143 that was developed into the Be-6, the R-1 provided a wealth of useful data for the Beriev Be-10. In operation, the R-1 was notable for its considerable jet efflux and wake when on the water.

Berkmans Speed Scout

Aware that the US military might soon need dedicated fighter aircraft, the brothers Emile and Maurice Berkmans began work on their **Speed Scout** in 1916. The aircraft was an unequal-span biplane of typical wire-braced wooden construction with fabric-covered flying surfaces and a fuselage of plywood semi-monocoque construction. The Speed Scout was planned with an armament of two synchronised 0.3-in (7.62-mm) fixed forward-firing machine-guns firing through the propeller disc, but it is thought that armament was never fitted. The prototype began its flight trials in the spring of 1918 and revealed good handling and climb performance, but was technically obsolescent and not considered for large-scale production.

A lack of official interest in modern theories of air warfare left US warplane development to the foresight of people such as the Berkmans brothers.

SPECIFICATION

Berkmans Speed Scout
Type: single-seat fighter
Powerplant: one Gnome Monosoupape rotary engine rated at 100 hp (75 kW)
Performance: maximum speed 115 mph (185 km/h) at sea level; initial climb rate 1,100 ft (335 m) per minute; service ceiling

22,000 ft (6705 m); endurance 2 hours 30 minutes
Weights: empty 820 lb (372 kg); maximum take-off 1,190 lb (540 kg)
Dimensions: wingspan 26 ft (7.92 m); length 18 ft 8 in (5.69 m); height 7 ft 10 in (2.39 m)
Armament: see above

Berliner-Joyce FJ, F2J and F3J

The Berliner-Joyce Aircraft Corporation was established in February 1929 at Dundalk, Maryland, acquiring the assets of the former Berliner Aircraft Company Inc. The new company had intended to produce the Berliner Monoplane, but instead became involved in the design of the P-16 two-seat fighter to meet a requirement of the USAAC.

The second type built by the company was the **Berliner-Joyce XFJ-1** fighter prototype. Ordered in May 1929, the XFJ-1 was first flown in May 1930, and was powered by a 450-hp (336-kW) Pratt & Whitney R-1340C Wasp radial engine. The aircraft was damaged in a crash landing and, as it had already revealed very poor landing qualities, was rebuilt to a revised standard as the **XFJ-2**.

The latter had a 500-hp (373-kW) R-1340-92 radial engine, enlarged vertical tail surface and, as first flown, the XFJ-2 had spatted wheels. Although faster, flight trials revealed that the XFJ-2 still exhibited instability, and further development was abandoned. The sole machine remained on strength up to 1934 however, and was probably operated as a station 'hack'.

In June 1931 the US Navy ordered the **XF2J-1** two-seat fighter prototype. The aircraft bore a familiar resemblance to the US Army's P-16, with an upper

Berliner-Joyce designed the XFJ-1 to the USN's Bureau of Aeronautics specification for Design No. 96. This called for a single-seat, short-span biplane of limited height, able to fit into an aircraft-carrier's hangar without the need for wing-folding.

wing 'gulled' into the line of the upper fuselage, but was powered by a Wright R-1510-92 experimental two-row radial engine rated at 625 hp (466 kW). The machine first flew in 1933 and revealed a maximum

speed of 196 mph (315 km/h), but the engine proved very troublesome and development was abandoned in favour of the Grumman XFF-1.

In June 1932 the USN ordered the fighter which

Featuring a severely staggered unequal-span biplane wing cellule, the single-bay XF3J-1 also offered an enclosed cockpit with a turtleback which extended rearward to the leading edge of the vertical tail.

had the dubious distinction of being its last biplane with fixed landing gear. This was the **XF3J-1** proto-type, of which the sole example first flew in January 1934, and was handed over for evaluation from April of the same year. The XF3J-1 was assessed as offering poorer capabilities than the rival

SPECIFICATION

Berliner-Joyce XF3J-1
Type: single-seat carrierborne fighter
Powerplant: one Wright R-1510-26 radial engine rated at 625 hp (466 kW)
Performance: maximum speed 209 mph (336 km/h) at 6,000 ft (1830 m); climb to 5,000 ft (1525 m) in 2 minutes 42 seconds; service ceiling 24,500 ft (7470 m); range 719 miles (1157 km)
Weights: empty 2,717 lb

(1233 kg); maximum take-off 4,409 lb (2000 kg)
Dimensions: wingspan 29 ft (8.84 m); length 22 ft 11 in (6.98 m); height 10 ft 9 in (3.28 m); wing area 239.60 sq ft (22.26 m²)
Armament: two 0.3-in (7.62-mm) Browning fixed forward-firing machine-guns in the forward fuselage, and two 116-lb (53-kg) bombs carried on hardpoints under the lower wing

Grumman XF2F-1, and was consequently scrapped at the end of 1935.

The failure of the XF3J-1 marked the end for Berliner-Joyce which, already suffering from the

effects of the USA's economic depression, ended its involvement with aviation and was absorbed by North American Aviation, its parent company.

Berliner-Joyce OJ

To meet a 1930 USN requirement for a lightweight shipboard observation biplane, Berliner-Joyce designed and produced its **XOJ-1** that secured a production contract in 1931.

A conventional two-seat biplane, the XOJ-1 had a

fabric-covered fuselage incorporating two open cockpits and its fixed tail-wheel-type landing gear could be replaced by one main centreline float and two smaller underwing stabilising floats. It was initially powered by one 300-hp (224-kW) Wright

SPECIFICATION

Berliner-Joyce OJ-2
Type: two-seat shipborne observation aircraft
Powerplant: one Pratt & Whitney R-985-A Wasp Junior radial engine rated at 400 hp (298 kW)
Performance: maximum speed 154 mph (248 km/h) at sea level; initial climb rate 1,350 ft (411 m) per minute; climb to 10,000 ft (3050 m) in 12 minutes 6 seconds; service ceiling 15,300 ft (4665 m); range 530 miles (853 km)
Weights: empty 2,323 lb (1054 kg); maximum take-off 3,713 lb (1684 kg)

Dimensions: wingspan 33 ft 8 in (10.26 m); length 25 ft 8 in (7.82 m); height 10 ft 10 in (3.30 m); wing area 284.20 sq ft (26.40 m²)
Armament: one 0.3-in (7.62-mm) Browning fixed forward-firing machine-gun in the leading edge of the starboard upper wing, and provision for one 0.3-in (7.62-mm) Browning trainable rearward-firing machine-gun in the rear cockpit, plus up to 500 lb (227 kg) of bombs carried on one underfuselage and two underwing hardpoints

R-975-A Whirlwind radial engine, and special equip-ment included attachments to permit launch from the catapults of light cruisers.

The production type resulting from the XOJ-1 was the **OJ-2**, of which 39 were built for the USN, which received the first such aircraft in 1933. The OJ-2s were operated by VS-5B and VS-6B squadrons. The machines

were withdrawn from front-line service in 1935 and the survivors were then operated up to the early 1940s at Naval Air Reserve bases.

This OJ-2 is depicted as it appeared with the US Navy's squadron VS-6B during 1933. The type was deployed on board two aircraft-carriers.

Variant

XOJ-3: one OJ-2 completed with a cockpit canopy and lengthened engine cowling. The machine crashed in March 1934 and was rebuilt to OJ-2 standard.

Berliner-Joyce P-16 and PB-1

The first product of the Berliner-Joyce company was a two-seat fighter to meet a requirement of the USAAC. The **Berliner-Joyce XP-16** prototype, first flown in October 1929, was based on a metal structure covered largely with fabric. The machine was a single-bay biplane with a distinctive gulled upper wing. Initial power-plant was one 600-hp (447-kW) Curtiss V-1570-A supercharged Vee engine.

Evaluation by the USAAC resulted in the award of two production contracts (totalling 15 and 10 aircraft, respectively) for the **Y1P-16** service test model. Delivered in 1932, these aircraft differed very little from the XP-16 except in their powerplant of one V-1570-25 engine. At the end of their trials the aircraft were accepted for service with the designation P-16,

but this was later changed to **PB-1** in the Pursuit Biplane category. In service, the aircraft were found to be low on perfor-mance and agility and, in combination with a tendency to nose-over very easily, this resulted in the type's premature with-drawal from service in January 1934.

Tandem open cockpits for the P-16's pilot and observer/gunner were located immediately to the rear of the upper wing's trailing edge.

An unpopular machine due to the poor visibility it afforded its pilot on landing, the P-16 nevertheless gained the colourful USAAC markings of the era.

SPECIFICATION

Berliner-Joyce P-16 (PB-1)
Type: two-seat fighter
Powerplant: one Curtiss V-1570-25 Vee engine rated at 600 hp (447 kW)
Performance: maximum speed 175 mph (282 km/h) at sea level; cruising speed 151 mph (243 km/h) at optimum altitude; initial climb rate 1,970 ft (600 m) per minute; climb to 15,000 ft (4570 m) in 8 minutes 48 seconds; service ceiling 29,000 ft (8840 m); range 650 miles (1046 km)
Weights: empty 2,803 lb

(1271 kg); maximum take-off 3,996 lb (1813 kg)
Dimensions: wingspan 34 ft (10.36 m); length 28 ft 2 in (8.59 m); height 9 ft (2.74 m); wing area 279.00 sq ft (25.92 m²)
Armament: two 0.3-in (7.62-mm) Browning fixed forward-firing machine-guns in the forward fuselage and one 0.3-in (7.62-mm) Browning trainable rearward-firing machine-gun in the rear cockpit, plus up to 244 lb (111 kg) of bombs carried externally

Bernard 12

The aircraft now generally known by the generic name Bernard were in fact produced by a number of companies successively created by the French manufacturer Adolphe Bernard. First, in the course of 1917, came the EAB (Etablissements Adolphe Bernard) whose first wholly original design was the **AB.1** two-seat night bomber. The **AB.2** was a higher-powered prototype, and the **AB.3** was a projected passenger transport development.

In 1922 the EAB was transformed into the SIMB (Société Industrielle des Métaux et du Bois), whose first original design by Jean Hubert, the new chief designer, was the **Bernard 10** low-wing cantilever monoplane fighter prototype. Finally, in 1926-7, the SIMB became the SAB (Société des Avions Bernard) whose first original design was the **Bernard 20**.

Owing much to the Bernard 10, the Bernard 12

differed most strongly in its more conventional main landing gear arrangement, its radial- rather than Vee-engined powerplant, and its heavy fixed forward-firing armament.

First flown in May 1926, the Bernard 12 was powered by a Gnome-Rhône (Bristol) Jupiter engine. The type was proposed for production in the C.1 (Chasse monoplace, or single-seat fighter) category with the uprated powerplant of one Hispano-Suiza or Lorraine water-cooled engine of 500 hp (373 kW). The

A main landing gear arrangement consisting of a through-axle carried at the closed ends of two Vee struts was employed on the 12, rather than the deep underfuselage pylon of the 10 which carried an auxiliary aerofoil incorporating the axle.

monoplane layout was generally distrusted in the French air arms during the 1920s, however, and as a result further development of the Bernard fighter was discontinued.

SPECIFICATION	
Bernard 12	**Dimensions:** wingspan 39 ft 4½ in (12.00 m); length 23 ft 7½ in (7.20 m); height 8 ft 10⅓ in (2.70 m); wing area 226.05 sq ft (21.00 m²)
Type: single-seat fighter **Powerplant:** one Gnome-Rhône (Bristol) Jupiter 9Ab radial engine rated at 420 hp (313 kW)	
Performance: maximum speed 165 mph (265 km/h) at optimum altitude; service ceiling 26,245 ft (8000 m)	**Armament:** two 0.303-in (7.7-mm) Vickers fixed forward-firing machine-guns in the forward fuselage, and two 0.303-in (7.7-mm) Vickers fixed forward-firing machine-guns in the leading edges of the wing
Weights: empty 2,006 lb (910 kg); normal take-off 3,395 lb (1540 kg)	

Bernard 14 and 15

Designed in response to official scepticism about the structural integrity of monoplanes, the **Bernard 14** was an all-new design in an effort to capture a production order for a fighter of Bernard origins. The company opted for a sesquiplane layout in the Bernard 14, which was of wooden construction and armed with four 0.303-in (7.7-mm) machine-guns, of which two were mounted in the wing above the fuselage and two were mounted in the fuselage nose.

The Bernard 14 was developed in parallel with the Bernard 12 and made its maiden flight at the end of 1925, but was destroyed

in February 1926 after structural failure of the upper wing. Further development was discontinued after this accident.

A sole prototype of the **Bernard 15** was flown during 1926 as the last fighter developed by the SIMB before the company closed at the end of 1926. The aircraft was a sesquiplane and therefore of basically similar layout to its numerical predecessor. The type had the same armament and powerplant as the Bernard 14, but differed principally in having a smaller wing. The Bernard 15 had a maximum speed of 168 mph (270 km/h).

Bernard 14

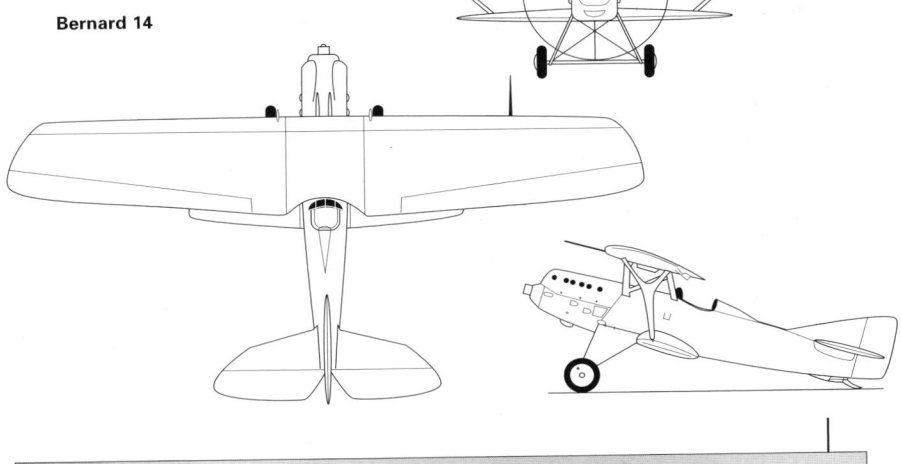

Designer Jean Hubert gave the Bernard 14 a sesquiplane layout to avoid the structural weight and aerodynamic drag of a full biplane layout.

SPECIFICATION	
Bernard 14	**Dimensions:** wingspan 41 ft ⅛ in (12.50 m); length 24 ft 3⅓ in (7.40m); height 10 ft 2 in (3.10 m); wing area 290.63 sq ft (27.00 m²)
Type: single-seat fighter **Powerplant:** one Hispano-Suiza 12Hb Vee engine rated at 500 hp (373 kW)	
Performance: maximum speed 165 mph (265 km/h) at optimum altitude; climb to 16,405 ft (5000 m) in 12 minutes	**Armament:** two 0.303-in (7.7-mm) Vickers fixed forward-firing machine-guns in the forward fuselage, and two 0.303-in (7.7-mm) Vickers fixed forward-firing machine-guns in the leading edges of the upper wing
Weights: empty 2,756 lb (1250 kg); normal take-off 3,968 lb (1800 kg)	

Bernard 20

A full-scale mock-up of the **Bernard 20** low-wing cantilever monoplane single-seat fighter was displayed at the Paris Salon de l'Aéronautique in 1928. Derived from the V.2 racer, the Bernard 20 was designed to meet an official requirement for an interceptor of the lightweight or 'Jockey' type, and was notable for its very high level of aerodynamic cleanliness and basically all-wood construction. The mock-up had been used for wind tunnel tests, record-

ing some excellent figures, and the sole prototype flew for the first time in the spring of 1929. At this time, however, the low-wing fighter was not highly regarded in French official circles, and the test and development programme was terminated after 18 months when the 'Jockey' programme was cancelled.

SPECIFICATION	
Bernard 20	3,020 lb (1370 kg)
Type: single-seat fighter **Powerplant:** one Hispano-Suiza 12Jb Vee engine rated at 400 hp (298 kW)	**Dimensions:** wingspan 35 ft 5⅓ in (10.80 m); length 24 ft 5⅓ in (7.45 m); height 8 ft 2½ in (2.50 m); wing area 179.76 sq ft (16.70 m²)
Performance: maximum speed 199 mph (320 km/h) at 13,135 ft (4000 m); service ceiling 19,685 ft (6000 m)	**Armament:** two 7.7-mm (0.303-in) Vickers fixed forward-firing machine-guns in the forward fuselage
Weights: empty 2,255 lb (1023 kg); normal take-off	

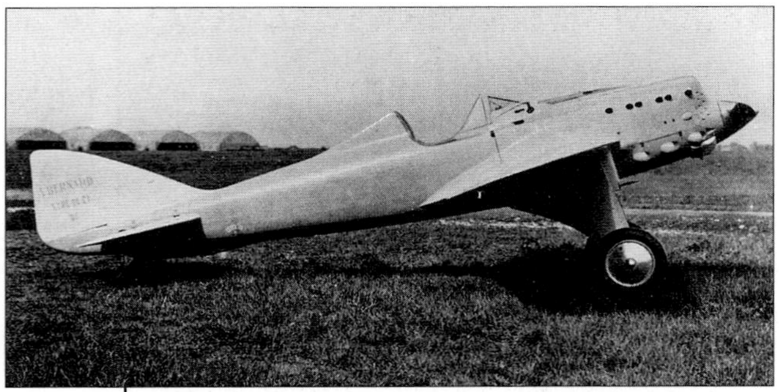

Louis Béchereau designed the exceptional Bernard 20 to meet an official French requirement. The aircraft performed well, but fell foul of indecision within the French military. The aircraft featured a small windscreen and prominent roll bar.

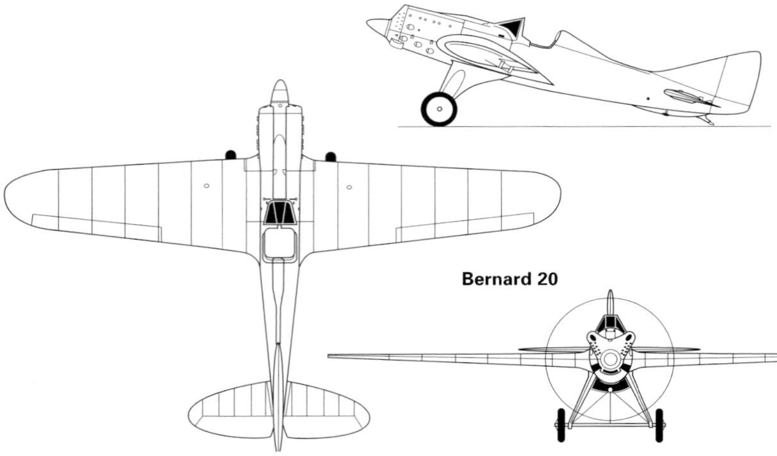

Bernard 70 series

The **Bernard 70** was a single-seat fighter that was projected but never built, but its basic design formed the basis for the **Bernard 72** racing monoplane, built to compete in the 1930 Coupe Michelin. Of wooden stressed-skin construction, the Bernard 72 was forced out of the race by lubrication problems with its Gnome-Rhône Titan radial engine. The machine was then re-engined with the more powerful Titan-Major, and in that form received the revised designation **Bernard 73**.

The basic design was retained for the **Bernard 74** single-seat lightweight fighter. The **Bernard 74.01**, the first of two prototypes, flew in February 1931 with one Gnome-Rhône 7Kbs radial engine, while the **Bernard 74.02** second prototype made its maiden flight in October of the same year, powered by one 360-hp (268-kW) Gnome-Rhône 7Kd radial engine. This machine demonstrated a maximum speed of 217 mph (350 km/h) at 13,125 ft (4000 m) and normal take-off weight of 2,734 lb (1240 kg).

Any production model would have been based on the Bernard 74.02, but no production order was placed. The Bernard 74.01, revised with a 500-hp (373-kW) Gnome-Rhône 9Kbrs Mistral radial engine and redesignated as the **Bernard 75**, was displayed at the 1932 Paris 'Salon' and ended its career as a pilot trainer for a private company.

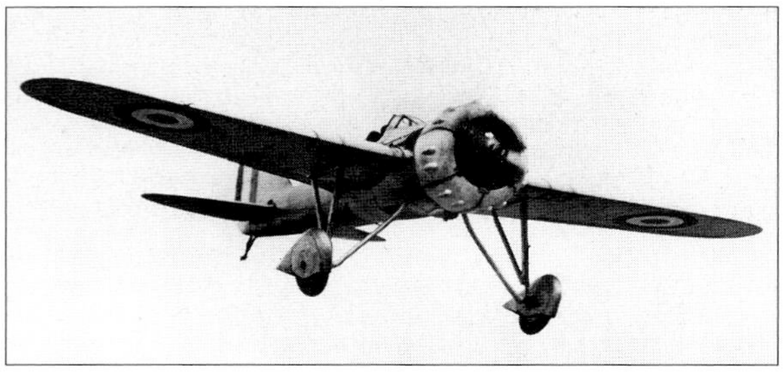

Both the Bernard 73 and 74 (illustrated) featured a closely-cowled radial engine with fairings over the cylinder heads.

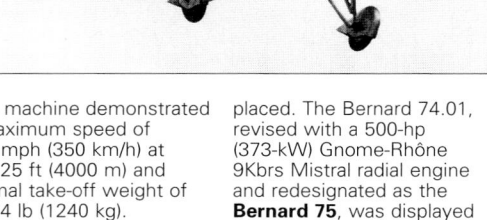

SPECIFICATION

Bernard 74.01
Type: single-seat lightweight fighter
Powerplant: one Gnome-Rhône 7Kbs Titan-Major radial engine rated at 280 hp (208 kW)
Performance: maximum speed 193 mph (310 km/h) at optimum altitude; service ceiling 26,245 ft (8000 m)
Weights: empty 1,819 lb (825 kg); normal take-off 2,438 lb (1106 kg)
Dimensions: wingspan 30 ft 2¼ in (9.20 m); length 22 ft 11⅝ in (7.00 m); height 8 ft 2⅜ in (2.50 m); wing area 144.78 sq ft (13.45 m²)
Armament: two 0.303-in (7.7-mm) Vickers fixed forward-firing machine-guns in the forward fuselage

Bernard 190

Bernard developed the **190T** as an enlarged and improved version of its **18T** 8-passenger airliner. The prototype 190T made its first flight in spring 1928 and some eight production aircraft were subsequently built. All served with the CIDNA (Compagnie Internationale de Navigation Aérienne) on its various European services. Compared with the Bernard 18T, the 190T had a larger cabin, although still configured for the carriage of eight passengers, an enclosed cockpit and redesigned tail surfaces. It retained the proven wooden construction and cantilever high-wing layout of its predecessor.

SPECIFICATION

Bernard 190T
Type: passenger transport
Powerplant: one Gnome-Rhône 9Ab Jupiter engine rated at 420 hp (313 kW)
Performance: maximum speed 134 mph (216 km/h); service ceiling 12,140 ft (3700 m); range 621 miles (1000 km)
Weights empty 4,312 lb (1956 kg); maximum take-off 7,496 lb (3400 kg)
Dimensions: wingspan 56 ft 9 in (17.30 m); length 41 ft 3¼ in (12.58 m); height 11 ft 9¼ in (3.59 m); wing area 461.79 sq ft (42.90 m²)

Variants

Bernard 191GR: three 600-hp (447-kW) Hispano-Suiza 12Lb-engined long-range aircraft built for various pioneering flights and record attempts
Bernard 192T: one-off transport built for Aéropostale, powered by one 480-hp (358-kW) Gnome-Rhône 9Kkx Jupiter
Bernard 193T: one-off transport version of 197GR, powered by one 450-hp (336-kW) Lorraine 12Eb engine
Bernard 197GR: ordered by the Société des Moteurs Lorraine to demonstrate its engine in a sales tour of South America. It flew the South Pacific before being used in a number of pioneering flights. It was lost off Rangoon on 26 February 1929

Wearing the famous Cicognes badge and named* Oiseau Canari *(Canary Bird), Bernard 191GR. 2 is preserved at the Musée de l'Air, Paris.

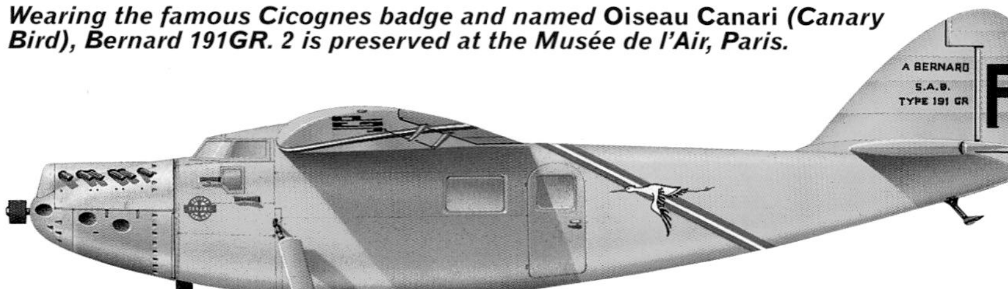

Bernard 260

Responding to a French air ministry requirement of 1931 for a single-seat fighter offering a maximum speed of 217 mph (350 km/h) at 16,405 ft (5000 m), Bernard offered the **Bernard 260**. This was a cantilever low-wing monoplane of all-metal construction and featured Handley Page slats. Other features of the type were divided main landing gear units that were notably long to provide adequate ground clearance for the large two-bladed propeller.

Flown for the first time in September 1932, the Bernard 260 prototype revealed a high degree of manoeuvrability. Engine cooling posed considerable problems, however, and a number of alternative radiator installations were used.

While the 260 was being tested, a fixed undernose radiator, a pair of radiators on the main gear units and a frontal radiator were all tried.

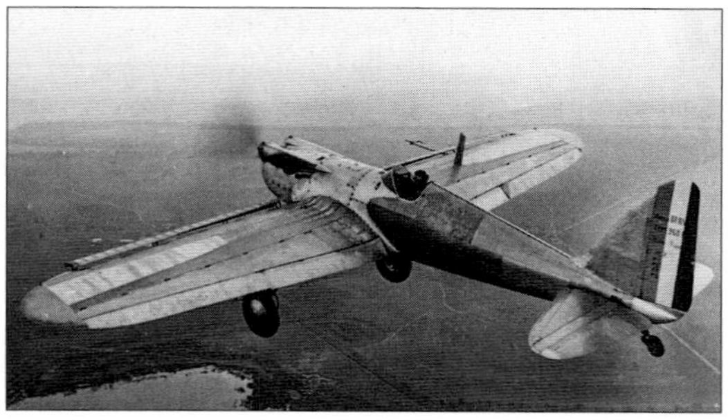

Bernard 260 continued

During the course of the type's development a large number of modifications was effected.

The official evaluation of the Bernard 260 showed that it was faster than competing designs, but had a relatively poor rate of climb. With the selection of the Dewoitine D.500 as the winning design, further development of the Bernard 260 was abandoned, but not before the slats and flaps had helped to avoid a catastrophe. On 6 July 1933, while flying at Villacoublay at an altitude of 3,935 ft (1200 m), the Bernard 260 shed its propeller: The pilot brought the aircraft down to a safe landing. The **Bernard 261**, a development with retractable landing gear, never flew.

SPECIFICATION

Bernard 260
Type: single-seat lightweight fighter
Powerplant: one Hispano-Suiza 12Xbrs Vee engine rated at 690 hp (514 kW)
Performance: maximum speed 224 mph (360 km/h) at 16,405 ft (5000 m); climb to 32,810 ft (10000 m) in 30 minutes
Weights: empty 2,992 lb (1357 kg); normal take-off 3,968 lb (1800 kg)
Dimensions: wingspan 37 ft 7/8 in (11.30 m); length 25 ft 7 in (7.80 m); height 12 ft 5½ in (3.79 m); wing area 195.91 sq ft (18.20 m²)
Armament: two 0.303-in (7.7-mm) Vickers fixed forward-firing machine-guns under the wing

Bernard H.52

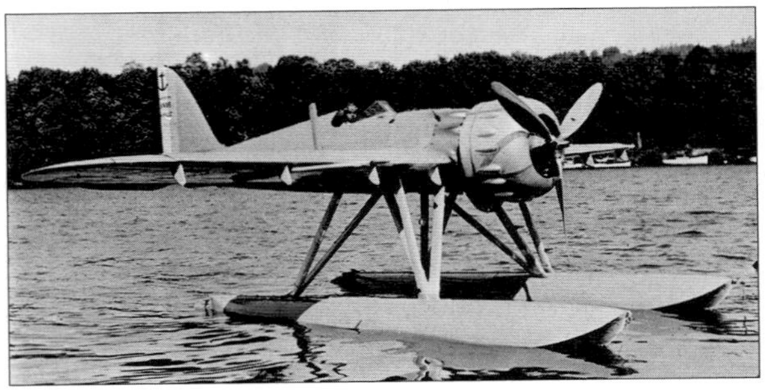

The **Bernard H.52**, a single-seat floatplane fighter of mid-wing cantilever monoplane configuration with an open cockpit, made its first flight on 16 June 1933. Built to a French navy requirement, it utilised the tailplane, wing and rear fuselage of the Bernard 260. The machine was of all-metal construction, retained the Handley Page leading-edge slats of the Bernard 260, had twin-float landing gear and had the central section of its fuselage built integral with the wing. A second example was test-flown in 1934, but no production ensued.

Two-, three- and four-bladed propellers were trialled on the H.52.

SPECIFICATION

Bernard H.52
Type: single-seat fighter floatplane
Powerplant: one Gnome-Rhône 9Kdrs Mistral radial engine rated at 500 hp (373 kW)
Performance: maximum speed 204 mph (329 km/h) at 13,125 ft (4000 m); climb to 13,125 ft (4000 m) in 9 minutes; range 373 miles (600 km)
Weights: empty 3,263 lb (1480 kg); maximum take-off 4,163 lb (1888 kg)
Dimensions: wingspan 37 ft 8¾ in (11.30 m); length 30 ft 6⅛ in (9.30 m); height 14 ft (4.27 m); wing area 195.91 sq ft (18.20 m²)
Armament: two 0.295-in (7.5-mm) Darne fixed forward-firing machine-guns under the wing

Bernard H.110

Bearing a close resemblance to the H.52, the **Bernard H.110** was a single-seat fighter floatplane powered by a licence-built Wright Cyclone radial engine. Basically of metal construction, it differed from its predecessor by having fabric-covered wings. By the time construction began, the Bernard firm had gone into liquidation, and the H.110 was built at the facility of the Société Schreck. Testing began in June 1935, but was soon abandoned as a result of Bernard's financial problems and thus the difficulties that any further development or production would have entailed.

SPECIFICATION

Bernard H.110
Type: single-seat fighter floatplane
Powerplant: one Hispano-Suiza 9Vbs radial engine rated at 710 hp (529 kW)
Performance: maximum speed 205 mph (330 km/h) at 8,200 ft (250 m)
Weights: maximum take-off 4,189 lb (1900 kg)
Dimensions: wingspan 38 ft ⅔ in (11.60 m); length 30 ft 6⅛ in (9.30 m); wing area 204.52 sq ft (19.00 m²)
Armament: two 0.295-in (7.5-mm) Darne fixed forward-firing machine-guns in the leading edge of the wing

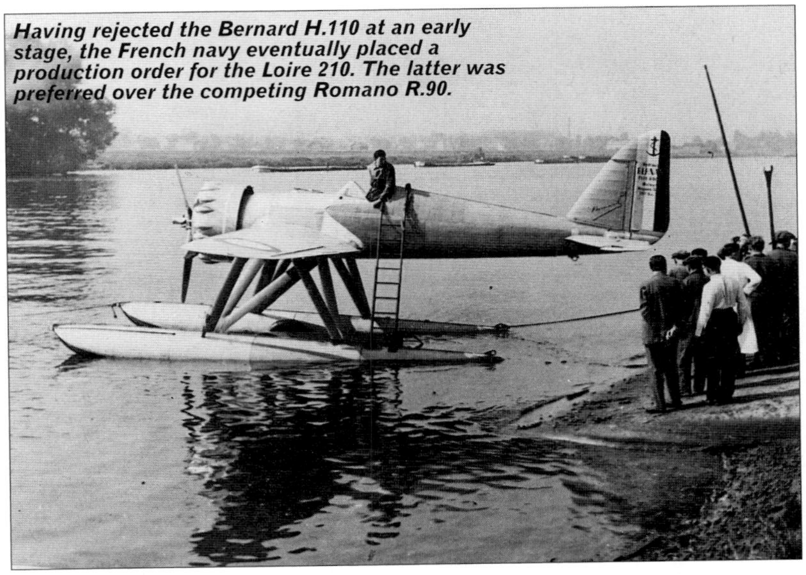

Having rejected the Bernard H.110 at an early stage, the French navy eventually placed a production order for the Loire 210. The latter was preferred over the competing Romano R.90.

Bernard V series

Designed for the 1924 Coupe Beaumont speed contest, the **Bernard V.1** (**Vitesse-1**, or speed no. 1) was completed in May 1924. Shortly after this, the aircraft was destroyed completely during take-off from Istres. Of wooden construction, the V.1 was a mid-wing cantilever monoplane with conventional fixed landing gear and its wing, set well forward on the fuselage, was of thin section and narrow chord.

Built originally alongside the V.1, the **V.2** was better known as the **Bernard-Ferbois** (the latter meaning iron and wood), and was modified continually in attempts to capture the world speed record for France. A second model, the **V.2.02**, was displayed at the 9th Paris Salon in 1924 but was never flown. The **V.2.01** differed from its sister ship in having an unusual bi-convex wing. The machine was used to establish a French speed record on 8 November 1924 and then, on 11 December 1924, Adjutant Florentin Bonnet made six high-speed runs with a much modified and more powerful machine. The result was a triumphant average speed of 278.48 mph (448.171 km/h), Adjutant Bonnet thus beating the existing landplane speed record by 11.8 mph (19 km/h). This record remained unbroken for several years afterwards.

A version of the V.2 with retractable landing gear was projected as the **SIMB V.3**, but was never built.

Adapted from the

In modified form, the V.2.01 had a reduced wing area, reshaped engine cowling and redesigned oil radiator. The power of the Hispano-Suiza 12Gb engine was boosted to 600 hp (447 kW).

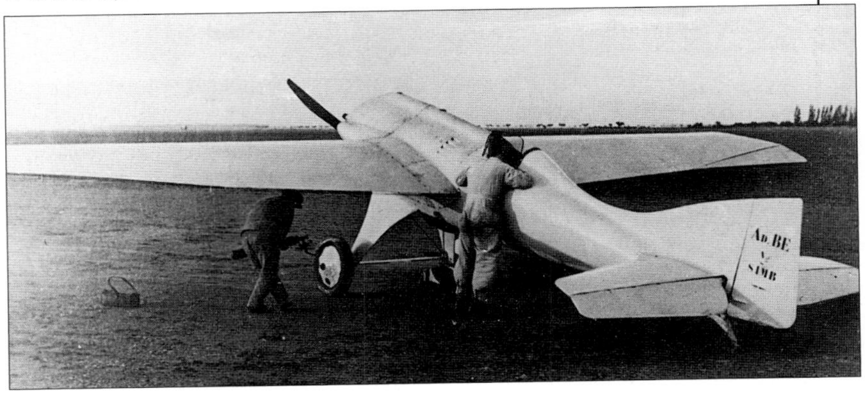

SPECIFICATION

Bernard V.2 (11 December 1924)
Type: single-seat racing aircraft
Powerplant: one Hispano-Suiza 12Gb Vee engine rated at 600 hp (447 kW)
Performance: maximum speed 291 mph (468 km/h) at optimum altitude
Weights: empty 2,127 lb (965 kg); maximum take-off 2,621 lb (1189 kg)
Dimensions: wingspan 29 ft 10¼ in (9.10 m); length 22 ft 3¾ in (6.80 m); height 7 ft 7¼ in (2.32 m); wing area 116.25 sq ft (10.80 m²)

HV.120 (Bernard's intended contender for the 1928 Schneider Trophy contest), the **V.4** appeared at the end of 1933. By then it featured widely spaced main landing gear legs, which were carefully faired, and streamlined wheel spats. The V.4 was transported to Istres late in December of the same year, and every effort was made to prepare it for flight by the end of the year. The date was critical, for the French air ministry had offered a prize of 500,000 francs for any French aircraft able to beat the landplane speed record of 304.52 mph (490.08 km/h).

Work proved very difficult, but it was hoped to make a first flight on 27 December 1933. Unfortunately, the prevailing mistral wind began to blow and the attempt on the record had to be postponed. In February 1934 further abortive efforts were made to prepare the V.4 for flight, but difficulties with the engine, coupled with the air ministry's failure to offer any financial assistance, led to the abandonment of the V.4 before it had flown.

BFW CL.I, CL.II and CL.III

The Bayerische Flugzeug-Werke AG came into existence during February 1916 as an organisation created by Albatros-Werke GmbH and incorporating the previous Otto-Werke GmbH. In 1917 the new company received an order for its **BFW CL.I** two-seat fighter, which was being designed as the **Type 17** to offer the same level of performance as the Halberstadt CL.II (for which BFW was negotiating licenced manufacture), but which would require 20 per cent fewer man hours to manufacture.

With a typical wire-braced wooden structure covered with plywood and fabric, the CL.I prototype made its first flight in April 1918 and was submitted for its official trials in June of the same year. The official report on the type then compared it unfavourably with the Hannover CL.V, and as a result BFW undertook to upgrade its prototype as the **CL.Ia**. This mainly involved the replacement of the original fuselage with a unit of lighter structure. Trials again proved disappointing, and BFW revised the machine to **CL.III** standard.

The second prototype of the CL.I was completed with a 175-hp (131-kW) MAN Mana.III inline engine and emerged as the Type 18 that was evaluated as the **CL.II** from May 1918.

Dimensionally identical to the CL.I, the CL.II was able to climb to 13,125 ft (4000 m) in just 5 minutes.

SPECIFICATION	
BFW CL.Ia	
Type: two-seat reconnaissance and escort fighter	**Dimensions:** wingspan 34 ft 10⅛ in (10.62 m); length 25 ft 7½ in (7.81 m)
Powerplant: one Mercedes D.III inline engine rated at 160 hp (119 kW)	**Armament:** one 0.312-in (7.92-mm) LMG 08/15 fixed forward-firing machine-gun in the nose, and one 0.312-in (7.92-mm) LMG 14 Parabellum trainable rearward-firing machine-gun in the rear cockpit
Performance: climb to 13,125 ft (4000 m) in 6 minutes 30 seconds	
Weights: empty 1,587 lb (720 kg); maximum take-off 2,337 lb (1060 kg)	

Blackburn early monoplanes

Robert Blackburn chose the monoplane configuration for his early designs. None of them was allocated a designation, but brief descriptions are given in chronological order.

The **Blackburn First Monoplane** was completed in April 1909 with a 35-hp (26-kW) Green inline engine, but would not fly, while the **Second Monoplane** (described as the **Light Type Monoplane**) used the new and untried 40-hp (30-kW) Isaacson radial engine. It flew from the sands at Filey in Yorkshire on 8 March 1911. Surviving damage on that occasion, it subsequently went on to achieve a number of flights, and marked the acceptance of Blackburn as a leading British designer.

The need to train pilots led Blackburn to develop a larger, two-seat monoplane which he christened **Mercury**. Isaacson provided a more powerful engine of 50 hp (37 kW) and the new machine, sometimes known as the **Mercury I**, joined the Second Monoplane at the Blackburn Flying School. Interest had been aroused in the Mercury by this time, and orders were received for eight such aircraft. The first two, known under the designation **Mercury II**, were single-seaters, each with a Gnome rotary engine rated at 50 hp (37 kW) and built for the *Daily Mail* Circuit of Britain contest which offered £10,000 in prize money. The first machine was lost in a take-off crash, while the second had an adventurous career, being converted into a two-seater and later being revised as a school machine with wings of greater span and the designation **Type B**. Of the remaining six Mercurys, the first (**Mercury Passenger Type** or **Mercury III**) had a 60-hp (45-kW) Renault engine, the second (Mercury III) a 50-hp (37-kW) Isaacson engine and of the other four Mercury III machines, three and one respectively had Gnome and Anzani engines of similar power.

Following the success of his early batch of wooden monoplanes, Blackburn turned his attention to steel construction when it became obvious that there was a military requirement for aircraft. In November 1911 the War Office issued a specification for a two-seat reconnaissance type, and one of the requirements for this was an ability to be dismantled for transportation in a crate between operating areas.

With only nine months before competitive trials were scheduled on Salisbury Plain, Blackburn built two monoplanes with the designation **Type E**. The first to be completed, in April 1912, was a single-seater powered by a 60-hp (45-kW) Green inline engine and built for a Lieutenant W. Lawrence for use in India, an idea which did not reach fruition. The Type E two-seater for the War Office trials was completed in June 1912, and powered by a 70-hp (52-kW) Renault Vee engine. Unfortunately, this second Type E proved too heavy for flight.

Blackburn's next design, known merely as the **Single-Seat Monoplane**, is the best known of his early aircraft, for although only one example was built, the aircraft survives in flying condition with the Shuttleworth Trust at Old Warden. Flown in 1912, it was powered by a 50-hp (37-kW) Gnome rotary engine and accumulated a considerable number of flying hours before it was almost destroyed in a crash in 1914. Restoration was undertaken at Old Warden, and the aircraft flew again in September 1949. It has the distinction of being the oldest airworthy British aircraft.

Developing the design, Blackburn built a two-seat version designated **Type I**, the first of these flying in August 1913. Powered by an 80-hp (60-kW) Gnome rotary engine, the Type I carried out a considerable amount of flying. Another Type I followed, a single-seater with the same engine, and in turn an **Improved Type I** appeared. It, too, saw much use, and was rebuilt eventually as a floatplane trainer with an Anzani radial engine for the Northern Aircraft Co. at Lake Windermere. Many pilots of the RNAS received their basic training on this **Land/Sea Monoplane** before it was written off on 1 April 1916.

Bearing a basic similarity to the Type I was the **White Falcon**, a single two-seat monoplane with a 100-hp (75-kW) Anzani engine. This machine was built for Blackburn's test pilot, W. Rowland Ding, during 1915, but its subsequent history is unknown.

Having given exemplary service, the Land/Sea monoplane was destroyed when it capsized at Bowness.

SPECIFICATION	
Blackburn Single-Seat Monoplane	
Type: single-seat touring aircraft	endurance 3 hours
Powerplant: one Gnome rotary engine rated at 50 hp (37 kW)	**Weights:** empty 550 lb (249 kg); maximum take-off 980 lb (445 kg)
Performance: maximum speed 60 mph (97 km/h) at sea level;	**Dimensions:** wingspan 32 ft 1 in (9.78 m); length 26 ft 3 in (8.00 m); height 8 ft 9 in (2.67 m); wing area 236.00 sq ft (21.92 m²)

Blackburn B-1 Segrave

Designed by the racing driver Sir Henry Segrave, who had been a fighter pilot in World War I, the **Blackburn B-1 Segrave** four-seat tourer was an advanced twin-engined low-wing cantilever monoplane. A wooden prototype, with the official designation **Saro Segrave Meteor I**, was built by Saunders-Roe and first flew in May 1930.

A demonstration in Rome before the Italian air minister resulted in an agreement for licensed production as the **Piaggio P.12**, but it seems probable that only two such aircraft were built. Space problems at Saunders-Roe's Cowes works, and the decision to build a metal version, resulted in the construction by Blackburn of two aircraft

designated **Blackburn C.A.18 Segrave I**, although these had Saro-built wooden wings. By the time these aircraft were completed, Blackburn had adopted a new type numbering system and the

Segrave became the **B-1**. No production orders were forthcoming and only a single further example, the **C.A.20 Segrave II**, was completed by Blackburn for tests concerning its wing structure.

G-AAXP was the Saro Segrave Meteor I prototype. Later, the B-1 undertook several tours throughout Europe, without arousing any serious sales interest in the aircraft.

SPECIFICATION

Blackburn B-1 Segrave I
Type: four-seat touring aircraft
Powerplant: two de Havilland Gipsy III inverted inline engines each rated at 120 hp (90 kW)
Performance: maximum speed 138 mph (222 km/h) at optimum altitude; cruising speed 112 mph (180 km/h) at optimum altitude; initial climb rate 800 ft (244 m) per minute; service ceiling 14,000 ft (4265 m); range 450 miles (724 km)
Weights: empty 2,246 lb (1019 kg); maximum take-off 3,300 lb (1497 kg)
Dimensions: wingspan 39 ft 6 in (12.04 m); length 28 ft 6 in (8.69 m); height 7 ft 9 in (2.36 m); wing area 230.00 sq ft (21.37 m²)

Blackburn B-2

The success of its Bluebird series of biplanes led Blackburn to develop a new type, the **Blackburn B-2**, with the same basic layout but with a semi-monocoque fuselage of all-metal construction and a single-bay biplane wing of steel and Dural construction with fabric covering. The prototype B-2, with a 120-hp (90-kW) de Havilland Gipsy III engine, flew at Brough on 10 December 1931. It subsequently took part, with the first production B-2, in the King's Cup Air Race during the following month.

A demonstration tour in Portugal, in which the B-2, de Havilland Tiger Moth, and two foreign aircraft competed for a government order, was won by the Tiger Moth as, apparently, the B-2's side-by-side seating

was not favoured. Orders in the UK were also hard to achieve, in spite of numerous demonstrations. Blackburn, however, continued to build airframes and to try different engine installations in the hope that the situation would improve.

A number of civil B-2s was built for Blackburn's flying schools at Hanworth in Middlesex and at Brough in Yorkshire and a total of 42 B-2s was built as trainers. All were for civil use except for the last three, which were bought by the Air Ministry in 1937 and issued to the Elementary and Reserve Flying Training School at Brough. On the outbreak of World War II, the B-2s of the Blackburn school at Hanworth were merged with those at Brough. In

1942, the aircraft were taken on charge by the RAF, which presented 24 of the surviving B-2s to the Air Training Corps as instructional airframes; two were retained by Blackburn. All 26 B-2s survived the war, but the eighth production example crashed in 1951.

Wearing standard wartime training colours, G-ACBJ was in service with the Blackburn flying schools. The aircraft became an ATC instructional airframe in February 1942.

SPECIFICATION

Blackburn B-2
Type: two-seat primary flying trainer
Powerplant: one de Havilland Gipsy Major 1 inverted inline engine rated at 130 hp (97 kW)
Performance: maximum speed 112 mph (180 km/h) at optimum altitude; cruising speed 95 mph (153 km/h) at optimum altitude; initial climb rate 600 ft (183 m) per minute; range 320 miles (515 km)
Weights: empty 1,175 lb (533 kg); maximum take-off 1,850 lb (839 kg)
Dimensions: wingspan 30 ft 2 in (9.19 m); length 24 ft 3 in (7.39 m); height 9 ft (2.74 m); wing area 246.00 sq ft (22.85 m²)

G-AEBJ, the only airworthy B-2 in the UK in the late 1990s, puts on a spirited low-level display. The type's unusual side-by-side seating is obvious in this view, with the pilot sitting to the left. The aircraft's all-metal construction is also evident.

Blackburn B-2

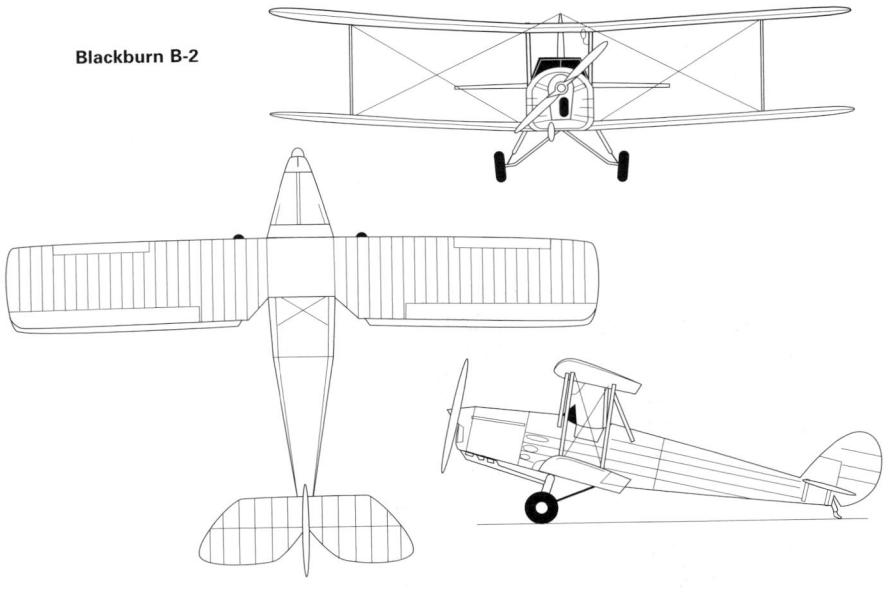

Blackburn B-5 Baffin

With the weight and power/weight ratio of radial engines going down and up respectively, Blackburn decided to follow the lead of the Finns, who used a variety of radial engines in their licence-built Ripons. One FAA Ripon was fitted with a 650-hp (485-kW) Armstrong Siddeley Tiger I engine, while a second received a 545-hp (406-kW) Bristol Pegasus IMS engine. The designation **T.5J Ripon Mk V** was applied to both machines,

which were otherwise known as the **B-4** and **B-5**, respectively.

Following competitive trials, the latter version was selected as a new first-line warplane, powered by a Pegasus IM3 engine, and two pre-production aircraft were ordered. Earlier Ripon Mk IIs were converted on the production line to the new standard and the name **Baffin** was approved. Three FAA units received the Baffin and more than 60 Ripons were subse-

quently re-engined to Baffin standard. Since the 'new' type's performance proved little better than that of its predecessor, however, the Baffin had a short front-line life, the last FAA aircraft finally being declared obsolete in 1937.

The Royal New Zealand Air Force then bought 12 Baffin aircraft. These were followed by a further 17, allowing the equipment of three squadrons, and these Baffins were the only examples of the type to serve in World War II. Most of them had been withdrawn by 1941.

K3589 was one of two pre-production Baffins. It was delivered for test work in 1933 and retained until sold for scrap in 1937.

Originally delivered to No. 810 Sqn FAA, in whose colours it is illustrated, S1573 was converted from a Ripon IIA and was later sold to New Zealand.

SPECIFICATION

Blackburn Baffin
Type: two-seat carrierborne and land-based torpedo bomber
Powerplant: one Bristol Pegasus IM3 radial engine rated at 565 hp (421 kW)
Performance: maximum speed 136 mph (219 km/h) at 6,500 ft (1981 m); initial climb rate 480 ft (146 m) per minute; service ceiling 15,000 ft (4570 m); range 450 miles (869 km)
Weights: empty 3,184 lb (1444 kg); maximum take-off 7,610 lb (3452 kg)

Dimensions: wingspan 45 ft 6½ in (13.88 m); length 38 ft 3¾ in (11.68 m); height 12 ft 10 in (3.91 m); wing area 683.00 sq ft (63.45 m²)
Armament: one 0.303-in (7.7-mm) Vickers fixed forward-firing machine-gun in the forward fuselage and one 0.303-in (7.7-mm) Lewis trainable rearward-firing machine-gun in the rear cockpit, plus one torpedo or up to 2,000 lb (907 kg) of bombs carried externally

Blackburn B-6 Shark

Begun as a private venture to meet Specification S.15/33, the **B-6** was based on the company's **B-3** torpedo-bomber prototype (designed to meet Specification M.1/30), which had first flown on 24 February 1933. The B-6 prototype made its maiden flight on 24 August 1933 and in November of the same year was flown to the A&AEE. Deck landing trials aboard HMS *Courageous* followed early in the following year and in August 1934 a contract for 16 aircraft was placed for the FAA.

The prototype was fitted with twin floats and undertook successful sea trials. Further contracts followed,

Apart from its narrow-chord cowling, the Shark prototype (illustrated) was similar to the production Mk I. Note the 1,500-lb (680-kg) torpedo.

and Blackburn eventually delivered 238 aircraft to the FAA in both seaplane and landplane configurations.

Like the prototype, the **Shark Mk I** was powered by one 710-hp (522-kW) Armstrong Siddeley Tiger IV radial engine. The Tiger VI engine was used in the **Shark Mk II**, production of which began in 1936, and the next production variant, the **Shark Mk III**, used an 800-hp (597-kW) Bristol

Pegasus III. Some 95 Shark Mk IIIs were delivered.

As the Shark was replaced by the Fairey Swordfish, the surviving

aircraft were relegated to second-line duties and a number were converted for target-towing.

Six **Shark Mk IIA** floatplanes were purchased by the Portuguese navy and delivered in March 1936. The only other customer was Canada which, in 1936, bought seven Shark Mk IIs for the RCAF. Such was the success of these

machines that Boeing Aircraft of Canada, a subsidiary of the US company, secured an agreement for licensed production at Vancouver, where 17 Shark Mk IIIs were built with 840-hp (626-kW) Pegasus IX engines. The Canadian-built Sharks served until 1944, when the last such aircraft were withdrawn.

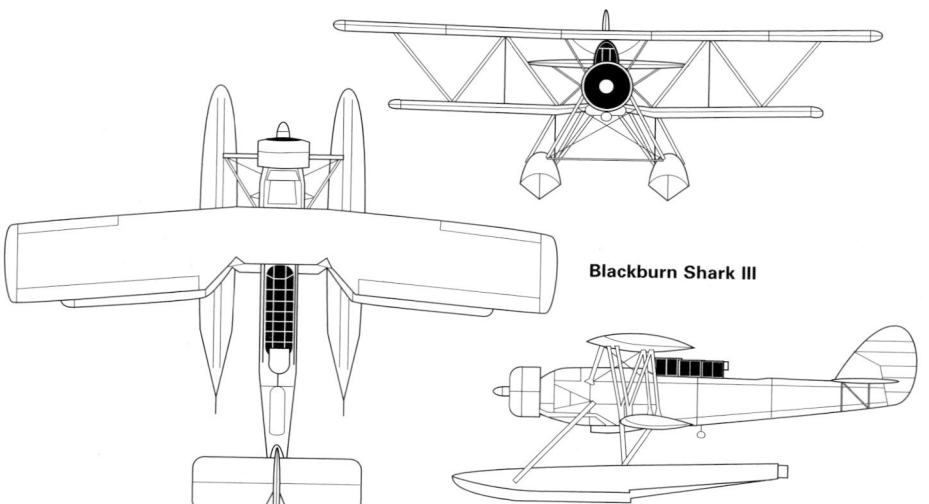

Blackburn Shark III

SPECIFICATION

Blackburn Shark Mk II (torpedo landplane)
Type: two/three-seat carrierborne, land-based and shore-based torpedo and reconnaissance bomber
Powerplant: one Armstrong Siddeley Tiger VI radial engine rated at 760 hp (567 kW)
Performance: maximum speed 150 mph (241 km/h) at sea level; cruising speed 118 mph (190 km/h) at optimum altitude; initial climb rate 895 ft (273 m) per minute; service ceiling 16,000 ft (4875 m); range 625 miles (1006 km)
Weights: empty 4,039 lb

(1832 kg); maximum take-off 8,050 lb (3651 kg)
Dimensions: wingspan 46 ft (14.02 m); length 35 ft 3 in (10.74 m); height 12 ft 1 in (3.68 m); wing area 489.00 sq ft (45.43 m²)
Armament: one 0.303-in (7.7-mm) Vickers fixed forward-firing machine-gun in the forward fuselage and one 0.303-in (7.7-mm) Lewis or Vickers gas-operated trainable rearward-firing machine-gun in the rear cockpit, plus one 1,500-lb (680-kg) torpedo or 2,000 lb (907 kg) of bombs carried externally

Blackburn B-9

In 1933 Blackburn projected a **Segrave III** eight-passenger transport for the Australian and Canadian markets. This came to nothing, but led to the **C.A.19/1** or **HST.8 (High Speed Transport No. 8)** project and then to the **C.A.21** project for a 10-passenger transport that could also be configured for the aerial survey role. The C.A.21 again failed to secure any orders, but led to the design of the larger **C.A.21A (HST.10)** with improvements such as retractable main landing gear units, hydraulically-operated trailing-edge flaps and two Napier Rapier H-type engines. Blackburn then unsuccessfully developed a military version of the C.A.21A as the **C.A.21B**.

By this time Blackburn had decided to manufacture a prototype as a private venture, and construction of this machine, later accorded the designation **Blackburn B-9**,

began in August 1934. The aircraft employed the tubular spar designed by F. Duncanson; this was a three-section Dural unit whose central part was sealed to serve as the main fuel tank and which carried at its ends the tubular steel mountings for the two Rapier engines. The B-9 was of all-metal construction covered with light alloy, except for the fin and control surfaces which were fabric covered. In configuration the B-9 was a low-wing cantilever monoplane with retractable main landing gear units and a curvaceous semi-monocoque fuselage incorporating a cockpit separate from the cabin.

Completion of the B-9 was delayed by slow delivery of materials and the increasing pressure placed on Blackburn for production of military aircraft. The prototype was completed in the middle of 1936, but was then abandoned. Early

in 1939 it entered use as an instructional airframe, in which role it served up to 1946, when it was scrapped.

Projected military variants of the B-9 included the **HSBT.10** coastal reconnaissance bomber and transport, the **HST.20** long-range bomber and the **HSNT.10** general-purpose aircraft.

Two air-cooled Napier Rapier H-type engines driving two-bladed wooden propellers powered the HST.10. The aircraft is shown wearing its Class B civil marking during 1936.

SPECIFICATION

Blackburn B-9
Type: two-crew light transport
Powerplant: two Napier Rapier VI H-type engines each rated at 365 hp (272 kW)
Performance: (estimated) maximum speed 204 mph (328 km/h) at 5,500 ft (1675 m); cruising speed 175 mph (282 km/h) at optimum altitude; initial climb rate 1,000 ft (305 m) per minute;

service ceiling 23,800 ft (7255 m); range 1,000 miles (1609 km)
Weights: empty 5,490 lb (2490 kg); maximum take-off 8,850 lb (4014 kg)
Dimensions: wingspan 57 ft 4 in (17.48 m); length 42 ft (12.80 m); height 12 ft (3.66 m); wing area 442.00 sq ft (41.06 m²)
Payload: up to 12 passengers

Blackburn B-20

When the Air Ministry issued Specification R.1/36 for a reconnaissance flying-boat for service with the RAF, Blackburn and Saunders-Roe both competed for the contract. The latter won with the

Lerwick, which was ultimately a disappointment once in service.

The other submission was the **Blackburn B-20**, an extremely original design which featured a retractable planing bottom

Seen here on its beaching gear, the Blackburn B-20 demonstrates its retractable hull (in the lowered position) and wingtip floats.

SPECIFICATION

Blackburn B-20
Type: eight/nine-seat coastal reconnaissance flying-boat
Powerplant: two Rolls-Royce Vulture X X-type engines each rated at 1,830 hp (1364 kW)
Performance: (estimated) maximum speed 306 mph (492 km/h) at 15,000 ft (4570 m); cruising speed 200 mph (322 km/h) at optimum altitude; range 1,500 miles (2414 km)
Weights: normal take-off 35,000 lb (15876 kg)
Dimensions: wingspan 82 ft 2 in (25.04 m); length 69 ft 7½ in (21.22 m); height 25 ft 2 in (7.67 m)

with planing bottom lowered and 11 ft 8 in (3.56 m) with planing bottom raised; wing area 1,066.00 sq ft (99.03 m²)
Armament: (proposed) two 0.303-in (7.7-mm) Browning trainable forward-firing machine-guns in the bow turret, two 0.303-in (7.7-mm) Browning trainable machine-guns in the dorsal turret and four 0.303-in (7.7 mm) Browning trainable rearward-firing machine-guns in the tail turret, plus up to 2,000 lb (907 kg) of bombs carried internally in the wing

to the hull. This gave a favourable wing incidence at take-off, and also kept the propellers clear of the water. Retracting the lower hull section in the air much reduced drag by comparison with that of a conventional hull and the aerodynamic cleanliness was further enhanced by the provision of underwing stabilising floats which retracted to form the wingtips. A prototype was ordered by the Air Ministry to test the practicality of the design, and two of the new Rolls-Royce Vulture X engines were provided to power it. In retrospect this was a poor choice since

the Vulture was later to prove a failure.

The B-20 was flown in late March or early April 1940, and the retractable hull worked well. A problem was experienced with aileron control and, unfortunately, the machine was lost on 7 April 1940, when it crashed into the sea

during high-speed trials, only one of the crew escaping.

With the retractable hull concept largely proven, Blackburn planned to use it on a floatplane fighter, the **B-44**, but development was overtaken by the pressing need to build Short Sunderland flying-boats.

Blackburn B-24 Skua

The **Blackburn B-24 Skua** monoplane fighter and dive-bomber of all-metal construction marked a radical departure from the RN's tradition of fabric-covered biplanes as it was the UK's first naval dive-bomber and the country's first deck-landing aircraft with trailing-edge flaps, retractable landing gear and a variable-pitch propeller.

The Skua competed with designs from Avro, Boulton Paul, Hawker and Vickers for the naval contract. Two prototypes were ordered in April 1935, and the first of

these made its maiden flight on 9 February 1937 with the powerplant of one 840-hp (626-kW) Bristol Mercury IX radial engine.

Orders for 190 Skuas had been placed six months before the prototype's maiden flight, and some subcontract work

was awarded to speed up production. Because all Mercury engines were required for the Bristol Blenheim light bomber, the

Skuas of No. 800 Sqn (illustrated) were involved in the successful attack on the Königsberg.

production version of the B-24 had the Bristol Perseus XII radial engine for service as the **Skua Mk II**. The first production aircraft flew on 28 August 1938, and few modifications to the basic design were required apart from fitting upturned wingtips and a modified tailwheel oleo to cure juddering. The entire production run of 190 aircraft was delivered between October 1938 and March 1940.

The first FAA units to receive the Skua in 1938 were Nos 800 and 803

Squadrons for service on HMS *Ark Royal*, replacing the Hawker Nimrod and Osprey. No. 801 Squadron aboard HMS *Furious* was then re-equipped, and the Skua also joined No. 806 Squadron before the outbreak of World War II.

As a fighter the Skua was already obsolete, but the type made its mark in the dive-bombing role early in the war when 16 aircraft from Nos 800 and 803 Squadrons sank the German cruiser *Königsberg* off Bergen at dawn on 10 April 1940.

Illustrated is a pair of No. 803 Sqn Skuas. The Skua was withdrawn from operational service in 1941, having proved moderately successful, although a number remained flying as target-tugs and on general training duties.

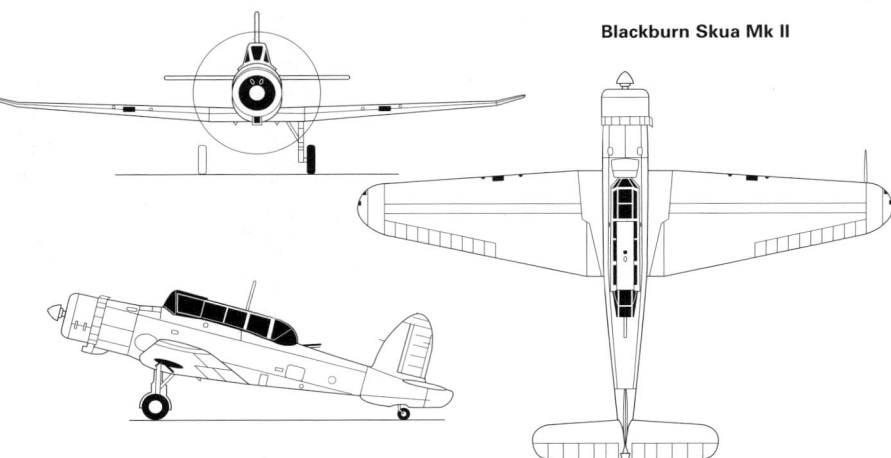

Blackburn Skua Mk II

SPECIFICATION

Blackburn Skua Mk II
Type: two-seat carrierborne and land-based fighter and dive-bomber
Powerplant: one Bristol Perseus XII radial engine rated at 890 hp (664 kW)
Performance: maximum speed 225 mph (362 km/h) at 6,500 ft (1980 m); cruising speed 165 mph (266 km/h) at 15,000 ft (4570 m); initial climb rate 1,580 ft (482 m) per minute; service ceiling 20,200 ft (6160 m); range 760 miles (1223 km)
Weights: empty 5,490 lb (2490 kg); maximum take-off 8,228 lb (3732 kg)

Dimensions: wingspan 46 ft 2 in (14.07 m); length 35 ft 7 in (10.85 m); height 12 ft 6 in (3.81 m); wing area 312.00 sq ft (28.98 m²)
Armament: four 0.303-in (7.7-mm) Browning fixed forward-firing machine-guns in the leading edge of the wing and one 0.303-in (7.7-mm) Lewis trainable rearward-firing machine-gun in the rear cockpit, plus one 500-lb (227-kg) bomb beneath the fuselage and eight 30-lb (14-kg) practice bombs on underwing racks

Blackburn B-25 Roc

Developed from the Skua dive-bomber, the **Blackburn B-25 Roc** was the first FAA aircraft to have a power-operated gun turret. The idea was that the turret's four guns would be used in broadside attacks on enemy bombers but the Roc, with its poor speed, is unlikely to have caught an enemy bomber.

Orders for 136 Roc fighters were received in April 1937 and, because of Blackburn's involvement with the Skua programme, production was undertaken by Boulton Paul, which was also the manufacturer of the type's electrically-powered turret. The first Roc made its maiden flight on 23 December 1938. Trials revealed that the heavy turret penalised the Roc by comparison with the Skua, but the former could still be held steady in

a steep dive with the use of dive-brakes. An enlarged propeller was fitted, and various other means of improving performance were tried without much success.

Four Rocs were flown as seaplanes with Blackburn Shark floats, and the weight and drag of these units reduced the aircraft's speed by another 30 mph (48 km/h); stability was also rather poor, and low-altitude turns had to be avoided. One Roc float-plane was tested as a target-tug, with a wind-driven winch in place of the turret, and subsequently a number of Roc landplanes was used as target-tugs.

After familiarisation with several Fleet Air Arm units, the first four Rocs to enter full service were delivered to No. 806 Squadron in February 1940, serving

alongside eight Skuas. Four months later six Rocs joined No. 801 Squadron, while No. 2 Anti-Aircraft Co-operation Unit received 16 Rocs in June 1940. The most unusual role for the Roc fell to four which were damaged in a Ju 87 raid on Gosport, and were used subsequently as machine-gun posts, with their turrets permanently manned.

Other Rocs were dispersed to various locations in the UK and even to Bermuda, and the type gradually faded away until the last two were withdrawn in August 1943 for lack of spares.

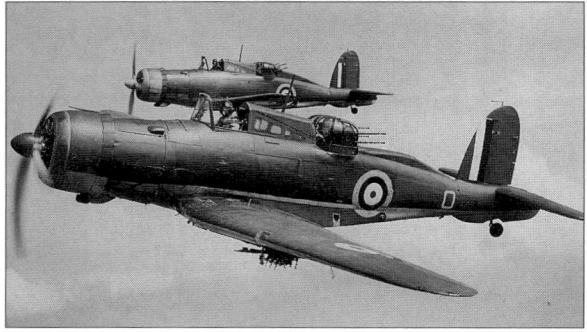

These production Rocs show the standard four-gun Boulton Paul turret. With the turret removed, a winch could be installed, capable of streaming a target with 6,000 ft (1830 m) of cable at an altitude of 10,000 ft (3050 m).

SPECIFICATION

B-25 Blackburn Roc
Type: two-seat carrierborne and land-based fighter and target-tug
Powerplant: one Bristol Perseus XII radial engine rated at 905 hp (675 kW)
Performance: maximum speed 223 mph (359 km/h) at 10,000 ft (3050 m); cruising speed 135 mph (217 km/h) at optimum altitude; initial climb rate 1,500 ft (457 m) per minute; service ceiling 18,000 ft (5485 m); range 810 miles

(1304 km)
Weights: empty 6,124 lb (2778 kg); maximum take-off 7,950 lb (3606 kg)
Dimensions: wingspan 46 ft (14.02 m); length 35 ft 7 in (10.85 m); height 12 ft 1 in (3.68 m); wing area 310.00 sq ft (28.80 m²)
Armament: four 0.303-in (7.7-mm) Browning trainable machine-guns in the dorsal turret

Blackburn Roc

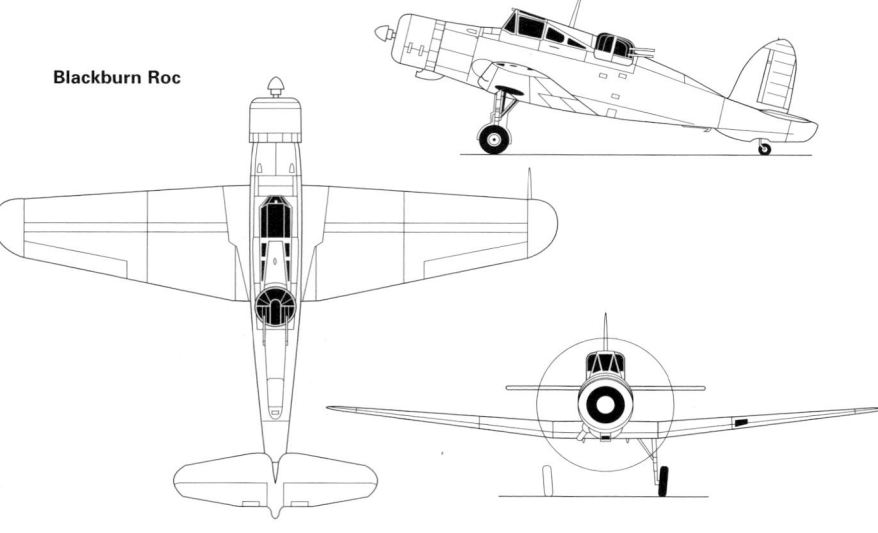

Blackburn B-26 Botha

When the Air Ministry issued Specification M.15/35 for a twin-engined reconnaissance bomber with three-seat accommodation and the ability to carry a torpedo, it attracted submissions from Blackburn and Bristol, each envisaging the use of a powerplant of two Bristol Perseus radial engines. A change in the requirement then increased the crew to four, leading to the new Specification 10/36, and both types were ordered as the **Blackburn B-26 Botha** and Bristol Beaufort.

Bristol employed the Taurus in its Beaufort, but this engine was in short supply and Blackburn was accordingly committed to using 880-hp (656-kW) Perseus X engines in the initial production version of the Botha.

Orders for 442 Bothas were placed in 1936, and the first production aircraft flew on 28 December 1938. Trials resulted in changes to the empennage to provide better longitudinal control. The first **Botha Mk I** delivered to the RAF was received on 12 December 1939.

A number of unexplained fatal accidents occurred in the first half of 1940 and the Botha was criticised for its shortcomings and the fact that it was underpowered. Consequently, Perseus Mk XA engines and some other improvements were incorporated.

The fact that the Botha was underpowered led to its relegation to training units, where it continued to suffer fatal accidents. A few Bothas were fitted with winch gear and used by the target towing unit at Abbotsinch as **Botha TT.Mk I** aircraft. Production was terminated after the delivery of 580 aircraft.

Although produced in some numbers, the Botha was a failure and was withdrawn from service in late 1944.

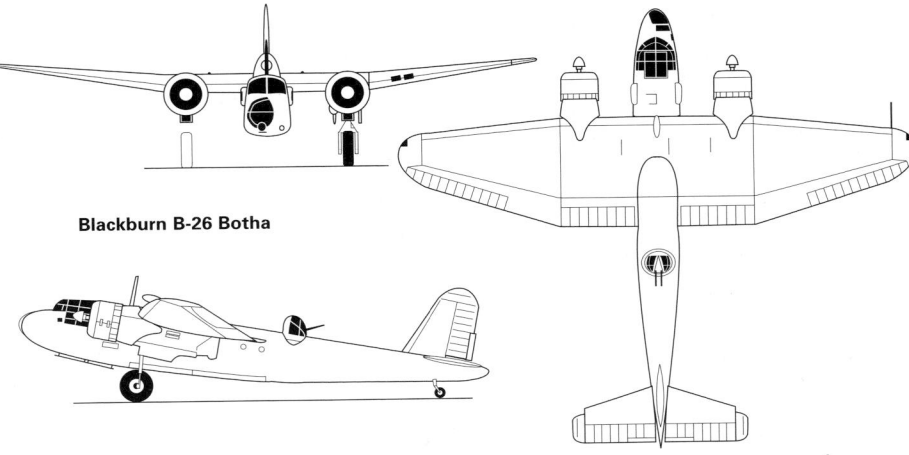

Blackburn B-26 Botha

SPECIFICATION

Blackburn Botha Mk I
Type: four-seat reconnaissance and torpedo bomber, and trainer
Powerplant: two Bristol Perseus XA radial piston engines each rated at 930 hp (694 kW)
Performance: maximum speed 249 mph (401 km/h) at 5,500 ft (1675 m); cruising speed 212 mph (341 km/h) at 15,000 ft (4570 m); initial climb rate 985 ft (300 m) per minute; service ceiling 17,500 ft (5335 m); range 1,270 miles (2044 km)
Weights: empty 11,830 lb (5366 kg); maximum take-off 18,450 lb (8369 kg)
Dimensions: wingspan 59 ft (17.98 m); length 51 ft ½ in (15.56 m); height 14 ft 7½ in (4.46 m); wing area 518.00 sq ft (48.12 m²)
Armament: one 0.303-in (7.7-mm) Vickers fixed forward-firing machine-gun in the forward fuselage and two 0.303-in (7.7-mm) Lewis trainable machine-guns in the dorsal turret, plus one torpedo, or bombs or depth charges up to a total weight of 2,000 lb (907 kg) carried internally

Blackburn B-37 Firebrand

The origins of the **Blackburn B-37 Firebrand** lay in Specification N.9/39, issued in December 1939 and detailing a single-seat fleet fighter with an armament of four 20-mm cannon. In January 1941 three prototypes were ordered to Specification N.11/40, and the first of these made its first flight on 27 February 1942. The second prototype, armed with four 20-mm Hispano cannon and with racks for two 500-lb (227-kg) bombs, made its maiden flight in July and the third machine followed in September. All three were powered by the 2,305-hp (1719-kW) Napier Sabre III engine, as were nine initial-production **Firebrand F.Mk I** fighters.

The second prototype undertook deck landing trials aboard HMS *Illustrious* in February 1943 and, following an accident, it was rebuilt as the **Firebrand TF.Mk II** prototype with a widened wing centre-section to allow the carriage of a 1,850-lb (839-kg) torpedo between the wheel bays. The first flight took place on 31 March 1943, and there followed 12 production machines. No. 708 Sqn at Lee-on-Solent was the Firebrand TF.Mk II trials unit and was the only squadron to receive Firebrands during World War II.

With Sabre engine production allocated to the Hawker Typhoon, the 2,400-hp (1790-kW) Bristol Centaurus VII was fitted in the **Firebrand TF.Mk III**, which first flew in prototype form on 21 December 1943. There followed a second prototype and

This Firebrand TF.Mk IV wears a typical standard FAA Extra-Dark Sea Grey over Sky colour scheme. EK621 was finally scrapped at Milnathort in 1965.

Pictured carrying a dummy torpedo, EK121 was the first production Firebrand TF.Mk IV. No. 813 Squadron re-formed at Ford in September 1945 to bring the TF.Mk IV into service.

SPECIFICATION

Blackburn Firebrand TF.Mk 5
Type: single-seat carrierborne and land-based torpedo strike fighter
Powerplant: one Bristol Centaurus IX radial engine rated at 2,520 hp (1879 kW)
Performance: maximum speed 340 mph (547 km/h) at 13,000 ft (3960 m); cruising speed 256 mph (412 km/h) at optimum altitude; initial climb rate 2,500 ft (762 m) per minute; service ceiling 28,500 ft (8685 m); range 740 miles (1191 km)
Weights: empty 11,835 lb (5368 kg); maximum take-off 17,500 lb (7938 kg)
Dimensions: wingspan 51 ft 3½ in (15.63 m); length 38 ft 9 in (11.81 m); height 13 ft 3 in (4.04 m); wing area 383.00 sq ft (35.58 m²)
Armament: four 20-mm Hispano Mk V fixed forward-firing cannon in the leading edge of the wing, plus one 1,850-lb (839-kg) torpedo carried under the fuselage or 16 60-lb (27-kg) unguided air-to-surface rockets carried under the wing

some 27 production machines. These suffered some directional instability on take-off, the fault being remedied by the introduction of a fin and rudder of increased area on the **Firebrand TF.Mk IV**, which also had wing dive brakes and a two-position torpedo carrier. The first of 102 Firebrand TF.Mk IVs flew on 17 May 1945, and the type entered service with No. 813 Squadron on 1 September 1945.

The final production variants were the **Firebrand TF.Mk 5** and **Firebrand TF.Mk 5A**, the latter having powered ailerons in addition to the horn-balanced rudder and elevators and the longer-span aileron tabs common to all Mk 5 aircraft. Sixty-eight of these machines were manufactured and saw service with Nos 813 and 827 Squadrons, FAA.

Blackburn B-48

Work on the **Blackburn B-48**, which was designed as a potential successor to the Firebrand, began in October 1943 in response to Specification S.28/43. This called for an improved Firebrand 'with redesigned wing and improved pilot's view', and the new aircraft was known by the unofficial name **Firecrest**, although its formal designation was **Y.A.1**.

The B-48 was based structurally and aerodynamically on the Firebrand, but differed mainly in its powerplant of one Bristol Centaurus 59 engine driving a five-bladed propeller, the movement of the cockpit both forward and upward, the relocation of the majority of the fuselage fuel tankage to a location aft of the cockpit and the introduction of a new wing.

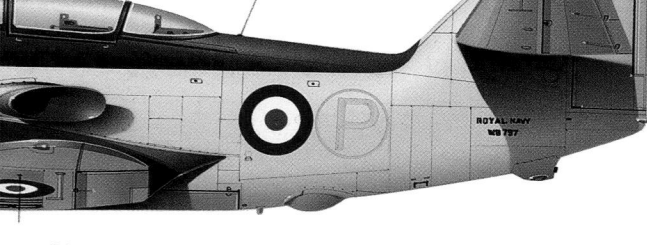

SPECIFICATION	
Blackburn B-48	(4769 kg); maximum take-off
Type: single-seat carrierborne and land-based torpedo strike fighter	15,280 lb (6931 kg)
Powerplant: one Bristol Centaurus 59 radial engine rated at 2,475 hp (1845 kW)	**Dimensions:** wingspan 44 ft 11½ in (13.70 m); length 39 ft 3½ in (11.98 m); height 14 ft 6 in (4.42 m); wing area 361.50 sq ft (33.58 m²)
Performance: maximum speed 380 mph (612 km/h) at 19,000 ft (5790 m); cruising speed 272 mph (438 km/h) at 10,000 ft (3050 m); initial climb rate 2,500 ft (762 m) per minute; service ceiling 31,600 ft (9630 m); range 900 miles (1448 km)	**Armament:** (planned) one 1,850-lb (839-kg) torpedo carried under the fuselage, or alternatively two 500-lb (227-kg) bombs, or 16 60-lb (27-kg) air-to-surface unguided rockets, or two 0.5-in (12.7-mm) machine-gun pods carried under the wing
Weights: empty 10,513 lb	

The anhedral of the wing's inner sections allowed the use of comparatively short and therefore lighter main landing gear legs, and the B-48 was given semi-STOL capability by the incorporation of four-section Fowler flaps with auxiliary flaps on the two outer sections.

Blackburn received an order for two prototypes, but in the event only the first was completed, and then only after the end of World War II. This machine made its maiden flight on

A wing of laminar-flow section and inverted-gull layout was designed for the B-48. It was planned to fold in two places to produce the smallest possible package for carrierborne stowage.

1 April 1947, and was followed by a specially ordered machine based closely on the B-48 prototype, but intended for research into the power-boosted ailerons then being introduced on the Firebrand TF.Mk 5A.

By this time the advent of the turbine engine had effectively killed development of the B-48. A turbo-prop-engined version with an Armstrong Siddeley Python, Bristol Proteus or Rolls-Royce Clyde turbo-prop engine was suggested but not built. The data recorded in the B-48 flight test programme proved very useful in the development of the B-54.

Blackburn B-54 and B-88

Specification GR.17/45 for a carrierborne anti-submarine aircraft attracted submissions from Blackburn, Fairey and Shorts. Blackburn's first offering was the **Blackburn B-54** (or **Y.A.7**), a two-seat gull-wing monoplane with acute dihedral on the tailplane and the powerplant of one 2,000-hp (1491-kW) Rolls-Royce Griffon 56 Vee engine driving a contra-rotating assembly of two three-bladed propellers. The original choice had been the aborted Napier Double Naiad turboprop, with the aircraft designated **Y.A.5**. The first B-54 prototype was flown initially, in Y.A.7 form, on 20 September 1949, deck landings taking place in the following February.

The second prototype was the **Y.A.8**, which was completed to a modified standard for the carriage of a three-man crew to meet a new naval requirement and, with changes to the wings and tail, first flew on 3 May 1950. Both the Y.A.7 and Y.A.8 were useful test aircraft, paving the way for the third prototype, the turboprop-powered **Y.B.1** which carried the Blackburn type number **B-88**. With an Armstrong Siddeley Double Mamba turboprop, again driving a contra-rotating propeller unit, this flew for the first time on 19 July 1950. The trials resulted in the production contract going to the Fairey entry, later named Gannet, and the Y.B.1 became a testbed with Armstrong Siddeley for the Double Mamba turboprop. The Y.A.7 and Y.A.8 served at RAE Farnborough for several years before being scrapped in the period 1956-57.

Blackburn's B-88 was a formidable naval aircraft, which lost out to the equally impressive Gannet.

SPECIFICATION	
Blackburn B-88	**Weights:** maximum take-off
Type: three-seat carrierborne anti-submarine aircraft	13,091 lb (5938 kg)
Powerplant: one Armstrong Siddeley Double Mamba turboprop engine rated at 2,950 ehp (2200 ekW)	**Dimensions:** wingspan 44 ft 2 in (13.46 m); length 42 ft 8 in (13.00 m); height 16 ft 9 in (5.11 m)
Performance: maximum speed 320 mph (515 km/h) at optimum altitude	**Armament:** (proposed) a wide variety of attack weapons carried internally, and air-to-surface unguided rockets or depth charges carried under the wing

Blackburn B-101 Beverley

The **Blackburn B-101 Beverley** transport originated with General Aircraft, which had made various studies for a large freight aircraft. When the Air Ministry's Specification C.3/46 called for a medium-range tactical transport, the **G.A.L.60 Universal Freighter** design was submitted. A contract was awarded for a single prototype and, to power it, a new version of the Bristol Hercules radial engine was developed. In configuration the G.A.L.60 was a simple unpressurised machine with fixed tricycle landing gear, and the prototype was built at the General Aircraft factory.

General Aircraft merged with Blackburn on 1 January 1949, forming Blackburn and General Aircraft Ltd, and the G.A.L.60 was taken to Brough, Yorkshire for its first flight on 20 June 1950.

Some changes were incorporated in a second prototype with Bristol Centaurus engines: new techniques in parachuting stores demanded a change in design of the rear doors; the tail boom was increased in size to provide passenger accommodation; and the large single mainwheels were replaced by four-wheel bogies. Designated **G.A.L.65** and **B-100**, the second machine flew in June 1953, by which time 20 had been ordered for the RAF's Transport Command as the **B-101**, subsequently named **Beverley C.Mk 1**.

Blackburn Beverley 101 (continued)

The first two production aircraft flew in January and March 1955 respectively and remained with Blackburn for tests and modifications, while the next two went to the A&AEE at Boscombe Down in Wiltshire for acceptance trials. Hot-weather trials in Tripoli were followed by cold-weather trials in Canada. The first squadron delivery was made to No. 47 Sqn on 12 March 1956 and the Beverley was, at the time, the largest aircraft to be delivered to the RAF.

In addition to the Beverley's main hold it featured a smaller forward hold. Tests with paradropped loads culminated in the drop of a 40,000-lb (18144-kg) load beneath eight parachutes. As a transport, the Beverley could carry 94 troops or 70 paratroops, of which 36 and 30 respectively were carried in the tail boom compartment.

In May 1954, an RAF order was placed for a further 27 Beverleys, and the type eventually served with five units. The RAF retired its last Beverleys at the end of 1967, when they were replaced by the Lockheed Hercules.

There were several projects for civil versions of the design, including a cross-Channel car ferry with two decks, but none of these materialised. The two prototypes and first two production aircraft were allocated civil markings but, apart from one recorded instance, they do not appear to have been used. The fourth machine used its civil identity late in 1955 when it carried heavy drilling equipment for the Iraq Petroleum Company.

XM103 was among the last batch of 27 Beverleys ordered. The aircraft was finished as illustrated prior to No. 84 Sqn's re-equipment with Andovers.

Wearing the scorpion badge of No. 84 Sqn, this Beverley C.Mk 1 was pictured after the unit retired its aircraft in 1967. The squadron served as a heavylift transport unit in the Middle East, hence the brown camouflage.

SPECIFICATION

Blackburn Beverley C.Mk 1
Type: four/six-crew medium-range transport
Powerplant: four Bristol Centaurus 273 radial engines each rated at 2,850 hp (2125 kW)
Performance: maximum speed 238 mph (383 km/h) at 5,700 ft (1735 m); cruising speed 173 mph (278 km/h) at 8,000 ft (2440 m); initial climb rate 760 ft (232 m) per minute; service ceiling 16,000 ft (4875 m); range 1,300 miles (2092 km)
Weights: empty 79,234 lb (35940 kg); maximum take-off 143,000 lb (64864 kg)
Dimensions: wingspan 162 ft (49.38 m); length 99 ft 5 in (30.30 m); height 38 ft 9 in (11.81 m); wing area 2,916.00 sq ft (270.90 m²)
Payload: maximum payload 55,770 lb (25297 kg)

Blackburn B-103 Buccaneer

In 1962 Blackburn was bought by the Hawker Siddeley Group, and in May 1963 became the Hawker Siddeley Aviation Ltd, Hawker Blackburn Division, a name which was changed to Hawker Siddeley Aviation Ltd, Brough, in April 1965. Then, in 1977, Hawker Siddeley merged with other British aerospace manufacturers to create British Aerospace, and thus the **Blackburn B-103 Buccaneer** was also known as a Hawker Siddeley and BAe product in the later parts of its career.

The B-103 proved by its long and distinguished service that it was a far better machine than many would have initially believed. Developed for the Royal Navy's **NA.39** requirement of the early 1950s, the B-103 was the world's first two-seat carrierborne low-level strike warplane to be built for the high-speed under-the-radar means of penetration of enemy airspace. In its basic design the airframe incorporated a number of advanced features including a full wing and tail boundary layer control system to give maximum lift, area-ruling of the bulky fuselage, a tailcone split vertically and hinged so that the two halves could be deployed as airbrakes, and a rotary bomb door carrying on its inner surface conventional or nuclear weapons. The door was rotated to expose the weapons for delivery, avoiding the drag penalty of conventional bomb doors that open into a high-speed airstream.

The B-103 design was chosen in 1955 to meet the NA.39 requirement, an order being placed in July of that year for an evaluation batch of 20 aircraft. Powerplant of the pre-production models, of which the first made its maiden flight on 30 April 1958, comprised two de Havilland Gyron Junior DGJ.1 turbojet engines each rated at 7,000 lb st (31.14 kN). The full naval 'kit' of folding wings and nose, arrester hook and catapult points was introduced on the fourth example, which carried out the first carrier compatibility trials. An order for 40 examples of the **Buccaneer S.Mk 1** was placed in October 1959, these machines being powered by the Gyron Junior 101 rated at 7,100 lb st (31.58 kN). The first of these aircraft made its maiden flight on 23 January 1962, and on 17 July of that year No. 801 Squadron, FAA was commissioned as the first operational Buccaneer squadron, embarking in HMS *Ark Royal* during the following January.

The Buccaneer S.Mk 1 was decidedly underpowered, and the Rolls-Royce Spey turbofan was selected as powerplant for the major production variant, the **Buccaneer S.Mk 2**, the first of 84 production examples making its initial flight on 5 June 1964. The Buccaneer S.Mk 2 had a much greater range than the Buccaneer S.Mk 1, for although the Spey engines provided some 30 per cent more power they also had a lower fuel consumption rate, and the Buccaneer S.Mk 2 was also equipped for inflight-refuelling. The variant entered FAA service in October 1965 and the last was retired in 1978.

Although scheduled for operation from shore bases, a fully navalised **Buccaneer Mk 50** version of the Buccaneer was supplied to the South African Air Force in 1965. These 16 aircraft were also fitted with a Bristol Siddeley BS.605 twin-chamber rocket motor in the rear of the fuselage, providing a 30-second boost of 8,000 lb st (35.59 kN) to complement

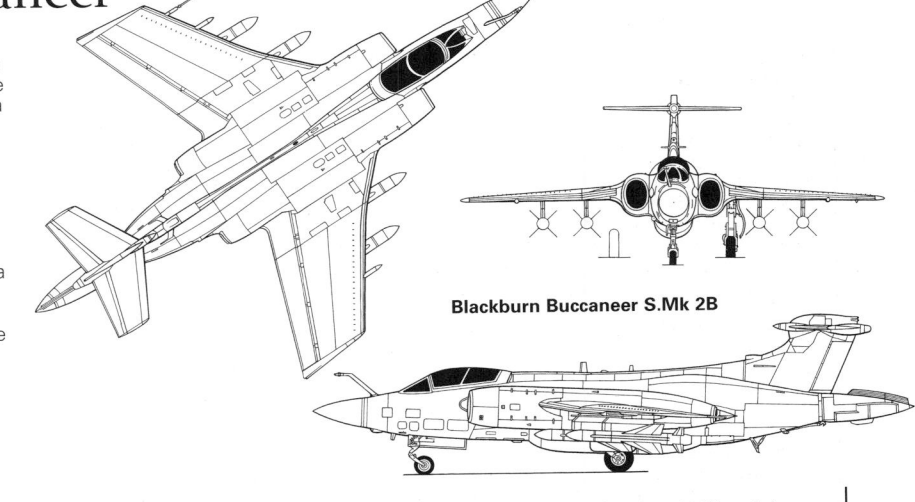

Blackburn Buccaneer S.Mk 2B

the standard powerplant for take-off from 'hot and high' airfields. The SAAF retired its last Buccaneers in 1991. The RN's Buccaneer S.Mk 2s were not retired when the progressive run-down of the UK's carrier force brought their withdrawal from FAA service. From 1969 onwards they were transferred to the RAF, with No. 12 Squadron the first to become operational on the Buccaneer S.Mk 2 in July 1970.

The first RAF aircraft were known unofficially as **'interim S.Mk 2Bs'**, having been given Mod 1188 which added Martel anti-ship missile capability, characterised by longer, shallower wing pylons. Other ex-Navy aircraft received some minor RAF-specific modifications under Mod 1499. In 1972 these non-Martel aircraft were retrospectively designated **S.Mk 2A** and were mostly used by the training unit. Most of these aircraft were upgraded with both modifications, being designated **S.Mk 2B**, and later receiving bulged bomb bay tanks. In addition to the foregoing, 43 new-production Buccaneer S.Mk 2Bs were ordered, the first making its initial flight on 8 January 1970. Before their retirement the remaining RN Buccaneers had undergone modifications comparable to those of the Buccaneer S.Mk 2B, receiving the revised designations **Buccaneer S.Mk 2C** and **S.Mk 2D** without and with Martel capability respectively.

Following the loss of a Buccaneer on 7 February 1980, investigation revealed that this accident was the result of a wing fatigue problem. The RAF fleet was therefore grounded pending detailed inspection, and a return to normal operations did not follow until late July of that same year. Subsequently, No. 216 Squadron was disbanded, and in late 1981 the type remained in service with No. 12 Sqn at Lossiemouth and with No. 237 OCU and No. 208 Squadron at Honington. The latter units were scheduled to disband in 1983 when replaced by Tornado squadrons, but the surviving Buccaneers were proving too useful to lose and the type was retained in service, finally in the anti-ship role, until 1994, having seen combat during the 1991 Gulf War.

No. XV Sqn reformed in 1970 as the RAF's second Buccaneer squadron. The unit flew its nuclear-armed S.Mk 2Bs from RAF Laarbruch until 1983.

XN974 was the first Buccaneer S.Mk 2. The variant eventually equipped Nos 800, 801, 803 and 809 Squadrons, operating from the aircraft-carriers Ark Royal, Eagle and Victorious.

SPECIFICATION

Blackburn Buccaneer S.Mk 2B
Type: two-seat carrierborne and land-based low-level strike aircraft
Powerplant: two Rolls-Royce Spey RB.168-1A Mk 101 turbofan engines each rated at 11,255 lb st (50.06 kN)
Performance: maximum speed 646 mph (1040 km/h) at 200 ft (61 m); initial climb rate 7,000 ft (2134 m) per minute; service ceiling more than 40,000 ft (12190 m); range 2,300 miles (3701 km) with typical weapons load
Weights: empty 29,980 lb (13599 kg); maximum take-off 62,000 lb (28123 kg)
Dimensions: wingspan 44 ft (13.41 m); length 63 ft 5 in (19.33 m); height 16 ft 3 in (4.97 m); wing area 514.70 sq ft (47.82 m²)
Armament: up to 16,000 lb (7258 kg) of a wide variety of disposable stores carried on the revolving door of the lower-fuselage weapons bay and on four underwing hardpoints, and including one free-fall nuclear weapon or four 1,000-lb (454-kg) conventional bombs internally, and up to 12 1,000-lb (454-kg) or 24 500-lb (227-kg) bombs, or four rocket-launcher pods, or three AJ.168 Martel ASMs and a Martel data-link pod, or four Sea Eagle anti-ship missiles carried externally

Blackburn Blackburd

In the autumn of 1917 the Blackburn Aircraft and Motor Co. Ltd was building the Sopwith Cuckoo when the Admiralty issued its Specification N.1B for a more capable torpedo bomber. Blackburn received a contract to design and build three prototypes of a larger warplane able to deliver the more destructive 18-in (457-mm) Mk VIII torpedo.

Intended for operation from HMS *Argus*, the world's first true aircraft-carrier, the **Blackburn Blackburd** was a large machine of typical construction for its period, with a wire-braced, largely wooden airframe, covered mainly with fabric. The landing gear provided anchorages for skid/hydrofoil surfaces intended to improve safety in the event of a ditching at sea. For the same reason, stabilising floats were installed under the lower wing on the second prototype, and flotation bags were fitted in the fuselage. The main wheels and their axle were jettisonable, which would have been an asset in any ditching, but the reason for this was to provide clearance for the release of the torpedo carried externally under the fuselage. The landing back on the carrier would therefore have had to be made on the skids.

Trials indicated that the Blackburd was superior to the rival Shorts Shirl, but offered poor performance and handling. The second and third Blackburds were completed with modifications to allow service in hotter climes. An order was then placed for 100 production examples, but this was later cancelled in favour of larger-scale production of the Cuckoo, which was deemed more survivable if less offensively capable than the Blackburd.

A man standing by the starboard undercarriage unit lends scale to the first Blackburd. Worthy of note are the type's constant-section fuselage and the impressive size of the torpedo.

SPECIFICATION

Blackburn Blackburd
Type: single-seat carrierborne and shore-based torpedo bomber
Powerplant: one Rolls-Royce Eagle VIII Vee engine rated at 350 hp (261 kW)
Performance: maximum speed 95 mph (153 km/h) at sea level; initial climb rate 845 ft (258 m) per minute; service ceiling 17,000 ft (5180 m); endurance 3 hours
Weights: empty 3,228 lb (1464 kg); maximum take-off 5,700 lb (2586 kg)
Dimensions: wingspan 52 ft 5 in (15.98 m); length 34 ft 10 in (10.62 m); height 12 ft 4¼ in (3.77 m); wing area 684.00 sq ft (63.54 m²)
Armament: one 1,423-lb (645-kg) Mk VIII torpedo carried under the fuselage

Blackburn BT.1 Beagle

Operating under considerable financial constraints, the Air Ministry issued Specification 24/25 in 1925. This called for a high-altitude bomber that could double, with much increased warload and much reduced performance, as a coast-defence torpedo bomber for the RAF. Blackburn responded with its **BT.1 Beagle**, which was revised before work on the prototype began, to meet the specification.

In December 1926 the Air Ministry contracted for a single prototype that began to take shape as a large single-bay biplane with the powerplant of one Bristol Jupiter VIIIF radial engine. The machine was of mixed construction under a covering largely of fabric.

Blackburn BT.1 Beagle (continued)

The prototype Beagle made its maiden flight on 18 February 1928, and was later delivered to the A&AEE at Martlesham Heath in Suffolk, for official trials and evaluation against its rivals, the Gloster Goring, Handley Page Hare, Hawker Harrier and Westland Witch. None of the prototypes was deemed adequate, and the Beagle was returned to its manufacturer for modification with the 590-hp (440-kW) Jupiter XF engine located in an installation offering better cooling. Further trials followed from March 1931, but no production order resulted and the machine was probably used as a 'hack' into the closing months of 1932.

Just one Beagle prototype was completed and the aircraft is illustrated in its original Jupiter VIIIF-engined form. Note the machine-gun and bomb rack installations.

SPECIFICATION

Blackburn BT.1 Beagle
Type: two-seat day bomber, reconnaissance and torpedo-bombing aircraft
Powerplant: one Bristol Jupiter VIIIF radial engine rated at 460 hp (343 kW)
Performance: maximum speed 140 mph (225 km/h) at 5,000 ft (1525 m); cruising speed 115 mph (185 km/h) at optimum altitude; climb rate at 5,000 ft (1525 m) 740 ft (226 m) per minute; service ceiling 16,000 ft (4875 m); endurance 8 hours 30 minutes
Weights: empty 3,495 lb (1585 kg); maximum take-off 7,750 lb (3515 kg)
Dimensions: wingspan 45 ft 6 in (13.87 m); length 33 ft 1 in (10.08 m); height 11 ft 9 in (3.58 m); wing area 570.00 sq ft (52.95 m²)
Armament: one 0.303-in (7.7-mm) Vickers fixed forward-firing machine-gun in the forward fuselage and one 0.303-in (7.7-mm) Lewis trainable rearward-firing machine-gun in the rear cockpit, plus one 1,850-lb (839-kg) torpedo or up to 920 lb (417 kg) of bombs carried externally

Blackburn CA.15 Monoplane and Biplane

The **Blackburn CA.15** was one of relatively few aircraft types to reach hardware form in the manufacturer's extensive series of CA (Commercial Aeroplane) projects and designs. Initially projected in 1929 as the **CA.15A** 11-passenger monoplane transport, it had the powerplant of three 240-hp (179-kW) Armstrong Siddeley Lynx IV radial engines. The design was optimised for use with wheeled landing or float alighting gear and with alternative monoplane and biplane wing arrangements. Further development of the basic concept led to the slightly smaller **CA.15B** and it was at this stage that the Air Ministry saw the opportunity for a complete assessment of the advan-

The CA.15 Monoplane's wing was in two halves, which extended from the upper fuselage. Its Jaguar radial engines were installed in leading-edge nacelles.

tages and disadvantages of the monoplane and biplane wing arrangement.
Blackburn was therefore asked to prepare the designs for a pair of 10-passenger transport aircraft that would differ only in their monoplane and biplane wings. The design of the resulting **CA.15C** was entrusted to B. A. Duncan, leading to the two aircraft being nicknamed 'The Duncan Sisters'. The aircraft were of metal construction covered with light alloy on their fuselage and fabric on their flying surfaces. The

biplane was of the two-bay type, while the monoplane had a wing of slightly larger area resulting from its increased span and chord.
The **CA.15C Biplane** and **CA.15C Monoplane** made their first flights on 10 June and 4 October 1932, respectively. The two machines were competitively evaluated by the A&AEE at Martlesham

The unstaggered wing cellule of the Biplane mounted the two Jaguar engines in nacelles carried by the inner sets of interplane struts.

Heath from the summer of 1933, and trials at the same maximum take-off weight revealed that the Biplane was slower, and the Monoplane was forced to carry only a smaller payload as a result of its higher structure weight. It had been intended that both aircraft would then be operated by Imperial Airways as part of its network in Africa, but the airline did not want the aircraft. The Biplane was therefore scrapped early in 1934, but the Monoplane survived to a time early in 1938 as the platform for automatic pilot, radio and other trials.

SPECIFICATION

Blackburn CA.15C Biplane
Type: two-crew light transport
Powerplant: two Armstrong Siddeley Jaguar IVC radial engines each rated at 400 hp (298 kW)
Performance: maximum speed 118 mph (190 km/h) at optimum altitude; cruising speed 110 mph (177 km/h) at optimum altitude; initial climb rate 535 ft (163 m) per minute; service ceiling 9,000 ft (2745 m); range 350 miles (563 km)
Weights: empty 7,931 lb (3598 kg); maximum take-off 12,150 lb (5511 kg)
Dimensions: wingspan 64 ft (19.51 m); length 55 ft (16.76 m); height 16 ft (4.88 m); wing area 1,037.00 sq ft (96.34 m²)

Payload: up to 10 passengers

Blackburn CA.15C Monoplane (as CA.15C Biplane unless otherwise stated)
Performance: maximum speed 128 mph (206 km/h) at optimum altitude; initial climb rate 665 ft (203 m) per minute; service ceiling 13,500 ft (4115 m);
Weights: empty 8,818 lb (4000 kg); maximum take-off 13,074 lb (5930 kg)
Dimensions: wingspan 86 ft (26.21 m); length 55 ft 3 in (16.84 m); height 16 ft 9 in (5.11 m); wing area 1,068.00 sq ft (99.22 m²)

Blackburn F.1 Turcock

The **Blackburn F.1 Turcock** was the only completed variant of the proposed **Blackcock** fighter series designed in 1926 to meet the requirements attached to Specifications F.9/26 and N.21/26. The type was schemed as a private-venture interceptor that could be built in six differently-named variants according to the specific type of air- or water-cooled engine installed. In overall terms, it was a commendably clean single-bay biplane with a staggered single-bay wing cellule and an all-metal structure covered largely with fabric.

The prototype was completed to an order from the Turkish government with the name Turcock and made its maiden flight on 14 November 1927. This machine was destroyed in

an accident in February of the following year, and no further development of the basic fighter concept was undertaken.

Major F. A. Bumpus and B. A. Duncan, designers of the Turcock, gave the aircraft a fixed tailskid landing gear with a main unit of the through-axle type.

SPECIFICATION

Blackburn F.1 Turcock
Type: single-seat fighter
Powerplant: one Armstrong Siddeley Jaguar VI radial engine rated at 446 hp (333 kW)
Performance: maximum speed 176 mph (283 km/h) at 15,000 ft (4570 m); initial climb rate 1,300 ft (396 m) per minute; climb to 10,000 ft (3050 m) in 8 minutes; service ceiling 27,500 ft (8380 m);
endurance 1 hour 45 minutes
Weights: empty 2,282 lb (1035 kg); maximum take-off 2,726 lb (1236 kg)
Dimensions: wingspan 31 ft (9.45 m); length 24 ft 4 in (7.41 m); height 8 ft 11 in (2.72 m)
Armament: (proposed) two 0.303-in (7.7-mm) Vickers fixed forward-firing machine-guns in the forward fuselage

Blackburn 2F.1 Nautilus

As indicated by its designation, the **Blackburn 2F.1 Nautilus** was the company's first two-seat fighter and was designed in response to the Air Ministry's Specification O.22/26 of June 1926 for a two-seat carrierborne fleet spotter with a limited secondary capability in the interception role. The task of designing such a type with excellent low-speed controllability, the strength for catapult launches and arrested landings, a wing-folding system, the ability to use float alighting gear as an alternative to wheeled landing gear, all in combination with fighter-type performance was difficult enough. Moreover, it was further complicated by the air ministry's indecision about the exact powerplant to be installed.

Thus it was not until 1929 that the Air Ministry was in a position to order prototypes in the form of two examples of the Short Gurnard and single examples each of the Nautilus, Fairey Fleetwing and Hawker Naval Hart. The engine that had finally been selected was the Rolls-Royce F.XIIMS Vee engine.

The Nautilus airframe was of all-metal construction covered largely with fabric, and included equal-span two-bay biplane wings. The fixed tailskid landing gear had divided main units that could also be fitted with floats, in the form of two medium-sized units or one large unit complemented by two underwing stabilising floats.

The Nautilus prototype made its first flight in May 1929, but encountered controllability problems and was somewhat revised before its second flight on 21 August 1929. Official trials late in 1929 led to the decision to undertake a carrierborne evaluation of the Nautilus, Fleetwing and Naval Hart in 1930. The Naval Hart emerged victorious from this process, and the Nautilus was then used mainly for communications, flying up to the beginning of 1933.

A streamlined fuselage could be achieved with the Rolls-Royce engine, which was much narrower than the Napier Lion that had originally been favoured.

SPECIFICATION

Blackburn 2F.1 Nautilus
Type: two-seat carrierborne and land-based spotter and fighter
Powerplant: one Rolls-Royce F.XIIMS Vee engine rated at 525 hp (391 kW)
Performance: maximum speed 154 mph (248 km/h) at 5,000 ft (1525 m); initial climb rate 1,260 ft (384 m) per minute; service ceiling 18,800 ft (5730 m); range 375 miles (604 km)
Weights: empty 3,223 lb (1462 kg); maximum take-off
4,750 lb (2155 kg)
Dimensions: wingspan 37 ft (11.28 m); length 31 ft 8 in (9.65 m); height 10 ft 10 in (3.30 m); wing area 458.00 sq ft (42.55 m²)
Armament: one 0.303-in (7.7-mm) Vickers fixed forward-firing machine-gun in the forward fuselage, and one 0.303-in (7.7-mm) Lewis trainable rearward-firing machine-gun in the rear cockpit, plus four 20-lb (9.1-kg) bombs carried externally

Blackburn F.2 Lincock

In 1928 Blackburn built its second single-seat fighter, the **Blackburn F.2**, as a private venture. The aircraft was a lightweight biplane of wooden construction and powered by a 240-hp (179-kW) Armstrong Siddeley Lynx IVC radial engine. The semi-monocoque fuselage was plywood-covered, but all other surfaces were fabric-covered and the type made its first public appearance in May 1928 as the **F.2 Lincock I**. In the course of the following year the Lincock made numerous appearances, creating a good impression with its high performance, but nonetheless failing to attract orders.

Interest shown by the Canadian government, and its insistence on metal construction, led to the metal **F.2A Lincock II** with a 255-hp (190-kW) Lynx IV geared engine. This machine was tested in Canada but turned down.

Production of the **F.2D Lincock III** totalled five aircraft: two each for Japan and China, and one demonstrator for Blackburn. The Lincock III was armed with two guns in troughs in the forward fuselage, firing through the propeller. Interest from the Italian government resulted in Piaggio acquiring a licence to produce a two-seat, aerobatic trainer version of the Lincock. Only one was built as the **Piaggio P.11**.

Easily distinguished, among Lincocks, as a Lincock III by its straight fin leading edge, this aircraft was one of five of the type completed.

SPECIFICATION

Blackburn F.2D Lincock III
Type: single-seat lightweight fighter
Powerplant: one Armstrong Siddeley Lynx Major radial engine rated at 270 hp (201 kW)
Performance: maximum speed 164 mph (264 km/h) at sea level; cruising speed 141 mph (227 km/h) at optimum altitude; initial climb rate 1,660 ft (506 m) per minute; service ceiling 23,000 ft (7010 m);
range 380 miles (612 km)
Weights: empty 1,326 lb (601 kg); maximum take-off 2,082 lb (944 kg)
Dimensions: wingspan 22 ft 6 in (6.86 m); length 19 ft 6 in (5.94 m); height 7 ft 4 in (2.24 m); wing area 170.00 sq ft (15.79 m²)
Armament: two 0.303-in (7.7-mm) Vickers fixed forward-firing machine-guns in the forward fuselage

Blackburn GP and SP

Its failure to win a production order for the twin-fuselage **TB** persuaded Blackburn to essay a more conventional type in its search for naval aircraft orders. The result was the **Blackburn GP (General Purpose)** patrol floatplane, which was intended primarily for the long-range anti-submarine role with bomb armament. It could also be configured for the shorter-range anti-ship role with torpedo armament. The machine was of typical wire-braced wooden structure covered with plywood on the small-section fuselage and with fabric on the flying surfaces. Power was provided by two 150-hp (112-kW) Sunbeam Nubian Vee engines.

The first of the two prototypes appeared in July 1916 in this form, and was followed later in the same year by the second prototype, which was completed to the revised **SP (Special Purpose)** standard with a strengthened airframe and the powerplant of two Rolls-Royce Falcon engines. Neither type secured a production order, but it is worth noting that the later, more successful, Kangaroo was little more than a landplane version of this floatplane type.

Blackburn GP and SP (continued)

SPECIFICATION

Blackburn SP
Type: three-seat patrol, anti-submarine bomber and torpedo-bomber floatplane
Powerplant: two Rolls-Royce Falcon Vee engines each rated at 190 hp (142 kW)
Performance: maximum speed 97 mph (156 km/h) at sea level; climb to 5,000 ft (1525 m) in 10 minutes; service ceiling 11,000 ft (3355 m); endurance 5 hours
Weights: empty 5,480 lb (2486 kg); maximum take-off 8,600 lb (3901 kg)
Dimensions: wingspan 74 ft 10¼ in (22.82 m); length 46 ft (14.02 m); height 16 ft 10 in (5.13 m); wing area 880.00 sq ft (81.75 m²)
Armament: single 0.303-in (7.7-mm) Lewis trainable machine-guns in the nose and dorsal positions, plus one 14-in (356-mm) torpedo carried under the fuselage or four 230-lb (104-kg) bombs carried under the lower wing

In configuration the GP was an unequal-span biplane with an unstaggered three-bay wing cellule in which the outer panels were sharply dihedralled and arranged to fold; ailerons were installed on the trailing edges of the longer-span upper wing.

Blackburn L.1 Bluebird

The side-by-side seating arrangement of the **Blackburn L.1 Bluebird** was unique among British two-seat lightplanes when this wooden biplane entered production in 1927. The L.1 prototype had been built as an entry for the 1924 Air Ministry Light Aeroplane trials at Lympne, and was powered by a 1100-cm³ (67.13-cu in) Blackburne Thrush radial engine. The machine was not completed in time to participate, but was re-engined with a 60-hp (45-kW) Armstrong Siddeley Genet radial for another competition in September 1926. Unfortunately, landing gear

problems eliminated the Bluebird. The spell of bad luck ended when it won the Grosvenor Cup Air Race a few days later at a speed of almost 85 mph (137 km/h). Other racing successes followed before the aircraft was destroyed in a fatal mid-air collision during June 1927.

The first production batch of 13 aircraft, bearing the designation **L.1A Bluebird II**, had an 80-hp (60-kW) Genet II radial engine and were delivered to several flying clubs in East Anglia and Yorkshire. One example, built for Major the Master of Sempill, had twin floats and became well known for a

flight around the coast of the UK. Two Bluebird IIs were sold to Brazil.

The **L.1B Bluebird III** appeared in 1927; the first machine would have been the 14th production Bluebird II, but was completed to the new standard with a plywood- rather than fabric-covered decking for the rear fuselage and a fuel tank in the centre section of the upper wing. Following a tour of various towns this machine was revised with the 90-hp (67-kW) ADC Cirrus III engine. A production batch of six Bluebird IIIs with the 60-hp (45-kW) Genet engine was laid down, but the final machine

was not completed.

With the final model, the **L.1C Bluebird IV**, a complete redesign was undertaken and the new type emerged in 1929 bearing no resemblance to its predecessors other than in basic layout. A greater power requirement led to the Bluebird IV being offered with a variety of engines and because of military commitments, Blackburn was initially able to build only three Bluebird IVs. Saunders-Roe at Cowes on the Isle of Wight undertook the manufacture of 55 aircraft though, in fact, the last 20 or so of these

were then completed by Blackburn.

The Bluebird IVs led eventful lives, and a number were used to undertake long-distance flights, the most notable being claimed as the first solo round-the-world flight by a light aircraft. This was achieved by Mrs Victor Bruce between 25 September 1930 and 20 February 1931 although it should be pointed out that the stages Tokyo-Seattle and New York-Le Havre were carried out aboard ship. The last surviving Bluebird was the 11th production machine, which was broken up in 1947.

In addition to its duralumin floats, the Bluebird II floatplane received a Fairey-Reed metal propeller, which was better able to withstand the rigours of waterborne operations than the usual wooden unit.

SPECIFICATION

Blackburn L.1C Bluebird IV
Type: two-seat touring aircraft
Powerplant: one de Havilland Gipsy I inverted inline engine rated at 100 hp (75 kW)
Performance: maximum speed 103 mph (166 km/h) at sea level; cruising speed 86 mph (138 km/h) at optimum altitude; initial climb
rate 720 ft (219 m) per minute; range 470 miles (756 km)
Weights: empty 1,040 lb (472 kg); maximum take-off 1,750 lb (794 kg)
Dimensions: wingspan 30 ft (9.14 m); length 23 ft 2 in (7.06 m); height 9 ft (2.74 m); wing area 270.00 sq ft (25.08 m²)

Blackburn Pellet

In March 1923 Blackburn announced its intention to produce a racing seaplane for participation in that year's Schneider Trophy contest, which was to be held off the southern coast of the UK. Time for the design and construction of this **Blackburn Pellet** was short, and the company

therefore decided to base its flying-boat on the hull of the **N.1B** flying-boat that had been held in storage since the end of World War I.

To this structural core were now added a single-bay biplane wing with two stabilising floats carried under the outboard section

of the lower wing. The Pellet was prepared for its first flight on 23 July 1923, but was caught by the tide as it was launched and turned over. The flying-boat was recovered and stripped down for drying out and repair, and then despatched by rail for assembly at Fairey's facility at Hamble.

Time before the contest was now very short, and the Pellet finally lifted off on its maiden flight on 26 September 1923, revealing itself to be very bow-heavy and lacking in adequate radiator cooling area. The first flight thus ended in a forced landing, after which the Pellet was towed back to base for overnight work to install

Pictured as it first appeared with a wooden propeller, the Pellet is prepared for launching early in September 1923. The aircraft had larger floats, following its early capsize.

SPECIFICATION

Blackburn Pellet
Type: single-seat racing flying-boat
Powerplant: one Napier Lion W-type engine rated at 450 hp (336 kW)
Performance: (estimated) maximum speed 161 mph
(259 km/h) at sea level
Weights: empty 2,150 lb (975 kg); maximum take-off 2,800 lb (1270 kg)
Dimensions: wingspan 34 ft (10.36 m); length 28 ft 7 in (8.71 m); height 10 ft 8 in (3.25 m)

additional radiators and fit a metal propeller in place of the original wooden unit. The following day was the start of the contest's navigability and flotation tests, and as the pilot taxied out he was forced to take avoiding action to miss a rowing boat. The Pellet started to porpoise, lifted off in a semi-stalled attitude, drifted to starboard as a result of propeller torque, hit the water and sank. The pilot managed to escape after more than one minute under the water, and the wreckage of the Pellet was recovered that night.

Blackburn R.1 Blackburn

When the Air Ministry issued a requirement for a carrierborne reconnaissance aircraft that would also be able to spot for the fleet's guns, Blackburn designed a new fuselage and mated it to the wings and tail surfaces (except rudder) of its Dart torpedo-bomber. Much of the structure followed the pattern of the earlier type, but the front of the fuselage was of truly elephantine appearance, completely filling the gap between the upper and lower wings and carrying the Napier Lion IIB engine. The pilot sat in an open cockpit above the engine, with the navigator inside the fuselage and the gunner occupying a position to the rear. The massive main landing gear arrangement was capable of being configured with two wheels or a side-by-side pair of floats.

Three prototypes of this **Blackburn R.1 Blackburn** in the company's new role-based designation system, in which R stood for reconnaissance, shared

flight-testing in 1922, and a production order for 12 aircraft was placed that year. Deliveries of the **Blackburn Mk I** began in April 1923, the aircraft being based at Gosport, and FAA Blackburns served on board HMS *Eagle* in the Mediterranean from 1923.

Further orders were placed in 1925-6 for 29 more Blackburns with a number of improvements as well as the revised powerplant of one 465-hp (347-kW) Lion V. In this form the type became the **Blackburn Mk II**, and in 1926 Mk IIs embarked on HMS *Furious*. By 1929 Blackburns were also carrier-based in the Far East on HMS *Argus*, while in the Mediterranean they served on board HMS *Courageous*. A few Blackburns were used as dual-control trainers, and most of the Mk Is were converted to Mk II standard before the type became obsolete in 1931 on its replacement by the Fairey IIIF.

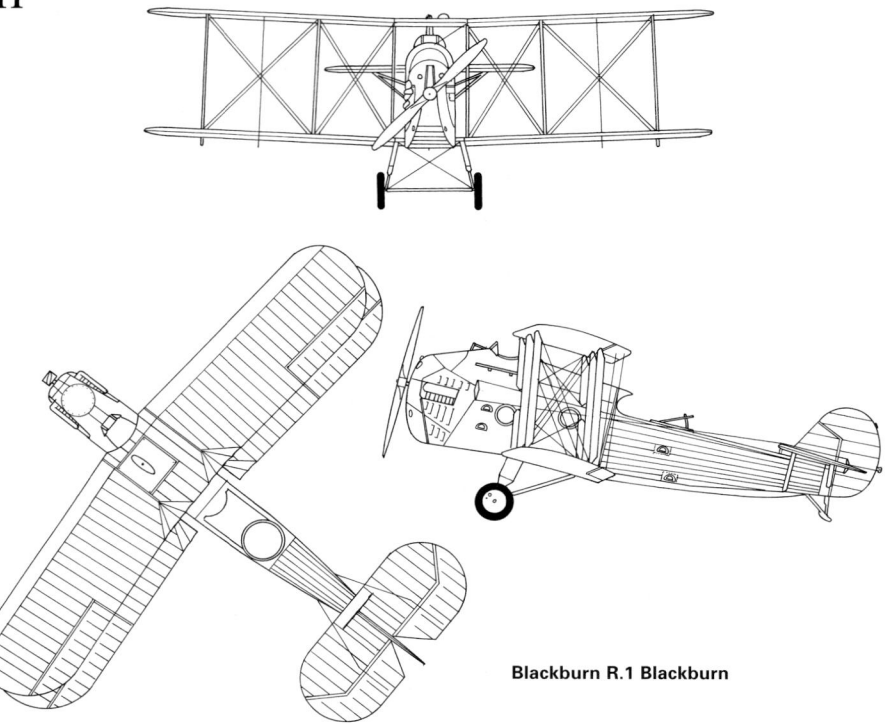

Blackburn R.1 Blackburn

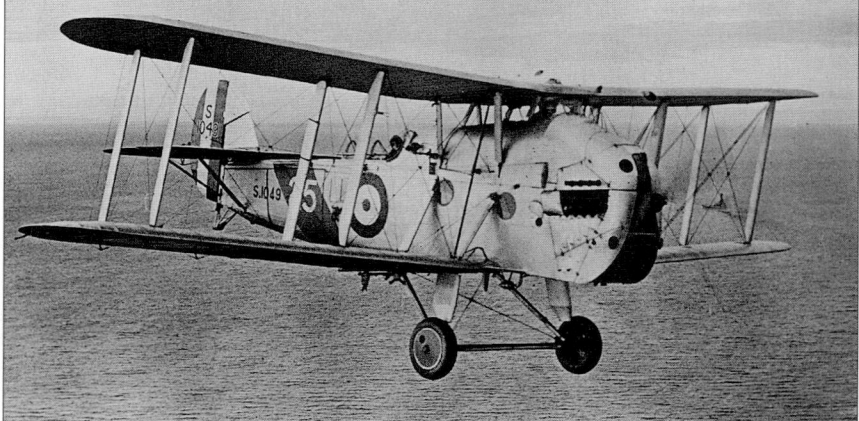

S1049 was part of a batch of 12 Blackburn Mk IIs ordered in October 1925. The Blackburn pilot was seated in an unusually lofty position, providing him with excellent visibility during carrier operations.

SPECIFICATION	
Blackburn Blackburn Mk I **Type:** three-seat carrierborne and land-based reconnaissance and spotter aircraft **Powerplant:** one Napier Lion IIB W-type engine rated at 450 hp (336 kW) **Performance:** maximum speed 122 mph (196 km/h) at 3,000 ft (915 m); cruising speed 112 mph (180 km/h) at 10,000 ft (3050 m); initial climb rate 690 ft (210 m) per minute; service ceiling 12,950 ft (3945 m); endurance 4 hours 15 minutes	**Weights:** empty 3,929 lb (1782 kg); maximum take-off 5,962 lb (2704 kg) **Dimensions:** wingspan 45 ft 6½ in (13.88 m); length 36 ft 2 in (11.02 m); height 12 ft 6 in (3.81 m); wing area 650.00 sq ft (60.39 m²) **Armament:** one 0.303-in (7.7-mm) Vickers fixed forward-firing machine-gun in the forward fuselage, and one 0.303-in (7.7-mm) Lewis trainable rearward-firing machine-gun in the rear cockpit

Blackburn R.2 Airedale

Designed by Major F. A. Bumpus, the **Blackburn R.2 Airedale** was the company's second reconnaissance type and was its response to the Air

Ministry's Specification R.37/22 for a three-seat carrierborne type to succeed the Blackburn R.1 Blackburn and Avro Type 555 Bison.

SPECIFICATION	
Blackburn R.2 Airedale **Type:** three-seat carrierborne and land-based reconnaissance and spotter aircraft **Powerplant:** one Armstrong Siddeley Jaguar III radial engine rated at 385 hp (287 kW) **Performance:** maximum speed 120 mph (193 km/h) at sea level **Weights:** maximum take-off 4,942 lb (2242 kg)	**Dimensions:** wingspan 46 ft (14.02 m); length 36 ft 4 in (11.07 m); height 14 ft 3 in (4.34 m) **Armament:** one 0.5-in (12.7-mm) Vickers fixed forward-firing machine-gun in the forward fuselage and one 0.303-in (7.7-mm) Lewis trainable rearward-firing machine-gun in the rear cockpit, plus light bombs carried under the fuselage

The first Airedale (illustrated) was lost when the service pilot entrusted with ferrying the machine to Martlesham Heath in Suffolk for its official trials crashed while attempting a cross-wind take-off.

Blackburn R.2 Airedale (continued)

An early decision that conditioned the layout of the Airedale was the use of a parasol wing to provide the crew with the best possible downward fields of vision, and while the selected engine was the Armstrong Siddeley Jaguar III radial, provision was made for the alternative installation of any radial engine of about the same power.

The oval-section fuselage was a semi-monocoque unit of plywood-covered wooden construction, and provided accommodation for the pilot in an open cockpit ahead of the wing, the navigator/radio operator in an enclosed cabin with access to an open observation position to the rear of the wing and the gunner in an open position still farther to the rear.

The wing was of typical Blackburn mixed metal and wood construction under a covering of fabric and was designed so that its halves could be folded back, to rest against the sides of the fuselage and so reduce hangarage requirements to a minimum.

The Air Ministry contracted for two Airedale prototypes for competitive evaluation against the

Hawker Hedgehog, and the first of these was seen publicly for the first time in October 1925. This Airedale was lost at the end of its manufacturer's trials. The second prototype was completed with a strengthened main landing gear unit and a modified tailplane. Officially tested in June 1926, this second prototype revealed the fact that the Airedale offered

insufficient improvement over the Blackburn and Bison to warrant production. Blackburn attributed the lack of a production order in part to the Air Ministry's well-known disapproval of the monoplane configuration, and therefore redesigned the Airedale as the **R.3** with a staggered biplane wing cellule, but nothing came of this idea.

Blackburn RB.1 Iris

Blackburn's first venture into large flying-boats came in response to the Air Ministry's Specification R.14/24, which called for a large long-range reconnaissance flying boat. The result was the **Blackburn RB.1 Iris**, the first machine in the RB (Reconnaissance Boat) section of the company's new designation system. This was a three-engined biplane of wooden construction with accommodation for a crew of five. First flown on 19 June 1926, the big flying-boat undertook trials at the Marine Aircraft Experimental Establishment (MAEE) later in that same summer. Blackburn had already decided to build a

new metal hull, and the Iris was returned to the factory during the following year to have this incorporated along with other improvements. The original 650-hp (485-kW) Rolls-Royce Condor III engines were replaced by 675-hp (503-kW) Condor IIIAs and in this revised form the single Iris was redesignated as the **RB.1A Iris II**.

Following trials by the RAF, the Iris II undertook demonstration tours in the Mediterranean, Middle East, India, and Scandinavia. As a result of the 'boat's impressive showing, the Air Ministry ordered the **RB.1B Iris III**, the first of three such 'boats flying in November

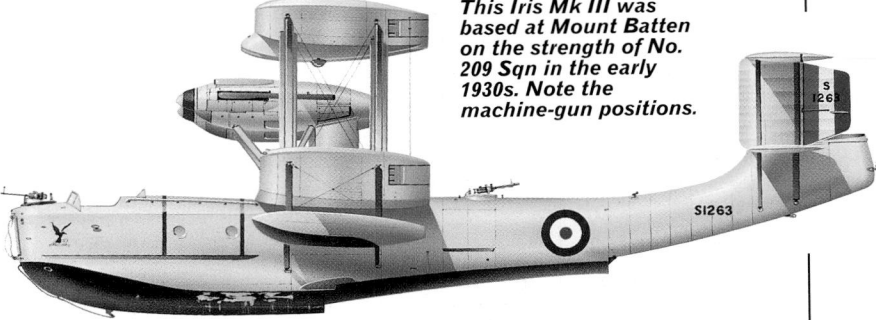

This Iris Mk III was based at Mount Batten on the strength of No. 209 Sqn in the early 1930s. Note the machine-gun positions.

Ordered in 1932, S1263 was the first of three RB.1D Iris Mk Vs. In addition to its revised powerplant, the Mk V introduced larger-diameter propellers and aluminium rather than steel fuel tanks.

1929. With a new Dural structure and other modifications, this version proved superior to its predecessor, and eventually the three aircraft were delivered to No. 209 Squadron, which had been re-formed at Mount Batten, Plymouth. Then the largest RAF aircraft, the Iris 'boats made a number of overseas tours, but in February 1931 one was lost in a fatal crash and

a replacement was ordered.

The **RB.1C Iris IV** was the Iris II re-engined with three 800-hp (597-kW) Armstrong Siddeley Leopard III radials, with the central unit mounted as a pusher and the other two as tractor units. This version showed an empty weight saving of 1,430 lb (649 kg) and an increase in speed to 130 mph (209 km/h) at sea level.

The final variant was the **RB.1D Iris V**, which did not involve any further production, but rather the installation in three Iris III

'boats of the new powerplant of 825-hp (615-kW) Rolls-Royce Buzzard IIMS engines; the first of these conversions flew in March 1932. The Iris V 'boats had only a short service life, two being lost in January 1933. The third was returned to Blackburn for use as a flying testbed for 720-hp (537-kW) Junkers Jumo IVC engines, built under licence in the UK as the Napier Culverin Series 1, and later used for anti-corrosion paint experiments.

SPECIFICATION	
Blackburn Iris III	(8640 kg); maximum take-off
Type: five-seat long-range reconnaissance flying-boat	29,489 lb (13376 kg)
Powerplant: three Rolls-Royce Condor IIIB Vee engines each rated at 675 hp (503 kW)	**Dimensions:** wingspan 97 ft (29.57 m); length 67 ft 4 in (20.54 m); height 25 ft 6 in (7.77 m); wing area 2,229.00 sq ft (207.07 m²)
Performance: maximum speed 118 mph (190 km/h) at sea level; cruising speed 97 mph (156 km/h) at optimum altitude; initial climb rate 503 ft (153 m) per minute; service ceiling 10,600 ft (3230 m); range 800 miles (1287 km)	**Armament:** single 0.303-in (7.7-mm) Lewis trainable machine-guns in each of the bow, dorsal and tail positions, plus up to 2,000 lb (907 kg) of bombs carried under the lower wing
Weights: empty 19,048 lb	

Blackburn RB.2 Sydney and CB.2 Nile

Designed in response to the Air Ministry's Specification R.5/27, the **Blackburn RB.2 Sydney** was clearly based on data derived from early RB.1 Iris variants. The Sydney was in effect a monoplane development of the Iris and a single prototype was ordered in June 1927 with the powerplant of three 510-hp (380-kW) Rolls-Royce Falcon X Vee engines, although the

company soon received instruction that these were to be replaced by three 525-hp (391-kW) Rolls-Royce F.XIIA Vee engines and finally by three F.XIIMS engines.

The Sydney was a substantial flying-boat of all-metal construction, based on a two-step hull with an enclosed flight-deck. In order to keep the engine thrust line in the same position relative to

the tailplane as in the Iris, the wing was located at the top of a Dural-covered steel pylon and braced on each side to the hull by two struts. The tail unit comprised a strut-braced horizontal surface and three vertical surfaces, each of the latter comprising a fin and rudder. The engines were located in nacelles on the leading edge of the wing's centre section. The Sydney made

its maiden flight on 18 July 1930, and there followed an official evaluation that was much hindered by a number of serviceability problems. Eventually, the decision was made not to proceed with any production of the Sydney or its revised Kestrel MS-engined **RB.2A** development. The sole 'boat was struck off charge in 1934.

In parallel with the design and construction of

the Sydney, Blackburn planned and partially built the **CB.2 Nile** as an airliner flying-boat in its Commercial Boat series. This differed from the Sydney mainly in the layout of its hull and its 515-hp (384-kW) Bristol Jupiter IX radial engine powerplant. This slightly lower-powered engine was chosen in view of its proven reliability and its reduced susceptibility to overheating in 'hot and high' conditions such as those in Africa, where the 'boat was likely to find its main employment.

Originally flown in silver, the Sydney was launched on 28 November 1930 in a dark-grey scheme.

The Nile was not completed, however, for the scheme of Cobham-Blackburn Air Lines Ltd to operate a flying-boat service between Alexandria and Cape Town was overtaken by the British government's decision that all Empire air mail should be carried by Imperial Airways. The Nile's hull was therefore stored and finally tested to destruction in 1935. Nothing came of the plan to build a **CB.2F** version for Canadian Airways, despite its early interest in the type.

SPECIFICATION

Blackburn RB.2 Sydney
Type: five-crew patrol and torpedo bomber flying-boat
Powerplant: three Rolls-Royce F.XIIMS Vee engines each rated at 525 hp (391 kW)
Performance: maximum speed 123 mph (198 km/h) at 5,000 ft (1525 m); cruising speed 100 mph (161 km/h) at optimum altitude; initial climb rate 390 ft (119 m) per minute; service ceiling 16,500 ft (5030 m); endurance 7 hours 30 minutes
Weights: empty 17,065 lb (7741 kg); maximum take-off 23,350 lb (10592 kg)
Dimensions: wingspan 100 ft (30.48 m); length 65 ft 7 in (19.99 m); height 20 ft 4 in (6.20 m); wing area 1,500.00 sq ft (139.35 m²)
Armament: single 0.303-in (7.7-mm) Lewis trainable machine-guns in the bow, dorsal and tail positions, plus two 1,850 lb (839-kg) Mk VIII or Mk X torpedoes or up to 1,100 lb (499 kg) of bombs carried under the wing

Blackburn RB.3 Perth

A development of the Iris, the **Blackburn RB.3A Perth** was built to replace the earlier flying-boat in service with No. 209 Squadron, RAF and differed from the Iris V primarily in having an enclosed cockpit and a hull covered with corrosion-resistant Alclad material. An improvement in armament was the installation of a 37-mm C.O.W. gun in the bow position for anti-shipping work, but there was also an alternative 0.303-in (7.7-mm) machine-gun as on the Iris.

The Perth first flew on 11 October 1933 and the type's service introduction came in January 1934, when the second such 'boat was delivered to Plymouth. At that time the first was still under test at Felixstowe, but by 31 May 1934 all three machines from the first contract had been delivered and were in service as the largest biplane flying-boats ever to operate with the RAF. A fourth Perth had been ordered subsequently and flew in April 1934, but this was retained at the MAEE at Felixstowe in Suffolk for experimental work.

Problems with the tail unit required the flying-boats to be modified, keeping them out of service for several months. The first Perth was lost in heavy seas during September 1935 when it lost a wing float, and two of the remaining three were eventually struck off charge in 1936. The last 'boat survived a further two years on test duties at Felixstowe.

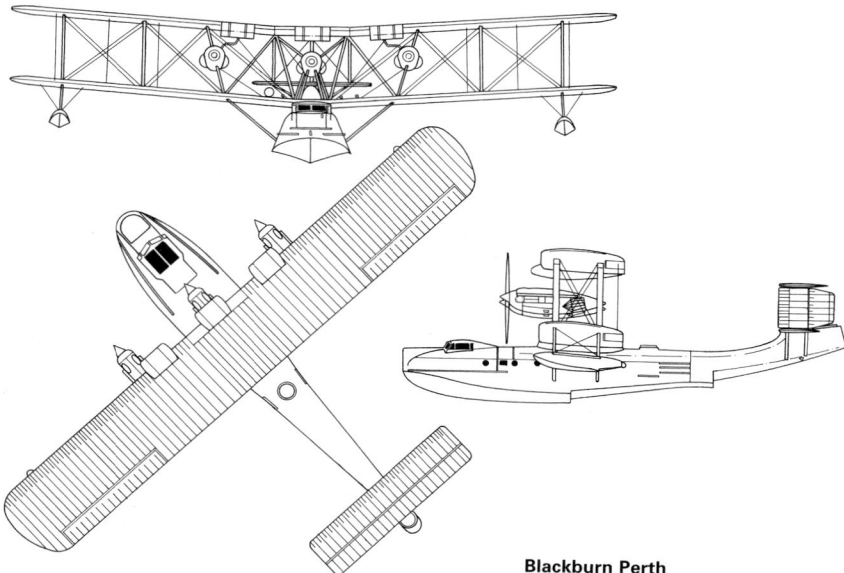

Blackburn Perth

SPECIFICATION

Blackburn RB.3A Perth
Type: five-seat long-range reconnaissance and bombing flying-boat
Powerplant: three Rolls-Royce Buzzard IIMS Vee engines each rated at 825 hp (615 kW)
Performance: maximum speed 132 mph (212 km/h) at sea level; cruising speed 109 mph (175 km/h) at optimum altitude; initial climb rate 800 ft (244 m) per minute; service ceiling 11,500 ft (3505 m); range 1,500 miles (2414 km)
Weights: empty 20,927 lb (9492 kg); maximum take-off 38,000 lb (17237 kg)
Dimensions: wingspan 97 ft (29.57 m); length 70 ft (21.34 m); height 26 ft 5½ in (8.06 m); wing area 2,511.00 sq ft (233.27 m²)
Armament: one 37-mm Coventry Ordnance Works trainable cannon and one 0.303-in (7.7-mm) Lewis trainable machine-gun in the bow position, one 0.303-in (7.7-mm) Lewis trainable machine-gun in the dorsal position, and one 0.303-in (7.7-mm) Lewis trainable machine-gun in the tail position, plus up to 2,000 lb (907 kg) of bombs carried under the lower wing

With its 37-mm C.O.W. gun removed, this Perth has the Lewis gun mounting in the bow position.

Blackburn RT.1 Kangaroo

The GP and SP led to a developed landplane version, the **Blackburn RT.1 Kangaroo (Reconnaissance-Torpedo No. 1)**. Powered by two 250-hp (186-kW) Falcon II engines, the Kangaroo prototype began official trials in January 1918. The report on its performance indicated some problems, but since production of a batch of 20 aircraft (originally intended to be GP floatplanes) had already begun, the company was allowed to go ahead.

B9976, delivered in May 1918, was one of 19 production military Kangaroos. RFC/RAF Kangaroos were intended for use on anti-submarine and night-bombing missions, but none ever flew in the latter role.

Blackburn RT.1 Kangaroo (continued)

In 1918, the first Kangaroo deliveries were made to No. 246 Squadron. From the sixth aircraft more powerful Rolls-Royce Falcon III engines were installed, and in the course of six months of wartime operations, the Kangaroos sank one U-boat and damaged four more.

With the coming of peace in November 1918, the surviving aircraft were sold on the civil market: three went to the Grahame White Aviation Co. at Hendon in May 1919, and eight to a Blackburn subsidiary, the North Sea Aerial Navigation Co. Ltd. As a civil type the Kangaroo could carry eight passengers and saw

considerable use. One Kangaroo was entered for the £10,000 England-Australia flight in 1919 but, damaged in an emergency landing on Crete, was withdrawn due to lack of

spares. The type's final role was as a dual-control trainer, used by RAF pilots taking refresher courses, but by 1929 the last Kangaroo had been withdrawn and scrapped.

G-EAIT was the first civil Kangaroo. A fully enclosed seven-passenger cabin was installed in the main fuselage, while the forward machine-gun position was also partially enclosed to accommodate an eighth, rather lonely, passenger.

SPECIFICATION	
Blackburn RT.1 Kangaroo	**Weights:** empty 5,284 lb
Type: three-seat long-range anti-submarine aircraft	(2397 kg); maximum take-off 6,287 lb (2852 kg)
Powerplant: two Rolls-Royce Falcon III Vee engines each rated at 270 hp (201 kW)	**Dimensions:** wingspan 74 ft 10¼ in (22.82 m); length 44 ft 2 in (13.46 m); height 16 ft 10 in
Performance: maximum speed 98 mph (158 km/h) at 6,500 ft (1980 m); cruising speed 86 mph (138 km/h) at 10,000 ft (3050 m); initial climb rate 480 ft (358 m) per minute; absolute ceiling 13,000 ft (3960 m); endurance 9 hours	(5.13 m); wing area 868.00 sq ft (80.64 m²)
	Armament: single 0.303-in (7.7-mm) Lewis trainable machine-guns in each of the nose and dorsal positions, plus up to 980 lb (445 kg) of bombs carried internally and externally

Blackburn T.1 Swift and T.2 Dart

In 1920 Blackburn built as a private venture the proto-type of a single-seat carrierborne torpedo aircraft to replace the Sopwith Cuckoo. Designated as the **Blackburn T.1 Swift** and powered by one Napier Lion IIB W-type engine, this prototype was submitted to the A&AEE for tests, following some redesign to correct a centre-of-gravity problem, and underwent development flying during May 1921. No British orders were placed for the Swift, but the Air Ministry

awarded a contract for three modified aircraft, with a shorter-span wing cellule, and the first of these **T.2 Dart** aircraft made its maiden flight in October 1921. Following successful trials, a production order for 26 Darts was placed, deliveries beginning the following March.

In 1924 the Dart entered service with two fleet torpedo flights on board HMS *Eagle* and HMS *Furious*, and in 1926 the first night landing at sea was carried out on the

Handley-Page slots were retrofitted to the Dart fleet from 1928, as evidenced by this aircraft being manhandled on a carrier deck in 1932.

Furious. Further orders were placed, and by the time production ended in 1928, 117 Darts had been supplied to the FAA, later aircraft having the 465-hp (347-kW) Lion V engine. The Darts in FAA service were eventually replaced by Blackburn Ripons.

Three two-seat civil examples of the Dart with floats were delivered to Blackburn's subsidiary, North Sea Aerial and General Transport Co. Ltd, for use on an Air Ministry contract that provided refresher courses for the RAF Reserve.

The export model of the Dart retained the name Swift and the 450-hp (336-kW) Lion engine. The first two of seven export

aircraft were delivered to the US Navy, which designated them **Swift F**, but following competitive trials the USN decided that torpedo aircraft were not suited to single-crew operation, and instead ordered the Douglas DT-2. Other export customers for the **Swift Mk II** were the Imperial Japanese navy and the Spanish navy, which received two and three such aircraft, respectively.

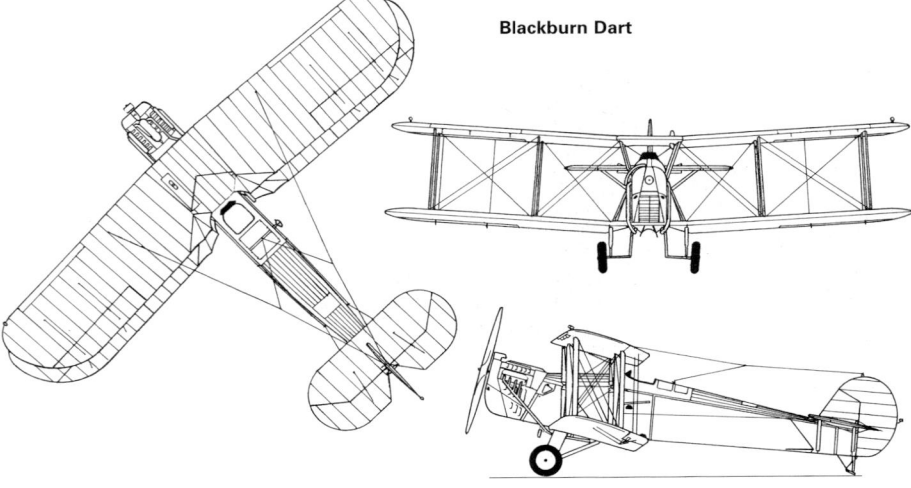

Blackburn Dart

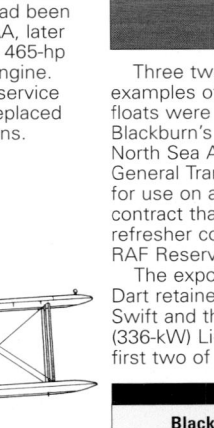

SPECIFICATION	
Blackburn T.2 Dart	**Weights:** empty 3,599 lb
Type: single-seat carrierborne and land-based torpedo carrier	(1632 kg); maximum take-off 6,383 lb (2895 kg)
Powerplant: one Napier Lion IIB W-type engine rated at 450 hp (336 kW)	**Dimensions:** wingspan 45 ft 5¾ in (13.86 m); length 35 ft 4½ in (10.78 m); height 12 ft 11 in (3.94 m); wing area 654.00 sq ft
Performance: maximum speed 107 mph (172 km/h) at 1,000 ft (305 m); cruising speed 104 mph (167 km/h) at 5,000 ft (1525 m); initial climb rate 600 ft (183 m) per minute; service ceiling 12,700 ft (3870 m); endurance 3 hours	(60.76 m²)
	Armament: one Mk VIII or Mk IX torpedo, or up to 1,040 lb (472 kg) of bombs carried under the fuselage

Blackburn T.3 Velos

In 1925 Blackburn developed the basic structure of its T.2 Dart into a two-seat type as the result of a Greek navy requirement for a coastal defence aircraft. The main differences between this aircraft and the Dart, apart from having floats, was that it was equipped as standard for

night flying, had improved communications systems and a second cockpit for a gunner. The resulting twin-

Unlike the Dart, the Velos was optimised for use as a twin-float seaplane. As such, its handling on the water was superb.

float seaplane was designated as the **Blackburn T.3 Velos**. In 1925 a small batch of these aircraft was built by Blackburn, and later in the same year production by Blackburn began in the Greek National Aircraft Factory, which the British company had built and was operating under a five-year contract. The first Greek-built Velos flew in March

1926 with wheeled landing gear and the second, completed as a floatplane, followed two weeks later. A total of twelve aircraft was built in Greece.

The **T.3A Velos** prototype, with metal rather than wooden floats, was built in the UK and completed a South American tour in 1927 without attracting any orders. The machine was

later converted into a two-seat trainer, the first of six for the North Sea Aerial and General Transport Co. Ltd, in whose service the type replaced the floatplane Dart, and these aircraft were eventually converted to landplane configuration.

By 1935 all the Velos aircraft had been withdrawn, the last surviving in a scrapyard until 1939.

SPECIFICATION

Blackburn T.3 Velos
Type: two-seat coastal defence warplane
Powerplant: one Napier Lion IIB W-type engine rated at 450 hp (336 kW)
Performance: maximum speed 107 mph (172 km/h) at optimum altitude; cruising speed 73 mph (117 km/h) at optimum altitude; initial climb rate 650 ft (198 m) per minute; service ceiling 14,100 ft (4300 m);

endurance 4 hours 30 minutes
Weights: empty 3,890 lb (1764 kg); maximum take-off 6,200 lb (2812 kg)
Dimensions: wingspan 48 ft 6 in (14.78 m); length 35 ft 6 in (10.82 m); height 12 ft 3 in (3.73 m); wing area 654.00 sq ft (60.76 m²)
Armament: one 0.303-in (7.7-mm) Lewis trainable machine-gun in the rear cockpit, plus one 18-in (457-mm) torpedo or four 230-lb (104-kg) bombs carried under the fuselage

Blackburn T.4 Cubaroo

First flown in prototype form during the summer of 1924, the **Blackburn T.4 Cubaroo I** was an extremely large single-engined torpedo bomber created in response to the Air Ministry's Specification 16/22 for a coastal defence warplane able to carry a 21-in (533-mm) torpedo. The other contender for the prospective production order was the Avro Type 557 Ava. The Cubaroo was related in structural terms

to the Swift, Dart and Blackburn, and as such was of steel tube construction covered largely with fabric.

In configuration, the Cubaroo was a three-bay biplane, with accommodation for the pilot and navigator in an open cockpit ahead of the upper wing, and a bomb-aimer and two gunners in the fuselage. The latter manned a pair of trainable machine-guns fired through rotating trap doors in the

The Cubaroo's original two-bladed wooden propeller was later replaced by a three-bladed metal unit. Twin-engined variants with Rolls-Royce Condor IV direct-drive or Condor III geared Vee engines were projected.

SPECIFICATION

Blackburn T.4 Cubaroo I
Type: four/five-seat torpedo bomber
Powerplant: one Napier Cub X-type engine rated at 1,000 hp (746 kW)
Performance: maximum speed 115 mph (185 km/h) at optimum altitude; absolute ceiling 11,800 ft (3595 m); range 1,800 miles (2897 km)
Weights: empty 9,632 lb

(4369 kg); maximum take-off 19,020 lb (8627 kg)
Dimensions: wingspan 88 ft (26.82 m); length 54 ft (16.46 m); height 19 ft 4 in (5.89 m)
Armament: single 0.303-in (7.7-mm) Lewis trainable machine-guns in the dorsal and two trap-door positions, plus one 3,000-lb (1361-kg) torpedo or four 550-lb (249-kg) bombs carried externally

lower sides of the fuselage adjacent to the lower wing's roots, from where they had good downward and rearward fields of fire. There was also another trainable machine-gun in the open dorsal position at the rear of the fuselage's raised upper line.

The wing cellule possessed folding outer wing panels for ease of hangarage and the powerplant was based on one Napier Cub X-type. The second prototype was virtu-

ally identical to the first, but was completed with a three-bladed propeller and was later revised with the 1,100-hp (820-kW) Beardmore Simoon I engine.

The Cubaroo handled well in the air and was in most respects a useful type, but no order was placed as the Air Ministry

decided in 1925 that for reliability reasons all its larger bombers would henceforward have a multi-engined powerplant. Blackburn schemed twin-engined developments of the T.4 as the **T.4A Cubaroo II**, **T.4B Cubaroo III** and **T.4C Cubaroo IV**, but nothing came of these.

Blackburn T.5 Ripon

The **Blackburn T.5 Ripon**, built to the Air Ministry's Specification 21/23 for a torpedo bomber that could double in the reconnaissance role with an endurance of 12 hours, was a further development of the Swift, Dart and Velos family. The first of two prototypes flew as a landplane in April 1926 while the second, completed as a floatplane, followed four months later.

The two **Ripon Mk I** prototypes were each

powered by one 467-hp (348-kW) Napier Lion V W-type engine and, as a result of competitive trials, a contract was placed for one further prototype and an initial production batch of 20 improved **Ripon Mk II** aircraft. The latter were aerodynamically 'cleaned up' and their performance was improved by installation of the 570-hp (425-kW) Lion XI engine. Service entry began in July 1929, when the Ripon Mk II began to replace the Dart.

Designed from the outset as a torpedo-bomber, the Ripon, as exemplified by this Mk IIC, could deliver a standard 18-in (457-mm) torpedo.

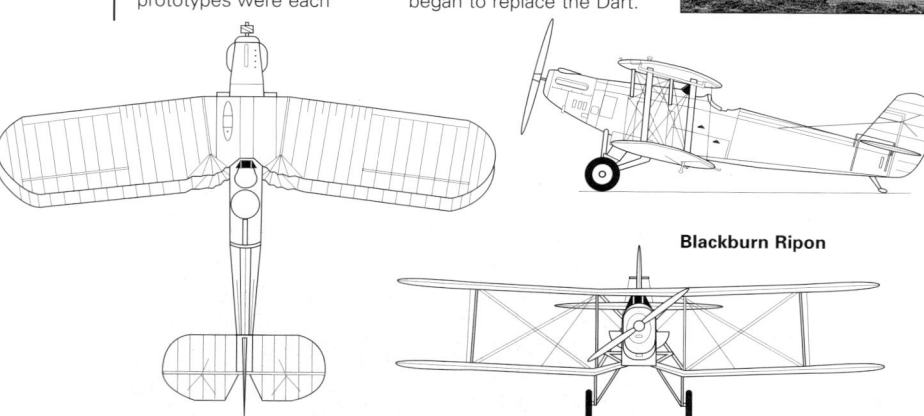

Blackburn Ripon

SPECIFICATION

Blackburn Ripon Mk IIA
Type: two-seat carrierborne and land-based torpedo bomber
Powerplant: one Napier Lion XIA W-type engine rated at 570 hp (425 kW)
Performance: maximum speed 132 mph (212 km/h) at sea level; cruising speed 109 mph (175 km/h) at optimum altitude; initial climb rate 800 ft (244 m) per minute; service ceiling 13,000 ft (3960 m); range 1,060 miles (1706 km)
Weights: empty 4,132 lb (1874 kg); maximum take-off

7,282 lb (3303 kg)
Dimensions: wingspan 44 ft 10 in (13.67 m); length 36 ft 9 in (11.20 m); height 12 ft 10 in (3.91 m); wing area 683.00 sq ft (63.45 m²)
Armament: one 0.303-in (7.7-mm) Vickers fixed forward-firing machine-gun in the forward fuselage and one 0.303-in (7.7-mm) Lewis trainable rearward-firing machine-gun in the rear cockpit, plus one torpedo or up to 1,650 lb (748 kg) of bombs carried externally

Blackburn T.5 Ripon (continued)

Further modification resulted in the main production version, the **Ripon Mk IIA**, of which 40 were ordered in early 1930. A variety of armament loads could be carried, including one torpedo. The final production version

was the **Ripon Mk IIC**, a variant which incorporated steel and Dural to replace wood in the wing construction and of which some 31 examples were built until 1932. A number of earlier aircraft was later converted to Ripon Mk IIC standard,

and some were also converted subsequently to a radial-engined form as Baffins. One all-metal **Ripon Mk III** was built, but no production of this variant followed.

The Ripon was offered for export with a wide vari-

ety of engine types, but Finland became the only other customer for the type. A **Ripon Mk IIF** with the 530-hp (395-kW) Bristol Jupiter VIII radial engine and interchangeable wheel/float landing gear was bought by the Finnish government as a pattern aircraft, and licensed production of 25

aircraft was undertaken by the National Aircraft Factory. All possessed a radial-engined powerplant, either the Gnome-Rhône Jupiter VI, Armstrong Siddeley Panther IIA or Bristol Pegasus IIM3. The last Ripon in Finnish service was struck off charge only on 15 December 1944.

Blackburn TB

Designed to an Admiralty specification for a long-range fighter floatplane to combat Zeppelin airships, the **Blackburn TB** (or **Twin Blackburn**) was a curious

twin-engined biplane which had the appearance of two single-seat aircraft joined by a centre section and combined tail unit. The TB was Blackburn's first twin-

engined design, but not its first biplane, which had been the single 130-hp (97-kW) Canton-Unné radial engined Type L twin-float seaplane, built in 1914 but damaged beyond repair in 1915. The engine chosen for the TB was a new

150-hp (112-kW) radial unit, designed by American J. W. Smith, but this proved unsatisfactory and the TB prototype first flew in August 1915 with the powerplant of two Gnome rotary engines. The Admiralty had ordered nine aircraft, and the Gnome engines were used in all

except the last, which had 110-hp (82-kW) Clerget 9B rotary engines.

By all accounts the TB was a dismal failure, with structural problems, a tendency to catch fire and a limited load, meaning that the aircraft saw little service before being broken up in August 1917.

Crews disliked the TB, since its structure flexed in flight and petrol often dripped onto the floats when the engines were primed, subsequently catching fire. In addition, the type's lack of power restricted its warload of steel darts to 70 lb (32 kg).

SPECIFICATION	
Blackburn TB	
Type: two-seat Zeppelin interceptor floatplane	**Weights:** empty 2,310 lb (1048 kg); maximum take-off 3,500 lb (1588 kg)
Powerplant: two Gnome Monosoupape rotary engines each rated at 100 hp (75 kW)	**Dimensions:** wingspan 60 ft 6 in (18.44 m); length 36 ft 8 in (11.13 m); height 13 ft 6 in (4.11 m); wing area 585.40 sq ft (54.35 m²)
Performance: maximum speed 86 mph (138 km/h) at sea level; climb to 5,000 ft (1525 m) in 12 minutes; endurance 4 hours	**Armament:** 70 lb (32 kg) of steel darts

Blackburn TR.1 Sprat

In an effort to reduce its costs in the financially strained 1920s, the Air Ministry sought whenever possible to procure dual-role aircraft. It was in this context that it issued Specification 5/24 for a two-seat aircraft with interchangeable wheel and float landing gear for service with the RAF as an advanced trainer and with the FAA as a deck-landing and floatplane conversion

trainer. Several designs were submitted, and of these the **Blackburn TR.1 Sprat**, Parnall Perch and Vickers Type 120 Vendace were selected for service evaluation.

As the first machine in Blackburn's TR (TRainer) category, the Sprat was in effect a scaled-down Velos with a downward-sloped forward decking to improve the pilot's field of vision in the landing mode. The

Sprat was of largely metal construction with a wooden rear fuselage, all under a covering of fabric except on the forward fuselage, which was skinned with light alloy. In configuration the Sprat was an equal-span biplane with a staggered single-bay wing cellule including outer

Another of Major Bumpus's designs, the Sprat was equipped with a sturdy fixed tailskid landing gear, including wide-track divided main units on which the wheels could be replaced by Dural floats.

panels that folded to the rear of the aircraft.

The sole Sprat prototype made its maiden flight on 24 April 1926, and in the prototype

competition was placed second to the Vendace, which was ordered into production and then cancelled as an economy measure.

SPECIFICATION	
Blackburn TR.1 Sprat	
Type: two-seat advanced flying and deck-landing trainer	per minute; service ceiling 17,500 ft (5335 m)
Powerplant: one Rolls-Royce Falcon III Vee engine rated at 275 hp (205 kW)	**Weights:** empty 2,318 lb (1051 kg); maximum take-off 3,220 lb (1461 kg)
Performance: maximum speed 115 mph (185 km/h) at sea level; initial climb rate 1,100 ft (335 m)	**Dimensions:** wingspan 34 ft 9 in (10.59 m); length 29 ft 3 in (8.92 m); height 11 ft (3.35 m); wing area 406.50 sq ft (37.76 m²)

Blackburn Triplane

Alongside its TB floatplanes, Blackburn was building two of the four prototypes of the Air Department Scout (later nicknamed Sparrow). This type was designed by Harris Booth for the Admiralty's Air Department as an interceptor that could be constructed simply and cheaply from readily avail-

able materials for the carriage of a 2-pdr Davis recoilless gun. The Scout was of extraordinary appearance and was powered by one 100-hp (75-kW) Gnome Monosoupape rotary engine installed at the rear of the central nacelle to drive a two-bladed pusher propeller.

The Scout proved to be flyable but wholly impractical, and Booth left the Admiralty in 1916 to work

The Blackburn Triplane is illustrated as it appeared later in its career, with a 100-hp (75-kW) Monosoupape engine and two-bladed propeller.

for Blackburn, for which his first design was the **Blackburn Triplane**. Bearing a number of conceptual similarities to the Scout, the Triplane was of typical construction for its period with a wire-braced wooden structure covered largely with fabric. In configuration it was an equal-span triplane with a staggered wing cellule notable for the large gaps between the wings and the use of strut-connected ailerons. The tail unit was carried by booms extending rearward from the trailing edges of the upper and lower wings, a pilot's nacelle extended forwards from the centre section of the middle wing, and a fixed tailskid landing gear with narrow-track main units extended from the lower corners of the central nacelle.

Only one prototype was built, and this made its maiden flight at the beginning of 1917 with a 110-hp (82-kW) Clerget 9Z rotary engine driving a four-bladed propeller, although this powerplant was later changed to one Gnome unit. Official trials at the Admiralty's establishment at Eastchurch indicated that the Triplane had no military value whatsoever, and the machine was therefore scrapped in March 1917.

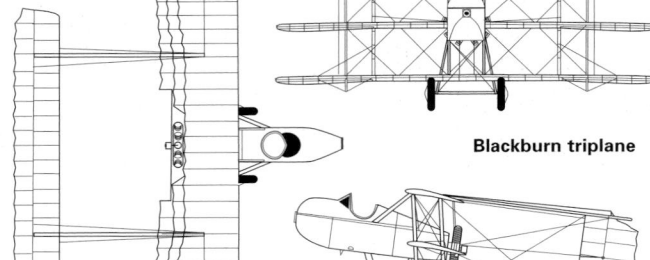

Blackburn triplane

SPECIFICATION	
Blackburn Triplane	maximum take-off 1,500 lb (680 kg)
Type: single-seat interceptor fighter	**Dimensions:** wingspan 24 ft (7.31 m); length 21 ft 5¼ in (6.53 m); height 8 ft 6 in (2.59 m); wing area 221.00 sq ft (20.53 m²)
Powerplant: one Gnome Monosoupape rotary engine rated at 100 hp (75 kW)	
Performance: maximum speed about 90 mph (145 km/h) at sea level	**Armament:** (proposed) one 2-pdr Davis fixed forward-firing recoilless gun in the nose of the nacelle
Weights: empty 1,011 lb (459 kg);	

Blackburn Type L

In 1912 the War Ministry responded to a spate of structural failures in monoplane aircraft by prohibiting such types from RFC service. There had been no problems with the Blackburn monoplanes, but even so Robert Blackburn decided that the move against the monoplane layout was not a trend his company could sensibly buck, and this led to the design and manufacture of the first Blackburn biplanes. The first of these was the twin-float **'Hydro Biplane'** of 1913 with the powerplant of one Gnome rotary engine or Anzani radial engine, but work was halted in favour of a larger and more capable type after the *Daily Mail* revealed its 1914 Circuit of Britain seaplane race with a first prize of £10,000.

The resulting machine was the **Blackburn Type L**,

The Type L's alighting gear was of the three-point type with a side-by-side pair of main floats and a small float strut-mounted under the tail unit. The units were of typical wire-braced layout.

SPECIFICATION	
Blackburn Type L	(716 km)
Type: two-seat coastal reconnaissance floatplane	**Weights:** empty 1,717 lb (779 kg); maximum take-off 2,475 lb (1123 kg)
Powerplant: one Canton-Unné 9 radial engine rated at 130 hp (97 kW)	**Dimensions:** wingspan 49 ft 6 in (15.09 m); length 32 ft 6 in (9.91 m); height 12 ft 6 in (3.81 m); wing area 481.00 sq ft (44.69 m²)
Performance: maximum speed 81 mph (130 km/h) at sea level; climb to 5,000 ft (1525 m) in 34 minutes; service ceiling 11,000 ft (3355 m); range 445 miles	**Armament:** one 0.303-in (7.7-mm) Lewis trainable machine-gun in the rear cockpit

which was an unequal-span biplane of wire-braced wooden construction covered largely with fabric. The machine had tandem two-seat accommodation in a pair of open cockpits, an unstaggered two-bay type wing cellule and the powerplant of one Canton-Unné 9 water-cooled radial engine. The Type L was completed shortly before the scheduled start of the race in August 1914, but events were then overtaken by the outbreak of World War I and the Type L was used for coastal reconnaissance from Blackburn's base at Scarborough in Yorkshire. A trainable machine-gun was later added in the rear cockpit, but the Type L was written off in a crash early in 1915.

Blériot XI

By the end of 1908 Louis Blériot had gained only limited success with his early monoplane designs, while contemporary biplanes seemed to enjoy greater manoeuvrability as well as superior performance. Then came the **Blériot XI**, the aircraft which has ensured its designer an important place in aviation history.

The Blériot XI was displayed with the **Blériot IX** and incomplete **Blériot X** at the Salon de l'Automobile et de l'Aéronautique held in Paris during December 1908. Thought to have been designed with the aid of Raymond Saulnier, the Blériot XI had a fuselage built largely of ash with supporting struts and wire ties, and the shoulder-mounted wing was a wire-braced unit that was also of wooden construction covered with rubberised fabric. For lateral control trailing-edge ailerons were later replaced by a wing-warping system. There was an odd fixed rudder (soon discarded) above the centre section, and the tail unit included a small central rudder and a low-set tailplane with tip-mounted elevators.

The first Blériot XI was built at the end of 1908, and, after the Salon had finished, made its first flight on 23 January 1909 with the powerplant of one 28-hp (21-kW) REP engine driving a primitive four-bladed REP propeller. In this original form the Blériot XI made 20 flights between January and March 1909, the best lasting only some three minutes, but was then taken in hand for modification to the so-called **Blériot XI (mod)** standard with a 25-hp (19-kW) Anzani radial driving a genuinely effective two-bladed Chauvière wooden propeller. Flying was resumed on 27 May 1909. On 26 June the machine established a new European endurance record of 36 minutes 55 seconds, and on 13 July won a cross-country prize.

The Blériot XI's main landing gear consisted of two large bicycle wheels, connected to a pair of steel tubes braced by wooden beams. The original tailwheel was later replaced by a skid (illustrated).

293

Blériot XI (continued)

With the confidence thus gained, Blériot decided to enter for the £1,000 prize offered by the *Daily Mail*, for the first flight in either direction across the English Channel. At 4.41 a.m. on 25 July 1909, Blériot took off from a field at Les Baraques near Calais and, maintaining an average altitude of 330 ft (100 m), landed on the cliffs by Dover Castle at 5.17 a.m.

Blériot at once became famous on both sides of the Channel, and a flood of orders for Blériot XIs followed: more than 100 aircraft had been ordered within two days of the flight. Blériot began quantity production, but from the outset had to call on the aid of subcontractors. Between 1909 and 1912, nearly every European aviation contest saw at least one Blériot XI among the winners, and the type was flown by most of the leading aviators throughout

After its leap to fame with Blériot's Channel crossing, the XI spawned a number of variants. The Blériot XI-3 seated three people in tandem and featured a more powerful engine than the XI.

Europe. Among them was Alphonse Pégoud, famous for his multiple loops at the Hendon aerodrome during 1913 and 1914. By the end of 1913 Blériot had delivered 800 aircraft of the total of 1,294 aircraft of all types built in France during that year.

The military saw in the Blériot XI an ideal general-purpose type and, even before the outbreak of World War I, the Blériot XI had been used operationally by the Italians in the Italo-Turkish War (1911-12), by the French in their struggle with nationalist elements in Morocco during March 1912 and also with nationalist elements in Tunisia and Algeria, and by both sides in the first and second Balkan Wars (1912-13 and 1913 respectively). The first Blériot XI variant to enter military service was the **Blériot XI Militaire** (military), which was a single-seater powered by one 50-hp (37-kW) Gnome rotary engine.

Standard models of the Blériot XI were flown by six escadrilles of the French army air service up to the middle of 1915, when they were relegated to secondary duties for another year or so. The aircraft were also operated by the British (including 104 licence-built aircraft), the Belgian air service, and six squadrons of the Italian army air service (70 built under licence). The parasol-wing version was flown by two French squadrons and also served in modest numbers with both the RFC and RNAS.

With its parasol, the Blériot XI Brevet Gouin provided its pilot with good downward visibility in the observation role. The aircraft illustrated is one of a handful used by British forces.

SPECIFICATION

Blériot XI Artillerie
Type: single-seat reconnaissance and artillery-spotting aircraft
Powerplant: one Gnome rotary engine rated at 50 hp (37 kW) for take-off
Performance: maximum speed 56 mph (90 km/h) at sea level; climb to 3,280 ft (1000 m) in 18 minutes; service ceiling 6,560 ft (2000 m); endurance 3 hours 45 minutes

Weights: empty 705 lb (320 kg); maximum take-off 1,764 lb (800 kg)
Dimensions: wingspan 29 ft 2½ in (8.90 m); length 25 ft 7 in (7.80 m); wing area 161.46 sq ft (15.00 m²)
Armament: generally none, although the pilot sometimes carried a rifle, carbine or pistol, and provision was later made for 55 lb (25 kg) of light bombs carried on the sides of the fuselage

Variants

Blériot XI Artillerie: single-seat artillery spotter variant of the Blériot XI Militaire
Blériot XI-2 Artillerie: two-seat artillery spotter with a more powerful engine
Blériot XI-2 Génie (engineer): slightly enlarged two-seater development of the Militaire with a 70-hp (52-kW) Gnome engine and modified landing gear
Blériot XI-3: enlarged development of the Blériot XI Militaire with three-seat accommodation and one 140-hp (104-kW) Gnome engine, among other changes
Blériot XI Brevet Gouin: parasol-wing development of the basic Blériot XI
Blériot XIE.1: single-seat trainer
Blériot XI-2 bis: side-by-side two-seater with a revised tail
Blériot XIR.1 Pingouin (penguin): a 'rouleur' or ground trainer with a clipped wing only partially covered so that take-off was impossible. The type was widely used by the French and later by the Americans in France

Blériot 110

In 1929 the French air ministry decided to order long-range aircraft from three French manufacturers for attempts on the world straight-line and closed-circuit distance records. The first company to respond to this call was Blériot, with its **Blériot 110**, which resembled a glider in its overall configuration and was of all-wood construction. Up to 1,320 Imp gal (6000 litres) of fuel could be carried in 10 tanks, six of them in the wing and the other four in the fuselage.

Unfortunately, a fuel supply problem cut short the aircraft's first flight on 16 May 1930, although no damage was sustained. After successful testing, the aircraft was transferred to Oran, in Algeria, where the record attempts were to be made. The Blériot 110 had been named *Joseph Le Brix* at the end of 1931 in memory of the navigator of the Dewoitine D.33, a rival to the Blériot, who had lost his life in a crash which brought another record attempt to a tragic end.

Between 15 November

The Blériot 110 had a long-span high wing with a trailing edge that tapered in a curve to pointed wingtips. The narrow-section fuselage was curved at the top and tapered to a keel-like undersurface onto which the undercarriage was mounted.

SPECIFICATION

Blériot 110
Type: two-crew long-distance aircraft
Powerplant: one Hispano-Suiza 12Lb Vee engine rated at 600 hp (447 kW)
Performance: maximum speed 137 mph (220 km/h) at optimum altitude; practical ceiling 6,560 ft (2000 m); estimated maximum

range 7,830 miles (12600 km)
Weights: empty 5,808 lb (2680 kg); maximum take-off 19,378 lb (8790 kg)
Dimensions: wingspan 86 ft 11¼ in (26.50 m); length 47 ft 9½ in (14.57 m); height 16 ft 1 in (4.90 m); wing area 871.91 sq ft (81.00 m²)

1930 and 26 March 1932, the Blériot 110 broke three world records, in the process covering a total distance of 36,206 miles (58268 km) in a flying time of 467 hours. The last of these records, created between 23 and 26 March 1932, was a world closed-circuit distance record of 6,587 miles (10601 km) in 76 hours 34 minutes of flight. On 5 August 1933, Paul Codes and Maurice

Rossi took off in the *Joseph Le Brix* from New York, overflew France, and landed at Rayak in Syria on 7 August: the distance of 5,657.4 miles (9104.7 km) was a world straight-line distance record that stood until broken by a Soviet

type, the Tupolev ANT-25, in July 1937. After further record attempts which, although unsuccessful, led to non-stop east-west crossings of both the North and South Atlantic, the Blériot 110 was scrapped in 1935.

Blériot 111

Designed by André Herbemont as a fast and comfortable executive transport, the **Blériot 111** was conceptually ahead of its time. The first version, designated as the **Blériot 111/1**, made its maiden flight on 24 January 1929 as a low-wing monoplane with a semi-cantilever wing. The machine was powered by a 280-hp (209-kW) Hispano-Suiza 6Mbr engine and had an enclosed cockpit for the pilot forward of the passen-

ger cabin. The **Blériot 111bis**, or **Blériot 111/2**, first flew in October 1929 with revised landing gear and wing struts. Re-engined with a Jupiter radial engine it became the **Blériot 111/3** and then, after modification to carry seven passengers, became the flagship of the *Patrouille Blériot*. The *Patrouille* gave exhibitions throughout France and northern Spain during the early 1930s in a similar manner to that of Sir Alan

During their unusual careers, the Blériot 111s appeared in a number of forms. The aircraft illustrated combines the retractable landing gear and engine of the 111/4 with an open cockpit.

Cobham's *Flying Circus* in the UK.

Revised with modified wing bracing, a more powerful Hispano-Suiza engine and retractable landing gear (the first fitted to a French aircraft), the Blériot 111/1 became the **Blériot 111/4** that made its maiden flight on 27 October 1930. The principal change in the **Blériot 111/5** was the relocation of the pilot's cockpit, now of the open type, to a position behind the five-passenger cabin, while its 500-hp (373-kW) Hispano-Suiza 12Mbr engine had a frontal radiator and a three-

bladed propeller. When re-engined with the Gnome-Rhône 14K radial engine, the Blériot 111/5 was named **Sagittaire** (Sagittarius). In 1934 this machine was further revised in an effort to improve performance, becoming the **Blériot 111/6** after it had received a wing of completely new design and a more powerful engine. The 111/6 was the only realistic French

entry in the October 1934 London to Melbourne MacRobertson race, but damage to the landing gear just two days before the starting day led to its withdrawal. The Blériot 111/6 ended its career with appearances at Blériot air shows during 1936. The basic design had seen its power tripled and its loaded weight increased by 50 per cent, but no commercial orders were received.

SPECIFICATION

Blériot 111/6
Type: one-crew executive transport
Powerplant: one Gnome-Rhône 14Kbrs radial engine rated at 840 hp (626 kW)
Performance: maximum speed 230 mph (370 km/h) at optimum altitude; practical ceiling 18,045 ft (5500 m); range 621 miles (1000 km)
Weights: empty 4,709 lb (2136 kg); maximum take-off 7,496 lb (3400 kg)
Dimensions: wingspan 55 ft 9¼ in (17.00 m); length 34 ft 11¾ in (10.66 m); height 13 ft 4¼ in (4.07 m); wing area 372.12 sq ft (34.57 m²)
Payload: four passengers carried in an enclosed cabin

Blériot 127 and Blériot 137

Re-engining its twin-fin **Blériot 117M** bomber escort fighter with more powerful Hispano-Suiza 12Gb units, and redesigning its empennage to include a large single fin-and-rudder unit, the company produced the **Blériot 127/1** prototype, which first flew on 7 May 1926. The modified **Blériot 127/2** second proto-

type, which made its maiden flight on 10 January 1928, had more powerful Hispano-Suiza 12Hb engines with radiators located under the wings to reduce drag. The pilot and co-pilot were located in open side-by-side cockpits with dual controls. After tests, some 42 aircraft were delivered.

The Blériot 127 was a mid-wing monoplane and of largely wooden construction. Its most unusual feature was provided by the gunners' positions: one was accommodated in the fuselage nose, while two additional positions were provided in rearward extensions of the underwing engine nacelles. The Blériot 127 was operated in the M.4 (four-seat multi-role aircraft) category intended for bombing and reconnaissance as well as escort duties. Entering service

from April 1929, the aircraft proved cumbersome and ineffective in service, but was not withdrawn from first-line duties until the end of 1934.

The **Blériot 127/3** was a single prototype of a night bomber version, and the **Blériot 127/4** was a 127/2 with its standard dual-wheel main landing gear units converted to take large single wheels, initially with large 'trouser' fairings.

The **Blériot 137** was an all-metal high-wing development of the 127 with the

earlier type's nacelle gun positions replaced by two midships gunners' cockpits. Two examples of the Blériot 137 were built: the first, powered by Hispano-Suiza engines, made its first flight on 21 December 1930 while the second, with Salmson engines, appeared a few months later. Of similar overall dimensions to its predecessor, although with more angular wing and tailplane outlines, the Blériot 137 had a maximum speed of 143 mph (230 km/h).

The Blériot 127 had gunners' positions in its nose and in the rear of its engine nacelles. Intended to provide a virtually unlimited field of fire to the rear, these latter positions could be reached from the fuselage during flight via the deep-section wing.

SPECIFICATION

Blériot 127/2M.4
Type: four-seat multi-role warplane
Powerplant: two Hispano-Suiza 12Hb engines each rated at 550 hp (410 kW)
Performance: maximum speed 124 mph (199 km/h) at 6,560 ft (2000 m); service ceiling 24,440 ft (7450 m); range 932 miles (1500 km)
Weights: empty 8,267 lb (3750 kg); maximum take-off
10,948 lb (4966 kg)
Dimensions: wingspan 76 ft 1¼ in (23.20 m); length 48 ft 2 in (14.68 m); height 11 ft 2¼ in (3.41 m); wing area 947.26 sq ft (88.00 m²)
Armament: two 0.303-in (7.7-mm) Lewis trainable machine-guns in each of the nose and two nacelle positions, plus up to 2,205 lb (1000 kg) of bombs carried internally

Blériot 165 and Blériot 175

Intended as a replacement for the Farman Goliath airliner, the **Blériot 165** was an equal-span biplane with a two-bay wing

cellule, a rectangular-section fuselage and power provided by two Gnome-Rhône Jupiter radial engines in nacelles strut-

mounted between the wings. The pilot and co-pilot were seated side-by-side in an open cockpit in the forward fuselage, and the enclosed cabin accommodated 16 passengers.

The first Blériot 165 made its maiden flight on 27 October 1926 and was followed by a second machine with two Renault engines and equipment for night flying. Designated as the **Blériot 175**, this second machine was then revised with Jupiter engines and

became the second Blériot 165. Both examples flew on the Air-Union 'Golden Ray' service between Paris and London.

Plans to build a military variant as the **Blériot 123** three-seat bomber and a

second Blériot 175 (for a long-distance flight to Tokyo) were abandoned.

Both Blériot 165s, Léonard de Vinci and Octave Chanute, served with Air Union.

SPECIFICATION

Blériot 165
Type: two-crew passenger transport
Powerplant: two Gnome-Rhône (Bristol) 9Ab Jupiter radial engines each rated at 420 hp (313 kW)
Performance: maximum speed 115 mph (185 km/h) at optimum altitude; practical ceiling 16,405 ft (5000 m); range 326 miles (525 km)
Weights: empty 6,435 lb (2919 kg); maximum take-off 12,346 lb (5600 kg)
Dimensions: wingspan 75 ft 5½ in (23.00 m) length 48 ft 8½ in (14.85 m); height 15 ft 11 in (4.85 m); wing area 1,282.02 sq ft (119.10 m²)
Payload: up to 16 passengers in an enclosed cabin

Blériot-SPAD S.33, S.46, S.56 and S.66

In August 1914 the Société Blériot-Aéronautique bought the organisation known as SPAD (Société Pour les Appareils Deperdussin) that was on the verge of liquidation after the conviction of its owner, Armand Deperdussin, for fraud. Blériot changed the full form of the SPAD acronym to the Société Anonyme Pour l'Aviation et ses Dérivés. For the duration of World War I Blériot was content to allow this subsidiary to produce aircraft under its own name, but this changed post-war and in 1921 SPAD was absorbed into the main company to become known as Blériot-SPAD.

The company's first venture into the transport aircraft field was the **S.27**, of which only a few examples were produced, and then the **Blériot-SPAD S.33** that first flew in prototype form on 12 December 1920. Both this and early production aircraft were powered by one 250-hp (186-kW) Salmson radial engine, but later aircraft switched to a more powerful version of the Salmson engine rated at 260 hp (194 kW). Enclosed accommodation was provided for four passengers, and behind this cabin in side-by-side open cockpits were a fifth passenger (to starboard) and the pilot. One S.33 was even modified as a blind-flying trainer, the pupil flying from within the blacked-out cabin.

The S.33 was a great success, 41 examples being built, and the S.33 and its developments dominated the field of smaller European transport aircraft right through the 1920s and into the early 1930s. The first of these developments was the **S.46**, which was developed to provide improved performance through use of a 370-hp (276-kW) Lorraine-Dietrich 12Da engine and longer-span wing. Following the first flight of the prototype on 16 June 1921, some 38 aircraft were delivered.

First flown on 3 February 1923, the **S.56** was a revision of the S.33 with a metal wing cellule and the one 380-hp (283-kW) Gnome-Rhône (Bristol) Jupiter radial engine. The cabin layout was also altered, with two pairs of side-by-side seats, and a second access door was provided. The prototype conversion was followed by the sole **S.56/2** with a 400-hp (298-kW) Jupiter, eight examples of the **S.56/3** with the 380-hp (283-kW) Jupiter and improved landing gear, and then the radically altered **S.56/4** with the pilot and 'open-air' passenger now moved forward to side-by-side cockpits immediately behind the 420-hp (313-kW) Jupiter engine, the six-passenger cabin moved farther aft, and wing modifications. Production of the S.56/4 totalled eight aircraft, and these were supplemented by two S.56/3 conversions. The **S.56/5** flew for the first time in 1928, and this had the cabin divided into forward and rear compartments for four and two passengers respectively, the rear compartment being convertible as a freight hold. Six S.56/3s were converted to S.56/5 standard. The final version was the **S.56/6**, of which two were built. These were four-passenger aircraft, with the pilot restored to a cockpit at the rear of the cabin, and were produced specially for the Air-Publicité company and intended for the towing of advertising banners.

Eight S.33s were later brought up to **S.66** standard, with faired headrests for the pilot and the open-cockpit passenger.

This S.33 is depicted as it appeared in the service of France's CIDNA (Compagnie Internationale de Navigation Aérienne) during 1933. The type formed the backbone of the company's European routes.

SPECIFICATION

Blériot-SPAD S.33
Type: one-crew passenger transport
Powerplant: one Salmson CM.9 radial engine rated at 260 hp (194 kW)
Performance: maximum speed 112 mph (180 km/h) at optimum altitude; cruising speed 99 mph (160 km/h) at optimum altitude; service ceiling 12,470 ft (3800 m); range 671 miles (1080 km)
Weights: empty 2,315 lb (1050 kg); maximum take-off 4,546 lb (2062 kg)
Dimensions: wingspan 38 ft 3 in (11.66 m); length 29 ft 9½ in (9.08 m); height 10 ft 6 in (3.20 m); wing area 454.04 sq ft (42.18 m²)
Payload: up to five passengers

Variants

S.48: one S.33 briefly fitted with a 275-hp (205-kW) Lorraine engine
S.50: two prototypes, with the powerplant of one 300-hp (224-kW) Hispano-Suiza 8Fb Vee engine, were followed by conversions of three S.33s. One of the prototypes, adapted with the wing cellule of the S.46, was flown as a ministerial transport
S.86: one S.66 re-engined in 1925 with one 450-hp (336-kW) Lorraine engine
S.116: the 32nd S.66 converted as the sole S.116 in 1928, with a 450-hp (336-kW) Renault 12Ja engine in place of the original Lorraine-Dietrich unit
S.126: the S.86 further revised in 1929 with a 450-hp (336-kW) Hispano-Suiza 12Ha engine

Blériot-SPAD S.51

Built to a French Aéronautique Militaire requirement of 1924 for a single-seat fighter to replace the Nieuport-Delage NiD.29C.1, André Herbemont's **Blériot-SPAD S.51/1** prototype flew for the first time on 16 June of the same year. It retained the classic Herbemont unequal-span biplane formula with swept-back upper wing and straight lower wing, with the wing cellule of fabric-covered metal construction.

The S.51/1 was rejected by the French authorities, but the modestly improved **S.51/2** that appeared in 1925 then secured an export order from Poland. Fifty such fighters were delivered in 1925-6 for service with the renowned 11th (Kosciusko) Squadron of the Polish air arm.

The sole **S.51/3** prototype was fitted with the first French variable-pitch propeller, which was designed by Herbemont, and recorded a speed 7.5 mph (12 km/h) greater than that of the S.51/2 with the same engine. The **S.51/4**, with a Gnome-Rhône 9Ab Jupiter engine boosted to give 600 hp (447 kW), appeared in 1928. Some 10 examples of this variant were completed, single examples going to Turkey and the USSR, with the revised armament of two Vickers machine-guns in the fuselage and two Darne machine-guns in the wing. Several of the French aircraft were later sold to private owners and flying clubs.

A single example of the Blériot-SPAD S.51/4 was exported to Turkey. The S.51/4 represented the final evolution of the design, but only 10 production aircraft were completed.

SPECIFICATION

Blériot-SPAD S.51/2
Type: single-seat fighter
Powerplant: one Gnome-Rhône (Bristol) Jupiter IV radial engine rated at 420 hp (313 kW)
Performance: maximum speed 143 mph (230 km/h) at optimum altitude; climb to 13,125 ft (4000 m) in 9 minutes 12 seconds; service ceiling 29,530 ft (9000 m)
Weights: empty 2,182 lb (990 kg); maximum take-off 2,998 lb (1360 kg)
Dimensions: wingspan 31 ft ⅞ in (9.47 m); length 21 ft 2 in (6.45 m); height 10 ft 2 in (3.10 m); wing area 257.80 sq ft (23.95 m²)
Armament: two 0.303-in (7.7-mm) Vickers fixed forward-firing machine-guns in the fuselage

Blériot-SPAD S.60 and S.70

In 1925 the French air ministry issued a requirement for a two-seat fighter, and in December of the same year Blériot-SPAD received an order for three prototypes of André Herbemont's **S.60** design. The planned fighter was based on what had by now become Herbemont's established formula and the first prototype made its maiden flight on 26 June 1926 with the prescribed powerplant of one 420-hp (313-kW) Gnome-Rhône (Bristol) 9Ab Jupiter radial engine and the planned armament of two 0.303-in (7.7-mm) Vickers fixed forward-firing machine-guns and two 0.303-in (7.7-mm) Lewis trainable rearward-firing machine-guns. The S.60 displayed very poor handling and stability in the air, and further development of the type was discontinued in favour of the **S.70**.

With the failure of the S.60 prototype, the other two prototypes ordered in December 1925 were completed to the improved

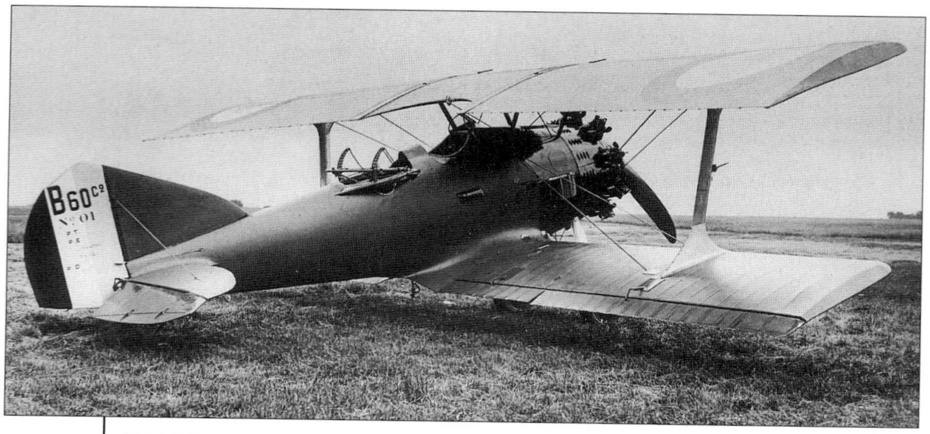

Neither the S.60 (illustrated) nor the S.70 proved successful.

S.70 standard with a revised tail unit and one turbocharged Lorraine-Dietrich engine. The first of the S.70s made the type's maiden flight on 21 April 1927, but its performance and handling were so little improved compared to the S.60 that development was soon terminated.

SPECIFICATION

Blériot-SPAD S.70
Type: single-seat fighter
Powerplant: one Lorraine-Dietrich 12 W-type engine rated at 450 hp (336 kW)
Performance: maximum speed 130 mph (210 km/h) at optimum altitude
Weights: empty 2,934 lb (1331 kg); maximum take-off 4,173 lb (1893 kg)
Dimensions: wingspan 37 ft ⅞ in (11.30 m); length 24 ft 7¼ in (7.50 m); height 10 ft 6⅜ in (3.21 m); wing area 393.37 sq ft (36.60 m²)
Armament: two 0.303-in (7.7-mm) Vickers fixed forward-firing machine-guns in the forward fuselage

Blériot-SPAD S.61

The sole example of the **Blériot-SPAD S.61/1** flew for the first time on 6 November 1923 after development in parallel with the S.51. The S.61 differed from the S.51 in having a straight wing. The S.61/1 was followed by the revised **S.61/2**, in which the original ventral radiator was replaced by a frontal radiator and the wings were of wooden rather than metal construction.

Although the French authorities placed no orders for the S.61, impressive export orders for 250 and 100 examples of the S.61/2 were obtained from Poland and Romania, respectively. In Poland 30 more machines were later built under licence by the CWL and PZL companies.

Four S.61/2s originally built for Poland were retained by Blériot-SPAD and used as the basis for a number of experimental versions. The first was the **S.61bis**, later converted into the **S.61/6**. Subvariants of the S.61/6 included the **S.61/6a** which had a Lorraine-Dietrich W-type engine. This same machine was redesignated as the **S.61/6b** after its fuel tankage had been increased and, piloted by the celebrated Pelletier d'Oisy, won the French Coupe Michelin cross-country air race on 25 June 1925. The **S.61/6c** was intended as a contender for a world speed-over-distance record, but was destroyed while making a record attempt. The **S.61/6d** replacement aircraft carried off the 1927 Coupe Michelin. Modified four months later to take a new Lorraine engine developing only 230 hp (172 kW), it was redesignated **S.61/9** and, although underpowered, took second place in the 1929 Coupe Michelin.

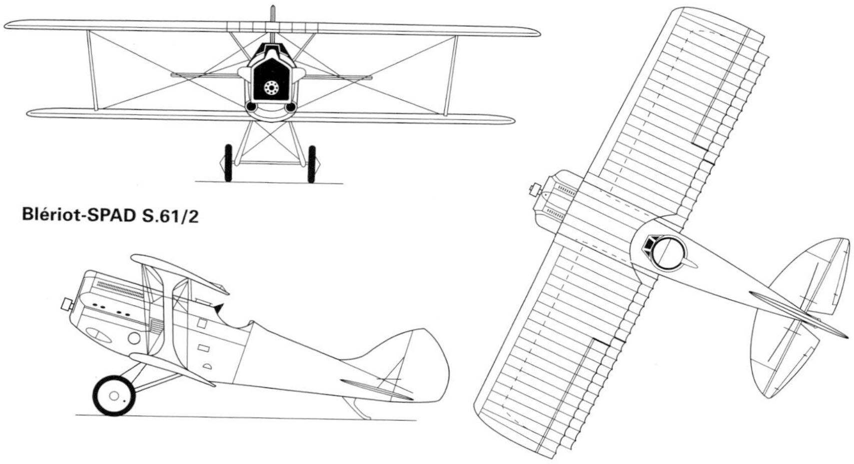

Blériot-SPAD S.61/2

Other experimental S.61 variants included the **S.61/3** with a reduced-span metal wing cellule and the **S.61/4** with a 480 hp (358-kW) Lorraine-Dietrich 12Ee W-type engine. Three examples of the **S.61/5** were built with the powerplant of one 450-hp (336-kW) Hispano-Suiza 12Gb engine, one being converted as the sole **S.61/8** with the 500-hp (373-kW) Hispano-Suiza 12Hb engine. The **S.61/7** was built for an attempt on the world altitude record with a wing cellule of increased span and its Lorraine-Dietrich engine boosted by a Rateau supercharger. Louis Blériot was unfortunate to pick as its pilot Jean Callizo, a self-made businessman who had been a wartime pilot. Callizo had already claimed the altitude record in a Gourdou-Leseurre GL-40 fighter, and he now boasted (with the aid of falsified instrument readings) to have broken that record again with the S.61/7. Suspicions had been aroused before the record attempt, however, and other instruments concealed in the aircraft showed that Callizo had made a wholly false claim: he was disgraced and stripped of the Légion d'Honneur awarded for his two 'records'. After this ill-fated venture the S.61/7, which had been damaged on landing, was unceremoniously scrapped.

The final version of the S.61 was the **S.61SES** with a redesigned sesquiplane wing cellule, and it was hoped that this would interest the Polish air force. Its performance showed no improvement over that of the S.61/2, however, and further development was abandoned.

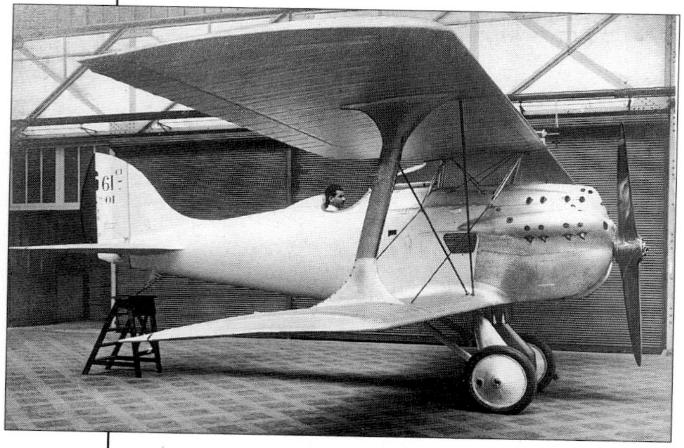

The S.61/2 went on to serve with Poland's 2nd, 3rd, 4th and 11th Fighter Regiments. A Polish S.61/2 gained second place in the 'Capitaine Echard' trophy race at the Zurich aerial meeting of 1927.

SPECIFICATION

Blériot-SPAD S.61/2
Type: single-seat fighter
Powerplant: one Lorraine-Dietrich 12Ew W-type engine rated at 450 hp (336 kW)
Performance: maximum speed 141 mph (227 km/h) at optimum altitude; climb to 13,125 ft (4000 m) in 9 minutes 39 seconds; service ceiling 24,605 ft (7500 m)
Weights: empty 2,326 lb (1055 kg); maximum take-off 3,450 lb (1565 kg)
Dimensions: wingspan 31 ft 4¾ in (9.57 m); length 22 ft 10⅞ in (6.98 m); height 9 ft 6⅛ in (2.90 m); wing area 315.39 sq ft (29.30 m²)
Armament: two 0.303-in (7.7-mm) Vickers fixed forward-firing machine-guns in the forward fuselage

Blériot-SPAD S.81

Preceding the S.51 and S.61 despite its higher designation number, the **Blériot-SPAD S.81.01** prototype made its maiden flight on 13 March 1923 as one of a number of fighter designs built to meet a French Aéronautique Militaire requirement of 1922. Official interest was shown in the parasol-wing Dewoitine D.1 and in the S.81, with none of the other designs getting past the prototype stage. While the D.1 was ahead in performance, it was ultimately rejected in favour of the S.81, which was considered a tougher and more reliable design with its wooden monocoque fuselage and fabric-covered metal wings.

Only two S.81 prototypes were built, the second being used for static tests. An official order then followed for 80 examples of the **S.81/1C.1** production fighter. Improvements made to the prototype during tests, including a lengthened fuselage and a larger vertical tail surface, were incorporated in the production series. The first **S.81/1** off the production line made its initial flight in September 1924 and was in service with 2e Régiment by the year end.

Experimental versions of the S.81 were the **S.81/2** and **S.81/3**, which made their first flights on 20 May and 18 August 1924 respectively and differed primarily in the type of radiator installed, and the **S.81/4** which had wings of wooden construction.

Blériot-SPAD S.81 (continued)

The **S.81bis** was a one-off development that first flew in the summer of 1923 with the same engine as the fighter, but with a wing cellule of reduced span and area as the machine was intended as a racer to compete in the Coupe Michelin cross-country speed contest. Its performance proved to be poor, and it was later converted into the **S.81/6** racer.

SPECIFICATION	
Blériot-SPAD S.81/1C.1	**Weights:** empty 1,865 lb (846 kg);
Type: single-seat fighter	maximum take-off 2,791 lb (1266 kg)
Powerplant: one Hispano-Suiza	**Dimensions:** wingspan 31 ft 6⅛ in
8Fb Vee engine rated at 300 hp	(9.61 m); length 20 ft 11⅞ in
(224 kW)	(6.40 m); height 9 ft 6¼ in (2.90 m);
Performance: maximum speed	wing area 322.93 sq ft (30.00 m²)
149 mph (240 km/h) at 1,640 ft	**Armament:** two 0.303-in (7.7-mm)
(500 m); climb to16,450 ft (5000 m)	Vickers fixed forward-firing
in 14 minutes; range 311 miles	machine-guns in the forward
(500 km)	fuselage

French fighters and racing aircraft of the early 1920s often featured twin Lamblin radiators, as on the S.81.

Blériot-SPAD S.91

By the mid-1920s the French air ministry was becoming concerned about the cost of new warplanes at a time when the bombers under development by potential foes seemed to pose a real threat. A possible way out of the resulting operational dilemma was found in the concept of the lightweight fighter, called the 'Jockey' fighter by the French. This would have been affordable in greater numbers than larger and generally more capable fighters, and yet would still offer a useful home-defence capability. The resulting requirement called for an armament of two machine-guns, a range of 249 miles (400 km), a high rate of climb and good agility.

The **Blériot-SPAD S.91**, which was the company's response to the requirement, was an equal-span biplane of all-metal construction covered with fabric everywhere except on the forward fuselage, where the engine cowling comprised a number of light alloy panels.

The **S.91 Léger** first prototype made its maiden flight on 23 August 1927 with the powerplant of one 500-hp (373-kW) Hispano-Suiza 12Hb engine. The **S.91/1** second prototype differed most importantly in having a frontal radiator, although it was later revised with the Hispano-Suiza 12Gb to become the **S.91/2** that made its first flight on 31 August 1928. The S.91/2 was demonstrated in Greece and Romania, and was then revised to **S.91/3** standard with one 420-hp (313-kW) Gnome-Rhône (Bristol) 9As Jupiter radial engine, and finally in 1931 to **S.91/5** standard with the 480-hp (358-kW) Gnome-Rhône 9Ae Jupiter engine. This much-developed prototype was lost on 10 May 1931.

Meanwhile, the first prototype had been converted into the **S.91/4** with a number of modifications as well as the powerplant of one 500-hp (373-kW) Hispano-Suiza 12Mb engine and first flew in this form on 4 July 1930. Later modifications that turned the S.91/4 into the **S.91/6**, which first flew on 10 November 1931, included rounded wingtips, a lengthening of the fuselage and empennage and other modifications.

Meanwhile the 'Jockey' programme had been abandoned, but Herbemont still felt that his S.91 was worthy of production in a further developed form, and in October 1930 designed a new variant that was based on the S.91/4 with a radically revised inverted sesquiplane wing cellule. This machine was built as the **S.91/7** and first flew on 23 December 1931 with the Hispano-Suiza 12Mc Vee engine. In this form it set a 500-km (311-mile) closed-circuit speed record of 308.8 km/h (191.9 mph). It was later modified again as the **S.91/8** that first flew on 20 August 1932 with the Hispano-Suiza 12Xbrs supercharged engine driving a Ratier variable-pitch propeller for a maximum speed of 224 mph (360 km/h).

The S.91/8 was then loaned to Hispano-Suiza for trials of a 20-mm cannon in a moteur-canon installation between the engine's cylinder banks and firing through the hollow propeller shaft. In this form the S.91/8 became the **Blériot-SPAD S.91/9.**

In configuration the S.91 was a single-bay biplane with straight wings of equal chord as well as span, an oval-section fuselage, a cantilever tail unit and fixed tailskid landing gear.

SPECIFICATION	
Blériot-SPAD S.91/7	(1093 kg); maximum take-off
Type: single-seat fighter	3,214 lb (1458 kg)
Powerplant: one Hispano-Suiza	**Dimensions:** wingspan 28 ft 4½ in
12Mc Vee engine rated at 500 hp	(8.65 m); length 20 ft 8⅛ in
(373 kW)	(6.30 m); height 9 ft 5 in (2.87 m);
Performance: maximum speed	wing area 191.60 sq ft (17.80 m²)
199 mph (320 km/h) at 13,125 ft	**Armament:** two 0.303-in (7.7-mm)
(4000 m); climb to 19,685 ft	Vickers fixed forward-firing
(6000 m) in 9 minutes 12 seconds;	machine-guns in the forward
range 311 miles (500 km)	fuselage
Weights: empty 2,410 lb	

Blériot-SPAD S.510

Developed from the experimental S.91 to meet a French air ministry requirement of 1930 for a new single-seat fighter, the **Blériot-SPAD S.510** was unique among the contenders built to meet the specification in being of biplane configuration.

The **S.510.01** prototype, which made its first flight on 6 January 1933, had an oval-section fuselage built of Dural and steel, the rear section being a Dural monocoque. The equal-span wings were of metal with fabric covering. Sweepback was incorporated in the upper wing only, and ailerons were provided on both the upper and lower wings. An open pilot's cockpit was located immediately below a cut-out in the upper-wing trailing edge. Flight trials led to a lengthening of the fuselage to improve directional and longitudinal stability, and the modification of the ailerons to improve lateral control.

The Dewoitine D.500 low-wing monoplane proved superior to the S.510 in speed, and won the design competition. However, ace pilot Louis Massotte then demonstrated the S.510 to the air minister, showing off the biplane's unsurpassed manoeuvrability and rate of climb. As a result, an order for 60 **S.510C.1** fighters was placed in August 1935, with production aircraft delivered from April 1937.

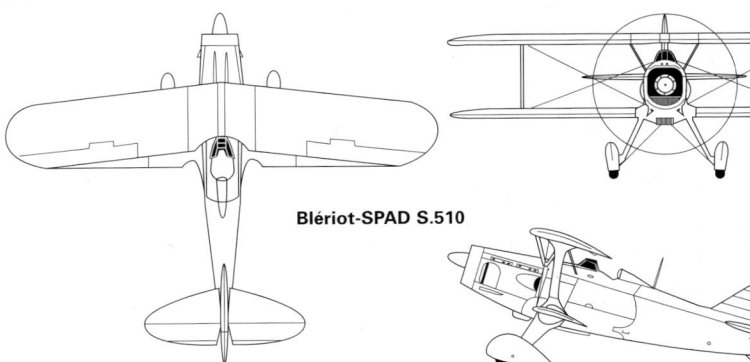

Blériot-SPAD S.510

By the outbreak of World War II the S.510 had been relegated to flying schools and the escadrilles régionales which had been established for target defence of cities and industrial complexes well behind the front line. Little was heard of the aircraft in action, however.

The final Blériot-SPAD fighter design was the **S.710**, of which only a single prototype was built. This was intended to meet the requirements of a 1934 fighter specification and, despite being a biplane in configuration, had many advanced design features, including a 'butterfly' type tail unit, retractable main landing gear units, and an enclosed pilot's cockpit. First flown in April 1937 with the powerplant of one 860-hp (641-kW) Hispano-Suiza 12Ycrs Vee engine for an estimated maximum speed of 292 mph (470 km/h), the S.710 prototype developed tail flutter and crashed on 15 June 1937, killing Massotte. Herbemont subsequently retired from aircraft design.

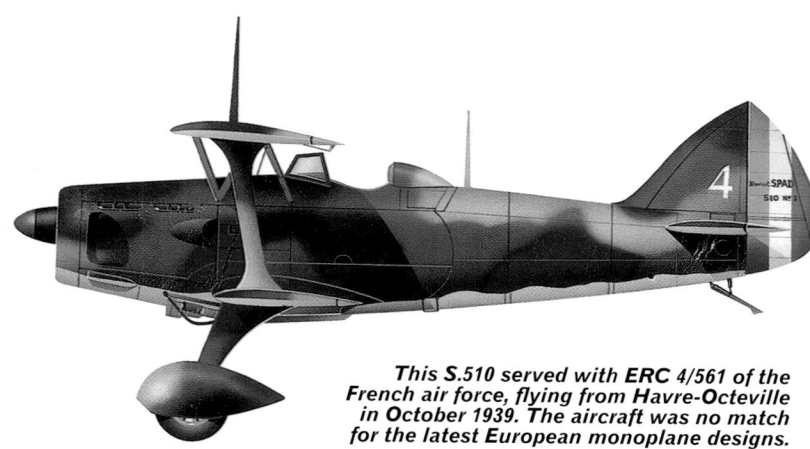

This S.510 served with ERC 4/561 of the French air force, flying from Havre-Octeville in October 1939. The aircraft was no match for the latest European monoplane designs.

SPECIFICATION

Blériot-SPAD S.510C.1
Type: single-seat fighter
Powerplant: one Hispano-Suiza 12Xbrs Vee engine rated at 690 hp (515 kW)
Performance: maximum speed 231 mph (372 km/h) at 13,125 ft (4000 m); climb to 13,125 ft (4000 m) in 4 minutes 31 seconds; service ceiling 34,450 ft (10500 m); range 543 miles (875 km)
Weights: empty 2,756 lb (1250 kg); maximum take-off 4,034 lb (1830 kg)
Dimensions: wingspan 29 ft (8.84 m); length 24 ft 5¾ in (7.46 m); height 12 ft 2½ in (3.72 m); wing area 236.81 sq ft (22.00 m²)
Armament: four 0.295-in (7.5-mm) MAC 1934 fixed forward-firing machine-guns in underwing gondolas

---

Bloch MB.130 and MB.131

Marcel Bloch's small factory at Courbevoie had been created at the time when the fledgling company was concerned mainly with the design and manufacture of lightplanes. Very shortly after settling into its premises, however, the company had the opportunity of creating a reconnaissance-bomber to satisfy a French air ministry BCR (Bombardement, Chasse et Reconnaissance) requirement.

First flown on 29 June 1934, the **Bloch MB.130.01** prototype for a multi-role warplane able to undertake the bomber, heavy (escort) fighter and reconnaissance roles, gained a contract for 40 production aircraft, despite its indifferent performance.

In order to solve the many problems of the MB.130, the company evolved the improved **MB.131**. The MB.130 contract was then amended to cover an equal number of MB.131s. An **MB.131.01** prototype flew for the first time on 16 August 1936 as an all-metal cantilever monoplane of low-wing configuration with a twin-engine powerplant.

The MB.131.01 was also disappointing, so an **MB.131.02** second proto-type was built for a maiden flight on 8 May 1937. This second machine differed by having a wing and tail unit of increased area, and a new fuselage. In this basic form the MB.131 entered production towards the end of 1937 when manufacture had been entrusted to the new nationalised SNCASO (Société Nationale de Constructions Aéronautiques du Sud-Ouest), which consisted of

Six France-based reconnaissance groups and one group stationed in North Africa were flying the MB.131 at the start of World War II. The type was easily outclassed by the Messerschmitt Bf 109 and by British fighters.

the previous Bloch and Blériot concerns.

The initial production version, of which 13 were built, was the **MB.131R.4**, a four-seat reconnaissance type, and there followed five examples of the **MB.131Ins** dual-control trainer version. The major production version was the **MB.131RB.4**, a reconnaissance-bomber evolved from the R.4 with an internal bomb bay and changes in equipment. Some 119 were built, and other variants included one **MB.133** prototype with a revised tail unit, and one **MB.134** prototype with 1,140-hp (850-kW) Gnome-Rhône 14N-48/49 radials.

Deliveries to the Armée de l'Air began in the autumn of 1938, and on the outbreak of World War II, seven reconnaissance groups were MB.131-equipped. It soon became apparent that the type was incapable of making daylight reconnaissance sorties without suffering unacceptable losses. The surviving aircraft were therefore restricted to night operations. At the time of the French collapse in June 1940, the only examples remaining in operational service were those which had been deployed overseas, although a few were subsequently operated in France by the Vichy French air force as target tugs.

SPECIFICATION

Bloch MB.131RB.4
Type: four-seat reconnaissance bomber
Powerplant: two Gnome-Rhône 14N-10/11 radial engines each rated at 950 hp (708 kW)
Performance: maximum speed 217 mph (350 km/h) at 12,300 ft (3750 m); cruising speed 168 mph (270 km/h) at 12,300 ft (3750 m); climb to 13,125 ft (4000 m) in 13 minutes; service ceiling 23,785 ft (7250 m); range 808 miles (1300 km)
Weights: empty 10,340 lb (4690 kg); maximum take-off 18,960 lb (8600 kg)
Dimensions: wingspan 66 ft 7¼ in (20.30 m); length 58 ft 6¾ in (17.85 m); height 13 ft 5½ in (4.10 m); wing area 581.25 sq ft (54.00 m²)
Armament: single 0.295-in (7.5-mm) MAC 1934 trainable machine-guns in the nose position, dorsal turret and ventral cupola, plus up to 1,764 lb (800 kg) of bombs carried internally

---

Bloch MB.150

In July 1934 Avions Marcel Bloch was a contender in a design competition resulting from a French air ministry specification for a new single-seat fighter, which also attracted submissions from Dewoitine, Loire, Morane-Saulnier and Nieuport. The Morane-Saulnier design was eventually selected as the winner, while the **Bloch MB.150.01** proto-type could not be induced to part company with the security of mother earth.

Nothing further happened for about six months until, early in 1937, it was decided to force the 'ugly duckling' into the air. This feat was achieved on 4 May 1937 after the replacement of the original wing and the revision of the main landing gear units as longer-stroke units. The original 930-hp (693-kW) Gnome-Rhône 14Kfs radial engine was then replaced by the 970-hp (723-kW) 14N-07. Further

Revised with a 14N-07 engine, the MB.150 was fitted with a constant-speed propeller. This was driven via a long propeller shaft so that a longer-chord cowling could be installed.

evolution of the prototype resulted in the replacement of the N-07 engine by the 14N-01 geared engine and finally in the adoption of the 1,030-hp (768-kW) 14N-21 engine, as well as a wing increased in span by 4¾ in (0.12 m).

In this form the MB.150 was finally deemed nearly adequate for full evaluation, and an order was placed for 25 pre-production aircraft. It then emerged that a complete structural redesign was required for large-scale production and, in combination with the need for the incorporation of several aerodynamic revisions, this led to the redesignation of the production model as the **Bloch MB.151**.

SPECIFICATION

Bloch MB.150.01
Type: single-seat fighter
Powerplant: one Gnome-Rhône 14N-07 radial engine rated at 970 hp (723 kW)
Performance: maximum speed 270 mph (434 km/h) at 8,530 ft (2600 m)
Weights: empty 3,748 lb (1700 kg); maximum take-off 5,071 lb (2300 kg)
Dimensions: wingspan 32 ft 10½ in (10.02 m); length 30 ft 10 in (9.40 m); height 10 ft 5½ in (3.19 m); wing area 165.77 sq ft (15.40 m²)
Armament: (proposed) two 20-mm Hispano-Suiza HS-404 fixed forward-firing cannon and two 0.295-in (7.5-mm) MAC 1934 fixed forward-firing machine-guns

Bloch MB.151 and MB.152

Revising the MB.150 with a wing of reduced area and a 920-hp (686-kW) Gnome-Rhône 14N-11 unit (later supplanted by the identically rated 14N-35), Bloch produced the **MB.151**. It was in this form that a new prototype, designated as the **Bloch MB.151.01**, flew for the first time on 18 August 1938. Construction of the balance of the pre-production order had already started by then, but only four of these aircraft had been delivered by April 1939.

At the same time the SNCASO design team had been working on an improved version, powered by the 1,030-hp (768-kW) 14N-21. First flown on 15 December 1938, the new MB.152.01 prototype was, in the event, powered by the 1,000-hp (746-kW) 14N-25 engine, and entered flight testing in February 1939. The improved performance of this version led to an initial order for 400 aircraft, of which 60 and 340 were to be completed to the **MB.151C.1** and **MB.152C.1** production standards, respectively.

Orders for the MB.151C.1 eventually reached 144 units. The aircraft were considered generally inferior to the MB.152C.1 and were used mainly for conversion and fighter training.

Production was dreadfully slow, however, and by the outbreak of World War II a combined total of only 120 MB.151C.1 and MB.152C.1 fighters had

been delivered. Even more unfortunately, not one of these could be used in action as all the aircraft lacked their reflector gun sights. Some 95 of them could not be used at all as they had been delivered without propellers. Even by the end of November, at which time 358 aircraft had been delivered, 157 were still without propellers and there were serious problems with engine overheating, which still needed attention.

Despite the problems, the Armée de l'Air did everything possible to speed up the introduction of what was potentially a valuable addition to its inventory. The fighter groups soon realised that their MB.151C.1 and MB.152C.1 fighters were fine warplanes, and it was tragic that indifference and political intrigue forced so many courageous pilots of the Armée de l'Air to lose their lives in obsolete aircraft, instead of being able to fight the Luftwaffe on more equal terms with capable machines such as the MB.152C.1.

Nine MB.151 fighters were supplied to the Greek air force and, after the collapse of France, six groups of the Vichy French air force flew MB.151C.1 and MB.152C.1 aircraft. When SNCASO production ended in May 1940, more than 600 MB.151C.1s and MB.152C.1s (144 and 482 respectively) had been built. When three of these groups were later re-equipped with

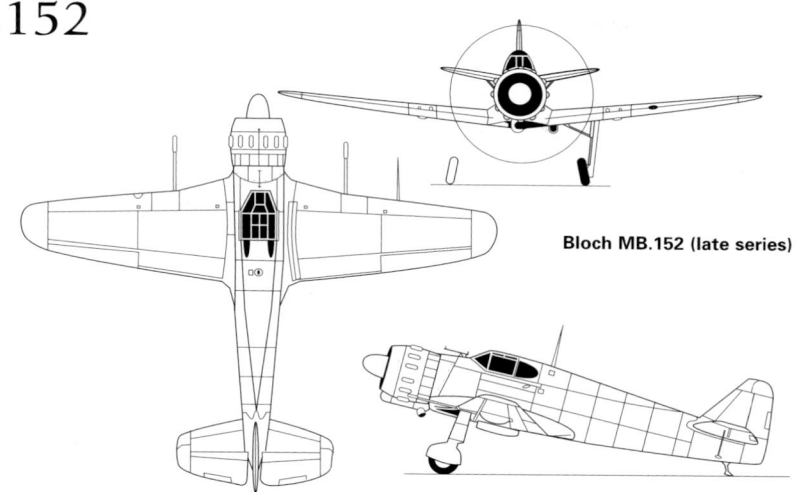

Bloch MB.152 (late series)

Dewoitine fighters, some 20 MB.152C.1 fighters were handed over to the Romanian air force.

The only variant of the basic type to fly was one **MB.153.01** prototype, which was an MB.152 re-engined with a 1,050-hp (783-kW) Pratt & Whitney R-1830-SC3G Twin Wasp

Although the MB.151 proved inferior to the later MB.152C.1, it had a maximum speed of 289 mph (465 km/h) at 16,405 ft (5000 m) and the ability to climb to 3,280 ft (1000 m) in 1 minute 57 seconds.

radial engine. This machine made its maiden flight on 8 April 1939 and was taken on French air force charge late in May 1940. It was lost in a landing accident a

couple of days later. The **MB.154** was a variant proposed with the Wright R-1820-G205A Cyclone radial unit, but no MB.154 was completed.

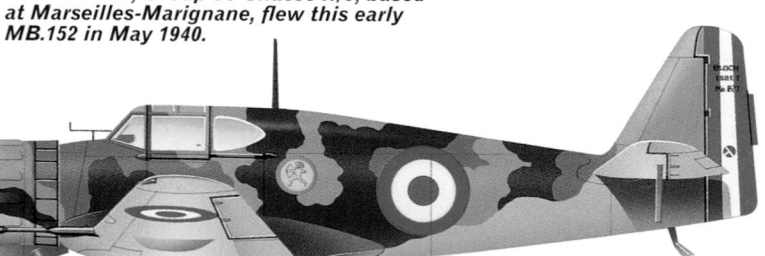

3e Escadrille, Group de Chasse II/9, based at Marseilles-Marignane, flew this early MB.152 in May 1940.

SPECIFICATION	
Bloch MB.152C.1	
Type: single-seat fighter	**Weights:** empty 4,758 lb (2158 kg); maximum take-off 6,173 lb (2800 kg)
Powerplant: one Gnome-Rhône 14N-25 radial engine rated at 1,080 hp (805 kW) or one Gnome-Rhône 14N-49 radial engine rated at 1,100 hp (820 kW)	**Dimensions:** wingspan 34 ft 7 in (10.54 m); length 29 ft 10¼ in (9.10 m); height 9 ft 11⅛ in (3.03 m); wing area 186.43 sq ft (17.32 m²)
Performance: maximum speed 316 mph (509 km/h) at 14,765 ft (4500 m); cruising speed 280 mph (450 km/h) at optimum altitude; climb to 6,560 ft (2000 m) in 3 minutes 24 seconds; service ceiling 32,810 ft (10000 m); range 373 miles (600 km)	**Armament:** two 20-mm Hispano-Suiza HS-404 fixed forward-firing cannon and two 0.295-in (7.5-mm) MAC 1934 fixed forward-firing machine-guns, or four 0.295-in (7.5-mm) MAC 1934 fixed forward-firing machine-guns

Bloch MB.155

SPECIFICATION	
Bloch MB.155C.1	6,393 lb (2900 kg)
Type: single-seat fighter	**Dimensions:** wingspan 34 ft 7 in (10.54 m); length 29 ft 8⅛ in (9.05 m); height 10 ft 6 in (3.21 m); wing area 186.43 sq ft (17.32 m²)
Powerplant: one Gnome-Rhône 14N-49 radial engine rated at 1,100 hp (820 kW)	**Armament:** two 20-mm Hispano-Suiza HS-404 fixed forward-firing cannon and two or four 0.295-in (7.5-mm) MAC 1934 fixed forward-firing machine-guns, or six 0.295-in (7.5-mm) MAC 1934 fixed forward-firing machine-guns
Performance: maximum speed 323 mph (520 km/h) at 14,765 ft (4500 m); climb to 13,125 ft (4000 m) in 6 minutes 55 seconds; service ceiling 32,810 ft (10000 m); range 652 miles (1050 km)	
Weights: empty 4,718 lb (2140 kg); maximum take-off	

With production of the MB.151 and MB.152 in progress, the SNCASO design team began the development of an improved version, for both company and official testing of the MB.152 fighter had left little doubt that the basic design had considerable potential.

Once again pressure of circumstance was to prevent any really significant improvement except in range, for the aim was to utilise most of the jigs and

France's desperate wartime situation denied the MB.155 any real chance of demonstrating its potential as a truly capable fighter.

tooling created for the MB.152. In this way, production could begin without extensive delays, a factor of some importance by late 1939. Providing extra fuel capacity required an extensive fuselage redesign to move the cockpit farther aft. In other respects the basic configuration remained unchanged.

Other modifications introduced in the **Bloch MB.155.01** prototype, which was produced as an MB.152 conversion and first flew on 3 December 1939, included increased wing chord and an improved lower-drag engine cowling. Following successful flight tests early in 1940, the type was put into production at the beginning of May under the designation **MB.155C.1**. Additional improvements on the production aircraft included extra armour and an armoured windscreen. Unfortunately, the French capitulation of 25 June came before any of the new fighters, of which 10 had been completed, had been delivered. Subsequently, after ratification of the French-German armistice, the MB.155C.1 fighters, of which 19 remained on the production line, were completed and delivered to the Vichy French air force. When, in November 1942, the Vichy French forces were disbanded, all remaining MB.155s were seized by the Germans.

Bloch MB.157

Representing the last of the fighter aircraft evolved directly from the MB.150, the **Bloch MB.157** combined the airframe of the MB.152 with a new and far more powerful Gnome-Rhône 14R, with a power output of 1,590 hp (1186 kW) for take-off, and possessing a supercharger that could provide a rating of 1,700 hp (1268 kW) at 26,245 ft (8000 m).

Unfortunately, the increased size and weight of the engine meant that the basic MB.152 airframe could not be modified, the company deciding to design a new fighter which would retain the same basic structural concepts and techniques.

Having postulated such a design philosophy, it was possible to formulate the details of the MB.157 very rapidly, for the basic design already existed. The result of this was that within just over six months of design initiation, the components of the prototype were ready for assembly. With German forces closing on

Paris, the components were loaded to be taken to a place of security, but the vehicle was intercepted by the Germans and ordered to proceed to an SNCASO establishment within the occupied zone.

The MB.157 was later assembled and, finally, in March 1942, made its maiden flight under German supervision, demonstrating superb performance before being flown to Orly where the

Potentially the best fighter produced by France in World War II, the MB.157 offered superb combat capability and had the potential for great reliability. The prototype was extensively tested by the Luftwaffe after its components were captured by advancing German forces in 1940.

powerplant was removed for wind-tunnel testing. This was the most interesting feature of the fighter as far as the Germans were concerned and, after tests had been completed, the engine was transported to Germany. SNCASO's airframe which, in conjunction with the Gnome-Rhône 14R engine, had demonstrated a degree of performance that was not to be attained elsewhere until later in World War II, was destroyed during an Allied air raid.

SPECIFICATION	
Bloch MB.157	(2388 kg); normal take-off 7,165 lb (3250 kg)
Type: single-seat fighter	**Dimensions:** wingspan 35 ft 1¼ in (10.70 m); length 30 ft ¼ in (9.15 m); height 14 ft 1¼ in (4.30 m); wing area 208.82 sq ft (19.40 m²)
Powerplant: one Gnome-Rhône 14R-4 radial engine rated at 1,590 hp (1186 kW)	
Performance: maximum speed 441 mph (710 km/h) at 25,755 ft (7850 m); cruising speed 248 mph (400 km/h); climb to 26,245 ft (8000 m) in 11 minutes; range 680 miles (1095 km)	**Armament:** (proposed) two 20-mm Hispano-Suiza HS-404 fixed forward-firing cannon and four 0.295-in (7.5-mm) MAC 1934 fixed forward-firing machine-guns
Weights: empty 5,265 lb	

Bloch MB.174

Late in 1936 the SNCASO initiated the design of a two/three-seat multi-role bomber which it identified as the **MB.170**, and the **MB.170.01** prototype flew for the first time on 15 February 1938. This was a monoplane of low-wing cantilever layout and was powered by two 950-hp (708-kW) Gnome-Rhône 14N-06/07 radial engines. The prototype featured an unusual cupola, beneath the fuselage, for the carriage of a camera in the reconnaissance role or alternatively to provide an additional position for a defensive gun. When the MB.170.01 prototype was damaged as the result of a crash landing, the flight test programme was taken up by a second, but rather different **MB.170.02** prototype that was configured mainly for the high-speed bomber role; the under-fuselage cupola was deleted, the undersurface of the forward fuselage was extensively glazed, and the tail unit carried fins of increased area.

Pictured below is an MB.174A.3 of the Groupe de Reconnaissance II/33 of the Vichy-controlled Armée de l'Air based at Tunis-El Aouina. The 2e Escadrille retained the MB.174 until June 1943.

While this programme had been in progress, the design team had evolved a series of variants for differing roles, and allocated them the identifications **MB.171**, **MB.172**, **MB.173** and **MB.174**. An **MB.174.01** prototype was flown for the first time on 5 January 1939, and differed yet again – the crew accommodation and glazed canopy were moved farther aft, the fuselage nose was extensively glazed, and it was fitted with two 1,030-hp (768-kW) 14N-20/21 engines. Six pre-production examples were ordered, followed by an additional order for 50 production aircraft.

The pre-production and production aircraft all had more powerful 14N-48/49 engines, but early testing of the first pre-production aircraft showed that engine cooling was only marginal, leading to a reduction in the diameter of the propeller spinners to allow an increased airflow to the engine cylinders. Just before the first examples were delivered to service units, it was decided to modify the defensive armament as a result of early combat experience with other types, and it was not until mid-March 1940 that the first **MB.174A.3** production aircraft were delivered, and were used operationally for the first time on 29 March 1940.

Early operational experience with these aircraft proved them to be first-class reconnaissance machines, with sufficient speed and manoeuvrability at altitude to be able to elude Luftwaffe interceptors. When the collapse of France was imminent, many of the MB.174A.3 aircraft were destroyed by their operating units to prevent their capture, but despite this fact, a number remained in service with the French air force (first Vichy French and then Free French) in Tunisia until after VE-Day in May 1945. Additionally, isolated examples were used for development projects for two or three years after the war's end.

SPECIFICATION	
Bloch MB.174A.3	**Dimensions:** wingspan 58 ft 8½ in (17.90 m); length 40 ft 2½ in (12.25 m); height 11 ft 7¾ in (3.55 m); wing area 409.03 sq ft (38.00 m²)
Type: three-seat reconnaissance and light bomber aircraft	
Powerplant: two Gnome-Rhône 14N-48/49 radial piston engines each rated at 1,100 hp (820 kW)	
Performance: maximum speed 329 mph (530 km/h) at 17,060 ft (5200 m); cruising speed 248 mph (400 km/h) at 13,125 ft (4000 m); climb to 26,245 ft (8000 m) in 11 minutes; service ceiling 36,090 ft (11000 m); range 1,025 miles (1650 km)	**Armament:** two 0.295-in (7.5-mm) MAC 1934 fixed forward-firing machine-guns in the leading edge of the wing, two 0.295-in (7.5-mm) MAC 1934 trainable rearward-firing machine-guns in the dorsal position, and three 0.295-in (7.5-mm) MAC 1934 trainable rearward-firing machine-guns on ventral wobble mounts, plus up to 1,102 lb (500 kg) of bombs
Weights: empty 12,346 lb (5600 kg); maximum take-off 15,784 lb (7160 kg)	

Bloch MB.175

The **MB.175** was developed as an improved version of the MB.174 for the light bomber and attack bomber roles.

The primary change involved the provision of a larger bomb bay. It was a problem easy to identify but difficult to solve, for the length of the MB.174's bomb bay was determined by the position of the wing spars, which continued through the fuselage. Evolution of the new version thus entailed the design of an entirely new wing centre-section, to increase the gap between the spars. In other respects the **Bloch MB.175.01** prototype, first flown in December 1939, differed little from its predecessor. Testing showed that the MB.175 retained the excellent performance and flying characteristics of the MB.174, and the type was immediately put into production to meet outstanding orders for more than 1,100 aircraft.

While the development of the MB.175 was progressing, SNCASO had also been working on the installation of the revised powerplant of two 1,050-hp (783-kW) Pratt & Whitney R-1830-SC3G Twin Wasp radial engines in an MB.174 airframe, with a view to easing the pressure on the hard-pressed French aero engine manufacturing capability. The resulting **MB.176.01** prototype was flown before the MB.175.01, in September 1939, but testing revealed a considerable fall-off in performance. Nevertheless, it was decided that this version should also go into production, but utilising the new MB.175 airframe. Thus the first production examples of these new aircraft, the **MB.175B.3** and **MB.176B.3**, initially flew in April and May 1940 respectively, but only 23 of the former and five of the latter had been completed when production was terminated on 25 June 1940, with the fall of France.

Approximately 200 airframes remained on the production lines, and a large proportion of the components for an additional batch of 200 had been manufactured. The occupying Germans then tested the MB.175, and authorised the completion of those on the line, but without armament. In fact only 56 aircraft were completed and dispatched to Germany for use as operational trainers. No further production of the MB.175 took place until after the end of World War II, when a total of 80 **MB.175T** torpedo-bombers was built for supply to the Aéronavale.

Completion of MB.175 aircraft for use as Luftwaffe trainers had ended after the seizure of all remaining Gnome-Rhône engines by the Germans. This led to the installation of two 830-hp (619-kW) Hispano-Suiza 12Y-31 Vee engines in an MB.175 airframe to create the **MB.177**. The new variant's abysmal performance, however, meant that only the one prototype was completed.

The MB.175B.3 entered service first with the Groupe de Reconnaissance II/52 in May 1940, and the aircraft of this group, plus additional MB.175s and one MB.176, were subsequently flown to North Africa, the majority being destroyed during an Allied ground attack on Oran-La Sénia in November 1942.

As French forces were forced out of their home country by the invading Germans, a number of units took their aircraft to North Africa. Several brand-new MB.175s, including the aircraft above, were included in this number.

SPECIFICATION	
Bloch MB.175B.3	
Type: three-seat light bomber	10¾ in (17.95 m); length 40 ft 9¼ in
Powerplant: two Gnome-Rhône 14N-48/44 radial engines each rated at 1,140 hp (850 kW)	(12.43 m); height 11 ft 7¾ in (3.55 m); wing area 413.29 sq ft (38.39 m²)
Performance: maximum speed 335 mph (540 km/h) at 17,060 ft (5200 m); cruising speed 245 mph (395 km/h) at 13,125 ft (4000 m); climb to 26,245 ft (8000 m) in 13 minutes 30 seconds; range 994 miles (1600 km)	**Armament:** two 0.295-in (7.5-mm) MAC 1934 fixed forward-firing machine-guns in the leading edge of the wing, two 0.295-in (7.5-mm) MAC 1934 trainable rearward-firing machine-guns in the dorsal position, and three 0.295-in
Weights: empty 12,478 lb (5660 kg); maximum take-off 17,688 lb (8023 kg)	(7.5-mm) MAC 1934 trainable rearward-firing machine-guns on wobble mounts in the ventral position, plus up to 1,323 lb
Dimensions: wingspan 58 ft	(600 kg) of bombs carried internally

Bloch MB.200

When, in 1932, the French air ministry circulated its specification for a five-seat night bomber, five companies submitted no fewer than eight proposals. Bloch and Farman were successful, although the resulting production aircraft were completed in differing bomber categories.

The Bloch type was finalised as a four-seat bomber, with a configuration and general appearance very similar to those of the Bristol Bombay and Handley Page Harrow. A high-wing cantilever monoplane of all-metal construction with fixed tailwheel landing gear, the **Bloch** **MB.200.01** prototype had the powerplant of two 760-hp (567-kW) Gnome-Rhône 14Krsd radial engines and was first flown in July 1933. An initial order for 25 aircraft was placed in January 1934, despite the fact that the prototype's maximum speed was 18 per cent below estimate.

When the **MB.200B.4** production type began to enter service towards the end of the year, it was found to be both reliable and viceless. The fact that it was dreadfully slow, even though production aircraft had more powerful Gnome-Rhône engines, was not then considered a matter of

These MB.200s of 2e Escadrille GB I/23 demonstrate the type's ungainly appearance. The MB.200 saw its last combat action during June 1941 in fighting between Vichy French and Allied forces in Syria. On 9 June, two MB.200s were shot down by RAF Hurricanes from No. 80 Sqn.

vital importance, and 208 such aircraft were eventually supplied to the Armée de l'Air from production by Bloch (4), Breguet (19), Hanriot (45), Loire (19), Potez (111) and SNCASO (10).

At the beginning of World War II seven front-line groupes de bombardement were still equipped with these obsolete aircraft but, at the time of the German offensive in May 1940, all had been relegated to the training role. The type had also been built under licence in Czechoslovakia, to the extent of 124 aircraft, by Aero and Avia and, in common with those captured in France, these were seized by the Germans, serving as crew trainers and for general duties. Many were passed on to German satellites.

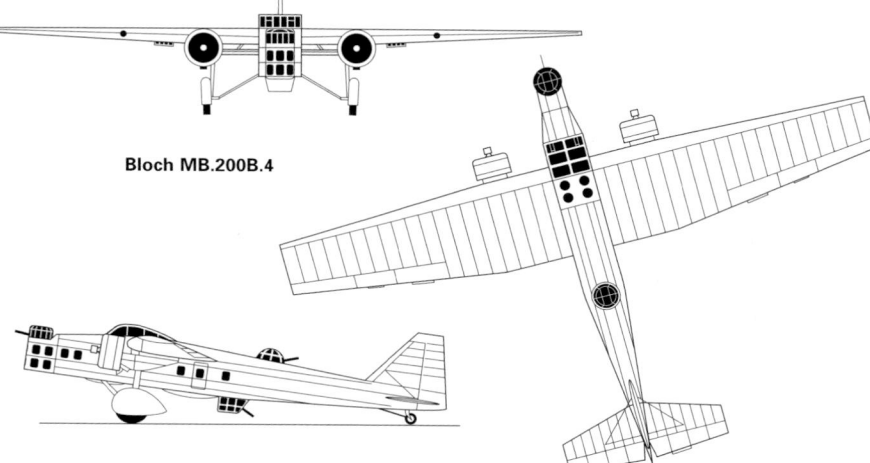

Bloch MB.200B.4

This Bloch MB.200 was marked No. 77 and served with l'Armée de l'Air's Section de Remorquage d'Otange in May 1940.

SPECIFICATION

Bloch MB.200B.4
Type: four-seat medium bomber
Powerplant: two Gnome-Rhône 14Kirs/Kjrs radial engines each rated at 870 hp (649 kW)
Performance: maximum speed 177 mph (285 km/h) at 14,110 ft (4300 m); climb to 19,685 ft (6000 m) in 23 minutes 6 seconds; service ceiling 26,245 ft (8000 m); range 621 miles (1000 km)
Weights: empty 9,840 lb

(4463 kg); maximum take-off 16,490 lb (7480 kg)
Dimensions: wingspan 73 ft 8 in (22.45 m); length 52 ft 6 in (16.00 m); height 12 ft 9½ in (3.90 m); wing area 721.18 sq ft (67.00 m²)
Armament: single 0.295-in (7.5-mm) MAC 1934 trainable machine-guns in the nose, dorsal and ventral positions, plus up to 2,646 lb (1200 kg) of bombs

Bloch MB.210

Although developed from the MB.200, the **Bloch MB.210** was in general appearance a very different machine. This was due to its switch to a cantilever monoplane wing in the low-rather than high-set position, and its introduction of retractable main landing gear units. Built as a private venture, the **MB.210.01** prototype was flown for the first time on 23 November 1934. The powerplant comprised two 800-hp (596-kW) Gnome-Rhône 14Kdrs/Kgrs radials. For comparative purposes, a second prototype was completed as the **MB.211.01** with two 860-hp (641-kW) Hispano-Suiza 12Y Vee engines, but this machine was not flown until 29 August 1935. Flight testing proved that the original engine installation was superior, with the result that no further examples of the MB.211 were built.

The MB.210.01 prototype had been built with fixed landing gear, but the first example of the **MB.210Bn.4** production model had the intended retractable main units and 870-hp (649-kW) 14Kirs/Kjrs engines. When first

flown on 12 December 1935, the second production example introduced increased dihedral on the outer wing panels and these wings were incorporated as standard on subsequent production aircraft. One more change came before the definitive model was realised, this resulting from the translation of the type from the Bn.4 to **Bn.5 (Bombardement, Nuit cinq-place**, or five-seat night bomber) category, and the first of these Hanriot-built bombers flew in November 1936.

Contracts were eventually placed for 257 production aircraft, with the MB.210 entering service from late in 1936, but squadron use showed that the engines were prone to overheating. All aircraft then in service were grounded pending installation of 14N-10/11 engines, which became the standard powerplant.

On the outbreak of World War II, 12 groupes de bombardement were equipped with the MB.210, but the type's best possible maximum speed of around 200 mph

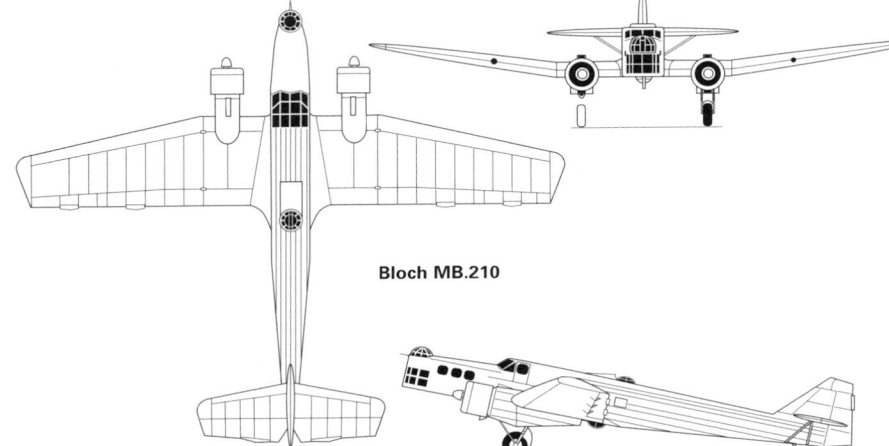

Bloch MB.210

(322 km/h) meant that it could be regarded as little more than a sitting target for Luftwaffe fighters. However, the slow receipt of more advanced aircraft meant that the type's relegation to a training role was nowhere near complete when the German campaign against France began on 10 May 1940. Thus, nine bomber groupes still included these obsolete aircraft among

their numbers, and these machines were used to make night attacks on German targets before all surviving airworthy aircraft were flown to North Africa on 17 June 1940.

Mention should be made of the MB.210.01 prototype which, fitted with

twin float alighting gear, was delivered to the Aéronavale for evaluation as a torpedo-bomber, a role in which the type failed to win a production contract. In addition, 24 MB.210 bombers were built for Romania, delivery being completed by mid-1938.

MB.210 production contracts were placed with ANF Les Mureaux (20), Bloch (25), Breguet (16), Hanriot (50), Potez-CAMS (35), Renault (35) and the nationalised SNCAC/SNCAO/SNCASO groups (76).

SPECIFICATION

Bloch MB.210Bn.5
Type: five-seat night bomber
Powerplant: two Gnome-Rhône 14N-10/11 radial engines each rated at 910 hp (679 kW)
Performance: maximum speed 199 mph (320 km/h) at 11,480 ft (3500 m); cruising speed 149 mph (240 km/h) at 11,480 ft (3500 m); climb to 13,125 ft (4000 m) in 12 minutes; service ceiling 32,480 ft (9900 m); range 1,056 miles (1700 km)
Weights: empty 14,109 lb

(6400 kg); maximum take-off 22,487 lb (10200 kg)
Dimensions: wingspan 74 ft 9½ in (22.80 m); length 62 ft (18.90 m); height 21 ft 11¾ in (6.69 m); wing area 672.76 sq ft (62.50 m²)
Armament: single 0.295-in (7.5-mm) MAC 1934 trainable machine-guns in the nose position and the retractable dorsal and ventral turrets, plus up to 3,527 lb (1600 kg) of bombs carried internally

Bloch MB.220 and MB.221

SPECIFICATION

Bloch MB.220
Type: four-crew transport aircraft
Powerplant: two Gnome-Rhône 14N-16/17 radial engines each rated at 985 hp (734 kW)
Performance: maximum speed 205 mph (330 km/h) at optimum altitude; cruising speed 174 mph (280 km/h) at optimum altitude; service ceiling 22,965 ft (7000 m);

range 870 miles (1400 km)
Weights: empty 15,007 lb (6807 kg); maximum take-off 20,944 lb (9500 kg)
Dimensions: wingspan 74 ft 10½ in (22.82 m); length 63 ft 1¾ in (19.25 m); wing area 807.29 sq ft (75.00 m²)
Payload: up to 16 passengers

As an all-metal low-wing cantilever monoplane with the powerplant of two Gnome-Rhône radial engines and fitted with retractable landing gear, the **Bloch MB.220** was the French equivalent of the American Douglas DC-2 and DC-3. It was, however, produced in only very limited quantities.

The first service by the MB.220 was flown on the Paris-London route on 27 March 1938. The scheduled time for the flight was cut to 1 hour 15 minutes with the new aircraft.

Bloch MB.220 and MB.221 (continued)

The prototype MB.220 flew in December 1935, followed by 16 production aircraft. Four crew could be accommodated, as well as 16 passengers on eight seats to each side of a central aisle. Cabin entry was gained via a door to port.

By mid-1938 some 10 MB.220s had been delivered, and the type was being utilised fully on Air France's European route network.

During World War II most of the MB.220s were initially mobilised for service with the Armée de l'Air's military transport units although examples were later operated in Deutsche Lufthansa, Free French and Vichy French colours in Europe, North Africa and the Middle East. At least five examples survived the war, being modified to **MB.221** standard with Wright R-1820-97 Cyclone radial engines. The MB.221s flew on Air France's short-range European routes, but by 1949 four had been sold off to Société Auxiliare de Navigation Aérienne and within about a year all had been retired.

Bloch MB.480

In August 1935 the French air ministry issued a requirement for a combat floatplane able to undertake the torpedo, bombing and reconnaissance roles and nearly every French aircraft manufacturer responded. Like Lioré-et-Olivier, Bloch took its inspiration from an existing bomber, in this case the MB.131. Bloch therefore began work on what became the **Bloch MB.480** twin-float type with a low-set cantilever wing and a high-set tail unit with endplate vertical surfaces. The Bloch contender was later than

Neither the MB.480.01 (illustrated) nor the MB.480.02 saw any operational service. One aircraft was destroyed when it collided with a pier.

other designs, and just two examples were ordered in May 1937.

The **MB.480.01** and **MB.480.02** first and second prototypes made their maiden flights in June and October 1939 respectively, and as a result of early trials the tail unit was raised to keep it clear of spray, and was also fitted with bracing struts to prevent flutter. The higher position of the tail unit limited the field of fire for the 20-mm cannon in the dorsal turret, and so the upper parts of the fins were considerably reduced in area.

The worsening international situation then persuaded the French navy that the MB.480's role could be better performed by landplanes such as the Lioré-et-Olivier LeO 451 and Martin Model 167, and further development of the aircraft was cancelled in December 1939.

SPECIFICATION	
Bloch MB.480	**Dimensions:** wingspan 77 ft 1⅛ in (13.50 m); length 62 ft 8 in (19.10 m); height 15 ft 1 in (4.60 m); wing area 884.79 sq ft (82.20 m²)
Type: four/five-seat reconnaissance, bomber and torpedo floatplane	
Powerplant: two Gnome-Rhône 14N-02/03 radial engines each rated at 1,060 hp (790 kW)	**Armament:** one 20-mm Hispano-Suiza HS-404 trainable rearward-firing cannon in the dorsal turret, and single 0.295-in (7.5-mm) Darne trainable machine-guns in the nose and ventral positions, plus up to 2,712 lb (1230 kg) of bombs or two 15¾-in (400-mm) torpedoes each weighing 1,477 lb (670 kg)
Performance: maximum speed 205 mph (330 km/h) at 4,920 ft (1500 m); cruising speed 174 mph (280 km/h) at optimum altitude; service ceiling 23,290 ft (7100 m); range 1,240 miles (1995 km)	
Weights: empty 15,476 lb (7020 kg); maximum take-off 26,455 lb (12000 kg)	

Bloch MB.700

In 1936 the French air ministry was becoming increasingly concerned about the apparent inability of the French aircraft manufacturing industry to create and build advanced monoplane fighters. In an effort to break this cycle of non-performance, which threatened the ability of France to protect itself from bomber attack, the air ministry issued a 1936 requirement for a lightweight fighter of wooden construction in a programme that echoed

The MB.700's close engine cowling and large spinner left only a small annular slot for the entry of cooling air.

the 'Jockey' lightweight fighter programme of the 1920s. As such, it was designed to create a fast-climbing home defence fighter capable of quick and simple construction.

The three fighter prototypes to emerge from this requirement were the Arsenal VG-30, **Bloch MB.700** and Caudron C.713. The Bloch contender was designed by André Herbemont of the Blériot-SPAD organisation that, on 1 January 1937, was absorbed into the newly created nationalised SNCASO (Société Nationale des Constructions Aéronautiques du Sud-Ouest) under the leadership of Marcel Bloch. The MB.700 was of largely wooden construction under a stressed plywood skin, and in configuration was a conventional low-wing cantilever monoplane.

No details of the type's career have survived, and the sole prototype was captured at Buc by the invading Germans in June 1940 and subsequently destroyed.

SPECIFICATION	
Bloch MB.700	**Dimensions:** wingspan 29 ft 1⅓ in (8.90 m); length 24 ft 1 in (7.34 m); height 11 ft 1¾ in (3.40 m); wing area 133.47 sq ft (12.40 m²)
Type: single-seat fighter	
Powerplant: one Gnome-Rhône 14N-06 radial engine rated at 700 hp (522 kW)	**Armament:** (proposed) two 20-mm Hispano-Suiza HS-404 fixed forward-firing cannon and two 0.295-in (7.5-mm) MAC 1934 fixed forward-firing machine-guns
Performance: maximum speed 342 mph (550 km/h) at optimum altitude; endurance 2 hours	
Weights: maximum take-off 4,078 lb (1850 kg)	

Blohm und Voss BV 40

In July 1933 the Blohm und Voss shipbuilding company of Hamburg established an aircraft manufacturing subsidiary as the Hamburger Flugzeugbau GmbH. In September 1937, however, this was absorbed into the parent group as the Schiffswerft Blohm und Voss, Abteilung Flugzeugbau. This change of organisation meant that aircraft designed up to and after September 1937 had the prefixes 'Ha' and 'BV', respectively.

Born of the necessity both to conserve strategic materials and to provide a gun platform of minimal frontal area for attacks on heavily armed Allied bombers, the **Blohm und Voss BV 40,** designed by Dr-Ing. Richard Vogt, was one of several designs submitted to the German air ministry in 1943. The elimination of the engine, it was argued, would provide

Piloting the BV 40 was accomplished in a prone position. Tests suggested that a dive speed of 560 mph (900 km/h) could be reached, although the ailerons would have been ineffective at this speed due to flutter.

a minimal cross-section, making an attacking fighter almost invisible from a head-on position, certainly until it was close enough to open fire with its own potent armament.

The result, therefore, was a glider fighter armed with two 30-mm cannon, one in each wingroot. The aircraft incorporated a heavily armoured cockpit section, a metal centre fuselage and wooden rear fuselage, wings and tail surfaces. The twin-wheel landing gear was jettisoned on take-off, a semi-retractable skid being provided for landing. The structure was comparatively simple, facilitating manufacture by craftsmen inexperienced in aircraft construction. A further advantage was an apparent requirement for little more than glider training for the single pilot.

The BV 40 was to be towed to altitude, either singly or in pairs, by a Messerschmitt Bf 109G fighter, the object being to attain a position above and ahead of the approaching bomber stream which would be attacked in a head-on 20° dive, this initial cannon attack being followed up by a secondary attack with a small explosive device suspended from the BV 40 on a wire cable. The use of the latter weapon necessitated the deletion of one of the cannon, however, and the idea was abandoned.

Nineteen prototypes and 200 production examples of the BV 40 were ordered, and the **BV 40 V1** first prototype made its maiden flight behind a Messerschmitt Bf 110 at the end of May 1944. Six prototypes took part in the test programme, which was almost complete when the project was abandoned in the autumn of 1944.

Blohm und Voss Ha 135

The first aircraft designed by the Hamburger Flugzeugbau was the **Ha 135**, created under the initial supervision of Reinhold Mewes before his departure to Fieseler. The unremarkable Ha 135 was a primary flying trainer of equal-span biplane layout, offering tandem accommodation for the pupil and instructor in open cockpits. First flown in the late spring of 1934, the prototype was the only example to be completed and was of mixed metal and wood structure, covered largely with fabric.

Key features of the Ha 135 were its staggered single-bay wing cellule, sturdy main landing gear and radial engine.

Blohm und Voss Ha 136 and Ha 137

The successor to Reinhold Mewes as Hamburger Flugzeugbau's chief designer was Dr-Ing. Richard Vogt, who had previously been chief designer at Kawasaki in Japan. Vogt's first new design was the **Ha 136** advanced flying trainer, which was a small low-wing cantilever monoplane of all-metal construction, with open single-seat accommodation.

Two prototypes of the Ha 136 were built for flight trials in 1934. The **Ha 136A** was powered by one 160-hp (119-kW) BMW-Bramo Sh.14A radial engine, while the **Ha 136B** featured a 135-hp (101-kW) Argus As 8R air-cooled inverted inline. Neither of the variants was accepted for production.

Much of the design philosophy of the Ha 136 was retained in the **Ha 137**, which also used the novel type of spar Vogt had developed for Kawasaki. This spar was of tapered cylindrical section and of welded steel and Dural construction to provide great strength and, as it was sealed, it could addi-tionally serve as the main fuel tankage.

The Ha 137 was schemed as a single-seat dive-bomber. In overall layout it was a low-wing cantilever monoplane based ultimately on the Kawasaki Ki-5 and thus characterised by open accommodation, faired landing gear units and all-metal construction. The **Ha 137 V1** first prototype made the type's maiden flight in April 1935, and was soon followed by the basically similar **Ha 137 V2** second prototype: both of these aircraft were powered by the 720-hp (537-kW) BMW 132A-3 (licence-built Pratt & Whitney Hornet) radial engine. As the aircraft were being completed, however, the German air ministry decided that it preferred a two-seat config-uration for the dive-bomber, so that a means of rear defence could be provided. Development of the Ha 137 was continued, however, as an insurance against the failure of the definitive dive-bomber prototypes and also as a possible attack fighter.

The Ha 137 V1 and V2 had been envisaged as the precursors of a possible **Ha 137A** production model, but the **Ha 137 V3** third prototype was completed as the first step toward a possible **Ha 137B** produc-tion model with a liquid-cooled powerplant, and was thus evaluated with one 640-hp (477-kW) Rolls-Royce Kestrel V Vee engine. The **Ha 137 V4**, **V5** and **V6** switched to a German Vee engine, the Junkers Jumo 210Aa.

In the event the dive-bomber order went to the Junkers Ju 87 and the attack fighter order to the Henschel Hs 123, and development of the Ha 137 ended. The existing aircraft were maintained in flying condition as testbeds for a number of experimental tasks, including test firings of RZ 65 air-to-air rockets.

The Ha 137's main spar was installed in the thickest part of the wing and naturally conformed to the wing's front elevation. The latter was of inverted gull shape to reduce the length of the main units of the fixed tailwheel landing gear.

Blohm und Voss BV 138

The first flying-boat design built by the Hamburger Flugzeugbau, was the **Ha 138**. The three prototypes of the original twin-engined design were each to have been powered by a different manufacturer's 1,000-hp (746-kW) engine for comparative evaluation, but development delays necessitated revision of the basic design to accept three 650-hp (485-kW) Junkers Jumo 205C Diesel engines. Almost two years after the completion of the mock-up, the **Ha 138 V1** first prototype lifted off on its maiden flight on 15 July 1937. The **Ha 138 V2** second prototype, with a modified hull

design, joined the test programme in November, but the two machines were soon found to be unstable in both hydrodynamic and aerodynamic terms. Modifications to the vertical tail surfaces failed to improve the performance adequately, and radical redesign was therefore undertaken. The result was the **BV 138A** in the designation system adopted after the absorption of the Hamburger Flugzeugbau into the Blohm und Voss parent company. The hull was much enlarged, its planing surfaces were improved, and the revised tail surfaces were carried by more substantial booms.

The prototype was followed by five more **BV 138A** pre-production 'boats, preceding production for the reconnaissance units of the Luftwaffe. It was with the Luftwaffe that the type first saw action during the Norwegian campaign of 1940, flying in supplies to support the invasion.

Above: 3./SAGr 125 operated this BV 138C-1 from its base at Constanza, Romania. As one of the final units to fly the BV 138, on 1 May 1945 one of 3./SAGr 125's aircraft was tasked with the collection of couriers carrying Hitler's will, but the pilot refused to embark the men due to their lack of identification and instead evacuated ten wounded soldiers.

Below: The distinctive fuselage shape of the BV 138 led to the popular nickname 'Die fliegende Holzschuh' (the flying clog).

SPECIFICATION

Blohm und Voss BV 138C-1
Type: five-seat maritime reconnaissance flying boat
Powerplant: three Junkers Jumo 205D vertically-opposed Diesel engines each rated at 880 hp (656 kW)
Performance: maximum speed 171 mph (275 km/h) at sea level; cruising speed 146 mph (235 km/h) at 3,280 ft (1000 m); climb to 10,390 ft (3165 m) in 24 minutes; service ceiling 16,405 ft (5000 m); range 3,107 miles (5000 km)
Weights: empty 17,857 lb (8100 kg); maximum take-off 32,408 lb (14700 kg)

Dimensions: wingspan 88 ft 7 in (27.00 m); length 65 ft 3½ in (19.90 m); height 21 ft 8 in (6.60 m), wing area 1,204.60 sq ft (112.00 m²)
Armament: single 20-mm MG 151 trainable cannon in the bow turret and in the rear hull position, and one 0.51-in (13-mm) MG 131 trainable machine-gun in the position at the rear of the central engine nacelle, plus three 110-lb (50-kg) bombs under the starboard wingroot, or (**BV 138C-1/U1**) six 110-lb (50-kg) bombs or four 331-lb (150-kg) depth charges

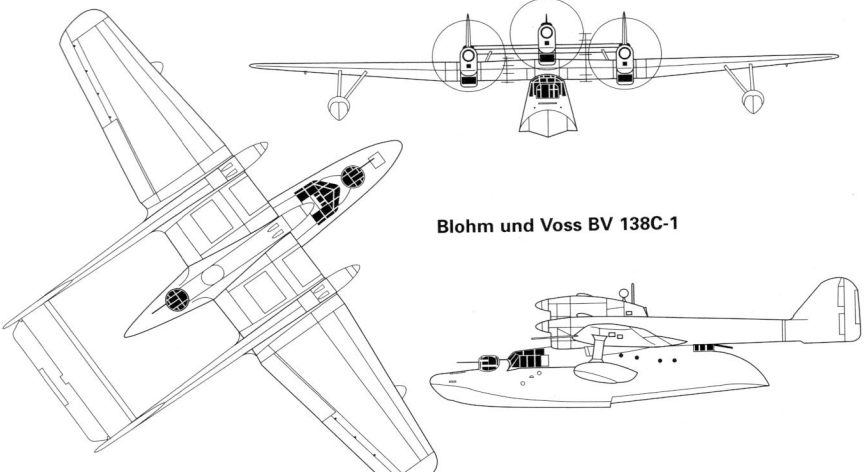

Blohm und Voss BV 138C-1

Variants

BV 138A-1: initial production version, first flown in April 1940. Total of 25 built with the armament of one 20-mm trainable cannon in the bow turret and two 0.312-in (7.92-mm) MG 15 trainable machine-guns, one in each of two open positions located behind the central engine nacelle and at the rear of the hull
BV 138B-1: structurally strengthened version developed following modification of the fourth BV 138A pre-production 'boat into the **BV 138B-0**. Total of 19 built, powered by three Jumo 205D engines and armed with a single 20-mm MG 151 trainable cannon in the bow turret and in the rear hull position as well as 331 lb (150 kg) of bombs beneath the starboard wingroot
BV 138C-1: further strengthened version introduced in March 1941 and built into 1943 to the extent of 227 'boats. Standard powerplant was three Jumo 205D engines (the central engine driving a four-bladed propeller and the two outer engines retaining three-bladed units). A 0.51-in (13-mm) MG 131 trainable machine-gun was added in the position behind the central engine nacelle
BV 138 MS (Minensuche, mine-search): minesweeping version converted from BV 138B-0 pre-production 'boats by the deletion of armament and the addition of a Dural degaussing loop and field-generating equipment

Blohm und Voss Ha 139

In 1935 Lufthansa issued a specification for a new seaplane for use on its newly established transatlantic postal service. The aircraft had to be capable of taking off and landing on rough water, to be suitable for catapult-launching, and to possess the ability to carry a 500-kg (1,102-lb) minimum payload for at least 5000 km (3,107 miles) at a cruising speed of 250 km/h (155 mph). Hamburger Flugzeugbau evolved a number of design

studies, including the **P.15** project for a twin-float seaplane that later became the subject of an order for three prototypes. The selected powerplant was the specially developed Junkers Jumo 205 Diesel unit that offered a specific fuel consumption almost 25 per cent lower than that of comparable petrol engines.
The **Ha 139 V1** first prototype made its maiden flight in the autumn of 1936, and by March 1937

the first two aircraft had been delivered to Lufthansa for service as **Ha 139A** machines on the route between Horta in the Azores and New York. During the period between August and November 1937, the floatplanes made seven crossings, operating in conjunction with the catapult-equipped depot ships *Friesenland* and *Schwabenland*. Operations were suspended in November to allow enlarged vertical tail

surfaces to be fitted to improve directional stability, and underwing radiators were added for all four engines in an effort to overcome cooling problems.
The heavier **Ha 139 V3** third prototype was slightly larger and became the **Ha 139B** when it entered service in mid-1938, after which it completed 13 crossings on the Horta-New York route between 21 July and 19 October 1938. During that year the three Ha 139 floatplanes amassed 597 flying hours, and the shortest recorded crossing times were

13 hours 40 minutes and 11 hours 53 minutes on the east/west and west/east trips respectively. The floatplanes were then switched to the South Atlantic route, linking Bathurst in the Gambia and Natal/Recife in Brazil.
Late in 1939 the Ha 139s and their crews were absorbed into the Luftwaffe, the third prototype being modified for reconnaissance duties. A lengthened glazed nose was fitted to accommodate an observer and, to compensate for this, the vertical tail surfaces were

again enlarged. Designated **Ha 139B/U** (**Umbau**, reconstructed), this machine was subsequently modified for the mine-sweeping role as the **Ha 139B/MS**. All three aircraft took part in the 1940 Norwegian campaign, the first two as troop transports.

An Ha 139 is craned, engines running, into the water.

SPECIFICATION

Blohm und Voss Ha 139B/U
Type: five-seat maritime reconnaissance floatplane
Powerplant: four Junkers Jumo 205C vertically-opposed Diesel engines each rated at 600 hp (447 kW)
Performance: maximum speed 179 mph (288 km/h) at 9,845 ft (3000 m); cruising speed 148 mph (238 km/h) at 6,560 ft (2000 m); service ceiling 16,405 ft (5000 m); range 3,076 miles (4950 km)

Weights: maximum take-off 41,888 lb (19000 kg)
Dimensions: wingspan 96 ft 9⅜ in (29.50 m); length 65 ft 10¼ in (20.07 m); height 15 ft 9 in (4.80 m); wing area 1,399.31 sq ft (130.00 m²)
Armament: single 0.312-in (7.92-mm) MG 15 trainable machine-guns in the nose, dorsal hatch and staggered twin beam positions

Blohm und Voss Ha 140

In the summer of 1935 the German air ministry issued a requirement to the Hamburger Flugzeugbau and to Heinkel for a twin-engined floatplane to meet the Luftwaffe's maritime reconnaissance and torpedo bombing needs. Dr-Ing. Vogt responded with a design that was offered in parallel forms as a seaplane or landplane. The type in this original form had an inverted-gull wing configuration and the powerplant of two Junkers Jumo 210 inverted-Vee engines.

Three prototypes were ordered. As the design was finalised, the wing was altered in size and configuration, and the need for greater power was reflected in the switch to a powerplant of two BMW 132K radial engines. The **Ha 140 V1** first prototype made its maiden flight on 30 September 1937, about one month later than the rival Heinkel He 115, as a mid-wing cantilever monoplane of all-metal construction.

The Ha 140 V1 was damaged when the forward part of its starboard float buckled upward in a landing on rough water, and was replaced in the official trials programme by the essentially similar **Ha 140 V2** second prototype. The **Ha 140 V3** third prototype, which was completed only in the last stages of 1938, differed from its predecessors in having a strengthened airframe, slats along the full span of the outer wing panels' leading edges, and the omission of the gun cupola that had been installed above the nose of the earlier floatplanes.

The Ha 140 programme was officially ended in September 1939 with the selection of the He 115 for service. The Ha 140s were then operated by Blohm und Voss for a number of experimental tasks.

SPECIFICATION

Blohm und Voss (Hamburger) Ha 140 V2
Type: three-seat coastal reconnaissance and torpedo bomber floatplane
Powerplant: two BMW 132K radial engines each rated at 830 hp (619 kW)
Performance: maximum speed 207 mph (333 km/h) at 9,845 ft (3000 m); cruising speed 183 mph (295 km/h) at sea level; climb to 9,845 ft (3000 m) in 11 minutes 30 seconds; service ceiling 16,405 ft (5000 m); range 1,243 miles (2000 km)

Weights: empty 13,889 lb (6300 kg); maximum take-off 20,342 lb (9227 kg)
Dimensions: wingspan 72 ft 2⅛ in (21.98 m); length 54 ft 11½ in (16.75 m); height 10 ft ¼ in (3.05 m); wing area 990.27 sq ft (92.00 m²)
Armament: single 0.312-in (7.92-mm) MG 15 trainable machine-guns in the nose cupola and dorsal hatch positions, plus one 2,095-lb (950-kg) torpedo or four 551-lb (250-kg) bombs carried internally

Seen in standard configuration, the clean lines of the Ha 140 are apparent. Later experimental tasks included testing a scale model of the BV 222 empennage, and flying with variable-incidence wings in a test programme for the BV 144.

Blohm und Voss BV 141

During 1937 the German air ministry issued a requirement for a single-engined warplane providing three-seat accommodation and good capability in the short-range battlefield reconnaissance and observation roles; the latter placed great emphasis on the provision of good all-round fields of vision. The requirement drew responses from Arado and Focke-Wulf as well as a radically novel design by Dr-Ing. Vogt. This unorthodox design featured an asymmetric layout, and the powerplant of one BMW 132N radial engine, rated at 865 hp (645 kW). The engine was installed at the forward end of a port-side boom that carried the tail unit at its rear and was balanced by an extensively glazed crew nacelle mounted to starboard of the centreline.

The official preference was for the Focke-Wulf Fw 189, but Hamburger Flugzeugbau built a private-venture **Ha 141-0** (later **BV 141 V2**) prototype which first flew on 25 February 1938. Two further prototypes appeared in the autumn of 1938 as the **BV 141 V1** and **V3**, both slightly larger than the first and with a completely redesigned crew nacelle. The third machine, with wider-track main landing gear units, was armed with two 0.312-in (7.92-mm) MG 17 fixed forward-firing machine-guns as well as two MG 15 trainable

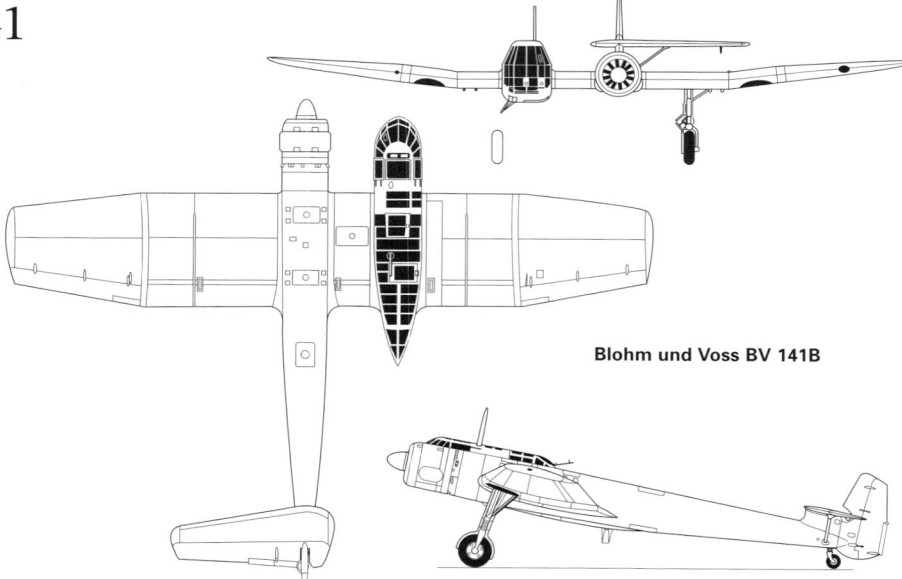

Blohm und Voss BV 141B

Variants

BV 141A: five pre-production aircraft with the wing increased in span and area, and the powerplant of one 1,000-hp (746-kW) BMW Bramo 323 radial engine
BV 141B: five extensively redesigned pre-production aircraft with external changes such as the introduction of equi-taper outer wing panels and an asymmetric horizontal tail surface to improve the field of fire from the rear gun position

machine-guns of the same calibre firing to the rear; the type could also carry a camera and racks for four 110-lb (50-kg) bombs, and was sufficiently successful in initial trials to attract an order for five pre-production **BV 141A** machines.

Official evaluation was completed satisfactorily, but plans for production were terminated in April 1940 as the type was considered to be underpowered. Although five examples of a redesigned, strengthened and more powerful **BV 141B** were ordered, the second of which undertook service trials with the Luftwaffe's Aufklärungsschule 1 (reconnaissance school no.1) in the autumn of 1941, development was delayed and finally discontinued in 1943.

Blohm und Voss BV 141 (continued)

SPECIFICATION	
Blohm und Voss BV 141B	**Dimensions:** wingspan 57 ft 3½ in
Type: three-seat short-range	(17.46 m); length 45 ft 9¼ in
reconnaissance and observation	(13.95 m); height 11 ft 9¾ in
aircraft	(3.60 m); wing area 570.51 sq ft
Powerplant: one BMW 801A-0	(53.00 m²)
radial engine rated at 1,560 hp	**Armament:** two 0.312-in
(1163 kW)	(7.92-mm) MG 17 fixed forward-
Performance: maximum speed	firing machine-guns in the front of
230 mph (370 km/h) at sea level;	the crew nacelle and two 0.312-in
service ceiling 32,810 ft (10000 m);	(7.92-mm) MG 15 trainable
range 746 miles (1200 km)	rearward-firing machine-guns in
Weights: empty 10,362 lb	the rear of the crew nacelle, plus
(4700 kg); maximum take-off	four 110-lb (50-kg) bombs carried
13,448 lb (6100 kg)	under the wing

Prototype V9 was the first BV 141B-0 machine. It differed from the A-0 aircraft by having its tailplane offset to port.

Blohm und Voss BV 142

Designed for transatlantic mail services and originally designated as the **Ha 142**, the **Blohm und Voss BV 142** was a direct derivative of the Ha 139 floatplane and incorporated maximum structural commonality with its forebear. Based on the Ha 139 V3 prototype, the new machine retained the inverted-gull wing but the original engines were replaced by four BMW 132H radial units in nacelles whose inboard members were lengthened to carry the landing gear's rearward-retracting main legs; the twin-wheel tail assembly was also retractable.

The **Ha 142 V1** prototype flew for the first time on 11 October 1938, followed closely by the **BV 142 V2** second machine. Two further BV 142 prototypes joined the test and evaluation programme, which included trials by Lufthansa, but no great interest was shown in the type, and by the time World War II began all four were back with the manufacturer. It was then decided to undertake the conversion of the first two prototypes for military use in the long-range maritime patrol and reconnaissance role. The main changes included the addition of a lengthened glazed nose, similar to that of the Ha 139B/U, and of armament in nose, dorsal and ventral positions. Delivered to the Luftwaffe late in 1940 as the BV 142 V1/U1 and V2/U1, the aircraft served with 2./Aufklärungsgruppe Oberbefehlshaber der Luftwaffe in France. The remaining prototypes were used as transports during the Norwegian invasion, but all had been withdrawn from use by 1942.

In service as a maritime patrol aircraft, the BV 142 proved very vulnerable, its performance being severely degraded with weapons on board.

SPECIFICATION	
Blohm und Voss BV 142 V2/U1	(11000 kg); maximum take-off
Type: long-range maritime patrol	36,376 lb (16500 kg)
and reconnaissance floatplane	**Dimensions:** wingspan 96 ft
Powerplant: four BMW 132H-1	10¾ in (29.53 m); length 67 ft 1 in
radial engines each rated at 880 hp	(20.45 m); height 14 ft 6¾ in
(656 kW)	(4.44 m); wing area 1,399.35 sq ft
Performance: maximum speed	(130.00 m²)
233 mph (375 km/h) at sea level;	**Armament:** single 0.312-in
cruising speed 202 mph (325 km/h)	(7.92-mm) MG 15 trainable
at 6,560 ft (2000 m); service ceiling	machine-guns in the nose position,
29,525 ft (9000 m); range	twin beam positions, ventral
2,423 miles (3900 km)	cupola and power-operated dorsal
Weights: empty 24,251 lb	turret

Blohm und Voss BV 144

In 1940, when German fortunes in World War II were very much in the ascendant, Lufthansa began to plan its post-war operations and foresaw a requirement for an 18-seat airliner to replace the Junkers Ju 52/3m.

Developed to meet such a specification, the **BV 144** was a high-wing monoplane of all-metal construction with retractable tricycle landing gear and the power-plant of two BMW 801MA radial engines. Its internal layout provided accommo-dation for two pilots, a radio operator and 18 to 23 passengers. The cabin included a toilet compart-ment, and there were forward and aft cargo holds.

The design featured a number of innovative features, of which the most notable was the variable-incidence wing. This could be rotated about its tubular main spar to change the angle of attack by up to 9°.

Two prototypes were ordered and, after the surrender of France in June 1940, the project was transferred to Breguet's factory near Bayonne, where the **BV 144 V1** first prototype was completed and flown for the first time prior to the liberation of France. Although French develop-ment continued for a while after the German with-drawal, the project was eventually discontinued.

Altering the BV 144's wing incidence varied the amount of lift it generated, while also keeping the fuselage level during landing and/or low-speed manoeuvres. Wing and tail unit leading edges were de-iced by hot air.

SPECIFICATION	
Blohm und Voss BV 144 V1	(9100 m); range 932 miles
Type: medium-range airliner	(1500 km); maximum take-off
Powerplant: two BMW 801MA	weight 28,660 lb (13000 kg)
radial engines each rated at	**Dimensions:** wingspan 88 ft 7 in
1,600 hp (1193 kW)	(27.00 m); length 71 ft 6¼ in
Performance: maximum speed	(21.80 m); wing area 947.25 sq ft
292 mph (470 km/h) at optimum	(88.00 m²)
altitude; service ceiling 29,855 ft	

Blohm und Voss BV 155

In the spring of 1942 the German authorities decided to press ahead with the completion of the aircraft carrier *Graf Zeppelin*, whose construction had been halted in May 1940. The Messerschmitt Bf 109T had been created as the fighter for the air wing to be carried by the aircraft-carrier, but this was now obsolete and the German air ministry instructed Messerschmitt to create a new carrier-borne fighter as the **Me 155** on the basis, wher-ever possible, of Bf 109G assemblies and compo-nents. In February 1943, however, all work on new surface vessels for the German navy was halted, and with this the need for the Me 155 in its original form disappeared.

Messerschmitt was unhappy to have the work of Ing. Waldemar Voigt's design team wasted, and reworked the concept as the **Me 155A** to meet an air ministry requirement for a long-range warplane able to undertake pinpoint attacks with a single 1000-kg (2,205-lb) bomb. By late 1942, however, the threat that would be posed by US heavy bombing forces was becoming fully apparent and Messerschmitt was asked to turn the Me 155A into the **Me 155B** high-altitude interceptor. The wingspan was increased by the inser-tion of a wide-span centre section of constant thick-ness and chord inboard of the standard Bf 109G-6 outer panels, suggesting a ceiling of 46,260 ft (14100 m) with the power provided by the Daimler-Benz DB 628 inverted-Vee engine. The latter was, in effect, the DB 605A with a two-stage supercharger. More development yielded the **Me 155B-1** design with a further increase in span and a DB 603A turbocharged engine that gave ceiling of 50,855 ft (15500 m).

At this stage in August 1943 the whole project was transferred to Blohm und Voss, whereupon the design was redesignated as the **BV 155**. Dr-Ing. Richard Vogt believed that the Messerschmitt design, drawing on elements of aircraft such as the Bf 109 and Me 209, would be inefficient and lacking in strength. Vogt therefore redesigned the aircraft, keeping only the basic

configuration of the Me 155B, as he created the BV 155. The most noticeable external changes were the enlarged tail unit, the replacement of the Me 155B's four shallow underwing radiators by two large overwing radiators, and the use of main landing gear units based on those of the Ju 87D dive-bomber.

The **BV 155 V1** first prototype made its maiden flight on 1 September 1944 with the DB 603A turbocharged engine driving a four-bladed propeller. The **BV 155 V2** second prototype joined the test programme on 8 February 1945. This machine had changes such as radiators under rather than over the wing, the movement of the pressurised cockpit to a position farther forward and its revision with a clear-vision canopy, further enlargement of the

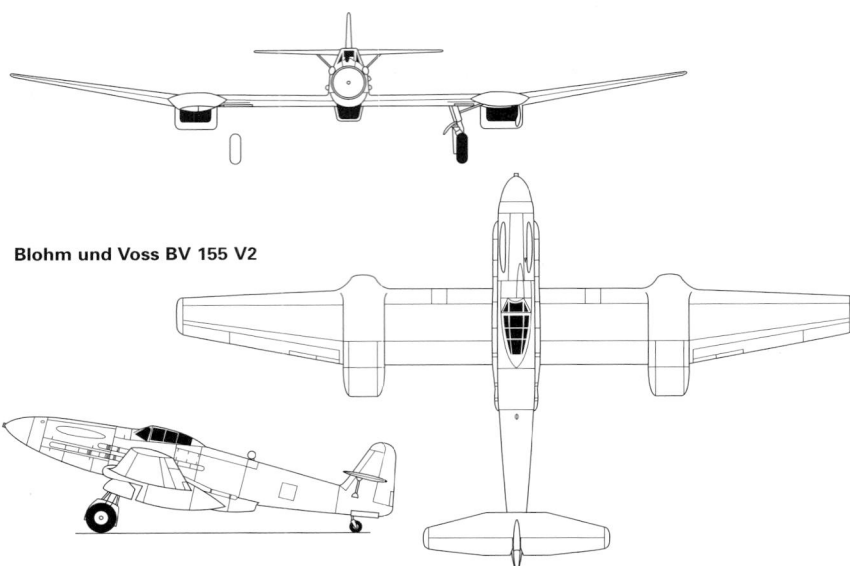

Blohm und Voss BV 155 V2

tail unit, and the addition of still more span to the wing. The **BV 155 V3** third prototype, differing from the V2 only in its

engine, was incomplete at the end of World War II. Work had only just begun on four further prototypes of the planned production

model, the **BV 155C**, that marked yet another radical redesign to a more conventional overall layout with an annular radiator.

Underwing radiators were installed in an attempt to cure the cooling problems of the BV 155 V1.

Blohm und Voss BV 222 Wiking

The largest flying-boat to achieve operational status during World War II, the **Blohm und Voss BV 222 Wiking** (viking) was designed originally by Dr-Ing. Vogt and Herr R. Schubert to meet a 1937 Lufthansa requirement for a long-range passenger transport. This was required to operate between Berlin and New York in a flight time of 20 hours with 16 passengers, or to accommodate up to 24 passengers on shorter routes.

Three prototypes, each with the powerplant of six 1,000-hp (746-kW) BMW-

Bramo Fafnir 323R radial engines, were ordered in September 1937 and work on the first began in January 1938. There were a number of notable features in the design, which clearly had military potential, including an extensive unobstructed floor area, made possible by a beam of almost 10 ft (3.05 m) and an absence of intermediate bulkheads above floor level. The wing incorporated a tubular main spar that also served to contain fuel and oil tankage in the manner typical of Vogt designs.

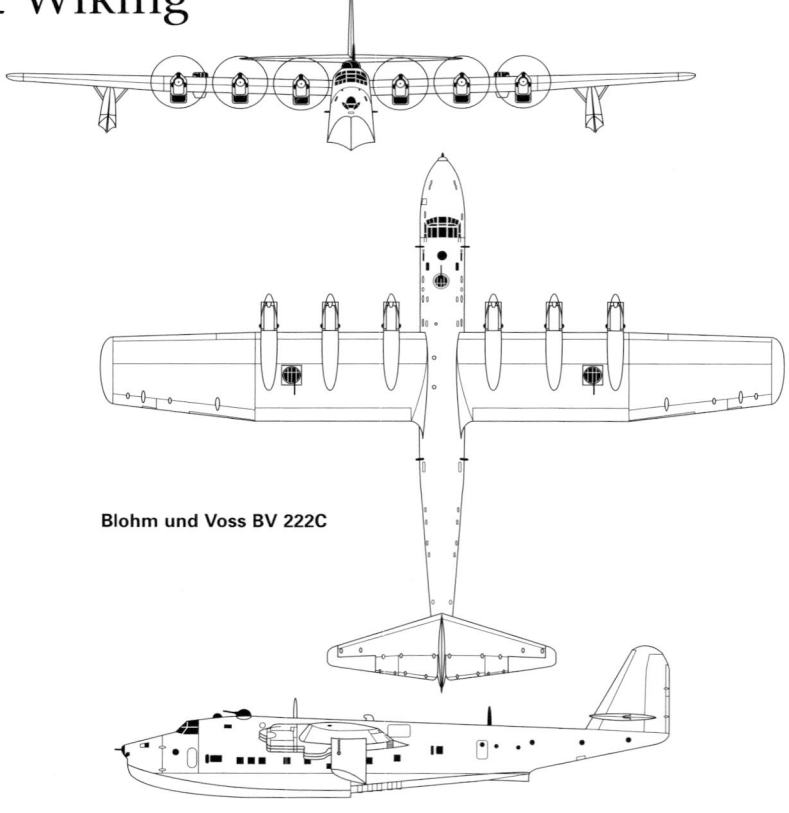

Blohm und Voss BV 222C

Blohm und Voss BV 222 Wiking (continued)

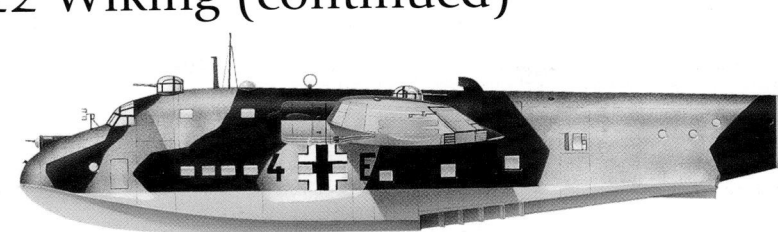

The BV 222's outboard stabilising floats each split into halves to retract sideways into the wing.

On 7 September 1940 the **BV 222 V1** first prototype made its maiden flight, and it was immediately clear that this huge flying-boat possessed considerable military potential. The 'boat was soon fitted with enlarged doors for transport duties with the Luftwaffe, undertaking its first sortie on 10 July 1941. After initial service in Norway the 'boat was transferred to the Mediterranean theatre,

where it was used to carry supplies for German forces in North Africa.

Armament was introduced on the **BV 222 V2** and **V3** second and third prototypes, first flown on 7 August and 28 November 1941, respectively. The V3 carried only a 0.312-in (7.92-mm) trainable MG 81 machine-gun in the bow, but the V2 was fitted additionally with a similar weapon in each of four waist positions and in two upper turrets, plus a pair of 0.51-in (13-mm) MG 131 trainable machine-guns in two gondolas beneath the

wing's centre section. The V1 was retrospectively equipped with similar bow and waist armament, and with an MG 131 in each of the upper turrets. On 10 May 1942 it became the first BV 222 to be delivered to Luft-Transportstaffel (See) 222, in whose service it was joined by the V2 in August of the same year after the 'boat's hull had been provided with a modified planing bottom to improve its hydrodynamic qualities.

At the end of 1942 it was decided to modify the BV 222 for service in the

Entering Luftwaffe service in autumn 1942, BV 222 V8 had been shot down by the end of the year. It was the last of the BV 222A aircraft.

This BV 222A-0 was on the strength of Luft-Transportstaffel (See) 222, flying from Petsamo, Finland early in 1943.

maritime reconnaissance role in the hands of a redesignated Aufklärungsstaffel (See) 222, and later with 1.(Fern) See-Aufklärungsgruppe 129 at Biscarosse in France. For this task four of the 'boats already delivered to the Luftwaffe were modified to

carry FuG 200 Hohentwiel search radar plus revised armament in the form of five power-operated turrets (three on the upper hull and the other two at quarter-span above the wing). Examples of the **BV 222C** production series also saw service in Norway.

Variants

BV 222A: four additional prototypes in Luftwaffe service, carrying freight or up to 76 equipped troops
BV 222B: proposed version with Junkers Jumo 208 engines
BV 222C: production 'boat, of which five were completed and flown. The seventh prototype was the development 'boat, and was first flown on 1 April 1943 with the powerplant of six 980-hp (731-kW) Junkers Jumo 207C Diesel engines and additional machine-guns installed in the nose and the sides of the hull

Blohm und Voss BV 238

Early in 1940, Dr-Ing. Vogt began work on the design of a very large, long-range flying-boat for service with Lufthansa. However, this project was shelved in early 1941 when the company received a German air ministry request to undertake the design of a multi-purpose flying-boat with very long range. The result was the **Blohm und Voss BV 238**, of which four prototypes were ordered in the form of three **BV 238A** and one **BV 238B** machines, each with six

engines but of the liquid-cooled and air-cooled types, respectively.

To ensure that as little financial risk as possible was involved in developing the aircraft, an approximately quarter-scale aerodynamic and hydrodynamic model with the powerplant of six 21-hp (16-kW) ILO F 12/400 engines was constructed. Built near Prague, the resulting **FGP 227** proved a complete financial loss, not flying until just a few months before the maiden

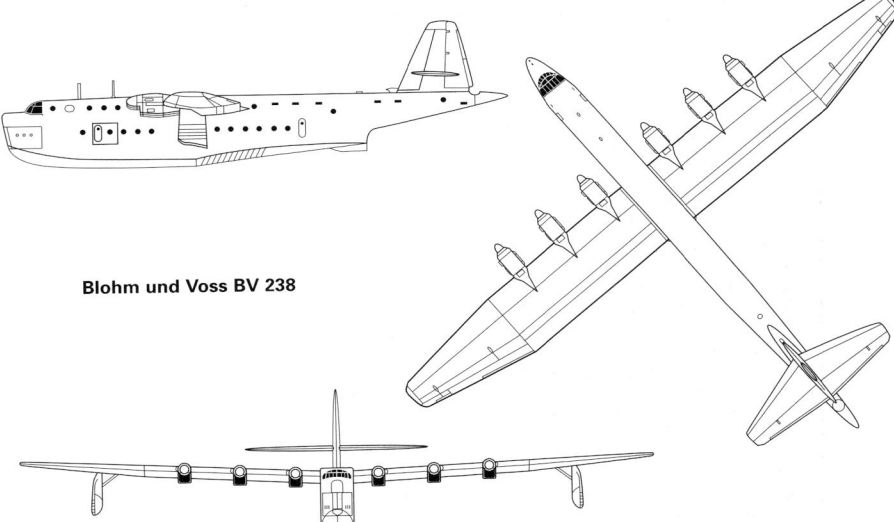

Blohm und Voss BV 238

SPECIFICATION

Blohm und Voss BV 238 V1
Type: long-range multi-role flying-boat
Powerplant: six Daimler-Benz DB 603A inverted-Vee engines each rated at 1,750 hp (1305 kW)
Performance: (estimated) maximum speed 264 mph (425 km/h) at 19,685 ft (6000 m); range 2,423 miles (3900 km)
Weights: empty 111,995 lb (50800 kg); maximum take-off 176,370 lb (80000 kg)
Dimensions: wingspan 197 ft 4¾ in (60.17 m); length 142 ft 8½ in (43.50 m); height 43 ft 11½ in (13.40 m); wing area

3,928.96 sq ft (365.00 m²)
Armament: (proposed) two 20-mm MG 151 trainable cannon in the dorsal turret, four 0.51-in (13-mm) MG 131 trainable machine-guns in each of the bow, tail and two wing-mounted turrets, and two 0.51-in (13-mm) MG 131 trainable machine-guns in each of the two beam positions, plus up to 11,023 lb (5000 kg) of bombs carried in the wing and up to 10,582 lb (4800 kg) of weapons carried under the wing and comprising four torpedoes, or four missiles, or two glide bombs

flight of the sole BV 238, and the machine provided no data whatsoever for the BV 238 programme.

Although considerably larger than the BV 222, the BV 238 was generally similar in configuration. It differed primarily by having a high- rather than shoul-

der-mounted wing, a modified tail unit, and one-piece rather than split retractable stabilising floats. Flown successfully in the spring of 1945, the **BV 238 V1**, the only prototype to be completed, was destroyed on Lake Schaal by strafing North American P-51

Mustang fighters a few days before the end of the war. Tests had shown it to be suitable for service use, but this was not to be and the BV 238's claim to fame lay in the fact that it was the largest military flying-boat to be built and flown during World War II.

Blume Bl.502 and Bl.503

Professor Walter Blume, formerly chief designer and managing director of Arado Flugzeugwerke GmbH,

started work during the mid-1950s on the design of a four-seat light cabin monoplane of all-metal

construction. Of low-wing cantilever configuration, with a conventional tail unit and retractable tricycle land-

ing gear, the **Blume Bl.500** prototype was built by Focke-Wulf and completed its maiden flight on 14 March 1957.

The two production variants were the **Bl.502** with the powerplant of one Avco

Lycoming O-320-A engine, similar to that which had powered the prototype, and the **Bl.503** with the uprated powerplant of one Avco Lycoming O-360-A1A engine rated at 180 hp (134 kW).

Building on his experience with the Arado company, Dipl.-Ing. Walter Blume hoped to break into the lightplane market with his Bl.502 (illustrated). The aircraft failed to gain significant orders, however.

SPECIFICATION

Blume Bl.502
Type: four-seat cabin monoplane
Powerplant: one Avco Lycoming O-320-A flat-four engine rated at 150 hp (112 kW)
Performance: maximum speed 155 mph (250 km/h) at sea level; cruising speed 137 mph (220 km/h) at optimum altitude; initial climb rate 1,050 ft (320 m) per minute;
service ceiling 15,750 ft (4800 m); range 559 miles (900 km)
Weights: empty 1,477 lb (670 kg); maximum take-off 2,469 lb (1120 kg)
Dimensions: wingspan 34 ft 5⅛ in (10.50 m); length 26 ft 8¾ in (8.15 m); height 7 ft 10½ in (2.40 m); wing area 161.46 sq ft (15.00 m²)

Boeing Model 1 (B & W)

In 1915 William E. Boeing, a major timberman and landowner of Seattle, Washington, and Commander G. Conrad Westervelt, an air-minded naval officer attached to the Seattle Navy Yard, decided to enter into a partnership for the design and manufacture of aircraft. This informal arrangement was formalised in July 1916, after Westervelt's departure on a posting to the eastern coast of the USA, as the Pacific Aero Products Company that subsequently became the Boeing Airplane Company in April 1917.

Worthy of brief mention as the very first of a long line of aircraft, the **Boeing Model 1** was also known as the **B & W** in reflection of its collaborative creation by Boeing and Westervelt. Of wooden construction, covered with fabric, the Model 1 was an unequal-span biplane. The fuselage had two open cockpits in tandem and the alighting gear included two single-step floats, strut-mounted and braced beneath the fuselage, and a small float under the tail.

The first of the two Model 1 machines made its maiden flight on 29 June 1916 and the aircraft were sold to the New Zealand Flying School. In December 1919 they were used to establish the country's first airmail service.

To celebrate Boeing's diamond jubilee in 1966, Boeing engineers built this Model 1 replica. The aircraft survives in The Museum of Flight, Seattle; the fate of the original aircraft has never been positively ascertained.

SPECIFICATION

Boeing Model 1 (B & W)
Type: two-seat floatplane
Powerplant: one Hall-Scott A-5 Vee engine rated at 125 hp (93 kW)
Performance: maximum speed 75 mph (121 km/h) at sea level; cruising speed 67 mph (108 km/h) at optimum altitude; initial climb rate 700 ft (213 m) per minute;
range 320 miles (515 km)
Weights: empty 2,100 lb (953 kg); maximum take-off 2,800 lb (1270 kg)
Dimensions: wingspan 52 ft (15.85 m); length 31 ft 2 in (9.50 m); wing area 580.0 sq ft (53.88 m²)

Boeing Model 2 (C-4) and Model 3 (C-5, C-6 and C-11)

Alternatively known as the **C-4** (as it was the fourth aircraft owned by Boeing, although only its third design), the **Boeing Model 2** retained an overall similarity in configuration to the Model 1. The wing introduced a large amount of forward stagger, increased dihedral, and considerably different interplane struts. The tail unit was completely revised in an arrangement in which the fixed tailplane was eliminated and the vertical surface was changed to a fixed fin and plain rudder, while the float under the tail also disappeared. Only one example was built, and this was dismantled after testing although it was reassembled and flown again in August 1918.

The **Model 3** was generally similar, differing primarily in having modified cabane struts. Three examples were built as the **C-5**, **C-6** and **C-11**, and the USN acquired two for evaluation as trainers.

SPECIFICATION

Boeing Model 3
Type: two-seat training floatplane
Powerplant: one Hall-Scott A-7A inline engine rated at 100 hp (75 kW)
Performance: maximum speed 73 mph (117 km/h) at sea level; cruising speed 65 mph (105 km/h) at optimum altitude; service ceiling
6,500 ft (1980 m); range 200 miles (322 km)
Weights: empty 1,898 lb (861 kg); maximum take-off 2,395 lb (1086 kg)
Dimensions: wingspan 43 ft 10 in (13.36 m); length 27 ft (8.23 m); height 12 ft 7 in (3.84 m); wing area 495.00 sq ft (45.99 m²)

William Boeing engages in a pre-flight discussion with a C-5 crewman.

Boeing Model 4 (EA)

Two examples of the **Boeing Model 4**, a revised version of the Model 3 and otherwise known as the **EA** (possibly E for Boeing's fifth design and A for army), were built for evaluation by the US Army as trainers. The most noticeable external change from the Model 3 was the replacement of the float alighting gear by fixed tailskid landing gear. The Model 4's also featured a single cockpit seating two side-by-side.

The Model 4 was the first Boeing type to introduce the more reliable Curtiss OXX series of engines. The aircraft were delivered in January 1917.

The EA's undercarriage included a single strut-mounted wheel, forward of the two main wheels, to minimise the danger of nosing over.

SPECIFICATION

Boeing Model 4
Type: two-seat trainer
Powerplant: one Curtiss OXX-3 or OXX-5 Vee engine rated at 100 hp (75 kW)
Performance: maximum speed 67 mph (108 km/h) at sea level; cruising speed 60 mph (97 km/h) at optimum altitude; initial climb rate
438 ft (134 m) per minute; service ceiling 7,000 ft (2135 m); range 280 miles (451 km)
Weights: empty 1,598 lb (725 kg); maximum take-off 2,185 lb (991 kg)
Dimensions: wingspan 48 ft 10 in (14.88 m); length 24 ft 10 in (7.57 m); wing area 479.00 sq ft (44.50 m²)

Boeing Model 5

The USN's success with the Model 3 led to an order for another 50 similar aircraft. Generally like the Model 3, these **Boeing Model 5** floatplanes were delivered to the USN during 1918. So much trouble was experienced with their Hall-Scott engines that the aircraft were virtually unused, and when disposed of as surplus after the end of World War I, the majority were still in their packing cases.

One additional example was acquired for evaluation with a single main float under the fuselage and two small stabilising floats under the tips of the lower wing. This machine was constructed from the dismantled airframe of the Model 2 and, with the

powerplant of one 100-hp (75-kW) Curtiss OXX-6 Vee engine, was identified as the **C-1F**, the portion of the designation after the hyphen indicating one float. No further examples were ordered.

The final example of the Model 5 was the **C-700**

Flying under the power of its OXX-6 engine, the C-1F demonstrates its revised float arrangement. The aircraft was doped overall medium grey, the standard US Navy finish of 1918.

built for William Boeing himself. On 3 March 1919 it was used by Boeing and Edward Hubbard to fly a trial mail route between

Vancouver and Seattle. It later inaugurated the first international contract air mail service between Seattle, and Victoria, BC.

SPECIFICATION	
Boeing Model 5	
Type: two-seat training floatplane	6,500 ft (1980 m); range 200 miles (322 km)
Powerplant: one Hall-Scott A-7A inline engine rated at 100 hp (75 kW)	**Weights:** empty 1,898 lb (861 kg); maximum take-off 2,395 lb (1086 kg)
Performance: maximum speed 73 mph (118 km/h) at sea level; cruising speed 65 mph (105 km/h) at optimum altitude; service ceiling	**Dimensions:** wingspan 43 ft 10 in (13.36 m); length 27 ft (8.23 m); height 12 ft 7 in (3.84 m); wing area 495.00 sq ft (45.99 m²)

Boeing Model 6 (B-1)

First flown on 27 December 1919, the **Boeing Model 6** (also known as **B-1** to indicate that it was Boeing's first commercial rather than private or military type) was a neat biplane flying-boat with a pusher powerplant. In its overall design and structure the Model 6 clearly drew heavily on Boeing's experience with the Curtiss HS-2L flying-boat which the company had built under licence in World War I.

The Model 6 was based on a single-step hull of

wood-planked construction, and provided accommodation for one pilot and two passengers in a tandem arrangement of two open cockpits located ahead of the staggered unequal-span biplane wing cellule. The wings and tail unit were of fabric-covered wooden construction. The Hall-Scott L-6 engine was mounted amid the cabane struts supporting the centre section of the upper wing. This engine proved unreliable and lacking in adequate power however, and was later replaced by a six-cylin-

der 400-hp (298-kW) Liberty 12 Vee engine.

The Model 6 was in every way a good flying-boat for its period, but only one machine was built as the market was being flooded with cheap ex-military aircraft released after the end of World War I. The 'boat was sold in 1920 to

Seen as it appeared towards the end of its career, the B-1 featured a Liberty engine with large frontal radiator and enlarged underwing floats. Ailerons, elevators and rudder were all horn-balanced.

Edward Hubbard and used up to 1928 on the international air mail service between Seattle, Washington, and Victoria, British Columbia. It

remained airworthy into the early 1930s, and was put on outdoor display in 1934. Stored during World War II, the aircraft was placed on indoor display in 1954.

SPECIFICATION	
Boeing Model 6 (B-1)	
Type: three-seat utility flying-boat	13,300 ft (4055 m); range 400 miles (644 km)
Powerplant: one Hall-Scott L-6 inline engine rated at 200 hp (149 kW)	**Weights:** empty 2,400 lb (1089 kg); maximum take-off 3,850 lb (1746 kg)
Performance: maximum speed 90 mph (145 km/h) at sea level; cruising speed 80 mph (129 km/h) at optimum altitude; service ceiling	**Dimensions:** wingspan 50 ft 3 in (15.32 m); length 31 ft 3 in (9.53 m); height 13 ft 4 in (4.06 m); wing area 492.00 sq ft (45.71 m²)

Boeing Model 6D (B-1D), Model 6E (B-1E) and Model 204

In the late 1920s Boeing built another eight flying-boats designated in the same sequence as the

Model 6 of 1919, although these later 'boats retained only a conceptual similarity to the earlier type and were

based on new structural ideas. The new 'boats were two **Model 6D** (or **B-1D**) and six **Model 6E** (or **B-1E**)

machines completed between May 1928 and April 1929.

The Model 6D was based on a single-step wooden hull with accommodation for the pilot and up to three

passengers in an enclosed cabin located ahead of the wing cellule, which was based on shortened Model 40 panels. The first Model 6D was completed in April 1928 and had the power-

Two B-1Es were finished to Model 204 standard with five-seat accommodation, as illustrated. The 'boat's hull was constructed with cross strips of wood veneer over wooden longerons and formers.

SPECIFICATION	
Boeing Model 6E (B-1E)	
Type: four-seat utility flying-boat	rate 1,000 ft (305 m) per minute; service ceiling 12,000 ft (3660 m); range 450 miles (724 km)
Powerplant: one Pratt & Whitney Wasp radial engine rated at 410 hp (306 kW)	**Weights:** empty 3,090 lb (1402 kg); maximum take-off 4,550 lb (2064 kg)
Performance: maximum speed 115 mph (185 km/h) at sea level; cruising speed 105 mph (169 km/h) at optimum altitude; initial climb	**Dimensions:** wingspan 39 ft 8¼ in (12.10 m); length 32 ft (9.75 m); height 12 ft (3.66 m); wing area 466.00 sq ft (43.29 m²)

plant of one 220-hp (164-kW) Wright Whirlwind J-5 radial engine. The second Model 6D was completed

with the considerably more potent powerplant of one 420-hp (313-kW) Pratt & Whitney Wasp radial engine

for improved performance.
The Model 6E was basically identical to the 6D (which, despite its lower

designation, was built marginally later), except for its somewhat heavier construction, its rudder of

revised shape, its increased fuel capacity and its Wasp powerplant. The first Model 6D flew on 4 March 1928.

Boeing Model 7 (BB-1)

First flown on 7 January 1920, the sole **Boeing Model 7** (or **BB-1**) was a touring and sporting flying-boat for the civil market. The type was clearly inspired by the Model 6 in its overall concept and configuration, but was

smaller than the earlier type and had open accommodation in a single cockpit for the pilot ahead of a side-by-side pair of passengers. It was sold to the Aircraft Manufacturing Company of Vancouver, British Columbia.

SPECIFICATION	
Boeing Model 7 (BB-1) **Type:** three-seat utility flying-boat **Powerplant:** one Hall-Scott L-4 inline engine rated at 130 hp (97 kW) **Performance:** maximum speed 84 mph (135 km/h) at sea level; cruising speed 75 mph (121 km/h) at optimum altitude; service ceiling	10,000 ft (3050 m); range 500 miles (805 km) **Weights:** empty 2,028 lb (920 kg); maximum take-off 2,699 lb (1224 kg) **Dimensions:** wingspan 45 ft 6 in (13.87 m); length 27 ft 8 in (8.43 m); height 11 ft 8 in (3.56 m); wing area 403.00 sq ft (37.44 m²)

The Model 7 was of wooden construction with a wood-planked single-step hull and fabric-covered flying surfaces, and was unusual among American aircraft in having a single fore-and-aft pair of transverse Vee-type interplane struts on each side.

Boeing Model 8 (BB-L6)

The alternative designation **BB-L6** rightly suggested a wing cellule based on that of the Model 7 (BB-1)

flying-boat and the use of a Hall-Scott L-6 engine; the **Boeing Model 8** was a landplane rather than a

flying-boat, and was built to the order of the company's first test pilot, Herb Munter. Munter had been inspired by the visit of the Italian Ansaldo A.1 Balilla fighter to Seattle. This aircraft had a mahogany plywood-covered fuselage whose cross-section changed from a rectangular

shape over its forward section to an inverted triangular shape to the rear of the cockpit.
A similar configuration was specified for the Model 8, which carried two side-by-side passengers

ahead of the pilot in a tandem arrangement of two open cockpits.
Making its maiden flight on 24 May 1920, the Model 8 survived to 1923, when it was burned in a hangar fire.

With its tandem cockpit layout, the BB-L6 established the standard layout for American-built three-seat open-cockpit biplanes.

SPECIFICATION	
Boeing model 8 (BB-L6) **Type:** three-seat utility aircraft **Powerplant:** one Hall-Scott L-6 Vee engine rated at 200 hp (149 kW) **Performance:** maximum speed 100 mph (161 km/h) at sea level; cruising speed 90 mph (145 km/h) at optimum altitude; service ceiling 15,000 ft (4570 m); range 450 miles	(724 km) **Weights:** empty 1,652 lb (749 kg); maximum take-off 2,632 lb (1194 kg) **Dimensions:** wingspan 44 ft 9 in (13.64 m); length 29 ft 3 in (8.92 m); height 10 ft 10 in (3.30 m); wing area 465.00 sq ft (43.20 m²)

Boeing Model 10 (GA-1)

Late in 1919, the US Air Service (soon to become the US Army Air Service) was starting to plan a new generation of warplanes based on experience in World War I. One of the concepts that had proved most successful in that war had been ground attack in support of the infantry, and the USAAS allocated the GA designation to this type of aircraft.

The task of designing the first such US aircraft was entrusted to the Engineering Division of the USAAS. The first of these types was the **GA-X**, an abbreviation of **Ground Attack - Experimental**, which was planned as a large machine that could cruise slowly over the battlefield, protected from ground fire by about 2,200 lb (998 kg) of armour

plate, to support the infantry with its powerful gun armament. As speed was not a primary consideration, aerodynamic cleanliness was sacrificed to fields of fire and a sturdy structure able to carry a heavy load of ammunition and armour. The result was an angular machine of wire-braced wooden construction with plywood and fabric covering. The

core of the structure was the rectangular-section fuselage, which carried three of the five-man crew: the forward gunner in an open nose position, the pilot in a semi-enclosed cockpit with armoured shutters for forward vision and the rear gunner in an open dorsal position.
This fuselage carried the substantial wire-braced tail unit and the massive three-bay triplane wing cellule. The engines were installed in nacelles on the middle wing; at the front of each nacelle was a gunner's position, where the gunner was protected by armour and sighted through armoured shutters.
The Engineering Division built the GA-X prototype in 1920, and after it had completed limited flight trials Boeing was the successful bidder for a production batch of 20 **GA-1** aircraft for more extensive testing and

limited service. The first GA-1 flew in May 1921. The production total was soon trimmed to a mere 10 aircraft, for the type was considerably overweight as a result of its armour protection, the fields of vision for the crew were wholly inadequate, and there were problems with the type's aerodynamics and the cooling of its engines.
Nevertheless, all 10 GA-1s were accepted for service and based at Kelly Field in Texas, from where they were used for operational trials in northern Mexico and then as much disliked trainers until their early retirement.
No Boeing designation was given to the **GA-2**, of which the company produced two examples to another Engineering Division design for an armoured ground-attack type crewed by one pilot and two gunners.

Structurally akin to the GA-1, the GA-2 biplane had a 750-hp (559-kW) Engineering Division W-18 W-type engine. It was armed with one 37-mm cannon and six 0.3-in (7.62-mm) machine-guns.

Boeing Model 10 (GA-1) continued

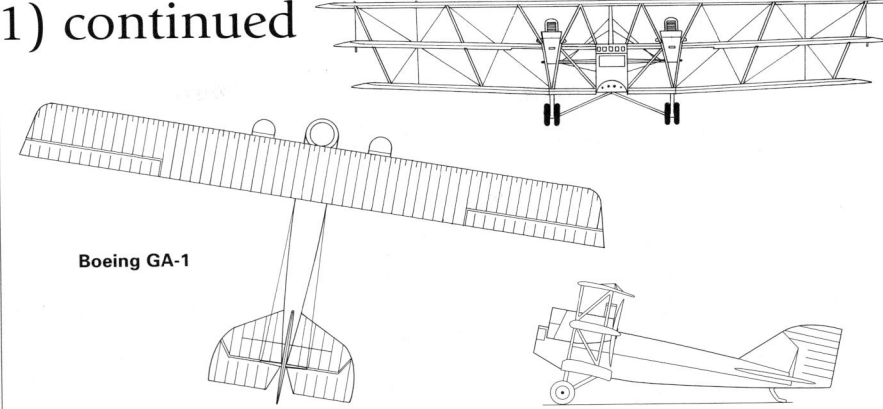

Boeing GA-1

SPECIFICATION

Boeing Model 10 (GA-1)
Type: four/five-seat ground-attack warplane
Powerplant: two Liberty 12A Vee engines each rated at 435 hp (324 kW)
Performance: maximum speed 105 mph (169 km/h) at sea level; cruising speed 95 mph (153 km/h) at optimum altitude; initial climb rate 600 ft (183 m) per minute; service ceiling 11,500 ft (3505 m); range 350 miles (563 km)
Weights: empty 7,834 lb (3553 kg); maximum take-off 10,426 lb (4729 kg)

Dimensions: wingspan 65 ft 6 in (19.96 m); length 33 ft 7 in (8.53 m); height 14 ft 3 in (4.34 m); wing area 1,016.00 sq ft (94.39 m²)
Armament: one 37-mm trainable forward-firing cannon in the nose position, and eight 0.3-in (7.62-mm) Browning machine-guns: two fixed rearward-firing in the lower fuselage, one trainable forward-firing in the nose position, one trainable rearward-firing in the dorsal position and two trainable forward-firing in each of the two nacelle positions

Boeing Models 15, 53, 54, 55, 58, 67, 68 (PW-9 and FB)

Using the experience gained from the subcontracted production of other manufacturers' aircraft, and in particular the Thomas-Morse MB-3A fighter, Boeing began the private-venture development of a single-seat fighter under the designation **Boeing Model 15**. First flown on 2 June 1923, this was a biplane with a staggered single-bay wing cellule in which the lower wing was of smaller span and chord than the upper wing. The wings were of fabric-covered wooden construction, the fuselage was made of welded steel tube under a skinning of light alloy forward and fabric aft, and the braced fabric-covered wooden tail unit featured a variable-incidence tailplane. The landing gear was of the fixed tailskid type with a main unit of the through-axle type, and the powerplant was based on one 435-hp (324-kW) Curtiss D-12 Vee piston engine.

The US Army had become interested in the Model 15 even before it had flown and, after early tests by the manufacturer, the prototype was evaluated under the designation

XPW-9 in competition against the Fokker XPW-7 and Curtiss XPW-8A. Its performance proved good enough to warrant an order for two XPW-9 additional prototypes for more extensive evaluation. These aircraft were delivered in May 1924, and the second machine differed in its main landing gear arrangement, which was of the divided type; it was this arrangement that was chosen for the 30 examples of the **PW-9** production-standard fighter ordered in 1925.

The USN was as keen as the Army to acquire examples of Boeing's new fighter, and the first of an order for 14 for service with the USMC, under the designation **FB-1**, was delivered on 1 December 1925. In the event, only 10 of the aircraft were delivered to FB-1 standard, which was virtually identical to the US Army's PW-9 configuration. The 11th and 12th aircraft of this order introduced the 510-hp (380-kW) Packard 1A-1500 Vee engine and were equipped with the through-axle landing gear unit and an arrester hook for operation from aircraft-carriers,

The 27 Boeing FB-5s ordered by the US Navy became the first fighters for that service intended from the outset for carrier operations. The aircraft in the foreground was operated by VF-1, and that unit's 'High Hat' emblem is visible above the lower wing.

with the designation **FB-2**. These aircraft were known to Boeing as the **Model 53**. The 13th machine was identical to the FB-2 except for its twin-float alighting gear, and was designated **FB-3 (Model 55)**. The 14th and last of the USN's initial order also had twin-float alighting gear, but introduced the 450-hp (336-kW) Wright P-1 radial engine and was designated the **FB-4 (Model 54)** or **FB-6** when revised with the 400-hp (298-kW) Pratt & Whitney Wasp radial engine.

Minor refinements left the PW-9 (below) indistinguishable from the PW-9. The USAAC received 25 aircraft over the period 19 June 1926-4 February 1927. Two aircraft were converted for other projects.

Variants

Model 15A: 24 of 25 fighters ordered by the US Army under the designation **PW-9A** with the improved D-12C engine (rated identically to the D-12) and fitted with duplicated flying and landing wires
Model 15B: the 25th of the US Army's PW-9As with the changed designation **PW-9B**, detail improvements and intended for testing of the D-12D engine. Some 15 of this subvariant were ordered, but none was built as such
Model 15C: 15 fighters ordered to PW-9B standard, but built as **PW-9C** machines with the D-12D engine and modified fittings for the flying and landing wires. An additional 25 of the same subvariant were ordered in August 1926
Model 15D: last of the 40 PW-9C fighters modified, with the changes to be introduced in a follow-on order for 16 **PW-9D** machines, these changes including an aerodynamically balanced rudder of increased area (fitted retrospectively to most in-service PW-9 aircraft) and other detail improvements
Model 58: the 30th of the original PW-9s, completed as an experimental fighter under the designation **XP-4** with changes such as a supercharged engine, and a lower wing of span and chord equal to those of the upper wing. No production examples were ordered
Model 67: Boeing's designation for the major production version of the Model 15 family, built for the USN under the designation **FB-5** with the Packard 2A-1500 engine, a redesigned landing gear structure and increased wing stagger. Some 27 examples were delivered by early 1926. The **Model 67A (FB-7)**, with the Pratt & Whitney Wasp engine, failed to materialise
Model 68: the 24th PW-9A was converted as an experimental advanced trainer with the designation **AT-3** and its original engine replaced by a 180-hp (134-kW) Wright-Hispano Model E Vee engine for much reduced performance, but also significantly lower purchase and operating costs. No production examples were built

SPECIFICATION

Boeing Model 67 (FB-5)
Type: single-seat carrierborne fighter
Powerplant: one Packard 2A-1500 Vee engine rated at 520 hp (388 kW)
Performance: maximum speed 176 mph (283 km/h) at sea level; cruising speed 150 mph (241 km/h) at optimum altitude; initial climb rate 2,100 ft (640 m) per minute; service ceiling 22,000 ft (6705 m); range 420 miles (676 km)

Weights: empty 2,458 lb (1115 kg); maximum take-off 3,249 lb (1474 kg)
Dimensions: wingspan 32 ft (9.75 m); length 23 ft 9 in (7.24 m); height 9 ft 5 in (2.87 m); wing area 241.00 sq ft (22.39 m²)
Armament: one 0.5-in (12.7-mm) and one 0.3-in (7.62-mm) Browning fixed forward-firing machine-gun, or two 0.3-in (7.62-mm) Browning fixed forward-firing machine-guns in the forward fuselage

Boeing Model 16 (DH-4 Liberty Plane and O2B)

Boeing's involvement with the **DH-4 Liberty Plane** resulted in the **Boeing Model 16** designation, and started in 1920 when the company was one of 10 selected to undertake the conversion of DH-4s to the tactically superior **DH-4B** standard. Boeing completed 111 such conversions for redelivery between March and July 1920, and 50 of these aircraft were cycled through Boeing's facility yet

again in 1923 for additional refurbishment.

In February 1923 the US Army contracted with Boeing for the conversion of three DH-4s with larger main wheels and a fuselage of fabric-covered welded steel tube construction in place of the original plywood-covered wooden structure. These three conversions were **DH-4M-1** (later **XDH-4M-1**) machines with an arc-welded fuselage, while

similar conversions by the Atlantic Aircraft Corporation, a Fokker subsidiary, used a gas-welded fuselage and had the designation **DH-4M-2**. The success of the prototype conversions, in whose designation the 'M' stood for '**Modernized**', resulted in the placement of orders in the summer of 1923 for 183 similar aircraft, mainly for the photographic reconnaissance and survey roles.

Some 163 examples were delivered to the US Army between January and September 1924, and 22 of the aircraft were subsequently converted by the US Army to the **DH-4M-1T** dual-control trainer standard, with a few more adapted to the target-towing role with the revised designation **DH-4M-1K**. The last 30 machines from the US Army's orders were diverted to the US Marine Corps, which accepted the

In 1917 the US Army selected the Airco (de Havilland) DH.4 to be produced under licence in the USA. Three US companies (Dayton-Wright, Fisher Body and Standard) built 4,846 examples, of which 111 were later converted by Boeing as the Model 16.

aircraft in March 1925, for service with the designation **O2B-1**. The last four of the aircraft were later converted by the USN to **O2B-2** standard for cross-

country operation by day and night, the changes including navigation lights, radio equipment, flares and improved crew accommodation.

SPECIFICATION	
Boeing Model 16 (DH-4M) **Type:** two-seat day bomber, reconnaissance, observation and training aircraft **Powerplant:** one Liberty 12A Vee engine rated at 420 hp (313 kW) **Performance:** maximum speed 118 mph (190 km/h) at optimum altitude; cruising speed 104 mph (167 km/h) at optimum altitude; initial climb rate 760 ft (232 m) per minute; service ceiling 12,800 ft (3900 m); range 330 miles (531 km) **Weights:** empty 2,939 lb	(1333 kg); maximum take-off 4,595 lb (2084 kg) **Dimensions:** wingspan 42 ft 5 in (12.93 m); length 29 ft 11 in (9.12 m); height 9 ft 8 in (2.95 m); wing area 440.00 sq ft (40.88 m²) **Armament:** two 0.3-in (7.62-mm) fixed forward-firing machine-guns in the forward fuselage and two 0.3-in (7.62-mm) trainable rearward-firing machine-guns in the rear cockpit, plus up to 400 lb (181 kg) of bombs carried under the fuselage

Boeing Model 21 (NB)

Boeing designed the **Model 21** to meet a USN requirement for a primary flying trainer. The aircraft

was an equal-span unstaggered two-bay biplane notable for the unusual width of its wing cellule's

centre section. The tailskid landing gear could be converted to float configuration, and the pilot and pupil were accommodated in tandem open cockpits. USN testing of the Model 21 was carried out with the prototype aircraft, under the not completely correct designation **VNB-1**.

From the potential operator's point of view, the type was unsuitable for the required role, being unspinnable and too easy to fly. On the understanding that modifications would be introduced to correct these problems, 41 production aircraft were ordered under the designation **NB-1**. The first of these was delivered on 5 December 1924, and it

was soon discovered that Boeing's spin modifications were too effective, since it was possible to get into a flat spin from which recovery was virtually impossible. Further modifications produced an acceptable compromise. Some NB-1 aircraft had Lawrance J-2 or J-4 engines, and several were later modified with the 220-hp (164-kW) Wright Whirlwind J-5 radial.

Following delivery of the NB-1s, an additional 30 machines were ordered to the **NB-2** standard that differed from that of the NB-1 only in having war-surplus 180-hp (134-kW) Wright-Hispano Type E-4 Vee engines. These were installed at the USN's request to utilise some of the very large number of these licence-built engines held in naval stores.

Variants

NB-3: in an attempt to effect a further improvement in the handling characteristics of the Model 21, the last two NB-1 aircraft were retained by Boeing for experimentation. The first of these became the NB-3 with a lengthened fuselage, tail unit modifications, and the Wright-Hispano Type E-4 engine. Testing in mid-1925 showed no significant improvement and the NB-3 was reworked and delivered to NB-1 standard
NB-4: used for the same purpose as the NB-3, the NB-4 had the same fuselage modifications, but incorporated the lighter Lawrance engine. The NB-4 also showed no improvement and was reworked and delivered as an NB-1

Boeing NB-2

In floatplane configuration, the NB-1 replaced the wide-track main wheels with a single large float supported by four struts and bracing wires. Stability was provided by floats positioned beneath the lower wing between the outboard strut and the wingtip.

SPECIFICATION	
Boeing Model 21 (NB-1) **Type:** two-seat primary flying trainer **Powerplant:** one Lawrance J-1 radial engine rated at 200 hp (149 kW) **Performance:** maximum speed 99 mph (160 km/h) at sea level; cruising speed 90 mph (145 km/h) at sea level; climb to 5,000 ft (1525 m) in 9 minutes 48 seconds; service ceiling 10,200 ft (3110 m); range 300 miles (483 km)	**Weights:** empty 2,136 lb (969 kg); maximum take-off 2,837 lb (1287 kg) **Dimensions:** wing span 36 ft 10 in (11.23 m); length 28 ft 9 in (8.76 m) as a floatplane; height 11 ft 8 in (3.56 m); wing area 344 sq ft (31.96 m²) **Armament:** (as gunner trainer) one 0.3-in (7.62-mm) trainable rearward-firing machine-gun in the rear cockpit

Boeing Model 40 and Model 95

To meet the requirements of the Air Mail Department of the US Post Office, which needed a new mailplane to replace its ageing DH-4s, Boeing designed the **Model 40**. It was required to compete against the submissions of other manufacturers, and the Post Office specification had stipulated the use of a Liberty engine as well as the ability to carry 1,000 lb (454 kg) of air mail. A fairly conventional unstaggered two-bay biplane, the Model 40 had a mail compartment in the forward fuselage and its pilot seated well aft in an open cockpit. First flown on 7 July 1925, the Model 40 was unsuccessful in the competition, in which the Douglas entry was declared the winner.

Boeing's design then gathered factory dust for some 18 months until, early in 1927, the US Post Office began the process

of turning the government air mail service over to private enterprise. Requiring an aircraft to operate on any of the routes for which it might bid, Boeing dusted off the Model 40, and began a process of redesign and conversion. The resulting **Model 40A** had three major changes: the Liberty engine was replaced by a Pratt & Whitney Wasp radial; the composite-structure fuselage gave place to one of steel tube with fabric covering; and better use was made of fuselage capacity. In addition, an enclosed cabin for two passengers was provided more or less directly over the lower wing, with cargo

and/or mail compartments between the pilot's cockpit and the cabin, and between the cabin and engine firewall.

Boeing was allocated the San Francisco-Chicago route and gained Approved Type Certificate No. 2 from the US Department of Commerce. Some 25 Model 40A aircraft were built, 24 for service with the new Boeing Air Transport Corporation, and one as an engine testbed for Pratt & Whitney. The first example of the Model 40A was flown initially on 20 May 1927, and all 24 for BATC had been delivered in time for inauguration of the company's first air mail service on 1 July 1927.

The Boeing Model 40A's two-person passenger cabin, seen here between the wings, allowed BATC to earn additional income on the San Francisco-Chicago mail route. The type underwent strict airworthiness tests under the newly implemented Department of Commerce certification process.

Variants

Model 40B: designation applied to 19 examples of the Model 40A after the replacement of the Wasp engine by the 525-hp (391-kW) Pratt & Whitney Hornet radial to give improved performance
Model 40B-2: designation applied retrospectively to the Model 40B to indicate seating for two passengers, following introduction of the four-passenger Model 40B-4
Model 40B-4: 38 new-build aircraft retaining the Hornet engine, but introducing improvements such as seating for four passengers, openable cabin windows, a tailwheel replacing the tailskid, and shielding to improve radio communication
Model 40B-4A: designation applied to one standard Model 40B-4 used as an engine testbed by Pratt & Whitney
Model 40C: designation of 10 aircraft, the first flown on 16 August 1928, with seating for four passengers but retaining the Wasp engine of the Model 40A. All but one were later converted to Model 40B-4 standard
Model 40H-4: four standard Model 40B-4s built by Boeing Aircraft of Canada. Two were exported to New Zealand
Model 40X: designation used for one special-order machine basically similar to the Model 40C, but with an enclosed cabin for only two passengers and a second open cockpit forward of the pilot
Model 40Y: special-order machine, generally similar to the Model 40X, but with the Wasp engine replaced by the more powerful Hornet engine
Model 95: retaining a basically similar configuration to the Model 40, the Model 95 was a more modern all-cargo/mail transport with a biplane wing cellule of wooden construction with fabric covering, and incorporated the bolted Dural fuselage structure developed for the Model 83 and Model 89 (XF4B-1) fighter prototypes. Externally, it was similar to the Model 89, but was considerably larger. The first Model 95 was flown on 29 December 1928, powered by a 525-hp (391-kW) Pratt & Whitney Hornet radial
Model 95A: designation applied to the 23rd machine off the production line as tested by Boeing, with a lower-powered Pratt & Whitney Wasp engine

SPECIFICATION

Boeing Model 40A
Type: one-crew passenger, freight and mail transport
Powerplant: one Pratt & Whitney Wasp radial engine rated at 420 hp (313 kW)
Performance: maximum speed 128 mph (206 km/h) at optimum altitude; cruising speed 105 mph (169 km/h) at optimum altitude; initial climb rate 770 ft (235 m) per minute; service ceiling 14,500 ft (4420 m); range 650 miles (1046 km)

Weights: empty 3,531 lb (1602 kg); maximum take-off 6,000 lb (2722 kg)
Dimensions: wingspan 44 ft 2¾ in (13.47 m); length 33 ft 2¾ in (10.12 m); height 12 ft 3¼ in (3.73 m); wing area 547.00 sq ft (50.82 m²)
Payload: two passengers plus freight and/or mail within the context of a 1,600-lb (726-kg) payload

Boeing Model 42 (CO-7)

DH-4B and DH-4M upgrades kept the DH-4 in useful service into the middle of the 1920s, but by this time the surviving aircraft were structurally old and aerodynamically obsolete. There were still large numbers of engines and considerable stocks of equipment in reserve, however, and the US Army therefore decided to undertake a last programme to wrest still further service from the DH-4. One of the

elements of this final round of modifications was entrusted to Boeing, which created its **Boeing Model 42** design as the combination of the powerplant, fuselage and vertical tail surface of the DH-4M-1 with a new horizontal tail surface, wing cellule and landing gear.

The US Army allocated three DH-4M-1s to Boeing for conversion to the revised **CO-7** standard as prototypes for a proposed

corps observation type. These machines were to be one **XCO-7** for static tests, one **XCO-7A** for flight trials, and one **XCO-7B** for flight trials with a revised tail unit and powerplant.

The XCO-7B differed from the XCO-7A only in its balanced elevator halves and inverted version of the

Liberty 12A engine with a high thrust line. After completion, both the XCO-7A and XCO-7B were transported by railroad to McCook Field, Ohio, where the first flight was recorded by the XCO-7A on 6 February 1925. Trials soon confirmed that, while the basic design was adequate in terms of performance and handling, it offered little in the way of

performance improvement over current types. No production plans were considered, therefore, and the US Army turned finally to the consideration of all-new designs.

The XCO-7A incorporated tapered wings, a Liberty engine, wider horizontal tail surfaces, and a new landing gear onto a DH-4M-1 fuselage.

SPECIFICATION

Boeing Model 42 (XCO-7A)
Type: two-seat corps observation aircraft
Powerplant: one Liberty 12A Vee engine rated at 420 hp (313 kW)
Performance: maximum speed 122 mph (196 km/h) at sea level; cruising speed 110 mph (177 km/h) at optimum altitude; initial climb rate 810 ft (247 m) per minute; service ceiling 13,050 ft (3980 m); range 420 miles (676 km)
Weights: empty 3,107 lb

(1409 kg); maximum take-off 4,665 lb (2116 kg)
Dimensions: wingspan 45 ft (13.72 m); length 29 ft 2 in (8.89 m); height 10 ft 8 in (3.25 m); wing area 440.00 sq ft (40.88 m²)
Armament: two 0.3-in (7.62-mm) Browning fixed forward-firing machine-guns in the forward fuselage, and two 0.3-in (7.62-mm) Browning trainable rearward-firing machine-guns in the rear cockpit

Boeing Model 50 (PB)

In September 1925 the US Navy issued a requirement for a reconnaissance and bombing flying-boat able to make the non-stop 2,400-mile (3860-km) crossing of the eastern Pacific between San Francisco, California and Hawaii. The Naval Aircraft

Factory therefore developed an advanced flying-boat to be built by Boeing. The new flying-boat, known to the company as the **Boeing Model 50**, was of conventional layout with the exception of its powerplant of two water-cooled

engines in a tandem push/pull arrangement. Internally, however, the aircraft was full of structural innovations that were to be important in later Boeing designs and the construction of the hull was most unusual in that the lower portion was of

metal construction, while the upper portion was wooden. In addition to the two-step hull, the Model 50 featured an unstaggered equal-span two-bay biplane wing cellule.

By the time that the Model 50 was complete and accepted by the USN as the **PB-1**, the first flight between California and Hawaii had been accom-

plished in September 1925 by a NAF PN-9, and the PB-1 was therefore used for experimental tasks.

In 1928 the PB-1 became the **XPB-2** after the water-cooled powerplant had been replaced by the NAF with an air-cooled arrangement of two 800-hp (597-kW) Pratt & Whitney R-1860 Hornet geared radial engines.

The PB-1 introduced the aerodynamic innovation of using auxiliary aerofoil sections above and ahead of the ailerons to serve as aerodynamic balances.

SPECIFICATION	
Boeing Model 50 (PB-1) **Type:** five-crew maritime reconnaissance flying boat **Powerplant:** two Packard 2A-2500 Vee engines each rated at 800 hp (597 kW) **Performance:** maximum speed 112 mph (180 km/h) at sea level; cruising speed 94 mph (151 km/h) at optimum altitude; initial climb rate 400 ft (122 m) per minute; service ceiling 9,000 ft (2745 m); range 2,500 miles (4023 km) **Weights:** empty 11,551 lb	(5240 kg); maximum take-off 26,882 lb (12194 kg) **Dimensions:** wingspan 87 ft 6 in (26.67 m); length 59 ft 4¾ in (18.10 m); height 20 ft 10¼ in (6.36 m); wing area 1,801.00 sq ft (167.31 m²) **Armament:** single 0.3-in (7.62-mm) Browning trainable machine-guns, one each in the bow and a side-by-side pair of dorsal positions, plus up to 400 lb (181 kg) of bombs carried under the lower wing

Boeing Model 63 (TB)

During the 1920s the US Navy's Bureau of Aeronautics carried out the basic design of new naval aircraft whose construction was then allocated to industrial contractors. The Bureau wanted to take its experience with Curtiss and Martin torpedo-bombers one step further, the result of this process being a large biplane

whose construction was contracted to Boeing for production with the company designation **Boeing Model 63**. The primary structure was of Dural light alloy type, and the main units of the fixed tailskid landing gear carried twin wheels. The single-bay wing cellule was unstaggered and the wheeled undercarriage

could be replaced by an arrangement of two single-step floats.

The first machine, identified as the **XTB-1**, made its maiden flight in May 1927, and all three aircraft were delivered to the USN in June of the same year. The type saw limited service, but even before delivery of the three aircraft the Navy had decided that overwater

The XTB-1 crew consisted of pilot and bombardier/navigator in a side-by-side cockpit, and a rear gunner in the top of the rear fuselage. When attacking, the bombardier moved to the aiming station seen clearly here in the base of the forward fuselage.

operations would be better served by a twin-engined powerplant, resulting in the limited production of the **TB**. The basic design was further adapted with a powerplant of two wing-

mounted Wright R-1750 Cyclone radial piston engines. This powerplant was evaluated in a single **XTN-1** prototype and then contracted to Douglas for production as the T2D.

SPECIFICATION	
Boeing Model 63 (TB-1) **Type:** three-seat land- or shore-based torpedo bomber **Powerplant:** one Packard 3A-2500 Vee engine rated at 730 hp (544 kW) **Performance:** maximum speed 115 mph (185 km/h) at optimum altitude; cruising speed 100 mph (161 km/h) at olo altitude; initial climb rate 754 ft (230 m) per minute; service ceiling 12,500 ft (3810 m); range 878 miles (1413 km) **Weights:** empty 5,640 lb (2558 kg); maximum take-off	9,786 lb (4339 kg) **Dimensions:** wingspan 55 ft (16.76 m); length 40 ft 10 in (12.45 m); height 13 ft 6 in (4.12 m); wing area 868.00 sq ft (80.64 m²) **Armament:** one 0.3-in (7.62-mm) Browning fixed forward-firing machine-gun in the forward fuselage, and one 0.3-in (7.62-mm) Browning trainable rearward-firing machine-gun in the rear cockpit, plus one 1,740-lb (789-kg) Bliss-Leavitt torpedo carried under the fuselage

Boeing Model 66 (XP-8) and Model 69 (F2B)

Given the imminent availability of the new Packard 2A-1500 inverted-Vee engine offering a very useful 600 hp (448 kW), the US Army decided that an experimental fighter should be designed and built for the evaluation of this engine. In April 1925 Boeing agreed to manufacture one example of its **Boeing Model 66** design for evaluation.

The aircraft was delivered in July 1927 for official trials with the unofficial

designation **XP-8** that became official only after the USAAC had bought the machine from Boeing in January 1928. The XP-8 failed to meet the USAAC's expectations in terms of its performance, and therefore was not ordered into production. Plans to revise the type with a powerplant of one Pratt & Whitney R-1690 radial piston engine were considered but then dropped, and the XP-8 was retired in June 1929.

After it had evaluated the

FB-4 with a Wright P-1 radial engine, the USN directed that this machine be further revised as the FB-6 with a Pratt & Whitney Wasp. The FB-6 was evaluated exhaustively and demonstrated the clear superiority of the Wasp over the P-1, and this led to the Navy's decision to combine the former engine with an airframe based on that of the Model 66, evaluated by the US Army as the XP-8. The result was the **Boeing Model 69**, which

made its maiden flight as the USN's **XF2B-1** prototype on 3 November 1926. It differed mainly in the span of its upper and lower wings being more nearly equal, and in the propeller having a large spinner.

Satisfactory testing of the prototype resulted in an

order for 32 production aircraft under the designation **F2B-1**, with deliveries beginning on 30 January 1928, and these served with US Navy's VF-1B (fighter) and VB-2B (bomber) squadrons on board the USS *Saratoga*. The F2B-1 differed from the prototype by deletion of the spinner and introduction of a balanced rudder.

Variant

Model 69B: under this designation two aircraft, generally similar to the USN's F2B-1, were built for export, one each to Brazil and Japan

Boeing Model 66 (XP-8) and Model 69 (F2B) (continued)

Production aircraft, known as F2B-1s, featured an enlarged balanced rudder and a revised and strengthened undercarriage. This aircraft was the personal aircraft of the commander of VB-2B.

Boeing Model 74 and Model 77 (F3B)

First flown in March 1927, the **Boeing Model 74** private-venture naval fighter prototype was based on the F2B-1. It had the main landing gear arrangement of the FB-5, the rudder of the XF2B-1 (later changed to that of the F2B) and provision for the standard wheeled landing gear to be replaced by float alighting gear. This took the form of a single main float under the fuselage and two stabilising floats under the lower wing. The USN evaluated

the Model 74 as the **XF3B-1**, but decided against the concept of the fighter floatplane, and none of these four prototypes entered production.

On return to Boeing, the Model 74 was rebuilt as the **Model 77** prototype with basically the same powerplant and fuselage, although the latter was lengthened, but a completely new wing cellule, tail unit and landing gear. As first flown in February 1928, the Model

77 was thus an unequal-span biplane of mixed metal and wood construction covered largely with fabric except on the tail unit and ailerons, which were covered with a corrugated light alloy skinning. The machine was powered by one 425-hp (317-kW) R-1340-80 Wasp radial engine which drove a two-bladed metal propeller.

The Model 77 was evaluated by the USN and then ordered to the extent of 73 aircraft, supplemented by the prototype for a total of 74 machines. Production aircraft differed from the prototype mainly in the elimination of the spreader bar arrangement of the

undercarriage and the revision of the vertical tail surface's shape. The **F3B-1** fighters were delivered between August and November 1928, the first aircraft going to the VF-2B squadron on USS *Langley* and later aircraft being allo-

cated to the VB-2B (later VF-6B) squadron on the USS *Saratoga* and the VF-3B and VB-1B squadrons on the USS *Lexington*. The aircraft remained in first-line service to 1932, and were then retained as 'hacks'.

The US Navy operated the F3B-1 in the fighter-bomber role for four years. This example was dedicated to the bombing role and was operated by VB-1B from the USS Lexington.

Boeing Model 80 and Model 226

The growth of operations on the Boeing Air Transport Corporation's San Francisco-Chicago route resulted in the design and development of a purpose-designed passenger transport, the **Boeing Model 80**. First flown during August 1928 as a large unequal-span biplane, the Model 80 had a

marginally staggered two-bay wing cellule of fabric-covered wooden construction, and a fuselage and tail unit of welded steel tube, also covered with fabric. The landing gear was

of the fixed tailwheel type with wide-track divided main units, and power was provided by three 410-hp (306-kW) Pratt & Whitney Wasp radial engines.

The main cabin accom-

modated 12 passengers, plus a flight stewardess. This was very much an innovation for, although some European airlines had introduced male stewards at an earlier date, Boeing stewardesses, who were all registered nurses, represented the first of the air

hostesses that are now an integral part of civil airline operations.

Another feature of the Model 80 was the provision of a separate enclosed flightdeck for the pilot and co-pilot/navigator, a development that was not accepted enthusiastically by

The first two Model 80As were completed with fully-cowled engines and a smaller vertical tail. Later Model 80As featured a larger vertical tail which was supplemented by two auxiliary rudders after conversion to 80A-1 standard.

Variants

Model 80A-1: designation of 10 Model 80As after a modification that introduced increased vertical tail area in the form of two auxiliary fins and rudders, mounted on the tailplane, one on each side of the original fin and rudder assembly

Model 80B-1: the 12th machine off the Model 80A production line was completed with open accommodation for the flight crew. Following evaluation of this machine by BATC flight crews, it was subsequently converted to Model 80A-1 configuration, after it had been agreed that an enclosed flightdeck made for more efficient operation

Model 226: designation of the 11th machine off the Model 80A production line, completed as an executive transport for the Standard Oil Company, and introducing the additional vertical tail surfaces applied to the Model 80

all flight crew. Four of these aircraft were built, entering service with BATC in the late summer of 1928.

The Model 80s were to have been followed by 12 examples of the much improved **Model 80A**, this type having more powerful Pratt & Whitney Hornets, reduced fuel capacity, refinements to the wing, improved streamlining and, because of the increased power available, a cabin layout to accommodate a maximum of 18 passen-gers. Only 10 of the aircraft were completed as such, the 11th and 12th

airframes becoming the **Model 226** and **Model 80B-1** respectively.

SPECIFICATION	
Boeing Model 80A-1	minute; service ceiling 14,000 ft (4265 m); range 460 miles (740 km)
Type: two/three-crew commercial transport	**Weights:** empty 10,582 lb (4800 kg); maximum take-off 17,500 lb (7938 kg)
Powerplant: three Pratt & Whitney Hornet radial engines each rated at 525 hp (391 kW)	**Dimensions:** wingspan 80 ft (24.38 m); length 56 ft 6 in (17.22 m); height 15 ft 3 in (4.65 m); wing area 1,220.00 sq ft (113.34 m²)
Performance: maximum speed 138 mph (222 km/h) at optimum altitude; cruising speed 125 mph (201 km/h) at optimum altitude; initial climb rate 900 ft (274 m) per	**Payload:** up to 18 passengers and 898 lb (407 kg) of freight

Boeing Model 81 (N2B)

When the Fairchild engine company introduced the Fairchild-Caminez four-cylinder radial piston engine, Boeing decided to develop a trainer to take advantage of this power-plant. The latter was an innovatory unit in which the pistons powered the crankshaft by means of cams to produce one complete power cycle per revolution rather than one complete power cycle per two revolutions in conven-tional radial engines. The result was the **Boeing Model 81**, which was developed from the Model 64 private-venture trainer prototype that the company had flown in 1926 and had offered unsuccessfully to the USN in two forms as a two-bay

biplane with a thin aerofoil section and as a single-bay biplane with a thick aerofoil section.

The Model 81 was an unequal-span single-bay biplane of mixed metal and wood construction with a welded steel tube fuselage and tail unit and wooden wings. It was delivered to the USN in June 1928 but was difficult to evaluate properly as a result of prob-lems with the experimental engine. In January 1930, therefore, the Navy sent the machine to the Wright Aeronautical Corporation for revision with a better engine, the Wright R-540 that was the service version of the Whirlwind J-6-5 radial unit and rated at 165 hp (123 kW). Despite improved performance, the USN did

not order the Model 81 into production.

Boeing built another Model 81 in an effort to secure civil orders. This machine was evaluated in several forms with different engines, the original being the **Model 81A** which was originally flown with the Fairchild-Caminez, that was then replaced by a 145-hp (108-kW) Axelson radial. The machine first flew on

27 December 1928 and was delivered to the Boeing School of Aeronautics at Oakland, California. The school found this engine unsuitable and revised the Model 81A to **Model 81B** standard with a 115-hp (86-kW) Axelson engine and then with a J-6-5 radial. The final

changes were a redesigned vertical tail surface and the powerplant of one 100-hp (75-kW) Kinner K-5 radial engine to turn the Model 81B into the **Model 81C**. This machine lasted for several years as an airwor-thy trainer, and was then relegated to classroom use up to 1942.

Seen here fitted with the original Fairchild-Caminez engine, this aircraft was the second of two Model 81s built. It was sold to the US Navy as the XN2B-1 and was operated from the test centre at Anacostia, Maryland from June 1928.

SPECIFICATION	
Boeing Model 81 (XN2B-1)	minute; service ceiling 12,000 ft (3660 m); range 335 miles (539 km);
Type: two-seat primary flying trainer	**Weights:** empty 1,652 lb (749 kg); maximum take-off 2,178 lb (988 kg)
Powerplant: one Fairchild-Caminez radial engine rated at 125 hp (93 kW)	**Dimensions:** wingspan 35 ft (10.67 m); length 25 ft 8 in (7.82 m); height 11 ft 2 in (3.40 m); wing area 295.00 sq ft (27.41 m²)
Performance: maximum speed 104 mph (168 km/h) at sea level; initial climb rate 515 ft (157 m) per	

Boeing Model 93 (P-7)

In a manner exactly analo-gous to that employed to create the XP-4 out of the last PW-9 for evaluation of the Packard 1A-1500 engine in a turbocharged installation, the sole **XP-7** was created out of the final PW-9D by Boeing at the request of the USAAC for

the evaluation of the Curtiss V-1570 Conqueror Vee piston engine.

The resulting prototype was known to its manufac-turer as the **Boeing Model 93** and to the USAAC as the XP-7, and was an unequal-span biplane that could be regarded as virtually a

sesquiplane as the lower wing was so much smaller than the upper wing. The machine was of largely fabric-covered mixed metal and wood construction with a staggered single-bay wing cellule. The engine was installed under a full light-alloy cowling, drove a two-bladed metal Curtiss-Reed tractor propeller, and

SPECIFICATION	
Boeing Model 93 (XP-7)	3,260 lb (1479 kg)
Type: single-seat fighter	**Dimensions:** wingspan 32 ft (9.75 m); length 24 ft (7.31 m); height 9 ft (2.74 m); wing area 241.00 sq ft (22.39 m²)
Powerplant: one Curtiss V-1570-1 Vee engine rated at 600 hp (447 kW)	
Performance: maximum speed 167 mph (269 km/h) at sea level; initial climb rate 1,867 ft (847 m) per minute	**Armament:** two 0.3-in (7.62-mm) Browning fixed forward-firing machine-guns in the forward fuselage, plus up to 244 lb (111 kg) of bombs carried under the lower wing
Weights: empty 2,323 lb (1053 kg); maximum take-off	

was cooled by a 'tunnel' radiator installation with controllable shutters at its front.

The XP-7 was delivered in September 1928 and in its flight trials proved the suitability of the V-1570 engine for the fighter task. The USAAC considered an order for four P-7 fighters

for a full operational evalu-ation of the improved fighter, but later decided to await the appearance of the more modern type that Boeing was develop-ing via the parallel Model 83 and Model 89 proto-types. The XP-7 was then converted to standard PW-9D configuration.

With the exception of the experimental XP-9, the Model 93 was the last Boeing fighter to utilise a liquid-cooled engine. The V-1570-1 engine gave the aircraft a modest increase in performance over the standard PW-9D.

Boeing Model 96 (P-9)

The first monoplane designed and built by Boeing, but beaten into the air by the Model 200 Monomail, the **Boeing Model 96** design resulted from a requirement issued by the USAAC in May 1928. The conceptual and structural novelty of the new type combined with the low priority accorded to

it by the USAAC to delay the completion of the sole machine from April 1929 to September 1930. Consequently, the maiden flight did not take place until 18 November 1930.

The **XP-9** was a braced high-wing monoplane of all-metal construction and initial trials indicated that it possessed very poor

handling characteristics. These problems were largely as a result of the small area of its tail unit, and an inadequate down-ward field of vision for landing due to the location of the cockpit above and behind the broad-chord wing. An enlarged vertical tail surface with smooth metal skinning was introduced, but failed to effect

any significant improve-ment, and this revised **XP-9** logged only 15 hours in the air before being grounded for use as an instructional airframe in August 1931. Preliminary

plans had been made for the exercise of an option for five **Y1P-9** service test aircraft to be produced under the P-12D contract, but this option was not taken up.

The XP-9's Curtiss SV-1570-15 Vee engine was installed inside an extensively louvered cowling, drove a two-bladed Curtiss-Reed metal propeller fitted with a spinner, and was cooled by a radiator neatly installed inside the cowling.

SPECIFICATION

Boeing Model 96 (XP-9)
Type: single-seat fighter
Powerplant: one Curtiss SV-1570-15 Vee engine rated at 600 hp (448 kW)
Performance: maximum speed 213 mph (343 km/h) at optimum altitude; cruising speed 180 mph (290 km/h) at optimum altitude; initial climb rate 1,560 ft (475 m) per minute; service ceiling 26,800 ft (8170 m); range 425 miles (684 km)
Weights: empty 2,669 lb

(1211 kg); maximum take-off 3,623 lb (1643 kg)
Dimensions: wingspan 36 ft 6 in (11.13 m); length 25 ft 1¾ in (7.66 m); height 9 ft 10¼ in (3.00 m); wing area 210.00 sq ft (19.51 m²)
Armament: two 0.5-in (12.7-mm) Browning fixed forward-firing machine-guns in the forward fuselage, plus up to 244 lb (111 kg) of bombs carried under the fuselage

Boeing Models 83, 89, 99, 100, 218, 223, 235, etc (F4B)

Under the initial designations **Model 83** and **Model 89**, Boeing developed as a private venture two single-seat fighter prototypes for evaluation by the USN. Intended as replacements for the F2B and F3B and, it was hoped, for the USAAC's PW-9, the proto-types retained the same Wasp engine and therefore relied upon design refine-ments to offer improved performance. Both proto-types were of single-bay biplane configuration, with

wings of wooden construc-tion under a fabric covering, a steel tube fuselage covered largely with fabric, and a conventional braced tail unit. Both prototypes' landing gear was of the fixed tailskid type: while that of the Model 83 had main units that incorpo-rated a spreader bar, as well as arrester gear, the Model 89 had divided main units as well as an under-fuselage hardpoint for one 550-lb (249-kg) bomb. Both prototypes were evaluated

by the USN during 1928 under the designation **XF4B-1**, and the Model 89 was also flight-tested by USAAC pilots.

As a result of naval eval-uation, 27 aircraft were ordered under the designa-tion **F4B-1**. These combined the arrester hook of the Model 83 with the landing gear of the Model 89, and were built with the company designation **Model 99**. The first produc-tion example was flown on 6 May 1929, and all were delivered within less than four months. Production of this family of aircraft even-tually totalled 586 and there were many variants.

For naval operations, an arrester hook, as clearly visible on this F4B-1, was standard equipment. This aircraft belonged to VB-1B 'Red Rippers' and was flown as a bomber.

SPECIFICATION

Boeing Model 235 (F4B-4)
Type: single-seat carrierborne fighter
Powerplant: one Pratt & Whitney R-1340-16 Wasp radial engine rated at 550 hp (410 kW)
Performance: maximum speed 188 mph (303 km/h) at 6,000 ft (1830 m); climb to 5,000 ft (1525 m) in 2 minutes 42 seconds; service ceiling 26,900 ft (8200 m); range 370 miles (595 km)

Weights: empty 2,354 lb (1068 kg); maximum take-off 3,611 lb (1638 kg)
Dimensions: wingspan 30 ft (9.14 m); length 20 ft 1 in (6.12 m); height 9 ft 4 in (2.84 m); wing area 227.50 sq ft (21.13 m²)
Armament: two 0.3-in (7.62-mm) Browning fixed forward-firing machine-guns in the forward-fuselage

Variants

Model 99: company designation of the fourth production F4B-1 following its conversion as the **F4B-1A** executive transport for the Assistant Secretary of the US Navy
Model 100: company designation of four examples, similar to the F4B-1, built as commercial and export aircraft
Model 100A: one special two-seat machine built originally for Howard Hughes
Model 218: one company-owned machine with a semi-monocoque metal fuselage structure, flown by the US Army and Navy as the prototype of the **P-12E** and **F4B-3**, respectively. The machine was subsequently sold to China
Model 223: company designation of 46 **F4B-2** fighters for the USN, built to the same basic standard as the US Army's **P-12C**, but fitted with a tailwheel
Model 235: company designation for the USN's **F4B-3** and **F4B-4** fighters, of which 21 and 92 respectively were delivered. The F4B-3 was generally similar to the USAAC's **P-12E** except for installed equipment, while the F4B-4 had a vertical fin of increased area, and the last 45 carried a life raft in the pilot's headrest. A number of P-12 fighters transferred from the USAAC to the USN in 1940 were all designated **F4B-4A**
Model 256: company designation of 14 aircraft, similar to the USN's F4B-4 in standard, supplied to Brazil in 1932 for landplane service without arrester gear or flotation equipment
Model 267: company designation of nine additional aircraft supplied to Brazil as the wing cellule of the P-12E with the rest of the F4B-3's airframe

Boeing Models 100, 101, 102, 222, 227, 234 and 251 (P-12)

In November 1928 the USAAC, impressed with the performance and handling of the Model 89, placed an initial order for 10 examples of the **P-12** land-

based fighter, a type which was built as the **Model 102** and was essentially identi-cal to the US Navy's F4B-1 apart from its naval equip-ment. The first of these

aircraft was delivered in February 1929 in non-stan-dard form for use on a goodwill flight into Central America, and was then returned to Boeing for revi-

sion to full P-12 standard. The first true P-12 made its maiden flight in April 1929 with a powerplant of one 450-hp (336-kW) Pratt & Whitney R-1340-7 radial

engine. The revised aircraft were considered as service test types, and the last of them was completed as the sole **Model 101** for use as the **XP-12A**, which first flew in April 1929 and was in effect the true prototype for the USAAC series.

Some of the changes effected in the XP-12A were adopted for the **Model 102B** which the USAAC placed in service as the **P-12B**. This type was ordered to the extent of 90 aircraft and was the first genuine production variant. The first P-12B was handed over in February 1930, and its only subvariant was the **XP-12G** experimental development with the Y1SR-1340-G/H turbocharged engine inside the type of ring cowling later adopted for the P-12B. The machine was returned to P-12B standard at the end of the engine trials.

A privately-funded development at this time was the **Model 218** prototype. It made its first flight in September 1930 as a development of the P-12B with a semi-monocoque metal fuselage structure based on a type pioneered in the Model 96, Model 202 and Model 205, revised main landing gear, and, soon after the start of the trials programme, a vertical tail surface of revised shape as pioneered in the XP-15 and XF4B-1. This prototype was evaluated by the USN and USAAC, the latter according it the designation **XP-925** with the R-1340-D engine that was later replaced by an R-1340-E engine to produce the revised designation **XP-925A**.

The **P-12C**, known to Boeing as the **Model 222**, was ordered in June 1930 when the USAAC issued a contract for 131 examples of an improved P-12B with a number of detail changes and a later engine. The most obvious external changes in this model were the reversion to the Model 83's type of through-axle main landing gear unit, and the adoption of a ring cowling for the 450-hp (336-kW) R-1340-9 engine. The USAAC received the disassembled aircraft in August 1930, and the type made its first flight in January 1931. In the event only 96 aircraft were delivered up to February 1931, the last 35 aircraft being completed to the improved **P-12D** standard. The P-12D, known to Boeing as the **Model 227**, was externally indistinguishable from the P-12C except for the relocation of the wiring harness from the back to the front of the engine and the removal of the P-12C's cowling struts. The initial 35 aircraft were diverted from the P-12C order, and were delivered in disassembled form for a first flight made in March 1931. Another 16 aircraft of this variant were later created as P-12C conversions, and the entire P-12C and P-12D force was later retrofitted with the vertical tail surface of the **P-12E**. The sole subvariant of the P-12D was the **XP-12H**, which was the 33rd machine, experimentally fitted with a

GISR-1340-E geared radial engine. Trials revealed the unsatisfactory performance of this engine, and the XP-12H was converted back to P-12D standard.

Impressed with the stronger fuselage structure, revised vertical tail unit and improved performance of the Model 218 prototype, the USAAC ordered a production derivative as the P-12E, to which the manufacturer accorded the designation **Model 234**. In other respects the P-12E was basically similar to the P-12D, with the exception of its uprated powerplant. The order was placed in March 1931 and covered 135 aircraft, of which 110 were delivered to P-12E standard, with a first flight recorded in October 1931. The designation **XP-12E** was used for the first P-12E when used for test work and, after passing through a number of other designation changes, the machine became a standard P-12E. The **P-12J** was another P-12E, modified in this instance with a special bomb sight and an SR-1340-H engine. With the XP-12E and five P-12E aircraft, this machine later became one of the seven **YP-12K** aircraft with the SR-1340-E fuel-injected engine; all these aircraft reverted to basic P-12E standard in June 1938. Before this time, the machine that had been the XP-12E became the sole

P-12Es flown by the US Army Air Corps were almost identical to the F4B-4s flown by the USN. The P-12E could be distinguished from other aircraft in the series by its faired headrest. On the F4B-4 this contained a life raft.

XP-12L between January 1934 and February 1937 when fitted with a Type F-7 turbocharger for its engine.

The **P-12F** was the last production variant of the P-12 family and was known to its manufacturer as the **Boeing Model 251**. These were the last 25 aircraft of the P-12E order, and were delivered between March and May 1932 with the powerplant of one 500-hp

(373-kW) Pratt & Whitney SR-1340-G engine. In a modification that was later retrofitted to the earlier aircraft as well as to all of the P-12Es, the last 10 aircraft were also delivered with a tailwheel in place of a tailskid. The very last machine, which was the final machine of the P-12 and F4B family, was also delivered with a fully enclosed cockpit with a rearward-sliding section for access. The surviving aircraft were finally retired for use as instructional airframes during 1941.

SPECIFICATION
Boeing Model 234 (P-12E)

Type: single-seat fighter
Powerplant: one Pratt & Whitney R-1340-17 radial engine rated at 500 hp (373 kW)
Performance: maximum speed 189 mph (304 km/h) at 7,000 ft (2135 m); cruising speed 160 mph (257 km/h) at optimum altitude; climb to 10,000 ft (3050 m) in 10 minutes 48 seconds; service ceiling 26,300 ft (8015 m); range 580 miles (933 km)
Weights: empty 1,999 lb (907 kg); maximum take-off 2,690 lb

(1220 kg)
Dimensions: wingspan 30 ft (9.14 m); length 20 ft 3 in (6.17 m); height 9 ft (2.74 m); wing area 227.50 sq ft (21.09 m²)
Armament: one 0.5-in (12.7-mm) Browning fixed forward-firing machine-gun and one 0.3-in (7.62-mm) Browning fixed forward-firing machine-gun, or two 0.3-in (7.62-mm) Browning fixed forward-firing machine-guns, in the forward fuselage, plus up to 700 lb (318 kg) of bombs carried under the fuselage and lower wing

At least one P-12B has been restored and flown in the markings of the 95th Attack Squadron of the 17th Attack Group, USAAC. The aircraft has the Olive Drab and yellow colours typical of the era.

Variants

Model 100E: two aircraft essentially identical to the P-12E for Thailand
Model 100F: single machine essentially identical to the P-12F and delivered to Pratt & Whitney as an engine testbed

Boeing Model 200 and Model 221 Monomail

With the continuing requirement for aircraft of the cargo/mail-carrying type, in 1929 Boeing began the development of a machine far more advanced than its current Model 40 and Model 95. A low-wing monoplane of all-metal construction, the **Boeing Model 200 Monomail** had

a performance that benefited from a number of new ideas: the cantilever wing eliminated drag-inducing struts and bracing wires, a semi-monocoque fuselage structure provided a more streamlined shape, semi-retractable tailwheel landing gear ensured that most of the main unit struc-

ture was retracted within the wing during cruising flight, and the radial engine was surrounded by a low-drag cowling.

Using the same engine as the Model 40B, the advanced Model 200 was able to demonstrate superior performance.

Boeing Model 200 and Model 221 Monomail (continued)

The Model 200 retained the open pilot's cockpit, situated well aft, and the forward cargo/mail compartments of the earlier Model 40.

First flown on 6 May 1930, the Monomail was used for a number of tests and experimental flights before entering service on Boeing Air Transport's San Francisco-Chicago route in July 1931.

Variants

Model 221 Monomail: a single machine, first flown on 18 August 1930, with its fuselage lengthened by 8 in (0.20 m), but its cargo/mail capacity reduced to provide accommodation for six passengers in an enclosed cabin
Model 221A Monomail: designation applied to the Model 200 and Model 221 following fuselage 'stretches' to provide accommodation for eight passengers. Both aircraft saw service on the Cheyenne-Chicago route of Boeing's newly formed United Air Lines subsidiary

Boeing Model 202 (P-15)

As soon as its P-12 and F4B fighters were under production, Boeing turned its attentions to the design of a more advanced fighter to supersede these classic biplanes. Boeing was already at work on two considerably more advanced aircraft, the Model 200 Monomail and the Model 96, but decided that it would be sensible also to adopt a lower-risk approach to fighter design by creating an interim type that was little more than the current type of biplane fighter revised to mono-plane configuration and upgraded with all the drag-reduction features that could be incorporated.

The design team's first thought in this direction was the **Model 97** design, which was to have been nothing more than the second prototype Model 89 adapted to monoplane configuration by the removal of the lower wing and the addition of lift struts to support the revised upper wing. Boeing then decided not to build this type, but to use the same basic concept in the **Model 202**, which was to be of basically all-metal construction with a semi-monocoque fuselage based on that of the Model 96. (The major jump in designation numbers, it should be noted, was not the result of a furious spate of activity by the aircraft design team, but rather the company's decision to assign the numbers between 103 and 199 to aerofoil designs.)

The Model 202 was built as a private venture and made its first flight in January 1930 as a parasol-wing monoplane with a powerplant based on one 450-hp (336-kW) Pratt & Whitney SR-1340-D Wasp radial engine.

After the completion of its manufacturer's trials, the Model 202 was transferred to Wright Field, Ohio, for official trials in March 1930. During these trials it received the unofficial designation **XP-15**, a narrow-chord ring cowling and a revised vertical tail surface. The USAAC found that the XP-15 had a higher level speed than the current P-12B fighter, but also that its landing speed, climb rate and agility all suffered from the loss of wing area.

The Model 202 was therefore not ordered into production, but nonetheless proved useful for the introduction of a number of design and constructional details that were adopted for later aircraft of the P-12 series. The Model 202 was lost in a crash during February 1931.

On 7 February 1931 the sole Model 202 was lost at the end of a high-speed run. A propeller blade separated from the hub, the subsequent vibration being so severe that the Wasp engine was thrown from the aircraft. The type's parasol wing is clearly evident in this view.

Boeing Model 203

In 1929 Boeing began the design of a low-powered biplane that could be used as a trainer at the Boeing School of Aeronautics. The forward cockpit was large enough to accommodate two passengers, however, and this made the machine suitable for secondary use as a general utility type. Designated as the **Boeing Model 203**, the new type was a single-bay biplane with wings of fabric-covered wooden construction, while the fuselage and braced tail unit were of welded steel tube construction, also covered with fabric.

Five of these aircraft were laid down, the first of them powered by the 145-hp (108-kW) Axelson radial engine and the last three by the 165-hp (123-kW) Axelson radial engine, while the second was completed to **Model 203A** standard with the Wright Whirlwind J-6-5 radial engine. The first Model 203 made its maiden flight on 1 July 1929, and all five aircraft were duly delivered to Boeing's flying school. The four Model 203s were subsequently converted to Model 203A standard by the installation of the Wright engine, and two additional Model 203As were built at the school. Most of them acquired tail-wheels to replace their tailskids at a later date.

The final designation **Model 204B** was applied to four of the Model 203As after their conversion to advanced trainer standard with the 220-hp (164-kW) Avco Lycoming R-680 radial engine, more comprehensive instrumentation and a blind-flying hood for the pupil's cockpit.

Bearing similarities in design to the Model 95 and the P-12/F4B, the Model 203 seated two passengers side-by-side in its forward cockpit, with the pilot situated aft. It was the last Boeing type to employ a welded steel fuselage.

Boeing Model 205 (F5B)

The **Boeing Model 205** was nothing more than a copy of the Model 202 with the revisions required to turn it into a carrierborne fighter and bomber, most notably an arrester hook, enlarged fuel capacity and provision for the carriage of a bombload under the fuselage. The sole prototype was manufactured by Boeing as a private venture, but delivered straight to the USN under a bailment contract for evaluation as the **XF5B-1** prototype. The type made its maiden flight in February 1930 without undertaking any preliminary manufacturer's trials, and was later revised with a narrow-chord ring cowling and a revised vertical tail.

The USN found that the machine was faster than the Model 202 at sea level because the engine was rated for optimum performance at low level, and that the range was greater. The Navy did not order the type into production as it offered no significant improvement over the current F4B, but later bought the prototype, whereupon the unofficial XF5B-1 designation became official. The XF5B-1 was then used for several experimental tasks before being destroyed in static structural tests in March 1936.

Compared to the Model 202, the Model 205 had the appearance of a much cleaner design thanks to its cowling and revised tail shape.

SPECIFICATION	
Boeing Model 205 (XF5B-1) **Type:** single-seat carrierborne fighter and bomber **Powerplant:** one Pratt & Whitney SR-1340-C Wasp radial engine rated at 480 hp (358 kW) **Performance:** maximum speed 171 mph (275 km/h) at sea level; cruising speed 145 mph (233 km/h) at optimum altitude; initial climb rate 1,850 ft (564 m) per minute; service ceiling 26,400 ft (8045 m); range 690 miles (1111 km)	**Weights:** empty 2,062 lb (935 kg); maximum take-off 3,419 lb (1551 kg) **Dimensions:** wingspan 30 ft 6 in (9.30 m); length 21 ft (6.40 m); height 9 ft 4 in (2.84 m); wing area 157.30 sq ft (14.61 m²) **Armament:** two 0.3-in (7.62-mm) Browning fixed forward-firing machine-guns in the forward fuselage, plus up to 500 lb (227 kg) of bombs carried under the fuselage

Boeing Model 214, Model 215 and Model 246 (B-9)

In 1930 Boeing began the private-venture development of a bomber. To achieve outstanding performance, the design was based on the revolutionary Model 200 and the resulting prototypes and service evaluation bombers were, in effect, scaled-up versions of this type. They differed by having a twin-engined powerplant and by adaptation of the slender fuselage to accommodate the crew and weapons. To provide the crew accommodation, the fuselage was extended well forward of the wing and the bombload could be divided between an internal bomb bay and underwing racks.

First to fly was the **Boeing Model 215**, which made its maiden flight on 13 April 1931 with the powerplant of two 575-hp (429-kW) Pratt & Whitney R-1860-13 Hornet radial engines. This was tested by the USAAC under the initial designation **XB-901** and satisfactory testing resulted in the purchase of this machine with the designation **YB-9**. At the same time the then-incomplete **Model 214** was contracted under the designation **Y1B-9**, plus five additional service test aircraft with the designation **Y1B-9A** (**Model 246**).

The Model 214, initially powered by two 600-hp (447-kW) Curtiss V-1570-29 Conqueror Vee engines, first flew on 5 November 1931, and was later re-engined with a supercharged version of the Pratt & Whitney Hornet radial engine. This powerplant was also used in the Y1B-9A service test aircraft, the first of which flew on 14 July 1932.

The Y1B-9A differed externally from the earlier prototypes in having modified vertical tail surfaces, and internally featured a number of equipment and structural changes to meet service requirements.

Subsequent testing, and evaluation against the Martin Model 123, resulted in orders for the Martin bomber as the B-10 and a considerable disappointment for Boeing.

SPECIFICATION	
Boeing Model 246 (Y1B-9A) **Type:** five-seat medium bomber **Powerplant:** two Pratt & Whitney SR-1860-11 radial engines each rated at 600 hp (447 kW) **Performance:** maximum speed 186 mph (299 km/h) at 6,000 ft (1830 m); cruising speed 165 mph (266 km/h) at optimum altitude; initial climb rate 900 ft (274 m) per minute; service ceiling 20,750 ft (6325 m); range 540 miles (869 km) **Weights:** empty 8,941 lb	(4056 kg); maximum take-off 14,320 lb (6495 kg) **Dimensions:** wingspan 76 ft 10 in (23.42 m); length 51 ft 9 in (15.77 m); height 12 ft (3.66 m); wing area 954.00 sq ft (88.63 m²) **Armament:** single 0.3-in (7.62-mm) Browning trainable machine-guns in the nose and dorsal positions, plus up to 2,260 lb (1025 kg) of bombs carried internally and externally

The USAAC's first all-metal cantilever bomber (Y1B-9A, foreground) and first production monoplane fighter (Boeing XP-936) formate.

Boeing Model 236 (F6B and BFB)

The **Boeing Model 236** was the last biplane fighter designed as such by Boeing, for higher designations were used only to describe developments of existing fighters. Another distinction held by the type was that of being the last biplane fighter designed for the US Navy with a fixed landing gear.

The spur for the design of the Model 236 was the advent of a new two-row radial engine, the Pratt & Whitney R-1535 Twin Wasp Junior unit that combined a high power output with a moderately small overall diameter. Indeed, Model 236 may be regarded as the ultimate expression of the design philosophy used in the F4B series of fighters, but with greater power, a basically all-metal primary structure, an improved main landing gear arrangement, and a number of detail refinements.

The **XF6B-1** made its maiden flight on 1 February 1933 and after completing its manufacturer's trials, was evaluated by the Navy.

The service decided that the XF6B-1 lacked the agility to merit production, but the prototype was retained for test work and in March 1934 received the revised designation **XBFB-1** in the new BF-for-Bomber Fighter category.

A single example of the Model 236 was completed. Flying originally as the XF6B-1, the aircraft was lost as the XBFB-1 in a landing accident in 1936.

SPECIFICATION	
Boeing Model 236 (XF6B-1) **Type:** single-seat carrierborne fighter **Powerplant:** one Pratt & Whitney R-1535-44 Twin Wasp Junior radial engine rated at 625 hp (466 kW) **Performance;** maximum speed 200 mph (322 km/h) at 6,000 ft (1830 m); cruising speed 170 mph (274 km/h) at optimum altitude; climb to 5,000 ft (1525 m) in 4 minutes 12 seconds; service ceiling 24,400 ft (7435 m); range 737 miles (1186 km)	**Weights:** empty 2,288 lb (1038 kg); maximum take-off 4,283 lb (1943 kg) **Dimensions:** wingspan 28 ft 6 in (8.69 m); length 22 ft 1½ in (6.74 m); height 10 ft 7 in (3.22 m); wing area 252.00 sq ft (23.41 m²) **Armament:** two 0.3 in (7.62 mm) Browning fixed forward-firing machine-guns in the forward fuselage, plus up to 500 lb (227 kg) of bombs carried under the fuselage

Boeing Model 247

On 8 February 1933 Boeing flew the prototype of a new airliner which was identified by the designation **Boeing Model 247**. The design team had evolved this machine in aerodynamic and structural terms from the Model 200 and Model 215.

A revolutionary aircraft, the Model 247 has since been regarded as a prototype for the modern airliner, for it was a clean low-wing cantilever monoplane of all-metal construction with a

twin-engined powerplant and tailwheel landing gear with retractable main units. In addition, it offered fully enclosed accommodation for a pilot, co-pilot, stewardess and 10 passengers. With one engine inoperative, the machine could climb and maintain altitude with a full load, and the type also introduced a new feature for a civil transport by being equipped with pneumatic de-icing boots on the leading edges of the wing and tail unit to

prevent ice accretion from reaching a dangerous level.

Sixty examples of the Model 247 were ordered 'off the drawing board' to re-equip the Boeing Air Transport System, shortly to become a major limb of United Air Lines, and another 15 were ordered subsequently for companies or individuals. That built for Roscoe Turner and Clyde Pangborn as a contender in the England-Australia MacRobertson air race of 1934 was provided with fuselage fuel tanks instead of the standard airline cabin equipment, and introduced drag-reducing NACA engine cowlings and controllable-pitch propellers with optimum settings for take-off and cruising performance.

When the USA became involved in World War II in December 1941, 27 Model 247Ds remaining in airline use were impressed for service with the USAAF under the designation **C-73**. It had been anticipated that the aircraft

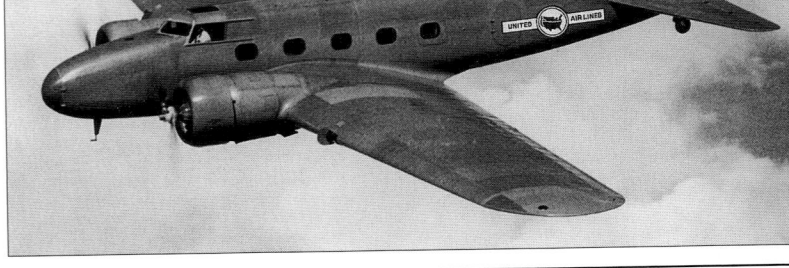

Variants

Model 247A: the 30th Model 247, adapted as an executive transport and testbed for Pratt & Whitney
Model 247E: designation applied to the first Model 247 when used by Boeing to test improvements that were incorporated in the Model 247D and retained after it entered airline service in Model 247D configuration
Model 247Y: after some service with United Air Lines, one Model 247D was converted under this designation as a private military aircraft for a customer in China, with the armament of two 0.5-in (12.7-mm) fixed forward-firing machine-guns, plus one gun of the same calibre on a trainable mounting in the dorsal position

These improvements were incorporated retrospectively on most airline Model 247s, thus elevating them to **Model 247D** standard, which also included a backward- rather than forward-sloped windscreen.

could be used for the carriage of cargo and troops, but it was discovered that the cabin doors were too small for this purpose. Instead, the C-73s were deployed to ferry aircrew and, later in the war, were used for training. In service they were revised with 600-hp (447-kW) Pratt & Whitney R-1340-AN-1 radial engines. When no longer required in late 1944, they were returned to civil airlines for further service.

SPECIFICATION	
Boeing Model 247D	25,400 ft (7740 m); range 745 miles (1199 m)
Type: three-crew civil transport	
Powerplant: two Pratt & Whitney S1H1C Wasp radial engines each rated at 550 hp (410 kW)	**Weights:** empty 9,144 lb (4148 kg); maximum take-off 13,650 lb (6192 kg)
Performance: maximum speed 200 mph (322 km/h) at optimum altitude; cruising speed 189 mph (304 km/h) at 8,000 ft (2440 m); initial climb rate 1,150 ft (351 m) per minute; service ceiling	**Dimensions:** wingspan 74 ft (22.56 m); length 51 ft 7 in (15.72 m); height 12 ft 1¾ in (3.60 m); wing area 836.13 sq ft (77.68 m²)
	Payload: up to 10 passengers and 400 lb (181 kg) of mail

Boeing Model 248, Model 266 and Model 281 (P-26)

Work on the company-funded **Boeing Model 248** prototype began in September 1931, although the USAAC contracted to supply engines and instruments for three trials aircraft which were designated **XP-936**. Destined to become the first all-metal production fighter and the first monoplane to serve with the USAAC in the pursuit role, the new fighter retained an open cockpit. In addition, despite Boeing's experience with retractable main landing gear units and cantilever wings, fixed landing gear and externally braced wings were employed.

The first XP-936 flew on

20 March 1932, and later completed an evaluation programme at Wright Field, Ohio, where the second airframe had been delivered for static tests. On 25 April the third was sent to Selfridge Field, Michigan, for tests with operational squadrons. Boeing subsequently received a production order for 111 (later increased to 136) of the **Model 266** production version, which had the USAAC designation **P-26A** and incorporated some improvements, including a

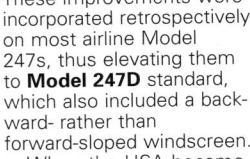

SPECIFICATION	
Boeing Model 266 (P-26A)	(1340 kg)
Type: single-seat fighter	
Powerplant: one Pratt & Whitney R-1340-27 radial engine rated at 500 hp (373 kW)	**Dimensions:** wingspan 27 ft 11⅜ in (8.52 m); length 23 ft 7 in (7.19 m); height 10 ft ⅜ in (3.06 m); wing area 149.50 sq ft (13.89 m²)
Performance: maximum speed 234 mph (377 km/h) at 7,500 ft (2285 m); cruising speed 200 mph (322 km/h) at optimum altitude; initial climb rate 2,360 ft (719 m) per minute; service ceiling 24,400 ft (8350 m); range 360 miles (579 km)	**Armament:** two 0.5-in (12.7-mm) Browning fixed forward-firing machine-guns or one 0.5-in (12.7-mm) and one 0.3-in (7.62-mm) Browning fixed forward-firing machine-guns in the forward fuselage, plus up to 200 lb (91 kg) of bombs carried externally
Weights: empty 2,197 lb (997 kg); maximum take-off 2,955 lb	

revised wing structure and the addition of flotation gear and radio; later aircraft also had higher headrests to protect the pilot in a roll-over crash. The first production P-26A made its maiden flight on 10 January 1934 and the last of the original 111 aircraft was delivered at the end of June 1934.

The need to reduce the landing speed of the P-26 resulted in the development of trailing-edge flaps which were fitted retrospectively to aircraft already in service and to those still on the production line. These included the additional order for 25 aircraft completed as the two **P-26B** (**Model 266A**) aircraft with the Pratt & Whitney R-1340-33 fuel-injected engine, and the 23 **P-26C** aircraft which had minor changes to the fuel system and carburation. Many were later converted to P-26B standard. Production was completed by 12 export examples of the **Boeing Model 281**, comprising 11 for China and one aircraft for Spain.

Operators of P-26 fighters surplus to US requirements included Guatemala and Panama. Although Boeing's diminutive fighter had been retired from front-line service by the time the USA entered World War II, the P-26 was among the aircraft ranged against the Japanese at Pearl Harbor, and machines of the Philippine army air force's 6th Pursuit Squadron were in action as Japanese forces fought their way through the archipelago.

Boeing Model 264 (P-29)

Even as it was developing its Model 248 prototype, Boeing was aware that its new fighter should be regarded at best as an interim type. For this reason, therefore, Boeing decided that it would undertake as a private venture, although with a large measure of USAAC support, a more advanced fighter prototype, and this improved type was allocated the company designation **Boeing Model 264**.

The Model 264 was clearly related to the Model 266 in conceptual and structural terms and also possessed the same powerplant and basically the same fuselage and tail unit. Where the new type differed from the Model 266, however, was in its enclosed cockpit, cantilever wing, and tailwheel landing gear. The main units of the latter retracted rearward into the undersurface of the wing, leaving the lower half of each wheel exposed. The powerplant was based on one 475-hp (354-kW) Pratt & Whitney R-1340-31 Wasp radial, installed inside a long-chord NACA cowling to drive a two-bladed propeller.

The first machine made its maiden flight on 20 January 1934. Only five days later the machine was flown to Wright Field, Ohio, for evaluation by the USAAC, with the experimental designation **XP-940**. The service felt that, while the new fighter might not be suitable as an operational type, it did point the way to the future. It therefore agreed to buy the machine as well as to purchase two more aircraft.

The first of the two new machines was the **YP-29**, which featured a revised tailwheel and cockpit enclosure, and uprated powerplant. The cockpit of the Model 264 had been criticised for its narrowness, and the YP-29 therefore featured a wider, longer 'glasshouse' enclosure. Trials revealed that the new cockpit was a major improvement, but poor take-off and landing performance resulted in the USAAC's decision to have the YP-29 revised with a one-piece split flap on the inboard sections of the wing's trailing edges and extending right across the underside of the fuselage.

In this form the machine was used for a number of experimental tasks, including trials with controllable-pitch propellers, and was eventually accorded the revised designation **P-29**.

The **YP-29A** designation was applied to the Model 264 prototype when it returned to USAAC service in April 1934 after purchase from Boeing and modification with an open cockpit, a pilot's headrest faired into the upper line of the rear fuselage, and a narrower-chord engine cowling. The **YP-29B** was the second machine ordered directly by the USAAC, and was completed to a standard that differed from that of the YP-29A only in the slightly greater dihedral of the outer wing panels, a one-piece split flap like that of the YP-29 under the fuselage and centre section, and a tailwheel unit like that of the YP-29.

All three aircraft eventually proved useful in a number of development and experimental tasks after initial consideration of a P-29A production version had been abandoned as a result of the fact that while the type was somewhat faster than the P-26A it had a lower service ceiling and poorer levels of agility.

In its XP-940 form (illustrated), the Model 264 had a relatively small cockpit enclosure compared to that of later variants. The lack of bracing for the cantilever wing allowed a noticeably cleaner design.

SPECIFICATION	
Boeing Model 264 (YP-29)	(1138 kg); maximum take-off
Type: single-seat fighter	3,518 lb (1596 kg)
Powerplant: one Pratt & Whitney R-1340-35 radial piston engine rated at 600 hp (448 kW)	**Dimensions:** wingspan 29 ft 4½ in (8.95 m); length 24 ft 11¾ in (7.61 m); height 7 ft 8 in (2.34 m); wing area 176.60 sq ft (16.41 m²)
Performance: maximum speed 250 mph (402 km/h) at optimum altitude; cruising speed 212 mph (341 km/h) at optimum altitude; climb rate at 10,000 ft (3050 m) 1,600 ft (488 m) per minute; service ceiling 26,000 ft (7925 m); range 800 miles (1288 km)	**Armament:** one 0.5-in (12.7-mm) Browning fixed forward-firing machine-gun and one 0.3-in (7.62-mm) Browning fixed forward-firing machine-gun in the forward fuselage, plus up to 10 17-lb (7.7-kg) fragmentation bombs carried internally
Weights: empty 2,509 lb	

Boeing Model 273 (F7B)

The **Boeing Model 273** was in fact schemed slightly before the Model 264 (P-29) and the two types differed mainly in details and the naval equipment installed in the Model 273. Resulting from a requirement issued by the USN's Bureau of Aeronautics in December 1932 for an advanced carrierborne fighter, the Model 273 was selected for prototype construction in preference to three other monoplane proposals. It represented a significant number of 'firsts' including the first cantilever low-wing monoplane fighter with retractable landing gear to be evaluated by the Navy and the first Boeing aircraft to be completed with a controllable-pitch propeller and flown with wing trailing-edge flaps.

The aircraft was mainly of Dural semi-monocoque construction and was powered by a Pratt & Whitney SR-1340-30 Wasp radial piston engine, which drove a two-bladed variable-pitch metal propeller.

The **XF7B-1** made its maiden flight on 14 September 1933 and, retrofitted with a long-chord NACA cowling, arrived for its official evaluation at Anacostia, Maryland, in November 1933. The trials showed that the XF7B-1's overall levels of performance were somewhat better than those of current biplane fighters, but the aircraft possessed poor agility by comparison with that of current biplane types. In addition, its configuration, high landing speed, and poor downward fields of vision all made the XF7B-1 unsuitable for carrierborne operations.

Boeing was able to improve the aircraft to a limited extent, but the combination of the XF7B-1's lack of agility and long landing run dictated that it would not enter production. The aircraft was retained as a test machine, however, and was eventually scrapped after an accident in March 1935. The cause of the crash was a windscreen collapse in the course of a terminal-velocity test dive, causing the pilot to pull out so sharply that the machine exceeded its 9-*g* loading limit by 3.1 *g*. The structure was so 'sprung' that the machine could not be flown again without expensive repairs being undertaken.

The Model 273's low-set thick-section wing made it difficult for a carrier landing signal officer to see the aircraft's tailplane to judge the approaching machine's attitude and speed during a carrier landing.

SPECIFICATION	
Boeing Model 273 (XF7B-1)	824 miles (1326 km)
Type: single-seat carrierborne fighter	**Weights:** empty 2,782 lb (1262 kg); maximum take-off 3,868 lb (1755 kg)
Powerplant: one Pratt & Whitney SR-1340-30 Wasp radial piston engine rated at 550 hp (410 kW)	**Dimensions:** wingspan 31 ft 11 in (9.73 m); length 27 ft 7 in (8.41 m); height 7 ft 5 in (2.26 m); wing area 213.00 sq ft (19.79 m²)
Performance: maximum speed 233 mph (375 km/h) at 10,000 ft (3050 m); cruising speed 200 mph (322 km/h) at optimum altitude; climb to 5,000 ft (1525 m) in 3 minutes 24 seconds; service ceiling 29,200 ft (8900 m); range	**Armament:** two 0.3-in (7.62-mm) Browning fixed forward-firing machine-guns in the forward fuselage

Boeing Model 294 (B-15 and C-105)

In 1930s America a number of radical thinkers, in both the US government and services, realised that the USA might eventually require an advanced strategic bomber. This thinking led to the introduction of the Boeing B-9, and the Martin B-10 and B-12. While it was appreciated that these did not represent the ideal, they did serve the purpose of

preparing the way for the procurement of a true strategic bomber.

In 1933 came the US Army's requirement for a design study of such a warplane, then identified as the XBLR-1 (Experimental Bomber Long Range no.1), that included in its requirements a range of 5,000 miles (8046 km). Both Boeing and Martin produced design studies,

In the US Army men like Colonels Hugh Knerr and C. W. Howard were working steadily away in the 1930s to ensure, to the best of their capability, that the US would have a strategic bombing capability.

but it was the former company which received the contract for construction and development of its **Boeing Model 294** under the designation **XB-15**. When this large monoplane flew for the first time on 15 October 1937, it was the largest aircraft built in the USA up to that time.

As might be expected, the XB-15 introduced a number of original features including internal passages within the wing to permit minor engine repairs or adjustments in flight; two auxiliary power units within the fuselage; sleeping bunks to allow for 'two-watch' operation and the introduction of a flight engi-

neer into the crew. The designed powerplant was four liquid-cooled double-Vee engines each rated at something in the order of 2,000 hp (1491 kW), but such engines did not materialise for some years and the actual powerplant comprised four 1,000-hp

(746-kW) units, which meant that performance was far below that estimated. The Model 294 was purely an experimental aircraft, but was provided with cargo doors and flown as a cargo transport during World War II under the designation **XC-105**.

SPECIFICATION

Boeing Model 294 (XB-15)
Type: 10-crew long-range bomber and transport
Powerplant: four Pratt & Whitney R-1830-11 radial engines each rated at 1,000 hp (746 kW)
Performance: maximum speed 195 mph (314 km/h) at 5,000 ft (1525 m); cruising speed 152 mph (245 km/h) at 6,000 ft (1830 m); service ceiling 18,900 ft (5760 m); range 5,130 miles (8256 km)
Weights: empty 37,709 lb (17105 kg); maximum take-off 92,000 lb (41731 kg)
Dimensions: wingspan 149 ft

(45.42 m); length 87 ft 7 in (26.70 m); height 18 ft 1 in (5.51 m); wing area 2,780.00 sq ft (258.26 m²)
Armament: (XB-15) single 0.5-in (12.7-mm) Browning trainable machine-guns in the nose position and dorsal turret, single 0.3-in (7.62-mm) Browning trainable machine-guns in each of the two ventral positions, and single 0.3-in (7.62-mm) Browning trainable machine-guns in each of the two beam positions, plus up to 8,000 lb (3629 kg) of bombs carried internally

Boeing Model 299 (B-17 Flying Fortress, B-40, BQ-7, etc)

In May 1934 the USAAC issued its specification for an advanced multi-engined bomber able to haul a 2,000-lb (907-kg) bombload over a range of between 1,020 miles (1640 km) and, somewhat optimistically, 2,200 miles (3540 km) at speeds of between 200 and 250 mph (322 and 402 km/h). So far as the USAAC was concerned, 'multi' meant more than one engine but Boeing, invited to submit its proposal for this requirement, elected to use four engines to power its **Model 299 Flying Fortress**, on which design work was initiated in mid-June 1934.

On 28 July 1935 the Model 299 flew for the first

time. Just over three weeks later it was flown non-stop to Wright Field, Ohio, to be handed over for official test and evaluation: the 2,100-mile (3380-km) flight being made at an average speed of 252 mph (406 km/h). The elation of the Boeing company was understandable, especially with confirmation that initial trials were progressing well. On 30 October 1935 these early hopes were partially dashed by the news that the prototype had crashed on take-off: subsequent investigation showed that the attempt to take-off had been made with the controls locked. However, in view of the satisfactory testing before this accident, the USAAC

decided on the procurement of 13 **YB-17** (later **Y1B-17**) service test aircraft as well as one further airframe for static testing.

The crashed prototype had been powered by four 750-hp (559-kW) Pratt & Whitney R-1680-E Hornet radial engines and in overall configuration the machine was a low-wing cantilever monoplane with the

In addition to the Fortress Mk Is of No. 90 Sqn (illustrated), the RAF operated variants of the Fortress B.Mk II (B-17F) and B.Mk IIA (B-17E), and Fortress B.Mk III (B-17G).

section of the wing at the roots so thick that it was equal to half the diameter of the circular-section fuselage. Other features of the design were wide-span flaps on the wing's trailing edge, fixed tailwheel landing gear with electrically retractable main units, and an armament that included five 0.3-in (7.62-mm) machine-guns and a maximum bomb load of 4,800 lb (2177 kg) carried in the fuselage bomb bay.

The initial Y1B-17 flew for the first time on 2 December 1936, and differed from the prototype by having 930-hp (694-kW) Wright GR-1820-39 radial engines, accommodation for a crew of nine, and minor detail changes. Twelve of the aircraft were delivered between January and August 1937, equipping the USAAC's 2nd Bombardment Group at Langley Field, Virginia. The thirteenth machine went to Wright Field for further tests and after one of the

Y1B-17s survived without damage the turbulence of a violent storm, it was decided that a further static test example should, instead, be completed as an operational bomber. Designated as the **Y1B-17A (Model 299F)**, this machine was powered by 1,000-hp (746-kW) GR-1820-51 engines with Moss/General Electric turbochargers. The machine first flew on 29 April 1938, and subsequent testing by the USAAC gave convincing proof of the superiority of the turbocharged engine over the normally aspirated unit, the first subsequently becoming standard on all future versions.

The order for Y1B-17s was followed by a contract for 39 examples of the **B-17B (Model 299E**, later **Model 299M)** variant, more or less identical to the Y1B-17A with turbocharged engines. The first of these flew on 27 June 1939, and all had been delivered by

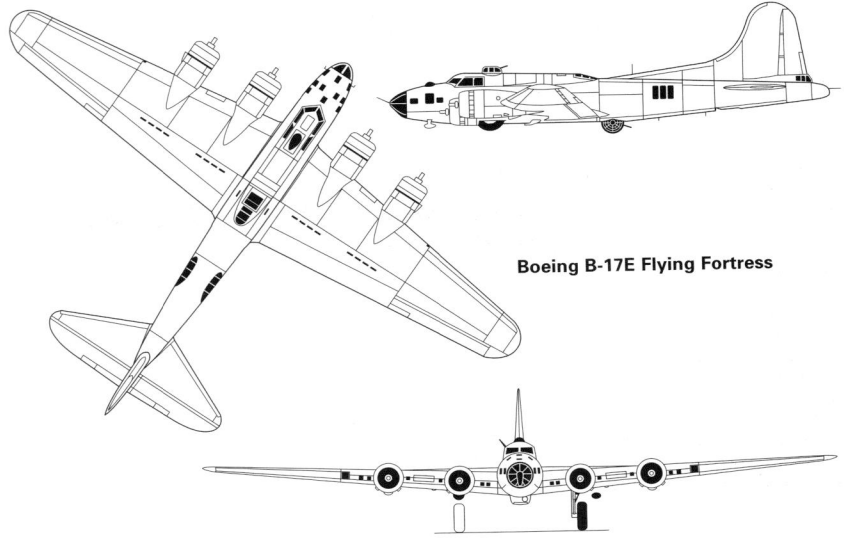

Boeing B-17E Flying Fortress

Variants

B-17H: designation of a small number of air/sea rescue aircraft with search radar and droppable lifeboat, and later redesignated as the **SB-17G**

B-40: bomber escort version originating from the **XB-40** prototype converted from a B-17F. Four **TB-40** trainers were built, and some **YB-40** aircraft carried up to 30 guns. The type was not operationally successful

BQ-7: radio controlled, pilotless flying bomb from which the crew of two parachuted after setting it on course. The type was inaccurate and little used

CB-17G and VB-17G: designations for B-17G bombers equipped as staff transports

DB-17P: drone director conversions

F-9: photo-reconnaissance version with different camera installations producing **F-9A**, **F-9B** and **F-9C** variants. Other designations for PR aircraft included **FB-17** and **RB-17G**

Model 299Z: two B-17Gs modified extensively to allow for the flight test of a turboprop powerplant installed in the fuselage nose

Model 299AB: having run through the alphabet on production aircraft and design studies, double letters followed the Model 299Z, and the Model 299AB was an executive transport conversion for TWA, which used the aircraft for survey and liaison when establishing its post-war Near East routes

PB-1: one B-17F and one B-17G used by the USN for various test projects

PB-1G: air/sea rescue type for service with the USCG, and comprising 17 B-17Gs with conversions similar to those of the USAAF's B-17H

PB-1W: 31 B-17Gs used by the USN in the ASW and AEW roles after conversion with APS-80 search radar with its antenna in a radome mounted above or below the fuselage

QB-17L and QB-17N: target drone conversions

TB-17G: special duty trainer conversions

XB-38: one aircraft equipped experimentally with Allison V-710-89 Vee engines

XC-108: transport conversion to accommodate 38 passengers

XC-108A: cargo transport with freight door on port side

XC-108B: experimental fuel tanker

YC-108: VIP transport

During the B-17G production run, Boeing built 4,035 aircraft, Douglas added another 2,395 and Lockheed Vega completed 2,250 examples.

March 1940. In 1939 the **B-17C** (**Model 299H**) was ordered, the first of the 38 on contract making its initial flight on 21 July 1940. This type differed in its 1,200-hp (895-kW) R-1820-65 engines and in the increase in its defensive firepower from five to seven machine-guns.

The B-17C was the first version supplied to the UK's RAF, which gave the designation **Fortress Mk I** to the 20 examples it received in early 1941. Equipping No.90 Squadron, the aircraft were used operationally for the first time

on 8 July 1941 when they undertook a high-altitude (30,000-ft/9145-m) attack on Wilhelmshaven. In the 26 attacks made on German targets during the next two months the Fortress Mk I proved unsatisfactory, although there was American criticism of the way in which it had been deployed. Nonetheless, the use of the Fortress in daylight over German territory had proved that the type's operating altitude was an inadequate defence in itself, and that the bomber needed more formidable

defensive armament. Until improvements in the Fortress were made, or a means of deploying them more effectively was found, the aircraft were withdrawn from operations over Europe.

Prior to this, during 1940, Boeing had received an order for 42 examples of the **B-17D**, which differed little from the B-17C and retained the same Boeing model number, but as a result of early reports of combat conditions in Europe was delivered with self-sealing tanks and additional armour for protection of the crew. The aircraft were delivered during 1941. The **B-17E**, **B-17F** and **B-17G** variants that followed (all **Model 299O**) had a redesigned and enlarged vertical tail surface with a large dorsal fin. The B-17E and B-17F were the first of these bombers to serve with the 8th AAF in Europe, and differed from each other primarily in armament and equipment. They were then the most advanced developments of the B-17, but in two major operations against German strategic targets, made on 17 August and 14 October 1943, a total of 120 aircraft was lost. Clearly the B-17 could not mount an adequate defence against determined and skilled fighter interception, no matter how cleverly

devised was the box formation in which the type flew. The hard truth was that without adequate long-range fighter escort the B-17 was very vulnerable to attack during mass daylight operations. Many of the losses were attributed to head-on attack, and the final major production version was planned to offset this shortcoming.

The B-17G therefore had a 'chin' turret housing two 0.5-in (12.7-mm) machine-guns beneath the forward fuselage, which meant that this version carried a total of 13 such guns. To increase the type's operational ceiling, later production examples had improved turbochargers.

Some 8,680 B-17Gs were eventually built.

Although used most extensively in Europe and the Middle East, the B-17 was operational in every theatre involving the US forces. In the Pacific theatre the type rendered invaluable service for maritime patrol, reconnaissance, and conventional and close-support bombing. A number of variants were also produced or converted for special purposes and operations. Almost 13,000 examples of all versions of the B-17 were built, but only a few hundred B-17Gs remained in USAAF service after the end of World War II, and these were soon made redundant.

SPECIFICATION	
Boeing Model 299O (B-17G Flying Fortress)	(16391 kg); maximum take-off 65,500 lb (29710 kg)
Type: nine/ten-crew long-range medium bomber	**Dimensions:** wingspan 103 ft 9 in (31.62 m); length 74 ft 4 in (22.66 m); height 19 ft 1 in (5.82 m); wing area 1,420.00 sq ft (131.92 m²)
Powerplant: four Wright R-1820-97 radial engines each rated at 1,200 hp (895 kW)	
Performance: maximum speed 287 mph (462 km/h) at 25,000 ft (7620 m); cruising speed 182 mph (293 km/h) at optimum altitude; climb to 20,000 ft (6095 m) in 37 minutes; service ceiling 35,800 ft (10850 m); range 2,000 miles (3219 km) with a 6,000-lb (2722-kg) bombload	**Armament:** two 0.5-in (12.7-mm) Browning trainable machine-guns in the chin, dorsal, ventral and tail turrets, and single 0.5-in (12.7-mm) Browning trainable machine-guns in the two waist, two cheek and single dorsal positions, plus up to 17,600 lb (7983 kg) of bombs carried internally and externally
Weights: empty 36,135 lb	

Boeing Model 307 Stratoliner (C-75)

The Model 299 prototype was developed in parallel with a civil version of the same basic design which had the company designation **Boeing Model 300**. The basic plan was for the two types to share a common wing, tail unit and powerplant, but from the beginning a more spacious fuselage had been designed for the civil version. As the design progressed, however, it was decided to provide a circular-section fuselage with moderate pressurisation and thereby permit the **Model 307**, as this final design was identified, to operate with passengers at 20,000 ft (6095 m), a height above

much of the turbulent weather. When, in due course, the Model 307 entered airline service, this 'high-altitude' operational capability resulted in selection of the name **Stratoliner**.

Ten Model 307s were built, the first making its maiden flight on 31 December 1938. Unfortunately, this machine was lost before it could be delivered to Pan American. Of the nine which remained, three went to Pan Am as **Model S-307** aircraft, five to Transcontinental & Western Air (TWA) as **Model SA-307B** aircraft, and one modified aircraft to Howard

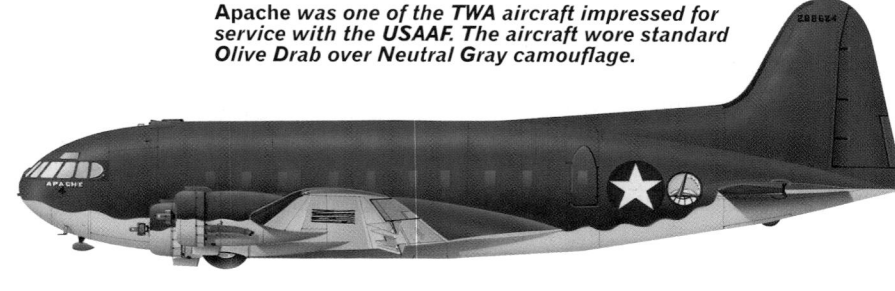

Apache was one of the TWA aircraft impressed for service with the USAAF. The aircraft wore standard Olive Drab over Neutral Gray camouflage.

Hughes as the sole **Model SB-307B** type.

In 1942 the TWA aircraft were impressed into service with the USAAF, which allocated the military designation **C-75**. With accommodation for 33 passengers as well as a

crew of five, the aircraft were operated by TWA under contract to the USAAF's Air Transport Command as VIP transports. After two and a half years' service, during which the five aircraft accumulated between them approxi-

mately 3,000 transatlantic crossings, some 45,000 flight hours and about 7.5 million miles (12 million km), they were released from military service and returned to Boeing for refurbishment and conversion back to airline standards.

Boeing Model 307 Stratoliner (C-75) (continued)

Returning the C-75s to civilian service required the incorporation of new wings and tail unit, and the installation of more powerful engines.

The Model 307's cabin pressure of 23 lb/sq in (0.18 kg/cm²) maintained a cabin altitude of 8,000 ft (2440 m) up to a height of 14,700 ft (4480 m).

Boeing Model 314 Clipper (C-98 and B-314)

In January 1935 Pan American Airways informed the US Bureau of Air Commerce of its wish to establish a transatlantic service and, despite its ownership of the large Martin M-130 and Sikorsky S-42 four-engined flying-boats, the airline wanted a new aircraft for the route.

Boeing submitted a successful tender and a contract for six **Boeing Model 314 Clipper** flying-boats was signed on 21 July 1936. The manufacturer used features of the XB-15 heavy bomber, adapting the wing and horizontal tail surface for this large flying-boat, which was schemed with a maximum take-off weight of 82,500 lb (37422 kg) including up to 74 passengers accommodated in four separate cabins. There was a major change in the powerplant, however, the XB-15's quartet of Pratt & Whitney R-1830 Twin Wasp radial engines being replaced by four Wright GR-2600 Double Cyclone radial engines for a maxi-

Some of the Model 314's 4,200 US gal (3,497 Imp gal; 15899 litres) of fuel was stored in the stabilising sponsons on the hull's waterline. These sponsons also acted as loading platforms.

mum speed of 193 mph (311 km/h) and a range of 3,500 miles (5633 km).

The first Model 314 lifted off for its maiden flight on 7 June 1939, this original version having a single vertical tail surface that was later replaced by twin vertical surfaces for improved directional stability. These surfaces also proved inadequate, however, and the original centreline unit was restored as a wholly fixed surface with no rudder. The Model 314 was certificated and entered transatlantic air mail service on 20 May 1939, passenger services starting on 21 June that year. At that time the Model 314 was the largest production airliner in regular passenger service.

Pan Am ordered another six 'boats to the improved **Model 314A** standard with 1,600-hp (1193-kW) Double Cyclone engines driving larger-diameter propellers, an additional 1,200 US gal (999 Imp gal; 4542 litres) of fuel capacity, and a revised interior. The first Model

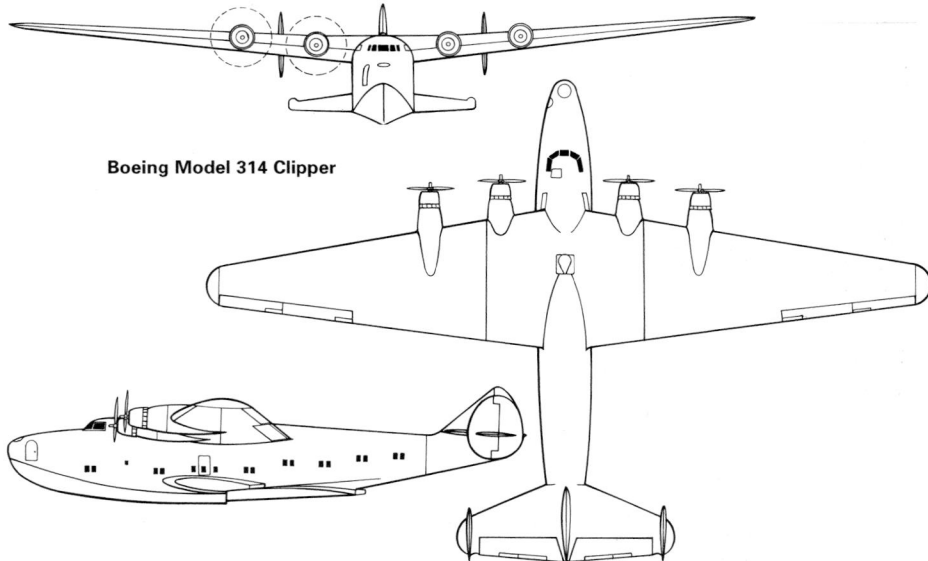

Boeing Model 314 Clipper

314A flew on 20 March 1941 and delivery of the six 'boats was complete by 20 January 1942. Five of the original order were sold, four were requisitioned by the US Army's Transport Command and given the military designation **C-98**. They were little used, however, and in November 1942 one was returned to the airline. The other three 'boats were transferred to the USN to

sector of the wartime 'Horseshoe Route'.

Of Pan Am's nine Model 314 and Model 314A 'boats, four were requisitioned by the US Army's Transport Command and given the military designation **C-98**. They were little used, however, and in November 1942 one was returned to the airline. The other three 'boats were transferred to the USN to

join two acquired direct from Pan Am: the airline provided crews for the type which was designated **B-314** in Navy service, where the partially camouflaged 'boats operated under civil registrations.

Both BOAC and Pan Am terminated Model 314 services in 1946 and the surviving 'boats were sold to various smaller American charter airlines.

retrospectively converted to Model 314A standard in 1942. Three of the repeat order were sold, before delivery, to BOAC for transatlantic service and use on the Foynes-Lagos

Boeing Model 344 (PBB Sea Ranger)

Early in World War II it became clear that Germany would make every effort to develop its fleet of submarines and surface raiders to interdict sea lanes to the UK. When the USA became actively

embroiled in the war, it was of great importance to both the UK and the USA that the North Atlantic link between them should be kept as free as possible of enemy warships, and this fact prompted the USN to

circulate its requirement for a patrol bomber possessing exceptional payload/range performance. The **Boeing Model 344** proposal was sufficiently impressive to win a contract for an **XPBB-1** prototype and 57

examples of the **PBB-1 Sea Ranger** production version.

A large all-metal flying boat, the Model 344 incorporated a new wing very similar to that used on the Boeing Model 345 (B-29 Superfortress), but featured

fixed underwing stabilising floats at about two-thirds span. The XPBB-1 prototype made its maiden flight on 9 July 1942, and at that time was the largest twin-engined flying boat to have been built and flown in

World War II. A change in policy then gave emphasis to land- rather than water-based aircraft, however, and no production examples of this magnificent 'boat were built.

In order to facilitate construction of its first 57 Sea Rangers, the USN built a new factory for Boeing at Renton. In the event, the flying-boat was cancelled and the facility was turned over to the USAAF for B-29 production.

SPECIFICATION

Boeing Model 344 (XPBB-1 Sea Ranger)
Type: 10-crew very-long-range maritime reconnaissance and bomber flying-boat
Powerplant: two Wright R-3350-8 Duplex Cyclone radial engines each rated at 2,300 hp (1715 kW)
Performance: maximum speed 228 mph (367 km/h) at 14,200 ft (4330 m); cruising speed 158 mph (254 km/h) at optimum altitude; initial climb rate 980 ft (299 m) per minute; service ceiling 22,400 ft (6830 m); range 6,300 miles (10139 km); maximum endurance 72 hours
Weights: empty 41,531 lb

(18838 kg); maximum take-off 101,130 ft (45873 kg)
Dimensions: wingspan 139 ft 8½ in (42.58 m); length 94 ft 9 in (28.88 m); height 34 ft 2 in (10.41 m); wing area 1,826.00 sq ft (169.64 m²)
Armament: two 0.5-in (12.7-mm) Browning trainable machine-guns in each of the bow, dorsal and tail turrets, and one or two 0.5-in (12.7-mm) Browning trainable machine guns in each of the two waist positions, plus up to 20,000 lb (9072 kg) of bombs, mines, depth charge and torpedoes in two wing bays

Boeing Model 345 (B-29 Superfortress)

The outbreak of World War II in Europe in 1939, made it essential that US Army Air Corps planners should at least consider long-range strategic bomber projects, and the initial identification used for such a type was **VHB** (**Very Heavy Bomber**). When it seemed likely that a VHB might have to be deployed over the vast reaches of the Pacific Ocean the identification **VLR** (**Very Long Range**) seemed more apt, and it was the VLR project which General Henry H. 'Hap' Arnold, head of the USAAC, got under way at the beginning of 1940.

Requests for proposals were sent to five US manufacturers on 29 January 1940: in due course design studies were submitted by Boeing, Consolidated, Douglas and Lockheed, these being allocated the designations **XB-29**, XB-32, XB-31 and XB-30 respectively. Douglas and Lockheed subsequently withdrew from the competition, and on 6 September 1940 contracts were awarded to Boeing and Consolidated (later Convair) for the construction and development of two (later three) prototypes of their designs. The XB-32

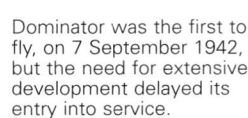

Dominator was the first to fly, on 7 September 1942, but the need for extensive development delayed its entry into service.

Because of its own foresight, Boeing was much further along the design road in 1940 and was therefore able to convince the USAAC that it would have production aircraft available within two or three years. The company therefore received orders for more than 1,500 aircraft before even a prototype had flown. The reason for the advanced design state of Boeing's proposal was the fact that as early as 1938 the company had offered to the USAAC its ideas for an improved B-17 with a pressurised cabin to make high-altitude operations less demanding on the crew. While there was

42-65210 Fay, was an early Martin-built B-29-5-MO. The aircraft was on the strength of the 874th Bomb Squadron, 498th Bomb Group, USAAF when its was lost in March 1945.

then no requirement for such a bomber, the USAAC had encouraged Boeing to keep the design updated to meet the changing conditions of war, and this had been reflected in successive designs identified as the **Models 316, 322, 333, 334** and **341**.

The design for the XB-29 prototype was the **Model 345** development of the Model 341, and the first of the prototypes made its maiden flight on 21 September 1942. The specification of the USAAC (now the US Army Air Forces/USAAF) had called for a speed of 400 mph (644 km/h), so the XB-29 had a high-aspect-ratio

cantilever monoplane wing mid-set on the circular-section fuselage. Because such a wing would entail a high landing speed, wide-span Fowler-type flaps were installed on the wing trailing edge. Electrically retractable tricycle landing gear was provided and, as originally proposed by Boeing, pressurised accommodation was included for the flight crew. In addition, a second pressurised compartment just aft of the wing provided accommodation for crew members who, in the third XB-29 and subsequent production aircraft, sighted defensive gun turrets from adjacent blister windows.

Variants

RB-29 and RB-29A: photo-reconnaissance versions of the B-29 and B-29A respectively, totalling 118 conversions originally under the designation **F-13**
SB-29: B-29 bombers converted for the air/sea rescue role with a lifeboat that could be dropped by parachute
B-29D: designation originally allocated to an improved version of the B-29 with Pratt & Whitney R-4360 engines. The type was not built as such, but was produced after World War II as the **B-50A**
XB-29E: a single B-29 conversion for testing of fire-control systems
B-29F: six specially winterised aircraft for use in cold weather tests in Alaska before reconversion to standard B-29 configuration
XB-29G: one aircraft modified to flight test General Electric turbojet engines. The engine was carried within the bomb bay and could be lowered into the slipstream for testing
XB-29H: one conversion from B-29A standard for special armament tests
RB-29J: conversions of some YB-29Js for use in the photo-reconnaissance role
YB-29J: a small number (believed to be six) of B-29s given Wright R-3350-CA-2 fuel-injected engines in improved nacelles
YKB-29J: two YB-29Js converted as inflight-refuelling tankers
B-29K: one B-29 operated as a cargo transport
B-29L: original designation of B-29s converted as inflight-refuelling tankers with a British-developed hose-and-drogue system
KB-29M: 92 B-29s converted into inflight-refuelling tankers using a hose-and-drogue system
B-29MR: 79 B-29s equipped as inflight-refuelling receiver aircraft
KB-29P: 116 B-29s converted as inflight-refuelling tankers, these being equipped with the Boeing-developed flying boom system
YKB-29T: one three-hose inflight-refuelling tanker, capable of dispensing fuel to three fighters simultaneously
XB-39: one B-29 converted as a testbed for the Allison V-3420 engine
XB-44: one B-29A following conversion by Pratt & Whitney as a testbed with its standard powerplant replaced by four 28-cylinder R-4360 engines in new nacelles. This was the prototype conversion for the intended B-29D, but was used post-war for the B-50A
P2B-1S: two B-29s used after World War II by the USN for anti-submarine and research projects
P2B-2S: two additional B-29s used by the USN as above
Washington B.Mk 1: 88 B-29s for the RAF, which received the aircraft on loan for a period of five years

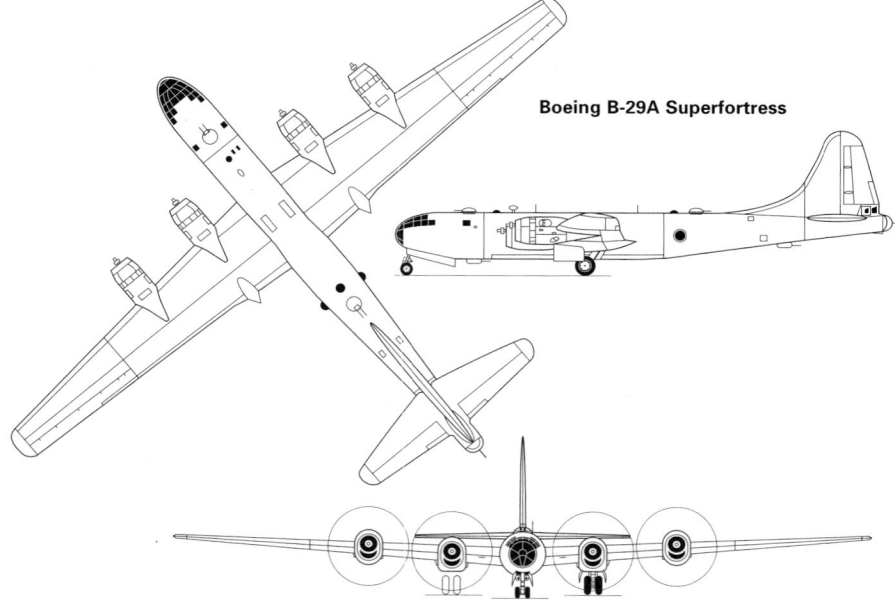

Boeing B-29A Superfortress

Boeing Model 345 (B-29 Superfortress) (continued)

The front and rear compartments of the B-29's fuselage were connected by a crawl-tunnel which passed over the fore and aft bomb bays. The tail gunner was accommodated in a pressurised compartment totally isolated from the other crew positions. The powerplant consisted of four Wright R-3350 Duplex Cyclone twin-row radial piston engines, each with two General Electric turbochargers mounted one in each side of the large engine nacelle.

The prototypes were followed by 14 **YB-29** service test aircraft, the first of these flying on 26 June 1943. Deliveries of YB-29s began almost immediately to the 58th Very Heavy Bombardment Wing (VHBW). **B-29 Superfortress** production was the most diverse aircraft manufacturing undertaken in the USA during World War II, with literally thousands of sub-contractors supplying components or assemblies to the four main production plants: Boeing at Renton, Washington, and Wichita, Kansas; Bell at Marietta, Georgia; and Martin at Omaha, Nebraska. B-29 production totalled 1,644 from Boeing's Wichita plant, 668 from Bell and 536 from Martin. Boeing's Renton plant produced only the **B-29A**, with slightly increased span and changes in fuel capacity and armament: production continued until May 1946 and totalled 1,122 aircraft.

The designation **B-29B** was applied to 311 of the aircraft built by Bell. These were reduced in weight by removal of all defensive armament except for the tail guns, which were installed in an unmanned installation aimed and fired automatically by an APG-15B radar-based fire-control system.

The production total of

Although the B-29 introduced a new era in complex and expensive, but supremely capable warplanes, the type will always be best remembered for its atomic missions against Japan.

almost 4,000 B-29s of all versions must be regarded as very large, having regard to the size and cost of these warplanes, and it is not surprising that the B-29 saw a wide variety of employment in the post-war years, when the type operated under several designations. The B-29 was widely used in the Pacific theatre during World War II, which it effectively ended with the atomic bombings of Hiroshima and Nagasaki on 6 and 9 August 1945, respectively, and was also used operationally during the Korean War.

SPECIFICATION

Boeing Model 345 (B-29 Superfortress)
Type: 10-crew long-range strategic bomber and reconnaissance aircraft
Powerplant: four Wright R-3350-23, -23A, -41 or -57 radial engines each rated at 2,200 hp (1641 kW)
Performance: maximum speed 358 mph (576 km/h) at 25,000 ft (7620 m); cruising speed 230 mph (370 km/h) at optimum altitude; climb to 20,000 ft (6095 m) in 38 minutes; service ceiling 31,850 ft (9710 m); range 3,250 miles (5230 km)
Weights: empty 70,140 lb (31815 kg); maximum take-off 124,000 lb (56245 kg)
Dimensions: wingspan 141 ft 3 in (43.05 m); length 99 ft (30.18 m); height 29 ft 7 in (9.02 m); wing area 1,736.00 sq ft (161.27 m²)
Armament: two 0.5-in (12.7-mm) Browning trainable machine-guns each in the two dorsal and two ventral barbettes, and three 0.5-in (12.7-mm) Browning trainable machine-guns or one 20-mm trainable cannon and two 0.5-in (12.7-mm) Browning trainable machine-guns in the tail turret, plus up to 20,000 lb (9072 kg) of bombs carried internally

---

Boeing Model 345-2 (B-50)

Seeking enhanced capability for the B-29, in 1944 Boeing took a standard B-29A and used it as the prototype for an improved **Model 345-2** which was given the provisional USAAF designation **B-29D**.

Increased power was considered to be essential and the chosen powerplant, comprising four 3,500-hp (2610-kW) Pratt & Whitney R-4360-45 radial engines mounted in redesigned nacelles, was test flown in another B-29 converted to **XB-44** standard. While this area of improvement was being investigated, Boeing got on with modification of the B-29A: this involved a new and somewhat lighter wing, strengthened but lighter landing gear and, to retain good directional stability despite an increase of almost 60 per cent in power, a revised vertical tail surface of greater area.

The lightening of the wing by 650 lb (295 kg) derived largely from the use of the 75ST light alloy in place of the previously standard 24ST, yet the new wing was 16 per cent stronger than that of the production B-29. The redesign of the landing gear made possible operations at higher weights, and the greater vertical tail surface area came from increasing the height of the fin and rudder by about 5 ft (1.52 m). This would have made it impossible to put the B-29D into standard hangars, a fact that made it necessary to provide for the fin and rudder to fold to starboard.

The USAAF ordered 200 B-29Ds, but with the end

SPECIFICATION

Boeing Model 345-2 (B-50A)
Type: 10-crew strategic heavy bomber
Powerplant: four Pratt & Whitney R-4360-35 radial engines each rated at 3,500 hp (2610 kW)
Performance: maximum speed 385 mph (620 km/h) at 25,000 ft (7620 m); cruising speed 235 mph (378 km/h) at optimum altitude; initial climb rate 2,225 ft (678 m) per minute; service ceiling 37,000 ft (11280 m); range 4,650 miles (7483 km)
Weights: empty 81,050 lb (36764 kg); maximum take-off 168,408 lb (76389 kg)
Dimensions: wingspan 141 ft 3 in (43.05 m); length 99 ft (30.18 m); height 32 ft 8 in (9.96 m); wing area 1,739.00 sq ft (161.55 m²)
Armament: four 0.5-in (12.7-mm) Browning trainable machine-guns in the forward dorsal barbette, two 0.5-in (12.7-mm) Browning trainable machine-guns in each of the rear dorsal and two ventral barbettes, and one 20-mm trainable cannon and two 0.5-in (12.7-mm) Browning trainable machine-guns in the tail turret, plus up to 20,000 lb (9072 kg) of bombs carried internally

A B-50D demonstrates the type's clear B-29 ancestry. Key recognition features compared to the earlier bomber were the B-50's taller vertical tail and revised engine nacelles.

Variants

KB-50: cover-all designation of all 132 B-50 conversions to initial inflight-refuelling tanker configuration with a three-point refuelling system
WB-50: B-50s modified for weather reconnaissance purposes
B-50A: first 59 production bombers
TB-50A: 11 B-50As modified to trainers for the Convair B-36
B-50B: 45 examples of an improved bomber version with the maximum take-off weight increased by 1,300 lb (590 kg) to 170,000 lb (77112 kg) and numerous improvements incorporated
EB-50B: a B-50B retained by Boeing for experimental purposes, including, at one time, investigation of tracked landing gear
RB-50B: all 44 in-service B-50Bs were modified to this standard with a rear bomb bay capsule for photographic and electronic equipment and the extra crew necessary
YB-50C: the 60th B-50A, taken in hand during construction for modification to improved standard with R-4360-51 turbo-compound engines to allow a maximum take-off weight of 207,000 lb (93895 kg). The conversion was not completed
B-50D: this **Model 345-9-6** was a revised production version (222 built) with its nose cone moulded from a single piece of Perspex, take-off weight raised to 173,000 lb (78473 kg), provision for underwing fuel tanks and, from the 16th machine onwards, provision for inflight-refuelling
DB-50D: B-50Ds modified as launch aircraft for the experimental Bell GAM-63 Rascal stand-off missile
TB-50D: 11 B-50Ds adapted as trainers for the Convair B-36
WB-50D: B-50D bombers modified as weather reconnaissance aircraft
RB-50E: 14 RB-50Bs modified for special photographic reconnaissance missions
RB-50F: 14 RB-50Bs modified to a special-mission standard with SHORAN navigation radar
RB-50G: 15 RB-50Bs modified to a standard similar to the RB-50F but with extra radar and the nose section of the B-50D
TB-50H: 24 new-built aircraft used as systems trainers for Boeing B-47 crews
WB-50H: conversions from TB-50H standard as weather-reconnaissance aircraft
KB-50J: 112 KB-50s modified to improved standard by Hayes Industries with extra fuel, a three-point refuelling system, no operational equipment and a pair of 5,200-lb st (23.13-kN) General Electric J47 turbojets in underwing nacelles to boost speed to 444 mph (715 km/h) for better compatibility with jet aircraft
KB-50K: TB-50H aircraft modified to a standard identical with the KB-50J
B-54A: proposed production version of the YB-50C
RB-54A: proposed reconnaissance bomber version of the YB-50

of war in the Pacific the total was trimmed to a mere 60 and the considerable airframe and powerplant changes then

spurred the decision to redesignate the new type as the **B-50**. The initial production **B-50A** flew for the first time on 25 June

1947 and demonstrated not only improved performance, by comparison with the B-29A, but also an increase of almost 20 per

cent in maximum take-off weight. Production of the B-50A eventually totalled 79 aircraft, and 57 of these were later converted as

inflight-refuelling tankers, a role in which the type saw service in the Vietnam War before being retired in the latter half of the 1960s.

Boeing Model 367 (C-97 and KC-97 Stratofreighter)

Early in 1942 Boeing initiated a design study to examine the feasibility of producing a transport version of its B-29 Superfortress bomber. In due course the company's proposal was submitted to the USAAF for consideration and, because at that time the long-range transport was a much-needed operational type, a contract for three prototypes was awarded on 23 January 1943. Identified by the company as the **Boeing Model 367** and designated **XC-97** by the USAAF, the first of these prototypes made its maiden flight on 15 November 1944.

The XC-97 had much in common with the B-29, including the entire wing and engine layout. At first view the fuselage, of 'double-bubble' cross

section, appeared to be entirely new, but in fact the lower 'bubble' was basically a B-29 structure, and so was the tail unit attached to the new upper 'bubble', which was of greater radius than its lower counterpart. In July 1945, following brief evaluation of the prototypes, 10 service test aircraft were ordered as six **YC-97** cargo transports, three **YC-97A** troop transports and one **YC-97B** with 80 airline-type passenger seats in its main cabin.

The first production contract, issued in March 1947, was for 27 **C-97A** aircraft with 3,250-hp (2425-kW) Pratt & Whitney R-4360-27 engines and specified accommodation for 134 troops or 53,000 lb (24040 kg) of freight. Two transport versions followed,

under the designation **C-97C** and **VC-97D**, and following trials with three **KC-97A** aircraft equipped with additional tankage and a Boeing-developed inflight-refuelling boom, the **KC-97E** flight-refuelling tanker went into production in 1951. This version was powered by 3,500-hp (2610-kW) R-4360-35C engines and the following **KC-97F** variant differed only in its R-4360-59B engines. Both the KC-97E and KC-97F were convertible tanker/transports, but for full transport capability the inflight-refuelling equip-

ment had to be removed. The most numerous variant, with 592 built, was the **KC-97G** which had full tanker or full transport capability without any onunit equipment change.

When production ended in 1956 a total of 888 C-97s of all versions had been built, and many were converted later for other duties. The **KC-97L** variant had boosted performance as a result of the addition

Boeing built the KC-97G at its Renton plant until 1956, when the type was ousted by the revolutionary KC-135A Stratotanker. Each of the 592 KC-97Gs built cost an average of $1,205,000.

of two 5,200-lb st (23.13-kN) General Electric J47-GE-23 turbojets in underwing nacelles to improve rendezvous compatibility with Boeing B-47 jet-powered bombers. KC-97Gs converted to allcargo configuration were redesignated **C-97G**, and in all-passenger configuration became **C-97K** machines. Search and rescue conversions were **HC-97G**, and three KC-97L aircraft went to the Spanish air force, which allocated the local designation **TK.1**. Several aircraft served in various roles with Israel's air force.

The chin radome, added to the C-97A (illustrated), housed an AN/APS-42 search radar and provided a useful point of recognition between this production aircraft and the near-identical YC-97A.

SPECIFICATION	
Boeing Model 367 (KC-97G Stratofreighter) **Type:** four/five-crew long-range transport or inflight-refuelling tanker **Powerplant:** four Pratt & Whitney R-4360-59B radial piston engines each rated at 3,500 hp (2610 kW) **Performance:** maximum speed 375 mph (604 km/h) at 25,000 ft (7620 m); cruising speed 300 mph (483 km/h) at optimum altitude; climb to 20,000 ft (6095 m) in	50 minutes; service ceiling 35,000 ft (10670 m); range 4,300 miles (6920 km) **Weights:** empty 82,500 lb (37421 kg); maximum take-off 175,000 lb (79379 kg) **Dimensions:** wingspan 141 ft 3 in (43.05 m); length 110 ft 4 in (33.63 m); height 38 ft 3 in (11.66 m); wing area 1,769.00 sq ft (164.34 m²) **Payload:** up to 96 troops, or 69 litters plus attendants, or freight

Variants

C-97D: the third YC-97A, the YC-97B and two C-97A aircraft following their conversion to a standard passenger configuration; the three VC-97D aircraft were subsequently redesignated C-97D
KC-97H: one KC-97F following modification for service trials as a tanker using the probe-and-drogue inflight-refuelling system developed in the UK
YC-97J: final designation of two KC-97Gs converted for USAF use as flying testbeds, each with four 5,700-shp (4250-kW) Pratt & Whitney YT43-P-5 turboprop engines

Boeing Model 377 Stratocruiser

The **Boeing Model 377 Stratocruiser** commercial transport was a development of the military Model 367, based on the improved-structure YC-97A with Pratt & Whitney R-4360 engines. The first flight of the **Model 377-10-19** prototype took place on 8 July 1947, and this machine was later delivered to Pan Am, which became the largest single operator of the **Stratocruiser**. There were a variety of interior configurations in the **Models 377-10-26, -28, -29, -30** and **-32** accommodating

from 55 to 112 passengers or, if equipped as a 'sleeper', 28 upper- and lower-berth units plus five seats. The main cabin was in the upper lobe of the fuselage, with a luxury lounge or cocktail bar seating 14 on the lower deck, which was reached via a spiral staircase.

Of the 55 Stratocruiser aircraft built, Pan Am was operating 27 at one time. Of these, 10 were given additional fuel capacity to make them suitable for transatlantic operations, and were known as **Super Stratocruiser** machines. At

One of five Stratocruisers flown by the Israel Defence Force/Air Force under a civilian registration, 4X-FPV was modified with a hinged rear fuselage for freight loading.

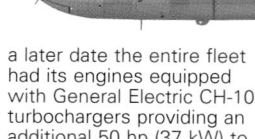

a later date the entire fleet had its engines equipped with General Electric CH-10 turbochargers providing an additional 50 hp (37 kW) to the output. British Overseas Airways Corporation also acquired a

fleet of 17 Stratocruisers: only six of these were original purchases from Boeing, the remainder being acquired from other airlines. After just over nine years' service with BOAC, 10 were sold to Transocean

Airlines in the USA during 1958. Of these, four were converted to 117-passenger high-density seating, the remainder each having an additional 12 seats added to their standard 63- and 84-seat layouts.

Boeing Model 377 Stratocruiser (continued)

Before the Stratocruiser disappeared from service during 1963, a few had been modified to a cargo configuration, but by far the strangest conversion resulted from those airframes acquired by Aero Spacelines Inc. Under the designation **B377-PG**, this company built an oversize cargo aircraft which it named **Pregnant Guppy**. The company subsequently built other examples, using both Model 367 and Model 377 airframes, under variations of the Guppy name.

Three Model 377s were finished in Boeing house colours during the testing and certification phase. The Stratocruiser was based on the 75ST structure of the YC-97A and all subsequent C-97s.

SPECIFICATION

Boeing Model 377 Stratocruiser
Type: five-crew commercial transport
Powerplant: four Pratt & Whitney R-4360 Wasp Major radial engines each rated at 3,500 hp (2610 kW)
Performance: maximum speed 375 mph (604 km/h) at 25,000 ft (7620 m); cruising speed 340 mph (547 km/h) at 25,000 ft (7620 m); initial climb rate 1,040 ft (317 m) per minute; service ceiling more than 32,000 ft (9755 m); range 4,200 miles (6759 km)
Weights: empty 83,500 lb (37875 kg); maximum take-off 145,800 lb (66134 kg)
Dimensions: wingspan 141 ft 3 in (43.05 m); length 110 ft 4 in (33.63 m); height 38 ft 3 in (11.66 m); wing area 1,769.00 sq ft (164.34 m²)
Payload: up to 112 passengers

Boeing Model 400 (F8B)

US Navy aircraft-carriers operating in the Pacific theatre during World War II were very vulnerable to air attack. With the emerging need to attack the Japanese home islands, concern was expressed at the need to sail within easy range of land-based aircraft. If, however, a long-range fighter and fighter-bomber were available, then it might be possible to engage the enemy without the need to bring the carriers within striking distance of land-based defence aircraft.

Boeing immediately began work on its **Model 400**. Submitted to the USN, the design study was awarded a contract in May 1943 for three **XF8B-1** prototypes. The first of these made its initial flight during November 1944 as the largest piston-engined single-seat fighter ever to have been built in the USA and, as events subsequently proved, one of the most powerful single-engined fighters developed by any nation involved in World War II.

Only the first prototype had been completed and flown before the end of World War II and although the remaining two prototypes were completed and handed over after VJ-Day, interest in turbine-powered fighters meant that the XF8B-1 was abandoned.

SPECIFICATION

Boeing Model 400 (XF8B-1)
Type: single-seat carrierborne long-range fighter and fighter-bomber
Powerplant: one Pratt & Whitney XR-4360-10 Wasp Major radial engine rated at 3,000 hp (2237 kW)
Performance: maximum speed 432 mph (695 km/h) at 26,900 ft (8200 m); cruising speed 190 mph (306 km/h) at optimum altitude; initial climb rate 3,660 ft (1116 m) per minute; service ceiling 37,500 ft (11430 m); range 2,800 miles (4506 km)
Weights: empty 13,519 lb (6132 kg); maximum take-off 20,508 lb (9302 kg)
Dimensions: wingspan 54 ft (16.46 m); length 43 ft 3 in (13.18 m); height 16 ft 3 in (4.95 m); wing area 489.00 sq ft (45.43 m²)
Armament: six 0.5-in (12.7-mm) Browning fixed forward-firing machine-guns or six 20-mm fixed forward-firing cannon in the leading edges of the wing, plus up to 3,200 lb (1451 kg) of bombs, mines, depth charges and torpedoes carried internally and externally

Two three-bladed contra-rotating metal propellers absorbed the power of the XF8B-1's four-row XR-4360-10 radial engine.

Boeing Model 450 (B-47 Stratojet)

This RB-47H was assigned to the 55th Strategic Reconnaissance Wing and was adorned with the characteristic radomes and aerials of the variant.

By early 1944, four companies were involved in the design of an aircraft to meet a jet bomber specification drawn up by the USAAF, but Boeing's initial **Model 424** submission to meet this requirement failed to arouse any interest. A **Model 432** second submission, with engines buried in the centre fuselage and a straight wing similar to that of the Model 424, was made in late 1944. This was awarded a contract covering design definition and the preparation of a mock-up. However, during this stage of development, Boeing learned of new German aerodynamic research data which were becoming available following the end of war in Europe.

German investigation into the benefit of swept wings led to the adoption by Boeing of a sweptback configuration for its **Model 448** proposal, with a total of six engines housed within the fuselage. This powerplant installation was not acceptable to the USAAF and the rejection of the Model 448 led to a fourth design proposal, the **Model 450**. This retained the swept wing but with the powerplant in podded nacelles under the wing. Boeing's mock-up was completed in this configuration, and official inspection in the spring of 1946 led to a contract for two **XB-47** (**Model 450-3-3**) proto-

types. These differed somewhat from the mock-up, incorporating changes that included increased wingspan and modified landing gear.

The first of the two prototypes made its maiden flight on 17 December 1947, immediately creating an impression of speed and efficiency. The XB-47 had a laminar-flow wing of high aspect ratio, in the high-set configuration, and the wing was so thin that it could not incorporate fuel tankage. In addition, there was no space in which wing-mounted main undercarriage units could be housed. Instead, retractable twin wheel tandem units were mounted on the centreline of the slender fuselage, and stability on the ground was provided by small outrigger wheels that retracted into the inboard engine nacelles. It was appreciated at an early stage that the well-spaced main units would make normal take-off rotation impossible and, as a result, the height of the two main

units was designed so that the aircraft stood on the runway in an attitude at which it would take off when flying speed was attained. Under each half of the wing were three engines, two of them in paired pods inboard and the third a short distance in from the tip: in the case of the prototype these engines were 3,750-lb st (16.68-kN) General Electric J35 turbojets. The fuselage provided accommodation for a crew of three; incorporated a large bomb bay that was intended to house

Variants

B-47B-II: B-47Bs after conversion to updated B-47E standard
B-47B/CL-52: one B-47B transferred to the RCAF, which loaned the aircraft to Canadair Ltd for use as a testbed for the Canadian-built Orenda Iroquois turbojet
DB-47B: conversions of B-47Bs as control aircraft, primarily for the QB-47E but also for other drones. The tail armament was removed and radio control equipment was installed
RB-47B: 24 B-47Bs (some designated **YRB-47B**) converted for the reconnaissance role, carrying eight cameras and other equipment in a specially heated compartment in the bomb bay
TB-47B: 66 standard B-47Bs modified by the addition of a fourth crew position for an instructor, and used for the conversion training of pilots and navigators
YDB-47B: one B-47B converted to carry, launch and control a Bell GAM-63 Rascal missile during initial dropping trials
XB-47D: two B-47Bs converted to serve as testbeds for the 9,710-eshp (7241-ekW) Wright YT49-W-1 turboprop engine installed in place of the paired J47 turbojets on each side, and with the single J47 in the outboard position retained
DB-47E: two B-47E conversions, plus two generally similar
YDB-47E aircraft, also for launch and control trials with Bell GAM-63 missiles
QB-47E: 14 B-47Es converted to radio-controlled drone configuration for use as targets, though not expendable because of their cost, and for use on tasks considered too hazardous for a human crew
RB-47E: major B-47 strategic photo-reconnaissance version, 240 aircraft being completed to this configuration on the production line. Bombing equipment was replaced by up to 11 cameras and associated equipment for night photography
WB-47E: 24 B-47Es converted for the weather reconnaissance role
YB-47F: single B-47B revised with an inflight-refuelling probe for use in probe-and-drogue refuelling tests
KB-47G: one B-47B modified and equipped as a hose tanker for probe-and-drogue inflight-refuelling experiments with the YB-47F
RB-47H: 32 B-47s completed in production for the electronic reconnaissance mission and therefore equipped with nose, underfuselage and wing radomes, and with the bomb bay converted as a compartment to accommodate equipment and three specialist operators
ERB-47H: three B-47Es converted for the same role as the RB-47H, but with a crew of five
YB-47J: one standard bomber converted as a testbed for the new MA-2 radar bombing/navigation system
RB-47K: 15 new RB-47E aircraft for use in the photo and weather reconnaissance roles at all altitudes
EB-47L: 35 B-47Es, following conversion during 1963, to serve as communications relay stations

This aircraft was the 171st B-47E manufactured by Lockheed at its Marietta, Georgia facility. A grand total of more than 1,800 Stratojets was completed, at one time equipping 28 SAC wings.

urgent was the requirement, in fact, that in addition to production by Boeing at Wichita, Kansas, Douglas and Lockheed also built the aircraft.

The first true production version, of which 399 were built (381 of them by Boeing), was the **B-47B** (**Model 450-11-10**). This version differed from the B-47A in its higher operational weights, in being equipped for inflight-refuelling, and in having provision for underwing fuel tanks. Later production aircraft, beginning with the 88th machine, had 5,800-lb st (25.80-kN) J47-GE-23 turbojet engines. The first B-47B flew on 26 April 1951, and the type entered service some two months later.

The most important production version was the **B-47E** (**Model 450-157-35**), of which more than 1,600 were built in bomber and reconnaissance versions. The variant incorporated strengthened landing gear for operation at higher weights, a modified nose section with an inflight-refuelling receptacle and ejection seats for the crew, a drag chute, tail armament changed from two 0.5-in (12.7-mm) Browning machine-guns to two 20-mm cannon, the internal RATO system replaced by a jettisonable external rack to carry up to 33 1,000-lb st (4.49-kN) rockets and J47-GE-25 engines with water injection were fitted. The first B-47E flew on

30 January 1953, and the variant entered service with the USAF's Strategic Air Command shortly after this.

It had been anticipated that a more advanced bomber would replace the B-47 by 1957, but it was soon appreciated that the B-47 would in fact have to continue in service until well into the 1960s. This factor, plus a requirement to adopt a low-altitude 'under the radar' approach to a target in response to the emergent threat posed by SAMs, caused wing fatigue problems. Low-altitude attack required the use of toss-bombing, but the B-47's wing had not been designed for such manoeuvres, or for the extended life that was being enforced upon it. As a result, massive sums of money were spent on wing structure revision and rein-

forcement. B-47Es so converted received the revised designation **B-47E-II**. More extensively modified B-47Bs, brought up to B-47E standard and having the wing structure modifications, received the designation **B-47B-II**.

This programme, and others involving equipment updates, ensured that the B-47 saw 15 years of first-line service before being withdrawn in 1966. Even then, examples continued in use for weather reconnaissance, with Military Airlift Command, until the end of 1969. The B-47 represented a great technological achievement for Boeing, and has an honoured place in USAF history as its, and indeed the world's, first swept-wing production turbojet bomber to be built on a large scale.

SPECIFICATION	
Boeing Model 450 **(B-47E-II Stratojet)** **Type:** three-crew strategic medium bomber **Powerplant:** six General Electric J47-GE-25 or -25A turbojet engines each rated at 7,200 lb st (32.03 kN) with water injection **Performance:** maximum speed 606 mph (975 km/h) at 16,300 ft (4970 m); cruising speed 557 mph (896 km/h) at 38,500 ft (11735 m); initial climb rate 4,660 ft (1420 m) per minute; service ceiling 40,500 ft (12345 m); range	4,000 miles (6437 km) **Weights:** empty 80,756 lb (36630 kg); maximum take-off 198,180 lb (89893 kg) **Dimensions:** wingspan 116 ft (35.36 m); length 109 ft 10 in (33.48 m); height 27 ft 11 in (8.51 in), wing area 1,428.00 sq ft (132.66 m²) **Armament:** two 20-mm trainable rearward-firing cannon in remotely-controlled tail turret, plus up to 20,000 lb (9071 kg) of bombs carried internally

the large and heavy nuclear bombs of that era, but which could be modified to carry 22,000-lb (9979-kg) of conventional bombs; had provision for the installation of RATO (rocket-assisted take-off) units; and was fitted with remotely-controlled defensive armament in the tail.

Evaluation of the XB-47 by the USAF resulted in a contract for 10 of the **B-47A (Model 450-10-9)** variant for larger-scale service testing and familiari-

sation. Generally similar to the prototypes, the B-47A differed in its powerplant of six 5,200-lb st (23.13-kN) J47-GE-11 turbojets and was used largely for the evaluation of the best form of tail armament and fire control. The first of the B-47As made its maiden flight on 25 June 1950, a day that also marked the beginning of the Korean War, a conflict that speeded the demand for large numbers of the USAF's new bomber. So

---

Boeing Model 451 Scout (L-15)

Under the designation **Boeing Model 451 Scout**, the company developed a somewhat uncharacteristic

design to meet a US Army requirement for a liaison and observation type. This was required to have good

low-speed handling characteristics and a better-than-average field of vision for its two occupants.

Design of the Model 451 was initiated in 1946 and two **XL-15** prototypes were ordered. Of high-wing monoplane configuration, the Model 451 had an all-metal basic wing structure, with flaps suspended below the trailing edge. These surfaces could be operated collectively as flaps, or differentially to augment the wing spoilers that served as ailerons.

SPECIFICATION	
Boeing Model 451 Scout **(XL-15)** **Type:** two-seat liaison and observation aircraft **Powerplant:** one Avco Lycoming O-290-7 flat-four engine rated at 125 hp (93 kW) **Performance:** maximum speed 112 mph (180 km/h) at optimum altitude; cruising speed 101 mph (163 km/h) at optimum altitude;	initial climb rate 628 ft (191 m) per minute; service ceiling 16,400 ft (5000 m); endurance 5 hours 30 minutes **Weights:** empty 1,509 lb (684 kg); maximum take-off 2,050 lb (930 kg) **Dimensions:** wingspan 40 ft (12.19 m); length 25 ft 3 in (7.70 m); height 8 ft 8½ in (2.65 m); wing area 269.00 sq ft (24.99 m²)

Prominent metal-framed, fabric-covered flaps were distinctive features of the L-15. The aircraft's unusual tailwheel undercarriage featured a rear unit of similar stroke to the main gear legs.

Boeing Model 451 Scout (L-15) (continued)

The Model 451 Scout's wing was mounted above a short fuselage pod that accommodated the pilot and observer in tandem, with the powerplant mounted in the nose. A slender boom, high on the rear part of the fuselage's forward pod section, carried a tail unit incorporating inverted endplate fins and rudders. The landing gear was of the fixed tail-wheel type, but the tailwheel unit was similar in length to the nosewheel unit of the tricycle landing gear so that the machine stood on the ground in what was virtually flying attitude.

Unusual features of Boeing's design made it easy to load the aircraft for transport by air or road and, in addition, the type could be dismantled and converted into a self-contained trailer for towing behind a road vehicle. Testing of the two proto-types resulted in a follow-up order for 10 similar **YL-15** aircraft for more comprehensive service trials, but no further orders followed, and the aircraft were later handed over to the US Forest Service.

Boeing Model 464 (B-52 Stratofortress)

By normal standards long since rendered obsolete due to its great vulnerability to SAMs, the mighty **Boeing B-52 Stratofortress** has seen two would-be successors fall by the wayside; remains a major element in one of the three US strategic deterrents; and will remain in valuable service until well into the 21st century.

The B-52 design began life in 1948 as a turboprop successor to the piston-engined B-50. The design team was faced with a quandary: the turbojet engines of the period were so thirsty that a huge airframe would be needed to carry all the fuel necessary for the required range, so the answer appeared to be to use turboprops. However, while the turbo-prop was the obvious answer, because it was more economical than the pure turbojet, it was also more complicated and less reliable. Then, in 1949, Pratt & Whitney brought out its J57 turbojet engine. Far and away superior to any other US powerplant, it was originally rated at 7,500 lb st (33.36 kN) and helped to change the philosophy of both Boeing and the USAF.

Boeing and its rival, Convair, fought bitterly to win the contract for the new USAF bomber. Convair had already provided the mammoth B-36 and so had a wealth of experience with heavyweight aircraft, but its proposed YB-60, though cheaper than the compet-ing B-52, could not equal its performance, and Boeing won the day.

The **XB-52** (**Model 464-67**) prototype took to the air for the first time on 15 April 1952. Its technol-ogy was based on the medium-range B-47 that had flown five years previ-ously. It therefore had a similar extremely thin, shoulder-mounted wing, with engines clustered in podded pairs below and ahead of the leading edge, and the same undercar-riage arrangement. The XB-52 offered tandem seat-ing for the pilots, a feature repeated in the **YB-52** second prototype.

The first three produc-tion aircraft were designated **B-52A** (**Model 464-201-0**) and spent their lives at Boeing as test and development machines, beginning an improvement programme that will continue beyond 2000. The first version to join the USAF was the **B-52B** (**Model 464-201-3**), which was virtually identical to the B-52A but with a naviga-tion/bombing system. Of the 50 built, 27 were converted as **RB-52B** reconnaissance aircraft.

The **B-52C** (**Model 464-201-6**) was substan-tially improved in performance and equip-ment, and was the first model (35 built) to have the white anti-radiation under-surface finish. It was succeeded by the **B-52D** (**Model 464-201-7**), of which 170 were built with an improved fire-control system for the tail arma-ment of four 0.5-in (12.7-mm) machine-guns. As the B-52Ds were being turned out by Boeing's plant at Wichita, Kansas, the USAF was thinking about the giant bomber's successor. This was to be the WS-110, later the Mach 3 North American B-70 Valkyrie. The B-70 was years in the future, however, and B-52 improvement continued with the **B-52E** (**Model 464-259**), whose 100 examples had a more advanced navigation and weapon delivery system. Continuing weight increases called for more power, especially at take-off, and the **B-52F** (**Model 464-260**), of which 89 were built, had a later, more powerful version of the J57, fitted like earlier versions with water injec-tion to boost power on take-off.

The **B-52G** (**Model 464-253**), which was planned initially as the final version pending arrival of the B-70, brought along a host of major improve-ments, and represented the biggest single advance of any model. The airframe was substantially redesigned to save weight and to make it safer; inte-gral wing-tanks greatly increased fuel capacity; the tail gunner was relocated in the crew compartment; the vertical tail surface was shortened and provision was made for launching ECM decoys and stand-off missiles. The decoy was a small jet aircraft known as the Quail, designed to have a radar signature similar to that of the bomber to confuse missile radars. Production of the B-52G totalled 193 aircraft, the last of them delivered in 1960. Missile armament took the form of the AGM-28 Hound Dog, which had a range of 750 miles (1207 km). The B-52G was, in fact, to be less a bomber than the first stage of a missile.

Meanwhile, Boeing and the USAF were planning the **B-52H** (**Model 464-261**), which really was the final production model. It was characterised by two major changes: a new engine type in the Pratt & Whitney TF33 turbofan, which gave greater thrust in concert with a consider-ably reduced specific fuel consumption, and structural changes which permitted the aircraft to fly at low alti-tudes without excessive fatigue problems. The B-52H also exchanged the four 0.5-in (12.7-mm) tail guns for a single fast-firing 20-mm 'Gatling' type gun, and was built to carry Skybolt ballistic missiles under the wings and Quail decoys in the bomb bay.

The final B-52H, which was also the last of 744 B-52 bombers, rolled out of Wichita in June 1962. The Skybolt missile was cancelled in December of the same year, while the B-70 project had already been terminated.

In 1963 the B-52D was studied as a CBC (conven-tional bomb carrier) and in the following year the process of rebuilding of B-52D bombers began at Wichita. This permitted the type to carry 105 'iron' bombs of 750-lb (340-kg) nominal weight, but actu-

This 2nd Air Force B-52D has Vietnam-era two-tone green and tan over gloss black camouflage. It also illustrates the tall fin associated with all models prior to the B-52G.

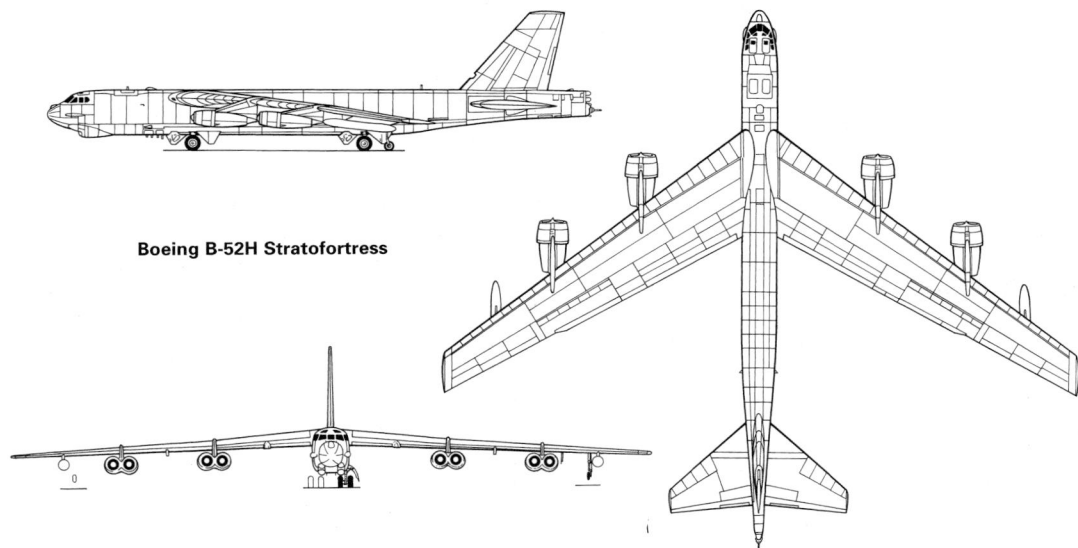

Boeing B-52H Stratofortress

Turrets containing sensors for the ALQ-151 EVS adorn the underside of this B-52G's nose. This system, combined with terrain avoidance radar, allows the crew to fly low-level missions in zero visibility.

ally weighing 825 lb (374 kg). In 1965 rebuilt CBC aircraft began operations over Vietnam. Through the late 1960s and early 1970s the bombers continued to rain bombs on Vietnam, aided by improved navigation and weapon-delivery techniques and to some extent

protected by increasingly sophisticated ECM devices. Used in an all-out attack on North Vietnam's capital and its port (Hanoi and Haiphong respectively) during late 1972, they caused tremendous destruction, but the USAF lost 15 of these giant aircraft to the SAM

defences. Soon afterwards, all US forces were withdrawn from the Southeast Asian theatre.

Ten years earlier the USAF had initiated defence studies that were to lead to the Advanced Manned Strategic Aircraft (AMSA) requirement of 1965. This was then envisaged as a low-altitude penetration bomber that would begin to replace SAC's B-52 bombers by 1980. In mid-1970, North American Rockwell was named as prime contractor for the B-1A, whose production was cancelled by President 'Jimmy' Carter in June 1977. This decision was reversed in September 1981 by President Ronald Reagan, and the development and production of 100 B-1Bs was authorised. Delivery of production aircraft began in July 1985, but the limited number of these penetration bombers meant that the veteran B-52 still had to shoulder a great deal of strategic responsibility.

This fact was reflected in the very large sums that were and are still being spent on programmes to improve and update the B-52 force. The Offensive Avionics System (OAS) was implemented to update the navigation and weapons delivery systems of B-52G and B-52H aircraft in USAF service, and a major milestone in this effort was the first OAS-equipped B-52G on 3 September 1980. With the completion of the programme in the early 1980s, the entire surviving fleet had an improved low-level penetration capability. Other upgrades were the ALQ-151 EVS (Electro-optical Viewing System) with low-light-level TV and forward-looking IR sensors in undernose turrets, and the Phase VI upgraded electronic countermeasures system package.

Of the 167 B-52Gs surviving into the early 1990s, 98 were fitted for the stand-off nuclear role, armed with the AGM-86B cruise missile, and the other 69 for the force-projection role with free-fall weapons.

As more updated B-52Hs became available, the B-52Gs of the stand-off nuclear type were reassigned to the force-projection role and the last B-52G had finally been

retired from service by the end of 1994.

Some 96 of the 102 B-52H bombers remained in service during the early 1990s with a primary armament of up to 20 AGM-69A SRAM stand-off nuclear missiles as a complement or alternative to the B61 and B83 thermonuclear free-fall bombs, but from 1991 the aircraft were retrofitted for the alternative stand-off nuclear and conventional bombing roles.

As the Rockwell B-1B Lancer increasingly assumed the free-fall nuclear role of the B-52H, this latter type has been reallocated to the force projection role, with weapons that now include the AGM-86C conventionally-armed counterpart of the AGM-86B nuclear-armed cruise missile. The importance of the B-52H to the USAF's continued need for warplanes with global reach while carrying very heavy warloads is demonstrated by the fact that, during the late 1990s, the Department of Defense was giving consideration to the possibility of revising the surviving B-52H bombers with the powerplant of four Rolls-Royce RB.211-524 turbofan engines for reduced long-term costs.

SPECIFICATION	
Boeing Model 464 (B-52H Stratofortress) **Type:** six-crew long-range strategic heavy bomber **Powerplant:** eight Pratt & Whitney TF33-P-3 turbofan engines each rated at 17,000 lb st (75.62 kN) **Performance:** maximum speed 595 mph (958 km/h) at optimum altitude; cruising speed 509 mph (819 km/h) at optimum altitude; service ceiling 55,000 ft (16765 m); range 10,000 miles (16093 km) without inflight-refuelling	**Weights:** maximum take-off 505,000 lb (229088 kg) **Dimensions:** wingspan 185 ft (56.39 m); length 160 ft 11 in (49.05 m); height 40 ft 8 in (12.40 m); wing area 4,000.00 sq ft (371.60 m²) **Armament:** one 20-mm General Electric M61 Vulcan trainable six-barrel cannon in the remotely-controlled tail barbette, plus up to 20 AGM-86B, -86C or AGM-129 cruise missiles, B61 or B83 nuclear free-fall bombs, or up to 51 750-lb (340-kg) bombs

Boeing Model 707

Boeing's 'Dash-80' prototype was almost devoid of cabin windows, since it was intended more as a military tanker/transport demonstrator than as a commercial airliner.

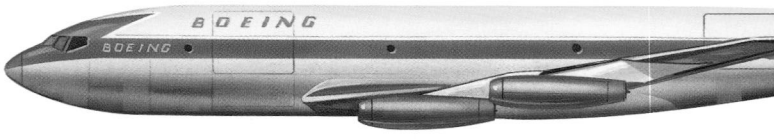

The Boeing company was the first American aircraft manufacturer to design and build a turbine-engined civil transport aircraft, and then to make it a success on the world airliner market. The process began when the company initiated studies for a turbojet- or turboprop-powered version of its C-97 Stratofreighter military transport. Little or no interest resulted from Boeing's proposals, and in August 1952 the company took the

bold step of gambling some $16 million to build the prototype of a completely new turbojet-powered civil

transport. To maintain a degree of secrecy for this project it was allocated the designation **Model 367-80**. The aircraft was known as **'Dash-80'** to Boeing employees, but higher echelons of the company knew that it would be marketed as the **Boeing Model 707**.

Boeing was sufficiently realistic to appreciate that its large private-venture investment was nowhere near the amount that would be needed if large-scale production of a civil airliner was to become a reality. Shrewdly, therefore, the company developed the initial design as a high-speed military transport and inflight-refuelling tanker, in the process banking on a military contract which would underwrite the tooling costs and provide finance for the development of a first-class modern civil airliner.

The Model 367-80, which was rolled out on 14 May 1954, had clearly been derived from two related piston-engined transports, the Model 377 Stratocruiser and C-97, but aerodynamically had a close relationship to the B-47. It retained the distinctive wing of the turbojet- powered bomber with its 35° sweep angle. The mounting of the inboard powerplant units of the B-47, with two turbojets paired in side-by-side nacelles carried on a cantilever underwing pylon, had received serious consideration for the 'Dash-80'. However, it was appreciated that under certain circumstances the failure of one unit of the pair could result in the need to shut down the remaining operative engine, seriously compromising reserve power, and it was decided

instead, as a safety measure, to install the engines in individual pylon-mounted pods.

Flown for the first time on 15 July 1954, the 'Dash-80' was powered by four 9,500-lb st (42.26-kN) Pratt & Whitney JT3P turbojet engines and, as originally flown, was primarily a military demonstrator. At an early stage in the programme the 'Dash-80' acquired a Boeing-designed inflight-refuelling boom. With this combination of a high-performance, large-capacity aircraft with inflight-refuelling tanker capability, Boeing was able to demonstrate effectively to the USAF the potential of the type for refuelling in-service and future aircraft at or near their operational altitudes, and at speeds which would not present any real problems for either of the aircraft involved.

Variants

Model 707-100B: development of the initial production version with more powerful turbofan engines, plus the aerodynamic improvements to the wing and tail unit introduced on the Model 720

Model 707-200: generally similar to original production version but with Pratt & Whitney JT4A-3 turbojet engines

Model 707-300 Intercontinental: long-range transoceanic version with increased wingspan and fuselage length, more powerful engines, and accommodation for 189 passengers

Model 707-300B Intercontinental: developed version of the Model 707-300 with more powerful turbofan engines and aerodynamic refinements

Model 707-300C Convertible: passenger, mixed passenger/freight, or freight version of the Model 707-320B with a cargo door and Boeing-developed freight-loading system. A maximum of 215 passengers could be carried in the all-passenger configuration

Model 707-300C Freighter: dedicated freight-carrying version of the Model 707-300C with all passenger facilities removed

Model 707-400 Intercontinental: generally similar to the Model 707-300 with the exception of its powerplant of four Rolls-Royce Conway Mk 508 turbofan engines

Boeing Model 707 (continued)

On 5 October 1954, less than three months after the Model 367-80's first flight, Boeing received an initial contract for 29 KC-135A tanker/transports.

With military interest secured, the 'Dash 80' was equipped as a civil demonstrator. It offered, initially to US airlines, a turbojet-powered airliner that would soon make obsolete the existing piston-engine airliners operating US domestic transcontinental routes. The first contract for the Model 707 was placed by Pan Am. On 13 October 1955, the airline ordered six examples of the first production version, which had the designation **Model 707-100**, often rendered unofficially as **Model 707-120** by Boeing. Just three months before that date, the USAF had given Boeing clearance to build civil developments of the 'Dash 80' simultaneously with the manufacture of military C/KC-135 aircraft, and no time was lost in establishing a production line for civil machines. Pan Am's first **Model 707-121** (using the Boeing designation) flew initially on 20 December 1957 and was delivered to the airline in the

following August. On 26 October 1958, it was used to inaugurate Pan Am's New York-London transatlantic jet airliner service despite the fact that the type was intended primarily for transcontinental rather than intercontinental services. This move was a flag-waving rather than practical operation, however, and Pan Am's aircraft soon reverted to the domestic routes for which they had been intended. It was not until the airline received its first true long-range versions of the Model 707, namely the **Model 707-300 Intercontinental**, that sustained scheduled transatlantic flights began on 10 October 1959.

Production of the Model 707 ended in the early 1980s after the delivery of 763 civil aircraft in a 25-year manufacturing effort.

Throughout the 25 years that the Model 707 was in production, there had been continuing development to enhance performance, operating economy, load-carrying capability and range. Moreover, the Model 707 was delivered with a variety of increasingly powerful engines, the net result of which is that the **Model 707-300C Intercontinental**, in all-cargo configuration, has a maximum take-off weight almost 34 per cent greater than that of the domestic **Model 707-200** of 1959.

These details of the Model 707 would be incomplete without a final mention of the 'Dash 80' which, in almost 18 years

of service, was probably the most extensively modified aircraft in aviation history. In addition to the changes associated with the continuing development of the Model 707, the 'Dash 80' was the subject of many major aerodynamic and structural modifications

to test new ideas and advanced features of later Boeing jet transports, included flying with a tail-mounted engine during 727 trials. On 25 April 1972, its test work complete, Boeing announced that the 'Dash 80' was being presented to the Smithsonian Institution.

SPECIFICATION

Boeing Model 707-300C Intercontinental

Type: three-crew long-range transport
Powerplant: four Pratt & Whitney JT3D-7 turbofan engines each rated at 19,000 lb st (84.52 kN)
Performance: maximum speed 627 mph (1009 km/h) at optimum altitude; cruising speed 605 mph (974 km/h) at 25,000 ft (7620 m); initial climb rate 4,000 ft (1219 m) per minute; service ceiling 39,000 ft (11890 m); range 5,755 miles (9262 km) with 147 passengers
Weights: empty 146,400 lb (66406 kg) or 141,100 lb (64002 kg) in passenger and freight layouts respectively; maximum take-off 333,600 lb (151318 kg)
Dimensions: wingspan 145 ft 9 in (44.42 m); length 152 ft 11 in (46.61 m); height 42 ft 5 in (12.93 m); wing area 3,050.0 sq ft (283.35 m²)
Payload: up to 189 passengers or 93,098 lb (42229 kg) of freight

Egyptair flew its last scheduled 707-300 passenger service in February 1994. The carrier began -300 operations in 1968, the aircraft initially replacing the Comet on the Cairo-London route.

Boeing Model 707 (C-137 and C-18)

Examples of this essentially civil type that entered service with the USAF received the basic **C-137** designation. They comprised three **Model 707-153** machines delivered in 1959 as **VC-137A** VIP transports with accommodation for 22 passengers and provision for use as airborne command posts. These aircraft were subsequently re-engined with TF33 turbofan engines to become **VC-137B** machines, and the first letter of the prefix was dropped in the late 1970s. The three aircraft served with the 89th Airlift Wing at Andrews AFB, and were supplemented by four more aircraft, with the final example being retired early in 1999.

The first pair of these additional transports were **Model 707-353C** machines, procured for use as presidential transports under the **VC-137C** designation. On replacement by the

This VC-137A is shown in its MATS colour scheme, with the original short fin. The aircraft was later converted to VC-137B standard.

MATS
86970

MILITARY AIR TRANSPORT SERVICE
U.S. AIR FORCE

VC-25A, the two **C-137C** aircraft joined the first three on general staff and VIP transport duties. In the late 1980s two more C-137C aircraft were added to the fleet operated by the 89th Airlift Wing, and in 1991 a **Model 707-355C** was issued to Central Command as a transport under the **EC-137D** designation, which was thus used for the second time, having previously been applied to the test aircraft for the E-3 programme.

Under the designation

C-18A, eight ex-American Airlines Model 707 airliners were purchased in 1981 for the fleet operated by the 4950th Test Wing. Two were left in their original configuration, although one was broken up for spares and the other was used for general trials and training work. Of the other six, four were modified to **EC-18B** standard for the ARIA (Advanced Range Instrumentation Aircraft) role, which involved the fitment of a large steerable telemetry-receiving antenna

in a giant nose radome as fitted to the EC-135E. The final pair was equipped as **EC-18D** CMMCA (Cruise

Missile Mission Control Aircraft) machines with APG-63 radar and a telemetry receiving system.

SPECIFICATION

Boeing Model 707 (C-137C)

Type: three-crew VIP transport
Powerplant: four Pratt & Whitney TF33 (JT3D-3) turbofan engines each rated at 18,000 lb st (80.07 kN)
Performance: maximum speed 628 mph (1011 km/h) at optimum altitude; cruising speed 599 mph (964 km/h) at 25,000 ft (7620 m); initial climb rate 3,550 ft (3155 m) per minute; service ceiling 42,000 ft (12800 m); range 7,611 miles (12248 km)
Weights: maximum take-off 327,000 lb (148325 kg)
Dimensions: wingspan 145 ft 9 in (44.42 m); length 152 ft 11 in (46.61 m); height 42 ft 5 in (12.93 m); wing area 3,010.00 sq ft (279.63 m²)
Payload: up to 51,615 lb (23413 kg)

Boeing Model 707 (E-3 Sentry, E-6 Mercury and E-8 J-STARS)

The requirement for an AWACS (Airborne Warning And Control System) aircraft was outlined by the USAF in 1963, at which time it was envisaged that a force of up to 64 aircraft

would be required. Economic considerations meant that a much smaller number was eventually built, however.

The resulting **Boeing E-3A Sentry** is essentially

a flexible, jamming-resistant, mobile and survivable radar station that also carries a command, communications and control centre. In addition to its long-range surveil-

lance capability, AWACS can provide all-weather identification and tracking over all kinds of terrain, and the 22nd and subsequent aircraft added a maritime surveillance capability.

Two main areas of use were planned by the USAF: firstly, the type would serve within TAC (Tactical Air Command) for airborne surveillance and as a command centre for the rapid deployment of TAC forces; and secondly, the type would serve within the ADC (Aerospace Defense Command) as a command and control post. Now flying under Air Combat Command, the two basic E-3 missions remain largely unaltered.

Boeing was the successful one of two contenders for the supply of an AWACS aircraft, being awarded a contract on 23 July 1970 to provide two prototypes under the designation **EC-137D**. The company's AWACS concept was based on the airframe of the Model 707-300B commercial transport, and the prototypes were modified in the first place to carry out comparative trials between the prototype surveillance radars designed by the Hughes Aircraft Company and those by the Westinghouse Electric Corporation. These tests continued into the autumn of 1972, and on 5 October the USAF announced that Westinghouse had been selected as prime radar contractor.

Very little modification of the basic airframe was needed to make it suitable for the new role. Most important was the addition of a large rotodome assembly carried on two wide-chord streamlined struts. The remainder of the essential avionics antennae was housed within the wing, fuselage and tail unit. New engine pylon fairings were provided for the more powerful turbofan engines of the pre-production aircraft and of the production machines which were designated **E-3A** and given the name **Sentry**. Internal modifications included the provision of SDCs (Situation Display Consoles) and other equipment bays, and the addition of a crew rest area. Basic operations were schemed as requiring a flight crew of four plus 13 AWACS specialist officers, but this number could be varied and other personnel could be carried for systems management and radar maintenance.

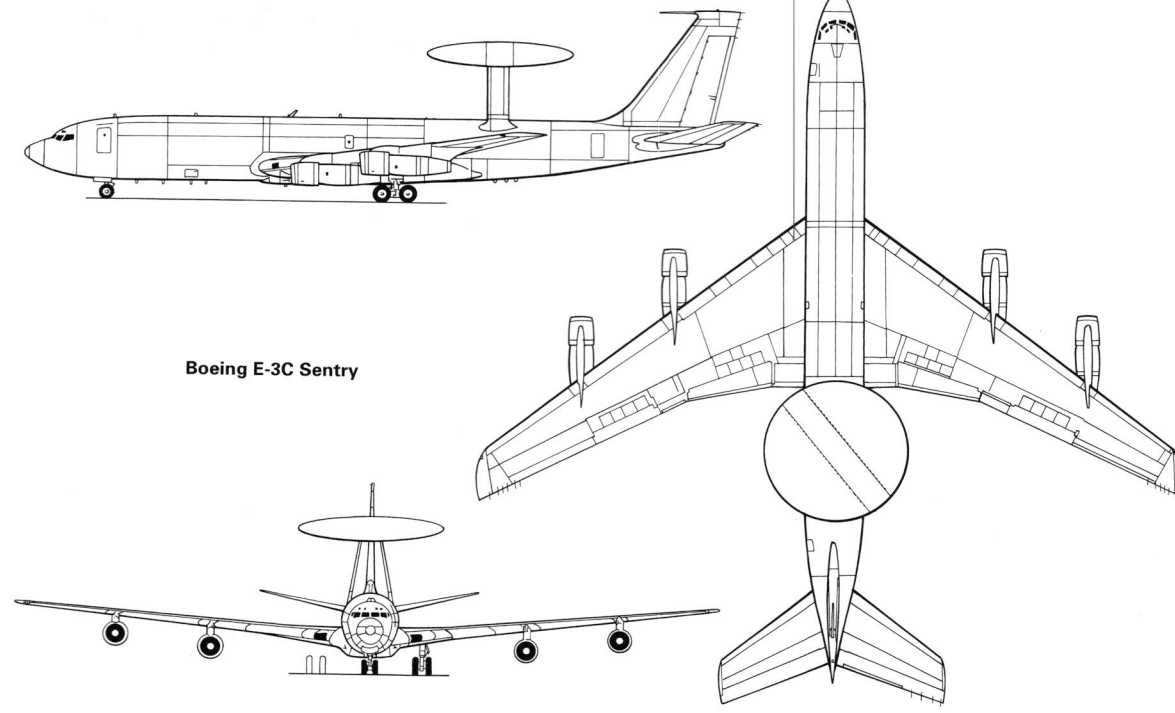

Boeing E-3C Sentry

Not surprisingly, the mass of avionics equipment required the installation of extensive cooling and wiring systems. There is also a large demand for electrical power, which is supplied by generators with a combined output of 600 kVA. The over-fuselage rotodome is 30 ft (9.14 m) in diameter and has a maximum depth of 6 ft (1.83 m). It originally carried the antennae for the APY-1 surveillance radar and IFF/TADIL C (Identification Friend or Foe/TActical Digital Intelligence Link – Command). When the radar is being used, the rotodome is driven hydraulically at 6 rpm, but in non-operational flight the rotodome is rotated at one twenty-fourth of this speed to ensure that low temperatures do not cause the bearing lubricant to congeal.

The APY-2 radar installed in the 25th example of the Sentry (and representing the standard to which the radar of the first 24 machines was then upgraded) can function as a pulse and/or pulse-Doppler radar, and is operable in six different modes. The data-processing capability of the first 23 E-3As was provided by an IBM 4 Pi CC-1 high-speed computer, while the more powerful IBM CC-2 computer was introduced on the 24th Sentry. Also introduced on this machine was the newly-developed JTIDS (Joint Tactical Information Distribution System), which provides a high-speed secure communications channel and is also less vulnerable to jamming than earlier systems.

The first production E-3A was delivered on 24 March 1977 and a total of 34 aircraft (including the two EC-137Ds upgraded to full production standard) had been delivered by June 1984. The first 24 of these were completed as **E-3A 'core'** machines, while the last 10 were completed as **E-3B 'standard'** machines for service from July 1984, with the APY-2 radar offering an

improved overwater capability, CC-2 computer, ECM-resistant voice communications, more radio equipment, five more situation display consoles (making a total of 14), and provision for the 'Have Quick' secure communications system and self-defence AAMs. The E-3As were then upgraded to E-3B standard, and in 1984 10 were then further modified to **E-3C** standard, with five more situation display consoles, more radio equipment and the 'Have Quick A-Nets' communications system.

One E-3C is used by Boeing as the **JE-3C** for development and integration of the AYR-1 ESM system. The USAF is currently considering upgrading its E-3s with the installation of the 'glass' flightdeck of the Next Generation Model 737 and the Eagle system for the detection and tracking of theatre ballistic missiles with an IR search-and-track sensor and a laser rangefinder. The service is

also planning or considering major upgrades to the radar, computer and navigation systems, the last with the aid of GPS update.

Another 18 aircraft of the E-3A 'standard' configuration were delivered from December 1981 for the use of NATO forces based in Europe, while Saudi Arabia received five aircraft in addition to eight **KE-3A** inflight-refuelling tankers. The latter are based on the same airframe and were built alongside the E-3. A further two export customers have purchased E-3s with the revised powerplant of four 24,000-lb st (106.76-kN) CFM International CFM56-2A turbofans. France received four **E-3F** aircraft in 1991-2, while the UK received seven **E-3D** machines in the same period for service with the local designation **Sentry AEW.Mk 1**. The last of the British aircraft was the 1,010th and final Model 707 airframe to be built.

Having operated a handful of NKC-135As on loan from the USAF, the USN decided to adopt the E-6A Mercury as a replacement for its EC-130Qs.

Boeing Model 707 (E-3 Sentry, E-6 Mercury and E-8) (cont.)

The **E-6A Mercury** was designed as successor to the Lockheed EC-130Q Hercules and is operated by the USN's VQ-3 and VQ-4 squadrons in the TACAMO (Take Charge And Move Out) role. In April 1983 Boeing was given the contract to develop the **TACAMO II** type and, as the platform for the new type, the company chose the airframe of its Model 707. This offered commonality with the E-3, but with the revised powerplant of four 22,000-lb st (97.84-kN) CFM International F108-CF-100 turbofan engines, offering outstanding fuel efficiency and resulting in ultra-long patrol endurance that can be extended by inflight-refuelling.

The first E-6A flew on 19 February 1987. Flight trials revealed a flaw in the structure which caused part of the fin to be lost in a high-speed dive. With suitable remedies, the first pair of E-6As was delivered to NAS Barbers Point, Hawaii, on 2 August 1989. The name **Hermes** was initially assigned but then changed to Mercury, and deliveries have totalled 16 aircraft.

The Mercury is packed with communications equipment, including UHF satellite communications, whose antennas are housed in the wingtip pods along with the antennas for the ALR-66(V)4 ESM (Electronic Support Measures) system. All communications equipment is secure against eavesdropping, and is hardened against the effects of EMP (electro-magnetic pulse).

The E-6A's principal task is the provision of a link between various national and military commands, including the E-4B presidential transport and command centre, and the USN's submarines. In order to communicate with the submarines, the E-6A uses two trailing-wire antennas: one is 4,000 ft (1219 m) long and deploys from the tail cone, and the other is 26,000 ft (7925 m) long and deploys from a position under the rear fuselage. With the E-6A flying a tight orbit, the antennas hang vertically, allowing VLF communications with submarines, which have a towed aerial array.

In May 1997 Raytheon redelivered the first E-6A upgraded to the **E-6B** standard that combines the original TACAMO role with the 'Looking Glass' airborne command post task previously undertaken by the USAF's EC-135. It is possible that another four aircraft will be converted to the E-6B standard.

The **E-8** developed by prime contractor Grumman (now Northrop Grumman), made a 'star' debut in 1991 during Operation Desert Storm long before it was considered operational. It represents a major advance in battlefield control, introducing the kind of capability for monitoring and controlling the land battle that the E-3 provides for the air battle. The E-8 is based on the Model 707-300 airframe, and no new-build aircraft are envisaged.

Two **E-8A** prototype conversions were fitted with a ventral canoe fairing that housed the APY-3 multimode side-looking radar. The cabin was reconfigured with operator consoles. A datalink provides the means to transmit gathered intelligence to the ground in near real-time. The radar allows the controllers to monitor the positions and movements of all ground vehicles, as well as serving other functions. It can also differentiate between wheeled and tracked vehicles.

The first of the two E-8As with **J-STARS** equipment flew on 22 December 1988, and in January 1991 both E-8As were deployed to Riyadh in Saudi Arabia to fly combat missions under the control of the hastily organised 4411th Joint STARS Squadron.

In service the system was to be have been carried by new-build **E-8Bs** with F108 turbofan engines, but the carrier is now the **E-8C**, based on converted Model 707 airliner airframes with the powerplant of four 18,000-lb st (80.05-kN) Pratt & Whitney JT3D-3B turbojets. The first of a required 19, later reduced to 13, E-8Cs was delivered in June 1996.

Boeing Model 717 (C-135 and KC-135 Stratotanker)

In September 1955 Boeing received the USAF's first order for the **KC-135A Stratotanker** inflight-refuelling tanker, following successful trials with the 'Dash 80' prototype after it had been configured with a Boeing-designed flying boom refuelling system under the rear fuselage. The USAF required that the cabin should have no windows and that the diameter of the fuselage should be increased by 12 in (0.305 m) by comparison with that of the 'Dash 80'. This gave the **Model 717** a fuselage diameter 4 in (0.10 m) less than that of the Model 707 civil transport. The whole refuelling package was installed in the lower fuselage.

Key dates in the Model 717 programme then included the first flight of a KC-135A on 31 August 1956 and a service debut with the 93rd ARS on 28 June 1957. Production of the KC-135A totalled 732 aircraft in a long and efficient manufacturing

programme. The first 582 aircraft were built with a short fin, but from the 583rd a taller fin (then retrofitted to earlier machines) was introduced to make the Stratotanker more stable during take-off. In addition, an early modification saw the addition of strengthening straps around the rear fuselage to dampen jet-induced resonance.

Internally, the KC-135A has 22 fuel tanks and the main cabin provides a considerable volume for freight, for which a side-loading door is fitted. The cabin can alternatively be fitted with seating for 80 troops. The refuelling boom operator works in a prone position in a fairing under the rear of the fuselage.

The **C-135A Stratolifter** differed from the KC-135A in being equipped specifically for the long-range transport role. Its cabin was outfitted for the carriage of up to 126 troops, or 44 litters and 54 seated casualties, or freight. Galley and toilet facilities were

provided at the rear of the cabin. The first C-135A flew on 19 May 1961 and was delivered to the MATS (Military Air Transport Service) from 8 June 1961, marking the belated move of this important service into jet-powered transport capability. After the delivery of 18 examples of the C-135A, Boeing's production line switched to the **C-135B**, of which 30 were completed with a tailplane of increased span and the revised powerplant of four 18,000-lb st (80.05-kN) TF33-P-5 turbofans. The service life of the C-135 in this original role was short, however, and the C-135s were soon used as the basis of conversions to other roles. Seventeen KC-135Bs had also been built, and were immediately adapted as EC-135C command post aircraft.

In the second half of 1998 the USAF still had

501 KC-135s available and virtually none of these is still in its original KC-135A form, for the type has been steadily upgraded over the years in a number of programmes. Some 56 were converted to **KC-135Q** standard with additional navigation and communications equipment to support the SR-71. The KC-135Qs were also modified for the carriage and transfer of the high-flash-point JP-7 fuel used by the SR-71 in addition to the regular JP-4/5 used by the tanker itself.

Other early tanker variants were the **C-135F** (a designation applied to 12 KC-135As supplied to France), and the **KC-135D**, of which four were converted from **RC-135A** survey aircraft. Between

1975 and 1988 Boeing replaced the lower wing skins of all surviving KC-135s to extend their useful lives to a time beyond 2020, and work also started on the re-engining of most surviving aircraft to replace the noisy and thirsty J57 turbojet engines with quieter, more fuel-economical and less maintenance-intensive turbofan engines.

Of the two re-engining programmes undertaken for the KC-135, the less ambitious was to upgrade the KC-135As of the ANG and Air Force Reserve (together with 21 special-mission EC/RC/NKC-135 aircraft). The USAF bought large numbers of surplus Model 707s and stripped off their JT3D-3B (military designation TF33) engines

As delivered, the original KC-135As featured short fins and J57 turbojets, as on this aircraft, which is finished in MATS colours.

SPECIFICATION	
Boeing Model 717 (KC-135A Stratotanker)	9,200 miles (14806 km); radius 3,455 miles (5560 km) to offload 24,000 lb (10886 kg) of fuel or 1,151 miles (1852 km) to offload 120,000 lb (54432 kg) of fuel
Type: four-crew inflight-refuelling tanker with secondary transport capability	
Powerplant: four Pratt & Whitney J57-P-59W turbojet engines each rated at 13,750 lb st (61.15 kN)	**Weights:** empty 106,306 lb (48220 kg); maximum take-off 316,000 lb (143338 kg)
Performance: maximum speed 610 mph (982 km/h) at optimum altitude; cruising speed 532 mph (856 km/h) at 35,000 ft (10668 m); initial climb rate 1,290 ft (393 m) per minute; service ceiling 45,000 ft (13716 m); range	**Dimensions:** wingspan 130 ft 10 in (39.88 m); length 136 ft 3 in (41.53 m); height 41 ft 8 in (12.70 m); wing area 2,433 sq ft (226.03 m²)
	Payload: up to 83,000 lb (37648 kg) of freight

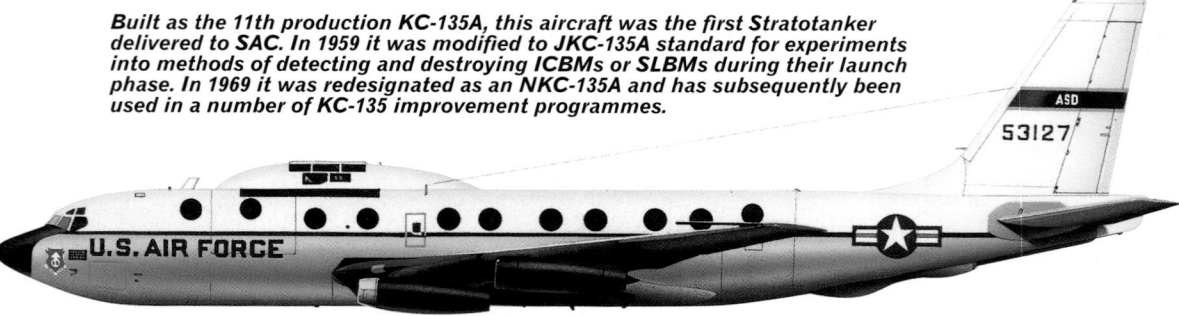

Built as the 11th production KC-135A, this aircraft was the first Stratotanker delivered to SAC. In 1959 it was modified to JKC-135A standard for experiments into methods of detecting and destroying ICBMs or SLBMs during their launch phase. In 1969 it was redesignated as an NKC-135A and has subsequently been used in a number of KC-135 improvement programmes.

for fitment to the tankers, which then received the revised designation **KC-135E**. At the same time the airliners' wider-span tailplanes were also fitted to the tankers to maintain stability with the greater thrust of the new engines. More than 160 KC-135As were modified, this total including the four KC-135Ds, which retain their original designation.

In 1980 Boeing announced a major upgrade programme for the KC-135, involving the installation of high-bypass-ratio turbofan engines. Under the company designation **KC-135RE**, the first conversion made its maiden flight on 4 August 1982. Designated in service as the **KC-135R** (the second time this had been applied, having previously been used by a reconnaissance variant of the KC-135A), the re-engined and upgraded

tanker is now the mainstay of the USAF's tanker fleet, and as more conversions are completed more units are dispensing with their older variants.

The engine selected for the KC-135R was the 22,000-lb st (97.84-kN) CFM International CFM56 (military designation F108-CF-100). The use of this engine gives the ability to offload 150 per cent more fuel than the KC-135A at a radius of 2,879 miles (4633 km). Other changes include fitment of an APU, characterised by intake and exhaust ports on the port side of the rear fuselage, to provide the KC-135R with the ability to undertake autonomous operations from austere locations, and many other systems were also upgraded during the conversion.

Delivery of the first KC-135R, to the SAC's

384th ARW, took place in July 1984, and the 200th aircraft was delivered in April 1990 with the prospect of the programme continuing to cover most of the active-duty tanker fleet. The 11 surviving C-135F tankers were also upgraded under this programme, in the process becoming **C-135FR**.

aircraft. The French machines were subsequently fitted with Adèle RWR and underwing pods for probe-and-drogue work.

The **KC-135R(RT)** designation is applied to a small number of aircraft, most of them trials or ex-special mission machines, fitted with a refuelling

receptacle, and these aircraft have been joined by the surviving KC-135Qs. The latter were fitted with refuelling receptacles as they underwent the re-engining conversion to emerge as **KC-135T** tankers with a primary role of supporting F-117 attack aircraft and other covert programmes. A feasibility study has also been undertaken to fit the KC-135R with underwing refuelling pods for the refuelling of probe-equipped aircraft from other US or foreign services. In addition, both Turkey and Singapore operate small numbers of ex-USAF KC-135R Stratotankers, although the Turkish aircraft were converted from previously stored KC-135As.

Boeing KC-135R Stratotanker

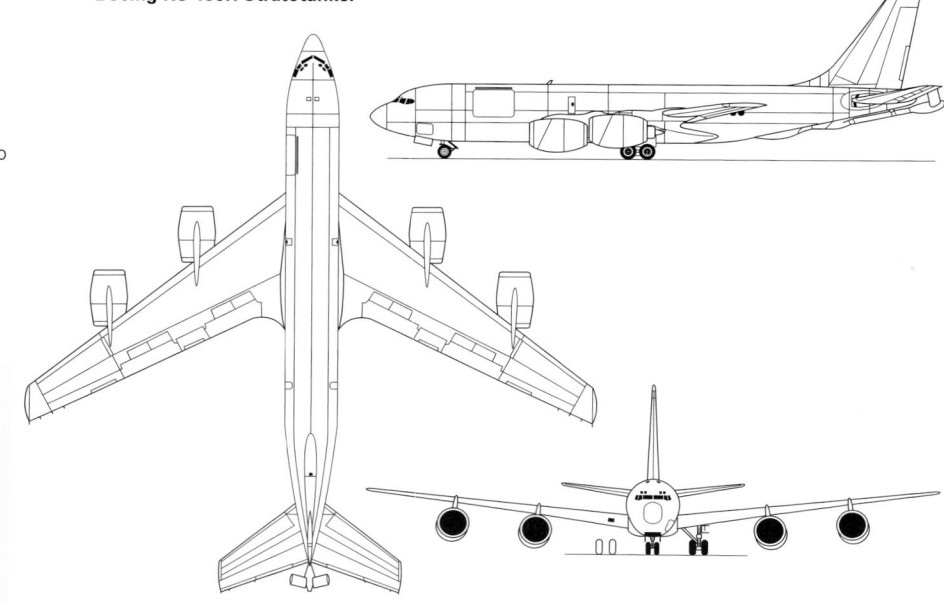

Variants

JC-135A and JKC-135A: at least four C-135A and KC-135A aircraft used for temporary tests
NC-135A and NKC-135A: at least 15 C-135A and KC-135A aircraft used for permanent tests
VC-135A: five C-135A and KC-135A aircraft converted as staff transports, while the unofficial designation **VKC-135A** was often used for two KC-135As also converted as staff transports but retaining their inflight-refuelling tanker capability
VC-135B: 11 C-135Bs converted as staff transports

Boeing Model 717 (EC-135)

It soon became obvious that the Model 717 would be ideally suited for conversion to the airborne command post and communications relay roles with the cabin revised for a command staff and a large quantity of advanced communications equipment. An initial five KC-135As were therefore converted in 1965 as

EC-135A flying command posts to serve within the context of the Post-Attack Command Control System as communications relay aircraft between SAC headquarters and the commanders of silo-based intercontinental ballistic missile forces.

With the end of the Cold War, the EC-135's original

command and control mission has become far less important and the inventory has been retired accordingly.

The EC-135s were equipped with comprehensive communications equipment, which allowed the airborne commander to link with national command authorities, theatre forces and other airborne command posts such as the USN's Boeing E-6 Mercury TACAMO fleet. A trailing-wire aerial was deployed from the lower fuselage and the airframe was liberally covered with antennas. An ARC-208(V) Milstars satellite communications antenna was accommodated in a large dorsal fairing on some aircraft.

Variants

EC-135B ARIA: four C-135B conversions for the **ARIA** (**Apollo Range Instrumentation Aircraft**, later **Advanced Range Instrumentation Aircraft**) role with a steerable antenna in a nose extended into a large 'platypus' radome section
EC-135C: 13 KC-135B airborne command post conversions for SAC's 'Looking Glass' Post-Attack Command Control System. The variant was characterised by antennas at the wingtips and below the fuselage, an inflight-refuelling receptacle above the fuselage, and the standard flying boom installation under the lower part of the rear fuselage: the EC-135C could therefore take fuel from boom-equipped tankers and, using its own flying boom, either hand off fuel to other receptacle-equipped aircraft or receive fuel from bombers by reverse action of its flying boom
EC-135E: four out of the eight EC-135Ns converted with TF33-P-102 turbofan engines and used for test purposes
EC-135G: four KC-135A conversions retaining tanker capability but revised with an inflight-refuelling receptacle and additional communications equipment (at the wingtips and on the fuselage) for service as airborne control centres for ICBM launch purposes, but also able to double as communications relay aircraft between SAC headquarters and missile field command posts

SPECIFICATION	
Boeing Model 717 (EC-135C) **Type:** 15/16-crew flying command post **Powerplant:** four Pratt & Whitney TF33-P-9 turbofan engines each rated at 18,000 lb st (80.05 kN) **Performance:** maximum speed 616 mph (991 km/h) at 25,000 ft (7620 m); cruising speed 560 mph (901 km/h) at 35,000 ft (10668 m);	service ceiling 40,600 ft (12375 m); range 5,654 miles (9099 km) **Weights:** empty 102,300 lb (46403 kg); maximum take-off 299,000 lb (135626 kg) **Dimensions:** wingspan 130 ft 10 in (39.88 m); length 136 ft 3 in (41.53 m); height 41 ft 8 in (12.70 m); wing area 2,433.0 sq ft (226.03 m²)

Boeing Model 717 (EC-135) (continued)

Used as part of the Apollo space programme, the EC-135N was a specialised spacecraft tracking platform. In 1985, this aircraft was converted to C-135N standard for use as a command post. It received TF33 engines in 1986.

The core of the 2nd ACCS's equipment was the **EC-135C**. Related variants were the **EC-135H**, **EC-135J**, **EC-135P** and **EC-135Y**. The **EC-135A**, **EC-135G** and **EC-135L** were radio relay platforms used to extend the effective range of the main command post. By 1992 most of the EC-135A/G/ H/L/P aircraft were in open storage at Davis-Monthan AFB, Arizona, along with two EC-135Cs and one EC-135J. The USAF's EC-135 force has now finally been retired in favour of the USN's E-6 Mercury.

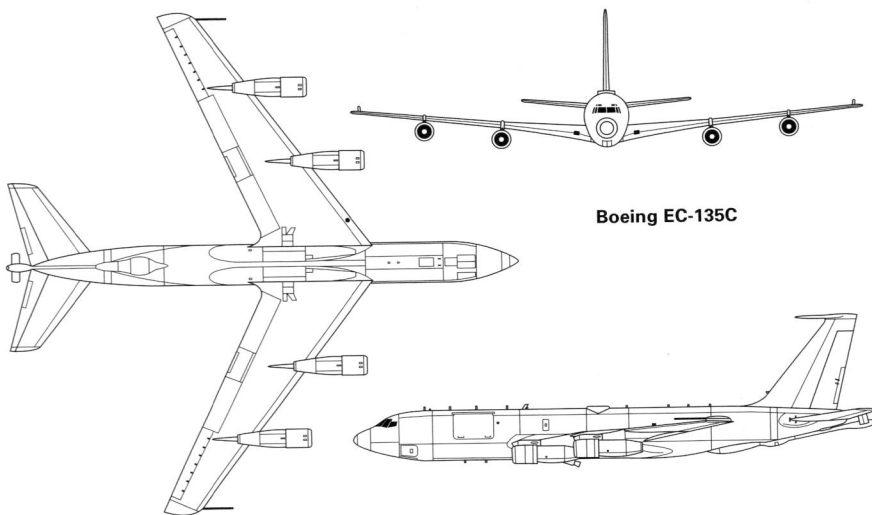

Boeing EC-135C

Variants continued

EC-135H: five airborne command post aircraft for United States Air Forces in Europe (USAFE), converted from one VC-135A and four KC-135As with an inflight-refuelling receptacle and additional communications equipment (including a long trailing-wire antenna). The designation remained unaltered even after the aircraft were revised with TF33-P-102 turbofans

EC-135J: four airborne command post aircraft for PACAF. The aircraft were originally three **National Emergency Airborne Command Posts (NEACPs)** converted from C-135C standard to a layout similar to that of the EC-135C, and after replacement in the NEACP role by Boeing E-4s were reallocated to the Pacific Air Force (PACAF), together with a fourth machine also converted from EC-135C standard. All four aircraft were characterised by the typical command post antennas at the wingtips and on the fuselage

EC-135K: two aircraft created as Tactical Air Command (TAC) airborne command post and navigation/deployment lead aircraft for fighters. Converted from KC-135A standard, but upgraded with a powerplant of four TF33 turbofan engines

EC-135L: eight KC-135As converted in 1965 to the **Post-Attack Command and Control System** role. The type retains the tanker boom, and as part of the conversion process was fitted with an inflight-refuelling receptacle

EC-135N: eight C-135As converted for **ARIA** spacecraft-tracking role

EC-135P: four aircraft were created for PACAF (later TAC) as airborne command post conversions of two KC-135As (already converted to EC-135A standard), one NKC-135A and one EC-135H with the appropriate communication equipment, an inflight-refuelling receptacle, and a reverse-action facility in the flying boom

EC-135Y: one NKC-135A and one EC-135N converted as a flying command post for the commander of the US Central Command

Boeing Model 717 (McDonnell Douglas MD-95)

By the early 1990s McDonnell Douglas felt that it should offer a modern replacement for the DC-9-30, based on a new powerplant, modern avionics and the combination of aerodynamic and structural improvements that had been pioneered in the later versions of the DC-9 as well as the later MD-80 series and the MD-90. The new type was schemed as the **McDonnell Douglas MD-95**, and this was announced at the 1991 Paris Air Show although the company had yet to formally launch the type. The MD-95 was planned as an advanced-technology equivalent of the DC-9-30 with its fuselage lengthened by some 3 ft 3 in (1 m) to allow the carriage of up to 106 passengers over regional airliner sectors. The configuration and structure of the MD-95 were basically the same as those of the MD-80 and MD-90, and the structure was schemed in aluminium alloy, with a measure of glassfibre, and was planned for extensive subcontracting.

The powerplant selected for the new airliner was an Anglo-German type, the BMW Rolls-Royce BR715 turbofan, with an option for uprating to 20,000 lb st (88.95 kN) in the higher-weight **MD-95-30ER** that was being planned as an extended-range derivative with greater fuel capacity.

McDonnell Douglas formally launched the MD-95 in October 1995 following the receipt of an initial order from ValuJet (now AirTran) for 50 aircraft. As work on the MD-95 was proceeding, McDonnell Douglas merged into Boeing in August 1997 and lost its separate identity. In January 1998 Boeing redesigned the MD-95 as the **Boeing Model 717**. At the same time, it confirmed that it intended to proceed with the programme, now shifted to the old Douglas facility at Long Beach, California, as it saw the Model 717 as a type to fill the gap in its product line in the capacity bracket below that of the Model 737-600 that was then its smallest-capacity airliner.

The first **Model 717-200** was rolled out on 10 June 1998, but the start of flight trials was delayed by final development problems with the BR715 engine. The Model 717-200 first flew on 2 September 1998, and AirTran will receive its first service aircraft in May 1999. Boeing is currently considering a reduced-capacity **Model 717-100X** for the carriage of 75 to 80 passengers, an increased capacity **Model 717-300X** for the carriage of up to 130 passengers in a two-class arrangement, and a corporate transport version similar to the BBJ corporate transport version of the Model 737.

The BR715 turbofan offers a high power/weight ratio, excellent fuel economy and low noise emissions.

SPECIFICATION

Boeing Model 717-200
Type: two-crew regional and short-range airliner
Powerplant: two BMW Rolls-Royce BR715 turbofans each rated at 18,500 lb st (82.27 kN)
Performance: maximum cruising speed 504 mph (811 km/h) at high altitude; range 1,726 miles (2778 km) with maximum payload
Weights: empty 70,640 lb (32042 kg); maximum take-off 113,750 lb (51597 kg)
Dimensions: wingspan 93 ft 3½ in (28.44 m); length 119 ft 3½ in (36.36 m); height 28 ft 2½ in (8.60 m); wing area 1,000.7 sq ft (92.97 m²)
Payload: up to 106 passengers within the context of a 26,885-lb (12195-kg) maximum payload

Boeing Model 720

The early success of its Model 707 civil transport led Boeing to proceed with the development of an intermediate-range version under the initial designation of **Boeing Model 707-020**. This revised type retained the same wing and tailplane span, but featured a modified wing profile with increased sweep and changes to the trailing edge at the wingroots. In terms of structure and weight however, the design was entirely new, resulting in the eventual allocation of the designation **Model 720** to add emphasis to the point that the type was not merely a re-engined 707.

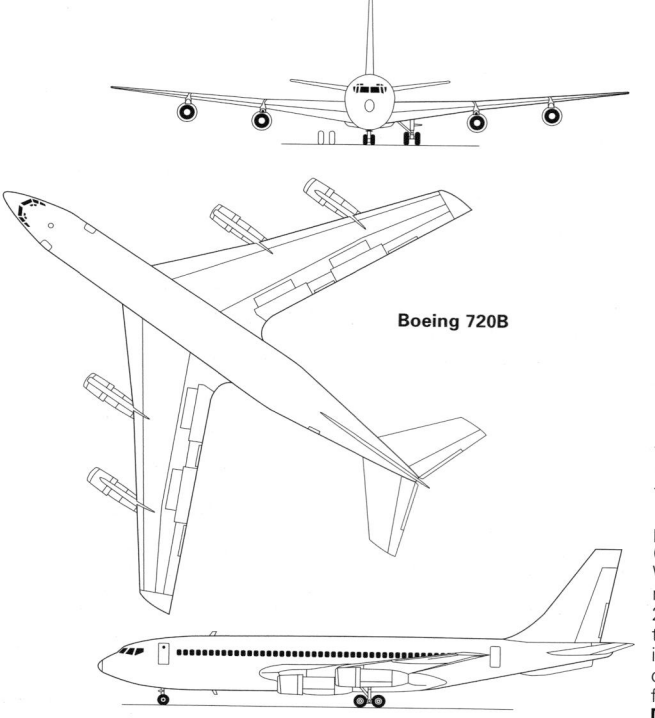

Boeing 720B

Most significant of the aerodynamic changes introduced on this new type were refinements to the wing leading edge, and these modifications were later introduced to the Model 707 family on the Model 707-100B variant; the changes improved take-off performance and cruising speed. The length of the fuselage was reduced by 7 ft 9 in (2.36 m) by comparison with that of the Model 707-100 and Model 707-200, and reduction of the standard fuel load made it possible to lighten the structure.

The basic Model 720, powered by four 12,500-lb (55.59-kN) thrust Pratt & Whitney JT3C-7 turbojets, made its maiden flight on 23 November 1959, and the type entered service initially with United Airlines on 5 July 1960. It was followed by the improved **Model 720B** which intro-

Air Malta used at least six different 720Bs between 1974 and 1984. The aircraft were obtained by a mixture of leasing and outright purchase and were replaced by far more economical 737s, Airbus A320s and Avro RJ70s.

duced Pratt & Whitney JT3D turbofan engines, initially the 17,000-lb st (75.6-kN) JT3D-1. These not only made it possible to operate from still shorter runways, but their greater efficiency allowed for some increase in range despite a higher payload. First flown on 6 October 1960, this version entered service with American Airlines on 12 March 1961. There was, however, only a limited demand for the smaller-capacity Model 720 and Model 720B, and production ended in 1969 after totals of 65 Model 720 and 89 Model 720B aircraft had been built and delivered.

SPECIFICATION	
Boeing Model 720B **Type:** three/four-crew intermediate-range transport **Powerplant:** four Pratt & Whitney JT3D-3 turbofan engines each rated at 18,000 lb st (80.05 kN) **Performance:** maximum speed 627 mph (1009 km/h) at optimum altitude; cruising speed 611 mph (983 km/h) at 25,000 ft (7620 m); initial climb rate 3,700 ft (1128 m) per minute; service ceiling 42,000 ft (12802 m); range	4,155 miles (6687 km) with maximum payload **Weights:** empty 112,883 lb (51204 kg); maximum take-off 234,000 lb (106142 kg) **Dimensions:** wingspan 130 ft 10 in (39.88 m); length 136 ft 9 in (41.68 m); height 40 ft 11 in (12.47 m); wing area 2,521 sq ft (234.20 m²) **Payload:** up to 112 passengers within the context of a 40,500-lb (18371-kg) payload

Boeing Model 727

Even before its Model 707 airliner was ready for service, Boeing had come to the conclusion that it would make commercial sense to complement its new longer-range transport with a new short/medium-range airliner. Boeing realised that its new airliner would need good take-off and landing characteristics for the length of average runway currently available. Operation over short-haul routes required an effective solution to a nasty problem: the provision of the highest possible cruising speed at the lowest possible altitude, with seat/mile costs kept to a minimum figure. Short stage lengths also meant a higher ratio of landings to flight hours, affecting not only the design of the landing gear, but also of servicing access to the airliner. In addition, the capability of operating into and out of smaller airports, often nearer to city centres, meant that noise had to be kept to a minimum.

Early estimates suggested that a potential market for in excess of 300 aircraft would exist and this factor emphasised the economic desirability of using as many Model 707 and Model 720 components and systems as possible. It was assumed that engines of suitable power would be available, regardless of the selection of a two-, three- or four-engined layout, but engine position was not easy to define. The need to develop an efficient wing would be simplified if it did not also have to serve as a mounting for the powerplant, and this encouraged the investigation of rear-engined configurations. Having opted for a three-engined layout, Boeing planned to use the Allison-built version of the Rolls-Royce Spey turbofan, but the Pratt & Whitney JT8D turbofan was finally selected. All three engines were fitted with thrust-reversers to help with short-field landing problems.

Of the utmost impor- tance to the success of this project was the design of an advanced wing to provide the necessary broad range of performance. Consequently, the detailed design and development of such a wing was started long before a decision was made to proceed with the new airliner, by then identified as the **Boeing Model 727**.

The new fuselage used the upper lobe that had been designed for the Model 707. The entirely new lower fuselage structure incorporated a hydraulically actuated ventral airstair, and an auxiliary power unit (APU), thus making the new type capable of independent operation at small, poorly-equipped airports or able to effect speedy turnarounds.

United Airlines showed a great deal of enthusiasm for the Model 727 from an early date.

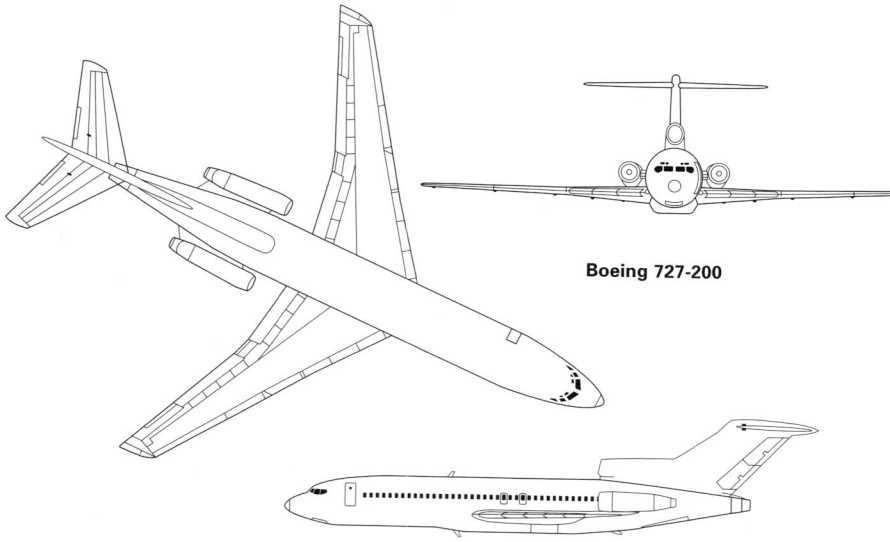

Boeing 727-200

Boeing Model 727 (continued)

United's requirements had considerable influence on the final configuration of the new airliner. Eastern Air Lines was also a potential customer, and with these two companies each expected to order 40 aircraft, the construction go-ahead was given in August 1960.

The first 727, a production aircraft in United insignia, made its maiden flight on 9 February 1963, some months behind schedule, and was followed by a Boeing demonstrator aircraft on 12 March, and two more production aircraft very shortly after this. These four aircraft completed the FAA certification programme by the end of the year, making good the time that had been lost and enabling the initial deliveries to Eastern and United to be made on time.

Airline services with the original **Model 727-100** were initiated by Eastern on 1 February 1964, with United following only five days later. Both companies discovered very quickly that the Model 727's economics were better than anticipated. United found the Model 727 cheaper to operate than its twin-engined Caravelles on even the shortest stage lengths. Despite such encouragement, orders for the new airliner totalled only 127 in the early spring of 1962 and were unchanged by the end of the year. Clearly, the airliner had to prove attractive to a wider range of operators. This resulted in the certification of versions with higher gross weights and various fuel options to provide the greatest possible operational flexibility.

However, by late 1964 it

had become clear that there was a growing demand for a higher-capacity short-range transport, and the decision to develop a 'stretched' version of the Model 727 proved the turning point in the programme. Designated as the **Model 727-200**, the new version had no significant differences from the earlier Model 727-100, except for the insertion of two fuselage plugs, one forward and one aft of the main landing gear wheel-well.

The first airline to order this new version, shortly after the initial announcement, was Northeast Airlines and the carrier flew the first 727-200 revenue service on 14 December 1967. With a little over 500 Model 727-100s having been built, production of this version ended in late 1973. Total production was 1,832 aircraft of all variants.

Variants

Model 727-100C: convertible version of the basic Model 727-100 incorporating strengthened flooring as well as the cargo door and freight-handling system developed for the Model 707-300C
Model 727-100QC: convertible version generally similar to above but with quick-change (QC) palletised passenger facilities
Model 727-200: lengthened-fuselage version with structural modifications for operation at higher weights. Standard and maximum passenger capacities are 163 and 189, respectively
Advanced Model 727-200: final production version, generally similar to Model 727-200 but with advanced features such as a performance data computer system to enhance economy and safety of operation, improved cabin interiors and equipment, and optional powerplants including the JT8D-17R with automatic performance reserve (APR), which ensures that if one of the engines suffers a significant loss in thrust during take-off or initial climb, the thrust of the other two engines is increased automatically
Model 727RE: designation of a project investigating the possibility of re-engining Model 727-200s with Pratt & Whitney PW2037 or Rolls-Royce RB.211-535 turbofans, so producing an aircraft with Model 757 capabilities at a fraction of the cost of the new airliner
C-22: designation of Model 727s bought from airlines by the US forces, and comprising one **C-22A** (ex-Lufthansa Model 727-100), four **C-22B** (ex-National/Pan am Model 727-100) machines, and one **C-22C** (ex-Singapore Airlines Model 727-200). Other ex-airline Model 727s have also been bought in small numbers by a number of other air arms

Eastern Airlines was the first carrier to place the 727 into regular service. At one time the airline's fleet peaked at 101 examples of the trijet.

SPECIFICATION	
Boeing Advanced Model 727-200	range 2,487 miles (4002 km) with maximum payload
Type: three-crew short/medium-range transport	**Weights:** empty 102,900 lb (46675 kg); maximum take-off 209,500 lb (45027 kg)
Powerplant: typically three Pratt & Whitney JT8D-9A turbofan engines each rated at 14,500 lb st (64.50 kN)	**Dimensions:** wingspan 108 ft (32.92 m); length 153 ft 2 in (46.69 m); height 34 ft (10.36 m); wing area 1,700.00 sq ft (157.93 m²)
Performance: maximum speed 621 mph (999 km/h) at 20,500 ft (6250 m); cruising speed 570 mph (917 km/h) at 24,700 ft (7530 m); service ceiling 33,000 ft (10060 m);	**Payload:** up to 189 passengers or 41,000 lb (18598 kg) of freight

Braniff flew a number of 727-100s and -200s, one of the latter being illustrated. Originally developed with a similar fuel load to the 727-100C, the 727-200 eventually reached a fuel capacity of 8,090 US gal (30624 litres).

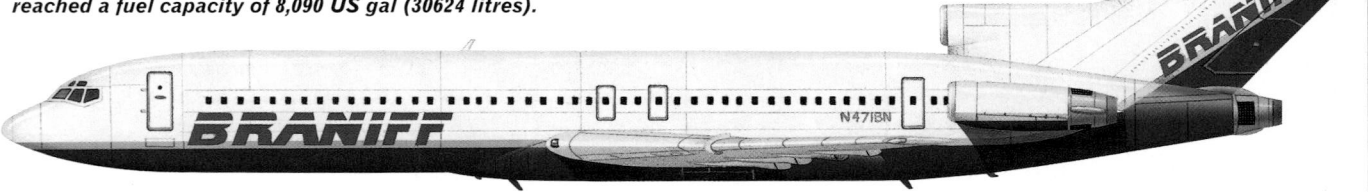

Boeing Model 737

On 19 February 1965 Boeing announced its intention to build the **Model 737** short-range transport with a powerplant of two turbofans, to complement its existing model line-up. The initial order had come from Lufthansa, the first foreign airline to be first on the order book for a new US airliner, and the carrier signed a contract for 21 aircraft, this being announced simultaneously with the Boeing production decision.

The family likeness of the Model 737 to the 707/727 was plain to see as a result largely of the retention of what was basically a Model 727 fuse-

lage and a tail unit which was of similar configuration to that of the Model 707. Accommodation for between 60 and 85 passengers was initially envisaged, but Lufthansa required seating capacity for 100 passengers, and the fuselage length was sized accordingly.

The wing incorporated much of the technology developed for the 727 and the major area of change concerned the powerplant. A wing-mounted powerplant was dictated, since space in the relatively short fuselage was at a premium and passengers could not be seated next to fuselage-mounted engines. The first engine choice was the

14,000-lb st (62.28-kN) Pratt & Whitney JT8D-1 turbofan, but by the time that the negotiations with Lufthansa had been completed, the JT8D-7 had been substituted as this was flat-rated to develop the same thrust at higher ambient temperatures. This engine became the standard powerplant for the **Model 737-100**, with the option available of the higher-rated 14,500-lb st (64.50-kN) JT8D-9.

The first Model 737-100 made its maiden flight on 9 April 1967 and Lufthansa inaugurated its services with the new type on 10 February 1968.

Less than two months after Boeing's launch of the Model 737, the company disclosed that the larger-capacity **Model 737-200**

variant was to be developed almost simultaneously. This rapidly became the initial standard model, the first of the type flying on 8 August 1967 and entering revenue service with United Airlines on 29 April 1968. The Model 737-200 had its fuselage lengthened by 6 ft (1.83 m) to increase the maximum accommodation to 130 passengers. The rapid growth in air travel, and consequently in seating capacity requirements, during this period meant that there was virtually no demand for the 100/103-seat 737-100, which went out of production after a mere 30 had been built.

The comparatively short take-off and landing distances of the 737 meant that the type was

able to operate into airfields with unpaved or gravel runways. Boeing therefore developed suitable FOD (foreign object damage) protection gear in kit form. Production of the Model 737-200 ended in 1988 after the completion of some 1,114 aircraft.

Later, two successive series of related variants emerged and their success has made the Model 737 into the best-selling airliner in history. Orders, up to March 1999, totalled 1,980 examples of the **'Classic'** series (**Model 737-300**, **Model 737-400** and **Model 737-500**) and 1132 examples of the **'Next Generation'** series (**Model 737-600**, **Model 737-700**, **Model 737-800** and **Model 737-900**), raising orders for the Model 737 series to a figure well past the 4,000 mark. It was in March 1981 that Boeing announced the Model 737-300 as an updated and slightly enlarged version equipped with new-generation 20,000-lb st (88.96-kN) CFM56-3 turbofans but later uprated to 22,000 lb st (97.86 kN), as well as other improvements. Subsequent additions to the 'Classic' series are the larger Model 737-400 and smaller Model 737-500 variants. Launched in November 1993, the 'Next Generation' series boasts a new and larger wing, higher cruising speeds and greater range.

Modest numbers of 737s have also been supplied to the USAF, to replace Convair T-29 navigation trainers. Boeing was contracted to supply 19 aircraft under the designation **T-43A**, now revised to

CT-43A. The military variant's first flight was made on 10 April 1973, and all had been delivered by the end of July 1974. Although the general configuration of the CT-43A is the same as that of the commercial 737-200, there are a number of detail and interior changes to fit the aircraft to its specific role. With the decline in the

USAF's need for dedicated navigators from the mid-1980s, many of the aircraft have been reassigned to the utility transport role.

The 'Classic' series, including the -400, is most easily distinguished from earlier 737s by its revised and repositioned engine nacelles.

Surviving CT-43As remain in service with the 562nd FTS at Randolph AFB, Texas. The aircraft were originally delivered following experience in the period of the Vietnam War, which revealed to the USAF that it had inadequate facilities for the training of navigators.

31152

U.S. AIR FORCE

Variants

Model 737-200C: convertible passenger/freight version of the 737-200
Model 737-200QC: quick-change convertible passenger/freight version of the 737-200 with palletised passenger facilities
Advanced Model 737-200: final production standard for the original 727-200 variant. First became available in 1971 with accommodation for a maximum of 130 passengers and the ability to operate at an optional maximum weight of 117,000 lb (53071 kg) and options for engines such as the JT8D-15, JT8D-17 or JT8D-17R
Advanced Model 737-200C/QC: convertible and quick-change convertible versions of Advanced Model 737-200 respectively
Advanced Model 737-200 Executive Jet: generally similar to the Advanced Model 737-200, but supplied in a form suitable for the installation of special business and executive luxury interiors to customer requirements
Advanced Model 737-200 High Gross Weight Structure: generally similar to Advanced 737-200, but available in two maximum-weight options
Model 737-200 SLAMMR or Surveiller: three aircraft for the Indonesian air force in the maritime surveillance/transport role with Motorola SLAMMR (Side-Looking Airborne Multi-Mission Radar) equipment
Model 737-300: first of the **'Classic'** series with a fuselage stretched by 8 ft 6 in (2.59 m) to provide accommodation for 128 passengers in a typical two-class layout. The first Model 737-300 flew in February 1984 and deliveries began to launch customers US Airways and Southwest Airlines in November 1984. The Model 737-300 was available in standard airliner and **Executive** 'bizjet' forms
Model 737-400: a further 10 ft (3.05 m) increase in fuselage length compared with the Model 737-300 for typical accommodation of 146 passengers in standard seating or 168 passengers in high-density seating. The first Model 737-400 flew in January 1988, and Piedmont Airlines received the first machine in September 1988. The type was offered in three maximum-weight forms
Model 737-500: smallest member of the 'Classic' series. The type first flew in June 1989, and Southwest Airlines received the first aircraft in February 1990 with accommodation for up to 108 passengers in a two-class arrangement
Model 737-600: first of the **'Next Generation'** series with a wing increased in span to 112 ft 7 in (34.31 m) as well as in chord for a greater area, and also increased fuel capacity, a new flightdeck with

liquid-crystal displays, and the uprated powerplant of two CFM56-7 turbofan engines each rated at 22,000, 24,000 and 26,200 lb st (97.86, 106.76 and 116.54 kN) in the Model 737-600, Model 737-700 and Model 737-800 respectively. The Model 737-600 replaces the Model 737-500 and offers similar accommodation. The first 737-600 flew in January 1998 and was delivered to SAS in September 1998
Model 737-700: successor to the 737-300, with similar accommodation. The type first flew in February 1997, and the initial delivery was made to Southwest Airlines in December of the same year
Model 737-800: successor to the model 737-400 with a fuselage 129 ft 6 in (39.47 m) long for the accommodation of up to 160 passengers in a typical two-class arrangement, or 189 passengers in a single-class arrangement with high-density seating. The type first flew in July 1997, and the initial delivery was made to Hapag-Lloyd in April 1998
Model 737-900: launched in November 1997 by an order from Alaska Airlines, and is in effect Boeing's direct counterpart to the Airbus A321. The fuselage is increased in length by 8 ft 8 in (2.64 m) over that of the 737-800 to provide seating for an additional 15 passengers, raising the typical two-class accommodation to 177 passengers. The first Model 737-900 should fly in 2000 for delivery in the following year
C-40A: 737-700 equipped with a forward-located side cargo door to meet a USN requirement for a modern type to replace the C-9 Nightingale; ordered as the **C-39A** although the designation was then changed for some unknown reason to C-40A. The first two aircraft are scheduled for delivery in 2001, and the overall requirement is for 27 such aircraft. A civil version equipped with a similar cargo door could also be developed
Boeing Business Jet: the **BBJ** is the dedicated 'bizjet' member of the 'New Generation' series with the 737-700's fuselage and the strengthened wing and powerplant of the 737-800. The first machine was delivered in the latter part of 1998

Boeing Model 739 (RC-135)

It was, to some extent, natural that the KC-135A Stratotanker and C-135 Stratolifter should be developed for a number of other applications including Elint, Sigint and Comint. The manufacturer allocated this series a different designation, **Boeing Model 739**, to indicate its considerable

avionics differences from the Model 717 derivatives. By the late 1990s all surviving aircraft had been brought under the control of the 55th Strategic Wing, Offutt AFB, Nebraska.

The first such variants were several KC-135As, modified with electronic recording equipment in the

early 1960s for use in the 'Iron Lung' and 'Briar Patch' programmes. At much the same time, several KC-135A-II and at least five JKC-135A conversions were effected in the 'Office Boy' and 'Nancy Rae' programmes to monitor Soviet ICBM test launches.

Boeing 739 (RC-135) (continued)

Variants

RC-135A: the first variant built specifically for the reconnaissance role, this was a photo-mapping and electronic reconnaissance type based on the C-135A and using the same powerplant. Four such aircraft were delivered in 1965 and 1966 with a fuel dump tube in the place occupied by the inflight-refuelling boom on the KC-135A, one forward fuselage tank removed, geodetic survey equipment installed internally, and a camera package located in a bay aft of the landing gear's nose unit. This last incorporated a sliding panel over the large, flat glass plate that was optically ground to provide the multiple cameras with optimum viewing conditions. The aircraft were later converted into KC-135D tankers

OC-135B: three **WC-135B** weather reconnaissance aircraft (10 C-135B conversions) adapted for the 'Open Skies' optical verification programme, with a crew of up to 38 and equipment including four cameras of three different types

TC-135B: sole WC-135B conversion for OC-135B training

RC-135C: 10 aircraft built with the designation **RC-135B** for the electronic reconnaissance role, based structurally on the C-135B, but with a powerplant of four TF33-P-9 turbofans. The aircraft were completed in 1964 and 1965, and before delivery were converted by Martin into RC-135Cs for a variety of electronic reconnaissance tasks. There was no standardisation in the electronics fit, which was optimised for the Sigint task with the ASD-1 automatic reconnaissance system and the QRC-259 fast-sweep analyser as the core units

RC-135D: four aircraft were Elint conversions of one KC-135A and three C-135A machines, effected in 1962 and 1963, with a fuel dump tube, an inflight-refuelling receptacle, a 'thimble' nose radome and other systems including tubular antennas projecting forward from the wingroots. The three survivors were converted to standard KC-135A standard between 1975 and 1979

RC-135E: sole RC-135E was a C-135B conversion similar to the RC-135C but with a wide fibreglass radome around the forward fuselage

RC-135M: six C/VC-135B conversions effected in 1967 and 1968 for electronic reconnaissance in the Rivet Card and Rivet Quick programmes. The aircraft were fitted with 'thimble' nose radomes, teardrop fairings on the fuselage sides forward of the tail, and twin-lobe ventral antennas

RC-135S: three C-135B conversions with numerous blister fairings and a dipole aerial as part of the Cobra Ball programme for the recording of foreign missile tests, including the re-entry of warheads, by both telemetry intercept and optical means. The aircraft each have a 'thimble' nose radome, electronic receivers located in cheek fairings, a teardrop fairing on the rear fuselage, and the RTOS (Real-Time Optical System) characterised by large circular windows in the fuselage for photography

TC-135S: one EC-135B converted into the sole TC-135S for Cobra Ball Telint training, without making demands on the limited flying hours available on the two surviving operational aircraft

RC-135T: converted originally from a C-135B in 1971 as the **RC-135R**,

this single machine featured a long fence-like antenna on top of the fuselage and was used by SAC for command support and training roles before conversion to KC-135A standard

RC-135U: two RC-135C conversions with SLAR and Elint systems, with their antennas on the fuselage and wingtips. The aircraft are associated with the Combat Pink and Combat Sent programmes and their primary equipment is the AEELS (Automatic Elint Emitter Locator System). The external signs of this and also the MUCELS equipment include two large cheek fairings for side-facing antennas and a 'farm' of downward-facing antennas under the fuselage

RC-135V: eight RC-135C conversions in the Rivet Card programme with cheek fairings, enlarged 'thimble' nose radomes, flat plate antennas under the centre section of the wings, and extensive antenna arrays under their fuselages for the Elint role

RC-135W: six RC-135Ms upgraded under the Rivet Joint programme to a standard basically similar to that of the RC-135 but with longer cheek fairings, that on the port side partially covering the crew door

TC-135W: single training machine produced as a C-135B conversion

RC-135X: single machine similar to the RC-135S but converted from C-135B standard under the Cobra Eye programme, with revised sensor equipment including fewer antennas and a single camera behind a sliding fuselage door

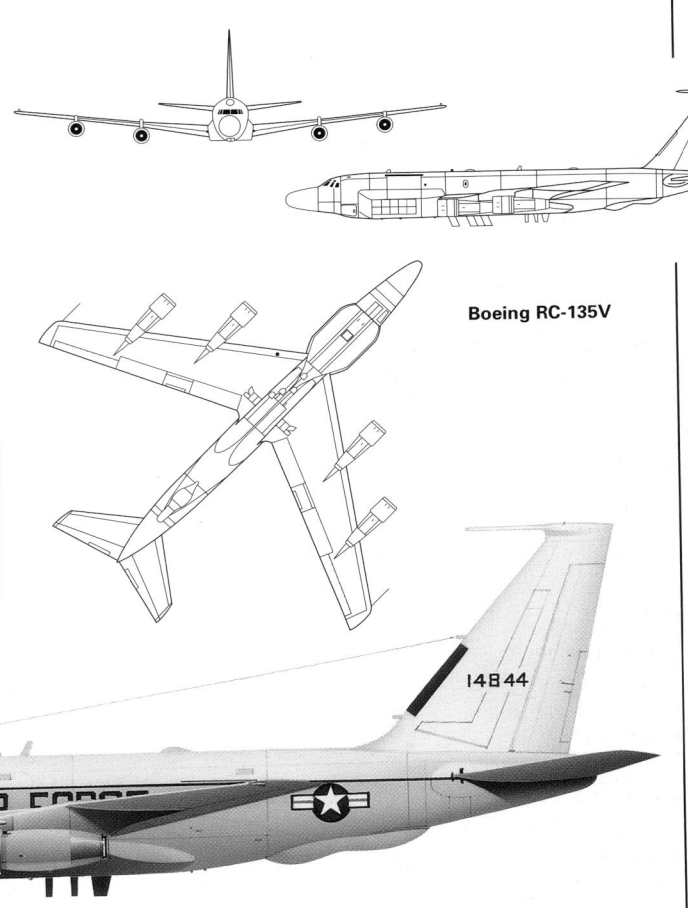

Boeing RC-135V

RC-135Vs have seen a great deal of operational service, including missions during US and NATO operations against Iraq and over Bosnia. The aircraft have been involved in the sustained NATO action against Serbia.

14844

Boeing Model 747

The USAF's CX-HLS (Cargo, Experimental – Heavy Logistics System) requirement led to a design competition initiated in May 1964. Design development contracts were issued to Boeing, Douglas and Lockheed, the last winning with its C-5 Galaxy.

Boeing was keenly disappointed to lose the military contract, but market research had shown that a large-capacity airliner would become

of interest to operators during the early 1970s, and even before the destination of the military contract had been announced, Boeing had set up a small design group, working to outline the details of a new civil transport.

Boeing was now able to concentrate on the design of what was identified from the outset as the **Boeing Model 747**. Initial studies covered aircraft up to a maximum weight of about

600,000 lb (272160 kg) and capable of accommodating as many as 430 passengers. A two-deck 'double-bubble' fuselage concept did not appeal to possible operators, so Boeing reappraised the project. This led, early in 1966, to the drafting of what was basically a 'big brother' to the Model 707, featuring a wing with advanced aerodynamic features but set in the same low-wing configuration, a somewhat similar conventional tail unit, and tricycle landing gear. The

fuselage was of almost circular section, with the flight deck located high on the forward fuselage within the now easily recognised 'hump' fairing, allowing the extension of the main passenger cabin beneath it right into the nose.

The most staggering feature of this fuselage was its size, providing a cabin 20 ft 1½ in (6.13 m) wide and 185 ft (56.39 m) long. Early plans provided accommodation for 368 mixed-class passengers in a typical layout. It had a maximum weight of

625,000 lb (283500 kg), which in turn meant that if the 747 was to operate from existing runways it would require landing gear that would support and distribute this mass effectively without causing damage to the runway. The resulting main units, four in total, each had a four-wheel bogie, and the nose unit had twin wheels.

It was with the design in this general form that Boeing began to seek prospective customers. Pan Am was considered to be the most likely first buyer,

Externally, the 747-400 (illustrated) is most easily distinguished from other 747 variants, especially the 747-300 which shares its SUD as standard, by its winglets.

but until there was positive airline interest, it was not feasible for the company to make a launch commitment, as the investment required represented too big a gamble for detail design and construction on a private-venture basis.

On 13 April 1966 it was announced simultaneously that the company had

designed and was to manufacture the Model 747 and that Pan Am had ordered 25 of these giant aircraft. It was not until additional orders had been received from JAL and Lufthansa, however, that the company finally made its 25 July 1966 decision to begin construction.

Pan Am's appraisal of

Boeing's design had resulted in the implementation of some detail changes and, not surprisingly, the first press reports that followed Boeing's announcement were well laced with adjectives which implied magnitude – very soon, the Model 747 had gained the popular and near-immortal nickname of '**Jumbo Jet**'.

No prototype of the 747 was built, the original production machine being intended as Boeing's demonstrator. This was rolled out on 30 September 1968 at Paine Field outside Everett, Washington, where the company had

established a completely new factory for the Model 747 production line. The first flight was completed on 9 February 1969 and, with the participation of the next four production aircraft as they became available, the certification programme was completed just before the end of 1969, FAA approval being granted on 30 December. On 22 January 1970 Pan Am inaugurated its first service with the type, introducing it on the New York-London route.

Shortening the fuselage and increasing the fuel capacity produced the 747SP. The aircraft offers a range of 7,658 miles (12324 km) with 305 passengers and 20,000 lb (9072 kg) of cargo.

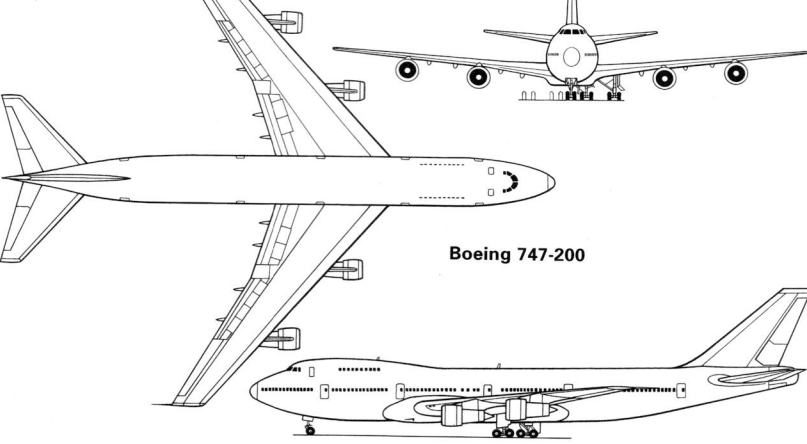

Boeing 747-200

SPECIFICATION
Boeing Model 747-200B **Type:** three-crew long-range heavy transport **Powerplant:** four General Electric CF6-50E2 turbofan engines each rated at 52,500 lb st (233.53 kN), or Pratt & Whitney JT9D-7R4G2 turbofan engines each rated at 54,750 lb st (243.54 kN), or Rolls-Royce RB.211-524D4 turbofan engines each rated at 53,110 lb st (236.24 kN) **Performance:** maximum speed 602 mph (969 km/h) at 30,000 ft (9145 m); cruising speed 584 mph	(940 km/h) at 35,000 ft (10670 m); service ceiling 45,000 ft (13715 m); range 7,082 miles (11397 km) with maximum passenger payload **Weights:** empty 375,170 lb (170,177 kg); maximum take-off 833,000 lb (377849 kg) **Dimensions:** wingspan 195 ft 8 in (59.64 m); length 231 ft 10 in (70.66 m); height 63 ft 5 in (19.33 m); wing area 5,500.00 sq ft (510.95 m²) **Payload:** up to 516 passengers within the context of a 151,500-lb (68720-kg) payload

Variants

Model 747-100B: version of the 747-100 with a strengthened fuselage, landing gear and wing structure
Model 747-200B: entering service in January 1971, this variant was generally similar to the 747-100B but with a choice of engines from three manufacturers and increased fuel capacity for a maximum take-off weight of up to 833,000 lb (377849 kg)
Model 747-200B Combi: version of the 747-200B with a port-side freight door as standard, allowing use of the type in all-passenger or passenger/freight configurations
Model 747-200B Convertible: version of the 747-200 equipped for operation in all-passenger or all-freight configuration, or in any one of five predetermined passenger/cargo variations
Model 747-200F Freighter: all-freight version of the 747-200 with the fuselage nose opening forward and upward to give clear and straight-in loading access to the main deck, plus a freight-loading system that can be operated by two people. A side freight door is optional, and the maximum payload is 248,000 lb (112493 kg)
Model 747SP: introduced by Pan Am in 1976, this **Special Performance** variant is a lighter-weight version for longer-range operations, with the fuselage length reduced by 47 ft 1 in (14.35 m) and a new tail unit with greater horizontal and vertical areas
Model 747SR: this **Short-Range** version of the Model 747-100B incorporated structural modifications to allow for a much higher frequency of operations
Model 747SUD: this **Stretched Upper Deck** variant, available optionally on 747-100B, Model 747-200B, Model 747-200B Combi and Model 747SR types, provides economy-class seating for 69 passengers on the lengthened upper deck as well as an additional seven seats on the lower deck following deletion of the original circular staircase
Model 747-300: first variant to be built and delivered with the extended upper deck, with its rear moved 23 ft 4 in (7.11 m) closer to the tail; the Model 747-300 entered service with Swissair early in 1983
Model 747-400: first flown on 29 April 1988 with the initial delivery made in January 1989 to Northwest Airlines, the Model 747-400 retains the fuselage dimensions of the Model 747-300, but differs in the modification of its wing, with winglets at its tips and an increase in span,

a two-crew EFIS flight deck, numerous aerodynamic enhancements, extensive use of composite materials for a significant reduction in empty weight, an optional fuel tank in the tailplane and engines that are both uprated and more efficient. The Model 747-400 is also available in subvariants such as the **Model 747-400 Combi**, **Model 747-400F** pure freighter, **Model 747-400D (Domestic)** for short routes in the Japanese domestic market with up to 568 passengers, the original wingspan and no winglets but with strengthening of the wing, fuselage and landing gear for a greater number of flight cycles, and **Model 747-400PIP (Performance Improvement Package)** for options including greater weight. Boeing has also considered a number of other improved versions, the **Model 747-500X** and **Model 747-600X** being ended in January 1998 but with work continuing on the **Model 747-400X** for possible service as the **Model 747-400ER** with range extended to 8,860 miles (14260 km), and the **Model 747-400Y** with a range of 8,965 miles (14430 km) with an additional 90 seats and a wing increased in span by 7 ft 6 in (2.29 m). Possible engines for this last variant include the General Electric/Pratt & Whitney Engine Alliance GP7000 and the Rolls-Royce Trent 600 each rated at some 68,000 lb st (302.5 kN)
E-4: AABNCP (Advanced Airborne National Command Post) or **NEACP (National Emergency Airborne Command Post)** type, based on the airframe of the Model 747-200B and equipped for the carriage of the president and his command staff in time of crisis. First flown on 13 June 1973 with the command and communications equipment stripped from an EC-135J, the three **E-4A** aircraft were delivered in 1974. A fourth machine was delivered in December 1979 as the **E-4B** with more advanced command and communications equipment, and the three E-4As were later upgraded to the same standard, which included the powerplant of four 52,500-lb st (233.53-kN) General Electric F103-GE-100 (CF6-50E) turbofans
C-19A: military designation of 747-200B civil aircraft earmarked for emergency military use under the Civil Reserve Aircraft Fleet concept
VC-25A: designation of two specially equipped 747-200B aircraft operated by the USAF as presidential transports
Model 747-123 Space Shuttle Carrier: designation of a single 747-100 acquired from AA by NASA and modified for carriage of a Space Shuttle Orbiter in a 'piggy-back' position over the fuselage

Boeing Model 747 (continued)

The period between the start of 747 construction and the receipt of certification had not been without its problems. Boeing's major difficulty had been to restrict weight growth, but in order to maintain the payload/range performance that had been specified, it was necessary to increase maximum take-off weight which, in the case of the initial **Model 747-100**, rose to 710,000 lb (322056 kg). The other major problem, and one closely related to weight, concerned the powerplant. Pan Am had opted for Pratt & Whitney engines, and the JT9D was an entirely new project which had been proposed for this aircraft at an initial rating of 41,000 lb st (182.38 kN). The engine not only suffered its own development problems, but as the weight of the airframe increased, it also became essential that the engine should be developed for greater thrust. This accelerated evolution of the new turbofan engine created great difficulties for Pratt & Whitney, and although a 43,000-lb st (192.27-kN) JT9D-3 was readied for production aircraft, it suffered innumerable teething troubles. Only when modified JT9D-3A engines were introduced later in 1970 were the problems overcome.

Boeing Model 757

In the early months of 1978, Boeing announced that it proposed to develop a new family of advanced-technology aircraft. Retaining the **7X7** designation formula, these three new twin-engined designs carried the designations **Model 757**, Model 767 and Model 777, the first of the three differing most significantly from the last two in retaining the same narrow-body fuselage section as the 727. The Model 757 was originally planned with the same type of T-tail and forward fuselage as the 727, but this was later changed to a more conventional low-set tailplane and a new forward fuselage allowing the incorporation of a flightdeck essentially identical to that of the 767.

A short/medium-range airliner, the Model 757 was intended to provide its operators with new standards of fuel efficiency. Boeing claimed that the 757 would be the world's most economical turbofan-powered airliner of the short/medium-range type. This was to result from the combination of a new advanced-technology wing, high-bypass ratio turbofan engines, and advanced avionics that would permit the aircraft to operate at optimum efficiency.

The first orders for the 757, which has the designation **Model 757-200** in its initial form with a longer fuselage than the proposed **757-100**

that was later abandoned, were announced on 31 August 1978 as 19 and 21 aircraft for British Airways and Eastern Air Lines respectively.

The powerplant options were to have been the Rolls-Royce RB.211-535 or General Electric CF6-32 turbofan engines. However, the latter was abandoned in the development stage and was replaced in Boeing's plans by the Pratt & Whitney PW2000 turbofan engine, initially in its PW2037 form but eventually in its higher-rated PW2040 form. The two launching airlines opted for the Rolls-Royce engine, marking the first time that Boeing had introduced a new airliner with a non-American powerplant. The Model 757 is operated by a flight crew of two, using a new-generation avionics control system which is capable of handling an entire flight from shortly after take-off, including the landing.

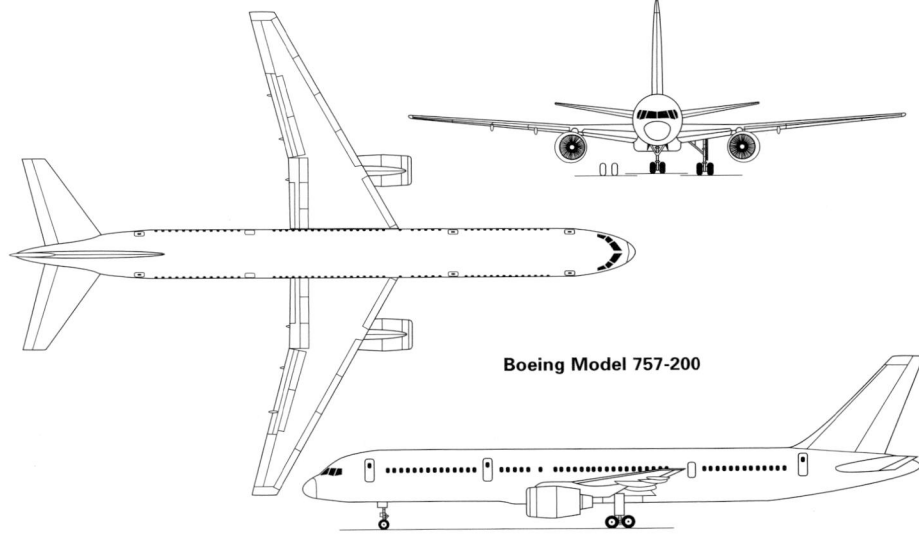

Boeing Model 757-200

The first flight of a 757 took place on 19 February 1982 and by March 1999 Boeing had received orders for 966 aircraft. The 757-200 entered revenue service with Eastern in January 1983.

SPECIFICATION

Boeing Model 757-200
Type: two-/three-crew short-/medium-range transport
Powerplant: two Rolls-Royce RB.211-535C or -535E4 turbofan engines each rated at 37,400 or 40,100 lb st (166.36 or 178.37 kN), or two Pratt & Whitney PW2037 or PW2040 turbofan engines each rated at 38,200 or 41,625 lb st (169.92 or 185.16 kN)
Performance: maximum speed 591 mph (951 km/h) at optimum altitude; cruising speed 582 mph (936 km/h) at 31,000 ft

(9450 m); service ceiling 38,000 ft (11580 m); range 3,662 miles (5893 km) with maximum payload
Weights: empty 126,250 lb (57267 kg); maximum take-off 240,000 lb (108864 kg)
Dimensions: wingspan 124 ft 10 in (38.05); length 155 ft 3 in (47.32 m); height 44 ft 6 in (13.56 m); wing area 1,994.00 sq ft (185.24 m²)
Payload: up to 239 passengers within the context of a 57,530-lb (26096-kg) payload

Variants

Model 757-200PF: Package Freighter variant developed for UPS with a large freight door forward and no cabin windows
Model 757-M Combi: mixed passenger/freight variant with a windowed cabin, port-side forward freight door and the ability to carry up to 150 passengers as well as three freight containers
Model 757-200F: freighter variant developed by Pemco Aeroplex as a conversion of existing aircraft, with a large freight door and provision for operation in all-freight, combi and quick-change configurations
Model 757-200X: extended-range development of the Model 757-200 under consideration by Boeing with the strengthened wing and components of the Model 757-300
Model 757-300: 'stretched' variant launched in 1996 on the basis of a firm order for 12 aircraft by Condor Flugdienst. The new variant is 23 ft 3 in (7.09 m) longer than the Model 757-200 and seats 280 in a high-density layout. The greater payload of the Model 757-300 required strengthening of the wing, landing gear and parts of the fuselage, as well as upgraded wheels and brakes. The longer fuselage also required the addition of a retractable tailskid. The first Model 757-300 flew in August 1998 with delivery beginning early in 1999
C-32A: four USAF VIP transports to replace C-137s, delivered from mid-1998 and based on the 757-200

With the 727 in decline, Boeing's 757 was without a serious rival in the short-/medium-range market until the arrival of the A321.

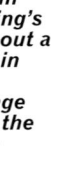
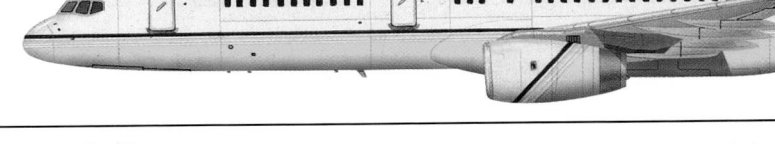

Boeing Model 767

The **Boeing Model 767** is the company's first wide-bodied transport of the twin-engined type, and was projected in the early and mid-1970s to provide Boeing with an offering to rival the Airbus A310. The

767 introduced a completely new fuselage structure, 4 ft 1 in (1.24 m) wider than that of the Model 757, providing seven- or eight-abreast seating with two aisles. High-density eight-abreast

accommodation is provided for a maximum of 289 passengers.

The go-ahead for the Model 767 programme was announced on 14 July 1978 following receipt of an order for 30 aircraft from United. By March 1999 orders had reached 864, with over 700 delivered.

Pratt & Whitney JT9D-7R4D and General

CAD techniques were used to speed the design work, the high accuracy of this process being of great benefit when, as in this case, a large amount of the component construction was carried out by other companies.

Electric CF6-80A/C turbofans were specified by those airlines which had placed orders by the summer of 1981. Boeing also considered the Rolls-Royce RB.211-524H as an optional powerplant and this became available in a longer-range subvariant of the **Model 767-300**.

Boeing planned initially to offer two versions as the **Model 767-100** with a shorter fuselage and accommodation for approximately 180 passengers, and the baseline **Model 767-200**. The company then decided to abandon the 767-100, and instead the 767-200 was developed in subvariants with alternative maximum weights. Thus the version which was ordered initially by United Airlines for US domestic service was the medium-range type with a maximum weight of 282,000 lb (127915 kg), but there is also the baseline type with a maximum weight of 300,000 lb (136080 kg), and a longer-range type with a maximum weight of 315,000 lb (142884 kg) for use on non-stop transcontinental services and also on many international routes.

With basically the same flightcrew and avionics as the 757, offering considerable advantages in maintenance and cross-rated crews, the 767 was expected to possess seat-mile costs some 32 per cent below those of current wide-bodied transport aircraft of the three-engined type. The 767 also provided a significant freight capacity.

The first Model 767-200 made its maiden flight on 26 September, which was

Boeing 767-219(ER) ZK-NBA, was the first 767-200ER delivered to Air New Zealand. The carrier received the aircraft in 1985 and in 1999 it remained in service alongside three other -200s and nine -300s.

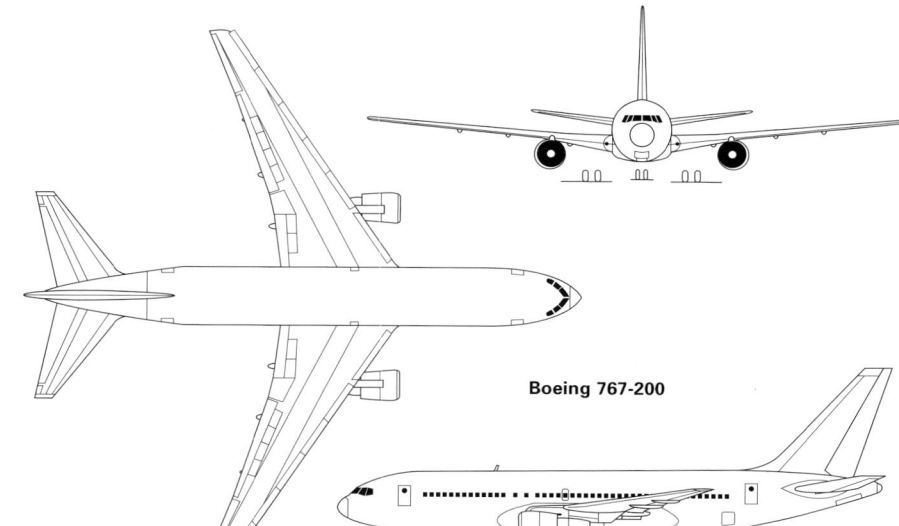

Boeing 767-200

Variants

Model 767-200ER: Extended-Range development of the 767-200, first flew on 6 March 1984 with changes such as centre-section fuel tankage and a maximum weight of 345,000 lb (156492 kg), with options for 351,000 lb (159214 kg), 380,000 lb (172368 kg) and 387,000 lb (175543 kg). The version entered service with Ethiopian Airlines in May 1984

Model 767-300: first flown in January 1986, this is a development of the 767-200 with the fuselage 'stretched' by 21 ft 1 in (6.43 m), and strengthening of the fuselage, wing and landing gear for operation with a maximum of 269 passengers at a maximum weight of some 351,000 lb (159214 kg) over a range of between 4,603 and 4,902 miles (7408 and 7889 km)

Model 767-300ER: in service with American Airlines from February 1988, this is the Extended-Range version of the 767-300 with further increased centre-section fuel tankage for take-off at optional maximum weights of 380,000 lb (172268 kg), 387,000 lb (175543 kg) and 400,000 lb (181440 kg) for a range of between 6,605 and 6,974 miles (10630 and 11223 km)

Model 767-300 Freighter: dedicated freight derivative of the 767-300 with a port-side forward freight door and strengthening of the cabin floor, wing and landing gear. UPS took delivery of the first Model 767-300 Freighter in October 1995

Model 767-400ER: launched early in 1997 after the receipt of orders from Delta Air Lines and Continental Airlines, this is a further lengthened version for a maximum of 303 passengers in a two-class seating arrangement and a maximum weight of 449,750 lb (204007 kg). Other changes include a strengthened and aerodynamically modified wing of increased span, fitted with raked tip extensions, longer landing gear legs carrying Model 777 wheels and brakes, and a new flightdeck based on that of the 737 'New Generation' series and the 777. The first flight of the Model 767-400ER is scheduled for August 1999, with deliveries from May 2000

E-767 AWACS: stemming mainly from a Japanese requirement, which resulted in an order for four aircraft of which the first two were delivered in March 1998, this is an AWACS development of the 767-200ER, with the upgraded systems developed for the E-3. Boeing is also offering and considering other military derivatives of the Model 767, including an advanced tanker/transport

a few days ahead of the target date set when the programme was launched in 1978. This Boeing-owned Model 767 was joined at an early date by the first three Model 767-200s off the production line, and all four aircraft were used in an intensive flight programme that resulted in certification in June and September 1982 with Pratt & Whitney and General Electric engines respectively. The Model 767-200 entered revenue service with Delta Air Lines in December 1982.

SAS maintains a fleet of 767-300(ER)s and a single -200(ER). The 767-300s (illustrated) are powered by Pratt & Whitney PW4060 turbofans, each rated at 60,000 lb st (267 kN). The PW4060 is only available on ER aircraft.

SPECIFICATION	
Boeing Model 767-200	39,700 ft (11795 and 12100 m)
Type: two/three-crew medium-range transport	depending on powerplant; range between 3,636 and 4,430 miles
Powerplant: two General Electric CF6-80A or Pratt & Whitney JT9D-7R4D turbofan engines each rated at 48,000 lb st (213.51 kN), or CF6-80A2, JT9D-7R4E, JT9D-7R4E4 or PW4050 turbofan engines each rated at 50,000 lb st (222.41 kN), or PW4052 turbofan engines each rated at 52,000 lb st (231.31 kN), or CF6-80C2B4 turbofan engines each rated at 52,500 lb st (233.53 kN)	(5852 and 7129 km) depending on powerplant and version **Weights:** empty 177,500 or 178,400 lb (80514 or 80922 kg) depending on powerplant and version; maximum take-off 300,000 or 315,000 lb (136080 or 142884 kg) depending on powerplant and version
Performance: maximum speed 568 mph (914 km/h) at optimum altitude; cruising speed 529 mph (851 km/h) at optimum altitude; service ceiling between 38,700 and	**Dimensions:** wingspan 156 ft 1 in (47.57 m); length 159 ft 2 in (48.51 m); height 52 ft (15.85 m); wing area 3,050.00 sq ft (283.35 m²) **Payload:** up to 290 passengers within the context of a 44,100-lb (20004-kg) payload

Boeing Model 777

At the end of 1986, Boeing began work on an airliner with a passenger capacity between that of its 767-300 and 747-400. The aircraft was seen within the company as a rival to the Airbus A330 and A340 as well as to the McDonnell Douglas MD-11. The **Model 777** (originally **Model 767-X**) was launched on 29 October 1990, after United Airlines had contracted for 34 of the aircraft. The new type made its maiden flight on 12 June 1994, and the **Boeing Model 777-200** entered revenue-earning service with United on 7 June 1995.

The 777 is a turbofan-powered long-haul airliner in which a major contribution comes from the Japanese aircraft industry. New aluminium alloys and weight-saving composite materials are employed in many components, and the two-man flightdeck was designed to be similar to that of the 747-400, with all the basic flying information appearing on six flat liquid-crystal screens. As a result of the proven reliability of the powerplant and on-board systems (including the company's first civil fly-by-wire control system), Boeing was able to achieve ETOPS (Extended-range Twin-engined OPerationS) certification for regular service; this certification demanded the ability to maintain level flight for three hours in single-engined configuration in order to reach a suitable landing site after suffering an inflight engine failure.

With a fuselage diameter of 20 ft 4 in (6.20 m), the 777 has an interior wider than that of every other airliner except the 747. Accommodation (with seats arranged between six- and 10-abreast) is provided for a maximum of 440 passengers.

Two versions are offered with the same trio of engine options.

Boeing Model 777 (continued)

The **Model 777-200 A Market** (later redesignated as the **Model 777-200**) has any of three maximum take-off weights between 506,000 lb (229522 kg) for a 375-passenger range of 4,568 miles (7352 km) and 535,000 lb (242676 kg) for a 375-passenger range of 5,546 miles (8926 km). The **Model 777-200 B Market** (later **Model 777-200IGW**, or **Increased Gross Weight** and finally the **Model 777-200ER**, or **Extended Range**) is a heavier type offering greater fuel capacity, more powerful engines and the option of three maximum take-off weights between 580,000 lb (263088 kg) for a 305-passenger range of 6,939 miles (11168 km) and 632,500 lb (286902 kg) for a 305-passenger range of 8,493 miles (13667 km). The **Model 777-200 C Market** is a development proposed for the ultra-long-range niche with a range of more than 8,061 miles (12972 km).

The wing design of the Model 777 depends on a high-efficiency aerofoil

section, and some customers wanted the aircraft to possess the capability to use the taxiways and passenger gates developed for the DC-10 and aircraft of similar size. Boeing therefore offers, as an option, a wing in which the outer 21 ft 3 in (6.48 m) on each side can be folded up into the vertical position. The 777 is offered with powerplant options that comprise the Rolls-Royce Trent 800, General Electric GE90 and Pratt & Whitney PW4000 series engines. In the case of the basic Model 777-200, these comprise those rated at between 71,000 and 74,000 lb st (315.8 and 329.2 kN) and in the case of the Model 777-200IGW those between 82,000 and 85,000 lb st (364.7 and 378.1 kN), through the incorporation in the engines of new wide-blade fans and an increase in bypass ratio from 6:1 to 9:1.

Boeing is also producing the **Model 777-300** (origi-

nally **Model 777 Stretch**) with a strengthened airframe and the fuselage lengthened by 33 ft 3 in (10.13 m). This type made its maiden flight in October 1997 and provides accommodation for up to 550 passengers at a maximum take-off weight of up to 660,000 lb (299376 kg) with engines each rated at up to some 98,000 lb st (436 kN). Further developments for service from early in the 21st century are the **Model 777-200X** and **Model 777-300X** with 101,000 lb st (449.3 kN)-class engines and greater fuel capacity for ranges in the order of 9,950 and 7,450 miles (16015 and 11990 km) respectively. The standard twin-engined powerplant would offer adequate flight performance, but to boost

By the end of 1999, 10 GE90-powered 777-200ERs will have joined the Air France fleet. Japan's Fuji, Kawasaki and Mitsubishi have a risk-sharing partnership with Boeing in the 777 programme, amounting to some 20 per cent of the airframe.

take-off capability, Boeing is considering the addition of a third engine in the form of a tail-mounted APTU (Auxiliary Power and Thrust Unit). This would provide additional thrust for take-off and climb and also double, as the acronym suggests, as an APU.

The proposed **Model 777-100X** 'shrink' version, with a shortened fuselage and accommodation for up to 254 passengers carried over a range of 9,942 miles (16000 km) appears to have been abandoned. In March 1999, orders for the Model 777 stood at 419.

Boeing's impressive 777-300 became the world's longest jetliner when it flew for the first time in 1997. Cathay Pacific became the first airline to receive the new type in May 1998.

SPECIFICATION	
Boeing Model 777-200 **Type:** two/three-crew long-range transport **Powerplant:** two Pratt & Whitney PW4074 turbofan engines each rated at 74,000 lb st (329.17 kN) **Performance:** maximum speed 588 mph (946 km/h) at optimum altitude; cruising speed 575 mph (925 km/h) at optimum altitude; service ceiling 43,100 ft (13135 m); range 4,840 miles (7785 km) with	363 passengers **Weights:** empty 298,900 lb (135,581 kg); maximum take-off 515,000 lb (233,604 kg) **Dimensions:** wingspan 199 ft 11 in (60.93 m); length 209 ft 1 in (63.73 m); height 60 ft 9 in (18.51 m); wing area 4,605.00 sq ft (427.8 m²) **Payload:** up to 440 passengers within the context of a 121,100-lb (54931-kg) payload

Boeing Model 953 (C-14)

In 1971 the USAF began to put together the specification of a new transport as a possible replacement for its fleet of turboprop-powered Lockheed C-130 Hercules. Early in 1972, requests for proposals were sent to nine US aircraft manufacturers. The prototype aircraft from Boeing and McDonnell Douglas were selected for competitive evaluation under the

respective designations **YC-14** and YC-15.

Before the allocation of designations, the USAF specification had the identification **AMST**, signifying **Advanced Military STOL Transport**, and the requirement emphasised to manufacturers the importance of STOL (Short Take-Off and Landing) capability. The **Boeing Model 953** design for

STOL performance was based on the use of a supercritical wing, which was developed by NASA. To this wing Boeing added an advanced wing upper-surface blowing concept with the two engines mounted above and largely ahead of the wing so that their efflux was exhausted over its upper surface; with the wing's leading-edge and Coanda-type trailing-edge flaps extended, the high-speed airflow from the engines tended to cling to the upper surface of the wing/flap system, and was thus directed downward to provide powered lift.

The first of two YC-14 service test aircraft made its maiden flight on 9 August 1976, and the type soon proved to have admirable performance. The maximum payload was 150 troops or 81,000 lb (36742 kg) of

An advanced and ultimately very effective STOL airlifter, the YC-14 competed closely with the equally impressive McDonnell Douglas YC-15.

freight in conventional operations while, for STOL operations from an airfield length of less than 625 yards (572 m), the payload was still a useful 27,000 lb (12247 kg). At the completion of testing in the

late summer of 1977, the YC-14s were returned to Boeing for continued development within the company, but no further government funding for development or procurement was made.

SPECIFICATION	
Boeing Model 953 (YC-14) **Type:** two/four-crew advanced STOL transport **Powerplant:** two General Electric YF103-GE-100 (CF6-50D) turbofan engines each rated at 51,000 lb st (226.86 kN) **Performance:** maximum speed 504 mph (811 km/h) at 30,000 ft (9145 m); cruising speed 472 mph (760 km/h) at optimum altitude; initial climb rate 6,350 ft (1935 m)	per minute; service ceiling 45,000 ft (13715 m); range 3,000 miles (4828 km) **Weights:** empty 117,500 lb (53297 kg); maximum take-off 170,000 lb (77111 kg) for STO or 237,000 lb (107501 kg) for CTO **Dimensions:** wingspan 129 ft (39.32 m); length 131 ft 8 in (40.13 m); height 48 ft 4 in (14.73 m); wing area 1,762.00 sq ft (163.69 m²)

Boeing X-32 (Joint Strike Fighter)

Both Boeing and Lockheed Martin were invited to proceed into the Concept Demonstration Programme phase of the **JSF (Joint Strike Fighter)** competition in 1996. The JSF concept involves a single basic type being procured in different variants for service in disparate roles by the USAF, USN, USMC and Britain's Fleet Air Arm. Both CTOL (Conventional Take-Off and Landing) and STOVL (Short Take-Off and Vertical Landing) versions are to be offered for operations from both land bases and ships, with the type earmarked to replace the F-16, F/A-18, AV-8B and Sea Harrier FA.Mk 2.

Other NATO operators may also select the JSF to replace their F-16 fleets in the first two decades of the 21st century, and at least two of these, Norway and the Netherlands, may join the UK in providing a contribution towards development costs. Current predictions suggest that as many as 2,800 aircraft may be produced for the US market alone, making the JSF by far the most valuable military aircraft project in the short to medium term.

Both JSF contenders will build demonstrators for a preliminary fly-off competition, scheduled to be concluded by 2001, at which stage the winning design will be announced. Boeing's design had previously featured a diamond-delta wing and forward swept underfuselage engine air intake, but in January 1999, the company announced its intention to adopt a more conventional swept wing, aft-swept air intake and all-moving tailplane. Nevertheless, Boeing's **X-32A** flight demonstrator will still be of the earlier design configuration, since Boeing considers that at this early stage any differences in performance between the X-32 and any prototype JSF will be insignificant. The aircraft will be powered, as will Lockheed Martin's X-35, by a single Pratt & Whitney F119 turbofan.

With first flights for the first of two X-32s and the competing X-35 due before the end of 1999, construction of the X-32A in USAF/USN CTOL configuration was well advanced by early 1999, while work on the STOVL **X-32B** for the USMC/FAA began three months ahead of schedule.

This artist's impression illustrates Boeing's JSF concept in its original CTOL form. The aircraft will carry its primary armament internally.

Boeing (McDonnell Douglas/Hughes) AH-64 Apache

Formulated in the early 1970s, the US Army's requirement for an AAH (Advanced Attack Helicopter) visualised a machine suitable for the day/night anti-armour role in all weather conditions. Bell and Hughes were selected to build two flight-test prototypes for competitive evaluation. These were the YAH-63 and **YAH-64A** respectively, and it was the latter, designed as the **Model 77** and first flown on 30 September 1975, that was declared the winning contender on 10 December 1976. A further four air vehicles (one ground test and three flight-test prototypes) were built for the second phase of the programme, and these were involved primarily with full engineering development and evaluation of the advanced avionics, electro-optical and fire-control systems. Noteworthy modifications to production standard included swept tips on the four blades of the main

rotor, an all-moving tailplane relocated to the low-set position, a fin of increased height, and adoption of a 'Black Hole' IR suppression system. On 26 March 1982 a US Army contract for an initial batch of 11 **Hughes AH-64A Apache** helicopters was finally issued.

The first production aircraft was subsequently delivered in January 1984, the month in which Hughes became a division of McDonnell Douglas; this move was confirmed by a change of name to the McDonnell Douglas Helicopter Company on 27 August 1985. In August 1997 McDonnell Douglas was merged into Boeing, and since that time the AH-64 has been a Boeing product.

The Apache is a tandem, two-seat conventional helicopter with advanced crew protection systems, avionics and electro-optics, plus weapon-control systems that include the nose-mounted Martin-Marietta AAQ-11 TADS/PNVS (Target

Acquisition and Designation Sight/Pilot Night-Vision Sensor). The co-pilot/gunner sits in the front seat, with the pilot 1 ft 7 in (0.49 m) higher in the rear cockpit. Both use various sophisticated sensors and systems for the detection and attack of targets, including the IHADSS (Integrated Helmet And Display Sight System), which provides a monocular helmet-mounted designator/sight. The co-pilot/gunner has primary responsibility for firing both the gun and any missiles, but can be overridden by the pilot in the back seat.

In combat, the AH-64A flies nap-of-the-earth, using terrain masking. In some scenarios, Bell OH-58C Kiowa or OH-58D Kiowa Warrior scout helicopters spot and designate targets for the Apache, and assist in communications to position AH-64A units to engage armour and other ground targets. In joint exercises the Apache has also worked effectively with USAF A-10As.

Survivability is enhanced by the use of armour, the design having been required to survive 0.5-in (12.7-mm) hits fired from anywhere in the helicopter's lower hemisphere plus 20°, and to remain airborne for 30 minutes after such a hit. Most critical systems are protected against 23-mm cannon hits. The crew is protected by lightweight boron armour shields, and the landing gear, cockpit and seats are designed to give a 95 per cent chance of surviving ground impacts at sink rates up to 42 ft (12.9 m) per second. The gun mounting is designed to

In AH-64D Longbow Apache guise, the AH-64 acquires a mast-mounted radar system, allowing it to fly and fight in all weathers.

collapse into the fuselage between the seats of the two crew members in the event of a crash landing. The turboshaft engines are widely separated and their key components are armour protected. The transmission can run for over an hour without oil and the gearboxes and shafts are designed to run for a similar time after ballistic damage. The helicopter is aerobatic and can be flown up to +3.5 g and down to -0.5 g.

Total AH-64A procurement by the US Army stands at 827 helicopters. From the 604th machine, 1,800-shp (1342-kW) General Electric T700-GE-701C engines, originally planned as part of an **AH-64B** upgrade, were installed.

The first fully-fledged Apache combat unit was the 3/6th Cavalry at Fort Hood, Texas, beginning in July 1986. The first combat deployment of the Apache came with the 82nd Airborne Division's 1st Aviation Battalion's participation in Operation Just Cause in Panama during December 1989 and January 1990. More recently, Apaches were employed to devastating effect during Operation Desert Storm against the Iraqi forces occupying

Kuwait. On 17 January 1992 it was AH-64 helicopters which fired the first shots of the campaign, attacking Iraqi radar sites and thus opening a radar-free corridor for Coalition air strikes against Baghdad and other targets.

The Apache's principal payload consists of up to 16 AGM-114A Hellfire long-range, laser-guided anti-tank missiles, carried in quartets on four hardpoints under the stub wing. Early plans to arm the AH-64 with TOW missiles were halted when development of the Hellfire proceeded more rapidly than expected. The other main disposable weapon is a pod carrying 19 2¾-in (70-mm) Hydra 70 air- to-surface unguided rockets, and the standard fixed armament comprises a 30-mm M230 Chain Gun cannon in a trainable under-fuselage mounting and supplied with 1,200 rounds of ammunition.

The Apache has also been tested with a variety of air-to-air weapons including the AIM-9L Sidewinder, FIM-92A Stinger, Matra Mistral and Shorts Starstreak. The air-to-air capability of the M230 cannon is also being improved. For defence suppression, the SideARM missile can be employed.

SPECIFICATION
Boeing (McDonnell Douglas/Hughes) AH-64A Apache

Type: two-seat attack helicopter
Powerplant: two General Electric T700-GE-701 turboshaft engines each rated at 1,696 shp (1265 kW)
Performance: maximum level and cruising speed 182 mph (293 km/h) at optimum altitude; initial vertical rate of climb 2,500 ft (762 m) per minute; service ceiling 21,000 ft (6400 m); hovering ceiling 15,000 ft (4570 m) in ground effect and 11,500 ft (3505 m) out of ground effect; range 1,180 miles (1899 km) with maximum internal and external fuel, or 300 miles (482 km)

with internal fuel
Weights: empty 11,387 lb (5165 kg); maximum take-off 21,000 lb (9525 kg)
Dimensions: main rotor diameter 48 ft (14.63 m); stub wing span 19 ft 1 in (5.82 m) over empty weapon racks; length overall 58 ft 3⅜ in (17.76 m) with rotors turning; height 15 ft 3½ in (4.66 m); main rotor disc area 1,809.56 sq ft (168.11 m²)
Armament: one 30-mm M230 Chain Gun trainable cannon in an underfuselage mounting, and up to 1,700 lb (771 kg) of disposable stores carried on four hardpoints under the stub wing

Boeing (McDonnell Douglas/Hughes) AH-64 Apache (cont.)

The **AH-64C** designation was to have been applied to some 540 examples of the AH-64A upgraded to **AH-64D** standard except for the omission of the latter's Longbow target-acquisition and fire-control system. This variant was abandoned early in 1994, however, so in the mid-1990s the AH-64D Apache became the second version of the Apache to enter service, although initially without the Northrop Grumman APG-78 Longbow radar/ missile system fitted to the definitive **AH-64D Longbow Apache** that followed from 1997. The US Army's initial plan for an upgraded

Apache fleet called for the conversion of 748 AH-64As to AH-64D standard, and of this total 227 were to be completed to the definitive Longbow Apache standard. During 1992 McDonnell Douglas converted four AH-64As with the Longbow millimetric-wavelength fire-control radar and AGM-114L Hellfire missile seekers, to act as proof-of-concept aircraft for the AH-64D. The prototype AH-64D Longbow Apache developmental aircraft subsequently made its first flight on 15 April 1992, although functioning radar was not flown until late in 1993 on the second proto-type. Two AH-64C

prototypes were also flown. Early in 1999 the US Army finally decided that 530 examples of the AH-64A would be upgraded to AH-64D standard, for which 500 Longbow systems would be procured, and that the other 218 surviving AH-64As would be passed to the ANG as a partial replacement for its AH-1s.

The Longbow system is readily identifiable by the mast-mounted location of the antenna for its APG-78 radar. The new radar allows the AGM-114L to be fired in an autonomous fire-and-forget mode, whereas the current laser-guided Hellfire requires

external designation (for example by an OH-58D) or use in conjunction with the TADS, and as such is a line-of-sight and non fire-and-forget weapon. The APG-78 radar can detect, classify and prioritise 12 targets simultaneously, placing them in six categories: tracked vehicle, wheeled vehicle, air defence, rotary-wing aircraft, fixed-wing aircraft and unknown. The radar can see through the fog and smoke that currently foils IR or TV sensors.

The AH-64D also incorporates a range of improvements in targeting, battle management, communications, weapons

and navigation systems. The cockpit has new glass displays, and electrical power generation is doubled. The forward avionics bay is expanded, and the landing gear fairings are extended forward to accommodate some of the new equipment.

The Apache has been exported widely, current and imminent operators including Egypt (AH-64A), Greece (AH-64A), Israel (AH-64A with the local designation **Pethen**, meaning 'cobra'), the Netherlands (AH-64D), Saudi Arabia (AH-64A), the UK (Westland-built WAH-64D) and the United Arab Emirates (AH-64A).

Boeing (McDonnell Douglas) C-17 Globemaster III

On 29 August 1981 McDonnell Douglas (since 1997 incorporated into Boeing) was selected to proceed with a design to fulfil the USAF's C-X requirement for a new heavy cargo transport. Although the aircraft reached initial operational capability only in January 1995, it is now revitalising the USA's strategic airlift capability.

McDonnell Douglas's winning design was designated **C-17A** and later received the name **Globemaster III**. It is based on the now-classic military transport aircraft configuration whose primary features are a high-set wing, large fuselage with an upswept rear section, rear-fuselage loading ramp, and housings on each side of the fuselage for the main landing gear units. The C-17 also incorporates advanced

technology features such as winglets, a supercritical wing section and high-performance turbofans. Short-field performance is aided to some extent by an externally blown flap system similar to that demonstrated on the McDonnell Douglas YC-15. The utility of these STOL features was negated to some extent when rough field capability was deleted as an economy measure. However, the C-17 can routinely operate from airfields previously denied to jet-powered transports. Reverse thrust on the F117 engines, which are similar to those which power the Boeing Model 757 airliner, allows the aircraft to reverse up a shallow slope or to turn around on a narrow runway.

The C-17 has a flight crew of two, a loadmaster, and provision for 102

*Internally, the **C-17A** has a cabin length of 88 ft (26.82 m) including the rear ramp, and has a minimum width and height of 18 ft (5.49 m) and 12 ft 4 in (3.76 m) respectively.*

troops/paratroops on stow-able seats in the cabin. The hold can also accommodate alternative loads such as 48 litters, three AH-64 Apaches, or air-droppable platforms up to a weight of 110,000 lb (49896 kg). The cockpit is state-of-the-art, with four multi-function displays, and a HUD for each pilot. Flight control is effected by a fly-by-wire system, and the pilots each have a control column rather than the conventional yoke.

After an earlier full-scale development schedule had been abandoned, the single prototype of the C-17A made its maiden flight on 15 September 1991. Deliveries to the 17th Airlift Squadron at Charleston AFB, South

Carolina, began in June 1993 to replace the C-141B StarLifter. There was continued opposition to the C-17 for political and financial reasons, which had already resulted in the trimming of the C-17A procurement programme from 210 aircraft to a planned total of 120 by 1991. However, by January 1991, the number had been cut to a minimum of 40 aircraft. The controlling and indeed radical reduction of production costs and the manifest capabilities of the new airlifter then resulted in an

increase to a total of 120 again for delivery by 2005, with a further 15 later added for the use of the US Special Forces, and the prospect of another 45 standard airlifters under possible consideration. In 1999 Boeing was working on a civil derivative of the type with the designation **MD-17** as a contender in the freight market, and there remains the possibility of small export orders, perhaps under leasing arrangements, to countries such as the UK, with the revised powerplant of four Rolls-Royce turbofans.

SPECIFICATION	
Boeing (McDonnell Douglas) C-17A Globemaster III	2,762 miles (4445 km) with a 160,000-lb (72576-kg) payload and no inflight refuelling
Type: three-crew heavy transport	
Powerplant: four Pratt & Whitney F117-PW-100 turbofan engines each rated at 40,700 lb st (181.04 kN)	**Weights:** empty 277,000 lb (125647 kg); maximum take-off 585,000 lb (265356 kg)
Performance: normal cruising speed 507 mph (816 km/h) at 28,000 ft (8535 m); service ceiling 45,000 ft (13715 m); range 5,408 miles (8704 km) on a ferry flight without inflight refuelling, or	**Dimensions:** wing span 169 ft 10 in (51.76 m) including winglets; length 174 ft (53.04 m); height 55 ft 1 in (16.79 m); wing area 3,800.00 sq ft (353.02 m²) **Payload:** up to a weight of 169,000 lb (76658 kg)

Boeing (McDonnell Douglas) F-15E, F-15I and F-15S Eagle

All **F-15** fighters were built by McDonnell Douglas, which was subsequently absorbed into Boeing. The aircraft were originally intended to be dual-role machines, but the ground-attack role was abandoned in 1975 and the relevant software was never incorporated. However, trials of

the F-15 in the air-to-ground role began during 1982 when McDonnell Douglas modified the second **TF-15A** two-seater as the '**Strike Eagle**', using company funds. The 'Strike Eagle' was conceived as an ETF (Enhanced Tactical Fighter) and as such was seen as a possible replace-

ment for the General Dynamics F-111, and in the resulting evaluation emerged as the winner over the rival type, the 'cranked-wing' F-16XL version of the General Dynamics F-16.

The first production example of the resulting **F-15E** made its maiden

flight on 11 December 1986. McDonnell Douglas's 'Strike Eagle' name was not adopted, though some unofficial epithets such as '**Beagle**' (Bomber Eagle) and '**Mud Hen**' have been used on occasion. With the new avionics and equipment for the 'mud-moving' role, the F-15E is very

much a second-generation **Eagle**. The aircraft also introduced redesigned controls, a wide field of vision HUD, and three CRTs that provide multi-purpose displays of navigation, weapons delivery and systems operations. The weapons system operator (WSO) in the rear cockpit

This F-15I demonstrates the camouflage scheme applied in Israeli service as well as its AIM-120 and indigenous Python 4 AAMs. As on the Saudi F-15S, some F-15I systems are downgraded.

in earlier aircraft.

In 1988 the 405th Tactical Training Wing at Luke AFB, Arizona, became the Tactical Air Command's replacement training unit for the F-15E and the first operational F-15Es were delivered to the 4th TFW, Seymour Johnson AFB, North Carolina. During Operation Desert Storm, the F-15E was assigned strike missions against a variety of targets, including five/six-hour sorties in search of 'Scud' missile launch sites. Two F-15E warplanes were lost in combat during 2,200 sorties totalling 7,700 hours.

The USAF procured 209 F-15Es, all of which had been delivered by July 1994. In 1991 the Secretary of Defense overruled USAF leaders who wanted to keep the F-15E Eagle in production, but orders were later placed for the first 12 of a required 24 attrition replacement aircraft. Although the F-15E is an exceedingly potent warplane for the strike/attack mission, critics point out that its low wing-loading produces a rough ride, especially for the back-seater, and that its payload is less than that of the F-111 it replaced.

The F-15E's primary mission is air-to-ground strike and attack, for which it carries a maximum of 24,250 lb (11000 kg) of tactical ordnance, including Mk 82 and Mk 84 bombs and GBU-10, -12 and -15 PGMs. The aircraft can also carry CBU-52, -58, -71, -87, -89, -90, -92 or -93 cluster bombs. Other guided weapons in the F-15E's inventory include the AGM-65 Maverick ASM and it is also capable of carrying up to five B57 or B61 free-fall nuclear bombs. Specialist weapons include the AGM-88 HARM and the AGM-130 powered version of the GBU-15. As a dual-role warplane, the F-15E has air-to-air capability and is able to engage enemy aircraft beyond visual range with four AIM-7M Sparrows or eight AIM-120 AMRAAMs. The F-15E also has four AIM-9 Sidewinder missiles and a 20-mm M61A1 Vulcan six-barrel cannon.

Since September 1995 Saudi Arabia has been receiving 72 examples of a new dual-role Eagle under the designation F-15S, with the last aircraft scheduled for delivery in 2000. All are two-seaters, based on the F-15E's airframe but with downgraded avionics and downgraded LANTIRN pods. The fuselage-mounted CFTs (Conformal Fuel Tanks) are deleted, thereby reducing the F-15S's combat radius and thus its threat to Israel. A similar variant, designated **F-15I Ra'am** (Thunder), gained an initial order for 25 from Israel, in the face of stiff competition from a modified, long-range strike version of the F-16D Fighting Falcon, and these aircraft have been delivered from November 1997. Israel is planning the purchase of another 40 to 60 aircraft offering the same level of capability, but these may be F-16D Block 50+ aircraft rather than more F-15I machines, or perhaps a mix of the two US types.

employs four multi-purpose CRT terminals for radar, weapon selection and monitoring of enemy tracking systems. The WSO also operates the Raytheon APG-70 synthetic aperture radar and the AAQ-13 navigation and AAQ-14 targeting pods of the Lockheed Martin LANTIRN nav/attack system. The navigation pod incorporates its own terrain-following radar, which can be linked to the aircraft's flight control system to allow automatic coupled terrain-following flight. The targeting pod allows the aircraft to self-designate GBU-10 and GBU-24 laser-guided bombs.

Power for the new variant was initially provided by two Pratt & Whitney F100-PW-220 turbofans with a digital engine control system, but this was soon replaced under the Improved Performance Engine programme by the F100-PW-229 and this was installed in all aircraft delivered from August 1991; the engine was also retrofitted

SPECIFICATION	
Boeing (McDonnell Douglas) F-15E Eagle	
Type: two-seat strike and attack warplane	
Powerplant: two Pratt & Whitney F100-PW-220 turbofan engines each rated at 23,830 lb st (106.00 kN) with afterburning	
Performance: maximum speed more than 1,650 mph (2655 km/h) or Mach 2.5 at high altitude; initial climb rate more than 50,000 ft (15240 m) per minute; service	ceiling 60,000 ft (18290 m); radius 790 miles (1271 km) on a typical mission with maximum warload
	Weights: empty 31,700 lb (14379 kg); maximum take-off 81,000 lb (36741 kg)
	Dimensions: wingspan 42 ft 9¾ in (13.05 m); length 63 ft 9 in (19.43 m); height 18 ft 5½ in (5.63 m); wing area 608.00 sq ft (56.48 m²)
	Armament: see above

Boeing (McDonnell Douglas) F/A-18A, B, C & D Hornet

Victorious in the USN's Air Combat Fighter programme that pitted the General Dynamics YF-16 against the **Northrop YF-17** in the mid-1970s, the **Hornet** was a more sophisticated navalised derivative of YF-17, which had originally been designed to meet the USAF's ACF (Air Combat Fighter) requirement. It was at first intended that the Hornet should be produced as the **F-18** fighter and the **A-18** strike/attack warplane. Eventually, however, it was realised that the match of the right airframe with a choice of two mission software packages would allow the procurement of a single type capable of undertaking both missions in succession to the McDonnell Douglas F-4 Phantom II and Vought A-7 Corsair II. The new type's dual-role capability was reflected in its new core designation of **F/A-18**. At one time it was also proposed that there should be a simplified **F/A-18L** land-based export model with carrier equipment deleted.

Under the original agreement McDonnell Douglas was to have design leadership and the larger workshare of the naval version, and Northrop that of the land-based versions. The export success of the naval F/A-18 to land-based customers eventually led to major disagreements and a lawsuit between the partners. Nevertheless, responsibility for development and production of the F/A-18 has always been shared by McDonnell Douglas (now incorporated into Boeing) and Northrop (now Northrop Grumman), with the former the dominant partner. To speed the development process, 11 aircraft were ordered for trials purposes and nine of these were completed as single-seaters. The first of these aircraft made its maiden flight on 18 November 1978, and the others had joined the test programme by March 1980.

Production of the initial **F/A-18A** single-seat version eventually totalled 371 aircraft that were delivered from May 1980, and the first fully operational Hornet unit was the USMC's VMFA-314 that was declared operational on 7 January 1983. The first US Navy unit was VFA-25 that received its aircraft from August 1983.

The F/A-18 offered much greater weapons delivery accuracy than its predecessors, and was a genuinely multi-role aircraft, able to out-bomb the A-7 and to out-turn the F-14. Suddenly, the fleet's attack aircraft was in many ways also its finest fighter. The aircraft's dogfighting capability is remarkable, the high-lift wing and leading-edge extensions conferring excellent high-Alpha capability and turn performance. Similarly, the Hughes (now Raytheon) APG-65 radar,

Prior to the full introduction of the F/A-18E and Dassault's Rafale M, the F/A-18C remains the most potent naval fighter extant. The type is gradually ousting the F-14 Tomcat from US Navy service.

which has become the benchmark fighter radar, is as effective at putting bombs on target as it is at detecting and engaging multiple airborne targets. In the air-to-ground role the F/A-18 can carry a laser spot tracker on the starboard underfuselage pylon, with an AAS-38 NITE Hawk FLIR or an AAR-50 TINS (Thermal Imaging Navigation System) pod on the port side station.

Two USN and two USMC F/A-18 units, on board the USS *Coral Sea*, participated in the El Dorado Canyon action against targets in Libya in April 1986, mainly employed in defence suppression. This marked the combat debut of both the F/A-18 and the AGM-88A HARM. In addition, Hornets from both the USN (nine squadrons) and USMC (seven squadrons) were heavily committed to action during Operation Desert Storm against Iraq in 1991.

Boeing (McDonnell Douglas) F/A-18A-D Hornet (cont.)

F/A-18A/B Hornets (a single-seat A is illustrated) remain in service with the US Navy's flight demonstration team, the Blue Angels. The aircraft have certain items of equipment, including the Vulcan cannon, removed in an effort to decrease weight and increase performance.

The F/A-18A was super-seded by the **F/A-18C**, which remained the princi-pal single-seat production model up to 1999, some 347 having been ordered for US service. The first F/A-18C made its maiden flight on 3 September 1986. Changes were made to the aircraft's weapons capabil-ity, so that the F/A-18C is compatible with the AIM-120 AMRAAM and with the imaging infra-red version of the AGM-65 Maverick. The F/A-18C was also designed with provi-sion for installation of the proposed (and cancelled) **RF-18A** interchangeable reconnaissance nose.

New avionics give the F/A-18C its only external distinguishing characteris-tics: a five-pronged antenna array for the ALR-67 RHAWS on the gun bay door, with small fairings on the sides of the nose and on the trailing edge of the fin, and similar ALQ-165 airborne self-protection jammer antennas on the gun bay access door, nose gear door, on top of the nose and behind the canopy. The F/A-18C also introduced the Martin-Baker NACES (naval aircrew common ejection seat) in place of the SJU-5/6 ejec-tion seat, and is fitted with small strakes above the LERXes, the former being designed to reduce buffet on the vertical fins and to improve yaw control at very high angles of attack. These strakes have since been retrofitted to virtually all surviving Hornets.

After 137 baseline F/A-18Cs had been deliv-ered, production switched to a version capable of the night attack role. This retains the F/A-18C desig-nation, but incorporates a package of equipment providing compatibility with GEC Cat's Eye pilot's night vision goggles, an AAR-50 TINS pod, Kaiser AVQ-28 raster HUD, externally carried AAS-38 FLIR target-ing pod, and colour multi-function displays. The last were joined by a new Honeywell colour digital moving map, which

replaced the projected moving map display used previously, freeing the aircraft from the need to be loaded with bulky film for projection. The first exam-ple of the night-attack Hornet was delivered on 1 November 1989.

The Hornet's versatility has led to substantial export sales. Canada was the first foreign customer, taking delivery of 98 single-seat aircraft known to their manufacturer and operator by the designations **CF-18A** and **CF-188A** respectively; it should be noted that the name Hornet is used only unofficially in Canada, as Frelon, the French language equivalent, could be confused with the Aérospatiale helicopter of the same name. Deliveries were accomplished between October 1982 and September 1988. The Canadian aircraft are virtually standard F/A-18As, except in being fitted with a spotlight on the port side of the nose for identification of aircraft during night intercepts, a new ILS (instrument landing system), and provision for the carriage of LAU-5003 rocket pods. The Canadian aircraft were followed by an Australian order negotiated in 1981, whereby local assembly, and later produc-tion, of 57 **AF-18A** aircraft was undertaken by ASTA. The Australian aircraft were handed over during 1985-90 as replacements for the Dassault Mirage IIIO. The aircraft are to be updated from 2000 to a virtual F/A-18C standard, and can launch AGM-65 ASMs, AGM-88 ARMs and Paveway II LGBs. Spain

purchased 60 examples of the **EF-18A** for the Ejercito del Aire, with delivery from 1986 to 1990. Spanish Hornets are operated under the local designation **C.15**. Like the Australian Hornets, the Spanish EF-18As are being upgraded to near F/A-18C standard. Subsequent export contracts have all been for the F/A-18C and comprise 32 **KAF-18C** aircraft for Kuwait, which were delivered by September 1993; 26 for Switzerland with deliveries starting in 1995; and 57 for Finland, delivered from 1995 in the form of knock-down kits for local assembly by Valmet.

The Hornet is equipped with nine external stores stations, enabling it to carry a wide range of ordnance. For air-to-air missions, the missile armament includes the AIM-120 AMRAAM, AIM-7 Sparrow and AIM-9 Sidewinder, in addition to a nose-mounted 20-mm M61A1 Vulcan six-barrel cannon. For the attack role AGM-65 Maverick, AGM-84E SLAM (Stand-off Land Attack Missile), AGM-62 Walleye, GBU-10, -12 and -16 PGMs, Mk 80 bombs, CBU-59 cluster bombs and fuel/air explo-sives are all available. For the anti-ship role the Hornet can carry two AGM-84 Harpoon missiles, and for the defence-suppression role two AGM-88 HARMs are employed. The aircraft can also operate in the

strike role with B57 and B61 nuclear free-fall bombs.

Development of a two-seat version of the Hornet was undertaken concur-rently with that of the single-seater. Thus two examples of the **TF-18A**, later redesignated as **F/A-18B**, featured in the original contract. Basically similar to the single-seater, the F/A-18B introduced a second seat, and possessed identical equipment and virtually identical combat capability, the latter being a factor in the change of designation. Procurement of the F/A-18B for the USN and USMC ended with the 40th example, and this version has never been employed by front-line forces.

The second two-seat version is the **F/A-18D**, which is broadly similar to the single-seat F/A-18C. Some 31 aircraft were completed to this baseline standard before production changed to the F/A-18D counterpart of the night-attack F/A-18C, and production amounted to 109 aircraft. The night-attack version of the F/A-18D has replaced the Grumman A-6 Intruder with the USMC's all-weather attack squadrons. Originally dubbed **F/A-18D+**, the

aircraft features 'uncou-pled' cockpits, usually with no control column in the rear cockpit (although this item can be refitted) but two sidestick weapons controllers.

Production of two-seat Hornets has also been undertaken for the export market, and all customers to date have ordered some of these aircraft for training purposes. Equipment and designations vary some-what, according to local needs, but these machines are basically similar to their US service equivalents. Deliveries were undertaken to Australia (18 examples of the **ATF-18A**, fundamentally an F/A-18B), Canada (40 examples of the **CF-18B** for service with the local desig-nation **CF-188B**), Kuwait (eight examples of the **KAF-18D**) and Spain (12 examples of the **EF-18B** operated as the **CE.15**). The F/A-18D variant has been ordered by F/A-18C opera-tors, these comprising Finland (seven) and Switzerland (eight), and Malaysia, which uniquely ordered only the two-seat variant in the form of eight F/A-18D aircraft. Thailand contracted for eight exam-ples of the F/A-18C/D but later cancelled its order.

Malaysia's small force of Harpoon-armed F/A-18Ds has given the country a powerful anti-shipping capability in a region where maritime strength is of great importance. The US has released the AIM-120 for the aircraft, making it one of the most potent interceptors in the area.

SPECIFICATION

Boeing (McDonnell Douglas) F/A-18C Hornet

Type: single-seat carrierborne and land-based fighter and strike/attack warplane

Powerplant: two General Electric F404-GE-402 turbofan engines each rated at 17,700 lb st (78.73 kN) with afterburning

Performance: maximum speed more than 1,190 mph (1915 km/h) or Mach 1.80 at high altitude; initial climb rate 45,000 ft (13715 m); combat ceiling about 50,000 ft (15240 m); range more than 2,073 miles (3336 km) for

ferry with drop tanks; radius more than 460 miles (740 km) on a fighter mission or 662 miles (1065 km) for an attack mission

Weights: empty 23,832 lb (10810 kg); maximum take-off 33,585 lb (15234 kg) for a fighter mission or 48,253 lb (21888 kg) for an attack mission

Dimensions: wingspan 37 ft 6 in (11.43 m) without tip-mounted missiles; length 56 ft (17.07 m); height 15 ft 3½ in (4.66 m); wing area 400.00 sq ft (37.16 m²)

Armament: see above

Boeing (McDonnell Douglas) F/A-18E/F Super Hornet

The first of McDonnell Douglas's (Boeing from 1997) Hornet upgrade concepts to reach fruition is the **F/A-18E Super Hornet** development of the F/A-18C. This was developed to fill the gap left by the 1991 cancellation of the General Dynamics/ McDonnell Douglas A-12 Avenger II carrierborne attack warplane. The first F/A-18E made its maiden flight in November 1995 at the start of a programme designed to see the delivery of the first production aircraft in 1998 and an initial operational capability in 2001. Major alterations from the F/A-18C are

upgraded avionics, a larger airframe with changes to reduce the radar cross section, increased internal and external fuel capacities and greater power from engines aspirated via larger inlets of revised parallelogram shape. The avionics upgrade is centred on the Raytheon APG-73 radar. Another advanced element of the Super Hornet's avionics systems is the IDECM (Integrated Defensive Electronic CounterMeasures) system whose three major elements will be the ALR-67(V)3 RWR, ALQ-214 radio-frequency countermeasures system and ALE-55 fibre-optic towed

decoy system; the last two are still under development, so the F/A-18E is initially being operated with the ALE-50 towed decoy system.

The enlarged airframe includes a fuselage lengthened by 2 ft 10 in (0.86 m), an enlarged wing characterised by a thicker section and two more hardpoints allowing an increase in the disposable load to 17,750 lb (8051 kg), enlarged LERXes, and horizontal and vertical tail surfaces. As well as being larger, the Super Hornet also has a structure extensively redesigned to reduce weight and cost without sacrifice of strength.

The greater power required for the Super Hornet is provided by two F414-GE-400 turbofans – the 'growth II plus' development of the Hornet's F404 with several features derived from the F412 – that was to have been used in the A-12 Avenger II.

The cockpit of the F/A-18E is similar to that of

Both the revised intake shape and additional underwing pylons (here mounting AGM-88 missiles) are evident on this F/A-18E.

the F/A-18C with the exception of a larger flat-panel display in place of the current three HDDs, and another change in the use of a quadruplex digital 'fly-by-wire' control system without the Hornet's mechanical back-up system. This last reduces weight and, to provide a 'get home' capability in the event of catastrophic damage to the 'fly-by-wire' system, a direct electrical linkage to the control surface actuators has been added. It is worth noting that the F/A-18E is seen as just one step in the Hornet's 'developability', which could later see the introduction of active-array radar, an IR search and track system, an advanced EW system and mission computer, and a digital map generator allowing passive terrain-reference navigation.

The **F/A-18F Super Hornet** is the two-seat

development of the F/A-18E, with the rear cockpit equipped with the same displays as the front cockpit and otherwise configured for alternative combat or training roles with hand controllers for the weapon system operator or stick and throttle for the instructor.

In addition, the **F/A-18F C²W** electronic combat version, which would be capable of both jamming and lethal SEAD, may be bought to replace US EA-6Bs from 2007.

The USN had originally planned to procure a total of 1,000 F/A-18Es and F/A-18Fs, but in 1997 the total was reduced to 548 in light of the capabilities offered by the JSF programme. Any delay in the service debut of the JSF to a time later than 2008-10, however, will see the number of Super Hornets rise to 748.

SPECIFICATION

Boeing (McDonnell Douglas) F/A-18E Super Hornet	(13864 kg); maximum take-off 66,000 lb (29937 kg)
Type: single-seat carrierborne and land-based multi-role fighter, attack and maritime air superiority warplane	**Dimensions:** wingspan 44 ft 8½ in (13.62 m) including tip-mounted AAMs; length 60 ft 1¼ in (18.31 m); height 16 ft (4.88 m); wing area 500.00 sq ft (46.45 m²)
Powerplant: two General Electric F414-GE-400 turbofan engines each rated at 22,000 lb st (97.86 kN) with afterburning	**Armament:** one 20-mm M61A2 Vulcan rotary six-barrel cannon with 570 rounds, plus up to 17,750 lb (8051 kg) of disposable stores, including the 10/20-kiloton B57 and 100/500-kiloton B61 free-fall nuclear weapons, AIM-120 AMRAAM, AIM-7 Sparrow and AIM-9 Sidewinder AAMs, AGM-88 HARM, AGM-65 Maverick ASM, AGM-84 Harpoon anti-ship missile, AGM-62 Walleye optronically-guided glide bomb, Paveway LGBs, Mk 80 series bombs, Rockeye and CBU-series cluster bombs, BLU-series napalm bombs and LAU-series multiple launchers for 70-mm air-to-surface unguided rockets
Performance: maximum speed more than 1,190 mph (1915 km/h) or Mach 1.80 at high altitude; service ceiling about 50,000 ft (15240 m); radius 681 miles (1095 km) on a hi-hi-hi interdiction mission with four 1,000-lb (454-kg) bombs, two AIM-9 Sidewinder AAMs and two drop tanks, or 560 miles (901 km) on a hi-lo-hi interdiction mission with the same stores, or 173 miles (278 km) on a 135-minute maritime air superiority mission with six AAMs and three drop tanks	
Weights: empty 30,564 lb	

Boeing (McDonnell Douglas) MD-11

McDonnell Douglas conceived the **McDonnell Douglas MD-11** as a development of its DC-10 wide-body airliner with increased passenger capacity in a completely restyled cabin, a revised wing with tip-mounted winglets, a modified horizontal tail surface, reduced leading-edge sweep, a lengthened tail cone ending in a vertical chisel edge, new-generation engines, and a modern two-

crew EFIS 'glass' digital flightdeck. McDonnell Douglas revealed the type at the Paris Air Show of 1985, and in December 1986 received its first order, from British Caledonian, for nine aircraft. This allowed the official launch of the MD-11 programme in December 1986, and the first of the new aircraft made its maiden flight on 10 January 1990. The first test programme was under-

taken by five aircraft, four of them with CF6-80C2D1F turbofans and one with the alternative powerplant of three 60,000-lb st (266.89-kN) Pratt & Whitney PW4460s.

The MD-11 entered service with Finnair on 20 December 1990, less than a month after the airline had received its first aircraft. There were a number of problems with the type, however, includ-

ing a shortfall in the guaranteed performance, and McDonnell Douglas was compelled to implement a major effort to reduce drag and weight through aerodynamic and structural changes so that the type could meet expectations in range. The delay and cost inherent in this effort had an adverse effect on the continuing rate of sales

success, and a further squeeze was imposed by the increasing availability of two rival types, the four-engined Airbus A340 and the twin-engined Boeing Model 777.

McDonnell Douglas produced its MD-11 airliner in five subvariants and planned at least another three developments. The basic MD-11, described in the specification below, was followed by the subvariants.

SPECIFICATION

Boeing (McDonnell Douglas) MD-11	(12569 km) with 323 passengers
Type: two-crew medium/long-range transport	**Weights:** empty 288,880 lb (131036 kg); maximum take-off 625,500 lb (283727 kg)
Powerplant: three General Electric CF6-80C2D1F turbofan engines each rated at 61,500 lb st (273.57 kN), or Pratt & Whitney PW4460 turbofan engines each rated at 60,000 lb st (266.89 kN)	**Dimensions:** wingspan 169 ft 10 in (51.77 m); length 201 ft 4 in (61.37 m) with General Electric engines or 200 ft 11 in (61.24 m) with Pratt & Whitney engines; height 57 ft 9 in (17.60 m); wing area 3,648.00 sq ft (338.90 m²)
Performance: maximum speed 588 mph (945 km/h) at 31,000 ft (9145 m); service ceiling 42,000 ft (12800 m); range 7,810 miles	**Payload:** up to 410 passengers within the context of a 112,564-lb (51059-kg) maximum payload

Externally, the most obvious feature of the MD-11, when compared to the earlier DC-10, is the inclusion of tip-mounted winglets.

Boeing (McDonnell Douglas) MD-11 (continued)

The five MD-11 subvariants include the **MD-11 PIP** resulting from the continuous **Performance Improvement Program** for greater range through drag reduction features and greater fuel capacity as well as a 2,250-lb (1021-kg) reduction in structure weight, the **MD-11 Combi** mixed passenger/freight model with accommodation for up to 240 passengers and 10 cargo pallets for a maximum payload of 144,300 lb (65454 kg), the **MD-11CF** convertible freighter, the **MD-11F** freighter with a maximum payload of 200,790 lb (91078 kg), and the **MD-11ER** extended-range subvariant with further increased fuel capacity for a maximum take-off weight of 630,500 lb (285995 kg) and an increase in range of 552 miles (889 km) or in payload of 6,000 lb (2722 kg).

Subvariants that were proposed but not built were the **MD-11LR** long-range version with 12-ft (3.66-m) wing extensions for a range of 9,206 miles (14816 km) with 300 passengers in a three-class arrangement, the **MD-11 'Simple Stretch'** with the fuselage lengthened by 22 ft (6.70 m) for the delivery of up to 365 passengers over a range of 6,213 miles (10000 km), and the **MD-11 'Twin-Jet'** medium-range derivative considered in a number of forms with just the two wing engines.

When McDonnell Douglas merged into Boeing during August 1997 production of the MD-11 continued, but in June 1998 Boeing announced that production of the MD-11 series would end in 2000 with the completion of the 195th example.

Boeing/BAe (McDonnell Douglas/BAe) T-45 Goshawk

In 1981 the USN selected a modified version of the **BAe Hawk** trainer as the aircraft component of its **T45 Training System**, a highly significant programme that was aimed at the production of up to 600 jet pilots annually throughout the 1990s and into the 21st century. As the Hawk was preparing for entry into service with the RAF, the USN began a three-year study into new trainer requirements that would, ideally, combine the handling qualities of the Rockwell T-2B/C Buckeye intermediate trainer and the McDonnell Douglas TA-4J Skyhawk advanced trainer. A saving in flight hours and costs was seen to be possible if the right aircraft was selected and, in 1978, an evaluation of available types was made with the intention of undertaking what had become the VTXTS (US NAvy experimental training system) programme. The Hawk was judged to be superior on a number of counts, including fuel consumption, to existing USN trainers and all its rivals, and in November 1981 the British trainer was duly selected. In May 1986 an engineering development contract was awarded to McDonnell Douglas, as the US prime

contractor. The principal subcontractor is BAe, which retains responsibility for the wing, centre and rear fuselage, fin, tailplane, windscreen, canopy and flying controls.

As first proposed, there were to have been two variants in the form of a 'wet' **T-45A** outfitted for carrierborne operation and a 'dry' **T-45B** restricted to land-based training and dummy carrier landing practice. Subsequent confirmation of the practicality of extending the lives of both the T-2 and TA-4J led to a USN decision to acquire only the T-45A with full carrier qualification.

In order to tailor the basic **Hawk Mk 60** airframe to stringent USN requirements, a number of changes was made. The airframe was strengthened to withstand the inevitable stresses of carrier operations. The forward fuselage has a deeper profile to accommodate a new and somewhat strengthened twin-wheel nose landing gear unit, which is also compatible with the USN's steam catapults. The main units were also redesigned with longer-stroke oleos. At the tail the height of the fin and the span of the tailplane was increased, and a single ventral fin was

While the standard T-45A (illustrated) is proving exemplary, the first of a projected 100 'Cockpit 21' T-45Cs with 'glass' cockpits are now entering service. These provide greater continuity in training with advanced aircraft such as the F/A-18E.

added. The Hawk's single ventral airbrake was replaced by two fuselage side-mounted units, while SMURFs (Side-Mounted Under Root Fins) were added ahead of and below the two halves of the horizontal tail surface to eliminate airbrake-related pitch-down during low-speed manoeuvres with the landing gear retracted. The T-45 has new electrically actuated and hydraulically operated full-span slats on the leading edges of its wing, and a new aileron/rudder interconnect. The aircraft is also provided with an arrester hook and USN standard cockpit instrumentation and radios. The aircraft's overall appearance is otherwise similar to that of other two-seat Hawks with the exception of its squared-off wingtips, which do not alter overall span, and a broader-span square-tipped horizontal tail surface.

Although the strengthening programme was necessary for the carrier role, the T-45A (renamed **Goshawk** to avoid confusion with the US Army's

MIM-23 Hawk surface-to-air missile) remains land-based, flying to a training carrier as required. The USN has stated that it expects each T-45A to undertake 38,000 field landings, 16,000 carrier landings and over 1,000 seaborne launchings. Initial carrier qualifications with the two full-scale F405-RR-400L (Adour 861-49)-powered development prototypes and the single F405-RR-401 (Adour 871)-powered pre-production aircraft began on board the USS *John F. Kennedy* on 4 December 1991. The first production T-45A made its maiden flight on 16 December 1991, but deliveries to the USN had begun when the prototypes went to NATC Patuxent River, Maryland, in October 1990. For many years plans to re-engine the aircraft with a variety of American-built candidate engines have been mooted and the AlliedSignal F124 turbofan was flight-tested in

September 1997, without the modification proceeding further. A much improved digital 'glass' cockpit, with two colour MFDs, was incorporated from the 73rd production machine and is being retrofitted to earlier aircraft. Provision is made for a single pylon under each wing for the carriage of a rack for practice bombs, rocket pods or extra fuel. The centreline pylon can also carry stores for use in the weapons training role.

The original total of 268 aircraft was later trimmed to 197 production Goshawks and with the introduction of the T-45, the training task is being accomplished with 25 per cent fewer flying hours using 42 per cent fewer aircraft and 46 per cent fewer personnel.

Since McDonnell Douglas's 1997 merger with Boeing, the T-45 Goshawk has been known as a joint Boeing and BAe product.

SPECIFICATION	
Boeing/BAe (McDonnell Douglas/BAe) T-45A Goshawk **Type:** two-seat land-based but carrier-compatible intermediate and advanced trainer **Powerplant:** one Rolls-Royce/Turboméca F405-RR-401 turbofan engine rated at 5,845 lb st (26.00 kN) **Performance:** maximum speed 620 mph (997 km/h) at 8,000 ft (2440 m); initial climb rate 6,982 ft	(2128 m) per minute; service ceiling 42,250 ft (12875 m); range 1,152 miles (1854 km) **Weights:** empty 9,399 lb (4263 kg); maximum take-off 12,758 lb (5787 kg) **Dimensions:** wingspan 30 ft 9¾ in (9.39 m); length 39 ft 3¼ in (11.97 m) including probe; height 14 ft (4.27 m); wing area 176.90 sq ft (16.69 m²) **Armament:** see above

Boeing Helicopters Model 114, 234 & 414 (H-47 Chinook)

Following the evaluation of submissions by five US helicopter manufacturers, in March 1959 the US Army selected the **Boeing Vertol Model 114** as the machine most closely meeting its requirements for a battlefield mobility helicopter. Such a helicopter was expected to be equipped for all-weather operations, lift a load of 4,000 lb (1814 kg) internally or 16,000 lb (7258 kg) suspended from an external sling, carry a maximum of 40 troops with full equipment, have straight-in rear loading, be suitable for the casualty evacuation role, and be able to airlift any component of the Martin Marietta Pershing surface-to-surface missile system. An initial contract for five **YHC-1B** pre-production examples was placed in June 1959, but soon after entering service these helicopters were redesigned as the **YCH-47A Chinook**.

The Model 114 was, in effect, a larger and more powerful version of the same company's Model 107 and key features included fixed quadricycle rather than tricycle landing gear, and a fuselage that

CH-47C Chinooks in service with the Italian army were licence-built in Italy by Elicotteri Meridionali. Surviving aircraft are used as heavy transports and in operations with Italian paratroops.

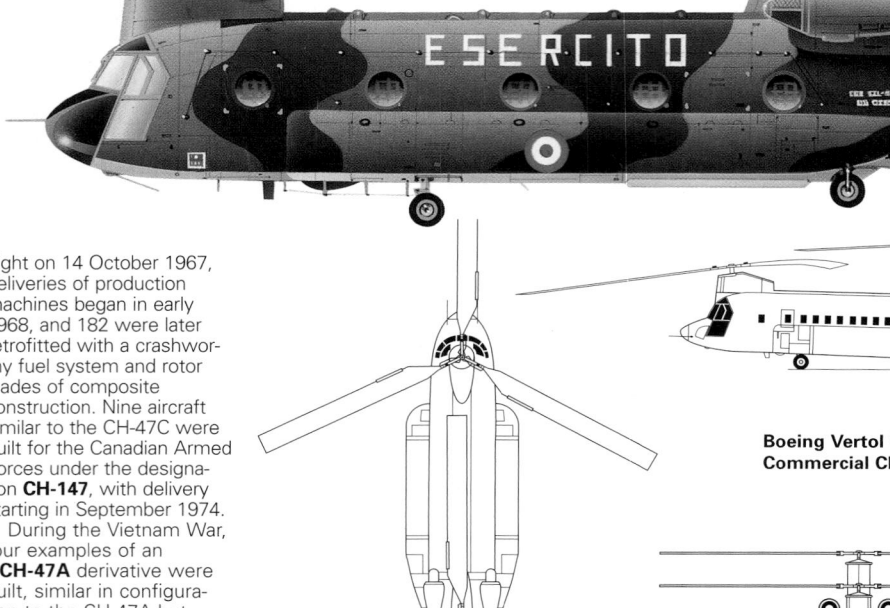

Boeing Vertol Model 234 Commercial Chinook

was sealed and fitted with compartmented fairing pods on each lower side to supplement the buoyancy of the sealed lower fuselage for water operations. The first YHC-1B made its initial flight on 21 September 1961, by which time the first contract for the **CH-47A** initial production helicopter had been placed. The CH-47A was powered by two 2,200-shp (1641-kW) Lycoming T55-L-5 turboshafts, which were later replaced by 2,650-shp (1976-kW) T55-L-7s, and the delivery of the 354 examples of the CH-47A began in August 1962.

Since that time a number of versions has been built. The first of these was the **CH-47B**, of which 108 were delivered with 2,850-shp (2125-kW) T55-L-7C engines, redesigned rotor blades and other detail refinements. The first of two prototypes made its maiden flight during October 1966, and deliveries began on 10 May 1967. The second improved model was the **CH-47C (Model 234)**, of which 270 were delivered with 3,750-shp (2796-kW) T55-L-11A engines, a strengthened transmission system, and increased fuel capacity. The first of these helicopters made its initial

flight on 14 October 1967, deliveries of production machines began in early 1968, and 182 were later retrofitted with a crashworthy fuel system and rotor blades of composite construction. Nine aircraft similar to the CH-47C were built for the Canadian Armed Forces under the designation **CH-147**, with delivery starting in September 1974.

During the Vietnam War, four examples of an **ACH-47A** derivative were built, similar in configuration to the CH-47A but equipped with armour and armament. The latter included a 40-mm grenade-launcher in the nose, a 20-mm forward-firing cannon and a 0.3-in (7.62-mm) machine-gun or a 19-round rocket pack mounted on a pylon, one on each side of the fuselage, plus five gun positions for air gunners stationed in the cabin, each having a 0.5-in (12.7-mm) or 0.3-in (7.62-mm) machine-gun on a trainable mounting. Three of these were evaluated in

Vietnam, but no further examples were built.

Chinooks operating in Southeast Asia proved themselves invaluable, not only for the transport of troops and supplies as well as for casualty evacuation, but also for the recovery of disabled aircraft and the airlift of refugees. Chinooks are still considered a vital component of the US Army's helicopter air logistic forces, and 472 surviving helicopters of the CH-47A, CH-47B and CH-47C marks were later modernised. Under a US Army development programme, one example each of the CH-47A, CH-47B and CH-47C versions were stripped down to the basic airframe and rebuilt to an improved standard to serve as **CH-47D** prototypes, of which the first flew on 26 February 1982 with more powerful 4,500-shp (3356-kW) T55-L-712 turboshaft engines driving a higher-rated transmission, redesigned avionics, many design refinements, an APU and a triple hook cargo-suspension system. Boeing was subsequently contracted for the remanufacture of older helicopters

Still the mainstay of US Army medium-lift helicopter operations, the CH-47 Chinook serves on in much-improved CH-47D guise.

to the CH-47D standard, and the first of these was delivered in May 1982.

Under the designation **Chinook HC.Mk 1**, the RAF ordered 33 helicopters to a standard based on the Canadian CH-147. These machines have British avionics and equipment, as well as a number of special provisions. The first was handed over in August 1980, and the number for British service was later increased to 41, of which the survivors were subsequently upgraded to **Chinook HC.Mk 1A** standard. Some 32 of the helicopters were later modernised to the **Chinook HC.Mk 2** (basically CH-47D) standard with a number of enhancements including T55-L-712F engines. Another 17 helicopters were later ordered, eight of them to the Chinook HC.Mk 2 standard and the others to the **Chinook HC.Mk 3** standard similar to the **MH-47E** in

US service for special operations missions.

Since 1970 Chinooks have been built in Italy for European and Middle East customers, following acquisition by Elicotteri Meridionali of co-production and marketing rights from Boeing Vertol.

Production by Boeing Vertol (later the Helicopter Division of the Boeing Company's Defense & Space Group that is now the Military Aircraft & Missiles Systems Group) of new military Chinooks is now limited to the **Model 414**, which is the **CH-47D International Chinook** export version. In addition to Canada and the UK, the Chinook has been sold to Argentina, Australia, Egypt, Greece, Iran, Italy (**CH-47C Plus** to an improved CH-47C standard), Japan (**CH-47J** licence-built by Kawasaki), Libya, Morocco, the Netherlands, Singapore, South Korea, Spain, Taiwan and Thailand.

SPECIFICATION	
Boeing Vertol CH-47C Chinook **Type:** two/three-crew twin-rotor medium transport helicopter **Powerplant:** two Avco Lycoming T55-L-11A turboshaft engines each rated at 3,750 shp (2796 kW) **Performance:** maximum speed 178 mph (286 km/h) at sea level; cruising speed 160 mph (257 km/h) at optimum altitude; service ceiling 10,800 ft (3290 m); radius 115 miles (185 km)	**Weights:** empty 21,464 lb (9736 kg); maximum take-off 38,500 lb (17463 kg) **Dimensions:** rotor diameter, each 60 ft (18.29 m); length overall, rotors turning 99 ft (30.18 m); height 18 ft 11 in (5.68 m); rotor disc area, total 5,654.86 sq ft (523.34 m²) **Payload:** up to 55 troops, or 24 litters or freight carried internally or externally

Boeing Helicopters Model 114, etc. (H-47 Chinook) (cont.)

In the late summer of 1978 the company announced the development of a civil counterpart to the military Chinook, intended for commercial service. Two basic versions were planned, the **Model 234LR (Long-Range)** variant to serve in all-passenger, 'combi' passenger/freight, or all-cargo roles; and the **Model 234UT (Utility Transport)** variant for more specialised tasks such as resources exploration and development, logging and general utility or heavy construction work.

The Model 234LR

programme was launched in November 1978, following the finalisation of a contract with British Airways Helicopters (BAH) for the supply of three aircraft (later increased to six), required primarily by BAH to carry passengers and priority cargo from points in Scotland to and from North Sea oil platforms. In full passenger configuration these Chinooks have four-abreast seating for a maximum of 44 passengers.

The rotors of the civil Chinook are powered by two Avco Lycoming AL 5512 turboshaft engines, via a combining gearbox and inter-

connecting shafts which enable both rotors to be driven in an emergency by either engine. Large external fuel tanks are accommodated within the fairings which extend along both sides of the lower fuselage. These fairings also provide a flotation capability that can ensure survival of the aircraft if forced down onto a sea surface with storm waves not exceeding 30 ft (9.15 m) in height.

The first Model 234LR made its maiden flight on 19 August 1980, and two additional aircraft took part in the development programme,

with the first example entering service with BAH on 1 July 1981.

Although Boeing is still studying a **CH-47F Advanced Chinook** with 5,000-shp (3729-kW) engines supplied with additional fuel and driving more advanced rotors, the most advanced model to have entered production by 1999 is the MH-47E Chinook, of which 51 are required for operation in support of the US Army's Special Forces. These machines, which operate in conjunction with CH-47Ds upgraded to a partial Special Forces stan-

dard with the designations **CH-47D Special Operations Aircraft** and **MH-47D SOA**, have T55-L-714 engines, armour protection, offensive and defensive weapons, and additional fuel and inflight-refuelling capability. Also fitted is a completely revised avionics suite with a number of defensive elements as well as an advanced all-weather day/night navigation system including night vision goggles, FLIR, GPS-updated INS and APQ-174 radar for terrain-following, terrain-avoidance, ground-mapping and air-to-ground ranging.

Boeing Vertol Model 76 (VZ-2)

Among the several vertical-lift concepts investigated by US forces in the late 1940s and 1950s was that of the tilt-wing configuration. A significant part in this programme was played by the **Vertol Model 76** (from 1960 the **Boeing**

Vertol Model 76), which was based on an open fuselage structure of alloy tube perched on a fixed tailwheel type landing gear and featuring at its nose a helicopter-type bubble canopy. In the centre was the tilt wing, transmission

Serving its last years solely under NASA control, the Model 76 was the world's first aircraft to employ the tilt-wing concept.

and turboshaft powerplant, while at the rear was a large-area T-tail. The two three-bladed rotors were located on the leading edges of the wing, and for additional control at low speeds, vertical and horizontal ducted fans were built into the tail.

The Model 76 first flew

in April 1957, and achieved its initial complete transition from vertical to horizontal flight on 23 July 1958. The trials programme for this

VZ-2A (**VZ-3A** after modifications) was conducted jointly by the US Army and NASA, and continued into the middle of the 1960s.

SPECIFICATION	
Boeing Vertol Model 76 (VZ-2A) **Type:** one/two-seat tilt-wing research aircraft **Powerplant:** one 850-shp (634-kW) Avco Lycoming YT53-L-1 turboshaft transmission-limited to	700 shp (522 kW) **Weights:** empty 3,700 lb (1678 kg) **Dimensions:** wingspan 24 ft 11 in (7.59 m); proprotor diameter, each 9 ft 6 in (2.90 m); length 26 ft 5 in (8.05 m); height 15 ft (4.57 m)

Boeing Vertol Model 107 (H-46 Sea Knight)

Shortly after the formation of the Vertol Aircraft Corporation in March 1956, the company initiated a design study for a twin-turbine commercial transport helicopter. In the formulation of the design, special attention was paid to the incorporation of features that would make the type suitable for military use in the event that the US armed forces showed an interest in the type's procurement.

Allocated the designation **Vertol Model 107**, a prototype entered construction in May 1957, and the first flight of this aircraft was recorded on 22 April 1958. Company testing and development progressed well, and an extensive demonstration tour aroused considerable interest, resulting in the sale of a few helicopters to commercial operators. The first of the armed forces wishing to evaluate the new helicopter was the US Army which, in July 1958, ordered 10 slightly modified aircraft under the designation **YHC-1A**. The first of these flew for the first time on 27 August 1959. By that time the US Army had

come to favour a larger and more powerful helicopter, which Vertol had developed from the Model 107 as the Model 114 and, in consequence, reduced its order to only three YCH-1A (later **YCH-46C**) machines. The company subsequently equipped the third of these with 1,050-shp (783-kW) General Electric T58-GE-6 turboshaft engines and rotors of increased diameter, and this derivative was fitted out with a commercial interior as the **Model 107-II** prototype, which first flew on 25 October 1960. By that time Vertol had become a division of The Boeing Company.

When the USMC showed an interest in this helicopter, one was modified as the **Model 107M** with the powerplant of two T58-GE-8 engines and this was successful in winning a contract for the **HRB-1** (changed to **CH-46** in 1962) production model, which was named as the **Sea Knight**. Since that time Sea Knights have been used extensively by both the USMC and the USN. The former uses them for troop transport, the latter mainly in the vertical replenishment role.

The first of 160 examples of the CH-46A flew on 16 October 1962, and test-

After much procrastination on the part of the Canadian government, SAR-dedicated CAF CH-113s are to be replaced by a variant of the Anglo-Italian EH101, to be known as the Cormorant.

ing continued late into 1964 so that the type did not enter full USMC service until a time early in 1965. Since then, a number of versions has been built, these including 266 examples of the **CH-46D** for the USMC to a standard generally similar to that of the CH-46A except for its 1,400-shp (1044-kW) T58-GE-10 turboshaft engines; 174 examples of the **CH-46F** for the USMC to a standard generally similar to that of the

CH-46D but with additional avionics; 14 examples of the **UH-46A Sea Knight**, similar to the CH-46A, for the USN with first deliveries to Utility Helicopter Squadron 1 in July 1964; and 10 examples of the **UH-46D** for the USN to a standard virtually identical to that of the CH-46D. The USMC updated 273 of its older Sea Knights to the **CH-46E** standard with 1,870-shp (1394-kW) General Electric T58-GE-16 turboshafts and other

A pair of CH-46Fs, one hauling an underslung load, engages in a vertical replenishment mission. The CH-46 is now an old design and is slated for retirement as the V-22 enters service.

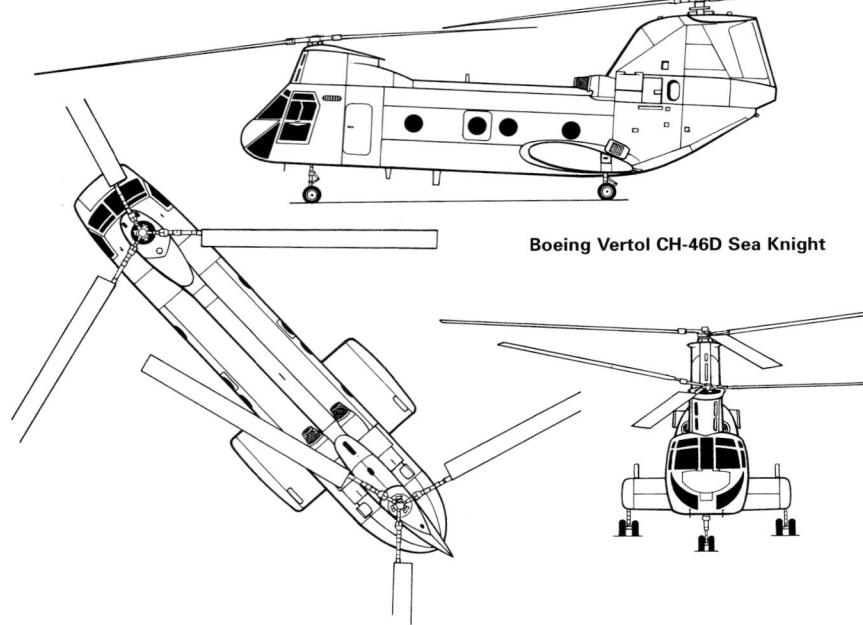

Boeing Vertol CH-46D Sea Knight

improvements including structural strengthening and glassfibre rotor blades.

Six utility helicopters, almost identical to the CH-46A, were delivered to the RCAF in 1963 under the designation **CH-113 Labrador**, and 12 similar aircraft were built for the Canadian Army during 1964-5, these being desig-

nated **CH-113A Voyageur**. In the Canadian Armed Forces' SARCUP (Search And Rescue Capability Upgrade Project), Boeing of Canada was later contracted to modify six CH-113 and five CH-113A helicopters to an improved SAR standard by mid-1984. In 1962-3 Boeing Vertol supplied Model 107-II helicopters to Sweden for service with the air force in the search and rescue role, and with the navy for ASW and minesweeping duties; both of these versions received the local designation **Hkp 4A**.

In 1965 Kawasaki in Japan acquired from Boeing Vertol the worldwide sales rights for the Model 107-II, and built the type up to about 1990 in several versions with the basic designation **Kawasaki-Vertol KV 107-II**. The type is now being retired from Japanese service.

Variants

RH-46A Sea Knight: a few CH-46As experimentally converted for minesweeping developments
HH-46D Sea Knight: a few UH-46Ds converted for the base rescue role

---

SPECIFICATION

Boeing Vertol CH-46A Sea Knight
Type: two/three-crew twin-rotor transport helicopter
Powerplant: two General Electric T58-GE-8B turboshaft engines each rated at 1,250 shp (932 kW)
Performance: maximum speed 155 mph (249 km/h) at sea level; cruising speed 151 mph (243 km/h) at 5,000 ft (1525 m); initial climb rate 1,440 ft (439 m) per minute; service ceiling 14,000 ft (4265 m); hovering ceiling 9,070 ft (2765 m) in ground effect and 5,600 ft (1707 m) out of ground effect;
range 265 miles (426 km) with maximum internal payload
Weights: empty 12,406 lb (5627 kg); maximum take-off 21,400 lb (9707 kg)
Dimensions: rotor diameter, each 50 ft (15.24 m); length overall, rotors turning 83 ft 4 in (25.40 m); height 16 ft 8½ in (5.09 m); rotor disc area, total 3,926.99 sq ft (364.82 m²)
Payload: up to 25 troops, or 4,000 lb (1814 kg) of freight carried internally or 6,330 lb (2871 kg) of freight carried externally

---

Boeing Vertol Model 179 (H-61)

In 1971 the US Department of Defense issued a requirement for a new UTTAS (Utility Tactical Transport Aircraft System) helicopter to replace the Bell UH-1 in service with the US Army. The requirement called for much the same payload volume and weight as those available with the UH-1, but this payload had to be carried to much greater altitudes and at considerably higher ambient temperatures. The two leading contenders for UTTAS hardware were the Sikorsky S-70 ordered for evaluation as the YUH-60A, and the **Boeing Vertol Model 179**, which was ordered for evaluation as the **YUH-61A**.

The Model 179 was the first Boeing Vertol design with a single main rotor, and this profited from the company's licensed production of the West German MBB BO 105 utility heli-copter. In addition to the crew of two or three, the cabin could accommodate 11 troops or an alternative freight load; there was also provision for the carriage of a slung load.

Three military proto-types were completed, the first of these making the type's maiden flight on 29 November 1974. A competitive evaluation of the YUH-60A and YUH-61A was conducted from 1975, and the Sikorsky entrant was judged the winner. Boeing Vertol completed a fourth prototype as the Model 179 civil demonstrator, with accommodation for between 14 and 20 passengers, but develop-ment of both types was later abandoned.

SPECIFICATION

Boeing Vertol Model 179 (YUH-61A)
Type: two/three-crew utility tactical transport helicopter
Powerplant: two General Electric YT700-GE-700 turboshaft engines each rated at 1,536 shp (1146 kW)
Performance: maximum speed 178 mph (287 km/h) at 4,000 ft (1220 m); cruising speed 167 mph (269 km/h) at 4,000 ft (1220 m); hovering ceiling 6,450 ft (1966 m) out of ground effect; range 372 miles (599 km)
Weights: empty 9,487 lb (4302 kg); maximum take-off 18,700 lb (8481 kg)
Dimensions: main rotor diameter 49 ft (14.93 m); length overall, rotors turning 59 ft 6 in (18.13 m); height 15 ft 2 in (4.63 m) with rotors turning; main rotor disc area 1,885.74 sq ft (175.19 m²)
Armament: provision was made for one or two 0.3-in (7.62-mm) trainable lateral-firing machine-guns to be pintle-mounted in the cabin doorways
Payload: 11 troops, or four litters plus attendants, or 8,000 lb (3620 kg) of freight carried in the cabin, or 10,000 lb (4536 kg) of freight carried as a slung load

---

The YUH-61A's fuselage structure utilised a great deal of glassfibre and honeycomb, both for strength and to reduce maintenance.

Boeing Vertol Model 360

First flown on 10 June 1987, the **Boeing Vertol Model 360** was designed and built as a private venture for the development and evaluation of advanced helicopter technologies. Laid out as a cargo-carrying type with much the same size and overall configuration as the Model 107, the Model 360 was based on an essen-

tially oval-section fuselage with a covering of Kevlar and Nomex honeycomb panels over a basic framework of graphite epoxy fuselage frames and longerons. It was supported on the ground by fully-retractable tricycle landing gear with twin wheels on each unit.

The powerplant was based on a side-by-side

Of advanced aerofoil section for improved high-speed performance and hovering efficiency, the Model 360's rotors had composite blades on glassfibre heads.

pair of ALF 5512 turboshafts installed in the sides of the rear fuselage in a low-drag installation and these engines drove the tandem arrangement of two interconnected four-bladed rotors.

The cabin floor was fitted with a cargo-handling roller system and supported the fuel tanks, and was suspended on sprung counterweights for maximum isolation from rotor-induced vibration. The same arrangement was

used on the flightdeck, from which the two primary members of the crew operated the helicopter by means of a Bendix integrated flight control and flight management system. The latter included six CRT displays

and incorporated a Honeywell digital automatic flight control system.

It was never intended that production of the purely experimental Model 360 would be undertaken, but the type remained airworthy into the early 1990s.

SPECIFICATION

Boeing Vertol Model 360
Type: two/three-crew technology demonstrator helicopter
Powerplant: two Textron Lycoming ALF 5512 turboshaft engines each rated at 4,200 shp (3132 kW)
Performance: (estimated) maximum design speed 270 mph

(435 km/h) at optimum altitude; cruising speed 207 mph (334 km/h) at optimum altitude
Weights: (estimated) maximum take-off 30,500 lb (13835 kg)
Dimensions: fuselage length 51 ft (15.54 m); height 19 ft 4¾ in (5.91 m)

Boeing/Sikorsky H-66 Comanche

In 1982 the US Army announced its extremely ambitious **LHX (Light Helicopter Experimental)** programme for an armed multi-role helicopter. Up to 5,000 of these were to be bought as replacements for the service's current forces of Bell UH-1 Iroquois, Bell AH-1 HueyCobra, and Hughes OH-6 Cayuse and Bell OH-58 Kiowa helicopters. As the complexity of the programme and the real cost of this advanced type became clearer, however, the procurement total was gradually whittled down, and by 1987 the projected total was 2,096 helicopters to operate only in the armed reconnaissance and scout roles in succession to the current force of 3,000 AH-1, OH-6 and OH-58 types. In 1998 the planned total was 1,292 helicopters with the possibility of 389 to be added later.

The US Army request for proposals was issued in June 1988, and 23-month demonstration and validation contracts were then placed with two industrial teamings, namely the 'Super Team' that combined Bell and McDonnell Douglas, and the 'First Team' involving Boeing and Sikorsky. The 'First Team' was selected as winner in April 1991 and

contracted to manufacture four flying prototypes for demonstration and validation purposes; the contract also included provision for two non-flying prototypes, one for use in static tests and the other as a propulsion system testbed. The number of flying prototypes was reduced to three and finally two in 1992 and 1994 respectively.

The engine specified for the new helicopter was selected in October 1988 as the LHTEC (Allison/ Garrett, now Allison/ AlliedSignal) T800 advanced turboshaft. In 1990 the LHX designation was changed to **LH**, and in April 1991 the combined service designation and name **RAH-66 Comanche** was selected, the LH prototype and service test helicopters then receiving the designation **YRAH-66**.

Development of the Comanche was slowed by technical considerations as well as political antipathy in several quarters and then the downturn in US funding of advanced military programmes. Then the US budget for 1993 delayed the development and production elements of the programme to an indefinite degree, with the object of ensuring that the Longbow radar would be installed

from the first rather than the fourth production batch. In January 1993 the programme was again revised, with three engineering and manufacturing development prototypes added for the 1998-2003 period, with production starting in 1999 and initial operational capability reached in 2003. A December 1993 critical design review led to the authorisation of production of three prototypes and urged further research and development cutbacks. In December 1994 the number of prototypes was again reduced to two, in this instance without the Longbow radar and AGM-114 Hellfire ASM, and production was again set further into the future. The definitive programme finally emerged in 1995, and called for two prototypes, six 'early operational capability' helicopters with reconnaissance equipment but no armament for trials from 2001, a production decision in 2003, the establishment of the first operational unit in 2007, and production encompassing 1,292 helicopters.

The Comanche is designed for minimum observability (electromagnetic, thermal, acoustic and visual) consonant with its operational tasks, and is therefore based on a 'stealthy' airframe offering a minimum of reflective surfaces and built largely of

composite materials. The twin-engined powerplant and associated gearboxes and transmission are located behind and to each side of the small pylon which carries the five-bladed main rotor. The latter is of composite construction with cuffed swept-tip blades emerging from the faired and bearingless rotor head. The T-tail has a vertical surface inclined to starboard and including an eight-blade shrouded anti-torque rotor. The landing gear is of the retractable tailwheel type while weapon stowage is internal, with a bay on each side of the lower fuselage below the main rotor. The very advanced avionics (designed for maximum commonality with the Lockheed Martin F-22 Raptor) include dual triplex fly-by-wire control systems with sidestick cyclic pitch controllers but conventional collective levers, a nav/ attack system with GPS update and FLIR, a 'glass' cockpit arrangement

with two large liquid-crystal displays in each cockpit, night vision equipment, crew helmet displays and sights, laser and radar warning receivers plus associated jammers, and provision for Longbow radar which is currently to be installed in only one out of three of the helicopters.

The armament is planned as a 20-mm three-barrel cannon with 500 rounds in an undernose turret, and up to three Hellfire ASMs or six Stinger AAMs on the launcher that can be extended from each of the two bays. Where 'stealthy' operations are less important, the Comanche can also be fitted with a stub wing above the weapons bays, this being capable of carrying up to eight Hellfires or 16 Stingers or drop tanks at its tips. Provision for other weapons will be added in due course.

The first YRAH-66 made its maiden flight on 4 January 1996, with IOC scheduled for 2006.

SPECIFICATION

Boeing/Sikorsky RAH-66 Comanche
Type: two-crew reconnaissance, attack and air combat helicopter
Powerplant: two LHTEC T800-LHT-801 turboshaft engines each rated at 1,432 shp (1068 kW)
Performance: (estimated) maximum speed 201 mph (324 km/h) at 4,000 ft (1220 m); initial vertical climb rate 1,418 ft (432 m) per minute; range 1,450 miles (2334 km) with drop

tanks; endurance 2 hours 30 minutes with standard fuel
Weights: (estimated) empty 7,765 lb (3522 kg); maximum take-off 17,408 lb (7896 kg)
Dimensions: main rotor diameter 39 ft ½ in (11.90 m); length overall, rotors turning 46 ft 10¼ in (14.28 m); height 11 ft ¾ in (3.37 m); main rotor disc area 1,197.04 sq ft (111.21 m²)
Armament: see above

Together, Comanche (foreground) and Longbow Apache will fly as part of a fully-integrated, digitally-controlled system within the US Army's Force XXI concept.

Boisavia aircraft

The French company Boisavia, which was established soon after the end of World War II, designed and built a small three-seat light aircraft as the **Boisavia B-50 Muscadet**. This was developed into the **B-60 Mercurey** four-seat cabin monoplane, which flew for the first time in prototype form on 3 April 1949 and was of similar configuration to the Piper Cub, with fixed tailwheel landing gear. Power for the prototype was provided by a Renault (later SNECMA) 4Pei

inverted inline engine. Built in modest numbers, variants of the B-60 (two aircraft only) found employment in the agricultural, glider-towing, touring and training roles.

A type that enjoyed less success was the **B-26 Anjou**, which first flew in **B-260** prototype form on 2 June 1956. This was a twin-engined four/five-seat cabin monoplane intended for the touring role, and in configuration was a low-wing cantilever monoplane with retractable tricycle

B-60 Variants

B-601 Mercurey: three examples of an agricultural version powered by the 190-hp (142-kW) Avco Lycoming O-435-1 engine
B-602 Mercurey: redesignation of one B-60 with a 165-hp (123-kW) Continental E165-4 engine
B-603 Mercurey-Spécial: glider-tug development with the 240-hp (179-kW) Salmson (Argus) As 10 engine
B-604 Mercurey-Spécial: more extensively developed glider-tug version with a lengthened fuselage, increased fin area, improved landing gear and a 230-hp (172-kW) Salmson 9Abc radial engine
B-605 Mercurey: version with the 170-hp (127-kW) SNECMA-Régnier 4L-02 engine

landing gear. Power was provided by two 170-hp (127-kW) SNECMA-Régnier 4L-02 inverted inline engines.

Only very small numbers of the B-26 were completed, and it is thought that a seven-seat development with the powerplant of two 220-hp (164-kW) Potez 4D-31 piston engines remained only a project.

Another Boisavia product was the **B-80 Chablis**, which was a lightweight parasol-wing monoplane with open accommodation to seat two in tandem.

Intended mainly for the home builder, the type was of plywood- and fabric-covered wooden construction with fixed tailwheel landing gear and utilised one 65-hp (49-kW) Continental E65 engine.

The B-60's all-wood wing was braced on each side by V-struts. Its cantilever tail unit was also of wood, but the fuselage was of welded steel tube with fabric covering.

SPECIFICATION	
Boisavia B-60 Mercurey	18,045 ft (5500 m); range 684 miles (1100 km)
Type: four-seat cabin monoplane **Powerplant:** one SNECMA 4Pei inverted inline engine rated at 140 hp (104 kW)	**Weights:** empty 1,146 lb (520 kg); maximum take-off 2,205 lb (1000 kg)
Performance: maximum speed 146 mph (235 km/h) at sea level; cruising speed 118 mph (190 km/h) at optimum altitude; service ceiling	**Dimensions:** wingspan 37 ft 4 in (11.38 m); length 23 ft 3 in (7.09 m); height 6 ft 10 in (2.08 m); wing area 193.76 sq ft (18.00 m²)

Bolkhovitinov DB-A

Viktor Fyedorovich Bolkhovitinov headed a team in the design of the **Bolkhovitinov DB-A (Dalnii Bombardirovschik – Akademia)**, a four-engined heavy bomber designed as successor to the Tupolev TB-3.

The DB-A was one of the first Soviet aircraft to

feature a stressed-skin monocoque fuselage structure and was a mid-wing monoplane of metal construction with tailwheel landing gear. The latter's main units semi-retracted into the bottoms of large and very deep 'trouser' fairings below the nacelles for the inner pair of engines.

The DB-A first prototype took to the air on its maiden flight on 5 March 1936 and was soon followed by the **DB-2A** second prototype which featured more powerful 1,000-hp (746-kW) AM-34RNV engines and revised radiators. At the end of 1936 and beginning of 1937, the DB-2A established several impressive world-class payload-to-

height and payload-over-range records.

Testing proceeded satisfactorily, and during 1938 a batch of 12 DB-A pre-production aircraft was delivered, with five entering experimental service and the others flying test duties. During 1938 the

DB-2A prototype was revised with 900-hp (671-kW) AM34FRN/TK turbocharged engines for improved performance at altitude. Further development of the basic design was then abandoned in favour of the rival Tupolev ANT-42.

Dural light alloy was employed throughout in the DB-A's structure, with the control surfaces being fabric covered.

SPECIFICATION	
Bolkhovitinov DB-A	**Dimensions:** wingspan 129 ft 7 in (39.50 m); length 80 ft ⅓ in (24.40 m); wing area 2,475.78 sq ft (230.00 m²)
Type: six/seven-seat heavy bomber **Powerplant:** four Mikulin AM-34RN Vee engines each rated at 970 hp (724 kW)	**Armament:** (DB-2A and proposed for production model) one 20-mm ShVAK trainable cannon in the nose position and six 0.3-in (7.62-mm) ShKAS trainable machine-guns in the dorsal, tail and 'trouser' positions, plus up to 11,023 lb (5000 kg) of bombs carried internally
Performance: maximum speed 205 mph (330 km/h) at 13,125 ft (4000 m); service ceiling 23,690 ft (7220 m); range about 2,858 miles (4600 km) **Weights:** empty 33,951 lb (15400 kg); maximum take-off 57,320 lb (26000 kg)	

Bölkow Bö 46

First flown on 30 January 1964, the **Bölkow Bö 46** was an experimental helicopter designed by Bölkow but using a very streamlined fuselage built by SIAT. Ordered to the extent of three prototypes, the Bö 46 was designed for the evaluation of the Derschmidt type of rotor as a means of securing the maximum

Wind tunnel tests had suggested that a helicopter equipped with the Derschmidt rotor might achieve a forward speed of up to 310 mph (499 km/h).

possible flight performance from a helicopter.

The Derschmidt lead-lag type of rotor was based on a relatively large star-shaped rigid hub. Glassfibre outer blade sections were attached to the hub section's five aerofoil-

shaped arms by means of hinges that permitted these sections to move forward and backward around their drag hinges so that any advancing blade was swept back relative to the airflow, thereby reducing the tips' Mach number.

SPECIFICATION	
Bölkow Bö 46	altitude; cruising speed 162 mph (261 km/h) at optimum altitude
Type: two-seat experimental high-speed helicopter **Powerplant:** one Turboméca Turmo IIIB turboshaft engine rated at 800 shp (597 kW)	**Weights:** maximum take-off more than 4,409 lb (2000 kg) **Dimensions:** main rotor diameter 32 ft 9¾ in (10.00 m); main rotor disc area 845.42 sq ft (78.54 m²)
Performance: maximum speed 198 mph (319 km/h) at optimum	

Bölkow Bö 46 (continued)

The Bö 46's unique rotor design reduced compressibility problems, and any retreating blade was swept forward relative to the airflow, thereby reducing the possibility of a tip stall. The outer sections worked in the same fashion as a resonant pendulum, with the result that the blade-movement mechanism needed power only to start and synchronise its motion.

The Bö 46 proved successful in technical terms, but all further work on the type was cancelled in 1966 before full evalua-tion with a pair of 882-lb st (3.92-kN) Turboméca Marboré II turbojet engines mounted on the fuselage sides. These boosted level speed to more than 249 mph (400 km/h).

Boulton & Paul P.3 Bobolink

Although built only in proto-type form, the **Boulton & Paul P.3 Bobolink** is worthy of mention as Boulton & Paul's first aircraft. The company had built other firms' aircraft under sub-contract during World War I and the Bobolink was the result of a design competition to find a Camel replacement.

The winner of the competition was the Sopwith Snipe, so the Boulton & Paul aircraft did not enter production. Three serial numbers were allocated for prototypes, but records suggest that only one machine was built. As might have been expected, the Bobolink bore a number of similarities to the Camel, although it had a two- rather than one-bay staggered biplane wing cellule. The performance of the Boulton & Paul aircraft was comparable with that of the Snipe, but the latter was considered to be more suitable for mass production.

An interesting feature of Boulton & Paul's Bobolink fighter was that the pilot could jettison the main fuel tanks in the event of an in-flight fire. Access to the Bobolink's cockpit was particularly difficult.

SPECIFICATION

Boulton & Paul P.3 Bobolink
Type: single-seat fighter
Powerplant: one Bentley B.R.2 rotary engine rated at 230 hp (172 kW)
Performance: maximum speed 125 mph (201 km/h) at 10,000 ft (3050 m); climb to 6,500 ft (1980 m) in 5 minutes 20 seconds; service ceiling 19,500 ft (5945 m); endurance 3 hours 15 minutes
Weights: empty 1,226 lb (557 kg);
maximum take-off 1,992 lb (904 kg)
Dimensions: wingspan 29 ft (8.84 m); length 20 ft (6.10 m); height 8 ft 4 in (2.54 m); wing area 266.00 sq ft (24.71 m²)
Armament: two 0.303-in (7.7-mm) Vickers fixed forward-firing machine-guns in the upper part of the forward fuselage, and provision for one 0.303-in (7.7-mm) Lewis machine-gun above the centre section of the upper wing

Boulton & Paul P.7 Bourges

Design of the **Boulton & Paul P.7 Bourges** twin-engined day reconnaissance bomber began in 1918 with the company's receipt of a contract for three prototypes.

The first airframe to be completed was powered by 230-hp (172-kW) Bentley B.R.2 rotary engines, since the problematic proposed ABC Dragonfly radial engines were not ready. In this original form the new type was designated **Bourges Mk IIA**; it later became the **Bourges Mk IA** when the Dragonfly engines were installed.

Of typical design and construction for its period, the P.7 had a primary structure of wire-braced wood covered largely with fabric, and an unstaggered equal-span biplane wing cellule.

Flight trials revealed that the Bourges was almost as manoeuvrable as contemporary single-engined fighters, but in an effort to improve the field of fire from the gunner's position, the upper wing was modified and, at the same time, the vertical tail surface was altered. In this form the machine became the **Bourges Mk IB**.

The third machine had 450-hp (336-kW) Napier Lion W-type engines installed in nacelles on the upper surface of the lower wing rather than in mid-gap. This change resulted in a speed increase of almost 7 mph (11 km/h). In spite of its fine performance, the Bourges was abandoned, as the large numbers of surplus aircraft available when World War I ended effectively stifled the emergence and manufacture of new designs.

SPECIFICATION

Boulton & Paul P.7 Bourges Mk IA
Type: three-seat reconnaissance bomber
Powerplant: two ABC Dragonfly I radial engines each rated at 320 hp (239 kW)
Performance: maximum speed 123 mph (198 km/h) at 6,500 ft (1980 m); climb to 6,500 ft (1980 m) in 7 minutes 40 seconds; service ceiling 20,000 ft (6095 m); endurance 9 hours 15 minutes
Weights: empty 3,820 lb (1733 kg); maximum take-off 6,326 lb (2869 kg)
Dimensions: wingspan 57 ft 4 in (17.48 m); length 37 ft (11.28 m); height 12 ft (3.66 m); wing area 738.00 sq ft (68.56 m²)
Armament: two 0.303-in (7.7-mm) Lewis trainable machine-guns in each of the nose and dorsal positions, plus up to 900 lb (408 kg) of bombs carried internally

Boulton & Paul P.8 Atlantic

After World War I Boulton & Paul decided that the best opportunity readily available to publicise itself was the prize of £10,000 offered by the *Daily Mail* before the war for the first non-stop flight across the Atlantic. The same notion appealed to several other manufacturers, so something of a race developed.

The company's contender was the **Boulton & Paul P.8 Atlantic**, of which two examples were to be built, based on the P.7 Bourges. Boulton & Paul bought the second P.7 prototype, badly damaged in a crash, from the Air Ministry and used this as the core of the first P.8 by fitting it with a modified wing and a wholly different powerplant, comprising two Napier Lion W-Type piston engines

The first P.8 was readied for its maiden flight in April 1919 but crashed on take-off due to the fact that the fuel system could not supply adequate fuel to both engines when these

Registered G-EAPE, the second Atlantic was completed as an airliner and also flew as an aerodynamic testbed. It could be loaded with a 500-lb (227-kg) box of mail.

SPECIFICATION

Boulton & Paul P.8 Atlantic
Type: three-seat long-distance record-breaking aircraft
Powerplant: two Napier Lion W-type engines each rated at 450 hp (336 kW)
Performance: maximum speed 149 mph (240 km/h) at sea level; climb to 10,000 ft (3050 m) in 8 minutes; service ceiling 25,000 ft
(7620 m); range 3,850 miles (6196 km)
Weights: empty 5,170 lb (2345 kg); maximum take-off 7,880 lb (3574 kg)
Dimensions: wingspan 60 ft 4 in (18.39 m); length 40 ft (12.19 m); height 12 ft 4 in (3.76 m); wing area 770.00 sq ft (71.53 m²)

were running at full throttle. The second machine was not ready when the first non-stop flight across the Atlantic was achieved by a Vickers Vimy in June 1919. Boulton & Paul therefore abandoned its attempt, although the second P.8 was completed and made its first flight on 10 May 1920 as an airliner prototype and aerodynamic test-bed. No orders were received for this type, largely because the de Havilland D.H.18 offered the same load-carrying capability on only half the power.

Boulton & Paul P.9

Following its production of the Sopwith Camel during World War I, Boulton & Paul used components of this aircraft in its **P.6**, a small two-seat biplane that was built to test different aerofoil sections. The company then retained the basic layout of the P.6 for the **Boulton & Paul P.9** which flew in early 1919, a few weeks after its predecessor. The P.9 prototype, built to an Australian order, was shipped to Tasmania where it inaugurated an air mail service between Hobart and Melbourne in December 1919.

The success of the P.9 in Australia prompted production of seven further examples, three of which went to Australian customers. The others were initially registered in the UK, but one was taken on a joyriding tour to the Cape of Good Hope in 1928. Another P.9, flown from Croydon to Switzerland, was damaged in February 1929 when it sank through the ice on a frozen lake, but was recovered and rebuilt.

This P.9 was retained by its manufacturer for use as a company transport until November 1920. What appear to be dark patches of fabric behind the aft cockpit are, in fact, integral suitcases.

SPECIFICATION	
Boulton & Paul P.9	8 minutes 30 seconds; service
Type: two-seat touring aircraft	ceiling 14,000 ft (4265 m); range
Powerplant: one Royal Aircraft	300 miles (483 km)
Factory 1A Vee engine rated at	**Weights:** empty 1,244 lb (564 kg);
90 hp (67 kW)	maximum take-off 1,770 lb (803 kg)
Performance: maximum speed	**Dimensions:** wingspan 27 ft 6 in
104 mph (167 km/h) at 1,000 ft	(8.38 m); length 24 ft 8 in (7.52 m);
(305 m); cruising speed 85 mph	height 10 ft (3.05 m); wing area
(137 km/h) at optimum altitude;	323.00 sq ft (30.01 m²)
climb to 5,000 ft (1525 m) in	

Boulton & Paul P.12 Bodmin

In the financially strained times that followed the end of World War I, the Air Ministry had to resort to subterfuges to secure funding for experimental aircraft. So, when it wanted to evaluate the concept of aircraft with their engines buried in a fuselage 'engine room' and driving the propellers by means of extension shafts and gearboxes, it invented the 'spares carrier' and 'postal' concepts to disguise bomber-type aircraft intended for experimental use. The latter covered medium and small aircraft and led to orders for the single-engined Parnall Possum and twin-engined **Boulton & Paul P.12 Bodmin**.

Ordered to the extent of two aircraft, the Bodmin was designed as a substantial biplane with a primary structure of steel tube under a covering of fabric. The engine room, located in the central fuselage and carrying two Napier Lion engines, was lit by natural and artificial light, contained full engine instrumentation, and allowed either engine to be shut down for maintenance or repair without causing asymmetric-thrust problems. This last resulted from the fact that the forward engine drove two counter-rotating tractor propellers while the rear unit powered two counter-rotating pusher propellers, either pair of which was sufficient for the maintenance of level flight.

The first of the two Bodmins made its maiden flight early in 1924, and flight trials were disappointing as both maximum speed and service ceiling were below the figures expected. Predictably, powerplant problems, including engine cooling and transmission difficulties, proved to be insurmountable.

The P.12's fixed tailskid landing gear included a main unit with two large main wheels under the lower wing's centre section, and two smaller forward wheels to prevent nose-over accidents.

SPECIFICATION	
Boulton & Paul P.12 Bodmin	(3593 kg); maximum take-off
Type: three-seat experimental	11,000 lb (4990 kg)
aircraft configured as a day bomber	**Dimensions:** wingspan 70 ft
Powerplant: two Napier Lion	(21.34 m); length 53 ft 4½ in
W-type engines each rated at	(16.27 m); wing area 1.204.00 sq ft
450 hp (336 kW)	(111.85 m²)
Performance: maximum speed	**Armament:** provision for one or
116 mph (187 km/h) at sea level;	two 0.303-in (7.7-mm) Lewis
climb to 6,500 ft (1980 m) in	trainable machine-guns in each of
8 minutes 9 seconds; service	the nose and dorsal positions
ceiling 16,000 ft (4875 m)	
Weights: empty 7,920 lb	

Boulton & Paul P.25 Bugle

Although it could not afford to order Boulton & Paul's experimental **P.15 Bolton** into production, the Air Ministry was fully aware of the potential of the aerodynamic and structural design incorporated in this all-metal machine. It therefore decided to help Boulton & Paul to improve its all-steel airframe concept with the aid of an order for two more prototypes, in this instance of the **Boulton & Paul P.25 Bugle**. The new design was clearly a linear descendant of the all-wood P.7 Bourges and all-steel P.15 Bolton, but embodied a number of conceptual and structural refinements.

The Jupiter engines were installed on mountings that could be hinged sideways to provide access to the rear of the engines for servicing and as, for safety reasons, the Air Ministry had turned against the concept of fuselage-mounted fuel tanks, fuel was carried in a pair of tanks under the upper wing between each engine and the fuselage. The fuselage was more angular than those of the Bugle's predecessors, but the location of the pilot's open cockpit above and behind the nose gunner's open position provided each of these men with a splendid field of vision.

The first of the two **Bugle Mk I** aircraft made its maiden flight on 30 June 1923, and the second prototype was completed in the same year. The potential of the type had been more fully recognised by this time, however, and an order had been placed for a third machine. This, too, was a Bugle Mk I, and was completed in 1924 to a standard revised with 436-hp (325-kW) Jupiter IV piston engines, four-seat accommodation, reduced span and increased fuel capacity. This third machine was used by No.25 Squadron, RAF, for comparison with the Vickers Virginia, and revealed a combination of lively performance, viceless handling and excellent manoeuvrability. Another two Bugle Mk I prototypes, basically similar to the third machine, were also built in 1924.

The following year saw the delivery of another two aircraft, these being completed to the **P.25a Bugle Mk II** standard with 450-hp (336-kW) Napier Lion W-type engines in nacelles on the lower wing, the fuel tankage relocated to the fuselage, and aerodynamic fairings added to the bomb carriers under the fuselage and lower-wing centre section. The seven Bugles excelled in service but, starved of funding, the RAF could not place production orders for the type.

Boulton & Paul P.25 Bugle (continued)

SPECIFICATION

Boulton & Paul P.25 Bugle
Type: three-seat day bomber
Powerplant: two Bristol Jupiter II/III radial engines each rated at 400 hp (298 kW)
Performance: maximum speed 120 mph (193 km/h) at sea level; climb to 10,000 ft (3050 m) in 15 minutes 30 seconds
Weights: empty 5,079 lb (2304 kg); maximum take-off 8,110 lb (3679 kg)

Dimensions: wingspan 65 ft ½ in (19.83 m); length 39 ft 9 in (12.12 m); height 15 ft 8 in (4.78 m); wing area 932.00 sq ft (86.58 m²)
Armament: one 0.303-in (7.7-mm) Lewis trainable machine-gun in each of the nose and dorsal positions, plus bombs carried externally under the fuselage and lower wing

Developed from the P.7 and P.15, the P.25 introduced a more advanced main landing gear arrangement as well as a revised powerplant of two air-cooled Bristol Jupiter II/III radial engines, each driving a two-bladed tractor propeller.

Boulton & Paul P.29 Sidestrand

Following its experience with the P.7, P.15 and P.25 twin-engined bombers, Boulton & Paul designed the **P.29 Sidestrand** to meet Specification 9/24 for a three/four-seat medium day bomber. The first of two **Sidestrand Mk I** prototypes flew in 1926 as a type that was clearly a direct descendant of the earlier types in its basic concept and the company subsequently received an order for 18 production aircraft.

Deliveries to the RAF's newly re-formed No. 101

Squadron began in 1928, the first batch of six aircraft being of the **Sidestrand Mk II** version with 425-hp (317-kW) Bristol Jupiter VI direct-drive engines as installed on the two prototypes. These aircraft were followed by nine examples of the **Sidestrand Mk III** version with Jupiter VIIIF geared engines, and the final three production aircraft were replacement Mk IIs.

The Sidestrand inherited the good manoeuvrability of its antecedents, but despite proving to be an

excellent aircraft for bombing and gunnery, only No. 101 Squadron was equipped. Three Sidestrand Mk III bombers were converted to the **Sidestrand Mk V** configuration that then received the revised name Overstrand, a type that began to replace its predecessor in December 1934.

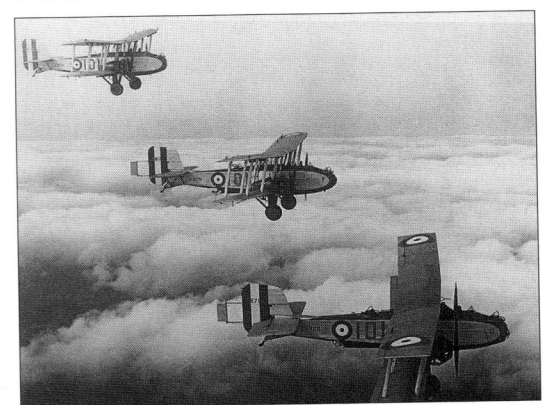

The P.29 Sidestrand used an equal-span, unstaggered three-bay biplane wing cellule.

Boulton & Paul P.29 Sidestrand

SPECIFICATION

Boulton & Paul Sidestrand Mk III
Type: three/four-seat medium bomber
Powerplant: two Bristol Jupiter VIIIF radial engines each rated at 460 hp (343 kW)
Performance: maximum speed 140 mph (225 km/h) at 10,000 ft (3050 m); climb to 15,000 ft (4570 m) in 19 minutes; service ceiling 24,000 ft (7315 m); range 500 miles (805 km)
Weights: empty 6,010 lb (2726 kg); maximum take-off 10,200 lb (4627 kg)

Dimensions: wingspan 71 ft 11 in (21.92 m); length 40 ft 8 in (12.40 m) increasing to 46 ft (14.02 m) when fitted with a servo-rudder mechanism; height 14 ft 10 in (4.52 m); wing area 980.00 sq ft (91.04 m²)
Armament: one 0.303-in (7.7-mm) Lewis trainable machine-gun in each of the nose, dorsal and ventral positions, plus up to 1,050 lb (476 kg) of bombs carried internally in the fuselage and externally under the centre section of the lower wing

Boulton & Paul P.31 Bittern

The Air Ministry's Specification 27/24 called for a single-seat night-fighter for use against formations of enemy bombers. Boulton & Paul's twin-engined monoplane proposal was so radical for the time that exceptional performance and agility were the only factors that would prevent an almost certain assurance of failure.

Two prototypes were built under the designation and name **P.31 Bittern**. The first had a strut-braced shoulder-set wing with two mid-set Armstrong Siddeley Lynx radial engines on its leading edge. The second

prototype differed in having a redesigned, longer-span wing, with Handley Page leading-edge slots on its leading edge. The engines of this machine were mounted much lower on the wing, within Townend rings and without a close cowling around their cylinders.

Despite the innovative ideas, both prototypes were revealed as seriously underpowered during the trials programme that started in 1927. As a result, when the prototypes were tested, their performance was so poor that further development of the type was abandoned.

The first Bittern had two 0.303-in (7.7-mm) Vickers fixed forward-firing machine-guns in the sides of the forward fuselage, while the second (illustrated) had single 0.303-in (7.7-mm) Lewis weapons in elevating barbettes on each side of the fuselage nose.

SPECIFICATION

Boulton & Paul P.31 Bittern (1st prototype)
Type: single-seat night-fighter
Powerplant: two Armstrong Siddeley Lynx radial engines each rated at 230 hp (172 kW)
Performance: maximum speed 145 mph (233 km/h) at optimum altitude

Weights: maximum take-off 4,500 lb (2041 kg)
Dimensions: wingspan 41 ft (12.50 m); length 32 ft (9.75 m)
Armament: two 0.303-in (7.7-mm) Vickers fixed forward-firing machine-guns in the forward fuselage

Boulton & Paul P.64 Mail-Carrier and P.71A

In 1929 Boulton & Paul built a twin-engined all-metal biplane, under a contract awarded by Imperial Airways in 1928, for a mailplane capable of carrying a 1,000-lb (454-kg) payload over a 1,000-mile (1609-km) range at reasonable speed. The company considered its **P.64 Mail-Carrier** to be the answer, but unfortunately the type was both expensive and unsatisfactory.

First flown in March 1933, the P.64 prototype was an equal-span, two-bay biplane with an oval-section fuselage which provided enclosed accommodation for the two-man crew as well as stowage for the mail payload. Power was provided by two 555-hp (414-kW) Bristol Pegasus IM2 radial engines carried in nine-sided nacelles attached to the underside of the upper wing.

The machine lasted barely seven months before it was destroyed in an unexplained fatal crash during trials at Martlesham Heath in October.

Development of the basic layout was continued, however, and the resulting **Boulton & Paul P.71A** was lighter, slimmer and longer. The P.71A employed

Armstrong Siddeley Jaguar VIA radial engines, and two aircraft were delivered to Imperial Airways at Croydon in February 1935. By then the airline had lost interest in the mail-carrying possibilities and the two aircraft, named *Boadicea* and *Britomart*, were converted with accommodation for 13 passengers.

As VIP transports they had seven seats, which were easily removable if the aircraft were required for use as light freighters. Unfortunately, both P.71As were lost within 19 months of delivery.

P.64 G-ABYK never entered Imperial service, but both P.71As did so. The first crashed on landing at Brussels in 1935, and the second disappeared over the English Channel in September 1936.

SPECIFICATION

Boulton & Paul P.71A
Type: two-crew light transport
Powerplant: two Armstrong Siddeley Jaguar VIA radial engines each rated at 490 hp (365 kW)
Performance: maximum speed 195 mph (314 km/h) at 5,000 ft (1525 m); cruising speed 166 mph (267 km/h) at 5,000 ft (1525 m); climb to 4,500 ft (1370 m) in 4 minutes 30 seconds; service ceiling 4,500 ft (1370 m) on one engine; range 600 miles (966 km)
Weights: empty 6,700 lb (3039 kg); maximum take-off 9,500 lb (4309 kg)
Dimensions: wingspan 54 ft 1½ in (16.50 m); length 44 ft 2 in (13.46 m); height 15 ft 2 in (4.62 m); wing area 718.00 sq ft (66.70 m²)
Payload: see above

Boulton Paul P.75 Overstrand

Generally known as a product of Boulton Paul rather than Boulton & Paul as the bulk of the type's service came after the Norwich-based Boulton & Paul had sold its aircraft division to become the completely separate Boulton Paul Aircraft Ltd with a factory in Wolverhampton, the **Boulton Paul P.75 Overstrand** was a development of the Sidestrand. The prototype first flew in 1933 and was a conversion of the eighth production Sidestrand. Three other conversions followed with the initial designation **Sidestrand Mk V**, but the name Overstrand was adopted in March 1934.

An order was placed for 24 production Overstrands to replace the Sidestrand in service with No. 101 Squadron, RAF, but the first aircraft to reach this unit in January 1935 was a Sidestrand conversion that was followed by another conversion in the following month. The first true Overstrands were not delivered until early the following year.

While the conversions were powered by 555-hp (414-kW) Bristol Pegasus I radial engines, the produc-

Fitting the Overstrand with a power-operated nose turret led a contemporary annual to comment that 'it is likely to lead to a revolution in air tactics'.

tion aircraft had Pegasus II engines. Apart from its uprated powerplant, the Overstrand differed from its predecessor in having a fully enclosed power-operated nose turret, the first in any RAF aircraft. In addition, the Overstrand also had an enclosed cockpit with a movable windscreen for the pilot and further evidence of its advanced design was the provision of an autopilot. Boulton Paul engine cowlings and exhaust collectors helped to reduce engine noise and minimise exhaust flame emission respectively, with considerable benefit during night operation.

All Overstrand bombers were built at Norwich, the last being delivered at the end of 1936. Four aircraft were loaned to No. 144 Squadron by their parent unit in January 1937, but were later for exchanged Avro Ansons. No. 101

Squadron phased out its Overstrands during 1937, and began to re-equip with the Bristol Blenheim Mk I in June 1938. A few Overstrands lingered on as gunnery trainers until about 1941.

A proposed develop-

ment, the **P.80 Superstrand**, was to have had retractable landing gear and a generally cleaned-up airframe, but the advent of more advanced and capable monoplane bombers killed this project.

Boulton Paul P.75 Overstrand

SPECIFICATION

Boulton Paul P.75 Overstrand Mk I
Type: five-seat medium bomber
Powerplant: two Bristol Pegasus IIM3 radial engines each rated at 580 hp (433 kW)
Performance: maximum speed 153 mph (246 km/h) at 6,500 ft (1980 m); rate of climb 1,110 ft (338 m) per minute at 5,000 ft (1525 m); service ceiling 22,500 ft (6860 m); range 545 miles (877 km)
Weights: empty 7,936 lb (3600 kg); maximum take-off 12,000 lb (5443 kg)
Dimensions: wingspan 72 ft (21.95 m); length 46 ft (14.02 m); height 15 ft 6 in (4.72 m); wing area 980.00 sq ft (91.04 m²)
Armament: one 0.303-in (7.7-mm) Lewis trainable machine-gun in each of the nose turret and dorsal and ventral positions, plus up to 1,600 lb (726 kg) of bombs carried internally and externally in and under the fuselage

Boulton Paul P.82 Defiant

A new tactical concept, first conceived in 1935, proposed the use of a power-operated multi-gun turret as the primary armament of a single-engined fighter. This appeared to have more than one advantage: firstly, it relieved the pilot of the dual task of flying the aircraft and concentrating on a target; and secondly, the weapons could be used offensively or defensively over a far greater field of fire than that possible for a fixed battery. Previously, Boulton Paul had built 59 Hawker Demons under subcontract, each fitted with a Frazer-Nash hydraulically operated turret.

When the Air Ministry issued Specification F.9/35 for a two-seat fighter with a power-operated gun turret, both Boulton Paul and Hawker made submissions. The Hawker Hotspur prototype was not pursued, however, because the Hawker factories had no production capacity available at that time.

The first of the **Boulton Paul P.82 Defiant** prototypes made its maiden flight on 11 August 1937 as a low-wing cantilever monoplane of all-metal construction with retractable tailwheel land-

ing gear and the power-plant of one 1,030-hp (768-kW) Rolls-Royce Merlin I Vee engine; the second prototype had a Merlin II engine. Both machines had the large and heavy four-gun turret mounted within the fuselage to the rear of the cockpit, and it was soon revealed that this installation's weight and drag imposed severe limits on speed and manoeuvrability.

The first of an eventual 713 production examples of the **Defiant Mk I** day fighter flew on 30 July 1939, and deliveries to No. 264 Squadron began in December of that year. It was this squadron which first deployed the type operationally, on 12 May 1940 over the beaches of Dunkirk, achieving complete tactical surprise. Fighters making conventional attacks on the tail of the Defiant were met with an unprecedented burst of fire from the turret's four machine-guns: in one day the squadron claimed 38 enemy aircraft destroyed, and by the end of May the total had increased to 65. It was, however, only a brief period of air superiority, for it took little time for Luftwaffe fighter pilots to discover that they could

attack head-on, or against the belly of the Defiant, with complete impunity.

Rising losses of the Defiant in the day fighter role soon persuaded the Air Ministry to redeploy the Defiant to the night-fighter task, and the comparatively new and highly secret AI (Air Interception) radar was installed in many of the Defiant Mk Is, this equipment comprising either the AI.Mk IV or AI.Mk VI, aircraft so fitted being designated **Defiant Mk IA**.

In an attempt to improve the Defiant's performance, two Mk Is were converted as **Defiant Mk II** prototypes. Apart from the installation of the more powerful Merlin XX engine, fuel capacity was increased, a rudder of greater area was provided and there were modifications to the engine installation. First flown on 20 June 1940, the Defiant Mk II was built to a total of 210 examples, of which

In service, the Defiant Mk I (illustrated) soon revealed its inherent vulnerability. Converted as a night-fighter, however, the aircraft recorded more 'kills' per interception in the winter of 1940-1 than any other contemporary night-fighter.

many were later converted as **Defiant TT.Mk I** target tugs. In addition, some 150 Mk I fighters were converted as **Defiant TT.Mk III** tugs, and 140 new production Defiant TT.Mk I aircraft were built to bring total construction, including prototypes, to 1,065 by the time production ended in 1943.

At the peak of its deployment as a night-fighter, the Defiant equipped 13 Royal Air Force squadrons. The type was used subsequently at home, in the Middle and Far East as a target-tug and, in addition, about 50 Mk I fighters were modified for use in the air/sea rescue role.

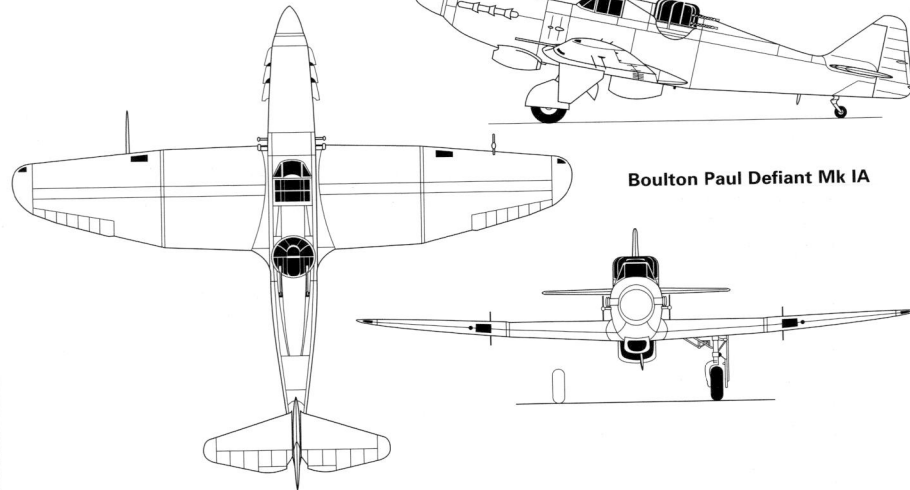

Boulton Paul Defiant Mk IA

SPECIFICATION

Boulton Paul Defiant Mk II
Type: two-seat night-fighter
Powerplant: one Rolls-Royce Merlin XX Vee engine rated at 1,280 hp (954 kW)
Performance: maximum speed 313 mph (504 km/h) at 19,000 ft (5790 m); cruising speed 260 mph (418 km/h) at optimum altitude; initial climb rate 1,900 ft (579 m) per minute; service ceiling 30,350 ft (9250 m); range 465 miles (748 km)

Weights: empty 6,282 lb (2849 kg); maximum take-off 8,424 lb (3821 kg)
Dimensions: wingspan 39 ft 4 in (11.99 m); length 35 ft 4 in (10.77 m); height 11 ft 4 in (3.45 m); wing area 250.00 sq ft (23.23 m²)
Armament: four 0.303-in (7.7-mm) Browning trainable machine-guns in a power-operated Boulton Paul Type A Mk IID dorsal turret

Boulton Paul P.108 Balliol

The Air Ministry's Specification T.7/45 called for a turboprop-powered advanced trainer with three-seat accommodation, and to meet this requirement Boulton Paul designed the **P.108 Balliol**. The airframe was ready before the engine, however, and the first flight

was made on 30 May 1947 with an 820-hp (611-kW) Bristol Mercury radial engine. Ten months later a second prototype flew with the chosen engine, namely the 1,000-shp (746-kW) Armstrong Siddeley Mamba. This prototype was the world's first single-turboprop aircraft to fly, and

the first P.108 was similarly re-engined at a later date.

Having specified a three-seat turboprop, the Air Ministry had second thoughts and decided instead that it needed a two-seat piston-engined trainer. A new Specification T.14/47 was drawn up, with the Rolls-Royce Merlin defined as the engine, and

Boulton Paul received a contract for four prototypes of the **Balliol T.Mk 2**, which had the same basic airframe as the earlier aircraft. In competition was the Avro Type 701 Athena, which was built to a lesser extent than the Balliol.

In its service trials the Balliol performed well, and sizeable contracts were

This Balliol T.Mk 2 was flown by the RAF's No. 7 Flying Training School from its base at RAF Cottesmore in the early 1950s.

awarded to allow the replacement of the North American Harvard. However, by 1951, the Air Ministry had again changed its mind, deciding instead to concentrate on all-through jet training, and orders were cut back. Sources differ on the number of Balliols constructed, but it seems

SPECIFICATION

Boulton Paul Balliol T.Mk 2
Type: two-seat advanced trainer
Powerplant: one Rolls-Royce Merlin 35 Vee engine rated at 1,245 hp (928 kW)
Performance: maximum speed 288 mph (463 km/h) at 9,000 ft (2745 m); initial climb rate 1,790 ft (546 m) per minute; climb to 10,000 ft (3050 m) in 6 minutes; service ceiling 32,500 ft (9905 m); range 660 miles (1062 km)
Weights: empty 6,730 lb

(3043 kg); maximum take-off 8,410 lb (3815 kg)
Dimensions: wingspan 30 ft 4 in (11.99 m); length 36 ft 6 in (11.13 m); height 12 ft 6 in (3.81 m); wing area 250.00 sq ft (23.23 m²)
Armament: one 0.303-in (7.7-mm) Browning fixed forward-firing machine-gun in the port wing and provision for four 60-lb (27-kg) rockets under the wings

probable that 175 production aircraft were built for the RAF. Some of the aircraft earmarked for the RAF were diverted to fulfil a contract for the Ceylon air force (variously reported as nine or 12 aircraft), and Boulton Paul had a civil demonstrator between 1954 and 1956.

Pre-production examples of the Balliol went to the Central Flying School, while production models were delivered to No. 7 Flying Training School and served later at the RAF College, Cranwell, until superseded by the de Havilland Vampire T.Mk 11 in 1956. The **Sea Balliol T.Mk 21** was ordered for the Fleet Air Arm, and the last of 30 aircraft was delivered in December 1954. The Sea Balliol introduced a smaller-diameter propeller, strengthened landing gear, an arrester hook for deck landing and other equipment changes. The type equipped No. 781 Squadron and No. 1843 Squadron of the Royal Navy Volunteer Reserve.

Boulton Paul P.111 and P.120

The **P.111** and **P.120** delta-wing research aircraft, built to Air Ministry Specifications E.27/46 and E.27/49 respectively, were used to investigate the high-speed characteristics of the delta wing.

The P.111 first flew on 10 October 1950 with the powerplant of one Rolls-Royce Nene RN.2 Mk 3 turbojet. The aircraft's fintip was detachable and it had no tailplane. After tests in its original form, the machine was fitted with a nose probe and four rectangular airbrakes around the front fuselage. Some internal modifications were also made, and in this new form the machine received the revised designation **P.111A**, recommencing flight tests in July 1953. The P.111A proved that it could become supersonic in a shallow dive.

The P.120, first flown on 6 August 1952, was similar in general layout to the P.111 but had an all-moving tailplane mounted high on a squat fin. Unfortunately, the new aircraft was lost on 29 August, in an accident thought to have been caused by tail flutter. The P.120 was the last aircraft designed and built by Boulton Paul.

The P.111's delta wing had a leading-edge sweep angle of 45° and its detachable wingtips made it easy to carry out comparative tests with blunt and pointed tips. The former reduced the span to 25 ft 8 in (7.82 m) and area to 269.25 sq ft (25.01 m²).

SPECIFICATION	
Boulton Paul P.111A	**Weights:** empty 6,500 lb
Type: single-seat transonic research aircraft	(2948 kg); maximum take-off 9,600 lb (4354 kg)
Powerplant: one Rolls-Royce Nene RN.2 Mk 3 turbojet engine rated at 5,100 lb st (22.69 kN)	**Dimensions:** (with wing and fin pointed tips) wingspan 33 ft 6 in (10.21 m); length 26 ft 1 in (7.95 m); height 12 ft 6 in (3.81 m); wing area 290.13 sq ft (26.95 m²)
Performance: maximum speed Mach 0.98; initial climb rate 9,400 ft (2865 m) per minute	

Brantly-Hynes Model B-2 and Model 305

In 1943 N. P. Brantly began the design of a lightweight helicopter, which was built and flown in 1946 under the designation **Brantly Model B-1**. Brantly used a co-axial twin-rotor configuration, but soon realised that his design was too heavy and complicated to appeal to the private pilot. An improved **Model B-2**, with a single main rotor and an anti-torque tail rotor, made its first flight on 21 February 1953, and a further improved second prototype flew on 14 August 1956.

The Model B-2 entered production in 1958, and the excellence of its basic design was reflected in the fact that the type remained in production into 1983, the final variant being the **Brantly-Hynes Model B-2B**. By this time changing fortunes had resulted in several different owners of the original Brantly interests, but this merely emphasised the wide appreciation of a good product, and of a steady demand for it. The last owner of the type certificates was Michael K. Hynes, who established Brantly-Hynes Helicopter Inc. on 1 January 1975, initially to provide product support for the large number of Brantly helicopters in use, but later to start production of the Model B-2B and also the larger **Model 305**.

The definitive Model B-2B offers side-by-side two-seat accommodation in an enclosed cabin with dual controls as standard. The Lycoming engine is mounted vertically in the fuselage, just to the rear of the cabin.

Basically a larger-scale version of the Model B-2B, the prototype of the original **Brantly Model 305** made its maiden flight in January 1964 and received its FAA certification in July of the following year, with deliveries to customers following shortly after this. Apart from its increased dimensions, it differed from its predecessor externally in having a small variable-incidence tailplane. Considerably more power was provided by an Avco Lycoming flat-six engine, and an enlarged cabin accommodated a total of five persons on a pair of side-by-side forward seats and an aft bench seat for three people.

The type was offered with wheel, ski or float landing gear, and its production record paralleled that of the Model B-2.

Large numbers of Model B-2Bs are still flying, the type featuring a three-bladed main rotor and two-bladed tail rotor, an all-metal fuselage structure, and provision for operation with skid, wheel or float landing gear.

SPECIFICATION	
Brantly-Hynes Model B-2B (skid landing gear)	service ceiling 10,800 ft (3290 m); hovering ceiling 6,700 ft (2042 m) in ground effect; range 250 miles (402 km)
Type: two-seat light helicopter	**Weights:** empty 1,020 lb (463 kg); maximum take-off 1,670 lb (757 kg)
Powerplant: one Avco Lycoming IVO-360-A1A flat-four engine rated at 180 hp (134 kW)	**Dimensions:** main rotor diameter 23 ft 9 in (7.24 m); length overall, rotors turning 28 ft (8.53 m); height 6 ft 9 in (2.06 m); main rotor disc area 443.00 sq ft (41.16 m²)
Performance: maximum speed 100 mph (161 km/h) at sea level; cruising speed 90 mph (145 km/h) at optimum altitude; initial climb rate 1,900 ft (579 m) per minute;	

Bratukhin helicopters

In spring 1940, Ivan Pavlovich Bratukhin became head of a rotary-wing design bureau at the Moscow Aviation Institute (TsAGI). Impressed by the performance of the German Focke-Achgelis Fa 61 helicopter, Bratukhin decided to adopt a similar configuration, based on a side-by-side pair of counter-rotating rotors carried on long outrigger arms, for the helicopter which he designed for the bureau. Bratukhin decided that a separate engine for each rotor would lead to a less complicated and more efficient design and the resulting prototype, designated as the **Omega** and also as the **2MG (twin-engined helicopter)**, had two 220-hp (164-kW) MV-6 inline engines.

Early hovering tests from August 1941 revealed a variety of problems, and the advance of German forces following their invasion of the USSR then resulted in a break in the helicopter's development of some six months from October 1941. During this period the design bureau was evacuated eastward, and it was mid-1942 before the Omega was once again coaxed into the air. Powerplant unreliability eventually brought the tests to an end, but by that time it had been decided that the basic concept was promising and that further development would continue.

Bratukhin helicopters (continued)

Variants

Omega II: otherwise known as the **G-2 (helicopter no. 2)**, this was a single improved version of the Omega with 330-hp (246-kW) MG-31F radial engines, structural strengthening and other improvements; first flown in September 1944 with considerable success in the following test programme, which included an altitude of 9,845 ft (3000 m) achieved in January 1945; the helicopter was used subsequently for pilot training

G-3: otherwise known as the **AK**, this was a development of the Omega II intended for operational service rather than experimental use; the type's main difference from the G-2 lay in its powerplant of two 450-hp (336-kW) Pratt & Whitney R-985-AN-1 Wasp Junior radial engines. Two prototypes were flown in 1945 and there followed an order for 10 production helicopters, of which possibly none or possibly a maximum of five were actually flown as research machines and one pilot training helicopter

G-4: very similar to the original Omega but with a powerplant of two 500-hp (373-kW) Ivchyenko AI-26GR radial units that were the first Soviet engines designed specifically for helicopter use; two prototypes (first flown in October 1947) and four production aircraft were built out of a batch of 10 that had been ordered

B-5: improved and larger design initiated in 1945 with the letter prefix

altered from G to B in honour of Bratukhin; the type was a scaled-up version of the G-4 with an uprated powerplant of two 550-hp (410-kW) AI-26GR(f) engines and eight-seat accommodation. The sole prototype was completed in 1947 for limited trials

B-9: generally similar to the B-5, except for its non-lifting wing and larger fuselage. Designed for the air ambulance role, but abandoned before it had flown following the failure of the B-5

B-10: otherwise designated as the **VNP (Vozdushnii Nabludatyelnii Punkt,** or air observation post) and retaining the general configuration of the B-5 and B-9, this had 575-hp (429-kW) AI-26GRF engines and a new Dural semi-monocoque fuselage configured for use in the artillery observation role. The type was also planned for use in the utility role but, although flown in 1947, development was abandoned as single-rotor helicopters were beginning to show greater promise

B-11: last of Bratukhin's twin-rotor helicopters before dissolution of his design bureau in 1951. It was generally similar to the B-5, but with an improved rotor system, a strut-braced lifting wing and revised fuselage and tail. The type was designed for evaluation against Mil and Yakovlev single-rotor helicopters and the two prototypes first flew in June and September 1948, one being lost in a fatal accident on 13 December 1948; the surviving prototype was given uprated engines as fitted in the B-10, but was then abandoned

SPECIFICATION

Bratukhin B-11
Type: three-seat communications and light transport helicopter
Powerplant: two Ivchyenko AI-26GRF radial engines each rated at 575 hp (429 kW)
Performance: maximum speed 96 mph (155 km/h) at 4,920 ft (1500 m); service ceiling 8,365 ft (2550 m); range 204 miles (328 km)
Weights: empty 7,491 lb (3398 kg); maximum take-off 9,149 lb (4150 kg)
Dimensions: rotor diameter, each 32 ft 10 in (10.00 m); length, fuselage 32 ft ¾ in (9.76 m); rotor disc area, total 1,690.84 sq ft (157.08 m²)

Bratukhin established his twin-engined helicopter layout with the Omega, mounting one engine at the end of each outrigger. The design of the rotor-drive system was sufficiently sophisticated to allow rotor auto-rotation and, in the case of a single engine failure, for both rotors to be driven by the remaining engine. The aircraft's similarity to Focke-Achgelis designs was readily apparent.

Breda A.7

The **A.7 LD** was a strut-braced parasol-wing monoplane with two-seat accommodation and fixed tailskid landing gear. Two prototypes were built, each with one 400-hp (298-kW) Lorraine-Dietrich engine, and these were followed by 12 production aircraft which entered service with reconnaissance units of the Regia Aeronautica in 1929. The production version of the A.7 was powered by an Isotta-Fraschini Asso engine.

SPECIFICATION

Breda A.7 Asso
Type: two-seat reconnaissance aircraft
Powerplant: one Isotta-Fraschini Asso Vee engine rated at 510 hp (380 kW)
Performance: maximum speed 146 mph (235 km/h) at optimum altitude; cruising speed 109 mph (175 km/h) at optimum altitude; climb to 6,560 ft (2000 m) in 7 minutes 11 seconds; service ceiling 21,325 ft (6500 m); range 746 miles (1200 km)
Weights: empty 3,307 lb (1500 kg); maximum take-off 5,511 lb (2500 kg)
Dimensions: wingspan 49 ft 9¾ in (15.18 m); length 30 ft 3 in (9.22 m); height 10 ft 3½ in (3.14 m); wing area 462.86 sq ft (43.00 m²)
Armament: one 0.303-in (7.7-mm) Lewis trainable machine-gun in the rear cockpit

Variants

A.16: known originally as the **A.7 Raid** (long range), this was a two-seat long-range reconnaissance monoplane, powered initially by an Asso 500 AQ engine; it was modified later as a three-seater powered by one Bristol Jupiter VII radial engine driving a four-bladed propeller; the type was rejected by the Regia Aeronautica

Engine cooling for the A.7 was by a single ventral radiator located just in front of the main landing-gear units, while the prototype employed twin lateral radiators. Production aircraft, as here, also had a revised empennage.

Breda Ba 19, Ba 25 and Ba 28

The first Breda **Ba 19** aerobatic trainer made its appearance in 1928, and this prototype was followed by 41 production aircraft, which were delivered to the Regia Aeronautica during 1931 and 1932. Almost all were single-seat aircraft, and they flew many impressive public displays throughout Italy during the 1930s, when formation flying by the Ba 19 units was unrivalled anywhere in the world.

The Ba 19 was a robust unequal-span biplane of mixed construction. Most aircraft were powered by the 220-hp (164-kW) Alfa Romeo (Armstrong Siddeley) Lynx radial engine, but at least one had a 240-hp (179-kW) Walter Castor engine. A handful of two-seat Ba 19 aircraft was built.

Breda's next important trainer was the **Ba 25**, which was the most important Italian basic flying trainer of the 1930s. The Ba 25 first flew in prototype form during 1931 as a two-seater that was later also evaluated in single-seat form. A single-bay unequal-span biplane of mixed construction, the definitive Ba 25 seated the pupil and instructor in tandem open cockpits.

The first operator of the Ba 25 was the civil flight training school at Cinisello Balsamo, in which Breda had a financial interest, but less than 100 production examples were built between 1931 and 1935. Then, expansion of the Regia Aeronautica between 1935 and 1938 led to a dramatic change, and in that period 481 examples of the Ba 25 were delivered for service use. Total production for the Regia

Aeronautica amounted to 719 machines, and others were sold to private owners and civil flying clubs in Italy. The type was also exported and built under licence by the CNA and SAI companies.

A number of different engine types was installed, including the Alfa Romeo (Armstrong Siddeley) Lynx to create a variant usually designated as the Ba 25/Lynx, the 240-hp (179-kW) Alfa Romeo D.2 to create the Ba 25/D.2,

This Ba 25-I is typical of the many Ba 25s which remained airworthy with the Italian forces and were captured by the Allies and pressed into service.

engine, which was the Italian licence-built version of the Gnome-Rhône 7K. The structure was generally refined, with ailerons incorporated in both upper and lower wings and the prototype was initially allocated a civil registration in June 1934. The type was sufficiently successful to gain a production contract for 50 examples for Italian service, and also attracted a number of orders from export customers. In Italian service the Ba 28 was not particularly successful, and was reported to be dangerous during more taxing aerobatic manoeuvres.

the 220-hp (164-kW) Isotta-Fraschini Asso 200 to create the Ba 25/Mezzo-Asso, and the 240-hp (179-kW) Walter Castor.

Developed from the Ba 25 for the advanced flying training role, the **Ba 28** had a more powerful Piaggio P.VII Z Stella radial

Variants

Ba 25 Ridotto: small number of aircraft produced in single-seat configuration with the wing reduced (hence Ridotto in the designation) in span and area; the Ba 25 Ridotto was used for aerobatic training and was very effective, the type being the favourite mount of several privileged pilots

Ba 25-I: this version, alternatively known as the **Ba 25 Idro**, was a twin-float seaplane; at least 42 were built, all for service as two-seat primary trainers at a number of seaplane training schools. Additionally, several standard Ba 25s were converted for operation on skis

Ba 26: intended exclusively for primary training, this differed from the basic Ba 25 in having the 130-hp (97-kW) Walter NZ engine and increased wingspan; the variant was not developed beyond the prototype stage

SPECIFICATION

Breda Ba 25/Lynx
Type: two-seat basic flying trainer
Powerplant: one Alfa Romeo (Armstrong Siddeley) Lynx radial engine rated at 200 hp (149 kW)
Performance: maximum speed 127 mph (205 km/h) at optimum altitude; climb to 16,405 ft (5000 m) in 29 minutes; service

ceiling 16,075 ft (4900 m); range 249 miles (400 km)
Weights: empty 1,653 lb (750 kg); maximum take-off 2,205 lb (1000 kg)
Dimensions: wingspan 31 ft 6 in (9.60 m) length 27 ft 2¾ in (8.30 m); height 9 ft 6¼ in (2.90 m); wing area 265.88 sq ft (24.70 m²)

Breda Ba 27

Inspired by the American Travel Air Model R, the **Ba 27** single-seat fighter was schemed as a wire-braced low-wing monoplane with a fuselage of steel tube construction under a covering of corrugated light alloy. The flying surfaces were all of wooden construction.

Two Ba 27 prototypes were built and entered flight test early in 1933 with the powerplant of one Bristol Mercury IVA radial engine, licence-built as the Alfa Romeo Mercurius.

Considerable criticism of the design led to revision of the wing in order to provide the pilot with better fields of vision. The aircraft emerged as the **Ba 27 Metallico**, with a more rounded fuselage, smooth rather than corrugated skinning, and the pilot's cockpit

Breda modified the Metallico's wing with a steel and Dural structure and a revised shape to improve the pilot's downward view.

moved forward and raised.

The sole Ba 27 Metallico prototype made its first flight in June 1934, and was later operated by the Italian air force up to December 1937. The Ba 27 Metallico was not accepted for production by the Italian authorities, but 18 examples were ordered by the Chinese government, which was anxious to obtain fighters to confront the invading Japanese. In the event, only 11 were delivered in the course of 1937, entering service with the 29th Pursuit Squadron at Canton.

SPECIFICATION

Breda Ba 27 Metallico
Type: single-seat fighter
Powerplant: one Alfa Romeo Mercurius (Bristol Mercury IVA) radial engine rated at 540 hp (403 kW)
Performance: maximum speed 236 mph (380 km/h) at 16,405 ft (5000 m); climb to 16,405 ft (5000 m) in 7 minutes 30 seconds; service ceiling 29,530 ft (9000 m); range 466 miles (750 km)

Weights: empty 2,910 lb (1320 kg); maximum take-off 4,078 lb (1850 kg)
Dimensions: wingspan 35 ft 5¼ in (10.80 m); length 25 ft 2 in (7.67 m); height 11 ft 1⅞ in (3.40 m); wing area 202.91 sq ft (18.85 m²)
Armament: two 0.5-in (12.7-mm) Breda-SAFAT fixed forward firing machine-guns in the forward fuselage

Breda Ba 33 and Ba 39

Designed in 1931, the **Ba 33** soon attracted international interest when, in the hands of Breda's chief pilot, Ambrogio Colombo, it was flown to victory that same year in the second Giro Aereo d'Italia. A lightweight low-wing monoplane accommodating two in tandem, the Ba 33 was of advanced concept for its time, with clean lines and a minimum of strut and wire bracing. In addition, the Ba 33 was the first of a series of Breda sporting and tour-

ing aircraft of mixed construction to incorporate on its wing both trailing-edge flaps and leading-edge automatic slats. The crew was normally housed under glazed canopies, but at least one example flew with open positions. The Ba 33 was powered by one 120-hp (90-kW) de Havilland Gipsy III engine and showed remarkable flying qualities, with an ability to achieve short take-offs and landings, and

an excellent rate of climb combined with economy and good overall performance.

Ba 33s achieved a number of important long-distance flights, including a seven-stage journey to Calcutta from London in 1933, and also carried off a number of sporting prizes. A batch of 10 Ba 33s was purchased by the Regia Aeronautica for liaison duties, and one was exported to Japan in 1932. A single-seat sport and racing version was also developed under the designation **Ba 33S**.

A larger and heavier development of the Ba 33, the **Ba 39** flew for the first time in September 1932

Although it had greater power than the Ba 33 and proved equally successful, the Ba 39 (illustrated) had a lower maximum speed as a result of its all-up weight which was 453 lb (205 kg) greater.

and soon revealed flying qualities even better than those of its predecessor. The Ba 39 achieved success in numerous sporting events, and examples made several outstanding distance flights.

Civil production was augmented by military orders after the type had been evaluated in the liaison role. Of the 60 aircraft delivered to the Italian air force, some 20 were specialised for use in the homeland with the designation **Ba 39 Met** (for **Metropolitano**) and another 20 for overseas deployment as the **Ba 39 Col** (for **Coloniale**).

Variants

Ba 39S: a 1934 version with three-seat accommodation
Ba 42: a small batch of this variant was built in 1934, with changes that included the powerplant of one NACA-cowled 180-hp (134-kW) Fiat A.70S radial engine and specially designed wing-valve slots in place of the previous leading-edge slats

SPECIFICATION

Breda Ba 39
Type: two-seat touring and liaison aircraft
Powerplant: one Colombo S.63 inverted inline engine rated at 140 hp (104 kW)
Performance: maximum speed 137 mph (220 km/h) at optimum altitude; climb to 13,125 ft (4000 m) in 21 minutes; service

ceiling 19,685 ft (6000 m); range 559 miles (900 km); endurance 3 hours 30 minutes
Weights: empty 1,235 lb (560 kg); maximum take-off 2,062 lb (935 kg)
Dimensions: wingspan 34 ft 2 in (10.41 m); length 24 ft 5 in (7.44 m); height 9 ft 8 in (2.95 m); wing area 188.37 sq ft (17.50 m²)

Breda Ba 64

Colonnello Amedeo Mecozzi was the main protagonist of Italy's Aviatione d'Assalto (assault aviation) in the early 1930s, and his enthusiasm for ground-attack aircraft led to the development of the **Breda Ba 64**. A low-wing cantilever monoplane of all-

metal construction, the first prototype flew in 1934 as a two-seater, with the pilot located in an open cockpit immediately behind the engine and the second crew member in a cockpit to the rear of the wing's trailing edge. The second prototype was completed in single-seat form. It also differed from its predecessor in having tailwheel landing gear, the main units of which retracted back-

Despite poor flight characteristics, the Ba 64 saw considerable service with the Regia Aeronautica's 5⁰ and 50⁰ Stormi (wings) during 1937 and 1938, supplying much photographic material for propaganda purposes.

wards into underwing nacelles, leaving the wheels partially exposed, whereas the first prototype had robust fixed landing gear.

Limited production of a definitive Ba 64 took place in 1936, a total of 42 aircraft being completed in

two subvariants as the **Ba 64 monoposto** and **Ba 64 biposto** with single- and two-seat accommodation respectively. The type was withdrawn from first-line service in 1939, and the last four were scrapped in April 1943.

Breda Ba 65

Intended as an aeroplano di combattimento (multi-role combat aircraft), capable of fulfilling the interceptor fighter, light bomber, reconnaissance and attack roles, the **Ba 65** first flew in prototype form during September 1935. It was a low-wing cantilever monoplane of all-metal construction with tailwheel landing gear, the main units of which retracted rearward into shallow underwing fairings. The basic structure of the fuselage and wing was of steel tube under a skinning of Dural with some fabric covering. The wing incorporated trailing-edge flaps and Handley Page leading-edge slats.

An initial production order was placed in 1936 for 81 Ba 65s with 700-hp (522-kW) Gnome-Rhône 14K engines. A batch of 13 of these aircraft equipped the 65[a]

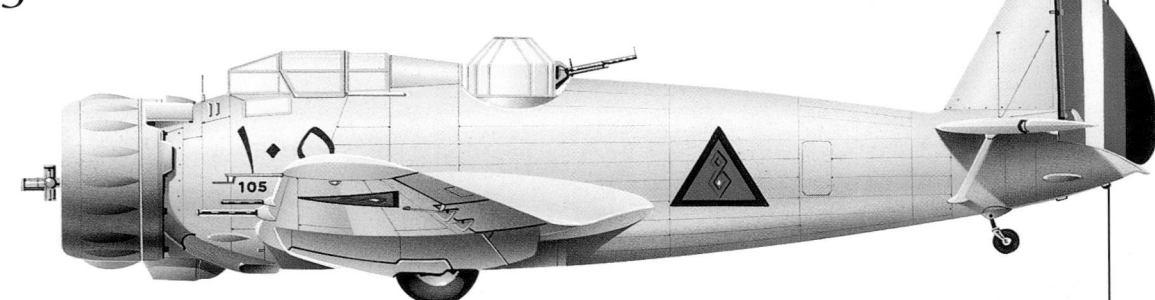

Iraq received 25 Fiat-powered two-seat Ba 65s in 1938 – two of them were dual-control trainers and the remainder had Breda L turrets. The aircraft saw limited action against the British during 1940-41.

Squadriglia of the Aviazione Legionaria, the Italian air contingent supporting the Fascist cause in the Spanish Civil War. The unit took part in operations at Santander in August 1937, then at Teruel, and in the battles for the River Ebro. Like the prototype, these were monoposto (single-seat) aircraft, with the pilot's cockpit fully enclosed by a glazed canopy.

Experience in Spain indicated that the Ba 65 was suited only to the attack role, and the type served thenceforth with the Regia Aeronautica's two assault wings. A second series of 137 aircraft was produced by July 1939. These machines were fitted with one Fiat A.80 engine, and six Fiat-powered Ba 65s and four more of the Gnome-Rhône aircraft were sent to the Aviazione Legionaria in Spain in 1938.

Following Italy's entry into World War II in June 1940, Ba 65s became involved in the fighting in North Africa against the British. The aircraft had a desperately low serviceability rate in desert conditions and put up an extremely unimpressive performance. The last serviceable aircraft were lost during the British offensive in Cyrenaica in February 1941.

A large number of the

Ba 65s serving with Italian units were of the biposto (two-seat) configuration, with an observer/gunner in an open cockpit above the trailing edge of the wing. A small number of this biposto subvariant had a Breda L turret, but in either case the observer/gunner operated a single 0.303-in (7.7-mm) machine-gun.

Exports included 25 Fiat-powered two-seaters to Iraq in 1938; 20 aircraft with the Piaggio P.XI C.40 engine to Chile later the same year, 17 of them in single-seat layout and the other three equipped as dual-control trainers; and 10 Fiat-powered two-seaters with Breda L turrets to Portugal in November 1939. A single Fiat-powered production aircraft was tested with an

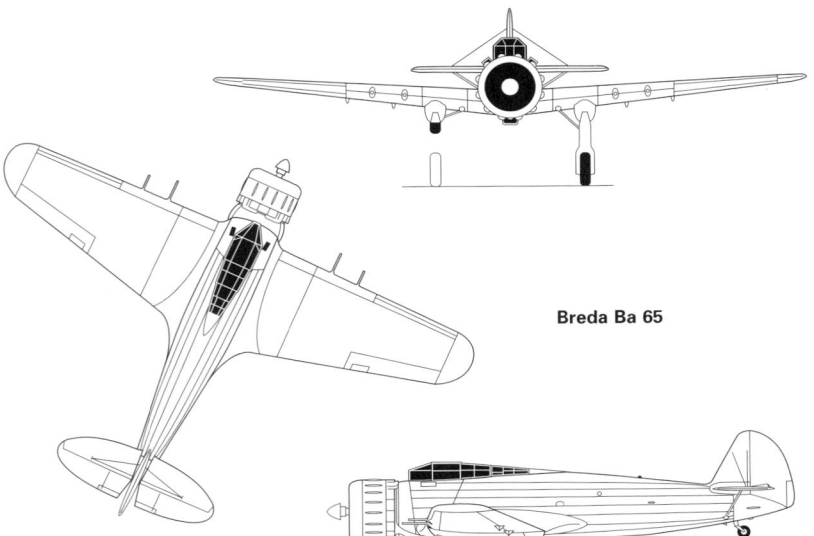

Breda Ba 65

American Pratt & Whitney R-1830 radial in June 1937 in anticipation of an order from the Chinese Nationalist government, but this did not materialise.

Based in concept and structure on the Ba 65, the **Breda Ba 75** was an experimental two-seat reconnaissance and ground-attack aircraft, of

which a single prototype was built and tested in 1939. Compared with the Ba 65, the Ba 75 was of larger overall dimensions, and otherwise differed in

having its wing moved from the low- to mid-set position, fixed tailwheel landing gear whose main wheels were fitted with rear fairings in an effort to

reduce drag, greater vertical tail area and extensive glazing along the lower sides and bottom of the fuselage for observation purposes.

Breda Ba 88 Lince

A propaganda triumph when its appearance was trumpeted by Mussolini's Fascist regime, the **Breda Ba 88 Lince** (lynx) was a sleek all-metal shoulder-wing monoplane with a twin-engined powerplant. The prototype, which had a single vertical tail surface, made its maiden flight during October 1936 in the hands of Furio Niclot, Breda's chief test pilot. In April 1937 Niclot established two world speed-over-distance records in the aircraft, bettering them in December of that year using the same machine.

The prototype, which had retractable tailwheel landing gear and the powerplant of two 900-hp (671-kW) Gnome-Rhône 14K radial engines, was then revised with a tail unit incorporating twin vertical surfaces. Regarded as an aeroplano di combattimento suitable for the attack, long-range reconnaissance and bombing roles, the Ba 88 was only then kitted out with its full complement of military equipment and weapons, resulting in an immediate degradation of performance and handling as a result of the extra weight and drag. Nevertheless, the first batch of 88 aircraft, including eight dual-control trainers, was completed between May and October 1939. Problems with the prototype led to a number of weight-saving modifications, and vitally needed additional power was provided by the installation of Piaggio P.XI RC.40 radial piston engines.

On 16 June 1940, a mere six days after Italy's declaration of war on France and its allies, the Ba 88 had its first taste of action: 12 aircraft from the Regia Aeronautica's 19°

Gruppo Autonomo made bombing and machine-gun attacks on the principal airfields of Corsica, and three days later nine Ba 88s made a repeat attack. Analysis of these operations showed that the Ba 88 had only limited value, and any remaining doubts were settled when Ba 88s of the 7° Gruppo Autonomo joined action in Libya against the British. Fitted with sand filters, their engines overheated and failed to deliver their designed power.

By mid-November 1940 most surviving Ba 88s had been stripped of useful equipment and were employed as decoys for attacking British aircraft. During this time, however, further batches of Ba 88 Lince machines were being delivered, most going straight to the scrap yard.

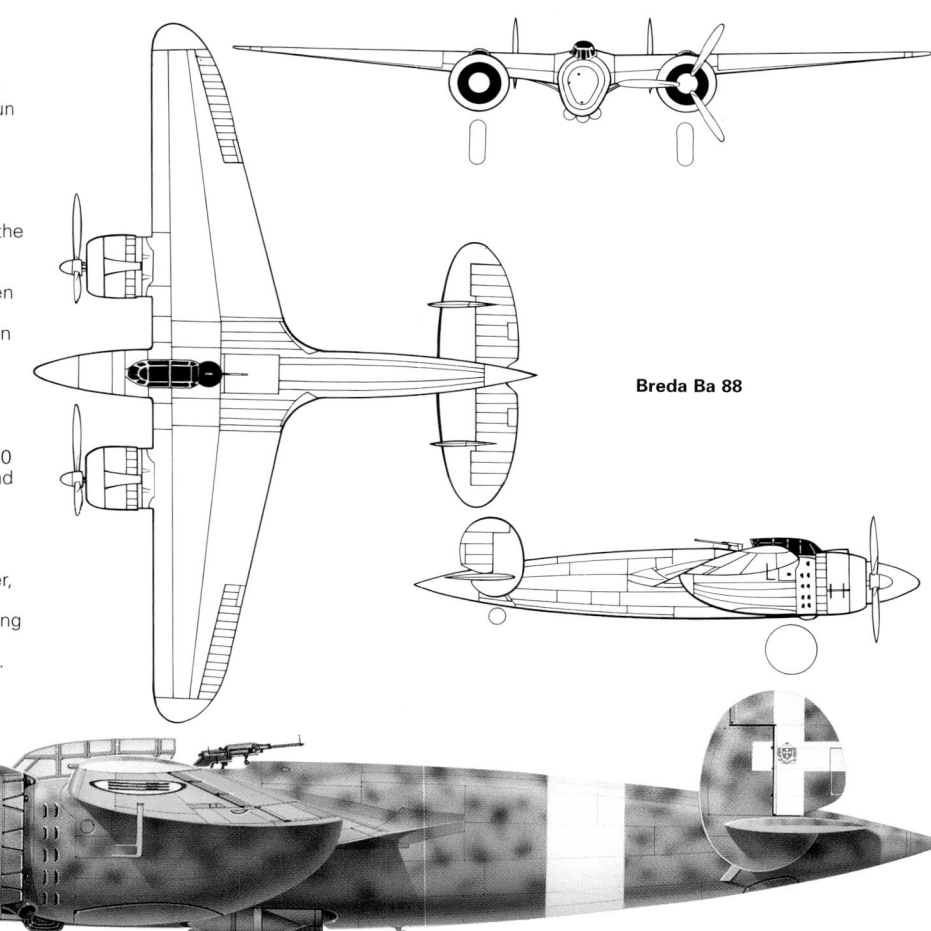

Breda Ba 88

Ba 88s of 7° Gruppo, 5° Stormo, had to abort attacks on targets at Sidi Barrani in September 1940 when the aircraft failed to gain sufficient altitude or maintain formation, and reached a speed less than half that claimed by Breda.

In 1942 Agusta modified three Ba 88s as dive-bombers. The wingspan was increased to reduce the wing loading, the original engines were replaced by lower-rated Fiat A.74 units, the nose armament was increased to four 0.5-in (12.7-mm) machine-guns, and dive-brakes were installed. These **Ba 88M** aircraft were delivered to

the 103° Gruppo Autonomo Tuffatori (independent dive-bombing group) on 7 September 1943. They were flight-tested by Luftwaffe pilots, but no further reports of the Ba 88 emerged. The machine represented perhaps the most remarkable failure of any aircraft that saw operational service in World War II.

SPECIFICATION	
Breda Ba 88 Lince	(15.60 m); length 35 ft 5 in
Type: two-seat attack, fighter-bomber and reconnaissance aircraft	(10.79 m); height 10 ft 2 in (3.10 m); wing area 358.88 sq ft (33.34 m²)
Powerplant: two Piaggio P.XI RC.40 radial engines each rated at 1,000 hp (746 kW)	**Armament:** three 0.5-in (12.7-mm) Breda-SAFAT fixed forward-firing machine-guns in the nose and one
Performance: maximum speed 304 mph (490 km/h) at 13,405 ft (4000 m); climb to 9,845 ft (3000 m) in 7 minutes 30 seconds; service ceiling 26,245 ft (8000 m); range 1,019 miles (1640 m)	0.303-in (7.7-mm) Breda-SAFAT trainable rearward-firing machine-gun in the rear cockpit, plus up to 2,205 lb (1000 kg) of bombs carried internally in a fuselage bomb bay or, alternatively, three 441-lb (200-kg) bombs carried semi-
Weights: empty 10,251 lb (4650 kg); maximum take-off 14,881 lb (6750 kg)	exposed in individual recesses in the fuselage belly
Dimensions: wingspan 51 ft 2 in	

Breguet BUM, BUC, BLM and BrM

Serving as a pilot in the first part of World War I, Louis Breguet soon realised that the aircraft of the period lacked the structural strength and engine power for anything but the reconnaissance role. By this time, however, Breguet was already well advanced with the design of two new military aircraft planned in

accordance with the dictates of Général Bernard, the Directeur de l'Aéronautique, who had called for warplanes in Categories A and B with tractor and pusher powerplants respectively. Breguet preferred the former type, and his contender in this category was an aircraft with a 160-hp (119-kW)

Gnome rotary engine. This machine entered limited production and service as the **AG4** (A for the category and G4 for the Gnome engine), but Breguet recognised the need for greater power and a larger, sturdier airframe.

Breguet then designed the **Type IV**, otherwise known by the military

designation **BU3**, as his first high-powered type in the B category in accordance with the demands of the French general staff that all new military aircraft of the two-seat type should have this configuration. This provided the observer in the front seat with an uninterrupted field of vision for his primary task, and also with good fields of fire for his 0.315-in (8-mm) Hotchkiss trainable machine-gun. The U3

portion of the designation indicated the powerplant of one 160-hp (119-kW) variant of the Salmson (Canton-Unné) water-cooled radial piston engine. The BU3 prototype was under construction at the time that the German advance into north-east France in the late summer of 1914 threatened the Breguet plant at Douai, and the prototype was therefore moved by road to Villacoublay outside Paris.

Breguet BUM, BUC, BLM and BrM (continued)

Finished late in 1914, the BU3 prototype was rushed into service as part of the extraordinary miscellany of aircraft operated by the *Escadrilles de Protection du Camp Retranché de Paris* (squadrons for the protection of the fortified base of Paris) at the time that the Germans were threatening the French capital in September 1914.

The prototype was demonstrated by Louis Breguet himself and had a partially armoured nacelle. The observer/gunner was located in the rear seat and had to stand up before he could fire his machine-gun over the pilot's head.

In November 1914 the brothers André and Edouard Michelin approached the French government with the offer to build 100 bombers for presentation to the French army air service. The BU3 was selected for production and there followed a period

of uncertainty as an element of the French army air service believed that the BU3 should be built without armour for service as a two-seat fighter. Sense prevailed however, and the BU3 was produced as a bomber.

The initial variant of the BU3 built by Michelin was the **BUM**, the designation signifying that it was a Category B aircraft with a Salmson (Canton-Unné) engine and built by Michelin. The type had a number of changes as a result of initial experience with the BU3, and was built for service in the Bombardement deux-place (two-seat bomber) category as the **BrM2B.2** with the Salmson (Canton-Unné) engine rated at 200 hp (149 kW). The **BLM** was the definitive Michelin-built version of the BU3 and entered service as the **BrM4B.2** with the uprated powerplant of one 220-hp

(164-kW) Renault 12Fb Vee engine.

Breguet had planned as early as 1914 to develop a smaller, lighter and faster version of the BU3 that would be capable of a level speed of 87 mph (140 km/h). After the first BUM unit had been created, the unit's commanding officer asked Breguet for a faster derivative of the BUM that could act as escort for the bombers. Breguet responded with the **BUC** whose designation indicated a Category B aircraft with a Salmson (Canton-Unné) engine but optimised for the Chasse (fighter) role. As Breguet was planning this type, the advent of the true fighter was still some months ahead, and the French designer therefore went along with the

perceived wisdom of the time in believing that the new warplane should be armed with a 37-mm cannon, which would allow the aircraft to cruise with the bomber forces and pick off German warplanes before they could close to machine-gun range.

The **BLC** was the light bomber and escort fighter counterpart of the BUC. The type was powered by the Renault 12Fb Vee piston engine. Neither the BUC nor BLM was extensively used, and both types were generally considered inadequate.

Breguet's BLC (illustrated) was dimensionally identical to the BUC. It also carried the same armament although the 37-mm cannon, as fitted to this aircraft, was later replaced by a 0.303-in (7.7-mm) Lewis trainable forward-firing machine-gun. A climb to 6,560 ft (2000 m) was achieved in about 16 minutes.

The **Breguet de Chasse** was a BUC variant for British service with the RNAS, which received 17 of the type. The main change in the alteration of the BUC into the Breguet de Chasse was the replacement of the 2M7 radial by the 225-hp (168-kW) Sunbeam Mohawk Vee engine or, in a couple of cases, the 250-hp (187-kW) Rolls-Royce Falcon Vee. The aircraft were used by No.5 Wing based at Dunkerque, but were withdrawn in June 1916 as a result of their poor performance.

SPECIFICATION

Breguet BUC
Type: two-seat light bomber and bomber escort
Powerplant: one Salmson (Canton-Unné) 2M7 radial engine rated at 200 hp (149 kW)
Performance: maximum speed 86 mph (138 km/h) at sea level; endurance 3 hours
Weights: empty 2,557 lb (1160 kg); maximum take-off 3,384 lb (1535 kg)
Dimensions: wingspan 53 ft 9¾ in

(16.40 m); length 31 ft 2 in (9.50 m); height 12 ft 1¾ in (3.70 m); wing area 581.27 sq ft (54.00 m²)
Armament: one 37-mm Hotchkiss trainable forward-firing cannon or one 0.303-in (7.7-mm) Lewis trainable forward-firing machine-gun in the front cockpit, plus up to 661 lb (300 kg) of disposable stores carried on two hardpoints under the lower wing

Breguet Bre.4, Bre.5, Bre.6 and Bre.12

In spring 1916 the French air force decided to categorise its aircraft into five types: Category A for army co-operation aircraft, Category B for fighting scouts, Category C for three-seat *avions de combat* (multi-role warplanes), Category D for *avions canon* (cannon-armed aircraft) and Category E for bombers. The weapon chosen for the Category D aircraft was the 37-mm Hotchkiss cannon. Machines with this primary weapon were divided into two subcategories: Category D.1 encompassed aircraft with a short-barrel version of the cannon and intended mainly for the air combat role, while Category D.2 covered aircraft with the long-barrel version of this weapon and intended mainly for attacks on German observation and gunnery-spotting balloons, trains and batteries of artillery.

Breguet had already decided to produce a warplane primarily designed for an escort role but he

also wanted something that could double as a light bomber. This accorded well with what was soon to become the Category C specification. The **Type IV** (later **Bre.4**) bomber had been designed with carriage of a 37-mm cannon in mind and was therefore the starting point for the new **Breguet Type V** (later **Bre.5**). The Type V prototype appeared late in 1915 with the gun armament limited to a single short-barrel 37-mm cannon operated by the observer/gunner in the front seat, but the prototype was soon revised to the Category C requirement with a Lewis rearward-firing machine-gun located above the centre section of the upper wing.

After acceptance trials in April 1916, the type entered limited production and service as the **Bre.5Ca.2**, the 'Ca' portion of the designation indicating that it was a Canon (cannon-armed) machine. The Bre.5Ca.2 never equipped a full squadron, but was instead allocated in flight

strength to bomber squadrons whose other flights would be escorted by the new type. Some later aircraft were completed with the 250-hp (187-kW) Renault 12Fbx or Fcx engine.

While the French used the Bre.5 mainly as an escort, the RNAS used 35 of the type as bombers. These machines were 25 aircraft ordered directly from the manufacturer, and 10 aircraft produced under licence in the UK as the **Grahame-White G.W.19** with 250-hp (187-kW) Rolls-Royce Falcon Vee engines.

As the Type V was entering production and service as the **Bre.5**, there were fears that supplies of the Renault 12 engine might be inadequate and Breguet accordingly produced a revised **Type VI** (**Bre.6**) powered by the 225-hp (168-kW) Salmson (Canton-Unné) A9 water-cooled radial engine. The Type VI entered production and service as the **Bre.6B.2** two-seat bomber and **Bre.6Ca.2** escort fighter with a 37-mm cannon.

No details of the Type VI's weights and performance have survived, but the type entered service as the Bre.6B.2 two-seat bomber (above) and Bre.6Ca.2 escort fighter with a 37-mm cannon.

SPECIFICATION

Breguet Bre.5Ca.2
Type: two-seat escort fighter and light bomber
Powerplant: one Renault 12Fb Vee engine rated at 220 hp (164 kW)
Performance: maximum speed 83 mph (136 km/h) at 6,560 ft (1999 m); climb to 6,560 ft (1999 m) in 28 minutes; endurance

6 hours 15 minutes
Weights: empty 2,970 lb (1347 kg); maximum take-off 4,158 lb (1886 kg)
Dimensions: wingspan 57 ft 7¾ in (17.50 m); length 32 ft 9¾ in (9.90 m); height 12 ft 9⅜ in (3.90 m); wing area 621.10 sq ft (57.70 m²)
Armament: see above left

As the Bre.5 series was phased out of service in favour of the Breguet Bre.14, the surviving aircraft were revised for nocturnal bombing operations as the **Bre.12B.2** with a twin-wheel nose unit like that of the BrM4B.2. A few other aircraft were built to a similar standard as **Bre.12Ca.2** night-fighters with one Renault 12Fb or Renault 12Fbx engine, the latter rated at 250 hp (187 kW), the 37-mm cannon adapted to carry a searchlight on its starboard side and an array of eight landing lights under the lower wing.

Breguet Bre.14

Initial work began on the **Bre.14** two-seat tractor biplane in the summer of 1916. The resulting type remained in production from March 1917 until 1928, and was not withdrawn from French service until 1932.

The prototype, designated **Breguet AV Type XIV**, made its first flight on 21 November 1916. The AV in the prototype designation stood for 'Avant' (before, or ahead of), indicating that the 12-cylinder Renault engine was at the front of the fuselage, contrary to the official Section Technique de l'Aéronautique's (STAE) preferences. The Type 14 (the Roman numerals were discarded at an early date) was immensely practical and tough. Its angular fabric-covered wings and fuselage were of Dural, steel and wooden construction. The pilot and observer/gunner were seated close together in open tandem cockpits. The authorities were sufficiently impressed to place a first order for 150 reconnaissance aircraft in the A.2 category on 6 March 1917. By the end of the year the type was being built in the B.2 bomber category as well as the A.2 reconnaissance form.

The **Bre.14A.2** reconnaissance version was equipped with a camera, a radio transmitter and racks for four light bombs. By comparison with the A.2 version, the bomber prototype, test flown in spring 1917, had flaps and ailerons on the lower wing, increased span, transparent panels in the sides of the observer's cockpit, and a small forward extension of a section of the lower-wing leading edges. This was designed to accommodate the Michelin bomb racks, which would otherwise interfere with the flaps. Both versions had sliding floor panels in the pilot's and observer's cockpits for ground observation.

The Bre.14A.2 was the first version to make its mark, beginning to replace the obsolescent Sopwith 1½-Strutter during the summer of 1917.

In 1918 horn-balanced ailerons were introduced in an effort to improve lateral control. At the same time the span of the Bre.14A.2's lower wing was increased, while the **Bre.14B.2** aircraft's lower wing was reduced and the shape of the wing tip revised. The flaps on the Bre.14B.2's lower wing were discarded, so there was no longer any need for the original leading-edge extensions to accommodate the Michelin bomb racks which, in the event, were replaced by racks of improved design.

Renault's 12F engine had been developed to give a reliable 300 hp (224 kW), but other alternative powerplants were tested and several fitted to production batches. These included the Renault 12K, Fiat A.12bis and the American Liberty 12. Plans to build Fiat and Liberty-powered Bre.14s for service in 1919 were abandoned with the end of World War I.

Other wartime versions

On its maiden flight, the AV Type XIV was piloted by Louis Breguet and the company's chief engineer, Louis Vullierme. In production Bre.14A.2 and B.2 (illustrated) forms, the type saw much action.

included the **Bre.14B.1** single-seat bomber, which did not go into large-scale production, and the **Bre.14S** ambulance. This latter **Sanitaire** model resulted from the experimental use of a Bre.14 for rapid evacuation of casualties from just behind the front line in 1917. In 1918 four Bre.14S ambulances, each equipped for the carriage of two litters, operated on the Aisne front.

The Bre.14 was also in service in Greece, Serbia and the Middle East at the end of 1918, but it was in the French overseas empire that the type was to achieve great distinction over more than a decade in the period between the two world wars. The version used in the more far-flung colonies was the **Bre.14TOE (Théatres des Operations Extérieures)**.

In overall terms, approximately 5,300 Bre.14s were built up to December 1918. Three Bre.14A.2 and six Bre.14B.2 escadrilles formed part of the French occupation force that was based in western Germany from 1919. Other Breguet Bre.14s supported the French intervention force in the Russian Civil War after the revolution of October 1917.

A small number of Fiat-powered Bre.14s was built, and 24 Bre.14A.2s powered by the Renault 12FeR (fitted with a Rateau supercharger for improved high-altitude performance) were delivered to the 34e Régiment d'Aviation at Le Bourget in 1921.

The Bre.14 was widely exported, and it played an active role in the French

forces' bloody battles against Syrian and Moroccan insurgents, which lasted through the 1920s – the struggle against the Riff rebels in Morocco was only concluded in 1934. Spain also flew the Bre.14 in violent fighting in its sector of Morocco, maintaining four Bre.14- equipped squadrons in 1922, and supplementing these with 40 more Bre.14s purchased in 1923. By September 1926 some 301 Bre.14A.2s, plus a number of Bre.14B.2s, were in service in French Morocco. They were supplemented by 52 **Bre.14Tbis Sanitaire** aircraft. France had persevered with the air ambulance for front-line casualty evacuation and had built this version of the 'civilianised' **Bre.14Tbis** in some numbers for overseas service.

The US Air Service in France, which in 1918 used the Bre.14 in its day bomber squadrons, also acquired a number of **Bre.14Et.2** trainers. The Bre.14 continued in the training role with the French Aéronautique Militaire on a considerable scale through the 1920s, the last examples being retired from service only in 1932.

Apart from its military exploits, the Bre.14 made a number of outstanding long-distance flights immediately after World War I. In January 1919, for example, Capitaine Coli and Lieutenant Roget made a double crossing of the Mediterranean, covering some 1,000 miles (1609 km) in the process. On 5 April the same year Roget flew from Lyons to Rome and then back to Nice, and Coli and Roget subsequently established a new French long-distance record with a distance of 1,180 miles (1899 km) between Le Bourget and Kenitra in Morocco.

Variants

Bre.14T.2 Salon: making its first flight in 1919, this civil conversion of the Bre.14 retained the rear cockpit for the pilot while the forward fuselage was deepened to provide a two-seat cabin accessed by a door in the starboard side; several of this version were used by the CMA airline
Breguet 14Tbis: this version appeared in 1921, having a much improved cabin with four windows on each side, above which were four portholes in the upper decking; fuel was carried in streamlined tanks; the Lignes Aériennes Latécoére operated over 100 Bre.14s in the early 1920s, most of them Bre.14Tbis machines, It is believed that service use of Bre.14s in floatplane form was restricted to a few Bre.14Tbis ambulances in the colonial territories; five Bre.14Tbis civil floatplanes were used for several years in French Guiana

SPECIFICATION		
Breguet Bre.14A.2		**Dimensions:** (with original
Type: two-seat reconnaissance aircraft		ailerons) wingspan, upper 47 ft 1¼ in (14.36 m) and lower 40 ft 8 in
Powerplant: one Renault 12Fe Vee engine rated at 300 hp (224 kW)		(12.40 m; length 29 ft 1¼ in (8.87 m); height 10 ft 10 in (3.30 m); wing area 511.30 sq ft (47.50 m²)
Performance: maximum speed 109 mph (175 km/h) at 6,560 ft (2000 m); climb to 6,560 ft (2000 m) in 6 minutes 50 seconds; service ceiling 19,685 ft (6000 m); endurance 2 hours 45 minutes		**Armament:** one 0.303-in (7.7-mm) Vickers fixed forward-firing machine-gun in the port side of the forward fuselage and two 0.303-in (7.7-mm) Lewis trainable rearward-firing machine-guns in observer's cockpit, plus a bomb load of up to 88 lb (40 kg)
Weights: empty 2,227 lb (1010 kg); maximum take-off 3,386 lb (1536 kg)		

Breguet Bre.16

Essentially an enlarged version of the Bre.14, the **Bre.16** was a two-seat tactical night bomber in the Bn.2 category. The prototype flew for the first time on 1 June 1918 with the powerplant of one 450-hp (336-kW) Renault 12Jb engine. It was planned to have the type available in large numbers in 1919, but the end of World War I slowed production, which started in 1919 for the delivery of aircraft with the considerably downrated powerplant of one Renault 12Fe engine and redesigned vertical tail surfaces of angular shape.

Examples of the Bre.16 were also flown with the American Liberty 12 unit and a French Panhard unit.

Several batches of **Bre.16Bn.2** warplanes were built.

Breguet Bre.16 (continued)

Most Bre.16s were constructed under licence up to 1923 and the type entered service in 1921, replacing the twin-engined Farman F.50. The Bre.16 proved more efficient than its Farman predecessor, carrying a similar bombload although only single-engined, and remained in service for five years until replaced by the twin-engined Farman Goliath during 1926. It is estimated that at least 200 were in

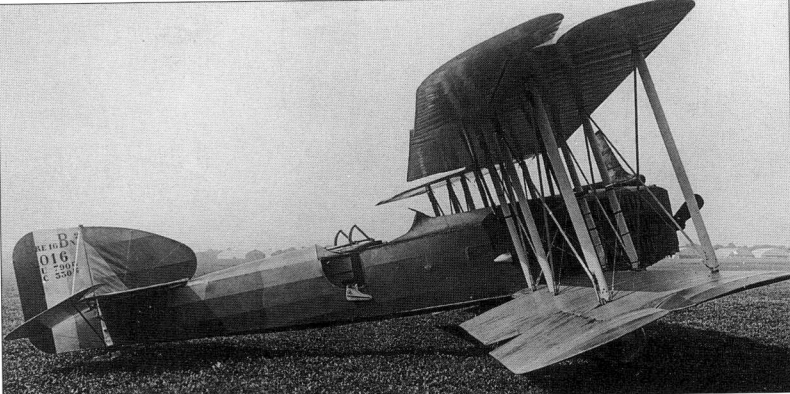

French service, some seeing operations in Syria and Morocco. Many were exported to China and Czechoslovakia.

Of similar basic structure to the Bre.14, the Bre.16 featured a wing cellule of the equal-span type and of three- rather than two-bay layout. In addition, horn-balanced ailerons were fitted to both the upper and lower wings.

SPECIFICATION

Breguet Bre.16Bn.2
Type: two-seat tactical night bomber
Powerplant: one Renault 12Fe piston engine rated at 300 hp (224 kW)
Performance: maximum speed 99 mph (160 km/h) at sea level; cruising speed 87 mph (140 km/h) at optimum altitude; service ceiling 15,090 ft (4600 m); range 559 miles (900 km)
Weights: empty 2,789 lb (1265 kg); maximum take-off 4,850 lb (2200 kg)
Dimensions: wingspan 55 ft 79 in (16.96 m); length 31 ft 4 in (9.55 m); height 10 ft 10¾ in (3.32 m); wing area 812.70 sq ft (75.50 m²)
Armament: one 0.303-in (7.7-mm) Vickers fixed forward-firing machine-gun in the forward fuselage and two 0.303-in (7.7-mm) Lewis trainable rearward-firing machine-guns in the observer's cockpit, plus up to 1,213 lb (550 kg) of bombs

Breguet Bre.17

The prototype of the **Bre.17** two-seater, a fighter in the C.2 category, flew in the summer of 1918. It had been intended to produce at least 1,000 series aircraft in 1919, but following the end of World War I the orders were cut back and the lack of urgency resulted in less than 100 being built during the early 1920s.

The **Bre.17C.2** was a very effective two-seat fighter for its time, and in aerodynamic and structural terms was in effect a scaled-down Bre.14, with greater performance and agility resulting from the type's more compact overall dimensions and more powerful engine. Like the Bre.14, the Bre.17 was an unequal-span biplane of the two-bay type, initially powered by one 420-hp (313-kW) Renault 12K engine. The prototype was tested as a night-fighter, but no further development in that role took place.

Production aircraft were powered by an engine of slightly higher power, and had a revised vertical tail surface.

The Bre.17C.2 flew with a number of French escadrilles, but did not form the sole equipment of any single unit.

For its period, the Bre.17 offered potent armament, which included two synchronised Vickers machine-guns mounted on top of the engine cowling, two Lewis machine-guns carried on a ring mount in the rear cockpit and a third Lewis gun firing through a trap in the fuselage floor.

SPECIFICATION

Breguet Bre.17C.2
Type: two-seat fighter
Powerplant: one Renault 12K1 Vee engine rated at 450 hp (336 kW)
Performance: maximum speed 135 mph (218 km/h) at 6,560 ft (2000 m); climb to 6,560 ft (2000 m) in 5 minutes 45 seconds; service ceiling 24,610 ft (7500 m)
Weights: maximum take-off 4,056 lb (1840 kg)
Dimensions: wingspan 46 ft 10 in (14.28 m); length 26 ft 7 in (8.10 m); height 11 ft 2½ in (3.42 m); wing area 466.09 sq ft (43.30 m²)
Armament: two 0.303-in (7.7-mm) Vickers fixed forward-firing machine-guns in the forward fuselage, two 0.303-in (7.7-mm) Lewis trainable rearward-firing machine-guns in the gunner's cockpit, and one 0.303-in (7.7-mm) Lewis trainable downward/rearward-firing machine-gun in the trap door position in the gunner's cockpit

Breguet Bre.19

Designed as a successor to the Bre.14, the **Breguet Bre.19** was intended for service as either a two-seat day bomber in the B.2 category or as a two-seat reconnaissance aircraft in the A.2 category. The **Bre.19.01** prototype was exhibited at the Paris Salon de l'Aéronautique in November 1921 with an experimental Breguet-Bugatti 16-cylinder engine, but was soon re-engined with a 450-hp (336-kW) Renault 12Kb engine. The Bre.19.01 subsequently made its maiden flight in March 1922.

There followed 11 evaluation aircraft, which were fitted with a variety of engines. Quantity production started in 1923, and by 1927 some 2,000 Bre.19s (divided almost equally between reconnaissance and bomber versions) had been delivered to the French Aviation Militaire.

The Bre.19 had an oval-section fuselage built up on a Dural tube primary structure, and was covered as far as the rear cockpit with Dural sheet and aft of this point with fabric. The fabric-covered biplane wing cellule was of the unequal-span type.

The first version to go into French service was the **Bre.19A.2** reconnaissance variant from the autumn of 1924. The **Bre.19B.2** bomber version first went into service in June 1926.

French-built Bre.19s were powered by 12-cylinder engines of the liquid-cooled type, in the forms of either the Renault 12K or the Lorraine 12D and 12E. While some structural strengthening was found necessary during its early career, the Bre.19 gave outstanding service. It equipped French units involved in hostilities against rebel Druze tribesmen in Syria and the Riff insurgents in Morocco, as well as forming the backbone of metropolitan day bomber and reconnaissance units for many years. Inevitably the type soldiered on into obsolescence, even equipping four night-fighter escadrilles, attempting a role for which it was quite unsuited. The type was finally relegated to reserve duty and training in 1934.

As early as 1923, Breguet embarked on an aggressive export campaign. The Bre.19.01 first prototype was displayed at an international competition organised by the Spanish war ministry, and soon afterwards the first **Bre.19.02** evaluation aircraft was supplied to Yugoslavia. As a result, Yugoslav military aviation took delivery of 400

Wearing the 5e Escadrille emblem, this Bre.19B.2 flew with the Aviation Militaire's 11e Régiment from Metz-Frecaty during 1928.

Variants

Bre.19GR: the Breguet company ensured that the Bre.19 remained in the headlines throughout the 1920s and early 1930s by developing a series of **Grand Raid** (GR) variants. The first was the Bre.19 no. 3, a standard early example powered by a Lorraine-Dietrich 12Db engine; flown by Pelletier d'Oisy and Bésin, and carrying auxiliary fuel tanks, this machine flew from Paris to Shanghai. Bre.19 no. 64, with additional internal fuel tanks, was flown by Lemaitre and Arrachart to capture the world distance record, flying from Etampes to Villa Cisneros in the Spanish Sahara on 3/4 February 1925. A Belgian GR was followed by the conversion of the two Japanese-owned Bre.19s to GR standard; bought by the Asahi Shimbun newspaper group, the second flew from Tokyo to Paris in the summer of 1925. Four more French GRs were built, one being converted to take a 600-hp (447-kW) Hispano-Suiza 12Lb engine; named *Nungesser-Coli*, it was flown around the world between October 1927 and April 1928 by Costes and Le Brix

Bre.19 Bidon: the Bidon (petrol can) variant was a logical development of the GR; built specifically for long-range flights, it incorporated more internal fuel tankage and a number of airframe changes. The first example was bought by Belgium, but the second established a world speed-over-distance record for France when, in May 1929, it covered a distance of 3,107 miles (5000 km) at an average of 116.88 mph (188.1 km/h). Two more Bidons were built by Breguet, one eventually being sold to China. At least one Bidon was built in Spain by CASA

Bre.19 Super Bidon: this final development was built to coax the maximum possible range out of the design, extra tankage being provided in the upper wing and the lengthened fuselage. The first example was built for France and named *Point d'Interrogation* (question mark or simply '?'); after an unsuccessful transatlantic attempt it was re-engined with a Hispano-Suiza 12Lb and flown in two days from Le Bourget to Manchuria, landing on 29 September 1929 and establishing a world straight-line distance record of 4,912 miles (7905 km). In September 1930 the same aircraft, crewed by Costes and Bellonte, achieved the first non-stop flight between Paris and New York. CASA built the only other Super Bidon, which differed from the original in having enclosed crew cockpits and auxiliary fins; it was lost on a flight from Seville to Latin America

Bre.19 seaplane: single examples of a twin-float version appeared, one built by Breguet and the other completed by Nakajima as a temporary conversion for an Imperial Japanese Navy competition

Bre.19ter: developed from the Bidon, this experimental military prototype was powered by a 600-hp (447-kW) Hispano-Suiza 12Lb engine and had elliptical wingtips and a curved vertical tail surface; the type was offered for export in 1928

Bre.19.7: five Yugoslav examples of the Bre.19 were returned to Breguet, which fitted the aircraft with semi-elliptical wingtips, four additional support struts between the fuselage and upper wing, 600-hp (447-kW) Hispano-Suiza 12Nb engines and lengthened their fuselages. They were redelivered to Yugoslavia in 1930; five similar aircraft were delivered to Romania, and all 10 participated in the Petite Entente military aircraft competition. The Yugoslav Bre.19.7 machines doing particularly well. A total of 125 Yugoslav Bre.19.7 warplanes were put into production, though a shortage of Hispano-Suiza engines meant that only 75 had been completed by 1933; a number of these aircraft took part in Yugoslavia's brief resistance to the Germans in the spring of 1941, several later being used by the Croat regime. Turkey ordered 50 Bre.19.7 aircraft in 1933, and these were the last Bre.19s to be built by Breguet

Bre.19.9: a re-engined Yugoslav Bre.19.7 with an 860-hp (641-kW) Hispano-Suiza 12Ybrs engine

Bre.19.10: one-off Yugoslav conversion of a Bre.19.7, with a 720-hp (537-kW) Lorraine 12Hfrs Petrel, and flown in 1935

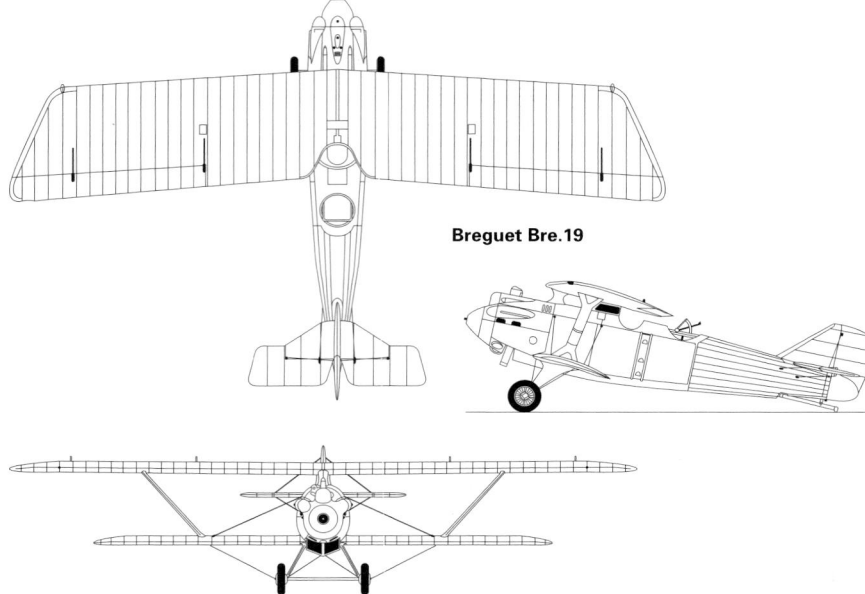

Breguet Bre.19

Bre.19s. The first 150 had Lorraine engines, the next 150 had 500-hp (373-kW) Hispano-Suiza 12Hb or 12Lb engines, and the final 100 had 420-hp (313-kW) Gnome-Rhône 9Ab Jupiter radial engines built under licence in Yugoslavia. When Yugoslavia was invaded in April 1941 the surviving Bre.19s saw limited action, but most were destroyed on the ground. About 40 were subsequently handed over to the puppet Croat regime for use against partisan units.

Spain imported 19 complete aircraft, the CASA company then assembling 26 aircraft from French components before building 177 Bre.19s. Of these, 127 were powered by Lorraine engines built under licence and the other 50 by imported Hispano-Suiza units. The Spanish Bre.19s first saw action against rebel tribes in Morocco, and at the beginning of the Spanish Civil War in 1936 some 135 were still on strength. Although obsolete, the Bre.19 was used by both sides in the war

and was employed largely against troops and ground targets, but also for coastal patrol.

Other foreign purchasers included Romania, Turkey and Poland, the last of whose machines were not withdrawn from service until just before the German invasion in 1939. The Chinese authorities obtained a total of 74 aircraft, which were employed against the Japanese in Manchuria. Surviving aircraft from 30 Bre.19s imported by the Greek government were expended in action against the invading Italians in October 1940. Belgium

bought six Bre.19B.2s in 1924, and then initiated licensed production by the SABCA company. The Bre.19 was also popular in Latin America, where Argentina obtained 25, Bolivia 15, Venezuela 12 and Brazil five. The Bolivian and Paraguayan Bre.19s saw action during the early 1930s.

The British, Italian and Persian governments each purchased two examples of the Bre.19 for technical evaluation. In Japan the Nakajima company also bought two aircraft, but subsequently abandoned plans for licensed production.

SPECIFICATION

Breguet Bre.19A.2
Type: two-seat reconnaissance aircraft
Powerplant: one Lorraine 12Ed W-type engine rated at 450 hp (336 kW)
Performance: maximum speed 133 mph (214 km/h) at sea level; climb to 16,405 ft (5000 m) in 29 minutes 50 seconds; service ceiling 22,640 ft (6901 m); range 497 miles (800 km)
Weights: empty 3,058 lb (1387 kg); maximum take-off 5,511 lb (2500 kg)
Dimensions: wingspan 48 ft 7¾ in (14.83 m); length 31 ft 6¼ in (9.61 m); height 12 ft 1¼ in (3.69 m); wing area 538.21 sq ft (50.00 m²)
Armament: one 0.303-in (7.7-mm) Vickers fixed forward-firing machine-gun in the forward fuselage and two 0.303-in (7.7-mm) Lewis trainable rearward-firing machine-guns in the observer's cockpit, plus up to 1,764 lb (800 kg) of bombs carried in two lower-fuselage weapons bays and on two hardpoints under the lower wing

Breguet Bre.270 and Bre.410

Built to a 1928 French air ministry requirement for a two-seat observation aircraft, the **Bre.270.01** all-metal sesquiplane prototype made its maiden flight on 23 February 1929.

Following early tests, the prototype was returned to the company, where the tail unit was redesigned. Nine further prototypes were completed under the **Bre.270** and **Bre.271** designations, two of these being displayed at the 1930 Paris Salon de l'Aéronautique.

Despite rather poor

performance in overall terms, the Bre.270 received orders for a total of 85 examples during 1930. In 1932, an order was placed for 45 examples of the Bre.271, powered by an engine delivering 150 hp (112 kW) more than the original Hispano-Suiza 12Hb, and capable of lifting an increased load. Several Bre.270s were subsequently modified for VIP liaison duties with a 'glasshouse' canopy covering both cockpits.

In 1932 the original prototype, fitted with a supplementary ventral fuel tank, made a long-distance flight across Africa to Madagascar. Besides small batches of Bre.270s bought by Brazil and Venezuela, 15 examples of the **Bre.273** reconnaissance bomber development were exported to Venezuela and another six to China.

Experimental versions of the basic design included the **Bre.272TOE** fitted with a radial engine and the **Bre.274** with a 760-hp

(567-kW) Gnome-Rhône 14K. Intended as a bomber, the latter was subsequently operated by the French sportswoman Maryse Hilsz, who flew it to victory in the 1936 Coupe Hélène Boucher contest at an average speed of 172 mph (277 km/h).

A series of experimental **Breguet Bre.410** twin-engined biplanes, which shared the same 'chassis' and tail boom construction as the Bre.270 series, met with initial success. They secured an Armée de l'Air order, which intended them for the 'multiplace de combat' role with capability

in the heavy fighter, bomber and reconnaissance tasks. With the appearance of more promising rival designs, however, the order was cancelled.

At the outbreak of World War II, a number of Groupes Aériens d'Observation had Bre.270s on charge; these units included GAO 509, GAO 543 and GAO 547, which lost a number of their wholly obsolete aircraft on reconnaissance patrols across the Rhine before the survivors were finally withdrawn from service at the end of 1939.

Breguet Bre.270 and Bre.410 (continued)

SPECIFICATION

Breguet Bre.270
Type: two-seat observation aircraft
Powerplant: one Hispano-Suiza 12Hb Vee engine rated at 500 hp (373 kW)
Performance: maximum speed 147 mph (236 km/h) at sea level; climb to 19,685 ft (6000 m) in 29 minutes; absolute ceiling 25,920 ft (7900 m); range 621 miles (1000 km)
Weights: empty 3,871 lb (1756 kg); maximum take-off 5,276 lb (2393 kg)

Dimensions: wingspan 55 ft 9¾ in (17.01); length 32 ft ¼ in (9.76 m); height 11 ft 5¾ in (3.55 m); wing area 534.66 sq ft (49.67 m²)
Armament: one 0.303-in (7.7-mm) Vickers fixed forward-firing machine-gun in the forward fuselage and two 0.303-in (7.7-mm) Lewis trainable rearward-firing machine-guns in the observer's cockpit, plus up to 264 lb (120 kg) of bombs carried externally under the lower wing

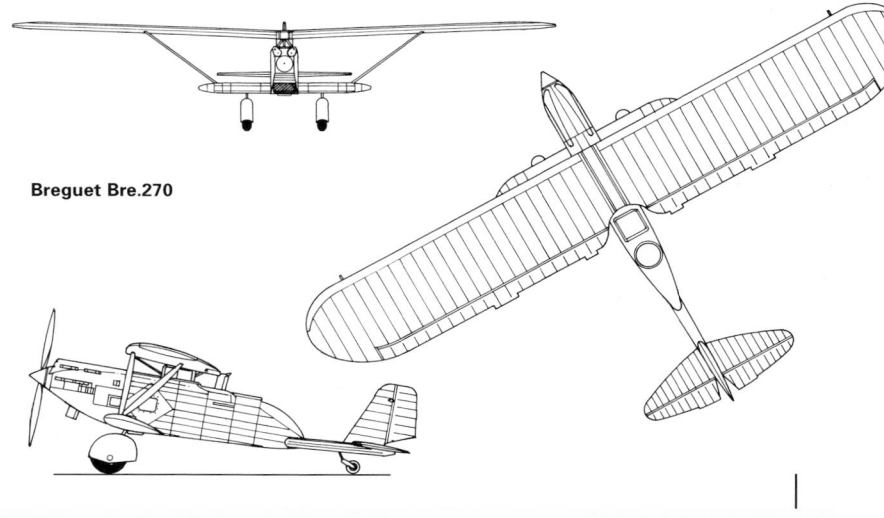

Breguet Bre.270

High-tensile steel replaced aluminium alloys in the Bre.270's structure, and the short fuselage, engine, lower wing and tail boom were all attached to a steel chassis, resulting in a very tough aircraft. The machine was a two-seat sesquiplane.

Variants

Bre.330: two prototypes were built to meet an official requirement of 1928 for a high-altitude reconnaissance machine; built in 1931, the aircraft had an enlarged fuselage and the powerplant of one 650-hp (485-kW) Hispano-Suiza 12Nb engine; the first, redesignated as the **Bre.330.01bis** and crewed by Codes and Robida, made a long-distance flight from Paris to Hanoi in January 1932, while the second made a publicity tour of France and then, redesignated as the **Bre.27S** and named *Joe III*, was flown by Maryse Hilsz to the Far East during 1934, in the process covering some 21,750 miles (35000 km)

Breguet Bre.280T

An unequal-span biplane with cabin accommodation for eight passengers, the **Breguet Bre.280T** was developed from the earlier **Bre.26T** transport. Four examples of the Bre.26T were built, two of them under licence by CASA, for the civil market, with accommodation for six passengers. Two examples of an ambulance version, the **Bre.26TSbis**, were delivered to the French Aviation Militaire.

Although the Bre.280T was generally similar to the Bre.26T, it was notable for its more refined contours, with an enclosed cabin for the two-man crew as well as rounded rather than angular tips to the wings and tailplane.

The Bre.280T first flew in prototype form during the autumn of 1928. The Bre.280T prototype was followed by eight series

aircraft, each powered by one 500-hp (373-kW) Renault 12Jb liquid-cooled engine. From 1929 onwards the aircraft flew with Air-Union on routes connecting Paris with the south of France and Switzerland. Less regularly, they were used on the company's service linking Paris and London. Surviving aircraft were taken over by Air France on its formation in 1933.

SPECIFICATION

Breguet Bre.280T
Type: two-crew passenger transport
Powerplant: one Renault 12Jb engine rated at 500 hp (373 kW)
Performance: maximum speed 137 mph (220 km/h) at optimum altitude; cruising speed 123 mph (198 km/h) at optimum altitude; service ceiling 15,420 ft (4700 m),

range 683 miles (1100 km)
Weights: empty 4,497 lb (2040 kg); maximum take-off 7,319 lb (3320 kg)
Dimensions: wingspan 56 ft 7¼ in (17.25 m); length 39 ft 9¼ in (12.12 m); wing area 601.29 sq ft (55.86 m²)
Payload: six passengers

Variants

Bre.281T: this version was powered by one 450-hp (336-kW) Lorraine-Dietrich 12Ed engine; two examples were built for Air-Union but were soon converted, one as a Bre.280T and the other as a **Bre.284T**
Bre.284T: the prototype of this variant flew shortly after that of the Bre.280T, its major difference being the use of the 580-hp (433-kW) Hispano-Suiza 12Lbrx engine; the Breguet company retained the prototype, but seven production examples of the Bre.284T were sold, five to Air-Union and two to Air-Orient, the latter operating the type on its services in the Far East; like the Bre.280Ts, surviving examples were eventually taken over by Air France

Breguet Bre.390, Bre.392 and Bre.393

Development of the **Breguet Bre.393T** three-engined passenger transport began with the **Bre.390T** prototype, an all-metal sesquiplane which made its first flight in February 1931. However, during a test flight on 3 July 1931, one of the propellers broke away and the machine was completely destroyed in the ensuing crash.

This Bre.393T flew on the Toulouse-Casablanca route with Air France during 1934. Each of the Bre.393T's passengers benefited from the provision of a comfortable armchair beside a large window.

A single example of the **Bre.392T** followed with 300-hp (224-kW) Hispano-Suiza 9Qc radial engines in place of the Bre.390T's 240-hp (179-kW) Gnome-Rhône 5Kd radials, and this machine was completed as a freight carrier. It was followed later in 1933 by the **Bre.393T** prototype,

which introduced a number of improvements. This aircraft was delivered to Air France in July 1934, and was followed by two more examples later in the same year. The remaining three aircraft for Air France were delivered in 1935.

The Bre.393T carried a crew of two and up to 10

passengers. The type flew regular routes between Toulouse and Casablanca, the Mediterranean leg of the route to South America, and later on the Natal-Buenos Aires stage in Brazil. The type's final employment was on European routes radiating from Paris.

SPECIFICATION

Breguet Bre.393T
Type: two-crew passenger transport
Powerplant: three Gnome-Rhône 7Kd Titan Major radial engines each rated at 350 hp (261 kW)
Performance: maximum speed 155 mph (249 km/h) at optimum altitude; cruising speed 146 mph (235 km/h) at optimum altitude; service ceiling 19,195 ft (5850 m); range 606 miles (975 km)
Weights: empty 8,743 lb (3966 kg); maximum take-off 13,228 lb (6000 kg)
Dimensions: wingspan 67 ft 11¼ in (20.71 m); length 48 ft 5 in (14.76 m); wing area 715.39 sq ft (66.46 m²)
Payload: 10 passengers

Breguet Bre.520 and Bre.521 Bizerte

In 1931 Breguet obtained a licence from Short Brothers of the UK for construction of the Calcutta biplane flying-boat. The company subsequently responded to a 1932 Aéronautique Maritime requirement for a long-range flying-boat for the maritime reconnaissance role, with its **Bre.520** proposal based on the design of the Calcutta. The **Breguet Bre.521 Bizerte**, as the flying-boat was to be designated in its definitive form, was based on an all-metal structure with stabilising floats strut-mounted beneath the lower wing, a strut-braced tail unit, and a powerplant of three engines strut-mounted between the upper and lower wings. The powerplant of the **Bre.521.01** prototype, which flew for the first time on 11 September 1933, comprised three

Flying with the Luftwaffe's 1. Seenotstaffel, this Bizerte was based at Brest-Hourtin during the winter of 1943-44.

uncowled 845-hp (630-kW) Gnome-Rhône 14Kdrs radial engines. The type's official trials began in

January 1934, by which time the revised engines had been enclosed in NACA-type cowlings. The French navy ordered three pre-production examples of the Bre.521 before the trials had been completed, and the first of these flew during 1935.

The second of the pre-production 'boats introduced a number of modifications which became standard on subsequent aircraft. These changes included deletion of the open bow gun position, a forward extension of the cockpit canopy, the provision of two new gun positions in blisters on the hull sides and a new tail position.

Deliveries of production 'boats began in 1935 and

continued at a steady pace into 1940, by which time 31 had been built, including the prototype. By October 1939, five squadrons were equipped with the type. Only two of these

squadrons survived to serve with the Vichy French naval air arm (four Bizertes going on to be operated by the Luftwaffe), the other units being disbanded in June 1940.

Variants

Bre.522: one Bre.521 re-engined with three 1,000-hp (746-kW) Hispano-Suiza 14AA radial engines
Bre.530 Saigon: civil passenger version of the Bizerte with three 785-hp (488-kW) Hispano-Suiza 12Ybr Vee engines; the pilot and co-pilot were seated under a raised canopy, and three cabins provided accommodation for 11 second-class, six first-class and three de luxe-class passengers. Only two Bre.530s were built and went into service on Air France's Marseilles-Ajaccio-Tunis route at the beginning of 1935

SPECIFICATION

Breguet Bre.521 Bizerte
Type: eight-seat long-range maritime reconnaissance flying boat
Powerplant: three Gnome-Rhône 14Kirs or 14N-11 radial engines each rated at 900 hp (671 kW)
Performance: maximum speed 152 mph (245 km/h) at 3,280 ft (1000 m); cruising speed 124 mph (200 km/h) at optimum altitude; climb to 6,560 ft (2000 m) in 8 minutes 46 seconds; service ceiling 19,685 ft (6000 m); range 1,864 miles (3000 km)
Weights: empty 20,878 lb (9470 kg); maximum take-off 36,597 lb (16600 kg)
Dimensions: wingspan 115 ft 4 in (35.15 m); length 67 ft 3 in (20.50 m); height 24 ft 5¼ in (7.45 m); wing area 1,750.27 sq ft (162.60 m²)
Armament: two 0.295-in (7.5-mm) Darne trainable machine-guns in each of the port and starboard dorsal positions, and one 0.295-in (7.5-mm) Darne trainable rearward-firing machine-gun in the tail position, plus up to 661 lb (300 kg) of bombs carried externally under the lower wing

Breguet Bre.690 series

In 1934 the French air ministry issued a requirement for a three-seat heavy fighter of twin-engined layout. Several manufacturers submitted design proposals to meet this requirement, the Potez 630 winning the contest and entering production. Breguet instead decided to build an aircraft that was both heavier and more powerfully engined, believing that its design would form the basis of a truly effective multi-role warplane. Design of the **Breguet Bre.690** began in 1935. The prototype was not completed until 1937, however, and with priority supply of Hispano-Suiza engines going to the Potez 630, it was not until

23 March 1938 that the **Bre.690.01** prototype flew for the first time with the powerplant of two 680-hp (507-kW) Hispano-Suiza 14AB-02/03 counter-rotating radial engines. Delivered for official trials in summer 1938, the Bre.690 was found to have a performance superior to that of the Potez 630, but late in August was returned to Breguet for modification of the landing gear.

During the year preceding the first flight of the Bre.690, the French air ministry had been giving considerable thought to the development of a two-seat attack bomber. The early factory trials of the Bre.690 seemed to crystallise official thinking with the result that, even before the proto-

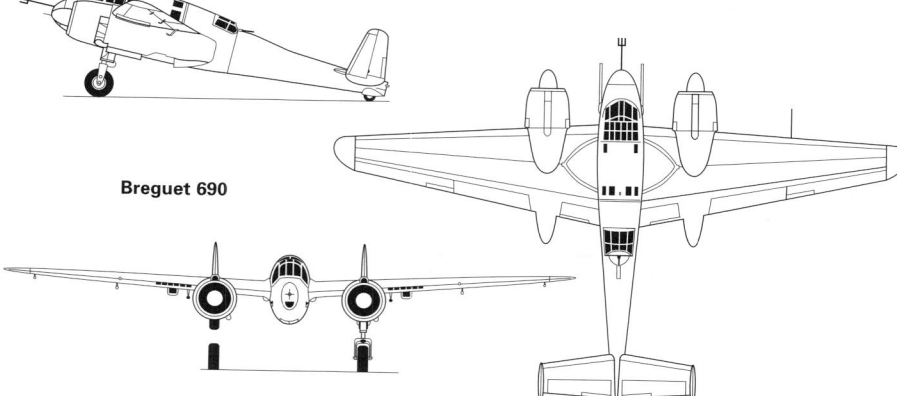

Breguet 690

type had begun testing, Breguet had received a contract for 100 examples in a form revised for the attack role. The result was the **Bre.691**, a mid-wing cantilever monoplane of all-

metal construction. To the rear of the wing, the fuselage tapered sharply to a tail unit which had twin endplate vertical surfaces. The landing gear was of the tailwheel type with

retractable main units and the prototype, which made its maiden flight on 22 March 1939, was powered by two 700-hp (522-kW) Hispano-Suiza 14AB-10/11 radial engines.

Breguet 690 series (continued)

The Bre.690's navigator position was deleted in the Bre.691 to provide a bomb bay for 882 lb (400 kg) of bombs, and considerable thought was given to the provision of gun armament which could be used for both the air-to-air and air-to-ground tasks.

The first production example of the **Bre.691AB.2** made its initial flight on 15 May 1939, and deliveries to GBA I/54 began in October 1939. More extensive experience with the Bre.691 revealed its Hispano-Suiza engines to be unreliable, leading to the modification of a production aircraft to accept two Gnome-Rhône 14M-6/7 engines. First flown on 25 October 1939 as the **Bre.693.01**, this version became the major production version of the Bre.690 series. The Gnome-Rhône engines were installed from the 79th airframe on the production line, and the 234 examples of the **Bre.693AB.2** were virtually identical in all other respects to the earlier production version. Late production aircraft, however, had two additional 0.295-in (7.5-mm) fixed rearward-firing machine-guns, one installed in the tail of each engine nacelle to improve rear defence.

Foreign interest in the Bre.690 series was cut short by the German invasion of France and the single **Bre.694.01** prototype, intended as the precursor first of a three-seat tactical

reconnaissance type and later a two/three-seat reconnaissance bomber, and which had appealed to Belgium and Sweden respectively, was delivered to the Aéronavale on 1 June 1940. The Bre.694.01 was generally similar to the original Bre.690, with the navigator's compartment restored, and was powered by two 710-hp (529-kW) Gnome-Rhône 14M-4/5 engines.

The final production version was the **Bre.695**, which was virtually identical to the Bre.693 except for a change in powerplant. This resulted from a French government policy designed to ensure that, in the event of the nation's engine-building factories being damaged by enemy action, it would be possible to introduce foreign-manufactured engines on certain production lines. The subsequent marriage of the Bre.693 airframe and the 825-hp (615-kW) Pratt & Whitney R-1535-SB4G Twin Wasp Junior radial engine was more difficult than had been anticipated. The **Bre.695.01** prototype flew for the first time in early

1940, however, and the first example of the **Bre.695AB.2** production version followed on 23 April 1940.

Two more prototypes were developed, although neither appeared in production form. Making its maiden flight on 3 November 1939, the first of these was the **Bre.696.01** two-seat light bomber. This was little changed from the Bre.693 from which it was derived except for some slight changes in gun armament and a slightly enlarged bomb bay. The second of these final prototypes was the **Bre.697.01**, which was intended as the basis of a two-seat heavily armed 'destroyer' which would have been known as the **Bre.700** in production form. The prototype first flew on 19 October 1939 with the powerplant of two 1,070-hp (798-kW) Gnome-Rhône 14N-48/49 radial engines providing a high rate of climb. During its trials the Bre.697.01 recorded a maximum speed of 354 mph (570 km/h). The machine was later destroyed to prevent its capture by the Germans.

Pratt & Whitney-powered Breguet Bre.695AB.2 of the 1ᵉ Escadrille, GBA I/51, of l'Armée de l'Air de l'Armistice, was based at Lézignan-Corbières in June 1942 and flew under German control.

The initial operational deployment of the Bre.693 on 12 May 1940, when the type was used in attacks on German columns advancing through Belgium, was little short of disastrous, with 10 out of the 11 aircraft destroyed in action or written off on landing. Subsequent use proved the type effective if given adequate fighter escort, or if a low-level approach was

made to the target. Nevertheless, by 25 June, almost half of the 106 Bre.693s which had been delivered had been destroyed. After the Franco-German armistice, two groupes continued to operate with the Bre.693 and Bre.695, but in November 1942 the aircraft were seized by the Germans and transferred to Italy for use as trainers.

SPECIFICATION

Breguet Bre.693AB.2
Type: two-seat attack bomber
Powerplant: two Gnome-Rhône 14M-6/7 radial engines each rated at 700 hp (522 kW)
Performance: maximum speed 304 mph (490 km/h) at 16,405 ft (5000 m); cruising speed 248 mph (400 km/h) at 13,125 ft (4000 m); climb to 13,125 ft (4000 m) in 7 minutes 12 seconds; range 839 miles (1350 km)
Weights: empty 6,636 lb (3010 kg); maximum take-off 10,803 lb (4900 kg)
Dimensions: wingspan 50 ft 5 in (15.37 m); length 31 ft 8¾ in (9.67 m); height 10 ft 5¾ in (3.19 m); wing area 314.32 sq ft

(29.20 m²)
Armament: one 20-mm Hispano-Suiza forward-firing cannon and two 0.295-in (7.5-mm) MAC 1934 forward-firing machine-guns in the nose, one 0.295-in (7.5-mm) MAC 1934 trainable rearward-firing machine-gun in the rear cockpit, one 0.295-in (7.5-mm) MAC 1934 fixed obliquely rearward/downward-firing machine-gun in the ventral position and (late aircraft) one 0.295-in (7.5-mm) MAC 1934 fixed rearward-firing machine-gun in the rear of each engine nacelle, plus up to 882 lb (400 kg) of bombs carried internally in the lower fuselage

Breguet Bre.730, Br.730 and Br.731

To meet a French Admiralty requirement of 1935 for a long-range maritime reconnaissance flying-boat, Breguet proposed the **Bre.710** as a large 'boat of gull-wing configuration. A change in the requirement led to considerable redesign, and construction of a prototype of the resulting **Bre.730** was initiated in

late 1936. The Bre.730 was of high-wing cantilever monoplane configuration, the wing mounting four radial piston engines in leading-edge nacelles and carrying beneath it a large fixed stabilising float on each side.

The **Breguet Bre.730.01** first prototype made its maiden flight on 4 April

1938, but just over three months later, in July, the hull was damaged severely in a shallow-water landing. Nevertheless, testing up to that time had been completely satisfactory and production of hulls had begun: four were virtually complete by the time of the French capitulation to Germany on 25 June 1940. Construction was subsequently resumed by the Vichy government, the Bre.730.1 combining the first of the four production hulls and the salvaged wing of the prototype, and this 'boat and three of about a dozen production hulls survived an Allied air attack in April 1944. It was not until the Germans had been expelled from France that, in December 1944, flight trials of the **Bre.730 No.1** finally began under the revised designation **Br.730 No.1**, Breguet's

Both Br.731 aircraft were delivered to Escadrille 33S. They were given the names Altair and Bellatrix during their brief period of service.

designation prefix having changed from Bre. to Br. in 1942. One of the three remaining hulls was completed to the same configuration, while the other two were completed to the Br.731 standard with a refined nose structure, modified stabilising

floats and the powerplant of four 1,350-hp (1007-kW) Gnome-Rhône 14R-200/201 radial engines. The 'boats saw a comparatively short period of service before being scrapped, and the Br.730.1 crashed in December 1948.

SPECIFICATION

Breguet Br.730.1
Type: 10-seat long-range maritime reconnaissance and transport flying boat
Powerplant: four Gnome-Rhône 14N-44/45 radial engines each rated at 1,120 hp (835 kW)
Performance: maximum speed 205 mph (330 km/h) at 4,920 ft (1500 m); cruising speed 143 mph (230 km/h) at optimum altitude; climb to 9,845 ft (3000 m) in 9 minutes; range 4,287 miles (6900 km); endurance 30 hours
Weights: empty 35,494 lb

(16100 kg); maximum take-off 62,831 lb (28500 kg)
Dimensions: wingspan 132 ft 5 in (40.35 m); length 79 ft 11½ in (24.35 m); height 28 ft 2⅔ in (8.60 m); wing area 1,862.22 sq ft (173.00 m²)
Armament: (proposed) one 25-mm Hispano-Suiza trainable cannon in the dorsal turret and one 0.295-in (7.5-mm) Darne trainable machine-guns in each of four hull positions, plus four 441-lb (200-kg) bombs
Payload: up to 19,180 lb (8700 kg) of freight

Breguet Br.761 Deux Ponts, Br.763 and Br.765 Sahara

The design of the **Breguet Br.761 Deux Ponts** (two decks) two-deck utility transport began in 1944, the resulting prototype being powered by four 1,580-hp (1178-kW) SNECMA-built Gnome-Rhône 14R radial engines and making its maiden flight on 15 February 1949. A mid-wing cantilever monoplane of all-metal construction, the Br.761 prototype featured a tailplane and elevator set high on the fuselage, with twin fins and rudders inset from the tips. Three **Br.761S** pre-production aircraft followed, with the powerplant of four 2,020-hp (1506-kW) Pratt &

Six ex-Air France Br.763s were operated by l'Armée de l'Air's 64e Escadre de Transport, together with the original three Br.761S pre-production aircraft and four Br.765 Sahara military transports.

Whitney R-2800-B31 Double Wasp radial engines, modified wingtips and the introduction of a third fin on the centreline. All four of these early Br.761s were laid out for operation by a crew of four. One of the Br.761S pre-production aircraft was leased for a time to Air Algérie, but in the mid-1950s all three were used by the Armée de l'Air for service trials.

Air France had shown interest in the Br.761, and in 1951 ordered 12 examples of an improved version known by the company designation **Br.763**. These introduced a revised wing, a flight deck rearranged for operation by a crew of three and an uprated powerplant. The first of these machines made its initial flight on 20 July

1951, and the type entered service from August 1952 under the class name *Provence*. As then operated by Air France, the Br.763 had accommodation for 59 and 48 passengers on the upper and lower decks respectively, but a maximum of 135 could be carried in a high-density seating arrangement. Alternative layouts could allow the type to operate in the mixed passenger/cargo, all-cargo, or air ferry roles.

During 1964 Air France transferred six of its Br.763s to the Armée de l'Air, these being given the military name **Sahara**. In

addition, four military-specific **Br.765 Sahara** transports were built, with accommodation for up to 146 fully-equipped troops, 85 litters plus medical attendants, or freight, vehicles and heavy equipment. They provided the Armée de l'Air with a valuable Escadre transport capability, and it was not until late 1972 that the last of them was retired from service. Air France also continued to operate its six Br.763s, but in a freighter rather than passenger role under the name **Universal**. These aircraft remained in service until 1971.

Breguet Bre.790 Nautilus

The first of two prototypes of this attractive three-seat flying-boat made its maiden flight in the summer of 1939. Flight tests proved the overall efficiency of its design, resulting in the placement of a contract for 75 production examples. This was subsequently reduced to just 45, but none of these had been built before French resistance to the German invasion came to an end in June 1940.

Power for the Bre.790 was provided by a single nacelle-mounted Hispano-Suiza engine, which was mounted above the hull on two sets of N-type struts and drove a pusher propeller.

Breguet Br.890H Mercure, Br.891 Mars and Br.892R Mercure

Foreseeing in 1948 that there could be considerable demand for a medium-capacity transport for the civil and military roles, Breguet began design of the **Br.890**. Intended primarily for the carriage of freight, one variant was nonetheless proposed for use in a convertible cargo/passenger role.

The basic prototype was the **Breguet Br.890H Mercure**, a high-wing cantilever monoplane of all-

metal construction with the exception of fabric-covered control surfaces on the tail unit. Power was provided by two 2,000-hp (1491-kW) Bristol Hercules 739 radial engines installed in nacelles on the leading edges of the wing. An advanced feature of the type was the provision of a swing-tail to allow easy access for vehicles via a loading ramp. Mobile lifting gear mounted on overhead rails was designed for

direct lifting from trucks either at the rear or through a side-loading door.

The **Br.891R Mars** was the military development of the above, retaining the folding tail and incorporating tip-up seats for 20 paratroops, parachute doors on each side of the fuselage, a floor chute for container-dropping, provision for the carriage of up to 28 stretchers, and a glider tow hook. Power

was provided by two 1,600-hp (1193-kW) Gnome-Rhône 14R-200 radial engines.

The **Br.892R Mercure** was a convertible cargo/passenger version of the Br.890H with four engines, a large cargo door to star-

board and two passenger doors on the port side of the fuselage, and provision for the carriage of up to 40 passengers on easily removable seats. Only a single prototype of each version was built and no production orders resulted.

The hydraulically-retractable tricycle landing gear of the Br.890 series had very stalky main units as a result of the high-wing configuration. The Br.890H Mercure is illustrated.

Breguet Br.940 Intégral and Br.941

Becoming convinced during the early 1950s that the future of air transport held an important niche for STOL aircraft, Breguet began work on a technology demonstrator under the designation **Br.940 Intégral** (whole, or entire). The resulting machine was of the configuration that was becoming increasingly standardised for utility transports and was of light alloy stressed-skin construction.

The key to the Br.940's STOL capability was the wing and powerplant. The wing was a low-aspect-ratio unit and the whole of its trailing edge was hinged to provide triple-slotted inboard flaps and double-slotted outboard flaps that created what was in effect a variable-camber wing. The whole of the wing and this powerful trailing-edge arrangement was 'blown' by the air streaming back

from the four slow-turning three-bladed propellers, which were driven by the four engines in nacelles placed across virtually the full span of the leading edge. The engines' gearboxes were interconnected by transverse shafts to ensure the synchronisation of the propellers (the inner and outer pairs turning clockwise and anti-clockwise respectively) and the continued rotation of all four propellers in the case of an engine failure.

The Br.940 made its first flight on 21 May 1958, and highly successful trials followed. In the course of these trials the Br.940 revealed the ability to take-off over a 50-ft (15-m) obstacle in only 625 ft (190 m) and to land over an obstacle of the same height in a mere 525 ft (160 m), while the landing speed was only 46 mph (75 km/h). The technical

As a military transport, the Br.941 incorporated retractable tricycle landing gear, with main units that retracted into fairings on each side of the fuselage, leaving the cabin unobstructed.

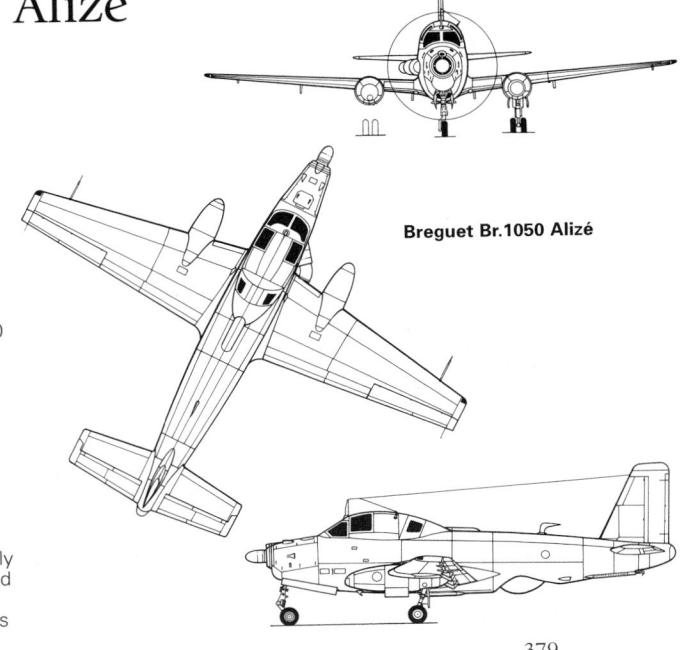

success of the Br.940 paved the way for the succeeding **Br.941**.

Using the systems and techniques proven by the Br.940, Breguet then designed a somewhat larger and considerably more refined STOL transport that it hoped would attract both civil and military orders.

Breguet's proposal appealed to the French air ministry, and a prototype was ordered on 22 February 1960. The powerplant comprised four Turboméca Turmo IIID turboprop engines, each rated at 1,200 shp (895 kW) and driving a slow-turning propeller of large diameter, in a similar arrangement to that of the Br.940.

The prototype flew for the first time on 1 June 1961 and subsequent testing resulted in a French government contract for the supply of four production transports under the designation **Br.941S**. These aircraft differed from the prototype in having more

The Intégral's fuselage was of rectangular section with a two-man flight deck in the nose, and a large cabin accessed by a rear ramp/door arrangement.

powerful Turmo engines, a longer nose to permit the installation of a large radome and modification of the rear cargo door to allow for the airdrop of heavy loads. Operated by a crew of two, these aircraft could provide accommodation for up to 57 civil passengers, or 40 fully-equipped troops, or 24 litters. The first Br.941S made its initial flight on 19 April 1967, and testing proved that, with an all-up weight of 48,502 lb (22000 kg), the Br.941S could become airborne in

only 607 ft (185 m). All four of the production aircraft entered service with the Armée de l'Air, but no additional examples were built. There had been hopes that, with assistance from the McDonnell Aircraft Corporation, orders might be generated in the USA, but despite a successful demonstration tour in America, no production orders were received for this unpressurised transport or its proposed **Breguet Br.942** pressurised derivative.

SPECIFICATION	
Breguet Br.941S **Type:** two/three-crew STOL transport **Powerplant:** four Turboméca Turmo IIID3 turboprop engines each rated at 1,500 shp (1119 kW) **Performance:** maximum speed 280 mph (450 km/h) at sea level; cruising speed 249 mph (400 km/h) at 9,845 ft (3000 m); service ceiling 31,170 ft (9500 m); range 621 miles (1000 km) with maximum payload	**Weights:** empty 32,408 lb (14700 kg); maximum take-off 58,422 lb (26500 kg) **Dimensions:** wingspan 76 ft 8½ in (23.40 m); length 77 ft 11 in (23.75 m); height 31 ft 8 in (9.65 m); wing area 902.05 sq ft (83.80 m²) **Payload:** see above within the context of a 22,046-lb (10000-kg) maximum payload weight

Breguet Br.960 Vultur and Br.1050 Alizé

At a comparatively early stage of turbine engine development, before the introduction of more economical by-pass or ducted fan engines, a mixed powerplant concept was selected by a number of designers of military aircraft. Such a system offered economical operation by the turboprop for long-range cruise, with the availability of a supplementary turbojet for take-off with heavy weaponloads or for high speed in combat. Breguet had chosen such a powerplant for the **Br.960 Vultur** naval strike aircraft, with an Armstrong Siddeley Mamba turboprop in the nose and a Hispano-Suiza Nene turbojet in the rear fuselage.

Experience with the Vultur, first flown on 3 August 1951, led the

French navy to abandon the idea of such a powerplant for a strike aircraft. Instead, Breguet was contracted to develop a three-seat carrier-based anti-submarine aircraft from the Vultur. The second prototype was duly modified to serve as an aerodynamic test vehicle for the new design, the 980-shp (731-kW) Mamba in the nose being replaced by an uprated 1,650-shp (1230-kW) Mamba, the turbojet engine in the rear fuselage being removed to make room for a large retractable 'dustbin' radome, and dummy streamlined nacelles being mounted beneath the monoplane wings. In a production version these nacelles would serve to house the main landing gear units and sonobuoy equipment. By the time

this aircraft had been flown and tested, Breguet had received an order for two full prototypes and three pre-production aircraft, these being designated **Br.1050** and named **Alizé** (trade wind). The first prototype made its maiden flight on 6 October 1956, and the first production example was handed over officially on 29 May 1959.

As finalised, the Br.1050 was a cantilever low-wing monoplane with hydraulically-folding outer wing panels, retractable tricycle undercarriage, arrester gear for carrier operation, and power provided by a Rolls-Royce Dart turboprop. The single-seat accommodation of the Vultur had been extensively modified to seat a pilot and two radar operators, and an underfuselage weapons

Breguet Br.1050 Alizé

379

In September 1952, the second prototype Vultur was built with more powerful Mamba ASMa.3 and Nene Mk 104 engines.

bay housed a torpedo or depth charges, with stores also being carried on underwing racks. Production totalled 75 for the French navy, the type initially equipping Flottilles 4F and 9F.

One of the most elderly combat aircraft regularly operating from aircraft-carrier decks in 1999, the Alizé is expected to serve with the Aéronavale beyond the year 2000.

Service use in France

has been reduced from a peak of three flottilles to one, 6F, for use in the anti-submarine role from the aircraft-carrier *Foch*. An upgrade programme initiated in 1980 introduced Thomson-CSF Iguane radar in the ventral radome, Omega Equinox navigation system, new communications equipment and ESM in the noses of the underwing stores panniers. This added 15 years to the expected service life, but a further modification programme for 24 surviving aircraft began in 1990 to introduce datalink, better decoy capability and other improvements to give a further service life extension. A few Alizés were flown by Escadrille 59E at Hyères for training and SAR, and with 10S at

St Raphael on miscella-neous test tasks.

With the Indian navy, an original 12 Alizés (supple-mented by later purchase of about a dozen ex-Aéronavale aircraft) served with INAS 310 'Cobras' squadron from the

Vikrant. The addition of ski-ramps to that carrier forced the remaining five Alizés ashore in 1987; a dwindling number continued in service until late 1992 from Dabolin, when the last example was withdrawn from service.

SPECIFICATION	
Breguet (Dassault Aviation Br.1050 Alizé) **Type:** three-seat, carrierborne ASW aircraft **Powerplant:** one Rolls-Royce Dart RDa.7 Mk 21 rated at 1,975 ehp (1473 ekW) **Performance:** maximum level speed 'clean' at 9,845 ft (3000 m) 323 mph (520 km/h); cruising speed at optimum altitude 230 mph (370 km/h); maximum rate of climb at sea level 1,380 ft (420 m) per minute; service ceiling more than 20,505 ft (6250 m); range 1,553 miles (2500 km) with standard fuel	**Weights:** empty 12,566 lb (5700 kg); maximum take-off 18,078 lb (8200 kg) **Dimensions:** wingspan 51 ft 2 in (15.60 m); length length 45 ft 6 in (13.86 m); height height 16 ft 4¾ in (5.00 m); wing area 387.51 sq ft (36.00 m²) **Armament:** underfuselage weapons bay accommodating one torpedo or three 353-lb (160-kg) depth charges; racks under inner wings for two 353-lb (160-kg) or 386-lb (175-kg) depth charges; racks beneath outer wings for six 5-in (127-mm) rockets or two AS12 ASMs

Breguet Br.1001 Taon and Br.1100

SPECIFICATION	
Breguet Br.1001 Taon **Type:** single-seat light attack fighter **Powerplant:** one Bristol Orpheus BOr.3 turbojet engine rated at 4,850 lb st (21.57 kN) **Performance:** maximum speed 742 mph (1194 km/h) at sea level **Weights:** normal take-off 11,023 lb (5000 kg) **Dimensions:** wingspan 22 ft 3¾ in (6.80 m); length 38 ft 3¾ in (3.70 m); height 12 ft 1¾ in (3.70 m); wing area 158.23 sq ft	(14.70 m²) **Armament:** (proposed) four 0.5-in (12.7-mm) Colt-Browning fixed forward-firing machine-guns in the forward fuselage, and up to 2,000 lb (907 kg) of disposable stores carried on four underwing hardpoints and generally comprising two or four 500-lb (227-kg) bombs, or two Nord 5110 (AS20) ASMs, or two Matra Type 116C multiple launchers each carrying 19 2.68-in (68-mm) unguided air-to-surface rockets

In response to a NATO requirement for a single-seat lightweight attack fighter suitable for operation from semi-prepared and even unprepared front-line airstrips, Breguet designed a small mid-wing mono-plane with swept flying surfaces. Retractable tricy-cle landing gear was provided, this being designed especially for operation on unprepared strips. The fuselage incorpo-rated some area ruling, accommodated the pilot on an ejection seat in an

enclosed cockpit and housed one Bristol Orpheus BOr.3 turbojet. In competi-tion with other proposals, the **Breguet Br.1001 Taon** (gadfly, and also an anagram of NATO) design won an order for three prototypes, the first of these making its maiden flight on 26 July 1957 as the **Br.1001.01**.

The **Br.1001.02** second prototype incorporated minor aerodynamic improve-ments and had a slightly lengthened fuselage. To enhance the type's high-speed performance, improved area ruling was provided by the introduction of aerodynamic bulges at the wingroots, these serv-ing also to house additional fuel. In this configuration the Br.1001.02 set an inter-

Variants

Br.1002: designation applied to a proposed missile-carrying interceptor version of the Taon
Br.1003: designation allocated for the production version of the Taon, of which none was built; it was planned that the Br.1003 would have a fully area-ruled fuselage and the powerplant of one Orpheus BOr.12 turbojet rated at 8,170 lb st (36.34 kN) with afterburning

national speed record for a 1000-km (621-mile) closed circuit, attaining a speed of 1046.65 km/h (650.36 mph) at 7620 m (25,000 ft) on 25 April 1958. Three months later, on 23 July, the Taon raised this figure again for the same record to 1075 km/h (667.98 mph). Despite this impressive high-speed performance, development was discontinued as the Fiat G.91 had been selected as winner of the competi-tion, and only two of the planned three prototypes were built.

Modelled broadly on the Br.1001, the **Br.1100** in fact preceded the Taon into the air as the prototype of a single-seat ground-attack and light tactical fighter. The completion of the latter had been delayed to allow the incorporation of area ruling, then only recently discov-ered, in its fuselage. Making

its maiden flight on 31 March 1957, the Br.1100 had been designed to meet a French air ministry require-ment demanding an armament fit including an internal pack of 15 2.68-in (68-mm) Brandt SNEB Type 22 rockets or two 30-mm DEFA cannon, and a power-plant based on two small turbojets such as the SNECMA R.105 Vesta, Hispano-Suiza R.800 or Turboméca Gabizo. Breguet selected the last in a form offering 2,668 lb st (11.87 kN) dry and 3,307 lb st (14.71 kN) with afterburning. The French air ministry ordered three prototypes, the third of them to be completed to a navalised standard, but only one machine was flown, the second and third being cancelled even though the second was almost complete.

Although it offered fine low-altitude performance, the Taon disappointed in both its short take-off and range capabilities.

Brewster B-38 (SBA and Naval Aircraft Factory SBN)

The Brewster Aeronautical Corporation was founded in the early 1930s, and for the first years of its existence concentrated on the manu-facture of components under subcontract to other manufacturers. It was not until 1934 that the company became involved in the construction of its first aircraft, a two-seat scout-bomber required by

the USN for service aboard the carriers USS *Enterprise* and USS *Yorktown*, which were scheduled for launch in 1936. Known to the manufacturer as the **Brewster B-38**, the sole **XSBA-1** prototype emerged as a mid-wing cantilever monoplane of all-metal construction except for its fabric-covered control surfaces.

The XSBA-1 flew for the first time on 15 April 1936, and flight testing indicated that more power was necessary to provide satis-factory performance. In 1937, therefore, an XR-1820-22 engine was installed, and after further evaluation of the prototype in this revised form the Navy ordered this improved **B-138** type into production.

At that time, however, Brewster had inadequate production facilities and it was therefore decided that the 30 aircraft order would be completed by the Naval Aircraft Factory (NAF).

The Brewster-designed scout/bomber built by the NAF was given the revised designation **Naval Aircraft Factory SBN-1** and deliver-ies extended from

November 1940 to March 1942. By that time more advanced designs were becoming available, and production of the SBN came to an end. The SBNs were used by VB-3 when they first entered service and most were employed for training at a later date. VT-8 used the SBN-I for training on board the USS *Hornet*.

Brewster B-38 (SBA and Naval Aircraft Factory SBN) (cont.)

SPECIFICATION

Brewster/NAF SBN-1

Type: two-seat carrierborne scout/bomber and trainer
Powerplant: one Wright XR-1820-22 Cyclone radial piston engine rated at 950 hp (708 kW)
Performance: maximum speed 254 mph (409 km/h) at 15,200 ft (4635 m); cruising speed 117 mph (188 km/h) at optimum altitude; service ceiling 28,300 ft (8625 m); range 1,015 miles (1633 km) with a 500-lb (227-kg) bombload
Weights: empty 4,503 lb

(2042 kg); maximum take-off 6,759 lb (3066 kg)
Dimensions: wingspan 39 ft (11.89 m); length 27 ft 8 in (8.43 m); height 12 ft 5 in (3.78 m); wing area 259.00 sq ft (24.06 m²)
Armament: one 0.5-in (12.7-mm) Browning fixed forward-firing machine-gun and one 0.3-in (7.62-mm) Browning trainable rearward-firing machine-gun in the rear cockpit, plus up to 500 lb (227 kg) of bombs carried internally

Brewster incorporated trailing-edge flaps and a lower fuselage weapons bay into its B-38 design. The former helped to simplify carrierborne operation by increasing lift at low speeds.

Brewster B-39 (F2A and Buffalo)

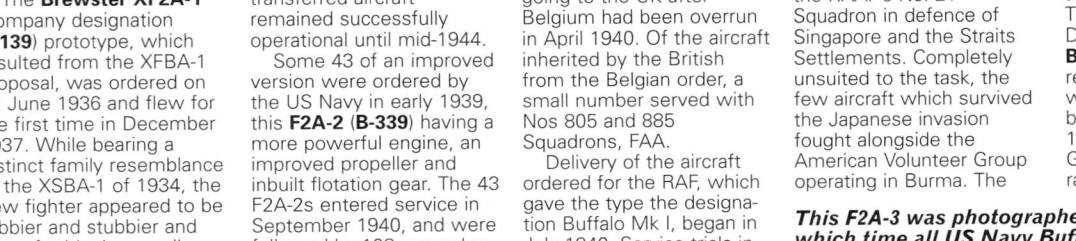

The first monoplane fighter to equip a USN squadron, the **Brewster B-39 Buffalo** originated from a requirement of 1936 for a new generation of carrier-based fighters. In requesting proposals from US manufacturers for such an aircraft, the US Navy indicated requirements which included a monoplane configuration, wing flaps, arrester gear, retractable landing gear and an enclosed cockpit.

Proposals were received from Brewster, whose design was allocated the designation **XFBA-1**, Grumman (XF4F-1) and Seversky (XFN-1), but of these the only significant aircraft in the long term was the Grumman design which became the F4F Wildcat.

The **Brewster XF2A-1** (company designation **B-139**) prototype, which resulted from the XFBA-1 proposal, was ordered on 22 June 1936 and flew for the first time in December 1937. While bearing a distinct family resemblance to the XSBA-1 of 1934, the new fighter appeared to be tubbier and stubbier and was of mid-wing cantilever monoplane configuration. The XF2A-1 was of all-metal construction except for the fabric covering of its control surfaces. Hydraulically-operated split flaps were provided, and the main units of the tail-

wheel landing gear retracted inward to be housed in fuselage wells. The powerplant consisted of one Wright XR-1820-22 Cyclone radial engine rated at 950 hp (708 kW).

Service testing of the prototype began in January 1938, with 54 examples of the **F2A-1** production model known to the company as the **B-239** being ordered. Delivery of these machines started 12 months later, nine aircraft going almost immediately to equip the US Navy's VF-3 squadron, with the balance of 45 aircraft being diverted to Finland, which was then fighting off the might of the USSR in the so-called 'Winter War'. Later equipping the Finnish air force's HLeLv 24 and HLeLv 26 units, these transferred aircraft remained successfully operational until mid-1944.

Some 43 of an improved version were ordered by the US Navy in early 1939, this **F2A-2** (**B-339**) having a more powerful engine, an improved propeller and inbuilt flotation gear. The 43 F2A-2s entered service in September 1940, and were followed by 108 examples of the **F2A-3** variant with more armour protection and a bulletproof windscreen. These two production versions equipped the US Navy's VF-2 and VF-3 squadrons as well as the US Marine

Corps' VFM-221 squadron. A number of the fighters were used operationally in the Pacific, but as the type was overweight, unstable and of poor manoeuvrability it was no match for opposing Japanese fighters.

Belgian and British purchasing missions ordered 40 **B-339B** and 170 **B-339E** aircraft respectively, most of the former going to the UK after Belgium had been overrun in April 1940. Of the aircraft inherited by the British from the Belgian order, a small number served with Nos 805 and 885 Squadrons, FAA.

Delivery of the aircraft ordered for the RAF, which gave the type the designation Buffalo Mk I, began in July 1940. Service trials in September immediately revealed that the Buffalo's performance was totally

Wearing Dark Green and Earth over Sky camouflage, this B-339 Buffalo Mk I served with No. 21 Sqn, RAAF. It was wearing the Dutch markings illustrated when it was captured by the Japanese at Andir in the Dutch East Indies in 1942.

inadequate for the type's effective deployment in the European theatre. Instead, the aircraft were sent to the Far East to equip the RAF's Nos 67, 146, 243, 453 and 488 Squadrons as well as the RAAF's No. 21 Squadron in defence of Singapore and the Straits Settlements. Completely unsuited to the task, the few aircraft which survived the Japanese invasion fought alongside the American Volunteer Group operating in Burma. The

Buffalo fighters with the most successful combat record were a small number out of almost 100 which had been ordered for the air arm of the Netherlands East Indies' army, which saw action in Java and Malaya. These had the Brewster Designations **B-339D** and **B-439** (72 and 20 aircraft respectively). The former was similar to the B-339E, but the B-439 had the 1,200-hp (895-kW) GR-1820-G205A Cyclone radial engine.

This F2A-3 was photographed in August 1942, by which time all US Navy Buffalos had been passed to the Marine Corps. Most export aircraft were to a similar standard, but with carrier-specific equipment deleted.

SPECIFICATION

Brewster F2A-3

Type: single-seat carrierborne and land-based fighter
Powerplant: one Wright R-1820-40 Cyclone radial engine rated at 1,200 hp (895 kW)
Performance: maximum speed 321 mph (517 km/h) at 16,500 ft (5030 m); cruising speed 258 mph (415 km/h); initial climb rate 2,290 ft (698 m) per minute; service ceiling 33,200 ft (10120 m); range 965 miles (1553 km)
Weights: empty 4,723 lb

(2146 kg); maximum take-off 7,159 lb (3247 kg)
Dimensions: wingspan 35 ft (10.67 m); length 26 ft 4 in (8.03 m); height 12 ft 1 in (3.68 m); wing area 208.9 sq ft (19.41 m²)
Armament: four 0.5-in (12.7-mm) Browning fixed forward-firing machine-guns in the upper part of the forward fuselage and leading edge of the wing, plus two 100-lb (45-kg) bombs carried under the wing

Brewster B-40 (SB2A Buccaneer and Bermuda)

With its first design, the B-38, entering production, Brewster was able to turn to the design of an improved version. The aim was to produce a more effective scout/bomber with heavier armament (including an increased bombload) and higher performance.

In configuration the new **Brewster B-40** was generally similar to the B-38, but differed primarily in having a larger bomb bay and main landing gear units that retracted inward wholly into the wing undersurface.

The first of two **XSB2A-1**

prototypes was ordered by the USN on 4 April 1939, and this **B-140** machine flew for the first time on 17 June 1941. By then the company had already received several production orders, comprising 140 for the USN, 162 for the Netherlands, and a total of 750 for the RAF. Procurement for the USAAF was also intended and the designation **A-34** was allocated, but the contract was cancelled before any production resulted.

The provision of heavier armament was realised without difficulty, the US Navy's **SB2A-1 Buccaneer**

(known to the manufacturer as the **B-240**) having some eight machine-guns. Unfortunately, however, the new type's performance was far below that anticipated and the larger, much heavier aircraft also lacked manoeuvrability. Despite this, the US Navy continued to procure small numbers, acquiring 80 of the **SB2A-2** (**B-340**) with armament changes, and then 60 of the **SB2A-3** variant. These last, intended for carrierborne operations, featured a folding wing and an arrester hook. The 162 **B-340D**

aircraft built for the Netherlands were also taken over by the USN, and these were given the designation **SB2A-4** and transferred to the USMC for use as trainers. In this role they served a useful purpose in establishing the Marines' first night-fighter squadron, VFM(N)-531.

Deliveries of **B-240E** aircraft to the RAF began in July 1942. Supplied under

Lend-Lease with the USN designation **SB2A-1B**, the type was identified in the UK as the **Bermuda Mk I**, but its performance was so poor that the aircraft was completely unsuitable for combat operations. As a result, most were converted for target-towing duties with the revised designation **Bermuda TT.Mk I**, and second-line deployment, so far as is known, was the fate of all the 771 aircraft produced by Brewster.

The only innovative feature proposed for the B-40 was the introduction of a power-operated gun turret in the rear cockpit. On the prototype this appeared only as a mock-up, however, and it did not materialise at all on production aircraft.

SPECIFICATION

Brewster SB2A-2 Buccaneer
Type: two-seat carrierborne and land-based scout/bomber and trainer
Powerplant: one Wright R-2600-8 Cyclone 14 radial engine rated at 1,700 hp (1268 kW)
Performance: maximum speed 274 mph (441 km/h) at 12,000 ft (3660 m); cruising speed 161 mph (259 km/h) at optimum altitude; initial climb rate 2,290 ft (698 m) per minute; service ceiling 24,900 ft (7590 m); range 1,675 miles (2696 km) without bombload
Weights: empty 9,924 lb (4501 kg); maximum take-off

14,289 lb (6481 kg)
Dimensions: wingspan 47 ft (14.33 m); length 39 ft 2 in (11.94 m); height 15 ft 5 in (4.70 m); wing area 379.00 sq ft (35.21 m²)
Armament: two 0.5-in (12.7-mm) Browning fixed forward-firing machine-guns in the upper part of the forward fuselage, two 0.3-in (7.62-mm) Browning fixed forward-firing machine-guns in the leading edge of the wing, and two 0.3-in (7.62-mm) Browning trainable rearward-firing machine-guns in the rear cockpit, plus up to 1,000 lb (454 kg) of bombs carried internally

Bristol Boxkite

In 1909 Sir George White, the Bristol-born millionaire who had made his fortune in the pioneering of electric trams for urban transport, decided that aircraft had reached the stage of practical development in which a major investment might well yield rich returns. There were already two British aviation companies, namely Short Brothers and Handley Page Ltd. White appreciated that these companies and a number of less formally established organisations had been created on the basis more

of enthusiasm than sound financial thinking, especially in terms of capitalisation.

In February 1910 therefore, White, his brother and his son created four companies. These were the Bristol Aeroplane Co. Ltd, the Bristol Aviation Co. Ltd, the British and Colonial Aeroplane Co. Ltd and the British and Colonial Aviation Co. Ltd. The first two and the last of these companies were designed for future development, while the third was to start immediately.

White determined that his new company should

cut its teeth on the licensed production of other companies' products and the decision went in favour of a French aircraft, the Zodiac pusher biplane designed by Gabriel Voisin. After the first of the type had failed to fly, however, the agreement was cancelled and Bristol decided to move forward to a type of its own. This was modelled closely on the Henry Farman pusher biplane powered by the Gnome rotary engine, for which Bristol also became the sole agent in the UK and all parts of the British Empire.

The first product of the new company, even then

known generally as Bristol, was therefore the **Bristol Boxkite** (derived from the name of the first machine, but otherwise the **1910 Biplane**). The first example, originally with a 50-hp (37-kW) Grégoire four-cylinder engine which proved to be unreliable and of inadequate power, was re-engined with a 50-hp (37-kW) Gnome rotary and flown successfully at Larkhill on 30 July 1910. The second was powered by a 50-hp (37-kW) ENV eight-cylinder engine. These machines formed the initial equipment of the newly established Bristol flying schools at Brooklands and Larkhill respectively. Four other Boxkites were shipped in pairs with air missions to Australia and India, arriving in December 1910, but the first overseas government order for British aircraft was one for eight Boxkites placed by Russia. Delivered

in April 1911, they were powered by 70-hp (52-kW) Gnome engines and featured enlarged fuel tanks, increased span and three rudders.

The initial British official order, placed by the War Office in March 1911, was for four aircraft, two of them with the 50-hp (37-kW) Gnome and the other two with the 60-hp (45-kW) Renault. The aircraft equipped the Larkhill-based No. 2 (Aeroplane) Company of the British army's Air Battalion, which was established on 1 April 1911. Two early Boxkites, one with a 70-hp (52-kW) Gnome, were used by the RNAS, and the Admiralty also ordered six for training duties.

In all, some 76 Boxkites were built, all but six of them at Filton; the exceptions were the first aircraft to emerge from the Brislington works.

Boxkites found gainful employment with Bristol's own flying schools and as trainers with the RNAS and the Admiralty. The latter based machines at Eastchurch, Chingford and other naval air stations.

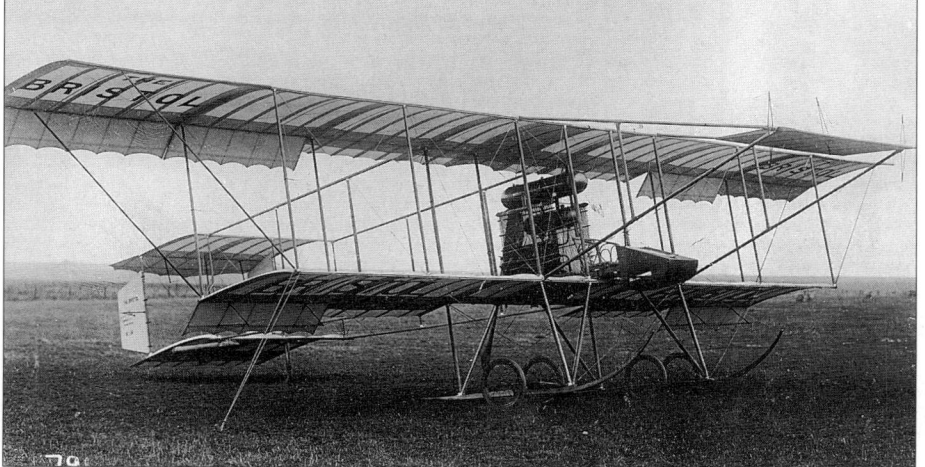

SPECIFICATION

Bristol Boxkite
Type: two-seat trainer
Powerplant: one Gnome rotary engine rated at 50 hp (37 kW)
Performance: maximum speed 40 mph (64 km/h) at sea level

Weights: empty 900 lb (408 kg); maximum take-off 1,150 lb (522 kg)
Dimensions: wingspan 46 ft 6 in (14.17 m); length 38 ft 6 in (11.73 m); height 11 ft (3.61 m); wing area 517.00 sq ft (48.03 m²)

Bristol Biplane Type T

Built initially for the French pilot Maurice Tabuteau, with the final letter of its designation reflecting this fact, the **Bristol Biplane Type T** was developed not so much directly from the Boxkite but rather with features of this type, which had already been produced in racing form with reduced-span wings. The Biplane Type T differed from the Boxkite in having an enclosed nacelle for the pilot, an extended skid structure forward of the main landing gear to prevent nosing-over, and a more powerful Gnome engine. In addition to the machine built for Tabuteau to fly in the 1911 Circuit de l'Europe race, four more examples were built to compete in the *Daily Mail*-sponsored Circuit of Britain race in the same year, but none of these five aircraft achieved success in their contests. At least one of the four Biplane Type T machines for the Circuit of Britain race was powered by a 60-hp (45-kW) Renault engine.

Variant

Challenger-England: Biplane Type T converted in 1911 by E. C. Gordon England to accommodate a 60-hp (45-kW) ENV engine

Tabuteau, in his Type T, at the very beginning of the Circuit de l'Europe race. The race included a Channel crossing.

SPECIFICATION

Bristol Biplane Type T
Type: single-seat sporting biplane
Powerplant: one Gnome rotary engine rated at 70 hp (52 kW)
Performance: maximum speed 55 mph (88 km/h) at sea level
Weights: empty 650 lb (295 kg); maximum take-off 850 lb (386 kg)
Dimensions: wingspan 35 ft (10.67 m); length 24 ft 6 in (7.47 m); wing area 350.00 sq ft (32.52 m²)

Bristol Type 1 to Type 5 Scout, S.S.A., G.B.1 and S.2A

When an Italian contract for Henri Coanda's **S.B.5** monoplane was cancelled in November 1913, the basic design was adapted to become the **Bristol Scout A** biplane. The incomplete fuselage of the S.B.5 was finished and fitted with a staggered single-bay biplane wing cellule and a redesigned tail unit. Powered by an 80-hp (60-kW) Gnome rotary engine, the aircraft flew trials in February 1914, and at the end of April the Scout returned to Filton to be fitted with a set of increased-span wings which improved its low-speed performance. In June 1914 Lord Carberry bought the machine and re-engined it with an 80-hp (60-kW) Le Rhône rotary engine. In this form the aircraft survived an accident during the London-Manchester Air Race on 20 June, but then

Some 74 Scout Cs were built for the Admiralty and 87 for the War Office. The first production order was placed in November 1914 and the last example was delivered in March 1916.

sank on the English Channel (Carberry being rescued) after running out of fuel on the second leg of the London-Paris-London Air Race on 7 July.

Two more almost identical airframes were completed during the summer of 1914. Given the designation **Scout B**, these aircraft were flown to Nos 3 and 5 Squadrons, RFC in France. Locally fitted armament consisted of two rifles in the former and a rifle, pistol and five rifle grenades in the latter. Although subsequent production orders were placed, few of the Scouts had really effective armament. In March 1916, however, one aircraft was fitted with a Vickers

machine-gun and in this form became the first British aircraft equipped with a synchronised weapon to see service in France. On 25 July 1915, Captain Lanoe G. Hawker flying a **Scout C**, shot down two Aviatik 'C' category biplanes and an Albatros, winning the first Victoria Cross awarded for aerial combat.

Scouts served with the RFC and the RNAS, mostly in small numbers with squadrons equipped principally with other types. The Scouts acted as escorts for reconnaissance two-seaters or, in the case of RNAS aircraft, for anti-Zeppelin patrols, a task in which they were armed with Rankin darts.

Variants

Type 1 Scout C: an improved Scout B, of which 161 were built. The 80-hp (60-kW) Gnome engine was originally specified and fitted to all the RNAS aircraft because of its greater reliability, but shortages of this engine led to the installation of the 80-hp (60-kW) Le Rhône rotary unit in the majority of those for the RFC
Types 2, 3, 4 and 5 Scout D: introduced in November 1915, this version featured revised fuel and oil tanks and a variety of engine types, and later examples introduced new wings and revised underwing skids. Some 130 examples of the Type 3 were delivered for the War Office, without engines, between February and September 1916: the first 50 retained the Scout C wings and the remainder were equipped with standardised gun mountings; 80 Scout Ds were delivered to the RNAS between April and December 1916, the first 60 of them to the Type 4 standard with the 100-hp (75-kW) Gnome Monosoupape engine and a cut-away wing centre section with a mounting for a trainable Lewis gun, and the last 20 to the Type 2 standard with the 80-hp (60-kW) Gnome engine for service with RNAS training schools; three Type 5s were fitted with the 110-hp (82-kW) Clerget rotary engine in response to RFC interest in a more powerful version
S.S.A.: designed by Coanda as a single-seat armoured biplane for the French government, this aircraft had a bulletproof sheet-steel 'bath' protecting the pilot, petrol/oil tanks, engine and propeller hub; powered by an 80-hp (60-kW) Clerget rotary, the S.S.A first flew on 8 May 1914 and was handed over to the French on 3 July 1914
G.B.1: unrealised project for a single-seat racer with a 100-hp (75-kW) Gnome Monosoupape
S.2A: two-seat derivative of the Scout D intended to meet an Admiralty requirement for a two-seat fighter with the powerplant of one 110-hp (82-kW) Clerget or 100-hp (75-kW) Gnome engine; two were eventually built as side-by-side two-seat advanced trainers

SPECIFICATION

Bristol Type 3 Scout D
Type: single-seat scout
Powerplant: one Le Rhône 9C rotary engine rated at 80 hp (60 kW)
Performance: maximum speed 100 mph (161 km/h) at sea level; initial climb rate 1,100 ft (335 m) per minute; climb to 10,000 ft (3050 m) in 18 minutes 30 seconds; service ceiling 15,500 ft (4725 m); endurance 2 hours
Weights: empty 760 lb (345 kg); maximum take-off 1,250 lb (567 kg)
Dimensions: wingspan 27 ft 4 in (8.33 m); length 19 ft 9 in (6.02 m); height 8 ft 6 in (2.59 m); wing area 198.0 sq ft (18.59 m²)
Armament: alternative arrangements of small arms and grenades in early aircraft, while later aircraft had one 0.303-in (7.7-mm) Lewis fixed forward-firing machine-gun

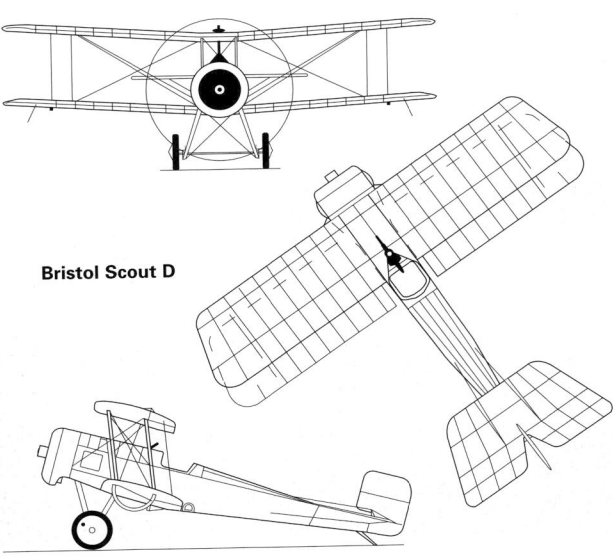

Bristol Scout D

Bristol Types 10, 11, 20 and 77 M.1 Monoplane Scout

The success of German Fokker 'E' category monoplanes against the poorly armed biplanes of the RFC underlined the latter's need for a manoeuvrable, high-performance single-seat fighter. Bristol's Frank Barnwell therefore designed such an aircraft around a rotary engine in a close-cowled installation with a large hemispherical spinner.

The **Bristol M.1A Monoplane Scout (Type 10)** prototype was built as a private venture and its maiden flight took place on 14 July 1916. Later that month the M.1A undertook trials at the CFS at Upavon and on 9 October the War Office issued a contract for purchase of the M.1A and for the manufacture of four more aircraft. The latter, designated **M.1B (Type 11)**, incorporated a number of minor modifications, including a Vickers gun mounted on the port upper longeron. The first two M.1Bs, handed over in December 1916 and January 1917, were fitted with 110-hp (82-kW) Clerget rotary engines but the third, taken on charge in February 1917, was powered by a 130-hp (97-kW) Clerget, and the fourth was delivered in March 1917 with a 150-hp (112-kW) Bentley A.R.I.

Adding a Lucifer engine to an M.1C airframe produced the M.1D Monoplane racer. The aircraft was flown with great success, until lost in a fatal crash during the 1923 Grosvenor Cup Race.

The trials at the CFS had revealed a landing speed of 49 mph (79 km/h), which was considered too high for the small airfields being used in France, so the Monoplane Scout never saw service on the Western Front. A production order was placed in August 1917, but fewer than 30 of the aircraft only partially equipped a small number of units in Macedonia, Palestine and Mesopotamia. Others were issued to flying schools or were used as personal aircraft by senior officers, and six were given to the Chilean government in 1917. Another six were converted for civil use after the end of World War I and one survives at Minalton, near Adelaide.

Variants

Type 20 M.1C Monoplane Scout: 125 production examples were ordered to this standard, powered by the 110-hp (82-kW) Le Rhône engine; the Vickers machine-gun was relocated to the centreline of the fuselage, in front of the pilot, and a cut-out was provided in the port wingroot
Type 77 M.1D Monoplane Scout: designation applied to one of the four M.1B prototypes after it had been rebuilt in 1922 with the 100-hp (75-kW) Bristol Lucifer radial engine

SPECIFICATION	
Bristol Type 20 M.1C Monoplane Scout **Type:** single-seat fighter **Powerplant:** one Le Rhône 9J rotary engine rated at 110 hp (82 kW) **Performance:** maximum speed 130 mph (209 km/h) at sea level; climb to 10,000 ft (3050 m) in 10 minutes 10 seconds; service ceiling 20,000 ft (6095 m);	endurance 1 hour 45 minutes **Weights:** empty 896 lb (406 kg); maximum take-off 1,348 lb (611 kg) **Dimensions:** wingspan 30 ft 9 in (9.37 m); length 20 ft 5½ in (6.24 m); height 7 ft 9½ in (2.37 m); wing area 145.00 sq ft (13.47 m²) **Armament:** one 0.303-in (7.7-mm) Vickers fixed forward-firing machine-gun on the upper part of the forward fuselage

Bristol Types 12, 14, 15, 16, 17, 22, 96 & O-1 (F.2 Fighter)

In March 1916 Frank Barnwell completed the design of a two-seat reconnaissance aircraft which was intended to compete with the Royal Aircraft Factory R.E.8 as a replacement for the RAF B.E.2. Designated as the **R.2A** (later **Type 9**), this was a two-bay, equal-span biplane powered by one 120-hp (90-kW) Beardmore inline engine. The later availability of the 150-hp (112-kW) Hispano-Suiza 8 Vee engine led to a second study, the **R.2B (Type 9A)**, before the advent of the 190-hp (142-kW) Rolls-Royce Falcon Vee engine resulted in redesign of the fuselage to accommodate either this

F.2Bs flew extensively with the RAF post-war. Other users included Australia, Canada, Greece, Mexico, New Zealand, Peru and Spain.

unit or the Hispano-Suiza engine. A prototype of each version was ordered on 28 August 1916 in a contract which also covered the manufacture of 50 production aircraft.

The first prototype, given the designation **F.2A (Type 12)** to denote its change to a fighter role, made its first flight on 9 September 1916. Production examples of the F.2A were all powered by the Falcon and featured revised cowlings and wings of a modified planform.

No. 48 Squadron was the first RFC unit to re-equip with the F.2A, receiving its first aircraft in February 1917 and flying to France on 8 March. The unit was based at Bellevue and on 5 April six F.2As took off to make the squadron's first offensive patrol. From this, only two aircraft returned, following an attack by an equal number of Albatros D.III single-seat fighters of Jagdstaffel 11 led by Freiherr Manfred von Richthofen. Similar disastrous encounters resulted from tactical errors, principally the use of the aircraft as a platform for the rear-gunner. As soon as pilots began to adopt single-seater tactics, using the forward-firing Vickers gun as the main offensive armament, the 'Brisfit' became one of the most effective fighters of World War I.

After World War I the F.2 Fighter was used as an army co-operation aircraft and as a trainer, remaining in overseas service with the RAF to a time as late as 1932. Production totalled 5,308 aircraft.

Variants

Type 14 F.2B Fighter: main production version, incorporating a number of improvements. The aircraft of the first production batch were powered by the 190-hp (142-kW) Falcon I engine, those of the second batch by the 220-hp (164-kW) Falcon II and the majority by the Falcon III; other engines, introduced when production outstripped the supply of Falcons, included the 200- and 300-hp (149- and 224-kW) versions of the Hispano-Suiza 8 Vee unit to create the **Type 16** and **Type 17** respectively, the 200-hp (149-kW) Sunbeam Arab Vee unit to create the **Type 15**, the 200-hp (149-kW) RAF 4d Vee unit, the 180-hp (134-kW) Wolseley Viper Vee unit, as well as the 230-hp (172-kW) Siddeley Puma inline
Type 22 F.2C Fighter: among experimental re-enginings of the F.2B were installations of the 200-hp (149-kW) Salmson radial to produce the Type 22 F.2C, the 300-hp (224-kW) ABC Dragonfly radial to produce the **Type 22A F.2C**, and the 230-hp (172-kW) Bentley B.R.2 rotary to produce the **Type 22B F.2C**
Type 14 F.2B Mk II: first flown in December 1919 for army co-operation duties, this developed version was fitted with desert equipment and a tropical cooling system; 435 were

produced, some as new-build machines and others as reconditioned aircraft
Type 96 Fighter Mk III: structurally strengthened version, 50 of which were delivered between October and December 1926, followed by 30 unarmed dual-control trainer aircraft between January and June 1927
Type 96A Fighter Mk IV: conversions of Mk III airframes with strengthened landing gear and structure for operation at higher gross weight; also fitted with enlarged fin, horn-balanced rudder and Handley Page automatic slots
O-1: the F.2B was one of the types chosen for American production after the USA had entered World War I in April 1917; 2,000 had been ordered from the Curtiss Aeroplane and Motor Company by December 1917, the first making its maiden flight on 5 March 1918 with one 400-hp (298-kW) Liberty 12 Vee engine. The engine/airframe combination proved to be unsuitable and the contract was cancelled in July 1918 in favour of a version with the 300-hp (224-kW) Wright-Hispano Vee engine, first flown in June in the form of two pattern airframes sent to the USA from the UK; the second of these was fitted with a 290-hp (216-kW) Liberty 8 engine but crashed before an official evaluation could be undertaken

Bristol Types 12, 14, 15, 16, 17, 22, 96 & O-1 (F.2 Fighter)(cont.)

The Royal New Zealand Air Force received its first two F.2B Fighters, which included H1557, in August 1919. These war-weary machines were joined by five refurbished aircraft in 1925-26.

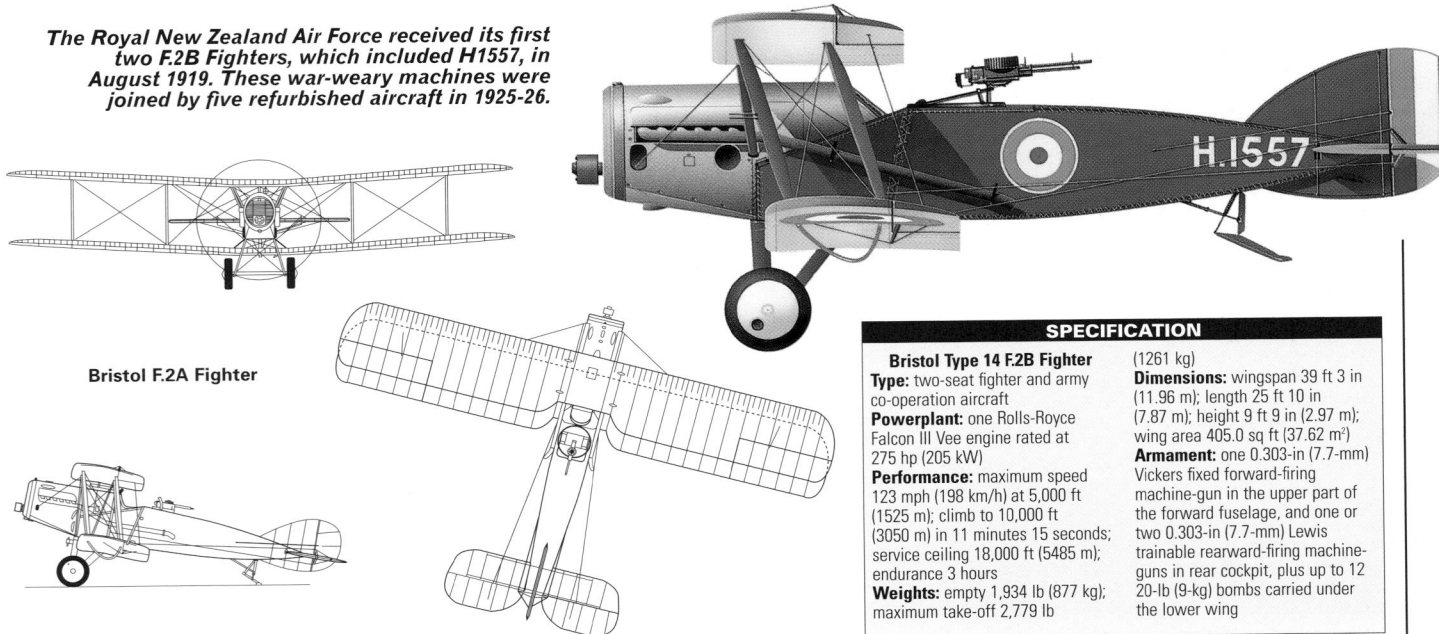

Bristol F.2A Fighter

SPECIFICATION	
Bristol Type 14 F.2B Fighter **Type:** two-seat fighter and army co-operation aircraft **Powerplant:** one Rolls-Royce Falcon III Vee engine rated at 275 hp (205 kW) **Performance:** maximum speed 123 mph (198 km/h) at 5,000 ft (1525 m); climb to 10,000 ft (3050 m) in 11 minutes 15 seconds; service ceiling 18,000 ft (5485 m); endurance 3 hours **Weights:** empty 1,934 lb (877 kg); maximum take-off 2,779 lb	(1261 kg) **Dimensions:** wingspan 39 ft 3 in (11.96 m); length 25 ft 10 in (7.87 m); height 9 ft 9 in (2.97 m); wing area 405.0 sq ft (37.62 m²) **Armament:** one 0.303-in (7.7-mm) Vickers fixed forward-firing machine-gun in the upper part of the forward fuselage, and one or two 0.303-in (7.7-mm) Lewis trainable rearward-firing machine-guns in rear cockpit, plus up to 12 20-lb (9-kg) bombs carried under the lower wing

Bristol Type 13 M.R.1

The **Bristol M.R.1** (retrospectively allocated the designation **Type 13**) was a fairly conventional two-seat biplane in configuration. Its design was initiated in 1916 in an attempt to satisfy two design aims. The first was to construct a practical all-metal aircraft and the second was to satisfy a need to find an alternative material to wood, as stocks of good quality timber were shrinking rapidly as aircraft production expanded with the demands of World War I. Following evaluation of the design two prototypes were ordered. Experiencing difficulty with the production of suitable all-metal wings, the company subcontracted the Steel Wing Company of Gloucester to build them. The first prototype was soon waiting for these wings, and to prevent unnecessary delay a set of wooden wings was built and installed.

This aircraft was test-flown successfully in October 1917 with one 140-hp (104-kW) Hispano-Suiza 8 Vee engine. The second machine received its metal wings and was

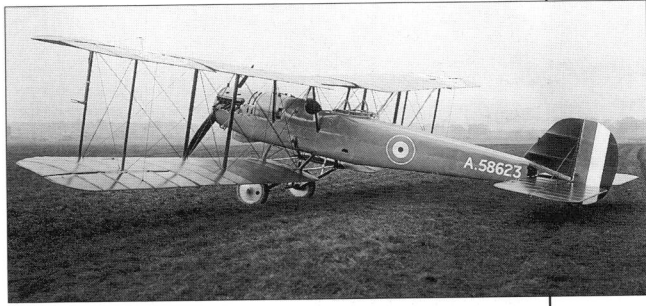

also flown successfully late in 1918, but no further examples were ordered. Nevertheless, the company had gained invaluable experience with an important structural material of the future.

Both prototypes had a Dural monocoque fuselage, and even with its metal wings the second prototype revealed satisfactory performance. No further examples were built.

SPECIFICATION	
Bristol M.R.1 (second prototype) **Type:** two-seat all-metal research aircraft **Powerplant:** one Wolseley Viper Vee engine rated at 180 hp (134 kW) **Performance:** maximum speed 110 mph (177 km/h) at optimum	altitude; endurance 5 hours **Weights:** empty 1,700 lb (771 kg); maximum take-off 2,811 lb (1275 kg) **Dimensions:** wingspan 42 ft 2 in (12.85 m); length 27 ft (8.23 m); height 10 ft 3 in (3.12 m); wing area 458.00 sq ft (42.55 m²)

Bristol Type 18 Scout E and Type 21 Scout F

In the autumn of 1916, even before the F.2 Fighter had been issued to the RFC in France, the British were making a determined effort to produce single-seat fighters able to better the latest generation of German fighters. The hitherto-standard rotary engine had almost reached its limit, so attention was focused on air- or water-cooled radial units and the water-cooled inline or Vee engines. The Vee engine on which greatest hopes had been pinned was the Hispano-Suiza 8, but in its initial forms this was unreliable and the limited stocks of reliable units were reserved for the S.E.5.

Frank Barnwell therefore began two designs around a proposed 10-cylinder 'Cruciform' engine, one of which was based loosely on the Scout D and was known as the **Scout E** (later awarded the retrospective designation **Type 18**). With the Cruciform engine subsequently being abandoned, Bristol was told that it would receive a few examples of the new, more powerful and, it was hoped, more reliable 200-hp (149-kW) Hispano-Suiza 8 engine. Barnwell therefore modified the design of the Scout E into the **Scout F** (later awarded the retrospective designation **Type 21**).

Bristol received the contract for six Scout F prototypes in June 1917, but this order specified the

The first Scout F demonstrates the very clean nose entry, which was made possible by the type's underfuselage radiator installation.

SPECIFICATION	
Bristol Type 21 Scout F **Type:** single-seat fighter **Powerplant:** one Sunbeam Arab Vee engine rated at 200 hp (149 kW) **Performance:** maximum speed 138 mph (222 km/h) at sea level; climb to 10,000 ft (3050 m) in 9 minutes 30 seconds **Weights:** empty 1,440 lb (653 kg);	maximum take-off 2,200 lb (998 kg) **Dimensions:** wingspan 29 ft 7 in (9.02 m); length 20 ft 10 in (6.35 m); height 8 ft 4 in (2.54 m); wing area 260.00 sq ft (24.15 m²) **Armament:** two 0.303-in (7.7-mm) Vickers fixed forward-firing machine-guns in the upper part of the forward fuselage

use of the Sunbeam Arab engine as there was an acute shortage of the Hispano-Suiza unit. The design was finalised only in November 1917 and, as by this time the early Arab engines had revealed apparently incurable vibration problems, it was decided that only the first two prototypes would use the Arab for initial trials.

The first of the two Scout F prototypes made its maiden flight in March 1918, and in their trials the two machines revealed excellent performance and handling. Despite the fact that the Hispano-Suiza engine was now available in larger numbers and was making a good reputation for itself, no consideration was given to the installation

of this engine in the Scout F as attention was now centred on a new radial engine, the 315-hp (270-kW) Cosmos Mercury. The engine manufacturer approached Bristol with the notion of using the Scout F as a testbed for the Mercury engine, and was favourably received as the basic airframe had originally been designed for a radial

engine. The third Scout F was accordingly modified to accept the Mercury with the revised designation **Scout F.1**. This machine made its first flight on 6 September 1918.

The Armistice ended any hope of orders for the Scout F.1, but even so the type was very successful in trials in late 1918 and early 1919, recording a maximum

speed of 145 mph (233 km/h) at sea level and a climb to 10,000 ft (3050 m) in 5 minutes, 24 seconds. No further evolution of the Scout F.1 was considered as work on the Mercury engine had been terminated. The fourth Scout F was completed as a spare airframe, but the last two prototypes were not completed.

Bristol Type 23 (F.2C Badger)

It was in February 1917 that the designation F.2C was first used, in this instance for a development of the F.2B fighter that was soon abandoned in favour of the F.2B. In October of the same year the designation was used once more, this time for a new two-seat biplane intended for the reconnaissance fighter role and optimised for simplicity (and therefore speed) of production.

This new **F.2C** was an unstaggered two-bay biplane, with its two-man crew located close together in cockpits set as high as possible to provide the best possible fighting

conditions. Power was to be provided by the 260-hp (194-kW) Salmson 9 engine.

By the end of November 1917 it had become clear that the Salmson engine would not be available in adequate numbers, so the design was again revised, with a wing cellule of smaller area and one 230-hp (172-kW) Bentley B.R.2 rotary engine. Even in this form the F.2C failed to find official approval as the intended powerplant could not provide adequate performance with the aircraft in maximum loaded condition.

In April 1918, therefore, Bristol offered a new F.2C

design using the 320-hp (239-kW) ABC Dragonfly, a new and apparently promising air-cooled radial engine. In its new form, the F.2C was a single-bay biplane which possessed a number of Scout F features and, in September 1918, an order was placed for three **F.2C Badger Mk I** prototypes. By this time the Dragonfly had been revealed as a notably unreliable engine, and the second machine was completed with a 400-hp (298-kW) Cosmos Jupiter radial.

With World War I at an end, only two of the original Badgers were completed. The first of these had the Dragonfly engine and made its first flight on 4 February 1919, suffering an engine failure on take-off and sustaining severe damage. The repaired and subsequently modified aircraft was then delivered for official trials. The second prototype made its first flight only on 24 May 1919 as a result of problems with the Jupiter engine that was later replaced by a Dragonfly.

Trials revealed inade-

The Badger seated its pilot under the upper-wing centre section, with his head protruding through a circular opening.

quate lateral control, so the third prototype was cancelled before delivery. Meanwhile, a simple rectangular fuselage of plywood-covered wooden construction had been designed and this was combined with a 240-hp (179-kW) Siddeley Puma inline engine. Mating this with a spare set of Badger wings, tail surfaces and landing gear produced the **Type 23X F.2C Badger X** (denoting a shortened form of **Experimental** rather than 10). This was a single-seat research aircraft whose flying qualities could

be directly compared with the data gathered in wind tunnel tests of a model. The Badger X made its first flight on 22 May 1919, but was damaged beyond economical repair only nine days later.

British officialdom had meanwhile been sufficiently impressed with the performance of the Jupiter engine to contract for another Badger, in this instance equipped to complete military standard. This was the **Type 23A F.2C Badger Mk II**, which was used for Jupiter development.

SPECIFICATION	
Bristol Type 23 F.2C Badger Mk I	maximum take-off 3,150 lb (1429 kg)
Type: two-seat reconnaissance fighter	**Dimensions:** wingspan 36 ft 9 in (11.20 m); length 23 ft 8 in (7.21 m); height 9 ft 1 in (2.77 m); wing area 357.00 sq ft (33.17 m²)
Powerplant: one ABC Dragonfly IA radial engine rated at 320 hp (239 kW)	
Performance: maximum speed 135 mph (217 km/h) at sea level; climb to 10,000 ft (3050 m) in 11 minutes; service ceiling 19,000 ft (5790 m); endurance 2 hours	**Armament:** (proposed) two 0.303-in (7.7-mm) Vickers fixed forward-firing machine-guns in the upper part of the forward fuselage, and two 0.303-in (7.7-mm) Lewis trainable machine-guns in the rear cockpit
Weights: empty 1,950 lb (885 kg);	

Bristol Type 24 and 25 Braemar, Type 26 and Type 37 Tramp

Designed late in World War I to provide a long-range heavy bomber for attacks on Germany, the first of two **Bristol Type 24 Braemar** triplanes made its maiden flight on 13 August 1918. Of wire-braced wooden construction under a covering of fabric, this large triplane had a slab-sided fuselage structure, biplane tail unit and four-wheel main landing gear. It

had been planned originally to have a powerplant of four engines in an internal engine room, but in the event, four 230-hp (171-kW) Siddeley Puma inline engines were used, mounted in tandem pairs on the centre wing. The Pumas were installed because the chosen powerplant of four 360-hp (268-kW) Rolls-Royce Eagle Vee engines was unavail-

Flown under the ownership of the Air Board, this Type 26 Pullman was tested at Martlesham Heath during 1920.

SPECIFICATION	
Bristol Type 25 Braemar Mk II	(15.70 m); height 20 ft (6.30 m); wing area 1,905.0 sq ft (176.97 m²)
Type: triplane heavy bomber	**Armament:** (planned) two 0.303-in (7.7-mm) Lewis trainable forward-firing machine-guns in the nose position and two 0.303-in (7.7-mm) Lewis trainable rearward-firing machine-guns in the dorsal position, plus one 3,300-lb (1497-kg) bomb, or six 230- or 250-lb (104- or 113-kg) bombs, or 12 112-lb (51-kg) plus five 40-lb (18-kg) bombs carried internally
Powerplant: four Liberty 12 Vee engines each rated at 400 hp (298 kW)	
Performance: maximum speed 122 mph (196 km/h) at optimum altitude; absolute ceiling 17,000 ft (5180 m)	
Weights: empty 11,208 lb (5084 kg); maximum take-off 16,512 lb (7490 kg)	
Dimensions: wingspan 81 ft 8 in (24.89 m); length 51 ft 6 in	

able; the resulting poor performance meant that the **Braemar Mk I** saw only limited experimental use before being scrapped in 1920. A second prototype, the **Type 25 Braemar Mk II**, powered by four Liberty Vee engines, was flown for the first time on 18 February 1919, but by then the bomber requirement no longer existed and the aircraft was used experimentally before being

wrecked in an accident in late 1920.

A third Braemar had been under construction, but this was completed as the **Type 26 Pullman**, a 14-passenger civil transport aircraft. Although creating something of a stir when exhibited in 1920, it was dismantled without entering service. One final attempt was made to produce something worthwhile from the basic

design. Two examples of the **Type 37 Tramp** were therefore built, the powerplant of four Puma engines being installed as originally intended in an internal engine room. So much trouble was experienced with the transmission system linking engines and propellers that neither of the Tramps was flown. A steam-turbine powered **Tramp Boat** never left the drawing board.

Bristol Types 27, 28, 29, 47 and 48 Tourer

The end of World War I and the curtailment of military orders naturally turned the thoughts of Bristol's chief designer, Frank Barnwell, to civil markets, and as a consequence he began work on a two/three-seat biplane. Known initially as the **Rancher** and later as the **Colonial**, this was to be powered by a 100-hp (75-kW) Cosmos Lucifer engine. The project made little progress, however, and the requirement was met by developments of the Bristol Fighter. In January 1919 three non-military Falcon-engined two-seaters were built for the Controller of Civil Aviation. They were each fitted with dual controls and additional fuel tankage to provide an endurance of five hours. A fourth aircraft, with a hinged cover over the passenger seat, was known as the **Bristol Coupé**, and in 1923

this received the retrospective designation **Type 27**. When the Puma engine of the Badger X was installed in an F.2B airframe, the F.2B entered service as an engine test-bed. Subsequently, as a company transport, it became known as the **Bristol Tourer**, later designated as the **Type 29**. A second aircraft, with a four-bladed propeller and a redesigned radiator, was built in September 1919.

In July 1919, Bristol received an enquiry for a Tourer capable of accommodating two passengers. A relatively simple modification allowed side-by-side seating and an optional coupé top. The open version later became the **Type 47** and that with the coupé top the **Type 28**. Two examples of a three-seat open-cockpit seaplane, later designated as the **Type 48**,

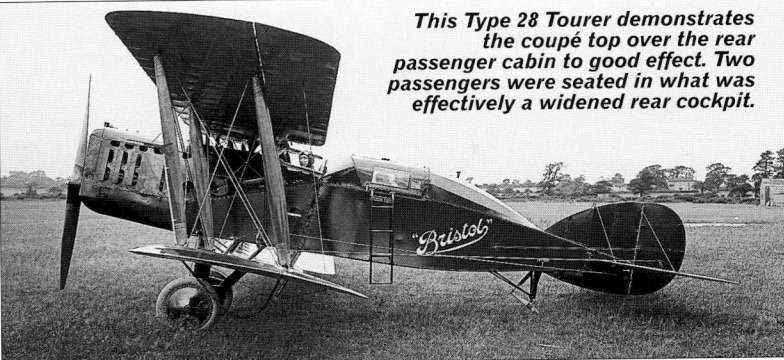
This Type 28 Tourer demonstrates the coupé top over the rear passenger cabin to good effect. Two passengers were seated in what was effectively a widened rear cockpit.

were subsequently built, and the first of these was flown on 15 October 1920. Most Tourers were exported, including aircraft dispatched to Australia, Newfoundland and Spain. Six Type 28 Tourers were acquired for Western Australian Airlines' Geraldton-Perth mail service, inaugurated on 4 December 1921. A locally-converted F.2B with a 300-hp (224-kW) Hispano Suiza Vee engine was flown by QANTAS, then by the Flying Doctor Service in the Northern Territories, and finally in the New Guinea gold fields, where it ended its days in April 1928.

Variants

Type 45 Scandinavian Tourer: version of Type 29 with alternative wheel/ski landing gear
Type 81 Puma Trainer: in 1922 the Tourer demonstrator was modified for evaluation as an advanced trainer; four were built for the Filton Reserve Flying School which opened on 15 May 1923; six of the modified **Type 81A** variant, with revised landing gear and empennage, were supplied to the Greek government in 1925, and were later re-engined with the Rolls-Royce Falcon III
Type 86 Greek Tourer: six 'civil' F.2Bs, with the Puma engine and other modifications, and convertible into fighters, were operated by the Greek government; in 1931 all six were modified by the Greek navy with the Falcon engine
Type 88 Bulgarian Tourer: for the Bulgarian Department of Posts and Telegraphs, a Tourer with a 180-hp (134-kW) Wolseley Viper engine was developed to overcome a Versailles Treaty clause which prohibited Bulgarian operation of aircraft powered by engines with an output of more than 200 hp (149 kW); two were delivered in April 1924, differing from the Puma Tourer in not having a centre-section fuel tank; three more further-developed aircraft were purchased in April 1926

SPECIFICATION

Bristol Type 28 Tourer Coupé
Type: two/three-seat touring and training aircraft
Powerplant: one Siddeley Puma inline engine rated at 240 hp (179 kW)
Performance: maximum speed 120 mph (193 km/h) at optimum altitude; service ceiling 20,000 ft (6095); range 400 miles (644 km)
Weights: empty 1,900 lb (862 kg); maximum take-off 3,000 lb (1361 kg)
Dimensions: wingspan 39 ft 5 in (12.01 m); length 26 ft 1 in (7.95 m); height 10 ft 1 in (3.07 m); wing area 407.0 sq ft (37.81 m²)

Bristol Types 52 and 53 Bullfinch

In July 1920 Bristol bought the design and production facilities for the Jupiter radial engine from the defunct Cosmos Engineering Company. It began work on the layout of the **MFA** single-seat fighter of all-metal cantilever monoplane design that could be converted as the **MFB** two-seat reconnaissance biplane. Bristol's new wind tunnel was used to establish the optimum aerofoil

section and fuselage contours for the new type, and Air Ministry Specification 2/21 was issued in April 1921 to cover the supply of three prototypes.

In February 1922 the name Pegasus was suggested for the MFA, but this did not fit with the Air Ministry's system of nomenclature, and in March the official name **Bullfinch** was assigned. Of the three prototypes, two

were completed as **Bristol Type 52** single-seat monoplanes with the official designation **Bullfinch Mk I** and finally delivered in April 1923. The third prototype was built as the **Type 53** and given the official designation **Bullfinch Mk II**. This

was a two-seat biplane with a separate cockpit for an observer/gunner, armed with a single 0.303-in (7.7-mm) Lewis trainable machine-gun.

All three prototypes of the Bullfinch were flown experimentally by the RAF, the first Bullfinch Mk I and the Bullfinch Mk II being evaluated by the A&AEE at

Martlesham Heath and the second Bullfinch Mk I being used for engine tests at Farnborough. The single-seat monoplane revealed good performance, but the two-seat biplane was too heavy and was unable to carry the required military load. No further orders were placed.

SPECIFICATION

Bristol Type 52 Bullfinch Mk I
Type: single-seat fighter
Powerplant: one Bristol Jupiter III or IV radial engine rated at 425 hp (317 kW)
Performance: maximum speed 135 mph (217 km/h) at 15,000 ft (4570 m); service ceiling 22,000 ft (6705 m); endurance 4 hours
Weights: empty 2,175 lb (986 kg);
maximum take-off 3,205 lb (1454 kg)
Dimensions: wingspan 38 ft 5 in (11.71 m); length 24 ft 5 in (7.44 m); height 10 ft 9 in (3.27 m); wing area 267.00 sq ft (24.80 m²)
Armament: two 0.303-in (7.7-mm) Vickers fixed forward-firing machine-guns in the forward fuselage

The Bullfinch Mk I's wing was built in two sections, connected at the centreline to a cabane arrangement of steel tube struts.

Bristol Type 62 Ten-Seater

Born of a British Treasury decision to subsidise the development of a number of approved air transport companies, the **Bristol Type 62 Ten-Seater** was originally to have been a six-passenger aircraft

powered by a Bristol Jupiter radial engine. Early in 1921, however, this powerplant had yet to receive type approval, and when a 450-hp (336-kW) Napier Lion W-type engine became available the basic design

was scaled up to carry a pilot and nine passengers. The first aircraft made its maiden flight on 21 June 1921. Manufacturer's trials followed, and the only major modification was the removal of the front set of

wheels. The aircraft flew a number of experimental services after its arrival at Croydon on 8 July 1921, and during the following month was flown to the A&AEE at Martlesham Heath. Purchased by the Air

Council in December, the aircraft was later taken over by the Instone Air Line for use on the London-Paris route, and was subsequently operated for a time by Handley Page Transport Ltd.

As originally conceived, the Type 62 had a main landing gear comprising two sets in tandem, the rear pair having brakes.

G-EAWY

Variants

Type 75: the Jupiter engine was awarded type approval in September 1921 and a hinged, easily-accessible 'power egg' installation was evolved for the second Ten-Seater, the **Type 75**. First flown in June 1922, this was purchased by the Instone Air Line in February 1924, together with the incomplete fourth airframe for use as spares; when Instone became part of the Imperial Airways organisation, which used only multi-engined aircraft for passenger services, it was converted for use as a freighter. It then re-entered service on the London-Cologne route on 22 July 1924, redesignated as the **Type 75A Express Freight Carrier**, but was withdrawn from use in 1926

Type 79 Brandon: the third airframe was also fitted with a Jupiter engine and was completed, after some redesign, as the Brandon troop-carrier and ambulance aircraft; it also featured a new reduced-span wing cellule and could carry two litters and four seated patients, or three litters plus a medical attendant

SPECIFICATION

Bristol Type 75
Type: passenger and cargo transport and ambulance
Powerplant: one Bristol Jupiter radial engine rated at 425 hp (317 kW)
Performance: maximum speed 110 mph (177 km/h) at optimum altitude; service ceiling 8,500 ft (2590 m); endurance 5 hours

30 minutes
Weights: empty 4,000 lb (1814 kg); maximum take-off 6,755 lb (3064 kg)
Dimensions: wingspan 56 ft (17.07 m); length 40 ft 6 in (12.34 m); height 11 ft (3.35 m); wing area 700.0 sq ft (65.03 m²)
Payload: see above

Bristol Type 73 Taxiplane and Type 83 PTM

Frank Barnwell's first design to use the Cosmos Lucifer radial engine was the Colonial three-seat biplane, but this had been abandoned when the Bristol Tourer was evolved from the F.2B Fighter. However, by July 1921,

Barnwell had completed a new design and the newly-certified Lucifer was chosen to power three examples of the **Bristol Type 73 Taxiplane**. Of wooden construction with plywood and fabric covering, the Taxiplane had a

hinged mounting for the Lucifer. The prototype flew for the first time on 13 February 1923, and in April it was flown to the Aircraft & Armament Experimental Establishment at Martlesham Heath for certification tests. It returned to Filton during the following month, having proved satisfactory as a two-seater, but over-weight in three-seat form. As a result, only two more examples were built.

Variants

Type 83A Primary Training Machine (PTM): a new two-seat fuselage, combined with the wing cellule, tail unit and landing gear of the Taxiplane; six were built as primary trainers for use at the Filton Reserve Flying School; another, delivered to Bulgaria in April 1926, was the first to have the enlarged rudder and elevators which were a feature of subsequent production aircraft
Type 83B Primary Training Machine: development of the Type 83A with the Lucifer IV engine rated at 120 hp (90 kW); 12 examples were supplied to Chile during February and March 1926, and five to Hungary in April of the same year
Type 83E Primary Training Machine: this was a substantially strengthened version built to meet the requirement for a testbed for the 210-hp (157-kW) Bristol Titan

SPECIFICATION

Bristol Type 83A Primary Training Machine
Type: two-seat primary flying trainer
Powerplant: one Bristol Lucifer radial engine rated at 100 hp (75 kW)
Performance: maximum speed

96 mph (154 km/h) at sea level
Weights: empty 1,340 lb (608 kg); maximum take-off 1,840 lb (835 kg)
Dimensions: wingspan 31 ft 1 in (9.47 m); length 24 ft (7.32 m); height 8 ft 10 in (2.69 m); wing area 291.00 sq ft (27.03 m²)

Bristol employed the wing design of its Taxiplane (illustrated) on the PTM, featuring identical upper and lower wings which were thus interchangeable. This view of the first Taxiplane shows the two-seat rear cockpit.

Bristol Type 76 Jupiter-Fighter & Type 89 Advanced Trainer

Bristol wanted to create a low-cost airframe in which its Jupiter engine could be demonstrated to potential customers. The obvious solution appeared to be the modification of a spare F.2B fighter airframe, and in January 1923 Wilfrid Reid, the company's chief designer after the departure of Frank Barnwell, gave his approval to the concept. The attractions of this cheap conversion effort were obvious, and the company decided to build one example of this **Type 76 Jupiter-Fighter**, in time for its participation in a Swedish air show in July 1923.

The conversion of the airframe into the Jupiter-Fighter was completed in April 1923. The company

then started work on a second conversion, with a decision soon made for the completion of a third conversion so that, while the first machine was undergoing its official evaluation, the second and third could be displayed at two Swedish venues. Then, in June, Bristol decided to use the third machine to evaluate the Jupiter engine running on alcohol fuel for comparison with a supercharged version of the Jupiter in the Bristol Seely.

The first machine made its maiden flight early in June 1923 and attained a maximum speed of 134 mph (216 km/h), a velocity at which the slip-stream was too rough for

the gunner to stand in the rear cockpit. It was also clear that the limited fuel capacity and the pilot's poor forward fields of vision meant that the type could not optimistically be offered as a fighter, but that it was an ideal machine in which to demonstrate the Jupiter. The second Jupiter-Fighter was displayed statically in Sweden, without armament but with a new type of aileron developed by another Bristol engineer, Leslie Frise. It was joined by the first machine for the flying display, in which it impressed all with its climb performance and agility.

Sweden then decided to buy the Jupiter-Fighter if it revealed adequate perfor-

mance under the harsh conditions typical of Swedish winter operations. After being fitted with ski landing gear and a carburet-tor heater, therefore, the second Jupiter-Fighter was sent to Lapland during November 1923. Though it was almost impossible to operate most aircraft this far north during the winter as engine oil froze solid, the Jupiter started without

problem after the aircraft had been left out in the open at -4° F (-20° C) with standard petrol and arctic motor oil. The Swedish government bought this machine, which became the longest-lived of the Jupiter-Fighters surviving until 1936.

The first Jupiter-Fighter crashed after its engine seized up at 20,000 ft (6095 m) in November 1923.

SPECIFICATION

Bristol Type 89 Advanced Trainer
Type: two-seat advanced trainer
Powerplant: one Bristol Jupiter IV (DR) or VI (DR) radial engine rated at 320 hp (239 kW)
Performance: maximum speed 110 mph (177 km/h) at optimum

altitude; range 340 miles (547 km)
Weights: empty 2,326 lb (1055 kg); maximum take-off 3,250 lb (1474 kg)
Dimensions: wingspan 39 ft 3 in (11.96 m); length 25 ft (7.62 m); height 9 ft 6 in (2.90 m); wing area 405.00 sq ft (37.625 m²)

Bristol Type 76 Jupiter-Fighter and Type 89 AT (continued)

First flown in March 1924, the third aircraft was fitted with a high-compression engine and a bi-fuel system with alcohol in a gravity-feed tank over the centre section of the upper wing. The machine lifted off on alcohol and the pilot switched over to petrol on reaching an altitude at which detonation would not occur, and for this system the Jupiter engine was fitted with a separate carburettor for each type of fuel. The Air Ministry soon decided not to pursue the bi-fuel system as there were problems of corrosion in the tank, and supercharging now clearly offered a better long-term prospect.

The success of the Jupiter-Fighter had persuaded Bristol to under-take the design of the **Type 89 Advanced Trainer** with the Jupiter engine, although in a form derated to 290 hp (216 kW) to avoid the higher premiums associated with the insurance of aircraft with engines rated at 300 hp (224 kW) or more. The fifth Puma Trainer was revised with the Jupiter III engine and made its first flight in this revised form on 14 April 1924, by which time a second Advanced Trainer was nearly complete and two more aircraft were under construction.

The Advanced Trainer had Frise ailerons and a revised vertical tail surface. Given the nature of their training task and their use of a higher-powered engine, the Advanced Trainers suffered a higher accident rate than the Lucifer-engined Primary Training Machines, and the occasional new machine was built for attrition replacement purposes. The Advanced Trainer was also used by the Beardmore Reserve School at Renfrew up to 1930.

From the tenth machine, which was delivered in October 1926, the aircraft were completed to the improved **Type 89A Advanced Trainer** standard with a stronger fuselage. Ten and three Type 89A aircraft were manufactured for the Filton and Renfrew schools respectively, the latter also assembling a final machine from spares and salvaged components. All the aircraft for Renfrew had the Jupiter VI engine, but those for use at Filton used surplus Jupiter IV engines that were cheaper and could be maintained by the factory. The aircraft at the Filton school were used for experimental work as well as for training, and the last machines were retired and scrapped only in April 1933 as the school switched to the Hawker Hart Trainer.

Finished with a black fuselage and silver doped wings, G-EBOC was the first Advanced Trainer delivered to the revised Type 89A standard. Of the ATs to be lost in accidents, five fell foul of collisions over Filton.

Bristol Type 84 Bloodhound

One of Bristol's objectives with the Type 52 Bullfinch had been the creation of a design that could be adapted as a two-seat reconnaissance fighter to replace the F.2B Fighter. With the failure of the two-seat Bullfinch, the F.2B continued to provide Bristol with useful work through much of the 1920s. In October 1921, however, the Air Ministry issued Specification 3/21 for an F.2B replacement with the Napier Lion W-type engine. Three Lion-engined basic designs in the form of two biplanes and one monoplane were therefore created. Continued opposition to the Lion engine within the company finally paid dividends, with the Air Ministry agreeing to consider a Jupiter-engined design if it met the requirement in all other respects. Accordingly, single biplane and monoplane designs were drafted and Bristol unsuccessfully offered these reconnaissance fighter designs to the Air Ministry in May 1922. The company was, however, heartened by the release in June 1922 of the new Specification 3/22 for a two-seat fighter with a supercharged engine. The Armstrong Siddeley Jaguar radial engine was already being offered with a super-charger, but the head of the company's aero engine branch, Roy Fedden, argued that the Jupiter could offer just as much power up to 10,000 ft (3050 m) through the use of alcohol fuel or higher compression, and could therefore avoid the cost, weight and mechanical complexity of a supercharger system.

Bristol offered its **Fighter 'C'** biplane and **Fighter 'D'** monoplane designs to the new requirement during July 1922, and in October decided to build one private-venture example of the biplane. Then the Air Ministry asked for a quotation for three prototypes with a supercharged engine. One of them had an all-metal structure and the other two had wooden flying surfaces including biplane wings that could be replaced by metal mono-plane wings when the latter became available.

Fedden offered Wilfred Reid, Bristol's chief designer, the Orion engine, a Jupiter derivative with a turbocharger offering 400 hp (298 kW) at 15,000 ft (4570 m), although this engine was never actually used. In February 1923 the Fighter 'C' design received the official name of **Bloodhound**, to which the company designation **Type 84** was retrospectively allocated. The prototype made its maiden flight in May 1923 and was soon modified with a larger vertical tail surface. Late in June Bristol received an order for three Bloodhounds for RAF evaluation against rival designs including the Hawker Duiker, Armstrong Whitworth Wolf and de Havilland Dormouse.

There were some minor problems with the Bloodhound prototype and, after he had rejoined Bristol in October 1923, Barnwell revised the type for greater stability. These changes improved the pilot's fields of vision and the handling of the aircraft, which reached a speed of 130 mph (209 km/h) and was delivered for official trials in January 1924. The three Bloodhounds ordered by the Air Ministry were built to basically the same standard as the revised first prototype.

The report of the Martlesham Heath test team revealed that the Dormouse had better performance, but that the Bloodhound offered superior handling and was probably the better fighter. The steel tube structure was thought unsuitable for a production type, however, and no further orders were placed. The aircraft were then used for racing and tests with a number of Jupiter variants, but their most important contribution to British aviation in the 1920s was a long-endurance test of the Jupiter, which was so successful that it persuaded Imperial Airways to adopt the type.

SPECIFICATION

Bristol Type 84 Bloodhound
Type: two-seat fighter
Powerplant: one Bristol Jupiter IV radial engine rated at 425 hp (317 kW)
Performance: maximum speed 130 mph (209 km/h) at optimum altitude; climb to 10,000 ft (3050 m) in 14 minutes 21 seconds; service ceiling 22,000 ft (6705 m); endurance 3 hours
Weights: empty 2,515 lb (1141 kg); maximum take-off

4,236 lb (1921 kg)
Dimensions: wingspan 40 ft 2 in (12.24 m); length 26 ft 6 in (8.08 m); height 10 ft 8 in (3.25 m); wing area 494.00 sq ft (45.89 m²)
Armament: two 0.303-in (7.7-mm) Vickers fixed forward-firing machine-guns in the forward fuselage, and one 0.303-in (7.7-mm) Lewis trainable rearward-firing machine-gun in the rear cockpit

By increasing the wing dihedral and tilting the engine's thrust line, Barnwell was able to improve the stability and handling of the Bloodhound.

Bristol Type 105 Bulldog

With a need to re-equip the RAF's fighter squadrons, which at the time lacked a warplane with the performance that would allow them to intercept and tackle the new generation of bombers such as the Fairey Fox, the Air Ministry drew up Specification F.9/26. This called for a single-seat day/night fighter powered by an air-cooled radial engine and armed with two Vickers machine-guns. A number of competing types resulted, with the **Bristol Type 105 Bulldog** winning narrowly from the Hawker Hawfinch.

The **Bulldog Mk I** prototype flew for the first time on 17 May 1927, and was subsequently modified with a larger-span wing cellule for an attempt on the altitude and climb-to-height records. The Bulldog Mk I had been superseded for test purposes by a length-ened-fuselage **Bulldog Mk II** prototype known to the manufacturer as the **Type 105A**, and it was the production version of this aircraft which entered service with the RAF's No. 3 Squadron at Upavon, Wiltshire, in June 1929. The Bulldog Mk II was an unequal-span biplane of the single-bay type based on an all-metal airframe covered largely with fabric, except on the forward fuselage where light alloy panels predominated. The power-plant of this version

This ex-Latvian Bulldog was flown by volunteer pilots in support of Basque forces during the Spanish Civil War.

Variants

Bulldog Mk IIA: major production version, generally similar to Mk II, but with the 490-hp (365-kW) Jupiter VIIF engine, a strengthened structure for operation at higher weights and wider-track main landing gear; later Mk IIAs had the tailskid replaced by a tailwheel, and brakes incorporated in the main wheels
Bulldog Mk IIIA: two interim aircraft with the 560-hp (418-kW) Mercury IVS.2 engine
Bulldog Mk IVA: final fighter production version with strengthened ailerons and one 640-hp (477-kW) Mercury VIS.2 engine
Bulldog TM: Training Machine version with a special removable rear fuselage incorporating a second cockpit, dual controls as standard, and no armament; the training rear fuselage could be replaced by a standard rear fuselage and there was provision for the installation of machine-guns so that the TM could be converted into a fighter

comprised one Bristol Jupiter VII radial engine.

The Bulldog was widely used by the RAF, a total of 312 of all versions equipping no fewer than 10 squadrons and remaining in service until 1937. In addition to those serving with the RAF, the Bulldog was also exported to Australia, Denmark, Estonia, Finland, Latvia, Siam and Sweden.

SPECIFICATION	
Bristol Type 105 Bulldog Mk II	(1094 kg); maximum take-off
Type: single-seat day/night fighter	3,530 lb (1601 kg)
Powerplant: one Bristol Jupiter VII radial engine rated at 440 hp (328 kW)	**Dimensions:** wingspan 33 ft 10 in (10.31 m); length 25 ft (7.62 m); height 9 ft 10 in (3.00 m); wing area 306.50 sq ft (28.47 m²)
Performance: maximum speed 178 mph (286 km/h) at 10,000 ft (3050 m); climb to 20,000 ft (6095 m) in 14 minutes 30 seconds; service ceiling 27,000 ft (8230 m); range 350 miles (563 km)	**Armament:** two 0.303-in (7.7-mm) Vickers fixed forward-firing machine-guns in the forward fuselage, and four 20-lb (9-kg) bombs carried under the lower wing
Weights: empty 2,412 lb	

Bristol Type 130 Bombay

Designed to meet the Air Ministry's Specification C.26/31 as a replacement for the Vickers Valentia serving in the Middle East and India, the **Type 130 Bombay** was intended primarily as a troop or cargo carrier. However, it also had to possess an effective self-defence capability and be capable of undertaking an important secondary role as a long-range bomber. A contract was awarded for one prototype in March 1933 and this made its first flight on 23 June 1935 with the powerplant of two 750-hp (559-kW) Bristol Pegasus III radial engines. Military trials were undertaken at the A&AEE and development testing resulted in the implementation of various improvements, including

No. 216 Sqn, RAF had this Type 130A Bombay Mk I on strength in Egypt during 1940-41. The Type 130A introduced revised tail surfaces.

the installation of more powerful Pegasus XXII radial engines.

A contract for one batch of 50 production aircraft was awarded to meet the revised Specification 47/36, but with Filton's production lines geared to the mass production of the higher-priority Blenheim, it was decided that Bombay production should be

undertaken in Belfast by Short Brothers & Harland at a new government-owned factory. The aircraft to be built was the slightly revised **Type 130 Mark II**, known in service as the **Type 130A Bombay Mk I**.

The first production example of the Bombay flew in March 1939, and the initial squadron to receive the type was No. 216 in Egypt during the following September. Other deliveries followed to Nos 117, 267 and 271 Squadrons and the Bombay fulfilled its dual transport and bomber roles during the Libyan campaign of 1940. Although few in numbers, the Bombays were very active, and among their achievements was the evacuation of the Greek royal family from Crete to Egypt. A few UK-based aircraft ferried

supplies across the English Channel before the collapse of France in 1940. The Bombay was eventually replaced by more modern types in the transport role as the

bomber/transport concept became outdated and the type passed quietly out of service in the mid-1940s, having achieved all and more than its designer had intended.

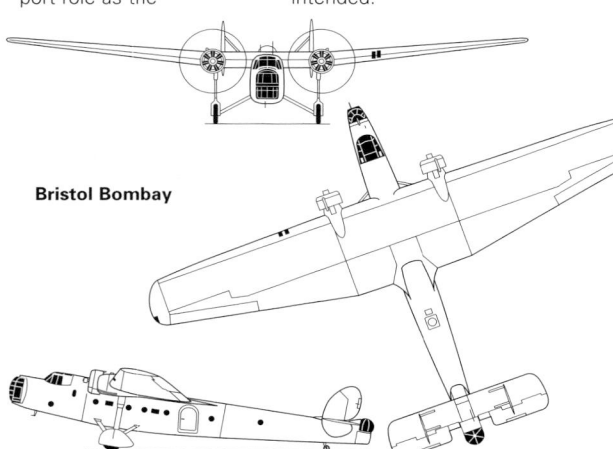

Bristol Bombay

SPECIFICATION	
Bristol Type 130 Bombay	with fuselage tanks
Type: three-crew bomber and transport	**Weights:** empty 13,800 lb (6260 kg); maximum take-off 20,000 lb (9072 kg)
Powerplant: two Bristol Pegasus XXII radial engines each rated at 1,010 hp (753 kW)	**Dimensions:** wingspan 95 ft 9 in (29.18 m); length 69 ft 3 in (21.11 m); height 19 ft 6 in (5.94 m); wing area 1,340.00 sq ft (124.49 m²)
Performance: maximum speed 192 mph (309 km/h) at 6,500 ft (1980 m); cruising speed 160 mph (257 km/h) at 10,000 ft (3050 m); initial climb rate 750 ft (340 m) per minute; service ceiling 25,000 ft (7620 m); range 880 miles (1416 km) or 2,230 miles (3589 km)	**Armament:** one 0.303-in (7.7-mm) Vickers 'K' trainable machine-gun in each of the nose and tail turrets, plus up to 2,000 lb (907 kg) of bombs carried under the fuselage

Bristol Type 138

On 11 April 1934 the Italian pilot Renato Donati, flying a Caproni Ca 131 biplane powered by a Bristol Pegasus engine, set a new world altitude record of 47,360 ft (14435 m), which was soon increased by the

Potez 506 to 48,698 ft (14843 m). Pressure then mounted for a British attempt to regain the record. In June Bristol received an invitation to tender for two prototypes of a suitable aircraft and,

working on the basis of his November 1933 proposal for a single-seat high-altitude research aircraft powered by a specially adapted Pegasus with a two-stage supercharger, Barnwell drafted an

improved version to meet the new Specification 2/34 and this received the company designation **Bristol Type 138A**.

The design was finalised in September as a low-wing monoplane of wooden construction in order to minimise weight. Simple, fixed landing gear was selected for the same

reason. Specially developed pressurised flying suits and oxygen pressure helmets were available for the crew. The key to success lay in the Pegasus PE.VIS engine, which incorporated a mechanical supercharger, but which could also drive an auxiliary supercharger mounted on the firewall, via a flexible shaft and clutch.

Bristol Type 138 (continued)

The first Type 138 was completed in early 1936 and Cyril Uwins, a previous holder of the altitude record, made the maiden flight at Filton on 11 May. A standard Pegasus IV, driving a three-bladed propeller, was fitted for this and further flights on 22 May and 16 July. Following a visit to Farnborough in

early August for trials with the oxygen equipment, the aircraft were returned to Filton on 15 August for installation of the special engine and its four-bladed propeller.

Squadron Leader F. R. D. Swain was selected as pilot for the attempt, and he collected the **Type 138A** from Filton on

Provision was made for a second crew position forward of the Type 138's pilot's cockpit.

5 September, returning to Farnborough. From that airfield he took off on 28 September to attain an FAI-homologated record height of 49,967 ft (15230 m) before landing at Netheravon. Although the Italians regained the record in May 1937 with a flight to 51,362 ft (15655 m) by the Caproni Ca 161, minor improvements were made to the Type 138A to enable Flight Lieutenant M. J. Adam to raise the record yet again, in this instance to 53,937 ft (16440 m) on 3 June 1937.

SPECIFICATION

Bristol Type 138A
Type: one/two-seat high-altitude research aircraft
Powerplant: one Bristol Pegasus PE.VIS radial engine rated at 500 hp (373 kW)
Performance: maximum speed 177 mph (285 km/h) at 45,000 ft (13715 m); climb rate 1,430 ft (436 m) per minute at 40,000 ft

(12190 m); design ceiling 54,000 ft (16459 m); endurance 2 hours 15 minutes
Weights: empty 4,391 lb (1992 kg); maximum take-off 5,310 lb (2409 kg)
Dimensions: wingspan 66 ft (20.12 m); length 44 ft (13.41 m); height 10 ft 3 in (3.12 m); wing area 568.0 sq ft (52.77 m²)

Variants

Type 138B: the second airframe was to have been powered by a 500-hp (373-kW) Rolls-Royce Kestrel supercharged engine for comparative tests, but although the aircraft was delivered to Farnborough in 1937 the engine installation was never completed

Bristol Types 142 Blenheim, 149 Bolingbroke and 160

In 1934 Lord Rothermere, the proprietor of the *Daily Mail* newspaper, required for his personal use a fast and spacious private aircraft. This aviation-minded organisation had already appreciated the potential of what is today called the business or corporate aircraft. Rothermere envisaged his requirements as a fast aircraft that would accommodate a crew of two and up to six passengers, and it just so happened that the Bristol Aeroplane Company had already drawn up the outline of a light transport in this category.

The new aircraft had been designed with the powerplant of two 500-hp (373-kW) Bristol Aquila I engines, but Rothermere's interest in a high-speed transport resulted in Barnwell's proposal to use two 650-hp (485-kW) Bristol Mercury VIS engines and this resulted in the **Bristol Type 142**. First flown at Filton on 12 April 1935, the Type 142 sparked off a hubbub of comment and excitement when it was found to be some 30 mph (48 km/h) faster than the prototype of the most recently procured British fighter. Named *Britain First*, the Type 142 was presented to the nation by Rothermere after the Air Ministry had requested that it might retain the machine for a period of testing to evaluate its potential as a light bomber. This, then, was the sire of the **Type 142M Blenheim**, which proved an important interim weapon at the beginning of World War II. The Aquila-engined **Type 143** was similar, and first flew in January 1936. Only limited

testing was undertaken, performance being severely curtailed by the non-availability of variable-pitch propellers.

Aware of Air Ministry interest in the Type 142, Bristol busied itself with the evolution of the Type 142M military version and in the summer of 1935 the Air Ministry decided to accept the company's proposal, placing a first order in September of the same year for an initial 150 aircraft to Specification 28/35. The new aircraft was very similar to the Type 142, but incorporated a bomb-aimer's station, a bomb bay and a dorsal gun turret. Little time was lost for, following the first flight of the prototype on 25 June 1936, initial deliveries to RAF squadrons began in March 1937, and in July 1937 a follow-on order was placed for 434 additional examples of the **Blenheim Mk I**, as the type had been named.

Of all-metal construction except for its fabric-covered control surfaces, the Blenheim Mk I was a mid-wing cantilever monoplane. The landing gear was of the tailwheel type with retractable main units, and the powerplant comprised two 840-hp (626-kW) Bristol Mercury VIII engines.

The first RAF squadron to receive the Blenheim Mk I was No. 114 and it was this unit which first demonstrated the new type officially to the public at the RAF's final Hendon Display in the summer of 1937. Production contracts immediately soared, necessitating the establishment of new production lines by A. V. Roe and Rootes Securities. Between them

the three lines built 1,552 examples of the Blenheim Mk I which, at its peak, equipped no fewer than 26 RAF squadrons.

By the outbreak of World War II in September 1939, however, few Blenheim Mk Is remained in service with home-based bomber squadrons, the type having been superseded in the bombing role by the **Blenheim Mk IV**, which incorporated the lessons learned by the squadrons while operating the Mk I. The Mk I's utility was by no means ended, however, many of the type continuing to serve as conversion trainers and, initially, as crew trainers in OTUs. More valuable by far were some 200 which were converted to serve as night-fighters, pioneering the newly conceived technique of AI (Airborne Interception) radar, carrying AI.Mk III or Mk IV. The single forward-firing machine-gun was totally inadequate for this role, of course, and a special underfuselage pack to house four 0.303-in

(7.7-mm) machine-guns was produced. So-equipped, a **Blenheim Mk IF** scored the first AI success against an enemy aircraft on the night of 23 July 1940.

The ultimate development of the basic Type 142M was the **Blenheim Mk II** prototype, which was a Mk I converted with extra tankage.

The Blenheim Mk I was exported before the war to Finland, Turkey and Yugoslavia, and was also built under licence by the first two nations. In addition, a small number had been supplied to Romania in 1939 as a diplomatic bribe. The result, of course, was that the Blenheim Mk I fought both for and against the Allies.

When, in August 1935, the Air Ministry had initiated Specification G.24/35 to find a successor to the Avro Anson in the coastal reconnaissance/light bomber role, Bristol had proposed its **Type 149**. Very similar to the Blenheim Mk I, this was schemed with the power-

plant of two Aquila engines to confer longer range with the existing fuel capacity, but this was unacceptable to the Air Ministry. Subsequently, renewed interest was shown in the Type 149 for the general reconnaissance role, and a prototype was built as a Blenheim Mk I conversion with the original powerplant of two Mercury VIII engines, but also with increased fuel capacity. The fuselage nose was lengthened to provide additional accommodation for the navigator/observer and his equipment, and this change was to grace the Mk I's successor, the Blenheim Mk IV.

The Air Ministry then had misgivings about the Type 149, fearing that its introduction and manufacture would interfere with the production of the Blenheim. Instead, the Type 149 was adopted by the RCAF for production in Canada as the **Bolingbroke Mk I**. The first Bolingbroke Mk I had Mercury VIII engines, but after 18 Bolingbroke Mk Is had

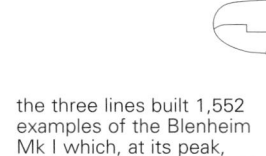

Bristol Blenheim Mk I

been built, production changed to the definitive Canadian version, the **Bolingbroke Mk IV** with Mercury XV engines and Canadian and US equipment. Later variants included a small number of **Bolingbroke Mk IV-W** aircraft with 1,200-hp (895-kW) Pratt & Whitney R-1830 Twin Wasp engines, and some **Bolingbroke Mk IV-T** multi-purpose trainers.

Having blown hot and then cold over the Type 149, the Air Ministry then developed a sudden renewal of interest in the type, primarily as an interim measure until the Type 152 torpedo-bomber, derived from the Blenheim, became available. The decision was taken, therefore, to introduce the longer nose and stepped windscreen of the Bolingbroke and to make provision for longer range by the introduction of increased-capacity wing tanks. The designation Type 149 was retained for this changed configuration, the new RAF designation being **Blenheim Mk IV**. The above changes took place on the production lines towards the end of 1938, although the first 68 Blenheim Mk IVs were built without the 'long-range wing'. The powerplant comprised two examples of the more powerful

Mercury XV engine, allowing an increased maximum take-off weight. No. 90 Squadron was the initial unit to be equipped with the Blenheim Mk IV in March 1939, the first of more than 70 squadrons to operate these aircraft. Inevitably, such extensive use brought changes in armament and equipment, but especially the former, for the armament of the first Blenheim Mk IVs was unchanged from the initial two-gun fit of the Mk I. Protective armour was also increased and, while it was not possible to enlarge the capacity of the bomb bay, provision was made for an additional 320 lb (145 kg) of bombs to be carried externally for short-range missions.

With so many squadrons operating the type it was inevitable that the Blenheim should notch up many wartime 'firsts' for the RAF. These included the first reconnaissance

mission over German territory, made on 3 September 1939 by a Blenheim Mk IV of No. 139 Squadron, and the first dropping of bombs on German targets, on 4 September 1939. From the beginning of the war, until replaced in home squadrons of Bomber Command by the Douglas Boston and de Havilland Mosquito during 1942, the Blenheim Mk IV was used extensively in the European theatre. Although vulnerable to fighter attack, the type was frequently used for unescorted daylight operations and undoubtedly the skill of its crews and the aircraft's ability to absorb a great deal of punishment were the primary reasons for its survival. In the overseas squadrons, the Blenheim continued to serve long after its usefulness in Europe had ended and, except in Singapore where it was no match for the Japanese fighters, it proved a valuable weapon. Some 3,983 Blenheim Mk IVs and Bolingbrokes had been built when production ended. In addition to serving with the RAF the Blenheim Mk IV had served with the French

This Canadian-built Bolingbroke Mk IV was relegated to the target-towing role. The aircraft served with No. 1 Training Command Bombing and Gunnery School, RCAF during 1944.

Free and South African air forces, and had been used in small numbers by Finland and Greece. The **Blenheim Mk IVF** was an interim night-fighter analogous to the Mk IF, and produced as conversions from existing Blenheim Mk IV airframes.

The last of the direct developments of the Blenheim design was the **Type 160**, known briefly as the **Bisley**, which entered service in the summer of 1942 as the **Blenheim Mk V**. Envisaged originally as a low-altitude bomber for the close-support role, with a 'solid' nose housing four machine-guns, the Blenheim Mk V was in fact built for deployment as a high-altitude bomber with the powerplant of two Mercury XV or XXV engines. Except for a changed nose, some alterations in detail and updated

equipment, these aircraft were basically the same as their predecessors. Some 945 were built, all produced by Rootes and the first unit to receive the Blenheim Mk V was No. 18 Squadron. The type equipped six squadrons in the Middle East and four in the Far East, where it was used without distinction. This resulted from an increase of over 17 per cent in maximum take-off weight which, without the introduction of more powerful engines, resulted in a serious fall in performance. It was only when the Blenheim Mk V was deployed in the Italian campaign, contending with the advanced fighters in service with the Luftwaffe, that losses rose to quite unacceptable proportions, and the type was at last withdrawn from front-line service.

All Blenheims sported a dorsal turret, armed either with single or twin Vickers machine-guns. Some Mk IVs (illustrated) carried a rearward-firing installation of two guns beneath their nose.

SPECIFICATION

Bristol Blenheim Mk IV
Type: three-seat light bomber
Powerplant: two Bristol Mercury XV radial engines each rated at 905 hp (675 kW)
Performance: maximum speed 266 mph (428 km/h) at 11,800 ft (3595 m); cruising speed 198 mph (319 km/h) at optimum altitude; initial climb rate 1,500 ft (457 m) per minute; service ceiling 27,260 ft (8310 m); range 1,460 miles (2350 km)
Weights: empty 9,790 lb (4441 kg); maximum take-off 14,400 lb (6532 kg)
Dimensions: wingspan 56 ft 4 in (17.17 m); length 42 ft 7 in

(12.98 m); height 9 ft 10 in (3.00 m); wing area 469.00 sq ft (43.57 m²)
Armament: one 0.303-in (7.7-mm) Vickers fixed forward-firing machine-gun in the leading edge of the port wing, two 0.303-in (7.7-mm) Browning trainable machine-guns in the power-operated Bristol dorsal turret, and two remotely controlled 0.303-in (7.7-mm) Browning trainable rearward-firing machine-guns in a power-operated Frazer-Nash mounting beneath nose, plus up to 1,000 lb (454 kg) of bombs carried internally and 320 lb (145 kg) of bombs carried externally

---

Bristol Type 148

In April 1935, the Air Ministry issued Specification A.39/34 calling for a monoplane to succeed the Hawker Audax and Hector biplanes that the RAF was currently flying in the army co-operation role. The resulting **Bristol Type 148** was conceptually related to the Type 146 and indeed made use of many of the same components and assemblies. Provision was made for automatic leading-edge slots on the outer parts of the wing, designed for interconnection with the

split trailing-edge flaps for improved lateral control at low speed, but these were not installed until 1939. The tandem two-seat cockpit was at first enclosed by a framed canopy that angled down over its rear section, where the gunner was provided with a 0.303-in (7.7-mm) Lewis trainable machine-gun. Later, the gun's obsolete ring mounting was replaced by a more modern pillar mounting, with the weight of the gun counter-balanced by that of the seated gunner, and

this demanded a sliding hood section in place of the tilting section. The cockpit also incorporated a prone bombing position on its floor. The equipment included the typical army-co-operation combination of radio equipment, a camera and a pick-up hook for messages.

The Air Ministry ordered two Type 148 prototypes in June 1935 and when, in October 1935, Bristol proposed the manufacture of a third but unarmed airframe for use as a testbed for its Hercules and Taurus engines, the Air Ministry complied. However, it later cancelled

this **Type 148A** machine on the grounds that it was importing a Northrop 2-L as a testbed for the Hercules. At much the same time the Air Ministry ordained that the second Type 148 should be completed to the revised **Type 148B** standard with the 1,050-hp (783-kW) Taurus II radial engine, in place of the Bristol Perseus engine originally specified.

The first Type 148 prototype was completed with one Bristol Mercury IX engine, and made its maiden flight on 15 October 1937. Trials revealed that, even without its slotted leading

edges, the Type 148 had an excellent speed range between a minimum of 62 mph (100 km/h) and a maximum of 255 mph (410 km/h). Pilots reported positively on the Type 148's handling characteristics, but in the event the Air Ministry preferred the rival Lysander. The Type 148 then suffered damage in an accident and while being repaired was revised with the 905-hp (675-kW) Perseus XII engine. The revised Type 148 and the Type 148B, which first flew in May 1938, were then used for development of the Perseus XII and Taurus II engines.

Bristol Type 148 (continued)

It is worth noting that work was also undertaken on the design of a related machine as the Type 147 in response to the Air Ministry's Specification F.9/35 for a two-seat night-fighter. The design of the Type 147 used essentially the same fuselage, flying surfaces and landing gear as the Type 148, together with a similar front cockpit, but carried its gunner in a revised rear cockpit section, from which he would control a flush-fitting dorsal barbette carrying four machine-guns. Bristol estimated good performance for the Type 147 with the Perseus engine, but the Air Ministry preferred the Boulton-Paul Defiant.

An unsuccessful challenger to the Boulton-Paul Defiant, Bristol's Type 148 incorporated many of the features of its predecessor, the Type 146. It was also considered and then rebuffed as a contender for an Air Ministry engine testbed.

SPECIFICATION

Bristol Type 148
Type: two-seat army co-operation warplane
Powerplant: one Bristol Mercury IX radial engine rated at 840 hp (626 kW)
Performance: maximum speed 255 mph (410 km/h) at optimum altitude; service ceiling 31,200 ft (9510 m)
Weights: empty 4,450 lb (2019 kg); maximum take-off 5,250 lb (2381 kg)
Dimensions: wingspan 40 ft (12.19 m); length 31 ft (9.45 m); height 10 ft 6 in (3.20 m); wing area 275.00 sq ft (25.55 m2)
Armament: two 0.303-in (7.7-mm) Browning fixed forward-firing machine-guns in the leading edge of the starboard wing and one 0.303-in (7.7-mm) Vickers 'K' trainable rearward-firing machine-gun in the rear of the cockpit, plus provision for light bombs carried under the wing

Bristol Type 152 Beaufort

In 1935 the Air Ministry had issued Specifications M.15/35 and G.24/35 detailing its requirements for a torpedo-bomber and a general reconnaissance/bomber respectively. The latter was met by the Bristol Type 149 Bolingbroke, while to meet the first requirement, Bristol began by considering an adaptation of the Blenheim, identifying its design as the Type 150. This proposal, which was concerned primarily with a change in fuselage design to accommodate a torpedo and the installation of more powerful engines, was submitted to the Air Ministry in November 1935.

Bristol then came to the conclusion that it would be possible to meet both specifications with a single aircraft evolved from the Blenheim, and immediately prepared a new design outline, the **Type 152**. By comparison with the Blenheim Mk IV, the new design was slightly longer to allow for the carriage of a torpedo in a semi-exposed position. The Type 152 was more attractive to the Air Ministry than the Type 150, but it was then decided that a crew of four was essential and the accommodation was redesigned to this end. The resulting high roof line became a distinguishing feature of the new aircraft, which was built to the Air Ministry's Specification 10/36 and subsequently named as the **Beaufort**.

Early analysis soon showed that the intended powerplant of two Bristol Perseus engines would provide insufficient power and instead the newly developed Taurus was selected for the Beaufort. The initial contract, for 78 aircraft, was placed in August 1936, but the first prototype did not fly until 15 October 1938. There had been a number of reasons for the delay, including engine overheating problems and the need to disperse Blenheim production before the Beaufort could be built.

Test-flying of the prototype revealed a number of shortcomings, leading to the provision of doors to enclose the retracted main landing gear units, repositioning of the engine exhausts, and an increase to two machine-guns in the dorsal turret. Allied with continuing teething problems with the new engine, these factors delayed the entry into service of the **Beaufort Mk I**, which started to equip No. 22 Squadron of Coastal Command in January 1940. It was this unit which, on the night of 15-16 April 1940, began the Beaufort's operational career by laying mines in enemy coastal waters, but in the following month all in-service aircraft were grounded until engine modifications could be carried out.

Earlier, the Australian government had shown interest in the Beaufort, and following the visit of a British Air Mission in early 1939, it was decided that Australian railway and industrial workshops could be adapted to produce these aircraft, resulting in the establishment of two assembly plants. At an early stage, the Australians decided that they did not want the Taurus power-plant, obtaining a licence from Pratt & Whitney to build the Twin Wasp, and this powered all of the 700 Australian-built Beauforts.

Australian production began in 1940, the first **Beaufort Mk V** off Australian production lines making its initial flight in May 1941. Apart from the change in powerplant, these aircraft were generally similar to their British counterparts except for an increase in fin area to improve stability with the more powerful Twin Wasp. In fact, engine and propeller changes accounted for most of the different variants produced by the Australian factories, including the **Beaufort Mk V**, **Beaufort Mk VA**, **Beaufort Mk VI**, **Beaufort Mk VII** and **Beaufort Mk VIII**. This last was the definitive production version, of which 520 were built up to the end of production in

Bristol Type 152 Beaufort Mk I

SPECIFICATION

Bristol Beaufort Mk I
Type: four-seat torpedo-bomber
Powerplant: two Bristol Taurus VI, XII or XVI radial engines each rated at 1,130 hp (843 kW)
Performance: maximum speed 260 mph (418 km/h) at 6,000 ft (1830 m); cruising speed 200 mph (322 km/h) at optimum altitude; service ceiling 16,500 ft (5030 m); range 1,035 miles (1666 km)
Weights: empty 13,107 lb (5945 kg); maximum take-off 21,230 lb (9630 kg)
Dimensions: wing span 57 ft 10 in (17.63 m); length 44 ft 7 in (13.59 m); height 12 ft 5 in (3.78 m); wing area 503.00 sq ft (46.73 m2)
Armament: two 0.303-in (7.7-mm) Vickers 'K' trainable forward-firing machine-guns in the nose position, two 0.303-in (7.7-mm) Vickers 'K' trainable rearward-firing machine-guns in the power-operated Bristol dorsal turret, and some aircraft had one 0.303-in (7.7-mm) Browning trainable rearward-firing machine-gun in the undernose blister position and one 0.303-in (7.7-mm) Vickers 'K' trainable lateral-firing machine-gun in each of the two beam positions, plus one 1,605-lb (728-kg) torpedo or up to 2,000 lb (907 kg) of bombs or mines

In March 1942 No. 22 Squadron left the UK, and its Beaufort Mk Is, such as this example, were shipped to Ceylon. The squadron continued to fly Beauforts on anti-shipping patrols and convoy escort duties until it re-equipped with the Beaufighter.

August 1944, and had additional fuel tankage, a Loran navigation system and variations in armament. Some 46 of the last production batch were subsequently converted to serve as unarmed transports. Designated as the Beaufort Mk IX, this variant had the dorsal turret removed and the resulting aperture faired in. The powerplant rating of all the Australian versions

was 1,200 hp (895 kW). The Beaufort was used extensively by the RAAF in the Pacific theatre, serving from the summer of 1942 until the end of World War II in 1945.

The early trials of the Beaufort Mk V with Twin Wasp engines induced the Air Ministry to specify this powerplant for the next contract, and a prototype with these American

engines was flown in November 1940. The first production **Beaufort Mk II** flew in September 1941 and, by comparison with the **Beaufort Mk I**, revealed much improved take-off performance. However, because of a shortage of Twin Wasp engines in the UK, only 164 production **Mk II**s were built before the **Mk I** with improved Taurus XII or XVI

engines was reintroduced on the line. In addition to the powerplant change, this version had structural strengthening, a changed gun turret, and ASV radar with Yagi aerials. When production of this version ended in 1944, well over 1,200 Beauforts had been built in the UK.

The final two designations, **Beaufort Mk III** and **Beaufort Mk IV**, related

respectively to a version with Rolls-Royce Merlin XX engines of which none was built, and a version with two 1,250-hp (932-kW) Taurus XX engines of which only a prototype was built.

The Beaufort was the standard torpedo-bomber in service with Coastal Command during 1940-3 and the type acquitted itself well until superseded by the Beaufighter.

Bristol Type 156 Beaufighter

The **Bristol Type 156** design, which subsequently received the name **Beaufighter**, was born of an improvisation forced upon Bristol in the wake of the Munich crisis of 1938, when the RAF was desperately short of modern fighters. Bristol had virtually completed design of the Beaufort and the improvisation that was now suggested was the use of major assemblies from this aircraft in a design that would yield a new long-range fighter in the shortest possible time. The proposal hinged upon the employment of the wing, tail unit and landing gear of the Beaufort, coupled with a powerplant comprising two Bristol Hercules sleeve-valve engines and requiring only a new fuselage to unite these assemblies. A draft proposal, knocked together in a few days and submitted to the Air Ministry in October 1938, resulted in an order for four prototypes. On 17 July 1939 the first of these made its maiden flight.

The Beaufighter emerged as mid-wing cantilever monoplane of all-metal construction except for the fabric covering of its control surfaces, and the four prototypes experimented with three different marks of Hercules engine, although the third and fourth both had Hercules II units.

Factory and service testing revealed few airframe problems, although some concern centred upon the engines, for the second prototype proved somewhat slower than the first. What was even more

disconcerting was that the aircraft were being flown without operational equipment, and Bristol realised that introduction of the 1,400-hp (1044-kW) Hercules III engine would provide little, if any, improvement. The only alternative engine available at short notice was the 1,500-hp (1119-kW) Hercules XI and it was decided to use this engine in the powerplant of the initial production versions.

Beaufighter armament varied somewhat according to the basic role in which a particular version was to operate. The **Beaufighter Mk IF** was visualised as a night-fighter, with bulky AI (Airborne Interception) radar, and this dictated a concentration of heavy fire in the nose. The standard armament of the Mk IF was thus four 20-mm cannon in the nose and four 0.303-in (7.7-mm) machine-guns in the leading edge of the starboard wing and two more such machine-guns in the leading edge of the port wing, although early production aircraft off the Filton line in fact had only the four cannon. The radar was the AI.Mk IV, which was installed in the fuselage nose, and this became the standard unit for Beaufighters for Fighter Command.

Three Beaufighter production lines were established and the first Beaufighters were handed over to the RAF on 27 July 1940. Nos 25 and 29 Squadrons each received their first example of the Beaufighter on 2 September 1940; by 17 September No. 29

Squadron was fully operational on the type, followed by Nos 25, 219, 600 and 640 Squadrons. It was this last squadron which recorded the first Beaufighter victory with the AI.Mk IV radar, on 19 November 1940 when a Ju 88 was damaged over Oxfordshire and crashed before it could cross the English Channel.

An alternative employment for the **Beaufighter Mk IF** arose even while the initial night-fighter squadrons were being equipped, for there was an urgent need for long-range day fighters to operate around the Mediterranean and in the Western Desert. To meet this demand about 80 **Beaufighter Mk IF**s were provided with desert equipment and an additional 50-Imp gal (227-litre)

fuel tank on the fuselage floor. At a later date additional tankage was provided in the outer panels of the wing, but this necessitated deletion of the machine-guns.

The provision of special Coastal Command radio and navigation facilities distinguished the initial Beaufighter Mk IC (Coastal) which entered service with No. 143 Squadron in the spring of 1941. This mark proved itself a valuable weapon from the outset, becoming gradually more important as its capability was more fully developed and expanded.

A heavy demand for the Hercules engine, which was also used on the Short Stirling bomber, led to experimentation with other engine types. Accordingly, two of three airframes

supplied to Rolls-Royce at Hucknall were provided with 1,075-hp (802-kW) Merlin X Vee engines, and in their trials these aircraft revealed slightly improved performance. There was also a slight change in the aircraft's centre of gravity, manifesting itself in some directional instability, and this was resolved by the introduction of a tailplane with 12° dihedral that was adopted both retrospectively and as standard on all subsequent production aircraft. The Merlin-engined version of the Beaufighter was the **Beaufighter Mk II**, and the first production **Beaufighter Mk IIF** with 1,280-hp (954-kW) Merlin XX engines made its initial flight on 22 March 1941. The **Beaufighter Mk IIF** was, in fact, the only Merlin-engined version to be built, and the type served primarily as a home-defence night-fighter, although it was also used by the Fleet Air Arm.

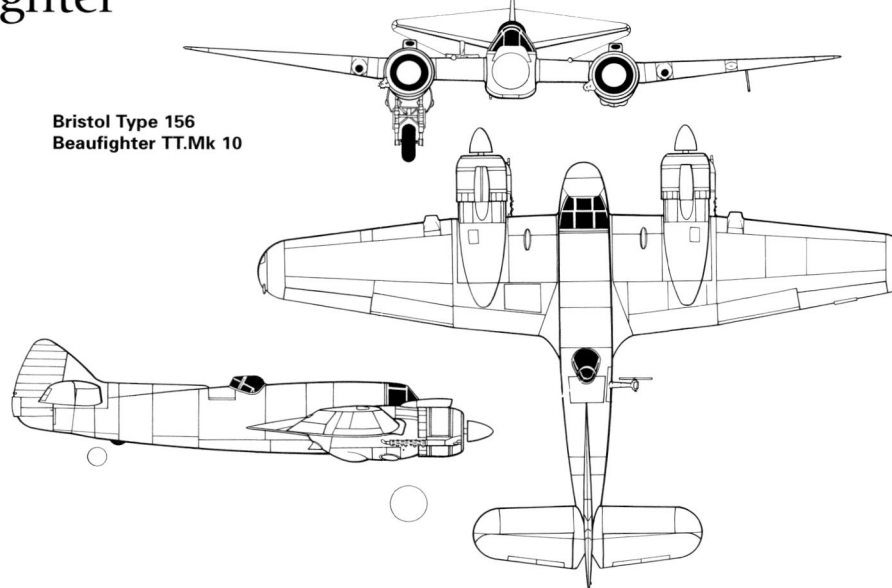

Bristol Type 156
Beaufighter TT.Mk 10

A Beaufighter Mk IF of No. 604 Sqn, RAF Fighter Command, shows off its overall black finish used by night fighters in 1942. Later production aircraft had a dihedral tailplane added to improve stability.

NG·F T4638

Bristol Type 156 Beaufighter (continued)

The only other variant to fly among the early marks was a single example of the **Beaufighter Mk V**. It was armed with only two 20-mm forward-firing cannon and, in place of the wing guns, four 0.303-in (7.7-mm) Browning machine-guns in a power-operated Boulton Paul turret mounted in the fuselage just aft of the pilot. But the weight and drag of the turret eroded performance so drastically that development was abandoned.

Fortunately, the feared shortage of Hercules engines did not materialise, and the more powerful Hercules VI, rated at 1,670 hp (1245 kW) at 7,500 ft (2286 m), became available for the Beaufighter. Following tests of three aircraft with this powerplant, the

Hercules VI and closely related Hercules XVI were accepted as standard. Airframes so powered received the designation **Beaufighter Mk VI**, supplanting both the **Mk I** and the **Mk II** on the production lines towards the end of 1941. The first **Beaufighter Mk VI** entered service with squadrons of Coastal and Fighter Commands at the beginning of 1942.

A far wider variation in equipment and weapons was made possible by the **Beaufighter Mk VI**'s more potent powerplant, expanding the variety of roles that this superb aircraft was able to undertake. The wing guns could be replaced by a 50-Imp gal (227-litre) tank to starboard and a 24-Imp gal (109-litre) tank to port for extended range; two 250-lb (113-kg)

bombs could be carried beneath the wing; eight 90-lb (41-kg) rocket projectiles could be carried in place of wing guns and an American- or British-made standard marine torpedo could be deployed. An initial batch of 16 **Beaufighter Mk VIC** aircraft was similarly converted to equip No. 254 Squadron, and the resulting 'Torbeau', as the type was unofficially nicknamed, carried out its first successful operation in early April 1943.

The **Beaufighter Mk VIF** was the first variant of the type to serve in the Burma-India theatre, where it was used initially by No. 176 Squadron in the defence of Calcutta. Mk VIFs were also used by four squadrons of the US Army Air Forces' 1st Tactical Air Command during operations in the Mediterranean theatre.

An anti-shipping strike version designated as the **Beaufighter TF.Mk X** supplemented the **Beaufighter Mk VIC** in Coastal Command service. This was powered by a modified version of the Hercules VI engine, designed to give peak output at low level, and was also the first to standardise on AI.Mk VIII radar mounted in a so-called 'thimble' nose. Other versions to serve with Coastal Command included 60 torpedo-carrying **Beaufighter Mk VIC** aircraft with Hercules XVI

The first squadron to be equipped with the Beaufighter Mk IC was No. 252 Squadron at Bircham Newton in November 1940. In April 1941 the squadron moved to Aldergrove, Northern Ireland for convoy patrols in the North Atlantic.

engines and eight underwing rockets in place of the wing guns. These were designated **Beaufighter Mk VI** Interim Torpedo Fighter (ITF), and were employed to swell the ranks pending delivery of the **TF.Mk X**. These 60 aircraft were subsequently converted to **Mk X** configuration. The final British production version was the **Beaufighter Mk XIC** for Coastal Command. This was similar to the **Mk X** but without the ability to carry a torpedo, and the 163 of this version brought total British construction to over 5,500 aircraft.

Of these, more than 50

had been supplied to Australia during 1941-2, and in 1944-5 Australia licence-built 364 aircraft, similar to the Beaufighter TF.Mk X, under the designation **Beaufighter Mk 21**. It was the Australian-flown Beaufighters which, blasting Japanese naval and merchant ships, earned for this outstanding machine the nickname 'Whispering Death'. After the end of World War II, many of the RAF's Beaufighters were converted to serve as target tugs under the designation **Beaufighter TT.Mk 10**, and the last example was only withdrawn from service in 1960.

SPECIFICATION

Bristol Beaufighter TF.Mk X
Type: two-seat anti-shipping strike fighter
Powerplant: two Bristol Hercules XVII radial engines each rated at 1,770 hp (1320 kW)
Performance: maximum speed 303 mph (488 km/h) at 1,300 ft (396 m); cruising speed 249 mph (401 km/h) at 5,000 ft (1524 m); climb to 5,000 ft (1524 m) in 3 minutes 30 seconds; service ceiling 15,000 ft (4572 m); range 1,470 miles (2366 km)
Weights: empty 15,600 lb (7076 kg); maximum take-off 25,200 lb (11431 kg)
Dimensions: wingspan 57 ft 10 in

(17.63 m); length 41 ft 8 in (12.70 m); height 15 ft 10 in (4.83 m); wing area 503.00 sq ft (46.73 m²)
Armament: four 20-mm Hispano fixed forward-firing cannon in the nose, six 0.303-in (7.7-mm) Browning fixed forward-firing machine-guns in the leading edges of the wing, and one 0.303-in (7.7-mm) Vickers 'K' trainable rearward-firing machine-gun in the dorsal position, plus one 2,127- or 1,650-lb (965- or 748-kg) torpedo carried under the fuselage and two 250-lb (113-kg) bombs or eight 90-lb (41-kg) air-to-surface unguided rockets carried under the wing

---

Bristol Type 163 Buckingham and Type 166 Buckmaster

When it started the design of a replacement for the Blenheim, Bristol had no means of knowing that its new tactical day bomber, the **Bristol Type 163 Buckingham**, was to be rendered obsolete, even before it had flown, by the superlative de Havilland Mosquito.

Bristol's earlier project to Specification B.2/41, the Type 162, itself schemed as a replacement for a

previous Beaufighter bomber scheme, the Type 161 Beaumont, was revised as a result of official delays in finalising the requirement. It was further delayed by teething troubles with the new Bristol Centaurus radial engine, and it was not until 4 February 1943 that the Buckingham prototype made its maiden flight in unarmed form. The second prototype, complete with

armament, followed shortly afterwards and was followed by two more prototypes, all powered by the Centaurus IV engine with high-altitude rating, although production aircraft were to have the medium-altitude Centaurus VII or XI.

Minor control modifications were made before the first production example of the **Buckingham B.Mk 1** flew on 12 February 1944, but after 10 aircraft had been completed changes were made to the tail surfaces to improve stability, particularly in single-engined flight.

Although outclassed by the Mosquito in European operations, it was felt that the Buckingham's superior

range would prove a great asset against the Japanese. But by the time production aircraft were being delivered the end of the Far East war was in sight and the original order was cut from 400 to 119, plus the four prototypes.

With the end of the Buckingham's potential usefulness as a bomber, it was decided to convert the aircraft as fast courier transports. The last batch of 65 on the line were completed as **Buckingham C.Mk 1** transports, and it was intended that the earlier **Buckingham B.Mk 1**s would be retrospectively

modified to the same standard. In this configuration, with extra tankage, seats for four passengers and a crew of three, the Buckingham had a range of 3,000 miles (4828 km) and was used on services to Malta and Egypt, although it was uneconomical with so small a passenger capacity. Although 54 of the bombers were returned to Filton for conversion, most were stored and eventually scrapped with very low hours.

Derived from the Type 163 Buckingham to undertake the advanced training role, the Bristol Type 166

SPECIFICATION

Bristol Buckingham B.Mk 1
Type: four-seat tactical day bomber
Powerplant: two 2,520-hp (1880-kW) Bristol Centaurus VII or XI radial piston engines each rated at 2,520 hp (1879 kW)
Performance: maximum speed 330 mph (531 km/h) at 12,000 ft (3658 m); cruising speed 285 mph (459 km/h) at optimum altitude; initial climb rate 1,700 ft (518 m) per minute; service ceiling 25,000 ft (7620 m); range 3,180 miles (5118 km)
Weights: empty 24,042 lb (10905 kg); maximum take-off

38,050 lb (17259 kg)
Dimensions: wingspan 71 ft 10 in (21.89 m); length 46 ft 10 in (14.27 m); height 17 ft 6 in (5.33 m); wing area 708.00 sq ft (65.77 m²)
Armament: four 0.303-in (7.7-mm) Browning fixed forward-firing machine-guns in the nose, four 0.303-in (7.7-mm) Browning trainable machine-guns in the power-operated Bristol turret and two 0.303-in (7.7-mm) Browning trainable rearward-firing machine-guns in the ventral position, plus up to 4,000 lb (1814 kg) of bombs carried internally

Designed as a light day-bomber, the Bristol Buckingham did not see service in this role – just a handful were used as high-speed transports by the Transport Command Development Unit.

Buckmaster had considerable commonality with its predecessor, and in fact the last 110 Buckingham aircraft were converted to Buckmaster standard by installation of dual controls and the implementation of other modifications.

The prototype Buckmaster flew from Filton on 27 October 1944, and a second prototype followed; both aircraft being conversions of partially completed Buckingham machines. Some 150 additional sets of Buckingham components had already been manufactured when the contract was cut back, and these were used for the manufacture of the **Buckmaster T.Mk 1**, the first of 110 production aircraft being completed in 1945.

Although several Buckmasters served with No. 8 Squadron at Aden on communications duties, most were delivered to OCUs to train Brigand pilots, and the Buckmaster had the distinction, at the time of its introduction, of being one of the fastest and most powerful trainers to serve with the RAF. Blind-flying instruction and instrument training could be undertaken.

The last Buckmasters in service with Training Command operated with No. 238 OCU into the mid-1950s, while one or two others were used on experimental work at Filton. One of these, probably the last survivor, was relegated to RAF Halton where it served as an instructional airframe until scrapped in 1958.

Bristol Type 164 Brigand

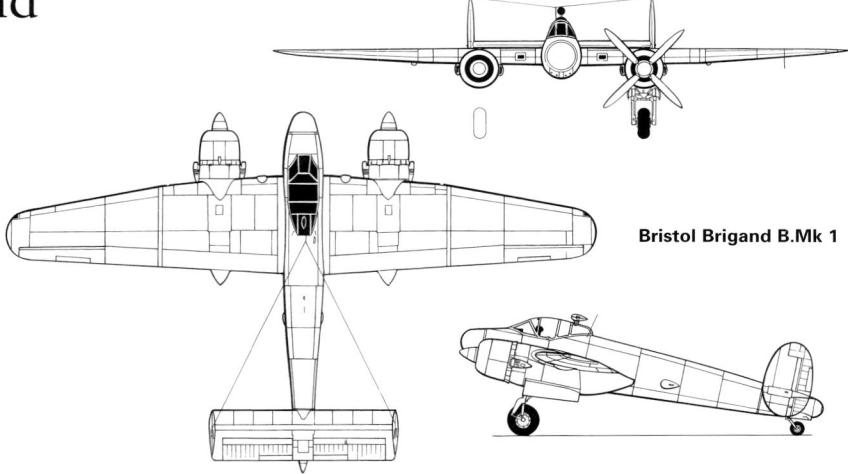

Bristol Brigand B.Mk 1

Following the success of the Beaufighter in the torpedo-bomber role, the Air Ministry issued Specification H.7/42 for a successor to the Beaufighter for service with Coastal Command. Bristol submitted the **Type 164**, later to become the **Brigand**. Four prototypes were ordered in April 1943, the first flying on 4 December of the following year, and production began using some jigs from the Buckingham.

The first 11 **Brigand TF.Mk 1** torpedo-bombers were delivered in 1946 to Nos 36 and 42 Squadrons and the Air/Sea Weapons Development Unit, Coastal Command, but by this time the requirement for coastal strike aircraft had ceased and the Brigands were eventually returned to Filton for conversion to fill a new RAF requirement for a light bomber to be used in Burma and Malaya.

In its new role the **Brigand B.Mk 1** was first delivered to No. 84 Squadron at Habbaniyah in Iraq early in 1949. Other Brigands went to No. 8 Squadron at Aden to replace that unit's Hawker Tempests. The RAF's last frontline Beaufighters were serving with No. 45 Squadron in Ceylon, which began to receive the Brigand in replacement during May 1949 shortly before moving to Malaya, and for the next five years these aircraft were in action against terrorists.

The **Brigand B.Mk 1** had armour plating, a redesigned cockpit and a one-piece transparent canopy, which could be jettisoned in emergency. Provision for the rear-firing gun was deleted, but the four 20-mm nose cannon remained in modified blast tubes. Sixteen unarmed aircraft were also delivered to No. 1301 Flight in Ceylon for the meteorological reconnaissance role under the designation **Brigand Met.Mk 3**. Two **Brigand B.Mk 1**s went to the Pakistan air force for evaluation in 1948; one crashed and the other returned, after a major overhaul, to the RAF, where it received a new serial number. A new **Brigand B.Mk 1** was built as an RAF replacement for the crashed aircraft.

Nine examples of a new radar trainer version, the **Brigand T.Mk 4**, were delivered to No. 228 Operation Conversion Unit (OCU) in 1950 and were used to train airborne interception (AI) radar operators. In 1955 the **Brigand T.Mk 5** appeared, differing in the AI installation and produced by converting **Brigand B.Mk 1**s and **T.Mk 4**s. The Brigand was phased out of service when No. 238 OCU was disbanded in March 1958. The Brigand was the RAF's last piston-engined attack aircraft, being replaced in this role by the turbojet-powered English Electric Canberra.

SPECIFICATION

Bristol Brigand B.Mk 1
Type: three-seat ground-attack bomber
Powerplant: two Bristol Centaurus 57 radial engines each rated at 2,470 hp (1843 kW)
Performance: maximum speed 358 mph (576 km/h) at 16,000 ft (4877 m); cruising speed 311 mph (500 km/h) at optimum altitude; initial climb rate 1,500 ft (457 m) per minute; service ceiling 26,000 ft (7925 m); range 2,800 miles (4506 km) with drop tanks

Weights: empty 25,598 lb (11611 kg); maximum take-off 39,000 lb (17690 kg)
Dimensions: wingspan 72 ft 4 in (22.05 m); length 46 ft 5 in (14.15 m); height 17 ft 6 in (5.33 m); wing area 718.00 sq ft (66.70 m²)
Armament: four 20-mm Hispano fixed forward-firing cannon in the nose, plus up to 2,000 lb (907 kg) of bombs or eight 60-lb (27-kg) air-to-surface unguided rockets carried under the wing

No. 84 Squadron was equipped with Brigands between January 1949 and February 1953. The squadron was used in an offensive role against insurgent forces in Malaya between 1950 and 1953.

Bristol Type 167 Brabazon

The post-war needs of civil aviation in the UK were the subject of a study undertaken by an Inter-Departmental Committee, chaired by Lord Brabazon of Tara. In 1943, the committee recommended the development of five types of transport aircraft, including a transatlantic airliner with the capability to operate non-stop between London and New York. Bristol was revealed on 11 March 1943 as the manufacturer selected to produce this potentially prestigious trans-oceanic aircraft, which was designated as the **Bristol Type 167 Brabazon I**, and which was intended to challenge the dominance of the USA in the long-range transport market.

After much detailed discussion to determine the size, capacity and performance of the aircraft, it was defined by Specification 2/44 as a 50-passenger transport with a maximum take-off weight of 250,000 lb (113400 kg). The basic layout had been finalised by November 1944, featuring, among other things, a fuselage with a maximum diameter of 16 ft 9 in (5.11 m), multi-wheel tricycle landing gear and a powerplant of four coupled pairs of Bristol Centaurus radial engines driving contra-rotating propeller units. Manufacture of the first prototype began in October 1945. The completed aircraft was rolled out in December 1948 and A. J. 'Bill' Pegg, Bristol's chief test pilot, made the first flight on 4 September 1949. A restricted certificate of airworthiness was issued on 14 June 1950.

SPECIFICATION

Bristol Brabazon I
Type: long-range passenger transport
Powerplant: eight Bristol Centaurus radial engines each rated at 2,500 hp (1865 kW)
Performance: maximum speed 300 mph (483 km/h) at optimum altitude; cruising speed 250 mph (402 km/h) at optimum altitude;

cruising altitude 25,000 ft (7620 m); range 5,000 miles (8046 km)
Weights: empty 145,100 lb (65816 kg); maximum take-off 290,000 lb (131544 kg)
Dimensions: wingspan 230 ft (70.10 m); length 177 ft (53.95 m); height 50 ft (15.24 m): wing area 5.317.00 sq ft (493.95 m²)
Payload: see above

Bristol Type 167 Brabazon (continued)

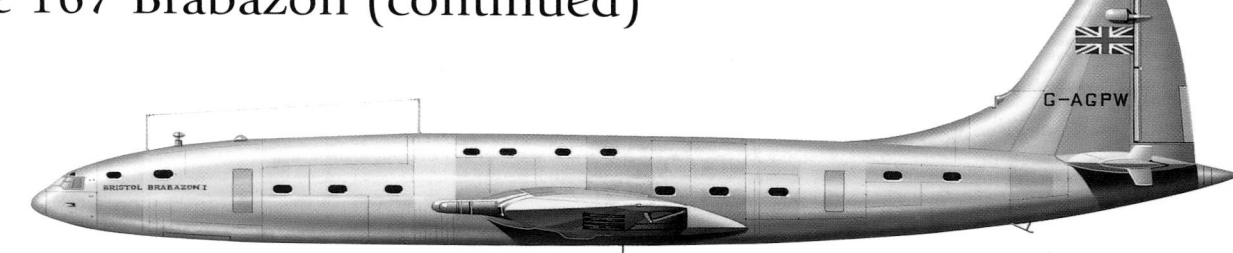

On the following day the **Brabazon I** undertook a number of demonstration flights at London Airport; the rear fuselage having been furnished with 30 seats for the occasion.

Fatigue cracks in the propeller mounting structure were a factor in the Air Registration Board's refusal to grant unrestricted approval for commercial passenger-carrying flights, preventing trial operation in a 180-seat layout on the London-Nice route of BEA.

After approximately £3 million had been spent on the UK's largest land-

The thin nacelles of the Brabazon Mk I indicate that they did not house the engines, but only the drive shafts for the contra-rotating propeller units, each driven by a pair of Bristol Centaurus radials buried in the wings.

plane the project was cancelled and the prototype was broken up at Filton in October 1953, having flown less than 400 hours.

Variant

Brabazon II: designed to Specification 2/46. This version was to have carried 100 passengers and been powered by four 7,000-shp (5220-kW) coupled pairs of Bristol Proteus 710 turboprop engines. Structural changes were introduced, as were four-wheel main landing gear bogies. The prototype, semi-complete when the programme was cancelled, was scrapped at Filton.

Bristol Type 170 Freighter

Bristol developed the **Type 170** short-range utility transport during the closing stages of the war. Its shape was largely determined by the British army's needs, which included the ability to airlift the standard three-ton truck. The design was finalised with a high-wing monoplane configuration; clamshell nose doors; flightdeck above the cargo hold/cabin; fixed tailwheel landing gear and a powerplant of two wing-mounted

Silver City's 'Superfreighter' aircraft could accommodate up to 23 passengers and three cars. In 1962, Air Charter and Silver City Airways were merged to form British United Air Ferries, which operated a combined fleet of 24 Type 170 aircraft, increasing to 41 by 1970.

Bristol Hercules sleeve-valve radial engines. Two civil prototypes were financed by the Ministry of Supply as the need for military transports appeared to be nearing an end, but the condition attached to this funding was that the company should cover tooling costs and also build two additional prototypes.

As a result, the company took the opportunity to construct its own examples as passenger/cargo vari-

ants. The MoS aircraft were known as the **Type 170 Mk I Freighter**, retaining the nose loading doors, while the company prototypes were of the **Type 170 Mk II Wayfarer** type, with a solid nose, side entrance/loading door, and an optional reinforced freight floor. The Freighters were true cargo-carriers, while the Wayfarers were available in several configurations, including one with a maximum of 32 passengers, with a galley and toilet.

The first to fly was one of the Freighter prototypes on 2 December 1945, followed by a Wayfarer in the 32-seat configuration on 30 April 1946. The first prototype was used for service trials at Boscombe Down, as a result of which the wingspan was extended to allow an increase in maximum take-off weight. This, in turn, required the installation of more powerful engines, and resulted in the version designated **Type 170**

Variants

Type 170 Freighter Mk IA: mixed-traffic variant of Mk I with 16 passenger seats and toilet to the back of the rear spar
Type 170 Freighter Mk IB: BEA version of Mk I
Type 170 Freighter Mk IC: BEA version of Mk IA
Type 170 Freighter Mk ID: BSAA version of Mk IA
Type 170 Wayfarer Mk IIA: version of Mk II with 32 seats, pantry and toilet
Type 170 Wayfarer Mk IIB: BEA version of Mk IIA with two toilets
Type 170 Wayfarer 1Mk IIC: version of Mk II with 20 seats in front of rear spar, baggage hold, and toilet
Type 170 Freighter Mk XI: version of Mk I with a wing spanning 108 ft (32.92 m) and extra tankage
Type 170 Freighter Mk XIA: mixed-traffic version of Mk XI
Type 170 Freighter Mk 21E: convertible version of the Mk 21 with cabin heating, soundproofing and 32 removable seats
Type 170 Freighter Mk 31: version of Mk 21 with dorsal fin
Type 170 Freighter Mk 31E: convertible version of Mk 31
Type 170 Freighter Mk 31M: military version of Mk 31 with provision for supply dropping
Type 179 Freighter: project for a twin-boom version
Type 179A Freighter: project for a version with upswept tail and ramp-loading door
Type 216 Freighter: project for a car ferry with two Dart turboprops

Freighter Mk 21. The best known variant was the **Type 170 Freighter Mk 32** with a lengthened fuselage. The variant was developed for Silver City Airways to provide increased passenger/car capacity for service on the operator's Channel

Air Bridge route. 'Super-Wayfarer' aircraft were acquired later, able to carry a maximum of 60 passengers. When production of Type 170 ended in early 1958, a total of 214 of all variants had been built.

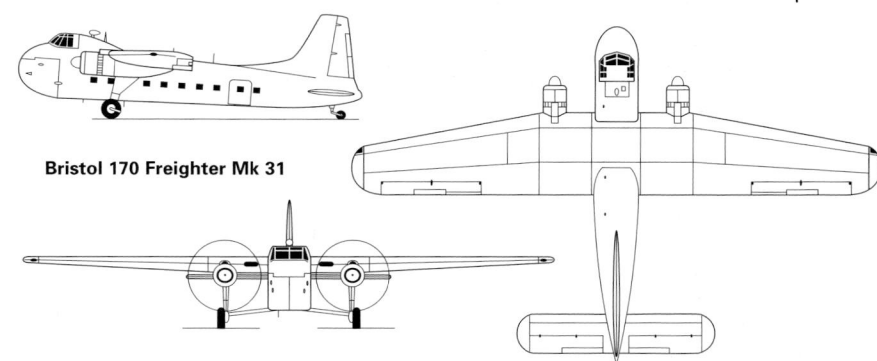

Bristol 170 Freighter Mk 31

SPECIFICATION	
Bristol Type 170 Freighter Mk 32	range 820 miles (1320 km) with maximum payload
Type: utility transport	**Weights:** empty 29,950 lb (13585 kg); maximum take-off 44,000 lb (19958 kg)
Powerplant: two Bristol Hercules 734 radial engines each rated at 1,980 hp (1477 kW)	**Dimensions:** wingspan 108 ft (32.92 m); length 73 ft 4 in (22.35 m); height 25 ft (7.62 m); wing area 1,487 sq ft (138.14 m²)
Performance: maximum speed 225 mph (362 km/h) at 3,000 ft (914 m); cruising speed 163 mph (262 km/h) at 5,000 ft (1524 m); service ceiling 24,500 ft (7467 m);	**Payload:** up to 12,000 lb (5443 kg)

Bristol Type 171 Sycamore

Late in 1944 Bristol formed a helicopter department at Filton and recruited Raoul Hafner from the Airborne Forces Experimental Establishment, where he had been leading a British rotorcraft development team. Drawing on pre-war experience with his A.R.III Gyroplane, Hafner started work on the **Bristol Type 171 Sycamore** as a single-engined four-seat

helicopter for civil and military applications. The lack of a sufficiently developed British engine of the required power led to the selection of the widely used 450-hp (336-kW) Pratt & Whitney Wasp

Junior radial engine for the first two **Type 171 Mk 1** prototypes that were developed to the Ministry of Supply's Specification E.20/45.

After extensive component testing, ground

Variants

Type 171 Mk 3: Airframe changes included a shortened nose and an increase in cabin width to accommodate three passengers on the rear seat. To maintain essential systems in the event of engine failure, the accessory drive was transferred from the engine to the rotor gearbox. The initial production batch included one Sycamore HC.Mk 10 and four Sycamore HC.Mk 11 ambulance and communications machines for evaluation by the AAC, and four Sycamore HR.Mk 12 helicopters for rescue duties with RAF Coastal Command. Two Mk 3A helicopters, with a freight hold behind the engine bay, were built for BEA.

Type 177 Mk 4: Main production version, incorporating modifications evolved from Mk 3 experience, including revised landing gear, four cabin doors and the pilot's position moved from port to starboard. Deliveries included three Sycamore HR.Mk 50 and seven Sycamore HC.Mk 51 helicopters for the RAN, three Sycamore Mk 14 helicopters for Belgian air force use in the Congo, and 50 Sycamore Mk 52 helicopters for the West German army and navy. The RAF received two Sycamore HR.Mk 13 and more than 80 Sycamore HR.Mk 14 helicopters, equipped with winches for air-sea rescue duties, initially with No. 275 Squadron of Fighter Command, which received its first helicopter on 13 April 1953; Sycamores also operated in light assault and reconnaissance roles in Malaya, Cyprus and Borneo.

The Sycamore HR.Mk 14 went into service in April 1953 with the RAF's No. 275 Squadron. This rescue example is demonstrating the use of its winch for air-sea rescue duties.

running of the completed airframe began on 9 May 1947, and the first flight was made by H. A. Marsh on 27 July. The second helicopter joined the test programme in February 1948. On 25 April 1949, to facilitate its flight to the Paris Salon de l'Aéronautique, it became the first British helicopter

to be granted a civil certificate of airworthiness. An Alvis Leonides radial was installed in the third airframe, which appeared in the static park at the 1948 Society of British Aircraft Constructors (SBAC) exhibition at Farnborough. Designated **Type 171 Mk 2**, this helicopter made a successful

first flight on 3 September 1949, although a second take-off attempt ended abruptly when the rotor disintegrated. After introducing a strengthened rotor, development flying was resumed while work continued on the assembly of 15 production examples of the **Type 171 Mk 3**.

SPECIFICATION

Bristol Type 171 Sycamore HR.Mk 14

Type: five-seat communications/ SAR/light troop-carrying helicopter
Powerplant: one Alvis Leonides 73 radial engine rated at 550 hp (410 kW)
Performance: maximum speed 127 mph (204 km/h) at sea level; cruising speed 105 mph (169 km/h) at optimum altitude; initial climb

rate 1,300 ft (396 m) per minute; endurance 3 hours
Weights: empty 3,810 lb (1728 kg); maximum take-off 5,600 lb (2540 kg)
Dimensions: main rotor diameter 48 ft 7 in (14.81 m); length 46 ft 2 in (14.07 m) with rotors folded; height 12 ft 2 in (3.71 m); main rotor disc area 1,853.80 sq ft (172.22 m²)

Bristol Type 173, Type 191 and Type 192 Belvedere

The first British tandem-rotor helicopter, the **Bristol Type 173** combined two sets of Sycamore rotors and control systems each powered by a 575-hp (429-kW) Alvis Leonides radial engine.

The first of two prototypes, developed to the Ministry of Supply's Specification E.4/47, made its first hovering flight on 3 January 1952. Problems delayed further progress until July; but this **Type 173 Mk 1** helicopter appeared at the SBAC Show in September. Evaluation by the RAF followed, and in 1953 naval trials were undertaken on board the aircraft carrier HMS *Eagle*. The first prototype was subsequently given four-bladed rotors and a low-set flat tailplane incorporatiing small fins at its tips.

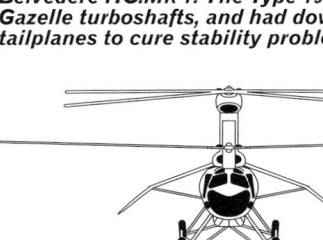

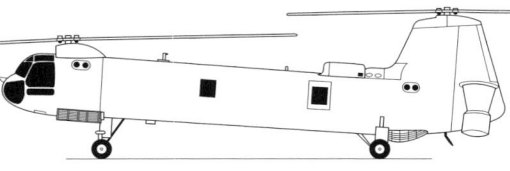

The RAF ordered the Type 192 Belvedere in April 1956 and its service designation was Belvedere HC.Mk 1. The Type 192 featured Gazelle turboshafts, and had downward-canted tailplanes to cure stability problems.

Bristol Type 192 Belvedere

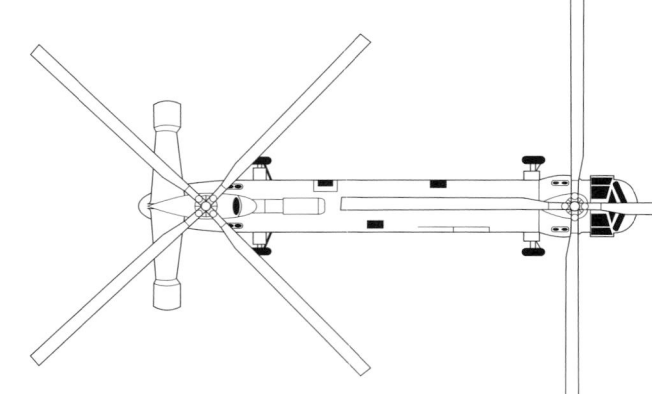

SPECIFICATION

Bristol Belvedere HC.Mk 1

Type: two/three-crew short-range tactical transport helicopter
Powerplant: two Napier Gazelle NGa.2 Mk 100 turboshaft engines each rated at 1,465 shp (1092 kW)
Performance: maximum cruising speed 138 mph (222 km/h) at optimum altitude; initial climb rate 1,350 ft (411 m) per minute; service ceiling 17,300 ft (5273 m); hovering ceiling 7,500 ft (2286 m) in ground effect; range 460 miles (740 km) on a ferry flight with

standard fuel or 75 miles (121 km) with a 6,000-lb (2722-kg) payload
Weights: empty 11,634 lb (5277 kg); maximum take-off 20,000 lb (9072 kg)
Dimensions: rotor diameter, each 48 ft 11 in (14.91 m); length 89 ft 9 in (27.36 m) with rotors turning; height 17 ft 3 in (5.26 m); rotor disc area, total 3,760 sq ft (349.30 m²)
Payload: up to 18 fully armed troops or 6,000 lb (2722 kg) of freight

Bristol Type 173, Type 191 and Type 192 Belvedere (cont.)

A tandem arrangement of two sets of stub wings, designed to offload the rotors in flight, characterised the second prototype, which also had castoring front wheels. Designated **Type 173 Mk 2**, this was first flown on 31 August 1953 and was transferred to the RAF in August 1954 for further naval trials, the forward stub wings having been removed and the rear set replaced by the upswept tailplane of the Mk 1. In August 1956 the helicopter was leased to BEA, but was withdrawn from use

following an accident at Filton on 16 September. Three further prototypes, designated **Type 173 Mk 3**, were built for the Ministry of Supply with 850-hp (634-kW) Leonides Major engines, four-bladed metal rotors, and a taller rear pylon. Only the first progressed beyond the ground-running stage, beginning hovering trials on 9 November 1956. The third had the shortened fuselage and long-stroke landing gear of the **Type 191** naval version, which in April 1956 secured an order (later cancelled) for

three Leonides Major-powered prototypes and 65 production examples with Napier Gazelle turboshaft engines.

The cancellation of the naval variant was not the end of the story, however. The RAF had a requirement for a personnel and paratroop transport helicopter, also possessing the capability to lift bulky loads on an external sling. An order for 22, later increased to 26, examples of the **Type 192** version was placed in April 1956, the contract specifying the use of the Gazelle turboshaft. The

prototype, first flown on 5 July 1958, was joined in the development programme by nine pre-production aircraft. These originally had wooden rotor blades and a tailplane with anhedral and endplate fins, but were later brought up to production standard for delivery to the RAF with metal rotor blades, a tailplane of compound anhedral, powered flying controls, sliding doors, improved air inlets and enlarged wheels with low-pressure tyres. The eleventh aircraft was completed as the first

production **Belvedere HC.Mk 1**, delivered to No. 66 Squadron at RAF Odiham in August 1961. This unit was also the last to operate the Belvedere, disbanding at RAF Seletar in March 1969. By the time that No. 66 Squadron had received its first Belvedere, Bristol's helicopter department had been acquired by Westland, becoming its Bristol Helicopter Division. It was this division which continued production of the RAF's Belvedere helicopters, and maintained product support while they remained in service.

Bristol Type 175 Britannia

Soon after the end of World War II, BOAC stated a requirement for a MRE (Medium-Range Empire) civil transport, and five British aircraft manufacturers, including Bristol, submitted a total of eight designs to the specification which had been advised. Most nearly meeting the requirement was the **Bristol Type 175**, a pressurised low-wing monoplane with tricycle landing gear, cabin accommodation for between 32 and 36 passengers, and the powerplant of four Bristol Centaurus sleeve-valve radial engines. This powerplant provided more power than was required by the planned payload, however, and it was decided to amend the design to accommodate between 40 and 44 passengers, this being increased again at a later stage to between 42 and 48 passengers. It was anticipated that BOAC would order this version, but in fact it was the UK's Ministry of Supply which ordered three prototypes on 5 July 1948.

More design changes followed and, when it made its maiden flight on 16 August 1952, the first prototype was of the same general configuration as the initial production **Britannia Series 100** aircraft which could accommodate a maximum of 90 tourist-class passengers. The powerplant of this prototype comprised four 2,800-ehp

(2088-ekW) Bristol Proteus turboprop engines, but the Series 100 production aircraft had the more developed 3,780-ehp (2819-ekW) Proteus 705. Fifteen of this version were built for BOAC, these being designated **Britannia 102**, and they first entered service on 1 February 1957 on BOAC's service to South Africa.

A larger-capacity version followed under the designation **Britannia Series 300**, the prototype **Britannia 301** making its first flight on 31 July 1956. This variant had its fuselage lengthened by 10 ft 3 in (3.12 m) for the accommodation of up to 133 tourist-class passengers and it also had non-stop transatlantic capability. Although seven aircraft were ordered by BOAC, they did not serve with the airline, being delivered instead to Aeronaves de Mexico (two **Britannia 302** aircraft), Transcontinental SA (two **Britannia 305** aircraft), Air Charter (two **Britannia 307** aircraft) and Ghana Airways (one **Britannia 309** machine).

BOAC had transferred its order to the **Britannia Series 300LR** (long-range) type with increased fuel tankage, and initially with 4,120-ehp (3072-ekW) Proteus 755 turboprops. The designation Britannia Series 300LR was later changed to **Britannia Series 310**, and the **Britannia 311** prototype first flew on 31 December

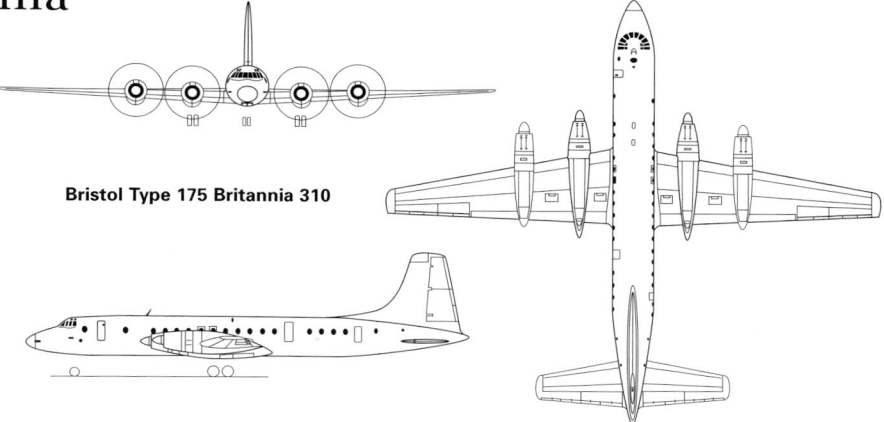

Bristol Type 175 Britannia 310

1956. BOAC's first **Britannia 312** was delivered on 10 September 1957 and used for proving flights over the North Atlantic.

Final development produced the **Britannia Series 320**, which differed primarily by having Proteus 765 turboprop engines each rated at 4,450 ehp (3318 ekW), but only two of these were built and leased to Canadian Pacific Air Lines (late CP Air).

It had seemed in the early days of Britannia production that this airliner might capture a significant bag of orders, but it was left behind in the wake of the new Boeing Model 707 and never recovered. Production of civil airliners totalled 60, and in addition a further 23 aircraft (three **Britannia 252** and 20 **Britannia 253** machines)

were completed for service with the RAF's Transport Command as the **Britannia C.Mk 2** and **Britannia C.Mk 1** respectively. Basically similar to the Series 310, these aircraft incorporated a large freight door; the 22 remaining in service in 1975 were then retired, and were acquired by small airlines in Africa, Europe, and the Middle East. About 10 of these remained in service in early 1982 but disappeared from service during the decade.

The last Britannia delivered from Filton, at the end of November 1960, was the original prototype which, by then, had an unusual powerplant: Proteus 705s in

the two inboard positions, one Proteus 755 in the starboard outer position and one 5,500-ehp (4101-ekW) Bristol Orion turboprop in the port outer position; the machine ended its days at RAF St Athan, where it served as an instructional airframe. This was not quite the end of the Britannia story, however, for a manufacturing licence had been granted in 1954 to Canadair. This company built initially 33 CL-28 Argus maritime reconnaissance aircraft, derived from the Britannia, for service with the RCAF, and then the CL-44 transport version for both military and civil use.

After the cancellation of the projected pure-jet Vickers V.1000 transport, the RAF ordered a militarised version of the Britannia. A total of 20 was eventually delivered, serving from 1959-1976.

SPECIFICATION	
Bristol Type 175 Britannia Series 310	range 4,268 miles (6869 km) with maximum payload
Type: long-range transport	**Weights:** empty 82,537 lb (37438 kg); maximum take-off 185,000 lb (83915 kg)
Powerplant: four Bristol Proteus 755 turboprop engines each rated at 4,120 ehp (3072 ekW)	**Dimensions:** wingspan 142 ft 3 in (43 m); length 124 ft 3 in (37 m), height 37 ft 6 in (11.43 m); wing area 2,075.00 sq ft (192.77 m²)
Performance: maximum speed 397 mph (639 km/h) at optimum altitude; cruising speed 357 mph (575 km/h) at optimum altitude; service ceiling 24,000 ft (7315 m);	**Payload:** up to 133 passengers

Bristol Type 188

The first turbojet-engined aircraft of Bristol design to reach the flight-test stage, the **Bristol Type 188** was developed in response to Specification ER.134, issued in February 1953. The requirement was for a research vehicle, capable of flight at twice the speed of sound, for investigation into the effects of kinetic heating on airframes.

Manufactured from stainless steel, the Type 188 was to have been powered by two Rolls-Royce Avon RA.24R engines, but the de Havilland Gyron DGJ.10 was substituted. The original order was for six aircraft, later reduced to three, one of which was a structural test airframe transported to Farnborough in May 1960. The first flying prototype was rolled out on 26 April 1961 but technical snags, including engine inlet design problems, delayed the maiden flight until 14 April 1962. Flown by chief test pilot Godfrey Auty, the Type 188 took off from Filton to land after 23 minutes at the A&AEE at Boscombe Down. The second prototype flew for the first time on 29 April 1963.

In 1960 Bristol Aircraft merged with the aviation interests of Vickers Ltd and the English Electric Co. to create the British Aircraft Corporation. In 1959 Bristol Aero-Engines merged with Armstrong Siddeley Motors Ltd to create Bristol Siddeley Engines Ltd and finally, in 1968, Bristol Siddeley became part of Rolls-Royce Ltd, the name Bristol disappearing as an independent manufacturer.

The Type 188's research career was short as, despite extensive fuselage tankage, the fuel consumption was so great that endurance was wholly inadequate.

SPECIFICATION	
Bristol Type 188	more than 1,240 mph (1995 km/h) or Mach 1.88 at high altitude
Type: single-seat high-speed research aircraft	**Weights:** empty 28,000 lb (12701 kg); maximum take-off 37,527 lb (17022 kg)
Powerplant: two Bristol Siddeley (de Havilland) Gyron Junior DGJ.10R turbojet engines each rated at 14,000 lb st (62.28 kN) with afterburning	**Dimensions:** wingspan 35 ft 1 in (10.69 m); length 71 ft (21.64 m); height 13 ft 4 in (4.06 m); wing area 396.00 sq ft (36.79 m²)
Performance: maximum speed	

Bristol Burney aircraft

Bristol was an early contender in the seaplane field with a series of conceptually very advanced seaplanes that were evaluated under conditions of great secrecy virtually up to the outbreak of World War I in August 1914. The origins of this extensive programme can be found in the series of flights completed during October 1911 by Howard Pixton. The machine employed was a Boxkite modified with flotation bags under its lower wing, with a naval officer, Lieutenant Charles Burney, flying as passenger. Burney then formulated a concept based on the use of hydrofoils after the pattern proposed by two Italian pioneers, Forlanini and Guidoni; this involved elevating the hulls of motor boats above the surface of the water to reduce drag and thus boost speed. On the advice of his father, an admiral in the Royal Navy, Burney approached Sir George White of Bristol with the idea of a joint development and exploitation programme.

Burney's overall concept for a ship-launched scout seaplane was based on the combination of several novel aspects. These included a sealed fuselage that was buoyant in the water, a folding wing, hydrofoils and separate air and water propellers.

Burney recommended as a starting point the conversion of the sole **Bristol G.E.1** biplane, then under construction. Its alighting gear comprised three 'hydropeds', which were each a leg fitted with a ladder of hydrofoil surfaces, as well as five pneumatic floats under the fuselage and lower wing for buoyancy.

At the end of 1911, Bristol established its secret 'X Department' to undertake the work under the supervision of Frank Barnwell, who had only recently joined the company. Burney's concept for the adapted G.E.1, now known as the **Bristol X.1**, was based on the use of a 60- to 80-hp (45- to 60-kW) ENV engine, with a clutch system allowing it to drive either the air propeller or the water propellers. Barnwell felt that Burney's design was too small and too 'draggy' to have any chance of success, however, and therefore recommended a monoplane design with a boat hull and buoyant wingtips.

The **X.2**, designed by Barnwell with a conventional wing and 'hydroped' legs, began to take shape with an 80-hp (60-kW) Canton-Unné water-cooled radial engine in the nose. Completed in May 1912, the X.2 soon showed that its water propellers provided good acceleration, but then the speed of the machine through the water ripped off the fairings round the 'hydroped' legs. Subsequent towing trials behind a torpedo boat revealed that the hydrofoils lifted the machine above the level of the water without problem, but that the X.2 was unstable. Stability was provided by airframe modifications which generated sufficient stability for towed trials, but when the water propellers were activated, unequal torque reactions caused the X.2 to heel; also noted was the tendency of the wingtip to touch the surface of the water, causing considerable drag, as well as a tendency of the aircraft to turn toward the submerged wingtip, requiring the addition of a small float under each tip.

In September 1912 reinforced streamlined fairings were added to the 'hydroped' legs. It was then decided that the first air tests would be undertaken with the X.2 towed to the speed at which the hydrofoil surface lifted the machine above the surface of the water; earlier trials had revealed a tendency for the engine to stall when both the water and air propellers were clutched in. The engine was removed and replaced by 500 lb (227 kg) of ballast, and in this form the X.2 first took off on 21 September after being towed to a speed of 21 mph (34 km/h) against a 14-mph (23-km/h) headwind. However, the X.2's controls were locked and as the X.2 climbed steeply in a nose-high attitude, the boat party slipped the tow, the X.2 then stalling and crashing.

The X.2 was damaged beyond economical repair, so in March 1913 Bristol began work on the improved **X.3**, with contrarotating water propellers whose torque reactions cancelled each other, as well as a number of other changes.

The first taxiing tests were done with an 80-hp (60-kW) Gnome rotary engine and float-carrying outriggers in place of the two halves of the wing. The main 'hydroped' legs had controllable water rudders and a water elevator. Stability under tow was good and the taxiing performance was satisfactory. It was discovered that the nose dropped when the air propeller was clutched in, however, and Barnwell overcame this tendency by the installation of a forward elevator just to the rear of the air propeller; as the air propeller was clutched in, this elevator automatically moved to keep the nose up. The wing and the Canton-Unné engine were then fitted, but in June 1914 the X.3 was badly damaged after it ran onto a submerged sandbank. At this stage the Admiralty withdrew its support and all further work on the X.3 was cancelled, the remains of the machine being scrapped in 1920.

The Bristol Burney X.2's hull was planked with thin mahogany veneer and covered with sailcloth before being varnished to provide good waterproof qualities. Here, the X.2 is seen taxiing at Dale in September 1912, using its underwater propellers.

SPECIFICATION	
Bristol Burney X.3	200 hp (149 kW)
Type: two-seat experimental hydrofoil seaplane	**Dimensions:** wingspan 57 ft 10 in (17.63 m); length 36 ft 8 in (11.18 m); wing area 500.00 sq ft (46.45 m²)
Powerplant: one Canton-Unné radial engine rated at around	

Bristol Coanda aircraft

Henri Coanda was a Romanian who had been educated in France as an engineer, largely under the supervision of Eiffel, who had built the first wind tunnel in Europe. At the Paris Salon de l'Aéronautique of 1910, Coanda exhibited an ambitious biplane with an engine that drove a small-diameter ducted fan rather than a conventional propeller. This biplane probably failed to fly, but Coanda must be credited with the invention of this type of propulsion arrangement. Coanda joined Bristol during January 1912, and his first design in the UK was a conventional two-seat monoplane powered by a 50-hp (37-kW) Gnome rotary engine.

The tandem seating arrangement of what became known as the **Bristol Coanda School Monoplane** was modified in the second example to provide side-by-side seating with dual controls in a widened fuselage. During 1913 there followed another 11 aircraft, five of them with tandem seating and the other six with side-by-side seating.

In May 1912 the War Office announced its stringent conditions for a standard type with which to equip the fledgling British army air arm, but stipulated that all the contenders had to be ready for inspection and evaluation in a mere two months. Clearly there was inadequate time for the creation of an all-new

design, especially as the prize money was limited to only £5,000 for any one entrant. Coanda was already well advanced with a new design for a military monoplane, however, and Bristol entered two of these, and also two Gordon England G.E.2 biplanes, in the competition. The two Coanda aircraft were each powered by one of the new 80-hp (60-kW) Gnome rotary engines and reflected Coanda's belief in the importance of reducing drag. Thus the usual pyramids of cabane struts were replaced by a pair of vertical wood-faired steel pylons on the fuselage centreline.

The Coanda Military Monoplane did moderately well in the trials and the War Office bought both aircraft, but one crashed during its delivery flight and the War Office immediately placed a ban (eventually lifted after five months) on the use of all monoplanes by the military wing of the RFC. The prohibition ended all short-term hopes of additional British sales, but 20 production aircraft were later completed with increased wingspan, and a number of these aircraft were sold to Italy and Romania as well as to the RFC.

A single and notably unsuccessful experimental variant, completed in September 1912, was known as 'The Elephant'. Intended as a rival to the sturdy Etrich and DFW monoplanes then used by

the Imperial German army air service, this machine had a 70-hp (52-kW) Daimler-Mercedes engine.

Having effectively removed Bristol's chance of securing a major British official order for the Coanda Military Monoplane, the Air Ministry partially compensated the company by the award of a contract for manufacture of the RAF B.E.2, which was clearly the best British aircraft of its type at that time. Coanda therefore decided to plan a biplane, spurred by the receipt in November 1913 of requests from Spain and Germany for long-range aircraft of the two-seat type; the aircraft would be powered by the Renault and Daimler-Mercedes engines rated at 70 and 90 hp (52 and 67 kW) respectively.

The result was the **B.R.70** biplane that was later redesignated as the **B.R.7**. Eight of these aircraft were built, one of them in Germany by Bristol's subsidiary at Halberstadt, the Deutsche Bristol-Werke, with the Daimler-Mercedes engine.

The most successful of the Bristol Coanda designs, the T.B.8 saw service with the RNAS mainly as a trainer. However, a small number, based in France, flew bombing missions against German positions.

The first machine was completed in February 1913, but Spain refused to accept the aircraft as they failed to deliver the guaranteed performance, and the aircraft had only a short and chequered career in the UK.

In January 1913 Coanda designed a two-seat seaplane, with its fuselage mounted midway between the biplane wings and alighting gear based on a single centreline float and two stabilising floats under the outboard ends of the lower wing. The machine was generally known as the **Hydro 120** as it was the 120th Bristol airframe. It first flew on 15 April 1913 but was lost during this flight after the engine overheated.

The Admiralty had also ordered a landplane derived from the Coanda Military Monoplane, of which one example was converted as the biplane prototype for what became known as the **T.B.8**. This was the most successful early Bristol aircraft type after the Boxkite, for production totalled 53 machines (including a number built under licence in France by

After initial tests at Filton, Bristol Coanda School monoplane No. 132 was delivered to Turin for service with the Italian military aviation school.

Breguet and some Coanda Military Monoplane conversions). Powerplants included 50- and 80-hp (37- and 60-kW) Gnome rotary units, 60- and 80-hp (45- and 60-kW) Le Rhône rotary units and the 100-hp (75-kW) Gnome Monosoupape rotary.

Single examples of the **T.B.8H** and the **G.B.75** variants were completed. The T.B.8H was a floatplane with the 80-hp (60-kW) Gnome engine. The G.B.75, produced to an order of Prince Cantacuzene of Romania, was a much improved development of the T.B.8 with far better streamlining and one 75-hp (56-kW) Gnome Monosoupape rotary. The type revealed for the first time the hand of Frank Barnwell, who had recently been employed by Bristol and was to become its greatest designer.

The completion of the G.B.75 was overtaken by the outbreak of World War I and the aircraft was delivered to the RFC with the 80-hp (60-kW) Gnome engine.

One final type worthy of mention as a Coanda biplane was the **P.B.8**, which was the designer's only biplane of the pusher configuration. Work on the design began in November 1913, but the aircraft was not completed until July 1914.

Bristol Prier aircraft

On 12 April 1911, Pierre Prier achieved the first non-stop flight from London to Paris. He was employed as the chief flying instructor of the Blériot school at Hendon and was a qualified engineer who wanted to design as well as to fly

aircraft. He seized the opportunity eagerly when approached in June 1911 to join the staff of the British and Colonial Aeroplane Co. Ltd. Prier's first design was for a single-seat, high-speed monoplane for participation in the annual

Gordon Bennett Cup race. The **Bristol Prier Type P-1** was not ready in this for this event, but two more generally similar aircraft were produced for the Circuit of Britain competition. However, both failed to participate in this contest as a result of accidents suffered by the pilots, including Prier himself.

The Type P-1 was powered by a 50-hp (37-kW) Gnome rotary

Prier adopted Blériot-type warping wings for his monoplane designs. Both the rudder and tailplane were all-moving surfaces.

engine and achieved a maximum speed of 70 mph (113 km/h). The technical success of the Type P-1 immediately suggested the creation of a two-seater development,

and the first of this type initially flew in September 1911. It was, in effect, the prototype of a series of successful military and training aircraft manufactured in quantity during

SPECIFICATION	
Bristol Prier Monoplane (Prier-Dickson type)	65 mph (105 km/h) at sea level
Type: two-seat training and sporting aircraft	**Weights:** empty 660 lb (299 kg); maximum take-off 1,080 lb (490 kg)
Powerplant: one Gnome rotary engine rated at 70 hp (52 kW)	**Dimensions:** wingspan 34 ft (10.36 m); length 26 ft (7.92 m); height 9 ft 9 in (2.97 m); wing area 200.00 sq ft (18.58 m²)
Performance: maximum speed	

1912. The type, among other things, succeeded the Boxkite in service at the three military flying schools of the UK as well as at other military flying schools in Germany, Italy and Spain. Production of the two-seater, which was sometimes nicknamed the 'Military', included a final batch of 10 which were completed to an improved standard pioneered by Captain Bertram Dickson. Two of the aircraft were sold to the Turkish government, and a third to the Bulgarian government.

The single-seat version was additionally developed as a low-powered type, sometimes known as the 'Popular', for pupils who had managed their first solo flights, fitted in this instance with a 35-hp (26-kW) Anzani radial. The first and third Type P-1 monoplanes were converted to this standard, to which seven new-build machines were also completed.

Prier left Bristol in 1912, being replaced by Henri Coanda. One of Coanda's first developments was a version of the **Prier-Dickson** type with side-by-side rather than tandem accommodation. Production of this 'Sociable' model totalled three aircraft, bringing the total of Prier monoplanes manufactured by Bristol between July 1911 and December 1912 to 34 aircraft.

British Aerospace (Handley Page/SA) Jetstream

Originally ordered for the RAF, 14 Jetstreams were converted to T.Mk 2 standard – characterised by a bulbous nose radome – for the Royal Navy.

The name of Handley Page, once an integral part of the British aviation industry, disappeared from the active scene into aviation history in early 1970, following celebration of the company's diamond jubilee on 17 June 1969. The straw which finally broke the camel's back was the Handley Page **H.P.137** project for a twin-turboprop executive/feederline transport, within the 12/20-seat capacity as originally envisaged. When, in January 1966, the company decided to begin work on the construction of four prototypes, the launch cost was estimated at £3 million and the H.P.137 prototype flew successfully on 18 August 1967. However, by the time the certification programme was well advanced, in August 1969, the cost had already exceeded £13 million and on 8 August the company went into voluntary liquidation. Following attempts to continue production with financial backing from the USA, as Handley Page Aircraft Ltd, and later by a newly formed Jetstream Aircraft Ltd, it was finally Scottish Aviation Ltd which continued manufacture of the aircraft. Then this company also lost its separate identity when, on 1 January 1978, it became the Scottish Aviation division of the British Aerospace Aircraft Group.

The first definitive civil version was the **Jetstream 200**, developed initially by Handley Page as a low-wing cantilever monoplane of all-metal, fail-safe construction. It had straight flying surfaces, a powerplant of two turboprop engines in slender wing-mounted nacelles whose bulged lower portions accommodated the main units of the retractable tricycle landing gear, a conventional empennage with the tailplane located about one-third of the way up the vertical tail surface, and a deep oval-section fuselage that offered pressurised accommodation for the flight crew of two (on a separate flightdeck). It also accommodated up to 18 passengers who enjoyed the unusual feature, in an aircraft of this class, of standing headroom. The powerplant of civil Jetstream 200 aircraft comprised two Turboméca Astazou XVI turboprop engines each rated at 965 shp (720 kW). However, modest numbers of the first version – which was the Jetstream 1 completed by Handley Page and supplied to International Jetstream Corporation in the USA – were powered by Astazou XIV engines each rated at 840 shp (626 kW). Many were subsequently converted by Riley Aircraft of Carlsbad, California, to Riley Jetstream configuration with Astazou XVI engines.

As early as 1967 there had been good prospects for military versions of the Jetstream following the receipt of an order from the US Air Force. This contract was for 11 examples of the **Jetstream 3M**, which would have been designated C-10A in USAF service, plus options for no fewer than 300 additional aircraft. This order was subsequently cancelled, but in February 1972 the Royal Air Force ordered 26 of the **Jetstream 201** variant. Similar to the civil **Jetstream 200**, this model differs in its powerplant of two Astazou XVID turboprop engines each rated at 996 ehp (743 ekW), new 'eyebrow' windows above the flightdeck, plus instrumentation and avionics to meet service requirements. The first of these aircraft flew on 13 April 1973, and all had been delivered by early 1976, although all the aircraft were placed in temporary storage pending a decision on their utilisation. In October of that year it was announced that eight were to be used by the RAF as **Jetstream T.Mk 1** multi-engined pilot trainers, and that 14 would be modified to serve with the Royal Navy as **Jetstream T.Mk 2** aircraft for observer training. The latter differed mainly from the RAF version by the installation of MEL E.190 weather and terrain-mapping radar in a nose radome.

On 5 December 1978 BAe announced its intention to develop a new version of the aircraft under the designation **Jetstream 31**. A development aircraft was converted from Jetstream 1 standard and first flew on 28 March 1980, and the most important features of the Jetstream 31 became evident. These included a wholly revised American powerplant, in the form of two Garrett (now AlliedSignal) TPE331-10 turboprop engines, each rated at 900 shp (671 kW) and driving four- rather than three-bladed propellers for much improved field performance and payload. The first production example was rolled out on 25 January 1982. An initial production batch of 10 aircraft was laid down, and production of the Jetstream 31 up to 1993 totalled 382 aircraft. This included 161 examples of the **Super 31**, also known as the **Jetstream 32**, with an uprated powerplant in the form of two TPE331-12 turboprop engines each rated at 1,020 shp (761 kW) for still further enhancement of performance. The Jetstream 31 was offered in three versions: as the Jetstream 31 Commuter designed to carry 18/19 passengers and baggage; the Jetstream 31 Corporate executive version seating 8/10 passengers; and the Jetstream 31 Special intended for such roles as airfield calibration, cargo, casualty evacuation, military communications, multi-engine training, and resources survey and protection.

The only two military operators of the Jetstream 31 have been the UK and Saudi Arabia. British military procurement of the variant totalled four Jetstream **T.Mk 3** radar observer trainers for the Fleet Air Arm with Doppler navigation, a TANS (Tactical Air Navigation System) computer and Racal ASR.360 multi-mode radar with its antenna in a radome under the fuselage. In other respects, the Jetstream T.Mk 3 differs from the Jetstream T.Mk 1 in details such as its powerplant of two TPE331-10UF turboprop engines each rated at 940 shp (701 kW), its maximum speed of 303 mph (488 km/h) at 15,000 ft (4570 m) and its initial climb rate of 2,230 ft (680 m) per minute.

SPECIFICATION

BAe (Scottish Aviation/Handley Page) Jetstream T.Mk 1
Type: two-crew multi-engined pilot trainer
Powerplant: two Turboméca Astazou XVID turboprop engines each rated at 996 ehp (743 ekW)
Performance: maximum speed 282 mph (454 km/h) at 10,000 ft (3050 m); cruising speed 282 mph (454 km/h) at 10,000 ft (3050 m); initial climb rate 2,500 ft (762 m) per minute; service ceiling 25,000 ft (7620 m); range 1,382 miles (2224 km)
Weights: empty 7,683 lb (3485 kg); maximum take-off 12,566 lb (5700 kg)
Dimensions: wingspan 52 ft (15.85 m); length 47 ft 1½ in (14.37 m); height 17 ft 5½ in (5.32 m); wing area 270.00 sq ft (25.08 m²)
Payload: one pupil on the flightdeck and four in the cabin

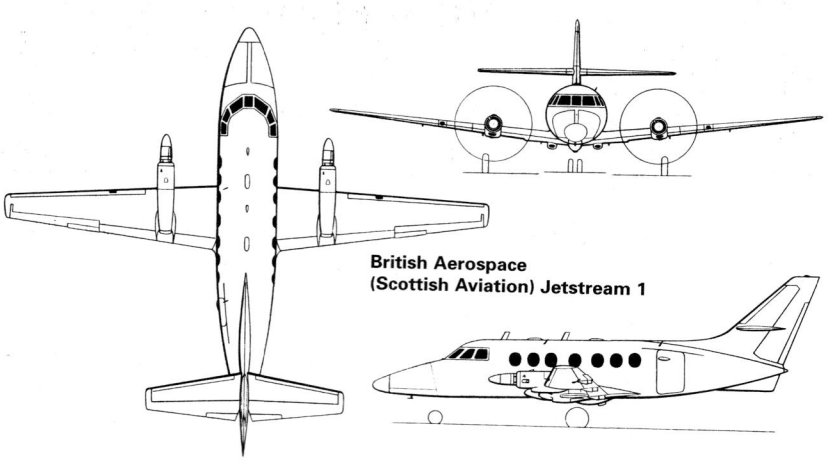

British Aerospace (Scottish Aviation) Jetstream 1

British Aerospace (Handley Page/SA) Jetstream (cont.)

The Jetstream T.Mk 3 has a service ceiling of 31,600 ft (9630 m), range of 1,226 miles (1973 km), empty weight of 9,600 lb (4355 kg) and maximum take-off weight of 15,212 lb (6900 kg).

Two Jetstream 31 aircraft with the avionics of the Panavia Tornado IDS were ordered by the Saudi Arabian air force's training academy for the training of navigators. These aircraft were delivered in 1987, and one was lost two years later in an accident.

The final variant was the **Jetstream 41**, which was developed as a version of the Jetstream 31 with its fuselage lengthened by 16 ft (4.88 m) to allow the type to operate in the regional airliner role with a maximum of 29 passengers. The wing was also increased in span by 8 ft (2.44 m) to 60 ft (18.29 m). Other changes included the uprated powerplant of two TPE331-14 turboprop engines each rated at 1,650 shp (1230 kW) in revised nacelles and driving a handed five-bladed propeller, increased fuel capacity, improved ailerons and flaps, a tail unit with rudder of increased chord and a tailplane of greater area. It was fitted with forward- rather than inward-retracting main landing gear units with two wheels rather than the original one wheel, and a revised flightdeck with Honeywell digital avionics including a four-display EFIS (Electronic Flight Instrumentation System).

The first Jetstream 41 made its maiden flight on 25 September 1992 for the start of deliveries in November of the same year. The initial steady flow of orders started to dry up in the mid-1990s, and in May 1997 BAe announced that production of the Jetstream family would end in 1997 after the completion of 103 Jetstream 41 aircraft including the prototype aircraft.

A total of 97 Jetstream 41s was delivered to 14 customers from November 1992 until production was terminated in July 1997.

British Aerospace (Hawker Siddeley) Hawk

When Air Staff Target (AST) 362 was issued in 1964 for a new trainer to replace the Hawker Siddeley Gnat in service with the Royal Air Force, the requirement was only partially filled by a small number of two-seat SEPECAT Jaguar aircraft. By 1968 the shortfall remained, and in that year Hawker Siddeley initiated studies for a subsonic

RAF Hawk trainers are now painted in this high-conspicuity gloss black colour scheme, helping to reduce the risk of mid-air collision.

trainer, the original high performance criteria for such an aircraft having been waived in the interim. The company's private venture P.1182 (later HS.1182) evolved into an advanced trainer formalised as **AST 397** in January 1970, Hawker Siddeley being awarded a production contract during the following October. The design team opted for a simple but robust low-wing layout for an aircraft of modest dimensions – although it was appreciably larger than the tiny Gnat – and with the powerplant of one Rolls-Royce/Turboméca Adour Mk 151-01 turbofan engine rated at 5,200 lb (23.13 kN). It was in the design of its cockpit that the new aircraft most impressed observers, for it elevated the instructor in the rear seat well above the pupil in the front seat to provide him with excellent forward fields of vision. The first **Hawker Siddeley Hawk T.Mk 1** made its maiden flight on 21 August 1971. An indication of the

integrity of the Hawk design was the fact that there were no prototypes or pre-production aircraft, and five of the six aircraft used for flight development were subsequently delivered to the RAF as part of the service order which totalled 175 Hawk T.Mk 1 aircraft.

In details of its construction the Hawk is entirely conventional: the fuselage incorporates skin, stringer and frame components; the one-piece wing is attached by three bolts on each side, which places the associated structure under compression for integral strength; inboard of the 'kink' in the leading edge, the wing encloses an integral fuel tank and pick-up points for the main landing gear units; and three hardpoints (one under the fuselage and two under the wing) were fitted as standard on RAF machines. The Hawk T.Mk 1 entered service in April 1976 with delivery of the first production aircraft to No. 4 FTS (Flying Training School) at RAF Valley. Students were

The Hawk has been a great export success for BAe. Sales have been particularly strong in the Middle East, where five air arms currently operate the type.

given a total of 75 hours dual and solo instruction on the Hawk, about 10 hours being eliminated from the advanced stages as the new aircraft was able to undertake the weapons phase previously handled by the Hawker Hunter. Valley's initial course of pilots trained on the Hawk graduated in November

1977. BAe completed deliveries of the Hawk T.Mk 1 by the end of 1976, other users being No. 1 Tactical Weapons Unit at RAF Brawdy, No. 2 TWU at RAF Lossiemouth and later RAF Chivenor, the Central Flying School at Valley (and later at RAF Scampton), the Empire Test Pilots School at Boscombe Down, and

SPECIFICATION

British Aerospace (Hawker Siddeley) Hawk T.Mk 1
Type: two-seat advanced flying and weapons trainer
Powerplant: one Rolls-Royce/Turboméca Adour Mk 151-01 turbofan engine rated at 5,200 lb st (23 kN) dry
Performance: maximum speed 645 mph (1038 km/h) at 11,000 ft (3355 m); cruising speed not available; initial climb rate 9,300 ft (2835 m) per minute; climb to 30,000 ft (9145 m) in 6 minutes 6 seconds; service ceiling 50,000 ft (15240 m); range 1,923 miles (3094 km) with two drop tanks or 1,509 miles (2428 km) with internal fuel
Weights: empty 8,040 lb (3647 kg); maximum take-off 12,566 lb (5700 kg)
Dimensions: wingspan 30 ft 9¾ in (9.39 m); length 36 ft 7¾ in (11.17 m) excluding probe; height 13 ft 1¼ in (3.99 m); wing area 179.60 sq ft (16.69 m²)
Armament: up to a normal 1,500 lb (680 kg) but maximum 6,800 lb (3084 kg) of disposable stores carried externally

British Aerospace Hawk T.Mk 1

the 'Red Arrows' aerobatic team based at Scampton.

In order to expand the Hawk's capability in the weapons training role, the MoD contracted for the modification of 89 aircraft in January 1983. The resulting aircraft was designated **Hawk T.Mk 1A**, the most significant difference to the earlier trainer variant being its ability to carry a pair of AIM-9L Sidewinder AAMs on underwing launchers. For close-in air combat or ground strafing, a single 30-mm gun pod could also be fitted under the fuselage. The Hawk T.Mk 1A

conversion programme was completed in May 1986, and the aircraft were intended as limited point-defence fighters for emergency use in the UK Defence Region as supplements to the McDonnell Douglas Phantoms and Panavia Tornado in the 'mixed fighter force'.

A number of Hawk T.Mk 1 aircraft have been rewinged, and of these aircraft a few were completed to a standard allowing the carriage of stores on two underwing hardpoints, but not on the centreline hardpoint. These

aircraft have the alternative designations **Hawk T.Mk 1W** and **Hawk T.Mk 1 FTS**.

Realisation of the Hawk's considerable development and export potential began in 1977 when BAe introduced the upgraded Hawk Mk 50 for an initial sale to Finland, whose 50 aircraft were delivered from December of the same year; the initial four British-built aircraft were followed by 46 assembled in Finland by Valmet, and a follow-on order for seven **Hawk Mk 51A** aircraft was placed in December 1990. During

1978, Kenya and Indonesia also purchased the Hawk in the form of 12 **Hawk Mk 52** and 20 **Hawk Mk 53** aircraft respectively. The following **Hawk Mk 60** introduced an uprated powerplant, the Adour Mk 861 engine rated at 5,700 lb st (25 kN) dry, additional wing leading-edge fences and four-position flaps to improve lift, anti-skid brakes and revised wheels and tyres. This improved model was the subject of a series of foreign orders, commencing in July 1982, to Zimbabwe (eight Hawk

Mk 60 aircraft and, later, five **Hawk Mk 60A** aircraft), Dubai (nine **Hawk Mk 61** aircraft), Abu Dhabi (16 Hawk Mk 60 aircraft of which 15 were later upgraded to Hawk **Mk 63A** standard and supplemented by four Hawk **Mk 63C** aircraft), Kuwait (12 Hawk **Mk 64** aircraft), Saudi Arabia (30 Hawk **Mk 65** aircraft), Switzerland (20 Hawk **Mk 66** aircraft including 19 assembled by F+W) and South Korea. (20 Hawk **Mk 67** 'long-nosed' aircraft equipped with ranging radar and nosewheel steering).

British Aerospace ATP and Jetstream 61

By the beginning of the 1980s the British Aerospace 748 was nearing the limit of its development and sales potential even in its most modern Super 748 form. In March 1984 British Aerospace announced that it had decided to press ahead with the development of an improved version of the 748, its primary task being to give BAe a continued foothold in the growing regional airliner market against offerings such as the Franco-Italian ATR 72.

The result was the **British Aerospace ATP (Advanced TurboProp)** that made its maiden flight on 6 August 1986 as a development of the 748 with a stretched fuselage, swept vertical tail surface, a

host of individually small but cumulatively large updated features, and a completely new powerplant. This last was based on two Pratt & Whitney Canada PW126A turboprop engines each rated at 2,653 shp (1979 kW) and turning BAe/Hamilton Standard six-bladed propellers, which were designed to turn slowly as a means of reducing noise. The propellers had reversible-pitch blades of composite construction, and all fuel was accommodated in two integral tanks in the wing for a maximum capacity of 1,400 Imp gal (6364 litres).

The landing gear by Dowty was of the tricycle type with twin wheels on each unit, and the main units retracted forward into

the undersides of the engine nacelles, whose downward bulges were of cleaner design than the equivalent elements on the 748. Provision was made for a crew of four (two pilots on a digital flight deck with an EFIS instrumentation system, and two attendants), and the cabin was laid out with pairs of seats to each side of the central aisle. The standard seating arrangement was for 64/68 passengers, but low- and high-density arrangements for 60 or 72 passengers were possible.

The first production aircraft flew on 20 February

1987, and the ATP received European and American certifications in March and August 1988 respectively. The first delivery was made to British Midland Airways, and the type operated its first revenue-earning service on 9 May 1988. Deliveries to Loganair and Manx Airlines, the other two members of the Airlines of Britain Group, swelled the group's ATP fleet to 16, and other aircraft were sold to operators in Europe, the Far

East, Africa and North America. Despite its updated features, however, the ATP found only a very modest market, and despite BAe's decision to redesignate the type as the **Jetstream 61** in an effort to capitalise on the success of the 'real' Jetstream series, production ended after the completion of only 60 aircraft.

A P.132 derivative, essentially an updated Coastguarder, was offered in the maritime warfare role, but found no customers.

Production of the ATP ceased at the end of 1993, the aircraft being remarketed as the Jetstream 61. Of the 58 ATPs delivered, this example was one of two received by Biman Bangladesh Airlines.

SPECIFICATION

British Aerospace ATP
Type: regional airliner
Powerplant: two Pratt & Whitney Canada PW126A turboprop engines each rated at 2,653 shp (1979 kW)
Performance: maximum cruising speed 306 mph (493 km/h) at 13,000 ft (3960 m); economical cruising speed 272 mph (437 km/h) at 18,000 ft (5485 m); initial climb rate not available; range 921 miles

(1482 km) with 68 passengers
Weights: empty 31,310 lb (14202 kg); maximum take-off 50,550 lb (22930 kg)
Dimensions: wingspan 100 ft 6 in (30.63 m); length 85 ft 4 in (26.00 m); height 24 ft 11 in (7.59 m); wing area 843.00 sq ft (78.32 m²)
Payload: up to 72 passengers within the context of a 15,490-lb (7026-kg) maximum payload

British Aerospace EAP

From the mid-1970s it was clear to the British aircraft industry, whose primary aircraft manufacturing elements were then the British Aircraft Corporation and Hawker Siddeley Aviation, that there would soon be a British, if not European, requirement for an advanced fighter. Such an aircraft would be needed to supplant obsolescent types such as the BAC (English Electric) Lightning and McDonnell Douglas F-4 Phantom II. In 1977 BAC, Hawker Siddeley and Scottish Aviation were nationalised and merged as

British Aerospace, and it was under the aegis of this new pan-British company that initial work started on the design of a new fighter offering performance and capabilities at least comparable to those of the General Dynamic F-16 Fighting Falcon. From an early stage the British government stated that it would not invest in the programme. However, such was its importance for the long-term viability of the British aircraft industry as a whole that BAe was joined by Dowty, Ferranti, GEC Avionics, Lucas, Rolls-

Royce and Smiths Industries to pursue the work as a private venture, that also received support from Aeritalia of Italy and MBB of West Germany.

The result of this embryonic European effort was the **British Aerospace ACA (Agile Combat Aircraft)** design, which was displayed as a full-scale mock-up at the 1982 Farnborough Air Show and the 1983 Paris Air Show. By this time the air staffs of France, Italy, Spain, the UK and West Germany were edging towards the establishment of a collaborative programme, analogous to those that had produced the Panavia Tornado and SEPECAT Jaguar, to design,

develop and manufacture an advanced multi-role fighter together with its engines and all major avionics items. As a result, therefore, the British government announced in 1982 that it would contribute funding to a development of the ACA

concept as the **British Aerospace EAP (Experimental Aircraft Programme)** prototype technology demonstrator for the anticipated European fighter, which became the European Fighter Aircraft in 1986.

SPECIFICATION

British Aerospace EAP
Type: single-seat technology demonstrator
Powerplant: two Turbo-Union RB199-34R Mk 104D turbofan engines each rated at about 17,000 lb st (75.62 kN) with afterburning
Performance: maximum speed more than 1,320 mph (2124 km/h) or Mach 2.0 at high altitude
Weights: empty, about 22,050 lb

(10002 kg); normal take-off 32,000 lb (14515 kg)
Dimensions: wingspan 38 ft 7 in (11.77 m); length 48 ft 2¾ in (14.70 m); height 18 ft 1½ in (5.52 m); wing area 560.00 sq ft (52.02 m²)
Armament: none, although four dummy air-to-air missiles were carried in semi-recessed positions under the fuselage and inboard wing panels

British Aerospace EAP (continued)

France withdrew from the programme in 1985, after which it became known as Eurofighter 2000 and finally the Eurofighter Typhoon. The object of the EAP effort was the integration of a number of new and advanced technologies in a single airframe to further any EFA programme.

In May 1983 the Ministry of Defence and BAe contracted for the design, construction and flight testing of the EAP aircraft for the validation of a number of concepts. These included advanced aerodynamics, an advanced structure making extensive use of advanced materials (carbonfibre composites

and aluminium-lithium alloys as well as titanium), active control technology for an aircraft of inherently unstable design, a power-plant with a full-authority digital engine control system and aspiration via a ventral inlet with a down-ward-hinging lower lip to ensure clean airflow at high angles of attack, a digital databus system for full integration of the avionics, and an advanced digital cockpit (multi-function displays and voice-acti-vated items).

The EAP first flew on 8 August 1986, reaching Mach 1.1 at 30,000 ft (9145 m) in the course of that flight, and was revealed as a close-coupled canard

The EAP had excellent high-alpha capability. At high angles of attack the lower lip of the sophisticated vari-cowl chin intake hinged down to ensure a clean, uninterrupted supply of air to the engine in all flight regimes.

type with a tall vertical tail surface incorporating an inset rudder, powerplant of side-by-side turbofan engines, tricycle landing gear with a single wheel on each unit, and high-set cockpit. The low-set dihedralled delta wing had compound sweep on its leading edge, and on each side its moving surfaces comprised two-section flaps and

two-section elevons on the leading and trailing edges respectively, while the anhedralled canard foreplane was of the all-moving type. Together with the rudder, these moving surfaces were controlled by means of a quadruplex 'fly-by-wire' system created by GEC

Avionics on the basis of that designed and validated in the Jaguar ACT programme.

The EAP programme lasted to 1 May 1991 and comprised 259 test flights that generated a mass of data for the EFA, which was designed to a generally similar configuration.

British Aerospace Hawk Mk 100

Having already developed an 'advanced' wing for the Hawk, BAe was able, during the mid-1980s, to offer a development of the Hawk trainer as a relatively cheap dedicated dual-role weapon systems trainer and fully combat-capable ground-attack aircraft based on the Hawk Mk 60. The uprated powerplant was the Adour Mk 871 turbofan rated at 5,845 lb st (26.00 kN) dry, and the wingspan was increased by 1 ft 9 in (0.53 m) to 32 ft

7 in (9.93 m), the extra length being at the tips to provide tip-mounted rails for two Sidewinder AAMs. Adaptation of the Hawk's wing to take a larger warload was aided by a modest degree of sweep-back (21.5° at the leading edge), which meant that the additional pylons to accommodate the heavier ordnance loads required in the ground-attack role did not affect the aircraft's centre of gravity. With the addition of an elongated

nose housing an optional FLIR and/or laser sensors, an advanced cockpit with multi-function displays and HOTAS, plus more sophisticated avionics to exploit its enhanced combat potential, the resulting **Hawk Mk 100** first flew in October 1987 as a converted development airframe. The wing, which is stressed for six pylons carrying a maximum of 6,614 lb (3000 kg) of stores, incorporates combat manoeuvre flaps. As well as wingtip AAMs, a single 30-mm ADEN cannon pod is an optional fitting on the fuselage centreline in place of a further stores station.

Abu Dhabi was the initial customer for the Hawk Mk 100 series (18 **Hawk Mk 102** aircraft with an RWR, wingtip launch rails and nose-mounted laser designator). Oman ordered four **Hawk Mk 103** aircraft in July 1990, and in December that year Malaysia ordered 10 **Hawk Mk 108** aircraft, of which the first was handed over in February 1994. The most substantial order for the Hawk Mk 100 came from Saudi Arabia which, under the post-Gulf War 'Al Yamamah II' contract signed for up to 60 Hawk Mk 100 aircraft. It was believed that Brunei had also ordered 19 aircraft, but this order was in fact not placed, or was postponed

or cancelled. Indonesia and Malaysia contracted for eight **Hawk Mk 109** and 10 Hawk Mk 108 aircraft respectively. In mid-1997 Australia ordered 33 Hawk Mk 100 series aircraft, to be delivered from 2000 as 12 British-built and 21 Australian-built aircraft, to operate as fighter lead-in trainers. The most recent order to mid-1999 was placed in 1998 by South Africa, with a contract for 24 Hawk Mk 100 series aircraft to operate as fighter lead-in trainers.

For offensive or defensive air-to-air missions, the Hawk 100 carries AIM-9 Sidewinder or MATRA Magic infra-red-guided missiles.

SPECIFICATION
British Aerospace Hawk Mk 100

Type: two-seat advanced flying and weapons trainer with air combat and ground-attack capability

Powerplant: one Rolls-Royce/Turboméca Adour Mk 871 turbofan engine rated at 5,845 lb st (26.00 kN)

Performance: maximum speed 645 mph (1038 km/h) at 36,000 ft (10975 m); initial climb rate 11,800 ft (3597 m) per minute; climb to 30,000 ft (9145 m) in 7 minutes 30 seconds; service ceiling 44,500 ft (13545 m); range more than

1,612 miles (2594 km) with two drop tanks; radius 760 miles (1223 km) on a hi-lo-hi mission with a 2,000-lb (907-kg) warload

Weights: empty 9,700 lb (4400 kg); maximum take-off 20,061 lb (9100 kg)

Dimensions: wingspan 30 ft 9¾ in (9.39 m) with normal tips or 32 ft 7 in (9.93 m) with missile-carrying tips; length 38 ft 4 in (11.68 m) excluding probe; height 13 ft 1¼ in (3.99 m); wing area 179.60 sq ft (16.69 m²)

Armament: up 6,614 lb (3000 kg) of disposable stores carried externally

British Aerospace Hawk Mk 200

The international success of the Hawk's two-seat models persuaded BAe to develop a single-seat variant which would attract new customers, particularly the smaller air arms requiring a relatively cheap air superiority fighter and ground-attack aircraft. The resulting **British Aerospace Hawk Mk 200** is a far more cost-effective package in the long term, compared to the short-term option of continual refurbishment of older aircraft. Moreover, a

single-seat type is more practical and desirable in some respects, not least because there is simply not a pool of trained navigators to occupy second seats.

In redesigning the Hawk's forward fuselage to accommodate a single cockpit, BAe also provided the volume for the incorporation, to customer requirement, of a modern radar and, under the cockpit floor, an inbuilt pair of 25-mm ADEN cannon that represent a significant

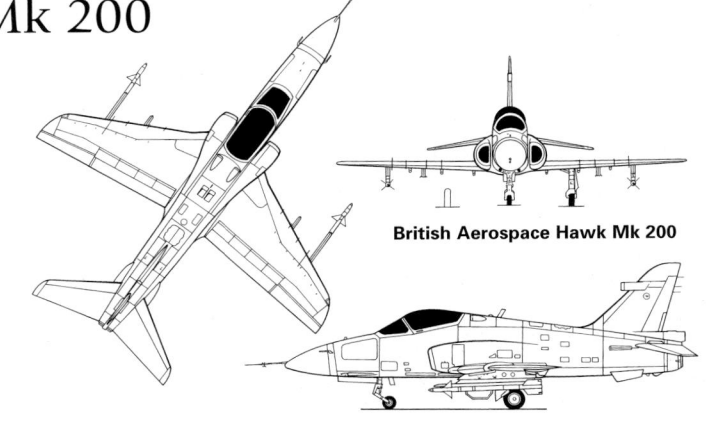

British Aerospace Hawk Mk 200

increase in combat capability. The provision of seven hardpoints (including wing-tip AAM launchers) enables the carriage of up to 6,614 lb (3000 kg) of stores, the same as the load of the Hawk Mk 100. Constructed of conventional aluminium alloy and having about 80 per cent commonality with the two-seat models, the Hawk Mk 200 is also powered by a single Adour Mk 871 turbofan. Even with additional equipment to tailor it for a multi-mission combat task, the aircraft has a maximum take-off weight of less than 21,000 lb (9527 kg). The Northrop Grumman (originally Westinghouse) APG-66H radar is a multi-mode equipment modified from that fitted in the Lockheed Martin (originally

General Dynamics) F-16. With the pilot's seat set farther aft than the forward position of other Hawks, the pilot faces a main instrument panel which includes a comms/navigation integration panel, HUD, multi-function CRT display, radar display configured for the most modern symbology, and a RHAW receiver.

The Hawk Mk 200 demonstrator made its maiden flight on 19 May 1986 and was later lost in an accident. The second Hawk Mk 200 flew on 24 April 1987 and, unlike the first aircraft, was fitted with full avionics but no radar and, later, a number of small but significant airframe revisions were made. To counteract any tendency for the tailplane of

the Hawk Mk 200 to stall, a condition belatedly revealed on the trainer in 1975, the aircraft eventually received the fuselage-mounted tailplane vanes, or SMURFs (Side-Mounted under Root Fin) developed for the US Navy's T-45 Goshawk trainer. These vanes throw a vortex over the tailplane to prevent undue travel caused by downwash from the flaps when the aircraft is in the low-speed configuration. In addition, an RWR was fitted to the fin leading edge, and the rear fuselage brake chute 'box' was deepened to house a chaff/flare dispenser and rearward-facing RWR antenna. The first APG-66-equipped **Hawk 200RDA** (Radar Development Aircraft) flew

Despite a slow start, hampered by the loss of the prototype, sales of the Hawk 200 are building. Like its two-seat counterpart, the Hawk 200 has sold particularly well in the Middle and Far East and is proving a potent aircraft in service.

on 13 February 1992.

Oman became the launch customer for the Hawk Mk 200 when it ordered 12 **Hawk Mk 203** aircraft on 31 July 1990, primarily as replacements for its ageing Hawker Hunters. Malaysia followed on 10 December 1990 with an order for 18 **Hawk Mk 208** aircraft. It was at one time though that Saudi Arabia's 'Al Yamamah II' order might have included an unconfirmed number of APG-66H-equipped **Hawk Mk 205** single-seaters within an overall buy of approximately 60 Hawks,

but no such aircraft has as yet been built. The Indonesian Hawk purchase of June 1993 combined both Hawk Mk 109 two-seat aircraft and **Hawk Mk 209** single-seat machines, the order for the latter eventually being finalised as 32 aircraft, not all of which may be delivered as a result of Indonesia's financial problems in the late 1990s and a measure of political antipathy to continued sales of arms to Indonesia as a result of its 'human rights' record.

SPECIFICATION

British Aerospace Hawk Mk 200

Type: single-seat air superiority and ground-attack warplane
Powerplant: one Rolls-Royce/Turboméca Adour Mk 871 turbofan engine rated at 5,845 lb st (26.00 kN)
Performance: maximum speed 632 mph (1017 km/h) at sea level; cruising speed 495 mph (796 km/h) at 41,000 ft (12495 m); initial climb rate 11,510 ft (3508 m) per minute; service ceiling 45,000 ft (13715 m); range 2,244 miles (3610 km) with three drop tanks; radius 587 miles (945 km) on a hi-lo-hi mission with

a 3,000-lb (1361-kg) warload
Weights: empty 9,810 lb (4450 kg); maximum take-off 20,061 lb (9100 kg)
Dimensions: wingspan 30 ft 9¾ in (9.39 m) with normal tips or 32 ft 7 in (9.93 m) with missile-carrying tips; length 37 ft 2 in (11.33 m) excluding probe; height 13 ft 8 in (4.16 m); wing area 179.60 sq ft (16.69 m²)
Armament: two 25-mm ADEN fixed forward-firing cannon in the lower part of the forward fuselage, plus up to 6,614 lb (3000 kg) of disposable stores carried externally

British Aerospace Sea Harrier

The **British Aerospace Sea Harrier** was developed from the Royal Air Force's Harrier close support and reconnaissance warplane, the world's first and, at that time, only STOVL aircraft. The Sea Harrier fortuitously filled the gap left by the phase-out of the McDonnell Douglas Phantom and the 1979 decommissioning of HMS *Ark Royal*, the last conventional aircraft-carrier in service with the Royal Navy. The advent of the Sea Harrier happily coincided with the introduction of a new generation of 20,000-ton light carriers intended primarily for the anti-submarine role. These three ships were intended to embark only helicopters, and the Sea Harrier was instrumental in retaining

some fixed-wing strike capability when the entire Fleet Air Arm was otherwise destined to become an all-helicopter force. Concurrent with the Royal Navy's receipt of HMS *Invincible*, dubbed a 'through-deck cruiser' rather than an aircraft-carrier to get it past UK Treasury scrutiny, the Sea Harrier became one of the most important types ever

procured by the FAA. The 1982 war in which the UK regained the Falkland Islands from Argentine occupation was then to prove the prudency of the decision to adopt the Sea Harrier.

Although a Harrier, in its original P.1127 form, had landed on the *Ark Royal* as early as 8 February 1963, the Royal Navy had initially evinced little interest in the

The only foreign customer of the Sea Harrier is the Indian navy which received a total of 23 Sea Harrier FRS.Mk 51s. This aircraft is from the first batch of six and was assigned to INAS 300 'White Tigers'.

programme despite the manufacturer's assurances that the engineering changes required to produce a navalised Harrier would be minimal. Naval interest gradually increased, spurred by the knowledge that no other fixed-wing aircraft could be ordered, and by a series of successful Harrier test deployments from seagoing platforms. This

The Sea Harrier FA.Mk 2 combines the well-respected Blue Vixen radar and AMRAAM missiles, producing a much more potent interceptor than the earlier FRS.Mk 1.

culminated in May 1975 in an initial order for 24 **Sea Harrier FRS.Mk 1** single-seat warplanes and one Harrier T.Mk 4A two-seat trainer, followed by a further 10 Sea Harrier FRS.Mk 1 aircraft in May 1978. The designation reflected the Sea Harrier's triple capability as a fleet defence fighter, reconnaissance platform and strike/attack aircraft. On 31 March 1980 the trials unit (No. 700A Squadron) was redesignated No. 899 Squadron as the operational HQ unit, and on the same day No. 800 Squadron formed, with four aircraft, on board the *Invincible*.

British Aerospace Sea Harrier (continued)

The main differences between the RAF's Harrier GR.Mk 3 and the Sea Harrier FRS.Mk 1 were the latter's front fuselage contours, with a painted radome covering a Ferranti Blue Fox pulse-modulated radar and its associated avionics bay. The cockpit was raised by 10 in (0.25 m) and the canopy was revised to give the pilot better fields of vision. An improved Rolls-Royce Pegasus Mk 104 turbofan engine, rated at 21,500 lb st (96 kN), was fitted. The underwing hard-points were stressed to take a wide variety of loads up to and including a lightweight version of the WE177 nuclear weapon. An autopilot was added, as was a revised nav/attack system and a new HUD. Magnesium was deleted from all airframe areas likely to be exposed to corrosion from salt water.

Embarking aboard HMS *Hermes* in June 1981, No. 800 Squadron had by then been joined by the second Sea Harrier unit, No. 801 Squadron. Both squadrons were subsequently deployed as part of the Royal Navy's modest fixed-wing air assets during the Falklands conflict. The Sea Harrier served with distinction, achieving a commendable 80 per cent serviceability record in an arduous operating environment. Expanded capability was provided for the Sea Harriers of both squadrons (and hastily re-formed No. 809 Squadron) on board the *Hermes* and *Invincible* for Operation Corporate, as

the British termed the Falklands War. Particularly significant was the supply from the USA of AIM-9L Sidewinder short-range AAMs, nullifying any disadvantage the Sea Harrier might have suffered relative to the higher-performance equipment of the Argentine air force. Scoring 22 confirmed victories, the Sea Harrier force lost six aircraft, all of them to causes other than aerial combat. Contributing greatly to the weapons load with which Sea Harriers were launched was the 'ski jump', a ramp fitted to carrier bows. First tested on land at an angle of 7°, this 'ski jump' was later increased in angle to 13°, which allowed 2,500 lb (1134 kg) to be added to the maximum take-off weight. Following the South Atlantic operation, 14 Sea Harrier FRS.Mk 1 aircraft were ordered as attrition replacements and, in 1984, nine more single-seat aircraft as well as three Harrier T.Mk 4(N) two-seat machines were added, bringing naval procurement up to 57 single-seaters and four trainers.

Combat operations had highlighted areas in which the Sea Harrier could be improved, and all these were addressed. They included the capability to carry up to four AIM-9L AAMs, installation of an improved radar and radar warning receiver, and stronger wing hardpoints to take larger-capacity drop tanks. At that time it appeared that the Soviet navy's growing carrier-build-

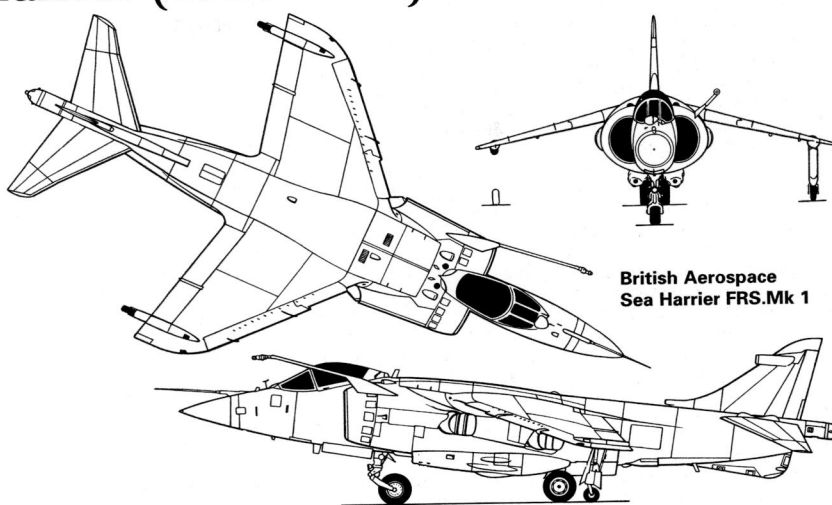

British Aerospace Sea Harrier FRS.Mk 1

ing programme might require NATO-assigned forces to be capable of launching ever more powerful AAMs to block any threat posed by low-flying bombers. An important addition to the Sea Harrier's inventory in this combat scenario was a current-generation fire-and-forget missile. These changes coincided with a mid-life update for the Sea Harrier, and the majority of the improvements recommended for the Sea Harrier FRS.Mk 1 were carried over to the new **Sea Harrier FRS.Mk 2**.

Late in 1978 the Indian navy became the second Sea Harrier operator, budgeting for up to 48 **Sea Harrier FRS.Mk 51** single-seat and **Harrier T.Mk 60** two-seat aircraft to a standard basically similar to that of the British aircraft except for their MATRA Magic rather than Sidewinder AAMs. Six single-seaters and two trainers were ordered in December 1979, and a second batch of 10 single-seaters and one trainer followed in November 1985; a third batch, ordered in October 1986, comprised seven single-seaters and one two-seater; a final order placed in the second half of 1997 covered two more Harrier T.Mk 60 aircraft for an overall total of 23 Sea Harrier FRS.Mk 51 and six Harrier T.Mk 60 machines.

In refining the Sea Harrier as a more capable interceptor while retaining its reconnaissance and strike/attack capability, BAe made some significant changes to the airframe.

The company received a contract in January 1985 for the project definition phase of the programme, which included two conversions of the Sea Harrier FRS.Mk 1 to the standard that was known as the Sea Harrier FRS.Mk 2 up to May 1994, when it was changed to the **Sea Harrier F/A.Mk 2** and **FA.Mk 2** in 1995. In 1984 it was reported that the Ministry of Defence planned to award a contract to BAe and Ferranti to cover a mid-life update of the entire Sea Harrier fleet, but these plans were substantially revised in 1985 to cover an upgrade of some 30 airframes with the Blue Vixen radar, an improved RWR, the JTIDS and provision for the AIM-120 AMRAAM. The original BAe proposal also covered the installation of wingtip Sidewinder rails. These additions, along with several other aerodynamic refinements, were eventually cut from the project, but a kinked wing leading edge and wing fence were retained.

The first of two prototype conversions flew on 19 September 1988. Despite the addition of an extra equipment bay and a recontoured nose to house the Blue Vixen radar which gives it more of an elongated appearance than its predecessor, the Sea Harrier FA.Mk 2 is actually nearly 2 ft (0.61 m) shorter overall due to the elimination of the extended pitot head probe of the earlier variant. No increase in wingspan was found to be necessary to carry additional stores, including a

pair of 190-Imp gal (864-litre) drop tanks plus AIM-120 AMRAAMs (or BAe ALARM anti-radar missiles) on each of the outer pylons, although ferry tips are available to increase span to 29 ft 8 in (9.04 m). The cockpit of the Sea Harrier FA.Mk 2 introduced new multi-function CRT displays and HOTAS controls to reduce pilot workload, and the type is powered by the Pegasus Mk 106 turbofan, a navalised version of the Mk 105 fitted to the AV-8B, but with no magnesium in its construction.

On 7 December 1988 a contract was awarded for the conversion of 31 Sea Harrier FRS.Mk 1 aircraft to the Mk 2 standard. On 6 March 1990 the Ministry of Defence revealed its intent to order at least 10 new-build Sea Harrier FRS.Mk 2 aircraft to augment the conversions, attrition having by that time reduced the Royal Navy's Sea Harrier inventory to 39 aircraft, and in January 1994 this intent was confirmed as an order for 18 Sea Harrier FRS.Mk 2s and an additional eight Sea Harrier FRS.Mk 1 conversions for a total of 57 Sea Harrier FA.Mk 2s.

In order to enhance pilot conversion training, a new two-seat **Harrier T.Mk 8** trainer was created, the four such aircraft supplementing the three surviving Harrier T.Mk 4N machines from 1996. Essentially a reconfigured Harrier T.Mk 4N, the Harrier T.Mk 8 duplicates the Sea Harrier FA.Mk 2's systems except for the radar.

SPECIFICATION	
British Aerospace Sea Harrier FRS.Mk 1	(7.70 m) with normal tips or 29 ft 8 in (9.04 m) with ferry tips; length 47 ft 7 in (14.50 m); height 12 ft 2 in (3.71 m); wing area 202.10 sq ft (18.68 m²)
Type: single-seat carrierborne STOVL fighter, reconnaissance and strike/attack warplane	**Armament:** up to a maximum of 8,000 lb (3629 kg) or normal 5,000 lb (2268 kg) of disposable stores for STO or VTO respectively, carried on three hardpoints under the fuselage and four hardpoints under the wing; typical loads comprise two 30-mm ADEN fixed forward-firing cannon in pods on the lateral underfuselage hardpoints, and one WE177 free-fall nuclear bomb (now withdrawn from inventory), 1,000-lb (454-kg) free-fall and retarded bombs, four multiple launchers for air-to-surface unguided rockets, two drop tanks, two Sea Eagle or AGM-84 Harpoon anti-ship missiles, and four AIM-9L Sidewinder AAMs
Powerplant: one Rolls-Royce Pegasus Mk 104 vectored-thrust turbofan engine rated at 21,500 lb st (96 kN)	
Performance: maximum speed more than 736 mph (1185 km/h) at low altitude; cruising speed more than 528 mph (850 km/h) at high altitude; initial climb rate about 50,000 ft (15240 m) per minute; service ceiling 51,000 ft (15545 m); radius 460 miles (750 km) on a hi-hi-hi-hi interception mission or 288 miles (463 km) on a hi-lo-hi attack mission	
Weights: empty 14,052 lb (6374 kg); maximum take-off 26,200 lb (11884 kg)	
Dimensions: wingspan 25 ft 3 in	

British Aircraft (British Klemm) B.K.1 Eagle

The **British Klemm B.K.1 Eagle** represented a new aircraft of British design. Like its predecessor, the

Swallow, it was of wooden construction with fabric-covered control surfaces, but differed in being a

three-seat cabin monoplane with manually retractable main landing gear units. The standard powerplant was

one de Havilland Gipsy Major inline engine rated at 130 hp (97 kW), and it was with this engine that the

prototype made its maiden flight early in 1934.

A so-called de luxe version, designated as the

Eagle 2, appeared after the company changed its title to the British Aircraft Manufacturing Co., and with specially prepared engines this type scored a number of successes in pre-war air races. Speed was not the only attribute of these aircraft, however – one was used to make a solo flight across the Tasman Sea from Australia to New Zealand, another made a record crossing of the South Atlantic, and a third was flown from Hanworth to Tokyo without incident by Katsutaro Ano. Production totalled 42 (five B.K.1 and 37 B.A.2 Eagle 2 aircraft), of which 17 were exported, and at least seven of the British aircraft were impressed for service with the Royal Air Force during World War II. Two other aircraft were impressed in India and one each in Kenya and Malaya.

Some 37 production Eagle 2s were completed, of which G-ACZT was the first. The aircraft was a more luxurious development of the B.K.1 Eagle.

British Aircraft (British Klemm) L.25 Swallow

The reliability, safety and excellent low-power performance of the Klemm L.25, a two-seat German lightplane, made it an extremely attractive proposition for private owners. The type was first flown in 1927, and British pilots had acquired 27 German-built aircraft by 1933, at which time the British Klemm Aeroplane Co. was established at Hanworth, Middlesex, to built the type in the UK. The British prototype made its maiden flight in November 1933, and differed from the original Klemm standard in having some structural reinforcement to meet UK airworthiness standards. A low-wing cantilever monoplane of all-wood construction except for its fabric-covered control surfaces, the L.25 had wings that could be folded to simplify storage. Two open cockpits in tandem, non-retractable tailskid landing gear, and a reliable low-powered engine completed the basic aircraft.

Regardless of the specific engine installation, the initial production version was designated as the **British Klemm L.25C 1A Swallow**, and the prototype and five other examples had the British Salmson A.D.9 radial engine rated at 75 hp (56 kW); all but one of the remainder had the Pobjoy Cataract II radial engine rated at 85 hp (64 kW). After 28 aircraft had been built, the wing, tailplane, fin and rudder were given angular lines to speed production, the fuselage top decking losing its smooth curve for the same reason. At the same time the company name changed to the British Aircraft Manufacturing Co., with the result that the modified Swallow was redesignated **British Aircraft Swallow 2**. More than 100 were built with the powerplant of one Cataract III or Blackburn Cirrus Minor 1 engine, each rated at 90 hp (67 kW). Some of these saw limited service during World War II as instructional airframes for the Air Training Corps and as unofficial 'hacks' for RAF station commanders.

G-ADDB was built as a Swallow, but appeared in May 1935 in modified form as the Swallow 2 prototype. In this form the aircraft featured simplified, more angular lines, as illustrated, to speed production.

British Aircraft IV Double Eagle

The type that followed the Eagle 2 off the drawing boards of the design team at the British Aircraft Manufacturing Co. was the **British Aircraft 3 Cupid**. This was a cantilever low-wing monoplane with fixed tailskid landing gear (including main units with nicely faired legs) and side-by-side two-seat accommodation under a low-drag canopy. Only one example of the type was completed, and this was registered in August 1935. The machine was powered by one de Havilland Gipsy Major inverted inline engine rated at 130 hp (97 kW), and its primary data included a maximum speed of more than 140 mph (225 km/h), wingspan of 35 ft (10.67 m) and length of 23 ft 4 in (7.11 m).

The B.A.3 was followed by the **British Aircraft IV Double Eagle**, which was the company's attempt to create a high-speed light transport. The Double Eagle was a cantilever shoulder-wing monoplane with an oval-section fuselage and tailwheel landing gear. The latter included single-wheel main units that retracted rearward into the underside of the nacelles for the two wing-mounted engines, which were de Havilland Gipsy Major inverted inline units each driving a two-bladed propeller. The fuselage was outfitted for the carriage of a pilot and up to five passengers.

The first of the three Double Eagle aircraft was registered in July 1936, and was powered by two Gipsy Major engines each rated at 130 hp (97 kW). It survived in the UK to July 1941, when it was impressed for service with the Royal Air Force to April 1944, when it was struck off charge. The second machine was also registered in July 1936 with the more potent powerplant of two Gipsy VI engines each rated at 200 hp (149 kW), and in July 1941 this machine was impressed for use as an instructional airframe. The third machine was completed in June 1936 to a South African order with the same powerplant as the first aircraft. This machine was operated in the aerial survey role up to 1940, when it was impressed for service with the South African Air Force.

This aircraft, the first Double Eagle, was impressed into RAF service for use in the communications role as ES949. It is illustrated pre-war, wearing a racing number.

British Taylorcraft Auster Mks I to V (Models E, G and J)

The RAF's initial evaluation of 24 impressed examples of the British Taylorcraft Model Plus C and Model Plus D served to confirm the utility of the two-seat braced high-wing mono-plane in the air observation post and communications roles. The Royal Air Force therefore placed an initial order for 100 generally similar aircraft for military use under the designation **British Taylorcraft Auster Mk I**. Other than the provision of split trailing-edge flaps to improve field performance as a means of enhancing the type's utility through the ability to use short and ill-prepared airstrips close behind the front line, the various Auster aircraft that now followed changed little throughout the rest of World War II. During this time more than 1,600 machines were built for service under the designations Auster Mk I, **Auster Mk III**, **Auster Mk IV** and **Auster Mk V**.

The Auster Mk I entered service with No. 654 Squadron in August 1942.

Only two examples of the **Auster Mk II**, with the 130-hp (97-kW) Lycoming O-290-3 engine, were built because of a shortage of this American powerplant. This led to the Auster Mk III, which was basically identical to the Auster Mk I except for its 130-hp (97-kW) de Havilland Gipsy Major I inverted inline engine. The 470 examples of the Auster Mk III were followed by 254 examples of the Auster Mk IV, which reverted to the Lycoming engine, and introduced a slightly larger cabin to provide volume for a third seat. The model built in largest numbers was the Auster Mk V, of which approximately 800 were built to a standard that differed from that of the Auster Mk IV by introducing blind-flying instrumentation.

At the height of their utilisation, Auster aircraft equipped 10 squadrons of the 2nd Tactical Air Force, and nine squadrons of the Desert Air Force. The type was also used in small numbers by associated

This Auster Mk I, once delivered to No. 651 Sqn, was based at RAF Dumfries in the autumn of 1942, before being shipped to North Africa. The squadron later flew in support of the 1st Army in Algeria. By August 1943, the Auster Mk III was replacing the Mk I in service.

Canadian and Dutch squadrons. The initial deployment of Auster aircraft in an operational role was during the North-West African campaign from November 1942, and aircraft of the type became an indispensable tool in the Sicilian and Italian campaigns. Just three weeks after D-Day in June 1944, these unarmed lightplanes were in the forefront of the action as the Allied armies advanced into France. Flown by British army officers, who had been trained by the RAF for service with the AOP squadrons, the Auster machines not only spotted for the artillery but, with suitable camera equipment, also provided photographic evidence of the effectiveness of the artillery action.

Numbers of the aircraft survived to be declared surplus to requirements in the years between 1945

and 1953, and many of these machines were sold onto an eager civil market. The most important models to achieve civil registration were the Auster Mk III of which at least 48 became **Auster 3** (otherwise **Model E**) aircraft, the Auster Mk IV of which at least 17 became **Auster 4** (otherwise **Model G**) aircraft, and the Auster Mk V of which at least 250 became **Auster 5** (otherwise **Model J**) aircraft. Responsibility for their continued support was vested in Auster Aircraft Ltd, as British Taylorcraft was renamed in March 1946 as it moved to Rearsby Aerodrome,

Leicestershire. Some of these aircraft were sub-variants such as the **Auster 5A** (one aircraft with a bench-type rear seat for two passengers), **Auster 5C** and **Auster 5D** (more than 29 aircraft with the 130-hp/97-kW Gipsy Major 1 or 1F engine), **Auster 5M** (two aircraft with provision for night advertising by means of neon tubes under the wing), and **Auster 5/150** (one aircraft with the 150-hp/112-kW Lycoming O-320-A2B flat-four engine). In 1956, Auster built 14 examples of the **Alpha 5**, which was basically to AOP standard but without the enlarged rear section to the cabin glazing.

SPECIFICATION

British Taylorcraft Auster Mk V
Type: two-seat air observation post and light liaison aircraft
Powerplant: one Lycoming O-290-3 flat-four engine rated at 130 hp (97 kW)
Performance: maximum speed 130 mph (209 km/h) at sea level; cruising speed 112 mph (180 km/h) at optimum altitude; initial climb
rate 950 ft (290 m) per minute; service ceiling 15,000 ft (4570 m); range 250 miles (402 km)
Weights: empty 1,100 lb (499 kg); maximum take-off 1,850 lb (839 kg)
Dimensions: wingspan 36 ft (10.97 m); length 22 ft 5 in (6.83 m); height 8 ft (2.44 m); wing area 167.00 sq ft (15.51 m²)

British Taylorcraft Auster AOP.Mk 6 (Model K)

The use of aircraft as air observation posts for the army had its origins in World War I, and in World War II a considerable number of American light aircraft types were pressed into service for this purpose. In the UK, developments of the pre-war US Taylorcraft design had resulted in a series of Auster aircraft from the British Taylorcraft company (renamed as Auster Aircraft Ltd in 1946), and the last of these types to enter service was the **Auster Mk V** with an American engine, the 130-hp (97-kW) Avco Lycoming O-290 unit.

As the end of World War II approached, however, the British authorities decided that the time was ripe for the development of a replacement for the Auster Mk V with a British engine, and the resulting **British Taylorcraft Model K** appeared in 1945 for service as the **Auster AOP.Mk 6**. The new type differed from its predecessor in having a strengthened rear fuselage,

a higher maximum take-off weight and an uprated British powerplant in the form of the 145-hp (108-kW) de Havilland Gipsy Major 7 inverted inline engine, driving a propeller whose greater diameter demanded the introduction of lengthened main landing gear legs. A significant difference in appearance was produced by the incorporation of external non-retractable aerofoil

flaps. Of light alloy construction, these last were mounted behind the wing on the sections of the trailing edge inboard of the flaps, and were intended to enhance the type's field performance, an objective that was not really achieved.

An initial production run of 296 Auster AOP.Mk 6 aircraft was completed in 1949, but further production began in 1952 and the total built by the end of the

run was around 400 machines. Of these, 22 ex-British aircraft were delivered to the Belgian air force and two were transferred to the Royal Hong Kong Auxiliary Air Force, while new aircraft were supplied to the Royal Canadian Air Force (36), South African Air Force (five) and Arab Legion (four). Operational experience revealed that, by comparison with the Auster

Mk V, the Auster AOP.Mk 6 was heavier and clumsier on the controls as well as possessing inferior take-off performance, but the Auster AOP.Mk 6 served for a number of years until it began to replaced from 1955 by the Auster AOP.Mk 9.

The **Auster T.Mk 7** was a dual-control version of the Auster AOP.Mk 6, and was quickly convertible to AOP standard. More than 80

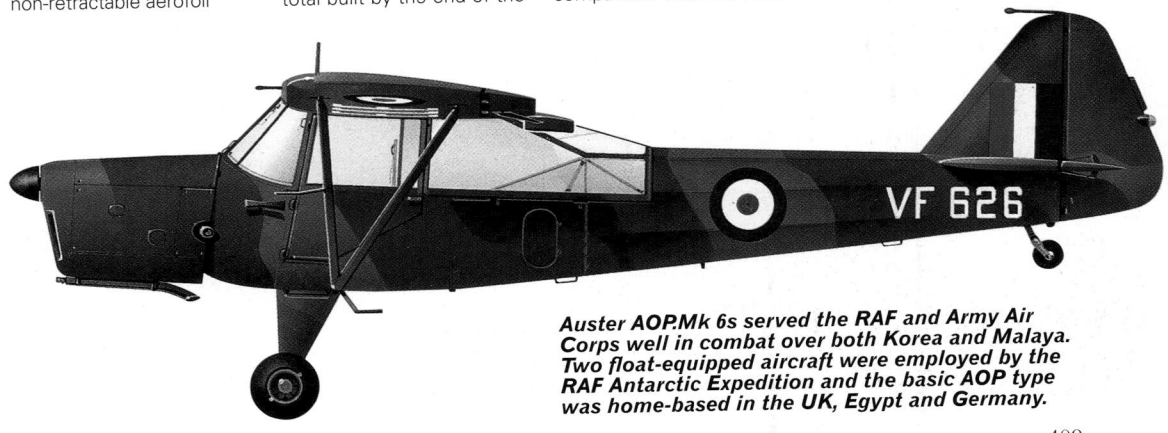

Auster AOP.Mk 6s served the RAF and Army Air Corps well in combat over both Korea and Malaya. Two float-equipped aircraft were employed by the RAF Antarctic Expedition and the basic AOP type was home-based in the UK, Egypt and Germany.

such aircraft were built after conversion of the Auster AOP.Mk 6 prototype as the Auster T.Mk 7 proto-

SPECIFICATION

British Taylorcraft Auster AOP.Mk 6
Type: two-seat air observation post aircraft
Powerplant: one de Havilland Gipsy Major 7 inverted inline engine rated at 145 hp (108 kW)
Performance: maximum speed 124 mph (200 km/h) at 1,000 ft (305 m); cruising speed 108 mph

(174 km/h) at optimum altitude; initial climb rate 810 ft (247 m) per minute; service ceiling 14,000 ft (4265 m); range 315 miles (507 km)
Weights: empty 1,413 lb (641 kg); maximum take-off 2,160 lb (980 kg)
Dimensions: wingspan 36 ft (10.97 m); length 23 ft 9 in (7.24 m); height 8 ft 4 in (2.55 m); wing area 184.00 sq ft (17.09 m²)

type, and overseas customers included the RCAF (six), Burmese air force (three) and Arab Legion (two).

As surplus Auster AOP.Mk 6 machines began to appear they were snapped up for conversion for civil use initially as the **Auster 6** and **Auster 6A Tugmaster** and, later, as the **Beagle A.61 Terrier**. The Auster 6 was a straightforward conversion

for the touring and sporting role, and 34 such conversions were effected largely in Canada and Belgium with smaller numbers produced in the UK, Australia and South Africa. The Tugmaster was intended primarily as a glider-tug, and differed from the baseline military model in its enlarged tail surfaces and the revision of the engine to 145-hp (108-kW) Gipsy Major 10

Mk 1-1 standard. Some 29 conversions were effected for use in the UK, Finland and Sweden. The Auster 6 and 6A were dimensionally identical to the Auster AOP.Mk 6, but differed in details such as their maximum speed of 121 mph (195 km/h), cruising speed of 105 mph (169 km/h), empty weight of 1,480 lb (671 kg) and maximum take-off weight of 2,200 lb (998 kg).

British Taylorcraft Model Plus C and Model Plus D

In 1936 the Taylorcraft Aviation Company (later the Taylor-Young Airplane Company and from 1940 the Taylorcraft Aviation Corporation) was formed in the USA for the design and manufacture of lightplanes for private use. The most successful of the pre-war aircraft to emanate from this company were designated as the **Models B, C** and **D**.

In the course of November 1938 Taylorcraft Aeroplanes (England) Ltd was established at Thurmaston, Leicestershire, to build these Taylorcraft aircraft under licence. Six examples of the **Model A** were imported into the UK, followed by one example of the Model B, and these were typical of the aircraft that were to be built by the new company. Of braced high-wing monoplane configuration, with a fabric-covered wing of mixed wood and metal construction, the aircraft had a fuselage and tail unit of fabric-covered welded steel tube construction, with

This aircraft was one of the nine Model Plus D aircraft which were completed to a standard similar to that of the Model Plus C, but with a more powerful engine for greater performance.

side-by-side seating in an enclosed cabin for two persons. The landing gear was of the fixed tailwheel type with main unit shock-absorption by rubber bungee. The powerplant of the imported Model A machines consisted of one 40-hp (30-kW) Continental A-40 flat-four engine, and the Model B differed in having a 50-hp (38-kW) A-50 engine from the same manufacturer.

The English-built equivalent to the Model A was originally designated as the **British Taylorcraft Model C**, but this was soon redesignated as the **Model Plus C** to reflect the improved performance resulting from installation of a 55-hp (41-kW) Lycoming O-145-A2 flat-four engine. Production of the Model

Plus C, including the prototype, was 23 aircraft. With the powerplant changed to one 90-hp (67-kW) Blackburn Cirrus Minor 1 inverted inline engine, the designation changed to **Model Plus D**, and nine civil aircraft were completed to this standard before the outbreak of World War II in late September 1939.

Of the 32 British-built aircraft mentioned above, 20 of the Model Plus C and four of the Model Plus D machines were then impressed for service with

the Royal Air Force. The Model Plus C aircraft, revised with the Cirrus Minor engine for RAF use, received the designation **Model Plus C.2**. Most of

these aircraft were used by No. 651 Squadron for evaluation of the type's suitability for the air observation post and communications roles.

SPECIFICATION

British Taylorcraft Model Plus C
Type: two-seat touring and sporting aircraft
Powerplant: one Avco Lycoming O-145-A2 flat-four engine rated at 55 hp (41 kW)
Performance: maximum speed 110 mph (177 km/h) at sea level; cruising speed 90 mph (67 km/h) at

optimum altitude; initial climb rate 550 ft (168 m) per minute; range 275 miles (443 km)
Weights: empty 720 lb (327 kg); maximum take-off 1,200 lb (544 kg)
Dimensions: wingspan 36 ft (10.97 m); length 22 ft 10 in (6.96 m); height 8 ft (2.44 m); wing area 167.00 sq ft (15.51 m²)

Britten-Norman BN-3 Nymph

Britten-Norman Ltd of Bembridge on the Isle of Wight started on the design of the **Britten-Norman BN-3 Nymph** in September 1968. Its intention was the creation of a four-seat lightplane which the company would develop and then produce in the form of kits that would be assembled by approved maintenance/repair and other such organisations.

The Nymph was of orthodox design and construction as a high-wing cabin monoplane of

the strut-braced type with fixed tricycle landing gear. The fuselage was of semi-monocoque construction in light alloy with a glassfibre engine cowling, and the cantilever tail unit was of light alloy construction and included a swept fin. The wing (foldable for reduced hangarage requirements) was based in concept on that of the BN-2 Islander light transport and was again of light alloy construction, with virtually the whole of its trailing edge occupied by outboard ailerons and

inboard flaps. The wing's bracing struts were angled backward from the wing's main spar to points on the sides of the lower fuselage toward the rear of the cabin. This created the space for the opening of the single door that was standard on the port side and optional on the starboard side. The cabin provided heated and ventilated accommodation for four persons in a fore-and-aft arrangement of paired seats.

Construction of the prototype started on 25 March 1969, and this machine made its first flight only eight weeks later, on 17 May 1969, with the powerplant of one Avco Lycoming O-235-C1B flat-four engine. An example of the same manufacturer's O-320 engine, rated at 160 hp (119 kW), was later fitted and the Rolls-Royce

Britten-Norman had planned that the Nymph would be suitable for construction in underdeveloped countries by means of a 'technology transfer' system, but these plans came to nothing. The design was later taken on by NDN as the NAC-1 Freelance, the prototype flying in 1984.

(Continental) O-200 engine was offered as an option at a rating of 130 hp (97 kW). The Nymph was exhibited at the Paris Air Show of the same year and gained an initial order for 100 aircraft for assembly by AESL in New Zealand for the Australian

and New Zealand markets. The order was not confirmed, however, and when Britten-Norman ran into financial problems in the early 1970s and was taken over by Fairey in August 1972, the Nymph programme was dropped.

SPECIFICATION

Britten-Norman BN-3 Nymph
Type: four-seat touring aircraft
Powerplant: one Avco Lycoming O-235-C1B flat-four engine rated at 115 hp (86 kW)
Performance: maximum speed 117 mph (188 km/h) at sea level; cruising speed 113 mph (182 km/h) at 7,500 ft (2285 m); initial climb

rate 600 ft (183 m) per minute; service ceiling 11,200 ft (3415 m); range 600 miles (966 km)
Weights: empty 1,140 lb (517 kg); maximum take-off 1,925 lb (873 kg)
Dimensions: wingspan 39 ft 8⅜ in (11.98 m); length 23 ft 7¾ in (7.20 m); height 9 ft 6 in (2.90 m); wing area 169.00 sq ft (15.70 m²)

Brochet aircraft

During the 1950s Avions Maurice Brochet, headed by Maurice Brochet, was well known in France for a series of lightplanes which Brochet designed for amateur construction, the most popular being those based on the **Brochet M.B.70**. This was a two-seat cabin

monoplane with a strut-braced high-set wooden wing, and a wooden fuselage and tail unit, all of which were covered with fabric. The landing gear was of the fixed tailwheel type, the main units having rubber-cord shock-absorption, and power was

Derived directly from the M.B.70 and M.B.80 airframes, the M.B.100 seated three people in its fully-enclosed cabin.

provided by a 45-hp (34-kW) Salmson 9Adb radial piston engine. The pilot and passenger/ pupil were accommodated in tandem inside an enclosed cabin, and dual controls were standard. Brochet's original aim

had been to make sure that the M.B.70 would be easy to build, but in refining his design for the type, he had worked to ensure that it would not only be easy to fly, but also simple to maintain. This high level of

practicality attracted the attention of the SFASA (Service de la Formation Aéronautique et des Sports Aériens), which ordered between 40 and 50 examples of various models for distribution to flying clubs.

SPECIFICATION

Brochet M.B.100
Type: three-seat training and touring aircraft
Powerplant: one Hirth HM 504A-2 inverted inline engine rated at 91 hp (68 kW)
Performance: maximum speed 112 mph (180 km/h) at optimum altitude; cruising speed 103 mph (165 km/h) at optimum altitude;

initial climb rate 590 ft (180 m) per minute; service ceiling 11,485 ft (3500 m); range 373 miles (600 km)
Weights: empty 1,025 lb (465 kg); maximum take-off 1,720 lb (780 kg)
Dimensions: wingspan 34 ft 11¼ in (10.65 m); length 21 ft 4 in (6.50 m); height 6 ft 6¾ in (2.00 m); wing area 153.40 sq ft (14.25 m²)

Variants

M.B.50 Pipistrelle: designed in 1947 for amateur construction, the two-seat Pipistrelle was of typical Brochet braced high-wing design, and its data included the powerplant of one Train 4A inverted inline engine rated at 45 hp (34 kW), maximum speed of 87 mph (140 km/h) at sea level, cruising speed of 71 mph (115 km/h) at optimum altitude, empty weight of 529 lb (240 kg), maximum take-off weight of 772 lb (350 kg), wingspan of 26 ft 2¾ in (8.00 m) and length of 16 ft (4.88 m)
M.B.80: generally similar to the M.B.70, but with the fuselage widened by 4 in (10.2 cm), balanced steel main landing-gear units, and a Minie 4DC.32B flat-four engine rated at 75 hp (56 kW).
M.B.84: development of the M.B.80 with the revised powerplant of one Continental A65-8 flat-four engine rated at 65 hp (49 kW), cruising speed of 96 mph (155 km/h) at optimum altitude, range of 311 miles (500 km), maximum take-off weight of 1,200 lb (545 kg),

wingspan of 34 ft 3 in (1.044 m) and length of 21 ft 7½ in (6.59 m)
M.B.100: three-seat development of the M.B.70 with landing gear similar to that of the M.B.80 and the powerplant of one Hirth inverted inline piston engine; this model was not intended for amateur construction and was produced with a welded steel-tube fuselage structure
M.B.101: this was a version of the M.B.100 with air filter and special external finish for service in North Africa
M.B.110: this was a four-seat cabin monoplane on similar lines to the preceding aircraft; it had the steel-tube fuselage structure of the M.B.100, covered mostly with fabric, and plywood skins for the wing and tail surfaces; the powerplant consisted of one SNECMA Regnier 4L-02 inverted inline engine rated at 170 hp (127 kW)
M.B.120: this was a two-seater combining the M.B.80's wing, M.B.100's fuselage in a form modified to seat two, and the powerplant of one Continental C90 flat-four engine rated at 90 hp (67 kW)

Bücker Bü 131 Jungmann

The first product of the Bücker Flugzeugbau GmbH, established at Johannisthal, Germany, during 1932, was a two-seat light trainer known as the **Bücker Bü 131 Jungmann** (youth). Designed by Anders Andersson, the company's Swedish chief engineer, the Jungmann was a conventional single-bay biplane with a staggered, swept and single-bay biplane wing cellule of fabric-covered wooden construction, a welded steel-tube fuselage that, with the exception of light alloy around the engine and cockpit, was also fabric-covered, and a wire-braced tail unit of similar construction to the fuselage. The fixed tail-

wheel type landing gear had rather stalky divided main units, and the prototype first flew on 27 April 1934 with the powerplant of one Hirth HM 60K inverted inline engine rated at 80 hp (60 kW).
The **Bü 131A**, as the initial production version was designated, proved to be very successful. The type was manufactured not only for civil flying schools in Germany, but was also built very extensively for the Luftwaffe, although production figures do not appear to have survived. Examples were also exported for service in some eight European countries, with the largest numbers going to Hungary (100) and Romania (150),

and in addition 75 aircraft were licence-built in Switzerland. The most extensive licensed construction was undertaken in Japan, where 1,037 **Nippon Kokusai Ki-86a** aircraft were built for service with the Imperial Japanese army air force under the designation **Type 4 Primary Trainer**. This followed the initiation of production for the Imperial Japanese navy air force, which operated the type as the **Navy Type 2 Trainer Model 11** (otherwise **K9W1 Momiji**, or maple), built by Hitachi and Kyushu. Production figures for the naval version differ according to source at between 217 and 339, but it seems reasonably certain

that more than 200 were used as the navy's standard trainer. The engine used in the two Japanese variants, which each had the Allied reporting name **'Cypress'**, was the 110-hp (82-kW) inverted inline engine known to the army as the Hitachi [Ha-47] 11 and to the navy as the Hitachi GK4A Hatsukaze 11. The sole **Ki-86B** was an experimental development with an all-wood airframe, but was somewhat heavier than the Ki-86a, with worse performance.

Used throughout World War II by the Luftwaffe, the Bü 131A was later displaced by the superior Bü 181, and many of the aircraft also saw service with auxiliary ground-attack squadrons. Carrying 2.2- and 4.4-lb (1 and 2-kg) bombs, they were used by night to maintain non-stop harassment over the Soviet lines. Like other classic trainers, many Bü 131 aircraft survived the war, and were even built by Aero in Czechoslovakia during the 1950s under the designation **C4**.

Variants

Bü 131B Jungmann: this was an improved version with the uprated Hirth HM 504A-2 engine
Bü 131C Jungmann: this was an experimental version, of which only a single example was built with the powerplant of one Cirrus Minor inverted inline engine rated at 90 hp (68 kW)

SPECIFICATION

Bücker Bü 131B Jungmann
Type: two-seat primary flying trainer with a secondary tasking for night harassment
Powerplant: one Hirth HM 504A-2 inverted inline engine rated at 105 hp (78 kW)
Performance: maximum speed 114 mph (183 km/h) at sea level; cruising speed 106 mph (170 km/h) at optimum altitude; climb to 3,280 ft (1000 m) in 6 minutes 18 seconds; service ceiling 9,845 ft (3000 m); range 404 miles (650 km)

Weights: empty 860 lb (390 kg); maximum take-off 1,499 lb (680 kg)
Dimensions: wingspan 24 ft 3⅓ in (7.40 m); length 21 ft 8 in (6.60 m); height 7 ft 4½ in (2.25 m); wing area 145.32 sq ft (13.50 m²)
Armament: generally none, although provision was later added for the occupant of the rear seat to drop light fragmentation bomblets, and finally for such weapons to be dropped from racks under the lower wing

The Bü 131 Jungmann is most easily distinguished from the later Bü 133 Jungmeister by means of its standard inline engine.

Bücker Bü 133 Jungmeister

Demand for the Bü 131 Jungmann was so great that Bücker's production facilities at Johannisthal were soon overwhelmed. A new factory was therefore established at Rangsdorf and there,

where it would be possible to expand production facilities, the company began development of a single-seat trainer based on the Bü 131 design. Generally similar in overall configuration and

construction, this **Bücker Bü 133 Jungmeister** (young champion) differed primarily in its smaller overall dimensions, which meant that the prototype, with the powerplant of one Hirth HM 6 inverted inline engine rated at 135 hp (101 kW), possessed excellent aerobatic performance. Testing by the Luftwaffe resulted in production aircraft being ordered for service in the advanced training role, including the early instruction of fighter pilots, and the initial production

In 1999, G-AYSJ was based at Duxford, Cambridgeshire, from where it was used to mount aerobatic displays on the UK air show circuit.

examples had the designation **Bü 133A**. No record of the number built for the Luftwaffe appears to have survived, but about 50 were manufactured by

Dornier-Werke in Switzerland for the Swiss air force, and a similar quantity by CASA in Spain for the Spanish air force.

SPECIFICATION

Bücker Bü 133C Jungmeister
Type: single-seat advanced flying and aerobatic trainer
Powerplant: one Siemens Sh 14A-4 radial engine rated at 160 hp (119 kW)
Performance: maximum speed 137 mph (220 km/h) at sea level; cruising speed 124 mph (200 km/h) at optimum altitude; climb to

3,280 ft (1000 m) in 2 minutes 48 seconds; service ceiling 14,765 ft (4500 m); range 311 miles (500 km)
Weights: empty 937 lb (425 kg); maximum take-off 1,290 lb (585 kg)
Dimensions: wingspan 21 ft 7¾ in (6.60 m); length 19 ft 9 in (6.00 m); height 7 ft 2½ in (2.20 m); wing area 129.17 sq ft (12.00 m²)

Variants

Bü 133B Jungmeister: this was the designation of licence-built aircraft with the more potent powerplant of one Hirth HM 506 inverted inline engine rated at 160 hp (119 kW)
Bü 133C Jungmeister: this was the designation of the major production version with the powerplant of one Siemens Sh 14A-4 radial engine

Bücker Bü 180 Student

After it had designed the Bü 133 and got this type into production, the company turned its attention to the development of the **Bücker Bü 134** as a two-seat cabin monoplane of high-wing configuration. The single prototype of this aircraft proved to be unsuccessful when tested, and its development was abandoned. Convinced that future trainers would need

Generally similar in design to the UK's Miles Magister, the Student seated an instructor and pupil in tandem. The first prototype Bü 180 flew in 1937.

to be of monoplane configuration, the company persevered and now designed another two-seat trainer of cantilever low-wing layout.

SPECIFICATION

Bücker Bü 180 Student
Type: two-seat sporting and training aircraft
Powerplant: one Walter Mikron II or Zundapp 9-092 inverted inline engine rated at 60 hp (45 kW)
Performance: maximum speed 109 mph (175 km/h) at sea level; cruising speed 99 mph (160 km/h) at optimum altitude; climb to

3,280 ft (1000 m) in 8 minutes 54 seconds; service ceiling 14,765 ft (4500 m); range 404 miles (650 km)
Weights: empty 650 lb (295 kg); maximum take-off 1,190 lb (540 kg)
Dimensions: wingspan 37 ft 8¾ in (11.50 m); length 23 ft 3½ in (7.10 m); height 6 ft ¾ in (1.85 m); wing area 161.46 sq ft (15.00 m²)

Designated **Bücker Bü 180**, and later named **Student**, this had a monoplane wing of wooden construction, covered partially with plywood and partially with fabric, and the tail unit was of similar construction. The forward fuselage was fabricated of welded steel tube and the

rear fuselage was a wooden monocoque, all covered by fabric except for light alloy panels around the engine. The fixed landing gear was of the tailskid type with divided main units, the powerplant was based on one Walter Mikron II or Zundapp 9-092 inverted

inline engine, and the two-seat accommodation was provided in a tandem arrangement of open cockpits. The prototype first flew in the autumn of 1937, and there then followed a small number of production aircraft intended for civil use.

Bücker Bü 181 Bestmann

Experience with the Bü 180 showed Bücker that, even with an engine of small power output, the

two-seat monoplane could offer quite good performance. With this encouragement the

company began the design of a new trainer that adopted the construction of the Bü 180 in combination with side-by-side seating in an enclosed cabin to provide ideal conditions for primary training. Identified as the **Bücker Bü 181**, and later named **Bestmann**, the new aircraft had wings of wooden basic construction with plywood and fabric covering, a tail unit of similar structure, and a fuselage with steel-tube

Several thousand Bü 181s were built. Aircraft not required for training were utilised in liaison, glider tug and anti-tank weapon transportation roles.

forward section and a wooden monocoque rear section. The landing gear was of the fixed tailwheel type with divided main units, and power was provided by a Hirth HM 504 inverted inline engine.

The prototype made its first flight early in 1939 and, following testing by the Luftwaffe, the type was ordered into full production as the **Bü 181A** for service as a standard basic trainer.

SPECIFICATION

Bücker Bü 181A Bestmann
Type: two-seat primary flying trainer
Powerplant: one Hirth HM 504A inverted inline engine rated at 105 hp (87 kW)
Performance: maximum speed 134 mph (215 km/h) at sea level; cruising speed 121 mph (195 km/h) at optimum altitude; climb to

3,280 ft (1000 m) in 5 minutes 18 seconds; service ceiling 16,405 ft (5000 m); range 497 miles (800 km)
Weights: empty 1,058 lb (480 kg); maximum take-off 1,653 lb (750 kg)
Dimensions: wingspan 34 ft 9¼ in (10.60 m); length 25 ft 9 in (7.85 m); height 6 ft 8¾ in (2.05 m); wing area 145.32 sq ft (13.50 m²)

Variant

Bü 181D Bestmann: this was a later production version with a number of detail improvements

Bücker Bü 181 Bestmann (continued)

Details of the number of Bü 181s constructed for the Luftwaffe are not accurately known, but it has been estimated that production must have run into many thousands. As the type became available in large numbers it was also used as a communications aircraft and, in smaller numbers, as a glider tug.

In addition to production by Bücker, 708 aircraft of this type were built by Fokker in the Netherlands during the war, and in 1944-6 125 machines were built in Sweden for that nation's air force under the designation **Sk 25**. Wartime production for German requirements had also been launched in occupied Czechoslovakia, where it continued after the war to yield the **Zlin Z-281** and **Z-381** for civil use as well as the **C.6** and **C.106** for military service. Under licence from Czechoslovakia, Egypt also manufactured a derivative of the Z-381 as the **Heliopolis Gomhouria** that was exported to several other Arab states.

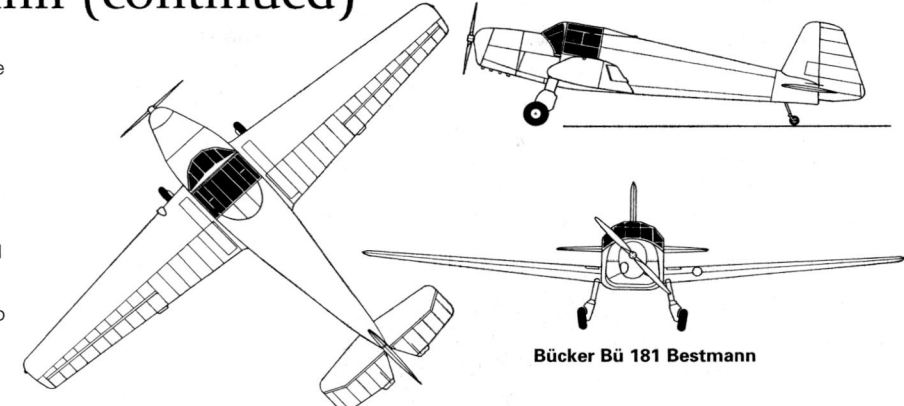

Bücker Bü 181 Bestmann

Budd Conestoga (RB)

The **Budd Conestoga** was probably the first large aircraft of original design to be fabricated from stainless steel. It reflected another approach to the desire felt early in World War II to ensure that alternative materials could be found for aircraft construction, to replace the extensively-used aluminium alloys of which a shortage had been predicted.

Intended for use as a cargo carrier or troop transport, the Conestoga was developed by the Budd Manufacturing Company in collaboration with the US Navy Bureau of Aeronautics. The high-set monoplane wing was primarily of stainless steel stressed-skin construction, but the trailing edges of the wing outer panels, trailing-edge flaps and ailerons were covered with fabric. The tail unit was similar, but the fuselage was wholly of stressed-skin construction. The upswept rear fuselage incorporated an electrically-operated ramp which allowed military vehicles to be driven directly into the hold, which was 8 ft (2.44 m) wide and 8 ft (2.44 m) high. Because the flightdeck was mounted high on the nose, the cargo compartment maintained the foregoing dimensions over a length of 25 ft (7.62 m). As an alternative to bulky cargo, 24 fully armed paratroops and equipment/supplies could be carried or, in a casualty evacuation role, 24 litters and 16 sitting patients. Power was provided by two Pratt & Whitney Twin Wasp radial engines in wing-mounted nacelles, and the landing gear was of the semi-retractable tricycle type.

In August 1942 the US Navy awarded a contract to the Budd company for 200 of these transports under the designation **RB-1**, and US Army Air Forces interest resulted in a contract for an additional 600 aircraft under the designation **C-93**. The prototype flew for the first time on 31 October 1943, but production delays, cost overruns and a realisation that there was unlikely to be a shortage of conventional light alloys resulted in cancellation of the USAAF contract. Shortly after this the US Navy contract was reduced to only 25 aircraft, and of these 17 were delivered before the war ended, but were not used. Sold as war surplus items, 14 were acquired by Robert Presscott and used to start a freight airline known originally as National Skyway Freight Corporation, but later as the Flying Tiger Line.

Very little use was made of the Conestoga by the US military although it was relatively successful in airline service. Advanced features included a rear-loading ramp and constant-section cabin. The main undercarriage remained semi-retracted in flight.

SPECIFICATION	
Budd RB-1 Conestoga **Type:** two/three-seat cargo and troop transport **Powerplant:** two Pratt & Whitney R-1830-92 Twin Wasp radial engines each rated at 1,200 hp (895 kW) **Performance:** maximum speed 197 mph (317 km/h) at 7,500 ft (2285 m); cruising speed 165 mph (266 km/h) at optimum altitude;	initial climb rate 850 ft (259 m) per minute; service ceiling 15,600 ft (4755 m); range 700 miles (1127 km) with maximum payload **Weights:** empty 20,156 lb (9143 kg); maximum take-off 33,860 lb (15359 kg) **Dimensions:** wingspan 100 ft (30.48 m); length 68 ft (20.73 m); height 31 ft 9 in (9.68 m); wing area 1,400.00 sq ft (130.06 m²)

Burgess Model HT

The **Burgess Model HT** was designed by W. Starling Burgess of the Burgess Company that was part of the Curtiss Aeroplane and Motor Corporation. The Model HT was designed in response to a requirement issued in the autumn of 1916 by the US Navy, which needed a fighter floatplane with a powerplant of one Gnome Monosoupape 9N rotary engine rated at 165 hp (123 kW) and a performance that included a maximum level speed of at least 95 mph (153 km/h) and an endurance of 2 hours 30 minutes.

The prototype was demonstrated to officers and officials of the US Navy in May 1917 and, although it failed to attain the required performance as it was powered by the Curtiss OXX-2 Vee engine rated at only 100 hp (75 kW) pending the availability of the intended rotary engine, it secured an order for six (later increased to eight) **Model HT-B** production aircraft as the service was impressed with the type's carefully considered design and high level of aerodynamic and hydrodynamic cleanliness.

The Model HT-B was a sesquiplane of fabric-covered and wire-braced wooden construction. The core of the structure was the fuselage, which was itself based on a wire-braced wooden primary structure of rectangular section faired out to a flat-bottomed oval shape with light frames and stringers before being covered. From front to back, the fuselage carried the powerplant, fuel and oil tanks, pilot's open cockpit, and tail unit. This last was based on single horizontal and vertical surfaces, the former comprising a tailplane that was strut-braced to the lower longeron on each side and carried plain elevator halves, and the latter comprising a wire-braced fin carrying an aerodynamically balanced rudder that was hinged at its lower end to the vertical knife-edge in which the fuselage terminated.

The wing cellule was of the single-bay type, and the upper wing was of considerably greater span than the lower wing, although both surfaces were of the same constant chord to their raked tips. The two halves of the flat lower wing extended from the lower longerons. The two outer panels of the flat upper wing, each with its tip supported by a kingpost-and-cable arrangement and carrying an inversely tapered aileron at the outboard end of its trailing edge, extended from a flat centre section that had a cut-out in its trailing edge above the pilot's head. This centre section was carried above the fuselage by two pairs of outward-canted cabane struts, the upper and lower wings were separated on each side by a sharply outward-canted K-type interplane strut, and the whole wing cellule was braced with the standard arrangement of flying and landing wires.

The airframe was completed by the alighting gear and powerplant. The alighting gear was based on a pair of single-step wooden floats connected by two horizontal members, carried side-by-side under the lower wing by struts extending downward and outward from the lower longerons, and braced laterally by struts rising upward and outward to the lower wing in line with the interplane struts: the interplane and float bracing struts formed a straight line in front elevation. The tail was supported by a small float carried by two vertical pairs of wire-braced struts. As noted above, the powerplant was based on one OXX-2 Vee engine installed in the front of the fuselage inside an essentially circular cowling, driving a two-bladed wooden propeller of the tractor type, and cooled by a circular frontal radiator.

The fact that the production model had to retain the lower-powered Curtiss engine meant that the planned armament was seldom, if ever, fitted, and the floatplanes were there-fore used mainly for the scouting and training roles after delivery from September 1917.

The revised designation **Model HT-2** was applied to another six aircraft delivered during the course of 1918 to a slightly improved standard.

The Burgess Company failed in December 1918, and it is believed that the Model HT-B and Model HT-2 floatplanes were discarded soon after this.

Also known as the Speed Scout, the HT-2 saw little in-service use. The aircraft utilised a number of distinctive features, including a spacious cockpit and single, broad-chord interplane struts.

SPECIFICATION	
Burgess Model HT-2	
Type: single-seat floatplane fighter used mainly as an advanced trainer	**Dimensions:** wingspan 34 ft 4 in (10.46 m); length 22 ft 3 in (6.87 m); height 10 ft 9 in (3.28 m)
Powerplant: one Curtiss OXX-2 Vee engine rated at 100 hp (75 kW)	**Armament:** generally none, although provision was made for one 0.3-in (7.62-mm) Marlin fixed forward-firing machine gun in the forward fuselage
Performance: maximum speed 85 mph (137 km/h) at 1,000 ft (305 m); endurance 2 hours	

Burnelli aircraft

Very soon after the end of World War I in 1918 Vincent Burnelli was formulating his ideas for an aircraft of new concept. He was convinced that the fuselage of an aircraft could, if properly designed, add a significant component of lift to that provided by the wings, and then devoted many years in attempts to develop and promote his ideas. The first fruit of this work was the biplane **Remington Burnelli Airliner** of 1920, followed by the **RB-2** biplane freighter in 1924. Typical of Burnelli's later adoption of the monoplane layout was the **Chapman-Burnelli CB-16** of 1928, its aerofoil-section fuselage providing what must surely have been the first truly practical wide-body transport, accommodating 20 passengers in a main cabin that was 18 ft (5.49 m) long, 11 ft 4 in (3.45 m) wide and 5 ft 6 in (1.68 m) in maximum height. The high-set braced monoplane wing and fuselage were all-metal, and the tail unit was of fabric-covered steel tube construction. The landing

gear was of the tailwheel type with manually-retractable main units, and the powerplant comprised two Curtiss GV-1550 Conqueror Vee engines each rated at 625 hp (466 kW) and mounted in the fuselage nose, one at each side.

Powered by two Packard Vee engines each rated at 800 hp (597 kW), the **Uppercu-Burnelli UB-20** was an essentially similar aircraft that differed mainly in its fixed landing gear and metal stressed-skin construction.

A year earlier, in 1929, Burnelli adopted his lifting-fuselage concept in a twin-engined experimental monoplane, the **GX-3**, to compete in the Guggenheim Safe Aircraft Competition. Other unusual features of this aircraft included a variable-camber wing, full-span flaps and a four-wheel landing gear. Power was provided by two American ADC Cirrus III inline engines each rated at 90 hp (67 kW).

Continuing his attempts to develop a commercially

attractive transport aircraft embodying the lifting-fuselage concept, Burnelli designed and built in 1934 the **UB-14**, in which the aerofoil-section fuselage was basically the centre-section of the wing. More graceful in form than the earlier designs, the UB-14 had a fuselage structure that incorporated upswept tail booms united by a wide-span tailplane and elevator that carried twin fins and rudders. By then, the landing gear was hydraulically retractable and power provided by two Pratt & Whitney radial engines. The pilot and co-pilot/navigator were accommodated in an enclosed cabin on the upper surface of the wing, well toward the nose, and 14 passengers were seated in the spacious comfort of a cabin 11 ft (3.55 m) long and 12 ft (3.66 m) wide with features such as thermo-statically controlled heating, ventilation, lighting, toilet and ample baggage space. The UB-14 was destroyed when it cartwheeled into the ground in 1935.

Burnelli then produced

the improved **UB-14B**. One further example of the Burnelli UB-14B transport was built in the UK by Cunliffe Owen Aircraft during 1938. A somewhat redesigned type, this had the designation **Cunliffe Owen OA-I**, but only this one aircraft was manufactured with the powerplant of two Bristol Perseus XIVC radial engines each rated at 710 hp (530 kW).

In 1935 Burnelli produced his A-1 bomber design, which did not progress beyond the stage of a wooden mock-up. But the type provided the basis for the **General Aircraft XCG-16A** transport glider. This was built in 1943, and was intended to carry up to 40 fully-equipped troops. Designed by Harley Bowlus, the XCG-16A was of wooden construction, spanned 92 ft (28.04 m), had a maximum weight of 19,000 lb (8618 kg) and could carry an alternative freight load of 8,800 lb (3992 kg). The XCG-16A was in every respect superior to the competing Waco XCG-13A, but was not ordered into production.

Burnelli's last lifting-body design was also his most successful. This was the **Cancargo CBY-3 Loadmaster**, produced just after World War II by the Cancargo Aircraft Manufacturing Company, a

subsidiary of the Canadian Car & Foundry Company. Construction was all-metal, and the initial powerplant comprised a pair of Pratt & Whitney R-1830 radial engines each rated at 1,200 hp (895 kW). The large lifting-body fuselage could accommodate 22 passengers and 700 cu ft (19.82 m³) of freight in a cabin 20 ft (6.10 m) wide, 26 ft 6 in (8.08 m) long and 7 ft (2.13 m) high, and the provision of a door in each side of the compartment allowed items up to 20 ft (6.10 m) long to be loaded. In a pure freight role the CBY-3 could uplift 2,070 cu ft (58.62 m³) of cargo. The CBY-3 underwent a varied career in the Americas, including re-engining with Wright R-2600 radial engines, and is now the only Burnelli aircraft in existence, as part of the collection of the Connecticut Aeronautical Historical Association.

Burnelli had no commercial success with any of his aircraft. Perhaps he suffered the penalty of being ahead of the state of the art, for modern research and development has shown lifting-body aircraft to be practical without the use of wings, leading to the unique and highly successful Space Shuttle. But this he did not know when he died in 1964.

A supremely advanced design, the UB-14 might have evolved into an eminently practical transport aircraft. Unfortunately, Burnelli's design was too radical to achieve general acceptance.

SPECIFICATION	
Burnelli UB-14B	
Type: transport aircraft	ceiling 22,000 ft (6705 m); range 1,240 miles (1996 km)
Powerplant: two Pratt & Whitney Hornet radial engines each rated at 750 hp (560 kW)	**Weights:** empty 9,200 lb (4173 kg); maximum take-off 17,500 lb (7938 kg)
Performance: maximum speed 210 mph (338 km/h) at sea level; cruising speed 205 mph (330 km/h) at 10,000 ft (3050 m); service	**Dimensions:** wingspan 71 ft (21.64 m); length 44 ft (13.41 m); height 10 ft (3.05 m); total lifting area 686.00 sq ft (63.73 m²)

Buscaylet aircraft

Buscaylet Père et Fils-Bobin et Cie, which had built aircraft under sub-contract during World War I, decided in the immediate post-war years to initiate the design and manufacture of its own products. Securing the services of Louis de Monge as its designer, the company built the prototype of a single-seat parasol-wing fighter designated as the **Buscaylet-de Monge 5/2**. This was derived from the **de Monge 5/1** racer which had crashed when flown in monoplane configuration during 1921. The basic structure of the 5/2 was of metal, with mixed wood and metal skinning, and the powerplant was based on one Hispano-Suiza 8Fb Vee engine rated at 300 hp (224 kW). An unusual feature of the design of the racer had been the provision of attachment for stub wings that could be used to convert the aircraft to a sesquiplane. This was intended to simplify the problems of early flight testing, but for high-speed performance the stub wings were to be removed. de Monge retained this feature for his fighter prototype, claiming that the sesquiplane wing could enhance its value, allowing it to double in the high-altitude role with the wing area increased from 258.34 sq ft (24.00 m²) to 344.46 sq ft (32.00 m²). The prototype flew for the first time during 1923, but when the French air arm evaluated the type for the fighter role it decided that the 5/2 was too advanced. As a result, all further development was abandoned.

The other data for the 5/2 included a maximum speed of 168 mph (270 km/h) at sea level, service ceiling of 24,605 ft (7500 m), maximum take-off weight of 2,976 lb (1350 kg), wingspan of 35 ft 9⅛ in (10.90 m), length of 23 ft 5½ in (7.15 m), height of 8 ft 10¼ in (2.70 m), and proposed armament of two 0.303-in (7.7-mm) Vickers fixed forward-firing machine-guns.

A large lifting surface was carried between the main undercarriage wheels of the Buscaylet-Béchereau 2, or BB.2. The aircraft offered inadequate performance for use in the front-line fighter role.

In 1923 the French air service issued a requirement for an advanced single-seat fighter, and the Buscaylet company responded with the **Buscaylet-Béchereau 2**, which was a development by Louis Béchereau of the **Letord-Béchereau 2**. The primary difference between the two types was the replacement of the earlier type's pair of broad-chord combined lifting surface/struts, between the outboard ends of the substantial main landing gear unit and the mid-points of the parasol wing's two halves, with two substantial struts on each side. Other features of the design were a basically circular-section fuselage with a long dorsal spine that gradually turned into the fin of the low-aspect-ratio vertical tail surface, an extensively louvered cowling over the two-row radial engine that was a water-cooled unit with a frontal radiator, a slightly swept parasol wing with full-span ailerons outboard of the cut-out in the trailing edge of the centre section, and a very substantial aerofoil-section central fairing carried by four large struts under the fuselage, and itself supporting the two main wheels of the fixed tailskid landing gear.

The **BB.2** first flew in 1924 and revealed poor performance and inadequate handling. Further development of the type as a single-seater was thereupon discontinued although, after his appointment as chief designer of the Salmson company, Béchereau later evolved the type into a two-seat fighter.

The company built and flew the **Buscaylet-de Monge 7/4** in 1923 and the **Buscaylet-de Monge 7/5** in 1925, but with neither design gaining any commercial success, the company suffered financial disaster and ceased to trade.

SPECIFICATION	
Buscaylet-Béchereau 2	3,876 lb (1758 kg)
Type: single-seat fighter	**Dimensions:** wingspan 45 ft 11⅓ in (14.00 m); length 32 ft 9⁹⁄₁₀ in (10.00 m); height 9 ft 10 in (3.00 m); wing area 419.81 sq ft (39.00 m²)
Powerplant: one Salmson 18Cm radial engine rated at 500 hp (373 kW)	
Performance: maximum speed 155 mph (250 km/h) at 9,845 ft (3000 m)	
Weights: empty 2,976 lb (1350 kg); maximum take-off	**Armament:** (proposed) two 0.303-in (7.7-mm) Vickers fixed forward-firing machine-guns in the upper part of the forward fuselage

Bushmaster 2000

In the mid-1960s William B. Stout, founder of the Stout Metal Airplane Company, itself a division of the Ford Motor Company, decided to modernise the Ford Tri-Motor to provide a simple and economical transport aircraft. The original Tri-Motor, derived from the Stout Pullman, had been flown during the latter half of the 1920s and, not surprisingly, the prototype of the new **Bushmaster 2000** was able to benefit from many developments in materials and constructional techniques.

The new prototype was completed during 1966 by Aircraft HydroForming Inc., rights to the type's production being acquired later by Bushmaster Aircraft Corporation. This new tri-motor aircraft introduced more powerful engines with modern constant-speed and fully-feathering propellers, lighter weight and stronger light alloy covering for the all-metal fuselage structure, controllable trim tabs, oleo-pneumatic shock absorbers, and a host of design refinements. In a high-density seating arrangement, it could have carried a pilot and 23 passengers. The Bushmaster 2000 was basically an aircraft from an earlier era, however, and failed to attract sales against more modern, higher-performance aircraft.

SPECIFICATION	
Bushmaster 2000	range 700 miles (1127 km)
Type: two-crew short-range commuter transport	**Weights:** empty 7,500 lb (3402 kg); maximum take-off 12,500 lb (5670 kg)
Powerplant: three Pratt & Whitney R-985-AN-1 Wasp Junior radial engines each rated at 450 hp (336 kW)	**Dimensions:** wingspan 77 ft 11 in (23.75 m); length 50 ft 8 in (15.44 m); height 13 ft 5 in (4.09 m); wing area 851.70 sq ft (79.12 m²)
Performance: maximum speed 125 mph (210 km/h) at sea level;	

Only one Bushmaster 2000 prototype was completed. The type failed to enter production in the face of competition from all-new transport aircraft designs.

CallAir Model A

In the late 1930s members of the Call family of air-minded ranchers in Wyoming combined their talents to design a basic and robust utility aircraft for use by farmers and ranchers. Finalised as the **Model A**, it was ready for production in 1940 but, with a major war raging in Europe, there was no opportunity of proceeding further at that time. Subsequently, the Call Aircraft Company was formed at Afton, Wyoming,

Variants

CallAir Model A-4 Model 150: two/three-seat cabin monoplane powered by the Lycoming O-320-A2A engine rated at 150 hp (112 kW)
CallAir Model A-5: agricultural duster/sprayer version of the Model A-4 Model 150 retaining the same powerplant
CallAir Model A-6: improved version of the Model A-5 with the Lycoming O-360-A1A engine rated at 180 hp (134 kW)
IMCO CallAir Model A-9: improved agricultural aircraft developed from the Models A-5 and A-6 with the powerplant of one Lycoming O-540-B2B5 engine rated at 235 hp (175 kW)
IMCO CallAir Model B-1: scaled-up development of the CallAir design with increased span, greater hopper capacity and the powerplant of one Lycoming IO-720-A1A engine rated at 400 hp (298 kW)
Ag Commander Model A-9: designation of the IMCO Model A-9 as produced by Aero Commander
Ag Commander Model A-9 Super: version of the Model A-9 with increased hopper capacity and the powerplant of one Lycoming IO-540 engine rated at 290 hp (216 kW)
Ag Commander Model B-1: designation of the IMCO model B-1 as produced by Aero Commander
Sparrow Commander: redesignation of the Ag Commander Model A-9 as built by North American Rockwell
Quail Commander: redesignation of the Ag Commander Model A-9 Super as built by North American Rockwell
Snipe Commander: redesignation of the Ag Commander Model B-1 as built by North American Rockwell; production of this version ended when Rockwell International came to an agreement with the Mexican company
AAMSA Model A9B-M Quail: designation of last production version of the Quail Commander; it incorporated a number of structural and aerodynamic refinements to improve maintenance and field performance
AAMSA Snipe: designation applied to Snipe Commander; production of this version was terminated at the end of 1975

but although a prototype of the **CallAir Model A** was built with the powerplant of one Continental A-80 engine rated at 80 hp (57 kW), it was not until 1946 that production of the **Model A-2** finally began. The designation **Model A-1** had been applied to the Model A prototype after it had been re-engined with a Lycoming O-235-A engine rated at 100 hp (75 kW), and it was in this form that the original type certification was gained on 26 July 1944.

The production Model A-2 was a braced low-wing monoplane with a wooden wing and welded steel tube fuselage and tail unit, all covered primarily with fabric. The landing gear was of the fixed tailwheel type, and the powerplant of the Model A-2 was a Lycoming O-280-A unit rated at 125 hp (93 kW). The Model A-2 was followed by the **Model A-3** with the Continental C-125-2 engine also rated at 125 hp (93 kW) and then the **Model A-4** with the Lycoming O-290-D2 engine rated at 135 hp (101 kW). Throughout the production of these three variants there had been little difference in basic design, and any changes, other than to the power-plant, were limited to refinements. The final versions to be developed by CallAir included the Model A-4 Model 150, Model A-5 and Model A-6.

In 1962, the IMCO

This Aero Commander-built CallAir Model A-9B demonstrates the type's classic agplane layout. N7799V remained in service in Colorado in mid-1999.

(Intermountain Manufacturing Company) acquired the Call Aircraft Company, and developed from the Models A-5 and A-6 a new agricultural aircraft, the **IMCO CallAir Model A-9**. A scaled-up development of this machine appeared in 1966 as the **IMCO CallAir Model B-1**.

Many changes followed: the Aero Commander Division of the Rockwell Standard Corporation acquired IMCO in December 1966, subsequently becoming the Aero Commander Division of the North American Rockwell Corporation. In 1971, what was now the Rockwell International Corporation entered into an agreement with Industrias Unidas SA of Mexico, and the resulting Aeronautica Agricola Mexicana SA then continued production of one of these aircraft as the AAMSA Model A9B-M Quail.

CAMS 30 and 31

The Chantiers Aéro-Maritimes de la Seine (CAMS) was founded by the Swiss engineer D. Lawrence Santoni in November 1920 for the manufacture of seaplanes and high-speed surface vessels. The new company's first products were licence-built examples of two Italian flying-boats, the SIAI S.9 and S.13. The designer of these SIAI 'boats, Rafaele Conflenti, then accepted Santoni's invitation to become technical director of the CAMS firm in 1921.

Conflenti's first successful design for his new employers was the **CAMS 30E**. Intended for the primary and intermediate training roles, with pupil and instructor seated side-by-side in open cockpits, this CAMS 30 was an equal-span biplane flying-boat of wooden construction, with its wings braced on each side by a single pair of parallel struts. It had a smoothly contoured hull and angular tailplane of typical Conflenti

The CAMS 31 represented a neat single-seat biplane design for use in the fighter role. Its poor performance and manoeuvrability made it entirely unsuited to air-to-air combat, however.

design, reminiscent of the earlier SIAI flying-boats. The Hispano-Suiza engine was mounted between the wings, drove a two-bladed pusher propeller, and was cooled by a single radiator mounted over the engine.

After exhibition at the 1922 Salon de l'Aéronautique in Paris, the CAMS 30E prototype was test-flown from the Seine early in 1923. Passed to the official Services Techniques de l'Aéronautique Maritime in March 1923, the type was soon adopted as equipment for the French navy's pilot school at Berre. Production for the French navy totalled 22 'boats, and seven more were exported to Yugoslavia, there they remained in naval service

for more than a decade. Series aircraft had twin radiators, located one on each side of the engine, in place of the single radiator of the prototype.

The data for the CAMS 30E included the powerplant of one Hispano-Suiza 8Aa Vee engine rated at 150 hp (112 kW), maximum speed of 95 mph (153 km/h), empty weight of 1,951 lb (885 kg), maximum take-off weight of 2,601 lb (1180 kg), wingspan of 40 ft 8¼ in (12.40 m), length of 30 ft 5¼ in (9.28 m), height of 10 ft 2¾ in (3.12 m), and wing area of 462.86 sq ft (43.00 m²).

The single **CAMS 30T** was a four-seat tourer development of the CAMS 30E built in the spring of 1923, and in August 1924 Ernest Burri captured the world speed record for passenger-carrying seaplanes with this 'boat.

One of the most unusual of the company's flying-boats was the **CAMS 31**, its aircraft being CAMS' only fighter flying-boat.

CAMS 30 and 31 (continued)

A single-seat 'boat with a two-bay, equal-span biplane wing cellule, the CAMS 31 was of wooden construction, carried two stabilising floats beneath the tips of the lower wing and had a conventional braced tail unit. The Hispano-Suiza engine was mounted between the wings, in a nacelle carried on hefty N-type struts above the hull, and drove a two-bladed pusher propeller. The pilot's open cockpit was located just forward of the lower wing, and the armament was a pair of fixed forward-firing machine-guns mounted in the bow. First flown in late 1922, this prototype was later identified as the **CAMS 31 Type 22** (for 1922) after a second prototype had been built and flown in 1923 as the **CAMS 31 Type 23**. This latter differed in its revised wing cellule of smaller span but increased chord, resulting in exactly the same wing area. Although both 'boats handled satisfactorily, their lack of performance and manoeuvrability made them totally unsuited to the fighter role, and no production aircraft resulted.

CAMS 33

In 1923 the French navy held a competition for flying-boats to be used in various categories. The winner of the section for coastal reconnaissance and bombing seaplanes was the **CAMS 33**, designed by Rafaele Conflenti. Powered by two Hispano-Suiza engines mounted in tandem between the equal-span wings, and driving one tractor and one pusher propeller, the CAMS 33 had a slim single-step hull. Two prototypes were built and flown in the spring of 1923. The first had a rounded bow section, while the **CAMS 33B** second prototype was fully militarised with an angular bow section housing the forward machine-gunner's position. The pilot and co-pilot were seated side-by-side in open cockpits somewhat forward of the wing leading edge, while a second gunner's cockpit was located in the dorsal position to the rear of the wing cellule. Each gunner operated a pair of 0.303-in (7.7-mm) machine-guns.

Construction of the CAMS 33B was in wood, the hull covered with plywood and the flying surfaces with fabric. The single-bay wing cellule was braced on each side by a pair of parallel struts and, as with Conflenti's previous designs, the upper wing was flat while the lower had considerable dihedral.

The 'boats of a small production batch went into service with the French navy's Escadrille 1R1, operating from Cherbourg-Chanyereyne. Yugoslavia maintained its interest in CAMS designs and purchased six examples in 1925.

Side-by-side cockpits identify this as a military CAMS 33. The civil 33C won a French contract for 12 militarised 'boats by flying for 18 hours with only one stop.

SPECIFICATION

CAMS 33B
Type: three/four-seat coastal reconnaissance and bombing flying boat
Powerplant: two Hispano-Suiza 8Fg Vee engines each rated at 275 hp (208 kW)
Performance: maximum speed 109 mph (175 km/h) at sea level; ceiling 16,405 ft (5000 m); range 510 miles (820 km)
Weights: maximum take-off 8,818 lb (4000 kg)
Dimensions: wingspan 57 ft 9¾ in (17.62 m); length 43 ft 5 in (13.23 m); height 16 ft (4.88 m)
Armament: two 0.303-in (7.7-mm) Lewis trainable machine-guns in each of the bow and dorsal positions, plus up to 661 lb (300 kg) of bombs carried under the lower wing

Variants

CAMS 33C: known sometimes under the alternative designation **CAMS 33T**, this was a transport version of the basic design; it participated in the same competition as the military CAMS 33B but was unsuccessful; though bearing a civil registration and test-flown over a substantial period, it was not put into passenger service; power was provided by two Hispano-Suiza 8Fd Vee engines each rated at 260 hp (194 kW), and there was cabin accommodation for seven passengers

CAMS 36

The original **CAMS 36** was a compact single-seat biplane flying-boat for the fighter role but then, in order that it could compete in the Schneider Trophy contests, the type was stripped of military equipment, the original pusher propeller arrangement for the single Hispano-Suiza 8Fd engine, rated at 320 hp (239 kW), was replaced by a tractor propeller configuration, and the conventional paired vertical interplane struts were replaced by I-type struts. However, a lack of funds meant that the two CAMS 36 racers prepared for the Schneider Trophy contest of 1922 were unable to participate.

Originally built as a fighter, the CAMS 36 was modified to emerge as a sleek racing flying-boat. The aircraft was denied its chance to compete in the 1922 Schneider Trophy.

SPECIFICATION

CAMS 36bis
Type: racing flying-boat
Powerplant: one Hispano-Suiza 8Fe Vee engine rated at 360 hp (239 kW)
Performance: maximum speed about 162 mph (260 km/h) at sea level; climb to 6,560 ft (2000 m) in 5 minutes 49 seconds; service ceiling 19,685 ft (6000 m); endurance 2 hours
Weights: empty 2,083 lb (945 kg); maximum take-off 2,778 lb (1260 kg)
Dimensions: wingspan 28 ft 2½ in (8.60 m); length 27 ft 3¾ in (8.32 m); height 9 ft ½ in (2.76 m); wing area 215.29 sq ft (20.00 m²)

Variant

CAMS 36bis: this modification was introduced for the 1923 Schneider Trophy contest to take place off Cowes, on the Isle of Wight; the CAMS 36bis had a more powerful Hispano-Suiza 8Fe engine, twin radiators attached to the engine support struts, and conventional pairs of struts in place of the single I-type struts. On the day of the contest Lieutenant Pelletier d'Oisy was taxiing the CAMS 36bis out to the starting point on the Solent when he collided with a yacht at anchor, the resulting damage prevented the aircraft from participating in the contest

CAMS 37

The engineer Maurice Hurel gave up his naval career to take up an appointment with the CAMS company in the summer of 1923. A year later he became chief designer when Rafaele Conflenti was recalled to Italy by the new Fascist regime headed by Benito Mussolini. Hurel's first design was the **CAMS 37**, the prototype of which was displayed on the French navy stand at the 1926 Paris Salon de l'Aéronautique. The CAMS 37 was a compact single-bay biplane flying-boat with the powerplant of one Lorraine 12 liquid-cooled engine driving a two-bladed pusher propeller. Two **CAMS 37A** amphibian prototypes followed, and it was this version which attracted the first production orders: the French navy obtained 15 such machines in 1926, and the Portuguese government purchased seven in 1929. Series aircraft retained the mixed construction and the general configuration of the prototypes, except that the original fin and rudder design was revised to a more angular square-shaped form of increased area. The pilot was seated in an open cockpit in the forward part of the hull, behind the bow gunner's position. In addition to the bow gunner's cockpit, there was a second open midships position.

Other versions of the CAMS 37 followed in quick succession. The **CAMS 37/2** was a pure flying-boat version of the CAMS 37A amphibian; the CAMS **37A/3** amphibian had a reinforced hull; the **CAMS 37A/6** (three built) had an enclosed cabin and was intended as an admiral's barge; the **CAMS 37A/7** or **CAMS 37Lia** was a 1930 liaison amphibian, again with an enclosed cabin, and

SPECIFICATION

CAMS 37/13
Type: general-purpose flying-boat
Powerplant: one Lorraine 12Ed engine rated at 450 hp (335 kW)
Performance: maximum speed 112 mph (180 km/h) at sea level; climb to 6,560 ft (2000 m) in 19 minutes; service ceiling 12,795 ft (3900 m); range 497 miles (800 km)
Weights: empty 4,740 lb (2150 kg); maximum take-off 6,790 lb (3080 kg)
Dimensions: wingspan 47 ft 6¾ in (14.50 m); length 37 ft 3¾ in (11.37 m); height 15 ft 5¾ in (4.72 m); wing area 644.78 sq ft (59.90 m²)
Armament: one 0.303-in (7.7-mm) Lewis trainable machine-gun in each of the bow and dorsal positions, plus up to 220 lb (100 kg) of bombs carried under the lower wing

was built in some numbers. Four examples of the metal-hulled **CAMS 37A/9** were used by the French navy as staff officer transports, and were followed on the production line by a batch of **CAMS 37/11**

unarmed trainers, most of which were delivered in 1937. They had four open cockpits in side-by-side pairs in the forward part of the hull. The final version of this long-lived maid-of-all-work type was the **CAMS**

37/13, otherwise known as the **CAMS 37bis**. This had a metal hull and was structurally strengthened to allow for catapult-launching from ships at sea. As with all members of the CAMS 37 family, this last variant

had folding wings for compact stowage.

The CAMS 37 served at every French naval air station, proving sturdy and reliable both on the water and in flight. Some were shipborne, and the CAMS

37/11 version flew from a number of major warships, proving itself adaptable to a wide range of roles, from ranging for the heavy guns of the fleet to casualty evacuation.

In both two and four-seat forms, the CAMS 37 family proved to be a most effective and versatile military aircraft. Dependent on variant, the machine could either be launched by ship's catapult or from the water.

Variants

CAMS 37/12: one-off four-seat private cabin flying-boat
CAMS 37A: two amphibians for the local aero club on the French West Indian island of Martinique, delivered in 1936
CAMS 37/10: two built especially for catapult-launching trials from the transatlantic liner *Isle de France*, for use in connection with attempts to provide a fast mail service between France and the USA
CAMS 37C or CAMS 37GR: Grand Raid (long-range) version flown by the famous pilot Guilbaud on a tour of Africa and the Mediterranean between October 1926 and March 1927, in which the 'boat covered more than 14,000 miles (22600 km) in 38 stages without incident or any damage to the machine

CAMS 38

One of Rafaele Conflenti's last designs for the CAMS company before he returned to his native Italy, the **CAMS 38** was built specially to participate in the 1923 Schneider Trophy contest. Based on a hull with a concave planing bottom, the new single-

seat flying-boat was an equal-span biplane with slight dihedral on the lower wing, and the upper and lower wings separated on each side by a single pair of interplane struts. The Hispano-Suiza 8Fd Spécial engine was faired carefully into the

undersurface of the upper wing's centre-section and drove a two-bladed pusher propeller. The engine was cooled by an arrangement similar to that of the CAMS 36bis, namely two Lamblin radiators attached to the forward struts that supported the engine above the hull. While in the CAMS 36 and 36bis, the pilot's cockpit was

located behind the wing cellule, whereas in the CAMS 38 it was immediately forward of the lower wing's leading edge.

Maurice Hurel, the company's chief pilot and also Conflenti's design assistant, was entrusted with the task of piloting the CAMS 38 in the 1923 Schneider Trophy contest. He completed the first lap

despite the fact that the 'boat had suffered damage from a wave before take-off, but engine vibration and loss of power then forced his withdrawal during the second circuit. For a period in 1923-4 the CAMS 38 was used for flight trials at the St Raphael testing station in the south of France before being scrapped.

After the failure of its CAMS 36 entry in the 1923 Schneider Trophy contest, CAMS had high hopes for the CAMS 38. This, too, was forced to retire, but did at least manage to join the race.

SPECIFICATION	
CAMS 38	(6000 m); endurance 2 hours
Type: single-seat racing flying-boat	**Weights:** empty 2,075 lb (941 kg),
Powerplant: one Hispano-Suiza	maximum take-off 2,765 lb
8Fd Spécial Vee engine rated at	(1254 kg)
360 hp (268 kW)	**Dimensions:** wingspan 28 ft 2½ in
Performance: maximum speed	(8.60 m); length 27 ft 3½ in
186 mph (300 km/h); climb to	(8.32 m); height 9 ft 1¾ in (2.79 m);
6,560 ft (2000 m) in 5 minutes	wing area 202.37 sq ft (18.80 m²)
25 seconds; service ceiling 19,685 ft	

CAMS 46, CAMS 53, CAMS 55 and CAMS 56

The **CAMS 46** training flying-boat was an improved version of the CAMS 30E, and appeared in two versions during 1926. The **CAMS 46ET**

was a basic trainer with a Hispano-Suiza 8Ab Vee engine rated at 180 hp (134 kW), whereas the **CAMS 46E** was a primary trainer with a Hispano-Suiza

SPECIFICATION	
CAMS 55/10	1,165 miles (1875 km)
Type: five-seat maritime	**Weights:** empty 10,119 lb
reconnaissance and bombing	(4590 kg); maximum take-off
flying-boat	15,212 lb (6900 kg)
Powerplant: two 500-hp (373-kW)	**Dimensions:** wingspan 66 ft
Gnome-Rhône Mistral 9Kbr radial	11¼ in (20.40 m); length 49 ft 3¾ in
engines each rated at 500 hp	(15.03 m); height 17 ft 9 in
(373 kW)	(5.41 m); wing area 1,221.21 sq ft
Performance: maximum speed	(113.45 m²)
121 mph (195 km/h) at sea level;	**Armament:** two 0.303-in (7.7-mm)
cruising speed 93 mph (150 km/h)	Lewis trainable machine-guns each
at optimum altitude; climb to	in the bow and midships positions,
3,280 ft (1000 m) in 7 minutes	two 165-lb (75-kg) bombs carried
30 seconds; service ceiling	under the lower wing
11,155 ft (3400 m); range	

8Aa engine rated at 150 hp (112 kW). The overall design was cleaner than that of the CAMS 30, with an enlarged and more rounded fin and rudder. Both versions had side-by-side seating for pupil and instructor, with dual controls. The CAMS 46ET had twin radiators, located one on each side of the engine. Only the ET version went into production for the French navy, one escadrille serving at the Hourtin training station for many years.

The other data for the CAMS 46ET two-seat basic trainer flying-boat included a maximum speed of 99 mph (160 km/h) at sea

level, service ceiling of 11,485 ft (3500 m), range of 280 miles (450 km), empty weight of 2,156 lb (978 kg), maximum take-off weight of 2,976 lb (1350 kg), wingspan of 39 ft 4½ in (12.00 m), length of 29 ft 9 in (9.07 m), height of 9 ft 9 in (2.97 m) and wing area of 398.28 sq ft (37.00 m²).

The most successful French civil flying-boat of its era, the **CAMS 53** first flew in prototype form during 1928. Designed, like the military **CAMS 55** series, by Maurice Hurel, it owed much to the earlier experimental CAMS 51. Its plywood-covered wooden hull was a two-step design

and accommodated pilot and co-pilot in an enclosed cabin forward of the single-bay biplane wing cellule, and the comfortable cabin had seats for four passengers. The wooden wings were covered with fabric, and power was provided by two 500-hp (373-kW) Hispano-Suiza 12Hbr engines mounted in tandem just below the upper wing and cooled by means of two Lamblin radiators, mounted one on each side of the engine.

Two examples of the original CAMS 53 went into service with the Aéropostale company on its Marseilles-Algiers route in the autumn of 1928, making scheduled Mediterranean crossings, carrying both passengers and mail.

CAMS 46, CAMS 53, CAMS 55 and CAMS 56 (cont.)

Five more examples of the CAMS 53 were built, and these were followed by 12 examples of the **CAMS 53/1**, six of the **CAMS 53/2**, two of the **CAMS 53/3** and two of the **CAMS 56**, the last being redesignated CAMS 53/3 'boats. The various versions of the CAMS 53 operated during the 1930s with Air-Union/Aéronavale between Marseilles, Ajaccio (Corsica) and Tunis and with Air-Union/Lignes de l'Orient on the staged route between Marseilles and Beirut in the Levant (now Lebanon), a route later extended to Baghdad. When Air France was formed in 1933, merging the various French air transport companies, it took over 23 CAMS 53 flying-boats which continued to operate accident-free services throughout the Mediterranean for the next three years, sporting a distinctive orange livery. On 15 May 1929 a CAMS 53 piloted by Paulin Paris established a world flying-boat class record, lifting a 4,409-lb (2000-kg) payload to an altitude of 15,837 ft (4827 m).

The variants mentioned above are worthy of slightly more detail. The CAMS 53/1 was a 1929 design with greater endurance, a strengthened hull and increased fuel capacity. Twelve 'boats were built as such, and one CAMS 56 plus all seven CAMS 53 'boats were brought up to CAMS 53/1 standard. The CAMS 53/2 had a modified hull shape, and in addition to six CAMS 53/2 'boats built as such, a seventh machine was created as a 1933 conversion of a CAMS 53/1 that had already been converted from CAMS 53 standard in 1931. The CAMS 56 was a 1928 development of the CAMS 53 with the powerplant of two 480-hp (358-kW) Gnome-Rhône Jupiter 9Akx radial engines; originally designated **CAMS 55/3**, the four examples built were known by the designation CAMS 56 in

This CAMS 55/2 flew with Escadrille 4S1 of the Aéronautique Maritime in North Africa during the 1930s. 4S1 survived, with its CAMS 55/2s, until 1 July 1940.

airline service. The **CAMS 53R** designation was used for a single CAMS 53 completed in 1929 with two 480-hp (358-kW) Renault 12Jb liquid-cooled engines; during construction the 'boat had received the provisional designation **CAMS 57**, but on completion was known as the CAMS 53R and did not go into regular airline service.

The data for the CAMS 53/1 passenger/mail-carrying flying-boat included the powerplant of two Hispano-Suiza 12Lbxr (later 12Lbr) engines each rated at 580 hp (433 kW), maximum speed of 132 mph (212 km/h) at optimum altitude, service ceiling of 18,700 ft (5700 m), range of 590 miles (950 km), empty weight of 10,362 lb (4700 kg), maximum take-off weight of 15,212 lb (6900 kg), wingspan of 66 ft 11¼ in (20.40 m), length of 48 ft 7½ in (14.82 m), height of 18 ft 1¼ in (5.52 m) and wing area of 1,237.89 sq ft (115.00 m²).

The origins of the CAMS 55 naval flying-boat can be traced to the CAMS 51 prototype for a twin-engined biplane 'boat for the R.3 (three-seat reconnaissance and limited bomber) role. This made its maiden flight in January 1927 with the powerplant of two 380-hp (283-kW) Gnome-Rhône Jupiter radial engines mounted in tandem on a pair of

N-struts over the hull and located just below the upper wing's centre-section. From this CAMS 51, and the long-range **CAMS 54GR** which made an abortive attempt to cross the North Atlantic from east to west in 1928, was developed the CAMS 55 bombing and reconnaissance flying-boat.

The **CAMS 55.001** prototype, with the powerplant of two 600-hp (447-kW) Hispano-Suiza 12Lbr engines mounted in tandem, first flew in 1928, piloted by its designer, Maurice Hurel. This machine was followed by four evaluation 'boats, two of them **CAMS 55J** 'boats with the powerplant of two Jupiter air-cooled engines and the other two **CAMS 55H** 'boats with the powerplant of two Hispano-Suiza liquid-cooled engines. The CAMS 55 was of the sturdy construction demanded by its primary role of maritime reconnaissance. The structure was of wood, the two-step hull being plywood-covered, with the forward step reinforced by a sheath of galvanised steel sheet. The single-bay biplane wing cellule was of wooden construction under a covering of fabric, and incorporated dihedral on the lower wing only. The upper bow section of the hull, surrounding the forward gunner's cockpit, was widened to form a balcony with small

windows set in the underside for downward observation; the open pilot's and co-pilot's cockpits were located side-by-side just forward of the wing cellule, with the wireless operator's cabin immediately to their rear; and behind the wing cellule was a midships gunner's position.

The Aéronautique Maritime was impressed by tests with the prototype and evaluation 'boats, and placed production orders for the **CAMS 55/1**, **CAMS 55/2** and **CAMS 55/10** variants. At one time no fewer than 15 escadrilles of the French naval air service had

the type on strength, but the first unit to receive the type was Escadrille 3E1 at Berre. It flew the experimental CAMS 55H and CAMS 55J boats in 1930, and then fully re-equipped with the CAMS 55/2 which replaced the unsatisfactory Latham 47. When the Breguet Bizerte flying-boat entered service from 1936 onward, the CAMS 55 was relegated to coastal patrol duties. A number served during the early part of World War II, the last operational 'boats flying with Escadrille 20S (formerly 8S5) from Tahiti in the French Pacific islands until scrapped in January 1941.

Variants

CAMS 55/1: this was the first production version, powered by two 600-hp (447-kW) Hispano-Suiza 12Lbr engines; 43 built
CAMS 55/2: powered by two 480-hp (358-kW) Gnome-Rhône Jupiter 9Akx radial engines; 29 built in parallel with CAMS 55/1
CAMS 55/3: only a single prototype of this version was completed; it featured an all-metal hull and was built for a 1932 French navy contest for a new long-range flying-boat; built at Saint-Denis, it was assembled and test-flown from the company's seaplane base at Sartrouville; after only limited testing the 'boat crashed into the Seine on take-off, on 4 January 1932, killing the pilot, Antoine Brunel
CAMS 55/6: this one-off prototype had all-metal wingtip floats and hull; it benefited from the use of Dural and Vedal alloys so that the hull was 882 lb (400 kg) lighter than that of the earlier wooden structure; financial stringencies prevented quantity production
CAMS 55/10: this version appeared in 1934, powered by two Gnome-Rhône Mistral 9Kbr radial engines with reduction gear; like its predecessors, it had folding wings, and additional fuel capacity was provided to give increased range; a total of 32 CAMS 55/10 'boats was built, four of them modified for colonial use
CAMS 55/14: this 1934 variant, with Gnome-Rhône engines, metal hull and wooden wingtip floats, did not go into production

CAMS 58

The four examples of the **CAMS 58** passenger and mail transport flying-boat represented three different

SPECIFICATION

CAMS 58/3

Type: commercial passenger and mail transport flying-boat
Powerplant: two Hispano-Suiza 12Nbr engines each rated at 650 hp (485 kW)
Performance: maximum speed 124 mph (200 km/h) at optimum altitude; service ceiling 14,765 ft (4500 m); range 590 miles (950 km)

Weights: empty 11,967 lb (5428 kg); maximum take-off 18,629 lb (8450 kg)
Dimensions: wingspan 79 ft 8¾ in (24.30 m); length 48 ft 11 in (14.91 m); height 20 ft 1¾ in (6.14 m); wing area 1,396.12 sq ft (129.70 m²)
Payload: up to four passengers plus mail carried internally

versions, differing widely from each other. The single **CAMS 58/0** had a hull of metal construction with alloy

sheet covering. Powered by two tandem-mounted 650-hp (485-kW) Hispano-Suiza

12Nbr liquid-cooled engines, it did not fly until 1933, three years after the start of

The push-pull arrangement of the CAMS 58/2's powerplant is evident in this view, as is the type's sesquiplane wing cellule. Although it never entered service, the 58/2 offered enclosed accommodation for a crew of three and 12 passengers.

design work. Neither the CAMS 58/0, nor the **CAMS 58/2** which followed, entered regular passenger service. The CAMS 58/2, which first flew in 1931, shared the sesquiplane configuration of the CAMS 58/0, but was powered by four 300-hp (224-kW) Lorraine Algol 9Na radial engines in tandem pairs. Two examples of the **CAMS 58/3** were completed for Air France in 1933 to a standard that included a wooden hull, accommodation for four passengers plus mail, and the powerplant of two tandem-mounted Hispano-Suiza engines. After relatively limited test-flying, they were discarded as uneconomic and withdrawn from service.

Canadair CL-2, CL-4, CL-5 (C-4/Argonaut/North Star, C-5)

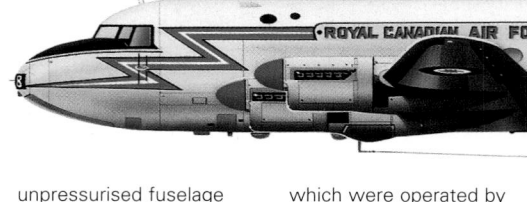

Canadair's North Star was most easily distinguished from the standard Douglas DC-4 by means of its engines. The large radial units of the DC-4 were replaced with more streamlined Merlin inline engines in narrower nacelles in all but the C-5 version.

While World War II was still in progress, Trans Canada Air Lines was already considering the most suitable aircraft with which to begin post-war long-range services. The final choice for an interim aircraft, until new-generation civil transports became available, was a version of the Douglas DC-4 with Rolls-Royce Merlin engines. So it was, in 1944, that the development of this **Canadair CL-2** became one of the first tasks of the new company, which was created by the Canadian government as Canadair Ltd to take over the assets and responsibilities of Canadian Vickers Ltd. The latter's British parent company had decided in summer 1944 to abandon further aircraft design and construction in Canada.

For early evaluation of the concept, a Douglas-built unpressurised fuselage was used for a conversion, this being powered by four Merlin 620 Vee engines each rated at 1,725 hp (1286 kW). Designated **Canadair DC-4M-X**, this was flown for the first time on 20 July 1946 and very quickly proved that Trans Canada's notion was good. Production aircraft included 23 unpressurised **C-54GM** aircraft, plus the prototype, which were operated by the Royal Canadian Air Force as **North Star Mk 1** transports or, in the case of the six aircraft used by TCA (see below) but subsequently returned to the RCAF, as **North Star Mk M1** transports. These machines saw extensive service in the logistics role during the Korean War, were later modified into passenger transports with the revised designations **North Star Mk 1 ST** and **North Star Mk M1 ST** respectively, and served until 1966 when the last four were withdrawn.

Trans Canada ordered 20 aircraft with a pressurised cabin that provided accommodation for between 40 and 62 passengers, according to class. But while awaiting the development and manufacture of this specifically civil variant, Trans Canada operated six of the unpressurised aircraft on loan from the RCAF, designating them **DC-4M-1** or **North Star M-1** in civil use. Delivery of Trans Canada's own aircraft began in October 1947, these having the designations **DC-4M-2/3** or **DC-4M-2/4** when powered by Merlin 622 engines, or **North Star M2-3** or **North Star M2-4** (company designation **CL-4**) when powered by Merlin 624 engines. Some of the latter aircraft were later adapted as freighters with the revised designation **DC-4M-2/4C** or **North Star M2-4C**.

The other major operator was BOAC, which acquired 22 CL-4 or **C-4** machines after failure of the Avro Tudor, operating the aircraft under the name **Argonaut** from 1949 to 1960. One other original order was received by Canadair, for the supply of four aircraft delivered to Canadian Pacific Air Lines under the designation **C-4-1** or **North Star C-4-1**, or **C-4-1C** or **North Star C-4-1C** after conversion as freighters. On their retirement from service with their original operators, these civil aircraft were gradually sold off to smaller operators, and examples remained in service late into the 1960s.

A final aircraft for the RCAF was the sole **CL-5**, otherwise known as the **C-5**; this was a development of the CL-4 with Pratt & Whitney R-2800 radial engines.

SPECIFICATION	
Canadair CL-2 (C-4)	range 3,200 miles (5150 km)
Type: four/five-crew transport	**Weights:** empty 46,832 lb
Powerplant: four Rolls-Royce	(21243 kg); maximum take-off
Merlin 626 Vee engines each rated	82,300 lb (37331 kg)
at 1,760 hp (1312 kW)	**Dimensions:** wingspan 117 ft 6 in
Performance: maximum speed	(35.81 m); length 93 ft 7½ in
325 mph (523 km/h) at 25,200 ft	(28.54 m); height 27 ft 6¼ in
(7680 m); cruising speed 289 mph	(8.39 m); wing area 1,460.00 sq ft
(465 km/h) at 12,200 ft (3720 m);	(135.63 m²)
service ceiling 29,500 ft (8990 m);	

Canadair CL-28 Argus

The **Canadair CL-28 Argus** (military designation **CP-107**) was designed to meet a 1952 requirement for a maritime patrol and anti-submarine warfare aircraft to succeed the Avro Lancaster Mk 10 and the Consolidated Catalina in service with the Royal Canadian Air Force's Maritime Air Command. The aircraft was based on the Bristol Britannia airliner, and while the wing, tail unit and landing gear were virtually identical on both types, the fuselage of the CL-28 was redesigned to incorporate two weapons bays, a piston- rather than turbine-engined powerplant was adopted, and pressurisa-

tion was eliminated as a feature unnecessary at the low altitudes customarily used by maritime reconnaissance aircraft.

The first **Argus Mk 1** made its maiden flight from Canadair's factory at Montreal, Quebec Province, on 28 March 1957, and was followed by 12 further aircraft built to Mk 1 standard, fitted with American APS-20 radar in a chin-mounted radome. The 20 examples of the **Argus Mk 2** that followed were fitted with British ASV.Mk 11 radar, mounted in a smaller radome. Production ended in July 1960 with the completion of the RCAF's last Argus Mk 2.

The normal crew complement of the Argus was 15, comprising three pilots, two flight engineers, three navigators and seven ASW systems operators.

Canadair completely redesigned the Britannia fuselage so that, although it resembled the airliner, the Argus was in fact a very different machine.

SPECIFICATION	
Canadair CL-28 Argus	(36741 kg); maximum take-off
Type: 15-crew long-range maritime	157,000 lb (71214 kg)
patrol aircraft	**Dimensions:** wingspan 142 ft
Powerplant: four Wright	3½ in (43.37 m); length 128 ft 9½ in
R-3350-TC981-EA1 Cyclone turbo-	(39.26 m); height 38 ft 8 in
compound radial engines each	(11.79 m); wing area 2,075.00 sq ft
rated at 3,700 hp (2759 kW)	(192.77 m²)
Performance: maximum speed	**Armament:** up to 8,000 lb
315 mph (507 km/h) at 10,000 ft	(3629 kg) of bombs, depth charges,
(3050 m); cruising speed 207 mph	homing torpedoes or mines carried
(333 km/h) at optimum altitude;	in two internal weapon bays, plus
initial climb rate 900 ft (274 m) per	up to 3,800 lb (1724 kg) of air-to-
minute; service ceiling 25,000 ft	surface missiles or free-fall
(7620 m); range 5,900 miles	weapons carried on underwing
(9495 km)	hardpoints
Weights: empty 81,000 lb	

Canadair CL-28 Argus (continued)

The Argus crew were able to work in shifts during a patrol which could last up to 20 hours, a crew rest area with bunks and a galley being provided.

The crew stations comprised an observer/bomb-aimer's position in the glazed nose; a flight deck with provision for pilot, co-pilot and flight engineer; behind them the routine navigator's and radio operator's positions; and a rear compartment housed six or seven members of the ASW team under a tactical co-ordinator, with two beam look-out positions behind

this compartment.

The ASW equipment carried by the Argus included search radar, a magnetic anomaly detector, electronic countermeasures and a diesel exhaust detector. Sonobuoys, flares and marine markers were carried in a rear fuselage compartment and offensive weapons, which could include acoustic homing torpedoes and depth charges, were carried in the two internal weapon bays. In addition to ASW and maritime patrol, the Argus could be used also for minelaying and, in emergency, as a transport.

After grounding of the fleet of aircraft in 1972

because of landing-gear problems, a specification was drawn up for a Long-Range Patrol Aircraft to replace the Argus in service as early as possible. This requirement was met by the CP-140 Aurora derivative of the US Navy's Lockheed P-3 Orion, and by 1981 all CP-107 aircraft had been withdrawn from service.

Canadair CL-41 Tutor

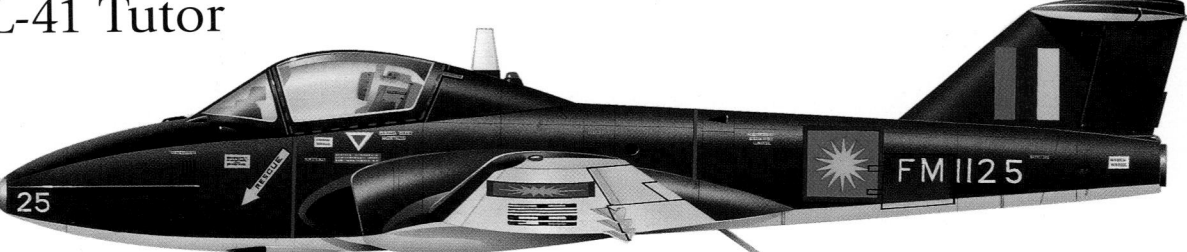

The development programme for the **Canadair CL-41 Tutor** was funded privately by the company because of the Canadian government's initial lack of interest in this basic jet trainer. Two prototypes were built, each with the powerplant of one Pratt & Whitney JT12A-5 turbojet rated at 2,400 lb st (10.68 kN). The first of these machines made its maiden flight on 13 January 1960. In September 1961 the Canadian government ordered 190 examples of the **CL-41A** for the Royal

Canadian Air Force (now the Canadian Armed Forces – Air Command), with the designation **CT-114 Tutor**. Features include side-by-side seats, an upward-opening canopy, lateral door-type airbrakes, a T-tail,

a steerable nosewheel and the standard powerplant of one General Electric J85-CAN-40 turbojet rated at 2,850 lb st (12.68 kN). Delivery took place from 1963-6.

Further development resulted in the **CL-41G-5** armament trainer and light-attack aircraft. This had an uprated engine and six underwing hardpoints; the landing gear was modified for soft-field operation, and zero-altitude automatic ejection seats were fitted. In addition, the second prototype Tutor was modified with F-104G avionics as the **CL-41R** experimental systems trainer. In March 1966 the Royal Malaysian Air Force ordered 20 aircraft, these having the

Malaysia's Tebuans were withdrawn in the mid-1980s, as a result of corrosion and fatigue problems. Nevertheless, six were retained in service in an airworthy condition for some years.

name **Tebuan** (wasp) in Malaysian service, and the first of these were delivered in 1967 for service into the mid-1980s.

The main operator of the CT-114 Tutor in Canadian service is the Training Command's No. 2 Flying Training School at Moose Jaw, Saskatchewan. After primary training, pupils do some 200 hours on the CT-114 to gain their 'wings' before proceeding to specialised training for combat jets, multi-engined types or helicopters. Ten Tutors were modified for

the *Golden Hawks* (later the *Snowbirds*) aerobatic team, and the type also serves with the Flying Instructors' School. These units share the Moose Jaw base with No. 2 FTS. In 1976 the CAF began a modification programme which included provision of external fuel tanks, upgrading of avionics, changes to the canopy electrical system and relocation of the engine ice-detector probe. In 1994 a further upgrade was instigated, in which wiring and other systems were replaced.

SPECIFICATION

Canadair CL-41G-5 Tebuan
Type: two-seat armament trainer and light-attack aircraft
Powerplant: one General Electric J85-CAN-J4 turbojet engine rated at 2,950 lb st (13.12 kN)
Performance: maximum speed 470 mph (755 km/h) at 28,500 ft (8685 m); initial climb rate of 4,250 ft (1295 m) per minute; service ceiling 42,200 ft (12860 m); range 1,340 miles (2157 km)
Weights: empty 5,296 lb (2402 kg); maximum take-off 11,288 lb (5120 kg)

Dimensions: wingspan 36 ft 6 in (11.13 m); length 32 ft (9.75 m); height 9 ft ¾ in (2.76 m); wing area 220.00 sq ft (20.44 m²)
Armament: up to 4,000 lb (1814 kg) of disposable stores carried on six underwing hardpoints, and generally comprising weapons such as 1,000-, 500- and 250-lb (454-, 227- and 113-kg) bombs, pods for 0.3-in (7.62-mm) machine-guns, and multiple launchers for unguided rockets

Canadair CL-44

In March 1954 Canadair negotiated a manufacturing licence for the Bristol Britannia long-range airliner from its British parent company. This licence covered, initially, a maritime reconnaissance version of the airliner for service with the Royal Canadian Air Force, the first being delivered in the autumn of 1957 under the designation CL-28 Argus. It differed from its parent aircraft in having a redesigned and unpressurised fuselage to make possible the inclusion of weapon bays, and it had economical turbo-compound piston engines to give the long range/endurance essential for the maritime role.

The RCAF also had a modest need for an aircraft which could be used in freight/troop-carrying roles, and to meet this requirement Canadair proposed another version of the

Britannia. To provide for the large capacity/payload that was needed, Canadair's design included greater wingspan and a lengthened fuselage, and alternative engine proposals included the Bristol Orion, Pratt & Whitney T34 or Rolls-Royce Tyne turboprop engines, as well as Wright R-3350 radial piston engines. The first of these engine types was selected by the RCAF, but development of this engine was then cancelled in the UK and the Tyne II, rated at 5,500 ehp (4101 ekW), was chosen as its replacement. The aircraft that resulted from this programme was designated as the Canadair **CL-44-6**, and 12 were built for the RCAF, with which they served as the **CC-106 Yukon**, the last of them being delivered in 1961.

These RCAF aircraft had what was then the conventional type of side-loading

capability, with large cargo doors in the fuselage, forward and aft of the wing. While the CL-44-6 was under development and construction, Canadair's design team proposed a then-revolutionary idea to simplify and speed cargo loading: the provision of a hinged aft fuselage section which would swing to one side, complete with tail unit, to permit straight-in loading or unloading of freight. This enabled large items of cargo, or palletised freight, to be transferred directly from trucks into the large cargo hold, and the **CL-44D4**, as this version was designated, became the world's first production-line cargo aircraft with such a capability.

The concept appealed to large cargo operators, and Canadair soon received orders from Seaboard World Airlines (**CL-44D4-1**), The Flying Tiger Line (**CL-44D4-2**) and Slick Airways (**CL-44D4-6**). The

Flying Tiger Line was an early recipient of the swing-tail CL-44D-4. The tail section was hinged just forward of the port tailplane and the fairings covering the two hinges are apparent in this view.

first CL-44D4 flew on 16 November 1960, American certification was gained seven months later, and in July 1961 Flying Tiger and Seaboard flew the first services with these aircraft. A fourth customer was Loftleidir of Iceland, its initial order for three aircraft being completed as civil trans-

ports with seating accommodation for a maximum of 178 passengers. Used to provide low-cost transatlantic services, this fleet was supplemented by a fourth aircraft in 1966. It differed from the earlier three aircraft by having a fuselage lengthened by 15 ft 2 in (4.62 m) to provide accommodation for a maximum of 214 passengers. Also known as the **Canadair 400**, this flew for the first time on 8 November 1965 and, after it had entered service, the operator's three 178-seat airliners were modified to the same **CL-44J** standard.

One other variant resulted when the Conroy Aircraft Corporation in the USA purchased a CL-44D4 from Flying Tiger for conversion as a large cargo transporter. This company's founder, Jack Conroy, had developed the original Pregnant Guppy and its successors, and considered the CL-44D4 suitable for a similar exercise. In its completed form, designated **CL-44-O** and first flown on 26 November 1969, it had a maximum internal height of 11 ft 4 in (3.45 m), and maximum width of 13 ft 11 in (4.24 m), and retained the swing-tail loading capability.

Production of civil CL-44 aircraft totalled 27, and the RCAF's CC-106 Yukon machines eventually came on to the civil market. Many of these have changed hands several times and some eight of the aircraft were still in service late in 1998.

SPECIFICATION

Canadair CL-44D4
Type: four/five-crew long-range cargo transport
Powerplant: four Rolls-Royce Tyne RTy.12 Mk 515/10 turboprop engines each rated at 5,730 ehp (4273 ekW)
Performance: cruising speed 386 mph (621 km/h) at 20,000 ft (6095 m) with typical payload; initial climb rate 1,190 ft (363 m) per minute; service ceiling 30,000 ft (9145 m); range 2,875 miles (4627 km) with maximum payload
Weights: empty 88,952 lb (40348 kg); maximum take-off 210,000 lb (95254 kg)
Dimensions: wingspan 142 ft 3½ in (43.37 m); length 136 ft 10¾ in (41.73 m); height 38 ft 8 in (11.79 m); wing area 2,075.00 sq ft (192.77 m²)
Payload: up to 63,272 lb (28725 kg) of freight

Canadair CL-84

Canadair's interest in V/STOL aircraft began in 1956, and in 1963 the company was joined by Canada's Department of Defense Production in the funding of a prototype of a tilt-wing research aircraft. Designated as the **Canadair CL-84**, this machine featured a conventional fuselage with crew positions for two and with internal capacity for test equipment or seats for up to 12 troops for possible military evaluation.

The wing could be tilted through an angle of 100°, effectively facilitating backward flight at 35 mph (56 km/h) in addition to forward and hovering flight. Krüger leading-edge flaps were fitted, together with full-span slotted trailing-edge flaps which could be operated differentially as ailerons. At tilt angles of up to 30°, the tailplane and wing were interconnected to adopt identical angles of incidence, but at higher angles the tailplane assumed a zero-incidence setting. At low speed, or in the hover, control in the pitch axis was maintained by the use of two small rotors mounted at the end of the fuselage.

The CL-84 made its first hovering flight on 7 May 1965, and then embarked upon a test and development programme in which it had accumulated

An extremely advanced aircraft for its period, the CL-84 provided much useful research data for future projects.

145 hours before crashing on 12 September 1967 in an accident attributed to malfunction of the pitch control of the port propeller. In July of the same year, however, the Canadian Department of Defense had ordered three examples of the improved **CL-84-1** (Canadian Armed Forces designation **CX-84**), with 1,500-shp (1118-kW) Lycoming LTC1K-4A turboprop engines in place of the 1,400-shp (1044-kW) units which powered the prototype. Internal fuel capacity was also increased, and two hard-points were provided beneath the fuselage to accommodate armament pods or drop tanks.

The first CL-84-1 made its maiden flight on 19 February 1970, this event preceding a 150-hour manufacturer's test programme which included gun-firing trials with a 0.3-in (7.62-mm) Minigun six-barrel rotary machine-gun in a General Electric SUU-11A/A pod. In 1972-3 the second aircraft was used for a joint American/British/Canadian V/STOL instrument flight programme, flown from the US Naval Air Test Center at NAS Patuxent River, Maryland. As a result of a demonstration to the US Navy in February 1972, during which it made a number of landings on the 'interim sea control ship' USS *Guam*, the first CL-84-1 was delivered to Patuxent River in July 1973 for an in-depth evaluation, but crashed during that month. The programme was completed by the second aircraft and included sea trials aboard USS *Guadalcanal* in March 1974.

SPECIFICATION

Canadair CL-84-1
Type: two-crew V/STOL research convertiplane
Powerplant: two Lycoming LTC1K-4A turboprop engines each rated at 1,500 shp (1118 kW)
Performance: maximum speed 321 mph (517 km/h) at optimum altitude; cruising speed 309 mph (497 km/h) at optimum altitude; initial climb rate 4,200 ft (1280 m) per minute; range 340 miles (547 km)
Weights: empty 8,775 lb (3980 kg); maximum take-off 12,600 lb (5715 kg) for VTO or 14,500 lb (6577 kg) for STO
Dimensions: wingspan 34 ft 8 in (10.56 m); length 53 ft 7½ in (16.34 m); height 14 ft 2¾ in (4.34 m) with wing horizontal or 17 ft 1½ in (5.22 m) with wing vertical; wing area 233.00 sq ft (21.65 m²)
Payload: see above within the context of a 2,315- or 4,215-lb (1050- or 1912-kg) maximum payload for VTO or STO respectively

Canadair CL-215/CL-215T

The **Canadair CL-215** was designed to meet a requirement for a firefighting amphibian which could replace the miscellany of types used in the 'water bombing' role during the 1960s. The Canadian Province of Quebec and the French Protection Civile were the first customers, respectively ordering 20 and 10 CL-215s to undertake a primary role of forest fire detection and suppression. However, the robust and versatile amphibian was also available to military customers for the SAR and utility roles.

From the outset, simplicity of design was a primary requirement, with ease of maintenance and reliability of equipment (achieved through the incorporation of proved systems wherever practicable) also receiving careful attention. Protection against saltwater corrosion was achieved through the use of corrosion-resistant materials and also by fully sealing components during assembly.

The CL-215 has a single-step hull, and fixed stabilising floats are mounted just inboard of the wingtips. The tricycle landing gear comprises a nose unit with twin wheels and main units with single wheels, the former retracting into the hull and the latter being raised to lie flat against the hull during operations from water.

The high-mounted wing and tailplane are single-piece structures, with ailerons and flaps occupying the entire wing trailing edge. All fuel is carried in flexible wing cells, and the engine nacelles are integral with the wing structure.

The piston-engined CL-215 has established an enviable reputation for water-bombing efficiency over three decades of operations.

SPECIFICATION

Canadair CL-215
Type: two/six-crew multi-purpose amphibian
Powerplant: two Pratt & Whitney R-2800-CA3 Double Wasp radial engines each rated at 2,100 hp (1566 kW)
Performance: cruising speed 181 mph (291 km/h) at 10,000 ft (3050 m); initial climb rate 1,000 ft (305 m) per minute; range 1,300 miles (2092 km) with a 3,500-lb (1587-kg) payload
Weights: empty 26,810 lb (12161 kg); maximum take-off 43,500 lb (19731 kg) from land or 37,700 lb (17100 kg) from water
Dimensions: wingspan 93 ft 10 in (28.60 m); length 65 ft ¼ in (19.82 m); height 29 ft 3 in (8.92 m); wing area 1,080.00 sq ft (100.33 m²)
Payload: up to 26 passengers or freight within the context of a 12,000-lb (5443-kg) maximum water payload or 8,518-lb (3864-kg) maximum utility payload

Canadair CL-215/CL-215T (continued)

For its firefighting role the CL-215 can lift 1,200 Imp gal (5455 litres) of water or retardant fluid in two fuselage tanks. The water is scooped from a convenient lake or river through two retractable inlets, mounted under the hull, while the CL-215 taxis across the surface. It then takes off and flies to the area of the fire, where the load is jettisoned in less than a second. The operation is repeated until the fire is under control. In most circumstances a load can be dropped at least every 10 minutes.

Configured for the SAR role, the CL-215 carries a crew of six. In addition to the pilot and co-pilot, a flight engineer is housed on the flight deck. The navigator's station is located farther back in the forward fuselage, and two observers are carried in the rear fuselage. The basic avionics are augmented by an AVQ-21 weather and search radar in the nose. The maximum endurance is 12 hours.

The maiden flight of the CL-215 took place on 23 October 1967, and deliveries to France began in May 1969. Production lasted into the early 1990s and included examples for the Canadian provinces of Québec (15) and Manitoba (2), and for France (15), Greece (11), Spain (17 equipped for SAR but suitable also for firefighting and other roles), Royal Thai navy (2), CVG Ferrominera Orinoco CA of Venezuela (2) and Yugoslavia (4).

A retrofit programme, resulting in the conversion of 17 aircraft up to August 1998, resulted in the **CL-215T** version with features of the CL-215 turboprop-powered development. The major change is the revised turboprop powerplant, and an option adopted by several customers is that of powered flight controls.

Canadair CL-415

In December 1986 Canadair Ltd was bought by Bombardier Inc., and in August 1988 merged with the parent group as the Canadair Group of Bombardier Inc. It was during this period that Canadair was considering the development of a derivative of its CL-215 amphibian flying-boat with a turboprop- rather than piston-engined powerplant for greater overall power, an improved power/weight ratio, and more ready availability of spares and fuel. In 1991 the improved type was designated as the **CL-415** to distinguish it from the CL-215T turboprop-powered conversion of the CL-215, and the official launch of the new model came in October 1991 with the receipt of an initial French order.

The first CL-415 made its maiden flight on 6 December 1993, and the type received its Canadian and US certifications in June and October 1994 respectively, allowing the delivery of the first machine to France in December 1994. An initial production batch of 50 aircraft was planned, and by August 1998 some 40 of these had been completed in a programme currently running at 10 'boats per year.

The CL-415 retains the proven airframe of the CL-215 in combination with a number of important changes. The most obvious of these changes is the new turboprop powerplant, with the two Pratt & Whitney Canada PW123AF engines located in slender nacelles above the wing for a higher thrust line with the new Hamilton Standard four-bladed propellers. Other highly evident external changes are the addition of small winglets at the tips of the flat wing for improved lateral stability. For improved directional and longitudinal stability after the movement of the engines' thrust lines, the tail unit has been modified with a 'bullet' fairing on the leading edge of the tailplane/fin junction. There are also two swept finlets (their leading edges offset to port) on the tailplane between the inner edges of the engine nacelles and the outer edges of the centre section. Less evident changes include powered flight controls, a pressure refuelling system, a new electrical system, a revised 'glass' flightdeck with air-conditioning, structural changes and strengthening for greater operational efficiency despite the type's higher weights, and a four-tank firefighting system with a water capacity increased to 1,351 Imp gal (6140 litres).

The standard CL-415 designation is used for the water-bombing and utility version. This has eight inward-facing seats as standard, but with the above-floor water tanks removed, can alternatively be operated with up to 30 forward-facing seats. With the above-floor tanks retained, the CL-415 can also be outfitted for the combi role with freight and 11 passenger seats respectively forward and to the rear of the tanks. Canadair is also considering a **CL-415M** derivative for the maritime patrol, special missions and SAR roles, with options such as radar, precision navigation and other mission-specific equipment.

SPECIFICATION

Canadair CL-415
Type: two/six-crew multi-role amphibian flying-boat
Powerplant: two Pratt & Whitney Canada PW123AF turboprop engines each rated at 2,380 shp (1775 kW)
Performance: maximum cruising speed 234 mph (376 km/h) at 10,000 ft (3050 m); initial climb rate 1,375 ft (419 m) per minute; range 1,507 miles (2426 km) with a 1,100-lb (499-kg) payload
Weights: empty 28,353 lb (12861 kg); maximum take-off 43,850 lb (19890 kg) from land or 37,850 lb (17168 kg) from water
Dimensions: wingspan 93 ft 11 in (28.63 m); length 65 ft ½ in (19.82 m); height 29 ft 5½ in (8.98 m); wing area 1,080.00 sq ft (100.33 m²)
Payload: up to 30 passengers or 8,375 lb (3799 kg) of freight in the utility role, or 13,500 lb (6123 kg) of water in the firefighting role

In addition to its fuselage water tanks, the CL-415 also has foam concentrate tanks and and a mixing system for the inflight production of foam/water retardant liquids.

Canadair CL-600 Challenger

Originating from the drawing board of Bill Lear, designer of the Lear Jet, this executive aircraft was at first named **LearStar 600**. However, when Lear sold the exclusive production rights to Canadair in April 1976, the type was redesignated as the **Canadair CL-600** and became known subsequently as the **Challenger**. Canadair's market research indicated a sales potential for some 1,000 business aircraft in this category and, believing it could capture some 40 per cent of this market, the company launched the Challenger development programme on 29 October 1976, at which time it had 53 firm orders and a government backing loan of Canadian $130 million.

Canadair introduced a number of changes in the basic design, the most noticeable being the movement of the tailplane from a position near the bottom of

SPECIFICATION

Canadair CL-601 Challenger 601-3R
Type: two-crew business transport and commuterliner
Powerplant: two General Electric CF34-3A1 turbofan engines each rated at 9,220 lb st (41 kN)
Performance: maximum cruising speed 548 mph (882 km/h) at optimum altitude; service ceiling 41,000 ft (12495 m); range 4,124 miles (6639 km) with five passengers
Weights: empty 25,760 lb (11684 kg); maximum take-off 45,100 lb (20457 kg)
Dimensions: wingspan 64 ft 4 in (19.61 m) over winglets; length 68 ft 5 in (20.85 m); height 20 ft 8 in (6.30 m); wing area 520.00 sq ft (48.31 m²) excluding winglets
Payload: up to 19 passengers within the context of a 5,240-lb (2377-kg) maximum payload

This Challenger 601-3A demonstrates the clean lines of the type. Even from outside, the Challenger's capacious fuselage is evident, allowing the type to boast one of the widest cabins in its class.

the fuselage to the tip of the swept fin. A major selling point for the Challenger is a fuselage of large cross-section, with a width of 8 ft 2 in (2.49 m) and height of 6 ft 1 in (1.85 m), providing a 'walk about' cabin of the type not shared by other purpose-built executive jets. The aircraft provides comfortable accommodation for a maximum of 18 passengers. Three pre-production aircraft were built, the first of them flying on 8 November 1978 with the powerplant of two Lycoming ALF502L-2 turbofan engines each rated at 7,500 lb st (33.36 kN), and the first production aircraft flew on 21 September 1979. Canadian and American certification were gained during August and November 1980 respectively. However, both imposed temporary restrictions, limiting gross weight to 33,000 lb (14969 kg) and speed to 365 mph (587 km/h), while flight into known icing conditions and the use of thrust reversers were prohibited.

To overcome these limitations, Canadair carried out a weight and drag reduction programme which, at the same time, offered a considerable increase in range capability. Full certification was gained and deliveries of production aircraft began at the beginning of 1981. By the end of the year, the company had firm orders and options for approximately 200 aircraft. Almost 150 were for the standard CL-600, with the remainder for the CL-601. By the middle of the 1990s, deliveries had exceeded 300 aircraft, with orders still coming in, and further developments of the basic type available and under development.

Variants

CL-600 Challenger 600: original model, of which 83 were built including 76 that were later retrofitted to **Challenger 600S** standard, with the drag-reducing winglets introduced on the Challenger 601-1A; deliveries started in December 1980, and 12 of the aircraft were handed over to the CAF as three **CC-144** VIP transports, three **CE-144A** ECM trainers, three coastal patrol machines, two general transports and one **CX-144** test machine

CL-601 Challenger 601-1A: first flown on 17 September 1982 and delivered from May 1983, this model introduced winglets and the revised powerplant of two 8,650-lb st (38.48-kN) General Electric CF34-1A turbofan engines for greater range and slightly lower operational noise levels; production totalled 66 aircraft, of which four were completed for CAF service with the same **CC-144** designation as the four **Challenger 600** VIP transports

CL-601 Challenger 601-3A: first flown on 28 September 1986 and delivered from May 1987 after the receipt of Canadian and American certification in April 1987, this model has been built to the extent of 134 aircraft; the type differs from the Challenger 601-1A in its uprated powerplant of two CF34-3A turbofan engines each rated at 9,220 lb st (41.01 kN), and a 'glass' cockpit with a fully integrated digital avionics suite, including flight guidance and flight management systems

CL-601 Challenger 601-3R: first flown on 8 November 1988 and delivered from July 1993 after the receipt of Canadian certification in March 1989; the type is an extended-range development with features that can be retrofitted to the Challenger 601-1A and Challenger 601-3A to create the **Challenger 601-1A/ER** and **Challenger 601-3A/ER** models; the Challenger 601-3R is visually identifiable by the replacement of its tail fairing by a conformal tailcone tank for an additional 153 Imp gal (697 litres) of fuel

CL-604 Challenger 604: first flown on 18 September 1994 and delivered from 1996, this model has two CF34-3B turbofan engines each rated at 8,730 lb st (38.83 kN) and fuel capacity further increased by 273 Imp gal (1242 litres) for a range of 4,603 miles (7408 km); other changes are new landing gear, strengthened tail unit, new wing/fuselage fairings, and a Collins Electronic Flight Instrumentation System

Canadair Global Express

In October 1991 Bombardier announced that its Canadair Group was about to launch a programme to design, develop, manufacture and market a wholly new corporate transport as the **Canadair Global Express**. The programme was formally initiated in December 1993 after the start of design work earlier in the same year. The three objectives set by Canadair for the Global Express were that it should have the highest speed and greatest range of any corporate transport, the largest and most versatile cabin of any aircraft in its class, and the highest possible despatch and mission reliability.

The key payload/range task required of the Global Express with a four-person crew was the non-stop carriage of eight passengers over the route linking New York and Tokyo, a distance of 7,485 miles (12046 km), to be covered at a cruising speed of Mach 0.8 and an altitude of 51,000 ft (15545 m). The cabin was sized for the carriage of up to 19 passengers over shorter ranges, and of prime importance were the ability to operate into and out of smaller airfields near the headquarters of purchasing companies and good field performance.

The Global Express was a 'clean sheet of paper', or rather 'blank computer screen' design, based nonetheless on the company's experience with other modern aircraft, notably the Challenger 'bizjet' and Regional Jet regional airliner. It was designed and manufactured with the aid of a CAD/CAM (Computer-Aided Design/Computer-Aided Manufacture) system. The Global Express therefore retained the same basic layout as its predecessors from the Canadair stable, namely a circular-section fuselage, a low-set swept wing and a swept T-tail. Also retained was a powerplant of two turbofan engines pod-mounted on the sides of the rear fuselage to leave the wing unobstructed for its primary task and also to keep this noise- and vibration-producing assembly behind the cabin's rear pressure bulkhead.

The speed and payload/range requirements of the new type demanded the development of an advanced wing, the use of modern turbofan engines, and the adoption of an advanced cockpit and control system. The main features of the high-aspect-ratio wing emerged as a 35° sweep angle, tip-mounted winglets, a supercritical aerofoil section and, among its moving surfaces, multi-segment slats on its leading edges, flaps on its trailing edges and multi-function spoilers on its upper surfaces. The engine selected for the new type was the BMW Rolls-Royce BR710. The cockpit is of the 'glass' type with digital avionics displaying their data on the six screens of the Honeywell Primus 200XP system, core of the advanced system providing airliner-type capabilities.

This combination of features provided the right field and flight performance, but just as important was the creation of a cabin that would be conducive to passenger rest and/or productivity while in transit. For this reason, therefore, Canadair opted for what was in effect a wide-body fuselage with a three-compartment cabin 48 ft (14.63 m) long, with a maximum width of 8 ft 2 in (2.49 m) and a maximum height of 6 ft 3 in (1.90 m). This cabin can be outfitted in a large number of different forms according to customer requirements, and the fuselage also carries a crew rest area, a large galley, at least one toilet compartment and a baggage compartment.

Canadair lined up a team of 11 other major aerospace companies for the task of designing, developing and building the Global Express. Among these, the most notable are Mitsubishi Heavy Industries of Japan, responsible for the manufacture of the central fuselage and wing, and Short Brothers of the UK, responsible for the design and manufacture of fuselage sections and the engine nacelles. The first example of the Global Express made its maiden flight on 13 August 1996 and received Canadian certification in July 1998, with deliveries starting soon after this.

In June 1999, Global Express was chosen as the platform for the UK government's ASTOR stand-off radar programme, with Raytheon-supplied mission equipment.

SPECIFICATION

Canadair Global Express
Type: three/four-crew long-range corporate transport
Powerplant: two BMW Rolls-Royce BR710-A2-20 turbofan engines each rated at 14,750 lb st (66 kN)
Performance: maximum cruising speed 678 mph (1091 km/h) at optimum altitude; typical cruising speed 647 mph (1041 km/h) at optimum altitude; service ceiling 51,000 ft (15545 m); range 7,485 miles (12046 km) with eight passengers
Weights: empty 41,000 lb (18598 kg); maximum take-off 93,750 lb (42525 kg)
Dimensions: wingspan 94 ft (28.65 m); length 99 ft 5 in (30.30 m); height 24 ft 10 in (7.57 m); wing area 1,022.00 sq ft (94.94 m²)
Payload: up to 19 passengers within the context of a 7,200-lb (3266-kg) maximum payload

While its basic airframe structure is of metal alloy, the Global Express does incorporate considerable amounts of composite in such components as the ailerons, flaps, spoilers, rudder and various fairings.

Canadair Regional Jet

The technical and commercial success of its Challenger 'bizjet' was one of the factors that prompted Canadair, then recently acquired by Bombardier Inc., to plan a regional airliner development in an effort to secure a major part of the market for high-speed regional airliners that was developing rapidly from the middle of the 1980s. This market came to include a growing number of 'hub-bypass' routes that became economically feasible only with the introduction of modern aircraft offering low operating costs.

Canadair started preliminary design work in the autumn of 1987 and was able to 'freeze' the basic design in June of the following year as what is, in essence, an enlarged version of the Challenger. The wing was increased in span by 5 ft 3 in (1.60 m) and the fuselage lengthened by 19 ft 5 in (5.92 m) to allow the incorporation of a cabin that is of basically the same cross-section as that of the Challenger but, with its length increased to 48 ft 5 in (14.76 m). A typical payload comprises 50 passengers in a 2+2 seating arrangement with a central aisle. Other changes include the option of higher weights (allowing the carriage of more fuel for increased range), more comprehensive digital avionics including the Collins Pro Line V integrated instrument system with provision for a head-up display, and a higher certificated ceiling.

The company announced the formal launch of the **Regional Jet** (otherwise known as the **RJ** or **CRJ**) at the end of April 1989, and started work on the manufacture of three development aircraft, of which the first made the type's maiden flight on 10 May 1991. All three aircraft were involved in the 1,400-hour flight test programme by November 1991, and the RJ received its Canadian certification at the end of July 1992. American and European certifications followed in January 1993, and the first delivery had already been made to Lufthansa CityLine of Germany in October 1992. By early 1999 Canadair had received orders for 628 aircraft and delivered 290 of these in a programme that is still securing major orders. In 1998 the programme was progressing at the rate of five aircraft per month, but accelerating to meet the increased rate and size of orders.

Three-section leading-edge slats, a higher window line and a lowered cabin floor level are all less obvious features of the stretched and re-engined CRJ 700.

SPECIFICATION	
Canadair Regional Jet Series 100	1,128 miles (1818 km) with maximum payload
Type: three/four-crew regional airliner	**Weights:** empty 30,100 lb (13653 kg); maximum take-off 47,450 lb (21523 kg)
Powerplant: two General Electric CF34-3A1 turbofan engines each rated at 9,220 lb st (41 kN)	**Dimensions:** wingspan 69 ft 7 in (21.21 m); length 87 ft 10 in (26.77 m); height 20 ft 5 in (6.22 m); wing area 587.10 sq ft (54.54 m²) excluding winglets
Performance: maximum cruising speed 529 mph (851 km/h) at 37,000 ft (11275 m); climb rate 3,700 ft (1128 m) per minute at 1,500 ft (457 m); service ceiling 41,000 ft (12495 m); range	**Payload:** up to 52 passengers within the context of a 12,100-lb (5488-kg) maximum payload

Variants

Regional Jet Series 100: this was the initial production model optimised for the carriage of up to 50 passengers over a range of 1,128 miles (1818 km)

Regional Jet Series 100ER: this is the extended-range development of the Regional Jet Series 100 that was announced in September 1990 with greater fuel capacity for a maximum take-off weight of 51,000 lb (23133 kg) and a range of 1,864 miles (3000 km) with a 13,878-lb (6295-kg) maximum payload

Regional Jet Series 100LR: this is the long-range development of the Regional Jet Series 100 that was announced in March 1994 and certificated in April of the same year with provision for still more fuel to permit take-off at a maximum weight of 53,000 lb (24041 kg) for the delivery of the maximum payload to a range of more than 2,267 miles (3648 km)

Regional Jet Series 200: this is a development of the Regional Jet Series 100 with the revised powerplant of two examples of the CF34-3B1 turbofan with the same rating as the CF34-3A1, but maintained to a temperature of 86°F (30°C); the Regional Jet Series 200 is available in standard, **Regional Jet Series 200ER** extended-range and **Regional Jet Series 200LR** long-range versions equivalent to the Regional Jet Series 100 subvariants

Regional Jet Series 700: the programme for this 70-seat derivative of the 50-seat Regional Jet Series 100/200, originally designated as the **RJ-X**, was launched on 17 January 1997 to meet the increasing demand for larger aircraft with superior operating economies on regional airline routes; the first aircraft was completed in the first quarter of 1999, with Canadian, American and European certification scheduled to follow in the third quarter of 2000 for the **'A'** and **'B'** models with 70- and 78-seat accommodation respectively; the Regional Jet Series 700 is offered in standard and **Regional Jet Series 700ER** extended-range versions with maximum-payload ranges of 1,959 and 2,338 miles (3152 and 3763 km) after take-off at weights of 72,500 and 75,000 lb (32886 and 34020 kg) respectively, and otherwise differ from the Regional Jet Series 100/200 mainly in their larger size and uprated powerplant; the span is increased by 6 ft (1.83 m) to 75 ft 6 in (23.01 m) by the introduction of wingroot plugs, and the overall length is increased by 19 ft (5.94 m) to produce an overall length of 106 ft 4 in (32.41 m), and the uprated powerplant comprises two CF34-8C1 turbofans each rated at 13,790 lb st (61.34 kN); other changes included an enlarged horizontal tail surface, an extended wing leading edge fitted with high-lift devices, longer main landing-gear units, and new wheels, tyres and brakes

Corporate Jetliner: this is the corporate shuttle version of the Regional Jet Series 200 with more comfortable cabin accommodation for between 18 and 30 passengers

Canadair Special Edition: this is a longer-range derivative of the Corporate Jetliner with more luxurious cabin accommodation for between 15 and 19 passengers

CANSA aircraft

In 1936 the Aeronautica Gabardini SA, established in 1913, changed its name to CANSA (Costruzioni Aeronautiche Novaresi S.A.) and in 1939 became a subsidiary of Fiat. Gabardini had specialised in light aircraft and trainers, and it is therefore unsurprising that most of the aircraft designed and built by CANSA, with the exception of the **FC.20** reconnaissance and attack bomber, were trainers intended mainly for military use.

Designed by Giacomo Mosso, the **CANSA C.5** light tourer and primary trainer flew in prototype form on 24 July 1939 as an open-cockpit biplane of fabric-covered mixed construction with a staggered, unequal-span single-bay wing cellule that was notable for its flat lower wing and sharply dihedralled upper wing. The landing gear was of the fixed tailskid type with divided main units carrying wheels fitted with brakes.

With Italy's entry into World War II only a matter of time, no civil orders were forthcoming but an initial service order of 23 October 1939 called for 12 aircraft in the form of six single-seat **C.5** machines with the Fiat A.50 radial engine rated at 85 hp (63 kW), one two-seat **C.5B** with the A.50 engine and five two-seat **C.5B/1** machines with the Alfa Romeo 110-I inline engine rated at 120 hp (90 kW). One single-seater and one of the Alfa Romeo-powered two-seaters were stressed for aerobatics.

A subsequent order covered 50 A.50-powered aircraft, all of which were delivered before the end of 1941. Most of these were single-seat C.5 machines but a few (total unspecified) were delivered to two-seat C.5B standard. Until the September 1943 armistice with the Allies, most of the C.5 and C.5B aircraft served with the RUNA, an organisation which undertook flying training for the Regia Aeronautica in association with local aero clubs.

Appearing in 1942, the **C.6** was a single-seat basic rather than primary flying trainer with the powerplant of one Isotta-Fraschini Beta RC.10 inverted inline engine rated at 280 hp (209 kW) and a single-bay biplane wing cellule with swept-back outer panels. Of fabric-covered mixed metal and wood construction, the C.6 had a maximum speed of 162 mph (260 km/h). Neither the C.6 nor its **C.6B** two-seat counterpart entered production.

Despite a designation apparently earlier than

A total of 67 C.5s was eventually completed. The aircraft served the pre-armistice Italian air force well as single-seat biplane trainers. The derived C.5B seated two in tandem.

those of the C.5 and C.6, the **C.4** also appeared in 1942 and was a two-seater with two open cockpits and a cantilever low-set wing. Again of mixed metal and wood construction under a covering of fabric, and featuring fixed tailskid landing gear, the C.4 was intended for the touring as well as the training role, and was powered by a CANSA C.80 inverted inline engine rated at 90 hp (67-kW). The C.4 did not enter production.

A cantilever low-wing monoplane, the **FC.12** of 1941 was originally intended as a trainer for the fighter and dive-bomber roles with tandem two-seat accommodation under a long framed canopy, but was later revised as a contender for orders as an operational type in the ground-attack role. The type had tailwheel landing gear with main units that retracted rearward into underwing fairings, and was powered by one Fiat

A.30 RA inverted-Vee engine rated at 600 hp (447 kW). The maximum speed was 261 mph (420 km/h), and the armament was planned as five 0.5-in (12.7-mm) Breda-SAFAT machine-guns, installed as four fixed forward-firing weapons (two in the wing and two in the fuselage) and one trainable rearward-firing weapon. No production order was placed for the FC.12.

Designed by Mosso, the first prototype of the **FC.20** made its maiden flight on 12 April 1941 as a twin-engined reconnaissance bomber with a long glazed nose and the powerplant of two Fiat A.74 RC.38 radial engines, each rated at 840 hp (626 kW), in nacelles on the leading edge of the wing. In 1942 there followed the **FC.20bis** that was akin to its predecessor in being a cantilever low-wing monoplane of all-metal construction (except for the fabric covering of its

control surfaces and the fuselage between the trailing edge of the wing and the tail cone), with twin endplate vertical surfaces on its dihedralled horizontal tail surface. The main landing gear units retracted into the nacelles for the two A.74 engines.

Intended as a low-level tank destroyer, the FC.20bis had the primary armament of one downward-canted 37-mm cannon, an adaptation of a Breda naval anti-aircraft gun, which was mounted in the lower section of a redesigned stubby nose. Additional armament comprised two wing-mounted 0.5-in (12.7-mm) Breda-SAFAT machine-guns plus a third weapon of the same type mounted in a Scotti dorsal turret. Up to 126 4.4-lb (2-kg) light bombs could also be carried in an internal weapon bay, and two 220-lb (100-kg) bombs could be accommodated on underwing racks.

During March and April 1943 the new prototype flew with the 22° Gruppo, which was based at Capua with the main task of inter-

cepting formations of Consolidated B-24 Liberator bombers, but the FC.20bis proved itself incapable of the task as it lacked manoeuvrability, displayed a tendency to spin, and was greatly underpowered. Consequently, the prototype rarely managed to bring a B-24 within range of its heavy cannon, and when this was managed the pilot had great difficulty in maintaining control of the aircraft whenever the cannon was fired.

Despite the lack of promise shown by the F.C.20bis prototype, production of an evaluation batch of 10 aircraft went ahead, none of them being delivered before Italy came to terms with the Allies in September 1943. Although they showed little improvement in flight characteristics, three were allocated to the Cerveteri-based 173ª Squadriglia Ricognizione Strategica, whose Fiat CR.25 aircraft had been giving a good account of themselves on convoy escorts in the Straits of Messina. However, the armistice of September 1943 intervened before the FC.20bis could be used in action by this squadron. One or two FC.20bis aircraft were impressed subsequently by the Germans, but nothing is known of their use or

ultimate fate.

The other data for the FC.20bis ground attack or anti-shipping aircraft included a maximum speed of 261 mph (420 km/h) at 14,765 ft (4500 m), cruising speed of 211 mph (340 km/h) at optimum altitude, service ceiling of 24,115 ft (7350 m), range of 715 miles (1150 km), empty weight of 10,516 lb (4770 kg), maximum take-off weight of 15,036 lb (6820 kg), wingspan of 52 ft 6 in (16.00 m), length of 39 ft 11½ in (12.18 m), height of 13 ft 2¾ in (4.03 m) and wing area of 430.57 sq ft (40.00 m²).

There were two further developments of the basic type. The **FC.20ter** was a dive-bomber derivative with air brakes and the uprated powerplant of two Fiat A.80 RC.41 radial engines each rated at 1,000 hp (746 kW). The **FC.20quater** was a development of the FC.20bis with two 20-mm Mauser cannon in place of the wing-mounted 0.5-in (12.7-mm) machine-guns, but the delayed delivery of its two Daimler-Benz DB 601 inverted-Vee engines, for an estimated maximum speed of more than 311 mph (500 km/h), meant that the prototype had not been completed at the time of the armistice.

SPECIFICATION	
CANSA C.5	range 398 miles (640 km)
Type: single-seat primary trainer	**Weights:** empty 999 lb (453 kg);
Powerplant: one Fiat A.50 radial engine rated at 85 hp (63 kW)	maximum take-off 1,462 lb (663 kg)
Performance: maximum speed 109 mph (175 km/h) at sea level; service ceiling 15,255 ft (4650 m);	**Dimensions:** wingspan 27 ft 10¾ in (8.50 m); length 20 ft 5 in (6.22 m); height 8 ft 3¼ in (2.52 m); wing area 193.76 sq ft (18.00 m²)

CANT Z.501 Gabbiano

In 1931 the Cantiere Navale Triestino was reorganised as the Cantieri Riuniti dell'Adriatico (CRDA) and Marshal Italo Balbo, then the Italian minister of aviation, persuaded Ing. Filippo Zappata to return home from France, where he was working for Blériot, to become the company's chief engineer.

Zappata's first design was the **CANT Z.501 Gabbiano** (seagull), a long-range reconnaissance bomber flying-boat of wooden construction, with fabric covering on the upper part of the hull and on the flying surfaces. These comprised a strut-mounted and strut-braced parasol wing and a strut-and wire-braced tail unit with single vertical and horizontal surfaces. The powerplant was based on one Isotta-Fraschini Asso XI R2C Vee engine, rated

This Z.501 was employed by 2ª Escuadrilla, Grupo num 62 of the Agrupación Española (Spanish Nationalist Air Force). The aircraft was based at Majorca in 1939.

at 900 hp (671 kW) and driving a two-bladed wood or three-bladed metal propeller. The engine was installed ahead of the wing's centre section in a nacelle extended rearward to include a cockpit for the flight engineer, who was also responsible for the

operation of a 0.303-in (7.7-mm) machine-gun. Two similar weapons were mounted in the open bow and dorsal positions. Racks were attached to the wing struts, inboard of the stabilising floats, for the carriage of a maximum load of 1,411 lb (640 kg) of bombs.

SPECIFICATION	
CANT Z.501 Gabbiano	**Weights:** empty 8,466 lb
Type: four/five-crew reconnaissance bomber flying-boat	(3840 kg); maximum take-off 15,510 lb (7035 kg)
Powerplant: one Isotta-Fraschini Asso XI R2C.15 Vee engine rated at 900 hp (671 kW)	**Dimensions:** wingspan 73 ft 10 in (22.50 m); length 46 ft 11 in (14.30 m); height 14 ft 6 in (4.42 m); wing area 667.38 sq ft (62.00 m²)
Performance: maximum speed 171 mph (275 km/h) at 8,200 ft (2500 m); cruising speed 149 mph (240 km/h) at 6,560 ft (2000 m); climb to 13,125 ft (4000 m) in 18 minutes; service ceiling 22,965 ft (7000 m); range 1,491 miles (2400 km)	**Armament:** one 0.303-in (7.7-mm) Breda-SAFAT trainable machine-gun in each of the bow, nacelle and dorsal positions, plus up to 1,411 lb (640 kg) of bombs

CANT Z.501 Gabbiano (continued)

The prototype of the Z.501 made its first flight on 7 February 1934, and in October of that year CANT's chief pilot, Mario Stoppani, flew the aircraft 2,560 miles (4120 km) from the company's base at Monfalcone near Trieste at the head of the Adriatic Sea to Massawa in Eritrea, a distance record for seaplanes. In July 1935, after France had taken the record, Stoppani regained it with a 3,080-mile (4957-km) flight to Berbera in British Somaliland.

The Z.501 entered squadron service with the Regia Aeronautica in 1937, and by the time Italy entered World War II on 10 June 1940 more than 200 formed the equipment of at least 17 squadrons and four flights. The Z.501's operational debut had already taken place by this time, and this event was recorded by a unit of the Aviazione Legionaria, based in Majorca and operating in support of the Nationalist forces in the Spanish Civil War. A small number of Z.501 'boats served with a coastal defence unit of the Romanian air force. A total of 454 such machines was delivered before production ended in 1943.

CANT Z.504

Completed in 1935 as a single prototype, the **CANT Z.504** was a two-seat fighter flying-boat that resembled a scaled-down Z.501 with a biplane wing cellule rather than parasol monoplane wing. Designed for the shipborne role and therefore stressed for catapult launches, the Z.504 was based on an extremely elegant hull with a two-step planing bottom and two open cockpits, one for the pilot ahead of the wing cellule and one for the observer/gunner behind it.

The upswept tail unit was nicely contoured and braced by struts and wires, and comprised single vertical and horizontal surfaces with balanced control surfaces. The lower wing of the unstaggered wing cellule extended from the upper sides of the hull, and the wing cellule was of the single-bay type with a single set of parallel interplane struts on each side, and ailerons were installed on the outboard ends of only the upper wing's trailing edge. The powerplant was based on a single radial engine installed in a nacelle attached to the underside of the upper wing's centre section, and drove a two-bladed tractor propeller. There were probably two 0.303-in (7.7-mm) fixed forward-firing machine-guns in the upper part of the bow for the use of the pilot, and the observer/gunner had one 0.303-in (7.7-mm) Breda-SAFAT trainable rearward-firing machine-gun. No other details of the Z.504, which was not adopted for service by the Regia Marina, appear to have survived.

CANT's Z.504 was an attractive, but ultimately unsuccessful, fighter flying-boat.

CANT Z.505 and Z.506 Airone

In July 1935 the prototype of a large twin-float seaplane of wooden construction except for its metal floats, and with the powerplant of three Isotta-Fraschini Asso XI RC.15 Vee engines each rated at 840 hp (626 kW) flew for the first time. This was the **CANT Z.505**, which had been designed as a mailplane of generally very clean concept with a low-set cantilever monoplane wing, a wire-braced tail unit and a maximum take-off weight of 28,207 lb (12795 kg).

On 19 August of the same year, Mario Stoppani undertook the first flight of the slightly smaller and lighter **Z.506**, which had been designed as a 12/14-passenger transport with the initial powerplant of three Piaggio Stella IX radial engines each rated at 610 hp (455 kW) and a wing of notably less dihedral than that of the Z.505. The type was put into production during 1936 as the **Z.506A** and entered service with the Italian airline Ala Littoria during that year on routes around the Mediterranean. With the revised and uprated powerplant of three Alfa Romeo 126 RC.34 radial engines each rated at 750 hp (559 kW) and generally flown by Stoppani, the Z.506A set several altitude, distance and speed records during 1936-8, including speeds of 191.539 mph (308.25 km/h), 198.7 mph (319.78 km/h) and 200.118 mph (322.06 km/h) over distances of 5000 km (3,107 miles), 2000 km (1,243 miles) and 1000 km (621 miles) respectively. The Z.506A carried a payload of 2000 kg (4,409 lb) to 25,623 ft (7810 m) and 5000 kg (11,023 lb) to 22,693 ft (6917 m), and later flew 3,345.225 miles (5383.6 km) over a closed circuit.

A military version, designated as the **Z.506B Airone** (heron), was displayed at the October 1937 Milan Aeronautical Exhibition, and during the following month this set a load-to-height record of 33,318 ft (10155 m) with a 1000-kg (2,205-lb) payload, and then flew 4,362 miles (7020 km) non-stop from Cadiz to Caravelas. This machine had the powerplant of three Alfa Romeo 126 RC.34 radial engines each rated at 750 hp (559 kW). Production of the Z.506B totalled 324 floatplanes including two prototypes, and these machines were supplied to the Regia Aeronautica and to the Regia Marina; the latter received more than

Variants

Z.606B Airone: this was a militarised version featuring a stepped, extensively-glazed tandem two-seat cockpit, and a ventral gondola which contained the bomb-aimer's position and the bomb bay, immediately behind which was a gunner's position with a single 0.303-in (7.7-mm) Breda-SAFAT trainable machine-gun; a 0.5-in (12.7-mm) Breda-SAFAT machine-gun was fitted in the Breda M.1 upper turret; the bomb bay could accommodate one 1,764-lb (800-kg) torpedo or a combination of smaller weapons to a similar total weight, while later versions were able to carry a bombload of 2,646 lb (1200 kg) and were equipped with two 0.303-in (7.7-mm) Breda-SAFAT machine-guns in waist positions and a Caproni Lanciani Delta E turret in place of the earlier aircraft's Breda turret; the Z.506B was built at CANT's Monfalcone and Finale Ligure factories, and by Piaggio under licence
Z.506S: this was the search-and-rescue version, including 20 Z.506B floatplanes converted by Savoia-Marchetti in 1948
Z.506 landplane: one Z.506 was specially prepared for an endurance record attempt by Stoppani, and for this task was converted to landplane configuration with fixed, spatted landing gear; the flight was at first postponed and then cancelled as a result of bad weather

29 aircraft, the balance of a Polish order for 30 which were not delivered as a result of the German invasion of September 1939 that started World War II. Five were delivered to the Nationalist forces in the Spanish Civil War late in 1938. A number of Airone aircraft, converted for the search-and-rescue role, remained in regular service as late as 1959.

The Z.505, of which I-ZAPP is the only known example, was longer than the Z.506. The aircraft was designed to achieve long range and offered accommodation for eight passengers alongside its load of mail.

SPECIFICATION	
CANT Z.506B Airone	**Weights:** empty 18,298 lb
Type: five-crew reconnaissance bomber and rescue floatplane	(8300 kg); maximum take-off 27,117 lb (12300 kg)
Powerplant: three Alfa Romeo 126 RC.34 radial engines each rated at 750 hp (559 kW)	**Dimensions:** wingspan 86 ft 1⅓ in (26.50 m); length 63 ft 1½ in (19.25 m); height 24 ft 5⅕ in (7.45 m); wing area 936.49 sq ft (87.00 m²)
Performance: maximum speed 227 mph (365 km/h) at optimum altitude; cruising speed 202 mph (325 km/h) at optimum altitude; climb to 13,125 ft (4000 m) in 14 minutes; service ceiling 26,245 ft (8000 m); range 1,705 miles (2745 km)	**Armament:** one or two 0.303-in (7.7-mm) Breda-SAFAT trainable machine-guns and one 0.5-in (12.7-mm) trainable machine-gun, plus up to 2,646 lb (1200 kg) of bombs or one torpedo

CANT Z.508

Built to the extent of a single prototype in 1936, the **CANT Z.508** was in concept a scaled-up version of the Z.501 for the heavy bomber role. The type was based on a substantial hull with a two-step planing bottom and a raised and fully-enclosed cockpit for the pilot and co-pilot. Enclosed compartments were provided in the hull forward and aft of the cockpit for other members of the crew, who included a bomb-aimer/gunner in a bow compartment with a glazed forward section for the bomb-aiming role and an open position for the gunnery role.

The monoplane wing was of the parasol type and of constant thickness and chord except for its semi-elliptical tips, which were thus tapered in thickness and chord and carried the large ailerons. The wing was carried over the hull by a pair of inward-canted N-type struts. A large cylindrical fairing was extended from each side of the hull in line with its upper surface by two sets of hull-mounted struts, and from this extended a parallel pair of wing-bracing struts that also provided the anchorage for two sets of auxiliary bracing struts as well as the two pairs of struts that carried the stabilising float.

The tail unit comprised single vertical and horizontal surfaces, the tailplane that carried balanced elevators and was located about three-fifths of the way up the vertical surface (fitted with a balanced rudder) with lower bracing struts and upper bracing wires. The 'boat was completed by its powerplant, which comprised three Isotta-Fraschini Asso XI Vee engines. These were installed in nacelles on the leading edges of the upper wing to drive three-bladed tractor propellers. The starboard engine was cooled with the aid of an assembly of three radiators extending from the leading edge onto the upper surface of the wing just inboard of the engine, while the central and port engines were cooled with the aid of an assembly of six similar radiators between the two engines.

The Z.508 was unsuitable for the bomber role, but was used for the establishment of a number of records during 1937. Flown by Mario Stoppani, the Z.508 lifted a payload of 10000 kg (22,046 lb) to an altitude of 6,560 ft (2000 m), and with a payload of 5000 kg (11,023 lb) recorded a speed of 154.26 mph (248.25 km/h) over a 2000-km (1,243-mile) course and a speed of 156.42 mph (251.73 km/h) over a 1000-km (621-mile) course.

Essentially a scaled-up Z.501 with three engines, the Z.508 showed little military potential and was restricted in its use to the establishment of a number of records.

SPECIFICATION	
CANT Z.508	196 mph (315 km/h) at optimum
Type: heavy bomber flying-boat	altitude
Powerplant: three Isotta-Fraschini Asso XI RC.40 Vee engines each rated at 840 hp (627 kW)	**Dimensions:** wingspan 98 ft 5 in (30.00 m); length 70 ft 5 in (21.45 m); height 18 ft 6⅝ in (5.65 m)
Performance: maximum speed	

CANT Z.509

Built to the extent of three machines, the **CANT Z.509** was in essence a scaled-up and somewhat heavier version of the Z.506A for the airline Ala Littoria's transatlantic postal service to South America. The greater drag and weight of the Z.509 were more than offset by the use of the uprated powerplant of three Fiat A.80 radial engines, and as a result the Z.509 was considerably faster than the Z.501, and also had a much enlarged fuel capacity for the considerably greater range demanded by transatlantic operation.

During 1938, the Z.509 was used to recapture for Italy several of the international seaplane speed records that had been captured by German machines in recent years, but further plans for the Z.509 were cut short by the outbreak of World War II in September 1939. Italy was neutral at that time, but planned to enter the war on Germany's side and now concentrated on the development of military aircraft.

The history of only one Z.509 has been recorded. Registered I-ATLA, the aircraft did not enter regular airline service, but was used in a number of record-breaking attempts.

SPECIFICATION	
CANT Z.509	14 minutes; service ceiling 26,245 ft (8000 m); range 2,486 miles (4000 km)
Type: long-range mail-carrying floatplane	
Powerplant: three Fiat A.80 RC.41 radial engines each rated at 1,000 hp (746 kW)	**Weights:** empty 22,002 lb (9980 kg); maximum take-off 35,196 lb (15965 kg)
Performance: maximum speed 264 mph (425 km/h) at 14,765 ft (4500 m); cruising speed 217 mph (350 km/h) at optimum altitude; climb to 14,765 ft (4500 m) in	**Dimensions:** wingspan 92 ft 11 in (28.32 m); length 62 ft 10 in (19.15 m); height 24 ft 8 in (7.52 m); wing area 1,076.43 sq ft (100.00 m²)

CANT Z.511

The world's largest floatplane, the **CANT Z.511** was designed by Zappata in 1939 as a four-engined commercial transport for operation across the South Atlantic. It was to have accommodation for crew and passengers on the upper deck, including sleeping berths for 16 people, and mail and freight compartments below.

The prototype made its maiden flight in September 1943 and, together with the second aircraft, was taken over by the Regia Aeronautica. One of the aircraft was damaged by Allied aircraft on Lake Trasimeno and the second was scrapped by the Germans, before the aircraft could be used for an anti-shipping raid on New York. For this the two aircraft were to have flown across the Atlantic, taxiing on the water for the last few miles to avoid radar detection before releasing several manned torpedoes against vessels in the harbour area.

A superb floatplane, the Z.511 featured wing leading-edge walkways for engineers to reach the engines in flight. Ladders in the float struts allowed spare parts stowed in the floats to be reached.

SPECIFICATION	
CANT Z.511	16 minutes; service ceiling 22,965 ft (7000 m); range 2,796 miles (4500 km)
Type: four/five-crew long-range passenger and mail floatplane	
Powerplant: four Piaggio P.XII RC.35 radial engines each rated at 1,500 hp (1118 kW)	**Weights:** empty 45,012 lb (20417 kg); maximum take-off 73,830 lb (33489 kg)
Performance: maximum speed 264 mph (425 km/h) at 13,125 ft (4000 m); cruising speed 205 mph (330 km/h) at optimum altitude; climb to 13,125 ft (4000 m) in	**Dimensions:** wingspan 131 ft 2¾ in (40.00 m); length 93 ft 6 in (28.50 m); height 36 ft 1 in (11.00 m); wing area 2,099.03 sq ft (195.00 m²)

CANT Z.1007 Alcione and Z.1015

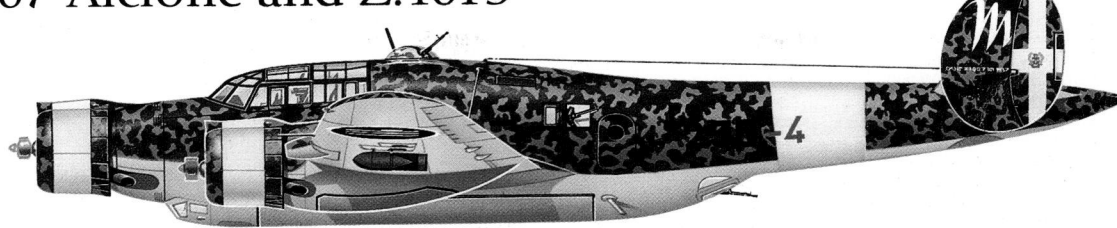

The design studies which culminated in the **CANT Z.1007bis Alcione** (kingfisher) began in 1935 and the **Z.1007** prototype, powered by three 825-hp (615-kW) Isotta-Fraschini Asso XI Vee engines, made its first flight in March 1937. Changes made during the initial flight test programme included the replacement of the two-bladed wooden propellers with three-bladed Piaggio metal units, and modifications to the ventral radiators. Annular radiators identified an interim production version, 34 of which were built.

In the meantime, a redesigned version powered by three Piaggio P.XI R2C.40 radial engines was built. Early examples had the tailplane mounted lower on the fin than had been the case with the prototype, and later aircraft, of the Serie IV-IX batch, introduced a revised horizontal tail surface with noticeable dihedral and oval endplate vertical surfaces. The first aircraft, in fact built as the 35th airframe off the production line, was first flown in 1938 as the **Z.1007bis**, and after a total of eight pre-production examples had been completed for service trials, the type entered quantity production. A total of 561 Z.1007s of all variants were completed.

This twin-fin aircraft was part of 230ª Squadriglia, 95º Gruppo of the 35º Stormo Bombardamento Terrestre of the Regia Aeronautica.

SPECIFICATION

CANT Z.1007bis Alcione
Type: five-crew medium bomber
Powerplant: three Piaggio P.XI R2C.40 radial engines each rated at 1,000 hp (746 kW)
Performance: maximum speed 289 mph (465 km/h) at 13,125 ft (4000 m); climb to 19,685 ft (6000 m) in 16 minutes eight seconds; service ceiling 24,605 ft (7500 m); range 1,115 miles (1795 km)
Weights: empty 20,712 lb (9395 kg); maximum take-off 30,027 lb (13620 kg)
Dimensions: wingspan 81 ft 4⅓ in
(24.80 m); length 60 ft 2⅓ in (18.35 m); height 17 ft 1½ in (5.22 m); wing area 807.32 sq ft (75.00 m²)
Armament: one 0.5-in (12.7-mm) Breda-SAFAT or Scotti trainable machine-gun in each of the dorsal turret and ventral position, one 0.303-in (7.7-mm) Breda-SAFAT trainable lateral-firing machine-gun in each of the two beam positions, plus up to 2,646 lb (1200 kg) of bombs carried internally or 2,205 lb (1000 kg) of bombs carried externally

Variants

Z.1007ter: improved Z.1007bis with three Piaggio P.XIX radial engines each rated at 1,150 hp (858 kW), and the bomb load reduced to 2,205 lb (1000 kg); the variant's maximum speed was 311 mph (500 km/h), range 1,398 miles (2250 km) and maximum take-off weight 23,071 lb (10465 kg)
Z.1015: prototype of long-range mailplane with the powerplant of three Piaggio P.XII RC.35 radial engines each rated at 1,500 hp (1118 kW), maximum speed of 348 mph (560 km/h), range of 1,864 miles (3000 km) and maximum take-off weight 29,982 lb (13600 kg); intended for further development as a bomber

CANT Z.1011

A contemporary of the Z.1007 and first flown in 1935, the **CANT Z.1011** was intended as a twin-engined medium bomber for the Regia Aeronautica, with a bomb-aimer's position in the long and angular glazed nose. As a plywood-covered wooden construction with a low-set cantilever monoplane wing, the aircraft was underpowered on its pair of Isotta-Fraschini Asso XI engines. Its inadequate performance resulted in cancellation of the project after the completion of another four prototypes. One of these was fitted with 800-hp (597-kW) Isotta-Fraschini K.14 (licence-made Gnome-Rhône 14K) radial engines and all five aircraft were used later as transports for high-ranking Italian government personnel and air force staff.

The engine nacelles of the Z.1011 also accommodated the retractable main units of the tailwheel landing gear. The aircraft was totally unsuccessful as a bomber due to the lack of power from its twin radial engines.

SPECIFICATION

CANT Z.1011
Type: medium bomber
Powerplant: two Isotta-Fraschini Asso XI RC.15 Vee engines each rated at 840 hp (626 kW)
Performance: maximum speed 230 mph (370 km/h) at 14,765 ft (4500 m); cruising speed 193 mph (310 km/h) at optimum altitude; climb to 9,845 ft (3000 m) in 11 minutes 42 seconds; service ceiling 26,245 ft (8000 m); range 1,243 miles (2000 km)
Weights: empty 12,540 lb (5688 kg)
Dimensions: wing span 92 ft ¼ in (28.05 m); length 55 ft 9 in (17.00 m); height 17 ft 3 in (5.25 m); wing area 861.14 sq ft (80.00 m²)
Armament: one 0.303-in (7.7-mm) Breda-SAFAT trainable forward-firing machine-gun in the nose position, and two 0.303-in (7.7-mm) Breda-SAFAT trainable machine-guns in each of the dorsal and ventral turrets

CANT Z.1018 Leone

The **CANT Z.1018 Leone** (*lion*) was the last design for CANT by Filippo Zappata before his departure to the Breda company, and was also the designer's first aircraft of all-metal construction. The prototype, which first flew in 1940, was built of wood and also featured a tail unit with twin endplate vertical surfaces. An all-metal prototype then followed. This incorporated major changes which included a single vertical tail surface and a lengthened fuselage with a revised cockpit position. The type had a twin-engined powerplant in which a number of different engine types were trialled, including the Piaggio P.XII RC.35, Piaggio P.XV RC.45, Alfa Romeo 135 RC.32 and Fiat RA.1050, the latter being a licence-built version of the Daimler-Benz DB 605A.

Some 300 examples of the Leone were ordered in 1941 but only five of these had been completed, together with 10 pre-production aircraft, by the time that production was halted by the Italian armistice. Nevertheless, a small number saw limited operational service. In overall terms, the Z.1018 was the first Italian bomber to offer performance and armament comparable to the best of contemporary Allied bombers of the same class. A projected version would have been a heavy day and night fighter with a fixed forward-firing armament of seven 20-mm cannon in the nose as well as three 0.5-in (12.7-mm) machine-guns plus. In its night-fighter form, the Z.1018 would have been equipped with German Lichtenstein SN-2 radar.

A handful of Leones served operationally with the 101º Gruppo of 47º Stormo Bombardimento Terrestre.

SPECIFICATION

CANT Z.1018 Leone
Type: five-crew medium bomber
Powerplant: two Alfa Romeo 135 RC.32 radial engines each rated at 1,400 hp (1044 kW)
Performance: maximum speed 323 mph (520 km/h) at optimum altitude; climb to 6,560 ft (2000 m) in three minutes 10 seconds; service ceiling 23,785 ft (7250 m); range 1,367 miles (2200 km)
Weights: empty 19,400 lb (8800 kg); maximum take-off 26,455 lb (12000 kg)
Dimensions: wingspan 73 ft 9¾ in
(22.50 m); length 57 ft 9 in (17.60 m); height 20 ft (6.10 m); wing area 673.15 sq ft (63.00 m²)
Armament: one 0.5-in (12.7-mm) Breda-SAFAT fixed forward-firing machine-gun in the starboard wing root, one 0.5-in (12.7-mm) Breda-SAFAT trainable machine-gun in each of the dorsal turret and ventral position, and one 0.303-in (7.7-mm) Breda-SAFAT trainable lateral-firing machine-gun in each of the two beam positions, plus up to 3,307 lb (1500 kg) of bombs carried internally

Cantilever Aero Bullet

Designed with the assistance of Vincent J. Burnelli by Dr William W. Christmas of the **Cantilever Aero Company** and built by the Continental Aircraft Company, the **Cantilever Aero Bullet** (otherwise known as the **Christmas Scout** and **Christmas Bullet**) was a fighter based on the latest aerodynamic and structural thinking in the later stages of World War I.

The first prototype of the Bullet was completed in mid-January 1919 with the Liberty 6 inline engine and

The Bullet was mainly of wooden construction, and in layout was a sesquiplane with fixed landing gear. The cantilever wings required neither interplane struts nor flying/landing wires.

was totally destroyed in a crash during the course of its first flight. The second prototype was completed with the Hall-Scott L-6 inline engine and, like its predecessor, was lost in a crash during its first flight in the summer of 1919. Further development of the Bullet was immediately cancelled.

The core of the Aero Bullet structure was the rectangular-section fuselage, which was very deep in its central section where the larger upper wing and smaller lower wing were attached to the lower and upper longerons respectively.

SPECIFICATION

Cantilever Aero Bullet (manufacturer's claim)
Type: single-seat fighter
Powerplant: one Liberty 6 inline engine rated at 185 hp (138 kW)
Performance: maximum speed 175 mph (282 km/h) at sea level; service ceiling 14,700 ft (4480 m); range 550 miles (885 km); **Weights:** empty 1,820 lb (839 kg); maximum take-off 2,100 lb (953 kg) **Dimensions:** wingspan 28 ft (8.53 m); length 21 ft (6.40 m); wing area 170.00 sq ft (15.79 m²)

Caproni Ca 1, Ca 2, Ca 3 and Ca 5

Alongside Russia, Italy was the only country to have designed and built a multi-engined bomber type in the period before World War I. After having been projected in 1913 as the **Caproni 260 hp**, to which the retrospective company designation **Ca 30** was afforded after the end of World War I, the Caproni 260 hp (**Ca 31**) prototype made its maiden flight in October 1914 with a powerplant of three Gnome rotary piston engines. The Ca 31 was a substantial three-bay biplane of completely orthodox construction and was of the twin-boom layout. The three engines were installed in tandem in the central nacelle: the rearmost unit drove a pusher propeller and the other two engines drove tractor propellers at the front of the two booms.

The Ca 31 was flyable but hardly practical, and its concept was therefore adapted in the new **Caproni 300 hp** prototype (retrospectively designated **Ca 32** after World War I) with two tractor engines installed at the front of the two booms to provide direct drive for the two tractor propellers. Other changes effected at this stage were a revised central nacelle, a modified

tail surface and revised wings.

The Italian air force ordered it into production after two prototypes (company designation **Ca 32**) had been built, for service as the **Ca 1** with the revised powerplant of three 100-hp (75-kW) Fiat A.10 inline piston engines. Some 160 of the aircraft were delivered between August 1915 and December 1916.

After the end of World War I a number of surplus aircraft were converted as **Ca 56** civil passenger transports with a payload of six passengers.

The **Ca 2**, of which nine were delivered over the same period as the Ca 1, with the contemporary company designation **Ca 350 hp**, was a simple evolution of the Ca 1 with

the central engine replaced by a 150-hp (112-kW) Isotta-Fraschini V.4B inline engine. Operations confirmed that there was nothing wrong with the basic airframe, but it soon became clear that greater capabilities would result from the adoption of a higher-rated powerplant.

This realisation led to the creation of the **Ca 3** as the uprated version of the Ca 2 that was tested in prototype form late in 1916 and entered production with the company designation **Caproni 450 hp** (later **Ca 33**). A total of 298 Italian aircraft was delivered between February 1917 and 1919.

The type was basically the Ca 2 with the two outboard engines replaced by a pair of Isotta-Fraschini V.4B engines. The aircraft served mainly with the Italian air force in the heavy bomber role, but the Italian navy also made limited use of the type in the torpedo bomber role, and modest numbers of the basic bomber were also supplied to France, where another 83 generally similar aircraft were built under licence by Robert Esnault-Pelterie with the designation Caproni-Esnault-Pelterie.

A number of surplus aircraft were converted as **Ca 56a** civil passenger transports with a payload of six passengers.

The **Ca 3 mod (modificato**, or modified) variant was known to Caproni as the **Ca 36** (sometimes **Ca 36M**), and was an improved and structurally simplified version of the Ca 3. Deliveries between 1923 and 1927 totalled 153 aircraft. The Ca 3 mod bombers saw some operational service in the first stages of the military effort undertaken by Mussolini's Fascist regime to 'restore Italy's lost colonies' in North Africa.

A few of the Ca 3 mod aircraft were later converted to **Ca 36S** air ambulance standard for air force use, and variants that failed to progress past the project or prototype stages included the **Ca 34**, **Ca 35** with tandem pilot seating, **Ca 36** with detachable outer wing panels, **Ca 37** single-engined two-seater for the ground-attack role, and **Ca 39** seaplane with side-by-side twin-float alighting gear.

By 1917 Caproni had come to the sensible conclusion that while its Ca 3 biplane and Ca 4 triplane bombers lacked

adequate outright performance for successful penetration of enemy airspace defended by modern fighters.

This paved the way for the biplane bomber known to the manufacturer as the **Caproni 600 hp** or **600/900 hp** (**Ca 44** series) and to the Italian air force as the **Ca 5**. The Ca 5 was in fact produced in two other subvariants known to the manufacturer as the **Caproni 750 hp** or **600/750 hp** (**Ca 45**) and **Caproni 900/1200 hp** (**Ca 46**). Production of these models totalled 659 aircraft in the period between 1918 and 1921.

In overall conceptual terms, the Caproni 600 hp was an updated Caproni 450 hp (Ca 3) with an uprated powerplant, new wings, revised nacelle and modified main landing gear.

The Caproni 600 hp prototype first flew in the second half of 1917 with a powerplant of three 200-hp (149-kW) Fiat A.12 inline engines but later replaced by three improved 250-hp (186-kW) A.12 engines. Large-scale orders were placed for 3,900 aircraft, later reduced to 3,650, of which one-third was earmarked for French service.

This Caproni Ca 31 was flown from Plateau de Malzéville by Escadrille CEP 115 of the Aéronautique Militaire (French air force) during 1916.

SPECIFICATION

Caproni Ca 3
Type: four-crew heavy bomber
Powerplant: three Isotta-Fraschini V.4B inline engines each rated at 150 hp (112 kW)
Performance: maximum speed 87 mph (140 km/h) at sea level; climb to 13,125 ft (4000 m) in 40 minutes; service ceiling 15,750 ft (4800 m); range 280 miles (450 km); endurance 3 hours 30 minutes **Weights:** empty 5,071 lb (2300 kg); maximum take-off 8,576 lb (2890 kg)
Dimensions: wingspan 72 ft 10 in (22.20 m); length 35 ft 9¾ in (10.90 m); height 12 ft 1½ in (3.70 m); wing area 1,029.50 sq ft (95.64 m²)
Armament: one 0.256-in (6.5-in) Revelli trainable forward-firing machine-gun in the nose position, and one, two or three 0.256-in (6.5-mm) Revelli trainable rearward-firing machine-guns in the dorsal position, plus up to 992 lb (450 kg) of bombs carried externally

Caproni Ca 1, Ca 2, Ca 3 and Ca 5 (continued)

Two French manufacturers, along with two American manufacturers, were involved in the panned production of 1,500 aircraft to be used by the US Air Service. The intervention of the Armistice led to the radical curtailment of these orders, and in fact no French aircraft were completed and American production totalled just three aircraft (two Ca 44 machines by Standard and one **Ca 46** machine by Fisher). Even so, **Ca 5** bombers of Italian manufacture were used operationally by the French and Americans as well as by the Italians.

The Ca 44 was powered by three A.12 or A.12bis engines each rated at 250 or 300 hp (186 or 224 kW) respectively, and was the major production model in 1917.

The Ca 44 was further developed into the **Ca 45**, which was the variant selected by France, with the revised powerplant of three 250-hp (186-kW) Isotta-Fraschini V.6 inline engines. The **Ca 46** was a further development along the same basic lines for production and service in 1918 with the maximum bomb load and range reduced, and the powerplant altered to three 360-hp (269-kW) Liberty 12 Vee piston engines.

A number of Ca 44 bombers were converted to **Ca 50** air ambulance machines with provision for the installation of one litter inside an aerodynamic fair-ing on each of the booms. After the end of World War I, a number of Ca 44s and Ca 45s surplus to Italian air force requirements were adapted for the civil transport market with the designation **Ca 57** (otherwise **Breda M-1**), with accommodation for eight passengers.

Known after the end of World War I as the **Ca 47**, the **I.Ca** was the seaplane conversion of the Ca 44 of which 10 were produced.

Caproni Ca 4

Caproni Ca 4 was the Italian military designation for the series of very large triplane bombers designed with the initial company designation **Caproni 600 hp (Ca 40)**.

The primary changes effected were a more refined nacelle carried on the central rather than lower wing, the replacement of the single dorsal gunner on the centreline with one, two or three weapons with two gunners in the booms immediately to the rear of the wing trailing edges, the carriage of the bombs below the central wing rather than above the lower wing, the replacement of the four-bay biplane wing cellule by a six-bay triplane wing cellule with a large faired frame on its centreline for the carriage of bombs and the alteration of the landing gear to the fixed tailskid type with wide-track main units each carrying eight wheels on two axles.

The prototype appeared in 1916 with the same type of nacelle and landing gear nosewheel arrangement as the Caproni 450 hp series and a powerplant of three 200-hp (149-kW) Fiat A.12 inline engines. This single-ton machine was followed in 1917 by three generally similar pilot production aircraft that were dimensionally identical to the prototype.

In 1918 there followed 35 full production Ca 4s that were differentiated after the war as 12, 17 and six examples of the **Ca 41**,

Ca 42 and Ca 52 respectively. The **Ca 41** introduced a more refined nacelle and revised landing gear.

In a very few cases a trio of 250-hp (186-kW) Isotta-Fraschini V.6 inline engines was used to produce a subvariant known to the manufacturer as the **Caproni 750 hp**. The **Ca 42** was known to the manufacturer as the **Caproni 1200 hp**, and differed from the Ca 41 in having three 400-hp (298-kW) Packard Liberty 12 Vee piston engines. The Ca 52 was basically similar to the Ca 42 and was the subvariant of the Caproni 1200 hp intended for use by the RNAS, which did not in the event use the aircraft operationally.

Variants that reached the prototype stage but did not enter production or service included: the **Ca 43** seaplane; that was a conversion of a Ca 43 with a powerplant of three A.12 engines and an alighting arrangement of two side-by-side floats; the **Ca 48** transport with a powerplant of three 360-hp (268-kW) Liberty 12 engines and accommodation for 23 passengers; the **Ca 51** with a powerplant of three 700-hp (522-kW) Fiat A.14 engines and a biplane tail unit including a tail gunner's position and the **Ca 58** (also planned in **Ca 59** export form) improved version of the **Ca 48** with a powerplant of three A.14 engines or three Isotta-Fraschini V.6 engines.

Caproni also considered more potent versions for the day and night bomber roles with a powerplant of three 500-hp (373-kW) Bugatti engines, or three 700-hp (522-kW) A.14 engines.

Given the serials N526 to N531, the six Caproni CA 41 bombers bought for Britain's Royal Naval Air Service were never used operationally.

SPECIFICATION	
Caproni Ca 4 (Ca 42)	(13.10 m); height 20 ft 8 in
Type: five-crew heavy bomber	(6.30 m); wing area 2,152.85 sq ft
Powerplant: three Packard Liberty	(200.00 m²)
12 Vee engines each rated at	**Armament:** two 0.256-in (6.5-mm)
400 hp (298 kW)	Revelli trainable forward-firing
Performance: maximum speed	machine-guns in the nose position,
87 mph (140 km/h) at sea level;	and one 0.256-in (6.5-mm) Revelli
climb to 9,845 ft (3000 m) in	trainable rearward-firing machine-
24 minutes; service ceiling 9,845 ft	gun in each of the two dorsal
(3000 m); endurance seven hours	positions above the booms, plus up
Weights: empty 8,818 lb	to 3,913 lb (1775 kg) of bombs
(4000 kg); maximum take-off	carried on the sides of a bomb
16,534 lb (7500 kg)	carrier on the centreline of the
Dimensions: wingspan 98 ft 1¼ in	bottom wing
(29.90 m); length 42 ft 11¾ in	

Caproni Ca 73

Designed in 1924, the **Caproni Ca 73** was of inverted sesquiplane configuration, built originally as a commercial transport to carry up to 10 passengers and a crew of two. The Ca 73 was powered by two 500-hp (373-kW) uncowled Isotta-Fraschini Asso Vee engines mounted in tandem on the cabane struts supporting the centre section of the upper wing. An essentially similar aircraft with two 400-hp (298-kW) Lorraine-Dietrich engines was the **Ca 73bis**, while a bomber version, with the Asso powerplant of the Ca 73, was designated as the **Ca 73ter** (but was also sometimes referred to as the **Ca 82**). This last featured machine-gun positions in the nose and in the upper fuselage, and could carry a 1,984-lb (900-kg) bombload.

The shorter-span upper wing of the Ca 73 did not incorporate ailerons and had a span of 59 ft ½ in (18.00 m). The aircraft's tail unit had a span of 20 ft 6 in (6.25 m).

SPECIFICATION	
Caproni Ca 73	11,883 lb (5390 kg)
Type: two-crew commercial	**Dimensions:** wingspan 82 ft
transport or four/five-crew light	(25.00 m); length 49 ft 6½ in
bomber	(15.10 m); height 18 ft 4¾ in
Powerplant: two Isotta-Fraschini	(5.60 m); wing area 1,539.29 sq ft
Asso Vee engines each rated at	(143.00 m²)
500 hp (373 kW)	**Armament:** one 0.303-in (7.7-mm)
Performance: maximum speed	Lewis trainable machine-gun in
112 mph (180 km/h) at optimum	each of the nose and dorsal
altitude; service ceiling 15,080 ft	positions, plus up to 1,984 lb
(4600 m); endurance three hours	(900 kg) of bombs
Weights: empty 7,496 lb	**Payload:** up to 10 passengers
(3400 kg); maximum take-off	

Variant

Ca 74: this designation was applied retrospectively to the **Ca 80**, which was powered by two Bristol Jupiter radial engines each rated at 400 hp (298 kW); the type was also built as the **Ca 80S** air ambulance and as the **Ca 88** and **Ca 89**, both of which featured fuselage modifications including the installation of a retractable ventral turret

Caproni Ca 90

When it appeared in 1929, the six-engined **Caproni Ca 90** heavy bomber was the world's largest aircraft and although the record, in terms of wingspan and weight, was taken by the incredible Dornier Do X flying boat later in the same year, the Ca 90 remained the largest land-plane until surpassed in 1934 by the Soviet Tupolev ANT-20 *Maksim Gorkii*. The wing cellule was of Caproni's favoured inverted sesquiplane type, with the lower wing carrying two tandem pairs of Isotta-Fraschini Asso W-type engines. Another pair of similar engines was mounted on struts above the fuselage.

After component testing, the Caproni Ca 90 embarked upon a test and evaluation programme which included a series of flights which set new records for altitude, endurance and payload.

The Ca 90's fuselage was of welded steel-tube construction covered with fabric except on the forward section, which was skinned with corrugated Dural.

SPECIFICATION	
Caproni Ca 90	66,138 lb (30000 kg)
Type: heavy bomber	**Dimensions:** wingspan 152 ft
Powerplant : six Isotta-Fraschini	10⅔ in (46.60 m); length 88 ft 5 in
Asso W-type engines each rated at	(26.95 m); height 35 ft 5 in
1,000 hp (746 kW)	(10.80 m); wing area 5,345.53 sq ft
Performance: maximum speed	(496.60 m²)
127 mph (205 km/h); service ceiling	**Armament:** number of 0.303-in
14,765 ft (4500 m); endurance	(7.7-mm) trainable machine-guns,
seven hours	plus up to 17,637 lb (8000 kg) of
Weights: empty 33,069 lb	bombs
(15000 kg); maximum take-off	

Caproni Ca 97

Designed in 1927, the **Caproni Ca 97** was built as a tri-motor type with the powerplant of three 130-hp (97-kW) Lorraine-Dietrich radial engines. A high-wing monoplane offering enclosed accommodation for six passengers, the Ca 97 was also manufactured with a one-or-two engine powerplant with a total power rating of 400 to 500 hp (298 to 373 kW).

The type was used as a civil and military transport, for training and air ambulance duties, and as a bomber and reconnaissance aircraft. A Jupiter-engined **Ca 97 Idro** twin-float seaplane was also built. Some 13 **Ca 97**s were built.

*In the bomber role the **Ca 97** was fitted with a dorsal machine-gun position aft of the wing and was powered by one Bristol Jupiter radial engine.*

SPECIFICATION	
Caproni Ca 97	(1500 kg); maximum take-off
Type: general-purpose aircraft	5,500 lb (2495 kg)
Powerplant: one Bristol Jupiter	**Dimensions:** wingspan 52 ft 4 in
radial engine rated at 500 hp	(15.95 m); length 35 ft 1⅔ in
(373 kW)	(10.70 m); height 11 ft (3.35 m);
Performance: maximum speed	wing area 430.57 sq ft (40.00 m²)
140 mph (225 km/h) at optimum	**Armament:** one 0.303-in (7.7-mm)
altitude; service ceiling 24,280 ft	Lewis or Breda-SAFAT trainable
(7400 m); range 621 miles	machine-gun in the dorsal position
(1000 km)	**Payload:** up to six passengers
Weights: empty 3,307 lb	

Caproni Ca 100 'Caproncino'

Based on the de Havilland DH.60 Moth but incorporating some minor differences in detail design, including an increased-span lower wing, the **Caproni Ca 100 'Caproncino'** was built in some numbers for civil and military use from 1929. Powered initially by the 85-hp (63-kW) de Havilland Gipsy inline engine, the Ca 100 was then fitted with a variety of engines of different output. A twin-float seaplane version, of which 30 were built, was known as the **Ca 100 Idro**, and in 1934 a light bombing trainer was built with the powerplant of one 130-hp (97-kW) radial engine and able to carry four small bombs. In 1931 a Ca 100 Idro flown by Antonini and Trevisan established a seaplane altitude record of 16,462 ft (5018 m).

In 1935, the Peruvian government signed a contract with Caproni which gave the company a 10-year monopoly for the manufacture and repair of military aircraft in that country. Several Ca 100s were supplied from Italy, and in May 1937 a factory was opened in Peru, charged with producing 25 Ca 100s within two years but actually building only 12 in that period.

The type was also manufactured by a Caproni subsidiary in Bulgaria as the **KN-1**.

Alternative powerplant choices for the Ca 100 included the 90-hp (67-kW) Blackburn Cirrus Minor, 115-hp (86-kW) Isotta-Fraschini Asso 80R, 145-hp (108-kW) Colombo S.63 and 85-hp (63.4-kW) Fiat A.50 engines. The aircraft illustrated is a Ca 100 Idro floatplane.

SPECIFICATION	
Caproni Ca 100 Caproncino	23 minutes 18 seconds; service
Type: two-seat trainer	ceiling 13,125 ft (4000 m); range
Powerplant: one de Havilland	435 miles (700 km)
Gipsy inline engine rated at 85 hp	**Weights:** empty 882 lb (400 kg);
(63 kW)	maximum take-off 1,499 lb (680 kg)
Performance: maximum speed	**Dimensions:** wingspan 32 ft 10 in
102 mph (165 km/h) at optimum	(10.00 m); length 23 ft 11 in
altitude; cruising speed 87 mph	(7.30 m); height 9 ft ¼ in (2.75 m);
(140 km/h) at optimum altitude;	wing area 262.65 sq ft (24.40 m²)
climb to 8,200 ft (2500 m) in	

Caproni Ca 101, Ca 102 and Ca 111

A scaled-up development of the **Ca 97**, the Caproni **Ca 101** also appeared in 1927, initially as a civil transport powered by three Armstrong Siddeley Lynx radial engines built under licence by Alfa Romeo and each rated at 200 hp (149 kW). The Ca 101 was later developed as a bomber with three 370-hp (276-kW) Piaggio Stella VII radial engines and in this form equipped night bomber units of the Regia Aeronautica. The aircraft took part in the campaign which followed the Italian invasion of Ethiopia on 3 October 1935. The Italian colonial administration in Italian East Africa used the Ca 101 in a variety of roles, including reconnaissance and casualty evacuation, some of these aircraft being powered by Walter Castor or Alfa Romeo D2 radial engines rated at 240 or 270 hp (179 or 201 kW) respectively.

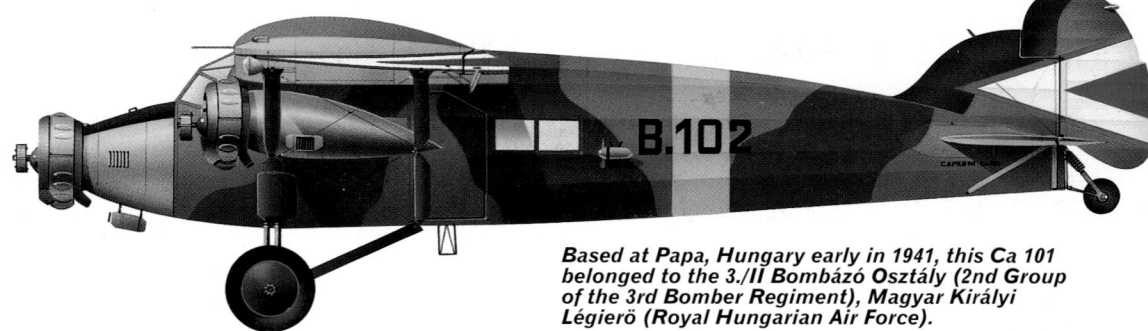

Based at Papa, Hungary early in 1941, this Ca 101 belonged to the 3./II Bombázó Osztály (2nd Group of the 3rd Bomber Regiment), Magyar Királyi Légierö (Royal Hungarian Air Force).

SPECIFICATION

Caproni Ca 111
Type: two/four-crew long-range reconnaissance aircraft
Powerplant: one Isotta-Fraschini Asso 750 RC radial engine rated at 830 hp (619 kW)
Performance: maximum speed 180 mph (290 km/h) at optimum altitude; cruising speed 158 mph (255 km/h) at optimum altitude; climb to 3,280 ft (1000 m) in five minutes 22 seconds; service ceiling 21,980 ft (6700 m); range 808 miles (1300 km)
Weights: empty 7,694 lb (3490 kg); maximum take-off 12,103 lb (5490 kg)
Dimensions: wingspan 64 ft 5½ in (19.65 m); length 50 ft 2½ in (15.30m); height 12 ft 7½ in (3.85 m); wing area 662.00 sq ft (61.50 m²)
Armament: one 0.303-in (7.7-mm) Breda-SAFAT trainable machine-gun in each of the dorsal, ventral and two beam positions, plus light bombs carried internally and externally

Variants

Ca 102: similar to the **Ca 101** but with two 500-hp (373-kW) Bristol Jupiter radial engines. The **Ca 102quater** was powered by two tandem pairs of engines
Ca 111: single-engined version, powered originally by one 750-hp (559-kW) Fiat engine and with increased wingspan; in 1934 a new wing was developed and an Isotta-Fraschini Asso 750RC was installed; the prototype and four pre-production aircraft were followed by 148 production machines, all of which were delivered to the Regia Aeronautica by 1936; 25 were completed as **Ca 111 Idro** twin-float seaplanes for use by long-range maritime reconnaissance units

Caproni Ca 113

Introduced in 1931 as a development of the Ca 109 biplane trainer, the **Ca 113** was a tandem two-seat advanced flying trainer. In its initial form the Ca 113 was powered by one 240-hp (179-kW) Walter Castor radial piston engine, but this unit was later replaced by one Piaggio Stella VII C.35. The Ca 113's prime achievement was the setting of a world altitude record of 47,352 ft (14433 m). This was established by Renato Donati on 11 April 1934 in a modified aircraft with greater wingspan and power provided by a 530-hp (395-kW) Alfa Romeo (Bristol) Pegasus supercharged radial piston engine driving a four-bladed propeller. The same modified machine was used in 1935 by Contessa Carina Negrone to set a women's altitude record of 39,402 ft (12010 m).

Variant

Ka.B.3: multi-role development of the **Ca 113** by Caproni's Bulgarian subsidiary; the type had two seats and the option of several radial engine types

Powerfully engined as standard, the Ca 113 was a useful trainer and excellent aerobatic mount. The type was used to win the Aerobatic Trophy at the 1931 Cleveland Air Races.

SPECIFICATION

Caproni Ca 113
Type: two-seat advanced flying trainer
Powerplant: one Piaggio Stella VII C.35 radial engine rated at 370 hp (276 kW)
Performance: maximum speed 155 mph (250 km/h) at optimum altitude; climb to 9,845 ft (3000 m) in five minutes 40 seconds; service ceiling 23,950 ft (7300 m); range 186 miles (300 km)
Weights: empty 1,874 lb (850 kg); maximum take-off 2,425 lb (1100 kg)
Dimensions: wingspan 34 ft 5 in (10.50 m); length 23 ft 11 in (7.30 m); height 8 ft 11 in (2.70 m); wing area 290.64 sq ft (27.00 m²)

Caproni Ca 114

Developed in 1933 to meet a Regia Aeronautica requirement for a single-seat fighter, the **Ca 114** was a single-bay equal-span staggered biplane of mixed wood and metal-construction. Although the Ca 114 was rejected for Italian service in favour of the Fiat CR.32 after official trials, it became the subject of an export order for the Cuerpo de Aeronautica del Peru. It is believed that 36 aircraft were delivered in three batches, the last of them in January 1935, and the type saw operational service in the 1941 conflict between Peru and Ecuador.

The Ca 114's wings were fabric-covered two-spar structures and the fuselage was of steel tube, covered with fabric and light alloy panels.

SPECIFICATION

Caproni Ca 114
Type: single-seat fighter
Powerplant: one Bristol Mercury IV radial engine rated at 530 hp (395 kW)
Performance: maximum speed 221 mph (355 km/h) at 16,405 ft (5000 m); cruising speed 143 mph (230 km/h) at optimum altitude; climb to 9,845 ft (3000 m) in four minutes; service ceiling 31,170 ft (9500 m); range 373 miles (600 km)
Weights: empty 2,888 lb (1310 kg); maximum take-off 3,660 lb (1660 kg)
Dimensions: wingspan 34 ft 5⅓ in (10.50 m); length 25 ft 2⅓ in (7.68 m); height 8 ft 4 in (2.54 m); wing area 276.43 sq ft (25.68 m²)
Armament: two 0.303-in (7.7-mm) Breda-SAFAT fixed forward-firing machine-guns in the forward fuselage

Caproni Ca 133 and Ca 148

Designed by Rodolfo Verduzio after his return to the Caproni company in 1934, the **Ca 133** was an improved version of the Ca 101. Of welded steel-tube construction with metal and fabric covering, the Ca 133 featured faired engine nacelles with NACA cowlings, spatted main wheels, flaps on the trailing edge of the high-set wing, and modified tail surfaces. The civil version, accommodating up to 16 passengers, was used by Ala Littoria, and the military version saw wide service with the Regia Aeronautica, particularly in Italian East Africa.

SPECIFICATION	
Caproni Ca 133	14,473 lb (6565 kg)
Type: three-crew passenger/troop transport and bomber	**Dimensions:** wingspan 69 ft 8½ in (21.25 m); length 50 ft 4¼ in (15.35 m); height 13 ft 1½ in (4.00 m), wing area 699.68 sq ft (65.00 m²)
Powerplant: three Piaggio Stella VII C.16 radial engines each rated at 460 hp (343 kW)	
Performance: maximum speed 174 mph (280 km/h) at optimum altitude; cruising speed 143 mph (230 km/h) at optimum altitude; service ceiling 18,045 ft (5500 m); range 839 miles (1350 km)	**Armament:** four 0.303-in (7.7-mm) Breda-SAFAT trainable machine-guns, plus up to 1,102 lb (500 kg) of bombs carried under the fuselage
Weights: empty 8,818 lb (4000 kg), maximum take-off	**Payload:** up to 18 passengers or troops

This brightly coloured Ca 133 served with Bomberstaffel 1B, Bombergeschwader, Fliegerregiment Nr 2 of the Österreichische Luftstretkräfte (Austrian air force) at Zeltweg in 1937.

Variants

Ca 133S: bomber aircraft converted for use in the air ambulance role
Ca 133T: a number of bomber aircraft deployed as military transports
Ca 148: introduced in 1938, this was an improved version of the **Ca 133**; a small number served in East Africa and some flew with the post-war Italian air force; changes included the forward movement of the cockpit, relocation of the main cabin door from its original position to the rear of the trailing edge, and the introduction of strengthened landing gear

Caproni Ca 164

Built in small numbers for use as a trainer and touring aircraft, the **Ca 164** was a biplane of Caproni's much-favoured inverted-sesquiplane configuration. The aircraft saw limited service in World War II for a number of roles including, for a short time, tactical reconnaissance in Croatia.

The Ca 164 featured a fabric-covered airframe that combined wooden wings with a fuselage and tail unit of welded steel tube and had fixed tailskid landing gear with divided main units.

SPECIFICATION	
Caproni Ca 164	nine minutes 10 seconds; service ceiling 13,780 ft (4200 m); range 329 miles (530 km)
Type: two-seat training and touring aircraft	**Weights:** empty 1,874 lb (850 kg); maximum take-off 2,590 lb (1175 kg)
Powerplant: one Alfa Romeo 115-I inverted inline engine rated at 185 hp (138 kW)	
Performance: maximum speed 143 mph (230 km/h) at optimum altitude; cruising speed 114 mph (183 km/h) at optimum altitude; climb to 6,560 ft (2000 m) in	**Dimensions:** wingspan 31 ft 11¾ in (9.75 m); length 25 ft 4¾ in (7.74 m); height 9 ft 10 in (3.00 m); wing area 241.12 sq ft (22.40 m²)

Caproni Bergamaschi Ca 135

The Cantieri Aeronautici Bergamaschi was established in 1927, but produced only a few training aircraft before it was taken over by Caproni in 1931 to become Caproni Aeronautica Bergamasca, better known as Caproni Bergamaschi. In 1933, the company secured the services of Cesare Pallavicino, previously of

SPECIFICATION	
Caproni Ca 135/P.XI	(6050 kg); maximum take-off 21,050 lb (9550 kg)
Type: four-crew medium bomber	**Dimensions:** wingspan 61 ft 8¼ in (18.80 m); length 47 ft 2 in (14.38 m); height 11 ft 1¾ in (3.40 m); wing area 645.86 sq ft (60.00 m²)
Powerplant: two Piaggio P.XI RC.40 radial engines each rated at 1,000 hp (746 kW)	
Performance: maximum speed 273 mph (440 km/h) at 15,750 ft (4800 m); cruising speed 230 mph (370 km/h) at optimum altitude; climb to 13,125 ft (4000 m) in 13 minutes 20 seconds; service ceiling 22,965 ft (7000 m); range 1,243 miles (2000 km)	**Armament:** one 0.5-in (12.7-mm) Breda-SAFAT trainable machine-gun in each of the nose, dorsal and ventral turrets, plus up to 3,527 lb (1600 kg) of bombs carried internally
Weights: empty 13,340 lb	

Breda, as its chief designer. It was under the stimulus of Pallavicino's work that Caproni Bergamaschi soon became a more important source of advanced aircraft than the parent company.

The first aircraft to come from the company under its new ownership was the **PL.3** two-seat long-range monoplane, which was powered by one 700-hp (522-kW) Fiat A.59 (licence-built Pratt & Whitney Hornet) radial engine. This machine was built in 1934 to participate in the MacRobertson race between London and Melbourne. A virtually contemporary design was the **PS.1** four-seat cabin monoplane.

The emphasis placed on

Eight Ca 135s were assigned to the Spanish Nationalists. Of these, three crashed in a storm during their delivery flight and the remainder were declined by the Spanish. The five remaining aircraft therefore joined Italian training units.

clean design was apparent in the **Caproni Ca 135**. The machine was conceived as a medium bomber, and the prototype made its maiden flight on 1 April 1935 with the powerplant of two 800-hp (596-kW) Asso XI RC radial engines.

Caproni Bergamaschi Ca 306, Ca 308, Ca 309 Ghibli

First revealed at the 1935 Milan Exhibition, the **Ca 306** was an elegant light transport with accommodation for a pilot and co-pilot plus six passengers. The Ca 306 was a low-wing cantilever monoplane, mainly of plywood-skinned wooden construction. Its powerplant comprised two inverted inline piston engines in the form of Walter Major 6, de Havilland Gipsy Six or Alfa

Romeo 115-I units. The Ca 306 entered production as the **Ca 308 Borea** (north wind) and was built to the extent of only eight aircraft (six for Ala Littoria and two for the Italian colonial administration of Libya), but nonetheless had considerable importance as the progenitor of a long line of military aircraft.

The first of these military descendants was the **Ca 309 Ghibli** (desert wind) that made its maiden

flight in October 1936 as the prototype of a variant intended for the general-purpose role in Italy's North and East African colonies. The Ca 309 switched to a mixed structure in which the flying surfaces of the Ca 306 were combined with a new fuselage of welded steel tube construction covered with light alloy panels and fabric. The fuselage of the Ca 309 retained the Ca 306's basically rectangular cross section, but introduced a revised forward section in which the cockpit was moved farther to the rear to allow the incorporation of a glazed bombardier position. The other major change

was effected in the powerplant and the main landing gear arrangement: the former became a pair of Alfa Romeo 115-I or -II engines each rated at 185 or 200 hp (138 or 149 kW), and the latter became a pair of faired cantilever units carrying spatted wheels.

The type offered a useful combination of performance, economy, sturdiness and reliability. It was accordingly ordered in modest numbers for service with the Aviazione Presidio Coloniale and Aviazione Sahariana in the

light bomber, reconnaissance, transport and close-support roles in the **Ca 309 Serie VI** final subvariant with one or two 20-mm forward-firing cannon in the fuselage. Production of the Ca 309 totalled 243 aircraft, and most of these were lost in the first campaigns of the North African war that started after Italy's June 1940 entry into World War II, when the 'colonial warplane' proved wholly lacking in the performance and armament required to survive against determined air opposition.

SPECIFICATION

Caproni Bergamaschi Ca 309 Ghibli
Type: three-crew light reconnaissance bomber
Powerplant: two Alfa Romeo 115-II inverted inline engines each rated at 200 hp (149 kW)
Performance: maximum speed 155 mph (250 km/h) at 2,460 ft (750 m); cruising speed 130 mph (210 km/h) at 4,920 ft (1500 m); climb to 9,845 ft (3000 m) in 17 minutes 30 seconds; service ceiling 14,765 ft (4500 m); range 416 miles (670 km)
Weights: empty 4,409 lb

(2000 kg); maximum take-off 6,603 lb (2995 kg)
Dimensions: wingspan 53 ft 1¾ in (16.20 m); length 43 ft 7½ in (13.30 m); height 10 ft 8 in (3.25 m); wing area 416.58 sq ft (38.70 m²)
Armament: two 0.303-in (7.7-mm) Breda-SAFAT fixed forward-firing machine-guns in the leading edges of the wingroots, and one 0.303-in (7.7-mm) Breda-SAFAT trainable forward-firing machine-gun in the nose position, plus up to 740 lb (335 kg) of bombs carried externally

In standard configuration, the Ca 308 seated its two-man crew side-by-side in an enclosed cockpit and could seat six passengers in the main cabin.

Caproni Bergamaschi Ca 310–Ca 316 Libeccio

It was appreciated that a more powerful version of the Ca 308/309 would have potential as a military aircraft. Caproni therefore developed this more potent type in parallel with the Ca 309.

The resulting **Ca 310 Libeccio** (south-west wind) flew in prototype form during April 1937. The only major changes from the Ca 309 were limited to the forward fuselage and the engine nacelles and in the retractable main landing-gear units. The uprated powerplant comprised two 430-hp (321-kW) Piaggio P.VII C.16 Stella radial engines.

The Ca 310 had been planned as an export model, but the Italian air force ordered a small batch for evaluation purposes: 16

of these aircraft were sent to Spain in July 1938 for operational trials in the hands of a reconnaissance bomber squadron of the Italian expeditionary force, operating alongside the Nationalist insurgents in the Spanish Civil War. Caproni soon captured orders from Peru, Yugoslavia, Hungary and Norway. Most of these countries soon discovered that the performance of the Ca 310 fell somewhat below expectations and, after taking four machines, Norway refused to accept any further deliveries. However, it then agreed to take 12 examples of the more powerful **Ca 312**. In the event, none of these 12 aircraft had been delivered before Norway was invaded by German forces in April 1940 and the

Norway took just four examples of the Ca 310 (illustrated). A subsequent British order for a generally improved aircraft was approved by Germany as late as March 1940, even though the UK and Germany were at war!

aircraft were taken on charge by the Italian air force. Hungary was also unhappy with its Ca 310s and in 1940 the surviving 33 machines were returned to Italy, where they were refurbished by Caproni and issued to the 50° Stormo d'Assalto as a temporary replacement for its Breda Ba 65s.

Potentially the most important customer for the Ca 310 was the UK, which was undertaking a major expansion of the RAF in a programme that was accelerated after the Munich crisis of October 1938. In its search for an effective crew trainer, Britain chose the Ca 310 and negotiations continued into the period after the outbreak of World War II, but the deal eventually came to nothing.

A version of the Ca 310

that did not proceed past the prototype stage was the **Ca 310 Idro** seaplane.

In 1938 Caproni flew the **Ca 310bis** prototype, which was a P.VII RC.35-engined Ca 310 with a completely glazed and heavily-framed nose. The new type was ordered into production as the **Ca 311** that first flew in prototype form during April 1939 with the dorsal turret moved to a position immediately behind the cockpit and additional fuselage glazing.

The Ca 311 began to replace the Meridionali Ro.37 biplane in Italian service from 1940, although full re-equipment

did not occur until 1941.

The sole subvariant of the Ca 311 was the **Ca 311M** (**Modificato**, or modified), which reverted to a more conventional forward fuselage. Total production of the Ca 311 and Ca 311M series for the Italian air force exceeded 320 aircraft, and these served with all but two of the Italian air force's gruppi osservazione aerea in theatres as diverse as North Africa and the USSR.

In addition to Norway's Ca 312s, another 12 or so aircraft were built to a revised **Ca 312M** standard as flying classroom and crew-training machines.

SPECIFICATION

Caproni Bergamaschi Ca 314A Libeccio
Type: three-seat light bomber and convoy escort warplane
Powerplant: two Isotta-Fraschini Delta RC.35I-DS Serie II inverted-Vee piston engines each rated at 730 hp (544 kW)
Performance: maximum speed 245 mph (395 km/h) at 13,125 ft (4000 m); cruising speed 199 mph (320 km/h) at 14,765 ft (4500 m); initial climb rate 797 ft (243 m) per minute; service ceiling 21,000 ft (6400 m); range 1,050 miles (1690 km)
Weights: empty 10,053 lb (4560 kg); maximum take-off 14,594 lb (6620 kg)
Dimensions: wingspan 54 ft 7½ in

(16.65 m); length 38 ft 8½ in (11.80 m); height 12 ft 1⅓ in (3.70 m); wing area 421.94 sq ft (39.20 m²)
Armament: two 0.5-in (12.7-mm) Scotti/Isotta-Fraschini fixed forward-firing machine-guns in the leading edges of the wingroots, one 0.5-in (12.7-mm) Scotti/Isotta-Fraschini trainable machine-gun in the Caproni-Lanciani Delta E dorsal turret, and one 0.303-in (7.7-mm) Breda-SAFAT trainable rearward-firing machine-gun in the ventral position, plus up to 661 lb (300 kg) of bombs carried in a lower-fuselage bay or up to 705 lb (320 kg) of bombs carried externally under the fuselage

435

Notable for its considerable length, the Italian 17.7-in (450-mm) torpedo offered the Ca 313RA a significant anti-shipping capability.

The only subvariants of the Ca 312 were not built even in prototype form; these were the **Ca 312bis** export model and the **Ca 312IS** (**Idro Siluranti**, or torpedo seaplane).

In an effort to improve the Ca 310's performance, Caproni decided to use an all-new powerplant. The prototype of this new development was a Ca 310 revised with a pair of Isotta-Fraschini A.120 IRCC.40 engines, and this made its first flight in December 1939. The other major change in this important model was the incorporation of heavier armament.

The initial production model was known to the Italians as the **Ca 313RPB.1**, the letter suffix indicating **Ricognizione Piccolo Bombardamento** (reconnaissance and light bombing). The version was slated for delivery against new contracts from the British, French and Swedes in subvariants known as the **Ca 313B**, **Ca 313F** and

Ca 313S. The British order was overtaken by events and not fulfilled; five aircraft were delivered to France before Italy entered the war, and the Swedish order was completed from November 1940, when orders for the type had risen to 84 aircraft. The problems that were to plague the Ca 313 became evident during the course of the Ca 313S's delivery programme. Before this was completed at the beginning of 1941, engine and other failings had caused the loss of two aircraft and the forced landings of other machines during the course of the flights from Italy to southern Sweden. The Ca 313 was seriously let down by poor design, which included the location of the fuel lines close to the engine exhausts, with the result that any fuel leak generally started an in-flight fire. Nevertheless, the Ca 313S served Sweden in the maritime patrol role through most of World War

II until it was supplanted by the Saab B 17. Most of the aircraft were modified to the **S 16A** and **S 16B** standards with local improvements and two of the aircraft were adapted as transports with the local designation **Tp 16**.

After it had completed the Swedish order, Caproni started work on the **Ca 313RPB.2** version for the Italian air force but, in the event, only the first 60 aircraft were delivered.

In 1940 the Luftwaffe expressed an interest in the Ca 313 as the basis for a crew trainer and Caproni delivered three **Ca 313G** prototypes in the course of 1941. This model was basically similar to the Ca 313RPB.2 except for its equipment and a revised nose, and in 1943 Germany ordered 905 aircraft of this

type. So poor was Caproni's production rate, however, that only 16 of the aircraft had been delivered before production of the Libeccio series was halted in 1944. The designation **Ca 315** was allocated to a version of the Ca 313G that was at one stage proposed for licensed production in Germany.

The other 60 aircraft of the Ca 313RPB.2 order were in fact completed as **Ca 313RA** (**Ricognizione Aerosiluranti**, or reconnaissance and air-launched torpedo) warplanes to a standard that was later redesignated **Ca 314 Libeccio**. The revised type was pioneered by the conversion of an eventual seven Ca 313RPB.2 warplanes to the interim **Ca 313RPB/S** standard with provision for a 17.7-in (450-mm) torpedo carried under the fuselage.

The **Ca 314A** was the convoy escort variant of the Ca 314 series, and was otherwise known as the **Ca 314Sc** in which the letter suffix stood for **Scorta** (escort). The type used Delta RC.35I-DS Serie II engines and had heavier

armament. The type entered service in 1942, but deliveries proved slow and erratic due to difficulties in production.

The **Ca 314B** was the torpedo bomber counterpart of the Ca 314A with provision under the fuselage for one 1,984-lb (900-kg) torpedo, one 1,102-lb (500-kg) bomb or two 551-lb (250-kg) bombs.

The **Ca 314C** was the attack bomber counterpart of the Ca 314A, and differed from the baseline model in its provision for two 0.5-in (12.7-mm) machine-guns to be added under the wing-roots and in its internal or external bomb load. Most Ca 314Cs were fitted with two 780-hp (582-kW) Delta RC.35I-DS Serie III engines.

After the Italian armistice of September 1943, the Ca 313 and Ca 314 fought on both sides. Surviving aircraft were retained in Italian service after World War II, but were finally retired in 1950 after some consideration had been given to production of the **Ca 313AVS** as an instrument flying trainer version of the Ca 313.

In addition to the mainstream variants, a handful of Ca 316 floatplane prototypes was produced. The aircraft were intended for maritime reconnaissance missions after a catapult launch.

Caproni Bergamaschi Ca 331 Raffica

The first of the company's machines with an all-metal structure, the **Ca 331 Raffica** (squall) was a low-wing cantilever monoplane that first flew in prototype form on 31 August 1940. Intended as a high-speed reconnaissance bomber, the aircraft had tailwheel landing gear with all three units retractable, and was powered by two 770-hp (574-kW) Isotta-Fraschini Delta RC.40 inverted-Vee engines.

In its official trials the Ca 331 revealed good performance and handling.

The Regia Aeronautica initially expressed no interest in the type, however, but the Luftwaffe was more enthusiastic and undertook its own trials during 1942. Initial plans for production to meet German needs were set aside for a number of reasons including an incipient shortage of aluminium alloy, however.

The initial model was the **Ca 331A** reconnaissance bomber, carrying up to 2,205 lb (1000 kg) of bombs internally. During 1941-2 the Regia

Aeronautica reconsidered the Ca 331 and decided that it now needed the type, albeit in modified form as the **Ca 331B** or **Ca 331CN** three-seat night-fighter. The second of the two Ca 331A prototypes was modified to this standard and made its maiden flight in the summer of 1942. The CA 331B was powered by two 840-hp (627-kW) Delta IV engines and introduced a revised forward fuselage with a 'solid' nose that was initially fitted with six 0.5-in (12.7-mm) fixed

forward-firing machine-guns, although this arrangement was later modified to two 0.5-in (12.7-mm) machine-guns and four 20-mm Mauser cannon. The second Ca 331B prototype, which was not flown, had the uprated engines later installed in the first prototype and its fixed forward-firing armament comprised four 0.5-in (12.7-mm) machine-guns and two 20-mm Ikaria cannon.

Plans were made for large-scale manufacture of

the Ca 331B, but the September 1943 armistice with the Allies ended all hope of production. The Germans subsequently disassembled the two night-fighter prototypes. Further development of the Ca 331 night-fighter at that time was centred on the use of an uprated powerplant of two 1,475-hp (1100-kW) Fiat RA.1050 RC.58 (licence-built Daimler-Benz DB 605A-1) inverted-Vee engines, for an estimated maximum speed of 401 mph (645 km/h), and the installation of a 37-mm cannon in a ventral fairing.

SPECIFICATION	
Caproni Bergamaschi Ca 331B Raffica	(4600 kg); maximum take-off 14,991 lb (6800 kg)
Type: three-seat night-fighter and night intruder	**Dimensions:** wingspan 53 ft 9⅔ in (16.40 m); length 38 ft 6¼ in (11.74 m); height 11 ft 5 in (3.48 m); wing area 413.35 sq ft (38.40 m²)
Powerplant: two Isotta-Fraschini Delta IV inverted-Vee engines each rated at 840 hp (627 kW)	
Performance: maximum speed 314 mph (505 km/h) at 17,390 ft (5300 m); cruising speed 280 mph (450 km/h) at optimum altitude; climb to 13,125 ft (4000 m) in 9 minutes 48 seconds; service ceiling 26,575 ft (8100 m); range 1,128 miles (1815 km)	**Armament:** various fixed forward-firing armament fits (see above) and one 0.5-in (12.7-mm) Breda-SAFAT trainable machine-gun in each of the Caproni-Lanciani dorsal turret and ventral positions, plus up to 2,646 lb (1200 kg) of bombs carried internally and externally
Weights: empty 10,141 lb	

Notable for the extreme cleanliness of its fuselage contours, the Ca 331 had an inverted gull wing and dihedralled horizontal tail surfaces.

Caproni Campini N.1

Ingeniere Secondo Campini founded a company in 1931 to undertake research into reaction propulsion. In 1939 he produced a power unit for installation in an airframe which he had induced Caproni to build for flight evaluation. Designated as the **Caproni Campini N.1**, and sometimes known inaccurately as the **CC.2**, this machine was a low-wing cantilever monoplane with a large tubular-section fuselage and

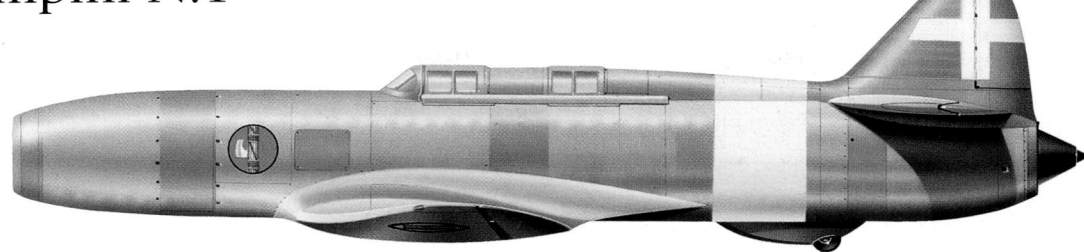

outward-retracting main landing gear units. It made its maiden flight at Taliedo

on 28 August 1940. An all-metal machine with tandem two-seat accommodation, the N.1 was powered by an Isotta-Fraschini radial engine buried in the forward fuselage and used to drive a variable-pitch ducted fan compressor. The compressed air from this unit was passed through a variable-area propelling nozzle at the rear of a

On 30 November 1941, Mario de Bernardi and Ingeniere Pedace flew the N.1 for a distance of 168 miles (270 km) from Taliedo to Guidonia at an average speed of just 130 mph (209 km/h). While it performed important pioneering work, the N.1 ultimately proved to be an evolutionary dead-end.

jetpipe in which fuel could be burned to increase thrust. However, even with the use of this primitive type of afterburning, the aircraft had a maximum speed of only 233 mph

(375 km/h). The aircraft was at the same time a pioneer of reaction propulsion but also a technical dead-end, and is today preserved in the Museo della Scienza Tecnica in Milan.

SPECIFICATION	
Caproni Campini N.1	altitude
Type: two-seat research aircraft	**Weights:** empty 8,024 lb
Powerplant: one Isotta-Fraschini	(3640 kg); maximum take-off
radial engine rated at 900 hp	9,250 lb (4195 kg)
(671 kW) and driving a three-stage	**Dimensions:** wingspan 52 ft
fan compressor	(15.85 m); length 43 ft (13.10 m);
Performance: maximum speed	wing area 387.51 sq ft (36.00 m²)
233 mph (375 km/h) at optimum	

Caproni Trento F-5

Caproni could not survive the economic problems that engulfed Europe after World War II and went bankrupt in 1950. The Caproni group had comprised more than 20 companies, and one of the

few surviving members of the collapse was Aeroplane Caproni Trento. In 1951, this company began the construction of a small turbojet-powered trainer of original design.

The resulting **F-5** was a

low-wing cantilever monoplane of all-wood construction, entirely skinned with plywood except for the fabric covering of the rudder and elevators. Power was provided by a French-built Palas turbojet engine, mounted low in the mid-fuselage.

The F-5 was Italy's first post-war lightweight jet-powered aircraft, but despite energetic sales efforts it failed to become a life-saver for the company, leaving the sailplane-building Caproni Vizzola as the last surviving unit of this once great company.

The F-5 had landing gear of tricycle type, with all three units retractable. The cabin was enclosed by jettisonable canopies and accommodated two in tandem with dual controls.

SPECIFICATION	
Caproni Trento F-5	at optimum altitude; service ceiling
Type: two-seat trainer	26,245 ft (8000 m)
Powerplant: one Turboméca Palas	**Weights:** empty 1,036 lb (470 kg);
turbojet engine rated at 331 lb st	maximum take-off 1,653 lb (750 kg)
(1.47 kN)	**Dimensions:** wingspan 25 ft 9 in
Performance: maximum speed	(7.85 m); length 21 ft 7¾ in
224 mph (360 km/h) at sea level;	(6.60 m); wing area 107.64 sq ft
cruising speed 242 mph (390 km/h)	(10.00 m²)

Caproni Vizzola C22J

On 21 July 1980, the long-established Italian company of Caproni Vizzola Costruzioni Aeronautiche SpA flew the prototype of a lightweight turbojet-

powered basic training aircraft designated as the **C22J**. Bearing some resemblance to the company's family of **Calif** sailplanes, the C22J shared

with the **Calif A-21SJ** jet-powered sailplane that aircraft's Microturbo TRS powerplant.

A shoulder-wing cantilever monoplane, the C22J had a tadpole-shaped fuselage structure designed as a lifting body, a T-tail

SPECIFICATION	
Caproni Vizzola C22J	(740 km)
Type: two-seat basic flying trainer	**Weights:** empty 1,587 lb (720 kg);
Powerplant: two Microturbo TRS	maximum take-off 2,502 lb
18-046 turbojet engines each rated	(1135 kg)
at 220 lb st (0.98 kN)	**Dimensions:** wingspan 32 ft 9¾ in
Performance: maximum cruising	(10.00 m); length 20 ft 3¾ in
speed 299 mph (482 km/h) at sea	(6.19 m); height 6 ft 2 in (1.88 m);
level; economic cruising speed	wing area 94.19 sq ft (8.75 m²)
202 mph (325 km/h) at 9,845 ft	**Armament:** provision for up to
(3000 m); initial climb rate 1,810 ft	441 lb (200 kg) of disposable stores
(552 m) per minute; service ceiling	carried on two or four underwing
24,930 ft (7600 m); range 460 miles	hardpoints

mounted on a slender tail boom, retractable tricycle landing gear, and its twin-engined powerplant mounted in the fuselage.

Considered suitable for a wide range of roles in addition to that of a trainer,

Largely of metal construction, the C22J used some glassfibre for fairings or skins in unstressed areas.

plans were later made by Agusta, which had acquired a 50 per cent interest in the C22J programme during 1981, to develop a **C22R** prototype for the evaluation of the type's potential for FAC, reconnaissance and tactical Elint. Nothing came of these plans, and the C22J did not enter large-scale production.

Caproni Vizzola F.4 and F.5

In 1937 Caproni Vizzola established its own design office and the first two aircraft to come from this

new design stable were the **Caproni Vizzola F.4** and **F.5** single-seat fighters. These two types were

developed in parallel on the basis of a common airframe of stressed-skin construction with a

plywood-covered wooden wing and light alloy-covered steel tube fuselage. The two types differed mainly in their planned powerplant, that for the F.4 being based on the 890-hp

(664-kW) Isotta-Fraschini Asso L.121 RC.40 inverted-Vee engine and that for the F.5 being based on the Fiat A.74 RC.38. It was decided subsequently to fit the F.4 with a 1,175-hp (876-kW)

Daimler-Benz DB 601A inverted-Vee unit, the delay caused by this change meaning that the prototype of the F.5 became the first to fly, an event that took place early in 1939. Testing resulted in an order for a pre-production batch of 14 aircraft, these differing from the prototype by having an enlarged vertical tail surface and a fixed tailwheel. Despite plans to build several developments of the F.5, none materialised and only the 14 pre-production aircraft were completed.

The F.4 was flown with its Daimler-Benz engine during 1940, but no production aircraft followed as it was decided to produce a more developed fighter as the **F.6**.

The F.4 (illustrated) and F.5 gave way to the F.6, which offered superb performance but was ultimately cancelled.

SPECIFICATION

Caproni Vizzola F.5
Type: single-seat fighter
Powerplant: one Fiat A.74 RC.38 radial engine rated at 870 hp (649 kW)
Performance: maximum speed 317 mph (510 km/h) at 9,845 ft (3000 m); cruising speed 292 mph (470 km/h) at optimum altitude; climb to 21,325 ft (6500 m) in 6 minutes 30 seconds; service ceiling 31,170 ft (9500 m); range 478 miles (770 km)
Weights: empty 4,078 lb (1850 kg); maximum take-off 5,181 lb (2350 kg)
Dimensions: wingspan 37 ft 1 in (11.30 m); length 25 ft 11 in (7.90 m); height 9 ft 10 in (3.00 m); wing area 189.45 sq ft (17.60 m²)
Armament: two 0.5-in (12.7-mm) Breda-SAFAT fixed forward-firing machine-guns in the sides of the forward fuselage

CASA 201 Alcotan

CASA, otherwise Construcciones Aeronáuticas SA, was founded in 1923 and work began in the following year with licensed production of Breguet reconnaissance bombers. CASA subsequently licence-built numerous types, including the Breguet Bre.19A.2, Dornier Do J Wal, Do R Super Wal, Vickers Vildebeeste, Gotha Go 145A (**CASA 1.145**), Bü 131 Jungmann (**CASA 1.131**), Bücker Bü 133 Jungmeister (**CASA 1.133**), Junkers Ju 52/3m (**CASA 352L**) and Heinkel He 111H-16 (**CASA 2.111**). The latter aircraft was powered by Rolls-Royce Merlin engines.

After World War II, design and manufacture of aircraft in Germany was banned for some years and CASA built the prototype of the Do 25 on behalf of Dr Claudius Dornier. CASA subsequently licence-built a batch of 50 Do 27 aircraft with the designation **CASA 127** for the Spanish air force.

CASA's most recent licence-built type was the Northrop F-5A Freedom Fighter. Seventy such aircraft were ordered, comprising 19 SF-5A and 17 RF-5A single-seaters as well as 34 SF-5B two-seaters. The first CASA-assembled aircraft flew in May 1968 and production ended in 1971.

Long before this, however, CASA had designed its own aircraft. The first of these was the CASA III parasol-wing sporting monoplane with tandem two-seat accommodation. The type was designed in 1929, and production totalled 10 aircraft with a variety of engine types.

The company's first transport was the twin-engined **CASA 201 Alcotan** (kestrel), whose prototype first flew in February 1949. This was a low-wing monoplane of basically all-metal construction with retractable tailwheel landing gear. Several versions were offered with alternative engine installations and, following the evaluation of five prototypes, the Spanish air force ordered an eventual 112 examples of the production version, which had the service designation **T.5**. Shortage of the specified engine, the 500-hp (373-kW) Sirio S.VIIA radial, necessitated the storage of some airframes, but others were completed with the 475-hp (354-kW) Armstrong Siddeley Cheetah 27 radial.

Variants

CASA 201A Alcotan: passenger transport version with Cheetah 27 engines
CASA 201B Alcotan: passenger transport version with Sirio S.VIIIA engines
CASA 201D Alcotan: blind-flying, multi-engine, navigation and radio trainer version with Cheetah 27 engines
CASA 201E Alcotan: bombing and photographic trainer with Cheetah 27 engines
CASA 201F Alcotan: blind-flying, multi-engine, navigation and radio trainer version with Sirio S.VIIA engines
CASA 201G Alcotan: bombing and photographic trainer with Sirio S.VIIA engines

As a transport, the Alcotan carried a crew of two and up to 10 passengers.

SPECIFICATION

CASA 201A/D/E Alcotan
Type: two-crew light transport and trainer
Powerplant: two Armstrong Siddeley Cheetah 27 radial engines each rated at 475 hp (354 kW)
Performance: maximum speed 202 mph (325 km/h) at optimum altitude; cruising speed 193 mph (310 km/h) at 6,560 ft (2000 m); service ceiling 18,370 ft (5600 m); range 621 miles (1000 km)
Weights: empty 7,826 lb (3550 kg); maximum take-off 11,283 lb (5095 kg)
Dimensions: wingspan 60 ft 4½ in (18.40 m); length 45 ft 3¼ in (13.80 m); height 12 ft 7½ in (3.85 m); wing area 449.95 sq ft (41.80 m²)
Payload: up to 10 passengers

CASA 202 Halcon

Designed primarily for use on Spain's internal air routes, the **CASA 202 Halcon** (falcon) first flew in May 1953, and 20 were subsequently ordered. Generally similar to, but slightly larger than the Alcotan, the Halcon differed in having tricycle landing gear and accommodation for a crew of three and 14 passengers in a heated and air-conditioned cabin.

However, the production examples of the Halcon were in fact delivered to the Spanish air force under the designation **T.6**.

The Halcon served for several years before being replaced by the C-207 Azor. Some CASA-built Junkers Ju 52/3m transports had been replaced by the Halcon; others soldiered on to be replaced by the Azor.

SPECIFICATION

CASA 202 Halcon
Type: three-crew transport
Powerplant: two Elizalde Beta 9C-29-750 radial engines each rated at 775 hp (578 kW)
Performance: maximum speed 214 mph (346 km/h) at 9,315 ft (2840 m); cruising speed 186 mph (300 km/h) at optimum altitude; service ceiling 24,770 ft (7550 m)
Weights: empty 11,618 lb (5270 kg); maximum take-off 17,086 lb (7750 kg)
Dimensions: wingspan 70 ft 8½ in (21.55 m); length 52 ft 6 in (16.00 m); height 12 ft 5½ in (3.80 m); wing area 617.33 sq ft (57.35 m²)
Payload: up to 14 passengers

CASA 207 Azor

The **CASA 207 Azor** was essentially a scaled-up development of the Halcon. The aircraft flew for the first time on 28 September 1955 as a contender originally for the domestic civil market. Having found no takers, it was rescued from obscurity by the Spanish government, which placed an initial order for 10 for the Ejército del Aire (Spanish air force).

Carrying a crew of four and providing cabin accommodation for up to 40 passengers, the **CASA 207A** initial model received the Spanish air force designation **T.7A** and entered service in 1960; two of the 10 were fitted experimentally with Pratt & Whitney Double Wasp radial engines. The aircraft of the original batch were followed by a further 10 aircraft, configured for either the paratroop transport or freight-carrying roles. Designated **CASA 207C** (military designation

The two CASA 207 prototypes, as well as the 20 production Azor aircraft, were used by the Spanish air force into the first half of the 1980s, in the hands of the 35th Wing of its Transport Command at Madrid-Getafe.

T.7B), these were distinguishable by the large cargo-loading double doors at the rear of their fuselage, and could transport up to 37 paratroops or freight. In 1973 CASA proposed a four-turboprop STOL design, known as the **CASA 401**, to replace the Azor, but this was eventually abandoned in favour of the CASA C.212 Aviocar.

SPECIFICATION

CASA 207 Azor
Type: three-crew short/medium-range troop and cargo transport
Powerplant: two Bristol Hercules 730 radial engines each rated at 2,040 hp (1522 kW)
Performance: maximum speed 261 mph (420 km/h) at 4,920 ft (1500 m); cruising speed 249 mph (400 km/h) at 12,340 ft (3760 m); initial climb rate 1,083 ft (330 m) per minute; service ceiling 26,245 ft (8000 m); range 1,460 miles (2350 km)
Weights: empty (207A) 23,370 lb (10600 kg); maximum take-off (207A) 35,275 lb (16000 kg) or (207C) 36,376 lb (16500 kg)
Dimensions: wingspan 91 ft 2½ in (27.80 m); length 68 ft 5 in (20.85 m); height 25 ft 5 in (17.75 m); wing area 923.15 sq ft (85.80 m²)
Payload: (207A) 6,806 lb (3087 kg) or (207C) 8,818 lb (4000 kg)

CASA C.101 Aviojet

Designed by CASA with assistance from MBB and Northrop, the **C.101 Aviojet** trainer and light attack aircraft has won orders from Spain, Chile, Honduras and Jordan.

The first and last of four prototypes made their maiden flights on 27 June 1977 and 17 April 1978 respectively, and all four aircraft were handed over to the Spanish air force for trials at the end of 1978. The C.101 is of modular construction, to reduce cost and complexity, and ample space was deliberately provided for avionics and equipment to meet any conceivable requirement. Features include straight horizontal flying surfaces but a swept vertical tail surface, a single turbofan of high bypass ratio for good fuel economy, lateral inlets above the wing, a tandem arrangement of vertically stepped Martin-Baker Mk 10L zero/zero ejection seats, a pressurised cockpit with separate canopies and slotted flaps. The most unusual feature is that all versions have a large fuselage bay beneath the rear cockpit in which armament, a reconnaissance camera, ECM jammer, laser designator or other devices can be housed.

An initial contract from the Spanish air force covered the purchase of 60 **C.101EB-01** trainers, which were given the local designation and name **E.25 Mirlo** (blackbird). The C.101EB-01 is powered by the 3,500-lb st (15.57-kN) TFE731-2-2J turbofan. A second contract covered another 28 aircraft and all the surviving machines received a nav/attack system modernisation between 1990 and 1992.

The C.101EB proved to have low-level performance that was somewhat better than predicted, but was disappointing at higher altitude. Thus the export **C.101BB** attack/trainer is powered by a TFE731-3-1J giving an extra 200 lb (0.89 kN) of thrust, and uses the aircraft's inbuilt provision for armament carried on six underwing pylons: the

The C.101 has now served the Spanish for two decades. An Aviojet variant submitted for the USAF/USN JPATS requirement was unsuccessful.

Spanish C.101EB aircraft have hardpoints, but these are not used. The C.101BB uses the underfuselage bay for quick-change reconnaissance, ECM, laser designator or twin 0.5-in (12.7-mm) machine-gun packs as an alternative to the 30-mm DEFA cannon pod mounted on the centreline.

The **C.101BB-02** was exported to Chile, which received four CASA-built aircraft and 10 partially manufactured and wholly assembled in Chile by ENAER. All are designated as **T-36 Halcon** (hawk) in service and, although intended for advanced training, were modified with ranging radar in the nose to serve as **A-36BB** tactical weapons trainers.

The **C.101CC** first flew on 16 November 1983 as a dedicated attack aircraft with one TFE731-5-1J turbofan. There is no increase in maximum weaponload since the pylons have not been changed, but an increase in maximum take-off weight allows more fuel to be carried with a given weaponload.

Chile placed an order for 23 **C.101CC-02** attack aircraft in 1984, of which one was built in Spain, three delivered in kit form and the remaining 19 manufactured under licence in Chile. Four very similar **C.101BB-03** aircraft were delivered to Honduras. The first A-36 briefly served as a demonstrator for the proposed **A-36M**, with dummy BAe Sea Eagle missiles underwing, but this project foundered. Sixteen examples of the **C.101CC-04** have been delivered to Jordan to serve as advanced trainers.

On 25 May 1985 CASA flew the TFE731-5-1J-engined **C.101DD** prototype with new avionics which include a HUD. The aircraft also has HOTAS controls and is compatible with the AGM-65 missile. Intended as an improved trainer and light attack aircraft, the variant has yet to win orders.

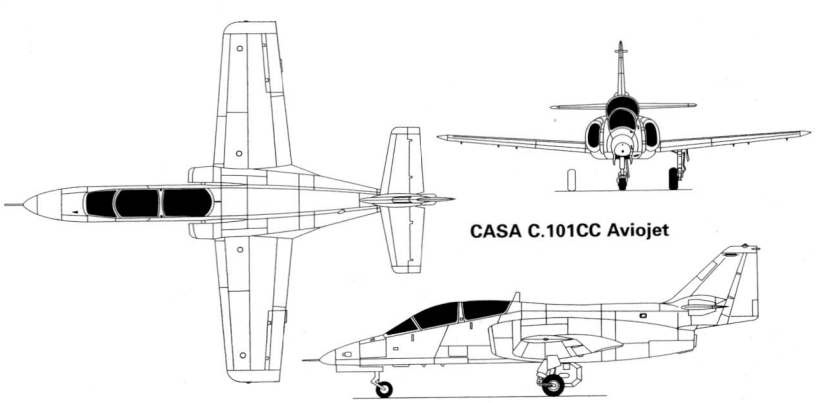

CASA C.101CC Aviojet

SPECIFICATION

CASA C.101CC Aviojet
Type: two-seat light attack and weapons training aircraft
Powerplant: one AlliedSignal TFE731-5-1J turbofan engine rated at 4,300 lb st (19.13 kN) and 4,700 lb st (20.91 kN) with military power reserve
Performance: maximum speed 501 mph (806 km/h) at 20,000 ft (6095 m); cruising speed 407 mph (656 km/h) at 30,000 ft (9145 m); initial climb rate 4,900 ft (1494 m) per minute at normal power and 6,100 ft (1859 m) per minute with MPR; climb to 25,000 ft (7620 m) in 6 minutes 30 seconds; service ceiling 42,000 ft (12800 m); combat radius 322 miles (519 km) on a lo-lo-lo interdiction mission with one cannon pod and four 551-lb (250-kg) bombs
Weights: empty 7,717 lb (3500 kg); maximum take-off 13,889 lb (6300 kg)
Dimensions: wingspan 34 ft 9⅜ in (10.60 m); length 41 ft (12.50 m); height 13 ft 11¼ in (4.25 m); wing area 215.29 sq ft (20.00 m²)
Armament: one 30-mm DEFA fixed forward-firing cannon under the fuselage or two 0.5-in (12.7-mm) Colt-Browning fixed forward-firing machine-guns in the lower-fuselage bay, plus up to 4,056 lb (1840 kg) of disposable stores carried under the wing

CASA C.212 Aviocar

CASA's **C.212 Aviocar** is a simple airlifter of modest performance which has proved attractive to a number of smaller air arms as well as civil operators. The aircraft has limited maintenance requirements, good STOL performance and a rear ramp/door. The freight capacity is often exchanged for accommodation for 15 paratroops and an instructor/dispatcher, or 12 litters and three seated casualties plus attendants, or 19 passengers.

The Aviocar has an all-metal structure including a basically rectangular-section fuselage with an upswept tail unit, a high-set wing carrying the two engines, and fixed tricycle landing gear. The type first flew on 26 March 1971 for a service debut in 1973, and Spanish production of the **C.212A** (later redesignated **C.212-5 Series 100**) and specifically military **C.212-5 Series 100M** (Spanish military designation **T.12B**, of which two were later converted to **D.3A** medevac standard) totalled 129 aircraft, while another 29 aircraft were made in Indonesia under the designation **IPTN (Nurtanio) NC.212-100 Aviocar**. Exports of the C.212-5 Series 100M military version were made to Chile

and Portugal.

The **C.212AV** is the VIP version of the C.212A, and is known to the Spanish military as the **T.12C**. Under the designation **C.212B**, six pre-production C.212A machines were converted to photo-survey standard with Wild RC-10 cameras and a darkroom in the hold, and this variant is known to the Spanish military as the **TR.12A**. The **C.212C** is the civil version of the C.212A Series 100, of which a few examples have entered military or paramilitary service as well as operating with a modest number of airlines. The **C.212D** was applied to the last two of the eight pre-production aircraft after modification as navigation trainers for service with the Spanish air force under the service designation **TE.12B**. Some production aircraft followed to the same standard.

Introduced in 1979, the **C.212 Series 200** is a stretched development of the C.212-5 Series 100 with the uprated power-plant of two TPE331-10-503C turboprop engines each flat-rated at 900 shp (671 kW) and an increased-length hold. The Indonesian-built version is the **NC.212-200**.

The **C.212 Series 200M** has been widely exported to

military operators, with Spain using **D.3B** SAR aircraft with APS-128 nose radar and **TR.12D** ECM trainers, and Swedish aircraft being designated **Tp.89**.

Substituting the C.212-5 Series 100's powerplant of two TPE331-5-251C turboprop engines each flat-rated at 755 ehp (563 ekW) for TPE-331-10R-513Cs produced the **C.212 Series 300**. First flown in September 1984, the **C.212-M Series 300** became the standard production version in 1987, and features Whitcomb winglets. The civil model is available in **C.212 Series 300 Airliner** and **C.212 Series 30 Utility** subvariants for the 26-passenger

The C.212 Series 300 Aviocar has found a ready export market. Like all variants of the type, the aircraft mounts its main undercarriage units on fuselage side sponsons.

airliner, or for the 23-passenger utility roles respectively. Another civil variant that has been offered but not yet taken up is the **C.212 Series 300P**, with the revised powerplant of two 1,100-shp (820-kW) Pratt & Whitney Canada PT6A-65 turboprop engines for improved 'hot-and-high' performance. The specifically military version of the C.212 Series 300 is the **C.212 Series 300M** which has again been widely exported.

The latest variant of the Aviocar is the **C.212**

Series 400, or **C.212 Series 400M** for any military development. The C.212 Series 400 first flew in April 1997 and differs from the Series 300 mainly in its increased weight, and modified flightdeck and cabin. The powerplant comprises two 1,100-shp (820-kW) TPE331-12RJ turboprop engines and the flightdeck has been revised with an EFIS. By the middle of 1998, CASA and IPTN had sold some 570 examples of the C.212, including special-mission variants.

SPECIFICATION

CASA C.212-M Series 300 Aviocar

Type: two-crew STOL utility medium transport with capability for armed roles such as light attack
Powerplant: two AlliedSignal TPE331-10R-513C turboprop engines each flat-rated at 900 shp (671 kW) without automatic power reserve and 925 shp (690 kW) with automatic power reserve
Performance: maximum speed 230 mph (370 km/h) at optimum altitude; cruising speed 220 mph (354 km/h) at 10,000 ft (3050 m); initial climb rate 1,630 ft (497 m) per minute; service ceiling 26,000 ft (7925 m); range 519 miles (1433 km) with maximum payload
Weights: empty 9,700 lb

(4400 kg); maximum take-off 17,637 lb (8000 kg)
Dimensions: wingspan 66 ft 6½ in (20.28 m); length 52 ft 11¾ in (16.15 m); height 21 ft 7¾ in (6.60 m); area 441.33 sq ft (41.00 m²)
Armament: provision is made for up to 1,102 lb (500 kg) of disposable stores carried on one hardpoint on each side of the fuselage, and generally comprising two machine-gun pods, or two multiple launchers for air-to-surface unguided rockets, or a combination of these weapons
Payload: up to 25 troops, or 24 paratroops, or 12 litters plus four attendants, or 6,217 lb (2820 kg) of freight

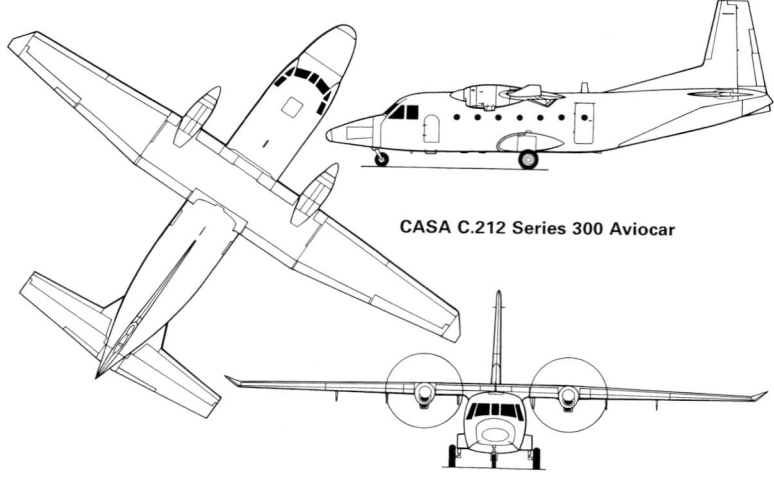

CASA C.212 Series 300 Aviocar

CASA C.212 Aviocar (Special-Mission Versions)

Since its introduction in 1979, three specialised variants of the **C.212 Series 200M Aviocar (Special Mission Variant)** have been developed: the **C.212-M Series 200M (ASW Version)**; **C.212 Series 200M (MP Version)**; and **C.212 Series 200M (DE Version)**, with a flight crew of two on the flightdeck and a mission crew generally of four in the modified cabin. The ASW Version is generally similar to the baseline Series 200M except for its electronic suite and arma-

ment. In the anti-submarine role, the primary sensors are search radar, sonobuoys, MAD, ESM and Stingray, Mk 46 and A 244/S lightweight torpedoes.

The MP Version is optimised for the maritime patrol and anti-ship tasks, and has as its primary sensor the Eaton-AIL APS-128 search radar (with its antenna in a nose radome to scan through an arc of 270°), used in conjunction with Sea Skua or AS15TT lightweight anti-ship missiles. In other respects, the Maritime Patrol

Version is basically similar to the ASW Version apart from its revised accommodation, lack of armament capability, modified avionics and carriage of a searchlight, smoke markers and a camera.

Typical of the MP Version in its late-production form are the three such aircraft built under licence by IPTN for the Indonesian navy's air arm with the Thomson-CSF AMASCOS (Airborne Maritime Situation Control System).

SPECIFICATION

CASA C.212 Patrullero (ASW Version)

Type: six-crew short/medium-range maritime reconnaissance and coastal reconnaissance aircraft with ASW capability
Powerplant: two AlliedSignal TPE331-10R-513C turboprop engines each flat-rated at 900 shp (671 kW) without automatic power reserve and 925 shp (690 kW) with automatic power reserve
Performance: maximum cruising speed 220 mph (354 km/h) at 10,000 ft (3050 m); economical cruising speed 186 mph (300 km/h) at 10,000 ft (3050 m); initial climb

rate 1,630 ft (497 m) per minute; service ceiling 26,000 ft (7925 m)
Weights: empty 8,333 lb (3780 kg); maximum take-off 17,637 lb (8000 kg)
Dimensions: wingspan 66 ft 6½ in (20.28 m); length dependent on version 20 ft 8 in (6.30 m); area 441.33 sq ft (41.00 m²)
Armament: up to 1,102 lb (500 kg) of disposable stores carried on one hardpoint on each side of the fuselage, and generally comprising two Stingray, Mk 46 or A 244/S lightweight torpedoes, or two AS15TT or Sea Skua lightweight anti-ship missiles

CASA C-212 Aviocar (Special-Mission Versions) (cont.)

The **DE Version** of the special-mission Aviocar (such as the four aircraft in service with the UAE) is optimised for the Elint/ECM role with its automatic signals interception, classification and localisation capability. Two similar aircraft in Portuguese service also possess a jamming capability.

The **C-212 Patrullero** (patroller), otherwise known as the **C-212 Series 300M (Special Mission Version)** is the special missions variant of the C-212 Series 300M and is available in the same three specialised variants as the C-212 Series 200M.

Spain's D.3B search and rescue aircraft carry the AN/APS-128 search radar in a distinctive extended nose radome. The radar has a 270° scan. The aircraft are based at Cuatro Vientos with 803 Squadron.

Caudron C.21, C.22 and C.23

The **Caudron C.21** twin-engined biplane made its appearance in November 1917. It was powered originally by 80-hp (60-kW) Le Rhône rotary engines, but was later re-engined with 120-hp (90-kW) units. The type found no service application during World War I. The design was then developed into the **C.21bis** for post-war commercial use, and the C.21 itself made a number of pioneering flights in the immediate post-war period.

The **C.22** night bomber in the BN.2 (two-seat night bomber) category followed, but this was underpowered and did not go into production. Deville then produced the **C.23** heavy bomber, a larger aircraft which was able to lift a substantial bombload. The C.23 appeared in February 1918, winning orders for 1,000 **C.23BN.2** operational examples, of which only 54 had been completed by the time of the armistice. Like the Handley Page O/400,

the C.23 was planned with the payload/range capability to bomb Berlin, but none of these aircraft saw operational service in World War I and no further production was undertaken. Most of the C.23s went to equip the French Aviation Militaire's 22e Régiment at Luxeuil in 1919. The machines proved too heavy and were also lacking in manoeuvrability, however, and were therefore withdrawn and scrapped in February 1920.

The C.23 was also used as an airliner after the war. The first version, used on the Paris-Brussels route,

had open-cockpit accommodation for 12 passengers, while the following **C.23bis** had an enclosed passenger cabin and was operated briefly between Paris and London.

As a night-bomber, the C.23 did not excel and enjoyed just one year of active service.

SPECIFICATION	
Caudron C.23BN.2	9,193 lb (4170 kg)
Type: two-seat night bomber	**Dimensions:** wingspan 80 ft 3½ in (24.47 m); length 42 ft 7 in (12.98 m); height 9 ft 10 in (3.00 m); wing area 1,141.01 sq ft (106.00 m²)
Powerplant: two Salmson (Canton-Unné) 9Z radial engines each rated at 240 hp (179 kW)	
Performance: maximum speed 90 mph (145 km/h) at 3,280 ft (1000 m); service ceiling 14,765 ft (4500 m); endurance 5 hours	**Armament:** one 0.303-in (7.7-mm) Lewis trainable machine-gun in the nose position, plus up to 1,323 lb (600 kg) of bombs carried under the fuselage
Weights: empty 5,161 lb (2341 kg); maximum take-off	

Caudron C.59 and C.60

The **Caudron C.59** intermediate trainer was a conventional unstaggered two-bay biplane of wooden construction with fabric

covering. The pupil was accommodated in an open cockpit under the centre section of the upper wing, with the instructor's cockpit

Ailerons were fitted only on the C.59's upper wing. The upper wing was of slightly greater span than the lower wing and only the lower unit incorporated dihedral. Two sets of interplane struts were used on each side, in keeping with the two-bay configuration.

immediately behind it and located beneath a cut-out in the upper wing's trailing edge. Power was provided by a Hispano-Suiza 8Ab engine, with its Lamblin radiator located under the fuselage just forward of the main landing gear.

The prototype flew for the first time in August 1921. After extensive official

tests, the C.59 was ordered on a large scale by the French Aviation Militaire for service in the official Et.2 (two-seat transitional trainer) category. Eventually, over 1,000 C.59s were delivered to the French army, with smaller batches going to the Aéronautique Maritime. The type remained in French service for 15 years, and on 1 January 1936 11 examples were still in use with the Armée de l'Air. Total production reached 1,800 aircraft, and many C.59s went to

French civil flying schools, while others were exported to several foreign air arms.

The **Caudron C.60** intermediate trainer was very similar to the C.59 except for its powerplant of one 130-hp (97-kW) Clerget 9B rotary engine installed in the forward fuselage under a horseshoe-type cowling. The C.60 was rejected by the French military, but found favour in French civil flying schools and was also exported in considerable numbers.

Variant

C.59/2: a single example with the powerplant of one 230-hp (172-kW) Lorraine 7Ma radial engine and incorporating redesigned landing gear with a wide-track main unit

SPECIFICATION	
Caudron C.59Et.2	endurance 3 hours 30 minutes
Type: two-seat intermediate flying trainer	**Weights:** empty 1,543 lb (700 kg); maximum take-off 2,178 lb (988 kg)
Powerplant: one Hispano-Suiza 8Ab Vee engine rated at 180 hp (134 kW)	**Dimensions:** wingspan 33 ft 7¼ in (10.24 m); length 25 ft 7 in (7.80 m); height 9 ft 6¼ in (2.90 m); wing area 279.87 sq ft (26.00 m²)
Performance: maximum speed 106 mph (170 km/h) at sea level;	

Caudron C.109

The **C.109** two-seat light monoplane had a parasol wing and a fuselage of light rectangular wooden structure with fabric covering. The entire wing was fabric-covered, and the outer panels could be folded rearward for transportation or storage. The pupil/passenger was accommodated in an open cockpit beneath the wing's centre section, with the pilot/instructor immediately to the rear in a cockpit beneath a cut-out in the wing's trailing edge. Dual controls could be installed as required.

The C.109 prototype flew for the first time during May 1925. It met with some success, being selected for staged long-distance flights by such celebrities of the time as Thoret and Delmotte. The type was also popular with French women fliers, including Maryse Bastié and Lena Bernstein.

Production totalled 24 aircraft, six of which were purchased by the French Aviation Militaire for liaison duties. A number of developments, differing only in minor detail, were built. Two examples of the **C.110** were followed by the one-off **C.112**, **C.113**, **C.114**, **C.116** and **C.117** types.

Four short vertical struts mounted around the forward cockpit supported the centre section of C.109's parasol wing, while its outer panels were braced to the lower fuselage longerons on each side by a pair of Dural struts.

Variant

C.109/2: the sole surviving C.109 (the sixth machine) became the C.109/2 in about 1950, when it was adapted to take a Salmson 5Aq radial engine rated at 85 hp (63 kW)

SPECIFICATION	
Caudron C.109	endurance 4 hours
Type: two-seat light sport and training aircraft	**Weights:** empty 723 lb (328 kg); maximum take-off 1,224 lb (555 kg)
Powerplant: one Salmson AD 9 radial engine rated at 40 hp (30 kW)	**Dimensions:** wingspan 37 ft 8¾ in (11.50 m); length 20 ft 2 in (6.15 m); height 7 ft 5½ in (2.27 m); wing area 215.59 sq ft (20.00 m²)
Performance: maximum speed 78 mph (126 km/h) at sea level;	

Caudron C.230 and C.270 Luciole

The **Caudron C.230 Luciole** prototype made its maiden flight in November 1930. It was a two-seat light biplane with equal-span unstaggered single-bay wings. The wooden fuselage structure was fabric-covered, and the cantilever tailplane had a wood frame and was plywood-covered.

The C.230 was powered by a 95-hp (71-kW) Salmson radial engine and enjoyed some success in the French market for light touring and sports aircraft.

Production totalled 15 machines to the baseline standard, followed by a number of variants. The C.230 series took part in practically every sporting aircraft rally or contest in France from 1931 onwards, and the type appeared frequently in other parts of Europe.

Developed from the C.230 series, the first **C.270 Luciole** appeared in 1931. It had a less complicated wing-folding arrangement than the earlier aircraft; featured modified ailerons, rudder and elevators; reverted to fabric covering for the fuselage; and had more refined landing gear. Production of the basic C.270, powered by a 95-hp (71-kW) Salmson 7Ac radial engine, totalled 82 out of an overall production figure of 725 for all versions of the Luciole series. After the outbreak of World War II in 1939, many examples of the **C.272/4** and **C.275** types were requisitioned for service use as liaison aircraft. In 1946 the surviving machines were used as glider tugs by the Ecole de l'Air.

The Luciole carried ailerons only on its upper wing. The upper wing's centre section was braced to the fuselage by four short vertical steel tube struts, and the outer panels, which could be folded, had a pair of vertical spruce interplane struts on each side.

SPECIFICATION	
Caudron C.272 Luciole	at optimum altitude; service ceiling
Type: two-seat sport and touring aircraft	13,125 ft (4000 m); range 311 miles (500 km)
Powerplant: one Renault 4Pb inline engine rated at 95 hp (71 kW)	**Weights:** empty 1,138 lb (516 kg); maximum take-off 1,720 lb (780 kg)
Performance: maximum speed 98 mph (158 km/h) at sea level; cruising speed 84 mph (135 km/h)	**Dimensions:** wingspan 32 ft 5¾ in (9.90 m); length 25 ft 2 in (7.67 m); height 9 ft ¾ in (2.76 m); wing area 258.34 sq ft (24.00 m²)

Variants

C.232: 50 of this version were built with one Renault 4Pb inline engine; the fuselage had plywood covering
C.232/2: three examples that differed from the C.232 only in having wheel brakes
C.232/4: seven completed to a standard identical to that of the C.232/2 except for improved equipment
C.233: single prototype to take unsuccessful Michel AM-16 engine but later fitted with a Salmson engine, thus becoming a C.230
C.235: one airframe fitted with a German 100-hp (75-kW) Argus As 8R inline engine for French air ministry tests of this engine
C.270/1 Luciole: development of the C.270 with an improved Salmson 7Ac2 engine
C.271 Luciole: one machine with a 120-hp (90-kW) Lorraine 5Pc engine driving a Ratier metal propeller
C.271/2 Luciole: five of this C.271 development with a 110-hp (82-kW) Lorraine 5Pb engine
C.272 Luciole: 52 aircraft with the Renault 4Pb engine
C.272/2 Luciole: 22 of a development with the Renault 4Pci engine; from the fifth example the aircraft were completed with a taller and more pointed vertical tail surface of a shape that characterised all later Luciole aircraft
C.272/3 Luciole: 15 of a version with the 120-hp (90-kW) Renault 4Pdi engine and fitted with Messier brakes
C.272/4 Luciole: 21 aircraft with 140-hp (104-kW) Renault 4Pei

engines and fitted with Messier wheel brakes; the luggage compartment forward of the cockpits was eliminated
C.272/5 Luciole: 80 aircraft with 100-hp (75-kW) Renault 4Pgi engines
C.273 Luciole: 14 aircraft with 100-hp (75-kW) Michel 4 A-14 engines driving Merville Series 402 propellers
C.274 Luciole: one displayed at the 1932 Paris Salon de l'Aéronautique with the unsuccessful 135-hp (101-kW) Chaise 4Ba inline engine
C.275 Luciole: 433 examples based on the C.272/5 but without wing-folding; it was by far the most popular version of the Luciole and, like the other versions, was sold to private owners in France and abroad and flew with the Caudron flying schools. Of the overall total, 296 were ordered by the French government for the Aviation Populaire movement, which was intended to train would-be pilots who were unable to afford the fees charged by flying clubs
C.276 Luciole: version powered by the 105-hp (79-kW) de Havilland Gipsy III inline engine and with brakes designed by the Charles company and a tailplane reminiscent of the earlier Luciole
C.276H Luciole: two C.276 aircraft re-engined in 1956 with the Hirth HM 504A-2 engine
C.277 Luciole: nine aircraft differing from the C.272/4 only in its non-folding wing cellule
C.277R Luciole: one C.275 re-engined with a Renault 4Po 3 engine in 1949
C.278 Luciole: one example with new landing gear and a 135-hp (101-kW) Salmson 9Nc radial engine

Caudron C.440 Goéland

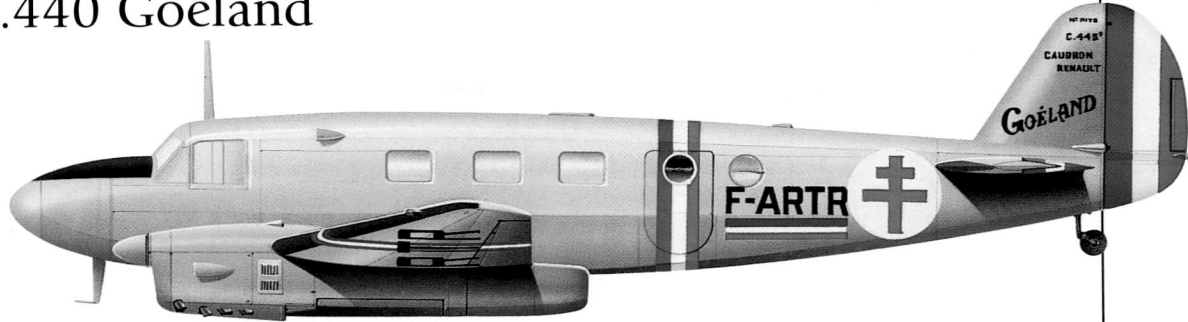

Developed to satisfy a need for a fast, economical and comfortable transport, the **C.440 Goéland** (seagull) appeared in 1934.

The wing was of spruce and plywood and carried ailerons and trailing-edge flaps. The fuselage was largely of wood and had plywood skinning except for the nose section and upper decking, which had stressed sheet metal covering. The prototype had fairings attached to the front of each main leg to cover the wheel wells when the landing gear was retracted, but the next two aircraft had two wheel well doors attached to the underside of each nacelle, this becoming a feature of all future Goélands.

In its basic passenger configuration the Goéland offered cabin accommodation for six passengers. Baggage holds were located forward and aft, and a toilet was situated at the rear of the cabin.

The Goéland remained in production up to the outbreak of World War II, the principal model being the **C.445**, which was also adopted by the Armée de l'Air as the **C.445M** and used for a variety of tasks,

including communications duties and crew training. Some C.445Ms were used by the Aéronavale. Civil users included Air France and several other French operators. The type was sold to Yugoslavia's Aeroput and also to operators in Bulgaria and Spain. In 1940, two C.445Ms were supplied to the Belgian Aéronautique Militaire.

Production continued during World War II, and after the German occupation of France, 44 C.445s and 10 C.445Ms were requisitioned, some flying on Lufthansa routes and others being operated by the Luftwaffe. Considerable numbers of C.445Ms and **C.449** aircraft were built for the Germans by Renault

and Caudron. The Germans used the Goéland as a pilot, radio and navigational trainer, and also for communications, and a small number of the aircraft had glazed noses for bomb-aimer training. In addition to the **C.447** specialised ambulance version, a few other Goélands were used for casualty transport.

Other Goélands served the French Vichy regime, while a number were scattered throughout France's overseas empire, most of them in North Africa. Several C.445s operated in the UK after June 1940.

In 1945 the Caudron plant was taken over by the French government as the Ateliers Aéronautiques d'Issy-les-Moulineaux. Here, production of the C.445M and C.449 continued under the designation AA.1. After the war, Goélands continued in service with Air France for postal flights and crew training. Other civil operators included SABENA and two French companies, Aigle Azur and CAT (Compagnie Air Transport). Goélands also continued to fly for a number of years

The Goéland combined economy with aerodynamic excellence and became one of the most successful of the contemporary aircraft in its class. This machine wears Free French roundels.

with the Armée de l'Air.

Production of all versions totalled 1,702. The production listing below totals 1,446; it has not been possible to verify the subtypes of the remaining 256 Goélands.

Variants

C.440 Goéland: prototype plus first two production aircraft
C.441 Goéland: four aircraft with two 220-hp (164-kW) Renault 6Q-01 engines, and 3° dihedral on the outer wing panels
C.444 Goéland: 17 of the first version to introduce counter-rotating engines (Renault 6Q-00 and 6Q-01) and propellers to overcome torque effects
C.445 Goéland: 119 aircraft similar to C.444 but with outer-wing dihedral increased to 4° and comprising 114 C.445, two **C.445/1** and three **C.445/2** aircraft
C.445M Goéland: 404 of the militarised version with an internal layout varying according to role
C.445R Goéland: one long-distance variant with additional fuel tanks in the passenger cabin
C.445/3 Goéland: 510 of one of the principal post-war versions, with counter-rotating Renault 6Q-10 and 6Q-11 engines
C.446 Super Goéland: one machine only
C.447 Goéland: 31 air ambulance aircraft with accommodation for four litters, and additional side windows
C.448 Goéland: seven of a version with supercharged Renault 6Q-02 and 6Q-03 engines each rated at 240 hp (179 kW), and increased maximum take-off weight of 8,157 lb (3700 kg)
C.449 Goéland: 349 of the final production model, many built after World War II and comprising 24 basic C.449 aircraft, 298 **C.449/1**, **C.449/2** and **C.449/3** aircraft, and 27 **C.449/4** and **C.449/5** machines; the C.449/4 was a specialised photographic type

SPECIFICATION

Caudron C.445M Goéland
Type: two-crew military transport and trainer
Powerplant: two Renault 6Q-00/01 or 6Q-08/09 Bengali 6 inverted inline engines each rated at 220 hp (164 kW)
Performance: maximum speed 186 mph (300 km/h) at sea level; cruising speed 162 mph (261 km/h) at optimum altitude; climb to 6,560 ft (2000 m) in 10 minutes

15 seconds; service ceiling 22,965 ft (7000 m); range 621 miles (1000 km)
Weights: empty 5,053 lb (2292 kg); maximum take-off 7,716 lb (3500 kg)
Dimensions: wingspan 57 ft 8½ in (17.59 m); length 44 ft 10½ in (13.68 m); height 11 ft 1¾ in (3.40 m); wing area 452.10 sq ft (42.00 m²)
Payload: up to six passengers

Caudron C.480 Frégate

Developed from the earlier **C.280 Phaléne**, the **Caudron C.480 Frégate** appeared in prototype form during 1935. The Frégate differed from the Phaléne in cabin layout, the pilot being

seated forward with two passengers seated side-by-side to his rear in a cabin accessed by a single door on each side. The high wing was of different planform with taper on the leading

Subtle airframe modifications, revised accommodation and greater power to cope with increased weights differentiated the C.480 from the C.280.

SPECIFICATION

Caudron C.480 Frégate
Type: three-seat touring aircraft
Powerplant: one Renault 4Pei Bengali inverted inline engine rated at 140 hp (104 kW)
Performance: maximum speed 130 mph (210 km/h) at optimum altitude; cruising speed 115 mph (185 km/h) at optimum altitude; service ceiling 14,765 ft (4500 m);

range 528 miles (850 km)
Weights: empty 1,323 lb (600 kg); maximum take-off 2,315 lb (1050 kg)
Dimensions: wingspan 39 ft ½ in (11.90 m); length 26 ft 10 in (8.18 m); height 6 ft 11½ in (2.12 m); wing area 215.29 sq ft (20.00 m²)

edge and a straight trailing edge, and was braced on each side by a Vee-strut.

Production totalled 27 aircraft, and 20 of the machines were requisitioned

by the French air ministry in 1939 for wartime duties with the Armée de l'Air.

Caudron C.510 Pélican

A further development of the Phaléne, the **C.510 Pélican** had a lengthened fuselage, enabling it to

accommodate a litter and attendant when flown in the air ambulance role. As a tourer the C.510 accom-

modated a pilot and up to three passengers. Its wing design (including wing folding) and fuselage structure followed closely those of the Phaléne, although the ailerons, fin

and rudder were both redesigned and enlarged. Dual controls could be fitted if required by the customer. Some 62 C.510s were built, some of these operating as air

ambulances and others as privately-owned touring aircraft. On the outbreak of World War II, a number of C.510s was impressed for service with the Armée de l'Air.

When extra range was required of the C.510, its cabin could be modified to accommodate two, rather than three, passengers and an auxiliary fuel tank.

Caudron C.600, C.601 and C.610 Aiglon

The Aiglon was especially popular with French women fliers: Mesdames Dupeyron and Lion flew an Aiglon to establish new women's straight-line distance records in 1937 and 1938.

The **Caudron C.600 Aiglon** (eaglet) light touring monoplane was the work of the outstanding French aircraft designer of the 1930s, Marcel Riffard.

The first of two C.600 prototypes made its maiden flight in March 1935. A low-wing cantilever monoplane with tandem open cockpits, the type had excellent aerodynamic qualities. The Aiglon proved itself with a number of outstanding flights. André Japy flew a single-seat **C.610** from Paris to Saigon between 12 and

16 December 1935 at an average speed of 80 mph (128 km/h).

Construction was entirely of wood, except for the fabric covering of the rudder and elevators, the monoplane wing including wide-span flaps on the trailing edge. There were variations in the shape of the vertical tail surface, three distinct types being used.

Total production of the Aiglon was 203 aircraft, of which some were fitted with a continuous glazed canopy over the cockpits. The type was particularly popular with French private owners and flying clubs. A number was sold abroad, 14 being exported to Spain, two to Argentina and one to Japan. With the outbreak of World War II, many Aiglons were requisitioned and used as liaison aircraft by the Armée de l'Air.

Variants

C.600G Aiglon: five aircraft powered by the de Havilland Gipsy Major inverted inline engine driving a Ratier metal propeller
C.601 Aiglon Senior: 18 aircraft with 140-hp (104-kW) Renault 4Pei engines
C.610: two of a special long-distance, single-seat version with increased fuel capacity

Caudron C.630 Simoun

An outstanding four-seat cabin touring monoplane of the 1930s, the **C.630 Simoun** (sandstorm) incorporated many technical features developed in designer Riffard's series of

racers for the Coupe Deutsch de la Meurthe contests. The experimental **C.500 Simoun IV** and **C.620 Simoun VI** were exhibited at the Paris Salon de l'Aéronautique in 1934.

The C.620 was intended for the Challenge Internationale de Tourisme competition, and its comfortable individual seats, deep windscreen and three large windows

on each side of the cabin found greater favour than the more conventional layout of the C.500. There was clearly a market for the Simoun and, apart from the one-off **C.520** and two long-range versions of the C.620 with extra fuel tanks in the cabin, the production **C.630** was the next version to appear.

The C.630 was an elegant low-wing cantilever monoplane of wooden construction, the wing being covered with plywood and fabric. The slab-sided fuselage had light alloy covering for the curved underside and roof.

The C.620 prototype made its maiden flight in October 1934. Only a few months later, in mid-1935,

delivery of the C.630 series began with the 180-hp (134-kW) Renault 6Pri (otherwise 6Q-07) engine. Orders for some 70 private tourers followed. Commercially, 12 examples of the C.630 established France's first regular air-mail service from 10 July 1935. When the service ceased in May 1939, over 45 million letters had been carried.

A number of variants followed the C.630, but only the **C.635** with the 6Q-01 or 6Q-09 engines, was built in quantity. Five of the type in red livery equipped the French VIP Escadrille Ministerielle while, during 1935-6, the French services placed initial orders for the militarised **C.635M** version. Other military and naval orders followed, the Simoun being used widely for liaison, as a general staff transport, and as a transition or navigation trainer.

As standard, the wheels and tailwheel of the Simoun were enclosed in streamlined fairings. Differential brakes were also standard.

Caudron C.630 Simoun (continued)

At the outbreak of World War II in 1939, some 60 civil Simouns were impressed by the Armée de l'Air for military service. Of 103 Simouns seized by the Germans in November 1942, 65 were used for training and liaison purposes. Large numbers of Simouns also flew with the French in North Africa.

Many well-known French pilots of the 1930s used the Simoun in long-distance attempts and a number of Simouns remained in a flying condition after World War II.

Variants

C.630 Simoun: 20 of the initial production version with the 180-hp (134-kW) Renault 6Pri engine
C.631 Simoun: three aircraft with the 220-hp (164-kW) Renault 6Q-01 engine
C.632 Simoun: one aircraft similar to the C.631
C.633 Simoun: six aircraft with a modified fuselage and the Renault 6Q-07 engine
C.634 Simoun: three aircraft with a modified wing, increased take-off weight and Renault 6Q-01 or 6Q-09 engine
C.635 Simoun: 46 aircraft with an improved cabin layout and Renault 6Q-01 or 6Q-09 engine; a number of earlier aircraft was also converted to this improved standard
C.635M Simoun: version of the C.635 with military equipment, detail modifications and the Renault 6Q-09 or 6Q-15 engine

SPECIFICATION

Caudron C.635M Simoun
Type: four-seat military liaison, light transport and training aircraft
Powerplant: one Renault 6Q-09 Bengali inverted inline engine rated at 220 hp (164 kW)
Performance: maximum speed 186 mph (300 km/h) at sea level; cruising speed 162 mph (260 km/h); service ceiling 19,685 ft (6000 m); range 932 miles (1500 km)
Weights: empty 1,664 lb (755 kg), maximum take-off 3,042 lb (1380 kg)
Dimensions: wingspan 34 ft 1½ in (10.40 m); length 29 ft 10¼ in (9.10 m); height 7 ft 6½ in (2.30 m); wing area 172.23 sq ft (16.00 m²)

Caudron C.640 Typhon

Owing a great deal in concept to the de Havilland DH.88 Comet, the **C.640 Typhon** (typhoon) was inspired by the French pioneer of long-range postal routes, Jean Mermoz. The C.640 was thus designed as a mailplane, offering high speed and long range.

The first C.640 made its debut in June 1935 as a low-wing cantilever monoplane of wooden construction. Its enclosed cabin accommodated two in tandem with dual controls and full wireless equipment. The variable-

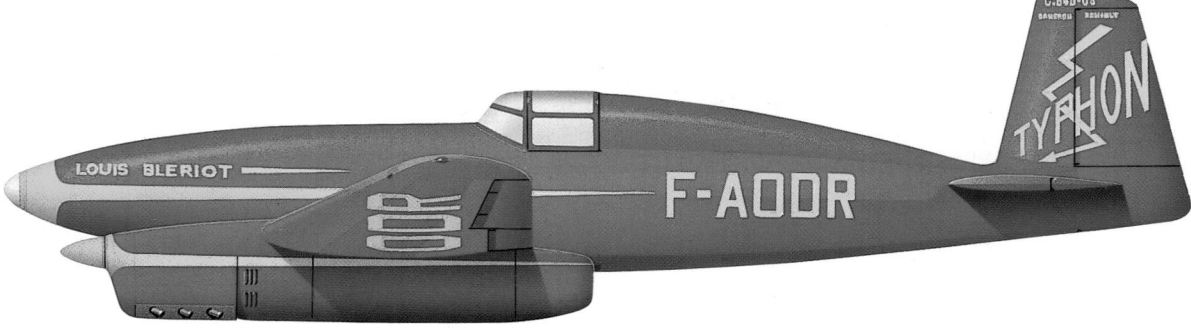

incidence tailplane was adjustable in flight.

Seven examples of the C.640 were constructed, the fourth and seventh machines having an enlarged fin. The Typhon established speed records over a 3,107-mile (5000-km) distance and participated in the celebrated Istres-Damascus-Paris race of August 1937. Unfortunately, the type was not very successful in service as its wing was too flexible, resulting in severe buffet problems that were never fully resolved.

Each main unit of the C.640's tailwheel landing gear retracted rearward to lie fully within the engine nacelles that were carefully faired into the underside of the wing. This aircraft was No. 5 out of the seven built.

SPECIFICATION

Caudron C.640 Typhon
Type: two-seat high-speed mailplane and record-breaking aircraft
Powerplant: two Renault 6Q Bengali inverted inline engines each rated at 220 hp (164 kW)
Performance: maximum speed 249 mph (400 km/h) at optimum altitude; cruising speed 230 mph (370 km/h) at optimum altitude; service ceiling 22,965 ft (7000 m); range 2,315 miles (3725 km)
Weights: empty 3,594 lb (1630 kg), maximum take-off 7,496 lb (3400 kg)
Dimensions: wingspan 47 ft 6¾ in (11.50 m); length 35 ft 11 in (10.95 m); height 9 ft 10 in (3.00 m); wing area 301.40 sq ft (28.00 m²)

Variants

C.641 Typhon: two examples (the second sold to Romania) of a single-seat record-breaking development, with the pilot seated in a cockpit under a raised canopy; the fuel capacity was almost doubled to provide a range of 4,163 miles (6700 km)
C.670 Typhon: one prototype of a high-speed bomber development, known as an avion de represailles (reprisal aircraft); first flown in March 1937, the C.670 carried a crew of three

Caudron C.690

With the same basic design characteristics as Riffard's lightweight, all-wood, low-wing cantilever monoplane racers, the **Caudron C.690** was designed as a trainer for pilots of single-seat fighters. It was similar to the earlier **C.720**, but was somewhat heavier and also had an uprated powerplant. The first prototype flew in early 1936 and was followed by the second on 18 February 1936. Both aircraft were demonstrated abroad, resulting in the purchase of single aircraft by the USSR and Japan. While undergoing official tests on 10 May 1937, the first prototype crashed, killing Caudron's chief test pilot, René Paulhan. Despite this disaster, official interest continued to

This C.690M, No. 2, was used as a Caudron company demonstrator in eastern and southern Europe in the late 1930s.

grow and a production series was ordered for the Armée de l'Air. These aircraft differed from the prototype in having a fin of triangular shape, longer landing-gear legs, and fixed leading-edge slots.

Production was slow to get under way, and the first **C.690M** did not begin flight tests until the beginning of April 1939. These military aircraft were unarmed but equipped with an OPL camera gun.

SPECIFICATION

Caudron C.690M
Type: single-seat fighter trainer
Powerplant: one Renault 6Q-05 Bengali Sport inverted inline engine rated at 220 hp (164 kW)
Performance: maximum speed 230 mph (370 km/h) at 6,560 ft (2000 m); cruising speed 199 mph (320 km/h) at optimum altitude; climb to 3,280 ft (1000 m) in 1 minute 30 seconds; service ceiling 31,825 ft (9700 m); range 684 miles (1100 km)
Weights: empty 1,482 lb (672 kg); maximum take-off 2,315 lb (1050 kg)
Dimensions: wingspan 25 ft 3¼ in (7.70 m); length 25 ft 7¾ in (7.82 m); height 8 ft 6¼ in (2.60 m); wing area 96.88 sq ft (9.00 m²)

Fifteen aircraft had been delivered by the end of May 1939, but none remained in flying condition after the French collapse in June 1940. The ninth machine was concealed from German forces and restored to flying condition after the war, taking to the air on 12 April 1945. After a subsequent accident, the aircraft was repaired to airworthy condition before disappearing from history.

Caudron C.714 Cyclone

The excellence of Riffards racers persuaded Caudron to start on the development a lightweight fighter.

This led to the **Caudron C.710** prototype which made its first flight on 18 July 1936. Despite its small size and weight, the C.710 soon revealed its development potential for, even with fixed landing gear and two 20-mm cannon, the 450 hp (336 kW) delivered by its Renault 12Ro I inverted-Vee engine was sufficient to provide a maximum speed that exceeded that of many contemporary fighters. An attempt to capitalise more effectively on this potential led to the **C.713 Cyclone**, first flown in December 1937. The C.713 was generally similar to the C.710, but introduced retractable tailwheel landing gear and a redesigned vertical tail surface. Further development of the concept paved the way for the **C.714** that first flew, in the form of the **C.714.01** initial prototype, in the summer of 1938.

In November 1938, an order for 100 C.714 production aircraft in the C.1 (single-seat fighter) category was placed.

Of low-wing cantilever monoplane configuration, the C.714 was of all-wood construction except for the control surfaces, which were of light alloy construction under a fabric covering. The wing section was too shallow to accommodate the machine-guns conventionally, and streamlined pods were therefore designed to carry a pair of guns beneath each wing.

Production began in the summer of 1939, and 50 of the aircraft which had been intended for service with the Armée de l'Air were diverted to the assistance of Finland, but only six of these had been delivered by 12 March 1940, the balance remaining in France. It is believed that about 40 C.714s were delivered to the French air force, which cancelled production

The Polish-manned Groupe de Chasse I./145 was known as the 'Warsaw Group', the unit seeing action against the Germans in the period 2-13 June 1940. This aircraft was based at Lyon-Brun.

after the completion of some 90 aircraft because of dissatisfaction with the type's climb rate. The C.714 was also used to equip an all-Polish squadron. Following the collapse of France, a small number of C.714s was used by the Vichy French and about 20 were seized by the Germans for use as fighter trainers.

SPECIFICATION	
Caudron C.714C.1 Cyclone **Type:** single-seat lightweight fighter **Powerplant:** one Renault 12Ro I inverted-Vee engine rated at 450 hp (336 kW) **Performance:** maximum speed 301 mph (485 km/h) at 13,125 ft (4000 m); cruising speed 199 mph (320 km/h) at optimum altitude; climb to 13,125 ft (4000 m) in 6 minutes 45 seconds; service ceiling 29,855 ft (9100 m); range	559 miles (900 km) **Weights:** empty 3,086 lb (1400 kg); maximum take-off 3,858 lb (1750 kg) **Dimensions:** wingspan 29 ft 5 in (8.97 m); length 27 ft 11 3/4 in (8.53 m); height 9 ft 5 in (2.87 m); wing area 134.55 sq ft (12.50 m²) **Armament:** four 0.295-in (7.5-mm) MAC 1934 fixed forward-firing machine-guns in fairings under the wing

Variants

C.720: trainer version of the C.714 with one 220-hp (164-kW) Renault 6Q Bengali six-cylinder inverted inline engine or one 100-hp (75-kW) Renault 4Pei four-cylinder inverted inline engine
C.760: prototype with one 750-hp (560-kW) Isotta-Fraschini Delta RC.40 engine
C.770: prototype with one 800-hp (597-kW) Renault 626 engine

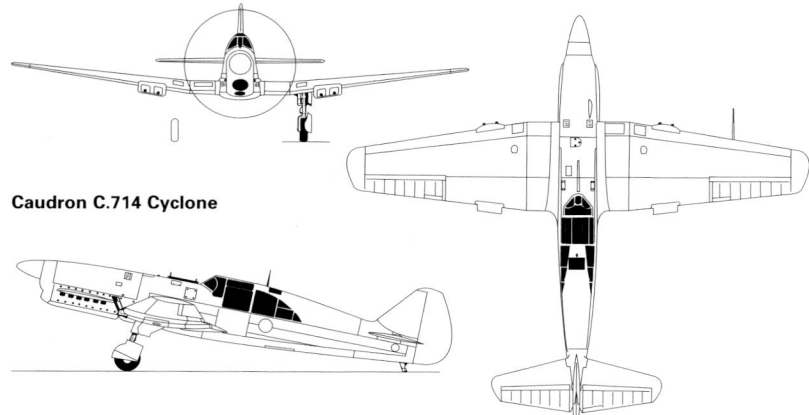

Caudron C.714 Cyclone

Caudron G.2 and G.3

The brothers René and Gaston Caudron had been designing aircraft for more than five years when their **Caudron G.3** (or **G.III**) made its first appearance in May 1914. It had been preceded by about 20 different designs and nearly 150 machines, and the new aircraft owed much to the earlier **Type B**.

The G.3 was a sesquiplane that employed wing-warping for lateral control, although in late production aircraft this system was replaced by ailerons fitted only on the upper wing. It was a general-purpose type, with the observer and pilot accommodated in tandem open cockpits in an abbreviated nacelle.

The G.3 had been developed from its immediate predecessor, the single-seat **G.2**, which had itself been built in some numbers and played a prominent role in air displays and meetings during 1913 and the early months of 1914.

Designed with a military role in mind, the G.3 was ordered into large-scale production when World War I broke out and the type was used widely in the first two years of the conflict for corps reconnaissance and artillery observation duties. The G.3 proved well-suited to its allotted tasks and, despite being unarmed, was popular with its crews. As the war progressed and enemy aircraft became more threatening, however, the slow speed and vulnerability of the G.3 began to tell against it. As a result, the French withdrew their G.3s from operational escadrilles in mid-1916.

Total French production of the G.3 in world War I was 2,450 aircraft. In addition, the British Caudron Co. Ltd manufactured 233 machines, and the AER company of Orbassano, near Turin, completed 166. The Italian air arm used the G.3 on a wide scale for reconnaissance until March 1917. British aircraft were also used in the reconnaissance and observation roles, although the RFC is credited with employing a number of G.3s fitted with a machine-gun and carrying light bombs for strafing attacks on German troops and emplacements. Of the British-built G.3s, 124 went to the RFC and 109 to the RNAS. The latter used the type from the outset for training, but early in the war it also operated a number of the type on abortive sorties against marauding German airships. The RFC did not dispense with its last operational G.3s until August 1917.

Of the main versions to enter service during the war, the standard artillery observation version, the **Cau 3A.2**, was used by the Allies (including Belgian units) on the Western Front, in Russia and in the Middle East. The **Cau 3D.2** was a dual-control trainer, and **Cau 3E.2** was the standard rotary-engined trainer. The number of G.3s used for training was greatly increased by the conversion of operational types as they were withdrawn from first-line service. Pilots who received their primary training on the type included members of the American Expeditionary Force in France, which received 192 French-built trainers during 1917 and 1918. One special type of trainer conversion, used only by the French and Americans, was the **Cau 3R.1**, the 'R' standing for **Rouleur** (taxi aircraft): the type was a single-seater with the fabric stripped off large areas of the wings so that it could not become airborne. It was used exclusively for ground training. The final important version of the G.3 was the **Cau 3.12**, in which the standard engine was replaced by a 100-hp (75-kW) Anzani radial.

After World War I the G.3 was kept in the public eye by a number of remarkable flights. In January 1919, wartime ace Jules Vedrines landed his G.3 on the roof of the famous Galeries Lafayette department store by the edge of the Seine in the heart of Paris and in the same month Madame de Laroche established a women's altitude record of 12,795 ft (3900 m).

Caudron G.2 and G.3 (continued)

Adrienne Bolland, a pioneering woman pilot, made a truly daring flight in a G.3, crossing the Andes from Tamarindos in Argentina to Santiago in Chile on 1 April 1921. The imagination of the French, however, was captured by Swiss pilot Francois Durafour, who landed a G.3 on the west slope of Mont Blanc on 31 July 1921, taking off from the mountainside successfully soon afterwards.

From 1919 onward, many G.3s surplus to military requirement, were sold to private owners,

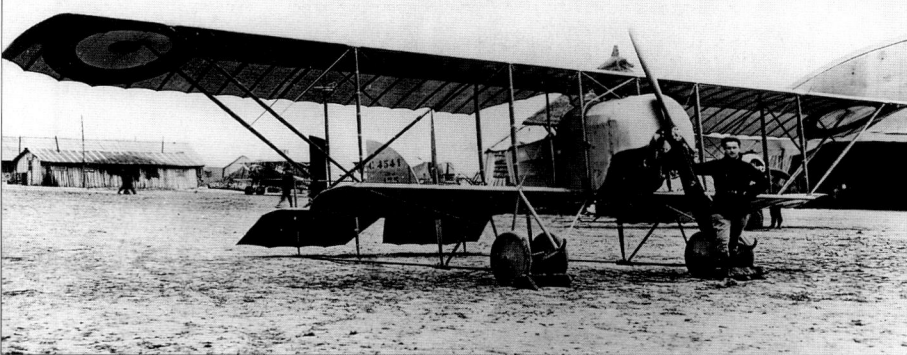

SPECIFICATION	
Caudron G3	30 minutes
Type: two-seat reconnaissance and training aircraft	**Weights:** empty 959 lb (435 kg); maximum take-off 1,565 lb (710 kg)
Powerplant: one Le Rhone rotary engine rated at 80 hp (60 kW)	**Dimensions:** wingspan 43 ft 6 in (13.26 m); length 22 ft 7¼ in (6.89 m); height 8 ft 6 in (2.59 m); wing area 304.31 sq ft (28.27 m²)
Performance: maximum speed 67 mph (108 km/h) at sea level; climb to 6,560 ft (2000 m) in 27 minutes; service ceiling 9,845 ft (3000 m); endurance 3 hours	**Armament:** usually none, although a rifle or a pistol was sometimes embarked for the observer

many of them ex-Aviation Militaire pilots. Other examples of the type were used by flying clubs for training and touring.

A Le Rhône rotary engine was mounted in the nose of the G.3's fuselage nacelle, to drive a a two-bladed tractor propeller. Some aircraft were built with alternative rotary engines (Gnome or Clerget) of the same power.

Caudron G.4

The impossibility of installing effective defensive armament in the G.3, and also the inability of this type to lift a worthwhile bomb load, led to the development of the twin-engined **Caudron G.4** (or **G.IV**), which first appeared in March 1915.

Structurally similar to its immediate predecessor, the G.4 had increased wingspan and four rather than two rudders. Power was provided either by two 80-hp (60-kW) Le Rhône rotary units with 'horseshoe' or circular cowlings, or uncowled

100-hp (75-kW) Anzani radial units without any type of cowling.

Two versions were built as the **Cau 4B.2** day bomber and the **Cau 4A.2** artillery observation and reconnaissance aircraft. Entering service with the Aviation Militaire in November 1915, the G.4 was the first Allied twin-engined type to equip first-line units in any quantity. However, increasing losses during the summer of 1916 led to withdrawal

of French **G.4B.2** (Cau 4B.2) bombers from first-line service during autumn of the same year.

Production of the G.4 in France totalled 1,358 aircraft. The RNAS purchased 55 of the type, 43 of them imported and the other 12 built by the British Caudron Co. Ltd. Flown by Nos 4 and 5 Wings, the aircraft were used during 1916 and early 1917 for attacks on German seaplane and airship bases in Belgium, one of the most important

raids being made by No. 7 Squadron, RNAS, on the Bruges area in February 1917. The Italian Aeronautica Militare received imported G.4s and 51 examples built in Italy. G.4s were also supplied to the Imperial Russian air service, with which they flew in the reconnaissance role.

The type was used for a number of notable post-war flights, and some hundreds were sold to private owners and flying clubs in France and Italy after World War I.

The G.4's short crew nacelle had an observer/gunner's cockpit in the nose, although the field of fire was limited by the proximity of the engines.

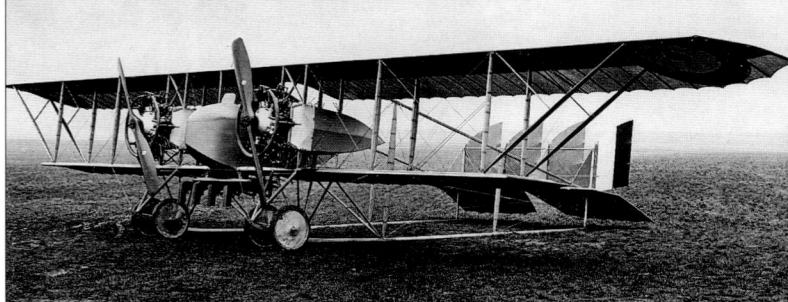

SPECIFICATION	
Caudron G.4	**Weights:** empty 1,616 lb (733 kg); maximum take-off 2,716 lb (1232 kg)
Type: two-seat bombing or reconnaissance aircraft	
Powerplant: two Le Rhône 9C rotary engines each rated at 80 hp (60 kW)	**Dimensions:** wingspan 55 ft 4¾ in (16.885 m); length 23 ft 7 in (7.19 m); height 8 ft 4½ in (2.55 m); wing area 396.45 sq ft (36.83 m²)
Performance: maximum speed 82 mph (132 km/h) at sea level; climb to 6,560 ft (2000 m) in 15 minutes; service ceiling 14,110 ft (4300 m); endurance 3 hours 30 minutes	**Armament:** one or two 0.303-in (7.7-mm) trainable machine-guns plus, in the G.4B.2 model, up to 220 lb (100 kg) of bombs carried externally

Caudron G.6

Paul Deville had flown in G.3s as an observer before going on to design the **Caudron G.6** (or **G.VI**) two-seat reconnaissance biplane. The type appeared in the summer of 1916 and went into service as the **Cau 6A.2** early in the following year. The prototype and early production aircraft were powered by two 80-hp (60-kW) Le Rhône rotary engines, but later machines had uprated powerplants.

While retaining the typical Caudron sesquiplane wing design, Deville abandoned the short central crew nacelle/tail boom configuration, selecting instead a conventional fuselage. The tail unit was also of simple configuration, with only a single vertical surface.

Total production of the G.6 amounted to 512 aircraft.

On one mission, with the renowned Jules Vedrines as pilot, a G.6 covered more than 200 miles (320 km), reaching its objective without difficulty after Vedrines had taken it above the clouds and navigated entirely by compass.

SPECIFICATION	
Caudron G.6	endurance 2 hours 30 minutes
Type: two-seat artillery observation and reconnaissance aircraft	**Weights:** empty 2,072 lb (940 kg); maximum take-off 3,164 lb (1435 kg)
Powerplant: two Le Rhône 9 rotary engines each rated at 130 hp (97 kW)	**Dimensions:** wingspan 56 ft 6 in (17.22 m); length 28 ft 2½ in (8.60 m); height 9 ft 8 in (2.95 m)
Performance: maximum speed 93 mph (150 km/h) at 6,560 ft (2000 m); climb to 6,560 ft (2000 m) in 7 minutes 35 seconds; service ceiling 15,500 ft (4725 m);	**Armament:** two 0.303-in (7.7-mm) Lewis trainable machine-guns in the rear cockpit, plus up to 220 lb (100 kg) of bombs carried externally

Caudron R.4

The **Caudron R.4** (or **R.IV**) appeared in prototype form in June 1915 and, for its time, was a remarkably clean aircraft.

The aircraft was a radical departure from its predecessors, with a full-length fuselage and single vertical tail surface. The unequal-span wing cellule was of the three-bay type, and ailerons were installed only on the upper wing. The three-man crew included nose and midships gunners.

The R.4 did well, defend-ing itself brilliantly against enemy interceptors and building up a considerable score of victories. Intended originally as a bomber, it served mainly as an A.3 category reconnaissance aircraft, frequently engaged in photographic work. The R.4's climb rate was not impressive, and a few aircraft were completed with two 150-hp (112-kW) Hispano-Suiza 8Aa Vee engines, in an attempt to improve performance.

Unfortunately, produc-tion aircraft began to reveal a certain amount of structural weakness. Among the crashes that resulted, the most disas-trous for the Caudron firm occurred on 12 December 1915, when a production aircraft under test was destroyed and Gaston Caudron, who was piloting the machine, was killed.

However, earlier in the type's career, Escadrille C.46 had claimed 34 German aircraft brought down with its R.4 warplanes in an eight-week period. Nevertheless, it was soon clear that, in addition to structural redesign, improved ceiling and greater manoeuvrability were highly desirable. The new Caudron chief designer, Paul Deville, accordingly set to work on a new improved development which was to emerge as the R.11. Production of the R.4 was terminated after the completion of 249 machines. In the reconnais-sance escadrilles the R.4 was replaced by the Letord 1 during 1917.

As well as the twin-wheel main landing gear units and tailskid, the R.4 also possessed a single nose wheel, intended to protect the propellers in the event of a rough landing.

SPECIFICATION	
Caudron R.4	**Weights:** empty 3,770 lb
Type: three-seat bomber or	(1710 kg); maximum take-off
photographic reconnaissance	5,137 lb (2330 kg)
aircraft	**Dimensions:** wingspan 69 ft 2¾ in
Powerplant: two Renault 12Db	(21.10 m); length 38 ft 8½ in
Vee engines each rated at 130 hp	(11.80 m); height 10 ft 6 in
(97 kW)	(3.20 m); wing area 753.50 sq ft
Performance: maximum speed	(70.00 m²)
85 mph (136 km/h) at sea level;	**Armament:** two 0.303-in (7.7-mm)
climb to 6,560 ft (2000 m) in	Lewis trainable machine-guns in
18 minutes ; service ceiling	each of the nose and dorsal
15,090 ft (4600 m); endurance	positions, plus up to 220 lb
3 hours	(100 kg) of bombs

Caudron R.11

Alongside the abortive **O.2** single-seat fighter and **R.5** and **R.10** reconnaissance bomber prototypes, there appeared in March 1917 the three-seat **Caudron R.11**. Intended originally for the French A.3 (Corps d'Armée trois-place) recon-naissance category, the twin-engined R.11 biplane owed much to the earlier R.4. The prototype was powered by two 200-hp (149-kW) Hispano-Suiza 8Ba Vee engines carried in streamlined, triangular nacelles located just above the lower wing. The type's one-piece lower wing was something of a structural achievement.

Orders were placed for 1,000 **R.11A.3** warplanes and the first aircraft were built in late 1917. Production was slow, however, only 20 R.11s being operational by

Escadrille C46 flew this R.11 for the protection of 13ᵉ Escadre's bombers, between February and November 1918. Note the aircraft's forward and midships gun emplacements.

April 1918. With the armistice, production ended abruptly after the comple-tion of only 370 aircraft. Pairs of aircraft were acquired by the British and US forces for evaluation.

In service, the R.11 was deployed as a formidable escort fighter used to protect formations of Bre.14B.2 day bombers. On attacks well behind enemy lines, the R.11 built up an impressive score at the expense of the German fighters.

No doubt the impact of the R.11 would have been much greater had more aircraft been available by the spring of 1918, but difficul-ties with the Hispano-Suiza geared engines were never fully overcome.

The R.11's fuel supply system had been arranged in such a way as to ensure that both engines could be fed from either main fuel tank if necessary, and late-production aircraft featured engine nacelles whose rear sections could be jetti-soned in flight, along with the fuel tanks they contained. Many of these later aircraft had the uprated powerplant of two 235-hp (175-kW) Hispano-Suiza 8Beb engines.

A number of two- and multi-seat aircraft had been lost in action when the pilot had been hit, and for this reason Caudron included dual controls for the rear gunner's cockpit. This was no doubt a contributory factor to the high morale among Caudron-equipped escadrilles.

The R.11A.3 continued to form the equipment of what were, by then, known as the Escadrilles de Protection of the 11ᵉ and 12ᵉ Régiments d'Aviation in the period after World War I. The last surviving aircraft were withdrawn from service and scrapped in July 1922.

SPECIFICATION	
Caudron R.11	4,777 lb (2167 kg)
Type: three-seat escort fighter	**Dimensions:** wingspan 58 ft 9⅓ in
Powerplant: two Hispano-Suiza	(17.92 m); length 36 ft 9½ in
8Bba Vee engines each rated at	(11.22 m); height 9 ft 2¼ in
215 hp (160 kW)	(2.80 m); wing area 583.96 sq ft
Performance: maximum speed	(54.25 m²)
114 mph (183 km/h) at 6,560 ft	**Armament:** two 0.303-in (7.7-mm)
(2000 m); climb to 6,560 ft	Lewis trainable machine-guns in
(2000 m) in 8 minutes 10 seconds;	each of the nose and dorsal
service ceiling 19,520 ft (5950 m);	positions, and one 0.303-in
endurance 3 hours	(7.7-mm) Lewis trainable machine-
Weights: empty 3,135 lb	gun in the undernose position
(1422 kg); maximum take-off	

Variants

R.12: experimental 1918 version of the R.11 with the powerplant of two 300-hp (224-kW) Hispano-Suiza 8Fb engines; development of the R.12 was terminated with the appearance of the more promising R.14
R.14: prototype of an enlarged development of the R.11. It appeared in August 1918 with the R.12's powerplant, but with a longer-span wing, revised armament, modified tail surfaces and other changes

Cavalier Mustang

During the 1960s Cavalier Aircraft Corporation of Sarasota, Florida, acquired the type certificate to the North American F-51 (origi-nally P-51) Mustang. From the design, Cavalier devel-oped a tandem two-seat business and sport conver-sion with a second seat added behind the pilot's seat in a cockpit modified with the canopy of the TF-51 trainer. This was marketed as the **Cavalier 2000**. The Cavalier 2000 gained two wingtip auxiliary fuel tanks and was powered by one 1,595-hp (1189-kW) Packard V-1650-7 Merlin Vee engine.

More importantly, however, Cavalier also gained a USAF contract to manufacture a version of the F-51D for supply to air forces receiving MAP assistance. The result was a new production programme, aircraft being assembled from a combination of new parts.

Cavalier Mustang (continued)

Other parts for the Cavalier Mustangs were taken from existing stocks; in addition, the new aircraft were delivered with many updated features, especially in the area of armament and avionics. While this programme was in progress, Cavalier developed as a private venture during 1967-68 an improved **Mustang II** specifically for use in the COIN (counter-insurgency) role. Reinforcement of the wings and fuselage, plus the installation of a more powerful version of the Merlin engine, developing

1,760 hp (1312 kW), made possible a higher take-off weight and the carriage of more armament.

At this stage the company decided to produce an even more advanced version with a Dart turboprop powerplant and a prototype was built as the **Turbo Mustang III**.

Development continued with the installation of a 2,445-ehp (2823-ekW) Lycoming T55-L-9 turboprop and this new aircraft had provision for cockpit armour and engine protection. It also introduced fire-suppressing reticulated

foam in the fuel tanks and the planned installation of a zero/zero escape system for the pilot.

Shortly after this stage of development, the programme was acquired by Piper Aircraft Corporation, which flew the Lycoming-engined prototype for the first time on 29 April 1971. Development of this aircraft, by now redesignated as the **Piper Enforcer** and featuring 10 underwing hardpoints, continued into the early 1980s but was then terminated for lack of any real military interest.

The length of the Dart engine combined with the right balance to keep the centre of gravity in the right position, despite the lower weight of this slimmer engine, required the design of an extended cowling for the Turbo Mustang III.

SPECIFICATION	
Cavalier Turbo Mustang III **Type:** single-seat close-support fighter **Powerplant:** one Rolls-Royce RDa.6 Dart Mk 510 turboprop engine rated at 1,740 ehp (1298 ekW) **Performance:** maximum speed 540 mph (869 km/h) at optimum altitude; cruising speed 380 mph (611 km/h) at optimum altitude; ferry range 2,300 miles (3701 km); radius more than 155 miles (250 km) with 2,000 lb (907 kg) of weapons and a loiter of 2 hours	30 minutes **Weights:** empty equipped 6,696 lb (3037 kg); maximum take-off 14,000 lb (6350 kg) **Dimensions:** wingspan 40 ft 1 in (12.22 m); length 32 ft 2¼ in (9.81 m); wing area 272.23 sq ft (25.29 m²) **Armament:** six 0.5-in (12.7-mm) Browning M2 or M3 fixed forward-firing machine-guns in the leading edge of the wing, plus up to 5,777 lb (2620 kg) of disposable stores carried on six underwing hardpoints

A re-built F-51D and the sole TF-51D formate. The modified machines featured the tall fin of the P-51H, while the two-seater also has a revised canopy shape. Two further two-seaters were F-51Ds, since they did not have dual controls as standard.

CERVA CE.43 Guépard

The **CE.43 Guépard** (cheetah) is an all-metal version of the **Wassmer WA.4/21**, itself a development of the WA.40 and WA.41 Baladou. Wassmer Aviation began work on its own range of light aircraft after 1955.

The WA.4/21 prototype flew in March 1967 and 25 had been built by 1970.

Construction was of steel tube with a fabric-covered fuselage and a plywood-covered wing, but in order to provide an alternative all-metal version, Wassmer Aviation and Siren SA formed a joint company in 1971, known as CERVA (Consortium Européen de Réalisation et de Ventes

d'Avions/European consortium for the manufacture and sale of aircraft).

A prototype of the resulting CE.43 was flown in May 1971, the second prototype was delivered to Service de la Formation Aéronautique (SFA) and a third airframe was used for static testing. Following its

receipt of certification on 1 June 1972, the CE.43 received a French government contract for five aircraft for the SFA and 18 for the Centre d'Essais en Vol (CEV). By early 1974 there were 12 CE.43s on the production line and the first deliveries to private customers were made during 1975.

The prototypes of two

new versions were flown under French government contract, the **CE.44 Couguar** (cougar) being powered by the 285-hp (213-kW) Continental Tiara engine and the **CE.45 Léopard** by the 310-hp (231-kW) Lycoming TIO-540, but all development ended when Wassmer went into liquidation during 1977.

SPECIFICATION	
CERVA CE.43 Guépard **Type:** four/five-seat light aircraft **Powerplant:** one Lycoming IO-540-C4B5 flat-six engine rated at 250 hp (186 kW) **Performance:** maximum speed 199 mph (320 km/h) at sea level; cruising speed 193 mph (310 km/h) at 6,560 ft (2000 m); initial climb rate 1,083 ft (330 m) per minute;	service ceiling 17,390 ft (5300 m); range 1,801 miles (2900 km) **Weights:** empty 1,863 lb (845 kg); maximum take-off 3,527 lb (1600 kg) **Dimensions:** wingspan 32 ft 9½ in (10.00 m); length 27 ft 9 in (8.40 m); height 9 ft 6 in (2.90 m); wing area 172.23 sq ft (16.00 m²)

When production ended late in 1976, 43 Guépards had been delivered. Components for the CE.43 were manufactured by Siren, while final assembly and flight testing were carried out by Wassmer.

Cessna Model A, Model AW and Model BW

In February 1911 Clyde V. Cessna, a farmer of Kansas, bought his first aircraft. This was a Blériot-type monoplane and Cessna suffered a series of accidents and mishaps before he had taught himself to fly competently by June 1911. By this time the aircraft had been totally rebuilt, and in the

summer of that year he successfully flew four exhibitions before rebuilding the aircraft once more.

The cycle of summer exhibition flying and winter rebuilding continued to 1916, when Cessna moved to Wichita, Kansas. Here, he was offered space at the Jones Motor Car Company in return for

painting an advertising slogan for the company's Jones Six car under the wing of his aircraft. Cessna built some 14 aircraft in Wichita, the first two of them comprising one improved version of his 'Blériot' and then the so-called **Comet**. The latter had the unusual feature of a semi-enclosed cockpit,

and in July 1917 set a US speed record of 124.6 mph (200.5 km/h).

The effects of the USA's entry into World War I now made themselves felt, and Cessna returned mainly to farming until February 1925 when, at the invitation of Walter Beech and Lloyd Stearman, he became president of the

Travel Air Manufacturing Company. Beech and Stearman were staunch adherents of the biplane layout while Cessna believed fervently in the monoplane layout. In 1926, therefore, Cessna left Travel Air. With Victor Roos, Cessna established the Cessna-Roos Aircraft Company in September

1927, founding the Cessna Aircraft Company Inc. in December 1927 following the departure of Roos.

The first Cessna design to enter series production was the **Cessna Model A**. A four-seater of mixed wood and steel-tube construction with fabric covering, the type was a cantilever monoplane with fixed tailskid landing gear, and 22 were built in **Model AA**, **Model AC**, **Model AF** and **Model AS** versions with different engines. Some 48 were of the definitive **Model AW** type that was produced through most of 1929 with a 125-hp (93-kW) Warner Scarab radial engine.

A three-seat version of the Model A with considerably greater power for very much improved performance was known as the **Model BW**, of which 13 were built with a 220-hp (164-kW) Wright Whirlwind J-5 engine.

Model A engines included the Anzani (AA), Comet (AC), 'Floco' (AF) and Siemens-Halske (AS) radials.

SPECIFICATION

Cessna Model AW
Type: four-seat touring aircraft
Powerplant: one Warner Scarab radial engine rated at 125 hp (93 kW)
Performance: maximum speed more than 125 mph (201 km/h) at sea level; cruising speed 105 mph (169 km/h) at optimum altitude; initial climb rate 620 ft (189 m) per minute; service ceiling 12,000 ft (3660 m); range 630 miles (1014 km)
Weights: empty 1,225 lb (556 kg); maximum take-off 2,260 lb (3637 kg)
Dimensions: wingspan 40 ft (12.19 m); length 24 ft 9 in (7.54 m); height 6 ft 11 in (2.11 m); wing area 224.00 sq ft (20.81 m²)

Cessna Model C (UC-77B/D) and Model C Airmaster (UC-94)

The first product of the Cessna company after reopening its factory in Wichita, Kansas, as the worst effects of the financial depression started to ebb in 1934, was the **Model C-34**. This was a high-wing cantilever type, which took full advantage of the latest aspects of structural and aerodynamic design. It completed its first flight in June 1935.

The Model C-34 was of mixed metal and wood construction covered with Dural on the forward fuselage, plywood on the forward parts of the flying surfaces, and fabric elsewhere. Options included a metal rather than wooden propeller, and Edo floats in place of the standard wheel undercarriage.

Some 42 of the aircraft were built, two later being impressed for service with the USAAF in World War II under the designation **UC-77B**.

The **Model C-37**, introduced during 1937, brought in minor improvements to the furnishing of a slightly wider cabin. Some 46 examples of the C-37 were built, and one impressed in 1942 was designated **UC-77C**.

Introduced in 1938, the Model C-38 Airmaster again featured minor improvements, with some of the previously optional equipment fitted as standard; airframe changes included the provision of wider-track landing gear and a large underfuselage flap which served as an airbrake to reduce landing speed. Production of the C-38 amounted to 16 aircraft.

The final Cessna four-seat models designed before World War II were the **C-145** and **C-165 Airmaster**. When first rolled out on 11 September 1938, the new type was initially designated as the **Model C-39**, but was very soon redesignated as the **Model C-145** with the numerical part of the designation now indicating engine horsepower rather than year of introduction. The C-145 was powered by the 145-hp (108-kW) Super Scarab radial engine, while the Model C-165 and slightly later **Model C-165D** differed only in having one Super Scarab engine rated at 165 or 175 hp (123 or 130 kW) respectively. By the time the manufacture of the Airmaster series ceased in 1941, production had reached 42 C-145, 34 C-165 and three C-165D aircraft. In 1942 three of the Model C-165s were impressed for USAAF service as **UC-94** aircraft.

A 145-hp (108-kW) Super Scarab radial engine, driving a two-bladed propeller, powered the four-seater Model C-34.

SPECIFICATION

Cessna Model C-38 Airmaster
Type: four-seat touring aircraft
Powerplant: one Warner Super Scarab Series 50 radial engine rated at 145 hp (108 kW)
Performance: maximum speed 162 mph (261 km/h) at sea level; cruising speed 150 mph (241 km/h) at 8,200 ft (2500 m); initial climb rate 800 ft (244 m) per minute; service ceiling 18,000 ft (5485 in); range 550 miles (885 km)
Weights: empty 1,370 lb (621 kg); maximum take-off 2,350 lb (1066 kg)
Dimensions: wingspan 34 ft 2 in (10.41 m); length 24 ft 8 in (7.52 m); height 7 ft (2.13 m); wing area 181.00 sq ft (16.81 m²)

Cessna CH-1 Skyhook (H-41 Seneca)

Cessna embarked on a relatively short flirtation with rotary-wing flight in March 1952 when it purchased the Seibel Helicopter Company. It was in the summer of 1952 that Cessna started work on the design of its first helicopter, which was in essence a development of the **Seibel S-3** that had first flown in 1947. A testbed first flew in July 1953, and paved the way for the **Cessna CH-1 Skyhook** that first flew in prototype form during July 1954.

This was a four-seat light helicopter of basically conventional appearance with a two-bladed main rotor and two-bladed tail rotor. The main rotor employed flexible steel sheet L-section hinges to attach the roots of the rotor blade to the hub, a system that permitted continuously-varying blade pitch angle without the need for pitch-change bearings.

The performance of the CH-1 was demonstrated in 1957 with the establishment of three records, including an altitude of 30,355 ft (9252 m) in two weight categories.

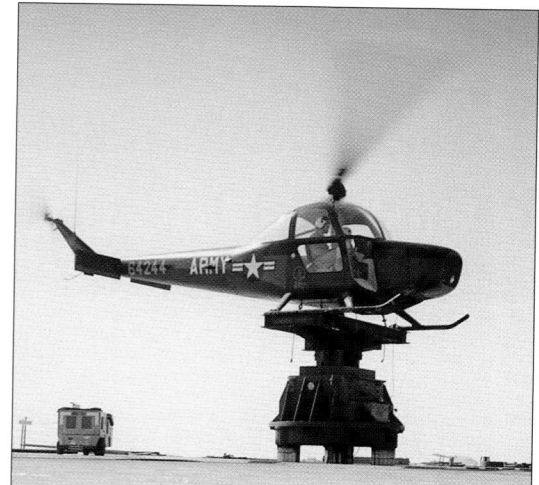

SPECIFICATION

Cessna CH-1C Skyhook
Type: one-pilot utility light helicopter
Powerplant: one Continental FSO-526-A flat-four engine rated at 270 hp (201 kW)
Performance: maximum speed 122 mph (196 km/h) at sea level; cruising speed 120 mph (193 km/h) at optimum altitude; climb rate 1,030 ft (314 m) per minute at 8,000 ft (2440 m); climb to 10,000 ft (3050 m) in 10 minutes 16 seconds; hovering ceiling 9,600 ft (2925 m) in ground effect; range 400 miles (644 km)
Weights: empty 2,080 lb (944 kg); maximum take-off 3,100 lb (1406 kg)
Dimensions: main rotor diameter 35 ft (10.67 m); length, rotors fore-and-aft 42 ft 8 in (13.00 m) and fuselage 29 ft 5 in (8.97 m); height 8 ft 5 in (2.57 m); main rotor disc area 962.11 sq ft (89.38 m²)
Payload: up to three passengers or 500 lb (227 kg) of freight

Cessna CH-1 Skyhook (H-41 Seneca) (continued)

Another unusual feature of the CH-1 was the installation of its 260-hp (194-kW) FSO-470-A air-cooled engine in the extreme nose. From this location it drove the main and anti-

torque rotors by means of a simplified transmission system with only three and two gears in the main rotor and anti-torque rotor drives respectively.

The CH-1 was of all-

metal construction with accommodation for two persons side-by-side, and the landing gear was of the fixed twin-skid type.

The CH-1 was followed by the improved **CH-1B**

with mechanical and aero-dynamic improvements, and the US Army evaluated a batch of 10 such helicopters under the designation **YH-41 Seneca**. The **CH-1C** was intended

as the definitive production variant for the civil market with four-seat accommodation, increased fuel capacity and all-weather instrumentation, but the programme was soon terminated.

Cessna Model CW-6 and Model DC-6 (UC-77A)

In November 1928 Cessna flew the first example of a new design, the **CW-6**, that featured fixed tailwheel rather than tailskid landing gear, and was of mixed metal and wood construction covered largely with fabric. Enclosed accommodation was provided for six persons. In this instance, the letter W in the designation stood not for Warner, as it had in the Model AW, but for Wright, as the new type was powered by one 220-hp (164-kW) Wright Whirlwind J-5 radial.

In the event, the Model CW-6 did not enter production as Cessna felt that

there would be a greater demand for a slightly scaled-down version with a four-seat cabin offering greater volume and comfort than those of the Model A series. The spur for the development of this type was the Curtiss Flying Service, which wanted to act as agent for the type in a form powered by a Curtiss engine. The promise of large sales was sufficient for Cessna to triple the size of its manufacturing facilities, and the initial result was the **Model DC-6** that first flew in February 1929 with the 170-hp (127-kW) Curtiss Challenger inline.

In the DC-6, the pilot sat in a cockpit ahead of the wing leading edge, and up to five passengers were accommodated in a cabin below the wing and fitted on each side with three windows. The cabin was placed over the aircraft's centre of gravity.

Disappointing performance resulted in the company revising the DC-6 with one Wright Whirlwind, which was available as the 300-hp (224-kW) nine-cylinder J-6-9 in the **Model DC-6A**, or the 225-hp (168-kW) seven-cylinder J-6-7 in the **Model DC-6B**.

The Depression, which followed the 'Wall Street crash' of 1929, restricted production of the two models to low figures. Production of the DC-6A is thought to have amounted to 20 aircraft, while that of

the cheaper Model DC-6B totalled at least 24 aircraft.

In 1942 the USAAF impressed four examples each of the Models DC-6A and DC-6B, with the service designations **UC-77** and **UC-77A** respectively.

In an attempt to keep the factory going during the Depression, Cessna designed and marketed the

CG-2 primary glider. Eldon Cessna, Clyde's son, also designed the single-seat **EC-1** with a 25-hp (19-kW) Cleone engine and the two-seat **EC-2** with a 30-hp (22-kW) E-107A engine. Only the glider achieved production status, however, before the company ceased operation, not to resume it until January 1934.

SPECIFICATION

Cessna Model DC-6B
Type: five/six-seat touring aircraft
Powerplant: one Wright Whirlwind J-6-7 radial engine rated at 225 hp (168 kW)
Performance: maximum speed 148 mph (238 km/h) at optimum altitude; cruising speed 125 mph (201 km/h) at optimum altitude; initial climb rate 900 ft (274 m) per

minute; service ceiling 17,500 ft (5335 m); range 685 miles (1102 km)
Weights: empty 1,871 lb (849 kg); maximum take-off 3,100 lb (1406 kg)
Dimensions: wingspan 41 ft (12.50 m); length 28 ft 2 in (8.59 m); height 7 ft 8 in (2.34 m); wing area 268.00 sq ft (24.90 m²)

Cessna Model T-50 (AT-8/17, UC-78, JRC and Crane)

Cessna's first twin-engined lightplane, built and first flown in 1939, was a five-seat commercial transport. This **Model T-50** was of low-wing cantilever monoplane configuration and of mixed construction. The wing and tail unit were of wood, the latter covered with fabric, while the fuselage was a welded steel-tube structure covered with fabric over lightweight wooden skinning.

In 1940 the military potential of this aircraft, as a trainer suitable for the conversion of pilots from single- to twin-engined types, became apparent almost simultaneously to two North American nations. First was Canada, which required a machine

of this type for the Commonwealth Joint Air Training Plan, and 550 Model T-50 aircraft were supplied under Lend-Lease, these receiving the local designation **Crane Mk IA**.

The second requirement was for the USAAC which, late in 1940, contracted for the supply of 33 Model T-50s for service evaluation under the designation **AT-8**. These were powered by two 295-hp (220-kW) Jacobs R-680-9 radials and proved over-powered for the training role, and less powerful engines were specified for service aircraft. The initial **AT-17** production version was fitted with two Jacobs R-755-9 engines driving wooden propellers. Some

JRC-1s, which were basically UC-78s, served with the US Navy. As with all members of the T-50 family, the JRC-1 had electrically-actuated retractable landing gear and flaps.

450 of this model were built, and these were followed into production by 223 of the generally similar **AT-17A**, which differed by having Hamilton Standard constant-speed metal propellers. The later **AT-17B** (466 built) had some equipment changes, and the **AT-17C** (60 built) had different radio equipment.

In 1942 what had, by now, become the USAAF decided that these aircraft would be valuable for liai-

son/communication purposes and as light personnel transports. Production of the Model T-50 for military service in the transport role totalled 1,287 machines, the aircraft being named **Bobcat** and given the designation **C-78**, later changed to **UC-78**. In addition, a few commercial Model T-50s were

impressed for USAAF service with the designation **UC-78A**.

The USAAF's requirement for the two-seat conversion trainers had been difficult to predict, and when it was discovered in late 1942 that procurement contracts very considerably exceeded the training

SPECIFICATION

Cessna UC-78 Bobcat
Type: five-seat light transport
Powerplant: two Jacobs R-755-9 radial engines each rated at 245 hp (183 kW)
Performance: maximum speed 195 mph (314 km/h) at sea level; cruising speed 175 mph (282 km/h) at sea level; initial climb rate 1,325 ft (404 m) per minute;

service ceiling 22,000 ft (6705 m); range 750 miles (1207 km)
Weights: empty 3,500 lb (1588 kg); maximum take-off 5,700 lb (2585 kg)
Dimensions: wingspan 41 ft 11 in (12.78 m); length 32 ft 9 in (9.98 m); height 9 ft 11 in (3.02 m); wing area 295.0 sq ft (27.41 m²)

requirement, Cessna was requested to fulfil the outstanding balance of the AT-17B and **AT-17D** models as **UC-78B** and **UC-78C** aircraft. The two subvariants were virtually identical, but differed from the original UC-78s in having two-bladed fixed-pitch wooden propellers and some minor equipment changes. Production of these two versions amounted to 1,806 UC-78Bs and 327 UC-78Cs.

In the period 1942-3, the USN had a requirement for a lightweight transport aircraft to carry ferry pilots between delivery points and their home bases, as well as for the movement of USN flight crews. This led to the procurement of 67 aircraft, generally similar to the UC-78, which entered service under the designation **JRC-1**.

Cessna Model 120 and Model 140

The **Cessna Model 120** prototype, first flown on 28 June 1945, represented the company's attempt to capture a major share of the market for personal lightplanes in the period following World War II. A two-seat cabin monoplane with a strut-braced high-set wing, the Model 120 was all-metal except for the wing, which was of fabric-covered wooden construction, the landing gear was of the fixed tail-wheel type introducing cantilever spring steel main units, and the enclosed cabin provided two seats side-by-side and dual controls as standard. The powerplant comprised an 85-hp (63-kW) C-85-12 flat-four engine, and the higher power of this unit by comparison with competing types, plus a low price tag, ensured that Cessna gained an unexpectedly large measure of sales success: production of the Model 120 eventually reached 2,172 units.

The Model 120 was a basic aircraft that was complemented by a 'de luxe' **Model 140**, which had manually-actuated flaps on the trailing edge of a wing that was now based on an all-metal structure, extra windows at the rear of the cabin, and a full electrical system. Like that of the Model 120, the production life of the Model 140 ended in 1950, and by this time 4,907 examples of the Model 140 had been completed, together with 525 examples of the **Model 140A**. The latter was introduced in 1949, with an all-metal wing braced on each side by a single strut and, in some aircraft, the uprated powerplant of one 90-hp (67-kW) C-90-12.

The trailing-edge flaps of the Cessna 140 are situated inboard of the wing struts and have a rippled surface texture. The lack of such a feature on this aircraft identifies it as a Model 120. Large numbers of both models remain airworthy.

SPECIFICATION
Cessna Model 140
Type: two-seat touring and sporting aircraft
Powerplant: one Continental C-85-12F flat-four engine rated at 85 hp (63 kW)
Performance: maximum speed 120 mph (193 km/h) at sea level; cruising speed 105 mph (169 km/h) at optimum altitude; initial climb
rate 680 ft (207 m) per minute; service ceiling 15,500 ft (4725 m); range 450 miles (724 km)
Weights: empty 900 lb (408 kg); maximum take-off 1,500 lb (680 kg)
Dimensions: wingspan 32 ft 10 in (10.01 m); length 21 ft (6.40 m); height 6 ft 3 in (1.91 m); wing area 159.60 sq ft (14.82 m²)

Cessna Model 150 and Model 152

When production of the Model 120 and Model 140 ended in 1950, Cessna concentrated on the development of four-seat aircraft of similar configuration. It was not until the first flight of the **Model 150** (originally designated as the **Model 142**), on 12 September 1957, that the company re-entered the market for two-seat lightplanes. A high-wing monoplane of all-metal construction with a single wing-bracing strut on each side, the Model 150 was of similar configuration to the Model 140A except for its fixed tailwheel-type landing gear. Dual controls were optional, the powerplant was based on one 100-hp (75-kW) O-200-A flat-four engine and production totalled 1,018 of this baseline variant.

Just before the end of production, the type had been available in **Model 150 Standard**, **Model 150 Commuter**, **Model 150 Commuter II** and **Model 150 Aerobat** versions. The differences between the first three represented varying standards of installed equipment, and there was also a wide range of optional avionics and equipment available. The Aerobat embodied structural changes, permitting a licence in the Aerobatic category for load factors of +6 g and -3 g at maximum weight.

Late in 1977 the Model 150 range was replaced in production by the **Model 152**, which was based on the **Model 150M,** but powered by the Lycoming O-235-L2C engine driving a new propeller. It otherwise differed from its predecessors in its electrical system, one-piece engine cowling and modified flaps.

SPECIFICATION
Cessna Model 152 Standard
Type: two-seat touring, sporting and training aircraft
Powerplant: one Lycoming O-235-L2C flat-four engine rated at 110 hp (82 kW)
Performance: maximum speed 127 mph (204 km/h) at sea level; cruising speed 123 mph (198 km/h) at 8,000 ft (2440 m); initial climb
rate 750 ft (229 m) per minute; service ceiling 14,700 ft (4480 m); range 794 miles (1278 km)
Weights: empty 1,107 lb (502 kg); maximum take-off 1,670 lb (757 kg)
Dimensions: wingspan 32 ft 8½ in (9.97 m); length 24 ft 1 in (7.34 m); height 8 ft 6 in (2.59 m); wing area 157.00 sq ft (14.59 m²)

Variants

Model 150A: 332 examples of a Model 150 development with a revised instrument panel, larger rear side windows and the main landing gear legs moved farther to the rear
Model 150B: 350 examples of Model 150A development with a number of enhancements including an improved propeller and spinner
Model 150C: 387 examples of a generally improved Model 150B with the option of a child seat
Model 150D: 681 examples of a major development of the Model 150C that first flew on 4 February 1963 with a cut-down rear fuselage allowing the incorporation of large windows in the rear of the cabin behind the trailing edge of the wing
Model 150E: 760 examples of a modestly upgraded development of the Model 150D
Model 150F: 3,000 examples of a significantly upgraded development of the Model 150E with a swept vertical tail surface, enlarged cabin doors and electrically-actuated trailing-edge flaps; this was the first variant built under licence by Reims in France, in this instance 67 aircraft with the designation **F150F**
Model 150G: 2,666 examples of a Model 150F development with a widened cabin and a new instrument panel; the 152 **F150G** aircraft were equivalent machines built in France
Model 150H: 2,110 examples of a slightly improved version of the Model 150G; the 170 **F150H** aircraft were equivalent machines built in France
Model 150J: 1,820 examples of a Model 150H development with revised landing gear; the 140 **F150J** aircraft were equivalent machines built in France
Model 150K: 875 examples of a Model 150J development with a revised cabin fitted with new seats, a trim tab on the lower part of the rudder's trailing edge, and cambered wingtips; the 129 **F150K** aircraft were equivalent machines built in France
Model 150L: 3,778 examples of a Model 150K development with an enlarged fin fairing, tubular steel landing-gear legs, an engine cowling of modified shape and, from 1974, new wheel spats; the 485 **F150L** aircraft were equivalent aircraft built in France, and the 39 **A150L** aircraft were equivalent machines built in Argentina by DINFIA
Model 150M: 3,624 examples of a Model 150L development with a taller but narrower-chord fin; the 285 **F150M** aircraft were equivalent machines built in France
Model A150 Aerobat: 734 examples of the aerobatic version of the Model 150 series, first flown on 2 January 1969 and produced in **Model A150K**, **Model A150L** and **Model A150M** subvariants with airframe-strengthening, full seat harnesses and quick-release doors; the 120 **FA150K/L** aircraft were equivalent machines built in France, the 141 **FRA150L** aircraft were built in France with the powerplant of one Rolls-Royce (Continental) O-240-A engine rated at 130 hp (97 kW), and the 75 **FRA150M** aircraft were built in France with the modified vertical tail surface of the F150M

Cessna Model 150 and Model 152 (continued)

Up to the time of its discontinuation in the mid-1980s, the Model 152 had been built to the extent of 7,584 aircraft. These included 315 examples of the **Model A152 Aerobat** development analogous to the Model A150, and 641 machines built in France with the designation **F152** (including 89 **FA152 Aerobat** machines). The Model 152 was available in Model 152, **Model 152 II**, **Model 152 Trainer** and **Model 152 Aerobat** versions.

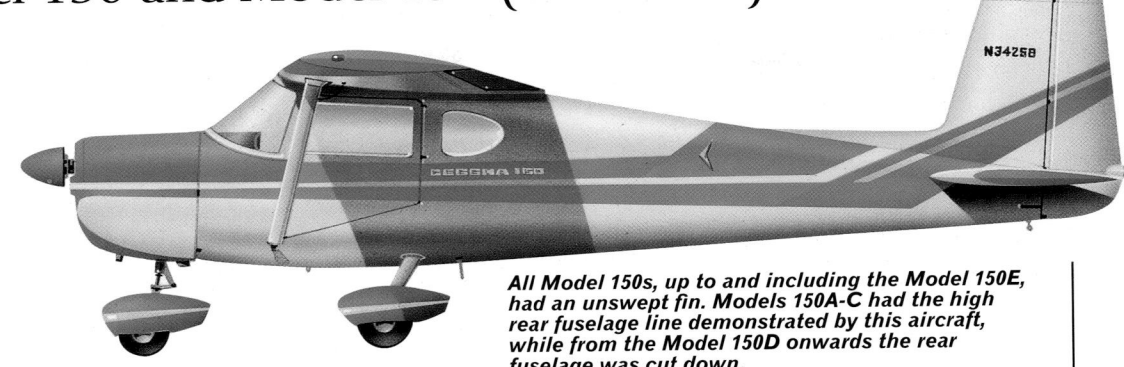

All Model 150s, up to and including the Model 150E, had an unswept fin. Models 150A-C had the high rear fuselage line demonstrated by this aircraft, while from the Model 150D onwards the rear fuselage was cut down.

Cessna Model 170, Model 172 Skyhawk, Hawk and Cutlass (T-41 Mescalero), and Model 175 Skylark

The **Cessna Model 170** was designed as a 'family' aircraft and was essentially a development of the Model 140 with a re-engineered airframe, incorporating a larger cabin providing accommodation for four persons. The success of Cessna's effort has led to the Model 170 and **Model 172** family of aircraft being built in larger numbers than any other aircraft yet produced.

The Model 170 prototype first flew in November 1947. The basic aircraft was a 'tail dragger', based on an all-metal fuselage and a fabric-covered aluminium wing. The prototype was powered by a 145-hp (108-kW) Continental C-145 flat-six engine.

Some 729 Model 170s were manufactured in 1948 before the production line turned over to the **Model 170A** that appeared on the market in 1949, with an all-metal wing of revised shape, single wing-bracing struts, and a large fin fillet. Wheel spats were first seen on newly-built Model 170As, but were later fitted to all members of the Model 170 family. A total of 1,536 Model 170As was built, followed by 2,907 examples of the **Model 170B** between 1952 and 1956. The Model 170B introduced the C-145-2 (later O-300) engine and thus had a distinctive split air intake on either side of the propeller, and also had slotted Fowler flaps.

Production of the Model 170 series thus totalled 5,172 aircraft in a nine-year production life.

The **Model 170C** prototype that first flew in January 1955 was the precursor of the Model 172. The prototype was a conversion from Model 170 standard with fixed tricycle landing gear that added

drag and adversely affected performance, but also facilitated taxiing as well as take-off and landing, and Cessna rightly appreciated that this was indeed the direction it must take. The true Model 172 prototype first flew in June 1955 with the O-300-C engine and was based on essentially the same airframe as the Model 170 except for its new squared-off vertical tail surface. Despite its adverse effect on performance, the new 'Land-O-Matic' landing gear with a steerable nose-wheel was a tremendous sales asset, and evidence of this fact was provided by the completion of 3,757 such aircraft up to 1960, when the Model 172 was replaced in production by the **Model 172A**, of which 994 were built.

Cessna liked to introduce new models at annual intervals (much like an automobile manufacturer) primarily for marketing reasons. The Model 172A had a swept vertical tail surface which was aesthetically pleasing, but again not a performance booster. In 1961 the **Model 172B Skyhawk** arrived, and production totalled 989 aircraft. The Model 172B had shortened landing gear units, a baggage door, and a redesigned engine cowl-

In 170A and 170B form, the Model 170 introduced single wing-bracing struts. Compared to the Model 140, the new aircraft featured a longer nose and an enlarged central cabin window on each side.

ing and propeller spinner. The **Model 172C** (810 built) had an increased maximum take-off weight. In 1963, the **Model 172D** (1,011 built) introduced a distinctive new shaping to the fuselage through the cutting down of the rear fuselage to permit the installation of an 'Omnivision' rear cabin window. It also featured an extended fin, one-piece windscreen and redesigned rear side windows. The **Model 172E** (1,209 built) had electrically actuated flaps. The **Model 172F** (1,400 built) had a more modern O-300-D engine and was followed by the **Model 172G** (1,474 built) with only minor changes. The **Model 172H** (1,586

built) had a redesigned nose gear with a spatted wheel, plus a new engine cowling and instrument panel. The Lycoming O-320-E2D engine, rated at 150 hp (112 kW), was introduced in the **Model 172I** (649 built). In 1971 the **Model 172K** (2,055 built) appeared with enlarged rear side windows, cambered wingtips and a straight dorsal fin fillet. The **Model 172L** (1,535 built) of

1972 had a larger fin fillet extended to the rear window, tubular steel landing-gear units and the landing light moved from the leading edge of the port wing to the engine cowling. A drooped (cambered) wing leading edge, which improved stall characteristics, was introduced in 1973 on the **Model 172M**, which also featured a recontoured tail and became immensely

Wearing its US military serial 69-7183 in large numerals on the fuselage side, this Greek T-41D is typical of those built for export. Note the characteristic lack of a spinner.

This Model R172K Hawk XP shows the classic lines of the 172 family, including the 'Omnivision' rear window.

popular, resulting in the construction of 6,825 aircraft. In 1977 the **Model 172N** was introduced, with the 160-hp (119-kW) Lycoming O-320-H2AD engine, but in 1981, this somewhat problematical engine was replaced in production aircraft by the -D2J version of the same basic unit. The Model **R172K Hawk XP** was developed from the Model 172N with the 195-hp (145-kW) Continental IO-360-K engine. In 1980, Cessna introduced the first Model 172 with retractable tricycle landing gear as the **Model 172RG Cutlass**, or **Cutlass RG**, of which 1,191 examples were manufactured with the 180-hp (134-kW) O-320-E20 engine driving a three-bladed propeller. A version with fixed landing gear, the

Model 172Q Cutlass (391 built), was introduced in 1982 to take further advantage of the new engine.

The Model 172 enjoyed 31 years of continuous production, but by the mid-1980s sales had slowed to a trickle as a result of US product liability laws, by which manufacturers could be held responsible for virtually any accidents involving their aircraft. Model 172 production ceased in 1986 but, following a long-awaited change in the law, was resumed in 1996. The sole current production model is the **Model 172R Skyhawk**, based on the Model 172N but with the 160-hp (119-kW) IO-360-L2A fuel-injected engine driving a two-bladed, fixed-pitch metal propeller and with new avionics. The first

delivery was made in 1997.

Licensed production of the Model 172 began in France during 1963 at the factory of Reims Aviation. French-built Skyhawk variants included the **F172D, F172E, F172F, F172G, F172H, F172K, F172L, F172M, F172N** and **F172P**. Reims also developed a higher-powered version of the F172, the **FR172 Reims Rocket** family, with a 210-hp (157-kW) engine. The prototype of the family, powered by a Continental IO-360-D engine, was flown by Cessna in 1962, and aircraft to this standard were later built as **T-41** machines in the USA.

Commercial models were built exclusively by Reims from 1971 to 1981 and the family included the **FR172E** based on the Model 172H, the **FR172F** based on the Model 172E, the **FR172F** based on the F172K, the **FR172G** based on the F172F, the **FR172H**

based on the F172L, the **FR172J** based on the F172M and the **FR172K Reims Hawk XP** based on the F172N.

Between 1966 and 1970, Cessna delivered a range of Model 172s for service with the US forces in the pilot screening and elementary flight training roles. The **T-41A**, based on the Model 172F and selected in July 1964, was built to the extent of 211 aircraft for the USAF. The **T-41B Mescalero**, based on the Model R172E, was built to the extent of 255 aircraft for the US Army with the IO-360-D engine. The **T-41C**, based on the Model R172E, was built to the extent of 52 examples for the USAF Academy with the IO-360-D engine driving a fixed- rather than variable-pitch propeller. The **T-41D**, basically similar to the T-41B except for its simplified avionics and 28-volt electrical system, was built to the extent of 238 aircraft for delivery under the terms of the Military Assistance

Program to countries such as Colombia, Ecuador, Greece, Honduras, Peru and Turkey. Model 170 and Model 172 aircraft were also bought 'off the shelf' by a number of military operators.

The **Model 175** first flew in December 1955 as the 'proof of concept' combination of an early Model 172 airframe with the 175-hp (131-kW) Continental GO-300 geared engine. A true prototype followed in April 1956, and early deliveries were based on the pre-Model 172D airframe. These 1,237 aircraft were followed from 1960 by 540 examples of the **Model 175A Skylark** with the GO-300-C engine, a swept vertical tail surface and a baggage door. From 1961 customers also had the option of the **Model 175B Skylark** and modestly improved **Model 175C Skylark**, of which 225 and 112 were delivered before rapidly declining sales led Cessna to terminate production in 1962.

SPECIFICATION	
Cessna T-41A	rate 645 ft (196 m) per minute;
Type: four-seat training and liaison aircraft	service ceiling 13,100 ft (3995 m); range 640 miles (1030 km)
Powerplant: one Continental O-300-C flat-six engine rated at 145 hp (108 kW)	**Weights:** empty 1,245 lb (565 kg); maximum take-off 2,300 lb (1043 kg)
Performance: maximum speed 139 mph (224 km/h) at sea level; cruising speed 131 mph (211 km/h) at 9,000 ft (2745 m); initial climb	**Dimensions:** wingspan 35 ft 7½ in (10.86 m); length 26 ft 11 in (8.20 m); height 8 ft 9½ in (2.68 m); wing area 174.00 sq ft (16.16 m²)

Cessna Model 177 Cardinal

Expanding its range of single-engined aircraft for what appeared to be an insatiable market, Cessna introduced the **Model 177** at the end of September 1967. The aim was to provide a successor to the Model 172 with more cabin volume, updated instrumentation, improved fields of vision for the pilot and a cantilever wing based on that of the Model 210. Other 'advanced' features included weight-saving integral wing fuel tanks, an improved version of Cessna's 'Land-O-Matic' landing gear, an all-moving tailplane, a wider-chord vertical tail surface, and what was regarded as an easy-handling control system.

The 'proof of concept' prototype first flew as the **Model 172J** on 15 July 1966. The Model 177 was the standard basic model: a de-luxe version, named **Cardinal**, included full blind-flying instrumentation, more extensive equipment, and luxurious interior appointments.

The powerplant of the **Model 177A** initial version (206 built) was based on the 180-hp (134-kW) IO-360-A2F. The **Model 177B** (1,381 built), introduced in 1969, had a constant-speed propeller, redesigned wing-roots and an engine cowling of new design.

By this time, the relatively high cost of the Model 177 family was adversely affecting sales of

a type offering only modest performance, and in an effort to reverse this trend, Cessna flew the first example of a development with retractable landing gear on 6 February 1970. This variant was delivered from the following year as the **Model 177RG Cardinal RG** with the IO-360-A1B6D engine and the same basic type was also made under licence in France as the **Reims**

F177RG. Later in 1971, the **Cardinal II** and **Cardinal RG II** versions appeared, these differing by having more comprehensive equipment as standard. In 1976 the Model 177 was withdrawn, the Cardinal becoming regarded as the

basic model of the remaining four versions. Two years later, the Cardinal also disappeared, the Cardinal II being renamed the **Cardinal Classic**. At the end of 1978, at which time more than 4,000 examples of the Model 177 and Cardinal versions had been built, all production was terminated.

The powerplant installation of the Model 177 marked the first time that a Lycoming horizontally-opposed engine had been used in a Cessna aircraft. The type's cantilever wing allowed it to dispense with wing-bracing struts.

SPECIFICATION	
Cessna Cardinal RG	rate 925 ft (282 m) per minute;
Type: four-seat touring and sporting aircraft	service ceiling 17,100 ft (5210 m); range 1,030 miles (1658 km)
Powerplant: one Lycoming IO-360-A1B6D flat-four engine rated at 200 hp (149 kW)	**Weights:** empty 1,680 lb (762 kg); maximum take-off 2,800 lb (1270 kg)
Performance: maximum speed 180 mph (290 km/h) at sea level; cruising speed 171 mph (275 km/h) at 7,000 ft (2135 m); initial climb	**Dimensions:** wingspan 35 ft 6 in (10.82 m); length 27 ft 3 in (8.31 m); height 8 ft 7 in (2.62 m); wing area 174.00 sq ft (16.16 m²)

Cessna Model 180, Model 185 Skywagon, AGcarryall (U-17)

Great operational versatility was conferred on both Model 185 versions by their ability to carry under the fuselage a detachable glassfibre Cargo-Pack, capable of carrying some 300 lb (136 kg), or Sorenson spray gear for agricultural work.

In May 1952 Cessna flew the first example of a more powerful-engined partner for the Model 170. Using the same all-metal wing and flap system as the Model 170B, the new **Model 180 Skywagon** featured a new fuselage and tail unit (including a square-topped vertical tail surface and an adjustable tailplane) as well as a 225-hp (168-kW) Continental O-470-A flat-six engine. Most significantly, the Model 180's additional power permitted a 350-lb (159-kg) increase in maximum take-off weight, with the same wing area.

The Model 180 was delivered from 1953 and proved very popular with all manner of pilots including those operating 'bushplane' services in the more remote areas of the USA and Canada, where the Model 180 was valued for its semi-STOL performance as well as its ability to operate on float or quadricycle amphibian float alighting gear. Production of the basic Model 180 totalled 3,000 aircraft, and later developments comprised the **Model 180A** (356 built), introduced in 1956 with the 230-hp (172-kW) O-470-K engine, the **Model 180B** (306 built), introduced in 1959 with a new instrument panel and a revised engine cowling, the **Model 180C** (250 built), with a constant-speed propeller and detail improvements, the **Model 180D** (152 built), an improved version of the Model 180C, the **Model 180E** (118 built), introduced in 1962 with a revised fuel system, the **Model 180F** (129 built), with an option for six-seat accommodation, the **Model 180G** (133 built),

with full six-seat accommodation and an extra window on each side of the cabin, the **Model 180H** (830 built and later named as the **Skywagon 180**), introduced in 1970 as an improved Model 180G, the **Model 180J** (486 built), introduced in 1973 with cowling-mounted landing and taxiing lights, and the **Model 180K** with the O-470-U engine.

Shortly before its disappearance from production, the Model 180 was available in two forms as the basic Model 180 Skywagon and the improved **Model 180 Skywagon II** with a factory-installed avionics package. Production of the Model 180 series ended in September 1981 after the delivery of more than 6,000 aircraft.

In July 1960 Cessna flew the prototype of the **Model 185 Skywagon**, later renamed as the **Skywagon 195**. This was in most respects similar to the Model 180, but had a strengthened airframe and landing gear as it was intended specifically as a utility 'bushplane' for service under difficult conditions. The main differ-

ences from the Model 180 were the larger fin fillet (to ensure directional stability when equipped with floats) and the extra power provided by the 260-hp (194-kW) IO-470-F engine. The Model 185 was a six-seater with an improved cabin possessing three rather than two windows on each side, and had the option of wheeled or ski landing gear, or pure float or amphibian float alighting gear. The type was offered in basic form as the Model 185 Skywagon and in more advanced form as the **Model 185 Skywagon II**.

The Model 185 (275 built) was introduced in 1960, and was followed by the **Model 185A** (275 built) with optional long-range tankage, and then the product-improved variants known as the **Model 185B** (78 built), **Model 185C** (89 built), **Model 185D** (108 built) and **Model 185E** (110 built). In 1971 Cessna introduced an extremely versatile version of the Model 185E in the form of the **Model A185E AGcarryall**, of which 723 were delivered. The type

was designed principally for the agricultural role in the widest possible sense, being able to demonstrate spraying procedures, to ferry people and equipment, serve as an agricultural pilot trainer and act as a back-up spray aircraft in peak periods. It could also operate as a light freighter as a result of its optional side-loading cargo door. The type was powered by the IO-520-D engine and, from 1972, was also produced as a dedicated spraying aircraft with spray bars under the wing and a chemical tank under the fuselage. The final version was the generally improved **Model A185F AGcarryall**, of

which some 2,538 were completed.

During 1962 the USAF was seeking a light utility aircraft suitable for supply to countries eligible for MAP aid. The Model 185 was selected 'off the shelf' and ordered under the designation **U-17**. More than 465 such aircraft were supplied in two variants as the **U-17A** (262 machines), based on the Model 185C with the IO-470-F engine rated at 260 hp (194 kW), and the improved **U-17B** (205 aircraft) with the uprated 300-hp (224-kW) IO-520-D engine. There were also seven examples of the **U-17C**, which was based on the Model 180H with the 230-hp (172-kW) O-470-L.

SPECIFICATION	
Cessna Model 185 Skywagon (landplane) **Type:** six-seat semi-STOL utility aircraft **Powerplant:** one Continental IO-470-F flat-six engine rated at 260 hp (194 kW) **Performance:** maximum speed 178 mph (286 km/h) at sea level; cruising speed 170 mph (274 km/h) at 7,000 ft (2135 m); initial climb	rate 1,010 ft (308 m) per minute; service ceiling 17,900 ft (5455 m); range 979 miles (1576 km) **Weights:** empty 1,696 lb (769 kg); maximum take-off 3,350 lb (1520 kg) **Dimensions:** wingspan 35 ft 10 in (10.92 m); length 25 ft 9 in (7.85 m); height 7 ft 9 in (2.36 m); wing area 174.00 sq ft (16.16 m²)

Cessna Model 190 and Model 195

The aircraft of the **Model 190** and **Model 195** series were unique among Cessna single-engined lightplanes of the period following World War II in being powered by radial engines. The two types were of high-wing cantilever monoplane configuration with fixed tailwheel landing gear and were produced in parallel

between 1947 and August 1954 to the extent of some 1,183 aircraft.

The Model 190 (233 built) first flew on 7 December 1945 with the powerplant of one 240-hp (179-kW) Continental R-670-23 radial. The two initial versions of the Model 195 were almost indistinguishable from the Model 190; the Model 195 was

powered by the Jacobs R-755-A2 radial engine, while the **Model 195A** had the 245-hp (183-kW) R-744-A2 engine. Production of the Model 195 and Model 195A totalled 860 aircraft, examples built in 1953 and 1954 identifiable by their close-cowled engines, the installation of a small propeller spinner, and an increase in flap area. There

were also 100 examples of the **Model 195B**, a development of the Model 190 with the powerplant of one 275-hp (205-kW) R-755-A2 engine. The Model 190 was also notable for the introduction of Cessna's now celebrated spring-steel landing-gear legs.

Many Model 190s and Model 195s remain airworthy, including this US-registered Model 195. Military 195s were designated LC-126A.

SPECIFICATION	
Cessna Model 195 **Type:** four/five-seat touring and sporting aircraft **Powerplant:** one Jacobs R-755-A2 radial engine rated at 300 hp (224 kW) **Performance:** maximum speed 180 mph (290 km/h) at sea level; cruising speed 159 mph (256 km/h) at 6,500 ft (1980 m); initial climb	rate 1,135 ft (346 m) per minute; service ceiling 18,300 ft (5580 m); range 700 miles (1127 km) **Weights:** empty 2,050 lb (930 kg); maximum take-off 3,350 lb (1520 kg) **Dimensions:** wingspan 36 ft 2 in (11.02 m); length 27 ft 4 in (8.33 m); height 7 ft 2 in (2.18 m); wing area 218.13 sq ft (20.26 m²)

Cessna Model 205 Super Skywagon

The **Model 205 Super Skywagon**, first flown on 15 January 1962, was developed from the Model 182. In appearance, it was a version of the Model C210 with fixed tricycle landing gear and, indeed, FAA certification of the type on 14 June 1962 was under the designation **Model 210-5**.

Deliveries began in August 1962, and in December 1963 Cessna introduced the **Model 205A** with detail improvements. Some 576 examples of the Model 205 and Model 205A series were built before the type was superseded at the end of 1963 by the Model 206 with a higher-rated engine. The Model 205 and Model 205A series was available with agricultural equipment and could be flown, like most of the single-engined aircraft of Cessna's high-wing range, with floats, skis or various sizes of wheels.

The Model 205 never achieved the popularity suggested by this Cessna publicity photograph.

SPECIFICATION

Cessna Model 205A
Type: six-seat passenger/utility transport
Powerplant: one Continental IO-460-S flat-six engine rated at 260 hp (194 kW)
Performance: maximum speed 173 mph (278 km/h) at sea level; cruising speed 162 mph (261 km/h) at 6,500 ft (1980 m); initial climb rate 965 ft (294 m) per minute; service ceiling 16,100 ft (4905 m); range 1,015 miles (1633 km)
Weights: empty 1,750 lb (794 kg); maximum take-off 3,300 lb (1497 kg)
Dimensions: wingspan 36 ft 7 in (11.15 m); length 27 ft 9 in (8.46 m); height 9 ft 9 in (2.97 m); wing area 175.5 sq ft (16.30 m²)

Cessna Model 206, Super Skylane and Stationair

The **Cessna Model 206 Super Skywagon** appeared in 1964 as a direct descendant of the Model 205. The Model 206 (275 built), was given a more powerful engine in the form of the 285-hp (213-kW) Continental IO-520-A six-cylinder unit, an enlarged tail unit, longer flaps and, most importantly, a double cargo door in the starboard side of the rear fuselage. The cabin could accommodate up to six passengers.

In 1965 Cessna split the Model 206 line, introducing the **Model U206 Super Skywagon** utility version (162 built) and the **Model P206 Super Skylane** passenger version (160 built); in the latter, the letter 'P' in the designation did not denote 'pressurised' as in some previous cases, but 'personal'. The Model P206 did not have the cargo door of the Model U206, and other changes included a 'de-luxe' passenger interior, a pointed spinner and main landing gear units carrying spatted wheels. The **Model P206A**

This float-equipped Model 206 has been modified by Soloy to have an Allison turboprop powerplant. The nose contours are considerably revised, with modified exhaust and intake configurations.

(146 built) and **Model U206A** (219 built) followed in 1966 as improved versions. Cessna also developed a **Model TU206A** variant with the TSIO-520-C turbocharged engine, and all the 'turbo' versions are distinguishable by an extra exhaust outlet pointing downward under the nose. A new instrument panel design was introduced in 1967 with the **Model P206B** (113 built) and **Model U206B** (258 built). Other small refinements were introduced on the virtually identical **Model P206C** (100 built) and **Model U206C** (319 built). Floatplane versions of the **Model U206D** (210 built in total) had an enlarged fin and rudder, but landplane **Model U206D** and **Model P206D** aircraft were little changed by comparison with their predecessors.

In 1970 Cessna introduced the **Model U206E Skywagon 206** (243 built) and the **Model P206E Super Skylane** (44 built); the Model U206E had a smoother, lowered-nose profile, but the Model P206E remained essentially the same as the Model P206D. In 1971 Cessna introduced the **Model U206F** (1,820 built), renaming it the **Stationair**. The Stationair had a three-bladed propeller (standard from 1975), a wing with cambered (drooped) leading edge, cowl-mounted landing lights, and increased baggage area. The **Stationair II**, introduced in 1975, had an improved avionics fit. The **Model U206G Stationair 6** (3,499 built) followed in 1978. Model 206 production continued until the 1986 cessation forced by product liability laws. When Cessna temporarily stopped building single-engined aircraft, a Model U206G was the very last machine off its production lines.

Several improved versions of the Model 206 have been developed by third-party firms. These include the **Soloy Turbine Pac** conversion, certified in 1984, with a 420-shp (313-kW) Allison 250-C20S turboshaft engine driving a three-bladed propeller, a longer nose, an enlarged fin and a ventral fin. The Robertson firm developed a **STOL 206** with wing-stall fences and a full-span flap/aileron system.

SPECIFICATION

Cessna Model U206G Stationair 6 (landplane)
Type: six-seat utility transport aircraft
Powerplant: one Continental IO-520-F flat-six engine rated at 300 hp (224 kW)
Performance: maximum speed 180 mph (290 km/h) at sea level; cruising speed 169 mph (272 km/h) at 6,500 ft (1980 m); initial climb rate 920 ft (280 m) per minute; service ceiling 14,800 ft (4510 m); range 1,036 miles (1667 km)
Weights: empty 1,896 lb (860 kg); maximum take-off 3,600 lb (1633 kg)
Dimensions: wingspan 35 ft 10 in (10.92 m); length 28 ft 3 in (8.61 m); height 9 ft 3½ in (2.83 m); wing area 174.00 sq ft (16.16 m²)

Cessna Model 207 Skywagon and Stationair

In 1967 Cessna started work on a stretched version of the Model 206D, designed to accommodate seven rather than six

Adding 2 ft 6 in (0.96 m) aft of the rear doorpost and 1 ft 6 in (0.46 m) forward of the engine firewall of the 206 produced the Model 207.

persons in the cabin. The changes also made a noticeable difference to the size and shape of the aircraft, and the new machine was designated as the **Cessna Model 207 Skywagon**, later revised to **Skywagon 7**. The wing and fuselage were strengthened, but the basic powerplant remained unaltered and was thus centred on the 285-hp (213-kW) IO-520 engine.

Cessna Model 207 Skywagon and Stationair (continued)

The Model 207 prototype first flew on 11 May 1968 and, in overall terms, the new type had a somewhat crude look, which may have contributed to its poor total of 362 sales. The **Model T207** was also developed with a TSIO-520-G turbocharged engine. Several small changes were made to the Model

207 over the following years but, in 1977, a larger-diameter propeller was introduced to create the **Model 207A** (426 built). In 1978, the line was overhauled and the versions with normally aspirated and turbocharged engines were renamed as the **Stationair 7** and **Turbo Stationair 7** respectively. In 1980 an

eighth seat was added to create the **Stationair 8** and **Turbo Stationair 8**.

The Model 207 was the only strut-braced Cessna design that was never certified for float operations, but several turboprop conversions were developed for it, most notably by the Soloy Corporation. Cessna production ceased in 1985.

SPECIFICATION

Cessna Model 207 Turbo Stationair 8
Type: eight-seat utility transport aircraft
Powerplant: one Continental TSIO-520-M flat-six engine rated at 310 hp (231 kW)
Performance: maximum speed 196 mph (315 km/h) at 17,000 ft (5180 m); cruising speed 185 mph (298 km/h) at 20,000 ft (6095 m);

initial climb rate 885 ft (270 m) per minute; service ceiling 26,000 ft (7925 m); range 702 miles (1130 m)
Weights: empty 2,199 lb (997 kg); maximum take-off 3,800 lb (1723 kg)
Dimensions: wingspan 35 ft 10 in (10.92 m); length 32 ft 2 in (9.80 m); height 9 ft 7 in (2.92 m); wing area 174.00 sq ft (16.16 m²)

Cessna Model 208 Caravan I (U-27)

The **Model 208 Caravan I** was developed as Cessna's ultimate 'bushplane', a 10-seat design aimed at securing a large proportion of the market for replacing the thousands of piston-engined bushplanes in service around the world. Preliminary design began in 1981 and among its objectives the design team listed a cabin 5 ft 2 in (1.57 m) wide to permit three-abreast seating, a port-side main cargo door divided horizontally rather than vertically and three additional access doors for cargo and passengers.

The Model 208 prototype made its first flight on 9 December 1982, and among the features of the

new aircraft were a capacious fuselage with a rectangular-section payload section, a tail unit with high-aspect-ratio straight horizontal and swept vertical surfaces, fixed tricycle landing gear and the powerplant of one PT6A-114 turboprop engine driving a McCauley three-bladed propeller.

Sixty-one examples of the basic Model 208 had been sold before the type started to achieve phenomenal sales success as a result of a Federal Express order for 177 of a specially developed version. This was the **Model 208A Cargomaster** tailored for all-freight operations with a Bendix/King avionics, a

revised fuselage without cabin windows and the starboard rear door, a taller vertical tail surface, an underfuselage cargo pannier, and extended exhausts to deflect the hot gases wide of the pannier. So successful was the Cargomaster that FedEx ordered the **Model 208B Super Cargomaster**, which has its fuselage lengthened by 4 ft (1.22 m) to allow the carriage of a 3,500-lb (1587-kg) payload with the aid of the 675-shp (503-kW) PT6A-114A engine. The Model 208B first flew on 3 March 1986 and deliveries began later in the same

year; to date more than 400 have been built.

From the Super Cargomaster, Cessna developed the **Model 208B Grand Caravan**, a similarly stretched version with windows and a quick-change cabin able to carry 14 passengers or freight.

The **U-27A** military version for the export market first appeared in 1986. It can accommodate a pilot and up to nine passengers and is intended for freight deliv-

ery, logistic support, paratroop and supply-dropping, medevac, electronic surveillance, FAC, troop transportation, maritime patrol and SAR missions. The U-27A possesses one centreline and six underwing hardpoints and has been proposed with a 360° FLIR turret and Stinger AAM self-defence armament to meet a USAF Special Operations Command gunship requirement. To date the military customers have included the Brazilian air force, Liberian army and Thai army.

With its underfuselage pannier and spacious cabin, the Grand Caravan is a versatile transport. This aircraft has weather radar in a pod on the right wing.

SPECIFICATION

Cessna Model 208 Caravan I
Type: 10-seat utility transport aircraft
Powerplant: one Pratt & Whitney Canada PT6A-114 turboprop engine flat-rated at 600 shp (448 kW)
Performance: maximum cruising speed 212 mph (341 km/h) at 10,000 ft (3050 m); maximum rate of climb at sea level 1,050 ft (320 m) per minute; maximum operating altitude 27,600 ft

(8410 m); range 1,578 miles (2539 km)
Weights: empty 3,800 lb (1724 kg); maximum take-off 7,300 lb (3311 kg)
Dimensions: wingspan 52 ft 1 in (15.88 m); length 37 ft 7 in (11.46 m); height 14 ft 2 in (4.32 m); wing area 279.40 sq ft (25.96 m²)
Payload: up to 3,000 lb (1361 kg)

Cessna Model 210 Centurion

The **Model 210** began life as a version of the Model 182 with retractable tricycle landing gear. It was the first single-engined Cessna aircraft designed with a fully retractable landing-gear arrangement, and the unusual 'downward and upward' stroke of its long-legged rear units is quite unique. The prototype was converted from a straight-finned Model 182, and made its maiden flight on 25 February 1957. At this early stage, the aircraft was referred to as the **Model 185**, but this designation was changed to Model 210 in 1958. A swept fin was then added to the design and a revised prototype first flew on 28 August 1958 with the 260-hp (194-kW) Continental IO-470-E engine.

The Model 210 has a

high-set wing with distinctive drooped wingtips (apart from the very final model). Early aircraft had a strut-braced wing, a faired-in cabin and squared-off nose. The first production version was the **Model C210** (575 built) of 1960, which closely resembled the Model 182 and had only two main cabin windows (with a small split side window for the pilot). It was followed in 1961 by the **Model C210A** (265 built) with a more spacious and comfortable cabin and an additional cabin window on each side. The **Model C210B** (280 built) of 1962 had a slightly longer fuselage allowing the carriage of more fuel, a wider cabin, Cessna's trademarked 'Omnivision' wraparound rear window, and the

powerplant of one 260-hp (194-kW) IO-470-S engine. The little-changed **Model C210C** (135 built) appeared in 1963, and this was followed in 1964 by the **Model C210D** (290 built) that introduced the name **Centurion**, which was applied to all subsequent versions; the type had the 285-hp (213-kW) IO-520-A engine, a widened horizontal tail surface, longer flaps and two small whip radio antennas above the cabin. The **Model C210E** (205 built) of 1965 was similar.

In 1966 another major change was introduced in the **Model T210F Turbo Centurion** (300 built), with a turbocharged engine, namely the 285-hp (213-kW) TSIO-520-C unit, and possessing the option of a three- rather than two-

bladed propeller, as well as a six-seat cabin option, a one-piece wraparound windscreen, a higher gross weight and an oxygen system for six passengers. Although it was expensive, the Model T210F (and its successors) were the fastest, highest-flying piston singles of their era and sold well.

A redesigned laminar-flow cantilever wing was introduced on the **Model C210G** and **Model T210G** (228 built) of 1967, which allowed the elimination of the wing struts. This wing had a distinct dihedral and was heavier than before, and to maintain the aircraft's centre of gravity in the correct position the wing was repositioned farther to the rear and the horizontal tail was further widened. The Model

C210G and later versions had a smaller, square window in the rear of the cabin in place of the 'Omnivision' unit. The **Model C210H** and **Model T210H** (210 built) were similar, but had a new flap system and cockpit changes. The **Model C210J** and **Model T210J** of 1969 had reduced dihedral and were the first Centurions to have a smooth, rounded engine cowling, without the 'chin' bump of the earlier variants. The **Model C210K** and **Model T210K** (303 built) of 1970 had an enlarged six-seat cabin with two side windows and two large radio antennas above the wing. They also had a new landing-gear arrangement with bulged doors in the lower fuselage. The **Model C210L** and **Model 210L** (2,070 built) of 1972 were similar to the Model C210K with two widely spaced nose-mounted landing lights, but introduced the **Centurion II** additional avionics option. The **Model C210M** and **Model T210M** (1,381 built) of 1977 and the **Model C210N** and **Model T210N** (1,943 built) of 1979 were very similar to the Model 210L, although the Model 210M did introduce the option of the TSIO-520-R engine driving a three-bladed propeller.

In 1978 Cessna introduced the first fully-pressurised Model 210, the **Model P210N Pressurized Centurion** (834 built) with the TSIO-520-P turbocharged engine. Noticeable changes included its four small, rounded cabin windows, additional air inlet scoops under the main engine intakes and a pair of close-set landing lights under the

spinner. The Model P210N and **Model T210N** of 1980 added an optional weather radar in a pod under the starboard half of the wing, and also longer exhaust stacks. No Model 210 machines were built in 1984, but in 1985 Cessna introduced the final variants, the **Model P210R** and **Model T210R** (112 built),

with a horizontal tail surface of increased span and new upswept wingtips; however, these proved to be prohibitively expensive and as a result production ceased in 1986.

SPECIFICATION	
Cessna Model T210M Turbo Centurion	minute; service ceiling 27,000 ft (8230 m); range 1,036 miles (1668 km)
Type: six-seat touring aircraft	
Powerplant: one Continental TSIO-520-R flat-six engine rated at 310 hp (231 kW)	**Weights:** empty 2,237 lb (1015 kg); maximum take-off 4,000 lb (1814 kg)
Performance: maximum speed 235 mph (378 km/h) at 17,000 ft (5180 m); cruising speed 222 mph (358 km/h) at 20,000 ft (6095 m); initial climb rate 930 ft (283 m) per	**Dimensions:** wingspan 36 ft 9 in (11.20 m); length 28 ft 2 in (8.59 m); height 9 ft 8 in (2.95 m); wing area 175.00 sq ft (16.26 m²)

Few Centurions found military buyers and, of the four T210Gs originally supplied to the Philippine air force, only one remained in service in late 1999. The aircraft flies with the 901st Weather Squadron.

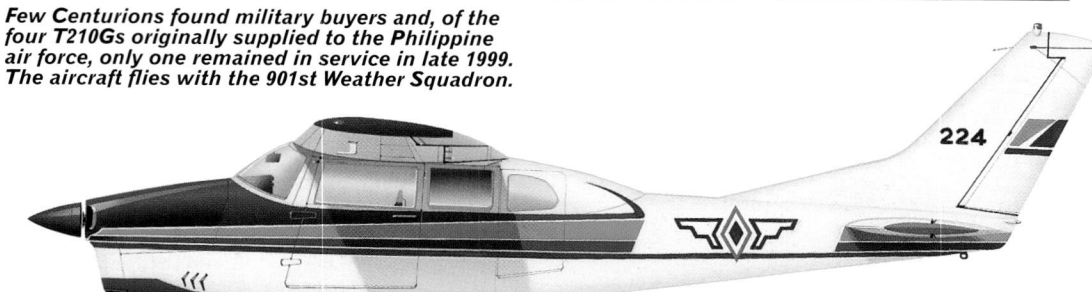

Cessna Model 303 Crusader

On 14 February 1978 Cessna flew the prototype of a new lightweight twin-engined aircraft which it then designated as the **Model 303 Clipper**. In this prototype form it was a four-seat aircraft of low-

The production Crusader, which was delivered from September 1981, was claimed by Cessna as the first lightweight twin of its class to have full IFR avionics and other equipment as standard.

wing cantilever monoplane configuration with a wing

of supercritical section. Other features included retractable tricycle landing gear, a swept vertical tail surface with a long dorsal fin, extensive use of bonded construction, and the powerplant of two 160-hp (119-kW) engines. Before the certification programme began, this prototype was superseded by a new **Model T303** which reverted to conventional construction,

the aircraft had six-seat accommodation, was powered by two turbocharged engines of increased output, and had acquired the new name **Crusader** because the

earlier title of Clipper infringed a US trademark.

Production of the Crusader was suspended in the mid-1980s after the delivery of about 300 such aircraft.

SPECIFICATION	
Cessna Model T303 Crusader	per minute; certificated ceiling 25,000 ft (7620 m); range 1,174 miles (1889 km)
Type: six-seat touring aircraft	
Powerplant: two Continental TSIO/LTSIO-520-AE flat-six engines each rated at 250 hp (186 kW)	**Weights:** empty 3,305 lb (1499 kg); maximum take-off 5,150 lb (2336 kg)
Performance: maximum speed 248 mph (400 km/h) at 18,000 ft (5485 m); cruising speed 225 mph (363 km/h) at 20,000 ft (6095 m); initial climb rate 1,480 ft (451 m)	**Dimensions:** wingspan 39 ft ½ in (11.90 m); length 30 ft 5 in (9.27 m); height 13 ft 4 in (4.06 m); wing area 189.20 sq ft (17.58 m²)

Cessna Model 305

In the late 1940s the US army issued a specification for a two-seat liaison and observation monoplane. From the submissions received from manufacturers, that of the Cessna Aircraft Company was declared the winner and in June 1950 an initial

contract was awarded for 418 examples of the aircraft, which the company identified as the **Cessna Model 305A**.

Cessna's design was based upon the successful Model 170, a lightweight strut-based high-wing monoplane, powered by a

145-hp (108 kW) Continental flat-six engine, which provided accommodation for a pilot and three passengers. The Model 305A differed by having the aft fuselage redesigned to give a clear view to the rear and by the provision of transparent panels in the wing centre-section, which formed the cabin roof. A wider access door gave

room to load a standard stretcher, for which support brackets were installed.

Deliveries of production aircraft began in December 1950, under the designation **L-19A** and with the name **Bird Dog**, and by October 1954 2,486 had been delivered, of which 60 were diverted to the US Marine Corps which designated them **OE-1**. An **L-19A-IT** instrument trainer version was developed in 1953, **TL-19D** trainers with constant-speed propellers appeared in 1956 and the improved **L-19E**, of higher gross weight, was the final version, to bring total production of Bird Dogs to 3,431. With redesignation in 1962, the US Army's L-19A, TL-19D and L-19E

aircraft became **O-1A**, **TO-1D** and **O-1E** respectively. The US Marines' OE-1 became **O-1B** and this service also acquired 25 of the higher-powered **O-1C**. US Army trainers, derived from standard production aircraft, had the designations **TO-1A** and **TO-1E**. Bird Dogs were operated in small numbers during the Korean War, but the US Air Force acquired many of the US Army's O-1s for use by forward air controllers in Vietnam; former TO-1Ds and O-1As were redesignated **O-1F** and **O-1G** respectively when equipped for this role. In addition to being supplied to many nations, O-1s were also built under licence by Fuji in Japan.

Vietnam-based O-1s usually flew with a pair of target marker rockets beneath each wing. The aircraft flew dangerous FAC missions throughout the war.

SPECIFICATION	
Cessna O-1E	530 miles (853 km)
Type: liaison and observation aircraft	**Weights:** empty 1,614 lb (732 kg), maximum take-off 2,400 lb (1089 kg)
Powerplant: one 213-hp (159-kW) Continental O-470-11 flat-six piston engine	**Dimensions:** wingspan 36 ft (10.97 m) length 25 ft 9 in (7.85 m); height 7 ft 3½ in (2.22 m); wing area 174.0 sq ft (16.16 m²)
Performance: maximum speed 130 mph (209 km/h); range	

Cessna Model 310 and Model 320 Executive Skyknight (U-3)

In 1952 Cessna started work on the design of a new five/six-seat light aircraft with a twin-engined powerplant. The result was the **Model 310** that first flew in prototype form on 3 January 1953, proving in production form to be a popular type that was manufactured up to 1981, when more than 5,500 examples had been built. Of low-wing cantilever monoplane configuration with retractable tricycle landing gear, the prototype was powered by two 225-hp (168-kW) Continental O-470-B engines and originally known as the **E225**. The use of this engine in the Model 310 was one of its first civil applications, and early production aircraft had the more powerful 240-hp (179-kW) O-470-M version of the engine.

Production Model 310 deliveries began in April 1954 and amounted to just 32 aircraft in this first year, but by the end of the following year had risen to 200. Steady product improvement continued from that time to yield variants up to the definitive **Model 310R** via major changes characterised by the following: the **Model 310B** of 1957, the **Model 310C** of 1959 with 260-hp (194-kW) engines, the **Model 310D** of 1960 with a more pointed nose as well as swept vertical tail surface in place of the origi-

nal upright unit, the **Model 310F** of 1961 with a large number of detail improvements including one more cabin window on each side, the **Model 310G** with the previously upright wingtip tanks canted outward and cabin alterations to increase accommodation from five to six, the **Model 310I** with the rear of the engine nacelles extended to create additional baggage compartments, the **Model 310K** of 1966 with a frameless windscreen as well as a number of airframe enhancements, the **Model 310L** of 1967 with two 260-hp (194-kW) IO-470-L fuel-injected engines as well as a package of improvements and the **Model 310P** with a ventral fin and 285-hp (213-kW) IO-520-M engines.

A de-luxe version with turbocharged engines and standard features such as air-conditioning and an oxygen system was introduced in 1966. This was known at the time as the **Turbo-System Executive Skyknight**, but was later redesignated for a short period as the **Model 320** and remained in production to the end of the series as the **Model T310**. The last versions were the basic **Model 310R** with 285-hp (213-kW) IO-520-MB engines, the structurally identical **Model 310 II** with a factory-installed avionics and equipment package,

the Model T310 with TSIO-520-BB engines, and the **Model T310 II** with the same additional equipment as the Model 310 II.

In the mid-1950s, following a competitive selection process, the Model 310B, a slightly modified version of the original Model 310A, was ordered for light freighting and liaison service with the USAF under the designation **L-27A**; this was changed to **U-3A** in the 1962 rationalisation of the US forces' designation systems. A total of 160 such aircraft was built, followed by 36 examples of the **Model 310M** (originally **Model 310E** and a development of the civil Model 310D) for service with the designation **L-27B** (later **U-3B**) with limited all-weather

A major identification feature of the Model 310 was the pair of wingtip fuel tanks, which in the early aircraft represented the entire fuel tankage, but was supplemented in later variants by wing tankage.

capability. A small number of Model 310s was supplied for service with the French air force, and to Argentina and the Philippines.

The Model 310 was also used as the basis for a number of improved models created by other

companies. The **Riley 65**, for instance, introduced a number of improvements, and two Riley developments with greater power were the **Rocket** with 290-hp (216-kW) Lycoming engines and the **Turbo-Rocket** with Lycoming turbocharged engines.

SPECIFICATION

Cessna Model 310R
Type: five/six-seat touring aircraft
Powerplant: two Continental IO-520-MB flat-six engines each rated at 285 hp (213 kW)
Performance: maximum speed 238 mph (383 km/h) at sea level; cruising speed 160 mph (257 km/h) at 10,000 ft (3050 m); initial climb rate 1,800 ft (549 m) per minute; service ceiling 19,750 ft (6020 m); range 1,765 miles (2840 km)
Weights: empty 3,358 lb (1523 kg); maximum take-off 5,500 lb (2495 kg)
Dimensions: wingspan 36 ft 11 in (11.25 m); length 36 ft 11½ in (9.74 m); height 10 ft 8 in (3.25 m); wing area 179.00 sq ft (16.63 m²)

Cessna Model 318 (T-37)

Designed to meet a 1952 USAF requirement for a jet-powered primary trainer, the **Model 318** was initially ordered in the form of two **XT-37** prototypes. The first of these flew on 12 October 1954 with the powerplant of two 940-lb st (4.18-kN) Continental YJ69-T-9 (licence-built Turboméca Marboré) turbojet engines installed in the roots of the straight wing. The aircraft had side-by-side seating for the crew under a one-piece canopy and behind a one-piece windscreen, with a central strengthening strip. Overall configuration was conventional, although the horizontal tailplane was

located about one-third of the way up the fin to remain clear of the jet exhaust. The manual controls had electric trimmers, while the flaps and landing gear (with wide-track main units) were hydraulically actuated.

An initial batch of 10 **T-37A** (**Model 318A**) aircraft was followed by 524 essentially similar machines with J69-T-9 engines. The first of these aircraft flew on 27 September 1955, but service entry was delayed until 1957 by the need for modifications. During 1959 production switched to the **T-37B** (**Model 318B**) variant with the powerplant of two J69-T-25 turbojets, as well

as enhancements such as improved navigation and communications equipment and provision for wingtip fuel tanks. A total of 466 such aircraft was built, some being exported. Forty-seven were funded by the Luftwaffe but remained in the USA, in USAF markings, for the training of Luftwaffe pilots. All surviving T-37As were also brought up to T-37B stan-

dard through modification. From April 1961, the USAF switched to 'straight-through' jet training on the T-37, as had been planned, but high costs forced the reintroduction of a 30-hour primary phase on the piston-engined Cessna T-41A in 1965. All-through jet training was briefly rein-

troduced, but today pilots are 'screened' on the T-41 and Slingsby T-3A.

The T-37 was to have been replaced by the Fairchild T-46A, but the development of this type was cancelled in 1986. A proposed T-37 derivative, the **T-48**, attracted little support, and from 1989 the

Over four decades of service the T-37 has proved to be a reliable, simple and versatile training aircraft. Nevertheless, the type is nearing the end of its useful life, even in the T-37B form illustrated, and the USAF is looking forward to its replacement.

SPECIFICATION

Cessna T-37B
Type: two-seat primary flying trainer
Powerplant: two Teledyne Continental J69-T-25 turbojet engines each rated at 1,025 lb (4.56 kN)
Performance: maximum speed 425 mph (684 km/h) at 25,000 ft (7620 m); cruising speed 380 mph (612 km/h) at 25,000 ft (7620 m);

initial climb rate 3,370 ft (1037 m) per minute; service ceiling 39,200 ft (11950 m); range 932 miles (1500 km)
Weights: empty 3,870 lb (1755 kg); maximum take-off 6,600 lb (2993 kg)
Dimensions: wingspan 33 ft 9⅓ in (10.30 m); length 29 ft 3 in (8.92 m); height 9 ft 2⅓ in (2.80 m); wing area 183.90 sq ft (17.09 m²)

Sabreliner Corporation began supplying modification kits to the USAF to allow its surviving T-37s to be structurally rebuilt for extended service. Current plans call for the T-37 to be replaced by the Raytheon T-6A Texan II.

The ultimate 'Tweet', as the T-37 was nicknamed in USAF service, was never used by the USAF, instead being built for export and for MAP (Military Aid Program) and FMS (Foreign Military Sales). Some 269 **T-37C** aircraft were built, all incorporating provision for a limited light attack capability with a K-14C gun sight, and underwing pylons (one on each wing) which can carry stores of up to 250-lb (113-kg) weight including a General Electric 0.5-in (12.7-mm) machine-gun pod. A survey or reconnaissance camera can be carried in the fuselage. The T-37C was supplied to Burma, Chile (which also received T-37Bs), Colombia, Greece (which also received T-37Bs), Pakistan (which also received T-37Bs), Peru (which also received T-37Bs), Portugal (30), Thailand (which also received T-37Bs) and Turkey.

Cessna Model 318E (A-37 Dragonfly)

A light attack derivative of the T-37, the **A-37 Dragonfly** flew on 22 October 1963 as the first of two **YAT-37D** prototype conversions from T-37B standard with the upgraded powerplant of two 2,400-lb st (10.67-kN) General Electric J85-GE-5 turbojet engines. Some 39 T-37B aircraft were then similarly converted, although with the powerplant of two J85-GE-17A engines, on the assembly line to become **A-37A** machines. Like the two YAT-37Ds, these featured armour protection, an internally housed 0.3-in (7.62-mm) Minigun, eight wing stores stations for ordnance and fuel, wingtip fuel tanks, ground-attack avionics and larger wheels and tyres.

Stressed to 6g rather than 5g, a full-production version was ordered by the USAF as the **A-37B**, which is known to its manufacturer as the **Model 318E**. This version introduced inflight-refuelling capability

and deliveries began in May 1968. The last of 577 examples were completed in 1975. The A-37B could carry up to 5,680 lb (2576 kg) of bombs, rocket launchers and stores dispensers, and at least 130 were retrospectively adapted to **OA-37B** forward air controller standard with modified avionics. The USAF retired its last Dragonfly in 1992.

Both the A-37B and OA-37B serve extensively with Latin American air arms. Chile has operated the A-37B since 1974, and has some 24 serving in the operational training and light attack roles. Colombia,

which has flown the Dragonfly since 1980, has about 26 A-37B and OA-37B aircraft. Ecuador has operated the A-37B since 1976, and currently disposes of some 24 such aircraft. Guatemala, the earliest Latin American operator of the Dragonfly, received its first A-37B aircraft in 1971, and eight remain operational. Honduras has flown the A-37B since 1975 and the OA-37B since 1984, and

This A-37B served with the USAF's 604th Special Operations Squadron at Bien Hoa during the Vietnam War. The type also flew with the Vietnamese air force and performed well.

Uruguay has 11 A-37B warplanes remaining from some 20 received through the 1970s and 1980s, and a further 16 obtained from surplus USAF stocks. The type is Uruguay's primary combat aircraft.

has 13 such aircraft. Peru has 23 A-37B machines remaining from 36 supplied in 1975-77. El Salvador has eight A-37Bs and OA-37Bs remaining from 19 A-37Bs and three OA-37Bs delivered since 1982.

Other operators of the A-37B in the late 1990s are South Korea and Thailand.

The former has some 27 ex-South Vietnamese aircraft received in September-October 1976, and until recently the latter had 12 A-37B and T-37 aircraft converted to a generally similar standard. Vietnam holds some A-37Bs in storage, these being ex-South Vietnamese aircraft captured at the end of the Vietnamese conflict and has unsuccessfully offered these for sale on several occasions.

SPECIFICATION	
Cessna OA-37B Dragonfly **Type:** two-seat light attack and forward air controller aircraft **Powerplant:** two General Electric J85-GE-17A turbojet engines each rated at 2,850 lb st (12.68 kN) **Performance:** maximum speed at 16,000 ft (4875 m) 507 mph (816 km/h); cruising speed 489 mph (787 km/h) at 25,000 ft (7620 m); initial climb rate 6,990 ft (2130 m) per minute; service ceiling 41,765 ft (12730 m); range 1,012 miles (1628 km) with maximum internal and external fuel, or 460 miles (740 km) with	maximum warload **Weights:** empty 5,843 lb (2650 kg); maximum take-off 14,000 lb (6350 kg) **Dimensions:** wingspan 35 ft 10½ in (10.93 m) with tip tanks; length 29 ft 3½ in (8.93 m) excluding probe; height 8 ft 10½ in (2.70 m); wing area 183.90 sq ft (17.09 m²) **Armament:** one 0.3-in (7.62-mm) Minigun fixed forward-firing machine-gun in the nose, plus up to 4,100 lb (1860 kg) of disposable stores carried under the wing

Cessna Model 335 and Model 340

In December 1971 Cessna announced the introduction of a pressurised transport, aimed primarily at the growing market for business aircraft, as the **Model 340** developed from the Model 310. This was in essence a hybrid type combining the wing and tricycle landing gear developed for the Model 414, a new pressurised fuselage of the fail-safe type, a tail unit based on that of the Model 310, and two 285-hp (213-kW) TSIO-520-K engines. Further development led to the **Model 340 II** with a factory-installed improved avionics package, and then the generally updated **Model 340A** that was ordered in two forms – as the basic Model 340A with two TSIO-520-NB engines, and the **Model 340A II** equivalent to the Model 340 II.

The Model 340 offered pressurised accommodation for six.

SPECIFICATION	
Cessna Model 340A **Type:** five/six-seat light executive transport **Powerplant:** two Continental TSIO-520-NB flat-six piston engines each rated at 310 hp (231 kW) **Performance:** maximum speed 281 mph (452 km/h) at 20,000 ft (6095 m); cruising speed 264 mph (425 km/h) at 24,500 ft (7470 m); initial climb rate 1,650 ft (503 m)	per minute; service ceiling 29,800 ft (9085 m); range 1,618 miles (2604 km) **Weights:** empty 3,948 lb (1791 kg); maximum take-off 5,990 lb (2717 kg) **Dimensions:** wingspan 38 ft 1⅛ in (11.62 m); length 34 ft 4 in (10.46 m); height 12 ft 7 in (3.84 m); wing area 184.00 sq ft (17.09 m²) **Payload:** up to four passengers

Cessna Model 335 and Model 340 (continued)

In 1978, Cessna introduced the **Model 340A III** cabin twin, with still further improved avionics.

Production of the Model 340 series ended in the mid-1980s, the type being yet another victim of the general aviation 'slump' that echoed an Arab hike in oil prices.

A lighter-weight unpressurised version of the Model 340 was introduced in 1979 as the **Model 335**, which was

also available in a **Model 335 II** version with a factory-installed avionics package, but production of the Model 335 ended during 1980, after only 45 had been built.

Cessna Model 336 Skymaster, Model 337 Super Skymaster (O-2), Reims F337 and Reims Milirole

The push/pull concept, with a tandem arrangement of engines driving one tractor and one pusher propeller, was adopted by Cessna in the late 1950s for a light, low cost, easy-to-fly twin-engined aircraft, and one obvious advantage over a normal twin layout was that, in the event of an engine failure, there would be no asymmetric thrust problems.

On 28 February 1961, the **Model 336 Skymaster** prototype made its maiden flight, with deliveries beginning in May 1963. Powered by two 210-hp (157-kW) Continental IO-360-A engines, the new machine had four-seat accommodation (alternative seating arrangements for up to six persons were available) with fixed tricycle landing gear. Fixed landing gear on light twins was becoming passé, however, and after 195 examples of the Model 336 had been built, the type was replaced on the production line early in 1965 by the **Model 337 Super Skymaster** with retractable landing gear. Volume for an additional 300 lb (136 kg) of baggage was available in an optional underfuselage glassfibre pack.

In 1969 Reims Aviation in France began licensed assembly of the Model

337, with primary structures supplied by Cessna and Continental engines built in the UK under licence by Rolls-Royce. The US and French production lines continued in parallel, the French version having the designation **Reims F337**. The name **Milirole** was applied to the basic unpressurised F337 for a short time. After 1974 Reims developed a special unpressurised STOL version, designated as the **FTB337**, which could be provided with a wide range of equipment to make it suitable for such duties as maritime or overland patrol and rescue. Detail improvements continued each year, and a turbocharged version, the **Model 337 Turbo-System Super Skymaster**, was introduced in 1970. The prototype of a pressurised **Model T337 Skymaster**, powered by 225-hp (168-kW) TSIO-360 engines, first flew in July 1971, by which time the word Super had been dropped.

O-2 military versions of the Model 337 were supplied to the USAF for various missions including forward air control over Vietnam. The Model 337 was selected 'off the shelf' during the later part of 1966 as being ideal for this role, and in its **Model 337M** mili-

tary form was equipped with four underwing pylons to carry flares, rocket-launcher pods and other light ordnance such as a 0.3-in (7.62-mm) Minigun machine-gun pod. These aircraft received the designation **O-2A**, and 501 were supplied to the USAF. In addition, a version equipped for the psychological warfare role entered USAF service under the designation **O-2B**. This carried a powerful air-to-ground broadcasting system using three 600-watt amplifiers and a battery of highly directional speakers, and was also equipped for leaflet drops. Total procurement of the O-2B amounted to 31 aircraft. Both the O-2A and O-2B versions carried advanced nav/com systems. Twelve O-2As were supplied to the Imperial Iranian air force early in 1970. A twin-turboprop **O-2T/O-2TT** did not proceed beyond USAF evaluation.

Production of a military version designated **Sentry O2-337** was started in 1980 by Summit Aviation Inc., but only very limited sales were achieved.

Manufacture of the

The O-2 was adopted after experience in Vietnam suggested that FAC sorties could be made more effective with aircraft operated by a pilot and a FAN (Forward Air Navigator), the latter being able to concentrate on the FAC mission without having to fly the aircraft.

Model 337 series by Cessna ended in mid-1980; by the beginning of that year 1,821 examples of the unpressurised Model 337 and 313 examples of the pressurised **Model T337**, as well as 544 military O-2s, had been delivered. Reims production figures were 66 F337 and 27 **F337P** aircraft before the French line switched solely to the **FTB337G**, of which 61 had been built by January 1981.

There have been numerous military operators of the Model 337 in both its baseline civil and more specifically military variants. Zimbabwe operates 15 survivors of 18 FTB337G aircraft obtained clandestinely in February 1976 by the Rhodesian air force. Locally named **Lynx**, these were fitted with turbocharged engines and were armed with two 0.3-in (7.62-mm) machine-guns above the cabin and various stores under the wing. They

undertook light strike, COIN and FAC duties during Rhodesia's long bush war and were fitted with redesigned heat-shielded exhausts as a counter to SA-7 SAMs.

The **Model 337D** commercial version is in service with the air forces of Burkina Faso and Togo, and other aircraft were delivered to the Sri Lankan air force; the navies of Ecuador, Mexico and Peru; the Chilean army and the Jamaica Defence Force's Air Wing. The Reims-built Super Skymaster was also delivered to the Burkina Faso and Togo air forces. The **Summit Sentry O2-337** derivative version was sold to the Haitian air corps and Thai air force. Ex-USAF O-2A machines found their way to the Costa Rican Public Security air section, the Dominican air force, the South Korean air force and the Salvadorean air force, of which the last also received one O-2B.

SPECIFICATION

Cessna Model 337 Super Skymaster
Type: six-seat touring and utility aircraft
Powerplant: two Continental IO-360-GB flat-six engines each rated at 210 hp (157 kW)
Performance: maximum speed 206 mph (332 km/h) at sea level; cruising speed 196 mph (315 km/h)

at 5,500 ft (1675 m); initial climb rate 1,200 ft (366 m) per minute; service ceiling 18,000 ft (5485 m); range 1,422 miles (2288 km)
Weights: empty 2,787 lb (1264 kg); maximum take-off 4,630 lb (2100 kg)
Dimensions: wingspan 38 ft 2 in (11.63 m); length 29 ft 9 in (9.07 m); height 9 ft 2 in (2.79 m); wing area 202.50 sq ft (18.81 m²)

Cessna Model 401 and Model 402

On 26 August 1965 Cessna flew the prototype of an aircraft generally similar to the Model 411, and this prototype served as the basis for two very closely related new types, the **Model 401** and **Model 402**. These two aircraft represented lower-cost versions of the Model 411, differing primarily by having two 300-hp (224-kW) Continental

TSIO-520-E flat-six engines and some reduction in basic installed equipment.

Production of the Model 401 was phased out in mid-1972, and further development was then concentrated on the Model 402 which, in December 1971, had been named **Utililiner**. At the same time a new version of the Model 402 was introduced

as the **Businessliner**, this having standard six- or optional eight-seat accommodation. Both versions remained available in 1982, the Model 402 Utililiner available optionally in a **Utililiner II** configuration with a factory-installed package of avionics and equipment. The Model 402 Businessliner was complemented by **Businessliner II**

SPECIFICATION

Cessna Model 402C Businessliner III
Type: one/two-crew light business transport
Powerplant: two Continental TSIO-520-VB flat-six piston engines each rated at 325 hp (242 kW)
Performance: maximum speed 266 mph (428 km/h) at 16,000 ft (4875 m); cruising speed 245 mph (394 km/h) at 20,000 ft (6095 m); initial climb rate 1,450 ft (442 m)

per minute; service ceiling 26,900 ft (8200 m); range 1,466 miles (2359 km)
Weights: empty 4,329 lb (1964 kg); maximum take-off 6,850 lb (3107 kg)
Dimensions: wingspan 44 ft 1½ in (13.45 m); length 36 ft 4½ in (11.09 m); height 11 ft 5½ in (3.49 m); wing area 225.80 sq ft (20.98 m²)
Payload: up to eight passengers

and **Businessliner III** versions, the Businessliner II having the same factory-installed package as the Utililiner II and the Businessliner III a more sophisticated avionics fit.

Production of the Model 402 totalled approximately 1,500 early in 1982, 12 of this number having been supplied to the Royal Malaysian air force during 1975. The type remained in production up to the end of 1987, at which time 1,540 examples had been

The Model 401 accommodated a crew of two and up to six passengers, but the Model 402 had a cabin layout which permitted a quick change from eight-seat commuter use to an all-cargo configuration.

completed in Model 402, **Model 402A**, **Model 402B** and **Model 402C** variants of the Utililiner and Businessliner.

Cessna Model 404 Titan

On 26 February 1975 Cessna flew the prototype of its new twin-engined **Model 404**, subsequently named as the **Titan**, of which initial deliveries

began in October 1976. In appearance the new type was generally similar to the turboprop-powered Conquest, which flew later, and the two aircraft

shared what was then a new feature for Cessna twins, a tailplane incorporating dihedral. Two versions were available initially, these being the **Titan Ambassador** passenger variant which was also offered with an alternative executive interior, and the **Titan Courier** utility version for freight or up to 10 passengers.

Early in 1982 seven variants were available in the

Total production of Titans stood at around 400 at the beginning of 1982, when production was suspended, never to be resumed. This aircraft is Brazil-registered.

forms of the Titan Ambassador in standard, **Titan Ambassador II** and **Titan Ambassador III** versions, the two latter having factory-installed avionics/equipment packages; the Titan Courier in standard and **Titan Courier II** versions, the latter with the same avion-

ics/equipment package as the Ambassador II; and the **Titan Freighter** in similar standard and **Titan Freighter II** versions. The Titan Freighter was a cargo version with impact-resistant polycarbonate interior features to protect the fuselage from damage by cargo.

SPECIFICATION	
Cessna Model 404 Titan Ambassador	per minute; service ceiling 26,000 ft (7925 m); range 2,119 miles (3410 km)
Type: one/two-crew passenger, executive or cargo transport	**Weights:** empty 4,834 lb (2192 kg); maximum take-off 8,400 lb (3810 kg)
Powerplant: two Continental GTSIO-520-M flat-six piston engines each rated at 375 hp (280 kW)	**Dimensions:** wingspan 46 ft 4 in (14.12 m); length 39 ft 6¼ in (12.04 m); height 13 ft 3 in (4.04 m); wing area 242.00 sq ft (22.48 m²)
Performance: maximum speed 267 mph (430 km/h) at 16,000 ft (4875 m); cruising speed 251 mph (404 km/h) at 20,000 ft (6095 m); initial climb rate 1,575 ft (480 m)	**Payload:** up to 10 passengers or freight

Cessna Model 411

When it took to the air for the first time on 18 July 1962, the **Cessna Model 411** represented what was currently the company's largest aircraft intended for the business market. Generally similar in overall configuration to

the Model 310, it differed from the earlier type by having a wing of slightly increased span and area, a fuselage that had been lengthened and a powerplant that had been upgraded and uprated. Production of the Model

411 was discontinued in June 1978, after the production of 400 examples, of which a small number had been supplied to the French air force.

The Model 411's powerplant was upgraded from that of the Model 310 to a pair of GTSIO-520 flat-six turbocharged engines, and accommodation was provided for a crew of two and up to six passengers, although four was a more normal figure for business operations.

SPECIFICATION	
Cessna Model 411	per minute; service ceiling 26,000 ft (7925 m)
Type: one/two-crew light business transport	**Weights:** empty 3,820 lb (1733 kg); maximum take-off 6,500 lb (2948 kg)
Powerplant: two Continental GTSIO-520 flat-six piston engines each rated at 340 hp (254 kW)	**Dimensions:** wingspan 39 ft 10¼ in (12.15 m); length 33 ft 5½ in (10.20 m); height 11 ft 6½ in (3.5 m); wing area 200.00 ft (18.58 m²)
Performance: maximum speed 268 mph (431 km/h) at 16,000 ft (4875 m); cruising speed 246 mph (396 km/h) at 20,000 ft (6095 m); initial climb rate 1,600 ft (488 m)	**Payload:** up to six passengers

Cessna Model 414 Chancellor

To boost is product line with a twin-engined pressurised transport, Cessna married the basic fuselage of the Model 421 with the wing developed for the Model 401. The resulting aircraft was the **Cessna Model 414**, and this first flew on 1 November 1968. A number of optional seating layouts for up to seven passengers, and a wide

range of cabin appointments were available, and new features introduced included engine cowlings with flush inlets to improve engine cooling and an accurate fuel monitoring system developed by Cessna to provide a better fuel management capability.

From the time of its introduction until 1976,

improvements introduced to the Model 402 were reflected in the Model 414, and in that year the name **Chancellor** was adopted. It was available for 1976 in standard and **Model 414 II** versions, the latter incorporating a package of factory-installed avionics and equipment. For 1978, after 513 of the original Model 414

machines had been built, an improved version was introduced as the **Model 414A**, whose major changes included a redesigned and increased-span wing incorporating integral fuel tanks and more baggage capacity in an extended nose. Versions available in early 1982 included the standard Model 414A Chancellor,

plus **Chancellor II** and **Chancellor III**, with differing factory-installed avionics/equipment packages. At that time, total production of all Model 414 and Model 414A versions was approximately 1,000 aircraft. Production of the Model 414 was suspended in the mid-1980s and never resumed.

Cessna Model 414 Chancellor (continued)

SPECIFICATION

Cessna Model 414A Chancellor
Type: one/two-crew light transport
Powerplant: two Continental
TSIO-520-NB flat-six piston
engines each rated at 310 hp
(231 kW)
Performance: maximum speed
271 mph (436 km/h) at 20,000 ft
(6095 m); cruising speed 259 mph
(417 km/h) at 24,500 ft (7470 m);
initial climb rate 1,580 ft (482 m)
per minute; service ceiling
30,800 ft (9390 m); range
1,528 miles (2459 km)
Weights: empty 4,356 lb
(1976 kg); maximum take-off
6,750 lb (2062 kg)
Dimensions: wingspan 44 ft 1⅝ in
(13.45 m); length 36 ft 4⅞ in
(11.09 m); height 11 ft 5⅝ in
(3.49 m); wing area 225.80 sq ft
(20.98 m²)
Payload: up to six passengers

In its Model 414A variant, the Chancellor omitted the tip tanks of the Model 414. Instead, the aircraft featured a redesigned wing incorporating integral fuel tanks, along with a reduced-chord tail, longer-span wing, longer nose and revised undercarriage.

Cessna Model 421 Golden Eagle

In October 1965 Cessna announced the development of a new twin-engined pressurised business aircraft designated as the **Model 421**, the prototype of which had flown for the first time on 14 October 1965. Derived from the Model 401 and Model 411, the Model 421 differed by having a fail-safe pressurised fuselage and an AiResearch air-conditioning and pressurisation system. Deliveries of initial production aircraft began in May 1967.

Two new versions of the Model 421 were introduced for 1970 as the **Model 421B Golden Eagle** and **Model 421B Executive Commuter**. Both had a number of improvements including a lengthened nose, an increase in wingspan, strengthened landing gear, and many detail refinements. The Executive Commuter was basically the same as the Golden Eagle except for the completion of its cabin with easily removable seating to provide alternative passenger/cargo configurations which could accommodate a maximum of 10 passengers. These two versions

were replaced in 1976 by the **Model 421C Golden Eagle**, which introduced some important changes including a new wing with integral fuel tanks that dispensed with the earlier types' distinctive wing tip tanks. Other changes provided increased area for the vertical tail surface and larger-capacity turbochargers. Four versions were available as the Model 421C Golden Eagle and **Model 421C Executive Commuter** that were each produced in **Model 421C II** versions with a factory-installed avionics/equipment package.

The Executive Commuter was discontinued for 1978, the Golden Eagle then being available in standard as well as Model 421C II and **Model 421C III** versions with differing avionics/equipment packages. By early 1982, some 2,000 Golden Eagles of all versions had been built, these including three examples for the RNZAF. Production was terminated in the mid-1980s.

SPECIFICATION

Cessna Model 421C Golden Eagle
Type: one/two-crew light transport
Powerplant: two Continental
GTSIO-520-N flat-six piston
engines each rated at 375 hp
(280 kW)
Performance: maximum speed
297 mph (478 km/h) at 20,000 ft
(6095 m); cruising speed 279 mph
(450 km/h) at 25,000 ft (7620 m);
initial climb rate 1,940 ft (591 m)
per minute; service ceiling
30,200 ft (9205 m); range
1,710 miles (2752 km)
Weights: empty 4,640 lb
(2105 kg); maximum take-off
7,450 lb (3379 kg)
Dimensions: wingspan 41 ft 1½ in
(12.53 m); length 36 ft 4⅞ in
(11.09 m); height 11 ft 5⅝ in
(3.49 m); wing area 215.00 sq ft
(19.97 m²)
Payload: up to six passengers

All but the earliest Model 421s featured a lengthened nose to provide more avionics and baggage capacity. This is a 1981 Golden Eagle.

Cessna Model 425 Corsair and Conquest I

Late in 1977 Cessna embarked on the design of a new turboprop-powered aircraft, and the prototype of the new type made its first flight on 12 September 1978. Introduced to service in 1980 as the **Model 425 Corsair**, this new pressurised business aircraft combined the airframe of the Model 421C Golden Eagle with the revised powerplant of two PT6A turboprops for an all-round improvement in performance including a higher cruising speed and better altitude performance at increased take-off weights. The Corsair offered similar accommodation to the Model 421, but featured a redesigned undercarriage

and rounded nose. As with most business aircraft in this class, it was extensively equipped as standard, but a wide range of optional avionics and equipment was also available.

Late in 1982, after the delivery of 132 aircraft, the Corsair was slightly improved, resulting in a 400-lb (181-kg) increase in maximum take-off weight, and renamed as the **Conquest I**. This revised aircraft remained in production for only a relatively short time before its production was ended in the mid-1980s as Cessna rationalised its product line at a time of rising fuel prices and climbing product liability costs.

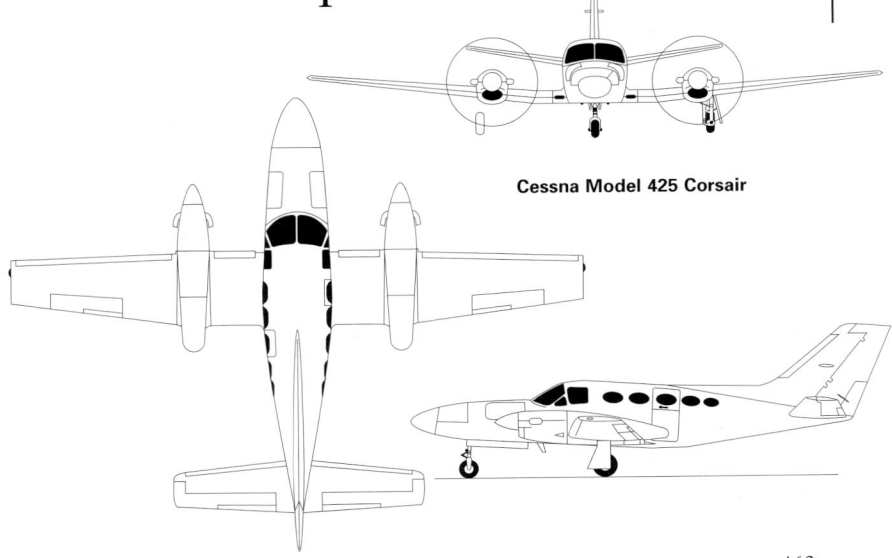

Cessna Model 425 Corsair

The major airframe feature distinguishing the Model 425 Corsair/Conquest from the Model 421 was a tail unit with the dihedralled tailplane first pioneered on the Model 404. By US business aircraft standards, the type's production run of 236 airframes was disappointing.

SPECIFICATION

Cessna Model 425 Corsair
Type: one/two-crew light transport
Powerplant: two Pratt & Whitney Canada PT6A-112 turboprop engines each flat-rated at 450 shp (336 kW)
Performance: maximum cruising speed 304 mph (489 km/h) at 17,700 ft (5395 m); economical cruising speed 242 mph (389 km/h) at 30,000 ft (9145 m); initial climb rate 2,027 ft (618 m) per minute;

service ceiling 34,700 ft (10575 m); range 1,854 miles (2984 km)
Weights: empty 4,870 lb (2209 kg); maximum take-off 8,200 lb (3720 kg)
Dimensions: wingspan 44 ft 1½ in (13.45 m); length 35 ft 10¼ in (10.93 m); height 12 ft 7¼ in (3.84 m); wing area 224.98 sq ft (20.90 m²)
Payload: up to six passengers

Cessna Model 441 Conquest II

On 15 November 1974 Cessna announced the development of a new turboprop-powered pressurised executive transport which it designated **Model 441**. The prototype

was flown for the first time on 26 August 1975 and, by the time initial deliveries began, the type had been given the name **Conquest II**.
Cessna had designed the

Conquest II in the hope that it would slot nicely into the potentially profitable twin-engined business aircraft market between current piston-engined and

turbojet-engined types. However, the company's marketing plans were delayed when problems arose in early 1978. One of the first production aircraft was involved in a crash and the type was grounded by Cessna as the problem was investigated and a cure developed. Modification of the tail unit was carried out before the type was recertificated, and existing aircraft were retrofitted with the new tailplane.

The Conquest was based on the wing and landing gear of the Model 404 Titan, but the span of the former was increased by the incorporation of wingtip extensions. The air-conditioned and pressurised cabin provided accommodation for one pilot and up to 10 passengers, but among the optional layouts was a de-luxe executive interior for four passengers. Production of the Conquest II was halted in the mid-1980s.

Garrett specifically developed the TPE331 turboprop engine to provide the high-altitude/high-speed performance that Cessna required for its 11-seat Model 441.

SPECIFICATION

Cessna Model 441 Conquest II
Type: one-crew executive transport
Powerplant: two Garrett TPE331-8-401S/402S turboprop engines each flat-rated at 636 shp (474 kW)
Performance: maximum speed 340 mph (547 km/h) at 16,000 ft (4875 m); cruising speed 298 mph (480 km/h) at 35,000 ft (10670 m); initial climb rate 2,435 ft (742 m)

per minute; service ceiling more than 35,000 ft (10670 m); range 2,638 miles (4245 km)
Weights: empty 5,706 lb (2588 kg); maximum take-off 9,850 lb (4468 kg)
Dimensions: wingspan 49 ft 4 in (15.04 m); length 39 ft ¼ in (11.89 m); height 13 ft 1¾ in (4.01 m); wing area 253.60 sq ft (23.56 m²)
Payload: up to 10 passengers

Cessna Model 500 Citation, Model 501 Citation I, Model 550 Citation II & Model 560 Citation V

The **Cessna Model 500 Citation** was one of the first of the new generation of turbofan-powered business jets, a response to growing pressure from environmentalists for quieter engines and from operators for better fuel economy. Its development represented a very large investment for the company, and the prototype **Fanjet 500**, as the type was then named, flew for the first time on 15 September 1969.

Renamed Citation shortly after its first flight, the eight-seat Model 500 had an overall configuration similar to that of other Cessna twin-engined aircraft except for its powerplant installation, which comprised two 2,200-lb st (9.78-kN) JT15D-1 turbofans each mounted in a pod, one on

each side of the rear fuselage just aft of the wing trailing edge. During development flying, a number of important changes were made, and it was not until late 1971 that initial deliveries were completed. Five years later, deliveries began of an improved **Model 501 Citation I** with increased wingspan and JT15D-1A engines. Soon after this, the type was also made available in a **Model 501 Citation I/SP** version certificated for single-pilot operation.

Small numbers of the Citation were procured by several air forces for the VIP and staff transport roles, while sales of the Citation I to military operators have included one example for the photo survey role with the Argentine army, and small numbers for the liaison and communication tasks with

the Chinese air force, the air forces of Mexico and Venezuela, and the Ecuadorian navy.

Development of the Citation continued with the **Citation II**, of which the prototype flew for the first time on 31 January 1977. This incorporated a

number of important changes including a wing of increased span, a lengthened fuselage to increase accommodation to 12, the uprated powerplant of two 2,500-lb st (11.12-kN) JT15D-4 turbofan engines, and greater fuel capacity. Deliveries

began in 1978 and, like the Citation I, it was followed by the **Model 551 Citation II/SP**, certificated for single-pilot operation. The Citation II serves with the Spanish navy and the air forces of Myanmar, Turkey and Venezuela.

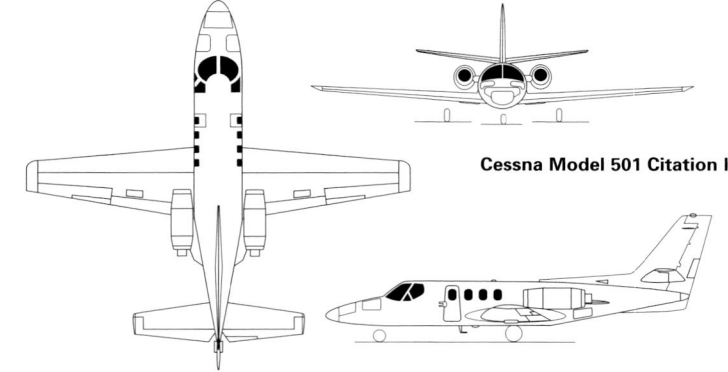

Cessna Model 501 Citation I

Cessna Model 500 Citation, Model 501 Citation I, Model 550 Citation II and Model 560 Citation V (cont.)

The **Model S550 Citation S/II** was first flown on 14 February 1984 and introduced a new aerofoil, wing leading-edge cuffs and JT15D-4B turbofans. A variant of this sub-type was adopted by the USN as a radar trainer; with a wing of reduced span and the powerplant of two 2,900-lb st (12.89-kN) JT15D-5 engines, this became the **Model 552**, known in service as the

T-47A. Fifteen were acquired by the service and were operated from NAS Pensacola by VT-86 until replaced by the Rockwell T-39 Sabreliner. The normal crew of the T-47A, generally known by the nickname 'Platypus', included a civilian pilot, a US Navy instructor and three students. A development of the Citation II, with the revised powerplant of two 2,750-lb st (12.23-kN) Pratt

& Whitney Canada PW530A turbofans, updated avionics and flight controls, and a cabin interior and seating based on those of the Citation V Ultra, is the **Citation Bravo.** This variant first flew on 25 April 1995 for delivery from June 1996, and by the late 1990s the sole military order for the type had been placed by the USAF, which in 1997 received five examples of the **OT-47B** for the tracker role with revisions that included the Northrop Grumman APG-66 radar and the Northrop Grumman

WF-360 IR tracking system.

A further development of the Citation S/II flew as an engineering prototype on 18 August 1987. Designated **Model 560 Citation V**, the type featured JT15D-5A engines and had a lengthened fuselage. Deliveries began in April 1989, and among the military operators of the Citation V have been the Moroccan air force, the Seychelles defence force, and the Venda Defence Force.

A development of the Citation V is the **Citation V Ultra** that first flew in August 1987. It introduces

a digital autopilot, an EFIS and two 3,045-lb st (13.55-kN) JT15D-5Ds. Among the military customers for this model are the Spanish air force, the US Army (up to 35 **UC-35A** aircraft for its medium-range transport requirement) and the USMC (**UC-35C**). The **Citation Excel** of 1997, combines Citation Ultra wings and tail with a shortened Citation X fuselage. The further improved **Citation Ultra Encore** will be delivered from 2000, with US Army aircraft to be known as **UC-35B**.

Seven cabin windows on each side identify this aircraft as a Citation V. The basic early Citation airframe has been modified and updated to produce a range of state-of-the art 'bizjets'.

SPECIFICATION	
Cessna Model 560 Citation V Ultra	certificated ceiling 45,000 ft (13715 m); range 2,255 miles (3630 km) with five passengers
Type: one/two-crew medium-range transport aircraft	**Weights:** empty 9,650 lb (4377 kg); maximum take-off 16,300 lb (7393 kg)
Powerplant: two Pratt & Whitney Canada JT15D-5D turbofan engines each rated at 3,045 lb st (13.55 kN)	**Dimensions:** wingspan 52 ft 2½ in (15.91 m); length 48 ft 10¾ in (14.90 m); height 15 ft (4.57 m); wing area 322.90 sq ft (30.00 m²)
Performance: maximum cruising speed 495 mph (796 km/h) at 35,000 ft (10670 m); initial climb rate 4,100 ft (1249 m) per minute;	**Payload:** up to eight passengers

Cessna Model 525 CitationJet, Citation CJ and Model 526

At the National Business Aircraft Association convention of 1989, Cessna announced its decision to proceed with the design and certification of a new light business transport in its Citation series. The new type was designated as the

Model 525 CitationJet, and it was to succeed the Citation and Citation I. One of the keys to the new type's capabilities was the FJ44 turbofan and this was first flown on a Citation during April 1990, the success of the engine

programme proving a useful fillip for the airframe programme.

The first of two CitationJet prototypes made its maiden flight on 29 April 1991, and the type received its FAA certification for single-pilot operation on 16 October 1992, allowing the start of commercial deliveries in March 1993 to a market that Cessna estimated at

1,000 such aircraft over a 10-year period. By March 1995 Cessna had completed 100 aircraft. Other than that involving the powerplant, the other primary changes compared to the Citation I included a new laminar-flow wing aerofoil of supercritical section, a new empennage with a tall T-tail, and main landing gear units of the

trailing-link type.

The CitationJet's avionics are based on the Honeywell SPZ-5000 three-axis autopilot and digital flight director, with a two-tube EFIS. Up to six passengers are accommodated, in a cabin laid out with two rearward-facing seats at the front and the other four in a club arrangement at the rear.

Cessna's Model 526 JPATS CitationJet represented a radical modification of the Model 525 'bizjet'. The aircraft was unsuccessful in competition with the Raytheon Beech T-6A Texan II and development was subsequently abandoned.

SPECIFICATION	
Cessna Model 525 CitationJet	range 1,708 miles (2749 km)
Type: one/two-crew business transport	**Weights:** empty 6,453 lb (2927 kg); maximum take-off 10,400 lb (4717 kg)
Powerplant: two Williams/Rolls-Royce FJ44-1A turbofan engines each rated at 1,900 lb st (8.45 kN)	**Dimensions:** wingspan 46 ft 9½ in (14.26 m); length 42 ft 7¼ in (12.98 m); height 13 ft 8½ in (4.18 m); wing area 240.00 sq ft (22.30 m²)
Performance: maximum cruising speed 430 mph (692 km/h) at 33,000 ft (10060 m); initial climb rate 3,311 ft (1009 m) per minute; service ceiling 41,000 ft (12495 m);	**Payload:** up to six passengers

Variants

Citation CJ1: Scheduled for delivery from the spring of 2000, the CJ1 was developed as the company's successor to the CitationJet, Cessna's best-selling entry-level business transport. The CJ1 is basically the CitationJet with a number of individually small, but collectively important, improvements made possible by technical developments, a 200-lb (91-kg) increase in maximum take-off weight for the carriage of additional fuel, and a revised flightdeck with avionics based on the Collins Pro Line 21 system
Citation CJ2: Due for certification and delivery from a time early in the 21st century, the CJ2 is a development of the CitationJet with a longer cabin and tailcone to carry more passengers and more baggage, increased wingspan, an enlarged swept horizontal tail

surface, new 2,300-lb st (10.23-kN) FJ44-2C turbofans and a modernised flightdeck with avionics based on the Collins Pro Line 21 system
Model 526 JPATS CitationJet: First flown on 21 December 1993 and supplemented from March 1994 by a second, essentially similar, prototype, the Model 526 was based closely on the CitationJet, retaining FJ44 turbofans, in their Williams International F129 military form. These engines were buried in a new fuselage with a blown canopy covering tandem cockpits, and other changes were simple D-section inlets for engine aspiration, a revised and strengthened wing of shorter span and a tail unit with a low-set tailplane. The JPATS CitationJet was the only twin-engined contender for the Joint Primary Aircraft Training System requirement issued by the USAF and USN, but was ultimately unsuccessful

Cessna Model 650 Citation III, Citation VI and Citation VII

With the first two members of its Citation series, Cessna had opted for the lower end of the market with small capacity and only modest performance. With the **Cessna Model 650 Citation III**, however, the company signalled its intention of entering the market for medium-capacity aircraft of greater performance. Cessna therefore opted for moderately swept flying surfaces including a high-aspect-ratio wing based on a NASA-developed super-

critical aerofoil section and a tall T-tail empennage. The new type was essentially of light alloy construction, with a low-set cantilever wing and a tricycle landing gear with a single-wheel nose unit and twin-wheel main units.

The first of two Citation III prototypes made the type's first flight on 30 May 1979, and the receipt of FAA certification in April 1982 allowed the start of deliveries in December of the same year. The standard powerplant was two

TFE731-3B-100S turbofans, the flightdeck was laid out for a two-person crew with avionics based on the Honeywell SPZ-650 integrated system and the separate cabin accommodated up to nine passengers.

In 1990 Cessna announced the **Citation VI** as a simplified and therefore cheaper version of the Citation III, and the first of the new type was rolled out on 2 January 1991 for the start of deliveries in 1992. The type retained the basic airframe of the Citation III with modification to features such as the flaps and spoilers, but the cabin was lengthened and reduced in height for the carriage of a maximum of 10 passengers. Cabin layouts to specific customer requirements were replaced by a few factory-installed layout options.

Also announced in 1990 was the **Citation VII** as a development of the Citation

VI with avionics based on the SPZ-8000 system and the powerplant changed to a pair of 4,140-lb st (18.41-kN) TFE731-4R-2S turbofans for a better cruising speed, climb rate and cruising altitude as well as a

six-passenger range of 2,554 miles (4111 km). The engineering prototype made its first flight in February 1991, certification followed in January 1992, and deliveries began three months later.

The Citation III, VI (illustrated) and VII feature a wing of two-spar construction with a quarter-chord sweep angle of 25°, and a trailing edge carrying three-section flaps.

SPECIFICATION	
Cessna Model 650 Citation VI **Type:** two-crew business transport **Powerplant:** two AlliedSignal (Garrett) TFE731-3B-100S turbofan engines each rated at 3,650 lb st (16.24 kN) **Performance:** maximum cruising speed 543 mph (874 km/h) at 35,000 ft (10670 m); initial climb rate 3,700 ft (1127 m) per minute; certificated ceiling 51,000 ft (15545 m); range 2,700 miles (4345 km)	**Weights:** empty 12,900 lb (5851 kg); maximum take-off 22,000 lb (9979 kg) **Dimensions:** wingspan 53 ft 6 in (16.31 m); length 55 ft 5½ in (16.90 m); height 16 ft 9½ in (5.12 m); wing area 312.00 sq ft (28.99 m²) **Payload:** up to 10 passengers within the context of a 3,489-lb (1583-kg) payload

Cessna Model 750 Citation X

The earlier types in its Citation series of business transports having offered, at best, an intra-continental range capability with modest payload, Cessna decided in the late 1980s to expand its product range with a more advanced

'bizjet'. This would provide both a larger payload and the combination of a higher cruising speed and much extended range for a full transcontinental or even transatlantic capability. The intended type was announced in October 1990

as the **Model 750 Citation X**, and the first of three prototype and pre-production aircraft made the type's maiden flight on 21 December 1993. FAA certification followed in June 1996 and the first deliveries to customers

were made later in the same year.

The Citation X is based on essentially the same layout as the middle series of Citation aircraft, the type's most notable feature being its 37° wing sweep at quarter chord. The wing is carried under the fuselage's primary structure in a large and very cleverly shaped fairing that accommodates much of the 13,000 lb (5897 kg) total fuel load. Each half of the wing's trailing edge is occupied by three-section flaps and an aileron, while virtually the full span of the leading edge is occupied by

a two-section slat. The T-tail has inset control surfaces, the fuselage is of circular section with a fail-safe structure in the section that is pressurised, and the tricycle landing gear has twin wheels on each unit.

The flight deck is laid out for a two-person crew with avionics based on the Honeywell Primus 2000 system. These include a five-tube EFIS with a PFD (Primary Flight Display) and an MFD (Multi-Function Display) for each of the two crew members, flanking the central screen for the EICAS (Engine Indication and Crew Alerting System).

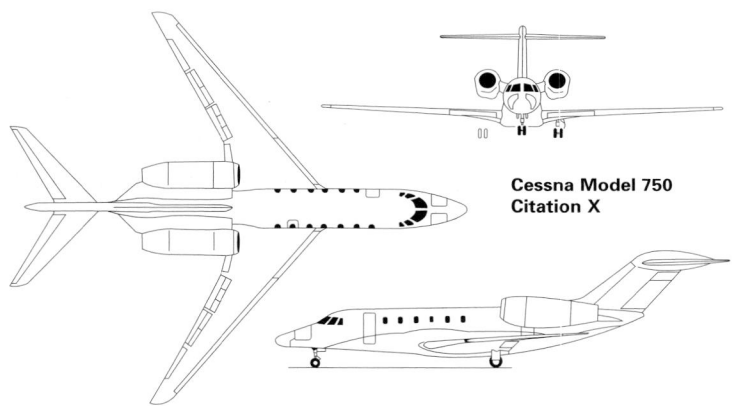

Cessna Model 750 Citation X

SPECIFICATION	
Cessna Model 750 Citation X **Type:** two-crew business transport **Powerplant:** two Allison AE3007C turbofan engines each rated at 6,442 lb st (28.66 kN) **Performance:** maximum cruising speed 589 mph (948 km/h) at 37,000 ft (11280 m); initial climb rate 4,000 ft (1219 m) per minute; service ceiling 51,000 ft (15545 m);	range 3,742 miles (6022 km) **Weights:** empty 21,450 lb (9730 kg); maximum take-off 35,700 lb (16194 kg) **Dimensions:** wingspan 63 ft 7 in (19.39 m); length 72 ft 4 in (22.05 m); height 19 ft 2 in (5.85 m); wing area 527.00 sq ft (48.96 m²) **Payload:** up to 12 passengers

Chase MS-7 Avitruk (C-122)

At the end of World War II, the USAAF lost virtually all interest in small and basically expendable assault gliders, but still saw a limited utility for the larger type of assault glider. The key to this capability was the carriage of a payload considerably heavier than that typical of World War II gliders, and this meant a larger airframe whose greater cost could only be

justified by a higher degree of durability and 'recoverability' for reuse.

The ideal starting point for a glider of this type was the **Chase CG-14**, whose good performance and payload could be enhanced by a scaling-up of the basic design and its revision with an all-metal rather than all-wood or mixed metal/wood structure. In January 1947 the USAAF contracted for a

single prototype, known to the manufacturer as the **Avitruk** and to the service as the **XCG-14B**; the order was soon increased to two aircraft and the type was redesignated **XCG-18A**. The initial XCG-18A made its maiden flight on 18 December 1947 as the first all-metal transport glider anywhere in the world. By this time, the USAAF had become the

USAF, and it was this service that in March 1948 placed a contract with Chase for an additional five aircraft and also altered the designation of the existing two machines to **XG-18A** in the revised G-for-Glider category. Four of the new aircraft were to be completed to this improved XG-18A standard for service trials and operational evaluation, while the

fifth was to be built as the sole example of the **MS-7** design as the **YC-122** for evaluation of the type in the light assault transport role with a powerplant of two Pratt & Whitney R-2000-11 radial piston engines.

The YC-122 was a cantilever high-wing monoplane of all-metal construction, based on a pod-and-boom fuselage and featuring a tricycle-type landing gear with a retractable nose unit and fixed main units.

Chase C-122 Avitruk (continued)

There followed two **YC-122A** service trials aircraft generally similar to the YC-122, the second of these aircraft becoming the sole **YC-122B** after it had been revised with two Wright R-1820-101 radials. Ordered to the extent of nine aircraft, the **YC-122C** was the definitive service trials type, modelled on the YC-122B. The type performed and handled well, but by this time the USAF had decided against the procurement of a small dedicated assault transport and no further production of the C-122 series followed. The YC-122C aircraft were operated in the utility role up to 1957 by the 16th and 316th Troop Carrier Groups of the 8th Air Force.

The C-122 had a fuselage of rectangular section with rounded-off corners and a rear ramp/door arrangement beneath its orthodox tail unit. The YC-122 is illustrated.

SPECIFICATION	
Chase YC-122C	(4667 km)
Type: two-crew utility transport	**Weight:** maximum take-off
Powerplant: two Wright R-1820-101 radial piston engines each rated at 1,425 hp (1063 kW)	32,000 lb (14515 kg)
Dimensions: wingspan 95 ft 8 in (29.16 m); length 61 ft 8 in (18.80 m)	
Performance: maximum speed 220 mph (354 km/h) at optimum altitude; range 2,900 miles	**Payload:** up to 30 troops or 8,000 lb (3629 kg) of freight

Chengdu F-7M Airguard

A much improved version of the licence-built J-7 II MiG-21 derivative intended for the export market, the **F-7M Airguard** dual-role fighter was developed in the early 1980s for delivery from 1984. It had an additional pair of underwing hardpoints (for the carriage of two PL-7 short-range AAMs or two drop tanks), a revised cockpit based on that of the J-7 II with its improved ejection seat and rear- rather than side-hinged canopy, and a number of other developments including a strengthened airframe, upgraded landing gear, and the pitot probe relocated from a position below the nose to a location above it. Most important, however, is the partial change from Chinese to Western avionics such as the HUDWASS, ranging radar with improved ECCM, air data computer, radar altimeter and multi-mode radios.

The type was considered for licensed manufacture in Pakistan as the **Sabre II**, possibly with a forward fuselage (complete with avionics etc.) manufactured in the USA by Grumman, which was also considering the feasibility of re-engining the type with a non-afterburning version of the General Electric F404 or Pratt & Whitney PW1120 turbofan. However, Pakistan finally opted for the **F-7P Skybolt** (the name later being dropped) derivative of the F-7M with a number of Western avionics features, the ability to carry both PL-5 and AIM-9 Sidewinder short-range AAMs, and the Martin-Baker Mk 10L zero/zero ejection seat instead of the basic Chengdu HTY-4 (Type IV) unit.

In 1988 the Chinese manufacturer began trials of the **F-7MP** version of the F-7P with engine improvements, a revised cockpit layout, and avionics enhancements, including installation of FIAR Grifo 7 fire-control radar in place of the original GEC-Marconi Type 226 Skyranger ranging radar. In an improved form, this Italian radar is also a possible option for the latest **F-7MR** version, with a full suite of Western avionics including the Marconi Super Skyranger multi-mode pulse-Doppler radar.

The **FT-7** is the two-seat advanced flying and armament trainer version of the F-7P for Pakistan, which operates the type in the conversion and continuation trainer roles.

Announced in 1988 as a collaborative venture between Chengdu, CATIC and Grumman, the **Super-7** was to have been the latest version of the Sabre II concept. It was to have the powerplant of one 17,000-lb st (75.62-kN) Turbo-Union RB.199 turbofan or alternatively one 18,000-lb st (80.07-kN) General Electric F404 turbofan (in the form of a licensed Volvo RM12) and aspirated in either case via lateral inlets so that a new nose could have been fitted with the Westinghouse APG-66 radar. The improved fighter was to have featured much of the F-16 Fighting Falcon's avionics (including the HUD) as well as the windscreen and canopy developed for the F-20 Tigershark. Extra fuel was to have been accommodated in a larger dorsal fin on the upper surface of a lengthened fuselage and other changes would have included an increased span with greater chord for increased wing area, leading-edge slats and combat flaps, two new inboard hardpoints each capable of carrying an AAM, an arrester hook, strengthened landing gear with larger wheels, and a new ejection seat.

In 1989 the project was shelved as a result of American displeasure with the communist party's suppression of democratic tendencies in China. Nevertheless, the project was revived for a short time in 1990 and 1991, when Chengdu started discussions with both British and Russian aero engine manufacturers.

In Pakistani service, all F-7s, whether to F-7P or F-7MP standard, are designated F-7P. The aircraft normally fly with a single pylon beneath each wing and armed, as illustrated, with AIM-9s.

SPECIFICATION	
Chengdu F-7M Airguard	mission with two 331-lb (150-kg) bombs and three drop tanks
Type: single-seat interceptor and ground-attack fighter	**Weights:** empty 11,629 lb (5275 kg); normal take-off 16,603 lb (7531 kg)
Powerplant: one Liyang (LMC) WP-7B(BM) turbojet engine rated at 13,448 lb st (59.82 kN) with afterburning	**Dimensions:** wingspan 23 ft 5⅝ in (7.154 m); length 48 ft 10 in (14.885 m) including probe; height 13 ft 5½ in (4.103 m); wing area 247.58 sq ft (23.00 m²)
Performance: maximum speed 1,350 mph (2175 km/h) or Mach 2.04 between 41,000 and 60,700 ft (12500 and 18500 m); initial climb rate 35,433 ft (10800 m) per minute; service ceiling 59,700 ft (18200 m); radius 373 miles (600 km) on a hi-lo-hi interdiction	**Armament:** two 30-mm Type 30-1 fixed forward-firing cannon, plus up to 5,511 lb (2500 kg) of disposable stores carried on five hardpoints

Chichester-Miles Leopard

Ian Chichester-Miles, formerly chief research engineer of BAe at Hatfield, established Chichester-Miles Consultants Ltd for the express purpose of designing and developing the **Chichester-Miles Leopard** as a four-seat light business aircraft with a powerplant of two light turbine engines pod-mounted on the sides of the rear fuselage. The design was completed in 1981, and work on the prototype, built under contract by Designability Ltd, began in the following year. This first prototype was unpressurised and made its maiden flight on 12 December 1988 with two 300-lb st (1.33-kN) Noel Penny Turbines NPT 301-3A turbojets. This was followed by a second, pressurised, prototype with a turbofan powerplant, a strengthened structure, new landing gear and a nose modified to allow the incorporation of EFIS avionics.

The Leopard is a cantilever low-wing monoplane with swept flying surfaces and tricycle landing gear, and particular features are an all-composite airframe, a laminar-flow wing of supercritical section, an all-moving vertical tail surface, and two all-moving independent tailplane sections. After disappearing from the aviation scene, the Leopard was actively promoted at the 1998 Farnborough Airshow.

An attractive light aircraft offering exceptional performance, the CMC Leopard is struggling to establish a market niche for itself. The turbojet-engined first prototype is illustrated.

Chrislea CH.3 Ace, Super Ace and Skyjeep

In the years immediately after World War II, several smaller British manufacturers designed new light aircraft in an attempt to compete with the spate of surplus military trainers, such as the Tiger Moth and Magister, that were available on the civil market. One such company was Chrislea Aircraft Ltd, whose designer, R. C. Christopherides, produced the four-seat **Chrislea CH.3 Ace**, a high-wing cabin monoplane. An innovation among British light aircraft of the period was its tricycle landing gear, and the powerplant was a 125-hp

(93-kW) Avco Lycoming, although it was intended that production models would use the new British 100-hp (75-kW) Monaco engine. The main difference, however, between this type and established British practice was in the control system, in which a single wheel on a universal joint replaced the conventional control column and rudder bar. The prototype Ace flew in September 1946 and within three weeks its single fin had been replaced by twin surfaces, each comprising a fin and rudder.
The first **CH.3 Series 2**

Super Ace flew in February 1948 and considerable criticism from flying instructors resulted in the unusual control system being replaced by a conventional installation. A number of Super Ace machines was sold abroad, but just 21 aircraft were flown.
In 1949 the prototype of the **CH.3 Series 4 Skyjeep** had been flown. This had a conventional control system, tailwheel

Of the Type CH.3 Series 2 Super Ace production aircraft, the sixth and seventh machines were exhibited at the 1948 SBAC Display at Farnborough. Although 21 aircraft were flown, four others were abandoned on the production line and two more were completed, but never flown.

landing gear and a 155-hp (116-kW) Blackburn Cirrus Major 3 engine. A removable top decking to the rear fuselage offered space for a stretcher or light freight. Two further Skyjeep aircraft were

completed and sold to customers in Argentina and Australia, while the prototype subsequently went to French Indo-China. Two other uncompleted aircraft were scrapped in 1952.

Chyeranovskii BICh-1 to BICh-11

Boris Ivanovich Chyeranovskii began studying the potential of the parabolic wing planform in 1921, completing and flying his first test vehicle, the **BICh-1** glider, in 1924. The wing of the BICh-1 took the form of a parabola, the straight trailing edge being occupied by elevons and flaps, and the pilot occupying a small nacelle aft of the wing leading edge.

There were no vertical surfaces, and the landing gear was of the monowheel type, with small stabilising skids. The BICh-1 proved uncontrollable and a modified development was built as the **BICh-2**, this introducing vertical tail surfaces and making 27 flights during the course of 1924.
Based on experience gained with the BICh-1 and

BICh-2, Chyeranovskii then built a small powered aircraft of similar parabolic wing configuration. This **BICh-3** was powered by a two-stroke engine, its pilot being seated farther aft and his open cockpit being faired into the vertical tail surface. Testing revealed the BICh-3 as controllable but fundamentally unstable.
During the period 1927-9, Chyeranovskii undertook a

number of design studies, all based on the use of the parabolic wing configuration, the most interesting being the **BICh-5**, which, tendered for an indeterminate military role, was to have been powered by two BMW VI engines. Less ambitious was the **BICh-7** tandem two-seater of 1929, which, based broadly on the BICh-3, was powered by a 100-hp (75-kW) Bristol Lucifer engine. Retaining the monowheel landing gear arrangement and featuring small wingtip rudders, the BICh-7 proved abortive, its pilot being unable to effect a take-off.

The design was extensively revised as the **BICh-7A**, an orthodox landing gear being fitted, both cockpits being enclosed and the wingtip rudders being discarded in favour of a more normal centrally-mounted surface. The BICh-7A was flown for the first time in 1932, the test pilot reporting unacceptably high stick loading. The wing control surfaces were modified until acceptable loading was achieved, the BICh-7A proving to possess good controllability, but flight testing being restricted by severe engine vibration.

The BICh-11 had a thick-section wing, a narrow central fuselage nacelle and small endplate fins with conventional rudders at the wingtips.

Chyeranovskii BICh-11 (continued)

Despite continued interest in the parabolic wing planform, Chyeranovskii adopted a trapezoidal wing for the **BICh-11**, completed in 1932. Of tailless configuration, the BICh-11 first appeared as a

glider, participating in the IX Glider Competition of 1933. In fact, the BICh-11 had been designed in collaboration with a Soviet rocket propulsion expert, with the primary purpose of flight

testing the OR-2 liquid-propellant rocket motor. Weighing 40 lb (18 kg) and developing 140 lb st (0.62 kN), the OR-2 was to be installed to the rear of the BICh-11's cockpit, with

the tanks for the jellied petroleum and liquid oxygen propellants faired into the wing on each side of the fuselage nacelle.

The OR-2 was fired on a test stand on 18 March 1933, but 10 days later Tsander, its designer, died and with him disappeared

the scheme to install the rocket motor in the BICh-11, with which it would have been known as the **RP-1** (**Raketnyii Planer-1**, or Rocket Glider no. 1). Subsequently, the BICh-11 was fitted with a Scorpion engine for further flight testing.

Chyeranovskii BICh-20 Pionyer

Yet another exotic wing planform was tested by Chyeranovskii with the **BICh-20 Pionyer**, this comprising a short-span centre section with straight leading edges and tapered trailing edges, coupled with semi-delta outer panels. Powered initially by a small

18-hp (13-kW) Blackburn Tomtit engine, but later by a slightly more potent Aubier-Dunne engine, the Pionyer was of tailless configuration, with the pilot seated in an enclosed cockpit forming an extension of the vertical fin. The Pionyer appeared in 1938, and proved stable

SPECIFICATION	
Chyeranovskii BICh-20 Pionyer **Type:** single-seat aerodynamic research aircraft **Powerplant:** one Aubier-Dunne piston engine rated at 20 hp (15 kW) **Performance:** maximum speed 103 mph (166 km/h) at sea level;	service ceiling 13,125 ft (4000 m); range 199 miles (320 km) **Weights:** empty 399 lb (181 kg); maximum take-off 633 lb (287 kg) **Dimensions:** wingspan 22 ft 8 in (6.90 m); length 11 ft 8¼ in (3.56 m); wing area 96.88 sq ft (9.00 m²)

and responsive during flight testing, providing data for the BICh-21 racing aircraft that followed.

The entire wing trailing edge of the BICh-20 was occupied by slotted flaps and elevons, while the landing gear was fixed and could be fitted with either wheels or skis.

Chyeranovskii BICh-21 (SG-1)

Derived from the BICh-20 Pionyer, the **BICh-21** was also known as the **SG-1** (**Samolyet Gonochnii-1**, or Racing Aircraft no. 1) and had a wing identical to that of its predecessor, apart from some gulling of the wingroots. Intended for competition flying, the

BICh-21 embodied considerable aerodynamic refinement as a result of wind tunnel testing, and was powered by a 220-hp (164-kW) engine. Construction of the prototype began in 1938, as soon as the Pionyer had demonstrated acceptable flight

SPECIFICATION	
Chyeranovskii BICh-21 **Type:** single-seat competition aircraft **Powerplant:** one MV-6 inline piston engine rated at 220 hp (164 kW) **Performance:** maximum speed	259 mph (417 km/h) at optimum altitude **Weights:** empty 1,160 lb (526 kg); maximum take-off 1,418 lb (643 kg) **Dimensions:** wingspan 22 ft 8 in (6.90 m); length 15 ft 5 in (4.70 m); wing area 96.88 sq ft (9.00 m²)

characteristics. The BICh-21 was not completed until 1940, the test programme commencing in 1941, but the German invasion interrupting its development.

In keeping with its racing role, the cockpit profile of the BICh-21 was lowered, and pneumatically retractable main landing gear units replaced the manually-operated units of the earlier BICh-20 Pionyer machine. The onset of war denied this promising machine success.

Chyetverikov MDR-6 (Chye-2)

Marking a noteworthy advance in Soviet flying-boat design from both aerodynamic and hydrodynamic points of view, the **MDR-6** was a three-seat coastal reconnaissance aircraft of all-metal

construction. The prototype, powered by 730-hp (544-kW) M-25E radial engines, was completed at Sevastopol in the summer of 1937, undergoing state trials in December of that year. With the revised

powerplant of two 1,100-hp (820-kW) M-63 radial engines, the flying-boat was ordered into production at Taganrog during 1938 as the **MDR-6A** (this designation being replaced by **Chye-2** after 1941), and 50 were built during 1939-41.

The completely redesigned hull contours of the later MDR-6s are clearly seen on this MDR-6B-4.

Refinement of the basic design resulted in the **MDR-6B-1** with an improved planing bottom, a redesigned bow from which the swivelling turret was eliminated, and new tail surfaces. Completed in December 1940, the MDR-6B-1 was powered by two 1,050-hp (783-kW) M-105 Vee engines, and the **MDR-6B-2** which

followed in 1941 was essentially similar, both embodying retractable underwing stabilising floats.

The **MDR-6B-3** differed in having 1,150-hp (857-kW) M-105PF engines in revised engine nacelles, and redesigned retractable stabilising floats. Despite dramatic improvements in performance over that of the MDR-6A, these 'boats

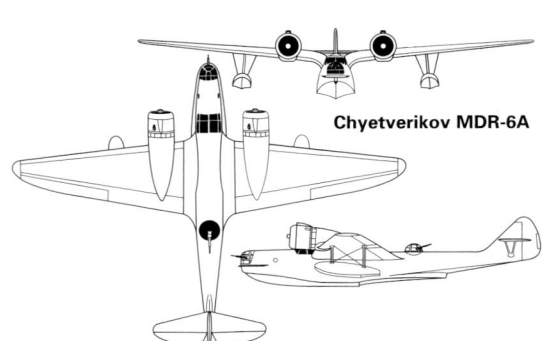

Chyetverikov MDR-6A

proved unacceptable to the Soviet navy on account of their inadequate rough-sea hydrodynamic performance. In consequence, a thoroughgoing hull redesign was undertaken by Chyetverikov, resulting during 1944 in the **MDR-6B-4**. Reverting to the fixed stabilising floats and retaining the M-105PF engines, the MDR-6B-4 had an appreciably deeper hull and added a central vertical fin to the tail assembly, lateral gun blisters also

being introduced. Deliveries of Consolidated PBY Catalina 'boats under the terms of the Lend-Lease Act militated against production of the MDR-6B-4.

Despite the Soviet navy's refusal to accept the successive B-series prototypes as the bases for production variants, Chyetverikov persisted with development of the basic design and, in 1946, tested the **MDR-6B-5** with 1,700-hp (1268-kW) VK-107

engines. Carrying a crew of four, this prototype featured a 20-mm B-20 cannon in the bow and a pair of similar weapons in an electrically operated dorsal turret. The MDR-6B-5 offered an excellent performance, but this time the Soviet navy concluded that the Chyetverikov flying-boat offered inadequate working space for crew members on long-duration patrols and further development was therefore discontinued.

Cierva autogiros

The Spanish pioneer Juan de la Cierva built his first autogiro, the **Cierva C.1**, at Madrid in 1920, using the fuselage of a Deperdussin monoplane, above which were mounted two four-bladed contra-rotating rotors, surmounted by a vertical surface to provide lateral control. Power was provided by a 60-hp (45-kW) Le Rhône, but the machine would not fly. In the following year Cierva tried again, this time with the **C.2**, which combined the fuselage of a Hanriot biplane with a three-bladed rotor. The C.2 was damaged and rebuilt nine times before Cierva gave up and began work on the **C.3**, which was ready to fly early in 1922. Use of a rotor with five rigid blades improved the lateral control, but the C.3 had a tendency to fall over on its side and had to be rebuilt four times.

Experimenting with models, Cierva now found that the secret of successful flight lay in flexible rotor blades, articulated to overcome the imbalance in lift between the advancing and retreating blades. Based on this theory, the **C.4** was built in 1922 with a four-bladed rotor articulated at the root. Initially this, too, was unsuccessful, but after some modifications, the machine made a first flight on 9 January 1923. Although this flight covered

only 600 ft (183 m), it proved the concept, and at the end of that month the C.4 achieved a 2.5-mile (4-km) closed-circuit flight in 4 minutes at a height of about 100 ft (30 m). Power for the C.4 was provided by a 110-hp (82-kW) Le Rhône 9Ja rotary engine. In July 1923 the similarly powered **C.5** was flown with a three-bladed rotor, and after this Cierva, who had previously financed his experiments from private sources, received subsidies from the Spanish government.

His next model, the **C.6**, was the beginning of a series of successful autogiros – a word coined by Cierva for his designs and which should be used with this spelling only for the machines of Cierva and his licensees.

The **C.6A**, using an Avro Type 504K fuselage and powered by a 110-hp (82-kW) Le Rhône 9Ja rotary engine, flew in May 1924. Ailerons were mounted on outrigger spars and the four-bladed rotor, with a diameter of 36 ft (10.97 m), had flapping hinges. By the use of a rope, the rotor could be spun up to 60 rpm on the ground, thereby shortening the take-off run and, when the machine was airborne, the rotational speed increased to 140 rpm. The first autogiro cross-country flight was made on 12 December 1924,

Based on an Avian IIIA fuselage and powered by an ADC Cirrus III engine, the C.17 was built as a smaller variant of the C.8L Mk III. However, even in a more powerful, re-engined form, the type ultimately proved unsuccessful.

Distinctive paddle-shaped rotor blades, stub wings mounted on outrigger-type pylons and an Avro 504K fuselage identify this as a C.6A.

between the two Madrid aerodromes of Cuatro Vientos and Getafé, a distance of 7.5 miles (12 km). A similarly-powered **C.6B** was also constructed.

Cierva brought the C.6A to England in October 1925 at the invitation of the Air Ministry's Director of Scientific Research and, following demonstrations at the RAE at Farnborough, the Ministry ordered several autogiros for evaluation by the RAF. The contract for their manufacture was given to A. V. Roe and, as a result of the British interest, the Cierva Autogiro Company was formed in the UK to hold Cierva's patents and grant construction licences.

The designations **Avro Type 574** and **Type 575** were allocated to the **Cierva C.6C** and **C.6D** respectively: each was powered by the 130-hp (97-kW) Clerget rotary engine, the first to fly being the C.6C on 19 June 1926, followed by the C.6D on 29 July. The C.6C was lost in a crash in January 1927,

when a rotor blade detached at a height of 120 ft (37 m), but the pilot was only slightly hurt. The C.6D was the first two-seat autogiro, and in September it was flown at Berlin by Ernst Udet.

The designation **C.7** was allocated to two Cierva-type autogiros built in Spain by Jorge Loring and flown in 1926. The powerplant was based on a 300-hp (224-kW) Hispano-Suiza Vee engine, and the C.7 was exhibited at the Madrid Air Show. Several **C.8** series autogiros, the most important up to that time, were built by Avro. The designation **C.8R (Avro Type 587)** was given to the C.6D after modification with paddle-shaped rotor blades and fitted with stub wings and, in the course of trials, it flew with both three- and two-bladed rotors. It was scrapped in 1929.

A two-seat Avro Type 552 fuselage with a 180-hp (134-kW) Wolseley Viper Vee engine was fitted with a similar rotor system to that of the C.8R, but had a dorsal fin. Flown in 1926, it became the **C.8V (Avro Type 586)** and subsequent experiments took place with different landing gear configurations. It was rebuilt in 1930 as an Avro Type 552.

Favourable results from experiments persuaded the Air Ministry to order another prototype autogiro from Avro. Based on a Type

504N fuselage with a 180-hp (134-kW) Armstrong Siddeley Lynx radial engine, it became the **C.8L (Avro Type 611)** and, piloted by H. J. Hinkler, first flew at Hamble in 1927. Juan de la Cierva had then recently qualified as a pilot and Hinkler converted him on to rotary-wing aircraft. Cierva was thus able to make the UK's first cross-country flight in this type of machine when he delivered the C.8L from the Hamble factory to the RAE at Farnborough on 30 September 1927. The C.8L spent almost three years there before crashing near Andover.

Air Commodore J. G. Weir, the Cierva company's chairman, ordered a civil **C.8L Mk II (Avro Type 617)**, which introduced a short-span fixed wing and was powered by a Lynx IV engine. Flown in May 1928, it subsequently took part in that year's King's Cup Air Race, but retired when it ran short of fuel. A demonstration tour by this autogiro began when Cierva flew it to Paris in September 1928. It continued to Berlin via Brussels and returned via Amsterdam to Paris, where it remains in the Musée de l'Air collection. Orders were received for two C.8Ls in the form of one **C.8L Mk III** for the Italian government and one **C.8L Mk IV** (designated **C.8W**) for the US aircraft manufacturer, Harold Pitcairn.

Cierva autogiros (continued)

The C.8W had a 225-hp (168-kW) Wright Whirlwind radial engine and made the first autogiro flight in the USA at Willow Grove in January 1929. Pitcairn bought the American rights and established the Pitcairn-Cierva Autogiro Co. in Pennsylvania; the C.8W is preserved in the Smithsonian Institution, Washington, DC.

The next autogiro in the Cierva numerical sequence was the **C.9**, this the first to change the pattern of using an existing fuselage. Two fuselages were built, a single-seater designated as the **Avro Type 576** and a two-seater designated as the **Avro Type 581**. The C.9, powered by a 70-hp (52-kW) Armstrong Siddeley Genet radial engine, was flown at Hamble in September 1927 and was subsequently tested by the RAE at Farnborough with half-length untapered blades; it was presented to the Science Museum in 1930.

Parnall built two single-seat autogiros, neither of which was successful; the **C.10** of 1927 crashed during comparative trials against the Avro-built C.9. The **Parnall C.11** of 1928 was similar, but powered by a 120-hp (90-kW) ADC Airdisco engine. Cierva wrecked the machine at Yale during an attempt to take off before the rotor had attained sufficient speed, but it was rebuilt with a simpler pylon and used later at Hamble as an instructional airframe.

The **C.12**, built by Avro, was based on an Avian fuselage and flown in 1929. It was later converted to single-seat configuration and mounted on Avian metal floats,

This Avro Rota Mk I was used by No. 529 Squadron in the period 1943-44. Used mostly for coastal radar calibration, the RAF's autogiros saw no combat service, even though they would have been almost immune to enemy fighters, thanks to their low speed and manoeuvrability.

becoming the first rotary-winged seaplane when it flew from Southampton Water in April 1930. Dubbed **Hydrogiro**, it was powered by a 100-hp (75-kW) Avro Alpha engine, but virtually nothing is known of its development or fate. In 1926 Short Brothers was given Specification 31/26, detailing a flying-boat autogiro designated **C.14**, but the project was subsequently dropped.

The designations **C.15** and **C.16** are believed to have been projects, and the next Cierva number was the **C.17** (**Avro Type 612**), a smaller version of the C.8L Mk III with a 90-hp (67-kW) Cirrus III engine and based on the Avian IIIA fuselage. Flown by Cierva in October 1928, it was found to be underpowered and a second version, the **C.17 Mk II**, was built with a 100-hp (75-kW) Alpha radial engine; this machine was equally unsuccessful and was converted to an Avian in 1935.

The designation **C.18** was allocated to a two-seat cabin autogiro built in France by Weymann-Lepère in 1929. Powered by an uncowled 195-hp (145-kW) Salmson AC7 radial engine, the only example was imported into the UK by the Cierva Autogiro Company and registered to it in June 1929. It is believed to have been taken to the USA.

The most prolific of the early Cierva designs was the **C.19**, which was built in a number of variants, mainly by Avro. The first three of these, designated **Avro Type 620**, had been laid down as C.17 Mk IIs, but were completed as **C.19 Mk I** autogiros. While Cierva had developed the rotor systems for previous models, Avro's airframes had been modified from those of existing fixed-wing types. The C.19 marked the beginning of the purpose-designed autogiro, and was the first to have automatic starting to get the rotor windmilling – a task undertaken previously with a length of rope. The three C.19 Mk I autogiros had 80-hp (60-kW) Genet II radial engines. They were

followed by three examples of the **C.19 Mk II**, one of the **C.19 Mk IIA** with an improved rotor head, six examples of the **C.19 Mk III**, 15 examples of the **C.19 Mk IVP** and one example of the experimental **C.19 Mk V**; all had the 105-hp (78.3-kW) Genet Major I engine.

A batch of **C.19 Mk IV** machines licence-built by Focke-Wulf in Germany had the 150-hp (112-kW) Siemens Sh.14B radial engine and carried the Cierva type number **C.20**. The designation **C.21** was allocated to a projected French C.19 Mk IV to be built by Lioré-et-Olivier, and the **C.22** and **C.23** are thought to have been projects only. The **C.24** two-seat cabin autogiro was designed and built by the de Havilland Aircraft Co. with rotor assemblies provided by Cierva. Powered by a 120-hp (90-kW) de Havilland Gipsy III engine, the only example was first flown by Cierva in September 1931 with a three-bladed rotor. Provided subsequently with a two-bladed rotor, and in this form redesignated as **C.26**, it completed a European tour in 1932 and was later preserved as a static exhibit.

The intervening **C.25** was one of the smallest autogiros, a single-seater built by Comper Aircraft and flown in early 1933. The fuselage appeared to be based on that of the Comper Swift lightplane, with modified tail surfaces and a low-set stub wing, and power was provided by an 85-hp (63-kW) Pobjoy Niagara R radial engine. Despite its high performance, the type received no orders.

In 1932 the French company Lioré-et-Olivier acquired a Cierva licence and, basing its design on detailed studies of the C.19 Mk IV, built the **C.27** with

the company designation **CL.10**, referring to Cierva and the French designer, Georges Lepère. The C.27 was a two-seat cabin autogiro with no wing, the powerplant of one 75-hp (60-kW) Pobjoy engine, and a three-bladed main rotor. Flown at Orly, it crashed after only a few flights.

Not strictly in chronological order, but convenient in the numbering sequence to mention at this point, is the **CL.20**, a two-seat cabin autogiro designed by Lepère and built by Westland. This flew at Hanworth on 5 February 1935 with a 90-hp (67-kW) Niagara III engine mounted in an enclosed cowling. No further development took place by Westland, but it is interesting to note that in 1937 Pitcairn in the USA proposed to build a version known as the **AC.35** with the 110-hp (82-kW) Pobjoy engine, while in 1956 Lepère was said to be working on a private venture development of his 1934 design for the French Giravia Company. Designated **L.30**, it was to have three seats and a 145-hp (108-kW) Continental engine.

G. & J. Weir in Glasgow built a single-seat autogiro which flew in the early summer of 1933. The Weir designation was **W-1** and, since it was built under a Cierva licence, the number **C.28** was allocated. Powered by a 40-hp (30-kW) Douglas Dryad engine, the autogiro had a two-bladed rotor with mechanical spin-up. Weir subsequently built other autogiros and the company's activities in this field were taken over by the Cierva company in 1945.

The idea of a larger than usual autogiro was tried with the **C.29** of 1934. A five-seat cabin aircraft with an uncowled 600-hp (447-kW) Armstrong

The sole C.24 was restored for display by the Mosquito Aircraft Museum in the UK, where it remains in late 1999. The fully-enclosed cabin accommodation of the type is clearly evident.

Siddeley Panther II radial engine, it was designed by Westland, with Cierva responsible for the rotor and its mechanism. Construction was of Dural tubing, but ground resonance during tests prevented it from flying and Juan de la Cierva's death in an air crash (not an autogiro) caused the design to be abandoned.

The next designation in the sequence, **C.30**, is the best known, since production took place in several countries. Following tests with a modified C.19 Mk V powered by a 100-hp (75-kW) Genet Major radial engine, and using a rotor head which could be tilted by use of a hanging control column, Avro commissioned National Flying Services to build a two-seat version which was designated C.30. It was flown in April 1933 and Avro obtained a manufacturing licence, subsequently allocating it the designation **Type 671**. The prototype of an improved model, the

C.30P with a 140 hp (104-kW) Major, was built in 1933 and featured folding rotor blades. Avro built three pre-production C.30P autogiros and obtained a licence to build examples of the **C.30A** production model. A batch of 12 was supplied to the RAF between August 1934 and May 1935, 10 of them serving initially with the School of Army Co-operation at Old Sarum under the service designation **Rota Mk I**. Of the remaining two, one was tested with floats and the other was fitted experimentally with a Civet Major engine at the RAE Farnborough. Civil C.30A production by Avro totalled 66, a number going to export customers, but many to UK purchasers. When World War II started, 13 of these machines were impressed into service alongside the surviving RAF aircraft, eventually serving with No. 529 Squadron at Halton, where their duties included radar calibration. A number survived the war to

return to civil ownership and at least six have been preserved.

Other European countries which built the C.30A included France, where Lioré-et-Olivier produced 25 with the designation **LeO C.301**, and Germany, where Focke-Wulf built some 40 examples.

Two Cierva projects came next in the sequence: the **C.31** of 1934 was to have been a two-seat coupé autogiro with retractable landing gear, while the similar **C.32** would have had greater performance. An Avro project, the **Type 665**, envisaged the combination of the four-seat fuselage of the Commodore biplane with a three-bladed rotor; the designation **C.33** was allocated, but the conversion was not completed.

The **C.34** of 1937 was built under licence by the Société Nationale de Constructions Aéronautiques du Sud-Est and had a 350-hp (261-kW)

Gnome-Rhône 7K radial engine.

The **C.35**, **C.36** and **C.38** appear to have been projects, and the **C.37** was a twin-engined cabin autogiro proposed by Avro as the **Type 668**, but which was not built. The **C.39** was a Cierva project for a two/three-seat fleet spotter for the FAA. This would have had a three-bladed rotor and a 600-hp (447-kW) Rolls-Royce Kestrel Vee engine.

The last Cierva autogiro number was **C.40**: this was a two-seat side-by-side development of the C.30 with a wooden fuselage and an internal metal structure. The powerplant was

based on one uncowled 175-hp (130-kW) Salmson 9Ng radial engine, and nine C.40 autogiros were assembled by the British Aircraft Manufacturing Co. at Hanworth in 1938. An improved rotor head enabled the autogiro to make a direct take-off; this was accomplished by accelerating the rotor beyond take-off revolutions with the blades at zero incidence, then putting them into positive pitch to create lift. Seven of the C.40 autogiros went to the RAF, the remaining two being civil-registered before they were impressed for military service.

SPECIFICATION	
Cierva C.30A	rate 700 ft (213 m) per minute;
Type: two-seat utility autogiro	service ceiling 8,000 ft (2440 m);
Powerplant: one Armstrong	range 285 miles (459 km)
Siddeley Genet Major IA radial	**Weights:** empty 1,220 lb (553 kg);
piston engine rated at 140 hp	maximum take-off 1,800 lb (816 kg)
(104 kW)	**Dimensions:** rotor diameter 37 ft
Performance: maximum speed	(11.28 m); length 19 ft 8½ in
110 mph (177 km/h) at sea level;	(6.01 m); height 11 ft 1 in (3.38 m);
cruising speed 95 mph (153 km/h)	rotor disc area 1,075.21 sq ft
at optimum altitude; initial climb	(99.89 m²)

Cierva W.11 Air Horse

The designation **W.10** was allocated to a project for a 4/5-seat single-engined helicopter, but the **Cierva W.11 Air Horse** was the largest helicopter in the world when it first flew on 7 December 1948. A single Merlin engine was mounted in the fuselage to drive three large three-bladed rotors mounted on outriggers projecting from the square fuselage.

As a passenger helicopter, the W.11 would have carried 24 persons, but other tasks that were envisaged included the air ambulance, aerial crane and crop sprayer roles. Cierva received a development contract for one W.11 in July 1946 and a second was ordered in early 1947.

With a payload of 6,720 lb (3048 kg) of insecticide, the W.11 would have made an impressive sprayer, and following its first flight,

The Air Horse carried its twin fins at the end of a mid-mounted tailplane on the rear fuselage and there was accommodation for a crew of three. Total Ministry of Supply development costs for the project were estimated at £350,000.

subsequent tests were promising. The Colonial Office made a grant of £45,000 to assist in the development costs since the type offered prospects of overseas use in the spraying role, but before the second W.11 had flown, the first crashed on 13 June 1950, killing the three members of the flight test crew; the second W.11 never flew and was scrapped in 1960. The designation **W.11T** was allocated to a project for an enlarged W.11 with two 1,620-hp (1208-kW) Rolls-Royce Merlin 502

engines, and the **W.12** was a projected freighter development with Rolls-Royce Dart turboprops: neither of these materialised since by that time Cierva, not having used the number W.13, was involved in development of the **W.14** which became the Skeeter and was eventually built by Saunders-Roe Ltd.

SPECIFICATION	
Cierva W.11 Air Horse	**Weights:** empty 12,140 lb
Type: two/three-crew multi-role	(5507 kg); maximum take-off
heavy helicopter	17,500 lb (7938 kg)
Powerplant: one Rolls-Royce	**Dimensions:** rotor diameter, each
Merlin 24 Vee piston engine rated	47 ft (14.33 m); width overall 95 ft
at 1,620 hp (1208 kW)	(28.96 m) with rotors turning;
Performance: maximum speed	length 88 ft 7 in (27.00 m) with
140 mph (225 km/h) at optimum	rotors turning; height 17 ft 9 in
altitude; cruising speed 95 mph	(5.41 m); rotor disc area, total
(153 km/h) at optimum altitude	5,204.83 sq ft (483.53 m²)
service ceiling 28,000 ft (8535 m);	**Payload:** see above
range 330 miles (531 km)	

CMASA aircraft

The company generally known as CMASA (Costruzioni Meccaniche Aeronautiche SA) was created in 1922 as the SCMP (Società di Costruzioni Meccaniche di Pisa) to take over the Gallinari works at Marina di Pisa, and initially concentrated on the licensed

production of Dornier aircraft. These included the Do E, Do F, Delfin and Wal. In 1929 the SCMP became a subsidiary of Fiat and in the following year its name was changed to CMASA. The company subsequently designed and built a number of its own designs.

An altogether conventional biplane flying-boat, the MF.10 was designed for launching by catapult from Italian navy ships.

CMASA aircraft (continued)

Nevertheless, CMASA's role in the Fiat empire gradually became the adaptation of standard Fiat aircraft with different engines and/or for different roles.

Under the leadership of Mario Stiavelli, however, CMASA was responsible for a series of **MF (Marina Fiat)** flying-boats. The first of the 'boats was the **CMASA MF.4**, a two/three-seat parasol-wing reconnaissance flying-boat that first flew in 1933 with the 600-hp (447-kW)

Piaggio Stella IX R radial engine installed as a tractor unit on the centre section of the wing. The **MF.5** civil flying-boat was a development of the Wal and also recorded its maiden flight in 1933 as a parasol-wing type with lateral sponsons for waterborne stability, provision for up to 10 passengers, and the powerplant of two 750-hp (559-kW) Fiat A.24R Vee engines installed as a tandem push/pull pair on the upper surface of the centre section. The **MF.6**

was a two-seat catapult-launched reconnaissance seaplane with a single main float, two auxiliary wingtip floats and the powerplant of one 575-hp (429-kW) Piaggio-built Bristol Jupiter VI radial engine.

The final example of the MF series was the **MF.10** that first flew in 1935 as the prototype for a reconnaissance flying-boat designed for catapult launch from the major surface vessels of the Italian navy. The MF.10 was a biplane with open

cockpits for the observer/gunner and pilot ahead of the unstaggered wing cellule, a two-step planing bottom for the hull, a tail unit with the strut-braced horizontal surface located

about two-thirds of the way up the vertical surface, and the single engine installed as a pusher unit on a nacelle incorporated in the centre section of the upper wing.

SPECIFICATION

CMASA MF.10
Type: two-seat reconnaissance flying-boat
Powerplant: one Fiat A.30RA Vee piston engine rated at 600 hp (447 kW)
Performance: maximum speed 171 mph (275 km/h) at optimum altitude; climb to 6,560 ft (2000 m) in 5 minutes; service ceiling 24,605 ft (7500 m)
Weights: empty 3,406 lb (1545 kg); maximum take-off 5,203 lb (2360 kg)
Dimensions: wingspan 38 ft 4⅗ in (11.70 m); length 30 ft 8 in (9.35); height 10 ft 7 in (3.23 m); wing area 382.13 sq ft (35.50 m²)
Armament: one 0.303-in (7.7-mm) Breda-SAFAT trainable forward-firing machine-gun

Cody aircraft

Samuel Franklin Cody, American cowboy, scout and gold prospector, first came to Europe with a Wild West show. He then became the most flamboyant of the UK's aviation pioneers, beginning his exploits by extensive experiments with man-lifting kites. Cody developed a unique form of kite which he patented in 1901, and three years later he was engaged by the British army to develop man-lifting kites for military use. To enable him to continue this development more easily, Cody was attached to the Balloon Factory at Farnborough, Hampshire, early in 1904, and as a result of his work, the first Kite Section of the Royal Engineers was established at Farnborough with, from 1906, Cody as the army's Chief Kiting Instructor.

While at Farnborough during 1905 Cody had built a single-seat biplane glider. A number of successful flights were made in this **Cody Kite-Glider** before, in 1907, he took the next step towards the achievement of manned flight. This was fundamentally a powered kite, one of his man-carriers being modified by the addition of a stabilising surface fore and aft of the biplane lifting surfaces. With wheeled landing gear and power provided by a 15-hp (11-kW) Buchet piston engine, the **Motor-Kite** was flown successfully without a pilot, but hanging from a wire, recording a

best flight of 4½ minutes.

It was in 1907 that Cody began construction of the **British Army Aeroplane No. 1 (Cody 1)** aircraft in which he was to make the first recognised powered and sustained flight in the UK. This occurred on 16 October 1908, and in configuration the British Army Aeroplane No. 1 was a biplane similar to that designed by the Wright brothers. It had a biplane wing cellule with booms fore and aft that mounted respectively the elevator and rudder. It did, however, have wheeled landing gear, and the power of the Antoinette engine was conveyed to two interplane pusher propellers. Cody's first flight covered only 1,390 ft (424 m), but progressive modification (**Cody 2**) plus the installation of a 60-hp (45-kW) ENV Type F Vee engine (**Cody 3**) enabled him to achieve a flight of 40 miles (64 km) on 8 September 1909.

Experience gained with the British Army Aeroplane No. 1 was embodied in an improved biplane built in 1910. Cody used this to compete in the contest for the British Empire Michelin Cup No. 1 and, in consequence, the machine is generally known as the **Michelin Cup Biplane**. The prize was to be awarded for the longest closed-circuit distance recorded during 1910, and on the last day of the year, in a flight of

4 hours 47 minutes, Cody was the victor with a recorded distance of just over 185 miles (298 km). In 1911 he built a new, but generally similar, aircraft, powered by a 60-hp (45-kW) Green inline engine, to compete in the 1,010-mile (1625-km) £10,000 Circuit of Britain contest sponsored by the *Daily Mail*. Cody's **Circuit of Britain Biplane** was the only British aircraft to complete the course, his finishing position being fourth. With this aircraft he also won the British Empire Michelin Cup for the second time, on 29 October 1911.

Cody turned to the monoplane configuration in his entry for the famous Military Trials of 1912. Like many other monoplanes of its period, the Cody design relied upon a kingpost and extensive wire bracing to maintain the integrity of the wing. Accommodation was provided for a crew of two, but despite Cody's confidence that he would win the trial contest, the opportunity never came: the **Monoplane** was

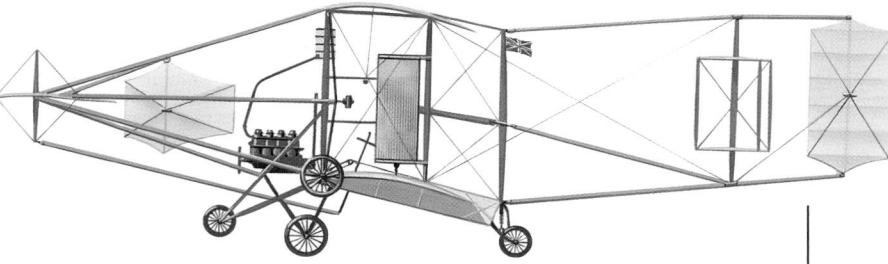

The British Army Aeroplane No. 1 is illustrated as it appeared in 1909. The power of the Antoinette engine was conveyed to two interplane pusher propellers by flat belts.

wrecked after colliding with a cow when landing during early tests. Cody wasted no time in salvaging its Austro-Daimler engine, which he then installed in a typical Cody biplane. Known as the **Military Trials Biplane**, this was declared the winner of the Military Trials of 1912. This was an ironic decision as the Farnborough B.E.2, piloted by Geoffrey de Havilland, gained the most qualifying points. However, the B.E.2 was a government-built aircraft and, with the superintendent of the Farnborough factory among the panel of judges, could not be awarded the £5,000 first prize. Cody was elated at his success and, with the Austro-Daimler engine replaced by a 100-hp (75-kW) Green unit to make the machine an all-British combination, went on to win the British Empire Michelin Cup for the third time. To compete in the 1913 Circuit of

Britain contest, for which the *Daily Mail* had put up a £5,000 first prize, Cody built a refined biplane based on his established configuration. Since the Circuit of Britain was around the coast, he equipped the biplane with float landing gear, this comprising a large central float with a balancer float beneath each lower wing. Reliability being essential, he selected the 100-hp (75-kW) Green engine to power the **Hydro-biplane**. After the successful completion of flotation tests, the floats were replaced by wheeled landing gear to allow a comprehensive series of flight tests to be completed before the contest. During one of these tests, on 7 August 1913, with Cody at the controls and accompanied by a passenger, the airframe began to break up in mid-air; both occupants were killed in the resulting crash, and the UK had lost one of its most colourful aviation pioneers.

The Monoplane's 120-hp (90-kW) Austro-Daimler inline engine drove a two-bladed tractor propeller by means of a chain.

SPECIFICATION

Cody Michelin Cup Biplane
Type: single-seat racing biplane
Powerplant: one ENV Type F Vee piston engine rated at 60 hp (45 kW)
Performance: maximum speed 65 mph (105 km/h) at sea level
Weights: maximum take-off 2,950 lb (1338 kg)
Dimensions: wingspan 46 ft (14.02 m) or 49 ft (14.94 m) including ailerons; length 38 ft 6 in (11.73 m); height 13 ft (3.96 m); wing area 640.00 sq ft (59.46 m²)

Commonwealth Aircraft CA-1 Wirraway

This CA-1 Wirraway was based in New Guinea with the RAAF's No. 5 Sqn during 1944. It was used in the army co-operation role.

The Commonwealth Aircraft Corporation Pty Ltd was formed in 1936 as the result of an Australian government scheme to establish an aircraft industry as part of the process to reduce the country's reliance on outside suppliers. A number of wealthy industrial firms contributed to the financing of the company and, following a visit by an Air Board Technical Commission to the USA in 1936, negotiations were concluded for licensed manufacture of the North American NA-16 two-seat general-purpose monoplane and its Pratt & Whitney Wasp engine. Tugan Aircraft Ltd was taken over by Commonwealth and its chief designer, Wing Commander Lawrence Wackett, became general manager of the new company. An initial order

was placed by the RAAF for 40 examples of the **NA-33**, as the licence-built version was designated by North American. The manufacturer's designation was **Commonwealth Aircraft CA-1**, indicating

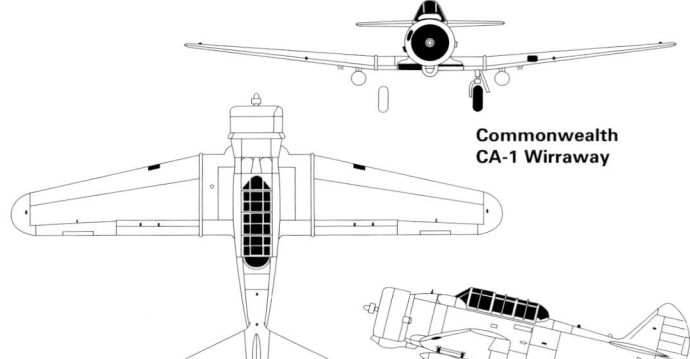

Commonwealth CA-1 Wirraway

that it was Commonwealth Aircraft's first product, and the name **Wirraway** was chosen.

The first Australian-built aircraft flew at Melbourne on 27 March 1939, and within four months the RAAF had accepted the first three aircraft. The outbreak of World War II in Europe led to increased orders for the Wirraway, and the British government also financed the purchase of aircraft for the Empire Air Training Scheme in Australia. By June 1942, Commonwealth had built 620 Wirraways, and the type continued in limited production until the 755th and last aircraft was delivered in 1946. There were a number of Commonwealth designations for the Wirraway: together with the number built, these were the CA-1 (40), **CA-3** (60), **CA-5** (32), **CA-7** (100), **CA-8** (200), **CA-9** (188) and **CA-16** (135). The **CA-10**

and **CA-10A** were to have been bomber and dive-bomber versions respectively, but were cancelled. The designation **CA-20** was allocated to Wirraways converted for use by the Royal Australian Navy in the post-war training role.

The Wirraway saw service on convoy patrol work from Darwin, in Malaya, New Britain and New Guinea before being

replaced by more warlike equipment, and by mid-1943 most first-line Wirraway squadrons had re-equipped with the Commonwealth Aircraft Boomerang. As they were withdrawn from service, almost 400 Wirraways were put into long-term storage and eventually a number of these were used as the basis for the CA-28 Ceres agricultural aircraft.

SPECIFICATION

Commonwealth Aircraft CA-1 Wirraway
Type: two-seat trainer and light bomber
Powerplant: one Commonwealth Aircraft (Pratt & Whitney) R-1340-S1H1G Wasp radial piston engine rated at 600 hp (447 kW)
Performance: maximum speed 220 mph (354 km/h) at 5,000 ft (1525 m); cruising speed 182 mph (293 km/h) at 5,000 ft (1525 m); initial climb rate 1,950 ft (594 m) per minute; service ceiling 23,000 ft (7010 m); range 720 miles (1159 km)

Weights: empty 3,992 lb (1811 kg); maximum take-off 6,595 lb (2991 kg)
Dimensions: wingspan 43 ft (13.11 m); length 27 ft 10 in (8.48 m); height 8 ft 8¾ in (2.66 m); wing area 255.70 sq ft (23.76 m²)
Armament: two 0.303-in (7.7-mm) Vickers Mk V fixed forward-firing machine-guns and one 0.303-in (7.7-mm) Vickers Mk I trainable rearward-firing machine-gun in the rear of the cockpit, plus up to 1,000 lb (454 kg) of bombs carried externally

Commonwealth Aircraft CA-2 and CA-6 Wackett Trainer

In October 1939, the Commonwealth Aircraft Corporation (CAC) tested the prototype of its first indigenous design, the **CA-2 Wackett Trainer**. Powered initially by a 140-hp (104-kW) de Havilland Gipsy Major II inline engine, the prototype was later revised with a 200-hp (149-kW) Gipsy Six engine. A second prototype followed, and both aircraft were then fitted with Warner Super

Scarab radial engines to become prototypes for the **CA-6**, which was the production version.

A number of Wackett Trainers survived to serve after World War II with civilian clubs and as agricultural aircraft. In 1947, 30 ex-RAAF Wacketts were bought for the Netherlands East Indies air force and based at Kalidjali. Improved engine cooling was achieved by removing the engine cowlings.

SPECIFICATION

Commonwealth Aircraft CA-6 Wackett Trainer
Type: two-seat basic flying trainer
Powerplant: one Warner R-500 Super Scarab 165D radial piston engine rated at 175 hp (130 kW)
Performance: maximum speed 110 mph (177 km/h) at sea level; cruising speed 97 mph (156 km/h) at

3,000 ft (915 m); initial climb rate 700 ft (213 m) per minute; service ceiling 16,000 ft (4875 m)
Weights: empty 1,806 lb (868 kg); maximum take-off 2,592 lb (1176 kg)
Dimensions: wingspan 37 ft (11.28 m); length 26 ft (7.92 m); height 6 ft 9 in (2.06 m); wing area 184.00 sq ft (17.09 m²)

CAC built 200 production CA-6s for delivery to the Royal Australian Air Force. They were built between May 1941 and April 1942 as intermediate trainers for pilots and wireless operators.

Commonwealth Aircraft Boomerang

Japan's December 1941 entry into World War II found Australia ill-prepared, the only fighters on strength with the RAAF being a few obsolescent Brewster Buffalos based in Malaya. However, the licence from North American, under which CAC built the Wirraway, permitted modifications to the design, and Lawrence Wackett used that aircraft's wing, landing gear and tail unit married to a new fuselage to produce a single-seat fighter, the **CA-12**, later named

Boomerang Mk I. An order was placed for 105 such fighters in February 1942, and because many Wirraway components were used, the prototype was built in only three months, the first making the type's maiden flight on 29 May of the same year.

Production of this first batch was completed in June 1943, and there followed a second batch of 95 **CA-13 Boomerang Mk II** aircraft, these incorporating a number of minor modifications. A single **CA-14** was built with its

engine boosted by a General Electric turbo-supercharger for improved high-altitude performance; it was later modified as the **CA-14A** with a squarer fin and rudder, but the availability of the faster Spitfire Mk VIII rendered these improvements unnecessary. The final production batch consisted of 49 **CA-19 Boomerang Mk II** aircraft, again with minor modifications, and the last of these was delivered in February 1945.

The Boomerang entered service in October 1942,

when the RAAF's No. 2 Operational Training Unit at Mildura, Victoria, received its first aircraft. It became operational with No. 84 Squadron, which was the first to receive the new fighters, in April 1943. Other squadrons followed, including Nos 4 and 5, in which the Boomerang replaced the Wirraway in the army co-operation role.

As higher-performance fighters became available, the Boomerang fighters were replaced, having proved to be extremely manoeuvrable, tough and blessed with a rapid climb rate. The type had acquitted itself well in roles for which it had not been designed, and was remembered with affection by its pilots.

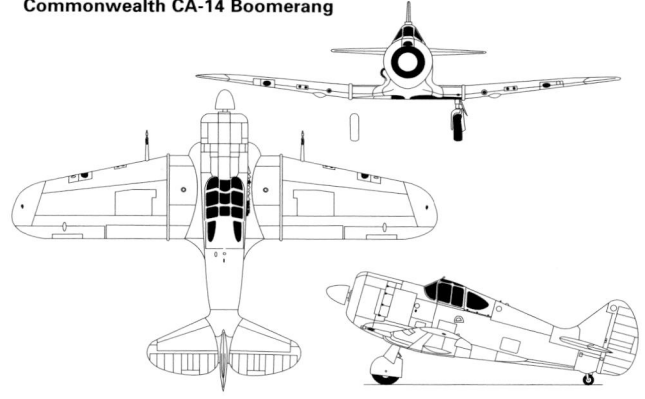

Commonwealth CA-14 Boomerang

Above: Named Sinbad II, *this CA-13 was flown by Flt Lt A. W. Clarke with the RAAF's No. 5 Sqn in March 1944. The aircraft was based in Queensland and was probably painted in Foliage Green and Earth over light blue.*

SPECIFICATION	
Commonwealth Aircraft CA-13 Boomerang Mk II	**Weights:** empty 5,373 lb (2437 kg); maximum take-off 8,249 lb (3742 kg)
Type: single-seat fighter and fighter-bomber	**Dimensions:** wingspan 36 ft (10.97 m); length 25 ft 6 in (7.77 m); height 9 ft 7 in (2.92 m): wing area 225.00 sq ft (20.90 m²)
Powerplant: one Pratt & Whitney R-1830-S3C4G Twin Wasp radial piston engine rated at 1,200 hp (895 kW)	**Armament:** two 20-mm Hispano Mk II fixed forward-firing cannon and four 0.303-in (7.7-mm) Browning Mk II fixed forward-firing machine-guns, plus up to 500 lb (227 kg) of disposable stores carried on one hardpoint under the fuselage
Performance: maximum speed 305 mph (491 km/h) at 15,500 ft (4725 m); cruising speed 190 mph (306 km/h) at optimum altitude; initial climb rate 2,940 ft (896 m) per minute; service ceiling 34,000 ft (10365 m); range 1,600 miles (2575 km)	

Left: Compact and manoeuvrable, the Boomerang, typified by this No. 5 Sqn CA-13 Boomerang Mk II, stood up well to Japanese fighters.

Commonwealth Aircraft CA-22 and CA-25 Winjeel

When the Royal Australian Air Force required a new elementary trainer to replace its current force of Tiger Moths and Wirraways, the CAC responded to a specification issued in 1948 with the **CA-22 Winjeel** (young eagle).

Two prototypes with 450-hp (336-kW) Wasp Junior engines were built, and the first of these flew in February 1951. It had been intended originally to use a new 420-hp (313-kW) radial engine, the Cicada, which was being developed by CAC's Engine Division, but this idea was dropped and production examples of the Winjeel had the R-985-AN-2 Wasp Junior engine. The first of 62 production aircraft,

designated **CA-25**, flew in February 1955 and was handed over to the RAAF on 16 September 1955. The last aircraft was delivered early in 1958.

In addition to its pilot training role, the Winjeel was used for communications and for the training of forward air controllers, the

last four aircraft in service being used in the latter role as late as 1980. The phasing out of the Winjeel in normal training service was completed in 1975 when it was replaced by the Aerospace CT4A Airtrainer. In 1979 a Winjeel flew from Point Cook, Victoria, to Papua, New Guinea – a

distance of 1,875 miles (3018 km) – where it was presented to the Port Moresby Technical College as a students' training aid.

In the same year, another Winjeel was acquired by enthusiasts and, following restoration, was flown again in February 1982.

CAC's Winjeel was a side-by-side two-seater with an optional third seat. It was similar in general configuration to the Percival Provost.

SPECIFICATION	
Commonwealth Aircraft CA-25 Winjeel	initial climb rate 1,500 ft (457 m) per minute; service ceiling 18,000 ft (5485 m); range 550 miles (885 km)
Type: two/three-seat basic flying trainer	**Weights:** empty 3,323 lb (1507 kg); maximum take-off 4,265 lb (1935 kg)
Powerplant: one Pratt & Whitney R-985-AN-2 Wasp Junior radial piston engine rated at 445 hp (332 kW)	**Dimensions:** wingspan 38 ft 7½ in (11.77 m); length 28 ft ½ in (8.55 m); height 9 ft 1 in (2.77 m); wing area 249.00 sq ft (23.13 m²)
Performance: maximum speed 186 mph (299 km/h) at optimum altitude; cruising speed 165 mph (266 km/h) at 8,500 ft (2590 m);	

Commonwealth Aircraft CA-27 Sabre

In 1950 the RAAF decided to replace its obsolescent Meteor fighters, which were unable to challenge the MiG-15 fighter in the Korean War, with a more modern turbojet-powered type. The service's initial intention was to procure a version of the Hawker P.1081 built in Australia. However, for a variety of reasons, the choice eventually settled on a version of the North American F-86F Sabre in a heavily modified form. Built under licence in Australia, the fighter was powered by a considerably more potent British engine (also licence-made in Australia) supplied from an enlarged internal fuel capacity, was armed with two heavy cannon of British design and piloted from a somewhat revised cockpit. The result was a fighter and fighter-bomber generally known as the **'Avon-Sabre'**, which was arguably the finest version of the whole prolific Sabre family by virtue of its heavier armament and improved performance; the latter was superior to that of all but some Canadair Sabre variants.

The Avon RA.7 engine was significantly more powerful than the General Electric J47 used in the baseline American fighter and required some 25 per cent more airflow, but was of basically the same overall dimensions and also about 400 lb (181 kg) lighter. The need to provide a larger flow of air and to keep the centre of gravity in the right position despite the engine's lighter weight meant considerable

revision of the fuselage, which thus retained a commonality of only some 40 per cent with that of the F-86F. The fuselage had to be deepened and also to be lengthened over its forward section, and the rear section had to be shortened slightly and modified to accept the engine in a position farther aft. Some 100 sets of components had been ordered from North American, but because of the changes, many of these kits were unusable.

The **CA-26** prototype made its maiden flight on 3 August 1953 with an imported British engine, and trials with this machine soon confirmed the performance advantages provided by the new engine. As the CAC's Engine Division was not yet in the position to deliver engines, the type was ordered into production as the **CA-27** with the imported Avon Mk 30 turbojet engine and the original type of F-86F slatted wing, carrying only two hardpoints. The CA-27 could therefore be regarded as a version of the early F-86F (complete with the 'all-flying' tailplane) except for its powerplant and fuselage, and in the latter the only essentially unaltered item was the cockpit, complete with its windscreen and canopy. The first **Sabre Mk 30** from the production line flew on 13 July 1954, and construction of this variant totalled 22 aircraft that were delivered to the RAAF from August 1954 for full service from March 1956.

The fighters of the next

Later in their RAAF careers, many of the surviving 'Avon-Sabres' were modified with the ability to carry and fire AIM-9B Sidewinder missiles. This aircraft totes more conventional rocket armament, however.

production batch were powered by the Australian-made Avon Mk 20 turbojet, and switched from the original type of slatted wing to the so-called '6-3' unslatted wing of extended chord that was also retrofitted on the Sabre Mk 30. The '6-3' wing had its leading-edge chord extended by 6 in (0.15 m) at the root and 3 in (0.076 m) at the tip, and offered a useful increase in maximum speed without sacrifice of high-altitude agility. The extended leading edges also contained additional fuel, and the two under-wing hardpoints could lift two drop tanks, or two bombs, or 16 5-in (127-mm) HVARs. Production totalled 20 aircraft, and surviving Sabre Mk 30s were later revised to **Mk 31** standard.

The **Sabre Mk 32** was the last version of the Australian-built Sabre series, and differed from its predecessors in having the Avon Mk 26 engine

(also retrofitted to earlier aircraft) and four under-wing hardpoints for four, rather than two, drop tanks and a greater load of unguided rockets in the ground-attack role. The initial production run of 28 aircraft was later supplemented by July 1957 and 1959 orders for 20 and 21 machines respectively to provide an effective stop-gap force after the RAAF had decided in 1957 not to procure the F-104 Starfighter, but to order the Dassault Mirage III – to be manufactured under

licence in Australia.

The Sabre was retired from Australian service in July 1971, but before this time surplus 'Avon-Sabres' had been sold to two regional allies. Malaysia received 18 aircraft from October 1969, and Indonesia received the same number of aircraft from February 1973. Malaysia retired its aircraft from service in the mid-1970s, and in July 1976 passed five of its aircraft to Indonesia, which retired the type only in the early part of the 1980s.

SPECIFICATION	
Commonwealth Aircraft CA-27 Sabre Mk 32 **Type:** single-seat fighter and fighter-bomber **Powerplant:** one Commonwealth (Rolls-Royce) Avon RA.7 Mk 26 turbojet engine rated at 7,500 lb st (33.36 kN) **Performance:** maximum speed 700 mph (1127 km/h) at sea level; initial climb rate 12,000 ft (3658 m) per minute; service ceiling 55,000 ft (16765 m); range 1,152 miles (1853 km) with drop	tanks **Weights:** empty 12,120 lb (5497 kg); maximum take-off 17,300 lb (7847 kg) **Dimensions:** wingspan 37 ft 1¼ in (11.31 m); length 37 ft 6 in (11.43 m); height 14 ft 4¾ in (4.39 m); wing area 302.26 sq ft (28.08 m²) **Armament:** two 30-mm ADEN Mk 4 fixed forward-firing cannon, plus up to 2,000 lb (907 kg) of disposable stores carried on four hardpoints under the wing

Commonwealth Aircraft CA-28 Ceres

The availability of a considerable quantity of spare Wirraway components led CAC to design the generally similar **CA-28 Ceres** for the agricultural role. The new type made its maiden flight in February 1958. In its spraying role, the Ceres was a single-seater, but a rear-facing passenger seat could be installed behind the pilot for crew-ferrying purposes. The last of 21 Ceres aircraft flew in July 1963, the type being operated in Australia and New Zealand.

A glassfibre-lined stainless steel hopper of 40-cu ft (1.13-m³) capacity was situated between the engine of the Ceres and its cockpit. The manually-operated slotted flaps were set half down during spraying or top-dressing operations.

SPECIFICATION	
Commonwealth Aircraft CA-28 Ceres **Type:** one/two-seat agricultural aircraft **Powerplant:** one Pratt & Whitney R-1340-S3H1G Wasp radial piston engine rated at 600 hp (447 kW) **Performance:** cruising speed 121 mph (195 km/h) at optimum altitude; operating speed 111 mph (179 km/h) at sea level; initial climb rate 725 ft (221 m) per	minute with maximum payload; ferry range 518 miles (834 km) **Weights:** empty 4,475 lb (2030 kg); maximum take-off 7,410 lb (3361 kg) **Dimensions:** wingspan 46 ft 11 in (14.30 m); length 30 ft 8½ in (9.36 m); height 9 ft (2.74 m); wing area 312.00 sq ft (28.98 m²) **Payload:** up to 2,380 lb (1080 kg) of liquid or dry chemicals

Comper CLA.7 Swift

In March 1929 the Comper Aircraft Company was formed by Flight Lieutenant Nicholas

Comper, formerly of the Royal Air Force, to build an aircraft of his own design. Designated

Comper CLA.7 and named **Swift**, the prototype made a first flight at Brooklands on 17 May 1930. A small and graceful single-seat aircraft for its period, the Swift was a

braced high-wing monoplane of wooden construction, with fabric and plywood covering. The wing was mounted directly on top of the fuselage and the pilot, in an

open cockpit immediately aft of its trailing edge, had a clear view forward. Power for the prototype was provided by a 40-hp (30-kW) A.B.C. Scorpion piston engine.

Comper CLA.7 Swift (continued)

Following successful testing of the prototype, seven more Swifts were completed during 1930, each powered by a 50-hp (37-kW) Salmson AD9 radial engine. A trial installation of a Pobjoy P prototype radial engine on the seventh of these production aircraft in preparation for an air race resulted in this unit being chosen as the standard engine, and most of the early construction Swifts were re-engined subsequently with the Pobjoy R.

It is interesting to note that the longest-lived Swift (G-ACTF), construction number S.32/9 and built in 1932, remained on the British civil aircraft register in 1999 and was located with the Shuttleworth Collection. At least two other Swifts survive in the UK with others extant abroad.

SPECIFICATION	
Comper CLA.7 Swift	ceiling 22,000 ft (6705 m), range
Type: single-seat sporting aircraft	380 miles (611 km)
Powerplant: one Pobjoy R radial	**Weights:** empty 540 lb (245 kg);
piston engine rated at 75 hp	maximum take-off 985 lb (447 kg)
(56 kW)	**Dimensions:** wingspan 24 ft
Performance: maximum speed	(7.32 m), length 17 ft 8½ in
140 mph (225 km/h): cruising	(5.40 m): height 5 ft 3½ in (1.61 m);
speed 120 mph (193 km/h); service	wing area 90.0 sq ft (8.36 m²)

The compact dimensions, high-wing arrangement and spatted undercarriage of the Swift are obvious in this view.

Comte AC-4 Gentleman

In 1927, under the designation **AC-4 Gentleman**, Comte produced the prototype of a two-seat cabin monoplane intended for sporting or training purposes. Of braced high-wing configuration, the AC-4 was of mixed construction covered largely with fabric, and had fixed tailskid landing gear.

SPECIFICATION	
Comte AC-4 Gentleman	at optimum altitude; service ceiling
Type: two-seat sporting and	13,125 ft (4000 m); range 435 miles
training aircraft	(700 km)
Powerplant: one Cirrus Hermes	**Weights:** empty 1,102 lb (500 kg);
inline piston engine rated at	maximum take-off 1,764 lb (800 kg)
115 hp (86 kW)	**Dimensions:** wingspan 39 ft 9½ in
Performance: maximum speed	(12.13 m); length 26 ft 5 in
109 mph (175 km/h) at sea level;	(8.05 m); height 9 ft 6 in (2.90 m);
cruising speed 87 mph (140 km/h)	wing area 21.5.29 sq ft (20.00 m²)

Power was provided by a 75-hp (56-kW) Cirrus II inline piston engine, although later production examples had the more powerful Cirrus Hermes or Genet Major inline engines.

Slightly staggered side-by-side seating for two was provided in the Gentleman's enclosed cabin, with dual controls available as an option.

Comte AC-8

Under the designation **AC-8**, Comte developed a light transport which adhered to the type of largely fabric-covered mixed construction that had become standard with this Swiss manufacturer. Similar in overall configuration to the AC-4, the AC-8 was a braced high-wing monoplane with conventional tail unit and fixed tailwheel landing gear incorporating hydraulic brakes. The AC-8 was available with either a Wright Whirlwind J-6 or 240-hp (179-kW) Lorraine radial engine. Production amounted to a mere three examples.

AC-8 passengers benefited from heated accommodation, while baggage was stowed behind the cabin.

SPECIFICATION	
Comte AC-8	(900 km)
Type: one-crew light transport	**Weights:** empty 2,458 lb
Powerplant: one Wright	(1115 kg); maximum take-off
Whirlwind J-6 radial piston engine	3,858 lb (1750 kg)
rated at 300 hp (224 kW)	**Dimensions:** wingspan 47 ft 6¾ in
Performance: maximum speed	(14.50 m); length 30 ft 2¼ in
133 mph (214 km/h) at sea level;	(9.20 m); height 9 ft 6 in (2.90 m);
cruising speed 109 mph (175 km/h)	wing area 301.40 sq ft (28.00 m²)
at optimum altitude; service ceiling	**Payload:** up to five passengers
16,405 ft (5000 m); range 559 miles	

Comte AC-12 Moskito

While adhering to the same overall layout and construction as Comte's earlier transports, the **AC-12 Moskito** was of cantilever high-wing monoplane configuration. The wing differed from that of its predecessors in being covered with plywood rather than fabric.

Dual controls were standard, but cabin heating and lighting were optional. Several engine types could be installed, such as the Argus As.8, the 120-hp (90-kW) de Havilland Gipsy III inline or the 140-hp (104-kW) Armstrong Siddeley Genet Major radial engine.

In addition to the structural revisions incorporated into the AC-12, Comte also supplied the aircraft with a more robust undercarriage than that of its predecessors.

SPECIFICATION	
Comte AC-12 Moskito	at optimum altitude; service ceiling
Type: three-seat light touring	16,405 ft (5000 m)
aircraft	**Weights:** empty 1,102 lb (500 kg);
Powerplant: one Argus As.8	maximum take-off 1,764 lb (800 kg)
inline piston engine rated at 95 hp	**Dimensions:** wingspan 38 ft ¾ in
(71 kW)	(11.60 m); length 24 ft 7¼ in
Performance: maximum speed	(7.50 m); height 7 ft 4½ in (2.25 m);
112 mph (180 km/h) at sea level;	wing area 170.08 sq ft
cruising speed 96 mph (155 km/h)	(15.80 m²)

Consolidated Model 1 (PT-1)

In 1921 Colonel Virginius Clark, chief designer of the Dayton-Wright Company, designed the Chummy sporting biplane. The airframe was advanced in its use of the new Clark Y thick-section aerofoil and of steel tubing in much of its structure.

By 1922 the company had built two such aircraft, one powered by a Le Rhône rotary piston engine and the other by a Clerget rotary. In 1921 the company had offered the design to the US Army Air Service as a replacement for its Curtiss JN-4D trainer, and in 1922 the service ordered three **TA-3 (Trainer, Air-cooled type 3)** machines for evaluation with the Le Rhône engine and dual controls. Evaluation showed that the type had the makings of a good trainer, but was somewhat lacking in power, so in 1923 Dayton-Wright re-engined one TA-3 with a more powerful 110-hp (82-kW) Le Rhône.

The USAAS then ordered 10 examples of this up-engined model, and these were the last US Army aircraft to be delivered with a rotary-engine. Appreciating that this type

of powerplant had passed its development peak, the USAAS then contracted for three examples of the **TW-3 (Trainer, Water-cooled type 3)** with a 150-hp (112-kW) Wright-Hispano I water-cooled Vee piston engine. The revised type clearly had greater long-term potential, and in June 1923 the USAAS contracted for 20 TW-3 production aircraft, together with enough spare parts for the construction of another three aircraft. At this time the General Motors Corporation was thinking of pulling out of the aircraft business and closing its Dayton-Wright subsidiary, so Reuben Fleet of the Gallaudet company secured rights to the Dayton-Wright trainer design. When the Gallaudet shareholders expressed disapproval at this move, Fleet left the company and established the Consolidated Aircraft Corporation.

It was to this new company that the TW-3 order went, and all the aircraft had been delivered by the end of 1923 with the uprated powerplant of one Wright-Hispano E (licence-built Hispano-Suiza 8) Vee piston engine. Once

the aircraft had entered service, Fleet continued to improve the TW-3, the most important change being the removal of the engine cowling to improve the occupants' forward and downward fields of vision. Visibility was still poor, so Fleet secured US Army permission to rebuild one TW-3 with a new, slimmer fuselage, providing tandem rather than side-by-side accommodation. This revised aircraft was generally known as the 'Camel' due to the hump between its two cockpits.

The 'Camel' may be regarded as the prototype of the Consolidated response to the USAAS's 1924 requirement for a new primary trainer. In the early summer of 1924, the USAAS tested a prototype unofficially designated **TW-8** (perhaps the Camel in 'modified' form), and then placed an order for 50 examples of the **Consolidated Model 1** production variant for service with the designation **PT-1**. Later orders raised the PT-1 total to 220 aircraft that acquired the nickname 'Trusty' for their excellent ability to make a quick and effective recov-

ery from a spin.

Whereas the TW-3 had supplemented the Curtiss JN-4D, the PT-1 supplanted this wholly obsolescent type and was responsible for a radical improvement in the safety record of US Army pilot training. One of the aircraft was diverted to the US

Navy for trials, and four other generally similar aircraft were delivered to Siam in 1928. From 1928 the PT-1 was replaced in first-line service by the PT-3, but then became a valuable implement in the National Guard flying programme until retired in the early 1930s.

The PT-1 was conceptually and structurally akin to the TW-3, and was therefore a conventional single-bay biplane of mixed construction.

SPECIFICATION	
Consolidated Model 1 (PT-1)	rate 690 ft (210 m) per minute;
Type: two-seat primary flying trainer	service ceiling 14,000 ft (4265 m); range 350 miles (563 km)
Powerplant: one Wright-Hispano E Vee piston engine rated at 180 hp (134 kW)	**Weights:** empty 1,805 lb (819 kg); maximum take-off 2,577 lb (1169 kg)
Performance: maximum speed 92 mph (148 km/h) at sea level; cruising speed 79 mph (127 km/h) at optimum altitude; initial climb	**Dimensions:** wingspan 34 ft 5½ in (10.50 m); length 27 ft 9¼ in (8.46 m); height 9 ft 10 in (3.00 m); wing area 284.00 sq ft (26.387 m²)

Consolidated Model 2 (NY and PT-3)

In 1925 a single PT-1 diverted to the USN won a naval flying trainer competition against 14 other designs. The type was ordered into production as the **Consolidated Model 2** for service as the **NY-1** with a 200-hp (149-kW) Wright Whirlwind J-4 radial engine. There is provision for the wheeled landing gear to be replaced by a single large float under the fuselage and two stabilising floats under the tips of the lower wing. The destabilising effect of the float alighting gear was coun-

tered by the provision of a larger vertical tail surface.

The initial USN contract called for 40 aircraft, but this total was later increased to 76. The first of these machines made its maiden flight in November 1925, with deliveries following from May 1926 with a Whirlwind engine of the R-790 naval type. In service, a number of NY-1 aircraft were modified to **NY-1A** gunnery training standard, with the rear cockpit adapted with a ring mounting for one 0.3-in (7.62-mm) trainable

machine-gun. Later still, a number of NY-1s were upgraded to **NY-2** standard under the designation **NY-1B**.

Naval experience suggested that, while the NY-1 had considerable potential, it was hampered by the high loading of its wing cellule. Consolidated therefore evolved a wing cellule extended in span, whose greater area resulted in a significantly lower wing loading. The new wing cellule was tested with complete success during the course of October 1926 and the US Navy ordered an improved trainer with this wing cellule and the uprated powerplant of one R-790-8 (Whirlwind J-5) radial engine. Production

totalled 181 aircraft. The sole variant on this basic theme was the **NY-2A** gunnery trainer, of which 25 were delivered.

Built to the extent of 20 aircraft delivered in 1929 for use mainly by USN and USMC reserve units, the **NY-3** was basically the NY-2 with the revised powerplant of one 240-hp (179-kW) R-790-94 radial engine. The NY series was gradually phased out of service from the mid-1930s, the number in useful service declining to 15 in 1937 and to just one in 1939, when the type was finally retired.

The Wright-Hispano E Vee piston engine was the American version of a French engine, the Hispano-Suiza 8, and had been manufactured during World War I in considerable numbers. By the time production was firmly established, however, engines of greater power were required for first-line aircraft, so existing stocks were placed in reserve for use in second-line applications such as trainers. As reserves of this reliable engine began to be exhausted, the US Army Air Corps (as the USAAS had become in 1926) started to consider an alternative for use in its next trainer.

Variants

XPT-4: projected PT-3 development with the experimental Fairchild-Caminez engine
XPT-5: the airframe of the XPT-3 was temporarily fitted in 1929 with the 170-hp (127-kW) Curtiss Challenger six-cylinder radial engine, but was later converted to PT-3 standard

Although generally similar to standard PT-3 training machines, this PT-3 was used in trials to assess the suitability of the Handley Page automatic slot on training types.

SPECIFICATION	
Consolidated Model 2 (NY-2 floatplane)	rate 865 ft (264 m) per minute; service ceiling 11,000 ft (3355 m); range 210 miles (338 km)
Type: two-seat primary flying trainer	**Weights:** empty 2,145 lb (973 kg); maximum take-off 2,843 lb (1290 kg)
Powerplant: one Wright R-790-8 Whirlwind radial piston engine rated at 220 hp (164 kW)	**Dimensions:** wingspan 40 ft (12.19 m); length 31 ft 4½ in (9.56 m); height 11 ft 10 in (3.61 m); wing area 370.00 sq ft (34.37 m²)
Performance: maximum speed 90 mph (145 km/h) at sea level; cruising speed 75 mph (121 km/h) at optimum altitude; initial climb	

Consolidated Model 2 (NY and PT-3) (continued)

The USN had already opted for an air-cooled radial piston engine in its own NY derivative of the PT-1, and the USAAC came to the conclusion that this type of powerplant was indeed ideal for a trainer as it was reliable and offered a good power/weight ratio. In 1927, therefore, one PT-1

was completed as the **XPT-2** with the modified powerplant of one 220-hp (164-kW) Whirlwind J-5 radial engine. Another aircraft was delivered as the **XPT-3** with revised wing panels and a vertical tail surface of revised shape.

The features pioneered in the XPT-2 and XPT-3

were combined in the Model 2 production variant, of which the USAAC ordered 130 examples for service from September 1927 with the designation **PT-3**. In 1928 Consolidated delivered four identical aircraft to Cuba; in the following year single examples were sold to Argentina,

Brazil and Peru, and a small number may also have been sold to Mexico.

Built to a total of 120 aircraft delivered from May 1928, the **PT-3A** was an improved version of the PT-3 with a number of minor equipment changes and a 225-hp (168-kW) R-790-3 radial engine. The

PT-3 and PT-3A were superseded as the USAAC's most important primary trainers by the Boeing (Stearman) PT-13 from 1937, but a number was still operational with the Spartan Flying School at Tulsa in Oklahoma during the early and middle stages of World War II.

Consolidated Models 2, 7, 8 & 15 Courier (O-17)

Evolved in parallel with the PT-3, the **O-17** resulted from a requirement issued by the USAAC on behalf of the National Guard for an advanced trainer suitable for cross-country flying training and gunnery, photographic and radio training. The **XO-17** prototype was a PT-3 conversion that first flew in April 1927 as the embodiment of the **Model**

2 Courier concept. It differed from the PT-3 in features such as a more streamlined fuselage with provision for a removable fairing (carrying a Scarff ring mounting for one 0.3-in/7.62-mm trainable machine-gun) to be installed over the rear cockpit, oleo-pneumatic shock absorbers, wheel brakes, and increased fuel capacity for the power-

plant of one Wright R-790-1 radial engine.

The type was then ordered into limited production for a mere 29 O-17 aircraft. The aircraft were delivered to National Guard units from the early summer of 1928, and another three generally similar aircraft were delivered to the RCAF as two **Model 7** landplanes and one **Model 8** floatplane, the latter with the same type of alighting gear as used in the NY series.

Despite its military-type designation, the sole **XO-17A** was a Consolidated prototype converted from PT-3 standard with the revised powerplant of one R-790-3

(Whirlwind J-5C) radial engine for use as a demonstrator, that failed to secure any orders. The **Model 15 Courier** was another demonstrator, in

this instance with the powerplant of one Pratt & Whitney R-1340 Wasp radial engine, that also failed to win contracts.

Variant

XPT-8: the airframe of the XO-17A, revised with a 225-hp (168-kW) Packard DR-980 Diesel engine, was flown under this designation

SPECIFICATION	
Consolidated Model 2 (O-17) **Type:** two-seat second-line observation aircraft used almost exclusively as a cross-country flying, gunnery, photographic and radio trainer **Powerplant:** one Wright R-790-1 radial piston engine rated at 225 hp (168 kW) **Performance:** maximum speed 118 mph (190 km/h) at sea level; cruising speed 100 mph (161 km/h) at optimum altitude; initial climb rate 865 ft (264 m) per minute;	service ceiling 12,000 ft (3660 m); range 550 miles (885 km) **Weights:** empty 1,881 lb (853 kg); maximum take-off 2,723 lb (1235 kg) **Dimensions:** wingspan 34 ft 5½ in (10.50 m); length 27 ft 11 in (8.51 m); height 9 ft 9 in (2.97 m); wing area 296.00 sq ft (27.50 m²) **Armament:** generally none, although provision was made for one 0.3-in (7.62-mm) Browning trainable rearward-firing machine-gun in the rear cockpit

This aircraft, 28-229, was originally a PT-3 trainer and was used as the XO-17 prototype. As such, it featured a more streamlined fuselage.

Consolidated Model 16 Commodore

Some time before it lost the production order for its **Admiral (PY)** flying-boat for the US Navy, Consolidated had gained contracts for a civil derivative, the **Model 16 Commodore**. Nothing had come of the suggestion of the Detroit and Cleveland Navigation Co. that it might start services with the Commodore by the spring of 1929 from Lake Erie between Detroit, Cleveland and Buffalo, and of the company's negotiations with Pan American Airways for the adoption of the type. However, greater things emerged from the negotiations which Reuben Fleet had been undertaking

with Ralph O'Neill, who was organising a South American airline service. In January 1929 there came the decision that Fleet,

together with James H. Rand Jr, would become involved with O'Neill in the opportunity, and six Commodore 'boats were ordered by Rand's own airline, Tri-Motor Safety Airways. In April came the decision to change the airline's name to the New York, Rio & Buenos Aires Line (NYRBA).

The main change effected in the change of the Admiral into the Commodore, which was powered by two 575-hp (429-kW) Pratt & Whitney R-1860 Hornet B radial engines driving three-

The Commodore embarked a crew of three, the two pilots in an open cockpit with a control column that could be swung over for the use of either man. Behind the cockpit were a lavatory, radio compartment and a cargo hold.

bladed metal propellers, was in the inside of the hull, which had passenger cabins 8 ft (2.44 m) wide and 5 ft (1.52 m) high. This arrangement allowed for a maximum of 32 passengers, although the normal load was 22 passengers in two eight-seat compartments and two three-seat drawing rooms.

The first of the 'boats was launched on the

Niagara River on 28 September 1929 and flown on the same day. It was later named as the *Buenos Aires*. During a demonstration flight, the hull was damaged as the 'boat bounded off heavy swells and, as a result, the hull of this and all later 'boats was strengthened. Another change was the introduction of a cockpit enclosure of plywood

SPECIFICATION	
Consolidated Model 16-1 Commodore **Type:** three-crew transport flying-boat **Powerplant:** two Pratt & Whitney R-1860 Hornet B radial piston engines each rated at 575 hp (429 kW) **Performance:** maximum speed 128 mph (206 km/h) at optimum altitude; cruising speed 108 mph (174 km/h) at optimum altitude; initial climb rate 675 ft (206 m) per	minute; service ceiling 11,250 ft (3430 m); range 1,000 miles (1609 km) **Weights:** empty 10,550 lb (4785 kg); maximum take-off 17,600 lb (7983 kg) **Dimensions:** wingspan 100 ft (30.48 m); length 61 ft 8 in (18.80 m); height 15 ft 8 in (4.76 m); wing area 1,110.00 sq ft (103.12 m²) **Payload:** up to 22 passengers and a small volume of freight

construction. The Commodore entered service on the route linking Buenos Aires and Rio de Janeiro, on 23 December 1929.

During June 1928 the NYRBA had ordered a second batch of six Commodores, another two being added in October of the same year. From the third 'boat, the designations for the type were the **Model 16-1** and the **Model 16-2**, the latter introduced

in 1930 on the 'shuttle service' across the estuary of the Plate river between Buenos Aires and Montevideo; it had 30-seat accommodation, but shorter range as the maximum take-off weight remained unaltered. To help speed deliveries during the winter months, when the water near Buffalo was frozen, Consolidated delivered assemblies to Langley Field, Virginia, where the 'boats were assembled and

test-flown from Chesapeake Bay.

By July the NYRBA had seven Commodores in service and had operated the entire 9,000-mile (14500-km) service from New York to South America through 15 countries for just four months when official pressure was applied on the NYRBA to merge with Pan American Airways. The official date of the acquisition was 15 September 1930, and

Pan Am took over 11 Commodores and also inherited the order for the last three of the NYRBA's aircraft.

Eight Commodores were subsequently returned to the USA, and Pan Am or its subsidiary companies operated the entire production run of 14 'boats (one was destroyed in a hangar fire during 1935) until starting to dispose of them in 1937. Among the later operators of the Commodore, which

was always notable for its reliability, were Miami-Key West Airways, Chamberlin Air Lines, China National Airways Corporation (a subsidiary of Pan Am) and the Brazilian air force. Pan Am at times recommissioned small numbers of the 'boats, especially during World War II, and converted one as the sole **Model 16T-2** navigation trainer. The last of the 'boats was retired and broken up only in 1949.

Consolidated Model 17, Model 18 and Model 20 Fleetster

Designed as a passenger and/or mail transport for the inland routes of the NYRBA airline, linking the coastal route operated by the Commodore from

Miami to Buenos Aires with the inland cities of Argentina, Bolivia, Chile, Paraguay and Uruguay, the **Model 17 Fleetster** had a streamlined all-metal

monocoque fuselage and a high-set cantilever wooden wing.

Type certificated on 23 January 1930 in both landplane and twin-float seaplane form, the Fleetster could seat a maximum of eight passengers (although the three NYRBA aircraft were normally fitted with two full-width bench seats, each for three persons) and the pilot's enclosed cockpit could accommodate an additional passenger seat if the space was not required for radio equipment. Sold to Pan American as part of the NYRBA sale on 15 September 1930, the **Model 17-1 Fleetster** remained in service until October 1934. A fourth aircraft was built for the US Assistant Secretary of War and served as the **Y1C-11** before being adapted to **Model 17-2** standard with six-seat accommodation and the 575-hp (429-kW) R-1820-1 engine for continued service as the **C-11A**. Three basically similar aircraft were procured for service with the designation **Y1C-22**.

Thanks to its overall aerodynamic cleanliness, the Model 17 achieved 180 mph (290 km/h) on the 575 hp (429 kW) delivered by its powerplant of one Pratt & Whitney R-1860 Hornet B radial engine.

Variants

Model 17AF Fleetster: nine-passenger development powered by a 575-hp (429-kW) R-1820E Cyclone engine. The Model 17AF received type certification on 6 January 1932 and three were built for Luddington Airline for its New York-to-Washington service; a 1,000-lb (454-kg) increase in maximum take-off weight allowed a payload increase of 700 lb (318 kg), and to compensate for this the wing was increased in span and area
Model 17-2C: one aircraft, type certificated on 29 September 1930. Generally similar to the Model 17-1, but powered by the R-1820E
Model 18: built in 1932 and evaluated as the **XBY-1**, the Model 18 was intended for carrierborne bomber operations; it had a metal fuselage and a cantilever wooden wing and, though unsuccessful, had the distinction of being the USN's first stressed-skin aircraft and the first aircraft with integral fuel tanks in the wing
Model 20-2: on 7 May 1930 Consolidated received type certification for a parasol-wing version of the Model 17, three of which were built for the NYRBA and one for a Canadian customer; the wing was supported by four short struts, and the pilot's cockpit was moved to the rear of the passenger cabin, its original location becoming a freight compartment
Model 20-A: developed to the order of Transcontinental & Western Air Inc., which ordered seven of the type, the Model 20-A was a development of the Model 20, type certificated on 15 September 1932 as a quick-change version with provision for the cabin layout to be adapted for the accommodation of varying passenger/cargo loads; the Model 20-A entered service in October 1932

SPECIFICATION	
Consolidated Model 17 Fleetster	per minute; service ceiling 18,000 ft (5485 m); range 675 miles (1086 km)
Type: one-crew light transport aircraft	**Weights:** empty 3,326 lb (1509 kg); maximum take-off 5,300 lb (2404 kg)
Powerplant: one Pratt & Whitney R-1860 Hornet B radial piston engine rated at 575 hp (429 kW)	**Dimensions:** wingspan 45 ft (13.72 m); length 31 ft 9 in (9.68 m); height 9 ft 2 in (2.79 m); wing area 313.50 sq ft (29.12 m²)
Performance: maximum speed 180 mph (290 km/h) at optimum altitude; cruising speed 153 mph (246 km/h) at optimum altitude; initial climb rate 1,200 ft (366 m)	**Payload:** up to nine passengers (five in floatplane form)

Consolidated Model 21 (PT-11, PT-12, BT-6, BT-7 & N4Y)

In 1930 the USAAC issued a requirement for a primary flying trainer to replace the PT-3, and Joe Gwinn, the company's chief designer, decided that a much-improved development of the Model 2 could win the resulting competition. This resulted in the **Model 21-A**, which had more elegant lines than the Model 2 and a

number of drag-reducing features. In February 1931, only eight weeks after the start of design work, the **Model 21** prototype took to the air with the powerplant of one 170-hp (127-kW) Kinner C-5 radial engine, although the airframe was stressed to cope with engines rated at up to 400 hp (298 kW). Moreover, the wings were

built with fittings to allow any changes that might be required to overcome stability problems with higher-rated engines.

The USAAC was impressed with the type's potential, and ordered four **Y1PT-11** aircraft for evaluation with a powerplant of one 165-hp (123-kW) Continental R-545-1 radial engine. All four of the aircraft were delivered in May 1931. Two were later revised to **PT-11D** standard; the third was revised with the 300-hp (224-kW) Wright R-975-1 (Whirlwind J-6-9) radial engine to become the sole **Y1BT-6** (later **BT-6**) in the basic trainer category, before being further revised to **PT-11D** standard. The last Y1PT-11 became the **Y1PT-11A** (later **PT-11A**)

after being re-engined with the 175-hp (131-kW) Curtiss R-600-1 radial engine, and was then revised to **Y1PT-11C** standard with the 180-hp (134-kW) Lycoming YR-680-1 radial engine.

After one of the Y1PT-11 aircraft had been temporarily revised to **Y1PT-11B** standard with the 210-hp (157-kW) Kinner YR-720-1 radial engine, six basically similar aircraft were delivered from July 1932. Five of these were subsequently accepted for full USAAC service with the designation **PT-11B**, and the sixth was transferred to the US Coast Guard with the 165-hp (123-kW) Whirlwind J-6-5 radial engine, before becoming the sole **N4Y-1** with the 220-hp (164-kW) R-680-3 radial engine.

Variant

Model 21-C: this was the civil counterpart of the military Model 21-A, and the sole sale to a military customer was made to Mexico, which received its 10 aircraft in November and December 1936; the aircraft were built by Fleet Aircraft in Canada, and their standard included a powerplant of one 420-hp (313-kW) R-985-SB Wasp Junior radial engine and an armament of two 0.3-in (7.62-mm) machine-guns installed as one fixed weapon in the forward fuselage and one trainable weapon located on a mounting in the rear cockpit

SPECIFICATION	
Consolidated Model 21 (PT-11D)	7 minutes 24 seconds; service ceiling 13,700 ft (4175 m)
Type: two-seat primary flying trainer	**Weights:** empty 1,918 lb (870 kg); maximum take-off 2,585 lb (1173 kg)
Powerplant: one Lycoming R-680-A radial piston engine rated at 200 hp (149 kW)	**Dimensions:** wingspan 31 ft 7 in (9.63 m); length 26 ft 11 in (8.20 m); height 9 ft 8 in (2.95 m); wing area 280.00 sq ft (26.01 m²)
Performance: maximum speed 118 mph (190 km/h) at sea level; climb to 5,000 ft (1525 m) in	

Consolidated Model 21 (PT-11, PT-12, BT-6 & BT-7) (cont.)

The designation **PT-11C** was applied to 18 aircraft of the **PT-11D** type delivered to the Colombian air force in July and August 1934 for service up to 1952. The aircraft had provision for alternative wheeled landing gear or floats, and the powerplant was one R-760-E7 (Whirlwind J-3) radial engine.

Delivered between May and July 1932 with a powerplant of one 220-hp (164-kW) R-680-3 radial engine, the 21 **Y1PT-11D** aircraft received the revised designation PT-11D after they had been accepted for full USAAC service. In 1934 the USN ordered three similar aircraft with the designation **XN4Y-1**. Ten aircraft were delivered in April and May 1932 to the **Y1PT-12** standard that differed from that of the PT-11D only in minor equipment changes and its powerplant of one 300-hp (224-kW) Pratt & Whitney R-985-1 radial engine. The aircraft were later accepted for full service with the designation **PT-12**, but were later allocated the revised designation **Y1BT-7**, that finally became **BT-7**.

The US Army Air Corps received just 10 PT-12 biplane trainers.

Consolidated Model 22 Ranger (P2Y)

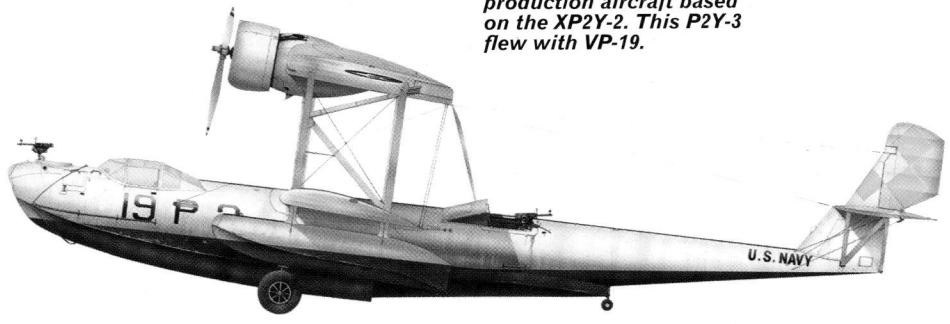

In addition to P2Y-2 conversions, the US Navy also received 23 P2Y-3 production aircraft based on the XP2Y-2. This P2Y-3 flew with VP-19.

In June 1929 a US Navy contract for a new patrol flying-boat went to the Martin company, rather than to Consolidated's **Model 9 Admiral**. Although it was unhappy with the loss of the production contract, Consolidated decided to capitalise on its Model 9 experience in the development of the improved **Model 22 Ranger**, which also incorporated some of the company's experience with the Model 16 Commodore in features such as the enclosed flightdeck.

Designed by Isaac M. 'Mac' Laddon, the new 'boat retained the fabric-covered wooden wing of the Model 9 as the upper wing of a new sesquiplane wing cellule. The lower wing was mounted in the high-set position on the hull, which was of all-metal construction with a two-step planing bottom, and carried stabilising floats under its outer ends. The upper wing carried the powerplant of three Wright R-1820-E1 Cyclone radial piston engines installed as two engines under the wing and the third strut-mounted on the centreline above the wing.

The US Navy ordered one **XP2Y-1** prototype in May 1931, and followed six weeks later with an order for 31 examples of the **P2Y-1** production version. The XP2Y-1 made its maiden flight in March 1932, and initial trials soon led to the removal of the centreline engine before service trials in May of the same year. These trials were successful, and Consolidated delivered all 31 examples of the P2Y-1 between December 1932 and June 1933 for use by the USN's VP-10 and VP-5 squadrons, which made a number of classic long-range formation flights in the type.

Two 'boats built for the export market were the **P2Y-1C**, delivered to Colombia in December 1932, and the **P2Y-1J**, delivered to Japan in January 1935.

In August 1933 the last P2Y-1 was modified as the **XP2Y-2** with R-1820-88 radial engines in NACA-cowled nacelles raised to the leading edges of the upper wing. The revised powerplant installation reduced drag by an appreciable degree, and the USN procured the kits from Consolidated. with which 21 of the P2Y-1s were modified to this standard for service with the designation **P2Y-2**.

In December 1933 the US Navy ordered an additional 23 'boats to this improved standard, based on the P2Y-2 but with R-1820-90 radial engines and tankage in the wings for additional fuel. The P2Y-3 aircraft were delivered from January 1935. All of the Navy's P2Ys had been withdrawn and placed in storage by the end of 1941. Production of the P2Y series was ended with a variant for Argentina, which received six of these **P2Y-3A** 'boats during August and September 1937. The P2Y-3As replaced Supermarine Southamptons, and were themselves replaced by Consolidated PBY-5A amphibians in 1947.

SPECIFICATION

Consolidated Model 22 Ranger (P2Y-3)
Type: five-seat maritime reconnaissance flying-boat
Powerplant: two Wright R-1820-90 Cyclone radial piston engines each rated at 750 hp (559 kW)
Performance: maximum speed 149 mph (240 km/h) at 4,000 ft (1220 m); cruising speed 118 mph (189 km/h) at optimum altitude; initial climb rate 650 ft (198 m) per minute; service ceiling 16,500 ft (5030 m); range 2,650 miles (4265 km)
Weights: empty 12,769 lb (5792 kg); maximum take-off 25,266 lb (11461 kg)
Dimensions: wingspan 100 ft (30.48 m); length 61 ft 9 in (18.82 m); height 16 ft 3 in (4.95 m); wing area 1,514.00 sq ft (140.65 m²)
Armament: one 0.3-in (7.62-mm) Browning trainable forward-firing machine-gun in the bow position, and one 0.3-in (7.62-mm) Browning trainable lateral/rearward-firing machine-gun in each of the two side-by-side dorsal positions, plus up to 2,000 lb (907 kg) of disposable stores carried on two hardpoints under the lower wing

Consolidated Model 25, Model 26 and Model 27

The Detroit Aircraft Corporation, of which Lockheed Aircraft Company was then a subsidiary, gave up its aviation activities during 1932. One of the company's designers joined Consolidated, and for this company continued the development of a military aircraft based on the Lockheed Altair. This interested the USAAC sufficiently to gain a contract for two prototypes, one of them the **Y1P-25** two-seat fighter known to the company as the **Model 25** and the other an attack version of the same aircraft, designated as the **Y1A-11** and known to the company as the **Model 27**. This differed from the fighter primarily in having two more 0.3-in (7.62-mm) fixed forward-firing machine-guns, and external provision for up to 400 lb (181 kg) of bombs.

A cantilever low-wing monoplane of all-metal construction, except for the fabric covering of the control surfaces on the tail unit, the Y1P-25 had tail-wheel landing gear with retractable main units, the powerplant of one Curtiss V-1570-27 Conqueror

SPECIFICATION

Consolidated Model 26 (PB-2A)
Type: two-seat fighter
Powerplant: one Curtiss V-1710-61 Vee piston engine rated at 700 hp (522 kW)
Performance: maximum speed 274 mph (441 km/h) at 25,000 ft (7620 m); cruising speed 215 mph (346 km/h) at optimum altitude; climb to 15,000 ft (4570 m) in 7 minutes 47 seconds; service ceiling 28,000 ft (8535 m); range 580 miles (818 km)
Weights: empty 4,306 lb (1953 kg); maximum take-off 5,643 lb (2560 kg)
Dimensions: wingspan 43 ft 11 in (13.39 m); length 30 ft (9.14 m); height 8 ft 3 in (2.51 m); wing area 297.00 sq ft (27.58 m²)
Armament: two 0.3-in (7.62-mm) Browning fixed forward-firing machine-guns, and one 0.3-in (7.62-mm) Browning trainable rearward-firing machine-gun in the rear of the cockpit

It is interesting to note the turbo-supercharger associated with the PB-2A's Curtiss engine, located just ahead of and above the port wingroot.

turbocharged Vee engine, and accommodation for a crew of two in tandem in an enclosed cockpit. First flown late in 1932, the Y1P-25 crashed on 13 January 1933, but in its short test life had shown sufficient promise for the USAAC to order four generally similar service test aircraft. They differed by

having the V-1710-57 Conqueror turbocharged engine, simplified landing gear and revised cockpit canopies. Tested in the summer of 1934 under the designation **P-30**, known to the company by the designation **Model 26**, the aircraft revealed performance sufficient to gain a contract for 50 **P-30A** fight-

ers in December 1934. These introduced the slightly more powerful V-1710-61 turbocharged engine and a variable-pitch propeller. Entering service in 1935, they had the distinction of being the only two-seat monoplane fighters to gain operational status with the USAAC during the period between

the world wars. Shortly after entering service, the P-30A was redesignated as the **PB-2A**; simultaneously, the surviving examples of the P-30 were reclassified as **PB-2** aircraft.
Development of the Y1A-11 continued with the procurement of four service test **A-11** aircraft. These differed from the P-30s by

having normally aspirated engines and two-bladed propellers, but although one was revised as the sole **XA-11A** with the 1,000-hp (746-kW) Allison XV-1710-7 Vee engine, no production aircraft were ordered.
The **YP-27** and **YP-28**, both with radial engines, were not built.

Consolidated Model 28 (PBY Catalina)

Seeking to fulfil a requirement for a patrol flying-boat offering somewhat greater range and load-carrying capability than the P2Y or Martin P3M, the USN contracted with Consolidated and Douglas during October 1933 to build competing **Consolidated XP3Y-1** and Douglas XP3D-1 prototypes. Only a single prototype of the Douglas design was built, but the XP3Y-1 paved the way for the most extensively built flying-boat in aviation history.

Consolidated identified its design as the **Model 28** and, like the P2Y which preceded it, this was based on a parasol-mounted wing. However, in the new design, the introduction of internal bracing resulted in a wing which was virtually a cantilever unit except for two small streamlined struts between hull and wing centre-section on each side. Another innovation adding to aerodynamic efficiency was the provision of stabilising floats which, when retracted in flight, formed streamlined wingtips. The two-step hull design was very similar to that of the P2Y, but the Model 28 had a clean cruciform cantilever tail unit. The powerplant of the prototype comprised two 825-hp (615-kW) R-1830-54 Twin Wasp engines mounted on the leading edges of the wing, and the armament comprised four 0.3-in (7.62-mm) trainable machine-guns and up to 2,000 lb (907 kg) of bombs carried externally.

First flown on 28 March 1935, the XP3Y-1 was soon

transferred to the US Navy for service trials, which confirmed a significant improvement in performance over current patrol flying-boats. The prototype's extended range and improved load-carrying capability caused the USN to request further development to bring this new aircraft into the category of a patrol bomber. Accordingly, in October 1935, the prototype was returned to Consolidated for the necessary work to be carried out – this included installation of 900-hp (671-kW) R-1830-64 engines which had been specified for the 60 examples of the **PBY-1** (a patrol bomber designation) which had been ordered on 29 June 1935. At the same time, redesigned vertical tail surfaces were introduced and the **XPBY-1**, as the prototype had by now been redesignated, flew for the first time on 19 May 1936. After completing its trials, this machine was delivered to the USN's VP-11F during October 1936, the month in which the first of the PBY-1 'boats also began to reach the unit.

Minor equipment changes brought the designation **PBY-2** for the second production order placed on 25 July 1936 for 50 **Model 28-2** 'boats, while the **PBY-3** (66 **Model 28-3** 'boats) ordered on 27 November 1936 and **PBY-4** (33 **Model 28-4** 'boats) on 18 December 1937 had 1,000-hp (746-kW) R-1830-66 and 1,050-hp (783-kW) R-1830-72 Twin Wasp engines, respectively. All

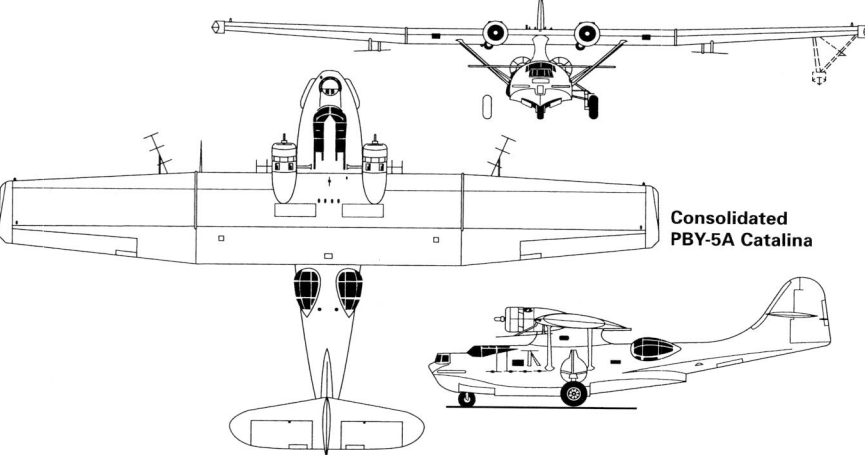

**Consolidated
PBY-5A Catalina**

but the first examples of the PBY-4 introduced large transparent blisters over the waist gun positions, in place of sliding hatches, and these blisters became a characteristic feature of all subsequent production 'boats.

In April 1939 the first example of the PBY-4 production aircraft was returned to the company for the installation of wheeled landing gear so that the machine could operate as an amphibian. When completed in November 1939, this machine emerged with the designation **XPBY-5A**. Testing confirmed the very considerable advantages of the amphibian configuration and the 33 aircraft outstanding on USN contracts for the **PBY-5** variant (in all, 684 **Model 28-5** machines completed with 1,200-hp/895-kW R-1830-82 or -92 engines and greater fuel capacity) were completed as **PBY-5A**

amphibians; an additional 134 PBY-5A amphibians were ordered on 25 November 1940.

Extensive service use of the PBY series had by now suggested that the hull would benefit from hydrodynamic improvement. The Naval Aircraft Factory carried out the necessary research and development work to achieve this end, receiving an order for 156 of these modified aircraft under the designation **PBN-1 Nomad** (155 machines). This course was adopted in order that the fairly extensive design and production changes would not interfere with the major production effort at Consolidated. However, when the final production version was built by Consolidated, to the extent of 175 **PBY-6A** machines between April 1944 and April 1945, the improvements of the NAF were among the package of changes incorporated.

From mid-1937, the PBY series was introduced rapidly into service with the US Navy, and by the time that the USA became involved in World War II, some 21 squadrons were equipped with the type. Before this, however, interest shown by the USSR had resulted in an order for three aircraft and the negotiation of a licence-production agreement. When these three machines were delivered, they were accompanied by a team of Consolidated engineers who assisted in establishment of the Soviet production facilities. Designated **GST**, these production aircraft were powered by Mikulin M-62 radial engines, a developed version of the M-25 (licence-built Wright R-1820 Cyclone), which had a power rating of 900-1,000 hp (671-746 kW). The first of the GST machines appeared late in 1939 and an unspecified number, certainly reaching 400 and possibly 1,000 or more, was built during World War II and possibly to a time as late as 1948 for service with the Soviet navy.

European interest started with purchase by the British of a single Model 28-5 for evaluation. The aircraft was allocated to the Marine Aircraft Experimental Establishment in July 1939. The outbreak of war anticipated the termination of trials, but with little doubt of the excellence of the design, a first batch of 50 was ordered under the designation **Catalina Mk I**.

PBY-5s were delivered to the Royal Australian Air Force, as typified by A24-10. This aircraft served with No. 11 Sqn in Queensland during 1942.

Consolidated Model 28 (PBY Catalina) (continued)

Initial deliveries of the Catalina to the RAF began early in 1941, these entering service with Nos 209 and 240 Squadrons of Coastal Command. The Catalina subsequently equipped nine squadrons of Coastal Command, as well as an additional 12 squadrons serving overseas. The RAF received about 700 of these aircraft which, with the exception of 11 PBY-5A machines diverted to the UK from USN contracts, were all non-amphibious flying-boats. They comprised 109 of the **Catalina Mk I**, equivalent to the USN's PBY-5, 14 of the Canadian-built **Catalina Mk IA** equivalent, 225 of the **Catalina Mk IB** (**PBY-5B**), six of the improved **Catalina Mk II**, 36 of the Canadian-built **Catalina Mk IIA**, 12 of the **Catalina Mk IIIA** (PBY-5A), 97 of the **Catalina Mk IVA** (PBY-5), 193 of the **Catalina Mk IVB**, which was built by Boeing Aircraft of Canada under the designation **PB2B-1** and was generally similar to the non-amphibious PBY-5, and 50 of the **Catalina Mk VI**, which was the Boeing-built **PB2B-2** with the taller vertical surfaces first introduced on

the PBN-1. No **Catalina Mk V** machines served with the RAF, this designation being allocated for potential supplies of the PBN-1, none of which was in the event sent to the UK.

Soon after the receipt of the UK's first production order, France ordered 30 aircraft. Allocated the company's identification **Model 28-5MF**, none of these was delivered before the collapse of French resistance. Other foreign orders received at about the same time covered 18 aircraft for the RAAF, and 48 ordered by the Dutch government for use in the Netherlands East Indies.

Canada had its own close association with the Catalina, as both manufacturer and customer. Under an agreement reached between the Canadian and US governments, production lines were laid down in Canada by Boeing Aircraft of Canada and by Canadian Vickers. Boeing Canada production totalled 362 aircraft, these comprising 240 PB2B-1s supplied to Australia, New Zealand and the UK; 50 PB2B-2s for the UK; 17 non-amphibious Catalinas for the RCAF, and

55 amphibians which, in RCAF service, were designated **Canso**. Aircraft produced by Canadian Vickers totalled 379 equivalent to the PBY-5A, of which 149 were supplied to the RCAF. From the balance of 230, the USN planned to acquire 183 under the designation **PBV-1A**, but in fact received none of these machines. The latter were all supplied to the USAAF, which had previously acquired 56 PBY-5As as a direct transfer from the USN for service with the revised designation **OA-10**. These were used throughout World War II for search and rescue, some carrying an air-dropped lifeboat beneath each wing. The 230 aircraft built by Canadian Vickers were designated **OA-10A** in USAAF service, and the final production aircraft to be received were 75 PBY-6As for service under the designation **OA-10B**.

The PBY series continued in service with a very large number of air arms after World War II, when machines surplus to American requirements were transferred to the Allies.

Boeing-Canada's PB2B-2 incorporated the taller tailfin introduced on the PBN-1 Nomad. The majority of PB2B-2s carried centimetre-wave radar in a pylon-mounted, neatly faired radome situated above the cockpit.

SPECIFICATION

Consolidated PBY-5A
Type: seven/nine-seat long-range maritime patrol bomber amphibian flying-boat
Powerplant: two Pratt & Whitney R-1830-92 Twin Wasp radial piston engines each rated at 1,200 hp (895 kW)
Performance: maximum speed 179 mph (288 km/h) at 7,000 ft (2135 m); cruising speed 117 mph (188 km/h) at optimum altitude; climb to 10,000 ft (3050 m) in 19 minutes 18 seconds; service ceiling 14,700 ft (4480 m); range 2,545 miles (4096 km)
Weights: empty 20,910 lb (9485 kg); maximum take-off

35,420 lb (16066 kg)
Dimensions: wingspan 104 ft (31.70 m); length 63 ft 10½ in (19.47 m); height 20 ft 2 in (6.15 m); wing area 1,400.00 sq ft (130.06 m²)
Armament: two 0.3-in (7.62-mm) Browning trainable forward-firing machine-guns in the bow turret, one 0.3-in (7.62-mm) Browning trainable rearward-firing machine-gun firing aft through a tunnel aft of the hull step, and one 0.5-in (12.7-mm) Browning trainable lateral-firing machine-gun in each of the two beam positions, plus up to 4,000 lb (1814 kg) of bombs or depth charges carried externally

Consolidated Model 29 (PB2Y Coronado)

Plans for the development of a maritime patrol bomber larger than the PBY were drawn up by the US Navy very soon after the first flight of the XPBY-1 prototype. The aim was to procure a patrol flying-boat with increased performance and good weapon-load capability, and Consolidated and Sikorsky each received a contract for the construction of a prototype for evaluation. The Sikorsky XPBS-1 flew for the first time on 13 August 1937, but despite introducing a number of new features it was the **Consolidated Model 29** which, when evaluated as the **XPB2Y-1** following a first flight on 17 December 1937, was regarded as the more suitable of the two for production. At the time, the US Navy had no funds for the immediate procurement of any of these large 'boats, so Consolidated had almost 15 months in which to rectify the shortcomings revealed by initial flight tests.

The most serious of the problems was lateral instability, which the company attempted to rectify by the addition of two oval-shaped fins, mounted one each end of the tailplane. Stability was still far from

With its four R-1830-92 engines giving it power equivalent to two PBY-5As, the PB2Y-5 was the ultimate patrol bomber variant of the Coronado. The engines gave maximum power at low altitude.

satisfactory, however, and this was resolved finally by the design of a new tail unit with endplate fin-and-rudder units similar to those of the B-24 Liberator. The other problem concerned the hydrodynamic performance of the flying-boat's hull, and here, fortunately, the delayed procurement allowed time for redesign, the new hull being deeper than that of the prototype with a much-changed nose profile.

Eventually, on 31 March 1939, the USN was able to order six of these aircraft under the designation **PB2Y-2** and the name **Coronado**, and delivery of

these to VP-13 began on 31 December 1940. They were impressive aircraft, powered by four radial engines mounted on the high-set cantilever wing. Construction was entirely of light alloy, and interesting features included stabilising floats which were retracted once the 'boat was airborne to become the wingtips, and bomb bays incorporated into the deep-section wing. Accommodation was provided for a crew of nine.

These PB2Y-2 'boats were used for service trials, leading to the procurement of the **PB2Y-3 Coronado**, following the conversion of

one of the PB2Y-2s as the **XPB2Y-3** prototype. The PB2Y-3 differed from the PB2Y-2 by having increased armament and the provision of self-sealing fuel tanks and armour. A total of 210 of this version was

built, late-production aircraft being equipped with ASV (Air to Surface Vessel) search radar. Ten of the aircraft, designated **PB2Y-3B**, were supplied to the RAF and based initially at Beaumaris, Anglesey, for

SPECIFICATION

Consolidated PB2Y-3 Coronado
Type: long-range flying-boat bomber
Powerplant: four Pratt & Whitney R-1830-88 Twin Wasp radial piston engines each rated at 1,200 hp (895 kW)
Performance: maximum speed 223 mph (359 km/h) at 20,000 ft (6095 m); cruising speed 141 mph (227 km/h) at 1,500 ft (460 m); climb to 10,000 ft (3050 m) in 21 minutes 30 seconds; service ceiling 20,500 ft (6250 m); range 1,370 miles (2205 km) with an 8,000-lb (3629-kg) bombload
Weights: empty 40,935 lb

(18568 kg); maximum take-off 68,000 lb (30844 kg)
Dimensions: wingspan 115 ft (35.05 m); length 79 ft 3 in (24.16 m); height 27 ft 6 in (8.38 m); wing area 1,780.00 sq ft (165.36 m²)
Armament: two 0.5-in (12.7-mm) Browning trainable machine-guns each in the bow, dorsal and tail turrets, and one 0.5-in (12.7-mm) Browning trainable lateral-firing machine-gun in each of two beam positions, plus up to 12,000 lb (5443 kg) of weapons including bombs, depth bombs and torpedoes in wing bomb bays

service with Coastal Command. Their stay there was only brief, for they were transferred to No. 231 Squadron of Transport Command and used from June 1944 to operate freight services.

Variants in US service, converted from PB2Y-3 standard, included 31 examples of the **PB2Y-3R** transport fitted with R-1830-92 single-stage supercharged engines; one **XPB2Y-4** converted by the experimental installation of Wright R-2600 Cyclone engines; a number of

PB2Y-5 conversions from PB2Y-3 standard with increased fuel capacity and R-1830-92 engines; and a number of **PB2Y-5H** casualty-evacuation machines which saw service in the Pacific theatre with accommodation for 25 litters.

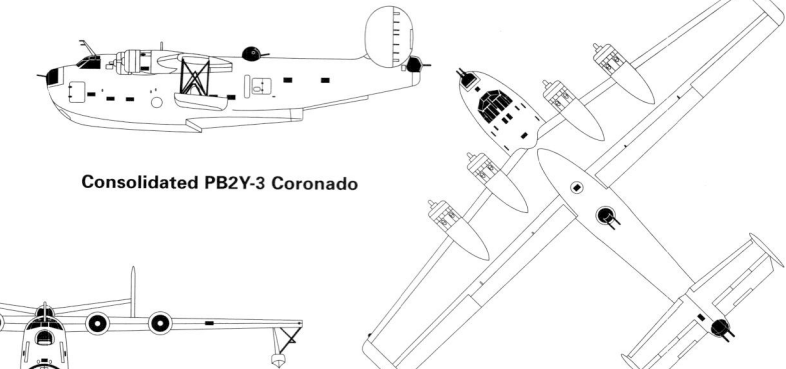

Consolidated PB2Y-3 Coronado

Consolidated Model 32 (B-24 Liberator)

In the European theatre of World War II, the **B-24 Liberator** was much overshadowed by the Boeing B-17 Flying Fortress, but regardless of this fact, the Consolidated warplane was built in considerably larger numbers and, despite the fact that it was a four-engined type, in larger numbers than any other American aircraft of World War II.

In January 1939, the USAAC invited Consolidated to prepare a design study for a heavy bomber with performance superior to that of the B-17. Consolidated wasted little time in submitting a design proposal, identifying it as its **Model 32**. Given the paramount nature of the range performance required on the new type, the Consolidated design team created the Model 32 around the high-aspect-ratio Davis wing, first introduced on the company's ultimately unsuccessful **Model 31** flying-boat design, of which a prototype was then nearing completion. The US Army awarded a contract to Consolidated on 30 March 1939, insisting that construction of the **XB-24** prototype must be completed by the end of the year. This was achieved by the company, for the XB-24 made its maiden flight on 29 December 1939.

In size, the XB-24 was marginally smaller than the Fortress except in wingspan, though the area of this wing was about 26 per cent less than that of the Boeing bomber. To ensure maximum capacity within the fuselage structure, the wing was located comparatively high in the shoulder-wing position, and to provide good low-speed handling characteristics and an acceptable landing speed, wide-span Fowler-type flaps were installed on the trailing edge of the wing. In basic construction, the fuselage was conventional, but deep in section

to allow for installation of a bomb-bay which could accommodate up to 8,000 lb (3629 kg) of bombs stowed vertically. The most unusual feature of the bomb-bay was the provision of unique 'roller shutter' doors which retracted within the fuselage when opened for attack, causing less drag than conventional bomb-bay doors. The tail unit, with its ovoid endplate fin-and-rudder units, was generally similar to that developed for the Model 31 flying-boat. Retractable tricycle landing gear and the powerplant of four 1,200-hp (895-kW) Pratt & Whitney R-1830-33 Twin Wasp engines in wing-mounted nacelles completed the basic configuration.

Consolidated had begun to receive orders for its new bomber even before the first flight of the prototype. These included seven of the service test **YB-24** and 36 of the initial production **B-24A** for the USAAC, and 120 aircraft 'off the drawing board' for the French. Early flight tests proved successful, but to meet the USAAC specification, some development was necessary to achieve higher speed. From the start, however, there was no doubt that the XB-24 was able to demonstrate excellent long-range capability. Furthermore, the large-volume fuselage lent itself to adaptation to other roles.

The XB-24 was followed during 1940 by the seven YB-24 service trials aircraft, the latter differing from the prototype by the provision

of pneumatic de-icing boots on the leading edges of the wings, tailplanes and fins. By the time that the first production aircraft began to come off the line at San Diego, France had already capitulated, and the aircraft of the French order were completed to British requirements, as specified in an order for 164 which had been placed soon after that of France. The RAF allocated the name **Liberator** to its new bomber, this being adopted later by the USAAF, and the first of these machines flew on 17 January 1941. The type was designated as the **LB-30A** by Consolidated, indicating Liberator to British specification, and the first six of these reached the UK during March 1941 after being flown directly across the North Atlantic. These initial aircraft were used as unarmed transports by BOAC, and later by RAF Ferry Command. The next batch, received in mid-1941, joined the RAF with the designation **Liberator Mk I** for service with Coastal Command. They were modified in the UK to equip them with an early form of ASV radar and to increase the standard armament of six 0.303-in (7.7-mm) trainable machine-guns to include an underfuselage gun pack housing four or six 20-mm fixed forward-firing cannon. The Liberator Mk I entered service with No. 120 Squadron of Coastal Command in June 1941, and was the first RAF aircraft with the range and endurance to close the

'Atlantic Gap', that area of the ocean in which, until that time, sea convoys were beyond the range of air support from either North America or the UK.

In the same month, the B-24 entered service with the Air Corps Ferrying Command that operated services across the North Atlantic, similar to those of RAF Ferry Command.

The first true operational bomber version, however, was the **Liberator Mk II** (company designation **LB-30**), for which there was no USAAF equivalent. This differed from the Liberator Mk I primarily by having an extended forward fuselage, by accommodating a maximum crew of 10, and by the installation of Boulton-Paul power-operated turrets, each with four 0.303-in (7.7-mm) Browning machine-guns, in

The Dragon and his Tail was a B-24J, flying against the Japanese mainland from the island of Ie Shima with the 43rd BG. The aircraft is depicted as it appeared in spring 1945. It was one of the last Liberators to enter combat.

the dorsal and tail positions. The RAF received 139 of this version, and when Nos 159 and 160 Squadrons began operations with their Liberators in the Middle East in June 1942, they were the first to deploy these aircraft in the bombing role. One aircraft of this batch became the personal transport of the British prime minister, Winston Churchill, operated with the name *Commando*.

In the USA the XB-24 prototype had meanwhile been modified to XB-24B standard with self-sealing fuel tanks and armour, but the most significant improvement was the installation of R-1830-41 turbocharged engines. This resulted in flatter oval-shaped nacelles, due to the relocation of the oil coolers into the sides of the cowlings.

SPECIFICATION	
Consolidated B-24H/J Liberator **Type:** 10-crew long-range bomber and reconnaissance aircraft **Powerplant:** four Pratt & Whitney R-1830-65 Twin Wasp radial piston engines each rated at 1,200 hp (895 kW) **Performance:** maximum speed 290 mph (467 km/h) at 25,000 ft (7620 m); cruising speed 215 mph (346 km/h) at optimum altitude; climb to 20,000 ft (6095 m) in 25 minutes; service ceiling 28,000 ft (8535 m); range 2,100 miles (3380 km) **Weights:** empty 36,500 lb	(16556 kg); maximum take-off 71,200 lb (32296 kg) **Dimensions:** wingspan 110 ft (33.53 m); length 67 ft 2 in (20.47 m); height 18 ft (5.49 m); wing area 1,048.00 sq ft (97.36 m²) **Armament:** two 0.5-in (12.7-mm) Browning trainable machine-guns in each of the nose, dorsal, ventral 'ball' and tail turrets, and one 0.5-in (12.7-mm) Browning trainable lateral-firing machine-gun in each of the two beam positions, plus up to 12,800 lb (5806 kg) of bombs carried internally and externally

Consolidated Model 32 (B-24 Liberator) (continued)

The XB-24B also introduced dorsal and tail turrets, each armed with two 0.5-in (12.7-mm) Browning machine-guns to supplement the original fit of hand-held guns in the beam and nose positions – nine aircraft were produced for the USAAF with the designation **B-24C**. These were followed by the **B-24D**, the first major production variant (2,696 completed) and the first to be employed operationally by USAAF bomber squadrons. This differed initially by the installation of R-1830-43 engines, but subsequent production batches introduced progressive changes in armament, provision of auxiliary fuel in the outer wing panels and bomb bay, increases in gross weight and bombload and, in some late production examples, external bomb racks below the inner wing for the carriage of two 4,000-lb (1814-kg) bombs. In RAF service the B-24D was designated as the **Liberator Mk III**, while the designation **Liberator Mk IIIA** was used to identify similar aircraft supplied under Lend-Lease with US armament and equipment. Most Liberator Mk III/IIIA aircraft served with Coastal Command, eventually equipping 12 squadrons. Some 122 of the aircraft were modified extensively in the UK, receiving ASV radar equipment including chin and retractable ventral radomes, a Leigh Light and increased fuel capacity, but reduced armament, armour and weapons load. These aircraft received the designation **Liberator GR.Mk V**, and some of them were provided with small stub wings on the forward fuselage for the carriage of eight rocket projectiles.

The USAAF also operated the B-24D in the anti-submarine role, and in 1942 the USN began to receive small numbers of this version under the designation **PB4Y-1**. However, at the end of August 1943, the USAAF disbanded its Anti-Submarine Command, handing over its aircraft to the US Navy in exchange for an equivalent number of aircraft of bomber configuration to be produced against outstanding US Navy orders. These ex-USAAF B-24 aircraft, which were equipped with ASV radar, were also designated PB4Y-1.

The deployment of the USAAF's B-24D to the Middle East began in June 1942, one of the first operations being launched by 13 aircraft against the

Romanian oilfields at Ploesti on 11/12 June 1942. All 13 aircraft completed what the USAAF described as 'an unsuccessful attack', its only success being to alert this strategic target to its vulnerability. Consequently, it was a very different story on 1 August 1943 when units of the 8th and 9th Air Forces sent 177 B-24s against the same target. Although rather more successful in terms of damage caused, the raid was very costly for the Liberator force.

By that time, of course, the B-24 was being built at an enormous rate by an industrial team that comprised Consolidated, Douglas and Ford. In mid-1942 the first true transport variants began to appear, with nose and tail gun positions deleted, a large cargo door installed in the port side of the fuselage, and accommodation for passengers or cargo. The USAAF acquired 276 such aircraft under the designation **C-87** with a crew of five and up to 20 passengers; 24 similar aircraft, with side windows, served with RAF Transport Command as the **Liberator C.Mk VII**, and examples flown by the USN were designated **RY-2**. Similar aircraft, but with R-1830-45 engines and equipped as VIP transports, were identified as the **RY-1** and **C-87A** by the US Navy and USAAF respectively. The US Navy also acquired 46 of a transport variant designated **RY-3**, and 27 similar aircraft were delivered in early 1945 for use by RAF Transport Command. One special logistics version was the **C-109** fuel tanker, used to ferry 2,900 US gal (10978 litres) of aviation fuel per load over the Himalayan 'hump' into China to supply the B-29 Superfortress force operating from forward bases in that country.

An **XF-7** prototype for a reconnaissance version was also produced in 1943, with bomb racks removed and extra fuel tanks

provided in the forward section of the bomb bay. This retained the normal defensive armament, and could also accommodate up to 11 cameras. The **F-7** production derivative was used extensively in the Pacific theatre, and later versions included the **F-7A** and **F-7B** with different camera installations.

The first production model to come from Ford was the **B-24E**, which was generally similar to the B-24D except for different propellers and detail changes. This version was also built by Consolidated and Douglas, some with R-1830-65 engines; total production was 801 aircraft. There followed 430 examples of the **B-24G**, all but the first 25 of which had a nose turret in a lengthened forward fuselage. This model came from a new production line operated by North American. Similar aircraft produced by Consolidated, and also by Douglas and Ford, were designated **B-24H**, of which 3,100 were completed.

The major production variant was the **B-24J**, of which 6,678 were completed by the five production lines. This differed from the B-24H in only minor details. The B-24H and B-24J supplied

Liberator GR.Mk VIs in service with the RAF had all the features of the B-24J, including a gun turret in the upper nose. They also featured a retractable ventral ASV radome in the rear fuselage.

to the RAF under Lend-Lease were designated **Liberator GR.Mk VI** when equipped for ASW/maritime reconnaissance by Coastal Command, or **Liberator B.Mk VI** when used as a heavy bomber in the Middle and Far East. Those used by the USN were identified as PB4Y-1s. The final production versions were the **B-24L**, similar to the B-24D with the tail turret replaced by two manually controlled 0.5-in (12.7-mm) machine-guns, of which Consolidated built 417 and Ford 1,250; and the **B-24M** which differed from the B-24J in its type of tail turret. Convair, as Consolidated was often known from 1943 after its merger with Vultee, built 916 of this latter version at San Diego and Ford produced another 1,677. Odd variants included a single B-24D with an experimental thermal de-icing system for evaluation as the **XB-24F**; the **XB-24K** prototype of

the version with a single vertical tail surface which it was intended should be produced in large numbers as the **B-24N**, although only the **XB-24N** prototype and seven **YB-24N** service test aircraft were built before production ended on 31 May 1945; and the single **XB-41** experimental bomber escort armed with 14 0.5-in (12.7-mm) machine-guns and converted for flight engineer training under the designation **AT-22** (later **TB-24**). Most of the USAAF's Liberators were declared surplus at the war's end, the very last being retired in 1953.

From first to last 18,482 members of the Liberator family had been built. In addition to those supplied to the RAF, USAAF and USN, others had been operated by units of the RAAF, RCAF and SAAF. Nowhere had they been of greater value than in the Pacific theatre, where their long range and versatility made them true 'maids of all work'.

This early Liberator Mk III shows off the glazed nose of this variant. All bomber Liberators up to the earliest B-24Gs had this shorter forward fuselage and glazing.

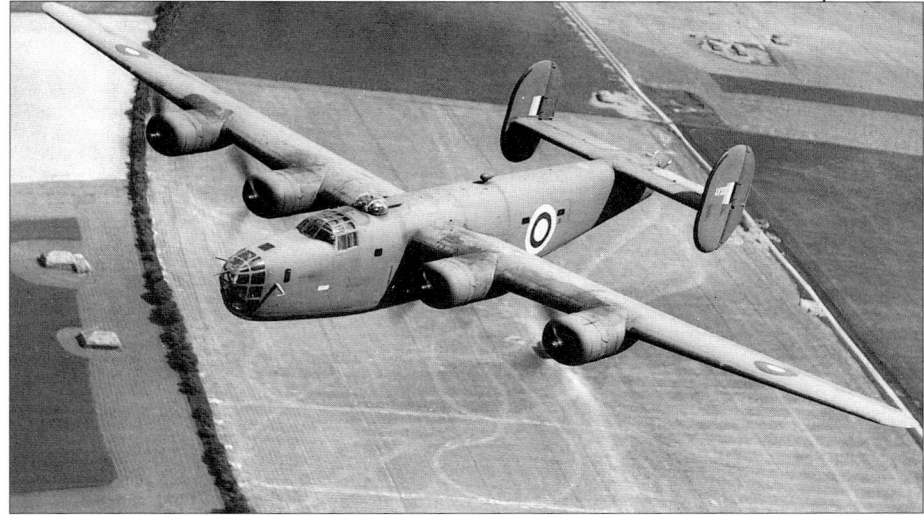

Consolidated Model 33 and Model 34 (B-32 Dominator)

For precisely the same requirement to which Boeing designed its B-29, Consolidated evolved a competing proposal as the **Model 33**. Each company was awarded a contract to build three prototypes, those from Consolidated being allocated the designation **XB-32**. The first prototype made its maiden flight on 7 September 1942, two weeks before the first XB-29, and the second and third prototypes followed on 2 July and 9 November 1943 respectively. Like the XB-29, the XB-32s featured pressurisation of the crew accommodation and remotely-controlled gun barbettes, but otherwise differed from each other in some fairly major aspects of their configurations: the first prototype had a rounded fuselage nose and

Hobo Queen II *was one of two B-32s jumped by 14 Japanese fighters during a photo-reconnaissance mission over Tokyo, probably on 18 August 1945. The action represented the last aerial combat of World War II and resulted in at least two Japanese fighters, and possibly four, being destroyed. One B-32 crewman in the second aircraft was killed and two wounded, but both aircraft returned safely to Okinawa.*

twin fin-and-rudder units based on those of the B-24, the second had a modified nose with a stepped windscreen for the flight deck, and the third retained this fuselage design, but introduced a large single fin-and-rudder unit. This last

was the layout finalised for **Model 34** production aircraft, ordered as the **B-32 Dominator**.

Somewhat smaller than the B-29, the B-32 was of cantilever high-wing monoplane configuration and powered by four Wright

R-3350 Duplex Cyclone radial engines of the same series as that used for the B-29. The landing gear was of the retractable tricycle type, and two cavernous bomb bays could carry 20,000 lb (9072 kg) of bombs. Consolidated experienced extensive problems in development of the B-32, to the extent that it was not possible to begin delivery of production examples until November 1944, almost eight months after B-29s had been deployed to forward bases in China.

Even then, production aircraft, of which 115 were built, had the intended pressurisation system and remotely controlled gun barbettes deleted. In the final analysis, only 15 of these aircraft became operational before VJ-Day, equipping the USAAF's 386th Bombardment Squadron based on Okinawa. Some 40 of a version designated **TB-32** were also produced for training purposes, but at the end of World War II both versions were soon withdrawn from service.

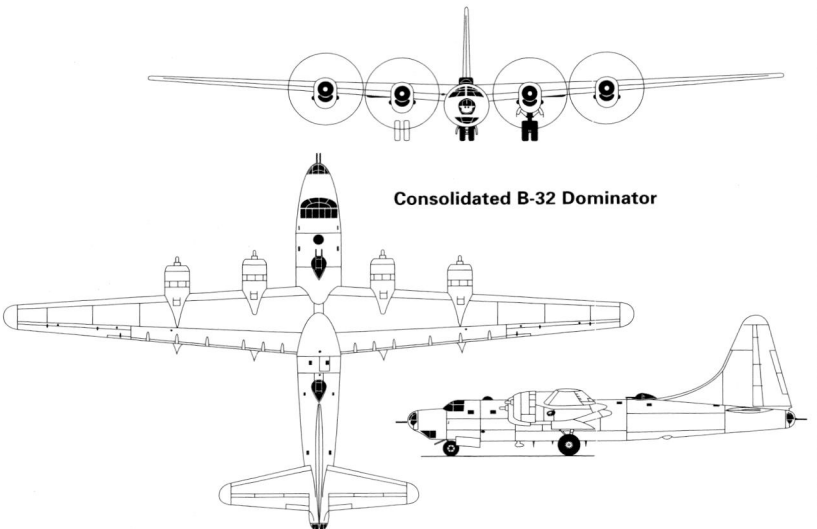

Consolidated B-32 Dominator

SPECIFICATION	
Consolidated Model 34 (B-32 Dominator)	**Weights:** empty 60,272 lb (27339 kg); maximum take-off 123,250 lb (55906 kg)
Type: eight-crew long-range strategic bomber	**Dimensions:** wingspan 135 ft (41.15 m); length 82 ft 1 in (25.02 m); height 32 ft 2 in (9.80 m); wing area 1,422.00 sq ft (132.10 m²)
Powerplant: four Wright R-3350-23A Duplex Cyclone radial piston engines each rated at 2,200 hp (1641 kW)	
Performance: maximum speed 357 mph (575 km/h) at 25,000 ft (7620 m); initial climb rate 1,050 ft (320 m) per minute; service ceiling 35,000 ft (10670 m); range 3,800 miles (6115 km)	**Armament:** two 0.5-in (12.7-mm) Browning trainable machine-guns in each of the nose, two dorsal, ventral and tail turrets, plus up to 20,000 lb (9072 kg) of bombs carried internally

Consolidated Model 39 Liberator-Liner (R2Y)

By 1943 many American aircraft manufacturers were considering how best to exploit their positions after the end of World War II, and in common with many others Consolidated felt that there would be a major boom in air transport. By 1943, therefore, the company had started to plan a pure transport based on the powerplant,

Restrictions were placed on the Model 39's operational capability by its wing carry-through structure, which divided the cabin into two sections.

wing and landing gear of the Model 32 and the single-fin tail unit under development for the Model 40, with a new circular-section fuselage.

The resulting **Model 39 Liberator-Liner** was a large shoulder-wing monoplane of light alloy construction with fabric-covered control surfaces and the powerplant of four 1,200-hp

(895-kW) R-1830-94 Twin Wasps. Consolidated built the fuselage of the prototype as a private venture and mated it with the tail unit of a PB4Y-2. It was at this stage that the USN placed a March 1944 order for 253 production aircraft to be delivered between August 1944 and March 1945 for service with the designation **R2Y-1**. Only one month later, however, the USN cancelled the order after inspecting a mock-up.

Consolidated then received permission from the USN to fly the prototype as the **XR2Y-1**, and this made the type's maiden flight on 15 April 1944. Consolidated then bought the first of the cancelled R2Y-1s and completed it as a second prototype with the powerplant of four R-1830-65

engines, with which it made its first flight in September 1944. The aircraft were used on a number of experimental services, but secured no production orders at a time when the market was flooded by less capable but also very considerably cheaper ex-military transport aircraft. They were scrapped late in 1945 after having flown their last missions as testbeds for

full-span flaps. In the later stages of their careers, the two aircraft were known within the company by the revised designation **Convair Model 104** in the sequence started by Vultee. This was a reflection of the shortened version of the Consolidated-Vultee name that had come into increasingly frequent use following the purchase of Reuben Fleet's holding in Consolidated by Vultee in December 1941 and then the full merger of the two companies in March 1943.

SPECIFICATION	
Consolidated Model 39 Liberator-Liner (XR2Y-1)	4,000 miles (6437 km)
Type: four-crew long-range medium transport	**Weights:** maximum take-off 64,000 lb (29030 kg)
Powerplant: four Pratt & Whitney R-1830-65 Twin Wasp radial piston engines each rated at 1,200 hp (895 kW)	**Dimensions:** wingspan 110 ft (33.53 m); length 90 ft (27.43 m); height 26 ft (7.925 m); wing area 1,048.00 sq ft (97.36 m²)
Performance: maximum cruising speed 202 mph (325 km/h) at optimum altitude; range	**Payload:** up to 48 day passengers, or 24 night passengers or 18,500 lb (8392 kg) of freight

Consolidated Model 40 (PB4Y Privateer), Model 101 (RY)

The B-24 was well suited for adaptation to the long-range maritime patrol bomber role, as shown by the PB4Y-1. Experience soon revealed that, while the aircraft were excellent machines in their new role, there was still considerable room for useful development in the purely naval tasking. This demanded the maximum possible endurance at medium and low altitudes, so the turbochargers fitted to the USAAF aircraft were superfluous to requirements and indeed so much dead weight and additional cost. In May 1943, therefore, Consolidated-Vultee received instructions to set aside three PB4Y-1s for conversion as **XP4Y-2** prototypes for the fully navalised patrol bomber that was initially known to the company as the **Model 40**, but later as the **Vultee Model 100**, and which received the initial name **Sea Liberator** that was later changed to **Privateer**. The major changes effected in the conversion were the replacement of the original tail unit by a revised empennage with a dihedralled tailplane and a single vertical surface of considerable height. The forward fuselage was lengthened and R-1830-94 radial engines fitted in modified nacelles. Revised armament was installed as single nose, single tail, two dorsal and two beam units.

The first of the prototypes made its maiden flight in September 1943, initially with the standard Liberator tail unit and powerplant; the second prototype was basically similar, while the third introduced the revised powerplant without turbochargers. All three aircraft were then modified with the revised tail unit in its first form with a comparatively short vertical surface that was replaced by the definitive surface before redelivery in February 1944. The potential of the modified type had already been confirmed, however, and in October 1943 the USN had placed an order for 660 **PB4Y-2** warplanes, with a contract for an additional 710 aircraft following one year later, for a planned total of 1,370 Privateers.

The first aircraft were completed in March 1944, but the end of World War II brought massive cancellations of all military equipment, and the last of 740 PB4Y-2s was delivered in October 1945. Deliveries to the US Navy began in June 1944, and the first two units to equip with the new type were VPB-118 and VPB-119, which received their aircraft in August of the same year. The first of these squadrons left for operational service from a base in the Marianas Islands in January 1945, and by the end of World War II 13 squadrons were fully

This PB4Y-2 Privateer shows the type's Liberator ancestry. The USN used its PB4Ys on patrol duties and also as Elint platforms, in which role one became the first Cold War shoot-down victim.

equipped with the Privateer, while another five operated a mix of Liberators and Privateers. The Privateer remained in service after World War II, the last aircraft being retired from first-line service only in 1954, their designation having been changed in 1951 to P4Y-2 Privateer. Some of the aircraft were transferred to the Chinese Nationalist air force, a few of them remaining operational into the 1960s, and three aircraft operated by the Honduran air force in the transport role were retired only in the early 1970s.

The designation **PB4Y-2B** was applied to at least 19 aircraft, adapted with underwing provision for two examples of the ASM-N-2 Bat anti-ship glide bomb, which weighed 1,880 lb (853 kg) and used radar guidance. The only use of this sophisticated weapon in World War II occurred in April 1945, when two such bombs were launched against Japanese shipping in the harbour of Balikpapan in Borneo. In 1951 the PB4Y-2B aircraft received the revised designation **P4Y-2B Privateer**. The designation **PB4Y-2G** was applied to nine aircraft transferred to the USCG for use in the search and rescue role, and the designation **PB4Y-2K** was used for aircraft modified as target drones, the surviving aircraft receiving the revised designation **P4Y-2K** in 1951 and

QP-4B in 1962. The **PB4Y-2M** aircraft were modifications for the meteorological research role, with the nose transparency of the B-24D, and in 1951 the surviving aircraft received the revised designation **P4Y-2M**. The **PB4Y-2P** machines were aircraft modified for the photo-reconnaissance role and in 1951 the designation was altered to **P4Y-2P**. Other aircraft were modified with special electronic equipment as Elint aircraft.

PB4Y-2S was the designation applied to PB4Y-2 aircraft adapted for the anti-submarine role, with radar designed to locate the periscopes and/or snorkels of such boats as they cruised just below the surface. In 1951 the surviving aircraft received the revised designation **P4Y-2S**. Some 10 of the aircraft were supplied to the French naval air arm from November 1950. These aircraft were allocated to Flottille 8F (later redesignated as Flottille 28F) for use from Tan Son Nhut in French Indo-China in the bomber role. The type suffered losses in operations against communist insurgents, and an additional 14 aircraft were later supplied. Flottille 28F and

the later Flottille 24F were transferred to Karouba in Tunisia after the French loss of Indo-China, and saw further action in the war of Algerian Independence (1954-62) and the Suez campaign (1956). The last French aircraft were scrapped in 1961, with the advent of the Lockheed P2V in French service.

Known to the parent company as the **Model 101**, the **RY-3** was the transport version of the Privateer, with a revised and further lengthened fuselage and providing accommodation for a crew of four plus 28 passengers or 25,641 lb (11631 kg) of freight supplemented by 1,600 lb (726 kg) of additional freight in a hinged nose section. The USN ordered 112 examples of this transport in March 1944, but only 34 were completed. Of these, one was retained by Convair, seven went to the USMC, and the other 26 were delivered from February 1945 to the RAF for service with the designation **Liberator C.Mk IX**. The RAF lost three aircraft in fatal crashes; doubts about the structural integrity of the type led to all surviving aircraft being grounded in April 1946.

SPECIFICATION	
Consolidated Model 40 (PB4Y-2 Privateer) **Type:** 11-crew maritime patrol bomber **Powerplant:** four Pratt & Whitney R-1830-94 Twin Wasp radial piston engines each rated at 1,350 hp (1007 kW) **Performance:** maximum speed 249 mph (400 km/h) at 12,000 ft (3660 m); cruising speed 158 mph (254 km/h) at optimum altitude; initial climb rate 1,180 ft (360 m) per minute; service ceiling 18,300 ft (5580 m); range 2,900 miles (4667 km) on a patrol mission or 2,630 miles (4233 km) with a bomb load of 4,000 lb	(1814 kg) **Weights:** empty 39,400 lb (17872 kg); maximum take-off 65,000 lb (29484 kg) **Dimensions:** wingspan 110 ft (33.53 m); length 74 ft 7 in (22.73 m); height 29 ft 1½ in (8.88 m); wing area 1,048.00 sq ft (97.36 m²) **Armament:** two 0.5-in (12.7-mm) Browning trainable machine-guns in each of the one nose, two dorsal, one tail and two beam turrets, plus up to 8,000 lb (3629 kg) of disposable stores carried in a lower-fuselage weapons bay

Consolidated TBY Sea Wolf

In April 1940 the Vought company received a USN contract for the prototype

of a three-seat torpedo-bomber. Designated XTBU-1, this was a mid-

wing cantilever monoplane with tailwheel landing gear, the powerplant of one Pratt & Whitney R-2800-22 radial engine, and a crew of three seated in tandem beneath a long 'greenhouse' canopy. Weapons were to be carried in a lower-fuselage weapons bay or on

Sea Wolf production was terminated after only 180 aircraft had been completed.

SPECIFICATION	
Consolidated TBY-2 Sea Wolf **Type:** three-seat carrierborne and land-based torpedo bomber **Powerplant:** one Pratt & Whitney R-2800-22 Double Wasp radial piston engine rated at 2,000 hp (1491 kW) **Performance:** maximum speed 312 mph (502 km/h) at 17,700 ft (5395 m); cruising speed 156 mph (251 km/h) at optimum altitude; initial climb rate 1,770 ft (539 m) per minute; service ceiling 29,400 ft (8960 m); range 1,025 miles (1650 km) with one torpedo **Weights:** empty 11,336 lb	(5142 kg); maximum take-off 18,940 lb (8591 kg) **Dimensions:** wingspan 56 ft 11 in (17.35 m); length 39 ft 2 in (11.94 m); height 15 ft 6 in (4.72 m); wing area 440.00 sq ft (40.88 m²) **Armament:** three 0.5-in (12.7-mm) Browning fixed forward-firing machine-guns, one 0.5-in (12.7-mm) trainable rearward-firing machine-gun in the dorsal turret and one 0.3-in (7.62-mm) Browning trainable rearward-firing machine-gun in the ventral position, plus up to 1,600 lb (726 kg) of disposable stores

two underwing hardpoints. Successful testing led to the US Navy decision for production of this type, but as Vought currently lacked

adequate production capacity, it was arranged instead that the type should be built by Consolidated.

Accordingly, a contract

for 1,100 examples of the **TBY-2** was placed with Consolidated in September 1943, the type soon gaining the name **Sea Wolf**. The

TBY-2 differed from the originally planned **TBY-1**, of which none was built, by having a radar pod mounted beneath the star-

board wing. Some 600 of an improved **TBY-3** version had been ordered by this time, but the order was cancelled.

Continental Copters El Tomcat

During 1959 Continental Copters Inc. of Fort Worth, Texas decided to design and develop a lightweight agricultural helicopter on the basis of the well-proved and readily available Bell Model 47G-2. The most important change in the design was a new forward fuselage to provide single-seat accommodation in an angular sealed enclosure, providing excellent fields of vision in the forward hemisphere. The resulting **El Tomcat Mk II** prototype first flew

in April 1959 with the 200-hp (149-kW) Lycoming VO-435-A1B engine.

There followed in April 1965 the first example of the improved **El Tomcat Mk III** that entered limited production, and the family later came to include a number of steadily improved subvariants. The **El Tomcat Mk IIIA** that first flew in January 1965 had a lower windscreen, two landing lights and one Franklin 6V flat-six engine in its 6V4-200-C32, 6V-335-A or 6V-350-A forms, rated

at 200, 210 and 235 hp (149, 157 and 175 kW) respectively. First flown in 1967 and generally powered by the 6V-350 engine, the **El Tomcat Mk IIIB** had a repositioned and further reduced windscreen, a modified glassfibre nose, a lower cockpit roof and a revised control system. First flown in May 1968 and possessing the same engine options as the Mk IIIA, the **El Tomcat Mk IIIC** was an improved Mk IIIB with a more refined nose profile, wraparound cabin side windows for improved rearward fields of vision, and an enhanced refuelling capability.

The **El Tomcat Mk V**, first flown in June 1968, had the 220-hp (164-kW) Lycoming VO-435 engine and paved the way for the last two subvariants, the **El Tomcat Mk V-A** and the **El Tomcat Mk V-B**. The first of these intro-

The El Tomcat Mk VI-B was photographed during certification flight trials. The aircraft was clearly based on the Bell 47, but its single-seat accommodation possibly restricted sales.

duced a large number of improvements including a fold-away jump seat, an improved ventilation system to minimise the ingress of toxic sprays and dry chemicals, and streamlined blister tanks alongside the sides of the

fuselage. The latter was basically an uprated version of the Mk V-A with the 265-hp (198-kW) VO-435-B1A engine.

In addition, the company also produced the **El Tomcat Mk VI-B** as a variant of the Bell 47-G5.

SPECIFICATION	
Continental Copters El Tomcat Mk V-A	(383 km)
Type: single-seat agricultural helicopter	**Weights:** empty 1,375 lb (623 kg) without specialist equipment; maximum take-off 2,450 lb (1111 kg)
Powerplant: one Lycoming VO-435-A1F flat-six piston engine 260 hp (194 kW)	**Dimensions:** main rotor diameter 37 ft 1½ in (11.32 m); length 31 ft 7 in (9.63 m) for fuselage; height 9 ft 5 in (2.87 m); main rotor disc area 1,082.49 sq ft (100.56 m²)
Performance: maximum speed 100 mph (161 km/h) at sea level; hovering ceiling 10,850 ft (3310 m) in ground effect; range 238 miles	

Convair CV-240 Convair-Liner, CV-340 and CV-440 (C-131 Samaritan, R4Y and T-29)

The creation of an effective DC-3 replacement fascinated aircraft manufacturers from the end of World War II until well into the 1980s. Consolidated Vultee, or Convair, hoped to gain success in this market and in 1954 became the Convair Division of the General Dynamics Corporation. It was this division which then provided continuing product support for the Convair piston-engined airliner series and its derivatives.

Although it achieved significant sales, the CV-240 could not match the success of the DC-3. This aircraft flew South American routes for Pan Am.

In 1945 American Airlines issued the specification for an airliner to replace the DC-3. In due course this led to the construction of the abortive **Model 110** 30-passenger prototype, which flew for the first time on 8 July 1946. Before this date, however, American Airlines had already decided that greater capacity and a pressurised cabin were necessary, and this led to the development of the **Model 240**, known later as the **Convair-Liner**. No

prototype was built as such, all the aircraft being completed to production standard, and the first of these machines made its maiden flight on 16 March 1947. While retaining the same powerplant of two 2,100-hp (1566-kW) R-2800-S1C3G radial engines and overall configuration as the Model 110, the new aircraft introduced a lengthened fuselage to allow standard accommodation of 40 passengers. The Model 240, generally known as the **CV-240**, entered service with American Airlines on 1 June 1948 and, of the total of 566 aircraft, 176 were delivered to civil operators and the other 390 to military operators.

To meet its requirement for a large 'flying classroom' type of trainer for the instruction of navigators and radar operators, the USAF ordered two **XAT-29** prototypes, these being based on the Model 240. The first XAT-29 made its initial flight on 22 September 1949 and, following successful evaluation by the USAF, a first production contract was placed for the **T-29A**, of which 46 were built. The T-29A had positions for

student navigators and four astrodomes in the upper fuselage, the **T-29B** was pressurised and provided for the simultaneous training of 10 navigators and four radar operators, and the **T-29C** was similar to the T-29B except for its more powerful engines. The **T-29D** was an advanced navigation/bombing trainer, with the 'K' system bomb sight and camera scoring equipment.

Development of an improved civil version, known as the **Model 340** (otherwise **CV-340**), was initiated in early 1951. It differed from the CV-240 in its powerplant of two 2,500-hp (1864-kW) R-2800-CB16 or -CB17 engines of 2,500 hp

(1864 kW), a wing of greater area to offset the higher operating weights of this model, and a further 'stretch' of the fuselage to increase standard accommodation to 44 passengers. The first example of this version made its maiden flight on 5 October 1951, and the initial delivery, to United Air Lines, was made on 28 March 1952. Production of the CV-340 for civil and military service totalled 311 aircraft.

Further refinement of the basic design led to the generally similar **Model 440** (**CV-440**), which incorporated aerodynamic and comfort improvements plus a high-density seating arrangement to accommodate a maximum of 52 passengers.

SPECIFICATION	
Convair CV-440	24,900 ft (7590 m); range 470 miles
Type: two/three-crew medium-range transport	(756 km) with maximum payload
Powerplant: two Pratt & Whitney R-2800-CB16 or -CB17 Double Wasp radial piston engines each rated at 2,500 hp (1864 kW)	**Weights:** empty 33,314 lb (15111 kg); maximum take-off 49,000 lb (22226 kg)
Performance: maximum speed 337 mph (542v km/h) at optimum altitude; cruising speed 299 mph (481 km/h) at 13,000 ft (3960 m); initial climb rate 1,260 ft (384 m) per minute; service ceiling	**Dimensions:** wingspan 105 ft 4 in (32.11 m); length 79 ft 2 in (24.13 m) or, with weather radar, 81 ft 6 in (24.84 m); height 28 ft 2 in (8.59 m); wing area 920.00 sq ft (85.47 m²)
	Payload: up to 52 passengers

Convair CV-240 Convair-Liner, CV-340 and CV-440 (C-131 Samaritan, R4Y and T-29) (continued)

The first CV-440 was produced by the conversion of a CV-340, and took to the air for its maiden flight on 6 October 1955. Production of the CV-440 for the civil market totalled 155 aircraft.

The first of the USAF's transport variants was the **C-131A Samaritan** for casualty evacuation. Based on the CV-240, this had large loading doors for litters or cargo, and was equipped to accommodate 27 litters or 37 sitting casualties.

Based on the CV-440, the R4Y-1 was the US Navy's basic transport version of the Convair piston-twin series. The Navy also operated a small number of T-29B aircraft transferred from the USAF.

The 26 examples of the C-131A were followed by 36 **C-131B** transport/electronic testbed aircraft; 33 **C-131D/VC-131D** transports, of which 27 and six were to CV-340 and CV-440 standards respectively; and finally 15 **C-131E** ECM trainers delivered during 1955-7. The **RC-131F** designation was applied to photo-survey conversions of **C-131E** aircraft, and the single similarly-derived **RC-131G** was equipped to check navigational aids. Two aircraft re-engined with turboprop engines to provide handling experience with this type of powerplant, and four similarly modified C-131D machines, were used as VIP transports under the designation **VC-131H**.

The US Navy received 36 **R4Y-1** (**C-131F**) cargo, personnel and evacuation transports, a single **R4Y-1Z** (**VC-131F**) VIP transport, and two **R4Y-2** (**C-131G**)

The T-29A (illustrated) differed from the CV-240 in being unpressurised. Otherwise, most of the T-29s procured for the USAF and the USN were generally similar, except for interior changes.

transport versions of the CV-440. The Canadian Armed Forces received eight aircraft similar to the USAF's VC-131H, designating them **CC-109**.

Metropolitan. A number of ex-civil CV-440 aircraft also entered service with the Bolivian, Italian, Spanish and West German air forces.

Convair CV-540, CV-580, CV-600 and CV-640

The development of turboprop engines offered an ideal opportunity for the replacement of large and complex air-cooled radial piston engines. The robust, well-designed structures of the Convair-Liner series allowed these aircraft to accept the considerably more powerful turboprop engines without undue airframe stress, the result being a new lease of life for the series.

The first such conversions came in 1954, when D. Napier & Sons in the UK installed two of its 3,060-ehp (2282-ekW) Eland NEl.1 turboprop engines in a CV-340, and this conversion flew for the first time on 9 February 1955. This, and five similar aircraft, entered service with Allegheny Airlines in America under the designation **CV-540**. Canadair converted three CV-440s to Eland power with the designation **Canadair 540**, and later built 10 new aircraft with this power-

plant for service with the RCAF under the designation **CL-66 Cosmopolitan**. All the aircraft were later re-engined with Allison 501 turboprops.

In the USA, PacAero Engineering Corporation of Santa Monica, California, initiated a conversion programme for CV-340s and CV-440s. This involved the installation of 3,750-shp (2796-kW) Allison 501-D13 turboprop engines, and provision of greater area for the control surfaces on the tail unit. Designated **CV-580**, and known sometimes as the **Super Convair**, the type had accommodation for 52 passengers, as CV-340 conversions included the installation of the additional eight seats of the CV-440's high-density arrangement. PacAero's first CV-580, of which 164 were created, made an initial flight on 19 January 1960, but it was not until June 1964 that the type began to enter airline service, with Frontier

Airlines the first operator.

The last of these first-generation conversion programmes was that initiated by Convair, which selected the 3,025-ehp (2256-ekW) Rolls-Royce RDa.10/1 Dart Mk 542 turboprop engine for installation in CV-240/340/440 aircraft. In addition to the provision of the revised powerplant, the programme also involved structural strengthening and the option of a 48-seat interior arrangement for the CV-240 conversions, and the option of a 56-seat interior arrangement for the CV-340 and CV-440 conversions. In their new form, these aircraft were designated **CV-240D**, **CV-340D** and **CV-440D**, this being changed later to **CV-600** for

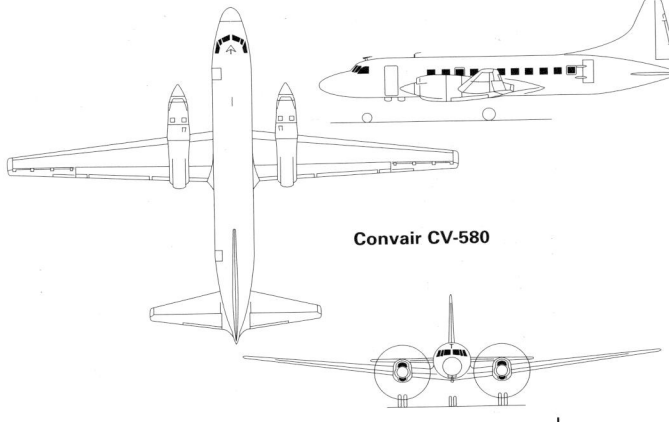

Convair CV-580

When development and production of the Eland came to an end in 1962, the five original Eland conversions reverted to the original type of piston-engined powerplant. One of the five is illustrated with Eland engines.

SPECIFICATION

Convair CV-580
Type: two-crew medium-range transport
Powerplant: two Allison 501-D13H turboprop engines each rated at 3,750 shp (2796 kW)
Performance: cruising speed 342 mph (550 km/h) at 20,000 ft (6095 m); initial climb rate more than 2,200 ft (671 m) per minute; range 2,268 miles (3651 km) with a 5,000-lb (2268-kg) payload

Weights: empty 30,275 lb (13733 kg); maximum take-off 58,140 lb (26372 kg)
Dimensions: wingspan 105 ft 4 in (32.11 m); length 81 ft 6 in (24.84 m); height 29 ft 2 in (8.89 m); wing area 920.00 sq ft (85.47 m²)
Payload: up to 52 passengers within the context of a maximum payload of 8,870 lb (4023 kg)

the CV-240D and **CV-640** for the other two. The first of 38 CV-600 conversions entered service with Central Airlines on 30 November 1965, and the first of 27 CV-640 conversions entered service with Caribair on 22 December 1965.

Kelowna Flightcraft of Canada has developed a stretched version of the CV-580, but available as a retrofit package for any member of the Convair-Liner series, as the **Kelowna CV5800**. This has a lengthened fuselage and a large port-side rear cargo door, a refurbished airframe extending the life to 100,000 hours, and modern Honeywell avionics including an autopilot, four-tube EFIS and weather radar as well as upgraded communications.

In mid-1999 there were still 126 examples of the CV-580 in service, together with 25 examples of the CV-600 and CV-640, most of them with operators in North and South America.

Convair Model 2 (F2Y Sea Dart)

By early 1948 two separate research programmes, namely those for the Convair blended hull/wing and the NACA hydro-ski concept, were beginning to offer such promise that a supersonic fighter seaplane seemed feasible to the USN's Bureau of Aeronautics. The resulting specification was issued in October 1948, and demanded among other things the ability to operate in waves up to 5 ft (1.52 m) high and a maximum air speed in the order of Mach 0.95. Two designs were submitted, one of them coming from the NACA and embodying the hydro-ski concept, and the other emanating from Convair and employing the blended hull/wing concept. Evaluation of the competing designs suggested that the Convair concept offered better climb rate and higher performance,

and given the fact that there was little hard data on the capabilities of the hydro-ski in high-speed take-off and landing operations, the design and development contract went to Convair. In January 1951, the company received a US Navy contract for two **Y2-2** prototypes based on its **Convair Model 2** design. The Y2-2 was based aerodynamically on the delta-winged F-102 Delta Dagger, but embodied two hydro-skis and was planned with a powerplant of two Westinghouse XJ46-WE-2 afterburning turbojet engines for an estimated maximum speed of Mach 1.5 and a maximum rate of climb at sea level of 30,000 ft (9145 m) per minute. Pending availability of the J46, the aircraft were to be completed with a lower-rated powerplant of two J34-WE-32 turbojets, and in August 1951 the

Y2-2 became the **XF2Y-1**.

The first XF2Y-1 was completed toward the end of 1952 and began taxiing trials during mid-December. The prototype encountered severe vibration and airframe pounding at waterborne speeds as low as 69 mph (111 km/h) as a result of the hydro-skis' blunt after ends, but the machine made an inadvertent hop of about 1,000 ft (305 m) in mid-January 1953. Considerable development of the hydro-skis and their extending mechanisms had to be undertaken before an official first flight was recorded in April 1953. The designed powerplant of two XJ46 turbojet engines was installed later in 1953, but these units failed to deliver their anticipated thrust. It rapidly became clear that, without a major redesign to incorporate the area-rule principle as a means of overcoming transonic drag, which was higher than anticipated, the XF2Y-1 would be incapable of exceeding Mach 1. Convair proposed such an area-ruled development as the **XF2Y-2** with a single hydro-ski and a powerplant of one Wright J67 turbojet engine rated at 12,000 lb st (53.38 kN) with afterburning or one Pratt & Whitney J75 turbojet engine rated at 15,000 lb st (66.72 kN) with afterburning. The need for a redesign of such magnitude persuaded the USN to question the whole programme, however, and

Finished in a flamboyant colour scheme, a YF2Y-1 machine taxies on its hydro-skis. The aircraft proved a technical failure, but it is difficult to imagine a combat scenario in which its unique capabilities would have been useful.

in October 1953 the BuAer ordered the completion of the second XF2Y-1 prototype to **YF2Y-1** standard.

As construction of the two XF2Y-1 prototypes was proceeding, in August 1952 the USN ordered 12 examples of the planned production model, the **F2Y-1**, with a fixed forward-firing armament of four 20-mm cannon together with an unrevealed number of 2.75-in (70-mm) FFAR unguided rockets. The contract was later amended to cover four YF2Y-1 pre-production and eight F2Y-1 production machines, and further change finally resulted in an order for 22 machines before the F2Y-1 programme was cancelled in March 1954. This left the USN with an eventual five flying-boats (one XF2Y-1, one XF2Y-1 completed to YF2Y-1 standard, and three YF2Y-1s built as such) as vehicles for aerodynamic testing

and high-speed research. The first YF2Y-1 was completed in the spring of 1954, and in August of the same year became the first (and to date the only) flying-boat to exceed Mach 1, an event that took place in a shallow dive. Considerable progress was made with the refinement of the hydro-ski arrangement, and the US Navy decided to reconsider its evaluation of the type. During a public demonstration flight in November 1954, however, the first YF2Y-1 broke up in the air as a result of structural failure following fatal pilot-induced pitch oscillation, and this effectively ended hopes for a production **Sea Dart** order. The other three YF2Y-1s were completed: two of these never flew and the other machine completed trials with single- and twin-ski arrangements before the Sea Dart research programme closed in 1957.

SPECIFICATION	
Convair Model 2 (XF2Y-1 Sea Dart)	
Type: single-seat experimental aircraft used as a fighter flying-boat prototype	Mach 1.5 at 35,000 ft (10670 m); initial climb rate 32,700 ft (9967 m) per minute; service ceiling 54,800 ft (16705 m); range 513 miles (826 km)
Powerplant: two Westinghouse J34-WE-32 turbojet engines each rated at 3,400 lb st (15.12 kN), later replaced by two Westinghouse XJ46-WE-2 turbojet engines each rated at 4,080 lb st (18.15 kN) dry and 6,100 lb st (27.13 kN) with afterburning but in fact delivering only 5,750 lb st (25.58 kN) with afterburning	**Weights:** empty 12,652 lb (5739 kg) with J34 engines; maximum take-off 16,527 lb (7497 kg) with J34 engines or 22,000 lb (9979 kg) with J46 engines
Performance: (estimated with fully-rated engines) maximum speed 994 mph (1600 km/h) or	**Dimensions:** wingspan 33 ft 8 in (10.26 m); length 52 ft 7 in (16.03 m); height 16 ft 2 in (4.93 m) with the hydro-skis retracted or 20 ft 9 in (6.32 m) with the hydro-skis extended; wing area 563.00 sq ft (52.30 m²)

Convair Model 3 (R3Y Tradewind)

Shortly after the establishment of Consolidated Vultee in 1948, the US Navy expressed interest in a new long-range multi-role flying-boat, and the company's proposal for its **Convair Model 3**, powered by four turboprop engines,

received a contract for two prototypes, awarded on 27 May 1946. Designated **XP5Y-1**, the new flying-boat featured an unusually slim fuselage for an aircraft of this class with a length:beam ratio of 10:1. It was powered by four

Allison T40-A-4 turboprop engines, each driving an arrangement of two contra-rotating propellers through a common gearbox. The type's main role was anti-submarine warfare, and it was to have been fitted with advanced radar, ECM and MAD equipment in addition to carrying a heavy load of bombs, mines, rockets and torpedoes. The first 'boat was flown from San Diego on 18 April 1950, and in August the type set a turboprop endurance

record of 8 hours 6 minutes. August was an eventful month for the XP5Y-1 as the USN decided to discontinue its development for the maritime patrol task, but to persevere with the basic design for use as a passenger and cargo aircraft.

SPECIFICATION	
Convair Model 3 (R3Y-1)	
Type: five-crew heavy transport flying-boat	2,785 miles (4482 km) with typical payload
Powerplant: four Allison T40-A-10 turboprop engines each rated at 5,850 shp (4362 kW)	**Weights:** empty 71,824 lb (32579 kg); maximum take-off 140,374 lb (63674 kg)
Performance: maximum speed 388 mph (624 km/h) at 30,000 ft (9145 m); cruising speed 300 mph (483 km/h) at optimum altitude; initial climb rate 3,310 ft (1009 m) per minute; service ceiling 39,700 ft (12100 m); range	**Dimensions:** wingspan 145 ft 9 in (44.42 m); length 139 ft 8 in (42.57 m); height 44 ft 10 in (13.67 m); wing area 2,102.00 sq ft (195.27 m²)
	Payload: up to 103 troops, or 92 litters plus 10 attendants, or 48,000 lb (21773 kg) of freight

In its R3Y-2 version, the Tradewind featured an upward-hinging nose for the rapid unloading of troops and equipment.

Convair Model 3 (R3Y Tradewind) (continued)

Work continued, despite the loss of an XP5Y-1 in a non-fatal crash off San Diego on 15 July 1953, and the first **R3Y-1 Tradewind** flew on 25 February 1955. Major changes included the deletion of all armament and of tailplane dihedral, the addition of a port-side cargo hatch aft of the wing, and the provision of redesigned engine nacelles to accept improved T40-A-10 engines.

The R3Y-1's performance was demonstrated on 24 February 1955 when one of the only five 'boats built flew coast-to-coast across the USA at an average speed of 403 mph (649 km/h) on delivery to the Navy Test Center at Patuxent River, Maryland. Similarly, on 18 October, a record flight of 6 hours 45 minutes at an average speed of 360 mph (579 km/h) was accomplished between Honolulu and Naval Air Station Alameda, California. The US Navy's VR-2 transport squadron received the first of its mixed fleet of R3Y-1 and **R3Y-2** 'boats on 31 March 1956, but financial considerations and continuing problems with the engine/propeller combination, culminating in two in-flight separations of propellers and the gearbox from an engine (on 10 May 1957 and 2 January 1958), led to a curtailment of Tradewind operations. Squadron strength was first cut to two R3Y-1 and two R3Y-2 'boats, and the unit was finally disbanded on 16 April 1958.

In R3Y-1 form, the Tradewind loaded cargo via a large side door. Technical problems and over-complexity plagued the type, limiting its use in service.

Variant

R3Y-2: six examples of this assault transport version of the R3Y-1 were built, featuring a hinged nose section which opened upward to provide an exit through which men and equipment could be landed directly onto the beach using the aircraft's built-in ramp; the R3Y-2 made its first flight on 22 December 1954 and in September 1956 one example, equipped as a tanker, made inflight-refuelling history by the simultaneous replenishment of four F9F-8 Cougars

Convair Model 4 (B-58 Hustler)

In March 1949 the USAF's Air Research and Development Command (ARDC) invited proposals for a supersonic strategic medium bomber. After the original submissions had been reduced to two, in the form of those from Boeing and Consolidated Vultee, the latter was selected in August 1952 to develop its **Model 4** design to the hardware stage under contract MX-1964. On 10 December 1952 the designation **B-58** was allocated and late in that year Convair received a contract for 18 aircraft, to be powered by the new J79 axial-flow turbojet engine, for which General Electric received a development contract at the same time. The performance requirement for the new aircraft demanded considerable advances in terms of aerodynamic, structural and materials thinking. The resulting machine, one of the first to incorporate the NACA/Whitcomb-developed area-rule concept, was a delta-winged aircraft with four engines in underslung pods, a slim fuselage and, perhaps its most novel feature, a 62-ft (18.90-m) long jettisonable underfuselage pod to carry the nuclear weapon and the fuel for the outward leg of any mission. The three-man crew, in individual tandem cockpits, were provided with jettisonable escape capsules.

In June 1954 the 18-aircraft order was reduced to two **XB-58** prototypes and 11 **YB-58A** service test examples, together with 31 pods. The first of the aircraft was rolled out on 31 August 1956 and made its first flight on 11 November of the same year. On 30 December, still without a pod, the XB-58 became the first bomber to exceed Mach 1. A further 17 YB-58A service test aircraft were ordered on 14 February 1958, together with 35 MB-1 bomb pods, to bring to 30 the number of aircraft available for the manufacturer's test programme and ARDC service trials with the 6592nd Test Squadron and the 3958th Operational Evaluation and Training Squadron at Carswell AFB.

Some 86 production **B-58A Hustler** bombers were ordered between September 1958 and 1960. This figure was supplemented by 10 YB-58A service test aircraft brought up to production standard to equip the 43rd BW, which activated as the first B-58 unit on 15 March 1960 and became operational on 1 August 1960. The 116th and last B-58A was delivered on 26 October 1962 and the type was withdrawn from SAC service on 31 January 1970.

SPECIFICATION

Convair Model 4 (B-58A Hustler)

Type: three-seat supersonic strategic medium-bomber
Powerplant: four General Electric J79-GE-5A turbojet engines each rated at 15,600 lb (69.39 kN) with afterburning
Performance: maximum speed 1,385 mph (2229 km/h) or Mach 2.1 at 40,000 ft (12190 m); cruising speed 611 mph (983 km/h) at 38,450 ft (11720 m); initial climb rate 17,830 ft (5435 m) per minute; service ceiling 63,400 ft (19235 m); radius 1,750 miles (2816 km) without inflight refuelling
Weights: empty 55,560 lb (25202 kg); maximum take-off 176,890 lb (802237 kg)
Dimensions: wingspan 56 ft 10 in (17.32 m); length 96 ft 9 in (29.49 m); height 31 ft 5 in (9.58 m); wing area 1,542.00 sq ft (143.25 m²)
Armament: one 20-mm T171 Vulcan trainable rearward-firing six-barrel rotary cannon in a radar-aimed tail barbette, plus up to 19,450 lb (8823 kg) of disposable nuclear or conventional bombs carried in disposable underfuselage pod

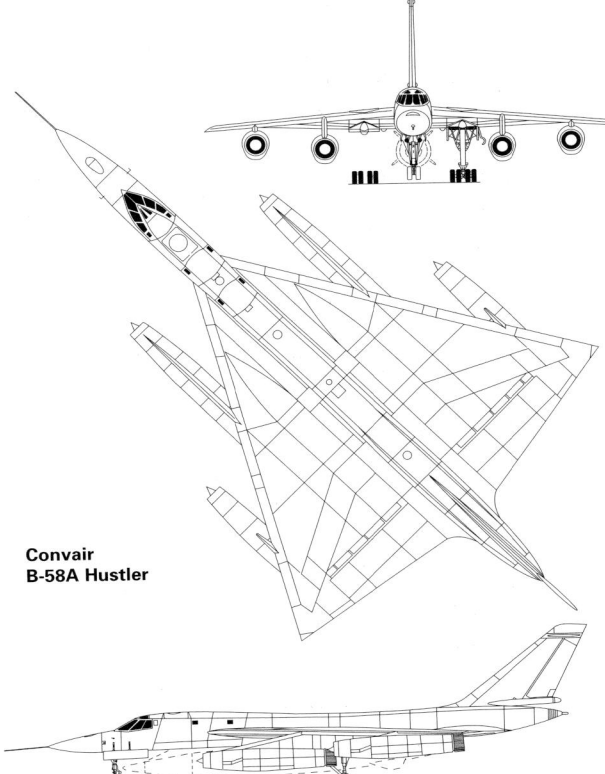

Convair B-58A Hustler

The unusual configuration of the B-58, with its delta wing and four underslung jet pods, is well illustrated in this view.

Variants

TB-58A Hustler: eight aircraft converted from the pre-production YB-58A standard for pilot conversion duties, with dual controls, a raised seat in the second cockpit and extended glazing to provide forward vision for the instructor; the inflight-refuelling equipment was retained but the ASQ-42V nav/attack, ECM and defence systems were removed; the first TB-58A flew on 10 May 1960 and was delivered on 13 August of the same year
NB-58A Hustler: one aircraft converted as a test vehicle for the General Electric J93 engine, intended for the North American B-70 Valkyrie and carried in a nacelle beneath the fuselage

Convair Model 5 (FY)

Contemporary with the Lockheed XFV-1, the **XFY-1** prototype was designed as the **Convair Model 5** for the same USN competition. This was intended to investigate the potential of a small single-seat tail-sitting VTOL fighter for operation from and to small platforms on a variety of ships. The fuselage served to accommodate the pilot's cockpit, and turboprop powerplant driving a contra-rotating propeller arrangement to obviate torque-reaction problems as well as to allow the generation of maximum forward thrust, and also carried the flying surfaces. The latter included a monoplane wing of modified delta planform and a large cruciform arrangement of tail surfaces. On the ground the XFY-1 rested on small castoring wheels at the tips of the horizontal and vertical tail surfaces.

Extensive tethered tests from a special rig were followed by a first vertical take-off and landing on 1 August 1954. Testing continued with a series of similar vertical flights before the first complete transition from vertical to horizontal flight and vice versa was accomplished on 2 November 1954. Although some 40 flight hours were accumulated by this experimental fighter, its development was abandoned as a result of major flight-control problems and the realisation of the type of problems the tail-sitter aircraft would encounter in carrier operations.

An interesting design concept, the tailsitting VTOL fighter possessed insurmountable operational drawbacks.

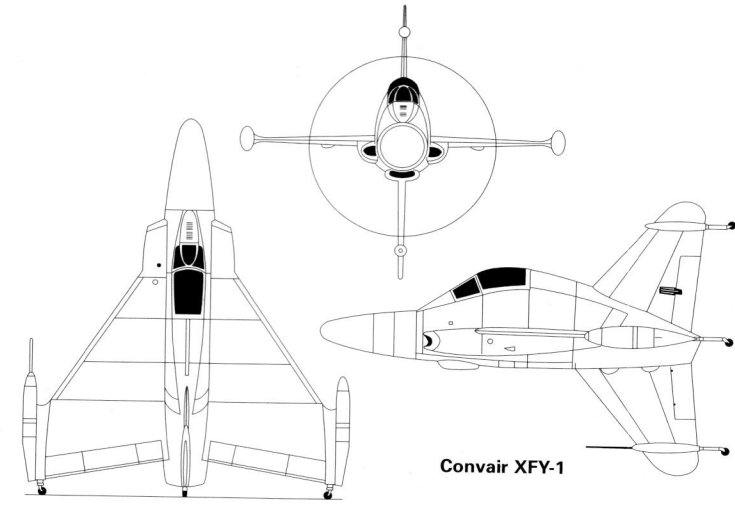

Convair XFY-1

SPECIFICATION	
Convair Model 5 (XFY-1)	(10670 m)
Type: single-seat experimental VTOL fighter	**Weights:** empty 11,784 lb (5345 kg); maximum take-off 16,250 lb (7371 kg)
Powerplant: one Allison YT40-A-6 turboprop engine rated at 5,850 ehp (4362 ekW)	**Dimensions:** wingspan 27 ft 7¾ in (8.43 m); length 34 ft 11¾ in (10.66 m); tailspan 22 ft 11 in (6.98 m); wing area 355.00 sq ft (32.98 m²)
Performance: maximum speed 610 mph (982 km/h) at 15,000 ft (4570 m); initial climb rate 10,500 ft (3200 m) per minute; service ceiling 43,700 ft (13320 m); endurance 1 hour at 35,000 ft	**Armament:** (proposed) four 20-mm cannon or 46 2.75-in (70-mm) FFARs in wing-tip pods

Convair Model 8 (F-102 Delta Dagger)

The **F-102 Delta Dagger** was developed as the **Model 8** on the basis of data derived from Convair's **Model 7-002 (XF-92A)** delta-wing research aircraft. Even before the contract for the Model 7-002 had been awarded, however, the USAF had formulated an Advanced Development Objective (ADO) for an interceptor which would possess performance considerably superior to that of the Soviet intercontinental jet bombers that were seen as its most likely adversary. This ADO was probably one of the most revolutionary in USAF history because, for the first time, it regarded this projected interceptor as a complete weapon system.

With this notion in mind, in June 1950 the USAF issued a request for proposals for a new interceptor, then identified as Project MX-1554. Four months later, the Hughes Aircraft Company was awarded a contract for development of Project MX-1179, this being the Electronic Control System (ECS) with which the MX-1554 airframe would be compatible. In spite of an extended development period of the design chosen to satisfy the MX-1554 concept, the MX-1179 failed to materialise within an acceptable timescale for this aircraft and was later abandoned. Instead, the Hughes E-9 (later redesignated MG-3) fire-control system was adopted, and finally replaced by the MG-10.

Six airframe manufacturers submitted proposals in January 1951, Convair, Lockheed and Republic later being chosen to develop their designs to mock-up stage. However, it did not take the USAF long to realise that it could not afford three parallel but separate projects, and on 11 September 1951 it gave Convair a contract which authorised use of the Westinghouse J40 turbojet pending availability of the more powerful Wright J67. A decision to proceed with production of the **Model 8-80** was made on 24 November 1951, this being regarded as an interim project until an 'Ultimate Interceptor' should reach fruition. The first **YF-102** prototype made its maiden flight on 24 October 1953, but was lost in an accident only nine days later. By that time, however, it had demonstrated that its performance was far below the required figures; this dismal forecast was confirmed by the YF-102 second prototype when this flew on 11 January 1954. There followed another eight prototypes to the same basic pattern.

It was not until there was a major redesign, incorporating the area-ruled fuselage concept, that a wasp-waisted prototype flew on 19 December 1954. Powered by the J57-P-23 turbojet of the type intended for production aircraft, this first of four **YF-102A** (**Model 8-90**) prototypes also introduced a lengthened fuselage, a revised canopy and a cambered leading edge on the wing, and the significance of these changes was revealed when the type achieved a speed of Mach 1.22 and altitude of 53,000 ft (16155 m) during its first flight. The type then went into production as the **F-102A** (**Model 8-10**), which entered service with Air Defense Command's 327th FIS at George Air Force Base in April 1956. Production finally totalled 875 aircraft. In addition, 111 **TF-102A** (**Model 8-12**) side-by-side two-seat trainers were built for the USAF, these retaining full operational armament and capability.

To represent the MiG-21 in aerial combat training, an initial six F-102As were converted, under a USAF contract awarded in April 1973, into two **QF-102A** piloted and four **PQM-102A** unpiloted target drones under the Pave Deuce programme, with further PQM-102A conversions following as manoeuvring targets for missile tests and the like. An improved **F-102B** materialised eventually as the F-106 Delta Dart.

A sleek and purposeful-looking aircraft, the F-102 was, in fact, something of a disappointment in service. Nevertheless, the type was an important component of the ConUS air defence network.

XF-92A proved the delta-wing concept for the subsequent F-102 interceptor.

SPECIFICATION	
Convair Model 8-10 (F-102A Delta Dagger)	(8641 kg); maximum take-off 31,276 lb (14187 kg)
Type: single-seat supersonic all-weather interceptor fighter	**Dimensions:** wingspan 38 ft 1½ in (11.62 m); length 68 ft 4½ in (20.84 m); height 21 ft 2½ in (6.46 m); wing area 661.50 sq ft (61.45 m²)
Powerplant: one Pratt & Whitney J57-P-23 or -25 turbojet engine rated at 17,200 lb st (76.51 kN) with afterburning	**Armament:** two AIM-26/26A Falcon, or one AIM-26/26A plus two AIM-4A Falcon, or one AIM-26/26A plus two AIM-4C/D, or six AIM-4A, or six AIM-4C/D air-to-air missiles carried internally plus 24 or 12 2.75-in (70-mm) FFARs in the missile bay doors
Performance: maximum speed 825 mph (1328 km/h) or Mach 1.25 at 36,000 ft (10970 m); initial climb rate 13,000 ft (3960 m) per minute; service ceiling 54,000 ft (16460 m); range 1,350 miles (2173 km)	
Weights: empty 19,050 lb	

Convair Model 8-24 (F-106 Delta Dart)

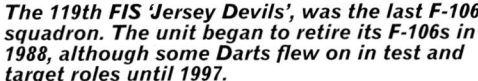

When evaluation of the YF-102A showed that the type offered real capability, even though this was not of the standard originally desired, the USAF ordered the type into production as the F-102A, and at the same time contracted for 17 examples of the F-102B. This took place in November 1955, by which time the MX-1179 ECS had found a creator, the Hughes Aircraft Company. Hughes designated it as the MA-1 fire-control system, and a mock-up of the proposed cockpit with radically new equipment and cockpit displays was available for inspection in December 1955.

On 17 June 1956 the F-102B was officially redesignated as the **F-106**, reflecting the fact that the original requirement had now changed considerably. When the initial details became known, on 28 September 1956, it was clear that the USAF had raised its sights somewhat. Convair was now required to produce an aircraft capable of intercepting enemy aircraft in all weathers at altitudes of up to 70,000 ft (21335 m) and within a radius of 430 miles (692 km). Armed with guided missiles and/or rockets with nuclear warheads, the F-106 was also expected to carry out interceptions at speeds of up to Mach 2.0 at heights of up to

An extension of the concept begun with the F-102, the F-106 defended the USAF for three decades, during the height of the Cold War.

35,000 ft (10670 m), under automatic guidance from SAGE (Semi-Automatic Ground Environment) installations integrating with the MA-1 fire control system via a data-link system.

Two **YF-106A (Model 8-24)** prototypes made their first flights on 26 December 1956 and 26 February 1957, but the results of the flight tests were disappointing, and it was painfully obvious that there were still many shortcomings. Maximum speed was some 15 per cent below the required figure, but causing greater concern was the slow rate of acceleration, and neither of these factors was helped by delays in the J57-P-9 turbojet which had been substituted for the Wright J67 originally selected (the production powerplant was the Pratt & Whitney J75). To aggravate the situation still further, the MA-1 ECS was not performing well, and a shortage of funds almost caused the USAF to scrap the entire F-106 programme.

To salvage something

from this difficult situation, the USAF decided to reduce its planned procurement of 1,000 F-106s to just 350 aircraft. So much had already been spent on the programme that it seemed sensible to continue development so that the USAF would eventually acquire a smaller, but high-quality, force of interceptors. The combination of engine inlet modifications and eradication of some of the bugs from the engine and avionics made it possible for the first deliveries of aircraft with an initial operational capability to be made to the 498th FIS at Geiger AFB, Washington, in October 1959. Production of 277 **F-106A** single-seat fighters and 63 **F-106B (Model 8-27)** tandem two-seat combat trainers, which retained a full combat capability, ended in December 1960. Improved **F-106C, F-106D** and **F-106X** variants were projected, but none was built.

Late-production examples of the F-106A differed from those which entered service in 1959, which meant that modification programmes to

The 119th FIS 'Jersey Devils', was the last F-106 squadron. The unit began to retire its F-106s in 1988, although some Darts flew on in test and target roles until 1997.

bring all aircraft to a common standard (**Model 8-31** for single-seaters and **Model 8-32** for two-seaters) were running concurrently with the production of new aircraft. Circumstances demanded that the F-106's first-line service life would

be much longer than originally anticipated, which meant that update programmes were almost continuous up to the type's retirement from service in July 1989, by which time the **Delta Dart** was operated only by the ANG.

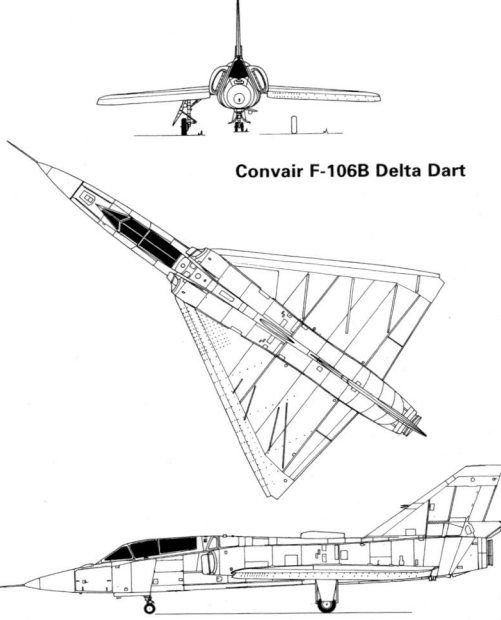

Convair F-106B Delta Dart

SPECIFICATION

Convair Model 8-24 (F-106A Delta Dart)

Type: single-seat supersonic all-weather interceptor fighter
Powerplant: one Pratt & Whitney J75-P-17 turbojet engine rated at 24,500 lb st (108.98 kN) with afterburning
Performance: maximum speed 1,525 mph (2454 km/h) or Mach 2.31 at 40,000 ft (12190 m); climb to 51,800 ft (15790 m) in 6 minutes 54 seconds; service ceiling 57,000 ft (17375 m); radius 729 miles (1173 km) with two drop tanks
Weights: empty 23,646 lb

(10728 kg); maximum take-off 41,831 lb (18995 kg)
Dimensions: wingspan 38 ft 3½ in (11.67 m); length 70 ft 8¾ in (21.56 m); height 20 ft 3 in (6.17 m); wing area 631.30 sq ft (58.65 m²)
Armament: one AIR-2A Genie or AIR-2B Super Genie nuclear-tipped air-to-air rocket and four AIM-4F/G Super Falcon air-to-air missiles carried in the internal weapons bay; many aircraft had one 20-mm M61 Vulcan fixed forward-firing six-barrel rotary cannon in place of the Genie

Convair Model 22 (CV-880), Model 30 (CV-990 Coronado)

In 1954 the news that Boeing and Douglas were building advanced airliners with turbojet propulsion came as a major challenge to Convair, which immediately embarked on a

programme to gain a share of the market that would otherwise fall to Boeing and Douglas by default. The company's interpretation of its market research led to a design that would

carry fewer passengers than the competing Boeing 707 and Douglas DC-8, but would offer higher performance, especially in terms of speed.

It was in April 1956 that

Convair made the public announcement of its intention to build a turbojet-powered airliner, simultaneously revealing the fact that Delta Air Lines and TWA had ordered 10 and 30

aircraft respectively. Few aircraft can have had as many designations as the **Model 22**, beginning with the name **Skylark**, later changed to **Golden Arrow**, **CV-600** and finally **CV-880**

Variant

UC-880: this is a single CV-880M operated since 1980 by the US Navy with an atypical designation for conversion as an inflight-refuelling tanker in support of the McDonnell Douglas (now Boeing) F/A-18 Hornet flight test programme; the aircraft was later adapted for trials of anti-submarine warfare systems

for the initial version, whose prototype flew for the first time on 27 January 1959. In general appearance this was very similar to the Model 707, with a low-set monoplane wing that had an equivalent 35° sweep angle, swept conventional tail surfaces, and tricycle landing gear with four-wheel bogies on each main unit. The powerplant comprised four 11,200-lb st (49.82-kN) General Electric CJ805-3 turbojet engines, and these were mounted in a fashion similar to the arrangement adopted in the Model 707. The fuselage was more slender than that of the Model 707's production version, however, and this limited the seating arrangement to a five-abreast layout that made provision for 88-110 passengers.

This original version of the CV-880 was intended for domestic use. Certification was gained on 1 May 1960, and Delta inaugurated its first service with the type exactly two weeks later. Despite a high cruising speed and range of close on 3,000 miles (4828 km) with full payload, the limited capacity of the CV-880 by comparison with that of the competing Boeing and Douglas airliners made the CV-880 a far less attractive proposition to potential operators. By

the time that production ended, therefore, only 48 of the aircraft had been built. Even with the introduction of the **Model 31** derivative which, with increased fuel capacity and several other improvements, was intended for intercontinental services, the restricted seating capacity resulted in minimal appeal to airlines, and as a consequence only 17 examples of this **CV-880M** variant were built.

Even before the CV-880 prototype had achieved its first flight, the company had decided to build a higher-performance version, offering increased capacity. It was, perhaps, unfortunate for Convair that an early order for this Model 30 version from American Airlines signalled a go-ahead for its production. Had there been more time in which to judge customer reaction to the CV-880, a major redesign of the fuselage might have received consideration. Instead, the Model 30 was given a lengthened fuselage to increase capacity to a mixed-class total of 90 or a one-class total of 149, but retained the original fuselage width that limited seating to the same inadequate five-abreast arrangement that had curtailed sales of the CV-880. Other improve-

ments were incorporated in the design of this **CV-990**, which was originally called the **CV-600** in deference to the demands of Howard Hughes, head of TWA, that there should not be a designation suggesting something better than the CV-880, a designation indicating the type's speed of 880 ft (268 m) per second, or 600 mph (966 km/h).

No prototype was built, and the first to fly on 24 January 1961 was one of the airliners ordered by American Airlines. FAA certification was not gained until December of that year, and American was the recipient of the first aircraft for airline service on 7 January 1962. Swissair also received an initial aircraft at much the same time and, introducing yet another name, gave its aircraft the name Coronado before undertaking the new type's first airline service during the following month. During the development flying that preceded certification, it was discovered that there were several aerodynamic shortcomings which eroded the CV-990's planned performance. Research and development to overcome these prob-

To cure the problems associated with supersonic air flowing over the CV-990's wings, the aircraft incorporated distinctive 'speed pods'.

lems paved the way for a series of aerodynamic improvements that was introduced retrospectively to all 37 CV-990 airliners that were produced, to create a variant redesignated as the **CV-990A**.

Convair's CV-880 and CV-990 programmes

proved themselves extremely costly ventures for the company, and as a result the aviation divisions of the General Dynamics Corporation, which had acquired Convair in 1953, confined their future activities to the field of military aviation.

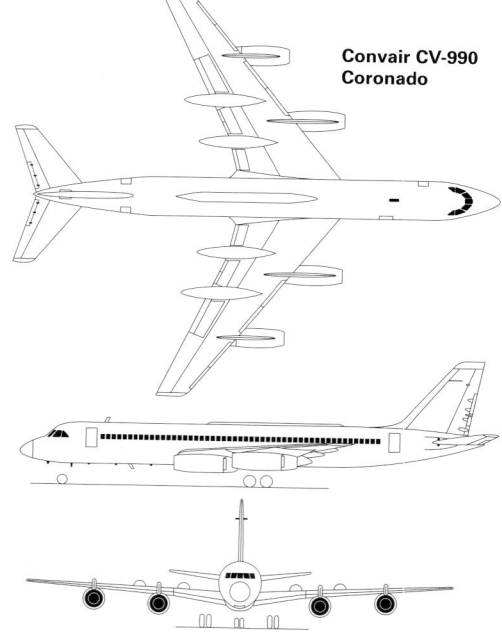

Convair CV-990 Coronado

Cathay Pacific chose the CV-880 on the basis of its small size. Rival aircraft, such as the DC-8 and 707, offered too many seats for Cathay's needs.

SPECIFICATION

Convair Model 30 (CV-990A)
Type: four/five-crew medium-range transport
Powerplant: four General Electric CJ805-23B turbofan engines each rated at 16,500 lb st (73.40 kN)
Performance: maximum cruising speed 625 mph (1006 km/h) at 21,200 ft (6460 m); service ceiling 41,000 ft (12495 m); range 3,800 miles (6116 km) with

maximum payload
Weights: empty 120,560 lb (54686 kg); maximum take-off 255,000 lb (115668 kg)
Dimensions: wingspan 120 ft (36.58 m); length 139 ft 5 in (42.49 m); height 39 ft 6 in (12.04 m); wing area 2,250.00 sq ft (209.03 m²)
Payload: up to 149 passengers

Convair Model 105 (L-13)

Late in World War II Convair developed a two/three-seat general-purpose monoplane suitable for service in the air ambulance, liaison, observation and photo-

graphic roles. Two prototypes of this **Model 105** design were ordered in 1945 for evaluation with the service designation **XL-13**, and extensive testing resulted in a production

order for 300 examples of the **L-13A** (48 of them for service with the Air National Guard). Delivery began in 1947.

A braced high-wing monoplane of all-metal

construction, the L-13A had a tailwheel landing gear which could be equipped optionally with floats or skis as alternatives to the standard wheels. The enclosed cabin, intended to accom-

modate three, could also carry a crew of two together with two litters or a maximum of six persons in an emergency. Twenty-eight of the L-13As were modified as **L-13B** machines for arctic use, the changes including the installation of a combustion heater.

Convair Model 105 (L-13) (continued)

Variants

Centaur 101: as the L-13s were retired from USAF service in the mid-1950s, a number was bought by civil operators for conversion as utility transports; the **Centaur 101** was a creation of the Longren Aircraft Co. as a 'bushplane' with six-seat accommodation and the powerplant of one 300-hp (224-kW) Lycoming R-680-E3 radial engine; the sole conversion was undertaken by ACME aircraft, which also built a small number of aircraft to the same standard
Centaur 102: this designation was applied to a few aircraft completed

with the Jacobs R-755-A2 radial engine
Husky I: this designation was applied to a number of L-13 conversions by Caribbean Traders Inc. with the Franklin O-425-9 flat-six engine
Husky II: this designation was applied to a number of L-13 conversions with the 300-hp (224-kW) R-680-13 radial engine
Husky III: this designation was applied to a number of L-13 conversions with the 450-hp (336-kW) Pratt & Whitney R-975-7 (Whirlwind J-6-9) radial engine

SPECIFICATION

Convair Model 102 (L-13A)
Type: two/three-seat utility aircraft
Powerplant: one Franklin O-425-9 flat-six piston engine rated at 245 hp (183 kW)
Performance: maximum speed 115 mph (185 km/h) at sea level; cruising speed 92 mph (148 km/h) at optimum altitude; initial climb rate 830 ft (253 m) per minute; service ceiling 15,000 ft (4570 m); range 368 miles (592 km)
Weights: empty 2,070 lb (939 kg); maximum take-off 2,900 lb (1315 kg)
Dimensions: wingspan 40 ft 5½ in (12.33 m); length 31 ft 9 in (9.68 m); height 8 ft 5 in (2.57 m); wing area 270.00 sq ft (25.08 m²)
Payload: see above

Both the tailplane and wing were braced by a single strut on each side of the fuselage. In addition, the L-13 had a foldable wing, incorporating high-lift devices that included leading-edge slats and slotted trailing-edge flaps.

Convair Model 109 (B-46)

Very shortly after the end of World War II Convair began the design of its **Model 109** as a turbojet-powered medium bomber, gaining a contract for

three **XB-46** prototypes from the USAAF. Of all-metal construction, the XB-46 was of high-wing cantilever monoplane configuration, had a slim

oval-section fuselage, a conventional tail unit and retractable tricycle landing gear. It was designed to accommodate a crew of three. First flown on 3 April 1947, the XB-46 was handed over to the newly formed US Air Force late in 1947, attaining an average speed of 533 mph (858 km/h) during its delivery flight to Wright

The XB-46 housed its four turbojet engines in side-by-side pairs within two underwing nacelles.

Field at Dayton, Ohio. Despite this performance, the XB-46 remained a one-off prototype, the

USAF instead ordering the more advanced Boeing B-47 Stratojet into production.

SPECIFICATION

Convair Model 109 (XB-46)
Type: three-seat medium bomber prototype
Powerplant: four Allison (General Electric) J35-A-3 turbojet engines each rated at 4,000 lb st (17.79 kN)
Performance: maximum speed 545 mph (877 km/h) at 15,000 ft (4570 m); cruising speed 439 mph (706 km/h) at 35,000 ft (10670 m); climb to 35,000 ft (10670 m) in 19 minutes; service ceiling 40,000 ft (12190 m); range 2,870 miles (4619 km) with an 8,000-lb (3629-kg) bombload
Weights: empty 48,018 lb (21781 kg); maximum take-off 95,600 lb (43364 kg)
Dimensions: wingspan 113 ft (34.44 m); length 105 ft 9 in (32.23 m); height 27 ft 11 in (8.51 m); wing area 1,285.00 sq ft (119.38 m²)
Armament: two 0.5-in (12.7-mm) Browning trainable rearward-firing machine-guns in a radar-directed tail barbette, plus up to 22,000 lb (9979 kg) of disposable stores carried in a lower-fuselage weapons bay

Convair (Consolidated Model 36) B-36 Peacemaker

This aircraft was the last of the 22 B-36As completed. Like all the B-36As, BM-025 was unarmed and used for crew training by the 7th Bomb Group (Heavy) of Strategic Air Command, based at Carswell Air Force Base, Texas.

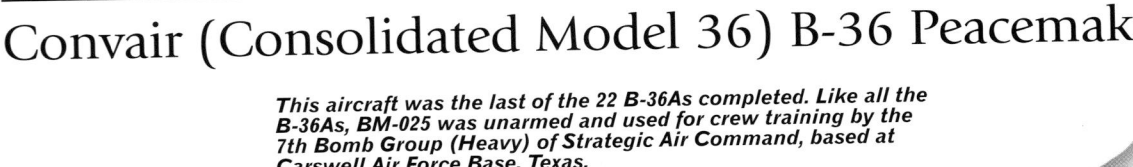

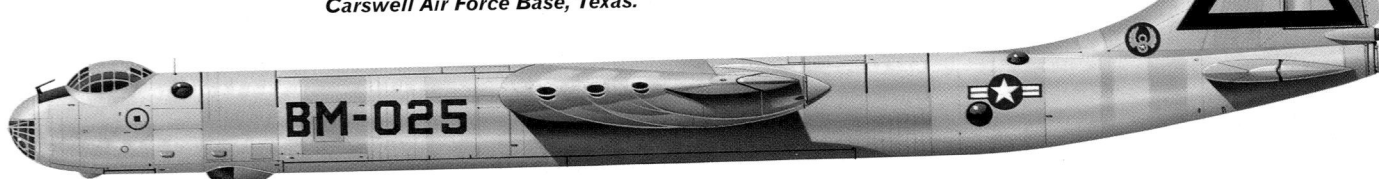

The first bomber with intercontinental capability, the **Convair B-36** originated from a specification issued by the USAAC on 11 April 1941 for an aircraft with the ability to carry a maximum bombload of 72,000 lb (32659 kg) and to deliver 10,000 lb (4536 kg) of bombs on European targets from bases in the continental USA. An unrefuelled range of 10,000 miles (16093 km) was a prime

requirement, with a maximum speed of 240-300 mph (386-483 km/h) and ceiling of 35,000 ft (10670 m). Selected from four competing designs, the **Model 36** featured a pressurised fuselage and a wingroot thickness of 6 ft (1.83 m) to permit inflight access to the powerplant of six radial engines, disposed as pusher units. The design originally featured twin fin-

and-rudder units, but by the time the **XB-36** prototype was ready to be rolled out at Fort Worth on 8 September 1945, a single vertical tail surface had been substituted.
First flown on 8 August 1946, the XB-36 had single main wheels. The **YB-36** second machine, intended for the service test role, also had the single-wheel main undercarriage, although these single

wheels were then each replaced by the type of four-wheel bogie adopted for the production aircraft. In this form the machine was known as the **YB-36A**, and also differed from the XB-36 by introducing a raised flightdeck roof.
On 23 July 1943 an order was placed for 100 aircraft, but it was more than four years before the first of the 22 **B-36A** aircraft, completed in

unarmed form for use as crew trainers, took off on its maiden flight on 28 August 1947. Production of the B-36, named as the **Peacemaker** and known as a Convair rather than Consolidated product, continued for almost seven years, the last example being delivered to SAC on 14 August 1954. The last of the type were retired on 12 February 1959.

Variants

B-36B: 73 aircraft with six 3,500-hp (2610-kW) R-4360 engines, maximum take-off weight of 328,000 lb (148778 kg) and a defensive armament of two 20-mm cannon in each of the six retractable and remotely-controlled fuselage barbettes and two similar weapons in each of the nose and tail turrets; the first example was flown on 8 July 1948
YB-36C: proposed version with R-4360-51 tractor engines
B-36D: first flown on 26 March 1949 as a B-36B conversion with additional power in the form of four Allison J35 turbojet engines, this version was cleared to operate at a weight of 358,000 lb (162386 kg), permitting an increase in maximum bombload to 84,000 lb (38102 kg); in addition, the maximum speed was raised to 435 mph (700 km/h) and the ceiling to more than 45,000 ft (13715 m); additional power for the 22 production B-36D aircraft (complemented by 64 B-36B conversions) was provided by two pairs of 5,200-lb st (23.23-kN) General Electric J47-GE-19 turbojet engines pod-mounted outboard of the main engines; deliveries of the B-36D began on 19 August 1950 and the type entered service with the 7th Bomb Wing at Carswell AFB
RB-36D: 17 new RB-36D aircraft and seven B-36B conversions were delivered for strategic reconnaissance duties, deliveries starting on 3 June 1950; operating with a crew of 22, the RB-36D was equipped with 14 cameras installed in the space occupied normally by two of the bomber version's four bomb bays
RB-36E: the YB-36A and 21 B-36A aircraft were converted to a standard similar to that of the RB-36D, the first flying on 18 December 1949
B-36F: similar to the B-36B but with uprated 3,800-hp (2834-kW) R-4360-53 engines, the B-36F was flown for the first time on 18 November 1950; production totalled 58 aircraft, including 24 examples of the RB-36F reconnaissance derivative with increased fuel capacity
GRB-36F: the US Air Force's FICON (Fighter Conveyance) parasite fighter programme, originally to have used the McDonnell XF-85 Goblin, was continued with the Republic GRF-84F; following successful trials, involving test drops from a trapeze-equipped GRB-36F in May 1953, at least 12 aircraft were converted to this standard; they were also used as control aircraft for guided missile development
B-36H: first flown on 5 April 1952, the B-36H introduced improvements to the flightdeck, and production totalled 156 aircraft, including 73 examples of the RB-36H reconnaissance derivative; one aircraft, designated **NB-36H**, had a nuclear reactor installed for an experimental programme to study radiation shielding methods and the effects of radiation on airframe and equipment; the first flight was made on 17 September 1955
B-36J: version with additional fuel tankage in the outer wing panels and with the landing gear strengthened for operation at 410,000 lb (185973 kg); production totalled 33 aircraft, of which the first made its maiden flight on 3 September 1953, and some of the aircraft were later modified by the deletion of all but the tail turret armament, reducing the crew complement to nine
YB-60: a turbojet-powered version of the B-36 was proposed under the designation **XB-36G**; a contract for two prototypes was awarded by the USAF on 15 March 1951, these being allocated the designation YB-60. The aircraft retained the basic fuselage of the B-36 with a modified nose and generally similar wing centre section and landing gear in combination with new swept outer wing panels, a new tail unit and the wholly different powerplant of eight 9,000-lb st (40.03-kN) Pratt & Whitney J57-P-3 turbojet engines pylon-mounted in podded pairs forward of the wing's leading edge; the first YB-60 flew on 18 April 1952, but the type failed to gain a production contract, the USAF instead ordering the Boeing B-52
X-6: proposed nuclear-powered version
XC-99 (Model 37): long-range heavy transport aircraft combining the powerplant, landing gear and flying surfaces of the B-36 with a new fuselage some 20 ft (6.10 m) longer than that of the bomber and providing two-deck accommodation for troops and/or freight. The XC-99 was the world's largest landplane at the time of its completion, and made its maiden flight on 23 November 1947. In an improved form, the XC-99 was delivered to the USAF in May 1949. The machine was then strengthened to permit a significant increase in its maximum take-off weight, and used for a weekly freight service along the west coast of the USA during the Korean War. The XC-99 left the USA only shortly before being retired in March 1957

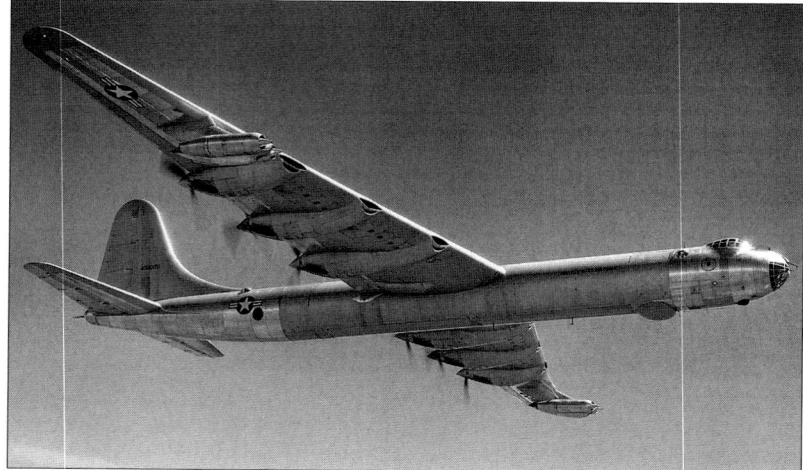

This B-36D, rebuilt from B-36B standard, demonstrates the two pairs of podded J47 turbojets mounted under the outer wings, as well as the type's pusher piston-engine arrangement.

SPECIFICATION

Convair B-36J Peacemaker
Type: 10-crew long-range strategic reconnaissance bomber
Powerplant: six Pratt & Whitney R-4360-53 radial piston engines each rated at 3,800 hp (2834 kW) and four General Electric J47-GE-19 turbojet engines each rated at 5,200 lb st (23.13 kN)
Performance: maximum speed 411 mph (661 km/h) at 36,400 ft (11095 m); cruising speed 391 mph (629 km/h) at optimum altitude; initial climb rate 1,920 ft (585 m) per minute; service ceiling 39,900 ft (12160 m); range 6,800 miles (10944 km) with a bombload of 10,000 lb (4536 kg)
Weights: empty 171,035 lb (77580 kg); maximum take-off 410,000 lb (185973 kg)
Dimensions: wingspan 230 ft (70.10 m); length 162 ft 1 in (49.40 m); height 46 ft 8 in (14.22 m); wing area 4,772.00 sq ft (443.32 m²)
Armament: two 20-mm M24A1 trainable cannon in each of the six retractable and remotely-controlled fuselage barbettes and the two manned nose and tail positions, plus up to 86,000 lb (39009 kg) of bombs carried internally

Couzinet aircraft

The Société des Avions René Couzinet was established in the late 1920s to build the **Couzinet 10 Arc-en-Ciel** (rainbow), a three-engined monoplane intended for an attempt on the world long-distance record and also as the basis for a transatlantic mailplane and/or passenger transport. Unfortunately, the Couzinet 10 was destroyed in an accident in August 1928, and a second machine was later destroyed by fire. However, via the improved **Couzinet 30**, a second Arc-en-Ciel was evolved, the **Couzinet 70**, for service on the Aéropostale's South Atlantic air mail service to destinations in South America.

Typically, the Couzinet 70 was of cantilever monoplane configuration with the wing, of thick section, set low on a fuselage that was of conventional rectangular section over its forward part. Over its rear part, however, it had an upper line that tapered upward into a raised knife edge to create a very low-aspect-ratio fin, carrying a plain rudder. The fixed tail-wheel landing gear featured speed fairings for each of the wheels, and the four-man crew was accommodated on the enclosed flightdeck and in the cabin. The whole aircraft was of plywood-covered wooden construction and the two wing-mounted engines were accessible in flight via crawlways in the wing. Following route-proving trials in 1933, a number of modifications was implemented, resulting in a change of designation to **Couzinet 71**.

The Couzinet 71 entered regular service with the Aéropostale in May 1934, but no further examples were built.

Two passenger-carrying aircraft of generally similar configuration were also built by Couzinet. These comprised single examples of the considerably smaller **Couzinet 101**, and the **Couzinet 110** with three 135-hp (101-kW) Salmson radial engines and accommodation for the pilot and co-pilot/passenger plus four passengers in a separate cabin.

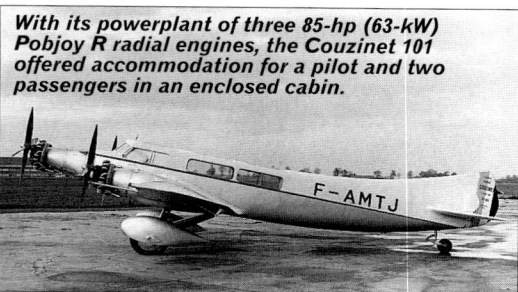

With its powerplant of three 85-hp (63-kW) Pobjoy R radial engines, the Couzinet 101 offered accommodation for a pilot and two passengers in an enclosed cabin.

SPECIFICATION

Couzinet 70
Type: four-crew long-range air mail transport
Powerplant: three Hispano Suiza 12Nb Vee piston engines each rated at 650 hp (485 kW)
Performance: maximum speed 174 mph (280 km/h) at optimum altitude; cruising speed 147 mph (236 km/h) at optimum altitude; range 4,225 miles (6800 km)
Weights: empty 16,116 lb (7310 kg); maximum take-off 37,015 lb (16790 kg)
Dimensions: wingspan 98 ft 5 in (30.00 m); length 52 ft 52 ft 11¾ in (16.15 m); height 13 ft 1½ in (4.00 m); wing area 968.78 sq ft (90.0 m²)
Payload: up to 1,323 lb (600 kg) of air mail and freight

Culver Cadet (A-8, PQ-8 and TDC)

In the early 1930s, while working for the Lambert Aircraft Corporation, Albert Mooney designed a small two-seat monoplane named originally as the **Monoprep G**, a name conforming with the Monocoupe/Monosport line built by Lambert. When this organisation ran into financial difficulties, Mooney left and, with K. K. Culver, formed the Dart Aircraft Company at Port Columbus, Ohio, acquiring from Lambert the design and manufacturing rights for the little two-seater which the new company called the **Dart Dart**. This was a graceful low-wing monoplane of mixed construction, relying upon its light weight and clean lines to provide remarkable performance despite the use of quite low-powered engines. The initial version was the **Dart G**, powered by the 90-hp (67-kW) Lambert R-266 radial, but when supplies of this engine became limited, a second version appeared as the **Dart GK**, with the similarly rated Ken-Royce engine. Finally came the **Dart GW** with a Warner Scarab Junior radial engine. Production totalled almost 50 aircraft, including two **Dart GW 'Special'** models, one with a 125-hp (93-kW) engine and the other with a 145-hp (108-kW) engine.

In 1939 the Dart organi-sation was renamed as the Culver Aircraft Company, its sole product then being renamed as the **Culver Dart**. Late in the following year the company moved to Wichita, Kansas, an event that brought increased prestige and success to the new company. After World War II, attempts were made to restart manufacture of this aircraft, but new post-war designs were beginning to appear, outclassing the little Dart that had seemed so advanced only seven years earlier.

Before the move of the Culver company from Port Columbus, Mooney had been working on the design of an improved version of the Dart that would offer equal or better performance on reduced power. Originally desig-nated as the **Culver Model L**, the new type flew for the first time on 2 December 1939 at Port Columbus, but it was not until the company had moved to Wichita that production really got under way. Similar in overall configuration to the Dart, the aircraft that acquired the definitive designation **Culver Cadet** differed from its predecessor, which had a welded steel tube fuse-lage, in having a wooden semi-monocoque fuselage and tailwheel landing gear with retractable main units.

The powerplant of the orig-inal **Cadet LCA** was a 75-hp (56-kW) Continental A75-8 flat-four engine. The **Cadet LFA** of 1941 intro-duced a number of refinements and more comprehensive equipment, and was available with either the Continental A80-8 or the Franklin 4AC-176-F3 engine, each of them rated at 80 hp (60-kW). A version known as the **Cadet LFA-90** was also available to special order, with the powerplant of one 90-hp (67-kW) Franklin 4AC-199-E3 flat-four engine.

Production of the Cadet far exceeded that of the Dart, but was brought to an end by the USA's entry into World War II. Just before that time, Walter Beech and an associate acquired control of the company, reorganisation making possible large-scale produc-tion of aircraft derived from the Cadet for wartime purposes.

In 1940 the USAAC selected the Cadet LCA lightplane as suitable for development into a radio-controlled target. The first of these acquired for test purposes was allocated the designation **A-8** (later **XPQ-8**). As a derivative of the Cadet, therefore, its **Cadet LAR-190** was a low-wing monoplane based on the original Cadet, but revised with the uprated

Culver's PQ-8A, which could be operated in manned form for delivery flights and testing, had a maximum speed of 116 mph (187 km/h).

powerplant of one 100-hp (75-kW) Continental O-200 flat-four engine. Successful testing resulted in a production order for 200 of the similar **PQ-8**, and at a later date an additional 200 were ordered as **PQ-8A** (later **Q-8A**) machines, this version being equipped with the uprated 125-hp (93-kW) O-200-1 engine.

A few aircraft were completed as Cadet LAR-190 or '**Lark 95**' machines for the civil market in 1941 with the 90-hp (67-kW) Franklin 4AC-199-E3 engine.

Others were bought for operation with this desig-nation when surplus aircraft were released after the end of World War II. Further iterations of the same design at later dates were the **Lambert Monosport** and **Dart Model G**.

The USN had a similar training requirement for the anti-aircraft gunners of its warships, and late in 1941 acquired a single example of the PQ-8A for evaluation. This paved the way for a 1942 order for 200 **TDC-2** essentially similar aircraft.

SPECIFICATION	
Culver Cadet LFA	initial climb rate 800 m (244 m) per minute; service ceiling 17,000 ft (5180 m); range 500 miles (805 km) **Weights:** empty 806 lb (366 kg); maximum take-off 1,305 lb (592 kg) **Dimensions:** wingspan 27 ft (8.23 m); length 17 ft 8 in (5.38 m); height 5 ft 6 in (1.68 m); wing area 120.00 sq ft (11.15 m²)
Type: two-seat lightplane **Powerplant:** one Franklin 4AC-176-F3 flat-four piston engine rated at 80 hp (60 kW) **Performance:** maximum speed 142 mph (229 km/h) at 3,000 ft (915 m); cruising speed 130 mph (209 km/h) at 7,000 ft (2135 m);	

Culver Model NRD (PQ-14 and TD2C)

The main problem associ-ated with the early Culver radio-controlled targets was that their maximum speed of 116 mph (187 km/h) was completely unrealistic in 1941-2, when attacking fighters and bombers could demonstrate speeds respectively three and two times that of the target aircraft type.

To meet the requirement that emerged in 1942 for a higher-performance target, Culver developed the **Model NRD**. With a general resemblance to the Cadet, the Model NRD possessed a single-seat cockpit for ferrying and testing duties. The primary changes were a higher-aspect-ratio wing, larger

A pilot serves to illustrate the small dimensions of this US Navy TD2C-1 target aircraft.

control surfaces to ensure much improved response and manoeuvrability, retractable tricycle landing gear, and the uprated powerplant of one Franklin O-300 flat-six engine.

Early in 1943 the USAAF acquired a single prototype conversion from PQ-8 stan-dard for evaluation as the **XPQ-14**. This machine proving satisfactory, 75 examples of the **YPQ-14A** production model were ordered for full service trials. The USAAF finally acquired 1,433 examples of

this **PQ-14A** (later **Q-14A**), of which 1,201 were trans-ferred to the US Navy for service with the revised designation **TD2C-1**. A heavier version was later built, the USAAF acquiring an initial batch of 25 for

service trials under the designation **YPQ-14B**, following with orders for 1,112 examples of the **PQ-14B** for training units. A single aircraft with a Franklin O-300-9 engine was designated **PQ-14C**.

SPECIFICATION	
Culver Model NRD (PQ-14A)	(244 m) per minute; range 512 miles (824 km) **Weights:** maximum take-off 1,820 lb (826 kg) **Dimensions:** wingspan 30 ft (9.14 m); length 19 ft 6 in (5.94 m); height 7 ft 11 in (2.41 m); wing area 103.00 sq ft (9.57 m²)
Type: single-seat and radio-controlled target aircraft **Powerplant:** one Franklin O-300-11 flat-six piston engine rated at 150 hp (112 kW) **Performance:** maximum speed 180 mph (290 km/h) at optimum altitude; initial climb rate 800 ft	

Curtiss/AEA Aerodrome aircraft

The AEA (Aerial Experiment Association), founded in September 1907 and funded by Dr and Mrs Alexander Graham Bell with the intention of developing heavier-than-air craft in North America, included

among its members the Americans Glenn Curtiss and Lieutenant T. E. Selfridge, and two Canadians, F. W. 'Casey' Baldwin and John A. D. McCurdy. Although Curtiss was responsible for the

design of only one of the four AEA aircraft, which were known to the organi-sation by the generic name **Aerodrome**, his engines were used in all four machines and it is there-fore sensible to consider

them under the Curtiss/ AEA banner.

Like the Wright brothers, Curtiss had a background as a cycle manufacturer. It was not long, however, before he had designed and built an engine to power the cycle, thus gain-ing a foothold in the motorcycle industry. The

capability of his lightweight petrol engines led to their use in powering a number of early airships, and it was this which brought an invi-tation to Curtiss to become a member of the AEA, which was formally estab-lished on 1 October 1907. Curtiss contributed signifi-cantly to the design and development of the four aircraft designated **Aerodromes Nos 1, 2, 3** and **4** and named respectively **Red Wing**, **White Wing**, **June Bug** and **Silver Dart**.

The aircraft were direct descendants of the Wright gliders, and their design drew extensively on the data provided by the Wright brothers to Selfridge. The latter became the first man to die in the crash of a powered, heavier-than-air craft when the Wright biplane in which he was a passenger crashed during September 1908 while being flown by Orville Wright. In configuration, all of the aircraft were pusher biplanes whose upper and lower wings converged toward each other at the tips in long bowed curves.

The first of the AEA aircraft to fly, on 12 March 1908, was the **Aerodrome No. 1**, **Red Wing**, attributed to Selfridge. The machine was flown by Baldwin off the ice of the frozen Lake Keuka at Hammondsport, New York. The Aerodrome No. 1 had no means of lateral control, and accomplished only two hop-flights before crash-landing; the longer of these

efforts was the first, which covered 319 ft (97 m).

In May 1908 various members of the AEA, including Baldwin to whom the design was attributed, flew the second machine, the **Aerodrome No. 2**, **White Wing**. The European influence of pioneers such as Esnault-Pelterie and Blériot was evident in the use of small ailerons for lateral control (the first appearance of such a feature in a non-European aircraft), and wheeled landing gear. The Aerodrome No. 2's longest flight was accomplished on 22 May 1908, when it covered 1,017 ft (310 m), and like the Aerodrome No. 1 was abandoned after suffering damage in a heavy landing.

The third AEA aircraft was the **Aerodrome No. 3**, **June Bug**, attributed to Curtiss. The Aerodrome No. 3 was more advanced in concept than it two predecessors, and between 21 June and 31 August 1908, it succeeded in making more than 30 take-offs in the hands of several AEA members, but most particularly Curtiss and McCurdy. Curtiss was awarded the *Scientific*

Among **June Bug's** *features were four triangular wingtip ailerons and a biplane tail unit. The best of its flights covered a distance of 2 miles (3.2 km) on 29 August 1908.*

American journal's prize for the first officially recognised flight of more than 1 km (1,095 yds) after covering 5,090 ft (1551 km) in a time of 1 minute 42½ seconds on 4 July. *June Bug* was later transformed into the *Loon* with a pair of pontoon floats to turn it into a seaplane, but this could not lift off the water.

As originally projected in July 1908, the **Aerodrome No. 4**, **Silver Dart**, attributed to McCurdy, was similar to *June Bug*. However, it was of enlarged size and had a 50-hp (37-kW) Curtiss engine installed between the upper and lower wings to drive two pusher propellers by means of a chain-belt drive. The machine had a tall single rudder as its only tail surface, and a monoplane forward elevator. As finalised in the middle of October, however, the

Aerodrome No. 4 had the engine located in line with the lower wing to drive a single pusher propeller on the centreline inboard of the converging sets of tail booms that carried the smaller rudder, and a biplane forward elevator. Like the earlier aircraft of the series, the Aerodrome No. 4 was built at Hammondsport, but it was taken to ice-covered Baddeck Bay in Nova Scotia for its first flight. Here, modifications were effected, including the relocation of the radiator farther forward, shortening of the tail booms by about 1 ft (0.305 m), and shortening the main landing gear legs in a process that reduced the wings' angle of incidence. On 23 February 1909, *Silver*

Dart made a maiden flight of some 880 yds (805 m) with McCurdy at the controls. On the following day, it made a flight of 4½ miles (7.24 km), and within a few weeks had achieved at least one flight of 12 miles (19.3 km).

Silver Dart was a dead end in purely aeronautical terms, and on the completion of this machine's test programme, the AEA was disbanded. McCurdy continued to fly *Silver Dart*, which completed some 200 or more flights in all as McCurdy honed his flying skills; in 1910 McCurdy created the CAC (Canadian Aerodrome Company), which built the **Baddeck 1** and **Baddeck 2** aircraft. Both of these later crashed, and the CAC went into liquidation.

SPECIFICATION	
AEA (Curtiss) Aerodrome No. 3 **June Bug**	about 40 mph (64 km/h) at sea level
Type: single-seat experimental aircraft	**Weights:** maximum take-off 615 lb (270 kg)
Powerplant: one Curtiss Vee piston engine rated at 40 hp (30 kW)	**Dimensions:** wingspan 42 ft 6 in (12.95 m); wing area 370.00 sq ft (34.37 m²)
Performance: maximum speed	

Curtiss early floatplanes

Despite the fact that it is a French pioneer, Henri Fabre, who is credited with the accomplishment of the first successful take-off from water in a powered aircraft, it is Curtiss who is seen as the real inventor of the practical seaplane. The original Curtiss floats were short and featured a flat bottom over their entire lengths, but the later Curtiss floats were somewhat longer and introduced the combination of a Vee-

bottom and a hydroplane step (located slightly behind the aircraft's centre of gravity) of the type that Curtiss had developed for his flying-boat in 1912. With regard to Curtiss seaplane developments, it is interesting to note that the pattern Curtiss established in 1911, with a single main float under the fuselage and two small stabilising floats under the wingtips, became standard for US Navy floatplanes up to their disappearance in 1961, whereas the twin-float pattern first trialled on the *Loon* (*June Bug* with floats) in 1918 is still standard for civil floatplanes.

Completed in June 1911 for a first flight on the last day of that month by Curtiss, the A-1 was handed over to Lieutenant Theodore G. Ellyson, Naval Aviator No. 1, later on the same day.

The first successful taxi, take-off and landing of a Curtiss floatplane, which at the time was called a hydroaeroplane, or just hydro, was achieved on 26 January 1911 in a **'Curtiss Pusher'**, modified with a clumsy arrangement of tandem floats. By 1 February, Curtiss had introduced a new alighting gear arrangement with a sled-shaped main float. Located under the pilot and powerplant, this float was long enough to provide longitudinal stability, while small floats were attached under the tips of the lower wing for lateral stability.

The second Curtiss hydro was a notable exception to the 'Curtiss Pusher' layout that was otherwise standard during

this period. The unnamed floatplane, generally designated as the **Tractor Hydro** in later histories, was an otherwise standard **'Curtiss Pusher' Type III** biplane with the forward elevator removed, the engine installed ahead of the wing as a tractor to keep the propeller out of the spray, and the pilot seated behind the wing cellule.

Once he had successfully developed the landplane into the floatplane, Curtiss almost inevitably proceeded to the creation of the amphibian floatplane. This the American pioneer achieved by the modification of a hydro with retractable main wheels under the lower wing and a nose wheel on the bow of the float.

SPECIFICATION	
Curtiss A-1	**Weights:** empty 975 lb (442 kg); maximum take-off 1,575 lb (714 kg)
Type: two-seat general-purpose floatplane	**Dimensions:** wingspan 37 ft (11.28 m) including the ailerons; length 27 ft 8 in (8.43 m); height 9 ft 4 in (2.84 m); wing area 331.00 sq ft (30.75 m²)
Powerplant: one Curtiss O Vee piston engine rated at 75 hp (56 kW)	
Performance: maximum speed 65 mph (104.5 km/h) at sea level	

Curtiss early floatplanes (continued)

This development process paved the way for the **A-1**, which was the first aircraft bought by the US Navy. The A-1, later redesignated as the **AH-1** in the system introduced by the USN during 1914, was variously flown as a landplane, float-plane and amphibian floatplane in a host of experimental evaluations. In the later form it was named *Triad*. It was struck off charge on 16 October 1914, after some 60 flights totalling 285 hours.

In the period between 1911 and 1914, the USN bought another 13 'Curtiss Pushers' with a number of detail differences. These were the **A-2**, **A-3**, **A-4**, **AH-8**, **AH-9**, and **AH-11** to **AH-18**. The **A-2** was delivered on 13 July 1911 in landplane configuration, but was then converted as a floatplane. In this latter configuration the machine achieved a flight of 6 hours 10 minutes on 6 October 1912. By October 1912 the A-2 had been further converted into a flying-boat by building a superstructure from the upper surface of the pontoon to enclose the crew. Retractable tricycle landing gear, similar to that of the *Triad* was fitted, and the designation of the modified machine was changed to **E-1**. This machine was also called the **OWL (Over Water and Land)** and was also briefly known as the **AX-1**.

The next two US Navy aircraft were the **A-3** and **A-4**, and these were also single-float 'Curtiss Pushers' with minor differences of detail. The A-3 achieved a measure of notoriety on 13 June 1913 when it set an American seaplane altitude record of 6,200 ft (1890 m).

The first two aircraft procured under the new USN designation system were **AH-8** and **AH-9**, both of which were referred to as **Type AH-8** in the manner of ships, where the first of a new class or design gave its name to the entire group. The two AH-8 floatplanes were followed by five more (**AH-11** to **AH-15**), and these were followed by a further three machines (**AH-16** to **AH-18**) that US Navy records designate as the AH-8 type.

Further designation changes took place within the procurement period of the 'Curtiss Pushers', the last 11 being ordered in a system in which every USN aircraft was identified by a consecutive serial number prefixed by A (Airplane). The USN had decided to designate its aircraft by the manufacturer's own name and model number, but since the Curtiss aircraft had no firm number at the factory, the last 11 of the basic design (A60 to A62 and A83 to A90) were designated as the Type AH-8. A83 was the AH-9 rebuilt, and A84 to A90 may have been similarly reassigned.

The original AH-8 had, meanwhile, been transferred to the US Army. It survived World War I and was then stored before being refurbished in 1928 and flown briefly by Captain Holden C. Richardson, Chief of the Design and Materiel Division, Bureau of Aeronautics, on 10 February of that year.

It is also worth noting that, by the autumn of 1911, Curtiss was advertising his hydro aircraft on the open market. The standardised float gear was available for an additional $500 when buying a standard Model D or E landplane. The hydros were nearly as popular as the landplanes and, during 1912, were licensed for construction by foreign manufacturers.

Curtiss early flying-boats

The first Curtiss flying-boat, tested at San Diego, California, on 10 January 1912, had no formal designation but is generally known to aviation historians as the **Flying-Boat No. 1**. It was more a hydro than a true flying-boat as it was based on an adaptation of the airframe of the standard Type III 'Curtiss Pusher' with no forward elevator or pusher engine. To the underside of this airframe's lower wing was attached a wide hull and the powerplant comprised one 60-hp (45-kW) Curtiss Vee engine installed in the hull, immediately ahead of the lower wing's leading edge, to drive a pair of tractor propellers. Side-by-side accommodation was provided in a cockpit behind the lower wing's trailing edge.

The Flying-Boat No. 1 proved incapable of taking off, but the **Flying-Boat No. 2**, known as the **Flying Fish**, was the world's first successful flying-boat. The machine had a full-length hull with a flat bottom, and this hull carried both the wing cellule and the tail unit. The Flying-Boat No. 2 was powered by a single 75-hp (56-kW) Curtiss O Vee engine installed in standard 'Curtiss Pusher' fashion, to drive a two-bladed wooden pusher propeller. The Flying-Boat No. 2 was subjected to considerable development and modification in a short time, and ended with the double-surfaced wing cellule of the Model E-75 landplane and no forward elevator.

In its initial form the high drag of the Flying-Boat No. 2's hull prevented it from reaching flying speed. Curtiss watched the take-off efforts from a motor boat, and then decided that a break in the straight line of the hull's bottom, creating a step just to the rear of the 'boat's centre of gravity, would provide a solution to the problem. The concept of the step worked so effectively that Curtiss took out a patent on it, together with vents that allowed air to bleed into the cavity behind the step as a further means of reducing drag in the approach to take-off speed. Revised with such a step, the Flying-Boat No. 2 achieved its maiden flight in July 1912.

Several other 'boats were built immediately after the Flying-Boat No. 2 for the evaluation of a number of features. These 'boats had no known designations and their constant modifications have complicated the problem of identifying them. The three most important of these machines were the **Freak Boat**, the **Tadpole** and the **OWL**.

The **Freak Boat** was based on a full-length hull, but the two pilots were seated in a completely exposed side-by-side arrangement as on the standard hydro, and the interplane gap was reduced. Extensive modification of the *Freak Boat* included entirely new tail surfaces and an unequal-span wing cellule of reduced span, and it was in this form that the 'boat was sold to the USN in November 1912 for service with the designation **C-1**, which was altered to **AB-1** in the course of March 1914. The single 'boat remains of historical importance as it was the first flying-boat operated by the USN, and also because of the fact that it achieved the first successful catapult launch of a flying-boat, an event that took place on 12 December 1912, at the Washington Navy Yard. The AB-1 made its last flight on 1 April 1914.

The **Tadpole** was a hybrid type, of which several others were created, in which a hydro-type long central float was built up into a 'hull' by the filling-in of the volume between the top of the float and the leading edge of the lower wing with a light fabric-covered superstructure in which the members of the crew were seated. The tail unit was carried above the rear of the hull on struts, and other unusual features of the *Tadpole* were a wing cellule pivoted on the rear spar of the lower wing to provide a variable-incidence capability.

The **OWL** (Over Water and Land) was a conversion of the A-2, the second aircraft bought by the US Navy and delivered on 13 July 1911 in stock Model E landplane configuration with an interim powerplant in the form of one 50-hp (37-kW) Curtiss inline engine. The machine was converted into a floatplane in June 1912, but was then further adapted during October 1912 with the *Tadpole's* type of forward superstructure, thus turning the A-2 into a short-hulled flying-boat. Further experimental development added retractable wheels to provide an amphibious capability, resulting in the unofficial designation *OWL*. The 'boat's official designation changed to **E-1** in September 1913 and finally to **AX-1** in March 1914. The 'boat was wrecked on 27 November 1915, after completing 91 flights.

It is also worth noting that the testing of the experimental flying-boats of 1912 soon resulted in a marketable design. The earliest production versions, which were undesignated, had hulls with strong lower structures and, as noted above, a light upper superstructure. This basic design proved eminently 'developable' and led to the **Model F**, which was extensively sold to private owners in the USA as well as to the American and foreign armed forces.

The 1913 initial variant of the Model F flying-boat used the early composite hull construction and what were essentially Model E-75 wings with strut-braced extensions on the upper wing. The core of the structure was the hull, which had a single step and

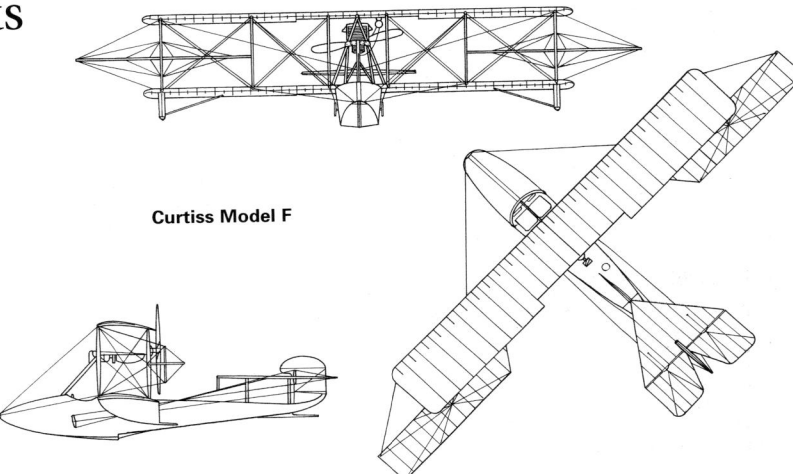

Curtiss Model F

SPECIFICATION	
Curtiss Model F (1917 Revision)	30 minutes
Type: two-seat training flying-boat	**Weights:** empty 1,860 lb (844 kg); maximum take-off 2,460 lb (1116 kg)
Powerplant: one Curtiss OXX-3 Vee piston engine rated at 100 hp (75 kW)	**Dimensions:** wingspan 45 ft 1⅛ in (13.75 m); length 27 ft 9¾ in (8.48 m); height 11 ft 2¾ in (3.43 m); wing area 387.00 sq ft (35.95 m²)
Performance: maximum speed 69 mph (111 km/h) at sea level; climb to 2,300 ft (700 m) in 10 minutes; service ceiling 4,500 ft (1370 m); endurance 5 hours	

side-by-side accommodation in an open cockpit for the pilot and co-pilot, pupil or passenger.

The US Navy bought five Model Fs of the 1913 variant as its 'C' class flying-boats that were designated as **C-1** to **C-5** (later **AB-1** to **AB-5**). Among the distinctions of these 'boats were the first flight under automatic control (the **C-2** on 30 August 1913 with a Sperry gyroscopic automatic pilot), the first catapult launch from a warship (the **AB-2** on 5 November 1915 from the battleship USS *North Carolina*), and the first US military aircraft to see action. This last involved the **AB-3** which, with one other 'boat, was transported to Vera Cruz on Mexico's eastern seaboard on board the cruiser USS *Birmingham*. On 25 April, Lieutenant (jg) P. N. L. Bellinger piloted the AB-3 on a reconnaissance mission over the city of Vera Cruz

In its modernised form, the Model F featured sponsons low down on the forward fuselage. These improved the 'boats hydrodynamic qualities.

The hull of the Model F carried all the flying surfaces, while its Curtiss O Vee engine was mounted beneath the lower wing. This aircraft has the standard 1913 configuration.

and surveyed the harbour for mines. This 'boat later had its wings cropped for use as a non-flying 'Penguin' taxiing trainer. The Aeronautical Section of the US Army's Signal Corps bought one example of the Model F in its 1913 variant.

The variant of the Model F flying-boat that was standardised in 1914 differed from the 1913 version in having a revised equal-span wing cellule, a hull with a full-depth primary structure

and a foredeck with rounded upper surface of wood veneer, and a diagonal strut from the engine mount to the lower forward hull structure to protect the crew from a falling engine in the event of a crash-alighting. On later examples of the Model F's 1914 variant, the original type of equal-span wing cellule was replaced by a more modern cellule, with the ailerons inset into the outboard ends of the trailing edge of the upper wing.

In its 1913 and 1914 forms, the basic Model F flying-boat was ordered to the extent of only eight

Variants

Model MF: known under the Curtiss company's retrospectively-applied numbering system of 1935 as the **Model 18**, this was one of a number of experimental developments of the Model F, but was the only one to be accepted for production. It was substantially improved structurally and incorporated sponsons on the side of the forward hull, and the MF designation implied **'Modernised Model F'**. The type was fitted experimentally with engines in the 150-hp (112-kW) class; the 22 Model MFs delivered to the USN and the 80 additional 'boats built by the Naval Aircraft Factory retained the 100-hp (75-kW) Curtiss OXX-3 engine. During the early 1920s some ex-USN Model MF 'boats were modified under the name **Seagull** for the civil market by Curtiss and Cox-Klemin, and others were built as new for private owners

Judson Triplane: produced late in 1916 or early in 1917, and later allocated the designation **Model 7**, this was a slightly scaled-up version of the Model F, built as a one-off for a Mr Judson; it was originally powered by a 150-hp (112-kW) Curtiss V-X engine, but was re-engined with a 400-hp (298-kW) Curtiss K-12 for post-war exploratory flights in South America

Model K: an enlarged 1915 development of the Model F, which proved only moderately successful in the USA, but was widely exported

'boats by the USN up to the end of 1916. After the USA's entry into the World War I during April 1917, however, orders were increased when the design was chosen as the USN's standard primary training flying-boat: procurement after April 1917 totalled 144 boats and production continued up to

the time of the Model F's replacement in production by the **Model MF** during 1918. The **Model F (Revised)** of 1917-8 was greatly improved over the 1914 model, the principal change being a redesign of the control system to delete the shoulder-yoke type of aileron control.

Curtiss Model D and Model E

By mid-1911 the 'Curtiss Pusher' had become virtually standardised and was being produced on a production-line basis. It was at this stage that Curtiss started to employ specific designations in its advertising. It is no longer known to what specific types the designations **Model A**, **Model B** and **Model C** were attached, if indeed they were attached, so the first properly designated Curtiss aircraft known to history are the **Model D**

and **Model E**.

The US Army and USN purchased 12 'Curtiss Pusher' aircraft of the landplane type in 1911 and 1912, but only one of these was a Model D, more specifically of the **Model D-8** subvariant; the other two subvariants of the Model D were the **Model D-4** with one 40-hp (30-kW) Curtiss four-cylinder inline engine and the **Model D-8-75** with one 75-hp (56-kW) Curtiss eight-cylinder Vee engine.

The sole Model D to enter military service was the US Army's second aircraft, and was an existing machine bought in March 1911 and delivered later in the same month for service as **Signal Corps Aeroplane No. 2**. The aircraft was soon revised with a lower-rated powerplant in the form of a 40-hp (30-kW) Curtiss engine, and later the forward elevator was removed. The machine ended as a so-called 'Penguin' ground trainer with cut-down wings after the US Army had grounded all its pusher training aircraft during February 1914.

The Model E was a slightly larger type, built as the **Model E-4**, **Model E-8** and **Model E-8-75** with the same engines as the equiv-

US Army Aeroplane No. 6, a Model E, was flown as a single-seater due to its low power.

alent Model D subvariants.

The US Army ordered three examples of the Model E-4 as its sixth, eighth and 23rd aircraft. The type was considered to be underpowered and was therefore generally flown in single-seat layout, and in an effort to improve performance, the 40-hp (30-kW) engine of the first machine was exchanged with the 60-hp (45-kW) engine of the

sole Model D-8 in military service. The second machine was later converted to seaplane configuration, and the third machine was sold out of the service in 1914. The aircraft were retired in 1914 as a result of their poor safety and reliability records at the US Army's flight training establishment at North Island outside San Diego, California.

Eugene Ely takes off from the deck of USS Birmingham in a Model D on 14 November 1910. This was the first time that an aircraft had taken off from a ship.

SPECIFICATION	
Curtiss Model D-8	
Type: single-seat aircraft	60 mph (96.5 km/h) at sea level
Powerplant: one Curtiss Vee piston engine rated at 60 hp (45 kW)	**Weights:** maximum take-off 650 lb (295 kg)
Performance: maximum speed	**Dimensions:** wingspan 33 ft 4 in (10.16 m); length 25 ft 9 in (7.85 m); height 7 ft 5½ in (2.27 m)

Curtiss Model G

The first Curtiss aircraft designed to the increasingly popular tractor configuration, the **Model G Tractor** was created in 1912 in direct response to the interest in such aircraft expressed by the US Army's Signal Corps. Production totalled just two aircraft delivered to the service in 1914 with differing details, but neither survived for more than a

few months.

As completed for its maiden flight in February 1913, the first machine (Signal Corps No. 21) had an unequal-span wing cellule, with balanced ailerons located in mid-gap. Its landing gear was of the fixed tricycle type, supplemented by a tailskid attached to the lower edge of the ventral fin, and the powerplant comprised one

In basic configuration the Model G was a biplane of the type of fabric-covered and wire-braced wooden construction typical of the era.

75-hp (56-kW) Curtiss Model O engine. The second machine was Signal Corps No. 22, and as completed this had a longer, equal-span wing cellule, a revised quadricycle main landing gear unit, and one Curtiss OX engine.

The US Army accepted SC No. 21 in June 1913 after it had been modified with a direct-drive propeller, a revised equal-span wing cellule of longer span with ailerons on the outboard ends of the upper wing's trailing edge, and tailskid landing gear. The wheels were later replaced

by floats so that the aircraft could be used in Hawaii, but its capabilities were wholly indifferent and the service sold the machine to a civilian in mid-1914. The SC No. 22 machine entered service in

December 1913 after it had been modified to unequal-span layout with a shortened lower wing and upper-wing ailerons, and after limited use as a trainer, this machine was discarded in October 1914.

SPECIFICATION

Curtiss Model G Tractor
Type: two-seat observation and training aircraft
Powerplant: one Curtiss OX Vee piston engine rated at 90 hp (67 kW)
Performance: maximum speed

54 mph (86 km/h) at sea level
Weights: maximum take-off 2,400 lb (1089 kg)
Dimensions: wingspan 41 ft (12.50 m); length 25 ft (7.62 m); wing area 390.00 sq ft (36.23 m²)

Curtiss Model 1 (Model J, Model N and Model JN 'Jenny' and 'Canuck')

The **Curtiss Model J** was designed by B. Douglas Thomas, formerly of the Sopwith Company. It was an equal-span tractor biplane powered by a 90-hp (67-kW) Curtiss O water-cooled engine. One of the two Model Js was tested as a single-float seaplane, and both were bought by the US Army's Signal Corps late in 1914. The Model J achieved a respectable 70 mph (113 km/h), but was handicapped by its outmoded shoulder-yoke aileron control system. Developed in parallel with the Model J, the **Model N** had the 100-hp (75-kW) Curtiss OXX engine and interplane ailerons. Despite a higher loaded weight, it was credited with a maximum speed of 82 mph (132 km/h), somewhat better than that of the Model J. Nevertheless, only one example was built.

It was from the Model J and Model N that the **Model JN** was created. In January 1915 the US Army ordered eight examples of what was described as the **Model J Modified**, although by the time the aircraft were delivered in the spring of 1915 they had the revised designation **JN-2**. Two aircraft were sent to the Mexican border early in 1916, where they flew observation missions against Mexican guerrillas and bandits led by Pancho Villa, thus becoming the first US Army aircraft to fly combat operations.

The JN-2 was an equal-span biplane with ailerons on both the upper and lower wings, and a tail unit with a distinctive rudder but no fixed vertical fin. The type proved unsuc-

cessful but was developed into the **JN-3** and finally the famous **JN-4**.

The JN-4 two-seat biplane soon acquired the nickname **'Jenny'** which was used widely during the interwar years, and it was without doubt one of the most significant American aircraft of its time. From April 1917, when the USA entered World War I, it was built in large numbers and used to train some 95 per cent of all American and Canadian pilots. It achieved renewed fame between 1919 and the late 1920s, when thousands were flown in the barnstorming era, thrilling spectators at travelling aerial pageants and shows throughout the USA.

The JN-4 was developed from the JN-2 via the interim JN-3. The UK and the US Army bought 91 and two examples of the JN-3 respectively, and several JN-2s were upgraded to JN-3 standard by the incorporation of JN-3 wings and vertical tail surfaces and by the installation of the 100-hp (75-kW) OXX engine. Total produc-

tion was no more than 100, a dozen of them built at the newly opened Curtiss factory at Toronto in Canada.

In its original form the JN-4 closely resembled the JN-3. It first appeared in July 1916 when 105 were sold to the UK and 21 to the US Army. Others were purchased by private owners and a number were operated by the Curtiss company's flying schools. As a result of British experience with the JN-3 and JN-4, Curtiss developed the **JN-4A** (retrospectively designated as the **Model 1** in the system that Curtiss introduced in 1935), which incorporated a number of improvements including a larger tailplane and engine downthrust. A total of 781 such aircraft was completed, 87 of them at the Canadian factory. The US Army bought 601 of these and the US Navy five, and the rest were exported to the UK. The **JN-4B** (**Model 1A**) appeared late in 1916, just before the JN-4A and differed in several design details – it introduced the

larger tailplane and used the OX-2 engine – and included among its customers a number of private purchasers and flying schools as well as 76 and nine aircraft for the US Army and USN respectively.

Two examples of the experimental **JN-4C** were followed by the very successful **JN-4 Can** and **JN-4D** (**Model 1C**). The former had been developed from the JN-3 by the Curtiss company's Canadian associate, Canadian Aeroplanes Ltd, and soon became known as the **'Canuck'**. Production totalled 1,260, of which 680 went to the US Army while the bulk of the remainder became the

standard Canadian primary trainer. The JN-4 Can served with the RCAF until 1924, while privately owned aircraft remained in use into the 1930s. John Ericson, chief engineer of Canadian Aeroplanes Ltd, assembled 127 aircraft in 1927, most of them reconditioned aircraft incorporating many parts which had been held in stock. Some had a third cockpit and were known under the designation **Ericson Special Three**.

The JN-4D appeared in June 1917 and went into large-scale production, 2,812 being built between November 1917 and January 1919. In view of the urgent need for efficient trainers in wartime conditions, the production programme involved six other US manufacturers. As well as several new features, the JN-4D combined the more

SPECIFICATION

Curtiss JN-4D
Type: two-seat primary trainer
Powerplant: one Curtiss OX-5 Vee piston engine rated at 90 hp (67 kW)
Performance: maximum speed 75 mph (121 km/h) at sea level; cruising speed 60 mph (97 km/h) at optimum altitude; climb to 2,000 ft (610 m) in 7 minutes 30 seconds;

service ceiling 6,500 ft (1980 m); range 250 miles (412 km)
Weights: empty 1,390 lb (630 kg); maximum take-off 1,920 lb (871 kg)
Dimensions: wingspan 43 ft 7⅞ in (13.30 m); length 27 ft 4 in (8.33 m); height 9 ft 10⅝ in (3.01 m); wing area 352.00 sq ft (32.70 m²)

This JN-4 Can 'Canuck' was flown by the School of Aerial Fighting in 1918. Late in 1919, a reconditioned, ex-military 'Canuck' could be purchased in the US for $2,600-3,000.

CITY OF TORONTO   C368

Variant

Twin JN: retrospectively designated as the **Model 1B**, the **Twin JN** appeared in April 1916 and was provisionally designated **JN-5**; it was an enlarged and twin-engined version of the JN-4 intended for the observation role; the standard wing cellule was used, though span was increased. The vertical tail surface was derived from that of the R-4 (Model 2); power was provided by two 90-hp (67-kW) OXX-2 engines mounted between the wings and production totalled eight

successful elements of the JN-4 Can and JN-4A designs (stick control of the former, in place of the Deperdussin system, and the lines and engine down-thrust of the latter). The end of World War I led to cancellation of contracts for 1,100 examples of a modified **JN-4D-2** version. In the event, only the prototype was delivered to the military authorities, although several were sold to civil operators in 1919.

In a bid to provide an advanced trainer to meet urgent wartime needs, the JN-4D was re-engined with a more powerful engine, the 150-hp (112-kW) Hispano-Suiza unit licence-built by the Wright company. The resulting **JN-4H** (**Model 1E**) was in production from the end of 1917 to the time of the Armistice, 929 being delivered to the US Army. The JN-4H was also built in **JN-4HT** dual-control, **JN-4HB** bombing and **JN-4HG** gunnery training versions.

The one-off **JN-5H** advanced trainer was built to a US Army requirement, but was rejected in favour of the Vought VE-7. It was developed into the **JN-6H** (**Model 1F**) which had a strengthened aileron control arrangement. The US Army purchased 1,035 examples of the JN-6H, subsequently passing five examples to the USN. The aircraft delivered to the US Army were built in subvariants specialised for different training functions as the **JN-6HB** single-control bomber trainer, **JN-6HG-1** dual-control trainer, **JN-6HG-2** single-control gunnery trainer, **JN-6HO** single-control observation trainer and **JN-6HP** single-control pursuit (fighter) trainer.

As part of the post-war economy drive the US Army was forced to modernise the 'Jenny' rather than purchase new designs. This task was allocated to the US Army's service depots, which upgraded many of the earlier aircraft in a programme that lasted to 1926. The revised aircraft all used Wright-built 180-hp (134-kW) Hispano-Suiza engines and were redesignated **JNS** (standing for **JN Standardised**). Between 200 and 300 JNS trainers were completed. The US Army used the JN-4A, JN-4D and JN-4 Can primary trainers until 1919. The higher powered JN-4H and JN-6H aircraft remained in service until they were phased out in the mid-1920s, the last 'Jennies' being withdrawn from Army service in 1927.

Meanwhile, from 1919 onward, more 'Jennies' had been sold to private owners, many of whom used their aircraft to earn a living as stunt pilots. Unhampered by regulations relating to their operation until the first restrictions were applied in 1927, the 'Jenny' became known to a whole generation of US citizens.

In the Twin JN, an 11-ft 4-in (3.45-m) section was added into the upper wing of the JN-4, with short panels joining the lower wing to the fuselage on each side.

Curtiss Model 6 (Model H-4 Small America, Models H-12 and H-16 Large America, and Model F-5L)

In 1913 the Daily Mail offered a prize of £10,000 (then $50,000) for the first aerial crossing of the Atlantic Ocean. Mr Rodman Wanamaker, the owner of department stores in New York and Philadelphia, wanted to ensure that the prize was won by an American aircraft, and in August 1913 he commissioned the design and construction of two aircraft, for which the name *America* had already been selected, from Curtiss.

In layout the resulting **Model H** adhered to the established pattern of previous Curtiss flying-boats, but was somewhat larger than its predecessors to carry the fuel required for a flight of 1,100 miles (1770 km), representing the length of the longest leg in the planned transatlantic

flight. It had a powerplant of two 90-hp (67-kW) Curtiss OX Vee engines installed in the interplane gap and driving pusher propellers, and carried a crew of three in an enclosed cabin.

In production, the H-4 was equivalent to the original America. RNAS aircraft, like that illustrated, had Anzani radial engines installed.

America was named in June 1914 and embarked on an extensive test programme. One of the early problems encountered was the tendency for the bow to bury itself in the water as engine power was increased. This phenomenon had not hitherto been apparent to any significant degree in earlier 'boats because of the relatively low power of their single-engined power-plants. The need was clearly for more buoyancy in the forward part of the hull, and this was met initially by the addition of planing surfaces on the sides of the hull forward of the step. These were soon replaced by larger structures that Curtiss called 'fins', and this feature came to be used on many flying-boats into the 1930s, with the name sponson rather than fin being used.

In this form *America* was finally deemed ready for the transatlantic flight, and the frequently post-poned effort was scheduled for 5 August

The F-5L was the ultimate military expression of the H-series. This aircraft served with the Atlantic Fleet Scouting Squadron, USN, in January 1924.

1914, but the flight was cancelled on the outbreak of World War I. Lieutenant John C. Porte, the British ex-naval officer who had been selected as pilot, was recalled to duty in the UK and was able to persuade the Admiralty first to impress and then to buy *America* and its sister, as the prototypes of a long line of twin-engined biplane flying-boats that would serve the UK and USA until well into World War II.

The original *America* gave its name to the class, and later developments up to the **Model H-16** were bought by the UK for service with the designations **Small America** and **Large America**.

Curtiss Model 6 (Model H-4 Small America, Models H-12 and H-16 Large America, and Model F-5L) (continued)

Until the introduction of the **Model H-12**, the only service customer for the Curtiss twin-engined flying-boats was the RNAS, which designated *America* and its successors as the **Model H-4 Small America** series that in 1935 received the retrospective Curtiss designation **Model 6**.

As a result of British experience, Curtiss found that the hulls of its 'boats possessed a number of significant structural and hydrodynamic failings. Late in 1915 Porte designed and built improved hulls and fitted them with standard Curtiss wings and tails. The improvements proved desirable, and the Model H series of large 'boats was produced with the new hulls and British-built Curtiss wings to become the standard patrol/bomber flying-boat of the RNAS and later the RAF.

The H-4 was given the retrospective British designation Small America after the **Model H-12 Large America** appeared. As delivered (four 'boats), the Model H-4 was fitted with a powerplant of two 90-hp (67-kW) OX-5 engines, but these were deemed to lack adequate power and were therefore replaced as the standard powerplant by a pair of 100-hp (75-kW) Anzani radials. With this powerplant the Model H-4 could carry an offensive load of only two 100-lb (45-kg) bombs, so later 'boats were completed

with the powerplant of two 110-hp (82-kW) Clerget 9 rotary engines to allow the carriage of a heavier warload. Curtiss built a total of 62 H-4s, eight of them being assembled in the UK.

Developed as a result of the RNAS's experience with the Model H-4, the **Model H-12** (company designation **Model 6A**) appeared in prototype form during the autumn of 1916. Larger and more powerful than its predecessor, it was powered by two 160-hp (119-kW) Curtiss V-X-X engines driving tractor propellers. After 84 H-12s had been delivered to the UK, a batch of 20 was ordered for the USN, these having 200-hp (149-kW) Curtiss V-2-3 engines.

While the H-12s were found to perform reasonably well on the water and in the air, they were considered underpowered. As a result the British replaced the original Curtiss engines with Rolls-Royce Eagle Vee engines, first the 275-hp (205-kW) Eagle I and then the 375-hp (280-kW) Eagle VIII to create the **Model H-12A** (**Model 6B**) and **Model H-12B** (**Model 6D**) respectively. The US Navy replaced the Curtiss engines with 360-hp (268-kW) Liberty low-compression Vee engines toward the end of 1917, the modified 'boats being redesignated **Model H-12L**.

These 'boats played an

This photograph of an H-16 illustrates the attachment of its wingtip floats directly beneath the outer surfaces of the lower wing.

important part in the battle against the U-boat menace and operated from a number of coastal bases in Britain and Ireland during 1916 and 1917. Problems with deterioration in their laminated wood hulls led to research by Lieutenant Porte, his work leading to production of the improved **F-5L** flying-boat. With availability of the improved **Curtiss H-16** the US Navy scrapped its surviving H-12Ls at the end of 1920.

Developed from the Model H-12, the Model H-16 (company designation **Model 6C**) had wings of slightly increased span, a hull that had been revised and strengthened structurally, and in the case of all the 'boats delivered to the USN, the powerplant of two 360-hp (268-kW) Liberty engines. Production totalled 150 H-16s by the NAF and 184 by the Curtiss company. Of the Curtiss-built aircraft, 60 were crated and sent to the UK, where they were assembled and given 345-hp (257-kW) Rolls-Royce Eagle IV engines. The other H-16s went to the USN, a number arriving at bases in the UK in time to see service alongside the British 'boats before the cessation of hostilities.

After World War I most surviving USN H-16s were

refitted with later 400-hp (298-kW) Liberty 12A engines, some also being modified by fitting parts from the successful Model F-5L 'boats. Two H-16s tested with pusher engines were designated as the **Model H-16-1** and **Model H-16-2**, the latter also having a revised wing cellule, but neither was successful.

The basic airframe of the Small America (Model H-4) and Large America (Model H-12 and -16) was further developed in the UK as, most importantly, the **Felixstowe F.2** that

combined a hull designed by Porte, Rolls-Royce Eagle engines, and the Curtiss flying surfaces. Highly successful in its own right, the F.2 led to the still better **F.5** and redesigned to US standards by the NAF, the F.5 became the Model F-5L in the US Navy's nomenclature, the L denoting the use of Liberty engines. Production totalled 60 by Curtiss, 138 by the NAF and 30 by Canadian Aeroplanes Ltd. In the early 1920s a number of F-5Ls was converted as 16/20-seat civil transports.

Variants

F-6: two NAF-built F-5Ls which were given redesigned vertical tail surfaces; all surviving F-5Ls were retrofitted to the same standard
PN-5: new designation applied to all F-5Ls in 1922
PN-7: two 'boats with a redesigned wing cellule and 525-hp (391-kW) Wright T-2 engines
PN-8: two 'boats generally similar to the PN-7 except for introduction of a metal hull and 475-hp (354-kW) Packard 1A-2500 engines
PN-9: conversion of one PN-8 with redesigned tail surfaces and engine nacelles
PN-10: two 'boats generally similar to the PN-9
PN-11: four 'boats with a redesigned and wider hull
PN-12: two 'boats ordered as PN-10s but completed with Wright R-1750 Cyclones and two Pratt & Whitney R-1850 Hornet units; the improved performance of these two 'boats led to the procurement of a new generation of 'boats derived from the F-5

SPECIFICATION

Curtiss Model F-5L
Type: four-seat maritime reconnaissance and patrol flying-boat
Powerplant: two Liberty 12A Vee piston engines each rated at 400 hp (298 kW)
Performance: maximum speed 90 mph (145 km/h) at sea level; climb to 2,200 ft (670 m) in 10 minutes; service ceiling 5,500 ft (1675 m); range 830 miles (1336 km)

Weights: empty 8,720 lb (3955 kg); maximum take-off 13,600 lb (6169 kg)
Dimensions: wingspan 103 ft 9¾ in (31.63 m); length 49 ft 3¾ in (15.03 m); height 18 ft 9¼ in (5.72 m); wing area 1,397.00 sq ft (129.78 m²)
Armament: six to eight 0.3-in (7.62-mm) Browning trainable machine-guns, plus up to 920 lb (417 kg) of bombs carried under the lower wing

Curtiss Model 17 Oriole

SPECIFICATION

Curtiss Model 17 Oriole (long-span variant)
Type: three-seat general-purpose aircraft
Powerplant: one Curtiss C-6 inline piston engine rated at 160 hp (119 kW)
Performance: maximum speed 97 mph (156 km/h) at optimum altitude; cruising speed 77 mph (124 km/h) at optimum altitude;

initial climb rate 700 ft (213 m) per minute; service ceiling 12,850 ft (3915 m); range 388 miles (624 km)
Weights: empty 1,732 lb (786 kg); maximum take-off 2,545 lb (1154 kg)
Dimensions: wingspan 40 ft (12.19 m); length 26 ft 1 in (7.95 m); height 10 ft 3 in (3.12 m); wing area 399.00 sq ft (37.07 m²)

The **Curtiss L-72** design, later named **Oriole** and retrospectively designated as the **Model 17**, inaugurated the Curtiss practice of allocating bird names to the

Great care was taken in the Oriole's fuselage design, resulting in beautifully rounded contours and laminated plywood skins.

company's designs. Appearing in June 1919, it represented an early bid for the US private aircraft market. Unfortunately, the glut of war-surplus aircraft resulted in relatively limited orders for the new biplane: the exact figure is not known, but production did not exceed 50 machines.

The Oriole had provision for the pilot in the front cockpit with two passengers in a large cockpit immediately beneath the cut-out in the centre section of the upper wing's trailing edge. These passenger seats were staggered to provide additional room, and a small door in the fuselage side provided easy access. Early examples of the Oriole were powered by a 90-hp (67-kW) Curtiss OX-5 engine which gave a maximum speed of 86 mph (138 km/h), while later aircraft were fitted with the Curtiss C-6 and had increased wingspan.

The Oriole participated in a number of air races during the 1920s and achieved some success. Particularly well known was the much-modified company-owned Oriole flown by Curtiss pilot, 'Casey' Jones. Several examples of the Oriole were sold in an incomplete state and used as the bases for new designs by small companies trying to gain a footing in the cut-throat US aircraft industry. These included the **Curtiss-Ireland Comet**, which married the Oriole's fuselage to a set of new single-bay wings; and the **Pitcairn Orowing** with the short-span wing cellule, tailplane and landing gear of the Oriole attached to a Pitcairn-designed lightweight fuselage.

Curtiss Model 19 Eagle

The first **Curtiss Eagle** (later **Model 19**) was a three-engined three-bay biplane, largely of wooden construction, built in 1919 in anticipation of a strong demand for new passenger-carrying designs. In the event, the limited American market after World War I was met largely by converted military types. Nevertheless, the Eagle set new standards with a carefully streamlined fuselage and wide-track double-bogie main landing gear units with metal wheel fairings. The fully enclosed cabin accommodated two pilots and up to six passengers in considerable comfort. Less than 20 examples of the Eagle were completed. One **Eagle II** was built with two 400-hp (298-kW) Curtiss C-12 Vee engines, while three examples of a single-engined **Eagle III** variant, powered by the 400-hp (298-kW) Liberty Vee engine, were used by the US Army as air ambulances and staff transports. While most of the batch of three-engined **Eagle I** aircraft (as they were retrospectively designated with the appearance of the Eagles II and III had 150-hp (112-kW) Curtiss K-6 engines, a few were powered by 160-hp (119-kW) C-6 inline units.

One of three single-engined Eagles in US Army service, this aircraft was modified for use in the ambulance role.

SPECIFICATION	
Curtiss Model 17 Eagle I	**Weights:** empty 5,130 lb (2327 kg); maximum take-off 7,450 lb (3379 kg)
Type: two-crew transport	
Powerplant: three Curtiss K-6 inline piston engines each rated at 150 hp (112 kW)	**Dimensions:** wingspan 61 ft 4 in (18.69 m); length 36 ft 9 in (11.20 m); height 12 ft 4 in (3.76 m); wing area 900.00 sq ft (83.61 m²)
Performance: maximum speed 107 mph (172 km/h) at optimum altitude; climb to 4,075 ft (1240 m) in 10 minutes; range 475 miles (764 km)	
	Payload: up to six passengers

Curtiss Model 23 (CR and R-6)

Curtiss first became involved in the design and construction of racing aircraft early in 1920, when the millionaire S. Cox approached the company to produce two aircraft to take part in the James Gordon Bennett Trophy race being held in France in September of that year. The two examples of the **Curtiss Cox Racer** (later **Model 22**) were named *Texas Wildcat* and *Cactus Kitten*, and were originally braced high-wing monoplanes, each powered by the 427-hp (318-kW) Curtiss C-12 Vee engine. Only the *Texas Wildcat* was tested before being dispatched to France where, again tested with its special thin racing wing, it was found to be unstable. A new biplane wing was designed hurriedly and installed, enabling the aircraft to take part in the race, but the machine was wrecked in a landing accident. The *Cactus Kitten* was returned to the USA without being flown, and was given a set of short-span triplane wings with which it gained second place in the 1921 Pulitzer Trophy race.

This race was won, in fact, by another Curtiss racer, one of the company's **Model 23** biplanes built for the US Navy under the designation **CR-1** (contemporary designation **L-17-1**) and **CR-2**. The US Navy had intended to compete but withdrew, and Curtiss borrowed the CR-2. Both the CR-1 and CR-2 were biplanes with fixed tailskid landing gear and the powerplant of one Curtiss CD-12 Vee engine, but differed in minor detail. They were converted subsequently to **CR-3** floatplane standard (**Model 23A**, contemporary designation **L-17-3**) to compete in the 1928 Schneider Trophy contest in the UK. Apart from the change from landing to alighting gear, the aircraft had new 465-hp (347-kW) Curtiss D-12 engines with Curtiss-Reed metal propellers, a significant combination which resulted in the two aircraft gaining first and second place in the Schneider Trophy contest.

Given the intense rivalry between US Army and US Navy, it is not surprising that the US Army decided it too must have racing aircraft and as a result ordered from Curtiss two examples of the **R-6** development of the US Navy's CR. The R-6 was considerably cleaner than its predecessors, and a major contribution to drag reduction was the introduction of wing surface radiators. With these two aircraft the US Army took the first two places in the 1922 Pulitzer air races, and twice raised the world air speed record, the second time to 236.587 mph (380.74 km/h).

Lieutenant Lester J. Maitland of the US Army Air Corps flew this R-6 into second place in the 1922 Pulitzer Trophy Race. Note the aircraft's extremely clean lines, especially around the nose.

SPECIFICATION	
Curtiss Model 23 (R-6)	altitude; range 283 miles (455 km)
Type: single-seat racing aircraft	**Weights:** empty 1,616 lb (733 kg); maximum take-off 2,121 lb (962 kg)
Powerplant: one Curtiss D-12 Special Vee piston engine rated at 460 hp (343 kW)	**Dimensions:** wingspan 19 ft (5.79 m); length 18 ft 10½ in (5.75 m); height 7 ft 7 in (2.31 m); wing area 135.91 sq ft (12.63 m²)
Performance: maximum speed 237 mph (381 km/h) at optimum	

Curtiss Model 26 (Orenco D)

During 1918 the US Air Service ordered four prototypes of the **Orenco Model D** biplane fighter designed by the Ordnance Engineering Company and, in keeping with the policy of the time, acquired the rights to the design. The first **Model D** flew in January 1919 with a powerplant of one 300-hp (224-kW) Wright-Hispano H

One Orenco D was used for the experimental development of a turbocharger installation for improved performance at higher altitudes, with an undernose radiator.

Vee engine, and although the Model D was not an exceptional type the USAS nonetheless decided to

purchase a production batch of 50 such aircraft. The production order went to Curtiss, this manufacturer revising the type as the **Curtiss Orenco D** (later **Model 26**) with a modified engine installation, dihedral on both the upper and

lower wings, and a longer-span upper wing carrying horn-balanced ailerons on the outboard ends of its trailing edge.

The first single-seat fighter of American design to enter full if somewhat limited production, the

Orenco D was an unequal-span staggered two-bay biplane of wooden construction covered with plywood and fabric. The Orenco D fighters were delivered from August 1921 and saw limited service into the mid-1920s.

SPECIFICATION

Curtiss Model 26 (Orenco D)
Type: single-seat fighter
Powerplant: one Wright-Hispano H Vee piston engine rated at 300 hp (224 kW)
Performance: maximum speed 139 mph (224 km/h) at sea level; cruising speed 133 mph (214 km/h) at optimum altitude; initial climb rate 1,140 ft (347 m) per minute; service ceiling 12,450 ft (3795 m); range 340 miles (547 km); endurance 2 hours 30 minutes
Weights: empty 1,908 lb (865 kg);

maximum take-off 2,820 lb (1279 kg)
Dimensions: wingspan 32 ft 11¾ in (10.05 m); length 21 ft 5½ in (6.54 m); height 8 ft 4 in (2.54 m); wing area 273.00 sq ft (25.36 m²)
Armament: one 0.5-in (12.7 mm) Browning fixed forward-firing machine-gun and one 0.3-in (7.62-mm) Browning fixed forward-firing machine-gun or two 0.3-in (7.62 mm) Browning fixed forward-firing machine-guns in the upper part of the forward fuselage

Curtiss Model 32 (R2C and R-8)

Determined to wrest back the Pulitzer Trophy, which the US Army had won in 1922 with the Curtiss R-6, the US Navy contracted in mid-1923 for two racing aircraft that Curtiss created under the company designation **L-111-1** (later **Model 32** in the revised system of nomenclature introduced in 1935). The US Navy had introduced its own definitive designation system in March 1923, and under this the L-111-1 was the **R2C** rather than **C2R** that would have been logical for a successor to the CR in the service's first system.

The L-111-1 was very much an evolutionary development of the L-19-1 (R-6), made possible by the evolution of an uprated version of the D-12 Vee

engine and continued aerodynamic and structural refinement. The engine was the D-12A, which resulted from a navy-funded programme to develop a more powerful version of the D-12 for its new generation of fighter aircraft, delivering 507 hp (378 kW).

The engine was installed in the forward fuselage inside a Dural cowling based on that of the R-6 and therefore shaped closely to the contours of the engine with its Vee arrangement of two cylinder banks; the engine drove a two-bladed propeller fitted with a spinner, and was cooled by surface radiators on the upper and lower surfaces of both wings. The first

R2C-1 achieved its maiden flight on 9 September 1923, and the machine was soon involved in a day-by-day speed contest with the rival Wright F2W-1, of which two examples had been built as racing aircraft, albeit with a fighter designation in an effort to avoid political and public antipathy, with a considerably more powerful engine, the 700-hp (522-kW) Wright T-3 Vee unit. This rivalry was excellent for the rapid fine-tuning of the aircraft and also for the improvement of the two engine

types, which featured strongly in the US Navy's plans of the period: the D-12A was to pave the way for a new generation of fighters, while the T-3 was seen as the engine for aircraft such as torpedo-bombers.

In the 1923 Pulitzer Trophy race the second and first R2C-1 racers took first and second places, in the hands of Lieutenant (jg) Alford J. 'Al' Williams and Lieutenant Harold J. Brow, at speeds of 243.67 mph (392.16 km/h) and 241.78 mph (389.11 km/h) respectively. Just under one month later Brow took the second machine to a world air speed record of

259.16 mph (417.06 km/h), and 10 days later Williams raised the record still further to 266.59 mph (429.025 km/h).

Late in 1923 the USN sold the first R2C-1 to the USAAS for a mere $1, and the machine was operated as the **R-8** until it crashed in September 1924 on a training flight for that year's Pulitzer Trophy race.

In 1924 the second R2C-1 was mounted on twin-float alighting gear for the use of the US Navy team contesting that year's Schneider Trophy race, and in this R2C-2 form received the company designation **H-18-2** that was later altered to **Model 32A**.

The 1924 Schneider Trophy race was cancelled after none of the European competitors reached the starting line. The R2C-2 was then used as a trainer for the 1925 and 1926 Schneider Trophy races.

SPECIFICATION

Curtiss Model 32 (R2C-1)
Type: single-seat racing aircraft
Powerplant: one Curtiss D-12A Vee piston engine rated at 507 hp (378 kW)
Performance: maximum speed 267 mph (429.5 km/h) at sea level; climb to 5,000 ft (1525 m) in 1 minute 36 seconds; service

ceiling 31,800 ft (9695 m); range 173 miles (279 km)
Weights: empty 1,692 lb (767 kg); maximum take-off 2,112 lb (958 kg)
Dimensions: wingspan 22 ft (6.71 m); length 19 ft 8½ in (6.01 m); height 6 ft 9¼ in (2.06 m); wing area 144.25 sq ft (13.40 m²)

Curtiss Model 34A/O Hawk (P-1, P-2, P-3 and P-5)

Successful testing of the **XPW-8B** (**Model 34**) experimental fighter, incorporating a new wing cellule and a number of other modifications, led to

an order for 15 production aircraft. Designated **P-1** (**Pursuit aircraft no. 1**) under a new identification system introduced by the US Army at that time,

10 of these **Model 34A Hawk** single-seat fighters entered service with the 27th and 94th Pursuit Squadrons. A third unit, the 17th Pursuit Squadron,

was equipped with the Hawk following delivery of 25 examples of the **P-1A** (**Model 34G**), which retained the new wing and redesigned tailplane of the

P-1 but included some detailed design improvements. An export version of the P-1A was later offered for sale, and eight were bought by Chile and a single example by Japan for delivery in 1926 and 1927 respectively.

Late in 1926 the US Army acquired 25 examples of the improved **P-1B** (**Model 34I**) with the powerplant of one 435-hp (324-kW) Curtiss V-1150-3 Vee engine in place of the previously standard Curtiss D-12. The P-1B had larger-diameter

wheels and a more rounded radiator. Chile also obtained eight of this version for delivery in 1927. The **P-1C** (**Model 34O**) incorporated wheel brakes and equipment changes which increased the overall weight, and delivery of 33 P-1C Hawk fighters to the US Army was completed by April 1929.

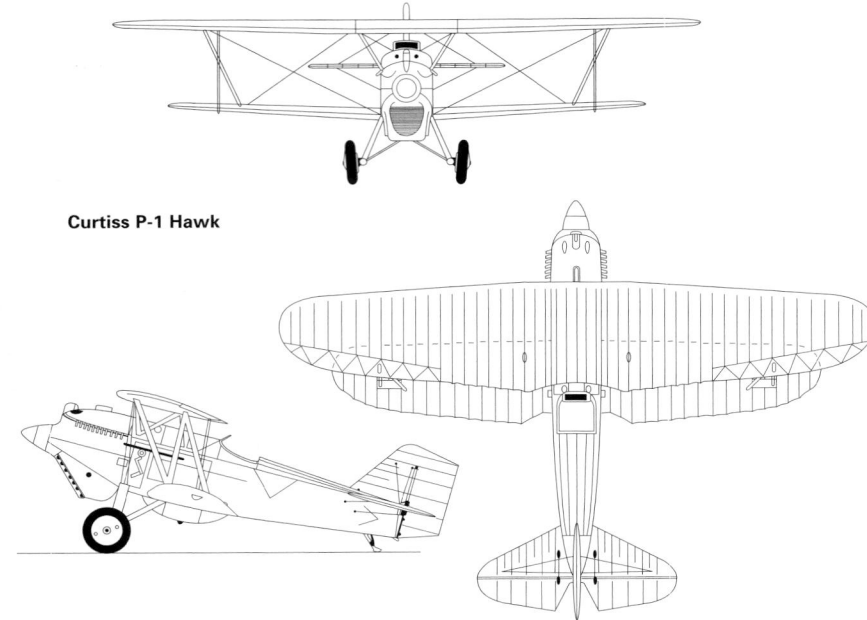

Curtiss P-1 Hawk

Variants

P-2: five aircraft of the original P-1 order were completed under the designation P-2 (**Model 34B**) with the 500-hp (373-kW) Curtiss V-1400 engine developed from the D-12; three were later converted to P-1S standard and another became the **XP-6** prototype

P-3A: designation of five **Model 34N** service test aircraft with the powerplant of one Pratt & Whitney Wasp air-cooled radial engine; one was redesignated as the **XP-3A** when used in connection with experiments to develop the NACA engine cowling, and a second XP-3A was a P-1A airframe powered by the 410-hp (306-kW) Pratt & Whitney R-1340-1 Wasp radial

P-5: this designation was applied to five examples of the **Model 34L** for evaluation in the high-altitude role

With the D-12F engine fitted with a side-mounted turbocharger, the P-5's service ceiling was raised to to 31,700 ft (9660 m). The characteristic frontal radiator installation of the Hawk series is evident.

SPECIFICATION	
Curtiss Model 340 Hawk (P-1C) **Type:** single-seat fighter **Powerplant:** one Curtiss V-1150-3 Vee piston engine rated at 435 hp (324 kW) **Performance:** maximum speed 155 mph (249 km/h) at optimum altitude; cruising speed 123 mph (198 km/h) at optimum altitude; initial climb rate 1,460 ft (445 m) per minute; service ceiling 20,800 ft (6340 m); range 300 miles	(483 km) **Weights:** empty 2,195 lb (996 kg); maximum take-off 2,973 lb (1349 kg) **Dimensions:** wingspan 31 ft 6 in (9.60 m); length 23 ft (7.01 m); height 8 ft 9 in (2.67 m); wing area 252.00 sq ft (23.41 m²) **Armament:** two 0.3-in (7.62-mm) Browning fixed forward-firing machine-guns in the upper part of the forward fuselage

Curtiss Model 34C/H Hawk (F6C)

In 1925 the US Navy ordered nine examples of the **Model 34C Hawk** fighter under the designation **F6C-1**. These aircraft were virtually identical to those of the US Army's P-1 series, and were intended originally for shore use by the US Marine Corps. In fact only five aircraft were delivered as F6C-1s, the remaining

four being completed to the **F6C-2** (**Model 34D**) standard, strengthened for carrierborne operations and therefore fitted with arrester hooks.

During 1927 the USN obtained 35 examples of the **F6C-3** (**Model 34E**), a modified version of the F6C-2. These aircraft were followed by 31 examples of the **F6C-4** (**Model 34H**),

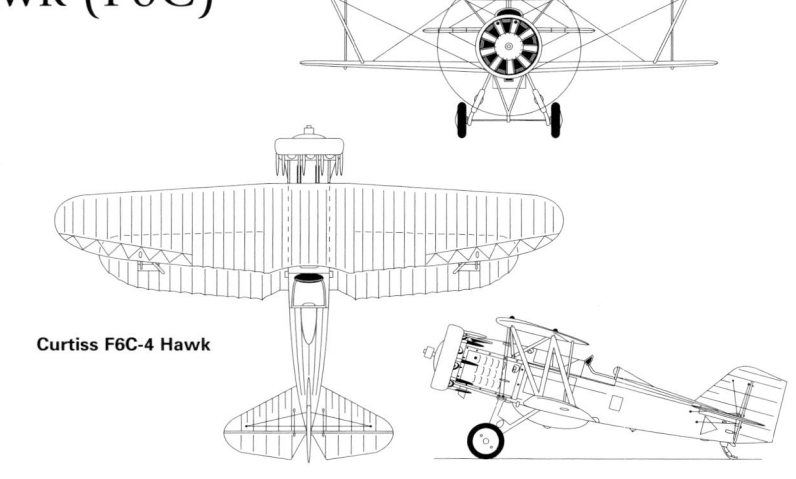

Curtiss F6C-4 Hawk

Variants

XF6C-5: one conversion from XF6C-4 standard (originally the first production F6C-1) to take the 525-hp (691-kW) Pratt & Whitney R-1690 Hornet radial engine

F6C-6: a single F6C-3 fighter adapted as a racing machine with its radiator relocated inside the fuselage, the rear fuselage given a more streamlined configuration and low-drag landing gear replacing the standard pattern

XF6C-6: the F6C-3 which had won the 1930 Curtiss Marine Trophy was converted to parasol wing monoplane configuration and given wing surface radiators; the wing was braced to each side of the fuselage by a single strut, and the main landing-gear units comprised single struts with large 'spat'-type fairings over the wheels; after achieving the fastest lap in the 1930 Thompson Trophy race, the XF6C-6 came to grief when its pilot was overcome by exhaust fumes

XF6C-7: designation of one F6C-4 converted temporarily in 1932 as a testbed for an experimental 350-hp (261-kW) Ranger SVG-770 air-cooled inverted-Vee engine

the first F6C-1 having been converted to take the 420-hp (313-kW) Pratt & Whitney Wasp air-cooled radial engine and serving as the prototype **XF6C-4**. The F6C-1 formed part of the equipment of the USMC's VF-9M squadron, while the F6C-2 fighters operated with the US Navy's VF-2 squadron on the carrier USS *Langley*.

SPECIFICATION	
Curtiss Model 34H Hawk (F6C-4) **Type:** single-seat carrierborne and land-based fighter **Powerplant:** one Pratt & Whitney R-1340 Wasp radial piston engine rated at 410 hp (306 kW) **Performance:** maximum speed 155 mph (249 km/h) at sea level; climb to 5,000 ft (1525 m) in 2 minutes 30 seconds; service ceiling 22,900 ft (6980 m); range 340 miles (547 km)	**Weights:** empty 1,980 lb (898 kg); maximum take-off 3,171 lb (1438 kg) **Dimensions:** wingspan 37 ft 6 in (11.43 m); length 22 ft 6 in (6.86 m); height 10 ft 11 in (3.33 m); wing area 252.00 sq ft (23.41 m²) **Armament:** two 0.3-in (7.62-mm) Browning fixed forward-firing machine-guns in the upper part of the forward fuselage, plus light bombs carried on underwing racks

Curtiss Model 34C/H Hawk (F6C) (continued)

The F6C-3 fighters were flown from 1928 by the VF-5S squadron, which became VB-1B in July of that year in deference to the Hawk's intended fighter-bomber role, on the carrier USS *Lexington*. For a short period VB-1B operated its F6C-3 machines as twin-float seaplanes. Other F6C-3 warplanes served with the shore-based VF-8M squadron of the US Marine Corps.

The USN decided that the maintenance of water-cooled engines on board carriers presented unwarranted problems, with the result that the radial-engined F6C-4 was used to equip the VF-2B squadron on the *Langley* until 1930. The aircraft were then passed to USMC units.

Four F6C-2s were converted from F6C-1 standard for carrier operations. This F6C-2 was photographed aboard Langley.

Curtiss Model 34P/Q, Model 35 and Model 63 Hawk (P-6, P-11, P-17, P-20, P-21, P-22, P-23, AT-4 and AT-5)

The first member of the Hawk series of Curtiss fighters to bear the **P-6** designation was modified from one of the original P-1 fighters. Powered by a Curtiss V-1570 Conqueror engine, the **XP-6** (**Model 34P**) prototype took second place in the 1927 US National Air Races. A second conversion that competed in this same contest was the **XP-6A** (**Model 34K**), also powered by the Conqueror engine, but with an untapered wing cellule similar to that of the experimental **PW-8** and including wing surface radiators to reduce drag; the XP-6A took first place with the then-remarkable speed of 201 mph (323 km/h).

The US Army was sufficiently impressed with the XP-6 to order an evaluation batch of 18 P-6 fighters, the main difference between the prototype and evaluation aircraft being the latter's improved fuselage contours and deeper, more rounded nose. Nine of the

This P-6E was retained by the 33rd Pursuit Squadron (PS) in 1938, long after re-equipment with P-12s and P-35s. The aircraft was probably assigned the role of squadron 'hack', the stylised badge on the fuselage side befitting this role.

18 aircraft, fitted with Prestone- rather than water-cooled V-1670 engines, had the revised designation **P-6A**. The **XP-6B**, which made a remarkable flight from the eastern part of the continental USA to Alaska, was a P-1C converted to take the V-1670 engine. One P-6A became the sole **XP-6D** after conversion to take a turbocharged version of the Conqueror engine. All of the P-6 and all but one of the P-6A aircraft were revised with

This P-6E wears the markings of the 17th PS of the 1st PG. The colour scheme was based on the snow owl depicted on the rear fuselage band.

Variants

XAT-1: one P-1A was converted in 1926 as the **Model 34J** for evaluation as an advanced trainer, the primary change being the down-rated powerplant of one 180-hp (134-kW) Wright-Hispano E Vee engine

AT-4: in 1927 Curtiss delivered 35 production versions of the **XAT-4** with the designation AT-4, but these were soon converted to P-1D standard with the D-12 Vee engine

AT-5: these were five **Model 34K** advanced trainers with the 220-hp (164-kW) Wright Whirlwind J-5 radial engine; ordered as AT-4s, they were later converted to P-1E standard with the D-12 engine

AT-5A: bearing a close resemblance to the AT-5, the AT-5A (**Model 34M**) had a lengthened fuselage; 31 were delivered, and these later became P-1F fighters after being re-engined with the D-12 engine

P-11: this designation was given to three machines that were ordered as combinations of the P-6 airframe and the untried powerplant of one 600-hp (447-kW) Curtiss H-1640 Chieftain engine; with the failure of this powerplant, two of the P-11 aircraft were completed as Conqueror-powered P-6 fighters, while the third became the **YP-20** powered by the Wright Cyclone radial engine; the YP-20 was later re-engined with the Conqueror engine, new landing gear and a new tailplane to become the sole **XP-6E** prototype for the P-6E series; further modified, with a supercharged engine and experimental enclosed cockpit for the pilot, it became the **XP-6F**

XP-17: the first P-1 was later revised as a testbed for the

experimental Wright V-1470 air-cooled inverted-Vee engine under the revised designation XP-17

XP-21: two conversions from XP-3A standard to test the 300-hp (224-kW) Pratt & Whitney R-985 Wasp Junior radial engine; one became the **XP-21A** when modified with the R-975 Wasp Junior, and the other was converted to P-1F standard

XP-22: temporary designation for a P-6A used to test the new radiator and air cooler installations for the V-1570-23 engine, and later reverted to P-6A standard

XP-23: produced by conversion of the unfinished last P-6E, the XP-23 (**Model 63**) had a light alloy monocoque fuselage, improved tail, and powerplant of one turbocharged and geared G1V-1570C Conqueror engine; only at high altitude was the type's performance better than that of the standard P-6E, and the machine became the YP-23 after the turbocharger had been removed

Hawk I: at first, no Curtiss designation was given to various export versions of the P-6; eight examples of a P-6D development with the Conqueror engine were sold to the Netherlands East Indies in 1930, and another eight of the type were built in the Netherlands; three **P-6S** fighters with the 450-hp (336-kW) Wasp radial were sold to Cuba and one of the same type to Japan in 1930; and the sole **Japan Hawk** of 1930 had the Conqueror, but may have been the same airframe as the Japanese P-6S; from 1932, after the introduction of the Hawk II, these export examples of the P-6 received the retrospective company designation Hawk I

the V-1570-C turbocharged engine in the spring of 1932, thereupon receiving the revised designation **P-6D**.

Ordered in July 1931 under the designation **Y1P-22**, the **Model 35** was the most illustrious and impressive of all the US Army's Hawk fighter biplanes, and deliveries of 46 such **P-6E** fighters

were completed in the winter of 1931-2. The P-6E possessed excellent manoeuvrability, and the type equipped the crack 17th and 33rd Pursuit Squadrons. The P-6E aircraft differed from the P-6D in having a slimmer forward fuselage with the engine radiator mounted just forward of the main landing gear arrangement.

The latter comprised single-strut main legs with 'spat'-type wheel fairings. One P-6E Hawk was powered by the V-1570F normally aspirated engine under the revised designation **XP-6G**, while a standard P-6E fighter was tested as the **XP-6H** with four 0.3-in (7.62-mm) machine-guns mounted in the wings.

Curtiss Model 37 and Model 38 Falcon (O-1, O-11, O-12, O-13, O-16, O-18, O-26 and O-39 series)

The first Curtiss biplane to bear the name **Falcon** was the Liberty-powered Curtiss L-113 (later **Model 37**) that appeared in 1924. It was unsuccessful when evaluated as the **XO-1** in competition with the Douglas XO-2 to meet a requirement for an observation type, but was accepted for production the following year when revised with the 510-hp (380-kW) Packard 1A-1500 engine. It was a conventional unequal-span biplane with a wing of wooden construction that incorporated considerable

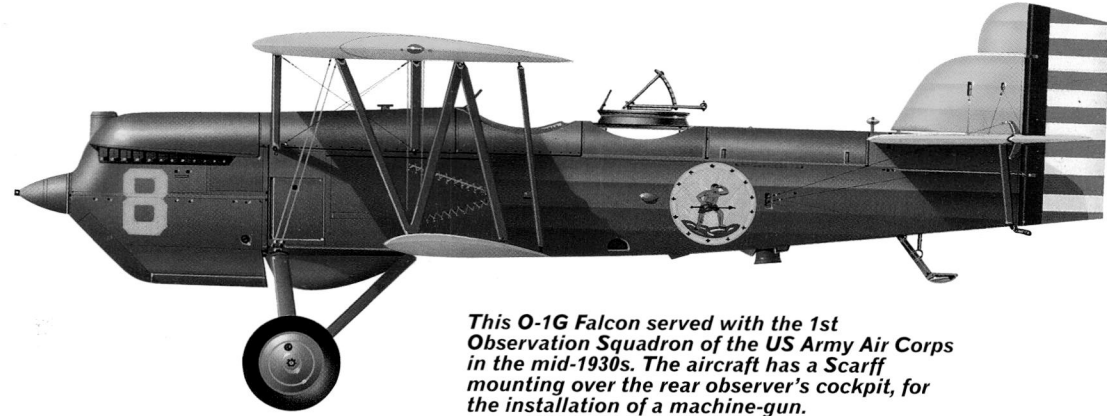

This O-1G Falcon served with the 1st Observation Squadron of the US Army Air Corps in the mid-1930s. The aircraft has a Scarff mounting over the rear observer's cockpit, for the installation of a machine-gun.

Variants

O-11: Model 37C version of the O-1 intended for National Guard units and powered by the government-surplus Liberty engine; the **XO-11** was an O-1 conversion and was followed by 66 O-11 production aircraft; one O-11 used for test purposes became a second XO-11, while another was fitted with modified tail surfaces, dual controls and other improvements to become the **O-11A**; the final O-11 became the **XO-12** with the new Pratt & Whitney R-1340 Wasp radial engine
XO-13: one O-1 was redesignated XO-13 when re-engined with the new Curtiss Conqueror engine, being entered for and competing successfully in the 1927 National Air Races; the **XO-13A** was another conversion to compete in these races, this having wing surface radiators to reduce drag; one O-1C became the **O-13B** when powered by a Conqueror engine and was evaluated for observation work, and three O-1E machines were redesignated **YO-13C (Model 37K)** when similarly re-engined; the sole **YO-13D** was an O-11 with the supercharged Conqueror engine; it was converted later as an **O-13C** and finally as an O-1B
XO-16: O-11 with a modified fuselage and Conqueror engine **(Model 37G)**
XO-18: O-1B used briefly to test the new Curtiss Chieftain engine
Y1O-26: O-1E with a Prestone-cooled Conqueror engine requiring a smaller radiator **(Model 37L)**
O-39: O-1G airframe with the Curtiss V-1570-25 Conqueror engine; 10 of this **Model 38A** type were built in 1931; these all had a radiator the size of that used in the P-6E fighter and were all fitted initially with wheel spats, while in-service changes included a reduction in rudder area and, on a number of the aircraft, a glazed canopy over the tandem cockpits
Civil Falcon: 20 civil aircraft were built, these machines including the **Conqueror Mailplane**, the **D-12 Mailplane**, the **Lindbergh Special** for Charles Lindbergh, and 14 examples of the **Liberty Mailplane**; this last was a single-seat mailplane with the Liberty engine, and was used for night mail flights by National Air Transport; of the survivors sold at a later date, at least two were used for smuggling spirits into the USA during the prohibition era

sweep on the outer panels of the upper wing. The fuselage was built up from aluminium tubing with steel tie-rod bracing.

The new biplane went into production as the **O-1 (Model 37A)** for observation duties with the US Army. The initial order was for 10 aircraft re-engined with the Curtiss D-12 engine. One of these was completed later as the **O-1A** with the Liberty engine, and the first O-1 was later converted to **O-1 Special** standard as a VIP transport. Forty-five examples of the **O-1B (Model 37B)** were ordered in 1927, this first major production version incorporating refinements such as wheel brakes and a ventral auxiliary fuel tank which could be jettisoned in flight. There followed four **O-1C** aircraft, part of the O-1B order, converted to serve as VIP transports by enlargement of the rear cockpit and the addition of a baggage compartment. (The designation **O-1D** was not used.)

In 1929 the US Army ordered 41 of the **O-1E**

(Model 37I) version with the V-1150E engine developed from the original D-12. Other improvements included the introduction of oleo-pneumatic shock-absorbers and horn-balanced elevators. One O-1E was later modified as a VIP transport with the revised designation **O-1F (Model 37J)**. The **XO-1G (Model 38)** replaced the earlier variants' defensive armament of two Lewis guns on a Scarff mounting with a single gun on a post mounting. Other modifications introduced redesigned horizontal tail surfaces and a steerable tailwheel. The XO-1G was originally an

O-1E which had been modified previously as the **XBT-4 (Model 46)** contender to meet a US Army basic trainer requirement, and successful evaluation of the XO-1G led to the construction of 30 examples of the **O-1G** production variant, bringing total O-1 manufacture for the US Army to 127.

The O-1 and its variants saw a decade of service with the observation squadrons of the US Army Air Corps, and ended their days with reserve National Guard units. There were also export versions and a number of commercial Falcons.

Curtiss Model 37D Falcon (F8C and OC)

The basic designation **F8C** in the US Navy's system covered two quite different types of aircraft, the earlier type being designated

Model 37C Falcon and the later type being designated **Model 49 Helldiver**.

The **Model 37D** resulted from a requirement issued

by the USN on behalf of the USMC for a two-seat land-based fighter with bombing and observation capabilities. Curtiss responded with a

substantial biplane based generally on the O-1, but more specifically combining features of the **XO-12** and **XA-14** with the heavier

fixed forward-firing machine-gun armament and underwing bomb racks of the A-3 and revised for a powerplant of one air-cooled radial piston engine, which was the type now mandatory for USN and USMC aircraft.

Curtiss Model 37D Falcon (F8C and OC) (continued)

The US Navy initially ordered two **XF8C-1** prototypes and four **F8C-1** production aircraft with the powerplant of one 432-hp (322-kW) R-1340-B Wasp engine at the front of the fuselage; the latter was lengthened over its forward section to maintain the centre of gravity in the right position despite the use of a lighter engine. All of these aircraft were delivered in January and February 1928.

The first XF8C-1 was delivered in February 1928,

and after the completion of their trials the two prototype aircraft lost their prototype status to become plain F8C-1 machines and were complemented by four aircraft delivered as such. Despite the fact that they had been intended for the attack and general-purpose roles, the aircraft had been ordered in the fighter category as the US Navy lacked any attack designation at this time. However, the poor performance of this comparatively heavy type

in the fighter role imposed upon it soon led to the redesignation of all six aircraft as **OC-1** machines in the observation category. The last of the aircraft was retired in April 1935.

The machine that had originally been the second XF8C-1 was later revised for testing of the Curtiss H-1640 Chieftain radial piston engine.

Delivered in February 1928, the sole **XF8C-3** was

basically similar to the F8C-1 apart from detail modifications and more military equipment that added slightly to the weight and therefore decreased climb, ceiling and range performance. At the end of its trials, the

XF8C-3 became an additional **F8C-3** to complement the 20 aircraft built to F8C-3 standard for delivery between February and April 1928, and all 21 F8C-3 machines soon received the revised designation **OC-2**.

This aircraft is one of four F8C-1s built for the USMC. The circular marking between the unit number (8) and aircraft number (9) denotes a Marine Corps aircraft, while the diagonal line within denotes an observation type.

SPECIFICATION

Curtiss Model 37D Falcon (F8C-3)
Type: two-seat fighter and attack aircraft
Powerplant: one Pratt & Whitney R-1340-B Wasp piston engine rated at 432 hp (322 kW)
Performance: maximum speed 144 mph (232 km/h) at sea level; cruising speed 109 mph (176 km/h) at optimum altitude; initial climb rate 1,010 ft (308 m) per minute; service ceiling 16,400 ft (5000 m); range 653 miles (1051 km)
Weights: empty 2,512 lb (1139 kg); maximum take-off 4,175 lb (1894 kg)
Dimensions: wingspan 38 ft (11.58 m); length 27 ft 11 in (8.51 m); height 10 ft 3 in (3.12 m); wing area 351.00 sq ft (32.61 m²)
Armament: two 0.3-in (7.62-mm) Browning fixed forward-firing machine-guns in the upper part of the forward fuselage, two 0.3-in (7.62-mm) Browning fixed forward-firing machine-guns in the leading edges of the lower wing, and one or two 0.3-in (7.62-mm) Browning trainable rearward-firing machine-guns in the rear cockpit, plus up to 200 lb (91 kg) of disposable stores carried on two hardpoints under the lower wing

---

Curtiss Model 37H and Model 44 Falcon (A-3 and A-4)

In the mid-1920s, the US Army decided to develop a type of warplane optimised for the close support of ground forces and this led to the introduction of the A-for-Attack category in 1926. The USAAC decided that it would be sensible in the short term to develop one of its two current types of observation aircraft for the

role. Both Curtiss and Douglas offered to develop their observation types to satisfy this requirement, but after trials with the Douglas XA-2 prototype conversion from O-2 standard, the USAAC decided that the O-1B version of the Curtiss Falcon series was ideal for adaptation to this role.

This led to the evolution of the **Model 44**, which was the retrospective company designation accorded by Curtiss in 1935 for the type accepted for USAAC service with the designation **A-3**. The changes involved in the transformation of the O-1 into the A-3 included the addition of racks for light bombs under the lower wing and the addition of two extra machine-guns in the lower wing. The rest of the airframe was therefore essentially similar to that of the O-1B, and as such was a biplane with a staggered single-bay wing cellule and fixed tailskid landing gear including divided main units.

Production of the A-3 reached 66 aircraft with the V-1150-3 military version of the Curtiss D-12E Vee engine, and the performance of the A-3 was basically similar to that of the O-1B. The designation **A-3A** was applied to six A-3 machines later revised as conversion trainers with dual controls.

Known to Curtiss as the **Model 37H**, the **A-3B** was the attack counterpart of the O-1E with the same aerodynamic and airframe improvements: these included an engine cowling of lower-drag shape, Frise rather than plain ailerons, horn-balanced elevators, and oleo-pneumatic rather than rubber compression disc shock absorbers. Production amounted to 78 aircraft, and all surviving A-3 aircraft were upgraded to A-3B standard. The last of

the aircraft was scrapped in October 1937. Delivered in December 1927, the **XA-4** prototype was a single A-3 conversion for evaluation of the 440-hp (328-kW) Pratt & Whitney R-1340-1 radial engine in an attack type. The engine installation, which required no water, radiator and associated 'plumbing', resulted in a reduced empty weight, but its higher drag meant a slight sacrifice of performance. The aircraft was scrapped in March 1932.

On the A-3, a single 0.3-in (7.62-mm) machine-gun was carried in each lower wing, positioned to fire just outboard of the propeller arc. The aircraft also carried a Scarff ring for the mounting of an observer's machine-gun.

SPECIFICATION

Curtiss Model 37H (A-3B)
Type: two-seat ground-attack warplane
Powerplant: one Curtiss V-1150-3 Vee piston engine rated at 426 hp (318 kW)
Performance: maximum speed 140 mph (224.5 km/h) at sea level; cruising speed 111 mph (179 km/h) at optimum altitude; initial climb rate 948 ft (289 m) per minute; service ceiling 14,400 ft (4390 m); range 647 miles (1041 km)
Weights: empty 2,902 lb (1316 kg); maximum take-off 4,476 lb (2030 kg)
Dimensions: wingspan 38 ft (11.58 m); length 27 ft 7 in (8.41 m); height 10 ft 3 in (3.12 m); wing area 351.00 sq ft (32.61 m²)
Armament: two 0.3-in (7.62-mm) Browning fixed forward-firing machine-guns in the upper part of the forward fuselage, two 0.3-in (7.62-mm) Browning fixed forward-firing machine-guns in the leading edges of the lower wing, and two 0.3-in (7.62-mm) Lewis or Browning trainable rearward-firing machine guns in the rear cockpit, plus up to 200 lb (91 kg) of disposable stores carried on two hardpoints under the lower wing

---

Curtiss Model 40 Carrier Pigeon

Built for a US Post Office mailplane competition, the **Carrier Pigeon** prototype (later **Model 40**), appeared in 1925 as a dumpy single-

bay biplane with an upper wing of less span than the lower, and a braced tail unit. The machine was of mixed construction, the

wings having wooden frameworks while the fuselage was built up of welded steel tubing. The need to land and take off

from ill-prepared fields was recognised in the fixed wide-track independent main landing gear units.

In 1926 some 10 examples of the Carrier Pigeon were built for the US National Air Transport

organisation, which also bought the prototype from the US Post Office. The **Carrier Pigeon II** was a 1929 design, three of which were built for National Air Transport. Like its predecessor, it was a single-seat mail carrier, but was otherwise a new design resembling the Falcon series and powered by a 600-hp (447-kW) Curtiss G1V-1570 liquid-cooled Vee engine.

SPECIFICATION

Curtiss Model 40 Carrier Pigeon I
Type: single-seat mailplane
Powerplant: one Liberty 12 Vee piston engine rated at 400 hp (298 kW)
Performance: maximum speed 125 mph (201 km/h) at optimum altitude; cruising speed 105 mph (169 km/h) at optimum altitude; initial climb rate 800 ft (244 m) per minute; service ceiling 12,800 ft (3900 m); range 525 miles (845 km)
Weights: empty 3,603 lb (1634 kg); maximum take-off 5,620 lb (2549 kg)
Dimensions: wingspan 41 ft 11 in (12.78 m); length 28 ft 9½ in (8.78 m); height 12 ft 1 in (3.68 m); wing area 505.00 sq ft (46.91 m²)
Payload: up to 1,000 lb (454 kg) of mail

The Carrier Pigeon had mail holds fore and aft of the pilot's open cockpit, which was located just behind the trailing edge of the wings.

Curtiss Model 42 (R3C)

The R3C-2 floatplane had a maximum speed of 246 mph (396 km/h) at sea level.

For the 1925 domestic air racing season, which was the last for which the American forces ordered new aircraft, the US Army and US Navy decided to collaborate in a move designed to maximise their potential at a time of shrinking financial resources. The services felt that the US Navy's R2C-1 was still highly competitive but could be improved by the application of more power, and the engine that could deliver this uprated output was available in the form of the new Curtiss V-1400 Vee engine. The USAAS and USN agreement for a joint racing campaign allowed the placement of an order for four aircraft to be delivered in September 1925. Three of the aircraft were funded by the USN and were intended for racing with the designation **R3C-1**, although the fighter designation F3C-1 was used on paper in an effort to secure the continuance of funding. The fourth was a jointly-funded static aircraft intended for testing to destruction. The arrangement for the three flying aircraft was for the first to be tested by pilots from

both services, the second and third to go to the USN and USAAS respectively for the 1925 Pulitzer Trophy race, and the first then to be allocated to the USN for revision as a twin-float seaplane for Schneider Trophy race preparations.

The new type received the company designation **L-114-1** (later **Model 42**), and was a development of the L-111-1 (R2C-1) with refinements such as a new and very thin aerofoil section optimised for maximum lift at the incidence angle that generated least drag. It also had its water expansion tank installed on the upper fuselage to serve as a fairing for the improved windscreen, the tailskid built integral with the rear fuselage, the trailing edges of the upper wing's roots cutaway to improve the pilot's downward fields of vision and a wider foot for the I-type interplane struts. In addition, the US Navy aircraft had, hinged metal 'breakaway' panels on the sides of the cockpit that could be activated rapidly to enlarge the cockpit opening and thereby facilitate the departure of a pilot wearing a parachute, which the USAAS thought impractical

in a low-level racing machine.

The first R3C-1 achieved its maiden flight on 11 September 1925, and just over one month later R3C-1 aircraft took first and second places in the Pulitzer Trophy race. The winner was the USAAS machine at the disappointing speed of 248.98 mph (400.69 km/h), while second place fell to the second USN machine. It is interesting to note that the third, fourth and fifth places also went to Curtiss aircraft, in this instance the P-1, PW-8B and PW-8B fighters.

After the Pulitzer Trophy race, all three R3C-1s were fitted with twin-float alighting gear for use in the campaign for the Schneider Trophy race, which took place only two weeks later. This alteration resulted in the **R3C-2** variant (later known to Curtiss as the **Model 42A**). The race was won by the USAAS machine, in the hands of 1st Lieutenant James H. Doolittle, at a speed of 232.57 mph (374.29 km/h),

while the two USN aircraft were forced to retire. Doolittle later used the same machine to raise the world air speed record for seaplanes to 245.7 mph (335.4 km/h), and in the 1926 Schneider Trophy race 1st Lieutenant Christian F. Schilt of the US Marine Corps placed second in the USAAS machine.

For the 1926 Schneider Trophy race, the first of the US Navy's aircraft was revised to the **R3C-3** standard with the 700-hp (522-kW) Packard 2A-1500 Vee engine. The machine was wrecked in a hard landing after a training flight in November 1926. The second of the USN's aircraft was revised to the **R3C-4** standard with the 736-hp (549-kW) Curtiss V-1550 Vee engine and improved floats, but failed to finish the race as a result of a fuel pump problem when lying second.

SPECIFICATION

Curtiss Model 42 (R3C-1)
Type: single-seat racing aircraft
Powerplant: one Curtiss V-1400 Vee piston engine rated at 565 hp (422 kW)
Performance: maximum speed 285 mph (458.5 km/h) at sea level; climb to 5,000 ft (1525 m) in 1 minute 28 seconds; service ceiling 26,400 ft (8045 m); endurance 50 minutes
Weights: empty 1,792 lb (813 kg); maximum take-off 2,181 lb (989 kg)
Dimensions: wingspan 22 ft (6.71 m); length 20 ft 1⅜ in (6.13 m); height 6 ft 9½ in (2.07 m); wing area 144.00 sq ft (13.38 m²)

Curtiss Model 43 Seahawk (F7C-1)

Built as a private venture to meet a US Navy requirement for a single-seat carrierborne fighter with an air-cooled radial engine, the **Curtiss Seahawk** prototype (later **Model 43**) flew for the first time on

28 February 1927. Evaluated as the **XF7C-1**, this prototype had an unequal-span staggered single-bay wing cellule, and the outer panels of the upper wing had considerable sweep on the lines of

the Falcon.

A 17-aircraft production series of the **F7C-1** Seahawk fighters followed, with production aircraft having a wing cellule of increased span and area. Whereas the prototype had been intended for operation as a landplane or seaplane (with one large central float and two small underwing stabilising floats), production machines were intended solely as landplanes for operation from shore bases. Delivered between August 1927 and the beginning of 1929, the F7C-1 force formed the equipment of the USMC's VF-6M squadron based at Quantico, Virginia.

Variants

XF7C-2: single F7C-1 conversion for evaluation with the 575-hp (429-kW) Wright Cyclone radial engine and full-span flaps
XF7C-3: a demonstration prototype for China with an armament of four 0.3-in (7.62-mm) machine-guns, I-type interplane struts, and ailerons on both the upper and lower wings rather than on just the upper wing; the type was superseded by the F11C

SPECIFICATION

Curtiss Model 43 Seahawk (F7C-1)
Type: single-seat fighter
Powerplant: one Pratt & Whitney R-1340-B Wasp radial piston engine rated at 450 hp (336 kW)
Performance: maximum speed 155 mph (249 km/h) at sea level; cruising speed 150 mph (241 km/h) at optimum altitude; initial climb rate 1,860 ft (567 m) per minute; service ceiling 22,100 ft (6735 m); range 355 miles (571 km)
Weights: empty 2,053 lb (931 kg); maximum take-off 2,782 lb (1262 kg)
Dimensions: wingspan 32 ft 8 in (9.34 m); length 22 ft 7¼ in (6.88 m); height 9 ft 8½ in (2.96 m); wing area 275.00 sq ft (25.55 m²)
Armament: two 0.3-in (7.62-mm) Browning fixed forward-firing machine-guns in the forward fuselage

The F7C-1's sturdy tailskid landing gear with divided main units, was designed with carrier operations in mind.

Curtiss Model 48 and Model 51 Fledgling (N2C)

Three **XN2C-1** prototypes were built in 1927 in response to a USN requirement for a new primary trainer. These **Fledgling** aircraft (later designated **Model 48**) were to a biplane design with an equal-span staggered two-bay wing cellule, with the pupil and instructor in tandem in open cockpits. There was provision for conversion to seaplane form with a single main float and two small stabilising floats under the outer parts of the lower wing.

The Fledgling was ordered into production for the USN as the **N2C-1**, retaining the exposed 220-hp (164-kW) Whirlwind J-5 radial engine of the prototypes. Some 31 N2C-1s were followed by 20 examples of the **N2C-2** (**Model 48A**), powered by the new 240-hp (179-kW) Whirlwind J-6-7 (R-760-94) radial engine.

The commercial version of the Fledgling was known as the **Model 51** and powered by the 170-hp (127-kW) Curtiss Challenger radial engine.

The Curtiss Flying Service flew a total of 109 Model 51 aircraft, most of them as trainers, and a small number of the type was exported.

The **Fledgling Junior** was a version of the Model 51 with a wing cellule of reduced span, but it was not successful and as a result no quantity production was undertaken.

Four examples of the commercial **Fledgling J-1**, equivalent to the naval N2C-1 and powered by the Whirlwind J-6-5 radial engine, appeared in 1929. They were followed by the **Fledgling J-2**, equivalent to the N2C-2 and employing the same engine. Two Model 51s were converted to Fledgling J-2 standard with the Whirlwind J-6-7 engine, and further Fledgling J-2s, built as such, were exported in small batches to Colombia and Brazil. The Fledgling soldiered on into the mid-1930s, during which period several N2C-2s were converted into pilotless drones for anti-aircraft gunnery training, these having fixed tricycle landing gear.

SPECIFICATION

Curtiss Model 48 Fledgling (N2C-1)
Type: two-seat primary flying trainer
Powerplant: one Wright R-760-8 Whirlwind radial piston engine rated at 220 hp (164 kW)
Performance: maximum speed 109 mph (175 km/h) at sea level; cruising speed 87 mph (140 km/h) at optimum altitude; initial climb rate 965 ft (294 m) per minute; service ceiling 15,100 ft (4600 m); range 366 miles (589 km)
Weights: empty 2,135 lb (968 kg); maximum take-off 2,832 lb (1285 kg)
Dimensions: wingspan 39 ft 2 in (11.93 m); length 27 ft 4 in (8.33 m); height 10 ft 4 in (3.15 m); wing area 365.00 sq ft (33.91 m²)

Curtiss Model 49 and Model 61 Helldiver (F8C, O2C, S3C)

Ordered by the US Navy at the same time as the two XF8C-1s, the **XF8C-2** was in fact the entirely new **Helldiver** (later **Model 49**) design produced specifically for the dive-bombing role. Externally, the XF8C-2 differed from the USN's Falcons in having its two forward-firing machine-guns moved from the lower to the upper wing, and in having the upper wing reduced in area and span. The XF8C-2 was destroyed when it crashed during a test dive in December 1928, and Curtiss replaced this machine with an identical aircraft delivered in August 1929, while a second prototype, delivered in April 1929, was the sole example of the **XF8C-4** (**Model 49A**). The second XF8C-2 and the XF8C-4 were each powered by a cowled Wasp engine and were capable of carrying a 500-lb (227-kg) bomb on a special rack which launched the weapon clear of the propeller area during a dive-bombing attack.

The Helldiver was based on a fuselage of welded steel tube construction, while the upper and lower wings of the staggered single-bay wing cellule were of

Seen in its original Model 49C form, this aircraft became the much modified and redesignated XF8C-8, O2C-2, XF10C-1 and XS3C-1.

SPECIFICATION

Curtiss Model 49A Helldiver (F8C-4)
Type: two-seat carrierborne and land-based dive-bomber
Powerplant: one Pratt & Whitney R-1340-88 Wasp radial piston engine rated at 450 hp (336 kW)
Performance: maximum speed 137 mph (221 km/h) at sea level; cruising speed 116 mph (187 km/h) at optimum altitude; initial climb rate 1,030 ft (314 m) per minute; service ceiling 19,800 ft (6035 m); range 452 miles (727 km)
Weights: empty 2,506 lb (1137 kg); maximum take-off 3,776 lb (1713 kg) as a fighter and 4,038 lb (1832 kg) as a bomber
Dimensions: wingspan 32 ft (9.75 m); length 25 ft 11⅞ in (7.92 m); height 10 ft 2 in (3.09 m); wing area 308.00 sq ft (28.61 m²)
Armament: two 0.3-in (7.62-mm) Browning fixed forward-firing machine-guns and two 0.3-in (7.62-mm) Browning trainable rearward-firing machine guns, plus up to 500 lb (227 kg) of bombs carried externally

wooden construction and had swept outer panels on the upper wing; the covering was largely of fabric. A total of 25 **F8C-4** (**Model 49B**) aircraft was built, these entering carrier service in 1930. The Helldiver was frequently in the spotlight and was used to obtain publicity for US naval aviation. Though tough and durable, its performance was not impressive and the last aircraft were withdrawn from reserve service just before World War II.

Variants

F8C-5: 63 examples were delivered to land-based observation USMC units from 1931 onwards; by then, dive-bombing had become regarded as a secondary mission and the F8C-5s soon received the revised designation **O2C-1**; the USN later obtained 30 more aircraft which were designated O2C-1 from the outset and, like the F8C-4s, many of them were relegated to reserve units in 1934

XF8C-6: two F8C-5s temporarily fitted with leading-edge slots and trailing-edge flaps

Cyclone Helldiver: two civil-registered and company-owned aircraft, later designated **Model 49C**, similar to the F8C-5 except for the powerplant of one Wright Cyclone radial engine and glazed crew canopies; both had USN markings from the outset, although they were bought by the USN only after considerable use by Curtiss; one, designated **XF8C-7** by the USN, then **XO2C-2** and finally **O2C-2**, was used as a VIP transport; the second company machine became the **XF8C-8**; two identical aircraft were bought by the USN and designated O2C-2

XS3C-1: one-off **Model 61** variant supplied to the USN to replace the XF8C-8 after it had crashed; modified extensively, the variant had a new tailplane, single-strut main landing-gear units, and one 650-hp (485-kW) Cyclone engine; it was considered for the two-seat fighter role and was known unofficially as the **XF10C-1**

Curtiss Model 50 Robin (C-10)

The **Curtiss Robin** (later **Model 50**), was a workmanlike cabin monoplane with a strut-braced high-set wing, and was built for the US private owner market. Of mixed construction, the Robin had a wooden wing and a fuselage built up of steel tubing. The cabin accommodated three, the two passengers seated side-by-side behind the pilot. The first of four prototypes made its maiden flight on 7 August 1928.

Initial production aircraft were powered by the Curtiss OX-5 engine, of which large numbers were available as stock surplus to requirements after large-scale production in World War I, in a successful effort to keep down costs and thereby boost

SPECIFICATION

Curtiss Model 50C (Robin C-1)
Type: three-seat touring aircraft
Powerplant: one Curtiss Challenger radial piston engine rated at 185 hp (138 kW)
Performance: maximum speed 120 mph (193 km/h) at sea level; cruising speed 102 mph (164 km/h) at optimum altitude; initial climb rate 640 ft (195 m) per minute; service ceiling 12,700 ft (3870 m); range 300 miles (483 km)
Weights: empty 1,700 lb (771 kg); maximum take-off 2,600 lb (1179 kg)
Dimensions: wingspan 41 ft (12.50 m); length 25 ft 1 in (7.65 m); height 8 ft (2.44 m); wing area 223.00 sq ft (20.72 m²)

sales. Early Robins were also distinguished by large flat fairings over the parallel diagonal wing-bracing struts; although claimed to give additional lift, they were found to be ineffective and were abandoned on later machines. The original landing gear had distinctive box-type housings for the bungee rubber cord shock absorbers attached to each of the main wheel units. Subsequent production series had oleo-pneumatic shock absorbers and a number of Robins were adapted as twin-float seaplanes.

Total production of the Robin was 769, the peak output being attained during 1929. Undoubtedly

one of the most popular private touring aircraft of its era, the Robin would have sold in greater quantities were it not for the economic depression of the early 1930s. Perhaps the most famous Robin was a **Model J-1**. Its young Irish-American pilot, Douglas Corrigan, installed additional fuel tanks and in July 1938, after announcing an attempted east-to-west flight from New York to Los Angeles, calmly made a successful east-to-west crossing of the North Atlantic from a point near Dublin in Ireland to New York. As a result the American press dubbed him 'Wrong Way' Corrigan!

A number of Robins are

still flying, most of them powered by post-World War II surplus Continental or Ranger engines.

The Challenger-engined Robin Cs had this distinctive, squared-off, engine cowling. The aircraft had a complicated arrangement of wing and undercarriage bracing struts.

Variants

Challenger Robin: early Robin variant (**Model 50A**) with the 165-hp (123-kW) Curtiss Challenger engine
Comet Robin: owner-conversion of 1937 with the 150-hp (112-kW) Comet radial in a **Robin J-1** airframe
Robin B: this version incorporated wheel brakes and a steerable tailwheel in place of the former tail skid; total production believed to have been 325
Robin B-2: powered by Wright engines in the 150/180-hp (112/134-kW) range; the variant was in production from late 1929 to late 1930
Robin C: modified version with 185-hp (138-kW) Challenger engine; about 50 built
Robin C-1: retaining the Challenger engine, this **Model 50C** variant had detail refinements, and was a popular version, of which more than 200 were built
Robin C-2: long-range **Model 50D** variant with extra fuel tank and the 170-hp (127-kW) Challenger engine; six completed
Robin 4C: one four-seat **Model 50E** version with the Challenger engine
Robin 4C-1: although this version had an enlarged fuselage section forward, intended to allow the accommodation of the pilot and up to three passengers, the three aircraft built were completed as

roomy three-seaters
Robin 4C-1A: the genuine four-seat **Model 50G** version, of which 11 were built with the enlarged forward fuselage of the Robin 4C-1, the additional passenger being seated next to the pilot but slightly to his rear
Robin CR: an experimental model with 120-hp (90-kW) Curtiss Crusader engine that proved a failure
Robin J-1: more than 40 J-1s, with the 165-hp (123-kW) Wright Whirlwind J-6-5 engine, were built as new, and others were converted to this **Model 50H** standard from earlier versions
Robin J-2: Model 50I long-range version of the J-1 with an extra fuel tank; two built
Robin M: the Milwaukee Tank company redesigned the OX-5 engine as the air-cooled V-502, developing 115 hp (86 kW); a small number of Robin B aircraft were revised with this new engine
Robin W: a few Robins were built in 1930 with the 110-hp (82-kW) Warner Scarab radial engine; these **Model 50J** machines were not particularly successful as the Scarab was not sufficiently powerful for an aircraft with the size and weight of the Robin; one Robin W, with increased dihedral and an enlarged vertical tail surface, was sold to the USAAC as the **XC-10**, and was used intermittently for pilotless radio-control tests

Curtiss Model 52 and Model 53 Condor (B-2)

In basic design, the **Condor** (later **Model 52**) was a traditional twin-engined, equal-span unstaggered three-bay biplane bomber. The type was evolved from the experimental **Curtiss NBS-1** (**Model 36**), which had first flown in 1924. The only unusual feature of the

Condor was, in fact, a particular feature of its predecessor: the engine nacelles extended behind the wings, and the extreme rear section of each contained a gunner's position.

The **XB-2** prototype was ordered for the US Army in 1926 and made its initial

Variants

B-2A: temporary designation of one B-2 fitted with dual controls
Condor 18: later known as the **Model 53**, this civil version of the B-2 had a redesigned and lengthened fuselage, with the pilot and co-pilot accommodated within an enclosed cabin in a modified nose; the wings were similar to those of the B-2, with dihedral on the lower wings only, and there was accommodation for 18 passengers. Following construction of three Condor 18 transports, there appeared a second batch of three aircraft, which differed in a number of respects including dihedral on the upper as well as the lower wing, engine nacelles that were smaller and more streamlined, vertical and horizontal tail surfaces that were enlarged, and a fuselage reduced in length; the first Condor 18 flew in June 1929, but by that time the market had already been captured largely by three-engined Ford and Fokker high-wing monoplanes, which offered better performance than the Condor 18's cruising speed of 125 mph (201 km/h). The Condor 18s were sold in 1931 for a sum only slightly greater than cost price to Eastern Airlines, which operated them for several years; late in the 1930s four of the aircraft were fitted with increased seating and used for joyrides during barnstorming tours

flight in July 1927. It had a biplane tail unit and wings with a thick aerofoil section, and vertical radiators for the Curtiss GV-1570 engines were mounted on top of the nacelles.

Despite the loss of the prototype in December 1927, the US Army proceeded with the acquisition of 12 examples of the **B-2** production version, in which the only externally visible change was the use of smaller radiators. Deliveries began in June 1929 and the B-2 formed the equipment of the 11th BS, the only heavy bomber unit of the US Army at that

time. The B-2 proved reliable, but of limited practical value. One example was used in 1930 for experiments with an early form of automatic pilot.

The B-2's crew of five included three gunners, including one in the nose of the aircraft, immediately above the bomb-aiming position.

SPECIFICATION	
Curtiss Model 52 Condor (B-2) **Type:** five-seat heavy bomber **Powerplant:** two Curtiss GV-1570 Vee piston engines each rated at 600 hp (447 kW) **Performance:** maximum speed 132 mph (212 km/h) at sea level; cruising speed 114 mph (184 km/h) at optimum altitude; initial climb rate 850 ft (259 m) per minute; service ceiling 17,100 ft (5210 m); range 805 miles (1296 km) **Weights:** empty 9,300 lb	(4218 kg); maximum take-off 16,591 lb (7526 kg) **Dimensions:** wingspan 90 ft (27.43 m); length 47 ft 4½ in (14.43 m); height 16 ft 3 in (4.95 m); wing area 1,496.00 sq ft (138.97 m²) **Armament:** two 0.3-in (7.62-mm) Browning trainable machine-guns in each of three positions, plus up to 2,508 lb (1138 kg) of bombs in a lower-fuselage weapons bay

Curtiss Model 55 Kingbird (RC)

The **Kingbird** (later **Model 55**) was a twin-engined high-wing monoplane of the strut-braced type with accommodation for between five and seven passengers. The Curtiss engineers introduced one unusual feature in the design, installing the two radial engines as close together as possible, with the propeller arcs just clearing each other ahead of the short nose section. This was a feature of a number of later designs by other companies, intended to ease asymmetric control problems in the event of an engine failure.

The **Kingbird C** prototype flew for the first time in May 1929 with the powerplant of two 185-hp (138-kW) Curtiss Challenger engines. There followed two examples of the **Kingbird D-1** powered by 225-hp (168-kW) Wright Whirlwind J-6-7 engines. The **Kingbird D-2** was the production version, 14 of the type being built for service with the Eastern Air Transport company; two Kingbird D-1s were later converted to D-2 standard. The single **Kingbird D-3** first flew in the summer of 1931 with the powerplant of two 330-hp (246-kW) Whirlwind J-6-9 engines.

Modifications were made to the first three Kingbird aircraft to be completed, the Kingbird C becoming the **Kingbird J-1** with 240-hp (179-kW) Whirlwind J-6-7 engines, the first Kingbird D-1 becoming the **Kingbird J-2** with Whirlwind J-6-7 engines and the second Kingbird D-1 becoming the **Kingbird J-3** with 300-hp (224-kW) Whirlwind J-6-9 engines and subsequently operating as a mail carrier. The only other Kingbird built was delivered to the USMC in March 1931 as the **RC-1** transport. Apart from internal modifications required by the USN, the RC-1 was a standard eight-seat Kingbird D-2.

As a result, in part at least, of the economic depression of the early 1930s, the Kingbird met with little success and had only a relatively short career. This aircraft was the third built.

SPECIFICATION

Curtiss Model 55 Kingbird D-2
Type: one-crew light transport
Powerplant: two Wright Whirlwind J-6-9 radial piston engines each rated at 300 hp (224 kW)
Performance: maximum speed 142 mph (229 km/h) at optimum altitude; cruising speed 112 mph (180 km/h) at optimum altitude; initial climb rate 1,000 ft (305 m) per minute; service ceiling 12,900 ft (3930 m); range 378 miles (608 km)
Weights: empty 3,877 lb (1759 kg); maximum take-off 6,115 lb (2774 kg)
Dimensions: wingspan 54 ft 6 in (16.61 m); length 34 ft 9 in (10.59 m); height 10 ft (3.05 m); wing area 405.00 sq ft (37.62 m²)
Payload: up to seven passengers

Curtiss Model 58 Sparrowhawk (F9C)

In 1930 the USN called for a new single-seat fighter for operation from aircraft carriers. At this time the navy wanted to increase the aircraft complement of its carriers without having to resort to the introduction of folding wings, and the requirement therefore specified aircraft of very small dimensions. After the evaluation of three contending prototypes, the Atlantic (Fokker) XFA-1, Berliner-Joyce XFJ-1 and **Curtiss XF9C-1** (named **Sparrowhawk** and retrospectively allocated the company designation **Model 58**), the USN decided that it was satisfied with none of them. All would have passed into oblivion if at that time there had not been another urgent problem requiring resolution: how to produce in a very short time a single-seat fighter able to operate from the USN's new giant rigid airship USS *Akron*. The *Akron* had a hangar within its envelope for four scouting aircraft to be launched and retrieved by means of a trapeze which could be lowered through the belly of the airship. A hook mounted above the fuselage of the scout could engage with the trapeze, allowing the aircraft to be drawn up inside the mother ship.

The wings of the XF9C-1 were small enough to pass through the opening between the *Akron's* hangar and the outside air, so the USN adapted it accordingly. The XF9C-1 was tested with a trapeze fitted to the airship USS *Los Angeles* in the autumn of 1931. A second prototype, financed by the company as the **Model 58A** and tested as the **XF9C-2**, was flown with simplified landing gear which had single-strut main legs and wheel spats.

Six examples of the **F9C-2** production version were delivered in 1932, and these aircraft differed from the prototypes in having an upper wing whose roots were gulled into the top of the fuselage rather than the flat wing attached directly to the upper fuselage which had been a feature of the prototypes. Although it was intended that they should have the revised landing gear of the XF9C-2, the aircraft in fact entered service aboard the *Akron* in September 1932 with standard main units as incorporated on the XF9C-1.

There were no F9C-2s aboard the *Akron* when the airship came down at sea in 1933, and the machines therefore went on to fly with its sister ship, the USS *Macon* (ZRS-5). The *Macon* was lost in 1935, and in this instance the airship took four F9C-2s down with it. During service aboard this latter airship, the fighters had been launched and hooked on with the main units of the landing gear removed and replaced by a 30-US gal (114-litre) auxiliary fuel tank.

During their relatively brief careers, the racy F9C-2s, with their colourful paint schemes and light-hearted unit insignia, caught the imagination of the American people. They gained publicity out of all proportion to their small numbers, as a result of the unique and dramatic scenario of single-seat warplanes operating from their huge, lighter-than-air mother ships. One F9C-2 has been preserved in the Smithsonian Institution, Washington, DC.

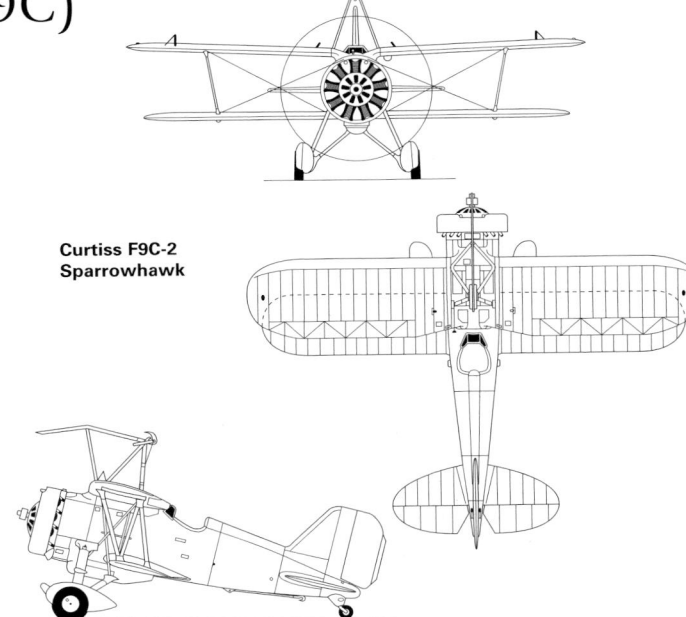

Curtiss F9C-2 Sparrowhawk

SPECIFICATION

Curtiss Model 58 Sparrowhawk (F9C-2)
Type: single-seat airship-based scouting aircraft
Powerplant: one Wright R-975-E Whirlwind radial piston engine rated at 438 hp (327 kW)
Performance: maximum speed 176 mph (283 km/h) at 4,000 ft (1220 m); cruising speed 138 mph (222 km/h) at optimum altitude; initial climb rate 1,690 ft (515 m) per minute; service ceiling 19,200 ft (5850 m); range 297 miles (478 km)
Weights: empty 2,089 lb (948 kg); maximum take-off 2,779 lb (1261 kg)
Dimensions: wingspan 25 ft 6 in (7.77 m); length 20 ft 1½ in (6.13 m); height 10 ft 7 in (3.23 m) with skyhook; wing area 172.80 sq ft (16.05 m²)
Armament: two 0.3-in (7.62-mm) Browning fixed forward-firing machine-guns in the forward fuselage

This F9C-2 was photographed as it hung from Macon's trapeze prior to launching.

Curtiss Model 59 & Model 60 Shrike (A-8, A-10, A-12, S2C)

The USAAC's need for attack warplanes of greater speed and overall capabilities paved the way for the 1929 issue of a requirement that resulted in the design and construction of two competing monoplane prototypes. The Atlantic (Fokker) XA-7 remained only a prototype. The **Curtiss XA-8** prototype, to the **Shrike** design that in 1935 received the company designation **Model 59**, made its maiden flight in June 1931 and made a considerable impact on the USAAC. It was indeed an impressive aircraft for its time, the first Curtiss machine of all-metal low-wing monoplane configuration with advanced features such as automatic leading-edge slots and trailing-edge flaps. The wing was strut- and wire-braced, and the main units of the fixed tailwheel landing gear comprised two fully enclosed 'trouser' units, these fairings also providing accommodation for four 0.3-in (7.62-mm) machine-guns. The pilot and observer/gunner were accommodated in widely separated cockpits, the former under a fully

enclosed canopy and the latter protected by an extended windscreen. Power was provided by a 600-hp (447-kW) Curtiss V-1570C Vee engine with a radiator beneath the nose, slightly forward of the wing leading edge.

Curtiss won a contract for five examples of the **YA-8** (**Model 59A**) service test version on 29 September 1931, and these were followed by eight **Y1A-8** machines in the following year. Both the YA-8 and Y1A-8 machines had an open pilot's cockpit. The designation **A-8** was applied to all but two of the aircraft after their acceptance for full service. The exceptions were one YA-8 which was reworked as the experimental **YA-10** (**Model 59B**) with the 625-hp (466-kW) Pratt & Whitney Hornet radial engine and one Y1A-8 which became the **Y1A-8A** with the 675-hp (503-kW) V-1570-57 geared engine and a redesigned wing. The USN ordered one aircraft similar to the YA-10, and this **Model 69** machine was delivered in December 1932 for evaluation as the **XS2C-1** with the power-

This aircraft is an inline-powered A-8. Note the widely separated cockpits, which limited the aircraft's effectiveness in service.

plant of one 625-hp (466-kW) Wright R-1510-28 Whirlwind radial engine. Possessing no carrierborne capability, this was the US Navy's first two-seat warplane, but remained only a prototype.

The A-8s, each powered by the Prestone-cooled V-1570-31 engine rated at 600 hp (447 kW), created something of a sensation in US aviation circles when they went into service with the 3rd Attack Group at Fort Crockett, Texas, in April 1932. At that time, all other standard equipment was of biplane configuration and the first US Army low-wing monoplane fighter, the Boeing P-26A, did not enter squadron service until eight months later.

The USAAC had, mean-

while, ordered a further 46 Shrikes under the designation **A-8B**, but maintenance problems with the liquid-cooled engine of the A-8 led to the new aircraft being completed with R-1820-21 air-cooled radial engines and the revised designation **A-12** (**Model 60**). These aircraft retained the open pilot's cockpit with faired headrest which had been introduced on the A-8 production batch, and carried the same machine-gun armament and bombload. In an attempt to improve co-operation between the pilot and the observer/gunner, a major modification was introduced, the rear cockpit being

moved forward sufficiently for its glazed covering to form a continuation of the fuselage decking immediately behind the pilot's cockpit.

After long service with the USAAC's attack group, the Shrikes were relegated to second-line units in 1939, but nine A-12s were still in service in Hawaii when the Japanese attacked Pearl Harbor. It is also worth noting that the Chinese nationalist government bought 20 examples of the **Export Shrike** version of the A-12 in 1936, and these machines saw some action against the Japanese in 1937-8.

With the Cyclone radial engine and revised cockpit layout, the A-12 Shrike was a more effective combat aircraft than the earlier Shrikes.

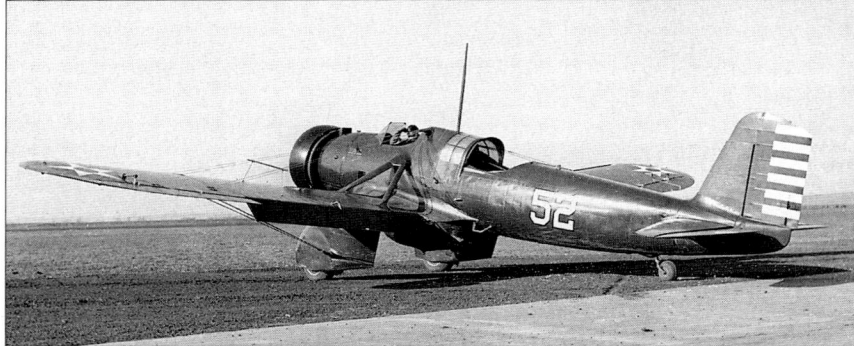

SPECIFICATION	
Curtiss Model 60 Shrike (A-12) **Type:** two-seat attack warplane **Powerplant:** one Wright R-1820-21 radial piston engine rated at 690 hp (515 kW) **Performance:** maximum speed 177 mph (285 km/h) at sea level; cruising speed 151 mph (243 km/h) at optimum altitude; initial climb rate 1,170 ft (357 m) per minute; service ceiling 15,150 ft (4620 m); range 510 miles (821 km) **Weights:** empty 3,898 lb (1768 kg); maximum take-off 5,756 lb (2611 kg)	**Dimensions:** wingspan 44 ft (13.41 m); length 32 ft 3 in (9.83 m); height 9 ft 4 in (2.84 m); wing area 284.00 sq ft (26.38 m²) **Armament:** four 0.3-in (7.62-mm) Browning forward-firing machine-guns in the landing-gear fairings with limited elevation capability, and one 0.3-in (7.62-mm) Browning trainable rearward-firing machine-gun in the rear cockpit, plus up to four 122-lb (55-kg) or 10 30-lb (13.6-kg) bombs carried on underwing racks

Curtiss Model 64 Goshawk (F11C-1/2 and BFC-1/2)

At much the same time in the early 1930s that Curtiss was planning the Hawk II (Model 35B), the US Navy contracted with the manufacturer for an improved derivative of the F6C as the **F11C**. It contained major changes that included the 600-hp (447-kW) Wright R-1510-98 engine, single-leg cantilever main landing-gear units, a slight increase in the interplane gap, metal- rather than fabric-covered control surfaces, and armament based on two 0.3-in (7.62-mm) fixed forward-firing machine-guns supplemented by a hardpoint under the fuselage for

the carriage of a nominal 500-lb (227-kg), but actual 474-lb (215-kg) bomb, or a ventral tank for auxiliary fuel. Curtiss designed the type as the **Goshawk**, later designated as the **Model 64** and in April 1932 the US Navy ordered one example with the designation **XF11C-1** (later **XBFC-1** after the adoption of the BF-for-Bomber Fighter category).

The machine was of fabric-covered metal construction, used the wing cellule of the dismantled YP-23, and was delivered in September 1932.

SPECIFICATION	
Curtiss Model 64 Goshawk **(F11C-2 and BFC-2)** **Type:** single-seat carrierborne fighter and fighter-bomber **Powerplant:** one Wright R-1820-78 Cyclone radial piston engine rated at 700 hp (522 kW) **Performance:** maximum speed 202 mph (325 km/h) at 8,000 ft (2440 m); cruising speed 150 mph (241 km/h) at optimum altitude; initial climb rate 2,300 ft (701 m) per minute as a fighter or 1,820 ft (555 m) per minute as a fighter-bomber; service ceiling 25,100 ft (7650 m) as a fighter or 20,700 ft (6310 m) as a fighter-bomber;	range 570 miles (917 km) with auxiliary fuel or 285 miles (459 km) with standard fuel **Weights:** empty 3,037 lb (1378 kg); maximum take-off 4,132 lb (1874 kg) **Dimensions:** wingspan 31 ft 6 in (9.60 m); length 22 ft 7 in (6.88 m); height 9 ft 8⅞ in (2.96 m); wing area 262.00 sq ft (24.34 m²) **Armament:** two 0.3-in (7.62-mm) Browning fixed forward-firing machine-guns in the upper part of the forward fuselage, plus up to 500 lb (227 kg) of disposable stores carried on three hardpoints

The F11C-2s remained on the strength of VF-1B (later redesignated VB-2B and finally VB-3B) until their retirement in 1938.

Curtiss Model 64 Goshawk (F11C-1/2 and BFC-1/2) (cont.)

Even before its delivery, however, the XF11C-1 had been overtaken by a naval derivative of the Hawk II for, shortly before ordering the XF11C-1, the USN had bought a company-owned Hawk II (**Model 64A**) demonstrator. This had one R-1820-78 engine, slightly longer main landing-gear legs carrying wheels with low-pressure tyres, a tail-wheel in place of the earlier tailskid, fabric-covered control surfaces on the tail unit, and external provision for underwing racks for light bombs as well as an underfuselage hardpoint for either a 50-US gal (189-litre) fuel tank or the crutch that would swing a medium-weight bomb clear of the propeller disc before release in a dive-bombing attack.

Flight trials of this **XF11C-2** (later redesignated as the **XBFC-2**) revealed the need for a small number of minor changes. After the implementation of required changes, the XF11C-2 came to be regarded as the prototype for the next version of the Hawk family to enter production for the USN. This was the **F11C-2**, of which 28 examples were ordered as dual-role fighters and fighter-bombers in October 1932.

The aircraft were delivered during February 1933 for the use of the VF-1B squadron on board the aircraft-carrier USS *Saratoga*. From March 1934 the aircraft were revised with a semi-enclosed cockpit and a number of other modifications before they received the revised designation **BFC-2** in recognition of their fighter-bomber or, as the USN would have it, bomber-fighter role.

Curtiss Model 67 Goshawk and Model 68 Hawk III

The fact that both the USN and Curtiss felt that the F11C-2 still possessed development potential was reflected by the USN's decision to procure a variant with retractable landing gear. This would thereby create a modest bridge across the performance gap that was beginning to open between the service's biplanes and the new monoplanes that were starting to appear in the land-based armouries of several countries during the first half of the 1930s. Thus, the fifth F11C-2 was revised to **XF11C-3** (later **Model 67A**) standard with a main landing-gear retraction system and a metal-framed upper wing. The retractable landing-gear arrangement was inspired by that of the Grumman XFF-1 carrier-borne fighter prototype, and was a manually operated system that raised the wheels into external wells in the lower sides of a considerably deepened forward fuselage.

The XF11C-3 was delivered to the USN in May 1933 with a powerplant based on one 700-hp (522-kW) R-1820-80 Cyclone radial engine, and in its trials revealed a 17-mph (27.5-km/h) increase in maximum level speed over the F11C-2. It was also noted, however, that the 370-lb (168-kg) increase in structure

weight had an unfortunate effect on the type's handling in the air. The XF11C-3 was later designated as the **XBF2C-1** when the BF-for-Bomber Fighter category was introduced for carrierborne fighters capable of delivering a useful bombload.

The US Navy felt that the poorer handling was more than offset by the increase in speed, however, and ordered 27 **BF2C-1** production aircraft to a standard based on that of the XBF2C-1 (modified with a raised rear turtledeck, a semi-enclosed cockpit and a metal-framed lower wing) as well as the same armament provisions as the F11C-2 (BFC-2). The BF2C-1s were delivered from October 1934, and were assigned to VB-5 on board the aircraft-carrier USS *Ranger*.

Hawk IIs supplied to Turkey were alternatively known as 'Turkeyhawks'. This aircraft has spat-mounted machine-guns and underwing weapons racks.

Right: Wearing Nationalist Chinese markings, this Hawk III was one of 102 supplied to China. Gear retraction problems suffered by US Navy Goshawks were not carried over to export Hawk IIIs.

SPECIFICATION

Curtiss Model 67 Goshawk (BF2C-1)

Type: single-seat carrierborne fighter and fighter-bomber
Powerplant: one Wright R-1820-4 Cyclone radial piston engine rated at 770 hp (574 kW)
Performance: maximum speed 225 mph (362 km/h) at 8,000 ft (2440 m); cruising speed 157 mph (253 km/h) at optimum altitude; initial climb rate 2,150 ft (655 m) per minute as a fighter and 1,950 ft (594 m) per minute as a fighter-bomber; service ceiling 27,000 ft (8230 m) as a fighter; range 725 miles (1167 km) with auxiliary fuel and 570 miles (917 km) with standard fuel
Weights: empty 3,326 lb (1509 kg); maximum take-off 4,552 lb (2065 kg)
Dimensions: wingspan 31 ft 6 in (9.60 m); length 24 ft 4 in (7.41 m); height 9 ft 11½ in (3.03 m); wing area 262.00 sq ft (24.34 m²)
Armament: two 0.3-in (7.62-mm) Browning fixed forward-firing machine-guns in the upper part of the forward fuselage, plus up to 500 lb (227 kg) of disposable stores carried on three hardpoints

Variants

Hawk II: Curtiss undertook a straightforward, but relatively major, development of the P-6E for export, with a number of detail refinements and two major changes in the form of cantilever main landing-gear legs (with spatted wheels) and the R-1820 Cyclone engine to create the Hawk II (later **Model 35 Goshawk**) that was initially built as a company demonstrator to display the Hawk II's capabilities to potential customers. Orders were placed for 126 aircraft from eight countries comprising Bolivia (nine delivered between December 1933 and June 1934), Chile (four aircraft supplemented by a number of locally licence-produced machines), China (50), Colombia (26 twin-float seaplanes), Cuba (four Model 35B aircraft), Germany (two aircraft delivered October 1933 after Ernst Udet had been impressed by a dive-bombing exhibition by the **Hawk 1A 'Gulfhawk'** privately owned by Gulf Oil and flown by Alford 'Al' Williams), Siam (12) and Turkey (19); in addition to these machines, one Hawk II demonstrator was later revised to the improved **Model 47** standard and sold to Norway in July 1934
Hawk III: this **Model 68** was the export version of the BF2C-1 with wooden rather than metal wings; deliveries were made to Argentina (10), China (102 **Model 68C** aircraft), Siam (24 **Model 68B** aircraft) and Turkey (one). The Chinese aircraft formed the backbone of that country's fighter capability when the 2nd Sino-Japanese War (1937-1945) broke out in July 1937, but were soon outclassed by Japanese monoplane fighters, and the survivors were retired to second-line duties in 1941; the Thai (previously Siamese) aircraft saw operational service against the French during the Thai invasion of Indo-China (January 1941) and the Japanese during the latter's invasion of Thailand (December 1941), but were later retired to second-line employment as advanced trainers before being retired in the late 1940s
Hawk IV: this **Model 79** was a Hawk III demonstrator revised with a fully enclosed cockpit and sold to Argentina in July 1936

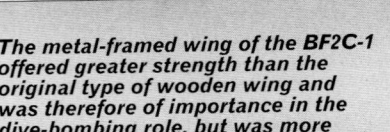

The metal-framed wing of the BF2C-1 offered greater strength than the original type of wooden wing and was therefore of importance in the dive-bombing role, but was more prone to vibration in flight.

Curtiss Model 71 Seagull (O3C and SOC/SON)

Last of the Curtiss biplanes to be used operationally by the US Navy, the **SOC** (**Model 71 Seagull**) originated in 1933 and remained operational until the end of World War II.

The USN's requirement for a new scouting/observation aircraft was circulated to US manufacturers early in 1933, resulting in proposals from Curtiss, Douglas and Vought, but it was the **XO3C-1** prototype, ordered on 19 June 1933 and first flown in April 1934, which was ordered into production as the **SOC-1** (**Model 71A**), the changed official designation reflecting the combination of scout and observation roles.

When first flown, the prototype was equipped with amphibious landing gear, twin main wheels being incorporated in the central main float. Standard production aircraft were built as floatplanes, however, with fixed tail-wheel landing gear optional. The pilot and gunner/observer were accommodated in tandem cockpits, enclosed by a continuous

The SOC had foldable wings and a tail unit of light alloy, while the fuselage was of welded steel-tube, all under a covering of light alloy and fabric.

transparent canopy with sliding sections for access. To provide a maximum field of fire for the trainable machine-gun in the rear cockpit, the turtleback could be retracted.

Deliveries of the SOC-1 began on 12 November 1935. These early aircraft were powered by the R-1340-18 engine, and production of 135 SOC-1s was followed by that of 40 **SOC-2** (**Model 71B**) machines with wheeled landing gear, detail improvements and the R-1340-22 engine. There followed 83 examples of the **SOC-3** (**Model 71E**), this being generally similar to the SOC-1. After modification in 1942 to install arrester gear, the SOC-2 and SOC-3 were redesignated as the **SOC-2A** and **SOC-3A** respectively. Curtiss also built three aircraft virtually

the same as the SOC-3 for service with the USCG: these **SOC-4** (**Model 71F**) aircraft were acquired by the USN in 1942 and equipped with arrester gear to bring them up to **SOC-3A** standard. In addition to the SOCs built by Curtiss, 44 were produced by the NAF. Basically the same as the Curtiss-built SOC-3, these machines were designated **SON-1** or, if fitted with arrester gear, **SON-1A**.

Following termination of SOC production early in 1938, Curtiss became involved in the development and manufacture of a successor, the Seamew, for service as the SO3C. When

its operational performance proved unsatisfactory, however, the SO3C was withdrawn from first-line service and all available SOC

aircraft then reverted to operational status, continuing to fulfil their appointed role until the end of World War II.

Variant

XSO2C-1: a single **Model 71C** evaluated as an improved SOC

SPECIFICATION

Curtiss Model 71E Seagull (SOC-3 floatplane)
Type: two-seat scout/observation aircraft
Powerplant: one Pratt & Whitney R-1340-22 Wasp radial piston engine rated at 600 hp (448 kW)
Performance: maximum speed 161 mph (259 km/h) at 5,000 ft (1525 m); cruising speed 131 mph (211 km/h) at optimum altitude; initial climb rate 915 ft (279 m) per minute; service ceiling 14,400 ft (4390 m); range 859 miles (1382 km)

Weights: empty 3,633 lb (1648 kg); maximum take-off 5,495 lb (2492 kg)
Dimensions: wingspan 36 ft (10.97 m); length 31 ft 1 in (9.47 m); height 14 ft 7 in (4.44 m); wing area 342.00 sq ft (31.77 m²)
Armament: one 0.3-in (7.62-mm) Browning fixed forward-firing machine-gun and one 0.3-in (7.62-mm) Browning trainable rearward-firing machine-gun, plus up to 650 lb (295 kg) of bombs carried under the wing

Curtiss Model 75 (P-36, P-37 and P-42)

In 1934 Curtiss undertook the private-venture development of a new monoplane pursuit (fighter) aircraft. Known as the **Model 75**, it had such advanced features as tailwheel landing gear with retractable main units and an enclosed cockpit. Curtiss believed that the

USAAC would consider the new type as a replacement for the lower-performance Boeing P-26.

The Model 75 prototype, powered by a 900-hp (671-kW) Wright XR-1670-5 radial engine, was submitted to the USAAC in May 1935 for evaluation in a

design competition for a single-seat fighter. The contest did not take place at the planned time as no competing designs were ready, and it was not until April 1936 that it finally began. By then, the Model 75 had been re-engined with an 850-hp (634-kW) R-1820 radial to become the **Model 75B**. Seversky won the USAAC's competition, but Curtiss gained some slight compensation by being awarded a contract for three examples of its design. Powered by a derated version of the 1,050-hp (783-kW) Pratt & Whitney R-1830-13 engine, these were used for test and evaluation under the designation **Y1P-36** (Model

75E). By comparison with the original Model 75 prototype, these had cockpit modifications to improve fore and aft view, and introduced a retractable tailwheel.

Service testing of the Y1P-36 was considered so successful that a contract for 210 examples of the production **P-36A** (**Model 75L**) fighter was awarded on 7 July 1937, and at that time this represented the USAAC's largest peacetime contract for fighter aircraft.

Variants

Model 75J: Model 75A demonstrator fitted with a mechanical supercharger for its R-1830 engine
Model 75K: unrealised project for a version with the Pratt & Whitney R-2180 Twin Hornet engine, finally produced as the **Model 75R** by conversion of the Model 75A demonstrator
P-37 (Model H75I): realising that the service life of the P-36 would be limited by the R-1830 air-cooled radial engine, Curtiss adapted the prototype Model 75/75B airframe with the 1,150-hp (858-kW) Allison V-1710-11 liquid-cooled Vee engine and the cockpit moved farther to the rear to create the **XP-37**; although the XP-37's engine/supercharger combination was quite troublesome, the USAAC realised the potential of the concept and ordered 13 **YP-37** service test aircraft with the V-1710-21 engine, revised nose contours, a 25-in (0.635-m) lengthening of the fuselage to the cockpit for balance and directional stability purposes, and most of the aerodynamic improvements worked out on the XP-37. The YP-37 was still plagued with supercharger problems, and all but one were out of service or retired by early 1942
P-42 (Model 75S): the fourth P-36A was redesignated as the **XP-42** and used for USAAC and NACA programmes intended to overcome the aerodynamic drag handicap of large radial engines by comparison with that of equivalent liquid-cooled types; delivered in March 1939, the XP-42 had a special 1,050-hp (783-kW) R-1830-31 engine fitted with a long extension shaft to drive a propeller. Fitted with a spinner, at the front of a lengthened and nicely tapered nose; the machine retained the XP-42 designation until scrapped in January 1947

SPECIFICATION

Curtiss Model 75 (P-36C)
Type: single-seat fighter
Powerplant: one Pratt & Whitney R-1830-17 radial piston engine rated at 1,200 hp (895 kW)
Performance: maximum speed 311 mph (500 km/h) at 10,000 ft (3050 m); cruising speed 270 mph (435 km/h) at optimum altitude; climb to 15,000 ft (4570 m) in 4 minutes 54 seconds; service ceiling 33,700 ft (10270 m); range 820 miles (1320 km)
Weights: empty 4,619 lb

(2095 kg); maximum take-off 5,829 lb (2644 kg)
Dimensions: wingspan 37 ft 3½ in (11.35 m); length 28 ft 10 in (8.78 m); height 9 ft 3 in (2.81 m); wing area 236.00 sq ft (21.92 m²)
Armament: two 0.3-in (7.62-mm) Browning fixed forward-firing machine-guns in the upper part of the forward fuselage, and two 0.3-in (7.62-mm) Browning fixed forward-firing machine-guns in the leading edge of the wing

Curtiss's XP-37 was the first US fighter to exceed 300 mph (483 km/h) in level flight.

Curtiss Model 75 (P-36, P-37 and P-42) (continued)

Delivery of the P-36A began in April 1938, but by late 1941 the type was already considered obsolete. Circumstances compelled limited use of the P-36A in the opening stage of hostilities with Japan, but the type was soon relegated to the training role.

Variants included a single **P-36B** with the 1,000-hp (746-kW) R-1830-25 engine, and the last 31 of the original production run were completed to the **P-36C** standard with the 1,200-hp (895-kW) R-1830-17 engines and the standard fuselage-mounted armament of two 0.3-in (7.62-mm) machine-guns supplemented by two 0.3-in (7.62-mm) machine-guns in the leading edges of the wing. The designations **XP-36D**, **XP-36E** and **XP-36F** were applied to experimental versions: the XP-36D was a P-36A conversion with four 0.3-in

(7.62-mm) machine-guns in the wing, the XP-36E was a P-36A conversion with six 0.3-in (7.62-mm) machine-guns in the wing, and the XP-36F was a P-36A conversion with two 23-mm Madsen cannon in gondolas under the wings. The designation **P-36G** was used for 30 **Model H75A-8** aircraft ordered by Norway, impressed by the USA after the fall of Norway and finally transferred to Peru in 1943.

Pictured as it appeared in US service in early 1942, this P-42C shows the type's more advanced features, which included a fully-retractable undercarriage.

Curtiss Model 76 Shrike II (A-14 and A-18)

The **Model 76** twin-engined attack monoplane was a private venture, contemporary with the Curtiss Hawk 75 prototype. The Model 76 prototype made its maiden flight in September 1935 with the powerplant of two experimental Wright XR-1510 twin-row radial engines. The weapons bay in the lower fuselage had provision for a total bombload of 600 lb (272 kg), and the gun armament comprised four 0.3-in (7.62-mm) fixed forward-firing machine-guns in the nose, and a similar weapon on a trainable rearward-firing mount in the rear cockpit for the use of the observer/gunner.

After USAAC appraisal, the Model 76 was returned to Curtiss and fitted with 775-hp (578-kW) Wright R-1670-5 Cyclone radial engines in revised nacelles and driving constant-speed propellers, in this form being accepted with the designation **XA-14**. The USAAC was sufficiently impressed to order 13 examples of the **Model 76A** (given the name **Shrike II** in July 1936) developed version as **Y1A-18** service test aircraft. All 13 had been delivered by October 1937 to a standard that was essentially a refined version of the Model 76, but with the powerplant of two R-1820-47 Cyclone engines driving three- rather than two-bladed propellers, and the weaponload of 600 lb (272 kg) revised by being carried in two smaller weapons bays in the wing and on two hardpoints under the wing for chemical smoke tanks or small bombs. The aircraft entered initial service with the 8th Attack Squadron,

aircraft (a number having been written off as a result of weaknesses in the landing gear) were retired from first-line service in 1940 and diverted to the 3rd Bombardment Group as A-18 operational trainers. The last A-18 in flying condition was grounded in 1943.

The Shrike II was a cantilever mid-wing monoplane of all-metal construction, except for fabric covering on the moving control surfaces and portions of the wing. The two-man crew was accommodated beneath a long cockpit enclosure.

SPECIFICATION	
Curtiss Model 76A Shrike II (Y1A-18)	13,170 lb (5974 kg)
Type: two-seat attack aircraft	**Dimensions:** wingspan 59 ft 6 in (18.14 m); length 41 ft (12.50 m); height 11 ft 6 in (3.51 m); wing area 526.00 sq ft (48.87 m²)
Powerplant: two Wright R-1820-47 Cyclone radial piston engines each rated at 850 hp (634 kW)	**Armament:** four 0.3-in (7.62-mm) Browning fixed forward-firing machine-guns in the nose and one 0.3-in (7.62-mm) Browning trainable rearward-firing machine-gun in the rear cockpit, plus up to 400 lb (272 kg) of bombs carried in two wing bays and 200 lb (91 kg) of bombs or chemical smoke tanks underwing
Performance: maximum speed 247 mph (398 km/h) at 2,500 ft (760 m); cruising speed 217 mph (349 km/h) at optimum altitude; service ceiling 28,650 ft (8370 m); range 651 miles (1048 km)	
Weights: empty 9,410 lb (4268 kg); maximum take-off	

of the 3rd Attack Group; with that unit the type pioneered low-flying formation attacks on ground targets, but for economy reasons no further **A-18** machines were ordered. Surviving

Curtiss Model 77 Helldiver (SBC)

*This **SBC-3** served with VS-5 in 1937. The blue fuselage bands and red tail surfaces indicate that this aircraft was flown by the leader of the 3rd section aboard USS Yorktown.*

Requiring a new two-seat fighter, the USN ordered a prototype from Curtiss in 1932 under the designation **XF12C-1**. This **Model 73** prototype flew for the first time during 1933 as a parasol-wing monoplane with retractable landing gear and the powerplant of one 625-hp (466-kW) Wright R-1510-92 Whirlwind 14 engine. When, at the end of the year, it was decided that the operational role of any production variant should be scouting rather than fighting, the designation was changed to **XS4C-1**. Following yet another change of heart in January 1934, the new type's role became that of

a scout-bomber, and an engine of greater power, in the form of the Wright R-1820 Cyclone, was installed. Extensive trials followed, and during a dive test in September 1934 there was structural failure of the wing and the **XSBC-1**, as the prototype was by now designated, was extensively damaged.

The parasol wing clearly lacked the strength for the dive-bombing role, and a new prototype was ordered as the **XSBC-2** that Curtiss designed as the **Model 77 Helldiver**. This was of mixed construction with tailwheel landing gear including retractable main

units, but had a staggered biplane wing cellule and the powerplant of one 700-hp (522-kW) R-1510-12 engine. When, in March 1936, this engine was replaced by a 700-hp (522-kW) Pratt & Whitney R-1535-82 Twin Wasp Junior, the designation changed yet again, this time to **XSBC-3**. The production version of the prototype in its definitive form had the company designation **Model 77A**, of which the USN ordered 83 examples on 29 August 1936 for service with the designation **SBC-3**. The first deliveries were made to VS-5 on 17 July 1937.

A late-production SBC-3 was used as the basis for the improved **XSBC-4** (**Model 77B**) prototype

that introduced the more powerful Wright R-1820-22 Cyclone engine. Following an initial contract of 5 January 1938, the first of 174 production examples of the **SBC-4** for the US Navy was delivered in March 1939. Because of

In RAF service, the Cleveland Mk I had a very limited flying career. Of note in this photograph are the gun sight protruding from the windscreen and the type's I-type interplane struts.

SPECIFICATION

Curtiss Model 77A Helldiver (SBC-4)

Type: two-seat carrierborne and land-based scout bomber
Powerplant: one Wright R-1820-34 Cyclone 9 radial piston engine rated at 900 hp (671 kW)
Performance: maximum speed 234 mph (377 km/h) at 15,200 ft (4635 m); cruising speed 175 mph (282 km/h) at optimum altitude; initial climb rate 1,630 ft (497 m) per minute; service ceiling 24,000 ft (7315 m); range 405 miles (652 km) with one 500-lb (227-kg) bomb
Weights: empty 4,552 lb (2065 kg); maximum take-off

7,080 lb (3211 kg)
Dimensions: wingspan 34 ft (10.36 m); length 28 ft 1½ in (8.57 m); height 10 ft 5 in (3.17 m); wing area 317.00 sq ft (29.45 m²)
Armament: one 0.5-in (12.7-mm) Browning fixed forward-firing machine-gun in the upper part of the forward fuselage and one 0.3-in (7.62-mm) Browning trainable rearward-firing machine-gun in the rear of the cockpit, plus up to 1,500 lb (680 kg) of disposable stores carried on one hardpoint under the fuselage and two hardpoints under the lower wing

the desperate situation in Europe in early 1940, the US Navy diverted 50 of its SBC-4 aircraft to France, but these were received too late to be used in combat. Five were recovered for use by the RAF, and these were issued to RAF Little Rissington for allocation as ground trainers under the designation **Cleveland Mk I**. The USN's deficiency of 50

aircraft was made good by delivery of 50 out of the 90 aircraft which had been placed in production for France. Retaining the SBC-4 designation, these differed from standard in having self-sealing fuel tanks. By the time the

USA became involved in World War II, the SBC-3 had become obsolescent, but the SBC-4 was still in service with VB-8 and VS-8, and also with the USMC's VMO-151. The last of these aircraft were retired in 1943.

Curtiss Model 81 and Model 87 Warhawk (P-40, Tomahawk and Kittyhawk)

Last of the famous Hawk line of fighters, the **P-40 Warhawk** has always been something of an enigma. By no stretch of the imagination could it be numbered among the great fighter aircraft of World War II yet, with the exceptions of the Republic P-47 and the North American P-51, it was the most extensively built US fighter, with almost 14,000 delivered before production ended in November 1944.

Evolution towards the **Model 81** began in 1937, when the airframe of the Model 75 prototype was modified to accept the 1,150-hp (858-kW) Allison V-1710-11 Vee engine to create the **Model 75I**, that was the first American fighter capable of a speed exceeding 300 mph (483 km/h). The USAAC

evaluated the Model 75I as the XP-37 and saw, despite engine and supercharger difficulties, that the concept had considerable potential and accordingly ordered 13 of the YP-37 service test model with a lengthened fuselage and the improved V-1710-21 engine with the new B-2 supercharger. The YP-37 continued to suffer powerplant problems, however, and a little later the tenth P-36A was revised with the 1,160-hp

(866-kW) Allison V-1710-19 engine in place of the original 1,050-hp (783-kW) Pratt & Whitney R-1830-13 radial engine, engine cooling being provided by a radiator initially located in the ventral position but gradually moved forward to a location under the engine. In other respects, this **Model 75P** differed little from the P-36A when it was flown for the first time on 14 October 1938. The USAAC evaluated the machine as the **XP-40**, and in May 1939 this prototype was flown in competition against other pursuit prototypes and then selected for production as the type most closely meeting the USAAC's requirements.

A total of 524 P-40 (Model 81) production aircraft was ordered on 27 April 1939, this then representing the USAAC's largest single order for fighters. Just under one year later, in April 1940, the first P-40s began to come off the production line, the initial three being used for service trials. These differed from the XP-40 in having the 1,090-hp (813-kW) V-1710-33 engine and two 0.3-in (7.62-mm) machine-guns in the leading edges of the wing to

This P-40M Kittyhawk III served with No. 250 Sqn, No. 239 Wing, No. 211 Group, RAF. It was based at El Assa, Tunisia, in March 1943. The P-40 proved most effective during desert operations.

supplement the two 0.5-in (12.7-mm) machine-guns in the upper part of the forward fuselage. By September 1940 a total of 200 of these aircraft had been delivered to the USAAC, the rest of the order being diverted to later variants; once they had entered service, the aircraft were upgraded with armour, bulletproof windscreens and self-sealing fuel tanks. Further important models for the USAAC and the USAAF, as the USAAC became in June 1941, started with the **P-40B** (**Model H81-B**), of which 131 were delivered from January 1941 with an additional two 0.3-in (7.62-mm) machine-guns in the leading edges of the wing. The 193 examples of the **P-40C** completed the original order for 524 aircraft; delivered from March 1943, these aircraft differed from the P-41B in having provision for a drop tank and fuel tanks with internal self-sealing capability rather than added covers.

More extensive changes

characterised the **P-40D** that received the revised company designation **Model H87-A2**, just 23 of the aircraft being constructed. Changes included the 1,150-hp (1007-kW) V-1710-39 engine and a shorter nose of the type that was retained for all subsequent aircraft; the armament was revised by the movement of the 0.5-in (12.7-mm) guns to a wing modified with provision for two 20-mm cannon (never installed); and the incorporation of three hardpoints allowed the carriage of one 500-lb (227-kg) bomb or a drop tank under the fuselage and six 20-lb (9.1-kg) bombs under the wing. The **P-40E**, of which 820 were built to **Model 87-B2** standard, was basically the P-40D with six 0.5-in (12.7-mm) guns in the wing and no provision for cannon. The **P-40E-1** (**Model 87-A4**) was a variant of the P-40E of which 1,500 were ordered for Lend-Lease delivery to the UK, although some were retained by the USAAF.

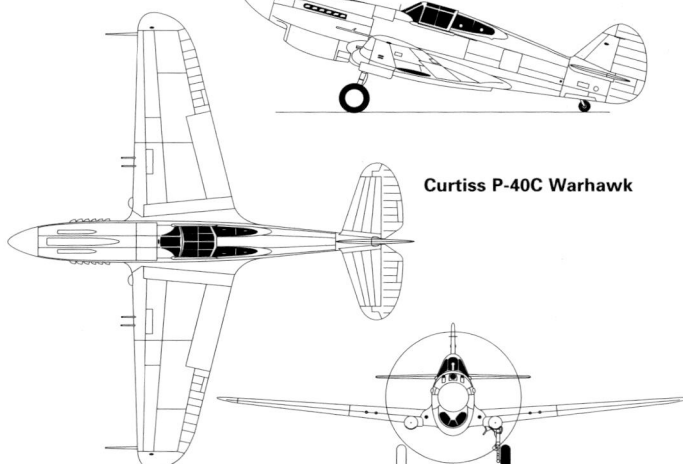

Curtiss P-40C Warhawk

Curtiss Model 81 and Model 87 Warhawk (P-40, Tomahawk and Kittyhawk) (continued)

It had been appreciated for some time that the P-40 was limited by its Allison engine, which provided adequate power only at low and medium altitudes. In June 1941 Curtiss flew the **XP-40F** (**Model 87-B3 Warhawk**) prototype conversion from P-40D standard with the 1,300-hp (969-kW) Rolls-Royce Merlin 28 Vee engine. Performance with the British engine was much enhanced, and Curtiss received orders for 1,311 examples of the **P-40F** production aircraft with the American-built version of the Merlin, in the form of the Packard V-1650-1, the armament of six 0.5-in

(12.7-mm) guns and, from the 700th aircraft, a lengthened rear fuselage for improved directional stability.

The 1,300 examples of the **P-40K** were to an improved P-40E standard with the V-1710-73 engine rated for optimum performance at higher altitudes, and were delivered from August 1942. Earlier aircraft had a dorsal fin fillet for improved directional stability, but later aircraft had the lengthened rear fuselage of the later P-40F aircraft and, like the P-40F, were built in subvariants according to the new block system introduced in 1942. The

P-40L, of which 700 were built to the **Model 97-A3** standard, was an improved **P-40F-5** with minor equipment changes, the 600 **P-40M** warplanes were in essence **P-40K-20** machines with the V-1710-81 engine, and the 5,220 examples of the **P-40N** (**Model 87V** and **Model 87W**) were the final production aircraft with the V-1710-81 engine, a lightened structure, decreased fuel capacity, increased armour, and the armament of four 0.5-in (12.7-mm) guns and only the under-fuselage hardpoint for one bomb or drop tank.

The P-40 was moder-

ately effective as a fighter up to the later stages of 1942, although only at low level. Thereafter, however, it was used almost exclusively in the

ground-attack role, in which its armament was little more than adequate, but its sturdiness and stability were decided assets.

SPECIFICATION	
Curtiss Model 87V/W (P-40N-1)	
Type: single-seat fighter-bomber	
Powerplant: one Allison V-1710-81 Vee piston engine rated at 1,200 hp (895 kW)	
Performance: maximum speed 350 mph (563 km/h) at 15,000 ft (4570 m); climb to 14,000 ft (4265 m) in 6 minutes 42 seconds; service ceiling 31,000 ft (9450 m); range 1,080 miles (1738 km) with auxiliary fuel and 360 miles (579 km) with standard fuel	
Weights: empty 6,000 lb	(2722 kg); maximum take-off 7,740 lb (3511 kg)
	Dimensions: wingspan 37 ft 3½ in (11.36 m); length 33 ft 4 in (10.16 m); height 12 ft 4 in (3.76 m); wing area 236.00 sq ft (21.92 m²)
	Armament: four 0.5-in (12.7-mm) Browning fixed forward-firing machine-guns in the leading edges of the wing, plus up to 700 lb (318 kg) of disposable stores carried on one underfuselage and two underwing hardpoints

Variants

P-40A: retrospective designation applied to a single P-40 adapted for the photo-reconnaissance role
YF-40F: unofficial designation of the third P-40F after conversion for evaluation of different radiator installations and larger vertical tail surfaces
XP-40G: unofficial designation of the **Model 81-AG** conversion of a single P-40 with the wing of the **Model H81-A2** (**Tomahawk Mk IA**)
P-40G: 43 P-40s revised in a fashion identical to that of the XP-40G
P-40J: projected version of the P-40E with a turbocharged engine
P-40P: 1,500 of a projected version with the V-1650-1 engine, but in fact built to P-40N standard
XP-40Q: two P-40Ks and one P-40N adapted to **Model 87X** standard with revised radiator systems, two-stage supercharger and, on two of the aircraft, a 'bubble' canopy
P-40R: designation reserved for a planned 600, but in actuality some 70 P-40F and 53 P-40L, aircraft converted for the training role with the V-1710-81 engine
TP-40: a number of P-40Ns adapted as dual-control trainers
Twin-Engined P-40: projected P-40C development with two V-1650 engines in wing-mounted nacelles
Tomahawk: 10 examples of P-40C used by the British
Tomahawk Mk I: 140 British aircraft to the **Model H81-A** standard basically similar to the P-40 except for the armament of four wing guns, and deemed unsuitable for operational service before being relegated to training use in Canada
Tomahawk Mk II: 110 British aircraft to the **Model H81-A2** standard basically similar to the P-40B, and including 23 transferred

to the USSR
Tomahawk Mk IIB: 930 British aircraft to the Model H81-A2 and Model H81-A3 standards basically similar to the P-40C; most of the aircraft were used by the British and South Africans in North Africa, but 23 were transferred to the USSR, 100 were released to the Chinese for the use of the American Volunteer Group, and others were passed to Egypt and Turkey
Kittyhawk Mk I: the name Kittyhawk was used by the British to designate Model 87 aircraft, which the British first adopted on take-over of outstanding French orders; the 560 Kittyhawk Mk I aircraft were the only machines directly purchased (later aircraft being under Lend-Lease) and were completed to the Model A87-A2 standard similar to the P-40D with the armament of four 0.5-in (12.7-mm) machine-guns; 72 and 17 of the aircraft were diverted to Canada and Turkey respectively
Kittyhawk Mk IA: 1,500 **Model H87-A3** and **Model H87-A4** aircraft were basically similar to the P-40E, and 163, 12 and 62 were diverted to Australia, Canada and New Zealand respectively
Kittyhawk Mk II: 330 **Model H87-B3** aircraft were 230 P-40F and 100 P-40L aircraft, of which the first 230 were later identified as
Kittyhawk Mk IIA warplanes; 81 of the aircraft were transferred to the USAAF overseas and another seven to the Free French
Kittyhawk Mk III: 616 aircraft comprising 192 P-40K, 160 P-40L and 264 P-40M machines, and the last 170 were transferred to the USSR; other transfers included 210 to Australia, 15 to Canada, and 58 to New Zealand
Kittyhawk Mk IV: 586 aircraft P-40Ns of which the last 130 were transferred to the USSR; other transfers were 468 to Australia, 35 to Canada and 172 to New Zealand

Curtiss Model 82 (SO3C Seamew)

In 1937 the US Navy invited proposals for the design of a scout monoplane which would offer performance better than that of the Curtiss Seagull. The new type was required for operation from either ships or land bases. From the proposals received, Curtiss and Vought were each awarded prototype contracts in May 1938 under the respective designations **XSO3C-1** and XOS2U-1. The **Curtiss Model 82** design emerged victorious and was therefore ordered into production, even though the XSO3C-1 had serious instability problems. These were finally resolved by the introduction of upturned

wingtips and increased area for the tail surfaces.

Of all-metal construction except for fabric-covered control surfaces, the XSO3C-1 had a crew of two accommodated in tandem enclosed cockpits. The XSO3C-1 prototype flew for the first time on 6 October 1939, and both this and the **Model 82A** production version, which entered service as the

SO3C-1 with the initial name **Seagull**, were powered by the 520-hp (388-kW) V-770-6 engine.

SO3C-1 production aircraft entered service in

July 1942, at first on board the cruiser USS *Cleveland*, and 300 such aircraft were completed before production switched to the **SO3C-2**. Known to the company as the **Model 82B**, this differed from its predecessor in having

equipment (including an arrester hook) for carrier-borne operation and, in landplane form, a centreline hardpoint for the carriage of a single 500-lb (227-kg) bomb. Production of this model totalled 456 aircraft, of which 250 were allo-

As a floatplane, the Seamew featured a single main float with underwing stabilising floats. Note the unusual way in which a section of fin slides forwards with the open canopy.

cated to the UK under Lend-Lease, although British records suggest that in fact only 100 aircraft were received. The designation of the subvariant initially intended for the Royal Navy was **SO3C-1B** (**Model 82C**), but the aircraft actually delivered were of the **SO3C-2C** subvariant with an uprated engine, hydraulic brakes and a number of other refinements. In British service the SO3C-2C received the designation **Seamew Mk I**, and the name was later adopted by the USN in place of the original Seagull. None of the aircraft was used operationally by the RN, which instead allocated them to Nos 744 and 745 Training Squadrons.

The unsatisfactory performance of the SO3C-1 in USN service led to the type's withdrawal from first-line service after only a comparatively short time. Many of the aircraft were converted as **SO3C-1K** radio-controlled target drones, of which 30 were transferred to the UK for use with the local designation **Queen Seamew**.

In an attempt to redress the unsatisfactory situation with the SO3C-1, Curtiss introduced the **Model 82C** development late in 1943. This had a lightened structure and the 500-hp (373-kW) V-770-8 engine, but only 39 examples of this variant, known to the USN as the **SO3C-3**, were completed before production ended in January 1944. At this stage plans for the production of a carrier-capable subvariant of the SO3C-3 were cancelled, as had been the notion that the SO3C-1 should be produced by the Ryan Aeronautical Corporation as the **SOR-1**.

Upturned wingtips and increased fin area were featured by the production Seamew in an attempt to solve earlier handling problems.

SPECIFICATION

Curtiss Model 82B Seamew (SO3C-2C)

Type: two-seat scout and observation floatplane
Powerplant: one Ranger V-770-6 inverted-Vee piston engine rated at 600 hp (448 kW)
Performance: maximum speed 172 mph (277 km/h) at 8,100 ft (2470 m); cruising speed 125 mph (201 km/h) at optimum altitude; initial climb rate 380 ft (116 m) per minute; service ceiling 15,800 ft (4815 m); range 1,150 miles (1851 km)
Weights: empty 4,284 lb (1943 kg); maximum take-off 5,729 lb (2599 kg)
Dimensions: wingspan 38 ft (11.58 m); length 36 ft 10 in (11.23 m); height 15 ft (4.57 m); wing area 290.00 sq ft (26.94 m²)
Armament: one 0.3-in (7.62-mm) Browning fixed forward-firing machine-gun and one 0.3-in (7.62-mm) or 0.5-in (12.7-mm) Browning trainable rearward-firing machine-gun, plus two 325-lb (147-kg) depth charges or 100-lb (45-kg) bombs carried under the wing

Curtiss Model 84 (SB2C Helldiver & A-25 Shrike)

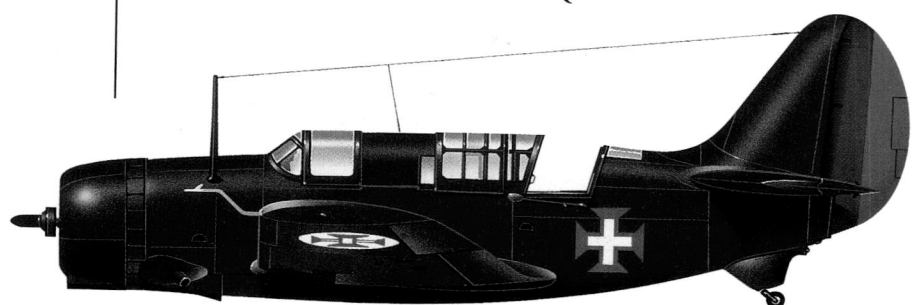

Post-war, a number of war-surplus Helldivers, including this Portuguese example, was exported.

Variants

SB2C-1C: 170 of the original order for 370 SB2C-1s were completed with the four wing-mounted machine-guns replaced by two 20-mm cannon, the suffix 'C' denoting cannon armament; the company designation was **Model 84A** and total production was 708 aircraft including the 170 from the SB2C-1 order
XSB2C-2: experimental long-range seaplane prototype in the form of one **Model 84C** conversion of an early production SB2C-1 with twin floats and specialised equipment
SB2C-3: second production version, the **Model 84E**, of which 1,112 were built with the 1,900-hp (1417-kW) R-2600-20 engine and detail improvements
SB2C-4: this **Model 84F** was the major production version, of which 1,985 were built, to a standard that differed from that of the SB2C-3 in having underwing racks for eight 5-in (127-mm) rockets or two 500-lb (227-kg) bombs
SB2C-4E: an unknown number of SB2C-4s equipped with radar for night operations
SB2C-5: this **Model 84G** was the final Curtiss production version with increased fuel capacity, and production totalled 970 aircraft
XSB2C-6: two **Model 84H** prototypes with the 2,100-hp (1566-kW) R-2600-22 engine, lengthened fuselage, square wingtips and extra fuel
SBF-1: the SBF designation was used for aircraft produced by the Fairchild Aircraft Corporation's Canadian division; the SBF-1, of which 50 were completed, was equivalent to the SB2C-1C
SBF-3: total of 150 built to basically the same standard as the SB2C-3
SBF-4E: total of 100 built to basically the same standard as the SB2C-4E
SBW-1: the SBW designation was used for aircraft produced by the Canadian Car & Foundry Company; the SBW-1, of which 40 were completed, was equivalent to the SB2C-1C
SBW-1E: 450 aircraft ordered of an SBW-1 subvariant for the Royal Navy; in the event only 26 were built and supplied as **Helldiver DB.Mk I** aircraft that did not become operational
SBW-3: total of 413 built to basically the same standard as the SB2C-3
SBW-4E: total of 96 built to basically the same standard as the SB2C-4E and supplemented by 174 of the SBW-1B order completed to SBW-4E standard

The last and most famous of the Helldiver line was the **SB2C Helldiver** of the early 1940s; this was the final combat aircraft built by Curtiss for the USMC and USN, and also the most extensively built of all US Navy dive-bombers.

In 1938, the US Navy began the process of procuring a new scout-bomber to replace the SBC, which was then still in production. From the proposals received, Brewster and Curtiss were awarded contracts for prototypes, the former being designated XSB2A-1 and later entering production as the SB2A Buccaneer. The Curtiss **Model 84** prototype, designated **XSB2C-1** by the USN, flew for the first time on 18 December 1940 but was destroyed in an accident early in January 1941. The USN already had great faith in this design, but it was not until 18 months later, in June 1942, that the first example of the **SB2C-1** initial production variant flew. The extended development period indicated by these dates resulted mainly from a USAAC order for 900

A-25A Shrike land-based aircraft in April 1941. The process of developing this **Model S84** caused delay as a result of the need to ensure maximum compatibility of design and equipment to satisfy both the USN and US Army. In the final analysis only a few of the A-25As entered US Army service, the majority being reassigned to the USMC under the designation **SB2C-1A**.

The SB2C-1 entered service with the US Navy from December 1942, initially with VS-9, but further protracted delays in finalising the details of the best combat configuration prevented the type's initial operational employment until late in 1943.

In configuration the SB2C was a low-wing cantilever monoplane largely of all-metal construction, the outer panels of the wings folding upward for carrier stowage. Arrester gear and catapult launching spools were standard, but the latter equipment and wing-folding capability were deleted from the A-25A. The powerplant of the prototype and SB2C-1 comprised one 1,700-hp (1268-kW) Wright R-2600-8 Cyclone 14 twin-row radial engine. The armament consisted of four 0.5-in (12.7-mm) fixed machine-guns in the leading edges of the wing and two 0.3-in (7.62-mm) trainable machine-guns in the rear cockpit, plus up to 1,000 lb (454 kg) of bombs in a lower-fuselage bay.

Production eventually totalled more than 7,000 examples and only 26 of these were used by any other country during World War II, for the type was of such great value in the Pacific theatre that the USN absorbed almost the entire production. Many continued in service with the USN in early post-war years, and some were eventually sold to other nations.

SPECIFICATION

Curtiss Model 84G Helldiver (SB2C-5)

Type: two-seat carrierborne and land-based scout-bomber
Powerplant: one Wright R-2600-20 Cyclone 14 radial piston engine rated at 1,900 hp (1417 kW)
Performance: maximum speed 260 mph (418 km/h) at 16,100 ft (4910 m); cruising speed 148 mph (238 km/h) at optimum altitude; climb to 10,000 ft (3050 m) in 8 minutes 54 seconds; service ceiling 26,400 ft (8045 m); range 1,805 miles (2905 km)
Weights: empty 10,580 lb (4799 kg); maximum take-off 15,918 lb (7220 kg) in the scout role with maximum fuel
Dimensions: wingspan 49 ft 8⅝ in (15.15 m); length 36 ft 8 in (11.18 m); height 13 ft 1½ in (4.01 m); wing area 422.00 sq ft (39.20 m²)
Armament: two 20-mm M2 fixed forward-firing cannon in the leading edges of the wing and two 0.3-in (7.62-mm) Browning trainable rearward-firing machine-guns in the rear of the cockpit, plus up to 2,000 lb (907 kg) of bombs or one torpedo in the lower-fuselage weapons bay and on underwing racks

Curtiss Model 85 (O-52 Owl)

A reconnaissance and observation aircraft of a concept similar to the Westland Lysander and Henschel Hs 126, the **Model 85 Owl** was a high-wing cabin mono- plane with a single bracing strut on each side. The design originated in 1939 and in many respects can be regarded as a mono- plane development of the Model 77 biplane. Without evaluating a prototype, the USAAC ordered 203 **O-52** production aircraft. Deliveries began in February 1941 and at the time of the Japanese attack on Pearl Harbor, a

few of the aircraft were deployed in the Pacific area. It is also reported that a small number was sent to the

USSR. By that time, however, most O-52s in the USA had been relegated to the training role.

Distinctive among the Owl's features were its extensively glazed cockpit, and the main units of its tailwheel landing gear, which retracted to lie with their wheels within the fuselage profile.

SPECIFICATION

Curtiss Model 85 Owl (O-52)
Type: two-seat observation and reconnaissance aircraft
Powerplant: one Pratt & Whitney R-1340-51 radial piston engine rated at 600 hp (448 kW)
Performance: maximum speed 220 mph (354 km/h) at optimum altitude; cruising speed 192 mph (309 km/h) at optimum altitude; climb to 10,000 ft (3050 m) in 8 minutes 12 seconds; service ceiling 21,000 ft (6400 m); range 700 miles (1127 km)

Weights: empty 4,231 lb (1919 kg); maximum take-off 5,364 lb (2433 kg)
Dimensions: wingspan 40 ft 9 in (12.42 m); length 26 ft 4¾ in (8.05 m); height 9 ft 11½ in (3.03 m); wing area 210.00 sq ft (19.50 m²)
Armament: one 0.3-in (7.62-mm) Browning fixed forward-firing machine-gun and one 0.3-in (7.62-mm) Browning trainable rearward-firing machine-gun in the rear of the cockpit

Curtiss Model 97 (SC Seahawk)

Development of the **SC Seahawk** began in June 1942, when the USN requested Curtiss to submit proposals for an advanced scout aircraft capable of easy conversion between wheeled landing gear and floats. This capa- bility was required so that the aircraft could be oper-

ated from aircraft-carriers and land bases, or be cata- pulted from battleships and cruisers in floatplane form. The new type was required to replace the rather similar SO3C Seamew and Vought OS2U Kingfisher. The **Model 97** design proposal was submitted on

1 August 1942, but it was not until 31 March 1943 that a contract was issued for two **XSC-1 (Model 97A)** prototypes.
The first prototype made its maiden flight on 16 February 1944, and the prototypes were followed by 500 **SC-1 (Model 97B)** production aircraft that had been ordered in June 1943. All the aircraft were delivered in landplane form, the floats being procured separately and installed by the USN on an 'as and when required' basis. Delivery of produc- tion aircraft began in October 1944, the first aircraft equipping the unit aboard the 'battle-cruiser' USS *Guam*. A second batch of 450 SC-1s was ordered, but of these only 66 had been delivered before the cancellation of the balance of the contract

Curtiss developed the Seahawk as a single-seater, the development of ASV radar and other sensors making the observer dispensable. The first operational Seahawks were assigned to USS Guam.

at VJ-Day.
An improved version was developed, changes including the 1,426-hp (1063-kW) R-1820-76 engine, provision of a clear blown canopy, and a jump seat behind the pilot. The successful evaluation of

the modified prototype, at first designated **XSC-1A** and then **XSC-2 (Model 97C)**, led to a contract for the **SC-2 (Model 97D)** production version, but only 10 of these had been delivered by the end of World War II.

SPECIFICATION

Curtiss Model 97B Seahawk (SC-1)
Type: single-seat scout and anti- submarine aircraft
Powerplant: one Wright R-1820-62 Cyclone radial piston engine rated at 1,360 hp (1007 kW)
Performance: maximum speed 313 mph (504 km/h) at 28,600 ft (8716 m); cruising speed 125 mph (201 km/h) at optimum altitude; initial climb rate 2,500 ft (762 m) per minute; service ceiling 37,300 ft 11370 m); range 625 miles (1006 km)

Weights: empty 6,320 lb (2867 kg); maximum take-off 9,000 lb (4082 kg)
Dimensions: wingspan 41 ft (12.50 m); length 36 ft 4½ in (11.09 m); height 12 ft 9 in (3.89 m); wing area 280.00 sq ft (26.01 m²)
Armament: two 0.5-in (12.7-mm) Browning fixed forward-firing machine-guns in the leading edges of the wing, plus two 325-lb (147-kg) depth charges or two 100-lb (45-kg) bombs carried under the wing

Curtiss-Wright CW-1 to CW-3 and CW-5 to CW-18

During 1928, Curtiss bought Robertson Airlines, and then established the Curtiss-Robertson Airplane Manufacturing Corporation. The first aircraft built by the new outfit were designed at the company's other establishments, but soon there began to appear aircraft designed at the new St Louis plant and also in Wichita, Kansas, the latter the home of the Travel Air Manufacturing Company that Curtiss bought in 1929. In 1930 Curtiss-Robertson and Travel Air were merged as the Curtiss-Wright Airplane Company, whose designs were then identi- fied by the CW prefix.
St Louis production also resulted in some anoma- lous designations: the **Curtiss-Wright CA-1** was a very attractive biplane amphibian, while Curtiss- Robertson produced two

designs, the **CR-1 Skeeter** and the **CR-2 Coupe**: the former was an ultra-light sporting aircraft and the latter was a two-seat cabin monoplane which also appeared in 1930.
Curtiss-Wright got into its stride with the **CW-1 Junior**, an improved version of the CR-1 Skeeter, which was further developed into the **CW-3 Duckling** amphibian. The designation **CW-2** was applied to an unbuilt two- seat monoplane project, **CW-4** to the **T-32 Condor II** and alternatively to the **Travel Air 4000**, **CW-5** to an unbuilt freighter project, and **CW-6** to **CW-11** to former Travel Air products (**Models 6000**, **7000**, **8000**, **9000**, **10** and **11** respec- tively).
The **CW-12 Sport Trainer** of 1930 was a handsome two-seat biplane

that was developed in a number of forms. The **CW-12K** was a high- performance model; the **CW-12B** was the most popular version with the powerplant of one 90-hp (67-kW) Curtiss-Wright Gipsy inline engine and built

to the extent of 27 examples; and the **CW-12W**, powered by the 110-hp (82-kW) Warner Scarab radial, reached 12 examples. The designation **CW-13** was not used, so the next model was the **CW-14**, developed from the

Travel Air 4000/4 – this was initially called the **Speedwing**, after the Travel Air design, but was later renamed as the **Sportsman**; **Osprey** was the name allocated to the two-seat military model for export. The single prototype

This Bolivian CW-C14B Osprey demonstrates the type's trainable rear machine-gun and synchronised forward-firing weapon. The Osprey's cockpits were moved slightly aft compared to those of the civilian CW-14.

was the **CW-14C** with the 185-hp (138-kW) Curtiss Challenger radial engine, and this was followed by the **CW-A14D** three-seater, of which five were built with the 240-hp (179-kW) Wright Whirlwind J-6-7 (R-760E) engine; the **CW-B14B Speedwing Deluxe**, of which two were produced with the 300-hp (224-kW) Whirlwind J-6-9 (R-975E); the **CW-B14R Special Speedwing Deluxe**, of which only one example was manufactured with accommodation for

one and powered by the 420-hp (313-kW) SR-975E supercharged radial engine; the **CW-C14B Osprey** military aircraft powered by the 300-hp (224-kW) R-975E and armed with two machine-guns (one fixed and one trainable) and a light bombload; and the **CW-C14R**, identical to the CW-C14B except for its J-6-9 engine.

The next design was the **CW-15 Sedan**, designed by an ex-Travel Air employee, and was not surprisingly similar to the

Travel Air Model 10. Total production amounted to 15 aircraft: nine of the **CW-15C**, three of the **CW-15D** and three of the **CW-15N**.

The **CW-16 Light Sport** was a three-seat version of the CW-12, and was available in three variants, namely the **CW-16E** (10 built) with the 165-hp (123-kW) J-6-5 engine, the **CW-16K** (11 built) with the 125-hp (93-kW) Kinner B-5 engine and the **CW-16W** (one built) with the 110-hp (82-kW) Scarab engine. The

CW-17R Pursuit Osprey was a version of the CW-B14B with a more powerful engine, the 420-hp (313-kW) J-6-9

radial unit, but it is uncertain whether or not even a prototype was built. Finally, the **CW-18** was a projected trainer for the USAAC.

Curtiss-Wright CW-4 (BT-32 Condor II)

The **CW-4** (sometimes referred to as the **Curtiss T-32 Condor II**) of 1933 was even more of an anachronism than its namesake, the Condor 18 of four years earlier. Its only concession to the then current modernity was the landing gear, its main units retracting into the engine nacelles. A two-bay biplane of mixed construction, with a strut-braced single fin and rudder tail assembly, the T-32 prototype made its first flight on 30 January 1933. The layout for most of the production batch of 21 aircraft that followed was as a luxury 12-passenger night sleeper transport, and a number of T-32s flew with Eastern Air Transport

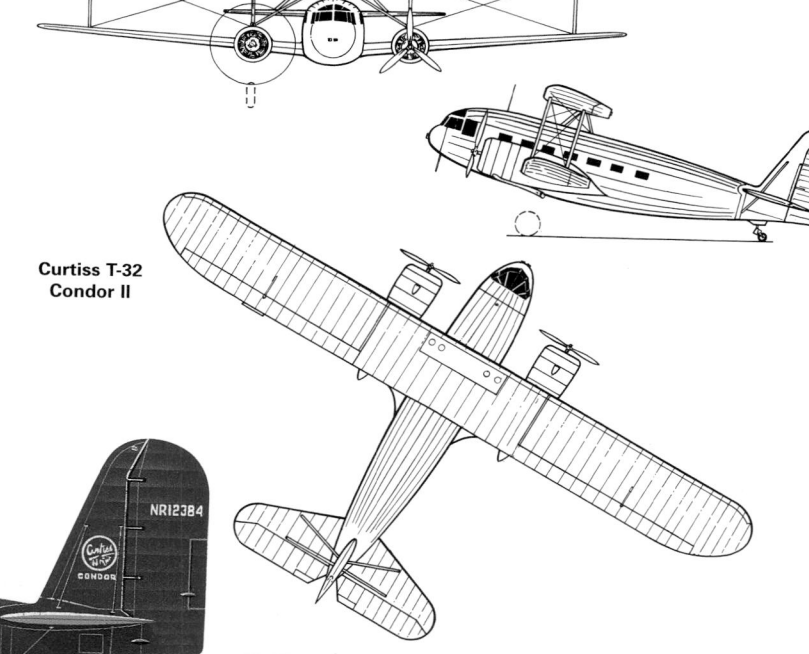

The prototype BT-32 was sold to China (illustrated), while three aircraft with twin floats were exported to Colombia and four landplanes went to Peru.

and American Airways during the following three years on regular night services.

Two modified T-32s were bought as transports for the US Army and operated

until 1938 under the designation **YC-30**.

Ten T-32s were ultimately converted to **AT-32**

standard, being redesignated **T-32C**. Four T-32s were being operated under British civil registra-

tions at the outbreak of World War II; these were impressed and flown by the RAF.

Variants

AT-32: this version differed from the original T-32 in detail and was provided with variable-pitch propellers; the engines had full NACA cowlings instead of the Townend rings of the T-32. The AT-32s were convertible from night sleepers into comfortable 15-passenger day transports and were built in **AT-32A** to **AT-32D** subvariants
AT-32A: three of an AT-32 sub-variant with 710-hp (529-kW) SCR-1820-23 Cyclones
AT-32B: three aircraft with 720-hp (537-kW) SCR-1820-F2s
AT-32C: one aircraft with SCR-1820-F2 engines
AT-32D: four aircraft with SCR-1820-23 engines
AT-32E: two aircraft for the US Navy, operated under the designation R4C-1 by the USN and USMC as 12-passenger de-luxe transports; both were used by the US Antarctic Survey, finally being abandoned in the Antarctic in 1941
BT-32: eight examples of this bomber development of the AT-32 were completed; defensive armament comprised five machine-guns with single guns located in manually-operated turrets in the nose and above the rear fuselage, the other guns being aimed through lateral ports and from an extensively glazed ventral position
CT-32: military cargo version with a large loading door in the starboard side of the fuselage, all three built went to Argentina

Curtiss T-32 Condor II

One Condor was completed with extra fuel tanks as a long-range version for use by the 1933 Byrd Antarctic Expedition. Equipped to operate with either twin floats or skis, it was unique in having fixed landing gear.

Curtiss-Wright CW-19 and CW-23

The **CW-19L Coupe** was designed by George Page as an advanced all-metal two-seat cantilever low-wing monoplane for the private owner. Built in 1935 and powered by a 90-hp (67-kW) Lambert R-266 radial engine, the CW-19L was revealed in its test programme to be manoeuvrable but underpowered.

The **CW-19W** retained the side-by-side cabin layout of the earlier machine, but replaced the Lambert engine with a 145-hp (108-kW) Warner Super Scarab radial engine.

The militarised **CW-19R** was a radical redesign intended for the export market. The two-man crew was accommodated in tandem under a long sliding canopy, and there was provision for machine-gun armament, with light bombs carried on underwing racks. Additional machine-guns for the ground-attack mission could be attached to the landing-gear fairings.

The Curtiss-Wright management believed the CW-19R would satisfy the need for a utility fighter, reconnaissance and ground-attack aircraft. In the event, sales were limited, comprising 20 aircraft purchased by China and three by Cuba. Power was greatly increased, with the 450-hp (336-kW) Whirlwind J-6-9 (R-975E) available as an alternative engine, and the aircraft demonstrated good flight characteristics and had an outstanding rate of climb.

An unarmed basic trainer version of the CW-19R was built as the **CW-A19R**. Flown in February 1937, this was evaluated by the USAAC, which placed no order. Three such aircraft were completed, one being converted later into a CW-22. The sole **CW-23** was developed from the CW-19R. It had a 600-hp (447-kW) Pratt & Whitney R-1340 Wasp radial engine and inward-retracting main landing-gear units, and was intended as a basic combat trainer for the USAAC. First flown in 1939, the type was rejected for production after the USAAC had evaluated the machine.

A feature common to the whole CW-19 series was the streamlined 'trouser' type of fairing, over each main unit of the fixed tailwheel landing gear.

SPECIFICATION

Curtiss-Wright CW-19R
Type: two-seat light fighter and attack aircraft
Powerplant: one Wright R-760E2 Whirlwind radial piston engine rated at 350 hp (261 kW)
Performance: maximum speed 185 mph (298 km/h) at optimum altitude; cruising speed 164 mph (264 km/h) at optimum altitude; initial climb rate 1,890 ft (576 m) per minute
Weights: empty 1,992 lb (904 kg); maximum take-off 3,500 lb (1588 kg)
Dimensions: wingspan 35 ft (10.67 m); length 26 ft 4 in (8.03 m); height 8 ft 2 in (2.49 m); wing area 174.00 sq ft (16.16 m²)
Armament: one 0.3-in (7.62-mm) fixed forward-firing machine-gun in the upper part of the forward fuselage and one 0.3-in (7.62-mm) trainable rearward-firing machine-gun in the rear of the cockpit, plus provision for two 0.3-in (7.62-mm) fixed forward-firing machine-guns on the outer sides of the landing gear fairings and light bombs carried on underwing racks

Variant

CW-B19R: unrealised project for a civil version of the CW-A19R

Curtiss-Wright CW-21 and CW-22 (SNC Falcon)

A lightweight interceptor development of the CW-19, the **CW-21** was an all-metal cantilever low-wing monoplane with tailwheel landing gear, whose main units retracted rearward into underwing fairings. Power was provided by a 1,000-hp (746-kW) Wright R-1820-G5 Cyclone radial engine, and the armament comprised two 0.3-in (7.62-mm) fixed forward-firing machine-guns. The prototype made its maiden flight on 22 September 1938 and was demonstrated in China during the following March, thereafter remaining in Chinese service. After prolonged negotiations, three production examples of the CW-21 were purchased by the Chinese, and these were followed by 27 more of the type to be built at Loiwing in China from components supplied by Curtiss-Wright. All three American-built CW-21 light fighters crashed during their delivery flight from Burma to Kunming, and available information indicates that none of the 27 aircraft to be built in China was ever completed.

For the **CW-21B**, Curtiss-Wright revised the landing gear with inward-retracting main units of the type developed for the one-off experimental CW-23. The Netherlands bought 24 examples of the CW-21B but, as they did not become available until five months after the home country had been overrun by the Germans, these aircraft were delivered to the Netherlands East Indies, where they arrived between October and December 1940. Hotly engaged in operations against attacking Imperial Japanese navy air force fighters and bombers during the early months of 1942, the CW-21Bs were immediately discovered to be very vulnerable as a result of their lack of self-sealing tanks and bulletproof windscreens. Most of the CW-21B fighters were shot down, but some fell into Japanese hands in a usable, airworthy condition.

Based on the same basic aerodynamic and structural concepts as the CW-21, the **CW-22** was designed during 1940 as a two-seat cantilever low-wing monoplane of all-metal construction for the general-purpose and advanced training roles. The two crewmembers were housed in tandem under a continuous glazed canopy, and the CW-22 revealed its lineage in its landing gear, which had main units retracting rearward into underwing fairings as on the CW-21. The CW-22 was sold to the total of 36 aircraft to the Netherlands East Indies, but as a result of the Japanese advance in that region in the first months of 1942, these aircraft were delivered to the Dutch in northern Australia during March 1942.

A **CW-22B** developed version was sold to Turkey, the Netherlands East Indies and various Latin American countries. Several Dutch aircraft were later captured and flown by the Japanese.

Both the CW-22 and CW-22B were armed with two machine-guns, one fixed and the other trainably mounted.

After a demonstrator had been tested by the USN, a **CW-22N** advanced training version went into production. The USN applied the designation **SNC-1 Falcon** to the type, a total of 455 being purchased. The aircraft of the third batch had a modified, higher cockpit canopy. Many SNC-1s were sold to private American owners after the end of World War II.

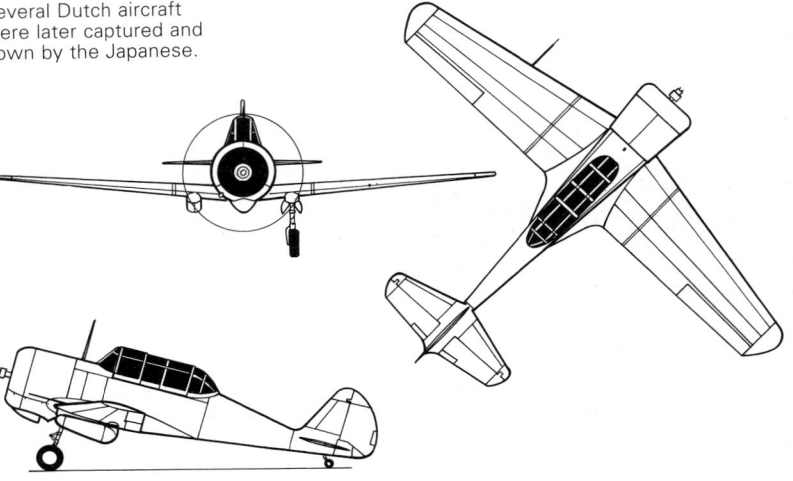

In combat, the Dutch CW-21Bs often became embroiled in dogfights, a type of air combat for which they had not been intended, having been designed for the point defence interception role.

SPECIFICATION

Curtiss-Wright CW-22N (SNC-1 Falcon)
Type: two-seat advanced flying and armament trainer
Powerplant: one Wright R-975-28 Whirlwind radial piston engine rated at 420 hp (313 kW)
Performance: maximum speed 198 mph (319 km/h) at sea level; initial climb rate 1,650 ft (503 m) per minute; service ceiling 21,800 ft (6645 m); range 780 miles (1255 km)
Weights: empty 2,736 lb (1241 kg); maximum take-off 3,788 lb (1718 kg)
Dimensions: wingspan 35 ft (10.67 m); length 27 ft (8.23 m); height 9 ft 11 in (3.02 m); wing area 173.70 sq ft (16.14 m²)
Armament: one 0.3-in (7.62-mm) Browning fixed forward-firing machine-gun and one 0.3-in (7.62-mm) Browning trainable rearward-firing machine-gun

Curtiss-Wright CW-20 (C-46 Commando)

On 26 March 1940 Curtiss-Wright flew the prototype of a 36-seat commercial airliner which had the company designation **CW-20**. Its large-capacity fuselage aroused US Army interest in the type for cargo/transport and casualty evacuation, and a militarised version with 2,000-hp (1491-kW) Pratt & Whitney R-2800-43 engines was ordered into production under the designation **C-46** and named **Commando**. When the first of these **CW-20B** models entered service in July 1942, they were the largest and heaviest twin-engined aircraft to serve with the USAAF, and proved such a valuable transport in the Pacific theatre of operations that well over 3,000 Commandos were built before production ended.

Apart from differing engines and few cabin windows, the original C-46s were generally similar to

This C-46 was flown by the Chinese Nationalist Air Force in standard USAAF camouflage. It took part in the 1949 evacuation to Taiwan.

the CW-20 prototype. The **C-46A** which followed had a large cargo door on the port side of the rear fuselage, a strengthened cargo floor, and folding seats for 40 troops. Pratt & Whitney R-2800-51 engines of equivalent power replaced the R-2800-43s of the C-46, these having better performance at altitude. This proved of great importance, and C-46As 'humping' vital

supplies over the Himalayas to China from India, after the loss of the 'Burma Road', were found to have better performance than the C-47 at the altitudes involved. They made a vital contribution to the success of this airlift of essential war materials into China.

In the Pacific the Commando played a significant role in the island-hopping operations which culminated in Japanese surrender, and 160 **R5C-1** aircraft (similar to the USAAF C-46As), supplied to the US Marine Corps, made an important contribution. Later versions for the USAAF included the **C-46D** (**CW-20B-2**) personnel version with an extra door on the starboard side (1,610 built); the **C-46E** (**CW-20B-3**) utility version with the door arrangement of the C-46A and the stepped windscreen of the XC-46B (17 built); the **C-46F** (**CW-20B-4**) cargo model with doors on both sides and square-cut wingtips; and a single **C-46G** (**CW-20B-5**) combin-

Never awarded the level of recognition enjoyed by the C-47, the C-46 nevertheless proved vital in the Far Eastern war.

ing a stepped windscreen and square wingtips. Commandos remained in service with both the USAAF/USAF and USMC after World War II had ended. The USAF employed C-46s opera-

tionally during the Korean War, as well as in the early stages of hostilities in Vietnam, and a very small number remains in service with civilian operators, chiefly freight-haulers in Central and South America.

Variants

CW-20T: original prototype with dihedralled tailplane, endplate vertical tail surfaces and 1,700-hp (1268-kW) Wright R-2600 Twin Cyclone radials
CW-20A: modification of the original prototype with straight tailplane, single fin and rudder assembly, and detail improvements; evaluated by the US Army as the **C-55**, it was then returned to Curtiss, who then sold it to BOAC
CW-20B-1: single conversion from a C-46A to evaluate a stepped windscreen design, powered by 2,100-hp (1567-kW) H-2800-34W radials and service designated **XC-46B**
CW-20E: project for an **AC-46K** version with 2,500-hp (1865-kW) Wright R-3350-BD radials
CW-20G: C-46G when converted as a testbed for the General Electric TG-100 turboprop, which was installed in the starboard nacelle, leaving the original R-2800-34W radial in the port nacelle. The service designation was originally **XC-46C**, but was changed to **XC-113**
CW-20H: three examples with Wright R-3350 radials delivered in 1945 under the service designation **XC-46L**

SPECIFICATION

Curtiss C-46A Commando **Type:** troop and freight transport **Powerplant:** two 2,000-hp (1492-kW) Pratt & Whitney R-2800-51 radial piston engines **Performance:** maximum speed 270 mph (435 km/h) at 15,000 ft (4570 m); cruising speed 173 mph (278 km/h); service ceiling 24,500 ft (7470 m); range at	173 mph (278 km/h) 3,150 miles (5069 km) **Weights:** empty 30,000 lb (13608 kg); maximum take-off 45,000 lb (20412 kg) **Dimensions:** wingspan 108 ft (32.91 m); length 76 ft 4 in (23.26 m); height 21 ft 9 in (6.62 m), wing area 1,360 sq ft (126.34 m²)

Curtiss-Wright CW-25 (AT-9 Jeep)

In 1940, the USAAC knew that it was essential to begin preparations for the very real possibility that the USA might become involved in World War II.

As a part of this general thinking, the USAAC had already begun evaluation of the Cessna Model T-50 as an 'off-the-shelf' twin-engined trainer.

For the more specific transition to the high-performance type of twin-engined bomber, the USAAC and its successor, the US Army Air Forces, considered that something less stable than the AT-8 (as the T-50 became) was needed. Curtiss-Wright had anticipated this requirement, however, and created the design of the **CW-25** as a twin-engined pilot transition trainer which had the take-off and landing characteristics of a light bomber. Based on a wider-span development of the

CW-19's wing, the CW-25 was a cantilever low-wing monoplane with tailwheel landing gear. The single prototype acquired for evaluation had a welded steel-tube fuselage structure and the covering was largely of fabric, but production aircraft were of aluminium alloy construction. The type was ordered into production under the designation **AT-9** and with the name **Jeep**. Manufacture of the AT-9 totalled 491 aircraft, and

there followed 300 examples of the generally similar **AT-9A** with R-980-13 engines and revised landing-gear retraction hydraulics. The aircraft remained in use for a comparatively short time, for the USA's involvement in World War II resulted in the early development of more effective training aircraft and also in the availability of early models of the B-25 Mitchell and B-26 Marauder bombers for adaptation to the training role.

Designed to train B-25 and B-26 crews, the AT-9 Jeep took its name from the character of a popular cartoon strip. This use of the Jeep name predated its use for the US Army vehicle.

SPECIFICATION

Curtiss-Wright CW-25 (AT-9 Jeep) **Type:** two-seat advanced conversion trainer **Powerplant:** two Lycoming R-680-9 radial piston engines each rated at 295 hp (220 kW) **Performance:** maximum speed 197 mph (317 km/h) at optimum altitude; cruising speed 175 mph (282 km/h) at optimum altitude;	climb to 10,000 ft (3050 m) in 8 minutes 48 seconds; service ceiling 19,000 ft (5790 m); range 750 miles (1207 km) **Weights:** empty 4,600 lb (2087 kg); maximum take-off 6,000 lb (2722 kg) **Dimensions:** wingspan 40 ft 4 in (12.29 m); length 31 ft 8 in (9.65 m); height 9 ft 10 in (3.00 m); wing area 233.00 sq ft (21.65 m²)

Curtiss-Wright Model 200 (X-19)

With the X-19 in the hover, its front nacelles were pointed slightly rearward from the vertical and its rear nacelles slightly forwards. Note that the flaps of the stub wings are also fully deflected.

SPECIFICATION

Curtiss-Wright Model 200 (X-19)
Type: two-crew experimental VTOL (vertical take-off and landing) aircraft
Powerplant: two Lycoming T55-L-5 turboshaft engines each rated at 2,200 shp (1640 kW)
Performance: maximum speed 460 mph (740 km/h) at 20,000 ft (6076 m); cruising speed 400 mph (644 km/h) at 15,000 ft (4572 m); initial climb rate 3,930 ft (1198 m) per minute; range 735 miles (1183 km) with a 1,000-lb (454-kg) payload
Weights: empty 9,750 lb (4423 kg); maximum take-off 13,660 lb (6196 kg) for VTO and 14,750 lb (6691 kg) for CTO (conventional take-off)
Dimensions: wingspan 34 ft 6 in (10.52 m) between the outer edges of the proprotors' swept discs; length 44 ft 5 in (13.54 m); height 17 ft ¼ in (5.19 m); wing area 154.60 sq ft (14.36 m²) for the front and rear wings combined; proprotor disc area, total 530.93 sq ft (49.32 m²)
Payload: four passengers, or 3,910 lb (1774 kg) of freight for VTO or 5,000 lb (2268 kg) of freight for CTO

In common with most US aircraft manufacturers, Curtiss-Wright was hit hard at the end of World War II by massive cancellations of outstanding military orders. Some manufacturers had a number of types readily convertible to transports for the civil market under construction. Others were leading the technological revolution bought about by the arrival of the jet engine, but neither of these factors worked to Curtiss-Wright's advantage. In 1946 the company closed all its manufacturing plants except for one in Columbus, Ohio, which was sold to North American Aviation, with the rights to all Curtiss and Curtiss-Wright designs.

Curtiss-Wright later produced a number of experimental designs, of which the two most significant were the **Model 200** (**X-19**) and **VZ-7**. Derived from the **Model X-100** vehicle, which had been powered by one 825-shp (615-kW) Lycoming YT53-L-1 turboshaft driving two 10-ft (3.05-m) diameter propellers to validate the company's 'radial lift force' concept, the Curtiss-Wright Model 200 was an experimental six-seat VTOL aircraft. It was powered by two Lycoming T55-L-5 turboshafts with an arrangement of extension shafts and gearboxes to drive four 13-ft (3.96-m) diameter 'proprotor' units in nacelles allowing them to be swivelled between the horizontal position in which they served as propellers with lift generated by the wings, and the vertical position in which they provided vertical lift. The Model 200 first flew on 26 June 1964, and it was evaluated by the USAF under the designation X-19 as a validation aircraft for Curtiss-Wright's proposed **LT-1** VTOL (vertical take-off and landing) logistic transport. Only limited flight testing was undertaken.

VZ-7 was another experimental design: a light transport platform built as part of the US Army's investigation of such 'aircraft'. Turbomeca Artouste's IIB turboshaft powered the VZ-7, driving four small horizontal propellers. Directional control was effected by a rudder in the engine exhaust. Flight trials took place in the late 1950s.

DAR aircraft

In order to establish a home-based aircraft manufacturing industry, despite limitations imposed by the treaty finalising Bulgaria's defeat in World War I, the

Other DAR types

DAR 1: twelve 1926 two-seat single-bay biplane intended for touring and primary training; built with one 60-hp (45-kW) Walter NZ radial engine; twelve of the **DAR 1A** variant followed with the 85-hp (63-kW) Walter Vega engine
DAR 2: adaptation of the Albatros C.III reconnaissance biplane; total of 12 aircraft built with the powerplant of one 160-hp (119-kW) Mercedes inline engine
DAR 3 Garvan (raven): reconnaissance biplane first tested in prototype form with the 420-hp (313-kW) Gnome-Rhône (Bristol) Jupiter radial and then with a 400-hp (298-kW) Lorraine-Dietrich engine; the DAR 3 production model followed in 1929 with the Lorraine-Dietrich engine or in later aircraft, the 480-hp (358-kW) Jupiter engine. In the mid-1930s, the **DAR 3a** appeared with recontoured vertical tail surfaces, redesigned landing gear, rounded wing tips and one 630-hp (470-kW) Wright Cyclone radial engine with Townend ring; the definitive **DAR 3b** of 1936 (also known as the **LAZ-3-3**) was Lazarov's work alone, and innovations included a glazed canopy for the two-man crew, faired landing gear struts with wheel spats, and one 750-hp (559-kW) Alfa-Romeo 126 RC 34 radial engine; 12 went into squadron service, flying alongside imported Heinkel He 45s, before being relegated to training, liaison and other second-line tasks
DAR 4: one example of this light passenger transport biplane was built; powered by three 145-hp (108-kW) Walter Mars radial engines, it carried a crew of two and four passengers; its narrow-track landing gear caused considerable problems; and overall performance was disappointing
DAR 5: one single-seat aerobatic trainer biplane, powered by a 145-hp (108-kW) Gnome-Rhône Titan engine

An impressive dive-bomber, the DAR 10 lost out because of the ready availability of the Ju 87D.

Bulgarian government founded the DAR (*Drjavna Aeroplanna Rabotilnitza*, or State Aircraft Workshops) at Bojourishtye on the outskirts of Sofia, in 1924. DAR repaired foreign-built aircraft and built a number of trainer and reconnaissance biplanes during the late 1920s.

The type produced in greatest numbers during the period between the two world wars was the Focke-Wulf Fw 44 Stieglitz primary trainer.

The final DAR design was the **DAR 11** single-seat fighter of 1941, which did not progress beyond the project stage. Ing. Zvetan Lazarov was chief designer of the DAR organisation in its later stages. Aircraft designed under his supervision were sometimes given the prefix LAZ, as a testement to his input, rather than DAR.

SPECIFICATION

DAR 10F
Type: two-seat light reconnaissance bomber and dive-bomber
Powerplant: one Fiat A.74 RC 38 radial piston engine rated at 960 hp (716 kW)
Performance: maximum speed 282 mph (454 km/h) at 16,405 ft (4890 m); climb to 16,405 ft (4890 m) in 8 minutes 30 seconds; service ceiling 29,530 ft (9001 m); range 870 miles (1400 km)
Weights: empty 4,475 lb (2030 kg); maximum take-off 7,540 lb (3420 kg)
Dimensions: wingspan 41 ft 6 in (12.65 m); length 32 ft 3 in (9.83 m); height 9 ft 9¾ in (3 m); wing area 246.28 sq ft (22.88 m²)
Armament: two 20-mm MG FF fixed forward-firing cannon in the leading edges of the wing and one 0.312-in (7.92-mm) MG 15 trainable rearward-firing machine-gun in the rear of the cockpit, plus provision for two 0.312-in (7.92-mm) MG 15 fixed forward-firing machine-guns in underwing packs and up to 1,102 lb (500 kg) of bombs carried under the fuselage and wing

Other DAR types continued

DAR 6 Sinigier (titmouse): two-seat trainer biplane, intended as a primary trainer when powered by an 85-hp (63-kW) Walter Vega engine and as a basic trainer with a 145-hp (108-kW) Walter Mars engine; the **DAR 6a** of 1937 had a redesigned landing gear, revised vertical tail surfaces and new powerplant, in the form of a 160-hp (112-kW) Siemens Sh.14 radial engine

DAR 8: single-bay two-seat sport or training biplane with a Walter Minor 4 inline engine; 12 were built; the single **DAR 8a** had a 145-hp

(108-kW) Walter Mars radial engine

DAR 10: designed as a two-seat multi-purpose aircraft capable of ground-attack, light bombing and reconnaissance roles, the DAR 10 was an impressive cantilever low-wing monoplane with a wooden wing covered with plywood, while the fuselage had a steel tube structure covered with light alloy panels forward and fabric aft. Only two prototypes were built: the **DAR 10F** powered by the A.74 RC 38 engine and the **DAR 10A** with the 950-hp (708-kW) Alfa Romeo 128 RC 21 engine; despite the promise of these prototypes, the Bulgarians decided to obtain the Junkers Ju 87D, which could be delivered direct from Germany

Dart aircraft

Founded by A. R. Weyl and E. P. Zander, and known originally as Zander and Weyl, and then as Dunstable Aircraft, Dart Aircraft Ltd's main experience was in glider construction, but it also built a few replicas of historic aircraft and advertised its ability to undertake sub-contracting

work for wood and metal aircraft parts.

The company's first venture into powered aircraft was the **Dart Pup**, a light single-seat monoplane with obvious glider ancestry. At the time of the aircraft's first flight in July 1936, the company was named Dunstable so the machine was called

the **Dunstable Dart**; when the company was renamed Dart Aircraft later that year the aircraft became the Dart Pup. In 1937 the sole Pup was modified, but crashed on take-off in August 1938.

Next was the single-seat **Flittermouse** ultra-light monoplane. The pilot was accommodated in a small pod, at the rear of which was installed a Scott Squirrel

motorcycle engine driving a pusher propeller.

Three booms carried the tail unit, extending from the trailing edges of the wing centre section and the base of the accommodation pod. The Flittermouse was delivered in 1936, but was soon sold to a new owner who added tricycle landing gear. The aircraft was scrapped in 1951.

Dart built a flying replica

of the Blériot Type XI cross-Channel aircraft with an original 25-hp (19-kW) Anzani engine in 1937 for the International Horseless Carriage Corporation; the aircraft was later used for demon-stration flying. The last type to emerge from Dart Aircraft was the **Kitten**, another single-seat ultra-light monoplane but with a low-set wing, no external bracing, and powered by a 27-hp (20-kW) Ava 4a-00 flat-four engine. The **Kitten I** first flew on 15 January 1937 and was delivered in August, resold in September and stored throughout World War II. It survived to fly again in 1949 at Broxbourne, where it was re-engined with an Aeronca-JAP J-99 engine; it was destroyed in a crash in November 1952. A second aircraft, the **Kitten II** was built with a J-99 and flew in spring 1937. It also survived World War II, reappearing at Southend, and was followed in 1951 by the **Kitten III**, which differed by having wheel brakes.

Above: The only Dart-designed aircraft to be constructed in the post-war era was the sole Kitten III G-AMJP. The aircraft is seen here in its second colour scheme in September 1965.

Left: G-AEXT, a Dart Kitten II, remained on the British civil aircraft register in late 1999. The aircraft's simplicity and petite size are evident.

SPECIFICATION	
Dart Kitten II/III	19,700 ft (6005 m); range
Type: single-seat lightplane	340 miles (547 km)
Powerplant: Aeronca-JAP J-99	**Weights:** empty 510 lb (231 kg);
flat-two piston engine rated at	maximum take-off 752 lb (341 kg)
36 hp (27 kW)	**Dimensions:** wingspan 31 ft 9 in
Performance: maximum speed	(9.68 m); length 21 ft 4 in (6.50 m);
95 mph (153 km/h) at sea level;	height 7 ft 11 in (2.41 m); wing
cruising speed 83 mph (134 km/h)	area 129.00 sq ft (11.98 m²)
at 2,000 ft (610 m); ceiling	

Dassault Atlantic 1

NATO's requirement in early 1958 for a long-range maritime patrol aircraft attracted 24 design submissions from aircraft manufacturers in nine countries. From these the **Breguet Br.1150** design study was selected for production at the end of 1958. The model was called **Atlantic**, later altered to

Atlantic 1 after the development of the **Atlantique 2**.

The Atlantic was the first combat aircraft to be designed and built as a multi-national project. Responsibility for production was given to the specially created SECBAT (*Société d'Etudes et de Construction du Breguet Atlantic*).

The original consortium members, led by Breguet (later Dassault-Breguet and now just Dassault), comprised Sud-Aviation, the Belgian ABAP grouping (Fairey, FN and SABCA), Dornier in Germany and Fokker in the Netherlands. Italy joined in 1968, with some of the work then being allocated to Aeritalia.

A similar multi-national organisation was set up to build the Rolls-Royce Tyne

turboprop engine, other members included FN in Belgium, MAN in Germany and SNECMA in France.

A cantilever mid-wing monoplane of all-metal construction, the Atlantic incorporates a 'double-bubble' fuselage with a pressurised upper deck and a MAD (magnetic anomaly detector) boom extending rearward from the tail, a conventional tail unit with an ECM

(electronic countermea-sures) pod at the tip of the fin; retractable tricycle land-ing gear with twin wheels on each unit; and two Tynes in wing-mounted nacelles.

Suitable for anti-ship, coastal reconnaissance, SAR, fleet escort, logistic support, freight and passenger transport and minelaying roles, the Atlantic was designed primarily for the ASW (air staff requirement) role.

Dassault Atlantic 1 (cont.)

A ventral radome and additional blade antenna identify this as one of the German Elint Atlantics. The aircraft were heavily engaged in electronic eavesdropping missions during the Cold War.

For the ASW role, the Atlantic is equipped with sonobuoys and Thomson-CSF search radar which can detect a conventional submarine's schnorkle at ranges of up to 47 miles (75 km). For attack the Atlantic carries bombs, depth charges and homing torpedoes in its weapons bay; additional capability is provided by the carriage of air-to-surface missiles or rockets on underwing attachments. The Atlantic's crew of 12 includes seven specialists to co-ordinate and direct the aircraft's operations.

The first prototype made its maiden flight on 21 October 1961 and the first of 40 aircraft for the French navy was delivered in July 1965, followed by 20 aircraft for the German navy. A second production batch included nine for the Netherlands navy and 18 for the Italian air force. Three of those supplied to

the French navy were transferred subsequently to Pakistan. Several advanced versions of the Atlantic were proposed, but it was not until July 1977 that the French government authorised design definition of an improved version, scheduled to enter service in the period 1985-90.

The Atlantic's sensors (search radar, MAD, ARAR 13A ESM, sonobuoys, etc.) are mainly of Thomson-CSF manufacture, and are computer-integrated on the display and control panels of the PLOTAC system in the tactical compartment. Useful updating has been achieved within the limitations of the 1950s-vintage electronics, but the Atlantic can now only be regarded as obsolescent; the French started to retire their aircraft in 1992, keeping in service only a modest number for the lower-intensity surveillance

task.

Five of the German naval air arm's 15 survivors were extensively converted as Sigint aircraft, with the E-Systems Peace Peek mission equipment installed by Vought and based on a Loral ESM suite with antennas in wingtip pods. The Italian aircraft were upgraded by Aeritalia with improved radar and navigation systems as well as the Selenia ALR-730 ESM system.

SPECIFICATION

Dassault Atlantic 1
Type: 12-crew maritime patrol aircraft
Powerplant: two Rolls-Royce Tyne RTy.20 Mk 21 turboprop engines each rated at 6,100 ehp (4549 ekW)
Performance: maximum speed 409 mph (658 km/h) at optimum altitude; cruising speed 345 mph (556 km/h) at 23,620 ft (7500 m); patrol speed 196 mph (315 km/h) at optimum altitude; service ceiling 32,810 ft (10000 m); range 5,592 miles (9000 km); maximum endurance 18 hours
Weights: empty 55,115 lb (25000 kg); maximum take-off 98,104 lb (44500 kg)
Dimensions: wingspan 119 ft 1 in (36.30 m); length 104 ft 2 in (31.75 m); height 37 ft 2 in (11.33 m); wing area 1,295.37 sq ft (120.34 m²)
Armament: up to 7,716 lb (3500 kg) of disposable stores (comprising bombs, depth charges, homing torpedoes, air-to-surface missiles including the AM39 Exocet anti-ship missile, and rockets) carried in the lower-fuselage weapons bay and on four underwing hardpoints

Dassault Atlantique 2

The Atlantique 2 is most easily recognised by its revised fintip shape and the larger air intake on the lower port side of the nose.

Originally called the **ANG (Atlantic Nouvelle Génération**, or new-generation Atlantic), the **Dassault Atlantique 2** was planned as a multi-national programme to replace the Atlantic (now called Atlantic 1) with its various users. France is currently the sole customer, although that country's requirement for 30 aircraft (originally 42) makes the project viable even if the rate of manufacture is too low for competitive costings.

After very prolonged studies, the Atlantique 2 was designed as a minimum-change type with totally new avionics, systems and equipment, packaged into an airframe differing from that of the original model only in ways to increase service life, reduce costs and minimise maintenance. In addition, an Astadyne gas-turbine auxiliary power unit is fitted, and production machines are fitted with Ratier/BAe

propellers with larger composite blades.

The Atlantique 2's sensors include the Thomson-CSF Iguane frequency-agile radar with a new interrogator and decoder, a SAT/TRT Tango FLIR in a chin turret, over 100 sonobuoys in the rear fuselage, a new Crouzet MAD receiver in the boom, extending rearward from the tail, and the Thomson-CSF ARAR 13 ESM installation with frequency analysis at the top of the fin and D/F in the new wingtip nacelles. All processors, data buses and sensor links are of standard digital form, navaids include an inertial system and Navstar satellite receiver, and every part of the avionics and communications has been upgraded. The main weapons bay can accommodate all NATO standard bombs and depth charges, as well as other weapon types including two air-to-

surface or anti-ship missiles, up to eight Mk 46 torpedoes or seven Franco-Italian MU39 Impact advanced torpedoes. The Atlantique has a rarely used secondary transport function, and could also be used in a limited overland electronic reconnaissance role.

The first Atlantique 2 flew in May 1981 and production deliveries began in 1989.

Proposed variants of the Atlantique 2 have included a BAe Nimrod replacement for the RAF, with additional turbofan engines in pods under the wing and with either Allison T406 or General Electric T407 turboprop engines replacing the Tynes; an **Atlantique 3** with further improvements; and the **Europatrol**, a derivative aimed at replacing NATO's P-3 Orions. A Tyne upgrade has also been proposed.

SPECIFICATION

Dassault Atlantique 2
Type: 10/12-crew long-range maritime patrol and anti-submarine/ship aircraft
Powerplant: two Rolls-Royce Tyne RTy.20 Mk 21 turboprop engines each rated at 6,100 ehp (4549 ekW)
Performance: maximum speed 402 mph (648 km/h) at optimum altitude; cruising speed 345 mph (555 km/h) at 23,620 ft (7200 m); patrol speed 196 mph (315 km/h) between sea level and 5,000 ft (1525 m); initial climb rate 2,900 ft (884 m) per minute; service ceiling 30,000 ft (9145 m); range 5,639 miles (9075 km); operational radius 2,071 miles (3333 km) for a
2-hour patrol in the ASV role with one AM39 Exocet missile, or 690 miles (1110 km) for an 8-hour patrol in the ASW role at low altitude; endurance 18 hours
Weights: empty 56,437 lb (25600 kg); maximum take-off 101,852 lb (46200 kg)
Dimensions: wingspan 122 ft 9¼ in (37.42 m) including wingtip ESM pods; length 103 ft 9 in (31.62 m); height 35 ft 8¾ in (10.89 m); wing area 1,295.37 sq ft (120.34 m²)
Armament: up to 13,228 lb (6000 kg) of disposable stores carried as 5,511 lb (2500 kg) internally and 7,717 lb (3500 kg) externally

Dassault Balzac V

The concept of aircraft capable of vertical take-off and landing has long attracted the enthusiasm of aircraft designers. VTOL was also a concept that appealed strongly to NATO, which had become increasingly worried during the 1950s about the vulnerability of its European airfields to Soviet pre-emptive attack. The two European nations that led the way were the UK and

France. By an eccentricity of fortune, the French did not favour the concept of thrust vectoring even though it had been conceived by a Frenchman, Michel Wibault, during the early 1950s. Instead, the French concentrated their efforts initially on the direct-lift engine and then on the hybrid lift/propulsion system.

Both the British and the French were working

toward the evolution of a VTOL strike and attack warplane offering supersonic flight capability, as finally demanded by the NATO Basic Military Requirement, issued some-

what belatedly in 1961 after many delays. The French had started to

consider a VTOL attack fighter to meet national requirements even before

Although the Balzac V proved the validity of the lift jet/propulsion jet system, it inevitably suffered from the weight and complexity problems inherent in using nine engines.

NBMR No. 3 had been drafted, their planned type being the **Mirage IIIV**, a VTOL development of the supersonic Mirage IIIE strike/attack fighter. This would be approached at the technical level via the **Balzac V** prototype that was designed to validate the lift/propulsion arrangement and the control system planned for the Mirage IIIV.

As the Balzac V was planned only as a research type, it was decided to rebuild an existing airframe to the new configuration, and the choice fell on the Mirage III.001 initial prototype of the Mirage III family. Under French government contract, this machine was revised by Sud-Aviation with a different Dassault-designed fuselage optimised for the hybrid powerplant. This comprised a Bristol Siddeley Orpheus propulsion turbojet engine in the rear fuselage, where it was aspirated via the standard lateral inlets and exhausted at the tail, and a battery of eight Rolls-Royce RB.108 lift turbojet engines. These were installed as four groups of two engines around the centre of gravity, where the groups were aspirated via four Venetian blind pop-up doors in the upper fuselage, and exhausted via fore-and-aft doors in the lower fuselage. The power delivered by the lift turbojets totalled 17,680 lb st (78.64 kN), enough to provide a thrust:weight ratio of 1.23:1 at the Balzac V's maximum take-off weight of 14,330 lb (6500 kg). Considerable thought went into the creation of the throttle system for the nine-engined powerplant; the system eventually adopted was a single power lever, controlling all eight RB.108 lift engines as a single unit, and also fitted with a switch throttling the Orpheus propulsion engine. This system allowed the pilot to take-off vertically and transition to wingborne flight (and later to reverse the process for a vertical landing) without taking his hand from the single lever. Another feature of the control system for the powerplant's lifting element was a button for use in the failure of any one engine: as soon as he detected an engine failure, the pilot pressed this button to cut out the symmetrically-opposed engine and thus restore dynamic balance; asymmetric thrust in the brief moment before the cutting of the second engine was balanced out by the 'puffer' reaction-control system.

The other main features to be validated in the Balzac V were the retractable dams ahead of the exhausts of the lift turbojet engines to improve lift and help prevent the reingestion of hot exhaust gases, the SNECMA automatic attitude control system, and the Dassault electro-hydraulic autopilot system.

For initial trials, the Balzac V was operated with fixed tricycle landing gear that provided a distinct nose-up attitude and was capable of dealing with a high sink rate. All was ready in the autumn of 1962, and the Balzac V made its first hovering flight in October of that year, while tethered in the gantry originally constructed for trials with the Coléoptére. The Balzac V made its first free hovering flight only six days later, and further trials paved the way for its first translation to wingborne flight in March 1963. The test programme continued at a moderately high rate to January 1964, when the aircraft suffered a major divergent lateral oscillation during a vertical descent and crashed, killing the pilot. The Balzac V was repaired for further trials, but again crashed with fatal results. What had emerged, however, was the viability of the hybrid powerplant arrangement, and the basic suitability of the SNECMA and Dassault stability and control systems.

SPECIFICATION

Dassault Balzac V
Type: single-seat experimental VTOL aircraft
Powerplant: one Bristol Siddeley BOr.3 Orpheus turbojet engine rated at 5,000 lb st (22.24 kN) for propulsion, and eight Rolls-Royce RB.108 Stage 1A turbojet engines each rated at 2,210 lb st (9.83 kN) for direct lift
Performance: maximum speed 687 mph (1105 km/h) at sea level; endurance about 20 minutes
Weights: maximum take-off 14,330 lb (6500 kg)
Dimensions: wingspan 26 ft 11½ in (8.22 m); length 45 ft (13.72 m); wing area 375.13 sq ft (34.85 m²)

Dassault Etendard II and Etendard VI

The vulnerability and cost factors associated with modern combat aircraft combined to create interest in lightweight attack warplanes at national as well as at NATO-wide level. In July 1953 the French air force issued a requirement for such a type. In April 1954 NATO issued a parallel NBMR-1 (NATO Basic Military Requirement No. 1) for a simple attack warplane possessing a maximum take-off weight of less than 10,000 lb (4536 kg), a very short turnaround time, optimisation for the low-altitude role, and ability to operate from short undamaged lengths of runway or, perhaps more importantly, from grass airstrips improvised in the countryside close behind a moving front line. The European aviation industry felt that there was considerable merit and potential in the NATO requirement, and nine designs were submitted (two British, five French and two Italian), and of these the Fiat G.91 was eventually selected for production.

As may be imagined from the number of French contenders, France was particularly enthusiastic as it felt that the NATO and French requirements could be met by variants of the same basic design. There were difficulties, however, for the NATO requirement specified a single-engined warplane, while the French requirement called for the use of two existing engines. Dassault responded with its closely related **Mystère XXII** twin-engined and **Mystère XXVI** single-engined designs that were soon renamed in the **Etendard** (battle standard, or national flag) series and projected in a number of variants. The variant optimised for the French requirement, which emphasised medium- as well as low-altitude capability, became the **Etendard II** with a pressurised cockpit, two 2,425-lb st (10.79-kN) Turboméca Gabizo turbojets, and an armament comprising two 30-mm cannon and a disposable armament of 992 lb (450 kg).

The variant optimised for NBMR-1 was the **Etendard VI** with an unpressurised cockpit and one 4,050-lb st (18.02-kN) Orpheus BOr.1 turbojet in the first prototype, which first flew on 15 March 1957, and one Orpheus BOr.3 engine in the second prototype. The inevitable weight escalation, as additional equipment was tacked onto the original requirement, meant that the Orpheus BOr.12 turbojet, rated at 6,810 lb st (30.29 kN) dry and 8,170 lb st (36.34 kN) with afterburning, was then substituted for these units in the third prototype. This prototype was planned, but then cancelled, as the precursor of the production version, which would also have been larger than the prototypes and had an area-ruled fuselage.

In the event, the G.91 was declared winner of the NBMR-1 competition, as noted above, and the Etendard VI did not enter production. Meanwhile, the French had been pressing ahead with their own versions of the type, which comprised one out of an initially planned three Etendard IIs and two out of an initially planned three Etendard VIs. The Etendard II had made its maiden flight on 23 July 1956, but was soon grounded as a result of the powerplant's unreliability. The two Etendard VIs were soon relegated to use in the development programme for the Etendard IV.

A 3-ft (1-m) extension of the basic Etendard II rear fuselage was necessary to accommodate the Etendard VI's Orpheus engine. The two Etendard VIs made their first flights on 15 March and 14 September 1957, respectively.

SPECIFICATION

Dassault Etendard VI
Type: single-seat lightweight tactical fighter
Powerplant: one Bristol Orpheus BOr.3 turbojet engine rated at 4,850 lb st (21.35 kN)
Performance: maximum speed 693 mph (1116 km/h) at sea level
Weights: empty 8,201 lb (3720 kg); maximum take-off 12,919 lb (5860 kg)
Dimensions: wingspan 26 ft 9¼ in (8.16 m); length 40 ft 8¾ in (12.40 m); wing area 226.04 sq ft (21.00 m²)
Armament: two 30-mm DEFA fixed forward-firing cannon, or four 0.5-in (12.7-mm) Browning fixed forward-firing machine-guns, or 55 2¾-in (70-mm) rockets in a lower-fuselage weapons bay, plus disposable stores carried on two underwing hardpoints

Dassault Etendard IVM/P

The original Dassault Etendard was the French company's entry in a NATO competition held in 1955 for a light strike fighter, able to operate from unpaved strips. Dassault developed subsequent versions, but these were deemed to be underpowered.

As a private venture, Dassault installed the much more powerful SNECMA Atar 08 turbojet and this version, which first flew on 24 July 1956, was designated the **Etendard IV**. After rejection by the NATO nations in favour of the Italian Fiat G.91, the Etendard underwent a protracted modification programme to meet an Aéronavale requirement for a carrier-based attack and reconnaissance aircraft and two versions were developed to fulfil these primary maritime roles.

Dassault Etendard IVM/P (cont.)

Both naval Etendard variants are equipped with such standard naval features as long-stroke undercarriage, arrester hook, catapult attachments and associated strengthening, folding wingtips and a high-lift system which combines leading-edge and trailing-edge flaps, as well as two perforated belly airbrakes.

The first version was designated **Etendard IVM** and deployed aboard the carriers *Foch* and *Clemenceau* (Flottilles 11F and 17F) along with the training unit 15F. The prototype of this variant flew for the first time on 21 May 1958, and was followed by six pre-production aircraft. The

first of 69 production Etendard IVMs for the French navy was delivered on 18 January 1962, and production was completed in 1964. The Etendard IVM was equipped with Aïda all-weather fire-control radar and a Saab toss-bombing computer. A unique nose-mounted underfin blade fairing contained the guidance aerial for the AS20 radio-command missile (now obsolete). The Etendard IVM was withdrawn from service in July 1991 and has been replaced by the Super Etendard.

The seventh Etendard was the prototype of the **Etendard IVP**, a reconnaissance/tanker version,

of which 21 were ordered. The first flight was made on 19 November 1960. The primary design changes include nose and ventral stations for three and two OMERA reconnaissance cameras (replacing attack avionics and guns respectively), an independent navigation system, a fixed nose probe for inflight refuelling, and a 'buddy-pack' hose-reel unit designed by Douglas to allow Etendard-to-Etendard refuelling. The Etendard IVP remains in Aéronavale service with Flottille 16F at Landivisiau and is due to be retired in 2000. The 10 survivors are used for carrierborne reconnaissance and as buddy tankers for the Super Etendard, having seen action over Bosnia and during the Allied Force offensive.

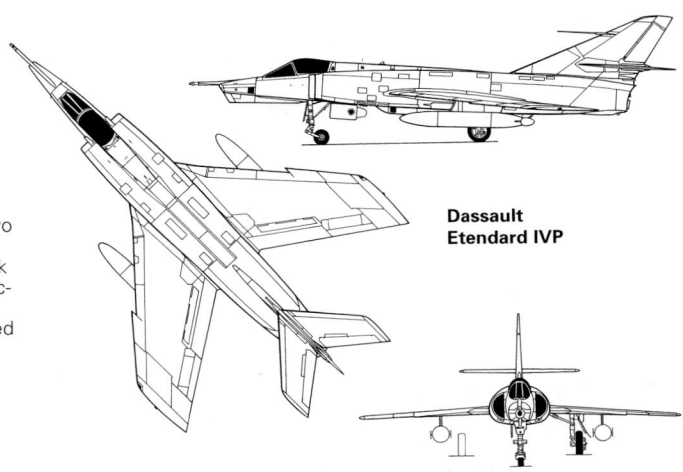

Dassault Etendard IVP

Dassault's Etendard IVM might have been replaced by the Jaguar M, but in the event gave way to the Super Etendard. The undernose AS20 air-to-ground missile guidance antenna is a prominent recognition feature.

SPECIFICATION

Dassault-Breguet Etendard IVP
Type: single-seat, carrier-based reconnaissance aircraft
Powerplant: one SNECMA Atar 8B turbojet rated at 9,700 lb (43.16 kN) thrust
Performance: maximum level speed 'clean' at optimum altitude Mach 1.08; maximum level speed 'clean' at sea level 683 mph (1099 km/h); maximum rate of climb at sea level 19,685 ft (6000 m) per minute; service ceiling 50,850 ft (15500 m)

Weights: empty 13,000 lb (5900 kg); maximum take-off 22,485 lb (10200 kg)
Dimensions: wingspan 31 ft 6 in (9.60 m); length 47 ft 3 in (14.40 m); height 14 ft 1 in (14.30 m); wing area 312 sq ft (29 m²)
Armament: two 132-Imp gal (600-litre) underwing tanks plus bombs or rockets for a maximum external ordnance load of 3,000 lb (1360 kg)

Dassault Mystère/Falcon 10/100

The baby of the **Dassault Mystère/Falcon** family of business jets, the **Mystère/Falcon 10** was conceived as the smaller but faster half-brother to the Mystère/Falcon 20, and was known at first as the **Minifalcon** when announced at the Paris Air Show of 1969. The Mystère/Falcon 10 has a wing of higher aspect ratio than that of the Mystère/Falcon 20, for greater efficiency in the cruise regime, and good field performance is provided by the combination of slats over the full span of

With the Falcon/Mystère family, Dassault has created a highly regarded family of biz-jets. The main recognition feature of the Falcon 10/100 compared to the other Falcons is the former's three cabin windows to each side.

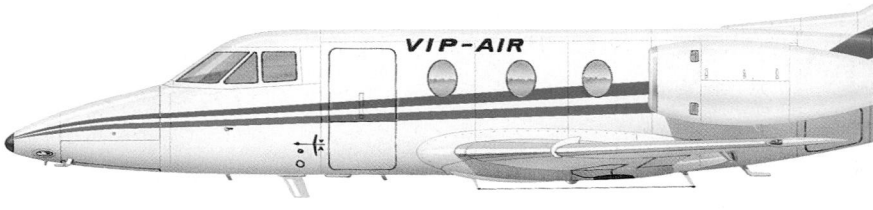

the leading edges and, inboard of the ailerons on the trailing edges, double-slotted flaps.

SPECIFICATION

Dassault Mystère/Falcon 10
Type: two-crew executive transport
Powerplant: two AlliedSignal (Garrett) TFE731-2 turbofan engines each rated at 3,230 lb st (14.37 kN)
Performance: maximum cruising speed 566 mph (912 km/h) at 25,000 ft (7620 m); service ceiling 45,000 ft (13715 m); range 2,212 miles (3560 km) with four passengers

Weights: empty 10,760 lb (4880 kg); maximum take-off 18,740 lb (8500 kg)
Dimensions: wingspan 42 ft 11 in (13.08 m); length 45 ft 5¾ in (13.86 m); height 15 ft 1½ in (4.61 m); wing area 259.42 sq ft (24.10 m²)
Payload: up to seven passengers within the context of a 2,400-lb (1090-kg) payload; four underwing hardpoints can be fitted for the carriage of electronic warfare pods

The first prototype made its maiden flight on 1 December 1970 with the powerplant of two General Electric CJ610 turbojet engines, but was soon revised with the definitive turbofan powerplant of two TFE731s. Six months after its first flight the prototype established a 1,000-km (621.4-mile) closed-circuit speed record for its class of 578.13 mph (930.4 km/h), and a companion record over a 2,000-km (1,243-mile) closed circuit was established by the third

prototype in May 1973, a month after the first production aircraft had flown. By mid-1982 sales of well over 200 aircraft had been achieved, and by the time production ended in 1990, some 226 aircraft had been delivered, the last examples being completed to the **Mystère/Falcon 100** standard with a number of minor improvements.

In addition to the normal executive transport role, the Mystère/Falcon 10 can be equipped for aerial photography, ambulance

duties, liaison, navigation/attack system training and radio navigation aid calibration. Seven of these aircraft were delivered to the Aéronavale for service under the designation **Falcon 10MER**. They are used in general communications and liaison duties, as well as to give training to Super Etendard pilots.

In this last role the Falcon 10MER has been found to make a good mock intruder, used not only to train interceptor pilots, but also ground control radar crews.

Dassault Falcon/Mystère 20/200 and HU-25 Guardian

Originally called the **Mystère 20**, the Dassault (originally Dassault-Breguet)

Falcon 20 twin-engined business jet first flew on 7 May 1963. Developed

from the outset as a 'top of the range' aircraft, the Falcon 20 featured exten-

sive integral tankage, fully powered controls and the powerplant of two General

Electric CF700 aft-fan engines each flat-rated at 4,200 lb st (18.58 kN) and

The standard Falcon 20/200 has five cabin windows on each side of the fuselage. The Gardian variant (illustrated) replaces the forward port cabin window with an enlarged observation window.

The Falcon 200 introduced the ATF3-6 engine of the HU-25A to the civil market. For home sales, Dassault's Falcon takes the Mystère name, while export aircraft are designated as Falcons.

fitted with target-type reversers. The cabin could be furnished for up to 12 passengers, although most of the aircraft sold onto the primary corporate transport market seated nine or fewer passengers. Initial US sales of what was at first called the Fan Jet

Falcon resulted from a link with PanAm (the later Falcon Jet Corporation is a Dassault subsidiary), and this helped sales of many specially equipped versions for military purposes. The type has a conventional metal fail-safe structure, manufacture of which is

shared with other companies in France and Spain. The leading-edge slats, slotted flaps, wing-mounted airbrakes, flight controls and twin-wheel landing gear units are all actuated hydraulically. Engine bleed air is used for wing and engine inlet de-icing.

In January 1977 the sale of 41 **Falcon 20G** aircraft to the US Coast Guard, which allocated the service designation **HU-25A Guardian**, introduced the unique three-spool ATF3-6 turbofan, which was fitted as standard from 1983 in the next production version, which was designated as the **Falcon 200** for the civil market. The fuselage of the HU-25A was modified to incorporate two observation windows and a drop hatch for rescue supplies. The HU-25A's primary tasks are medium-range all-weather SAR, maritime surveillance and environmental protection. In its

original configuration, the type was given a sophisticated array of equipment including an APS-127 radar, very extensive communications capabilities, and advanced navaids including an inertial platform, Omega, R-nav system and TACAN. The HU-25A has four fuselage hardpoints to carry rescue packs and four underwing hardpoints for sensor pods.

Today, just over half of the Guardians delivered remain in their original configuration. Seven of the aircraft have been modified to **HU-25B** standard with a Motorola APS-131 SLAR in a fuselage pod offset slightly to starboard, a Texas Instruments RS-18C IR linescan unit in another pod under the starboard wing and a laser-illuminated TV under the port wing. The Coast Guard operates these Guardians on surveillance duties with responsibility for detection of maritime pollution. A further nine aircraft have been modified for service from May 1988 on drug interdiction duties (pursuit and identification of suspect aircraft) under the designation **HU-25C Interceptor** with APG-66 search radar in the nose, turret-mounted WF-360

FLIR sensor and new secure communications equipment.

The **Falcon 20H** maritime surveillance version is operated under the name **Gardian** (guardian) by the French Aéronavale in the Pacific. Two aircraft are tasked with patrol and SAR duties within French territorial economic zones in the Pacific. The Gardian has extremely comprehensive avionics including Thomson-CSF Varan radar and VLF Omega navigation, and is characterised by an extra-large observation window in the port side of the fuselage.

The **Gardian 2** version, based on the Falcon 200, was a simplified export version marketed for Exocet attack, ESM/ECM, target designation and target-towing, but is now cancelled. However, the basic Falcon 200 is offered with equipment for every kind of specialised role. The Libyan and French air forces use the **Falcon 20 SNA** version with Mirage radar and electronics for training in low-level attack, while the UK (Royal Navy) and Norway are among seven users of EW/ECM versions. Other Falcon aircraft in French service have radar for the training of Mirage 2000, Mirage IVP and Mirage F1CR crews, and Dassault itself operates a Falcon 20 to test the Rafale's RBE2 radar. The majority of military and para-military operators, however, fly their small numbers of Falcon 20 and Falcon 200 aircraft on VIP and staff transport duties. Dassault ended production of all Falcon 20 and Falcon 200 variants in 1988, although there have since been several upgrade programmes.

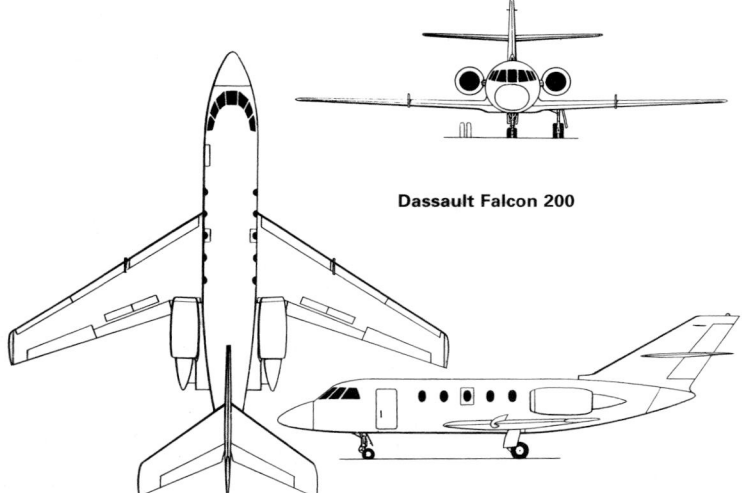

Dassault Falcon 200

SPECIFICATION	
Dassault Falcon/Mystère 200 **Type:** two-crew corporate and executive business transport **Powerplant:** two AlliedSignal (Garrett) ATF3-6A-4C turbofan engines each rated at 5,200 lb st (23.13 kN) **Performance:** maximum cruising speed 541 mph (870 km/h) at 32,020 ft (9150 m); economical cruising speed 485 mph (780 km/h) at 41,010 ft (12500 m); service ceiling 45,000 ft (13715 m); range	2,889 miles (4650 km) with eight passengers and maximum fuel **Weights:** empty 18,188 lb (8250 kg); maximum take-off 32,000 lb (14515 kg) **Dimensions:** wingspan 53 ft 6½ in (16.32 m); length 56 ft 3 in (17.15 m); height 17 ft 5 in (5.32 m); wing area 441.33 sq ft (41.00 m²) **Payload:** up to 14 passengers within the context of a 4,134-lb (1875-kg) payload

Dassault Falcon/Mystère 50

In the mid-1970s, Dassault decided to produce an aircraft offering the same cabin cross-section as the Falcon 20 in combination with a revised powerplant and enlarged fuel tankage for considerably greater range. The immediate objective was a trans-USA capability with a typical

corporate payload of two crew and nine passengers, and this requirement was fully met by the Dassault design. The original prototype of the Falcon/Mystère 50 flew for the first time on 7 November 1976, and was followed by the first production aircraft on 2 March 1979.

The Falcon 50 has the same external fuselage cross-section as the Falcon 20, but this fuselage has been extensively redesigned with area ruling, for combination with an advanced new wing featuring compound leading-edge sweep and a fully optimised supercritical aerofoil section.

The innovative decision was taken to fit three engines, the choice falling on an uprated version of the TFE731 geared turbofan engine used in the Falcon 10 and 100. The third engine duct extends well forward of the fin's leading edge above the rear fuselage, the inlet being faired into a vertical tail surface less acutely swept than that of previous Falcons. The wing is fitted

with full-span slats on its leading edges and double-slotted flaps on its trailing edges, giving a maximum lift coefficient greater than that of previous Falcons and providing a field length similar to that of the Falcon 20 and derived Gardian.

A total of 241 Falcon 50s had been sold by early 1995, with sales continuing at a satisfactory rate after this time into the late 1990s.

Dassault Falcon/Mystère 50 (continued)

VIP versions of the Falcon 50, usually for four/five passengers, have been bought by several governments including those of Djibouti, France, Iraq, Italy (three convertible to air ambulance configuration), Jordan, Morocco, Portugal, Rwanda, Spain (operated under the designation **T.16**), Sudan and Yugoslavia.

A typical Falcon 50 cabin layout seats eight or nine passengers, with an aft passenger lavatory as well as a forward crew lavatory, galley and wardrobe.

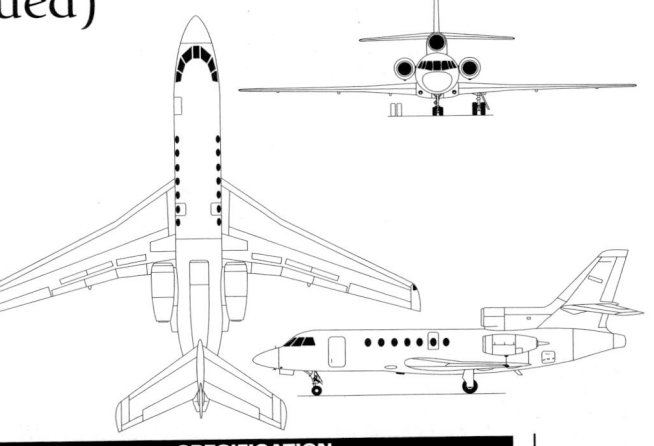

SPECIFICATION

Dassault Falcon/Mystère 50
Type: two/three-crew long-range business and VIP transport aircraft
Powerplant: three AlliedSignal (Garrett) TFE731-3 turbofan engines each rated at 3,700 lb st (16.46 kN)
Performance: maximum cruising speed 497 mph (800 km/h) at optimum altitude; certificated altitude 45,000 ft (13,715 m); range 4,027 miles (6480 km) with eight passengers

Weights: empty 20,172 lb (9150 kg); maximum take-off 38,801 lb (17600 kg) standard or 40,785 lb (18500 kg) optional
Dimensions: wingspan 61 ft 10½ in (18.86 m); length 60 ft 9¼ in (18.52 m); height 22 ft 10½ in (6.97 m); wing area 504.09 sq ft (46.83 m²)
Payload: up to 12 passengers within the context of a 3,461-lb (1570-kg) standard or 4,784-lb (2170-kg) maximum payload

Dassault Falcon/Mystère 900

The **Falcon 900** (**Mystère 900** in France), stretched version of the Falcon 50 Falcon tri-jet, has a fuselage of greater cross-section providing an additional 3 in (8 cm) of passenger headroom, an uprated powerplant, and a slightly modified wing of greater span and area. Intended primarily for civilian use, the first Falcon/Mystère 900 flew on 21 September 1984 and, following the receipt of French and US certification in March 1986, deliveries were made mainly to civil customers in a programme that saw sales of 142 aircraft to

operators in 30 countries by the beginning of 1995.

The initial model, which was delivered up to 1992, was the Falcon/Mystère 900, powered by three 4,500-lb st (20.02-kN) TFE731-5AR-1C turbofans. Receiving British and French certification at the end of 1991 for delivery from the following year, the succeeding **Falcon/Mystère 900B** is cleared for operations from unpaved airfields and for Category II approaches, and is powered by uprated engines for a slight improvement in performance, especially in range.

The latest civil variant is the **Falcon/Mystère 900EX** with 5,000-lb st (22.24-kN) TFE731-60 engines providing an 8 per cent reduction in specific fuel consumption in the cruise regime, greater fuel capacity, a large measure of redesign in certain airframe features and completely updated Honeywell Primus 2000 avionics including a five-screen colour EFIS.

The first of two VVIP Mystère 900 aircraft was delivered to the French air force's Groupe de Liaisons Aériennes Ministérielles in November 1987. Similarly tasked machines have been bought by Algeria, Australia, Gabon, Malaysia, Nigeria and Spain, the latter assigning the local designation **T.18**. Two Falcon 900s

were delivered to the JASDF for long-range maritime surveillance duties. These aircraft are fitted with US search radar, operations control station, special communications radio, HU-25A Guardian-style observation windows and a drop hatch for sonobuoys, flares and markers.

The Falcon 900B introduced uprated engines which allow the type to reach a cruising altitude of 39,000 ft (11855 m) as well as giving compliance with FAR 36 Part III noise regulations.

SPECIFICATION

Dassault Falcon/Mystère 900B
Type: two/three-crew long-range executive and VIP transport aircraft
Powerplant: three AlliedSignal (Garrett) TFE731-5BR-1C turbofan engines each rated at 4,750 lb st (21.13 kN)
Performance: maximum cruising speed 575 mph (927 km/h) at 27,000 ft (8230 m); certificated ceiling 51,000 ft (15550 m); range 4,603 miles (7408 km) with eight

passengers
Weights: empty 23,348 lb (10545 kg); maximum take-off 45,503 lb (20640 kg)
Dimensions: wingspan 63 ft 5 in (19.33 m); length 66 ft 3¾ in (20.21 m); height 24 ft 9¼ in (7.55 m); wing area 527.75 sq ft (49.03 m²)
Payload: up to 19 passengers within the context of a 4,817-lb (2185-kg) payload

Dassault Falcon 2000

First announced at the Paris Air Show of 1989 as the company's successor to the Falcon 20 and 200 series, the **Dassault Falcon 2000** is a corporate transport optimised for the transcontinental role. The

type was originally designated as the **Falcon X**, but became the Falcon 2000 in October 1990 after the company's receipt of the first orders for the aircraft. Milestones in the Falcon 2000's history was the

April 1990 selection of the CFE738 turbofan as the core of a twin-engined powerplant which also included Dee Howard thrust reversers, and the February 1991 adherence of Alenia (with Piaggio as

a subcontractor) as a 25 per cent risk-sharing partner with primary responsibility for the rear fuselage, pylons and engine nacelles.

The Falcon 2000 has a fuselage with the same cross-section as the Falcon 900, although in this instance shortened by

6 ft 6 in (1.98 m), and also the wing of the Falcon 900 with a modified leading edge carrying no inboard slats. In overall terms the structure of the Falcon 2000 is conventional, based on light alloys with a relatively high proportion of composite materials.

Cabin accommodation is

provided for a maximum of 19 passengers, although the standard seating is four seats in a forward cabin and four seats plus a two-person sofa in a rear cabin. The standard flightdeck complement is two, and the avionics are based on the Collins Pro Line IV

suite with colour weather radar, an autopilot, a four-screen electronic flight instrumentation system and the Honeywell FMZ-2000 flight management system.

The first Falcon 2000 flew on 4 March 1990, when the sole prototype took to the air. The Falcon

2000 received European and American certifications in November 1994 and February 1995 respectively. The first delivery was made to a south

African customer in February 1995, and since that time a steady procession of deliveries has been made to corporate and fractional operators.

Falcon 2000 is currently the ultimate Dassault biz-jet, although the company is interested in a supersonic corporate jet project.

SPECIFICATION

Dassault Falcon 2000
Type: two-crew corporate transport
Powerplant: two General Electric/ AlliedSignal CFE738-1-1B turbofan engines each rated at 6,000 lb st (26.69 kN)
Performance: maximum cruising speed 555 mph (893 km/h) at optimum altitude; economical cruising speed 495 mph (430 km/h) at optimum altitude; certificated ceiling 47,000 ft (14325 m); range

3,596 miles (5787 km) with eight passengers and reserves
Weights: empty 19,700 lb (8936 kg); maximum take-off 35,800 lb (16239 kg)
Dimensions: wingspan 63 ft 5 in (19.33 m); length 66 ft 4½ in (20.23 m); height 22 ft 10¾ in (6.98 m); wing area 527.65 sq ft (49.02 m²)
Payload: up to 19 passengers within the context of a 3,064-lb (1390-kg) payload

Dassault M.D.303, M.D.311, M.D.312 & M.D.315 Flamant

The portly **M.D.315 Flamant** (flamingo) had a long career as a utility transport and aircrew trainer, and its prototype made its maiden flight on 10 February 1947. This machine had the designation **M.D.303**, and was evaluated successfully later in that same year. Production examples of the Flamant, the first of which flew in January 1949, were intended mainly for service with the

Armee de l'Air in France's overseas territories, and deliveries to AOF (Afrique Occidentale Française) squadrons began in October 1950. There were three main versions: first of these was the **M.D.311** bombing, navigation and photography trainer, of which 39 were built; more

numerous, and longer-serving, were the six-seat **M.D.312** military liaison/communications type and the 10-seat **M.D.315** light utility transport. These latter two models (production totals 142 and 137 respectively) were used over a long period by the Armée de

l'Air and, in the case of the M.D.312, by the Aéronavale. Convertible from passenger to cargo or aeromedical transport, several were passed on to other air forces such as those of Cambodia (later Kampuchea), Madagascar, Tunisia and Vietnam as they were withdrawn from French service.

One M.D.315 was converted as the **M.D.316**

with 820-hp (611-kW) SNECMA 14X Super Mars radial engines; this flew on 17 July 1952. A single-finned second prototype, the **M.D.316T**, had 800-hp (597-kW) Wright R-1300-CB7A1 Cyclone radials. These new models were intended for crew training and commercial transport operation, but neither reached production status.

Over 200 Flamants were still in service in the mid-1960s, but the type thereafter declined in importance and the last aircraft were retired in 1982. The aircraft illustrated is an M.D.312.

SPECIFICATION

Dassault M.D.315 Flamant
Type: one/two-crew multi-purpose transport
Powerplant: two SNECMA (Renault) 12S 02-201 inverted-Vee piston engines; each rated at 580 hp (433 kW)
Performance: maximum speed 236 mph (380 km/h) at 3,280 ft (1000 m); cruising speed 186 mph (300 km/h) at optimum altitude; initial climb rate 984 ft (300 m) per minute; service ceiling 26,245 ft

(8000 m); range 755 miles (1215 km)
Weights: empty 9,370 lb (4250 kg); maximum take-off 12,787 lb (5800 kg)
Dimensions: wingspan 67 ft 11 in (12.50 m); length 41 ft ¼ in (12.50 m); height 14 ft 9¾ in (4.50 m); wing area 508.06 sq ft (47.20 m²)
Payload: up to 10 passengers or freight

Dassault M.D.450 Ouragan

Dassault's **M.D.450 Ouragan** (hurricane), France's first post-war jet fighter to enter service, is now extinct – the last survivors having been a dozen or so ex-Israeli air force aircraft refurbished and sold to El Salvador in the mid-1970s for service, it is thought, into the middle part of the 1990s. The private-venture prototype of the Ouragan first flew on 28 February 1949, without the armament, pressurised cockpit and wing-tip fuel tanks that became standard on production aircraft. Three prototypes and 12 pre-production Ouragans were followed by an initial contract for 150 production aircraft, subsequently increased to 350. The first production Ouragan flew

Proving among the best of the early jet fighters, the Ouragan possessed excellent handling and fighting capabilities. The former were appreciated by the Patrouille de France.

on 5 December 1951, and the last was completed in mid-1954. Deliveries to the Armée de l'Air began in 1952: three escadres (groups) received the type, but began phasing the fighter out in favour of its improved descendant, the Mystère IVA, in May 1955. However, the last Ouragan

did not disappear from a French operational unit until six years later, and 50 or so still served as advanced trainers in the mid-1960s. Four **Barougan** aircraft were Ouragans fitted with a twin-wheel 'diabolo' main landing gear arrangement and a brake parachute: between 1954

and 1957 this arrangement was evaluated for possible use from Algerian desert strips, but the idea was not adopted.

Some 75 Ouragans were acquired by the Israeli air force from 1955 in the form of 24 new and 51 ex-Armée de l'Air aircraft. In the Suez and

later Middle East campaigns, the type proved an agile and stable weapons platform, particularly for the ground-attack task. An earlier customer was the Indian air force, to which 104 **Toofani** (the Hindi word for hurricane) fighters were delivered from 1953.

Dassault M.D.450 Ouragan (continued)

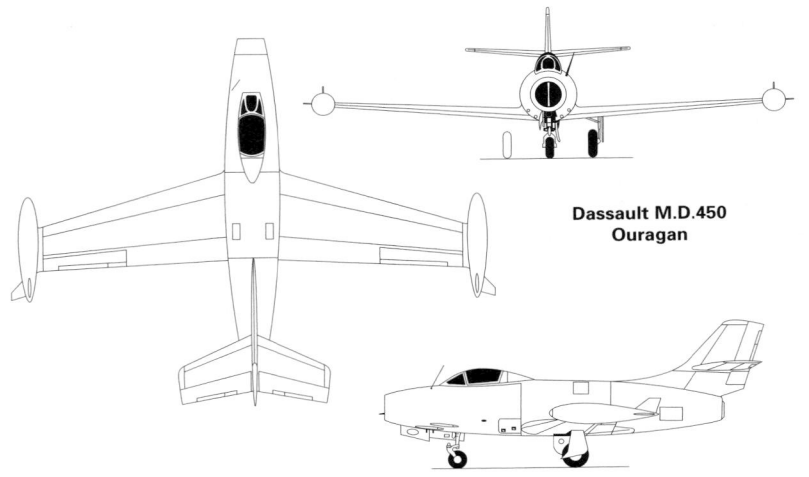

Dassault M.D.450 Ouragan

Variants

M.D.450R: single example of a reconnaissance variant
M.D.450-30L: single example with two 30-mm DEFA cannon and the Atar 101B turbojet aspirated via lateral inlets

SPECIFICATION

Dassault M.D.450 Ouragan
Type: single-seat fighter and ground-attack aircraft
Powerplant: one Hispano (Rolls-Royce) Nene Mk 104B turbojet engine rated at 5,004 lb st (22.26 kN)
Performance: maximum speed 584 mph (940 km/h) at sea level; initial climb rate 7,874 ft (2400 m) per minute; service ceiling 42,650 ft (1300 m); range 572 miles (920 km); radius 280 miles (450 km) on an interception mission
Weights: empty 9,132 lb (4142 kg); maximum take-off 17,416 lb (7900 kg)
Dimensions: wingspan 43 ft 2 in (13.16 m) including tip tanks; length 35 ft 2⅝ in (10.74 m); height 13 ft 7 in (4.14 m); wing area 256.18 sq ft (23.80 m²)
Armament: four 20-mm Hispano-Suiza HS-404 Modéle 50 fixed forward-firing cannon in the underside of the forward fuselage, plus up to 2,000 lb (907 kg) of bombs, rockets or napalm tanks carried under the wing

Dassault M.D.452 Mystère II & III and M.D.453 Mystère IIIN

Dassault rightly appreciated that the straight-winged Ouragan was only the beginning of a major design road, and the next steps were the adoption of a swept wing and the introduction of a larger percentage of French equipment in the **M.D.452 Mystère** (mystery). First flown on 23 February 1951, the **Mystère I,** first prototype of the improved fighter series, was basically an Ouragan with a new wing swept at an angle of 30°. There followed three **Mystère IIA** prototypes that first flew in the middle part of 1952, two of them

with the 6,283-lb st (27.95-kN) Hispano-Suiza (Rolls-Royce) Tay Mk 250 turbojet and one with the 5,511-lb st (24.51-kN) SNECMA Atar 101C turbojet, followed by 16 pre-production aircraft in the form of 11 (soon reduced to 10) machines ordered in April 1951, and then the first six of the production version. These latter were now completed as four **Mystère IIB** machines with a powerplant of one Tay Mk 250 engine but an armament of two 30-mm DEFA 541 cannon, nine **Mystère IIC** machines

with a powerplant of one SNECMA Atar 101C or Atar 101D turbojet, revised inlet trunking, rearranged fuel tankage and two DEFA 551 cannon, and finally two more Mystère IICs powered by one 8,378-lb st (37.27-kN) Atar 101F-2 afterburning turbojet.

These last two machines were experimental, and the type ordered into production was the Mystère IIC with a powerplant of one Atar 101D non-afterburning turbojet. There followed 124 full-production examples of the Mystère IIC in the form of the balance of the initial order for 40 aircraft and a second order for 90 aircraft, and these aircraft were delivered between October 1954 and January 1957, with more sharply swept tail

surfaces and an uprated version of the Atar 101D. The Mystère IIC offered a number of handling and performance advantages over the Ouragan, but enjoyed only a comparatively short career, as the superior Dassault Mystère

IV series appeared very soon after the Mystère II. The aircraft had all been retired by the late 1950s. Israel ordered a batch of 24 aircraft, but these were not delivered and were diverted to the French air force.

Variants

M.D.453 Mystère IIIN: this night-fighter development of the Mystère IIC was developed as successor to the cancelled M.D.450-30-L version of the Ouragan; as first flown on 18 July 1952, the first of a planned three prototypes, (the other two later being cancelled), was basically the Mystère IIC with the powerplant installation rearranged with lateral inlets to provide for the later installation of air interception radar in the nose; in the event nothing came of the type. After the completion of a short evaluation period, the sole M.D.453 was used for ejection seat trials

SPECIFICATION

Dassault M.D.452 Mystère IIC
Type: single-seat interceptor fighter
Powerplant: one SNECMA Atar 101D-2/3 turbojet engine rated at 6,173 lb st (27.46 kN)
Performance: maximum speed 646 mph (1040 km/h) at sea level; initial climb rate 4,528 ft (1380 m) per minute; service ceiling 59,055 ft (18000 m); range 746 miles (1200 km)
Weights: empty 12,809 lb (5810 kg); normal take-off 16,424 lb (7450 kg)
Dimensions: wingspan 37 ft 2 in (11.33 m); length 40 ft 1¾ in (12.24 m); height 14 ft 9⅛ in (4.40 m); wing area 325.93 sq ft (30.28 m²)
Armament: two 30-mm DEFA 551 fixed forward-firing cannon in the underside of the forward fuselage

The Mystère II series used the DEFA 30-mm cannon, which was evolved from a wartime German weapon, the Mauser MG 213 revolver-type gun.

Dassault M.D.454 Mystère IV

Although it was based on the same aerodynamic thinking, and resembled the M.D.452 Mystère II in general appearance, the **M.D.454 Mystère IV** was a completely fresh design with a wing possessing a quarter-chord sweep angle of 38°, an oval- rather than circular-section fuselage that was stronger, deeper and longer, a taller and more sharply-swept vertical tail surface, an all-moving 'slab' horizontal tail surface (rather than a tailplane with separate elevators), fully powered rather than

French Mystère IVAs fought in the 1956 Suez campaign, Indian aircraft flew against Pakistan in 1965, and the Israelis flew the type in the 1967 'Six-Day War'.

boosted flight control surfaces and, perhaps most importantly of all, flying

surfaces of considerably reduced thickness/chord ratio for marginally super-

sonic speed in a shallow dive. Design work on this considerably more advanced

type began in 1951. Dassault was still heavily involved in prototype trials

Variants

M.D.454 Mystère IVB: sharing only the wing, tailplane and main landing gear units of the Mystère IVA, this was schemed as an aerodynamically refined model and first flew in prototype form on 16 December 1953 with the powerplant of one 9,546-lb st (44.67-kN) Rolls-Royce Avon RA.7R afterburning turbojet in a slimmer fuselage (made possible by the use of an axial-flow turbojet in place of the Mystère IVA's centrifugal-flow turbojet); the second prototype had the SNECMA Atar 101F-12 engine while the third was powered by the 9,921-lb st (44.13-kN) Atar G-2 afterburning engine in preparation for the higher-rated Atar 101G-31 planned for the production model but cancelled as better all-round capabilities were offered by the Super Mystère B2
M.D.454 Mystère IVN: developed in parallel with the Mystère IVB and first flown on 16 July 1954 with the Avon RA.7R afterburning turbojet, this was the two-seat prototype of a planned night-fighter with a lengthened fuselage, APG-33 air intercept radar in a radome above the nose inlet, and an armament of two 30-mm DEFA 551 cannon and an extending pack of 52 2.68-in (68-mm) rockets; the type's development was discontinued in favour of that of the superior Sud-Aviation Vautour

The Mystère IVA was phased out of first-line service from 1975, but France retained a useful number as advanced combat and weapon trainers until the early 1980s.

with the first Mystère IIs, and another major decision – to use a different French powerplant, in this instance the Hispano-Suiza Verdon, a much improved development of the Tay and whose construction Hispano-Suiza had licensed from Rolls-Royce. The Mystère IV prototype first flew on 28 September 1952 (just before the Mystère IIB proved its ability to exceed Mach 1 in a shallow dive) with the powerplant of one 6,283-lb st (27.95-kN) Tay Mk 250A turbojet. Trials revealed the need for modifications: a longer rear fuselage, a taller vertical tail surface and a dorsal spine, and these were among the

60 changes that were effected in the nine Mystère IVA pre-production aircraft that paved the way for the attractive and highly effective Mystère IVA production model.

The Mystère IVA received its first production order in April 1953, when an American offshore order was placed for 225 aircraft destined for the French air force. The first 50 of these aircraft were delivered with the Tay Mk 250A engine for a maximum take-off weight of 15,983 lb (7250 kg) and a

maximum speed 683.5 mph (1110 km/h) or Mach 1.035, but all later aircraft had the more powerful Verdon 350 for improved performance and a greater maximum take-off weight with under-wing stores for the fighter-bomber role. The initial American-funded order for France was later supplemented by a domestic and export orders, raising the total of Mystère IVA fighters built to 421 (including 110 for India and 60 for Israel), all completed by October 1958.

Dassault Mercure

The early sales success of its Mystère/Falcon 20 series led Dassault to investigate the market prospects for a new short-range airliner, one in very much the same class as the Boeing Model 737. The enormous sales of this American aircraft have confirmed the accuracy of the basic market research, but Dassault was unsuccessful in attracting more than one customer for its new venture, known as the **Mercure** (mercury).

Generally similar in size and external configuration to the Model 737, Dassault's aircraft was of low-wing monoplane configuration with a circular-section pressurised fuselage providing accommodation for between 120 and 150 passengers, or

a maximum of 162 passengers in a high-density arrangement. The tail unit was entirely conventional, and the tricycle landing gear had twin wheels on each unit. Like the Model 737, the Mercure had the powerplant of two Pratt & Whitney JT8D turbofan engines, these being of the Dash-15 series which was one of the options available for the Model 737.

The cost of launching such a project was formidable and Dassault obtained from the French government loan support amounting to 56 per cent of the estimated initial cost (Dassault putting in 14 per cent of the total and the balance of 30 per cent coming from risk-sharing partners).

The initial Mercure

Beset by unacceptably high operating costs and very short range, the Mercure was never in a position to challenge the Boeing 737.

prototype flew for the first time on 28 May 1971, with the registration F-WTCC; the last three letters of this specially chosen registration representing Transport Court-Courrier (short-range transport). This machine had the powerplant of two 15,000-lb st (66.72-kN) JT8D-11 engines, but the second prototype first flew on 7 September 1972 with the definitive JT8D-15

engines. It had been the initial intention to give the go-ahead for manufacture only after receipt of orders for 50 aircraft. Somewhat imprudently, however, production began after the receipt of an order for 10 **Mercure 100** aircraft from Air Inter – a French domestic airline – on 29 January 1972. This company, which

received the first of its fleet on 16 May 1974, remained the sole customer and could operate the aircraft only with the aid of an annual subsidy from the French government to offset the extremely high cost of spares which resulted from production ending so rapidly.

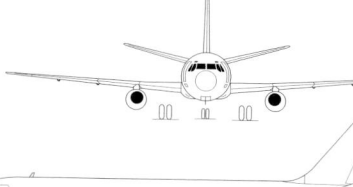

Dassault Mercure 100

Dassault Mirage I and Mirage III

Designed in response to a 1954 Armée de l'Air requirement for a small all-weather interceptor with a level speed of more than Mach 1 and the ability to attain an altitude of 59,055 ft (18000 m) in less than 6 minutes, the **M.D.550 Mystère-Delta** prototype first flew on 25 June 1955. As then flown, this single-seat machine had a delta wing set low on the fuselage, a triangular vertical tail surface, retractable tricycle landing gear, and the powerplant of two Dassault M.D.30 (Armstrong Siddeley Viper) turbojet engines. The prototype was later revised as the **Mirage I**, with a swept vertical tail surface. When flown on 17 December 1956, with M.D.30R after-burning engines and a supplementary SEPR 66 rocket motor, the Mirage I reached a speed of Mach 1.3 in level flight with turbojet power alone, rising to Mach 1.6 with the rocket motor ignited.

Later evaluation of this prototype led to the conclusion that this initial Mirage was too small to carry a significant military load, suggested at the time as a single Matra or Nord AAM carried externally under the fuselage. This led to consideration of a larger **Mirage II** version with increased power in the form of two Turbomeca Gabizo turbojet engines. Both the Mirage I and the Mirage II project were then

abandoned in favour of the far more ambitious **Mirage III**.

The success of this later design was legendary; the prototype Mirage III first flew on 17 December 1956, but the last of 1,422 related Mirage III, Mirage 5 and Mirage 50 warplanes was not completed until 1992. Even then, several air forces had just completed or were in the process of upgrading their Mirage III aircraft for further service.

Discounting some anomalies, the designation Mirage III covers aircraft equipped with nose radar, the first of which for the Armée de l'Air were 10 **Mirage IIIA** pre-production machines and, entering service in July 1961, 95 **Mirage IIIC** interceptors. These had a rocket motor in the rear fuselage to assist the 13,227-lb st (58.84-kN) SNECMA Atar 9B-3 afterburning turbojet in high-altitude missions, although the facility was little used. The Mirage IIIC has been withdrawn, as have most of the **Mirage IIIB** two-seat trainers including, as a final stage, the few **Mirage IIIB-I** test beds and **Mirage IIIB-RV** inflight refuelling trainers. The survivors of the single-seat **Mirage IIICZ** fighters exported to South Africa were withdrawn in October 1990, but 19 **Mirage IIICJ** veterans of Middle East wars were transferred from Israel to Argentina in 1982 and were retired in the mid-1990s.

On 22 October 1999, Switzerland retired its Mirage IIIS fighters. Its Mirage IIIRS reconnaissance aircraft and Mirage IIIBS/BD trainers will remain in service until at least 2003, however.

The second phase of Mirage III development was represented by the **Mirage IIIE**, which first flew on 5 April 1961 as a development of the Mirage IIIC optimised for strike and attack as well as intercep-tion. Retaining the Thomson-CSF Cyrano II radar and with the engine modestly uprated, the Mirage IIIE series intro-duced an avionics bay behind the cockpit, Doppler navigation and slight land-ing gear changes to allow the carriage a 15-kT AN52 nuclear free-fall bomb or large drop tank on the fuse-lage centreline. France received 183 such aircraft as well as 20 examples of the equivalent **Mirage IIIBE** trainer. The Mirage IIIE's nuclear tasking passed to the Mirage 2000N in 1988 and by 1994 only one French squadron remained – in the defence-suppression and conventional attack roles – with retirement

Variants

Mirage IIIT: one aircraft that served as a test bed for the 19,841-lb st (88.26-kN) SNECMA TF-106 turbofan engine
Mirage Milan: a Mirage IIIE conversion with the Atar 9K-50 turbojet engine and retractable 'moustache' foreplanes for investigation into means of alleviating the longitudinal controllability of the tail-less delta-wing configuration

following in the same year. With a camera nose, the Mirage IIIE became the **Mirage IIIR**, of which 70 were delivered to the French air force, the last 20 to **Mirage IIIRD** standard with Doppler navigation. All have now been supplanted by the Mirage F1CR.

Abroad, Argentina received 17 examples of the **Mirage IIIEA** for inter-ception, armed with the Matra R530 radar-homing and R550 Magic heat-seek-

ing AAMs. Brazil acquired 16 examples of the **Mirage IIIEBR** and, from 1988, six ex-French aircraft upgraded with foreplanes and new avionics, to which standard 10 older aircraft were raised. In Lebanon, the 10 **Mirage IIIEL** warplanes have long been in storage, while Pakistan is expanding its fleet by rebuilding many of the 50 **Mirage IIIO** machines it bought in 1990 after Australia withdrew the survivors of its fleet of 100 aircraft. These have joined the 27 survivors of 18 **Mirage IIIEP** multi-role warplanes and 13 **Mirage IIIRP** reconnaissance aircraft bought new.

Four more countries have chosen extensive Mirage update programmes, but that for Spain's **Mirage IIIEE** (locally designated **C.11**) aircraft fell victim to funding cuts in

Serving with l'Armée de l'Air's EC 3/10 'Vexin' at BA 188 in Djibouti, this Mirage IIIC is illustrated as it appeared in 1980. The camouflage scheme illustrated was officially described as sand and chestnut.

SPECIFICATION

Dassault Mirage IIIE
Type: single-seat strike and attack fighter with interception capability
Powerplant: one SNECMA Atar 9C-3 afterburning turbojet engine rated at 13,668 lb st (60.80 kN), and provision for one jettisonable SEPR 844 rocket booster rated at 3,307 lb st (14.71 kN)
Performance: maximum speed 1,460 mph (2350 km/h) or Mach 2.21 at 39,370 ft (12000 m); cruising speed 594 mph (956 km/h) at 36,090 ft (11000 m); initial climb rate more than 16,405 ft (5000 m) per minute; climb to 36,090 ft (11000 m) in 3 minutes; service ceiling 55,775 ft (17000 m) with turbojet or 75,460 ft (23000 m) with turbojet and rocket; ferry

range 2,486 miles (4000 km) with three drop tanks; combat radius 746 miles (1200 km) on a hi-hi-hi mission with a very small warload
Weights: empty 15,542 lb (7050 kg); maximum take-off 30,203 lb (13700 kg)
Dimensions: wingspan 26 ft 11¾ in (8.22 m); length 49 ft 3½ in (15.03 m); height 14 ft 9 in (4.50 m); wing area 376.75 sq ft (35.00 m²)
Armament: two 30-mm DEFA 552 fixed forward-firing cannon in the underside of the forward fuselage, plus up to 8,818 lb (4000 kg) of disposable stores carried on one underfuselage and four underwing hardpoints

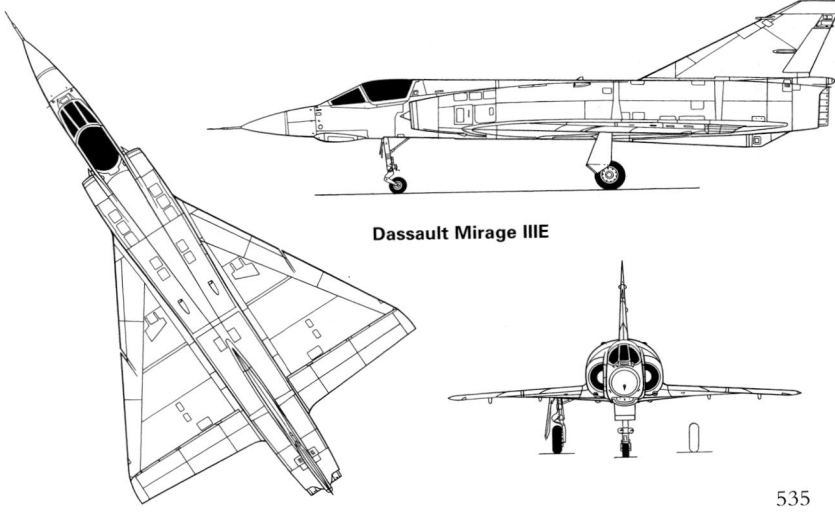

Dassault Mirage IIIE

1992 and they were withdrawn. South Africa bought 17 **Mirage IIIEZ**, four **Mirage RZ** and four **Mirage R2Z** aircraft, the last-mentioned fitted with the 15,873-lb st (70.61-kN)

Atar 9K-50 afterburning engine: several were later upgraded to Atlas (now Denel) Cheetah standard, following similar conversion of **Mirage IIIDZ** and **Mirage IIID2Z** two-seat

trainers. Switzerland received 36 **Mirage IIIS** and 18 **Mirage IIIRS** aircraft, which were later fitted with new avionics and canards. Since its introduction the Mirage IIIS has

been equipped with the Hughes TARAN 18 radar and navigation suite for compatibility with the Hughes Falcon AAM. Venezuela bought seven examples of the **Mirage**

IIIEV, followed by Mirage 5s, all of which have been upgraded to Mirage 50EV configuration. All Mirage IIIE operators fly two-seat **Mirage IIID** conversion trainers.

Dassault Mirage IV

The French government decided in 1954 to create a Force de Frappe (strike force) as the main element of a national nuclear deterrent capability designed to maintain France in the forefront of the world's powers. A key element of this capability was a manned bomber to deliver the AN22 weapon, a French-developed free-fall nuclear bomb with a 60 kiloton warhead. At this time Dassault was involved with the design of the Mirage III interceptor with a powerplant of one SNECMA Atar 101G-1 turbojet engine and one SEPR booster rocket, and the **Mirage IV** heavy fighter with a powerplant of two Atar 9 turbojet engines. Ultimately, all proposed variants of the Mirage IV fighter were abandoned, but the company's work was not wasted as the **Mirage IVC** became the basis for the medium strategic bomber required by the French air force. After a year of work trying to turn the Mirage IVC into such a warplane, Dassault rightly opined that greater size and weight were necessary to provide the warload, speed and range demanded by the French air force. This enlarged type would have had a powerplant of two large Pratt & Whitney J75-B turbojet engines, but the French air force then decided that inflight refuelling offered greater capabilities, and this led to the purchase of 12 Boeing

C-135F tankers to support pairs of bombers, of which one would carry the nuclear weapon and the other additional fuel and a 'buddy' refuelling pack.

The bomber finally developed for this role was the **Mirage IVA**, which first flew on 17 June 1959 as a large warplane with a low/mid-set delta wing, the navigator/systems operator in a small and virtually unglazed cabin behind the pilot's cockpit, a powerplant of two Atar 9 afterburning turbojet engines located side-by-side in the rear fuselage, and retractable tricycle landing gear. This last was optimised for the Mirage IVA's dispersed-site role, which envisaged RATO-boosted take-off from unprepared strips hardened by spray application of a quick-setting chemical compound, and comprised a twin-wheel nose unit and two main units each carrying a four-wheel bogie.

The prototype was followed by three slightly larger pre-production aircraft. The first of these flew in October 1961 with a powerplant of two 14,109-lb st (62.76-kN) Atar 9C afterburning turbojets, and the third of them flew in January 1963 to a standard fully representative of the Mirage IVA production type with Atar 9K-50 turbojets, an inflight-refuelling probe on the nose, full operational equipment, and provision for armament. The first of 62 Mirage IVA bombers entered service in

1964, comprising the 91e, 93e and 94e Escadres de Bombardement, each bomber being equipped with Thomson-CSF DRAA 8A surveillance radar, Marconi Doppler navigation, Dassault mission computer, and provision for one AN22 free-fall nuclear weapon semi-recessed into the lower fuselage on intermediate-range sorties at a maximum weight of 73,799 lb (33475 kg). Alternative loads were 16 992-lb (450-kg) conventional bombs or four AS37 Martel ASMs.

During the mid- and late 1980s, with their free-fall bombing capability now obsolete, 19 Mirage IVA bombers were converted to carry the 150/300-kiloton

In recent actions over Bosnia and Kosovo the veteran Mirage IV proved its worth in the reconnaissance role. The type's high-speed and -altitude capabilities made it relatively immune to interception, while its large sensor payload allowed high-resolution images to be obtained.

ASMP short-range missile with the revised designation **Mirage IVP**. This type was optimised for low-level penetration with the aid of new Thomson-CSF Arcana radar, upgraded nav/attack and EW equipment including the Thomson-CSF Serval RWR, dual Sagem Uliss INS, and flare/chaff dispensers on the outboard underwing hardpoints.

Some 12 Mirage IVPs were converted for the high/low-level strategic reconnaissance role with special navaids, revised

EW system and specific sensor systems including the CT52 pod designed to fit the underfuselage recess previously used for the free-fall nuclear weapon, and carrying vertical, oblique and forward cameras (typically three low-level Omera 35 and three high-level Omera 36 units) or a SAT Super Cyclone IR linescanner in place of the Omera 36 cameras. Between four and five of these aircraft remained active at any one time late in 1999.

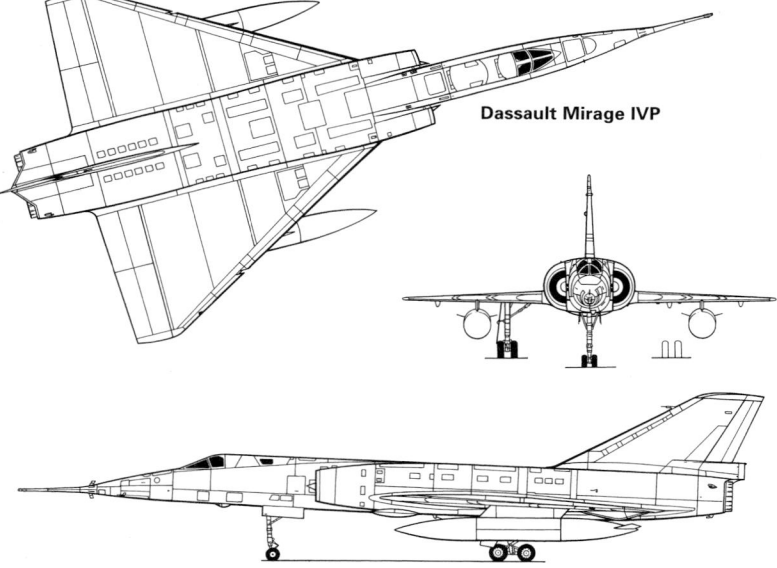

Dassault Mirage IVP

<table>
<tr><td colspan="2" align="center">**SPECIFICATION**</td></tr>
<tr><td colspan="2" align="center">**Dassault Mirage IVP**</td></tr>
<tr><td>**Type:** two-seat penetration missile-launch warplane
Powerplant: two SNECMA Atar 9K-50 turbojet engines each rated at 15,873 lb st (70.61 kN) with afterburning
Performance: maximum speed 1,453 mph (2338 km/h) or Mach 2.20 at 36,090 ft (11000 m); cruising speed 1,189 mph (1913 km) or Mach 1.80 at 36,090 ft (11000 m) for penetration; climb to 36,090 ft (11000 m) in 4 minutes 15 seconds; service ceiling 65,615 ft (20000 m);</td><td>range 2,486 miles (4000 km) with drop tanks; radius 771 miles (1240 km)
Weights: empty 31,966 lb (14500 kg); maximum take-off 73,799 lb (33475 kg)
Dimensions: wingspan 38 ft 10½ in (11.85 m); length 77 ft 1⅛ in (23.50 m); height 18 ft 6¾ in (5.65 m); wing area 839.61 sq ft (78.00 m²)
Armament: up to 15,873 lb (7200 kg) of disposable stores carried on one underfuselage or four underwing hardpoints</td></tr>
</table>

Dassault Mirage 5 and Mirage 50

In 1966 the Israeli air force asked Dassault to build a simplified version of the Mirage IIIE optimised for the daytime VFR ground-attack

mission. The basic changes implemented in the development of this **Mirage 5** were the movement of the avionics racking from its original

location behind the cockpit to the nose – which was now largely unoccupied after the removal of the radar – the reprofiling of the

nose into a much slimmer unit, and the addition of additional fuel tankage in the fuselage volume freed by the movement of the avionics racking. At the same time, two outward-canted underfuselage weapons

pylons were added so that a maximum of 8,818 lb (4000 kg) of stores could be carried in addition to 220 Imp gal (1000 litres) of fuel, although such a configuration demanded a long runway for take-off.

Dassault Mirage 5 and Mirage 50 (continued)

Late in 1999, only a handful of Chile's Mirage 50 aircraft remained in the original form illustrated. The majority have been considerably upgraded to Pantera standard.

As an alternative to ground-attack, the Mirage 5 could be used in the daytime fighter role with IR-guided AAMs (air-to-air missile), cannon and up to 1,034 Imp gal (4700 litres) of external fuel.

The prototype first flew on 19 May 1967, but delivery of the 50 **Mirage 5J** aircraft, ordered by Israel, was embargoed by President de Gaulle. The stored aircraft were finally delivered to the Armée de l'Air for service with the revised designation, **Mirage 5F**. The survivors flew with the 13e Escadre de Chasse, whose two components: EC 2/13 (which was eventually disbanded), and EC 3/13, that subsequently converted to the Dassault Mirage F1CT.

Following the initial order, the Mirage 5 proved popular with many customers requiring a cheap but potent fighter-bomber. Dassault also produced **Mirage 5D**, two-seat trainer, and **Mirage 5R**, single-seat reconnaissance aircraft, to complement the basic model. As the production run of 525 aircraft progressed, the original no-frills standard was developed into more capable forms made possible by the introduction of transistorised rather than thermionic avionics, which were smaller and lighter as well as more capable. This process allowed the optional reintroduction of radar such as the Cyrano IV, Agave or Aïda II, or the addition of a laser rangefinder. Indeed, Dassault could mix and match a wide range of avionics to suit any nation's specific requirements, and many aircraft have also been radically upgraded during their service lives. Identification of the delta-winged Mirage warplanes is a highly confusing topic, made all the worse by radical upgrade programmes led by both Dassault and IAI (Israel Aircraft Industries Ltd.), and further complicated by IAI's own construction/ upgrading programme which encompasses the Nesher, Dagger, Kfir and Nammer variants.

A derived programme of considerable importance resulted in the **Mirage 50**, which introduced the Atar 9K-50 turbojet engine as developed for the Mirage F1. The greater thrust of this unit endows the aircraft with better runway performance, faster acceleration, larger weapon load, and improved manoeuvrability. The Mirage 50 prototype made its maiden flight on 15 April 1979, and Chile was the first customer with an order for 16 aircraft (four Mirage IIIR2Z had already been delivered to South Africa with the Atar 9K-50 engine). The Mirage 50 package is also available as a conversion of both Mirage III and Mirage 5 aircraft, and the complete avionics/ weapons range of the Mirage III and Mirage 5 is available on the Mirage 50, thereby bringing together the two separate development strands of the Dassault early delta-winged aircraft, but at the same time creating further confusion concerning designations.

Over half of the Mirage III, Mirage 5 and Mirage 50 operators have at times opted for update programmes, pursued either with indigenous systems integrators or with help from Dassault or IAI. Important modifications applied to many of the upgraded aircraft included the addition of an inflight refuelling probe, the introduction of improved nav/attack avionics and the addition of canard foreplanes to improve manoeuvrability and runway performance.

Abu Dhabi took **Mirage 5AD** fighters, **Mirage 5RAD** reconnaissance aircraft and **Mirage 5DAD** trainers, for which no upgrade programme has been announced. Argentina received **Mirage 5P** interceptors in addition to IAI Daggers, and these have been updated with a laser rangefinder, HUD (head-up display) and inflight refuelling probe. Belgium took **Mirage 5BA** ground-attack aircraft, **Mirage 5BD** two-seaters and **Mirage 5BR** reconnaissance aircraft, and of these, 15 Mirage 5BA and five Mirage 5BD aircraft

were being upgraded with HUD, laser rangefinder and canards, although all were retired in December 1993. Interest in the purchase of these well-maintained machines was then expressed by Chile and the Philippines, the aircraft eventually going to the former as **Mirage 5MA/MD Elkan** warplanes. Chile also took delivery of the **Mirage 50C** and **Mirage 50DC** and, with IAI assistance, ENAER (Chile) upgraded these to **Mirage 50CN Pantera** standard, with canard foreplanes and Israeli avionics. Colombia received **Mirage 5COA** aircraft in the fighter role, **Mirage 5COR** aircraft for reconnaissance and **Mirage 5COD** two-seat trainers. Later, IAI (which also supplied the Kfir to Colombia), completed the conversion of the Mirage 5COD aircraft with some Kfir avionics and 50 per cent canards, while the remainder of the fleet was converted with 75 per cent canards in Colombia to become **Mirage 50M** warplanes. Egypt has completed a minor update programme on some of its aircraft, which comprise **Mirage 5SDE** and **Mirage 5SSE** interceptors, **Mirage 5SDR** reconnaissance platforms, **Mirage 5SDD** trainers and **Mirage 5E-II** attack aircraft. Gabon took delivery of **Mirage 5G** interceptors, **Mirage 5G-II** attack aircraft and **Mirage 5DG** two-seaters. Libya received **Mirage 5D** attack aircraft, **Mirage 5E** fighters, **Mirage 5DR** reconnaissance machines and **Mirage 5DD** trainers. Pakistan has updated its Mirage fleet with new avionics; aircraft in service at the end of the 1990s include various Mirage III

SPECIFICATION

Dassault Mirage 50M
Type: single-seat multi-role fighter
Powerplant: one SNECMA Atar 9K-50 turbojet engine rated at 15,873 lb st (70.82 kN) with afterburning
Performance: maximum speed 1,451 mph (2335 km/h) or Mach 2.2 at 39,370 ft (12000 m); cruising speed 594 mph (956 km/h) at 36,090 ft (11000 m); initial climb rate 36,614 ft (11160 m) per minute; service ceiling 59,055 ft (18000 m); combat radius of 817 miles (1315 km) on a hi-hi-hi interception mission with two

AAMs and three drop tanks
Weights: empty 15,763 lb (7150 kg); maximum take-off 32,407 lb (14700 kg)
Dimensions: wingspan 26 ft 11¾ in (8.22 m); length 51 ft ⅛ in (15.55 m); height 14 ft 9 in (4.50 m); wing area 376.75 sq ft (35.00 m²)
Armament: two 30-mm DEFA 552A fixed forward-firing cannon in the undersides of the inlets, plus up to 8,818 lb (4000 kg) of disposable stores carried on three underfuselage and four underwing hardpoints

models as well as **Mirage 5PA** and Cyrano- or Agave-equipped **Mirage 5PA-II** and **Mirage 5PA-III** fighter-bombers with anti-ship capability, plus **Mirage 5DPA** and **Mirage 5DPA-II** aircraft for conversion. Peru has upgraded its fleet with an inflight refuelling probe and a laser rangefinder. Its aircraft included the **Mirage 5P-IV** and **Mirage 5DP-IV**. Venezuela has re-engined both single- and two-seat aircraft with the Atar 9K-50 – raising their designation

to **Mirage 50EV** and **Mirage 50DV** respectively – for service alongside new-build aircraft of both variants and second-hand aircraft upgraded to Mirage 50EV standard. Features of the Venezuelan aircraft include canard foreplanes, an inflight refuelling probe, Cyrano IVM-3 radar and Exocet capability. Zaïre has not upgraded its aircraft, and operates **Mirage 5M** single-seaters and one **Mirage 5DM** two-seater.

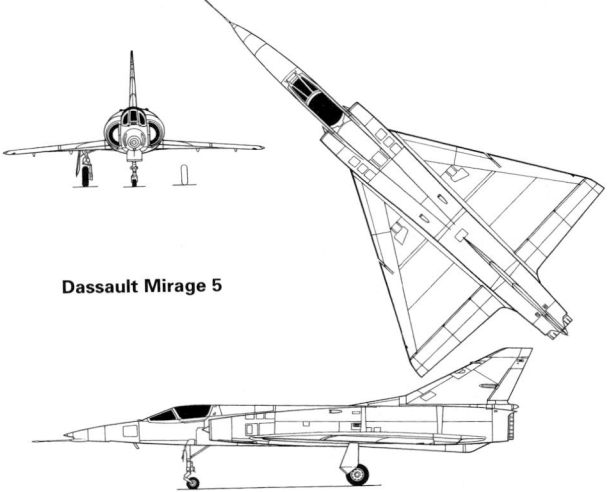

Dassault Mirage 5

Belgium's Mirage 5 fleet had just entered an upgrade programme when the decision was made to abandon the type on economic grounds. The Mirage 5BR aircraft were replaced by reconnaissance pod-equipped F-16s.

Dassault Mirage 2000

For the third generation of its Mirage warplane series, Dassault returned to the delta configuration – using negative longitudinal stability and a fly-by-wire flight control system – to eliminate many of the shortcomings of a conventionally controlled delta. The **Mirage 2000** was therefore designed with its predecessor's large high-lift wing, considerable internal volume (for fuel and avionics) and low wave drag, but included the improved agility, low-speed handling and more docile landing speed available from a computer- controlled, naturally unstable aircraft. Conceived in 1972 as the low-key **Delta 1000** project, the type moved up several gears from December 1975, when cancellation of the projected **Dassault Avion de Combat Futur** left the Armée de l'Air without a new in-development interceptor. The official specification was written for the aircraft in March 1976, and a high-priority development programme was launched to ensure a service debut in 1982.

The Mirage 2000 has a large and lightly loaded wing fitted with automatic leading-edge manoeuvring slats and two-piece elevons on the trailing edge. Its air inlets for the SNECMA M53 afterburning turbofan are of the traditional Mirage type with movable half-cone centrebodies and, on the outside, small vortex-generating strakes. Construction is largely of traditional alloys with sparing use of carbonfibre. Powered by the 18,839-lb st (83.36-kN) M53-2 afterburning turbofan, the first of five Mirage 2000 prototypes became airborne at Istres on 10 March 1978. A fin of broader chord with less complex leading-edge shape and trailing-edge root

fairings was introduced during the test programme. It also characterised the first production-standard **Mirage 2000C** on its initial flight on 20 November 1982. As with the 36 machines which followed, power was increased to 19,842 lb st (88.26 kN) through the installation of the uprated M53-5 engine.

Delivery of the Mirage 2000C single-seat interceptor began in April 1983 for an initial operational capability in July 1984. Eventually, three squadrons of EC 2 were equipped with early production aircraft fitted with the M53-5 engine and Thomson-CSF RDM (Radar Doppler Modulations) radar; some 37 of these early aircraft were upgraded to **Mirage 2000-5** standard in 1994-97. The 38th Mirage 2000C introduced the definitive initial standard with the 21,384-lb st (95.12-kN) M53-P2 engine and, in the nose, the Thomson-CSF/Dassault Electronique RDI (Radar Doppler Impulsions) radar optimised for look-down/shoot-down intercepts with Super 530D semi-active radar-homing AAM. Two Super 530 medium-range AAMs are normally carried on the inboard wing pylons, accompanied by a pair of IR-guided R550 Magic 2 short-range AAMs on the outboard pylons. The standard gun armament comprises two 30-mm DEFA 554 fixed forward-firing cannon. The RDM-equipped initial Mirage 2000C interceptors carried Super 530F and Magic 1 missiles. Both subvariants of the Mirage 2000C can be fitted with a detachable inflight-refuelling probe.

Production of the Mirage 2000C for France totalled 121 aircraft. Similar aircraft were also manufactured for export with the designation **Mirage 2000E** and the

combination of the M53-P2 engine and the RDM radar modified with a continuous-wave illuminator for the Super 530D missile in the interceptor role, or up to 13,889 lb (6300 kg) of stores including the ARMAT anti-radar missile and AS30L laser-guided ASM, for use in the attack role. Greece took delivery of 36 **Mirage 2000EG** aircraft in 1988-92. The Egyptian aircraft, delivered in 1986-88, comprised 16 **Mirage 2000EM** single-seat and four **Mirage 2000BM** two-seat aircraft. India ordered 42 **Mirage 2000H** aircraft, delivered in 1985-88, with the M53-5 engine – later replaced by the M53-P2 turbofan – and compatible with Super 530D missiles; perhaps confirming reports that RDM radar is fitted. Peru obtained 10 **Mirage 2000P** aircraft in 1986-87. In the period 1989-90 Abu Dhabi took delivery of 22 **Mirage 2000EAD** multi-role fighters with provision for US weapons, and eight **Mirage 2000RAD** reconnaissance aircraft: the **Mirage 2000R** has a radar nose and carries its

sensors in the form of centreline pods. Greece took delivery of 36 **Mirage 2000EG** aircraft in 1988-92. Two countries which wanted the type but failed to secure it because of financial or political considerations were Jordan and Pakistan.

A programme to enhance the Mirage 2000C/E series was launched in 1986 with a view to improving export prospects. Two trials aircraft tested elements of the new programme: the **Mirage 2000-3** had a five-screen pilot's display from the Rafale, replacing the original instrumentation, and the **Mirage 2000-4** integrated the new MICA medium-range AAM – four of which could be carried in a rectangular pattern beneath the inner parts of the wing – augmented by a pair of Magic 2 short-range AAMs outboard. These

features, when added to a Thomson-CSF RDY multi-mode radar, a new central processing unit, a holographic HUD, an ICMS Mk 2 countermeasures suite and an additional electrical generator, produced the **Dassault Mirage 2000-5** multi-role warplane. A two-seat trainer prototype flew on 24 October 1990, and was followed by a single-seat equivalent on 27 April 1991. Options available include Super 530 or Sky Flash AAMs in place of the MICAs and (from 1995) the uprated M53-P20 turbofan. The standard radar is the RDY, optimised for air interception but also possessing good air-to-surface capabilities with weapons as diverse as the AM39 Exocet anti-ship missile, ARMAT, AS30L laser-guided ASM, laser-guided bombs and APACHE stand-off weapons dispenser.

Abu Dhabi operates this Mirage 2000EAD. Its Mirage 2000 fleet is to be upgraded to a standard known as Mirage 2000-9 with RDY radar. New 2000-9s are also on order.

Mirage 2000-5 adds true multi-role capability to the already outstanding Mirage 2000. The aircraft competes head-to-head with the latest F-16 and F/A-18 variants for export orders.

Dassault Mirage 2000C

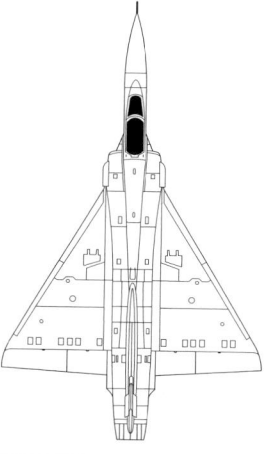

SPECIFICATION

Dassault Mirage 2000-5
Type: single-seat multi-role fighter
Powerplant: one SNECMA M53-P20 turbofan engine rated at 22,046 lb st (98.06 kN) with afterburning
Performance: maximum speed 1,451 mph (2335 km/h) or Mach 2.2 at high altitude; initial climb rate 56,000 ft (17070 m) per minute; service ceiling 54,000 ft (16460 m); range 2,071 miles (3333 km) with drop tanks or 1,151 miles (1850 km) on a hi-hi-hi mission

Weights: empty 16,534 lb (7500 kg); maximum take-off 33,069 lb (15000 kg)
Dimensions: wingspan 29 ft 11½ in (9.13 m); length 47 ft 1¼ in (14.36 m); height 17 ft ¾ in (5.20 m); wing area 441.33 sq ft (41.00 m²)
Armament: two 30-mm DEFA 554 fixed forward-firing cannon in the lower part of the forward fuselage, plus up to 13,889 lb (6300 kg) of disposable stores carried on five underfuselage and four underwing hardpoints

Dassault Mirage 2000 (continued)

In 1992, Dassault received a commitment from Taiwan for 48 **Mirage 2000-5Ei** aircraft for delivery in 1996-98. The second customer for the Mirage 2000-5 was Qatar, which in July 1994 ordered nine **Mirage 2000-5EDA** delivered from 1997. In addition to these newly-build aircraft, the Armée de l'Air's first 37 Mirage 2000C fighters were upgraded to this standard between 1994 and 1997 in a programme that also updated the cockpit. In the spring of 1999, Greece ordered 15 examples of the improved **Mirage 2000-5 Mk II** – a redesignation of the **Mirage 2000-9**, with the M53-P2 engine and the same type of stand-off attack capability. The United Aran Emirates requested 30 of these to complement their existing aircraft converted to the same standard. The new Greek aircraft are also being supplemented by the conversion of 10 of the 35 surviving Mirage 2000EGs.

Designed to provide the Armée de l'Air with a two-seat conversion trainer equivalent of the Mirage 2000C, the **Mirage 2000B** first flew, in production form, on 7 August 1983. Increased in length by only 7½ in (19 cm), the Mirage 2000B sacrificed a little internal fuel capacity and both cannon in order provide for a second Martin-Baker Mk 10 zero/zero ejection seat in the lengthened cockpit. The aircraft is fitted with an RDI radar (although this was not present on the first

15 examples) and all trainers have the M53-5 engine. Mirage 2000Bs and Cs in French service are sometimes, and confusingly, referred to jointly as **Mirage 2000DA** machines, the letter suffix standing for **Défense Aérienne** (air defence). Orders were terminated in 1991 as an economy measure after the completion of 32 aircraft.

The export version of the Mirage 2000B, with the RDM radar and M53-P2 engine, is the **Mirage 2000ED**, and customers for the type have been Egypt (four **Mirage 2000BM** aircraft in 1986-88), India (seven **Mirage 2000TH** aircraft delivered in 1985-88 and later revised with the M53-P2 turbofan), Peru (two **Mirage 2000DP** aircraft in 1986-87), Abu Dhabi (six **Mirage 2000DAD** aircraft in 1989-90), Greece (four **Mirage 2000BG** aircraft in 1988-92), Taiwan (12 **Mirage 2000-5Di** aircraft in 1996-1998) and Qatar (three **Mirage 2000DDi** aircraft in 1997-2000).

In 1979 Dassault was contracted to produce two prototypes of what was then designated as the **Mirage 2000P** (**Pénétration**) but soon became the **Mirage 2000N** (**Nucléaire**). This strike version of the Mirage 2000B has a strengthened airframe for high-speed, low-level flight, and considerable differences in avionics. Most significant among the latter is a Dassault Electronique/Thomson-CSF Antilope 5 nose radar; optimised for

terrain following, ground mapping and navigation, but with additional air-to-air and air-to-sea modes. The radar displays information in the pilot's HUD and on a three-colour head-down display with moving-map overlay, and provides automatic terrain following down to 300 ft (91 m) at speeds up to 691 mph (1112 km/h). The weapons system operator in the rear seat has twin inertial navigation systems, two altimeters and an additional moving map.

The Mirage 2000N is equipped to carry alternative loads of conventional ordnance including the AS30L laser-guided ASM (air-to-surface missile) and BGL laser-guided guided bomb, the APACHE stand-off munitions dispenser, the AM39 Exocet anti-ship missile, and the ARMAT anti-radar missile. The first 31 Mirage 2000Ns to enter French service, however, were not equipped with these modifications. In service, the ASMP- (French air-to-surface, medium-range weapon) only aircraft are known as **Mirage 2000N-K1** machines while the dual-role aircraft have the designation **Mirage 2000N-K2**.

Initially flown on 3 February 1983, the Mirage 2000N achieved initial operational capability in July 1988, when the first of an eventual three squadrons in EC 4 reformed with the type. Orders for the Mirage 2000N were reduced as a result of lessening tensions in Europe, but delays with the Dassault Rafale programme then generated

a requirement for more aircraft with only a conventional weapons capability. This resulted in the **Mirage 2000N'** (**N Prime**), a confusing designation which was then amended to **Mirage 2000D**. When further orders were curtailed in 1991, France had ordered 75 Mirage 2000N (31 K1 and 44 K2) and 75 Mirage 2000D warplanes, the first of which flew on 19 February 1991. All versions have provision for an inflight-refuelling probe and the Mirage 2000D was delivered from 1993 onwards.

Dassault announced in 1989 that an export version of the Mirage 2000D would be available from 1994 as the **Mirage 2000S** (**Strike**), the variant was subsequently dropped.

Armed with ASMP, the Mirage 2000N has taken over the nuclear deterrent role formerly assigned to the Mirage IVP.

Dassault Mirage F1

Ecuador equips its Mirage F1s with French missiles for the air-to-air role and Israeli bombs for air-to-ground missions. The aircraft fly with Escuadrón de Caza 2112.

FAE 802

The **Mirage F1** was Dassault's successor to its Mirage III and Mirage 5. Employing a high-mounted swept wing and conventional tail surfaces, the private-venture prototype flew on 23 December 1966. It was officially adopted in May 1967, when three prototypes were ordered. With greater power available from the 15,873-lb st (70.61-kN) SNECMA Atar 9K-50 afterburning turbojet, the Mirage F1 easily outperformed the Mirage III.

To meet the French air force's primary requirement for an all-weather interceptor, the **Mirage F1C** initial production model was equipped with a Thomson-CSF Cyrano IV monopulse radar, the later Cyrano IV-1 standard adding limited look-down capability. The Mirage F1C – delivery of which began in May 1973 –

was initially restricted in armament to its two internal 30-mm cannon. In 1976, however, the R530 medium-range AAM (air-to-air missile) was issued, and one year late this was followed into service by the R550 Magic.

The Armée de l'Air acquired 83 basic Mirage F1Cs, of which the final 13 were fitted with the Thomson-CSF Type BF radar warning receiver. Another 79 aircraft, delivered between March 1977 and December 1983, were

of the **Mirage F1C-200** subvariant with a fixed inflight-refuelling probe. Provision for the probe required a very small 'plug' in the forward fuselage, increasing the aircraft's length by 2¾ in (7 cm).

There is also an operational conversion unit with the **Mirage F1B** two-seater of which the Armée de l'Air ordered 20, and were delivered between October 1980 and March 1983. Incorporation of a lengthened cockpit, featuring a second ejection seat

together with controls and instruments, added only 11⅞ in (0.30 m) to the standard F1C's length but required deletion of the fuselage fuel tank and both internal cannon. Empty weight increased by 441 lb (200 kg), partially as a result of the installation of two Martin-Baker Mk 10 zero/zero ejection seats rather than the Mirage F1C's Mk 4 seat with a forward speed limitation. In other respects the Mirage F1B is combat-capable and can compensate for its

internal deficiencies by carrying cannon pods and drop tanks.

Exports of the Mirage F1C were made to six countries. South Africa received the first of 16 **Mirage F1CZ** warplanes in 1975. Morocco received 30 **Mirage F1CH** warplanes from 1978. Jordan received 17 **Mirage F1CJ** aircraft in 1981, and also two **Mirage F1BJ** trainers. Kuwait received 18 **Mirage F1CK** machines from 1976 and then nine **Mirage F1CK-II** machines from 1984 – the

Dassault's Mirage F1CR provides l'Armée de l'Air with a most capable tactical reconnaissance platform. The aircraft are on strength with ER 1/33 and ER 2/33 (illustrated) and fly alongside two Mirage F1CT squadrons and a single F1B/F1C-equipped conversion unit.

Mirage F1CK-II standard, to which all survivors were upgraded, included air-to-surface capability with ARMAT anti-radar missiles. Kuwait was also ahead of France in ordering the two-seat version, the first of its six **Mirage F1BK** aircraft (two Mirage F1BK and four **Mirage F1BK-II** machines) flying on 26 May 1976. Greece took delivery of 40 **Mirage F1CG** fighters from August 1975. Spain bought 45 **Mirage F1CE** fighters with the local designation **C.14A** for delivery from 1975, and also six **Mirage F1BE** two-seat trainers.

As soon as it had become clear that the Mirage F1 would support a major production run, Dassault studied a dedicated reconnaissance version, the major potential customer being the Armée de l'Air. With the escalating price of combat aircraft, however, a strong case existed for the development of pods that could be carried by non-dedicated aircraft. Some Armée de l'Air Mirage F1s, as well as those of some export customers (notably Iraq's **F1EQ** warplanes), have in fact been seen with various centreline reconnaissance pods. The development of a dedicated tactical reconnaissance platform for the Armée de l'Air did continue,

however, and the first **Mirage F1CR-200** flew on 20 November 1981. The Mirage F1CR carries a wealth of reconnaissance equipment both internally and externally: a SAT SCM2400 Super Cyclope IR linescan unit is installed in place of the cannon, an undernose fairing houses either a Thomson-TRT 40 panoramic camera or Thomson-TRT 33 vertical camera, the Cyrano IVM-R radar features extra ground-mapping and contour-mapping modes. Additional optical and electronic sensors are carried in various centreline pods, and an inflight-refuelling probe is fitted on the starboard side of the nose.

Sixty-four examples of the Mirage F1CR were ordered, of which the first flew on 10 November 1982. The first unit became operational in July 1983.

The **Mirage F1CT** derives its designation from being a tactical (tactique) air-to-ground version of the Mirage F1C-200. The two prototypes were conversions. The first flew on 3 May 1991, and 55 more followed from air force workshops by 1995. The Mirage F1CT programme upgraded the Mirage F1C to a standard similar to that of the Mirage F1CR: the radar was changed from the Cyrano IV

to the Cyrano IVM-R, and other elements of the programme included an upgraded nav/attack system including a laser rangefinder, Mk 10 ejection seat, improved radar warning receiver, chaff/flare dispensers, secure radio and provision for a wide range of weapons.

While most export customers for the Mirage F1 interceptor series were content to specify aircraft based on the original Mirage F1C, the SAAF recognised the advantages of a simplified version for day visual attack missions. This resulted in the development of the **Mirage F1A** bearing the same relationship to the Mirage F1C as the Mirage 5 to the Mirage III. The resulting Mirage F1A has a slender conical nose over the smaller Aïda II ranging radar, and the large instrument boom, housing the pitot/static heads, is attached on the underside of the nose. The main avionics racking was moved from a position behind the cockpit to the nose, making room for an extra fuselage tank. Other additions were a Doppler navigation radar and a retractable inflight refuelling probe. The Mirage F1A was bought by Libya (16) and South Africa, which received 32 **Mirage F1AZ** aircraft with a laser rangefinder.

On 22 December 1974 Dassault flew the **Mirage F1E** prototype powered by the new SNECMA M53 turbofan engine. Designed for potential export to Belgium, Denmark, the Netherlands and Norway – as successor to the obso-

lescent Lockheed F-104G Starfighter – the aircraft failed to win an order and was abandoned. This allowed the use of the designation for an upgraded multi-role fighter/attack version with the Atar 9K-50 turbojet engine, but with a more capable nav/attack system.

The **Mirage F1D** trainer is essentially similar to the F1B. It differs only in being based on the Mirage F1E and in having Mk 10 zero/zero ejection seats with command ejection. The trainers are fully combat capable and were bought in small numbers by some Mirage F1E operators. Deliveries of the Mirage F1E totalled 16 **Mirage F1JA** single-seaters and two **Mirage F1JE** two-seat trainers to Ecuador, 93 **Mirage F1EQ** machines to Iraq, 17 **Mirage F1EJ** machines to Jordan, 16 **Mirage F1ED** machines to Libya, 14 **Mirage F1EH** and six **Mirage F1EH-200** (with an inflight-refuelling probe) to Morocco, 12 **Mirage F1EDA** single-seaters and two **Mirage F1DDA** two-seaters to Qatar, and 22 **Mirage F1EE-200** (local designation **C.14B**) machines to Spain.

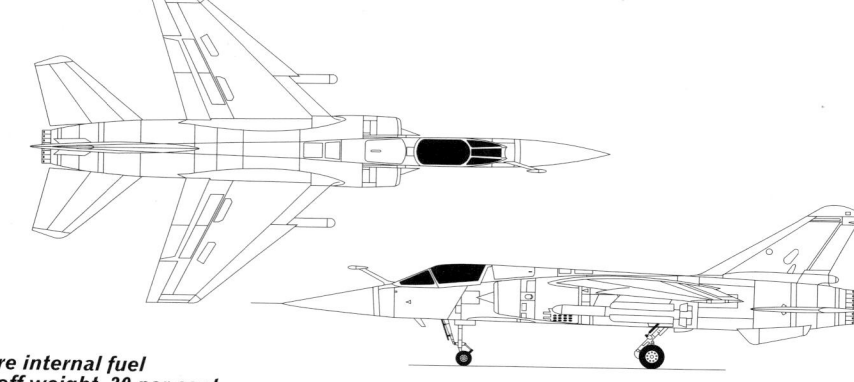

Compared to the Mirage III, the F1 offers 43 per cent more internal fuel capacity, a 5,511-lb (2500-kg) increase in maximum take-off weight, 30 per cent shorter take-off run, 25 per cent slower approach speed and improved manoeuvrability at all speeds.

Dassault Mirage F1C-200

SPECIFICATION

Dassault Mirage F1C
Type: single-seat fighter and attack warplane
Powerplant: one SNECMA Atar 9K-50 turbojet engine rated at 15,785 lb st (70.21 kN) with afterburning
Performance: maximum speed 1,451 mph (2335 km/h) or Mach 2.2 at 36,090 ft (11000 m); initial climb rate 41,930 ft (12780 m) per minute; service ceiling 65,615 ft (20000 m); combat radius 264 miles (425 km) on a hi-lo-hi attack mission with 14 551-lb (250-kg) bombs

Weights: empty 16,314 lb (7400 kg); maximum take-off 35,715 lb (16200 kg)
Dimensions: wingspan 27 ft 6¾ in (8.40 m) without tip stores; length 50 ft 2½ in (15.30 m); height 14 ft 9 in (4.50 m); wing area 269.11 sq ft (25.00 m²)
Armament: two 30-mm DEFA 553 fixed forward-firing cannon in the underside of the forward fuselage, plus up to 13,889 lb (6300 kg) of disposable stores carried on one underfuselage and four underwing hardpoints as well as two wing-tip missile rails

Dassault Mirage G

In the mid-1960s the French and British governments laid plans for the collaborative design, development and production of a variable-geometry strike warplane. The French government also decided to order an all-French prototype that was in essence a development of the earlier **Dassault Mirage F2** strike and attack fighter, with a variable-geometry wing and the powerplant of one 20,503-lb st (91.20-kN) SNECMA TF-306E afterburning turbofan engine. Dassault received its order in October 1965, and retained – in modified form – the fuselage, tail unit and tricycle landing gear of the Mirage F2 but combined it with a more powerful engine and a wing whose variable geometry was similar to that of the American General Dynamics F-111.

The prototype was completed in May 1967, and made its first flight on 18 November of the same year. Flight trials proceeded rapidly and smoothly – the maximum sweep angle of 70° being used within one week and a maximum speed of 1,388 mph (2233 km/h) or Mach 2.1 being reached within two months. The Mirage G clearly possessed considerable operational potential but, after a trials programme involving some 400 hours in the air during 316 flights, was lost during a flight in January 1971. Further development of the type's variable-geometry wing was entrusted to the **Mirage G8** derivative with a twin-engined powerplant.

Ordered during late 1968 in the form of two experimental combat aircraft prototypes, the Mirage G8 was a derivative of the Mirage G, from which it differed primarily in the powerplant of two SNECMA Atar 9K-50 afterburning turbojets and the enhanced avionics based on those of the Dassault Milan. The Mirage G8 had a shoulder-set wing capable of movement between minimum and maximum sweep angles of 23° and 70° respectively.

The first prototype – the **Mirage G8.01** (completed in two-seat configuration) – made its maiden flight on 8 May 1971. The second prototype – the single-seat **Mirage G8.02** – followed on 13 July 1972. The two aircraft were flown in an intensive test programme that yielded valuable information in a number of areas, including the variable-geometry wing. So successful was the programme that a production derivative was projected as the **Mirage F8** (later **Super Mirage**) to meet the French air force's requirement for an **ACF** (**Avion de Combat Futur**, or future combat aircraft). The Super Mirage would have had a powerplant of two 18,739-lb st (83.35-kN) SNECMA M53 afterburning turbofan engines, and a wing of fixed sweep. The French air force later concluded that the variable-geometry wing's cost, weight and maintenance requirements outweighed any operational advantages. A fixed leading-edge sweep angle of 55° was therefore planned instead, as this had proved best in trials with the two Mirage G8 prototypes. The Super Mirage was not ordered into production, however, so the lasting value of the Mirage G series was to be found in the Mirage 2000 and Super Mirage 4000 programmes.

The Mirage G8 wing had no ailerons – lateral control was entrusted at low speed to the upper-surface spoilers located forward of the trailing-edge flaps, and at high speed to differential movement of the taileron surfaces. Both the single-seat G8.02 and two-seat G8.01 are illustrated.

SPECIFICATION

Dassault Mirage G8.01
Type: two-seat experimental variable-geometry strike/attack warplane
Powerplant: two SNECMA Atar 9K-50 turbojet engines each rated at 15,873 lb st (70.61 kN) with afterburning
Performance; maximum speed 1,550 mph (2494 km/h) or Mach 2.35 at high altitude; initial climb rate 45,930 ft (14000 m) per minute; service ceiling 65,615 ft (20000 m); range about 4,039 miles (6500 km) with drop tanks
Weights: empty 22,046 lb (10000 kg); maximum take-off 52,469 lb (23800 kg)
Dimensions: wingspan 42 ft 7¾ in (13.00 m) spread; length 55 ft 1⅜ in (16.80 m); height 17 ft 6½ in (5.35 m); wing area 398.28 sq ft (37.00 m²) spread

Dassault Rafale

The **ACX** (**Avion de Combat Experimentale**) was designed by Dassault in the early 1980s (before France's August 1985 withdrawal from the multi-national EFA – European Fighter Aircraft – project) as a technology demonstrator for a national combat aircraft programme. France's withdrawal from the EFA was prompted ostensibly because the French forces, especially the navy, wanted a smaller and therefore lighter design weighing just over 17,637 lb (8000 kg). While emerging with a 20,945-lb (9500-kg) basic empty weight, the ACX demonstrator, first flown on 4 July 1986, helped to establish the basic aerodynamic design, configuration, performance, fly-by-wire control system, and composite-based structure of the planned **ACT** (**Avion de Combat Tactique**) that became the **Dassault Rafale**.

The **ACX**, later renamed **Rafale A**, was initially powered by two 15,422-lb st (68.60-kN) General Electric F404-GE-400 turbofan engines, but after 460 initial test sorties, including touch-and-go deck-landings on the French carrier *Clemenceau*, the port F404 was replaced by one of 15 flight development examples of the 16,523-lb st (73.50-kN) SNECMA M88-2 turbofan engine under development for the Rafale (squall).

The **Rafale C** single-seat prototype made its first flight on 19 May 1991, revealing a supercruise (supersonic flight with dry thrust) capability in the course of this sortie. It was the only such prototype of the air force single-seater. The **Rafale B** two-seat dual-control prototype first flew on 30 April 1993 with the Thomson-CSF/Detexis RBE2 multi-mode radar and Thomson-CSF/Matra Spectra defensive aids package. Originally envisaged as a combat-capable conversion trainer for the single-seater, the two-seat variant is now being developed as the principal Armée de l'Air operational variant – manned by a pilot with or without a weapons system operator.

In its definitive production forms, due to enter service from 2002, the Rafale multi-role warplane will replace up to half a dozen French air force interceptor, strike/attack and reconnaissance types. While retaining the ACX's main design features, the generic **Rafale D** (**Discret**, or stealthy) – prototype for the Armée de l'Air versions – is slightly smaller and lighter, with an empty weight below 19,841 lb (9000 kg). Changes to reduce the radar cross-section include more rounded wingroot fairings, an internally gold-coated canopy, radar-absorbing dark grey paint and a reprofiled rear-fuselage/fin junction. The fin itself is lower and topped by an ECM fairing to house the Rafale's Spectra system's RWR and lateral IR missile-launch detector windows. The fairings over the mountings for the Rafale D's canard foreplanes have small forward extensions to house more Spectra antennas, while the canard surfaces (linked with landing gear extension to tilt 20° upward to provide extra lift for landing) are larger than those of the ACX and fabricated from superplastic-formed titanium instead of carbon composites. Composites and other new materials comprise over 50 per cent of the definitive Rafale's airframe weight. An aerodynamic addition from the ACX is a small curved strake from the wingroot leading edge to the outer intake wall above the muzzle port, for the 30-mm cannon in the starboard fuselage. The armament capability of the Rafale also includes provision for disposable stores on 14 wing and fuselage hardpoints.

Five of the stores stations are plumbed for drop tanks. Among the advanced weapons that can be carried are the MICA medium-range AAM in semi-active radar-guided and IR-homing versions, AS30L laser-guided ASM, APACHE (now Scalp) stand-off munitions dispenser, ASMP nuclear medium-range missile, and AM39 Exocet anti-ship missile. These operate in conjunction with the RBE2 radar, the first in Europe with two-plane electronic scanning. Other elements of the avionics are a wide-angle Sextant HUD, a head-level tactical awareness display, and two head-down multi-

The Rafale A made its 865th and last flight on 24 January 1994. Some 30 per cent of the machine's airframe consisted of composites.

Rafale M is desperately needed by the Aéronavale to replace the Crusader (now retired). In time, the aircraft will also replace Dassault's own Super Etendard.

ACM (Avion de Combat Marine), the first proto-type of the **Rafale M** single-seat multi-role carrierborne warplane made its initial flight on 12 December 1991. The main changes differentiating the Rafale M from its land-based counterparts weigh some 1,653 lb (750 kg) and include major reinforcement of the Messier-Bugatti landing gear (whose nosewheel unit also became the first in France to require attachment of a take-off catapult bar) plus provision of a 'jump-strut' for automatic unstick rotation. Other changes include 13 rather than 14 hardpoints, and a maximum take-off weight reduced by 4,409 lb (2000 kg) to 42,989 lb (19500 kg). The Aéronavale's Rafale M requirement remains unchanged at 86 single-seat interceptor and strike/attack aircraft, but it seems that procurement will initially be limited to 60 aircraft for delivery from 2001.

functional displays in a cockpit with HOTAS controls and a pilot's helmet with sight and display. Voice command capability will be added at a later stage.

The Rafale D – of which the Armée de l'Air is scheduled to receive 212 (reduced from 250 and then 234) examples,

Dassault flew the first production Rafale, B 301, on 24 November 1998. In l'Armée de l'Air service, Rafale will initially replace the Jaguar and the oldest Mirage 2000Cs.

including about 130 in two- rather than one-seat form for improved operational capability – is to enter service as the **Rafale F**. The first production machine was delivered in December 1998. The early aircraft are to the **Rafale F1** standard, optimised for the air-to-air role but lack

ASMP capability and certain other systems of the definitive aircraft (such as the Spectra, helmet-mounted sight and automatic terrain-following systems). Later standards include the **Rafale F2,** for delivery from about 2003, with improved air-to-surface capability. This will include Scalp, a jam-resistant passive optronic surveillance and imaging system with a laser rangefinder or an Optronique Secteur

Frontale IR search-and-track system mounted forward of the cockpit and supplementing the radar for passive multi-target identification and tracking, and the MIDS data-link. The definitive **Rafale F3,** with improved radar able to undertake simultaneous air search and terrain following. At some stage in the programme, the standard engine will become the 20,907-lb st (93.00-kN) M88-3 turbofan.

Originally known as the

SPECIFICATION	
Dassault Rafale D	**Weights:** empty equipped
Type: single-seat multi-role warplane	19,973 lb (9060 kg); maximum take-off 42,989 lb (19500 kg)
Powerplant: two SNECMA M88-3 turbofan engines each rated at 16,861 lb st (75.00 kN) with afterburning	increasing to 54,012 lb (24500 kg) in later-production aircraft
Performance: maximum speed 1,189 mph (1913 km/h) or Mach 1.8 at 36,090 ft (11000 m); maximum climb rate at sea level 60,000 ft (18290 m) per minute; service ceiling 55,000 ft (16765 m); radius of action on a low-level penetration mission with 12 551-lb (250-kg) bombs, four MICA AAMs and three drop tanks 655 miles (1055 km)	**Dimensions:** wingspan 35 ft 5¼ in (10.80 m) with tip-mounted AAMs; length 50 ft 1¼ in (15.27 m); height 17 ft 6¼ in (5.34 m); wing area 491.93 sq ft (45.70 m²)
	Armament: one 30-mm GIAT/ DEFA M791B fixed forward-firing cannon in the starboard side of the forward fuselage, plus up to 20,944 lb (9500 kg) of disposable stores carried on 14 underfuselage, underwing and wingtip hardpoints

Dassault Super Etendard

A French naval requirement of the early 1970s for 100 new carrierborne strike/attack fighters (for which procurement of the navalised Jaguar M was originally planned) eventually resulted in a 1973 contract to Dassault-Breguet for 60 examples of a development of its current Etendard IV warplane. The upgraded **Super Etendard** (super standard) was planned with the powerplant of one 11,023-lb st (49.03-kN) SNECMA Atar 8K-50 turbojet and some 90 per cent airframe commonality. A new wing leading-edge profile and redesigned flaps ensured a mainly unchanged carrier deck performance despite heavier operating weights.

To widen its anti-ship attack and air-to-air capabilities, the Super Etendard also featured a new ETNA nav/attack system and an

Agave monopulse search and fire-control radar, an SKN602 INS, Crouzet 66 air data computer (and associated Crouzet 97 navigation display and armament system), and a HUD. A retractable inflight-refuelling probe was also fitted forward of the cockpit.

Three Etendard IVM airframes were converted as prototypes, flying from 29 October 1974. Production of 71 Super Etendards was then undertaken, the first of them flying on 24 November 1977. The new type began to replace Etendard IVs and some Vought F-8E(FN) Crusader interceptors from June 1978.

By the time the Falklands War started in April 1982, the Argentine navy (sole Super Etendard export customer) had received the first five of

14 aircraft on order to equip its air arm's 2ª Escuadrilla, together with five AM39 Exocet anti-ship missiles. These aircraft made their operational debut on 4 May 1982, sinking HMS *Sheffield* off the Falklands, followed on 25 May by the destruction of the supply ship *Atlantic Conveyor*. The squadron suffered no wartime losses, but has since lost three of its 14 aircraft. In October 1983 the Iraqi air force leased five Super Etendards and bought a substantial number of AM39 missiles for use against Iranian tankers in the Iran/Iraq war, scoring many successes.

A mid-1980s upgrade programme was planned to extend the long-range and anti-ship attack capabilities of the Aéronavale's surviving force of nearly 60 Super Etendards (some 53 of which had already been

modified to launch the ASMP stand-off nuclear missile). The main changes were: modernisation of the avionics, a revised cockpit with new instrumentation and HOTAS controls, and the new Anemone radar – incorporating track-while-scan, air-to-surface ranging, ground mapping and search functions. New systems included a wide-angle HUD with TV or IR imaging, Sherloc RWR and a VCN65 ECM display together with

the Barem jammer pod, a more modern INS, a weapons and air data computer with more processing capacity, and provision for night-vision goggles. Airframe changes have helped to extend the Super Etendard's service life to about 2008.

The prototype of the upgraded Super Etendard Modernisé first flew on 5 October 1990, Dassault modifying two more for operational development.

SPECIFICATION	
Dassault Super Etendard	**Weights:** empty 14,330 lb (6500 kg); maximum take-off 26,455 lb (12000 kg)
Type: single-seat carrierborne strike and attack warplane	
Powerplant: one SNECMA Atar 8K-50 turbojet engine rated at 11,023 lb st (49.03 kN)	**Dimensions:** wingspan 31 ft 6 in (9.60 m); length 46 ft 11½ in (14.31 m); height 12 ft 8 in (3.86 m); wing area 305.71 sq ft (28.40 m²)
Performance: maximum speed 857 mph (1380 km/h) or Mach 1.30 at 36,090 ft (11000 m); initial climb rate 19,685 ft (6000 m) per minute; service ceiling more than 44,950 ft (13700 m); combat radius 528 miles (850 km) on a hi-lo-hi anti-ship mission with one AM39 Exocet missile and two drop tanks	**Armament:** two 30-mm DEFA 553 fixed forward-firing cannon in the underside of the air inlets, plus up to 4,630 lb (2100 kg) carried on two underfuselage and four underwing hardpoints

Dassault Super Etendard (cont.)

Following disbandment of Flottille 14F in July 1991, pending its eventual re-equipment as the Aéronavale's first Rafale M unit, its Super Etendards were used to replace the last 11 Etendard IVP recon- naissance types equipping Escadrille 59S at Hyères. The Super Etendards were used for the operational conversion of French naval pilots after deck-landing training in Aérospatiale Zéphyr aircraft at the same base. Flottilles 11F and 17F comprise the Aéronavale's remaining front-line Super Etendard squadrons in late 1999, flying Modernisé aircraft, and will operate the machines until they are replaced by Rafale Ms.

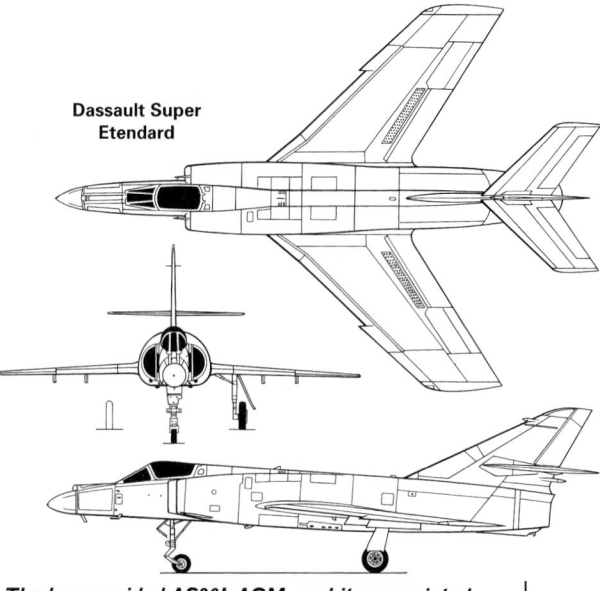

Dassault Super Etendard

The laser-guided AS30L AGM, and its associated ATLIS designator pod, give the Super Etendard a powerful precision attack capability.

Dassault Mirage 4000

Essentially a scaled-up version of the Mirage 2000 in structural and aerody- namic terms, the **Mirage 4000** (originally **Super Mirage Delta** and then **Super Mirage 4000**) was conceived from the early 1970s, after the cancella- tion of the **ACF** (**Avion de Combat Futur**) programme as a private venture in an effort to give Dassault a slice of the anticipated market for advanced multi- role warplanes. The Mirage 4000 was therefore designed to undertake both the low-altitude penetration and high-altitude intercep- tion roles with equal capa- bility, and the result was a comparatively large delta- winged aircraft with two turbofan engines located side-by-side in the rear fuselage, swept variable- incidence canard foreplanes on the upper sides of the air inlets, an advanced structure including boron and carbonfibre composite materials, and a fly-by-wire control system to allow the use of an unstable design with a rear centre of gravity.

The Mirage 4000 proto- type first flew on 9 March 1979 with the powerplant of two 18,739-lb st (83.36-kN) SNECMA M53-2 afterburn- ing turbofan engines, reaching Mach 1.6 on this initial foray into the air and Mach 2.2 five weeks later. These engines were later replaced by higher-rated M53-5 units, and although the Mirage 4000 clearly possessed considerable potential, no orders were placed as a result of its high cost with a twin-engined powerplant and advanced avionics, the latter including in the prototype the RDM multi-mode radar developed for the Mirage 2000. The programme was effectively terminated in the middle part of the 1980s, but the prototype was used for a number of development tasks including trials of the M53-P2 engine required for the Dassault Rafale programme.

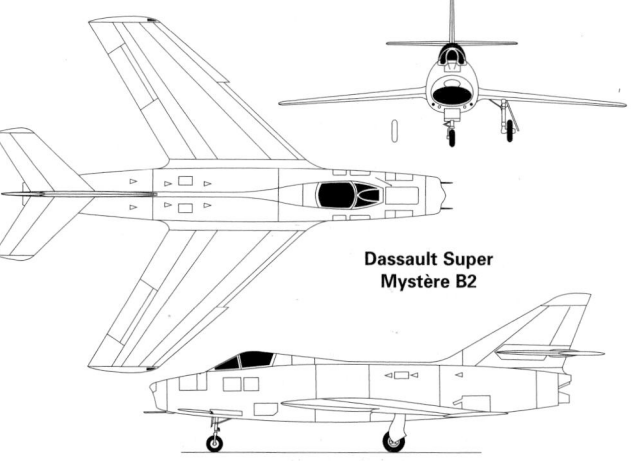

Dassault's Mirage 4000 represented a warplane of extreme capability, but at a price that was too costly for all but the most wealthy air arms.

SPECIFICATION

Dassault Mirage 4000
Type: single-seat multi-role warplane
Powerplant: two SNECMA M53-5 turbofan engines each rated at 19,378 lb st (86.20 kN) with afterburning
Performance: maximum speed 1,520 mph (2445 km/h) or Mach 2.3 at 39,370 ft (12000 m); initial climb rate 60,040 ft (18300 m) per minute; climb to 49,215 ft (15000 m) in 3 minutes; service ceiling 65,615 ft (20000 m); radius more than 1,243 miles (2000 km) with drop tanks as well as external weapons
Weights: empty about 28,660 lb (13000 kg); normal take-off 35,494 lb (16100 kg)
Dimensions: wingspan 39 ft 4½ in (12.00 m); length 61 ft 4¼ in (18.70 m); wing area 785.79 sq ft (73.00 m²)
Armament: two 30-mm DEFA 553 fixed forward-firing cannon in the undersides of the air inlets, plus up to 17,637 lb (8000 kg) of disposable stores carried on 11 hardpoints under the fuselage and wing

Dassault Super Mystère B2

The **Dassault Super Mystère B1** prototype, which first took to the air on 2 March 1955, shortly after this date exceeded the speed of sound in level flight, subsequently becoming the first European aircraft with a Mach 1+ performance to enter full-scale service. Developed from Dassault's earlier Mystère IVA via the interim Mystère IVB, the Super Mystère differed chiefly in having a new thinner-section wing with more marked sweep, a flat oval air intake and a larger and more swept fin-and- rudder assembly.

Production began in 1956, the first series-built **Super Mystère B2** making its maiden flight on 26 February 1957. Deliveries to the Armée de l'Air began later in that same year. Production totalled 180 aircraft, exclud- ing five pre-production machines, but including 36 aircraft for the Israeli air force. Those in French service had, in addition to the armament listed, a capability to fire the AIM-9 Sidewinder short-range AAM. In February 1958 Dassault flew a prototype

Super Mystère B4, powered by the 13,228-lb st (58.84-kN) Atar 9B afterburning turbojet, but this programme was overshadowed by the greater promise of the Mirage III and the Super Mystère B4 did not go into production.

By the late 1970s only a few Mystère B2 warplanes

Dassault Super Mystère B2

SPECIFICATION

Dassault Super Mystère B.2
Type: single-seat fighter and fighter-bomber
Powerplant: one SNECMA Atar 101G-2/-3 turbojet engine rated at 9,832 lb st (43.74 kN) with afterburning
Performance: maximum speed 739 mph (1189 km/h) or Mach 1.12 at 39,370 ft (12000 m); initial climb rate 17,505 ft (5335 m) per minute; service ceiling 55,775 ft (17000 m); range 1,112 miles (1790 km) with drop tanks and 540 miles (870 km) with standard fuel
Weights: empty 15,282 lb (6932 kg); maximum take-off 22,046 lb (10000 kg)
Dimensions: wingspan 34 ft 5¾ in (10.51 m); length 45 ft 9 in (13.95 m); height 14 ft 11¼ in (4.55 m); wing area 378.36 sq ft (35.15 m²)
Armament: two 30-mm DEFA 552 fixed forward-firing cannon in the underside of the forward fuselage and provision for one Matra 101bis pack with 35 2.68-in (68-mm) rockets in an extending underfuselage installation, plus up to 2,205 lb (1000 kg) of disposable stores carried on two underwing hardpoints

remained in French service, most having been replaced by Mirage F1s, but the type then still served with the Israeli air force, which had revised its surviving aircraft with the 9,300-lb st (41.37-kN) Pratt & Whitney J52-P-8A non-afterburning turbojet engine as the **Sa'ar** (storm). In 1977 Israel supplied Honduras with 18 examples of this revised version for service up to 1996. Despite its lack of an afterburner, this version had a considerably longer rear fuselage than the standard Super Mystère, and could carry a wider variety of external stores. It first appeared in the early 1970s and was used with some success in the Yom Kippur War of October 1973. In 1998, Honduras announced plans to return some of its Sa'ars to service.

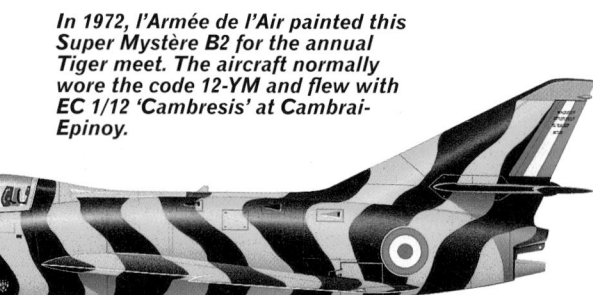

In 1972, l'Armée de l'Air painted this Super Mystère B2 for the annual Tiger meet. The aircraft normally wore the code 12-YM and flew with EC 1/12 'Cambresis' at Cambrai-Epinoy.

Dassault/Dornier Alpha Jet

Following Franco-West German studies of the early and mid-1960s for an advanced trainer, the two national specifications were merged in 1968 and a joint programme agreed in July 1969 for the manufacture of 400 **Alpha Jet** aircraft in the form of 200 machines for each country from national assembly lines. In July 1970 the **TA501** project submitted by Dassault, Breguet and Dornier was selected as superior to the rival **Aérospatiale/MBB E.650 Eurotrainer** and **VFW-Fokker VFT-291**. All three proposals were based on the powerplant of two 2,469-lb st (10.98-kN) SNECMA/Turboméca Larzac 02 (later higher-rated Larzac 04) turbofan engines; a major driving force for this powerplant was Germany's desire for no further high-performance aircraft with a single engine following heavy losses of the single-engined Lockheed F-104.

The Alpha Jet, ultimately derived from the **Breguet Br.126** and **Dornier P.375** projects, has a shoulder-set swept wing and stepped tandem cockpits, Martin-Baker AJRM4 and Stencel S-III-S3 ejection seats in the aircraft for France and Germany respectively, and stowage of the short mainwheel units (each carrying a low-pressure tyre) of the tricycle landing gear in the lateral engine nacelles. The French and German equipment fits differed considerably as a result of the fact that the Luftwaffe had by then decided to continue military pilot training in the USA. The Luftwaffe therefore now wanted a replacement for the Fiat (later Aeritalia) G.91R/3 in the light ground-attack role with an advanced nav/attack system including a Lear-Siegler twin-gyro INS, Litton Doppler navigation radar and Kaiser/VDO HUD, as well as a 27-mm Mauser BK 27 cannon in a ventrally-mounted pod rather than the French fit of one DEFA 553 cannon.

Alpha Jet development was approved in February 1972, two prototypes being ordered in each country from newly combined Dassault-Breguet and from Dornier. The first was a French machine that flew on 26 October 1973, while the second was a German aircraft that followed on 9 January 1974. During development the Larzac 04-C1 engines were replaced by Larzac 04-C6 units. Other changes included outer wing leading-edge extensions, single-slotted Fowler flaps and hydraulic servo-powered control surfaces, these combining with the uprated powerplant to provide transonic performance as well as a modest approach speed. The Luftwaffe's Alpha Jets were later re-engined with 3,175-lb st (14.12-kN) Larzac 04-C20 engines.

The first **Alpha Jet E** (**Ecole**, or school) from the French production line flew on 4 November 1977, and six aircraft were delivered for service trials in 1978. Replacement of Lockheed- and Canadair-built T-33s in Armée de l'Air training units started in May 1979 with Groupement Ecole (training wing) 314 at Tours, and 12 Alpha Jets then equipped the *Patrouille de France* national aerobatic team in the same year. The first **Alpha Jet A** (**Appui**, or attack) from the German production line flew on 12 April 1978, and was alternatively called the **Alpha Jet Close Support Version**. The type eventually equipped three Jagdbombergeschwadern (fighter-bomber wings) as well as the 18-aircraft 'shadow' training unit at Beja in Portugal. France and Germany eventually received 176 and 175 aircraft respectively, and the last German aircraft was delivered in January 1983.

From a time late in 1992 the survivors of these West German aircraft were withdrawn for possible disposal to France, Portugal and Turkey, apart from 45 machines to be retained by JBG 49 for lead-in fighter training. By a time early in 1994 only 50 of the aircraft had been delivered to Portugal. The other aircraft were mothballed, and their future remained uncertain to 1999, when Thailand decided to take 50 (soon reduced to 25) machines and the UK decided to take 12 for experimental work (some to be flown and others for cannibalisation), releasing BAe Hawks for the training role. At the same time the Luftwaffe revealed that it was negotiating with France and a Middle Eastern country for the sale of another 64 of its aircraft.

Egypt assembled 26 **Alpha Jet MS1** trainers at Helwan from September 1982 onwards, following receipt of four machines completed by Dassault.

In 1980 work began on the **Alpha Jet Alternative Close Support Version**, which first flew on 9 April 1982. In addition to light attack and anti-helicopter roles, the new version had improved potential for the lead-in fighter training role through the introduction of new avionics based on a digital databus and including a SAGEM ULISS 81 INS, Thomson-CSF VE.110 HUD and TMV630 laser rangefinder in a modified nose. Customers for this variant were Egypt (with the designation **Alpha Jet MS2**) and Cameroon. As with the Alpha Jet MS1, Egypt received the first four of its MS2s from Dassault and co-produced the other 11.

Other variants that reached the prototype stage but did not enter production were the **Alpha Jet NGEA** and the **Alpha Jet 3**. The Alpha Jet NGEA (**Nouvelle Génération Ecole/Appui**), later known as the **Alpha Jet 2**, was a development of the Alpha Jet MS2 and, in addition to new avionics, featured provision for Magic 2 short-range AAMs as well as the uprated powerplant of two Larzac 04-C20 engines. The **Alpha Jet 3 Advanced Training System** (later **Lancier**) was derived from the Alpha Jet MS2 with twin multi-function cockpit displays for mission training with such sensors as Agave or Anemone radar, FLIR, laser, video and ECM systems, plus advanced weapons. Dassault also proposed a naval trainer version to replace the Zéphyr.

The operators of the Alpha Jet have included Belgium (Alpha Jet E), Cameroon (Alpha Jet Close Support Version), Egypt (Alpha Jet MS1 and MS2), France (Alpha Jet E), Germany (Alpha Jet A), Ivory Coast (Alpha Jet E), Morocco (Alpha Jet E), Nigeria (Alpha Jet E), Portugal (Alpha Jet A), Qatar (Alpha Jet E), Thailand (Alpha Jet A) and Togo (Alpha Jet E).

The Alpha Jet E continues to serve with three Belgian air force units at Beauvechain. Students fly the SF.260D/M before moving onto the Alpha Jet, which was bought to replace the T-33 and Magister.

Germany's Alpha Jet As potentially represent a potent attack force for any smaller air force looking to purchase a relatively low-houred fleet of light attack aircraft. Thailand will use its aircraft to replace OV-10 Broncos in the border patrol role.

SPECIFICATION

Dassault/Dornier Alpha Jet E
Type: two-seat advanced flying and weapons training aircraft with light attack capability
Powerplant: two SNECMA/Turboméca Larzac 04-C6 turbofan engines each rated at 2,976 lb st (13.24 kN)
Performance: maximum speed 621 mph (1000 km/h) at sea level; initial climb rate 12,008 ft (3660 m) per minute; climb to 30,020 ft (9150 m) in less than 7 minutes; service ceiling 48,000 ft (14630 m); range more than 2,486 miles (4000 km) with four drop tanks; operational radius 416 miles (670 km) on a lo-lo-lo training mission with two drop tanks
Weights: empty 7,374 lb (3345 kg); maximum take-off 17,637 lb (8000 kg)
Dimensions: wingspan 29 ft 10¾ in (9.11 m); length 38 ft 6½ in (11.75 m); height 13 ft 9 in (4.19 m); wing area 188.37 sq ft (17.50 m²)
Armament: one 30-mm DEFA 553 fixed forward-firing cannon in an underfuselage pod, plus up to 5,511 lb (2500 kg) of disposable stores carried on four underwing hardpoints

de Havilland DH.16

The end of World War I was not a good time for the appearance of new civil designs onto a market flooded by cheap military aircraft now surplus to requirements. Instead, many conversions of military models were attempted, but the **DH.16** was a redesign of the DH.9A with a wider fuselage to allow the accommodation of four passengers in an enclosed cabin. Following its first flight at Hendon in March 1919, the DH.16 was sold to Aircraft Transport & Travel Ltd, which utilised it

Five of AT&T's stored DH.16s were broken up in 1922, the other two being sold for newspaper delivery flights. One of these was lost in a fatal crash in 1923, however, and the remaining machine was subsequently withdrawn and scrapped.

for pleasure flying before using the machine to inaugurate a service between London and Paris on 25 August 1919.

Total production of the DH.16 was nine aircraft, all but one of them for the use

of AT&T. The sole exception was the machine sold to a customer in Buenos Aires, where it operated a service to Montevideo. The first six DH.16s were powered by the 320-hp (239-kW) Rolls-Royce Eagle

VIII engine, while the last three had the more powerful Napier Lion engine. AT&T closed in December 1920 and its seven remaining DH.16s (one had been lost in a crash) were placed in storage.

SPECIFICATION

de Havilland DH.16
Type: single-crew light transport
Powerplant: one Napier Lion W-type piston engine rated at 450 hp (336 kW)
Performance: maximum speed 136 mph (219 km/h) at optimum altitude; cruising speed 100 mph (161 km/h) at optimum altitude; initial climb rate 1,000 ft (305 m) per minute; service ceiling 21,000 ft (6400 m); range 425 miles (684 km)
Weights: empty 3,155 lb (1431 kg); maximum take-off 4,750 lb (2155 kg)
Dimensions: wingspan 46 ft 5⅞ in (14.17 m); length 31 ft 9 in (9.68 m); height 11 ft 4 in (3.45 m); wing area 489.75 sq ft (45.50 m²)
Payload: up to four passengers

de Havilland DH.18

The designation **DH.18**, was allocated to a large single-engined biplane accommodating eight passengers in an enclosed cabin, and the pilot in an open cockpit behind the wing cellule. Built at Hendon, the DH.18 first flew in February 1920 and was delivered to Aircraft Transport & Travel Ltd for

use on the airline's service linking Croydon and Paris. However, this DH.18 had a short life, terminated by a forced landing near Croydon in August of the same year.

During 1920, Airco, which had been building de Havilland designs, was re-formed as the de Havilland Aircraft Co. Ltd.

The new organisation built an initial two modified **DH.18A** aircraft for Instone Air Line, which later received a third aircraft of the same type. These were kept busy on continental services until the first, having accumulated high flying hours, was withdrawn from use in September 1921; another was lost in a crash only two months after delivery. The third production DH.18A, delivered to Instone in June 1921, was passed to Daimler Hire Ltd in April 1922, only to be destroyed over France a few days later in a mid-air collision with a Farman Goliath.

The last two aircraft were designated **DH.18B**, and had plywood- rather than fabric-covered fuselages and weights increased to an empty

G-EARO, the first production DH.18 (built as a DH.18A), served with AT&T, before going to Instone. It ended its days with the RAE at Farnborough.

figure of 4,310 lb (1955 kg) and a maximum take-off figure of 7,116 lb (3228 kg). The machines served with Instone for a short time before the second was dismantled in 1923. The first was used in Air Ministry flotation tests, being deliberately landed in

the North Sea off Felixstowe in Suffolk during May 1924. Strangely, the last surviving DH.18 was the first production aircraft which, following its withdrawal from Instone's use in 1921, was delivered to the RAE for test purposes. It was scrapped in 1927.

SPECIFICATION

de Havilland DH.18A
Type: one-crew light transport
Powerplant: one Napier Lion W-type piston engine rated at 450 hp (336 kW)
Performance: maximum speed 128 mph (206 km/h) at optimum altitude; cruising speed 100 mph (161 km/h) at optimum altitude; initial climb rate 660 ft (201 m) per minute; service ceiling 16,000 ft (4875 m); range 400 miles (644 km)
Weights: empty 4,040 lb (1833 kg); maximum take-off 6,516 lb (2956 kg)
Dimensions: wingspan 51 ft 3 in (15.62 m); length 39 ft (11.89 m); height 13 ft (3.96 m); wing area 621.25 sq ft (57.71 m²)
Payload: up to eight passengers or freight

de Havilland DH.34

Building on commercial experience obtained with the DH.18 and structural experience with the two **DH.29** long-range aircraft, the company began work in 1921 on a new type, which became known as the **DH.32**. Considerable progress was made, and plans were announced for construction of the first aircraft. The new design showed great promise, but since the main customers would be Instone and Daimler Hire, who were already using Napier Lion-powered DH.18s, de Havilland bowed to their wishes and redesigned the aircraft to use that engine. The result was the **DH.34**, the company's most successful aircraft of the period immediately following the end of World War I.

The first of 11 aircraft flew on 26 March 1922, and made an inaugural

flight between Croydon and Paris on 2 April of the same year. Daimler Hire eventually used six DH.34s and Instone four, while one was sold to Dobrolet, the Soviet airline. When Imperial Airways was formed in 1924 it took over seven DH.34 transports from its predecessors and used them over the next two years before deciding to re-equip with larger aircraft.

There can be no doubt that the DH.34 made an impressive mark on the air transport scene during the four years or so in which the type served. Some 8,000 hours had been recorded by December 1922, less than nine months after the prototype's appearance, and over 100,000 miles (160934 km) flown without overhaul by the second Daimler aircraft. However, no fewer than

six DH.34s were lost in accidents, several of them fatal. An early stalling crash led to the addition of extensions to the top wing to increase its area, this modification giving rise to the designation **DH.34B**. The last four DH.34s in UK service were scrapped in 1926.

The DH.34 was an equal-span biplane of the two-bay type, with fixed tailskid landing gear and a wooden structure covered with plywood and fabric. Its three-person crew included a cabin boy. Daimler Airways inaugurated its services with the aircraft illustrated.

SPECIFICATION

de Havilland DH.34
Type: three-crew transport
Powerplant: one Napier Lion W-type piston engine rated at 450 hp (336 kW)
Performance: maximum speed 128 mph (206 km/h) at sea level; cruising speed 105 mph (169 km/h) at optimum altitude; service ceiling 10,000 ft (3050 m); range 365 miles (587 km)
Weights: empty 4,574 lb (2075 kg); maximum take-off 7,200 lb (3266 kg)
Dimensions: wingspan 51 ft 4 in (15.65 m); length 39 ft (11.89 m); height 12 ft (3.66 m); wing area 590.00 sq ft (54.81 m²)
Payload: up to eight passengers carried in an enclosed cabin

de Havilland DH.37

The de Havilland company's first venture into the field of private-owner aircraft was the **de Havilland DH.37**, seating two passengers side-by-side in an open cockpit (covered by a sliding hatch when unoccu- pied) ahead of that occu- pied by the pilot. The first of the two aircraft flew in June 1922 and the second in 1924, the latter being sold to Australia. The first machine was used exten- sively over the next five years, and in 1927 its Falcon III engine was exchanged for a 300-hp (224-kW) ADC Nimbus, the aircraft being converted to single-seat configuration for racing as the **DH.37A**.

However, in June that year it crashed while flying as a two-seater, killing the passenger and injuring the pilot. The Australian DH.37 had a longer life, being used initially by the controller of civil aviation and later by the Guinea Gold Company in New Guinea, being the first aircraft in that country. It crashed in New South Wales during March 1932.

Sylvia *was the first of the DH.37s and was converted into two-seat racing configuration later in its life, with the name* **Lois.**

SPECIFICATION

de Havilland DH.37
Type: three-seat touring aircraft
Powerplant: one Rolls-Royce Falcon III Vee piston engine rated at 275 hp (205 kW)
Performance: maximum speed 122 mph (196 km/h) at sea level; cruising speed 105 mph (168 km/h) at optimum altitude; initial climb rate 1,000 ft (305 m) per minute;
service ceiling 21,000 ft (6400 m); range 500 miles (805 km);
Weights: empty 2,118 lb (961 kg); maximum take-off 3,318 lb (1505 kg)
Dimensions: wingspan 37 ft (11.28 m); length 28 ft (8.53 m); height 11 ft 2 in (3.40 m); wing area 398.00 sq ft (36.97 m²)

de Havilland DH.50

Realising in 1922 that war- surplus DH.9Cs could not be expected to serve much longer, de Havilland used the experience gained in their operation to design a replacement as the **DH.50**, which carried four passengers in an enclosed cabin between the wings, with the pilot to the rear of this cabin in an open cockpit. The DH.9C's Siddeley Puma engine was retained and the result was a reliable and economical light transport.

First flown on 3 August 1923, the DH.50 made an excellent start to its career when, four days later, it was piloted by Alan Cobham to win first prize in the reliability trials which were being flown daily between Copenhagen in Denmark and Gothenburg in Sweden from 7-12 August. Cobham made several long-distance flights with the prototype before using the second aircraft, powered by a 385-hp (287-kW) Armstrong

Siddeley Jaguar radial engine and redesignated **DH.50J**, for a 16,000-mile (25749-km) flight from Croydon to Cape Town, completed between 16 November 1925 and 17 February 1926. This was followed later in 1926 by a survey flight to Australia and back, for which twin floats were fitted.

A number of orders was placed for the DH.50, and 16 production aircraft were built by de Havilland. Australian licensed produc- tion was carried out by QANTAS, which built four **DH.50A** and three DH.50J aircraft; by West Australian Airways, which produced three DH.50As; and by the Larkin Aircraft Supply Company, which manufac- tured a single DH.50A. European licences were granted to SABCA for construction of three DH.50As at Brussels for use in the Belgian Congo, and to Aero at Prague for

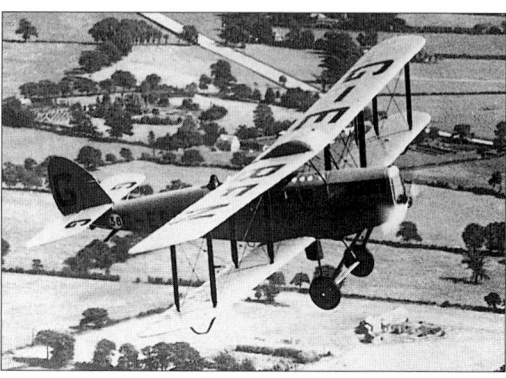

A wide variety of engines was used to power the de Havilland DH.50, including the ADC Nimbus, Bristol Jupiter IV, Jupiter VI, Jupiter XI, Pratt & Whitney Wasp C and, in the Czech-built versions, the Walter W-4.

seven aircraft.
Of the total de Havilland production of 17 aircraft, only four were based in the UK, two of them with Imperial Airways. One went to the Czech government, 11 to Australia and one to

New Zealand. The longest- lived survivor was the 15th British production machine, delivered in 1928 to the Australian controller of civil aviation and destroyed by Japanese action in New Guinea during 1942.

SPECIFICATION

de Havilland DH.50
Type: one-crew light transport
Powerplant: one Siddeley Puma inline piston engine rated at 230 hp (112 kW)
Performance: maximum speed 112 mph (180 km/h) at sea level; cruising speed 95 mph (153 km/h) at optimum altitude; initial climb rate 605 ft (184 m) per minute;
service ceiling 14,600 ft (4450 m); range 380 miles (612 km)
Weights: empty 2,352 lb (1022 kg); maximum take-off 3,900 lb (1769 kg)
Dimensions: wingspan 42 ft 9 in (13.03 m); length 29 ft 9 in (9.07 m); height 11 ft (3.35 m); wing area 434.00 sq ft (40.32 m²)
Payload: up to four passengers carried in an enclosed cabin

de Havilland DH.51

Following the DH.37 three-seat tourer, de Havilland's next type in this category was the **DH.51**. However, in this case, economy of opera- tion was a major criterion and the design was devel- oped around the 90-hp (67-kW) RAF 1A inline engine, of which war- surplus supplies were available at knock-down prices.

First flown in July 1924 by Geoffrey de Havilland, the DH.51 proved to be satisfactory, but since the engine did not have dual ignition, a certificate of airworthiness was refused. Ten hours of airborne testing would have been required with the single-ignition RAF 1A, but de Havilland decided that the cost of this was not justified. As things turned out, this was prob-

ably a major error of judgement, since once certificated the type might have gone on to achieve the fame which was to come later with the de Havilland DH.60, the first of the Moth family.

It was decided to re- engine the DH.51 with an Airdisco engine and this move, although conferring considerably enhanced performance, took the aircraft well outside the economic operating bracket for which it had been designed. As a result, only three DH.51s were built: the first two enjoyed reasonably long and active lives, being written off in 1931 and scrapped in 1933 respec- tively; the third machine, built in 1925 and shipped to Kenya, became the first aircraft on that country's civil register. Dismantled

Maintained in airworthy configuration and named **Miss Kenya,** *G-EBIR is flown regularly by the Shuttleworth Trust. The aircraft made its first post- restoration flight on 15 March 1973.*

during World War II, it survived to fly again and now, after several rebuilds, is again back in the coun- try of its birth, maintained by the Shuttleworth Trust at Old Warden, Bedfordshire as the oldest airworthy design of the de Havilland Aircraft Co.

SPECIFICATION

de Havilland DH.51
Type: three-seat touring aircraft
Powerplant: one Airdisco inline piston engine rated at 120 hp (90 kW)
Performance: maximum speed 108 mph (174 km/h) at sea level; initial climb rate 960 ft (293 m) per
minute; service ceiling 15,000 ft (4570 m)
Weights: empty 1,342 lb (609 kg); maximum take-off 2,240 lb (1016 kg)
Dimensions: wingspan 37 ft (11.28 m); length 26 ft 6 in (8.08 m); height 9 ft 9 in (2.97 m); wing area 325.00 sq ft (30.19 m²)

de Havilland DH.53 Humming Bird

The remains of the Shuttleworth Trust's Humming Bird were found in a private garden in 1955 and restored with the help of the de Havilland Technical School.

SPECIFICATION	
de Havilland DH.53 Humming Bird **Type:** single-seat ultra-light aircraft **Powerplant:** one Blackburne Tomtit Vee piston engine rated at 26 hp (19 kW) **Performance:** maximum speed 73 mph (117 km/h) at sea level; cruising speed 60 mph (97 km/h) at	optimum altitude; initial climb rate 225 ft (69 m) per minute; service ceiling 15,000 ft (4570 m); range 150 miles (241 km) **Weights:** empty 326 lb (148 kg); maximum take-off 565 lb (256 kg) **Dimensions:** wingspan 30 ft 1 in (9.17 m); length 19 ft 8 in (5.99 m); height 7 ft 3 in (2.21 m); wing area 125.00 sq ft (11.61 m²)

De Havilland entered the field of ultra-light aircraft with the **DH.53 Humming Bird**, which was built for the *Daily Mail* light aircraft trials held at Lympne, Kent, in October 1923. Two examples of the little braced monoplane were built with the powerplant of one 45.77-cu in (750-cc) Douglas motorcycle engine, and the first of these

machines recorded its maiden flight in September 1923. In spite of considerable problems with the engine, both aircraft did well in the trials.

In an effort to make the type more reliable, a Blackburne Tomtit engine was installed and other detail changes made before the first Humming Bird was flown to the

Brussels Aero Show in 1923. It later took part in several air races together with the second aircraft, owned by a group of RAF officers who re-engined it with a 35-hp (26-kW) ABC Scorpion engine, which proved unreliable.

Because of its economical performance, the first Humming Bird had secured an Air Ministry order for

eight aircraft for communications and flying practice. Five others were built for civil customers, three going to Australia, one to Czechoslovakia and one to the USSR. The last two of the RAF's Humming Birds were used in experiments which involved their launch from the airship R-33 and then their recovery in the air. Following the disposal of all

eight aircraft by the RAF in 1927, six were civil-registered and flown for several years. One survives with the Shuttleworth Trust at Old Warden, having been rebuilt with a number of new components after World War II. It was flown on occasion, but following extensive damage is no longer airworthy and is maintained as a static exhibit.

de Havilland DH.60 Moth

The idea of cheap flying for the man in the street has attracted aircraft manufacturers throughout the history of flight. One of the earliest examples of a successful design to this concept was the **DH.60 Moth**, the forerunner of a whole family of Moth aircraft which revolutionised the flying scene in the UK during the 1920s and 1930s. First flown on 22 February 1925, the DH.60 prototype had a 60-hp (45-kW) ADC (Airdisco) Cirrus I inline engine, a new powerplant which was in fact half a 120-hp (90-kW) Airdisco Vee engine. Such was the immediate success of the type that the Air Ministry was persuaded to subsidise five flying clubs equipped with the Moth, and the first of these aircraft was delivered to the Lancashire Aero Club in July 1925, a bare five months after the flight of the prototype. Some 20 DH.60s were built in that year, and 35 in the following year. Orders flowed in, British customers being complemented by purchasers in Australia and Japan, and evidence of military interest was provided by orders from the Air Ministry and the Irish Air Corps. Following the delivery by Alan Cobham of a floatplane Moth to the USA, an agreement was reached for production in that country.

During 1926 the Cirrus engine was improved to give 85 hp (63 kW), in which form it became the Cirrus II and supplemented

the earlier model. A one-off lightweight DH.60 built for the 1926 Air Ministry light aircraft trials at Lympne had a 75-hp (60-kW) Armstrong Siddeley Genet radial engine, and was later used for aerobatics. The next year's model had further improvements, including an increase in span, and carried the official designation **DH.60X** that was later changed to **Cirrus II Moth**.

Records were set, long-distance flights were undertaken, and the orders continued to roll in. The RAF's Central Flying School bought six Genet-engined models and the Irish Air Corps another two. Examples of the Cirrus II Moth were also delivered to innumerable export customers.

The designation DH.60X was reintroduced for the next variant, introduced in 1928 with the powerplant of one 90-hp (67-kW) Cirrus III engine. This model also pioneered a main landing gear unit of the split- rather than through-axle type, and by the end of that year a total of 403 Moths had been built. Additionally, production licences had been agreed with the General Aircraft Company in Australia and with two companies in Finland, namely the Government Aircraft Factory and Veljekset Karhumäki. Twenty-two Cirrus II Moths were supplied to the Finnish air force. Quantity production of the DH.60X ended in September 1928 when newer models were introduced, but a few more were built to special order.

One is preserved in flying condition by the Shuttleworth Trust at Old Warden.

Although the power of the DH.60's engine had been increased by 50 per cent, the weight of the aircraft had also gone up considerably, if not quite to the same extent. To cope better with this increase, and to make up for the dwindling supplies of Cirrus engines, de Havilland decided to build its own engine. In 1927 the company therefore asked Major Frank Halford, who had designed the Cirrus engine for ADC, to design a Cirrus replacement. His answer was the 100-hp (75-kW) Gipsy, a design which was later developed through a whole range of engines bearing this famous name, one which paved the way for the entire Moth family. Delivered in June 1928, the new engine was flown initially in a DH.60X test airframe; the revised powerplant greatly improved the already good performance of the Moth,

This view illustrates the DH.60's characteristic unstaggered wing cellule. Its Australian registration hints at the type's export success.

and the re-engined design was designated as the **DH.60G** but, for obvious reasons, was forever after this called the **Gipsy Moth**. A prototype Gipsy engine was installed in one of the **DH.71** monoplane racers which was to compete in the 1927 King's Cup Air Race, but the aircraft was withdrawn and

used subsequently for record-breaking flights.

The first production example of the DH.60G, flown by W. L. Hope, won the 1928 King's Cup air race at 105 mph (169 km/h), and several other Gipsy Moths were used in the establishment of new records. A reliability test, carried out over nine

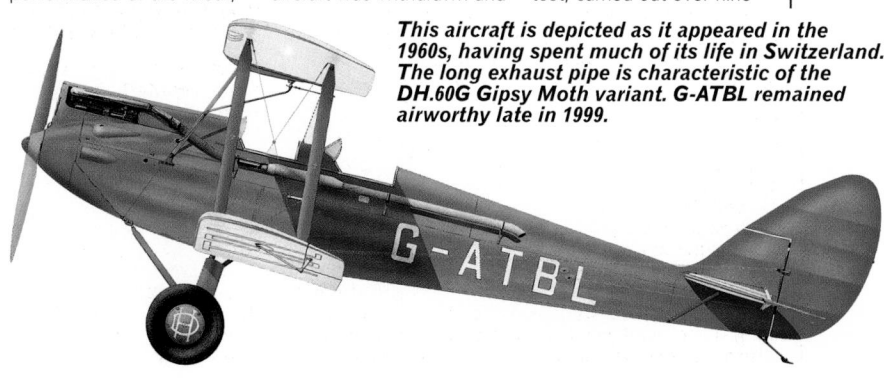

This aircraft is depicted as it appeared in the 1960s, having spent much of its life in Switzerland. The long exhaust pipe is characteristic of the DH.60G Gipsy Moth variant. G-ATBL remained airworthy late in 1999.

When powered by an Armstrong Siddeley Genet engine, the DH.60 was inevitably known as the Genet Moth.

months beginning in late December 1928, involved a DH.60G Moth flying for 600 hours with only routine servicing; the machine emerged from the test with flying colours, having completed 51,000 miles (82076 km) of trouble-free flight.

With this remarkable proof of reliability, the DH.60G became a favourite mount for long-distance fliers. In this respect, Amy Johnson's 20-day epic solo flight in May 1930 between Croydon and Darwin in northern Australia in the famous DH.60G *Jason* (preserved in the London Science Museum), and Francis Chichester's flight over a similar route in January of that year and his subsequent travels in the Pacific area have become

part of aviation history. Variants were legion and too many to record here. Among the aircraft were a pair of amphibian conversions with one large central float and two small underwing stabilising floats; one of these Moths had a Gipsy engine and the other a 105-hp (78-kW) Cirrus Hermes I engine. A few examples of a coupé version were flown, but this variant did not prove popular.

Total DH.60G production by de Havilland reached 595 before it ended in 1934, but 40 more aircraft were built in France by Morane-Saulnier, where they were known as **Morane Moth** machines, 18 by the Moth Aircraft Corporation in USA, and 32 by the Larkin Aircraft Supply Co. Ltd in Australia.

While the wooden-structure DH.60G was suitable for use in many countries, there were others, particularly where aircraft had to operate in remote areas, in which a strengthened and more easily repaired version was required. To fill this requirement de Havilland produced in 1928 the **DH.60M** variant with a fuselage of welded steel tube construction among other modifications, but retaining the same engine as the DH.60G. Production in the UK totalled 535, while 40 were assembled by de Havilland Aircraft of Canada, 10 in Norway and 161 by the Moth Aircraft Corporation in the USA. A large number of DH.60Ms went to service customers, in particular the RAF and the air forces of Canada,

Iraq and Sweden, as well as to the Norwegian army and Danish naval air service.

Since de Havilland was now building its own engines, it was logical that engine and airframe development went side-by-side. The 120-hp (90-kW) Gipsy II engine appeared in 1931 as a development of the Gipsy I, and was then developed into the Gipsy III with internal modifications to allow it to operate in the inverted position. The introduction of the Gipsy III gave the pilot improved fields of vision and also enhanced the streamlining to the forward fuselage. The installation of this engine in a new airframe and a first flight in March 1932 signalled the birth of another variant, the **DH.60GIII** which, like its predecessors, attracted

considerable interest and worldwide orders. Thirty such aircraft were built before the 133-hp (99-kW) Gipsy Major IIIA engine was installed to produce the version named as the **Moth Major**; 87 of this model were built.

The final development of the DH.60 series came when a modified DH.60M appeared as the **DH.60T Moth Trainer**, intended for military use and powered by the Gipsy II engine. This development marked the beginning of the evolutionary path toward the most famous Moth of all, the DH.82 Tiger Moth. All the orders received were from overseas military customers, comprising Brazil (40), China (1), Egypt (6), Iraq (5) and Sweden (10), making a total of 64, including two sold during 1931 to an unspecified country.

SPECIFICATION	
de Havilland DH.60G Gipsy Moth	
Type: two-seat touring and sporting aircraft	at optimum altitude; initial climb rate 500 ft (152 m) per minute; service ceiling 14,500 ft (4420 m); range 320 miles (515 km)
Powerplant: one de Havilland Gipsy I inline piston engine rated at 100 hp (75 kW)	**Weights:** empty 920 lb (417 kg); maximum take-off 1,650 lb (748 kg)
Performance: maximum speed 102 mph (164 km/h) at sea level; cruising speed 85 mph (137 km/h)	**Dimensions:** wingspan 30 ft (9.14 m); length 23 ft 11 in (7.29 m); height 8 ft 9½ in (2.68 m); wing area 243.00 sq ft (22.57 m²)

de Havilland DH.61 Giant Moth

SPECIFICATION	
de Havilland DH.61 Giant Moth	service ceiling 18,000 ft (5485 m); range 450 miles (724 km)
Type: one-crew transport aircraft	**Weights:** empty 3,650 lb (1656 kg); maximum take-off 7,000 lb (3175 kg)
Powerplant: one Bristol Jupiter XI radial piston engine rated at 500 hp (373 kW)	**Dimensions:** wingspan 52 ft (15.85 m); length 39 ft (11.89 m); height 13 ft 1 in (3.99 m); wing area 613.00 sq ft (56.95 m²)
Performance: maximum speed 132 mph (212 km/h) at sea level; cruising speed 110 mph (177 km/h) at optimum altitude; initial climb rate 500 ft (152 m) per minute;	**Payload:** up to 10 passengers carried in an enclosed cabin

Following the success of its DH.50 in Australia, the company was asked to design a larger replacement with a 450-hp (336-kW) Bristol Jupiter engine, a passenger cabin for up to eight people and, as before, the pilot accommodated in an open cockpit behind the wing cellule. The design and drawings took a mere 10 weeks, and the prototype **DH.61 Giant Moth** first flew in December 1927. Following trials in the UK, the proto-

type was shipped to de Havilland Aircraft Pty at Melbourne for assembly, flying again on 2 March 1928. Shortly after this, MacRobertson Miller Aviation placed the aircraft in scheduled service between Adelaide and Broken Hill.

Although the engine had not been available for the prototype, production examples of the Giant Moth were fitted with the Jupiter XI geared engine; two aircraft for Canada had

Short-built float alighting gear. Total production amounted to 10, including one assembled in Canada from components, and this aircraft was modified to take a 525-hp (391-kW) Pratt & Whitney Hornet geared radial engine. Of the four Giant Moth machines registered in Canada, one is known to have survived until 1941. Five found their way onto the Australian register, and the longest-lasting of these crashed in New

Guinea in May 1938. Three were registered in the UK, two of them later being sold to Australia and included in the Australian total above. The other British aircraft, named

Youth of Britain, was used by Alan Cobham in an aviation promotional tour of the UK in 1929. This machine had 10 seats for short-distance work and one 500-hp (373-kW) Armstrong Siddeley Jaguar VIC radial engine. Following the tour it was flown by Cobham to Southern Rhodesia in January 1930 for delivery to Imperial Airways, but lasted only two weeks before being damaged beyond repair in a crash landing at Broken Hill.

Geraldine *was used by the* **Daily Mail** *as a flying newsroom. The aircraft carried a motorcycle, allowing rapid transport to the story scene as soon as* **Geraldine** *had landed, a darkroom for processing film and a folding desk for a typewriter.*

de Havilland DH.66 Hercules

The need of a replacement for the DH.10s used on the RAF's air-mail service between Cairo and Baghdad, coupled with an agreement reached in 1925 for Imperial Airways to take over the service, led to the issue of a requirement met by the **DH.66 Hercules**, a three-engined biplane.

The prototype flew on 30 September 1926 following receipt of an order for five aircraft from Imperial Airways. Such was the speed and comparative simplicity of procedures in those days that the proto-type carried out acceptance

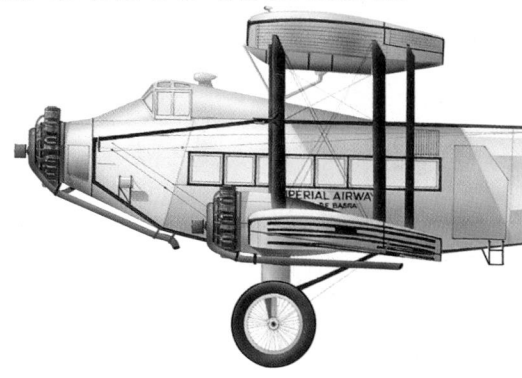

The DH.66 was equipped with a 155-cu ft (4.39-m³) baggage compartment, 465-cu ft (13.17-m³) air mail compartment, a cabin for seven passengers, and a three-man crew.

flights, took part in some crew training and was deliv-ered to Cairo by

mid-December. An inaugural flight between Croydon and India left England on 27 December and arrived in Delhi on 8 January 1927. The fifth aircraft was deliv-ered to Cairo in March 1927. The performance of these aircraft impressed West Australia Airways, then using the DH.50, and this operator then ordered four examples of the Hercules, the first of these flying in March 1929 and the type entering service with WAA on the route linking Perth and Adelaide on 2 June. By

that time Imperial Airways had ordered a sixth aircraft, and its seventh and final machine of this type followed in February 1930.

Imperial Airways' sixth Hercules had an enclosed pilots' cockpit, a modifica-tion which later became standard on the remaining aircraft. The airline's need for these last two Hercules followed the loss of three of the earlier aircraft in crashes between September 1929 and April 1931, but only the first caused fatalities. Aircraft shortage led to the

purchase by Imperial Airways of two Hercules from WAA in 1930-1. One of these crashed in Southern Rhodesia during November 1935 and Imperial Airways eventually withdrew its last aircraft from service in December 1935, having sold three to the SAAF. Their eventual history is not known, but the longest surviving Hercules was prob-ably one of the two former WAA aircraft, which was used in New Guinea until destroyed by Japanese action in 1942.

SPECIFICATION

de Havilland DH.66 Hercules
Type: two-crew medium transport aircraft
Powerplant: three Bristol Jupiter VI radial piston engines each rated at 420 hp (313 kW)
Performance: maximum speed 128 mph (206 km/h) at optimum altitude; cruising speed 110 mph (177 km/h) at optimum altitude; initial climb rate 765 ft (233 m) per minute; service ceiling 13,000 ft

(3960 m); range 525 miles (845 km)
Weights: empty 9,060 lb (4110 kg); maximum take-off 15,600 lb (7076 kg)
Dimensions: wingspan 79 ft 6 in (16.92 m); length 55 ft 6 in (16.92 m); height 18 ft 3 in (5.56 m); wing area 1,547.00 sq ft (143.72 m²)
Payload: up to 14 passengers and mail carried in enclosed compartments

de Havilland DH.71 Tiger Moth

In order to carry out research on high-speed flight and to test engines that could be used to replace the ADC Cirrus, in 1927 the company built two small single-seat

DH.71 Tiger Moth mono-planes. The first of the two aircraft flew on 24 June 1927, and the two machines were then entered for the King's Cup air race as it seemed

accepted that any new light aircraft of that time were required to prove them-selves in this way. However, one of the DH.71s was scratched before the race, while the other, powered by a Cirrus II engine, was withdrawn during the race as a result of bumpy conditions.

In August 1927 the first DH.71, then with an alterna-tive wing spanning only 19 ft (5.69 m) and powered

Such was the degree of streamlining required, that the DH.71 airframe was tailored to the size of the test pilot, Hubert Broad.

by the new 135-hp (101-kW) de Havilland Gipsy engine, was flown to a new 100-km (62.1-mile) closed-circuit class record of 186.47 mph (300.09 km/h). Five days later, test pilot Hubert Broad made an attempt on the world class altitude record, but having no oxygen the limitation was on man and not machine: Broad reached 19,191 ft (5849 m) before

having to give up, although the aircraft was still climb-ing at over 1,000 ft (305 m) per minute.

In 1930 the first DH.71 was taken to Australia, but crashed fatally during prac-tice for an air race after suffering engine failure on take-off. The second airframe, minus engine, was destroyed at Hatfield in an air raid during October 1940.

SPECIFICATION °

de Havilland D.H.71 Tiger Moth (standard configuration)
Type: single-seat high-speed research aircraft
Powerplant: one ADC Cirrus II inline piston engine rated at 85 hp (63 kW)
Performance: maximum speed

166 mph (267 km/h) at optimum altitude
Weights: empty 618 lb (280 kg); maximum take-off 905 lb (411 kg)
Dimensions: wingspan 22 ft 6 in (6.86 m); length 18 ft 7 in (5.66 m); height 7 ft (2.13 m); wing area 76.50 sq ft (7.11 m²)

de Havilland DH.75 Hawk Moth

The first of the high-wing monoplane Moths, the **DH.75 Hawk Moth** had a fabric-covered steel-tube fuselage that provided accommodation for four, a fabric-covered wooden wing extending from the upper corners of the cabin and braced on each side by a pair of parallel struts, a typical de Havilland tail unit with a strut-braced horizon-tal surface, and fixed tailwheel landing gear with divided main units. The prototype, first flown on 7 December 1928, was powered by the 200-hp (149-kW) de Havilland Ghost vee engine devel-oped by Major Frank B.

Halford as the combination of two four-cylinder Gipsy I engines on a common crankcase. The aircraft was underpowered, however, and in order to improve performance, the 240-hp (179-kW) Armstrong Siddeley Lynx VIA radial engine was used in subse-quent examples. Structural changes included a wing of increased span and chord, and in this form the type was redesignated as the **DH.75A**.

In December 1929 the first DH.75A was demon-strated in Canada, being flown with wheel and ski landing gear and, following trials with the second

aircraft on Short floats at Rochester, the Canadian government ordered three examples for civil use. The first of these (the original demonstration machine) had no doors on the port

Variant

DH.75B Hawk Moth: designation of the eighth and final Hawk Moth airframe, completed in May 1930 and powered by a 300-hp (224-kW) Wright R-975 radial engine

In prototype form, illustrated, the Hawk Moth featured a Ghost engine, in a rather untidy installation.

side and was not permitted to be flown in seaplane form, but this omission was remedied on the other two, which also had variable-pitch propellers. A de Havilland Canada test pilot carried out further tests on 4 October 1930, but although clearance for

float operations was given, the payload was restricted and the Hawk Moth was therefore flown subsequently only with wheels or skis. Three more Hawk Moth aircraft were built, two of them for export to Australia. One of the latter was used by Amy Johnson, in substitution

for her damaged Moth *Jason*, to fly from Brisbane to Sydney on 3 June 1930. Twice in its later career this aircraft was re-engined: in 1935 with a 300-hp (224-kW) Wright Whirlwind J-5 and then in 1943 with a 350-hp (261-kW) Armstrong Siddeley Cheetah IX.

de Havilland DH.80 Puss Moth

Developed to provide the growing numbers of affluent private pilots with a touring and sporting aircraft offering cabin comfort, the **DH.80** first flew in prototype form on 9 September 1929. It introduced the de Havilland Gipsy II engine in an inverted installation that significantly improved the pilot's fields of vision over the nose. It had a slab-sided plywood-covered fuselage accommodating the pilot (forward) and two passengers side-by-side at the rear of the cabin. Production aircraft began to appear in March 1930 with the designation **DH.80A Puss Moth** to indicate changes including a new fuselage of welded steel-tube construction under a covering of fabric. A notable feature of the type was the use of main landing gear

shock-absorber fairings that could be turned broadside to the airflow to act as airbrakes. Other changes included single doors on each side of the fuselage, and installation of the improved Gipsy III specifically intended for inverted running, although later aircraft were powered by the 130-hp (97-kW) Gipsy Major engine. Some 259 aircraft were manufactured in the UK, the last leaving Stag Lane in March 1933, and many of these machines were used for pioneering flights. Another 25 aircraft were built by de Havilland Aircraft of Canada.

During July 1931 Amy Johnson used a Puss Moth named *Jason II* to fly from Lympne to Tokyo in 8 days 22 hours 35 minutes, and in 1932

Jim Mollison flew another Puss Moth from Lympne to Cape Town in 4 days 17 hours 19 minutes. Mollison's second Puss Moth, *The Heart's Content*, had a 160-Imp gal (727-litre) fuel tank installed in the front of the cabin and additional windows in the rear, its range of 3,600 miles (5794 km) enabling him to make the first solo crossing of the North Atlantic from east to west as he lifted off from Portmarnock Strand, Dublin, on 18 August 1932 and arrived 31 hours 20 minutes later at Penfield Ridge, New Brunswick. On 6 February 1933, Mollison took off from Lympne en route to Natal, Brazil and became the first man to make a solo crossing of the South Atlantic.

This immaculate Puss Moth remained on the British civil register at the end of 1999. The aircraft is fully airworthy.

de Havilland DH.82 Tiger Moth

The success of the DH.60 Moth as a civil trainer led, inevitably, to the development of a military version known as the DH.60T Moth Trainer. Compared with the earliest civil versions, the DH.60T was strengthened to allow it to operate at a higher weight, it could be fitted with a rack for four 20-lb (9.1-kg) practice bombs under the fuselage, and it could also be fitted with a camera gun or various types of reconnaissance camera; the Moth Trainer was therefore suitable for service in a number of training roles. To aid escape from the front cockpit in an emergency, the rear flying wires were angled forward to the front wingroot fitting, and the cockpit doors were deepened. The centre section struts still surrounded the front cockpit, however, and in a new trainer which was developed to Specification 15/31 these struts were moved forward to provide improved egress. The effect of the centre-of-gravity changes caused by this staggering of the wings was offset by giving the mainplanes a small amount of sweep. A 120-hp (90-kW) Gipsy III inverted inline engine was installed, the

sloping line of the engine cowling providing improved visibility from the cockpit.

Eight pre-production aircraft were built with the same DH.60T designation, but bearing the name **Tiger Moth**. These aircraft were followed by a machine with increased lower wing dihedral and sweep, and this **DH.82 Tiger Moth** first flew on 26 October 1931. An order for 35 was placed to Specification T.23/31, and first deliveries of what was later the **Tiger Moth Mk I** were made to the RAF's No. 3 FTS in November 1931. Others went to the CFS in May 1932, and a team of five CFS pilots displayed their skill and the inverted flying capability of this new trainer at the 1932 Hendon display. Similar machines were supplied to the air forces of Brazil, Denmark, Persia, Portugal and Sweden. Two additional aircraft, with twin floats supplied by Short Brothers, were built to specification T.6/33 for RAF evaluation.

De Havilland then developed an improved version with the 130-hp (97-kW) Gipsy Major I engine and plywood- rather than fabric-covered rear fuselage

decking, and this **DH.82A** was named as the **Tiger Moth Mk II** by the RAF, which ordered 50 such aircraft to Specification T.26/33. The Tiger Moth Mk II had a hood which could be positioned over the rear cockpit for instrument flying instruction, and the first such aircraft were delivered to Kenley between November 1934 and January 1935. Others were supplied to the Bristol Aeroplane Company, the de Havilland School of Flying, Brooklands Aviation Ltd, Phillips and Powis School of Flying, Reid and Sigrist Ltd, Airwork Ltd and Scottish Aviation Ltd for use at the Elementary and Reserve Flying Schools which these companies operated under the RAF expansion scheme. No fewer than 44 such schools were in operation by August 1939, although 20 of them closed when hostilities began.

Licensed manufacture of the Tiger Moth before World War II included aircraft built in Norway, Portugal and Sweden, and by de Havilland Aircraft of Canada, whose pre-war output included 227 DH.82As. The company later built 1,520 of the

This Tiger Moth Mk II formation hailed from the Oxford University Air Squadron and was photographed in 1947.

DH.82C winterised version with the 145-hp (108-kW) Gipsy Major IC engine with a revised cowling, sliding cockpit canopies, cockpit heating, wheel brakes and a tailwheel in place of the standard skid. Skis or floats could be fitted if required, and some examples were powered by the 160-hp

(119-kW) Menasco Pirate D.4 engine when supplies of the Gipsy Major engine were exceeded by airframe production. A batch of 200 DH.82Cs was ordered by the USAAF with the designation **PT-24**, although these machines were diverted for use by the RCAF.

de Havilland DH.82 Tiger Moth (continued)

The outbreak of World War II saw civil machines impressed for RAF communications and training duties, and larger orders were placed for RAF service. A further 795 aircraft were built at Hatfield before the factory was turned over to production of the Mosquito, whereupon the Tiger Moth line was re-established at the Cowley works of Morris Motors Ltd, where some 3,500 machines were manufactured. De Havilland Aircraft of New Zealand built a further 345, and in Australia de Havilland Aircraft Pty produced a total of 1,085.

On 17 September 1939, just two weeks after war had been declared, 'A' Flight of the British Expeditionary Force Communications Squadron (later No. 81 Squadron) was despatched to France. Throughout the winter and the following spring, the unit's Tiger Moths operated in northern France, providing a valuable communications capability until the Dunkirk evacuation of June 1940, when surviving aircraft were flown back to England.

Preparations were also made for the Tiger Moth to be used in an offensive role, to combat the threatened German invasion. Racks designed to carry eight 20-lb (9.1-kg) bombs were fitted under the rear cockpit or, more suitably, beneath the lower wing. Although some 1,500 sets of racks were made and distributed to the flying schools, none was used operationally. Rather earlier, in December 1939, six

coastal patrol squadrons had been formed, five of them equipped with the Tiger Moth. However futile this may seem, it was considered that, despite an inability to attack, the sound of any engine might deter a U-boat commander from running on the surface and thus reduce his capacity to attack shipping. In the Far East a small number of Tiger Moths was converted for use as ambulance aircraft, the luggage locker lid being enlarged and a hinged lid cut into the rear fuselage decking, providing a compartment some 6 ft (1.83 m) long which could accommodate one casualty.

It was in the wartime trainer role, however, that the Tiger Moth made its greatest contribution. The type equipped no fewer than 28 Elementary Flying Training Schools in the UK, 25 in Canada (plus four Wireless Schools), 12 in Australia, four in Rhodesia (plus a Flying Instructors' School), seven in South Africa, and two in India.

Mention should also be made of the **DH.82B Queen Bee** radio-controlled target aircraft, which was essentially a version of the Tiger Moth with a basic structure of wood: it had the Moth Major fuselage, Tiger Moth wings, Gipsy Major engine, a wind-driven generator to provide electrical power, and a larger-capacity fuel tank. The prototype was flown manually on 5 January 1935, and 380 were then built for service use.

More than 8,000 Tiger Moths had been built by the end of World War II and large numbers were released onto the civil market as war-surplus stock. The RAF transferred many for civil and military

use to Belgium, France and the Netherlands, but in the UK and elsewhere they became available in quantity on the civil market. In addition to obvious use as trainers, or for sport and pleasure, they found unexpected employment. Many gave valuable service in the agricultural duster/sprayer role, a task which proved to be of great importance to New Zealand. A number of aircraft were the subject of conversion schemes, usually to provide enclosed accommodation. The most ambitious was

that carried out by the British company Jackaroo Aircraft Ltd, which involved widening the fuselage to seat four passengers in side-by-side pairs. Open-cockpit and enclosed-cabin variants were included in the 19 **Thruxton Jackaroo** conversions completed in the period 1957-9. It was once said that the initials DH. stood for 'Durable and Hefficient', and this is particularly true of the Tiger Moth. In the late 1990s moderately large numbers remained in use worldwide.

This colourful Swedish air force DH.82A is preserved in airworthy condition at the Air Force Museum at Malmen. Sweden built three DH.82s and 20 DH.82As under licence.

Note the anti-spin strakes fitted ahead of the tailfin of this preserved Tiger Moth. Many civilian operators removed these RAF-specified modifications post-war.

SPECIFICATION	
de Havilland DH.82C Tiger Moth	(145 km/h) at optimum altitude; initial climb rate 750 ft (229 m) per minute; service ceiling 14,600 ft (4450 m); range 275 miles (443 km)
Type: two-seat training and sporting aircraft	**Weights:** empty 1,115 lb (506 kg); maximum take-off 1,825 lb (828 kg)
Powerplant: one de Havilland Gipsy Major IC inline piston engine rated at 145 hp (108 kW)	**Dimensions:** wingspan 29 ft 4 in (8.94 m); length 23 ft 11 in (7.29 m); height 8 ft 10 in (2.69 m); wing area 239.00 sq ft (22.20 m²)
Performance: maximum speed 107 mph (172 km/h) at optimum altitude; cruising speed 90 mph	

de Havilland DH.83 Fox Moth

In 1932 de Havilland's chief designer, A. E. Hagg, evolved the **DH.83 Fox Moth** to meet a perceived need for a light transport aircraft offering good performance in combination with low purchase cost and economical operation. To standard Tiger Moth components (including the wings, tail unit, landing gear and engine mounting) he added a new plywood-covered

wooden fuselage carrying the pilot in an open cockpit above and behind an enclosed cabin which accommodated three passengers. The prototype, powered by a 120-hp (90-kW) Gipsy III engine, first flew on 29 January 1932. This machine was later shipped to Canada for trials on floats and skis, undertaken in service with Canadian Airways Ltd. The

success of these trials can be deduced from the fact that eight of the 98 British-built Fox Moths were exported to Canada between 1932 and 1935, and two more examples

Both the unusual position of the pilot and the DH.83's similarity to the Tiger Moth are clearly evident in this view of the preserved Fox Moth G-ACEJ.

were built by de Havilland Aircraft of Australia.

Many of these aircraft were powered by the Gipsy Major engine and some had a sliding hood over the cockpit. A single Japanese-built copy, powered by a 150-hp (112-kW) radial engine and

known as the **Chidorigo**, was flown by the Japanese Aerial Transport Company. After the end of World War II, de Havilland Canada built 52 examples of the **DH.83C**, which had a number of small improvements including a trim tab on the elevators,

an enlarged clear-view hood over the cockpit and the uprated powerplant of one 145-hp (108-kW) Gipsy Major IC engine. Another example of the DH.83C (there were no **DH.83A** or **DH.83B** variants) was completed by Leavens Bros Ltd in 1948.

SPECIFICATION	
de Havilland DH.83 Fox Moth **Type:** one-crew light transport **Powerplant:** one de Havilland Gipsy Major inverted inline piston engine rated at 130 hp (97 kW) **Performance:** maximum speed 113 mph (182 km/h) at optimum altitude; cruising speed 96 mph (154 km/h) at optimum altitude; initial climb rate 605 ft (184 m) per	minute; service ceiling 12,700 ft (3870 m); range 360 miles (579 km) **Weights:** empty 1,100 lb (499 kg); maximum take-off 2,070 lb (939 kg) **Dimensions:** wingspan 30 ft 10⅞ in (9.41 m); length 25 ft 9 in (7.85 m); height 8 ft 9½ in (2.68 m); wing area 261.00 sq ft (24.25 m²) **Payload:** up to three passengers carried in an enclosed cabin

de Havilland DH.84 Dragon

The **DH.84 Dragon** was designed in response to the request of Edward Hillman, head of Hillmans Airways Ltd that already operated the DH.83 Fox Moth, for a twin-engined aircraft to be used on a proposed service linking southern England and Paris. The type of slab-sided plywood box used successfully in the Fox Moth was adopted for the fuselage of the new design, a two-bay biplane with wings that could be folded outboard of the two

Gipsy Major engines. The pilot was provided with a separate compartment in the extreme nose, and the main cabin could seat six passengers. The prototype made its maiden flight on 12 November 1932, and was later delivered to Hillmans Airways at Maylands, Essex together with three examples of the **Dragon Mk 1** production model, whose availability facilitated inauguration of the Paris route in April 1933. British production totalled 115 aircraft built at

Stag Lane and, from 1934, at de Havilland's new facility at Hatfield. A further 87 were built in Australia during World War II, the de Havilland Australian factory at Bankstown, Sydney producing these aircraft as radio and navigation trainers for the RAAF; the first of these Australian-built aircraft flew on 29 September 1942.

Variants

Dragon Mk 2: the 63rd aircraft was the first of an improved version with the glasshouse cabin windows replaced by individual framed transparencies, and with main landing gear fairings

DH.84M Dragon: militarised version with a dorsal fin fillet and armament in the form of two machine-guns (one in the nose and the other on a dorsal gun ring) and up to 16 20-lb (9.1-kg) bombs; the type was supplied to Denmark, Iraq and Portugal to the extent of two, eight and three aircraft respectively

Wearing the blue and white colours of Hillmans Airways, G-ACAN, the prototype Dragon, was delivered for service on 24 November 1932. With its luggage compartment removed, the type could seat eight passengers.

SPECIFICATION	
de Havilland DH.84 Dragon Mk 2 **Type:** one-crew medium transport aircraft **Powerplant:** two de Havilland Gipsy Major I inverted inline piston engines each rated at 130 hp (97 kW) **Performance:** maximum speed 134 mph (216 km/h) at optimum altitude; cruising speed 114 mph (183 km/h) at optimum altitude;	initial climb rate 565 ft (172 m) per minute; service ceiling 14,500 ft (4420 m); range 545 miles (877 km) **Weights:** empty 2,336 lb (1060 kg); maximum take-off 4,500 lb (2041 kg) **Dimensions:** wingspan 47 ft 4 in (14.43 m); length 34 ft 6 in (10.52 m); height 10 ft 1 in (3.07 m); wing area 376.00 sq ft (34.93 m²) **Payload:** up to eight passengers

de Havilland DH.85 Leopard Moth

Introduced in 1933 as a successor to the DH.83 Puss Moth, the **DH.85 Leopard Moth** bore a superficial resemblance to the earlier type but incorporated a number of major changes, not least of which was a revised fuselage

construction. The steel-tube structure of the Puss Moth was replaced by the spruce and plywood box which was becoming a standard de Havilland feature, and this provided accommodation for the pilot and two passengers,

the latter seated side-by-side in the rear of the cabin. The prototype made its first flight on 27 May 1933 at Stag Lane, and just two weeks later won that year's King's Cup air race at Hatfield, two similar aircraft finishing third and sixth.

Variant

DH.85A Leopard Moth: designation of the prototype after revision as a testbed for the 230-hp (172-kW) de Havilland Gipsy Six R engine driving a variable-pitch propeller

This auspicious start ensured commercial success, and three years'

production, initially at Stag Lane and then at Hatfield, totalled 132 examples.

Other changes introduced in the de Havilland DH.85 Leopard Moth, compared to the DH.83 Puss Moth, included a new tapered and foldable wing with swept leading edges and relocated upper attachment points for the main landing-gear units' shock-absorbers.

SPECIFICATION	
de Havilland DH.85 Leopard Moth **Type:** three-seat touring and sporting aircraft **Powerplant:** one de Havilland Gipsy Major inverted inline piston engine rated at 130 hp (97 kW) **Performance:** maximum speed 137 mph (220 km/h) at optimum altitude; cruising speed 119 mph (192 km/h) at optimum altitude;	initial climb rate 550 ft (168 m) per minute; service ceiling 21,500 ft (6555 m); range 715 miles (1151 km) **Weights:** empty 1,405 lb (637 kg); maximum take-off 2,225 lb (1009 kg) **Dimensions:** wingspan 37 ft 6 in (11.43 m); length 24 ft 6 in (7.47 m); height 8 ft 9 in (2.67 m); wing area 206.00 sq ft (19.14 m²)

de Havilland DH.86

Designed and built in response to an Australian government requirement for a multi-engined aircraft to be used by QANTAS for service across the Timor Sea between Singapore and Australia, the **DH.86** was awarded its certificate

of airworthiness on 30 January 1934, only four months after work had commenced on the project. The aircraft was of wooden construction with fabric covering, and was a two-bay biplane with elegant tapered wings

and fixed tailskid landing gear, including main units that extended below the inboard engine nacelles in long-chord fairings.

The DH.86's four Gipsy Six engines were housed in nacelles along the leading edge of the lower wing.

de Havilland DH.86 (continued)

The DH.86 recorded its first flight on 14 January 1934, and the prototype and two identical aircraft were

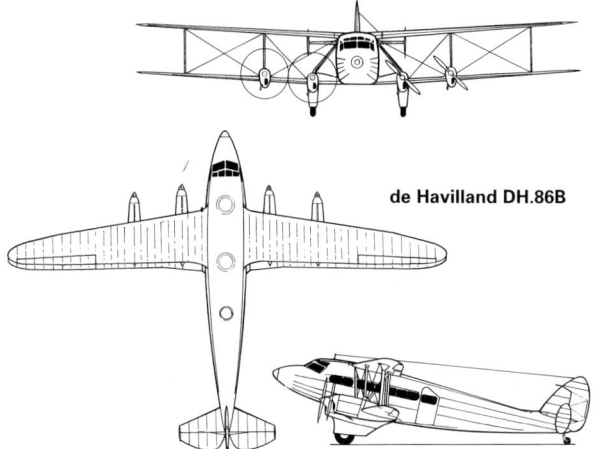

de Havilland DH.86B

equipped for single-pilot operation. The latter were used by Railway Air Services from 21 August

1934 on a new route linking Croydon with Glasgow via Birmingham, Manchester and Belfast. A second crew member (navigator/wireless operator) was carried behind the pilot.

QANTAS and Imperial Airways required that two pilots should be seated side-by-side, however, and in August 1934 the prototype re-emerged from the Stag Lane factory with a longer and wider nose to provide the necessary accommodation.

The first of 29 production examples was one of four flown by Holyman Airways in Australia, and other operators comprised QANTAS (six), Imperial Airways (five), Jersey Airways (six), Misr Airwork of Egypt (four), Hillmans Airways (three) and Wrightways (one).

Variants

DH.86A: introduced late in 1935, this version featured a modified windscreen, metal rudder, pneumatic landing-gear legs, larger brakes and a tailwheel; 20 were built, most of them being converted to DH.86B standard in 1937; production included four RAF aircraft in the form of two for the RAF Radio School at Cranwell and two for No. 24 Squadron at Hendon; others were impressed for service in World War II
DH.86B: conversion from DH.86A standard with auxiliary endplate finlets, fitted following an accident in September 1936 which resulted in an investigation at Martlesham Heath and a subsequent report criticising rudder and aileron control; newly-built DH.86Bs also had tailplanes with increased chord at the tips and higher gearing in the aileron circuit

de Havilland DH.87 Hornet Moth

For devotees of the biplane configuration with the desire for the comfort that could be provided only by cabin accommodation, the company designed the **DH.87 Hornet Moth** as an enclosed side-by-side two-seater, structurally similar to the DH.86. It had a single-bay biplane wing cellule with fabric-covered wooden wings of tapered planform, a spruce/plywood box fuselage with external longerons, stringers and fabric cover-

ing, and fixed tailwheel landing gear with divided main units. The prototype, first flown at Hatfield on 9 May 1934, was joined in a year-long test programme by two similar aircraft, preparing for production deliveries that began in August 1935 under the revised designation **DH.87A Leopard Moth**. Rather more than 60 aircraft were manufactured to this standard with a new wing cellule of increased taper and span, but in 1936

Another vintage de Havilland aircraft to survive into the 1990s is the DH.87B Hornet Moth G-ADLY. The type offers two-seat accommodation.

yet another set of wings was introduced, first fitted retrospectively to the second production example of the Hornet Moth. These new mainplanes, virtually without taper and with almost square tips, were made available to existing owners on a trade-in basis and were also fitted to

virtually 100 new aircraft, which had the designation **DH.87B Leopard Moth**. Following development of a floatplane version by de Havilland Aircraft of Canada, four examples

were acquired by the Air Ministry in 1937 for evaluation as seaplane trainers. Hornet Moth production, including the prototype, came to a total of 165 aircraft.

de Havilland DH.88 Comet

Designed specifically for the 1934 Victorian Centenary Air Race from Mildenhall to Melbourne in southern Australia, for which the prize money was donated by Sir MacPherson Robertson, the **DH.88 Comet** attracted three orders before the February 1934 deadline which had been stipulated by the manufacturer for guaranteed delivery before the race in October. The purchasers were Mr A. O. Edwards, managing director of the Grosvenor House Hotel, Bernard Rubin, and Jim and Amy Mollison. The Comet was

Grosvenor House *returned to the air briefly in the late 1980s, before being damaged in an accident. Housed in airworthy condition by the Shuttleworth Trust in 1999, the aircraft is likely to fly again when the Trust lengthens its presently inadequate runway.*

of wooden construction throughout, the front section of the fuselage containing three large fuel tanks, behind which was the tandem arrangement of two seats for the pilot and co-pilot. Two high-compres-

sion Gipsy Six R engines were installed, these units driving Ratier two-position propellers whose blades were set to fine pitch

before each take-off; the blades went into coarse pitch automatically at 150 mph (241 km/h) when a sealing disc in the spinner

opened to release the unit's internal pressure and thus activate the control mechanism. Other notable features included tailskid landing gear whose main units could be manually retracted into the underside of the two engine nacelles, and split trailing-edge flaps.

Hubert Broad flew the first Comet, that intended for the Mollisons, at Hatfield on 8 September 1934. The machine's certificate of airworthiness was issued on 9 October and certificates for the other two aircraft on 12 October, just eight days before the race. Dawn on 20 October saw the departure of the first contestants of the

MacRobertson race, including the Mollisons' *Black Magic*, Owen Cathcart-Jones' and Ken Waller's G-ACSR (owned by Rubin), and C. W. A. Scott and T. Campbell Black's *Grosvenor House*. *Black Magic* successfully completed the non-stop leg between London and Baghdad, but was forced to retire with engine trouble at Allahabad. Cathcart-Jones and Waller, after getting lost and being forced to land in Persia, struggled through to Melbourne to

finish fourth in the speed section before flying straight back, with mail and film, to set an out-and-return record of 13½ days. Scott and Black were the speed section winners, covering the course in 70 hours 51 minutes: *Grosvenor House* is now preserved by the Shuttleworth Trust at Old Warden, Bedfordshire.

Two more Comets were built, one as a mailplane for the French government and the other for Mr Cyril Nicholson, who sponsored

two unsuccessful attempts on the record between London and Cape Town. During the second

attempt the crew bailed out over Sudan on 22 September 1935, and the aircraft was lost.

SPECIFICATION	
de Havilland DH.88 Comet	initial climb rate 900 ft (274 m) per minute; service ceiling 19,000 ft (5790 m); range 2,925 miles (4707 km)
Type: two-seat racing aircraft and mailplane	
Powerplant: two de Havilland Gipsy Six R inverted inline piston engines each rated at 230 hp (172 kW)	**Weights:** empty 2,840 lb (1288 kg); maximum take-off 5,320 lb (2413 kg)
Performance: maximum speed 237 mph (381 km/h) at optimum altitude; cruising speed 220 mph (354 km/h) at optimum altitude;	**Dimensions:** wingspan 44 ft (13.41 m); length 29 ft (8.84 m); height 10 ft (3.05 m); wing area 212.00 sq ft (19.69 m²)

de Havilland DH.89 Dragon Rapide and Dominie

Designed in the light of experience gained from production and operation of the DH.84 Dragon and DH.86 light transports, the **DH.89 Dragon Six**, powered by two 200-hp (149-kW) Gipsy Six engines, first flew in prototype form at Stag Lane on 17 April 1934. Production aircraft, which had the revised name **Dragon Rapide**, were delivered from July 1934, the first customers including Hillmans Airways, Railway Air Services and Olley Air Service. From March 1937 small flaps were fitted to the trailing edges of the lower wing, outboard of the engine nacelles, the type then being redesignated **DH.89A**. Civil examples of the Dragon Rapide were soon in large-scale use with operators around the world, some even entering service in Canada on floats and skis. The reliability and economy of the type generated significant sales for the mid- and late 1930s, and by the outbreak of World War II in 1939 almost 200 had been delivered to civil operators.

A **DH.89M** militarised version was developed to meet the Air Ministry's G.18/35 specification for a general reconnaissance aircraft to be operated by the RAF's Coastal Command. A fixed forward-firing machine-gun was mounted in the nose, to the right of the pilot's seat, and a ring mounting for a trainable machine-gun was installed in the roof, aft of the cabin door. The Air Ministry's large-scale production contract was awarded to the more advanced Avro Anson, but two examples of the DH.89M were built for Lithuania and three more aircraft with additional modifications were delivered to the Spanish government for counter-insurgency service in Morocco. The latter aircraft had additional armament in the form of an extra ventral gun to fire downward through the floor, plus an underfuselage rack for 12 26½-lb (12-kg) bombs.

Although the DH.89M did not gain an Air Ministry contract as a coastal reconnaissance aircraft, the

Dragon Rapide was selected as a communications aircraft, the first being purchased for use by the Air Council and operated by No. 24 Squadron at Hendon. Civil examples of the Dragon Rapide were used to supply British forces in France in the spring and early summer of 1940, and many were impressed for communications duties, particularly with the Air Transport Auxiliary. In 1939, three DH.89s had been acquired as wireless trainers to the Air Ministry's T.29/38 specification, and these were followed by a further 14 for use by No. 2 Electrical and Wireless School. The first two of these DH.89As, also for No. 2 E&WS, were delivered in September 1939. The trainer version was identifiable by the direction-finding loop in the cabin roof, and was later designated as the **Dominie Mk I**, the communications version being the **Dominie Mk II**.

Of the 728 Dragon Rapides built before production ended in July 1946, 521 were to British military contracts, mostly under the designation **DH.89B**. Some 186 were built at Hatfield before pressure of work on other aircraft resulted in the transfer of production to Brush Coachworks Ltd at Loughborough, Leicestershire. The military

The classic lines of the Dragon Rapide have ensured its lasting popularity. This aircraft was photographed in South Africa, but several examples remain airworthy worldwide.

DH.89 figure includes 65 aircraft used by the Royal Navy, between 1940 and 1958, when the last was retired; some were impressed civil machines, some supplied new, and others transferred from the RAF. Soon after hostilities had ended in 1945, several hundred war-surplus Dominies were supplied to overseas air forces such as those of Belgium and the Netherlands, or were stripped of military equipment for sale to civil buyers. In this way the aircraft came to be used in

almost every country of the free world. Additionally, the last 100 production aircraft, built by Brush Coachworks, but undelivered because of the war's end, were finished to the requirements of civil operators by de Havilland's repair unit at Witney. They became the initial post-war equipment of operators including Iraqi Airways, Jersey Airways and KLM. At one period, during the 1950s, BEA operated a large fleet of Dragon Rapides on its services to the islands around the UK's coast.

This aircraft was the original DH.89M, delivered to specification G.18/35 for a coastal reconnaissance type. The machine was flown on test work at Farnborough between 1937 and 1938.

Variants

DH.89A Dragon Rapide Mk 4: conversion with Gipsy Queen 2 engines and constant-speed propellers; prototype conversion was made in 1953, and many aircraft were subsequently modified to this standard, which allowed an increased take-off weight and gave improved performance
DH.89A Dragon Rapide Mk 5: one-off conversion made by the company to one of its own communications aircraft, involving the installation of special Gipsy Queen 3 engines with manually operated variable-pitch propellers
DH.89A Dragon Rapide Mk 6: aircraft with standard engines but modified by addition of Fairey X5 fixed-pitch metal propellers

SPECIFICATION	
de Havilland DH.89A Dragon Rapide Mk 4	per minute; service ceiling 16,000 ft (4875 m); range 520 miles (837 km)
Type: one/two-crew light transport aircraft	**Weights:** empty 3,230 lb (1465 kg); maximum take-off 6,000 lb (2722 kg)
Powerplant: two de Havilland Gipsy Queen 2 inverted inline piston engines each rated at 200 hp (149 kW)	**Dimensions:** wingspan 48 ft (14.63 m); length 34 ft 6 in (10.52 m); height 10 ft 3 in (3.12 m); wing area 336.00 sq ft (31.21 m²)
Performance: maximum speed 150 mph (241 km/h) at optimum altitude; cruising speed 140 mph (225 km/h) at optimum altitude; initial climb rate 1,200 ft (366 m)	**Payload:** up to eight passengers carried in an enclosed cabin

de Havilland DH.90 Dragonfly

The external similarity of the **DH.90 Dragonfly** to the DH.89 Dragon Rapide belied its very different internal structure, the earlier type's spruce and plywood box fuselage being replaced by a pre-formed plywood monocoque shell strengthened with spruce stringers. The centre section of the lower wing was strengthened, making possible deletion of the nacelle/wing root bracing struts and inner bay rigging wires, which facilitated access to a cabin that provided accommodation for a pilot and up to four passengers. Powered by two Gipsy Major engines, the prototype made its first flight at Hatfield on 12 August 1935 and the first **DH.90A** production aircraft, which introduced Gipsy Major II engines, flew in February 1936. Production totalled 66 aircraft and military buyers included Canada, Denmark and Sweden.

The DH.90 was initially popular with the prominent private owners of the time, both in the UK and abroad, but most were eventually used for commercial purposes.

SPECIFICATION

de Havilland DH.90A Dragonfly
Type: one-crew light transport aircraft
Powerplant: two de Havilland Gipsy Major II inverted inline piston engines each rated at 130 hp (97 kW)
Performance: maximum speed 144 mph (232 km/h) at optimum altitude; cruising speed 125 mph (201 km/h) at optimum altitude; initial climb rate 730 ft (223 m) per minute; service ceiling 18,100 ft (5515 m); range 625 miles (1006 km)
Weights: empty 2,487 lb (1128 kg); maximum take-off 4,000 lb (1814 kg)
Dimensions: wingspan 43 ft (13.11 m); length 31 ft 8 in (9.65 m); height 9 ft 2 in (2.79 m); wing area 256.00 sq ft (23.78 m²)
Payload: up to four passengers in an enclosed cabin

de Havilland DH.91 Albatross

Designed by A. E. Hagg to an Air Ministry specification for a transatlantic mailplane, the **DH.91 Albatross** was aerodynamically and aesthetically one of the outstanding commercial aircraft of the period immediately preceding the outbreak of World War II. Of wooden construction, the DH.91 introduced the ply/balsa/ply sandwich fuselage structure later used so successfully for the Mosquito, and had a one-piece wing similar to that of the DH.88. The powerplant consisted of four Gipsy Twelve engines driving constant-speed propellers, and the main units of the tailwheel landing gear were electrically retractable into wells in the underside of the inboard wing panels. The prototype, initially with twin fin-and-rudder units mounted at mid-span on the tailplane, flew for the first time at Hatfield on 20 May 1937. Flight test results indicated that the vertical tail surfaces were unsatisfactory, and the redesigned tail unit incorporated endplate fins with unbalanced rudders and trim tabs.

Problems with the landing gear retraction system resulted in a wheels-up landing for the first prototype on 31 March 1938, and a structural weakness in the rear fuselage was revealed when the second prototype broke into two a few months later when landing during overload trials. Effective modifications were soon evolved, and the two prototypes were repaired and used experimentally by Imperial Airways. Their 3,330-mile (5359-km) maximum range made them particularly useful for a shuttle service between the UK and Iceland, however, and the aircraft were impressed for RAF service by No. 271 Sqn from September 1940. Five Albatross aircraft, with reduced capacity, additional cabin windows and slotted flaps replacing the split trailing-edge flaps, were delivered to Imperial Airways between October 1938 and June 1939. Providing accommodation for 22 passengers as well as the crew of four, the machines saw wartime service on the routes linking Bristol in the west of England with Shannon in Ireland and Lisbon in Portugal. With numbers reduced to two by enemy action or accidents, the survivors were scrapped in September 1943.

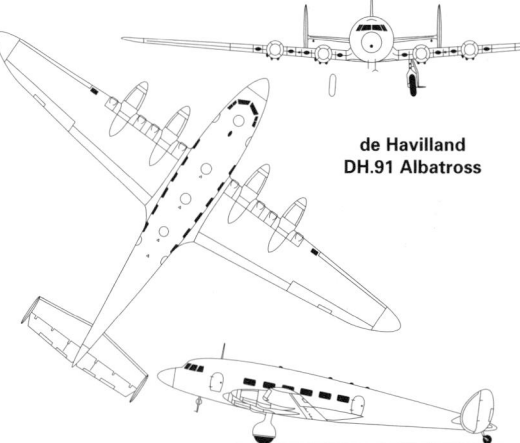

de Havilland
DH.91 Albatross

Fiona and Falcon were the last two remaining Albatross airliners. Tragically, both were broken up in the second half of 1943.

SPECIFICATION

de Havilland DH.91 Albatross (passenger version)
Type: four-crew long-range transport aircraft
Powerplant: four de Havilland Gipsy Twelve 1 inverted-Vee piston engines each rated at 525 hp (391 kW)
Performance: maximum speed 225 mph (362 km/h) at optimum altitude; cruising speed 210 mph (338 km/h) at optimum altitude; initial climb rate 700 ft (213 m) per minute; service ceiling 17,900 ft (5455 m); range (with passengers) 1,040 miles (1674 km)
Weights: empty 21,230 lb (9630 kg); maximum take-off 29,500 lb (13381 kg)
Dimensions: wingspan 105 ft (32.00 m); length 71 ft 6 in (21.79 m); height 22 ft 3 in (6.78 m); wing area 1,078.00 sq ft (100.15 m²)
Payload: up to 22 passengers in an enclosed cabin

de Havilland DH.93 Don

The de Havilland Gipsy Twelve inverted-Vee engine, originally used in the DH.91, was renamed as the Gipsy King for military use and was selected to power a multi-role trainer designed to the Air Ministry's Specification T.6/36. This **DH.93 Don** was a low-wing cantilever monoplane of wooden stressed-skin construction with enclosed accommo-dation and tailwheel landing gear including retractable main units. It was intended for use as a pilot, radio and gunnery trainer. The prototype made its first flight on 18 June 1937, and follow-ing manufacturer's initial trials, in the course of which small auxiliary fins were fitted beneath the tailplane, the aircraft was transferred to Martlesham Heath for official evalua-tion. The modifications that were then required led to an increase in weight, and as a result heavy equipment (includ-ing the Armstrong Whitworth turret) had to be removed. Of the origi-nal order for 250 Dons only 50 airframes were completed: of this total 20 were delivered as engine-less airframes and the remainder were converted for communications duties with No. 24 Squadron and a number of station flights.

L2391 was the fifth Don completed. The small auxiliary fins added beneath the tailplane are just visible in this photograph.

SPECIFICATION

de Havilland DH.93 Don
Type: one/two-crew communications aircraft
Powerplant: one de Havilland Gipsy King I inverted-Vee piston engine rated at 525 hp (391 kW)
Performance: maximum speed 189 mph (304 km/h) at 8,750 ft (2665 m); initial climb rate 820 ft (250 m) per minute; service ceiling 23,300 ft (7100 m); range 890 miles (1432 km)
Weights: empty 5,050 lb (2291 kg); maximum take-off 6,860 lb (3112 kg)
Dimensions: wingspan 47 ft 6 in (14.48 m); length 37 ft 4 in (11.38 m); height 9 ft 5 in (2.87 m); wing area 304.00 sq ft (28.24 m²)
Payload: up to three passengers

de Havilland DH.94 Moth Minor

The inherent stability of the Moth Minor is clearly demonstrated in this illustration, where both crew members have their hands off the controls.

On 24 August 1931 the company had flown the only example of the **DH.81 Swallow Moth**, a low-wing open-cockpit two-seater powered by an 80-hp (60-kW) Gipsy IV engine. With production capacity filled by orders for various models of the Moth, the project was then discontinued, to be resurrected some years later when advantage could be taken of some structural techniques used in the DH.88 and Albatross. Of wooden construction throughout, the prototype of the resulting **DH.94 Moth Minor** first flew at Hatfield on 22 June 1937. Production followed, and by the outbreak of World War II in 1939 some 71 examples had been completed, including nine examples of the **Moth Minor Coupé** variant with a built-up rear fuselage and hinged cabin top. Early in 1940, when Hatfield's production capacity was required urgently for aircraft more vital to the war effort, the Moth Minor's drawings, jigs, components and finished but undelivered airframes were delivered to de Havilland Aircraft Pty Ltd at Bankstown, Sydney, and more than 40 aircraft were then supplied to the RAAF.

SPECIFICATION

de Havilland DH.94 Moth Minor
Type: two-seat touring and training aircraft
Powerplant: one de Havilland Gipsy Minor inverted inline piston engine rated at 90 hp (67 kW)
Performance: maximum speed 118 mph (190 km/h) at optimum altitude; cruising speed 100 mph (161 km/h) at optimum altitude; initial climb rate 590 ft (180 m) per minute; service ceiling 16,500 ft (5030 m); range 300 miles (483 km)
Weights: empty 983 lb (446 kg); maximum take-off 1,550 lb (703 kg)
Dimensions: wingspan 36 ft 7 in (11.15 m); length 24 ft 5 in (7.44 m); height 6 ft 4 in (1.93 m); wing area 162.00 sq ft (15.05 m²)

de Havilland DH.95 Flamingo

The company's first aircraft of all-metal stressed-skin construction, the **de Havilland DH.95 Flamingo** was designed by R. E. Bishop as a medium-range transport to carry between 12 and 17 passengers as well as a crew of three. The DH.95 featured hydraulically retractable landing gear and split trailing-edge flaps, and was powered initially by two 890-hp (664-kW) Bristol Perseus XIIC radial engines. The prototype was first flown by de Havilland's chief test pilot, Geoffrey de Havilland Jr, at Hatfield on 28 December 1938, and during subsequent testing a centreline third fin was fitted temporarily to complement the original pair of endplate vertical tail surfaces. In May 1939 this aircraft was delivered to Guernsey & Jersey Airways Ltd for route-proving trials, linking Heston and Southampton's Eastleigh Airport with the two main Channel Islands.

The outbreak of World War II in 1939 precluded full commercial operation but the Royal Air Force had ordered three Flamingos (two for communications duties with No. 24 Squadron and one for The King's Flight), the last of these being delivered at Benson on 7 September 1940. This machine was transferred from The King's Flight to No. 24 Squadron in February 1941, the unit also having acquired the prototype, two aircraft ordered by civilian customers and the fifth airframe which had been used by the manufacturer for development with the Bristol Perseus XVI radial. This engine was fitted to all subsequent examples, including one used by the Royal Navy's No. 782 Squadron at Donibristle for communications flights to the Orkney and Shetland Islands and to Northern Ireland, and eight flown by BOAC on Middle East services, based at Cairo. The Royal Navy's Flamingo was the only aircraft to return to civil use after World War II, seeing limited service with British Air Transport at Redhill, where it was scrapped in 1954. Flamingo production totalled 16 aircraft.

Variant

Hertfordshire: this was to have been a fully militarised version to Specification 19/39 for the carriage of up to 22 paratroops; only the prototype was completed (becoming one of the aircraft used by No. 24 Squadron) and a production order for 40 was subsequently cancelled

Guernsey and Jersey Airways Ltd used the Flamingo prototype for route-proving, but never used the type on scheduled services.

SPECIFICATION

de Havilland DH.95 Flamingo
Type: three-crew medium transport
Powerplant: two Bristol Perseus XVI radial piston engines each rated at 930 hp (694 kW)
Performance: maximum speed 239 mph (385 km/h) at optimum altitude; cruising speed 184 mph (296 km/h) at optimum altitude; initial climb rate 1,470 ft (448 m) per minute; service ceiling 20,900 ft (6370 m); range 1,210 miles (1947 km)
Weights: empty 11,325 lb (5137 kg); maximum take-off 17,600 lb (7983 kg)
Dimensions: wingspan 70 ft (21.34 m); length 51 ft 7 in (15.72 m); height 15 ft 3 in (4.65 m); wing area 639.00 sq ft (59.36 m²)
Payload: up to 20 passengers carried in an enclosed cabin

de Havilland DH.98 Mosquito

Planned and designed as a private venture in the autumn of 1938, the **DH.98 Mosquito** was schemed as an unarmed bomber and reconnaissance aircraft, one that would fly so fast and so high that defensive armament would be superfluous. The powerplant was to comprise two Rolls-Royce Merlin engines, and to save on the use of strategic materials all-wood construction was chosen. This combination of features represented too many imponderables, and the Air Ministry filed de Havilland's proposal in the 'pending' tray. It was not until World War II had started in 1939 that the Air Ministry finally gave serious thought to the possibility that light alloys might come into short supply. In such circumstances an all-wood warplane might be a useful ace up the sleeve. Even then, the committal to proceed was only to the extent of authorising detail design, and de Havilland's design team began work at the end of December 1939, resulting in an order on 1 March 1940 for 50 aircraft against the Air Ministry's B.1/40 specification. However, in the bleak days after the evacuation from Dunkirk in mid-1940 it was decided to concentrate industrial effort on the manufacture of a few existing combat aircraft types, and de Havilland's new bomber was temporarily postponed.

Photo-reconnaissance was always a primary Mosquito role. This No. 140 Sqn PR.Mk XVI was based at Melsbroek, Belgium during the last seven months of war.

de Havilland Mosquito B.Mk 35

de Havilland DH.98 Mosquito (continued)

In due course the Mosquito programme was reinstated and eventually, on 25 November 1940, the prototype **Mosquito Mk I** was flown for the first time with the powerplant of two 1,460-hp (1089-kW) Merlin 21 engines. There was little doubt from factory testing that this new bomber was capable of development into an outstanding aircraft, comfortably exceeding the performance margins of the specification. When demonstrated to military and government officials shortly afterwards, these sceptical functionaries discovered that the new

bomber had the agility of a fighter as well as a dashing high speed that was not far short of 400 mph (644 km/h), and were also staggered to see the prototype performing smooth climbing rolls on the power of one engine, the propeller of the second engine 'feathered' to prevent windmilling and to cut drag to a minimum.

Official trials followed immediately, beginning on 19 February 1941 and leading to the initiation of priority production by July of that year. Three prototypes were built and the last of these to fly, on

This Mosquito TR.Mk 33 flew with 771 Sqn, FAA at Lee-on-Solent in 1947. The variant was fully navalised.

10 June 1941, was of the photo-reconnaissance (PR) version that was the first of these new aircraft to enter operational service. The initial sortie, a daylight reconnaissance over Brest, La Pallice and Bordeaux, was made on

20 September 1941, and immediately confirmed the concept of high speed and no armament as being correct, for during this initial deployment the lone **Mosquito PR.Mk I** was easily able to outpace three Messerschmitt Bf 109 fighters which attempted to intercept.

Next into service was the bomber version, the first being designated **Mosquito B.Mk IV** and powered by Merlin 21 or later Merlin 23 engines. Production totalled 273 aircraft, and deliveries to the RAF's No. 2 Group began in November 1941, the Mosquito bombers

going first to No. 105 Squadron at Swanton Morley, Norfolk. The winter months were spent in familiarisation and working up, for the Mosquito was a warplane very different from the Bristol Blenheim which it was replacing. This pioneering squadron had not only to learn how to handle a very much faster and more manoeuvrable aircraft, but also how best to deploy it in its offensive role. At that time there must have been some doubt among the crews that were to fly these aircraft of just how this 'plywood' bomber would withstand combat, but the

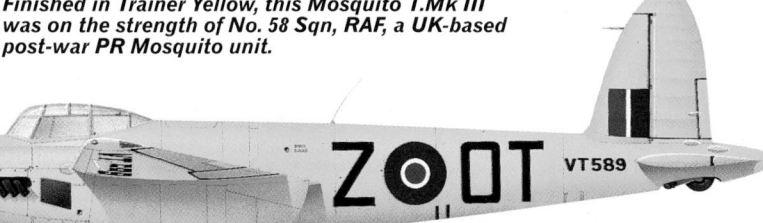

Finished in Trainer Yellow, this Mosquito T.Mk III was on the strength of No. 58 Sqn, RAF, a UK-based post-war PR Mosquito unit.

Variants

Mosquito PR.Mk IV: reconnaissance conversion from B.Mk IV standard with provision for up to four cameras (32 conversions)
Mosquito B.Mk V: prototype development of B.Mk IV with underwing hardpoints (one built)
Mosquito FB.Mk VI: most extensively built version. A fighter-bomber/intruder developed from the F.Mk II fighter prototype with provision for internal and underwing bombs and, from 1944, rocket projectiles; the powerplant was two 1,460-hp (1089-kW) Merlin 21 or 23 engines, or two 1,635-hp (1219-kW) Merlin 25 engines (2,718 built)
Mosquito B.Mk VII: Canadian-built version based on the B.Mk V with 1,418-hp (1057-kW) Packard-built Merlin 31 engines (25 built)
Mosquito PR.Mk VIII: reconnaissance version similar to the PR.Mk IV but powered by Merlin 61 engines with two-stage superchargers (five aircraft)
Mosquito B.Mk IX: high-altitude bomber equivalent of PR.Mk IX, some being modified from 1944 with provision to carry one 4,000-lb (1814-kg) HC bomb of the type also carried by 54 B.Mk IV conversions; the aircraft were powered by 1,680-hp (1253-kW) Merlin 72 engines (54 built)
Mosquito PR.Mk IX: reconnaissance version based on the B.Mk IX with 1,680-hp (1253-kW) Merlin 72 engines fitted with two-stage superchargers and increased fuel capacity (90 built)
Mosquito FB.Mk X: unbuilt fighter-bomber variant
Mosquito NF.Mk X: unbuilt night-fighter variant with two-stage engines
Mosquito FB.Mk XI: unbuilt fighter-bomber variant with two-stage engines
Mosquito NF.Mk XII: redesignation of NF.Mk II conversions following installation of AI.Mk VIII centimetric radar (97 conversions)
Mosquito NF.Mk XIII: new production night-fighters, equivalent to the NF.Mk XII but with a modified wing and greater fuel capacity (270 built)
Mosquito NF.Mk XIV: unbuilt NF.Mk XIII variant with two-stage engines
Mosquito NF.Mk XV: high-altitude night-fighter with increased wingspan, pressure cabin, AI.Mk VIII radar, a four-gun ventral pack, and two-stage engines (five B.Mk IV conversions)
Mosquito B.Mk XVI: B.Mk IX development with pressurised cabin and most with provision to carry a 4,000-lb (1814-kg) bomb; the powerplant was two 1,680-hp (1253-kW) Merlin 72 engines (1,200 built)
Mosquito PR.Mk XVI: reconnaissance variant of the B.Mk XVI, introducing a small astrodome; first pressurised PR version (432 built)
Mosquito NF.Mk XVII: redesignation of NF.Mk II conversions following installation of American-developed AI.Mk X radar (100 conversions)
Mosquito FB.Mk XVIII: development of the FB.Mk VI with 1,635-hp (1219-kW) Merlin 25 engines, a 57-mm Molins anti-tank gun in the forward fuselage (in place of the cannon), rocket projectiles and increased armour protection; used primarily for attacks on U-boats and shipping (25 built)

Mosquito NF.Mk XIX: night-fighter development of NF.Mk XIII with 'universal' nose to accept American or British AI radar (220 built)
Mosquito B.Mk XX: Canadian-built bomber equivalent of the B.Mk IV with American equipment (145 built, of which 40 were converted to **F-8** photo-reconnaissance standard for the USAAF)
Mosquito FB.Mk 21: Canadian-built equivalent of the FB.Mk VI with 1,460-hp (1089-kW) Merlin 31 engines (three built)
Mosquito T.Mk 22: Canadian-built equivalent of the T.Mk III
Mosquito B.Mk 23: unbuilt Canadian equivalent of the B.Mk IX
Mosquito FB.Mk 24: Canadian-built fighter-bomber with 1,620-hp (1208-kW) Merlin 301 engines with two-stage superchargers (two built)
Mosquito B.Mk 25: Canadian-built development of B.Mk XX with 1,620-hp (1208-kW) Packard Merlin 225 engines (400 built)
Mosquito FB.Mk 26: Canadian-built development of FB.Mk 21 with 1,620-hp (1208-kW) Packard Merlin 225 engines (338 built)
Mosquito T.Mk 27: Canadian-built development of T.Mk 22 with Packard Merlin engines
Mosquito T.Mk 29: trainers converted from FB.Mk 26 standard
Mosquito NF.Mk 30: high-altitude night-fighter with 1,710-hp (1275-kW) Merlin 76 engines with two-stage superchargers, and carrying some early ECM equipment (526 built)
Mosquito NF.Mk 31: unbuilt NF.Mk 30 variant with Packard Merlin engines
Mosquito PR.Mk 32: high-altitude reconnaissance version similar to NF.Mk XV with a lightened airframe and two 1,690-hp (1260-kW) Merlin 113 engines (five conversions)
Mosquito TR.Mk 33: naval torpedo-reconnaissance fighter (**Sea Mosquito**) for carrier-based operations; similar to FB.Mk VI but including folding wings, arrester gear and detail changes
Mosquito PR.Mk 34: very-long-range reconnaissance version of the PR.Mk 32 with additional fuel in the bulged 'bomb bay'; main PR type in post-war RAF service (50 built)
Mosquito B.Mk 35: long-range/high-altitude development of B.Mk XVI with pressurised cabin; post-war service only (122 built)
Mosquito NF.Mk 36: generally similar to NF.Mk 30, but with American AI.Mk X radar and 1,690-hp (1260-kW) Merlin 113/114 engines rated for operation at higher altitudes (266 built)
Mosquito TR.Mk 37: variant of TR.Mk 33, equipped with British-built radar (50 built)
Mosquito NF.Mk 38: similar to NF.Mk 30 but equipped with British AI.Mk IX radar (50 built)
Mosquito TT.Mk 39: redesignation of B.Mk XVI bombers following conversion to target tugs for service with the RN
Mosquito FB.Mk 40: Australian-built version of the FB.Mk VI with 1,460-hp (1089-kW) Merlin 31 engines (178 built)
Mosquito PR.Mk 40: Australian reconnaissance conversions from FB.Mk 40 standard
Mosquito FB.Mk 41: Australian-built fighter-bomber prototype, similar to FB.Mk 40 but with two-stage engines (one built)
Mosquito PR.Mk 41: Australian-built reconnaissance aircraft, a development of the PR.Mk 40 but with two-stage engines
Mosquito FB.Mk 42: Australian conversion from FB.Mk 40 with Merlin 69 engines (one conversion)

In November 1944, the 416th Night Fighter Squadron of the 12th Air Force, USAAF flew this Mosquito NF.Mk XXX on operations in Italy. Both the 416th, and the 9th AF's UK-based, 425th NFS, flew the British aircraft while awaiting delivery of the delayed P-61 Black Widow.

end of World War II. PR examples of the Mosquito were used extensively in the Middle and Far East, and No. 81 Squadron in Malaya was the last unit to use the type operationally, late in 1955. The last bomber versions were displaced by the English Electric Canberra in 1952-3, some then being used in a training role and others being converted for photo-reconnaissance or target tug duties. In this latter role some remained in service until 1961. Fighter versions, however, disappeared in the early 1950s, their role taken over by the new generation of turbine-powered fighters.

crews soon discovered that the Mosquito had an enormous capacity to absorb punishment. By no means did it consist only of plywood, but the strength and flexibility of this material was exploited to the full in its construction. The mid-set cantilever wing was a one-piece assembly, with plywood used for the spar webs and all skins. Tail unit structure was similar, but the fuselage was entirely different. This consisted of a plywood/balsa/plywood sandwich, built up onto spruce formers, and was constructed in two halves which were completely equipped individually with their appropriate control, pipe and wiring runs before the two halves were united. The retractable tail-wheel landing gear was

unusual in that shock absorption dispensed with costly oleo-pneumatic struts, substituting rubber-in-compression springing. All versions of the Mosquito had accommodation for a crew of two, seated side-by-side.

The **Mosquito Mk II** second prototype, first flown on 15 May 1941 with Merlin 21 engines, was equipped as a night fighter with AI.Mk IV radar and a nose armament of four 20-mm cannon and four 0.303-in (7.7-mm) machine-guns. Designated **Mosquito NF.Mk II**, of which 467 production examples were completed, the type began to enter service first with No. 157 Squadron, which made its first operational sortie on the night of 27-28 April

1942. The type equipped No. 23 Squadron shortly after this time, and this was the first unit to operate the type in the Mediterranean theatre when based at Luqa, Malta, from December 1942. The Mosquito fighters were deployed not only as dedicated night-fighters, but also in the day and night intruder role, making their first night intruder sortie on 30-31 December 1942.

Last of the basic variants was the **Mosquito T.Mk III**, which was a dual-control conversion trainer and 343 of these were constructed with Merlin 21 engines. The Mosquito was built not only in the UK, but also by the de Havilland factories in Australia and Canada, and when production finally

ended a total of 7,785 aircraft had been built. Many examples of the Mosquito continued to give valuable service with the RAF during the years immediately following the

SPECIFICATION

de Havilland Mosquito FB.Mk VI
Type: two-seat fighter-bomber
Powerplant: two Rolls-Royce Merlin 25 Vee piston engines each rated at 1,635 hp (1219 kW)
Performance: maximum speed 380 mph (611 km/h) at 13,000 ft (3960 m); cruising speed 325 mph (523 km/h) at 15,000 ft (4570 m); initial climb rate 2,850 ft (869 m) per minute; service ceiling 33,000 ft (10060 m); range 1,650 miles (2655 km) with an internal bombload
Weights: empty 14,300 lb (6486 kg); maximum take-off 22,300 lb (10115 kg)

Dimensions: wingspan 54 ft 2 in (16.51 m); length 40 ft 6 in (12.34 m); height 12 ft 6 in (3.81 m); wing area 452.00 sq ft (41.99 m²)
Armament: four 20-mm Hispano fixed forward-firing cannon and four 0.303-in (7.7-mm) Browning fixed forward-firing machine-guns in the nose, plus up to 2,000 lb (907 kg) of bombs carried in the lower-fuselage weapons bay and on two underwing hardpoints, or 1,000 lb (454 kg) of bombs carried in the lower-fuselage weapons bay and eight 60-lb (27-kg) rockets carried under the wing

de Havilland DH.100, DH.113 and DH.115 Vampire

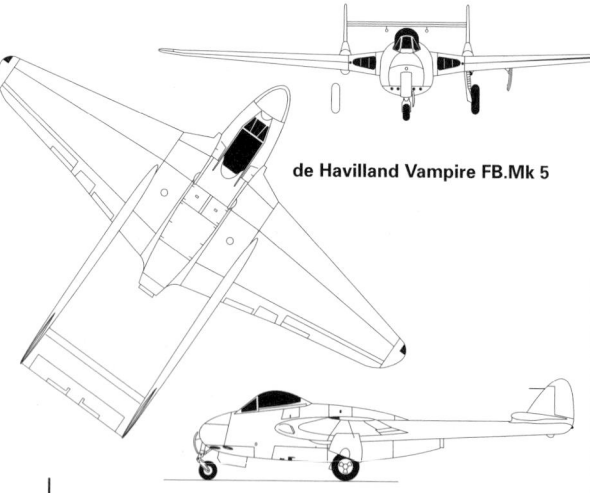

de Havilland Vampire FB.Mk 5

South Africa built up a sizeable Vampire fleet, which at one time included 21 T.Mk 55s (illustrated). FB.Mk 5, FB.Mk 9 and FB.Mk 52 aircraft were also on strength.

The **DH.100 Vampire** was the UK's first single-jet fighter, the prototype flying at Hatfield on 20 September 1943 in the hands of Geoffrey de Havilland, a mere 16 months after the start of the detail design process. The type entered service with the RAF in 1946 as the **Vampire F.Mk 1** with the 3,100-lb st (13.79-kN) de Havilland Goblin DGn.3 turbojet, and a number of this early variant were also used for experimental and trials work.

Development led to the **Vampire F.Mk 3**, which eventually replaced the

Vampire F.Mk 1 in RAF service. The Vampire F.Mk 3 was also the basis for a series of export Vampires, four going to Norway and 85 to Canada. Arrangements were made for production of the Vampire in Australia, where 80 **Vampire FB.Mk 30** aircraft were built by de Havilland Aircraft Pty Ltd with the powerplant of one Australian-built Rolls-Royce Nene engine. (Three Vampire F.Mk 1s fitted with Nene engines in the UK had been intended as prototypes for the proposed **Vampire F.Mk 2**.)

A ground-attack version of

the Vampire F.Mk 3, with strengthened wing and reduced span, entered production as the **Vampire FB.Mk 5**, and this attracted a number of export orders from countries including Egypt, Finland, France, Iraq, Lebanon, New Zealand, Norway, Sweden and Venezuela. Some standard Vampire FB.Mk 5s were also supplied to the Indian and South African air forces, and production licences were negotiated successfully with a number of countries. In Italy, Macchi built 80 examples of the **Vampire FB.Mk 52A**, while Switzerland produced 178 examples of the **Vampire F.Mk 6**, and France manufactured 67 examples of the Vampire FB.Mk 5. These last were assembled by SNCASE from British-made components, but SNCASE then undertook the manufacture of 183 Goblin-powered Vampire FB.Mk 5 and 250 **Vampire FB.Mk 53** aircraft

with French-built Nene engines, in which form they were designated **Sud-Est SE.535 Mistral**. The naval version of the Vampire FB.Mk 5 was the **Sea Vampire F.Mk 20**, of which 30 were delivered to the FAA. The **Sea Vampire F.Mk 21**, of which six were produced by conversion from Vampire F.Mk 3 standard, had a strengthened belly for trials with wheel-less landings on flexible decks.

The last single-seat Vampire variant to see service with the RAF was the **Vampire FB.Mk 9**, a version of the Vampire FB.Mk 5 with cockpit air-conditioning for use in hot climates; the Vampire FB.Mk 9 was also delivered to Ceylon (now Sri Lanka), Jordan and Rhodesia (now Zimbabwe).

This Vampire FB.Mk 5 demonstrates the type's distinctive twin-boom layout to good effect. Such a design enabled thrust losses to be kept to a minimum by using as short a jet pipe as possible.

de Havilland DH.100, D.H.113 and D.H.115 Vampire (cont.)

Total UK production of single-seat Vampire aircraft had reached more than 1,900 when the line closed in December 1953. The last single-seaters in military service into the early part of the 1980s were a handful of **Vampire FB.Mk 50** machines in the Dominican Republic, about 20 Vampire FB.Mk 6 aircraft in Switzerland and possibly a small number of Vampire FB.Mk 9s in Zimbabwe.

Brief mention must be made of the **DH.113** variant, known in service as the **Vampire NF.Mk 10**, which was a two-seat night-fighter development of which 95 were built, mainly for the RAF. A few were delivered to Italy under the designation **Vampire NF.Mk 54**, and 29 ex-RAF aircraft were later sold to the Indian air force between 1954 and 1958.

Experience with the wide side-by-side seating of the Vampire NF.Mk 10

proved invaluable in the development of the **DH.115 Vampire Trainer**, first flown on 15 November 1950 as a private venture with Martin-Baker ejection seats. The foresight of de Havilland was rewarded by production orders from the RAF and RN. The first deliveries to the RAF were made in 1952 while those of the RN's version, which was basically similar, began in 1954: the designations of these two variants were **Vampire T.Mk 11** and **Sea Vampire T.Mk 22** respectively. More than 530 went to the RAF and 73 to the RN from a total UK production total of 804, completed in 1958. Export deliveries of the closely related **Vampire T.Mk 55** were made to Austria (5), Burma (8), Ceylon/Sri Lanka (5), Chile (5), Egypt (12), Finland (5), India (5), Indonesia (8), Iraq (6), Ireland (6), Lebanon (3), New Zealand (12), Norway

(4), Portugal (2), South Africa (21), Sweden (57), Switzerland (39), Syria (2) and Venezuela (6). Ex-RAF Vampire T.Mk 11 aircraft were supplied to Jordan (2) and Rhodesia/Zimbabwe (4). Additionally, 109 generally similar aircraft were built in Australia under the designations Vampire **T.Mks 33**, **34** and **35**, and some 50 aircraft were assembled in India. It is believed that three or four Vampire T.Mk 55 trainers were still in service with Chile and Zimbabwe and about 15 remained active in Switzerland up to the early 1990s.

No. 112 Sqn RAF re-formed at Fassberg, Germany on 12 May 1951 to fly the Vampire FB.Mk 5. The aircraft remained very much in the front line until replaced by the Sabres in January 1954.

SPECIFICATION	
de Havilland DH. 100 Vampire (Vampire FB.Mk 6)	12,390 lb (5620 kg)
Type: single-seat fighter-bomber	**Dimensions:** wingspan 38 ft (11.58 m); length 30 ft 9 in (9.37 m); height 8 ft 10 in (2.69 m); wing area 262.00 sq ft (24.34 m²)
Powerplant: one de Havilland Goblin DGn.3 turbojet engine rated at 3,350 lb st (14.90 kN)	
Performance: maximum speed 548 mph (882 km/h) at 30,000 ft (9145 m); initial climb rate 4,800 ft (1463 m) per minute; service ceiling 42,800 ft (13045 m); range 1,220 miles (1963 km)	**Armament:** four 20-mm Hispano fixed forward-firing cannon in the lower part of the nose, plus up to 2,000 lb (907 kg) of disposable stores on two underwing hardpoints and generally comprising two 1,000-lb (454-kg) bombs, or eight 60-lb (27-kg) rockets, or two drop tanks
Weights: empty 7,283 lb (3304 kg); maximum take-off	

de Havilland DH.103 Hornet and Sea Hornet

De Havilland's Hornet, especially in the F.Mk 1 form illustrated, was a much lighter and more streamlined aircraft than the Mosquito.

Schemed as a scaled-down version of the Mosquito and retaining its ply/balsa/ply method of fuselage construction, but with a new wood and metal wing, the **DH.103 Hornet** was evolved as a long-range fighter, principally for use against the Japanese. The F.12/43 specification was

written around the original private-venture design, and work began in June 1943. The prototype flew for the first time at Hatfield on 28 July 1944 with the powerplant of two Rolls-Royce Merlin 130/131 engines, which were of reduced frontal area by comparison with earlier

versions of the same engine. In addition, each turned its four-bladed de Havilland Hydromatic propeller inward to overcome the normal tendency of an aircraft to swing during take-off or landing. Initial deliveries to the RAF were made in April 1945 and the first unit, No. 64 Squadron, was formed at RAF Horsham St Faith in May 1946. Although too late to see active service during World War II, the Hornet was used as a ground-attack aircraft during anti-terrorist operations in Malaysia, entering service in this role with No. 33 Squadron in March 1951. The last RAF Hornet unit, No. 45 Squadron, re-equipped with the Vampire in June 1955.

A naval version of the

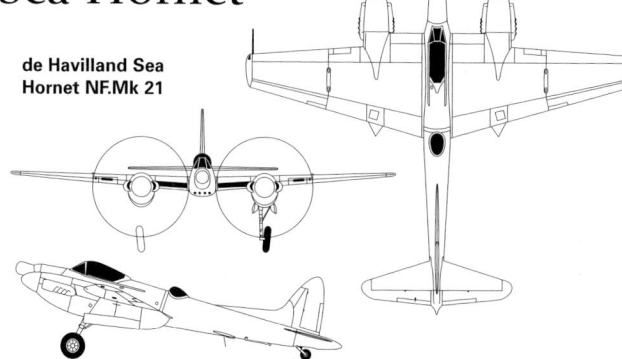

de Havilland Sea Hornet NF.Mk 21

Hornet was included in early project planning, and this **Sea Hornet** became the first British twin-engined single-seat carrierborne fighter. Three Sea Hornet prototypes were converted from **Hornet F.Mk 1** airframes, the first of these making its maiden flight on 19 April 1945. The first fully navalised prototype (the last of the three) was engineered by the Heston Aircraft Co. Ltd to the N.5/44 specification and featured folding outer wing

panels, revised main landing gear units designed to absorb the high sink rates associated with carrierborne operations, an arrester hook, tail-down accelerator gear and naval radio and radar. Operational trials were carried out by No. 703 Squadron, and the first front-line unit was No. 801 Squadron, which was commissioned at RNAS Ford on 1 June 1947. The Sea Hornet remained in service with Fleet Requirements Units as late as 1955.

Variants

Hornet F.Mk 1: initial production version (60 built), of which the first was delivered to Boscombe Down on 28 February 1945
Hornet PR.Mk 2: one F.Mk 1 photo-reconnaissance conversion with cameras mounted in the rear fuselage
Hornet F.Mk 3: the most prolific of the land-based Hornets with a dorsal fillet (later fitted retrospectively to earlier marks), enlarged internal fuel capacity, attachment points under each half of the wing for a drop tank, a 1,000-lb (454-kg) bomb or four 60-lb (27-kg) rocket projectiles; 120 built
Hornet FR.Mk 4: the last Hornet F.Mk 3s were completed to this reconnaissance fighter standard with the rear-fuselage fuel tank removed to provide volume for the accommodation of a single F.52 camera
Sea Hornet F.Mk 20: 78 production aircraft with similar armament to that carried by the Hornet F.Mk 3; the first was flown on 13 August 1946 and the last delivery was made on 12 June 1951
Sea Hornet NF.Mk 21: two-seat night-fighter version, also operated as an attack formation lead aircraft; the first prototype was a Hornet F.Mk 1 conversion with non-folding wings but with ASH radar nose and flame-damped exhausts; first flown on 9 July 1946; production totalled 79 aircraft, the last in November 1950
Sea Hornet PR.Mk 22: 43 aircraft similar to the Sea Hornet F.Mk 20, but with two F.52 cameras or one Fairchild K-19B camera, the latter for night photography

SPECIFICATION	
de Havilland D.H.103 Hornet (Hornet F.Mk 3)	**Dimensions:** wingspan 45 ft (13.72 m); length 36 ft 8 in (11.18 m); height 14 ft 2 in (4.32 m); wing area 361.00 sq ft (33.54 m²)
Type: single-seat fighter	
Powerplant: two Rolls-Royce Merlin 130/131 Vee piston engines each rated at 2,070 hp (1544 kW)	**Armament:** four 20-mm Hispano fixed forward-firing cannon in the underside of the forward fuselage, plus up to 2,000 lb (907 kg) of disposable stores on two underwing hardpoints and generally comprising two 1,000-lb (454-kg) bombs, or eight 60-lb (27-kg) rocket projectiles, or two drop tanks
Performance: maximum speed 472 mph (760 km/h) at 22,000 ft (671 m); initial climb rate 4,650 ft (1417 m) per minute; service ceiling 35,000 ft (10670 m); range 3,000 miles (4828 km)	
Weights: empty 12,880 lb (5842 kg); maximum take-off 20,900 lb (9480 kg)	

de Havilland DH.104 Dove

Proudly displaying the St Andrew's Cross on its fin, this Sea Devon C.Mk 20 belonged to the RNAS Prestwick Station Communications Flight.

Variants

Dove 1: initial production version for up to 11 passengers
Dove 1B: Dove 1 aircraft retrofitted with uprated powerplant
Dove 2: first executive version, with seating for six passengers
Dove 2B: Dove 2 aircraft retrofitted with uprated powerplant
Dove 3: projected high-altitude survey version
Dove 4: company designation for 39 examples of the RAF's **Devon C.Mk 1**, 13 examples of the RN's **Sea Devon C.Mk 20**, and others for export
Dove 5: uprated equivalent of Dove 1 with maximum take-off weight increased to 8,800 lb (3992 kg) and payload boosted by 20 per cent on 500-mile (805-km) stages
Dove 6: uprated equivalent of Dove 2 with same performance gains as the Dove 5
Dove 6B: version of Dove 6 cleared to a maximum of 8,500 lb (3856 kg)
Dove 7: up-engined version of Dove 1
Dove 8: up-engined version of Dove 2
Dove 8A: version of Dove 8 for the US market, for which it was designated **Custom Dove 600**

To provide a successor to its Dragon Rapide in the period after World War II, the company's design team under the leadership of R. E. Bishop, started work during 1944 on a low-wing cantilever monoplane which, with the exception of fabric-covered elevators and rudder, was to be of all-metal construction. The powerplant consisted of two Gipsy Queen engines, and their fully feathering constant-speed and reversible-pitch propellers made the **DH.104 Dove** the first British transport

aircraft to use reversible-pitch propellers for braking assistance. The standard accommodation was for between eight and 11 passengers.

First flown on 25 September 1945, the prototype soon demonstrated that there was little wrong with the basic design. Apart from the addition of a dorsal fin at an early stage of development to improve stability in single-engined flight, and much later of a redesigned elevator and of a domed roof to give a little more

headroom on the flight deck, production aircraft were generally similar to the original prototype.

The Dove production variants were characterised by the different marks of Gipsy Queen engines installed, these including the 330-hp (246-kW) Gipsy Queen 70 and 70-3 powering the prototype and **Dove 1/2** respectively, 340-hp (254-kW) Gipsy Queen 70-4 in the **Dove 1B/2B**, 380-hp (283-kW) Gipsy Queen 70 Mk 2 in the **Dove 5/6**, and 400-hp (298-kW) Gipsy Queen 70 Mk 3 in the **Dove 7/8**. A number of Dove conversions later effected by Riley Aircraft in the USA as the **Riley Turbo Executive 400** introduced 400-hp (298-kW) Lycoming IO-720-A1A flat-eight piston engines. A more ambitious conversion by Carstedt Inc. at Long Beach, California introduced two 605-ehp (451-ekW) Garrett AirResearch TPE331 turboprop engines and a lengthened fuselage to accommodate 18 commuter passengers: this **Carstedt Jet Liner 600**

was supplied primarily to Apache Airlines of Phoenix, Arizona.

Like the Dragon Rapide, which it superseded and supplemented, the Dove proved to be reliable and popular, and well over 542 were built before production ended in 1968. Of these just over 100 were supplied under the name

Devon to many air forces, including the RAF, and a small number also went to the RN with the name **Sea Devon**. In addition to the light transport role for which it had been designed, the Dove was also employed in moderately large numbers as a business, executive, and VIP aircraft.

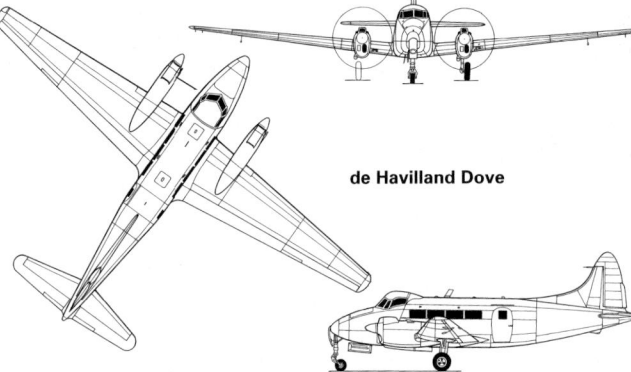

de Havilland Dove

SPECIFICATION

de Havilland DH.104 Dove 7 & 8
Type: two-crew light transport aircraft
Powerplant: two de Havilland Gipsy Queen 70 Mk 3 inverted inline piston engines each rated at 400 hp (298 kW)
Performance: maximum speed 235 mph (378 km/h) at optimum altitude; cruising speed 162 mph (261 km/h) at optimum altitude; initial climb rate 1,420 ft (433 m) per minute; service ceiling 21,700 ft (6615 m); range 1,175 miles (1891 km)
Weights: empty 6,580 lb (2985 kg); maximum take-off 8,950 lb (4060 kg)
Dimensions: wingspan 57 ft (17.37 m); length 39 ft 4 in (11.99 m); height 13 ft 4 in (4.06 m); wing area 335.00 sq ft (31.12 m²)
Payload: between seven and 11 passengers carried in an enclosed cabin

de Havilland DH.106 Comet

Specification IV drafted by the Brabazon Committee for a post-war jet airliner met with an initial response from de Havilland in 1944, although it was to be 27 July 1949 before John Cunningham lifted the first prototype **DH.106 Comet** from the Hatfield runway on a 31-minute maiden flight. Of all-metal stressed-skin construction and powered by four of the newly certificated 4,450-lb st (19.79-kN) Ghost 50 Mk 1 centrifugal-flow turbojet engines, the

aircraft began an intensive programme of test flights, among which were a number of overseas trips. These included London-Castel Benito on 25 October 1949 and London-Rome, London-Copenhagen and London-Cairo early in 1950. Tropical tests were undertaken at Khartoum, and high-altitude take-off tests at Nairobi. The second prototype was flown on 27 July 1950, and in April 1951 the machine was delivered to BOAC's Comet Unit at Hurn, with

flights to Johannesburg, Delhi and Singapore contributing to a 500-hour programme of proving flights and crew training.

BOAC's nine examples of the **Comet 1**, with multi-wheel bogies replacing the two prototypes' single main wheels, were delivered between January 1951 and September 1952. After the start of scheduled services to South Africa (with freight only) in January 1952, following the issue of a certificate of airworthiness on 22 January, the world's first jet passenger service was inaugurated between London and Johannesburg on 2 May 1952. London-Tokyo became a Comet route on 3 April 1953. Tragically, however, just a month later, on 2 May 1953, a Comet crashed in unexplained circumstances soon after take-off from Calcutta.

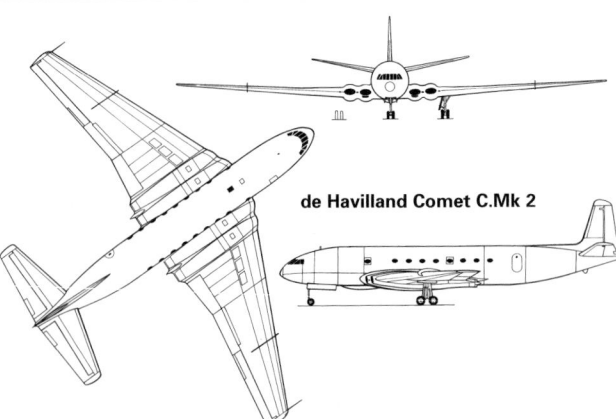

de Havilland Comet C.Mk 2

No. 192 Sqn RAF, later No. 51 Sqn, employed its Comet R.Mk 2s on regular Elint missions. The aircraft differed from C.Mk 2s in having more antennas and underfuselage radomes.

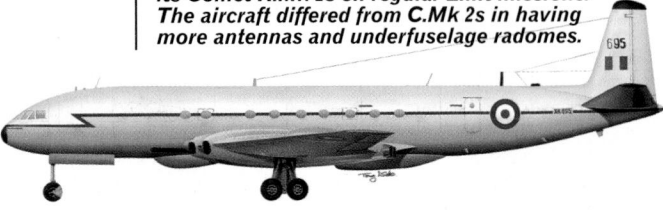

SPECIFICATION

de Havilland DH.106 Comet 4
Type: three-crew long-range passenger transport aircraft
Powerplant: four Rolls-Royce Avon 524 turbojet engines each rated at 10,500 lb st (46.71 kN)
Performance: cruising speed 503 mph (809 km/h) at high altitude; cruising altitude 42,000 ft (12800 m); range 3,225 miles (5190 km) with maximum payload
Weights: empty 75,424 lb (34212 kg); maximum take-off 162,000 lb (73482 kg)
Dimensions: wingspan 114 ft 10 in (35.00 m); length 111 ft 6 in (33.99 m); height 29 ft 6 in (8.99 m); wing area 2,121.00 sq ft (197.04 m²)
Payload: up to 81 passengers carried in the enclosed cabin

de Havilland DH.106 Comet (cont.)

Following two similar accidents, on 10 January and 8 April 1954, in which the Comets crashed into the Mediterranean, the fleet was grounded. A subsequent investigation revealed the cause to be structural failure of the pressure cabin, and although the Comet 2 already under construction for BOAC was modified for RAF service, more than four years elapsed before the revised Comet 4 was able to resume commercial operations.

Middle East Airlines received four Comet 4Cs, allowing the option on a fifth to lapse. Later, the carrier leased two Comet 4Cs to replace three aircraft lost in a 1968 Israeli commando attack on Beirut airport.

Variants

Comet 1A: basically as Comet 1 but with increased fuel capacity and with provision for water/methanol injection of the 5,000-lb st (22.24-kN) Ghost 50 Mk 2 engines; 10 aircraft were built, including two each for Canadian Pacific Airlines and the RCAF and three each for Air France and Union Aéromaritime de Transport

Comet 2X: a Comet 1 airframe powered by 6,600-lb st (29.36-kN) Rolls-Royce Avon Mk 502 axial-flow turbojet engines and first flown on 16 February 1952 as a development aircraft for the Comet 2

Comet 2: incorporating a 3-ft (0.91-m) fuselage 'stretch' and increased fuel capacity to increase the range by some 350 miles (563 km), the 44-seat Comet 2 was powered by four 7,300-lb st (32.47-kN) Avon Mk 503 engines; the first of 12 ordered by BOAC was flown on 27 August 1953, but following the Comet 1 crashes the completed airframes were rebuilt with rounded cabin windows and heavier-gauge skinning; 10 were delivered to RAF Transport Command for use by No. 216 Squadron, comprising two **Comet T.Mk 2** crew trainers and eight **Comet C.Mk 2** transports; three more were fitted with specialised electronics and served with Nos 51 and 192 Squadrons of No. 90 Group; RAF Comet Mk 2s were withdrawn in April 1967

Comet 2E: two aircraft with 7,330-lb st (32.61-kN) Avon 504 engines in the inner nacelles and 10,500-lb st (46.71-kN) Avon 524 engines in the outer positions, used by BOAC for proving flights from 1957-8, pending certification and delivery of the Comet 4

Comet 3: first flown on 19 July 1954 and powered by 10,000-lb st (44.48-kN) Avon 523 engines; an increase of 18 ft 6 in (5.64 m) in fuselage length allowed up to 78 passengers to be carried and additional fuel capacity was provided in the form of pinion tanks on the wings; it served later as a development aircraft for the cropped-wing Comet

Comet 4: production version of the Comet 3 for North Atlantic operations, powered by 10,500-lb st (46.71-kN) Avon 524 engines and seating up to 78 passengers; 19 Comet 4 aircraft were ordered by BOAC and the first made its maiden flight on 27 April 1958; eastbound and westbound services linking London and New York were inaugurated simultaneously on 4 October 1958; production totalled 27, including six for Aerolineas Argentinas and two for East African Airways

Comet 4B: designed for operation over shorter-stage lengths, this had a fuselage increased in length to 118 ft (35.97 m) for the accommodation of up to 99 passengers, a clipped wing spanning 107 ft 10 in (32.87 m), and no pinion tanks; the Comet 4B was built for British European Airways (14) and Olympic Airways (four), the first example flying on 27 June 1959

Comet 4C: final production version, combining the stretched fuselage of the Comet 4B with the wing of the Comet 4; the first of three for Mexicana was used for certification and development flying and had its maiden flight on 31 October 1959; other customers comprised Aerolineas Argentinas (1), East African Airways (1), King Ibn Saud (1), Kuwait Airways (2), Middle East Airlines (4), Misrair (9), RAE (1), RAF (5) and Sudan Airways (2); two additional aircraft were converted as prototypes for the Nimrod maritime patrol aircraft

de Havilland DH.108

Built to the Air Ministry's E.18/45 specification, the **DH.108** was developed to conduct research into the characteristics of swept wings in support of the DH.106 Comet and DH.110 programmes. The first prototype was a standard Vampire fuselage complete with the 3,000-lb st (13.50-kN) de Havilland Goblin DGn.2 turbojet engine, and mounting a mid-set wing with a sweep angle of 43° and elevons which acted as elevators and ailerons (there being no horizontal tail surfaces); it was was a low-speed test vehicle with a maximum speed of 280 mph (451 km/h). It had anti-spin parachutes in wingtip containers and fixed Handley Page leading-edge slots, both precautions against loss of lateral control at low speeds. It was first flown by Geoffrey de Havilland Jnr on 15 May 1946 at Woodbridge, Suffolk. A modified 45° swept wing with powered flying controls and automatic slats was fitted to the second prototype, which was flown in June 1946 and was intended to explore the transonic area of the flight envelope. Sadly, the aircraft broke up in flight on 27 September and Geoffrey de Havilland Jnr was killed.

A third DH.108, powered by the 3,750-lb st (16.68-kN) Goblin DGn.4 engine, made its first flight at Hatfield on 24 July 1947, piloted by de Havilland's new chief test pilot, John Cunningham. Identifiable by its longer, pointed nose and more streamlined cockpit canopy, this aircraft, flown by John

Derry on 9 September 1948, became the first machine in the UK to exceed the speed of sound. Earlier, on 12 April 1948, the same pilot had flown it in a successful attempt on the 100-km (62.1-mile) closed-circuit speed record, raising this to 605.23 mph (974.02 km/h). It was destroyed in a fatal crash on 15 February 1950, as was the first prototype on 1 May.

VW120 was the third of the DH.108s. The type was called Swallow by the Under Secretary of the Ministry of Supply, but being an experimental type, was not named by the manufacturer.

SPECIFICATION	
de Havilland DH.108 (second prototype)	640 mph (1030 km/h) at optimum altitude
Type: single-seat research aircraft	**Weights:** maximum take-off 8,960 lb (4064 kg)
Powerplant: one de Havilland Goblin DGn.3 turbojet engine rated at 3,300 lb st (14.68 kN)	**Dimensions:** wingspan 39 ft (11.89 m); length 24 ft 6 in (7.47 m); wing area 328.00 sq ft (30.47 m²)
Performance: maximum speed	

de Havilland DH.110 Sea Vixen

Designed originally as a land-based all-weather fighter for the RAF, in competition with the delta-winged Gloster Javelin, the **DH.110** was flown in prototype form on 26 September 1951, a second aircraft joining the programme on 25 July 1952. In the autumn of 1954 the latter aircraft undertook 'touch-and-go' trials on HMS *Albion*, and the first naval order for what now became the **DH.110 Sea Vixen** was placed in January 1955. The de Havilland factory at Christchurch was entrusted with the development and manufacturing programme, and a partially navalised prototype was first flown on 20 June 1955. It made the first full-stop arrested landing on board HMS *Ark Royal* on 5 April 1956. The

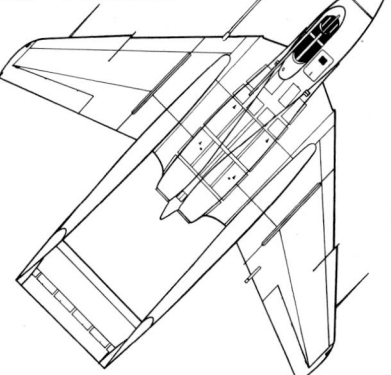

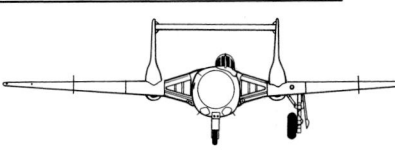

de Havilland Sea Vixen FAW.Mk 1

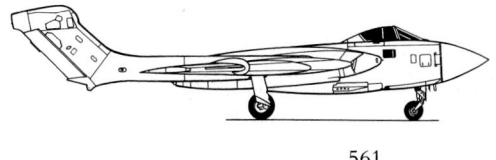

first of the initial production order for 45 **Sea Vixen FAW.Mk 1** all-weather fighters introduced a hinged and pointed radome, power-folding wings and a hydraulically steerable nosewheel, and this aircraft flew for the first time on 20 March 1957. Following service trials

with 'Y' Flight of No. 700 Squadron in November 1958 on board HMS *Victorious* and HMS *Centaur*, the type then became operational with No. 892 Squadron, which was formed at Yeovilton on 2 July 1959 and went to sea operationally in HMS *Ark Royal* in March 1960.

Variant

DH.110 Sea Vixen FAW.Mk 2: developed version with additional fuel capacity in the forward sections of the tail booms, which were extended forward of the wings, and provision for four Red Top short-range AAMs in place of the Firestreak AAMs carried by the Mk 1; two development aircraft, converted from Mk 1 standard, were flown on 1 June and 17 August 1962, and were later brought up to full Sea Vixen FAW.Mk 2 standard; 14 Mk 1s were completed to Mk 2 standard on the production line, the first flying on 8 March 1963, and 15 aircraft were newly built – these 31 aircraft were complemented by 67 Mk 1 conversions; the Sea Vixen FAW.Mk 2 entered service in December 1963 with No. 899 Squadron, which embarked in HMS *Eagle* a year later, and which was a component of its air group when it was decommissioned in 1972

In 1968, an aerobatic team, Simon's Sircus, was formed with five Sea Vixen FAW.Mk 2s from No. 892 Sqn. Nos 893 and 899 Sqns also flew the type operationally.

SPECIFICATION	
de Havilland DH.110 Sea Vixen (Sea Vixen FAW.Mk 2) **Type:** two-seat all-weather carrierborne attack fighter **Powerplant:** two Rolls-Royce Avon Mk 208 turbojet engines each rated at 11,230 lb st (49.95 kN) **Performance:** maximum speed 690 mph (1110 km/h) at sea level; climb to 10,000 ft (3050 m) in 1 minute 30 seconds; service ceiling 48,000 ft (21790 m) **Weights:** maximum take-off	41,575 lb (18858 kg) **Dimensions:** wingspan 51 ft (15.54 m); length 55 ft 7 in (17.02 m); height 10 ft 9 in (3.28 m); wing area 648.00 sq ft (60.20 m²) **Armament:** four Red Top short-range AAMs and two retractable nose packs each with 14 2-in (51-mm) rocket projectiles, plus up to 2,000 lb (907 kg) of disposable stores carried on four underwing hardpoints

de Havilland DH.112 Venom and Sea Venom

Developed from the Vampire, the **DH.112 Venom** single-seat fighter-bomber was intended to gain maximum performance benefit from the installation of higher-thrust versions of the Ghost

turbojet. Known initially as the **Vampire FB.Mk 8**, the new type was later redesignated as a result of extensive changes in the design, and was readily distinguishable from its predecessor by one conspicuous feature, a new wing. This had a straight trailing edge rather than the Vampire's tapered trailing edge, was of thinner section and, as another feature facilitating identification, was equipped to carry jettisonable wingtip fuel tanks.

The first Venom prototype was flown at Hatfield on 2 September 1949, and the **Venom FB.Mk 1** became operational with the RAF just under three years later, in August 1952. The type saw service in Germany, the Near East and the Far East, equipping 18 squadrons, as well as

No. 14 Squadron of the RNZAF. Two-seat **Venom NF.Mk 2** and **NF.Mk 3** night-fighters served between 1953 and 1957, and the Royal Swedish Air Force flew the type until 1960. Foreign users of the Venom in its baseline fighter-bomber form included Iraq and Venezuela.

Following successful manufacture and use of the Vampire FB.Mk 6, Switzerland negotiated a licence to build the Venom. Using the same consortium that had produced the Vampire, comprising the Federal Aircraft Factory (EFW) at Emmen, Pilatus at Stens, and the Flug und Fahrzeugwerke at Altenrhein, work began in 1953 on a batch of 150 **Venom FB.Mk 50** aircraft completed to FB.Mk 1 standard. A further batch

of 100 aircraft, in this instance to **FB.Mk 4** standard, was completed by 1957. Of this total of 250 aircraft, 90 remained in service with the Swiss air force into the 1980s but were then on the verge of replacement, the last aircraft being retired toward the end of 1983. Few would disagree that these Swiss aircraft had given remarkable service, and, operating from airfields in mountain valleys up to 4,500 ft (1400 m) above sea level, the Venom's manoeuvrability was a great asset. Modifications introduced by the Swiss included a redesigned nose housing UHF communications, strengthening of the inner wing sections to allow the use of rocket-launchers, and introduction of link collectors beneath the cannon.

Variants

Venom FB.Mk 1: initial production version for the RAF with the 4,850-lb st (21.57-kN) Ghost Mk 103 engine
Venom NF.Mk 2: night-fighter version of Venom FB.Mk 1 incorporating a new fuselage of wider section to accommodate the pilot and radar operator side-by-side; the new fuselage also had an extended nose to house AI radar
Venom NF.Mk 2A: redesignation of Venom NF.Mk 2 aircraft following incorporation of a clear-view canopy and tail unit modifications
Venom NF.Mk 3: improved version of Venom NF.Mk 2 with power-operated ailerons, tail unit modifications, powered jettison system for canopy and the 4,950-lb st (22.02-kN) Ghost Mk 104 engine
Venom FB.Mk 4: improved version of the Venom FB.Mk 1 with power-operated ailerons, redesigned tail unit and ejection seat
Venom FB.Mk 50: export version of the Venom FB.Mk 1, supplied to Iraq and Italy, and 150 built in Switzerland under licence for Swiss air force
Venom NF.Mk 51: version of Venom NF.Mk 2 built for the Royal Swedish Air Force (which designated the type as the **J 33**), and powered by the Ghost engine built by Svenska Flygmotor in Sweden
Sea Venom FAW.Mk 20: initial version of Sea Venom
Sea Venom FAW.Mk 21: improved version of Sea Venom FAW.Mk 20 with power-operated ailerons, clear-view jettisonable canopy, uprated Ghost Mk 104 engine, ejection seats and long-stroke landing gear
Sea Venom FAW.Mk 22: improved version of Sea Venom FAW.Mk 21 with 5,300-lb st (23.58-kN) Ghost Mk 105 engine, AAMs and ejection seats
Sea Venom Mk 52: British designation of version built in France for the Aéronavale (see Aquilon below)
Sea Venom FAW.Mk 58: designation of Sea Venom for service with RAN; generally similar to Sea Venom FAW.Mk 21, with radar and equipment to RAN requirements
Sud-Est Aquilon 20: designation of four Sea Venom FAW.Mk 20s assembled in France and powered by Fiat-built Ghost Mk 48 engines rated at 4,840 lb st (21.53 kN)
Sud-Est Aquilon 201: one-off French licence-built prototype with short-stroke landing gear and ejection seats
Sud-Est Aquilon 202: French licence-built production version with long-stroke landing gear
Sud-Est Aquilon 203: French licence-built production version with short-stroke landing gear, single-seat accommodation and fire-control radar
Sud-Est Aquilon 204: French licence-built two-seat trainer version

This No. 839 Sqn, FAA Sea Venom FAW.Mk 21 is illustrated as it appeared aboard HMS Eagle after the application of 'Suez stripes' in 1956.

de Havilland
Venom NF.Mk 2

de Havilland DH.112 Venom and Sea Venom (cont.)

RN evaluation of the Venom led to development of a two-seat carrierborne all-weather fighter, the initial production version being designated **Sea**

Venom FAW.Mk 20. This had strengthening for catapult take-offs, power-operated folding outer wing panels, arrester gear and naval equipment.

Entering FAA service in 1954, the type also saw service with the Royal Australian Navy and with the French Aéronavale.

Iraq received 15 Venom FB.Mk 50s. The aircraft flew with No. 6 Sqn and shared their attack role with Vampire FB.Mk 52s, Hawker Furies and F-84s.

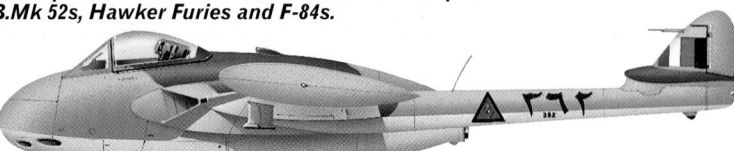

SPECIFICATION	
de Havilland DH.112 Sea Venom (Sea Venom FAW.Mk 22)	**Dimensions:** wingspan 42 ft 11 in (13.08 m); length 36 ft 7 in (11.15 m); height 8 ft 6¼ in (2.60 m); wing area 279.75 sq ft (25.99 m²)
Type: two-seat carrierborne all-weather fighter	**Armament:** four 20-mm Hispano fixed forward-firing cannon in the underside of the forward fuselage, plus up to 2,000 lb (907 kg) of disposable stores on two underwing hardpoints and generally comprising two Firestreak short-range AAMs, or two 1,000-lb (454-kg) bombs, or eight 60-lb (27-kg) rocket projectiles
Powerplant: one de Havilland Ghost Mk 105 turbojet engine rated at 5,300 lb st (23.58 kN)	
Performance: maximum speed 575 mph (925 km/h) at sea level; initial climb rate 5,750 ft (1753 m) per minute; service ceiling 40,000 ft (12190 m); range 705 miles (1135 km)	
Weights: empty 11,300 lb (5126 kg); maximum take-off 15,800 lb (7167 kg)	

de Havilland DH.114 Heron

Adopting the same philosophy that had produced the highly successful four-engined DH.86B after the twin-engined DH.84 Dragon, de Havilland continued the success of the twin-engined Dove by designing a scaled-up and four-engined version designated as the **DH.114 Heron**. Simplicity and reliability were the keynotes for the new aircraft, which provided accommodation for a crew of two and up to 14 passengers (17 if no lavatory was installed). Fixed tricycle landing gear eliminated the complications of a hydraulic system, and excellent short-field performance was assured by good wing design coupled with the use of variable-pitch propellers. These were driven by the powerplant of four Gipsy Queen 30 engines, which had a long operating period between overhauls.

The prototype recorded the new type's maiden

flight on 10 May 1950. The first production **Heron 1** was acquired by New Zealand National Airways, this and all subsequent aircraft having a tailplane with considerable dihedral. The seventh production example served as the prototype for the **Heron 2**, incorporating retractable landing gear which gave an increase in speed and a reduction in fuel consumption. This proved to be the most popular version, representing almost 70 per cent of the 150 examples of the Heron that were built. Despite these relatively small production figures, the Heron saw service in 30 countries, some of them with major airlines and many others as luxury transports (including four operated by The Queen's Flight at RAF Benson). About 25 of the total were used as communications aircraft by nine military services.

In its later years the

Heron was the subject of a number of modification programmes, the **Riley Turbo Skyliner** produced by the Riley Turbostream Corporation in the USA being typical of re-engined aircraft. This replaced the standard powerplant with 290-hp (216-kW) Lycoming IO-540 flat-eight engines, with or without turbochargers according to customer requirements. Far more ambitious was the conversion carried out by Saunders Aircraft Corporation of Gimli, Manitoba. Designated as the **Saunders ST-27**, this had a lengthened fuselage to provide accommodation for a maximum of 23 passengers, the wing rebuilt to incorporate a redesigned main spar, and the four Gipsy engines replaced by two 750-shp (559-kW) Pratt & Whitney Canada PT6A-34 turboprop engines. A total of 12 ST-27 conversions was completed and the prototype of an improved **ST-28** had been completed before Saunders went into receivership.

At the end of 1959, it should be noted, the general consolidation of the

British aviation industry of this period, saw the full merger of de Havilland into the Hawker Siddeley Group to become the de Havilland Division of Hawker Siddeley Aviation. De Havilland soon lost its separate identity so that the last aircraft of de Havilland design, the **DH.121** three-engined airliner and **DH.125** twin-engined business jet, came to be known as Hawker Siddeley (and then BAe) products.

Saunders ST-27

Variants

Heron 1B: Heron 1 version certificated for operation at the higher take-off weight of 13,000 lb (5897 kg)
Heron 2A: single Heron 2 sold in the USA
Heron 2B: Heron 2 version operating at the same take-off weight as the Heron 1B
Heron 2C: redesignation of Heron 2Bs with optional fully-feathering propellers
Heron 2D: aircraft with luxury interiors and certificated at a take-off weight of 13,500 lb (6123 kg)
Heron 2E: a custom-built aircraft with special VIP interior
Heron 3: two VIP aircraft for The Queen's Flight
Heron 4: one VIP aircraft for The Queen's Flight
Sea Heron C.Mk 20: Royal Navy designation of ex-civil Heron 2s and Heron 2Bs (three and two aircraft respectively) acquired in 1961

SPECIFICATION	
de Havilland DH.114 Heron 2D	18,500 ft (5640 m); range 915 miles (1473 km)
Type: two-crew light transport aircraft	**Weights:** empty 8,150 lb (3697 kg); maximum take-off 13,500 lb (6123 kg)
Powerplant: four de Havilland Gipsy Queen 30 Mk 2 inverted inline piston engines each rated at 250 hp (186 kW)	**Dimensions:** wingspan 71 ft 6 in (14.78 m); length 48 ft 6 in (14.78 m); height 15 ft 7 in (4.75 m); wing area 499.00 sq ft (46.36 m²)
Performance: cruising speed 183 mph (295 km/h) at 8,000 ft (2438 m); initial climb rate 1,140 ft (517 m) per minute; service ceiling	**Payload:** up to 14 passengers

A number of local companies undertook the basic conversion of the Heron to Lycoming power although this is a Riley aircraft. It belonged to the Sri Lankan air force.

de Havilland Australia DHA.3 Drover

Needing a larger aircraft for the Flying Doctor Service after World War II, the FDS turned to the de Havilland Aircraft Company (Pty) Ltd, which had been established in 1927 and was generally known as de Havilland Australia. The company had initially

concentrated on the maintenance and repair of de Havilland aircraft imported from the UK, but embarked on the design of aircraft during World War II, when licensed production was also undertaken. The **DHA G.1** was designed in 1942 as a troop-carrying

Lycoming-powered ZK-DDD was the only Drover ever registered in New Zealand. The aircraft was photographed in April 1977, while in use by a parachute club. It subsequently returned to Australia.

glider, but was unbuilt as the design was refined into the **G.2**, of which a mere six were completed.

The company's first powered design to see the light of day was the **DHA.3 Drover** light transport with accommodation for eight passengers as well as a crew of two, and it was this type that was selected for FDS use. The Drover was based broadly on the DH.104 Dove, but had three 145-hp (108-kW)

Gipsy Major 10 Mk 2 inverted engines and fixed tailwheel landing gear. The Drover first flew on 23 January 1948, and versions were offered with variable- and fixed-pitch propellers as the **Drover Mk 1** and **Drover Mk 1F** respectively; the **Drover Mk 2** had double-slotted flaps. Limited construction began in 1949, and 20 aircraft had been built when production ended in September 1953.

Customers for the Drover included Qantas, Trans-Australia Airlines and Fiji Airways, the last being the only export customer. In service with what was now the Royal Flying Doctor Service, the Drover carried two medical staff and two litters; all six aircraft were converted in 1960 to have Lycoming O-360 engines and Hartzell airscrews for improved performance and a higher maximum take-off weight,

under the revised designation **Drover Mk 3**. The last

aircraft were retired from RFDS use in 1970.

SPECIFICATION

de Havilland Australia DHA.3 Drover Mk 3
Type: two-crew utility transport
Powerplant: three Lycoming O-360-A1A flat-four piston engines each rated at 180 hp (134 kW)
Performance: maximum speed 158 mph (254 km/h) at optimum altitude; cruising speed 140 mph (225 km/h) at optimum altitude; initial climb rate 1,040 ft (317 m) per

minute; absolute ceiling 20,000 ft (6095 m); range 900 miles (1448 km)
Weights: empty 4,100 lb (1860 kg); maximum take-off 6,500 lb (2948 kg)
Dimensions: wingspan 57 ft (17.37 m); length 36 ft 6 in (11.13 m); height 10 ft 9 in (3.28 m); wing area 325.00 sq ft (30.19 m²)
Payload: up to eight passengers

de Havilland Canada DHC-1 Chipmunk

The company known formally as de Havilland Aircraft of Canada Ltd, but generally as de Havilland Canada, was created in March 1928 to undertake the assembly, maintenance and repair of de Havilland aircraft imported to Canada, and later embarked on the licensed production of de Havilland aircraft. Towards the end of World War II the company turned its attention to the design of its own aircraft, and the first result of this process was the **DHC-1 Chipmunk**, designed under the supervision of W. Jakimiuk to succeed the classic DH.82 Tiger Moth. Flying for the first time at Downsview, Toronto, on 22 May 1946, the DHC-1 was a tandem-seat stressed-skin monoplane powered by a 145-hp (108-kW) de Havilland Gipsy Major 1C inverted inline engine.

Chipmunks built to the prototype's specification received the designation **DHC-1B-1**, while those with a Gipsy Major 10-3 engine were **DHC-1B-2**

machines. Most Canadian-built Chipmunks had a bubble canopy. Downsview built 218 Chipmunks, the last of them being completed in 1951.

Two aircraft were evaluated by the A&AEE at Boscombe Down in the UK, and as a result, the fully aerobatic Chipmunk was ordered from de Havilland's Hatfield and Chester factories to Specification 8/48 as an *ab initio* trainer for the RAF, which received 735 of the 1,014 Chipmunk aircraft manufactured in the UK. The first Chipmunks to wear RAF roundels were flown by the Oxford UAS from February 1950, and thereafter the type replaced the Tiger Moth with all 17 University Air Squadrons, as well as equipping many RAF Volunteer Reserve flying schools in the early 1950s. National service pilots underwent their initial training on the **'Chippie'**, which served intermittently at the RAF College, Cranwell. A few Chipmunks of No. 114

Squadron were pressed into service in Cyprus on internal security flights during the troubles of 1958.

Under an agreement concluded between de Havilland and the General Aeronautical Material Workshops (OGMA) of Portugal, 60 examples of the Chipmunk were licence-manufactured from 1955 for the Portuguese air force. Other air services that operated the type included those of Burma, Ceylon, Chile, Colombia, Denmark, Egypt,

Iraq, Ireland, Jordan, Lebanon, Malaya, Saudi Arabia, Syria, Thailand and

Uruguay. Small numbers of this now-venerable type are still in service.

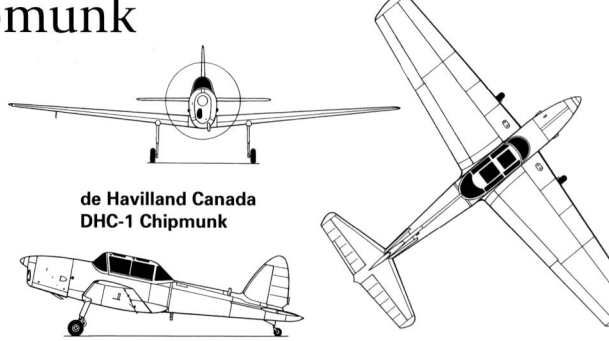

de Havilland Canada DHC-1 Chipmunk

Having received some aircraft direct from de Havilland's Hatfield factory, Portugal went on to licence-build its own Chipmunks.

Variants

DHC-1A-1 Chipmunk: partially aerobatic model with the Gipsy Major 1C engine; designated **Chipmunk T.Mk 1** by the RCAF
DHC-1A-2 Chipmunk: partially aerobatic model with the Gipsy Major 10 engine
DHC-1B-1 Chipmunk: fully aerobatic model with the Gipsy Major 1C engine
DHC-1B-2 Chipmunk: fully aerobatic with the Gipsy Major 10 engine
DHC-1B-2-S1 Chipmunk: model with the Gipsy Major 10 engine for the Royal Egyptian air force
DHC-1B-2-S2 Chipmunk: model with the Gipsy Major 10 engine for Royal Thai air force
DHC-1B-2-S3 Chipmunk: model with the Gipsy Major 10 for RCAF refresher training by Royal Canadian Flying Clubs with the service designation **Chipmunk T.Mk 2**
DHC-1B-2-S4 Chipmunk: Chilean version
DHC-1B-2-S5 Chipmunk: model with the Gipsy Major 10 engine for RCAF under the designation Chipmunk T. Mk 2
Chipmunk T. Mk 10: British-built model with the Gipsy Major 8 engine for the RAF (735 completed)
Chipmunk Mk 20: British-built export version of the Chipmunk T. Mk 10, but with the Gipsy Major 10 Series 2 engine (217 completed)
Chipmunk Mk 21: British-built model as the Mk 20 but to civil requirements (28 completed)
Chipmunk Mk 22: conversion of Chipmunk T.Mk 10s to civil standard with Mk 20 powerplant
Chipmunk Mk 22A: as Mk 22 but with extra fuel tankage
Chipmunk Mk 23: two conversions from Chipmunk T.Mk 10 standard with Mk 20 powerplant and agricultural spray equipment
Aerostructures Sundowner: single Australian-converted Chipmunk with 180-hp (134-kW) Lycoming O-360 flat-four engine, wingtip tanks, clear-view canopy and metal wing-skinning; several Canadian aircraft were also fitted with Lycoming engines
Masefield Variant: Bristol Aircraft conversion possible on Chipmunks Mks 20, 21, 22 and 22A, and comprising blown canopy, luggage compartments in the wings, landing-gear fairings and greater fuel capacity
Sasin SA-29 Spraymaster: several Australian conversions similar to the Chipmunk Mk 23
Super Chipmunk: specially converted aerobatic aircraft fitted with the 260-hp (194-kW) Lycoming GO-435 flat-six engine, revised flying surfaces and retractable landing gear; the sole example was flown in American colours for the 1970 world aerobatic championships

A pair of Chipmunk T.Mk 10s demonstrates the colour scheme worn by the type in the latter part of its RAF career.

SPECIFICATION

de Havilland Canada DHC-1 Chipmunk (Chipmunk T.Mk 10)
Type: two-seat primary flying trainer
Powerplant: one de Havilland Gipsy Major 8 inverted inline piston engine rated at 145 hp (108 kW)
Performance: maximum speed 138 mph (222 km/h) at sea level; cruising speed 116 mph (187 km/h)

at optimum altitude; initial climb rate 800 ft (244 m) per minute; service ceiling 15,800 ft (4815 m); range 280 miles (451 km)
Weights: empty 1,425 lb (646 kg); maximum take-off 2,014 lb (914 kg)
Dimensions: wingspan 34 ft 4 in (10.46 m); length 25 ft 5 in (7.75 m); height 7 ft (2.13 m); wing area 172.00 sq ft (15.97 m²)

de Havilland Canada DHC-2 Beaver

Design work on the **DHC-2 Beaver** light transport began in Toronto late in 1946. The concept behind this first of de Havilland Canada's line of effective STOL transports was influenced by the specific requirements of the Ontario Department of Lands and Forests. The resulting aircraft also suited the exacting requirements of 'bush' pilots in North America and elsewhere in the world for an effective, rugged and reliable STOL utility transport.

The prototype flew for the first time on 16 August 1947, and the type was certificated in Canada during March 1948. Large-scale production had already begun, and the **Beaver I** was soon in service. Basic accommodation was provided for the pilot and up to seven passengers, the latter replaceable by up to 1,500 lb (680 kg) of freight in the cabin.

Great operational flexibility was bestowed on the Beaver by its ability to operate on float, amphibious float or ski landing gear as alternatives to the otherwise standard wheels. Of the 1,657 Beaver Is built, no fewer than 980 went to the US forces (**YL-20** service test, **L-20A** and **L-20B** production aircraft, redesignated **U-6** in 1962) and 46 to the British army. There followed a single **Beaver II** with the Alvis Leonides radial engine and, in 1964, a few examples of the 10-passenger **Turbo-Beaver III** with the 578-ehp (431-ekW) United Aircraft of Canada Ltd (later Pratt & Whitney Aircraft of Canada) PT6A-6 or -20 turboprop. Most of the Turbo-Beavers were used by civil operators. In New Zealand one Beaver was converted with the AiResearch TPE331 turboprop engine. Production ended in the mid-1960s as de Havilland Canada decided to concentrate on the development of more ambitious projects.

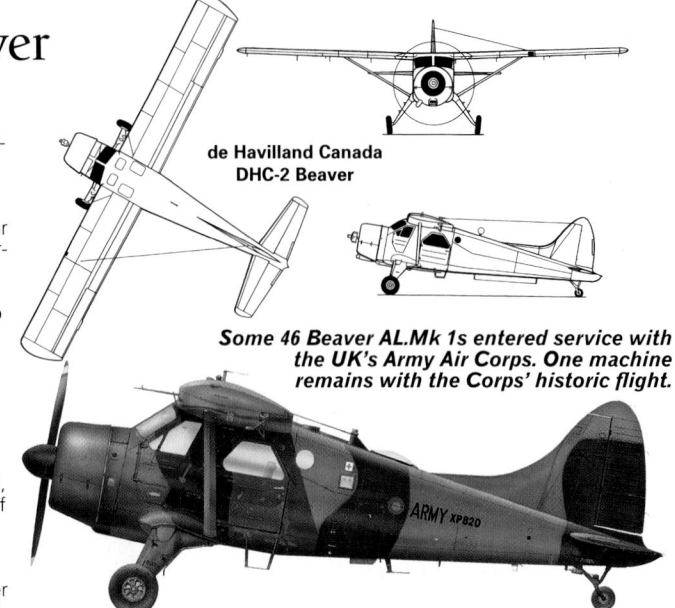

de Havilland Canada
DHC-2 Beaver

Some 46 Beaver AL.Mk 1s entered service with the UK's Army Air Corps. One machine remains with the Corps' historic flight.

de Havilland Canada DHC-3 Otter

Success with the Beaver persuaded de Havilland Canada in the late 1940s that there was room in the STOL utility market for a larger version of the aircraft, with cabin space for some 14 passengers or a freight load of up to 2,240 lb (1016 kg), although the latter was later increased. The company therefore developed the **DHC-3 Otter**, which was in essence a scaled-up Beaver, with an all-metal airframe and a Wasp radial engine, and which was initially known as the **King Beaver**. The choice of a single engine for an aircraft designed to operate in Canada's harsh climate and sparsely populated hinterland regions may seem lacking in forethought, but successful operations by the Beaver and other single-engined types had confirmed that the well-proven Pratt & Whitney radial engines were more than adequate for the task: these engines were both universally familiar and, more importantly, extremely reliable.

Notable for its parallel-chord wing with double-slotted flaps for good STOL performance, the Otter is an attractive high-wing monoplane with a single bracing strut on each side. The prototype first flew on 12 December 1951, and first deliveries were made in 1952. When production ceased in 1968, some 460 had been built, including 66 for the RCAF and 227 for the US armed forces in the form of 223 **U-1A** machines for the US Army and four **UC-1** (changed to **U-1B** in 1962) aircraft for the US Navy. When released by military operators, many examples of the Otter joined those already on the civil market, where again the type had found ready acceptance for its versatility.

Despite its already impressive STOL performance, the Otter was selected as the basis for a Canadian experiment in advanced STOL characteristics, a programme undertaken by the company in conjunction with the Defense Research Board. As part of this programme an Otter was fitted with extremely large flaps inboard of the strut/wing junction points; this also necessitated an enlargement of the tail surfaces, and ground stability was ensured by the replacement of the original tailwheel landing gear with a float chassis fitted with quadricycle wheels instead of the floats. The STOL modifications reduced the Otter's stalling speed by some 10 mph (16 km/h). The flaps were then removed, and a 2,450-lb st (10.90-kN) General Electric J85-GE-7 turbojet engine was installed in the fuselage aft of the wing with adjustable nozzles protruding one through each side of the fuselage. This arrangement permitted far greater control of speed, and allowed spot landings.

Finally, the single Wasp radial engine was replaced by a pair of wing-mounted Pratt & Whitney Canada PT6 turboprop engines, whose slipstream was found beneficial to the controllability of the aircraft.

Under the designation **DHC-3-T Turbo-Otter**, one aircraft was modified by Cox Air Resources to turboprop power, a 662-hp (494-kW) PT6A-27 replacing the standard Wasp. Empty weight was thus reduced to 4,100 lb (1861 kg), resulting in a useful payload increment.

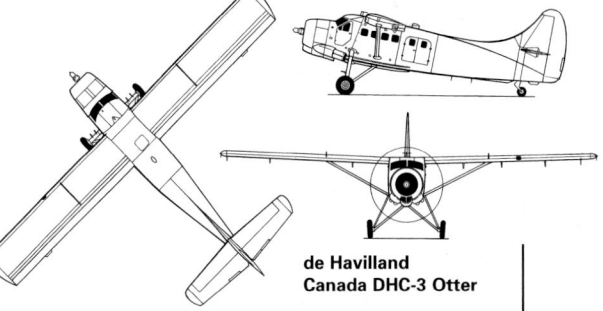

de Havilland
Canada DHC-3 Otter

Like the Beaver, the Otter can operate on wheel, ski, float or amphibious float landing gear. This aircraft is fitted with Edo floats and has the characteristic cabin access ladders.

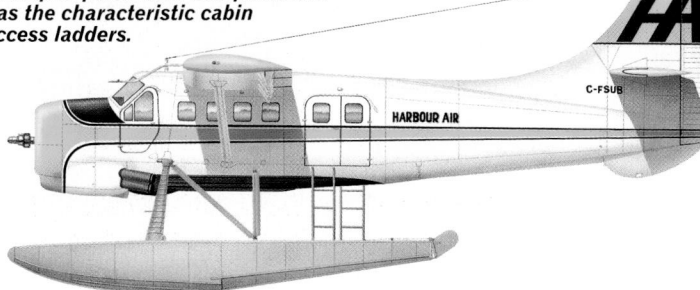

de Havilland Canada DHC-4 Caribou

The decision to build the DHC-4 Caribou was taken in 1956, the object being to develop an aircraft combining the load-carrying capability of the Douglas DC-3 with the type of STOL performance offered by the Beaver and Otter. The Canadian army placed an order for two aircraft and the US Army followed with a contract for five machines, the US Secretary of Defense waiving a restriction which limited the US Army to fixed-wing aircraft with an empty

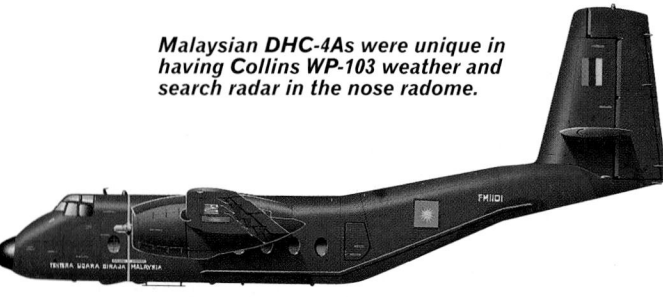

Malaysian DHC-4As were unique in having Collins WP-103 weather and search radar in the nose radome.

weight less than 5,000 lb (2268 kg).

The prototype flew in July 1958, its high wing having a characteristic centre-section with marked anhedral. The rear door was designed as a ramp for items weighing up to 6,720 lb (3048 kg). In the trooping role up to 32 soldiers could be carried. The Caribou served with the RCAF as the CC-108 and with the US Army as the AC-1 (1962 designation CV-2A). As a result of its evaluation of its first

Caribous served in Vietnam with both the US Army and the RAAF. Later, US aircraft passed to the ANG and AFRES (illustrated).

five aircraft, the US Army adopted the Caribou as standard equipment and placed orders for 159 machines. The second batch of aircraft had the designation CV-2B. Following tension on the border between China and India, the US Army handed over two Caribou aircraft to the Indian air force early in 1963. In January 1967 the 134 Caribous still in service with the US Army were transferred to USAF charge as C-7A and C-7B transports. The aircraft was a general sales success and examples flew not only with air forces throughout the world, but also with civil operators. In Canadian service the Caribou was replaced by the DHC-5 Buffalo and surplus examples were sold to a number of nations including Colombia, Oman and Tanzania. Many of the Canadian aircraft had also been loaned to the United Nations, seeing extensive international service.

Production ended in 1973 after the completion of 307 aircraft. The

DHC-4A model supplanted the DHC-4 on the production line from the 24th aircraft; the two models are very similar apart from the later model's increase in weight, the maximum take-off weight of the DHC-4 being 26,000 lb (11793 kg).

DHC-4A, CF-UYM, was delivered to Malaysia. Only 23 DHC-4s were completed before production switched to the DHC-4A.

SPECIFICATION

de Havilland Canada DHC-4A Caribou

Type: two-crew STOL tactical transport
Powerplant: two Pratt & Whitney R-2000-7M2 Twin Wasp radial piston engines each rated at 1,450 hp (1081 kW)
Performance: maximum speed 216 mph (348 km/h) at 6,500 ft (1980 m); cruising speed 182 mph (293 km/h) at 7,500 ft (2285 m); initial climb rate 1,355 ft (413 m) per minute; service ceiling 24,800 ft (7560 m); range 242 miles (389 km) with maximum payload
Weights: empty 18,260 lb (8283 kg); maximum take-off 28,500 lb (12927 kg)
Dimensions: wingspan 95 ft 7½ in (29.15 m); length 72 ft 8 in (22.12 m); height 31 ft 9 in (9.68 m); wing area 912.00 sq ft (84.72 m²)
Payload: up to 32 troops, or 26 paratroops, or 22 litters and four seated casualties plus four attendants, or 8,740 lb (3964 kg) of freight

de Havilland Canada DHC-5 Buffalo

Developed on the conceptual level from the DHC-4 Caribou, being a version of that type with an enlarged fuselage and turboprop-engined powerplant, the **DHC-5 Buffalo** was known originally as the **Caribou II**.

Buffalos fly on with No. 442 Sqn, Canadian Armed Forces, where their STOL performance is utilised to the full during SAR operations in British Columbia.

Variants

DHC-5B Buffalo: proposed version with CT64-P4C engines
DHC-5C Buffalo: proposed version with Rolls-Royce Dart RDa.12 engines
NASA/DITC XC-8A: designation of C-8A following conversion for use as an augmentor wing research aircraft; extensively modified, it had clipped wings, fixed landing gear and two Rolls-Royce Spey turbofan engines with vectored nozzles complementing the augmentor wings
XC-8A ACLS: redesignation of C-8A following conversion for use as an Air-Cushion Landing System research aircraft; instead of conventional landing gear it had an inflatable but perforated rubber air cushion which permitted operation from and to almost any type of surface, including ice, rough airfields, soft soils, snow, swamps and water
NASA/Boeing QSRA: redesignation of C-8A following conversion for use as a Quiet Short-haul Research Aircraft; this aircraft had a new wing incorporating upper-surface blowing and boundary-layer control, and the revised powerplant of four Lycoming F102 turbofan engines

Four were ordered for evaluation by the US Army, the development cost being shared by the US Army, the Canadian government and the company, and the first of these transports made its maiden flight on 9 April 1964. The DHC-5 had been developed to meet the requirements of the US Army for a transport that would be able to carry loads such as the Pershing missile, a 105-mm (4.13-in) Howitzer or 9-ton truck. The DHC-5's maximum payload was 10,630 lb (4822 kg) that could include, as an alternative to freight, up to 41 troops, or 35 paratroops, or 24 litters and six seated casualties/ attendants. The powerplant comprised two 2,850-ehp (2125-ekW) General Electric T64-GE-10 turboprop engines.

No further orders resulted from US Army evaluation of the DHC-5 (designated originally **YAC-2** by the US Army, and later **C-8A**), but the CAF acquired 15 of the **DHC-5A**, which it designated as the **CC-115**; six of the aircraft were later converted for use in the maritime patrol role. The primary changes in the DHC-5A were an increase in payload to 13,843 lb (6279 kg) and the powerplant of two 3,055-ehp (2278-ekW) General Electric CT64-810-1 turboprop engines. Following delivery of 24 and 16 aircraft respectively to the Brazilian and

Peruvian air forces, the production line was closed. In 1974, however, the company realised that there was a continuing demand for the Buffalo and launched production of an improved **DHC-5D**. This has more powerful engines which permit operation at a higher gross weight and offer improved performance. Overall production totalled 123 aircraft, and was completed in February 1987 with the delivery of the last two aircraft to Kenya. Other armed forces to operate the type included those of Cameroun, Ecuador, Egypt, Mauritania, Mexico, Oman, Sudan, Tanzania, Togo, the United Arab Emirates, Zaire and Zambia.

In response to the interest shown by some civil operators, the company developed a **DHC-5E Transporter** version which gained Canadian certification during 1981. Generally similar to the military Buffalo, it provided accommodation for 44 passengers in a standard utility layout, but was also offered with quick-change passenger/cargo and VIP/executive interiors. No sales were made.

Six out of 10 DHC-5D Buffalos originally delivered to the Kenyan air force remained in service at the dawn of the 21st century. The machines were received in two batches in 1977/78 and 1986/87.

SPECIFICATION

de Havilland Canada DHC-5D Buffalo

Type: three-crew STOL utility transport
Powerplant: two General Electric CT64-820-4 turboprop engines each flat-rated at 3,133 shp (2336 kW)
Performance: maximum cruising speed for STOL transport mission 261 mph (420 km/h) at 10,000 ft (3050 m); initial climb rate 2,330 ft (710 m) per minute; service ceiling 31,000 ft (9450 m); range 259 miles (416 km) with maximum payload
Weights: empty 25,160 lb (11412 kg); maximum take-off 49,200 lb (22317 kg)
Dimensions: wingspan 96 ft (29.26 m); length 79 ft (24.08 m); height 28 ft 8 in (8.73 m); wing area 945.00 sq ft (87.79 m²)
Payload: up to 41 troops, or 35 paratroops, or 24 litters plus six attendants, or 18,000 lb (8165 kg) of freight

de Havilland Canada DHC-6 Twin Otter

Originally designed in the early 1960s and first flown on 20 May 1965, the **DHC-6 Twin Otter** was initially powered by two 579-ehp (432-ekW) PT6A-6 turboprop engines, and was intended to extend the transport potential of the popular single-engined DHC-3 Otter, while retaining the efficient high-lift wing for STOL performance. The new 13/18-seat transport retained no more than the original basic wing structure, with the full span of the trailing edge occupied by double-slotted flaps and ailerons, and from the fourth aircraft onwards the **DHC-6 Series 100** adopted PT6A-20 engines. Optional conversion from fixed tricycle-wheel landing gear to floats or skis was available.

American certification was gained in 1966 and quickly led to commercial orders, but military interest was slow to materialise. Nevertheless, eight aircraft were delivered to the CAF as **CC-138** search and rescue aircraft, and after 115 Series 100 aircraft had been completed production switched to the **DHC-6 Series 200** with a lengthened nose and increased baggage capacity. Some 115 examples of this version were also produced, only a few of them for military customers, before the manufacturer embarked on the final **DHC-6 Series 300**, in which the introduction of more powerful PT6A-27 engines allowed capacity to be increased to 20 passengers at a maximum take-off weight increased by 1,000 lb (454 kg).

Production of the Twin Otter series ended in December 1988 after the completion of 844 aircraft.

Currently proving moderately popular is a conversion by Field Aviation of Canada with Hartzell propellers for reduced external and internal noise levels, and a revised cabin with lightweight seats and fire-retardant composite panelling.

Military operators of the Twin Otter series have been numerous and a total of 10 DHC-6s was supplied to the US forces for service with the core designation **V-18 Twin Otter**. Three survivors are currently operated, in the form of **UV-18B** machines flown at the USAF Academy for parachute training, six **UV-18A** aircraft having been retired in recent times from use by the Alaska Army National Guard.

In 1982 DHC, now part of the Bombardier group, offered three dedicated military Twin Otter variants: the **DHC-6 Series 300M** was a 15-troop transport convertible to 20 seats, with capability for paratroop or ambulance layout; the **DHC-6 Series 300M(COIN)** was a counter-insurgency variant with provision for armour protection, a cabin-mounted machine-gun and underwing ordnance; and the **DHC-6 Series 300MR** was a maritime reconnaissance model with search radar under the nose and underwing searchlight pod. A single DHC-6-300MR was purchased by the Senegal Department of Fisheries.

Above: 440 Transport and Rescue Squadron, CAF, maintains a fleet of four CC-138 Twin Otters at Yellowknife, Northwest Territories, Canada.

This DHC-6 Series 300 is one of several modified with cabin windows as the Vistaliner for sightseeing tours.

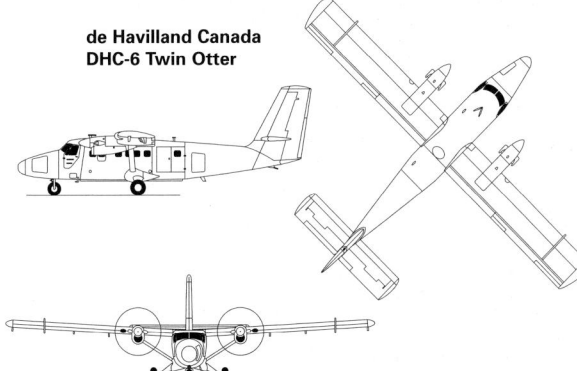

**de Havilland Canada
DHC-6 Twin Otter**

SPECIFICATION	
de Havilland Canada DHC-6 Series 300 Twin Otter	2,500-lb (1134-kg) payload
Type: two-crew light STOL transport	**Weights:** empty 7,415 lb (3363 kg) including two crew; maximum take-off 12,500 lb (5670 kg)
Powerplant: two Pratt & Whitney Canada PT6A-27 turboprop engines each rated at 620 shp (462 kW)	**Dimensions:** wingspan 65 ft (19.81 m); length 51 ft 9 in (15.77 m); height 19 ft 6 in (5.94 m); wing area 420.00 sq ft (39.02 m²)
Performance: maximum cruising speed 210 mph (338 km/h) at 10,000 ft (3050 m); initial climb rate 1,600 ft (488 m) per minute; service ceiling 26,700 ft (8140 m); range 806 miles (1297 km) with a	**Payload:** up to 20 passengers within the context of a 4,280-lb (1941-kg) maximum payload

de Havilland Canada DHC-7 Dash 7

Representing a courageous attempt to exploit the demand of third-level airlines for an economical medium-capacity transport by extending the unrivalled experience of de Havilland Canada (now Bombardier) in the design, development and manufacture of STOL transports, the **DHC-7 Dash 7** first flew on 27 March 1975, gaining its type certification 25 months later. Four turboprop engines drive large-diameter propellers at low speed to yield slow blade-tip speeds for quiet operations. The high-mounted, high-aspect-ratio wing is equipped with large double-slotted flaps and includes a pair of inboard spoilers acting as lift-dumpers on landing and an outboard pair acting differentially in flight to assist aileron control.

The ability of the DHC-7 to operate from short, austere, strips won it an enthusiastic, if limited, customer base.

Accommodation in the initial **DHC-7 Series 100** is for up to 50 passengers in a circular-section pressurised fuselage, or mixed freight/seats in the **DHC-7 Series 101**. The only later variants before production ceased after the completion of a mere 113 aircraft were the **DHC-7 Series 150** and **DHC-7 Series 151**, which were counterparts of the Series 100 and Series 101 variants with a greater fuel capacity and higher operating weights.

Field Aviation of Canada, a specialist in the refurbishment of de Havilland Canada transport aircraft, offers updates for still further enlarged fuel capacity and/or a cargo door.

The DHC-7 sold in only small quantities to military users. Two aircraft, designated **CC-132**, were supplied to the CAF: these were one VIP 32-seater and one DHC-7 Series 101 with mixed cargo and passenger layout. Both aircraft were flown by No. 412 Squadron of the CAF, based at Lahr in West Germany, and were later replaced by DHC-8s. One DHC-7 is operated by the Venezuelan navy on maritime patrol duties, and three **RC-7B** aircraft serve with the US Army as AR-LM (Airborne Reconnaissance-Low Multifunction) machines under the Grizzly Hunter programme. The latter use advanced sensors, including a Raytheon SLAR, in the drug interdiction and battlefield surveillance roles.

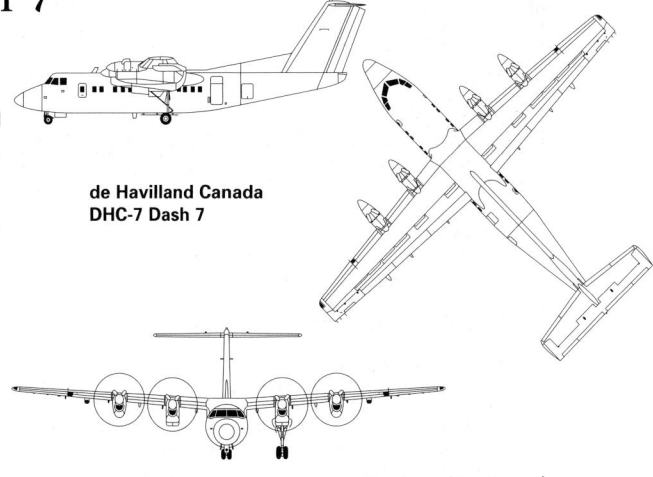

**de Havilland Canada
DHC-7 Dash 7**

SPECIFICATION	
de Havilland Canada DHC-7 Series 100 Dash 7	range 795 miles (1279 km) with 50 passengers
Type: two/three-crew medium STOL transport	**Weights:** empty 27,000 lb (12247 kg); maximum take-off 44,000 lb (19958 kg)
Powerplant: four Pratt & Whitney Canada PT6A-50 turboprop engines each flat-rated at 1,120 shp (835 kW)	**Dimensions:** wingspan 93 ft (28.35 m); length 80 ft 7⁷⁄₁₀ in (24.58 m); height 26 ft 2 in (7.98 m); wing area 860.00 sq ft (79.90 m²)
Performance: maximum cruising speed 266 mph (428 km/h) at 8,000 ft (2440 m); initial climb rate 1,220 ft (372 m) per minute; service ceiling 21,000 ft (6400 m);	**Payload:** up to 50 passengers or freight within the context of an 11,310-lb (5130-kg) maximum payload

de Havilland Canada DHC-8 Dash 8

Market research in the late 1970s by de Havilland Canada resulted in the conclusion that a 30/40-seat short-haul transport, filling the capacity gap between the company's existing 19-seat Twin Otter and 50-seat Dash 7, could prove a profitable venture. This paved the way for the design of the **DHC-8 Dash 8**, followed by the construction of four flying prototypes, of which the first made its maiden flight on 20 June 1983. These four prototypes saw extensive flying in a test programme that led to certification by Canada and the USA before the end of 1984.

The DHC-8 is in many respects a twin-engined and reduced-scale version of the DHC-7, but with less emphasis on STOL performance. Its configuration includes a high-set wing to optimise cabin space, and a T-tail carrying the horizontal surface well clear of the slipstream from the constant-speed propellers with four reversible-pitch blades. The landing gear is of the retractable tricycle type with twin wheels on each unit, the main units being housed in the engine nacelles when raised. As configured for commuter use, the cabin seats 36 passengers, but other options include layouts for up to 40 passengers, or mixed passenger/cargo traffic, or a 17-seat corporate interior. The initial-production **DHC-8 Series 100** was available in **Commuter** and **Corporate** versions, the latter typically carrying 17 passengers over a range of 1,520 miles (2446 km) with full IFR reserves in a cabin

which, like the flight deck, is both pressurised and air-conditioned. This variant was superseded in 1990 by the **DHC-8 Series 100A** with the option of PW123 engines and a revised cabin with greater aisle headroom, and in 1992 there followed the **DHC-8 Series 100B** with further improvements and PW121 engines for improved field and climb performance.

In 1992 the **DHC-8 Series 200** introduced uprated PW123C engines among other improvements, and was further developed as the **DHC-8 Series 200A** (certificated in March 1995) for improved payload/range performance with PW123C engines, and then as the **DHC-8 Series 200B** with PW123D engines offering full power at higher ambient temperatures. First flown on 15 May 1987 and delivered from February 1989, the **DHC-8 Series 300** is a stretched variant with its wing extended by 5 ft (1.52 m) and its fuselage lengthened by 11 ft 3 in (3.43 m) through the insertion of 'plugs' forward and aft of the wing. This provides a maximum capacity for up to 56 passengers carried over a range of 955 miles (1537 km) on the powerplant of two 2,380-shp (1775-kW) PW123 engines. The DHC-8 Series 300 was certificated in February 1989 and delivered from the same month, and has since spawned variants such as the **DHC-8 Series 300A** of 1990 with the improvements of the DHC-8 Series 100A and the powerplant of two

2,380-shp (1775-kW) PW123A engines, the **DHC-8 Series 300B** of 1992 with two 2,500-shp (1864-kW) PW123B engines, and the **DHC-8 Series 300E** of 1994 that is basically similar to the DHC-8 Series 300A except for the improved 'hot and high' performance provided by the powerplant of two PW123E engines each maintaining its rating of 2,380 shp (1775 kW) up to a higher ambient temperature.

The **DHC-8 Series 400** was launched in June 1995 for a maiden flight on 31 January 1998 and a service entry early in 1999 with the wing further increased in span and the fuselage lengthened for the carriage of a maximum load of 78 passengers over a range of 597 miles (961 km). A new powerplant of two 5,067-shp (3778-kW) PW150A turboprops is fitted, the engines running at a lower speed for reduced noise levels, with the new Dowty propellers having six all-composite blades. The DHC-8 Series 400 also has an active Ultra Electronics NVS (Noise and Vibration System) to reduce interior noise and vibration. Since 1998 the Dash 8 has been known as the **Dash 8/Q** to signify the incorporation of NVS, resulting in the designations **Dash 8 Q100, Dash 8 Q200, Dash 8 Q300** and **Dash 8 Q400**.

By mid-1999 the manufacturer had received orders for 615 examples of the DHC-8 series including small numbers of **DHC-8 Dash 8M** aircraft for military service with three air forces. Canada acquired six **DHC-8 Series 100M** machines as two **CC-142** transports for No. 412 Squadron and four **CT-142** navigation trainers with mapping radar in an extended nose. Two aircraft are operated by the USAF from Tyndall Air Force Base in Florida: designated **E-9A**, they are used for range support with equipment including a large electronically steered phased-array radar on the starboard side of the fuselage, APS-128 surveillance radar in a large underfuselage fairing, and

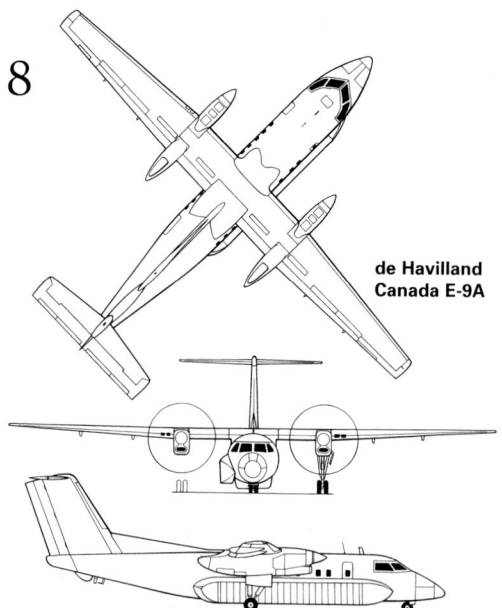

de Havilland Canada E-9A

In the Dash 8 Series 400, the wing spans 92 ft 3 in (28.12 m), while greater passenger capacity is provided by the 103-ft 8-in (31.60-m) long fuselage.

telemetry/communications relay equipment. The Kenyan air force operates three standard DHC-8 Series 100 aircraft on transport duties.

A distinctive revised nose shape differentiates the CT-142 navigation trainer from the similarly painted CC-142 transport aircraft.

SPECIFICATION
de Havilland Canada DHC-8 Dash 8 Series 100A

Type: three-crew short-range medium transport
Powerplant: two Pratt & Whitney Canada PW120A turboprop engines each rated at 2,000 shp (1491 kW)
Performance: maximum cruising speed 305 mph (491 km/h) at 15,000 ft (4570 m); initial climb rate 1,475 ft (450 m) per minute; certificated ceiling 25,000 ft

(7620 m); range 960 miles (1546 km) with maximum passenger payload
Weights: empty 22,600 lb (10251 kg); maximum take-off 34,500 lb (15649 kg)
Dimensions: wingspan 85 ft (25.91 m); length 73 ft (22.25 m); height 24 ft 7 in (7.49 m); wing area 585.00 sq ft (54.35 m²)
Payload: up to 39 passengers or freight within the context of an 8,400-lb (3810-kg) maximum payload

Deperdussin Monocoque Racer

Wealthy French silk merchant Armand Deperdussin founded the aircraft manufacturing organisation known as the Société Pour les Appareils Deperdussin (SPAD) at Betheny, near Reims, during 1910. Louis

Bechereau was to be responsible for the running of the company, alongside a young engineering graduate named André Herbemont. These two brought undying fame to the original short-lived SPAD organisation, which went into liquidation

in 1913 after Deperdussin had been arrested for embezzlement.

Deperdussin won recognition in Europe and North America with its Monocoque Racer monoplane.

Deperdussin Monocoque Racer (cont.)

Bechereau designed a series of monoplanes of increasing capability, perfecting a monocoque form of fuselage construction that combined a low-drag circular cross section with light weight and considerable strength. Lateral control of the **Deperdussin Monocoque Racer** was by wing-warping and power was provided for most of the range by Gnome rotary piston engines.

A first major success came on 9 September 1912, when a Deperdussin powered by a 160-hp (119-kW) Gnome and piloted by Jules Védrines won the fourth James Gordon Bennett Aviation Cup race at Chicago, Illinois. Even greater were the achievements of 1913, Maurice Prévost winning the first Schneider Trophy race at Monaco on 16 April, the Gordon Bennett Cup at Reims on 29 September,

and setting a world absolute speed record of 126.67 mph (203.86 km/h) on the same date. To complete the year's achievements, a Deperdussin piloted by Eugéne Gilbert won the Henry Deutsch de la Meurthe air race around Paris on 27 October. Thus, in a few months, Bechereau and Herbemont had created for Deperdussin the world's fastest aircraft of the period before World War I; from

this pinnacle came the collapse of the Deperdussin company, which was taken over by Louis Blériot and renamed initially as the Société Provisoire des

Aéroplanes Deperdussin and then as the Société Pour l'Aviation et ses Dérivés (thereby retaining the celebrated SPAD acronym), which gained immortal fame for its products during World War I.

SPECIFICATION	
Deperdussin Monocoque Racer (1913 version)	127 mph (204 km/h) at sea level
Type: single-seat racing aircraft	**Weights:** maximum take-off 992 lb (450 kg)
Powerplant: one Gnome rotary piston engine rated at 160 hp (119 kW)	**Dimensions:** wingspan 21 ft 9¾ in (6.65 m); length 20 ft ⅛ in (6.10 m); height 7 ft 6½ in (2.30 m); wing area 103.98 sq ft (9.66 m²)
Performance: maximum speed	

Deperdussin Type B and Type TT

Under the designation **Model TT**, Deperdussin produced during 1912 what was in effect a two-seat version of its earlier **Type B**, but intended specifically for the military market. The type entered service during the same year, initially with the air service of the French army and then with the air services of the British army and the Royal Navy, the later designating the type as the **Deperdussin Monoplane**. Such was the potential of the type, it was believed in the UK, that the British Deperdussin Aeroplane Co. Ltd was established, as successor to the British Deperdussin Aeroplane

Syndicate import agency, to manufacture and further develop the type for sale in the UK and British empire. The aircraft operated by the RN's air service was flown in both landplane and floatplane forms.

Generally similar in configuration to the Deperdussin racing aircraft of the period, although with a fuselage of more simple construction based on that of the Type B but with full covering including a rounded upper decking, the Type TT had accommodation for a passenger and pilot in a tandem arrangement of open cockpits. Powered by Anzani radial or Gnome rotary engines in

the power range from 60-100 hp (45-75 kW), these aircraft saw limited use for observation and patrol, some being deployed in the early days of World War I. It is interesting to note that an attempt was made early in 1914 to create an armed variant of the Type TT. The front cockpit was fitted with a built-up steel-tube 'pulpit', allowing the observer to stand and fire a trainable machine-gun over the top of the propeller disc; such were the weight and drag of the installation, however, that the type's already indifferent performance was degraded to a dangerous degree and the concept was abandoned.

Deperdussin developed the Type TT from the basically civil Type B. A British-built military Type TT is illustrated.

SPECIFICATION	
Deperdussin Type TT (British-built)	3 minutes 45 seconds; endurance 2 hours 30 minutes
Type: two-seat general-purpose aircraft	**Weights:** empty 1,226 lb (556 kg) equipped; maximum take-off 2,037 lb (924 kg)
Powerplant: Gnome rotary piston engine rated at 100 hp (75 kW)	**Dimensions:** wingspan 39 ft 6 in (12.04 m); length 24 ft 6 in (7.47 m); height 8 ft 10 in (2.69 m); wing area 236.00 sq ft (21.92 m²)
Performance: maximum speed 68 mph (109 km/h) at sea level; climb to 1,000 ft (305 m) in	

Dewoitine D.1 and D.9

The first design by Frenchman Emile Dewoitine after establishing his own company in October 1920 was a single-seat monoplane fighter of the high-wing type. This **D.1** was created in response to a 1921 French Service Technique de l'Aéronautique requirement and the initial stages of the programme were somewhat protracted as a result of changes in official policy. The **D.1.01** first prototype finally took to the air on its maiden flight on 18 November 1922. The prototype was powered by a 300-hp (224-kW) Hispano-Suiza 8Fb engine with twin Lamblin radiators under the nose. There was criticism of the forward field of vision for the pilot, and the

D.1.01 was therefore developed into the **D.1bis**, with the original faired cabane strut arrangement replaced by a centreline pylon to carry the wing of what now became a parasol monoplane. The transformation of the D.1.01 into the D.1bis was accomplished in August 1923, and by this time Dewoitine had already completed three of a contract for 10 pre-production aircraft to the original standard: two of these were lost in accidents, and the third was converted to D.1bis standard. The next five aircraft were completed to the D.1bis standard, and comprised single aircraft for Czechoslovakia, Italy and Japan as well as two for

Switzerland. There was continued criticism of the pilot's forward fields of vision, so the original prototype was converted to **D.1ter** standard with a cabane arrangement of short inverted-Vee struts, and the two Swiss aircraft as well as the last two of the French pre-production order were also completed to this standard. It also included a wing of reduced span but increased chord, and the radiators attached to the forward legs of the fixed tailskid landing gear's main unit arrangement.

Demonstrations of the D.1 in a number of countries by Dewoitine company pilot Marcel Doret resulted in the placement of additional orders. Yugoslavia ordered 60 aircraft (later reduced to 44) and Italy selected the D.1 over the Dornier Do H Falke, Ansaldo securing a licence to manufacture the D.1ter as the **A.C.2**, of which 112 examples were delivered to the Regia Aeronautica for first-line service until 1929. Although finally rejected for service with the French

Aviation Militaire, which had nonetheless ordered and received 20 such fighters, the D.1ter entered French service with the Marine Nationale, which had contracted in November 1923 for 44 D.1ter fighters to be built by SECM (Société d'Emboutissage et de Constructions Mécaniques). The first of these aircraft flew on 18 January 1925, 15 of them equipping Escadrille 7C1, operating from the aircraft-carrier *Béarn*.

The **D.9** single-seat fighter was of the same basic configuration as the D.1, but with its wingspan increased by 4 ft 3¼ in (1.30 m). Resulting from a 1923 requirement in the C.1 (single-seat fighter) category, the **D.9.01** prototype first flew in June 1924 with the powerplant of one

Gnome-Rhône (Bristol) Jupiter radial. The D.9 was also rejected by the French army air service and despite being lost in an accident during October 1925, went on to attain some export success. Belgium and Yugoslavia bought one and six aircraft respectively, and the Swiss EKW factory assembled three machines from parts supplied by the Dewoitine workshops. Most important, however, was a Regia Aeronautica order for 150 aircraft that were built under licence in Italy by Ansaldo with the local designation **A.C.3**. After service with fighter squadriglie of the Italian air force, the A.C.3s survived into the 1930s as the equipment for the newly formed 5° Stormo Assalto, a ground-attack unit based at Ciampino.

With the D.1, Dewoitine established its parasol-wing configuration.

SPECIFICATION	
Dewoitine D.1ter	**Weights:** empty 1,808 lb (820 kg); maximum take-off 2,734 lb (1240 kg)
Type: single-seat fighter	
Powerplant: one 300-hp (224-kW) Hispano-Suiza 8Fb Vee piston engine	**Dimensions:** wingspan 37 ft 8¾ in (11.50 m); length 24 ft 7¼ in (7.50 m); height 9 ft (2.75 m); wing area 215.29 sq ft (20.00 m²)
Performance: maximum speed 155 mph (250 km/h) at 6,560 ft (2000 m); initial climb rate 1,476 ft (450 m) per minute; service ceiling 26,245 ft (8000 m); range 249 miles (400 km)	**Armament:** two 0.303-in (7.7-mm) Vickers fixed forward-firing machine-guns in the upper part of the forward fuselage

Dewoitine D.21

The **D.21** prototype first flew in January 1926, and was in fact the second prototype of the unsuccessful **D.12** fighter prototype revised with the Hispano-Suiza 12Gb engine. With this engine the performance of the type was generally improved, and this fact was reflected in the receipt of a Turkish order for two aircraft for a full evaluation that paved the way for a later order for 10 more, which were delivered in 1928-29. Further orders were placed by Argentina and Czechoslovakia for 18 (plus the prototype) and three aircraft respectively and, of these, seven and three were built by EKW in Switzerland.

Both Argentina and Czechoslovakia then acquired licences for local manufacture of the type: the Argentine programme was allocated to the FMA, and 40 D.21s were built in the period 1930-31 with Madsen machine-guns and a licence-built version of the Lorraine-Dietrich 12Eb, which effectively made them D.12s; and the Czechoslovak programme was allocated to Skoda, which produced 26 **Skoda D 1** fighters in the period 1928-29 with the 562-hp (419-kW) Skoda L engine that was based on the Hispano-Suiza 12G engine.

SPECIFICATION	
Dewoitine D.21	
Type: single-seat fighter	**Dimensions:** wingspan 4 ft 11⅞ in (12.80 m); length 25 ft ¾ in (7.64 m); height 9 ft 10 in (3.00 m); wing area 266.95 sq ft (24.80 m²)
Powerplant: one Hispano-Suiza 12Gb Vee piston engine rated at 500 hp (373 kW)	
Performance: maximum speed 168 mph (270 km/h) at sea level; initial climb rate 1,968 ft (600 m) per minute; range 249 miles (400 km)	**Armament:** two 0.303-in (7.7-mm) Vickers fixed forward-firing machine-guns in the upper part of the forward fuselage and (not always installed) two 0.295-in (7.5-mm) Darne modèle 19 fixed forward-firing machine-guns in the leading edges of the wing
Weights: empty 2,403 lb (1090 kg); maximum take-off 3,483 lb (1580 kg)	

Re-engining the D.12 as the D.21, Dewoitine managed to achieve limited sales success on the export market.

Dewoitine D.26 and D.27

The most famous of the Dewoitine parasol-wing monoplane fighters, the **D.27** was developed in response to a French official requirement of 1926 for a lightweight C.1 (single-seat fighter) warplane, but like the previous designs from the Dewoitine stable this was rejected by the Aviation Militaire. Following the end of the Construction Aéronautique E. Dewoitine company in France during January 1927, work on the D.27 was transferred to Switzerland, where the D.27 prototype was built by the Thun workshops of the EKW organisation for a first flight on 3 June 1928 with the powerplant of one Hispano-Suiza 12Mb Vee engine. Later bought by the Fliegertruppe, the Swiss army air service, for competitive evaluation against the Comte AC-1, the prototype was a straightforward development of the earlier types with a considerable measure of aerodynamic refinement to reduce drag and thus boost performance, and revised landing gear.

In the autumn of 1928 EKW decided to build a pre-production series of 12 D.27s with the wing reduced in area and the original type of angular vertical tail surface, inherited from earlier Dewoitine fighters, replaced by an entirely redesigned and less angular tail assembly. By the end of 1928, small orders for the D.27 had been placed by Argentina, Romania and Yugoslavia, which had contracted for one, three and three aircraft respectively for evaluation; the Yugoslav order called for one complete D.27 and kits for two aircraft that would be assembled by Zmaj. No further orders for the type were placed despite the fact that at one time it had seemed more than likely that both Romania and Yugoslavia would take the D.27 in some numbers.

At the end of 1929, however, the Swiss army air arm decided to adopt the D.27 as its new fighter and started with an order for five **D.27 III** pre-production aircraft, which were delivered in 1931. There followed orders for an additional 15 pre-production and 45 production aircraft all delivered by 1932, the year in which 15 of the D.27 IIIs were revised with wheel spats and had their Hispano-Suiza 12Mb engines replaced by more powerful Hispano-Suiza 12Mc units, although these were soon abandoned in favour of the original engines. The Swiss D.27s remained in first-line service to 1940, thereafter equipping flying schools until finally scrapped in 1944.

The French authorities bought the second and third examples of the Swiss-built pre-production type, the aircraft being delivered in April 1929: the first of these was revised as the **D.272** with the 400-hp (298-kW) Hispano-Suiza 12Jb engine for use as an aerobatic display machine, and the second was submitted to an official evaluation with the armament of two 0.295-in (7.5-mm) Darne modèle 19 machine-guns. The French later ordered another four of the aircraft for assembly by Lioré-et-Olivier.

Emile Dewoitine had meanwhile re-established himself in France during March 1928 in the form of the Société Aéronautique

This reconditioned D.27 shows to good effect the type's parasol layout and retractable undernose radiator installation.

Française (Avions Dewoitine), which offered the D.27 for French service in two forms, neither of which was accepted: the **D.271** was to have been powered by the 500-hp (373-kW) Hispano-Suiza 12Hb engine, and the **D.273** was to have been powered by the Gnome-Rhône (Bristol) Jupiter VII radial engine fitted with a turbocharger to provide 425 hp (317 kW) at 13,125 ft (4000 m).

Ordered by the KTA (military technical service) of the Swiss army at the same time as the D.27 fighter, the **D.26** was a single-seat fighter trainer of construction similar to that of the D.27, but with a lower-powered engine in an uncowled installation. Nine examples of the D.26 were delivered in 1931, and these aircraft were intended mainly for training in gunnery and formation flight. Shortly after this, two more D.26s were purchased with the uprated powerplant of one 300-hp (224-kW) Wright 9Qe engine, and these last two machines were intended specifically for training in air-to-air combat, a task for which they were fitted with wing-mounted camera guns.

The aircraft were notable for their longevity, nearly all of them flying with training schools until 1948, when they were handed over to the Swiss Aero Club that subsequently used them for many years as glider tugs. The last machine was not retired until 1970, and is now on display at the Military Aeronautical Museum at Dubendorf.

D.27 fighters formed an important part of Switzerland's front-line fighter force through most of the 1930s and into 1940. The country was perhaps the manufacturer's most important customer in its pre-war years.

SPECIFICATION	
Dewoitine D.27	
Type: single-seat fighter	**Dimensions:** wingspan 4 ft 11⅞ in (12.80 m); length 25 ft ¾ in (7.64 m); height 9 ft 10 in (3.00 m); wing area 266.95 sq ft (24.80 m²)
Powerplant: one Hispano-Suiza 12Gb Vee piston engine rated at 500 hp (373 kW)	
Performance: maximum speed 168 mph (270 km/h) at sea level; initial climb rate 1,968 ft (600 m) per minute; range 249 miles (400 km)	**Armament:** two 0.303-in (7.7-mm) Vickers fixed forward-firing machine-guns in the upper part of the forward fuselage and (not always installed) two 0.295-in (7.5-mm) Darne modèle 19 fixed forward-firing machine-guns in the leading edges of the wing
Weights: empty 2,403 lb (1090 kg); maximum take-off 3,483 lb (1580 kg)	

Dewoitine D.33

In 1929, the French air ministry issued a requirement for an 'avion de grand raid' (long-distance aircraft), offering a substantial monetary prize to the manufacturer whose aircraft could cover a distance of 10000 km (6,214 miles) without refuelling. In response to this requirement Dewoitine produced the **D.33** as an all-metal low-wing cantilever monoplane with fixed tailskid landing gear including divided wide-track main units with spatted wheels. The long, sharply-tapering wing contained no fewer than 16 fuel tanks, with considerable wing dihedral, providing gravity feed to fuselage collector tanks which in turn supplied the maximum of 13,228 lb (6000 kg) of fuel to the engine.

The **D.33.01** first proto-type made its initial flight on 21 November 1930 in the hands of the company's chief test pilot, Marcel Doret. Named *Trait d'Union* (hyphen), this machine established a distance record of 6,445 miles (10372 km) at an average speed of 92.6 mph (149 km/h) during June 1931. On 21 July 1931, with a tricolour flag emblazoned on its tail unit, the aircraft took off for its 6,214-mile (10000-km) attempt on the non-stop record, with Tokyo as the target. The crew comprised pilots Le Brix and Doret with Masmin as radio operator. When the D.33.01 was some 310 miles (500 km) north-west of Irkutsk in Siberia, the engine seized and Doret made a crash landing after his companions had escaped by parachute.

The second aircraft, the **D.33.02**, also named as the *Trait d'Union*, was already complete. With a large red, white and blue roundel on the vertical tail surface, this aircraft lifted off with the same crew on 11 September 1931, Tokyo again being the objective. After some 24 hours of flight, however, the aircraft suffered violent turbulence while traversing the foothills of the Ural mountains. It was thrown into an uncontrollable dive, Doret escaping by parachute at low altitude, but both his comrades being killed as the aircraft crashed. An official investigation exonerated the company and its design, the powerplant again being blamed for the crash, but further development of the design was abandoned.

The D.33's pilots sat side-by-side in an enclosed cabin, with the radio operator in a compartment immediately behind. The first aircraft is illustrated.

SPECIFICATION	
Dewoitine D.33	theoretical maximum range
Type: three-crew long-range record-breaking aircraft	6,835 miles (11000 km)
Powerplant: one Hispano-Suiza 12Nb Vee piston engine rated at 650 hp (485 kW)	**Weights:** empty 6,834 lb (3100 kg); maximum take-off 21,605 lb (9800 kg)
Performance: maximum speed 152 mph (245 km/h) at optimum altitude; cruising speed 109 mph (175 km/h) at optimum altitude;	**Dimensions:** wingspan 91 ft 10¼ in (28.00 m); length 47 ft 3 in (14.40 m); height 16 ft 4¾ in (5.00 m); wing area 839.61 sq ft (78.00 m²)

Dewoitine D.332 series

An all-metal monoplane of the low-wing cantilever configuration, the **D.332** was an eight-passenger transport that made its maiden flight on 11 July 1933, piloted by Marcel Doret. The pilot and co-pilot were accommodated side-by-side in a cabin located forward of the wing leading edge, with the radio operator's compartment immediately behind them. The passenger cabin was roomy, well heated and ventilated, and had seats which could be folded down into bunk beds for night-flying comfort. Power was provided by three 575-hp (429-kW) Wright Cyclone radial engines, licence-built as Hispano-Suiza 9V units.

Named *Emeraude* (emerald), the new transport made a number of impressive demonstration flights to various European capitals, and gained a world class record on 7 September 1933 when it completed a 621-mile

(1000-km) course with a useful load of 4,409 lb (2000 kg) at an average speed of 161.3 mph (259.56 km/h).

Intended for use on Air France's proposed regular service to Saigon in French Indo-China, the D.332 set off on 22 December 1933 for a trail-blazing flight to that destination, which it reached on 28 December 1933 in a flying time of

Powered by three 650-hp (485-kW) 9V-16/17 radial engines, the D.338 had a maximum speed of 187 mph (301 km/h).

48 hours. When only some 249 miles (400 km) from Le Bourget airport on the return flight, *Emeraude* struck a hill near Corbigny during a violent snowstorm and all aboard were killed in the ensuing fire.

Variants

D.333: Air France ordered three examples of the D.333, a heavier and strengthened development of the D.332, accommodating up to 10 passengers; the aircraft were used to operate the Toulouse-Dakar (West Africa) sector of the Air France South American route for several years

D.338: following the first flight of a D.338 prototype in 1936, Air France bought 30 production aircraft; these had retractable landing gear, a wing of slightly increased span and a fuselage lengthened by 10 ft 5¼ in (3.18 m) by comparison with that of the D.332; on short- and medium-distance routes the D.338 had provision for up to 22 passengers, while aircraft operated on the Far Eastern service had 12 luxury seats, six of which could be converted as sleeping berths; the D.338s achieved a high reputation for reliability, many of them flying passenger routes in French overseas possessions during World War II; nine aircraft which remained airworthy operated the Paris-Nice service for several months after the end of the war

D.342: a single machine built in 1939, this had improved lines, accommodated 24 passengers, and was powered by three 915-hp (682-kW) Gnome-Rhône 14N radial engines; it was delivered to Air France during 1942

D.620: D.338 development with three supercharged 880-hp (666-kW) Gnome-Rhône 14Krsd radial engines and provision for 30 passengers; the only example built was never delivered for airline service and its ultimate fate is unknown

SPECIFICATION	
Dewoitine D.332	**Weights:** empty 11,640 lb (5280 kg); maximum take-off 20,613 lb (9350 kg)
Type: three-crew transport aircraft	
Powerplant: three Hispano-Suiza 9V radial piston engines each rated at 575 hp (429 kW)	**Dimensions:** wingspan 95 ft 1¾ in (29.00 m); length 62 ft 2 in (18.95 m); wing area 861.14 sq ft (80.00 m²)
Performance: maximum speed 186 mph (300 km/h) at optimum altitude; cruising speed 155 mph (250 km/h) at optimum altitude; service ceiling 20,670 ft (6300 m); range 1,243 miles (2000 km)	**Payload:** up to eight passengers within the context of a 3,933-lb (1784-kg) payload

Dewoitine D.370 series

Developed at about the same time as the D.500 in response to an official French requirement of 1930 for a C.1 (single-seat fighter) warplane, the **D.37** marked the culmination of the Dewoitine parasol-wing monoplane fighter concept. Completed by the Lioré-et-Olivier company, as Dewoitine was already overburdened by the D.500 programme, the **D.37.01** prototype first flew on 1 October 1931 with the powerplant of one 700-hp (522-kW) Gnome-Rhône 14Kbrs Mistral-Major radial engine. The D.37.01 prototype showed sufficient promise to merit further development and was revised with the 14Kbs and then the 800-hp (597-kW) 14Kds engine, and other changes included a modified engine cowling, changed landing gear and a

The D.371 had an all-metal monocoque fuselage and a fabric-covered metal wing, braced on each side by a pair of parallel struts.

wing revised with dihedral and reduced chord. There then appeared the **D.371.01** second prototype that first flew in February 1934 with further alteration.

In the spring of 1935 the Armée de l'Air ordered a batch of 28 D.371 fighters to a standard that differed from that of the prototype mainly in their powerplant of one close-cowled Gnome-Rhône 14Kfs radial. Lithuania also ordered the type in the form of 14 **D.372** fighters with the revised armament of two 0.303-in (7.7-mm) Browning machine-guns in the fuselage and two 0.303-in (7.7-mm) Darne

machine-guns in the leading edges of the wing. In November 1934 the French navy ordered an initial 20 examples of the **D.373** with flotation equipment, the wing reduced in span and fitted with trailing-edge flaps, an arrester hook allowing operation on the aircraft-carrier *Béarn*. An additional 25 examples of the **D.376** were subsequently ordered, differing from the D.373s in having outer wing panels that folded to the rear. The French navy in fact received its aircraft before the Armée de l'Air, the last aircraft for French service being delivered in December 1935. The

D.373 and D.376 (13 and nine aircraft respectively) still formed the equipment of naval Escadrille AC1 at the outbreak of World War II, but had been retired before the end of 1939.

Meanwhile, Lithuania had decided to accept seven examples each of the D.500 and cannon-armed D.501 in place of its D.372 fighters, which were therefore available to join 10 D.371 fighters that were diverted from the Armée de l'Air order to the Spanish Republican government during 1936. Shortly afterwards two more D.372s, ordered in the name of the Saudi Arabian government in

order to avoid open French identification with the Spanish Republican cause, were delivered at Barcelona. All the Spanish aircraft were armed eventually with two 0.303-in (7.7-mm) Vickers machine-guns. They

claimed 21 Nationalist aircraft destroyed in two months' fighting during the early stages of the Spanish Civil War, but thereafter were relegated to the coastal protection and advanced training roles.

SPECIFICATION

Dewoitine D.371C.1
Type: single-seat fighter
Powerplant: one Gnome-Rhône 14Kfs Mistral-Major radial piston engine rated at 930 hp (693 kW)
Performance: maximum speed 236 mph (380 km/h) at 14,435 ft (4400 m); climb to 14,765 ft (4500 m) in 5 minutes 12 seconds; absolute ceiling 36,090 ft (11000 m); range 559 miles (900 km)

Weights: empty 2,910 lb (1320 kg); maximum take-off 4,153 lb (1884 kg)
Dimensions: wingspan 36 ft 9¾ in (11.22 m); length 24 ft 4 in (7.44 m); height 11 ft 1¾ in (3.40 m); wing area 187.83 sq ft (17.45 m²)
Armament: four 0.295-in (7.5-mm) Darne fixed forward-firing machine-guns under the leading edges of the wing

Dewoitine D.500 and D.501

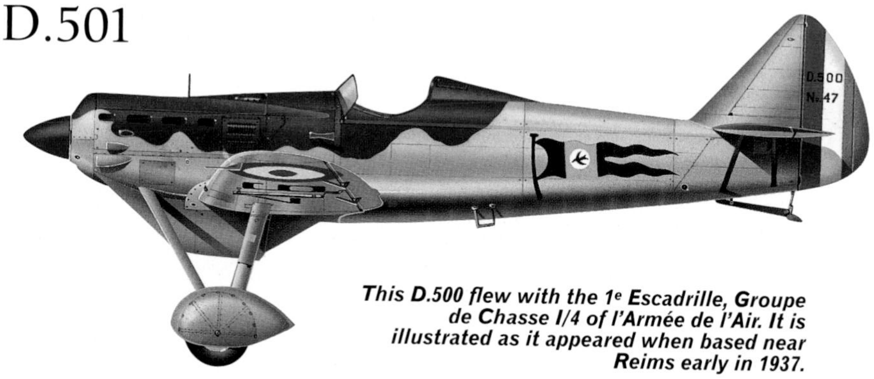

Designed to satisfy a French air ministry requirement of 1930 for a C.1 warplane to replace the Nieuport-Delage Ni-D.62 and Ni-D.622, the **D.500** was Dewoitine's first monoplane fighter not of the parasol-wing configuration. This antiquated structural concept, with its multiplicity of drag-inducing struts and bracing wires, was now replaced by a clean cantilever monoplane wing in the low-set position. The structure was all-metal, including the skinning, and the construction of the wing, fuselage and tail unit (including a strut-braced horizontal surface) was entirely conventional. The fixed tailwheel landing gear was strongly reminiscent of that of the D.37 series, and the powerplant of the **D.500.01** prototype, which flew for the first time on 19 June 1932, was based on the 660-hp (492-kW) Hispano-Suiza 12Xbrs Vee engine. The armament was initially two 0.303-in (7.7-mm) Vickers machine-guns in the fuselage, but these were soon replaced by 0.295-in (7.5-mm) Darne weapons, and provision was made at

much the same time for the installation of two further Darne machine-guns in the leading edges of the wing.

In November 1933 an order was placed for 60 examples of the D.500's production variant, of which 15 were to be produced by Dewoitine and the other 45 by Lioré-et-Olivier. In the event only 58 of the aircraft were built, the other two being completed to the somewhat different **D.510** standard; of the 58 machines that were completed, 48 were to the **D.500C.1** standard based on the prototype in its definitive form and thus powered by the Hispano-Suiza 12Xbrs engine, while the other 10 were manufactured to the **D.501C.1** standard, with the Hispano-Suiza 12Xcrs engine allowing the installation between the cylinder banks of a 20-mm Hispano-Suiza S7 cannon. The D.501C.1 also had two Darne machine-guns in the wing. The first example of the D.500C.1 flew on 29 November 1934, by which time orders had been placed for an additional 130 aircraft

(50 D.500C.1 and 80 D.501C.1 fighters) to be manufactured by Lioré-et-Olivier, and 60 D.501C.1 fighters by Ateliers et Chantiers de la Loire.

Deliveries of the D.500 series to the Armée de l'Air began in May 1935, and production for this service eventually reached 100 and 133 examples of the D.500C.1 and D.501C.1 respectively. The Aéronautique Navale, the air arm of the French navy, also received 30 D.501C.1s, and export sales were made to Lithuania and Venezuela, which received 14 D.501 and three D.500 fighters in 1936 and July 1935 respectively.

At the outbreak of

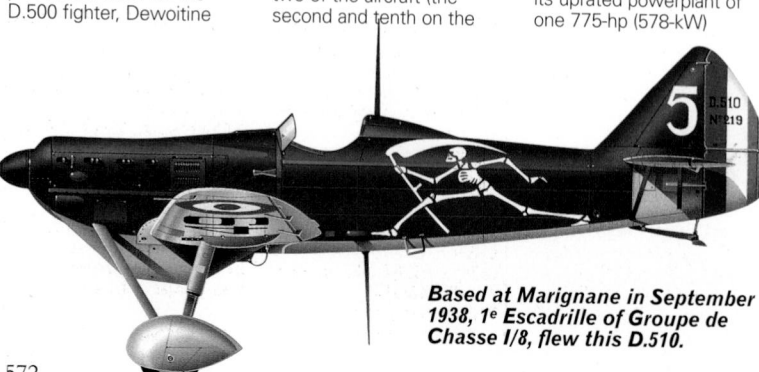

This D.500 flew with the 1e Escadrille, Groupe de Chasse I/4 of l'Armée de l'Air. It is illustrated as it appeared when based near Reims early in 1937.

World War II in September 1939, limited numbers of wholly obsolescent D.500C.1 and D.501C.1 aircraft were still in second-line service with the escadrilles régionales de chasse

(regional fighter squadrons) for the point defence of important military and industrial targets in areas well behind the front line, but they had all been retired to training roles by the end of 1939.

SPECIFICATION

Dewoitine D.501C.1
Type: single-seat fighter
Powerplant: one Hispano-Suiza 12Xcrs Vee piston engine rated at 660 hp (492 kW)
Performance: maximum speed 228 mph (367 km/h) at 16,405 ft (5000 m); cruising speed 140 mph (225 km/h) at optimum altitude; climb to 3,280 ft (1000 m) in 1 minute 21 seconds; service ceiling 33,465 ft (10200 m); range 541 miles (870 km)
Weights: empty 2,837 lb (1287 kg); maximum take-off

3,940 lb (1787 kg)
Dimensions: wingspan 39 ft 8 in (12.09 m); length 24 ft 9⅝ in (7.56 m); height 8 ft 10½ in (2.70 m); wing area 177.61 sq ft (16.50 m²)
Armament: one 20-mm Hispano-Suiza (Oerlikon) S7 fixed forward-firing cannon between the cylinder banks to fire through the propeller hub and two 0.295-in (7.5-mm) Darne fixed forward-firing machine-guns in the leading edges of the wing

Dewoitine D.510

After it had received its first production order for the D.500 fighter, Dewoitine

was instructed to complete two of the aircraft (the second and tenth on the

production line) to the revised **D.510** standard that differed from that of the D.500 and D.501 mainly in its uprated powerplant of one 775-hp (578-kW)

Hispano-Suiza 12Ycrs Vee engine, although other modifications increased the fuel capacity and altered the main landing-gear units. The new engine was both longer and heavier than the Hispano-Suiza 12Xcrs unit it replaced, demanding the lengthening of the forward fuselage, but had the same provision for the installation of a cannon between its cylinder banks to fire through the hollow propeller shaft. The first of the two prototype conversions made the new type's maiden flight 14 August 1934, and was followed into the air by the second

conversion in December of the same year.

The D.510 revealed better performance than the D.500 and D.501 without any appreciable degradation of agility, and was ordered into production by a contract of May 1935, which called for the delivery of an initial 35 (later trimmed to 25) aircraft. Deliveries of the **D.510C.1** started in October 1936, and another seven aircraft were then added to the initial order as replacements for the seven D.501 fighters that had been diverted to Lithuania from French orders.

Based at Marignane in September 1938, 1e Escadrille of Groupe de Chasse I/8, flew this D.510.

Dewoitine D.510 (continued)

Later contracts called for 80 more aircraft including 24 **D.510C** and 36 **D.510T** fighters for the air forces of the Chinese central government and Turkey; the former were delivered, but the latter were not and passed into French service. Others were placed by Japan, the UK and the USSR for one, two and one aircraft respectively for evaluations that led to no production orders. Two of the aircraft from the cancelled Turkish order eventually arrived in Spain after being sold, it was claimed, to the Hejaz (now Saudi Arabia) and were there revised with a Soviet engine type, the Klimov M-100 licence-built version of the Hispano-Suiza 12Ybrs, after the

French government demanded the return of the illegally exported French engines. By the outbreak of World War II in September 1939 the D.510C.1 was obsolete but still equipped three first-line groupes de chasse (fighter wings), which received more modern

equipment in the first months of the war. Some of the aircraft were allocated to two escadrilles régionales de chasse (regional fighter squadrons) in north Africa and others to a pair of Aéronautique Navale squadrons created in December 1939 and May 1940.

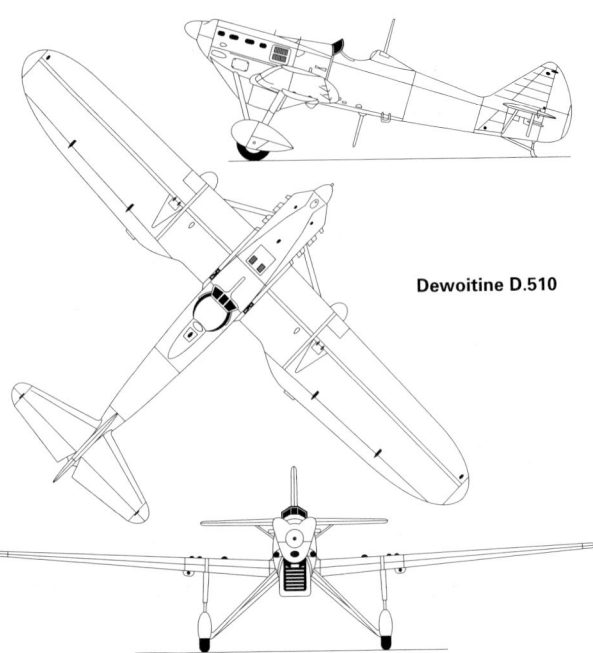

Dewoitine D.510

Dewoitine D.520

With development of the unpromising **D.513** fighter terminated, Dewoitine used the lessons learned in the construction of these prototypes to produce the more modern-looking **D.520**, the first of whose three prototypes made its maiden flight on 2 October 1938. A cantilever low-wing monoplane, the D.520 looked from the cockpit aft very similar to the D.513. Forward of the cockpit, however, was a wing of new planform with increased dihedral and a

After the French capitulation D.520 production continued, with aircraft finding their way into German, Hungarian, Italian and Vichy French hands. This aircraft flew with JG 105 from Chartres in May 1944.

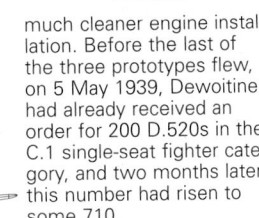

Dewoitine D.520C.1

D.520 No. 408 was delivered two days after the French surrender. It fought against the Allies in the Vichy French air force, but survived the war and was restored to airworthy condition in 1977-80.

revised planform with straight-tapered rather than semi-elliptical leading and trailing edges, as well as a

much cleaner engine installation. Before the last of the three prototypes flew, on 5 May 1939, Dewoitine had already received an order for 200 D.520s in the C.1 single-seat fighter category, and two months later this number had risen to some 710.

By then, the last details had been finalised for production aircraft, which were to be powered by the Hispano-Suiza 12Y-45 engine with a Szydlowski supercharger, and the first of these **D.520C.1** machines flew on 31 October 1939. Without doubt the most capable fighter of French origin available to the Armée de l'Air early in World War II, the D.520C.1 had been delivered to the extent of only some 300 aircraft by mid-June 1940 and just 403 machines had been taken on charge by the time of the French armistice with Germany on 25 June 1940. Continued

production of the D.520 was authorised in Vichy France, 474 being built before and after the German occupation of Vichy France in November 1942. Captured aircraft

plus production aircraft were delivered to Germany's allies, including Bulgaria, Italy and Romania, and were used also by the Luftwaffe as fighter trainers.

Variants

D.521: one D.520 following installation of the 1,030-hp (768-kW) Rolls-Royce Merlin III Vee engine; production of this version had been planned but was subsequently cancelled, and in any case the heavy Merlin engine proved unsatisfactory

D.524: designation allocated for the D.521 following removal of the Merlin engine and installation of a 1,200-hp (895-kW) Hispano Suiza 12Z; the development of this type was abandoned with the fall of France in June 1940

DFS 230

Variants

DFS 230A-2: dual-control version of the DFS 230A-1
DFS 230B-1: generally similar to DFS 230A but structurally strengthened, fitted with armament, and provided with a braking parachute
DFS 230B-2: dual-control version of the DFS 230B-1
DFS 230C-1: generally similar to DFS 230B-1 but with redesigned nose incorporating three braking rockets
DFS 230D-1: one prototype converted to DFS 230C-1 configuration
DFS 230 V7: prototype conversion to the planned **DFS 230F-1** standard for the carriage of up to 15 troops; no production examples were built

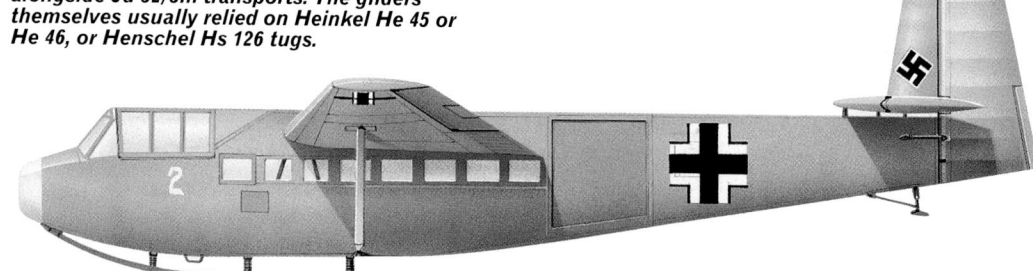

DFS 230 assault transport gliders were often flown alongside Ju 52/3m transports. The gliders themselves usually relied on Heinkel He 45 or He 46, or Henschel Hs 126 tugs.

Following military interest in a research glider being developed by DFS, a contract was awarded for the construction of an initial six prototypes. Demonstrated successfully during 1937, the resulting type was ordered into limited production by Gothaer Waggonfabrik as the **DFS 230A-1**. Production of the DFS was undertaken by Erla and Hartig as well as Gotha in Germany, and by Mars in occupied Czechoslovakia, where 410 machines were completed; total production was about 1,510 aircraft. A braced high-wing monoplane of mixed construction, the DFS 230 provided accommodation for a crew of two and eight fully armed troops. Towable by a variety of Luftwaffe aircraft, the DFS 230 used jettisonable landing gear for take-off and landed on a central skid mounted beneath the fuselage. The DFS 230 mounted the world's first operation by gliderborne troops when the Belgian fort of Eben-Emael was captured on 10 May 1940. DFS 230 gliders were also used in large numbers for the invasion of Crete, and in very small numbers for the surprise rescue of Benito Mussolini after he had been imprisoned. The type also saw extensive service in supply missions on the Eastern Front.

SPECIFICATION

DFS 230B-1

Type: two-crew assault transport glider
Performance: maximum gliding speed 180 mph (290 km/h); normal towing speed 112 mph (180 km/h)
Weights: empty 1,896 lb (860 kg); maximum take-off 4,630 lb (2100 kg)
Dimensions: wingspan 72 ft 1¼ in (21.98 m); length 36 ft 10½ in (11.24 m); height 9 ft (2.74 m); wing area 444.56 sq ft (41.30 m²)
Armament: two 0.312-in (7.92-mm) MG 34 fixed forward-firing machine-guns in the nose, and one 0.312-in (7.92-mm) MG 15 trainable machine-gun in the upper fuselage decking
Payload: up to eight troops or freight

DFW 'B' and 'C' series aircraft

Licensed builders of the C V included Automobil und Aviatik AG, Halberstädter Flugzeug GmbH and Luft-Verkehrs-Gesellschaft GmbH.

Under the abbreviation DFW, the German company Deutsche Flugzeug-Werke GmbH, which had been established by Bernard Meyer at Lindenthal near Leipzig in 1910, built a number of interesting aircraft. Like many other manufacturers, DFW started in business by the licence-production of French-designed aircraft, in this case the biplane types of Maurice Farman design.

The company's first original design had the name **DFW Mars** and was built in both monoplane and biplane configurations. Common to both versions was the fuselage (providing accommodation for two in a tandem arrangement of open cockpits), the tail unit and the tailskid landing gear. The wing of the Mars monoplane was wire-braced to landing gear attachments and to a king-post forward of the front cockpit, and the aircraft was powered by one 95-hp (71-kW) NAG inline engine. The unequal-span Mars biplane had conventional strut and wire bracing, large ailerons at the wingtips and the power-plant of one 90-hp (67-kW) Mercedes-Daimler inline engine. Pre-war production also included copies of the Etrich Taube and of the Jeannin Taube monoplanes.

With the outbreak of World War I in 1914, DFW began the design and construction of a series of aircraft, only one of which achieved conspicuous success. They included two-seat aircraft in the 'B' (unarmed) and 'C' (armed) general-purpose biplane categories, single-seat fighters in the 'D' (biplane) and 'Dr' (triplane) categories, and 'R' category multi-engined bombers. First, for the reconnaissance and trainer roles, came the **B I** equal-span biplane, whose fuselage and tail unit revealed a family affinity to the earlier Mars; the B I was powered by a 100-hp (75-kW) Mercedes D.I inline engine. The generally similar but reduced-span **B II** of 1915 was intended more specifically as a trainer, and was powered by a Mercedes inline engine in the form of either the 100-hp (75-kW) D.I or 120-hp (90-kW) D.II unit. An experimental 'C'-type biplane of 1916, distinguished by a single-bay wing cellule with I-type interplane struts, was followed in the same year by the armed general-purpose **C I** and **C II**, powered by one 150-hp (112-kW) Benz Bz.III inline engine. The two biplane types differed in the disposition of their crews: in the

C I the pilot sat behind the observer/gunner, but in the C II this arrangement was reversed to give the observer/gunner better fields of vision and fire.

Also developed in 1916 was the **C IV** with a single-bay biplane wing cellule, a refined fuselage and the powerplant of one Bz.IV engine or alternatively one 185-hp (148-kW) Conrad C.III NAG inline, whose installation meant a reduction in performance. The C IV led to the **C V** that was by far the most successful of DFW's aircraft, and which was built in substantial numbers by DFW as well as a team of licensees. The C V was used over the Western Front until well into 1918 and over the Italian front until the end of the war. Small numbers were also transferred to Turkey, and after World War I's end, Belgium, one of the victorious Allies, pressed into service 30 examples of the same type surrendered by the Germans.

The last of DFW's 'C' category aircraft was the single **C VI** of 1918, a heavier and more refined biplane powered by a 220-hp (164-kW) Benz Bz.IVa engine.

SPECIFICATION

DFW C V

Type: two-seat reconnaissance, artillery observation and general-purpose aircraft
Powerplant: one Benz Bz.IV inline piston engine rated at 200 hp (149 kW)
Performance: maximum speed 97 mph (155 mph) at sea level; climb to 3,280 ft (1000 m) in 4 minutes; service ceiling 16,405 ft (5000 m); endurance 3 hours 30 minutes
Weights: empty 2,138 lb (970 kg); maximum take-off 3,153 lb (1430 kg)
Dimensions: wingspan 43 ft 6⅞ in (13.27 m); length 25 ft 10¼ in (7.875 m); height 10 ft 8 in (3.25 m); wing area 457.48 sq ft (42.50 m²)
Armament: one 0.312-in (7.92-mm) LMG 08/15 fixed forward-firing machine-gun in the upper part of the forward-fuselage and one 0.312-in (7.92-mm) LMG 14 Parabellum trainable rearward-firing machine-gun in the rear cockpit, plus up to 220 lb (100 kg) of bombs carried under the lower wing

---

Dorand AR.1 and AR.2

During 1916 Colonel Dorand, then head of the French army's Section Technique de l'Aéronautique, designed a two-seat reconnaissance biplane. This was built in considerable numbers by the government's factory at Chalais-Meudon, as well as by Farman and Letord under sub-contract. Of fairly conventional construction for its day, it was unusual in having backward-staggered wings with the fuselage set well above the lower wing; both wings incorporated large cut-outs in their trailing edges. Robust fixed tailskid landing gear was provided for operation from rough airfields, and the powerplant of the first production version, the **Dorand AR.1A.2**, was the Renault 8Bd Vee engine. The **AR.2A.2** second production version was generally similar except for its reduced wingspan and the powerplant of one 200-hp (149-kW) Renault 8Ge engine.

Dorand AR.1 and AR.2 (continued)

Built in large numbers for the Aviation Militaire, which used the types on the Western and Italian Fronts from the spring of 1917 until a time early in 1918, the AR.1A.2 and AR.2A.2 were also acquired by the Air Service of the American Expeditionary Force, which thus obtained 22 and 120 examples of the two variants for use as trainers and advanced trainers respectively.

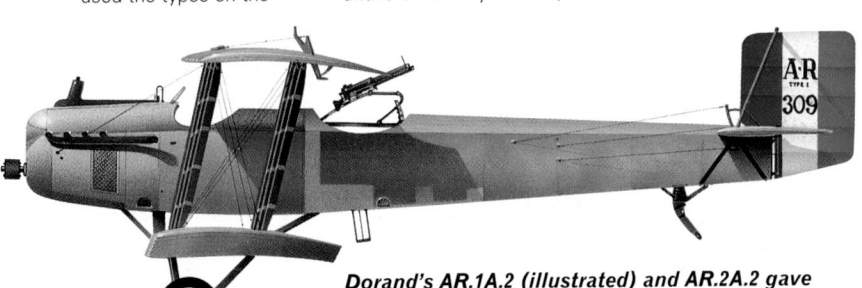

Dorand's AR.1A.2 (illustrated) and AR.2A.2 gave faithful, if somewhat unglamorous, service. Their most distinctive feature was their backward-staggered wings.

SPECIFICATION	
Dorand AR.1A.2 **Type:** two-seat artillery observation aircraft **Powerplant:** one Renault 8Bd Vee piston engine rated at 190 hp (142 kW) **Performance:** maximum speed 92 mph (148 km/h) at 6,560 ft (2000 m); climb to 6,560 ft (2000 m) in 13 minutes; service ceiling 18,045 ft (5500 m); endurance 3 hours **Weights:** empty 1,786 lb (810 kg); maximum take-off 2,756 lb (1250 kg)	**Dimensions:** wingspan 43 ft 6½ in (13.27 m); length 29 ft 11¾ in (9.14 m); height 10 ft 10 in (3.30 m); wing area 542.09 sq ft (50.36 m²) **Armament:** one 0.303-in (7.7-mm) Vickers fixed forward-firing machine-gun on the port side of the forward fuselage and one or two 0.303-in (7.7-mm) Lewis trainable machine-guns in the rear cockpit, plus up to 176 lb (80 kg) of bombs carried in a lower-fuselage weapons bay

Dornier Do B Merkur, Do C Komet III, Do D and Do T

The final variant of the Komet series of landplane transports was the **Do C Komet III**, which first flew on 7 December 1924. This appeared to be a refined and enlarged version of the Komet II, but was in fact a totally new type that bore the same relationship to the Delphin III flying-boat as the Komet I and II aircraft had borne to the Delphin I and II 'boats. The Komet III was powered by the 360-hp (268-kW) Rolls-Royce Eagle IX engine, although later aircraft had the option of the 400-hp (298-kW) Liberty 12 and 450-hp (336-kW) Napier Lion engines, and the type provided accommodation for six passengers as well as a two-man crew. The Komet III saw service with German airlines and also with operators in Denmark, Switzerland and the Ukraine. A small number was also built under licence in Japan by Kawasaki with Eagle IX, Lorraine-Dietrich 12 and Kawasaki-made BMW engines.

The first example of the generally similar **Do B Merkur I** (mercury I) made its maiden flight on 10 February 1925. It differed from the Komet III in having an increased span wing and incorporating a cut-out on the centreline of its trailing edge, an unbraced tail unit incorporating a fixed vertical surface of greater area and a more powerful engine in the form of the BMW VI rated at between 450 and 600 hp (336 and 447 kW) to create the Merkur I and **Merkur II** variants. A number of Komet III aircraft was then re-engined to a comparable standard, some having the 450-hp (336-kW) BMW IV engine without reduction gear and others the 500-hp (373-kW) BMW VI with reduction gear. The situation was further complicated by the fact that re-engined Komet III aircraft were henceforward known as Merkurs. The Merkur I and II each had accommodation for a crew of two and between six to eight passengers, but the Merkur II was certificated for operation at a higher weight that was further increased in the **Do B Bal** Merkur II variant that became the **Do B Bal 2 Merkur II** when fitted with the 640-hp (477-kW) BMW VIu high-compression engine.

The largest operator of the Merkur was undoubtedly DLH which, including converted Komet IIIs, may have had more than 30 in service at one period, but the type was also used by operators in China, Japan and Switzerland. In addition, Brazil and Colombia each had one Merkur in floatplane configuration.

The **Do C** was developed as a multi-role derivative of the Komet III. The core of the machine was the fuselage, providing an open cockpit for the crew of two (pupil and instructor) seated side-by-side and an enclosed cabin capable of accommodating six persons (trainees and instructors) with access by a port-side door.

Details of the Do C are scarce in number and generally conflicting in nature, but it is known that several of these aircraft, some of them in bomber form, were operated by the Chilean air force in around 1930.

The **Do D** was the twin-float seaplane version of the Do C, and it is known that the type was built as a torpedo bomber for Yugoslavia in 1927. The **Do T** was the landplane air ambulance version of the series, and it is possible that a small number of aircraft entered military service.

The Merkur carried its braced wing above the fuselage on four short struts. The crew of two was carried in an open cockpit, located just below the leading edge of the wing and offset to port. Enclosed accommodation was provided for six passengers.

SPECIFICATION	
Dornier Do B Merkur II **(landplane)** **Type:** two-crew transport aircraft **Powerplant:** one BMW VI Vee piston engine rated at 600 hp (447 kW) **Performance:** maximum speed 124 mph (200 km/h) at optimum altitude; cruising speed 112 mph (180 km/h) at optimum altitude;	service ceiling 17,060 ft (52000 m) **Weights:** empty 4,630 lb (2100 kg); maximum take-off 7,936 lb (3600 kg) **Dimensions:** wingspan 64 ft 3½ in (19.60 m); length 41 ft ⅛ in (12.50 m); height 11 ft 8½ in (3.56 m); wing area 667.38 sq ft (62.00 m²) **Payload:** up to eight passengers

Dornier Do C Delphin I, II and III, and Komet I and II

During 1920-1 Dornier developed a commercial flying-boat which was clearly derived from the Libelle. Later designated as the **Do Cs II Delphin I** (dolphin I) but originally known as the **Do L 1 Delphin I**, this new flying-boat was of the same general configuration and was constructed of steel and Dural, but differed in having a raised hull to provide an enclosed cabin. The wing was mounted directly above the cabin roof and braced on each side to the stabilising spon-son by a pair of parallel struts. The powerplant, of one 185-hp (138-kW) BMW IIIa inline engine, was nacelle-mounted above the bow immediately ahead of the pilot's open cockpit, which provided the pilot with very poor fields of vision. The engine itself, was located above and ahead of the cabin for four passengers.

In 1922 the type was improved as the **Do L 1a** with the rear part of the hull lengthened, the bow extended farther forward

Among the most ungainly aircraft designs ever flown, the Dornier Delphin nevertheless gave useful commercial service. A 1924-vintage Do L 2 Delphin II is illustrated.

to keep spray off the propeller, a pair of stiffening strakes added along the sides of the hull, the nose cut back slightly to present a less bluff nose entry, the rudder altered from the plain to the balanced type, and the wingspan increased. Another example of the Do L 1a was produced with an engine that was fully cowled in a form that that was extended to the rear to provide a roof for the cockpit. In addition to very limited commercial sales, the Delphin I also achieved the distinction of a single sale to the US Navy, which wished to evaluate the type's metal construction.

The shortcomings of the Delphin I were still evident, and in 1923 Dornier started work on the **Do L 2 Delphin II**, which first flew on 15 February 1924. This was powered by either a 250-hp (186-kW) BMW IV or 260-hp (194-kW) Rolls-Royce Falcon III engine,

and provided enclosed cabin accommodation for a crew of one or two and up to six or seven passengers. The commercial success of the Delphin II, even though it was built in only small numbers (probably two each for German and Spanish operators), paved the way for the development of the somewhat larger **Do L 3** or **Do L Bas Delphin III** during 1927-8, the first example flying on 30 March 1928. Powered by the BMW VI engine, this version accommodated the two-man crew in a compartment at the forward end of the cabin, which seated a maximum of 11 passengers and was separated from the flight deck by a bulkhead. The undersurface of the hull was provided with steel strakes so that, if necessary, take-offs and landings could be accomplished on ice surfaces. The type was produced, again only in small numbers, in two sub-

variants characterised by their round or square cabin windows.

Retaining a resemblance to earlier members of the family, the **Do C III Komet I** (comet I) was first flown in 1921. It had a deep fuselage, fixed tail-skid landing gear, conventional braced tail unit and a very large strut-braced wing of the constant-chord type, and as such was readily discernible as a landplane development of the Delphin I flying-boat, with the hull's planing bottom and stabilising sponsons replaced by the lower line of a conventional landplane with fixed tailskid landing gear. The revision of the forward fuselage allowed the relocation of the engine into a standard installation in the nose. The engine used in this installation was originally the 185-hp (138-kW) BMW IIIa, although this resulted in a service ceiling higher than the altitude permitted to German aircraft by the

Allied control commission, and later aircraft were therefore powered by the 180-hp (134-kW) BMW III engine. Accommodation was provided for four passengers in an enclosed cabin under the wing, and the pilot sat in an open cockpit on the upper surface of the fuselage, just to the rear of the wing's trailing edge. Surviving records leave doubts as to the number built, complicated by the fact that some of the aircraft were later converted to Merkur standard, but examples of the Komet I served initially with Deutsche Luft-

Reederei, later with Deutsche Aero Lloyd and finally with Deutsche Luft Hansa (DLH) when it was formed in 1926.

The improved **Komet II**, first flown on 9 October 1922, was built in larger numbers and served with airline operators in Colombia, Spain, Switzerland, the Ukraine and the USSR, as well as with DLH in Germany. It differed in having a lengthened fuselage, seating the same number of passengers but accommodated a crew of two, and was powered by the 250-hp (186-kW) BMW IV engine.

SPECIFICATION	
Do L 3 Delphin III	(4500 m); range 497 miles (500 km)
Type: two-crew transport flying-boat	**Weights:** empty 6,393 lb (2900 kg); maximum take-off 8,598 lb (3900 kg)
Powerplant: one BMW VI Vee piston engine rated at 600 hp (447 kW)	**Dimensions:** wingspan 64 ft 3½ in (19.60 m); length 47 ft 1 in (14.35 m); height 13 ft 3½ in (4.05 m); wing area 667.38 sq ft (62.00 m²)
Performance: maximum speed 112 mph (180 km/h) at optimum altitude; cruising speed 93 mph (150 km/h) at optimum altitude; service ceiling about 14,765 ft	**Payload:** up to 11 passengers

Dornier Do F, Do P, Do Y and Do 11

In March 1935, the Nazi government of Germany revealed the existence of a small, but nonetheless fully fledged, German air force that had been created in direct contravention of the Treaty of Versailles. Many of the aircraft now confirmed as the initial equipment of the Luftwaffe were already known to the world at large, for they had earlier been shown off in the guise of civil aircraft. Typical of these 'new'

warplanes was the **Do 11** bomber, which had first been announced as a transport produced by Dornier's subsidiary at Altenrhein in Switzerland. This subsidiary had produced its first bomber prototype as the **Do P** shoulder-wing monoplane of all-metal construction with fixed tailwheel landing gear and a powerplant of four 500-hp (373-kW) Bristol Jupiter radial engines mounted above the wing in tandem

push/pull pairs.

The first of two Do P prototypes flew in March 1930, and was followed in October 1931 by the first of two **Do Y** prototypes that had a powerplant of three 500-hp (373-kW) Jupiter VI engines, installed as two units in wing leading-edge nacelles and a third unit in a nacelle strut-mounted above the central fuselage. These four aircraft were presented to the world at large as freighter prototypes, but were in fact evolutionary steps in the process of creating the **Do F** (later **Do 11a**), which

was the prototype of the Do 11 that became the Luftwaffe's first operational heavy bomber.

First flown in May 1932, the Do F was as angular as its predecessors and, retaining the same type of basically all-metal construction, was thus a semi-cantilever monoplane with a metal-skinned fuselage and a shoulder-set wing of fabric-covered metal construction. Points on which the Do F differed from its predecessors, however, were its twin-engined powerplant and tailwheel landing gear with retractable main units. The powerplant comprised two Jupiter radial engines located in the wing leading edges; the Jupiter variant used in the Do F was built under licence in Germany as the Siemens und Halske Sh.22 with a rating of 550 hp (410 kW). The undercarriage retraction system was originally electrically operated but, proving both unreliable and underpowered, was replaced by a manual system.

With its internal bomb stowage and retractable landing gear, the five-man Do F was the equal of any European bomber of its period and was therefore ordered into production at Dornier's main production facility at Friedrichshafen in southern Germany. Production began in 1932, and deliveries of the **Do 11C** initial production model were scheduled to

begin in the following year with a powerplant of two Sh.22B-2 engines. In fact it was only in the early part of 1934 that the Do 11C entered service with the Behelfs bomber geschwader (auxiliary bomber group) that was the nucleus of the Luftwaffe's new bomber arm but currently masqueraded as Deutsche Lufthansa's traffic inspectorate. It then flew with the supposed air freight branch of the German national rail authority, which in fact provided navigational and night-flying experience. The German rail authority did also use the Do 11C for freight and air mail services linking Germany with the free port of Danzig, an ethnically German enclave in Poland, and Königsberg in East Prussia, but each aircraft was delivered with crates of 'spares' that in fact contained the bombing equipment (sight and racks) as well as the defensive guns and their mountings.

Gradually the Do 11C replaced the Junkers Ju 52/3mge interim bomber, and German air ministry plans called for the delivery of 372 Do 11s during 1934. This target proved impossible to attain, however, for the Do 11C was beset by a number of major problems including inferior handling characteristics, poor stability and, under certain conditions, wing vibration so severe that it threatened to cause structural failure.

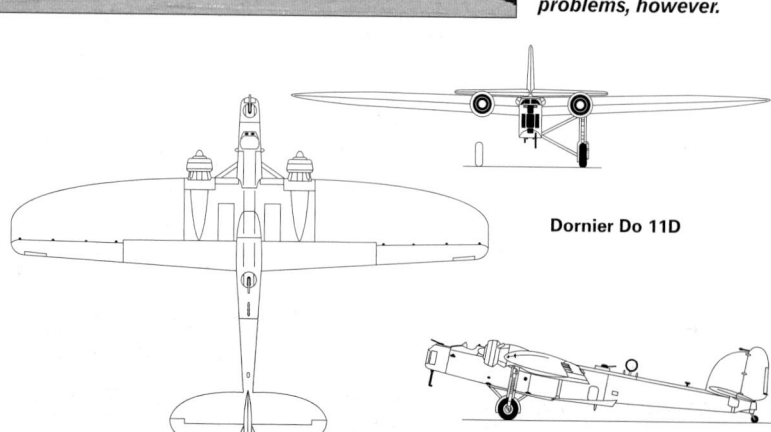

An advanced design for its era, the Do 11 (seen here in Do F prototype form) featured a retractable undercarriage and all-metal construction. The type was beset by structural problems, however.

Dornier Do 11D

Dornier Do F, Do P, Do Y and Do 11 (continued)

The instability of the Do 11 was cured by a redesign of the vertical tail surface with a larger rudder and small auxiliary finlets under the tailplane. The wing vibration was reduced, but not eliminated, by redesign of the wingtips and a reduction in span. The vertical tail and wing modifications were effected on all surviving Do 11C bombers. The designation **Do 11D** was applied to aircraft built to the revised Do 11C standard, which was the main production standard for the Do 11 series. Production of the Do 11C and Do 11D totalled only 150 aircraft,

the programme being curtailed because of continued problems, including main landing gear retraction difficulties that led to these units being locked in the extended position on all in-service aircraft. The inherently poor handling of the Do 11 compounded the type's structural problems: losses in the two operational units (the Gruppen Tutow and Fassberg) were high, but losses in the two bomber training schools equipped with the type were higher still.

The Do 11 therefore enjoyed only a short operational career, being phased

out of German service from the autumn of 1935 as supplies of the Do 23 became available. The type was then relegated to training and other second-line tasks for a short time longer, and 12 aircraft were transferred in 1937 to Bulgaria, a pro-German state also involved in the creation of a clandestine arm in defiance of the structures imposed on it by the Treaty of Neuilly, signed in 1919 to end Bulgaria's involvement on the losing side in World War I. The last aircraft were retired from Bulgarian service in 1940.

SPECIFICATION

Dornier Do 11D
Type: four-seat heavy day- and night-bomber
Powerplant: two Siemens Sh.22B-2 (Bristol Jupiter) radial piston engines each rated at 650 hp (485 kW)
Performance: maximum speed 162 mph (260 km/h) at sea level; cruising speed 140 mph (225 km/h) at 3,280 ft (1000 m); climb to 9,845 ft (3000 m) in 36 minutes; service ceiling 13,450 ft (4100 m); range 597 miles (960 km)
Weights: empty 13,173 lb (5975 kg); maximum take-off 18,078 lb (8200 kg)
Dimensions: wingspan 86 ft 3½ in (31.56 m); length 61 ft 8 in (18.80 m); height 18 ft ½ in (5.50 m); wing area 1,160.39 sq ft (107.80 m²)
Armament: one 0.312-in (7.92-mm) MG 15 trainable forward-firing machine-gun in the nose position, one 0.312-in (7.92-mm) MG 15 trainable machine-gun in the dorsal position, and one 0.312-in (7.92-mm) MG 15 trainable rearward-firing machine-gun in the ventral position, plus up to 2,205 lb (1000 kg) of bombs carried in a lower-fuselage weapons bay

Dornier Do J, Do R, Do 15 Wal and Super Wal

In the years after World War I, when Germany was prohibited from the manufacture of all but the smallest aircraft, Dr Claudius Dornier of the Zeppelin-Werke Lindau GmbH (from 1922 the Dornier Metallbauten GmbH to reflect the name of the chief designer and its emphasis on aircraft of all-metal construction) maintained a design capability in Germany. He also established production facilities in several European countries, most notably the Costruzioni Meccaniche Aeronautiche S.A. (CMASA) at Marina di Pisa in Italy during 1922 and the AG für Dornier-Flugzeuge at Altenrhein in Switzerland during 1926. The main output of Zeppelin-Werke Lindau in World War I had been giant flying-boats of Dornier design, and it was on the flying-boat that Dornier continued to concentrate after the war. In their definitive form, the Dornier 'boats were all-metal machines with a hull of high length/beam ratio and a two-step planing bottom in which the rear step was a vertical knife-

edge, waterborne stability provided by lateral sponsons extending from the hull just above the waterline, a semi-cantilever or cantilever wing carried in the parasol-wing position and multiple engines installed in tandem push/pull nacelles above the wing. The large-capacity hull provided for a variety of accommodation according to the Wal's employment in civil or military service, with a pilot and co-pilot seated side-by-side in a forward compartment. Behind them were navigation and radio compartments, still leaving a volume of hull that could be used for cargo, mail or passengers.

The first of these classic 'boats was the **Do J** built in prototype form by CMASA for a maiden flight on 6 November 1922. The type proved extremely successful for military, civil and record-breaking use, and was generally known as the **Wal** (whale). CMASA continued to be the main production source for Wals (although licensed production was also undertaken by Piaggio in Italy,

Based in the Balearic Islands in the late 1930s, this Do J Wal flew with Grupo 1-G-70 of the Agrupación Española (Spanish Nationalist air force).

Kawasaki in Japan, Aviolanda in the Netherlands and CASA in Spain), until Dornier started to make the type at Friedrichshafen in southern Germany during 1932. Before production ended in 1935 some 300 such 'boats had been delivered in a wide variety of forms. In its Italian-built form, the Wal received four increases in wingspan and area, was powered by at least 20 different types of engine and increased in maximum take-off weight from 8,818 lb (4000 kg) to 22,046 lb (10000 kg).

In 1924-5 CMASA produced a number of Wals for the Spanish navy, these being powered by 360-hp (268-kW) Rolls-Royce Eagle

IX engines. The load-carrying capability of the Wal/Eagle combination was demonstrated conclusively during February 1925 when 20 world-class records were established with payloads of 551 to 4,409 lb (250 to 2000 kg). In the same year two Wals were acquired by the Norwegian polar explorer Roald Amundsen for an expedition from Spitzbergen to the North Pole. One of these 'boats was lost in the pack ice, but following repair under the most difficult conditions the second returned to Spitzbergen in June 1926. It was subsequently overhauled and re-engined for a planned Atlantic crossing by a British pilot. When this failed to materialise the 'boat was acquired in 1928 by Wolfgang von Gronau for use in the German Commercial Flying School (DVS). Following overhaul and the installation of BMW VI engines it was used at the DVS for many long-distance overwater training flights. In this aircraft, on 18 August 1930, von Gronau and crew took off from List (on the island of Sylt) en route for New York via the Faroes, Iceland, Greenland and Labrador. After a flying time of 44 hours 25 minutes, the Wal landed safely in New York harbour to mark a great achievement. The Wal also featured in a round-the-world flight

during 1932. By this time Deutsche Luft Hansa, which was planning to establish an air mail service to South America, decided to unite the proven Wal with a specially-converted cargo vessel to serve as a mid-ocean refuelling base. The first of these vessels, the *Westfalen*, was equipped to take the Wal aboard, refuel it and then relaunch it into the air by catapult. After trial flights during 1933, the first scheduled flight from Germany to South America began on 3 February 1934. The success of this operation can be judged from the fact that the planned fortnightly schedule was very soon converted into a regular weekly service.

Given the success of the Wal series, it was inevitable that the type should be selected for service as a maritime reconnaissance flying-boat when the German war ministry decided in the early 1930s to create a naval air arm. The variant selected for this role was the **Militär-Wal 33** that later received the designation Do 15 and was a derivative of the earlier **'8-Tonnen Wal'**, so named for its maximum take-off weight of 8 tonnes (17,637 lb). The '8-Tonnen Wal' first flew in 1931, and the initial example of the Militär-Wal 33 flew in 1933 as a derivative of the civil model with military equip-

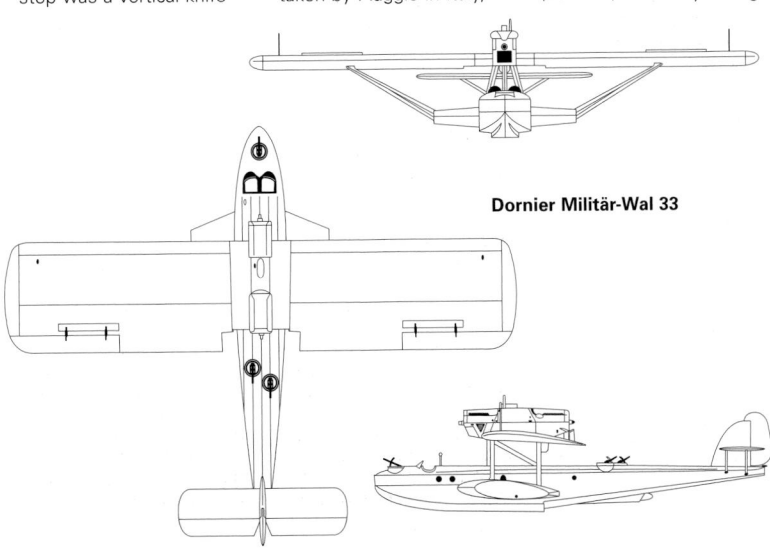

Dornier Militär-Wal 33

ment and the provision of defensive weapons that were later supplemented by limited offensive capability in the form of up to four light bombs. The Militär-Wal 33 conformed to the basic description above, and its parasol wing was based on a constant-chord centre section supported above the hull on a side-by-side pair of N-struts; this centre section was comparatively thin and supported the tandem push/pull engines in a long over-wing nacelle, and carried the constant-chord outer wing panels that were braced to the tips of the stabilising sponsons by outward-canted parallel struts.

Deliveries started late in 1933, and production of some 30 such 'boats was completed by 1935, when the Luftwaffe decided to forego further deliveries of the type as the much-improved Do 18 was imminent. The 'boats remained in first-line service to 1938, and continued in second-line service into the opening phases of World War II.

Before the end of Wal production in the mid-1930s, the type had been supplemented by the **Do R Super Wal**, produced at Friedrichshafen following the maiden flight of the first **Do R2** in September 1926. Featuring a wing of

increased span and a hull of greater length, the Super Wal had two cabins to accommodate a total of 19 passengers and was operated by a crew of four. The Do R2 was of similar overall configuration to the contemporary Wal, and its powerplant comprised a tandem arrangement of two 650-hp (485-kW) Rolls-Royce Condor engines. However, the **Do R4** of 1927 benefited from the power of four Siemens-built Bristol Jupiter radial engines, these being mounted in two tandem pairs and providing gross weight and speed increases of some 33 per cent and 16 per cent

respectively. The Super Wal was also licence-built in several countries, and the type gave valuable service to a number of

airlines including, of course, Deutsche Luft Hansa. In 1934 the Wal series was redesignated as the **Do 15**.

SPECIFICATION

Dornier Do 15 Wal (Militär-Wal 33)
Type: four-seat maritime reconnaissance flying-boat
Powerplant: two BMW VI Vee piston engines each rated at 750 hp (559 kW)
Performance: maximum speed 137 mph (220 km/h) at sea level; cruising speed 124 mph (200 km/h) at optimum altitude; climb to 9,845 ft (3000 m) in 35 minutes; service ceiling 9,845 ft (3000 m); range 1,367 miles (2200 km)
Weights: empty 11,872 lb (5385 kg); maximum take-off

17,637 lb (8000 kg)
Dimensions: wingspan 76 ft 1½ in (23.20 m); length 60 ft ½ in (18.30 m); height 17 ft 6⅝ in (5.35 m); wing area 1,033.34 sq ft (96.00 m²)
Armament: one 0.312-in (7.92-mm) MG 15 trainable forward-firing machine-gun in the bow position and one 0.312-in (7.92-mm) MG 15 trainable rearward-firing machine-gun in each of the two staggered side-by-side dorsal positions, plus up to 440 lb (200 kg) of bombs carried on four hardpoints under the wing

Dornier Do X

The largest aircraft in the world when it made its first flight from the Bodensee on 25 July 1929, the **Do X** was the product of the Altenrhein-based Swiss element of the Dornier company. Work on the design, which was the ultimate development of the Wal series, began in 1927, and the aircraft was intended to carry up to 100 passengers across the Atlantic in a level of comfort comparable with that offered by ocean liners. Of all-metal construction and powered initially by six tandem pairs of 500-hp (373-kW) Siemens-built Bristol Jupiter radial engines, the Do X had individual sleeping cabins, a lounge, a smoking room, a bathroom, a kitchen and a dining room arranged on three decks in the 131-ft (40-m) long hull. On the enclosed flight deck there was a crew comprising two pilots, a navigator and a radio operator, but the throttles were the responsibility of a flight engineer whose position was sufficiently far to the rear of the cockpit area to make power adjustments an interesting exercise in communications! The flight engineer was also able to inspect the powerplant in flight by using access tunnels in the very thick wing. The original Siemens engines developed insufficient power, and were therefore replaced by 12 Curtiss engines, but cooling problems continued to

The impressive Do X is illustrated here with its original Jupiter radial-engine powerplant. Note the faired-in engine supports.

reduce the output of the rear engines. Even so, proof of the 'boat's load-carrying ability was provided by a flight on 31 October 1929, when stowaways increased the number of persons on board to 170, 10 more than the planned maximum of 160 passengers and crew.

On 2 November 1930 the Do X left Friedrichshafen on the Bodensee for a flight to the USA via Amsterdam, Calshot and Lisbon. The flight was not without incident. At Lisbon, fire in a fuel tank damaged one of the wings, necessitating a delay of a month for repairs. Then, when attempting a take-off at Las Palmas in the Canary Islands, the Do X suffered hull damage which resulted in a further delay of some three months. The aircraft was lightened by the removal of non-essential equipment and fittings, and operated with a reduced crew for its next attempt. Although still unable to reach normal operating altitude for much of the crossing, the modified Do X completed the next stage to Natal (Brazil) via Portuguese Guinea, the Cape Verde Islands and Fernando Noronha. The Do X then flew to Rio de Janeiro before heading

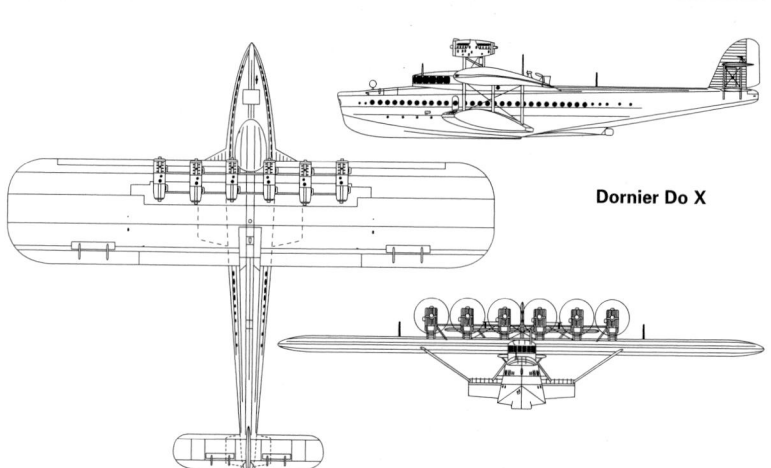

Dornier Do X

initially north-east round the coast of South America on its way to the USA. The 'boat reached New York, via the West Indies and Miami, on 27 August 1931. The return flight began on 19 May 1932, the Do X reaching Berlin on 24 May 1932 after a successful flight via Harbour Grace, Horta, Vigo and Calshot.

The flying-boat was among the aircraft destroyed when the Berlin Museum was severely

damaged by bombs during World War II. Two further examples of the Do X were built, with Fiat

engines, and were used experimentally by the Italian air force before being scrapped.

SPECIFICATION

Dornier Do X
Type: five-crew transoceanic flying-boat
Powerplant: 12 Curtiss V-1570 Conqueror Vee piston engines each rated at 640 hp (477 kW)
Performance: maximum speed 130 mph (210 km/h) at sea level; cruising speed 109 mph (175 km/h) at optimum altitude; service ceiling

4,100 ft (1250 m); range 1,367 miles (2200 km)
Weights: empty 72,036 lb (32675 kg); maximum take-off 123,459 lb (56000 kg)
Dimensions: wingspan 157 ft 5¾ in (48.00 m); length 131 ft 4 in (40.00 m); height 33 ft 1½ in (10.10 m) wing area 4,843.92 sq ft (450.00 m²)

Dornier Do 13 and Do 23

The troublesome nature of the Do 11 was reflected in Dornier's decision before the end of 1932 to undertake the development of a simplified version with

fixed landing gear and the Junkers type of 'double-wing' flaps extending right across the span of the wing trailing edges to serve collectively as camber-

changing flaps and, differentially on their outboard ends, as slotted ailerons. This revised type first flew in February 1933 as the **Do 13** prototype, which

had faired main landing gear units carrying spatted wheels, but revealed serious instability as well as the same type of wing vibration that was being

encountered on the Do 11. There followed two improved prototypes, the **Do 13b** and **Do 13c**, the latter adopting the reduced-span wing of the Do 11D and the revised powerplant of two 750-hp (559-kW) BMW VI Vee engines.

Dornier Do 13 and Do 23 (cont.)

The Do 13c proved the better of the two improved prototypes, and orders for the last 222 Do 11 bombers were transferred to the **Do 13C** production version of the Do 13c.

Deliveries of the Do 13C were much delayed by engine-cooling problems that were finally solved by the addition of flush radiators on the underside of the engine nacelles in place of the supplementary underwing radiators that had originally been evaluated but found to produce excessive drag. The Do 13C finally entered service in the autumn of 1934, and almost immediately there followed a number of losses as a result of structural failure. Production was therefore halted after the delivery of 12 aircraft.

As a consequence of these problems, Dornier undertook a complete restressing of the structure, with particular emphasis on the fuselage, and also incorporated a number of revisions into the wing, which was reduced in span. The immediate result of this process was the **Do 13e** prototype that made its maiden flight in September 1934 and, despite an increase of 981 lb (445 kg) in empty weight and a reduction in wing area, was finally deemed acceptable by the German air ministry. The ministry thus ordered that unfulfilled orders for the Do 11 and Do 13 should be transferred to the **Do 23**, the change in designation being thought sensible to avoid the stigma now attached to the Do 13.

The initial production model was the **Do 23F** with a powerplant of two BMW VIu engines. Only a very few Do 23Fs were completed before production was switched to the **Do 23G**, that differed only in the use of ethylene glycol rather than water for engine cooling. Construction of the Do 23F and Do 23G totalled about 210 aircraft in all, and the Do 23 series entered service in the summer of 1935. The type was delivered first to bomber training schools, and then entered operational service. In service the Do 23 proved disappointing and production of the limited but trouble-free Junkers Ju 52/3mge interim bomber, which was to have been replaced by the Do 11, Do 13 and finally Do 23, continued. So disappointing was the Do 23, indeed, that the type was phased out of first-line service from the summer of 1936, although a number of the aircraft survived in second-line tasks until the beginning of World War II. A few Do 23s were then pressed into service as aerial mine-detectors until the advent of more suitable aircraft.

In structural terms the Do 23 (illustrated) was virtually identical to the Do 11 and Do 13, being a semi-cantilever, shoulder-wing monoplane.

SPECIFICATION

Dornier Do 23G
Type: four-seat heavy day- and night-bomber
Powerplant: two BMW VIu Vee piston engines each rated at 750 hp (559 kW)
Performance: maximum speed 162 mph (260 km/h) at optimum altitude; cruising speed 130 mph (209 km/h) at optimum altitude; initial climb rate 886 ft (270 m) per minute; climb to 3,280 ft (1000 m) in 4 minutes; service ceiling 13,780 ft (4200 m); range 839 miles (1350 km); endurance 7 hours 30 minutes
Weights: empty 12,346 lb (5600 kg); maximum take-off

20,282 lb (9200 kg)
Dimensions: wingspan 83 ft 11⅛ in (25.60 m); length 61 ft 8⅛ in (18.80 m); height 17 ft 8½ in (5.40 m); wing area 1,147.43 sq ft (106.60 m²)
Armament: one 0.312-in (7.92-mm) MG 15 trainable forward-firing machine-gun in the nose position, one 0.312-in (7.92-mm) MG 15 trainable machine-gun in the dorsal position, and one 0.312-in (7.92-mm) MG 15 trainable rearward-firing machine-gun in the ventral position, plus up to 2,205 lb (1000 kg) of bombs carried in a lower-fuselage weapons bay

Dornier Do 17

Although Germany developed most of its warplanes of the early and mid-1930s in the guise of civil aircraft, the **Do 17** was virtually unique in being designed as a civil transport and only later being developed into a multi-role warplane. The origins of the type can be traced to a requirement issued in 1933 by Deutsche Lufthansa for a high-speed mailplane that could also offer accommodation for up to six passengers on the operator's European express services. Dornier responded with a design notable for its aerodynamic cleanliness and its powerplant of two 660-hp (492-kW) BMW VI 6,0 engines, the most powerful German engine of its period.

The core of the design was the extremely thin circular-section fuselage whose line was broken only by the cockpit's stepped windscreen; this slenderness inevitably led to the nickname 'Flying Pencil'. Oddly enough, this slenderness was not replicated in the wing, which was of broad chord and comparatively low aspect ratio; the leading and trailing edges of this wing were faired into the lines of the fuselage by extensive fillets that gave the central fuselage a distinct appearance in planform. The fuselage was of conventional metal construction with a covering of light alloy panel, and the shoulder-set cantilever wing was of Dural construction with light alloy skinning except on the undersurface between the two spars, which was covered with fabric. The tail was a cantilever unit with a single vertical surface, and the tailwheel landing gear was of the fully-retractable type, with the main units retracting rearward into the underside of the two wing-mounted engine nacelles, with the lowest portion of each wheel exposed.

The **Do 17 V1** made its first flight in the autumn of 1934, and before the end of the year had been supplemented in the flight test programme by the **Do 17 V2** and **V3** second and third prototypes. The aircraft were handed over to DLH in 1935 for evaluation, and the airline soon concluded that, while the Do 17 fully met its requirement in terms of performance, it was nonetheless an impractical type for the passenger transport role as the accommodation was wholly inadequate. Shoe-horned into the slender fuselage, this accommodation comprised a two-passenger compartment immediately aft of the two-man cockpit and a four-passenger compartment aft of the wing; as well as being cramped, these compartments could be entered only by passengers possessing considerable agility! DLH returned the three prototypes to Dornier, and it is probable that the

type would have been abandoned at this stage except for a fortuitous occurrence, namely a visit by a former Dornier test pilot who was now a DLH pilot and the airline's liaison officer with the German air ministry. Flugkapitän Untucht decided to fly one of the Do 17 prototypes, and as a result of this experience came to the conclusion that the type's performance and handling characteristics made it suitable for further development as a bomber. Dornier was sceptical, but a German air ministry evaluation confirmed Untucht's assessment and Dornier was ordered to produce a fourth prototype for military trials.

This **Do 17 V4** was completed in the summer of 1935 and differed externally mainly in its lack of cabin windows and the replacement of the single vertical surface by twin endplate surfaces to provide greater directional stability. Internally, it differed in the provision of a radio operator's position in place of the passenger compartment and the addition of a lower-fuselage weapons bay starting immediately to the rear of the front spar line. Two more prototypes, the **Do 17 V5** and **Do 17 V6**, joined the military flight

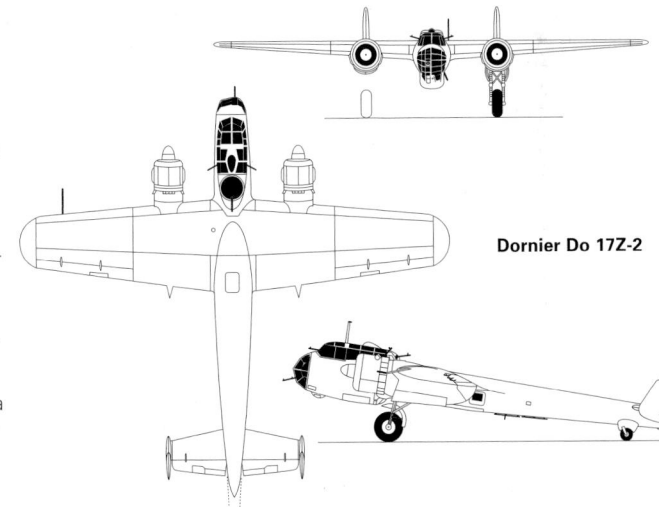

Several Do 17E-1 bombers like that illustrated, along with Do 17F-1 recce aircraft, survived the Spanish Civil War to serve on into the 1940s.

Dornier Do 17Z-2

During July 1940, 9./KG 76 flew this Do 17Z during the unit's heavy commitment to attacks against RAF bases in Kent. The unit was based at Cormeilles-en-Vexin.

test programme during the autumn of 1935; the latter was virtually identical to the Do 17 V4, but the Do 17 V5 had a powerplant of two 860-hp (641-kW) Hispano-Suiza 12Ybrs engines. No provision had been made for defensive armament in these early machines, for

German tactical thinking of the day suggested that the Do 17 bomber would be too fast for any contemporary fighter to intercept. However, more sanguine thinking then intervened and the **Do 17 V7** introduced a single defensive machine-gun in a blister fairing above the fuselage,

from where it was operated by the radio operator; this prototype also introduced a true bombardier nose with a glazed hemispherical nose cap and glazed panels in the underside of the nose section. Two further prototypes followed: the **Do 17 V8** was retained by Dornier as

a development aircraft, while the **Do 17 V9** was in effect the prototype for the first operational model, the **Do 17E-1** bomber. In the Do 17 V9, overall length, already reduced from that of the civil prototypes in the Do 17 V4, was further reduced, the nose glazing was considerably enlarged and provided with optically flat panels for bomb-aiming purposes, more glazing was added on the starboard side of the nose, the defensive gun blister was refined, the twin vertical tail surfaces were revised and enlarged, and full military equipment was fitted. The final prototype was the **Do 17 V10**, used for engine development purposes and completed with two 750-hp (559-kW) BMW VI 7,3 high-compression engines.

As final work on the prototypes was proceeding, Dornier had been preparing production lines at three of its factories for the large orders already placed for the two initial models, the Do 17E-1 bomber and **Do 17F-1** reconnaissance type that were to be produced in parallel. The Do 17E-1 had the same defensive arma-

ment as the Do 17F-1, namely single 0.312-in (7.92-mm) MG 15 trainable rearward-firing machine-guns in the dorsal and ventral hatch positions. It was also fully equipped for the bomber role, with a bomb sight in the glazed nose and bomb racks in the lower-fuselage weapons bay for a standard disposable load of 1,102 lb (500 kg) that could be increased to 1,653 lb (750 kg) for short-range missions.

The first Do 17E-1 bombers became available in the early months of 1937, and the first units to equip with the type were the I. Gruppen (wings) of Kampfgeschwadern (bomber groups) 153 and 155. These were followed later in the same year by II. and III./KG 153 and by II. and III./KG 155, the latter formation later becoming KG 158. Two other Kampfgeschwadern that later formed with the type were KG 252 and KG 255. Production of the Do 17 eventually totalled about 1,200 aircraft of all variants, and the type remained in first-line service into the closing stages of 1942

Variants

Do 17E-1: initial production bomber
Do 17F-1: photographic reconnaissance aircraft with two cameras and increased fuel
Do 17K: 70 or more aircraft, including 20 built in Germany and the others under licence by the Drjavna Fabrika Aviona at Kraljevo, this variant was for Yugoslavia; the type was based on the Do 17M but powered by two 980-hp (731-kW) Gnome-Rhône 14N-1/2 radial engines; the three subvariants were the **Do 17Kb-1** bomber, the **Do 17Ka-2** reconnaissance bomber, and the **Do 17Ka-3** reconnaissance bomber with different equipment
Do 17L: two prototypes of a proposed four-seat pathfinder version powered by two 900-hp (671-kW) Bramo 323A-1 radial engines
Do 17M: the 13th and 14th prototypes, powered by Bramo 323A-1 engines, were used to develop the airframe/engine combination for the production **Do 17M-1**, which could carry a 2,205-lb (1000-kg) bombload and was armed with three 0.312-in (7.92-mm) MG 15 machine-guns, in dorsal and ventral positions and one firing through the starboard side of the windscreen
Do 17P: photo-reconnaissance version of the Do 17M with two 875-hp (652-kW) BMW 132N radial engines and fitted with Rb20/30 and Rb50/30 or Rb20/8 and Rb50/8 cameras in the **Do 17P-1** production model
Do 17R: two engine testbeds, one with 950-hp (708-kW) Daimler-Benz DB 600G inverted-Vee engines and the other with 1,000-hp (746-kW) DB 601As
Do 17S: three DB 600G-powered high-speed reconnaissance aircraft for trials with a prone gunner's position in the underside of the forward fuselage, housing a rearward-firing MG 15 machine-gun; the nose was extensively glazed
Do 17U: 15 **Do 17U-0** and **Do 17U-1** aircraft were built to this standard as pathfinders, carrying two radio operators among the five-man crew
Do 17Z: the most numerous of the Do 17 series, some 525 aircraft being built between 1939 and 1940; the Do 17Z appeared in several versions; the sole **Do 17Z-0** was similar to the Do 17S with two 900-hp (671-kW) Bramo 323A-1 engines and the defensive armament of three MG 15 machine-guns; the **Do 17Z-1** had an additional nose-mounted MG 15 but was underpowered and able to carry only a 1,102-lb (500-kg) bombload; the substitution of 1,000-hp (746-kW) Bramo 323P engines in the **Do 17Z-2** restored the bombload to 2,205 lb (1000 kg) and up to eight MG 15 machine-guns were fitted – production of the Do 17Z-1 and Z-2 totalled 500 aircraft; 22 **Do 17Z-3** aircraft were built for reconnaissance duties with Rb50/30 or Rb20/30 cameras; the **Do 17Z-4** was a dual-control conversion trainer, and the **Do 17Z-5** was essentially a Do 17Z-2 with flotation bags in the fuselage and the rear of the engine bays; a single **Do 17Z-6 Kauz I** (screech owl I) long-range intruder and night-fighter was produced, incorporating the nose of the Ju 88C-2 with the fixed forward-firing armament of one 20-mm MG FF cannon and three 0.312-in (7.92-mm) MG 17 machine-guns; a new nose was developed for the nine **Do 17Z-10 Kauz II** conversions, this nose carrying four 0.312-in (7.92-mm) MG 17 machine-guns and four 20-mm MG FF cannon; for night-fighter duties they were equipped with Lichtenstein C1 radar and Spänner-II-Anlage infra-red detection apparatus

SPECIFICATION

Dornier Do 17Z-2
Type: four-seat medium bomber
Powerplant: two Bramo 323P Fafnir radial piston engines each rated at 1,000 hp (746 kW)
Performance: maximum speed 255 mph (410 km/h) at 4,000 ft (1220 m); cruising speed 186 mph (300 km/h) at 13,125 ft (4000 m); climb to 3,280 ft (1000 m) in 3 minutes 18 seconds; service ceiling 26,905 ft (8200 m); range 721 miles (1160 km)
Weights: empty 11,488 lb

(5210 kg); maximum take-off 18,940 lb (8590 kg)
Dimensions: wingspan 59 ft 1 in (18.00 m); length 51 ft 10 in (15.80 m); height 14 ft 11 in (4.55 m); wing area 592.03 sq ft (55.00 m²)
Armament: four or optionally up to eight 0.312-in (7.92-mm) MG 15 trainable machine-guns in the windscreen, nose, dorsal and ventral positions, plus up to 2,205 lb (1000 kg) of bombs carried in a lower-fuselage weapons bay

Dornier Do 18

This Do 18G-1 flew in the air-sea rescue role with 6./Seenotstaffel in the central Mediterranean during 1941-2.

Successor to the Wal flying-boats, the **Do 18** was developed as a transoceanic mailplane for Deutsche Lufthansa in the course of 1934. It retained the basic metal hull and stabilising sponsons which had characterised the earlier aircraft, but was aerodynamically more efficient. Powered by two 540-hp (403-kW) Junkers Jumo 5 Diesel engines, the **Do 18a** prototype first flew on 15 March 1935 and was followed by four of the **Do 18E** version with improved 600-hp (447-kW) Jumo 205C engines. Lufthansa's sixth 'boat was the sole **Do 18F**, first flown on 11 June 1937 and which from 27-29 March 1938 established a non-stop straight-line seaplane distance record of

5,214 miles (8391 km) in 43 hours, flying from England to Brazil. This 'boat later became the **Do 18L** when modified with the powerplant of two 880-hp (656-kW) BMW 132N radial engines, and made its first flight in this form on 21 November 1939.

The Do 18 was also adopted for service with the Luftwaffe's coastal reconnaissance units, and entered service in September 1938. The first German aircraft to be brought down by British forces in World War II was a Do 18 of 2./Küstenfliegergruppe 106 which, on 26 September 1939, was forced down by Lieutenant B. S. McEwen of the FAA's No. 803 Sqn, operating from HMS *Ark Royal* in the North Sea.

Variants

Do 18D: first military production version, the initial **Do 18D-1** being powered by Jumo 205C engines and armed with single 0.312-in (7.92-mm) MG 15 trainable machine-guns in open bow and dorsal positions; equipment changes led to the **Do 18D-2** and **Do 18D-3** in 1938; production of the Do 18D totalled about 75 'boats
Do 18G: improved version of the Do 18D, the sole model being the **Do 18G-1** with 880-hp (656-kW) Jumo 205D engines and a 0.51-in (13-mm) MG 131 machine-gun in the bow and a 20-mm MG 151 cannon in a power-operated dorsal turret
Do 18H: small number of six-seat unarmed trainers with dual controls; the sole model was the **Do 18H-1**; production of the Do 18G and H totalled 71 'boats
Do 18N: unarmed air-sea rescue aircraft converted from Do 18G standard for service with the designation **Do 18N-1**

Dornier Do 18 (cont.)

Production of just over 150 Do 18 flying-boats was completed in 1940. Following their replacement in first-line service by the Blohm und Voss BV 138, the last front-line Do 18G-1s were withdrawn from Norway-based 3./KüFlGr 406 and 3./KüFlGr 906 by August 1941. All had been relegated to air-sea rescue duties by 1942.

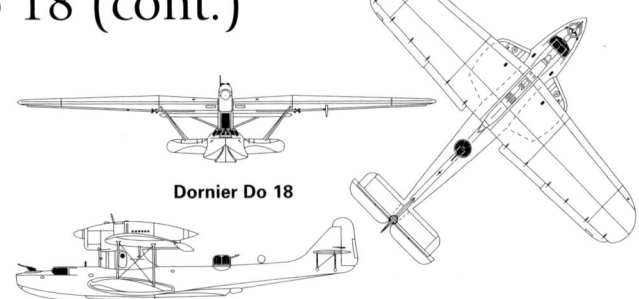

Dornier Do 18

SPECIFICATION	
Dornier Do 18G-1	
Type: four-seat coastal reconnaissance flying-boat	(5850 kg); maximum take-off 22,046 lb (10000 kg)
Powerplant: two Junkers Jumo 205D Diesel engines each rated at 880 hp (656 kW)	**Dimensions:** wingspan 77 ft 9¼ in (23.70 m); length 63 ft 7 in (19.37 m); height 17 ft 5½ in (5.32 m); wing area 1054.89 sq ft (98.00 m²)
Performance: maximum speed 162 mph (260 km/h) at 6,560 ft (2000 m); cruising speed 137 mph (220 km/h) at optimum altitude; climb to 3,280 ft (1000 m) in 7 minutes 48 seconds; service ceiling 13,780 ft (4200 m); range 2,175 miles (3500 km)	**Armament:** one 0.51-in (13-mm) MG 131 trainable forward-firing machine-gun in the bow position and one 20-mm MG 151 trainable cannon in the dorsal turret, plus two 110-lb (50-kg) bombs carried under the starboard wing
Weights: empty 12,897 lb	

Dornier Do 22

Development of the **Dornier Do 22** floatplane was the responsibility of Dornier's Altenrhein factory in Switzerland, where two prototypes were built. Of all-metal construction covered with fabric except on the metal-skinned forward fuselage, the Do 22 was powered by a Hispano-Suiza 12Ybrs engine driving a three-bladed propeller and carried a crew of three. Provision was made for an armament of four rifle-calibre machine-guns installed as one fixed forward-firing weapon in the forward fuselage above the engine, one trainable rearward-firing weapon in the ventral position and two trainable rearward-firing weapons in the rear cockpit. The type was not ordered by the Luftwaffe, but approxi-

The Do 22's rear cockpit housed a gunner and a radio operator, whose position in the front half of this cockpit was protected by a glazed canopy.

mately 30 aircraft were built at Friedrichshafen and the first production aircraft was flown on 15 July 1938. Do 22 floatplanes were

supplied to the Greek, Yugoslav and Latvian air forces as the **Do 22Kg**, **Do 22Kj** and **Do 22Kl** respectively.

Variant

Do 22L: single example of the landplane version with fixed spatted landing gear, which was first flown on 10 March 1939

Yugoslavia used its Do 22Kj floatplanes operationally from RAF Aboukir between 3 June 1941 and 23 April 1942.

SPECIFICATION	
Dornier Do 22K	
Type: three-seat utility floatplane	**Weights:** empty 5,734 lb (2600 kg); maximum take-off 8,820 lb (4000 kg)
Powerplant: one Hispano-Suiza 12Ybrs Vee piston engine rated at 860 hp (641 kW)	**Dimensions:** wingspan 53 ft 2 in (16.20 m); length 43 ft ½ in (13.12 m); height 15 ft 11 in (4.85 m); wing area 484.39 sq ft (45.00 m²)
Performance: maximum speed 217 mph (350 km/h) at 9,845 ft (3000 m); cruising speed 186 mph (300 km/h) at 13,125 ft (4000 m); climb to 16,405 ft (5000 m) in 15 minutes; service ceiling 29,830 ft (9000 m); range 1,429 miles (2300 km)	**Armament:** four machine-guns (see above), plus one 1,764-lb (800-kg) torpedo or four 110-lb (50-kg) bombs carried under the fuselage

Dornier Do 24

The **Do 24** originated from a Dutch navy requirement of 1935 for a flying-boat to replace the Wal 'boats operated at that time in the Netherlands East Indies. An all-metal monoplane with a shallow, broad-beamed hull and stabilising sponsons, the Do 24 had a strut-mounted wing which

carried a three-engined powerplant. The first two prototypes were powered by 600-hp (447-kW) Junkers Jumo 205C Diesel engines while the third prototype, which on 3 July 1937 became the first of the 'boats to fly, and the fourth prototype, were powered by 875-hp

This Do 24T-2 flew with 7. Seenotstaffel/ SBK XI in the Aegean during 1942. The aircraft carries white Mediterranean theatre bands.

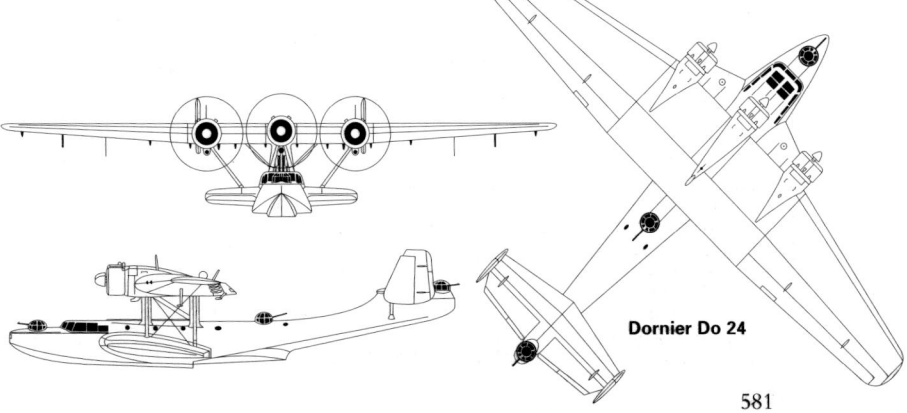

Variants

Do 24N-1: 11 Dutch-built Do 24K-2 'boats were completed to this standard as air-sea rescue machines for the Luftwaffe, retaining the Wright R-1820-G102 engines; the first was delivered in August 1941
Do 24T: 159 Do 24T-1, Do 24T-2 and Do 24T-3 aircraft, differing only in their equipment standards, were manufactured during the German occupation of the Netherlands; the 'boats were each powered by three 1,000-hp (746-kW) BMW-Bramo 323B-2 Fafnir radial engines and served principally with 1., 2. and 3./Seenotgruppe based at Biscarosse near Bordeaux and Berre near Marseilles on the west and south coasts of France respectively
Do 24TT: during the early 1980s a Do 24TT prototype was built with the TNT advanced-technology wing developed for the Do 228 commuter airliner and with the radically revised powerplant of three Pratt & Whitney Canada PT6A-45 turboprop engines
Do 318: a single prototype modified in 1944 by Weser with an Arado-designed boundary-layer control system; tests were very successful, but the 'boat was scuttled in Lake Constance in 1945

(652-kW) Wright R-1820-F52 Cyclone radial engines in order to meet the Dutch desire to use the same engine as those fitted to their Martin Model 139 bombers. On successful completion of the test programme, the rest of the Dutch order for 12

Do 24K-1 'boats was completed at Altenrhein. Licensed production of a further 48 **Do 24K-2** aircraft, with 1,000-hp (746-kW) R-1820-G102 engines, was undertaken by Aviolanda in the Netherlands, de Schelde building the

wings, but only 25 of these machines had been delivered before the German conquest of the Netherlands in May 1940.
Three completed aircraft and a number of partly-built airframes were transferred

Dornier Do 24

to Germany for evaluation in the air/sea rescue role and, as a result, the Dutch line was re-established under the control of the German company Weser Flugzeugbau, its production totalling 170 aircraft. A further 48 **Do 24T-1** aircraft

were built for the Luftwaffe at the SNCA du Nord plant at Sartrouville in France between 1942 and August 1944, and 40 more were delivered to the French navy after the liberation of 1944. Twelve **Do 24T-3** aircraft were

Post-war, Dornier's Do 24 proved its worth by flying on in the SAR role with the Spanish air force.

supplied to Spain under the designation **HR.5**, deliveries starting in June 1944, to provide search and rescue cover in the

Mediterranean for aircrew of both sides. The type remained in Spanish

service, based at Pollensa, Majorca until well into the 1970s.

SPECIFICATION

Dornier Do 24T-1
Type: six-seat maritime patrol and air/sea rescue flying-boat
Powerplant: three 1,000-hp (746-kW) BMW-Bramo 323B-2 radial piston engines
Performance: maximum speed 211 mph (340 km/h) at 9,845 ft (3000 m); cruising speed 183 mph (295 km/h) at 8,530 ft (2600 m); climb to 13,125 ft (4000 m) in 13 minutes 12 seconds; service ceiling 19,355 ft (5900 m); range 1,802 miles (2900 km)
Weights: empty 20,286 lb

(9200 kg); maximum take-off 40,565 lb (18400 kg)
Dimensions: wingspan 88 ft 7 in (27.00 m); length 72 ft 4 in (22.00 m); height 18 ft 10¼ in (5.75 m); wing area 1,162.54 sq ft (108.00 m²)
Armament: one 0.312-in (7.92-mm) MG 15 trainable machine-gun each in the bow and tail positions, and one 20-mm MG 151 or Hispano-Suiza HS-404 trainable cannon in the power-operated dorsal turret

Dornier Do 26

In aerodynamic terms the cleanest of the company's flying-boats, the all-metal **Dornier Do 26** was developed for transatlantic mail services, which were to be undertaken with a crew of four and 1,102 lb (500 kg) of mail on the route between Lisbon and New York. The mid-span stabilising floats retracted

completely into the wings, and the rear units of the two tandem pairs of 600-hp (447-kW) Junkers Jumo 205C Diesel engines could be given an upward tilt of 10° on take-off so that their three-bladed metal propellers were clear of the spray from the hull. Three examples of the Do 26, stressed for catapult

launching from support ships, were ordered by Deutsche Lufthansa in 1937, and the first of these flew on 21 May 1938. Two of the three 'boats were completed before the outbreak of World War II and delivered to the airline under the designation **Do 26A**. They were never used as intended, across the North Atlantic, and made just 18 crossings of the South Atlantic.

SPECIFICATION

Dornier Do 26D-0
Type: four-crew coastal patrol and transport flying-boat
Powerplant: four Junkers Jumo 205D Diesel engines each rated at 800 hp (597 kW)
Performance: maximum speed 201 mph (323 km/h) at 8,530 ft (2600 m); cruising speed 160 mph (257 km/h) at optimum altitude; climb to 6,560 ft (2000 m) in 16 minutes 30 seconds; service ceiling 14,760 ft (4500 m); range 2,980 miles (4800 km)
Weights: empty 24,912 lb

(11300 kg); maximum take-off 49,603 lb (22500 kg)
Dimensions: wingspan 98 ft 5 in (30.00 m); length 80 ft 8½ in (24.60 m); height 22 ft 5¾ in (6.85 m); wing area 1,291.71 sq ft (120.00 m²)
Armament: one 20-mm MG 151/20 trainable cannon in the bow turret, and one 0.312-in (7.92-mm) MG 15 trainable machine-gun in each of the two waist and one ventral positions
Payload: up to 12 troops

Variants

Do 26B: designation originally applied to the third 'boat, which was to have been built with an enlarged cabin seating four passengers; it was completed as the first Do 26D
Do 26D: four **Do 26D-0** 'boats were built for the Luftwaffe with an uprated powerplant and defensive armament; by April 1940 these 'boats, together with the two Lufthansa machines, were being used as transports in the Norwegian campaign; the Do 26D 'boats served with the Transozean Staffel and later with Küstenfliegergruppe 406

V5 was the prototype of an eight-seat Do 26C, but was impressed into Luftwaffe service.

Dornier Do 27

The **Do 27** was the first aircraft to enter production in Germany after World War II. Dr Claudius Dornier recommenced aviation activities in Spain in 1949, his Oficinas Tecnicas Dornier working closely with the Spanish company, CASA. The initial fruits of this collaboration became evident with the first flight of the **Do 25** four-seat prototype in June 1954. Prepared to meet a Spanish air ministry specification, this STOL light transport was powered by a single 150-hp (112-kW) ENMA Tigre engine.

A development of the

Do 25, the Do 27 first flew in prototype form on 8 April 1955 with a basically all-metal structure. Production took place in Germany at Dornier-Werke, the first example flying in October 1956, although in Spain CASA produced 50 generally similar aircraft under the designation **CASA C-127**. A high-wing cantilever monoplane with amazing STOL capability provided by large double-slotted flaps on the trailing edges of the wing inboard of the ailerons, a large 'wraparound' windscreen offering good forward and downward fields of vision,

fixed tailwheel landing gear with cantilever main units, and generous five-seat accommodation with the location of the strutless wing offering easy access for the loading of passengers and/or freight, the **Do 27A** proved popular.

Deliveries began at the rate of 20 aircraft per month, and the initial models aimed primarily at the military market were the generally similar Do 27A (four subvariants between the **Do 27A-1** and **A-4** with different maximum weights) and dual-control **Do 27B** (**Do 27B-1** and **B-2** subvariants). More than 620 aircraft had been built before production ended during 1965. By far the largest user was the Federal German Republic, which received 432 examples of the Do 27A and Do 27B; another early customer was the Swiss Flugwaffe, whose initial seven aircraft had wheel/ski landing gear. Other aircraft, either new-build or surplus to West German requirement, were supplied to the

Variants

Do 27H: civil or military version powered by the 340-hp (254-kW) Lycoming GSO-480-B1B6 engine driving a three- rather than two-bladed propeller
Do 27Q-5: civil version similar to Do 27A but with provision for the installation of quick conversion kits allowing the type's use in the advanced training, ambulance, glider-towing and photographic survey roles
Do 27Q-5(R): restricted-category version of Q-5, equipped for operation by pilot only in agricultural or forest dusting/spraying roles
Do 27Q-6: basically similar to the Q-5 but completed to the certification requirements of the USA's Federal Aviation Administration
Do 27S: twin floatplane version of which only a single prototype was built
Do 27T: single prototype powered by a Turboméca Astazou II turboprop engine

Belgian (**Do 27J-1**), Congolese, Israeli, Nigerian, Portuguese (**Do 27K-1** and **Do 27K-2**), Swedish, South African and Turkish air

forces, as well as the air arms of countries as diverse as Belize, Burundi, Guinea-Bissau, Rwanda and Sudan.

SPECIFICATION

Dornier Do 27A
Type: five-seat general-purpose light transport
Powerplant: one Lycoming GO-480-B1A6 flat-six piston engine rated at 270 hp (201 kW)
Performance: maximum speed 141 mph (227 km/h) at 3,280 ft (1000 m); cruising speed 109 mph (175 km/h) at 3,280 ft (1000 m); climb to 6,560 ft (2000 m) in

6 minutes 30 seconds; service ceiling 10,825 ft (3300 m); range 684 miles (1100 km)
Weights: empty 2,491 lb (1130 kg); maximum take-off 4,079 lb (1850 kg)
Dimensions: wingspan 39 ft 4½ in (12.00 m); length 31 ft 6 in (9.60 m); height 9 ft 2¼ in (2.80 m); wing area 208.83 sq ft (19.40 m²)

Having served in some numbers, the Do 27 has now passed out of Luftwaffe service.

Dornier Do 28

The success of its Do 27 persuaded Dornier that there could be a market for a twin-engined development of this single-engined type, offering greater performance and payload. This was the spur for the creation of the **Do 28** that first flew in **Do 28A** prototype form on 29 April 1959 with the wing, rear fuselage and tail unit of the Do 27 married to a new forward fuselage. This had a conventional nose and accommodated eight persons, and also carried a low-set stub wing supporting at its tips the nacelles for the powerplant of two 180-hp (134-kW) Lycoming O-360-A1A flat-four piston engines, as well as the cantilever main units of the new landing gear. This was still of the fixed tailwheel type but with wider-track cantilever main units.

Prototype trials convinced Dornier that a measure of redesign was needed, and this resulted in the use of more powerful engines and the adoption of a revised airframe with a longer-span wing of greater area. In this revised form the aircraft entered production, mainly for the executive transport market, as the **Do 28A-1**. This model's primary differences from the **Do 28B-1** included a powerplant of two 240-hp (186-kW) Textron Lycoming O-540 flat-six piston engines and generally improved performance. Production totalled 60 aircraft. The **Do 28B-1** was an improved Do 28A-1 with an uprated powerplant, wingtip auxiliary tanks, a larger tailplane, and electrically-operated flaps. This variant entered production in 1963, and production again totalled 60 aircraft, including a small number of the

Do 28B-2 variant with TIO-540 turbocharged piston engines.

Several Do 28s were used by the Nigerian and Katangan forces during the conflicts in those African countries. Other military users have been the Turkish army (three) and the Israel Defence Force/Air Force.

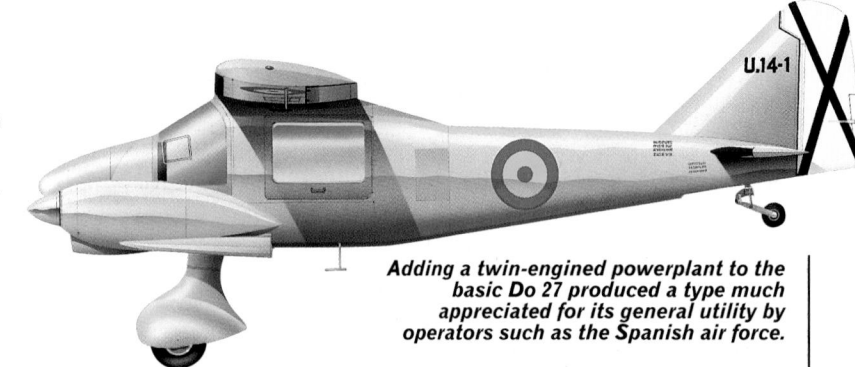

Adding a twin-engined powerplant to the basic Do 27 produced a type much appreciated for its general utility by operators such as the Spanish air force.

SPECIFICATION

Dornier Do 28B-1
Type: one-crew short-range utility transport aircraft
Powerplant: two Lycoming IO-540-A flat-six piston engines each rated at 290 hp (216 kW)
Performance: maximum speed 184 mph (290 km/h) at sea level; cruising speed 174 mph (274 km/h) at sea level; initial climb rate 1,400 ft (427 m) per minute; service ceiling 19,355 ft (5900 m);

ferry range 1,044 miles (1680 km) with auxiliary fuel; range 767 miles (1235 km) with maximum payload
Weights: empty 3,968 lb (1800 kg); maximum take-off 5,996 lb (2720 kg)
Dimensions: wingspan 45 ft 3½ in (13.80 m); length 29 ft 6 in (9.00 m); height 9 ft 2 in (2.80 m); wing area 241.12 sq ft (22.40 m²)
Payload: up to seven passengers, or two litters, or freight

Dornier Do 28D Skyservant and 128 Turbo-Skyservant

The original Do 28 series did not provide any more internal volume than the Do 27 and was therefore restricted in payload. Financial assistance provided by the West German ministry of economics then helped Dornier to develop the basic concept of the Do 28 into a bulkier, higher-powered STOL transport which could carry up to 13 passengers. This redesigned version was designated as the **Dornier Do 28D**, and was later named **Skyservant**. The redesign was so drastic that, apart from the layout and designation, the Do 28D bore little resemblance to the Do 28B. The prototype made its maiden flight on 23 February 1966, receiving type approval a year later, but only six production examples of the Do 28D had been completed before

the company introduced the improved **Do 28D-1** with the wingspan and maximum weight increased.

The Do 28D-1 secured FAA certification on 19 April 1968 and military type approval in January 1970. Orders for 178 machines were placed for the West German air force and navy, the Luftwaffe and Bundesmarine, that took 54 Do 28D-1 aircraft for staff transport and 124 **Do 28D-2** aircraft for light transport and communications. The Do 28D-2 had a number of significant internal alterations that increased the cabin length by 6 in (0.15 m), increased the fuel capacity and allowed the maximum weight to climb first to 8,370 lb (3800 kg) and finally to 8,844 lb (4015 kg). Other military deliveries were made to Cameroun, Ethiopia, Israel,

In Marineflieger service, the Do 28D has been replaced by the Dornier 228-212. The type was employed in the liaison and general transport roles.

Kenya, Malawi, Morocco, Nigeria, Somalia, Thailand, Turkey and Zambia. Production of the Do 28D-2 totalled 172 aircraft, and later recipients of the type from ex-West German stocks were Greece and Turkey.

A Do 28D-1 set several class records for piston-engined business aircraft in 1972, including an altitude

of 28,294 ft (8624 m) with a 2,205-lb (1000-kg) payload, as well as several time-to-height records. In 1980, a Luftwaffe Do 28D-2 was re-engined with Lycoming TIGO-540 turbocharged engines under a West German ministry of defence contract to validate a programme to upgrade that country's military

Skyservants under the revised designation **Do 28D-2T**.

Further development of the basic Do 28D design continued under a new designation, namely **128 Turbo-Skyservant**, the 'Do' prefix being dropped. The two basic variants were the **128-2** and **128-6**, both with accommodation for 10 passengers, but

Combining STOL performance with useful cargo/passenger capacity, the Do 28D continues to be a popular utility type.

Dornier Do 28D Skyservant

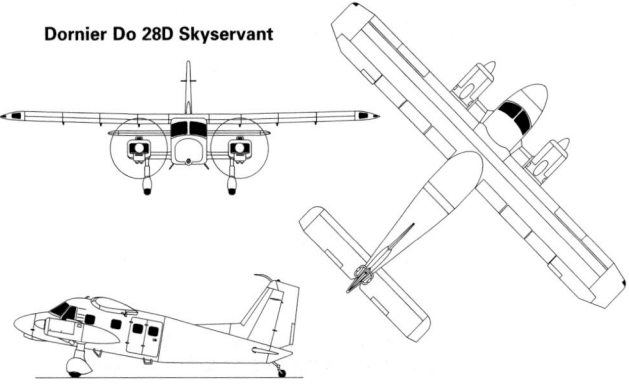

differing mainly in their powerplants, the 128-2 having two IGSO-540 piston engines and the 128-6 two 400-shp (298-kW) Pratt & Whitney PT6A-110 turboprop engines. The latter had first been seen in prototype form as the **Do 28D-5X TurboSky**, and first flown on 9 April 1978 with a pair of

600-shp (447-kW) Lycoming LTP101-600-1A turboprop engines flat-rated at 400 shp (298 kW), but then revised to **Do 28D-6X** standard with the definitive PT6A powerplant. The 128-6 also had a new fuel tank, reinforcements to the underwing engine supports, and other modifications. Orders and

options for 30 Do 128-6 aircraft from African customers had been announced by the autumn of 1982, 16 of these going to the Nigerian air force. A variant of the 128-6 has been delivered to Cameroun for the coastal patrol role in a form equipped with a 360° MEL Marec surveillance radar.

SPECIFICATION

Dornier 128-2 Skyservant
Type: two-crew STOL utility transport
Powerplant: two Lycoming IGSO-540-A1E flat six piston engines each rated at 380 hp (283 kW)
Performance: maximum speed 202 mph (325 km/h) at 10,000 ft (3050 m); cruising speed 131 mph (211 km/h) at 10,000 ft; initial climb rate 1,025 ft (312 m) per

minute; service ceiling 25,195 ft (7680 kg); range 399 miles (642 km) with maximum payload
Weights: empty 5,172 lb (2346 kg); maximum take-off 8,470 lb (3842 kg)
Dimensions: wingspan 51 ft ¼ in (15.55 m); length 37 ft 5¼ in (11.41 m); height 12 ft 10 in (3.90 m); wing area 312.16 sq ft (29.00 m²)
Payload: up to 10 passengers or freight

Dornier Do 29

With experience in the design and construction of STOL aircraft behind it, Dornier was well equipped to carry out a research programme sponsored by the Deutsche Versuchsanstalt für Luftfahrt into STOL and VTOL flight. The result was a trio of **Do 29** experimental aircraft. Based broadly on the Do 27's airframe, the Do 29 had the powerplant of two GO-480 piston engines, driving Hartzell propellers,

mounted behind the wing in a pusher configuration: these propellers turned in opposite directions to eliminate torque reaction and, more significantly, could be pivoted downward to a maximum of 90° for V/STOL flight. The first Do 29 flew in December 1958, and the three aircraft provided much useful information in their flight test programme. The first aircraft is preserved in the helicopter museum at Buckeburg in Germany.

The Do 29's pilot was accommodated in the nose of the fuselage, on a Martin-Baker ejection seat.

SPECIFICATION

Dornier Do 29
Type: single-seat STOL research aircraft
Powerplant: two Lycoming GO-480-B1A6 flat-six piston engines each rated at 270 hp (201 kW)

Performance: cruising speed 180 mph (290 km/h)
Weights: maximum take-off 5,511 lb (2500 kg)
Dimensions: wingspan 43 ft 4 in (13.20 m); length 31 ft 2 in (9.50 m); wing area 234.66 sq ft (21.80 m²)

Dornier Do 31

During the 1960s much thought was being given to the problems of vertical take-off and landing (VTOL). The UK's Hawker P.1127 series had already flown to demonstrate the possibility of a VTOL ground-attack fighter, and there was now talk of VTOL transports capable of supporting such fighters in the field. Dornier flew the first of two **Do 31E** experimental V/STOL transports on 10 February 1967. The primary element of the powerplant was the Rolls-Royce (Bristol) Pegasus vectored-thrust turbofan engine, one such unit being mounted beneath each half of the wing, while for direct lift a large pod at each wing tip contained four Rolls-Royce RB.162 turbojet engines.

The first Do 31E flew with only the Pegasus engines but the second,

first flown on 14 July 1967, had all 10 engines, making its first transition from vertical take-off to horizontal flight on 16 December 1967, and transitioning the other way five days later. Although ungainly in appearance, the Do 31 was no slouch and established several new class records for jet lift aircraft on its journey from Munich to the 1969 Paris Air Show. In addition to the two flying aircraft, a third was completed for static tests. During 1969-70 the type was involved in an evaluation programme in the USA as a result of agreements concluded between Dornier, the West German government and NASA.

The West German government considered a number of designs for a V/STOL civil jet transport and selected a Dornier

Do 31E-type aircraft would have proved costly to maintain in service. Harrier operators have found helicopters to be a far more acceptable alternative.

project, the **Do 231**, for further consideration. Based broadly on the layout of the Do 31, the new design would have had two 24,000-lb st (106.76-kN) RB.220 turbofan engines beneath the wing for forward flight and 12 13,100-lb st (58.27-kN) RB.202 lift fans, housed in the front and rear fuselage and two large pods in the outer parts of the wing. The **Do 231C** civil version would have accommodated 100 passengers, while the **Do 231M** military model would have had modified landing gear and a longer rear fuselage with rear-loading ramp. However, nothing further came of these interesting projects.

SPECIFICATION

Dornier Do 31E
Type: two-crew V/STOL experimental jet transport
Powerplant: two Rolls-Royce (Bristol) Pegasus 5-2 vectored-thrust turbofan engines each rated at 15,500 lb st (68.95-kN) and eight Rolls-Royce RB.162-4D turbojet engines each rated at 4,400 lb st (19.57 kN)
Performance: cruising speed 400 mph (644 km/h) at 20,000 ft

(6095 m); service ceiling 34,500 ft (10515 m)
Weights: empty 49,500 lb (22453 kg); maximum take-off 60,500 lb (27442 kg)
Dimensions: wingspan 59 ft 3 in (18.06 m); length 68 ft 6 in (20.88 m); height 28 ft (8.53 m); wing area 613.56 sq ft (57.00 m²)
Payload: up to 34 troops, or 24 litters, or 11,000 lb (4990 kg) of freight

Dornier Do 215

Considerable international interest in the Do 17 bomber had resulted from the success of the Do 17 V4 prototype at the 1937 Zürich international aviation meeting for military aircraft and in the following year, the advent of the generally improved Do 17Z again raised interest in the type. Dornier was given permission to negotiate export sales of a version

designated as the **Do 215** even though it was to all intents and purposes identical to the Luftwaffe's Do 17Z except for details of the equipment that would be specified by the ordering country. To aid in the sales effort, one of the Do 17Z-0 pre-production warplanes was redesignated as the **Do 215 V1** and used as a demonstration machine.

The main feature distinguishing the Do 215 from the otherwise similar Dornier Do 17 was its inline-engined powerplant.

Dornier Do 215 (continued)

The first country to express serious interest in the Do 215 was Yugoslavia, and Dornier therefore revised another Do 17Z-0 with a powerplant of two Gnome-Rhône 14N-1/2 radial piston engines as used in the Yugoslavs' Do 17Ks. However, with this powerplant the **Do 215 V2** was little better than the Do 17K and Dornier therefore completed a third aircraft as the **Do 215 V3** with two 1,075-hp (802-kW) DB 601A inverted-Vee engines driving three-bladed VDM metal propellers of the variable-pitch type. This third prototype made its first flight in the opening part of 1939, and soon revealed performance significantly higher than that offered by the two previous prototypes as well as any variant of the Do 17 series.

Several nations considered a purchase of the Do 215, but the only order placed before the outbreak of World War II was that from Sweden, which had recently had its order for the Breguet Bre.694 bomber cancelled by the French government. The Swedish air force ordered 18 examples of the four-man **Do 215A-1** variant that was based closely on the Do 215 V3 and designed to carry a maximum bombload of 2,205 lb (1000 kg). Dornier had just started work on these aircraft when the German authorities embargoed the type's export and ordered the completion of the current aircraft as long-range reconnaissance machines with the designations **Do 215B-0** for the pre-production aircraft and **Do 215B-1** for the production aircraft. Delivered from January 1940, the aircraft were allocated to the 3. Aufklärungsstaffel (reconnaissance squadron) of the Luftwaffe high command in the strategic reconnaissance role. During April 1940 this squadron was moved to Norway, which the Germans had just invaded, for reconnaissance over northern and eastern Europe. The Luftwaffe had meanwhile decided that the Do 215 had the potential to replace the Do 17, and ordered continued development and production. The **Do 215B-2** was a pure bomber variant that proceeded no further than the project stage and the designation **Do 215B-3** was applied to two aircraft supplied to the USSR under the German-Soviet non-aggression pact of 1939, so the next model to see service was the **Do 215B-4**.

Entering service in March 1940, this was a development of the Do 215B-1 with a different camera arrangement in the form of one Rb 50/30 camera below the lower gun position and one Rb 20/30 camera in the crew entry hatch under the forward fuselage. The Do 215B-4 was a reconnaissance bomber, and its two weapon bays could carry a maximum of two 250-kg (551-lb) SC250 bombs or 10 50-kg (110-lb) SC50 bombs on short-range missions, these figures being halved on medium-range missions or omitted entirely on the long-range reconnaissance missions, when an auxiliary fuel tank was carried in the weapons bays. Production of the Do 215B-1 and Do 215B-4 for the Luftwaffe lasted to a point early in 1941 and totalled 72 out of a planned 92 aircraft that served almost exclusively with reconnaissance units. The Do 215B-1 and Do 215B-4 were phased out of German service from the autumn of 1941, and early in 1942 four Do 215B-4s were transferred to the Hungarian air force as long-range reconnaissance aircraft, remaining in service only to the closing stages of 1942.

As production and service of the Do 215B continued, the modest success of the Do 17Z Kauz II night-intruder conversion of the Do 17Z-3 suggested that a comparable conversion from Do 215B standard could produce a night-fighter with usefully higher performance than the Kauz II, whose indifferent speed meant that it was better suited to the offensive night intruder than to the defensive night interceptor role. In the late autumn of 1940, therefore, the Do 215B-4 was earmarked for conversion with the same type of nose as the Kauz II, namely a solid unit that replaced the glazed bombardier nose and was fitted with fixed forward-firing gun armament (two 20-mm MG FF cannon and four 0.312-in/7.92-mm MG 17 machine-guns) as well as the sensor for the Spänner-Anlage IR system that was used to detect aircraft by the heat plumes of their engine exhausts. The Spänner-Anlage combined oversensitivity, unreliability, short range and inability to provide directional information, however, and was soon replaced by the FuG 202 Lichtenstein BC airborne interception radar, which used the Matratze (mattress) array of four 'stag's horn' antennas on the extreme nose to provide detection of targets at a range of between 220 and 4,375 yards (200 and 4000 m) as well as the target's bearing in azimuth and elevation. Installation of this radar in the Do 215B-4 conversion resulted in the definitive **Do 215B-5** night-fighter whose maximum level speed was reduced by 15½ mph (25 km/h) as a result of the drag produced by the radar antennas.

The Do 215B-5 scored its first radar-aided 'kill' in August 1941. All 20 Do 215B-5s were produced as conversions of the last Do 215B-4s on the production line, and were delivered to II Gruppe (wing) of Nachtschlacht-geschwader 1 in a process that was completed only late in 1942 as a result of delays in the delivery of the radar equipments. The last of these aircraft were retired only in the early part of 1944.

SPECIFICATION

Dornier Do 215B-1

Type: four-seat medium reconnaissance bomber

Powerplant: two Daimler-Benz DB 601Aa inverted-Vee piston engines each rated at 1,100 hp (820 kW)

Performance: maximum speed 292 mph (470 km/h) at 16,405 ft (5000 m); cruising speed 255 mph (410 km/h) at 13,125 ft (4000 m); initial climb rate 1,197 ft (365 m) per minute; service ceiling 29,530 ft (9000 m); range 1,519 miles (2445 km) with auxiliary fuel; radius 236 miles (380 km) with maximum bombload

Weights: empty 12,731 lb (5775 kg); maximum take-off 19,400 lb (8800 kg)

Dimensions: wingspan 59 ft ⅓ in (18.00 m); length 51 ft 9⅔ in (15.80 m); height 14 ft 11½ in (4.55 m); wing area 592.03 sq ft (55.00 m^2)

Armament: two 0.312-in (7.92-mm) MG 15 fixed or trainable forward-firing machine-guns in the windscreen, one or two 0.312-in (7.92-mm) MG 15 trainable forward-firing machine-guns in the nose position, two 0.312-in (7.92-mm) MG 15 trainable lateral-firing machine-guns in the side windows, one 0.312-in (7.92-mm) MG 15 trainable rearward-firing machine-gun in the dorsal position, and one 0.312-in (7.92-mm) MG 15 trainable rearward-firing machine-gun in the ventral position, plus up to 2,205 lb (1000 kg) of bombs carried in two lower-fuselage weapons bays

Dornier Do 217

Essentially an enlarged Do 17, the **Do 217** first flew in **Do 217 V1** prototype form during August 1938 with the powerplant of two 1,075-hp (802-kW) Daimler-Benz DB 601A engines. Although this aircraft soon crashed, the programme was continued by three prototypes powered by 960-hp (708-kW) Junkers Jumo 211A engines. The last of these was the armed **Do 217 V4** which, to improve stability, had enlarged vertical tail surfaces and modified dive brakes, whose four segments when closed formed the tail cone. A further three Jumo-engined aircraft were

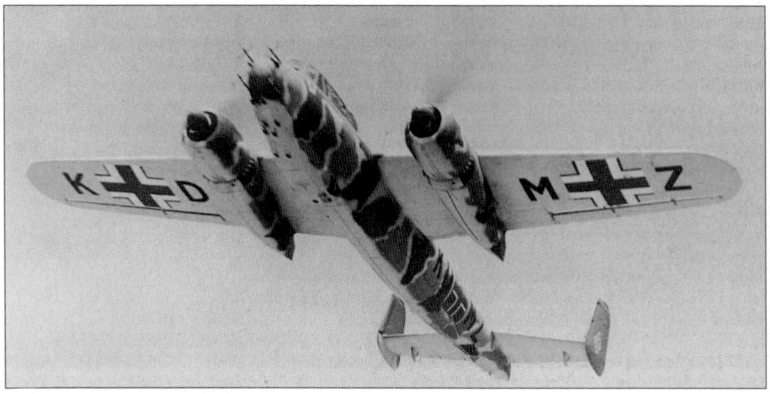

First of the truly effective Do 217 night-fighters, the Do 217J-2 featured radar and a powerful nose-mounted armament.

Variants

Do 217A: eight 217A-0 reconnaissance aircraft were built, each carrying two cameras and armed with three 0.312-in (7.92-mm) MG 15 machine-guns

Do 217C: five examples of this bomber version were built, the first (**Do 217C V1**) with Jumo 211A engines and the remainder (**Do 217C-0**) with DB 601A engines; all were armed with one 15-mm MG 151/15 cannon and five 0.312-in (7.92-mm) MG 15 machine-guns plus a 6,614-lb (3000-kg) bombload

Do 217E: the first series production variant, the **Do 217E-1** could carry a 6,614-lb (3000-kg) bombload and was armed with one 15-mm MG 151 cannon and five 0.312-in (7.92-mm) MG 15 machine-guns; the **Do 217E-2** introduced a dorsal turret with a 13-mm (0.51-in) MG 131 machine-gun, a similar gun mounted ventrally, three 0.312-in (7.92-mm) MG 15 machine-guns in the forward fuselage, and a 15-mm MG 151/15 cannon in the nose. Developed for anti-shipping operations over the Atlantic, the **Do 217E-3** carried additional armour-plating to provide crew protection, two additional

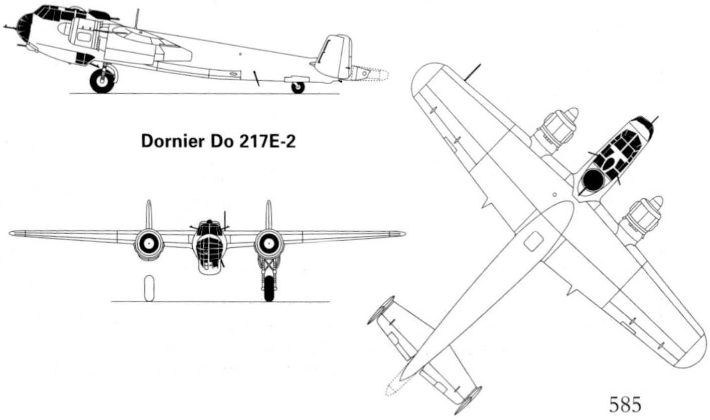

Dornier Do 217E-2

fuel tanks with a capacity of 165 Imp gal (750 litres) in the bomb bay, and seven MG 15 machine-guns supplementing a single 20-mm MG FF cannon in the nose; the **Do 217E-4** was the 1941 version of the Do 217E-2 with BMW 801C engines and cable-cutters in the leading edges of the wings; some 65 **Do 217E-5** aircraft were manufactured, these having underwing racks for the carriage of two Henschel Hs 293 missiles

Variants (Continued)

Do 217H: 21st Do 217E when fitted with DB 601 turbocharged engines for trial purposes

Do 217J: starting in 1942, 157 aircraft were built to the **Do 217J-1** and **Do 217J-2** standards; the former was a fighter-bomber, with a nose similar to that of the Do 17Z-10 with four 0.312-in (7.92-mm) MG 17 machine-guns and four 20-mm MG FF cannon, in addition to the dorsal and ventral positions each with a pair of 0.51-in (13-mm) MG 131 guns; the Do 217J-2 was a night-fighter with 20-mm MG 151/20 cannon replacing the MG FF weapons of the Do 217J-1 and fitted with FuG 212 Lichtenstein BC radar

Do 217K: introduced in the autumn of 1942, the **Do 217K-1** bomber had a new glazed nose with an unstepped cockpit; two SD-1400X (Fritz-X) guided bombs were carried beneath the wing of the **Do 217K-2**, which carried the associated FuG 203a and FuG 230a guidance equipment in the fuselage. It was a missile launched by a Do 217K-2 of III./KG 100, operating from Marseilles, that sank the Italian battleship *Roma* on 14 September 1943 when the Italian fleet broke out from La Spezia to join the Allies; either the SD-1400X or Hs 293 missile could be carried by the **Do 217K-3**

Do 217L: two experimental developments of the Do 217K with modified cockpit and defensive dispositions

Do 217M: the **Do 217M-1** was essentially the Do 217K-1 revised with the powerplant of two DB 603A engines; the otherwise similar **Do 217M-5** was equipped with an underfuselage rack for an Hs 293 missile; the **Do 217M-3** was the DB 603A-engined equivalent of the Do 217K-3; the **Do 217M-11** was an extended-span missile carrier equivalent to the Do 217K-2

Do 217N: a nose similar to that of the Do 217J-2 was incorporated in the Do 217M airframe to produce the **Do 217N-1** night-fighter, which was quickly replaced in production by the **Do 217N-2**, identified by deletion of the dorsal turret

Do 217P: the first prototype Do 217 V1, flown in June 1942, was developed as a high-altitude reconnaissance aircraft with a pressure cabin and two 1,750-hp (1305-kW) DB 603B engines, boosted by a two-stage supercharger driven by a 1,475-hp (1100-kW) DB 605T engine mounted in the bomb bay; the armament comprised four 0.312-in (7.92-mm) MG 81 machine-guns, and one Rb20/30 and two Rb75/30 cameras were installed in the three **Do 217P-0** pre-production aircraft

Do 217R: five conversions from Do 317 standard with DB 603 engines and the equipment to carry two Hs 293 missiles

followed by two machines with 1,550-hp (1156-kW) BMW 139 radial engines in an attempt to improve performance; the improved BMW 801, introduced in late 1939, was adopted for the production **Do 217A** recon-naissance aircraft, which entered service with the Aufklärungsgruppe Oberbefehlshaber der Luftwaffe in 1940. The first major production version, however, was the **Do 217E** that appeared in 1940 with a deepened fuselage and enlarged bomb bay which could accept larger bombs or a torpedo. The Do 217E became operational in the reconnaissance role with 3.(F)/11 in the closing months of 1940 and as a bomber with II./KG 40 during the spring of 1941. Some 1,730 Do 217s were built.

SPECIFICATION

Dornier Do 217M-1

Type: four-seat medium bomber

Powerplant: two Daimler-Benz DB 603A inverted-Vee piston engines each rated at 1,750 hp (1305 kW)

Performance: maximum speed 348 mph (560 km/h) at 18,700 ft (5700 m); cruising speed 248 mph (400 km/h) at optimum altitude; climb to 6,560 ft (2000 m) in 6 minutes 42 seconds; service ceiling 31,170 ft (9,500 m); range 1,336 miles (2150 km)

Weights: empty 19,489 lb (8840 kg); maximum take-off 36,817 lb (16700 kg)

Dimensions: wingspan 62 ft 4 in (19.00 m); length 55 ft 9¼ in (16.90 m); height 16 ft 4¾ in (5.00 m); wing area 613.54 sq ft (57.00 m²)

Armament: one 0.51-in (13-mm) MG 131 trainable machine-gun in the power-operated dorsal turret, one 0.51-in (13-mm) MG 131 trainable rearward-firing machine-gun in the ventral step position, one 0.312-in (7.92-mm) MG 81z trainable forward-firing two-barrel machine-gun in the nose, and two 0.312-in (7.92-mm) MG 81 trainable lateral-firing machine-guns mounted singly in the cockpit side windows, plus up to 8,818 lb (4000 kg) of disposable stores carried in a lower-fuselage weapons bay and on up to two underwing hardpoints, and generally comprising an internal load of two 1000-kg (2,205-lb) SC1000 bombs and two 250-kg (551-lb) SC250 bombs, or four 500-kg (1,102-lb) SC500 bombs, or eight 250-kg (551-lb) SC250 bombs and one 1800-kg (3,968-lb) SC1800 bomb or L5 torpedo, or two 2,304-lb (1045-kg) Hs 293A anti-ship missiles or 3,461-lb (1570-kg) FX-1400 Fritz-X anti-ship guided bombs, or two 551-lb (250-kg) SC250 bombs externally

---

Dornier Do 317

In July 1939 the German air ministry issued its 'Bomber B' requirement to a number of carefully selected aircraft manufacturers; the require-ment was designed to lead to an advanced medium bomber that would not only succeed types such as the Heinkel He 111 and Junkers Ju 88, but would also open a new era in medium bomber design and capabili-ties. The specification attached to the requirement therefore called for very high performance and also stipulated a number of notably advanced features. The operational scenario for the 'Bomber B' envisaged attacks on targets anywhere in the UK from bases in France and/or Norway, so a range of 2,237 miles (3600 km) was demanded, together with a maximum speed of 373 mph (600 km/h) at an altitude of between 19,685 and 22,965 ft (6000 and 7000 m) so that the bomber would be able to deal with the attentions of modern British fighters. Other require-ments were a 4,409-lb (2000-kg) disposable weaponload, a crew of three or four, a powerplant of two DB 604 or Junkers Jumo 222 24-cylinder engines and, most taxingly of all, pressurised accom-modation and a defensive armament system based

entirely on remotely controlled barbettes. The requirement was initially issued to Arado, Dornier, Focke-Wulf and Junkers, although Henschel was added when the extent of the company's experience with pressure cabins became evident.

The design submissions reached the German air ministry in July 1940; the Arado Ar 340 was soon knocked out of the running, but prototypes were ordered of the **Dornier Do 317**, the Fw 191 and the Ju 288. The Do 317 was based conceptually on the Do 217 and made provision for a four-man crew in a detachable and extensively glazed nose section that was pres-surised by air tapped from the superchargers of the two DB 604 engines. As detailed design work of the three companies' offerings continued, the German air ministry came to the conclusion that greater promise was provided by the Fw 191 and Ju 288, and therefore ordered Dornier to incorporate some of the ideas of the Do 317 into a planned high-altitude version of the Do 217 while continuing work on the Do 317 at a lower level of priority. In 1940 the German air ministry inspected the

Do 317 mock-up and told Dornier to cease work on this project so that greater effort could be put into development of the Do 217P high-altitude reconnaissance bomber, which had a pressure cabin based on that of the Do 317. During 1941, however, the Do 317 was offered a new lease of life as possible successor to the Do 217 and two pres-surised versions were now proposed: the **Do 317A** with a powerplant of two DB 603A inverted-Vee engines for medium-alti-tude operations with a conventional defensive armament scheme, and the **Do 317B** with a powerplant of two 2,870-hp (2140-kW) DB 610 inverted-Vee engines for high-altitude operations with an extended-span wing and a more advanced defensive armament scheme based on remotely-controlled barbettes.

The German air ministry ordered six Do 317A proto-types to a final design that was based on a shoulder-wing cantilever monoplane layout of all-metal construc-tion. The **Do 317 V1** first prototype made its maiden flight in 1943 without the defensive armament planned for the production version, and proved to have performance that was little better than that of the Do 217P. It was therefore decided that the other five

prototypes currently under construction should be completed without pres-surisation as launch platforms for the Henschel Hs 293A anti-ship missile, and in this form the aircraft received the revised desig-nation **Do 217R** when they served with III Gruppe (wing) of Kampfgesch-wader 100, based at Orléans in France.

The Do 317B, which had by that time reached the stage of a full-scale mock-up with increased span, was then cancelled. The offensive load of the Do 317B would have comprised up to 20,282 lb (9200 kg) of disposable stores carried in a lower-fuselage weapons bay and on two underwing hardpoints.

The Do 317 V1 shows off the type's tailfin and rudder shape, which was revised from that of the Do 217.

SPECIFICATION

Dornier Do 317A

Type: four-seat medium/heavy bomber

Powerplant: two Daimler-Benz DB 603 inverted-Vee piston engines each rated at 1,750 hp (1305 kW)

Performance: maximum speed 416 mph (670 km/h) at 24,935 ft (7600 m); cruising speed 336 mph (540 km/h) at optimum altitude; service ceiling 34,450 ft (10500 m); range 2,486 miles (4000 km) with auxiliary fuel and 2,237 miles (3600 km) with standard fuel

Weights: maximum take-off 52,910 lb (24000 kg)

Dimensions: wingspan 67 ft 8¾ in (20.65 m); length 55 ft 1½ in (16.80 m); height 17 ft 10½ in (5.45 m)

Armament: one 15-mm MG 151/15 fixed forward-firing cannon in the lower port side of the nose, one 13-mm (0.51-in) MG 131 trainable machine-gun in the power-operated dorsal turret, one 13-mm (0.51-in) MG 131 trainable rearward-firing machine-gun in the rear of the cockpit, one 13-mm (0.51-in) MG 131 trainable rearward-firing machine-gun in the ventral step position, and two 0.312-in (7.92-mm) MG 81 trainable forward-firing machine-guns on the starboard side of the nose, plus up to 6,614 lb (3000 kg) of disposable stores carried in a lower-fuselage weapons bay

Dornier Do 335 Pfeil

Following feasibility trials with the experimental Göppingen Gö 9 research aircraft, designed by Ulrich Hütter and built by Schempp-Hirth in 1939, the unconventional tandem engine layout patented by Dr Claudius Dornier in 1937 was adopted by the German air ministry for a bomber under the project number **Do P.231**, despite the fact that Dornier's original design proposal was for a fighter! When work was at an advanced stage the project was cancelled, but an emerging need for a high-performance fighter resulted in the reactivation

of Dornier's plans for an interceptor. A low-wing cantilever monoplane of all-metal construction with a cruciform tail unit, tricycle landing gear and the powerplant of two 1,800-hp (1342-kW) Daimler-Benz DB 603 engines, one buried in the rear fuselage and driving a three-bladed pusher propeller via an extension shaft and the other in the conventional nose position with a three-bladed tractor propeller, the first prototype of the **Do 335 Pfeil** (arrow) made its maiden flight during September 1943. The type was built

in a number of versions, albeit in small numbers, but the closest it came to service was with operational test unit Erprobungskommando 335 in the spring of 1945. Three major derivatives of the basic design were projected but failed to materialise. These comprised the **Do 435** two-seat night-fighter, the **Do 535** to be developed in conjunction with Heinkel with the rear piston engine replaced by a turbojet of Heinkel design, and the long-range reconnaissance **Do 635** which would have united two Do 335 airframes by means of a new wing centre-section.

Ten pre-production Do 335A-0 fighter-bombers were completed, the second (illustrated) being evaluated in the US post-war.

SPECIFICATION	
Dornier Do 335A-1 **Type:** single-seat fighter-bomber **Powerplant:** two Daimler-Benz DB 603A-2 inverted Vee piston engines each rated at 1,750 hp (1305 kW) **Performance:** maximum speed 478 mph (770 km/h) at 21,000 ft (6400 m); cruising speed 426 mph (685 km/h) at 23,295 ft (7100 m); climb to 26,245 ft (8000 m) in 14 minutes 30 seconds; service ceiling 37,400 ft (11400 m); range 857 miles (1380 km) **Weights:** empty 16,314 lb (7400 kg); maximum take-off 21,164 lb (9600 kg)	**Dimensions:** wingspan 45 ft 3¼ in (13.80 m); length 45 ft 5¼ in (13.85 m); height 16 ft 4¾ in (5.00 m); wing area 414.42 sq ft (38.50 m²) **Armament:** one 30-mm MK 103 fixed forward-firing cannon between the cylinder banks of the forward engine and two 15-mm MG 151/15 fixed forward-firing cannon in the upper part of the forward fuselage, plus one 500-kg (1,102-lb) SC500 or two 250-kg (551-lb) SC250 bombs carried in a lower-fuselage weapons bay and two 250-kg (551-lb) SC250 bombs carried under the wing

During initial tests at Oberpfaffenhofen and Rechlin, the Do 335 V1 demonstrated superb acceleration and generally good handling.

Dornier Libelle

Throughout World War I, Dr Claudius Dornier had been in charge of design and construction at the Zeppelin-Werke Lindau company located at Friedrichshafen in southern Germany. During the course of the war this organisation produced a series of aircraft (including the C I, C II, CS I, D I, Rs I, Rs II, Rs III, Rs IV and V 1). After the war the works were transferred to Manzell, near Friedrichshafen, and later renamed as the Dornier Metallbauten GmbH for which, during the early 1920s, Dornier designed and developed a number of interesting civil aircraft.

The first of these was the **Dornier Libelle I** (dragonfly I), a three-seat sports/trainer flying-boat which first flew on 16 August 1921. Of all-metal construction, except for fabric covering on part of the

Right: The Libelle's flat-bottomed hull had sponsons of aerofoil section projecting from each side to provide stability on the water.

wing and all the control surfaces, the Libelle I was a parasol-wing monoplane with its constant-chord foldable wing strut-mounted above the hull. An open cockpit beneath the wing provided accommodation for a pilot and one passenger forward, with a second passenger seated behind them, and dual controls were standard. Power was provided by a Siemens-

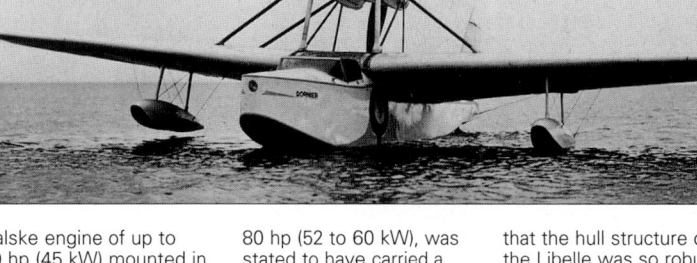

Halske engine of up to 60 hp (45 kW) mounted in a neat nacelle on the upper surface of the wing's centre section. A later **Libelle II**, of increased dimensions and powered by a similar engine of 70 to

80 hp (52 to 60 kW), was stated to have carried a pilot and four passengers without difficulty although only intended as a three-seater. It was also reported

that the hull structure of the Libelle was so robust that take-offs and landings had been performed on ice-covered surfaces. The type was extensively produced.

Variant

Spatz (sparrow): virtually a landplane version of the Libelle without the hull sponsons but with fixed tailskid landing gear; an 80-hp (60-kW) Siemens-Halske engine was standard, but a 100-hp (75-kW) engine and an open cockpit or enclosed cabin were optional

SPECIFICATION	
Dornier Libelle I **Type:** three-seat sporting and training flying-boat **Powerplant:** one Siemens-Halske radial piston engine rated at between 50 and 60 hp (37 and 45 kW) **Performance:** maximum speed about 75 mph (120 km/h) at	optimum altitude; service ceiling about 5,250 ft (1600 m) **Weights:** empty 882 lb (400 kg); maximum take-off 1,433 lb (650 kg) **Dimensions:** wingspan 27 ft 10½ in (8.50 m); length 23 ft 6½ in (7.18 m); height 7 ft 5¼ in (2.27 m); wing area 150.70 sq ft (14.00 m²)

Douglas A2D Skyshark

Interest in the efficiency of the turboprop engine at the end of World War II resulted in the receipt by Douglas of a contract for a

prototype version of the company's AD-1 Skyraider with a turboprop replacing its standard piston-engined powerplant. This apparently

Two Skyshark prototypes – of which the second is illustrated – were built and flown, along with six preliminary production aircraft. Four other production machines were built but never flown and a contract for a further 339 aircraft was cancelled.

simple conversion failed to materialise because the Allison XT40 turboprop had more than twice the power output of the piston engine it was intended to replace, and this required considerable redesign of the airframe. Two prototypes were therefore ordered under the designation **Douglas XA2D-1**, the first of these flying on 26 May 1950. The XA2D-1 retained the same overall configuration as the AD-1, but had a new tail unit, modified and strengthened landing gear, and the fuselage redesigned to accommodate the Allison XT40 engine. This consisted of two separate turbines driving a pair of contra-rotating propellers through the medium of a common gearbox. Early testing showed great promise, and 10 preliminary production aircraft were ordered under the designation **A2D-1 Skyshark**. In production form, the aircraft offered half as much warload again as the Skyraider, had twice the service ceiling and climbed over three times more quickly. Problems with the powerplant and gearbox led to delays, however, and two aircraft were lost in powerplant-related accidents. As a result of these problems and of the promise shown by the XA4D-1, the Skyshark programme was cancelled.

Douglas A3D (A-3) Skywarrior

The largest and heaviest aircraft designed for operation from an aircraft-carrier when Douglas completed the project design in 1949, the **A3D Skywarrior** originated from a US Navy requirement of 1947 for an attack bomber with strategic strike capability. The type was tailored to deployment on board the giant new aircraft-carriers that were ultimately to materialise, after prolonged opposition from the US Air Force, as the four ships of the 'Forrestal' class.

The Douglas design was a high-wing cantilever monoplane with retractable tricycle landing gear, two podded turbojet engines beneath the wing, and a large internal weapons bay to accommodate up to 12,000 lb (5443 kg) of varied weapons. The wing was swept back at 36° and was of the high aspect ratio type for maximum cruise efficiency and therefore long range. All the tail surfaces were swept, and the outer wing panels and vertical tail surface folded to facilitate flight and hangar deck accommodation.

The first of two **XA3D-1** prototypes made its maiden flight on 28 October 1952 with the powerplant of two 7,000-lb st (31.13-kN) Westinghouse XJ40-WE-3 engines. The failure of the J40 meant that the 9,700-lb st (43.18-kN) Pratt & Whitney J57-P-6 was used to power the sole **YA3D-1** production prototype and **A3D-1** initial production model. The first of the 49 A3D-1 aircraft flew on 16 September 1953, and deliveries to the US Navy's VAH-1 attack squadron began on 31 March 1956. In 1962 the core designation was changed from A3D to A-3, the initial three-seat production version thereupon becoming the **A-3A**. Six of these aircraft were later modified for the ECM role with seven-seat accommodation and a mass of specialised equipment under the revised designation **EA-3A**.

The **A3D-2** (from 1962 **A-3B**) entered service in 1957 with the uprated powerplant of two J57-P-10 engines and an inflight-refuelling probe. Surviving examples of these 164 aircraft were later modified, the radar-controlled tail turret (two 20-mm cannon) being replaced by ECM equipment including a chaff dispenser, the nose radome being modified for accommodation of an improved nav/attack radar, and the structure being strengthened to allow use of the LABS (Low-Altitude Bombing System). A reconnaissance variant with cameras in the weapons bay was designated **A3D-2P** (from 1962 **RA-3B**), and these 30 aircraft had the erstwhile weapons bay adapted for the carriage of two operators, 12 vertical and oblique cameras, and photoflash bombs. Later, eight A-3s were modified for use in the electronic aggressor role, as the **ERA-3B**.

The designation **A3D-2Q** (from 1962 **EA-3B**) identified 25 aircraft built specifically for the ECM role, with the weapons bay turned into a pressurised compartment accommodating four operators and their specialist equipment; the type also had forward- and side-looking radar, and a number of IR sensors. The only other new-build model was the **A3D-2T**, a designation used for 12 aircraft that received the revised designation **TA-3B** in 1962 and were operated as eight-seat navigator/bombardier trainers, with the weapons bay volume revised for an instructor and up to six pupils.

The A3B/A-3 series was also the basis of a number of conversions. The designation **A3D-2Z** was employed for two A-3B conversions that received the revised designation **VA-3B** in 1962 and were operated in the staff transport role with a well-appointed fuselage compartment for two officers. The final variants in US Navy service were the **KA-3B** inflight-refuelling tankers and at least 30 **EKA-3B** tanker/countermeasures aircraft. The EKA-3B remained a standard US Navy Reserve aircraft into the early 1990s.

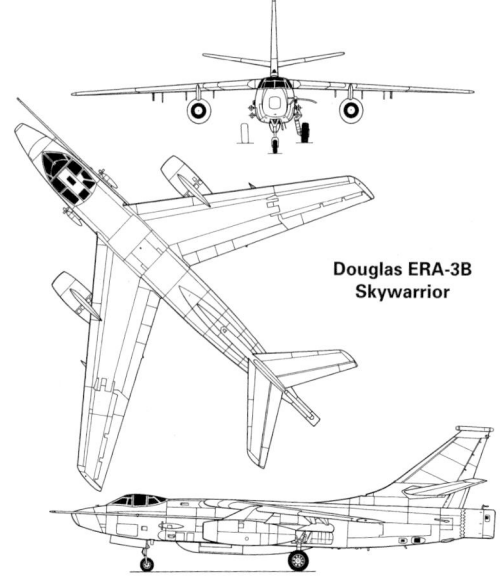

Douglas ERA-3B Skywarrior

Folding wings were essential for a carrier-based aircraft of the Skywarrior's size. The A-3 survived to see combat in the 1991 Gulf War.

EA-3Bs of VQ-1 flew electronic reconnaissance and Comint missions during the Vietnam War. The aircraft flew alongside EC-121 Constellations and EP-3 Orions.

Douglas A-4 Skyhawk

One of the most successful post-World War II aircraft to serve with the US Navy, the **A-4 Skyhawk** originated as a private-venture design under a team headed by Ed Heinemann.

Thus, when the US Navy began the search for a turbine-powered successor to the AD-1 (A-1) Skyraider, the company was able to propose a new attack aircraft with a gross weight of about half that of the official specification and one which was considerably faster. Of monoplane configuration, with a low-set delta wing incorporating integral fuel tanks, the design had a fuselage which accommodated avionics in the nose, additional fuel aft of the pilot's cockpit, and the Wright J65 turbojet (a licence-built Armstrong Siddeley Sapphire) in the centre fuselage. Ordered during the Korean War, the prototype was flown on 22 June 1954 and the first pre-production aircraft on 14 August 1954, with initial deliveries to US Navy Attack Squadron VA-72 beginning on 26 October 1956. Three months later, in January 1957, VMA-224 became the first US Marine

Corps squadron to receive Skyhawks.

It was a fortunate period in which to introduce this sparkling new attack aircraft, for by the time the US Navy and US Marines became involved in operations in Vietnam, both of these services were able to deploy the Skyhawk with the greatest confidence in its capability; indeed, such was its effectiveness that steadily improving A-4s remained in production until February 1979, built to a total of 2,960 aircraft including trainers, and exported to the armed forces of several nations. In 2000, Skyhawks remain in service in a variety of original and upgraded forms with Argentina, Brazil, Indonesia, Israel, New Zealand, Singapore and the US Navy. Indeed, Argentina's A-4 fleet has been augmented by 32 radically updated ex-USMC A-4Ms under the designation **A-4AR Fightinghawk**, along with four OA-4M-based **TA-4R** machines. Features of these Lockheed Martin-produced conversions include AN/APG-66 radar and HOTAS controls.

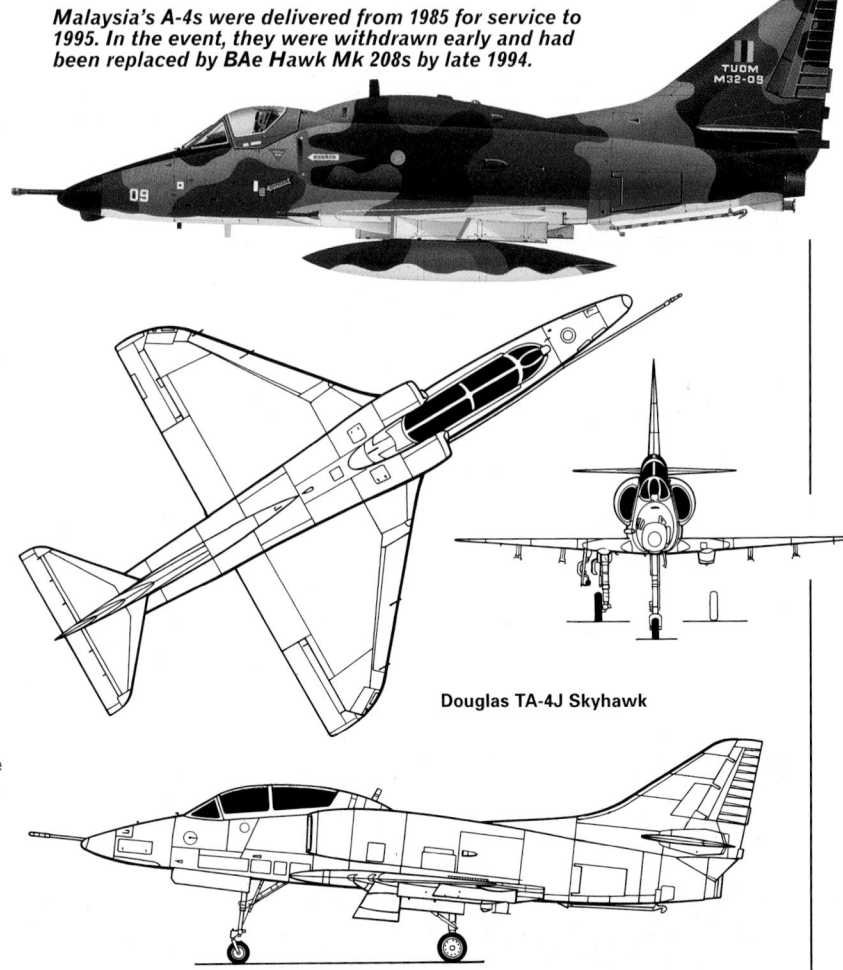

Malaysia's A-4s were delivered from 1985 for service to 1995. In the event, they were withdrawn early and had been replaced by BAe Hawk Mk 208s by late 1994.

Douglas TA-4J Skyhawk

Variants

XA4D-1: designation of one prototype, powered by a 7,200-lb (32.02-kN) thrust Wright J65-W-2 turbojet
YA4D-1 (later YA-4A and then A-4A): designation of 19 pre-production aircraft generally similar to XA4D-1; introduced the 7,700-lb (34.25-kN) thrust J65-W-4 or J65-W-4B turbojet and armament of two 20-mm cannon and up to 5,000 lb (2268 kg) of weapons on an underfuselage and two underwing hardpoints
A4D-1 (later A-4A): production aircraft, as YA4D-1; 146 built
A4D-2 (later A-4B): production version with strengthened rear fuselage, inflight-refuelling equipment, and the 7,800-lb (34.69-kN) thrust J65-W-16A turbojet; 542 built
A4D-2N (later A-4C): production version introducing terrain-following radar, autopilot and a number of other improvements; J65-W-16A engines, later uprated to 8,500-lb (37.80-kN) thrust with designation change to J65-W-16C; 638 built
A4D-3: proposed all-weather version with Pratt & Whitney turbojet; not built
A4D-5 (later A-4E): improved production version, introducing the 8,500-lb (37.80-kN) thrust Pratt & Whitney J52-P-6A turbojet and two additional underwing hardpoints to allow maximum weaponload of 8,200 lb (3719 kg); 494 built
A4D-6: proposed development with 11,500-lb (51.14-kN) thrust Pratt & Whitney TF30 turbofan installed in an enlarged airframe; not built
TA-4E: designation of two production prototypes of a two-seat trainer version; generally as A4D-5, but with fuselage lengthened by 2 ft 6 in (0.76 m) and reduced internal fuel
TA-4F: production version of TA-4E with the 9,300-lb (41.35-kN) thrust J52-P-8A turbojet; 240 built
A-4F: final attack production version for US Navy; introduced the J52-P-8A engine, and additional avionics in a hump-back fairing on the rear fuselage; 146 built
EA-4F: four TA-4Fs converted to carry stores simulating Soviet missile and aircraft signatures for dissimilar air combat training
A-4G: version similar to A-4F but with the avionics hump removed; eight built for Royal Australian Navy, later supplemented by eight refurbished A-4Fs; survivors later upgraded and passed to RNZAF as A-4Ks
TA-4G: two two-seat trainers for RAN, later supplemented by two refurbished TA-4Fs; generally similar to the TA-4F
A-4H: production version for the Israeli air force; generally similar to A4D-5 but with J52-P-8A engine; introduced a braking parachute, and replaced 20-mm guns by two of 30-mm calibre; 90 built

TA-4H: two-seat trainer version of the A-4H for Israel; 10 built
TA-4J: two-seat trainer for the USN, similar to TA-4F, but with reduced tactical systems, and armament of only one 20-mm cannon (not always fitted), and powered by 8,500-lb (37.80-kN) thrust J52-P-6 engine; 291 built
A-4K: version generally similar to A-4F for RNZAF, but incorporating a braking parachute; 10 built; survivors later upgraded with AN/APG-66 radar as **A-4K (Kahu)** aircraft
TA-4K: two-seat version of A-4K for RNZAF; four built; survivors later upgraded with AN/APG-66 radar as **TA-4K (Kahu)** aircraft
A-4KU: production version for Kuwait government, generally similar to A-4M; 30 built
TA-4KU: two-seat trainer version of A-4KU for Kuwait; six built
A-4L: redesignation of A-4Cs after withdrawal from first-line use and upgrading for use by reserve squadrons; all with J65-W-16C engines
A-4M Skyhawk II: production version for the USMC, introducing a number of improvements, equipped with braking parachute and the more powerful J52-P-408A engine; 162 built
OA-4M: conversion of TA-4F for USMC fast FAC role
A-4N Skyhawk II: production version for Israeli air force; generally similar to A-4M but with advanced avionics and systems, and 30-mm cannon; 117 built
A-4P: redesignation of ex-USN A-4Cs refurbished for service with the air force of Argentina
A-4PTM: redesignation of 25 ex-USN A-4Cs and 63 A-4Ls refurbished for the Royal Malaysian Air Force
TA-4PTM: two-seaters produced for the RMAF using A-4C and A-4E components
A-4Q: redesignation of ex-USN A-4Bs refurbished for service with Argentina's naval air arm
A-4S: redesignation of ex-USN A-4Bs overhauled and updated for service with the Republic of Singapore Air Force
A-4Y: provisional designation for all A-4Ms upgraded with revised cockpits and avionics. Designation not adopted in service
TA-4S: two-seat trainer version of A-4S for Republic of Singapore Air Force (two separate canopies)
Singapore Aircraft Industries A-4SU Super Skyhawk: comprehensively upgraded variant of the A-4S for the Republic of Singapore Air Force
Singapore Aircraft Industries TA-4SU Super Skyhawk: comprehensively upgraded variant of the TA-4S for the Republic of Singapore Air Force

SPECIFICATION

McDonnell Douglas A-4M Skyhawk
Type: single-seat carrier-based attack-bomber
Powerplant: one Pratt & Whitney J52-P-408A turbojet rated at 11,200 lb st (49.80 kN)
Performance: maximum speed 685 mph (1102 km/h) at sea level; maximum rate of climb at sea level 10,300 ft (3140 m) per minute; service ceiling 38,700 ft (11795 m); combat radius 345 miles (547 km)
with a 4,000-lb (1814-kg) warload
Weights: empty 10,465 lb (4747 kg); maximum take-off 24,500 lb (11113 kg)
Dimensions: wingspan 27 ft 6 in (8.38 m); length 40 ft 3½ in (12.29 m) height 15 ft (4.57 m); wing area 260.0 sq ft (24.15 m²)
Armament: two 20-mm cannon, plus up to 9,155 lb (4153 kg) of weapons on five external hardpoints

The Blue Angels A-4Fs introduced the P-408 engine and a brake 'chute to Skyhawk production. The aircraft replaced F-4Js from 1974.

Douglas A-20, DB-7, P-70 Boston and Havoc

The **A-20** (company designation **DB-7**) was one of the most extensively built light bombers of World War II. It was a ubiquitous warplane, used in a variety of roles and performing well, no matter where it was deployed. The basic design originated in 1936, when the Northrop Corporation, already partially owned by the Douglas Aircraft Corporation and fully absorbed in April 1937, began to consider the creation of an attack aircraft that would be an effective replacement for the single-engined light bombers then in service. By discussion with engineering staff of the USAAC it became possible to outline a fairly advanced specification, leading to the company project identified as the **Northrop Model 7A**.

Redesign in 1938 produced the **Model 7B**, also of twin-engined configuration, but with the proposed 425-hp (317-kW) Pratt & Whitney R-985 Wasp Junior radial engines replaced by two 1,100-hp (820-kW) Pratt & Whitney R-1830 Twin Wasp radial engines. Of shoulder-wing monoplane configuration, the Model 7B had an upswept rear fuselage carrying a conventional tail unit, the landing gear was of the then-radical tricycle type, and an unusual feature was the introduction of interchangeable fuselage nose sections that would make for easy production of either attack or bomber versions. First flown in this form on 26 October 1938, the Model 7B evinced the characteristics of a thoroughbred: it was fast, highly manoeuvrable and, in fact, could be regarded as a 'pilot's aircraft'.

Immediately it realised the potential of the new warplane, the company offered the type for export as the USAAC currently had no requirement for such a machine. The first order, for 100 aircraft, came

from a French purchasing mission in February 1939. The French required modifications to render the aircraft more suitable for deployment in Europe, where advanced aircraft in service with the Luftwaffe had demonstrated their potential in the Spanish Civil War. So extensive were the modifications that even the basic configuration of the Model 7B was changed. The fuselage was deepened to increase internal bomb capacity and fuel tankage, and its cross-section was reduced; the wing was lowered from the shoulder- to the mid-wing position; a longer oleo-strut for the nosewheel was introduced; armour protection for the crew and fuel tanks was provided; and uprated 1,200-hp (895-kW) Twin Wasp engines were installed. In view of the foregoing changes, the resulting aircraft was redesignated as the **DB-7** (**Douglas Bomber no. 7**), whose production prototype first flew on 17 August 1939. Despite efforts made by Douglas to complete manufacture of the initial 100 DB-7s by the end of 1939, the French had only just over 60 in service at the time of the German attack in May 1940, and only 12 aircraft of the 2e Groupement de Bombardement were used operationally, on 31 May 1940, in low-level attacks against German armoured columns.

During the period when

Douglas was developing the DB-7, a French order for an improved version was received. Required to operate at a gross weight some 24 per cent greater than that of the DB-7 as a result of additional equipment, this **DB-7A** model needed more powerful R-2600 Cyclone 14 radial engines in revised nacelles. Moreover, because the DB-7 had revealed marginal directional stability, the vertical tail surface was increased in area to ensure adequate directional stability and control with the higher-powered engines. When it was clear that the collapse of France was imminent, steps were taken to arrange for the UK to take over the balance of the French orders, plus a small quantity which had been ordered by Belgium. Thus some 15 to 20 DB-7s entered service with the RAF, which allo-

cated the name **Boston Mk I**, for service as conversion trainers. The next batch to be received, comprising about 125 DB-7s, was originally allocated the designation **Boston Mk II**.

The load-carrying and high-speed capability of the Boston Mk II suggested its suitability for conversion as

a desperately needed night-fighter, however, and in the winter of 1940 these machines were revised with AI (Airborne Interception) radar, additional armour, eight 0.303-in (7.7-mm) machine-guns in the nose, flame-damping exhaust systems, and an overall matt black finish.

The A-20G-20 introduced a dorsal turret to supplement the A-20G's already heavy gun armament. It also had provision for four 500-lb (227-kg) bombs underwing.

SPECIFICATION

Douglas A-20G-20 Havoc
Type: three-seat light attack bomber
Powerplant: two Wright R-2600-23 radial piston engines each rated at 1,600 hp (1193 kW)
Performance: maximum speed 317 mph (510 km/h) at 10,700 ft (3260 m); cruising speed 256 mph (412 km/h) at optimum altitude; climb to 10,000 ft (3050 m) in 8 minutes 48 seconds; service ceiling 23,700 ft (7225 m); range 945 miles (1521 km) with maximum warload
Weights: empty 16,993 lb
(7708 kg); maximum take-off 24,127 lb (10964 kg)
Dimensions: wingspan 61 ft 4 in (18.69 m); length 47 ft 11¾ in (14.63 m); height 17 ft 7 in (5.36 m); wing area 465.00 sq ft (43.20 m²)
Armament: six 0.5-in (12.7-mm) Browning M2 fixed forward-firing machine-guns, plus two similar weapons in the power-operated dorsal turret, and one rearward-firing through a ventral tunnel, plus up to 4,000 lb (1814 kg) of bombs carried in the lower-fuselage weapons bay and on four underwing hardpoints

The Soviet Union received large numbers of Boston Mk IIIAs/A-20Cs, as typified by this aircraft of the Northern Fleet Air Force (VVS SF), on the Arctic Front in spring 1944.

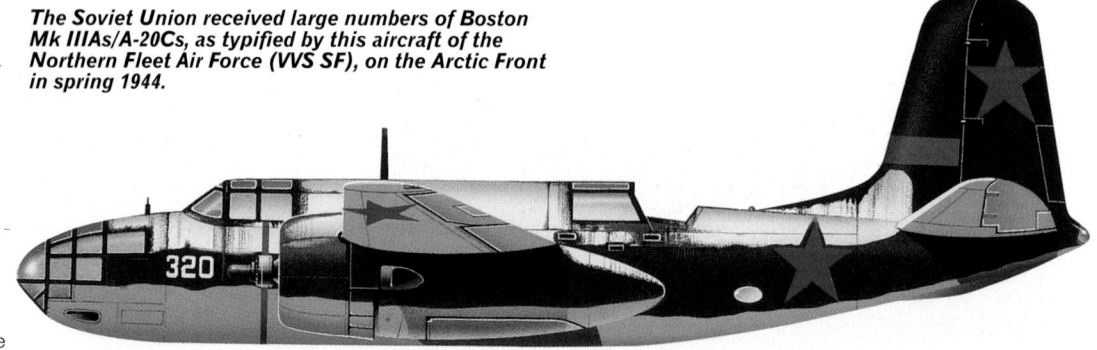

Douglas A-20, DB-7, P-70 Boston and Havoc (continued)

One unusual addition to the Boston Mk II was the provision of basic dual flying controls in the gunner's position; as no crew member could get to the pilot's aid in an emergency, this provision provided a long-odds chance that the gunner might achieve a non-calamitous landing. First delivered to the RAF in December 1940 under the designation **Havoc Mk I**, the type became operational with No. 86 Squadron on 7 April 1941. A second batch of about 100 DB-7As was converted to the **Havoc Mk II** standard that differed only in its armament of 12 nose-mounted machine-guns. About 40 DB-7s were modified to serve as night intruders, retaining the bomb-aimer's nose and able to accommodate up to 2,400 lb (1089 kg) of bombs; a gun armament of four 0.303-in (7.7-mm) machine-guns was mounted beneath the nose. Named officially **Havoc Mk I (Intruder)**, the type also acquired such unofficial names as 'Moonfighter', 'Ranger' and 'Havoc Mk IV'.

In order to enhance the somewhat limited capability of the AI radar installed in the Havoc Mk I, 21 aircraft were each equipped with a Helmore/GEC searchlight with an intensity of some 2,700 million candlepower. Designated **Havoc Mk I (Turbinlite)**, the aircraft were used with little success in an effort to illuminate German aircraft, which would then be attacked by Hurricane fighters accompanying the illuminator aircraft. Some 39 conversions of Havoc Mk IIs were also made under the designation **Havoc Mk II (Turbinlite)**. The name Havoc was adopted subsequently by the USAAF, as the general name for its A-20s of all versions.

In addition to the 2,700-million candlepower illumination in the nose, the Havoc Mk I (Turbinlite) aircraft retained their AI Mk IV radar, as evidenced by the wing and nose antennas on this machine.

A few DB-7As were retained for use in a light bomber role under the designation **Boston Mk III**, but the UK had meanwhile ordered an improved version, the **DB-7B**, with changed electric and hydraulic systems as well as instrumentation which conformed to RAF requirements and layout. These were also designated **Boston Mk III**, and carried four 0.303-in (7.7-mm) machine-guns in the nose, two on a high-speed mounting on the aft cockpit, and a seventh gun firing through a ventral tunnel, plus a bombload of up to 2,000 lb (907 kg). These Boston Mk IIIs were used extensively by squadrons of No. 2 Group, and served also in North Africa from a time early in 1942, in succession to the Blenheim.

Initial USAAC contracts for the DB-7, placed in May 1939, resulted in 63 A-20s with R-2600-7 turbocharged engines. Of these, three were converted to serve in the photo-reconnaissance role; the remainder became the **XP-70** prototype and 59 **P-70** production night-fighters, the prototype with R-2600-11 unsupercharged engines, and all with British-built AI radar and an armament of four 20-mm cannon mounted beneath the fuselage. These night-fighters were used primarily in the training role so that USAAC crews could become conversant with the newly developed technique of radar interception.

The first bomber version to serve with the USAAC was the **A-20A**, which was powered by R-2600-3 unsupercharged engines and with armament as for the DB-7B except that the machine-guns were of 0.3-in (7.62-mm) calibre. In addition, two remotely controlled aft-firing guns were mounted in the rear of each engine nacelle,

and the bombload was 1,100 lb (499 kg). One **XA-20B** prototype was modified from A-20A standard with changed armament based on three remotely controlled turrets. This was not adopted for the production **A-20B**, which had two 0.5-in (12.7-mm) machine-guns in the nose but was otherwise generally similar to the DB-7A.

Large-scale production dictated more standardisation, and as a result the RAF's Boston Mk III and USAAC's **A-20C** were one and the same, equipped with R-2600-23 engines. To boost production, Douglas granted a licence to Boeing and the latter produced 140 examples of the A-20C for supply to the RAF under Lend-Lease as **Boston Mk IIIA** aircraft, which differed in their electrical system and in some changes to the engines' ancillary equipment. DB-7s of this version were also supplied to the USSR under Lend-Lease during 1942. Boston Mk IIIs of the RAF's No. 226 Squadron provided training facilities for crews of the USAAF's 15th BS, which arrived in the UK during May 1942 as the vanguard of the US 8th Army Air Force. Six crews of this squadron, together with six British crews, made the first mission by the 8th AAF from England on 4 July 1942.

The next major production variant was the **A-20G**, of which 2,850 were built by Douglas at Santa Monica. These also had R-2600-23 engines, and were some 8 in (0.203 m) longer to provide a nose armament comprising two 0.5-in (12.7-in) machine-guns and four 20-mm cannon, complemented by either two 0.5-in (12.7-mm) guns or one 0.5-in (12.7-mm) and one 0.3-in (7.62-mm) gun in the rear cockpit. Most of the early production examples of the A-20G in this configuration were supplied to the USSR; the next A-20G variant had the 20-mm cannon

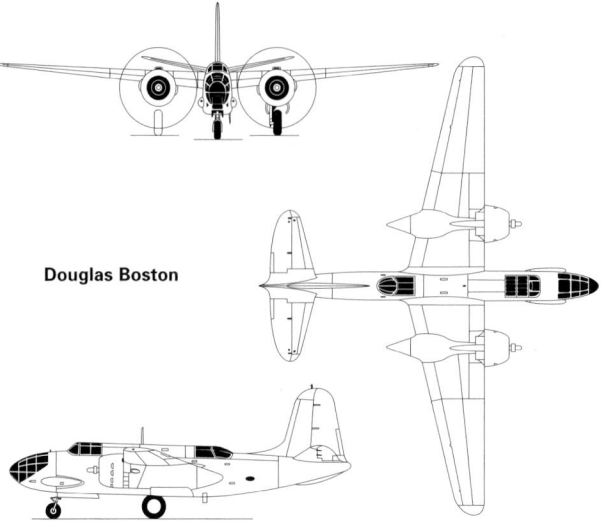

Douglas Boston

replaced by 0.5-in (12.7-mm) machine-guns; and the final variant introduced a rear fuselage 6 in (0.15 m) wider to accommodate an electrically-operated dorsal turret with two 0.5-in (12.7-mm) guns, as well as having under-wing bomb racks to accept an additional 2,000 lb (907 kg) of bombs, extra fuel tanks in the bomb bay, and provision for an under-fuselage drop tank to provide a ferry range of more than 2,000 miles (3219 km). These last two

capabilities were, of course, vital for the type's deployment in the Pacific theatre, where its arrival in 1942 came as something of a mixed blessing to Major General George C. Kenney's 5th Army Air Force, struggling to defeat the Japanese threat to New Guinea. As delivered, the aircraft were considered to be too lightly armed, so the basic armament was supplemented by four 0.5-in (12.7-mm) guns, and as there were no bombs available as required

Variants

A-20D: projected lightweight version with R-2600-7 turbocharged engines fed from larger fuel tanks of non-self-sealing design

A-20E: 17 examples of the A-20A with internal modifications of a minor nature

XA-20F: one A-20A modified to test two twin 0.5-in (12.7-mm) General Electric turrets in the dorsal and ventral positions; the aircraft was later modified again to incorporate a 37-mm cannon in the nose

XF-3: three prototype reconnaissance aircraft converted from A-20 standard

YF-3: two experimental reconnaissance aircraft similar to the XF-3 but fitted with R-2600-23 engines and a manned turret with two 0.5-in (12.7-mm) guns

F-3A: 46 reconnaissance aircraft converted from A-20J and A-20K standards

O-53: heavy observation variant equivalent to the A-20B; 1,489 were ordered in October 1940, but the contract was cancelled before a single aircraft had been completed

P-70A-1: 39 night-fighter conversions from A-20C standard produced in 1943 with six 0.5-in (12.7-mm) guns in the nose and two pivoted at the rear, with improved radar

P-70A-2: 65 night-fighter conversions from A-20G standard, equivalent to the P-70A-1 but without rear guns

P-70B-1: single experimental conversion from A-20G standard with SCR-720 radar and six 0.5-in (12.7-mm) guns in three blisters on each side of the nose

P-70B-2: 105 night-fighter trainers produced by conversion of A-20G and A-20J aircraft with SCR-720 or SCR-729 radar and provision (not always taken up) for a nose/ventral installation of six or eight 0.5-in (12.7-mm) guns

Havoc Mk I (Pandora): about 20 Havoc Mk I (Intruder) aircraft modified to carry the Long Aerial Mine, an abortive parachute weapon for use against bomber streams

Havoc Mk III: original designation for Havoc Mk I (Pandora)

Boston Mk III (Intruder): designation of Boston Mk IIIs modified for intruder missions with a pack of four 20-mm cannon under the fuselage

Boston Mk III (Turbinlite): three conversions similar to the Havoc Mks I and II (Turbinlite)

for their employment in a close-support role, Kenney suggested the provision of 23-lb (10-kg) fragmentation bombs with small parachutes attached. Each able to carry 40 of these 'parafrag' bombs, the aircraft played a vital role in dislodging the enemy from Buna. Other improvements introduced gradually to the A-20G included better

armour, navigation and bomb-aiming equipment, and winterisation accessories for aircraft to be operated in low-temperature zones.

Also produced were 412 of the **A-20H** model with little change except for the installation of 1,700-hp (1268-kW) R-2600-29 engines. Neither the A-20 nor the A-20H served with

the RAF, but the **A-20J** and **A-20K**, which were bomb-leader versions of the A-20G and A-20H respectively, were built for both the USAAF and RAF, with the designations **Boston Mk IV** and **Boston Mk V** respectively for the RAF aircraft. They differed only by having a frameless transparent nose to accommodate the bomb-aimer.

When production ended, on 20 September 1944, Douglas had built 7,385 DB-7s and its derivatives of all versions, and these had been used by the USAAF and its allies in the widest imaginable number of roles. The type had also been supplied to Brazil, the Netherlands and the USSR, and small numbers from those received by the UK

had been diverted to serve with the Royal Australian, Royal Canadian, Royal New Zealand and South African Air Forces. In addition, one A-20A had been supplied to the US Navy for evaluation under the designation **BD-1**, and in 1942 eight examples of the A-20B were procured for use as target tugs under the designation **BD-2**.

Douglas A-26 and B-26 Invader

When, in 1940, the USAAC issued a requirement for an attack aircraft, it had little or no information on World War II combat operations in Europe, and as a result the three prototypes of what became the **A-26 Invader** were ordered in differing configurations: the **XA-26** was an attack bomber with a bomb-aimer's position in the nose; the **XA-26A** was a heavily armed night fighter; and the **XA-26B** was an attack aircraft with a 75-mm cannon. After flight-testing and careful examination of reports from Europe and the Pacific, where the USA was now actively involved, the **A-26B Invader** was ordered into production and initial deliveries of the 1,355 built were made in April 1944.

Heavily armed and armoured, and able to carry an internal bombload of up

to 4,000 lb (1814 kg) of bombs, the A-26B was potentially a formidable weapon. Moreover, its two R-2800 engines conferred a maximum speed of 355 mph (571 km/h), making the A-26B the fastest US bomber of World War II. The Invader remained in service with the USAF until well into the 1970s.

Missions with the 9th AAF in Europe began in November 1944, and at the

same time the type became operational in the Pacific. The **A-26C**, with a bomb-aimer's position and only two guns in the nose, entered service in 1945, but saw only limited use before the end of World War II. A-26C production totalled 1,091. With little employment ahead of them, so far as anyone could see, one A-26B and one A-26C were converted to **XJD-1** configuration, this pair being followed by 150 A-26C machines converted as target tugs for the US Navy with the designation **JD-1**; some were later converted to launch and control missile test vehicles and drones under the designation **JD-1D**. These designations became **UB-26J** and **DB-26J** respectively in 1962.

The A-26B and A-26C became the **B-26B** and **B-26C** in 1948, and retained this designation up to 1962. Both versions saw extensive service in the Korean War, and were again used in the COIN (counter-insurgency) role in Vietnam. A special COIN version with very heavy armament and extra power was developed by On Mark Engineering in 1963, the prototype being designated as the **YB-26K** and named **Counter Invader**. Subsequently, about 70 B-26s were converted to the **B-26K** standard, 40 later being redesignated **A-26A**. Some were deployed in Vietnam, and others were supplied to friendly nations under the Military Assistance Program. The B-26 was also used for training (**TB-26B** and **TB-26C**), transport (**CB-26B** freighter and **VB-26B** staff transport), remotely-piloted

Stinky, wearing the 'RG' codes of the formerly B-26 Marauder-equipped 552nd BS, 386th BG, was an A-26B-15-DT. The aircraft was based at Beaumont-sur-Oise, France in April 1945.

vehicle (RPV) control (**DB-26C**), night reconnaissance (**FA-26C**, from 1948 redesignated **RB-26C**), and missile guidance research (**EB-26C**). After World War II, many Douglas

A-26s were declared surplus to requirements and snapped up by specialist companies for conversion into executive, survey, photographic and even fire-fighting aircraft.

For their new service careers, B-26Ks were allocated new serial numbers. The primary recognition feature of the K was its optional wingtip tanks, although it also had greater power and reinforced wings.

Variants

XA-26C: projected version with four 20-mm cannon in the nose; with the abandonment of the project, the 'C' suffix was reallocated to the transparent-nose version of the Invader
XA-26D: single prototype powered by two 2,100-hp (1567-kW) Chevrolet-built R-2800-83 engines as the precursor of the proposed **A-26D** production model, 750 of which were cancelled after VJ-Day
XA-26E: single prototype powered by two 2,100-hp (1567-kW) R-2800-83 engines as the precursor of a planned production batch of 1,250 **A-26E** transparent-nose aircraft cancelled after VJ-Day
XA-26F: single prototype (later redesignated **XB-26F**) with two R-2800-83 engines and a 1,600-lb st (7.12-kN) thrust General Electric J31 turbojet in the tail to boost performance; the maximum speed was 435 mph (700 km/h) at 15,000 ft (4570 m), an insufficient performance gain to warrant production
A-26Z: Douglas designation for a proposed post-war model to have been built as the **A-26G** and **A-26H** with unglazed and glazed noses respectively; improvements included a raised pilot's canopy and wingtip drop tanks
Invader Mk I: RAF designation of 140 A-26Cs received under Lend-Lease in 1944
On Mark Marketeer: unpressurised version of the Marksman C
On Mark Marksman A: pressurised executive transport produced by On Mark Engineering on an almost production-line basis; powered by 2,100-hp (1567-kW) R-2800-83AM3 engines
On Mark Marksman B: similar to the Marksman A apart from the provision of wingtip tanks and R-2800-83AM4A engines
On Mark Marksman C: similar to the Marksman A apart from extra fuel tankage in the wings and 2,500-hp (1865-kW) R-2800-CB16/17 engines
Smith Biscayne 26: high-speed transport version developed by the L. B. Smith Company and able to seat up to 15 passengers
Smith Super 26: standard Invader airframe converted with wingtip tanks and an executive interior
Smith Tempo I: unpressurised executive conversion with R-2800 B-series engines
Smith Tempo II: pressurised executive conversion with a new fuselage 9 ft 7½ in (2.93 m) longer than standard and able to seat up to 13 passengers

SPECIFICATION	
Douglas A-26B-15 Invader	area 540.00 sq ft (50.17 m²)
Type: three-seat light attack bomber	**Armament:** six 0.5-in (12.7-mm) Browning M2 fixed forward-firing
Powerplant: two Pratt & Whitney R-2800-27 or -79 radial piston engines each rated at 2,000 hp (1491 kW)	machine-guns in the forward fuselage, two 0.5-in (12.7-mm) Browning M2 trainable machine-guns in the dorsal barbette that could be locked to fire directly
Performance: maximum speed 355 mph (571 km/h) at 15,000 ft (4570 m); cruising speed 284 mph (457 km/h) at optimum altitude; climb to 10,000 ft (3050 m) in 8 minutes 6 seconds; service ceiling 22,100 ft (6735 m); range 1,400 miles (2253 km) with standard fuel and warload	forward under pilot control, two 0.5-in (12.7-mm) Browning M2 trainable rearward-firing machine-guns in the optional ventral barbette, and provision for eight 0.5-in (12.7-mm) Browning M2 fixed forward-firing machine-guns installed in four two-gun packs under the outboard wing panels,
Weights: empty 22,370 lb (10147 kg); maximum take-off 35,000 lb (15876 kg)	plus up to 6,000 lb (2722 kg) of disposable stores carried in two lower-fuselage weapons bays and
Dimensions: wingspan 70 ft (21.34 m); length 50 ft (15.24 m); height 18 ft 6 in (5.64 m); wing	on four underwing hardpoints

Douglas AD and A-1 Skyraider

Ed Heinemann, chief engineer at Douglas El Segundo, was so unimpressed by his XBTD series that he took it upon himself to design a simpler machine which he judged would be considerably more useful. Designated **XBT2D-1** when first flown on 18 March 1945, this aircraft became the **AD-1 Skyraider**, and enjoyed an amazingly long and varied career. Crewed by a pilot only, the AD-1 was at the time the largest single-seat warplane in production. Of low-wing cantilever monoplane configuration with tail-wheel landing gear including full carrierborne capability, the design was

based on the Wright R-3350 radial engine, smaller than the R-4360 of other competing prototypes. Although there was plenty of internal space this was not used for weapons; instead the wing, whose outer panels folded to reduce the type's carrierborne 'footprint', was given no fewer than seven hardpoints on each side, and a robust structure gave the Skyraider great integrity. Experience in World War II had shown that the most important characteristic for an aircraft in this category was the ability to deliver a wide range of weapons and such was the new type's basic versatility that 3,180 had been built

before production ended in 1957.

Just too late for World War II, the AD-1 proved a valuable weapon in the Korean War, when its heavy weapons load and endurance of up to 10 hours contrasted sharply with the payload/endurance performance of the jet-powered warplanes used in that conflict, and again proved its worth over Vietnam. The AD-1 to AD-4 versions differed in detail, but the AD-5 had a wider cockpit providing two-seat side-by-side accommodation, and several early versions had APS-20A radar and a rear cabin for two/three operators for the increasingly important AEW mission. The AD-5 also introduced conversion kits for ambulance, freight, transport or target-towing. The AD-6 and AD-7 were improved single-seaters.

Large numbers of single-seat versions were used by the French Armée de l'Air in Algeria. During 1962 existing versions of the AD family were redesignated in the new A-1 series, and in South Vietnam the USAF's 1st Air Commando Group of the Tactical Air Command used the A-1E,

A-1H and A-1J versions with great success, continuing to use them after the USN had withdrawn its last Skyraiders from that theatre. Nicknamed 'Sandy' or 'The Spad', A-1 versions were among the most hard-worked and versatile aircraft deployed in Vietnam.

This A-1H was the personal mount of Commander Bill Phillips during his time as the head of VA-52 aboard USS Ticonderoga. VA-52 undertook two tours of duty over Vietnam between 1964 and 1966.

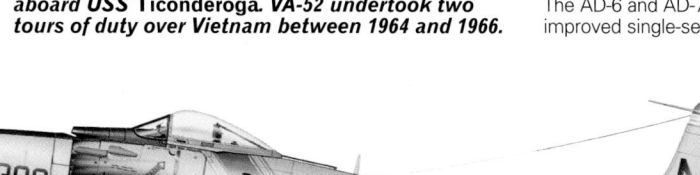

SPECIFICATION	
Douglas AD-7 (A-1J) Skyraider **Type:** single-seat carrierborne and land-based attack aircraft **Powerplant:** one Wright R-3350-26WB Duplex Cyclone radial piston engine rated at 2,800 hp (2088 kW) **Performance:** maximum speed 343 mph (552 m) at 20,000 ft (6095 m); cruising speed 195 mph (314 km/h) at 6,000 ft (1830 m); initial climb rate 3,230 ft (985 m) per minute; service ceiling 25,400 ft (7740 m); range 900 miles (1448 km) with maximum warload	**Weights:** empty 12,094 lb (5486 kg); maximum take-off 25,000 (11340 kg) **Dimensions:** wingspan 50 ft ¼ in (15.25 m); length 38 ft 10 in (11.84 m); height 15 ft 8¼ in (4.78 m); wing area 400.33 sq ft (37.19 m²) **Armament:** four 20-mm M3 cannon in the leading edges of the wing, plus up to 8,000 lb (3629 kg) of weapons carried on one underfuselage and 14 underwing hardpoints

Built primarily as a naval ASW aircraft, the A-1E carried a crew of two – pilot and systems operator. Over Vietnam (below), the aircraft was employed as an attack aircraft, often with a single pilot.

Variants

XBT2D-1N: two of the 25 XBT2D-1 prototype and service test aircraft modified as three-seat night attack prototypes with two radar operators (in a fuselage compartment behind the pilot's high-set cockpit), radar in a pod under the port wing and a searchlight in a pod under the starboard wing

XBT2D-1P: single XBT2D-1 converted as a photo-reconnaissance prototype

XBT2D-1Q: single XBT2D-1 converted as a two-seat electronic countermeasures aircraft; the electronics operator was located within the fuselage, and the radar and chaff pods were installed under the port and starboard halves of the wing respectively

AD-1: initial production version with the 2,500-hp (1864-kW) R-3350-24W engine and an armament of two 20-mm cannon and provision for up to 8,000 lb (3629 kg) of disposable stores (242 built)

AD-1Q: two-seat electronic countermeasures aircraft based on the XBT2D-1Q (35 built)

XAD-1W: single XBT2D-1 converted as a three-seat airborne early warning prototype, with two radar operators in the main cabin behind the pilot, and search radar in a bulky fairing under the fuselage

XAD-2: single XBT2D-1 converted as the prototype of an upgraded attack model; this was at first designated **BT2D-2**, and was powered by the 2,700-hp (2014-kW) R-3350-26W engine

AD-2: improved attack model evaluated by means of an AD-1 modified with wheel well covers, greater fuel capacity and other detail alterations (156 built)

AD-2D: unofficial designation for AD-2s used as remotely-controlled aircraft to gather radioactive material in the air after nuclear tests

AD-2Q: two-seat electronic countermeasures version of the AD-2 (21 built)

AD-2QU: AD-1Q fitted to tow an aerial target (1 built)

AD-3: proposed turbine-powered version, for which were considered the General Electric TG-100, two Allison 500, two Westinghouse 24C or two Westinghouse 19XB engines, or even a suggested Douglas-designed twin-turbine powerplant; this project was eventually redesignated A2D Skyshark

AD-3: an improved model of the AD-2 after the turbine-powered version became the A2D; compared with the AD-2 various improvements (longer-stroke landing gear, redesigned canopy, improved propeller, etc) were incorporated (125 built)

AD-3E and AD-3S: versions produced as the two components of an aerial anti-submarine team, with the AD-3E operating as the search aircraft and the AD-3S as the attack aircraft; two AD-3Ws were converted into the AD-3E aircraft and two AD-3Ns into the pair of AD-3S aircraft; though the feasibility of the system was proved, the later conversion of one AD-3S into a hunter-killer (with APS-81 radar in a pod under the port wing, and useful capacity left for offensive stores) showed the way for later production models

AD-3N: three-seat night attack version of the AD-3 (15 built)

AD-3QU: target-towing version of the AD-3 rendered superfluous by the success of the AD-2QU; the aircraft were thus delivered as **AD-3Q** electronic countermeasures machines, though provision for the Mk 22 target was retained (23 built)

AD-3W: three-seat airborne early warning version of the AD-3 with systems based on those of the XAD-1W (31 built)

AD-4: major production model of the Skyraider series; the type was fitted with the 2,700-hp (2014-kW) R-3350-26WA engine, an autopilot and a further improved canopy (372 built)

AD-4B: specialised AD-4 variant with the provision for a nuclear weapon launched using the over-the-shoulder 'toss bombing' technique; wing armament was increased to four 20-mm cannon in this version (28 conversions from AD-4 standard and 165 built from new)

AD-4L: version of the AD-4 fitted with anti-icing and de-icing equipment for winter operations in Korea; wing armament also increased to four 20-mm cannon (63 conversions)

AD-4N: three-seat night attack version of the AD-4, delivered or retrofitted with 'S' equipment to suit them for the submarine hunter/killer role (307 built)

AD-4NA: 100 AD-4Ns stripped of night attack equipment to permit heavier bombloads for Korean operations; fitted with four 20-mm cannon; designated A-1D after 1962

AD-4NL: version of the AD-4N equivalent to the AD-4L (36 conversions)

AD-4Q: two-seat electronic countermeasures version of the AD-4 (39 built)

AD-4W: three-seat airborne early warning version of the AD-4; 50 were transferred to the Royal Navy under the designation **Skyraider AEW.Mk 1**, and the 118 remaining in USN service were fitted for the 'E' search part of the anti-submarine mission (168 built)

Variants (continued)

AD-5: the initial AD-5 proposed by Douglas was a 1948 development with the R-3350 Turbo-Compound engine, but as this would have needed a considerable amount of fuselage redesign the USN refused development funds; the AD-5 designation thus went to a variant that combined within one airframe the submarine hunter and killer roles, the two crew being seated side-by-side in a widened forward fuselage; at the same time the length of the fuselage was increased by 1 ft 11 in (0.58 m), the fuselage dive brakes were eliminated, and the vertical tail surface was increased in area; wing armament was four 20-mm cannon; the overall utility of the version was recognised at an early stage, and AD-5s were delivered with kits enabling them to be converted for casevac with provision for four litters, troop transport with seating for 12 on bench seats, staff/VIP transport with four rearward-facing seats, cargo transport for up to 2,000 lb (907 kg) of freight, target-towing and photo-reconnaissance; in 1953 Douglas developed an inflight-refuelling store to be carried externally (212 built); redesignated **A-1E** in 1962
AD-5N: four-seat night attack version of the AD-5 (239 built); redesignated **A-1G** in 1962
AD-5Q: four-seat electronic countermeasures version of the AD-5N (54 conversions); redesignated **EA-1F** in 1962
AD-5S: one experimental aircraft evaluated in the anti-submarine role with MAD gear
AD-5W: four-seat airborne early warning version of the AD-5 (218 built); redesignated **EA-1E** in 1962
AD-6: improved version of the AD-4B single-seat attack aircraft with special equipment for accurate low-level bombing (713 built); redesignated **A-1H** in 1962

AD-7: final production version of the Skyraider, the AD-7 differed from the AD-6 in having the R-3350-26WB instead of the R-3350-26WA engine as well as local strengthening of the engine mounting, landing gear and outer wing panels (72 built); redesignated **A-1J** in 1962
UA-1E: 1962 redesignation of the AD-5 in the utility role with conversion kits

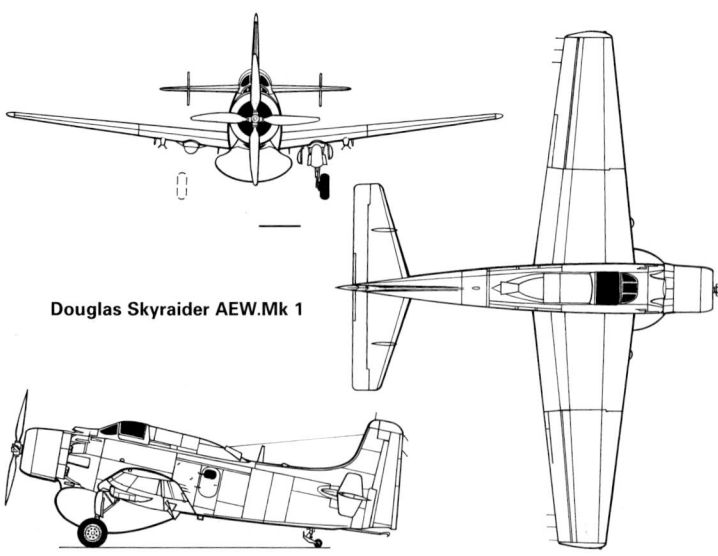

Douglas Skyraider AEW.Mk 1

Douglas B-7 and O-35

In the late 1920s the US War Department was taking careful note of recent developments in aircraft design, such as the technical revolution created by the appearance of all-metal cantilever monoplanes with retractable landing gear. It was decided initially to adopt such features in twin-engined aircraft intended for fast long-range reconnaissance, and the War Department accordingly ordered two Fokker XO-27 prototypes in this category. Fearing it might lose a valuable source of revenue, Douglas designed an aircraft incorporating the required features and in March 1930 received an order for one example each of the **Douglas XO-35** and **Douglas XO-36**; it was intended that these would differ only in their Curtiss V-1570 Conqueror engines, the former having a geared engine and the latter a direct-drive version of the same engine. In the event, the XO-36 was redesig-nated as the **XB-7** and built as a bomber, and in a paral-lel development the second of the Fokker XO-27 proto-types was completed as the XB-8 bomber. Later, six

YO-27 and six Y1O-27 service test aircraft were delivered to the US Army.
    The Douglas XO-35 was test-flown from the spring of 1931, causing quite a stir among a public used to seeing the USAAC's lumbering twin-engined biplanes. Based on a very slender fuselage covered with corrugated metal skinning, the XO-35 was a gull-wing monoplane with its wing set high on the fuselage. There were open gunners' cockpits in the nose and dorsal positions, the pilot's open cockpit was located immediately forward of the wing's lead-ing edge, and the fourth crew member was the radio operator accommo-dated in an enclosed compartment behind the pilot's position.

The XB-7 was almost identical, but had under-fuselage racks for up to 1,200 lb (544 kg) of bombs. During the US Fiscal Year 1932, orders were placed for seven **Y1B-7** and five **Y1O-35** service test aircraft. These differed from the prototypes mainly in having smooth metal sheet covering for the fuselages, and strut- rather than wire-braced horizontal tail surfaces. The Y1B-7 aircraft, later redesignated as a **B-7** machine, were attached to the two USAAC bomber squadrons based at March Field, California, while the **O-35** (previously Y1O-35) aircraft flew with observation units. In February 1931 the five O-35, six surviving B-7 and XO-35 prototype machines were all assigned to the air mail route linking Wyoming with the west coast of the USA.

Operations at night and in bad weather took their toll and in the four-month emergency period during which the USAAC ran the nation's air mail service no fewer than four of the B-7s

SPECIFICATION	
Douglas B-7	
Type: four-seat medium bomber	(2503 kg); maximum take-off 11,177 lb (5070 kg)
Powerplant: two Curtiss V-1570-53 Vee piston engines each rated at 675 hp (503 kW)	**Dimensions:** wingspan 65 ft (19.81 m); length 45 ft 11 in (14.00 m); height 11 ft 7 in (3.53 m); wing area 621.20 sq ft (57.71 m²)
Performance: maximum speed 182 mph (293 km/h) at sea level; cruising speed 158 mph (254 km/h) at optimum altitude; climb to 10,000 ft (3050 m) in 8 minutes 42 seconds; service ceiling 20,400 ft (6220 m); range 411 miles (661 km)	**Armament:** one 0.3-in (7.62-mm) Browning trainable machine-gun in each of the nose and dorsal positions, plus up to 1,200 lb (544 kg) of bombs carried on underfuselage hardpoints
Weights: empty 5,519 lb	

were lost in crashes. Soon after this the remaining B-7s and O-35s were rele-gated to second-line duties, an O-35 being the last to be grounded in February 1939.

Wearing the markings carried for the 1933 US Army Air Corps anti-aircraft exercises, this Y1B-7 served with the 31st Bomb Group. The main units of the tailwheel landing gear retracted into the undersides of the nacelles, leaving the lower part of each wheel exposed.

Douglas B-18 Bolo

Faced with a requirement issued by the USAAC early in 1934 for a bomber with virtually double the bombload and range capabil-ity of the Martin B-10, which was then the USAAC's stan-dard bomber, Douglas had little doubt that it could draw

upon engineering experi-ence and design technology of the DC-2 commercial transport which was then on the point of making its first flight. Private-venture proto-types to meet the USAAC's requirements were evalu-ated at Wright Field, Ohio in

August 1935, these includ-ing the Boeing Model 299, **Douglas DB-1** and Martin Model 146. The first was built as the B-17 Flying Fortress, the last was produced as an export vari-ant of the B-10/B-12 series, and the Douglas DB-1 (**Douglas Bomber no. 1**) was ordered into immediate production under the desig-

nation **B-18** in January 1936. The DB-1 prototype retained a basically similar wing, tail unit and powerplant to the DC-2. There were two differ-ences in the wing, however, for while it retained the same basic planform as that of the DC-2, the wing of the DB-1 had its span increased and was mounted in the mid- rather than low-wing

position on an entirely new fuselage. The latter was somewhat deeper than that of the commercial transport to provide adequate accommodation for a crew of six, to include nose and dorsal turrets as well as a bomb-aimer's position, and to provide volume for an inter-nal weapons bay.

Douglas B-18 Bolo (continued)

This Bolo served with the 18th Reconnaissance Squadron, USAAC. Some 350 B-18 aircraft were procured by comparison with almost 13,000 examples of the B-17 Flying Fortress.

The B-18 had, in addition, a third gunner's position, with a ventral gun discharging via a tunnel in the structure of the lower fuselage. The powerplant comprised two 930-hp (694-kW) R-1820-45 Cyclone 9 engines. A total of 133 B-18 bombers was covered by the first contract, this number including the single DB-1 which had served as a prototype. True production aircraft, which had the type name Bolo, introduced a number of equipment changes, producing an increase in the normal loaded weight, and more powerful R-1820-45 engines. The last B-18 to come off the production line differed in having a power-operated nose turret, and carried the company identification **DB-2**, but this feature did not become standard on subsequent production aircraft.

The next contracts, covering 217 **B-18A** aircraft, were placed in June 1937 and mid-1938 for 177 and 40 aircraft respectively. The B-18A differed from the B-18 in having the bomb-aimer's position extended forward and over the nose gunner's station, and in being fitted with more powerful R-1820-53 engines. Most of the USAAC's bomber squadrons were equipped with B-18s or B-18As in 1940, and the majority of the 33 B-18As which equipped the USAAC's 5th and 11th Bomb Groups, based on Hawaiian airfields, were destroyed when the Japanese launched their attack on Pearl Harbor.

When the B-18 series was replaced in first-line service by the B-17 in the course of 1942, some 122 B-18As were equipped with search radar and MAD (magnetic anomaly detection) equipment for deployment in the Caribbean on anti-submarine patrol under the designation **B-18B**. The RCAF also acquired 20 examples of the B-18A which, under the designation **Digby Mk I**, were also employed on maritime patrol. The designation **B-18C** was applied to another pair of aircraft reconfigured for anti-submarine patrol. Two more aircraft were converted for use as transports under the designation **C-58**, but many others were used similarly without conversion or redesignation.

SPECIFICATION

Douglas B-18 Bolo
Type: six-seat medium bomber and anti-submarine aircraft
Powerplant: two Wright R-1820-53 radial piston engines each rated at 1,000 hp (746 kW)
Performance: maximum speed 217 mph (349 km/h) at 10,000 ft (3050 m); cruising speed 167 mph (269 km/h) at optimum altitude; climb to 10,000 ft (3050 m) in 9 minutes 6 seconds; service ceiling 24,200 ft (7375 m); range 850 miles (1368 km) with standard fuel and warload
Weights: empty 15,750 lb (7144 kg); maximum take-off 27,097 lb (12286 kg)
Dimensions: wingspan 89 ft 6 in (27.28 m); length 56 ft 8 in (17.27 m); height 15 ft 2 in (4.62 m); wing area 959.00 sq ft (89.09 m²)
Armament: one 0.3-in (7.62-mm) Browning trainable machine-guns in each of the nose, dorsal and ventral positions, plus up to 4,400 lb (1996 kg) of bombs carried in a lower-fuselage weapons bay

Variants

B-18AM: 18 B-18As modified as trainers during World War II by the removal of bomb gear
B-18M: 22 B-18s modified as trainers in 1942 in the same way as the B-18AM
B-22: projected development of the B-18A with 1,600-hp (1193-kW) R-2600-3 radial engines

Douglas B-23 Dragon and UC-67

The B-18, which had been designed to meet a USAAC requirement of 1934 for a high-performance medium bomber, was clearly not in the same league as the B-17 Flying Fortress, which had been designed to the same specification. In an attempt to rectify the shortcomings of its DB-1 design, in 1938 Douglas developed an improved version, and the proposal seemed sufficiently attractive for the USAAC to award a contract for 38 of these aircraft under the designation **B-23** and the name **Dragon**.

Although in overall configuration it was similar to the B-18, the B-23 was virtually a new design. The wingspan was increased, the fuselage was entirely different and of much

A radically changed design born out of an effort to reverse the B-18's failure to compete effectively with the Flying Fortress, the B-23 failed to show any improvement in performance over the B-17E.

improved aerodynamic form, and the tail unit had a much higher vertical surface. The landing gear was the same tailwheel type, although with fully-retractable main units, but the engine nacelles were extended so that, when the main units were lowered in flight, they were faired by the nacelle extensions and created far less drag. Greatly improved performance was expected from these refinements in combination with 60 per cent more power provided by the powerplant of two R-2600-3 Cyclone 14 engines. An innovation was the provision of a tail gun position, this being the first US bomber to introduce such a feature when first flown on 27 July 1939 as a production-standard machine.

All the B-23s were delivered to the US Army during 1939. Early evaluation had shown that performance and flight characteristics were disappointing. Furthermore, information received from the European theatre during 1940 made it clear that development would be unlikely to result in range, bombload and defensive armament capabilities to compare with the bomber aircraft then in service with the combatant nations, or already beginning to emerge in the USA. As a result the B-23 saw only limited service in the maritime patrol mission along the USA's Pacific coastline before being relegated to training duties. During 1942 about 15 of these aircraft were converted as utility transports under the designation **UC-67**, and some of the remainder were used for a variety of purposes including engine-testing, glider-towing experiments and weapons evaluation.

Following the end of World War II many surplus B-23 and UC-67 machines were acquired by civil operators for conversion as corporate aircraft. The majority were modified by Pan American's Engineering Department with accommodation for a crew of two and up to 12 passengers. Some of the converted aircraft remained in civil use for about 30 years.

SPECIFICATION

Douglas B-23 Dragon
Type: four/five-seat medium bomber
Powerplant: two Wright R-2600-3 Cyclone 14 radial piston engines each rated at 1,600 hp (1193 kW)
Performance: maximum speed 282 mph (454 km/h) at 12,000 ft (3660 m); cruising speed 210 mph (338 km/h) at optimum altitude; climb to 10,000 ft (3050 m) in 6 minutes 42 seconds; service ceiling 31,600 ft (9630 m); range 1,400 miles (2253 km) with standard fuel and warload
Weights: empty 19,089 lb (8659 kg); maximum take-off 32,400 lb (14696 kg)
Dimensions: wingspan 92 ft (28.04 m); length 58 ft 4¾ in (17.80 m); height 18 ft 5½ in (5.63 m); wing area 993.00 sq ft (92.25 m²)
Armament: one 0.5-in (12.7-mm) Browning trainable machine-gun in the tail position and one 0.3-in (7.62-mm) Browning trainable machine-gun in each of the nose, dorsal and ventral positions, plus up to 4,400 lb (1996 kg) of disposable stores in a lower-fuselage weapons bay

Douglas B-66 Destroyer

US Air Force involvement in the Korean War highlighted the service's urgent need for a high-performance day/night tactical bomber. To speed the introduction of such a warplane, it was decided to procure a land-based version of the A3D Skywarrior then being developed for the US Navy. To this end, Douglas was given a contract for five pre-production **RB-66A Destroyer** all-weather/night photo-reconnaissance aircraft, the first of which was flown on 28 June 1954 at the company's Long Beach plant.

Although retaining the basic overall configuration of the A3D, the RB-66A dispensed with the arrester gear, strengthened landing gear and wing-folding of the naval version, and at the same time introduced aerodynamic changes in the wing design, revised accommodation for the three-man crew all seated on ejection seats, and detail changes in equipment including the installation of multiple cameras and the provision of bombing and navigation radar. Power for this initial version was provided by two 9,570-lb st

An early RB-66B-DT demonstrates the contemporary 'natural metal' finish and buzz-number. Note the aircraft's twin-gun tail installation and lack of arrester gear.

(42.57-kN) Allison YJ71-A-9 turbojet engines. Successful testing of the RB-66As then led to a contract for the first full-production version, the **RB-66B**, powered by 10,200-lb st (45.37-kN) J71-A-11 or -13 engines. The first of 145 RB-66Bs

flew in March 1955, and deliveries to the USAF began on 1 February 1956.

Production versions of the Destroyer also included the **B-66B** bomber (72 built), with the same powerplant as the RB-66B but provision for up to 15,000 lb (6804 kg) of bombs in place of recon-

naissance equipment; the **RB-66C** electronic reconnaissance and ECM type (36 built), with J71-A-11 or -13 engines and a crew of seven including five specialist radar operators, four of them accommodated in what had initially been the weapons bay; and the **WB-66D** combat area weather reconnaissance machine (36 built) with J71-A-13 engines and a

Variants

EB-66B: ECM (radar-jamming) version, of which 13 were converted from B-66B standard
NB-66B: two joint-services aircraft converted from B-66B standard for the high-altitude test paradropping of items such as Gemini and Apollo spacecraft
EB-66C: redesignation of RB-66Cs following installation of advanced ECM equipment
EB-66E: ECM version, of which 52 were converted from RB-66B standard with equipment similar to that of the EB-66B
X-21A: two WB-66D machines used by Northrop Corporation in a research programme involving the substitution of a new laminar-flow wing and, to ensure that the aerodynamic characteristics of the wing were not compromised by wing-mounted engines, the revised powerplant of two 9,490-lb st (42.21-kN) General Electric XJ79-GE-13 turbojet engines pod-mounted one on either side of the rear fuselage

crew of five (two plus equipment in the bomb bay). ECM versions of the B-66 and RB-66 proved of great value during operations in Vietnam for the

location, classification and jamming of enemy radar, but withdrawal of US forces from Southeast Asia led to the retirement of these aircraft.

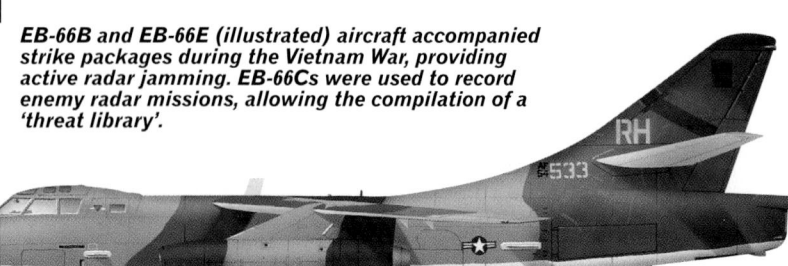

EB-66B and EB-66E (illustrated) aircraft accompanied strike packages during the Vietnam War, providing active radar jamming. EB-66Cs were used to record enemy radar missions, allowing the compilation of a 'threat library'.

SPECIFICATION	
Douglas RB-66B Destroyer	925 miles (1489 km) with standard
Type: three-seat all-weather day/night reconnaissance aircraft	fuel and warload
Powerplant: two Allison J71-A-11 or -13 turbojet engines each rated at 10,200 lb st (45.37 kN)	**Weights:** empty 43,476 lb (19720 kg); maximum take-off 83,000 lb (37648 kg)
Performance: maximum speed 631 mph (1015 km/h) at 6,000 ft (1830 m); cruising speed 525 mph (845 km/h) at optimum altitude; initial climb rate 4,840 ft (1475 m) per minute; service ceiling 38,900 ft (11855 m); combat radius	**Dimensions:** wingspan 72 ft 6 in (22.10 m); length 75 ft 2 in (22.91 m); height 23 ft 7 in (7.19 wing area 780.00 sq ft (72.46 m²) **Armament:** two 20-mm trainable rearward-firing cannon in radar-controlled tail barbette

Douglas BT and A-4

The excellent flight characteristics of the Douglas O-2 family led in 1930 to the conversion of 40 examples of the O-2K as basic flying trainers for the US Army; the conversion

process to the **BT-1** standard involved the installation of dual controls and the removal of the armament. In a similar process the sole O-32 was fitted with dual controls,

A tricycle undercarriage, red fuselage and silver wings distinguished the A-4. The revised landing gear, which included a steerable nose wheel, greatly facilitated landings under remote control.

Variants

BT-2BI: this designation was accorded in 1932 to 58 examples of the BT-2B provided with a folding blind-flying hood over the rear cockpit
BT-2C: an order for 20 BT-2Cs was received by Douglas at the end of 1930; these differed from the BT-2B in having slightly shorter fuselages and revised landing gear; 13 of them were converted later to instrument training standard with the revised designation **BT-2CI**; in 1940 seven BT-2C aircraft were modified as control aircraft for Douglas A-4 aerial targets and received the further revised designation **BT-2CR**
A-4: in 1940 two BT-2BI and 15 BT-2B aircraft were revised with fixed tricycle landing gear and were modified as radio-controlled anti-aircraft gun targets, sporting a bright red fuselage; designated originally **BT-2BG** and **BT-2BR**, all the aircraft later received the definitive designation A-4

also in 1930, and thus became the only **BT-2**. Thirty examples of the O-32A were modified in a fashion similar to that used for the O-2Ks to become **BT-2A** machines that saw service with US Army and National Guard units for basic training. Some 146 **BT-2B** aircraft were built as such, the

first of these appearing in 1931. The aircraft survived many years in basic training units.

The BT-2, here exemplified by a BT-2B, provided outstanding service in the training role. The aircraft were also heavily employed on air mail flights during 1931.

SPECIFICATION	
Douglas BT-2B	service ceiling 19,200 ft (5850 m);
Type: two-seat basic flying trainer	range 320 miles (515 km)
Powerplant: one Pratt & Whitney R-1340-11 radial piston engine rated at 450 hp (336 kW)	**Weights:** empty 2,918 lb (1324 kg); maximum take-off 4,067 lb (1845 kg)
Performance: maximum speed 134 mph (216 km/h) at sea level; cruising speed 117 mph (188 km/h) at optimum altitude; initial climb rate 1,130 ft (344 m) per minute;	**Dimensions:** wingspan 40 ft (12.19 m); length 31 ft 2 in (9.50 m); height 10 ft 10 in (3.30 m); wing area 362.00 sq ft (33.63 m²)

Douglas SB2D and BTD Destroyer

Early service use of the SBD Dauntless had convinced the US Navy of its capability as a dive-bomber. Long before that date, however, the USN had initiated the procurement of a more advanced dive-bomber. Douglas designed a two-seat aircraft in this category, and in June 1941 the USN ordered two **Douglas**

XSB2D-1 Destroyer prototypes. The first of these made its initial flight on 8 April 1943 but, despite trials which revealed that the new Douglas type was significantly better than the rival Curtiss SB2C Helldiver that had already been ordered into production, the Destroyer was not ordered into production,

but used rather as the basis for a new aircraft which the cut and thrust of war in the Pacific had shown to be more essential.

The Douglas XSB2D-1 prototype was a clean and purposeful-looking two-seat dive-bomber, introducing an internal bomb bay and, for the first time for an aircraft to operate from an aircraft-carrier, retractable tricycle landing gear. The USN's new requirement was for a single-seat torpedo/dive-bomber, and the XSB2D-1 was therefore modified for this new role by conversion to a single-seat cockpit, the addition of two 20-mm wing-mounted cannon, enlargement of the bomb bay, increased fuel capacity and air brakes on each side of the fuselage.

A contract on 31 August 1943 increased earlier orders for this aircraft, designated **BTD-1** and retaining the name

Two XSB2D-1 aircraft were completed. This example shows the type's full array of gun armament in the form of dorsal and ventral turrets, plus twin wing-mounted cannon.

Destroyer, to 358. Deliveries of production aircraft began in June 1944, but only 28 had been delivered before the balance of the contract was cancelled soon after VJ-Day. The Destroyer's performance was disappointing and, so far as is known, the type was not used operationally. Two aircraft were provided experimentally with a mixed powerplant, a 1,500-lb st (6.67-kN) Westinghouse WE-19XA

turbojet engine being fitted in the rear fuselage and fed with air through a dorsal inlet to the rear of the cockpit. These two **XBTD-2** aircraft were the first jet-powered machines built by Douglas and flown by the US Navy. A first flight was made in May 1945, but at speeds over 200 mph (322 km/h) the downward-angled turbojet could not be used. Further work on the project was cancelled late in 1945.

SPECIFICATION	
Douglas BTD-1 Destroyer **Type:** single-seat carrierborne torpedo/dive-bomber **Powerplant:** one Wright R-3350-14 Duplex Cyclone radial piston engine rated at 2,300 hp (1715 kW) **Performance:** maximum speed 344 mph (554 km/h) at 16,100 ft (4905 m); cruising speed 188 mph (303 km/h) at optimum altitude; initial climb rate 1,650 ft (503 m) per minute; service ceiling 23,600 ft (7195 m); range 2,140 miles (3444 km) with maximum fuel and no warload, and	1,480 miles (2382 km) with standard fuel and warload **Weights:** empty 11,561 lb (5244 kg); maximum take-off 19,000 lb (8618 kg) **Dimensions:** wingspan 45 ft (13.72 m); length 38 ft 7 in (11.76 m); height 16 ft 7 in (5.05 m); wing area 373.00 sq ft (34.65 m²) **Armament:** two 20-mm fixed forward-firing cannon in the leading edges of the wing, plus one torpedo or up to 3,200 lb (1451 kg) of bombs carried in the lower-fuselage weapons bay

Douglas C-1

The US Army Air Service made its first serious attempt to acquire a viable transport aircraft late in 1924 when it placed an order with Douglas for nine large single-engined **C-1** aircraft, the first of which made its maiden flight on 2 May 1925. Power was provided by a single V-1650-1 Liberty water-cooled engine.

The C-1 had a roomy enclosed cabin with three porthole-type windows on each side, located to the rear of the open cockpit for the pilot and co-pilot or flight mechanic, who were seated side-by-side. Seats for six to eight passengers were provided, and these could be removed to provide a freight hold of 160 cu. ft (4.53 m³). Passenger access to the cabin was by a door in the starboard side of the fuselage, and bulky freight

could be loaded through a trap in the cabin floor.

The C-1s were attached to US Army airfields and depots, and were often used for freight transport in addition to carrying personnel. They were successful in service, although attracting little public attention except when one of the aircraft was used as an aerial tanker in 1929 during highly publicised inflight-refuelling experiments

Photographed on 28 April 1926, this C-1 was typical of the type in military service. The C-1 received a civil type certificate in late 1927, but may not have entered civil employ.

with the Fokker C-2A three-engined transport, *Question Mark*. Later orders for developed versions brought total production to 26, many of the type surviving in US Army service until they were finally scrapped in 1936.

SPECIFICATION	
Douglas C-1 **Type:** two-crew transport aircraft **Powerplant:** one V-1650-1 Liberty Vee piston engine rated at 435 hp (324 kW) **Performance:** maximum speed 116 mph (187 km/h) at sea level; cruising speed 85 mph (137 km/h) at optimum altitude; initial climb rate 645 ft (197 m) per minute; service ceiling 14,850 ft (4525 m);	range 385 miles (620 km) **Weights:** empty 3,836 lb (1740 kg); maximum take-off 6,443 lb (2922 kg) **Dimensions:** wingspan 56 ft 7 in (17.25 m); length 35 ft 4 in (10.77 m); height 14 ft (4.27 m); wing area 805.00 sq ft (74.78 m²) **Payload:** up to eight passengers or 2,500 lb (1134 kg) of freight

Variants

C-1A: designation of a C-1 tested with a variety of engine installations and cowlings, and used finally for experiments with ski landing gear before being returned to normal C-1 configuration
C-1C: no **C-1B** aircraft were built, but 17 C-1C machines were manufactured in two batches, the second batch being delivered to the US Army by the end of 1927; they had a higher loaded weight, increased dimensions, a balanced rather than plain rudder, modified landing gear, and a metal rather than wooden cabin floor

Douglas C-47 Skytrain/Dakota, C-53 Skytrooper & R4D

The capability revealed by the DC-2 convinced the US Army of the excellence of the basic transport's design and construction, and a study of the improved DC-3 enabled the US Army to outline the modifications required for the DC-3's use as a military transport. These changes included more powerful engines, strengthening of the rear fuselage and cabin floor, provision of large loading doors, replacement of the airline-type interior by utility

seats lining the cabin walls, and adoption of a powerplant comprising two R-1830-92 radials. Ordered in large numbers in 1940, this type received the designation **C-47 Skytrain**, and was the precursor of an enormous and diverse military series that included the **C-53 Skytrooper** dedicated troop transport with 28 seats.

The C-47 was a notable glider tug, being involved in actions in Sicily, Burma, Normandy, Arnhem and

the Rhine crossing. Many of those supplied to the UK under Lend-Lease were involved in the D-Day operations in Normandy, and these aircraft were named **Dakota** in British service. Aircraft of the C-47 series later took part in the Berlin Airlift, were involved in the Korean War and, under the designation **AC-47D**, were deployed as well-armed gunships in Vietnam. The US Navy and US Marine Corps also used the type under a number of desig-

nations, although the original and basic identification was **R4D**; in 1962 those continuing in service acquired the tri-service C-47 designations. Like the US Army, the USN and USMC initially operated the R4D primarily for personnel and cargo transport, while later utilisation included radar countermeasures, air-sea warfare training and, with ski-modified landing gear, operations in the Arctic and Antarctic.

Throughout the entire

period of production there was little significant change in airframe design. The same was not true of the powerplant for, as improved and/or more powerful engines became available, they were installed to provide enhanced performance or load-carrying capability. Manufacturer's lists show six variants of the Wright SGR-1820 Cyclone engine with ratings from 900 to 1,000 hp (671 to 746 kW), and also six variants of the

R-1830 Twin Wasp engine with ratings from 1,000 to 1,100 hp (746 to 820 kW). After World War II large numbers of the military and naval versions of the DC-3 were declared surplus to requirements and sold onto the civil market, and so acute was the shortage of aircraft suitable for the resumption of civil passenger and cargo services that many were operated without any alteration to the military interior. The majority, however, was taken in hand for modification with internal furnishings and equipment, making the aircraft acceptable by airline standards, and some were even provided with executive and VIP interior layouts.

Many efforts have been made to enhance the performance of the C-47, as well as to prolong its service life and to extend its utility. In particular, a number of turboprop installations has been made, of which the latest and apparently most successful, in

In South Africa, the Dakota served on as a transport and even as a maritime patrol aircraft into the 1990s. In 2000, the type remains only in C-47TP form.

military applications, is that developed by Basler Turbo Conversions Inc. The **Basler Turbo-67** introduces two Pratt & Whitney Canada PT6A-67R turboprop engines each rated at 1,424 shp (1061 kW) and driving Hartzell five-bladed propellers, and a lengthening of the forward fuselage by 3 ft 4 in (1.02 m) to bring the pilots forward of the plane of the propellers. The modification also preserves the centre of gravity within acceptable limits despite the lighter weight of the turbine powerplant. Revisions in the cabin layout increase the seating capacity to a maximum of 34 troops or five LD3 cargo containers. Deliveries of the Turbo-67 began in 1990, recipients including the air forces of Colombia, Bolivia,

Guatemala and Salvador (with an AC-47 gunship conversion as well as a standard transport).

Early in 1992, the South African Air Force began to accept the **C-47TP Super Dakota** conversion by

Professional Aviation, which is similar in almost all respects to the Basler Turbo-67. Production conversion lines set up by the SAAF at the Swartkop and Ysterplaat bases were to convert the entire fleet of

over 40 Dakotas to this standard, with the first assigned to No. 35 Squadron at Cape Town in 1992 for SAR duty, but from the mid-1990s this programme was scaled down quite considerably.

This C-47A-65-DL has modifications suiting it to the aerial retrieval of landed gliders. The hook along the fuselage side was lowered in flight, with the aircraft just a few feet above ground level. The tow line of the glider was held above the ground on a temporary framework, so that it could be engaged by the hook trailing from the C-47. Many valuable assault gliders were retrieved in this manner for re-use.

2100444

Variants

C-41A: initial military model, essentially a version of the DC-3A with military instrumentation, swivelling seats and R-1830-21 engines; the type was used as a command transport (1 built)
C-47: initial military production model with span increased by 6 in (0.15 m), revised fuel tankage, R-1830-92 engines, small astrodome and accommodation for 6,000 lb (2722 kg) of freight, or 28 paratroops, or 14 casualties and three attendants (965 built)
C-47A: improved C-47 with 24- rather than 12-volt electrical system (5,253 built)
RC-47A: post-war modification used in Korea for limited reconnaissance missions and flare-dropping in support of tactical combat aircraft
SC-47A: post-war air/sea rescue variant (**HC-47A** from 1962)
VC-47A: post-war modification to staff transport standard with conventional seating
C-47B: version developed for operations 'over the hump' of the eastern Himalayas between India and China, with better heating and R-1830-90C engines fitted with two-stage blowers; the type proved only marginally successful, and many were later converted to C-47D standard (3,232 built)
TC-47B: specialised navigation trainer (133 built)
VC-47B: conversion of the C-47B to staff transport standard
XV-47C: experimental model mounted on twin Edo Model 78 amphibious floats, each able to carry some 300 US gal (1136 litres) of fuel; no production was undertaken, but 150 sets of floats were delivered for field installation (1 built)
C-47D: designation of C-47Bs after the removal of the high blower
AC-47D: designation of 26 airways check versions operated by the Military Air Transport Service from 1953 to 1962, when they were redesignated **EC-47D**
AC-47D: 1965 designation for gunship conversions with three 0.3-in (7.62-mm) General Electric Miniguns firing through the fourth and fifth windows and from the open door on the port side of the fuselage

RC-47D: reconnaissance version
SC-47D: air/sea rescue variant (**HC-47D** from 1962)
TC-47D: trainer modification
VC-47D: staff transport conversion
C-47E: designation initially intended for C-47s modernised and fitted with 1,475-hp (1100-kW) R-1820-80 engines, but used instead for eight aircraft modified for the USAAF by Pan American with 1,290-hp (962-kW) R-2000-4 radial engines for use as airways check aircraft
C-47M: **C-47H** and **C-47J** aircraft fitted with special electronic equipment for use in the Vietnam War
EC-47N: C-47A specially fitted for electronic reconnaissance in Vietnam
EC-47P: C-47D specially fitted for electronic reconnaissance in Vietnam
EC-47Q: version with R-2000-4 engines specially fitted for electronic reconnaissance in Vietnam
C-48: one DC-3A taken over from United Air Lines while under construction
C-48A: three DC-3As taken over while under construction
C-48B: 16 impressed aircraft
C-48C: seven DC-3As taken over from Pan American while under construction, and nine impressed aircraft
C-49: six DC-3s taken over from TWA while under construction
C-49A: one DC-3 taken over from Delta while under construction
C-49B: three DC-3s taken over from Eastern while under construction
C-49C: two DC-3s taken over from Delta while under construction
C-49D: six DC-3s taken over from Eastern while under construction, and five impressed aircraft
C-49E: 22 impressed aircraft
C-49F: nine impressed aircraft
C-49G: eight impressed aircraft
C-49H: 19 impressed aircraft
C-49J: 34 DC-3s taken over while under construction
C-49K: 23 DC-3s taken over while under construction
C-50: four DC-3s taken over from American while under construction

Douglas C-47 Skytrain, C-53 Skytrooper & R4D (cont.)

Variants (continued)

C-50A: two DC-3s taken over from American while under construction
C-50B: three DC-3s taken over from Braniff while under construction
C-50C: one DC-3 taken over from Penn Central while under construction
C-50D: four DC-3s taken over from Penn Central while under construction
C-51: one DC-3 taken over from Canadian Colonial while under construction
C-52: one DC-3A taken over from United while under construction
C-52A: one DC-3A taken over from Western while under construction
C-52B: two DC-3As taken over from United while under construction
C-52C: one DC-3A taken over from Eastern while under construction
C-52D: one impressed aircraft
C-53: dedicated troop transport version with 28 seats, glider-towing cleat, no freight door and power provided by R-1830-92 engines (221 built)
XC-53A: C-53 modified in 1942 with full-span slotted flaps and hot-air rather than pneumatic-boot de-icing
C-53B: eight C-53s modified in 1942 for Arctic operations with winterised equipment and extra fuel tankage
C-53C: 17 airline-ordered aircraft impressed while under construction
C-53D: identical to the C-53 apart from having side seats rather than seats in rows (159 built)
C-68: two impressed DC-3As
C-84: four impressed aircraft
C-117A: staff transport with 21 seats and generally similar to the C-47B (17 built)
C-117B: 11 C-117As modified by the removal of the high blowers for their R-1830-90C engines
C-117C: VC-47s upgraded to C-117B standard
XCG-17: experimental troop-carrying glider conversion, produced by removing the engines and fairing over the nacelles of a C-47; surprisingly enough, the XCG-17 had excellent glide performance, but by the time tests were completed in 1944, only limited requirement for gliders was felt by the USAAF and no production followed
R4D-1: initial freight model for the USN, generally similar to the C-47 apart from the use of naval instrumentation (100 built)
R4D-2: two DC-3s taken over from Eastern while under construction and used by the USN as staff transports; they were later designated **R4D-2F** and **R4D-2Z**
R4D-3: 20 C-53s received from the USAAF
R4D-4: 10 DC-3s taken over from Pan American while still under construction, and used by the USN as personnel transports; some were later modified for electronic countermeasures under the revised designation **R4D-4Q**

R4D-5: 238 C-47As received by the USN from USAAF contracts (**C-47H** from 1962)
R4D-5E: R4D-5s modified for special electronic operations
R4D-5L: R4D-5s modified for operations in the Arctic and Antarctic (**LC-47H** from 1962)
R4D-5Q: R4D-5s modified for radar countermeasures (**EC-47H** from 1962)
R4D-5R: R4D-5s modified as personnel transports (**TC-47H** from 1962)
R4D-5S: R4D-5s modified for air-sea warfare training (**SC-47H** from 1962)
R4D-5T: R4D-5s modified for navigation training
R4D-5Z: R4D-5s modified as staff transports (**VC-47H** from 1962)
R4D-6: 150 C-47Bs received by the USN from USAAF contracts (**C-47J** from 1962); versions equivalent to various R4D-5 variants were identified as the **R4D-6E**, **R4D-6L** (**LC-47J**), **R4D-6Q** (**EC-47J**), **R4D-6R** (**TC-47J**), **R4D-6S** (**SC-47J**), **R4D-6T** and **R4D-6Z** (**VC-47J**)
R4D-7: some 47 TC-47Bs received by the USN from USAAF contracts (**TC-47K** from 1962)
Dakota Mk I: RAF equivalent of the C-47 (52 aircraft supplied under Lend-Lease and one built from spares)
Dakota Mk II: RAF equivalent of the C-53 (nine aircraft supplied under Lend-Lease)
Dakota Mk III: RAF equivalent of the C-47A (12 supplied by the USAAF and 950 supplied under Lend-Lease)
Dakota Mk IV: RAF equivalent of the C-47B (896 supplied under Lend-Lease)
Lisunov Li-2: Soviet licence-built version, originally powered by 900-hp (671-kW) Shvetsov M-62 radial engines in the **PS-84** first version, but later fitted with uprated Shvetsov ASh-62 radials; production comprised a number of variants, some of them armed with turreted armament; the **Li-2G** freighter, **Li-2P** personnel transport, **Li-2PG** convertible model and the **Li-2V** high-altitude model are the best known of the variants (2,000 or more built in the USSR and supplemented by 707 Lend-Lease aircraft)
Showa L2D: in 1938 Mitsui acquired a licence to produce the DC-3 in Japan and Manchukuo (Manchuria), and also bought 13 DC-3 and seven DC-3A aircraft; Mitsui subcontracted production of the DC-3 to Showa, which built 414 L2D transports for the Imperial Japanese navy air force as **L2D2** personnel transports with 1,000-hp (746-kW) Mitsubishi Kinsei 43 radial engines, **L2D3** personnel transports with 1,300-hp (970-kW) Kinsei 51 engines, **L2D3a** personnel transports with 1,300-hp (970-kW) Kinsei 53 engines, **L2D3-1** freighters with Kinsei 51 engines, **L2D3-1a** freighters with Kinsei 53 engines, **L2D4** personnel transports with a 0.52-in (13.2-mm) trainable machine-gun in a dorsal turret and powered by Kinsei 51 engines, **L2D4-1** freighter versions of the L2D4, and **L2D5** personnel transports based on the L2D4 but built partially of wood and steel, and powered by 1,560-hp (1164-kW) Kinsei 62 engines; another 71 L2D2 aircraft were built by Nakajima

Douglas C-117

SPECIFICATION	
Douglas C-47A Skytrain **Type:** two/three-crew short/ medium-range transport **Powerplant:** two Pratt & Whitney R-1830-92 radial piston engines each rated at 1,200 hp (895 kW) **Performance:** maximum speed 230 mph (370 km/h) at 8,800 ft (2680 m); cruising speed 160 mph (257 km/h) at optimum altitude; climb to 10,000 ft (3050 m) in 9 minutes 36 seconds; service ceiling 24,000 ft (7315 m); range 3,800 miles (6115 km) with	maximum fuel and no payload, and 1,600 miles (2575 km) with standard fuel and payload **Weights:** empty 17,865 lb (8103 kg); maximum take-off 26,000 lb (11793 kg) **Dimensions:** wingspan 95 ft 6 in (29.11 m); length 63 ft 9 in (19.43 m); height 17 ft (5.18 m); wing area 987.00 sq ft (91.69 m²) **Payload:** up to 28 troops or paratroops, or 14 litters and three attendants, or 6,000 lb (2722 kg) of freight

Dakotas served extensively with the RAF during and after World War II, many subsequently finding their way into service with other Commonwealth nations. This Indian aircraft has a basic bare-metal finish, with an area of white paint applied above the cockpit in an attempt to cool the interior.

Douglas C-74 Globemaster I

As a consequence of the initial American involvement against Japanese forces in the Pacific, it was clear that transport aircraft

would be of vital importance to the US war effort. Because of the theatre of operations envisaged, such aircraft would require both

long range and great load-carrying capability, and early in 1942 Douglas began development of an aircraft to meet this requirement.

Designated as the **C-74 Globemaster I**, the first of 50 aircraft ordered by the US Army Air Forces did not fly until 5 September 1945.

Variant

DC-7: proposed civil version of C-74, of which Pan Am ordered 26 examples in 1944; later cancelled

SPECIFICATION

Douglas C-74 Globemaster I
Type: four/five-crew heavy transport aircraft
Powerplant: four Pratt & Whitney R-4360-69 radial piston engines each rated at 3,250 hp (2423 kW)
Performance: maximum speed 328 mph (528 km/h) at 10,000 ft (3050 m); cruising speed 212 mph (341 km/h) at optimum altitude; initial climb rate 2,605 ft (794 m) per minute; service ceiling 21,300 ft (6490 m); range

3,400 miles (5472 km) with standard fuel and payload
Weights: empty 86,172 lb (39087 kg); maximum take-off 172,000 lb (78018 kg)
Dimensions: wingspan 173 ft 3 in (52.81 m); length 124 ft 2 in (37.85 m); height 43 ft 9 in (13.34 m); wing area 2,510.00 sq ft (233.18 m²)
Payload: up to 125 troops, or 115 litters and medical attendants, or 48,150 lb (21841 kg) of freight

The Globemaster I suffered contract cancellations typical of the period following VJ-Day, and only 14 of the aircraft were completed. One of these, with 103 passengers and crew, flew from the USA to the UK on 18 November 1949, in the

process becoming the first aircraft to fly across the North Atlantic with more than 100 persons on board.

When the Globemaster I aircraft ended their useful service life, some were acquired by civil cargo operators.

The C-74 was a low-wing cantilever monoplane of all-metal construction, with a conventional tail unit, retractable tricycle landing gear with twin wheels on each unit, and four R-4360 engines.

Douglas C-124 Globemaster II

When, in late 1947, the newly formed US Air Force decided it needed a heavy strategic cargo transport, discussions between the USAF and Douglas resulted in development of the **C-124 Globemaster II**, which was based on the C-74. In fact, the **YC-124** service test prototype was basically the fifth C-74 revised with a new deeper fuselage, strengthened landing gear and the powerplant of four 3,500-hp (2610-kW)

R-4360-49 engines.

The YC-124 made its maiden flight on 27 November 1949, and the type entered production as the **C-124A**. Production totalled 204 aircraft, the first of them entering service with the USAF in May 1950. The next and final production version was the **C-124C**, with more powerful R-4360 engines, weather radar in a distinctive nose radome and, equally useful recognition points, wingtip fairings

Variant

YKC-124B: single aircraft with 5,550-eshp (4139-ekW) Pratt & Whitney YT34-P-1 turboprop engines and intended as the prototype of a tanker version
YC-124B: redesignation of the YKC-124B when its development as a tanker was abandoned

housing combustion heaters to de-ice the leading edges of the wing and tailplane and to heat the cabin. Production of the C-124C totalled 243, the last machine being delivered during May 1955. The fuselage of the Cargomaster II had clamshell nose loading doors with an associated inbuilt loading ramp, an electric hoist amidships (a carry-over from the C-74), and two 16,000-lb (7257-kg) capacity overhead cranes that could traverse the entire length of the cargo hold, which was 77 ft (23.47 m) long. The flight deck, accommodating a crew of five, was mounted

In September 1974, the 158th MAS, Georgia ANG retired the last C-124Cs from service. The type was nicknamed 'Old Shakey'.

SPECIFICATION

Douglas C-124C Globemaster II
Type: five-crew heavy transport aircraft
Powerplant: four Pratt & Whitney R-4360-63A radial piston engines each rated at 3,800 hp (2834 kW)
Performance: maximum speed 304 mph (489 mph) at 20,800 ft (6340 m); cruising speed 230 mph (370 km/h) at 10,000 ft (3050 m); initial climb rate 760 m (232 m) per minute; service ceiling 21,800 ft (6645 m); range 4,030 miles (6486 km) with standard fuel and a

26,375-lb (11963-kg) payload
Weights: empty 101,165 lb (45888 kg); maximum take-off 194,500 lb (88224 kg)
Dimensions: wingspan 174 ft 1½ in (39.75 m) length 130 ft 5 in (39.75 m); height 48 ft 3½ in (14.72 m); wing area 2,506.00 sq ft (232.81 m²)
Payload: up to 200 troops, or 123 litters plus 45 ambulatory patients and 15 medical attendants, or 74,000 lb (33566 kg) of freight

high in the nose over the clamshell doors.

Serving with the USAF's Air Materiel Command, Far Eastern Air Force, Military Air Transport Service, Strategic Air Command and Tactical Air Command, and used in conjunction with the C-133, the Globemaster

II remained in service until replaced by the C-5A Galaxy during 1970.

Douglas C-133 Cargomaster

The Berlin Airlift and Korean War added greater emphasis to the importance of heavy transport aircraft, and in the early 1950s Douglas received from the USAF development contracts for two new turboprop-powered transports, the **C-132** and **C-133**. The giant C-132 did not progress

beyond the mock-up stage, but the smaller C-133, which was designed to meet the requirements of the USAF's Logistic Carrier Supporting System SS402L, won an initial contract for 12 aircraft. No prototype was built, and the first production example of the **C-133A**, later named

Cargomaster, made its maiden flight on 23 April 1956.

The C-133A differed considerably from the C-74 and C-124 that had preceded it, for the new transport was based on a design that incorporated a high-mounted cantilever wing and tricycle landing

gear with main units that retracted into external pods, one on each side of the fuselage, ensuring that access to, and the volume of, the cargo hold was not compromised by these structures. The circular-section fuselage provided a cargo hold 90 ft (27.43 m) long, and the hold was pressurised, heated and ventilated. The hold was loaded via a two-section

rear door, whose lower section formed a ramp, or by a cargo door on the port side of the forward fuselage. It was possible for vehicles up to 12 ft (3.66 m) in height to be driven up the rear ramp direct into the cargo hold, and the C-133 Cargomaster was able to accept practically every type of contemporary vehicle in service with the US Army.

Douglas C-133 Cargomaster (continued)

The first C-133A transports were delivered to the Military Air Transport Service in August 1957, and production totalled just 35 aircraft. The early examples were each powered by a quartet of 6,000-eshp (4474-ekW) Pratt & Whitney T34-P-3 turboprop engines, while later production aircraft switched to T34-P-7W engines which, with water injection, had a maximum rating of 7,100 eshp (5294 ekW). The last three aircraft had clamshell rear-loading doors which increased the hold length by 3 ft (0.91 m), making it possible to airlift completely assembled Titan missiles. These were followed by 15 **C-133B** aircraft that retained the clamshell doors and incorporated more powerful T34-P-9W engines.

The fleet of 50 aircraft proved itself invaluable during the US involvement in Vietnam, but fatigue problems led to their withdrawal from service during 1971; the aircraft were then placed in storage. A few machines were later released onto the civil market.

The Cargomaster, depicted here by a C-133A-35-DL, was conceptually similar to the Lockheed Hercules. The C-133 was, however, a much larger and more powerful aircraft of far greater capacity.

SPECIFICATION

Douglas C-133B Cargomaster
Type: 10-crew strategic heavy transport
Powerplant: four Pratt & Whitney T34-P-9W turboprop engines each rated at 7,500 eshp (5593 ekW)
Performance: maximum speed 359 mph (578 km/h) at 8,700 ft (2650 m); cruising speed 323 mph (520 km/h) at optimum altitude; initial climb rate 1,280 ft (390 m) per minute; service ceiling 29,950 ft (9130 m); range more than 4,000 miles (6437 km) with a 52,000-lb (23587-kg) payload
Weights: empty 120,263 lb (54550 kg); maximum take-off 286,000 lb (129727 kg)
Dimensions: wingspan 179 ft 7¾ in (54.77 m) length 157 ft 6½ in (48.02 m) height 48 ft 3 in (14.71 m); wing area 2,673.00 sq ft (248.32 m²)
Payload: up to 110,000 lb (49896 kg) of freight

Douglas Cloudster

The one-off **Cloudster** is worthy of mention as the very first aircraft to be designed and built by the Davis-Douglas Company, which had been established in Los Angeles, California during July 1920. In fact, the Cloudster was itself the raison d'être for the formation of the company, David R. Davis being prepared to capitalise a new company in partnership with Donald Douglas on the understanding that the latter would design and build an aircraft with which the former could make the first non-stop flight coast-to-coast across the USA. A neat single-bay equal-span biplane of wooden construction, fabric-covered except for the forward section of the fuselage on which light alloy panels were used, the Cloudster was developed into the DT and World Cruiser, and was powered by the readily available Liberty engine that was both powerful and reliable.

First flown successfully on 24 February 1921, the Cloudster attempted its coast-to-coast flight in June of that same year, but was thwarted by engine failure. In 1923 the Cloudster was sold for use as a passenger transport, and experienced several new owners and modifications before force-landing in shallow water off the California coast late in 1926. The aircraft was damaged beyond repair by the incoming tide before it could be pulled ashore.

In June 1920, Donald Douglas single-handedly began the design of the Cloudster in the rear of a barber's shop in Los Angeles.

SPECIFICATION

Douglas Cloudster
Type: two-seat long-range aircraft
Powerplant: one Liberty 12 Vee piston engine rated at 400 hp (298 kW)
Performance: maximum speed 120 mph (193 km/h) at sea level; cruising speed 85 mph (137 km/h) at optimum altitude; absolute ceiling 19,160 ft (5840 m); range 2,800 miles (4506 km)
Weights: maximum take-off 9,600 lb (4354 kg)
Dimensions: wingspan 55 ft 11 in (17.04 m); length 36 ft 9 in (11.20 m); height 12 ft (3.66 m)

Douglas D-558-1 Skystreak

Conceived in 1945, the **D-558-1 Skystreak** was designed to meet the requirements of the US Navy's Bureau of Aeronautics and of NACA (NASA's predecessor) for a high-speed research aircraft. It was required to accumulate air/load measurements in free flight at speeds from Mach 0.75 to 0.85 and at heights between sea level and 40,000 ft (12190 m), data which at that time were unobtainable from wind tunnels.

The aircraft's design was kept as simple as possible, and the result was a low-wing cantilever monoplane with a small wing, a slender circular-section fuselage, and a tail unit that comprised a large-area vertical surface with the horizontal surface mounted approximately one-third of the way up the fin. The landing gear was of the retractable tricycle type and the fuselage, incorporating a single-seat cockpit, carried the powerplant based on one J35 turbojet engine. An unusual feature was the pilot's escape system, Douglas considering that the pilot might not survive a conventional ejection. The entire nose section of the aircraft, from the rear of the pilot's seat forward, was jettisonable in emergency; it was intended that the pilot should bale out conventionally from this nose section after it had slowed sufficiently after separation. To gather the data for which the Skystreak was designed, an automatic pressure recording system was installed, with connections to 400 measuring points on the airframe; additionally, strain gauges were attached to selected positions on the wings and tail unit.

Three examples of the D-558-1 were built, the first of these flying on 15 April 1947, and on 20 August 1947 establishing a new world speed record of 640.66 mph (1031.04 km/h), a figure raised five days later to 650.80 mph (1047.36 km/h). On 3 May 1948 the second Skystreak was lost in an accident when its engine compressor disintegrated just after take-off. The pilot, Howard Lilly, became the first NACA pilot to die while on active duty. After an enquiry had cleared the Skystreak of any blame for the accident, the third aircraft was returned to flight status. On 10 June 1953, this aircraft successfully completed a series of 82 flights, having been sustained in this programme by spares and components taken from the first prototype. Early in 2000, the first aircraft was preserved at the Naval Aviation Museum, Pensacola, Florida, while the third machine was latterly at MCAS Quantico, Virginia.

SPECIFICATION

Douglas D-558-1 Skystreak
Type: single-seat research aircraft
Powerplant: one Allison J35-A-11 turbojet engine rated at 5,000 lb st (22.24 kN)
Performance: maximum speed 651 mph (1048 km/h) at sea level
Weights: maximum take-off 10,105 lb (4584 kg)
Dimensions: wingspan 25 ft (7.62 m); length 35 ft 8½ in (10.88 m); height 12 ft 1¾ in (3.70 m); wing area 150.70 sq ft (14.00 m²)

BuNo. 37970 was the first Skystreak. It was flown in this striking bright-red colour scheme from the start, but was modified later in its career to include the canopy and windscreen shapes illustrated.

Douglas D-558-2 Skyrocket

To progress beyond the capabilities offered by the D-558-1 Skystreak, it had at first been planned that the powerplant of this type would be modified, the turbojet engine being one of smaller dimensions to leave volume for the addition of a rocket motor. Before this stage was reached, however, it was also decided to investigate the nature of a swept wing planform and this led to the design of 'Ed' Heinemann's new research aircraft, the **D-558-2 Skyrocket**. To accommodate the mixed powerplant, a larger-diameter fuselage was designed, retaining the jettisonable nose-section of the Skystreak and also its tricycle landing gear. The mid-set wing, swept at 35°, and a tail unit with swept horizontal and vertical surfaces replaced the more conventional straight surfaces of the earlier aircraft. Following evaluation of the design by the US Navy and NACA, three of these aircraft were ordered and the first was flown on 4 February 1948. In the course of a highly successful test

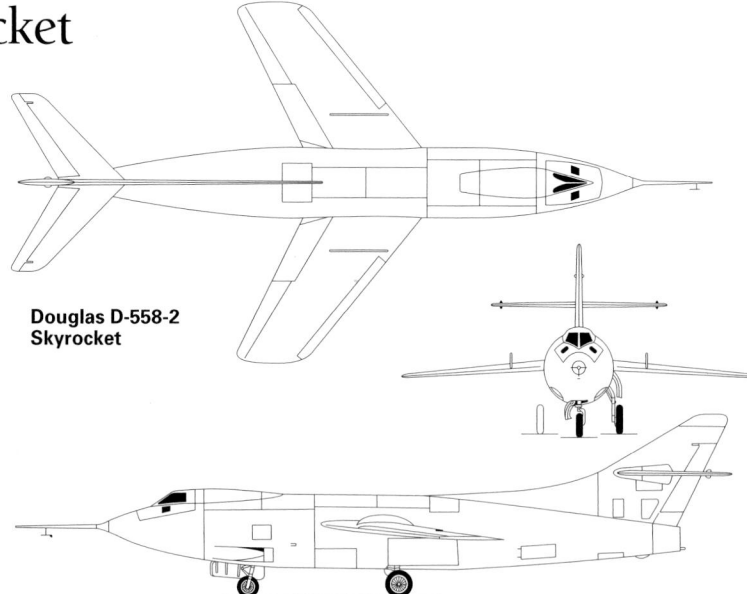

**Douglas D-558-2
Skyrocket**

Variant

D-558-3: project by designer/aerodynamicist Kermit E. Van Every for a hypersonic development with a very thin, straight wing and rocket power alone; anticipated performance maxima were a speed of 6,050 mph (9735 km/h) or Mach 9 and an absolute altitude of 750,000 ft (228600 m) or 142 miles (228.6 km); this ambitious project was abandoned in favour of the multi-agency North American X-15

Early on in the Skyrocket programme, before the adoption of an all-rocket powerplant, self launches were possible.

programme one of the aircraft in August 1951 attained a speed of 1,238 mph (1992 km/h) on rocket power alone following aerial launch from a Boeing P2B-1S mother-plane. A few days later the same aircraft attained an altitude of 79,491 ft (24230 m), exceeded by a height of 83,235 ft (25370 m) on 31 August 1953, and just less than three months later, on 20 November, a speed of Mach 2.05 was recorded, making the Skyrocket the first piloted aircraft in the world to be flown at twice the speed of sound. The

SPECIFICATION
Douglas D-558-2 Skyrocket **Type:** single-seat swept-wing research aircraft **Powerplant:** one Westinghouse J34-WE-22 turbojet engine rated at 3,000 lb st (13.34 kN) and one Reaction Motors XLR-8 rocket motor rated at 6,000 lb st (26.69 kN) **Performance:** maximum speed 585 mph (941 km/h) at 20,000 ft (6095 m) with turbojet alone, 720 mph (1159 km/h) at 40,000 ft (12190 m) with both engines after	a land take-off, and 1,250 mph (2012 km/h) at 67,500 ft (20575 m) with rocket motor alone after an air launch **Weights:** maximum take-off 10,572 lb (4795 kg) with turbojet alone, 15,266 lb (6925 kg) with both engines, and 15,787 lb (7171 kg) with rocket motor alone **Dimensions:** wingspan 25 ft (7.62 m); length 45 ft 3 in (13.79 m) including probe; height 12 ft 8 in (3.86 m); wing area 175.00 sq ft (16.26 m²)

Skyrocket programme ended in December 1956. The second, record-breaking, Skyrocket, is preserved at the Smithsonian's National Air and Space Museum, Washington, D.C.

Douglas DC-1 and DC-2

When TWA, faced with an urgent need to replace its obsolescent Fokker airliners, found itself behind United Air Lines in the queue for the Boeing Model 247, the airline drew up a specification for a three-engined airliner of all-metal construction with seats for at least 12 passengers for release to the US industry on 2 August 1932. Donald W. Douglas responded within a fortnight to this specification and a contract was signed on 20 September, Douglas having convinced TWA's technical adviser, Charles Lindbergh, that the required performance could be achieved safely on only two engines. The resulting **DC-1 (Douglas Commercial no. 1)** prototype was rolled out on 22 June 1933 and, powered by two R-1820 radial engines, made its maiden flight on 1 July of the same year.

Despite initial problems with the engines' carburettors, the test programme was completed successfully and the aircraft was handed over to TWA at Los Angeles Municipal Airport in December 1933. The DC-1 did not enter service, however, being used instead for promotional purposes by TWA; these included a coast-to-coast record flight of 13 hours 4 minutes through the night of 18-19 February 1934. TWA signed an initial contract for 25 production aircraft, which differed from the DC-1 in having more powerful engines and the fuselage lengthened by 2 ft (0.61 m) to provide accommodation for 14 passengers. These changes produced the **DC-2**, which was soon adopted by other US operators including American Airlines, Eastern Air Lines, General Air Lines, Panagra and Pan American. The DC-2 was also used in Europe by airlines including KLM, Lineas Aéreas Postales Españolas (LAPE) and Swissair. The most famous of these aircraft was KLM's Uiver which, flown by K. D. Parmentier and J. J. Moll, was winner in the transport division of the 1934 MacRobertson air race between England and Australia. In fact, its flight time of 90 hours 13 minutes 36 seconds was beaten only by the outright winner, the de Havilland DH.88 Comet dedicated racer, flown without a payload.

Such performance capability made the DC-2 worthy of military interest, the US Navy leading the way with a single **R2D-1** transport in 1934, supplemented later by four more basically similar aircraft.

Originally delivered to the Austrian government as the personal transport of Chancellor Engelbert Dollfuss, EC-AAA was soon sold to Lineas Aéreas Postales Españolas (LAPE). The aircraft was later flown by the Republican forces during the Spanish Civil War, having been re-registered EC-AGA in 1936.

Douglas DC-1 and DC-2 (continued)

The US Army Air Corps opened its purchases for Fiscal Year 1936 with a 16-seat DC-2, which was evaluated as the **XC-32** and paved the way to orders for two externally similar **YC-34** (later **C-34**) passenger transports and 18 **C-33** freight transports, the latter with an enlarged vertical tail surface and a cargo door. In 1937 one C-33 was fitted with the tail unit of a DC-3 and redesignated as the **C-33A** (later **C-38**); from it was developed the **C-39**, with other DC-3 components, including the wing centre-section and landing gear, and the powerplant of two 975-hp (727-kW) R-1820-55 engines. Thirty-five of this type were ordered for the US Army's transport groups, entering service in 1939. The fourth and fifth C-39 aircraft were converted while still on the production line to **C-41** and **C-42** standards respectively. The first was fitted with 1,200-hp (895-kW) R-1830-21 engines and cleared to operate at a gross weight of 25,000 lb (11340 kg) as the aircraft of the USAAC chief-of-staff, while the second was similarly powered and cleared at 23,624 lb (10716 kg) as the aircraft of the Air Force GHQ's commanding general. Two more C-39s were later converted to C-42 standard.

The DC-2s in military service were used extensively in the early years of World War II, and are remembered especially for their role in carrying US survivors of Japanese aggression from the Philippines to Australia from December 1941. A number of DC-2s, acquired for wartime service by the Royal Air Force, were used by No. 31 Squadron in India. Total Douglas DC-2 production, of all variants, was 193 aircraft.

Variants

DC-2A: two civil aircraft with Pratt & Whitney Hornet engines
DC-2B: two aircraft acquired by the Polish airline LOT with the powerplant of two 750-hp (559-kW) Bristol Pegasus VI radial engines
C-32A: military designation applied to 24 civil DC-2 machines impressed by the USAAF in 1942; these transports were without cargo doors

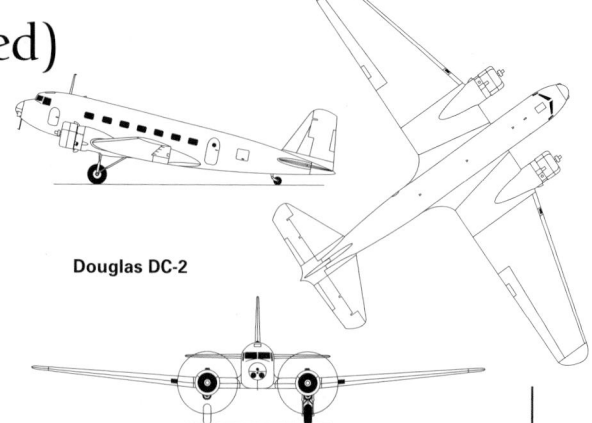

Douglas DC-2

SPECIFICATION	
Douglas DC-2	22,450 ft (6845 m); range
Type: two-crew transport aircraft	1,000 miles (1609 km)
Powerplant: two Wright SGR-1820-F52 Cyclone radial piston engines each rated at 875 hp (652 kW)	**Weights:** empty 12,408 lb (5628 kg); maximum take-off 18,560 lb (8419 kg)
Performance: maximum speed 210 mph (338 km/h) at 8,000 ft (2440 m); cruising speed 190 mph (306 km/h) at 8,000 ft (2440 m); initial climb rate 1,000 ft (305 m) per minute; service ceiling	**Dimensions:** wingspan 85 ft (25.91 m) length 61 ft 11¾ in (18.89 m) height 16 ft 3¾ in (4.97 m); wing area 939.00 sq ft (87.23 m²)
	Payload: up to 14 passengers

Douglas DC-3

Undoubtedly a classic airliner, and almost certainly as well known to travellers all over the world as to the aviation enthusiasts, by the beginning of 2000 the **Douglas DC-3**, as a type, had been in service continuously for over 63 years. Few can have appreciated the potential longevity of this design when, in 1934, the Douglas Aircraft Company was requested by American Airlines to develop an enlarged version of the DC-2 to provide a 'sleeper' that could be used on transcontinental flights within the USA. This resulted in the **DST (Douglas Sleeper Transport)** with 14 sleeping berths, first flown on 17 December 1935. It was, however, the 21-28-seat day version of this airliner, designated DC-3, which became so important a part of aviation history. Before

US involvement in World War II, when production of the type against civil orders was halted after the delivery of 430 aircraft to a few export customers as well as many American operators, the DC-3 had gained a dominant position in the USA's airlines, and its rugged reliability also appealed to military planners as soon as the requirement for large numbers of transport aircraft was appreciated.

The DC-3's robust construction meant that very large numbers of the type survived the war, and when these were disposed of as war surplus items, operators all over the world acquired them as fast as they could lay hands on them. Used in the passenger-carrying and utility roles, the DC-3 played a significant part in establishing many new airlines and

By 1939, KLM had a fleet of 22 21-seat DC-3s, operating to 61 destinations in 29 countries. In the same year the type carried a total of 98,000 passengers. A few KLM DC-3s escaped to the UK during the German invasion of the Netherlands, surviving to fly with BOAC on the Bristol-Lisbon route.

air services.

Of low-wing cantilever configuration, the DC-3 is of all-metal construction except for its fabric-covered control surfaces. A feature of the wing is its multi-spar structure, derived from that of the DC-1, which has played a significant part in the long service life of these aircraft. The all-metal fuselage is almost circular in cross-section, and the landing gear is of the tailwheel type, with a fully-castoring tailwheel and main units that retract into the underside of the engine nacelles, leaving the lower part of each wheel exposed; the cantilever tail unit is of metal construction.

Civil DC-3s delivered to US airlines before the nation became involved in World War II played a most important part in the development of reliable

Variants

DST: original model with accommodation for 28 day or 14 night passengers, and powered by Wright Cyclone radials (21 built)
DST-A: similar to the DST but powered by Twin Wasp radials (19 built)
DC-3: basic day passenger transport with accommodation for between 21 and 28 passengers, and power provided by Cyclones (266 built)
DC-3A: basic day passenger transport similar to the DC-3 but powered by Twin Wasp engines (114 built)
DC-3B: convertible model with seat/berths in the forward cabin and seats in the after cabin for 28 day passengers and fewer night passengers; recognisable by small extra windows on each side over the first and third main windows (10 built)

national air routes. It has been recorded that, in the period 1936-41, national passenger mileage in the USA increased by almost 600 per cent, a growth that was very largely due to the Douglas DC-3, which was the primary equipment of most US airlines in this period and whose safety record has

become almost legendary. Civil models (including the DST) were built in five series, and the standard powerplant was either the Wright SGR-1820 Cyclone or the Pratt & Whitney Twin Wasp, in ratings between 1,000 and 1,200 hp (746 and 895 kW) for various maximum take-off weights.

SPECIFICATION	
Douglas DC-3A	23,200 ft (7070 m); range
Type: two-crew medium transport aircraft	2,125 miles (3420 km)
Powerplant: two Pratt & Whitney S1C3G Twin Wasp radial piston engines each rated at 1,200 hp (895 kW)	**Weights:** empty 16,865 lb (7650 kg); maximum take-off 25,200 lb (11431 kg)
Performance: maximum speed 230 mph (370 km/h) at 8,500 ft (2590 m); cruising speed 207 mph (307 km/h) at optimum altitude; initial climb rate 1,130 ft (344 m) per minute; service ceiling	**Dimensions:** wingspan 95 ft (28.96 m); length 64 ft 5½ in (19.65 m); height 16 ft 11⅛ in (5.16 m); wing area 987.00 sq ft (91.69 m²)
	Payload: up to 28 passengers carried in an enclosed cabin

Douglas DC-4E, DC-4, C-54 Skymaster and R5D

Under the initial designation **DC-4**, subsequently changed to **DC-4E (DC-4 Experimental)**, Douglas designed and built the prototype of a new advanced civil transport to supersede the DC-3. This costly project was financed by Douglas together with five US airlines, which each contributed $100,000. The DC-4E emerged as an all-metal low-wing monoplane with a large circular-section fuselage, a tail unit incorporating a central fin-and-rudder assembly plus endplate fin-and-rudder assemblies, and retractable tricycle landing gear with very large single main wheels retracting inwards into the wing. The powerplant comprised four R-2180 radial engines in outward-angled nacelles on the leading edges of the wing.

This prototype made its maiden flight on 7 June 1938, by which time two of the financing airlines (Pan American and TWA) had withdrawn. The performance and operating economics of the new transport proved disappointing, largely as a result of the fact that the type was pushing the state of the art a little too far in its use of features such as power-boosted controls, an auxiliary power system, AC electrical power and provision for pressurisation. This led to the decision by Douglas and the remaining three airlines (American, Eastern and United) to embark on the alternative course of developing another transport that would be less complex and less costly; this emerged

as the **DC-4** and **C-54** family. The sole DC-4E prototype was later sold to Japan, where it received the designation **LXD1 (Navy Experimental Type D Transport)** and was used by Nakajima as the basis of the G5N heavy bomber.

The new DC-4 of 1939 was almost a different design, considerably lighter in construction and possessing a new high-aspect-ratio wing, a conventional tail unit with a single fin-and-rudder assembly, and retractable tricycle landing gear with twin wheels on each of the main units. Initial powerplant selection had been for four engines each of around 1,000 hp (746 kW), but after discussion with

interested airlines the type was put into production without even the prior construction of a prototype with four 1,450-hp (1081-kW) R-2000-2SD1G Twin Wasp radial engines.

Before the first aircraft had flown, the USA became embroiled in World War II. This meant that the aircraft on the production line were completed for the USAAF under the designation **C-54 Skymaster**, the first of these flying with military markings on 14 February 1942. These aircraft were virtually drab-painted civil airliners, but production contracts were soon drawn up for militarised versions capable of deployment for the transport of troops, cargo and

This aircraft was the first C-54D to be built. It was later converted by Convair to the SC-54D standard illustrated.

casualties. First of these variants for the USAAF was the **C-54A** with a strengthened floor, a cargo door and handling equipment, followed by other military models, with development progressing along the line of maximum seating capacity (50) for short/medium-range operations and restricted seating (20) for long-range flights. The DC-4 was also built for the US Navy as the **R5D** in many variants, construction for the two US services exceeding 1,000 aircraft.

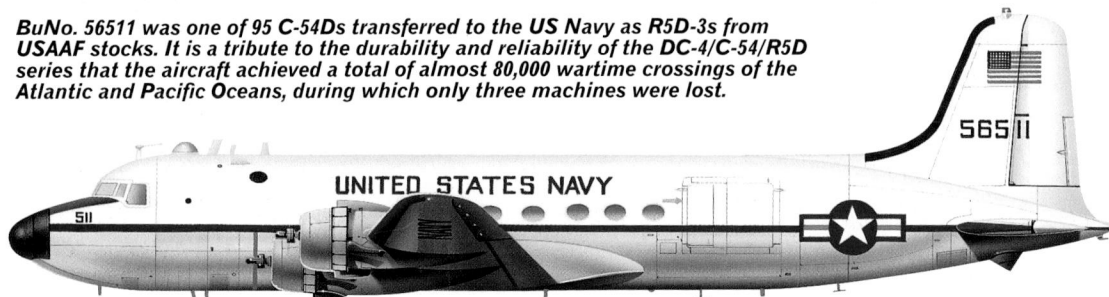

BuNo. 56511 was one of 95 C-54Ds transferred to the US Navy as R5D-3s from USAAF stocks. It is a tribute to the durability and reliability of the DC-4/C-54/R5D series that the aircraft achieved a total of almost 80,000 wartime crossings of the Atlantic and Pacific Oceans, during which only three machines were lost.

Variants

C-54: initial personnel transport with accommodation for 26 and powerplant of four 1,350-hp (1007-kW) R-2000-3 radial engines (24 built)

C-54A: fully militarised version capable of lifting 50 troops or 32,500 lb (14742 kg) of freight on the power of four 1,350-hp (1007-kW) R-2000-7 engines (252 built)

C-54B: similar to the C-54A apart from the deletion of two auxiliary fuel tanks in the cabin in favour of integral tankage in the wings; early aircraft had R-2000-3 engines and later aircraft R-2000-7 engines (220 built)

VC-54C: one C-54A modified as the personal transport of President Franklin D. Roosevelt, and named *Sacred Cow*

C-54D: major Skymaster production version, basically similar to the C-54B but powered by four 1,350-hp (1007-kW) R-2000-11 engines (380 built)

AC-54D: small number of C-54Ds modified with special electronic and communication gear to check air routes

EC-54D: 1962 redesignation of the AC-54D

HC-54D: 1962 redesignation of the SC-54D

JC-54D: nine C-54D machines modified for operations concerned with missile nosecone recovery

SC-54D: 38 aircraft modified by Convair for service with the MATS Air Rescue Service with special radar and observation blisters

TC-54D: C-54Ds modified to serve as multi-engine trainers

VC-54D: C-54Ds modified to serve as staff transports

C-54E: C-54D with the final two cabin fuel tanks replaced by bag tanks in the inner sections of the wing; the cabin was specially designed to facilitate rapid conversion between roles (passenger with 50 seats, freighter for 32,500 lb/14742 kg, and staff transport with 44 seats); by this time total fuel capacity had decreased from the 3,620 US gal (13703 litres) of the C-54 to the 3,520 US gal (13324 litres) of the C-54E (125 built)

XC-54F: one C-54B experimentally fitted with twin paratroop doors as the prototype of the proposed C-54F, based on the airframe of the C-54D

C-54G: troop-carrier version based on the C-54E with R-2000-9 engines (162 built)

VC-54G: C-54Gs converted as staff transports

C-54GM: designation of the DC-4 derivative produced by Canadair

C-54H: projected paratroop version with four R-2000-9 engines

C-54J: projected staff transport version based on the C-54G but without provision for freighting

XC-54K: one C-54E fitted experimentally with four 1,425-hp (1063-kW) Wright R-1820-HD Cyclone radial engines

C-54L: one C-54A modified with a revised fuel system

C-54M: designation of 38 C-54E aircraft stripped out to serve as coal-carriers during the Berlin Airlift; payload was increased by 2,500 lb (1134 kg)

MC-54M: 30 C-54Es fitted out as casevac aircraft with accommodation for 30 litters plus medical attendants, and used in the Korean War

EC-54U: post-1962 designation of R5D-4s modified with ECM equipment for evaluation and training

XC-112: projected version with cabin pressurisation and four Pratt & Whitney R-2800-22W radials

XC-114: prototype based on the C-54E with a fuselage stretch of 6 ft 9 in (2.06 m) and the powerplant of four 1,620-hp (1209-kW) Allison V-1710-131 Vee engines

XC-115: proposed version based on the XC-114 with four 1,650-hp (1231-kW) Packard V-1650-209 engines

XC-116: one prototype similar to the XC-114 but having thermal rather than pneumatic-boot de-icing

R5D-1: 56 C-54A aircraft transferred to the USN

R5C-1C: R5D-1s modified in service with a fuel system based on that of the C-54B

R5D-1F: staff transport version of the R5D-1, after 1962 designated **VC-54N**

R5D-1Z: interim designation for the R5D-1F/VC-54N model

R5D-2: 30 C-54Bs transferred to the USN

R5D-2F: staff transport version of the R5D-2, after 1962 designated **VC-54P**

R5D-2Z: interim designation of the R5D-2F/VC-54P model

R5D-3: designation of 95 C-54Ds transferred to the USN, after 1962 designated **C-54Q** (basic transport), **RC-54V** (photographic aircraft) and **VC-54Q** (staff transport), the last having served under the interim designation **R5D-3Z**

R5D-4: designation of 20 C-54Es transferred to the USN

R5D-4R: personnel transport version of the R5D-4, after 1962 designated **C-54R**

R5D-5: 13 naval equivalents of the C-54G used mainly by the US Coast Guard, and after 1962 designated **C-54S**

R5D-5R: personnel transport version of the R5D-5, after 1962 designated **VC-54T**

R5D-5Z: staff transport version of the R5D-5, after 1962 designated **VC-54S**

R5D-6: projected model equivalent to the C-54J

DC-4-1009: post-war civil model intended for passenger operations with maximum accommodation for 44 passengers, later increased to 86

DC-4-1037: post-war civil model intended for freight operations, and so retaining the large door of the C-54 series

Skymaster Mk I: RAF designation of one C-54B and 22 C-54D machines received under Lend-Lease

Douglas DC-4E, DC-4, C-54 Skymaster and R5D (cont.)

At the end of military production Douglas built 79 examples of the DC-4 for the civil market and these, together with large numbers of demilitarised C-54 aircraft, gave valuable service on long-range passenger and cargo routes until the new-generation airliners became available. Specialised derivatives of the DC-4 included 21 aircraft with 1,725-hp (1286-kW) Rolls-Royce Merlin Vee engines, devel-

Douglas abandoned the DC-4E as over-complex. The machine featured a distinctive triple-fin and rudder tail arrangement.

oped by Canadair in Montreal for service with the RCAF, which allocated the name **North Star** to the type. There followed production of the **DC-4M** for civil operators. Another DC-4 derivative was the **Aviation Traders Carvair**.

Accommodation on

these different DC-4s varied considerably. The basic version provided for a crew of four and 44 passengers with plenty of

room between the seats, and this enabled some operators to introduce as many as 86 seats in high-density layouts. The DC-4M carried up to 62 economy-class passengers.

Apart from many record-breaking flights, the DC-4 is remembered in aviation

history for its very considerable contribution to the Berlin Airlift of 1948-9. The use of the series by major airlines dwindled fairly rapidly as more advanced aircraft became available, but a small number remained in service into 2000.

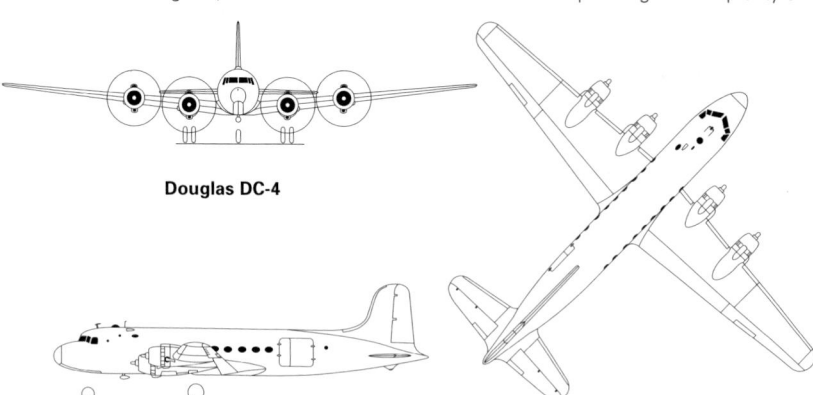

Douglas DC-4

SPECIFICATION	
Douglas DC-4-1009	range 2,500 miles (4023 km) with
Type: four-crew transport aircraft	an 11,440-lb (5189-kg) payload
Powerplant: four Pratt & Whitney	**Weights:** empty 43,300 lb
R-2000-2SD13G Twin Wasp radial	(19640 kg); maximum take-off
piston engines each rated at	73,000 lb (33112 kg)
1,450 hp (1081 kW)	**Dimensions:** wingspan 117 ft 6 in
Performance: maximum speed	(35.81 m); length 93 ft 10 in
280 mph (451 km/h) at 14,000 ft	(28.60 m); height 27 ft 6 in
(4265 m); cruising speed 227 mph	(8.38 m); wing area 1,460.00 sq ft
(365 km/h) at 10,000 ft (3050 m);	(135.63 m²)
service ceiling 22,300 ft (6800 m);	**Payload:** up to 86 passengers

Douglas DC-5 and R3D

Created by the El Segundo facility of the Douglas company, the **DC-5** was designed and developed as a 16/22-passenger commercial transport for local service operations out of smaller airports. Interestingly, at a time when the low-wing configuration was in the ascendant, the DC-5 was a high-wing monoplane, although it also featured tricycle landing gear, which was then relatively novel. With a design gross weight of 18,500 lb (8391 kg), the DC-5 was offered with the powerplant of two Pratt & Whitney R-1690 Hornet or Wright R-1820 Cyclone radial engines.

The prototype was powered by 850-hp (634-kW) GR-1820-F62 engines and flew for the first time on 20 February 1939. Orders for the new type were placed by KLM,

Pennsylvania Central Airways and SCADTA of Colombia for four, six and two aircraft respectively, but the programme was overtaken by the outbreak of World War II and only the KLM aircraft were delivered. Although intended for service in Europe, two went first to the Netherlands West Indies to link Curaçao and Surinam and the other two to Batavia in the Netherlands East Indies. All four were used to evacuate civilians from Java to Australia in 1942 and one, damaged at Kemajoran airport outside Batavia on 9 February 1942, was captured by the Japanese and extensively test-flown at Tachikawa air force base. The three surviving DC-5s were operated in Australia by the Allied Directorate of Air Transport and were given the US Army Air Forces'

designation **C-110**.

The earliest DC-5 military operations, however, were by the US Navy which had ordered seven examples in 1939. Three were **R3D-1** 18-seat personnel transports, the first of which crashed before delivery, and the other four were **R3D-2** aircraft for the US Marine Corps with R-1820-44 engines, a large sliding cargo door, and bucket seats for 22 paratroops. The prototype, after certification and development flying had been completed, was sold with a 16-seat executive interior to William E. Boeing, and was later impressed for USN use as the sole **R3D-3**.

Derived from the DB-7, the DC-5 was dramatically superior to the DC-3 designed at the company's Santa Monica facility. Nevertheless, the designer, 'Ed' Heinemann, was told

With its low-slung fuselage and tricycle landing gear, the DC-5 was an eminently more practical transport design than the DC-3/C-47.

by General H. H. Arnold to cancel the programme

because of the USAAF's selection of the C-47.

SPECIFICATION	
Douglas R3D-2	23,700 ft (7225 m); range 935 miles
Type: two-crew transport aircraft	(1505 km)
Powerplant: two Wright	**Weights:** empty 13,863 lb
R-1820-44 Cyclone radial piston	(6288 kg); maximum take-off
engines each rated at 1,000 hp	21,000 lb (9525 kg)
(746 kW)	**Dimensions:** wingspan 78 ft
Performance: maximum speed	(23.77 m); length 62 ft 2 in
221 mph (356 km/h) at 7,700 ft	(18.96 m); height 22 ft 7 in
(2345 m); cruising speed 202 mph	(6.88 m); wing area 824.00 sq ft
(325 km/h) at 10,000 ft (3050 m);	(76.55 m²)
initial climb rate 1,000 ft (305 m)	**Payload:** up to 22 paratroops or
per minute; service ceiling	freight

Douglas DC-6, C-118 Liftmaster and R6D

Given its major involvement during World War II in a war whose main theatres were on the other sides of the North Atlantic and, perhaps more taxingly, the Pacific, the US Army Air Forces understandably became very interested in long-range landplanes. The excellent record of the C-54 induced the USAAF to look for a larger-capacity transport from the same source,

and the first of these to fly, on 15 February 1946, had the designation **XC-112A**. By then, of course, World War II had been over for six months, the US forces were not in the short term interested in the acquisition of expensive new transport aircraft, and the new type was therefore developed for service with post-war airlines under the company identification **DC-6**.

The DC-6 retained the same wing as its predecessor, but had a pressurised fuselage that was lengthened by 6 ft 9 in (2.06 m) to give increased passenger capacity. Seating for 48 to 52 was standard, but a high-density layout could accommodate 86. The powerplant of the initial DC-6 comprised four 2,100-hp (1566-kW)

R-2800-CA15 Double Wasp radial engines, and the first of 50 airliners ordered by American Airlines made its initial flight on 29 June 1946. The DC-6 entered service in April 1947, initially on the New York-Chicago route of American Airlines.

During 1948 the company began development of an increased-capacity version with its

fuselage lengthened by 5 ft (1.52 m) and powered by 2,400-hp (1790-kW) R-2800-CB16 engines. Offered initially in an all-cargo version as the **DC-6A**, with two freight doors on the port side (one forward and one aft of the wing), no windows, and strengthened flooring, the DC-6A was followed by the generally similar **DC-6B** passenger transport. In

Delivered as logistics transports, the US Navy's R6D-1s were ordered before similar machines were ordered by the USAF. Forty R6D-1s were transferred to the USAF in 1962.

early production examples the standard seating capacity was 54, but high-density layouts for up to 102 passengers were introduced at a later time.

Civil DC-6s were built alongside 166 aircraft for the US Air Force and Navy, partially to support operations of the Military Air Transport Service (MATS). Those which served with the USAF had the designation **C-118A** and could accommodate 74 passengers, or 27,000 lb (12247 kg) of cargo, or 60 stretcher cases. The 29th DC-6 was given a VIP interior for the use of President Harry S. Truman as the **VC-118** that was named as *The Independence* and possessed a cabin for 24 passengers, or night accommodation for 12, and an executive stateroom. The DC-6s in USN service included 61 **R6D-1** and four **R6D-1Z** aircraft, the latter with VIP interiors; these became **C-118B** and **VC-118B** machines in 1962. Other military

services also acquired DC-6s, the majority of them ex-civil aircraft.

Last of the civil designations was **DC-6C**, this designation being applicable to a convertible cargo/passenger version that was generally similar to the DC-6A but with standard cabin windows. Construction of DC-6 civil and XC-112A/C-118/R6D military aircraft totalled 704. Among variants were two DC-6Bs modified by Sabena with a swing-tail arrangement to simplify the direct in-loading of bulky cargo. There were also a number of DC-6Bs converted with a 3,000-US gal (11356-litre) capacity underfuselage tank to carry fire-retardant chemicals, and these continue to see considerable service in Canada and the USA during periods of high fire risk in national timberlands.

The DC-6 came to be regarded as a worthy example of the reliable and efficient piston-engined airliners that

were soon displaced by first-generation turboprop- and turbojet-powered aircraft. As they became surplus to the requirements of major users, DC-6 transports were eagerly sought by operators in the lower echelons of air transport. They, too, benefited from the DC-6's excellence, and the type remains in declining service into the beginning of the 21st century.

Douglas DC-7

The design and subsequent development of the **DC-7** was prompted by American Airlines, which was seeking an aircraft superior in performance to the Lockheed Super Constellation being used by TWA. The Super 'Connie' benefited from the use of new Wright Turbo-Compound engines, and to meet American Airlines' requirement, the Douglas design team decided to develop an improved version of the DC-6B using this new engine.

The initial DC-7 was a direct development of the DC-6B with the fuselage lengthened by 3 ft 4 in (1.02 m) to allow for the inclusion of an additional row of seats, and the installation of 3,250-hp (2424-kW) R-3350 Turbo-Compound engines made possible an increase in

gross weight of 15,200 lb (6895 kg), which in turn required some strengthening of the landing gear. There were also some minor changes in detail, but externally the DC-7 appeared little different from the DC-6B when it made its first flight on 18 May 1953 for a service debut in November of the same year. A total of 105 DC-7s was built, and the 112 **DC-7B** which followed had only minor changes. Most importantly, the engine nacelles were extended farther aft to permit the installation of saddle tanks within the rear of nacelles that were made of titanium, then a new material.

Not all operators opted for this additional fuel capacity, but those which did, such as Pan American which inaugurated non-stop services between

The first DC-7 demonstrates the type's similarity to the DC-6 and the shorter overwing section of the engine nacelles on this initial version.

New York and London with the DC-7B on 13 June 1955, soon discovered that fuel capacity was marginal for North Atlantic services. In fact, with a full load and normal headwinds, the DC-7Bs used to operate the east to west service frequently had to divert for a refuelling stop. This was clearly unsatisfactory and indeed potentially dangerous, so Douglas set about the task of developing a version of the DC-7B with greater range.

The third version was the **DC-7C**, and this introduced a wing of increased span to provide for greater fuel capacity. This was achieved by inserting a new parallel-chord section of wing between the fuselage and the inboard engine nacelles, and this had the added advantage of improving the cabin environment by reducing engine noise. During the development of the DC-7C, Curtiss-Wright was able to offer a further increase in engine power and, as a result, the fuselage was lengthened by the insertion of a 'plug' 3 ft 4 in (1.02 m) long to provide accommodation for up to 105 passengers. Production of the DC-7C totalled 120, and the alphanumeric suffix of this version became corrupted most appropriately to **Seven Seas**, for this aircraft was able to take

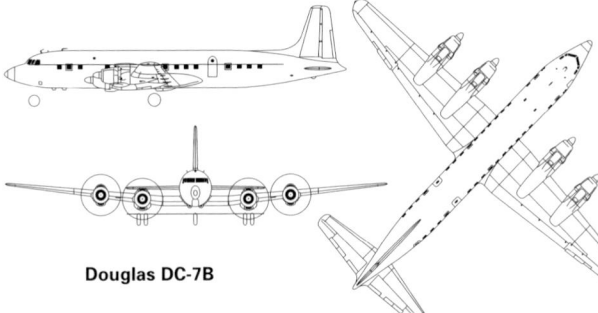

Douglas DC-7B

the oceans in its stride without any problems. The DC-7C was not only used on the North Atlantic and Pacific Ocean services, but also made possible non-stop scheduled operations across the continental USA, and was additionally used by SAS to inaugurate a route between Europe and the Far East over the North Pole.

An improved **DC-7D** was planned with four 5,730-eshp (4273-ekW)

Rolls-Royce Tyne turboprops, but the emergence of the new generation of turbojet-powered airliners, such as the Boeing 707 and the company's own DC-8, meant that this project remained unfulfilled. Because the Turbo-Compound engine increased operating costs, the DC-7 series of fine airliners disappeared quickly from the aviation scene when replaced by the first turboprop- and turbojet-powered airliners.

Douglas DC-8

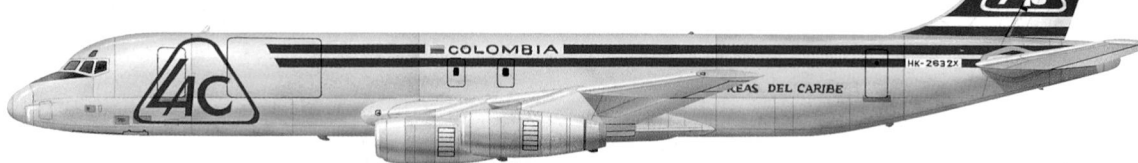

VIASA received this aircraft new in November 1965 as a DC-8 Series 53 airliner. It subsequently passed between several owners before being converted to Series 54F configuration by the manufacturer in 1977. It joined LAC Colombia as a dedicated freighter in 1981 with the name Mary de Donado.

Aware that Boeing was well advanced with its Model 707 long-range airliner and anxious to maintain a substantial share of the market for civil transports, Douglas announced on 7 June 1955 its intention of developing a turbojet-powered airliner to supersede the DC-7. The design of the DC-8 went ahead without delay, and the sole prototype/ demonstrator made the new type's first flight on 30 May 1958. In external features the DC-8 was very similar to the Model 707; it was of the same basic configuration with swept flying surfaces in the form of a low-set wing carrying four pylon-mounted turbojet engines and a tail unit with single horizontal and vertical surfaces. The tricycle landing gear had a steerable nose unit with twin wheels and two main units each with a four-wheel bogie whose two rear wheels were free castoring to make possible small-radius turns.

Nine aircraft took part in the certification programme, this total comprising three, four and two machines with JT3C turbojet engines, JT4A turbojet engines and Rolls-Royce Conway turbofan engines respectively. This seems a lot of development aircraft but, conscious of Boeing's lead, the Douglas company wanted to gain FAA approval for the DC-8 at the earliest possible date. The required certification was awarded on 31 August 1959, when Delta Airlines and United Air Lines became the recipients of the first aircraft.

During the following nine years Douglas built a total of 294 examples of the transports, produced in five series and all of the same overall dimensions with a fuselage measuring 150 ft 6 in (45.87 m) in length and providing accommodation for a typical payload of 150 passengers. They comprised the **DC-8 Series 10**, which was the original domestic version powered by four 13,500-lb st (60.05-kN) JT3C-6 engines; the generally similar **DC-8 Series 20** with more powerful engines for operation from hot and/or high airfields; the long-range intercontinental **DC-8 Series 30** with, typically, 16,800-lb st (74.73-kN) JT4A-9 engines; the basically similar intercontinental **DC-8 Series 40** with 17,500-lb st (77.84-kN) Conway Mk 509 turbofan engines; and the **DC-8 Series 50** with JT3Ds and a rearranged cabin interior to provide accommodation for a maximum of 189 passengers. A major improvement developed subsequently for these versions of the DC-8 was a new leading edge: this changed the wing profile, reducing drag and improving both speed and range. Standard on all late-production DC-8s, this leading edge was retrofitted to many early aircraft. Series 50 aircraft were available also as **DC-8F Jet Traders** in **AF** (all-cargo) or **CF** (convertible passenger/ cargo) versions.

The foregoing were followed from 1967 by three variants of the **DC-8 Super Sixty** subclass, of which 262 were built. These variants comprised the **DC-8 Super 61** with a fuselage extended by 36 ft 8 in (11.18 m) and able to carry up to 219 passengers; the ultra long-range **DC-8 Super 62** with wingspan increased by 6 ft (1.83 m) and with standard seating for 189 passengers in a fuselage lengthened by 6 ft 8 in (2.03 m); and the **DC-8 Super 63** combining the long fuselage of the Super 61 with the aerodynamic improvements of the Super 62. All versions of the Super Sixty series were available in all-cargo or convertible cargo/ passenger configurations.

In 1979 the Douglas Aircraft Company, now a division of the McDonnell Douglas Corporation, announced plans to re-engine Series 61, 62 and 63 aircraft with advanced-technology engines as the **DC-8 Super Seventy** series, numbered 71, 72 and 73 respectively. This programme involved installation of four General Electric/SNECMA CFM56 advanced turbofan engines, each rated at 22,000 lb st (97.86 kN), and certification of the **DC-8 Super 71** with this powerplant was gained during April 1982. Similarly powered, the first **DC-8 Super 72** and **DC-8 Super 73** conversions made their initial flights on 5 December 1981 and 4 March 1982 respectively, gaining certification later in the same year. Overall management of this re-engining programme was handled by Cammacorp of Los Angeles and the programme ended in March 1986 after the conversion of 110 aircraft. The more advanced powerplant was considerably quieter than that of existing DC-8s, and the Super Seventy family also demonstrated significant improvements in performance and operating costs.

The French Armée de l'Air was the first of the small number of military operators of the DC-8, acquiring one **Series 55CF** new and several others ex-airline. The of the French fleet eventually comprised one Series 55 and three Series 72 (ex-Series 62) aircraft for long-range strategic transport and VIP work. A fifth DC-8, a **Series 53** machine, remains the only aircraft in service, flying in the ECM/ Elint role in the hands of the 51 Escadron Electronique 'Aubrac' at Evreux.

Two ex-Swissair **DC-8 Series 62CF** aircraft, equipping the Escuadrilla Presidencial of the Fuerza Aérea Peruana, are the only other aircraft of this type remaining in military service for the transport role. More specialised was the single ex-United Airlines **Series 54F** freighter flown by the US Navy as the **EC-24A** from 1987. This unique aircraft, which was retired in 1999, had an extensive electronic suite and served with the Fleet Electronic Warfare Support Group (FEWSG) to simulate the C³ threat in fleet exercises.

N787FT was delivered to Flying Tiger Line as a Series 63AF in 1968. It is illustrated in Series 73AF form after conversion in 1982.

Douglas DC-9

Although facing a considerable degree of competition, Douglas initiated the design of a completely new short-range twin-jet transport at the beginning of the 1960s. With confidence in the design, construction of this aircraft began on 26 July 1963 and the first **Douglas DC-9**, as the type was designated, made its maiden flight on 25 February 1965. At that time Douglas had received orders for only 58 DC-9s, and an anxious period ensued before the company began to feel that its investment might be recouped. It is unlikely that it could have then believed that the DC-9 would prove to be the company's greatest commercial aircraft success. A cantilever low-wing monoplane with swept wings and a T-tail with all-swept surfaces, the initial **DC-9 Series 10 Model 11** production aircraft accommodated a flight crew of two, cabin attendants, and between

In its Series 15 form, the short-fuselage DC-9 gained extra power.

Variants

DC-9 Series 10 Model 15: as Series 10 Model 11, except for installation of 14,000-lb (62.26-kN) thrust JT8D-1 turbofan engines for operation at a higher gross weight
DC-9 Series 20: version for hot/high use with 4-ft (1.22-m) increase in wingspan, two 14,500-lb (64.48-kN) thrust JT8D-9 turbofans and accommodation for up to 90 passengers
DC-9 Series 30: developed version with fuselage lengthened by 14 ft 10¾ in (4.54 m) to accommodate 105 to 119 passengers, wingspan as Series 20, and initially with 14,000-lb (62.26-kN) thrust JT8D-7 turbofans; later available with engines of 14,500- to 16,000-lb (64.48- to 71.15-kN) thrust
DC-9 Series 40: lengthened fuselage (by 6 ft 3¾ in/1.92 m) version of Series 30 seating up to 132 passengers; produced only with engines of 14,500- to 16,000-lb (64.48- to 71.15-kN) thrust
DC-9 Series 50: short-/medium-range development of Series 30, with fuselage lengthened by an additional 8 ft (2.44 m) to seat a maximum of 139 passengers; redesigned cabin interior and produced with 15,500- to 16,000-lb (68.93- to 71.15-kN) thrust turbofans only
C-9A Nightingale: aeromedical transport version of DC-9 Series 30 in service with the US Air Force; 21 built
C-9B Skytrain II: fleet logistic transport combining features of the DC-9 Series 30 and 40; in service with the US Navy and Marines (15 built) and Kuwait (2 built, known as **C-9K** aircraft)
C-9C: VIP transport, based on the DC-9 Series 30, in service with the USAF's 99th Airlift Squadron; 3 built

80 and 90 passengers according to layout. Power was provided by two 12,250-lb (54.48-kN) thrust Pratt & Whitney JT8D-5 turbofans, pod mounted one on each side of the rear fuselage, and it was this version that first entered service with Delta Airlines on 8 December 1965. It was the company's intention from the outset to produce and market the DC-9 in several versions, to meet the differing requirements of civil operators, and the series was extended by special conversions for military use. **DC-9 Series 30** and subsequent versions were made available in specialised sub-variants comprising freight (**F**), convertible (**CF**), and passenger/freight (**RC**) configurations.

SPECIFICATION	
Douglas DC-9 Series 50	97 passengers 2,067 miles (3327 km)
Type: short/medium-range airliner	
Powerplant: two Pratt & Whitney JT8D-17 turbofans each rated at 16,000-lb st (71.15-kN)	**Weights:** empty 61,880 lb (28068 kg); maximum take-off 121,000 lb (54885 kg)
Performance: maximum cruising speed 558 mph (898 km/h); long-range cruising speed 510 mph (821 km/h); maximum range with	**Dimensions:** wingspan 93 ft 5 in (28.47 m); length 133 ft 7¼ in (40.72 m); height 28 ft (8.53 m); wing area 1,000.7 sq ft (92.97 m²)

Douglas DC-10 and McDonnell Douglas KC-10A Extender

Design of the **Douglas DC-10** began in 1966, to meet a requirement of American Airlines for a large-capacity civil transport. With the receipt of an order for 25 plus 25 options from American Airlines and 30 plus 30 options from United Airlines, the DC-10 was put into production in April 1968. Of low-set swept-wing monoplane

Swissair was the first carrier to introduce the DC-10 on over-water services, using the DC-10-30 (illustrated) on its Zürich-Montreal-Chicago route. The airline also used two DC-10-30ERs.

Variants

DC-10 Series 10: initial production version, seating a maximum 380 passengers, and powered by General Electric CF6-6D or CF6-6D1 turbofan engines of 40,000-lb (177.88-kN) or 41,000-lb (182.32-kN) thrust respectively; 122 built
DC-10 Series 10CF: convertible passenger/cargo version of the Series 10; 9 built
DC-10 Series 15: basically similar to Series 10, but with CF6-50C2F engines, each of 46,500-lb (206.79-kN) thrust, permitting higher gross weight; 7 built
DC-10 Series 30: extended-range intercontinental version; wingspan increased by 10 ft (3.05 m), increased fuel capacity, standard landing gear supplemented by a two-wheel main gear unit beneath the fuselage, and power provided by CF6-50A or CF6-50C turbofan engines, each of 49,000-lb (217.90-kN) or 51,000-lb (226.80-kN) thrust respectively; 156 built
DC-10 Series 30CF: convertible passenger/cargo version of Series 30, late production with 52,500-lb (233.47-kN) thrust CF6-50C1 engines; 26 built
DC-10 Series 30ER: extended-range version of Series 30, with additional fuel and 54,000-lb (240.14-kN) thrust CF6-50C2B engines; five built
DC-10 Series 40: intercontinental-range version, similar to Series 30, but first 22 aircraft with 49,400-lb (219.68-kN) thrust Pratt & Whitney JT9D-20 turbofans and subsequent aircraft with JT9D-59A engines each of 53,000-lb (235.69-kN) thrust; 42 built
KC-10A Extender: under this designation the USAF selected the DC-10 in late 1977 to meet its Advanced Tanker/Cargo Aircraft requirement. Basically a conversion of the DC-10 Series 30CF, the KC-10A has additional fuel cells in the lower fuselage, an inflight-refuelling boom, boom operator's station, inflight refuelling receptacle and an improved cargo-handling system; a total of 60 KC-10As was delivered, the first of them being flown on 12 July 1980; initial deliveries to the USAF began on 17 March 1981
MD-10: under this designation Boeing is converting ex-airline DC-10s with two-crew EFIS cockpits for freighter use by FedEx

configuration, and with all-swept tail surfaces, the DC-10 adopted a 'conventional' three-engine configuration, with one engine pylon-mounted beneath each wing and the third engine installed at the base of the fin. The initial production **DC-10 Series 10** was flown first on 29 August 1970, and following receipt of certification, on 29 July 1971, American Airlines introduced the type into

revenue service one week later, on 5 August. By the spring of 1983 the company had received orders for a total of 367 civil DC-10s, all of which had been delivered, but the production line remained open in autumn 1983 for manufacture of the generally similar **McDonnell Douglas KC-10A Extender** inflight-refuelling and cargo aircraft for the US Air Force.

SPECIFICATION	
Douglas DC-10 Series 30	**Weights:** empty 267,197 lb (121199 kg); maximum take-off 680,000 lb (263084 kg)
Type: commercial transport	
Powerplant: three General Electric CF6-50C turbofans each rated at 51,000 lb (226.80 kN) thrust	**Dimensions:** wingspan 165 ft 4½ in (50.41 m); length 182 ft 1 in (55.50 m); height 58 ft 1 in (17.70 m); wing area 3,958.0 sq ft (367.70 m²)
Performance: maximum cruising speed 564 mph (908 km/h) at 30,000 ft (9145 m); service ceiling at average cruise weight 33,400 ft (10180 m); range with maximum payload 4,605 miles (7411 km)	**Accommodation:** standard seating for between 255 and 270 passengers, with a maximum of 380 in all-economy configuration

Douglas DF

With increasing airline interest during the 1930s in the use of flying-boats for long-range passenger services, Douglas developed as a private venture the prototype of a twin-engined aircraft of this type. The **Douglas DF (Douglas Flying-boat)** was a high-wing cantilever monoplane that featured a wing carrying retractable stabilising floats. The 'boat had a deep and broad hull, upswept at the rear to mount a conventional tail unit. Construction was all-metal, except for the fabric-covered control surfaces, and this attractive machine was powered by two Wright SGR-1820-G2 Cyclone radial engines in nacelles mounted on the leading edges of the wing. There was also space for galleys, two toilets and a volume of baggage and cargo. Accommodation was provided for a maximum of 32 passengers.

SPECIFICATION	
Douglas DF	minute; service ceiling 13,900 ft (12927 kg); range 1,500 miles (2414 km) with 32 passengers
Type: four-crew transport flying-boat	
Powerplant: two Wright SGR-1820-G2 Cyclone radial piston engines each rated at 1,000 hp (746 kW)	**Weights:** empty 17,315 lb (7854 kg); maximum take-off 28,500 lb (12927 kg)
Performance: maximum speed 178 mph (286 km/h) at 6,800 ft (2075 m); cruising speed 160 mph (257 km/h) at optimum altitude; initial climb rate 800 ft (244 m) per	**Dimensions:** wingspan 95 ft (28.96 m); length 69 ft 10½ in (21.30 m); height 24 ft 6 in (7.47 m); wing area 1,295.00 sq ft (120.31 m²)
	Payload: up to 32 passengers

Douglas DF (cont.)

J-ANES was the DF-151 evaluated by the Japanese military as the **HXD-1**. In Aeroflot service, the last DF-195 served the Leningrad-Sebastopol route until 1940.

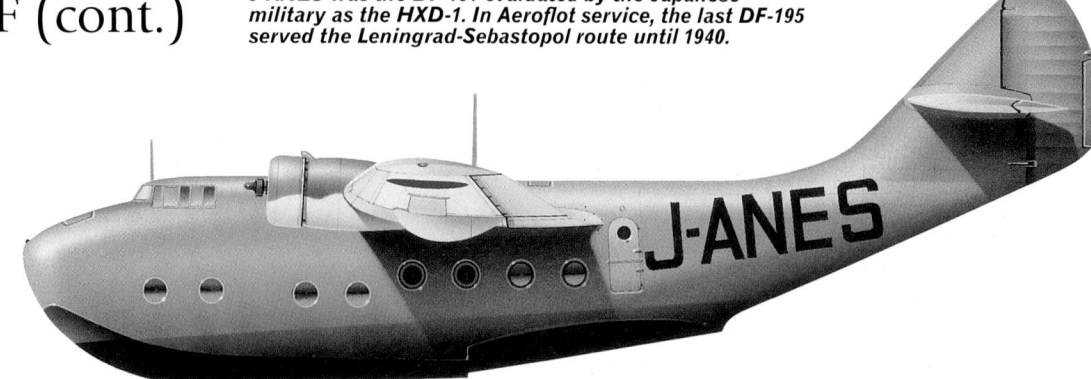

First flown in September 1936, the DF completed its flight test programme satisfactorily, but Douglas was unable to obtain a US buyer for the prototype and three other production 'boats that were under construction. Two of them were completed to the **DF-195** standard and sold to the USSR, while the other two were completed to the **DF-151** standard and sold to Japan. The latter were ostensibly for the Greater Japan Air Lines, but were taken for use by the Imperial Japanese navy air force under the designation **HXD-1** and **HXD-2 (Navy Experimental Type D Flying-Boat)**. One of the 'boats was transferred to Kawanishi for the company to disassemble and thus gain knowledge of current US constructional techniques, and the other was retained by the Japanese navy for flight evaluation, being used until it crashed during August 1938. One Soviet aircraft remained in service into 1940.

Douglas Dolphin and Sinbad (C-21, C-26, C-29 and R2D)

The **Dolphin** high-wing cantilever monoplane amphibian flying-boat was developed from the **Sinbad**, a flying-boat powered by two 300-hp (224-kW) Wright Whirlwind J-5C radials and which had flown for the first time in July 1930. The only example of the Sinbad served with the US Coast Guard from 1931 to 1939. The Dolphin and the Sinbad had the same engine layout: two radial engines, each driving a tractor propeller, mounted in the Dolphin on a complex arrangement of struts over the wing. The landing gear introduced on the Dolphin comprised main units attached to the hull by hinged Vee struts and to the undersurfaces of the wing by oleo legs. While the Sinbad had a tail-skid for use in conjunction with its detachable beaching gear, the Dolphin had a tail wheel, located at the rear of the second hull step. In flight or for operations from water, the main wheels were retracted above the waterline. The pilot and co-pilot were seated side-by-side in a fully enclosed cockpit just forward of the leading edge of the wing, with the passenger cabin immediately behind them.

The Dolphin was characterised by an auxiliary aerofoil surface, extending across the tops of the engine nacelles, to overcome turbulence problems. Early examples also had a pair of auxiliary fins to provide additional directional stability. The construction of the Dolphin was similar to that of the Sinbad, with an all-metal hull and a plywood-covered wooden wing, but the bow of the Dolphin's hull was redesigned.

Total production of the Dolphin was 58 'boats, but the type achieved a remarkable reputation for dependability, and several sea rescue successes by Dolphin 'boats of the USCG and USN caught the public imagination. There were no fewer than 17 versions of the Dolphin, these differing mainly in their engine installations and passenger cabin layouts. The main

*The Dolphin's distinctive auxiliary aerofoil surface is well illustrated by this **US Coast Guard OA-4B**. The undercarriage main wheels retracted upwards to lie exposed at an angle beneath the wing.*

Variants

Y1C-21: eight ordered in 1931 for the US Army Air Corps, and intended originally to escort bombardment units on over-sea flights, providing navigational and, if necessary, rescue assistance; the speed of the Martin B-10 and B-12 bombers coming into service rendered this policy impracticable and the 'boats, by then designated **C-21**, were used for staff transport duties in coastal areas; later they were loaned to the US Treasury (temporarily designated **FP-1**) for anti-smuggling border patrols to enforce Prohibition; although later redesignated **OA-3** (Observation Amphibian), the aircraft were used towards the end of their USAAC careers mainly as transports
Y1C-26: two delivered to the USAAC in 1933; these were the first Dolphins to feature the enlarged fin-and-rudder assembly and so dispense with the auxiliary fins; they were later redesignated **C-26** and then **OA-4**, and also **FP-2** when temporarily used by the US Treasury; later fitted with stainless steel wings and 400-hp (298-kW) Pratt & Whitney R-985-9 engines as **OA-4C**
C-26A: eight 'boats, differing only slightly from the C-26, were delivered soon after the Y1C-26s, and had the temporary US Treasury designation **FP-2A**; four were modernised on the same lines as the C-26 machines in 1936 and also redesignated OA-4C
C-26B: four 'boats were delivered to the USAAC in 1933 with the powerplant of two R-985-9 engines, and were later redesignated **OA-4B**; one was used for experiments with a fixed tricycle landing gear, while another was later converted to OA-4C standard
C-29: two built for the USAAC in 1933 with the powerplant of two 550-hp (410-kW) Pratt & Whitney R-1340-29 radial engines; when on loan to US Treasury the type was known as **FP-2B**
XRD-1: one 'boat delivered to the USN in August 1931; powered by two 435-hp (324-kW) Wright R-975E Whirlwind radial engines; used for seven years as a staff transport
RD: one civil **Model 1 Special** acquired for USCG patrol duties in August 1932; served until 1939

RD-2: of these four 'boats the first was of the same basic design as the C-26 and was delivered to the USCG with the powerplant of two 500-hp (373-kW) R-1340-10 Wasp Junior radial engines, while the last three 'boats were more similar to the C-26A; one was used as five-passenger luxury transport for President Franklin D. Roosevelt from June 1933, with the powerplant of two 410-hp (307-kW) R-1340-1 engines, later replaced by 500-hp (373-kW) R-1340-10 engines, and relegated to other duties in 1939; two others with 450-hp (336-kW) R-1340-29 engines were less luxurious and were used as naval staff transports until March 1940
RD-3: six delivered to the USN in 1935-6 as utility transport versions of the RD-2
RD-4: 10 built to a standard similar to that of the RD-3 but with 420-hp (313-kW) R-985-C1 engines; all were delivered to the USCG and employed mainly on air/sea rescue duties; four surviving 'boats were used for security coastal patrol when the USCG was taken over directly by the USN on American entry into World War II; all had been withdrawn from active service by June 1943
Civil Dolphin: apart from the first two Dolphins delivered, 10 more civil examples of the Dolphin were built; the sole **Model 3** was a four-seat luxury 'boat built for an American millionaire in 1931; it was then sold to an Australian owner and later taken over by the Royal Australian Air Force for liaison work during 1942-5; the remaining civil machines resembled the USCG's RD-4; one, with 550-hp (410-kW) Wasp S1D1 engines, was sold to a French owner, while another six were all built to the individual order of wealthy Americans; one of them was bought by William E. Boeing, founder of the Boeing company; another was used on the Los Angeles-Santa Catalina airline. The last two Dolphins went to the China National Aviation Corporation (a Pan Am subsidiary) and operated between Shanghai and Canton for a number of years

design change came with the 14th 'boat built, the fin-and-rudder assembly being redesigned with greater area, thus permitting the deletion of the auxiliary fins. The wing area was also increased in area and the hull length-ened.

The first two Dolphin 'boats were built for the Wilmington-Catalina Airline, linking the Los Angeles area with Santa Catalina Island, a distance of just 20 miles (32 km). Powered by 300-hp (224-kW) J-5C engines, these 'boats were known originally as **Model 1** aircraft, with accommodation for two pilots and six passengers; these two machines were later modified as **Model 1 Special** 'boats, with accommodation increased to eight passengers. Production of the Dolphin continued into 1935, most examples going to the US Army, US Navy and US Coast Guard. Few of the 'boats survived World War II.

SPECIFICATION	
Douglas C-21	
Type: two-crew staff transport and observation (air/sea rescue) amphibian flying-boat	10,000 ft (3050 m) in 18 minutes 30 seconds; service ceiling 14,200 ft (4330 m); range 550 miles (885 km)
Powerplant: two Wright R-975-3 radial piston engines each rated at 350 hp (261 kW)	**Weights:** empty 5,861 lb (2659 kg); maximum take-off 8,583 lb (3893 kg)
Performance: maximum speed 140 mph (225 km/h) at sea level; cruising speed 119 mph (192 km/h) at optimum altitude; climb to	**Dimensions:** wingspan 60 ft (18.29 m); length 43 ft 10 in (13.36 m); height 14 ft 1 in (4.29 m); wing area 562.00 sq ft (52.21 m²)
	Payload: up to eight passengers

Douglas DT

Following failure of the Cloudster to complete the US coast-to-coast flight, David R. Davis lost interest in the Davis-Douglas Company and withdrew his financial support. Thus, after some difficulty in gaining backing, Donald Douglas established the Douglas Company (later the Douglas Aircraft Company) in July 1921.

One of the reasons that this then little-known designer/engineer was able to gain the backing needed to form the new company was his torpedo-bomber design that in April 1921 gained a US Navy contract for three prototypes for evaluation under the designation **DT-1**. It was to prove an historic design: it was the first military aircraft produced by the new Douglas company, and one of the USN's first successful torpedo-bombers. Retaining in its wings and fuselage a family likeness to the earlier Cloudster, the single-seat DT-1 differed from its predecessor in being of composite construction: the folding wing cellule had wings of wooden construction covered with fabric, the fuselage was of welded steel tube with light alloy covering forward and fabric covering aft, and on the tail unit the vertical surfaces were of wood and the horizontal surfaces of steel tube, both covered with fabric. The fixed tailskid landing gear had wide-track main units that could be fitted with wheels or floats, and the powerplant was based on one 400-hp (298-kW) Liberty engine.

The first DT-1 made its maiden flight at the beginning of November 1921 and completed its acceptance trials during the following month. However, the USN decided that two-seat accommodation would be more suitable for an aircraft in this category and instructed the company to modify the remaining two aircraft with

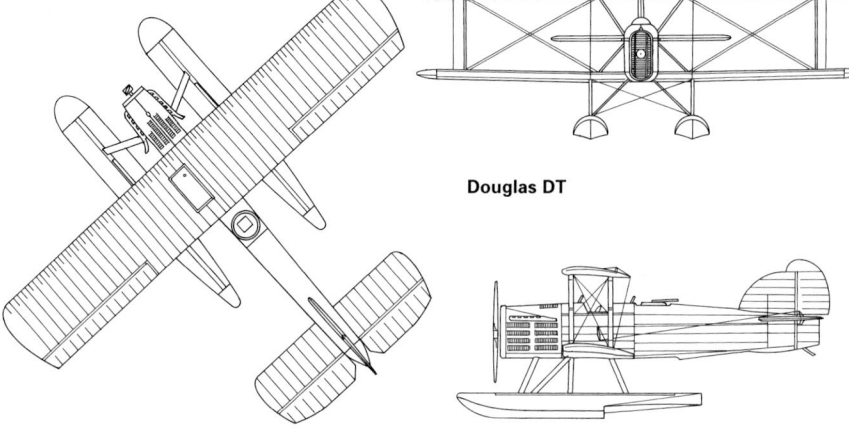

Douglas DT

Variants

DT-2B: one Liberty-engined DT-2 supplied to the Norwegian government; seven similar aircraft were built under licence in Norway, and some remained in second-line service in 1940
DT-3: proposed improved version of DT-2; not built
DT-4: bomber version of which four were created as DT-2 conversions by the NAF with the direct-drive 650-hp (523-kW) Wright T-2 Vee engine
DT-5: redesignation of two DT-4s following the installation of geared 650-hp (523-kW) Wright T-2B engines
DT-6: single DT-2 following the experimental installation of the 450-hp (336-kW) Wright P-1 radial engine
DTB: four aircraft with the 650-hp (523-kW) Wright Typhoon Vee engine for the Peruvian navy
SDW-1: three DT-2 aircraft modified by the Dayton-Wright company as long-range scout floatplanes; they had a deeper central fuselage section accommodating additional fuel tanks

As well as pioneering torpedo-dropping techniques, the DT was also extensively used in take-off trials aboard ship. The latter involved both catapult and conventional launches.

this seating under the revised designation **DT-2**. Even before these were received, the DT-1 had shown itself to be superior to competing designs, resulting in further orders for Douglas. The company built 38 DT-2s in addition to the two modified DT-1s, and 26 more were built by the Naval Aircraft Factory (6) and the LWF Engineering Company (20).

In addition to its torpedo-bombing role, in which it proved valuable in the development of the air-launched torpedo concept, the DT-2 was also used for gunnery practice, observation and scouting. Before they were retired from service in 1926, one float-equipped machine had been used in 1925 for early catapult launch tests from the USS *Langley*.

SPECIFICATION	
Douglas DT-2 (landplane)	
Type: two-seat torpedo-bomber	**Weights:** empty 3,737 lb (1695 kg); maximum take-off 6,502 lb (2949 kg)
Powerplant: one Liberty Vee piston engine rated at 450 hp (336 kW)	**Dimensions:** wingspan 50 ft (15.24 m); length 34 ft 2 in (10.41 m); height 13 ft 7 in (4.14 m); wing area 707.00 sq ft (65.68 m²)
Performance: maximum speed 101 mph (163 km/h) at sea level; climb to 5,000 ft (1525 m) in 13 minutes 36 seconds; service ceiling 7,800 ft (2,375 ft); range 293 miles (472 km)	**Armament:** one 1,835-lb (832-kg) torpedo carried under the fuselage

Douglas DWC

Early in 1923 the United States Army Air Service became interested in the possibility of making a round-the-world flight using a small formation of aircraft. A suitable aircraft had to be robust and reliable, possess good range capability, and be suitable for easy conversion between wheeled landing gear and float alighting gear. Initial interest was shown in the Cloudster, but Douglas instead proposed a version of the US Navy's DT-2 incorporating modifications that would provide a maximum extension of range. The proposal was accepted by the US Army, which thereupon ordered a **DWC (Douglas World Cruiser)** prototype in the late summer of 1923.

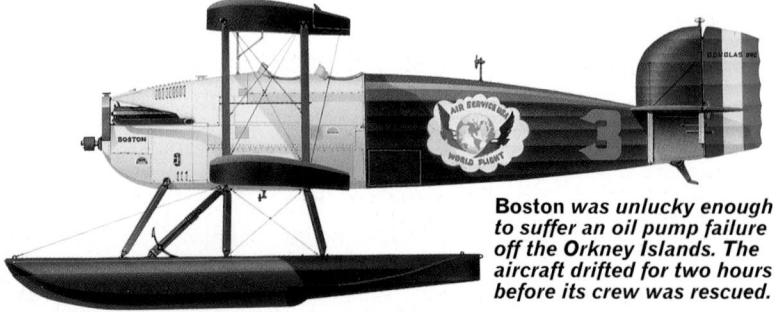

Boston was unlucky enough to suffer an oil pump failure off the Orkney Islands. The aircraft drifted for two hours before its crew was rescued.

Douglas DWC (cont.)

Because it was basically a DT-2 airframe, the first DWC was built and had completed its service trials (with both wheel and float landing gear) so quickly that a go-ahead for the flight was given on 19 November 1923. Three more DWCs were ordered, and the last of these was delivered in March 1924. The aircraft were completed to a standard that differed from that of the DT-2 in having almost six times the fuel capacity, which replaced the military equipment of the USN aircraft, and with a modified engine cooling system to allow an easy interchange of small- or large-capacity cooling radiators to suit operations in cold and hot regions respectively.

The four aircraft, numbered 1 to 4 and named respectively *Seattle*, *Chicago*, *Boston* and *New Orleans*, began their epic journey on 4 April 1924. Their round-the-world route was from east to west via Canada and Alaska, where *Seattle* was destroyed in a crash. The route continued via Japan, Korea, the coast of China, Indo-China, Thailand, India, Middle East, southern Europe, France and the UK. After suffering an engine failure *Boston* sank off the Faroe Islands while under tow, but *Chicago* and *New Orleans* crossed the North Atlantic via Iceland and Greenland to reach North America at Picton in Nova Scotia before flying across the USA to Seattle, successfully completing their truly remarkable journey on 28 September 1924 after flying 28,945 miles (46582 km). In so doing they had also achieved the first staged crossing of the Pacific Ocean, a point which is not generally appreciated.

Variant

DOS: initial designation of six aircraft, generally similar to the DWC machines, ordered by the USAAS for service as observation seaplanes; later designated **O-5**, they differed from the DWCs by having a standard fuel system and armament of two trainable machine-guns on a mounting in the rear cockpit

SPECIFICATION

Douglas DWC
Type: two-seat long-range aircraft
Powerplant: one Liberty Vee piston engine rated at 420 hp (313 kW)
Performance: (landplane) maximum speed 103 mph (166 km/h) at sea level; economical cruising speed 53 mph (85 km/h) at optimum altitude; service ceiling 10,000 ft (3050 m); range 2,200 miles (3541 km)
Weights: empty 4,300 lb (1950 kg); maximum take-off 6,915 lb (3137 kg)
Dimensions: wingspan 50 ft (15.24 m); length 35 ft 6 in (10.82 m); height 13 ft 7 in (4.14 m); wing area 707.00 sq ft (65.68 m²)

Douglas F3D and F-10 Skyknight

A US Navy requirement for a turbojet-powered carrier-based night fighter resulted in the receipt by Douglas of a contract for three prototype aircraft in this category under the designation **XF3D-1**. The type emerged as a mid-wing cantilever monoplane of all metal construction, the wings incorporating hydraulic folding for carrier stowage. The circular-section fuselage carried hydraulically actuated speed brakes, provided side-by-side pressurised accommodation for the pilot and radar operator, and carried at its rear a tail unit very similar to that of the D-558-1 Skystreak. An unusual feature was a crew escape tunnel, extending from the rear of the cabin to the underside of the fuselage. The landing gear was of retractable tricycle type, and the prototypes' powerplant comprised two 3,000-lb st (13.35-kN) J34-WE-24 turbojet engines mounted on the lower edges of the forward fuselage, beneath the wingroots.

The first prototype made its maiden flight on 23 March 1948, and while company testing was still in progress an initial contract for the construction of 28 **F3D-1 Skyknight** production aircraft was placed. The first of these was flown on 13 February 1950 and the type entered service early in 1951. The F3D-1 differed from the prototypes in having improved avionics and equipment and, as initially delivered, the powerplant of two 3,000-lb st (13.35-kN) J34-WE-32 turbojets that were later upgraded to -34 standard at a rating of 3,250 lb st (14.46 kN).

Before delivery of the first F3D-1, Douglas had received a contract for production of an improved **F3D-2**, which was to be the major and indeed ultimate production version, with a total of 237 built. It

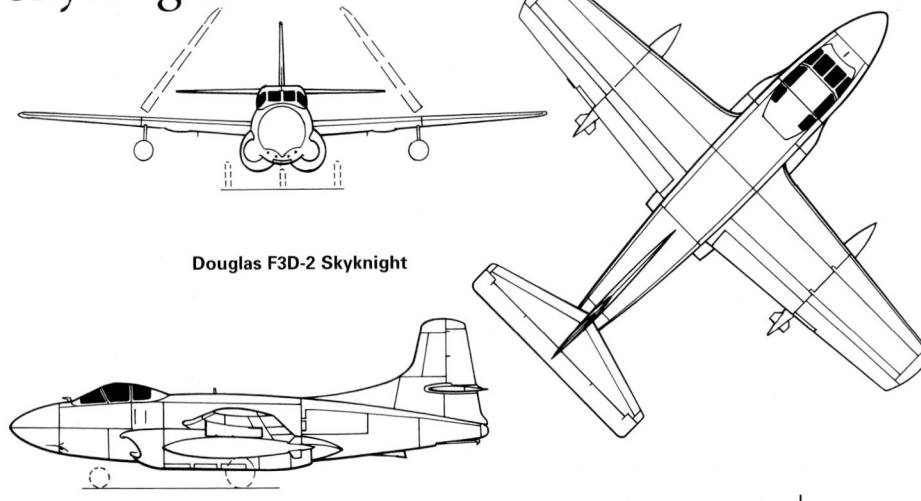

Douglas F3D-2 Skyknight

was intended that the F3D-2 should be powered by two 4,600-lb st (20.46-kN) J46-WE-3 turbojets, but development of this engine was abandoned and the aircraft were instead fitted with two -36 engines. Improvements included the provision of an autopilot and a general updating of the systems and equipment. The first of these F3D-2 night-fighters flew on 14 February 1951 and all of the aircraft had been delivered by a time just over one year later.

The Skyknight saw extensive use in the Korean War, this all-weather fighter accounting for the majority of the victories scored by the USN and US Marine Corps. The first combat victory came on 2 November 1952, being the first occasion that one jet aircraft had destroyed another (in this case a MiG-15) in a night inter-ception. The surviving F3D-1 and F3D-2 aircraft were redesignated **F-10A** and **F-10B** respectively with introduction of the new US tri-service desig-nation system in September 1962. Some Skyknight aircraft had been retired by 1965, but many ECM versions were operating in front-line roles over Vietnam until 1969.

In the EF-10B, ECM equipment replaced the radar. Three USMC units flew the type, VMCJ-1, -2 (illustrated) and -3.

Variants

F3D-1M (MF-10A): 12 F3D-1s following modification as test vehicles for Sparrow guided missiles
F3D-2B: redesignation of one F3D-2 while used during 1952 for special armament tests
F3D-2M (MF-10B): 16 F3D-2s following conversion to carry Sparrow missiles
F3D-2Q (EF-10B): 35 F3D-2s following conversion for the ECM role
F3D-2T: five F3D-2s converted as night-fighter trainers
F3D-2T2 (TF-10B): 55 F3D-2s adapted as radar operator trainers and electronic warfare aircraft
F3D-3: projected advanced version with a swept wing

SPECIFICATION

Douglas F3D-2 Skyknight
Type: two-seat carrierborne and land-based all-weather fighter
Powerplant: two Westinghouse J34-WE-36/-36A turbojet engines each rated at 3,400 lb st (15.12 kN)
Performance: maximum speed 565 mph (909 km/h) at 20,000 ft (6095 m); cruising speed 390 mph (628 km/h) at optimum altitude; initial climb rate 4,000 ft (1220 m) per minute; service ceiling 38,200 ft (11645 m); range 1,200 miles (1931 km)
Weights: empty 18,160 lb (8237 kg); maximum take-off 26,850 lb (12179 kg)
Dimensions: wingspan 50 ft (15.24 m); length 45 ft 6 in (13.97 m); height 16 ft (4.88 m); wing area 400.00 sq ft (37.16 m²)
Armament: four 20-mm fixed forward-firing cannon in the underside of the forward fuselage

Douglas F4D and F-6 Skyray

US Navy interest in German delta-wing research during World War II led, in 1947, to the design by Douglas of a carrierborne interceptor which embodied a variation of the pure delta wing. Approval of the design was signified by the award of a contract for two **Douglas XF4D-1** prototypes on 16 December 1948, the first making its maiden flight on 23 January 1951 with the powerplant of one 5,000-lb st (22.24-kN) Allison J35-A-17 turbojet engine. This represented an emergency solution to the delays that were being experienced in development of the Westinghouse J40 turbojet that had been the planned engine. Both prototypes were later flown with the XJ40-WE-6 rated at 7,000 lb st (31.14 kN) dry and the XJ40-WE-8 rated at 11,600 lb st (51.60 kN) with afterburning, but problems with the entire J40 engine programme finally led to selection of

the Pratt & Whitney J57 for production aircraft.

The F4D Skyray was a mid-wing cantilever monoplane, the wing being of modified delta configuration with its trailing edges carrying elevons that operated collectively as elevators or differentially as ailerons. The tail unit comprised only a swept vertical surface, the landing gear was of the retractable tricycle type, and the pilot was accommodated well forward of the wing in an enclosed cockpit that provided excellent fields of vision.

The potential of the F4D was demonstrated effectively on 3 October 1953 by the second prototype which, with the XJ40-WE-8 engine, set a new world speed record of 752.9 mph (1211.746 km/h). The first example of the F4D-1 production version flew on 5 June 1954 with the powerplant of one J57-P-2 turbojet developing 13,500 lb st (60.05 kN) with afterburning, but it

was not until 16 April 1956 that deliveries began, initially to USN's VC-3 squadron. The 419th and last production aircraft was delivered on 22 December 1958, but in the intervening period a change had been made by installation of the higher-rated J57-P-8 engine. All aircraft retained the F4D-1 designation, the popular nickname for the type being 'Ford'.

At the peak of its utilisation, the Skyray equipped 11 USN, six US Marine and three reserve squadrons, but none was used operationally. The type survived in first-line service until the late 1960s, with two front-line squadrons converting to the type not until 1964. The Skyray was redesignated as the **F-6A** in September 1962.

A proposed development designated **F4D-2N** with improved all-weather capability was eventually built as the **F5D-1 Skylancer**. Two prototypes were ordered in 1953, with wings of much reduced thickness/chord ratio, a lengthened fuselage, a revised vertical tail surface, and a new cockpit canopy. The first of these revised aircraft recorded its maiden flight on 21 April 1956.

By then, nine pre-production and 51 production examples had been ordered, but following early flight testing the programme was cancelled except for two of the pre-production aircraft. This termination resulted not from any shortcomings in the aircraft but rather from

With 16,000 lb st (71.17 kN) available from its afterburning J57-P-8 turbojet, the Skylancer could reach 1,098 mph (1767 km/h) at 10,000 ft (3050 m).

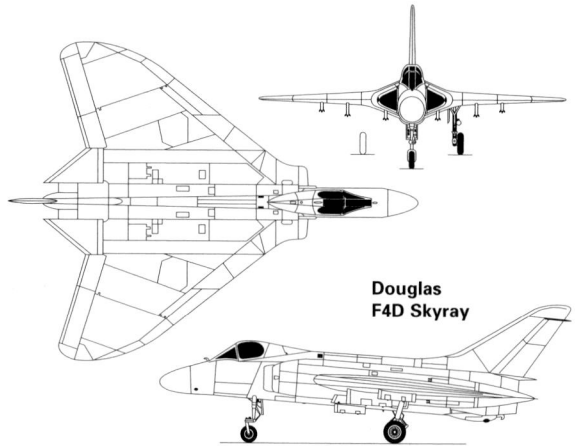

Douglas
F4D Skyray

the realisation that the performance of the F5D was little better than that of the Vought F8U-1 Crusader that was on the point of entering service. However, the four F5D-1s

fulfilled a useful role as they were used by the USN as flying testbeds for a variety of equipment before they were handed over to NASA.

It was the US Navy's desire to experiment with the delta-wing layout that led to the Skyray. In service, the type proved something of a disappointment.

SPECIFICATION	
Douglas F4D-1 Skyray	**Weights:** empty 16,024 lb
Type: single-seat carrierborne fighter	(7268 kg); maximum take-off 25,000 lb (11340 kg)
Powerplant: one Pratt & Whitney J57-P-8B turbojet engine rated at 14,500 lb st (64.50 kN) with afterburning	**Dimensions:** wingspan 33 ft 6 in (10.21 m); length 45 ft 8¼ in (13.93 m); height 13 ft (3.96 m); wing area 557.00 sq ft (51.75 m²)
Performance: maximum speed 722 mph (1162 km/h) at sea level; cruising speed 520 mph (837 km/h) at optimum altitude; initial climb rate 18,300 ft (5580 m) per minute; service ceiling 55,000 ft (16765 m); range 1,200 miles (1931 km)	**Armament:** four 20-mm fixed forward-firing cannon in the leading edges of the wing, plus up to 4,000 lb (1814 kg) of disposable stores carried on six underwing hardpoints

Douglas M series

The US Post Office was responsible for US internal air mail routes from 1918, and in 1925 decided that the various types of DH-4 biplane which had been the primary equipment since the inception of the service were worn out. A decision was therefore made to order a conversion of the Douglas O-2 observation biplane. This **DAM-1 (Douglas Air Mail no. 1)**, quickly shortened to **M-1**, was test-flown during the spring of 1925. It had twice the payload of the DH-4, but made use of the same tried and tested Liberty engine, of which large numbers were in store and readily available. The M-1 was a straightforward conversion of the O-2 with the forward cockpit covered in sheet aluminium to form a reinforced mail compartment

with access through two deck hatches, the pilot being located in what had been the O-2's rear (observer's) cockpit. During tests extended exhaust piping was installed to keep fumes away from the pilot. The M-1 was deemed successful, but Douglas received no production order.

With the introduction of Contract Air Mail (CAM) routes, however, the newly formed Western Air Express Company (later Western Airlines) ordered six Douglas mailplanes. Designated **M-2**, they differed from the M-1 mainly in the use of a frontal radiator in place of the original tunnel type. Provision was also made for quick conversion of the freight section to permit carriage of a passenger in place of mail. A month

before Western Air Express inaugurated its Los Angeles-Salt Lake City service in April 1926, the US Post Office ordered 50 of the **M-3** version for its major routes.

The Douglas company's chief engineer, J. H. 'Dutch' Kindelberger, then redesigned the M-3 with the aim of doubling its payload. The main change in this new **M-4** was an entirely new 'stretched' wing and the type lacked the cut-out in the trailing edge of the upper wing inherited from the O-2. The Post Office was sufficiently impressed to arrange for 40 of the 50-aircraft order for the M-3 to be delivered in M-4 configuration. A single M-4 bought by Western Air Express was designated **M-4A** by Douglas to differentiate it from the aircraft of the Post Office order. With the leasing of the CAM-8 route, linking Chicago and Dallas, to

National Air Transport ordered the ultimate M-4 model, the M-4S. This had accommodation for three and a Wasp radial engine.

National Air Transport (NAT) in October 1925, there emerged a need for more mailplanes. NAT at first used the Curtiss Carrier Pigeon and then, having acquired the important route linking Chicago and New York, bought at auction all 10 M-3 and eight M-4 machines from the Post Office when, during July 1926, that department relinquished all its routes to private operators. NAT introduced the Douglas

mailplanes on 1 September 1927, and phased the aircraft out of service during 1930 in favour of three-engined Ford Tri-Motors. In their three years of service the Douglas mailplanes performed admirably in all weathers and in the most difficult flying conditions. NAT had bought other M-4 aircraft from a variety of sources, and at one stage had as many as 24 Douglas mailplanes in operation.

Douglas M series (continued)

Among the aircraft bought by NAT was a privately owned aircraft which had been confiscated by the US Treasury while illegally smuggling liquor from Cuba to Florida during Prohibition; it became known as the 'Booze Ship'. NAT M-3s were flown with new long-span wings from the spring of 1928 onwards; for economic reasons these had been designed and constructed by the company's own engineering department. One M-4 was converted by NAT to take a 525-hp (391-kW) Pratt & Whitney Hornet radial engine.

A total of 57 Douglas mailplanes was built, but with the advent of the Ford and other three-engined types they were soon withdrawn from air mail services. A few were sold to private owners but the majority were scrapped. One long-wing M-4 which survived was restored to flying condition by Western Airlines

With the M-3 came the introduction of streamlined flying and bracing wires, revised engine installation and improved night-flying equipment.

(successor to Western Air Express) in the old authentic colours of red and silver to commemorate the company's 30th anniversary in 1956.

SPECIFICATION	
Douglas M-4	range 700 miles (1127 km)
Type: single-seat mailplane	**Weights:** empty 3,405 lb
Powerplant: one Liberty 12 Vee	(1544 kg); maximum take-off
piston engine rated at 400 hp	4,900 lb (2223 kg)
(298 kW)	**Dimensions:** wingspan 44 ft 6 in
Performance: maximum speed	(13.56 m); length 28 ft 11 in
140 mph (225 km/h) at sea level;	(8.81 m); height 10 ft 1 in (3.07 m);
cruising speed 110 mph (177 km/h)	wing area 411.00 sq ft (38.18 m²)
at optimum altitude; initial climb	**Payload:** up to 1,000 lb (454 kg) of
rate 1,000 ft (305 m) per minute;	mail
service ceiling 16,500 ft (5030 m);	

Douglas observation biplanes

The important family of Douglas observation aircraft sprang from two **XO-2** prototypes, the first of which was powered by the 420-hp (313-kW) Liberty V-1650-1 Vee engine and test-flown in the autumn of 1924. The second XO-2 was powered by the 510-hp (380-kW) Packard 1A-1500 Vee engine, which proved unreliable. The US Army ordered 45 **O-2** production aircraft in 1925, these retaining the XO-2's welded steel tube fuselage, wooden wings and overall fabric covering but at the same time introducing aluminium panels on the forward fuselage. The XO-2 had been flown with short- and long-span wings, the latter giving improved handling and therefore being specified for the production aircraft. The fixed tailskid landing gear included a main unit of the divided type, the horizontal

Variants

O-2C: the success of the O-2 in US Army observation squadrons led to orders for 46 O-2Cs in 1926; these differed from the O-2 in having frontal radiators for their Liberty engines and modified oleo-strut landing gear; the US Army Air Corps (USAAC) took delivery of 19 aircraft, while the remaining 27 went to reserve National Guard units
O-2D: two unarmed staff transport versions of the O-2C
O-2E: one-off machine which replaced the wire link between upper- and lower-wing ailerons of production aircraft by rigid struts
O-2H: realising that the basic O-2 design was nearing the end of its useful life, Douglas engineers in 1926 produced a radically revised aircraft in the O-2H; the fuselage was redesigned and a new tailplane was fitted, while the wings, which were of unequal span with considerable stagger (as opposed to the equal-span, unstaggered structure of all previous models) incorporated the rigid-strut aileron interconnections of the O-2E; an improved split-axle landing gear was standard; between 1928 and 1930 the USAAC received 90 O-2Hs and the National Guard a further 50
O-2J: three unarmed O-2Hs for service as USAAC staff transports
O-2K: a slightly modified version of the O-2J for US Army staff transport and liaison duties; total production was 37 for the USAAC and 20 for the National Guard
XO-6: five all-metal O-2s, built in the mid-1920s by Thomas-Morse
XO-6B: radically altered (smaller and lighter) version of the XO-6, precursor of the Thomas-Morse O-19 series
O-7: three O-2s with the 510-hp (380-kW) Packard 1A-1500 direct-drive engine; later converted to O-2 (two) and O-2C (one) standards
O-8: one aircraft with the 400-hp (298-kW) Curtiss R-1454 radial engine instead of the intended Packard inverted-Vee engine; later became an O-2A
O-9: one aircraft with the 500-hp (373-kW) Packard 1A-1500 geared engine; it resembled the O-7 but had a four- rather than two-bladed propeller; later became an O-2A
XO-14: one reduced-scale version of an O-2H and the first Douglas aircraft with wheel brakes
O-22: two built to a standard that differed from that of the O-2H in having N-type interplane struts, sweepback on the upper wing, metal-covered vertical tail surfaces, and the 450-hp (336-kW) Pratt & Whitney R-1340-9 radial engine with a Townend ring; a tailwheel replaced the previous tailskid
O-25: one O-2H revised with the 600-hp (447-kW) Curtiss V-1570-5 Vee engine; new type of machine-gun mounting fitted for the observer; later flown as the **XO-25A** with Prestone cooling system
O-25A: production version of O-25 in the form of 50 aircraft for the USAAC with the powerplant of one 600-hp (447-kW) Curtiss V-1570-7 geared engine; incorporated a tailwheel similar to that on the O-22
O-25B: three unarmed examples of the O-25A with dual controls for use as staff transports
O-25C: developed from the XO-25A, with the same Prestone-cooled Curtiss Conqueror geared engine; radiator located farther back beneath the forward fuselage; the USAAC took delivery of 30 O-25Cs

O-29: one aircraft similar to the O-2K but with the Wright R-1750 air-cooled radial engine; originally designated **Y1O-29A** and finally **O-29A**
O-32: similar to final version of experimental O-29 but with the 450-hp (336-kW) Pratt & Whitney R-1340-3 radial engine
O-32A: production version of O-32, of which 30 were built for the USAAC
YO-34: one machine similar to the O-22 but fitted with the Curtiss Conqueror engine
O-38: derivative of the O-25 but with the 525-hp (391-kW) Pratt & Whitney R-1690-3 radial engine and Townend ring; the National Guard received all 44 production aircraft
O-38A: single unarmed O-38 staff liaison machine for the National Guard
O-38B: derivative of the O-38 with the R-1690-5 engine; total production was 63, comprising 30 for USAAC observation squadrons and 33 for the National Guard
O-38C: single aircraft similar to the O-38B for use by US Coast Guard
O-38E: model with a wider and deeper fuselage on the lines of the private-venture O-38S, with a sliding canopy over the cockpits and the powerplant of one 625-hp (466-kW) R-1690-3 radial engine driving a metal propeller; could be operated on twin Edo floats; the National Guard took delivery of 37 such aircraft
O-38F: eight unarmed staff liaison aircraft delivered to the National Guard in 1933 with the powerplant of one R-1690-9 engine and a revised, fully enclosed canopy
O-38S: private-venture development of the O-38 with a wider and deeper fuselage, crew canopy and smooth-cowled 575-hp (429-kW) Wright R-1820-E Cyclone radial engine; in effect was the prototype of the O-38E
Observation biplanes for export: eight examples of the O-2C were purchased by Mexico, which followed in 1929 with an order for eight examples of the **O-2M**, a version of the O-32A but with the 525-hp (391-kW) Hornet radial engine; six examples of the **O-38P**, a version of the O-38E which could have wheel or float landing gear, were delivered to Peru's naval air arm during 1932; Chinese orders were impressive, totalling 82 aircraft in a six-year period beginning in 1930 with 10 **O-2MC** aircraft, closely resembling the O-38 except for the powerplant of one Hornet engine; these were followed by 20 examples of the **O-2MC-2**, which had the cylinders of their Hornet engines surrounded by a Townend ring, five of the **O-2MC-3** variant with the uprated powerplant of one 575-hp (429-kW) Hornet, 12 each of the **O-2MC-4** and **O-2MC-5** variants with the less powerful 420-hp (313-kW) Wasp C1 engine, 22 of the **O-2MC-6** variant with the 575-hp (429-kW) R-1820-E engine, and one **O-2MC-10** with the 670-hp (500-kW) R-1820-F21 engine
XA-2: the 46th aircraft of the original O-2 contract was completed as an attack machine with the powerplant of one 420-hp (313-kW) V-1410 Liberty inverted-Vee engine, and with a total of eight machine-guns (two in the engine cowling, two each in the upper and lower wings, and two on a ring-mounting operated by the observer) was remarkably well armed for its day; it competed against the Curtiss A-3 in 1926 but was not selected for production
OD-1: two O-2Cs for service with the US Marine Corps from 1929

tail surface was strut-braced, and the engine was cooled by a tunnel radiator.

The O-2 proved to be a conventional but very reliable biplane which soon attracted orders for 25 more aircraft: 18 **O-2A** machines equipped for night flying and six **O-2B** dual-control command aircraft for the US Army, plus one civil **O-2BS** modified specially for James McKee, who made a remarkable solo trans-Canada flight in September 1926. In 1927 the O-2BS was adapted as a three-seater with a radial engine. There followed large

numbers of variants and a considerable total of production aircraft.

Although an unremarkable design, the O-2 proved rugged and dependable in service. This O-2H was on the strength of the 91st Observation Squadron.

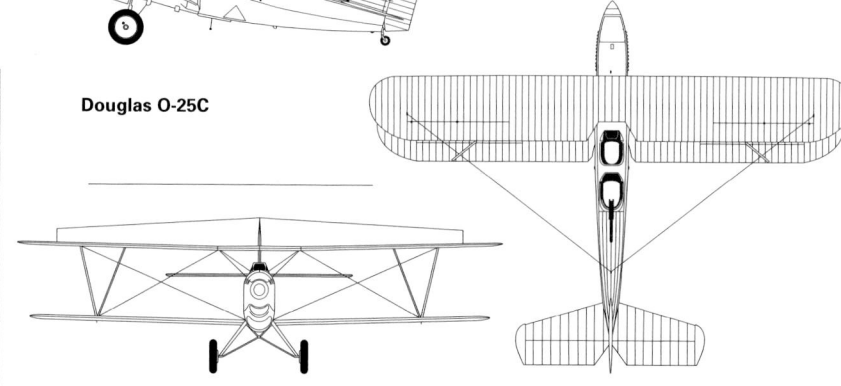

Douglas O-25C

SPECIFICATION	
Douglas O-2	4,785 lb (2170 kg)
Type: two-seat observation aircraft	**Dimensions:** wingspan 39 ft 8 in
Powerplant: one V-1650-1 Liberty	(12.09 m); length 28 ft 9 in
Vee piston engine rated at 420 hp	(8.76 m); height 10 ft 6 in (3.20 m);
(313 kW)	wing area 411.00 sq ft (38.18 m²)
Performance: maximum speed	**Armament:** one 0.3-in (7.62-mm)
128 mph (206 km/h) at sea level;	Browning fixed forward-firing
cruising speed 103 mph (166 km/h)	machine-gun in the forward
at optimum altitude; initial climb	fuselage and one 0.3-in (7.62-mm)
rate 807 ft (246 m) per minute;	Browning trainable rearward-firing
service ceiling 16,275 ft (4960 m);	machine-gun in the rear cockpit,
range 360 miles (579 km)	plus up to 400 lb (181 kg) of
Weights: empty 3,032 lb	disposable stores carried under the
(1375 kg); maximum take-off	lower wing

Douglas O-31, O-43 and O-46

Anxious to retain its position as chief supplier of observation aircraft to the US Army Air Corps, Douglas developed a proposal for a high-wing monoplane succesor to the O-2. A contract was signed in January 1930 for two **XO-31** prototype aircraft, the first of them being flown in December of that same year. A gull-wing monoplane, the XO-31 had a slim fuselage carrying a tandem arrangement of open cockpits for the pilot and observer, the power-plant of one 600-hp (447-kW) Curtiss V-1570-25 Conqueror Vee engine, and fixed tailwheel landing gear with a main unit of the split-axle type and provision for

large wheel fairings.

The XO-31 suffered from directional instability and experiments were therefore made with various fin and rudder shapes, as well as with auxiliary fins, in an effort to cure the problem. The second aircraft was completed as the **YO-31**, differing mainly in having a geared version of the Conqueror engine and an enlarged fin. Four **YO-31A** aircraft delivered during the first half of 1932 were modified radically with an elliptical wing planform, a new tail assembly, a semi-monocoque fuselage and a canopy over the cockpits. The aircraft appeared with a variety of tail units, the final

version (redesignated **O-31A**) featuring a very tall pointed fin with an inset rudder. The single **YO-31B** was an unarmed staff transport and the sole **YO-31C** had cantilever main landing gear units and a ventral bulge in the fuselage, which enabled the observer to operate his single 0.3-in (7.62-mm) machine-gun more effectively from a standing position.

Five **Y1O-31A** service-test aircraft were ordered in the summer of 1931, these being delivered to the USAAC in the spring of 1933 under the designation **Y1O-43**. They differed considerably from the final configuration of the O-31A, with a wire-braced parasol wing and a revised tail unit with a new fin and rudder. The aircraft went into service under the designation **O-43**. An order for 23 **O-43A** aircraft was completed during 1934, this variant having a deepened fuselage, which obviated the need for the ventral bulge under the gunner's position, together with an enlarged fin carrying an inset rudder similar to that of the O-31A. The canopy was enlarged, and fully enclosed both cockpits. The O-43 and O-43A served with USAAC observation squadrons for several years before being assigned to reserve National Guard units.

The 24th airframe of the O-43A contract was

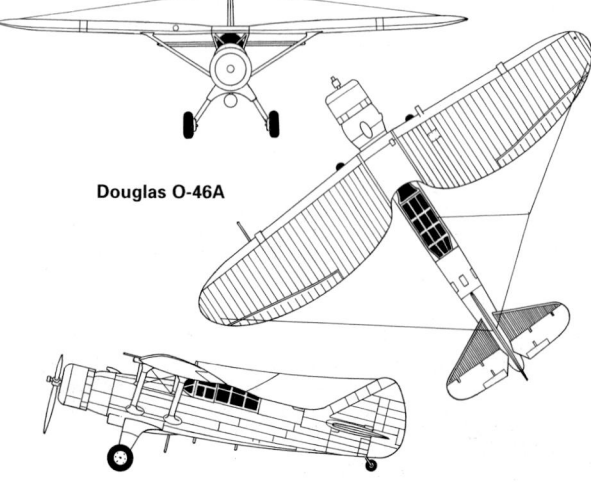

Douglas O-46A

completed as the **XO-46** prototype, which differed from the O-43A in having its wing braced on each side by parallel streamlined struts. And, for the first time, the previously favoured Vee-engined powerplant was replaced by one based on a radial engine, the R-1535-7. The XO-46 passed its tests with flying colours and an order for 71 **O-46A** production aircraft was subsequently increased to 90 machines that were delivered between May 1936 and April 1937. The

Corrugated fuselage skinning was very much a feature of the XO-31. This feature was dropped by the semi-monocoque, smooth-skinned YO-31.

O-46A differed externally from the XO-46 in having the canopies faired into the raised rear fuselage decking. The O-46A served with USAAC observation squadrons until 1940, when most were transferred to National Guard units before being withdrawn for training duties in 1942. The last first-line USAAC O-46A unit was the 2nd Observation Squadron, which still had several on charge when the Japanese attacked its base in the Philippines in December 1941.

SPECIFICATION	
Douglas O-46A	maximum take-off 6,639 lb (3011 kg)
Type: two-seat observation aircraft	**Dimensions:** wingspan 45 ft 9 in
Powerplant: one Pratt & Whitney	(13.94 m); length 34 ft 6¾ in
R-1535-7 radial piston engine rated	(10.53 m); height 10 ft 8 in (3.25 m);
at 725 hp (541 kW)	wing area 332.00 sq ft (30.84 m²)
Performance: maximum speed	**Armament:** one 0.3-in (7.62-mm)
200 mph (322 km/h) at 4,000 ft	Browning fixed forward-firing
(1220 m); cruising speed 171 mph	machine-gun in the leading edge of
(275 km/h) at optimum altitude;	starboard wing and one 0.3-in
initial climb rate 1,765 ft (541 m)	(7.62-mm) Browning trainable
per minute; service ceiling 24,150 ft	rearward-firing machine-gun in the
(7360 m); range 435 miles (700 km)	rear cockpit
Weights: empty 4,776 lb (2166 kg);	

Douglas SBD Dauntless and A-24

Without any doubt the **SBD Dauntless** must be regarded as the most successful dive-bomber produced by the American aviation industry during World War II. The type was successful in terms of both achievement and longevity, blunting the might of the Japanese navy in actions such as those of the Coral Sea and Midway and also during the Solomons campaign. It also continued to offer a valuable contribution to US Navy and US Marine Corps operations until a time late in 1944, long after contemporary creations had disappeared from the aviation scene.

A product of John Northrop's influence, the Dauntless stemmed from the **Northrop BT-1** which entered service with the USN in spring 1938. One of the BT-1s served as the prototype for a new naval dive-bomber allocated the designation **XBT-2**, although by the time this entered production in 1940 Northrop had become a division of the Douglas Company, resulting in the revised **SBD** designation. The chief designer throughout was 'Ed' Heinemann. There had been structural and engine changes, and while the SBD retained a general family likeness to its progenitor, it was really a very different aircraft. Of low-wing cantilever monoplane configuration, it was of all-metal construction except for fabric-covered control surfaces. Fuselage construction included a number of watertight compartments, the tail unit was conventional, the main units of the tailwheel landing gear retracted inward, and an arrester hook was provided for carrierborne operation. The two-man crew was accommodated in tandem beneath a continuous transparent, but framed, canopy, and was provided with dual controls. The powerplant of the prototype was based on one 1,000-hp (746-kW) Wright XR-1820-32 Cyclone radial engine. Testing of the prototype

showed not only its superiority over the earlier BT-1, but performance and flight characteristics that immediately singled it out as an exceptional aircraft. Initial production orders for 57 **SBD-1** and 87 **SBD-2** aircraft were placed on 8 April 1939, the SBD-2 differing in having increased fuel capacity and revised armament. The SBD-1 entered service with the US Marine Corps late in 1940, equipping VMB-2, with deliveries to VMB-1 following early in 1941. The **SBD-2** went to the US Navy, and by the end of 1941 was serving aboard the USS *Enterprise* with VB-6 and VS-6 as well as with VB-2 on the USS *Lexington*.

An improved version entered service as the **SBD-3** in March 1941, introducing larger-capacity self-sealing fuel tanks, armour protection, a bullet-proof windscreen, the 1,000-hp (746-kW) R-1820-52 engine, and armament changes that initiated the standard of two 0.5-in (12.7-mm) and two 0.3-in (7.62-mm) machine-guns. The SBD-3 was followed into production by the **SBD-4**, which differed only in having a 24- rather than 12-volt electrical system. Production of these two versions totalled 1,364 units, making possible a wider distribution of these much-needed and important aircraft to operational squadrons. Some 16 SBD-4s were later modified as reconnaissance aircraft with the revised designation **SBD-4P**.

The most extensively built version was the **SBD-5**, produced in a new, Douglas-operated factory at Tulsa, Oklahoma. This differed from earlier versions in its powerplant of one 1,200-hp (895-kW) R-1820-60 engine, its increased ammunition capacities, and its introduction of illuminated sights for both the fixed forward-firing and trainable rearward-firing machine-guns. A total of 2,409 was built for the USN before Douglas turned to

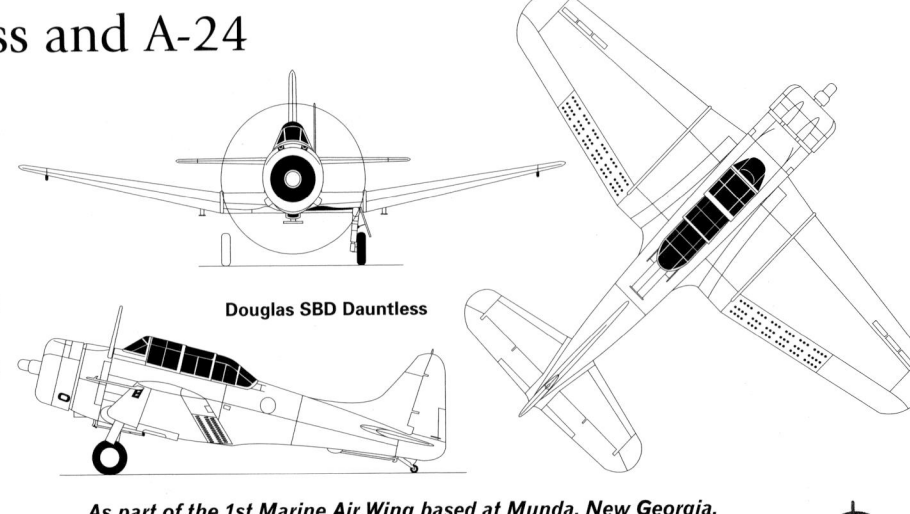

Douglas SBD Dauntless

As part of the 1st Marine Air Wing based at Munda, New Georgia, Marine Corps Scout Bomber Squadron VMSB-243 wasted no time in painting the new US national marking on its SBD-4s from July 1943.

the final production variant, the **SBD-6**, with the still more powerful R-1820-66 engine and increased fuel tankage. Also supplied to the USN in small numbers were photo-reconnaissance variants of the earlier production versions, as eight **SBD-1P**, at least 15 **SBD-2P** and 47 **SBD-3P** aircraft. Nine examples of the SBD-5 version were supplied for service with the Royal Navy's Fleet Air Arm in January 1945, these being designated **Dauntless DB.Mk I**, but none was used operationally. Another small quantity was supplied to Mexico. Although the first-line use of the SBD by the USN and USMC tailed off late in 1944, many late-version aircraft remained in use for some years after the end of World War II.

The success of the Junkers Ju 87 as a dive-bomber in the tactical support role, as Germany's armoured columns raced over much of north-western Europe in 1940, made the US Army Air Corps (the US Army Air Forces from mid-1941)

conscious of the fact that it possessed no significant aircraft of this type. Accordingly, 168 of the SBD-3s were ordered as a matter of some urgency, these being delivered in the summer of 1941 under the designation **A-24**. The variant was virtually identical to the SBD-3 (in contracts the designation **SBD-3A** was used), except for the deletion of the arrester hook and the provision of an inflated tailwheel tyre instead of the solid rubber one favoured by the US Navy. About a third of these aircraft were despatched to the Philippines in November 1941 for service with the USAAF's 27th Bombardment Group, but were still in transit at sea when Pearl Harbor was attacked and were diverted instead to Australia, equipping the 91st BS (from February 1942) and later the 8th BS. Both of these units found the A-24 lacking in performance and range for operational deployment in the South-East Asia theatre.

Despite these apparent shortcomings, the US Army continued to procure the A-24, during 1942 receiving first 170 **A-24A** aircraft equivalent to the SBD-4 (and contractually designated **SBD-4A**) and then 615 **A-24B** (**SBD-5A**) aircraft. These machines met with no significant success, confirming the experience of Ju 87 operations in Europe and North Africa, i.e. that their role was strictly confined: within that limited role, of course, they were indeed the 'tool for the job'. The failure of the dive-bomber in USAAF service resulted from the fact that there was no identical job for it to do. Despite this, a number remained in USAAF (later, US Air Force) service for some years after World War II. One A-24A was converted into the sole **RA-24A** radio-controlled drone, and when in 1948 all surviving A-24As received the revised designation **F-24A**, this aircraft became the **QF-24A**. At the same time the A-25B became the **F-24B**, a single drone-director being the **DF-24B**.

SPECIFICATION

Douglas SBD-6 Dauntless
Type: two-seat carrierborne and land-based scout/dive-bomber
Powerplant: one Wright R-1820-66 Cyclone radial piston engine rated at 1,200 hp (895 kW)
Performance: maximum speed 262 mph (422 km/h) at 18,500 ft (5640 m); cruising speed 143 mph (230 km/h) at optimum altitude; initial climb rate 1,710 ft (521 m) per minute; service ceiling 28,600 ft (8715 m); range 1,700 miles (2736 km) with maximum fuel and 773 miles (1244 km) as a scout bomber
Weights: empty 6,554 lb

(2973 kg); maximum take-off 10,882 lb (4936 kg)
Dimensions: wingspan 41 ft 6½ in (12.66 m); length 33 ft 1¼ in (10.09 m); height 13 ft 7 in (4.14 m); wing area 325.00 sq ft (30.19 m²)
Armament: two 0.5-in (12.7-mm) Browning fixed forward-firing machine-guns in the upper part of the forward fuselage two 0.3-in (7.62-mm) Browning trainable machine-guns in the rear of the cockpit, plus up to 2,250 lb (1021 kg) of bombs in the form of one 1,600-lb (726-kg) weapon under the fuselage and 650 lb (295 kg) of weapons underwing

Along with New Zealand, the Free French Air Force also flew the Dauntless in combat. In the case of the French, the aircraft were A-24Bs, flown in support of French and US forces along the French Atlantic coast and in the French Alps. This machine flew with GCB 1.18 'Vendée' from Vannes, France in November 1944.

Douglas Super DC-3, R4D-8 and C-117D

The continuing use and popularity of the DC-3 and its derivatives after World War II encouraged Douglas to evolve a suitable replacement. To save time and cost it was decided to modernise the existing type, and Douglas therefore bought two second-hand DC-3 transports which were upgraded with strengthening and extension of the fuselage to provide a cabin holding between 30 and 38 passengers, the addition of extra windows, and the incorporation of an airstair cabin door. Some changes were made to the flying surfaces (the wing was reduced in span, moved farther to the rear and given slightly swept outer panels, while the tail unit was redesigned) to improve handling and stability, and the retracted mainwheel units were totally enclosed in neat fair-

ings. The powerplant of the first prototype comprised two 1,475-hp (1100-kW) R-1820-C9HE Cyclone radial engines, while the second had two 1,450-hp (1081-kW) Pratt & Whitney R-2000-D7 radial piston engines.

Designated as the **DC-3S**, or **Super DC-3**, the first of these revised aircraft flew on 23 June 1949. Testing gave excellent results, demonstrating much improved performance over the basic

DC-3. It was too late for a mere improvement of an existing type, however, for faster and more comfortable aircraft of more modern design were already available, and the company's gamble failed to pay off, the only civil sales being of the second prototype to a construction company and three other aircraft to Capital Airlines. Slightly greater success attended the company's effort to secure military interest.

Ski-modified undercarriage was a distinctive feature of the LC-117D. The aircraft were used on polar-supply flights by the US Navy.

SPECIFICATION

Douglas R4D-8
Type: three-crew transport aircraft
Powerplant: two Wright R-1820-80 Cyclone radial piston engines each rated at 1,535 hp (1145 kW)
Performance: maximum speed 270 mph (432 km/h) at 5,900 ft (1800 m); cruising speed 251 mph (401 km/h) at optimum altitude; initial climb rate 1,300 ft (396 m)

per minute; range 2,500 miles (4023 km)
Weights: empty 19,537 lb (8870 kg); maximum take-off 31,000 lb (14075 kg)
Dimensions: wingspan 90 ft (27.43 m); length 67 ft 9 in (20.75 m); height 18 ft 3 in (5.56 m); wing area 969.00 sq ft (90.02 m²)
Payload: up to 33 passengers

Variants

YC-47F: one Super DC-3 evaluated by the US Air Force, initially under the designation **YC-129**
R4D-8X: US Navy designation for the prototype YC-129/YC-47F when evaluated for naval use
R4D-8 (C-117D from 1962): designation of 100 R4D-5, R4D-6 and R4D-7 aircraft modified to Super DC-3 standard; some aircraft were also modified for special roles as **R4D-8T (TC-117D)** trainers, **R4D-8Z (VC-117D)** staff transports and **R4D-8L (LC-117D)** winterised transports; some remained in service until well into the 1970s

Douglas T2D and P2D

In July 1925 the US Navy Bureau of Aeronautics ordered three prototypes of a new twin-engined torpedo-bomber and general-purpose warplane under the designation **Douglas XT2D-1**. The type had to be capable of operation with wheeled landing gear and float alighting gear, and also to be compatible with the USN's aircraft-carriers. Two months earlier a single XTN-1, with similar general characteristics, had been

ordered from the US Naval Aircraft Factory. The first XT2D-1 prototype flew on 27 January 1927 in landplane configuration, and soon after this its two 500-hp (373-kW) Wright P-2 radial engines were replaced by R-1750 Cyclone radial engines; the other two prototypes were similarly re-engined. The three aircraft participated successfully in trials with the USN's VT-2 torpedo-bomber squadron in the spring of 1927 and, in

consequence, nine examples of the **T2D** production model were purchased.

The basic configuration of the XT2D-1 prototypes was retained, although the fuselage of the T2D-1 was 2 ft 11½ in (0.90 m) shorter than that of the XT2D-1, and the engine nacelles were repositioned. A crew of four was carried, the pilot and co-pilot in tandem open cockpits, with the gunner/ bomb-aimer in the nose and the radio-operator/ gunner in the fourth cockpit amidships.

The T2D-1 performed satisfactorily in service, operating from aircraft-carriers (the first twin-engined aircraft to do so) during the 1928 USN fleet exercises. However, its size precluded embarkation of the carrier's full aircraft complement and, as a result, the type was re-allocated to patrol

The T2D-1s (illustrated) and P2D-1s were characterised by their bluff noses with angled bomb- or torpedo-aiming panels.

squadrons. The T2D-1 then flew with VP-1 and VP-2 from Pearl Harbor, Hawaii, operating on wheels or twin floats as required until scrapped in 1933.

Variant

P2D-1: in June 1930 Douglas received an order for 18 aircraft based on the T2D-1, but intended specifically for over-water patrol duties; these new P2D-1s had twin fin-and-rudder assemblies to ensure better flight characteristics, particularly with one engine inoperative, and were powered by 575-hp (429-kW) Wright R-1820-E radial engines; deliveries were completed by the end of 1931; the P2D-1s, almost always in twin-float configuration, flew with VP-3 stationed in the Panama Canal Zone until withdrawn from first-line service in 1937

SPECIFICATION

Douglas T2D-1 (landplane)
Type: four-seat torpedo-bomber and general-purpose warplane
Powerplant: two Wright R-1750 Cyclone radial piston engines each rated at 525 hp (391 kW)
Performance: maximum speed 125 mph (201 km/h) at sea level; climb to 5,000 ft (1525 m) in 5 minutes 54 seconds; service ceiling 13,830 ft (4215 m); range 457 miles (735 km)
Weights: empty 6,011 lb

(2726 kg); maximum take-off 10,523 lb (4773 kg)
Dimensions: wingspan 57 ft (17.37 m); length 42 ft (12.80 m); height 15 ft 11 in (4.85 m); wing area 886.00 sq ft (82.31 m²)
Armament: one 0.3-in (7.62-mm) Browning trainable machine-gun in each of the nose and dorsal positions, plus one 1,618-lb (734-kg) torpedo or equivalent weight in bombs carried under the fuselage

Douglas TBD Devastator

Early in 1934 the US Navy initiated a design competition for a new torpedo-bomber required for service on board aircraft-carriers and, in particular, on the USS *Ranger* which was due to be commissioned during the year. From the proposals received, prototypes were ordered from Douglas and the Great Lakes Aircraft Corporation; the **Douglas XTBD-1** represented the first carrierborne aircraft of monoplane configuration to be produced for the USN.

On the other hand, the Great Lakes XTBG-1, of which only a single prototype was built, was the last torpedo-bomber biplane to be procured by the USN.

The XTBD-1 prototype, which flew for the first time on 15 April 1935, was of fairly conventional configuration and construction. The low-set cantilever monoplane wing could be folded mechanically at approximately mid-span, and construction was all-metal except for the fabric cover-

ing of the rudder and elevators. The deep fuselage housed an internal weapons bay which could accommodate a torpedo or

a large armour-piercing bomb. Only the main units of the tailwheel landing gear were retractable, the wheels of the folded main

units remaining half-exposed below the wing; an arrester hook was mounted forward of the tail-wheel.

This TBD-1 was aircraft number 1 of the US Navy's VT-6. It is pictured in pre-war markings, the aircraft adopting camouflage for combat duties.

Douglas TBD Devastator (continued)

The TBD prototype's powerplant consisted of one 800-hp (597-kW) XR-1830-60 Twin Wasp radial engine, and accommodation was provided for a crew of three (pilot, bomb-aimer/navigator and gunner) in a cockpit under a long, transparent but heavily framed cockpit enclosure. Initial testing of the prototype went so well that within nine days of the first flight Douglas was able to deliver the machine to the USN for service trials, which were carried out over

a period of nine months and led to contracts for a total of 129 **TBD-1 Devastator** production aircraft. When delivery of the aircraft began on 25 June 1937, the USN had in its possession what was then without doubt the most advanced torpedo-bomber in the world. The first unit to receive the TBD-1, on 5 October 1937, was VT-3, VT-2, VT-5 and VT-6 equipping with the new type during the following year. The TBD-1 remained in first-line service until after the

Battle of Midway in whose main clash, on 4 June 1942, 35 TBD-1s were shot to pieces when they were caught between blistering anti-aircraft fire and the guns of A6M carrierborne fighters. Withdrawn from combat service as no longer capable of survival against the more potent weapons which were already in service, let alone under development, the surviving TBD-1s were used for some time for communications and training duties.

Douglas X-3 Stiletto

Under direction of the US Air Force's Air Research and Development Command, and sponsored jointly by the US Navy, USAF and NACA, Douglas designed and developed a high-speed research aircraft under the designation **X-3**, later named **Stiletto** after its lines. Intended primarily for research into the problems of high-altitude, high-speed flight and the effects of kinetic heating, the X-3 began its design life in 1945. The complexity of this programme is indicated by the fact that more than three years elapsed before approval was given for construction of a mock-up, in August 1948, and it was not until late June 1949 that Douglas received a contract for two flying prototypes and one static test airframe; in fact, only one prototype was built.

First flown on 20 October 1952, the X-3 had a slender, needle-nosed fuselage, a low-set cantilever monoplane wing

of very short span, a conventional tail unit, retractable tricycle landing gear, and the powerplant of two J34 turbojets mounted side-by-side in the fuselage. The pilot was accommodated in a pressurised cockpit on a downward-firing ejection seat that served also as an electric lift to provide access from the ground. Design of the X-3 was of unprecedented complexity, because of the high-speed requirement, involving advanced aerodynamics and the use of new constructional methods and materials. They included, in particular, the development of fabrication and construction techniques involving the use of titanium. Additionally, the airframe had more than 850 pinhole orifices distributed over its surface to record pressures, 185 strain gauges to record air loads and stresses, and 150 temperature-recording points. Testing proved

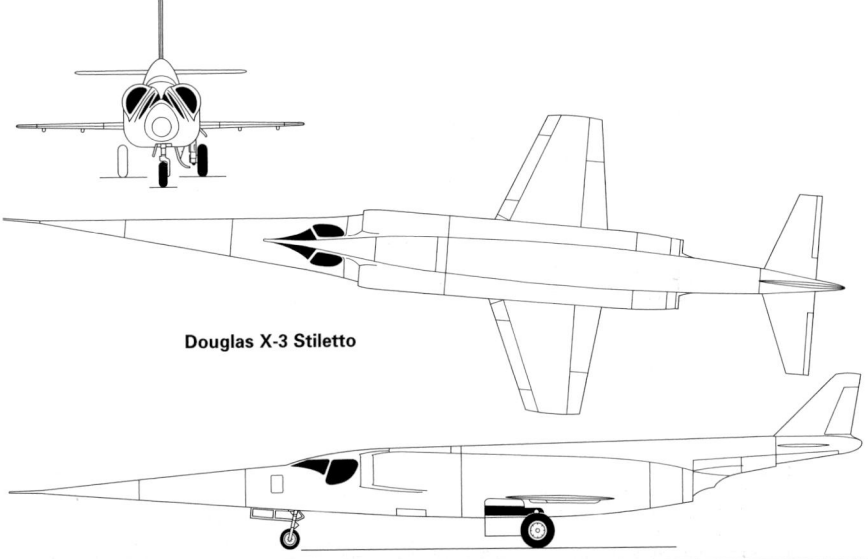

Douglas X-3 Stiletto

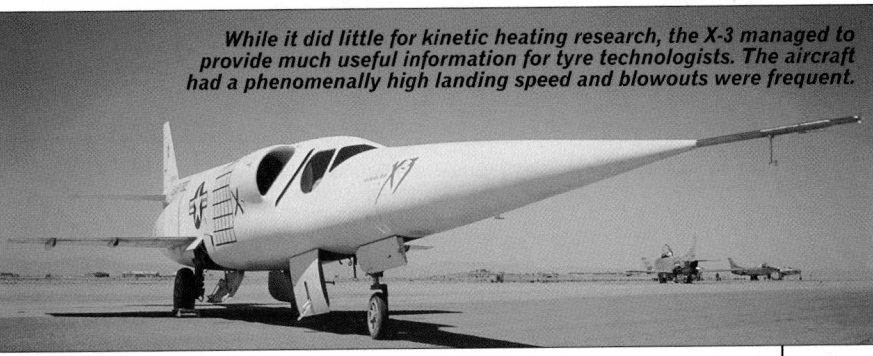

While it did little for kinetic heating research, the X-3 managed to provide much useful information for tyre technologists. The aircraft had a phenomenally high landing speed and blowouts were frequent.

disappointing, the aircraft being radically underpowered and able to achieve only some 50 per cent of its design speed of Mach 2.2; on one occasion Mach 1.21 was attained in a

dive. With virtually no hope of improving performance, the USAF cancelled the programme after only six flights and the aircraft was handed over to NACA. However, the X-3 was not

regarded as a failure, for it had made important contributions to titanium technology, and features of its design were used later in the Lockheed F-104 Starfighter.

After the USAF had discarded the Stiletto, the aircraft was taken on by NACA's High Speed Flight Station at Edwards AFB. Much useful information was gathered in a series of 20 subsequent flights and this was disseminated throughout the US aircraft industry, most notably influencing the F-104. The X-3 was preserved for display at the Air Force Museum, Wright-Patterson AFB.

Druine aircraft

Roger Druine died in 1958 at the age of 37, but in a comparatively short career this Frenchman had revealed himself as a highly talented designer of light aircraft for the home builder, generally working on the basis of a Druine-supplied kit; some of his types were also manufactured in the UK by Rollason Aircraft and Engines Ltd and in West Germany by Flugzeugbau Stark. Druine's three most important lightplanes, all of the low-wing cantilever monoplane layout with fixed tailskid landing gear including divided main units that generally carried plain wheels (though spatted wheels and floats were also seen at times), were the single-seat **Druine D.3 Turbulent**, the tandem two-seat **D.5 Turbi** and the side-by-side, two-seat **D.6 Condor**.

The D.3 was of very simple design and construction, with a flat-sided fuselage carrying a rounded upper decking to the front and rear of the pilot's open cockpit, a plain tail unit including vertical surfaces comprising only a very small fin and a large aerodynamically balanced rudder, a dihedralled wing of constant thickness and chord to its slightly rounded tips and incorporating ailerons but not

flaps, and main landing-gear units each based on a Vee strut extending outward and downward from the lower longerons to carry a single wheel on each side. The type was designed to be powered by any of several types of small air-cooled engine, the most popular choice being the 186-cu in (73-cc) Volkswagen car engine rated at between 25 and 35 hp (19 and 26 kW). The **D.31** was a version with the cockpit enclosed by a clear-view canopy and powered by the 45-hp (34-kW) Ardem 4 CO2 Mk 4 engine, and a subvariant

was the **D.31A** with the Ardem 4 CO2 Mk 10 engine and a strengthened main spar to allow operation at a weight of up to 700 lb (318 kg). The data for a typical D.3 with the 30-hp (22-kW) Ardem 4 CO2 conversion of the Volkswagen engine include a maximum speed of 87 mph (140 km/h) at sea level, initial climb rate of 492 ft (150 m) per minute and an endurance of 4 hours 30 minutes.

The **D.5** was basically an enlarged version of the D.3 to provide two-seat accommodation in a tandem arrangement of open cockpits. It was also designed for an assortment of air-cooled engine

types in variants between the **D.50** and **D.54**, some of them with a long enclosure over the cockpit.

The **D.6** was intended for primary flying training as well as sport and light touring use, and was basically a development of the D.5 mainly for factory production (by Borea et Fils in France and Rollason in the UK) with a wider fuselage to provide side-by-side seating under a full canopy. The prototype was the **D.60** with the 60-hp (45-kW) CNAD 4 engine, and the main variants were the **D.61** with the

65-hp (49-kW) Continental A65 engine, the **D.62** with the 90-hp (67-kW) Continental C90 engine, the **D.62A** with the 100-hp (75-kW) Continental O-200-A engine built under licence by Rolls-Royce, the **D.62B** improved version of the D.62A with the fuselage shortened and all but the first four with flaps, and the **D.62C** glider tug with the 130-hp (97-kW) Continental O-240 engine also made under licence by Rolls-Royce, as well as larger wheels and a raised canopy.

All of Druine's designs were of wooden construction with a plywood-covered fuselage and fabric-covered flying surfaces. A D.3 is illustrated.

Dufaux aircraft

The brothers Armand and Henri Dufaux of Geneva made the first aircraft in Switzerland during 1908, this machine being a triplane of clumsy appearance with three sets of three wings mounted one behind the other. In the following year they produced the **Dufaux 4** (history does not record the missing numbers) as a more orthodox single-seat biplane with an Antoinette Vee engine, but when this machine was demonstrated to the Swiss military commission in May 1910 it was judged to be unsuitable for military purposes. It survived, however, and is preserved at the Swiss Museum of Transport and

Communications in Lucerne. An improved version, the **Dufaux 5**, was built in the same year, and this aircraft was chartered by the Swiss commission for reconnaissance during the autumn manoeuvres. The Dufaux 5 was a two-seater with a 70-hp (52-kW) Gnome rotary engine. The resulting operational evaluation of the aircraft was deemed to be successful; in spite of several mishaps to the aircraft, the experience gained led to formation of the Swiss air arm in August 1914. The Dufaux 5 had a maximum speed of 52 mph (84 km/h), service ceiling of 1,970 ft (600 m) and range of 37 miles (60 km).

Other Dufaux types

Dufaux helicopter: flown during 1905 in tethered flights, this was a four-rotor design of which little is known

Dufaux single-engined fighter: designed and built by Armand Dufaux's Société pour la Construction et l'Entretien d'Avions in Paris, this was an extraordinary machine designed to overcome the 1915 non-availability of gun synchronisers; the fighter had its engine set into the fuselage behind the cockpit (for the staggered side-by-side seating of the two members of the crew), the engine driving driving a two-bladed pusher propeller whose two annular hubs connected the forward and aft sections of the fuselage, which were divided by the propeller; this odd arrangement, which presented all manner of problems, left the nose free for the observer's Lewis machine-gun; by the time the fighter appeared in the spring of 1916, adequate synchronising systems had appeared and no further development was undertaken

Dufaux Avion-Canon: project for a single-seat fighter armed with a single 37-mm Hotchkiss cannon (suggested by the ace Charles Nungesser) firing through the hollow shaft of the propeller, the latter driven by two inward-facing rotary engines by means of bevel gears; the aircraft was not built, and Armand Dufaux left aviation due to ill health

The single-engined fighter's bizarre powerplant arrangement made it thoroughly impractical as a warplane.

SPECIFICATION	
Dufaux single-engined fighter **Type:** single-seat fighter **Powerplant:** one Le Rhône 9J rotary piston engine rated at 110 hp (82 kW) **Performance:** maximum speed 87 mph (110 km/h) at sea level; climb to 6,560 ft (2000 m) in 13 minutes 9 seconds; endurance 2 hours	**Weights:** empty 1,168 lb (530 kg); maximum take-off 1,631 lb (740 kg) **Dimensions:** wingspan 26 ft 1⅔ in (7.96 m); length 20 ft (6.10 m); height 9 ft 1¼ in (2.80 m) **Armament:** one 0.303-in (7.7-mm) Lewis trainable forward-firing machine-gun in the starboard cockpit

Eagle Aircraft Eagle 220 and Eagle 300

The Eagle Aircraft Company was formed at Boise, Idaho, during the mid-1970s to develop an agricultural aircraft of advanced design. Of braced single-bay biplane configuration, the **Eagle Aircraft Eagle** introduced wings based on those developed for high-performance sailplanes, and these were of high aspect ratio and of wooden construction with fabric covering. Spray booms for liquid chemicals formed the trailing edge of the lower wing, and control in roll was shared by ailerons on the upper wing and spoilers in the upper surface of the lower wing. A 250-US gal

(946-litre) chemical hopper was mounted in the fuselage between the engine bay and the single-seat enclosed cockpit.

The precise designation of the aircraft was determined by the powerplant, the **Eagle 220** having a 220-hp (164-kW) conversion of a Continental W-670-6 radial engine, and the **Eagle 300** a 300-hp (224-kW) Lycoming flat-six engine. A total of 50 of these aircraft had been built by a time early in 1982, but the company went out of business toward the middle of the 1980s.

The Eagle's airframe was mainly of conventional construction, the fuselage having a basic steel tube structure, and including a wire-braced tail unit. An Eagle 220 is illustrated.

SPECIFICATION	
Eagle Aircraft Eagle 300 **Type:** single-seat agricultural aircraft **Powerplant:** one Lycoming IO-540-M1B5D flat-six piston engine rated at 300 hp (224 kW) **Performance:** maximum working speed 115 mph (185 km/h) at sea level; minimum working speed	65 mph (105 km/h) at sea level **Weights:** empty 2,650 lb (1202 kg); maximum take-off 5,400 lb (2449 kg) **Dimensions:** wingspan 55 ft (16.76 m); length 27 ft 6 in (8.38 m); height 10 ft 11 in (3.33 m); wing area 386.00 sq ft (35.86 m²)

Edgar Percival E.P.9 and Lancashire Prospector

Edgar Percival's name was made in the 1930s when he designed the Gull series of light aircraft. The Percival company went on to build the Prentice and Provost trainers after World War II, and was acquired eventually by the Hunting Group, which itself later became part of British Aircraft Corporation and thus British Aerospace and the current BAE Systems. In 1954 this Australian-born designer founded a new company, Edgar Percival Aircraft Ltd, at Stapleford airfield, UK, and here built as a private venture a high-wing utility aircraft known as the **Edgar Percival E.P.9**. Intended as a multi-role workhorse for the crop-spraying and light transport roles, the prototype first flew on 21 December 1955, and construction of a first batch of 20 production aircraft began soon after this. An Australian demonstration tour by the fourth certificated aircraft earned orders for four E.P.9 machines from that country: two were delivered by air in September 1957 to Super Spread Aviation (Pty) Ltd of Melbourne, and two others in the following month to Skyspread Ltd of Sydney. Other overseas customers were found in Canada, France, New Zealand and Tasmania, and a number of British-registered E.P.9s operated abroad on spraying and freight work. Two were bought by the British army in March 1958 for evaluation, and served for several years before being put up for civil disposal.

Samlesbury Engineering Ltd acquired rights to the E.P.9 in 1958, and these included some assembled and partly-assembled aircraft. The company was then renamed as the Lancashire Aircraft Co. Ltd, which completed three aircraft with the 295-hp (220-kW) GO-480-G1A6 engine, and in this form the designation **Lancashire Prospector Mk I** was applied. A further five aircraft were completed before production stopped with the 27th airframe. Mention should also be made of a Skyspread E.P.9 re-engined with the 375-hp (280-kW) Armstrong Siddeley Cheetah 10 radial engine in 1959; a similar engine was used on the last Lancashire-built aircraft in 1960, to create the **Prospector Mk II**.

With its radial-engine powerplant, the final Lancashire Prospector, a Mk II, was not withdrawn from use until 1982.

SPECIFICATION	
Edgar Percival E.P.9 **Type:** one-crew light utility aircraft **Powerplant:** one Lycoming GO-480-B1B flat-six piston engine rated at 270 hp (201 kW) **Performance:** maximum speed 146 mph (235 km/h) at sea level; cruising speed 128 mph (206 km/h) at optimum altitude; initial climb rate 1,100 ft (335 m) per minute; service ceiling 17,500 ft (5335 m); range 580 miles (933 km)	**Weights:** empty 2,010 lb (912 kg); maximum take-off 3,980 lb (1805 kg) **Dimensions:** wingspan 43 ft 6 in (13.26 m); length 29 ft 6 in (8.99 m); height 8 ft 9 in (2.67 m); wing area 227.6 sq ft (21.14 m²) **Payload:** up to five passengers, or two passengers and two litters, or one passenger and 185 cu ft (5.24 m³) of freight, or 170 Imp gal (773 litres) of spray chemicals

EKW C-35

Following its 1933 purchase of Fokker C.VE biplanes for service in a variety of roles, the Swiss air arm asked the Eidgenössische Konstruktions Werkstätte (EKW) factory at Thun to design a multi-purpose aircraft, initially to supplement and then to replace the Fokker design. EKW offered two projects, the **C-35** biplane and the **C-36**, the latter an advanced low-wing monoplane with twin fin-and-rudder assemblies which was eventually developed into the effective F + W C-3600 series. However, initial caution led the Swiss to select the C-35, which bore some similarity to Fokker's newer design, the C.X. The C-35 was a conventional biplane that proved to have a better performance than the C.VE and, after the conclusion of successful trials with two prototypes, an order for 40 production aircraft was placed in 1936, this order soon being doubled.

Delivery of the C-35s began in May 1937, continuing to the end of the following year, and proof that the aircraft were continuing to give good service came in 1941-2, when a further eight were assembled from spares.

From 1943 the C-35s were withdrawn from front-line units as they were replaced by examples of the C-3603, and were issued to night-flying units where they served until 1954. One example survives in the Verkehrshaus museum in Lucerne.

SPECIFICATION	
EKW C-35 **Type:** two-seat reconnaissance and ground-attack aircraft **Powerplant:** one Saurer/SLM HS-77 (Hispano-Suiza 12Y-31) Vee piston engine rated at 860 hp (641 kW) **Performance:** maximum speed 208 mph (335 km/h) at 13,125 ft (4000 m); initial climb rate 2,265 ft (690 m) per minute; service ceiling 26,245 ft (8000 m); range 466 miles (750 km) **Weights:** empty 4,828 lb (2190 kg); maximum take-off 6,900 lb (3130 kg) **Dimensions:** wingspan 42 ft 11 in (13.08 m); length 31 ft 3½ in	(9.54 m); height 12 ft 3½ in (3.75 m); wing area 344.46 sq ft (32.00 m²) **Armament:** one 20-mm Hispano-Suiza fixed forward-firing cannon in a moteur-canon installation firing through the propeller shaft, two 0.295-in (7.5-mm) fixed forward-firing machine-guns in the leading edges of the lower wing, and one 0.295-in (7.5-mm) trainable rearward-firing machine-gun in the rear cockpit, plus up to 220 lb (100 kg) of disposable stores carried on two hardpoints under the lower wing, and generally comprising ten 22-lb (10-kg) bombs

Elias aircraft

The American company of G. Elias & Brother Inc. was established in Buffalo, New York, during 1881, but did not embark on the construction of aircraft until after the end of World War I at a time when, like many post-war aircraft builders, the Elias brothers found their hopes defeated by the acute depression of 1930. The company nevertheless designed and developed a small number of aircraft for the US Army, and these types included three conventionally constructed **Elias TA-1 (Trainer Air-cooled type 1)** machines delivered during 1921 for evaluation purposes. Two-seat biplanes, the aircraft varied in their radial-engined powerplants: two had the 140-hp (104-kW) Lawrance R-I, while the other had the 170-hp (127-kW) ABC Wasp. Trials revealed that the Elias type was inferior in performance to the Dayton-Wright TA-3, which was also under evaluation, and no further examples were built.

The US Army also ordered from the company in 1922 a single example of an **XNBS-3 (Night Bomber, Short distance type 3)**. Powered by two 425-hp (317-kW) Liberty 12A Vee engines, this had a fabric-covered steel-tube fuselage and wooden wings. Carrying a crew of four, it would have been armed with five 0.3-in (7.62-mm) machine-guns and have carried up to 2,000 lb (907-kg) of bombs, but failed to pass the service test part of its programme.

The attempts of Elias to break into the civil aviation field also met with little success. These attempts included a parasol-wing monoplane known as the **EC-1 Aircoupe**, powered by an 80-hp (60-kW) Anzani radial engine, and providing an open or optionally enclosed cockpit. A single-seat mail-carrying equal-span biplane was also built and flown. Known as the **AJE Air Express** and also as the **Type M-1**, it was powered by a 400-hp (298-kW) Liberty engine. Space for mail was provided in a 65-cu ft (1.84-m³) Dural-lined compartment.

Perhaps the company's greatest success came after evaluation by the US Navy and US Marine Corps of an **EM-1** prototype designed to meet a US Marine Corps require-ment for a 'Marine Expeditionary' aircraft; this was required for multi-role operation at advanced locations on either wheel or float landing gear. A two-seat unequal-span biplane powered by a 300-hp (224-kW) Wright-Hispano H engine, the prototype later had its wings modified to equal-span configuration, and was also tested with float landing gear; it was deliv-ered to the USMC during 1922. There followed

Although the Elias company was sufficiently far-sighted to suggest that its AJE mailplane design could be used alternatively to carry survey cameras or crop-dusting chemicals, the type still failed to gain a market.

production of six EM-2 aircraft, these incorporat-ing the equal-span wing modification. One was delivered to the USMC and the others to the USN; of the five which went to the USN, one was completed specifically as an observation aircraft and carried the designation **EO-1**.

SPECIFICATION	
Elias EM-2 **Type:** two-seat utility aircraft **Powerplant:** one Liberty 12 Vee piston engine rated at 400 hp (298 kW) **Performance:** maximum speed 111 mph (179 km/h) at sea level **Weights:** maximum take-off 4,233 lb (1920 kg)	**Dimensions:** wingspan 39 ft 8 in (12.09 m); length 28 ft 6 in (8.69 m); height 10 ft 9 in (3.28 m) **Armament:** one 0.3-in (7.62-mm) Lewis or Browning trainable rearward-firing machine-gun in the rear cockpit, plus a not available weight of light bombs carried under the lower wing

Emair MA-1 Paymaster and Diablo 1200

Late in 1968 Air New Zealand began construction of a newly designed agri-cultural aircraft based upon the airframe of the Boeing (Stearman) Model 75 'Kaydet'. This work was undertaken on behalf of Murrayair Ltd of Hawaii, and by comparison with its predecessor the new aircraft had a wing cellule of increased span, a forward fuselage modified to accommodate the pilot

(plus a loader/mechanic on short-range flights) and the chemical hopper, strength-ened landing gear, and a more powerful engine in the form of the 600-hp (447-kW) Pratt & Whitney R-1340-AN1 Wasp radial unit. This machine made its first flight in New Zealand on 27 July 1969, and was then dismantled and trans-ferred to Honolulu, where it was flown within the context of a development

programme that led to FAA certification in April 1970.

Following certification, production of what was known as **Emair MA-1 Paymaster** was initiated at Harlingen, Texas by Emair, a division of the Murrayair company. A combination of role and company title then resulted in the use of the designation **Agronemair MA-1 Paymaster** for a short time, but after 25 aircraft had been built production was brought to an end in January 1976.

The Paymaster was superseded by the **MA-1B Diablo 1200**, whose test-ing had begun in August 1975. Generally similar to the Paymaster, the Diablo 1200 differed mainly in the installation of a more powerful Wright R-1820

In addition to its more powerful engine, the Diablo 1200 also benefited from the use of a larger-diameter and slower-turning propeller, which resulted in much lower operating noise levels.

SPECIFICATION	
Emair MA-1B Diablo 1200 **Type:** one/two-seat heavy-duty agricultural aircraft **Powerplant:** one 1,200-hp (895-kW) Wright R-1820 Cyclone radial piston engine derated to 900 hp (671 kW) **Performance:** maximum operating speed 117 mph (188 km/h) at sea	level **Weights:** empty 4,250 lb (1928 kg); maximum take-off 8,400 lb (3810 kg) **Dimensions:** wingspan 41 ft 8 in (12.70 m); length 30 ft (9.14 m); height 11 ft 9 in (3.58 m); wing area 400.00 sq ft (37.16 m²)

Cyclone radial engine. Although the maximum take-off weight was unchanged, the use of this engine allowed the carriage of a greater payload under hot-and-high conditions, and also opera-

tion from short or water-logged fields. By the end of 1980 a total of 48 Diablos had been deliv-ered, at which time the company suspended oper-ations as a result of the low level of demand.

EMBRAER EMB-110 Bandeirante and EMB-111 Patrulha

The aircraft design which launched EMBRAER (Empresa Brasileira de Aeronáutica SA) as a signifi-cant force among aerospace manufacturers made its maiden flight on 19 August 1972, and resulted from a require-ment for a light transport issued by the Força Aérea Brasileira (Brazilian air force) and the country's airlines. A nine-seat prede-

cessor with the same basic features (low-wing cantilever monoplane configuration, retractable tricycle landing gear and powerplant of two Pratt & Whitney PT6A turboprops) had been tested in proto-type form as the

EMBRAER EMB-100 (mili-tary designation **YC-95**), but the **EMBRAER EMB-110 Bandeirante** (pioneer) featured a much larger cabin which found favour with civil operators overseas, as well as with the Brazilian military.

Many examples of the Bandeirante were sold to third-level and feeder operators throughout the world. This EMB-110P1 is typical of such aircraft. It was flown by the British airline, Genair.

EMBRAER EMB-110 Bandeirante and EMB-111 Patrulha (cont.)

The first three of 80 Bandeirantes ordered by the Brazilian air force were delivered in February 1973 and the type rapidly became the mainstay of the service's transport force. The 60 **C-95** models were 12-seat versions, and were supplemented by 20 **C-95A (EMB-110K1)** freighters with a stretch of 2 ft 9½ in (0.85 m) ahead of the wing, uprated PT6A-34 turboprops in place of the C-95's PT6A-27s and a 71 x 56-in (1.80 x 1.42-m) freight door. This door incorporated an opening to facilitate air dropping or for use as an emergency exit. These machines were followed by 31 examples of the **C-95B**, a military version of the improved **EMB-110P** civil model, two of which were also bought by Gabon.

The Uruguayan air force took delivery of five 15-seat **EMB-110C** aircraft in 1975, and the Chilean navy bought three **EMB-110CN** navalised aircraft in the following year.

Four specialised versions also entered Brazilian military service. The first of these to join the Brazilian air force was the eight-seat **EC-95** for checking and calibration of navigation aids. Four of these (designated **EMB-110A** by the manufacturer) are in service. These aircraft serve with the Grupo Especial de Inspeção em Vôo (special inspection and checking group) at Santos Dumont.

The EC-95 was followed by six examples of the seven-seat **R-95 (EMB-110B)** photographic survey version. This model has apertures in the cabin floor to accommodate a Zeiss camera and associated equipment; Doppler and inertial navigation systems are also fitted. The R-95 serves with the 6º Grupo of the Comando Costeiro (COMCOS, or coastal command) at Recife. One example of the EMB-110B was also acquired by Uruguay. Two previously undelivered **EMB-110P1A** civilian transports were bought by the Colombian air force along with three for the Peruvian

government in the following year.

COMCOS also operates the **P-95** maritime surveillance version which the company designates **EMB-111A**. Twenty-one of these joined the two squadrons of 7º Grupo, which had been inactive since its last Lockheed P-2 Neptune aircraft were retired in 1976. An Eaton-AIL AN/APS-128 Sea Patrol search radar is housed in a large nose radome, and is fully integrated with the aircraft's inertial navigation system. A high-power searchlight, signal cartridge launcher and an ESM system are also carried, and rockets can be launched from four underwing pylons. Wingtip fuel tanks increase the aircraft's endurance to nine hours.

The Brazilian P-95s are locally known by the name **Bandeirulha**, a contraction of **Bandeirante Patrulha** (patrol pioneer). Brazil later bought a second batch of improved **P-95B** aircraft with upgraded avionics and strengthened airframes, a standard to which the P-95

machines were upgraded. Six **EMB-111AN** aircraft were delivered to the Chilean navy, and a single example to the Gabonese air force. The Chilean navy's EMB-111ANs were delivered in place of four surplus Lockheed SP-2E Neptune machines whose delivery was embargoed by the US government, and are used by VP-3 in the maritime patrol role. Two EMB-111As are also operated by the air force of Angola.

A SAR version is designated **SC-95B**, or

Two EMB-110P transports (above) were delivered to Gabon in 1980. The aircraft fly alongside a single EMB-111A, which is used for maritime patrol.

EMB-110P1(K). Deliveries began in late 1981 of eight to the 10º Grupo of COMCOS at Campo Grande; the type has a bubble window on each side of the fuselage, and can carry six litters in addition to observation and rescue personnel. One machine of the same basic type was also delivered to Senegambia.

Production of the Bandeirante for the civil as well as military markets lasted to 1990, and amounted to a total of 500 aircraft.

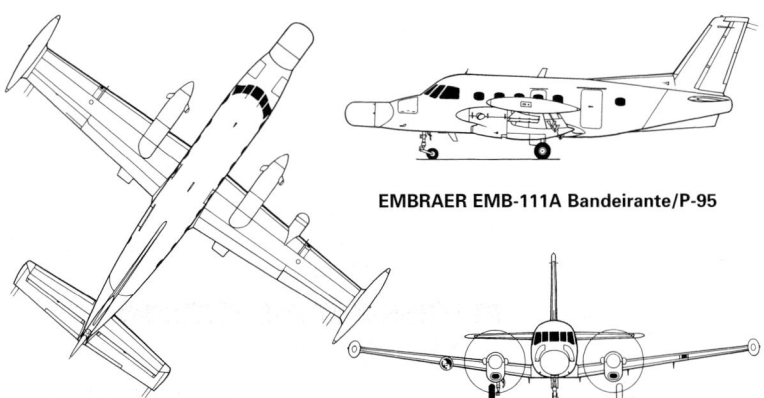

EMBRAER EMB-111A Bandeirante/P-95

SPECIFICATION	
EMBRAER EMB-111 Bandeirante Patrulha (P-95A)	15,432 lb (7000 kg)
Type: six/seven-seat coastal patrol and SAR aircraft	**Dimensions:** wingspan 52 ft 4 in (15.95 m) with tip tanks; length 48 ft 11 in (14.91 m); height 16 ft
Powerplant: two Pratt & Whitney Canada PT6A-34 turboprop engines each rated at 750 shp (559 kW)	1¼ in (4.91 m); wing area 313.23 sq ft (29.10 m²)
Performance: maximum cruising speed 223 mph (360 km/h) at 10,000 ft (3050 m); initial climb rate 1,190 ft (362 m) per minute; service ceiling 25,500 ft (7770 m); range 1,830 miles (2945 km)	**Armament:** up to 2,205 lb (1000 kg) of disposable stores carried on four underwing hardpoints and generally comprising eight 5-in (127-mm) air-to-surface unguided rockets or four multiple launchers each carrying seven 2.75-in (70-mm) air-to-surface unguided rockets
Weights: empty 8,289 lb (3760 kg); maximum take-off	

EMBRAER EMB-120 Brasilia

The success of the Bandeirante persuaded the Brazilian manufacturer to develop a much improved, stretched development. From its inception in 1979, the resulting **EMB-120 Brasilia** progressed towards its maiden flight on 27 July 1983, becoming one of the first of the 'new generation' of commuter aircraft to appear in the 1980s. The Brasilia was designed for two-crew operation with a payload of 30 passengers. The EMB-120 received Brazilian certification in May 1985 with the powerplant of two 1,590-shp (1195-kW) Pratt & Whitney Canada PW115 engines. The first civilian delivery was made to Atlantic Southeast Airways in the USA in June 1985, and by the middle of 1999 the company had delivered

348 out of 353 aircraft ordered up to that time.

The Brazilian air force has so far been the only military customer for the EMB-120. Five of a VIP transport version designated as the **VC-97** were delivered between 1987 and 1988, but one was written off in a training accident in July 1988. The VC-97 is equivalent to the **EMB-120RT (Reduced Take-off)**, the standard production version introduced from the fourth aircraft with the revised powerplant of two 1,800-shp (1342-kW) PW118s each driving a Hamilton Standard four-bladed propeller. A 'hot-and-high' version, powered by PW118A engines, has also been available since 1986, together with its all-cargo,

mixed passenger/cargo and quick-change counterparts. These are respectively the **EMB-120 Cargo** with a payload of 4,000 lb (1814 kg), the **EMB-120 Combi** with a typical payload of 19 passengers and 2,425 lb (1100 kg) of cargo, and the **EMB-120QC** quick-change convertible between a payload of 30 passengers and 7,716 lb (3500 kg) of freight and delivered from May 1993. The next version was the extended-range **EMB-120ER Brasilia Advanced** introduced in 1994 with increased maximum take-off weight without any need for major structural changes, a fact that permits earlier aircraft to be easily brought up to this standard. The longer-legged EMB-120ER was initially developed from

1992 as the **EMB-120X** (provisional), otherwise known as the **Improved Brasilia**, and in its production form incorporates many detail and style changes along with new avionics and an improved cabin.

The two last developments of the Brasilia were

planned as military variants, the **EMB-120EW** and the **EMB-120RS**. The EMB-120EW is an early warning and remote sensing type, of which the Brazilian air force ordered five for its SIVAM (Sistema de Vigilancia da Amazonia). The type has a number of changes including an

In basic concept, the EMB-120 is a low-wing cantilever monoplane with a T-tail, semi-monocoque fuselage and retractable tricycle landing gear. A VC-97 is illustrated.

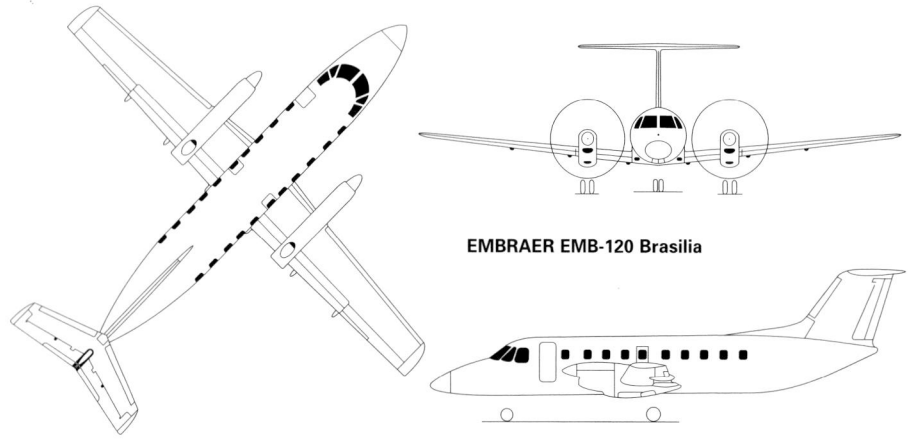

EMBRAER EMB-120 Brasilia

SPECIFICATION	
EMBRAER EMB-120ER Brasilia Advanced	32,000 ft (9755 m); range 1,874 miles (3017 km) with 20 passengers
Type: two-crew medium-range transport aircraft	**Weights:** empty 16,667 lb (7560 kg); maximum take-off 26,433 lb (11990 kg)
Powerplant: two Pratt & Whitney Canada PW118A turboprop engines each rated at 1,800 shp (1342 kW)	**Dimensions:** wingspan 64 ft 10¾ in (19.78 m); length 65 ft 10¼ in (20.07 m); height 20 ft 10 in (6.35 m); wing area 424.42 sq ft (39.43 m²)
Performance: maximum speed 378 mph (608 km/h) at 20,000 ft (6095 m); cruising speed 345 mph (555 km/h) at 25,000 ft (7620 m); initial climb rate 2,500 ft (762 m) per minute; service ceiling	**Payload:** up to 30 passengers within the context of a 7,363-lb (3340-kg) maximum payload

Ericsson Erieye side-looking airborne radar with its antenna in a longitudinal radome above the fuselage, a secure data downlink, new avionics and flight management systems, extra fuel capacity and a number of other enhancements. The EMB-120RS was schemed as the remote-sensing counterpart of the EMB-120EW, and an initial three aircraft were ordered with the same improvements as the EMB-120EW, but with a Canadian MacDonald Detwiler IRIS (Integrated Radar Imaging System) synthetic-aperture radar with its antenna in an underfuselage fairing for the resources exploitation, river pollution control and ground surveillance roles. Both orders were later switched to developments of the ERJ-145 regional jet.

EMBRAER EMB-121 Xingu

Between 1976 and 1987 EMBRAER built 105 examples of the **EMB-121 Xingu**. Conceived as a corporate transport derived from the Bandeirante, the Xingu's wing/powerplant installation was based on those of the former type. Powered by two Pratt & Whitney PT6A-28 turboprop engines and with a gross weight of 11,466 lb (5200 kg), the Xingu prototype entered flight test on 10 October 1976, followed by a pre-production aircraft on 20 May 1977 with the increased maximum weight of 12,500 lb (5670 kg).

The first six production examples of the **Xingu I** were delivered to the Força Aérea Brasileira as **VU-9** machines to be operated as VIP transports. Six more aircraft were later acquired, together with two ex-civil examples, with the new designation **EC-9**.

In September 1980 the French defence ministry selected the Xingu to serve in both the Armée de l'Air and Aéronavale as a multi-engine trainer and fast communications aircraft. An order was placed for 41 examples of the Xingu: some 25 **EMB-121AA** machines for the Armée de l'Air and 16 **EMB-121AN** machines for the Aéronavale. Deliveries began in March 1982 and were completed by the end of 1983.

A revised **EMB-121A1 Xingu II** with 750-shp (559-kW) PT6A-135 engines was offered as a new aircraft or upgrade from 1982. A further-developed, stretched **EMB-121B Xingu III** flew for the first time on 26 July 1980, but the project came to little. The last Xingu was delivered on 19 August 1987.

Featuring a T-tail and ventral fin, the Xingu I and II offered comfortable seating for six passengers in a pressurised fuselage. More than half of those built went to military operators.

EMBRAER EMB-121A1 Xingu II

SPECIFICATION	
EMBRAER EMB-121 Xingu	(610-kg) payload
Type: two-crew executive transport aircraft	**Weights:** empty 7,984 lb (3620 kg); maximum take-off 12,500 lb (5670 kg)
Powerplant: two Pratt & Whitney Canada PT6A-28 turboprop engines each rated at 680 shp (507 kW)	**Dimensions:** wingspan 47 ft 5 in (14.45 m); length 40 ft 2¼ in (12.25 m); height 15 ft 6½ in (4.74 m); wing area 296.00 sq ft (27.50 m²)
Performance: cruising speed 280 mph (450 km/h) at 11,000 ft (3355 m); initial climb rate 1,400 ft (426 m) per minute; service ceiling 26,000 ft (7925 m); range 1,462 miles (2353 km) with maximum fuel and a 1,345-lb	**Payload:** up to six passengers within the context of a 1,896-lb (860-kg) maximum payload

EMBRAER ERJ-145

At the Paris Air Show of June 1989 EMBRAER announced the development of a 45/48-seat turbofan-powered regional airliner based on its turboprop-powered EMB-120 Brasilia. A minimum-change design process led initially to the **EMB-145 Amazon** in which a modified version of the EMB-120's airframe (with a lengthened fuselage) was combined with the revised powerplant of two 7,000-lb st (31.14-kN) Allison AE 3007 turbofans in nacelles located above the wingroots, with their inlets slightly ahead of the wings' leading edge. This concept was adopted in an effort to keep the development costs, estimated at about US $200 million, as low as possible and to achieve operating costs comparable with those of large turboprop-powered aircraft. EMBRAER envisaged that the Amazon would have between 70 and 75 per cent commonality with the earlier Brasilia.

Wind-tunnel tests in the third quarter of 1990 revealed several shortcomings, however, so the design was reworked between October 1990 and March 1991 to implement a number of changes to the wings, landing gear and powerplant installation.

Both the EMB-145RS (foreground) remote-sensing aircraft and the EMB-145SA AEW are illustrated here. Three RS and five SA machines have been ordered for Brazil as the R-99A(SA) and R-99B(RS).

EMBRAER ERJ-145 (continued)

The CTA testing and research laboratory in São José dos Campos then carried out further tests, which were subsequently verified in the Boeing wind-tunnel in Seattle, and as a result a series of additional changes was announced in April 1991: the previous straight wing planform was replaced by a shorter and stiffer wing of supercritical section and swept at 22° 20', the engines were housed in pylon-mounted nacelles under the wing, and the forward fuselage was lengthened so that a longer nosewheel unit could be incorporated. Still further changes were announced in October 1991 after the engine installation had been altered to nacelles pylon-mounted on the sides of the rear fuselage. Subsonic and transonic wind-tunnel tests confirmed the sound nature of these changes and indicated a significant improvement in performance, and the design was finally frozen in July 1992. It is worth noting that a first flight late in 1991 had originally been envisaged.

In February 1993 Parker-Hannifin of the USA and GAMESA of Spain joined the programme as risk-sharing partners: the first was responsible for the control surfaces and provision of on-board systems, while the latter took on the development and construction of the wing and engine nacelles. Companies that

later became involved in the programme included Sonaca of Belgium (centre and rear fuselage sections plus engine pylons), ENAER of Chile (tail unit), Norton of the USA (nose radome), and C & D Interiors of the USA (passenger cabin and baggage compartment interiors).

The first flight of the prototype was achieved on 11 August 1995, and with the use of the prototype and three production aircraft the test and certification programme of 1,100 flights was completed by December 1996, when the EMB-145 entered service with Continental Express in the USA. In 1997 the EMB-145 was redesignated as the ERJ-145, and the type's main operators are two American airlines, Continental Express and AMR Eagle (now American Eagle), which between them have lodged orders and options for 267 aircraft. Firm orders stood at the figure of 293 aircraft in mid-1999, by which time deliveries amounted to 132 machines. The total includes orders from a number of European and Asiatic airlines, raising the ERJ-145's profile with operations undertaken or in prospect by a current 13 airlines in eight countries.

The ERJ-145 has two civil subvariants in the form of the extended-range ERJ-145ER with AE3007-A1 engines, and

the long-range ERJ-145LR with greater fuel capacity and AE3007-A3 engines flat-rated at 7,430-lb st (33.05 kN) for a maximum-payload range of 1,887 miles (3037 km).

The two last developments of the EMB-120 Brasilia were planned as military variants, the EMB-120EW and the EMB-120RS, but the Brazilian air force's orders for the two types were then switched to sub-variants of the ERJ-145. The EMB-145SA (originally EMB-120EW) is the early warning type, of which the Brazilian air force ordered five examples for delivery from 2002 for its SIVAM (Sistema de Vigilancia da Amazonia) programme designed to provide surveillance of the Amazon basin. The type has a number of changes including a crew of five to seven, an Ericsson Erieye side-looking airborne radar with its antenna in a longitudinal radome above the fuselage, a secure data downlink, new avionics and flight management systems, extra fuel capacity and a number of other enhancements. In December 1998 Greece also ordered the type, placing a contract for four generally similar aircraft. The EMB-145RS (originally EMB-120RS) is the remote-sensing counterpart of the EMB-145SA, and an initial three aircraft were ordered for delivery from 2001 with

Rheintalflug uses its six ERJ-145s on its scheduled route network in Austria and in Germany as part of Team Lufthansa. The ERJ-145 is making significant inroads into the European regional market.

the same improvements as the EMB-145SA, but with a Canadian MacDonald Dettwiler IRIS (Integrated Radar Imaging System) synthetic-aperture radar with its antenna in an underfuselage fairing, a

Versatron Skyball TV/FLIR, and a Daedalus UV/visible light/IR linescanner. The type is designed for service in the resources exploitation, river pollution control and ground surveillance roles.

SPECIFICATION

EMBRAER ERJ-145ER
Type: three/four-crew regional airliner
Powerplant: two Rolls-Royce Allison AE3007-A1 turbofan engines each rated at 7,040 lb st (31.32 kN)
Performance: maximum cruising speed 511 mph (823 km/h) at 37,000 ft (11280 m); economical cruising speed 423 mph (680 km/h) at 32,000 ft (9755 m); initial climb rate 2,379 ft (725 m) per minute;

service ceiling 37,000 ft (11280 m); range 975 miles (1569 km) with maximum payload
Weights: empty 25,772 lb (11690 kg); maximum take-off 42,328 lb (19200 kg)
Dimensions: wingspan 65 ft 9 in (20.04 m); length 98 ft (29.87 m); height 22 ft 1¾ in (6.75 m); area 550.91 sq ft (51.18 m²)
Payload: up to 50 passengers within the context of an 11,926-lb (5410-kg) maximum payload

EMBRAER ERJ-135, ERJ-170 and ERJ-190

In 1997 EMBRAER decided to capitalise on the probable success of the ERJ-145, for which sizeable orders were being received, by the introduction of a short-fuselage version optimised for the movement of up to 37 passengers over the same type of regional routes as the ERJ-145. The programme for the EMBRAER ERJ-135 was officially launched in September 1997, and the two prototypes were conversions of ERJ-145 pre-production aircraft, the first of them making the new type's maiden flight on 4 July 1998. The first customer was Continental Express of the USA, which received the first production aircraft in July 1999, by which time EMBRAER had received orders and options for 139 such aircraft.

The ERJ-135 retains a 90 per cent commonality with the ERJ-145 and has basically the same wing, tail unit, flight deck and primary

systems. The main changes were effected in the fuselage, which is shortened by 11 ft 7 in (3.53 m) in comparison with that of the ERJ-145 through the use of shorter frames in front of and behind the wing. The same 2+1 type of seating arrangement is retained, and the commonality of the ERJ-135 with the ERJ-145 means that there are very considerable advantages in operational aspects such as spares holding and crew ratings.

It is worth noting at this stage, even though neither of the two types is expected to fly until some time early in the 21st century, that EMBRAER has also been working in the opposite direction to create larger aircraft to partner the ERJ-145 and ERJ-135 in the creation of a family of regional airliners, offering a full spectrum of capacities between 39 and 90 or more passengers. The two larger types – to an essentially new design with a low-set

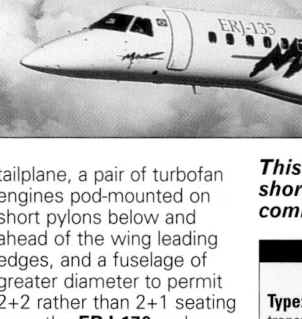

tailplane, a pair of turbofan engines pod-mounted on short pylons below and ahead of the wing leading edges, and a fuselage of greater diameter to permit 2+2 rather than 2+1 seating – are the ERJ-170 and ERJ-190. These two types were launched in June 1999 after the company had secured orders and options for up to 160 such aircraft from Crossair of Switzerland, the launch customer which at that time contracted for the firm delivery of 70 aircraft.

This photograph ably demonstrates both the shorter fuselage of the ERJ-135 and its great commonality with the ERJ-145.

SPECIFICATION

EMBRAER ERJ-135
Type: three-crew regional transport aircraft
Powerplant: two Rolls-Royce Allison AE3007-A3 turbofan engines each rated at 7,040 lb st (31.32 kN)
Performance: maximum cruising speed 511 mph (822 km/h) at optimum altitude; service ceiling 35,000 ft (10670 m); range 1,818 miles (2926 km) with maximum fuel and 1,599 miles

(2574 km) with maximum payload
Weights: empty 24,691 lb (11200 kg); maximum take-off 42,108 lb (19100 kg)
Dimensions: wingspan 65 ft 9 in (20.04 m); length 86 ft 4½ in (26.33 m); height 22 ft 1¾ in (6.75 m); wing area 550.90 sq ft (51.18 m²)
Payload: up to 37 passengers within the context of a 9,700-lb (4400-kg) maximum payload

EMBRAER EMB-200/201/802 Ipanema

The design of an agricultural aircraft, to meet a specification issued by the Brazilian ministry of agriculture, was initiated in May 1969 by the Departemento de Aeronaves of the nation's Centro Téchnico de Aeronãutica. Following the establishment of EMBRAER on 2 January 1970 to promote the development of an indigenous Brazilian aircraft industry, responsibility for development of this new single-seat agricultural aircraft was transferred to EMBRAER and the prototype made its maiden flight on 30 July 1970. Originally designated as the **EMB-200 Ipanema**, the aircraft was a low-wing cantilever monoplane of all-metal construction with fixed tailwheel landing gear and the powerplant of one 260-hp (194-kW) Lycoming O-540-H2B5D engine.

The EMB-200 gained Brazilian type certification on 14 December 1971, and this paved the way for the manufacture of the initial versions, which were the

EMB-200 and **EMB-200A**, which differed in having fixed-pitch and variable-pitch propellers respectively. In 1974, after the completion of 73 EMB-200 series aircraft, EMBRAER switched to production of the improved **EMB-201**, which differed from its predecessors in its powerplant of one 300-hp (224-kW) IO-540-K1J5D engine driving a constant-speed propeller, and in the introduction of detail improvements. A total of 200 EMB-201s had been built before, in 1977, a further improved **EMB-201A** entered production. This introduced a new wing profile, improved systems and revisions in cockpit layout. The EMB-201A remained in production up to 1992, manufacture from the middle of 1981 being the responsibility of the Industria Aeronãutica Neiva SA, which had become a wholly-owned subsidiary of EMBRAER in March 1980 and late in 1988 introduced an improved version of the

EMB-201A. Production of the EMB-201A totalled 402 aircraft, and there were also three **EMB-201R** glider-tugs (all delivered to the air force academy gliding club for use under the designation **U-19**) with the wing and tailplane reduced in span, agricultural equipment deleted and a tow hook added.

From October 1992 the standard production model has been the **EMB-802** with a choice of Continental or Lycoming engine, the wing increased slightly in span, and a larger payload hopper.

This EMB-201A demonstrates the downturned wingtips that were introduced as standard with this variant. Revised aerodynamics and a modified cockpit layout were also incorporated.

SPECIFICATION

EMBRAER EMB-802
Type: single-seat agricultural aircraft
Powerplant: one Lycoming IO-540-K1J5D flat-six piston engine or one Continental IO-550-D flat-six piston engine, each rated at 300 hp (224 kW)
Performance: maximum speed 143 mph (230 km/h) at sea level; cruising speed 132 mph (213 km/h) at 6,000 ft (1830 m); initial climb rate 930 ft (283 m) per minute; service ceiling 11,380 ft (3470 m);
range 583 miles (938 km)
Weights: empty 2,249 lb (1020 kg); maximum take-off 3,968 lb (1800 kg)
Dimensions: wingspan 38 ft 4¼ in (11.69 m); length 24 ft 4½ in (7.43 m) with the tail up; height 7 ft 2½ in (2.20 m) with the tail down; wing area 214.64 sq ft (19.94 m²)
Payload: up to 1,653 lb (750 kg) of dry chemicals or 209 Imp gal (950 litres) of liquid chemicals

EMBRAER EMB-312 Tucano and EMB-314 Super Tucano

Design of the turboprop-powered **EMB-312 Tucano** (toucan) high-performance trainer started in 1978 in response to a Força Aerea Brasileira (Brazilian air force) specification for an indigenously designed type to replace the Cessna T-37. First flown on 16 August 1980 the initial Tucano, of some 133 for Brazil, was delivered to the Air Force Academy near São Paulo in September 1983 for service with the designation **T-27**.

Designed from the outset to provide jet-like flying experience, the Tucano has a long cockpit with vertically staggered ejection seats and a single power lever governing both propeller pitch and the engine rpm.

The Brazilian air force's formation aerobatic team, the Escuadron de Fumaca (smoke squadron), received T-27 aircraft to replace its ageing North American Harvard machines, and has displayed extensively throughout the American continent.

An export order for 134 Tucanos was concluded with Egypt in September 1983, and all but the first 10 of these were licence-assembled at Helwan. The Egyptian air force itself operates only 54 locally assembled machines, and the other 80 were supplied to the Iraqi air force. These were followed by deliveries

(including current firm orders) to the air forces of Argentina, Colombia, Honduras, Iran, Paraguay, Peru, Venezuela and an undisclosed customer. Another major order was placed in July 1990 when France announced its intention to purchase 80 (later reduced to 50) Brazilian-built **EMB-312F** aircraft for

delivery from July 1993.

This French version boasts an increased fatigue life, a ventral airbrake, propeller and canopy de-icing, French-built avionics and a number of other improvements.

The Tucano's most notable export success came in March 1985, when it won a hotly contested British order for aircraft to replace the Royal Air Force's BAe (Hunting) Jet Provost turbojet-powered

trainers. The resulting, much modified **Tucano T.Mk 1**, was produced under licence in the Northern Ireland city of Belfast by Shorts, which manufactured 130 for the RAF and additionally produced aircraft to the same standard for the air forces of Kenya and Kuwait. By 1999 total firm orders, including the Shorts-built version, stood at 650 aircraft, of which the majority had been delivered.

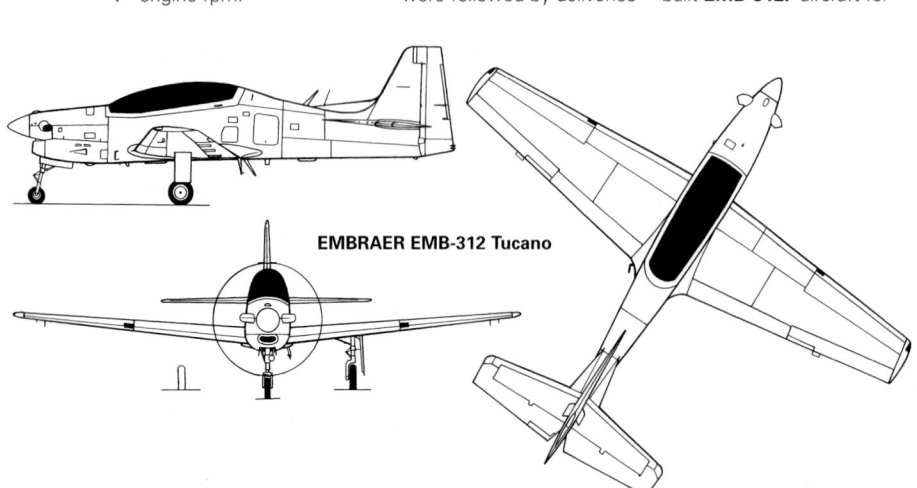

EMBRAER EMB-312 Tucano

Some 18 T-27 basic trainers entered service with the Fuerza Aérea Venezolana, alongside 12 AT-27 advanced and weapons trainers.

EMBRAER EMB-312 & EMB-314 Super Tucano (cont.)

In June 1991 EMBRAER announced the **EMB-312H** (later **EMB-314**) **Super Tucano** with an uprated PT6A engine driving a five-rather than three-bladed Hartzell propeller, the whole package being optimised for higher performance and greater agility as well as the ability to carry a heavier load. The EMB-312H concept was characterised by the three subvariants of the PT6A engine that were proposed, and these subvariants were the basic EMB-312H with the

powerplant of one 1,600-shp (1193-kW) PT6A-67R engine, the **EMB-312HJ** proposed unsuccessfully in partnership with Northrop Grumman for the US services' JPATS (Joint Primary Aircraft Training System) competition with the 1,300-shp (969-kW) PT6A-68A engine, and the **ALX** border patrol version with the 1,250-shp (932-kW) PT6A-68-1 engine. To accommodate the longer engine and to preserve the centre of gravity in the correct posi-

tion, the fuselage has been lengthened by the insertion of 'plugs' forward and aft of the cockpit and strengthened for the incorporation of a centreline hardpoint. Other revisions include airframe strengthening for a longer fatigue life and the ability to sustain higher loads when manoeuvring, a new wing accommodating the fixed forward-firing armament of two 0.5-in (12.7-mm) machine-guns, pressure refuelling, an onboard oxygen-generating system, cockpit pressurisation, HOTAS controls, a new canopy of the clamshell type in place of the original starboard-hinged type,

Martin-Baker Mk 10 zero/zero ejection seats, a 'glass' cockpit, propeller and canopy de-icing, and a ventral airbrake.

The EMB-312H first flew in May 1996, and the first customer for the EMB-314 was Bombardier, the Canadian group that has developed a private-venture training operation for NATO and allied pilots, but the order was later switched to the Raytheon Beech Texan II.

In August 1995 the Brazilian air force contracted with EMBRAER for the full development of the ALX light attack and weapons

training type for delivery from 1999 with the PT6A-68-5 engine. For its Amazon surveillance programme, the Brazilian air force intends to operate some 99 examples of the type in the form of 49 examples of the single-seat **A-29** for the dedicated attack role with a fuselage 34 ft 6½ in (10.53 m) long, 20 examples of the two-seat **AT-29** with the full-length EMB-314 fuselage and provision for a FLIR turret for night targeting capability, and 30 of the AT-29 with dual controls as advanced trainers to replace the Xavante.

With a respectable underwing weaponload and internal machine-guns, the ALX represents a potent COIN and light-attack platform.

SPECIFICATION

EMBRAER EMB-312 Tucano
Type: two-seat basic flying and armament trainer
Powerplant: one Pratt & Whitney Canada PT6A-25C turboprop engine rated at 750 shp (559 kW)
Performance: maximum speed 278 mph (448 km/h) at 10,000 ft (3050 m); cruising speed 255 mph (411 km/h) at 10,000 ft (3050 m); initial climb rate 2,231 ft (680 m) per minute; service ceiling 30,000 ft

(9145 m); typical range 1,145 miles (1844 km) with internal fuel
Weights: empty 3,991 lb (1810 kg); maximum take-off 7,000 lb (3175 kg)
Dimensions: wingspan 36 ft 6½ in (11.14 m); length 32 ft 4¼ in (9.86 m); height 11 ft 1¾ in (3.40 m);); wing area 208.82 sq ft (19.40 m²)
Armament: up to 2,205 lb (1000 kg) of stores carried on four underwing hardpoints

ENAER T-35 Pillán

ENAER's Pillán met with considerable success in Chile and won export orders from Spain. The aircraft follows the classic modern trainer layout, but uses as its basis a light cabin aircraft.

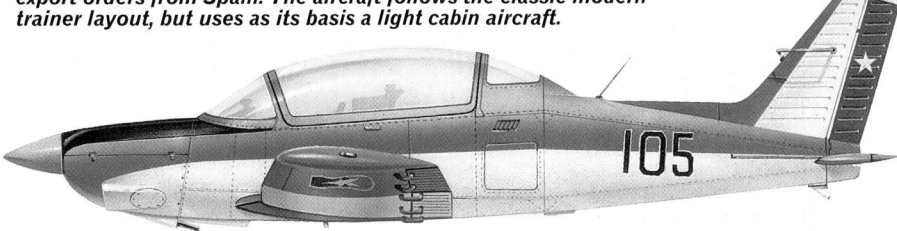

From 1980 ENAER assembled some 28 examples of the Piper PA-28 Dakota for local flying clubs and also for the Chilean air force. The latter was impressed with the capabilities of this basically civil type as a primary flying trainer, but wanted a more capable type for the aerobatic training role, with two seats in the vertically stepped tandem arrangement becoming standard for military trainers. The **ENAER Pillán** (devil) that resulted from this requirement was first flown on 6 March 1981 in the USA after development by Piper as the **PA-28R-300**, which was based on the PA-32 Saratoga series of lightplanes with a new central fuselage/wing centre section assembly as well as strengthened outer wing

panels and an uprated powerplant. The type is a useful trainer and counter-insurgency type intended for local manufacture by ENAER, the most important single component of the developing Chilean aerospace industry.

The two American-built prototypes had an all-moving tailplane that was replaced in production machines by an adjustable tailplane with separate elevators, and the production model also introduced a deeper cockpit canopy and larger rudder mass balance. The first production-standard Pillán flew in December 1984 and the type entered service in July 1985. The Pillán has been produced in several basically similar subvariants as the **T-35A** primary flying trainer for Chile, the **T-35B**

instrument trainer for Chile with more comprehensive instrumentation, the **T-35C** flying trainer for Spain assembled by CASA from Chilean-supplied kits (known locally by the designation **E.26 Tamiz**), and the **T-35D** flying and instrument trainer for Panama and Paraguay. The **T-35S** is the single-seat version of the T-35 intended for aerobatic display purposes. Developed as a turboprop-powered version powered by the 420-shp (313-kW) Allison 250-B17D turboprop engine and first flown as the **T-35TX**, the **T-35DT**

Turbo-Pillán variant offers significantly improved performance and payload, especially in the armed role. The development programme looked promising, but was discontinued in 1987 despite earlier plans to start production of the **T-35T Aucan** (blithe spirit) in 1988, but was then reinstated during 1991 as a conversion from standard T-35 configuration before being cancelled once more. At the beginning of the 21st century ENAER was trying to raise interest in the **Pillán 2000** updated version of the basic Pillán,

its primary hope being the Chilean air force whose inventory of basic Pillán trainers has been depleted by the sale of 10 and five T-35B aircraft to El Salvador and Guatemala respectively. The Pillán 2000 concept is based on the combination of the T-35's standard fuselage, tail unit and powerplant with a new wing (designed by two Russian companies) of greater span but lighter weight, for a lower wing-loading and thus improved climb rate and service ceiling in combination with greater agility.

SPECIFICATION

ENAER T-35A Pillán
Type: two-seat basic and intermediate flying and armament trainer with counter-insurgency capability
Powerplant: one Lycoming IO-540-K1K5 flat-six piston engine rated at 300 hp (224 kW)
Performance: maximum speed 193 mph (311 km/h) at sea level; cruising speed 166 mph (266 km/h) at 8,800 ft (2680 m); initial climb rate 1,525 ft (465 m) per minute; service ceiling 19,160 ft (5840 m); range 748 miles (1204 km)
Weights: empty 2,050 lb (930 kg); maximum take-off 2,900 lb

(1315 kg) for aerobatics or 2,950 lb (1338 kg) with external stores
Dimensions: wingspan 29 ft (8.84 m); length 26 ft 3 in (8.00 m); height 8 ft 8 in (2.64 m); wing area 147.34 sq ft (13.69 m²)
Armament: up to 1,102 lb (500 kg) of disposable stores carried on two underwing hardpoints, and generally comprising two 550- or 500-lb (250- or 227-kg) free-fall bombs, or two pods each carrying one 0.5-in (12.7-mm) machine-gun, or two multiple launchers each carrying four or seven 2.75-in (70-mm) air-to-surface unguided rockets

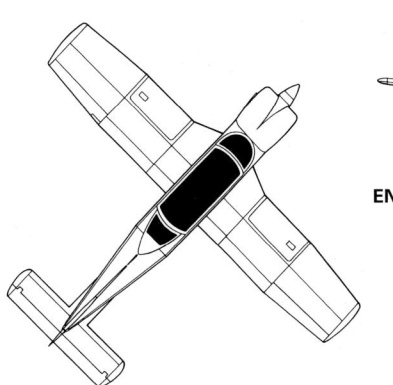

ENAER T-35A Pillán

English Electric P.5 Cork and Kingston

The Phoenix Dynamo Manufacturing Company became part of the English Electric Company in 1918, and while the flying-boat now known as the **English Electric P.5 Cork** should more correctly be designated as the **Phoenix P.5 Cork**, it is included here because of its obvious relationship with the English Electric designs which followed. The series of Porte flying-boats developed in the middle part of World War I had been generally successful, and in 1917 the Admiralty decided to order two 'boats for the evaluation of a new monocoque hull designed by Lieutenant Commander Linton Hope. The hulls were built by a Southampton company (May, Harden and May Ltd.) at its works on the River Thames at Hampton Wick, while Phoenix at Bradford was contracted to build the remainder of the airframe and to carry out final assembly. The two hulls differed in shape, and the **P.5 Cork Mk I** first 'boat was assembled at Brough, being completed in early August 1918.

Official trials began at the Isle of Grain later in that same month, but as a result of problems with varnish on their fabric covering, the wings had to be returned for re-covering and the wings of the **P.5A Cork Mk II** second 'boat were substituted. The opportunity was taken on the second aircraft to improve its performance on the water by raising the lower wing slightly above the hull and mounting it on pylons, and enlarging the rudder; the type also had a pair of nacelles on the upper wing, each carrying two 0.303-in (7.7-mm) Lewis trainable machine-guns. The Armistice killed any chances of a production order, but the two prototypes continued on experimental work for several years. The second Cork was eventually fitted with two 450-hp (336-kW) Napier Lion engines as the **Cork Mk III** and as such formed the basis for the next design, the Kingston.

Carrying the same basic design designation as the Cork, the **P.5 Kingston** was a redesign of the earlier flying-boat in its Mk III form, but incorporating a number of improvements. The first Kingston flew in 1924 with the powerplant of two Napier Lion engines which had been tried in the second Phoenix, and a small production batch of five such 'boats was ordered. These had redesigned wingtip floats, extended upper-wing ailerons and a larger fin-and-rudder assembly than their predecessor, together with a similar hull with the waist gun positions removed.

The first production example of the Kingston was lost during trials at Felixstowe in April 1925, but the crew escaped. The fourth production 'boat, fitted with a new Dural hull, became the **Kingston Mk II**, while the final variant was the **Kingston Mk III**, a designation applied to the last production Kingston which had yet another new hull, this time reverting to wooden construction and conferring a considerable improvement in the 'boat's take-off performance. The Kingston Mk III first flew

This aircraft, the third Kingston, was completed as a Mk I. The upper-fuselage bulge visible just behind the lower wing housed a dinghy.

in 1926, but in March of that year, with no further orders in prospect, English Electric closed its aircraft department and it was to be 23 years before the company's next aircraft, the classic Canberra jet-powered bomber, appeared.

SPECIFICATION	
English Electric P.5 Kingston Mk III	14,981 lb (6795 kg)
Type: multi-seat maritime reconnaissance and anti-submarine flying-boat	**Dimensions:** wingspan 85 ft 6 in (26.06 m); length 57 ft 1½ in (17.41 m); height 21 ft 6½ in (6.57 m); wing area 1,282.50 sq ft (119.14 m²)
Powerplant: two Napier Lion W-type piston engines each rated at 450 hp (336 kW)	**Armament:** one 0.303-in (7.7-mm) Lewis trainable machine-guns in each of the bow and fore-and-aft pair of upper-wing nacelle positions, plus up to 1,040 lb (472 kg) of disposable stores carried under the lower wing, and generally comprising two 520-lb (236-kg) or four 230-lb (104-kg) bombs
Performance: maximum speed 105 mph (169 km/h) at sea level; climb to 5,000 ft (1525 m) in 12 minutes 37 seconds; service ceiling 9,180 ft (2800 m); range 520 miles (837 km)	
Weights: empty 9,559 lb (4336 kg); maximum take-off	

English Electric Canberra

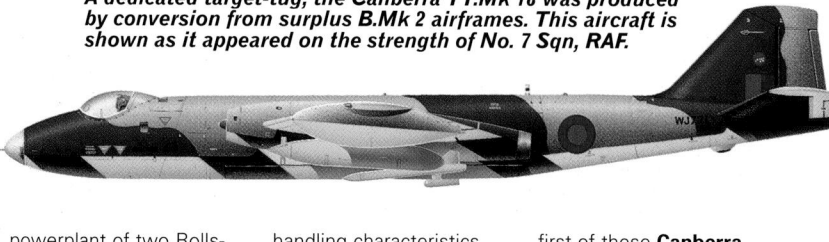

A dedicated target-tug, the Canberra TT.Mk 18 was produced by conversion from surplus B.Mk 2 airframes. This aircraft is shown as it appeared on the strength of No. 7 Sqn, RAF.

Before leaving Westland Aircraft, the company established by his family, the brilliant designer W. E. W. 'Teddy' Petter had been formulating the design of an advanced turbojet-powered bomber. On taking up his new appointment as chief designer of the English Electric Company, Petter was soon involved in the development of an aircraft type that not only became the first British jet bomber, but one that was still operating at the beginning of the 21st century.

Before the design of what was initially desig-

nated as the **English Electric A.1** was finalised, however, Petter had been forced to make extensive revisions to his original concept for this machine. One of the key factors in the success of the design lay in the particular wing planform chosen: discarding swept wings, with their associated higher wing loadings, Petter adopted a broad parallel-chord centre section and comparatively short-span tapered panels outboard of the nacelles, which were partially submerged in the wing at the junction of the centre section and the outer panels, for the

powerplant of two Rolls-Royce Avon axial-flow turbojets. The combination of this potent powerplant and a low-aspect-ratio and lightly loaded wing resulted in great manoeuvrability at high altitude, excellent low-speed performance, and good fuel economy. The rest of the A.1's airframe comprised a conventional tail unit, retractable tricycle landing gear, and an elegant circular-section fuselage carrying, in a forward location that provided good fields of vision, a pressurised cockpit for the crew of two (pilot and navigator) on a side-by-side pair of ejection seats. In this form, and with the powerplant of Avon RA.2 turbojets each rated at 6,000 lb st (26.69 kN), the prototype made the maiden flight of the Canberra series on 13 May 1949, revealing virtually trouble-free operation and delightful

handling characteristics.

As work was progressing on this prototype, the machine was being developed to the requirements of Specification B.3/45. Three additional prototypes were built, the first of these with two Rolls-Royce Nene RNe.2 centrifugal-flow turbojets each rated at 5,000 lb st (22.24 kN) as a temporary alternative, for the validation of such a powerplant in the event that there were development delays with the Avon engine. The next two prototypes were powered by Avon engines, and all four prototypes in due course received the designation **Canberra B.Mk 1**. It had been intended that the Canberra would use a radar bomb-aiming system, but delay in the development of this system resulted in an initial order for a tactical day bomber version with optical bomb-aiming under Specification B.5/47. The

first of these **Canberra B.Mk 2** aircraft made its initial flight on 23 April 1950 with the powerplant of two Avon RA.3 Mk 101 turbojets each rated at 6,500 lb st (28.91 kN), and provision for a crew of three including a bomb-aimer. The first of these aircraft was delivered to the Royal Air Force's No. 101 Squadron at Binbrook in Lincolnshire, UK on 25 May 1951, and this unit became the first of Bomber Command's jet bomber squadrons. Manufacture of the Canberra B.Mk 2 reached a figure of 415.

When replaced in British service by later models, many of the B.Mk 2s were refurbished for export, and specific variants of this series included the **Canberra B.Mk 52** for Ethiopia, **Canberra B.Mk 62** for Argentina, **Canberra B.Mk 72** for Peru and **Canberra B.Mk 82** for Venezuela.

IF1029 was one of 10 refurbished RAF B.Mk 15/16 airframes delivered to the Indian air force as Canberra B(I).Mk 66 aircraft in 1970-71.

English Electric Canberra (continued)

Development of the superb Canberra continued apace, and production eventually reached 1,352 aircraft before manufacture came to an end. Of the overall figure, 901 machines were built by English Electric and its sub-contractors (Avro, Handley Page and Short); 48 were built under licence for service with the Royal Australian Air Force by Australia's Department of Defence Production; and in the USA the Martin Company of Baltimore, Maryland, built an additional 403 somewhat revised aircraft under licence, with the company designation **Model 272** and the

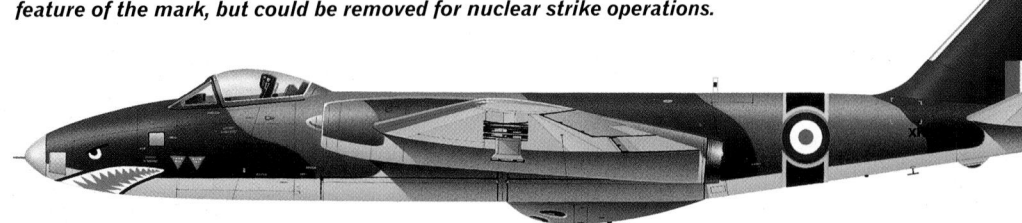

This Canberra B(I).Mk 8 flew with the RAF's No. 16 Squadron from RAF Wildenrath, West Germany. The underbelly gun pack was a key feature of the mark, but could be removed for nuclear strike operations.

service designation **B-57**. In 1963 the British Aircraft Corporation came into existence as a merger of Bristol, English Electric, Hunting and Vickers-Armstrongs, and the Canberra thereupon became a BAC responsibility until 1977, when BAC was merged with Hawker Siddeley and Scottish Aviation to create British Aerospace.

Like the de Havilland Mosquito of World War II, the Canberra was designed to operate at a speed and ceiling fast and high enough to allow the omission of all defensive armament. Such capability meant, inevitably, that the Canberra was capable of capturing a number of records, especially a number of officially recognised point-to-point speed records. A Canberra with Bristol Olympus turbojets established a world altitude record of 65,876 ft (20079 m) on 29 August 1955, capped on 28 August 1957 with a height of 70,000 ft (21336 m). This was accomplished by a Canberra with two Avon turbojets supplemented by a Napier Double Scorpion rocket motor.

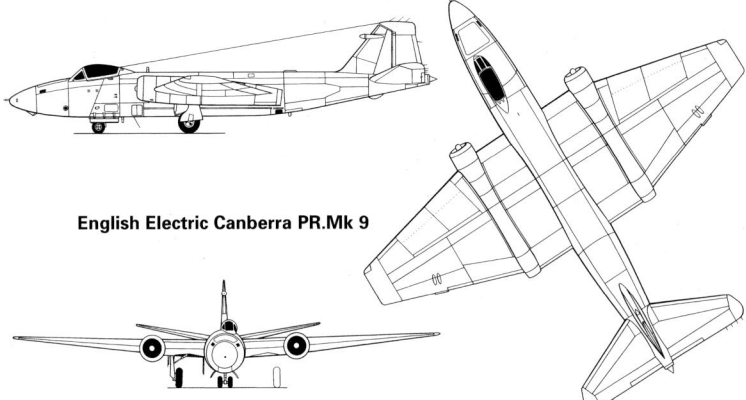

English Electric Canberra PR.Mk 9

SPECIFICATION

BAC Canberra B(I).Mk 8
Type: two-seat intruder
Powerplant: two Rolls-Royce Avon RA.7 Mk 109 turbojet engines each rated at 7,400 lb st (32.92 kN)
Performance: maximum speed 541 mph (871 km/h) at 40,000 ft (12190 m); initial climb rate 3,400 ft (1036 m) per minute; service ceiling 48,000 ft (14630 m); range 3,630 miles (5842 km) with maximum fuel or 806 miles (1297 km) on a lo-lo-lo mission

with maximum warload
Weights: empty 29,750 lb (12678 kg); maximum take-off 54,950 lb (24925 kg)
Dimensions: wingspan 63 ft 11½ in (19.50 m) without tip tanks; length 65 ft 6 in (19.96 m); height 15 ft 8 in (4.78 m); wing area 960.00 sq ft (89.16 m²)
Armament: up to 6,000 lb (2722 kg) of bombs carried internally plus an additional 2,000 lb (907 kg) of ordnance carried on underwing pylons

---

Variants

Canberra PR.Mk 3: generally similar to the B.Mk 2 but equipped for high-altitude photographic reconnaissance (37 aircraft); another two aircraft were built for Venezuela with the designation **Canberra PR.Mk 83**
Canberra T.Mk 4: generally similar to B.Mk 2 but equipped as trainers with dual controls and still carrying a navigator (67 aircraft); aircraft surplus to RAF requirements were later refurbished for the export market, whose specific models included the **Canberra T.Mk 13** for New Zealand, **Canberra T.Mk 54** for India, **Canberra T.Mk 64** for Argentina and **Canberra T.Mk 84** for Venezuela
Canberra B.Mk 5: target-marker version of B.Mk 2 having solid nose and optically flat bomb-aimer's panel (one prototype)
Canberra B.Mk 6: similar to B.Mk 2 but with increased fuel capacity and Avon Mk 109 turbojets each rated at 7,400 lb st (32.92 kN) (103 aircraft)
Canberra B(I).Mk 6: interim night interdictor version of B.Mk 6 with underwing weapons and an underfuselage gun pack (22 aircraft); when declared surplus to British requirements, 20 of the aircraft were refurbished for sale in equal numbers to India and Peru as the **Canberra B(I).Mk 66** and **Canberra B(I).Mk 56** respectively
Canberra PR.Mk 7: generally similar to PR.Mk 3 but with the uprated Avon Mk 109 turbojets introduced on the B.Mk 6 (75 aircraft plus **Canberra PR.Mk 57** aircraft for India, which later received four refurbished ex-RAF aircraft as two more Canberra PR.Mk 57s and two **Canberra PR.Mk 67** aircraft, the latter with slightly revised equipment)
Canberra B(I).Mk 8: multi-role version (long-range night interdictor/high-altitude bomber/target marker) and, in the case of RAF aircraft from 1963, equipped to carry air-to-surface missiles (73 aircraft); the type was also built for India, Peru and Venezuela with the designations **Canberra B(I).Mk 58**, **Canberra B(I).Mk 68** and **Canberra B(I).Mk 82** respectively, and when released from British service one machine was refurbished for Peru with the same **Canberra B(I).Mk 56** designation that had earlier been used for Peru's 10 conversions from Canberra B(I).Mk 6 standard
Canberra PR.Mk 9: high-altitude photo-reconnaissance version with a centre section of increased chord and outer-wing panels of greater span for an overall span of 67 ft 10 in (20.68 m) and a service ceiling of 58,000 ft (17680 m), powered controls, navigator's position in nose, and Avon Mk 206 turbojets each rated at 11,000 lb st (48.93 kN) (one prototype conversion and 23 production aircraft)

Canberra U.Mk 10: conversions from B.Mk 2 standard for service as unmanned target aircraft that later received the revised designation **Canberra D.Mk 10**
Canberra T.Mk 11: modification of B.Mk 2 with AI.Mk 17 radar equipment in fuselage nose and accommodation for crew of two and two pupils; developed to train pilots and navigators of all-weather fighters in the use of AI radar (seven conversions)
Canberra B(I).Mk 12: modification of B(I).Mk 8 for service with Royal New Zealand Air Force and South African Air Force (10 and six aircraft respectively)
Canberra T.Mk 13: version of T.Mk 4 for RNZAF (two aircraft)
Canberra U.Mk 14: conversions by Shorts, later redesignated **Canberra D.Mk 14**, from Canberra D.Mk 10 standard for use as targets in the trials of the Shorts Sea Cat naval SAM system
Canberra B.Mk 15: modification of B.Mk 6 with underwing attachments for two 1,000-lb (454-kg) bombs or packs of unguided rockets, plus more advanced nav/com equipment (38 conversions)
Canberra E.Mk 15: B.Mk 15 conversions for the high-altitude calibration of ground-based navaids with special navaids and recorders
Canberra B.Mk 16: similar to B.Mk 15 with addition of Blue Shadow equipment (20 conversions)
Canberra T.Mk 17: produced by BAC to the extent of 24 aircraft, this was an ECM trainer conversion of the B.Mk 2 with the Whittaker ARI.23363 and ARI.23379 Yellow Veil radar jammer and the GTE Dragonfly communications surveillance/jamming equipment in the nose, chaff dispensers in the bomb bay, and RWRs in the nose and tail; six of the RAF's 12 surviving aircraft were upgraded in the late 1980s to **Canberra T.Mk 17A** standard with modernised and expanded jammers for enhanced ECM capability
Canberra TT.Mk 18: produced by BAC to the extent of 18 aircraft, this was a conversion from B.Mk 2 standard with a target-towing installation under each wing
Canberra T.Mk 19: electronically silent target version produced as eight Marshalls conversions of T.Mk 11 night-fighter trainers with concrete in place of the radar
Canberra B.Mk 20: Australian licence-built tactical bomber with Australian-built Avon Mk 109 turbojets (48 aircraft)
Canberra T.Mk 21: trainer conversions made in Australia (seven aircraft in the form of five and two Mk 20 and Mk 2 conversions)
Canberra T.Mk 22: produced by BAC to the extent of seven aircraft, this was a conversion from PR.Mk 7 standard with Blue Parrot radar and other systems for the training of Fleet Air Arm crews

English Electric Lightning

Becoming a responsibility of the British Aircraft Corporation in 1963, the **English Electric Lightning** interceptor entered service during 1960 and in the process heralded a new era for the Royal Air Force. The prime mover behind the project was W. E. W. 'Teddy' Petter, whose far-sighted basic design was responsible for English Electric's receipt of a 1947 study contract for a super-sonic research aircraft. The resulting **P.1A** flew on 4 August 1954, and later exceeded Mach 1 on its powerplant of two rather basic and non-afterburning Bristol Siddeley Sapphire turbojet engines. Three research prototypes were built, two for intensive flight trials and one for test-ing to destruction in a ground rig, and these initial aircraft were readily identifi-able by the elliptical air inlet in their noses.

In 1954 the design underwent extensive change to turn it into a practical type for service deployment in the fast-climbing interceptor role. Three **P.1B** operational prototypes, with a power-plant of two Rolls-Royce Avon turbojet engines aspi-rated via a circular inlet fitted with a centrebody shock cone, were built. The first of these made its maiden flight on 4 April 1957, the name Lightning being allocated by the Air Ministry some 19 months later, and on 25 November 1958 a P.1B exceeded Mach 2 for the first time after being fitted with two Avon engines incorporating crude afterburner units. After a further 20 pre-production aircraft had been built and proved (this was a radically new aircraft to the Air Ministry), the Lightning was finally cleared to enter service in 1960. The RAF now had a highly supersonic all-weather interceptor, but it also had maintenance headaches the likes of which it had not previously seen. But perform the Lightning certainly did. The type had Ferranti AI.Mk 23 AIRPASS interception radar and associated fire-control system with its antenna in the inlet centrebody, an armament of two IR-homing Firestreak short-range AAMs on the sides of the fuselage, and truly supersonic performance.

The first production example of the **Lightning F.Mk 1** initial operational version flew on 29 October 1959 with Avon Mk 200R engines incorporating simple on/off afterburners, and deliveries to the RAF's No. 74 Squadron began in the following summer, with additional aircraft then following to Nos 56 and 111 Squadrons. The final production aircraft of the F.Mk 1 model (68 aircraft including the 20 pre-production machines and one F.Mk 1 static airframe) were the 28 **Lightning F.Mk 1A** aircraft with provision for a remov-able inflight-refuelling probe and a number of improve-ments such as UHF radio and a better windscreen rain-dispersal arrangement. The next variant, of which 44 were completed, was the **Lightning F.Mk 2** with better range, ceiling and speed, more advanced electronics, a liquid-oxygen breathing system, steer-able nosewheel, and Avon Mk 210 engines with fully-variable afterburner units. The first F.Mk 2 flew on 11 July 1961, and the type later equipped Nos 19 and 92 Squadrons in Germany.

The **Lightning F.Mk 3**, a further development of which 70 examples were built, was powered by two Avon Mk 301 engines each rated at 16,360 lb st (72.77 kN) with afterburn-ing. It had no guns, relying instead on an all-aspect Red Top missiles, and for long-range ferrying could be fitted with two large over-wing jettisonable fuel tanks along with an inflight-refu-elling probe under the port wing. The first F.Mk 3, also incorporating a larger, square-topped fin and AI.Mk 23B collision-course fire-control radar, flew on 16 July 1962 and the type entered service with No. 74 Squadron in mid-1964, subsequently re-equipping also Nos 23, 29, 56 and 111 Squadrons.

The ultimate **Lightning F.Mk 6** was the result of a long-overdue decision in 1965 to follow the advice of the British Aircraft Corporation in two impor-tant aspects. Firstly, the fuel capacity was almost doubled, and secondly the cambered, kinked wing leading edge was fitted – this had first been flown nine years earlier and allowed operation at greater weights. Increased fuel capacity (in the form of a much enlarged ventral tank) combined with the low subsonic drag of the new leading edge to provide the F.Mk 6 with a tremendous improvement in effective-ness. (The F.Mk 6 was built to the extent of 39 aircraft that were preceded by 16 **Lightning F.Mk 3A** machines to an interim F.Mk 6 standard that was later upgraded to the full F.Mk 6 standard.) Saudi Arabia and Kuwait bought a developed version of the F.Mk 6 for service with the designations **Lightning F.Mk 53** and **Lightning F.Mk 53K** respectively: the former comprised one F.Mk 3 conversion and 34 production aircraft, and the latter 12 production aircraft. Saudi Arabia also purchased five **Lightning F.Mk 52** conversions from F.Mk 2 standard.

The Lightning was phased out of RAF service in June 1988, and disap-peared from Kuwait and Saudi Arabian service in 1977 and in December 1985 respectively.

These No. 92 Sqn, RAF Lightning F.Mk 2s demonstrate the original fin shape and small underbelly fuel tank.

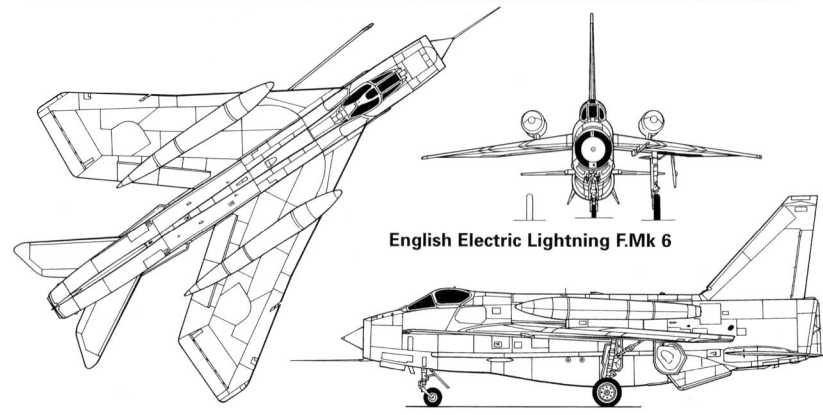

English Electric Lightning F.Mk 6

SPECIFICATION

BAC Lightning F.Mk 6
Type: single-seat supersonic all-weather interceptor
Powerplant: two Rolls-Royce Avon RB.136 Mk 301 turbojet engines each rated at 12,690 lb st (56.45 kN) dry and 16,360 lb st (72.77 kN) with afterburning
Performance: maximum speed 1,500 mph (2415 km/h) or Mach 2.30 at 40,000 ft (12190 m); cruising speed 595 mph (958 km/h) at optimum altitude; initial climb rate 50,000 ft (15240 m) per minute; service ceiling 60,000 ft (18290 m); range 800 miles (1287 km) with internal fuel
Weights: empty 28,040 lb (12719 kg); maximum take-off 41,700 lb (18915 kg)
Dimensions: wingspan 34 ft 10 in (10.61 m); length 55 ft 3 in (16.84 m); height 19 ft 7 in (5.97 m); wing area 458.50 sq ft (42.60 m²)
Armament: large, two-portion ventral pack contained fuel tank in the rear, and at the front either more fuel or a pack housing two 30-mm ADEN fixed forward-firing cannon; operational packs mounted ahead of ventral bay included two Firestreak or Red Top AAMs, or 44 2-in (51-mm) spin-stabilised rockets. Provision was made for five Vinten 360 70-mm cameras, or (night reconnaissance) cameras and linescan equipment and underwing flares; underwing/ overwing hardpoints could carry up to 144 rockets or six 1,000-lb (454-kg) bombs

Variants

Lightning T.Mk 4: RAF side-by-side two-seat operational trainer based on the F.Mk 1A (22 aircraft)
Lightning T.Mk 5: RAF side-by-side two-seat operational trainer based on the F.Mk 3 (22 aircraft)
Lightning T.Mk 54: ex-RAF T.Mk 4 trainers supplied to Saudi Arabia (two aircraft)
Lightning T.Mk 55: Saudi Arabian trainer version (seven aircraft including one T.Mk 5 conversion)
Lightning T.Mk 55K: Kuwaiti trainer version (two aircraft)

No RAF two-seaters were built with the larger ventral fuel/weapons pack, unlike the Saudi T.Mk 55, which might have formed the basis of a truly capable multi-role warplane. The aircraft illustrated is a Lightning T.Mk 5.

Enstrom Model F-28 and Model 280 Shark

The first **Model F-28** light helicopter, designed and built by Rudy J. Enstrom, made its maiden flight on 12 November 1960 as a two-seat experimental type with a two-bladed main rotor and an unskinned rear fuselage. On 26 May 1962 there followed the first of two pre-production examples with three-seat accommodation, and then in the autumn of 1963 the first Model F-28 production helicopter with a fully enclosed fuselage (light alloy- and glassfibre-covered main section and light alloy semi-monocoque boom) and the powerplant of one 180-hp (134-kW) Lycoming O-360-A1A engine driving a three-bladed main rotor. Since then more than 1,000 examples have been built in successive models.

Introduced in 1968, the **Model F-28A** was powered by the 205-hp (153-kW) HIO-360-C1A engine. Production was discontinued in February 1970, when the R. J. Enstrom Corporation ceased operations, but resumed in 1971 when the organisation was re-formed as the Enstrom Helicopter Corporation. A development of the Model F-28A with fixed tricycle landing gear and the revised powerplant of one 420-shp (313-kW) Allison 250-C20B turboshaft engine derated to 240 shp (179 kW), the **Spitfire**

Helicopter Spitfire Mk I gained the advantage of having an empty weight reduced by 200 lb (91 kg) and greater internal volume for fuel or payload. Developed in 1973 and certificated in September 1974 as a luxury version of the Model F-28A, the **Model 280 Shark** introduced a more streamlined cabin section, greater fuel capacity, dorsal and ventral vertical tail surfaces, and a small horizontal tail surface with small endplate fins. The **Model F-28C** and **Model 280C** were improved versions with the 205-hp (153-kW) HIO-360-E1AD engine fitted with a Rajay turbocharger, and the tail rotor relocated to the port side of the fuselage, with its direction of rotation reversed; the **Model F-28C-2** introduced a one-piece windscreen and a pedestal central instrument console for improved forward and downward vision. Certificated in January 1981, the **Model F-28F** and **Model 280F** were powered by the 225-hp (168-kW) HIO-360-F1AD turbocharged engine. Work on the design of the **Model 280L Hawk**, a four-seat version of the Enstrom 280C, began in January 1978 and the prototype first flew on 27 December 1978 with a main rotor increased in diameter by

2 ft (0.61 m) and the fuse-lage lengthened by 3 ft (0.91 m). The **Model 280L** had the same engine as the Model F-28F and Model 280F, supplied with fuel from a larger tank.

The **Model F-28F Falcon** is the current basic utility model, certificated in December 1980 and fitted with the 225-hp (168-kW) HIO-360-F1AD turbocharged engine. The similarly powered **Model 280FX Shark** was certificated in January 1985 with a number of refinements such as a redesigned air inlet system, fully faired skid landing gear, covered tail rotor shaft, tail rotor guard and a new tailplane with endplate fins. A dedicated police patrol version of the Model F-28F is the **Model F-28F-P Sentinel** that was delivered from October 1986 as a development of the standard Model F-28F with provision for any of three types of searchlight, a FLIR and specialised police radio equipment.

The first military sale was not made until 1989, when 15 examples of the Model 280FX were supplied to the Chilean army for primary training. Subsequently, the Peruvian army acquired 10 Model F-28F helicopters. In 1994 Colombia received 12 examples of the Model F-28F.

The Model 280FX also

As a basic three-seat utility helicopter, the smart-looking Model F-28F has found a ready market. Note this example's ground-handling wheels.

served as the basis for the four/five-seat **Model 480**, which became the company's **TH-28** entrant for the US Army's NTH (New Training Helicopter) competition. After a Model 280FX modified with the Allison 250 turboshaft had made its first flight in December 1988, the first true 'wide-body' Model 480

with five seats took to the air in October 1989, with deliveries to customers starting in 1994. The TH-28 was certified in September 1992 and four aircraft embarked on a 1,500-hour test programme. Intended as a basic trainer and light patrol helicopter, the TH-28 lost to the Bell TH-67 in the NTH competition.

SPECIFICATION	
Enstrom Model F-28F Falcon **Type:** three-seat light utility helicopter **Powerplant:** one Lycoming HIO-360-F1AD flat-four piston engine rated at 225 hp (168 kW) **Performance:** maximum speed 112 mph (180 km/h) between sea level and 3,000 ft (915 m); cruising speed 102 mph (165 km/h) at optimum altitude; initial climb rate 1,450 ft (442 m) per minute; certificated ceiling 12,000 ft	(3660 m); hovering ceiling 7,700 ft (2345 m) in ground effect and 8,700 ft (2650 m) out of ground effect; range 263 miles (423 km) **Weights:** empty 1,570 lb (712 kg); maximum take-off 2,600 lb (1179 kg) **Dimensions:** main rotor diameter 32 ft (9.75 m); length overall 29 ft 3 in (8.92 m) with rotors stationary; height 9 ft 2 in (2.79 m) to top of rotor head; main rotor disc area 804.25 sq ft (74.71 m²)

Entwicklungsring-Sud VJ 101C

In 1959 the design teams of the German companies Bölkow, Heinkel and Messerschmitt were formed into a consortium named Entwicklungsring-Sud to develop a Mach 2 VTOL interceptor for the West German defence ministry. During 1964 Heinkel left the consortium, which in the following year was re-formed as a company with the title Entwicklungsring-Sud GmbH, known more usually as EWR. There followed two prototypes of

the **VJ 101C** single-seat experimental VTOL aircraft. The powerplant comprised six RB.145 turbojet engines, developed jointly by Rolls-Royce and MAN-Turbomotoren: two were mounted vertically in the fuselage, immediately to the rear of the cockpit, and the other four were paired in a swivelling pod at each wingtip. Those in the fuselage provided only vertical lift and were used only for VTOL and low-speed flight, while those in the wingtip

pods could provide anything between vertical lift and horizontal thrust and were therefore operated for VTOL, low-speed flight, transition from vertical to horizontal flight and vice versa, and high-speed flight. Control of the aircraft in flight had been explored by a hovering rig powered by three Rolls-Royce RB.108 lift turbojets, and by May 1963 this had made a total of 70 flights.

The **VJ 101C X1** prototype was flown for the first

time in free hovering flight on 10 April 1963. It had exceeded a speed of Mach 1 several times before it crashed, following a vertical take-off, on 14 September 1964. The **VJ 101C X2** differed only in having afterburning engines in the wingtip pods, providing greater power for take-off and landing, and this made its first hovering flight on 12 June 1965. Four months later, on 22 October, the VJ 101C X2 achieved the first full transitions from vertical to horizontal flight and vice versa, but development was discontinued

soon after this.

Production of a single-seat interceptor was planned under the designation **EWR VJ 101D**, but this would have differed considerably from the research prototypes. VTOL lift would have been provided by a battery of Rolls-Royce/MAN RB.162 lift turbojets in the fuselage, but primary propulsion would have come from two Rolls-Royce/MAN RB.153 turbofan engines mounted in the rear fuselage, these relying upon thrust vectoring for control purposes. However, none of these aircraft was built.

Nicknamed 'Traumjäger' ('dream fighter') for its futuristic looks, the VJ 101 emerged as a pure research aircraft, having been scaled down to suit the available engines. The type proved a dead end as far as its potential as a warplane was concerned.

SPECIFICATION	
Entwicklungsring-Sud VJ 101C **Type:** single-seat VTOL research aircraft **Powerplant:** six Rolls-Royce/MAN RB.145 turbojet engines each rated at 2,750 lb st (12.23 kN) dry or, in the wingtip pods of the X2, 3,550 lb st (15.79 kN) with afterburning **Performance:** maximum speed	(X1) 713 mph (1147 km/h) or Mach 1.08 at high altitude **Weights:** maximum take-off (X1) 13,228 lb (6000 kg) and (X2) 17,637 lb (8000 kg) **Dimensions:** wingspan 21 ft 8¼ in (6.61 m); length 51 ft 6 in (15.70 m); height 13 ft 6½ in (4.13 m)

Erco Model 415 Ercoupe, Forney Fornair & Alon Aircoupe

The **Model 415 Ercoupe**, by any standards a classic American lightplane, has a long history as the type was designed by the Engineering and Research Corporation that was founded in 1930. Created to bring a high level of simplicity and safety into light aviation by the adoption of a flight control system that did away with separate rudder controls, the **Model 415-C Ercoupe** did not fly until 1937, and represented an advanced design for its era. The type was then built in very large numbers. A low-wing cantilever monoplane, the Model 415-C had a wing of all-metal construction with the exception of its fabric-covered outer panels. The fuselage and tail unit were all-metal structures, the cantilever tailplane being mounted high on the fuselage and carrying twin endplate fin-and-rudder assemblies. The fixed tricycle landing gear had oleo-pneumatic shock absorbers on all three faired units, and power was provided by a Continental A65 flat-four engine.

The most unusual feature of the Ercoupe was its much-advertised 'easy-to-fly' two-control system, which eliminated rudder pedals unless an individual customer opted for a conventional set of controls. The Erco system linked the ailerons, rudders and nosewheel so that turns in the air, or on the ground, were made by movement of a control wheel to remove the pilot's need to co-ordinate aileron and rudder movements in banked turns; the elevator operation was perfectly conventional.

Production of the Ercoupe ended with the outbreak of World War II, but was resumed after the war's end to create an improved Model 415-C with the 75-hp (56-kW) C75-12 engine that led to the **Model 415-D** of 1947 with a number of detail improvements, the **Model 415-E** of 1948 with the 85-hp (63-kW) C85-12 engine, the **Model 415-F** with the C85-12J fuel-injected engine, the **Model 415-G** de luxe model and the **Model 415-H** with a wide

Alon's Model A-2 differed from the original Ercoupe in having an all-metal structure, improved landing gear, a refined cockpit canopy and a 90-hp (67-kW) C90-16F engine.

assortment of optional equipment to create a range of price options. Production of some 6,000 aircraft (including more than 4,000 in 1947 alone) was marketed under the names **AirCoupe** and Ercoupe as well as **Forney Fornair**. Erco eventually ceased to operate, and all assets of Ercoupe were acquired by a new company, Alon Inc., incorporated on the last day of 1963. In due course an improved version of the Ercoupe was marketed as the **Alon Model A-2 Aircoupe**, the first example making its initial flight on

24 October 1964. The two- or three-control system remained optional, and the Aircoupe continued in

production as such until the company merged with Mooney Aircraft Inc. in 1967.

SPECIFICATION	
Erco Model 415-E Ercoupe **Type:** two-seat light aircraft **Powerplant:** one Continental C85-12 flat-four piston engine rated at 85 hp (63 kW) **Performance:** maximum speed 122 mph (196 km/h) at 2,000 ft (610 m); cruising speed 110 mph (177 km/h) at 2,000 ft (610 m);	initial climb rate 580 ft (177 m) per minute; service ceiling 12,000 ft (3660 m); range 450 miles (724 km) **Weights:** empty 814 lb (369 kg); maximum take-off 1,400 lb (635 kg) **Dimensions:** wingspan 30 ft (9.14 m); length 20 ft 9 in (6.32 m); height 5 ft 11 in (1.80 m); wing area 142.60 sq ft (13.25 m²)

Esnault-Pelterie aircraft

Robert Esnault-Pelterie, who was one of the most important pioneers of early aviation in France, began in 1904 by building and testing a glider similar in configuration to the Wright 1902 glider. Dissatisfied with its wing warping for its era, he introduced an elementary aileron system believed to be the first application of such a control surface in aviation history. It was not until November and December 1907 that Esnault-Pelterie achieved

several short flights in an aircraft of his own design, the **Esnault-Pelterie REP No. 1**. This was a tapered-wing monoplane with a short but distinctive fuselage that did little to aid longitudinal stability. Another unusual feature was the machine's landing gear, which comprised a strut-mounted monowheel beneath the forward fuselage, a tailwheel, and balancer wheels at the wingtips. Power was provided by a 25-hp

(19-kW) engine of Esnault-Pelterie's own design. Perhaps the strangest factor was a reversion to wing warping for lateral control.

A generally similar but improved **REP No. 2** was flying early in 1908. It was 'generally similar' because most pioneers of the period attempted to develop their aircraft by the incorporation of experimental 'improvements' in small stages. The **REP No. 2bis** which followed was the most successful of Esnault-Pelterie's early designs. Flown for the first time on 15 February 1909, it was powered by a 30-hp (22-kW) version of his

semi-radial (fan-type) engine, and in May of that year it achieved a flight of 5 miles (8 km).

More practical landing gear and more powerful engines were the major developments to follow, and in 1911 the Vickers company of the UK negotiated licensed production rights with Esnault-Pelterie, subsequently building a small number of monoplanes based on his design. Established at Billancourt, Seine, production of REP monoplanes continued and included by 1912 single- and two-seat civil aircraft (the **REP Type D** with a 60-hp/45-kW REP engine and the **REP Type K** with

an 80-hp/60-kW Gnome engine) and a three-seat military monoplane. In the following year a two-seat hydro-monoplane appeared, this having float alighting gear that comprised a single large central float and a balancer float at the tail. A few examples of REP monoplane types (notably the **REP Type N** and **REP Parasol**) saw service at the beginning of World War I, but by then Esnault-Pelterie had lost interest in conventional aircraft, turning instead to the potentialities of rocketry and space flight as his company concentrated on the licensed manufacture of other companies' aircraft.

Esnault-Pelterie did much to advance aviation technology. His Type N and Parasol served on into the early stages of World War I.

SPECIFICATION	
Esnault-Pelterie REP No. 2bis **Type:** single-seat monoplane **Powerplant:** one REP seven-cylinder semi-radial piston engine rated at 30 hp (22 kW) **Performance:** maximum speed about 50 mph (80 km/h)	**Weights:** maximum take-off 772 lb (350 kg) **Dimensions:** (approximate) wingspan 28 ft 2½ in (8.60 m); length 22 ft 5¾ in (6.85 m); height 8 ft 2½ in (2.50 m); wing area 169.54 sq ft (15.75 m²)

Etrich Taube

A citizen of the Austro-Hungarian empire, Doktor Igo Etrich was an enthusiast of flight from the later part of the 19th century and was convinced that the monoplane flying-wing layout offered the greatest chance for successful and safe flight. Etrich became involved in the practical side

of aviation during 1904 when, in collaboration with Franz Wels, he built and tested a model of his flying-wing glider, whose success led to the construction and flight-testing during 1907 of a man-carrying glider of the same configuration. Etrich and Wels then attempted to turn the 1907 glider into a

powered type with a 24-hp (18-kW) Antoinette engine driving a two-bladed wooden tractor propeller. Success with these endeavours evaded the two pioneers and it was only in 1909, after Wels had departed to seek aviation success elsewhere, that Etrich finally achieved limited success after modifying the powered aircraft with a rudder and frontal elevator.

This early Taube was pictured in 1910. Such was the popularity of the type that large numbers were used throughout Europe.

Etrich Taube (continued)

Although still convinced that it was with the flying-wing that the future of aviation would finally be secured, Etrich was practical enough to see that control in three dimensions currently required a fuselage to carry the fin/rudder and tailplane/elevator assemblies. The difficulty of making a monoplane wing structure that was both light and rigid enough to carry ailerons for control in the lateral plane without fear of aileron reversal also encouraged the use of warping for this purpose. This accorded well with Etrich's belief that the aerodynamic features required for the ideal wing configuration could be found in the winged seed of a tropical palm, the *Zanonia macrocarpa* with its swept-back and washed-out tips.

Etrich built his first aircraft with such a wing planform during 1909, and successful trials in November of the same year led to his design of the **Etrich Taube** (dove) in 1910. The name was highly appropriate given the planform of the wing and the graceful nature of the aircraft's progress and appearance in the air. The popularity of the Taube led to production in Austria-Hungary and in Germany. The two models of the Taube in service with the Imperial Austro-Hungarian army air service from 1912 were the **Taube A-I** with a powerplant of one 85-hp (63-kW) Austro-Daimler engine cooled by two radiators attached to the outer sides of the upper wing-supporting kingpost, and a tailskid landing gear arrangement with a central skid to prevent a nose-over accident during the landing run; and the **Taube A-II** with a powerplant of one 120-hp (90-kW) Austro-Daimler engine cooled by a frontal radiator, and a tailwheel landing gear arrangement with a main unit modelled on that of the Blériot Type XI. These variants were deemed obsolescent by the outbreak of World War I and were therefore used for training up to 1916.

In Germany, Etrich initially granted a licence to Rumpler, but after an acrimonious dispute, Etrich decided to forego his copyright to the design and Taube-type aircraft were eventually built by Albatros, DFW, Gotha, Halberstadt, Jeannin, Kondor, Krieger, LVG and Lübeck-Travemünde, in addition to Rumpler. These German aircraft were built with a large number of variations in size and details from the Austro-Hungarian norm, and production totalled some 500 aircraft, of which virtually all surviving examples were either bought by the Imperial German army air service or impressed for military service after the outbreak of World War I. Although the Taubes were technically obsolescent at this time, their reliability and ready availability meant that they remained in front-line German service up to the middle of 1915, and thereafter enjoyed a fruitful secondary career in the training role.

The **Albatros DE** was a German-built Taube powered by the 100-hp (75-kW) Mercedes D.I inline engine. Known as the **Stahltaube** (steel dove) as a result of the fact that it had a fuselage of steel tube construction, the DFW German-built Taube was also powered by the Mercedes D.I engine. Gotha produced four Taube-type designs, the **LE.1** and **LE.2** appearing in 1913 and the **LE.3** and **LE.4** in 1914. The LE.1 and LE.2 were basically similar apart from their main landing-gear units: the LE.1 had the Blériot type of unit, while the LE.2 had the Vee-strut type of unit. Both models were available with a number of different inline engine types. The LE.3 and LE.4 (possibly redesignated as the **A I** and **A II** respectively during the opening phase of the war) were powered by the Mercedes D.I engine, but differed in their radiator installations.

The **Halberstadt A I** variant on the basic theme was similarly powered by the Mercedes D.I engine. The **Jeannin Stahltaube** was one of the most elegant of all pre-war Taube types and was designed by Emil Jeannin with the 120-hp (90-kW) Argus As.II engine. There was little remarkable about the **Kondor Taube**, which was powered by the Mercedes D.I, while the most remarkable thing about the **Krieger Taube**, which was powered by the 100-hp (75-kW) Benz Bz.I or 110-hp (82-kW) Bz.II engine, was the circular-section fuselage that was of semi-monocoque plywood construction. Built in larger numbers than any other of the German-built Taubes, the **Rumpler Taube** was powered by the Mercedes D.I engine.

SPECIFICATION

Etrich Taube A-II
Type: two-seat reconnaissance aircraft
Powerplant: one Austro-Daimler inline piston engine rated at 120 hp (90 kW)
Performance: maximum speed 71.50 mph (115 km/h) at sea level; service ceiling 9,845 ft (3000 m); endurance 4 hours
Weights: empty 1,246 lb (565 kg); maximum take-off 2,094 lb (950 kg)
Dimensions: wingspan 47 ft 1 in (14.35 m); length 32 ft 3¾ in (9.85 m); height 10 ft 4 ⅛ in (3.15 m); wing area about 375.14 sq ft (34.85 m²)

Euler D I and D II

The **Euler D I** was one of a large number of fighter prototypes that emerged in Germany in response to the success enjoyed by the Nieuport Nie.11 sesquiplane fighter after its introduction by the French in January 1916. As was later to be repeated with the Sopwith Triplane, the German response to the new threat was based on the adoption of the same basic concept. As a result, the D I was a lightweight sesquiplane of wooden construction covered largely with fabric, and was powered by a rotary engine, in this instance the Oberursel U.0 unit derived from Le Rhône practice. The first of a probable two D I prototypes recorded the new fighter's maiden flight in the autumn of 1916 as little more than a Germanised version of the Nie.11, and although the type's full evaluation was not completed until January of the following year, Euler had received an order for 50 production aircraft as early as October 1916. The aircraft were already obsolete as production began, however, and were used only as fighter trainers.

The **D II** was little more than the D I with its wing cellule reduced in span, the fuselage length increased and its performance slightly boosted by the use of a more powerful engine, the 100-hp (75-kW) Oberursel U.I rotary unit. The German authorities ordered an initial 30 such fighters in April 1917, but the type was obsolete by the time deliveries started in December of the same year, so the aircraft were used only as fighter trainers.

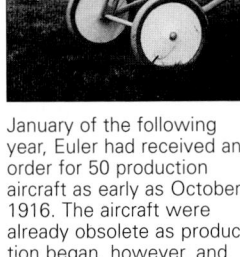

A second batch of 50 D I aircraft was ordered, but some of these were completed to the improved D II standard, which included parallel-chord wings. The aircraft illustrated is a D I.

SPECIFICATION

Euler D I
Type: single-seat fighter and fighter trainer
Powerplant: one Oberursel U.0 rotary piston engine rated at 80 hp (60 kW)
Performance: maximum speed 87 mph (140 km/h) at sea level; climb to 6,560 ft (2000 m) in 12 minutes 30 seconds
Weights: empty 838 lb (380 kg); maximum take-off 1,323 lb (600 kg)
Dimensions: wingspan 26 ft 6⅞ in (8.10 m); length 19 ft 5⅞ in (5.94 m); height 9 ft (2.75 m)
Armament: one 0.312-in (7.92-mm) LMG 08/15 fixed forward-firing machine-gun in the upper part of the forward fuselage

Eurocopter Deutschland BO 105 and EC Super Five

The parentage of the **BO 105** series of German helicopters is somewhat tortuous, for the type was first conceived by Bölkow-Entwicklungen KG that became Bölkow GmbH in 1962 after Boeing had bought a minority interest in the company. Then in the course of 1968 Bölkow GmbH merged with Messerschmitt Werke-Flugzeug-Union Sud GmbH to create Messerschmitt-Bölkow GmbH, and in 1969 this became Messerschmitt-Bölkow-Blohm GmbH (MBB) as Messerschmitt-Bölkow GmbH merged with Hamburger Flugzeugbau GmbH. In 1989 MBB became a subsidiary of Deutsche Aerospace AG (later Daimler-Benz Aerospace AG in January 1995 and then DaimlerChrysler Aerospace AG), which in January 1992 merged its helicopter division with that of Aérospatiale, the nationalised French aerospace company, to create Eurocopter. Within this organisation the helicopter divisions of MBB and Aérospatiale became Eurocopter Deutschland and Eurocopter France respectively, and are now to be the Eurocopter division of EADS (European Aeronautics, Defence and Space) Corporation to be created during 2000 by the merger of Aérospatiale Matra of France, DaimlerChrysler Aerospace of Germany and CASA of Spain.

Eurocopter Deutschland's most important in-production

Variants

BO 105LSA-3: Eurocopter Canada version with two 550-shp (410-kW) Allison 250-C28C turboshaft engines for improved 'hot-and-high' capability
BO 105LSA-3 Super Lifter: subvariant of the BO 105LSA-3 optimised for the carriage of external loads at a maximum take-off weight of 6,283 lb (2850 kg)
EC Super Five: certificated in 1993, this is an upgraded development of the BO 105CBS with the improvements incorporated in the PAH-1A1

The high-performance BO 105 has found employment in several civilian special-purpose roles. These include police (illustrated) and emergency medical service (EMS) uses.

helicopter is the BO 105, whose origins can be traced to 1962, when Bölkow saw a niche for a high-performance utility helicopter optimised for the executive and air taxi roles. The company accordingly started work on an advanced type based on the standard pod-and-boom fuselage with fixed twin-skid landing gear, but lifted by a four-bladed rigid rotor (with blades of glassfibre-reinforced plastic construction attached to a forged titanium hub) driven by a powerplant of two reliable and fuel-economical turboshaft engines; the result is a very high level of agility, which is particularly important in the military and naval derivatives of the basic helicopter. Much of the required development capital was provided by the West German government, and after the loss of the

first prototype to ground resonance problems with its Westland Scout main rotor, the first flight of a BO 105 with the definitive rigid rotor was made on 16 February 1967 by the second of an eventual three prototypes. One of these was powered by the MAN-Turbo 6022 turboshaft engine and the other two by the Allison 250-C18 turboshaft engine.

The success of the second and third prototypes proved the overall capabilities of the BO 105, and the type entered production as the **BO 105C** five-seater with a powerplant of two 400-shp (298-kW) Allison 250-C20 turboshaft engines. This and other basically civil variants have been assembled under licence by IPTN in Indonesia, CASA in Spain and Eurocopter Canada, many going to military customers in roles such as

maritime patrol and SAR. The basic BO 105C and **BO 105CB** (introduced in 1975) can carry five passengers in addition to the pilot, and the **BO 105CBS** is a slightly stretched version carrying six. The **BO 105LS** is a 'hot-and-high' version with uprated Allison 250-C28Cs, and was developed by Eurocopter Canada.

By far the most important customer was the German army air service, which bought 100 **BO 105M** helicopters for the scout role under the designation **VBH (Verbindungs und Beobachtungs Hubschrauber)**, and 212 **BO 105P** helicopters for the anti-armour role under the designation **PAH-1 (Panzerabwehr-hubschrauber-1)**. Three update programmes were proposed for the PAH-1, the first of which led to the **PAH-1A1** with new rotor blades and improved the cooling and intakes, and helicopters modified to this standard re-entered service in 1991. The **PAH-1A2** programme was to have added a night-fighting capability with a roof-mounted

German PAH helicopters are armed with six tube-launched Euromissile HOT ATMs, aimed by means of a roof-mounted stabilised sight system.

IR sight and digital HOT 2 missiles on lightweight, 'diagonally' staggered pylons. Finally, consideration was given to the conversion of 54 PAH-1 helicopters to **BSH (Begleitschütz-hubschrauber)** standard for use as escorts by the addition of four Stinger air-to-air missiles. The **BO 105/Ophelia** was a trials helicopter for the evaluation of mast- and helmet-mounted sighting systems. Neither of these upgrades went ahead.

The BO 105 also achieved substantial export sales, proving able to fulfil a number of role requirements, including short-range SAR, utility and VIP transport, light attack, scouting and anti-armour work. Of the current operators, Spain is the most important numerically with about 60 locally assembled aircraft, followed by Iraq which operates around 40.

The Spanish army operates three variants, comprising 28 anti-armour **BO 105ATH** (designated **HA.15**) machines with HOT missiles, 18 armed reconnaissance **BO 105GSH** (**HR.15**) machines with 20-mm Rheinmetall cannon, and 14 unarmed **BO 105LOH** (also **HR.15**) machines for observation duties. The BO 105LOH helicopters were subsequently modified with two 0.3-in (7.62-mm) machine-guns to become **BO 105GSH** machines.

Since 1977 IPTN in Indonesia has manufactured the BO 105 under licence as the **NBO-105CB**, with rotors and transmissions supplied from Germany. The current production version, from the 101st helicopter, is the stretched **NBO-105CBS**, also produced as the **NBO-105MPDS (Multi-Purpose Delivery System)** with a number of weapon options. Sweden operates ESCO Helitow-equipped BO 105CBS helicopters in the anti-tank role and unarmed SAR aircraft as the **HKP 9B**.

SPECIFICATION	
Eurocopter Deutschland BO 105CB	(2560 m) in ground effect and 5,300 ft (1615 m) out of ground effect; range 409 miles (658 km) with maximum payload
Type: one-crew utility light helicopter	
Powerplant: two Allison (now Rolls-Royce Allison) 250-C20B turboshaft engines each rated at 420 shp (313 kW)	**Weights:** empty 2,813 lb (1276 kg); maximum take-off 5,511 lb (2500 kg)
Performance: maximum cruising speed 150 mph (242 km/h) at sea level; initial climb rate 1,575 ft (480 m) per minute; maximum operating altitude 17,000 ft (5180 m); hovering ceiling 8,400 ft	**Dimensions:** main rotor diameter 32 ft 3½ in (9.84 m); length 38 ft 11 in (11.86 m) with the rotors turning; height 9 ft 10 in (3.00 m); main rotor disc area 818.62 sq ft (76.05 m²)
	Payload: up to five passengers

Eurocopter Deutschland/Kawasaki BK 117 and EC 145

In February 1977 MBB (now Eurocopter Deutschland) and Kawasaki agreed to undertake the collaborative design, development and production of

an advanced multi-purpose light helicopter that made use of many BO 105 components and accessories as well as the transmission developed for

the Kawasaki KH-7 design. The design matured as that of a typical utility helicopter with a pod-and-boom fuselage, twin-skid landing gear, and a dynamic

system in which paired turboshaft engines (installed side-by-side behind the main gearbox and thus above the rear part of the payload compartment) drove a four-bladed rigid main rotor and two-bladed tail rotor. The payload compartment was planned with a forward six/seven-passenger compartment accessed by a large sliding and jettisonable door on each side, and a rear freight compartment accessed by clamshell rear doors at the rear of the pod section.

Two assembly lines were

established, one each in West Germany and Japan, and while MBB was allocated responsibility for the rotors, tail boom, tail unit, landing gear, engine firewall and cowlings, hydraulic system, power-amplified controls and systems integration, Kawasaki was given responsibility for the fuselage, transmission, electrical and fuel systems, and standard items of equipment. The first of four prototypes flew on 13 June 1979, and the first full-production helicopter took to the air in December 1981.

At the beginning of the 21st century, the BK 117 continues to sell steadily. The type has proven especially useful in the EMS role.

Eurocopter Deutschland/Kawasaki BK 117 & EC 145 (cont.)

The initial **BK 117A** series was produced in three subvariants, all with a powerplant of two 600-shp (447-kW) Lycoming LTS101-750B-1 turboshaft engines: the **BK 117A-1** has a maximum take-off weight of 6,283 lb (2850 kg), the **BK 117A-3** has a larger tail rotor and a maximum take-off weight of 7,055 lb (3200 kg), and the **BK 117A-4** has an uprated transmission and greater fuel capacity. In 1987 production switched to the **BK 117B** with an improved version of the LTS101-750B-1 turboshaft engine for better hovering performance with greater payload. The BK 117B was produced in two sub-variants as the initial **BK 117B-1** at a maximum

take-off weight of 7,055 lb (3200 kg) and the later **BK 117B-2** with maximum take-off weight increased to 7,385 lb (3350 kg). The latest model was certificated in 1992 as the German-built **BK 117C** with a new cockpit and a power-plant of two 708-shp (528-kW) Turboméca Arriel 1E turboshaft engines. The two subvariants are the basic **BK 117C-1** and the improved **BK 117C-2** that first flew in June 1999 with features of the EC 135 including its avionics and tail rotor, as well as an enlarged cabin; the **BK 117C-2** is now known as the **EC 145**. Three examples of the BK 117 were produced under licence in Indonesia with the designa-

tion **IPTN NBK-117**. A few examples of these basically civil helicopters have entered military service as liaison machines and VIP transports.

The **BK 117M** is the specifically military variant, and was thus developed by the German half of the partnership without any input from Kawasaki which, like all other Japanese companies, is prohibited by the national constitution from participation in military developments for the export market. The BK 117M was revealed in 1985, and in addition to its armament has a digital fire-control system and defensive electronics. No examples have yet been ordered.

SPECIFICATION

Eurocopter Deutschland BK 117M

Type: one/two-crew military light utility helicopter
Powerplant: two Lycoming LTS101-750B-1 turboshaft engines each rated at 592 shp (442 kW)
Performance: maximum cruising speed 154 mph (248 km/h) at sea level; initial climb rate 1,910 ft (582 m) per minute; service ceiling 10,000 ft (3050 m); hovering ceiling 9,600 ft (2925 m) in ground effect and 7,500 ft (2285 m) out of ground effect; range 460 miles (740 km) with auxiliary fuel and 354 miles (570 km) with standard fuel
Weights: empty 5,644 lb (2560 kg); maximum take-off 7,055 lb (3200 kg)
Dimensions: main rotor diameter 36 ft 1 in (11.00 m); length 42 ft 8 in (13.00 m) with the rotors turning; height 12 ft 7½ in (3.85 m) with the rotors turning; main rotor

disc area 1,022.93 sq ft (95.03 m²)
Armament: generally none, although there is provision for one 0.5-in (12.7-mm) Colt-Browning M2-3 trainable machine-gun with 750 rounds in an underfuselage Lucas turret controlled by a helmet-mounted sight, or one 20-mm fixed forward-firing cannon on the side of the fuselage, or one 0.5-in (12.7-mm) Browning M2 trainable lateral-firing machine-gun mounted in a cabin door, plus up to a not available weight of disposable stores carried on two hardpoints at the ends of a transverse load-carrying beam, and generally comprising eight HOT 2 or BGM-71 TOW anti-tank missiles, short-range AAMs, machine-gun pods, and multiple launchers for unguided rockets
Payload: up to 11 passengers or freight carried in the rear of the cabin

Eurocopter Deutschland EC 135 and EC 635

Resulting from a programme launched in the mid-1980s for a technology-development helicopter, the **BO 108** first flew in 15 October 1988 with the powerplant of two Allison 250-C20R turboshaft engines. The powerplant drove a dynamic system that included a four-bladed main rotor derived from that of the BO 105 and a conventional tail rotor, although a new all-composite tail rotor of the bearingless type was introduced in 1990. In January 1991 the manufacturer announced that the BO 108 would be used as the basis of a helicopter to succeed the BO 105 in the light utility role with only 75 per cent of the earlier type's operating costs. In January 1992 the type became the **Eurocopter Deutschland EC 135** to reflect the merger of the helicopter divisions of Aérospatiale and MBB as Eurocopter.

The first true prototype flew on 5 June 1991 with the powerplant of two Turboméca TM319-1B Arrius turboshaft engines, and the primary changes effected during the development programme were an increase in the maximum seating capacity to seven persons, and the replacement of the tail rotor by a shrouded multi-bladed rotor

of the French 'fenestron' type. This was used in conjunction with a bearingless main rotor with composite blades. There followed two pre-production prototypes that recorded their maiden flights on 15 February and 16 April 1994 with different power-plants of the types proposed as alternatives for the production model: the first machine had 583-shp (435-kW) Arrius 2B engines while the second had 621-shp (463-kW) Pratt & Whitney Canada PW206B engines. A third pre-production prototype was subsequently built, and these three machines undertook the bulk of the development programme that led to preliminary European and US certification in June and July 1996, respectively. The first production helicopter was delivered in July 1996, and by December 1998 the EC 135 had been cleared for IFR as well as VFR operation. The primary models of the EC 135 are the **EC 135P1** with PW206B engines, the **EC 135T1** with Turboméca engines in their initial Arrius 2B and later Arrius 2B1 models, the **EC 135 ACT/FHS (Active Control Technology/Flying Helicopter Simulator)** model within the German programme to develop

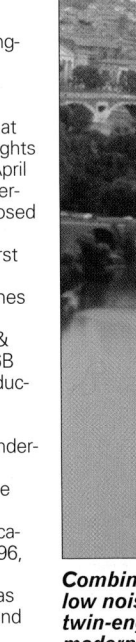

Combining its relatively low noise signature with twin-engined safety and modern design, the EC 135 is proving popular for operations which regularly take the aircraft over urban areas.

'fly-by-light' technology, the **EC 135 Police** with options for different sensor and equipment fits, and the **EC 635** military version with a more austere interior and provision for a wide assortment of equipment and weapon fits.

SPECIFICATION

Eurocopter Deutschland EC 135T1

Type: single-crew utility light helicopter
Powerplant: two Turboméca Arrius 2B1 turboshaft engines each rated at 670 shp (500 kW)
Performance: maximum cruising speed 160 mph (257 km/h) at sea level; initial climb rate 1,653 ft (504 m) per minute; service ceiling 20,000 ft (6095 m); hovering ceiling 13,260 ft (4040 m) in ground effect and 10,180 ft (3100 m) out of ground effect; range 545 miles

(878 km) with auxiliary fuel and 462 miles (745 km) with standard fuel
Weights: empty 3,230 lb (1465 kg); maximum take-off 6,393 lb (2900 kg)
Dimensions: rotor diameter 33 ft 5½ in (10.20 m); length 39 ft 10¾ in (12.16 m) with the rotor turning; height 11 ft 10½ in (3.62 m) with the rotor turning; rotor disc area 879.58 sq ft (81.71 m²)
Payload: up to seven passengers or freight including a 2,777-lb (1260-kg) maximum external load

Eurocopter France AS 332 Super Puma and AS 532 Cougar

Logically, if unimaginatively, known as the **Super Puma** when first proposed in 1974, the **Aérospatiale AS 332** was devised as a successor to the SA 330 Puma. Retaining the Puma's overall appearance,

including retractable tricycle landing gear, but profiting from the introduction of more advanced features made possible by developments in glassfibre rotor technology, the Super Puma is most readily identi-

fiable by its prominent ventral fin and nose radome for the optional Bendix/King RDR 1400 or Honeywell Primus 500 weather radar. Aimed primarily at the civil market, the helicopter nevertheless

incorporates features of value to military operators, including a gearbox operable for one hour without lubricant and rotors which remain safe for 40 hours after hits by 0.5-in (12.7-mm) small-arms fire.

The Puma's Turmo engines were replaced by Makila 1A units each delivering 1,780 shp (1327 kW) and able to wind up from idle to full power in just 1.5 seconds.

First flown on

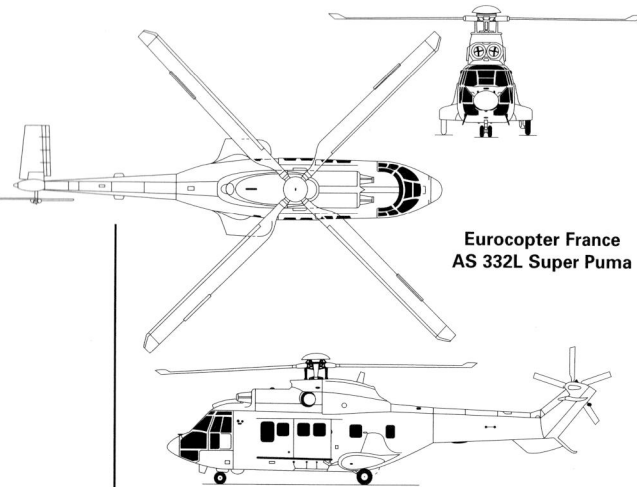

Eurocopter France
AS 332L Super Puma

With the AS 332L2 comes a full EFIS flightdeck, with two hours of emergency electrical generation available in the event of primary systems failure.

13 September 1978 with the above features as well as changes such as multi-purpose air inlets, lightweight Starflex rotor head, uprated transmission, thermally de-iced main rotor blades, and wider-track main landing-gear units with single wheels, the Super Puma entered service in 1981 as the military **AS 332B** and civilian **AS 332C**. Both these initial variants retained the Puma's cabin with a volume of 402.60 cu ft (11.40 m³), providing accommodation for 12-15 fully-equipped troops or 21 passengers. During the following year delivery began of the 'stretched' civil **AS 332L** and military **AS 332M** lengthened by 2 ft 6 in (0.76 m) to boost the cabin volume to 469.70 cu ft (13.30 m³) and so permit the carriage of four extra passengers.

In January 1990 the military variants were renamed **Cougar** (later **Cougar Mk I**), renumbered **AS 532** and accorded new variant

suffixes: the **AS 532AC** and **AS 532UC** were the armed and unarmed short-fuselage helicopters, the **AS 532AL** and **AS 532UL** were the armed and unarmed long-fuselage helicopters, the **AS 532MC** was the unarmed naval SAR and surveillance helicopter, and the **AS 532SC** was the armed naval ASW/AShW helicopter. Both maritime models had previously been known by the designation **AS 332F**, there being no long-fuselage maritime model. Civil production was concentrated on the AS 332L Super Puma, mainly for the oil exploration support role. The current production version for civil use is the **AS 332L1** with the long fuselage and accommodation for 20 airline-standard passengers, and a further improved version is the **AS 332L Tiger** developed for North Sea oil support operator Bristow Helicopters. Later examples of the Cougar Mk I have 1,877-shp (1400-kW)

Makila 1A1 engines.

It was on 6 February 1987 that the development prototype of the **Cougar Mk II**, known in its civil form as the **AS 332L2 Super Puma Mk II**, made its first flight with the powerplant of two 2,104-shp (1569-kW) Makila 1A2 engines, Spheriflex main and tail rotor heads with elastomeric bearings, longer main rotor blades, larger lateral sponsons carrying additional fuel, life rafts, etc., and a further 'stretch' of the fuselage to provide accommodation for 28 passengers. The Mk II version of the Super Puma and Cougar entered service in 1992 and was to have been used as the platform for French army aviation's HORIZON (Hélicoptère d'Observation Radar et d'Investigation sur ZONe) battlefield surveillance radar in the late 1990s. The French army originally requested 20 helicopters equipped with the Orchidée system, which had been trialled on an AS 330B fitted with the small Orphée radar. The combination of the Orchidée system and the Cougar Mk II proved prohibitively expensive and

was cancelled in 1990, only to be resurrected for Operation Daguet (the French element of the 1991 operation against Iraq). The experience gained from its 24 operational missions led to the HORIZON system. Eurocopter received a development contract in October 1992 for two aircraft, combining the capabilities of Orchidée with the endurance of the AS 532UL, and the first fully-equipped flight took place on 8 December 1992, allowing the delivery of the first of six such helicopters in April 1994. The French army is also replacing its original AS 330 helicopters with AS 532 Cougars, the first 22 aircraft being delivered to the Force d'Action Rapide by the end of 1991.

While armament options for the army

Cougar are restricted to gun and rocket pods, the naval AS 532SC has provision for a pair of AM39 Exocet anti-ship missiles or homing torpedoes. Operation from ship platforms is also possible, using hauldown gear to permit flying in rough seas. Large sponsons with inflatable floats are standard naval equipment, and are optional on other models. Having produced the standard AS 330 Puma under licence during the early 1980s, IPTN (Eurocopter) in Indonesia moved to production of the AS 332C and AS 332L as the **NAS-332**, rolling out its first aircraft for a civilian customer in April 1983. Other foreign service designations include Brazil (**CH-34**), Spain (**HD.21** for SAR and **HT.21** for VIP transport) and Sweden (**HKP 10**).

Variants

AS 532UB Cougar 100: simplified and therefore cheaper military Cougar Mk I for the unarmed tactical transport role with fixed landing gear and a maximum take-off weight of 19,841 lb (9000 kg)
AS 532AB Cougar Mk I: armed version of the AS 532UB
AS 532U2 Cougar Mk II: unarmed military tactical transport with accommodation for two crew and 29 troops
AS 532A2 Cougar Mk II: armed version of the AS 532U2

At least four AS 532A2 Cougar MK II helicopters have been ordered by l'Armée de l'Air for use in the CSAR role. The aircraft are named Cougar RESCO (Recherche et Sauvetage en Combat) in service and will be introduced during 2000.

SPECIFICATION

Eurocopter France AS 532UC Cougar Mk I
Type: two/three-crew general-purpose tactical medium helicopter
Powerplant: two Turboméca Makila 1A1 turboshaft engines each rated at 1,877 shp (1400 kW)
Performance: maximum cruising speed 163 mph (262 km/h) at sea level; initial climb rate 1,378 ft (420 m) per minute; service ceiling 13,450 ft (4100 m); hovering ceiling 8,860 ft (2700 m) in ground effect and 5,250 ft (1600 m) out of ground

effect; range 384 miles (618 km) with standard fuel
Weights: empty 9,546 lb (4330 kg); maximum take-off 20,615 lb (9350 kg)
Dimensions: main rotor diameter 51 ft 2¼ in (15.60 m); length 61 ft 4¼ in (18.70 m) with the rotors turning; height 16 ft 1¾ in (4.92 m); main rotor disc area 2,057.42 sq ft (191.13 m²)
Payload: up to 21 troops or 9,921 lb (4500 kg) of freight carried as an internal or external load

Eurocopter France AS 355 Ecureuil 2 and AS 555 Fennec

The helicopter now known as the **Eurocopter France AS 355**

Ecureuil 2 (Squirrel 2) or, in North America as the **TwinStar**, or as the

AS 555 Fennec in military form, first flew in prototype form on

28 September 1979 after straightforward creation by Aérospatiale as a twin-

engined development of the single-engined AS 350 Ecureuil.

Eurocopter France AS 355 Ecureuil 2 and AS 555 Fennec (cont.)

The Ecureuil 2 was intended mainly for the civil market as the **AS 355E** with two 420-shp (313-kW) Allison 250-C20F turboshaft engines and the **AS 355F** with wider-chord main rotor blades and a number of other improved features. The type fulfilled the manufacturer's expectations in appealing mainly to the civil market, but the French air force operates 10 examples of the **AS 355F1** version (delivered from January 1984) for surveillance around major air bases. The **AS 355F2** is an upgraded model delivered from the end of 1985 with an empty weight of 2,877 lb (1305 kg). Following the creation of Eurocopter, the purely military version of the AS 355 was redesignated as the **AS 555 Fennec** (desert fox).

Developed from the AS 355F as the twin-engined equivalent of the AS 350L1 with a beefed-up airframe, reinforced landing gear and improved instrumentation, the **AS 355M** (later **AS 555M**) possesses the same armament provisions as the AS 550 Fennec and can be subjected to comparable modifications for improved operational reliability. The version used by France has an armament of MATRA Mistral short-range AAMs, TOW anti-tank missiles, pintle-mounted machine-guns, and podded machine-guns or a 20-mm M621 cannon. An export variant was offered as the **AS 355M2**.

The **AS 355N** and **AS 555N** are civil and military versions capable of better overall performance at higher weights as a result of the introduction of an uprated powerplant, namely a pair of 456-shp (340-kW) Turboméca TM 319 Arrius 1M turboshafts. The specifically military variants of this model are now known as the **AS 555AN** armed helicopter with a T-100 sight, a centreline cannon and provision for two rocket launchers, the **AS 555CN** missile-armed helicopter, the **AS 555MN** unarmed naval helicopter with provision for surveillance radar with its antenna in an under-nose radome for 360° coverage, the **AS 555SN** armed naval helicopter, and the **AS 555UN** utility and trainer helicopter. The AS 555SN has Bendix/King RDR 1500 search radar, Sextant Avionique Mk 3 MAD, Sextant Avionique Nadir Mk 10 navigation system, Dassault Electronique RDN 85 Doppler navigation, and

With the extra power and safety provided by two engines, the Ecureuil 2 is able to lift a heavy load of special mission equipment. An AS 355N is shown.

provision for armament that includes the cannon and rocket launchers of the land-based model as well as two lightweight homing torpedoes.

The **Helibras HB 355F-2 Esquilo** is the Brazilian licence-built version of the **AS 355F-2 Ecureuil**, operated in Brazil with the service designations **CH-55** (air force light transport), **UH-12** (naval utility transport) and **VH-55** (air force utility transport).

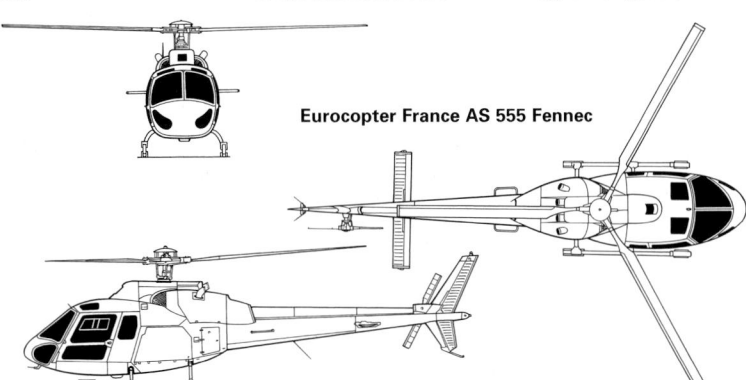

Eurocopter France AS 555 Fennec

SPECIFICATION	
Eurocopter France AS 555M Fennec	effect; range 437 miles (703 km)
Type: one-crew utility light helicopter	**Weights:** empty 2,998 lb (1360 kg); maximum take-off 5,732 lb (2600 kg)
Powerplant: two Allison 250-C20F turboshaft engines each rated at 420 shp (313 kW)	**Dimensions:** main rotor diameter 35 ft ¾ in (10.69 m); length 42 ft 5½ in (12.94 m) with the rotors turning; height 10 ft 11½ in (3.34 m); main rotor disc area 966.09 sq ft (89.75 m²)
Performance: maximum cruising speed 139 mph (224 km/h) at sea level; initial climb rate 1,280 ft (390 m) per minute; service ceiling 11,150 ft (3400 m); hovering ceiling 5,905 ft (1800 m) in ground effect and 4,430 ft (1350 m) out of ground	**Payload:** up to five passengers or 1,984 lb (900 kg) of freight carried in the cabin, or 2,502 lb (1135 kg) of freight carried as a slung load

Eurocopter France AS 565 Panther

The SA 360 Dauphin single-engined helicopter never achieved anything more than modest civil and very limited military sales, and was therefore developed into a twin-engined model, the **Aérospatiale SA 365C Dauphin 2** that first flew in prototype form on 24 January 1975 with a powerplant of two 650-shp (485-kW) Turboméca Arriel turboshaft engines. There was considerably greater sales interest in this model, which offered both higher performance and greater in-flight reliability factors, and the type entered production later in the decade with a powerplant of two 660-shp (492-kW) Arriel 1A or, in the improved **SA 365N** version that first flew on 31 March 1979, 710-shp (529-kW) Arriel 1C turboshaft engines. The SA 365N also introduced a large degree of composite construction and retractable tricycle landing gear as well as a number of improvements suggested by operational use of the earlier variants. Further

developments included the **SA 365N1** with two 724-shp (540-kW) Arriel 1C1 engines driving an improved rotor system with an 11-blade 'fenestron', and the **SA 365N2** with the revised powerplant of two Arriel 1C2 engines and provision for a 'glass' cockpit of the EFIS type. In January 1990 Aérospatiale decided to standardise its redesignation of helicopters currently in production: the original letter prefix was therefore altered from 'SA' for Sud-Aviation to 'AS' for Aérospatiale, and in this process the SA 365N became the **AS 365N**.

The **AS 365F** is the versatile naval development of the AS 365N, intended primarily for the anti-ship role with Agrion-15 search radar, MAD with a towed 'bird', an armament of two or four AS15TT short-range anti-ship missiles, and the avionics for mid-course targeting update of ship-launched Otomat long-range anti-ship missiles. The type is also available in SAR configuration with Omera-Segid ORB 32 search radar (or, in the unarmed Irish version, Bendix RDR 1500 search radar), a five-screen EFIS flightdeck, an autostabilisation system, a rescue winch, an automatic navigation system (Crouzet ONS-200A long-range navigation system, Crouzet Nadir Mk II navigation computer and Cina-B Doppler navigation in the Irish helicopters) and a hover/transition coupler. The manufacturer also offers a more advanced anti-submarine capability in a derivative with Thomson-Sintra (Alcatel) ASM HS 312 dunking sonar, Sextant Avionique (Crouzet) DHAX 3 MAD, and an armament of two lightweight homing torpedoes.

The first order for the type was placed by Saudi Arabia, which received 24 examples in two sub-variants now designated in the **Eurocopter France AS 565 Panther** military series as the **AS 565SC** (four for the SAR role with ORB 32

With its distinctive undernose radar, the AS 565SB Panther is a capable light naval helicopter. This example was photographed while test-firing an AS15TT missile.

radar, and later redesignated as the **AS 565MB**) and the **AS 565SA** (20 helicopters for the anti-ship role with Agrion-15 radar and four AS15TT missiles, and later redesignated as the **AS 565SB**). Small numbers of the AS 365F were also bought by other countries including Abu Dhabi (seven AS 565SB anti-ship helicopters) and Israel (up to 20 AS 565SAs for service with the local name **Atalef**, or bat).

Following on its development of the SA 361H military prototype on the basis of the single-engined SA 360, Aérospatiale capitalised on this work with a dedicated military version of its twin-engined SA 365. The first step in this direction was the **AS 365M** prototype that first flew on 29 February 1984 and revealed the ability to carry up to 12 troops or alternatively an armament of up to eight HOT anti-tank missiles or 44 2.68-in (68-mm) SNEB air-to-surface unguided rockets. Further development resulted in the April 1986 appearance of the **AS 365K** prototype, to which the name **Panther** was then allocated. The name was retained for the subsequent military developments, which are now listed in the AS 565 series. Other features of the Panther include greater use of composite materials, a longer fuselage fitted with armoured seats, cable-cutters for safer low-altitude flight capability, a strengthened cabin floor and landing gear, sliding rather than hinged doors, crash-resistant fuel tanks, IR-reducing exhausts, and the use of composite materials and special paints to reduce electromagnetic and thermal signatures.

The Panther has been offered in two basic forms for the land warfare and naval roles. The land-

warfare form has been offered in three subvariants as the **AS 565AA** (from 1997 **AS 565AB**) armed model, the **AS 565CA** anti-tank model and the **AS 565UA** (from 1997 **AS 565UB**) unarmed utility model. The AS 565AA/AB has two lateral outriggers, each carrying a single hardpoint for the carriage of two multiple launchers for air-to-surface unguided rockets, or two NC 20M621 pods, each carrying one 20-mm GIAT M621 cannon with 180 rounds, or four two-round packs of MATRA Mistral short-range AAMs. The AS 565CA carries two four-tube launchers for HOT ATMs aimed via a Viviane day/night unit. The AS 565UA utility subvariant lacks armament capability and is designed to carry eight or 10 assault

troops, or alternatively freight in the form of an internal or slung payload. The only operator of the AS 565K series is Brazil, with 36 AS 565AA helicopters operated under the local designation **HM-1**. The **AS 565 Panther 800**, first flown in prototype form during June 1992, is a derivative of the AS 565 with the considerably uprated powerplant of two 1,322-shp (986-kW) LHTEC T800-LHT-800 turboshaft engines, and also an IBM suite of integrated avionics.

Apart from the two naval developments of the SA 365F listed above, Eurocopter France's other two navalised variants of the AS 565 are the unarmed **AS 565MA** (replaced from 1997 by the **AS 565MB**) equivalent of the AS 565SC for the

SAR and sea surveillance roles, and the **AS 565SB** development of the AS 565SA for the anti-submarine as well as anti-ship roles. Chile operates four examples of the latter with Dassault Varan

radar, Thomson-CSF tactical radar and warning receiver, and provision for the AM39 Exocet AShM or MU90 Impact anti-submarine torpedo, and France has ordered 18 AS 565MAs.

SPECIFICATION

Eurocopter France AS 565SA Panther
Type: two-seat light naval utility helicopter optimised for the anti-ship and anti-submarine roles
Powerplant: two Turboméca Arriel 1M1 turboshaft engines each rated at 749 shp (558 kW)
Performance: maximum cruising speed 170 mph (274 km/h) at sea level; initial climb rate 1,378 ft (420 m) per minute; service ceiling 15,010 ft (4575 m); hovering ceiling 8,530 ft (2600 m) in ground effect and 6,100 ft (1860 m) out of ground effect; radius 155 miles (250 km) on an anti-ship mission with four missiles
Weights: empty 4,938 lb (2240 kg); maximum take-off

9,370 lb (4250 kg)
Dimensions: main rotor diameter 39 ft 2 in (11.94 m); length 44 ft 10⅝ in (13.68 m) with rotor turning; height 13 ft ¾ in (3.98 m); main rotor disc area 1,205.26 sq ft (111.97 m²)
Armament: up to 1,323 lb (600 kg) of disposable stores carried on four hardpoints under the two outrigger arms, and generally comprising four AS15TT light anti-ship missiles replaceable by two Mk 46 lightweight anti-submarine torpedoes
Payload: up to 10 passengers or 3,748 lb (1700 kg) of freight carried in the rear of the cabin, or 3,527 lb (1600 kg) of freight carried as a slung load

Eurocopter France EC 155B

It was in September 1996 that Eurocopter France launched its programme to take the development of the AS 365 Dauphin helicopter to a new stage, and it was at the Paris Air

Show of 1997 that the **AS 365N4 Dauphin 2** was formally announced; in February 1998 the designation was changed from AS 365N4 Dauphin 2 to **Eurocopter France**

EC 155B. The changes effected in the transformation of the AS 365N into the EC 155B were the introduction of a new cabin with bulged doors, revised windows and 40 per cent more floor area, and the adoption of a revised dynamic system with a five-bladed main rotor of the Spheriflex type and a 10-blade 'fenestron' shrouded tail rotor with the blades located at unequal intervals to reduce vibration.

The new type first flew on 17 June 1997 as a prototype conversion from AS 356N standard, and the first EC 155B

SPECIFICATION

Eurocopter France EC 155B
Type: one/two-crew utility light/medium helicopter
Powerplant: two Turboméca Arriel 2C1 turboshaft engines each rated at 851 shp (635 kW)
Performance: maximum cruising speed 165 mph (265 km/h) at sea level; service ceiling 16,765 ft (5110 m); hovering ceiling 6,210 ft (1893 m) in ground effect and 2,840 ft (866 m) out of ground

effect; range 511 miles (830 km)
Weights: empty 5,187 lb (2353 kg); maximum take-off 11,023 lb (5000 kg)
Dimensions: rotor diameter 41 ft 4 in (12.60 m); length 47 ft 4 in (14.43 m) with the rotor turning; height 14 ft 3¼ in (4.35 m); rotor disc area 1,342.19 sq ft (124.69 m²)
Payload: up to 14 passengers, or six litters or freight carried in the cabin or freight carried as a slung load

Germany's border police placed a 13-aircraft order for the EC 155B, for delivery from late 1998. In that year, the basic helicopter cost US $5.5 million.

was a production-standard helicopter that recorded its maiden flight on 11 March 1998. The

type received European certification late in 1998, and deliveries started shortly after this time.

Eurocopter EC 665 Tigre and Tiger

The **EC 665**, known in France as the **Tigre** and in Germany as the **Tiger**, was planned to meet French and German requirements for an advanced multi-role type for battlefield operations in the typical European scenario. It originated from a 1984 memorandum of understanding that reflected West Germany's need for a successor to the PAH-1 and France's requirement for a similar helicopter to bolster the capabilities of its ground forces. The original development was halted in 1986 because of rapidly escalating costs and to provide time for a reappraisal of the overall specification as the cost basis was recalculated. It was relaunched during March 1987 in basically common French and West German anti-tank models as well as a somewhat

different French escort model. The programme was largely responsible for the eventual creation of Eurocopter out of the original Eurocopter Tiger, created in September 1985. In November 1989 Eurocopter Tiger received a contract for an initial five helicopters, of which three were to be unarmed aerodynamic prototypes and the other two armed prototypes for the basically similar Tiger and Tigre anti-tank variants required by Germany and France (one prototype), and for the **Gerfaut** escort helicopter needed by France (one prototype).

The airframe is built largely of composite materials, and the type is of typical attack helicopter configuration, with a basically rectangular-section forward fuselage carrying an oval-section tail boom.

The four-bladed main rotor is of the semi-rigid type with a titanium and composite hub, elastomeric bearing and fibre elastomer blades. The airframe is completed by the stub wing and the landing gear. Survivability over the modern battlefield was a factor that drove a considerable part of the overall design in terms of structural factors and the location of key components, and survivability is further enhanced by redundancy in the electrical, fuel and hydraulic systems. Another factor deemed essential was the development of the avionics on the basis of a MIL 1553B digital databus to allow full integration of the current avionics and to facilitate the introduction of later generations of sensors and weapons during the course of the helicopter's service.

In its HAP combat support/escort form, the Tigre dispenses with the mast-mounted sight of the anti-tank variant. It does, however, feature an SFIM/TRT STRIX gyro-stabilised roof-mounted sight.

Eurocopter EC 665 Tigre and Tiger (continued)

The first of the five proto-type and development helicopters flew on 29 April 1991. **Tigre HAC** (**Hélicoptère Anti-Char**, or anti-tank helicopter) is for the French army, which requires 100 (originally 140) such helicopters. The primary armament is planned as a maximum of eight anti-tank missiles (all HOT 2 or Trigat weapons or four of each type, all aimed via the Osiris mast-mounted sight) on the inner underwing hardpoints and four MATRA Mistral short-range AAMs on the outer underwing hardpoints.

Named Gerfaut (gerfalcon) up to 1993, the **Tigre HAP** is the HAP (**Hélicoptère d'Appui et de Protection**, or attack and

protection helicopter) for the French army, which requires 115 (originally 75) such helicopters. This model carries an undernose turret armed with one 30-mm GIAT M30/781B cannon supplied with between 150 and 450 rounds of ammunition and, on the underwing hard-points, two multiple launchers each carrying 22 2.68-in (68-mm) air-to-surface unguided rockets and either four MATRA Mistral short-range AAMs or two multiple launchers each carrying 12 2.68-in (68-mm) rockets. The sensors of this variant include a roof-mounted combination of TV and FLIR optics, direct optics and a laser rangefinder.

Originally ordered as the **PAH-2** (**Panzerabwehr-hubschrauber-2**, or anti-tank helicopter no. 2), the **Tiger UHU** (**Unterstützungs-hubschrauber**, or support helicopter) is for the German army, which requires 212 such heli-copters to a standard that is now known as the **UHT** (**Unterstützungs-hubschrauber Tiger**). The model is basically similar to the HAC Tigre apart from its ability to carry Stinger 2 short-range AAMs on the outboard underwing hard-points in place of the French variant's Mistrals.

In common with France, Germany has constantly reviewed the nature and extent of the programme

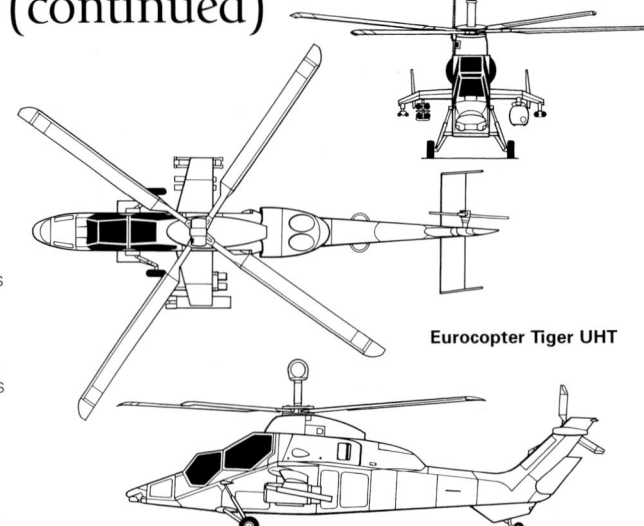

Eurocopter Tiger UHT

since the early 1990s, the driving forces being rising development and procure-ment costs as well as the demise of the Warsaw Pact threat that this battlefield

helicopter was intended to tackle. It is thought that the first Tiger and Tigre heli-copters will enter German and French service in 2001 and 2003 respectively.

The Osiris mast-mounted sight system employed by the Tigre HAC and Tiger UHT combines a TV, FLIR and laser rangefinder – feeding data and imagery to the co-pilot/gunner – while the pilot uses a nose-mounted FLIR as his primary night-vision sensor.

SPECIFICATION

Eurocopter UHT
Type: two-seat anti-tank and close support helicopter
Powerplant: two MTU/Turboméca/Rolls-Royce MTR 390 turboshaft engines each rated at 1,285 shp (958 kW) for take-off
Performance: maximum speed 167 mph (269 km/h) at optimum altitude; cruising speed 143 mph (230 km/h) at optimum altitude; initial climb rate 2,106 ft (642 m) per minute; hovering ceiling 10,500 ft (3200 m) out of ground

effect; range 497 miles (800 km) with standard fuel; endurance 3 hours 25 minutes
Weights: empty 7,275 lb (3300 kg); maximum take-off 13,448 lb (6100 kg)
Dimensions: main rotor diameter 42 ft 7¾ in (13.00 m); length 51 ft 10 in (15.80 m) with the rotors turning; height 17 ft ¾ in (5.20 m) to top of mast-mounted sight; main rotor disc area 1,428.76 sq ft (132.73 m²)
Armament: see above

Eurocopter France/CATIC/ST Aero EC 120B Colibri

The **EC 120B Colibri** is a five-seat light helicopter designed, developed and produced as a collaborative venture between Eurocopter France (overall leadership with 61 per cent as well as the dynamic system, seats, final assem-bly, flight test and certification), the China

National Aero-Technology Import and Export Corporation (24 per cent in the form of the Harbin Aircraft Manufacturing Corporation for the cabin, landing gear and fuel system) and Singapore Aerospace Technologies (15 per cent for the boom, fins, doors and instrument

pedestal). The type was initially planned as the **P120L** from February 1990, but was then extensively revised to trim 1,102 lb (500 kg) from the maxi-mum take-off weight. The development contract was signed in October 1992, the helicopter was redesig-nated as the **EC 120** in January 1993, assembly of the two prototypes started early in 1995, and the first prototype recorded its maiden flight on 9 June of the same year.

The influence of Eurocopter is very evident in the overall concept of this trim light helicopter, which combines light alloy

Eurocopter estimates a market for 1,600-2,000 Colibris (hummingbirds) up to 2010.

and composite material in a pod-and-boom fuselage and other elements of the airframe, which include twin-skid alighting gear, a three-bladed main rotor (titanium alloy Spheriflex head and composite blades of wide chord) and a tail unit (horizontal surface ahead of the large

vertical surface incorporat-ing the eight-blade advanced 'fenestron' shrouded tail rotor). The EC 120B Colibri received its European and American certifications in July 1997 and January 1998 respec-tively, and delivery of production helicopters began in January 1998.

SPECIFICATION

Eurocopter France/CATIC/ST Aero EC 120B Colibri
Type: one-crew light utility helicopter
Powerplant: one Turbomeca TM 319 Arrius 2F turboshaft engine rated at 504 shp (376 kW)
Performance: maximum cruising speed 142 mph (228 km/h) at optimum altitude; initial climb rate 1,325 ft (404 m) per minute; service ceiling 17,600 ft (5365 m); hovering ceiling 10,000 ft (3050 m) in ground effect and 8,300 ft

(2530 m) out of ground effect; range 454 miles (731 km)
Weights: empty 2,094 lb (950 kg); maximum take-off 3,902 lb (1770 kg)
Dimensions: rotor diameter 32 ft 9¾ in (10.00 m); length 37 ft 9½ in (11.52 m) with the rotor turning; height 11 ft 1¾ in (3.40 m); rotor disc area 845.42 sq ft (78.54 m²)
Payload: up to four passengers or freight carried in the cabin, or 1,543 lb (700 kg) of freight carried as a slung load

Eurofighter Typhoon

Given the general success of the collaborative design, development and produc-tion programme for the Panavia Tornado multi-role warplane, it seemed sensi-

ble in the mid-1980s to plan a similar type of European effort to produce a highly capable air-superiority fighter for service from the late

1990s. In June 1986, there-fore, the Eurofighter consortium was formed by the same three countries, namely Germany, Italy and the UK, that were soon joined by Spain. Other European nations, most notably France, had been

involved in earlier **EFA** (**European Fighter Aircraft**) discussions, but then dropped out of the collaborative effort to seek a solution to their require-ments from other sources or, in the case of France, in a purely national effort that

has yielded the Dassault Rafale.

Much experience was gained with the main concepts for the EFA, including an unstable aero-dynamic configuration with canard foreplanes, active digital 'fly-by-wire' control

Typhoon is vitally important for the future of British, German, Italian and Spanish air defence. In the RAF, the type will first replace the Tornado F.Mk 3, before going on to oust the Jaguar.

SPECIFICATION

Eurofighter Typhoon
Type: single-seat air combat fighter with attack capability
Powerplant: two Eurojet EJ200 turbofan engines each rated at about 13,490 lb st (60.00 kN) dry and 20,250 lb st (90.00 kN) with afterburning
Performance: maximum speed 1,321 mph (2125 km/h) or Mach 2.00 at 36,090 ft (11000 m); climb to 35,000 ft (10670 m) and Mach 1.5 in 2 minutes 30 seconds; service ceiling 47,570 ft (14500 m); radius 864 miles (1390 km) on an air-superiority mission with three drop tanks for a 10-minute combat air patrol
Weights: empty 24,239 lb (10995 kg); maximum take-off 50,705 lb (23000 kg)
Dimensions: wingspan 35 ft 11 in (10.95 m) over tip-mounted ECM pods; length 52 ft 4¼ in (15.96 m); height 17 ft 4 in (5.28 m); wing area 538.21 sq ft (50.00 m²)
Armament: one 27-mm Mauser BK27 fixed forward-firing cannon in the starboard side of the forward fuselage, plus up to 17,637 lb (8000 kg) of disposable stores carried on four semi-recessed missile stations under the fuselage and on 13 hardpoints (five under the fuselage and eight under the wing), and generally comprising four medium-range and six short-range AAMs plus three drop tanks in the air-to-air role, or three medium-range and two short-range AAMs, four Paveway III laser-guided bombs, one targeting pod and three drop tanks in the air-to-surface role, or four medium-range and two short-range AAMs, four anti-ship missiles and three drop tanks in the anti-ship role; other weapons can include ASMs, anti-radar missiles, optronically or laser-guided bombs, free-fall and retarded bombs, stand-off guided bombs and missiles, cluster bombs, bomblet dispensers, and multiple launchers for unguided rockets

system, a HOTAS cockpit, highly capable though complex avionics, multi-function cockpit displays, carbonfibre composite materials, extensive use of advanced 'conventional' materials such as aluminium-lithium and titanium alloys, and even direct voice command input, from the BAe EAP (Experimental Aircraft Programme) technology demonstrator.

As finalised in September 1987, the EFA European Staff Requirement for Development called for a relatively light but technically sophisticated single-seat fighter with the smallest possible radar cross-section, high supersonic performance, considerable agility, care-free handling capability, a powerplant of two turbo-fan engines, the ability to operate without difficulty from short and austerely equipped airstrips, and optimisation for the primary BVR (Beyond Visual Range) and close air combat roles together with a secondary air-to-surface capability. Germany and Italy were interested only in the air-to-air role, but nonetheless accepted the joint specification for a warplane possessing an empty weight of less than 21,495 lb (9750 kg), a gross wing area of 538.21 sq ft (50.00 m²), and a powerplant based on two examples of a new turbofan engine rated at 20,237 lb st (90.00 kN) with afterburning. This last was the EJ200 two-spool unit designed by the companion Eurojet consortium that comprised Rolls-Royce in the UK, MTU in Germany, Fiat Avio in Italy and SENER (now ITP) in Spain.

Signed in November 1988, the initial contract covered the design, construction and testing of eight prototypes (including a pair of two-seat aircraft) in a programme lasting to 1999; the prototypes were to be built in all of the partner countries, with the UK, Germany, Italy and Spain manufacturing three, two, two and one aircraft respectively. Funding was divided in proportion to the various national industrial participations, which themselves corresponded to the planned national purchases of the new warplane: 33 per cent each by BAe (now BAE Systems) and MBB (now DaimlerChrysler Aerospace), 21 per cent by Aeritalia (now Alenia), and 13 per cent by CASA. DaimlerChrysler and CASA are to became part of the EADS grouping with Aérospatiale during 2000. The planned national purchases, envisaged as taking place from 1996, totalled 765 aircraft, in the form of 250 each for the Royal Air Force and Luftwaffe, 165 for the Italian air force, and 100 for the Spanish air force.

After considerable political and financial in-fighting between the various national ministries and industries, it was decided in May 1990 that the new ECR90 multi-mode pulse-Doppler 'look-up/ look-down' fire-control radar with multiple target search and detection should be developed by GEC Ferranti of the UK with support from FIAR of Italy and INISEL of Spain. The ECR90 is optimised for use in the air-superiority role with the active radar-homing Hughes AIM-120 AMRAAM medium-range AAM, but also provides continuous-wave illumination of the target for semi-active radar guided AAMs such as the BAe Sky Flash and Selenia Aspide. The primary missile armament was planned as four of these medium-range AAMs carried semi-recessed into the lower fuselage for minimum drag, while other weapons could be carried on nine hardpoints (one under the fuselage and four under each half of the wing), of which the under-

fuselage and two underwing units were to be plumbed for the carriage of drop tanks. The total disposable weaponload was planned as 14,330 lb (6500 kg), and the armament was to be completed by a 27-mm Mauser BK27 cannon in the starboard side of the fuselage.

The ECR90 is the new fighter's primary active sensor, but it was fully clear by this time that an alternative sensor of the entirely passive type was required for multi-target tracking and imaging; the task of developing the required IRST (Infra-Red Search and Tracking) system was allocated to the Eurofirst team comprising FIAR of Italy, Thorn-EMI Electronics of the UK and Eurotronica of Spain. The contract for the design and development of the IRST was issued in the middle of 1992, and followed that for the highly advanced DASS (Defensive Aids Sub-System) that was granted to Marconi Defence Systems of the UK and Elettronica of Italy. The DASS contract specified the design and development of an integrated package of missile approach, laser and radar warning elements together with tip-mounted ESM and ECM pods and fuselage-mounted chaff/ flare dispensers and a towed decoy system. Germany and Spain felt that the DASS offered capabilities they did not need and could not afford, and therefore opted for use of

cheaper 'off-the-shelf' units for their own defensive systems.

A decision on production investment was originally scheduled for a time early in 1993, but Germany's continued fears about the unit and overall life-cycle costs of the EFA programme, at a time in which the country's financial position had deteriorated, then led to a series of postponements and, at times, threats of withdrawal. This led to a four-nation review of the whole EFA effort and, after the consideration of seven mostly single-engined alternatives, the decision late in 1992 to pursue the final development of a slightly less capable but somewhat cheaper **New EFA**, which became known as the **Eurofighter 2000** with options, for countries such as Germany, for the use of less capable electronic equipment as a means of reducing procurement cost. Late in 1999, the requirements for the new warplane stood at 232 for the UK, 180 for Germany, 121 for Italy and some 87 for Spain.

The first two Eurofighter 2000 prototypes, completed in Germany and the UK as **DA.1** and **DA.2** respectively, undertook their maiden flights on 27 March and 6 April 1994

with the interim powerplant of two RB.199-22 turbofan engines. The British-assembled DA.2 was in fact ready for flight before the German-assembled DA.1, but BAe was committed to waiting for the German machine to make the new fighter's first flight. The first prototype with the definitive powerplant of two Eurojet 200 turbofan engines was the Italian-built **DA.3** that was delayed by problems in the integration of the digital engine control system designed by DASA and MTU. The **DA.4** prototype was assembled by BAe as the first two-seat prototype, and is also the development prototype for the ECR90 radar; the DASA-assembled **DA.5** is used for avionics and weapons integration; and as a result of cuts in the programme the last two prototypes are the Spanish-assembled **DA.6** two-seat machine and the Italian-assembled **DA.7** single-seat machine.

Eurofighter has passed through a turbulent period of financial and technical problems, the latter centring mainly on the flight-control software developed initially in Germany, but is now beginning to reveal considerable potential as an advanced warplane that in 1998 received the name **Typhoon**.

In two-seat form, Typhoon remains fully combat-capable. Greece has already signed up for 60 Typhoons and Norway may also make a purchase.

EH Industries EH 101 Merlin, Cormorant & Heliliner

The **EH 101** has its roots in the **Westland WG.34** design that was adopted in late 1978 to meet the UK's Naval Staff Requirement 6646 for a replacement for the Westland Sea King. Work on the WG.34 was cancelled before a prototype had been completed, however, opening the way for revision of the design to meet Italian navy as well as Royal Navy requirements. Negotiations between Westland and Agusta began in November 1979, and the success of these talks led to the establishment of European Helicopter Industries Ltd, which was given a formal go-ahead in February 1984 when the two governments agreed to fund nine prototypes and subsequent development of what now became the **EH 101**, so designated as a result of a typing error in what should have been **EHI 01**.

Although replacement of the Sea King was the primary objective, therefore determining the size and weight of the EH 101, several other potential roles were planned from the outset, these roles including transport (both military and civil) and utility duties. Some roles can be performed using the same basic fuselage as the naval helicopter but, alternatively, the EH 101 can be fitted with a modified rear fuselage incorporating a ventral ramp/door. The nine prototypes ordered were assigned specific tasks concerned with the basic dynamics, specific British

and Italian anti-submarine equipment fits, the military tactical/logistic transport, the civil utility version and the commercial **Heliliner**.

The EH 101 is a three-engined helicopter with a single main rotor carrying five blades of composite construction with BERP-derived high-speed tips. Much use is made of composites throughout, although the fuselage itself is mainly of aluminium alloy. Systems and equipment vary with role and customer. For the Royal Navy, which calls its initial variant of the EH 101 the **Merlin HM.Mk 1**, IBM is the prime contractor in association with Westland and provides equipment as well as overall management and integration; other avionics include GEC Ferranti Blue Kestrel 360° search radar, GEC Avionics AQS-903 processing and display system, Racal Orange Reaper ESM and Ferranti/Thomson-CSF dipping sonar. Armament on the Merlin comprises four Marconi Sting Ray torpedoes, and there are also two sonobuoy dispensers. Options include the Exocet, Harpoon, Sea Eagle and Marte Mk 2 anti-ship missiles.

The initial Royal Navy requirement for 50 Merlins to operate from Type 23-class frigates, 'Invincible'-class aircraft carriers, ships of the Royal Fleet Auxiliary and other ships or land bases has been reduced to 44, with delivery starting late in 1998 rather than in 1996, as hoped. These

British helicopters are each powered by RTM 322 turboshafts, whereas the Italian helicopters (16 on order and eight on option) each have the alternative powerplant of three 1,714-shp (1278-kW) General Electric T700-GE-T6A turboshafts, assembled in Italy. Earlier CT7 commercial variants of the General Electric engine were used to power the prototypes, the first of which was a Westland-built machine that achieved its maiden flight on 9 October 1987. A similar Agusta-built basic model flew in Italy on 26 November 1987. Next to fly in Italy, on 26 April 1989, was a prototype of the Italian ASW version, followed in the UK by a basic ASW version on 15 June and then the definitive Merlin prototype on 24 October of the same year. The third and eighth prototypes were both finished as Heliliners.

The second prototype was lost in an accident on 21 January 1993, resulting in a suspension of all flight-testing until 24 June that year. The RTM 322 engines were first flown in the fourth prototype during July 1993, and subsequently fitted to the fifth prototype. The Italian seventh prototype, fitted with the ramp/door arrangement, first flew on 18 December 1989, representing the military utility variant, of which an initial 22 were ordered as the Royal Air Force's next medium-lift helicopter, its service designation being **Merlin HC.Mk 3**.

The first customer for the utility variant was to have been Canada, which ordered 15 EH 101s for SAR duties; replacing 13 CH-113A Labradors, these were to have been designated **CH-149 Chimo**. Canada also ordered 35 of the naval version, in this instance with the designation **CH-148 Petrel**, to meet its New Shipborne

EH Industries sees a market for the Heliliner in feeder and offshore passenger transport roles. The aircraft offers a three-engined safety margin.

Variant

Merlin HM.Mk 2: designation reserved for a development of the **Merlin HM.Mk 1** anti-ship helicopter with capability provided by a new-generation anti-ship missile, more advanced electronics, and more powerful engines driving a higher-rated transmission system

Aircraft requirement for a Sea King replacement. Assembled and fitted out by IMP Group Ltd in Canada, these EH 101s were to have been powered by 1,920-shp (1432-kW) CT7-6A1 turboshaft engines. The deal was hard-fought, subject to constant scrutiny and not unimportant to the chances of the EH 101's long-term success. Deliveries were scheduled to begin late in 1997 for the CH-148 and early in 1998 for the CH-149. However, an increasingly bitter argument over the costs versus acquisition of less complex aircraft saw the EH 101

become a campaign issue in the Canadian elections of 1993. The pro-EH 101 Conservative government was ousted in favour of a Liberal administration which, true to its election pledge, cancelled the entire programme. Then, in January 1998, the Canadian government placed a new order for 15 examples of the revised **AW320 Cormorant** version in the SAR role, for delivery between 2000 and 2003.

Further development of the EH 101 could result in an airborne early warning version of the type required by both the Italian navy and Royal Navy.

SPECIFICATION

European Helicopter Industries Merlin HM.Mk 1

Type: one/two-crew shipborne and land-based anti-submarine and utility helicopter

Powerplant: three Rolls-Royce/Turboméca RTM 322-01 turboshaft engines each rated at 2,312 shp (1724 kW)

Performance: cruising speed 173 mph (278 km) at optimum altitude; hovering ceiling 12,500 ft (3810 m) in ground effect; range 656 miles (1056 km)

Weights: empty 23,149 lb (10500 kg); maximum take-off

32,188 lb (14600 kg)

Dimensions: main rotor diameter 61 ft (18.59 m); length 74 ft 10 in (22.81 m) with the rotors turning; height 21 ft 10 in (6.65 m) with the rotors turning; main rotor disc area 2,922.60 sq ft (271.51 m²)

Armament: up to 2,116 lb (960 kg) of disposable stores carried on the lower sides of the fuselage, and generally comprising four homing torpedoes

Payload: up to 45 troops, or up to 16 litters plus a medical team, or up to 12,000 lb (3660 kg) of freight carried internally or as a slung load

The first Canadian Cormorant made its maiden flight from Agusta's Vergiate factory on 7 March 2000. The type should be in service from early 2001.

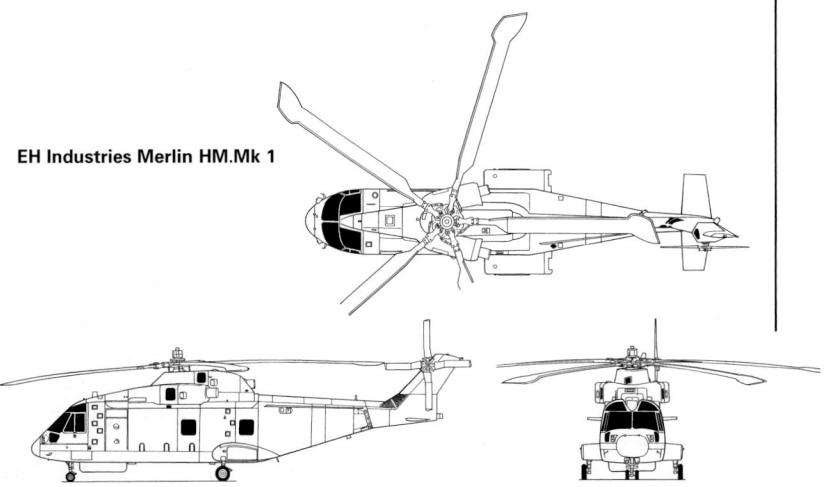

EH Industries Merlin HM.Mk 1

Extra 230

Walter Extra established the Extra-Flugzeugbau GmbH at Dinslaken for the design, development and manufacture (of kits as well as complete aircraft) of highly aerobatic aircraft for the training and competition roles.

His first type to enter production was the single-seat **Extra 230** competition machine, which first flew on 14 July 1983 as a mid-wing monoplane based on a fuselage and wire-braced tail unit of steel tube construction and a wing of wooden construction. The forward fuselage is covered with light alloy panels, while the rest of the airframe is skinned with doped Dacron fabric. The Extra 230 is stressed to 10 *g*, and very lively control responses are ensured by the use of large control surfaces (including three-quarter span ailerons), all capable of 26° deflection.

SPECIFICATION

Extra 230
Type: single-seat aerobatic aircraft
Engine: one Lycoming AEIO-360-A1E (DeMars modification) flat-four piston engine rated at 200 hp (149 kW)
Performance: maximum speed 218 mph (352 km/h) at optimum altitude; initial climb rate 2,950 ft (900 m) per minute; endurance 2 hours 30 minutes
Weights: empty 970 lb (440 kg); maximum take-off 1,234 lb (560 kg)
Dimensions: wingspan 24 ft 3⅛ in (7.40 m); length 19 ft 1¼ in (5.82 m); height 5 ft 8¼ in (1.73 m)

Extra 300, Extra 330 & Extra 200

First flown on 6 May 1988 as a specialised aerobatic aircraft, the **Extra 300** is based on a fuselage of steel tube construction covered with light alloy and fabric. The tail unit is a cantilever structure, fabricated from carbon composite materials and covered with fibreglass shells. The mid-set wing is flat and has a symmetrical aerofoil section, and is of carbon composites under fibreglass shells. The landing gear is of the fixed tailwheel type with a main unit of composite construction carrying spatted wheels, the cockpit is covered by a long clear-view canopy, and the engine generally drives a three-bladed Mühlbauer constant-speed propeller fitted with a spinner, although a four-bladed propeller from the same manufacturer is optional. The machine is stressed for ±8 *g*, and good control responses are ensured by the incorporation of large control surfaces including almost full-span ailerons for excellent roll rate.

The Extra 300 is the standard two-seat version with a tandem seating arrangement, and other members of the family include the **Extra 300L**, **Extra 300S** and **Extra 330**. The Extra 300L is a two-seater with a lower-set wing (for improved fields of vision and simpler installation of full IFR instrumentation in a more comfortable cockpit) with its span reduced from 26 ft 3 in (8.00 m) to 25 ft 3 in (7.70 m. Revised ailerons are incorporated for a roll rate boosted to almost 400° per second, and its fuselage is shortened from 23 ft 4¼ in (7.12 m) to 22 ft 9¼ in (6.94 m). The Extra 300S is the single-seat version of the basic Extra 300 with the wing reduced in span by 1 ft 7½ in (0.50 m) and fitted with improved ailerons. The Extra 330 is a development of the Extra 300S with a strengthened structure, larger control surfaces (including a wider-chord rudder with an enlarged balance area) and the uprated powerplant of one AEIO-580 flat-six engine rated at 330 hp (246 kW).

First flown on 2 April 1996 as what may be considered a two-seat development of the Extra 300 for the training and lower-standard competition roles, the **Extra 200** is stressed for ±10 *g*.

SPECIFICATION

Extra 300L
Type: two-seat aerobatic aircraft
Powerplant: one Lycoming AEIO-540-L1B5 flat-six piston engine rated at 300 hp (149 kW)
Performance: manoeuvring speed 182 mph (293 km/h) at optimum altitude; cruising speed 196 mph (315 km/h) at 8,000 ft (2440 m); initial climb rate 3,200 ft (975 m) per minute; service ceiling 16,000 ft (4875 m); range 586 miles (944 km) with auxiliary fuel and 477 miles (768 km) with standard fuel
Weights: empty 1,199 lb (544 kg); maximum take-off 1,340 lb (608 kg) for single-seat aerobatic use or 1,914 lb (868 kg) for two-seat normal use
Dimensions: wingspan 25 ft 3 in (7.70 m); length 22 ft 9¼ in (6.94 m); height 8 ft 7¼ in (2.62 m); wing area 115.18 sq ft (10.70 m²)

Walter Extra's aircraft (here a 300L) combine powerful engines with a lightweight airframe, and have proven to be world-beating aerobatic mounts.

Extra 400

Announced in February 1993 as something of a departure for a company that had hitherto produced aircraft only for the highly specialised aerobatic role, the **Extra 400** was designed by Extra in collaboration with Delft University for the high-performance touring and business transport roles. It first flew on 4 April 1996 with the second aircraft – which introduced downward-turned wingtips, a shallow ventral strake and NACA flush inlets on the sides of the nose – following in April 1998. The Extra 400 gained initial German certification in April 1997 for flight in VFR conditions, and the type later received certification for flight in IFR and icing conditions. From 1997 the manufacturer was considering the viability of a development with a turboprop- rather than piston-engined powerplant.

The Extra 400 is manufactured mostly of composite material and the fuselage is of basically circular section, which facilitated the incorporation of pressurised accommodation in a cabin seating the pilot and up to five passengers. The latter enter and depart the cabin by means of a port-side airstair door and enjoy the benefits of a design optimised for low internal and external noise levels. The aircraft is flown with the aid of an AlliedSignal Silver Crown two-tube EFIS (Electronic Flight Instrumentation System), with GPS-aided navigation.

In layout, the Extra 400 is a high-wing cantilever monoplane with a T-tail and retractable tricycle landing gear. The nosewheel and two main units retract rearward and forward respectively into the underside of the fuselage.

SPECIFICATION

Extra 400
Type: one-crew touring and business transport aircraft
Powerplant: one Continental Voyager TSIOL-550-A flat-six piston engine rated at 350 hp (261 kW)
Performance: maximum speed 298 mph (480 km/h) at optimum altitude; cruising speed 280 mph (450 km/h) at 25,000 ft (7620 m); certificated altitude 25,000 ft (7620 m); range 1,615 miles (2600 km) with four passengers
Weights: empty 2,653 lb (1203 kg); maximum take-off 4,290 lb (1946 kg)
Dimensions: wingspan 37 ft 8¾ in (11.50 m); length 30 ft 9¾ in (9.39 m); height 10 ft 1¾ in (3.09 m); wing area 153.95 sq ft (14.30 m²)
Payload: up to five passengers within the context of a 1,217-lb (552-kg) maximum payload

F+W C-3602, C-3603, C-3604 and C-3605

Development of the **Farner-Werke C-3605** two-seat target-tug can be traced back to the **Fabrique Fédérale C-3602**, two prototypes of which were built in 1939-40 for the long-range reconnaissance and ground-attack roles. The flight test programme indicated the need for modifications, and an initial batch of 10 aircraft entered production with the designation **C-3603**. After these had been subjected to a thorough service evaluation, a further 142 machines followed, serving with the Swiss air force between 1942 and 1952 in the combat role. Two other aircraft were produced for training and parachute tests with the designation **C-3603-1 TR**. In 1945 a C-3603-1 was converted for target-towing and, after considerable flight-testing, a successful installation was evolved and fitted to 20 other aircraft within a year.

Further improvements followed, and in 1946 Farner-Werke at Grenchen converted a C-3603-1 into a more advanced target-tug. A long tube was fitted from the rear cockpit to eject the target sleeve above the tailplane and between the twin vertical tail surfaces, with a cable-cutting device available to the pilot. Twenty C-3603 aircraft were converted to this standard.

Development of the basic airframe had meanwhile continued with the **C-3604**, a version using the 1,250-hp (933-kW) Saurer YS-2 engine in place of the 1,000-hp (746-kW) Hispano-Suiza used in earlier models. A prototype and 12 production examples of the C-3604 were built, the type entering service in 1947-48. The availability of unused spares produced for the C-3603 enabled a further six C-3603-1 aircraft to be assembled in 1948.

During the early 1950s a requirement for an aircraft to tow illuminated targets at night was met with the conversion of a C-3603-1, and this machine remained in service until replaced by the **C-3605** in 1972. Conversions of a further 40 C-3603-1s to target-tugs began in 1953, while another aircraft was fitted beneath one wing with a winch built by ML Aviation in the UK for high-speed towing, and a ballast tank beneath the other wing. In the same year, 20 more C-3603-1s were converted by the military at Dübendorf for catastrophe relief with underwing supply containers. The ultimate development of the C-3603 airframe came when the Hispano-Suiza engines of the 40 C-3603-1 conversions began to wear out. Various types of foreign aircraft were considered as replacements, but all were rejected for various reasons and a proposal to re-engine the C-3603-1 with the T53 turboprop was accepted. A prototype was first flown on 19 August 1968, and this was handed over to the Swiss air force in December 1968 for acceptance trials. The latter were satisfactory and, with a few modifications, a series of 23 aircraft was re-engined and given the new designation **C-3605**. The first C-3605 conversions entered service in 1971 and the last was delivered in January 1973.

This C-3603 demonstrates the type's original nose shape. The C-3605 featured a 6-ft (1.82-m) increase in the length of the nose.

SPECIFICATION

F+W C-3605
Type: two-seat target tug
Powerplant: one Lycoming T53-L-7 turboprop engine rated at 1,100 shp (820 kW)
Performance: maximum speed 268 mph (432 km/h) at 10,000 ft (3050 m); cruising speed 217 mph (350 km/h) at 20,000 ft (6095 m); initial climb rate 2,470 ft (753 m) per minute; service ceiling 32,810 ft (10000 m); range 605 miles (980 km)
Weights: empty 5,806 lb (2634 kg); maximum take-off 8,192 lb (3716 kg)
Dimensions: wingspan 45 ft 1 in (13.74 m); length 40 ft 8¼ in (12.40 m); height 13 ft 3½ in (4.05 m); wing area 308.93 sq ft (28.70 m²)

Fairchild AT-13, AT-14 and AT-21 Gunner

The growing importance of heavy defensive/offensive armament for its bomber aircraft had not been fully appreciated by US Army Air Corps planners until early in World War II, when information on combat experience in Europe became available to them. It was rapidly seen that the large numbers of bombers and the greater numbers of weapons installed in each of them would require the creation of considerably larger numbers of air crews and specially trained air gunners.

The USAAC therefore lost little time in ordering two specialised trainer prototypes from Fairchild. The first was the **XAT-13** intended to provide team training for a bomber's entire crew, and this aircraft was powered by two 450-hp (336-kW) Pratt & Whitney R-1340-AN-1 nine-cylinder radial engines.

The second prototype was the **XAT-14**, of similar layout but powered by two 520-hp (388-kW) Ranger V-770-6 inverted-Vee engines. The XAT-14 was then adapted as the **XAT-14A** specialised trainer for bombardiers, with its defensive guns removed. Testing and evaluation of these aircraft resulted in the procurement of a specialised gunnery trainer under the designation **AT-21 Gunner**.

A mid-wing cantilever monoplane of mixed construction, the AT-21 provided accommodation for a crew of five, including pilot, co-pilot/gunnery instructor and three pupils. Of the 175 AT-21s constructed, 106 were built by Fairchild and, to speed deliveries to the USAAF, the other 69 were produced as 39 by Bellanca and 30 by McDonnell. Entering service with newly established air gunnery schools, the AT-21 remained in service until 1944, when the surviving aircraft were displaced by training examples of the operational aircraft in which the air gunners would eventually serve. Many of these surplus aircraft were then converted for use as target tugs.

Variant

XBQ-3: designation of one AT-21 following conversion for evaluation as a flying-bomb, equipped with a radio control system and a 4,000-lb (1814-kg) explosive charge

The AT-21 had a deep oval-section fuselage, a tail unit with twin fin-and-rudder assemblies and retractable tricycle landing gear.

SPECIFICATION

Fairchild AT-21 Gunner
Type: five-seat air gunnery trainer
Powerplant: two Ranger V-770-11/15 inverted-Vee piston engines each rated at 520 hp (388 kW)
Performance: maximum speed 225 mph (362 km/h) at 12,000 ft (3660 m); cruising speed 196 mph (315 km/h) at 12,000 ft (3660 m); initial climb rate 930 ft (283 m) per minute; service ceiling 22,150 ft (6750 m); range 910 miles (1464 km)
Weights: empty 8,654 lb (3925 kg); maximum take-off 11,288 lb (5129 kg)
Dimensions: wingspan 52 ft 8 in (16.05 m); length 38 ft (11.58 m); height 13 ft 1½ in (4.00 m); wing area 378.00 sq ft (35.12 m²)
Armament: one 0.3-in (7.62-mm) Browning trainable machine-gun in the nose position and two 0.3-in (7.62-mm) Browning trainable machine-guns in the power-operated dorsal turret

Fairchild AU-23 Peacemaker

Under licence from Pilatus Flugzeugwerke AG of Switzerland, Fairchild (then known as Fairchild Hiller) began the production of a batch of Turbo-Porter utility aircraft. The first of these, named originally as the **Heli-Porter** but subsequently known as the Porter, was rolled out on 3 June 1966. Early production aircraft were powered by a 550-shp (410-kW) Pratt & Whitney Canada PT6A-20 turboprop.

In the late 1960s Fairchild began development of a specialised version for the counter-

While it was primarily used in the utility, COIN and psywar roles, the AU-23 was also trialled as a mini gunship. The aircraft became synonymous with covert Air America operations.

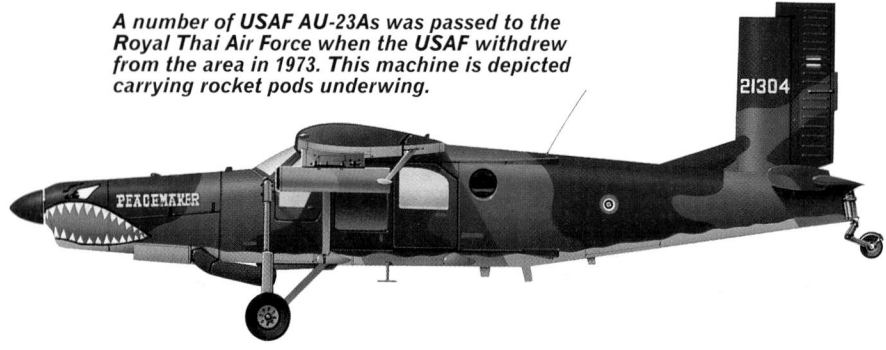

A number of USAF AU-23As was passed to the Royal Thai Air Force when the USAF withdrew from the area in 1973. This machine is depicted carrying rocket pods underwing.

SPECIFICATION	
Fairchild AU-23 Peacemaker	6,100 lb (2767 kg)
Type: two-crew COIN and multi-role aircraft	**Dimensions:** wingspan 49 ft 8 in (15.14 m); length 36 ft 10 in (11.23 m); height 12 ft 3 in (3.73 m); wing area 310.01 sq ft (28.80 m²)
Powerplant: one Garrett TPE331-1-101F turboprop engine rated at 665 shp (496 kW)	
Performance: maximum speed 174 mph (280 km/h) at optimum altitude; cruising speed 163 mph (262 km/h) at optimum altitude; initial climb rate 1,500 ft (457 m) per minute; service ceiling 22,800 ft (6950 m); range 558 miles (898 km)	**Armament:** up to 1,990 lb (903 kg) of disposable stores carried on one underfuselage and four underwing hardpoints, and generally comprising bombs, cannon, Miniguns, napalm, rockets and smoke grenades
Weights: maximum take-off	**Payload:** up to 10 troops or freight

insurgency (COIN) role. Originally known as the **Armed Porter**, this differed primarily in having one underfuselage and four underwing hardpoints.

In addition, this version was powered by the TPE331-1-101F turboprop, its main landing-gear units each carried a wheel fitted with a high-flotation tyre for rough-field operations, and a complete military nav/com system and an armament control system were installed. A total of 36 such aircraft was acquired by the US Air Force under the designation **AU-23A Peacemaker**, of which 28 and five were supplied to the Thai air force and Thai air police respectively. Stores that could be carried included reconnaissance cameras and a public address system with a pod containing 20 speakers.

Fairchild C-82 Packet, C-119 Flying Boxcar & R4Q

Fairchild C-119G Flying Boxcar

A distinctly longer nose ahead of the cockpit was a key recognition feature of the C-82. Production aircraft were equipped for glider-towing.

To meet a US Army Air Forces' requirement for a specialised military freighter, Fairchild began work on its **Model F-78** design. Following approval of the design and a mock-up in 1942, a contract for a single prototype was awarded and the designation **XC-82** allocated. First flown on 10 September 1944, the XC-82 was a high-wing cantilever monoplane of all-metal construction. The roomy central nacelle incorporated a flight deck for a crew of five and a large cabin/cargo hold with clamshell doors at the rear to provide easy access for wheeled or tracked vehicles. The rear doors could be removed completely for the deployment of heavy loads by

This Indian air force C-119 was one of those modified by Hindustan with an Orpheus turbojet engine pod-mounted above the fuselage. The turbojet allowed greater payloads to be carried, especially in 'hot and high' conditions.

parachute-extraction techniques. The fuselage was supported on the ground by robust retractable tricycle landing gear, and the powerplant was based on two 2,100-hp (1566-kW) Pratt & Whitney R-2800-34 18-cylinder radial engines in wing-mounted nacelles. Extending rearward from these nacelles was a pair of booms carrying twin fin-and-rudder assemblies and united at the rear by the tailplane carrying a single elevator.

The USAAF placed an initial contract for 100 **C-82A Packet** production aircraft. The first of these were delivered for evaluation in 1945 and a contract for 100 more followed. Because of wartime demands a second production line was laid down by North American Aviation at Dallas, Texas but, of a contract for 792 **C-82N** aircraft from this source, only three were completed before the general rash of contract cancellations that followed VJ-Day. Fairchild eventually built a total of 220 aircraft, deliveries ending in 1948.

Based on the C-119C, the R4Q-1 was delivered to the US Marine Corps as a tactical transport. The aircraft displaced R4Ds and a range of other small transport types and was extensively used during the conflict in Korea.

Fairchild C-82 Packet, C-119 Flying Boxcar and R4Q (cont.)

Although too late to operate during World War II, the Packet provided valuable service to the Tactical Air Command and Military Air Transport Service of what had meanwhile become the US Air Force before the type was retired in 1954.

During 1947 Fairchild developed an improved version of the C-82, the **XC-82B** (later **XC-119A**) prototype being a conversion from a production C-82A. It differed primarily in having the flight deck resited into the nose of the aircraft and the powerplant uprated to a pair of 2,650-hp (1976-kW) Pratt & Whitney R-4360-4 28-cylinder radial engines.

Following service tests the improved type was

ordered into production as the **C-119B Flying Boxcar** (55 built), these having a wider fuselage, structural strengthening for operation at higher gross weights, and more powerful R-4360-20 engines. Accommodating up to 62 paratroops, and with increased cargo capacity, the C-119 gave excellent service during operations in the Korean and Vietnam Wars, as well as in a wide variety of other heavy transport applications. The C-119 also served with the air forces of Belgium, Brazil, Ethiopia, India, Italy, South Vietnam and Taiwan. In addition, some surplus military aircraft, of both the C-82 and C-119 models, were acquired by civil oper-

SPECIFICATION

Fairchild C-119G Flying Boxcar
Type: four/five-crew cargo and troop transport
Powerplant: two Wright R-3350-85 radial piston engines each rated at 3,500 hp (2610 kW)
Performance: maximum speed 296 mph (476 km/h) at 17,000 ft (5180 m); cruising speed 200 mph (322 km/h) at optimum altitude; initial climb rate 750 ft (229 m) per minute; range 2,280 miles (3669 km)

Weights: empty 39,982 lb (18136 kg); maximum take-off 74,400 lb (33748 kg)
Dimensions: wingspan 109 ft 3 in (33.30 m); length 86 ft 6 in (26.37 m); height 26 ft 3 in (8.00 m); wing area 1,447.00 sq ft (134.43 m²)
Payload: up to 78 passengers, or 62 paratroops, or 35 litters plus medical attendants, or 28,000 lb (12701 kg) of freight

Variants

EC-82A: redesignation of one C-82A after being equipped with tracked landing-gear units
XC-119A (later C-119A): designation of XC-82B after modification to intended production standard
EC-119A: redesignation of the C-119A after conversion to serve as an ECM testbed
C-119C: production version (303 built) with revised tail unit
YC-119F: one service-test aircraft with two 3,500-hp (2610-kW) Wright R-3350 18-cylinder radial engines
C-119F: production version (212 built) with further tail revision
C-119G: production version (480 built) with propeller, equipment and powerplant changes
AC-119G: 26 gunship conversions from C-119G standard with four 0.3-in (7.62-mm) six-barrel Miniguns, armour protection and flare-launchers
YC-119H Skyvan: one conversion from C-119C with increased wing and tailplane span, revised tail surfaces, underwing fuel tanks and two R-3350 engines
C-119J: redesignation of 62 C-119F/Gs following incorporation of inflight openable door in rear fuselage
EC-119J: designation of about six C-119Js converted for satellite tracking
YC-119K: designation of one C-119G converted with two 3,700-hp (2759-kW) R-3350 engines and two underwing 2,850-lb st (12.68-kN) General Electric J85-GE-17 turbojet engines
C-119K: designation of five C-119Gs converted to the YC-119K standard plus incorporation of brake anti-skid units
AC-119K: designation of 26 C-119Gs converted originally to AC-119G standard, but later upgraded by the addition of two 20-mm cannon, improved avionics and two underwing J85-GE-17 turbojet engines
C-119L: designation of 22 C-119Gs following updating and installation of new propellers
R4Q-1: C-119C for US Marine Corps, which received 39 such aircraft
R4Q-2: C-119F for USMC, which received 58 such aircraft
XC-120 Packplane: conversion of one C-119B to meet a USAF requirement for an experimental detachable-fuselage transport created by the combination of the C-119B's flying surfaces with a new upper-fuselage component with a flat undersurface to mate with a detachable lower component with a flat upper surface and incorporating a cargo compartment; the flight deck was located in the upper component; the type could be flown with or without pack and it was intended that various packs for different military operations would be provided; no production contract followed military evaluation

ators. In 1961 Steward-Davis Inc. of Long Beach, California developed the Jet-Pak conversion for the C-119. This involved the installation of a 3,400-lb st (15.12-kN) Westinghouse

J34-WE-36 turbojet in a specially developed nacelle mounted on the upper surface of the wing's centre-section. At least 26 C-119s of the Indian air force had a more powerful

Bristol Siddeley Orpheus turbojet engine, built under licence by Hindustan Aeronautics, in a pod to enable them to operate with large payloads under 'hot-and-high' conditions.

Fairchild C-123 Provider

Just one US Air National Guard unit flew the jet-augmented, ski-equipped C-123J. The Alaska ANG's 144th Tactical Airlift Squadron received the type in June 1960 and continued to fly it for a further 16 years.

In 1943 the Chase Aircraft Company was founded to undertake the design, development and production of a heavy assault cargo glider for the US Army Air Forces. Following successful demonstration of an **XCG-18A** cargo glider prototype, there followed five examples of the **YCG-18A** service test model. One of these was later converted to **YC-122** standard as a light assault transport by the addition of two wing-mounted radial engines. There followed **YC-122A/B/C** aircraft for service trials, leading to construction of two prototypes of an even larger troop/cargo transport glider, the **XCG-20** (later **XG-20**). One of these was subsequently redesignated as the **XC-123** when fitted with two 2,200-hp (1641-kW) R-2800-23 18-cylinder radial engines. The XC-123 first flew on 14 October 1949, and in 1952 Chase received a contract for five **C-123B Provider** pre-production transports which were built and flown in 1953. In that year the Kaiser-Frazer Corporation acquired a majority holding in Chase, and was awarded a US Air Force contract for 300 examples of the C-123B in

its full operational form. This contract was cancelled in mid-1953 because of delays in the production effort and re-awarded to Fairchild, which then assumed responsibility for continued development and production of the C-123.

A high-wing cantilever monoplane of all-metal construction, the C-123 had a large-capacity fuselage upswept at the rear and incorporating a loading door in the undersurface that could be lowered to serve as a ramp. Other features of the configuration were a conventional but tall tail unit and retractable tricycle landing

gear. As an alternative to cargo, the main cabin could accommodate 60 fully-equipped troops, or 50 litters and six seated casualties plus six medical attendants. Fairchild's interest in development of this aircraft brought the introduction of a large dorsal fin to improve directional stability.

The company's first production C-123B made its initial flight on 1 September 1954, and production by Fairchild totalled 302 aircraft, including one static test airframe and 24 for delivery to Saudi Arabia (6) and Venezuela (18). At a later date C-123B transports

Variants

HC-123B: designation sometimes applied to 11 C-123Bs transferred to the US Coast Guard
UC-123B: a small number of C-123Bs converted for use as crop destruction/forest defoliation aircraft in Vietnam
VC-123C: command transport proposal from by Kaiser-Frazer
YC-124H: evaluation prototype with special wide-track landing gear; later tested with auxiliary power provided by two 2,850-lb st (12.68-kN) General Electric J85-GE-17 turbojet engines in underwing pods
C-123J: redesignation of 10 C-123Bs for operation under Arctic conditions following installation of Fairchild J44 auxiliary turbojet engines in wingtip pods with eyelid doors
C-123K: 183 C-123Bs converted with two J85-GE-17 auxiliary turbojet engines in underwing pods, larger wheels and an anti-skid braking system
NC-123K: two C-123Ks after conversion for armed night surveillance; sometimes known as **AC-123K**
UC-123K: 34 C-123Ks converted for forest defoliation missions in Vietnam
VC-123K: one C-123K following conversion as a VIP transport

This C-123 flew with the 63rd TAS, 439 TAW, Air Force Reserve from Westover AFB, Massachusetts after 1974. It wears SEA theatre camouflage.

Fairchild C-123B Provider
Type: two-crew tactical transport
Powerplant: two Pratt & Whitney R-2800-99W radial piston engines each rated at 2,300 hp (1715 kW)
Performance: maximum speed 253 mph (407 km/h) at optimum altitude; cruising speed 205 mph (330 km/h) at optimum altitude; initial climb rate 875 ft (267 m) per minute; service ceiling 24,000 ft (7315 m); range 1,340 miles (2156 km) with a 16,000-lb (7258-kg) payload

Weights: empty 29,900 lb (13562 kg); maximum take-off 60,000 lb (27216 kg)
Dimensions: wingspan 110 ft (33.53 m); length 75 ft 9 in (23.09 m); height 34 ft 1 in (10.39 m); wing area 1,223.00 sq ft (113.62 m²)
Payload: up to 60 troops, or 50 litters and six seated casualties plus six medical attendants, or freight up to the size of a 155-mm Howitzer and its towing vehicle

surplus to USAF requirement were supplied to the Philippines, Taiwan and South Vietnam.

Three experimental versions were built for USAF evaluation by the Stroukoff Aircraft Corporation whose president, Michael Stroukoff, had been Chase's chief engineer. These were the **YC-123D**, similar to a C-123B but with a boundary-layer control system; the **YC-123E** with a revised fin and rudder and a Stroukoff 'Pantobase' landing system incorporating retractable land and water skis, wheels and wingtip floats for operation from a wide variety of surfaces; and the **YC-134A**, incorporating both of the above systems.

Fairchild F-27 & FH-227

In April 1956 Fokker concluded an agreement with Fairchild for the latter to manufacture the F27 Friendship then under development by the Dutch company. Thus Fairchild became responsible for production and marketing in North America of the **F-27** series of aircraft that corresponded to some of those built by the Dutch company. However, when Fokker developed a 'stretched' version known as the F27 Mk 500, Fairchild decided to design its own version with a lengthened fuselage, and this was identified as the **Fairchild Hiller FH-227**. The FH-227 differed from the standard F-27 in having a fuselage 'stretch' of 6 ft (1.83 m) to provide accommodation for a maximum of 52 passengers, with increased baggage and cargo space, and in the

Such was the success of the FH-227 – the second aircraft being illustrated – that Fairchild halted F-27 production.

installation of 2,250-eshp (1678-ekW) Rolls-Royce Dart RDa.7 Mk 532-7 turboprop engines. The first of two FH-227 prototypes made its initial flight on 27 January 1966, and production of the FH-227 and its variants had reached 79 when production ended. About 24 of these transport aircraft were still in service, mainly in Central and South America, in the late 1990s.

Fairchild Hiller FH-227B
Type: three-crew passenger transport
Powerplant: two Rolls-Royce Dart RDa.7 Mk 532-7L turboprop engines each rated at 2,300 eshp (1715 ekW)
Performance: maximum cruising speed 294 mph (473 km/h) at 20,000 ft (6095 m); economic cruising speed 270 mph (453 km/h) at 25,000 ft (7620 m); service

ceiling 28,000 ft (8535 m); range 606 miles (975 km) with maximum payload
Weights: empty 23,200 lb (10523 kg); maximum take-off 45,000 lb (20638 kg)
Dimensions: wingspan 95 ft 2 in (29.01 m); length 83 ft 8 in (25.50 m); height 27 ft 7 in (8.41 m); wing area 754.00 sq ft (70.05 m²)
Payload: up to 52 passengers

Variants

FH-227B: certificated in June 1967, this version had structural strengthening for operation at a higher gross weight, uprated engines driving larger-diameter propellers, and a redesigned windscreen
FH-227C: standard FH-227 with the larger-diameter propeller of the FH-227B
FH-227D: introduced anti-skid braking units, an intermediate flap setting for take-off, and Dart RDa.7 Mk 532-7L engines
FH-227E: basically an FH-227C with FH-227D improvements

Fairchild Kreider-Reisner aircraft

Established in 1923 at Hagerstown, Maryland, the Kreider-Reisner Aircraft Company began its association with aviation as a sub-contractor. By 1925 it was operating a general flying service and in 1926 designed and built a lightplane, the **Kreider-Reisner Midget**, which gained some success in competition flying. This induced the company to design an improved three-seat biplane for use by its own flying service and, because it seemed more economical to build the new type itself than to contract it to

another company, this marked the company's beginning as a manufacturer of aircraft.

This first commercial aircraft was the **C-2 Challenger**, a conventional biplane of mixed construction with tandem open cockpits seating two passengers (forward) and pilot (rear), a braced tail unit, tailskid landing gear and power provided by a 90-hp (67-kW) Curtiss OX-5 Vee engine. The basic type was later produced in a variety of **C-3** and **C-4** variants with detail changes and a number of different

engines as requested by individual buyers.

Late in 1928 Kreider-Reisner introduced a new and slightly smaller two-seat **C-6 Challenger** biplane that benefited from some of the improvements introduced into the C-3 and C-4 models. Then, during 1929, the Fairchild Airplane Manufacturing Corporation of New York City acquired the Kreider-Reisner company, continuing

production and marketing of the latter company's successful Challenger aircraft. The C-4 and C-6 were redesignated as the **Fairchild KR-34** and **KR-21** respectively, and for continued support but not manufacture the original C-2 became known as the **KR-31**. As the company needed a testbed for a new air-cooled inline engine identified as the Fairchild 6-390, later the well-known Ranger, a KR-21 airframe was modified for the purpose. To cater for the

new engine, the geometry of the wing cellule and landing gear was revised, this being in addition to the fuselage modifications needed to allow for installation of the engine. In this form the aircraft was redesignated as the **KR-125**. In 1931 a similar engine was installed in a KR-21 airframe without the changes to wing and landing gear geometry. This proved to be a more pleasant aircraft to fly and a few were built and sold under the designation **KR-135**.

Fairchild KR-34C
Type: three-seat utility aircraft
Powerplant: one Wright Whirlwind J-6-5 radial piston engine rated at 165 hp (123 kW)
Performance: maximum speed 120 mph (193 km/h) at optimum altitude; cruising speed 102 mph (164 km/h) at optimum altitude;

initial climb rate 800 ft (244 m) per minute; service ceiling 14,000 ft (4265 m); range 510 miles (821 km)
Weights: empty 1,524 lb (691 kg); maximum take-off 2,368 lb (1074 kg)
Dimensions: wingspan 30 ft 1 in (9.17 m); length 23 ft 2 in (7.06 m); height 9 ft 3 in (2.82 m); wing area 285.00 sq ft (26.48 m²)

A neat single-bay biplane, the KR-34 offered open accommodation for three people. This restored KR-34C was photographed in 1966.

Fairchild Model F-11 Husky

During 1945 Fairchild Aircraft in Canada began the design of a utility aircraft which the company hoped would find a large-scale market in the period following the end of World War II. A braced high-wing monoplane, following the general lines of the many single-engined aircraft in this category that had been developed by the company and its American parent, the **Model F-11 Husky** differed in having an upswept rear fuselage to allow for a large rear-loading door that would make it easy to accommodate long items of cargo. Of all-metal construction, except for some fabric covering, the 12 examples built by the company before it went out of business had float or ski landing gear; tricycle landing gear had been planned but was not developed. The maiden flight of the prototype was made on 14 June 1946.

Husky Aircraft of Vancouver later acquired the design and sales rights, developing a new engine installation to provide more power. Six aircraft were converted to this new **Model F-11-2** standard with one 550-hp (410-kW) Alvis Leonides Mk 503/8 or Mk 514/880 nine-cylinder radial engine driving a three-bladed propeller. Following these conversions the six original aircraft were identified as **Model F-11-1** aircraft.

Power for the Husky was provided by a Wasp Junior engine driving a two-bladed propeller, while a maximum of seven or eight passengers was seated on bench seats. The F-11-1 prototype is illustrated.

SPECIFICATION	
Fairchild Model F-11-1 (floatplane configuration) **Type:** two-crew utility transport **Powerplant:** one Pratt & Whitney R-985-T1B3 or SB3 Wasp Junior radial piston engine rated at 450 hp (336 kW) **Performance:** maximum speed 138 mph (222 km/h) at 2,300 ft (700 m); cruising speed 121 mph (195 km/h) at 10,000 ft (3050 m); initial climb rate 675 ft (206 m) per	minute; service ceiling 15,500 ft (4725 m) **Weights:** empty 3,900 lb (1769 kg); maximum take-off 6,800 lb (3084 kg) **Dimensions:** wingspan 54 ft 9 in (16.69 m); length 37 ft 5 in (11.40 m); height 16 ft 3½ in (4.97 m); wing area 355.00 sq ft (32.98 m²) **Payload:** up to eight passengers or freight carried in the cabin

Fairchild Model FC-1, FC-2 (C-96 and JQ) and Model 51

During the early 1920s Sherman Fairchild was engaged actively in the new business of aerial photography and survey. He operated a variety of aircraft for this purpose, all of them possessing a number of shortcomings, so Fairchild designed what he considered to be an ideal aircraft for the aerial photography role. Tenders for construction of a number of these aircraft produced what appeared to be prohibitive prices, so Fairchild decided to build the aircraft 'in house'. Thus Fairchild acquired premises at Farmingdale, Long Island, in which to begin aircraft manufacture.

As first flown in mid-1926, the **Model FC-1** was of braced high-wing monoplane configuration with a wing that could be folded for storage, a braced tail unit, tailskid landing gear and the powerplant of one 90-hp (67-kW) Curtiss OX-5 Vee engine. The fuselage provided enclosed cabin accommodation for a pilot and one or two passengers, and there were ample windows and ports for easy use of cameras. After extensive testing during 1926 the Model FC-1 was re-engined with a 200-hp (149-kW) Wright Whirlwind J-4 nine-cylinder radial and in this form became known as the **Model FC-1A**. Further tests followed into 1927 before a decision was made to put the aircraft into production for general sales under the designation **Model FC-2**. This version differed in having increased cabin volume to seat a pilot plus four

Variants

Model FC-2W: generally similar to the Model FC-2 but intended more specifically as a cargo-carrier; modified windows, increased wingspan and area, and more powerful 400-hp (298-kW) Pratt & Whitney Wasp nine-cylinder radial engine
Model FC-2W2: generally similar to the Model FC-2W but with its fuselage lengthened by 2 ft 2 in (0.66 m) and the interior revised to accommodate a pilot and up to six passengers; seats easily removed for cargo-carrying; the most famous Model FC-2W2 was *Stars and Stripes*, which was used by the Byrd Antarctic Expedition of 1928
Model FC-2C (Challenger): small number of five-seat Model FC-2s built for the Curtiss Flying Service and powered by the 160-hp (119-kW) Curtiss C-6 Challenger six-cylinder inline piston engine
Model 51: this development of the Model FC-2 was created to provide Fairchild with a type to rival later transports with more powerful engines, and the aircraft were produced as conversions from Model FC-2s with a number of aerodynamic revisions as well as the uprated powerplant of one 300-hp (224-kW) Wright R-975 Whirlwind radial engine to create the Model 51 or one identically-rated Pratt & Whitney R-985 Wasp Junior radial engine to create the **Model 51A**
C-96: designation allocated by the USAAF in 1942 to three impressed Model FC-2W2s
JQ: under this core designation the US Navy acquired a single example of the Model FC-2 for evaluation as the **XJQ-1**; the machine was later re-engined with a 450-hp (336-kW) R-985 Wasp Junior nine-cylinder radial to become the **XJQ-2**, later **XRQ-2**

passengers, and a new J-5 engine as standard (with the Curtiss C-6 engine as an option). The Model FC-2 was also available with float or ski landing gear in place of the standard main wheels. A total of 56 Model FC-2s was built over an eight-month period from 1 June 1927.

Extensive cabin glazing and a strut-braced, high-wing characterised the FC-1 and FC-2. The aircraft illustrated is an FC-2 engaged in air mail services.

SPECIFICATION	
Fairchild Model FC-2 **Type:** one-crew utility aircraft **Powerplant:** one Wright Whirlwind J-5 radial piston engine rated at 200 hp (149 kW) **Performance:** maximum speed 122 mph (196 km/h) at optimum altitude; cruising speed 105 mph (169 km/h) at optimum altitude; initial climb rate 565 ft (173 m) per minute; service ceiling 11,500 ft	(3505 m); range 700 miles (1127 km) **Weights:** empty 2,160 lb (980 kg); maximum take-off 3,600 lb (1633 kg) **Dimensions:** wingspan 44 ft (13.41 m); length 31 ft (9.45 m); height 9 ft (2.74 m); wing area 290.00 sq ft (26.94 m²) **Payload:** up to four passengers or 820 lb (372 kg) of freight carried in the cabin

Fairchild Model 22

The rise of conglomerates in the USA during 1929 led to the American Aviation Corporation gaining a controlling interest in the Fairchild Aviation Corporation. This arrangement was not happy as far as Sherman Fairchild was concerned, and in 1931 he resigned and acquired with the proceeds of his shareholding the Kreider-Reisner subsidiary, which he later renamed the Fairchild Aircraft Corporation.

During the period of these negotiations the Kreider-Reisner subsidiary began the development of a new two-seat sporting/training aircraft, and this was marketed as the **Fairchild Model 22-C7** following certification in March 1931. The aim had been to produce a light-plane that would be cheap to buy and economical to

A braced parasol-wing monoplane of mixed construction, the Model 22 had a braced tail unit, tailskid landing gear and tandem open cockpits.

SPECIFICATION	
Fairchild Model 22-C7F **Type:** two-seat touring and training aircraft **Powerplant:** one Warner Super Scarab radial piston engine rated at 145 hp (108 kW) **Performance:** maximum speed 138 mph (222 km/h) at optimum altitude; cruising speed 118 mph (190 km/h) at optimum altitude;	initial climb rate 840 ft (256 m) per minute; service ceiling 19,400 ft (5915 m); range 630 miles (1014 km) **Weights:** empty 1,133 lb (514 kg); maximum take-off 1,750 lb (794 kg) **Dimensions:** wingspan 32 ft 10 in (10.00 m); length 22 ft (6.71 m); height 7 ft 11 in (2.41 m); wing area 170.00 sq ft (15.79 m²)

operate, in the hope of capturing a major share of a rapidly dwindling market. As first flown it was powered by an 80-hp (60-kW) Armstrong Siddeley Genet five-cylin-

der radial engine, but after extensive flight testing the production Model 22-C7 appeared with a 75-hp (56-kW) Michigan Rover four-cylinder inverted inline engine.

Only about 12 production examples of the Model 22-C7 were built, almost certainly as a result of the prevailing economic climate rather than any shortcomings in the

design, but the aircraft proved an excellent advertising medium and subsequent subvariants (the **Model 22-C7A**, **B**, **D**,

E, **F** and **G** with different engines up to the 145-hp/108-kW Warner radial unit) sold in greater numbers.

Fairchild Model 24 (C-61 Forwarder, J2K and Argus)

The mounting sales of the Model 22-C7 series induced Fairchild to produce what was basically a version of that aircraft with an enclosed cabin. To achieve this, the configuration was changed to that of a braced high-wing monoplane, the resulting cabin providing two-seat side-by-

side accommodation. Other changes included the introduction of a tailwheel in place of the original tailskid, and the initial **Model 22-C8** was powered by a licence-built British engine in the form of the 95-hp (71-kW) ACE Cirrus Hi-Ace four-cylinder inverted inline unit. Most variants were

available with optional float or ski landing gear. Certificated during April 1932, the basic Fairchild **Model 24-C8** was produced to the extent of only 10 aircraft, but these modest numbers, like those of the initial Model 22-C7, soon created interest and new orders.

Some 976 UC-61s were ordered by the USAAF, with 670 being passed to the RAF, with which the type served extensively. A UC-61A is illustrated.

Built in 1946 as a Model 24W, this aircraft remained on the US civil register into the 21st century. The aircraft has been re-engined with a Ranger unit.

SPECIFICATION	
Fairchild 24-G **Type:** three/four-seat light transport **Powerplant:** one Warner Super Scarab Series 50 radial piston engine rated at 145 hp (108 kW) **Performance:** maximum speed 130 mph (209 km/h) at sea level; cruising speed 118 mph (190 km/h) at sea level; initial climb rate	675 ft (206 m) per minute; service ceiling 16,500 ft (5030 m); range 475 miles (764 km) **Weights:** empty 1,475 lb (669 kg); maximum take-off 2,400 lb (1089 kg) **Dimensions:** wingspan 36 ft 4 in (11.07 m); length 23 ft 10 in (7.26 m); height 7 ft 4 in (2.24 m); wing area 173.16 sq ft (16.09 m²)

Variants

Model 24-C8A: about 25 of a version generally similar to the C8 but with a radial-engined powerplant; the prototype was flown with the 110-hp (82-kW) Warner Scarab 11-cylinder engine, but production aircraft had a 125-hp (93-kW) version of this engine
Model 24-C8B: two examples of a version almost identical to the original C8 but with the 125-hp (93-kW) Menasco Pirate four-cylinder inverted inline engine
Model 24-C8C: about 130 of a version that retained the same general configuration but in a form which was slightly scaled up to provide three-seat accommodation; it was powered by a 145-hp (108-kW) Super Scarab seven-cylinder radial engine, and was first certificated in April 1934
Model 24-C8D: about 14 of a three-seat version similar to the C8C but with the radial engine replaced by a 145-hp (108-kW) Ranger 6-390B six-cylinder inverted inline engine
Model 24-C8E: about 50 of a version of the C8C with improved equipment and a number of refinements
Model 24-C8F: about 40 of a version of the Model C8D with improved equipment and a number of refinements
Model 24-G: about 100 of a C8E development available in two versions as a three-seat de luxe or four-seat utility model
Model 24-H: about 25 of what was basically a de luxe version of the C8D but with the 150-hp (112-kW) Ranger 6-390D-3 engine
Model 24-J: about 40 of a version of the Model 24-G and available in de luxe and utility versions, each offering four-seat capacity
Model 24-K: about 34 of a version similar to Model 24-H but available in de luxe and utility versions and powered by the 150-hp (112-kW) Ranger 6-410B six-cylinder inverted inline engine
Model 24R9: about 35 of a refined version of the Model 24-K, available in de luxe and utility versions but with the 165-hp (123-kW) Ranger 6-

410B-1 engine
Model 24R40: about 25 of a version generally similar to the Model 24R9 but available only to order in de luxe form
Model 24W9: about 40 of a refined version of the Model 24-J, available in de luxe and utility models
Model 24W40: about 75 of a version similar to the Model 24W9 but available only in a utility model
Model 24W41: about 40 of a version similar to the Model 24W40 but with the Super Scarab Series 50A engine
Model 24W41A: about 10 of a version similar to the Model 24W41 but with the 165-hp (123-kW) Super Scarab 165D engine
C-61 (later UC-61): US Army Air Forces' designation of its version of the Model 24W41 with the 145-hp (108-kW) R-500-1 Super Scarab engine; 161 aircraft of this type were built, and two impressed civil aircraft were also given this designation
C-61A (later UC-61A): USAAF designation of its version of the Model 24W41A with radio and system revisions; 509 aircraft of this type were built, and three impressed civil aircraft were also given this designation
GK-1: US Navy designation of 13 impressed Model 24W40s
JK-1: USN designation of two impressed Model 24-Hs
J2K-1: US Coast Guard designation of two impressed Model 24Rs
J2K-2: USCG designation of two additional but slightly differing impressed Model 24Rs
UC-61B to UC-61J: designations allocated to 14 civil aircraft impressed for military use
UC-61K Forwarder: 306 of the final production version of World War II with the 200-hp (149-kW) Ranger L-440-7 six-cylinder inline engine
UC-86: USAAF designation for nine impressed Model 24R40s
Argus Mk I: Royal Air Force designation of UC-61s supplied under Lend-Lease
Argus Mk II: RAF designation of Lend-Lease UC-61As
Argus Mk III: RAF designation of Lend-Lease UC-61Ks

Fairchild Model 62 (PT-19, PT-23, PT-26 and Cornell)

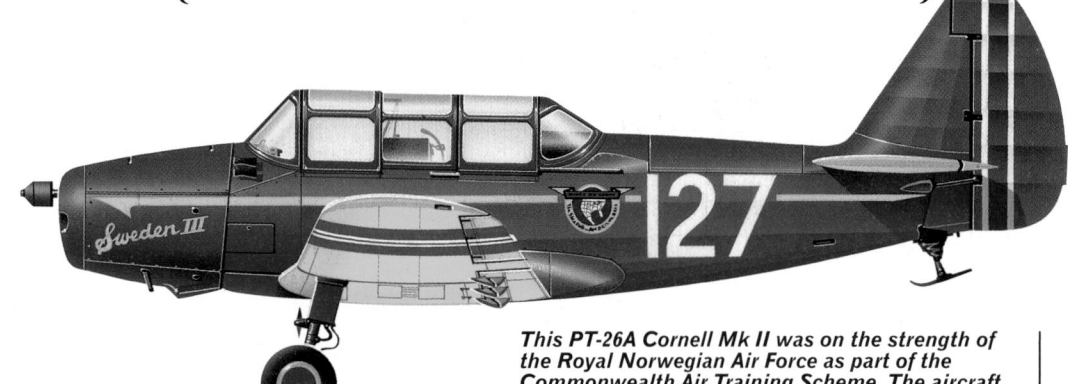

For many years before the outbreak of World War II it had been traditional to use docile, light two-seat biplanes for primary flying training. It was now suggested, however, that this could breed over-confidence, making the next stage of training more difficult. Many experienced instructors believed that a monoplane trainer, with a higher wing loading and which therefore needed to be flown thoughtfully for more of the time, could ensure that the step to be climbed between primary and advanced training was not quite so high.

This line of thought led to a need for more primary training aircraft and, in 1939, the USAAC carried out an evaluation of the **Fairchild Model 62** two-seat monoplane. By comparison with the USAAC's most advanced in-service biplane trainer, the Stearman PT-13, the maximum speed, rate of climb and service ceiling offered by the Model 62 were very nearly the same. However, the monoplane's wing loading was almost 43 per cent higher, which meant that the stalling speed was also higher and the low-speed handling characteristics just that little more critical. It seemed to be exactly what was needed, and in 1940 an initial order was placed for these trainers under the designation **PT-19**.

A low-wing cantilever monoplane of mixed construction, the Model 62 had a conventional tail unit, tailwheel landing gear and a powerplant based on the 175-hp (130-kW) Ranger L-440-1 eight-cylinder inverted inline engine. The instructor and pupil were accommodated in tandem cockpits enclosed by a sliding transparent canopy.

Delivery of the PT-19 began in 1940, and the aircraft soon proved that they were not lethal instruments of destruction in the hands of embryo pilots. With the expansion of flying training in 1941 Fairchild rapidly discovered that it had contracts for more aircraft than could be built in its existing factory. Steps were taken to double the factory's capacity, and arrange-ments were also made with Aeronca and the St Louis Aircraft Corporation to initiate production on Fairchild's behalf. At a later stage the Howard Aircraft Corporation provided an additional source of production.

A total of 270 PT-19s was built before a new **PT-19A** (**Model 62A**) version was introduced on the production lines of Fairchild, Aeronca and St Louis, these companies turning out 3,182, 432 and 44 respectively of the improved type. The only significant change was the introduction of the slightly more powerful L-440-3 engine and some detail refinements. Like the original model, the PT-19A had only basic instrumentation and so was unsuitable for blind-flying or instrument flight training. This short-coming was rectified in the subsequent **PT-19B**, which had full blind-flying instrumentation and a hood to cover the pupil's front cock-pit when such training was in progress. Production totalled 774 and 143 aircraft by Fairchild and Aeronca respectively.

The urgency of the demands of the US Army Air Forces, combined with production contracts for numbers far in excess of those which Fairchild had anticipated resulted in 1942 in a famine of Ranger engines. To resolve the situation the company produced an **XPT-23** (**Model 62A**) prototype by the installation of an uncowled 220-hp (164-kW) Continental R-670-5 seven-cylinder radial engine. After a successful evaluation, this variant was placed in production as the **PT-23**. A total of 869 such aircraft was built by Fairchild (2), Aeronca (375), Howard (199) and St Louis (200), all with the R-670-11 engine, as well as 93 by Fleet Aircraft Ltd of Fort Erie, Ontario, for use in the Commonwealth Air Training Scheme (CATS) which had been established in

Canada. A version of the PT-23 with the blind-flying instrumentation and hood introduced on the PT-19B was built by Howard (150) and St Louis (106) as the **PT-23A**. This was the last version to be built for the USAAF in America, with almost 6,000 delivered before the production lines closed down. The PT-23 trainer which Fleet had built in Canada resulted in the request for a slightly more advanced version, and this reverted to the L-440-3 engine. Improvements included the duplication of all controls and blind-flight and navigation instruments in each cockpit, plus the provision of cockpit heat-ing. Construction of this **Model 62A-3** totalled 1,727 aircraft, of which Fairchild in the USA built 670. These had the desig-nation **PT-26** and were supplied under Lend-Lease to the RCAF, which named the type as the **Cornell Mk I**. Fleet in Canada produced 807 **PT-26A** aircraft with the 200-hp (149-kW) L-440-7 engine, identified by the RCAF as the **Cornell Mk II**, and 250 generally similar **PT-26B** aircraft which the RCAF used as the **Cornell Mk III**.

This PT-26A Cornell Mk II was on the strength of the Royal Norwegian Air Force as part of the Commonwealth Air Training Scheme. The aircraft was based at Little Norway, Ontario in around 1943.

SPECIFICATION

Fairchild PT-26 (Cornell Mk I)
Type: two-seat primary flying trainer
Powerplant: one Ranger L-440-3 inverted piston engine rated at 200 hp (149 kW)
Performance: maximum speed 126 mph (203 km/h) at optimum altitude; cruising speed 114 mph (184 km/h) at optimum altitude; initial climb rate 675 ft (206 m) per minute; service ceiling 17,300 ft (5275 m); range 450 miles (724 km)
Weights: empty 2,022 lb (917 kg); maximum take-off 2,741 lb (1243 kg)
Dimensions: wingspan 36 ft (10.97 m); length 27 ft 8½ in (8.45 m); height 7 ft 7½ in (2.32 m); wing area 200.00 sq ft (18.58 m²)

This PT-19B is typical of the type in US service. The prominent roll-over bar between the two open cockpits is worthy of note.

Fairchild Model 71 (C-8 and R2Q) and Model 51/71

Basically an updated version of the FC-2W2, the **Model 71** incorporated many improvements derived from experience with the FC-2 and its vari-ants. Providing comfortable seating for a pilot and up to six passengers, the Model 71 was powered by the 420-hp (313-kW) Wasp nine-cylinder radial. The type was manufactured in modest numbers from 1928 until 1930, when it was replaced in production by the **Model 71A**, which differed primarily in having a few degrees of sweepback on the wing and introducing a number of refinements to the interior.

Though civil operators acquired most of the Model 71 and Model 71A aircraft, the US Army Air Corps acquired one Model 71 for evaluation as a light transport under the designation **XC-8**. After

This Canadian-built Model 71C later became the only one of its type to be exported. It was sold to an owner in Newfoundland and was subsequently used to fly surveys for Imperial Airways.

adaptation for the photographic role, the aircraft was redesignated **XF-1**. Eight service-test aircraft were ordered under the designation **YF-1**, but all nine aircraft were later redesignated **C-8**. Six production examples of the Model 71A followed with the designation **F-1A**, later changed to **C-8A**. The US Navy also acquired a single example for service

test under the designation **XJ2Q-1**, later redesignated **R2Q-1**.

In 1930 Fairchild established a Canadian branch of the company at Longueuil near Quebec as Fairchild Aircraft Ltd. In addition to providing support for Fairchild aircraft operating in Canada, it began production of the Model 71 for the Canadian Department of National

Defence. These aircraft differed from standard by the removal of the features introduced for passenger comfort, and were equipped specifically for aerial photography. A commercial **Model 71C** was later built and marketed, and this was also available as the **Model 71CM** with a metal-skinned fuselage.

Produced by the

Canadian Fairchild company, the **Model 51/71** was a combination of the wing of the Model 51 with the rest of the airframe of the Model 71 and a powerplant based on one 400-hp (298-kW) R-985-T1B Wasp Junior radial engine derated to 330 hp (246 kW). The company,

in fact, built only one such machine with the smooth cowling of the Model 71C and the divided windscreen of the Model 71CM, although another was created by Austin Airways by the combination of elements from single Model 51 and Model 71 aircraft.

SPECIFICATION

Fairchild Model 71C
Type: one-crew transport aircraft
Powerplant: one Pratt & Whitney R-1340C Wasp radial piston engine rated at 420 hp (313 kW)
Performance: maximum speed 132 mph (212 km/h) at optimum altitude; cruising speed 106 mph (171 km/h) at optimum altitude; initial climb rate 600 ft (183 m) per minute; service ceiling 11,000 ft

(3355 m)
Weights: empty 3,168 lb (1437 kg); maximum take-off 6,000 lb (2722 kg)
Dimensions: wingspan 50 ft 6 in (15.24 m); length 35 ft 10½ in (10.93 m); height 9 ft 4 in (2.84 m); wing area 309.60 sq ft (28.76 m²)
Payload: up to six passengers or freight carried in the cabin

Fairchild Model 82 and Model 34-42 Niska

In 1935-6 Fairchild Aircraft Ltd in Canada, concerned that its **Super 71** development of the Model 71 was not selling well, decided to press ahead with the development of an improved version of the

Model 71C as the larger-capacity **Model 82**. Like that of the **Super 71P**, the fuselage of the Model 82 incorporated an enclosed cockpit (in this instance for the pilot and co-pilot seated side-by-side)

forward of the wing leading edge in combination with a separate passenger cabin which, in this case, could seat a maximum of nine persons; large doors were provided on each side to make easy the loading of cargo as an alternative.

The first Model 82 took to the air on its maiden flight on 6 July 1935, and production of 23 such aircraft was completed in the form of 12 **Model 82A** aircraft, eight **Model 82B** aircraft with the 600-hp (447-kW) Wasp engine in

either its R-1340-S2H1 or -S3H1 forms, and three **Model 82D** aircraft with a higher empty weight, the last being complemented by one **Model 34-42** conversion. Seven of the aircraft were exported (one to Mexico, three to Venezuela and three to the Argentine navy) and the remainder were operated by Canadian airlines.

The **Model 34-42 Niska** (the name of an Indian

tribe of northern British Columbia) was a variant of the Model 82 reflecting the advent of N. F. Vanderlipp from Bellanca, whose designation system was adopted to indicate one tenth of the wing area and the engine power. First flown in March 1937, the sole Niska resembled the Model 82 except for its larger fin-and-rudder assembly and its revised powerplant of one 420-hp (313-kW) Ranger SVG-770-A-3 inverted inline engine.

Following the same general lines as its Model 71 predecessor, the Model 82 featured fixed tailwheel landing gear which could be replaced by floats or skis. CF-AXB was a Model 82A.

SPECIFICATION

Fairchild Model 82A
Type: two-crew general-purpose light transport
Powerplant: one Pratt & Whitney R-1340-T1D1 Wasp radial piston engine rated at 525 hp (391 kW)
Performance: maximum speed 155 mph (249 km/h) at 5,000 ft (1525 m); cruising speed 141 mph (227 km/h) at 5,000 ft (1525 m); climb to 9,000 ft (2745 m) in

10 minutes; service ceiling 15,650 ft (4770 m); range 655 miles (1054 km)
Weights: empty 3,060 lb (1388 kg); maximum take-off 6,325 lb (2869 kg)
Dimensions: wingspan 51 ft (15.54 m); length 36 ft 10¾ in (11.25 m); height 9 ft 4½ in (2.86 m); wing area 343.00 sq ft (31.86 m²)
Payload: up to nine passengers or freight carried in the cabin

Fairchild Model 91 and Model A-942

To meet a requirement of Pan American Airways for an amphibian flying-boat suitable for commercial services in South America and China (especially the routes along the Amazon and Yangtse rivers respectively), Fairchild began the design of the **Model 91** during 1934. Pan American dropped its Chinese

requirement and the Model 91 was therefore optimised for the operations of a service some 900 miles (1450 km) in length up the Amazon river into the interior of Brazil, and as a result the Model 91 emerged as a rugged and reliable machine. The first made its maiden flight on 5 April

1935, and was then identified as the **Model A-942-A**, a high-wing cantilever monoplane with a stabilising float strut-mounted under each half of the wing, a two-step hull of all-metal construction, and tailwheel landing gear of which all three units retracted.

The Model A-942-A, of which six were ordered by Pan American, was powered by one 800-hp (597-kW) Hornet radial engine mounted in a nacelle above the wing and driving a tractor propeller. After two of the 'boats had been delivered, however, the airline cancelled the balance of the order. Of the four airframes still under

construction, one was completed as another Model A-942-A and the other three as **Model A-942-B** 'boats, each powered by one 875-hp (652-kW) Wright GR-1820-F52 Cyclone nine-cylinder radial engine. The two 'boats acquired by

Pan Am gave excellent service over the Amazon route, operating purely as flying-boats with their wheeled landing gear removed to allow a greater payload; their capability made the four extra aircraft superfluous. Two of the four were sold to private buyers (one later served with the RAF in Egypt) and two went to Japan.

The prototype Model 91 was later sent to Spain for service with the Republicans. It was captured by the Nationalists, however, remaining in their hands until 1938.

VIRGEN DE CHAMORRO
63-1

SPECIFICATION

Fairchild Model A-942-A
Type: two-crew amphibian flying-boat
Powerplant: one Pratt & Whitney R-1690-S2EG Hornet radial piston engine rated at 800 hp (597 kW)
Performance: maximum speed 167 mph (269 km/h) at 2,500 ft (760 m); cruising speed 137 mph (220 km/h) at 2,500 ft (760 m); initial climb rate 840 ft (256 m) per minute; service ceiling 15,600 ft

(4755 m); range 665 miles (1070 km)
Weights: empty 6,596 lb (2992 kg); maximum take-off 10,500 lb (4763 kg)
Dimensions: wingspan 56 ft (17.07 m); length 42 ft 8 in (13.00 m); height 14 ft 8 in (4.47 m); wing area 483.00 sq ft (44.87 m²)
Payload: up to eight passengers carried in the hull

Fairchild Model 100 Pilgrim (C-24)

The **Model 100 Pilgrim** reflected the concern of Sherman Fairchild that aircraft should have a utilitarian efficiency rather than aesthetic grace, and was thus a thoroughly practical high-wing transport designed by Virginius E. Clark for the carriage of a 2,800-lb (1270-kg) payload.

The Model 100 first flew in 1930, and only one example had been completed before the

Fairchild Aircraft Manufacturing Corporation was revised as the American Airplane & Engine Corporation, a division of the Aviation Corporation. The Model 100 was a braced high-wing monoplane of basically all-metal construction, and was based on a fuselage of rectangular section built of welded steel tube and Dural covered with fabric. The

Dural- and fabric-covered wing halves were designed to fold to the rear for reduced hangarage 'footprint'. The landing gear was of the fixed tailwheel type with divided main units and the powerplant was based on one 575-hp (429-kW) Pratt & Whitney R-1690-B Hornet radial engine inside a narrow-chord Townend ring cowling to drive a two-bladed Hamilton Standard

metal propeller.

The type entered service in 1931 and was developed from the baseline Model 100 variant, of which only one was completed, through the **Model 100A** (16 built) with a much more corpulent fuselage and the **Model 100B** (six built for the civil market) development of the Model 100A with the Wright Cyclone radial engine. In 1932 the US Army Air Corps ordered

four examples of the Model 100B for evaluation with the designation **Y1C-24**, and these aircraft differed from their civil counterparts mainly in lacking the ventral freight bay. After the completion of their trials the aircraft were redesignated as **C-24** machines and allocated to bases in the continental USA for utility transport tasks such as the movement of spare parts and personnel.

The Model 100, here seen in prototype form, carried its payload in the form of freight and/or up to nine passengers in a ventral freight bay and/or cabin accessed by two rear doors and with a row of four glazed windows on each side.

SPECIFICATION

Fairchild Model 100B Pilgrim
Type: one-crew utility transport aircraft
Powerplant: one Wright R-1820E Cyclone radial engine rated at 575 hp (429 kW)
Performance: maximum speed 136 mph (219 km/h) at optimum altitude; cruising speed 118 mph (190 km/h) at optimum altitude; initial climb rate 800 ft (244 m) per minute; service ceiling 13,600 ft

(4145 m); range 510 miles (821 km)
Weights: empty 4,437 lb (2013 kg); maximum take-off 7,750 lb (3515 kg)
Dimensions: wingspan 57 ft (17.37 m); length 38 ft (11.58 m); height 12 ft 3 in (3.73 m); wing area 459.00 sq ft (42.64 m²)
Payload: up to nine passengers or 2,513 lb (1140 kg) of freight carried in the cabin

Fairchild Aerospace Do 328JET

By the mid-1980s the world's airline industry had come to the belief that one of the major markets of the near future would be regional transport of the type that would deliver passengers between outlying airports and the major hub airports. The market for regional transport aircraft was served almost exclusively by turboprop-powered types.

The anticipated growth in the regional transport market was immediately attractive to many manufacturers, especially the smaller companies which felt that they could gain a major slice of an important world market without the huge capital outlay required for any type of larger aircraft. Thus, there began major Brazilian, Canadian and German efforts to create a new generation of regional transports based on airframes possessing considerable 'stretch' potential – to allow increases in passenger capacity and installed power as the market evolved – and offering the lowest possible operating costs.

An early victim in this process was the turboprop engine, for manufacturers and operators were generally united in the belief that

the new generation of regional transports should have turbofan power for a higher cruising speed and altitude as well as greater acceptability to passengers.

With a modern turboprop-powered and pressurised regional transport already in production as the Do 328, Dornier decided that this could form the basis of a more profitable type with the two turboprop engines replaced by fuel-efficient but quiet turbofan engines. Fortunately for Dornier, such a change would be facilitated by the basic design of the Do 328. Its high-mounted wing allowed the turboprops to be replaced comparatively simply by turbofans in nacelles pylon-mounted below and ahead of the leading edges. Even so, the cost of the programme to create, certificate and manufacture what was initially known as the **Do 328-300**, but later became the **Dornier Do 328JET**, was really beyond the capabilities of Dornier.

Daimler-Benz (later DASA) held a 57.56 per cent stake in Dornier, with the remaining 42.44 per cent held in equal shares by two members of the Dornier family. Worried

about the almost inevitable escalation of the cost of the programme, DASA brokered a deal in which Fairchild Aircraft Inc. of the USA bought 80 per cent of the company (the other 20 per cent remaining in DASA's hands), and the company then became Fairchild-Dornier Germany, a subsidiary of the Fairchild Aerospace Corporation, and now the real parent of the Do 328JET and its derivatives.

Fairchild-Dornier decided to proceed with the Do 328JET during 1996, and officially launched the programme at the Paris Air Show of the following year. The second prototype Do 328 was re-engined with Pratt & Whitney Canada PW306/9 turbofans, each rated at 6,050 lb st (26.91 kN), the powerplant having been selected in January 1997, and this machine completed its maiden

flight on 20 January 1998.

The second Do 328JET, an all-new aircraft, first flew in May 1998 and the third followed in July. Early flight tests revealed problems with a tailplane shockwave at high speed, but these were eliminated by the addition of a fin-like fence below the tailplane. The wing/fuselage fairings were also redesigned as the original units caused Mach buffet in a significant element of the flight envelope. Other changes included a strengthening of the wing to carry the new powerplant, an increase of 3.94 in (0.10 m) in wing chord by alteration of the flaps, the introduction of a yaw damper to cure a Dutch-roll tendency, and improvement in lateral control by modification of the ailerons. Currently, thrust reversers are not a feature, but could become a future option.

Four aircraft were employed in the 1,200-hour certification programme, which

resulted in certification in July 1999 to allow the type to enter service the following month with the launch customer, Proteus Airlines, a French regional operator. By the end of 1999, Fairchild Aerospace could boast 173 orders and options for the type.

Fairchild-Dornier offers a corporate transport version known as the **Envoy 3** (originally **Do 328 Business Jet**). This has accommodation for a maximum of 19 passengers, but more typically between 12 and 14 passengers.

In May 1998 Fairchild-Dornier formally launched the **Do 428JET** at the Berlin air show. This variant is a comparatively simple development of the Do 328JET and is a stretched 42/44-seat derivative. It was originally designated as the **Do 328-700** before receiving the interim designation **Do 528JET**. Changes include uprated PW308 engines each rated at 6,575 lb st (29.25 kN), a fuselage lengthened to

With a minimum of structural changes, Fairchild Aerospace has produced an attractive jet commuterliner from the turboprop Do 328.

82 ft 5¼ in (25.13 m) and a wing with span increased to 76 ft 8½ in (23.38 m). The final assembly of both the initial variants of the JET family will be performed at Oberpfaffenhofen in Germany.

At the May 1998 Berlin air show, Fairchild-Dornier also launched a new family of related turbofan-powered transport aircraft with a fly-by-wire control system and between 55 and 95 seats.

This level of seating capacity would elevate the three members of this family from the regional jet niche toward the small airliner market. The basic model is the 70-seat **Do 728JET**, and this is flanked in the company's marketing efforts by the **Do 828JET** with 85-seat accommodation and the larger **Do 928JET** with 90/95-seat accommodation.

The Do 728JET is powered by General Electric CF34-8D turbofans each rated at 10,500 lb st (46.71 kN). The Do 728JET was scheduled for a first flight in March 2000. Certification and deliveries are scheduled to start in mid-2001.

Certification of the 55-seat Do 528JET was planned for 14 months after that of the Do 728JET, and that of the Do 928JET a further 14 months later. It is also anticipated that the Do 928JET could be subjected to a further fuselage stretch to provide 110-seat accommodation in the proposed **Do 1128JET**.

Fairchild Aerospace is lining up a series of risk-sharing partners for the three later members of the JET family, resulting in a diversified programme for the manufacture of major assemblies and components that would be delivered to Oberpfaffenhofen for final assembly at a projected rate of five aircraft per month from 2001.

SPECIFICATION	
Fairchild-Dornier Do 328JET **Type:** twin-turbofan 34-seat regional transport **Powerplant:** two Pratt & Whitney Canada PW306/9 turbofan engines each rated at 6,050 lb st (26.91 kN) **Performance:** maximum cruising speed 460 mph (741 km/h) at 25,000 ft (7620 m); cruising ceiling 31,000 ft (9450 m) with an option for 35,000 ft (10670 m); range 1,035 miles (1666 km) with 32 passengers	**Weights:** empty 20,282 lb (9200 kg); maximum take-off 33,047 lb (14990 kg) with an option for 33,510 lb (15200 kg) **Dimensions:** wingspan 68 ft 10 in (20.98 m); length 69 ft 9¾ in (21.28 m); height 23 ft 8¾ in (7.23 m); wing area 430.57 sq ft (40.00 m²) **Payload:** up to 34 passengers within the context of a maximum payload of 7,518 lb (3410 kg)

Fairchild-Dornier Do 228

A high wing and rugged construction make the Do 228 ideal for third-level operations from relatively austere airfields.

When Dornier adopted the designation **Do 128-2** and **Do 128-6** for Skyservant variants previously known as the **Do 28D-2** and **Do 28D-6**, two further derivatives of the basic twin-engined transport were in the project phase as the **Do 28E-1** and **Do 28E-2**. Given a go-ahead in November 1979, these then became the **Dornier 228-100** and **228-200** respectively, differing essentially only in fuselage length and operational weights.

Using the same fuselage cross-section as the Skyservant, the Dornier 228-100 was sized to seat 15 passengers, while the longer 228-200 would seat 19. Prototypes of the two variants made their maiden flights on 28 March and 9 May 1981, respectively,

and delivery of civil aircraft began in 1982. Of the 243 Do 228s ordered by mid-1998, the majority was for commercial use. The type has proved to be a useful and economical feederliner.

HAL in India also acquired a licence to assemble and produce the type. After Dornier had delivered eight examples of the **Do 228-201** (three and five for coast guard and airline service respectively), HAL flew the first Indian-assembled aircraft on 31 January 1986. The Indian Coast Guard began to operate the first of 36 Do 228-201s in July of that year. These aircraft are fitted with MEL Marec II radar, a Swedish IR/UV linescan sensor and other special features. Further deliveries comprised 43 for the Indian Air Force, and 30 for the Indian navy.

One Do 228-201 was evaluated by both the Bundesmarine and Luftwaffe, this later becoming a Luftwaffe hack, while the former acquired four other aircraft to provide two machines fully equipped for maritime pollution control (by MFG 3) and another two for liaison.

Other military users have included Finland (multi-sensor aircraft for para-military Frontier Guard), Malawi (three Do 228-201 and one **Do 228-202**), Niger (one Do 228-201 delivered in April 1986), Nigeria (one Do 228-100 transport and two Do 228-200 VIP transports), the Royal Oman police air wing (two Do 228-100s), and the Royal Thai navy (three MR aircraft).

This Dornier design became a Fairchild-Dornier product in 1996, when Fairchild took an 80 per cent stake in the Dornier company. Do 228 production ended in 1998.

SPECIFICATION	
Dornier Do 228 Maritime Patrol Version A **Type:** two-crew fishery protection and coastal patrol aircraft **Powerplant:** two AlliedSignal (Garrett) TPE331-5-252D turboprops each rated at 715 shp (533 kW) **Performance:** cruising speed 190 mph (305 km/h) at optimum altitude; initial climb rate 1,910 ft (582 m) per minute; service ceiling 28,000 ft (8535 m); range	1,982 miles (1740 km) **Weights:** empty 8,675 lb (3935 kg); maximum take-off 13,183 lb (5980 kg) **Dimensions:** wingspan 55 ft 8 in (16.97 m); length 49 ft 4¼ in (15.04 m); height 15 ft 11½ in (4.86 m); wing area 344.46 sq ft (32.00 m²) **Payload:** mission crew of three or freight within the context of a maximum payload of 4,667 lb (2117 kg)

Dornier Do 228 variants

Do 228-100: basic 15-seat feederliner
Do 228-200: stretched variant of Series 100 with 776-shp (579-kW) Garrett TPE331-5-252D turboprops
Do 228-101 and Do 228-201: variants fitted with engines of Do 228-200, plus fuselage strengthening and different tyres for operation at higher weights with a heavier payload
Do 228-202: modified payload/range parameters
Do 228-203F: pure freighter variant
Do 228-212: extended-range version powered by 778-shp (580-kW) TPE331-5A engines
Do 228 (Military): model marketed as the **Do 228 Troop** with accommodation for 17, 20 or 22 troops depending on specific variant, or as the **Do 228 Paratroop** with accommodation for 16, 19 or 21 paratroops depending on specific variant
Do 228 Maritime Patrol Version A: fishery protection and anti-smuggling patrol variant, equipped with 360° scan Bendix/King RDR-1500B surveillance radar (optional radars include Litton APS-504[V]5, Eaton-AIL APS-128 and Thorn EMI Super Searcher), Honeywell FLIR, stabilised long-range observation system, night-vision goggles, searchlight, and Wulfsberg GNS-500-5 navigation system with optional GPS receiver
Do 228 Maritime Patrol Version B: anti-pollution patrol variant fitted with Ericsson SLAR, Daedalus AADS 1221 IR/UV scanner and laser fluorescent sensor

Fairchild-Dornier 328

After deciding in 1986 to develop a 30-seat regional transport under the designation **Do 328**, Dornier backed away from the project and it was only in August 1988 that the company relaunched the programme for the current Dornier Do 328,

which is now more properly known as a Fairchild-Dornier product after Fairchild's acquisition of Dornier in mid-1996.

The Do 328 that emerged from this effort was conceived as an advanced development of the basic concept embodied in the Do 228. It

combined essentially the same TNT (*tragflügels neuer technologie*, or new-technology wing) advanced supercritical-section wing with a new T-tail and, for a high-altitude cruise capability, a pressurised circular-section fuselage derived from the lessons of the company's NRT (*neue rumpf technologien*, or new fuselage technologies) programme.

Design goals for the Do 328 included a level of field and climb performance similar to that of the Do 228 in concert with much improved speed and altitude performance. Its enlarged cabin offers standing headroom in the aisle and greater seat width than the Boeing Models 727 and 737. The Do 328 is mainly of light alloy

construction except for the rear fuselage, tail unit, nose and tail cones, and wing trailing edges, which are all largely of carbonfibre-reinforced plastics construction. The main units of the undercarriage retract into large external blister fairings. The high-set wing has high-lift devices almost along the full span of its trailing edge.

Fairchild-Dornier 328 (continued)

These devices comprise outboard drooping ailerons and inboard two-section single-slotted Fowler flaps; an option is three spoilers (one for lateral control and two for ground operation) ahead of each aileron.

The first Do 328 made its maiden flight on 6 December 1991, and was followed by two development aircraft before the first production example took to the air for its initial flight on 23 January 1993. European and American certification were awarded in October and November 1993 respectively, and the first delivery was made to Air Engiadina on 21 October of the same year.

The baseline version is the **Do 328-100** which has standard accommodation for 30 to 33 passengers in a 2+1 seating arrangement inside a cabin that also incorporates a galley and a toilet. There is provision for one or two cabin attendants, and the standard flight crew is two. The flightdeck is equipped with

the Honeywell Primus 2000 avionics system (with a five-display electronic flight instrumentation system), including an automatic flight control system, a flight management system, and an electronic indication, caution and advisory system. Options include colour rather than monochrome weather radar, a traffic alert and collision avoidance system, and an upgraded navigation system using either a GPS receiver or a laser inertial reference system.

The Do 328-100 has been followed by three improved variants. The **Do 328-110** has a maximum weight increased to 30,843 lb (13990 kg) for a full-load range of 1,150 miles (1853 km). The **Do 328-120** features thermodynamically enhanced 2,180-hp (1625-kW) PW119C engines driving slightly larger propellers for improved field performance. The **Do 328-130** is a development of the Do 328-120 with PW119C engines, a rudder-enhanced

deflection system, and additional flap settings for further improved field performance.

Dornier has also proposed the **Do 328-200** series in **-210**, **-220** and **-230** subvariants, equivalent to the Do 328-100 subvariants, for the high-density short-haul market. These variants can seat up to 39 passengers in four-abreast accommodation.

The **Do 328-500** (originally **Do 328 S**) was a more radically altered proposal with Pratt & Whitney Canada PW150/2 turboprop engines, a wing with span increased to 76 ft 9¼ in (23.40 m), and the fuselage lengthened by plugs fore and aft of the wing to provide accommodation for up to 50 passengers. Fairchild-Dornier has also proposed a hydrogen power testbed with Pratt & Whitney Canada PW119 turboprops adapted to run on hydrogen and oxygen.

Fairchild-Dornier Do 328 production ceased early in 2000, with the 105th and last airframe.

With its EFIS cockpit and comprehensive avionics suite, the Do 328 has even managed to break into the fiercely competitive US market.

SPECIFICATION	
Fairchild-Dornier Do 328-110 **Type:** 30-33 seat twin-turboprop regional transport **Powerplant:** two Pratt & Whitney PW119B turboprop engines each rated at 2,180 shp (1625 kW) **Performance:** maximum cruising speed 388 mph (620 km/h) at 20,000 ft (6095 m); cruising ceiling 25,000 ft (7620 m) normal and 31,000 ft (9450 m) optional; range 1,150 miles (1853 km) with	30 passengers **Weights:** empty 19,665 lb (8920 kg); maximum take-off 30,843 lb (13990 kg) **Dimensions:** wingspan 68 ft 10 in (20.98 m); length 69 ft 9¾ in (21.28 m); height 23 ft 9 in (7.24 m); wing area 430.57 sq ft (40.00 m²) **Payload:** up to 33 passengers within the context of a maximum payload of 8,135 lb (3690 kg)

Fairchild-Dornier (Swearingen) Merlin and Metro (C-26)

The Swearingen Aviation Corporation became a wholly-owned subsidiary of Fairchild Industries in 1979, and early in 1981 became known as the Fairchild Swearingen Corporation. Ed J. Swearingen had built up his business initially by building prototypes for other companies, and by designing and marketing improved versions of Beech Queen Air and Twin Bonanza aircraft. In 1964 Swearingen began the development of an aircraft known as the **Swearingen Merlin IIA**. This was a turboprop-powered eight-seat executive aircraft, which combined a new fuselage of Swearingen design with a modified Queen Air wing and Twin Bonanza landing gear. First flown on 13 April 1965, the Merlin IIA proved a tractable design and deliveries began in August 1966 shortly after the receipt of certification.

The Merlin IIA was powered by two 550-shp (410-kW) Pratt & Whitney (then United Aircraft of Canada) PT6A-20 turboprop engines, but in June 1968 it was superseded by the improved **Merlin IIB** with a pair of 665-shp (496-kW) Garrett TPE331-1-151G turboprop engines. Shortly after this the new **Merlin III** was introduced with its fuselage lengthened by 2 ft ½ in (0.62 m) and incorporating a wing, tail unit and

landing gear of Swearingen design plus two 840-shp (626-kW) TPE331-303G turboprop engines. Developed more or less simultaneously with the Merlin III was the **SA 226TC Metro** 20-passenger commuter airliner with the same powerplant but possessing a lengthened fuselage to provide the necessary accommodation. Introduced at the same time was the **Merlin IV**, a corporate version of the Metro which differed by accommodating only 12 passengers in a more luxurious interior.

The Merlin IIB was discontinued in 1972, but development of the Merlin and Metro continued after that time. In 1983 the versions available were the 8/11-seat **Merlin IIIC** executive transport with 900-shp (671-kW) TPE331-10U-503G turboprops, the **Merlin IVC** 13/16-seat corporate aircraft, and the generally similar **Metro III** 20-passenger commuter transport. A new version of this aircraft was delivered from 1983 as the **Metro IIIA** that differed from the Metro III primarily in its powerplant of two PT6A-45R turboprop engines each flat-rated at 1,100 shp (820 kW). On 10 March 1982 a Metro III was the 500th Swearingen turboprop aircraft to be delivered. Further develop-

ment continued, and at the end of the 20th century the versions available were the **SA 227CC** and **SA 227DC** version of what is now the **Metro 23** with TPE331-11U-612G and TPE331-12-UAR-701G engines respectively, the **Metro 23E** with an EFIS flightdeck, the **Merlin 23** business equivalent of the Metro 23, the **Expediter I** all-freight version introduced in the mid-1980s with a maximum payload of more than 5,000 lb (2268 kg), and the **Expediter 23** introduced in 1991 with a maximum payload of 5,500 lb (2495 kg).

In March 1988 the US Air Force selected the Metro III to replace the Convair C-131s used by the Air National Guard, and in March 1989 delivery began of 13 such aircraft under

Both the US Air Force and Army make use of the C-26. This anonymous looking C-26B is on strength with the US Army.

the designation **C-26A**. These serve in the ANG Operational Support Aircraft (ANGOSA) role with quick-change interiors for passengers, litters or freight. A further contract awarded in January 1991 provided for up to 53 **C-26B** aircraft with delivery starting January 1992; these are fitted with TCAS II, GPS and microwave landing systems, the first US military aircraft to be so equipped. A single **UC-26C** serves with the Texas ANG on anti-drug missions, fitted with APG-66 radar and a FLIR for the detection of low-flying aircraft.

Fairchild has also marketed the Metro as a **Special Mission Aircraft (SMA)**, with various configurations for maritime patrol,

submarine detection, flight inspection, photo reconnaissance, AEW and Elint roles. The Swedish air force acquired a **Merlin IVC** (Metro III equivalent) for use as a VIP transport under the designation **TP 88**, and took delivery in 1987 of a second, splinter-camouflaged, TP 88 for development of an AEW aircraft. This aircraft has been fitted with a large dorsal planar radar antenna housing for the Ericsson PS-890 Erieye radar, with which it first flew (with operational radar) in May 1991.

Fairchild-Dornier has now flown and exhibited its Metro 23-derived **Multi-Mission Surveillance Aircraft (MMSA)**. This is a rapidly configurable

This SA 226TC Metro exemplifies the type in service. The Metro differs little from the Merlin externally, the major differences being in internal layout.

airframe, capable of undertaking survey, surveillance, Elint and conventional reconnaissance duties while retaining its transport, VIP and air ambulance

capabilities. Along with Lockheed Fort Worth, Fairchild has developed a centreline systems pod for the MMSA, along with C³I consoles in the cabin, a dedicated surveillance radar fit and accompanying cockpit systems. The pod can house a Loral FLIR and infra-red line scan, electro-optical cameras, LOROP (LOng Range OPtical) gear, and air-to-air and sea surveillance radar. Fitting of the GEC-Marconi Seaspray 2000 radar is under investigation. A Mitsubishi FLIR

can also be provided for the pilot. Aircraft will be built, and fitted out, on demand.

SPECIFICATION	
Fairchild-Dornier (Swearingen) C-26A	range 1,224 miles (1970 km) with maximum payload
Type: two-crew utility transport	**Weights:** empty 9,180 lb (4164 kg); maximum take-off 16,000 lb (7257 kg)
Powerplant: two Honeywell TPE331-121UAR turboprop engines each rated at 1,119 shp (834 kW)	**Dimensions:** wingspan 57 ft (17.37 m); length 59 ft 4¼ in (18.09 m); height 16 ft 8 in (5.08 m); wing area 309.00 sq ft (28.71 m²)
Performance: maximum cruising speed 321 mph (517 km/h) at 15,000 ft (4570 m); economical cruising speed 290 mph (467 km/h) at 25,000 ft (7620 m); initial climb rate 2,370 ft (722 m) per minute; service ceiling 27,500 ft (8380 m);	**Payload:** up to 19 passengers or 5,000 lb (2268 kg) of freight carried in the cabin

Fairchild Republic A-10 Thunderbolt II

Originally conceived as a counter-insurgency aircraft to help the American war effort in Southeast Asia, the **A-10A Thunderbolt II** emerged as a dedicated close air support aircraft, with the primary role of destroying enemy armour. Two **YA-10A** service test aircraft were built for competitive evaluation in the US Air Force's AX competition. The Fairchild Republic type was judged the winner on 18 January 1973 after evaluation against the **Northrop YA-9A**, and there followed six pre-production aircraft. The first of these was subsequently converted into the sole two-seat **YA-10B**, or **N/AW A-10**, intended for the dedicated night/adverse weather role through the incorporation of provision for a weapons system officer and more advanced avionics. This programme was cancelled, but 707 examples of the A-10A production model followed the eight development machines.

'**Warthog**' is a nickname that has stuck with the A-10, largely as a result of its awkward looks. The design, however, is central to the ability of the A-10 to operate effectively in a lethal battlefield environment. Until the later introduction of an autopilot, the A-10A

had to be flown 'hands-on' by the pilot. This had obvious disadvantages for long flights, but bestowed outstanding agility on the aircraft, enabling it to jink and weave at very low level. Survivability factors were the keys to the design of the A-10's configuration, the widely spaced lateral pair of engines being mounted high on the rear fuselage where they are shrouded from ground fire from most angles by either the wing or the tailplane. A strong structure and system redundancy ensures that the A-10 can stay aloft with large amounts of battle damage, including an engine or fin shot away. A titanium armour 'bathtub' protects both the pilot and the ammunition tank. Furthermore, the aircraft was designed for rapid and easy maintenance. In

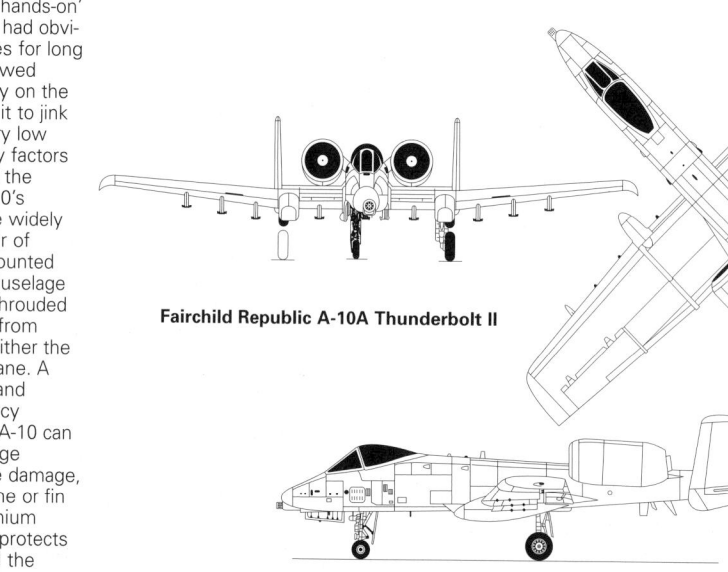

This A-10A is depicted as it appeared on the strength of the USAFE's 10th TFW based at Alconbury, UK in the late 1980s.

Fairchild Republic A-10A Thunderbolt II

the anticipated combat scenario, the A-10 would fly a large number of short sorties, spending the minimum amount of time on the ground while refuelling and re-arming. Rapid maintenance and repair could also be effected during this time thanks to the simplicity of the systems and the incorporation of many ready-access panels.

In terms of ordnance, the A-10 is designed around the enormous GAU-8/A 30-mm seven-barrel rotary cannon, which is the world's most powerful airborne gun.

This AFRES A-10A demonstrates the grey scheme that was adopted later in the type's career.

However, the principal weapon of the A-10 is the AGM-65 Maverick missile, which has either TV- or IR-guidance. This provides good stand-off range for the anti-armour role or against other 'hard' targets. Various cluster and free-fall bombs can also be carried, although use of these would force an overflight of the target, which is likely to be in the thick of a heavily-gunned battlefield, and so are rarely employed.

The avionics of the A-10 remained very basic for the type's early career. A HUD was provided, and a screen for displaying images from Maverick ASMs. A 'Pave Penny' seeker on a pylon under the forward fuselage spot-

ted targets designated by laser. No laser designator or rangefinder is fitted. Most current aircraft have received the LASTE (low-altitude safety and target enhancement) modification, which finally adds an autopilot to relieve the arduous task of keeping the A-10 straight and level throughout the flight. LASTE also improves gun accuracy considerably.

Entering service at Davis-Monthan Air Force Base, Arizona, the A-10A was first flown by the 355th Tactical Fighter Training Wing, and was later issued to the 23rd and 354th Tactical Fighter Wings and various USAF Reserve and Air National Guard units in the continental USA, and to units in South Korea and Alaska.

Fairchild Republic A-10 (cont.)

By far the A-10A's most important theatre was Europe, where the 81st TFW flew six squadrons from the twin bases at Woodbridge and Bentwaters in England.

There was considerable debate about the vulnerability of the A-10, and it was finally decided to start a gradual withdrawal of the type in favour of the F-16 Fighting Falcon. At the same time, redundant A-10As became available to replace the venerable OV-10 Bronco in the forward air control role. Without any change to the aircraft and its avionics, the A-10A was redesignated as

the OA-10A for the FAC role and distributed to tactical air support squadrons. For the FAC role the OA-10A is armed with AIM-9 Sidewinder short-range AAMs for self-defence and rocket pods for marking targets. While the A-10 force was put into decline, as a result of both USAF policy and a more general force cutback resulting from the 'peace dividend' following the collapse of the USSR as a credible threat in the early 1990s, the 'Warthog' suddenly found itself at war. Under the auspices of the 354th TFW (Provisional), 144 A-10s

from the USA and UK flew many missions in the Desert Storm campaign against Iraq in 1991. These missions included anti-armour work, air defence suppression and 'Scud' hunting. Throughout the conflict, the A-10 performed admirably, resulting in the destruction of huge numbers of tanks, artillery pieces and vehicles, and at the same time ensuring its longer-term survival as a warplane of proven utility. The A-10 remains on USAF strength in some numbers and is likely to remain an important combat type well into the 21st century.

SPECIFICATION

Fairchild Republic A-10A Thunderbolt II

Type: single-seat close air support and anti-tank warplane

Powerplant: two General Electric TF34-GE-100 turbofan engines each rated at 9,065 lb st (40.32 kN)

Performance: maximum speed 439 mph (706 km/h) at sea level; initial climb rate 6,000 ft (1829 m) per minute; range 2,454 miles (3949 km) with drop tanks; radius 620 miles (1000 km) on a deep attack mission or 288 miles (463 km) on a close air support mission with a 1-hour 42-minute loiter

Weights: empty 24,959 lb (11321 kg); maximum take-off 50,000 lb (22680 kg)

Dimensions: wingspan 57 ft 6 in (17.53 m); length 53 ft 4 in

(16.26 m); height 14 ft 8 in (4.47 m); wing area 506.00 sq ft (47.01 m²)

Armament: one 30-mm General Electric GAU-8/A Avenger fixed forward-firing seven-barrel rotary cannon, plus up to 16,000 lb (7257 kg) of disposable stores carried on three underfuselage and eight underwing hardpoints, and generally comprising six AGM-65 Maverick ASMs, 'Paveway' laser-guided bombs, 2,000-lb (907-kg) GBU-15 optronically guided bombs, 2,000-, 1,000- and 500-lb (907-, 454- and 227-kg) free-fall or retarded bombs, BLU-1 or BLU-27 napalm bombs, Rockeye II cluster bombs, CBU-52 or CBU-71 bomb dispensers, LAU-68 multiple rocket launchers, and SUU-23 20-mm cannon pods

Fairchild Republic T-46 Eaglet

First flown in October 1985, the **Fairchild Republic T-46 Eaglet** won the US Air Force's NGT (New-Generation Trainer) award to replace the Cessna T-37 as its jet-powered primary and basic flying trainer. The aircraft was a low-wing cantilever monoplane of all-metal construction with retractable tricycle landing gear, a tail unit with a straight horizontal surface and swept endplate vertical surfaces, a wide forward fuselage for a pressurised cockpit accommodating a crew of two side-by-side on McDonnell Douglas ACES II ejection seats, and a powerplant of two fuel-economical turbofan engines in nacelles under the roots of the anhedralled wing. One of the programme aspects that won the award for Fairchild Republic was the thorough

Of distinctive layout, the T-46A might well have been in a position to replace the USAF's aging fleet of T-37s from the mid-1980s. Instead, the ultimate T-37 replacement, Raytheon's Texan II, was only just entering service trials in April 2000.

preparation of its concept, this including the subcontracted manufacture by the Ames Industrial Corporation of the **Scale NGT**, a 62 per cent scaled version of the NGT with an all-composite structure, single-seat accommodation and the powerplant of two 220-lb st (0.98-kN) Microturbo TRS 18-046 turbojet engines. The Scale NGT was rolled out in August 1981, and its flight test programme was very useful in the finalisa-

tion of the NGT effort.

On 2 July 1982 Fairchild received a $104 million contract to cover two prototypes and two test specimens, plus an option on the first 54 aircraft. The Garrett Turbine Engine Company received $121.2 million for 29 purpose-designed TFE76-4A (F109-GA-100) engines, with an option on 119. The first metal was cut in April 1983, and in February 1984 $6 million

was released to cover long-lead items for the first production aircraft, due to fly in May 1986. A further 649 aircraft were required by the USAF. The first flight of the **T-46A** had been delayed by about six months because of late deliveries from subcontractors. The flight test programme then revealed a number of problems, but these were well on the way to solution when, largely for financial reasons, the US Congress cancelled the entire programme early

in 1986 at a time when the first 10 production aircraft were nearing completion.

The manufacturer had revealed in 1983 its intention to develop an export derivative, known within the company as the **FRC-225 Full Spectrum Trainer** or **AT-46A**. This was to feature a head-up display and stores management system, as well as four underwing hardpoints capable of carrying up to 1,320 lb (599 kg) of gun pods, bombs, rockets or tanks.

This aircraft was the only production T-46A to reach the USAF, nine other airframes being broken up from an incomplete state on the production line.

SPECIFICATION

Fairchild Republic T-46A Eaglet

Type: two-seat primary and basic flying trainer

Powerplant: two Garrett F109-GA-100 turbofan engines each rated at 1,330 lb st (5.92 kN)

Performance: maximum speed 460 mph (740 km/h) at 35,000 ft (10670 m); cruising speed 383 mph (616 km/h) at 45,000 ft (13715 m); initial climb rate 4,470 ft (1362 m)

per minute; service ceiling 46,500 ft (14175 m); range 1,370 miles (2205 km)

Weights: empty 5,184 lb (2351 kg); maximum take-off 6,817 lb (3092 kg)

Dimensions: wingspan 38 ft 7¾ in (11.78 m); length 29 ft 6 in (8.99 m); height 9 ft 11¾ in (3.04 m); wing area 160.90 sq ft (14.95 m²)

Fairey III

The fact that a **Fairey IIIF** was still in service in 1941 despite the fact that the basic design has its origins in 1917 provides a convincing illustration of the basic soundness of what was possibly Fairey's most successful aircraft in terms of service usage. Late in 1917 the **Fairey N.10**

seaplane was modified to landplane configuration and designated **Fairey IIIA**. Fifty were ordered as carrier-based two-seat bombers to replace the Sopwith 1½-Strutter in service with the Royal Naval Air Service, and the first production example of the Fairey IIIA flew at Northolt in June 1918. The end of World War I prevented the aircraft from

seeing much service, and the type was declared obsolete in 1919.

Another variant, the **Fairey IIIB**, using the same fuselage and horizontal tail

Little more than a landplane conversion of the 1917-vintage N.10 prototype, the Fairey IIIA was powered by a Maori engine and had unstaggered wings.

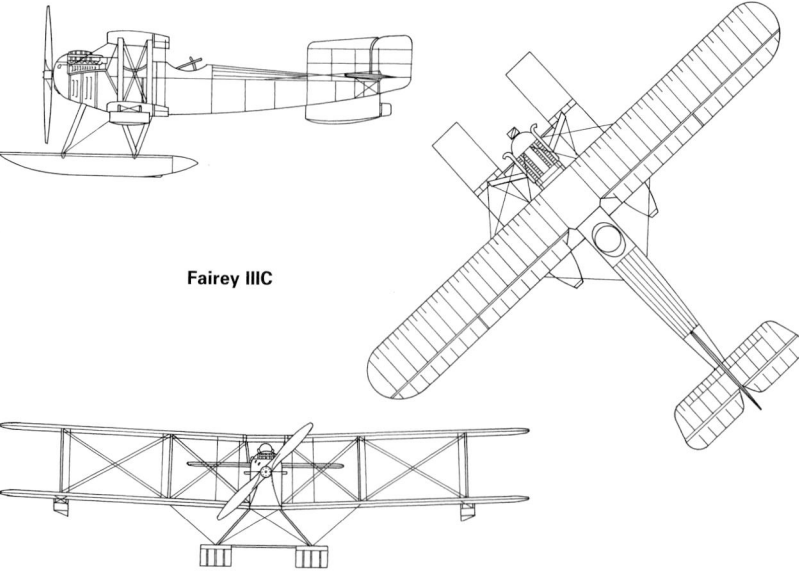

Fairey IIIC

Originally referred to as the 'IIIC (Improved)', the Fairey IIID was available in Mk I and Mk II forms. The latter – illustrated – had Lion V and VA engines.

surface combined with a wing cellule and vertical tail surface of greater area, entered small-scale production as a floatplane and saw some service on mine-spotting patrols from coastal bases. Production totalled 25 aircraft, of which the first flew in August 1918. Like the Fairey IIIA, the Fairey IIIB was powered by the 260-hp (194-kW) Sunbeam Maori engine. Sixty serial numbers had been allocated for Fairey IIIB production, and the last 30 plus a few from the previous batch were converted on the production line into **Fairey IIIC** aircraft.

This version was similar to the Fairey IIIB, but reverted to the equal-span wing cellule of the Fairey IIIA. A great improvement in performance resulted from use of the 375-hp (280-kW) Rolls-Royce Eagle VIII engine. The first production deliveries were made in November 1918 to No. 229 Squadron at Great Yarmouth, Norfolk, UK and others went to No. 267 Squadron on Malta. The only aircraft to see active service did so with the North Russian Expeditionary Force in 1919, transported by the seaplane carrier HMS *Pegasus*. The reliability of the Eagle engine earned the Fairey IIIC a great reputation, but only 35 such aircraft were built, replacing the earlier type in service with the RAF from 1921. Several Fairey IIICs survived to enter civilian service: one, fitted with sliding canopies and long-range tanks, was shipped to Newfoundland in March 1920 for a projected transatlantic flight which never materialised. It had formerly been used as a civil two-seat seaplane demonstrator by Fairey, and following damage in Canada was returned to the manufacturer for rebuild and resale.

The next derivative in the series was the **Fairey IIID**,

a direct development of the Fairey IIIC incorporating a number of improvements as a result of experience with the earlier models. In its landplane form the Fairey IIID was the first aircraft to be fitted with oleo-pneumatic landing gear, flying for the first time in August 1920. Air Ministry contracts to Specification 38/22 were placed, and total production for the RAF amounted to 207, of which 56 had the Eagle engine and the remainder the 450-hp (336-kW) Napier Lion in various marks. The majority of the Fairey IIIDs served in floatplane form with the Fleet Air Arm, operating from shore stations or from catapults on warships. Nos 441 and 444 Flights were the first to receive the Fairey IIID, in 1924. On 30 October 1925 one of these earned the distinction of being the first FAA seaplane to be catapulted from a ship at sea. In FAA service the Fairey IIID replaced the Parnall Panther and Supermarine Seagull amphibians, and eventually served with nine flights ranging from Leuchars in Fife, Scotland to the Far East. Fairey IIID aircraft in naval service were normally three-seaters, but some two-seat trainers were built and another two-seater was used for target-towing. As a landplane, the Fairey IIID's major contribution to RAF history occurred in 1926, when four aircraft flew from Heliopolis to Cape Town, returning to England via Greece, Italy and France without any mechanical failures. The aircraft covered a distance of 13,901 miles (22371 km) and were converted to seaplanes at Aboukir for the flight home to Lee-on-Solent. The only RAF squadron to receive the Fairey IIID was No. 202 Squadron, which had formerly been No. 481 Flight of the FAA.

The sterling qualities of

the Fairey IIID attracted several export orders. One from Australia was for six Eagle-engined aircraft, the first of which was handed over at Hamble on 12 August 1921. The third Australian Fairey IIID flew round that country's coast-line, a distance of 8,568 miles (13789 km), in 1924, earning the Britannia Trophy for its crew. Eleven Fairey IIIDs were supplied to the Portuguese government, the first four with Eagle engines and the others with Lion engines. Two were lost in long-distance flight attempts, but a third completed the journey begun by the others from Lisbon to Rio de Janeiro. Two Fairey IIIDs were sold to Sweden, and four to the Royal Netherlands naval air service for operations in the Dutch East Indies. A civil Fairey IIID with an Eagle IX engine was modified for ambulance work in British Guiana in 1924 and another civil aircraft was used in 1927 as a four-seat replacement for the de Havilland DH.50J on a service between Khartoum and Kisumu: it lasted barely a month, being damaged beyond repair during salvage operations following landing-gear collapse.

The designation **Fairey**

IIIE does not appear to have been allocated, although some sources ascribe it to the all-metal **Ferret**. The final, and most prolific, variant of the series was the **Fairey IIIF**, which was a mainstay of the RAF and FAA between the two world wars. Intended as a replacement for the Fairey IIID, the Fairey IIIF was built to Specification 19/24, which called for a land-based two-seat general-purpose aircraft for the RAF and a three-seat spotter-reconnaissance aircraft for the FAA. The prototype, which flew in March 1926, had wooden wings with a composite wood/metal fuselage, but production aircraft had an all-metal fuselage and later versions had all-metal wings. The Fairey IIIF had four basic marks, but within those were a multiplicity of subvariants denoting type of construction (composite or all-metal) and equipment fits. A pre-production batch of 10 followed the two prototypes, and the FAA received a total of 352 aircraft, of which the first 50 comprised the early batch plus 40 **Fairey IIIF Mk I** aircraft, all with the Napier Lion VA engine, while the remainder consisted of 33 **Fairey IIIF Mk II** and 269 **Fairey IIIF**

Mk III aircraft of various types, all with the Lion XIA. RAF aircraft totalled 243, all of them variants of the basic **Fairey IIIF Mk IV**.

The first Fairey IIIFs to enter service were RAF machines although, from the FAA pre-production batch, six went to No. 47 Squadron at Khartoum in 1927 as Bristol Fighter replacements. The first aircraft actually built for the RAF were a batch of 43 Fairey IIIF Mk IV and **Mk IVCM** aircraft delivered in January 1928 to No. 207 Squadron, replacing elderly DH.9As. A number of outstanding flights was made by RAF Fairey IIIFs and the type was eventually replaced by the Fairey Gordon, a radial-engined development known originally as the **Fairey IIIF Mk V**. The FAA took delivery of its first Fairey IIIFs in 1928, when No. 440 Flight received its aircraft to replace the Fairey IIID. Twelve flights eventually operated the Fairey IIIF, which also replaced Avro Bison, and Blackburn Blackburd and Ripon machines. The type served with every aircraft-carrier of the period and on every naval air station, and in floatplane form also equipped battleships and cruisers.

Fairey built the IIIF in a variety of materials. The 'M' in the designation of this RAF Fairey IIIF Mk IIIM denoted an all-metal structure.

Fairey III (continued)

Among the experiments carried out with the Fairey IIIF, one of the more interesting was the modification of three aircraft to autopilot/radio control for use as gunnery targets, in which form the type was known as the **Queen IIIF**. The first two aircraft were launched by catapult from HMS *Valiant* in January and April 1932 but crashed after flights of just 18 and 25 seconds respectively, while the third flew successfully in September of that year and in January 1933 was launched for its first test as a target. The Queen IIIF survived, while the fleet failed miserably in its attempts, which lasted for two hours and

exhausted the ammunition! However, in May 1933 the Royal Navy had the last laugh when the Queen IIIF was shot down near Malta after 20 minutes of flight at 8,000 ft (2440 m).

In its floatplane form, the Fairey IIIF was replaced by the Hawker Osprey from November 1932, the re-equipment programme being completed by 1935. Other Fairey IIIFs were gradually replaced from 1933 by the Fairey Seal, the FAA's equivalent of the Gordon. Known export sales of the Fairey IIIF included three to the Irish Army Air Corps, six to Argentina, two to New Zealand, 10 to Greece and one to Chile. A number of

engine installations was used on the Fairey IIIF, including the 460-hp (343-kW) Armstrong Siddeley Jaguar VI radial unit and the 450-hp (336-kW) Lorraine 12Ed water-cooled engine which was specified for the Argentine aircraft. These were later re-engined by the customer with 550-hp (410-kW) Armstrong Siddeley Panther VI radial engines. Other engines fitted for experimental work included the 635-hp (474-kW) Rolls-Royce Kestrel II, 525-hp (391-kW) Panther IIA, 520-hp (388-kW) Bristol Jupiter VIII and the Napier Culverin, a licence-built Junkers Jumo 205C Diesel engine. Several Fairey IIIFs were civil-registered, the first of them a **Mk IIIM** aircraft

used as a demonstrator by Fairey; it later competed in the MacRobertson England to Australia race of 1934, remained in Australia following re-registration, and was last recorded in

1936 in New Guinea. Two Mk IIIMs were bought new by Air Survey Co. Ltd. in 1930. One was lost during that year; the other carried out aerial mapping until it was retired in 1934.

SPECIFICATION

Fairey IIIF Mk IIIM/B (floatplane)
Type: two/three-seat spotter, reconnaissance and general-purpose aircraft
Powerplant: one Napier Lion XIA W-type piston engine rated at 570 hp (425 kW)
Performance: maximum speed 130 mph (209 km/h) at 10,000 ft (3050 m); climb to 5,000 ft (1525 m) in 6 minutes 42 seconds; service ceiling 20,000 ft (6095 m); endurance 4 hours
Weights: empty 3,923 lb (1779 kg); maximum take-off 6,300 lb (2858 kg)
Dimensions: wingspan 45 ft 9 in (13.94 m); length 35 ft 6 in (10.82 m); height 14 ft (4.26 m); wing area 443.50 sq ft (41.20 m²)
Armament: one 0.303-in (7.7-mm) Vickers fixed forward-firing machine-gun in the forward fuselage and one 0.303-in (7.7-mm) Lewis trainable rearward-firing machine-gun in the rear cockpit, plus up to 580 lb (263 kg) of disposable stores carried on three underwing hardpoints and generally comprising two 250-lb (113-kg) bombs, or two 230-lb (104-kg) bombs, or four 112-lb (51-kg) bombs, in each case with four 20-lb (9.1-kg) bombs

Fairey Albacore

As a replacement for the antiquated Swordfish, the **Albacore** appeared to have everything going for it: neat in appearance and with an enclosed cabin providing such luxuries as heating, a windscreen wiper and automatic emergency dinghy ejection, the Albacore nevertheless failed to come up to expectations. Far from supplanting the Swordfish, it merely complemented the older biplane and, ironically, was outlived by the latter in service. Designed to Specification S.41/36, the Albacore was ordered off the drawing board in May 1937, the Air Ministry placing a contract for two prototypes and 98 production aircraft. The first prototype flew on 12 December 1938, and production began in 1939. The prototype was tested on floats in 1940, but the results did not justify further development along these lines.

Later in the same year the first production aircraft underwent tests at the Aircraft & Armament Experimental

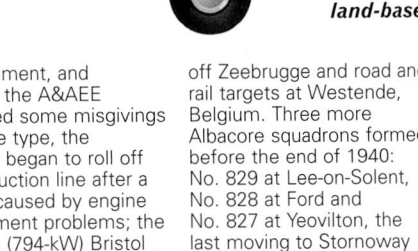

Establishment, and although the A&AEE expressed some misgivings about the type, the Albacore began to roll off the production line after a hold-up caused by engine development problems; the 1,065-hp (794-kW) Bristol Taurus II installed in early aircraft was later replaced by the Taurus XII. No. 826 Squadron was formed at Ford, Sussex, specially to fly the Albacore, and received 12 aircraft on 15 March 1940, first using the type in action on 31 May, attacking E-boats

off Zeebrugge and road and rail targets at Westende, Belgium. Three more Albacore squadrons formed before the end of 1940: No. 829 at Lee-on-Solent, No. 828 at Ford and No. 827 at Yeovilton, the last moving to Stornoway for anti-submarine patrols.

The Albacore finally went to sea when Nos 826 and 829 Squadrons joined HMS *Formidable* on 26 November 1940, for convoy escort duty to Cape Town. Aircraft from these squadrons took part in the Battle of Cape Matapan in March 1941, pressing home their torpedo attacks in true Swordfish tradition

against the Italian battleship *Vittorio Veneto*, the first occasion on which the Albacore had used the torpedo in action. By mid-1942 some 15 Fleet Air Arm squadrons were equipped with the Albacore, operating from the Arctic Circle on Russian convoys, to the Western Desert, the Mediterranean and the Indian Ocean. In November 1942 Albacores of Nos 817, 820, 822 and 832 Squadrons were in action during the Allied invasion of North Africa, flying anti-submarine patrols and bombing enemy coastal guns. The type had

reached its zenith in 1942, and in the following year the Barracuda began to replace the Albacore in all squadrons except No. 832, which was to be equipped with the Grumman Avenger. The last two squadrons to give up their Albacores were Nos 820 and 841 in November 1943, aircraft from the latter unit being passed to No. 415 Squadron, Royal Canadian Air Force, at Manston for use in English Channel operations on D-Day. Total Albacore production between 1939 and 1943 amounted to 800, including two prototypes.

Having formed at Ford in March 1940, No. 826 Squadron moved to Bircham Newton, Norfolk in the following month to make night attacks, lay mines and bomb shipping. The squadron went to sea in Formidable from November 1940 to April 1941 and was subsequently land-based in the eastern Mediterranean and Western Desert.

SPECIFICATION

Fairey Albacore
Type: three-seat carrierborne and land-based torpedo bomber
Powerplant: one Bristol Taurus XII radial piston engine rated at 1,130 hp (843 kW)
Performance: maximum speed 161 mph (259 km/h) at 4,500 ft (1370 m); cruising speed 116 mph (187 km/h) at 6,000 ft (1830 m); climb to 15,000 ft (4570 m) in 16 minutes 12 seconds; service ceiling 20,700 ft (6310 m); range 930 miles (1497 km) with a 1,600-lb (726-kg) weaponload
Weights: empty 7,250 lb (3289 kg); maximum take-off 10,460 lb (4745 kg)
Dimensions: wingspan 50 ft (15.24 m); length 39 ft 10 in (12.14 m); height 14 ft 2 in (4.32 m); wing area 623.00 sq ft (57.88 m²)
Armament: one 0.303-in (7.7-mm) Browning fixed forward-firing machine-gun in the leading edge of the starboard wing and two 0.303-in (7.7-mm) Vickers 'K' trainable rearward-firing machine-guns in the rear of the cockpit, plus up to 2,000 lb (9007 kg) of disposable stores carried on one underfuselage and four underwing hardpoints, and generally comprising one 1,610-lb (730-kg) torpedo beneath the fuselage, or six 250-lb (113-kg) or four 500-lb (227-kg) bombs under the lower wing

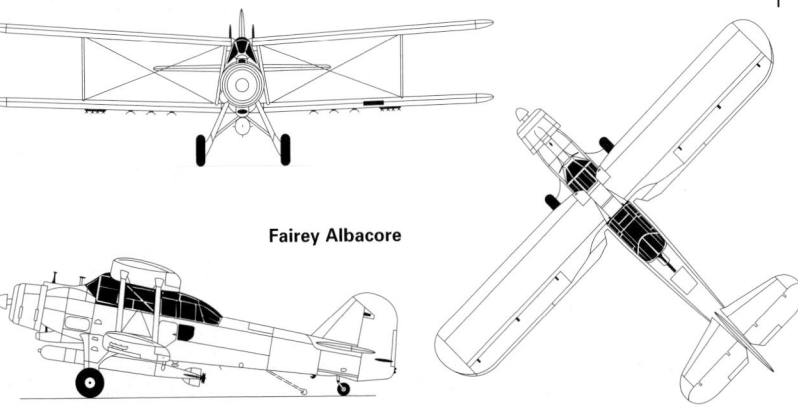

Fairey Albacore

Fairey Barracuda

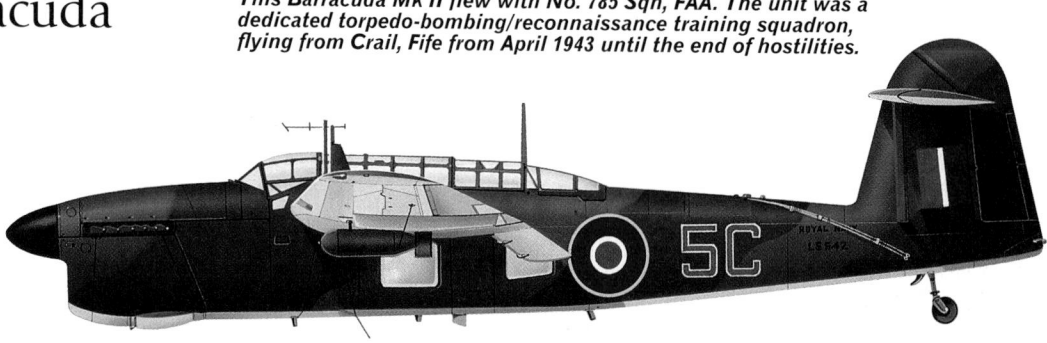

This Barracuda Mk II flew with No. 785 Sqn, FAA. The unit was a dedicated torpedo-bombing/reconnaissance training squadron, flying from Crail, Fife from April 1943 until the end of hostilities.

The **Barracuda** carrierborne torpedo and dive-bomber originated from Specification S.24/37 to which six companies tendered, Fairey gaining an order for two prototypes in July 1938. The engine originally selected was the 1,200-hp (895-kW) Rolls-Royce Exe unit but, after the development of this engine was halted in favour of the Merlin, Peregrine and Vulture, it was decided to use the 1,300-hp (969-kW) Merlin 30 to power the **Barracuda Mk I**.

When flown on 7 December 1940, the first prototype was seen to be a shoulder-wing cantilever monoplane of all-metal construction, the foldable wings incorporating Fairey-Youngman trailing-edge flaps that gave the aircraft performance much improved over that of its predecessors. The fuselage accommodated a crew of three in tandem in a long cockpit enclosed by a long 'greenhouse' canopy, and housed the main units of the tailwheel landing gear when retracted. Flight testing revealed that the low-set tailplane was badly positioned and a strut-based horizontal surface mounted high on a taller and narrower fin was designed for the second prototype. Because of the priority afforded to the construction of fighters and

bombers, this aircraft did not fly until 29 June 1941, and it was not until February 1942 that service trials and evaluation were completed.

These showed the need for airframe strengthening which, together with the addition of equipment not included in the original specification, resulted in the Barracuda suffering a weight problem that persisted through its service life. It played havoc with take-off and climb performance and after the completion of 30 Barracuda Mk Is, there appeared the **Barracuda Mk II** with the 1,640-hp (1223-kW) Merlin 32.

Barracudas built by Blackburn and Boulton Paul began to enter service in the spring of 1943, and although additional orders were placed, some of these were cancelled with the end of the war in Europe. In all, 1,688 Barracuda Mk IIs were built

in addition to the 30 Barracuda Mk Is and two prototypes.

The **Barracuda Mk III** was evolved to take a new ASV radar installation, with a blister radome beneath the rear fuselage. The prototype, converted from a Barracuda Mk II, flew first in 1943. Following orders placed that year, production of this version began in early 1944. Built alongside the Barracuda Mk II, the 852 Barracuda Mk III aircraft were manufactured by Boulton Paul and Fairey.

The final production variant was the **Barracuda Mk V** (the **Mk IV** being an unbuilt project), and this differed considerably in appearance although the basic structure was unchanged. The shortfall in power of the Merlins available in 1941 made the designers consider alternatives, and the decision was taken to use the Rolls-Royce Griffon. Initial

development was slow and the first Griffon-powered aircraft, converted from a Barracuda Mk II, did not fly until 16 November 1944. In production form the Barracuda Mk V had a longer, squarer wing than earlier versions, enlarged fin area to counteract the greater torque of the 2,030-hp (1514-kW) Griffon 37, and increased fuel capacity. This development had come too late, however, and of the 140 Barracuda Mk Vs ordered, only 30 had been delivered before the end of the war brought cancellation of the outstanding balance.

The Barracuda's operational service life began when No. 827 Squadron received 12 Barracuda Mk IIs on being re-formed during 10 January 1943. A conspicuous action came when 42 aircraft dive-bombed the German battleship *Tirpitz* on 3 April 1944, inflicting heavy

damage, and further attacks were made on the same target during the next four months. The Barracuda squadrons of HMS *Illustrious*, Nos 810 and 847, introduced the type to the Pacific theatre in April 1944, supporting US Navy dive-bombers in an attack on Japanese installations in Sumatra. The Barracuda flew from small escort carriers on anti-submarine patrols in European operations, using rocket-assisted take-off gear for lift-off from these carriers' short decks. Most squadrons were disbanded soon after VJ-Day, or re-equipped with other aircraft, and after some shuffling within squadrons the last Barracudas in front-line service were replaced in 1953 by Grumman Avengers.

The Barracuda Mk Vs never entered front-line service, being used for training until 1950.

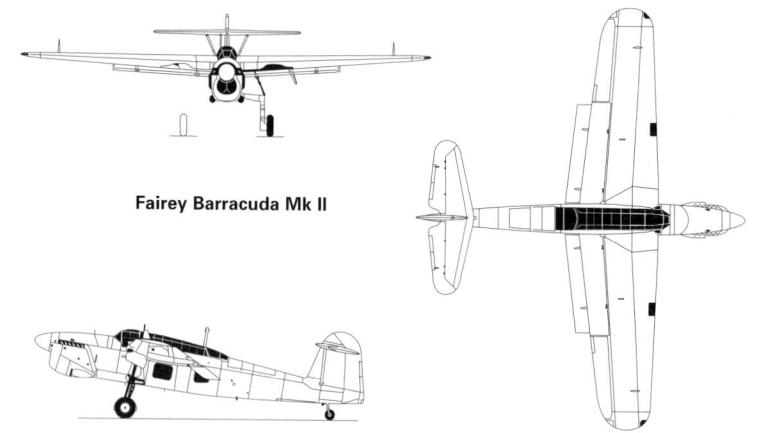

Fairey Barracuda Mk II

SPECIFICATION	
Fairey Barracuda Mk II	(34.09 m²)
Type: three-seat carrierborne torpedo and dive-bomber	**Armament:** two 0.303-in (7.7-mm) Browning trainable rearward-firing machine-guns in the rear of the cockpit, plus up to 2,000 lb (907 kg) of disposable stores carried on one underfuselage and six underwing hardpoints, and generally comprising one 1,572-lb (713-kg) 18-in (457-mm) Mk XIIA torpedo, or 1,600-lb (726-kg) bomb or 1,500-lb (680-kg) mine carried under the fuselage, or three 500-lb (227-kg) bombs carried under the fuselage and inner underwing hardpoints, or four 450-lb (204-kg) Mk VIII or 285-lb (120-kg) Mk XI depth charges carried on the inner underwing hardpoints, or six 250-lb (113-kg) bombs carried on the underwing hardpoints
Powerplant: one Rolls-Royce Merlin 32 Vee piston engine rated at 1,640 hp (1223 kW)	
Performance: maximum speed 228 mph (367 km/h) at 1,750 ft (535 m); cruising speed 193 mph (311 km/h) at 5,000 ft (1525 m); climb to 5,000 ft (1525 m) in 6 minutes; service ceiling 16,600 ft (5060 m); range 684 miles (1101 km) with torpedo armament	
Weights: empty 9,350 lb (4241 kg); maximum take-off 14,100 lb (6396 kg)	
Dimensions: wingspan 49 ft 2 in (14.99 m); length 39 ft 9 in (12.12 m); height 15 ft 1 in (4.60 m); wing area 367.00 sq ft	

Fairey Battle

First flown on 10 March 1936, the prototype of the **Fairey Day Bomber**, as the type was then known, originated as the company's submission to Specification P.27/32 for a two-seat single-engined monoplane bomber. This was required to carry 1,000 lb (454 kg) of bombs for 1,000 miles (1609 km) at a speed of 200 mph (322 km/h). The prototype exceeded the required performance and

won the competition against design proposals

from Armstrong Whitworth, Bristol and Hawker. A first production contract for 155 aircraft, to the revised Specification P.23/35, had

in fact been placed in 1935, before the prototype had flown. The first production example of the **Battle**, as the type was named, was

built at Hayes, Middlesex, but the second and subsequent Fairey-built aircraft came from a new factory at Heaton Chapel, Stockport.

This Battle (T) trainer was used by No. 3 Bombing and Gunnery School at Macdonald, Canada in 1943. Dreadful losses over occupied Europe soon saw the type relegated to secondary roles.

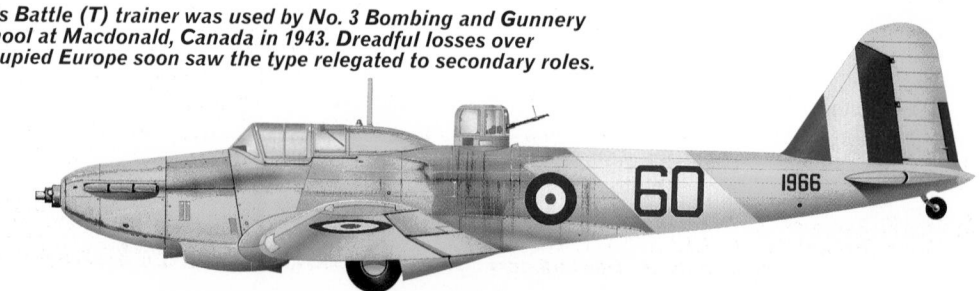

Fairey Battle (cont.)

It was to power the Battle that Rolls-Royce received the launch order for its famous 1,030-hp (768-kW) Merlin I engine, which powered the first 136 Fairey-built **Battle Mk I** aircraft. The introduction of Mk II to V versions of the Merlin engine identified equivalent **Battle Mk II** to **Battle Mk V** aircraft.

A cantilever low-wing monoplane of all-metal construction, except for some fabric covering on the control surfaces, the Battle had tailwheel landing gear with retractable main units that left their wheels partly exposed when retracted, and a fuselage incorporating tandem accommodation for the pilot and gunner in a long cockpit under a framed canopy. By the end of 1937 Fairey had completed some 85 Battles, the first going to No. 63 Squadron at Upwood in May 1937. As new orders for Battles were placed, production sub-contracts were awarded to Austin Motors. Meanwhile, the last 19 Battles of the initial Fairey order were provided with Merlin II engines, and these were also fitted to the Austin-built aircraft. The first Battle from the

Longbridge factory flew in July 1938, and 29 had been completed there by the end of the year. After 60 Austin-built Battles had been completed, the Merlin III engine was introduced on the production line.

By the outbreak of World War II more than 1,000 Battles had been delivered, and machines of No. 226 Squadron were the first to be sent to France as part of the Advanced Air Striking Force. It was here that the Battle's inability to defend itself against fighter attack became obvious. On armed daylight reconnaissance missions the type occasionally tangled with Bf 109 fighters, and although one of the latter was destroyed by a Battle's rear gunner in September 1940, the light bombers invariably suffered heavy casualties. As the period of the so-called 'phoney war' came to an end, the Battle squadrons were thrown into the fray on 10 May 1940 to try to stop the advancing German ground forces. Without fighter escort, and attacking from a height of only 250 ft (76 m) with delayed-action bombs, the Battle force came under heavy ground fire, losing 13 of the 32 aircraft sent on the

mission, all the others being damaged. The next day, seven out of eight aircraft were lost, and on 12 May five machines of No. 12 Squadron, flown by volunteer crews, attacked two vital road bridges over the Albert Canal; in the face of extremely heavy ground fire the attack was pressed home and one bridge seriously damaged, but at a cost of all five aircraft. Further heavy losses came on 14 May, when 35 out of 63 Battles failed to return from attacks against bridges and troop concentrations. This marked the end of the aircraft's career as a day bomber, and although a few remained in front-line service until late 1940 the survivors were mostly diverted to other duties. The most important of these was training, and 100 **Battle (T)** aircraft were built as dual-control trainers with separate cockpits, while 266 examples of the **Battle (TT)** target-towing variant were also supplied to supplement conversions.

The last production aircraft was an Austin-built **Battle TT.Mk I** delivered on 2 September 1940. This brought total Battle production to 2,203 aircraft including the proto-type.

Canada used a large

number of Battles for training and target towing in the Commonwealth Air Training Plan, the first being supplied to the RCAF at Camp Borden in August 1939. These were the vanguard of 739 of these aircraft, this total including seven airframes for instructional purposes. The RAAF received four British-built Battle machines and assembled 360 in Australia, including 30 target tugs, while other customers were Belgium (18 built under licence by

Avions Fairey), Turkey (29), South Africa (190 or more) and Ireland, where an RAF aircraft which landed at Waterford in 1941 was interned and later taken over by the Air Corps. Several Battles were used as testbeds for such engines as the Napier Dagger and Sabre, the Bristol Hercules and Taurus, the Rolls-Royce Exe and Merlin XII, and the Fairey Prince. Other aircraft were used for experiments with various types of propellers.

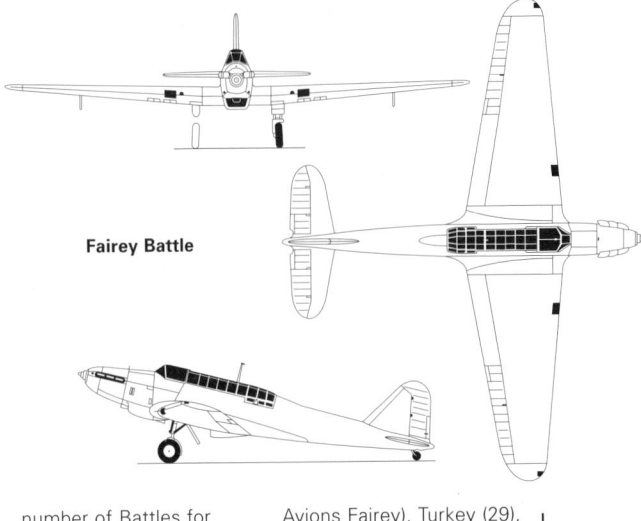

Fairey Battle

SPECIFICATION	
Fairey Battle Mk I	(12.90 m); height 15 ft 6 in
Type: three-seat light bomber	(4.72 m); wing area 422.00 sq ft
Powerplant: one Rolls-Royce	(39.20 m²)
Merlin I Vee piston engine rated at	**Armament:** one 0.303-in (7.7-mm)
1,030 hp (768 kW)	Vickers fixed forward-firing
Performance: maximum speed	machine-gun in the leading edge of
257 mph (414 km/h) at 15,000 ft	the starboard wing and one
(4570 m); cruising speed 210 mph	0.303-in (7.7-mm) Vickers 'K'
(338 km/h) at optimum altitude;	trainable rearward-firing machine-
climb to 5,000 ft (1525 m) in	gun in the rear of the cockpit, plus
4 minutes 6 seconds; service	up to 1,500 lb (680 kg) of
ceiling 25,000 ft (7620 m); range	disposable stores carried in two
1,000 miles (1609 km)	wing weapons bays and on two
Weights: empty 6,647 lb	underwing hardpoints, and
(3015 kg); maximum take-off	generally comprising four 250-lb
10,792 lb (4895 kg)	(113-kg) bombs carried internally
Dimensions: wingspan 54 ft	and two 250-lb (113-kg) bombs
(16.46 m); length 42 ft 4 in	carried externally

No. 63 Sqn, RAF was flying its Battle Mk Is from RAF Benson during November 1939. The unit provided operational training for Battle crews.

Fairey Campania

In October 1914 the Admiralty bought the former 20,000-ton Cunard liner *Campania* for recon-struction as a seaplane carrier with a 120-ft (36.60-m) flight deck; the seaplanes took off from this surface by means of a wheeled trolley, which was left behind when the aircraft became airborne, and were later recovered from the sea by crane. Early trials with a Sopwith Schneider showed that a deck extension was

needed for the operation of larger seaplanes, and a further 80 ft (24.40 m) was added before the ship re-entered service in April 1916. To equip the *Campania* the Admiralty ordered an initial batch of 10 twin-float seaplanes from Fairey, and the type became known as the **Fairey Campania**. The first prototype was the **F.16 Campania** that made its maiden flight in February 1917 with the 250-hp (186-kW) Rolls-Royce

Sydney Pickles took the Campania prototype aloft for its first flight on 16 February 1917. Note the nose-mounted slab radiators.

Mk IV (later Eagle IV) engine, while the second, representing the definitive aircraft, was the **F.17 Campania** that followed in June of that same year with the Eagle V engine. Production totalled 62 of the machines, of which 50 were built by Fairey and the remainder under subcontract by Barclay, Curie & Co. at Clydeside.

By the time the Campania was entering production, the demand for Rolls-Royce engines had led to the adoption for some aircraft of an alternative, the 260-hp (194-kW) Sunbeam Maori II unit, which required some modifications in the cooling and exhaust arrangements. The Maori engine was installed in 25 Fairey-built **F.22 Campania** aircraft operated from shore stations. In addition to the parent ship, the Campania flew from the light aircraft-carriers *Nairana* and *Pegasus*, and also saw action with the British North Russian Expeditionary Force at Arkhangyelsk in 1919. A few aircraft were later fitted with the 345-hp (257-kW) Eagle VIII or 325-hp (242-kW) Eagle VII engines, but despite the higher power the heavier engines brought no increase in performance.

SPECIFICATION

Fairey F.17 Campania
Type: two-seat coastal patrol and carrierborne reconnaissance floatplane
Powerplant: one Rolls-Royce Eagle V Vee piston engine rated at 275 hp (206 kW)
Performance: maximum speed 89 mph (143 km/h) at sea level; cruising speed 78 mph (126 km/h) at 6,500 ft (1980 m); climb to 6,500 ft (1980 m) in 34 minutes 15 seconds; service ceiling 7,000 ft (2135 m); endurance 5 hours
Weights: empty 3,713 lb (1684 kg); maximum take-off 4,263 lb (1934 kg)
Dimensions: wingspan 61 ft 7 in (18.77 m); length 43 ft 1 in (13.13 m); height 15 ft 1 in (4.60 m); wing area 674.60 sq ft (62.67 m²)
Armament: one 0.303-in (7.7-mm) trainable rearward-firing Lewis gun in the rear cockpit, plus up to 672 lb (305 kg) of disposable stores carried on hardpoints under the fuselage and lower wing, and generally comprising six 112- or 100-lb (51- or 45- kg) bombs

Fairey F.D.2

The first F.D.2, or Fairey Delta 2 as it was also known, is illustrated here carrying titles to celebrate its impressive World Speed record success.

Following its experiments with vertically launched delta-wing models during 1947, Fairey was asked if these could be made to fly supersonically and, since this would have been worthwhile only if a piloted supersonic aircraft was under consideration, the company anticipated that something might be in the wind and began studies. In fact, the Ministry of Supply was interested in supersonic flight: Specification E.R.103 was issued for a research aircraft and accepted by Fairey and English Electric, which were each to build two aircraft. The latter eventually produced the twin-engined P.1 which, in its developed form, became the Lightning, while the former built the **Fairey F.D.2** as a needle-nosed delta-wing aircraft powered by one turbojet engine. The contract was signed in October 1950, but because the Gannet was a priority programme,

the F.D.2 had to take second place, with manufacture beginning only at the end of 1952.

The first aircraft flew at Boscombe Down in October 1954 and built up a number of flights before it was damaged on landing after the loss of engine and hydraulic power, which prevented the pilot from powering the landing gear. The F.D.2 flew again in August 1955, becoming supersonic for the first time in October, and in subsequent flights the speed was gradually increased until, in November, the aircraft reached 1,028 mph (1654 km/h) or Mach 1.56 at an altitude of more than

36,000 ft (10975 m). With its potential thus revealed, the F.D.2 was rightly seen as a contender for the world absolute speed record, then held by the North American F-100 Super Sabre at 822 mph (1323 km/h). A great deal of work had to be done on the precise calibration of the aircraft and the cameras, but this work was rewarded on 10 March 1956 by an average speed over two runs over a 9.70-mile (15.60-km) course of 1,132 mph (1822 km/h) at 38,000 ft (11580 m).

The second F.D.2 flew at Boscombe Down in February 1956, and both aircraft were used in a

wide variety of research work. The first eventually went to the British Aircraft Corporation and, as the **BAC.221**, was fitted with a completely new ogival wing for practical confirmation of wind tunnel tests on the shape which was eventually to fly on the Aérospatiale/BAC

Concorde supersonic airliner. The F.D.2 and BAC.221 had noses which could be lowered to improve visibility when landing and taking off, and this feature was incorporated in Concorde. Both the research aircraft survived and are preserved.

SPECIFICATION

Fairey F.D.2
Type: single-seat supersonic research aircraft
Powerplant: one Rolls-Royce Avon Mk 200 turbojet engine rated at 12,000 lb st (53.38 kN) with afterburning
Performance: maximum speed more than 1,300 mph (2092 km/h) at 38,000 ft (11580 m); climb to
40,000 ft (12190 m) in 2 minutes 30 seconds; range 830 miles (1336 km)
Weights: empty 11,000 lb (4990 kg); maximum take-off 13,884 lb (6298 kg)
Dimensions: wingspan 26 ft 10 in (8.18 m); length 51 ft 7½ in (15.74 m); height 11 ft (3.35 m); wing area 360.00 sq ft (33.44 m²)

Fairey Firefly

Designed to the Admiralty's Specification N.5/40 calling for a two-seat reconnaissance fighter, the Firefly represented a considerable advance over the Fairey's earlier Fulmar used in the same basic role. A low-wing cantilever monoplane of all-metal construction, the **Firefly** had a conventional tail unit, retractable

tailwheel landing gear and accommodation for the pilot and navigator/radio-operator in separate enclosed cockpits. Power was provided by one 1,730-hp (1290-kW) Griffon IIB engine, but later examples of the **Firefly F.Mk I** initial production model had the 1,990-hp (1484-kW) Griffon XII.

The first of four development aircraft was flown on 22 December 1941, and the first production Firefly F.Mk Is were delivered in March 1943. A total of 459 of this version was built. The addition of ASH radar beneath the engine identified the **Firefly FR.Mk I**, of which 236 were built, and a number of F.Mk Is modified to FR.Mk I standard had the designation **Firefly F.Mk IA**.

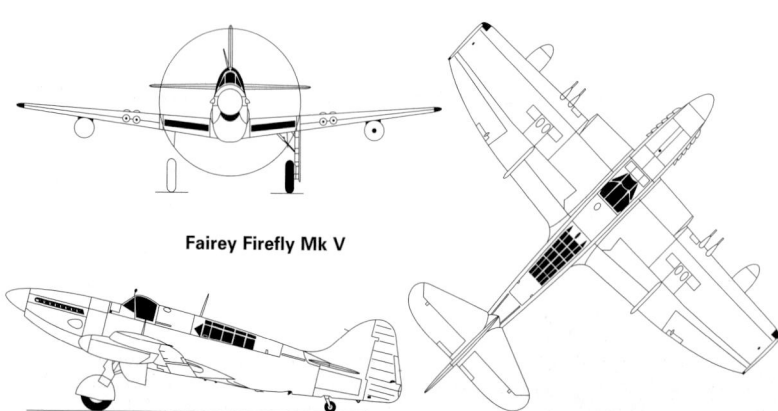

Fairey Firefly Mk V

This late-production Firefly Mk I shows the type's four-cannon fixed armament to advantage. All pre-Mk 4 aircraft had three-bladed propellers.

Fairey Firefly (continued)

A **Firefly NF.Mk II** night-fighter version was developed, but when it was realised that its AI.Mk 10 radar could be pod-mounted beneath the engine, as with the ASH radar of the FR.Mk I, the planned 328-aircraft programme was cancelled. Instead, 140 examples of the Firefly FR.Mk I were modified on the production line to **Firefly NF.Mk I** configuration, the 37 Firefly NF.Mk II aircraft that had been built being converted back to Mk I standard. Conversions of Mk Is after World War II included the unarmed dual-control **Firefly T.Mk 1** pilot trainer, the cannon-armed **Firefly T.Mk 2** operational trainer and the **Firefly T.Mk 3** used for training in ASW operations. A few aircraft were also converted as **Firefly TT.Mk 1** target tugs.

Only a prototype of the **Firefly F.Mk III** with the Griffon 61 engine was built, development being concentrated instead on the **Firefly F.Mk IV**. This had the 2,100-hp (1566-kW) Griffon 74 engine and new outer wing nacelles that could both carry fuel, or an ASH scanner to port and fuel to starboard. About 160 of this model were built, and the first **Firefly FR.Mk 4** was delivered in July 1946; some aircraft were converted later to **Firefly TT.Mk 4** standard. The **Firefly Mk 5** and **Firefly Mk 6** were similar externally to the Mk 4, the first aircraft of each variant flying in December 1947 and March 1949 respectively. Some 352 Mk 5s were built in versions designated **Firefly FR.Mk 5**, **Firefly NF.Mk 5**

and **Firefly AS.Mk 5**, the last with American sonobuoys and equipment that distinguished it from the British-equipped **Firefly AS.Mk 6D**, of which 133 were built. A few examples of the **Firefly T.Mk 5** trainer and the **Firefly TT.Mk 5** and **Firefly TT.Mk 6** target tugs were converted in Australia from Firefly AS.Mk 5 standard.

The first production example of the **Firefly AS.Mk 7** with the Griffon 59 engine flew in October 1951, this variant reintroducing the beard radiator that had caused problems with the sole Mk III. Intended as an ASW aircraft and providing accommodation for two radar operators as well as the pilot, the AS.Mk 7 saw only limited production in this original form, the majority being completed as **Firefly T.Mk 7** ASW trainers within a Mk 7 production of 151 machines. Later conversions to pilotless target aircraft were carried out by Fairey, these including 34 **Firefly U.Mk 8** aircraft

converted from T.Mk 7 standard, and 40 similar **Firefly U.Mk 9** conversions from Mk 4 and Mk 5 aircraft. These aircraft were used for missile development, and by the Royal Navy as targets for its Firestreak-armed fighters and Seaslug-carrying ships.

The Firefly first entered service with No. 1770 Squadron at Yeovilton, Somerset, on 1 October 1943. Later embarked on HMS *Indefatigable*, the type was active in operations against the German battleship *Tirpitz* in Norway during July 1944. The Firefly also saw action against Japanese oil refineries in Sumatra, in attacks on the Carolines and against shipping and ground targets in the Japanese home islands. In 1950, after war had broken out in Korea, Firefly Mk 5s were operated from Australian and British light fleet carriers, and in 1954 the type was in action in the attack role in Malaya. Just over two years later, the Firefly was retired after 13 years of valuable service.

An ex-RAN aircraft, the Royal Navy Historic Flight's Firefly Mk 5 was restored to airworthy condition in 1972. After several years' work by BAE Systems, the machine should return to air show flying in 2000.

SPECIFICATION	
Fairey Firefly AS.Mk 5 **Type:** two-seat carrierborne anti-submarine reconnaissance and strike aircraft **Powerplant:** one Rolls-Royce Griffon 74 Vee piston engine rated at 2,250 hp (1678 kW) **Performance:** maximum speed 386 mph (621 km/h) at 14,000 ft (4265 m); cruising speed 220 mph (354 km/h) at optimum altitude; climb to 10,000 ft (3050 m) in 6 minutes 50 seconds; service ceiling 28,400 ft (8655 m); range 1,300 miles (2092 km)	**Weights:** empty 9,674 lb (4388 kg); maximum take-off 16,096 lb (7301 kg) **Dimensions:** wingspan 41 ft 2 in (12.55 m); length 37 ft 11 in (8.51 m); height 14 ft 4 in (4.37 m); wing area 330.00 sq ft (30.66 m²) **Armament:** four 20-mm Hispano fixed forward-firing cannon in the leading edges of the wing, plus up to 2,000 lb (907 kg) of disposable stores carried under the wing, and generally comprising two 1,000-lb (454-kg) bombs or 16 60-lb (27-kg) air-to-surface unguided rockets

No. 739 Sqn was one of five units to fly the Firefly T.Mk 7 in service. The others were 719, 750, 796 and 1840 Sqns. The aircraft was used for observer training.

Fairey Firefly (biplane)

On 9 November 1925 Fairey flew the prototype of the **Firefly I** single-seat fighter, which it had designed and manufactured as a private venture. A conventional biplane, primarily of wooden construction covered with fabric, the Firefly I was a design in which Fairey was attempting to capitalise further on the possibility of low-drag installations of the 430-hp (321-kW) Curtiss D-12 engine, an American unit which the company had introduced to the UK in the Fox day bomber. Although the Firefly I demonstrated good performance, its American powerplant meant that it did not win a Royal Air Force contract. Instead, its design served as the basis for an improved and rather

different **Firefly II**, powered by the 480-hp (358-kW) Rolls-Royce Kestrel engine.

First flown on 5 February 1929, the Firefly II took part in an Air Ministry fighter competition in which it lost to the Hawker Fury. The Firefly II was later rebuilt with an all-metal structure, revised engine cooling and redesigned tail surfaces

under the modified designation **Firefly IIM**. In this form it won a contract in 1930 for 25 aircraft to serve with the Belgian air force under the designation **Firefly II**, and an additional 62 such aircraft were built in Belgium at the Avions Fairey factory at Gosselies for the Belgian service, plus one additional aircraft for supply to the USSR.

Variants

Firefly III: ship-based derivative of the Firefly II with an increased-area wing cellule and a different mark of Rolls-Royce engine

Firefly IIIM: redesignation of the Firefly III after it had been rebuilt with a metal structure and strengthening for catapult-launching; the machine was used on floats as a practice/trainer aircraft for the RAF's High-Speed Flight competing in the Schneider Trophy contests

Firefly IV: redesignation of two Firefly II aircraft following the installation by Avions Fairey of the 785-hp (585-kW) Hispano-Suiza 12Xbrs

SPECIFICATION	
Fairey Firefly IIM **Type:** single-seat fighter **Powerplant:** one Rolls-Royce Kestrel IIS Vee piston engine rated at 480 hp (358 kW) **Performance:** maximum speed 223 mph (359 km/h) at 13,125 ft (4000 m); climb to 19,685 ft (6000 m) in 10 minutes 54 seconds; service ceiling 30,840 ft (9400 m)	**Weights:** empty 2,387 lb (1083 kg); maximum take-off 3,285 lb (1490 kg) **Dimensions:** wingspan 31 ft 6 in (9.60 m); length 24 ft 8 in (7.52 m); height 9 ft 4 in (2.85 m); wing area 236.81 sq ft (22.00 m²) **Armament:** two 0.303-in (7.7-mm) Vickers fixed forward-firing machine-guns in the sides of the forward fuselage

As originally built, the Firefly II had a retractable radiator and a squared-off fin and rudder assembly. The type's clean lines are readily apparent.

Fairey Flycatcher I

In 1922 the Air Ministry's Specification 6/22 called for a naval single-seat fighter to replace the Nieuport Nightjar in carrierborne service. Alternative land-plane, floatplane and amphibian configurations were required, and the powerplant was to be based on one radial engine, for which the Bristol Jupiter and Armstrong Siddeley Jaguar were specified. Two designs were selected, the **Fairey Flycatcher** (redesignated as the **Flycatcher I** after the appearance of the **Flycatcher II**) and the Parnall Plover, each being ordered to the extent of three prototypes. Parnall later built 10 production examples of its Plover, but although the aircraft was far superior in looks to the angular Flycatcher I, it was no match in other respects to the Fairey biplane and lasted barely a year in naval service.

The first prototype of the Flycatcher I, with the 400-hp (298-kW) Jaguar II engine, made its maiden flight on 28 November 1922 as a landplane, and was subsequently re-engined with the identically rated Jupiter IV engine for the 1923 RAF Display. The second prototype was also completed with the Jaguar II engine but with float alighting gear, and first flew from Hamble in May 1923, while the third prototype was an amphibian. Like most other Fairey aircraft, the Flycatcher I had the camber-changing mechanism which gave an extremely short take-off, and an ability to fly onto carrier decks without using arrester wires. Another advantage in carrier operations was the aircraft's short span, which enabled it to be taken down on the lift without any need for wing-folding.

The first unit to equip with the production version was No. 402 Flight of the Fleet Air Arm in 1923, and thereafter the Flycatcher I continued to replace earlier types on all the aircraft-carriers and as a turret platform fighter in some capital ships. Total production, including the three prototypes, amounted to 196. The Flycatcher I continued to serve with the fleet until 1934 when the last aircraft, floatplanes operating with No. 406 Flight attached to the East Indies Squadron, were replaced by Hawker Ospreys.

Although angular in appearance, the Flycatcher I was extremely popular with its pilots. It was very responsive and strong in spite of its mixed wood and metal construction under a covering largely of fabric, and could be dived vertically at full throttle. It was aerobatic, even in floatplane form. No export sales of the Flycatcher I were made, and no genuine aircraft survives, although a full-scale replica has been built and is currently flying in the UK, albeit with a non-standard engine.

The **Flycatcher II** was a completely unrelated Jaguar-powered, naval-fighter prototype of 1926. Later, a Bristol Mercury engine was fitted but by this time the Air Ministry had switched its allegiance to liquid-cooled Vee engines for use in fighter powerplants, and Flycatcher II development was halted. The machine was written off after the engine failed at take-off in May 1929.

An unusual feature of the Flycatcher's construction was that the airframe was designed to be dismantled easily, with no section more than 13 ft 6 in (4.11 m) long. The carrier is HMS Eagle.

SPECIFICATION	
Fairey Flycatcher I (landplane) **Type:** single-seat carrierborne fighter **Powerplant:** one Armstrong Siddeley Jaguar III or IV radial piston engine rated at 400 hp (298 kW) **Performance:** maximum speed 134 mph (216 km/h) at 5,000 ft (1525 m); initial climb rate 1,090 ft (332 m) per minute; climb to 10,000 ft (3050 m) in 9 minutes 29 seconds; service ceiling 19,000 ft (5790 m); range 311 miles	(500 km) **Weights:** empty 2,038 lb (924 kg), maximum take-off 3,028 lb (1372 kg) **Dimensions:** wingspan 29 ft (8.84 m); length 23 ft (7.01 m); height 12 ft (3.66 m); wing area 288.00 sq ft (26.76 m²) **Armament:** two 0.303-in (7.7-mm) Vickers fixed forward-firing machine-guns in the sides of the forward fuselage, plus up to four 20-lb (9-kg) bombs carried under the lower wing

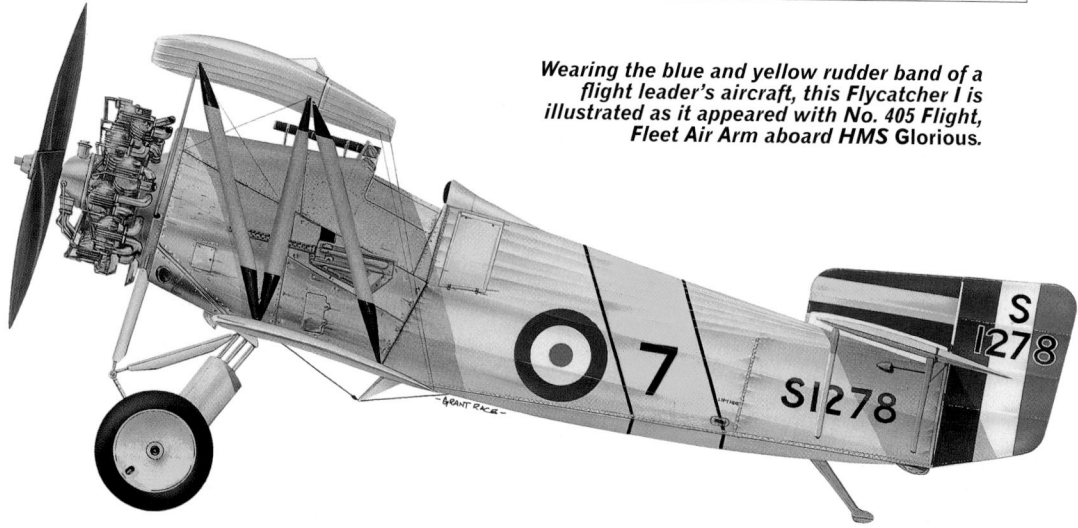

Wearing the blue and yellow rudder band of a flight leader's aircraft, this Flycatcher I is illustrated as it appeared with No. 405 Flight, Fleet Air Arm aboard HMS Glorious.

Fairey Fox

Inspired by the 450-hp (336-kW) Curtiss D-12 Vee engine that powered the US Navy's Curtiss CR-3 racing floatplane in the 1923 Schneider Trophy contest, Richard Fairey acquired from the Curtiss company a D-12 engine and the rights to manufacture it in the UK, as well as the British rights to the Curtiss-Reed metal propeller and the CR-3's high-efficiency aerofoil sections and wing surface radiators. The engine manufacturing licence was not taken up, but about 50 D-12 engines were imported for development as the Fairey Felix and use in the **Fox** day bomber.

First flown on 3 January 1925, the Fox prototype revealed a number of inadequacies, but also a maximum speed of 158 mph (254 km/h), which was about 40 mph (64 km/h) faster than the contemporary Fawn. However, the fact that the Fox was powered by a US engine caused some problems in Fairey's search for a British military order. An initial contract for 18 aircraft to Specification 21/25 was eventually placed, the first **Fox Mk I** being flown on 10 December 1925 and early deliveries to No. 12 Sqn being made later that same month to replace Fawns.

Later Fox production was of the Fox IA, with the Kestrel IIA engine. J9026 was among the final batch of four Foxes completed.

Fairey Fox (continued)

Another nine examples of the Fox were later ordered, and eventually the availability of the Rolls-Royce F.XIIA (later named Kestrel) engine opened the way for the Fox bombers to be re-engined, with the revised designation **Fox Mk IA**. The first of these flew on 29 August 1927 with the first Rolls-Royce F.XI engine, while the first fully developed F.XIIA engine flew in December 1928.

The **Fox Mk IIM** first flew on 25 October 1929 as a development of the Fox Mk I with a fabric-covered metal structure and the powerplant of one 480-hp (358-kW) F.XIB (later Kestrel IB) engine. The Fox Mk IIM was offered to the Royal Air Force, but the Hawker Hart had already been ordered to fill the day bomber role. Consequently, the Fox Mk IIM was offered for sale abroad and accepted by Belgium. Twelve aircraft were ordered in January 1931, the first three aircraft being delivered to Brussels-Evere airfield on 10 January 1932. A new factory was built at Gosselies, near Charleroi, for the British company's Belgian associ-ate, Avions Fairey, which had been established for licensed construction of the Fox. The first Belgian-assembled Fox flew on 21 April 1933, and the company's official records show the completion of 177 Fox-derived aircraft up to 1939. These 177 machines comprised 11 different versions with engines such as the Kestrel IIS and Hispano-Suiza 12Y. The most significant of the Belgian-built Fox types was the **Fox Mk VI** powered by an 860-hp (641-kW) Hispano-Suiza engine, as well as having a cockpit canopy and landing-gear fairings, for a maximum speed of more than 220 mph (354 km/h) and a climb to 20,000 ft (6095 m) in only 8 minutes 20 seconds. The Belgian air force still had 98 examples of various Fox models in first-line service when Germany invaded Belgium on 10 May 1940, and during the 18 days of Belgium's courageous but futile defence of its territory the obsolete Fox warplanes were continually in action.

Some further Fox aircraft were built in the UK, these including six floatplanes for Peru, but the exact numbers are not known. The few Fox aircraft acquired by the RAF remained in service until 1931, when they were replaced by Hawker Hart bombers.

SPECIFICATION

Fairey Fox Mk I
Type: two-seat day bomber
Powerplant: one Fairey Felix Vee piston engine rated at 480 hp (358 kW)
Performance: maximum speed 158 mph (254 km/h) at sea level; climb to 15,000 ft (4570 m) in 21 minutes 30 seconds; service ceiling 17,000 ft (5180 m); range 650 miles (1046 km)
Weights: empty 2,609 lb (1183 kg); maximum take-off 4,117 lb (1867 kg)
Dimensions: wingspan 38 ft (11.58 m); length 31 ft 2 in (9.50 m); height 10 ft 8 in (3.25 m); wing area 324.00 sq ft (30.10 m²)
Armament: one 0.303-in (7.7-mm) Vickers fixed forward-firing machine-gun on the port side of the forward fuselage and one 0.303-in (7.7-mm) Lewis trainable rearward-firing machine-gun in the rear cockpit, plus up to 500 lb (227 kg) of disposable stores carried on four underwing hardpoints, and generally comprising two 230-lb (104-kg) bombs, or four 112-lb (51-kg) bombs, or eight 20-lb (9.10-kg) bombs

Variants

Fox Mk III: privately funded demonstrator which later became the sole Fox Mk IV
Fox Mk III Trainer: single derivative of the Fox Mk II as a dual-control trainer with the 360-hp (269-kW) Armstrong Siddeley Serval radial engine; in 1934 it emerged from the Gosselies factory as the **Fox Mk IIIS** with the Kestrel IIMS supercharged engine; another five Fox Mk IIIS aircraft were built
Fox Mk III: 13 Belgian-built two-seat reconnaissance fighters with an additional 0.3-in (7.62-mm) FN-Browning forward-firing machine-gun
Fox Mk IIIC: two-seat reconnaissance/army co-operation aircraft with secondary bombing capability; the production total of 48 such aircraft, all powered by the Kestrel IIS, included one **Fox Mk IIICS** dual-control trainer, and all of these aircraft were characterised by an enclosed cockpit
Fox Mk IV: a development aircraft with a 775-hp (578-kW) Hispano-Suiza engine
Fox Mk IV Floatplane: six aircraft to a Peruvian order
Fox Mk V: the Fox Mk IV when fitted by the parent company with an enclosed cockpit and wheel spats for the long-range fighter role with only a pilot aboard; on its return to Belgium, the Fox Mk V was fitted with the 830-hp (619-kW) Hispano-Suiza 12Ydrs engine, had its wheel spats removed and was redesignated Fox Mk VIR as a reconnaissance prototype
Fox Mk VIC: 52 aircraft produced as two-seat fighter equivalents to the Fox Mk VIR
Fox Mk VIR: reconnaissance-fighter version of the basic Fox Mk VI series
Fox Mk VII: single-seat fighter development of the Fox Mk VIR with six machine-guns; only two were built, and these were known unofficially under the name **Kangourou**, reflecting the rearward movement and pouch-like appearance of the radiator bath
Fox Mk VIII: 15 examples of an improved version of the Fox Mk VIR with two 0.3-in (7.62-mm) FN-Browning machine-guns in the leading edges of the upper wing

Fairey Fulmar

In the mid-1930s the Fleet Air Arm was in desperate need of new aircraft to replace its antiquated biplanes, but the philosophy of the period dictated that if the Royal Navy was to acquire a high-performance fighter, a crew of two was desirable to cope with the growing sophistication of navigational aids. Inevitably, the extra size and weight imposed a performance penalty, but until the arrival of the Sea Hurricane and Seafire, the Fulmar was the best aircraft available.

Two prototypes of a light bomber to specification P.4/34 had been flown, the first of them on 13 January 1937, and from their design emerged, with comparatively few modifications, the **Fairey Fulmar** to the requirement of Specification O.8/38. The P.4/34 was smaller and lighter than the contemporary Fairey Battle and was stressed for dive-bombing. The second prototype was used as the flying mock-up of a fleet fighter, with certain changes to meet naval requirements and Specification O.8/38. Within seven weeks of receiving the detailed specification, on 16 March 1938, Fairey confirmed to the Admiralty that a modified version of the P.4/34 would meet the requirements, and an initial order was placed for 127 aircraft to be known as the Fulmar. This was increased to 250 at the time of the Munich crisis in September 1938, but Fairey warned that production could not begin until its new factory at Heaton Chapel, Stockport, was completed.

The P.4/34 had been powered by the 1,030-hp (768-kW) Rolls-Royce Merlin II, but it was planned that the initial production Fulmar would have the Merlin VIII. However, the first aircraft flew at Ringway on 4 January 1940 with a modified Merlin III, and it was not until 6 April 1940 that the first was flown with the intended Merlin VIII engine. After that production proceeded smoothly and by the end of 1940 a total of 159 Fulmars had been delivered. No. 808 Squadron at Worthy Down was the first to receive **Fulmar Mk I** aircraft in June 1940 and, as production increased, so squadrons were formed or re-equipped, but by 1943 the Fulmar was being replaced by the Seafire and Fairey Firefly. The last of 602 Fulmars was delivered to the Fleet Air Arm in February 1943. Of this total, the first 250 were Fulmar Mk I aircraft, while subsequent aircraft were to the **Fulmar Mk II** standard. These had the 1,300-hp (969-kW) Merlin 30 engine, a new propeller, tropical equipment and various other changes. A useful weight reduction of 350 lb (159 kg) had also been achieved, and although the

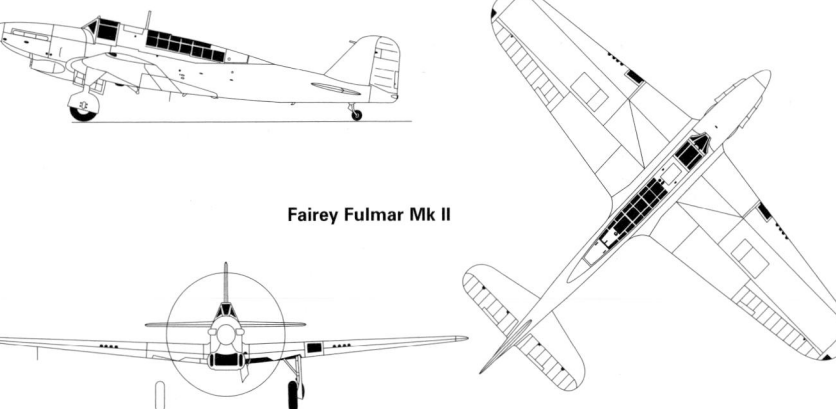

Fairey Fulmar Mk II

The Fulmar first saw action with the Fleet Air Arm, defending the Malta convoys against the Italian air force in September/October 1940. This early production Fulmar Mk I served with No. 806 Sqn from June 1940. Soon afterwards, it embarked in HMS Illustrious.

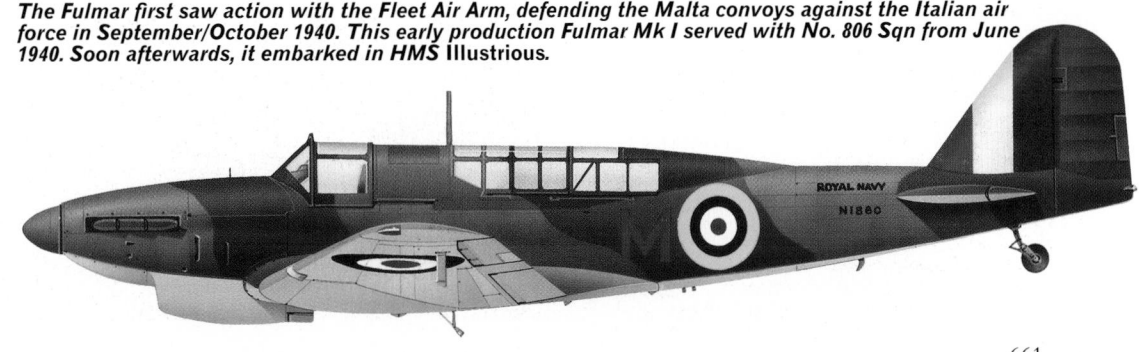

Fulmar Mk II DR673 was fitted with the later Merlin Mk 30 engine and tropical equipment. Note the extensive glazing of the observer's cockpit.

Fulmar Mk II was only a little faster than the Fulmar Mk I, it had a much better climb rate.

Tests with a night-fighter model began in 1941, following a series of night attacks on the Mediterranean Fleet by Italian air force torpedo-bombers. Installation of Air Interception Mk VI (AI.Mk VI) radar was carried out on a Fulmar Mk II at Lee-on-Solent, but the poor results led to this equip-ment's replacement by a modified AI.Mk IV radar. Extra drag and other prob-lems held up the issue to front-line squadrons until February 1944, but this version was used from June 1942 to train night-fighter crews in preparation for the Fairey Firefly. About 100 Fulmar Mk II fighters were converted to night-fighter standard, in more or less equal numbers for operational and training purposes. Moreover, the arrival of a new lightweight, high-frequency wireless telegraphy set, in early 1942, enabled the Fulmar to operate effectively as long-range reconnaissance aircraft over the expanse of Indian Ocean.

The Fulmar figured briefly in the early stages of experiments to prove the feasibility of the cata-pult-launching of fighters from armed merchant ships. Intended to provide some protection for convoys, such an operation was invariably a one-way trip as there was nowhere to land back on board. After combat the pilot had to bale out and hope to be picked up by one of the convoy.

As the Firefly began to enter service in 1943, so the Fulmar was withdrawn until the only remaining example, by coincidence the first one built, returned to Fairey as a communica-tions aircraft. Later, for a short time, it flew in its original colours before being grounded, and is now preserved in the Fleet Air Arm Museum at RNAS Yeovilton.

SPECIFICATION	
Fairey Fulmar Mk I	
Type: two-seat carrierborne fighter **Powerplant:** one Rolls-Royce Merlin VIII Vee piston engine rated at 1,080 hp (805 kW) **Performance:** maximum speed 247 mph (398 km/h) at 9,000 ft (2745 m); cruising speed 235 mph (378 km/h) at optimum altitude; initial climb rate 1,105 ft (337 m) per minute; service ceiling 21,500 ft (6555 m); range 830 miles (1336 km); patrol endurance 4 hours	**Weights:** empty 6,915 lb (3137 kg); normal take-off 9,672 lb (4387 kg) **Dimensions:** wingspan 46 ft 4½ in (14.14 m); length 40 ft 2 in (12.24 m); height 14 ft (4.27 m); wing area 342.00 sq ft (31.77 m²) **Armament:** eight 0.303-in (7.7-mm) Browning fixed forward-firing machine-guns in the leading edges of the wing and, on some aircraft, one 0.303-in (7.7-mm) Vickers 'K' trainable rearward-firing machine-gun in the rear of the cockpit

Fairey Gannet

This Gannet AS.Mk 1 is depicted as it appeared when serving aboard HMS Ark Royal with 815 Sqn in the late 1950s.

Specification GR.17/45 for a carrierborne anti-subma-rine/attack aircraft attracted tenders from Fairey and Blackburn, which received contracts for two and three proto-types respectively. The Blackburn aircraft comprised the Y.A.7 and Y.A.8, both with Rolls-Royce Griffon piston engines, and the Y.A.5. The latter had been designed for the projected Napier Naiad coupled turboprop engine but, on the discontinuation of this engine, it was redesigned as the Y.B.1 to take the Armstrong Siddeley Double Mamba coupled turboprop engine. The **Fairey Gannet** was also designed around the Double Mamba. This engine had a number of advantages over conven-tional powerplants: each half could be controlled independently, enabling an aircraft to cruise on one half while the other was shut down, thereby reduc-ing fuel consumption and extending range; and each engine drove a four-bladed propeller, these turning in opposite directions, so that there was no question of the asymmetric-thrust problem usually associated with twin-engined aircraft.

The Gannet prototype, then known as the Fairey 17, first flew on 19 September 1949 at Aldermaston, with the second following on 6 July 1950. Both were two-seat aircraft, but a three-seat prototype, subsequently added to the contract, flew in May 1951, two months after a production order had been placed. In June 1950 the first proto-type became the first turboprop-engined aircraft to land on an aircraft-carrier when it began trials with HMS *Illustrious*. The first production example of the **Gannet AS.Mk 1** flew in June 1953, and the type entered service with No. 703 Service Trials Squadron at Ford, when four production aircraft were delivered in April 1954. The first operational unit was No. 826 Squadron at Lee-on-Solent, which formed in January 1955.

Development of the Double Mamba engine resulted in an uprated version, the Mk 101, which provided 3,035 eshp (2263 ekW), and the intro-duction of this powerplant, together with some detail changes in equipment, produced the **Gannet AS.Mk 4** which supplanted the AS.Mk 1 on the production line. Total build for the two vari-ants was 255, the majority being Gannet AS.Mk 1s, and this completed the Fleet Air Arm's anti-submarine re-equipment programme, permitting replacement of the remaining Firefly aircraft and Grumman Avengers.

The requirement for trainers led to the **Gannet T.Mk 2** and **Gannet T.Mk 5**, which were versions of the Gannet AS.Mk 1 and Gannet AS.Mk 4 respectively. These had dual controls, and the retractable radar radome under the fuselage was not fitted. The prototype Gannet T.Mk 2 was a converted Gannet AS.Mk 1, and production totalled 37 Gannet T.Mk 2s and eight Gannet T.Mk 5s.

The FAA's need for an airborne early warning aircraft to replace its Skyraiders led in 1957 to the **Gannet AEW.Mk 3**: the prototype first flew in August 1958 and was followed by 43 production aircraft with the 3,875-eshp (2890-ekW) Double Mamba Mk 112 engine. The AEW.Mk 3 was a major redesign, incorporating a completely new fuselage and longer-stroke landing gear to provide clearance for the radome, and entered service in 1960. The variant equipped only one unit, No. 849 Sqn, and had the dubious distinction of being the last Fairey aircraft to serve with the Royal Navy.

Left: With the modification of the Gannet airframe to AEW.Mk 3 standard came the addition of a huge radome beneath the forward fuselage.

Below: This aircraft was the first of 15 Gannet AS.Mk 4s for the West German navy. Note the open bomb bay doors and the feathered forward propeller.

Fairey Gannet (cont.)

The Royal Navy's Gannets were also the last conventional fixed-wing aircraft to serve with the FAA in the carrierborne role and the last Gannet AEW.Mk 3 was retired late in 1978. The Gannet AS.Mk 1 and Gannet AS.Mk 4 had been replaced by Westland Wessex helicopters by July 1960, although a few Gannet AS.Mk 4s were fitted with new radar and electronics in a refurbishment programme during 1961 to become **Gannet AS.Mk 6** aircraft and serving with No. 831 Squadron.

The West German navy's air arm bought 15 Gannet AS.Mk 4s and one Gannet T.Mk 5 in 1958, and the following year the Indonesian naval air arm ordered 18 Gannet AS.Mk 4 and T.Mk 5 machines. Two squadrons of the Royal Australian Navy received Gannets at Culdrose in August 1955, returning to Australia on HMS *Melbourne*: the RAN's total force was 33 Gannet AS.Mk 1s and three Gannet T.Mk 2s. A number of Gannets has survived in museums, but perhaps the most surprising sale was a Gannet AEW.Mk 3 to a US private owner in 1982.

SPECIFICATION

Fairey Gannet AS.Mk 1
Type: three-seat carrierborne anti-submarine aircraft
Powerplant: one Armstrong Siddeley Double Mamba ASMD.1 Mk 100 turboprop engine rated at 2,950 ehp (2200 ekW)
Performance: maximum speed 311 mph (500 km/h) at optimum altitude; cruising speed 299 mph (481 km/h) at optimum altitude; service ceiling 25,000 ft (7620 m); range 662 miles (1066 km)
Weights: empty 15,069 lb (6835 kg); maximum take-off 21,600 lb (9798 kg)
Dimensions: wingspan 54 ft 4 in (16.56 m); length 43 ft (13.11 m); height 13 ft 8½ in (4.18 m); wing area 482.80 sq ft (44.85 m²)
Armament: up to 2,000 lb (907 kg) of disposable stores carried in a lower-fuselage weapons bay and generally comprising two homing torpedoes, depth charges or mines, and up to 16 60-lb (27-kg) air-to-surface unguided rockets carried under the wing

Fairey Gordon and Seal

When the time came to replace the ubiquitous Fairey IIIF, it was decided that the best replacement would, in fact, be an improved Fairey IIIF. Thus the prototype, initially identified as the **Fairey IIIF Mk V** but later named as the **Gordon**, was a conversion from a Fairey IIIF Mk IVM with the powerplant of one 525-hp (391-kW) Armstrong Siddeley Panther IIA radial engine instead of the original 570-hp (425-kW) Napier Lion. While the resulting reduction in available power might seem to have been a retrograde step, the Gordon had a loaded weight some 400 lb (181 kg) less than that of the Fairey IIIF Mk IVM and therefore possessed superior performance, particularly on take-off. Other changes were made in the electrical, fuel and oil systems, and in the mounting of the forward-firing machine-gun.

Ordered to Specification 18/30 for a two-seat day bomber and general-purpose aircraft, the first Gordon flew on 3 March 1931. Construction records appear to be a little unreliable, but about 185 Gordons were built for the Royal Air Force before production ended in 1934,

this total including a small number of trainers and the last 24 first-line aircraft to the **Gordon Mk II** standard with detail improvements and a taller vertical tail surface. Around 90 in-service Fairey IIIFs were also converted to Gordon standard. In addition, about 20 aircraft were exported, these being delivered to Brazil and China.

The first deliveries of Gordon Mk Is to the RAF were made in April 1931, the initial unit to receive the new type being No. 40 Squadron at Upper Heyford, and the first overseas squadron to be equipped was No. 6, a former Bristol Fighter unit, in the Middle East. Aircraft from Nos 35 and 207 Squadrons formed part of the RAF reinforcement of the Middle East during the Abyssinian crisis of 1935. The Gordon was still serving with first-line squadrons at home and overseas in 1938, and many were used for target-towing duties on

the outbreak of World War II. The last surviving example was still on charge as late as September 1941, but before this time a number of ex-RAF Gordons had been handed over to Egypt and New Zealand.

Contemporary with the Gordon was the FAA's **Seal**, of which the prototype was also a Fairey IIIF conversion, in this instance a Mk IIIB, originally designated as the **Fairey IIIF Mk VI**. Some 91 aircraft of this type were ordered, but possibly only 90 of these were completed, and delivery of the first Seals off the production line began in 1933, the process continuing to March 1935. Basically similar to the Gordon, the Seal differed primarily in its accommodation for a crew of three and its naval equipment. This latter included optional float or wheel landing gear, including a tailwheel and mainwheel brakes, an arrester hook, catapult attachment points,

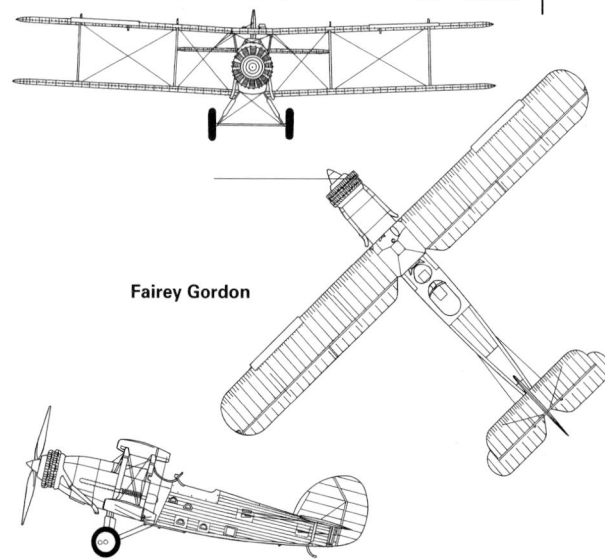

Fairey Gordon

flotation bags and slinging gear. The first units to be equipped were Nos 820 and 821 Squadrons, on board HMS *Courageous*, and the Seal remained in FAA use until the outbreak of World War II. The last Seals were operated by No. 273 Squadron of the

RAF, based in Ceylon, flying patrols over the Indian Ocean from August 1939 to April 1942. In addition to those built for the FAA, the Seal was produced to meet export orders placed by Argentina, Chile, Latvia and Peru.

Optional floats enabled the Seal to be deployed on warships in its catapult-launched floatplane configuration.

SPECIFICATION

Fairey Gordon Mk I
Type: two-seat day bomber and general-purpose aircraft
Powerplant: one Armstrong Siddeley Panther IIA radial piston engine rated at 525 hp (391 kW)
Performance: maximum speed 145 mph (233 km/h) at 3,000 ft (915 m); cruising speed 110 mph (177 km/h) at optimum altitude; initial climb rate 1,000 ft (305 m) per minute; service ceiling 22,000 ft (6705 m); range 600 miles (966 km)
Weights: empty 3,500 lb (1588 kg); maximum take-off 5,906 lb (2679 kg)
Dimensions: wingspan 45 ft 9 in (13.94 m); length 36 ft 9 in (11.20 m); height 14 ft 2 in (4.32 m); wing area 438.0 sq ft (40.69 m²)
Armament: one 0.303-in (7.7-mm) Vickers fixed forward-firing machine-gun in the forward fuselage and one 0.303-in (7.7-mm) Lewis trainable rearward-firing machine-gun in the rear cockpit, plus up to 500 lb (227 kg) of disposable stores carried on hardpoints under the lower wing, and generally comprising free-fall bombs

Fairey Gyrodyne and Jet Gyrodyne

In April 1946 Fairey announced a private-venture project for a rotary-wing aircraft to be built to a new concept originated by Dr J. A. J. Bennett, who had joined the company the previous year. Dr Bennett had assumed control of the Cierva Autogyro Company in 1936, following the death of Juan de la Cierva, and his ideas were based on the combination of a

lifting rotor plus a single asymmetric propeller mounted on a stub wing which would counteract yaw and provide thrust, lessening the loading of the main rotor.

A government contract to Specification E.4/46 was awarded for two prototypes, and the first

Gyrodyne was exhibited almost complete at White Waltham on 7 December 1946, and continued to build up flying time until March 1948 when it was dismantled for a thorough examination. The second prototype, basically similar to the first but with more comfortable interior

The Gyrodyne was a novel attempt at producing a helicopter, with a fixed propeller fulfilling both propulsive and anti-torque functions.

Although scheduled for scrapping in 1961, the Jet Gyrodyne was rescued and, after a somewhat chequered history, has been preserved.

furnishings befitting its role as a passenger demonstrator, was flying by the time of the next Farnborough air display in September 1948.

The first Gyrodyne was reassembled and, following further test-flying, it was decided to use this machine for an attempt on the world helicopter straight-line speed record. On 28 June 1948, flown by test pilot Basil Arkell, the Gyrodyne made two flights in each direction over a 3-km (1.86-mile)

course at White Waltham, achieving an average of 124.30 mph (200 km/h), enough to secure the record. An attempt was to be made in April 1949 to set a 100-km (62.10-mile) closed-circuit record, but two days before the date selected a rotor head fatigue failure resulted in the crash of the aircraft, killing the pilot and his observer. The subsequent grounding of the second Gyrodyne for an investigation was only to be expected, and the aircraft

did not appear again until 1953. By then, it had been completely redesigned to provide data on Fairey's big helicopter project, the Rotodyne.

The **Jet Gyrodyne**, as the machine had been redesignated, was the subject of a Ministry of Supply research contract. Its function was to continue testing the tip-jet principle and develop procedures for the compound helicopter concept epitomised by the Rotodyne. While the Jet Gyrodyne retained the basic

appearance and engine of the earlier model, it had a two-bladed main rotor with a diameter of 60 ft (18.29 m) and pressure burners at the tips, in place of the Gyrodyne's conventional three-bladed rotor, and at each end of the stub wing was a Fairey variable-pitch pusher propeller. These two propellers were driven by the Leonides engine, which no longer drove the main rotor; instead, two Rolls-Royce

Merlin compressors pumped air under pressure to the rotor tips, where it was mixed with fuel and burned to produce thrust.

Tethered flights at White Waltham were followed by the first free flight in January 1954, but a full transition to horizontal from vertical flight was not achieved until March 1955. By September 1956 some 190 transitions and 140 autorotative landings had been made.

SPECIFICATION	
Fairey Gyrodyne	range 250 miles (401 km)
Type: four/five-seat experimental helicopter	**Weights:** empty 3,600 lb (1633 kg); maximum take-off 4,800 lb (2177 kg)
Powerplant: one Alvis Leonides radial piston engine rated at 520 hp (388 kW)	**Dimensions:** rotor diameter 51 ft 9 in (15.77 m); stub wing span 16 ft 8 in (5.08 m); fuselage length 25 ft (7.62 m); height 10 ft 2 in (3.10 m); rotor disc area 2,103.35 sq ft (195.40 m²)
Performance: maximum speed 140 mph (225 km/h) at optimum altitude; cruising speed 110 mph (177 km/h) at optimum altitude;	

Fairey Hendon

The Air Ministry's Specification B.19/27 for a heavy night bomber resulted in contracts for two contrasting aircraft: the Handley Page Heyford biplane and the **Hendon** metal/fabric monoplane. The latter was a more advanced design with superior overall performance, but various problems during test-flying necessitated some redesign, and as a result the bulk of the production orders went to the Heyford, of which 121 were built against just 14 examples of the Hendon.

The type first flew in **Hendon Mk I** prototype form with two Bristol Jupiter air-cooled

radial engines on 17 November 1931: reports do not agree on the powerplant, one saying 460-hp (343-kW) Jupiter VIII engines and another 525-hp (391-kW) Jupiter XFs. In the event, the Jupiter engines were replaced the following year with 480-hp (358-kW) Rolls-Royce Kestrel IIIS liquid-cooled Vee engines, but these were replaced on the production **Hendon Mk II** by Kestrel VIs. Production aircraft were built between September 1936 and March 1937, the first entering service in November 1936. The type equipped only one unit, No. 38 Squadron, where the Hendon replaced the

Pictured here in prototype form, the Hendon took on an unusual tail-high attitude in cruising flight.

Heyford, although one flight was detached to form No. 115 Sqn.

The Hendon was the RAF's first monoplane to enter squadron service. It was also Fairey's first conventional twin-engined aircraft if one discounts the F.2 of 1917, and had a number of interesting features. The bombs and fuel were carried internally and a catwalk linked the tail and nose gun positions; the crew had enclosed cockpits, a feature planned originally for the prototype but later dropped in favour of open ones and reinstated for production aircraft. Additional contracts for 62 more Hendons were placed but later cancelled; these were to Specification B.20/34 and would have incorporated

695-hp (518-kW) Kestrel VI supercharged engines, a rotating nose turret and other improvements.

Only two Hendons were lost in accidents (one of them involving an aircraft

flown by a member of ground crew who had never before sat in an aircraft) before the type was replaced by the Vickers Wellington, from November 1938.

SPECIFICATION	
Fairey Hendon Mk II	**Dimensions:** wingspan 101 ft 9 in (31.01 m); length 60 ft 9 in (18.52 m); height 18 ft 9 in (5.72 m); wing area 1,447.00 sq ft (134.43 m²)
Type: five-seat heavy bomber	
Powerplant: two Rolls-Royce Kestrel VI Vee piston engines each rated at 600 hp (448 kW)	
Performance: maximum speed 155 mph (249 km/h) at 15,000 ft (4570 m); cruising speed 133 mph (214 km/h) at 15,000 ft (4570 m); initial climb rate 940 ft (287 m) per minute; service ceiling 21,400 ft (6525 m); range 1,360 miles (2189 km)	**Armament:** one 0.303-in (7.7-mm) Lewis trainable machine-gun in each of the nose, dorsal and tail positions, plus up to 1,660 lb (753 kg) of disposable stores in a lower-fuselage weapons bay and on two underfuselage hardpoints, and generally comprising one 1,000-lb (454-kg), or six 250-lb (113-kg) or 12 112-lb (51-kg) bombs carried internally and eight 20-lb (9.1-kg) bombs carried externally
Weights: empty 12,773 lb (5794 kg); maximum take-off 20,000 lb (9072 kg)	

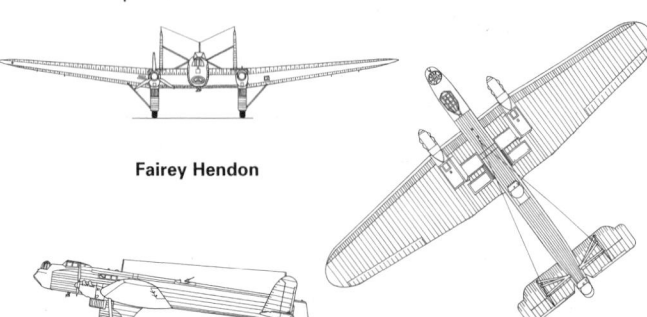

Fairey Hendon

Fairey Long-Range Monoplane

In the period between the two world wars there was much prestige to be gained from successful record-breaking flights: the Schneider Trophy contests led the way in speed, but there were many individual aircraft used in attempts to

set new long-distance records. The aircraft varied from modified production airframes to new types designed specifically for the task. The **Fairey Long-Range Monoplane** was in the latter category, two being built for the Air

Ministry to Specification 33/27. Wind tunnel tests with models had convinced Fairey that a high-wing cantilever layout would be the most advantageous, and the first Monoplane flew at Northolt on 14 November 1928 with

the powerplant of one 570-hp (425-kW) Napier Lion XIA W-type engine. The specification required a range of around 5,000 miles (8045 km), and by the time the Monoplane flew, the world's absolute distance record in a straight line was 4,466 miles (7187 km), set by a Savoia S.64. A number of problems was encoun-

tered with the Monoplane's engine, which delayed a 24-hour endurance flight to Cairo until March 1929, more than three months later than intended. The original record attempt was to have been made between Cranwell and Cape Town, but the delays also caused this to be cancelled.

Fairey Long-Range Monoplane (continued)

By April 1929, when the delays had finally been overcome, the weather on the South African route was unsuitable. Instead, it was decided to try for Bangalore in southern India. But various problems were encountered before and during the flight, which ended at Karachi. A distance of 4,130 miles (6647 km) had been covered in 50 hours 37 minutes, but there was insufficient fuel to complete the flight which was, nevertheless, the first non-stop flight from the UK to India. In December 1929 the Monoplane left Cranwell for Cape Town, in an attempt to better a 4,912-mile (7905-km) record established by a Breguet Bre.19 between Paris and Manchuria, but the flight ended in tragedy when the Monoplane, for reasons never established,

flew into high ground near Tunis, killing both pilots.

As a result of experience with the first aircraft, a revised Specification 14/30 was issued for the second, which was much better equipped. This **Long-Range Monoplane II** first flew on 30 June 1931 and was handed over to the RAF a month later. An automatic pilot developed by RAE Farnborough was installed, together with an impressive array of instrumentation. On return from a proving flight to Egypt the aircraft was slightly damaged in a forced landing, but repairs were effected and on 6 February 1933 the aircraft left Cranwell and flew 5,410 miles (8707 km) to Walvis Bay, South-West Africa, in 57 hours 25 minutes to set a new record; the great circle distance was 5,341 miles (8595 km). Three months

later that record was smashed by the Blériot-Zappata 110, which flew a great circle route of 5,657 miles (9104 km) between New York and Syria. Thoughts of re-engining the Monoplane in 1934 with a Junkers Diesel engine, for an estimated range of up to 8,300 miles (13358 km), came to nothing.

The final fate of the Long-Range Monoplane II does not seem to have been recorded. Note that the aircraft featured large wheel spats.

SPECIFICATION	
Fairey Long-Range Monoplane II	5,550 miles (8932 km)
Type: two-seat long-range aircraft	**Weights:** maximum take-off 17,500 lb (7938 kg)
Powerplant: one Napier Lion IXA W-type piston engine rated at 570-hp (425 kW)	**Dimensions:** wingspan 82 ft (24.99 m); length 48 ft 6 in (14.78 m); height 12 ft (3.66 m); wing area 850.00 sq ft (78.97 m²)
Performance: cruising speed 110 mph (177 km/h); still-air range	

Fairey Pintail and Fawn

An Air Ministry specification of May 1919 for a two-seat amphibian floatplane that would also be capable of operation from the flight decks of aircraft-carriers, attracted two designs in the forms of the Parnall Puffin and **Fairey Pintail**. The latter was the first wholly new aircraft designed by Fairey after World War I. The **Pintail Mk I**, the first of three prototypes, flew on 7 July 1920, with the **Pintail Mk II** and **Pintail Mk III** following on 25 May and 8 November 1921 respectively. There were minor differences in fuselage

lengths and the type of amphibian gear, the latter having given some problems and therefore becoming the subject of several modifications before it was decided not to retract the wheels but to leave them partly protruding from the floats, with shrouds ahead of them to help water operations.

While no British order was forthcoming, the Imperial Japanese navy ordered three aircraft in August 1923. The first of these flew a year later and all three were delivered in November 1924. Some changes were made in the

Japanese aircraft, known under the designation **Pintail Mk IV**, including an increase in the gap between the wing and fuselage.

Although only six examples of its Pintail had been built, Fairey felt that there was considerable development potential in the basic concept and thus proceeded with the development of a landplane version as the **Fairey Fawn**, which was put forward to meet Specification 5/21 for an army co-operation biplane. Ironically, the design was eventually produced as a day bomber to a later specification, the prototype Fawn flying in March 1923. Trials showed that a longer fuselage was needed and the next two Fawns were 'stretched' to create the **Fawn Mk II** version. Two more prototypes followed, and the first production example of the Fawn flew in January 1924.

Fifty production aircraft were ordered as Fawn Mk IIs, and these were followed by two more batches totalling 20 examples of the **Fawn Mk III**,

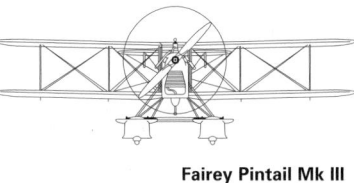
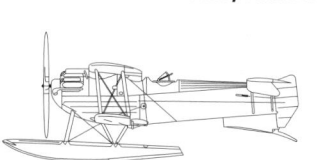

Fairey Pintail Mk III

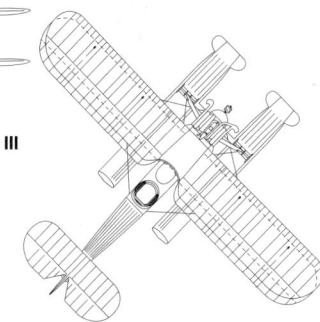

SPECIFICATION	
Fairey Fawn Mk II	**Dimensions:** wingspan 49 ft 11 in (15.21 m); length 32 ft 1 in (9.78 m); height 11 ft 11 in (3.63 m); wing area 550.00 sq ft (51.10 m²)
Type: two-seat day bomber	
Powerplant: one Napier Lion II W-type piston engine rated at 470 hp (350 kW)	
Performance: maximum speed 114 mph (183 km/h) at sea level; cruising speed 93 mph (150 km/h) at 10,000 ft (3050 m); climb to 10,000 ft (3050 m) in 17 minutes 24 seconds; service ceiling 13,850 ft (4220 m); range 650 miles (1046 km)	**Armament:** one 0.303-in (7.7-mm) Vickers fixed forward-firing machine-gun on the port side of the forward fuselage and two 0.303-in (7.7-mm) Lewis trainable rearward-firing machine-guns in the rear cockpit, plus up to 460 lb (209 kg) of disposable stores carried under the lower wing, and generally comprising bombs
Weights: empty 3,481 lb (1579 kg); maximum take-off 5,834 lb (2646 kg)	

The Fawn served with five UK-based bomber units, namely Nos 11, 12, 100, 503 and 602 Squadrons. A Fawn Mk II is illustrated.

which had the Napier Lion V rather than Lion II engine. Some of the later Fawns had turbocharged Lion VI

engines, although these did not enter squadron service and were instead used for test work.

Fairey Rotodyne

With the concept of the convertible helicopter proved on a small scale with the Jet Gyrodyne, the proposal put forward by Dr J. A. J. Bennett and Captain A. G. Forsyth in 1947 for a large compound helicopter looked viable, and various designs were considered. In December

1951 British European Airways issued a specification for a 30/40-seat passenger aircraft for short/medium-haul routes, and Fairey submitted a proposal along with other manufacturers. The layout corresponded roughly with Fairey's ideas, and in 1953 the company received a

Ministry of Supply research contract for a single prototype.

Test rigs were established at White Waltham and Boscombe Down, where an elaborate installation eventually comprised the rotor assembly, both engines, stub wings, etc., with all controls in a hut where the aircraft's nose would have been. Extensive testing was

carried out while the prototype was under construction. The **Rotodyne** made its first flight as a helicopter on 6 November 1957, and it was not until April 1958 that the first transition to normal flight was made.

The basic layout of the Rotodyne was a square-section fuselage with an untapered stub wing on which were mounted two

Eland turboprops for forward propulsion. The main wheels of the tricycle landing gear retracted forward into the nacelles and the nosewheel forward into the fuselage below the cockpit. Twin fin-and-rudder assemblies, later supplemented by a central fin, were mounted on an untapered tailplane set on top of the rear fuselage. A large four-bladed rotor for vertical take-off and landing was driven by tip jets which received compressed air from the Eland engines via a compressor; each engine fed air to two opposing rotor blades to ensure that, in the event of an engine failure, there would be enough pressure in the remaining engine to keep two of the four tip jets burning.

Following its success in establishing a world speed record with the Gyrodyne, Fairey decided that the Rotodyne's performance would enable it to emulate this feat, and on 5 January 1959 it set a record in the compound helicopter class with an average speed of 190.90 mph (307.20 km/h) over a 100-km (62.10-mile) closed circuit; this record stood until October 1961, when the Soviets beat it with the Kamov Ka-22.

At this stage the Rotodyne's future looked bright: during 1958 the Kaman Aircraft Corporation of the USA had secured a licensing agreement for sales and service in the USA with a possibility of manufacture there. Okanagan Helicopters of Vancouver was interested in three and

Japan Air Lines was considering the type for domestic routes; and the biggest potential customer was New York Airways, which joined with Kaman in a letter of intent for five plus options on 10 aircraft, for delivery in 1964, to an enlarged standard with 54/65-seat accommodation and Rolls-Royce Tyne turboprop engines.

Fairey needed up to £10 million to develop this version, and was offered 50 per cent of this by the government if BEA would

place a firm order; the government contribution was to be a loan repayable by a sales levy. In 1960 Fairey merged with Westland and although initially the Rotodyne project looked secure, it was not. In April 1960 Okanagan cancelled its order because of the long delivery dates, and five months later New York Airways expressed similar concern over the delay in production plans. Westland was then involved in taking over Bristol's helicopter programme as well

as other work in hand, and these factors combined with the ever-increasing weight of the Rotodyne, which reached a stage at which the Eland could no longer be

Only a single Rotodyne was completed and flown. But for development problems, the type might have formed the basis of a revolutionary, if complex, transport aircraft.

developed and the Tyne could not be afforded, to cause the withdrawal of government support. The project was therefore cancelled in February 1962.

SPECIFICATION	
Fairey Rotodyne	**Weights:** maximum take-off
Type: two-crew experimental	33,000 lb (14969 kg)
compound helicopter	**Dimensions:** rotor diameter 90 ft
Powerplant: two Napier Eland	(27.43 m); wingspan 46 ft 6 in
NEl.7 turboprop engines each rated	(14.17 m); length 58 ft 8 in
at 2,800 shp (2088 kW)	(17.88 m); height 22 ft 2 in
Performance: maximum speed	(6.76 m); rotor disc area
185 mph (298 km/h) at optimum	6,361.72 sq ft (591.00 m²)
altitude; range 450 miles (724 km)	**Payload:** up to 40 passengers

Fairey Seafox

Two of the less glamorous but necessary tasks performed by Fleet Air Arm aircraft in the period between the two world wars were the fleet gunnery-spotting and reconnaissance roles, undertaken by aircraft catapulted from capital ships. Specification S.11/32 for such an aircraft attracted a tender from Fairey for a biplane floatplane with a crew of two. The design was unusual in that the pilot sat in an open cockpit while the observer/gunner was in an enclosed rear cockpit. This arrangement allowed the pilot an excellent view during catapult launches and also gave him freedom of movement during the

subsequent recovery of the aircraft from the sea by crane. Construction was mixed, the fuselage being a metal monocoque and the wings being fabric-covered. Fairey's bid was accepted, and a contract for 49 **Seafox** aircraft was awarded in January 1936, with a follow-on contract for a further 15 in September of the same year.

As originally designed, the Seafox was to have had a 500-hp (373-kW) Bristol Aquila radial engine, but for some obscure reason the Napier Rapier air-cooled 16-cylinder H-type engine of only 395 hp (295 kW) was then chosen, and the Seafox was consequently under-

FAA units equipped with the Seafox were Nos 702, 713, 714, 716 and 718 Flights, and in January 1940 these flights were pooled to form No. 700 Squadron. The type also served with Nos 753 and 754 Squadrons in the training role.

powered throughout its life. The first prototype flew at Hamble on 27 May 1936, while the second, with wheeled landing gear, followed on 5 November 1936 although this machine was later converted to floatplane configuration.

The Seafox began to come off the production line in 1937, the first being delivered on 23 April. Catapult tests at the Royal Aircraft Establishment in March 1937 were followed by trials on board HMS *Neptune* off Gibraltar and, as they became available, production aircraft were formed into catapult flights. At the outbreak of World War II, the Seafox aircraft equipped a number of cruisers, sharing their task with Supermarine Walrus amphibians and Fairey Swordfish floatplanes, and it was not long before they

were in action against the German pocket battleship *Admiral Graf Spee* during the action in the River Plate in December 1939. One of the two Seafoxes from the cruiser HMS *Ajax* was catapulted and spotted for the guns, winning for its pilot, Lieutenant E. D. G. Lewin, the Distinguished Service

Cross as the first Fleet Air Arm decoration of the war.

Seafox production ended in 1938, but the type continued in front-line service until about 1942, when it was replaced on ships' catapults by the Vought Kingfisher. Even then, a few Seafoxes lingered on in the training role until July 1943.

SPECIFICATION	
Fairey Seafox	maximum take-off 5,420 lb (2458 kg)
Type: two-seat spotter and	**Dimensions:** wingspan 40 ft
reconnaissance floatplane	(10.81 m); length 35 ft 5½ in
Powerplant: one Napier Rapier VI	(10.81 m); height 12 ft 1 in (3.68 m);
H-type piston engine rated at	wing area 434.00 sq ft (40.32 m²)
395 hp (295 kW)	**Armament:** one 0.303-in (7.7-mm)
Performance: maximum speed	Lewis trainable rearward-firing
124 mph (200 km/h) at 5,860 ft	machine-gun in the rear cockpit,
(1,785 m); cruising speed 106 mph	plus up to 360 lb (163 kg) of
(171 km/h) at optimum altitude;	disposable stores carried on four
climb to 5,000 ft (1525 m) in	underwing hardpoints, and
15 minutes 30 seconds; service	generally comprising two 100-lb
ceiling 9,700 ft (2955 m); range	(45-kg) anti-submarine bombs and
440 miles (708 km)	eight 20-lb (9.10-kg) bombs
Weights: empty 3,805 lb (1726 kg);	

All the Seafoxes were built as floatplanes except the second prototype, which was completed and flown as a landplane. In 1937, it was modified to floatplane configuration for trials.

Fairey Swordfish

The origins of the **Fairey Swordfish** lie within the **S.9/30**, designed in response to a fleet spotter-reconnaissance specification issued in June 1930, to which the Gloster FS.36 was the other contender. The first S.9/30 was flown on 22 February 1934, and by this time the original specification had been abandoned. The Rolls-Royce Kestrel-powered S.9/30 was, however, tested experimentally in both landplane and float-plane form between 1933-4.

However, Fairey had already built the private-venture **TSR I**, a torpedo-spotter-reconnaissance aircraft intended for the Greek navy, in 1932-3. Completed almost a year before the S.9/30, the Armstrong Siddeley Panther-powered TSR I made its first flight on 21 March 1933. Aside from its radial engine, the TSR I was superficially similar to the S.9/30. After being refitted with a Bristol Pegasus engine, the TSR I was lost in an accident in September 1933, but the promise it had displayed led to the first **TSR II** (K4190), the prototype for the **Swordfish**.

The TSR II made its maiden flight on 17 April 1934, less than two months after the original S.9/30 had flown. Designed to meet the specification S.15/33 for a torpedo-spotter-reconnaissance aircraft, the TSR II was externally similar to the TSR I, and incorporated a Bristol Pegasus IIIM3 nine-cylinder radial engine. In June 1934 the TSR II began catapult trials at RAE Farnborough, followed by deck-landing tests on HMS *Courageous*. The aircraft was then fitted with floats for waterborne

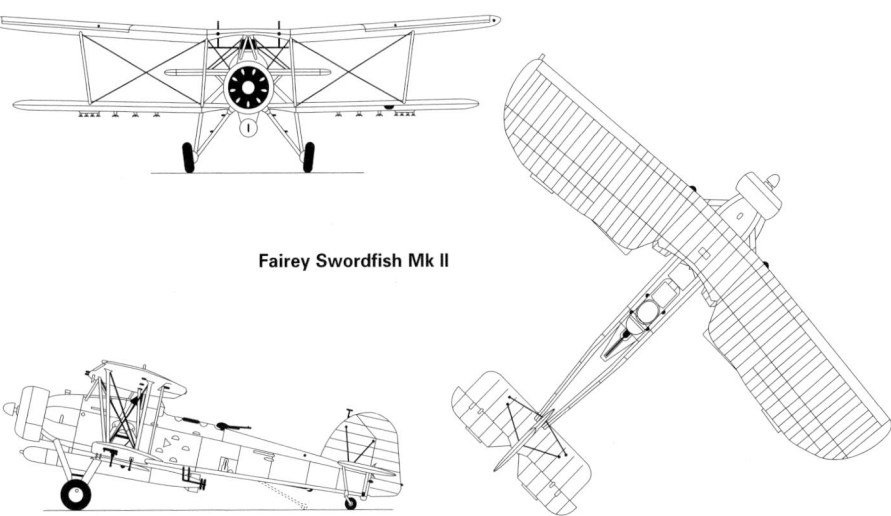

With 'invasion stripes' partly obscuring its 'Royal Navy' titles and serial number, this Swordfish Mk II is armed with eight 60-lb (27-kg) RPs. Note also the extended arrester hook.

Fairey Swordfish Mk II

tests, and then went to the Torpedo Trials Unit at Gosport, where it later crashed.

Favourable test reports completed in April 1935 led to a production aircraft, the **Swordfish Mk I**, for which orders for three development aircraft, and a production batch of 86 were placed in April-May 1935. The first Swordfish Mk Is began to reach Fleet air Arm squadrons in July 1936, when No. 825 Sqn took them on in place of their Fairey Seals, and operated them from HMS *Glorious* into the war. By 1938, the Swordfish Mk I had become the FAA's sole operational torpedo-bomber, replacing Blackburn Sharks and Blackburn Baffins as well as Seals.

At the outbreak of the war, the FAA was equipped with 13 front-line Swordfish squadrons, and a further 12 were activated during the conflict. There were additionally 22 wartime second- line squadrons, and 11 catapult flights (two with float-equipped Swordfish). The latter units were later formed into No. 700 Sqn. During the war, the FAA's

Swordfish first saw action in the Norwegian campaign, and went on to see service in the Mediterranean, the Western desert, Iraq, the Battle of the Atlantic, and in support of convoys bound for Russia. The Swordfish was instrumental in the destruction of among others, the U-boat *U-64* (the first German submarine to be claimed by the FAA during the

war), much of the French fleet at Oran in July 1940 following the D-Day evacuation, the Italian fleet at Taranto, and the German battleship *Bismarck*. The Swordfish is credited with the destruction of a greater tonnage of enemy shipping than any other Allied aircraft during World War II. However, the abortive attack on the German battle-cruisers *Scharnhorst* and

Gneisenau and the heavy cruiser *Prinz Eugen* in the English Channel in February 1942 marked the last use of the Swordfish in its original torpedo-bomber role. Thereafter, the Swordfish was primarily used in the anti-submarine role, acting as a hunter with ASV radar, and as a killer with depth charges, and later under-wing rockets, operating mainly from merchant aircraft-carriers and escort carriers.

The Swordfish Mk I was followed in 1943 by the **Swordfish Mk II**, introducing a strengthened lower wing, metal-skin under-surfaces, and rocket-projectile capability. The same year saw the introduction of the **Swordfish Mk III**, with a modified lower wing as well as RATO capability, and an air-to-surface-vessel (ASV) Mk X radar in a radome between the undercarriage legs. The final production version, the **Swordfish Mk IV** was a Mk II with a cockpit enclosure for training in Canada. All Mk Is and some Mk IIs were powered by the Pegasus IIIM3 as utilised by the initial production batch, while remaining Mk IIs and Mk IIIs employed

As a torpedo-bombing platform, the Swordfish was without peer. Its stability and responsive controls allowed accurate weapon deployment, although the aircraft was woefully vulnerable throughout the torpedo run.

Swordfish Mk I L2742 shows the type's optional float installation to advantage. This aircraft belonged to No. 701 Catapult Flight in 1938.

the more powerful Pegasus 30.

Following 692 Fairey-built Swordfish Mk Is, from late 1940 Blackburn was responsible for the remaining planned production of 1,700 (comprising 300 Mk Is, 1,080 Mk IIs and 320 Mk IIIs), making a grand total of 2,392. A total of 99 Mk IIs and six Mk IIIs were delivered to the Royal Canadian Navy. RAF Coastal Command was another Swordfish operator, with No. 812 Sqn beginning shore-based mine-laying duties from April 1940. The last operational Swordfish squadron within the FAA, No. 836, was finally disbanded on 21 May 1945.

SPECIFICATION

Fairey Swordfish Mk I (landplane)
Type: two/three-seat carrierborne and land-based torpedo bomber and reconnaissance aircraft
Powerplant: one Bristol Pegasus IIIM radial piston engine rated at 690 hp (515 kW)
Performance: maximum speed 139 mph (224 km/h) at 4,750 ft (1450 m); cruising speed 128 mph (206 km/h) at 5,000 ft (1525 m); climb to 5,000 ft (1525 m) in 10 minutes 30 seconds; service ceiling 12,400 ft (3780 m); range 1,030 miles (1657 km) with auxiliary fuel and 546 miles (878 km) with a 1,500-lb (680-kg) bombload
Weights: empty 5,200 lb (2359 kg); maximum take-off 9,250 lb (4196 kg)
Dimensions: wingspan 45 ft 6 in (13.87 m); length 36 ft 1 in (11.00 m) with the tail down; height 12 ft 10½ in (3.92 m) with the tail down; wing area 607.00 sq ft (56.39 m²)
Armament: one 0.303-in (7.7-mm) Vickers Mk V fixed forward-firing machine-gun in the starboard side of the forward fuselage and one 0.303-in (7.7-mm) Vickers 'K' or Lewis trainable rearward-firing machine-gun in the rear cockpit, plus up to 1,610 lb (739 kg) of disposable stores carried on one underfuselage and eight underwing hardpoints, and generally comprising one 1,610-lb (739-kg) 18-in (457-mm) torpedo or one 1,500-lb (680-kg) mine carried under the fuselage, or up to 1,500 lb (680 kg) of weapons, including 500-lb (227-kg), 250-lb (113-kg) and 20-lb (9-kg) bombs, carried under the fuselage and lower wing

Farman M.F.7 'Longhorn'

Although Henry and Maurice Farman had established a collaborative business, each retained independent activities and ideas in respect of design. This accounts for designations prefixed by the differing H.F. and M.F. initials. Maurice began in 1909 by developing his own ideas for modification and improvement of the basic Voisin design, but when tested this proved to he unsatisfactory. However, experimentation during 1910 led to a successful biplane in 1911 that was the forerunner of the **Farman M.F.7**, which first appeared in 1913 and was often called the **Type 1913**.

An unequal-span biplane, with the multiplic-ity of struts and bracing wires that were then an essential component of an aircraft's structure, the M.F.7 had a central fuse-lage nacelle with open accommodation for a crew of two. Directly behind them the engine was mounted to drive a pusher propeller, its blades turning between four slender fuselage struts that served to mount the biplane tail unit. Landing gear was of the tailskid type, and extending forward from the main landing-gear structure and braced from the wings were outriggers that carried the elevator, well forward of the nose of the fuselage nacelle. An excellent identification feature, these outriggers

Two long, upward-curving supports extended from the M.F.7's lower undercarriage members to support the elevator – these gave rise to the 'Longhorn' appellation.

brought the nickname **'Longhorn'**, one that in many reference books has pre-eminence over the official M.F.7 designa-tion. Original powerplant was a 70-hp (52-kW) Renault engine, but many later models had more powerful Renaults and a proportion of the consid-erable number licence-built in the UK during World War I had a 75-hp (56-kW) Rolls-Royce Hawk 6-cylinder inline piston engine.

SPECIFICATION

Farman M.F.7
Type: two-seat utility aircraft
Powerplant: one 70-hp (52-kW) Renault 8-cylinder Vee piston engine
Performance: maximum speed about 59 mph (95 km/h); service ceiling 13,125 ft (4000 m); endurance 3 hours 15 minutes
Weights: empty 1,279 lb (580 kg); maximum take-off 1,885 lb (855 kg)
Dimensions: wingspan 50 ft 10¼ in (15.50 m); length 39 ft 9¼ in (12.00 m) height 11 ft 4 in (3.45 m); wing area 645.86 sq ft (60.00 m²)

Like many aircraft developed in the years 1912-14, the M.F.7 was adopted for use in communications and patrol duties when World War I began. But it was in the continuing role as an elementary trainer that the 'Longhorn' became best known, large numbers of Allied pilots gaining their introduction to flight in it. Over 350 were built.

Farman M.F.11 'Shorthorn' and HF.20

While retaining a similar basic configuration to the M.F.7, Maurice Farman's later development intro-duced a number of refinements but had one major difference: it dispensed with the forward elevator. Instead, what would now be regarded as a conventional elevator was adopted, this being a hinged appendage of the monoplane tailplane; the twin rudders were replaced by neat twin fins and rudders. Instead of being mounted on the lower wing, the fuselage nacelle was between the wings, and without the outriggers that had mounted the elevator on the M.F.7, the new **M.F.11** looked a more workmanlike machine. It did, however, have a skid extending forward of the main wheels to reduce the danger of nosing-over on rough surfaces and this, by comparison with the outriggers, was sufficient to gain for the aircraft the nickname **'Shorthorn'**. Power was usually provided by Renault engines of 70 or 100 hp (52 or 75 kW), but at least one was reported to have flown with a 130-hp (97-kW) Canton-Unné and it seems likely that other engines may have been used.

Available with wheeled or float landing gear, the M.F.11 was used more extensively than the M.F.7 for bombing, reconnais-sance and training roles, and was built under licence by several manu-facturers. The Royal Naval Air Service, for example, received about 90 M.F.11s, and many of them were used in a bombing role, able to carry a number of light bombs on underwing racks. In an attack launched against enemy guns near Ostend, the 'Shorthorn' recorded on 21 December 1914 the first operational night flight to be made by either side during World War I.

This restored M.F.11 was photographed while overflying the 1937 RAF display at Hendon. Note the type's revised layout compared to the M.F.7.

SPECIFICATION

Farman M.F.11
Type: two-seat utility aircraft
Powerplant: one 70-hp (52-kW) Renault 8-cylinder Vee piston engine
Performance: maximum speed 62 mph (100 km/h); service ceiling 12,470 ft (3800 m); endurance 3 hours 45 minutes
Weights: empty 1,213 lb (550 kg); maximum take-off 1,874 lb (840 kg)
Dimensions: wingspan 53 ft (16.15 m); length 31 ft 2 in (9.50 m); height 12 ft 9½ in (3.90 m); wing area 613.56 sq ft (57.00 m²)
Armament: up to 18 16-lb (7.30-kg) bombs on underwing racks, and (optionally) one machine-gun for the observer

Farman M.F.11 'Shorthorn' and HF.20 (continued)

The Farman HF.20, a two-seat reconnaissance, training and occasional bomber aircraft, was the first Farman production machine to show a combination of the previously separate design ideas developed by the two Farman brothers. Basically a refined version of the MF.11 'Shorthorn', the **HF.20** had fixed tailskid landing gear similar to that of the earlier Maurice Farman aircraft, but dispensed completely with the precautionary skids forward of the four main wheels. Three-float alighting gear was an option.

The HF.20 and its derivatives were used quite extensively by the Allies in the early stages of World War I, and many were built under licence for the British armed forces by Airco, Grahame-White and others. In attempts to improve performance an 80-hp (60-kW) Le Rhône was substituted in the **HF. 21**, but as this version showed virtually no improvement its further development was discontinued. The **HF.22** floatplane saw service with the RNAS in Belgium but, also proving to be underpowered and slow, the surviving examples returned to the UK. However, the **HF.27** with the 140-hp (104-kW) or 160-hp (119-kW) Canton-Unné engine proved far more successful, seeing service on several fronts. The more powerful engine increased the type's load-carrying capability, with the result that on occasions HF.27s were used as bombers against submarines and Zeppelin sheds. By the end of 1915, however, the type was no longer suitable for front-line use and the majority ended their days as primary trainers. Production in France, Belgium, Italy, Russia and the UK exceeded 3,300 aircraft with eight known types of engine.

Farman F.40

The **F.40** was a two-seat pusher biplane with an unequal-span, unstaggered wing cellule of the three-bay type, representing an amalgam of the earlier Henry Farman (as typified by the HF.22) and Maurice Farman (MF.11) design features. The crew nacelle, located in mid-gap between the upper and lower wings, of which only the former was fitted with ailerons, had a smoother and more streamlined outline than those of the earlier aircraft. The upper pair of tail booms supported the angular horizontal tailplane and the large curved single fin was reminiscent of that used in the Henry Farman series.

The new type, known popularly as the **'Horace' Farman**, appeared at the end of 1915 and went into large-scale production for eventual service with more than 40 first-line Corps d'Armée deux-place (A.2 category) escadrilles of the French Aviation Militaire from early 1916. Versions of the F.40 were legion, and included the **F.40P** adapted to fire Le Prieur rockets, the **F.41** with shorter-span wings and a more angular crew nacelle,

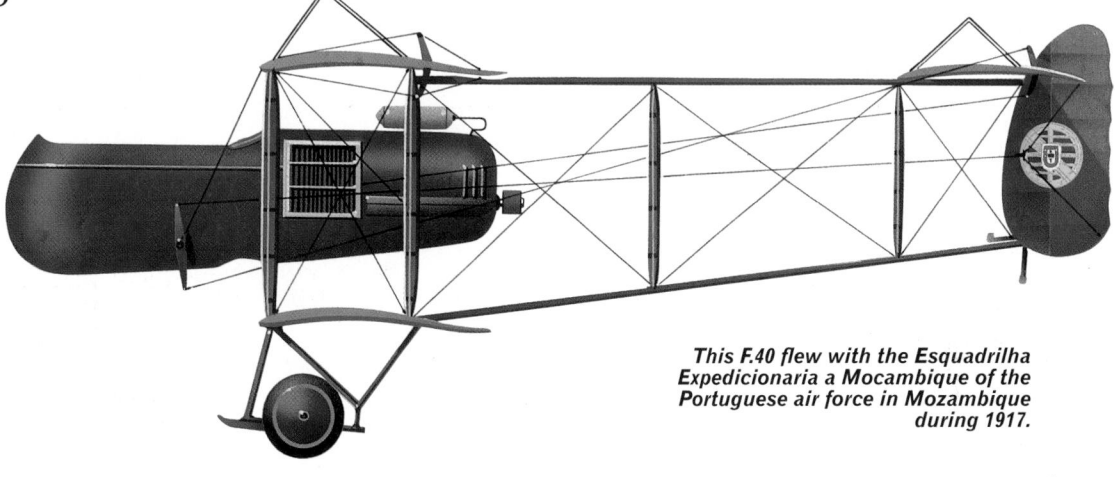

This F.40 flew with the Esquadrilha Expedicionaria a Mocambique of the Portuguese air force in Mozambique during 1917.

the **F.56** similar to the F.41 but with a 170-hp (127-kW) Renault engine, the **F.60** that combined the F.40's airframe with a 190-hp (142-kW) Renault engine, and the **F.61** that combined the F.41's airframe and the 190-hp (142-kW) engine.

'Horace' Farman aircraft also flew with the RNAS. Some of the 50 aircraft purchased from the Farman company operated with No. 5 Wing in France in 1916, and a small number was flown from British coastal stations, including Great Yarmouth.

Other F.40s flew with the Belgian forces in France, alongside F.41s and F.56s, and the F.40 was also operated by the Russians. French escadrilles relinquished their 'Horace' Farmans on the Western Front early in 1917, after just over a year's operations. The type soldiered on with French units in Macedonia and Serbia and a few were adapted for night bombing, although their bombload was very limited.

The Italian Savoia company built a version of the 'Horace' Farman under licence, its normal powerplant being a 100-hp (75-kW) Colombo engine. Italian-built Farmans were used in police operations against rebel tribesmen in Libya up to 1922.

SPECIFICATION	
Farman F.40A.2	maximum take-off 2,469 lb (1120 kg)
Type: two-seat corps reconnaissance and observation aircraft	**Dimensions:** wingspan 57 ft 9 in (17.60 m); length 30 ft 4¼ in (9.25 m); height 12 ft 9½ in (3.90 m); wing area 559.74 sq ft (52.00 m²)
Powerplant: one Renault 12 Vee piston engine rated at 135 hp (101 kW)	
Performance: maximum speed 84 mph (135 km/h) at 6,560 ft (2000 m); service ceiling 13,125 ft (4000 m); endurance 2 hours 20 minutes	**Armament:** one or two 0.303-in (7.7-mm) Lewis trainable forward-firing machine-guns in the front of the cockpit, plus light bombs carried under the lower wing or 10 Le Prieur unguided rockets carried on the interplane struts
Weights: empty 1,649 lb (748 kg);	

Farman F.60 Goliath series

Numerically the most important twin-engined aircraft in the world during the decade following the end of World War I, the **F.60 Goliath** was built as an airliner, of which more than 60 examples were used on scheduled European and South American air routes, and as a night bomber or torpedo-carrier, of which some 300 examples were built for service with the French forces and export customers.

The original **FF.60** (FF for Farman Frères) was designed in 1918 as a bomber that was schemed as the spearhead of the French contribution to the Allied efforts that were being planned for the campaigns of 1919. When fighting ceased in November 1918, the two prototypes nearing completion were converted to civil configuration, with cabins in the nose section and amidships, accommodating four and eight passengers respectively. The first example was exhibited publicly in January 1919, its maiden flight taking place later in that same month. On 8 February 1919 it was flown by Lieutenant Bossoutrot from Toussus-le-Noble to RAF Kenley in Surrey with 11 military personnel as passengers. This remarkable achievement, so soon after the first test flight, has on occasion been claimed erroneously as the first scheduled international passenger flight.

While a bomber version was undergoing tests, the civil F.60 went into production. Several impressive flights were made including, during August 1919, a trip of 1,274 miles (2050 km) from Paris to Casablanca in French Morocco in a flying time of 18 hours 23 minutes, with a crew of six. The F.60 went into service with the Compagnie des Grands Express Aériens between Le Bourget and Croydon on

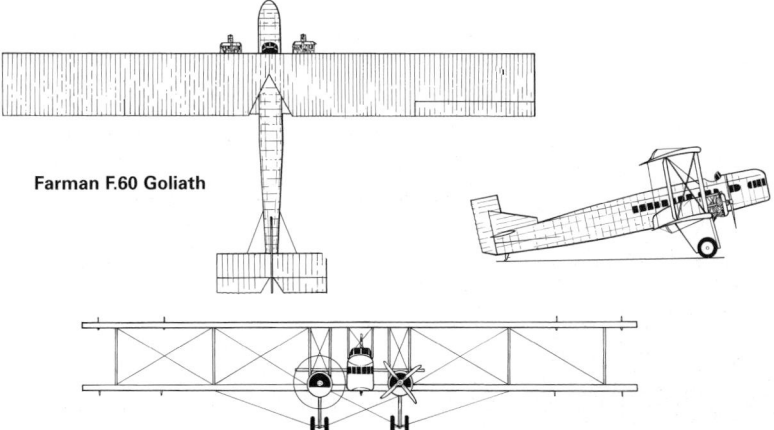

Farman F.60 Goliath

29 March 1920. Less than four months later Lignes Farman, an associate of the aircraft manufacturing company, inaugurated a route linking Paris and Brussels which, by the end of 1921, had been extended via Amsterdam to Berlin. By that time, a second French operator, Compagnie des Messageries Aériennes, was using the Goliath on the service linking Paris and London. The fourth French company to employ the Goliath was the Compagnie Aérienne Française, while the Romanian LARES airline flew Goliaths with British Armstrong Siddeley Jaguar radial engines, and SNETA (forerunner of the Belgian SABENA line) operated six aircraft. Other Goliaths were sold to South American operators.

In Czechoslovakia, Avia and Letov built a batch of Goliaths under licence, some with Bristol Jupiter radial engines manufactured under licence by the Walter company and others with Lorraine-Dietrich engines. Five were acquired by the Czech national airline CSA and a sixth aircraft was used by the Czech air arm as a VIP transport. An experimental Goliath ambulance was built with accommodation for 12 stretcher patients, a doctor and nurse, but is thought not to have gone into service.

The bomber version of the F.60 entered production in 1922, and the first such aircraft were

procured by the French Aéronautique Militaire, which took delivery of enough machines to equip six escadrilles. Later versions of the Goliath were also built for the French army and navy and, in addition, were exported in some numbers to equip pioneering night-bombing units in Poland and the USSR. Examples were also purchased by Italy and Japan.

In basic configuration the Goliath underwent remarkably few changes throughout its decade of development. A classic equal-span biplane of its era, of wooden construction with fabric covering, it had an unstaggered three-bay wing cellule, a wire-braced tail unit, fixed tailskid landing gear with wide-track, twin-wheel main units under the engine nacelles, and a slab-sided fuselage. One feature that did alter considerably, however, was the shape of the nose, which evolved steadily to cater for the varied crew layouts of

Air Union's F.60 fleet included this baseline F.60 with Salmson engines. The aircraft was named Normandie. Note the open cockpit for the aircrew.

This F.168 torpedo-bomber ably demonstrates the revised upper forward fuselage shape which allowed the crew a much improved forward view.

different military variants. A variety of powerplants was also to be seen on the Goliath aircraft, usually nacelle-mounted on each half of the lower wing.

Among the best customers for the Goliath was the French navy, which operated a number of variants, all of which could be fitted either with a 'trousered' wheeled landing gear or with large wooden twin floats supplemented by small auxiliary wingtip floats. Both French army and navy Goliath aircraft saw

action against the formidable Riff tribesmen in Morocco between 1925 and 1927.

SPECIFICATION	
Farman F.60	
Type: two-crew transport aircraft	**Weights:** empty 5,511 lb (2500 kg); maximum take-off 10,516 lb (4770 kg)
Powerplant: two Salmson CM.9 radial piston engines each rated at 260 hp (194 kW)	**Dimensions:** wingspan 86 ft 11¼ in (26.50 m); length 47 ft ¼ in (14.33 m); height 16 ft 1¼ in (4.91 m); wing area 1,733.05 sq ft (161.00 m²)
Performance: maximum speed 87 mph (140 km/h) at sea level; cruising speed 74½ mph (120 km/h) at 6,560 ft (2000 m); service ceiling 13,125 ft (4000 m); range 249 miles (400 km)	**Payload:** up to 12 passengers carried in two cabins

Variants

FF.60: three prototypes, believed to be two civil and one military, completed early in 1919
F.60: principal civil version, of which early examples were powered by two Salmson Z.9 radial engines and later examples by two 260-hp (194-kW) Salmson CM.9 radial engines; over 60 civil Goliaths were built, most of them to the basic F.60 standard; one civil F.60 was used by the French navy to carry out tests of a twin-float alighting gear installation
F.60bis: civil version powered by two 300-hp (224-kW) Salmson 9Az engines
F.60BN.2: principal early night bomber version with two Salmson 9Az engines; despite the BN.2 (two-seat night bomber) suffix, it had a crew of three; the armament comprised three 0.303-in (7.7-mm) Lewis trainable machine-guns and up to 2,293 lb (1040 kg) of bombs; the type was operated by the air arms of the French army and navy, and one was supplied to Japan for experimental use by the army air force
F.60Torp: torpedo-carrying variant with float alighting gear, redesigned nose section, open gunner's position with minimal glazing and two Gnome-Rhône (Bristol) Jupiter radial engines; 24 built
F.60M: blunt-nosed bomber of 1923 with 310-hp (231-kW) Renault 12Fy engines; pilot and co-pilot in side-by-side open cockpits behind a single windscreen; some F.60Ms had a glazed bomb-aiming panel projecting forward from lower part of nose; used by Aviation Militaire from 1926; one aircraft supplied to Japanese army
F.61: civil version powered by 300-hp (224-kW) Renault 12Fe engines
F.62BN.4: export version of the F.60M with 450-hp (336-kW) Lorraine-Dietrich engines and otherwise differing from the F.60M in having a nose balcony for the forward gunner's position; acquired by USSR to equip two night bomber eskadrilas but saw little front-line service, being relegated to training role in 1926
F.63BN.4: similar to export F.62BN.4 but powered by 450-hp (336-kW) Gnome-Rhône Jupiter radial engines; the Aviation Militaire acquired 42, but the aircraft suffered from airframe defects

F.65: version for the Aéronautique Maritime with interchangeable wheel landing gear and float alighting gear, as well as a blunt nose similar to those of the F.60Torp and F.60M; about 100 delivered from 1925; five of them were used in conjunction with French army Goliaths to make bombing attacks against Riff insurgents in Morocco during 1925-7
F.66BN.3: Jupiter-powered variant for Romania; at least one built
F.68BN.4: 32 Jupiter-powered bombers for Poland; used briefly as bombers but found ineffective and relegated to parachute training
F.4X: one special Goliath with four Salmson radial engines in tandem pairs, built for the 1923 Grand Prix des Avions Transports
F.140 Super Goliath: a TGP (Très Gros Porteur) super-heavy bomber prototype powered by four 500-hp (373-kW) Farman engines in tandem pairs on the lower wing, with an armament of trainable machine-guns in the nose, dorsal and ventral positions plus up to 3,307 lb (1500 kg) of bombs; six production examples served with the Aviation Militaire; the loss of one as a result of structural failure in August 1930 led to the scrapping of all surviving examples of this version and all of the French army's F.60, F.63 and F.160 aircraft
F.160BN.4: slightly developed version of F.60 with two 500-hp (373-kW) Farman engines; small number supplied to Aviation Militaire and one each to Italy and Japan; similar **F.161** not built
F.166: strengthened development of F.60 built for the Aéronautique Maritime with optional wheeled landing gear and float alighting gear, redesigned fin, and powerplant of two 500-hp (373-kW) Gnome-Rhône Jupiter radial engines; twin machine-guns in nose and dorsal positions, plus provision for a torpedo or bombs on underfuselage racks; contemporary and generally similar **F.162** not developed beyond prototype stage
F.168: Jupiter-engined torpedo-bomber floatplane which, together with the similar **F.167**, served with the Aéronautique Maritime from 1928 to 1936; fuselage revisions were introduced to improve the field of visibility for the pilot and co-pilot; about 60 entered service
F.169: improved Goliath version which entered service with Lignes Farman in 1929 with aerodynamic improvements and redesigned landing gear incorporating independent single-wheel main units

Farman F.190 series

The most popular example of the strut-braced high-wing cabin monoplane for the touring and air taxi roles that were very much in vogue in France during the late 1920s and early 1930s, the **F.190** was first flown in prototype form during 1928. An enclosed pilot's cockpit was located at the leading edge of the wing and behind this was a cabin seating up to four passengers. Access to the cabin was by a door on the right, immediately to the rear of the pilot's seat. The wide-track divided units of the fixed tailskid landing gear ensured successful operation of this robust monoplane from even low-grade flying

fields, and the tail unit was of typical Farman design. With a basic structure of wood, under a mixed fabric and plywood covering, the F.190 was built to the extent of 100 or more in all versions, and of this total more than half comprised the original version with single Gnome-Rhône 5Ba radial engine. An ambulance version known as the **F.197S** (**Sanitaire**) had provision for two litters and a medical attendant.

As well as private owners and air taxi companies, a number of established airlines in France and abroad used aircraft of the F.190 series. The main operator was the

Farman line with 14 aircraft, while Air Union had seven and other French operators included Air Orient and Air Afrique. When Air France was formed in 1933 it took over 15 F.190s from the various companies it had absorbed. Export customers of the commercial type included CIDNA in Prague and LARES in Bucharest.

The basic design appeared with a considerable variety of powerplants, each main variant bearing a different sub-type designation as follows: the **F.192** was powered by the 230-hp (172-kW) Salmson 9Ab, the **F.193** by the 230-hp (172-kW) Farman 9Ea, the **F.194** by the

With more than 50 per cent of all F.190 series aircraft having the Titan engine, other variants were relatively rare. An F.198 is illustrated.

250-hp (186-kW) Hispano-Suiza 6Mb, the **F.197** by the 240-hp (179-kW) Lorraine 7Me, the **F.198** by

the 250-hp (186-kW) Renault 9A, and the **F.199** by the 325-hp (242-kW) Lorraine 9Na.

SPECIFICATION

Farman F.190
Type: five-seat light transport aircraft
Powerplant: one Gnome-Rhône 5Ba radial piston engine rated at 230 hp (172 kW)
Performance: maximum speed 115 mph (185 km/h) at sea level; cruising speed 99 mph (160 km/h)

at optimum altitude; service ceiling 16,895 ft (5150 m); range 528 miles (850 km)
Weights: empty 2,041 lb (926 kg); maximum take-off 3,968 lb (1800 kg)
Dimensions: wingspan 47 ft 3 in (14.40 m); length 34 ft 3½ in (10.45 m); height 9 ft 10 in (3.00 m); wing area 432.72 sq ft (40.20 m²)

Farman F.220, F.221 and F.222

The **F.211** and **F.212** prototypes established a configuration that was retained in a series of four-engined heavy bomber designs over the next decade: a typical Farman high-set wing of considerable chord and thickness was united with an angular slab-sided fuselage, and the power-plant comprised four engines arranged in tandem pairs, mounted at the extremities of a pair of stub wings projecting from the lower fuselage, to drive two tractor and two pusher propellers. These prototypes were produced in response to an official requirement for a Bombardier Très Gros Porteur, a bomber capable of carrying heavy offensive loads over what were then regarded as medium and long ranges.

The F.211 and F.212 were developed into the **F.220.01** which first flew on 26 May 1932. Powered by four 600-hp (447-kW) Hispano-Suiza 12Lbr engines, the F.220 retained the basic concept of its predecessors, including the enclosed pilots' cabin, balcony nose gunner's position and fixed main landing-gear units of the wide-track divided type, but incorporated a number of detailed refinements. Later converted for civil use as *Le Centaure*, the sole F.220 was used as a pioneer long-range passenger/mail carrier over the South Atlantic route, making its first non-stop flight from Dakar in West Africa to Natal in Brazil on 3 June 1935.

In May 1933 the **F.221.01** prototype took

This F.222.1 served with the 2e Escadrille of l'Armée de l'Air's Groupement de Bombardement I/15. The aircraft was based at Reims-Courcy in May 1940.

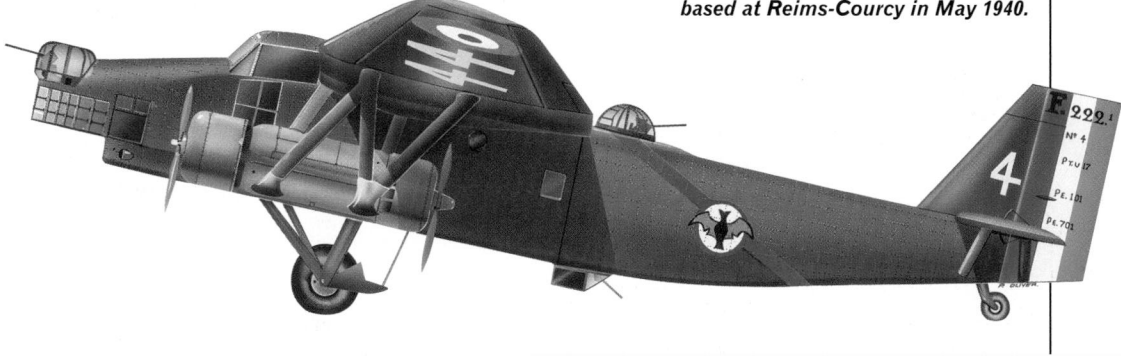

off on its maiden flight. It differed from the F.220 mainly in having a redesigned vertical tail surface, Gnome-Rhône Mistral Major radial engines, and the nose and ventral gunners' cockpits fully enclosed. A small production batch of **F.221** bombers followed, with redesigned nose sections, including a manually operated gun turret and revised glazing for the bomb-aimer's station. The dorsal gun was housed under a domed hand-operated turret, and the ventral position was semi-retractable. Whereas only the forward engines of the F.221.01 were

cowled, the series aircraft had long-chord cowlings on all four engines. Four civil variants, designated **F.2200**, appeared between 1936 and 1938 and were used by Air France on the South American service.

The F.221.01 prototype was modified as the **F.220.01** during the second half of 1935. The main change was the introduction of main landing-gear units which retracted forward into the engine nacelles. **F.222.1** production aircraft were followed by two batches of **F.222.2** bombers with redesigned nose sections eliminating the balcony of the earlier bombers and

Variants

F.221: 10 series aircraft delivered to Armée de l'Air between June 1936 and January 1937; they constituted the only effective four-engined bomber force in the world at that time, except in the USSR which fielded large numbers of Tupolev TB-3 machines; single prototype built and flown in May 1933
F.222.1: known originally as the F.222 but redesignated with the appearance of the F.222.2 version; it had increased fuel capacity; 11 series aircraft built, construction of first aircraft beginning in April 1936 and the last aircraft being completed in October 1937; the prototype F.222 was conversion of original F.221 prototype
F.222.2: two batches built by the Société Nationale de Constructions Aéronautiques du Centre, the nationalised group that incorporated Farman, the first of eight and the second of 16. A redesigned nose section gave much improved fuselage contours by comparison with those of the F.221 and F.222.1; no prototype built as such, aircraft no. 13 being the first F.222.2 completed

Having proven to have insufficient performance as an airliner, the F.224 machines were delivered to the Armée de l'Air to the F.224TT standard illustrated.

cut down to provide the pilot with improved visibility. The F.222.2 also featured additional dihedral on the outer wing sections. One civil F.222.1 was completed as the **F.2220** *Ville de Dalzar* and delivered to Air France in October 1937.

The Farman bombers, all in the **BN.5** (five-seat night bomber) category, were delivered to the 15e Escadre de Bombardement, which was specifically formed for the purpose at Avord in July 1935. By the beginning of 1938 there were 18 examples of the F.221 and F.222.1 in service, and two months earlier deliveries of the F.222.2 had started, the last of these aircraft being delivered in July 1938. On 16 August 1939 the disposition of the Farman bombers included four machines in Indo-China, eight in France's African colonies and 30 in metropolitan France, including 20 in first-line service with the 15e Escadre. Between the outbreak of World War II in September 1939 and the beginning of May 1940, the F.221 and F.222

bombers were engaged on leaflet-dropping night operations over Germany and Bohemia. During the Blitzkrieg on France in May and June 1940, the Farman bombers of the Armée de l'Air made 63 effective night sorties over western Germany and the occupied areas of north-east France. Three F.222.2 machines with additional fuel capacity were transferred to the French navy's newly formed Escadrille 10E, intended for long-range bombing and maritime patrol.

After the June 1940 armistice between Germany and France, Groupement 15, as the Farman-equipped unit was by then known, was re-formed as Groupe de Transport 15, comprising two escadrilles with a total of two F.221, two F.222.1 and six F.222.2 machines. They served the French Vichy regime, playing an important part in the transfer of Armée de l'Air units to Syria during the fighting in that country.

Farman also developed the **F.224** from the F.222

bomber, with a new fuselage of deep section designed to maximise volume for the accommodation of 40 passengers. It also introduced a tail unit with twin fin-and-rudder assemblies. A mock-up was exhibited at the 1937 Paris Salon de l'Aéronautique and resulted in an order for six such aircraft from Air France. The aircraft were in fact built by the SNCAC (Société Nationale de Constructions Aéronautiques du Centre), the nationalised company created by the forced merger of Farman and other manufacturers.

The first aircraft was tested by Air France but found incapable of maintaining straight flight on the power of only two engines, and also required very considerable runway length for take-off and landing. As a result of Air France's dissatisfaction, a deal was made whereby the F.224s, which had originally been intended for the route linking Paris and London, would be delivered to the Armée de

l'Air as **F.224TT** troop transports. As part of the same deal, an existing order for 10 Dewoitine D.339TT troop transports was altered to eight D.338 three-engined airliners for Air France.

The Armée de l'Air took delivery of the F.224 transports in 1938, but then returned the machines to the manufacturer for conversion to carry 39 paratroops with their equipment. During this process a defensive armament of two light

machine-guns was fitted, and a bomb bay was incorporated to allow the internal carriage of an 882-lb (400-kg) offensive load. The F.224s finally went into service between April and August 1939, operating with the GIA (Groupements d'Infanterie de l'Air) I/601 and I/602 units in 1940. A number of the aircraft survived the defeat of France in May and June 1940 to remain in service with the Vichy French air force.

SPECIFICATION

Farman (Centre) F.222.2BN.5
Type: five-crew heavy night bomber
Powerplant: four Gnome-Rhône 14N-11/15 radial piston engines each rated at 970 hp (723 kW)
Performance: maximum speed 224 mph (360 km/h) at 13,125 ft; cruising speed 174 mph (280 km/h) at 13,125 ft (4000 m); climb to 13,125 ft (4000 m) in 13 minutes 30 seconds; service ceiling 26,245 ft (8000 m); range 1,243 miles (2000 km) with a 5,511-lb (2500-kg) bombload
Weights: empty 23,810 lb (10800 kg); maximum take-off 41,226 lb (18700 kg)
Dimensions: wingspan 118 ft 1¼ in (36.00 m); length 70 ft 4½ in

(21.45 m); height 17 ft ⅓ in (5.19 m); wing area 2,002.08 sq ft (186.00 m²)
Armament: one 0.295-in (7.5-mm) MAC 1934 trainable forward-firing machine-gun in the nose turret, one 0.295-in (7.5-mm) MAC 1934 trainable machine-gun in the dorsal turret, one 0.295-in (7.5-mm) MAC 1934 trainable rearward-firing machine-gun in the ventral 'dustbin' position, plus up to 9,259 lb (4200 kg) of disposable stores carried in a lower-fuselage weapons bay, and generally comprising 20 441-lb (200-kg) bombs, or 40 220-lb (100-kg) bombs, or a mix of these weapons and 110-lb (50-kg) bombs

Farman NC.223

Like the NC.223.3 bomber, the NC.223.4 had a slim tapering high-aspect ratio wing, with the engines supported on struts. The latter's nose incorporated considerable aerodynamic refinement, however, and the tail unit, with twin fin-and-rudder assemblies, was of greater area.

Retaining the powerplant configuration of the earlier Farman four-engined bombers but incorporating a new stressed-skin metal wing of high aspect ratio, the **F.223** was intended as a bomber offering higher performance than the F.222 series. It had a more refined, though still angular, fuselage and a tail unit with twin fin-and-rudder units. However, the first example to fly, in June 1937, was a long-distance mail-carrier which was subsequently named *Laurent Guerrero* and flown on the South Atlantic route between West Africa and Brazil. This had the designation **NC.223.1** as the Farman company had by this time been absorbed, during March 1937, into the newly-formed nationalised company, the SNCAC (Société Nationale de Constructions Aéronautiques du Centre). The NC.223.1 soon established a reputation by establishing a new world distance-with-payload record in October 1937.

The **NC.223.01** bomber prototype flew for the first time on 18 January 1938. It differed from the civil machine chiefly in its powerplant, which comprised four Hispano-Suiza radial engines in place of the Hispano-Suiza 12Xirs-1 Vee engines of

the civil transport, and in its military equipment and armament. The proposed **NC.223.2BN.5** (five-seat night bomber) with Gnome-Rhône 14N radial engines was not built.

Eight **NC.223.3BN.5s** were ordered, and these entered service with the Armée de l'Air in May and June 1940, during the course of the German Blitzkrieg on France. The aircraft were powered by four Hispano-Suiza 12Y-29 Vee engines and armed defensively with a nose-mounted 0.295-in (7.5-mm) MAC 1934 machine-gun as well as single 20-mm Hispano-Suiza HS-404 cannon in power-operated dorsal and ventral turrets. The bombload, carried in four bays, was up to 9,240 lb (4191 kg). The NC 223.3s flew alongside the earlier Farman bombers with the Groupement de Bombardement 15 before being withdrawn to North Africa. Three were later

converted as long-range mail/passenger aircraft, while the other machines were flown by the Groupe de Transport I/15 in France's North African territories.

The **NC.223.4** was developed in parallel with the NC.223.3 and was intended from the outset as a high-speed mail-carrier. Three aircraft were built with the names *Camille Flammarion*, *Jules Verne* and *Le Verrier*.

In October 1939, soon after the outbreak of World War II, *Camille Flammarion* took part in the search for the German pocket battleship *Graf Spee* in the South Atlantic. Then, in May 1940, the French Aéronavale formed Escadrille B5 at Orly to operate the three NC.223.4s as long-range bomber and reconnaissance aircraft. In the event, only *Jules Verne* received military equipment, in the form of racks for up to eight 551-lb (250-kg)

bombs and provision for a 0.295-in (7.5-mm) MAC 1934 machine-gun on a gimbal mount attached to the rear entry door. The machine carried out a number of night operations, the most remarkable taking place on the night of 7-8 June 1940, when Berlin was attacked by means of a long and circuitous route

over the North Sea and the Baltic. Later, the three NC.223.4 aircraft made several attacks on Italian targets, but after the June 1940 armistice with Germany they were returned to passenger and mail operations. *Le Verrier* was shot down over the Mediterranean on 27 November 1940.

SPECIFICATION

Farman NC.223.3BN.5
Type: five-crew heavy night bomber
Powerplant: four Hispano-Suiza 12Y-29 Vee piston engines each rated at 920 hp (686 kW)
Performance: maximum speed 249 mph (400 km/h) at 13,125 ft (4000 m); cruising speed 174 mph (280 km/h) at 13,125 ft (4000 m); climb to 13,125 ft (4000 m) 10 minutes; service ceiling 26,245 ft (8000 m); range 1,491 miles (2400 km)
Weights: empty 23,259 lb (10550 kg); maximum take-off 42,329 lb (19200 kg)
Dimensions: wingspan 110 ft 2 in (33.58 m); length 72 ft 2 in (22.00 m); height 16 ft 8 in

(5.08 m); wing area 1425.19 sq ft (132.40 m²)
Armament: one 0.295-in (7.5-mm) MAC 1934 trainable forward-firing machine-gun in the nose, one 20-mm Hispano-Suiza HS-404 trainable cannon in the power-operated dorsal turret and one 20-mm Hispano-Suiza HS-404 trainable cannon in the powered-operated and semi-retractable ventral turret, plus up to 9,240 lb (4191 kg) of disposable stores carried in four internal bays and generally comprising 20 441 lb (200 kg) bombs, or 40 220 lb (100 kg) bombs, or a combination of these weapons with 110-lb (50-kg) bombs

Faucett F-19

The Compañia de Aviación Faucett S.A. was established in Peru on 15 September 1928 with its headquarters in Lima.

The airline, which has an unbroken history to the present, is the oldest in Peru. In the early 1930s Faucett established work-shops for the maintenance and repair of its own and other aircraft operating within the country, and in the later years of that decade began construction of a number of transport aircraft for its own use.

Based on the design of the Stinson Detroiter, modified by the company to meet its own particular requirements, the result-ing **Faucett F-19** provided accommodation for a crew of two and six passengers. In landplane configuration the F-19 was powered by one Pratt & Whitney Hornet radial engine, but the seaplane had a lower-powered engine, the 600-hp (447-kW) Pratt & Whitney Wasp S1H1-G radial unit.

Faucett at first constructed F-19 aircraft for its own airline, but subsequently built a number for the Peruvian government, the last example being produced in 1947.

Faucett's F-19 was a braced high-wing monoplane of mixed construction with a conventional tail unit. It had provision for fixed tailwheel landing gear with wide-track divided main units or for twin-float alighting gear.

SPECIFICATION

Faucett F-19 (landplane)
Type: two-crew light transport aircraft
Powerplant: one Pratt & Whitney Hornet S1E3-C radial piston engine rated at 875 hp (652 kW)
Performance: maximum speed 180 mph (290 km/h) at 8,000 ft (2440 m); cruising speed 140 mph (225 km/h) at 11,000 ft (3355 m); initial climb rate 1,000 ft (305 m) per minute; service ceiling 22,000 ft (6705 m)
Weights: empty 5,688 lb (2580 kg); maximum take-off 9,061 lb (4110 kg)
Dimensions: wingspan 58 ft ¾ in (17.70 m); length 38 ft 8½ in (11.80 m); height 14 ft 3¼ in (4.35 m); wing area 435.95 sq ft (40.50 m²)
Payload: up to eight passengers

FBA Type 290 series

The experimental **FBA Type 270HM.2** flying-boat of 1929 and **Type 271 HMT.2** amphibian flying-boat of 1930 were designed and built as possi-ble successors to the same company's **Type 17** for French naval service in the liaison and training roles. Neither of these types was ordered, however, and the FBA design team of Payonne and Perez was asked instead to produce a four-seat development of the basic concept. The **Type 290** prototype resulted from this, was exhibited at the 1930 Paris Salon de l'Aéronautique and flew for the first time in April 1931. The pilot and three passengers were accommodated in a well-glazed cabin in the forward section of the hull.

The Type 290, powered by a 300-hp (224-kW) Lorraine engine, was followed by another one-off civil machine, the **Type 291** four-seat amphibian, which had a Gnome-Rhône engine of the same power. The French navy, which was looking for aircraft that could be used as comfort-able 'admiral's barges', ordered eight amphibian developments of the Type 291: the six **Type 293** 'boats were each powered by one Lorraine Algol 9Na radial engine, while the two **Type 294** 'boats each had one Gnome-Rhône 7Kb Titan radial engine. Both versions performed yeoman service attached to the naval staff and principal naval air stations at Brest, Orly and Rochefort.

The 290 series were single-bay biplanes with their straight upper wings of less span than the dihedralled lower wing. A Type 293 is illustrated.

SPECIFICATION

FBA Type 293
Type: one-crew liaison and VIP transport amphibian flying-boat
Powerplant: one Lorraine Algol 9Na radial piston engine rated at 300 hp (224 kW)
Performance: maximum speed 109 mph (176 km/h) at optimum altitude; service ceiling 13,125 ft (4000 m); range 326 miles (525 km)
Weights: empty 2,866 lb (1300 kg); maximum take-off 4,630 lb (2100 kg)
Dimensions: wingspan 42 ft 11¾ in (13.10 m); length 31 ft ¾ in (9.47 m); height 13 ft 3 in (4.04 m); wing area 432.19 sq ft (40.15 m²)
Payload: three passengers carried in the cabin

Felixstowe F.1 and F.2

Squadron Commander John Porte of the Royal Naval Air Service had been interested in aviation as early as 1909, joining Glenn H. Curtiss in the USA at the beginning of 1914 to participate in the design of a transatlantic flying-boat. Returning to the UK at the outbreak of World War I, Porte influ-enced the Admiralty in acquiring flying-boats of Curtiss design. During the first year of the war, Porte gained operational experi-ence with some of these 'boats and, during September 1915, decided to devise modifications to these machines to improve their operational capability.

Modifications to the hulls of the Curtiss flying-boats then in service met with mixed success, but the experience gained enabled Porte to design a completely new single-step hull which was to become known as the Porte I. With the wings and tail unit of a standard Curtiss H-4 flying-boat and with power provided by two Hispano-Suiza engines, this was flown under the designa-tion **Felixstowe F.1**. Modifications made to the hull as a result of flight testing included the addi-tion of two more steps, and in this form the F.1 can be regarded as the proto-type of the family of 'F' 'boats that followed.

The range and payload of the H-4 were inadequate for North Sea patrols, and Porte induced Curtiss to develop the larger H-12 or Large America. The first of 50 such 'boats ordered by the Admiralty was deliv-ered to Felixstowe in July

Just under 100 examples of the F.2A were built, the type remaining in operational use until the end of World War I in 1918. Note the type's open cockpits and unequal-span wings.

1916 with the powerplant of two 160-hp (119-kW) Curtiss engines. This powerplant was deemed insufficient, and the engines were replaced by two 250-hp (186-kW) Rolls-Royce Eagle I units, the resulting conversion being redesignated H-12A. Although the type's performance in the air was satisfactory, it was soon discovered that the original hull was unsuited to operations in the North Sea. Porte designed a new two-step hull based on that of the F.1 and this, combined with a revised tail unit, the wing cellule of the H-12 and the Eagle engines, provided a much improved flying-boat, designated as the **Felixstowe F.2**. Testing showed that some slight modifications and more powerful engines would make it an ideal patrol 'boat, and with Eagle VIII engines the modified type entered production as the **F.2A**.

A single example of one variant appeared, this being designated as the **F.2C**. It had a modified hull of lighter construction and was powered initially by two 275-hp (205-kW) Eagle II engines. These were replaced subsequently by two 322-hp (240-kW) Eagle VI engines, and although tests showed that in this form the performance of the 'boat was marginally better than that of the F.2A, the F.2C did not enter production. There were no **F.2B** aircraft.

SPECIFICATION

Felixstowe F.2A
Type: four-seat patrol and escort flying-boat
Powerplant: two Rolls-Royce Eagle VIII Vee piston engines each rated at 345 hp (257 kW)
Performance: maximum speed 95.5 mph (153 km/h) at sea level; climb to 6,500 ft (1980 m) in 16 minutes 40 seconds; service ceiling 9,600 ft (2925 m); endurance 6 hours
Weights: empty 7,549 lb (3424 kg); maximum take-off 10,978 lb (4980 kg)
Dimensions: wingspan 95 ft 7½ in (29.15 m); length 46 ft 3 in (14.10 m); height 17 ft 6 in (5.33 m); wing area 1,133.00 sq ft (105.26 m²)
Armament: one or two 0.303-in (7.7-mm) Lewis trainable forward-firing machine-guns in the open bow position, one or two 0.303-in (7.7-mm) Lewis trainable rearward-firing machine-guns in the open dorsal position, and one 0.303-in (7.7-mm) Lewis trainable lateral-firing machine-gun in each of the two beam positions, plus up to 460 lb (209 kg) of disposable stores carried on two hardpoints under the lower wing, and generally comprising two 230-lb (104-kg) bombs

Felixstowe F.3

In February 1917 there flew the prototype of a new flying-boat developed from the F.2A. Generally similar in external appearance to its predecessor, this **Felixstowe F.3** differed from this type primarily in its slight increase in length and span, and was intended to offer more range and greater load-carrying capability. This was achieved, but as the F.3 had the same Eagle VIII powerplant as the F.2A, the improvements were not gained without cost. Thus

the F.2 was slower and less manoeuvrable than its predecessor and, as a result, lost the F.2A's capability for the engagement of German fighter seaplanes and Zeppelin airships. In consequence it was not popular with crews and because of its limitations was used mainly for anti-submarine patrols.

The prototype had flown originally with two 320-hp (239-kW) Sunbeam Cossack engines, probably because of the general shortage of the Eagle VIII engine, but the Eagle VIII

Although it was somewhat lacking in outright performance compared to the F.2A, the F.3 offered its crew the comfort of enclosed accommodation.

was installed in production examples. Orders for the aircraft, eventually totalling 263, considerably exceeded those for the higher-performance F.2A, probably because the type could carry double the bombload. However, only about 100 'boats had been completed by the end of World War I in 1918, although some were later completed to the improved F.5 standard for delivery to the Royal Air Force.

Operational use of the F.2A was confined to British home stations, and it is interesting to record that the F.3 was used extensively in the Mediterranean theatre. In fact, so urgent was the requirement for these flying-boats in that area that 18 were built under sub-contract by the Dockyard Constructional Unit at Malta.

SPECIFICATION

Felixstowe F.3
Type: four-seat patrol and anti-submarine flying-boat
Powerplant: two Rolls-Royce Eagle VIII Vee piston engines each rated at 345 hp (257 kW)
Performance: maximum speed 93 mph (149.5 km/h) at 2,000 ft (610 m); climb to 6,500 ft (1980 m) in 12 minutes 55 seconds; service ceiling 12,500 ft (3810 m); endurance 6 hours
Weights: empty 7,958 lb (3610 kg); maximum take-off 13,281 lb (6024 kg)
Dimensions: wingspan 102 ft (31.09 m); length 49 ft 2 in (14.99 m); height 18 ft 8 in (5.69 m); wing area 1,432.00 sq ft (133.03 m²)
Armament: one or two 0.303-in (7.7-mm) Lewis trainable forward-firing machine-guns in the open bow position, one or two 0.303-in (7.7-mm) Lewis trainable rearward-firing machine-guns in the open dorsal position, and one 0.303-in (7.7-mm) Lewis trainable lateral-firing machine-gun in each of the two beam positions, plus up to 920 lb (417 kg) of disposable stores carried on four hardpoints under the lower wing, and generally comprising four 230-lb (104-kg) bombs

Felixstowe F.5

First appearing early in 1918, the **F.5** was intended as a development of the F.3 incorporating the improvements and refinements deemed desirable as a result of experience with the F.3 and F.2A. Although externally similar to the F.3, the F.5 differed in having a slightly deeper hull with open cockpits for the crew plus an entirely new wing cellule of greater span. The basic powerplant of the prototype was unchanged, but slightly uprated 350-hp (261-kW) Eagle VIII engines were installed. Flight testing of this prototype revealed performance significantly improved over that of the F.3.

Unfortunately, however, it was decided that economic considerations would not allow the introduction of this new type and, instead, the production version of the F.5 introduced a hull that was similar to that of the prototype in combination with a wing cellule based on that of the F.3; as many F.3 components as possible

No. 230 Sqn was responsible for RAF F.5 operations. The unit was renumbered as No. 480 Flight late in 1922, retaining its F.5s until it was disestablished in April 1923.

were used in production of the F.5. Flight tests showed that performance of the production F.5 was inferior to that of the F.3, but this was hardly surprising, for the type was powered by 325-hp (242-kW) Eagle VII engines while Eagle VIII units were in short supply, and in this form the new 'boat's performance was distinctly disappointing.

Entering service too late to be used operationally during World War I, the F.5 became the RAF's standard post-war flying-boat until replaced by the Supermarine Southampton in August 1925. It should be noted that it was by the efforts of John Porte that the F.5 had been developed from the Curtiss H-8 and H-12 Large America 'boats. In 1918 Curtiss began building a flying-boat that was an improved foreign version of one of its own designs. Under the designation **F-5L**, this new aircraft remained the US Navy's standard patrol flying-boat until the late 1920s.

SPECIFICATION

Felixstowe F.5
Type: four-seat reconnaissance and anti-submarine flying-boat
Powerplant: two Rolls-Royce Eagle VIII Vee piston engines each rated at 350 hp (261 kW)
Performance: maximum speed 88 mph (142.5 km/h) at 2,000 ft (610 m); climb to 6,500 ft (1980 m) in 16 minutes 30 seconds; service ceiling 10,000 ft (3050 m); endurance 7 hours
Weights: empty 9,100 lb (4128 kg); maximum take-off 12,682 lb (5752 kg)
Dimensions: wingspan 103 ft 8 in (31.60 m); length 49 ft 3 in (15.01 m); height 18 ft 9 in (5.72 m); wing area 1,409.00 sq ft (130.90 m²)
Armament: one 0.303-in (7.7 mm) Lewis trainable forward-firing machine-gun in the open bow position, one 0.303-in (7.7-mm) Lewis trainable rearward-firing machine-gun in the open dorsal position, and one 0.303-in (7.7 mm) Lewis trainable lateral-firing machine-gun in each of the two open waist positions, plus up to 920 lb (417 kg) of disposable stores carried on four hardpoints under the lower wing, and generally comprising four 230-lb (104-kg) bombs

FFA AS 202 Bravo and FFT Eurotrainer 2000A

Originally known as the A.G. für Dornier Flugzeuge when it was created as the Swiss subsidiary of the West German company Dornier, this concern later became fully Swiss-owned and was then renamed FFA (Flug- und Fahrzeugwerke A.G. Altenrhein) before the 1980 reorganisation that turned it into FWA (Flugzeugwerke Altenrhein A.G.). In 1967 FFA reached agreement with the Italian company SIAI-Marchetti for the joint development and manufacture of the latter's **SA 202 Bravo** fully aerobatic lightplane design. The first prototype was a Swiss-built machine that made its initial flight in March 1969, and the original agreement called for FFA to build the fuselage and tail unit while SIAI-Marchetti constructed the wings.

The Italian company then ran out of production capacity and the agreement was amended for FFA to produce the Bravo on its own. The Bravo is of conventional all-metal design with a cantilever low-set wing with manu-

ally operated slotted trailing-edge flaps, fixed tricycle landing gear, and a large cockpit under a rearward-sliding blown canopy.

The first model to enter production (just 32 aircraft) was the **AS 202/15 Bravo** with the 150-hp (112-kW) Lycoming O-320-E2A flat-four engine driving a fixed-pitch propeller and drawing its fuel from tanks in the wing's leading edges. In August 1974 FFA flew the first example of the improved **AS 202/18A** with a more powerful engine driving a constant-speed propeller and drawing its fuel from bag tanks in the wings. Sales

of the AS 202/18A have been made in variants such as the **AS 202/18A-1 Bravo** baseline model (18 and eight delivered to Morocco and Uganda respectively), **AS 202/18A 2 Bravo** with a maximum take-off weight of 2,160 lb (980 kg), longer canopy and an electric trim system (48 aircraft delivered to Iraq, which later transferred between 10 and 12 machines to Jordan), **AS 202/18A-3 Bravo** with a mechanical trim system and 24- rather than 12-volt electrical system (40 aircraft delivered to Indonesia), and **AS 202/18A-4 Bravo** with a maximum take-off weight

Indonesian student pilots receive their basic training on gliders and AS 202/18A Bravos. The aircraft serve with Skwadron Pendidikan 101.

of 2,226 lb (1010 kg) and a more sophisticated level of instrumentation (four aircraft delivered to Oman).

FFA also developed a high-powered version as the **AS 202/26A** with the 260-hp (194-kW) Lycoming

O-540 flat-six engine, but this model did not enter production. The same fate befell the **FFT Eurotrainer** that was created in the early 1990s as an updated version of the standard type.

SPECIFICATION

FFA AS 202/18A Bravo
Type: two/three-seat primary flying trainer
Powerplant: one Lycoming AEIO-360-B1F flat-four piston engine rated at 180 hp (134 kW)
Performance: maximum speed 150 mph (241 km/h) at sea level; cruising speed 141 mph (226 km/h) at 8,000 ft (2440 m); initial climb rate 800 ft (244 m) per minute; service ceiling 17,000 ft (5180 m); range 707 miles (1140 km)
Weights: empty 1,565 lb (710 kg); maximum take-off 2,381 lb (1080 kg)
Dimensions: wingspan 31 ft 11¾ in (9.75 m); length 24 ft 7¼ in (7.50 m); height 9 ft 2¾ in (2.81 m); wing area 149.19 sq ft (13.86 m²)

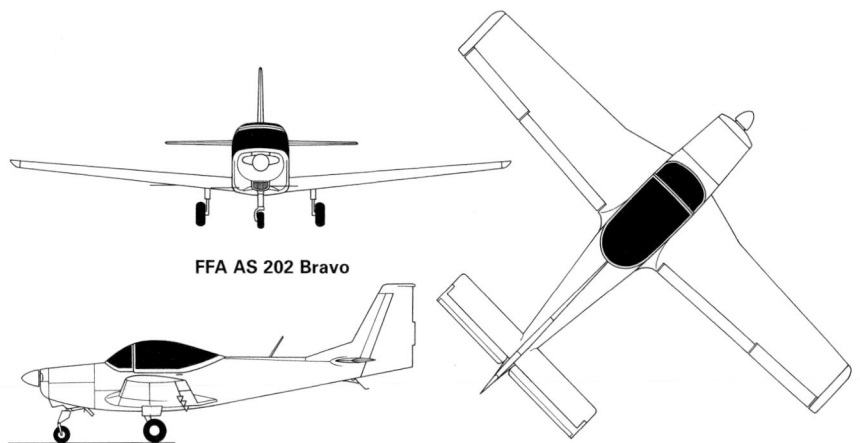

FFA AS 202 Bravo

Based on the Bravo airframe, the Eurotrainer offered accommodation for four. It featured retractable undercarriage, a full IFR instrument fit and was offered with Lycoming or Porsche engines.

Fiat AS.1, AS.2 and TR.1

Developed in a matter of weeks, the prototype **AS.1** two-seat touring aircraft first flew in the summer of 1928. A very basic monoplane of the strut-braced parasol configuration, the AS.1 was powered in its prototype form by a 90-hp (67-kW) Walter radial engine of Czechoslovak origin. The outer panels of the wing could be folded for towing or storage. Construction was of the mixed type under a covering of plywood and fabric except for the light alloy panelling immediately behind the engine. The standard powerplant of the production-standard AS.1 was based on the Fiat A.50 engine.

The two crew members had dual controls and were

seated in tandem open cockpits, each protected by a small windscreen. The occupants had additional protection from a larger windscreen built integral with the forward cabane struts and from some angles this gave the AS.1 the appearance of a fully enclosed cabin aircraft.

The **AS.2** development of 1929 had a strengthened structure and the 100-hp (75-kW) Fiat A.50S engine. Later versions of both the

Included among the AS.1's meritorious exploits was a flight from Vercelli to Tokyo by Lombardi and Capannini, between 13 and 22 July 1930.

AS.1 and AS.2 were built with fully enclosed accommodation. The **AS.1 Idro** was a twin-float seaplane version and the **AS.1 Sci** had ski landing gear, and both of these variants were introduced in 1930.

AS.1s made headlines throughout 1929 and 1930. In August 1929 eight of the aircraft won the Challenge Internationale de Tourisme team event. Donati and Capannini flew their AS.1 in January 1930 to establish world distance and endurance records for touring aircraft: the figures

were 1,706.29 miles (2746 km) and 29 hours 4 minutes respectively. During the same month the same two men set the world tourer altitude record at 22,250 ft (6782 m). In February Francis Lombardi flew from home to Mogadishu (East Africa), a distance of over 5,000

Variant

TR.1: of similar configuration to the AS.1 but with a fabric-covered metal airframe, wide-track main landing-gear arrangement, a fully enclosed two-seat cabin faired into the rear upper fuselage decking and the powerplant of one A.50S radial rated at 100 hp (75 kW), the TR.1 was flown for the first time in 1930, and won a number of sporting events in 1931, including the team event in the Giro Aereo d'Italia

miles (8047 km), in seven days. These achievements did not end the AS.1's career as a record-breaker. On 28 December 1932 an

AS.1 Idro reached an altitude of 24,157 ft (7363 m), powered by a CNA C7 engine, to establish a world height record for

touring seaplanes. Two days later the same aircraft, with the CNA engine but wheeled landing gear, attained 30,453 ft (9282 m) to set a world height record for touring landplanes.

During 1929 the AS.1 production programme accelerated rapidly for the AS.1. Already very popular among private owners, it was selected by the Regia Aeronautica as a liaison and courier aircraft and for

training reserve pilots. It appears that at least 500 examples of the AS.1 were built, plus some 50

examples of the AS.2, Italian air ministry orders alone totalling 276 AS.1 and 36 AS.2 aircraft.

SPECIFICATION	
Fiat AS.1	
Type: two-seat touring and training aircraft	(1000 km); endurance 5 hours 30 minutes
Powerplant: one Fiat A.50 radial piston engine rated at 90 hp (67 kW)	**Weights:** empty 992 lb (450 kg); maximum take-off 1,521 lb (690 kg)
Performance: maximum speed 98 mph (158 km/h) at optimum altitude; service ceiling 22,310 ft (6800 m); range 621 miles	**Dimensions:** wingspan 34 ft 1½ in (10.40 m); length 20 ft ¼ in (6.10 m); height 8 ft 3½ in (2.53 m); wing area 188.37 sq ft (17.50 m²)

Fiat BR, BR.1, BR.2, BR.3 and BR.4

In 1918 Celestino Rosatelli began work in the design bureau of the Società Italiana Aviazione, the aircraft manufacturing section of the giant Fiat complex. His initial task was development of the **SIA 9** reconnaissance biplane; great hopes had been set on this type,

which had then proved to be structurally unsound. The new design emerged as a light bomber biplane, and this **Fiat BR** (the letters standing for **Bombardiere Rosatelli**) appeared in 1919, by which time the SIA had reverted to the name Fiat. In April 1919 the BR estab-

lished a number of world records, lifting three passengers, although it was only a two-seat aircraft, to an altitude of 23,763 ft (7240 m) and attaining a maximum speed of 167.8 mph (270 km/h) with one passenger.

The BR completed its service trials successfully at the Montecello test centre in 1922 and went into production for the Aeronautica Militare, reorganised under the 1923 Fascist regime as the Regia Aeronautica.

In the October 1931 Coupe Bibesco military aircraft contest, a BR.3 covered 708 miles (1140 km) at an average speed of 156.60 mph (252 km/h). Remarkably, the type survived in Regia Aeronautica service into 1940.

Compared with the SIA 9, the BR had improved lines and a more robust structure. While retaining the two-bay biplane configuration of its predecessor, the BR introduced a revised and strengthened wing structure, and a tailplane of new design with a vertical tail surface shape which was to characterise

Rosatelli designs for the next decade. The pilot's open cockpit was located immediately below a cut-out in the upper wing's trailing edge, and the observer/gunner's cockpit was close behind it. Power for the BR was provided by the 700-hp (522-kW) A.14 Vee engine.

Two BRs were sold to Sweden, where they were given the service designation **B 1**.

SPECIFICATION	
Fiat BR.2	
Type: two-seat bomber	(10.66 m); length 34 ft 11¾ in (10.66 m); height 12 ft 10 in (3.91 m); wing area 755.87 sq ft (70.22 m²)
Powerplant: one Fiat A.25 Vee piston engine rated at 1,090 hp (813 kW)	
Performance: maximum speed 140 mph (240 km/h) at optimum altitude; climb to 13,125 ft (4000 m) in 15 minutes 46 seconds; service ceiling 20,505 ft (6250 m); range 621 miles (1000 km)	**Armament:** one 0.303-in (7.7-mm) Vickers fixed forward-firing machine-gun in the forward fuselage and one 0.303-in (7.7-mm) Lewis trainable rearward-firing machine-gun in the rear cockpit, plus up to 1,587 lb (720 kg) of disposable stores carried in a lower-fuselage weapons bay, and generally comprising free-fall bombs
Weights: empty 5,833 lb (2646 kg); maximum take-off 9,248 lb (4195 kg)	
Dimensions: wingspan 56 ft 9 in	

Variants

BR.1: Rosatelli set about improving the design of the BR in 1923, the resulting BR.1 going into Regia Aeronautica service in the following year; differing mainly in having Warren-type W-form interplane bracing struts, a feature characteristic of all subsequent Rosatelli biplanes, the BR.1 had a new double-track main landing-gear arrangement with two independent units; the A.14 engine was retained but its frontal radiator was replaced by one of more advanced type; the new bomber demonstrated improved performance and an increased bombload by comparison with those of the BR; the type also established a new world record, lifting a 3,307-lb (1500-kg) payload to an altitude of 18,097 ft (5516 m); the BR.1 became involved in tests with a new revolving cylinder-type bomb rack and was used also for torpedo dropping experiments; some 150 BR.1s were built, almost all of them going into service with the Regia Aeronautica; the Swedish air arm bought two examples which were designated **B 2** in Flygvapen service
BR.2: the first flight of the prototype BR.2 took place in 1925; it had a more powerful Fiat A.25 engine, and other improvements included a strengthened structure, greater instrumentation and increased fuel capacity; the landing gear was also redesigned and improved; in 1930

some 15 Regia Aeronautica light bomber squadrons were equipped with the BR.2, but by then the type had become obsolescent
BR.3: the BR.3 was largely an update of the BR.2, appearing in 1930, and some 100 examples were built for Italian light bomber squadrons; Hungary obtained a single example. In outward appearance the BR.3 differed little from the BR.2 which had gone into service some five years before; the A.25 engine was retained, albeit in a more developed version; the landing gear was again modified, simplified and strengthened; equipment fitted for the first time included a radio transmitter/receiver and a panoramic camera; later production aircraft had Handley Page leading-edge slats; in the mid-1930s the BR.3 was relegated to training units, with which a number of examples were still serving in 1940
BR.4: last of Rosatelli's single-engined biplane bombers, the BR.4 made its maiden flight in 1934; a complete redesign, it had a chin-type tunnel radiator similar to that of the CR.30 and CR.32, the A.25 engine was retained and the divided landing gear had large, streamlined spat-type fairings; despite considerable aerodynamic refinement, the BR.4 was too slow to compete with the new generation of light twin-engined low-wing monoplanes under development, and only a single prototype was built

Fiat BR.20 Cicogna

Flown for the first time from the Fiat company airfield in Turin by Enrico Rolandi on 10 February 1936, the prototype of the **BR.20 Cicogna** (stork) immediately made a favourable impression. Before long this medium bomber was being publicised throughout the aeronautical world by the efficient propaganda

machine of Benito Mussolini's Fascist government.

The BR.20 was a low-wing cantilever monoplane, its slab-sided fuselage having a mixed covering of Dural sheet and fabric. The wing was skinned with metal, and the fabric-covered tail assembly included twin fin-and-rudder assemblies. The nose

included a manually operated gun turret, and below it was a glazed section for the bomb-aimer/navigator. The weapons bay was located in the forward fuselage between the flight deck and the wireless operator's compartment. A retractable Tipo DR dorsal turret (replaced by a Tipo M.1 turret from the 21st production BR.20) and a ventral gun position completed the defensive armament.

In the spring of 1937 two special **BR.20A** long-range civil aircraft appeared. They had rounded noses, were stripped of all military equipment and had no break in the fuselage underside as with the bomber. The aircraft were specially built to take part in the prestigious air race between Istres in southern France and Damascus in Syria, in which they were able to gain only

sixth and seventh places. One other civilianised BR.20 was built, the **BR.20L** named *Santo Francesco*, that first flew early in 1939. It had an elongated streamlined nose section and additional fuel tanks, enabling it to make a non-stop flight from Rome to Addis Ababa on 6 March 1939, the three-man crew led by Maner Lualdi achieving an average speed of 251 mph (404 km/h).

Fiat BR.20 Cicogna (continued)

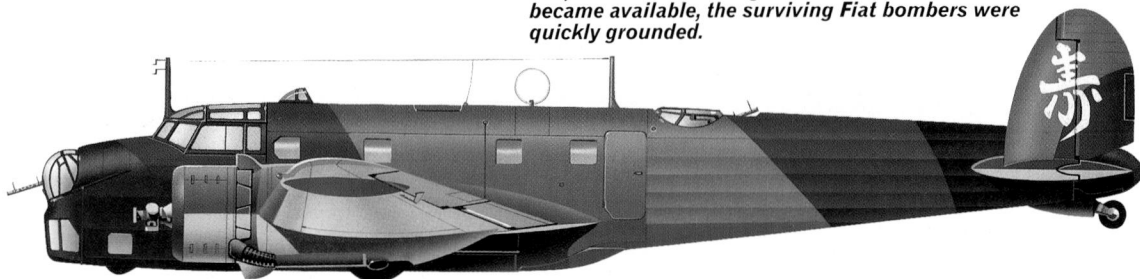

The Imperial Japanese army air force apparently did not find its BR.20 bombers particularly effective and, as soon as the long-awaited Mitsubishi Ki-21 became available, the surviving Fiat bombers were quickly grounded.

The first unit to equip with the BR.20 bomber was the 13° Stormo Bombardamento Terrestre at Lonate Pozzolo, in the autumn of 1936. The original BR.20 remained in production until February 1940, a total of 233 being completed. Of these, a single example went to Venezuela and 85 were sold to Japan. The Japanese BR.20 bombers, known as the **Type I**, were based at first in the Chinese coastal areas and were used to attack inland cities still in Chinese hands. Later, they were used in the border fighting against the Soviets at Nomanhan.

A number of BR.20s operated with the Italian Aviazione Legionaria supporting the Franco-led Nationalist faction in the Spanish Civil War. Arriving from the summer of 1937, the aircraft took part in day and night raids over the Teruel and Ebro fronts, frequently attacking troop and vehicle concentrations, as well as Republican-held cities. Nine BR.20s survived to take part in the Nationalist aviation victory parade at Madrid-Barajas on 12 May 1939. When the Italian personnel left for home, the BR.20s were handed over to Spain.

When Italy entered World War II on 10 June 1940, a new version of the basic design, the **BR.20M** (**Modificato**, or modified) had been in production for some six months. It differed from the original BR.20 in having a nose section of entirely new design and smoother outline. In all, 264 examples of the BR.20M were constructed, production ending in the spring of 1942.

In June 1940 the Regia Aeronautica had 172 examples of the BR.20 series in service, with a further 47 in reserve or under repair. The Fiat bombers took part in the brief campaign against France until 23 June 1940. Then, 80 factory-fresh BR.20Ms were allocated to the 13° and 43° Stormi and sent to Belgian bases to participate in the Italian effort

against the UK as part of the Corpo Aereo Italiano, which supported the Luftwaffe in the later stages of the Battle of Britain. They were involved in day and night raids against the ports of Harwich and Ramsgate and the industrial centre of Ipswich, between October and December 1940, when the survivors were withdrawn. The BR.20 was then involved in the campaigns in North Africa, Greece, Yugoslavia and in the attacks against Malta. Some missions were flown in the long-range reconnaissance role and this type of operation

became more usual as the war progressed, the BR.20 carrying out many such missions against partisan areas in the Balkans. At the time of the armistice between Italy and the Allies in September 1943, 81 BR.20s were still in first-line service with units in Italy, Yugoslavia, Albania and Greece, but by that time most surviving aircraft were attached to bomber training schools. During the final years of World War II a very few BR.20s remained in flying condition as trainers or transports.

Experimental versions tested included the **BR.20C**

The BR.20's wireless operator was seated in a compartment just in front of the main access door on the port side of the fuselage, just aft of the wing.

SPECIFICATION

Fiat BR.20

Type: five-seat medium bomber
Powerplant: two Fiat A.80 RC.41 radial piston engines each rated at 1,000 hp (746 kW)
Performance: maximum speed 268 mph (432 km/h) at 16,405 ft (5000 m); cruising speed 213 mph (343 km/h) at 15,910 ft (4850 m); climb to 16,405 ft (4000 m) in 17 minutes 56 seconds; service ceiling 23,620 ft (7200 m); range 1,864 miles (3000 km)
Weights: empty 14,110 lb (6400 kg); maximum take-off 21,826 lb (9900 kg)
Dimensions: wingspan 70 ft 8¾ in (21.56 m); length 52 ft 9¾ in (16.10 m); height 14 ft 1¼ in (4.30 m); wing area 796.56 sq ft (74.00 m²)

Armament: one 0.303-in (7.7-mm) Breda-SAFAT trainable forward-firing machine-gun in the Breda Tipo H nose turret, two 0.303-in (7.7-mm) Breda-SAFAT trainable rearward-firing machine-guns in the Breda Tipo DR dorsal turret or one 0.5-in (12.7-mm) Breda-SAFAT trainable rearward-firing machine-gun in the Breda Tipo M.1 dorsal turret, and one 0.303-in (7.7-mm) Breda-SAFAT trainable rearward-firing machine-gun in the ventral hatch position, plus up to 3,527 lb (1600 kg) of disposable stores carried in a lower-fuselage weapons bay, and generally comprising two 1,764-lb (800-kg) bombs, or two 1,102-lb (500-kg) bombs, or four 551-lb (250-kg) bombs or 12 441-lb (200-kg) bombs

with a powerful 37-mm cannon in the nose section and another BR.20 flown with tricycle landing gear. The final version to go into production was the **BR.20bis**, a complete redesign with a rounded fully glazed nose, more graceful fuselage contours,

a retractable tailwheel and pointed vertical tail surfaces. The main improvements were in engine power and defensive armament. Between March and July 1943 15 BR.20bis aircraft were built, but there is no record of their operational use.

This 3ª Squadriglia, 13° Stormo BR.20M was based at Pugli, southern Italy in April 1941. It is illustrated as it appeared just before it was transferred to North Africa. It carries mission symbols for eight raids against the UK during the Battle of Britain and six raids against Greece.

Fiat CR, CR.1, CR.2, CR.5 and CR.10

Two single-seat fighter prototypes, serialled MM.1 and MM.2 under the newly formed Regia Aeronautica's numbering system, were built and tested in 1923. Designated **Fiat CR** (**Caccia Rosatelli**, or Rosatelli fighter), and designed under the leadership of Celestino Rosatelli, these were compact biplanes of inverted-sesqui-

plane configuration. Of mixed wood and steel construction under a covering largely of fabric, the CR had rigid Warren-type W-form wing bracing and conventional fixed tailskid landing gear. The two prototypes differed in tail configuration, one having a rounded balanced rudder, and in the shape of the cowling for the Hispano-

Suiza engine.

The decision was made to build the CR in quantity as trials had revealed that the type surpassed its nearest rival, the SIAI S.52, in terms of manoeuvrability

Seemingly known under the alternative designations CR.5 or CR.10, this aircraft had an A.20 engine.

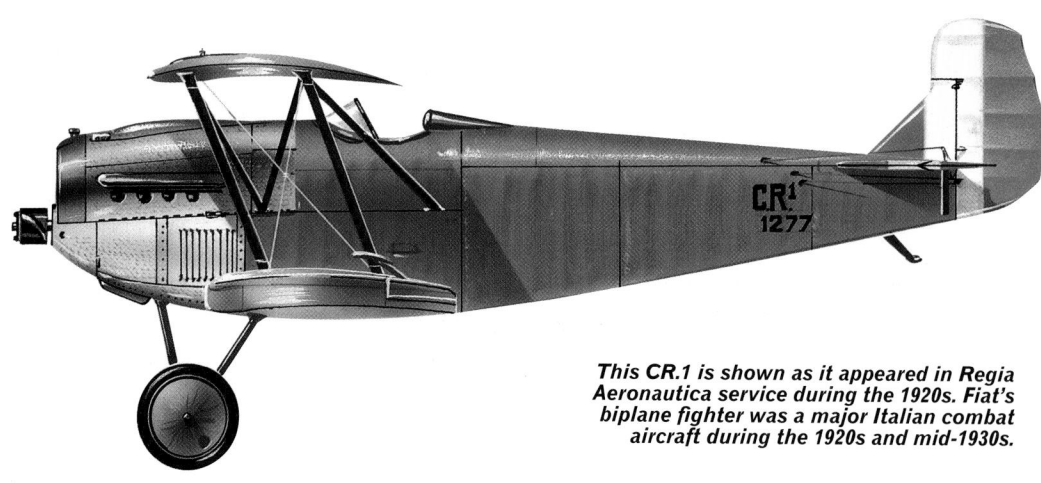

This CR.1 is shown as it appeared in Regia Aeronautica service during the 1920s. Fiat's biplane fighter was a major Italian combat aircraft during the 1920s and mid-1930s.

Liepaja. These aircraft were not withdrawn from service until 1936.

Variants of the CR.1 which were tested but did not enter production included one powered by a Fiat A.20 engine cooled by two Lamblin radiators, and another with an Alfa Romeo (Bristol) Jupiter radial. These were both **CR.5** aircraft, although some reports indicate that the designation **CR.10** may have been used for the A.20-engined aircraft. In 1928 the sole CR.2 was flight-tested with a 200-hp (149-kW) Armstrong Siddeley Lynx radial engine.

and speed even though the S.52 had the edge in climb rate. Production aircraft had the designation **CR.1**, but considerable care was taken in developing the type for squadron service, two further prototypes being tested under the CR.1 designation with a slight reduction in wing area and a revised radiator. These were followed by three production batches

from 1923, for a total of 240 aircraft.

During the 1930s a number of CR.1s was modified to take the 440-hp (328-kW) Isotta-Fraschini Asso Caccia engine. These re-engined machines were quite successful and revealed greatly improved performance. The Asso-powered CR.1 was withdrawn from service only in 1937.

A single CR.1 was purchased for the Belgian air arm and, after rejection of the type as squadron equipment, this was used by the 1e Escadrille de Chasse. Another example was tested by the Polish authorities, but the sole production order for the export market was placed by Latvia for nine CR.1s which equipped the naval fighter unit based at

SPECIFICATION	
Fiat CR.1	(840 kg); maximum take-off 2,546 lb (1155 kg)
Type: single-seat fighter	**Dimensions:** wingspan 29 ft 4⅓ in (8.95 m); length 20 ft 6 in (6.25 m); height 7 ft 10½ in (2.40 m); wing area 247.58 sq ft (23.00 m²)
Powerplant: one Hispano-Suiza 42-8 Vee piston engine rated at 300 hp (224 kW)	
Performance: maximum speed 169 mph (272 km/h) at optimum altitude; climb to 16,405 ft (5000 m) in 16 minutes 27 seconds; service ceiling 24,440 ft (7450 m); endurance 2 hours 35 minutes	**Armament:** two 0.303-in (7.7-mm) Vickers fixed forward-firing machine-guns in the upper part of the forward fuselage
Weights: empty 1,852 lb	

Fiat CR.20

The **Fiat CR.20** single-seat fighter was produced in considerable numbers for its time. It formed the equipment of the famous Regia Aeronautica aerobatic team and took part in the final stages of the Italian conquest of Libya, then in the campaign against the Emperor Haile Selassie in Abyssinia which ended in Italian victory in 1936. As there was no air opposition, the CR.20 was used for ground-attack duties in both campaigns. The various versions of the CR.20 ended their days in training units in the late 1930s.

This classic biplane had an unequal-span wing cellule and a carefully contoured fuselage. It was largely of metal construction with varnished fabric covering, except for light alloy panels over the forward fuselage. It was designed for the new Fiat A.20 engine, and four prototypes were built and tested, the first flight being made at Turin on 19 June 1926. In the following autumn the new fighter made a considerable impression at the Paris Salon de l'Aéronautique, where it was readily apparent as a Fiat product as a result of its W-type interplane struts and distinctive tail unit, both features of Celestino Rosatelli's drawing board.

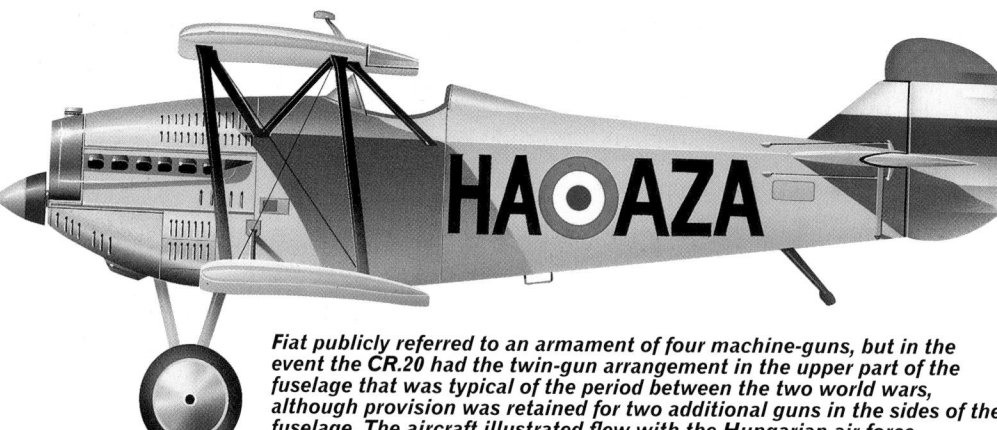

Fiat publicly referred to an armament of four machine-guns, but in the event the CR.20 had the twin-gun arrangement in the upper part of the fuselage that was typical of the period between the two world wars, although provision was retained for two additional guns in the sides of the fuselage. The aircraft illustrated flew with the Hungarian air force.

The fighter entered production in 1927, and 124 such warplanes were delivered between 1927 and 1929: of these, 107 were delivered to the Regia Aeronautica (88 Fiat-built and 19 CMASA-built aircraft) and the other 15 to Lithuania. A closely related model, built by Macchi in 1928 to the extent of 17 aircraft, was the **CR.20 Idro** (otherwise **ICR.20**) twin-float seaplane fighter. The two-seat trainer version of the CR.20 was the **CR.20B** that appeared in 1927, and this model entered service with the Regia Aeronautica as well as securing export orders from Austria and Hungary, which each received four such aircraft.

The CR.20 landplane

fighters were handicapped by a rather crude fixed tail-skid landing gear. As a result the **CR.20bis** appeared in 1929 with an entirely new divided main landing-gear arrangement incorporating oleo-pneumatic shock absorbers and wheel brakes, and the wing cellule of this model

was also modified slightly. Between 1920 and 1921 Fiat produced 211 examples of the CR.20bis model, including an unknown number of its **CR.20AQ** subvariant with the 425-hp (317-kW) A.20AQ engine. The latter provided a higher service ceiling and better perfor-

mance at altitude, but its increased fuel consumption meant reduced range and endurance. Countries that imported the CR.20bis included Austria (16 CR.20bis and 16 CR.20AQ aircraft, of which two crashed during their delivery flights), Hungary (12) and Paraguay (five).

In ICR.20 form, the type was deeply unpopular. The floats made for vicious handling inadequacies, including a tendency to fall out of loops.

Fiat CR.20 (continued)

The final production version of this single-seat fighter was the **CR.Asso**, which was the airframe of the CR.20bis married to the 450-hp (336-kW) Isotta-Fraschini Asso Caccia engine, an air-cooled unit which was housed in a distinctive and elegant cowling. The only major structural modification was a redesigned tailplane with increased horizontal surface area. A total of 204 examples of the CR.Asso was produced in 1932-3. The CR.Asso proved popular

with the squadriglie di caccia (fighter squadrons) and replaced the CR.20bis in aerobatic teams. The CR.20 family was also used in a variety of experimental roles, including the testing of the Handley Page leading-edge slat.

Some mystery surrounds a single CR.20 reported as sold to the USSR and four aircraft apparently used by Poland in the August 1929 fighter competition held between that country and other nations of the 'Little Entente' powers

(Czechoslovakia, Romania and Yugoslavia). In Hungarian service the CR.20bis remained in service from 1932 to 1936, when it was replaced by the CR.32 fighter, and the CR.20bis and CR.20AQ were still in Austrian service at the time of the 1938 annexation of the country by Germany, after which a number of the surviving aircraft were painted in Luftwaffe markings and used briefly at German training schools. Paraguay flew its five CR.20bis fighters operationally in the Gran Chaco War against Bolivia

between 1932 and 1935.

It was with the Regia Aeronautica, however, that the CR.20 played a dominant role. For a number of years virtually all the fighter squadrons were equipped

with various versions of the type and, in addition, the CR.20 Idro formed the strength of the uniquely Italian seaplane fighter units, the squadriglie di caccia marittima.

SPECIFICATION	
Fiat CR.20bis	**Weights:** empty 2,160 lb (980 kg); maximum take-off 3,086 lb (1400 kg)
Type: single-seat fighter	
Powerplant: one Fiat A.20 Vee piston engine rated at 410 hp (306 kW)	**Dimensions:** wingspan 32 ft 1¾ in (9.80 m); length 21 ft 11¾ in (6.70 m); height 9 ft (2.75 m); wing area 276.10 sq ft (25.65 m²)
Performance: maximum speed 168 mph (270 km/h) at sea level; climb to 16,405 ft (5000 m) in 13 minutes 37 seconds; service ceiling 27,885 ft (8500 m); endurance 3 hours	**Armament:** two 0.303-in (7.7-mm) Vickers fixed forward-firing machine-guns in the upper part of the forward fuselage

Fiat CR.25

The **CR.25** prototype flew for the first time on 22 July 1937 and immediately displayed excellent flying characteristics. A low-wing cantilever monoplane of all-metal construction with retractable tailwheel landing gear, it accommodated a crew of three comprising the pilot, observer/bomb-aimer and radio operator/gunner. The Italian air minister decided early in 1938 to use this twin-engined aircraft for land-based strategic reconnaissance combined with the role of long-range escort fighter. However, an original order for 40 aircraft was reduced in 1939 to just 10 aircraft, all completed by the begin-

ning of 1940. Nine of these, designated **CR.25bis**, were allocated to the 173ª Squadriglia Ricognizione Strategica Marittima (maritime strategic reconnaissance squadron) based at Palermo-Boccadifalco in Sicily. From there the type distinguished itself during escort missions for convoys bound to and from Libya. When on the leg which did not require escort work, the CR.25 aircraft carried out over-sea reconnaissance, often in the vicinity of Malta.

Despite a lack of spares, the small CR.25 force maintained a high level of operational efficiency, but attrition eventually took its

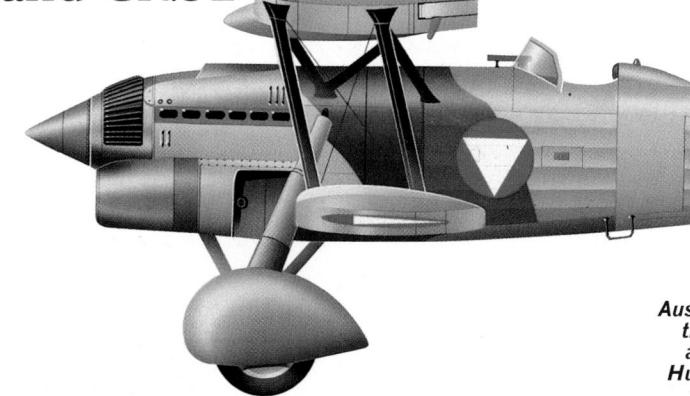

Similar in concept to the Mitsubishi Ki-46, the CR.25 gave exceptional service, despite being available only in limited numbers.

toll and surviving aircraft were withdrawn to northern Italy at the beginning of 1943. The tenth production aircraft was the sole **CR.25D**, which was used by the Italian air attaché in Berlin, where it was interned after Italy's armistice with the Allies on 8 September 1943.

Variant

CR.25quater: development of the CR.25bis with slightly increased wing area and more powerful armament; prototype testing was undertaken but no further development followed

SPECIFICATION	
Fiat CR.25bis	14,385 lb (6525 kg)
Type: three-seat strategic reconnaissance aircraft and long-range escort fighter	**Dimensions:** wingspan 52 ft 6 in (16.00 m); length 44 ft 5¾ in (13.56 m); height 11 ft 1¾ in (3.40 m); wing area 421.96 sq ft (39.20 m²)
Powerplant: two Fiat A.74 RC.38 radial piston engines each rated at 840 hp (626 kW)	**Armament:** two 0.5-in (12.7-mm) Breda-SAFAT fixed forward-firing machine-guns in the nose and one 0.5-in (12.7-mm) Breda-SAFAT trainable machine-gun in the power-operated dorsal turret, plus up to 1,543 lb (700 kg) of disposable stores carried in a lower-fuselage weapons bay, and generally comprising free-fall bombs
Performance: maximum speed 286 mph (460 km/h) at 18,045 ft (5500 m); cruising speed 245 mph (395 km/h) at optimum altitude; climb to 19,685 ft (6000 m) in 16 minutes 40 seconds; service ceiling 26,575 ft (8100 m); range 1,305 miles (2100 km)	
Weights: empty 9,645 lb (4375 kg); maximum take-off	

Fiat CR.30 and CR.32

In his **CR.30**, Celestino Rosatelli produced a completely new single-seat fighter design. The first of four prototypes flew in March 1932. The rounded wingtips and tail surfaces, together with the carefully cowled A.30 RA engine and wide-track divided main units of the fixed tailwheel landing gear combined to give a distinctive and workmanlike appearance to the CR.30, which retained W-form interplane bracing. Two of the prototypes participated in the Zurich international meeting in July 1932, creating widespread interest when they carried off the speed circuit contest at average speeds of 211.30 mph (340 km/h) and 205 mph (330 km/h). This success and others led to orders from the Regia Aeronautica for 121 examples of the

production-standard CR.30 for service with the squadriglie di caccia. Production lasted from 1932 to 1935, and the last first-line CR.30 fighters were retired from the 2º Stormo, then serving in Libya, in 1938.

The conversion of a pair of prototypes to two-seat

configuration proved a great success, and a large number of single-seat aircraft was later converted as **CR.30B** two-seat 'refresher' trainers and station hacks. That they filled an important gap is shown by the fact that the CANSA works received an order in World War II for 20

examples of the CR.30B to replace losses.

Two CR.30 fighters were converted as seaplanes by fitting twin floats and these were flown as trainers at the Scuola d'Alta Velocitá at Desenzano under the designation **CR.30 Idro** (otherwise **ICR.30**).

The main foreign opera-

tor of the CR.30 was the Hungarian air arm, which received two single-seat machines in the summer of 1936, followed by an ex-Regia Aeronautica aircraft in 1938 plus 10 CR.30B two-seaters. The Germans later passed two ex-Austrian CR.30s to Hungary. Austria had

Austria's CR.32 force was absorbed into the Luftwaffe soon after delivery. The aircraft were eventually passed on to Hungary by their new German owners.

At least 380 CR.32s took part in the air battles fought over Spain, proving formidable adversaries to the Soviet I-15 and I-16 machines which formed the backbone of the Republican fighter arm.

received three CR.30s and three CR.30Bs in 1936. Two CR.30s were sent to the Spanish Nationalists in 1938, but before that two had served with the Chinese 3rd Air Corps from 1934, and Paraguay had purchased two in 1937 as aerobatic trainers. A single CR.30 was handed over to Venezuela at the beginning of 1938 by an Italian aeronautical mission visiting that country. Total production of all versions was 176.

Not content with the excellent agility displayed by the CR.30 and determined to achieve an overall improvement in performance, Rosatelli produced a new fighter closely resembling the CR.30 but somewhat refined and with reduced overall dimensions. Manoeuvrability was enhanced by a judicious redistribution of loading, achieved mainly through relocation of fuel tanks. The resulting **CR.32** prototype took to the air for the first time on 28 April 1933. It

was an instant success, the first production order being received in March 1934. Production aircraft had variable-pitch propellers and could be equipped with a radio transmitter/receiver, panoramic camera or bomb racks. Modified versions for the Regia Aeronautica were built up to 1939, each designed to reduce all-up weight and improve performance. In addition, the CR.32 was demonstrated widely abroad and attracted considerable export orders.

Like the earlier CR.30, the CR.32 was widely used for aerobatic displays, many of them in Italy. On the occasion of visits by foreign statesmen, the 4° Stormo, based at Rome, invariably put on impressive shows with formations of five or 10 aircraft. During 1936 displays were given in other European capitals and major cities, and in 1937 throughout South America. The team's return to Europe culminated in a brilliant display at Berlin. The remarkable aerobatic quali-

ties of the CR.32 and its undoubted success in Spain misled the Italian air ministry, which formed the view that a fighter biplane still had potential as a weapon of war, with the result that the CR.42, developed from the CR.32, was already an outdated concept before the prototype made its first flight. The CR.32 itself soldiered on into World War II, and when Italy declared war, in June 1940, 324 were still in first-line service despite the fact that the type was by then hopelessly outclassed. Some aircraft were adapted as night-fighters, while those operated by units in Libya were used largely in the ground-attack role against British troops. The greatest wartime successes achieved by the CR.32 were in Italian East Africa, aircraft of the 410ᵃ and 411ᵃ Squadriglie destroying a number of British and South African aircraft before the final Italian surrender.

The first customer for

the CR.32 was China, which ordered 16 in 1933; armed with two 0.303-in (7.7-mm) Vickers machine-guns, these aircraft gave a good account of themselves against the invading Japanese. They were regarded as superior to the Curtiss Hawk biplanes which equipped most Chinese fighter units in the period 1934-6.

The Hungarian air arm received 76 CR.32s in 1935-6. These were used largely as fighter trainers, but fired their guns in anger when Hungary moved against the German puppet regime in March 1939. The Hungarians experimented with a CR.32 powered by a 750-hp (559-kW) Gnome-Rhône 11 Mars radial engine; the modified aircraft achieved an impressive maximum speed of 261 mph (420 km/h) at 13,125 ft (4000 m), but the Hungarian government's inability to obtain more Gnome-Rhônes thwarted

the plan to re-engine all available CR.32s. Austria ordered 45 CR.32bis fighters in the spring of 1936 to equip Jagdgeschwader II at Wiener Neustadt. In March 1938 the Austrian units were absorbed into Luftwaffe fighter groups, but after a brief period the 36 remaining aircraft were handed over to Hungary. When the Spanish Civil War ended in the spring of 1939, survivors of the CR.32s operated by the Italian Aviazione Legionaria were handed over to Spain, joining 60 **CR.32bis** supplied direct to Spain in 1937 and 27 **CR.32quater** fighters received by France in 1938. In addition, Spain acquired a manufacturing licence in 1938 and by the end of 1942 Hispano Aviación of Seville had completed 100 machines under the designation **HA-132-L Chirri**. Some of these remained in service as **C.1** aerobatic trainers up to 1953.

SPECIFICATION

Fiat CR.32ter

Type: single-seat fighter
Powerplant: one Fiat A.30 RA bis Vee piston engine rated at 600 hp (447 kW)
Performance: maximum speed 220 mph (354 km/h) at 9,845 ft (3000 m); cruising speed 196 mph (315 km/h) at optimum altitude; climb to 3,280 ft (1000 m) in 1 minute 35 seconds; service ceiling 28,870 ft (8800 m); range 485 miles (780 km)
Weights: empty 3,205 lb (1454 kg); maximum take-off 4,220 lb (1914 kg)
Dimensions: wingspan 31 ft 2 in

(9.50 m); length 24 ft 5¼ in (7.45 m); height 8 ft 7½ in (2.63 m); wing area 237.89 sq ft (22.10 m²)
Armament: two 0.5-in (12.7-mm) Breda-SAFAT fixed forward-firing machine-guns in the upper part of the forward fuselage and two 0.303-in (7.7-mm) Breda-SAFAT fixed forward-firing machine guns in the leading edges of the lower wing, plus up to 220 lb (100 kg) of disposable stores carried on one hardpoint under the fuselage, and generally comprising one 220-lb (100-kg) bomb or two 110-lb (50-kg) bombs

Variants

CR.32: original version; supplied to Regia Aeronautica (291, including prototypes), Hungary (76) and China (16)
CR.32bis: produced from 1935 with provision for two forward-firing 0.303-in (7.7-mm) SAFAT machine-guns in the leading edges of the lower wing in addition to the standard pair of fuselage-mounted guns; total production was 328, the Regia Aeronautica receiving 283 and Austria 45; the extra weight of the wing-mounted weapons often led to them being discarded
CR.32ter: version with only the two fuselage-mounted weapons, these being 0.5-in (12.7-mm) machine-guns; a total of 103 was built and all served in Spain, 60 of them with the Spanish air arm
CR.32quater: lighter than any version other than the original CR.32 but with the same armament as the CR.32ter; 398 were built, of which 105 served with the Italian Aviazione Legionaria in Spain; 27 went direct to Spain, 10 to Venezuela and (estimated) four to Paraguay; the balance was delivered to the Regia Aeronautica; this brought total Italian production to 1,212 aircraft

CR.33: version with the 700-hp (522-kW) Fiat A.33 RC.35 engine; the first prototype flew during 1935 with two others following in 1937, but no production aircraft were built
CR.40: short-nosed prototype powered by a 525-hp (391-kW) Bristol Mercury IV radial engine; built in parallel with the CR.32 prototype and test-flown in 1934; the upper wing was gulled and attached directly to the top of the fuselage, this arrangement giving the pilot a good forward and upward view
CR.40bis: prototype with the same wing configuration as the CR.40 but powered by the 700-hp (522-kW) Fiat A.59R radial engine; a disappointing maximum speed ensured that no production was undertaken
CR.41: similar to the CR.40 in general appearance, the CR.41 was powered by the 900-hp (671-kW) Gnome-Rhône 14Kfs radial engine; modified and enlarged vertical tail surfaces were used to maintain directional stability, and the maximum speed was 237 mph (381 km/h) at 16,405 ft (5000 m); tested during 1936 and 1937, the CR.41 was abandoned in favour of the CR.42

Fiat CR.42 Falco

Developed by Rosatelli to a requirement of the Italian air ministry, the **CR.42 Falco** (falcon) resulted from the belief that there was still a role for the highly manoeuvrable fighter biplane. This belief had been strengthened by

the achievements of biplane fighters involved in the air war which had been raging in Spain since 1936, and thus it was on 23 May 1938 that the prototype of this new biplane fighter first flew, at a time when every other major

European air force had or was in the process of adopting the 'modern' monoplane fighter. The CR.42 was derived from the CR.32, from which it retained the unequal-span wing configuration, and the experimental CR.40 and CR.41 fighters which had introduced a radial engine. The basic structure was of

metal, with mixed fabric and light alloy covering, and the wide-track divided main units of the fixed tail-wheel landing gear incorporated oleo-pneumatic shock absorbers and had both leg and wheel fairings. Power was provided by a A.74 R1C.38 radial engine in a long-chord cowling.

Following a successful series of test flights, the air ministry ordered 200 production machines, and the first of these series aircraft left the Turin factory during February 1939. Ironically, the tenth Fiat G.50 low-wing monoplane fighter had just left the production line just two months earlier.

Fiat CR.42 Falco (continued)

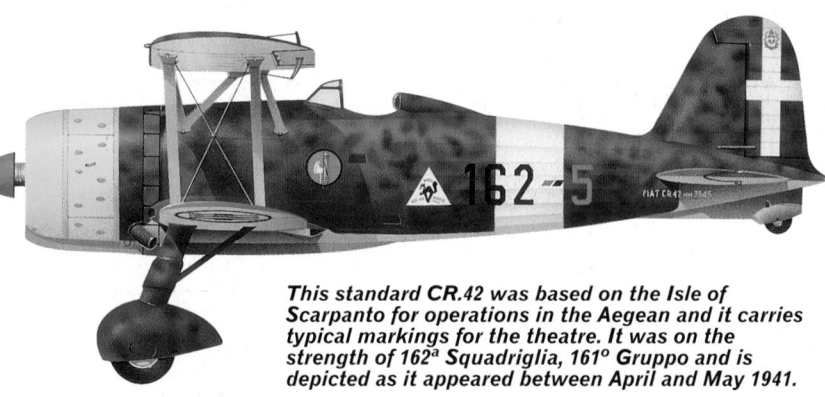

This standard CR.42 was based on the Isle of Scarpanto for operations in the Aegean and it carries typical markings for the theatre. It was on the strength of 162ª Squadriglia, 161º Gruppo and is depicted as it appeared between April and May 1941.

SPECIFICATION

Fiat CR.42AS Falco
Type: single-seat fighter and fighter-bomber
Powerplant: one Fiat A.74 R1C.38 radial piston engine rated at 840 hp (626 kW)
Performance: maximum speed 267 mph (430 km/h) at 16,405 ft (5000 m); cruising speed 235 mph (378 km/h) at 19,685 ft (6000 m); climb to 13,125 ft (4000 m) in 5 minutes 26 seconds; service ceiling 33,300 ft (10150 m); range 631 miles (1015 km) with auxiliary fuel or 488 miles (785 km) with standard fuel
Weights: empty 3,765 lb (1708 kg); normal take-off 5,033 lb (2283 kg)

Dimensions: wingspan 31 ft 10 in (9.70 m); length 27 ft 1⅜ in (8.27 m); height 11 ft 9⅓ in (3.59 m); wing area 241.12 sq ft (22.40 m²)
Armament: two 0.5-in (12.7-mm) Breda-SAFAT fixed forward-firing machine-guns in the upper part of the forward fuselage and, in some aircraft, two 0.5-in (12.7-mm) Breda-SAFAT fixed forward-firing machine-guns in blister fairings under the leading edges of the lower wing, plus up to 441 lb (200 kg) of disposable stores carried on two hardpoints under the lower wing, and generally comprising two 220-lb (110-kg) bombs

Final figures for CR.42 production according to the Fiat company show a total of 1,781 of all versions, including some 150 machines built for night ground-attack duties with the Luftwaffe during 1943-4.

Belgium ordered 40 CR.42s at the end of 1939, and by the time of the German onslaught on 10 May 1940 had taken 24 of the type on charge: these were operational with the 3e and 4e Escadrilles of the Aeronautic Militaire, and most were lost on the ground. Hungary ordered 68 CR.42s, and these were delivered during 1939-40. They participated in the campaign against Yugoslavia and were in action during the invasion of the USSR in the summer of 1941 before the survivors were withdrawn from front-line service at the end of 1941. Neutral Sweden took delivery of the first five of a contract for 72 CR.42s in February 1940, although final deliveries were not made until September 1941. In Flygvapen service the type was designated **J 11**, and was based at Gothenburg with Flygflottilj 9.

When Italy declared war on 10 June 1940, 272 CR.42s were on the strength of the fighter squadriglie. Aircraft of the 3º Stormo attacked targets in southern France and escorted bombing missions until the armistice with the French was signed on 24 June. CR.42s of the Corpo Aereo Italiano operated alongside Luftwaffe units from Belgian bases between September and November 1940. This participation in the Battle of Britain was sporadic and not particularly effective: the 50 CR.42 aircraft of the 18º Gruppo suffered heavy losses and on 3 January 1941 the CAI was recalled to Italy. The CR.42 then entered action in the Greek campaign, over the Aegean and also over Libya. Two fighter squadrons based in Italian East Africa, the 412ª and 413ª Squadriglie, received their CR.42 fighters in May 1940, but despite the type's robust qualities it was soon apparent that an effective fighter force in that theatre of operations could be maintained only if more fighters could be transferred from Italy. A great airlift over 2,485 miles (4000 km) of enemy territory was organised and, over a nine-month period from August 1940, SM.82 transports flew 51 dismantled CR.42s into East Africa as well as additional engines and spare parts. The last resistance in this theatre was provided by two surviving CR.42s until the Italians surrendered to the Allies in November 1941.

Variant

CR.42CB: this **Caccia Bombardiere** was an early conversion to carry a 441-lb (200-kg) bombload for ground attack; it joined operations in North Africa in spring 1941, and had two underwing racks for 110-lb (50-kg) or 220-lb (100-kg) bombs
CR.42AS: developed fighter-bomber with tropical carburettor, dust filter and racks for two 220-lb (100-kg) bombs; built in numbers from May 1941
CR.42CN: Caccia Notturna (night-fighter) version with exhaust flame dampers, radio, and small underwing searchlights
CR.42DB: flown in March 1941, this one-off prototype had a 1,160-hp (865-kW) Daimler-Benz DB 601E engine, demonstrating a maximum speed of over 320 mph (515 km/h)
ICR.42: otherwise known as the **CR.42 Idro**, this was a CR.42 mounted on twin floats as a development by CMASA, Fiat's subsidiary specialising in seaplanes; the variant was tested in 1940 but did not enter production
CR.42LW: night harassment and anti-partisan version; produced by Fiat for the Luftwaffe after the Italian aircraft industry in northern Italy had come under German control; the bombload was as for the CR.42AS
CR.42 two-seater: a small number of Swedish CR.42s survived World War II and was modified as target tugs; several Italian aircraft were converted as two-seat liaison aircraft with a second open cockpit immediately behind that of the pilot

Fiat CR.42

During early operations over Libya the CR.42 proved itself effective against both the aircraft of the Royal Air Force and ground targets, but as British forces built up the CR.42 was restricted more and more to ground-support activities. In July 1941 the first examples of the **CR.42AS** (**Africa Settentrionale**, or North Africa), optimised for the North African theatre, began to arrive in Libya. This variant had a tropical dust filter and was fitted with racks for two 220-lb (100-kg) bombs. From September 1942 losses became very heavy and only 82 CR.42s survived to be evacuated to Italy in January 1943.

Thereafter, the CR.42 continued in operational service in Greece, Albania and Yugoslavia, and the type was also based on Sicily for action against Malta, and on Sicily and on the Italian mainland for use in a fighter role. Despite continuing production, only 64 CR.42s remained serviceable at the time of the Italian armistice with the Allies in September 1943; few were flown by Italian units thereafter. The Luftwaffe continued small-scale production and about 150 of a night harassment version were delivered to the Germans and flown against the Allies from bases in northern Italy, Yugoslavia and Austria. The CR.42's last operations were flown in May 1945.

Fiat G.5

Fiat's G.5 was of low-wing cantilever monoplane configuration, and had fixed tailskid landing gear with wide-track divided main units carrying spatted wheels. I-BFFI was a G.5bis.

Designed by Gabrielli for use as a two-seat light aerobatic trainer, the **G.5** (**G.5/1** after the advent of later variants) was created in 1933 and powered by the A.54 radial engine with a Townend ring. In appearance it was typical of monoplane trainer types of

the period. The instructor and pupil were seated in tandem open cockpits, and the wing design incorporated Handley Page leading-edge slats. A small number of this original version appeared for use by private owners and flying clubs.

The following **G.5/2**, which did not progress beyond the prototype stage, differed mainly in having a 140-hp (104-kW) Fiat A.60 inverted inline engine. The final development of the basic design was the **Fiat G.5bis**, which had a more powerful

200-hp (149-kW) Fiat A.70 radial piston engine. Several were built and a number, converted to single-seat configuration, were still maintained in airworthy condition by private owners during the period following World War II.

SPECIFICATION	
Fiat G.5/1	
Type: two-seat aerobatic touring and training aircraft	climb to 6,560 ft (2000 m) in 9 minutes 22 seconds; service ceiling 18,865 ft (5750 m); range 491 miles (7905 km)
Powerplant: one Fiat A.54 radial piston engine rated at 135 hp (101 kW)	**Weights:** empty 1,323 lb (600 kg); maximum take-off 1,940 lb (880 kg)
Performance: maximum speed 140 mph (225 km/h) at optimum altitude; cruising speed 121 mph (195 km/h) at optimum altitude;	**Dimensions:** wingspan 34 ft 3¾ in (10.46 m); length 26 ft ¼ in (7.93 m); height 8 ft (2.44 m); wing area 184.93 sq ft (17.18 m²)

Fiat G.12

Originally ordered for service on the passenger routes of the Ala Littoria and Avio Linee Italiane airlines, the prototype of the **G.12C** (**Civile**, or civil) airliner did not fly until 15 September 1940, when Italy was already involved in World War II. As a result the G.12C 14-passenger transports delivered from 1941 onwards went directly to the Servizi Aerei Speciali, a military organisation co-ordinating the remaining functions of the civil air routes. G.12Cs operated between Milan and Bucharest, Budapest and

Tirana, and later provided support for the campaigns in Greece and Libya.

The **G.12 Gondar** was a special long-range version intended to maintain a physical communication capability with Italian East Africa, cut off by hundreds of miles of Allied-controlled territory. It was followed by three **G.12GA** (**Grande Autonomia**, or long range) transports, also fitted with additional fuel tanks. Late in 1942 and early 1943 single examples of the **G.12RT** and **G.12RTbis**, intended for liaison flights between Rome and Tokyo, were built: the two aircraft had ranges of 4,970 and 5,590 miles (8000 and

The G.12, illustrated in G.12T form, had a beautifully contoured fuselage. The landing gear was of the retractable tailwheel type, and power was provided by three Fiat radial engines.

Variant

G.12LCA: long-range civil model of which a few were completed for LATI (Linee Aeree Transcontinentale Italiane) with 750-hp (559-kW) Alfa Romeo 126 RC.34 radial engines and a maximum take-off weight of 34,116 lb (15475 kg)
G.212: enlarged version of the G.12 developed after World War II for a first flight on 19 February 1947; the prototype, which was taken over by the Aeronautica Militare in December 1947, was the sole **G.212CA** with a wingspan of 96 ft 3 in (29.34 m), Alfa Romeo 128 engines and accommodation for 24, 30 or 40 passengers according to seating arrangements; the **G.212CP** followed with Pratt & Whitney engines, and was known as the **Monterosa** or **Aeropullman**; a total of 18 was built, the type being operated primarily by the Avio Linee Italiane on routes from Rome and Milan to Switzerland, Belgium, Greece, Spain and Turkey; later, a few G.212s were sold to French operators and others were used by the Egyptian based Fiat-subsidiary, Societá Servizi Aerei Internationale d'Egitto, for passenger charter trips; the Aeronautica Militare bought six examples of the G.212CP, of which one was modified internally to provide a flying conference room for four plus a cabin for 14; the last two G.212 aircraft delivered to the military were used from 1951 onwards as flying classrooms

9000 km) respectively.

The principal military version built was the **G.12T**, intended as a transport for troops and freight. Its tasks included transport flights between Italy and North Africa and the carriage of fuel in Libya. As such, the G.12T accommodated 22 military personnel or an equivalent load of freight. Before the Italian armistice of September 1943 with the Allies, Fiat had supplied five G.12 aircraft to the Hungarian government, and after the armistice only one G.12 was used by the Italian Co-Belligerent Air Force although a considerable number remained operational in northern Italy, many of them used by the Luftwaffe.

After World War II surviving G.12s were used on the Corriere Aerei Militari (military courier services) of the Aeronautica Militare.

Production continued, the final versions to be built comprising the **G.12CA** civil airliner with 850-hp (634-kW) Alfa Romeo 128 RC.18 radial engines and the **G.12L** with 870-hp (649-kW) Fiat A.74 RC.42 radial engines, a lengthened fuselage and accommodation for 18 passengers: two subvari-

ants of the **G.18L** series were the **G.18LP** with 1,065-hp (794-kW) Pratt & Whitney R-1830-S1G3G Twin Wasp radial engines and the **G.18LB** with 730-hp (544-kW) Bristol Pegasus 48 radial engines. A total of 104 of all versions had been built when production ended in 1949.

SPECIFICATION	
Fiat G.12C	
Type: three/four-crew transport aircraft	range 1,081 miles (1740 km)
Powerplant: three Fiat A.74 RC.42 radial piston engines each rated at 770 hp (574 kW)	**Weights:** empty 19,599 lb (8890 kg); maximum take-off 28,219 lb (12800 kg)
Performance: maximum speed 246 mph (396 km/h) at 16,075 ft (4900 m); cruising speed 191 mph (308 km/h) at 11,155 ft (3400 m); service ceiling 26,245 ft (8000 m);	**Dimensions:** wingspan 93 ft 10 in (28.60 m); length 66 ft 1¾ in (20.16 m); height 16 ft 1 in (4.90 m); wing area 1,221.74 sq ft (113.50 m²)
	Payload: up to 14 passengers carried in the enclosed cabin

Fiat G.18

Designed by Giuseppe Gabrielli as potential equipment for Fiat's own airline, Avio Linee Italiane, the **G.18** prototype made its maiden flight on 18 March 1935. It was Gabrielli's answer to the DC-1 and DC-2, being a low-wing cantilever monoplane of all-metal construction which owed a great deal to a brief period of study undertaken

in the USA by Gabrielli. The main landing-gear legs retracted into the nacelles of the two 700-hp (522-kW) A.59R radials, leaving the wheels partially exposed, and there was accommodation for 18 passengers plus a three-man crew.

Tests with the prototype were disappointing, and after three G.18s had entered service with ALI in the first months of 1936 it was decided that the type was underpowered. ALI

therefore demanded a more powerful version. The resulting **G.18V**, first flown on 11 March 1937, had uprated A.80 RC.41 radials, redesigned vertical tail surfaces and a ventral strake which ran nearly the entire length of the fuselage undersurface. A total of six G.18Vs was built and delivered to ALI, which operated the variant on routes connecting Rome, Turin, Milan and Venice with nine European countries, achieving an excellent serviceability record.

On Italy's entry into World War II in June 1940, the airline was brought under military control and its flying personnel given Regia Aeronautica ranks. Renamed Nucleo Comunicazioni Avio Linee, the airline flew its G.18 and G.18V transports on a variety of tasks, including the ferrying of troops and equipment to Albania in

One of the more powerful G.18V aircraft is shown here, wearing the pre-war markings of the Avio Linee Italiane airline.

November 1940 as support for the Italian campaign against Greece. After the armistice between Italy and the Allies in September 1943, one aircraft remained operational with the Italian Co-Belligerent Air Force, operating between southern Italy and Albania. The Luftwaffe took over three aircraft discovered in the part of Italy Germany occupied, and transferred them to Germany. A fifth aircraft

was used by the Italian Fascist air arm co-operating with the German forces, and was the last to make a recorded flight by the type, on 29 April 1944. On the following day, as it was about to take off with a load which included ammunition, it was destroyed in an explosion which caused considerable damage to the airfield at Bresso, bringing a graphic end to the history of the G.18.

SPECIFICATION	
Fiat G.18V	
Type: three-crew transport aircraft	1,041 miles (1675 km)
Powerplant: two Fiat A.80 RC.41 radial piston engines each rated at 1,000 hp (746 kW)	**Weights:** empty 15,873 lb (7200 kg); maximum take-off 23,810 lb (10800 kg)
Performance: maximum speed 249 mph (400 km/h) at 15,090 ft (4600 m); cruising speed 211 mph (340 km/h) at optimum altitude; climb to 9,845 ft (3000 m) in 10 minutes 25 seconds; service ceiling 28,545 ft (8700 m); range	**Dimensions:** wingspan 82 ft ½ in (25.00 m); length 61 ft 8½ in (18.81 m); height 16 ft 5¼ in (5.01 m); wing area 950.05 sq ft (88.25 m²)
	Payload: up to 18 passengers in the enclosed cabin

Fiat G.46

The first new single-engined Fiat design built after World War II, the **G.46**, was projected as an intermediate trainer in 1946 and the **G.46B** prototype was flown for the first time in the summer of 1947. An all-metal cantilever low-wing monoplane, the G.46 incorporated inward-retracting landing gear and a glazed canopy for the tandem-seated pupil and instructor. Early tests revealed excellent flight characteristics, combining good manoeuvrability and an ability to perform aerobatics with a high degree

of safety.

The G.46 was accepted for quantity production and orders followed both for the Aeronautica Militare and for export. Two-seat versions built in quantity included the **G.46-1B** with a 195-hp (145-kW) Alfa Romeo 115bis engine; **G.46-2B** with a 250-hp (186-kW) de Havilland Gipsy Queen engine; and

by the 570-hp (425-kW) Alvis Leonides 502/4 Mk 24 radial engine, while the **G.49-2** had an R-1340

G.46-3B and **G.46-4B** differing in detailed equipment but both having the Alfa Romeo 115ter engine. A single-seat variant was built as the **G.46-A**, powered by the Alfa 115ter, and sub-variants designated **G.46-3A** and **G.46-4A** differed only in detail.

Some 150 of all versions were delivered to

SPECIFICATION	
Fiat G.46-4B	(500 km)
Type: two-seat intermediate trainer	**Weights:** empty equipped 2,425 lb (1100 kg); maximum take-off 3,109 lb (1410 kg)
Powerplant: one 215-hp (160-kW) Alfa Romeo 115ter 6-cylinder inverted inline piston engine	**Dimensions:** wingspan 34 ft 1½ in (10.40 m); length 27 ft 9¾ in (8.48 m); height 7 ft 10½ in (2.40 m); wing area 172.23 sq ft (16.00 m²)
Performance: maximum speed 194 mph (312 km/h); service ceiling 19,850 ft (6050 m), range 310 miles	

In mid-2000, this aircraft remained airworthy on the US civil register. The aircraft is a G.46-B and is operated by its New York owner as a display mount. The type's long cockpit canopy is evident.

the Italian air arm and 70 aircraft were exported. Production terminated in 1952, but G.46s remained at Italian military training schools for a number of years, before the survivors were relegated to civil

aero clubs where they were used for aerobatic training. The final version built, the **G.46-5B**, was a specialised two-seat navigation trainer that did not advance beyond the prototype stage.

Fiat G.49

The **G.49** was built in two versions and was intended as a replacement for the North American T-6 Texan basic trainer which in the early 1950s was still in service with many of the members of the NATO alliance. A low-wing cantilever monoplane with inward-retracting main landing-gear units, the G.49 was designed by Gabrielli around the need to keep the design simple and light. First flown at the end of September 1952, the **G.49-1** was powered

Wasp radial. Both versions had a raised canopy for the pupil and instructor, seated in tandem.

This all-metal, two-seat design was ultimately commercially unsuccessful and only a limited number

of Fiat G.49-2s went into service as trainers with Italy's Aeronautica Militare.

SPECIFICATION	
Fiat G.49-2	(2240 kg); maximum take-off 6,305 lb (2860 kg)
Type: two-seat basic flying trainer	**Dimensions:** wingspan 42 ft 7¾ in (13.00 m); length 31 ft 2 in (9.50 m); height 8 ft 8¼ in (2.65 m); wing area 262.43 sq ft (24.38 m²)
Powerplant: one Pratt & Whitney R-1340-S3H1 Wasp radial piston engine rated at 610 hp (455 kW)	
Performance: maximum speed 230 mph (370 km/h) at 4,920 ft (1500 m); cruising speed 122 mph (196 km/h) at optimum altitude; initial climb rate 1,300 ft (396 m) per minute; service ceiling 22,310 ft (6800 m); range 1,181 miles (1900 km)	**Armament:** one 0.5-in (12.7-mm) Breda-SAFAT fixed forward-firing machine-gun in the leading edge of the starboard wing, plus disposable stores on two underwing hardpoints, generally comprising practice bombs or eight air-to-surface unguided rockets
Weights: empty 4,938 lb	

An attractive design, the G.49 failed to find either a ready civil or military market. I-FIAT was a P&W-powered G.49-2.

Fiat G.50 Freccia, G.51 and G.52

Design of the **G.50 Freccia** (arrow) low-wing cantilever monoplane was launched by Gabrielli in April 1935. After extensive modifications, many ordered by the Italian authorities, the first of two prototypes made its maiden flight at Marina di Pisa on 26 February 1937. Test pilot Giovanni de Briganti reported a tendency to spin and this problem continued even after series production had begun. The G.50 was an all-metal aircraft, only the control surfaces being fabric-covered, with tailwheel landing gear including wide-track main units that retracted inward;

the tailwheel was originally fitted with a streamlined fairing, but this was often discarded in service use.

The prototypes and first pre-production batch of 45 aircraft had an enclosed cockpit with a rearward sliding canopy, but later production machines had either an open or partially enclosed cockpit. Apart from the two prototypes, a total of 778 machines was built, 428 of them at the CMASA works and the others by Fiat, which started production of the type only in November 1940. The final production machines left the Fiat assembly lines in the spring

of 1942.

Twelve pre-production G.50s formed the Gruppo Sperimentale de Caccia, which operated in Spain with the Italian Aviazione Legionaria for a few weeks before the Republican surrender to General Franco's Nationalist forces in 1939. When Italy entered World War II, 97 G.50s were in service. They took part in the fighting in southern France in June 1940 and then flew with the Corpo Aereo Italiano in Belgium for operations against the UK between September 1940 and January 1941. However, the very limited range of the G.50 reduced it to an almost non-existent role with the CAI. Subsequently, the G.50-equipped 24° and

154° Gruppi moved to Albania for operations against Greece. Some G.50s were converted as fighter-bombers with under-wing racks for bombs, including anti-personnel weapons, and this version equipped the 50° Stormo in North Africa.

The **G.50bis**, whose first example recorded its maiden flight on 9 September 1940, incorporated increased fuel tankage, a redesigned vertical tail surface, and glazed cockpit side panels to protect the pilot from the slipstream. This model

This G.50 carries the markings of 352ª Stormo, 20° Gruppo while it was serving with the CAI (Corpo Aereo Italiano) in Belgium in 1940-41.

Variant

G.50 prototype and pre-production aircraft: two prototypes and 45 pre-production aircraft with enclosed cockpits; suffered some instability in flight

G.50 initial production aircraft: characterised by modified flaps, reshaped vertical tail surface and an open cockpit; 206 built by CMASA and six by Fiat; 35 machines to Finland and 10 to Croatia

G.50bis: vertical tail surface further modified, folding transparent panels on sides of cockpit and greater fuel capacity; 421 built, 77 of them by CMASA

G.50ter: single example first flown in July 1941 with the new 1,000-hp (746-kW) A.76 radial engine for a maximum speed of 329 mph (530 km/h)

G.50V: single example powered by the 1,175-hp (876-kW) Daimler-Benz DB 601A inverted-Vee engine for a maximum speed of 360 mph (580 km/h) in flight trials from August 1941

G.50bisA/N: single prototype of a two-seat fighter-bomber variant intended for operation on the aircraft-carriers *Aquila* and *Sparviero* (conversions from merchant ships, neither of which was completed); test-flown for the first time on 3 October 1942 and planned with the armament of four 0.5-in (12.7-mm) machine-guns and one 551-lb (250-kg) bomb

G.50B: two-seat dual-control fighter trainer development of the G.50, of which CMASA built 100 examples between 1940 and 1943; prototype flown for first time on 30 April 1940; long glazed canopy, but top of section over rear cockpit left open

G.51: planned as the production version of the G.50V to be manufactured by CMASA, but was then cancelled in favour of the G.55

G.52: version proposed with the A.75 RC.53 radial engine

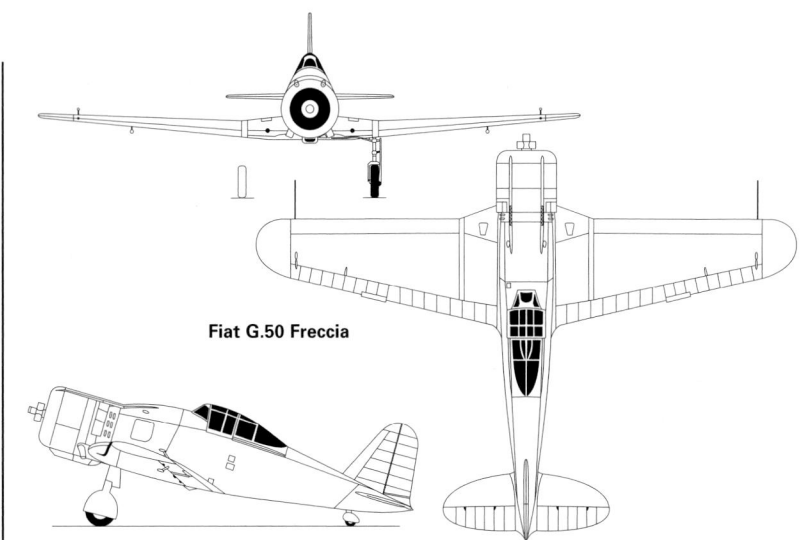

Fiat G.50 Freccia

SPECIFICATION	
Fiat G.50 Freccia	416 miles (670 km)
Type: single-seat fighter	**Weights:** empty 4,354 lb
Powerplant: one Fiat A.74 RC.38	(1975 kg); maximum take-off
radial piston engine rated at	5,324 lb (2415 kg)
870 hp (649 kW)	**Dimensions:** wingspan 35 ft
Performance: maximum speed	11½ in (10.96 m); length 25 ft 6¾ in
293 mph (472 km/h) at 19,685 ft	(7.79 m); height 9 ft 8½ in (2.96 m);
(6000 m); cruising speed 258 mph	wing area 195.37 sq ft (18.15 m²)
(415 km/h) at optimum altitude;	**Armament:** two 0.5-in (12.7-mm)
climb to 19,685 ft (6000 m) in	Breda-SAFAT fixed forward-firing
7 minutes 30 seconds; service	machine-guns in the upper part of
ceiling 32,265 ft (9835 m); range	the forward fuselage

was used in Croatia, but most of the type went to North Africa with the 2° and 155° Gruppi, whose aircraft were equipped with carburettor sand filters. After the September 1943

armistice, only four G.50s remained in flying condition, and these were used as trainers by the air arm of the Fascist republic still fighting alongside Germany.

Cpt. Olli Puhakka scored 13 kills with the G.50. As commander of 3/LeLv 26 of the Finnish air force he flew FA-25, chalking up five victories in the aircraft. His machine is illustrated as it appeared in December 1942.

Apart from the 12 pre-production aircraft flown in Spain and the 10 G.50s supplied to the air force of the puppet Croatian government, the only aircraft of the series to be exported were 35 G.50s bought by Finland in 1939. They were received too late for service in the 1939-40 Winter War with the USSR, but flew with some distinction against the Soviet forces during the Continuation War of 1941-44. Several aircraft survived the war after being used against the Germans in 1944-5, the last example being grounded in 1947.

Fiat G.55 Centauro

The **G.55 Centauro** (centaur) was a low-wing cantilever monoplane of all-metal construction, and was designed as a single-seat fighter by Gabrielli. It represented a great improvement by comparison with the G.50. Great care was taken to blend an aerodynamically advanced airframe with a structure which was robust and would lend itself to mass production. The configuration of the G.55 included

fully retractable landing gear and a raised cockpit providing excellent fields of vision. Fast and manoeuvrable, the type proved popular with its pilots.

The first of three prototypes flew on 30 April 1942. The third machine was the only prototype to carry armament, comprising one engine-mounted cannon and four fuselage-mounted machine-guns. The G.55 was evaluated under operational conditions

Fiat G.55/I Centauro

from March 1943, but by then the Italian air ministry had already decided on the type's mass production. However, only 16 **G.55/0** pre-production and 15 **G.55/I** initial production aircraft had been delivered to the Regia Aeronautica by September 1943, when Italy signed an armistice with the Allied forces, and subsequent production was undertaken for the Fascist air arm flying alongside the Luftwaffe in efforts to hold

the northern half of Italy. Before wartime production ended, 274 more G.55s had been completed and a further 37 were abandoned at an advanced stage of their construction.

Before the September 1943 armistice, the G.55 had been involved in the defence of Rome with the 353ª Squadriglia of the

Regia Aeronautica. Post-armistice operations were mainly with the Fascist air arm's Squadriglia 'Montefusco', based at Venetia Reale, and then with the three squadrons which formed the 2° Gruppo Caccia Terrestre: the G.55's losses were heavy, mainly in Allied attacks on airfields.

Variant

G.55A: Fiat reinstated the G.55 assembly line post-war, using assemblies and components manufactured during the conflict; the G.55A was a single-seat fighter/advanced trainer, the prototype first flying on 5 September 1946; it differed from the G.55 only in instrumentation and armament, the latter comprising either two wing-mounted plus two fuselage-mounted 0.5-in (12.7-mm) machine-guns, or two 20-mm Hispano-Suiza wing-mounted cannon plus two 0.5-in (12.7-mm) fuselage-mounted machine-guns; the Aeronautica Militare obtained 19 G.55As, and another 30 were supplied to Argentina, which in 1948 returned 17 of the aircraft for resale to Egypt with the armament of four 0.5-in (12.7-mm) Breda-SAFAT machine-guns

G.55B: two-seat advanced trainer variant, the prototype first flying on 12 February 1946; 10 were used by the Aeronautica Militare and 15 were sold to Argentina in 1948

G.56: developed from the G.55 to take the more powerful Daimler-Benz DB 603A engine; two prototypes were built in the spring of 1944 with minor changes in structure and the fuselage-mounted machine-guns deleted; the first prototype survived the war and was used subsequently by Fiat as a testbed

The revised canopy and rear fuselage contours of the two-seat G.55B compared to the G.55/I are readily apparent in this view of one of the former.

Fiat G.55 Centauro (continued)

With a DB 603 inline engine installed, the G.56 was flight-tested in Luftwaffe markings. No production followed.

SPECIFICATION

Fiat G.55/I Centauro
Type: single-seat fighter and fighter-bomber
Powerplant: one Fiat RA.1050 RC.58 Tifone (licence-built DB 605A) inverted-Vee piston engine rated at 1,475 hp (1100 kW)
Performance: maximum speed 391 mph (630 km/h) at 26,245 ft (8000 m); cruising speed 348 mph (560 km/h) at optimum altitude; climb to 19,685 ft (6000 m) in 7 minutes 12 seconds; service ceiling 41,665 ft (12700 m); range 746 miles (1200 km)
Weights: empty 5,798 lb (2630 kg); maximum take-off 8,197 lb (3718 kg)
Dimensions: wingspan 38 ft 10½ in (11.85 m); length 30 ft 9 in (9.37 m); height 10 ft 3¼ in (3.13 m); wing area 227.23 sq ft (21.11 m²)
Armament: one engine-mounted 20-mm MG 151/20 fixed forward-firing cannon, two 20-mm MG 151/20 fixed forward-firing cannon in the leading edges of the wing and two 0.5-in (12.7-mm) Breda-SAFAT fixed forward-firing machine-guns in the upper part of the forward fuselage, plus up to 705 lb (320 kg) of disposable stores carried on two underwing hardpoints, and generally comprising two 353-lb (160-kg) bombs

Fiat G.59

Known at the project stage as the **G.55M**, the **G.59** was in fact a revamped version of the G.55 wartime fighter, powered by a 1,420-hp (1059-kW) Rolls-Royce Merlin 500/20 piston engine. The first prototype comprised a G.55 airframe converted to two-seat configuration with a Packard-built engine taken from a North American P-51D Mustang.

Like the G.46, the G.59 was used for advanced high-speed and aerobatic training and was built in two-seat (B) and single-seat (A) configuration. It was used in limited numbers by the Aeronautica Militare and was exported to Syria. A number of ex-Aeronautica Militare single-seaters was subsequently sold abroad.

An unusually powerful and high-performing trainer, the G.59 served in Italy and abroad in respectable numbers.

Variant

G.59-1A: single-seater which entered service at Lecce flying school in 1950
G.59-1B: two-seater which entered service at Lecce flying school in 1950
G.59-2A: single-seater with four wing-mounted 20-mm cannon and underwing racks for bombs or auxiliary fuel tanks; 30 built, of which 26 sold to Syria and one to Argentina
G.59-2B: two-seater which followed the G.59-1B in production, 19 built, of which four sold to Syria
G.59-3A: single navigation trainer prototype
G.59-4A: single-seater of 1951 with bubble canopy and cut-down rear fuselage; 30 built, of which 20 went to the Aeronautica Militare
G.59-4B: two-seater produced in parallel with G.594A; 85 built

SPECIFICATION

Fiat G.59-4A
Type: single-seat advanced trainer
Powerplant: one 1,420-hp (1059-kW) Rolls-Royce Merlin 500/20 12-cylinder Vee piston engine
Performance: maximum speed 368 mph (593 km/h); climb to 22,965 ft (7000 m) in 8 minutes; service ceiling 37,730 ft (11500 m);
range 882 miles (1420 km)
Weights: empty equipped 6,283 lb (2850 kg); maximum take-off 7,628 lb (3460 kg)
Dimensions: wingspan 38 ft (11.58 m); length 31 ft ¾ in (9.47 m); height 12 ft ¾ in (3.68 m)
Armament: two or four machine-guns

Fiat RS.14

Designed at the CMASA works at Marina di Pisa by Manlio Stiavelli, the **RS.14 (Ricognizione Stiavelli**, or Stiavelli reconnaissance) was a long-range floatplane for the maritime reconnaissance role. The first of two prototypes recorded its maiden flight during May 1939 as a four/five-seat low/mid-wing cantilever monoplane of all-metal construction with the powerplant of two A.74 RC.38 radials. The fuselage had an almost perfectly streamlined shape, terminating in a cantilever tail unit incorporating a tall fin-

and-rudder assembly, and was mounted on a side-by-side pair of large floats by struts that were smoothly faired to cause minimum drag. These features were retained in the 186 series aircraft built by CMASA between May 1941 and September 1943.

The amply glazed, pointed nose section housed the observer/bomb-aimer, who also operated an AGR 90 camera in the rear fuselage. The flight deck accommodated the pilot and co-pilot on side-by-side seats, and the wireless operator's compartment was located immediately behind the flight deck.

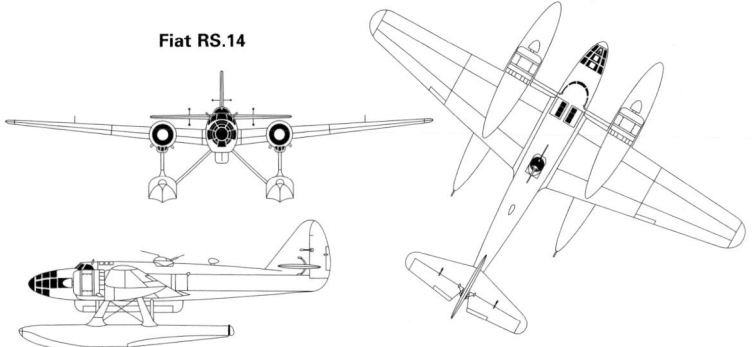

Fiat RS.14

The RS.14 formed the equipment of a number of squadriglie da ricognizione strategica marittima

(maritime strategic reconnaissance squadrons), located at bases round the coast of the Italian mainland and also of of Sicily and Sardinia. The RS.14 performed useful convoy escort work and covered enormous distances on anti-submarine patrols. A small number survived after Italy's September 1943 armistice with the Allies to operate with units of the Italian Co-Belligerent Air

Force. After World War II, surviving RS.14s were used for liaison between Italy mainland and outlying points in the Mediterranean, each carrying a maximum of four passengers.

A development of the basic design was the **AS.14 (Assalto Stiavelli**, or Stiavelli attacker), which was a twin-engined land-plane with retractable landing gear. Intended for

In a bombing role the RS.14 could carry a long ventral gondola to accommodate various combinations of anti-submarine bombs up to a maximum weight of 882 lb (400 kg).

the ground-attack task, the AS.14 was to have been armed in production form with a 37-mm cannon and two 0.5-in (12.7-mm) machine-guns in the nose, as well as two 0.5-in (12.7-mm) machine-guns firing from a ventral position. Despite the weight of the armament and armour protection, the maximum speed was a very respectable 273 mph (440 km/h). The prototype first flew on 11 August 1943, but no production was undertaken.

In AS.14 form, Fiat's twin-engined warplane was a dedicated ground-attack landplane. Like the RS.14, it employed a Caproni-Lanciani 'E' dorsal turret.

SPECIFICATION

Fiat RS.14
Type: five-seat long-range maritime reconnaissance floatplane
Powerplant: two Fiat A.74 RC.38 radial piston engines each rated at 840 hp (626 kW)
Performance: maximum speed 242 mph (390 km/h) at 13,125 ft (4000 m); cruising speed 205 mph (330 km/h) at optimum altitude; climb to 16,405 ft (5000 m) in 15 minutes; service ceiling 16,405 ft (5000 m); range 1,553 miles (2500 km)
Weights: empty 12,059 lb (5470 kg); maximum take-off 18,673 lb (8470 kg)
Dimensions: wingspan 64 ft 1¼ in (19.54 m); length 46 ft 3¾ in (14.10 m); height 18 ft 5¾ in (5.63 m); wing area 538.21 sq ft (50.00 m^2)
Armament: one 0.5-in (12.7-mm) Scotti trainable machine-gun in the dorsal turret and one 0.303-in (7.7-mm) Breda-SAFAT trainable lateral-firing machine-gun in each of the two beam positions, plus up to 882 lb (400 kg) of disposable stores carried in a detachable ventral tray, and generally comprising two 353-lb (160-kg) depth charges, or four 220-lb (100-kg) bombs, or six 110- or 88-lb (50- or 40-kg) bombs

Fieseler Fi 103 (V-1) and Fi 103 Reichenberg

After aiming his missile at the target, the Fi 103R-IV pilot was expected to bale out. This action was certain to result in his being sucked into the engine intake.

The first guided missile to be used operationally in large numbers, the **Fi 103** was a pilotless flying-bomb for the area bombardment of large urban areas. Development of the weapon was authorised in June 1942, and the Fi 103 began to take shape under the leadership of Dipl.-Ing. Robert Lusser as an aircraft-configured weapon with a circular-section fuselage. A small propeller, whose rotation measured the distance flown by the weapon before commanding a cut-off of the fuel and a dive after a pre-set distance had been covered, was installed at the fuselage nose. The fuselage itself contained the master magnetic compass, the warhead, the fuel tank, the two high-pressure air tanks used to power the control surfaces and feed the fuel to the engine, the battery, the master gyro assembly and guidance package, and the pneumatic servos controlling the elevators and rudder. The rest of the airframe comprised the cantilever mid-set wing and a plain tail unit whose vertical surface provided the rear support for the pulse-jet engine whose forward end was carried by a pylon over the battery section.

The first unpowered test vehicle was launched from an Fw 200 Condor motherplane in December 1942, and the first powered ground launch took place later in the same month. There were a number of development problems, but the weapon was ready for use in the summer of 1944 after some 300 Fi 103s had been fired in trials. The weapon was dubbed **V-1** (**Vergeltungswaffe-1**, or reprisal weapon-1) by the Nazi party, and the first was fired against London on 12 June 1944 from a fixed 'ski site' launcher ramp in which a powered piston accelerated the weapon to flying speed. The V-1 had a a range of 149 miles (240 km) with a 1,874-lb (850-kg) HE warhead.

The offensive that followed saw the Luftwaffe launch 8,617 standard missiles against London and other British targets in the period up to the end of August 1944, when the programme was taken over by the German army, which fired 11,988 weapons against a range of European targets in the period up to the end of March 1945. Another version of the weapon had a wooden wing and a smaller warhead for longer-range attacks, and 275 of these weapons were fired by the SS against British targets between January and March 1945. Finally, the Luftwaffe fired 865 missiles from adapted He 111 bombers between September 1944 and March 1945.

From a time late in 1943, German planners had started to consider the use of piloted missiles to make precision attacks on high-priority targets, a policy that developed quite independently of the Japanese *kamikaze* attacks. With a deteriorating war situation, Adolf Hitler gave the go-ahead for such a project in March 1944, and the Fi 103 was adopted for this programme in a version designated as the **Fi 103R** (**Reichenberg**). Four versions were planned initially: an unpowered **Fi 103R-I** for early flight tests, powered **Fi 103R-II** and **Fi 103R-III** to serve as basic and advanced two-seat trainers respectively, and the operational **Fi 103R-IV**. The last of these differed from the V-1 in having a pilot's cockpit (built round the forward support for the pulse-jet) as well as conventional controls and control surfaces. It was intended that, after launch from a motherplane, the pilot would aim his R-IV at the target and then bale out, descending by parachute, as the missile continued to its impact point. About 175 R-IVs were produced, but their continued development and planned use was abandoned in late 1944.

SPECIFICATION

Fieseler Fi 103R-IV
Type: single-seat piloted missile
Powerplant: one Argus 109-014 pulse-jet engine rated at 661 lb st (2.95 kN)
Performance: maximum speed 497 mph (800 km/h) at 8,200 ft (2500 m); range 205 miles (330 km) from a launch at 8,200 ft (2500 m); powered endurance 32 minutes
Weights: maximum launch 4,960 lb (2250 kg)
Dimensions: wingspan 18 ft 9¼ in (5.72 m); length 26 ft 3 in (8.00 m)

Fieseler Fi 156 Storch

Best-known of all the Fieseler designs because of its extensive use during World War II, the **Fi 156 Storch** (Stork) was a remarkable STOL (short take-off and landing) aircraft that was first flown during the early months of 1936. A braced high-wing monoplane of mixed construction, with a conventional braced tail unit and fixed tailskid landing gear with long-stroke main units, the Fi 156 was powered by an Argus inverted Vee piston engine, and its extensively glazed cabin provided an excellent view for its three-man crew. As with the earlier one-off **Fi 97** low-wing monoplane, the key to the success of this aircraft was its wing. This incorporated the company's high-lift devices and comprised, in the initial production series, a fixed slat extending over the entire span of the wing leading edge, with slotted ailerons and slotted camber-changing flaps occupying the entire trailing edge. Flight-testing of the first three prototypes (**Fi 156 V1**, **V2** and **V3**) showed that the capability of this aircraft more than exceeded its STOL expectations for, with little more than a light breeze blowing, it needed a take-off run of only about 200 ft (60 m) and could land in about a third of that distance.

Built to compete against fixed-wing submissions from Messerschmitt and Siebel and an autogyro from Focke-Wulf, the three prototypes were followed by the ski-equipped **Fi 156 V4** for winter trials, a pre-production **Fi 156 V5** and, in early 1937, by 10 **Fi 156A-0** aircraft for service evaluation. One of these was demonstrated publicly for the first time at an international flying meeting at the end of July 1937.

This view of an Fi 156C shows some of the type's key features. Among these was the extensive cockpit glazing, which overhung the fuselage sides to give the crew excellent downward visibility. Note also the rear-mounted machine-gun.

SPECIFICATION

Fieseler Fi 156C-2
Type: two-seat army co-operation/ reconnaissance aircraft
Powerplant: one 240-hp (179-kW) Argus As 10C-3 8-cylinder inverted Vee piston engine
Performance: maximum speed 109 mph (175 km/h) at sea level, economical cruising speed 81 mph (130 km/h), service ceiling 15,090 ft (4600 m), range 239 miles (385 km)
Weights: empty 2,050 lb (930 kg); maximum take-off 2,921 lb (1325 kg)
Dimensions: wingspan 46 ft 9 in (14.25 m), length 32 ft 5¾ in (9.90 m), height 10 ft (3.05 m), wing area 279.87 sq ft (26.00 m^2)
Armament: one rear-firing 0.31-in (7.92-mm) machine-gun on pivoted mount

Fieseler Fi 156 Storch (continued)

By the time of its first public demonstration, the general-purpose **Fi 156AA** was in production. Service tests confirmed that Germany's armed forces had acquired a 'go-anywhere' aircraft, and for the remainder of the war the Storch was found virtually wherever German forces were operating, production of all variants totalling almost 2,900 aircraft.

Because of their capability, Fi 156s were used in some remarkable exploits. Best known are the rescue of Benito Mussolini from imprisonment in a hotel amid the Apennine mountains, on 12 September 1943, and the flight made by Hanna Reitsch into the ruins of Berlin on 26 April 1945, carrying General Ritter von Greim to be appointed by Adolf Hitler as his new Commander of the Luftwaffe.

During the war the Fi 156 was built for the Luftwaffe by Morane-Saulnier in France and by Mraz in Czechoslovakia. These two companies continued production after the war, Morane-Saulnier producing **M.S.500** variants and Mraz the **K-65 Cap**.

Morane-Saulnier built the M.S.500 Criquet in three variants, the basic M.S.500 (illustrated) which equated to the Fi 156C, the M.S.501 and the M.S.502, which differed in engine type.

Fieseler Fi 156C-1

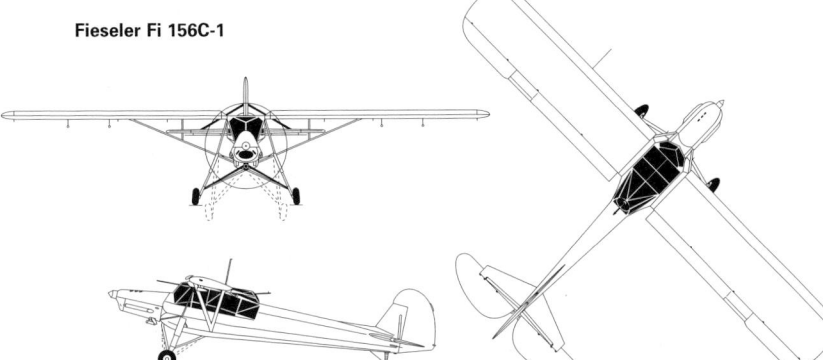

Variant

Fi 156B: projected variant with movable leading-edge slats, not built
Fi 156C-0: pre-production version of an improved Fi 156A-1 with raised rear-cabin glazing to allow installation of a rear-firing 0.31-in (7.92-mm) machine-gun
Fi 156C-1: liaison and staff transport version
Fi 156C-2: reconnaissance version with one camera and two-man crew; some later examples equipped to carry one stretcher for casualty evacuation
Fi 156C-3: general-purpose version, some with improved Argus As 10P engine
Fi 156C-3/Trop: tropicalised version of the Fi 156C-3 with engine dust/sand filters
Fi 156C-5: similar to Fi 156C-3 but with Argus As 10P engine as standard and provision to carry an underfuselage drop tank or camera installation
Fi 156C-5/Trop: tropicalised version of the C-5
Fi 156D-0: pre-production ambulance version with improved accommodation for one stretcher and an enlarged loading/unloading hatch; powered by Argus As 10C engine
Fi 156D-1: production version of the D-0 with Argus As 10P engine as standard
Fi 156E-0: designation of 10 pre-production aircraft with a form of tracked landing gear; no further production
Fi 256: two examples of a larger capacity (5-seat) civil version, built by Morane-Saulnier in France during 1943-44

Fieseler Fi 167

To meet a requirement for a two-seat torpedo-bomber and reconnaissance aircraft for service on the aircraft-carrier that the German navy was planning, proposals were submitted to the RLM by Arado and Fieseler. The latter's design was created under the supervision of Reinhold Mewes with emphasis on ease of production and maintenance as well as good STOL capability. Prototypes of both aircraft were built, but testing in late 1938 soon showed that the Ar 195 could not meet the requirement, whereas the **Fi 167 V1** considerably exceeded the specification. In configuration the Fi 167 was a two-bay biplane with rearward-folding outer wing panels, metal construction with a measure of fabric in the covering, fixed tail-wheel landing gear with tall jettisonable main units and a conventional braced tail unit. The two-man crew was accommodated in tandem beneath a long glazed canopy that possessed an opening rear section to facilitate the gunner's use of his trainable machine-gun.

As with the Fi 156, Fieseler's new aircraft had exceptional low-speed handling characteristics, achieved in this case by the provision on both the upper and lower wings of large ailerons on the outward ends of the trailing edges and automatic leading-edge slats on the leading edges of the outer panels, and on the lower wing of large-area flaps on the trailing edges. The effect of these surfaces, allied with the lift of the biplane wing cellules, made it possible for the aircraft to sink slowly and almost vertically under complete control.

The Fi 167 was intended for service on board the German aircraft-carrier *Graf Zeppelin*, was launched on 8 December 1938 and, following the completion of the **Fi 167 V2** second prototype, a batch of 12 **Fi 167A-0** pre-production aircraft was built. These incorporated some refinements considered desirable after service testing, including the addition of a two-man dinghy. When construction of the

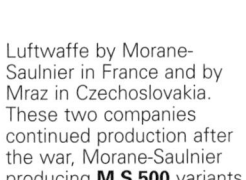

Erprobungsstaffel 167 used the Fi 167A-0 aircraft on various test duties in the Netherlands from summer 1940. Subsequently, nine of the airframes were sold to Romania.

SPECIFICATION

Fieseler Fi 167A-0
Type: two-seat land-based and possibly carrierborne torpedo-bomber and reconnaissance aircraft
Powerplant: one Daimler-Benz 601B inverted Vee piston engine rated at 1,100 hp (820 kW)
Performance: (reconnaissance) maximum speed 202 mph (325 km/h) at optimum altitude; cruising speed 168 mph (270 km/h) at optimum altitude; climb to 3,280 ft (1000 m) in 2 minutes 42 seconds; service ceiling 26,905 ft (8200 m); range 932 miles (1500 km)
Weights: empty 6,173 lb (2800 m); maximum take-off 10,692 lb (4850 kg)

Dimensions: wingspan 44 ft 3½ in (13.50 m); length 37 ft 4¾ in (11.40 m); height 15 ft 9 in (4.80 m); wing area 489.77 sq ft (45.50 m²)
Armament: one 0.312-in (7.92-mm) MG 17 fixed forward-firing machine-gun in the starboard upper part of the forward fuselage and one 0.312-in (7.92-mm) MG 15 trainable rearward-firing machine-gun in the rear of the cockpit, plus up to 2,204 lb (1000 kg) of disposable stores carried on one hardpoint under the underfuselage and four hardpoints under the lower wing, and generally comprising bombs or one 1,687-lb (765-kg) LT F5b torpedo under the fuselage, and four 110-lb (50-kg) SC50 bombs under the wing

Graf Zeppelin was stopped in 1940, the role for which the Fi 167 had been designed no longer existed. However, it was expected that when work on the aircraft-carrier was resumed, manufacture of the Fi 167 would also go ahead; this was not to be the case for when, in 1942, orders were given for construction of the aircraft-carrier to be restarted, it was decided that a version of the Junkers Ju 87 would amply meet requirements and no further examples of the Fi 167 were built.

Fisher P-75 Eagle

In 1942, when the US Army Air Force was desperately in need of a single-seat fighter with a high rate of climb, the Fisher Body Division of the General Motors Corporation came up with an unusual proposal. Evolved by the company's design team, under the leadership of Don Berlin, the proposal from Fisher Body was that assemblies of aircraft already in large-scale production could be combined with the most powerful engine then available to produce a new high-performance fighter. As a result approval was given for the construction of two **XP-75** prototypes with a new fuselage and wing centre-section that would unite P-51 Mustang outer wing panels, an A-24 tail unit and F4U Corsair retractable tailwheel landing gear to form the airframe. It was decided subsequently to use instead the outer wing panels of the Curtiss P-40. Power was provided by a

2,600-hp (1939-kW) Allison V-3420-19 engine mounted within the fuselage, aft of the cockpit, and driving two contra-rotating propellers via an extended shaft and reduction gearbox in the nose section.

Before the first prototype was flown on 17 November 1943, it had already been decided that the requirement emphasis had shifted and that long-range escort fighters were more urgently needed than interceptors. This brought a new contract for six long-range **XP-75A** aircraft, plus a conditional order for 2,500 production examples of the **P-75A Eagle**, the latter order being subject to the prototype aircraft meeting all requirements. The XP-75As introduced a number of changes brought about by the revised role and as a result of tests with the XP-75 prototype. They included a new cockpit canopy, a redesigned tail unit and the installation of a different mark of the

This machine was one of just six P-75A production-standard aircraft completed.

V-3420 engine. However, by the time the first production P-75A was ready for testing, in September 1944, the requirement for this aircraft no longer existed and only five were completed and used subsequently for test purposes.

SPECIFICATION	
Fisher P-75A Eagle	**Weights:** empty 11,495 lb
Type: single-seat long-range escort fighter	(5214 kg); maximum take-off 18,210 lb (8260 kg)
Powerplant: one 2,885-hp (2151-kW) Allison V-3420-23 24-cylinder double-banked Vee piston engine	**Dimensions:** wingspan 49 ft 4 in (15.04 m); length 40 ft 5 in (12.32 m); height 15 ft 6 in (4.72 m); wing area 347.0 sq ft (32.24 m²)
Performance: (approximate) maximum speed 400 mph (644 km/h); cruising speed 310 mph (499 km/h); service ceiling 36,000 ft (10975 m); range with maximum fuel 3,000 miles (4828 km)	**Armament:** ten 0.5-in (12.7-mm) forward-firing Browning machine-guns (six in wings and four in fuselage), plus two 500-lb (227-kg) bombs on racks beneath the wing centre-section

Fleet Models 1-6, 7 (Fawn), 8, 9, 10 and 16 (Finch)

The Consolidated PT-3, which was being delivered to the US Army Air Corps in 1928, clearly possessed considerable sales potential in a rapidly expanding civil market. Retaining the same general lines as the PT-3, the new civil version was designated as the Consolidated Model 14 and was named Husky Junior. Almost before the first example was completed, Consolidated decided that it did not want to become involved in the civil market, and this induced the company's president, Major Reuben H. Fleet, to acquire the rights for the Husky Junior design and to establish Fleet Aircraft Inc. at Buffalo, New York, to build and market it. Within about six months Consolidated had a change of heart, buying Fleet Aircraft Inc. to continue production in the USA, and in 1930 establishing a Canadian manufacturing and sales outlet by forming Fleet Aircraft of Canada Ltd at

Fort Erie, Ontario.

With a new start it was decided not to retain the name of Husky Junior and the designation **Fleet Model 1** was adopted. This aircraft differed little from its predecessor, having the same 110-hp (82-kW) Scarab radial engine and a basically similar airframe. The only major change was in the accommodation, the Model 1 having a tandem arrangement of two separate cockpits. The Model 1 was followed by the generally similar **Model 2** with detail improvements and power provided by a 100-hp (75-kW) Kinner K5 radial engine, but only a small number was built before the designation was changed to **Model 7** with

installation of the 125-hp (93-kW) Kinner B5 engine. This variant was known as the **Model 7B** in Canada, and examples in service with the Royal Canadian Air Force had the designation **Fawn Mk I**.

The Model 2 was the first version built in Canada, initial production being assisted by the receipt of at least three fuselage frames built in the US factory. As in the USA, only small numbers of Model 2s were built before production of the Model 7 was initiated. The type was seen in service, especially in Canada, with float and ski installations, and with more than one type of cockpit enclosure.

Variants

Model 10A: basic version with the 100-hp (75-kW) K5 radial engine
Model 10B: as the Model 10A but with the 125-hp (93-kW) B5 radial engine
Model 10D: as the Model 10A but with the 160-hp (119-kW) R5 radial engine
Model 10-32D: as the Model 10D but with 4-ft (1.22-m) increase in wingspan
Model 10E: as the Model 10A but with the 125-hp (93-kW) Scarab radial
Model 10F: as the Model 10A but with the 145-hp (108-kW) Super Scarab radial
Model 10G: as the Model 10A but with the 130-hp (97-kW) Gipsy Major inverted inline engine
Model 16B: structurally strengthened version of the Model 10A with the B5 engine for service as the RCAF's **Finch Mk II**
Model 16D: as the Model 16B but with the R5 engine
Model 16F: as the Model 16B but with the Super Scarab engine

Fleet's Model 7B had a maximum speed of 115 mph (185 km/h) and a service ceiling of 14,000 ft (4265 m). Its range was 298 miles (480 km) and maximum take-off weight was 1,742 lb (790 kg).

Fleet Models 1-6, 7 (Fawn), 8, 9, 10 and 16 (Finch) (cont.)

There were several variants of this basic theme. The **Model 3**, of which two examples were completed, had the 165-hp (123-kW) Wright J-6 radial engine, while two test aircraft were one **Model 4** with the 170-hp (127-kW) Curtiss Challenger radial engine and one **Model 5** with the 90-hp (67-kW) Brownback C-400 two-row radial engine. The **Model 6** was a single machine of uncertain configuration, although it is believed to have been a Model 2 with a trapeze above the upper wing for 'hook-on' experiments with military airships. **Model 7C** was the designation of versions powered by the 140-hp (104-kW) Armstrong Siddeley Civet I radial engine for service with the RCAF under the designation **Fawn Mk II**. **Model 7G** was the redesignation of one RCAF Model 7B following installation of the 120-hp (89-kW) de Havilland Gipsy III inline engine; the machine later reverted to Model 7B configuration. Under the designation **XPT-6** the

USAAC acquired one Model 7 for service test with the 100-hp (75-kW) Kinner R-370-1 (Kinner K5) engine. The service later bought 10 **YPT-6** aircraft virtually identical to the XPT-6 for more extensive service, and also five **YPT-6A** aircraft with an enlarged cockpit.

Built in only small numbers, probably as a result of their higher price tags, the **Model 8** and **Model 9** were produced only by the US company. The two types had a much improved fuselage that was fully faired to give a more rotund appearance, and was both deeper and wider to provide a more comfortable interior. This made it possible for the Model 8 to be regarded as a three-seater (the forward cockpit providing accommodation for two) when no baggage was carried, while the Model 9 was a conventional two-seater. Both types were powered by the Kinner B5, and examples of each appeared with a rudder of different shape.

Toward the end of 1934, the

by which time Consolidated had absorbed the US Fleet Aircraft Inc. operation as a cost-saving exercise, an order was received from China for a number of Model 7s, and these were built by the Canadian company. By this time the design included a tailwheel landing gear with wheel brakes, a revised tail unit and a number of detail improvements, resulting in the revised designation **Model 10**. Some 36 aircraft were built for China and despatched in mid-1935, together with components and materials for the assembly in China of an additional 20 aircraft. Fleet 10 variants were also exported to Argentina, the Dominican Republic, Iraq, Mexico, Nicaragua, Portugal, Venezuela and Yugoslavia.

In September 1938, following evaluation of a **Model 10D** by the RCAF, Fleet was requested to develop a trainer suitable for aerobatics carrying full military equipment. This resulted in production of the **Model 16** which

retained the same basic configuration as the Model 10 but was structurally strengthened. More than 400 of these aircraft were supplied between 1939 and 1941 for use by the RCAF and in the British Commonwealth Air Training Plan under the designations **Finch Mk I** and **Finch Mk II**. Post-war many of these surplus aircraft came onto the civil market, the majority acquired by buyers in Canada and the USA.

Consolidated also developed the **Model 21**. Fleet subsequently received an order for 10 Model 21s for Mexico, and built the aircraft (as well as a demonstrator) under the designation **Model 21M**.

Very similar in external appearance to the American-built Model 8 and Model 9, the Model 21M was of mixed construction and in layout was a conventional two-seat biplane with fixed tailwheel landing gear and open cockpits. However, it had a considerably more potent powerplant in the form of a neatly cowled 400-hp (298-kW) Pratt & Whitney R-985 Wasp Junior radial engine. The 10 aircraft were completed and delivered during 1937, and the company's demonstrator was later sold to a private buyer as the **Model 21K** with the revised powerplant of one 330-hp (246-kW) Jacobs L-6MB radial.

SPECIFICATION	
Fleet Model 16B	1,000 ft (305 m) in 2 minutes 18 seconds; service ceiling 10,500 ft (3200 m)
Type: two-seat elementary and primary flying trainer	
Powerplant: one Kinner B5 radial piston engine rated at 125 hp (93 kW)	**Weights:** empty 1,122 lb (509 kg); maximum take-off 2,000 lb (907 kg)
Performance: maximum speed 104 mph (167 km/h) at sea level; cruising speed 85 mph (137 km/h) at optimum altitude; climb to	**Dimensions:** wingspan 28 ft (8.53 m); length 21 ft 8 in (6.60 m); height 7 ft 9 in (2.36 m); wing area 194.40 sq ft (18.06 m²)

Fleet Model 60 Fort

In 1938, Fleet designed a completely new two-seat trainer as a private venture. Of all-metal construction, except for some fabric covering, this **Model 60** was a braced low-wing monoplane with a conventional tail unit, fixed tailwheel landing gear and accommodation for the instructor and pupil in a tandem arrangement of separate cockpits, each enclosed by a transparent canopy. Unusual features included a reinforced fin that could support the aircraft if it turned over on landing, and retractable fair-

ings on the main units of the fixed tailwheel landing gear to familiarise the pupil with the concept of retraction: if the pupil failed to lower the fairings before landing no damage would be caused.

First flown on 22 March 1940, the prototype was used for evaluation by the Royal Canadian Air Force, and there followed an order for 200 **Model 60K** production aircraft, plus the prototype, for service with the designation **Fort Mk I**. The first two machines were delivered in the spring of 1941, but by then

the RCAF had decided to reduce the order by 100, and the 101st Fort was delivered in mid-1942. Early in 1942 it was decided that instead of using the Fort for intermediate flying training, it would be re-equipped for use in the wireless training role and had the landing-gear fairings removed. All but one of these revised **Fort Mk II** aircraft had been retired from service use by 1945.

The Fort's raised rear cockpit gave the instructor a good view forwards over the student's cockpit.

SPECIFICATION	
Fleet Model 60K (Fort Mk I)	54 seconds; service ceiling 15,000 ft (4570 m); range 600 miles (966 km)
Type: two-seat intermediate flying trainer	
Powerplant: one Jacobs L-6MB radial piston engine rated at 330 hp (246 kW)	**Weights:** empty 2,530 lb (1148 kg); maximum take-off 3,500 lb (1588 kg)
Performance: maximum speed 162 mph (261 km/h) at optimum altitude; cruising speed 135 mph (217 km/h) at optimum altitude; climb to 1,000 ft (305 m) in	**Dimensions:** wingspan 36 ft (10.97 m); length 26 ft 10 in (8.18m); height 8 ft 3 in (2.51 m); wing area 216.00 sq ft (20.07 m²)

Variants

Model 60L: unrealised version with the 225-hp (168-kW) L-4MB radial engine for use as a primary flying trainer
Model 60: unrealised version with the 360-hp (269-kW) Jacobs L-7 radial engine for use as an advanced flying trainer

Fleet Model 80 and Model 81 Canuck

The last aircraft to be produced by Fleet Aircraft, before it ran into financial problems and takeover after World War II, was the **Model 80** two-seat lightplane. This originated from

the **Noury N-75** prototype, designed and first flown by Noury Aircraft Ltd of Stoney Creek, Ontario during 1944. Design and manufacturing rights were acquired by Fleet Aircraft,

A thoroughly utilitarian design, the Model 80 was available with landing gear able to carry wheels, skis or floats.

the company flying the prototype in modified pre-production form on 26 September 1945. The changes required in this process had been small, the most important of them introducing a redesigned fin-and-rudder assembly, and in this form the aircraft was designated as the **Model 80 Canuck**.

A three-seat **Model 81** was developed, baggage compartment space being used to accommodate a third person, but only a single example was built.

Looking externally somewhat like a Piper Cub or Taylorcraft Tandem, the Model 80 was built in reasonable numbers, including 24 machines

exported to Argentina, Brazil, Portugal and the USA. After the company ran into financial problems the design and production rights to the Model 80 design were sold to a company known as Leavens Brothers in Toronto, which built 26 more Canucks, largely from Fleet components.

SPECIFICATION

Fleet Model 80 Canuck	
Type: two-seat sporting and touring aircraft	initial climb rate 550 ft (158 m) per minute; service ceiling 12,000 ft (3660 m); range 298 miles (480 km)
Powerplant: one Continental C85-12J flat-four piston engine rated at 85 hp (63 kW)	**Weights:** empty 859 lb (390 kg); maximum take-off 1,422 lb (645 kg)
Performance: maximum speed 112 mph (180 km/h) at 3,000 ft (915 m); cruising speed 81 mph (180 km/h) at 3,000 ft (915 m);	**Dimensions:** wingspan 34 ft (10.35 m); length 22 ft 5 in (6.83 m); height 7 ft 1 in (2.16 m); wing area 173.50 sq ft (16.12 m²)

Fleetwings Model 23 (BT-12)

The Japanese attack on Pearl Harbor in December 1941 found the US Army Air Force largely unprepared for a major war. The desperate need for more and yet more aircraft resulted in unex-

pected manufacturers producing aircraft in equally unexpected materials. One of these manufacturers was Fleetwings, and because the company was a specialist fabricator in sheet stainless

steel, the **Model 23** basic trainer, of which a prototype was ordered by the USAAF under the designation **XBT-12**, had a structure that incorporated a large percentage of this material.

Of cantilever low-wing monoplane configuration, the Model 23 had a conventional tail unit, fixed tailwheel landing gear and a Pratt & Whitney Wasp Junior engine. Accommodation was provided for instructor and pupil in separate fully-dupli-cated cockpits with a single continuous canopy covering both. Following evaluation

Prior to building its BT-12, Fleetwings had gained considerable aerospace experience in the manufacture of stainless steel components for the US aircraft industry.

SPECIFICATION

Fleetwings Model 23/BT-12	
Type: two-seat military basic trainer	ceiling 23,800 ft (7255 m), range 550 miles (885 km)
Powerplant: one 450-hp (336-kW) Pratt & Whitney R-985-AN-1 Wasp Junior 9-cylinder radial piston engine	**Weights:** empty 3,173 lb (1439 kg), maximum take-off 4,410 lb (2000 kg)
Performance: maximum speed 195 mph (314 km/h); cruising speed 175 mph (282 km/h); service	**Dimensions:** wingspan 40 ft (12.19 m); length 29 ft 2 in (8.89 m); height 8 ft 8 in (2.64 m), wing area 240.40 sq ft (22.33 m²)

of the XBT-12 prototype, a contract for an additional 200 BT-12 aircraft was awarded, 24 of these being

completed and delivered in the period 1942-43 before the balance of the contract was cancelled.

Fletcher FU-24 and FD-25 Defender

In July 1954 Fletcher flew its **FU-24** prototype, a single-seat utility aircraft which the company had designed primarily for agri-cultural use. A cantilever low-wing monoplane of all-metal construction, it had a tail unit incorporating an all-moving tailplane, fixed tricycle landing gear and an enclosed cockpit for the pilot. Power was provided by a 225-hp (168-kW) Continental 0-470-8 flat-six engine.

The FU-24 must be regarded as the company's only real success in the field of aircraft design and construction, the first significant event being an agreement with Air Parts (NZ) Ltd of New Zealand to assemble 100 aircraft for use in topdressing opera-tions in that country. Fletcher subsequently developed the prototype of a six-seat passenger/cargo version under the designa-

tion **FU-24A Utility**. However, in 1964 Fletcher sold all manufacturing and sales rights of the FU-24 to the New Zealand company, which continued its devel-opment and production. When, in early 1973, Air Parts merged with Acre Engine Services Ltd to form New Zealand Aerospace Industries Ltd (NZAI), it was decided to expand production of the FU-24 as much as possible and the improved **FU24-950** was available in two-seat agricultural and eight-seat utility models. This resulted in a strange reversal, with FU24-950s being manufactured in New Zealand and supplied in assembly/component form to Frontier-Aerospace Inc. of Long Beach, California, for assembly and marketing in the USA under the name **TaskMaster**. Frontier-Aerospace also developed a utility military

version of the FU-24 which it named **Pegasus 1**.

By early 1982 NZAI was in serious financial difficul-ties. Subsequently reformed as Pacific Aerospace Corporation (PAC), the company was 75.1 per cent owned by AeroSpace Technologies of Australia (ASTA) until 1995. Aeromotive, a privately-owned New Zealand company, then bought ASTA's stake in PAC.

FU24 production has continued, somewhat sporadically, since. The further improved **FU24-954** model was launched during the 1980s and by late 1998 a total of 300 FU24s, including the original 100, had been built. Of these about 180 were still in use, 110 in New Zealand and the remainder in Australia, Bangladesh, Dubai, Malaysia, Pakistan, Sudan, Syria, Thailand, Turkey, Uruguay and Venezuela.

Undaunted by the failure of its **FL-23** military liaison aircraft, Fletcher also designed and built the prototype of a single-seat light ground-attack aircraft based on the FU-24 airframe under the designa-tion **FD-25B Defender**. A cantilever low-wing mono-plane of all-metal construction, the FD-25B had a conventional tail unit, fixed tailwheel landing gear, the pilot's cockpit enclosed by an acrylic canopy and power provided by a Continental E225 engine. For

Neither the six-seat US-designed FU-24A Utility (illustrated) nor the eight-seat variant of the New Zealand-designed FU24-950 found customers.

SPECIFICATION

PAC FU24-954	
Type: two-seat agricultural aircraft	16,000 ft (4875 m); range 441 miles (710 km)
Powerplant: one 298-kW (400-hp) Avco Lycoming IO-720-A1A or -A1B flat-eight piston engine	**Weights:** empty equipped 2,620 lb (1188 kg); maximum take-off 5,430 lb (2463 kg)
Performance: maximum speed 145 mph (233 km/h) at sea level; spraying speed 104-132 mph (167-212 km/h); service ceiling	**Dimensions:** wingspan 42 ft (12.80 m); length 31 ft 10 in (9.70 m); height 9 ft 4 in (2.84 m), wing area 294.0 sq ft (27.31 m²)

A potentially useful light attack and COIN aircraft, the FD-25B included bombs, napalm tanks and folding-fin rockets among its disposable stores.

ground-attack two forward-firing machine-guns were mounted in the

wings, and underwing racks were provided for the carriage of weapons.

Most FU24s still in use are new-build FU24-950s (pictured) or re-engined -950Ms. All are powered by the 400-hp (298-kW) Lycoming IO-720 engine.

Flettner Fl 184, Fl 185 and Fl 265

The pioneering work carried out in the field of rotary-wing aircraft by a German, Anton Flettner, is often overlooked and, perhaps for that reason, is particularly interesting. Seeking a way to overcome the torque induced when a rotor is driven from an airframe-mounted power source, Flettner explored the idea of putting a 30-hp (22-kW) Anzani engine and tractor propeller on the leading edge of each blade of a two-bladed rotor with a diameter of 98 ft (29.87 m). This prototype helicopter made a successful tethered flight in 1932, but was destroyed shortly after on the ground when it overturned during a gale.

Flettner then built the two-seat **Fl 184** autogyro with a three-bladed auto-rotating rotor and power provided by a 140-hp (104-kW) Siemens-Halske Sh.14 radial engine driving

a tractor propeller. This, too, was destroyed before it could be evaluated and the prototype **Fl 185** followed. This was a combined autogyro and helicopter. Its Sh.14A engine, mounted at the front of the fuselage, could be used to drive two anti-torque propellers mounted on outriggers, one on each side of the fuselage, but the main rotor was powered only when required for operation in a helicopter mode. When the Fl 185 was flown as an autogyro, the propellers on the outriggers were both set to act as pusher units and the main rotor auto-rotated, but for helicopter flight the main rotor was powered from the engine and the outrigger propellers set so that one acted as a tractor and the other as a pusher to offset rotor torque.

The Fl 185 was flown

only a few times before Flettner began construction, in 1937, of his **Fl 265 V1** prototype that first flew in May 1939. This had an airframe configuration similar to that of the Fl 185, but dispensed with the outriggers and propellers and introduced a counter-rotating assembly of two closely spaced, side-by-side, two-bladed intermeshing and synchronised rotors which, because they were rotating in opposite directions, each cancelled the effects of the other's torque. To simplify control problems there was a tail unit that incorporated an adjustable tailplane for trimming purposes, and for steering a large fin-and-rudder assembly to augment the use of differential collective-pitch change on the two rotors. This helicopter was lost in an accident some three months later when the counter-rotating blades struck each other, but the **Fl 265 V2** second prototype was used successfully for a variety of military trials. In all, six prototypes were built under contract to the German navy before, in 1940, an order was

Above: Note the twin rotorheads of this Fl 265, a configuration which resulted from its use of intermeshing main rotors.

Mounting its two propellers on outrigger arms to either side of the fuselage, the Fl 185 could be flown either as a helicopter or as an autogyro.

placed for quantity production. By that time, however, Flettner had designed a more advanced two-seat heli-

copter and it was therefore decided to proceed with the development and manufacture of this improved machine.

SPECIFICATION	
Flettner Fl 265	**Weights:** empty 1,764 lb (800 kg); maximum take-off 2,205 lb (1000 kg)
Type: single-seat helicopter	
Powerplant: one Siemens-Halske (Bramo) Sh.14A radial piston engine rated at 160 hp (119 kW)	**Dimensions:** rotor diameter, each 40 ft 4¼ in (12.30 m); rotor disc area, total 2,558.08 sq ft (237.65 m²)
Performance: maximum speed 99 mph (160 km/h)	

Flettner Fl 282 Kolibri

Fl 282 V21 (also known as the Fl 282B) is illustrated as it appeared while under evaluation in 1943. Allied bombing prevented mass production of this excellent helicopter.

Flettner's improved helicopter was the two-seat **Fl 282 Kolibri** (hummingbird), and to speed the development of a helicopter that could prove valuable for naval use a total of 30 prototypes and 15 pre-production examples were ordered in early 1940. Although the basic fuselage configuration was similar to that of its predecessor, the Fl 282 differed in one important respect. Its Sh.14A engine was mounted in the centre of the fuselage and the pilot was accommodated in the nose with enclosed, semi-enclosed and open cockpits provided in variety over the 24 prototypes that were built. Not all of these were two-seaters, but those which were accommodated an observer to the rear of the rotor pylon, seated so that his view was to the rear of the machine.

In 1942 the German navy began its Fl 282 trials, find-

ing the type extremely manoeuvrable, stable in poor weather conditions, and so reliable that in 1943 about 20 of the 24 prototypes were operating from warships in the Aegean and Mediterranean for convoy protection duties. It was discovered that, as pilots gained experience, the Fl 282 could be flown in

really bad weather, leading to an order for 1,000 production helicopters. As a result of Allied bombing attacks on the BMW and Flettner works, these helicopters were not built, and only three of the prototypes survived at VE-Day, the remainder having been destroyed to prevent them being captured.

SPECIFICATION	
Flettner Fl 282 V21	985 ft (300 m); range 106 miles (170 km)
Type: single-seat helicopter	
Powerplant: one Bramo Sh.14A radial piston engine rated at 160 hp (119 kW)	**Weights:** empty 1,676 lb (760 kg); maximum take-off 2,205 lb (1000 kg)
Performance: maximum speed 93 mph (150 km/h) at sea level; initial vertical climb rate 300 ft (91 m) per minute; service ceiling 10,825 ft (3300 m); hovering ceiling	**Dimensions:** rotor diameter, each 39 ft 2¾ in (11.96 m); fuselage length 21 ft 6¼ in (6.56 m); height 7 ft 2½ in (2.20 m); rotor disc area, total 2,418.61 sq ft (224.69 m²)

FLS (Edgley) Optica

Combining the fields of vision seldom offered by anything other than a helicopter with outstanding slow-flying capabilities, the original concept for the

Edgley EA7 Optica was as a three-seat touring aircraft. John Edgley, at that time a post-graduate student at the Imperial College of Science & Technology,

London, began the final aerodynamic design in 1974 and a model was tested in a wind tunnel during 1975. Construction of a prototype began in 1976 in London, and final assembly was carried out at the College of

Aeronautics, Cranfield. The first flight was made on 14 December 1979 with a 160-hp (119-kW) Lycoming O-320 engine, but this engine was later changed to a 180-hp (134-kW) IO-360 unit. The engine drives a five-bladed fixed-

pitch ducted fan, and the Optica was claimed to be the world's quietest powered aircraft.

Mounting the whole cockpit assembly ahead of the fan and engine gives the pilot and passengers 270° panoramic fields of vision plus almost vertical downward vision, and the design of the cockpit canopy allows photography through the panels. The tricycle landing gear is fixed and unfaired, with maintenance-free solid suspension, and the airframe is of all-metal construction. The internal cabin width of 5 ft 6 in (1.68 m) permits three-abreast seating, while baggage space and positions for mounting specialised observation equipment are provided behind the seats and in the unrestricted floor area in front of the two passenger seats.

Roles for the Optica are virtually unlimited, from the obvious aerial photography and surveillance patrols to traffic reporting, powerline inspection etc., and the Optica has the ability to perform much of a helicopter's type of work with fixed-wing economy and range. Considerable interest was shown in the Optica from the time of its first appearance, and at the 1981 Paris Air Show the announcement of a first production order was

made. A total of 25 Optica aircraft was ordered by the Australian distributor H. C. Sleigh Aviation in the initial production form powered by one IO-360 flat-four piston engine rated at 200 hp (149 kW) or one 210-hp (156-kW) TO-360 flat-four piston engine rated at 210 hp (156 kW).

With £2.3 million of funding from leading City of London institutions, Edgley bought Old Sarum airfield, near Salisbury, UK from the Ministry of Defence and set up a production line in existing hangars. Initial plans covered the construction of 200 aircraft, beginning in mid-1983, with first production models available towards the end of that year. The first Optica was completed in August 1984 and was delivered in April 1985 after the receipt of VFR and IFR certification. Edgley Aircraft then encountered financial problems and was reconstituted as Optica Industries Ltd, which relaunched Optica production in January 1986, but then suffered a major blow when fire destroyed its premises, the prototype

and nine completed aircraft in January 1987. Optica Industries then became Brooklands Aircraft Co. Ltd. (later Brooklands Aerospace Group) in April 1987. The Optica was then renamed as the **Optica Scout**, and an electronic surveillance derivative was offered as the **Scoutmaster** in **Mk I** and **Mk II** forms with different equipment. By a time early in 1989 Brooklands had delivered five aircraft, but in July 1990 was taken over by FLS Aerospace (Light Aircraft) Ltd. FLS transferred all work to Lovaux near Bournemouth for the

A seeming lack of buyer confidence in the radical Optica has led to the design struggling for its survival in spite of its unique capabilities.

creation of the improved **OA7-300 Optica**, and planned to have the type manufactured in Malaysia by Gegasi Industries.

Nothing came of this plan, and in mid-2000 FLS Aerospace was still seeking a buyer for the whole Optica programme.

SPECIFICATION	
Brooklands Optica Scout	(191 km/h) at optimum altitude;
Type: three-seat observation aircraft	initial climb rate 810 ft (247 m) per minute; service ceiling 14,000 ft
Powerplant: one Textron Lycoming IO-540-V4A5D flat-six piston engine rated at 260 hp (194 kW) driving a ducted fan	(4275 m); range 656 miles (1056 km) **Weights:** empty 2,090 lb (948 kg); maximum take-off 2,900 lb (1315 kg)
Performance: maximum speed 132 mph (213 km/h) at optimum altitude; cruising speed 119 mph	**Dimensions:** wingspan 39 ft 4 in (12.00 m); length 26 ft 9 in (8.15 m); height 7 ft 7 in (2.31 m); wing area 170.50 sq ft (15.84 m²)

FLS (Trago Mills) Sprint

Since the end of World War II, the British light aircraft industry has sought to develop a lightplane that would rival current American and, to a lesser extent, French aircraft of

the same class in terms of popularity. A type for which very considerable hopes were entertained was the **Trago Mills SAH-1**, designed by Sydney Holloway as a trim low-

wing cantilever monoplane that first flew in prototype form on 23 August 1983.

Design of this machine as a fully aerobatic sporting and touring aircraft had been launched in October 1977, and the result was a machine of light alloy construction with the flying surfaces stabilised by internal PVC foam. It had fixed tailwheel landing gear including wide-track cantilever main units, and side-by-side two-seat accommodation in a high-set cockpit behind a fixed windscreen and under a bubble canopy that slid to the rear to provide access and egress.

The SAH-1 received its British certification on 12 December 1985, and in August 1988 Norman

Whale joined members of Trago Mills' staff in organising a buy-out of the SAH-1 programme, which was now to be run by Orca Aircraft Ltd, with deliveries of production aircraft scheduled for 1990 after the completion of a small number of pre-production machines.

Orca ran into financial difficulties in the early 1990s before the production programme had been fully established, and in

October 1991 FLS Aerospace (Light Aircraft) Ltd bought the SAH-1 programme. FLS was unable to secure sufficient sales of the SAH-1, which it had renamed as the **Sprint**, to warrant the re-creation of the production line, and the company has offered for sale the whole package, which includes six airframes as well as all the jigs, tooling and a number of engines and much associated equipment.

Ease of manufacture and maintenance was a key element of the SAH-1 design, and for this reason the only moving surfaces were the ailerons, single-slotted flaps, elevators and rudder.

SPECIFICATION	
FLS Sprint	915 ft (279 m) per minute; service
Type: two-seat sporting and touring aircraft	ceiling 16,400 ft (5000 m); range 714 miles (1149 km)
Powerplant: one Lycoming O-235-L2A flat-four piston engine rated at 118 hp (88 kW)	**Weights:** empty 1,100 lb (499 kg); maximum take-off 1,750 lb (794 kg) **Dimensions:** wingspan 30 ft 8⅜ in
Performance: maximum speed 140 mph (226 km/h) at sea level; cruising speed 127 mph (204 km/h) at sea level; initial climb rate	(9.36 m); length 21 ft 7¼ in (6.58 m); height 7 ft 7½ in (2.32 m); wing area 120.00 sq ft (11.15 m²)

FMA AeC.1, AeC.2/3 and AeMO.1

The Fabrica Militar de Aviones (FMA, or Military Aircraft Factory) was founded in the Argentine city of Cordoba on

10 October 1927, and was intended then as the national organisation for aircraft research and production. In 1943, FMA was

renamed as the Institute Aerotécnico and in 1952 became Industrias Aeronauticas y Mecánicas del Estado (IAME, or State

Aeronautical and Mechanical Industries). Five years later it was given the new title Dirección Nacional de Fabricaciones e Investigaciones Aeronauticas (DINFIA, or National Directorate of Aeronautical Manufacture and Research), but in 1968 came a reversion to the original title as FMA became a component of the Area de Material Cordoba division of the Fuerza Aérea Argentina. FMA was later privatised,

and in July 1995 passed into the management control of Lockheed Martin, with the revised designation Lockheed Martin Aircraft Argentina SA.

Following the establishment of FMA in 1927, construction during its first four years was limited to licensed production of foreign aircraft. Thereafter, it began to build aircraft of indigenous design, the first being the **AeC.1** three-seat cabin monoplane.

A raised fairing carrying a ring mounting and a single trainable machine-gun distinguished the armed military AeMO.1.

FMA AeC.1, AeC.2/3 and AeMO.1 (continued)

Of mixed construction, the AeC.1 was of low-wing cantilever configuration with a braced tail unit, fixed tailskid landing gear, and a powerplant based on one Armstrong Siddeley Genet Major or Mongoose radial engine rated at 140 or 150 hp (104 or 112 kW) respectively. It is believed that only a small number of these aircraft were built for domestic use.

By the time FMA had got the AeC.1 airborne, there were already some 14 or 15 flying clubs in Argentina. Sponsored by

the government, and assisted either by financial grants or the provision of aircraft, these clubs had an acute need for an efficient two-seat trainer of national design and manufacture. FMA responded to this requirement with the **AeC.2** low-wing cantilever monoplane. Of mixed construction, the AeC.2 had a braced tail unit, fixed tailskid landing gear, tandem open cockpit accommodation for the pilot and pupil with dual controls standard, and a powerplant based on one

Wright Whirlwind radial engine. A lower-performance but generally similar two-seat trainer and tourer, designated **AeC.3**, differed primarily by having a 140-hp (104-kW) Armstrong Siddeley Genet Major radial engine.

Successful use of the AeC.2 in civil aero clubs led to the development of a specifically military model, the **AeMO.1** whose principal difference was a much more powerful engine in the form of a 240-hp (179-kW) Wright Whirlwind, and provision for the rear

cockpit to be adapted for the air-to-air gunnery role. AeMO.1s were acquired in some numbers by the Servicio Aeronautico del Ejercito (Army Aviation

Service), which also took a number of AeC.3s for use as elementary trainers. At a slightly later date the naval air arm, the Comando de Aviaciun Naval Argentina (Argentina Naval Aviation Command) also acquired AeC.3s for similar use.

SPECIFICATION	
FMA AeC.2	16,405 ft (5000 m); range 715 miles (1150 km)
Type: two-seat elementary and basic flying trainer	**Weights:** empty 1,653 lb (750 kg); maximum take-off 2,712 lb (1230 kg)
Powerplant: one Wright Whirlwind radial engine rated at 165 hp (123 kW)	**Dimensions:** wingspan 39 ft 4½ in (12.00 m); length 25 ft 11 in (7.90 m); height 8 ft 6¼ in (2.60 m); wing area 204.52 sq ft (19.00 m²)
Performance: maximum speed 137 mph (220 km/h) at sea level; cruising speed 106 mph (170 km/h) at optimum altitude; service ceiling	

FMA AeMB.1 and AeMB.2

On 9 October 1935 there flew the **AeMB.1** prototype of a new light bomber, which was a moderately advanced type of low-wing

cantilever configuration with a structure of light alloy.

The wing was tapered in thickness and chord with

rounded tips and ailerons on the outboard ends of its trailing edges, and also carried the wide-track main units of the fixed tailwheel landing gear. The aircraft was powered by one Cyclone engine, which was installed in the nose inside a narrow-chord ring cowling and drove a three-bladed metal propeller.

The **AeMB.2** was the production version of the AeMB.1 with a number of airframe modifications as well as a manually operated dorsal turret, and production of 15 aircraft was completed in 1936, the

year in which the type entered service. At least one of the aircraft was completed to observation

standard without the dorsal turret, and the type remained in service up to 1945.

The AeMB.2's oval-section fuselage provided accommodation for a pilot and navigator/bombardier. The gunner's dorsal position was deleted on the aircraft illustrated – the machine was employed solely in an observation role.

SPECIFICATION	
FMA AeMB.2	(17.20 m); length 35 ft 9¼ in (10.90 m); height 9 ft 2¼ in (2.80 m)
Type: three-seat day bomber and reconnaissance aircraft	**Armament:** one 0.301-in (7.65-mm) Madsen fixed forward-firing machine-gun in the forward fuselage, two 0.301-in (7.65-mm) Madsen trainable machine-guns in the manually operated dorsal turret, and one 0.45-in (11.35-mm) trainable rearward-firing machine-gun in the ventral position, plus up to 882 lb (400 kg) of disposable stores
Powerplant: one Wright SGR-1820-F3 Cyclone radial piston engine rated at 715 hp (533 kW)	
Performance: maximum speed 177 mph (285 km/h) at 6,890 ft (2100 m); service ceiling 19,685 ft (6000 m); range 373 miles (600 km)	
Weight: maximum take-off 7,716 lb (3500 kg)	
Dimensions: wingspan 56 ft 5¼ in	

FMA IAeDL.22

Design, development and production of FMA aircraft in the post-World War II period was the responsibil-

ity of the Instituto Aerotécnico. The first of these designs was a two-seat advanced flying

trainer, the **IAeDL.22** low-wing cantilever monoplane that was basically of wooden construction. The aircraft was clearly inspired in aerodynamic terms by the North

American AT-6 but employed wooden construction to suit Argentina's industrial capabilities. Power was provided by an indigenous IAe.16 supercharged radial engine. The type served in some numbers with the

Argentine air force in both its baseline model and the **IAeDL.22-C** subvariant that differed mainly in its revised powerplant of one 475-hp (354-kW) Armstrong Siddeley Cheetah 25 radial piston engine.

SPECIFICATION	
FMA IAeDL.22	service ceiling 17,060 ft (5200 m); range 746 miles (1200 km)
Type: two-seat advanced flying trainer	**Weights:** empty 3,351 lb (1520 kg); maximum take-off 4,894 lb (2220 kg)
Powerplant: one IAe.16 El Gaucho radial piston engine rated at 450 hp (336 kW)	**Dimensions:** wingspan 41 ft 4 in (12.60 m); length 30 ft 2¼ in (9.20 m); height 9 ft 3 in (2.82 m); wing area 249.73 sq ft (24.20 m²)
Performance: maximum speed 180 mph (290 km/h) at 1,475 ft (450 m); cruising speed 162 mph (260 km/h) at optimum altitude;	

Accommodation for the pupil and instructor was provided in the IAeDL.22's tandem cockpits, beneath a long 'greenhouse' canopy.

FMA IAe.24 Calquin

Clearly inspired by the de Havilland DH.98 Mosquito multi-role warplane in its basic design and largely wooden construction, the **IAe.24 Calquin** (royal eagle) light attack bomber was the first twin-engined warplane developed in Argentina. The machine was designed by Brigadier San Martin as a mid-wing

cantilever monoplane, and its structural core was the oval-section fuselage, which was a semi-monocoque unit of ply/balsa/ply construction. A glazed bombardier position with a bomb-aiming panel was incorporated above and between the two pairs of forward-firing cannon in the nose and the aircraft incor-

porated a lower-fuselage weapons bay.

The wing was of wooden construction covered with ply/balsa/ply

Key features of the Calquin were its forward-firing guns in the underside of the nose and the high-set cockpit for the two-man crew, who were seated side-by-side under a framed canopy.

sandwich material, and the dihedralled halves of this wing extended from the sides of the fuselage above the weapons bay. Virtually the full span of their trailing edges was occupied by outboard ailerons and inboard flaps. The landing gear was of the tailwheel type with a single wheel on each unit, the tailwheel unit retracting into the underside of the rear fuselage and the mainwheel units retracting rearward into the under-

side of the two engine nacelles. The powerplant was planned as two Rolls-Royce Merlin Vee engines, but Argentina was unable to obtain supplies of this engine and the IAe.24 was therefore completed with the powerplant of two R-1830-SCG Twin Wasp radial engines. These were installed at the front of two wing-mounted nacelles inside circular light alloy cowlings and drove three-bladed constant-speed Hamilton

Standard metal propellers.
The prototype made its maiden flight on 5 June 1946, and by this time the decision had been taken to press ahead with the construction of 100 aircraft. The first of the production aircraft recorded its initial flight on 4 July 1947, and all 100 had been delivered by 1950. The aircraft remained in service up to 1961, despite a number of problems with the wooden structure.

FMA IA-58 Pucará

Meeting a Fuerza Aérea Argentina (FAA) requirement for a close air support, reconnaissance and counter-insurgency aircraft, the **Pucará** was an indifferent performer in the 1982 Falklands War with the United Kingdom and consequently suffered a loss of support for its *modus operandi*. The Pucará concept originated in the early 1960s, when anti-guerrilla and counter-insurgency were the types of warfare anticipated by Argentina. FMA produced the **IA-58** design with twin turboprops and all-metal construction. The prototype flew on 20 August 1969, powered by a pair of 904-ehp (674-kW) Garrett TPE331-U-303 turboprops, but the production version utilised 1,022-ehp (762-kW) Turboméca Astazou XVIGs, which powered the second aircraft for its maiden flight on 6 September 1970.
Named for the stone forts built by the indigenous South American people, the Pucará is a manoeuvrable and rugged aircraft able to operate from short, rough airstrips – 262 ft (80 m) is enough when helped by three JATO bottles. A tall, retractable tricycle undercarriage provides ample clearance for weapons and the generous propeller ground clearance necessary for flights from uneven surfaces. The crew is provided with Martin-Baker Mk 6 zero/zero ejection seats, the rear occupant

having full dual controls and a raised cockpit floor. The forward windscreen is armoured, as is the cabin floor. In practice, a second crew member is rarely necessary for COIN missions and the aircraft is usually flown with the rear seat empty.
The first production **IA-58A** flew on 8 November 1974 and deliveries began to the FAA in 1976. Early action was seen late in 1976 against rebel forces in north-west Argentina. An initial order for 60 was augmented by a follow-on batch of 48, but the last 22 of these were not accepted by the FAA and offered for sale. Furthermore, a total of 40 surplus aircraft were made available for export in 1986, as soon as production had ended. All 24 aircraft deployed to the Falkland Islands in 1982 were lost to sabotage, ground fire and bombing, or were captured by British forces, one of these latter later flying in

British military markings for evaluation. Another was lost operating from Comodoro Rivadavia, although a Pucará shot down a Westland Scout helicopter. Prior to the conflict, in October 1981, the first of six aircraft diverted from FAA orders had been delivered to Uruguay. Colombia was presented with three for drugs interdiction operations in late 1989. In mid-2000, Argentina had 40 Pucarás in two squadrons. Some have the rear cockpit deleted in favour of additional fuel. Work on installation of a new navigation and attack system began in the late 1980s, but was soon terminated due to financial problems.
More ambitious upgrades also failed to gain acceptance. **IA-58B** was the designation for a single prototype, flown on 15 May 1979, with two 30-mm DEFA 553 cannon, a deeper forward fuselage and improved avionics. The

Still remaining in front-line service with Argentina, the Pucará is undoubtedly a capable type, but was unsuited to operations in the Falklands War.

planned 40 aircraft emerged as IA-58As. Taking aboard the lessons of the Falklands War, the **IA-58C** 'Pucará Charlie' was a proposed rebuild of IA-58As with the DEFA 553s in addition to the six 20-mm and 0.30-in (7.62-mm) weapons, the front cockpit faired over, the rear cockpit enlarged and protected by further armour, and weapon options expanded with Martin Pescador ASMs and MATRA Magic self-defence AAMs. Additional avionics were also added, while the engines gained self-start capability and modified exhausts to reduce infra-red emissions. Only one prototype was produced, and flew on 30 December 1985. It has been suggested that the FAA is considering retrofitting its surviving Pucarás to IA-58C standard, but no progress has been made.
IA-66 was the designa-

tion of a sixth prototype Pucará which flew in 1980, powered by 1,000-ehp (746-kW) Garrett TPE331-11-601W engines driving Dowty Rotol propellers. The latter were replaced by McCaulley units in 1983, but no production aircraft were ordered. Four ex-FAA IA-58As were delivered to the Sri Lankan air force in 1993. One each was lost in 1995 and 1997, while in late 1999, one of the remaining two airframes was being cannabalised for spares to keep the fourth flying. Several reported contracts for IA-58As have failed to materialise, such as 50 for Egypt and 12 for the Central African Republic, although one of six aircraft for Mauritania was actually painted before the 1978 order was cancelled. Iraq requested 20 in 1985, but was turned down by the Argentine government.

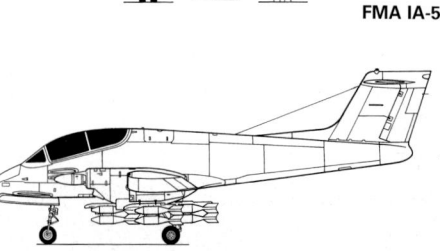

FMA IA-58A Pucará

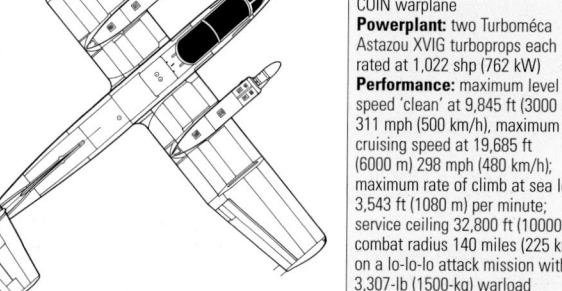

FMA IA-63 Pampa

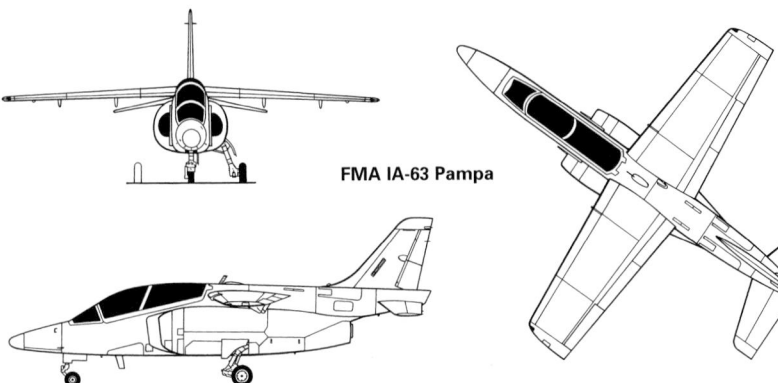

FMA IA-63 Pampa

FMA began **IA-63** development in 1979 to replace the FAA's ageing licence-built four-seat FMA Morane-Saulnier MS.760 Paris II light armed trainers. FMA received technical assistance with the design of the **Pampa** from Dornier, based on its Alpha Jet experience, and the Pampa was selected after the evaluation of seven joint project studies. It retained an Alpha Jet-type configuration, although with unswept wings and tailplane in a lighter airframe powered by a single TFE731-1-2-2N turbofan. The student and instructor are accommodated in stepped tandem UPC (Stencel) S-III-S311A63 lightweight zero/zero ejection seats in the pressurised cockpit.

Dornier also built the wings and tailplanes of the three flying and two static test prototypes, the first of which (EX-01) made its initial flight on 6 October 1984. Plans did not materialise for a fourth prototype, powered by a single 2,900-lb st (12.90-kN) Pratt & Whitney JT15D-5 turbofan.

The first of 18 IA-63s, comprising three pre-series and 15 initial production Pampas from a planned batch of 64, were delivered to the FAA from March 1988 to provide advanced training and weapons instruction. In the latter role and for light attack duties, for which most FAA Pampas are being upgraded, the IA-63 has four underwing and one fuselage weapons pylons.

FAA plans for Pampa procurement included a requirement for 46 more aircraft for front-line units, but severe funding problems have delayed further production deliveries. Similar problems have been encountered with a dock-training version in which the Argentine navy was interested for its carrier, *25 de Mayo*.

A version of the IA-63, known as the **Pampa 2000 International**, was offered for the US JPATS programme by FMA in conjunction with the Vought Aircraft Company. The second prototype (EX-02) and two production aircraft were sent to the US for modification to Pampa 2000 International standard, but no orders were forthcoming.

In 1997, FMA announced two 'New-Generation' versions of the Pampa design. **Pampa NG A** has upgraded avionics for the advanced training role, while **Pampa NG B** has the upgraded avionics, an uprated engine and is suitable for combat use. Both aircraft have been offered to the FAA and Argentine navy, but without success.

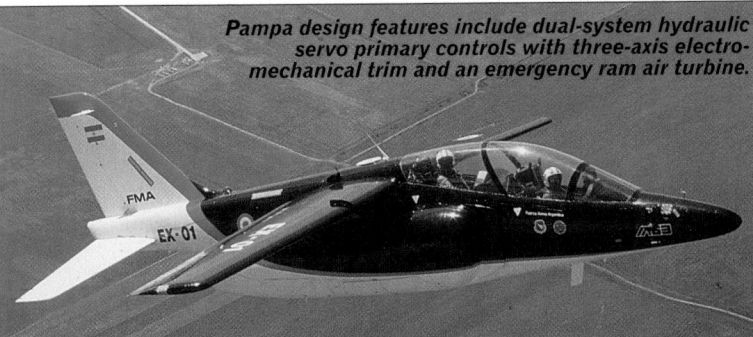

Pampa design features include dual-system hydraulic servo primary controls with three-axis electro-mechanical trim and an emergency ram air turbine.

SPECIFICATION

FMA IA-63 Pampa
Type: armed trainer
Powerplant: one Garrett TFE731-2-2N rated at 3,500 lb st (15.57 kN)
Performance: maximum level speed 'clean' at 22,965 ft (7000 m) 509 mph (819 km/h); cruising speed at 13,125 ft (4000 m) 464 mph (747 km/h); maximum rate of climb at sea level 5,118 ft (1560 m) per minute, service ceiling 42,325 ft (12900 m); range 932 miles (1500 km)
Weights: empty equipped 6,219 lb (2821 kg); maximum take-off 11,023 lb (5000 kg)
Dimensions: wingspan 31 ft 9¼ in (9.69 m); length 35 ft 10¼ in (10.93 m); height 14 ft 1 in (4.29 m); wing area 168.27 sq ft (15.63 m²)
Armament: up to 3,417 lb (1550 kg) of ordnance, including a ventral 30-mm DEFA cannon pod with 145 rounds and up to six Mk 81 250-lb (114-kg) bombs or two Mk 81s and two 500-lb Mk 82 (227-kg) bombs

Focke-Achgelis Fa 223 Drache

The layout of the **Fw 61** (later **Fa 61**), with a side-by-side pair of rotors carried on the ends of long outriggers, was retained by Heinrich Focke for a scaled-up six-passenger version designated **Focke-Achgelis Fa 266 Hornisse** (hornet), developed under contract from Deutsche Lufthansa. The prototype completed its ground running and tethered hovering programme during the summer of 1940 and the first free flight took place in August of that year. By then, however, the project had acquired military importance and development continued under the designation **Fa 223 Drache** (kite), 39 of the type being ordered by the German air ministry for evaluation in a variety of roles, including those of training, transport, rescue and anti-submarine patrol. Equipment varied according to role and included an MG 15 trainable machine-gun and two 551-lb (250-kg) bombs, a rescue winch and cradle, a reconnaissance camera and a 66-Imp gal (300-litre) auxiliary fuel tank.

Ten of the 30 pre-production Fa 223 helicopters were completed at the Bremen factory before it was bombed, and a further seven were built at the company's new factory at Laupheim, near Stuttgart. Another plant, this time located in Berlin, had completed just one example by the time the war ended. Only a small number of Fa 223s was actually flown, and two were acquired by the US forces during May 1945 at Ainring, Austria, where they had been in service with Lufttransportstaffel 40. In September one of them, flown by its German crew, became the first helicopter to cross the English Channel, en route to the Airborne Forces Experimental Establishment at RAF Beaulieu for evaluation: in October the helicopter was destroyed in a crash, the result of mechanical failure. After the war two Fa 223s were built in Czechoslovakia from German-manufactured components and development was also continued in France under the designation **Sud-Est SE.3000**, an example of which first flew on 23 October 1948.

Above: Fa 223 V14 was destroyed before providing any useful data during testing in the UK. It crashed vertically from an altitude of 60 ft (18.29 m).

Right: The Fa 223's widely spaced rotors and their outrigger mountings are graphically illustrated in this head-on view.

SPECIFICATION

Focke-Achgelis Fa 223 Drache
Type: two-crew transport, rescue and reconnaissance helicopter
Powerplant: one BMW 301R radial piston engine rated at 1,000 hp (746 kW)
Performance: maximum speed 109 mph (175 km/h) at sea level; cruising speed 75 mph (120 km/h) at optimum altitude; initial climb rate 1,100 ft (336 m) per minute; service ceiling 16,010 ft (4880 m); range 435 miles (700 km) with auxiliary fuel
Weights: empty 7,000 lb (3175 kg); maximum take-off 9,502 lb (4310 kg)
Dimensions: rotor diameter, each 39 ft 4½ in (12.00 m); span over rotors 80 ft 4¾ in (24.50 m); length 40 ft 2¼ in (12.25 m); height 14 ft 3¼ in (4.35 m); rotor disc area, total 2,434.82 sq ft (226.19 m²)
Payload: up to 2,820 lb (1280 kg) of freight

Focke-Wulf A 16, A 17, A 29 and A 38 Möwe

The first successful aircraft designed and built by Heinrich Focke and Georg Wulf, assisted by their colleague Herr Kolthoff, was the **A-5** single-seat mid-wing monoplane which, powered by a 50-hp (37-kW) Argus engine, which was flown in late 1912. The two principals served in the German army air service during World War I and their collaboration was resumed after hostilities had ceased, initially in the form of the Argus-powered **A 7 Storch** (stork), a tandem two-seat wood and fabric mid-wing monoplane which flew in

November 1921. In 1922, following damage sustained in a storm, the A 7 was rebuilt with a 55-hp (41-kW) Siemens Sh.10 radial engine and successful demonstration to local businessmen in Bremen led to backing being provided for the formation of Focke-Wulf Flugzeugbau AG on 1 January 1924. The new company's first design was the **A 16** all-wood, three/four-passenger airliner, powered by a 75-hp (56-kW) Siemens Sh.11 radial, which was first flown by Wulf on 23 June 1924. Rather more than 20

A 16s were built.
Introduced in 1927, the **A 17 Möwe** (gull) was essentially a scaled-up and improved A 16 with a

This A 16c served with Deutsche Lufthansa as D 659 Borkum. The aircraft had a roll-over protection pylon fitted behind the cockpit.

Variants

A 16a: with one 100-hp (75-kW) Mercedes D.1 engine
A 16b: with one 85-hp (63-kW) Junkers L.1a engine
A 16c: with one 100-hp (75-kW) Siemens engine
A 16d: with one 120-hp (89-kW) Mercedes D.11
A 26: one A 17a following conversion for use as an engine test-bed by the Deutsche Versuchsanstalt für Luftfahrt at Berlin-Adlershof
A 21: one photographic/mapping aircraft with a large aperture in the side of the fuselage, flown in 1927; powered by a 450-hp (336-kW) BMW V1 engine
A 29: in 1929 Focke-Wulf introduced a more powerful version of the A 17, powered by a 650-hp (485-kW) BMW V1 engine; four were delivered to Deutsche Lufthansa and a fifth was supplied to the Deutsche Verkehrsfliegerschule and used for commercial pilot training
A 38: four A 38s were built for Deutsche Lufthansa in 1931, the A 29 wing being mated to a new welded steel-tube fuselage with fabric covering and accommodating 10 passengers, two pilots and a radio operator; strengthened landing gear was introduced, a tailwheel replacing the skid of earlier versions; the original engine was the 400-hp (298-kW) Siemens Jupiter radial, but all four were later given 500-hp (373-kW) Siemens Sh.20a radials, becoming redesignated **A 38b**

welded steel-tube fuselage which was plywood-covered around the cabin area and fabric-covered aft. Accommodation was provided for eight passengers and a crew of two. The wing was of wooden construction with plywood covering, and the prototype was powered by a 420-hp (313-kW) Gnome-Rhône Jupiter 9Ab uncowled radial engine. After a period of service with Norddeutsche

Luftyerkehr, to which airline it was delivered in 1928, it was operated by Lufthansa which also acquired 10 of the 11 production examples. These aircraft had increased rudder area and some were powered by a 480-hp (358-kW) Siemens Jupiter radial, resulting in redesignation as **A 17a**. One aircraft with a 520-hp (388-kW) Junkers Jumo 5 diesel engine became the sole **A 17c**.

SPECIFICATION

Focke-Wulf A 16
Type: light passenger transport
Powerplant: one 75-hp (56-kW) Siemens Sh.11 7-cylinder radial piston engine
Performance: maximum speed 84 mph (135 km/h); service ceiling 8,200 ft (2500 m); range 342 miles (550 km)
Weights: empty 1,256 (570 kg); maximum take-off 2,138 lb (970 kg)
Dimensions: wingspan 45 ft 7¼ in (13.90 m); length 27 ft 10¾ in (8.50 m); height 7 ft 6½ in (2.30 m)

Focke-Wulf A 43 Falke

Designed in 1931, the **A 43 Falke** (falcon) marked a return to the lighter-weight category of general aviation aircraft. A braced high-wing monoplane with a Vee bracing strut on each side, the Falke had very clean lines. The wide-track main units of the tailskid landing gear had both strut and wheel fairings and the unusual tailskid incorporated a hard rubber roller in its contact face. This made manhandling and taxiing easier on both hard and soft surfaces. The enclosed cabin provided a high standard of accommodation for the pilot and two passengers, and included a ventilation system.

Focke-Wulf's Falke had a wing of wooden construction with mixed plywood and fabric covering, while the fuselage was of welded steel tube with fabric covering. This aircraft belonged to Norddeutsche Luftverkehr in the 1930s.

SPECIFICATION

Focke-Wulf A 43 Falke
Type: three-seat cabin monoplane
Powerplant: one 220-hp (164-kW) Argus As 10 8-cylinder inverted Vee piston engine
Performance: maximum speed 158 mph (255 km/h); cruising speed 134 mph (215 km/h); service ceiling 16,730 ft (5100 m); range
652 miles (1050 km)
Weights: empty 1,598 lb (725 kg); maximum take-off 2,480 lb (1125 kg)
Dimensions: wingspan 32 ft 9½ in (10.00 m); length 27 ft 2¾ in (8.30 m); height 7 ft 6½ in (2.30 m); wing area 150.70 sq ft (14.00 m²)

Focke-Wulf F 19 Ente

Heinrich Focke's proposal for a radical twin-engine canard transport aircraft was submitted to the Deutsche Versuchsanstalt für Luftfahrt (DVL) in the mid-1920s and wind tunnel tests were conducted at Göttingen prior to work beginning on the construction of a prototype.

Later in its career, the second F 19 acquired civil certification and ended its days as a test aircraft at the DVL's Berlin-Adlershof base. It flew on into 1939, carrying the registration D-1960.

Focke-Wulf F 19 Ente (continued)

The **F 19 Ente** (duck) was a shoulder-wing monoplane with a fabric-covered welded steel-tube fuselage which incorporated a small two-seat cabin in addition to the open cockpit for the two pilots. Conventional vertical tail

surfaces were fitted but the horizontal surfaces took the form of a 17-ft ¾-in (5.20-m) span fore-plane strut-mounted (forward of the cockpit. Power was supplied by two 75-hp (56-kW) Siemens Sh.11 radials. Georg Wulf was the pilot

for the maiden flight which took place on 2 September 1927, but he lost his life just 27 days later when a control rod broke during a single-engine flight demonstration and the Ente spun into the ground. A second aircraft,

SPECIFICATION

Focke-Wulf F 19 Ente
Type: light transport
Powerplant: two 110-hp (82-kW) Siemens Sh.14 radial piston engines
Performance: maximum speed 88 mph (142 km/h); service ceiling 9,842 ft (3000 m)

Weights: empty 2,590 lb (1175 kg); maximum take-off 3,638 lb (1650 kg)
Dimensions: wingspan 32 ft 9 in (10.00 m); length 34 ft 6½ in (10.53 m); height 13 ft 7¼ in (4.15 m); wing area 317.55 sq ft (29.50 m²)

with Sh.14 engines, reduced-span wings and auxiliary winglets

outboard of the engines, was flown by Cornelius Edzard late in 1930.

Focke-Wulf Fw 44 Stieglitz

Provision was made in the Fw 44's cockpit for the wearing of seat parachutes, while the instructor's seat could be folded forward for access to a baggage compartment.

Second only to the Fw 190 as the most prolific Focke-Wulf design, the **A 44** (**Fw 44**) **Stieglitz** (goldfinch) trainer appeared in 1932, the prototype making its first flight in the late summer of that year in the hands of Gerd Achgelis. Powered by a Siemens Sh.14a radial, the aircraft was a single-bay biplane with a fabric-covered welded steel-tube fuselage and wooden wings with fabric and plywood covering. In its original form it had a number of unacceptable flight characteristics, but these were eradicated following an extensive test programme undertaken by Kurt Tank, who had joined the company in November 1931 from BFW and headed the design and flight test departments of Focke-Wulf when Heinrich Focke became pre-occupied with his rotary-wing activities. The Stieglitz became an

outstanding aerobatic mount, particularly in the hands of Achgelis, Emil Kropf and Ernst Udet, and it won export orders from Bolivia, Chile, China, Czechoslovakia, Finland, Romania, Switzerland and Turkey; licence production was undertaken in Argentina, Austria, Brazil, Bulgaria and Sweden. The Stieglitz was also built in substantial numbers for the Luftwaffe, serving as a trainer until the end of World War II, and was also used by the pre-war Deutsche Verkehrsfliegerschule and the Deutsche Luftsportverband.

SPECIFICATION

Focke-Wulf Fw 44C
Type: two-seat trainer
Powerplant: one 150-hp (112-kW) Siemens Sh.14a 7-cylinder radial piston engine
Performance: maximum speed 115 mph (184 km/h); cruising speed 107 mph (172 km/h); service

ceiling 12,795 ft (3900 m); range 419 miles (675 km)
Weights: empty 1,157 lb (525 kg); maximum take-off 1,985 lb (900 kg)
Dimensions: wingspan 29 ft 6½ in (9,00 m); length 23 ft 11½ in (7.30 m); height 8 ft 10¼ in (2.70 m); wing area 215.29 sq ft (20.00 m²)

Variants

Fw 44B/E: two further prototypes were fitted with the 135-hp (101-kW) Argus As 8 inline engine and small numbers were delivered to the Luftwaffe
Fw 44C/D/F: major production versions, with minor equipment changes, all powered by the Siemens Sh.14a
Fw 44J: final production version, also powered by the Siemens Sh.14a

Focke-Wulf Fw 47

Developed to meet the requirements of the German meteorological service, the prototype **A 47** weather reconnaissance aircraft vas first flown in June 1931, the pilot being Cornelius Edzard. Powered by an As 10 engine, the A 47 was a parasol-wing

monoplane with a wing of wooden construction and a fabric-covered steel-tube fuselage. It was tested extensively by the Reichsverband der Deutschen Luftfahrt-indus-trie (predecessor of the present BDLI, or Federation of the German

Aerospace Industries) and then evaluated opera-tionally at the Hamburg weather centre, beginning in December 1932. Successful completion of the programme led to production orders for more than a score of aircraft, delivered between 1934 and 1936, and used by the meteorological service all over Germany.

SPECIFICATION

Focke-Wulf Fw 47C
Type: two-seat meteorological aircraft
Powerplant: one 240-hp (179-kW) Argus As 10C 8-cylinder inverted Vee piston engine
Performance: maximum speed 118 mph (190 km/h); service ceiling 18,375 ft (5600 m); range 398 miles

(640 km)
Weights: empty 2,348 (1065 kg); maximum take-off 3,484 lb (1580 kg)
Dimensions: wingspan 58 ft 3 in (17.75 m); length 34 ft 7¼ in (10.55 m); height 9 ft 11¾ in (3.04 m)

Variants

Fw 47C: initial production version with radio, modified rear cockpit with a windscreen and As 10c engine
Fw 47M: at least 11 aircraft, built between January and April 1938, powered by the Argus As 10e engine; at least one was fitted with skis

An aircraft of unusual configuration thanks to its large-area parasol wing, the Fw 47 was developed specifically to suit the requirements of the meteorological reconnaissance role.

Focke-Wulf Fw 56 Stösser

The first Focke-Wulf design for which Kurt Tank had responsibility from its beginning, the **Fw 56 Stösser** (falcon) was evolved to meet a Reichsluftfahrtministerium specification for an advanced trainer powered by the Argus As 10C

engine. Tank's design incor-porated a steel-tube fuselage with metal panels forward and fabric covering aft, and a wing of wooden construction with plywood covering back to the rear spar and fabric to the trail-ing edge. The first **Fw 56a** prototype was flown in

November 1933 and, after initial testing had revealed landing gear deficiencies, the **Fw 56 V2** second machine had new main landing gear units. It also featured an all-metal wing and was without the origi-nal faired headrest behind the cockpit. The **Fw 56 V3**

Variants

Fw 56A-0: three pre-production aircraft with minor wing and engine cowling modifications; the first two carried 0.31-in (7.92-mm) MG 17s in the upper fuselage decking and had a rack for three 22-lb (10-kg) practice bombs; the third had a single MG 17
Fw 56A-1: major production version, with provision for one or two MG 17 machine-guns

third aircraft, flown in February 1934, introduced further modified landing

gear and had a wooden wing similar to that of the first.

Fw 56 V4, the first of the pre-production Fw 56A-0 aircraft, incorporated a number of changes compared to the earlier machines. These included a revised exhaust arrangement to prevent noxious gases from entering the cockpit.

SPECIFICATION

Focke-Wulf Fw 56A-1
Type: single-seat advanced trainer
Powerplant: one 240-hp (179-kW) Argus As 10c 8-cylinder inverted Vee piston engine
Performance: maximum speed 173 mph (278 km/h) at sea level; service ceiling 20,340 ft (6200 m); range 249 miles (400 km)

Weights: empty 1,532 lb (695 kg); maximum take-off 2,194 lb (995 kg)
Dimensions: wingspan 34 ft 5½ in (10.50 m); length 25 ft 3 in (7.70 m); height 11 ft 7¾ in (3.55 m); wing area 150.70 sq ft (14.00 m²)
Armament: two 0.31-in (7.92-mm) MG 17 machine-guns

The Stösser was evaluated competitively at Rechlin in the summer of 1935 and was selected, in preference to the Arado Ar 76 and Heinkel He 74, for use as a Luftwaffe advanced trainer. It also played a part in the development of Ernst Udet's ideas on the techniques of dive-bombing, later used so effectively by Junkers Ju 87 Stuka units. In late 1936 Udet flew the second prototype at Berlin-Johannisthal, and at his instigation it was fitted with a bomb rack beneath both wings, each carrying three 2.20-lb (1-kg) smoke bombs. It was flown to great effect by Flugkapitiin Wolfgang Stein and substantial production orders were placed to equip the fighter and dive-bomber pilot schools of the Luftwaffe. Austria and Hungary also ordered the Stösser, and a small number was delivered to civil pilots, including Gerd Acligelis. Total production was around 1,000 aircraft.

Focke-Wulf Fw 58 Weihe

This Fw 58B served with Bomberstaffel 1/B of the Bombergeschwader of Fliegerregiment 2 of the Austrian air force in 1938.

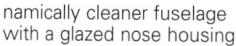

Destined to see extensive service with the Luftwaffe as a crew trainer, light transport and communications aircraft, the **Fw 58 Weihe** (kite) had a welded steel-tube fuselage with mixed metal and fabric covering, and a low-set braced monoplane wing of metal construction, with fabric covering aft of the main spar. Two Argus As 10C engines were mounted beneath the wing roots, one on each side of the fuselage, the main landing gear units retracting into the rear of their nacelles. The **Fw 58 V1** first prototype was first flown in the summer of 1935, as a six-seat transport, and the **Fw 58 V2** second prototype had two open gunner's positions, each with a single 0.31-in (7.92-mm) MG 15 machine-gun, in the nose and behind the cockpit. The **Fw 58 V4** fourth prototype had an aerodynamically cleaner fuselage with a glazed nose housing a single MG 15, and was the forerunner of the **Fw 58B** initial production version. Foreign operators of the Weihe included Argentina, Bulgaria, China, Hungary, the Netherlands, Romania and Sweden. Production totalled about 1,350 aircraft.

Variants

Fw 58B-1: production aircraft for the Luftwaffe, used in training, communications and casualty evacuation roles
Fw 58B-2: version with glazed nose and MG 15s for gunnery training; 25 were built under licence by Fabrica de Galleao in Brazil
Fw 58W: twin-float seaplane
Fw 58C: major production version introduced in 1938 and powered either by As 10C or 260-hp (194-kW) Hirth HM508D engines. Production included four of each model built for Deutsche Lufthansa in 1938-39

SPECIFICATION

Focke-Wulf Fw 58B-1
Type: light transport/gunnery trainer
Powerplant: two 240-hp (179-kW) Argus As 10c 8-cylinder inverted Vee piston engines
Performance: maximum speed 168 mph (270 km/h); service ceiling 18,375 ft (5600 m); range 497 miles (800 km)

Weights: empty 5,291 lb (2400 kg); maximum take-off 7,936 lb (3600 kg)
Dimensions: wingspan 68 ft 11 in (21.00 m); length 45 ft 11 in (14.00 m); height 12 ft 9½ in (3.90 m); wing area 505.92 sq ft (47.00 m²)
Armament: one 0.31-in (7.92-mm) MG 15 machine-gun

Focke-Wulf Fw 61/Fa 61

Heinrich Focke's rotary-wing experience was gained initially from licence production of Cierva C.19 and C.30 autogyros, leading to development of the **Fw 61** helicopter. The fuselage was similar to that of a light fixed-wing aircraft with a 160-hp (119-kW) Bramo Sh.14A radial engine mounted in the nose, the primary purpose of this powerplant being to drive two outrigger-mounted three-bladed counter-rotating rotors; it also turned a small-diameter conventional propeller for engine cooling purposes. The rotors were fully articulated and control was achieved by the use of cyclic pitch, differential pitch and differential collective pitch in the longitudinal, directional and lateral axes respectively. Vertical control was achieved by varying rotor revolutions through the use of the throttle, in contrast to the present method of maintaining reasonably constant rotor speed and altering the pitch of the blades.

Following a maiden flight on 26 June 1936, one that is usually reported as lasting for 28 seconds, but which is recorded in Heinrich Focke's log book as 45 seconds, the Fw 61 prototype completed its initial development programme and then established a number of world rotorcraft records. On 25 June 1937 Ewald Rohlfs flew it to a height of 8,000 ft (2440 m) and remained airborne for 1 hour 20 minutes 49 seconds. Next day he set a straight line distance record of 10.19 miles (16.40 km), a closed-circuit speed record of 76.15 mph (122.55 km/h) and a closed-circuit distance record of 50.09 miles (80.60 km). Perhaps the most publicised flight was that made by Hanna Reitsch in the Deutschlandhalle during February 1938. Such achievements encouraged Deutsche Lufthansa to order a passenger-carrying development of this helicopter, leading to the Fa 223 and Fa 266. By then Heinrich Focke had formed the new company Focke-Achgelis & Co. GmbH to concentrate on his interest in rotary-wing aircraft, this explaining the redesignation of the Fw 61 as the **Fa 61**.

SPECIFICATION

Focke-Wulf Fw 61 (as fully developed)
Type: single-seat experimental helicopter
Powerplant: one 160-hp (119-kW) Bramo Sh.14A 7-cylinder radial piston engine
Performance: maximum speed 76 mph (112 km/h) at sea level; cruising speed 62 mph (100 km/h);

service ceiling 8,600 ft (2620 m); range 143 miles (230 km)
Weights: empty 1,764 lb (800 kg); maximum take-off 2,094 lb (950 kg)
Dimensions: rotor diameter, each 22 ft 11½ in (7.00 m); length 23 ft 11½ in (7.30 m); height 8 ft 8¼ in (2.65 m); rotor disc area, total 828.51 sq ft (76.97 m²)

In essence merely an experimental design, the Fw 61/Fa 61 showed great promise. The outbreak of World War II put paid to plans for a more powerful Fa 224 two-seat sporting helicopter.

Focke-Wulf Fw 187 Falke

Kurt Tank's **Fw 187 Falke** (falcon) single-seat fighter proposal was evolved originally in 1936 as a private venture, based on two Daimler-Benz DB 600 engines which were then under development. The Reichsluftfahrtministerium was persuaded to sanction the manufacture of the aircraft and detail design was entrusted to Tank's assistant, Obering. R. Blaser. Of all-metal construction, the Fw 187 had an exceptionally slim fuselage with a cockpit so small that some instruments had to be located on the inboard sections of the engine cowlings where they could be seen by the pilot.

The specified DB 600s were in short supply and RLM approval for construction had been given on condition that the Jumo 210 would be substituted. Thus powered, the **Fw 187 V1** first prototype made its maiden flight during late spring 1937, in the hands

of Flugkapitän Hans Sander. The 680 hp (507 kW) provided by each of the Jumo 210 Da engines was considerably below the power of the DB 600 but the aircraft nevertheless achieved a very creditable 325 mph (523 km/h), compared with the projected 348 mph (560 km/h) with the original powerplant. Changes were made during initial tests: VDM propellers were introduced in place of the original Junkers-Hamilton variable-pitch units, and twin wheels were installed on each main gear leg; a 0.31-in (7.92-mm) MG 17 machine-gun was subsequently mounted on each side of the cockpit. The **Fw 187 V2** second prototype, flown in the summer of 1937, was similar but with Jumo 210G engines and a reduced-chord rudder.

The **Fw 187 V3** third aircraft was completed, at Udet's request, as a two-

seat interdictor, necessitating fuselage redesign, longer engine bearers and revised engine nacelles. Armed with two 20-mm MG FF cannon, it was flown in the spring of 1938, followed by two similar aircraft in the summer and autumn. All three had full-span flaps. Despite the loss of the first prototype on 14 May 1938, the programme continued and a pair of 1,000-hp (746-kW) DB 600As was supplied to Focke-Wulf for installation in the **Fw 187 V6** sixth prototype which achieved a maximum speed of 395 mph (636 km/h). Three **Fw 187A-0** pre-production examples were built, armed with four MG 17s and two MG FFs, and these were used to defend Focke-Wulf's factory at Bremen during the summer of 1940. During the winter they served (unofficially) with 13.(Zerstörer) Staffel of JG 77 in Norway.

Though the Fw 187 demonstrated excellent performance, the RLM refused to proceed with the type, ordering only three pre-production models.

SPECIFICATION	
Focke-Wulf Fw 187A-0	(3700 kg); maximum take-off
Type: single-seat day fighter	11,023 lb (5000 kg)
Powerplant: two 700-hp (522-kW)	**Dimensions:** wingspan 50 ft 2¼ in
Junkers Jumo 210G 12-cylinder	(15.30 m); length 36 ft 5 in
inverted Vee piston engines	(11.10 m); height 12 ft 7½ in
Performance: maximum speed	(3.85 m); wing area 327.23 sq ft
329 mph (529 km/h) at 3,280 ft	(30.40 m²)
(1000 m); service ceiling 32,810 ft	**Armament:** four 0.31-in (7.92-mm)
(10000 m)	MG 17 machine-guns and two
Weights: empty 8,157 lb	20-mm MG FF cannon

Focke-Wulf Fw 189 Uhu

In February 1937 a Reichsluftfahrtministerium specification for a short-range reconnaissance aircraft was issued to Arado, Hamburger Flugzeugbau and Focke-Wulf. Kurt Tank responded with the **Fw 189 Uhu** (eagle owl), an all-metal stressed-skin low-wing monoplane that had an extensively glazed fuselage pod, and twin booms carrying the tail surfaces. The mainwheels retracted to the rear, into the booms. The crew nacelle provided accommodation for pilot, navigator/radio operator and engineer/gunner, and power for the prototype was supplied by two 430-hp (321-kW) Argus As 410 engines. Construction of this aircraft began in April 1937 and Tank performed the first flight in July 1938. The **Fw 187 V2** second prototype, flown in August, was armed with one 0.31-in (7.92-mm) MG 15 machine-gun in each

of the nose, dorsal and rear positions, two fixed MG 17 weapons in the wingroots, and four underwing racks each carrying a 110-lb (50-kg) bomb. A third, unarmed, prototype was flown in September, this **Fw 189 V3** aircraft's engines driving Argus-designed air-pressure-actuated variable-pitch propellers.

The award of a development contract was followed by the first flight of a fourth prototype, forerunner of the production **Fw 189A**, which

Seen here is a Focke-Wulf Fw 189 Uhu (eagle owl) of Nachtkette/NAGr 15, which operated from Naglowitz in Poland in October 1944.

For the ground attack role, the Fw 189 V1b's crew nacelle was replaced by a tiny two-seat cockpit, made almost entirely from armour-plating.

Variants

Fw 189A-0: 10 pre-production aircraft built at Bremen in 1940, some delivered to 9.(H)/LG 2 for operational trials
Fw 189A-1: initial production version, with single flexible MG 15 machine-guns in dorsal and rear positions, an MG 17 in each wingroot and four underwing bomb racks, and carrying an Rb 20/30 or Rb 50/30 camera; further developments included the **Fw 189A-1/Trop** with desert survival equipment, and the **Fw 189A-1/U2** and
Fw 189A-1/U3 VIP transports used by Kesselring and Jeschonnek
Fw 189A-2: developed from the ninth prototype, with the flexible MG 15s replaced by twin MG 81Zs, introduced in 1942
Fw 189A-3: two-seat dual-control trainer, built in limited numbers
Fw 189A-4: introduced in late 1942, this light ground-attack version featured 20-mm MG 151/20 cannon mounted in the wingroots, and armour plate protection for the underside of the fuselage, engines and fuel tanks
Fw 189B: developed from the fifth prototype; three **Fw 189B-0** and

10 **Fw 189B-1** five-seat crew trainers preceded the Fw 189As, and some were used as conversion trainers by 9.(H)/LS 2 during the spring and summer of 1940
Fw 189C: proposed close-support version, based on the modified first prototype and the sixth prototype; development abandoned in favour of the Henschel Hs 129
Fw 189D: proposed twin-float trainer; the seventh prototype, intended as the development aircraft, was completed instead as an Fw 189B-0
Fw 189E: proposed version with two 700-hp (522-kW) Gnome-Rhône 14M radial engines; one French-built Fw 189A-4 airframe modified, using drawings supplied by SNCASO at Chatillon-sur-Seine, but the aircraft crashed near Nancy in north eastern France when being transferred to Germany for evaluation
Fw 189F: produced in **Fw 189F-1** and **Fw 189F-2** versions, the former being basically a re-engined Fw 189A-2 and the latter introducing electrically operated landing gear, increased fuel capacity and additional armour plating; both versions were powered by two 580-hp (433-kW) Argus As 411MA-1 engines

Introduced into service in 1941 as a short-range reconnaissance aircraft, the Fw 189 replaced the Henschel Hs 126. Later, the type was diverted to other roles, this example flying as an interim night-fighter with the Stab/Nachtjagdgeschwader 100 at Greifswald, in February 1945. Note the nose-mounted radar antennas.

SPECIFICATION

Focke-Wulf Fw 189A-1
Type: two-seat short-range reconnaissance aircraft
Powerplant: two 465-hp (347-kW) Argus As 410A-1 12-cylinder inverted Vee piston engines
Performance: maximum speed 208 mph (335 km/h); cruising speed 196 mph (315 km/h); service ceiling 22,965 ft (7000 m); range 416 miles (670 km)
Weights: empty 6,185 lb (2805 kg); maximum take-off 8,708 lb (3950 kg)
Dimensions: wingspan 60 ft 4½ in (18.40 m); length 39 ft 5½ in (12.03 m); height 10 ft 2 in (3.10 m); wing area 409.04 sq ft (38.00 m²)
Armament: two flexible 0.31-in (7.92-mm) MG 15 machine-guns, two 0.31-in (7.92-mm) MG 17 machine-guns and four 110-lb (50-kg) bombs

was powered by two Argus As 410A-1 engines and armed with only two MG 15s. The fifth prototype was representative of the proposed **Fw 189B** dual-control trainer, its redesigned fuselage nacelle having a stepped cockpit and much reduced glazing. An even more fundamental redesign was applied to the first prototype, which flew again in the spring of 1939 as the **Fw 189 V1b** with the crew nacelle replaced by a minute two-seat cockpit mounted on the centre-section and manufactured almost entirely from armour plating; this variant's proposed role was ground attack. Total production of the Fw 189 amounted to 864 aircraft, including a number built between 1940 and 1943 at the Aero factory in Prague and by SNCASO at Bordeaux-Mérignac.

Focke-Wulf Fw 190

Generally acknowledged by pilots to be a superior aircraft to the Luftwaffe's other main fighter of World War II, the Messerschmitt Bf 109, the **Fw 190** was developed under a contract placed by the German air ministry in the autumn of 1937. Kurt Tank submitted two proposals, one powered by a Daimler-Benz DB 601 liquid-cooled inverted-Vee engine and the other by the new BMW 139 air-cooled radial. The latter was selected, and detail design work began in the summer of 1938 under the leadership of Obering. R. Blaser.

A low-wing cantilever monoplane of light alloy stressed-skin construction, the **Fw 190 V1** first prototype was rolled out in May 1939 and recorded its maiden flight on 1 June of the same year.

When the Focke-Wulf Fw 190 first appeared in action in 1941, it was undoubtedly the most advanced fighter aircraft in the world, and was unofficially named Würger (Butcher Bird).

Variants

Fw 190A-1: initial production model with the 1,660-hp (1238-kW) BMW 801C-1 radial engine, long-span wing, FuG 7a radio and inadequate armament of four 0.312-in (7.92-mm) MG 17s
Fw 190A-2: following a prototype installation of two MG 17 machine-guns mounted above the engine and two 20-mm MG FF cannon in the wingroots, this version was introduced with similar armament, often augmented by two MG 17 guns in the outer wing panels; power was supplied by the improved BMW 801C-2 engine
Fw 190A-3: MG FF cannon moved to the outer wing panels and their original locations used for faster-firing MG 151 weapons; introduced in the autumn of 1941, the A-3 was powered by the 1,800-hp (1342-kW) BMW 801Dg engine; conversions included the **Fw 190A-3/U1** and **Fw 190A-3/U3** close-support aircraft and the **Fw 190A-3/U4** reconnaissance fighter; these conversions usually involved removal of the outboard MG FF cannon and the addition of Rb 12 cameras or ETC 500 bomb racks
Fw 190A-4: delivered from the summer of 1942, this version had FuG 16Z radio with a fin-mounted radio mast, and its BMW 801D-2 engine had provision for MW-50 water/methanol fuel injection to boost output to 2,100 hp (1566 kW) for short periods and thus raise the maximum speed to 416 mph (670 km/h) at 21,000 ft (6400 m); the **Fw 190A-4/Trop** had tropical filters for service in the Mediterranean theatre and also carried a 551-lb (250-kg) bomb beneath the fuselage; MW-50 fuel injection was deleted from the **Fw 190A-4/R6**, which could carry two underwing 8.27-cm (3¾-in) WGr.21 rocket tubes; with fixed armament reduced to two MG 151 cannon, the **Fw 190A-4/U5** could carry a 66-Imp gal (300-litre) drop tank beneath each wing and a 1,102-lb (500-kg) bomb under the fuselage
Fw 190A-5: introduced in early 1943, this version featured a new engine mounting which positioned the engine almost 6 in (15 cm) farther forward; used for a variety of roles, versions included the **Fw 190A-5/U2** with flame-damping equipment for night operations, two MG 151/20 cannon, an underfuselage ETC 501 bomb rack and two 66-Imp gal (300-litre) drop tanks; the similar **Fw 190A-5/U3** could carry a 1,102-lb (500-kg) bomb beneath the fuselage and two 254-lb (115-kg) bombs under the wing; and the **Fw 190A-3/U4** had two Rb 12 cameras for reconnaissance duties; fighter-bomber versions included the **Fw 190A-5/U6** and the long-range **Fw 190A-5/U7** while the **Fw 190A-5/U11** close-support aircraft carried a 30-mm MK 103 cannon under each half of the wing; the **Fw 190A-5/U12** featured the fixed armament of two MG 151/20 cannon and two MG 17 machine-guns supplemented by two WB 151A pods each carrying a pair of MG 151/20 cannon; torpedo-carrying models were the **Fw 190A-5/U14** and **Fw 190A-5/U15** carrying the LT F5b and LT 950 torpedo respectively; a 30-mm MK 108 cannon in the outboard wing position was standard for the **Fw 190A-5/U16**
Fw 190A-6: appearing in June 1943 and derived from the experimental **Fw 190A-5/U10**, this version introduced a new lighter wing which could accommodate four 20-mm MG 151/20 cannon; the

Fw 190A-6/R1 had six 20-mm MG 151/20 cannon, the **Fw 190A-6/R2** a 30-mm MK 108 in the outboard wing position, and the **Fw 190A-6/R3** two MK 103 cannon under the wings; the **Fw 190A-6/R6** carried WGr.21 rocket tubes
Fw 190A-7: this version entered production in December 1943, and was similar to the Fw 190A-6 except for the replacement of the fuselage-mounted MG 17s by 0.51-in (13-mm) MG 131 machine-guns
Fw 190A-8: in this basic model internal fuel was increased by 25 Imp gal (114 litres) and versions were similar to those produced under the Fw 190A-6 designation; also produced were the **Fw 190A-8/R7** with an armoured cockpit and the **Fw 190A-8/R11** all-weather fighter with heated canopy and PKS 12 radio navigation equipment; the **Fw 190A-8/U1** was a two-seat conversion trainer, while the **Fw 190A-8/U3** was the director component of the Fw 190/Ta 154 Mistel composite aircraft
Fw 190B: as part of the programme to improve high-altitude performance, three **Fw 190A-0** aircraft were modified in various ways; the **Fw 190 V13** was given a wing of increased area and a pressurised cockpit, and its BMW 801D-2 engine had a GM-1 power boost system, while the **Fw 190 V16** and **Fw 190 V18** were similar but had the standard wing and were armed with two MG 17 machine-guns and two MG 151/20 cannon; the Daimler-Benz DB 603 inverted-Vee engine with annular radiator was then substituted for the radial, and further development of the type was concentrated on the similar **Fw 190C**
Fw 190C: a small number of development aircraft was built with the 1,750-hp (1304-kW) DB 603 engine boosted by either the DVL-developed TK 11 or Hirth 2281 turbocharger in a large ventral fairing which gave rise to the nickname 'Kanguruh'; development was discontinued in favour of the Fw 190D
Fw 190D-9: late in 1943 several Fw 190A-7s were modified with the Jumo 213A inverted-Vee engine as **Fw 190D-0** prototypes for the Fw 190D-9, the use of this engine necessitating the inclusion of a 1-ft 7¾-in (0.50-m) rear-fuselage plug to compensate for the nose's additional 2 ft (0.60 m) of length; the fin was increased in area for the same reason; known popularly as the 'long-nose 190' or **'Dora 9'**, the Fw 190D-9 was armed with two wing-mounted MG 151/20 cannon and two MG 131 machine-guns above the engine, and had MW-50 water/methanol fuel injection to boost emergency power output to 2,240 hp (1670 kW); a 66-Imp gal (300-litre) drop tank or a 551-lb (250-kg) bomb could also be carried on each underwing rack; later aircraft were fitted with bubble canopies, as introduced earlier on the Fw 190F
Fw 190D-10: two Fw 190D-9s were converted to this standard with the Jumo 213C engine and a 30-mm MK 108 cannon firing through the spinner instead of the two MG 131 machine-guns
Fw 190D-11: seven prototypes with the Jumo 213F engine, two MG 151/20 cannon in the wingroots and two MK 108 cannon farther outboard in the wing
Fw 190D-12: essentially a ground-attack version with the engine-mounted MK 108 and two MG 151/20 cannon in the wing, with additional armour protection for the engine

Focke-Wulf Fw 190 (continued)

Variants (continued)

Fw 190D-13: similar to the D-12 but with an MG 151/20 in place of the MK 108 cannon

Fw 190E: proposed reconnaissance fighter whose development was abandoned

Fw 190F-1: preceding the Fw 190D and developed as a specialised ground-attack variant, this was introduced early in 1943 as a development of the Fw 190A-4 with the engine and cockpit given additional armour protection, the outboard 20-mm cannon removed and an ETC 501 bomb rack added beneath the fuselage

Fw 190F-2: similarly based on the Fw 190A-5 but introduced a bubble cockpit canopy

Fw 190F-3: developed from the Fw 190A-6, this variant could carry a 66-Imp gal (300-litre) drop tank or a 551-lb (250-kg) bomb beneath the fuselage and, in the **Fw 190F-3/R1** and **Fw 190F-3/R3** versions, four ETC 50 underwing bomb racks or two similarly located 30-mm MK 103 cannon respectively

Fw 190F-8: this was based similarly on the Fw 190A-8 but with two fuselage-mounted MG 131 machine-guns and four ETC 50 bomb racks; the **Fw 190F-8/U2** and **Fw 190F-8/U3** versions were fitted with the TSA bomb sight for anti-ship attack and a 1,543-lb (700-kg) BT 700 or 3,086-lb (1400-kg) BT 1400 torpedoes respectively

Fw 190F-9: this was a variant, introduced in mid-1944, similar to the Fw 190F-8 but powered by the BMW 801 TS/TH engine

Fw 190G-1: fighter-bomber derived from the A-5. It could carry a 3,968-lb (1800-kg) bomb which required strengthened landing gear; the wing-mounted armament was reduced to two MG 151/20 cannon, and Junkers-designed underwing racks accommodated two 66-Imp gal (300-litre) drop tanks

Fw 190G-2: similar to the G-1 but with Messerschmitt racks for the drop tanks

Fw 190G-3: introduced late in the summer of 1943 with Focke-Wulf racks and PKS 11 autopilot

Fw 190G-8: final G-series production version incorporating Fw 190A-8 modifications and powered by the 1,800-hp (1342-kW) BMW 801D-2 engine

In June 1942, JG 1 received the Fw 190A-3/U-1, which had an ETC 501 bomb rack capable of carrying a 500-kg (1,100-lb) SC 500 bomb.

The **Fw 190 V2** second prototype took to the air in October 1939 with the armament of two 0.51-in (13-mm) MG 131 and two 0.312-in (7.92-mm) MG 17 machine-guns. Both of these prototypes were fitted with large ducted spinners to reduce drag, but overheating problems were experienced with the engine and a NACA cowling was substituted. Even before the first prototype's initial flight, a decision had been taken to replace the BMW 139 with the more powerful but longer and heavier BMW 801 radial engine. This necessitated a number of major changes including structural strengthening and relocation of the cockpit to a position farther to the rear; the latter solved a centre of gravity problem and, as a bonus, reduced pilot discomfort from fumes and overheating resulting from the proximity of engine to cockpit with the BMW 139 installation.

The third and fourth prototypes were abandoned, and the **Fw 190 V5** with the new engine was completed early in 1940. Later in the year the machine was fitted with a wing spanning 3 ft 3½ in (1.00 m) more than the original 31 ft 2 in (9.50 m), and although some 6 mph (10 km) slower, this **Fw 190 V5g** was both more manoeuvrable and superior in climb performance to the short-span version that was now redesignated as the **Fw 190 V5k**. Of a pre-production batch of **Fw 190A-0** aircraft the first

Illustrated is a Focke-Wulf Fw 190A-5/U-12 'Red 13' of Leutnant Erich Hondt, Staffelkapitän of 2./JG 11, based at Husum in October 1943. Note the underwing gondolas, each containing a pair of 20-mm MG 151 cannon.

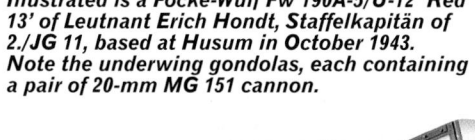

seven had the original wing but the remainder featured the longer-span unit.

During February 1941, the first aircraft were delivered to Erprobungs-kommando 190 for service evaluation, and in March Jagdgeschwader 26 in northern France began to prepare for the new fighter's introduction into full Luftwaffe service. The first operational unit, 6./JG 26 at Le Bourget, was equipped with the type in August 1941 and when the first clashes between Fw 190 and Supermarine Spitfire fighters took place soon after this, the superiority of the Fw 190 over the Spitfire was immediately apparent. This was

the beginning of a truly impressive service career which was to involve almost 20,000 aircraft, built in many versions by

Focke-Wulf, Ago, Arado, Fieseler and Dornier. Sixty-four examples of the **Fw 190A-8** were also built by the SNCAC in France

during 1945 for service with the revived French air force with the designation **NC.900**.

Focke-Wulf Fw 190A-8

Focke-Wulf Fw 190D-9 'Black Double Chevron' of Oberleutnant Oskar Romm, IV./JG 3, operated from Prenzlau in March 1945. Romm's wartime career ended in a crash on 24 April 1945, in which he was severely injured, his score at the time totalling 92 victories.

Focke-Wulf Fw 200 Condor

Kurt Tank's idea for the **Fw 200 Condor**, a new airliner for Deutsche Lufthansa, was submitted to the directors of the airline on 16 July 1936 with a promise that the first example would fly within a year. In fact the **Fw 200 V1**, the first of three prototypes, on which work had started in the autumn of 1936, recorded its maiden flight on 27 July 1937, and this was still a very creditable performance. A low-wing cantilever monoplane of light alloy construction, the Fw 200 was powered initially by four 875-hp (652-kW) Pratt & Whitney Hornet radial engines and was designed to provide accommodation for up to 26 passengers in two cabins. Two further prototypes, the second of which became Adolf Hitler's personal transport, were each powered by four 720-hp (537-kW) BMW 132G-1 radial engines. The second prototype and four examples of the **Fw 200A** initial production model were delivered to Lufthansa, two to DDL Danish Air Lines and two to Sindicato Condor, Lufthansa's Brazilian associate.

The prototype, redesignated as the **Fw 200S-1** and named *Brandenburg*, made a number of record flights in the latter half of 1938, beginning on 10 August when a Lufthansa crew flew non-stop from Berlin to New York in a time of 24 hours 56 minutes, returning on 13 August in 19 hours 55 minutes. Further aircraft

Fw 200 V3 was flown by the Luftwaffe as Hitler's personal transport – the Führermaschine. It was named **Immelmann III** *and went through three changes of colour scheme before adopting the camouflage illustrated.*

Known as the 'Scourge of the Atlantic', the Condor was notorious in Britain as one of Germany's most potent anti-shipping weapons.

were supplied to Lufthansa before the outbreak of World War II, and on 14 April 1945 a survivor flew the airline's last scheduled service, from Barcelona to Berlin, before the cessation of hostilities.

The prototype's flight to Tokyo had resulted in an order for five airliners from Dai Nippon K.K. and a single maritime reconnaissance aircraft for the Imperial Japanese Navy. Neither type was delivered to Japan, but the **Fw 200 V10** military prototype which resulted had increased fuel capacity and armament comprising single 0.312-in (7.92-mm) MG 15 trainable machine-guns in a dorsal turret and in

the front and rear positions of a ventral gondola. From this model was developed the **Fw 200C**, which first entered service as a transport with the KGrzbV 104 unit during the Norwegian campaign of April 1940, but was more usefully developed for the long-range maritime reconnaissance bomber role. The Condor soon became the scourge of Allied shipping following its operational debut with the Fernauflärungsstaffel (later 1./KG 40) on 8 April 1940, but throughout its career was plagued by a weakness in the fuselage just to the rear of the wing as a result of operations at higher weights than had originally

been intended. Operations in the maritime role were finally discontinued in the autumn of 1944, and the surviving Condors were used during the closing stages of World War II as transports by units including the 5. and 200.Transportstaffeln and the

Führer Kürierstaffel. This last unit's inventory included the **Fw 200C-4/U1** allocated to Heinrich Himmler and equipped with an armour-plated seat for the use of the head of the SS. Approximately 280 Condors were built.

Famous as a pre-war airliner, with a number of formidable long-distance flights and records to its credit, the Condor was designed by Kurt Tank in 1936. Lufthansa's Westfalen *was the second Fw 200 prototype.*

SPECIFICATION

Focke-Wulf Fw 200C-3/U4 Condor
Type: six-seat long-range maritime reconnaissance bomber
Powerplant: four Bramo 323R radial piston engines each rated at 1,200 hp (895 kW)
Performance: maximum speed 224 mph (360 km/h) at 15,750 ft (4800 m); cruising speed 208 mph (335 km/h) at 13,125 ft (4000 m); service ceiling 19,685 ft (6000 m); range 2,212 miles (3560 km); endurance 14 hours
Weights: empty 37,490 lb (17005 kg); maximum take-off 50,057 lb (24520 kg)
Dimensions: wingspan 107 ft 9¼ in (32.85 m); length 76 ft 11¼ in (23.45 m); height 20 ft 8 in (3.30 m); wing area 1,290.10 sq ft (119.85 m²)
Armament: one 20-mm MG 151/20 trainable forward-firing cannon in the forward ventral gondola position, one

0.51-in (13-mm) MG 131 trainable rearward-firing machine-gun in the rear dorsal position, one 0.51-in (13-mm) MG 131 trainable lateral-firing machine-gun in each of the two beam positions, one 0.312-in (7.92-mm) MG 15 trainable rearward-firing machine-gun in the rear ventral gondola position, and one 0.312-in (7.92-mm) MG 15 trainable machine-gun in the power-operated Fw 19 forward dorsal turret, plus up to 4,630 lb (2100 kg) of disposable stores carried in a ventral gondola weapons bay, two hardpoints under the outboard engine nacelles and two hardpoints under the outer wing panels, and generally comprising two 500-kg (1,102-lb) SC 500 bombs under the outboard engine nacelles, two 250-kg (551-lb) SC 250 bombs under the outer wing panels, and 12 50-kg (110-lb) SC 50 bombs in the weapons bay

---

Variants

Fw 200B-1: one aircraft for Lufthansa, powered by four 850-hp (634-kW) BMW 132DCs
Fw 200B-2: five ordered by Dai Nippon K.K. and two by Aero Oy of Finland with 830-hp (619-kW) BMW 132H radial engines; three were completed and diverted to Lufthansa, passing to KGrzbV 105 at Kiel-Holtenau in April 1940, together with the single Fw 200B-1
Fw 200C-0: 10 delivered in September 1939 as four unarmed aircraft (which served with KGrzbV 105) and six with armament which comprised one 0.312-in (7.92-mm) MG 15 machine-gun in each of forward and aft dorsal turrets and a third weapon firing through a ventral hatch
Fw 200C-1: initial production reconnaissance version with one 20-mm MG FF cannon in the nose, one MG 15 in a ventral gondola, a similar weapon in a forward dorsal position and a third in a rear dorsal position; offensive armament also included four 551-lb (250-kg) bombs on underwing racks
Fw 200C-2: similar to the Fw 200C-1 but with the rear of the outboard engine nacelles cut away to accommodate streamlined bomb racks

Fw 200C-3: introduced in 1941, this was a structurally strengthened version powered by Bramo 323R-2 radial engines; the **Fw 200C-3/U1** version had a 15-mm MG 151 cannon in a revised forward turret and a 20-mm MG 151/20 cannon to replace the ventral MG FF weapon; in the **Fw 200C-3/U2**, the ventral MG 151/20 was replaced by a 0.51-in (13-mm) MG 131 machine-gun to permit installation of the Lofte 7D bomb sight, and the **Fw 200C-3/U3** carried an MG 131 in each of the front and rear positions; the final **Fw 200C-3/U4** version carried an extra gunner and two additional beam-mounted MG 131s
Fw 200C-4: entering production in 1942, this model was fitted with FuG Rostock (later FuG 200 Hohentwiel) search radar and armed with an MG 151 cannon in the forward dorsal turret, a ventral MG 151/20 or (with Lofte 7D bomb sight) MG 131, and MG 15 machine-guns at the other stations; single examples of the **Fw 200C-4/U1** and **Fw 200C-4/U2** transports were also built
Fw 200C-6: standard to which a number of C-3/U1 and C-3/U2 aircraft were modified as interim missile carriers with two underwing Henschel Hs 293A rocket-propelled guided bombs and FuG 203b Kehl missile control equipment; this version entered service with III./KG 40 in November 1943
Fw 200C-8: definitive version of Fw 200C-6 with Hohentwiel radar

Focke-Wulf Ta 152 and Ta 153

Further improvement of the airframe used in the Fw 190D series to provide even better performance at high altitude led to the introduction of the **Ta 152** and **Ta 153**. The latter was built only as a development prototype, powered by the Daimler-Benz DB 603 engine, and introduced an entirely new high-aspect-ratio wing of increased span, together with revision of the fuselage structure, tail surfaces and internal systems. It was abandoned to avoid disruption of existing Fw 190 production.

As originally conceived, the Ta 152 was structurally closer to the Fw 190D except that the flap and landing-gear systems were hydraulically and not electrically actuated. In the autumn of 1944 a prototype

Variants

Ta 152C: the development prototype for the Ta 152C first flew on 19 November 1944 with the 2,100-hp (1566-kW) DB 603LA engine, the length of this unit requiring a compensating rear fuselage plug and enlarged tail surfaces; the wingspan was increased to 36 ft 1 in (11.00 m), and the armament for the **Ta 152C-1** and **Ta 152C-2** (the latter with improved radio equipment) was a 30-mm MK 108 engine-mounted cannon and four 20-mm MG 151/20 cannon; in the **Ta 152C-3**, the MK 108 was replaced by an MK 103
Ta 152E: photographic reconnaissance version of the Ta 152C with the standard wing in **Ta 152E-1** form; the **Ta 152E-2** was a high-altitude aircraft with the H-series wing; the engine was the Jumo 213E
Ta 152H: high-altitude fighter with pressurised cabin and a wing increased in span to 47 ft 6¾ in (14.50 m); the **Ta 152H-0** pre-production aircraft were mostly rebuilt from Fw 190A-1 airframes and had the Jumo 213E engine with MW-50 water/methanol fuel injection; **Ta 152H-1** production aircraft began to leave the Cottbus lines in November 1944

appeared with the Jumo 213E engine and a long-

span wing of high aspect ratio, and although this

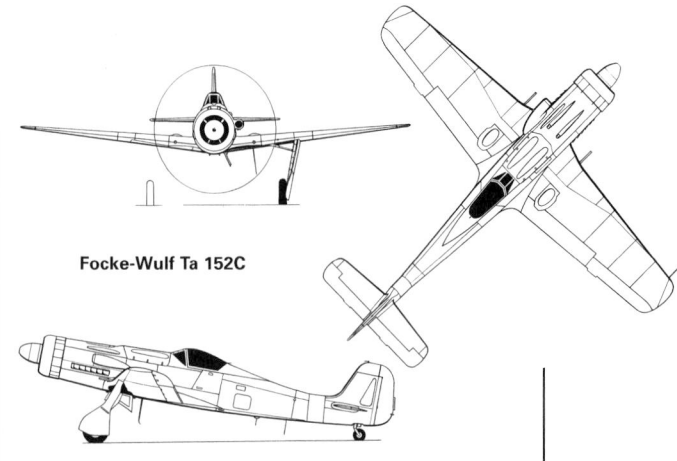

Focke-Wulf Ta 152C

prototype crashed on 8 October its replacement in the **Ta 152H** test programme had the Jumo engine but the standard Fw 190 wing. The first of 20 **Ta 152H-0** pre-production aircraft, built at Focke-Wulf's Cottbus factory, flew in October 1944. Service trials were

undertaken by Erprobungskommando 152 at Rechlin before the type's operational debut with JG 301. This unit was tasked with the protection of bases used by the Messerschmitt Me 262 jet fighter, which was particularly vulnerable during take-off and landing.

Kurt Tank's Fw 190 design had been so successful that the RLM allowed him to use the first letters of his surname to prefix all subsequent Focke-Wulf designs.

SPECIFICATION	
Focke-Wulf Ta 152H-1 **Type:** single-seat high-altitude fighter **Powerplant:** one Junkers Jumo 213E inverted-Vee piston engine rated at 1,750 hp (1305 kW) **Performance:** maximum speed 472 mph (760 km/h) at 41,010 ft (12500 m) with MW-50 water/methanol fuel injection and GM-1 power boost; cruising speed 373 mph (600 km/h) at optimum altitude; initial climb rate 3,445 ft (1050 m) per minute with MW-50;	service ceiling 48,555 ft (14800 m); range 746 miles (1200 km) **Weights:** empty 8,643 lb (3920 kg); maximum take-off 10,472 lb (4750 kg) **Dimensions:** wingspan 47 ft 6¾ in (14.50 m); length 35 ft 5½ in (10.80 m); height 13 ft 1½ in (4.00 m); wing area 252.96 sq ft (23.50 m²) **Armament:** one 30-mm MK 108 fixed forward-firing cannon in a Motorkannon installation, and two 20-mm MG 151/20E fixed forward-firing cannon in the wingroots

Focke-Wulf Ta 154

In order to combat the nightly bombing raids against German urban and industrial centres by the warplanes of the Royal Air Force's Bomber Command, the German air ministry ordered the development of a two-seat night-fighter in

Variants

Ta 154A-1: first production model, of which 250 had been ordered soon after the start of the flight test programme although, in the event, only some 50 or slightly more production aircraft were built before production was cancelled; the aircraft had FuG 212 Lichtenstein C-1 radar
Ta 152A-2: proposed single-seat production model; the designation **Ta 154A-2/U3** was used for six A-0 aircraft each adapted as the lower component of a Mistel composite aircraft with a 4,409-lb (2000-kg) warhead and attachment points for an Fw 190 to be used as the control element
Ta 154A-3: proposed two-seat conversion trainer
Ta 154A-4: variant of the Ta 154A-1 with Jumo 211N engines and FuG 220 or FuG 218 Neptun radar; the type saw limited service with 1./NJG 3 and Nachtschlachtgruppe 10
Ta 154C: proposed development with an armament of six MG 151/20 cannon and the fuselage lengthened by 3 ft 7¼ in (1.10 m) to allow the inclusion of more fuel tankage for the projected **Ta 154C-1** two-seat night-fighter and **Ta 154C-2** single-seat day fighter subvariants, and the **Ta 154C-3** with the same lengthened fuselage but a wing increased in area by 30 per cent to allow the carriage of a truly extraordinary fixed forward-firing battery of eight 30-mm MK 108 cannon
Ta 254: proposed high-altitude model

trained woodworkers. Powered by two 1,480-hp (1104-kW) Junkers Jumo 211F engines, the **Ta 154 V1** first prototype recorded its initial flight on 1 July 1943, and was soon joined by the similarly powered **Ta 154 V2** second prototype in handling and performance trials, during the course of which the machine was revised with 1,520-hp (1133-kW) Jumo 211N engines. The V2 also introduced the FuG 202 Lichtenstein BC-1 radar. The **Ta 154 V3** third prototype, first flown on 25 November 1943, was the forerunner of the **Ta 154A-0** pre-production model and was armed with four 20-mm MG 151/20 cannon in the sides of the fuselage below the cockpit.

Four more prototypes were flown between January and March 1944, the Ta 154 V4 introducing the proposed production-standard armament of two MG 151/20 and two 30-mm MK 108 cannon. The remaining eight aircraft of the original order were assembled within the context of orders for 22 Ta 154A-0 pre-production aircraft, four of them with 1,776-hp (1324-kW) Jumo 213A engines. In armed and radar-equipped configuration the Ta 154A had the impres-

August 1942. The resulting contenders were the all-metal Heinkel He 219 and the Focke-Wulf Ta 154, the latter designed by Tank as a twin-engined shoulder-wing monoplane of wooden construction throughout in order to utilise the skills of

The Ta 154 V3 was the first 'Moskito' to be fitted with radar equipment and became the prototype for the Ta 154A-0/U-1 night fighter.

sive maximum speed of more than 400 mph (644 km/h), but the programme was cancelled late in August 1944 following structural failures in two early production aircraft on 28 and 30 June 1944, the result of an adverse reaction between the adhesive and

the plywood it was bonding. The prototype and pre-production aircraft had used Tego-Film adhesive, but after the factory which produced it had been bombed, an alternative adhesive was used, and it was the latter that brought disastrous results.

SPECIFICATION	
Focke-Wulf Ta 154A-4 **Type:** two-seat night-fighter **Powerplant:** two Junkers Jumo 211N inverted-Vee piston engines each rated at 1,520 hp (1133 kW) **Performance:** maximum speed 382 mph (615 km/h) at 19,000 ft (5790 m); climb to 26,245 ft (8000 m) in 16 minutes; service ceiling 35,760 ft (10900 m); range 851 miles (1370 km) **Weights:** empty 13,933 lb	(6320 kg) without radar and armament; maximum take-off 18,188 lb (8250 kg) **Dimensions:** wingspan 52 ft 6 in (16.00 m); length 40 ft 10¼ in (12.45 m) without antennas; height 11 ft 1½ in (3.50 m); wing area 348.76 sq ft (32.40 m²) **Armament:** two 30-mm MK 108 and two 20-mm MG 151/20 fixed forward-firing cannon in the nose

Fokker 50 and 60

The **Fokker 50** is a comprehensively modernised version of the F27 Friendship Mk 500, and after being announced in November 1983, first flew on 27 December 1985. It was subsequently marketed in passenger, freight and combi passenger/freight models. The development programme used two prototypes and led to certification in May 1987, leading to deliveries (initially to Lufthansa CityLine) from August of the same year. Until Fokker went into bankruptcy in March 1996, the type was offered on the civil market in three basic variants, namely the **F50 Series 100** with the powerplant of two PW125B turboprops and accommodation for between 46 and 58 passengers in **F50-100** four-door and **F50-120** three-door subvariants, the **F50 Series 300** (otherwise **F50 High Performance**) for 'hot-and-high' operations with the powerplant of two PW127B turboprops each flat-rated at 2,750 shp (2050 kW) and available in **F50-300** four-door and **F50-320** three-door subvariants, and the **F50 Utility** based on the **F50-1120** with a heavy-duty floor and a large freight door. In the mid-1990s Fokker was planning the **F50 Series 400** with its fuselage lengthened by 7 ft

10½ in (2.40 m) for 68 passengers in **F50-400** four-door and **F50-420** three-door subvariants, but further progress in this direction was made moot by the company's financial collapse.

The F50-100 baseline model is externally similar to the F27, but features a host of structural and system improvements (the latter including digital avionics and an EFIS flight-deck) as well as greater use of composite materials in the airframe. Its PW125Bs drive six- rather than four-bladed propellers.

The basic type was also offered in a military variant with the designation **Troopship Mk 2** with the forward fuselage lengthened by 2 ft 11½ in (0.90 m) to allow the insertion of a starboard-side freight door and the carriage of a payload of 11,023 lb (5000 kg) including 54 passengers, or 50 troops, or paratroops, or 24 litters and a number of seated casualties plus attendants, or freight over a range of more than 1,612 miles (2595 km). The Troopship Mk 2 found its first purchaser early in 1994 when the Singaporean air force ordered four aircraft (with options on another three) as replacements for its Shorts SC.7 Skyvans.

The F50 was also

offered in the same three EW variants as the F27, although only one of these models found a purchaser. This is the **F50 Black Crow Mk 2**, of which a single example was ordered by an undisclosed customer for the Comint/Sigint role with an endurance of 14 hours. The **Kingbird Mk 2** was offered for the AEW and airborne command/ control roles, and would have been capable of flying an eight-hour patrol at a radius of 345 miles (555 km) with a mission suite that would have included a phased-array surveillance radar and an ESM system; a subvariant offered in 1992 was the **Kingbird Mk 2E** with

A thorough re-working of the basic F27 design, the Fokker 50 is most easily distinguished from its forerunner by it six-bladed propellers.

Ericsson FSR-890 Erieye radar (using a flat-plate antenna array located longitudinally above the fuselage) and the Teledyne ASN-150(V)8 central tactical system. The **Sentinel Mk 2** was designed for the border surveillance and reconnaissance role, and would have been outfitted with a mission suite including Motorola APS-135(V) SLAR, Texas Instruments APS-134(V)7 synthetic-aperture radar, and a pod-mounted Itek Eagle Eye optronic imaging system.

The **F50 Maritime Mk 2** was to have been a considerably developed version of the Maritime, with a flightcrew of two or three, a mission crew of between two and four, and a mission suite that included an IR detection system and the Texas Instruments APS-134 surveillance radar with its antenna in a ventral radome. The **F50 Maritime Enforcer Mk 2** was a considerably developed version of the F27MPA Maritime Enforcer, based on the airframe and powerplant of the F50. The Maritime Enforcer Mk 2 had basically the same airframe as the F27MPA Maritime Enforcer but with aerodynamic refinements, flight deck improvements, and a

powerplant of two PW125B turboprops. The avionics suite was basically an improved version of that to be carried by the F50 Maritime Mk 2. The weapons capability was increased to 8,664 lb (3930 kg) of disposable stores carried on eight hardpoints (two under the fuselage and six under the wing), allowing the carriage of up to eight torpedoes and/or depth bombs, or two or four AGM-84 Harpoon or AM39 Exocet anti-ship missiles, or a mixed load of torpedoes and missiles; more typical loads were four torpedoes, or two anti-ship missiles. Singapore was the only customer for the type, buying four.

Procured by the Dutch air force to the extent of four aircraft, the **F60 Utility** is a development of the F50 with its fuselage lengthened by 5 ft 4 in (1.62 m) to allow the incorporation of a large port-side freight door providing access to the cabin for large cargo items as an alternative to the standard accommodation for 55 paratroops or 6,007 lb (2725 kg) of freight.

The last F50 was delivered in May 1997, ending production of the F50 and F60 series at 212 aircraft.

The Maritime Enforcer Mk 2 was developed from the Fokker 50-100 for anti-submarine and anti-surface unit warfare, and is equipped with an impressive array of sophisticated avionics.

Left: Seen here landing at Schiphol after the first test flight, the Fokker 60 Utility is a 'stretched' military version of the Fokker 50, incorporating a large freight door on the port side.

SPECIFICATION	
Fokker 50-100	776 miles (1249 km) at standard
Type: two/three-crew short-range transport	maximum take-off weight with 50 passengers
Powerplant: two Pratt & Whitney Canada PW125B turboprop engines each flat-rated at 2,500 shp (1864 kW)	**Weights:** empty 27,886 lb (12650 kg); standard maximum take-off 41,865 lb (18990 kg)
Performance: cruising speed 325 mph (522 km/h) at optimum altitude; maximum operating altitude 25,000 ft (7620 m); range	**Dimensions:** wingspan 95 ft 1¾ in (29.00 m); length 82 ft 10 in (25.25 m); height 27 ft 3¼ in (8.317 m); wing area 753.50 sq ft (70.00 m²)
	Payload: see above

Fokker 70 and 100

First flown on 30 November 1986 after being announced at the same time as the Fokker 50 in November 1983, the **Fokker 100** is a development of the F28 Fellowship Mk 4000 twin-turbofan airliner, updated along the lines of the F50. The type was first flown with the powerplant of two Rolls-Royce Tay Mk 620 turbofan engines, but an option was later added for the 15,100-lb st (67.17-kN) Tay Mk 650 engine. As well as updated avionics (including an EFIS cockpit) and a general modernisation of systems, the **F100** also introduced a large measure of composite materials in the structure, a revised wing of greater span and improved aerofoil section for better cruising performance and high subsonic speeds, and a lengthening of the fuselage to allow the carriage of up to 107 passengers in a five-abreast seating arrangement inside a redesigned cabin.

The type was offered at three maximum take-off weight options with differing fuel quantities, and deliveries began in February 1988 (the first machine going to Swissair) after the flight test programme with two development aircraft had led to the F100's certification in November 1987. Production was undertaken in collaboration with Daimler-Benz Aerospace Airbus (fuselage sections and tail unit), Shorts (wing) and Northrop Grumman (engine nacelles and thrust reversers). The primary variant was the standard F100, although other models offered included the **F100QC** quick-change model with a large port-side door in the forward fuselage for a maximum freight payload of 25,353 kg (11500 kg), and the **Executive Jet 100** VIP and corporate shuttle.

At the time of Fokker's bankruptcy, the last of 277 F100s was delivered to TAM Brasil.

A lower-capacity version of the F100 was developed as the **Fokker 70**, with its fuselage reduced in length by 15 ft 2 in (4.62 m) for the carriage of up to 79 passengers. The F70 programme was launched in June 1993, and the first example was converted from the F100's second prototype for a first flight on 2 April 1993. The F70 received its certification in October 1994 and delivery of the first machine was made to the Ford Motor Company in the same month, with Sempati Air of Indonesia becoming the first airline to operate the type in March 1995. The last of 47 F70s was delivered in April 1997 to CityHopper. Variants that had been offered by the time of Fokker's collapse included the standard F70, the **F70A** for the North American market with an additional main deck cargo hold reducing seating capacity to 70, the **Executive Jet 70** for the VIP and corporate market,

and the **Executive Jet 70ER** extended-range executive transport.

Early in 1998, Rekkof Restart (Rekkof being Fokker spelled backwards) was created in an effort to resume manufacture of the F70 and F100 series. The company bought the production facilities for the two aircraft, but by the first half of 2000 there had been no resumption of manufacture.

In summer 2000, British Midland listed three leased Fokker 70s within its mainline fleet. The aircraft are configured for 74 passengers.

SPECIFICATION

Fokker 100
Type: two-crew short-range transport
Powerplant: two Rolls-Royce Tay Mk 620 turbofan engines each rated at 13,850 lb st (61.61 kN)
Performance: cruising speed 532 mph (856 km/h) at 25,500 ft (7770 m); maximum operating altitude 35,000 ft (10670 m); range between 1,484 and 1,933 miles (2389 and 3111 km) with 50 passengers depending on maximum take-off weight option
Weights: empty between 54,217 and 54,558 lb (24593 and 24747 kg) depending on weight option; maximum take-off between 95,000 and 101,000 lb (43090 and 45810 kg) depending on weight option
Dimensions: wingspan 92 ft 1½ in (28.08 m); length 116 ft 6¾ in (35.53 m); height 27 ft 10½ in (8.51 m); wing area 1,006.46 sq ft (93.50 m²)
Payload: see above. Maximum payload between 24,486 and 26,442 lb (11108 and 11993 kg) depending on weight option

Easily distinguished from the Fokker 70 by its longer fuselage and twin overwing passenger escape doors, the F100 remains a popular airliner.

Fokker C I, C.I, C.II and C.III

The **C I**, a compact unequal-span two-seat biplane of mixed construction for the reconnaissance role, was in effect an enlarged development of the D.VII single-seat fighter. Tested as the **U.38** at Schwerin in 1918, it was placed in immediate production but World War I ended before any deliveries could be made to the German air arm. Fokker arranged to have all the German-built C Is transferred to the Netherlands, where production continued under the very slightly revised designation **C.I** and

eventually more than 250 such aircraft were built. The powerplant was initially based on the BMW IIIa inline engine, but other installations included the 220-hp (164-kW) BMW IV, 160-hp (119-kW) Oberursel, 260-hp (194-kW) Mercedes and 200-hp (149-kW) Armstrong Siddeley Lynx units. The C.I was easily recognisable by a fuel tank mounted on the landing gear axle, where it was protected by a streamlined fairing which was claimed by the manufacturers to provide additional lift.

The USSR purchased 42

C.Is, while Denmark acquired two and built three more under licence, and one Danish C.I was still flying as a trainer in 1940; the Dutch army air corps procured a total of 62 C.Is which proved very reliable and were transferred eventually from first-line reconnaissance units to training units where, fitted with dual controls and rear cockpit folding hoods, they were often used as blind-flying trainers; and Dutch naval aviation obtained 16 C.Is, the last serving as a trainer up to 1938.

Variants

C.Ia: designation of modernised version of 1929 with the 200-hp (149-kW) Armstrong Siddeley Lynx radial engine and redesigned vertical tail surfaces; 21 Dutch army air corps C.Is were modified to this standard
C.I-W: experimental twin-float version flown by the Fokker company at Schwerin in 1919, and intended for naval reconnaissance and advanced training
C.II: three-seat passenger version of the C.I retaining the BMW IIIa engine in a revised oval-fronted cowling; behind the pilot's open cockpit were two more cockpits enclosed in a glazed canopy; the variant was built in small numbers in 1919-20 and sold in Canada, the Netherlands, South America and the USA; some C.IIs were converted to take the 230-hp (171-kW) Armstrong Siddeley Puma engine
C.III: advanced trainer version of the C.I sold to Spain; it resembled the C.I except that power was provided by a 220-hp (164-kW) Hispano-Suiza engine

This C.I is illustrated as it appeared in Soviet service in the 1920s. The undercarriage-mounted fuel tank was prone to splitting during heavy landings.

SPECIFICATION

Fokker C.I
Type: two-seat reconnaissance aircraft
Powerplant: one BMW IIIa inline piston engine rated at 185 hp (138 kW)
Performance: maximum speed 109 mph (175 km/h) at optimum altitude; service ceiling 13,125 ft (4000 m); range 385 miles (620 km)
Weights: empty 1,885 lb (855 kg); maximum take-off 2,767 lb (1255 kg)
Dimensions: wingspan 34 ft 5½ in (10.50 m); length 23 ft 8¾ in (7.23 m); height 9 ft 5 in (2.87 m); wing area 282.56 sq ft (26.25 m²)
Armament: one 0.303-in (7.7-mm) fixed forward-firing machine-gun in the upper part of the forward fuselage and one 0.303-in (7.7-mm) trainable rearward-firing machine-gun in the rear cockpit, plus up to 110 lb (50 kg) of disposable stores carried under the lower wing, and generally comprising four 27½-lb (12.50-kg) bombs

Fokker C.IV

At a time when sales of military aircraft were at a low ebb worldwide, the **C.IV** proved a remarkable commercial success. The first example flew in 1923 and production deliveries began in 1924. Developed from the C.I, the C.IV was a larger and more robust machine. The Napier Lion engine which powered the 30 aircraft supplied to the LVA (Dutch army air corps) and the 10 flown by the LA (Dutch East Indies army) had a pair of retractable side radiators attached to the forward fuselage. By comparison with those of the C.I, the fuselage and the track of the cross-axle landing gear were both wider.

C.IV production totalled 159 aircraft, of which 20 were licence-built in Spain by the Jorge Loring firm. The Spanish C.IVs operated with the Spanish army of Africa in action against the Riff tribesmen in Morocco. Other customers included the USSR, which bought 55 machines, Argentina and the US Army Air Service. At least one example was tested in Italy.

Like many other Fokker designs, the C.IV was renowned for its longevity. After a number of years as reconnaissance aircraft, the C.IVs were operated as trainers well into the 1930s in several parts of the world.

Variants

C.IVa: version with a reduced-span wing cellule and the maximum take-off weight trimmed to 4,444 lb (2016 kg); it was this version which was flown in the Dutch East Indies (10 aircraft)
C.IVb: version powered by either the 360-hp (268-kW) Rolls-Royce Eagle engine or the 420-hp (313-kW) Liberty 12 engine; some of this version were used by the Dutch army
C.IVc: long-range reconnaissance version with a wing cellule spanning 46 ft 9¾ in (14.27 m) and retaining the Napier Lion engine; some of this version were used by the Dutch army
C.IV-W: twin-float convertible seaplane version with the Lion engine and the wingspan of the C.IVc; the related **C.IVH** *Ciudad de Buenos Aires* was piloted by the Argentine Major Zanni from Amsterdam to Tokyo in 1924
CO-4: US Army Air Corps' version for evaluation at McCook Field, Ohio; three experimental **XCO-4** aircraft were followed by five **CO-4A** machines, all powered by the 420-hp (313-kW) Liberty 12A engine; the CO-4A had twin side radiators and its fuselage lengthened by 9½ in (0.24 m)

SPECIFICATION	
Fokker C.IV	5,004 lb (2270 kg)
Type: two-seat reconnaissance aircraft	**Dimensions:** wingspan 42 ft 3¾ in (12.90 m); length 30 ft 2¼ in (9.20 m); height 11 ft 1¾ in (3.40 m); wing area 421.96 sq ft (39.20 m²)
Powerplant: one Napier Lion W-type piston engine rated at 450 hp (336 kW)	
Performance: maximum speed 133 mph (214 km/h) at optimum altitude; service ceiling 18,045 ft (5500 m); range 746 miles (1200 km)	**Armament:** one or two 0.303-in (7.7-mm) fixed forward-firing machine-guns in the upper part of the forward fuselage, and two 0.303-in (7.7-mm) trainable rearward-firing machine-guns in the rear cockpit
Weights: empty 3,197 lb (1450 kg); maximum take-off	

Argentine Servicio Aeronautico de Ejercito pilot Major Zanni attempted a round-the-world flight in this Fokker C.IVH in 1924. On 11 October, his flight was cut short at Tokyo, but he had nevertheless completed a most meritorious solo journey to the Japanese capital, having taken off from Amsterdam on 26 June. His aircraft, Ciudad de Buenos Aires, was configured as a landplane.

Fokker C.V and C.VI

There can be no doubt that the **C.V** was one of the world's most successful military aircraft of the 1920s and 1930s. Originating with the C.V prototype which first flew in May 1924, the series proliferated with the possibility of different engines and five types of wing. The **C.V-A**, **C.V-B** and **C.V-C** had parallel-chord wings possessing areas of 403.66 sq ft (37.50 m²), 439.18 sq ft (40.80 m²) and 496.23 sq ft (46.10 m²) respectively, while the **C.V-D** and **C.V-E** had tapered sesquiplane wings, those of the C.V-D having V-struts and an area of 310.01 sq ft (28.80 m²), and those of the C.V-E having N-struts and an area of 423.04 sq ft (39.30 m²). Only the C.V-D and C.V-E were available after January 1926. In every case the C.V was of mixed construction, with a steel-tube fuselage and wooden wings. The type won early recognition as an outstanding multi-purpose aircraft. It was claimed that wings and engines could be changed in an hour, and a wide range of engines in the power range from 350 to 730 hp (261 to 544 kW) could be installed.

Early customers for the C.V-E included the Dutch naval air service and Bolivia; the former also received 10 **C.V-W** float-planes which were later converted to C.V-C standard as landplanes. These early C.V versions were usually powered by the 450-hp (336-kW) Hispano-Suiza engine, although a few had the 400-hp (298-kW) Lorraine-Dietrich engine. Mass production centred on the C.V-D and C.V-E. The C.V-D with short-span wings was a fighter/army co-operation version, while the C.V-E was intended as a reconnaissance bomber. Most Dutch army air corps C.V-Ds had either the 350- or 450-hp (261- or 336-kW) Hispano-Suiza liquid-cooled Vee engines, but some had the 450-hp (336-kW) Armstrong Siddeley Jaguar air-cooled radial engine.

Export aircraft included a batch for Denmark, one of which had a 730-hp (544-kW) Bristol Pegasus radial engine, resulting in the purchase of another 13 and licensed production of 36 of this version. Some of these Danish aircraft, captured by the Germans in April 1940, were used by the Luftwaffe for night operations on the Eastern Front during summer 1944.

Switzerland's C.V-Es served out their days as target tugs, a role which allowed them to become the world's oldest in-service examples of the type.

Basically a re-engined version of the C.V-D, the C.VI served in limited numbers with the Dutch army air corps.

Fokker C.V and C.VI (continued)

Norway built a batch of C.V-Es of which some remained in service until 1940; Sweden bought eight C.V-E warplanes from Fokker and licence-built another 46 with the Pegasus engine. Finland used 19 C.V-Ds and C.V-Es, some acquired as new, as well as three C.V-Es from Sweden and two C.V-Ds from Norway after their internment. The Swiss air force bought six new C.V-Es and built 49 under licence between 1932 and 1936, but Italy was proba-bly the largest licensed manufacturer of two versions known as the

Meridionali Ro.1 with the 420-hp (313-kW) Bristol Jupiter radial engine or the **Ro.1bis** with the 550-hp (410-kW) Piaggio-built Jupiter VIII engine.

Manfred Weiss in Hungary bought three C.Vs from Fokker and subse-quently licence-built at least 100 under the name **WM Budapest 9** with the Jupiter engine and **Budapest 11** or **Budapest 14** with Hungarian-built 870-hp (649-kW) WM K-14 (Gnome Rhône 14K) engines. A modified Weiss version, known as the **WM 21 Sólyom**, saw service in World War II.

A few other C.V versions also saw service during that conflict, in Finland and in the Netherlands, where 28 C.Vs were available on 10 May 1940 at the time of the German invasion. Many of the aircraft were destroyed on the ground, but the surviving airframes were used in the ground-attack role until the Dutch resistance ended five days later. The longest surviving aircraft of the series were the C.V-Es of neutral Switzerland, where the last aircraft were retired only in 1954 after ending their careers as target tugs.

Variant

C.VI: this unofficial designation was applied to 26 examples of the C.V-D converted by the Dutch army air corps with the 350-hp (261-kW) Hispano-Suiza engine

SPECIFICATION

Fokker C.V-D
Type: two-seat reconnaissance aircraft, escort fighter and light bomber
Powerplant: one 450-hp (336-kW) Hispano-Suiza Vee piston engine rated at 450 hp (336 kW)
Performance: maximum speed 140 mph (225 km/h) at 13,125 ft (4000 m); cruising speed 115 mph (185 km/h) at optimum altitude; service ceiling 18,045 ft (5500 m); range 478 miles (770 km)
Weights: empty 2,756 lb (1250 kg); maximum take-off 4,079 lb (1850 kg)

Dimensions: wingspan 41 ft (12.50 m); length 31 ft 2 in (9.50 m); height 11 ft 5¾ in (3.50 m); wing area 310.01 sq ft (28.80 m²)
Armament: one or two 0.31-in (7.9-mm) fixed forward-firing machine-guns in the upper part of the forward fuselage, one or two 0.31-in (7.9-mm) trainable rearward-firing machine-guns in the rear cockpit and occasionally a further similar weapon in the floor of the rear cockpit, plus up to 441 lb (200 kg) of disposable stores carried under the lower wing

Fokker C.VII-W

In 1928 the Dutch navy began to take delivery of a batch of **C.VII-W** twin-float seaplanes for use in the advanced training and reconnaissance roles. A total of 30 was built, these floatplanes being powered by the Armstrong Siddeley Lynx radial engine, although the design was capable of using other air-cooled engines of similar power. Some late production examples had the 280-hp (209-kW) Lorraine-Dietrich Mizar engine. Construction of the C.VII-W single-bay biplane included wooden wings with plywood and fabric covering, and a fabric-covered welded steel tube fuselage.

SPECIFICATION

Fokker C.VII-W
Type: two-seat light reconnaissance and training floatplane
Powerplant: one Armstrong Siddeley Lynx radial piston engine rated at 225 hp (168 kW)
Performance: maximum speed 99 mph (160 km/h) at sea level; cruising speed 81 mph (130 km/h) at optimum altitude; climb to 6,560 ft (2000 m) in 27 minutes; service ceiling 7,875 ft (2400 m); range 621 miles (1000 km)
Weights: empty 2,646 lb (1200 kg); maximum take-off

3,748 lb (1700 kg)
Dimensions: wingspan 42 ft 4 in (12.90 m); length 31 ft 2 in (9.50 m); height 13 ft 1½ in (4.00 m); wing area 398.28 sq ft (37.00 m²)
Armament: one 0.31-in (7.9-mm) fixed forward-firing machine-gun in the upper part of the forward fuselage, and one or two 0.31-in (7.9-mm) trainable rearward-firing machine-guns in rear cockpit, plus disposable stores carried on hardpoints under the rear fuselage, and generally comprising light bombs

Although the type was built in relatively small numbers, a few C.VII-W aircraft were still in service at the beginning of World War II.

Fokker C.VIII-W

In 1928 Fokker built a single example of the **C.VIII**, a single-engined light reconnaissance bomber with the 670-hp (500-kW) Hispano-Suiza 12Lb engine. The Dutch army air corps accepted the aircraft but placed no

production order for the C.VIII. However, when the Dutch navy required a reconnaissance floatplane in the following year, Fokker adapted the basic design and scaled it up to the new configuration as the **C.VIII-W**, flying the first

SPECIFICATION

Fokker C.VIII-W
Type: three-seat reconnaissance floatplane
Powerplant: one Lorraine-Dietrich W-type piston engine rated at 450 hp (336 kW)
Performance: maximum speed 121 mph (195 km/h) at sea level; cruising speed 99 mph (160 km/h) at optimum altitude; service ceiling 14,110 ft (4300 m); range 559 miles (900 km)
Weights: empty 4,222 lb (1915 kg); maximum take-off

6,063 lb (2750 kg)
Dimensions: wingspan 59 ft 4½ in (18.10 m); length 37 ft 8¾ in (11.50 m); height 12 ft 5½ in (3.80 m); wing area 473.63 sq ft (44.00 m²)
Armament: two 0.31-in (7.9-mm) trainable rearward-firing machine-guns in the rear cockpit, and one 0.31-in (7.9-mm) trainable rearward-firing machine-gun in the centre cockpit ventral hatch position

example of the revised type on 15 November 1929 and then receiving an order for nine to be delivered in 1930.

A few C.VIII-Ws were still in service at the time of the German invasion of May 1940, and were flown to France along with other surviving Fokker float-planes. The aircraft

patrolled the French coast in the Cherbourg area for a few days, then 26 float-planes, including five C.VIII-Ws, flew to Calshot on the south coast of England on 22 May. The aircraft were later trans-

This aircraft was the first of the Dutch navy's C.VIII-Ws. The type featured more closely-spaced cockpits than the C.VIII.

ferred to the Marine Aircraft Experimental Establishment at Felixstowe, but their advancing years and lack of spares back-up brought their rapid withdrawal from service.

Fokker C.X

Following the outstanding success of its C.V, in 1933 Fokker initiated the design of a successor.

The first **C.X**, powered by a Hispano-Suiza engine, made its initial flight in 1934 and was presented at that year's Paris air show. Of basically similar layout to its predecessor, the C.X had considerably higher performance in production form by virtue of its powerplant of one 650-hp (485-kW) Rolls-Royce Kestrel V engine.

A production line was established in 1935, the

first customer being the Dutch East Indies army air service, which had ordered 12 aircraft. Deliveries began in 1937, by which time 20 aircraft had also been ordered by the Dutch army air corps. While the first 17 aircraft, for service in the East Indies and Europe, had open cockpits and tailskid landing gear, the last 15 for European service had an enclosed pilot's cockpit and tailwheel landing gear. Dutch production totalled 36 aircraft, including four aircraft ordered by the Finnish air force in 1936. The type proved so successful in Finland that a licensed production agreement was negotiated to allow the Finnish State Aircraft Factory to manufacture 30 of this version in 1936-37, with another five following in 1942. The Dutch-built aircraft were known as **C.X Srs I** aircraft, the four sold to Finland were **C.X Srs II** machines, and

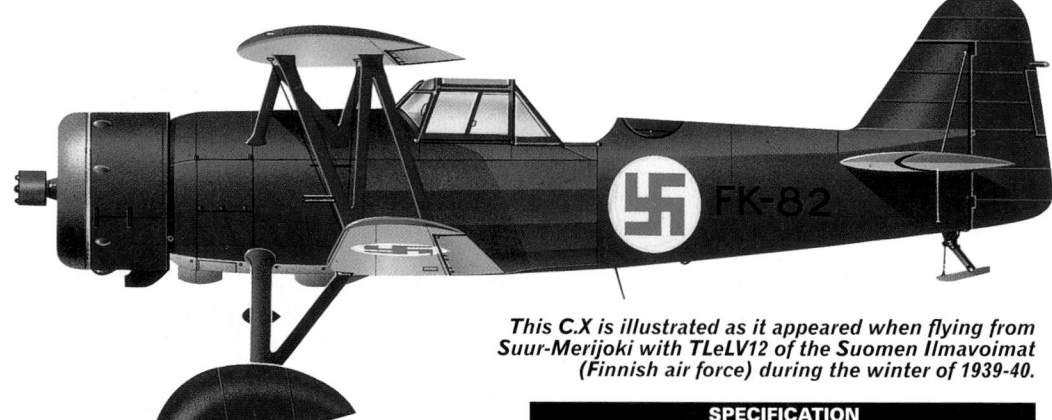

This C.X is illustrated as it appeared when flying from Suur-Merijoki with TLeLV12 of the Suomen Ilmavoimat (Finnish air force) during the winter of 1939-40.

the subsequent two Finnish-built batches were **C.X Srs III** and **C.X Srs IV** warplanes respectively.

At the outbreak of World War II the C.X was serving with three Finnish air force squadrons. At least one survived the war and flew until it crashed in 1958. When Germany attacked the

Netherlands on 10 May 1940, 10 C.Xs were in action, but were completely outclassed by the Luftwaffe's modern aircraft. Even so, one C.X achieved a minor 'first' on the last day of the Netherlands' resistance when two Dutchmen flew it to England to become the first members of the Free Dutch forces.

SPECIFICATION

Fokker C.X (Finnish-built)
Type: two-seat reconnaissance aircraft and bomber
Powerplant: one Bristol Pegasus XII or XXI radial piston engine rated at 835 hp (623 kW)
Performance: maximum speed 208 mph (335 km/h) at 6,070 ft (1850 m); cruising speed 171 mph (275 km/h) at 5,740 ft (1750 m); climb to 9,845 ft (3000 m) in 6 minutes; service ceiling 26,575 ft (8100 m); range 559 miles (900 km)
Weights: empty 3,417 lb (1550 kg); maximum take-off

6,393 lb (2900 kg)
Dimensions: wingspan 39 ft 4½ in (12.00 m); length 30 ft 2¼ in (9.20 m); height 10 ft 10 in (3.30 m); wing area 341.23 sq ft (31.70 m²)
Armament: one 0.30-in (7.62-mm) L-33 fixed forward-firing machine-gun in the upper part of the forward fuselage and one 0.30-in (7.62-mm) L-33 trainable rearward-firing machine-gun in the rear cockpit, plus up to 1,102 lb (500 kg) of disposable stores carried on two underwing hardpoints

Fokker C.XI-W

A requirement of the Dutch navy for a two-seat seaplane reconnaissance floatplane, able to operate from shore bases or the catapult of a warship, led in 1935 to the **C.XI-W**. With a fabric-covered steel-tube fuselage and a single-bay biplane wing cellule

covered partly in plywood and partly in fabric, the C.XI-W could carry a small bombload and had one forward-firing and one rear-firing gun. Prototype tests with a catapult installation took place in northern Germany, resulting in the qualification of the type for

use on the catapults of the Dutch cruisers *Tromp* and *De Ruyter*. Built initially with open cockpits, the aircraft were later modified with the same type of enclosed pilot's cockpit used on later examples of the C.X.

Fourteen C.XI-Ws were built, and the last surviving operational machine flew to England with other Fokker

floatplanes on 22 May 1940. Together with 12 C.XIV-W floatplanes, it was crated and shipped to Surabaya for use by the Dutch navy in the Netherlands East Indies.

There the machines were operated primarily in a reconnaissance role during the Japanese invasion of Java, but none is believed to have survived after March 1942.

SPECIFICATION

Fokker C.XI-W
Type: two-seat reconnaissance floatplane
Powerplant: one Wright SR-1820-F52 Cyclone radial piston engine rated at 775 hp (578 kW)
Performance: maximum speed 174 mph (280 km/h) at 5,740 ft (1750 m); cruising speed 146 mph (235 km/h) at 5,740 ft (1750 m); climb to 16,405 ft (5000 m) in 17 minutes 30 seconds; service ceiling 20,995 ft (6400 m); range 454 miles (730 km)
Weights: empty 3,781 lb

(1715 kg); maximum take-off 5,611 lb (2545 kg)
Dimensions: wingspan 42 ft 7¾ in (13.00 m); length 34 ft 1½ in (10.40 m); height 14 ft 9¾ in (4.50 m); wing area 430.57 sq ft (40.00 m²)
Armament: one 0.31-in (7.90-mm) FN-Browning fixed forward-firing machine-gun in the upper part of the forward fuselage and one 0.31-in (7.90-mm) FN-Browning trainable rearward-firing machine-gun in the rear cockpit

W-1, the C.XI-W prototype, was originally flown with open cockpits for both the pilot and gunner, before being fitted with a partial cockpit canopy for the pilot. The aircraft's floats were of Duralumin and Alclad construction.

Fokker C.XIV-W

Slightly smaller than the C.XI-W and fitted with a lower-powered engine, the **C.XIV-W** twin-float seaplane first appeared in

1937 and was used for training. Twenty-four such aircraft were built for the Dutch navy, 11 of them earmarked for the Dutch

East Indies. The 12 aircraft which were still serviceable after the German invasion of the Netherlands in May 1940 formed part of the group of 26 Fokker float-planes which escaped to England on 22 May. The 12

C.XIV-Ws were shipped to the Dutch navy in Surabaya, where they were

subsequently destroyed during the Japanese invasion of 1942.

SPECIFICATION

Fokker C.XIV-W
Type: two-seat training and reconnaissance floatplane
Powerplant: one Wright R-975-E3 Whirlwind radial piston engine rated at 450 hp (336 kW)
Performance: maximum speed 143 mph (230 km/h) at optimum altitude; cruising speed 121 mph (195 km/h) at optimum altitude; climb to 9,845 ft (3000 m) in 14 minutes 54 seconds; service ceiling 15,750 ft (4800 m); range 590 miles (950 km)
Weights: empty 2,903 lb

(1315 kg); maximum take-off 4,288 lb (1945 kg)
Dimensions: wingspan 39 ft 6½ in (12.05 m); length 31 ft 4 in (9.55 m); height 13 ft 11¾ in (4.25 m); wing area 341.23 sq ft (31.70 m²)
Armament: provision for one 0.31-in (7.9-mm) FN-Browning fixed forward-firing machine-gun in the upper part of the forward fuselage and one 0.31-in (7.9-mm) FN-Browning trainable rearward-firing machine-gun in the rear cockpit

As the first of the C.XIV-Ws, this aircraft is shown without the sliding cockpit canopy that was later added to the type.

Fokker D.X

Following the unsuccessful **D.IX** biplane fighter that was basically an updated version of the D VII fighter of World War I, Reinhold Platz produced a slim parasol-wing monoplane that was in essence an updated version of the D VIII fighter. The latter was based on the **V.41** prototype that was not completed in

World War I but shipped to the Netherlands in Fokker's post-war escape and there completed with a considerably more potent engine and a number of other improvements. The **D.X** parasol-fighter first flew in 1921 and was of typical Platz-inspired Fokker construction. The wing was a cantilever structure over

In common with a number of other contemporary parasol-wing types, the D.X occasionally suffered from catastrophic wing flutter at speed.

most of its span, and other features of the fighter were fixed tailskid landing gear and a curved balanced rudder without any fixed fin. The performance of the D.X attracted several foreign governments, and despite the fact that the

prototype crashed in that country during 1922 while being demonstrated, Spain became the sole customer for series-built aircraft,

acquiring 10 production aircraft. The aircraft were delivered in 1923, and the same year Fokker supplied one D.X to Finland.

SPECIFICATION

Fokker D.X
Type: single-seat fighter
Powerplant: one Hispano-Suiza 8Fb Vee piston engine rated at 300 hp (224 kW)
Performance: maximum speed 140 mph (225 km/h) at sea level; climb to 16,405 ft (5000 m) in 16 minutes

Weights: empty 1,896 lb (860 kg); maximum take-off 2,745 lb (1245 kg)
Dimensions: wingspan 45 ft 1⅓ in (13.75 m); length 26 ft 3⅗ in (8.00 m); height 9 ft 8 in (2.95 m)
Armament: two 0.303-in (7.7-mm) Vickers fixed forward-firing machine-guns in the upper part of the forward fuselage

Fokker D.XI (PW-7)

The sleek **D.XI** single-seat sesquiplane-fighter designed by Reinhold Platz attracted considerable attention when it first flew on 5 May 1923. No Dutch orders were placed, but

186 D.XIs were built for export. The D.XI was developed throughout its production life and versions built for different countries varied in design detail.

The principal customer

for the D.XI was the USSR, which flew 125 examples in its first-line fighter units until 1929. Other operators included Argentina with six aircraft for its naval air arm, Romania that received 50 aircraft that had originally been ordered by a German financier for use at the

clandestine German training establishment at Lipetsk in the USSR, Spain that received an indeterminate number of aircraft from a considerably cutback order, Switzerland with two and the USA with three. These last were evaluated with the designation

PW-7 after being revised with the 440-hp (328-kW) Curtiss V-1150 (otherwise D-12) Vee engine; the first machine had the standard plywood-covered wings and V-struts, while the second pair of aircraft had fabric-covered wings and N-struts.

This machine was one of three Fokker PW-7s. One of these aircraft was flown by 'Jimmy' Doolittle in experiments to determine its stress limits.

SPECIFICATION

Fokker D.XI
Type: single-seat fighter
Powerplant: one Hispano-Suiza 8Fb Vee piston engine rated at 300 hp (224 kW)
Performance: maximum speed 140 mph (225 km/h) at sea level; initial climb rate 1,595 ft (486 m) per minute; service ceiling 22,965 ft (7000 m); range 273 miles (440 km)

Weights: empty 1,907 lb (865 kg); maximum take-off 2,756 lb (1250 kg)
Dimensions: wingspan 38 ft 3½ in (11.67 m); length 24 ft 7¼ in (7.50 m); height 10 ft 6 in (3.20 m); wing area 234.66 sq ft (21.80 m²)
Armament: two 0.303-in (7.7-mm) fixed forward-firing machine-guns in the upper part of the forward fuselage

Fokker D.XIII

Following the unsuccessful **D.XII** single-seat fighter, the **D.XIII** fighter prototype recorded its maiden flight on 12 September 1924.

Designed in an effort to satisfy the requirement of the clandestine German army air service, the D.XIII was developed from the

D.XI with the revised powerplant of one Napier Lion engine. The prototype was characterised by good lines and possessed what was, for the time, outstanding performance.

One of the first of the 50 production examples of the D.XIII was flown on 16 July 1925 in a series of successful attempts on various world speed and load records. The production aircraft were delivered by a circuitous route to the training centre established with great secrecy by the German army at Lipetsk in the USSR. When the Germans withdrew from this base in 1933 they

In what might today be described as a 'black programme', the D.XIII, then the world's fastest fighter, was designed for the German army.

handed over the surviving 30 aircraft (including two

attrition-replacement machines) to the USSR.

SPECIFICATION

Fokker D.XIII
Type: single-seat fighter
Powerplant: one Napier Lion XI W-type piston engine rated at 570 hp (425 kW)
Performance: maximum speed 168 mph (270 km/h) at optimum altitude; cruising speed 137 mph (220 km/h) at optimum altitude; climb to 3,280 ft (1000 m) in 1 minute 42 seconds; service ceiling 26,245 ft (8000 m); range

373 miles (600 km)
Weights: empty 2,690 lb (1220 kg); maximum take-off 3,638 lb (1650 kg)
Dimensions: wingspan 36 ft 1 in (11.00 m); length 25 ft 11 in (7.90 m); height 9 ft 6 in (2.90 m); wing area 231.11 sq ft (21.47 m²)
Armament: two 0.312-in (7.92-mm) LMG 08/15 fixed forward-firing machine-guns in the upper part of the forward fuselage

Fokker D.XVI

The **D.XVI** was designed to meet a Dutch army air corps requirement for a fighter to succeed its elderly D VIIs. It was in essence a development of the sesquiplane concept embodied in the preceding

D.XI and D.XIII and optimised for service as a light and manoeuvrable fighter. As such, the D.XVI was an attractively proportioned sesquiplane of Fokker's typical mixed metal and wood construction covered

with fabric and plywood.

The first D.XVI flew in 1929 with the Jaguar radial engine, and the Dutch army air corps then received 14 production aircraft with divided main landing-gear units in place of the proto-

type cross-axle unit. One of the aircraft was later revised with a Bristol Mercury radial piston engine for use in aerobatic displays. Single D.XVIs were also delivered to China and Italy for evaluation purposes, and Hungary received four of a version powered by one Gnome-

Rhône (Bristol) Jupiter radial piston engine. One other airframe was completed with one Curtiss V-1570 Conqueror Vee piston engine as the prototype of a development to meet the requirement of the Dutch East Indies army air corps, but no production followed.

Fokker's sesquiplane D.XVI fighter saw only limited service with the Dutch air force, with a similarly limited number of examples being exported.

SPECIFICATION	
Fokker D.XVI	maximum take-off 3,086 lb
Type: single-seat fighter	(1400 kg)
Powerplant: one Armstrong	**Dimensions:** wingspan 30 ft 10 in
Siddeley Jaguar radial piston	(9.40 m); length 23 ft 7½ in
engine rated at 460 hp (343 kW)	(7.20 m); height 8 ft 10¼ in
Performance: maximum speed	(2.70 m); wing area 199.14 sq ft
205 mph (330 km/h) at 14,765 ft	(18,50 m²)
(4500 m); cruising speed 168 mph	**Armament:** two 0.31-in (7.9-mm)
(270 km/h) at optimum altitude;	fixed forward-firing machine-guns
range 398 miles (640 km)	in the upper part of the forward
Weights: empty 2,183 lb (990 kg);	fuselage

Fokker D.XVII

The **D.XVII** single-seat fighter was a development of the D.XVI with the Curtiss V-1570 Conqueror Vee engine and a number of aerodynamic and structural refinements, and as such was originally intended to satisfy a requirement of the Dutch East Indies army air corps. However, when the prototype appeared in 1932 this force had no funds, and the machine was instead evaluated by the Dutch army air corps, which subsequently ordered 11 production aircraft that were eventually supplemented by the prototype restored to production standard after being extensively damaged in an accident in the East Indies. Despite this small number, the aircraft were flown with three different engine types: the 690-hp (515-kW) Hispano-Suiza 12Xbrs, the 790-hp (589-kW) Lorraine-Dietrich 12Hfrs Petrel and, most commonly, the Rolls-Royce Kestrel IIS units. In spite of this powerplant miscellany, the D.XVII was well liked by its pilots.

Had it not been for the success of the D.XXI monoplane, which replaced the D.XVII in first-line service, the D.XVIIs would have been modified to incorporate an enclosed cockpit, but this idea was abandoned. Six D.XVII aircraft were based at the Dutch army's flying school on the island of Texel when the Germans invaded the Netherlands on 10 May 1940, but in the desperate situation which then existed the aircraft were used as fighter escorts to the C.V and C.X two-seaters which were making attacks on German armoured columns.

Among the D.XVII's more distinctive features were the fairings over the Vee cylinder banks of its Kestrel engine, and its large radiator, which was carried in an underfuselage box.

SPECIFICATION	
Fokker D.XVII	**Weights:** empty 2,425 lb
Type: single-seat fighter	(1100 kg); maximum take-off
Powerplant: one Rolls-Royce	3,263 lb (1480 kg)
Kestrel IIS Vee piston engine rated	**Dimensions:** wingspan 31 ft 6 in
at 595 hp (444 kW)	(9.60 m); length 23 ft 9½ in
Performance: maximum speed	(7.25 m); height 10 ft 2 in (3.10 m);
217 mph (350 km/h) at 13,125 ft	wing area 215.29 sq ft (20.00 m²)
(4000 m); cruising speed 180 mph	**Armament:** two 0.31-in (7.9-mm)
(290 km/h) at 13,125 ft (4000 m);	M.36 fixed forward-firing machine-
service ceiling 28,705 ft (8750 m);	guns in the upper part of the
range 528 miles (850 km)	forward fuselage

Fokker D.XXI

The **D.XXI** represented a complete break from previous Fokker designs as it was a low-wing cantilever monoplane of altogether more modern concept, albeit still with fixed tail-wheel landing gear even though the main units were of the wide-track cantilever type with faired legs and large drag-reducing spats on the main wheels.

The Dutch army air corps contracted for a prototype in 1935 to evaluate the type's potential for use in the Dutch East Indies, and although it was planned originally to use the 650-hp (485-kW) Rolls-Royce Kestrel IV liquid-cooled Vee engine, the prototype flew on 27 March 1936 with the 645-hp (481-kW) Bristol Mercury VIS air-cooled radial engine. At this time the Dutch government was inclined more toward bombers than fighters for home use, but a change in policy in the summer of 1937 led to an order for 36 examples of the D.XXI powered by the Mercury

Captain Veikko Karu, as commander of the Finnish air force's 2/LeLv 30, scored five kills in this D.XXI. In addition to air-to-air work, his unit also undertook anti-shipping work with the D.XXI, with notable success.

VIII engine and fitted with four 0.31-in (7.9-mm) M.36 machine-guns in the leading edges of the wing.

In the same year seven Mercury VIII-powered D.XXIs were ordered for the Finnish air force, all being delivered in the same year, and a licensed production arrangement was also concluded for the Finnish State Aircraft Factory at Tampere to manufacture 35 more aircraft. The Finnish standard included the Mercury VII engine (licence-built in Finland by Tampella or in Poland by PZL) and the armament of four 0.303-in (7.7-mm) Browning machine-guns installed as two in the fuselage and two in the wing. These aircraft were completed in 1938.

Two Dutch-built aircraft were delivered to Denmark, where another 10 were manufactured under licence by the Royal Army Aircraft Factory. These Danish aircraft had the Mercury VIS engine and the armament of two 0.31-in (7.9-mm) machine-guns and two 20-mm Madsen cannon, the latter in fairings under the wing. Licensed Spanish production of the D.XXI was also begun by the Republican government, but the production facilities were captured by the Nationalist army after only one aircraft, completed with the Soviet M-25 radial engine, had been finished: the Nationalists captured 25 fuselage and landing-gear sets together with 50 wings, but themselves completed no aircraft. In the Netherlands, meanwhile, the first D.XXI for the Dutch army air corps flew on 20 July 1938, and the last of the 36 aircraft was delivered on 8 September 1939. When Germany invaded the Netherlands on 10 May 1940, there were 28 D.XXIs operational. In the five days before the surrender of the Netherlands, the D.XXI fighters gave a moderately good account of themselves, largely as a result of their agility in the air, but in overall terms were so overwhelmed by sheer weight of numbers that only eight remained airworthy at the time of the capitulation. The type's greatest victory in Dutch colours came on 10 May, when D.XXIs destroyed 37 out of a formation of 55 Junkers Ju 52/3m transport aircraft which crossed the Dutch border in the early morning.

Fokker D.XXI (continued)

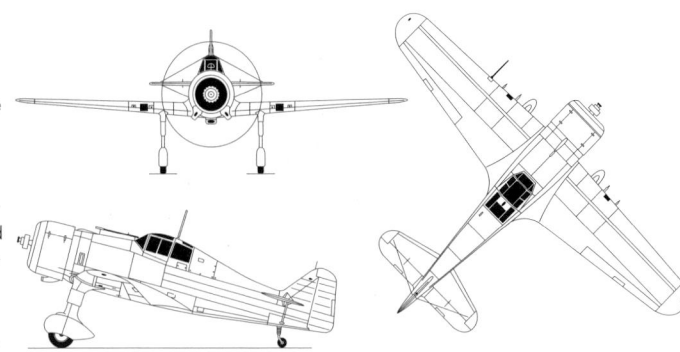

When Finland capitulated to the Soviets on 12 March 1940, ending the so-called Winter War, its air force had 29 D.XXIs on strength. The Finnish government then decided that another 55 such fighters should be manufactured with the 825-hp (615-kW) Pratt & Whitney R-1535-SB4-C/G Twin Wasp Junior radial engine, of which the country had bought 80 examples. Other changes included the installation of all four machine-guns in the wing, the revision of the cockpit canopy with the glazing extended farther to the rear, and enlargement of the vertical tail surfaces. The first American-powered D.XXI flew in January 1941, and proved to be slower and less agile than the Mercury-engined model. The last Mercury- and Twin Wasp Junior-engined aircraft were completed with retractable main landing-gear units, but these were not a success and the aircraft were converted to the original standard. When Finland resumed hostilities with the USSR in June 1941, its air force thus had a useful number of D.XXIs on strength. Partial replacement by the not altogether successful VL Myrsky began in the early autumn of 1944, the year in which D.XXI production ended, but the last D.XXIs were not retired from operational service until 1948 and from training service until 1951.

Before World War II several Dutch D.XXIs served as testbeds for engines such as the Rolls-Royce Kestrel V and Hispano-Suiza 12Y, and plans were in hand for versions with the Bristol Hercules (**Project 150**), Rolls-Royce Merlin (**Project 151**) and Daimler-Benz DB 600H (**Project 152**), all with retractable main landing gear and aerodynamic improvements.

Although it retained anachronistic fixed main undercarriage units, the D.XXI gave a reasonably good account of itself, especially in Finnish hands.

SPECIFICATION	
Fokker D.XXI (Dutch-built)	(1450 kg); maximum take-off
Type: single-seat fighter	4,519 lb (2050 kg)
Powerplant: one Bristol Mercury VIII radial piston engine rated at 830 hp (619 kW)	**Dimensions:** wingspan 36 ft 1 in (11.00 m); length 26 ft 10¾ in (8.20 m); height 9 ft 8 in (2.95 m); wing area 174.38 sq ft (16.20 m²)
Performance: maximum speed 286 mph (460 km/h) at 14,500 ft (4420 m); cruising speed 239 mph (385 km/h) at optimum altitude; climb to 3,280 ft (1000 m) in 1 minute 27 seconds; service ceiling 36,090 ft (11000 m); range 590 miles (950 km)	**Armament:** two 0.31-in (7.9-mm) FN-Browning M.36 fixed forward-firing machine-guns in the upper part of the forward fuselage, and two 0.31-in (7.9-mm) FN-Browning M.36 fixed forward-firing machine-guns in the leading edges of the wing
Weights: empty 3,197 lb	

Fokker DC.I

Designed by Reinhold Platz and first flown in 1923, the **DC.I** was a development of the C.IV for the reconnaissance fighter role with a shorter-span wing cellule. The DC.I, in whose designation the letters of the prefix indicated the fighter and reconnaissance tasks respectively, featured tandem accommodation in open cockpits and fixed tailskid landing gear. The DC.I prototype was demonstrated to the Spanish army air service, which then ordered the larger C.IV, and the sole purchaser of the DC.I was thus the Dutch East Indies army air service, which received a total of just 10 aircraft for service between 1925 and 1934.

SPECIFICATION	
Fokker DC.I	4,034 lb (1830 kg)
Type: two-seat fighter and reconnaissance aircraft	**Dimensions:** wingspan 38 ft 6½ in (11.75 m); length 29 ft ½ in (8.85 m); height 11 ft 1¾ in (3.40 m); wing area 371.91 sq ft (34.55 m²)
Powerplant: one Napier Lion W-type piston engine rated at 450 hp (336 kW)	
Performance: maximum speed 152 mph (245 km/h) at optimum altitude; service ceiling 26,245 ft (8000 m); endurance 3 hours	**Armament:** two 0.303-in (7.7-mm) fixed forward-firing machine-guns in the upper part of the forward fuselage and one 0.303-in (7.7-mm) trainable rearward-firing machine-gun in the rear cockpit
Weights: empty 3,086 lb (1400 kg); maximum take-off	

Based on the C.I, the DC.I was an unequal-span, single-bay biplane of mixed steel tube and wood construction, covered with plywood and fabric.

Fokker F.I and F.II

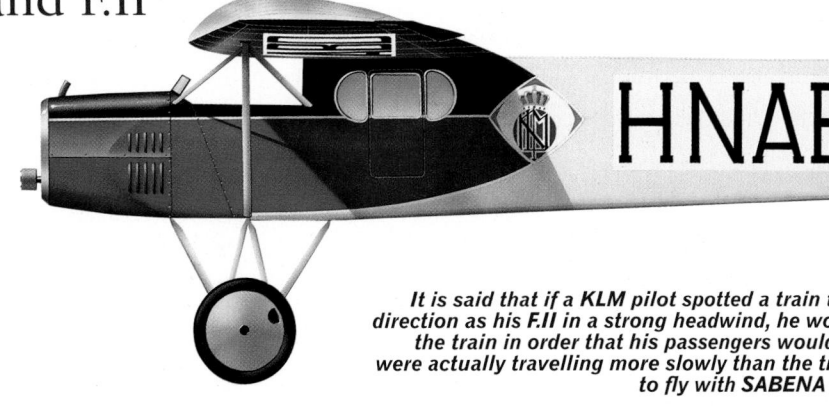

The first commercial aircraft designed by Reinhold Platz was the **F.I**, a parasol-wing monoplane with open cockpits for the pilot and passengers. Realising the need for better passenger accommodation, Platz abandoned development of the F.I and moved instead to the design of the improved **F.II**. Like the F.I (also known in prototype form as the **V.44**), the F.II (**V.45**) was built at the Fokker works at Schwerin in Germany, making its first flight in October 1919. After Anthony Fokker had decided to relocate his business from Germany to his native Netherlands, the F.II prototype was illegally flown out of Germany on 20 March 1920.

The F.II proved to be one of the first practical passenger transport aircraft in the world, and some 30 such aircraft were built, most of them under licence by Grulich in Germany, but some at the Netherlands Aircraft Factories in north Amsterdam and at Fokker's new Veere factory. It is believed that another three machines were completed at Schwerin.

The thick-section

It is said that if a KLM pilot spotted a train travelling in the same direction as his F.II in a strong headwind, he would fly directly above the train in order that his passengers would not realise that they were actually travelling more slowly than the train. HNABD went on to fly with SABENA after its KLM service.

The fuselage of the F.II was of fabric-covered welded steel tube construction and tapered in width to the strut-braced horizontal tailplane.

cantilever wing, of plywood-covered wooden construction and originally created for the F.I, was bolted directly to the top of the F.II's rectangular-section fuselage. There was no fixed fin, and the rudder was of relatively small area. Four passengers were accommodated in a cabin beneath the wing, while the pilot and a fifth passenger were located in an open cockpit immediately forward of the cabin. The F.II's fixed tailskid landing gear included a main unit of the cross-axle type with rubber-cord shock absorbers.

The Fokker-Grulich F.II, of which at least 19 were built, had an improved cockpit layout, redesigned cabin windows and strengthened landing gear. Ing. Karl Grulich was technical manager of Deutsche Aero Lloyd and his version of the F.II was flown by that airline. The wings of the **Grulich F.II** were built by Albatros and the fuselage by DAL, which also undertook the final assembly.

Veere- and Schwerin-built F.IIs had the BMW IIIa engine, but the Grulich-built versions initially had the 250-hp (186-kW) BMW IV engine, although most were later re-engined with the 320-hp (239-kW) BMW Va and given the revised designation **F.IIb**. The three Schwerin-built F.II aircraft were registered in the Free City of Danzig and used by the Deutsche Luftreederei airline. Dutch-built F.IIs flew from 1920 to 1927 with the national airline KLM, and two were sold to the Belgian airline SABENA for a service between Brussels and Antwerp.

One Dutch-built F.II had the 240-hp (179-kW) Armstrong Siddeley Puma engine, and one was flown briefly with a BMW IV engine. Longest-lived were the Fokker-Grulich F.IIbs; taken over with some F.IIs by the newly formed Deutsche Lufthansa in 1926, 10 still remained in service on feeder routes linking Köln with Aachen, Essen, Krefeld and Mülheim in the Ruhr up to 1934.

SPECIFICATION

Fokker F.II
Type: one-crew transport aircraft
Powerplant: one BMW IIIa inline piston engine rated at 185 hp (138 kW)
Performance: maximum speed 93 mph (150 km/h) at sea level; cruising speed 75 mph (120 km/h) at optimum altitude; range 746 miles (1200 km)
Weights: empty 2,646 lb (1200 kg); maximum take-off 4,189 lb (1900 kg)
Dimensions: wingspan 52 ft 9¾ in (16.10 m); length 38 ft 2¾ in (11.65 m); height 10 ft 6 in (3.20 m); wing area 411.19 sq ft (38.20 m²)
Payload: up to five passengers carried as four in the enclosed cabin and one in the open cockpit

Fokker F.III

Developed from the F.II, the **F.III** had a fuselage of reduced length and increased width, with a cabin accommodating five passengers in upholstered comfort. The pilot was seated in an open cockpit offset to starboard, its rear recessed into the leading edge of the high-set cantilever wing, which was of thick section and of Fokker's standard plywood-covered wooden construction. The fixed tail-skid landing gear had a cross-axle main unit with single wheels and, by comparison with that of the F.II, the rudder was of increased height.

The prototype, powered by the 185-hp (138-kW) BMW IIIa engine, first flew at Schwerin early in April 1921, and on 14 April inaugurated KLM flights for the year. The type was also exhibited at the 1921 Paris Salon de l'Aéronautique, where it met with a mixed reception as a result of Fokker's association with the German cause during World War I. Soon, however, the F.III became one of the most important European aircraft of the mid-1920s.

Of 31 F.IIIs built by Fokker, 12 were supplied to KLM with the 240-hp (179-kW) Armstrong Siddeley Puma engine. The aircraft were used heavily from 1921 onward. Other customers were Deutsche Luft-Reederei of Germany, which used a Danzig-registered machine with the BMW IIa engine, and the MALERT company of Hungary, which operated six F.IIIs (four with the BMW IIIa engine and two with the 230-hp/172-kW Hiero engine) on routes from Budapest to Vienna and Graz. One F.III was demonstrated in North America, but only two aircraft were sold there.

Later F.IIIs, powered by the 360-hp (268-kW) Rolls-Royce Eagle engine, had the pilot's cockpit offset to port, and some of these machines were completed as strut-braced parasol-wing monoplanes. The Deruluft airline, owned jointly by the USSR and Germany, acquired 10 of these Eagle-powered F.III aircraft, and two were taken into service by KLM in 1922. The latter were re-engined with 400-hp (298-kW) Gnome-Rhône (Bristol) Jupiter VI radial engines in 1925 and used on the route linking Amsterdam and Paris. In 1926 five surviving F.IIIs were sold to the Balair company of Switzerland and made a formation delivery flight to Basel on 28 April.

In 1923 production of the F.III began in Germany at the Staaken works, and the Deutsche Aero Lloyd airline acquired at least 20 of these so-called **Fokker-Grulich F.III** aircraft. Some were powered by the 250-hp (186-kW) BMW IV engine, while others had the Puma. Several of the machines were later re-engined with the 320-hp (239-kW) BMW Va engine for service under the revised designation **F.IIIc**. When Deutsche Lufthansa was formed in 1926 it took over 16 F.IIIs that were then operating services between Hamburg and Amsterdam, and transferred them to short routes linking north German coastal resorts; they were later used on internal freight services. In 1929 two F.IIIs were sold to British Air Lines Ltd., a company then based at Croydon Airport.

Interestingly, Fokker built two F.IIIs registered H-NABL. Both aircraft went to KLM as illustrated, but the second was later used as a parts source for a third F.III. In addition to Fokker-built F.IIIs in KLM service, the airline also built its own airframes. At least one aircraft was produced from spare parts, combined with sections of the second H-NABL, while a second may also have been assembled in this way.

Variants

Grulich V 1: the V 1 had a redesigned fuselage, tailplane and landing gear; powered initially by the Rolls-Royce Eagle VIII engine, it was later revised with an uncowled Gnome-Rhône radial to receive the revised designation V 1a; the type was used by the Deruluft airline
Grulich V 2: similar to the V 1 except for its F.III landing gear; believed to have been powered by the BMW IV engine

SPECIFICATION

Fokker F.III
Type: one-crew transport aircraft
Powerplant: one Armstrong Siddeley Puma inline piston engine rated at 240 hp (179 kW)
Performance: maximum speed 93 mph (150 km/h) at sea level; cruising speed 84 mph (135 km/h) at optimum altitude; endurance 5 hours
Weights: empty 2,645 lb (1200 kg); maximum take-off 4,409 lb (2000 kg)
Dimensions: wingspan 57 ft 9¾ in (17.62 m); length 36 ft 3¾ in (11.07 m); height 12 ft (3.66 m); wing area 420.88 sq ft (39.10 m²)
Payload: up to five passengers carried in an enclosed cabin

Fokker F.VII

The next transport type after the unsuccessful **F.V** was the **F.VII** that paved the way for a series that was built in many forms and large numbers, and which may be regarded as the most important transport aircraft of the 1920s.

The F.VII was designed along orthodox Platz lines by Ing. Walther Rethel as a six-passenger transport with a crew of two in an enclosed cockpit under the leading edge of the wing and a powerplant of one 360-hp (268-kW) Rolls-Royce Eagle Vee engine.

Fokker F.VII (continued)

The F.VII was intended for the long-range role, including KLM's service between Amsterdam in the Netherlands and Batavia in the Dutch East Indies, and combined a fabric-covered welded steel tube fuselage, a plywood-covered high-set wooden wing, a strut-braced triangular tailplane carrying aerodynamically balanced elevators, an aerodynamically balanced rudder hinged at its lower end to the vertical knife-edge in which the fuselage terminated and fixed tailskid landing gear.

Designed in 1923 and first flown in 1924, the F.VII was built to the extent of five aircraft for KLM with the powerplant of one Eagle or 450-hp (336-kW) Napier Lion W-type engine. The F.VII was a worthy but not exceptional machine, and the way to improve its capabilities, and therefore its commercial fortunes, was obvious: an increase in engine power and a decrease in wing area would yield a type able to fly faster with a larger payload and thus reduce operating costs.

The revised type was introduced as the **F.VIIa**, which first flew early in 1925 with one 480-hp (358-kW) Bristol Jupiter radial engine, a reduced-span wing, ailerons that were now incorporated within the basic wing planform rather than trailing-edge extensions with large overhanging horn balances, a more modern vertical tail surface arrangement with a fixed fin and balanced rudder rather than just a balanced rudder, and revised main landing-gear units whose original spidery appearance was much improved (and also reduced in drag) by the replacement of the original multi-strut arrangement by a simple arrangement of three struts.

The effect of these changes was that, while the passenger payload remained unaltered at eight persons, the maximum speed increased from 96 to 118 mph (155 to 190 km/h). Fokker built 42 F.VIIas for use by Czechoslovak, Danish, Dutch, French, Hungarian, Polish and Swiss operators, and other aircraft were built under licence with a variety of engine types in several other countries. Several of these aircraft later passed to military operators at the end of their civil careers.

In the summer of 1924 KLM issued a requirement for an airliner able to carry 10 passengers and main-

tain altitude with one of its engines stopped. The airline therefore suggested a powerplant of three Armstrong Siddeley Puma inline piston engines, but Fokker had an eye on the potential of the US market and therefore decided to evolve a variant of the F.VIIa with a powerplant of three 200-hp (149-kW) Wright Whirlwind J-4 radial engines. One of these was installed in the standard nose position, and although Fokker himself wanted to have the other two fitted in wing leading-edge nacelles, Platz decided for reasons of balance and thrust-line axis to install their nacelles on the vertical member of each main landing-gear unit with additional bracing to the wing and fuselage, and with the propellers turning in front of the wing leading edges. The first such machine made its maiden flight in September 1925 and after successful trials was dismantled for shipment to the USA and the forthcoming Ford Reliability Tour. This **F.VIIa-3m** won the

tour without difficulty, and was then bought by Edsel Ford for use by Commander Richard E. Byrd's scientific expedition to the Arctic. The machine had its engines revised with rear exhaust collector rings in place of the original clumsy arrangement of crude collectors in front of the engine to exhaust under the nose and over the wings in the case of the central and two outboard engines respectively, and in this form made the world's first claimed (but now disproved) flight over the North Pole in May 1926.

By this time the F.VIIa-3m was in production in the Netherlands and USA, and agreements for licensed construction were negotiated with SABCA in Belgium, Avia in Czechoslovakia, Meridionali in Italy, Lublin in Poland, and A. V. Roe in the UK, where aircraft were built with a number of different powerplants, of which the most popular was a trio of 220-hp (164-kW) Armstrong Siddeley Lynx

radial engines.

The **F.VIIa-3m/M** was the military version of the F.VIIa-3m transport, combining a bomber capability with the civil variant's transport role. First flown in 1928, the F.VIIa-3m/M was dimensionally identical to the civil transport, but was powered by three 220-hp (164-kW) Lynx radial engines, and had provision for two defensive machine-guns (trainably mounted in the single-gun ventral and dorsal positions) as well as bombs carried on racks under the fuselage. The prototype was produced in the Netherlands as an F.VIIa-3m conversion and used by the Dutch army air service, but no production followed.

In 1926 two Dutch-built transport aircraft were ordered for Sir Hubert Wilkins's expedition to the Antarctic. One of these was a standard F.VIIa with a Packard Liberty Vee

piston engine, and the other was the first example of the **F.VIIb-3m** with a new type of enlarged wing that soon became the standard type for Fokker tri-motor transports. This enlarged wing was designed to provide the capability for take-off at higher weights with a greater fuel load. The wing was retrofitted on a number of F.VIIa aircraft, and was offered on production aircraft from 1928, usually in conjunction with the uprated powerplant of three Whirlwind J-6 radial engines in variants each rated at between 300 and 330 hp (224 and 246 kW), although alternative powerplants in the power range between 200 and 350 hp (149 and 261 kW) were possible and included the Lynx, Gnome-Rhône Titan and Walter Castor radial engines. Production by the parent company up to 1933

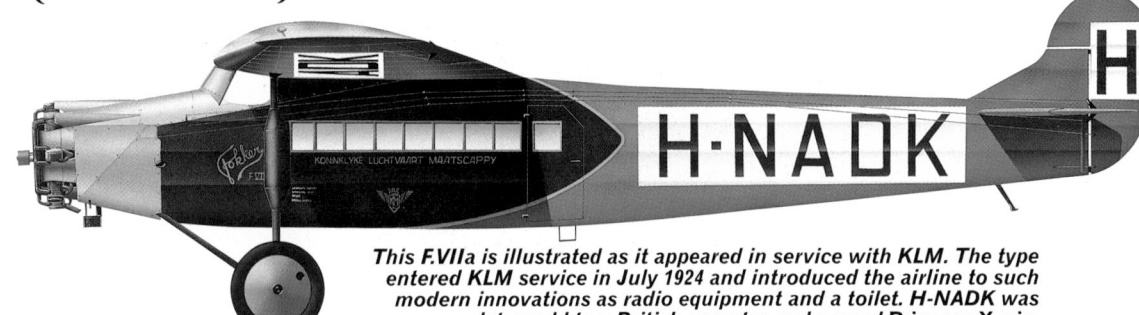

This F.VIIa is illustrated as it appeared in service with KLM. The type entered KLM service in July 1924 and introduced the airline to such modern innovations as radio equipment and a toilet. H-NADK was later sold to a British operator and named **Princess Xenia.**

The F.VII's introduced a new type of wide-track main undercarriage unit based on lateral arrangements of multiple steel tubes extending from the upper and lower longerons on each side.

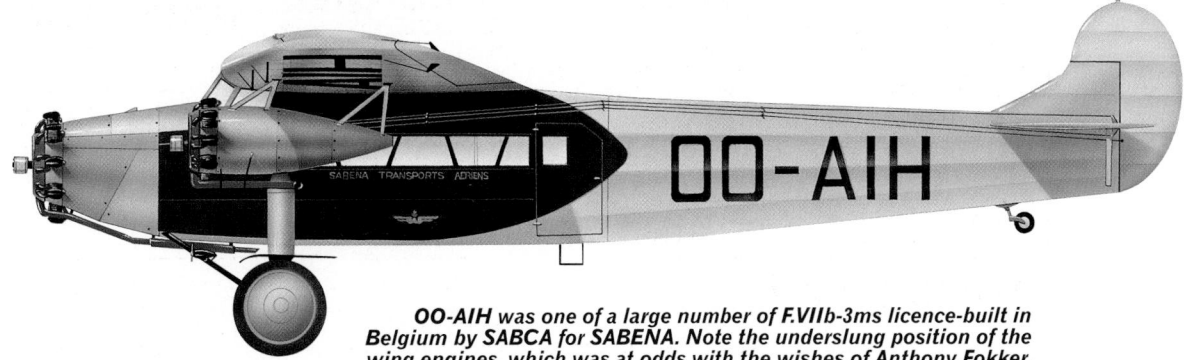

OO-AIH was one of a large number of F.VIIb-3ms licence-built in Belgium by SABCA for SABENA. Note the underslung position of the wing engines, which was at odds with the wishes of Anthony Fokker.

totalled 147 aircraft (74 by Fokker in the Netherlands and 73 by Atlantic in the USA), and further examples were built by Fokker's licensees in Belgium, Czechoslovakia, France, Italy, Poland and the UK for service in these countries as well as in Australia, Canada, Japan, Spain and Switzerland.

The variant with a powerplant of three 215-hp (160-kW) Lynx engines driving two-bladed fixed-pitch wooden propellers, may be taken as typical of commercial variants of the F.VIIb-3m. As with the F.VIIa-3m, not inconsiderable numbers of the F.VIIb-3m entered military service, sometimes at the end of their civil careers.

The **F.VIIb-3m/M** was the military version of the F.VIIb-3m transport analogous to the F.VIIa-3m/M military version of the F.VIIa-3m transport, and therefore combining a bomber capability with the civil variant's transport role. First flown in 1928 and produced in small numbers, the F.VIIb-3m/M was dimensionally identical to the civil transport, but was powered by three 325-hp (242-kW) Wright R-975 Whirlwind radial engines, and had provision for two defensive machine-guns as well as bombs carried on racks under the fuselage. Fokker built about 10 such aircraft, and some 24 more aircraft were produced in Poland and Spain as 21 Lublin-built machines and three machines respectively.

SPECIFICATION

Fokker F.VIIb-3m/M
Type: three-crew medium transport aircraft with bombing capability
Powerplant: three Wright R-975 Whirlwind J-6 radial piston engines each rated at 325 hp (242 kW)
Performance: maximum speed 129 mph (207 km/h) at 9,845 ft (3000 m); service ceiling 10,170 ft (3100 m); range 528 miles (850 km)
Weights: empty 6,722 lb (3050 kg); maximum take-off 11,422 lb (5190 kg)
Dimensions: wingspan 71 ft 2½ in (21.71 m); length 47 ft 8¾ in (14.55 m); height 12 ft 9½ in (3.90 m); wing area 727.66 sq ft (67.60 m^2)
Armament: one 0.303-in (7.7-mm) Lewis trainable rearward-firing machine-gun in the ventral position and one 0.303-in (7.7-mm) Lewis trainable machine-gun in the dorsal position, plus up to 2,205 lb (1000 kg) of disposable stores carried on hardpoints under the fuselage, and generally comprising free-fall bombs or one torpedo
Payload: up to 10 passengers or six litters carried in the enclosed cabin

Fokker F.VIII

Designed to meet a KLM requirement for a transport aircraft offering greater payload than the F.VII in its single-engined form, the **F.VIII** first flew in prototype form on 12 March 1927. While of similar general layout to its predecessors, the new aircraft had a wider fuselage capable of carrying 15 passengers and a crew of two. The nose contained a hinged baggage compartment, and the two 480-hp (358-kW) Jupiter VI engines were slung beneath the wing.

The prototype and six production examples were delivered to KLM in 1927-8. Another was delivered to the Hungarian airline MALERT in 1928, and Manfred Weiss in Budapest built two more for MALERT under licence. The KLM aircraft were later re-engined, various aircraft being powered by two 500-hp (373-kW) Pratt & Whitney Wasp radial engines or, as **F.VIIIa** aircraft, two 690-hp (515-kW) Wright R-1820 Cyclone radial engine in leading-edge nacelles.

The only F.VIII to see service in military markings was the last Dutch production aircraft, sold by KLM to British Airways in 1936. It went to Sweden in 1939, and was subsequently donated to the Finnish air force, with which it served in the 'Continuation War' with the USSR from 1941.

H-NAED, the first production F.VIII for KLM, was completed with Gnome-Rhône engines driving two-bladed metal propellers. KLM's last F.VIII was destroyed in May 1940.

SPECIFICATION

Fokker F.VIII
Type: two-crew transport aircraft
Powerplant: two Gnome-Rhône (Bristol) Jupiter VI radial piston engines each rated at 480 hp (358 kW)
Performance: maximum speed 124 mph (200 km/h) at optimum altitude; cruising speed 106 mph (170 km/h) at optimum altitude; service ceiling 18,045 ft (5500 m); range 649 miles (1045 km)
Weights: empty 8,124 lb (3685 kg) maximum take-off 12,566 lb (5700 kg)
Dimensions: wingspan 75 ft 5½ in (25.00 m); length 54 ft 11½ in (23.00 m); height 13 ft 9¼ in (4.20 m); wing area 893.43 sq ft (83.00 m^2)
Payload: up to 15 passengers carried in an enclosed cabin

Fokker F.IX and F.39

The **F.IX** high-wing monoplane transport resembled an enlarged F.VIII-3m and, powered by three Jupiter radials, accommodated 18 passengers for European services or between four and six passengers in greater comfort and with sleeping berths for services between the Netherlands and the Dutch East Indies. The first F.IX made its initial flight on 26 August 1929, entering service with KLM on 8 May 1930 with the name *Adelaar* (eagle). A second F.IX with a modified, lengthened nose and enlarged 20-seat passenger cabin was exhibited at the 1930 Paris Salon de l'Aéronautique, and this was delivered to KLM in January 1931.

Although the first F.IX made several flights to the Far East, it eventually went into regular service with 17-seat passenger capacity on the route linking Amsterdam and London. After being re-engined it was sold to the French Air Tropic company in October 1936 and finally went to the Spanish Republican government, by then engaged in the Civil War against General Franco's Nationalist forces.

Two examples of the F.IX were built under licence by Avia in Czechoslovakia and flew with that country's CSA airline with the designation **F.39** and three 635-hp (474-kW) Walter Pegasus radial engines. A military version was also developed by Avia with the same basic powerplant, and 12 examples of this bomber variant were delivered to the Czech air arm with the designation **F.IXM** and two to Yugoslavia as F.39s.

As the largest of Fokker's tri-motor transport designs, the F.IX met with only limited success and was built in small numbers.

SPECIFICATION

Fokker F.IX (original version)
Type: two/three-crew transport aircraft
Powerplant: three Gnome-Rhône (Bristol) Jupiter VI radial piston engines each rated at 500 hp (373 kW)
Performance: maximum speed 132 mph (212 km/h) at optimum altitude; cruising speed 109 mph (175 km/h) at optimum altitude; service ceiling 11,810 ft (3600 m); endurance 6 hours 30 minutes
Weights: empty 11,795 lb (5350 kg); maximum take-off 19,841 lb (9000 kg)
Dimensions: wingspan 89 ft ½ in (18.50 m); length 60 ft 8¾ in (27.14 m); height 15 ft 11 in (4.85 m); wing area 1,108.68 sq ft (103.00 m^2)
Payload: up to 18 passengers carried in an enclosed cabin

Fokker F.XII

Another development of the F.VII-3m, but smaller than the F.IX, the first **F.XII** recorded its maiden flight at the beginning of 1930 and entered service on the KLM route to Batavia in the Dutch East Indies during March 1931. Ten more such aircraft were built by Fokker, all for operation by KLM and its Far Eastern subsidiary KNILM, except for the final machine which was sold to Sweden and operated by AB Aerotransport.

The Dutch-operated F.XIIs maintained KLM's routes to the Far East for two years, and were then switched to the European services connecting Amsterdam with London, Paris, Berlin and other principal cities.

On the European runs the F.XII carried a crew of two and 16 passengers, but on the Far East route only four passengers were carried in a fair degree of comfort on fully-reclining seats.

Fokker F.XII (cont.)

The Danish Orlogsvaerftet built two F.XIIs under licence for use by DDL, the national airline, on the route linking Copenhagen and Berlin. The second of the aircraft, delivered in May 1935, was designated **F.XIIM** and introduced a measure of aerodynamic refinement resulting in improved performance.

Six Dutch F.XIIs were later sold to British operators, and four of these British machines were later re-sold to the Spanish government, which had already bought the last KLM-operated aircraft. All of these machines were flown in the Spanish Civil War and were lost during the course of that conflict. The last F.XIIs were the Swedish aircraft and the Danish F.XIIM, the first being scrapped in 1946 and the second a year later.

SPECIFICATION

Fokker F.XII
Type: two-crew transport aircraft
Powerplant: three Pratt & Whitney Wasp C radial piston engines each rated at 425 hp (317 kW)
Performance: maximum speed 143 mph (230 km/h) at optimum altitude; cruising speed 127 mph (205 km/h) at optimum altitude; service ceiling 11,155 ft (3400 m); range 808 miles (1300 km)
Weights: empty 9,590 lb (4350 kg); maximum take-off 15,984 lb (7250 kg)
Dimensions: wingspan 75 ft 6¼ in (17.80 m); length 58 ft 4¾ in (17.80 m); height 15 ft 6 in (4.72 m); wing area 893.43 sq ft (83.00 m²)
Payload: up to 16 passengers in an enclosed cabin

Fokker F.XVIII

A developed and enlarged version of the F.XII, the **F.XVIII** retained the same basic design with a metal fuselage structure and a high-set cantilever wing of wooden construction. The F.XVIII also possessed rather better lines and a number of detail design improvements by comparison with earlier Fokker tri-motor transports. Five F.XVIIIs were built in 1932 and all entered service on the route linking Amsterdam and Batavia in the Dutch East Indies. On this route the cabin was laid out for four passengers on seats that could be converted to berths for the nocturnal parts of the service; the cabin also provided accommodation for the wireless operator and the navigator.

F.XVIII aircraft achieved several notable flights on this route. For example, PH-AIP *Pelikaan* (pelican) carried the Christmas mail from Amsterdam to Batavia in December 1933 in a flying time of 73 hours 34 minutes; and between 15 and 22 December of the following year PH-AIS *Snip* (snipe), re-engined with Pratt & Whitney Wasp T1D1 radial engines driving controllable-pitch propellers, covered 6,400 miles (10300 km) from Amsterdam to Curaçao in a flight time of 55 hours 58 minutes carrying 220 lb (100 kg) of mail. The F.XVIIIs were withdrawn from the long-distance routes in 1935. One aircraft remained in the Caribbean where it was joined by a second, and both aircraft stayed in service until 1946. One of these was converted for military use during the war period and carried a defensive machine-gun.

Two F.XVIIIs were sold to the Czech national line CSA and operated the route from Prague to Berlin and Vienna, normally carrying 13 passengers. Another of the type was sold to a Palestine freight operator and the famous *Pelikaan* was bought in October 1936 by Air Tropic, a French company acting for the Spanish government; it is believed that this machine ended its days on military liaison and transport duties during the Spanish Civil War.

The designation **F.XIX** was used in 1931-32 for a small airliner that was projected with the powerplant of four 250-hp (186-kW) Gnome-Rhône Titan radial engines.

KLM gave each of its five F.XVIIIs a name. PH-AIS was Snip, -AIO was Oehoe (eared owl), -AIP was Pelikaan, -AIQ was Kwartel (quail) and -AIR was Rijstvogel (rice bird). After their service with KLM, the machines were dispersed across Europe, South America and the West Indies.

SPECIFICATION

Fokker F.XVIII
Type: two/four-crew transport aircraft
Powerplant: three Pratt & Whitney Wasp C radial piston engines each rated at 420 hp (313 kW)
Performance: maximum speed 149 mph (240 km/h) at optimum altitude; cruising speed 130 mph (210 km/h) at optimum altitude; service ceiling 15,750 ft (4800 m); range 1,131 miles (1820 km)
Weights: empty 10,192 lb (4623 kg); maximum take-off 17,306 lb (7850 kg)
Dimensions: wingspan 80 ft 4½ in (24.50 m); length 60 ft 8¼ in (18.50 m); wing area 904.20 sq ft (84.00 m²)
Payload: up to 13 passengers carried in an enclosed cabin

Fokker F.XX

The **F.XX** 12-passenger transport pioneered three major innovations in Fokker civil aircraft as it had a fuselage of elliptical cross-section instead of the rectangular section of the company's previous transports, a wing with both dihedral and trailing-edge flaps, and retractable landing-gear units. Power was provided by three Wright R-1820-F Cyclone radial engines, one mounted in the nose and the other two in nacelles carried by strut assemblies under the wing. The main units of the tailwheel landing-gear units retracted rearward into the engine nacelles. The F.XX was the first Fokker transport aircraft to have retractable landing gear, and the whole design showed much greater attention to aerodynamic refinement. Named *Zilvermeeuw* (silver gull), the new transport flew for the first time in 1933 and was handed over to KLM for operation on services from Amsterdam to London and Berlin.

The F.XX was much more modern in design than previous Fokker high-wing monoplane transports, but the advent of a new generation of twin-engined low-wing transports to a concept pioneered by the Boeing Model 247 and Douglas DC-1 soon rendered the F.XX obsolete and as a result only a single example was built. This machine was later sold via Air Tropic to the Spanish Republican government and used to maintain liaison between Madrid and Paris during 1937. Its ultimate fate is unknown.

SPECIFICATION

Fokker F.XX
Type: three-crew transport aircraft
Powerplant: three Wright R-1820-F Cyclone radial piston engines each rated at 640 hp (477 kW)
Performance: maximum speed 190 mph (305 km/h) at optimum altitude; cruising speed 155 mph (250 km/h) at optimum altitude; service ceiling 20,340 ft (6200 m); range 876 miles (1410 km)
Weights: empty 14,231 lb (6455 kg); maximum take-off 20,723 lb (9400 kg)
Dimensions: wingspan 84 ft 3¾ in (25.70 m); length 54 ft 9½ in (16.70 m); height 15 ft 9 in (4.80 m); wing area 1,033.37 sq ft (96.00 m²)
Payload: up to 12 passengers carried in an enclosed cabin

By 1 May 1937, the F.XX had been camouflaged prior to its service in Spain. The undercarriage doors shown here were later removed.

Fokker F.XXII (F.22)

Based conceptually on the somewhat larger 32-passenger F.XXXVI airliner that had first flown in June 1934, the 22-passenger F.XXII (from 1936 the **F.22**) first flew early in 1935 and was of typical Fokker design and construction for the period. The flying surfaces comprised a cantilever tail unit of fabric-covered welded steel tube construction, and a cantilever high-set wing of plywood-

The F.XXII had a typical Fokker structure, having an oval-section fuselage of fabric-covered welded steel tube construction.

covered wooden construction carrying the now-standard trailing-edge arrangement of inboard flaps and outboard ailerons. The airframe was completed, in a somewhat obsolescent fashion, by fixed tailwheel landing gear. The powerplant was installed in leading-edge nacelles and comprised four Wasp radials each driving a two-bladed variable-pitch metal propeller. The first machine and a further two aircraft were sold to KLM, and a fourth machine was delivered to a Swedish operator, AB Aerotransport.

One of the Dutch aircraft crashed in July 1935, the sole Swedish machine was lost in June 1936, and the two surviving aircraft were

sold to British operators in the forms of British American Air Services and Scottish Aviation, the latter then acquiring the former's machine for use as a flying classroom in the training of navigators at No. 12 Elementary Flying Training School. Both the aircraft were moved to No. 1 Air Observers' Navigation School in 1940, and were finally impressed into RAF service during October 1941 as crew training and transport aircraft. One of the impressed machines was lost to an inflight fire, but the other survived (albeit in damaged and therefore grounded form) for a return to the civil register in 1945 and service on the air route linking Prestwick and

Belfast between December 1946 and August 1947.

The designation **F.XXIII** was used for a development of the F.XXII that was projected in 1937 with a crew of four or five, up to 22 passengers and the powerplant of four Gnome-Rhône radial engines in nacelles on the leading edges of the wing. The designation **F.XXIV** was used for a larger and more advanced high-wing airliner that was projected in 1939 with an all-metal structure, provision for either 22 or 36 passengers depending on the route being operated, and the powerplant of two 750-hp (559-kW) Wright R-1820 Cyclone radial engines on the leading edges of a wing spanning

108 ft 3 in (33.00 m). It was intended as Fokker's response to types such as the Douglas DC-2 and DC-3, and performance estimates suggested a maximum speed of 292 mph (470 km/h). Tooling up for the construction of an initial four aircraft began in 1939 but was cancelled after the outbreak of World War II. During the

German occupation of the Netherlands from May 1940, the design was improved but after the liberation of the Netherlands the completion of aircraft could not have been accomplished before 1949 and KLM, in urgent need of advanced aircraft, opted in 1946-47 for the purchase of American airliners already in production.

SPECIFICATION

Fokker F.XXII (F.22)
Type: four-crew transport aircraft
Powerplant: four Pratt & Whitney R-1340-T1D1 Wasp radial piston engines each rated at 500 hp (373 kW)
Performance: maximum speed 177 mph (285 km/h) at optimum altitude; cruising speed 134 mph (215 km/h) at optimum altitude; service ceiling 16,075 ft (4900 m);
range 839 miles (1350 km)
Weights: empty 17,857 lb (8100 kg); maximum take-off 28,660 lb (13000 kg)
Dimensions: wingspan 98 ft 5¼ in (30.00 m); length 70 ft 7¼ in (21.52 m); height 16 ft 1 in (4.90 m); wing area 1,399.35 sq ft (130.00 m²)
Payload: up to 22 passengers or freight carried in the cabin

Fokker F.25 Promoter

After the liberation of the Netherlands in 1945, the Fokker company was eager to resume the design and production of its own aircraft to succeed the German aircraft it had been compelled to manufacture during the German occupation. One of the first aircraft to result from this effort was the **F.25 Promoter**, which was conceived as a four-seat light aircraft for the touring role, and first flew in 1946.

The F.25 was a low-wing cantilever monoplane of mixed metal and wood construction, and in configuration was a based on a central nacelle carrying the cabin at the front. An unusual feature of the design was the hinged nose, which could be opened to facilitate the loading of lengthy items such as a litter or skis.

Behind the cabin was the air-cooled engine driving a pusher propeller. The latter turned between the oval-section booms that extended rearward from the wing to carry the tail unit, which comprised two fin-and-rudder units and the single tailplane-and-elevator assembly.

The first F.25 was completed with a 190-hp (142-kW) Lycoming flat-six engine, but an option in the 20 production aircraft, which had more pointed vertical tail surfaces, was the 185-hp (138-kW) Continental E185 flat-four engine. Production ended in 1948.

A related design that proceeded no further than the project stage in 1946 was the **P-1 Partner** that was in essence a scaled-down version of the F.25 with two-seat accommodation under a canopy that

folded forward for access and egress. Another project, and one that was very much ahead of its time. was the **F.26 Phantom**. This was schemed as a small all-metal airliner with pressurised accommodation for a crew of three and up to 17 passengers carried at an estimated maximum speed of 500 mph (805 km/h) by two 5,000-lb st (22.24-kN) Rolls-Royce Nene turbojet engines.

Access to the F.25's two pairs of seats was via car-type doors. The tricycle landing gear was fully retractable, with a single wheel on each unit.

SPECIFICATION

Fokker F.25 Promoter
Type: four-seat touring aircraft
Powerplant: one Lycoming O-435-A flat-six piston engine rated at 190 hp (142 kW)
Performance: maximum speed 140 mph (225 km/h) at sea level; cruising speed 130 mph (210 km/h) at 3,280 ft (1000 m); service ceiling
11,155 ft (3400 m); range 590 miles (950 km)
Weights: empty 2,116 lb (960 kg); maximum take-off 3,142 lb (1425 kg)
Dimensions: wingspan 39 ft 4¼ in (12.00); length 28 ft (8.53 m); height 7 ft 10½ in (2.40 m); wing area 193.22 sq ft (17.95 m²)

Fokker F27 Friendship

With the end of World War II, Fokker lost little time in formulating the design of a new medium-range airliner. The company's design study of 1950 was for a 32-seat transport to be powered by two Rolls-Royce Dart turboprop engines. Known at the project stage as the **P.275**, the aircraft was then enlarged slightly and modified to incorporate a circular-section pressurised fuselage by 1952, when Dutch government backing was sought for construction and development.

The type was then designated as the **F27 Friendship**, and the first of two prototypes made its maiden flight on 24 November 1955 with the powerplant of two Dart Mk 507 engines. Of high-wing monoplane

configuration, the all-metal F.27 has a pressurised fuselage, retractable tricycle landing gear, and accommodation for 28 passengers. The second prototype, with Dart Mk 511 engines and its fuselage lengthened by 3 ft (0.91 m) to seat 32 passengers, was flown on 31 January 1957.

Above: This F27 Mk 600 was delivered to Swift Aire in 1980. It subsequently passed through a number of owners, before crashing in Bolivia on 22 December 1994.

Left: Spain's three Fokker F27-200MARs (local designation D.2) fly SAR missions with 802 Escuadrón from their base at Gando, on Gran Canaria.

Fokker F27 Friendship (continued)

Between the initial flights of the two prototypes, Fokker concluded an agreement with the Fairchild Engine and Airplane Corporation of the USA for the latter to manufacture and market the F27 in North America, where it was known as the **Fairchild F-27**.

Fokker's first production-standard F27 entered service with Aer Lingus in December 1958, but Fairchild had been a little quicker off the mark, its F-27 entering service with West Coast Airlines three months earlier. The American company had modified the interior layout to seat 40, increased the fuel capacity, and made provision for weather radar in a lengthened nose; Fokker adopted similar improvements at a later date. The initial Dutch production version was designated **F27 Friendship Mk 100** (Fairchild F-27) and was powered by two 1,715-shp (1279-kW) Dart RDa.6 Mk 514-7 engines. It was followed by the similar **F27 Friendship Mk 200 (F-27A)** with 2,140-shp

(1596-kW) Dart RDa.7 Mk 532-7R engines. Both airliners had standard accommodation for 40 passengers, but a high-density arrangement provided for a maximum payload of 52 passengers. An executive version of the Mk 200 was available with the interior design to customer requirements.

Subsequent production versions included the **F27 Friendship Mk 300 Combiplane (F-27B)** as a passenger/cargo aircraft with the Mk 100's power-plant, a reinforced cabin floor, cargo tie-down rings and a large cargo door forward of the wing on the port side. A similar **Combiplane** version of the Mk 200 had the designation **F27 Friendship Mk 400**, of which no equivalent version was produced by Fairchild. Fokker next developed a variant of the Mk 200 with its fuselage lengthened by 4 ft 11 in (1.50 m), and while this **F27 Friendship Mk 500** initially failed to appeal to airline operators, 15 were acquired by the French government for service

with the nation's Postale de Nuit. Mk 500s that later entered airline service provided standard accommodation for 52 passengers and high-density seating for 60. Fairchild produced its own stretched variant as the **FH-227**.

The last production version was the **F27 Friendship Mk 600**, which combined the fuselage of the Mk 200 (without the reinforced cabin floor) with the cargo door of the Mk 300 and Mk 400 Combiplanes. The Mk 600 also introduced an optional roller-track quick-change interior so that the type could be used in the passenger or cargo roles. Other production versions included the **F27 Friendship Mk 400M** and **F27 Friendship Mk 500M** military aircraft, the **F27 Mk 400M** aerial survey version and the **F27 Maritime (F27MPA)** for the coastal patrol, fishery protection and search and rescue roles. The last production aircraft had an updated flight deck and cabin interior, and manufac-

Fokker/Conair F27 Friendship firebomber conversion

ture was shared by Dassault-Breguet in France, MBB in West Germany and SABCA in Belgium. Production continued up to 1987, when the type was replaced by the updated

Fokker 50 derivative, and eventually totalled 786 aircraft in the form of 579 F27, 128 F-27 and 79 FH-227 machines, of which some 444 were still in service in mid-1999.

SPECIFICATION

Fokker F27 Friendship Mk 200
Type: two-crew short/medium-range transport aircraft
Powerplant: two Rolls-Royce Dart RDa.7 Mk 532-7R turboprop engines each rated at 2,140 eshp (1596 ekW) plus 525 lb (2.36 kN) thrust for take-off
Performance: cruising speed 298 mph (480 km/h) at 20,000 ft (6095 m); initial climb rate 1,480 ft (451 m) per minute; service ceiling 29,500 ft (8990 m); range

1,197 miles (1926 km) with 44 passengers
Weights: empty 26,781 lb (12148 kg); maximum take-off 44,996 lb (20410 kg)
Dimensions: wingspan 95 ft 1¾ in (29.00 m); length 77 ft 3½ in (23.56 m); height 27 ft 10½ in (8.50 m); wing area 753.50 sq ft (70.00 m²)
Payload: up to 52 passengers within the context of a 10,340-lb (4690-kg) maximum payload

Fokker F28 Fellowship

Fokker's marketing and sales experience with the F27 Friendship indicated airline needs for a higher-performance airliner of slightly greater capacity. In 1960, therefore, the company began design studies for such an aircraft. First details of the new **F28 Fellowship** were released in April 1962 and, with financial backing from the Netherlands government and risk-sharing support from MBB in West Germany and Shorts in the UK, a decision was made

in 1964 to begin development and production of this new jet airliner.

Of low/mid-wing cantilever monoplane configuration with a circular-section pressurised fuselage, a T-tail unit with swept surfaces and retractable tricycle landing gear with twin wheels on each unit, the F28 was designed for the power-plant of two Rolls-Royce RB.183 Spey turbofan engines. The first of three prototypes made its maiden flight on 9 May

1967, and certification and delivery of the initial production aircraft was achieved on 24 February 1969. This **F28 Fellowship Mk 1000** short-fuselage version could seat between 55 and 65 passengers, and was powered by two 9,850-lb st (43.81-kN) RB.183-2 Mk 555-15 turbofans. This variant was available optionally as the **F28 Fellowship Mk 1000C** for all-cargo or mixed passenger/cargo operations with a large cargo door incorporated in the port side of the forward fuselage to the rear of the standard passenger door.

The generally similar **F28 Fellowship Mk 2000** differed only in having the fuselage lengthened by 7 ft 3 in (2.21 m) to provide accommodation for a maximum of 79 passengers. Later (and in fact the last) production versions were the **F28 Fellowship Mk 3000** and **F28 Fellowship Mk 4000** with the fuselage lengths of the Mk 1000 and Mk 2000 respectively. The Mk 3000

Air Gabon received this F28 Mk 2000 in 1974, as part of a four-aircraft order. In summer 2000, the airline still listed a single Mk 2000 in its fleet.

Variants

F.28 Fellowship Mk 5000: projected version combining the fuselage of the Mk 3000 with a slatted wing of increased span
F.28 Fellowship Mk 6000: version combining the lengthened fuselage of the Mk 2000 with a slatted wing of increased span; two examples only, one of them a conversion of the first F28 prototype
F.28 Fellowship Mk 6600: projected version of Mk 6000 with a 7-ft 3-in (2.21-m) fuselage stretch to accommodate up to 100 passengers

was also available optionally with a 15-seat executive interior, and the Mk 4000 had maximum seating capacity of 85 passengers. Production of the Fellowship ended in

1987, once the updated Fokker 100 version had become available, after the completion of 241 aircraft, of which 188 were still in service in the middle of 1999.

SPECIFICATION

Fokker F28 Fellowship Mk 3000
Type: two-crew short/medium-range transport aircraft
Powerplant: two Rolls-Royce RB.183-2 Mk 555-15P Spey turbofan engines each rated at 9,900 lb st (44.04 kN)
Performance: maximum cruising speed 524 mph (843 km/h) at 22,965 ft (7000 m); economic cruising speed 421 mph (678 km/h) at 30,020 ft (9150 m); maximum cruising altitude 35,005 ft

(10670 m); range 1,704 miles (2743 km) with 65 passengers
Weights: empty 36,994 lb (16780 kg); maximum take-off 72,995 lb (33110 kg)
Dimensions: wingspan 82 ft 3 in (25.07 m); length 89 ft 10¾ in (27.40 m); height 27 ft 9½ in (8.47 m); wing area 850.38 sq ft (79.00 m²)
Payload: up to 65 passengers carried in an enclosed cabin

Fokker F.XXXVI (F.36)

The first four-engined Fokker airliner design to reach the production stage in the Netherlands, and still the largest aircraft to have been constructed in that country, the **F.XXXVI** (from

1936 **F.36**) had accommodation for a crew of four and up to 32 passengers, the resulting total giving rise to the numerical portion of the type's designation. The origins of the

type can be traced to a KLM requirement for a comfortable and reliable airliner for use on its route between the Netherlands and the Dutch East Indies. At this time Fokker was working on the design of a small four-engined airliner, the F.XIX, but now discon-

tinued work on this type to concentrate its civil design efforts on the altogether larger F.XXXVI. First flown in June 1934 with a power-plant of four 750-hp (559-kW) Wright SGR-1820-F2 Cyclone radial engines, each installed in a circular nacelle on the lead-

ing edge of the wing and driving a three-bladed metal propeller of the variable-pitch type, the F.XXXVI was of typical Fokker design and construction for the period, and therefore somewhat obsolescent by comparison with American airliners such as the

Arend (eagle), the only F.XXXVI, flew the Berlin-London, via Amsterdam, route with KLM. The aircraft first visited the UK on 28 September 1934 and ultimately joined the UK civil register in 1939 as G-AFZR.

during May 1940.

Other Fokker transport aircraft projected in the period before the outbreak of World War II in September 1939 were the **F.XXXVII** and **F.LVI**. The F.XXXVII (or **F.37**) was projected in 1937 as an all-metal monoplane with the powerplant of four 750-hp (559-kW) Cyclone radial engines and accommodation for 32 day or 16 night passengers. The F.LVI (or **F.56**) was also projected in 1937, and in this instance would have been an all-metal monoplane with the powerplant of four Hispano-Suiza engines and accommodation for 56 day or 28 night passengers.

Douglas DC-2.

The F.XXXVI was based on an oval-section fuselage of welded steel tube construction covered with fabric except over the nose section, which was skinned in plywood. The fuselage carried the high-set flight-deck, the four passenger cabins, the galley, the stewards' compartment, two lavatories and a dressing compartment, and also supported the flying surfaces. The latter comprised a cantilever tail unit of fabric-covered welded steel tube

construction, and a cantilever high-set wing of plywood-covered wooden construction with the standard trailing-edge combination of inboard flaps and outboard ailerons. The airframe was completed, in a somewhat obsolescent fashion, by fixed tailwheel landing gear.

Although KLM had evinced an interest in buying six examples of the F.XXXVI, in the event the airline took only the first machine as the new airliner's technical and structural obsolescence

had become more than clear when KLM's first DC-2 won the handicap section of the 1934 MacRobertson air race. The F.36 was used on a number of KLM's European services before being sold in September 1939 to Scottish Aviation, which was responsible for the operation of No. 12 Elementary Flying Training School, at which navigators were trained. Under pressure to increase the numbers of pupils completing their training in any given period, Scottish

Aviation bought the F.36 and also the two surviving F.22 airliners. The F.36 was lost in a take-off accident

SPECIFICATION	
Fokker F.XXXVI (F.36)	**Weights:** empty 21,825 lb (9900 kg); maximum take-off 36,376 lb (16500 kg)
Type: four-crew transport aircraft	
Powerplant: four Wright SGR-1820-F2 Cyclone radial piston engines each rated at 750 hp (559 kW)	**Dimensions:** wingspan 108 ft 3¼ in (33.00 m); length 78 ft 9 in (24.00 m); height 19 ft 8 in (6.00 m); wing area 1,829.925 sq ft (170.00 m²)
Performance: maximum speed 180 mph (290 km/h) at optimum altitude; cruising speed 149 mph (240 km/h) at optimum altitude; service ceiling 14,435 ft (4400 m); range 838 miles (1350 km)	**Payload:** up to 32 passengers carried in four eight-passenger enclosed cabins

Fokker G.I

G.I test-flying continued under German control after the fall of the Netherlands. As with many enemy aircraft captured during the German onslaught, a number of G.Is was used by the Luftwaffe in a training role.

In November 1936 the **G.I** heavy fighter prototype caused a sensation when exhibited at the Paris Air Show. The concept of a twin-engined twin-boom fighter, later adopted for the Lockheed P-38 Lightning, was revolutionary at the time, and the new aircraft was the centre of much critical appraisal. After the show the G.I was taken back to the Netherlands and recorded its first flight on 16 March 1937. At that time the G.I was powered by two 820-hp (611-kW) Hispano-Suiza 14Ab engines driving propellers that turned in opposite directions, but problems with these proto-type units resulted in a change to 825-hp (615-kW) Pratt & Whitney R-15350-SB4-G Twin Wasp Junior radial engines as the prototype was rebuilt after suffering brake failure

and ramming a hangar on 4 July 1937.

Demonstrations had already been given to the Netherlands army air corps, and considerable interest was shown, resulting at the end of the year in an order for 36 aircraft that received the retrospective designation **G.IA**. In order to ease the spares situation, it was stipulated that these must have Bristol Mercury VIII radial engines, which were also to power two other Fokker warplanes on order at that time, namely the T.V

bomber and D.XXI fighter. This decision resulted in delay, for though G.IA production began immediately to a standard that included an enlarged airframe and three- rather than two-seat accommodation, there was a hold-up in the supply of engines. Thus the first production aircraft to fly, actually the second of the batch, became airborne only on 11 April 1939. It remained with the maker for production testing and modifications, and the first aircraft was deliv-

ered to the Dutch army air corps on 10 July 1939. Only the first four aircraft were completed to the three-seat standard, the other machines being delivered as two-seaters.

In March 1940 Sweden ordered 18 **G.IB** aircraft together with an option for a further 77 aircraft including 12 to be completed as reconnaissance machines with an extensively glazed ventral gondola, but the fall of the Netherlands to Germany in May 1940 meant that the order could not be implemented. In 1939 Denmark and Hungary became the two other countries to order the G.IB, in both instances for licensed production, but in the event no aircraft resulted from the two agreements.

The possibility of export orders for the original two-seat variant with Hispano-Suiza engines followed the prototype's appearance at Paris, and a number of

foreign pilots came to Fokker to fly and evaluate the planned G.IB export version. An initial order for 25 aircraft was placed by the Republican government of Spain, but the Dutch government then banned the export of weapons to the participants in the Spanish Civil War and decided to take the aircraft already under construction. Estonia ordered nine aircraft, and Fokker had completed six of these machines before the imposition of a Dutch government embargo in October 1939. Ten aircraft for Spain had been completed before the imposition of the export ban, but of these only three entered Dutch army air corps service with the improvised nose-mounted armament of four 0.31-in (7.9-mm) machine-guns.

When Germany attacked the Netherlands on 10 May 1940, there were 23 G.Is in service.

At the time of the German attack on the Netherlands, 12 and 11 aircraft respectively were serving with the 4th Fighter Group at Alkmaar and the 3rd Fighter Group at Rotterdam/Waalhaven.

Fokker G.I (continued)

The handful of G.Is put up to combat the German invasion forces were successful in destroying several Junkers Ju 52/3m tri-motor transports during the early stages of the German invasion, but by the fifth day, when Dutch resistance ended, only a single example remained airworthy. The Germans occupied the Fokker factory, ordering completion of the other aircraft which had been ordered by Spain and, together with at least five repaired Mercury-engined G.IA aircraft, about 12 G.IB machines were later used by the Luftwaffe as fighter trainers. Test flights from the factory were made under German supervision, but on 5 May 1941 two Dutch pilots succeeded in evading an escorting German-flown G.I fighter and escaped to England. Their intact G.IB was taken to the Royal Aircraft Establishment, Farnborough for examination, and used subsequently by Phillips and Powis (Miles Aircraft) at Reading, Berkshire for research into wooden construction. It is believed that a total of 62 G.Is was built, and none of these machines survived World War II.

SPECIFICATION

Fokker G.IA
Type: two/three-seat heavy fighter and close-support aircraft
Powerplant: two Bristol Mercury VIII radial piston engines each rated at 830 hp (619 kW)
Performance: maximum speed 295 mph (475 km/h) at 9,020 ft (2750 m); cruising speed 221 mph (355 km/h) at 9,020 ft (2750 m); initial climb rate 2,736 ft (834 m) per minute; climb to 16,405 ft (5000 m) in 8 minutes; service ceiling 30,500 ft (9300 m); range 870 miles (1400 km)
Weights: empty 7,341 lb (3330 kg); maximum take-off 11,023 lb (5000 kg)
Dimensions: wingspan 56 ft 3⅗ in (17.15 m); length 35 ft 8 in (10.87 m); height 12 ft 5⅗ in (3.80 m); wing area 412.26 sq ft (38.30 m^2)
Armament: eight 0.31-in (7.9-mm) FN-Browning M.36 fixed forward-firing machine-guns in the nose and one M.36 trainable rearward-firing machine-gun in the nacelle tailcone position, plus up to 882 lb (400 kg) of disposable stores carried on four underwing hardpoints, and generally comprising four 220-lb (100-kg) bombs

Fokker Spin and M.1 to M.4

It was in 1908 that a fascination with flight was first instilled in Anthony Fokker, an 18-year old student, by the visit of Wilbur Wright to France. Fokker had to wait for two years, until after he had completed his military service, before he could start to build his first aircraft. At the Automobil Fachschule at Zalbach, near Mainz in Germany, Fokker teamed with Franz von Daum, a former officer in the German army but now a fellow student despite being some 30 years older than Fokker, to design and finance a first machine. Von Daum supplied the 50-hp (37-W) Argus engine for the **Fokker-Daum Spin** (spider), so named for the web of bracing wires used to ensure the structural integrity of this otherwise very frail low-wing monoplane. Construction commenced in the autumn of 1910 in the workshop of the school at Wiesbaden, possibly with assistance from the factory of Jacob Goedecker, a local manufacturer of Taube-type monoplanes.

Testing of the Spin probably started during November 1910, and after initial taxiing trials, a rudder was added to improve directional control. Lateral control was entrusted to differential warping of the sharply dihedralled wing, which was then revised with a modest degree of sweep to improve stability, and the trailing edge of the tailplane was warped by wires to serve as an elevator. By December Fokker was able to make a hop-flight of about 330 ft (100 m), but during the Dutchman's absence in the Christmas holiday, von Daum decided to fly the Spin. All that von Daum managed, however, was to taxi the aircraft into a tree, in the process virtually writing it off.

The two men took the opportunity to construct a new machine from the wreckage. They were aided by the fact that the engine had survived intact, and also by the fact that Goedecker played a more significant part in the design as well as building the resulting machine, the **Spin II**. The latter differed from the original machine (now known as the **Spin I**) in a number of important respects including greater use of steel tube as the primary structural medium, lateral control by ailerons, a tail unit with conventional hinged rudder and elevators, and a much simplified landing gear arrangement. It was on the Spin II that, on 16 May 1911, Fokker secured his pilot's brevet. Von Daum was keen to emulate his younger colleague, but crashed and wrecked the Spin II.

Fokker now terminated his association with von Daum and, after teaming with Goedecker, designed and built the **Spin III** with the same Argus engine. As completed during August 1911, the Spin III was somewhat smaller than the Spin II and, at Fokker's demand, had wing warping for lateral control. The Spin III could carry a passenger in addition to the pilot, performed more impressively than its two predecessors, and was inherently stable in calm weather. (When Fokker transported this aircraft to the Netherlands in August 1911 it received the nickname **'Haarlem Spin'** (Haarlem spider). It is worth noting at this stage that, while this machine is sometimes known as the Spin III, suggesting that the two earlier aircraft had been the Spin I and Spin II, it was in fact the first to be named and was therefore the Spin, the alternative appellations being used as a convenience to differentiate the first three aircraft

This B-1912 Spin demonstrates the level of refinement that had been reached by 1912. Note the faired cockpit nacelle and mass of bracing wires.

In February 1912 Fokker established the Fokker Aeroplanbau G.m.b.H. at Johannisthal bei Berlin, and here the company assembled some 25 Spin-type monoplanes from Goedecker-built components. The first model was the **A-1912** two-seater and later in the same year there appeared variants with the 60- and 70-hp (45- and 52-kW) Argus engines. Then came the **B-1912** with the 100-hp (75-kW) Argus engine, and while a few examples of the Spin had the 70-hp (52-kW) Renault engine, one was fitted with a 95-hp (71-kW) Mercedes engine for military trials and another was flown for experimental purposes with the 50-hp (37-kW) Gnome rotary engine. There were two 1913 variants of what was now known as the **M.1**, both of them with a tandem two-seat layout: the first was powered by the 50-hp (37-kW) Argus engine and had a completely open fuselage, while the second had the 100-hp (75-kW) Argus or Mercedes engine and a nacelle body. Six of the first variant were produced as trainers for the Fokker civil flying school, while at least five of the second variant were built for private owners, the Fokker military flying school at Schwerin, and the German army, by which the type was known as the **M.I**. The aircraft were completed with different types of seat fairings or fuselage shells to provide the type of protection required by the purchaser. Production examples of the Spin had stick- rather than wheel-operated controls, and the rear cabane pylon was located farther to the rear, in line with the tailplane's leading edge.

Further orders followed in July and August 1913, Fokker building 10 aircraft derived from the M.1 as the **M.2** (military **M.II**) with the 100-hp (75-kW) Argus or Mercedes engine, a circular-section fuselage, a tail unit with swept elevator halves and a swept rudder without a fin, and features to optimise ease of assembly/disassembly as a means of facilitating transport by road or rail. The less streamlined **M.3** had a slab-sided fuselage and either the 100-hp (75-kW) Mercedes or 70-hp (52-kW) Renault engine, the **M.3a** was a development with better streamlining as well as rudders above and below the rear of the fuselage, and the **M.4** was a shoulder-wing monoplane with ailerons and the 90-hp (71-kW) Mercedes engine. None of these three types was successful, the M.3a crashing while its Russian purchaser was learning to fly in Germany, but greater success was to attend subsequent Fokker aircraft as a new chief designer now appeared in the form of Martin Kreutzer.

SPECIFICATION

Fokker A-1912 Spin
Type: two-seat utility aircraft
Powerplant: one Argus inline piston engine rated at 50 hp (37 kW)
Performance: maximum speed 56 mph (90 km/h) at sea level
Weights: maximum take-off 882 lb (400 kg)
Dimensions: wingspan 36 ft 1 in (11.00 m); length 25 ft 5⅛ in (7.75 m); height 9 ft 10⅛ in (3.00 m); wing area 236.81 sq ft (22.00 m^2)

Fokker E series

On 19 April 1915 a French Morane-Saulnier Type L was forced down behind German lines after being hit by anti-aircraft fire. This event was significant in the development of fighter aircraft and their weapons for its pilot, Frenchman Roland Garros, had devised a scheme that allowed his single Hotchkiss machine-gun to be fired forward through the propeller disc: wedge-shaped steel plates attached to the rear of the propeller blades deflected any bullets that might endanger them.

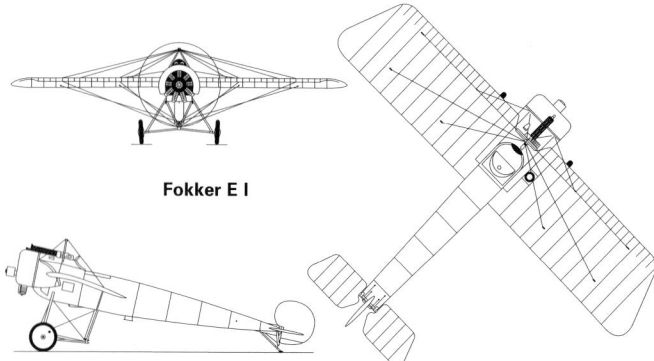

Fokker E I

German officers examining the damaged Type L saw immediately the significance of a fixed forward-firing machine-gun that could be aimed easily by the pilot. It resulted in Fokker being approached to develop a more sophisticated means of arriving at the same result, leading to the interrupter gear that 'timed' the bullets to pass harmlessly between the spinning propeller blades. Early tests of this device were carried out on the **Fokker M.5k/IMG**, production versions of this aircraft with an interrupter gear for its Maxim-type LIMG 08/15 'Spandau' machine-gun having the designation **Fokker E I** (E for **Eindecker**, or monoplane).

Of braced mid-wing configuration, the single-seat E I had tailskid landing gear, a conventional tail unit and was powered by one 80-hp (60-kW) Oberursel U.0 rotary engine. The E I was superseded by the generally similar but refined and strengthened **E II** (company designation **M.14**) with a more powerful engine, and the **E III** (company designation M.14 also) which only differed in detail from the E II. Final production version was the heavier but less successful **E IV** (company designation **M.15**), which was basically an E III with a 160-hp (119-kW) Oberursel U.III engine and two machine-guns. Production of all four versions is believed to have totalled about 300 aircraft.

It was early Fokker E-types that brought the so-called 'Fokker Scourge' when, from the autumn of 1915 to the spring of 1916, they played havoc with the unfortunate B.E.2c units of the Royal Flying Corps.

Although not an outstanding design, the Fokker E-series, here represented by an E.III, gained notoriety through skilful use of its newly-perfected weapons system.

SPECIFICATION

Fokker E series
Type: single-seat escort fighter/scout
Powerplant: one 100-hp (75-kW) Oberursel U.I 9-cylinder rotary piston engine
Performance: maximum speed 87 mph (140 km/h); climb to 9,845 ft (3000 m) in 30 minutes; service ceiling 11,480 ft (3500 m), endurance 1 hour 30 minutes
Weights: empty 880 lb (399 kg); maximum take-off 1,345 lb (610 kg)
Dimensions: wingspan 31 ft 2¾ in (9.50 m); length 23 ft 7½ in (7.20 m); height 7 ft 10½ in (2.40 m); wing area 172.23 sq ft (16.00 m²)
Armament: one fixed forward-firing 0.31-in (7.92-mm) LIMG 08/15 machine-gun

Fokker M.17 (D II)

Designed by Martin Kreutzer in parallel with the **M.16** series of fighter prototypes, the related **M.17** and **M.18** series of single-seat fighters differed from each other mainly in their powerplants, the M.17 having an air-cooled rotary engine and the M.18 a water-cooled inline engine. The M.17 prototype was first flown with the 80-hp (60-kW) Oberursel U.0 rotary engine as an equal-span biplane with an unstaggered single-bay wing cellule and a fuselage that completely filled the interplane gap. However, it was later revised with a fuselage whose upper line had been cut down, the 100-hp (75-kW) U.I rotary engine, a staggered wing cellule that was tested in one- and two-bay forms to create the **M.17e** and **M.17z** subvariants as they were retrospectively designated in Fokker's post-war system of nomenclature, and a 'comma' type of balanced rudder in place of the original balanced trapezoidal rudder above the rear fuselage.

Despite the fact that its service designation, **D II**, was later than that of the **D I**, the M.17 was ordered into production before the M.18, and in its production form resembled the M.17z, with either type of engine although the latter was preferred by service pilots, and an armament of one fixed forward-firing machine-gun with synchronisation equipment to fire through the propeller disc. The M.17 entered service in April 1916, the first recipient being the Imperial Austro-Hungarian army air service that took 62 of the aircraft (42 of them manufactured under licence by MAG) with the U.0 engine and a single-bay wing cellule. These aircraft entered service with the local designation **B II** (also used for the earlier **M.10** series of Fokker reconnaissance aircraft). Although the majority were unarmed and used in the training role, some of the aircraft were operated in the fighter role after being fitted with a single 0.32-in (8-mm) Schwarzlose machine-gun on top of the upper-wing centre section to fire straight ahead over the propeller disc.

The D II entered German service in July 1916 and, whenever possible, was fitted with the U.I engine, but soon revealed itself to be an indifferent fighter as a result of its comparatively long-span wings and inadequate power/weight ratio. Deliveries amounted to 181 aircraft that were generally retired from first-line service after only a short operational career, and the surviving aircraft were then used more effectively as advanced flying and fighter trainers.

Fokker built the M.17 in two basic variants. In two-bay form (above) the aircraft was designated M.17z by the company, while in a single-bay layout (below) the aircraft was known as the M.17e. The service-standard D II was close to the M.17z in configuration and achieved moderate sales.

SPECIFICATION

Fokker D II
Type: single-seat fighter
Powerplant: one Oberursel U.I rotary piston engine rated at 100 hp (75 kW)
Performance: maximum speed 93 mph (150 km/h) at sea level; climb to 6,560 ft (2000 m) in 8 minutes; service ceiling 13,125 ft (4000 m); range 124 miles (200 km); endurance 1 hour
30 minutes
Weights: empty 847 lb (384 kg); maximum take-off 1,268 lb (575 kg)
Dimensions: wingspan 28 ft 8½ in (8.75 m); length 20 ft 11¾ in (6.40 m); height 8 ft 4⅓ in (2.55 m); wing area 193.76 sq ft (18.00 m²)
Armament: one 0.31-in (7.92-mm) LMG 08/15 fixed forward-firing machine-gun on the starboard upper part of the forward fuselage

Fokker M.18 (D I) and M.21 (D IV)

In parallel with the M.16, Martin Kreutzer developed the M.17 and M.18 series of single-seat fighters that differed from each other mainly in their powerplants. The **M.18** was powered by a water-cooled inline piston engine and led to the **D I** fighter. The M.18 prototype was powered by the 100-hp (75-kW) Mercedes D.I inline engine and was first flown as an equal-span biplane with an unstaggered single-bay wing cellule and a fuselage that completely filled the interplane gap. The prototype was later revised with a fuselage typified by a cut-down upper line, a staggered wing cellule that was tested in one- and two-bay forms to create the **M.18e** and **M.18z** subvariants, and with a balanced trapezoidal rudder above the rear fuse-

The D I was an equal-span biplane of mixed metal and wood construction.

lage in place of the original 'comma' type of balanced rudder.

The M.18 was ordered into production for service as the D I with the cut-down fuselage, the two-bay staggered wing cellule, the 'comma' type of rudder, the 120-hp (90-kW) Mercedes D.II inline engine cooled by a pair of lateral radiators, and the armament of one 0.312-in (7.92-mm) MG 08/15 fixed forward-firing machine-gun on the starboard side of the upper fuselage with synchronisation equipment to fire through the propeller disc.

Fokker M.18 (D I) and M.21 (D IV) (continued)

The D I entered service in July 1916, but soon revealed itself to be a poor fighter as a result of its long-span wings and inadequate power/weight ratio. Deliveries amounted to only 112 aircraft for the Imperial German army air service (90 machines), Imperial German navy air service (six machines) and Imperial Austro-Hungarian army air service (16 machines). The type's general indifference led to its retirement from first-line service after only a short operational career, and the surviving aircraft were then used more effectively as advanced flying and fighter trainers.

The **M.21** was the last Fokker aircraft designed wholly by Kreutzer, and was an attempt to create an improved version of the D I by doubling the fixed forward-firing armament, providing better performance by installing the 160-hp (119-kW) Mercedes D.III engine, extending the span and, in the fighter's definitive form, replacing the wing-warping system used for lateral control in the original **M.21zf** subvariant by modifying the outboard ends of the upper wing's trailing edges with horn-balanced ailerons to create the **M.21zk**.

The first such **D IV** aircraft were delivered in August 1916, but performance was so poor with two machine-guns that the aircraft were generally flown with just one gun. Even so, the type lacked both the performance and agility of the more modern fighters being introduced

Fokker's D IV marked no significant improvement over the D III.

on both sides of the Western Front by this time, and production was limited to a mere 60 aircraft.

Fokker M.19 (D III)

The poor performance of the D II persuaded Kreutzer to develop the M.19 as a development of the M.17 with the fixed forward-firing armament doubled to a pair of 0.312-in (7.92-mm) machine-guns and the performance enhanced by the adoption of an uprated engine, the Oberursel U.III.

The resulting **D III** fighter reached the Western Front in August 1916, and production totalled 210 aircraft for the Imperial German army air force from Fokker as well as eight aircraft for the Imperial Austro-Hungarian army air service built under licence in Hungary by MAG. The later German-built aircraft were completed to a slightly improved standard with lateral control not by wing warping but by horn-balanced ailerons on the outboard ends of the upper wing's trailing edges to create a subvariant retrospectively known to Fokker as the **M.19zk** as opposed to **M.19zf** for the original version with control by wing warping. Another 10 aileron-equipped aircraft

Compared to the D II, the D III had a two-row rotary engine in a longer-chord cowling with a smaller downward step to the line of the lower fuselage.

were produced for the Dutch army air corps for delivery from October 1917.

The D III was theoretically a superior warplane to the D II, but was severely hampered by its engine's lack of reliability and therefore quickly relegated to the training and home-defence roles after only a short time over the Western Front.

Fokker M.22 (D V)

Drawn by Kreutzer just before his death during June 1916 in the crash of a D I fighter he was test-flying, the **M.22** was completed by Reinhold Platz. Powered by the Oberursel U.I rotary engine installed in a circular cowling without the lower-quadrant gap usual for engines of this type, the M.22 was basically an improved version of the M.19 (D III). It employed the same type of thin aerofoil section much favoured at the time by virtually all designers but Platz, who would soon introduce a much thicker section on his designs for Fokker, but also paid considerably greater attention to detail design features as a means of reducing drag and thus boosting performance with a moderately low-powered engine. The M.22 was thus an equal-span biplane of mixed construction covered largely with fabric. The single-bay wing cellule had a straight lower wing and a slightly swept upper wing, the latter carrying horn-balanced ailerons, and the tail unit was of the standard Fokker type for the period with no fixed surfaces and the 'comma' type of balanced rudder.

The M.22 was ordered into production as the **D V**. However, even before the first such aircraft were delivered in September 1916, it had become clear that the type was obsolescent in the fighter role by the standards prevailing over the Western Front, and the D V was then earmarked for use in the advanced flying and fighter training roles. Production totalled 216 aircraft, and despite the early decision to use the type in the training role, a few aircraft were apparently used from the time of the D V's operational debut in February 1917 by units of the Imperial German army and navy air services, including the former's Jasta 6, operating over the Western Front.

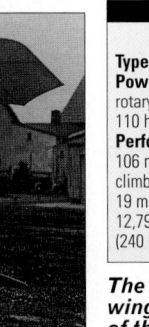

The D V's improved aerodynamic design included a wing cellule of greater stagger, and modest sweep of the upper wing's outer panels.

Fokker S.IX

Designed as a replacement for the S.IV basic trainer, the **Fokker S.IX** was suitable also for acrobatic training. The S.IX was built in two versions. The first, designated **S.IX/1**, was powered by an Armstrong Siddeley Genet Major radial engine. First flown in 1937, the type was used by the Netherlands army air force from 1938 to 1940 as a standard basic trainer, and

a number of S.IX/1s was built by the Dutch manufacturer Kromhout. The second version, designated **S.IX/2**, was powered by a 168-hp (125-kW) Menasco Buccaneer inline engine. A total of 27 S.IX/2s was ordered for the Netherlands navy air force, but only 15 had been delivered when production was terminated by the German invasion. Army orders for the S.IX/1

In addition to its design role of basic training, the two-seat S.IX/1 biplane was also capable of limited aerobatic training.

SPECIFICATION	
Fokker S.IX/1	ceiling 14,110 ft (4300 m), range
Type: two-seat primary trainer	441 miles (710 km)
Powerplant: one 165-hp (123-kW)	**Weights:** empty 1,532 lb (695 kg);
Armstrong Siddeley Genet Major	maximum take-off 2,150 lb (975 kg)
5-cylinder radial piston engine	**Dimensions:** wingspan 31 ft 4 in
Performance: maximum speed	(9.55 m); length 25 ft 1 in (7.65 m),
115 mph (185 km/h); cruising	height 9 ft 6 in (2.90 m); wing area
speed 93 mph (150 km/h); service	247.58 sq ft (23.00 m²)

totalled 24, but there is some uncertainty about whether or not all of these were built and delivered for, according to Fokker records, only 20 were completed.

Like many lightplanes used in service training schools in the desperate circumstances which

existed at the time of the German invasion, the S.IXs were called upon to carry out roles for which they had never been intended, and S.IXs of both services were in use for liaison and

evacuation duties until the end of Dutch resistance.

Fokker built three S.IX/1s after World War II had ended, these being powered by Kromhout-built Genet Major engines.

Fokker S.11 Instructor

Although the Fokker factory at Amsterdam was practically destroyed in World War II, its technical staff was maintained virtually intact. The factory was rebuilt in the space of a year after the end of hostilities and a simple low-wing trainer, the **Fokker S.11**

Instructor, was selected as the company's first postwar product. The S.11 prototype made its maiden flight during 1947. A cantilever low-wing monoplane, basically of metal construction but with some fabric covering, it had a braced tail unit, fixed tail-

wheel landing gear and power provided by an Avco Lycoming O-435-A engine.

The Royal Netherlands air force bought 40, Israel 41 and Italy's Macchi company built 150 under licence, designated **Macchi 416** in Italian air force service. Meanwhile, Fokker Industria Aeronautica SA was established at Rio de Janeiro's Galeao Airport in 1954. The first Brazilian-produced S.11 was accepted by the Brazilian air force on 29 December 1955 and a total of 100 was built.

The **S.12** with tricycle landing gear was also manufactured in Brazil, 50 being delivered. Little modification was needed to accommodate the new

In S.11 form, the S.11/S.12 featured tailwheel landing gear. Note that the main undercarriage was forward-racked and unfaired.

wheel arrangement as the wing had been stressed to support the gear in either position.

The 40 instructors of the Royal Netherlands air force provided elementary flying

training with No. 5 Instruction Squadron at Gilze-Rijen. With the introduction of more modern primary trainers in the 1970s, many S.11s were released to the civil market.

The S.12 employed a tricycle undercarriage. The large canopy allowed the installation of a jump seat for a third crew member in the rear of the cockpit.

SPECIFICATION	
Fokker S.11	service ceiling 13,125 ft (4000 m),
Type: two/three-seat primary	range 432 miles (695 km)
trainer	**Weights:** empty 1,786 lb (810 kg);
Powerplant: one 190-hp (142-kW)	maximum take-off 2,425 lb (1100 kg)
Avco Lycoming O-435-A flat-six	**Dimensions:** wingspan 36 ft 1 in
piston engine	(11.00 m); length 26 ft 8¾ in
Performance: maximum speed	(8.15 m); height 7 ft 10½ in
130 mph (210 km/h) at sea level;	(2.40 m); wing area 199.14 sq ft
cruising speed 103 mph (165 km/h);	(18.50 m²)

Fokker S.14 Mach-Trainer

The **Fokker S.14 Mach-Trainer** secured its place in aviation history by being the first Fokker-designed jet aircraft, the first jet-propelled trainer designed

as such, and the first aircraft of its type to enter production.

The low-wing all-metal S.14 was powered by a Rolls-Royce Derwent turbo-

jet with a bifurcated inlet in the nose. The outlet was in the extreme tail, aft of the horizontal tail surfaces, which were set somewhat aft of the fin and rudder. The

nosewheel of the tricycle landing gear retracted forwards into the underside of the nose, while the main units retracted inwards into the undersides of the wings. Pupil and instructor were seated side-by-side under a short, broad raised canopy

set well forward on the circular-section fuselage. Martin-Baker ejection seats were standard.

Test pilot Gerben Sonderman made the first test flight on 19 May 1951. On a second flight during the same day the landing gear failed and the prototype was damaged in the subsequent belly landing. However, the aircraft was repaired and displayed at the 1951 Paris Salon in June of that year.

A series of 20 S.14s was ordered by the Royal Dutch air arm, the Koninklike Luchtmacht, the first being flown initially on 15 January 1955. The prototype bore the serial K-1 and was powered by a Derwent V engine, while the production machines were serialled from LA to L-20 and had Derwent VIIIs.

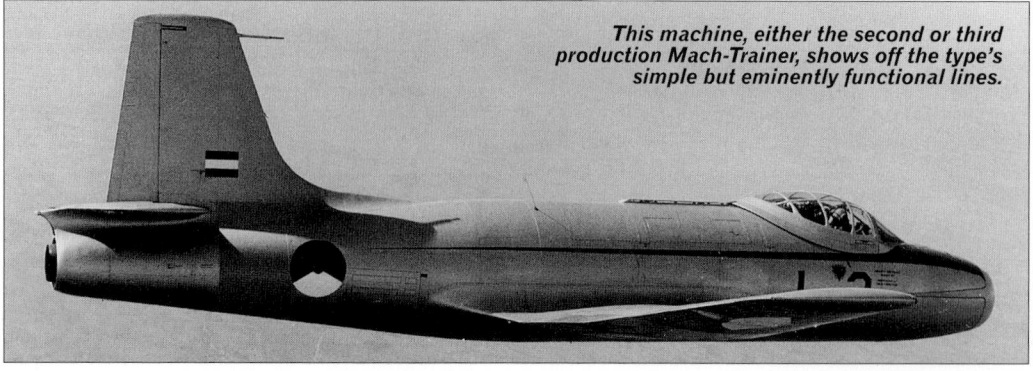

This machine, either the second or third production Mach-Trainer, shows off the type's simple but eminently functional lines.

Fokker S.14 Mach-Trainer (cont.)

S.14 aircraft L-4 was demonstrated in the USA during 1955, but crashed on 20 October that year at Hagerstown, Maryland. Aircraft L-8 took part in the London-Paris air race, known as the 'Arch to Arc' since it started at Marble Arch and ended at the Arc

de Triomphe. The last two S.14s were withdrawn from Dutch service on 29 March 1965 and preserved in Dutch air museums.

The original K-1 prototype was re-engined with a 5,100-lb (22.68-kN) thrust Rolls-Royce Nene 3 engine in 1953 and given

the specially selected civil registration PH-XIV on 24 October 1960. It was then used by the Lucht en Ruuimtevaart Laboratorium (Dutch National Aeronautical and Space Laboratory) until scrapped on 4 March 1966.

SPECIFICATION	
Fokker S.14 Mach-Trainer **Type:** two-seat advanced jet trainer **Powerplant:** one Rolls-Royce Derwent VIII turbojet rated at 3,472 lb st (15.44 kN) **Performance:** maximum speed 454 mph (730 km/h); normal cruising speed 354 mph (570 km/h); service ceiling	36,745 ft (11200 m); range 600 miles (965 km) **Weights:** empty equipped 8,300 lb (3765 kg) maximum take-off 11,795 lb (5350 kg) **Dimensions:** wingspan 39 ft 4½ in (12.00 m); length 43 ft 7½ in (13.30 m), height 15 ft 5 in (4.70 m); wing area 342.30 sq ft (31.80 m²)

Fokker T.IV

One of the ugliest Fokker designs, the **T.IVA** twin-engined torpedo-bomber/reconnaissance floatplane was a progressive development of the 1927 **T.IV**, of which 18 had been built for service at home and in the Netherlands East Indies. Portugal also acquired three of these aircraft.

The T.IVA differed from its predecessor mainly in powerplant, having Wright Cyclone SR-1820-F2 radial engines in place of the

T.IV's 450-hp (336-kW) Lorraine-Dietrich W-type engines. The more powerful units required a strengthened airframe; at the same time an enclosed cockpit, as well as bow, dorsal and ventral gun positions, were installed. Twelve of these new aircraft were ordered for the Netherlands East Indies naval air force, and in

1936 the surviving T.IVs were brought up to T.IVA standard.

Coastal and sea reconnaissance operations in the Netherlands East Indies were still being flown when the Japanese invasion began in 1942, and the T.IVA was also used for air-sea rescue work, proving to be reliable and seaworthy.

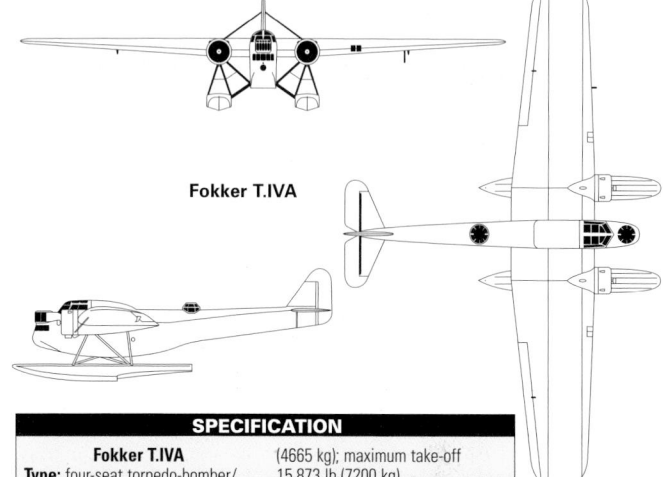

Fokker T.IVA

A torpedo-bomber, reconnaissance platform and SAR aircraft of some distinction, the T.IVA gave sterling service in the Dutch East Indies.

SPECIFICATION	
Fokker T.IVA **Type:** four-seat torpedo-bomber/reconnaissance aircraft **Powerplant:** two 750-hp (559-kW) Wright Cyclone SR-1820-F2 9-cylinder radial piston engines **Performance:** maximum speed 162 mph (260 km/h) at 2,625 ft (800 m), cruising speed 134 mph (215 km/h); service ceiling 19,355 ft (5900 m), range 969 miles (1560 km) **Weights:** empty 10,285 lb	(4665 kg); maximum take-off 15,873 lb (7200 kg) **Dimensions:** wingspan 85 ft 11½ in (26.20 m); length 57 ft 8¾ in (17.60 m), height 19 ft 8¼ in (6.00 m); wing area 1,052.74 sq ft (97.80 m²) **Armament:** single 7.9-mm (0.31-in) machine-guns in nose, dorsal and ventral positions, plus up to 1,764 lb (800 kg) of bombs internally or one torpedo externally beneath the fuselage

Fokker T.VIII-W

Designed to Dutch naval air service specifications for a torpedo-bomber and reconnaissance aircraft suitable for home and Netherlands East Indies service, the T.VIII-W floatplane was built in three versions: the **T.VIII-Wg** of mixed wood and metal construction, the all-metal **T.VIII-Wm** and the **T.VIII-Wc**, a larger version of mixed construction.

An initial order for five aircraft was placed, and all were completed by June 1939, when a further batch of 26 was ordered, most of them intended as replacements for T.IVs in the East Indies, but none was delivered there. Some 19 T.VIII-Wgs, five T.VIII-Wcs and 12 T.VIII-Wms, were built, including five against a Finnish order which was not

UK-based T.VIII-Ws wore RAF markings, plus a small triangular Dutch badge. German navy T.VIII-W operations were confined mostly to patrol work in the Mediterranean.

completed. The latter were of the larger T.VIII-Wc variant which was powered by 890-hp (664-kW) Bristol Mercury XI engines. In the event, the Fokker factory was overrun by the Germans before completion of this order, but the aircraft were finished and subsequently delivered to Germany along with 20 ex-

Dutch navy aircraft. A one-off landplane variant, the **T.VIII-L** built for Finland, was also seized by the Germans. Meanwhile, eight T.VIII-Ws had been flown to England along with other Dutch floatplanes on 14 May 1940, and on 1 June 1940 No. 320 (Dutch) Sqn RAF was formed at Pembroke Dock, to operate

the T.VIII-Ws on convoy escort work. Three of the aircraft were lost, and with no spares available the remaining aircraft were flown to Felixstowe for storage. They were joined by another in May 1941, when four Dutchmen escaped from Amsterdam and brought their T.VIII-W down on the sea near Broadstairs.

SPECIFICATION	
Fokker T.VIII-Wg **Type:** three-seat torpedo-bomber/reconnaissance floatplane **Powerplant:** two 450-hp (336-kW) Wright Whirlwind R-975-E3 9-cylinder radial piston engines **Performance:** maximum speed 177 mph (285 km/h), cruising speed 137 mph (220 km/h), service ceiling 22,310 ft (6800 m); range 1,709 miles (2750 km) **Weights:** empty 6,834 lb	(3100 kg); maximum take-off 11,023 lb (5000 kg) **Dimensions:** wingspan 59 ft ½ in (18.00 m); length 42 ft 8 in (13.00 m); height 16 ft 5 in (5.00 m); wing area 473.63 sq ft (44.00 m²) **Armament:** one 0.31-in (7.9-mm) forward-firing machine-gun on port side of fuselage and one similar single gun on pivoted mount in rear cockpit, plus up to 1,334 lb (605 kg) of bombs, or one torpedo

Fokker V.4 and V.5 (F I and Dr I)

German pilots serving on the Western Front were quick to appreciate the high rate of climb and remarkable manoeuvrability of the

Sopwith Triplane which the RNAS was operating in the spring of 1917. Consequently, Germany's aircraft manufacturers lost

little time in developing experimental triplanes.

Fokker's chief designer, Martin Kreutzer, was killed on 27 June 1916 while

testing a D I and was replaced by Reinhold Platz, who was thus responsible for the design and development of the company's new triplane. The origins of the **V.4** can be found in an order placed in May 1917

by the Imperial Austro-Hungarian army air service for a single-seat biplane fighter, but this concept was then revised to a triplane layout with three small cantilever wings wholly free of interplane

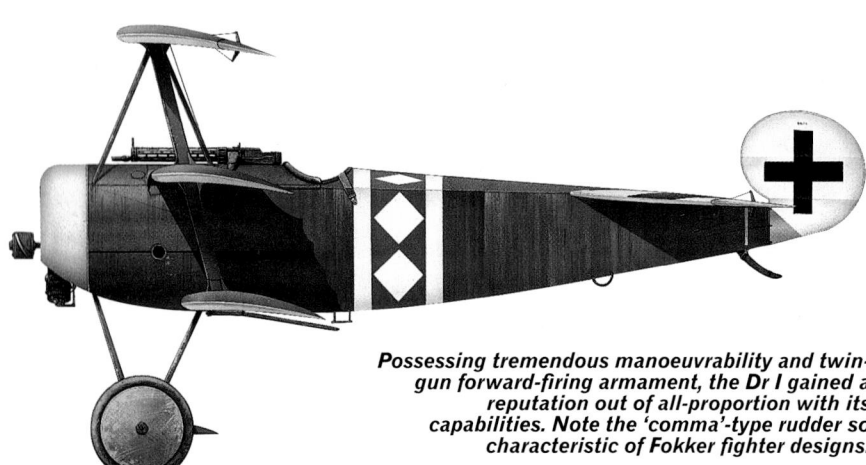

Possessing tremendous manoeuvrability and twin-gun forward-firing armament, the Dr I gained a reputation out of all-proportion with its capabilities. Note the 'comma'-type rudder so characteristic of Fokker fighter designs.

SPECIFICATION

Fokker Dr I

Type: single-seat fighter
Powerplant: one Thulin-built Le Rhône 9 or Oberursel U.II rotary piston engine each rated at 110 hp (82 kW)
Performance: maximum speed 115 mph (185 km/h) at sea level; climb to 3,280 ft (1000 m) in 2 minutes 54 seconds; service ceiling 20,000 ft (6095 m);

endurance 1 hour 30 minutes
Weights: empty 895 lb (406 kg); maximum take-off 1,292 lb (586 kg)
Dimensions: wingspan 23 ft 7 in (7.19 m); length 18 ft 11 in (5.77 m); height 9 ft 8 in (2.95 m); wing area 200.86 sq ft (18.66 m²)
Armament: two 0.312-in (7.92-mm) LMG 08/15 fixed forward-firing machine-guns in the upper part of the forward fuselage

struts. The other main features of the prototype were a slab-sided fuselage, a tail unit with a strut-braced triangular tailplane, plain elevators and a 'comma' rudder without a fin, and fixed tailskid landing gear whose through-axle was enclosed in an aerofoil-section fairing.

The V.4 first flew in the later part of May 1917 with the 120-hp (90-kW) Le Rhône 9 rotary engine, and it was immediately discovered that the wings vibrated badly. The type was therefore revised with a single I-type interplane strut on each side as well as horn-balanced ailerons and elevators. It was in this form that the first V.4 was delivered to Austria-Hungary in August 1917. Fokker had meanwhile received a German contract for another V.4 as well two **V.5** prototypes with a central wing intermediate in span between the upper and lower wings and a powerplant based on the 110-hp (82-kW) Le Rhône engine that was entering production in Germany as the Oberursel U.II.

The V.5 was ordered into production for service with the designation **F I** that was soon changed to **Dr I** in recognition of its

Dreidecker (triplane) layout. The Dr I was powered by a Thulin licence-built Le Rhône rotary or by the U.II unlicensed copy of the same French engine. The Dr I soon gained an exaggerated reputation of capability, probably because it was used by a number of major aces including the legendary 'Red Baron', who favoured the type for its superb manoeuvrability and high rate of climb. So far as maximum speed was concerned, however, the Dr I was inferior to contemporary Allied fighters, and a number was also lost as a result of wing structural failure. At one period, late in 1917, the type was grounded while wing-strengthening modifications were carried out. When production ended in May 1918 some 320 such aircraft had been built, and the Dr I remained in front-line service until the summer of 1918.

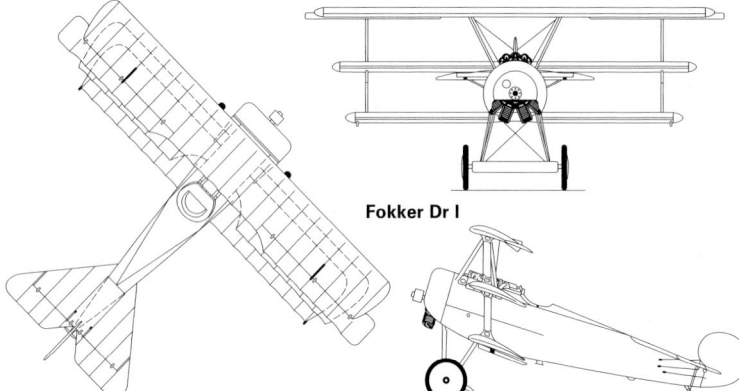

Fokker Dr I

Variants

V.6: Ordered in July 1917 and developed in parallel with the V.5 with the wholly different powerplant of one 160-hp (119-kW) Mercedes D.III inline engine, a water- rather than air-cooled unit whose greater weight led Platz to lengthen the fuselage and increase the area of the wing cellule; the depth of the fuselage was also increased, allowing greater interplane gaps; trials revealed that the V.6 had agility considerably inferior to that of the smaller V.5
V.7: Designation of a quartet of development aircraft with uprated engines; one of the machines was fitted with the 145-hp (108-kW) Oberursel U.III rotary engine and flown in the first D-category fighter competition of January 1918; two other aircraft were delivered to Austria-Hungary, one of them with the 160-hp (119-kW) Siemens-Halske Sh.III geared rotary engine and the other with the 145-hp (108-kW) Steyr-built Le Rhône 9 rotary engine; the fourth machine was used in Germany for evaluation of the 170-hp (127-kW) Goebel

Goe.III rotary engine
V.8: this extraordinary prototype was in essence a development of the V.6, equally describable as a quintuplane or a tandem-wing machine; the fuselage was considerably lengthened to allow the installation at the extreme nose of an unstaggered equal-span triplane cellule with the upper and lower wings above and below the fuselage respectively, and immediately to the rear of the cockpit an unstaggered biplane cellule; the upper wings of the two cellules each carried a pair of balanced ailerons, and there was a conventional tail unit; Fokker himself first flew the V.8 in October 1917, but further development of this extreme machine was soon terminated
V.9: experimental biplane of autumn 1917 using mostly Dr I components and with its upper wing's centre section supported on pairs of tripod cabane struts on each side; power was provided by the 80-hp (60-kW) Oberursel U.0 rotary engine
V.10: standard Dr I fitted with the 145-hp (108-kW) Oberursel U.III engine and possessing the phenomenal ceiling of 31,170 ft (9500 m)

Fokker V.11 and V.18 (D VII)

To compete in Germany's first single-seat fighter competition of 1918, Platz developed a new prototype, the **V.11**, which incorporated much of the design of the successful Dr I triplane. Its fuselage was similar in profile and construction, the tail unit was revised, but the landing gear was virtually unchanged. The intention to use a more powerful and heavier engine to attain a new level of performance meant that by comparison with the contemporary **V.13** prototype (ordered as the **D VI**), a staggered single-bay biplane wing cellule of greater span and area was required. The construction

of these wings was similar to that adopted for the cantilever wings designed for the Dr I but, being considerably larger, had a two- rather than one-spar basis. The powerplant of the prototype and early production aircraft was based on the 160-hp (119-kW) Mercedes D.III inline engine, but the later **D VIIF** subvariant had the more powerful BMW IIIa engine which gave improved performance.

This D VII replica demonstrates the classic lines of one of World War I's most capable fighter aircraft.

Fokker V.11 and V.18 (D VII) (continued)

Ordered in September 1917, the V.11 first flew in December 1917 and revealed generally good performance and agility but a measure of directional instability as well as other problems. The problems were cured by changes that included the lengthening of the fuselage and the modification of the wing cellule with reduced gap and stagger. As a result of the January 1918 fighter competition, in which the V.11 competed alongside the generally similar **V.18** that differed mainly in the introduction of a fixed fin, the type was ordered into large-scale production for service as the D VII, and the overall capability of the new fighter was so much better than that of the Albatros D V that Albatros Werke G.m.b.H. was ordered to build the Fokker fighter under subcontract at both of its factories. Within three months of the competition the D VII was in operational use, its performance matched only by the British Sopwith Snipe and the French SPAD S.13. By the time of the Armistice, Fokker had completed 877 D VIIs (of which six and the **V.22** prototype were transferred to Austria-Hungary as pattern aircraft for licensed production by MAG, which completed 12 aircraft after World War I) and Albatros had manufactured the more impressive total of 1,749 machines. Such was the impression that the type had made on the Allies that the Germans were required to hand over all machines of this type to the Allied Control Commission; the D VII and all surviving Zeppelin airships were the only German aircraft singled out in this fashion.

Fokker managed to smuggle D VII fighters as well as components for the type out of Germany and into his native Netherlands, where he set up a new aircraft factory. Of the 148 aircraft that resulted from this effort, 98 were used by the Netherlands (72 by the army air corps, 20 by the naval air service and six by the Dutch East Indies army air corps) and the other 50 were sold to the USSR. Switzerland bought eight D VII and two D VIIF aircraft from the Allied Control Commission, one of the aircraft later becoming a **D VIIS** after being re-engined with the Hispano-Suiza 8Fb Vee engine, then another six overhauled aircraft from Compte in 1925, and finally eight new-build aircraft also from Compte in 1928-29. The Americans shipped 142 examples of the D VII back to the USA for a thorough evaluation, many of the aircraft later being revised with American engines, and in 1920 the Americans bought several more D VII fighters from Fokker. Other countries that bought D VII fighters included Belgium (75 war-reparation aircraft, of which 35 entered service), Denmark, Finland, Hungary (50 aircraft), Poland, Romania and Sweden.

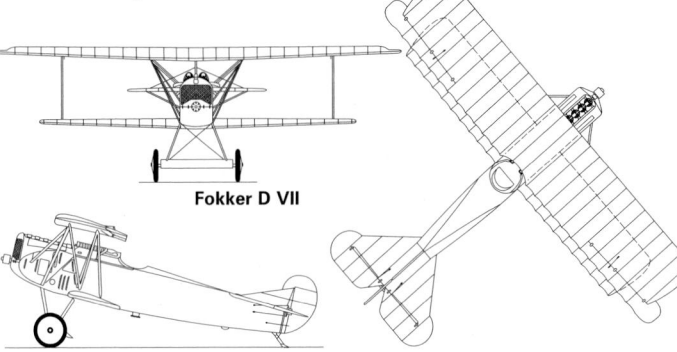

Fokker D VII

Variants

V.21: variant of the D VII with tapered wing panels and the 160-hp (119-kW) Mercedes D.III engine; flown in the second D-type competition of May and June 1918
V.22: pre-production prototype of the D VII, combining all the best features of the V.11, V.18 and V.21, and powered by the 160-hp (119-kW) Mercedes D.III engine
V.24: D VII experimentally fitted with the 240-hp (179-kW) Benz Bz.IV Vee engine
V.31: standard D VII fitted with a hook to tow the V.30 glider
V.34: prototype fitted with a V.33-type empennage (including the balanced rudder of more modern shape), an upper wing possessing no cut-out in the centre of its trailing edge, and a BMW IIIa engine in a neater cowling characterised by an oval radiator
V.35: this designation is believed to have been applied to a two-seat development of the D VIIF for long-distance flying
V.36: this was basically similar to the V.34 except for its D VII-type vertical tail surface and the relocation of the fuel tank from the fuselage to the axle fairing

SPECIFICATION	
Fokker D VIIF	
Type: single-seat fighter	**Weights:** empty 1,508 lb (684 kg); maximum take-off 2,006 lb (910 kg)
Powerplant: one BMW IIIa inline piston engine rated at 185 hp (138 kW)	**Dimensions:** wingspan 29 ft 2⅓ in (8.90 m); length 22 ft 9⅗ in (6.95 m); height 9 ft (2.75 m) with the tail up; wing area 217.44 sq ft (20.20 m²)
Performance: maximum speed 124 mph (200 km/h) at 3,280 ft (1000 m); climb to 6,560 ft (2000 m) in 5 minutes 15 seconds; service ceiling 21,325 ft (6500 m); endurance about 1 hour 20 minutes	**Armament:** two 0.312-in (7.92-mm) LMG 08/15 fixed forward-firing machine-guns in the upper part of the forward fuselage

Fokker V.28 (E V and D VIII)

The **E V** took part in the Imperial German army air service's second D-category competition of May and June 1918 despite the fact that it was not strictly eligible, being a parasol-wing monoplane rather than a biplane. In fact, the type had already been ordered into production, the first such fighter being delivered about two weeks before the competition ended. The E V was the production development of the **V.28** prototype, which combined several features of earlier aircraft. The fuselage with single-seat accommodation was similar to that of the D VII, while the horizontal tail surface and powerplant were the same as those of the Dr I. The E V differed in having a cantilever monoplane wing strut-mounted in the parasol-wing position. The V.28 performed well in the fighter competition, and particularly impressed both officials and service pilots with its manoeuvrability, take-off and climb performance.

An enormous spinner was the key recognition feature of the experimental V.37 trench-fighter. The aircraft employed extensive armour protection.

Variants

V.26: produced in parallel with the V.27 and V.28, the V.26 was essentially a version of the V.28 with the 110-hp (82-kW) Le Rhône nine-cylinder rotary engine
V.27: a participant in the second D-category fighter competition, the V.27 was essentially a scaled-up version of the V.26 and V.28 to accept a water-cooled stationary engine rather than an air-cooled rotary engine, in this instance the 200-hp (149-kW) Benz Bz.IIIb Vee unit
V.28: also flown in the second D-category competition, the V.28 was powered initially by the 110-hp (82-kW) Oberursel U.II rotary engine, but later by the 145-hp (108-kW) Oberursel U.III and finally the 140-hp (104-kW) Goebel Goe.III rotary engines; for the third D-category competition the V.28 was re-engined with the Siemens-Halske Sh.III geared rotary unit
V.29: parasol-wing fighter prototype similar to the V.27 except for its 160-hp (119-kW) Mercedes D.III inline piston engine
V.30: variant of the V.27 with the 180-hp (134-kW) Benz Bz.IIIa inline engine; the designation was re-used after World War I for a glider

based on V.26 components with the pilot seated in the extreme nose for centre-of-gravity reasons
V.37: development of the V.27 with sheet armour protection for the pilot, engine and fuel tanks as precursor to a proposed trench-fighter development; the type was fitted with a very large spinner (requiring cheek pieces on the sides of the fuselage to its rear) to improve streamlining, and the need to ensure adequate engine cooling meant that a large fan was added behind the propeller
V.39: created by Fokker immediately after the end of World War I, this was intended as the prototype of a light single-seat sporting machine scaled-down from the D VIII and powered by the 110-hp (82-kW) Le Rhône rotary engine, although other rotary engines were also envisaged
V.40: scaled-down ultra-light development of the V.39 intended for sport flying and powered by the 35-hp (26-kW) Anzani three-cylinder radial engine

Early use by combat units revealed problems with engine lubrication and the structural integrity of the wing, leading to a temporary suspension of both production and operational use. However, remedial action was taken very quickly and production resumed under the new designation **D VIII**, but the Armistice came shortly after this and, as a result, comparatively few D VIIIs saw operational service. Plans had been formulated for the development of the basic type with more powerful engines, but none of these entered production. Manufacture of the E V totalled 139 aircraft, while that of the D VIII was 150 aircraft, 53 of the latter being delivered after the Armistice without engines.

Fokker's D VIII was a neat parasol-wing fighter monoplane.

SPECIFICATION	
Fokker D VIII	186 miles (300 km); endurance
Type: single-seat fighter	1 hour 30 minutes
Powerplant: one Oberursel U.II	**Weights:** empty 847 lb (384 kg);
rotary piston engine rated at	maximum take-off 1,265 lb (574 kg)
110 hp (82 kW) or, in only 26	**Dimensions:** wingspan 27 ft 4⅘ in
aircraft, one Oberursel U.III rotary	(8.34 m); length 19 ft 5 in (5.92 m);
piston engine rated at 145 hp	height 8 ft 6⅓ in (2.60 m); wing
(108 kW)	area 115.18 sq ft (10.70 m²)
Performance: maximum speed	**Armament:** two 0.312-in
115 mph (185 km/h) at sea level;	(7.92-mm) LMG 08/15 fixed
climb to 6,560 ft (2000 m) in	forward-firing machine-guns in the
5 minutes 6 seconds; service	upper part of the forward fuselage
ceiling 19,685 ft (6000 m); range	

Fokker (America) F.14 (C-14 and C-15)

The **F.14** of 1929 was built at the New Jersey factory of the Fokker Aircraft Corporation of America as a seven/nine-passenger transport. The fuselage and wing were of normal Fokker design, although the upper fuselage decking was of corrugated Dural.

The F.14 differed principally from other Fokker transports in having a parasol wing carried on short struts above the fuselage.

SPECIFICATION	
Fokker F.14	**Weights:** empty 4,346 lb
Type: one-crew transport	(1971 kg); maximum take-off
Powerplant: one Pratt & Whitney	7,200 lb (3266 kg)
R-1750-3 Hornet A radial piston	**Dimensions:** wingspan 59 ft 5 in
engine rated at 525 hp (391 kW)	(18.11 m); length 43 ft 3 in
Performance: maximum speed	(13.18 m); height 12 ft 4 in
137 mph (220 km/h) at optimum	(3.76 m); wing area 551.00 sq ft
altitude; cruising speed 116 mph	(51.19 m²)
(187 km/h) at optimum altitude;	**Payload:** up to nine passengers
initial climb rate 810 ft (247 m) per	carried in an enclosed cabin within
minute; service ceiling 14,500 ft	the context of a 1,560-lb (708-kg)
(4420 m); range 690 miles (1110 km)	maximum payload

Variants

F.14A: civil development with the 575-hp (429-kW) Pratt & Whitney Hornet radial engine
Y1C-14: designation of 20 examples of a military transport version of the F.14 procured by the US Army in 1931 and fitted with the same powerplant as the F.14; as with later versions described, the Y1 prefix was dropped from the designation in due course, and the aircraft thus became plain **C-14** machines

Y1C-14A: designation of last machine delivered out of the batch of 20, which was powered by the 575-hp (429-kW) Wright R-1820-7 Cyclone engine
Y1C-14B: redesignation following installation of the 525-hp (391-kW) Pratt & Whitney R-1690-5 Hornet engine
Y1C-15: conversion of the ninth Y1C-14 as an air ambulance able to transport four litters and one medical attendant
Y1C-15A: redesignation of the Y1C-15 air ambulance following installation of the 575-hp (429-kW) Wright R-1820 Cyclone engine

Fokker (America) F.32

The **F.32** four-engined passenger transport was the last Fokker design to be built in the USA, and caused widespread interest when it appeared in 1929. The '32' in the designation indicated its passenger capacity, but as a sleeper for night operations this accommodation was halved to 16 berths.

The F.32 was a large snub-nosed, high-wing cantilever monoplane, its fixed wide-track landing gear having fairings over the main wheels. The crew cabin was well forward of the wing leading edge, and the passenger accommodation was located below the wing and extended into the rear fuselage. The power-plant comprised four Pratt & Whitney Hornet radial engines mounted in two tandem pairs below the wing, two of the engines operating as tractor units and the other two as pusher units.

Production of the F.32 totalled 10 aircraft, several of these going into service with California-based Western Air Express in 1930. Problems with cooling of the rear engines soon became evident and were never fully resolved, so the active career of the F.32 aircraft was relatively short. One of the machines was evaluated by the US Army Air Corps under the designation **YC-20**, but never received a USAAC serial number and was not bought by the service.

SPECIFICATION	
Fokker F.32	**Weights:** empty 15,080 lb
Type: five-crew transport	(6840 kg); maximum take-off
Powerplant: four Pratt & Whitney	24,250 lb (11000 kg)
Hornet B radial piston engines	**Dimensions:** wingspan 99 ft
each rated at 575 hp (429 kW)	(30.18 m); length 69 ft 10 in
Performance: maximum speed	(21.29 m); height 16 ft 6 in
140 mph (225 km/h) at optimum	(5.03 m); wing area 1,350.00 sq ft
altitude; cruising speed 123 mph	(125.42 m²)
(198 km/h) at optimum altitude;	**Payload:** up to 32 day or 16 night
initial climb rate 1,000 ft (305 m)	passengers within the context of a
per minute; service ceiling 13,500 ft	5,630-lb (2554-kg) maximum
(4115 m); range 740 miles (1191 km)	payload

Western Air Express used its F.32s on services between San Francisco and Los Angeles. The distinctive empennage comprised a single horizontal surface and two vertical surfaces.

Fokker (America) O-27 and B-8

In the latter part of the 1920s the US Army Air Corps became increasingly interested in the evaluation of advanced aircraft for tasks such as high-speed observation over the battle-field. One result of this interest was the **O-27** ordered from the Fokker Aircraft Corporation, as the Atlantic Aircraft Corporation had become in September 1925 in recognition of the fact that Anthony Fokker and his company were no longer badly tainted by their adherence to the German cause in World War I.

Although of typical Fokker construction, with fabric-covered welded steel tube for the fuselage and tail unit, and plywood-covered wood for the wing, the three-seat O-27 was somewhat different from other Fokker aircraft of the period in the shoulder-set position of its wing and the details of the wide-track

divided main units of its sturdy fixed tailwheel land-ing gear. Two **XO-27** prototypes were ordered, and the first of these flew in 1929. The second proto-type was completed with a lengthened and redesigned nose section and provision for a bombload under the new designation **XB-8**.

Six service test **YO-27** and six **YB-8** aircraft were ordered in 1931, but all 12 were completed as obser-vation aircraft, the machines ordered under the YB-8 designation being known as **Y1O-27** aircraft. The O-27s (as they were all subsequently redesignated) differed from the prototype in having enclosed canopies for the pilots' cockpits and improved, revised tail surfaces. There was an open gunner's cockpit in the nose with a glazed navigator's position beneath it, and a second open gunner's position was

located in the dorsal posi-tion.

The XO-27 was fitted with Curtiss V-1570 geared inline engines in 1932 to become the **XO-27A**, and the O-27s flew for several years with USAAC first-line units.

SPECIFICATION

Fokker O-27

Type: three-seat observation aircraft
Powerplant: two Curtiss V-1570-29 Vee piston engines each rated at 600 hp (447 kW)
Performance: maximum speed 160 mph (257 km/h) at optimum altitude
Weight: maximum take-off 8,918 lb (4045 kg)

Dimensions: wingspan 64 ft (19.51 m); length 47 ft 4 in (14.43 m); height 15 ft (4.57 m); wing area 619.00 sq ft (57.51 m²)
Armament: one 0.3-in (7.62-mm) Browning trainable forward-firing machine-gun in the nose position and one 0.3-in (7.62-mm) Browning trainable machine-gun in the dorsal position

*Fokker's **O-27** resulted from the USAAC's belief that the use of twin-engined monoplane aircraft could offer the possibility of a higher level of survivability than was achievable with its then-current generation of considerably slower single-engined biplanes.*

Fokker (America) F.9 Universal and Standard Universal

The **F.9 Universal** was the first American-designed Fokker aircraft, conceived in 1925 by R. B. C. Noorduyn, the manager of Fokker's US subsidiary, at that time known as the Atlantic Aircraft Corporation. A strut-braced high-wing monoplane with wide-track divided landing gear, the Universal was of typi-cal Fokker construction

and carried its one or two pilots in an open (later enclosed) cockpit just forward of the wing and its four passengers in an enclosed cabin in the fuse-lage under the wing. Powered by a 220-hp (164-kW) Wright Whirlwind J-5 radial engine, the Universal was placed in production in 1926 and a number was delivered, particularly to

SPECIFICATION

Fokker F.9 Standard Universal
Type: one/two-crew transport
Powerplant: one Wright Whirlwind J-6-9 radial piston engine rated at 300 hp (224 kW)
Performance: maximum speed 130 mph (209 km/h) at sea level; cruising speed 110 mph (177 km/h) at optimum altitude; initial climb rate 830 ft (253 m) per minute; service ceiling 14,000 ft (4265 m); range 500 miles (805 km)

Weights: empty 2,482 lb (1126 kg); maximum take-off 4,300 lb (1950 kg)
Dimensions: wingspan 47 ft 9 in (14.55 m); length 33 ft 6 in (10.21 m); height 8 ft 9 in (2.67 m); wing area 341.00 sq ft (31.68 m²)
Payload: up to six passengers carried in an enclosed cabin within the context of a 1,140-lb (517-kg) maximum payload

Canadian buyers, with twin-float alighting gear replacing the wheeled landing gear. In the follow-ing year there appeared the **Standard Universal** version with the 300-hp (224-kW) Whirlwind J-6 engine, allowing an increase in the passenger capacity to six persons.

Structural details of the Universal included a fabric-covered welded steel tube fuselage and a plywood-covered wooden wing.

This variant was also built in some numbers and was operated by several US and Canadian airlines on regular routes as well as for charter services. An unusual feature of both

variants was a control system, which provided the pilot and optional co-pilot with separate rudder bars but included only one control column for the pilot.

Fokker (America) F.18 Super Universal (JA)

The **F.18 Super Universal** was a somewhat enlarged and more robust version of the Universal with tougher, refined landing gear. Like its predecessor, the Super Universal could be operated on either wheeled landing gear or float alighting gear. Accommodating a crew of two and six passengers, the Super Universal was powered by a single Wasp radial engine, and the canopy over the pilots' cock-

pit was similar in design to that of the **F.10** and **F.10A** transports. A single Super Universal was tested briefly by the US Navy under the designation **XJA-1**.

The Super Universal was built in quantity by the Nakajima Aircraft Company in Japan after 10 had been imported in 1929. Nakajima built 47 of the type for civil operation between 1931 and 1936, these being used on regular routes for a number of years by both Japanese Air Transport Ltd and Manchurian Air Lines.

Based on the airframe of the earlier Universal, the Super Universal proved to be an equally rugged and utilitarian transport.

Two specialised ambulance variants were purchased by popular subscription for the Imperial Japanese army air force, the first in 1932 and the second, with a cowled engine, in 1938.

The Japanese Imperial navy air force took delivery of 20 Super Universals between 1933 and 1934 under the designation **Nakajima C2N1**, or **Nakajima-Fokker Navy**

Reconnaissance Aircraft. These had uncowled Bristol Jupiter radial engines and the defensive armament of a single 0.303-in (7.7-mm) trainable machine-gun on a ring mounting over an open dorsal cockpit. The aircraft were used in China and the homeland largely on liaison and transport duties.

The final version of the Super Universal to be built in any numbers was the

Nakajima Ki-6, or **Army Type 95-2 Crew Trainer**. Powered by an uncowled 580-hp (432-kW) Nakajima Kotobuki (Jupiter) radial engine, the Ki-6 carried a crew of six. Twenty examples were delivered by the end of 1935. Like the C2N1, the Ki-6 had a dorsal gun position (for training in air-to-air gunnery), but had the additional refinement of spat-type wheel fairings.

Folland Fo.108

Folland Aircraft Ltd could trace its origins to February 1936 at Hamble, Hampshire, when the British Marine Aircraft Ltd was formed with the intention of producing the Sikorsky S-42A flying-boat under licence. This scheme came to nothing and in May 1937 the company underwent a complete reorganisation and change of name. H. P. Folland, formerly chief designer of the Gloster Aircraft Company, became managing director, and the firm initially undertook sub-contract work.

A series of projects beginning with the **Fo.101** remained paper designs only, and the firm's first concept to reach hardware form was the **Fo.108**, designed to meet Specification 43/37 for an engine testbed. Percival and General Aircraft also tendered, but Folland won the contract for a batch of 12 aircraft. A large, single-engined low-wing monoplane with fixed landing gear, the Fo.108 was as big as a Bristol Beaufort and considerably taller. Resembling a scaled-up Hurricane, it accommo-

Among the aerodynamic features of the unusual Fo.108 were split trailing-edge flaps and automatic wingtip slots.

dated a pilot and two observers in a large cabin with complete instrumentation for monitoring engine performance in flight. Construction was mixed, the semi-monocoque fuselage being of light alloy construction while the wing and tail were covered with plywood.

Testbed aircraft lack the glamour of operational types, but the Fo.108 accomplished a wealth of interesting test programmes. Engine installations included different versions of the Napier Sabre, the Bristol Hercules and Centaurus, and the

Rolls-Royce Griffon. The fifth aircraft was later operated by de Havilland for propeller tests.

The first was delivered in 1940, and the first recorded loss was on 28 April 1944 when the eighth aircraft crashed on take-off from Heston during tests with the Centaurus IV. Tests of the Centaurus I and IV rapidly disposed of three more Fo.108s in only three weeks, the third, first and second aircraft being lost on 28 August and 14 and

18 September 1944 respectively. The sixth aircraft was also lost on 14 September while fitted with a Sabre I. The only other recorded fates are two struck off charge in 1945: the eleventh on 5 March after testing the Hercules XI and the fifth on 27 March after Griffon tests. Because of the variety of engines, weights and performance would have been variable and the only recorded details are noted at left.

Folland Fo.139 Midge

As fighter design became more complex and the resulting aircraft both heavier and costlier, W. E. W. 'Teddy' Petter, Folland's managing director and chief designer, concluded that the new small jet engines

then being developed would make possible the design of an effective lightweight fighter. In 1951 he therefore began design of the **Fo.141** on the basis of the 3,800-lb st (16.90-kN) Bristol BE.22 Saturn

turbojet engine, but termination of this unit's development resulted in substitution of the 4,520-lb st (20.11-kN) Bristol BE.26 Orpheus turbojet engine.

To prove the concept embodied in the Gnat, the **Fo.139 Midge** prototype was built with the 1,640-lb st (7.30-kN)

Armstrong Siddeley Viper turbojet engine, and this recorded its first flight at Boscombe Down, Wiltshire, on 11 August 1954. Extensive flight testing (nine hours in the first 13 days) included a supersonic dive, which was quite an achievement considering the low power of the prototype's engine and a tribute to its clean design.

Overseas pilots who flew the Midge came from the Royal Canadian Navy, Royal New Zealand Air Force, Indian air force, US Air Force and Jordanian air

force, and the aircraft was praised for its ease of handling and simplicity of design. A total of 220 flights totalling 110 hours 33 minutes had been made before the Midge was destroyed in a fatal crash at Chilbolton on 26 September 1955 while being flown by a Swiss pilot. Examination of the wreckage showed no fault with the aircraft.

By the time of the crash the lightweight concept had been proved, however, and the first Orpheus-powered Gnat F.Mk 1 had successfully flown.

Only by considering the relative size of the pilot can the tiny dimensions of the remarkable Midge be fully appreciated.

Folland Fo.141 and Fo.144 Gnat

Renowned for its service with the Red Arrows, the Gnat had previously acted as the mount for the RAF's Yellowjacks. The latter was dissolved to make way for the Red Arrows in 1965.

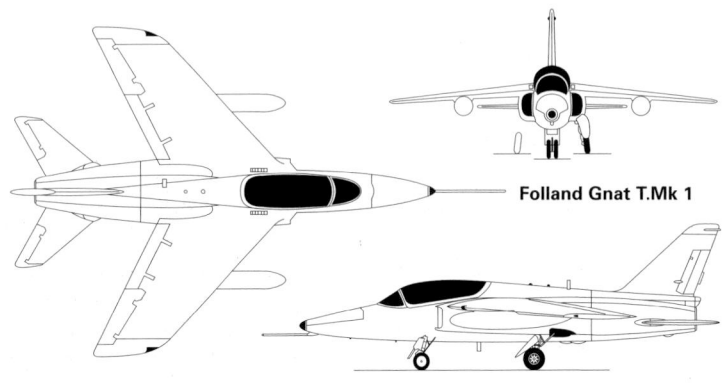

Perhaps the most widely known of the RAF's early jet trainers as a result of its outstanding performances in the hands of the pilots of the *Red Arrows* aerobatic team, the diminutive **Fo.141 Gnat** was designed originally as a lightweight fighter. The private-venture Gnat prototype, piloted by Folland's chief test pilot, Squadron Leader E. A. Tennant, flew at the Aeroplane and Armament Experimental Establishment at Boscombe Down on 18 July 1955. The aircraft's newly developed 3,285-lb st (14.61-kN) Bristol Orpheus BOr.1 turbojet engine was also airborne for the first time and a more powerful version, rated at 4,000 lb st (17.79 kN), was installed on 30 August in readiness for the Gnat's debut at that year's SBAC flying display and exhibition at Farnborough. Six (later increased to eight) development aircraft were ordered by the Ministry of Supply in August 1955, the first flying on 26 May 1956 with the 4,520-lb st (20.11-kN) Orpheus BOr.2 Mk 701 engine, and these were used for a variety of trials at Boscombe Down, including firing of the 30-mm Aden Mk 4 cannon, one of which was fitted in the lip of each intake; the Gnat fighter could also carry two 500-lb (454-kg) bombs or 12 3-in (76-mm) air-to-surface unguided rockets on two underwing hardpoints. Evaluation in the ground-attack role was undertaken in Aden, in competition with a modified Hawker Hunter which was ordered subsequently as the Hunter FGA.Mk 9.

Although the RAF had lost interest in the Gnat as a fighter, the Finnish air force took delivery of 13 **Gnat F.Mk 1** aircraft in 1958-9 and these remained in service until 1972 when they were replaced by Saab Drakens. Two of the Finnish aircraft were fitted with camera noses for fighter reconnaissance duties. The Yugoslav government also bought two aircraft for evaluation, but the major export order was from India: 25 complete aircraft were delivered from the UK together with components for the local assembly of a further 20 aircraft all with the 4,705-lb st (20.93-kN) Orpheus Mk 701-01 turbojet engine, and licensed production was undertaken by Hindustan Aeronautics (later Aircraft) Ltd at Bangalore, where 195 aircraft were built up to January 1974. The Gnat entered Indian Air Force service in the spring of 1958, when the Gnat Handling Flight was first formed, and ultimately eight squadrons were equipped. Although the RAF had not selected the Gnat for service in a front-line role, it did have a requirement for an unarmed two-seat advanced trainer to replace the de Havilland Vampire T.Mk 11 and to follow the Hunting Jet Provost sections of the all-through jet training programme. Folland undertook a private-venture investigation of the changes necessary to install a second seat and to bring the landing speed down to less than 115 mph (185 km/h). The most significant of these changes was a new wing, increased in area by 40 sq ft (3.72 m²) and providing additional fuel capacity, which reduced the fuel storage requirement in the fuselage, making room for additional equipment. The forward fuselage was increased slightly in length, the tail surfaces were enlarged, and outboard ailerons and conventional inboard flaps replaced the fighter's inboard ailerons. Power was to be supplied by the 4,230-lb st (18.82-kN) Orpheus BOr.4 Mk 100.

A Ministry of Supply design study contract was awarded in the autumn of 1956, and in August 1957 a batch of 14 pre-production **Fo.144 Gnat Trainer** aircraft was ordered, the first of these flying on 31 August 1959. It became clear, however, that no production order would be placed while Folland remained outside the major manufacturing groupings which the government favoured, and Folland therefore merged into Hawker Siddeley Aviation, becoming its Hamble Division. Contracts for 30, 20 and 41 aircraft were awarded in February 1960, July 1961 and March 1962 respectively. The last production **Gnat T.Mk 1** flew on 9 April 1965 and was delivered to the RAF on 14 May, in the all-red scheme of the *Red Arrows*. The Central Flying School first introduced the type in February 1962 but the major operator was No. 4 Flying Training School at Valley, which took its first aircraft on strength in November 1962 and which, in 1964, introduced the Gnat to the formation aerobatic scene, operating five all-yellow Gnats in a team known as the *Yellowjacks*. The team re-formed as the *Red Arrows* in 1965 under the control of the Central Flying School, and its Gnats were finally withdrawn at the end of the 1979 display season, to be replaced in 1980 by the British Aerospace Hawk T.Mk 1.

Folland Gnat T.Mk 1

In service as the RAF's advanced flying trainer, the Gnat T.Mk 1 proved fast and manoeuvrable. Its small cockpit dimensions meant that taller students could not be trained on the aircraft, however, the Hawker Hunter T.Mk 7 with its side-by-side seating being utilised on these occasions.

SPECIFICATION

Folland (Hawker Siddeley) Gnat T.Mk 1

Type: two-seat advanced flying trainer

Powerplant: one Bristol Siddeley Orpheus BOr.4 Mk 100 turbojet engine rated at 4,230 lb st (18.82 kN)

Performance: maximum speed 636 mph (1024 km/h) at 31,000 ft (9450 m); climb to 40,000 ft (1290 m) in 7 minutes; service ceiling 48,000 ft (14630 m); range 1,151 miles (1852 km) with two drop tanks; endurance 2 hours 15 minutes with two drop tanks

Weights: empty 5,140 lb (2331 kg); maximum take-off 8,630 lb (3915 kg)

Dimensions: wingspan 24 ft (7.32 m); length 31 ft 9 in (9.68 m); height 9 ft 7½ in (2.93 m); wing area 175.00 sq ft (16.26 m²)

This Finnish Gnat F.Mk 1 was modified for tactical reconnaissance duties, with an oblique camera mounted behind a lower forward fuselage window. So impressed was Finland with the Gnat that the country chose the aircraft over the cheaper option of buying US-surplus F-86 Sabres.

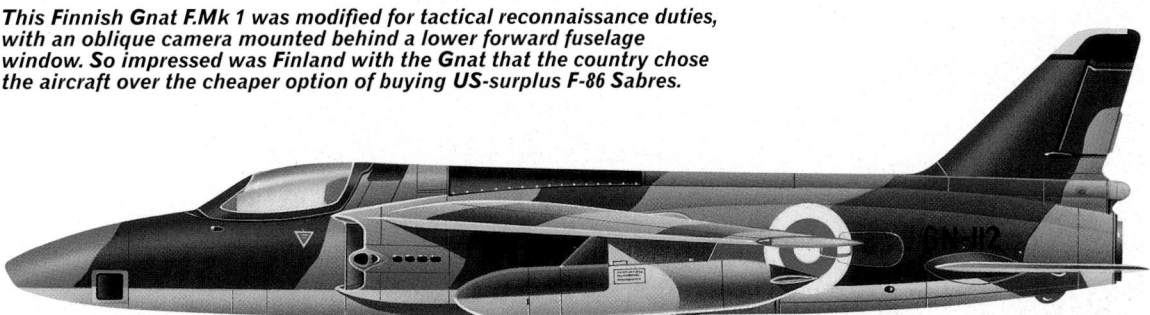

Ford Tri-Motor

For many years aviation enthusiasts have argued whether William B. Stout was the designer of the historic **Ford Tri-Motor**. There is, of course, no doubt that he designed the **2-AT Pullman** which the Stout Metal Airplane Company was producing in early 1925. In August of that year Stout's organisation was acquired by the Ford Motor Company, of which it became a division, and almost immediately development of a three-engined version of the Pullman was initiated under the designation **Ford 3-AT Tri-Motor**. This particular tri-motor was clearly derived directly from the Pullman: a high-wing cantilever monoplane of all-metal construction, it incorporated the type of corrugated metal skin used on the 2-AT and which was a feature of the Ford series. However, whereas the 2-AT with its single Liberty engine had been a good-looking machine, the one-off 3-AT, with three uncowled radial engines mounted one on each wing and one low on a modified nose, must be numbered among the category of ugly air transports. Not surprisingly no more were built.

The following **4-AT** differed very considerably, though its derivation from the Pullman was still discernible in the retention of the 2-AT's unusually shaped cabin windows. First flown on 11 June 1926, the 4-AT was of the same basic airframe configuration, with a braced tail unit and fixed tailskid landing gear that introduced much refined main units. Accommodation was provided for a crew of two in an open cockpit forward of the wing, with eight passengers in an enclosed cabin. One of the three 200-hp (149-kW) Wright Whirlwind J-4 radial engines was mounted neatly in the nose of the fuselage and the other two in strut-braced nacelles, one beneath each wing. This configuration remained virtually unchanged until production ended in 1933, but a considerable number of variants were produced in the two main production versions, the 4-AT and the larger-capacity **5-AT** introduced in 1928.

Dubbed the 'Tin Goose', the Tri-Motor also appeared with a variety of official and unofficial modifications, and the type was operated with wheel, float and ski landing gear. The machine also served with the US Army under the designations **XC-3**, **C-3**, **C-3A**, **C-4**, **C-4A**, **C-4B** and **C-9** (total of 13 aircraft) and the US Navy/Marine Corps as **XJR-1**, **JR-2**, **JR-3**, **RR-1**, **RR-2**, **RR-3**, **RR-4** and **RR-5** (total of nine aircraft). If proof of the Tri-Motor's longevity were needed, it is sufficient to remember that there were examples of the Tri-Motor still in revenue-earning service during the 1980s.

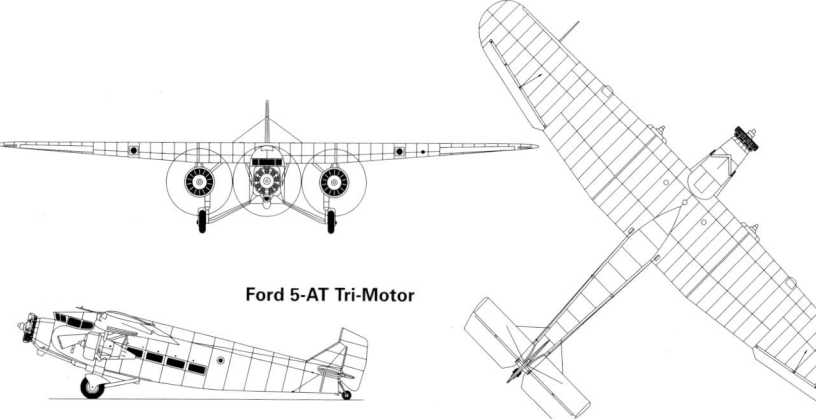

Ford 5-AT Tri-Motor

Above: This C-4A is typical of Tri-Motors in USAAC service. The aircraft were rugged and dependable freight and personnel transports.

Below: The 5-AI-CS variant of the Tri-Motor required increased keel area, a need satisfied by the addition of a ventral fin at the tail.

Scenic Airways of Las Vegas, Nevada, flew this 5-AT into the 1980s. Its duties included sightseeing flights over the Grand Canyon and it may well have become the last commercially active Tri-motor on the US civil register.

SPECIFICATION	
Ford 5-AT-D Tri-Motor	(5640 m); range 550 miles (885 km)
Type: one/two-crew transport	**Weights:** empty 7,840 lb
Powerplant: three Pratt & Whitney R-1340-C1 or -SC1 Wasp radial piston engines each rated at 420 hp (313 kW)	(3556 kg); maximum take-off 13,500 lb (6123 kg)
Performance: maximum speed 150 mph (241 km/h) at optimum altitude; cruising speed 122 mph (196 km/h) at optimum altitude; initial climb rate 1,100 ft (335 m) per minute; service ceiling 18,500 ft	**Dimensions:** wingspan 77 ft 10 in (23.72 m); length 50 ft 3 in (15.32 m); height 12 ft 8 in (3.86 m); wing area 835.00 sq ft (77.57 m²)
	Payload: up to 17 passengers carried in an enclosed cabin within the context of a 3,743-lb (1698-kg) maximum payload

Variants

4-AT-A: original production version; 14 built
4-AT-B: 1927 version with 220-hp (177-kW) Whirlwind J-5 engines and seating for up to 12 passengers; 39 built
4-AT-C: as 4-AT-B but with nose engine replaced by one 400-hp (298-kW) Pratt & Whitney Wasp radial; one built
4-AT-D: three aircraft similar to 4-AT-B but each with different engines and minor modifications
4-AT-E: generally as 4-AT-B but with three 300-hp (224-kW) Whirlwind J-6-9 engines; 24 built
4-AT-F: one aerodynamically refined aircraft based on the 4-AT-E
5-AT-A: production version introduced in 1928 with the wing span increased by 3 ft 10 in (1.17 m), seating for 13 passengers and power provided by three 420-hp (313-kW) Wasp radials; three built
5-AT-B: similar to 5-AT-A but with seats for 15 passengers, 41 built
5-AT-C: similar to 5-AT-A but with seats for 17 passengers; 51 built
5-AT-CS: seaplane version (with two Edo floats) of 5-AT-C; one built
5-AT-D: introduced a major change from the 5-AT-C by having the wing mounted 8 in (0.20 m) higher to increase cabin headroom but otherwise generally similar; 20 built
5-AT-DS: seaplane version (Edo floats) of 5-AT-D; one built
5-AT-E: proposed version with outboard engines relocated to the wing's leading edges

6-AT-A: equivalent to 5-AT-C except for having three 300-hp (224-kW) Whirlwind J-6-9 engines; three built
6-AT-AS: seaplane version (Edo floats) of 6-AT-A; one built
7-AT-A: redesignation of one 6-AT-A following installation of a 420-hp (313-kW) Wasp engine in the nose; later converted to 5-AT-C configuration
8-AT: freighter conversion of one 5-AT-C with the two outer engines removed
9-AT: redesignation of one 4-AT-B following installation of three 300-hp (224-kW) Wasp Junior engines
11-AT: redesignation of one 4-AT-E following installation of three 225-hp (168-kW) Packard Diesel engines; later converted to 4-AT-B configuration
13-A: redesignation of one 5-AT-D following installation of one 575-hp (429-kW) Wright Cyclone in the nose position and two 300-hp (224-kW) Whirlwind J-6-9 engines outboard; later restored to 5-AT-D standard
14-A: started life as four-engined **10-A** but redesignated when fitted with one 1,100-hp (820-kW) and two 715-hp (533-kW) Hispano-Suiza engines; accommodation for 40 passengers; a single machine was built but not flown
XB-906: designation of a single 5-AT-C modified as a bomber; crashed during manufacturer's trials

Fouga CM.8

The first aircraft in the Fouga CM.8 family was the **CM.8R-13 Sylphe**. This was a development of the **CM.8-13** glider with the powerplant of one 243-lb st (1.08-kN) Turboméca Piméné turbojet engine, and the first flight on 14 July 1949 was also the first flight of any Turboméca engine. A refined version was the **CM.8R-9.8 Cyclope**, which first flew on 31 January 1951 and featured a wing of reduced span. Many versions of the Cyclope were built, these including the **Cyclope II** and **Cyclope III** with the 353-lb st (1.57-kN) Palas turbojet engine. Then came an important development: the **CM.8R-8.3 Midjet** was a competition and aerobatic

Variants

Gemeaux II: designation when powered by one 606-lb st (2.70-kN) Turboméca Marboré I turbojet; first flown 16 June 1951
Gemeaux III: designation when powered by one Marboré II turbojet engine; flown on 24 August 1951 with prototype developing 772 lb st (3.43 kN), and on 2 January 1952 with production engine developing 882 lb st (3.92 kN)
Gemeaux IV: designation with one 441-lb st (1.96-kN) Turboméca Aspin I turbofan installed; first flown on 6 November 1951
Gemeaux V: final designation when powered by one 794-lb st (3.53-kN) Aspin II turbofan engine; first flown on 21 June 1952

SPECIFICATION

Fouga CM.88-R Gemeaux III
Type: single-seat engine test-bed aircraft
Powerplant: one Turboméca Marboré II turbojet engine rated at 882 lb st (3.92 kN)
Performance: maximum speed 249 mph (400 km/h) at sea level; cruising speed 186 mph (300 km/h) at optimum altitude; service ceiling 32,810 ft (10000 m); endurance 1 hour
Weights: empty 1962 lb (890 kg); maximum take-off 2,579 lb (1170 kg)
Dimensions: wingspan 35 ft 3½ in (10.76 m); length 21 ft 10¼ in (6.66 m); height 6 ft 4 in (1.93 m); wing area 137.78 sq ft (12.80 m²)

type of which 12 were built with the Palas engine but the wingspan further reduced from 28 ft 9 in (8.76 m) to 23 ft 2 in (7.06 m).

To provide a quickly-built aircraft to serve as a test-bed for a number of Turboméca engines, Fouga decided to combine two CM.8R-9.8 airframes. Using port and starboard outer wing panels, the airframes were united forward by a new wing centre-section and at the rear by the inboard sections of their butterfly tail units. This **CM.88-R Gemeaux I** first flew on 6 March 1951, power being provided by two 220-lb st (0.96-kN) Piméné turbojets, giving this version a maximum

The Cyclope featured a pylon-mounted turbojet above the fuselage and 'tooth-like' airbrakes which extended upwards from the upper wing surfaces.

In its original Gemeaux I form, the CM.88-R was powered by a pair of small turbojets, but later forms featured a single, centrally-mounted, engine.

level speed of 177 mph (285 km/h). Development is believed to have ended soon after the **Gemeaux V** version had finished its series of tests.

Fouga CM.170 Magister and CM.175 Zéphyr

Notable as the first jet trainer to enter service anywhere in the world, and also for its use of a butterfly tail, the aircraft later known as the **Aérospatiale Magister** was the result of a requirement issued by the French air force, and was designed and initially built by the Fouga company.

The result of the new design exercise was a trim monoplane of light alloy semi-monocoque construction. The core of the machine was the oval section fuselage, which carried the pupil and instructor in tandem in a pressurised cockpit under a large and heavily framed canopy with hinged sections for access and

egress. The powerplant of two small turbojets was attached to the sides of the fuselage. The mid-set wing was of high aspect ratio and without dihedral, and its two panels were tapered in thickness and chord, carried fuel tanks at their tips to supplement the internal capacity in two fuselage tanks, and had outboard ailerons and inboard flaps along the full span of their trailing edges. The airframe was completed by the landing gear, which was of the tricycle type with main units that retracted inward into the underside of the inner wings and a nose unit that folded neatly into the forward fuselage.

Following the maiden

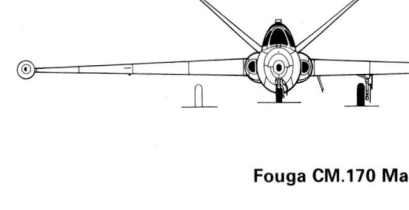

Fouga CM.170 Magister

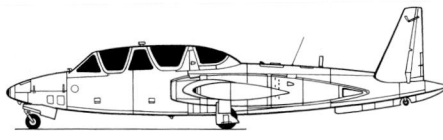

flight of the first of three **CM.170 Magister** prototypes on 23 July 1952, orders were placed in June 1953 for 10 pre-production aircraft and then in January 1954 for quantity production. In 1958, the Potez group assumed responsibility for Fouga activities and continued both production and development of the CM.170. This activity was, in turn, taken over by Sud-Aviation in

Above: In addition to its arrester hook, the Zéphyr was fitted with rearward-sliding canopies rather than the rearward-hinging items of the Magister.

Right: A variation on the Magister theme was the four-seat CM.191. The type was not a practical rival to existing executive aircraft types.

Above: In a market already satisfied with the Magister and other contemporary training aircraft, the Super Magister failed to pick up sales.

Right: Bangladesh had replaced all of its Magisters with another veteran jet trainer – the Cessna T-37 – by 1997.

April 1967, and production of the Magister continued into 1970, by which time Sud-Aviation had been absorbed into Aérospatiale.

First flown on 7 July 1954, the pre-production type was to the **CM.170-1 Magister** standard that was continued into the early production aircraft, of which the first made its maiden flight on 29 February 1956. Production of the CM.170 in France totalled 622 to meet orders from the French air force (400) and navy (32) as well as export sales to the air forces of Austria, Belgium, Brazil, Cambodia, Congo Léopoldville, Finland, the Federal Republic of Germany, Israel and Lebanon. In addition, the Flugzeug Union Süd organisation in Germany built 188, Valmet in Finland built 62 and IAI in Israel built 36, bringing overall production including prototypes to some 921.

The CM.170-1 had the powerplant of two Turboméca Marboré IIA engines, but these were replaced in the **CM.170-2** by Marboré VIC engines each rated at 1,058 lb st (4.71 kN). Differences that then distinguished the **CM.170-3**, first flown on 8 June 1964 and later redesignated as the **CM.173 Super Magister**, included an enlarged fuel capacity and Martin-Baker ejection seats under a modified canopy. The variant for the Aéronavale was the carrier-capable **CM.175 Zéphyr**, which was based on the CM.170-1 but had an arrester hook among other changes. The first of two prototypes flew on 30 May 1959.

Some 150 Magister aircraft remained in service up to the mid-1990s with the Armée de l'Air for initial flight training of career officers, and for miscellaneous duties including communications/ liaison in base flights and at squadron level. Similarly, in 2000, about 10 still remain operational with

the Force Aérienne Belge for communications and continuation flying duties.

The withdrawal from service of Magisters by their original purchasers, led to the acquisition of small quantities of used CM.170s by several other air forces for use in the basic training and/or light attack roles, the latter with an underwing armament of bombs and/or gun and rocket pods. Current or recent among these operators are Algeria, Bangladesh, Cameroon, Gabon, Ireland, Libya, Morocco, El Salvador, Senegambia and Togo.

The Israeli Defence Force/Air Force retains the Magister in a training role, after adding nine ex-Belgian and possibly other second-hand examples to its original import purchase and indigenous production of 82 machines. Between 1981 and 1986, some 80 were modernised by Bedek Division of IAI to have uprated Marboré VI engines, new avionics and other upgrades, being then renamed **Tzukit** (thrush) in the Advanced Multi-mission Improved Trainer (AMIT) programme.

An interesting development of the basic type that proceeded no further than the prototype stage was the **Potez-Heinkel CM.191** that made its

maiden flight on 19 March 1962 as a Super Magister development with a revised and wider forward fuselage providing four-seat accommodation under a single-piece canopy. The type was offered in the **CM.191-A** military form for the training, liaison and reconnaissance roles, and the **CM.191-B** civil form for the touring and executive roles.

SPECIFICATION	
Aérospatiale CM.170-1 Magister	fuel
Type: multi-role flying and weapons training aircraft with light attack capability	**Weights:** empty 4,750 lb (2150 kg); maximum take-off 7,055 lb (3200 kg)
Powerplant: two Turboméca Marboré IIA turbojets each rated at 882 lb st (3.92 kN)	**Dimensions:** wingspan 39 ft 10 in (12.15 m) with tip tanks; length 33 ft (10.06 m); height 9 ft 2 in (2.80 m); wing area 186.22 sq ft (17.30 m²)
Performance: maximum speed 444 mph (715 km/h) at 29,525 ft (9000 m); initial climb rate 3,346 ft (1020 m) per minute; service ceiling 36,070 ft (11000 m); range 746 miles (1200 km) with auxiliary	**Armament:** provision for two fixed forward-firing machine guns in the nose, and up to 220 lb (100 kg) of disposable stores carried on two underwing hardpoints

Found aircraft

Found Brothers Aviation was formed at Malton, Ontario during 1948 to produce the **Found FBA-1A** four-seat cabin monoplane designed by Captain S. R. Found. Powered by a 140-hp (104-kW) de Havilland Gipsy Major engine, the FBA-1A recorded its

maiden flight on 13 July 1949. At a much later date the FBA-1A was developed into the all-metal four/five-seat **FBA-2** which, when flown in prototype form on 11 August 1960, had the fixed tricycle landing gear intended as standard for the production **FBA-2B**. However, it was with

conventional tailwheel landing gear that the redesignated **FBA-2C** production version first flew on 9 May 1962. Available with float or ski alighting gear as optional alternatives to the standard wheeled landing gear, the FBA-2C introduced a more powerful engine, a slight increase in cabin length, and enlarged rear cabin doors to simplify the handling of cargo. When

production ended in favour of an improved version known as the **Centennial 100**, a total of 34 had been built.

Detail design work on the Centennial 100 began in October 1966 and the prototype, powered by the 290-hp (216-kW) Lycoming IO-540-G1D5 engine, lifted off on its first flight during 7 April 1967. Three prototypes and two production examples of the Centennial took part in the flight test programme, but shortly after award of the type's certification in July 1968 the Found company went out of business.

In the 1990s the

company returned to existence as Found Aircraft Canada Inc., and in November 1996 flew the first example of the improved FBA-2C as the **FBA-2C Bush Hawk-260** with the 260-hp (194-kW) Lycoming IO-540-D4A5 engine. This development received its Canadian certification in 1998 in a form that allowed an increase in maximum take-off weight and also the use of the 300-hp (224-kW) IO-540-L1C5 engine to create the **FBA-2C Bush Hawk-300**. Production of the two models began in the late 1990s.

SPECIFICATION	
Found FBA-2C	per minute; service ceiling 16,000 ft (4875 m); range 600 miles (966 km)
Type: four/five-seat light transport	
Powerplant: one Lycoming O-540-A1D flat-six piston engine rated at 250 hp (186 kW)	**Weights:** empty 1,550 lb (703 kg); maximum take-off 2,950 lb (1338 kg)
Performance: maximum speed 147 mph (237 km/h) at 5,000 ft (1525 m); cruising speed 142 mph (229 km/h) at optimum altitude; initial climb rate 1,100 ft (335 m)	**Dimensions:** wingspan 36 ft (10.97 m); length 25 ft 6 in (7.77 m); height 7 ft 9½ in (2.37 m); wing area 180.00 sq ft (16.72 m²)

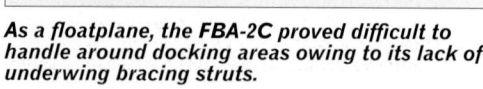

As a floatplane, the FBA-2C proved difficult to handle around docking areas owing to its lack of underwing bracing struts.

Fournier aircraft

In 1960 René Fournier designed and built a single-seat ultra-light aircraft which he designated as the **Fournier RF-01**. The designer's intention was to combine the characteristics of a light sporting aircraft with those of a sailplane, and the RF-01 was of extremely clean design and powered by a 25-hp (19-kW) modified Volkswagen flat-four car engine. Successful testing of the prototype brought French government support for the establishment of a production line. A second RF-01 prototype and two **RF-2** pre-production aircraft were followed by the first **RF-3** production machine that initially took to the air in March 1963. This model gained certification in June of the same year, allowing the delivery of production aircraft from November of that year.

Before this time Fournier had entered into partnership with Alpavia SA, which became responsible for manufacture of the RF-3. Some 95 RF-3s were built before development of an improved **RF-4D** superseded it. A further production change came in 1966, when Sportavia-Putzer was formed in West Germany to take over production of Fournier designs. A total of 160 RF-4Ds was built, and several of these machines

achieved notable flights: in May 1969, for example, Miro Slovak flew an RF-4D across the North Atlantic in 175 hours 42 minutes 7.11 seconds.

Later developments of the basic RF-4 design included a 'stretched' **RF-5** two-seater and the **Sportavia SFS 31 Milan** which combined the fuselage and tail unit of the RF-4 with the 49-ft 2½-in (15.00-m) span wing of the Scheibe SF-27M sailplane.

In December 1970 Fournier began the design of a side-by-side two-seat lightplane under the designation **RF-6**; this was later developed into the **Sportavia RS 180 Sportsman**. In the early 1970s Fournier established Avions Fournier at Nitray, near Montlouis, and at this new facility developed a slightly smaller version with a less powerful engine, although still seating two side-by-side, as the **RF-6B Club**. The prototype first flew on 12 March 1974 with the powerplant of one 90-hp (67-kW) O-200-E engine. The RF-6B was designed for training, including aerobatic training, and its structure was stressed to limits of +6 *g* and -3 *g*. The first of five pre-production aircraft recorded its maiden flight on 4 March 1976, its O-200-A engine being

adopted for all subsequent **RF-6B-100** aircraft produced by Avions Fournier. Production ended in 1980 after the completion of 45 aircraft, one additional airframe being used as an **RF-6B-120** development machine that first flew on 14 August 1980 with the uprated powerplant of one 118-hp (88-kW) Lycoming O-235-L2A engine.

Subsequently, Slingsby Engineering Ltd in the UK (long known as a designer and builder of sailplanes, and from 5 July 1982 known as Slingsby Aviation Ltd) gained a manufacturing and marketing licence from Avions Fournier. Slingsby then concentrated on development of the RF-6B-120 under the designation **T67**, and the first of a batch of 10 **T67A** aircraft with the O-235-L2A engine first flew on

The RF-4 (background) and two-seat RF-5 have been the most widely-produced Fournier designs. Over 100 examples of each have been built.

15 May 1981. Further developments of the RF-6 are listed under the Slingsby company. Later Fournier designs include the **RF-9** whose production is undertaken in Germany

by Gomolzig, and the **RF-10** whose production is undertaken in France by Aérostructure and in Brazil by Aeromot under the revised designation **Ximango**.

SPECIFICATION

Fournier RF-6B-100
Type: two-seat training and touring aircraft
Powerplant: one Rolls-Royce (Continental) O-200-A flat-four piston engine rated at 100 hp (75 kW)
Performance: maximum speed 124 mph (200 km/h) at sea level;

cruising speed 112 mph (180 km/h) at sea level; service ceiling 13,125 ft (4000 m); range 404 miles (650 km)
Weights: empty 1,102 lb (500 kg); maximum take-off 1,653 lb (750 kg)
Dimensions: wingspan 34 ft 5½ in (10.50 m); length 22 ft 11¾ in (7.00 m); height 8 ft 3 in (2.52 m); wing area 139.94 sq ft (13.00 m²)

Above: Fournier's first aircraft – the RF-01 – was a small aircraft powered by a Volkswagen car engine. Note the characteristic high-aspect ratio wings.

Left: A fixed tricycle undercarriage was a feature of the fully-aerobatic RF-6B. Around 45 were completed before production was halted.

Friedrichshafen FF 33 and FF 39

Derived from the two-seat **FF 29** patrol/reconnaissance floatplane, the initial Friedrichshafen **FF 33** was flown towards the end of 1914. Generally similar in construction and configuration to its predecessor, except for revised floats, the FF 33 shared also the 120-hp (89-kW) Mercedes D.11 powerplant. As in the FF 29, the pilot occupied the rear cockpit. Only six FF

33s were built for the German navy, being followed by five **FF 33b** aircraft which incorporated a number of changes. In this version the pilot's and observer's positions were reversed, the latter also being provided with a machine-gun on a pivoted mount; two-step floats were introduced; and the Mercedes D.11 was replaced by the more

The Friedrichshafen FF 33 family of floatplanes may be divided into two distinct groups – the scout variants with a three-bay wing format (pictured), and the armed scouts with a two-bay wing.

powerful 160-hp (119-kW) Maybach inline engine.

The most extensively-built version was the **FF 33e**, which introduced the Benz Bz.111 inline engine, longer twin floats which allowed the undertail central float to be deleted and replaced by a ventral fin, and a radio transmitter at the expense of armament. Almost 190 FF 33es are believed to have been built, the final production batch delivered from late 1917 being equipped with dual controls. It was followed by the **FF 33j**, which incorporated a number of aerodynamic refinements and the provision of a radio transmitter and receiver, and the last of the reconnaissance FF 33s was the dual-control **FF 33s** trainer. One FF 33e was operated as a scouting aircraft by the

German auxiliary cruiser, *Wolf*. The forward reconnaissance capability and radio transmitter of this aircraft, named *Wölfchen*, enabled the *Wolf* to gain some notable success against Allied shipping.

The FF 33 was developed also for scout/fighter patrols, the initial **FF 33f** being basically an FF 33e, of reduced span and length but with a machine-gun on a pivoted mount for the observer. Only five were built before production switched to the **FF 33h** (about 50 built) with aerodynamic refinement and the duplication of some inboard wing-bay bracing cables as a safeguard if the observer were compelled to fire his machine-gun forward between the wings. The major production version was the **FF 33l** (about 130 built) which had some further dimensional reduc-

tions to improve manoeuvrability, plus additional refinements to increase performance. One example of the FF 33l was completed with wheeled landing gear for evaluation as a general-purpose biplane under the designation **C.I**. Continued development of the patrol/reconnaissance two-seaters followed with the **FF 39** (14 built), which was basically a refined version of the FF 33e with its 150-hp (112-kW) powerplant replaced by a 200-hp (149-kW) Benz Bz.1V engine. The performance offered by this higher-powered unit resulted in production of the further-improved **FF 49c** with the same Bz.1V engine, a strengthened structure, balanced controls, a radio receiver and transmitter, and a machine-gun for the observer. Introduced in mid-1917, the FF 49c proved

so effective that it remained in service until the end of the war, with between 200 and 250 built by the company and two other sub-contractors. Twenty-five examples of an **FF 49b** bomber variant were built, which differed in having the crew positions reversed, deletion of the observer's machine-gun, and provision for carrying a light bombload.

Final development of the FF 33 family came with the **FF 59c** introduced in

mid-1918. This was basically a version of the FF 39 with a modified tail unit, the wing interplane struts placed further apart, and the inner-bay bracing wires deleted to make it less hazardous for the observer to fire his machine-gun forwards between the wings. The FF 59c had been preceded by single examples of the **FF 59a** and **FF 59b** development aircraft with differing tail units.

Friedrichshafen FF 38 (G II), FF 45 (G III) and FF 62 (G IV)

Although it was best known for its floatplanes, Friedrichshafen was also persuaded by Kober, its chief engineer, to embark on the design of a series of large landplane bombers. The first of these, which appeared in 1915, was the **FF 30** four-bay biplane with a biplane tail unit, a crew of three, and a powerplant of two 150-hp (112-kW) Benz Bz.III engines each driving a two-bladed pusher propeller. The FF 30 was evaluated as the **G I** but was not ordered into production.

A better fate awaited the **G II** that appeared in the first half of 1916 as the **FF 38** development of the G I with a three-bay wing cellule, monoplane tail unit, defensive armament of two 0.31-in (7.92-mm) LMG 14 Parabellum trainable machine-guns, offensive armament of 2,205 lb (1000 kg) of bombs and powerplant of two 200-hp (149-kW) Benz Bz.IV engines each driving a two-bladed pusher propeller. A small batch of G II produc-

tion aircraft was completed, most of them by Daimler Motorengesellschaft Werke.

Developed from the FF 38 as the **FF 45** with outer wing panels derived from those of the FF 30, the **G III** was the partner of the Gotha G V in constituting the main strength of the German Bombengeschwadern (bomber groups) on the Western Front from a time early in 1917 to the end of World War I in November 1918. The G III was thus a four-bay biplane of mixed metal and wood construc-

tion with fixed tailskid landing gear and the powerplant of two 260-hp (194-kW) Mercedes D.IVa engines, each driving a two-bladed wooden propeller of the pusher type, in substantial nacelles with frontal radiators. These nacelles were installed in mid-gap in the Vee-type interplane struts between the outboard ends of the upper- and lower-wing centre sections.

The **G IIIa** was a simple derivative of the G III with slightly less raked wingtips and a compound tail with

Together with the Gotha G.V, the Friedrichshafen G.III formed the backbone of the German night bomber force during 1917-18. Targets included Paris.

biplane horizontal surfaces and twin vertical surfaces. The G III and G IIIa were built by the parent company and also under licence by Daimler Motorengesellschaft Werke (245 G III and G IIIa bombers) and Hanseatische Flugzeug-Werke (93 G III and G IIIa bombers). The G III and G IIIa saw extensive use on the Western Front, which was their sole operational area. The types' greatest asset was their ability to cover long ranges with a sizeable bombload, and the aircraft were there-

fore often used to bomb Paris and were probably also involved in the German bomber offensive against England.

The **G IV**, produced only in small numbers during 1918, was the **FF 62** derivative of the G IIIa with a shortened nose (ending just forward of the centre sections' leading edges), defensive armament limited to just one 0.31-in (7.92-mm) LMG 14 trainable machine-gun in the dorsal position, tractor rather than pusher engines, and reduced dimensions.

The G.IIIa derivative was built exclusively under licence by the Daimler Works and Hanseatische Flugzeug-Werke. Note the twin vertical tailfins.

Fuji LM and KM Nikko (TL-1, T-3, T-5 and T-7)

Fuji's KM-2B primary trainer represents an interesting design concept. Rather than creating an all-new design, Fuji combined the basic airframe of its KM-2 with the tandem two-seat cockpit of the T-34.

81-5502

502

With the end of World War II, the development and manufacture of aircraft in Japan was prohibited under the country's surrender terms, and it was not until April 1952 that approval was given for revival of the nation's aircraft industry. In July 1953 Fuji Heavy Industries was established as successor to the well-known Nakajima company, its aviation division being initiated by licensed construction of the Beech Model 45 Mentor. From the Mentor the company developed the **LM-1 Nikko** liaison and general-purpose aircraft, which differed primarily in the removal of military equipment and the provision of a four/five-seat interior and increased fuel capacity. The LM-1 was powered by the 225-hp (168-kW) Continental O-470-13 engine, but introduction of the more powerful 340-hp (254-kW) Lycoming IGSO-480 resulted in the revised designation **LM-2**. Both the LM-1 and LM-2 entered service with the Japan Ground Self-Defence Force to the extent of 27 and two re-engined LM-1 aircraft respectively, the last of these machines being retired during 1981–82.

Contemporary with the LM-1 was the generally similar four-seat civil **KM**, which differed in having a version of the 340-hp (254-kW) Lycoming IGSO-480 engine that was introduced in the LM-2. A number of KMs was supplied to the Japanese government for use in its civil pilot training

programme. Development for military use followed with the first flight of the **KM-2 Super Nikko** on 16 July 1962. A two-seat trainer with side-by-side accommodation and an IGSO-480 engine, the type entered service with the Japan Maritime Self-Defence Force during September 1962, a total of 32 such aircraft eventually being procured with the designation **Kornadori** (robin). Two examples were ordered by the JGSDF under the designation **Fuji TL-I**, and both of these aircraft were delivered during 1981.

Needing a replacement in the primary flight training role for its T-34As, the Japanese Air Self-Defence Force opted for the **KM-2B**, which combined the airframe and powerplant of the KM-2 with the two-seat cockpit of the T-34. The first such machine flew in September 1974 and 50 production aircraft were delivered between March 1978 and February 1982 to the JASDF, which operates the type with the designation **T-3**.

The **KM-2 Kai** is basically a turboprop-powered version of the KM-2 for the JMSDF. The **KM-2D** prototype was a KM-2 converted with the Allison 250-B17D turboprop engine flat-rated at 350 shp (261 kW), and

first flew in June 1984. Other improvements include a modernised cockpit under a sliding canopy and a slightly swept vertical tail surface, and significant improvements were also achieved in fields of vision, payload and cockpit volume.

The JMSDF ordered an initial 24 aircraft in March 1987, the first production standard KM-2 Kai flew in April 1988, and deliveries began in August of the

same year to the JMSDF, which operates the type with the designation **T-5**. Production totalled some 34 aircraft.

Ordered to the extent of 50 aircraft delivered from 2000 for service as the JASDF's next-generation basic flying trainer, the **T-7** is a development of the T-3 with the considerably revised powerplant of one 400-shp (298-kW) Rolls-Royce Allison 250 turboprop engine.

A side-by-side two-seat cockpit arrangement distinguished the original KM-2. The cockpit canopy slid backwards for access.

SPECIFICATION

Fuji KM-2B
Type: two-seat primary flying trainer
Powerplant: one Lycoming IGSO-480-A1F6 flat-six piston engine rated at 340 hp (254 kW)
Performance: maximum speed 228 mph (367 km/h) at 8,000 ft (2440 m); cruising speed 158 mph (254 km/h) at 8,000 ft (2440 m);

service ceiling 26,800 ft (8170 m); range 600 miles (966 km)
Weights: empty 2,469 lb (1120 kg); maximum take-off 3,400 lb (1542 kg)
Dimensions: wingspan 32 ft 10 in (10.01 m); length 26 ft 4¼ in (8.03 m); height 9 ft 11 in (3.02 m); wing area 177.61 sq ft (16.50 m²)

Fuji T1F (T-1 Hatsutaka)

Fuji was already well advanced in the design of a small axial-flow turbojet, the JO-1, when the Japanese Air Self-Defence Force issued a requirement for a turbojet-powered successor to its T-6G Texan advanced trainers. Fuji's response was a very attractive type clearly inspired in its basic design by the North American F-86 Sabre, though the fuselage was of longer and finer line, and incorporated a tandem-seat cockpit section under a rear-hinged clamshell canopy. The requirement also elicited responses from Kawasaki and Shin Meiwa, but in July 1956 the JASDF contracted with Fuji for the construction of two prototypes of its **T1F**.

Development of the JO-3 turbojet planned for the type had meanwhile been transferred to Ishikawajima-Harima with the revised

designation J3, but as this engine was suffering development problems, the initial model was revised as the **T1F2** with an imported British engine, the Bristol Aero Engines (later Bristol Siddeley) Orpheus turbojet.

The first T1F2 prototype flew in January 1958 with the 4,050-lb st (18.02-kN) Orpheus BOr.1 turbojet, while the second prototype had the Orpheus BOr.3 engine. The type soon showed itself to be well suited to the JASDF's needs, and was ordered in two batches, each of 22

aircraft, for service under the designation **T-1A Hatsutaka** (young hawk), the name later being dropped. Deliveries of the two batches were completed in June 1961 and July 1962.

In May 1960 Fuji flew a **T1F2** prototype converted to T1F1 standard with the 2.646-lb st (11.77-kN) Ishikawajima-Harima J3-IHI-3 turbojet. Flight trials confirmed that the new variant was viable, despite its reduced power and thus its lower performance, and a production batch of 20 aircraft was ordered for service under the designation **T-1B**. These aircraft

were delivered between September 1962 and June 1963.

In April 1965 Fuji flew a **T1F3** prototype with the powerplant of one 3,086-lb (13.73-kN) J3-IHI-7 turbojet, and as this engine provided a considerable boost in performance, the JASDF decided to re-engine its whole T-1 fleet for service with the designation **T-1C**. Only three aircraft had been converted, however, before the service decided to terminate the programme.

Clearly inspired by the F-86 Sabre, the Fuji T-1 proved to be an excellent trainer.

SPECIFICATION

Fuji T1F2 (T-1A Hatsutaka)
Type: two-seat intermediate flying and armament trainer
Powerplant: one Rolls-Royce (Bristol Siddeley) Orpheus BOr.3 Mk 805 turbojet engine rated at 4,000 lb st (17.79 kN)
Performance: maximum speed 575 mph (925 km/h) at 36,000 ft (10975 m) but limited in practice to 534 mph (859 km/h); cruising speed 385 mph (620 km/h) at 30,000 ft (9145 m); maximum rate of climb at sea level 6,500 ft (1981 m) per minute; service ceiling 47,245 ft (14400 m); range 1,156 miles (1860 km) with drop tanks
Weights: empty 5,335 lb (2420 kg); maximum take-off

11,023 lb (5000 kg)
Dimensions: wingspan 34 ft 5 in (10.49 m); length 39 ft 9¼ in (12.12 m); height 13 ft 4½ in (4.08 m); wing area 239.18 sq ft (22.22 m²)
Armament: one 0.5-in (12.7-mm) Browning M53-2 fixed forward-firing machine-gun in the nose, plus up to 1,500 lb (680 kg) of disposable stores carried on two underwing hardpoints, and generally comprising two AIM-9 AAMs, or two free-fall bombs, or two napalm tanks, or four 5-in (127-mm) rockets, or two multiple launchers each carrying seven 2¾-in (70-mm) air-to-surface unguided rockets, or two 0.5-in (12.7-mm) machine-gun pods

Fuji FA-300 and Rockwell Commander 700 and 710

In collaboration with Fuji Heavy Industries in Japan, Rockwell International's General Aviation Division was involved in the development of a twin-engined six/eight-seat light transport aircraft. Design work began in Japan during 1971, the aircraft then having the designation **Fuji FA-300**, and on 28 June 1974 Fuji and Rockwell signed an agreement covering this machine's development as a joint venture, with Rockwell designating the aircraft **Rockwell Commander 700** for marketing efforts in North America.

Of low-wing cantilever monoplane configuration, the Commander 700 had a fuselage constructed for pressurisation, a conventional tail unit with a swept vertical surface, and retractable tricycle landing gear. The powerplant comprised two Lycoming turbocharged engines, these being wing-mounted in well-streamlined nacelles. The first of five prototypes made its initial flight in Japan on

13 November 1975 while the second, assembled by Rockwell, flew on 25 February 1976. Japanese certification was gained on 19 May 1977, and American certification followed on 31 October 1977.

Development of a generally similar aircraft proceeded simultaneously. This **Commander 710** differed mainly in its uprated powerplant of two 450-hp (336-kW) engines. The first of two prototypes flew in Japan on 22 December 1976, and Japanese certification was gained early in 1979. Later in the year it was reported that development was being continued, the Model 710 then being flown with winglets at the tips of its wing. Then Rockwell's decision late in 1979 to sell off its General Aviation Division to Gulfstream American Corporation brought termination of the collaboration agreement with Fuji. At that time Rockwell had delivered 25 Commander 700s and, under the termination agreement, Fuji

The FA-300/Rockwell Commander offered standard accommodation for a pilot and co-pilot plus four passengers, all in a pressurised, air-conditioned, heated and ventilated environment.

acquired worldwide manufacturing and marketing rights for these aircraft. It was then believed that if production was initiated by the Japanese company, efforts would be concentrated on the Commander 710, but in the event Fuji did not persevere with the type, and production of the series ended in the early 1980s.

SPECIFICATION	
Fuji/Rockwell Commander 700 **Type:** two-crew light transport **Powerplant:** two Lycoming TIO-549-R2AD flat-six piston engines each rated at 340 hp (254 kW) **Performance:** maximum speed 254 mph (409 km/h) at 17,000 ft (5180 m); cruising speed 244 mph (393 km/h) at 21,500 ft (6555 m); initial climb rate 1,633 ft (498 m) per minute; service ceiling	27,400 ft (8350 m); range 1,384 miles (2227 km) **Weights:** empty 4,704 lb (2134 kg); maximum take-off 6,947 lb (3151 kg) **Dimensions:** wingspan 42 ft 5½ in (12.94 m); length 39 ft 5¾ in (12.03 m); height 13 ft 3½ in (4.05 m); wing area 200.20 sq ft (18.60 m²) **Payload:** up to six passengers carried in an enclosed cabin

Funk Model B

Funk's Model B was of typical lightplane layout, with a braced high-set wing, a conventional tail unit and fixed tailwheel landing gear.

The brothers Howard and Joe Funk of Kansas City, Missouri, who had gained experience of aircraft design and construction as home builders of gliders and sailplanes, in 1934 embarked on the design of a small two-seat cabin monoplane. Identified as the **Model B**, the aircraft was similar in configuration to the well-known Piper Cub. Its major difference from other lightplanes of the period lay in its powerplant, which was based on the 63-hp (47-kW) Funk E engine, which was an extensively modified Ford motor car engine.

Successful testing of the prototype led to the establishment in 1939 of the Akron Aircraft Company Inc. at Akron, Ohio, to produce the Model B. By

the time that quantity construction was in progress, however, it had been decided to switch to the 75-hp (56-kW) Lycoming GO-145-C2 flat-four engine to create the **Model B-75-L**. During 1941 the company moved to Coffeyville, Kansas, continuing production there as the Funk Aircraft Company until after the USA's December 1941 involvement in World War

II. One Model B-75-L was impressed into service by the USAAF under the designation **UC-92**.

Production of the Model B restarted in 1946, the introduction of some small refinements and the Continental C85-12 engine resulting in the revised designation **Model B-85-C** and the name **Bee**. Declining sales brought an end to the company's activities in 1948, by which time more than 300 Model Bs of all versions had been built.

SPECIFICATION	
Funk Model B-85-C **Type:** two-seat lightplane **Powerplant:** one Continental C85-12F flat-four piston engine rated at 85 hp (63 kW) **Performance:** maximum speed 117 mph (188 km/h) at sea level; maximum cruising speed 105 mph (169 km/h) at optimum altitude;	initial climb rate 810 ft (247 m) per minute; service ceiling 15,500 ft (4725 m); range 365 miles (587 km) **Weights:** empty 870 lb (395 kg); maximum take off 1,350 lb (612 kg) **Dimensions:** wingspan 35 ft (10.67 m); length 20 ft 2 in (6.15 m); height 6 ft 1 in (1.85 m); wing area 169.00 sq ft (15.70 m²)

General Aircraft G.A.L.38 Fleet Shadower

Working to meet the Admiralty requirement that also resulted in the Airspeed AS.39 Fleet Shadower, General Aircraft was no more successful than Airspeed in producing an effective carrierborne aircraft which could provide the capability for remaining in contact with an enemy naval force by night. As a result, only a single prototype of the unusually-

Comparable to the AS.39 Fleet Shadower in terms of its general ugliness, the General Aircraft G.A.L.38 differed most significantly from its rival in having a tricycle undercarriage. Neither design won any production orders.

configured **General Aircraft G.A.L.38 Fleet Shadower** was built.

General Aircraft G.A.L.38 Fleet Shadower (continued)

General Aircraft adopted a sesquiplane configuration for its Fleet Shadower, the lower wing having about one-third of the span of the upper. Of all-wooden construction, the G.A.L.38 had a conventional tail unit with a tall fin and rudder, fixed tricycle landing gear and the powerplant of four Pobjoy Niagara V engines mounted in nacelles on the leading edge of the foldable upper wing. The fuselage accommodated the pilot in a high-set enclosed cockpit forward of the wing, the observer in an extensively glazed compartment located in the extreme nose, and the radio operator in a compartment below and behind the pilot.

Both contending companies used similar blown-flap techniques (the 'blowing' being provided by propeller slipstream) to attain the desired minimum control speed, which was 39 mph (63 km/h) in the case of the G.A.L.38 and, in addition, this type had full-span split trailing-edge flaps on the lower wing.

SPECIFICATION	
General Aircraft G.A.L.38 Fleet Shadower	(1830 m); endurance 11 hours
Type: three-seat carrierborne patrol aircraft	**Weights:** empty 6,153 lb (2791 kg); maximum take-off 9,458 lb (4290 kg)
Powerplant: four Pobjoy Niagara V radial piston engines each rated at 130 hp (97 kW)	**Dimensions:** wingspan 55 ft 10 in (17.02 m); length 36 ft 1 in (11.00 m); height 12 ft 8 in
Performance: maximum speed 115 mph (185 km/h) at optimum altitude; service ceiling 6,000 ft	(3.86 m); wing area 472 sq ft (43.85 m²)

General Aircraft G.A.L.42 Cygnet II

When C.W. Aircraft (Chronander and Waddington) collapsed for lack of finance in 1938, General Aircraft acquired all rights to its **Cygnet** two-seat light monoplane, the first stressed-skin lightplane of all-metal construction to be built and flown in the UK. A conventional cantilever low-wing monoplane with fixed tailwheel landing gear, the **General Aircraft G.A.L.42 Cygnet II** was the company's modified version of the Cygnet prototype with twin fin-and-rudder unit and, later, fixed tricycle landing gear. Production of the Cygnet II began in 1939, but plans to build the type in large numbers were frustrated by the outbreak of World War II. Thus only about 10 such aircraft were completed, five of them being impressed for service with the RAF to familiarise pilots with the take-off and landing qualities of aircraft with tricycle landing gear.

SPECIFICATION	
General Aircraft G.A.L.42 Cygnet II	(185 km/h) at optimum altitude; initial climb rate 800 ft (244 m) per minute; service ceiling 14,000 ft (4265 m); range 445 miles (716 km)
Type: two-seat training and sporting aircraft	
Powerplant: one Blackburn Cirrus Major II inverted inline piston engine rated at 150 hp (112 kW)	**Weights:** empty 1,475 lb (669 kg); maximum take-off 2,200 lb (998 kg)
Performance: maximum speed 135 mph (217 km/h) at optimum altitude; cruising speed 115 mph	**Dimensions:** wingspan 34 ft 6 in (10.52 m); length 23 ft 3 in (7.09 m); height 7 ft (2.13 m); wing area 179.00 sq ft (16.63 m²)

Bearing a passing resemblance to the Miles Messenger (the latter had a third, central fin), the Cygnet II saw limited service with the RAF.

General Aircraft G.A.L.48 Hotspur

The design of the **G.A.L.48 Hotspur** was drawn up to meet the requirements of Air Ministry Specification 10/40. This called for an assault glider that could carry a pilot and seven passengers for a distance of 100 miles (161 km) following release from its tug at a height of 20,000 ft (6095 m). A mid-wing cantilever monoplane of wooden construction, the resultant **Hotspur Mk I** was first flown in November 1940, and in its flight trials revealed its inability to meet the specified performance. Thus only about 20 examples of the Hotspur Mk I were built, although development of the basic concept led to the more successful **Hotspur Mk II** and **Hotspur Mk III** training versions for use by UK military glider training schools.

The Hotspur Mk II differed from the initial version in having a wing reduced in span by 16 ft (4.88 m) and fitted with modified ailerons as well as trailing-edge flaps, a revised cockpit canopy and entrance door, and dual controls. The Hotspur Mk III differed in having an externally braced tail assembly and some changes in equipment. There also appeared the prototype of a **Twin Hotspur**, uniting two standard fuselages by means of a new wing centre-section and tail unit: this was intended for the carriage of 16 airborne troops.

Becoming the primary training glider used by British forces during World War II, more than 1,000 Hotspur Mk II and III gliders were built, mostly by the furniture manufacturer Harris Lebus of Tottenham in north London.

In its Mk I form, the Hotspur fell some 17 miles (27 km) short of its specified gliding range from release at 20,000 ft (6095 m).

SPECIFICATION	
General Aircraft G.A.L.48 Hotspur Mk II	(1632 kg)
Type: one-crew training glider	**Dimensions:** wingspan 45 ft 10¾ in (13.99 m); length 39 ft 3½ in (11.98 m); height 10 ft 10 in (3.30 m); wing area 272.00 sq ft (25.27 m²)
Performance: towing speed 130 mph (209 km/h); gliding speed 90 mph (145 km/h); landing speed 56 mph (90 km/h)	
Weights: empty 1,661 lb (753 kg); maximum tow-off weight 3,598 lb	**Payload:** up to seven troops carried in an enclosed cabin

General Aircraft built only one prototype of the distinctive Twin Hotspur. The aircraft offered more than double the capacity of the Hotspur.

General Aircraft G.A.L.49 and G.A.L.58 Hamilcar

The **G.A.L.49 Hamilcar Mk I** was designed to meet an Air Ministry specification for a transport glider to carry the heavy support equipment needed by airborne troops. General Aircraft was successful in gaining the contract, and there followed 412 exam-

Produced to Air Ministry specification X.4/44, the Hamilcar Mk X could augment the power of its tug with its own Mercury radials.

As the largest Allied glider of the war, the Hamilcar Mk I had a loaded weight which was about 7,000 lb (3175 kg) less than the payload of the Me 321.

SPECIFICATION	
General Aircraft G.A.L.58 Hamilcar Mk X (untowed)	(1135 km) with standard fuel
Type: two-crew power-assisted heavy transport glider	**Weights:** empty 25,510 lb (11571 kg); maximum take-off 32,500 lb (14742 kg)
Powerplant: two Bristol Mercury 31 radial piston engines each rated at 965 hp (720 kW)	**Dimensions:** wingspan 110 ft (33.53 m); length 68 ft (20.73 m); height 20 ft 3 in (6.17 m); wing area 1,657.50 sq ft (153.98 m²)
Performance: maximum speed 145 mph (233 km/h) at optimum altitude; cruising speed 120 mph (193 km/h) at optimum altitude; service ceiling 13,000 ft (3960 m); range 1,675 miles (2696 km) with auxiliary fuel or 705 miles	**Payload:** up to 6,990 lb (3171 kg) of freight carried in an enclosed hold after powered take-off or 17,500 lb (7938 kg) of freight carried in an enclosed hold after assisted take-off

ples of the Hamilcar Mk I, the majority of them constructed under subcontract, to provide the Allies with their largest glider to see service during World War II.

Germany had also developed a large transport glider, the Messerschmitt Me 321, and subsequently decided to power it. General Aircraft made simi-

lar plans for the Hamilcar, so that it could operate as a conventional aircraft with less than half its normal payload, or use its engines to assist take-off at overload weights up to 47,500 lb (21546 kg). Of high-wing cantilever monoplane configuration and having a structure of wood under a skinning of plywood and fabric, the

powered **G.A.L.58 Hamilcar Mk X** differed from the glider only in having structural strengthening, the provision of essential systems, and the installation of two Bristol Mercury engines in nacelles on the wing's leading edges. It was planned to build the type in quantity for use against Japanese forces in the Pacific

theatre, but only 22 had been produced by conversion of Hamilcar Mk Is

before the war ended, and the Hamilcar Mk X was not used in action.

General Aircraft ST-1, ST-2 and Monospar ST-3 to ST-12

General Aircraft Ltd was formed in 1934 to take over the assets of the Monospar Wing Co. Ltd. The main asset, the Monospar wing, determined the course of the new company's early history, which began with design and construction of the four-seat **General Aircraft Monospar ST-4**. Before that, an experimental Monospar wing had been built for Air Ministry testing under the designation **ST-1**, followed by an **ST-2** second structure, fabricated by the Gloster Aircraft Company, for flight testing on the Ministry's Fokker F.VIIb-3m.

The first light aircraft designed specifically to use the wing was the three-seat **Experimental Monospar ST-3**, also built by the Gloster company. A small low-wing monoplane with fabric covering and powered by two 50-hp (37-kW) Salmson radial engines, the Experimental Monospar ST-3 was tested extensively and successfully, leading to the decision to set up General Aircraft Ltd as the manufacturer of

aircraft based on this type of wing structure. Designed by a Swiss engineer, H. J. Steiger, this strong and light single-spar (hence Monospar) wing was able to resist bending loads and had a pyramidal wire bracing system to take the torsional loads.

The four-seat Monospar ST-4 prototype was an attractive monoplane with fixed tailwheel landing gear and the powerplant of two 85-hp (63-kW) Pobjoy R radial engines. An initial batch of five Monospar ST-4 production aircraft was followed by about 30 **Monospar ST-4 II** aircraft with marginal differences. In 1933 there appeared a generally similar **Monospar ST-6** prototype which differed in having manually retractable main landing-gear units. One other production example of the Monospar ST-6 was built, and there were also two conversions from Monospar ST-4 II standard. Early in 1934 came the next development of the type, the externally similar **Monospar ST-10** which introduced 90-hp (67-kW) Pobjoy

Niagara engines, a revised fuel system and aerodynamic refinements. This combination proved good enough for the Monospar ST-10 prototype to win the 1934 King's Cup Race. Despite this achievement, only one more Monospar ST-10 was built, followed by two generally similar **Monospar ST-11** machines with de Havilland Gipsy Major engines and tailwheel landing gear including manually retractable main units.

Development of this early family of Monospar-winged aircraft ended with 10 examples of the

Monospar ST-12 to a standard that differed from that

of the ST-11 only in having fixed landing gear.

SPECIFICATION	
General Aircraft Monospar ST-12	(229 km/h) at optimum altitude; initial climb rate 1,233 ft (376 m) per minute; service ceiling 21,000 ft (6400 m); range 410 miles (660 km)
Type: four-seat light touring and transport aircraft	
Powerplant: two de Havilland Gipsy Major inverted inline piston engines each rated at 130 hp (97 kW)	**Weights:** empty 1,840 lb (835 kg); maximum take-off 2,875 lb (1304 kg)
Performance: maximum speed 158 mph (254 km/h) at optimum altitude; cruising speed 142 mph	**Dimensions:** wingspan 40 ft 2 in (12.24 m); length 26 ft 4 in (8.03 m); height 7 ft 10 in (2.39 m); wing area 217.00 sq ft (20.16 m²)

This Monospar ST-4 was delivered to its Swiss owner in November 1932. It was then sold on twice, eventually passing to a buyer in France.

General Aircraft Monospar ST-25 Jubilee and Universal

In 1935 General Aircraft flew the prototype of a new aircraft which carried the designation **Monospar ST-25**, this advanced type number and the name **Jubilee** being allocated to mark the Silver Jubilee of King George V's reign. The ST-25 was, to all intents and purposes, an updated version of the ST-10. It differed in having a folding seat at the rear to accommodate a fifth passenger when required, cabin windows extended farther to the rear, and a powerplant based on two Pobjoy Niagara II radial engines. The Monospar ST-25 was

a popular aircraft and production continued until 1939. During that time there were few changes in the basic design until late 1936 when, to improve directional stability in an engine-out situation, the standard tail unit was replaced by one of new design incorporating twin endplate fin-and-rudder units. No change was made in the type number, but new aircraft to this configuration had the name **Universal** and also introduced more powerful Niagara III engines. Production totalled 59 aircraft in the form of 30 Jubilee and some 29 Universal machines.

Florence Nightingale was the first example of the ST-25 Ambulance. A stretcher could be loaded via a large door on the starboard side. The entire Ambulance production run was exported.

General Aircraft Monospar ST-25 (continued)

An ambulance version of the Monospar ST-25 was developed, incorporating a large door on the starboard side to ease the loading of a stretcher patient, and a seat was provided for a medical attendant. The first example was used throughout the UK as a company demonstrator. As well as a number of the **Ambulance** version produced for export, five **Freighter** aircraft, retaining the large starboard door but otherwise to standard, were also sold to a Canadian customer.

Variants

Monospar ST-25 De Luxe: one aircraft of Jubilee configuration with controllable trim tabs, an enlarged fin and Niagara III engines with electric starters; converted subsequently to Universal standard
G.A.L.26: one Monospar ST-25 Jubilee flown experimentally with two 90-hp (67-kW) Blackburn Cirrus Minor inverted inline engines
G.A.L.41: designation of one Monospar ST-25 flown with an experimental pressurised cabin that utilised a 27-hp (20-kW) Douglas Sprite motorcycle engine with a supercharger fan to provide pressurisation air
T42: one Monospar ST-25 Universal flown experimentally during 1937 with tricycle landing gear

SPECIFICATION

General Aircraft Monospar ST-25 Universal
Type: four/five-seat light transport
Powerplant: two Pobjoy Niagara III radial piston engines each rated at 95 hp (71 kW)
Performance: maximum speed 131 mph (211 km/h) at optimum altitude; cruising speed 115 mph (185 km/h) at optimum altitude; initial climb rate 710 ft (216 m) per minute; service ceiling 15,300 ft (4665 m); range 420 miles (676 km)
Weights: empty 1,818 lb (825 kg); maximum take-off 2,875 lb (1304 kg)
Dimensions: wingspan 40 ft 2 in (12.24 m); length 25 ft 4 in (7.72 m); height 7 ft 10 in (2.39 m); wing area 217.00 sq ft (20.16 m²)

General Dynamics F-111 Aardvark

The major advantages offered by a variable-geometry planform are high supersonic performance with the wing swept back, economical subsonic cruising speed with the wing fully spread, a long operational or ferry range, and relatively short take-off and landing runs at very high weights. So when in 1960 the US Air Force's Tactical Air Command was seeking a strike and interdiction warplane to replace the Republic F-105 Thunderchief, it was very interested in the results of experiments with variable-geometry wing configurations that had been conducted by NASA's Langley Research Center at Hampton, Virginia. At the same time the US Navy was looking for a fleet air-defence fighter to succeed the McDonnell F4H Phantom II, and eventually the Department of Defense decreed that the two streams of thought should be combined in a single programme known as TFX, or Tactical Fighter, Experimental.

The Secretary of Defense, Robert McNamara, stuck to this decision despite strong objections from both services, and this led to the **General Dynamics F-111 Aardvark**, the last a long-standing nickname that was formally adopted at the time of the F-111's disappearance from US service. On 24 November 1962 a development contract for 23 aircraft was awarded to General Dynamics: 18 of these were to be **F-111A** tactical warplanes for the USAF and the other five **F-111B** aircraft developed primarily by Grumman for the US Navy. The F-111B began to run into trouble almost immediately, and despite a long and intensive flight development programme the type was cancelled in July 1968. The type had consistently proved over-weight and unable to meet the required performance, and only seven aircraft were completed in the form of the five development machines plus two of the 231 production F-111B fighters which the US Navy had planned to order.

The F-111A, on which all subsequent models were based, had an almost equally unhappy early history after its first flight on 21 December 1964, but was eventually cleared for service, with deliveries of 141 production examples beginning in October 1967 to the 474th Tactical Fighter Wing at Nellis AFB, Nevada. On 15 March 1968 the 428th Tactical Fighter Squadron detached six of its F-111A warplanes to Thailand for operational deployment over Vietnam, losing three of them in four weeks. Groundings and modifications followed, and when 48 more F-111As were sent to Vietnam in 1972-73, they flew more than 4,000 combat sorties in seven months for the loss of only six aircraft. Thus it was only comparatively late in its career that the F-111 reached full maturity and emerged as arguably the world's best long-range interdictor of the 1980s.

Among the many innovations introduced by the F-111, the most notable was of course the variable-geometry wing, which was the first on an operational warplane. The wing sweeps between a minimum of 16° and a maximum of 72° 30', conferring the ability to take off with a heavy load of fuel and weapons, yet achieve supersonic speed at low level and up to Mach 2.5 at altitude. A 'clean' F-111 has the ability to 'supercruise' (fly supersonically without afterburner), and power is provided by a pair of fuel-efficient Pratt & Whitney TF30 turbofans, although in the early versions the thrust was considered

A heavy weaponload, long range and high low-level penetration speed made the FB-111A a formidable Cold War nuclear bomber.

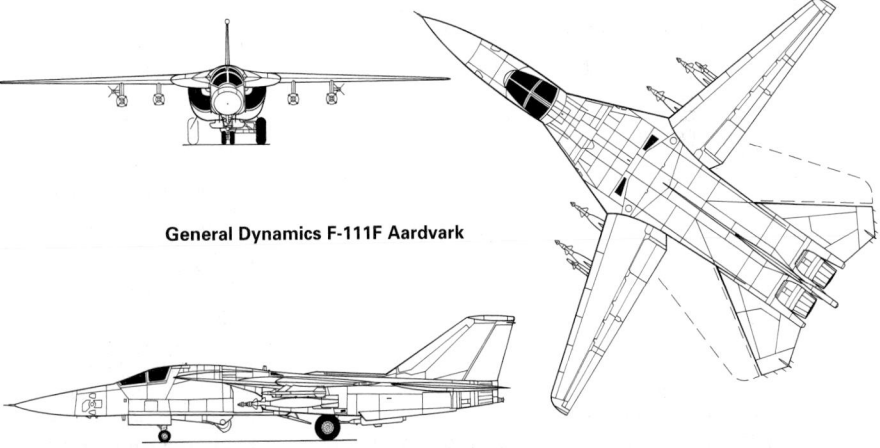

General Dynamics F-111F Aardvark

Overweight and possessing handling that made approaching an aircraft-carrier difficult even in perfect weather and in daylight, the F-111B was always destined to be an abject failure.

In RAAF service the F-111C continues to represent a potent strike force, thanks to an ongoing series of upgrades.

SPECIFICATION
General Dynamics F-111F Aardvark **Type:** two-seat long-range multi-role interdiction and attack warplane **Powerplant:** two Pratt & Whitney TF30-P-100 turbofan engines each rated at 25,100 lb st (111.65 kN) with afterburning **Performance:** maximum speed 1,650 mph (2655 km/h) or Mach 2.50 at 36,000 ft (10975 m); cruising speed 571 mph (919 km/h) at high altitude; service ceiling 60,000 ft (18290 m); range more than 2,925 miles (4707 km) with internal fuel **Weights:** empty 47,481 lb (21537 kg); maximum take-off 100,000 lb (145360 kg) **Dimensions:** wingspan 63 ft (19.20 m) spread and 31 ft 11⅜ in (9.74 m) swept; length 73 ft 6 in (22.40 m), height 17 ft 1⅜ in (5.22 m); wing area 525.00 sq ft (48.77 m²) spread and 657.07 sq ft (61.07 m²) spread **Armament:** provision for one 20-mm General Electric M61A1 Vulcan fixed forward-firing six-barrel rotary cannon in an optional weapons bay installation, plus up to 31,500 lb (14228 kg) of disposable stores carried in a lower-fuselage weapons bay and on six underwing hardpoints, and generally comprising operational loads such as up to three 1-megaton B43, or 10/20-kiloton B57 or 100/500-kiloton B61 nuclear weapons, or tactical loads such as varying numbers and combinations of 2,000-, 1,000-, 750- and 500-lb (907-, 454-, 340- and 227-kg) free-fall or retarded bombs, Paveway I, Paveway II and Paveway III laser-guided bombs, GBU-15 optronically guided bombs, AGM-65 Maverick ASMs, CBU-series bomb dispensers, and AIM-9 Sidewinder short-range AAMs

insufficient. Although there is a weapons bay, most ordnance is carried on the wing pylons. Another novelty is the fact that the side-by-side crew occupy a cockpit escape capsule, which ejects in one piece.

The F-111A, powered by two 18,500-lb st (82.29-kN) TF30-P-3 turbofan engines, was followed by the second production variant, the **F-111E**, of which 94 were completed with improved air inlets and slightly upgraded avionics. These aircraft served for most of their career at Upper Heyford in England. Then came the **F-111D**, of which 96 were built with more powerful 19,600-lb st (87.19-kN) TF30-P-9 engines and a radically updated avionics system. When it worked, this system was by far the most capable fitted to any F-111, but it was maintenance-intensive and ultimately proved over-ambitious. The F-111D served with the 27th TFW at Cannon AFB, New Mexico, until final retirement in late 1992.

The Strategic Air Command purchased the **FB-111A** model, which was equipped for strategic nuclear missions. This featured a wing increased in span by 7 ft (2.13 m) for additional fuel- and weapons-carrying capability. When the survivors of

these 76 aircraft, which also had strengthened landing gear and 20,150-lb st (89.63-kN) TF30-P-7 engines, were retired, some 51 of them were reworked for the 27th TFW as **F-111G** machines, and these served in a training role until 1993.

Export sales were limited to Australia, although the Royal Air Force ordered (and subsequently cancelled) the **F-111K** variant. Australia's aircraft were delivered in 1973 after a prolonged wrangle over technical difficulties. Featuring the long-span wing of the FB-111A but the lower-powered engines and avionics of the F-111A, the **F-111C** was purchased for service with No. 82 Wing at RAAF Amberley, Queensland, which received 24 such aircraft. Four ex-USAF examples of the F-111A were purchased as attrition replacements and modified to F-111C standard, and in the early 1990s the RAAF purchased 15 examples of the F-111G (ex-FB-111A). Originally, these were to be held in storage for use as the current F-111C fleet reached the end of its fatigue life, but the first examples have already entered service. Four of the RAAF aircraft operate in **RF-111C** reconnaissance form with a multi-sensor

reconnaissance pallet mounted in the former weapons bay.

Last of the F-111's production variants, the **F-111F** was also the last in operational service with the US Air Force, flying with the 522nd, 523rd and 524th Fighter Squadrons of the 27th Fighter Wing at Cannon AFB, New Mexico up to 1996. Production of the F-111F totalled 106 aircraft, initial deliveries going to Mountain Home AFB, Idaho, from 1972. Between 1977 and 1992 the force was deployed to Lakenheath in England with the 48th TFW. Although not as capable in avionics terms as the F-111D, the F-111F nevertheless proved much easier to maintain. Mk IIB avionics, as developed for the FB-111A, were combined with the

Weapons Control Panel from the F-111E. By far the most important improvement introduced by the F-111F, however, was the uprated powerplant of two TF30-P-100 turbofan engines which raised thrust/weight ratio from 0.39 in the early variants to 0.53. Thus, the F-111F was the only version not considered to be underpowered.

The F-111F was built (like all Aardvarks except the FB-111A) with provision

for a 20-mm Vulcan cannon in the weapons bay, but this was never used. For self-defence the F-111F routinely carried the AIM-9P Sidewinder, and the weapons bay was used primarily for the carriage of the AVQ-26 Pave Tack pod, which incorporates a FLIR sensor and bore-sighted laser rangefinder/designator. This provided the F-111F with the capability for the autonomous delivery of laser-guided bombs.

The Pave Tack pod is clearly visible in the bomb bay of this 48th TFW F-111F. The pod was extended (as illustrated) when in use and semi-retracted at other times. This aircraft is armed with 2,000-lb (907-kg) Mk 84-based Paveway II LGBs.

Globe GC-1 Swift

Shortly before World War II, Globe aircraft designed and developed a two-seat light cabin monoplane designated **Swift Model GC-1**. Its production was frustrated not only by disappointing performance as a result of low power but also, of course, by US involvement in World War II. A cantilever low-wing

monoplane, the Model GC-1 incorporated Duraloid bonded plywood in its wing and tail structure, but had a welded steel-tube fuselage with fabric covering. Retractable tailwheel landing gear was standard, and power for the prototype was provided initially by a 65-hp (48-kW) Continental A65 engine. First flown in

early 1941, the GC-1 was found to be seriously underpowered, leading to installation of a 80-hp (60-kW) Continental A80. It was with this latter powerplant that the aircraft was certificated in early 1942. Engines of 90 to 100 hp (67 to 75 kW) were to be

offered as optional for definitive aircraft, but no production followed and it was not until 1946 that the programme was revived.

This GC-1B Swift joined the UK civil register, having originally been registered in Rhodesia. The type offered good performance on low power.

Globe GC-1 Swift (continued)

While of the same general configuration, the post-war **Swift Model GC-1A** was of all-metal construction and of much improved overall design. Unfortunately, Globe started on the wrong foot by giving the almost 20 per cent heavier Model GC-1A the powerplant of one 85-hp (63-kW) Continental C85 engine. Despite the resulting docility of performance, almost 400 were built before installation of a more powerful engine created the **Model GC-1B**, which was a really sporty aircraft built in large numbers by Globe and under subcontract by Temco (Texas Engineering & Manufacturing Co.). The latter company acquired the Model GC-1's production and sales rights when Globe ran into financial difficulties in 1947, and production as the **Temco Swift** continued until 1951.

SPECIFICATION	
Globe Swift Model GC-1B	rate 850 ft (259 m) per minute;
Type: two-seat sporting and touring aircraft	service ceiling 14,200 ft (4330 m); range 420 miles (676 km)
Powerplant: one Continental C-125-2 flat-six piston engine rated at 125 hp (93 kW)	**Weights:** empty 1,110 lb (503 kg): maximum take-off 1,670 lb (758 kg)
Performance: maximum speed 145 mph (233 km/h) at sea level; cruising speed 132 mph (212 km/h) at 7,000 ft (2135 m); initial climb	**Dimensions:** wingspan 29 ft 4 in (8.94 m); length 20 ft 11 in (6.38 m); height 6 ft 2 in (1.88 m); wing area 131.60 sq ft (12.23 m²)

Gloster Mars I and Gloster I and II

The Gloucestershire Aircraft Company was established in mid-1917, its name being changed to Gloster Aircraft Company late in 1926 because of the company's concern about the peculiarities of English pronunciation and the effect that the original name might have on export sales.

The post-World War I scarcity of orders resulted in the company's conclusion that conspicuous success in competitive events might convince the Air Ministry that Gloster was the only worthwhile source for high-speed fighter aircraft. Thus was born the **Mars I** single-seat racer, nicknamed

'Bamel', in which no efforts were spared by Henry Folland to achieve genuinely high performance. The 'Bamel' was a remarkably clean biplane with a single-bay biplane wing cellule and the powerplant of one 450-hp (336-kW) Napier Lion engine in an unusually neat installation. An odd feature was a faired cabane structure to house the fuel and water header tanks, preventing direct forward view. First flown on 20 June 1921, the 'Bamel' won the annual Aerial Derby during the following month and, modified and improved, progressively established a British speed record of 196.40 mph (316.10 km/h)

on 12 December 1921 before winning the Aerial Derby again in 1922.

Early in 1923 the Mars I was given extensively modified wings, had the fuel and water header tanks transferred to tanks inside the fuselage so that the view-limiting cabane could be removed, and was fitted with a more powerful Lion engine. This created the **Gloster I**. After winning the Aerial Derby of 1923, the machine was acquired by the Royal Air Force and, revised with with twin-float alighting gear, was used by the RAF's High-Speed Flight for training purposes.

Gloster's policy of developing high-performance aircraft brought an order from the Air Ministry early in 1924 for two **Gloster II** aircraft to compete in the 1924 Schneider Trophy contest. Similar to the Gloster I, but with a wing cellule of increased stagger, the Gloster II was powered by the 585-hp (436-kW) Lion VA engine driving a

The Mars I is shown above as it appeared when first flown, with square radiator, uncowled centre cylinder bank of the Lion engine, and Nighthawk-type tail unit.

Fairey-Reed metal propeller, and featured remarkably clean floats and extensive fairing to improve aerodynamic efficiency. The first of these floatplanes was taken to RAF Felixstowe for flight testing on 12 September 1924. About a week later, while the aircraft was being flown by Hubert Broad, a forward float strut collapsed as the machine touched down on roughish water. Almost immediately the

machine sank and was a complete loss although, fortunately, Broad escaped without injury. Shortly after this event the 1924 Schneider Trophy contest was cancelled and the second Gloster II was completed with wheeled landing gear for high-speed flight development. It, too, was wrecked in a landing accident in mid-1925 and no further examples were built.

SPECIFICATION	
Gloster I (landplane)	4 minutes 18 seconds
Type: single-seat racing aircraft	**Weights:** empty 1,970 lb (894 kg); maximum take-off 2,650 lb (1202 kg)
Powerplant: one Napier Lion W-type piston engine rated at 530 hp (395 kW)	**Dimensions:** wingspan 20 ft (6.10 m); length 23 ft (7.01 m); height 9 ft 4 in (2.84 m); wing area 165.00 sq ft (15.33 m²)
Performance: maximum speed 220 mph (354 km/h) at sea level; climb to 10,000 ft (3050 m) in	

Gloster III

In February 1925, Gloster received from the Air Ministry an order for two examples of a new racing biplane, designated as the **Gloster III**, to compete in the 1925 Schneider Trophy contest. The new machine was derived from the Gloster II, and Henry Folland spared no efforts to achieve a clean airframe and a small frontal area, and also adopted a mono-

coque fuselage structure with plywood skinning for strength and light weight. The wings were of fabric-covered wooden construction, and the twin floats were mounted on wire-braced streamlined struts. The Napier Lion VII engine was adopted, making the Gloster III the smallest British aircraft to have so high-powered an engine. Flight testing of the

first machine showed that there was some directional instability so, with little time for the introduction of major modifications, the wing cellule was re-rigged and the area of the dorsal and ventral fins was increased. With these changes the aircraft was redesignated as the **Gloster IIIA**.

Flown by Hubert Broad, the Gloster IIIA gained second place in the Schneider Trophy contest at Baltimore, USA. The second aircraft, flying in Gloster III form, was unfortunate, being damaged in practice before the race. After its return to the UK, the Gloster IIIA was transferred to RAF Felixstowe, but the Gloster III was repaired and at the same time modified with wing

The Gloster IIIA N194 is pictured at Felixstowe, after modification of the tail unit. N194 was flown to second place in the 1925 Schneider Trophy race.

surface radiators, a new tail unit and several other small changes. In this form, it became the **Gloster IIIB** that was also

delivered to RAF Felixstowe, where both were used as trainers for pilots of the RAF's High-Speed Flight.

SPECIFICATION	
Gloster IIIB	**Weights:** empty 2,278 lb (1033 kg); maximum take-off 2,962 lb (1343 kg)
Type: single-seat racing floatplane	**Dimensions:** wingspan 20 ft (6.10 m); length 26 ft 10 in (8.18 m); height 9 ft 8 in (2.95m); wing area 152.00 sq ft (14.12 m²)
Powerplant: one Napier Lion VII W-type piston engine rated at 700 hp (522 kW)	
Performance: maximum speed 252 mph (405 km/h) at sea level	

Gloster IV

Gloster produced no contender for the 1926 Schneider Trophy contest, but early in 1926 Henry Folland and his team were already working on the

design of a successor to the Gloster III, adhering to the biplane configuration which, in Folland's opinion, provided the ideal combination of light weight and

structural integrity. To gain the desired increase in performance for this new **Gloster IV** a still more powerful version of the Lion engine was chosen, and every possible aerodynamic refinement was incorporated to reduce drag

to the absolute minimum. Wing surface radiators were employed for engine cooling and, for the first time, the company designed and built its own floats for the three aircraft: these floats also had cooling radiators, these being

fitted on the floats' upper surfaces. The dissipation of heat from the powerful engines that were then being developed brought problems to all designers of competing aircraft, and in order to keep the lubricating oil at an effective

The Gloster IVA N222 (pictured) was shipped to Venice on 16 August 1927, together with Gloster IVB N223, the latter taking part in that year's Schneider Trophy contest, won by a Supermarine S.5.

temperature, the Gloster IV also featured a combined oil tank/cooler in the under-surface of the nose and additional cooling surfaces on the fuselage sides.

The three aircraft comprised the Gloster IV with a 900-hp (671-kW) Napier Lion VIIA direct-drive engine, the **Gloster IVA** with reduced wingspan, a cruciform tail unit and the same powerplant, and the **Gloster IVB** which was the same as the Gloster IVA except for its powerplant of one Lion VIIB engine, driving its propeller by means of a reduction gear.

It was the IVB which was chosen to compete in the contest as the third member of the British team, but it was forced to retire during the sixth lap. Subsequently, the Gloster IV was sold, but the other two floatplanes remained in use by the RAF for high-speed flight research and training.

SPECIFICATION	
Gloster IVB	
Type: single-seat racing floatplane	**Weights:** empty 2,613 lb (1185 kg); maximum take-off 3,305 lb (1499 kg)
Powerplant: one Napier Lion VIIB W-type piston engine rated at 885 hp (660 kW)	**Dimensions:** wingspan 22 ft 7½ in (6.90 m); length 26 ft 4 in (8.03 m); height 9 ft 2 in (2.79 m); wing area 139.00 sq ft (12.91 m²)
Performance: maximum speed 295 mph (475 km/h) at sea level	

Gloster VI

The design of a **Gloster V** racing floatplane was projected but the type failed to materialise, and it was not until a time early in 1928 that Henry Folland and his team began the design of a new monoplane, rather than biplane, contender to compete in the Schneider Trophy contest of 1929. A wire-braced low-wing monoplane, the **Gloster VI** had a wing and cantilever tail unit of wooden construction, and a fuselage and floats of light alloy construction. The surfaces of the wing were almost entirely covered by coolers for the liquid-cooling system of the Lion VIID engine, and surface oil cool-ers, conforming to the fuselage contours to the rear of the cockpit, could be

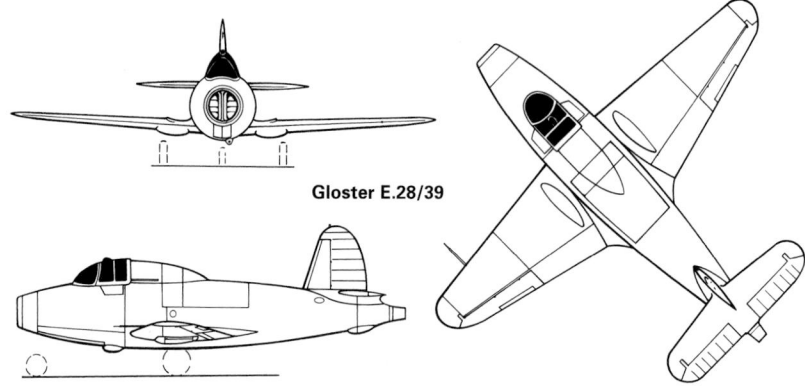

SPECIFICATION	
Gloster VI	
Type: single-seat racing floatplane	**Weights:** empty 2,284 lb (1036 kg); maximum take-off 3,680 lb (1669 kg)
Powerplant: one Napier Lion VIID W-type piston engine rated at 1,320 hp (984 kW)	**Dimensions:** wingspan 26 ft (7.92 m); length 27 ft (8.23 m); height 10 ft 9½ in (3.29 m); wing area 106.00 sq ft (9.85 m²)
Performance: maximum recorded speed 351 mph (565 km/h) at 100 ft (30 m)	

supplemented if needed by auxiliary oil coolers on the upper surface of the floats.

Two examples of the Gloster VI were built, but when tested at Calshot in August 1929 their highly boosted and supercharged Lion VIID engines proved to

N249, the first Gloster VI, pictured at Calshot, briefly held an absolute speed record when, on 10 September 1929, it achieved an average speed of 336.30 mph (541.21 km/h).

be too temperamental and they were withdrawn from the contest. Both ended their days at RAF Felixstowe, but extensive work to resolve their engine problems was unsuccessful, with the result that they saw little use.

Gloster E.28/39

The pioneering W.1 gas turbine designed by Frank Whittle, and built by Power Jets Ltd. under an Air Ministry contract awarded in March 1938, needed an airframe for testing in the air, and the Air Ministry therefore issued Specification E.28/39 to Gloster on 3 February 1940. The design was to be based on fighter requirements, with provision for the weight and space that would be needed by four 0.303-in (7.7-mm) Browning machine-guns, although these would not be fitted in the test aircraft. Two **Gloster E.28/39** prototypes were covered by the contract, these aircraft being required to have tricycle landing gear with a steer-able nosewheel.

Just over one year later the first of the Gloster E.28/39 prototypes was ready for taxiing tests, which were undertaken at Gloster's Hucclecote airfield by the chief test pilot, P. E. G. Sayer, on

Gloster E.28/39

7 April 1941. The following day the machine made a few short hops, after which a new nosewheel unit was fitted before the type was dismantled and taken by road to Cranwell, Lincolnshire, for flight trials as it was felt that the longer runways there would be an advantage. In fact, the E.28/39 was airborne in about 1,800 ft (550 m) on the thrust of 860 lb (3.83 kN) delivered by the Power Jets W.1 engine installed for initial flight tests, in the process becoming the UK's first jet-powered aircraft.

The first flight, made on 15 May 1941, lasted for 17 minutes and was completely successful. Ten more hours of flying were achieved in the following 13 days before the proto-type was returned to the factory to await the new and more powerful 1,160-lb st (5.16-kN) W.1A engine. A new series of tests began on 4 February 1942 at Edgehill, Warwickshire, but there were problems with the engine and the prototype was slightly damaged.

WW4041, the first E.28/39, employed heat-sensitive paint strips on the rear fuselage sides, and a fabric-covered rudder. Note the small-diameter jet-pipe.

Gloster E.28/39 (cont.)

Pilots of the Royal Aircraft Establishment at Farnborough also flew the aircraft, and during one of these flights, on 30 July, with the first prototype then powered by the new 1,526-lb st (6.79-kN) Rover W.2B engine, the ailerons jammed at 37,000 ft (11280 m), putting the aircraft into an inverted spin: Squadron Leader Davie managed to bale out

SPECIFICATION

Gloster E.28/39
Type: single-seat turbojet-powered research aircraft
Powerplant: one Power Jets W.2/500 turbojet engine rated at 1,760 lb st (7.83 kN)
Performance: maximum speed 466 mph (750 km/h) at 10,000 ft (3050 m); climb to 30,000 ft (9145 m) in 22 minutes; service ceiling 32,000 ft (9755 m)
Weights: empty 2,886 lb (1309 kg); maximum take-off 3,748 lb (1700 kg)
Dimensions: wingspan 29 ft (8.84 m); length 25 ft 3¾ in (7.72 m); height 9 ft 3 in (2.82 m); wing area 146.50 sq ft (13.61 m²)

at 33,000 ft (10060 m) but the E.28/39 was lost.

The second prototype had been re-engined with the 1,700-lb st (7.56-kN) Power Jets W.2/500 engine and testing continued, concluding with more flying

The E.28/39 quickly proved itself in flight tests, accumulating 10 hours of flying during the first 13 days of trials, and attaining 25,000 ft (7620 m).

at the RAE to obtain aerodynamic data. By this time an improved Power Jets W.2/500 engine had been installed. At the end of its test programme this aircraft was placed in the Science Museum, South Kensington, for permanent exhibition.

Gloster Gambet

Requiring a replacement for its Gloster Sparrowhawk fighters, early in 1926 the Imperial Japanese navy requested Aichi, Mitsubishi and Nakajima to submit designs for a new single-seat ship-based fighter. Nakajima was sufficiently astute to request Gloster to design a suitable aircraft, the result being the

Gambet which Henry Folland was already developing as a private venture on the basis of the Gamecock. A biplane with an unequal-span single-bay wing cellule, the single-seat Gambet was largely of wooden construction covered with fabric, and had fixed tailskid landing gear, arrester hooks, flotation gear and armament of two 0.303-in (7.7-mm) Vickers machine-guns. Nakajima bought the prototype and production rights in July 1927, and a team led by Engineer Takao Yoshida introduced modifications that would enable it to meet the IJN's specific requirements and, at the same time, make it more suitable for production in

The Gambet pattern aircraft, loosely based on the Gamecock, with arrester jaws and oleo landing gear, was bought by Nakajima Hikoki K.K.

Japan. A total of 150 aircraft was built by Nakajima in two versions as the **A1N1** (50) and **A1N2** (100), or **Type 3 Carrier-Based Fighter**.

SPECIFICATION

Gloster Gambet
Type: single-seat carrierborne fighter
Powerplant: one Bristol Jupiter VI radial piston engine rated at 420 hp (313 kW)
Performance: maximum speed 152 mph (245 km/h) at 5,000 ft (1525 m); climb to 10,000 ft (3050 m) in 7 minutes; service ceiling 23,200 ft (7070 m); endurance 3 hours 45 minutes
Weights: empty 2,010 lb (912 kg);

maximum take-off 3,075 lb (1395 kg)
Dimensions: wingspan 31 ft (9.70 m); length 21 ft 3½ in (6.49 m); height 10 ft 8 in (3.25 m); wing area 284.00 sq ft (26.38 m²)
Armament: two 0.303-in (7.7-mm) Vickers fixed forward-firing machine-guns in the sides of the forward fuselage, plus up to 80 lb (36 kg) of disposable stores carried under the lower wing and generally comprising four 20-lb (9.10-kg) bombs

Gloster Gamecock

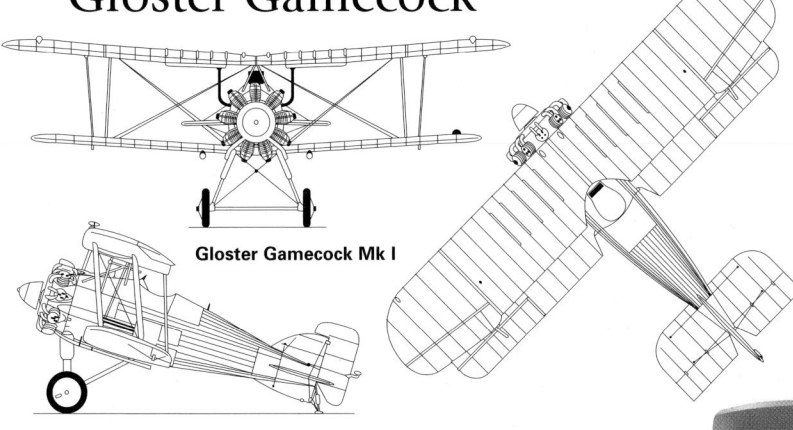

Gloster Gamecock Mk I

The **Gamecock**, built to the Air Ministry's Specification 27/23 calling for a single-seat fighter, was another development of the successful Grouse/Grebe family. It differed primarily in having a Bristol Jupiter engine to replace the Armstrong Siddeley Jaguar unit, whose unreliability had caused problems. Other changes included improved ailerons, refined fuselage contours and internal mounting of the two machine-guns. First flown

during February 1925, the Gamecock moved rapidly to service tests, which resulted in modification of the tail unit. With such modifications this first of three prototypes proved good enough to win an order for 30 production examples of the **Gamecock Mk I** fighter, the first of which entered service with No. 23 Squadron in May 1926, remaining operational until July 1931.

The Royal Air Force

Variant

Gamecock Mk III: redesignation of one RAF Gamecock Mk II, used for spinning trials following modifications to reduce its spinning tendency

SPECIFICATION

Gloster Gamecock Mk I
Type: single-seat fighter
Powerplant: one Bristol Jupiter VI radial piston engine rated at 425 hp (317 kW)
Performance: maximum speed 155 mph (249 km/h) at 5,000 ft (1525 m); climb to 10,000 ft (3050 m) in 7 minutes 35 seconds; service ceiling 22,000 ft (6705 m); endurance 2 hours

Weights: empty 1,930 lb (875 kg); maximum take-off 2,863 lb (1299 kg)
Dimensions: wingspan 29 ft 9½ in (9.08 m); length 19 ft 8 in (5.99 m); height 9 ft 8 in (2.95 m); wing area 264.00 sq ft (24.53 m²)
Armament: two 0.303-in (7.7-mm) Vickers Mk I fixed forward-firing machine-guns in the sides of the forward fuselage

Seen above is a Gloster Gamecock Mk I of No. 32 Sqn, RAF, based at Kenley between September 1926 and April 1928. Blessed with outstanding agility, the Gamecock was a favourite aerobatic mount.

acquired almost 100 Gamecocks, this number including three late-development **Gamecock Mk II** aircraft with a revised upper-wing centre section and other improvements. In addition to Gamecock fighters for the RAF, Gloster supplied three Gamecock Mk II machines to Finland, where 15 more were built under licence in 1929-30. Named **Kukko**, these were in first-line service with the Finnish air force from 1929 to 1935, and were subsequently used as trainers until the last was retired in 1941.

Gloster Gauntlet

The **Gauntlet**, which in 1937 equipped no fewer than 14 squadrons of the Royal Air Force's Fighter Command for the defence of the British Isles against air attack, stemmed from the Air Ministry's Specification F.9/26, against which the company had originally but unsuccessfully submitted its **Goldfinch** design. This failure spurred Gloster into the effort to produce a new aircraft fully meeting the specification, but before this was completed, the new Specification F.20/27 was drawn up for a single-seat high-altitude interceptor fighter. Gloster's submission to this was the **SS.18** biplane with an equal-span two-bay wing cellule, an all-metal basic structure covered with fabric and light alloy, fixed tailskid landing gear and a powerplant based on the unreliable 450-hp (336-kW) Bristol Mercury IIA radial engine. Despite this engine's poor showing, the SS.18 was only narrowly beaten during service trials.

Encouraged by the prototype's potential, Gloster continued development of the SS.18 by installation of a 480-hp (358-kW) Bristol Jupiter VIIF radial engine to create the **SS.18A**, and the aircraft was flown later with a 560-hp (418-kW) Armstrong Siddeley

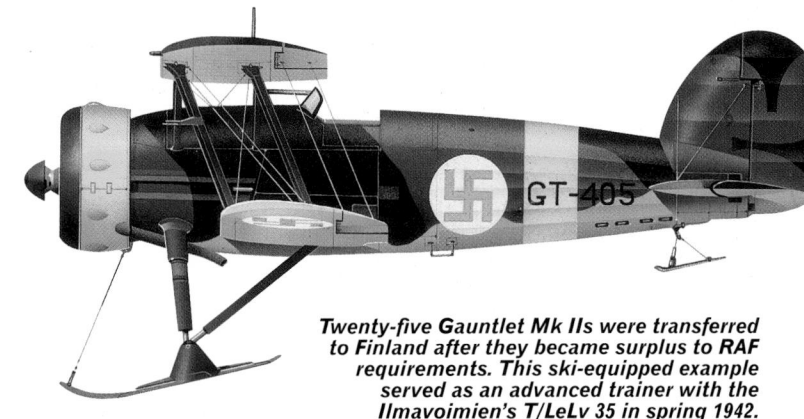

Twenty-five Gauntlet Mk IIs were transferred to Finland after they became surplus to RAF requirements. This ski-equipped example served as an advanced trainer with the Ilmavoimien's T/LeLv 35 in spring 1942.

Panther III radial engine with the further revised designation **SS.18B**. This twin-row engine was heavy and caused some handling problems, so Gloster decided to revert to the Jupiter engine in the **SS.19**. During 1931 the SS.19 gained spats for its main wheels and also a spatted tailwheel to become the **SS.19A**. The installation of a 536-hp (400-kW) Mercury VIS engine in October 1932 created the **SS.19B** and eventually, in 1934, the type was ordered into production with a contract for 24 **Gauntlet Mk I** fighters powered by the Mercury VIS2 engine.

Initial deliveries to the RAF's No. 19 Squadron were made on 25 May 1935. Hawker Aircraft Ltd had taken over the Gloster company during 1934, with the result that the major production version, the **Gauntlet Mk II**, of which 204 were built, embodied Hawker construction techniques in the fuselage structure but was otherwise generally similar to the Gauntlet Mk I. In addition to the aircraft produced for the RAF, which were the last open-cockpit biplane fighters used by this service, 17 machines were built under licence in Denmark and, at a later date, ex-RAF Gauntlet Mk II fighters were supplied to the Royal Australian Air Force (six), Finland (25), Rhodesia (three) and South Africa (six).

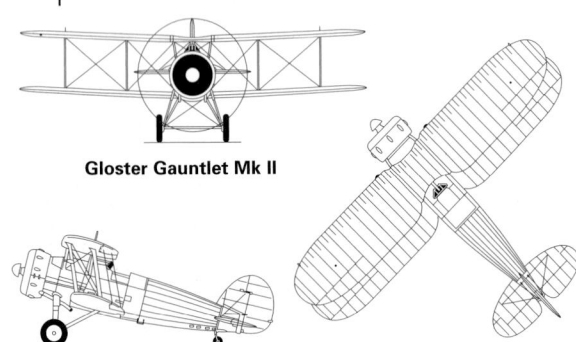

Gloster Gauntlet Mk II

SPECIFICATION

Gloster Gauntlet Mk II
Type: single-seat fighter
Powerplant: one Bristol Mercury VIS2 radial piston engine rated at 640 hp (477 kW)
Performance: maximum speed 230 mph (370 km/h) at 15,800 ft (4815 m); climb to 20,000 ft (6095 m) in 9 minutes 30 seconds; service ceiling 33,500 ft (10210 m); range 460 miles (740 km)

Weights: empty 2,770 lb (1256 kg); maximum take-off 3,970 lb (1801 kg)
Dimensions: wingspan 32 ft 3½ in (9.99 m); length 26 ft 5 in (8.05 m); height 10 ft 3 in (3.12 m); wing area 315.00 sq ft (29.26 m²)
Armament: two 0.303-in (7.7-mm) Vickers Mk V fixed forward-firing machine-guns in the sides of the forward fuselage

---

Gauntlet Mk II K7817, one of a batch of 100, was originally delivered to No. 54 Sqn, RAF, on 8 October 1936. Eight months later it was passed to No. 74 Sqn, in whose tiger stripes it is illustrated.

Gloster Gladiator

The inability of British manufacturers to produce an adequate replacement for the Bristol Bulldog by the mid-1930s led to further orders for the Gloster Gauntlet to equip the extra squadrons proposed under the 1935 expansion scheme for the Royal Air Force. Although design studies for monoplane fighters were showing considerable promise, Henry Folland, Gloster's chief designer, conducted a detailed examination of the Gauntlet's design to define the extent to which performance might be improved: the wing cellule was redesigned as a single-bay structure and the main landing-gear arrangement was revised to a pair of cantilever legs each carrying one Dowty internally-sprung wheel. Both changes reduced drag, promising an increase of between 10 and 15 mph (16 and 24 km/h) in maximum speed.

Gloster built a prototype of this design as a private venture under the designation **SS.37**, and this recorded its maiden flight on 12 September 1934 in the hands of the company's chief test pilot, Flight Lieutenant P. E. G. Sayer. The use of a Bristol Mercury IV engine produced a maximum speed of 236 mph (380 km/h), and this was increased to 242 mph (389 km/h) after the fitting of the 645-hp (481-kW) Mercury VIS in November 1934. With the Gauntlet's two Vickers Mk III fuselage-mounted machine-guns supplemented by two Lewis machine-guns under the lower wing, the SS.37 met Air Ministry armament requirements, and the prototype was flown to RAF Martlesham Heath early in 1935 for official evaluation.

Gloster's design was submitted to the Air Ministry in June 1935 and Specification F.14/35 was written around it; an order for 23 aircraft followed, the name **Gladiator** being announced on 1 July.

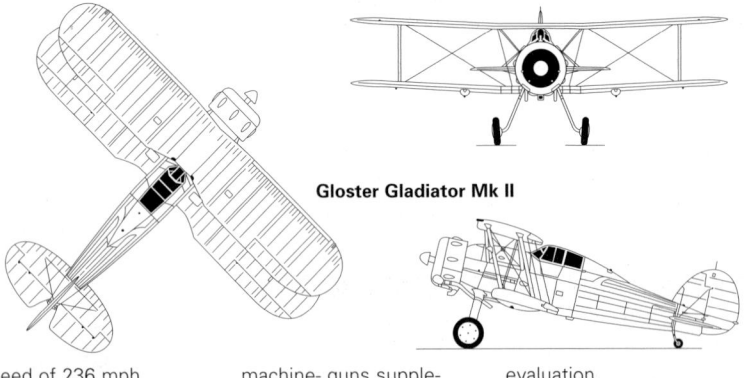

Gloster Gladiator Mk II

Gloster Gladiator (continued)

The 840-hp (626-kW) Mercury IX engine was specified for the Gladiator, and other changes included an enclosed cockpit, minor landing-gear modifications, a revised tail unit, and the fitting of improved Vickers Mk V machine-guns in the fuselage. The first production batch of 23 **Gladiator Mk I** fighters, delivered in February and March 1937, carried Lewis machine-guns under the wings, as did the first 37 of the second order for 180 aircraft. All of this second batch was fitted with a universal armament mounting under each wing, capable of accepting any Vickers or Lewis gun or, indeed, the licence-built Colt-Browning which was installed in fuselage and wing positions in the majority of aircraft delivered in 1938. A third order, in this instance for 28 machines, brought the RAF's Gladiator Mk I procurement to 231 aircraft, of which some were later converted to **Gladiator Mk II** standard.

The RAF later received 252 new Gladiator Mk IIs

built to Specification F.36/57, with the 830-hp (619-kW) Mercury VIIIA engine fitted with automatic mixture control, an electric starter and a Vokes air filter in the carburettor intake. Some 38 of the aircraft were fitted with arrester hooks and transferred to the Fleet Air Arm in December 1938, these being an interim replacement for Hawker Nimrod and Osprey fighters until the delivery of 60 fully navalised **Sea Gladiator** fighters. The latter had an arrester hook, catapult points and a ventral dinghy stowage fairing. Gladiator production totalled 746, with orders from Belgium, China, Ireland, Greece, Latvia, Lithuania, Norway and Sweden covering 147 and 18 examples of the Gladiator Mks I and II respectively.

The Gladiator was first issued in February 1937 to No. 72 Squadron at Church Fenton, Yorkshire, and although most of the squadrons that received the type had been re-equipped with the Hawker Hurricane or Supermarine Spitfire by September

1939, some of their aircraft had been reissued to home-based auxiliary units, four of which were fully operational when World War II broke out in September 1939. Two of these units, Nos 601 and 615 Squadrons, were posted to France in November 1939 as part of the Advanced Air Striking

Force. No. 263 Squadron, together with the Fleet Air Arm's No. 804 Sqn, participated in the Norwegian campaign, and the handful of aircraft of the Hal Far Fighter Flight and of No. 261 Sqn took part in the defence of Malta between April and June 1940. In the Balkans and Middle East the Gladiator

saw service during the war with Nos 6, 33, 80, 94, 112 and 127 Squadrons and also with No. 3 Sqn of the Royal Australian Air Force. After its withdrawal from first-line service, the Gladiator continued in RAF use for communications, liaison and meteorological reconnaissance duties until 1944.

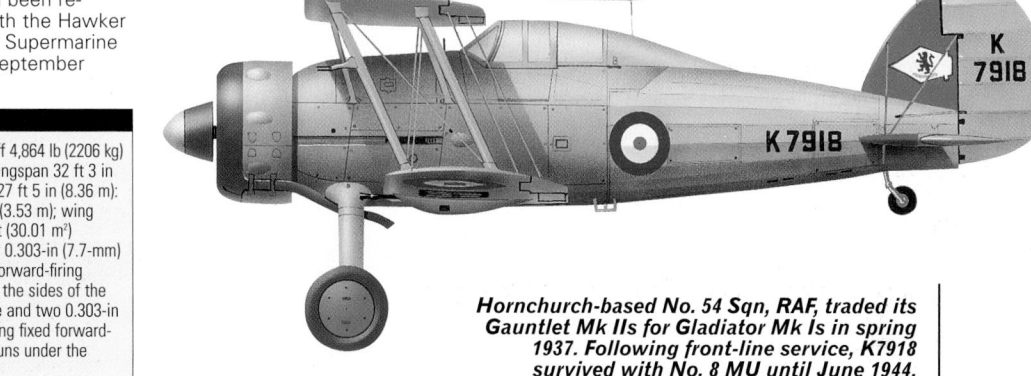

Pictured above is a Gloster Gladiator Mk II of the Esquadrilha de Caça Expedicionaria No. 2 of the Arma de Aeronáutica (Portuguese air force), based in the Azores in August 1941.

SPECIFICATION

Gloster Gladiator Mk II
Type: single-seat fighter
Powerplant: one Bristol Mercury VIIIA or VIIIA air-cooled radial engine rated at 830 hp (619 kW)
Performance: maximum speed 257 mph (414 km/h) at 14,600 ft (4450 m); climb to 10,000 ft (3050 m) in 4 minutes 45 seconds; service ceiling 33,500 ft (10210 m); range 440 miles (708 km)
Weights: empty 3,444 lb (1562 kg);

maximum take-off 4,864 lb (2206 kg)
Dimensions: wingspan 32 ft 3 in (9.83 m); length 27 ft 5 in (8.36 m): height 11 ft 7 in (3.53 m); wing area 323.00 sq ft (30.01 m²)
Armament: four 0.303-in (7.7-mm) Browning forward-firing machine-guns in the sides of the forward fuselage and two 0.303-in (7.7-mm) Browning fixed forward-firing machine-guns under the lower wing

Hornchurch-based No. 54 Sqn, RAF, traded its Gauntlet Mk IIs for Gladiator Mk Is in spring 1937. Following front-line service, K7918 survived with No. 8 MU until June 1944.

Gloster Grebe

The Grebe single-seat fighter was, with the Hawker Woodcock and Armstrong Whitworth Siskin, the first new fighter to be selected for re-equipment of the Royal Air Force in the years between the two world wars. The Grebe was derived from the **Grouse** research biplane, whose potential was so great that the Air Ministry undertook a service evaluation of the type. This was so success-

ful that the Air Ministry ordered three prototypes, the first of them becoming the Grebe prototype (subsequently designated as the **Grebe Mk I**) with the powerplant of one 325-hp (242-kW) Armstrong Siddeley Jaguar III radial engine. Service trials of this machine resulted in a production order for the **Grebe Mk II**, incorporating a number of improvements. These included more advanced

Designed by H. P. Folland, the Grouse-derived Gloster Grebe betrayed the influence of Folland's SE.5. This example, a Grebe Mk II, served with No. 25 Sqn, RAF.

SPECIFICATION

Gloster Grebe Mk II
Type: single-seat fighter
Powerplant: one Armstrong Siddeley Jaguar IV radial piston engine rated at 400 hp (298 kW)
Performance: maximum speed 151 mph (243 km/h) at sea level; climb to 20,000 ft (6095 m) in 23 minutes; service ceiling 23,000 ft (7010 m); endurance 2 hours 45 minutes

Weights: empty 1,720 lb (780 kg); maximum take-off 2,622 lb (1189 kg)
Dimensions: wingspan 29 ft 4 in (8.94 m); length 20 ft 3 in (6.17 m); height 9 ft 3 in (2.82 m); wing area 254.00 sq ft (23.60 m²)
Armament: two 0.303-in (7.7-mm) Vickers fixed forward-firing machine-guns in the upper part of the forward fuselage

landing gear with a steerable tailskid, and the uprated powerplant of one Jaguar IV engine.

The RAF received about 120 Grebe Mk IIs, a number of them operating as **Grebe (Dual)** two-seat trainers with dual controls, and the first aircraft entered service in October

1923. The Grebe remained in front-line use with the RAF for almost five years, during which time some took part in a number of unusual flight test programmes. One of these resulted in the Grebe Mk II becoming the first RAF fighter to notch up a successful 240-mph

(386-km/h) terminal-velocity dive, and two of the aircraft with special attachments on the upper wing were used for air-launching experiments from the British airship *R33*. During 1928 three Grebes were acquired by New Zealand for service with the nation's air force.

Gloster Javelin

When production examples of the **Javelin** entered service with No. 46 Squadron of the Royal Air Force in February 1956, they were the first delta-winged aircraft to be operated by the service. The new interceptor was also an advanced aircraft, the service's first all-weather fighter to be designed as such from the outset. Developed to meet the requirements of Air Ministry Specification F.4/48, the **GA.5** design featured all-metal construction and its lightly loaded, large-area delta wing ensured good high-altitude performance. Most delta-wing aircraft are devoid of conventional tail surfaces, resulting in a very high angle of attack for approach and landing but, as this was considered to be hazardous for all-weather/night operations, the design of the Javelin incorporated a T-tail with all-swept surfaces; in conjunction with wing trailing-edge flaps, this allowed landings to be made at almost normal angles of

attack. Retractable tricycle landing gear, a powerplant of two Armstrong Siddeley Sapphire ASSa.6 turbojet engines, a fuselage seating a crew of two in pressurised tandem-seat accommodation, and massive airborne interception radar in the nose completed the basic configuration of this aircraft.

The first of seven prototypes recorded its maiden flight on 26 November 1951, and on 7 July 1952 the new all-weather interceptor was ordered into production as the **Javelin F(AW).Mk 1**. The first production example flew on 22 July 1954, and there was a protracted development period before, on 29 February 1956, the first three Javelin interceptors were delivered to No. 46 Sqn. The type was finally withdrawn from RAF service in May 1968, and was also the last Gloster-designed aircraft to be built before the company lost its separate identity on full absorption into the Hawker Siddeley Group.

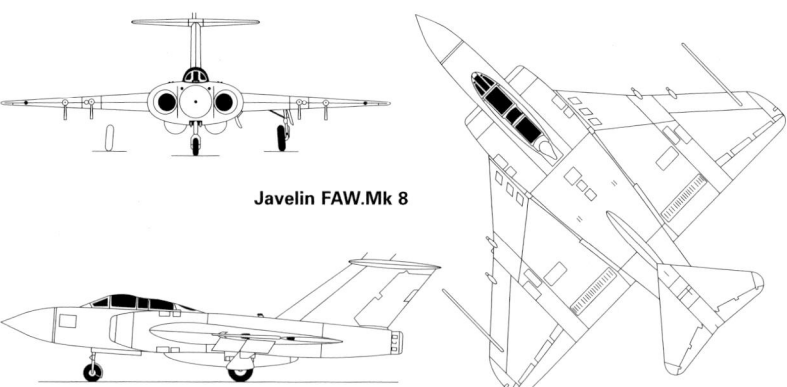

Javelin FAW.Mk 8

Variants

Javelin F(AW).Mk 1: initial production version with British AI.Mk 17 radar; 40 built
Javelin F(AW).Mk 2: differed primarily in having US-built APQ-43 radar; 30 built, the first of which was flown on 31 October 1955
Javelin T.Mk 3: dual-control trainer version with a 44-in (1.12-m) insert in the forward fuselage to offset the rearward movement of the centre-of-gravity position caused by removal of the radar; 23 built, of which the first flew on 6 January 1958
Javelin F(AW).Mk 4: introduced a fully-powered, all-moving tailplane; 50 built, of which the first flew on 19 September 1955
Javelin F(AW).Mk 5: incorporated a modified wing with increased internal fuel capacity, and with provision to carry four de Havilland Firestreak AAMs on underwing pylons; 64 built, of which the first flew on 26 July 1956
Javelin F(AW).Mk 6: counterpart of the F(AW).Mk 5 in the same manner as the F(AW).Mk 2 to the F(AW).Mk 1, and thus possessing American APQ-43 radar; 33 built, of which the first flew on 14 December 1956
Javelin F (AW).Mk 7: major production version (142 built with a first flight on 9 November 1956) featuring 11,000-lb st (48.93-kN) Sapphire ASSa.7 engines, modified flying-control system, and revised armament comprising two 30-mm ADEN cannon and four Firestreak AAMs
Javelin F(AW).Mk 8: final production version (47 built with a first flight on 9 May 1958) featuring Sapphire ASSa.7R engines with limited afterburning to provide 12,300 lb st (54.71 kN) above 20,000 ft (6095 m), US APQ-43 radar, and a Sperry autopilot
Javelin F(AW).Mk 9: redesignation of 76 F(AW).Mk 7s following upgrade to F(AW).Mk 8 standard; additionally, 22 of these aircraft were provided with an inflight-refuelling probe

Javelin FAW.Mk 9 XH768 is seen with the standard ventral fuel tanks. With superior armament to the Hunter, the Javelin also climbed more quickly to 50,000 ft (15240 m).

SPECIFICATION

Gloster Javelin F(AW).Mk 1
Type: two-seat all-weather fighter
Powerplant: two Armstrong Siddeley Sapphire ASSa.6 turbojet engines each rated at 8,000 lb st (35.59 kN)
Performance: maximum speed 709 mph (1141 km/h) at sea level; climb to 45,000 ft (13715 m) in 9 minutes 48 seconds; service ceiling 52,500 ft (16000 m)

Weights: empty 24,000 lb (10886 kg); maximum take-off 36,690 lb (16642 kg)
Dimensions: wingspan 52 ft (15.85 m); length 56 ft 3 in (17.15 m); height 16 ft (4.88 m); wing area 927.00 sq ft (86.12 m²)
Armament: four 30-mm ADEN fixed forward-firing cannon in the leading edges of the wing

Primary armament for later models of the Javelin, including this FAW.Mk 7, was the de Havilland Firestreak (initially codenamed Blue Jay) infra-red heat-seeking AAM, the first such weapon to enter service with the RAF.

Gloster Mars, Nighthawk, Nightjar and Sparrowhawk

Gloster's Mars I/'Bamel', which had led to the Gloster I and II, was derived from the Nieuport Nighthawk designed by Henry Folland. From this came a further family of early Gloster aircraft, beginning with the **Mars II**, which was developed as a single-seat fighter for the Imperial Japanese Navy following the visit to Japan of a British air mission in January 1921. Advice given by the British mission on

the equipment desirable for the development of a naval air arm resulted in an order for 50 aircraft based on the Nighthawk.

An equal-span biplane with a fabric-covered structure of wood, in its production form as the **Mars Mk II** the type had a tail unit incorporating dorsal and ventral fins, fixed tail-skid landing gear and a powerplant based on the 230-hp (172-kW) Bentley BR.2 rotary engine.

In IJN service, Sparrowhawks were launched from 30-ft (10-m) long platforms mounted above the gun turrets of various warships.

Gloster Mars, Nighthawk, Nightjar & Sparrowhawk (cont.)

Production of the Mars Mk II totalled 30 aircraft, and was followed by that of the generally similar **Mars Mk III**, of which 10 were built to a standard that differed from that of the Mars Mk II in having two open cockpits in tandem, with dual controls for use as trainers. The **Mars Mk IV**, of which 10 were completed, had arrester gear, flotation bags and strut-mounted paravanes forward of the main landing gear (to reduce the danger of the aircraft overturning if an emergency landing was made on water), and was intended for service as a carrierborne fighter. These

three production variants were later redesignated as the **Sparrowhawk Mk I**, **Sparrowhawk Mk II** and **Sparrowhawk Mk III** respectively. All proved highly successful with the IJN, remaining in service until 1928. In addition to the 10 Mars Mk III (later Sparrowhawk Mk II) aircraft for Japan, Gloster built a single example for use as a company demonstrator.

Under the designation **Mars Mk VI Nighthawk**, Gloster produced a small number of single-seat fighters for experimental use by the Royal Air Force. The Mars Mk VI Nighthawk was

basically the airframe of the Nighthawk revised with the 325-hp (242-kW) Armstrong Siddeley Jaguar II or Bristol Jupiter III radial, or the 385-hp (287-kW) Jupiter IV radial engine. In addition to the aircraft supplied to the RAF, 25 aircraft powered by the Jaguar engine were supplied to the army air force of Greece, with which they remained in first-line service until 1938 and belated relegation to training duties.

The final derivative of the Nighthawk airframe was the **Mars Mk X Nightjar**, a single-seat naval fighter for service with the Fleet Air Arm. This was basically a

navalised version of the RAF's Nighthawk with a reversion to the Bentley BR.2 engine. In addition the Mars Mk X Nightjar had new wide-track and longer-stroke landing gear and arrester jaws to engage fore and aft

wires on an aircraft-carrier's deck. From a holding of 22 Nightjars the RAF kept 12 in Fleet Air Arm service for a period of two years from July 1922, when the type was replaced by the Fairey Flycatcher.

SPECIFICATION

Gloster Mars Mk X Nightjar
Type: single-seat carrierborne fighter
Powerplant: one Bentley BR.2 rotary piston engine rated at 230 hp (172 kW)
Performance: maximum speed 120 mph (193 km/h) at sea level; climb to 15,000 ft (4570 m) in 20 minutes; service ceiling 19,000 ft (5790 m); endurance

2 hours
Weights: empty 1,765 lb (801 kg); maximum take-off 2,165 lb (982 kg)
Dimensions: wingspan 28 ft (8.53 m); length 18 ft 4 in (5.59 m); height 9 ft (2.74 m); wing area 270.00 sq ft (25.08 m²)
Armament: two 0.303-in (7.7-mm) Vickers Mk I fixed forward-firing machine-guns in the upper part of the forward fuselage

Gloster Meteor

The only Allied turbojet-powered warplane to see action during World War II, the **Meteor** was designed by George Carter, whose preliminary study gained Air Ministry approval in November 1940 under Specification F.9/40. It is worth noting that the designation **G.41**, often used as a 'company designation', is in fact spurious, being one of a sequence invented by the company's publicity department in 1948. The Meteor's twin-engined layout was determined by the low thrust produced by the turbojet engines then available. On 7 February 1941 an order was placed for 12 prototypes, although only eight were built. The first was fitted with 1,000-lb st (4.45-kN) Rover W.2B engines, and taxiing trials began at Newmarket Heath in July 1942. Delays in the production of flight-standard engines meant that the fifth airframe, with alternative 1,600-lb st (7.12-kN) de Havilland (Halford) H.1 engines, recorded the Meteor's maiden flight on 5 March 1943 at Cranwell, Lincolnshire.

Modified W.2B/23 engines then became available and were installed in the first and fourth prototypes, whose first flight dates were 12 June and 24 July 1943 respectively. On 13 November the third prototype made its maiden flight at Farnborough with

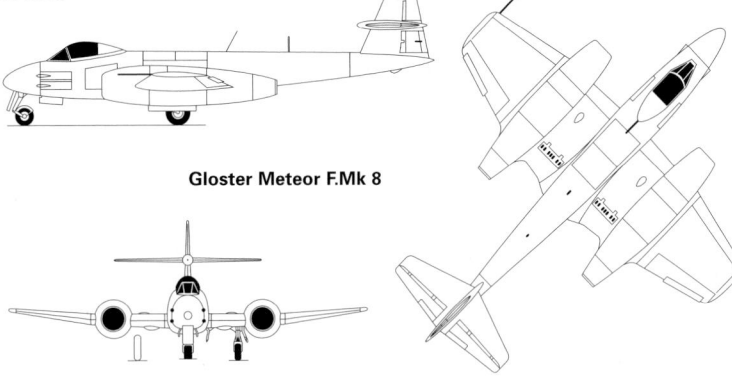

Gloster Meteor F.Mk 8

the powerplant of two Metrovick F.2 engines in underslung nacelles, and in the same month the second prototype flew, initially with Power Jets W.2/500 turbojet engines. The sixth aircraft later became the prototype **Meteor F.Mk II** with two 2,700-lb st (12.01-kN) de Havilland Goblin engines, and first flew on 24 July 1945. This machine was in fact preceded by the seventh prototype, which was used for trials with dive brakes as well as a modified vertical tail surface from 20 January 1944. The eighth prototype was powered by Rolls-Royce W.2B/37 Derwent I engines and posted its first flight on 18 April 1944.

Twenty **Meteor F.Mk I** fighters comprised the first production batch, these being powered by W.2B/23C Welland engines and incorporating minor

airframe improvements including a clear-view canopy. After a first flight on 12 January 1944, the first Meteor Mk I was delivered to the USA in February of that same year in exchange for a Bell YP-59A Airacomet, the first American jet aircraft. Others were used for airframe and engine development, and the 18th later became the **Trent-Meteor**, the world's first turboprop-powered aircraft, which recorded its maiden flight

on 20 September 1945: the Trent was basically a Derwent turbojet adapted with reduction gearing and a drive shaft that turned a five-bladed Rotol propeller of 7-ft 11-in (2.41-m) diameter, necessitating the introduction of longer-stroke landing gear to provide tip clearance; each engine delivered 750 shp (559 kW) with a residual thrust of 1,000 lb (4.45 kW).

The first operational jet fighter unit was No. 616

SPECIFICATION

Gloster Meteor F.Mk I
Type: single-seat fighter
Powerplant: two Rolls-Royce W.2B/23C Welland turbojet engines each rated at 1,700 lb st (7.56 kN)
Performance: maximum speed 415 mph (668 km/h) at 10,000 ft (3050 m); climb to 30,000 ft (9145 m) in 15 minutes; service ceiling 40,000 ft (12190 m)

Weights: empty 8,140 lb (2692 kg); maximum take-off 13,795 lb (6257 kg)
Dimensions: wingspan 43 ft (13.11 m); length 41 ft 3 in (12.57 m); height 13 ft 6 in (3.96 m); wing area 374.00 sq ft (34.74 m²)
Armament: four 20-mm Hispano fixed forward-firing cannon in the nose

Above: WL364 was typical of the Meteor T.Mk 7. This particular aircraft was retained by Gloster for some time as the mount for air-to-air photography during aerobatic manoeuvres.

Six Danish Meteor NF.Mk 11s were converted to TT.Mk 20 standard by Armstrong Whitworth in 1958. Four of the aircraft, including SE-DCH, were sold on to Sweden's Swedair. They served from August 1962 to April 1965, at which point two were sold on and two were retired.

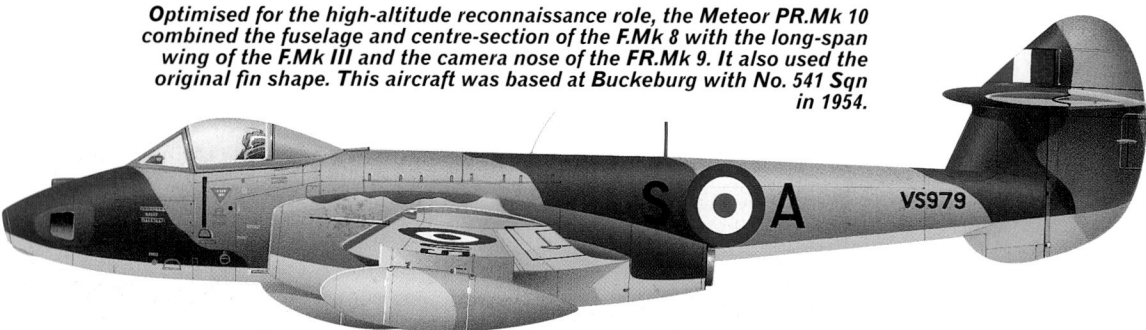

Optimised for the high-altitude reconnaissance role, the Meteor PR.Mk 10 combined the fuselage and centre-section of the F.Mk 8 with the long-span wing of the F.Mk III and the camera nose of the FR.Mk 9. It also used the original fin shape. This aircraft was based at Buckeburg with No. 541 Sqn in 1954.

Sqn based at Culmhead, Somerset, and equipped with Spitfire F.Mk VIIs when its first two Meteor F.Mk Is arrived on 12 July 1944. On 21 July the squadron moved to Manston, Kent, receiving more Meteors on 23 July to form a detached flight of seven. The first operational sorties were flown on 27 July, and on 4 August, near Tonbridge, F/O Dean destroyed the first V-1 flying bomb claimed by a jet fighter, using the Meteor's wingtip to roll it over into a spin after the Meteor's four 20-mm cannon had jammed. On the same day, F/O Roger shot down a second V-1 near Tenterden.

Conversion to the Meteor was completed towards the end of August, and the autumn was spent preparing for operations on the continent. Between 10 and 17 October, however, four Meteor fighters were detached to Debden, to take part in an exercise with the USAAF 2nd Bombardment Division and 65th Fighter Wing designed to provide the data that would permit the creation of tactics to be used against the Luftwaffe's Messerschmitt Me 163 and Me 262 reaction-powered fighters. The first Meteor F.Mk III aircraft were delivered to Manston on 18 December, and on 17 January the squadron moved to Colerne, Wiltshire, where the remaining Meteor F.Mk Is were replaced. On 20 January 1945 one flight of No. 616 Sqn's fighters joined No. 84 Group of the 2nd Tactical Air Force in Belgium, and in March No. 504 Squadron became the second Meteor F.Mk III unit to operate on the other side of the English Channel.

The Meteor **F.Mk III**, the second and last mark to see operational service during World War II, had increased fuel capacity and a sliding bubble canopy in place of the sideways-opening hood of the Meteor F.Mk I. Fifteen Meteor F.Mk IIIs were completed with Welland engines and 195 with Derwent engines, some in lengthened nacelles. The Derwent also powered the **Meteor F.Mk IV** (subsequently **Meteor F.Mk 4**), later examples of which were modified by a 5-ft 10-in (1.78-m) reduction in wingspan. Of the 657 such aircraft built, 465 were supplied to the RAF, allowing the surviving Meteor F.Mk IIIs to be passed to auxiliary units.

A 2-ft 6-in (0.76-m) fuselage extension, to accommodate a second cockpit in the Meteor F.Mk IV airframe, was a feature of Gloster's private-venture **Meteor Trainer**, first flown on 19 March 1948. Unarmed and fitted with dual controls, the aircraft was ordered for RAF use as the **Meteor T.Mk 7**, of which production totalled 712 including aircraft for the Royal Navy's Fleet Air Arm and also for overseas air forces.

The most prolific variant, however, was the **Meteor F.Mk 8** which had a lengthened fuselage, a redesigned tail unit, an additional 95-Imp gal (432-litre) fuel tank, and a bubble canopy over the cockpit. Extra equipment included a gyro gun sight and a Martin-Baker ejection seat, and 3,600-lb st (16.01-kN) Derwent 8 turbojet engines were installed to confer a top speed of almost 600 mph (966 km/h). The first of 1,183 Meteor F.Mk 8s flew on 12 October 1948. For low-level tactical reconnaissance the **Meteor FR.Mk 9** was developed from the Meteor F.Mk 8, carrying a camera nose and retaining the nose arma-

ment. The first of 126 examples was flown on 22 March 1950. This model was followed by an unarmed high-altitude version, the **Meteor PR.Mk 10**, which was a hybrid with the wing of the F.Mk III, the tail unit of the F.Mk 4 and the front fuselage of the FR.Mk 9. The first of 58 made its initial flight on 29 March 1950.

Development of a night-fighter version to Specification F.24/48 was assigned to Armstrong Whitworth in 1949. The cockpit section of the T.Mk 7 and an extended forward fuselage to accommodate American SCR-720 (AI.Mk 10) radar were mated to the F.Mk 8's rear fuselage and tail unit together with a wing similar to that of the F.Mk I, but redesigned to house the four 20-mm cannon displaced from the nose. The definitive **Meteor NF.Mk 11** prototype first flew on 31 May 1950, while a tropicalised version, the **Meteor NF.Mk 13**, first flew on 23 December 1952 and was used only by two Middle East squadrons. The **Meteor NF.Mk 12**, flown for the first time on 21 April 1953, had a higher limiting Mach number than its predecessors, American-built APS-81 radar and fin leading-edge fairings. A revised clear-view canopy and some minor aerodynamic and equipment changes identified the final night-fighter variant, the **Meteor NF.Mk 14**.

Conversions included the **Meteor U.Mk 15** and **Meteor U.Mk 16** pilotless target aircraft adapted from F.Mk 4 and F.Mk 8 airframes respectively. The **Meteor U.Mk 21** was a similar F.Mk 8 conversion for use at the Woomera range in Australia. NF.Mk 11s equipped for target-towing duties with the Royal Navy were designated Meteor **TT.Mk 20**.

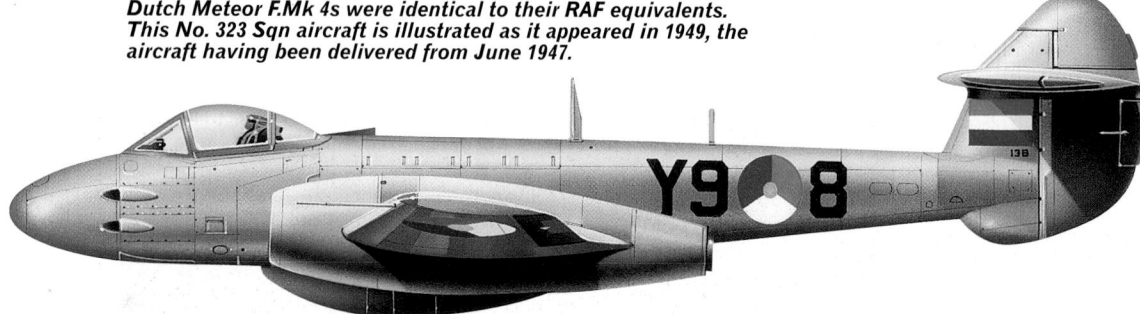

Dutch Meteor F.Mk 4s were identical to their RAF equivalents. This No. 323 Sqn aircraft is illustrated as it appeared in 1949, the aircraft having been delivered from June 1947.

Goodyear GA-1 and GA-2 Duck

In September 1944, just under one year before the end of World War II, the Goodyear Aircraft Corporation of Akron, Ohio, began the design of a small amphibian flying-boat. The first result of this effort was the **GA-1** prototype, which had two-seat accommodation. Of high-wing cantilever monoplane configuration with underwing stabilising floats, the GA-1 had a fabric-covered metal wing, all-metal hull with a single-step planning bottom, cruciform tail unit, retractable tailwheel landing gear and the powerplant of one 113-hp (84-kW) engine, pylon-mounted above the hull to drive a pusher propeller.

Successful evaluation of the GA-1 paved the company's way for the construction of about 20 pre-production aircraft for use as demonstrators, none of which was offered for sale. Generally similar to the prototype, these demonstrators differed mainly in their accommodation, which seated the pilot and two passengers. About 15 of these were completed under the designation **GA-2 Duck** with the uprated powerplant of one 145-hp (108-kW) Franklin 6A4-145-A3 engine, while the other aircraft were completed to the **GA-2B Duck** standard with a still more potent engine. By the time that the test programme had been completed and the demonstration 'boats had been evaluated on a worldwide scale, costs had escalated to a point where it would not be possible to market the 'boat on a sensible economic basis to the private pilots for which it had been intended, and the project was abandoned.

An attractive amphibian design, the GA-2 Duck failed to find favour with private buyers, mostly on account of its prohibitively high price. Note the streamlining of the underwing floats.

SPECIFICATION

Goodyear GA-2B Duck
Type: three-seat general-purpose amphibian flying-boat
Powerplant: one Franklin 6A4-165-B3 flat-four piston engine rated at 165 hp (123 kW)
Performance: maximum speed 125 mph (201 km/h) at 1,000 ft (305 m); cruising speed 112 mph (180 km/h) at 1,000 ft (305 m); initial climb rate 700 ft (213 m) per minute; service ceiling 15,000 ft (4570 m); range 300 miles (483 km)
Weights: empty 1,600 lb (726 kg); maximum take-off 2,300 lb (1043 kg)
Dimensions: wingspan 36 ft (10.97 m); length 26 ft (7.92 m); height 9 ft 6 in (2.90 m) on wheels; wing area 178.20 sq ft (16.55 m²)

Gotha G series

During 1917 and 1918 British people generally, and those who lived in London particularly, came to dread air attacks by the 'Gothas', a name which they applied indiscriminately to all German bombers making day or night raids. Development by Gotha of aircraft in this class had started during 1915, and the first of these twin-engined bombers were the **Gotha G.II** and **G.III** of 1916. Built in only small numbers they were generally similar, differing only in internal detail, but early experience of these aircraft operating in Europe brought development during 1916 of the longer-range **G.IV**. Of mixed wood and steel construction, with plywood and fabric covering, the G.IV was of three-bay biplane configuration with a basically square-section fuselage, braced tail unit and tailskid landing gear incorporating twin-wheel main units. The twin-engined powerplant, comprising two Mercedes D.IVa inlines strut-mounted between the wings, directly above the main landing gear, was arranged to drive pusher propellers, a large cut-out being provided in the trailing edge of the upper wing to give the necessary propeller clear-

ance. The G.IV was followed by an improved **G.V** that was basically the same, but introduced improved equipment and a number of refinements, including cleaner, more streamlined engine nacelles.

Daylight raids on England began on 25 May 1917 with a mass attack by 21 Gothas on Folkestone and Shorncliffe in Kent, followed by the first daylight raid on London on 13 June 1917. In this first attack on the capital a total of 162 people were killed and more than 400 injured, the largest number of fatalities of any World War I raid on the UK. It, and subsequent attacks during June and July, made without any significant opposition, brought a public outcry, which resulted in formation of the Royal Air Force as a completely independent service, unshackled by the British Army or Royal Navy. Interim measures taken to combat the Gothas included the withdrawal of some operational fighter squadrons from the Western Front, these proving sufficiently effective to make daylight raids too costly, and compelling Bombengeschwader 3, which had responsibility for these attacks, to shift to night operations: these

continued until May 1918. In the course of the 22 attacks made on the UK, the Gothas had dropped a total of more than 83 tons of bombs, no mean achievement for bomber aircraft of that era.

A number of Gotha G series aircraft followed the G.V, mostly built in ones or twos. They included the unusual **G.VI**, but with the fuselage offset to port and mounting one of two 194-kW (260-hp) Mercedes D.IVa engines in its nose, the other installed in a nacelle to starboard. The following **G.VII** was a twin-engined biplane, the prototype beautifully streamlined for its period, also powered by Mercedes D.IVas. Intended for the long-range reconnaissance

Variant

G.Vb: version of the standard G.V with a pair of auxiliary wheels mounted forward of each main landing gear unit to reduce the danger of nosing-over during night operations

role, the three or four production examples built were very considerably changed and lost the sleek lines. The **G.VIII** appears to have been little more than an increased-span version of the G.VII, but introduced 245-hp (183-kW) Maybach Mb.IV engines, and the **G.IX** was a similarly powered twin, built by Luft-Verkehrs Gesellschaft, of which virtually nothing

has been recorded. Last of the G series twins was the **G.X**, a smaller and lighterweight reconnaissance aircraft powered by two 180-hp (134-kW) BMW IIa engines.

As the earliest incarnation of Gotha's G-series twin-engined bomber designs, the G.II was of little real operational value.

SPECIFICATION

Gotha G.V
Type: three-seat long-range bomber
Powerplant: two 260-hp (194-kW) Mercedes D.IVa 6-cylinder inline piston engines
Performance: maximum speed 87 mph (140 km/h); service ceiling 21,325 ft (6500 m); range 311 miles (500 km)
Weights: empty 6,041 lb (2740 kg), maximum take-off

8,763 lb (3975 kg)
Dimensions: wingspan 77 ft 9 in (23.70 m); length 38 ft 11 in (11.86 m); height 14 ft 1¼ in (4.30 m); wing area 963.40 sq ft (89.50 m²)
Armament: two 0.31-in (7.92-mm) Parabellum machine-guns on pivoted mounts in nose and dorsal positions, and a bombload of 661 to 1,102 lb (300 to 500 kg) according to range of mission

Gotha Go 145

The Gotha company, which had been closed down in 1919 under the terms of the Treaty of Versailles, was re-formed on 2 October 1933. The first product of the revived company was the **Go 145** trainer, which was a single-bay biplane of fabric-covered wooden construc-

tion with a powerplant based on the Argus As 10C engine. The prototype first flew in February 1934 and the type entered service with the Luftwaffe during the following year. Although used originally as a pilot training aircraft, the Go 145 served also with the Störkampfstaffeln.

These were established from December 1942, when the Luftwaffe decided to emulate the Soviets' use of the Polikarpov Po-2 as a 'nuisance raider' during the hours of darkness. In October 1943 the German units were redesignated Nachtschlachtgruppen, and remained operational on the Eastern Front until the end of World War II. Just

under 10,000 Go 145 aircraft were built by Gotha, Ago, BFW and Focke-Wulf in Germany,

and the type was also produced under licence in Spain as the **CASA 1145-L**, and in Turkey.

Variants

Go 145A: initial production dual-control trainer
Go 145B: this 1935 model introduced an enclosed cockpit and landing-gear spats
Go 145C: air-to-air gunnery trainer with a 0.312-in (7.92-mm) MG 15 trainable machine-gun in the rear cockpit

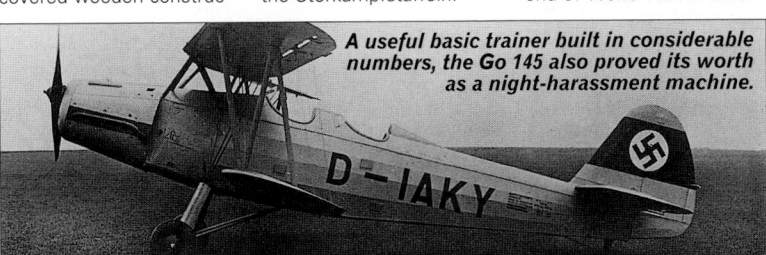

SPECIFICATION

Gotha Go 145A
Type: two-seat basic flying trainer
Powerplant: one Argus As 10C inverted-Vee piston engine rated at 240 hp (179 kW)
Performance: maximum speed 132 mph (212 km/h) at sea level; cruising speed 112 mph (180 km/h) at optimum altitude; climb to 3,280 ft (1000 m) in 5 minutes

30 seconds; service ceiling 12,140 ft (3700 m); range 391 miles (630 km)
Weights: empty 1,940 lb (880 kg); maximum take-off 3,043 lb (1380 kg)
Dimensions: wingspan 29 ft 6¼ in (9.00 m); length 28 ft 2⅜ in (8.60 m); height 9 ft 5¾ in (2.89 m); wing area 234.12 sq ft (21.75 m²)

Gotha Ho 229 (Horten Ho IX)

Among the most unusual warplanes schemed in World War II was the **Horten Ho IX** flying-wing design for a turbojet-powered fighter. Designed under the supervision of the brothers Reimar and Walter Horten, who had made their name with the creation of advanced flying-wing gliders, the Ho IX first saw the light of day in the form of the **Ho IX V1** glider prototype that recorded its maiden flight on 1 March 1944. The programme was then delayed as the **Ho IX V2** second prototype awaited the delivery of its powerplant of two flight-cleared BMW 003 turbojet engines, which were then replaced by 1,962-lb st (8.73-kN) Junkers Jumo 004B engines, to allow a first flight shortly before Christmas 1944.

The Ho IX was of mixed construction – welded steel tube for the centre section and wood elsewhere under a covering of plywood. There was no vertical tail surface, and the landing

gear was of the retractable tricycle type with a notably large nose wheel.

The Ho IX V2 was lost in mid-February 1945, but the programme continued as the German air ministry had contracted with Gotha for the 'productionisation' of the **Ho IX (8-229)** design as what has come to be known, erroneously, as the **Gotha Go 229** that would thus have been an intermediate step to the **Horten Ho 229** production version using Klemm-built wing panels. Gotha and Horten

then concentrated on the construction of more prototypes and 20 pre-production aircraft with revisions including an alteration of the air inlets' geometry and, to cure a centre-of-gravity problem, the forward movement of the two engines. The **8-229 V3** was intended as the precursor of the first single-seat production model, while the structurally redesigned **8-229 V6** was planned as the precursor of the definitive single-seat fighter. The **8-229 V4** and **V5** were projected as the

first steps toward a two-seat night-fighter model.

As late as March 1945 the 8-229 programme was confirmed within Luftwaffe

Not only did the Go 229 represent an outstanding jet fighter design, but the aircraft also successfully embodied the flying-wing concept. In addition, its design would have given it a degree of what is known today as 'stealth'.

plans, but less than two months later Germany had surrendered before the first **Ho 229A** production aircraft had been started.

SPECIFICATION	
Gotha (Horten) Ho 229A	
Type: single-seat fighter	**Weights:** empty 10,141 lb (4600 kg); maximum take-off 17,857 lb (8100 kg)
Powerplant: two Junkers Jumo 004B turbojet engines each rated at 1,962 lb st (8.73 kN)	**Dimensions:** wingspan 54 ft 11¾ in (16.;76 m); length 24 ft 6 in (7.47 m); height 9 ft 2¼ in (2.81 m); wing area 540.37 sq ft (50.20 m²)
Performance: maximum speed 607 mph (977 km/h) at 39,370 ft (12000 m); initial climb rate 4,331 ft (1320 m) per minute; range 1,181 miles (1900 km)	**Armament:** two 30-mm fixed forward-firing cannon

Gotha Go 242/244

The work of Dipl. Ing Albert Kalkert, the **Go 242** assault glider was developed with the approval of the Reichsluftfahrtministerium since it offered almost three times the troop-carrying capacity of the DFS 230 then in use. The fuselage pod was of steel tubular construction with fabric covering, and carried jettisonable landing gear and two retractable skids, and the wings were made of wood with fabric and plywood covering. The

aircraft could carry 21 fully-equipped troops, or the equivalent weight in military loads, such as a Kübelwagen utility vehicle loaded through the hinged rear fuselage. Two prototypes were flown in 1941 and production followed without delay, permitting entry into service in 1942. The type's operational debut was made in the Mediterranean and Aegean theatres, Go 242 units being based in Greece, Sicily and North Africa.

Gotha Go 244B-1

Right: These three Go 242A-1 gliders, wearing two distinctly different camouflage schemes, were photographed on a resupply mission on the southern sector of the Eastern Front in 1942.

Below: The powered Go 244 saw only limited service thanks to its largely inadequate performance. A standard Go 244B-1 is illustrated.

Variants

Go 242A: initial production version with deepened booms and, although essentially a cargo glider, the **Go 242A-1** could be armed with up to four 0.31-in (7.92-mm) MG 15 machine-guns; the **Go 242A-2** was the troop-carrying equivalent
Go 242B: introduced in 1942, with jettisonable nose wheel landing gear, the two initial versions were the **Go 242B-1** and **Go 242B-2** which differed principally in the design of the main landing gear; troop-carrying equivalents were the **Go 242B-3** and **Go 242B-4**, both with double rear doors; the **Go 242B-5** incorporated dual controls for pilot training
Go 242C-1: developed for marine attacks, in particular for a raid on the British fleet anchorage at Scapa Flow, the C-1 had a planing hull and underwing stabilising floats, it was to have carried a small assault boat with an explosive charge but the type was not used operationally, although a number was delivered to 6/KG 200 in 1944

Gotha Go 242/244 (continued)

Heinkel He 111 tugs were usually employed for the Go 242 and rocket-assisted take-off equipment could be fitted to the gliders, the variety of propulsion units including four 1,102-lb (4.90-kN) Rheinmetall-Borsig Rl-502 solid fuel rockets. Production totalled 1,528 aircraft.

After the fall of France,

the French Gnome-Rhône 14M radial engine became available to the Germans in large numbers, and the Go 242 was modified to serve as the **Go 244** twin-engined transport, each of the twin booms being extended forward of the leading edge of the wing to mount one of these engines; at the same

time fixed tricycle landing gear was installed. A total of 133 conversions was made from the five Go 242B variants and these were designated correspondingly **Go 244B-1** to **B-5**. First deliveries were made in March 1942 to the Greece-based KGrzbV 104 and to KGrzbV 106 in Crete, but the aircraft proved to

be relatively easy targets for Allied fighters and had been withdrawn by November 1942. Some

Go 244s had 660-hp (492-kW) BMW 132Z or captured 750-hp (559-kW) Russian Shvetsov M-25As.

SPECIFICATION	
Gotha Go 244B-2	**Weights:** empty 11,243 lb (5100 kg); maximum take-off 17,196 lb (7800 kg)
Type: assault/troop transport	**Dimensions:** wingspan 80 ft 4½ in (24.50 m); length 51 ft 10 in (15.80 m); height 15 ft 5 in (4.70 m); wing area 693.22 sq ft (64.40 m²)
Powerplant: two 700-hp (522-kW) Gnome-Rhône 14M 14-cylinder radial piston engines	
Performance: maximum speed 180 mph (290 km/h); service ceiling 24,605 ft (7500 m); range 373 miles (600 km)	**Armament:** four 0.31-in (7.92-mm) MG 15 machine-guns optional

Gotha LE series

Gotha was one of the many German aircraft manufacturers that decided in the pre-World War I period to launch onto the commercial market a series of Taube (dove) aircraft, with the type of monoplane wing pioneered by Igo Etrich. The result

was the **Gotha LE** (**Land Eindecker**, or land monoplane) series of aircraft.

In the event Gotha produced four Taube-type designs, the **LE 1** and **LE 2** appearing in 1913 and the **LE 3** and **LE 4** in 1914. The LE 1 and LE 2 were basically similar apart from

their main landing-gear units: the LE 1 had the Blériot type of unit, while the LE 2 had the Vee-strut type of unit. Both of these two-seat models were available with a number of different inline engine types, most notably the 70- and 85-hp (52- and 63-kW) Austro-Daimler units, the 100-hp (75-kW) Mercedes, 100-hp (75-kW) Rapp, and 70-, 100- and 120-hp (52-, 75- and 90-kW) Argus units.

The LE 3 and LE 4 (possibly redesignated as the **A I** and **A II** respectively during the opening phase of the war) each had a main landing-gear arrangement based on a two-wheel axle carried at

Performance details of the LE 1 and LE 2 included a maximum speed of about 57 mph (92 km/h) at sea level and a climb to 2,625 ft (800 m) in 20 minutes.

the closed ends of two Vee struts extending downward and outward from the lower longerons and were each powered by the 100-hp (75-kW)

Mercedes D.I inline engine; while the engine of the LE 3 was cooled by two lateral radiators, that of the LE 4 was cooled by a neat frontal radiator.

SPECIFICATION	
Gotha LE 3	climb to 2,625 ft (800 m) in 12 minutes; endurance 4 hours
Type: two-seat reconnaissance aircraft	**Weights:** empty 1,521 lb (690 kg); maximum take-off 2,262 lb (1026 kg)
Powerplant: one Mercedes D.I inline piston engine rated at 100 hp (75 kW)	**Dimensions:** wingspan 47 ft 6⅞ in (14.50 m); length 33 ft 7½ in (10.25 m); wing area 360.60 sq ft (33.50 m²)
Performance: maximum speed 59.5 mph (96 km/h) at sea level;	

Gotha WD series

In parallel with its **LD** series of landplanes, Gotha developed a family of floatplanes as the **WD** (**Wasser Doppeldecker**, or water biplane) series. Initially, the relationship between the two series was readily apparent, but whereas the reconnaissance landplane series faded from service by mid-1916, the floatplane series continued in development and the final version was the truly giant **WD 27** of 1918.

The series started with the **WD 1** and **WD 1a** that appeared before the outbreak of war in August 1914 as fabric-covered wooden biplanes with two-seat open-cockpit accommodation, and a twin-float main alighting gear arrangement supplemented by a small float beneath the tail unit. Powered by the 100-hp (75-kW) Gnome rotary engine, a few of these floatplanes were used by the Imperial German

navy air service for coastal patrol duties during the opening stages of the war. The following **WD 2** was a slightly larger floatplane of generally similar configuration but without the small float beneath the tail unit. Powered by the 150-hp (112-kW) Benz Bz.III inline engine, it was built for the German navy and also for Turkey, those for the latter having a single machine-gun on the top surface of the upper-wing centre section. One WD 2, modified by a reduction in wingspan and the installation of the 160-hp (119-kW) Mercedes D.III engine, was redesignated as the **WD 5**. From this one-off machine was developed the **WD 9** which differed primarily in having a single trainable machine-gun in the rear cockpit. Only one example was supplied to the German navy, but several were built for Turkey, these having the same Bz.III engine as the

WD 2 delivered earlier.

When pure observation and reconnaissance aircraft began to give way to scout or fighter aircraft, one of the early solutions to provide an effective means of mounting a forward-firing weapon was the introduction of a central nacelle incorporating a rear-mounted engine with

Apart from its carriage of a fuel tank in place of a torpedo, the WD 20 (illustrated) was identical to the WD 14. The wings could be folded just outboard of the engines.

pusher propeller. This configuration was adopted by Gotha for the **WD 3**, the central nacelle being flanked by twin booms, each carrying a single fin-and-rudder assembly and joined at the rear by a tailplane-and-elevator unit. Power was provided by the 160-hp (119-kW) Mercedes D.III engine mounted in the rear of the nacelle to drive a pusher propeller, and a single machine-gun was installed on a trainable mounting in the nose. After

this single unorthodox design, Gotha reverted to a development of the WD 9 to produce the slightly larger one-off and unarmed **WD 12** which was supplied to the German navy; it was also built for Turkey, the machines delivered to that nation being the first it had received with Mercedes engines. A similar armed patrol floatplane, developed from the WD 9, was built for Turkey under the designation **WD 13**, and this model reverted to the Bz.III

Four engines, comprising two Mercedes D.IIIs driving tractor propellers and two Mercedes D.Is driving pusher propellers, powered the WD 22.

powerplant. The last of these single-engined WD floatplanes built for the German navy was the unarmed **WD 15** developed from the WD 12: these two floatplanes had refined lines, a plywood-covered fuselage and a powerplant based on the 260-hp (194-kW) Mercedes D.IVa engine.

Gotha's twin-engined floatplane designs had originated in 1916 with the **WD 7**, which was of the same general lines and size as the WD 2 but with two 120-hp (90-kW) Mercedes D.II inline engines mounted on the lower wing, one on each side of the fuselage. Eight were built for the German navy, which used them as torpedo-bombing trainers. An armed reconnaissance variant of the WD 7 was built and this, strangely, had only a single engine; only one example was completed. It was followed by the much larger **WD 11** of the same general configuration, but which differed in having a tail unit incorporating twin fins and rudders and its two Mercedes D.III engines arranged to drive

pusher propellers. About 12 of these torpedo-bombers were built and delivered to the German navy, each able to carry one torpedo and armed with a single trainable machine-gun in the nose.

Only one of Gotha's twin-engined torpedo-bombers was built in significant numbers, this being the **WD 14** which was a slightly scaled-up development of the WD 11. Two more powerful Bz.IV engines were mounted on the lower wing to drive tractor propellers, and two trainable machine-guns were installed in nose and rear positions. Some 69 of these aircraft were built, but they saw only very limited use in their intended role as their low speed when carrying a torpedo made them extremely vulnerable to attack.

The three **WD 20** long-range reconnaissance floatplanes were completed to a standard that differed from that of the WD 14 only in the carriage of an auxiliary fuel tank in place of a torpedo,

As the first of Gotha's WD floatplane series, the WD 1 saw limited service at the very start of World War I.

and the two long-range patrol and reconnaissance **WD 22** machines of 1918 were basically similar except for having four engines mounted in tandem pairs. Last of the line of Gotha multi-engined floatplanes were the three giant **WD 27** long-range bomber and patrol aircraft with a span of 101 ft 8½ in (31.00 m). The aircraft were powered by four Mercedes D.III engines mounted in tandem pairs.

SPECIFICATION	
Gotha WD 14	10,234 lb (4642 kg)
Type: three-seat torpedo-bomber floatplane	**Dimensions:** wingspan 83 ft 8 in (25.50 m); length 47 ft 5 in
Powerplant: two Benz Bz.IV inline piston engines each rated at 200 hp (149 kW)	(14.45 m); height 16 ft 4¾ in (5.00 m); wing area 1,420.88 sq ft (132.00 m²)
Performance: maximum speed 81 mph (130 km/h) at sea level; climb to 3,280 ft (1000 m) in 13 minutes 6 seconds; endurance 8 hours	**Armament:** one 0.312-in (7.92-mm) LMG 14 Parabellum trainable machine-gun in each of the nose and dorsal positions, plus one torpedo carried beneath the fuselage
Weights: empty 6,945 lb (3150 kg), maximum take-off	

Gourdou-Leseurre GL-1, -2, -21, -22, -23 & GL-24

In the summer of 1917 the engineers Charles Edouard Pierre Gourdou and Jean Adolphe Leseurre became partners and set about the design of a single-seat fighter for the French Aéronautique Militaire. An official order followed and the resulting **Gourdou-Leseurre GL-1** (otherwise known as the **Type A**) was built in Paris at the workshops of the Wassmer company, normally a manufacturer of aircraft propellers.

The GL-1 prototype was a neat parasol-wing monoplane of mixed steel and wood construction under a covering mainly of fabric. The fuselage was of circular cross-section, the tail unit had a large distinctive fin

and-rudder assembly, the landing gear was of the simple robust fixed tailskid type, and the powerplant was based on one 180-hp (134-kW) Hispano-Suiza 8Ab Vee engine with a frontal radiator. Official flight testing began in May 1918 and revealed that, while the GL-1's structure was too heavy, it nonetheless offered performance generally superior to that of current biplane fighters with a 300-hp (224-kW) engine and including a maximum speed of 150 mph (242 km/h) at 3,280 ft (1000 m). An order for 100 production aircraft was cancelled, however, as a result of official insistence on a programme of struc-

tural lightening in concert with an improved and strengthened wing structure and bracing.

This led to the **GL-2** (otherwise **Type B**) with a new and stronger wing braced by four rather than two struts, a revised tail unit with the tailplane moved farther up the fuselage and the rudder modified, and improved landing gear. But the end of World War I meant loss of official interest after the delivery, from

Four struts on each side of the fuselage supported the wing of the GL-2. These struts were braced to each other, both with further struts and rigging.

November 1918, of 20 **GL-2C.1** production aircraft manufactured by Mayen et Zodiac with a larger fin and taller rudder to overcome a directional instability problem. Gourdou and Leseurre then joined the technical

office of the Compagnie Aérienne Française, but anxious to have their own workshops, they set up business in 1921 at St Maur-les-Fossés, on the south-eastern outskirts of Paris.

Finland received 19 GL-21C.1 fighters direct from France and a 20th was assembled from spares. The aircraft were not retired until 1931.

Variants

GL-23C.1: this 1925 single-seat fighter prototype, otherwise known as the **Type B4**, combined the basic GL-22C.1 airframe with the increased-span wing of the ET; seven were built and two with wings of different aerofoil section were used for comparative tests
GL-23TS: designation of one GL-23 after conversion by lengthening the fuselage and installing a porthole-type window in each side; the TS suffix stood for **Transport Sanitaire** (medical transport), and a pair of doors in the starboard side of the rear fuselage gave access for a single litter; the GL-23TS was demonstrated on 24 April 1925 at Le Bourget on the occasion of an international medical congress, but the small production order was won by the rival Hanriot HD-14S and only one more GL-23TS was built in 1926
GL-24: one-off machine built in 1925 as a two-seat dual-control trainer version of the GL-22; in the following year it was redesignated **GL-24X** after conversion to single-seat layout, and the machine was used for research into the effects of g during tight manoeuvres; in 1934 one GL-21 was revised with the 350-hp (261-kW) Hispano-Suiza 9Qd engine and, used for aerobatic flying, was also redesignated GL-24 although it was a single-seat aircraft

Gourdou-Leseurre GL-1, -2, -21, -22, -23 and GL-24 (cont.)

The GL-2 took part in the Coupe Deutsch de la Meurthe speed contest in 1919, and attained an average of 133.13 mph (214.26 km/h) over the 124-mile (200-km) cross-country course.

Gourdou and Leseurre then developed the GL-2 into the **GL-21** (otherwise **Type B2**) that was first exhibited at the Salon de l'Aéronautique in Paris during 1920. The GL-21 differed in detail and also dispensed with the GL-2's horn-balanced broad-chord ailerons in favour of narrower-chord plain ailerons of longer span. The GL-21 was followed in 1925 by the **GL-22** (otherwise **Type B3**) with steel instead of Dural bracing struts, a redesigned

longer-span wing, horizontal tailplane and landing gear, and a new 'beehive' type frontal radiator.

The principal customer for the **GL-21C.1** production version of the GL-21 single-seat fighter was Finland, which acquired a pattern machine in 1923 and built another 18 such machines in 1924 (later supplemented by another machine assembled from spare parts) for service up to 1931. Total production of the GL-21 was 30 aircraft, the balance of 10 machines, modified over the years, being flown by French private owners. The **GL-22C.1** was sold in small batches to Czechoslovakia, Estonia and Latvia, production amounting to only 20 aircraft for these three

As a clean parasol-wing monoplane, the GL-2 could achieve a maximum straight-line speed of 152 mph (245 km/h) at sea level.

customers. The **Type B5** or **GL-22ET.1**, more commonly known as the **ET**, was a single-seat advanced trainer version of the basic Type B3 with the span of its wing increased: of the 30 such aircraft completed, most served with the French navy, one being used for take-off and landing trials on the aircraft carrier *Béarn*, while the other flew with French army aviation training units.

One civil example of the Type B3, with a wing of enlarged area, was flown by the firm's test pilot,

André Christiany, to win the 1923 Coupe Michelin speed competition. Three civilianised ETs were flown by Georges Madon and pilots Bapt and Picard as a propaganda unit (painted overall in the red, white and blue of the tricolore) to give displays at air shows in France and North Africa during 1923. Various Type B3s continued to give outstanding displays and win competitions into the

1930s. One with modified landing gear was redesignated as the **Type B6**, and the **Type B7** was a GL-21C.1 with reinforced struts, new divided main landing-gear units and the uprated powerplant of one 300-hp (224-kW) Lorraine Algol radial engine. At least two aircraft were built for aerobatic demonstrations, one being flown by the celebrated French aviatrix Adrienne Bolland.

SPECIFICATION

Gourdou-Leseurre GL-22C.1 (Type B3)
Type: single-seat fighter
Powerplant: one Hispano-Suiza 8Ab Vee piston engine rated at 180 hp (134 kW)
Performance: maximum speed 153 mph (257 km/h) at sea level; climb to 16,405 ft (5000 m) in 17 minutes 30 seconds; service ceiling 24,605 ft (7500 m); range

280 miles (450 km)
Weights: empty 1,301 lb (590 kg); maximum take-off 1,940 lb (880 kg)
Dimensions: wingspan 30 ft 10 in (9.40 m); length 21 ft 3¾ in (6.50 m); height 8 ft 4¼ in (2.52 m); wing area 198.06 sq ft (18.40 m²)
Armament: one or two 0.303-in (7.7-mm) Vickers fixed forward-firing machine-guns in the upper part of the forward fuselage

Gourdou-Leseurre GL-810/811/812/813

Apart from brief flirtations with two flying-boat designs, the **M-2** twin-engined patrol biplane of 1926 and the 10-passenger **GL-710** of 1934, Gourdou-Leseurre concentrated its marine aircraft production on twin-float seaplanes.

The **L-2** prototype, built in 1926-27, had a steel-tube fuselage and rectangular wooden wings, both covered with fabric. Of low-wing monoplane configuration, the L-2 had the twin floats of its alighting gear connected to the fuselage and wing by a multiplicity

of struts. The prototype of an impressive series of three-seat observation and reconnaissance float-planes, the L-2 was flown to Copenhagen to take part in the international aeronautical exhibition held there in August 1927. There followed six **L-3** pre-production floatplanes with a 420-hp (313-kW) Gnome-Rhône (Bristol) Jupiter radial engine in place of the 380-hp (283-kW) Jupiter of the L-2, steel instead of wood spars, and strengthened struts. These changes made the L-3 suitable for shipboard catapult launch-

ing. Like the earlier L-2, the L-3 built in 1928 had two triangular fins, one above and one below the fuselage, and a single curved rudder.

Successful testing of the L-3 led to a production order from the French navy for production of the first 24 of an eventual 86 floatplanes of the **GL-810Hy** series. They were to be built at the firm's St Maur workshops with the floats manufactured at Les Mureaux, and were intended for deployment on the French navy's capital ships and cruisers, as well as the seaplane

carrier *Commandant Teste*. The first production example of the GL-810Hy took off from the Seine river at Les Mureaux on 23 September 1930, and differed from the earlier machines in having enlarged vertical tail surfaces of similar shape, and in the location of its three-man crew: the three tandem open cockpits of the L-2 and L-3 had accommodated pilot, observer and gunner in that order, but in the GL-810Hy and later variants the positions of the observer and gunner were exchanged.

In September 1931 the French naval air service ordered 20 examples of the improved **GL-811Hy**. This differed from the GL-810Hy in having dual controls, folding wings, a water rudder at the rear of the starboard float and radio equipment. They were intended specifically for operation from the *Commandant Teste*. Further orders, for 29 **GL-812Hy** and 13 **GL-813Hy** aircraft, followed in 1933-34. These had vertical tail surfaces of new design (more rounded and of greater surface area) and rounded wingtips, and were fitted with two-bladed metal propellers. The GL-813Hy was identical to the GL-812Hy except that it was fitted with dual controls. During 1936, 11 GL-810Hy, 13 GL-811Hy and six GL-813Hy float-planes were converted to GL-812Hy standard. Before this, however, the French navy had organised a competition for a replacement three-seat

One of the L-2's most notable features was the huge extent of bracing for its floats. After being exhibited in Denmark, the aircraft was demonstrated to several European naval air arms without success.

observation seaplane. Gourdou-Leseurre built the **GL-820Hy** with a 730-hp (544-kW) Hispano-Suiza radial engine with a Townend ring, a similar **GL-821.01Hy** for the torpedo-bombing role and therefore possessing a strengthened structure, and finally the **GL-821.02Hy** with improved lines and glazed canopies over the crew cockpits. However, these types did not win any production orders, which

went instead to the successful contender, the Loire 130 flying-boat.

The GL-810 family of floatplanes equipped Escadrille 7S2 aboard the *Commandant Teste* and Escadrille 7S3, which distributed its aircraft among the cruisers of the French fleet. Other units which flew these float-planes in all corners of the world up to 1937 included Escadrilles 1S1, 2S1, 2S4, 3S1, 3S2, 3S3, 3S6. 8S2

and 8S5. Although the Gourdou-Leseurre float-planes had mostly been replaced in first-line units by 1939, surviving machines were brought together at the time of the August mobilisation before World War II to equip the reactivated Escadrilles 1S2 at Cherbourg and 3S3 at Berre near Marseilles. Both of these units operated coastal anti- submarine patrols for the following 10 months.

Gourdou-Leseurre GL-832

Built in response to a 1930 French navy requirement for a light coastal patrol seaplane, for use principally in French overseas colonies, the **GL-831Hy** prototype was a modification of the firm's **GL-830Hy** with a 250-hp (186-kW) Hispano-Suiza radial engine in place of the 350-hp (261-kW) 9Qdr engine of the earlier aircraft. The GL-831HY flew for the first time on 23 December 1931 and in 1933 Gourdou-Leseurre received a production order for 22 **GL-832Hy** floatplanes. These were powered by the Hispano-Suiza 9Qb radial in place of the slightly more powerful Hispano-Suiza 9Wa engine of the prototype. A low-wing monoplane of metal construction covered with fabric, the GL-832Hy was stressed for catapult launching and had a very

large parallel-chord wing with cut-outs in its trailing edges at their junctions with the fuselage, and was arranged to fold for stowage purposes. The curved vertical tail surfaces were more conventional than those of the GL-810Hy series, but the horizontal tailplane was most unusual in its location, being attached to the underside of the rear fuselage, to which it was braced on each side by a pair of short struts. The two-man crew was located in tandem open cockpits, each with an individual windscreen.

The first and last production examples of the GL-832Hy recorded their maiden flights on 17 December 1934 and 12 February 1936 respectively. Placed in service on second-line cruisers such as the *Emile Bertin* and *Primauguet*, and on colonial

The French navy denied requests from Gourdou-Leseurre to fit a more powerful engine in the GL-832 at an early stage in the type's development.

sloops which were without catapults and had to launch their aircraft by lowering them on to the sea by crane, the GL-832Hy was still in service at the outbreak of World War II in September 1939, operator units comprising Escadrille 7S4 (later HS5) with the 1st Cruiser Division, Escadrille 8S2 based at Fort de France on the West Indian island of Martinique from September 1939, Escadrille 8S4 at Tripoli in the Levant, and Escadrille 7S4 in the Pacific. Remarkably, the last of the floatplanes were still active with Escadrille 7S4 at the time of the Japanese attack on Pearl Harbor in December 1941.

In 1937 the partnership between Leseurre and Gourdou was dissolved, but Gourdou still main-

tained his aviation interests, employing Georges Bruner as his chief engineer. Although several new projects were designed, only one prototype was actually built. This was the **Gourdou G-120Hy**, built to meet a requirement for a new light two-seat ship-board reconnaissance seaplane that would be suitable for catapult launching. It was a mid-wing monoplane with very cleanly installed twin-float alighting gear and the powerplant of two 140-hp (104-kW) Renault 4P-01 inverted inline engines, glazing for the nose and the two crew positions, and a strut-braced tail unit

with two endplate vertical surfaces. The wing incorporated revolutionary multiple flaps designed by Bruner and Gourdou, which were claimed to give excellent control at take-off and landing as well as in flight. A full-size mock-up appeared in 1939 and the prototype itself made two flights on 1 and 2 June 1940, demonstrating the effectiveness of the flaps. Unfortunately, the aircraft had to be broken up on 10 June to prevent it from falling into German hands. The proposed armament was two 0.3-in (7.62-mm) Darne machine-guns and the estimated maximum speed was 132 mph (212 km/h).

Gourdou-Leseurre LGL-32

The next Gourdou-Leseurre design to go into production after the GL-21 series was another single-seat fighter, the **GL-32** that became known as the **LGL-32** to reflect the fact that from 1925 to 1928 Gourdou-Leseurre was a subsidiary of a major ship-building company, the Ateliers et Chantiers de la Loire. The LGL-32 was built to participate in a competition to meet the Aéronautique Militaire's 1923 single-seat fighter programme requirement, and against tough competition it gained second place in a prolonged series of

tests. The **LGL-32.01** prototype flew for the first time in the spring of 1925, and the company received an initial order for five evaluation and 20 pre-production aircraft in January 1927. Three of the evaluation aircraft were later used as demonstrators, giving impressive performances in France and a number of foreign countries, and as a result the company gained considerable export orders.

The **LGL-32C.1** production fighter was of mixed metal and wood construction, with metal panels over the forward fuselage and fabric covering elsewhere.

Power was provided by a Gnome-Rhône (Bristol) 9Ady Jupiter radial engine. The new fighter's greatest

A parasol-wing monoplane in the Gourdou-Leseurre tradition, the LGL-32 featured a pair of parallel wing-bracing struts on each side and also incorporated a newly-designed tailplane with a curved leading edge.

shortcoming was its rather frail fixed tailskid landing gear, and as a result the type became all too well

known for a number of mishaps on landing, sometimes leading to aircraft up-ending on their noses.

Gourdou-Leseurre LGL-32 (cont.)

Positive factors of the LGL-32's performance were a good rate of climb and excellent manoeuvrability, these two qualities more than compensating for the fighter's fairly modest speed.

Total production of the LGL-32C.1 was 479. The type entered service with the Aéronautique Militaire at the end of 1927, equipping 12 first-line metropolitan-based fighter escadrilles until 1934, as well as two fighter regiments based at Sidi Ahmed in Tunisia and the Cercle de Chasse de Paris, the latter a volunteer reserve unit based at Le Bourget and responsible for defence of the French capital. In addition, the LGL-32C.1 equipped Escadrilles 3C1 and 3C2 of the French navy's Aviation Maritime. Good flying qualities and reasonable range led to the use of the LGL-32C.1 in numerous formation flights by fighter escadrilles, all of which helped to promote the

cause of French service aviation. Late production machines had redesigned landing gear, with wider-track independent main units and Messier shock absorbers. After 1934 attrition escalated, however, and by January 1936, of some 380 of the type which had been in French service only 135 remained, these being used for training duties and as ground instruction airframes for Armée de l'Air mechanics.

Romania took delivery of 50 LGL-32C.1s, the last being delivered in November 1928. After some indecision Turkey bought 12 aircraft, designated **LGL-32-T**, and Japan received one machine. It is reported, but remains unconfirmed, that in 1936 some four (or perhaps 12) LGL-32C.1s retired by the Armée de l'Air were sold to the Spanish Republican government, anxious to obtain aircraft from any source at the outset of the Spanish Civil War. Little is known of the fate of these

particular aircraft, which possibly reached Catalonia on 4 August 1936. Early in 1937, however, the Basque government (allied to the Republicans) followed its initial purchase of four ex-French LGL-32C.1s in October and November of the previous year with a contract for 12 (possibly 15) new-build aircraft with the divided main landing-gear arrangement of the **GL-410** fighter prototype. Ineffective as fighters and adapted as dive-bombers, some of the aircraft were modified to carry two 110-lb (50-kg) bombs on racks attached to the wing struts, an alternative being one 220-lb (100-kg) bomb under the fuselage. A dive-bombing attack led by Miguel Zambudio scored decisive hits on the Nationalist battleship *Espaniola* in April 1937. The battleship finally sank, much credit going to the LGL-32C.1 at a late stage in its career.

As a type which attracted little in the way of military interest, the LGL-32Hy managed to grab the headlines on 28 March 1927 when it was used to establish a world seaplane altitude record.

SPECIFICATION	
Gourdou-Leseurre LGL-32C.1	(500 km)
Type: single-seat fighter	**Weights:** empty 2,123 lb (963 kg);
Powerplant: one Gnome-Rhône	maximum take-off 3,033 lb (1376 kg)
9Ady Jupiter radial piston engine	**Dimensions:** wingspan 40 ft ¼ in
rated at 420 hp (313 kW)	(12.20 m); length 24 ft 9⅝ in
Performance: maximum speed	(7.55 m); height 9 ft 8¼ in (2.95 m);
155 mph (250 km/h) at sea level;	wing area 268.03 sq ft (24.90 m²)
climb to 16,405 ft (5000 m) in	**Armament:** two 0.303-in (7.7-mm)
12 minutes; service ceiling	Vickers fixed forward-firing
31,825 ft (9700 m); range 311 miles	machine-guns

Variants

LGL-32Hy: early in 1927 the LGL-32.01 prototype was revised with twin-float alighting gear in place of its original wheeled landing gear; the type aroused little interest in terms of sales prospects
LGL-321: the first evaluation aircraft converted to take a 600-hp (447-kW) Jupiter engine. It took part in an air display at Orly in March 1929; it was scrapped in 1931
LGL-323 and LGL-324: a standard LGL-32 was converted to take a 500-hp (373-kW) Jupiter VII radial engine fitted with a supercharger for high-altitude operation; as the LGL-323 this machine made several unsuccessful record attempts before being further modified as the LGL-324, with which, on 23 May 1929, Lemoigne set a world landplane altitude record, with a 1,102-lb (500-kg) payload, of 31,500 ft (9600 m); on 24 October Albert Lécrivain established a world altitude without payload record of 36,090 ft (11000 m)
LGL-33C.1: one example of this version flew in April 1925 to a standard that differed from the LGL-32 mainly in having a closely cowled 450-hp (336-kW) Lorraine 12Eb engine but also in revisions to its wing struts, main landing gear and vertical tail surface; demonstrated in Romania during April 1927, this machine was written

off in France during July 1927 while making an emergency landing
LGL-34C.1: merely an LGL-32C.1 with the standard Jupiter engine replaced by a 500-hp (373-kW) Hispano-Suiza 12Gb unit; after a number of public displays this modified aircraft was scrapped during 1929
LGL-341C.1: the first such machine had a small increase in wing area by comparison with the standard fighter and was powered by the 500-hp (373-kW) Hispano-Suiza 12Hb engine with a frontal radiator; the second machine, initially flown in May 1928, had twin radiators on the forward landing-gear struts in place of the frontal radiator; the LGL-341 offered good performance but no production was undertaken
LGL-390: in June 1934 a standard LGL-32 was re-engined with a 575-hp (429-kW) Hispano-Suiza 9Va radial and tested unsuccessfully as a night-fighter prototype
GL-633: one of the GL-32C.1 fighters built for the Basque government in 1937 was converted as a single-seat dive-bomber carrying a 1,102-lb (500-kg) bomb under the fuselage; considerably modified compared with standard aircraft, it had rounded wingtips, a curved fin and new wide-track landing gear; powered by the Gnome-Rhône 9Ady Jupiter engine, it attained a maximum speed of 174 mph (280 km/h)

Grahame-White Baby and New Baby

Claude Grahame-White was one of the most important of British aviation pioneers, not least because his enthusiasm for flight in particular was more than matched by his dedication to the concept of aviation in general, as expressed by his development of the major airfield at Hendon in the northern outskirts of London. A motor trader by occupation, Grahame-White caught the aviation 'bug' at the great Reims air meeting in northern France, learned to fly and entered several air races, in the process winning considerable sums of money. In 1910 Graham-White bought an area of pasture for the creation of his airfield, and here established, as the

commercial vehicle for his career in aviation, the Grahame-White Aviation Company Ltd. The company's first endeavour was a Wright-type pusher biplane, complete with a forward elevator, produced in 1910 for a planned flight from London to Paris. The type was evidently unsuccessful, and no data for the machine have survived.

The type of aircraft most successful in Europe at that

time was the boxkite, and later in 1910 there appeared the **Grahame-White Baby** of this configuration. This was a two-seat biplane powered by the 50-hp (37-kW) Gnome rotary engine driving a pusher propeller turning between the four pole booms that extended from the trailing edges of the wing cellule to carry the biplane tail unit. In the following year there

SPECIFICATION	
Grahame-White New Baby	endurance 3 to 4 hours
Type: two-seat general-purpose	**Weights:** empty 420 lb (191 kg);
aircraft	maximum take-off 655 lb (297 kg)
Powerplant: one Gnome rotary	**Dimensions:** wingspan 27 ft
piston engine rated at 50 or 70 hp	(8.23 m); length 32 ft 3 in (9.83 m);
(37 or 52 kW)	height 8 ft 6 in (2.59 m); wing area
Performance: maximum speed	235.00 sq ft (21.83 m²)
55 mph (89 km/h) at sea level;	

Grahame-White's New Baby employed a the frail-looking structure so typical of its period. Note the ailerons on both the top and bottom wings.

appeared the **New Baby** with a number of detail improvements as well as a forward elevator to supplement the tail unit, ailerons on both the upper and lower wings, and a choice of Gnome engines.

Grahame-White Type XV

Of the **Type XV** virtually nothing is known other than what can be gleaned from photographs. The aircraft was a development of the same organisation's **Box-kite** of 1912, which was clearly inspired by the Henry Farman type of biplane. The type appeared in two forms that differed from each other quite considerably in the same sort of way as the Farman MF.7 'Longhorn' and MF.11 'Shorthorn', and although there are some indications that the earlier variant was initially known as the **Type XII**, both variants were later known as Type XV aircraft.

The 1912 Box-kite was based on an equal-span biplane wing cellule in which the flat upper and lower wings were essentially identical. Hanging ailerons were set inboard of the outboard ends of both wings' trailing edges. The upper and lower wings were separated on each side by four sets of parallel interplane struts, and the whole wing cellule was wire braced. The forward and rear booms extended from the second set of interplane struts out from the inboard section: the rear booms were parallel in side elevation but converged in top elevation, while the forward booms converged in side elevation but were parallel in top elevation. The rear booms supported a high-set rectangular tailplane carrying a large plain elevator, and to the rear of the aftermost vertical spacer was hinged the plain rudder. The junction of the upper and lower members of the forward booms carried the pivot points for the forward elevator. Accommodation comprised provision for two people side-by-side in a completely exposed position on a very simple frame installed on the upper surface of the lower wing, with partial dual controls. The powerplant was based on one 50-hp (37-kW) Gnome rotary engine

For Grahame-White the Box-kite formed the basis of a small family of aircraft types and, ultimately, the Type XV military trainer.

installed on the upper surface of the lower wing to drive a two-bladed wooden pusher propeller.

In this form the Box-kite saw some service with the Grahame-White Flying School and was then bought by the Royal Flying Corps in March 1913 and survived into the later part of the same year.

From this machine was developed the Type XV that first appeared in 1913 as a simple development of the original Box-kite with rear booms that remained parallel in top elevation to support a tail unit that comprised two rudders and a tailplane carrying a rectangular elevator. The first of these aircraft was used for the initial British air-to-surface firing trials of the Lewis machine-gun in November 1913, and entered production for service with the Grahame-White flying school in August 1914, serving with this organisation as well as the Royal Naval Air Service after the start of World War I.

The production aircraft from 1914 onward were all built with revised aileron and wing installations. The final production variant, which first appeared in November 1914 and always had the

upper-wing extensions of the later Type XV, was analogous to the MF.11 development of the MF.7 in that the forward elevator and its booms were removed. Other changes in this variant were the use of an uprated powerplant in the form of the 80-hp (60-kW) Gnome or Le Rhône rotary engine, the adoption of double-acting ailerons, and the introduction of a central nacelle for the two crew members, who sat in tandem and were provided with full dual controls.

Production of the Type XV for the British military flying services totalled 135 aircraft in the form of 85 machines for the RNAS (which designated them Type 1600 in service) and 50 machines for the RFC, delivered as 23 in 1916 and 27 in 1917, when the aircraft were decidedly obsolete, even in the training role. Even so, some of the aircraft remained serviceable up to 1918.

Type XVs in RNAS service carried the designation Type 1600. The latter was derived from the serial number of the Type XV prototype (illustrated), which was the first of the type in RNAS service.

Grahame-White Type X Charabanc

The efforts of Claude Grahame-White to popularise flying at his airfield, opened during October 1910 in the north London suburb of Hendon, were so successful in the later stages of the period leading up to the outbreak of World War I in August 1914 that his company needed greater passenger-carrying capability to satisfy demand. John D. North responded with the **Type X**, which was designed to carry, in addition to the pilot in the front of the long open cockpit, the standard payload of up to four passengers, in two side-by-side pairs of wicker seats.

The Type X adhered to structural practices of the time, and was therefore a wire-braced wooden aircraft covered largely with fabric. In configuration it was an unequal-span three-bay biplane with a complex tail unit (twin horizontal surfaces and triple vertical surfaces) carried by four booms extending rearward from the wings. The airframe was completed by the central nacelle, which was mounted just above the upper surface of the lower-wing centre section and carried the occupants at the front and the powerplant at the rear.

The Type X recorded its maiden flight in the summer of 1913, and on 22 September of the same year established a world payload record by taking off with seven passengers and remaining in the air for almost 17 minutes 30 seconds. On 2 October, just over one week later, the Type X lifted off with nine passengers and remained aloft for just over 19 minutes 45 seconds. Another notable success for the Type X was as the platform from which the first British parachute descent was made on 9 May 1914. The Type X was also used for long-distance races in all-British form with the standard Austro-Daimler engine replaced by a 100-hp (75-kW) Green engine.

SPECIFICATION	
Grahame-White Type X Charabanc	**Weights:** empty 2,000 lb (907 kg); maximum take-off 3,100 lb (1406 kg)
Type: one-crew joyriding aircraft	**Dimensions:** wingspan 62 ft 6 in (19.05 m); length 37 ft 6 in (11.43 m); wing area 790.00 sq ft (73.39 m²)
Powerplant: one Austro-Daimler inline piston engine rated at 120 hp (90 kW)	
Performance: maximum speed 51 mph (82 km/h) at sea level; cruising speed 45 mph (73 km/h) at sea level	**Payload:** standard load of five passengers or nine passengers under overload conditions

The Type X utilised a fixed tailskid landing gear featuring twin-wheel main units, each of which was fitted with two anti-nose over skids.

Granville Brothers aircraft

The decade from 1925 to 1935 saw exciting attempts to wring more and more speed from often frail aircraft structures, the enthusiasm for these attempts being engendered by the rapidly growing sport/spectacle that began in the USA and was known as pylon racing. The classic in this category was the Thomson Trophy, first flown in 1929, and the races of 1931 and 1932 were won by **Granville Gee Bee** machines, strange looking barrel-shaped aircraft that had the minimum amount of airframe needed to get the pilot and a powerful radial engine into the air.

Designed and built by the five Granville brothers, hence the popular name Gee Bee (or **GB**), the **Model R Super Sportster** was typical of their concept of the racing machine at the peak of its development.

A wire-braced low/mid-wing monoplane with fixed tailwheel landing gear, the main units extensively faired and carrying spatted

wheels, the Model R had a barrel-shaped fuselage dictated by the diameter of the radial-engined power-plant. Two aircraft were built in the forms of the **Model R-1** with the 800-hp (597-kW) Pratt & Whitney Wasp engine and the **Model R-2** with, in its initial form, greater fuel capacity and a 550-hp (410-kW) Wasp Junior engine. Both were entered for the 1933 Bendix Trophy, the Model R-1 by then fitted with a 900-hp (671-kW) Pratt & Whitney Hornet engine and the Model R-2 with the Wasp unit that had previously been installed in the Model R-1.

The legendary 'Jimmy' Doolittle had flown a Gee Bee to win the Thomson Trophy of 1932, and on 3 September 1932 he set a world landplane speed record of 296.287 mph (476.830 km/h) in the Model R-1. However, within a year both the Model R-1 and the Model R-2 had crashed, the remnants being used for a hybrid machine, the **Model R-1/R-2**, that was raced

under the name of *Intestudinal Fortitude*. In 1934 the eldest of the five brothers, Zantford (nicknamed 'Granny') was killed in another accident and, with the driving force missing, Granville Brothers slipped into bankruptcy.

There had been an attempt to market a less potent version of the design for the sportsman pilot, this version stemming from the one-off **Model X Sportster** (110-hp/82-kW American Cirrus engine) of 1930 as a basic single-seat airframe that could be readily adapted for the installation of any of several engine types. The result was the **Sportster** range, which was built only in very small numbers, but including the **Model B** with a 110-hp (82-kW) Cirrus Ensign engine, the **Model C** with a 95-hp (71-kW) Menasco B-4 Pirate engine, the **Model D** with a 125-hp (93-kW) Menasco C-4 Pirate engine and, the only variant with a radial engine, the **Model E** with a 110-hp (82-kW) Warner Scarab

Not surprisingly, the achievements of the Gee Bee racers, such as this Model Z which could achieve nearly 300 mph (483 km/h), have become a part of the folklore of American aviation of this period.

unit. The **Model Y Senior Sportster** was an expansion of the Model X philosophy to provide two-seat accommodation, and two of this version were built. The **Model Z Super Sportster**, precursor of the **Model R**, was a one-off racer evolved from the Models X and Y, and was powered by the 535-hp (399-kW) Wasp Junior and had a maximum speed of 270 mph (435 km/h). For an attempt on the world land-plane speed record a 750-hp (560-kW) Wasp was fitted, but on 5 December

1931 the overstressed aircraft started to disintegrate in the air, the aircraft rolling into the ground with fatal results for the pilot after one wing had folded back. Another Granville type of the same basic layout was the **Q.E.D.** of 1934: this was a long-range two-seater with the Pratt & Whitney Hornet engine. The type was plagued by mechanical problems, but in 1939 achieved a non-stop flight from Mexico City to New York. On the return flight the machine crashed, killing the pilot.

SPECIFICATION	
Granville Brothers (Gee Bee) Sportster Model E	rate 1,500 ft (457 m) per minute; service ceiling 19,000 ft (5790 m); range 550 miles (885 km)
Type: single-seat sporting aircraft	
Powerplant: one Warner Scarab radial piston engine rated at 110 hp (82 kW)	**Weights:** empty 912 lb (414 kg); maximum take-off 1,400 lb (636 kg)
Performance: maximum speed 148 mph (238 km/h) at sea level; cruising speed 127 mph (204 km/h) at optimum altitude; initial climb	**Dimensions:** wingspan 25 ft (7.62 m); length 16 ft 9 in (5.11 m); height 6 ft (1.83 m); wing area 95.00 sq ft (8.83 m²)

Although it was a sporty-looking, attractive type, the Sportster Model E suffered from high costs of ownership – a problem which was compounded by the economically lean years of the 1930s.

Great Lakes 2-T-1

The Great Lakes Aircraft Corporation, established in late 1928 on the Cleveland, Ohio site lately vacated by the Glenn L. Martin Company, began by building two examples of an eight-seat commercial aircraft called the **Miss Great Lakes**. This design

was derived from the Martin T4M-1, but failing to gain little more than a flicker of interest for its eight-seat transport, the company concentrated on the development of a two-seat sports/trainer biplane designated as the **Great Lakes 2-T-1**. The prototype,

first flown in March 1929, was a single-bay biplane of fabric-covered mixed construction with a single-bay staggered wing cellule and fixed tailskid landing gear. Power was provided by an 85-hp (63-kW) Cirrus Mk III engine, and two open cockpits in tandem were provided for the pilot and passenger/pupil. Flight testing revealed that the

aircraft was excessively tail heavy and, after three more had been built, the upper wing was given a pronounced sweepback to overcome this problem.

It is believed that about 40 aircraft were built before production shifted to a generally similar **2-T-1A**, which introduced the 90-hp (67-kW) American-built Cirrus engine, slightly enlarged tail surfaces and a number of refinements.

The 2-T-1A was ordered in very large numbers before the financial recession of late 1929 brought large-scale cancellations, but about 200 are thought to have been built. The final version, in production until 1933, was the **2-T-1E** that introduced a new version of the American-built Cirrus engine and some slight refinement in lines. Only about a dozen were built.

SPECIFICATION	
Great Lakes 2-T-1E	at optimum altitude; service ceiling 12,000 ft (3660 m); range 375 miles (604 km)
Type: two-seat sporting/training aircraft	
Powerplant: one American Cirrus inverted inline piston engine rated at 95 hp (71 kW)	**Weights:** empty 1,012 lb (459 kg); maximum take-off 1,580 lb (717 kg)
Performance: maximum speed 110 mph (177 km/h) at sea level; cruising speed 95 mph (153 km/h)	**Dimensions:** wingspan 26 ft 8 in (8.13 m); length 21 ft (6.40 m); height 7 ft 10 in (2.39 m); wing area 187.60 sq ft (17.43 m²)

A number of 2-T-1 aircraft survive on the US civil register in the 21st century. Many, like this Warner-engined machine, have been highly modified.

Great Lakes BG

With a requirement in 1932 for a new two-seat carrier-borne dive-bomber. able to carry a 1,000-lb (454-kg) bomb beneath its fuselage, the US Navy contracted with the Consolidated Aircraft Corporation and the Great Lakes Aircraft Corporation to build competitive prototypes. The resulting **Great Lakes XBG-1** was an unequal-span biplane with tapered single-bay wings, fixed tail-wheel landing gear, a tandem arrangement of open cockpits for the pilot and the observer/ gunner,

and a powerplant based on the 750-hp (560-kW) R-1535-64 Twin Wasp Junior radial engine. Following its completion in mid-1933, the XBG-1 was tested by the US Navy and, when flown in competition against the Consolidated XB2Y-1, was found to be the better machine. The type was therefore ordered into production during November 1933 as the **BG-1**, which differed from the prototype in having an elongated canopy to enclose the two cockpits. Production totalled 61

aircraft including the prototype, and initial aircraft entered service with operational units in the autumn of 1934.

The BG-1 remained in

first-line service with the US Navy until 1938, then continuing in use as a general-purpose aircraft with second-line operators for several more years.

About half of the production aircraft were allocated to the US Marine Corps, remaining operational with some units until 1940.

SPECIFICATION

Great Lakes BG-1
Type: two-seat carrierborne dive-bomber
Powerplant: one Pratt & Whitney R-1535-82 Twin Wasp Junior radial piston engine rated at 750 hp (560 kW)
Performance: maximum speed 188 mph (303 km/h) at 8,900 ft (2715 m); climb to 5,000 ft (1525 m) in 5 minutes 30 seconds; service ceiling 20,100 ft (6125 m); range 540 miles (869 km) with maximum payload
Weights: empty 3,903 lb (1770 kg); maximum take-off

6,350 lb (2880 kg)
Dimensions: wingspan 36 ft (10.97 m); length 28 ft 9 in (8.76 m); height 11 ft (3.35 m); wing area 384.00 sq ft (35.67 m²)
Armament: one 0.3-in (7.62-mm) Browning fixed forward-firing machine-gun in the forward fuselage and one 0.3-in (7.62-mm) Browning trainable rearward-firing machine-gun in the rear of the cockpit, plus up to 1,000 lb (454 kg) of disposable stores carried under the fuselage, and generally comprising one 1,000- or 500-lb (454- or 227-kg) bomb

BG-1s flew with VB-4M (later VMB-2) from 1935 and VB-6M (later VMB-1) from 1936. Both units retained their aircraft until 1940, at which time VMS-1 (illustrated) was also operating a handful.

Variant

XB2G-1: a single example of a more developed version of the BG-1 was built for evaluation but failed to gain a production contract; it had retractable main landing-gear units and a deeper fuselage to provide an internal bay for a 1,000-lb (454-kg) bomb

Grigorovich I-Z

The Soviet authorities initiated the so-called 'Z' programme in mid-1930 with the object of developing a fighter to carry the new 3-in (76.2-mm) Kurchyevskii recoilless cannon. The OMOS (department of marine experimental aircraft construction) design team nominated for the task was led by Grigorovich and, quite naturally, he drew heavily on features of the I-5 single-seat biplane fighter on

which he had worked in collaboration with Nikolai Polikarpov. The majority of the single-seat fuselage was a semi-monocoque structure of Dural construction, Grigorovich adopting a low-wing configuration with the fabric-covered metal wing. The large vertical fin had a curved leading edge, and the braced horizontal tail surfaces were mounted high on the fin to avoid any interference from the exhaust gases of the large-

bore cannon. These two DRP weapons were mounted below the wing, outboard of the fixed tailskid landing gear's main units, and were single-shot cannon. They were complemented by a single machine-gun, mounted in the fuselage, to provide a means of registering fire on the target before the main weapons were fired.

Two prototypes of the new **Grigorovich I-Z** fighter were built, the first flying for the first time in the summer of 1931. The **I-Zbis** second prototype introduced a

number of modifications and structural strengthening, and appeared at the beginning of 1932. Both were powered by the 525-hp (391-kW) Gnome-Rhône Jupiter VI radial engine. The design bureau designation of the type was **TsKB-7**.

An order for 21 evaluation aircraft, powered by the Soviet 480-hp (358-kW) M-22 radial engine enclosed by a Townend ring, was received in 1933. The metal wing structure of the prototypes was now rejected in

favour of a wooden structure. Some 50 more I-Zs were later built, but the fighter's flight characteristics were not good and the heavy-calibre one-shot cannon was not a success. As a result, most of the aircraft were used for flight testing and experimental work. One example was used in the Vakhmistrov 'Zvyeno' parasite fighter trials. Series aircraft had a maximum speed which was 25 mph (40 km/h) lower than that of the prototypes.

SPECIFICATION

Grigorovich I-Z
Type: single-seat fighter
Powerplant: one M-22 radial piston engine rated at 480 hp (358 kW)
Performance: maximum speed 186 mph (300 km/h) at 9,845 ft (3000 m); climb to 16,405 ft (5000 m) in 14 minutes; service ceiling 22,965 ft (7000 m); range 373 miles (600 km)
Weights: empty 2,601 lb (1180 kg);

maximum take-off 3,633 lb (1648 kg)
Dimensions: wingspan 37 ft 8¾ in (11.50 m); length 25 ft 1¼ in (7.65 m); wing area 209.90 sq ft (19.50 m²)
Armament: two 3-in (76.2-mm) Kurchyevskii DRP fixed forward-firing cannon under the wing and one 0.3-in (7.62-mm) PV-1 fixed forward-firing machine-gun in the upper part of the forward fuselage

The forward fuselage and engine installation of the I-Z, including the helmeted cylinder head cowlings, were similar to those of the second I-5 prototype.

Grigorovich IP-1, IP-4, DG-55, DG-56 and DG-58

Developed during 1934 under the Grigorovich design bureau designation **DG-52**, the **IP-1 (Istrebitel Pushyechnii-1**, or cannon fighter-1) was a cantilever low-wing, all-metal monoplane, the prototype flying for the first time early in

1935. A single-seat cannon fighter, its pilot was seated in an open cockpit and had a faired headrest. Power was provided by a 640-hp (477-kW) Wright Cyclone radial engine, and the design incorporated tailskid landing gear with main units that

retracted rearward into bath-tub-type underwing fairings.

Like the I-Z, the IP-1 was developed to use the Kurchyevskii cannon, two 3-in (76.2-mm) APK-4 weapons being mounted underwing. Each of these cannon could fire five

rounds. The additional armament of two 0.3-in (7.62-mm) machine-guns was intended to assist the pilot in aiming the cannon.

The IP-1 was ordered into production, but the series version was much modified by comparison with the

prototype: the Kurchyevskii cannon were abandoned and replaced by two 20-mm ShVAK cannon in the wing-roots and by six 0.3-in (7.62-mm) ShKAS machine-guns in two three-gun trays mounted farther outboard under the wing.

Grigorovich IP-1, IP-4, DG-55, DG-56 and DG-58 (cont.)

A large dorsal fin was added to improve lateral stability, and this was extended forward to blend into the fairing of the pilot's head rest. Some 90 IP-1s were completed between 1936 and 1937, but they were overshadowed by the Polikarpov I-16 which met all the needs of the Soviet air arm at that time. This led to the temporary eclipse of single-seat fighters of all-metal construction in favour of the wooden Polikarpov designs. Production examples of the IP-1 were powered by the Soviet M-25 radial.

The **IP-4** (otherwise **DG-53**) development of the IP-1 appeared at the end of 1934 with the primary fixed forward-firing armament of four 45-mm Kurchyevskii APK-11 cannon aimed with

the aid of two light machine-guns. Like the IP-1 prototype the IP-4 was powered by the Cyclone engine. A second prototype, with two ShVAK cannon in place of the Kurchyevskii weapons, was projected, but not completed.

Although the IP-1 was the last of his designs to be built in quantity, Grigorovich produced several other notable aircraft before he became seriously ill in 1937. One of these was the **IP-2** (otherwise **DG-54**), powered by an 830-hp (619-kW) Hispano-Suiza 12Xbrs engine and armed with a ShVAK engine-mounted cannon and no fewer than 10 ShKAS wing-mounted machine-guns. The IP-2 was almost complete

when development was abandoned in 1936. Other designs included the **E-2 Kometa** (otherwise **DG-55**), a smooth-contoured low-wing cantilever mono-plane with tandem accommodation in a two-seat glazed cabin and powered by two 120-hp (90-kW) Cirrus Hermes engines and intended as a long-range racing aircraft. Clearly inspired by the de Havilland DH.88 Comet, the sole example was used from 1935 onward as a long-range mail and courier aircraft.

The remaining Grigorovich projects were the **DG-56** or **LK-3** (**Legkii Kreyser-3**, or light cruiser-3) of 1936, for possible production as a three-seat long-range escort fighter with two Hispano-Suiza

A large dorsal fin was added to the IP-1 (DG-52) to aid spin recovery; its centre-of-gravity had moved rearwards after changes to the aircraft's armament.

12Ybrs engines, and the **DG-58** or **PB-1** (**Pikiriyushchii Bombardirovshchik-1**, or dive-bomber-1) of 1937 planned as a two-seat low-wing dive-bomber powered by a single M-85 (Soviet version of the Gnome-Rhône 14K) radial engine. The developed

DG-58bis or **DG-58R** version was intended for the 'Ivanov' reconnaissance aircraft competition, but all work on this type ceased on the death of Grigorovich in July 1938. It was estimated that these developed versions would have a maximum speed of 280 mph (450 km/h).

SPECIFICATION	
Grigorovich IP-1	maximum take-off 4.145 lb (1880 kg)
Type: single-seat heavy fighter	**Dimensions:** wingspan 36 ft
Powerplant: one M-25 radial	(10.97 m); length 23 ft 8¾ in (7.23 m);
piston engine rated at 710 hp	wing area 215.07 sq ft (19.98 m²)
(529 kW)	**Armament:** two 20-mm ShVAK
Performance: maximum speed	fixed forward-firing cannon in the
255 mph (410 km/h) at 9,845 ft	wing roots and eight 0.3-in
(3000 m); climb to 3,280 ft	(7.62-mm) ShKAS fixed forward-
(1000 m) in 1 minute 18 seconds;	firing machine-guns as two in the
service ceiling 27,230 ft (8300 m);	upper part of the forward fuselage
range 373 miles (600 km)	and six in trays under the leading
Weights: empty 2,646 lb (1200 kg);	edges of the wing

Remarkably similar to the de Havilland DH.88 Comet, the sole Grigorovich E-2 was passed to Osoaviakhim and used for courier flights.

Grigorovich M-5

Born in 1883, Dmitrii Pavlovich Grigorovich began his distinguished design career in 1913 with the Shchyetinin and Shchyerbakov company in St Petersburg (later Leningrad before reverting to its original name). His successful repairs to the flying-boat of D. M. Aleksandrov decided Grigorovich to set up on his own, and after the establishment of the USSR following the revolutions of 1917, Grigorovich became head of the OMOS (department of marine aircraft experimental construction).

The Grigorovich M-1 two-seat flying-boat, powered by a 50-hp (37.3-kW) Gnome rotary engine driving a pusher propeller,

appeared in 1913 and was the repaired and improved Aleksandrov flying-boat, and was followed in the following year by the M-2 with the 80-hp (59.6-kW) Clerget rotary engine and then in 1914 by the M-3 with the 100-hp (74.6-kW) Gnome Monosoupape rotary engine. Grigorovich's first successful flying-boat was the M-4 (alternative designation ShchM-4), of which four were built in 1914-15 for the Imperial Russian navy, which allocated two of the 'boats to the Baltic and the other two to the Black Sea. The M-4 was followed during 1915 by the **M-5** (alternative designation ShchM-5). An unequal-span biplane flying-boat with a two-bay wing cellule and a

single-step hull, the M-5 was of wooden construction, the hull being covered with plywood and the flying surfaces with fabric. To the rear of the step, the hull tapered sharply into little more than a boom, supporting a characteristic single fin and rudder tail unit, which was braced by means of a complexity of struts and wires. The Gnome Monosoupape engine was mounted as a pusher unit between the wings, and the pilot and observer were accommodated side-by-side in a large cockpit forward of the wing cellule, the observer being provided with a single machine-gun on a trainable mounting.

Some 300 examples of the M-5 were built, most of them serving in the Baltic

and Black Seas, initially with the Imperial Russian naval air arm and then with both sides in the Russian Civil War. A few were still in flying condition with the

Soviet air arms in the mid-1920s. The type proved tough and effective, frequently riding out rough weather and withstanding heavy seas.

SPECIFICATION	
Grigorovich M-5	maximum take-off 2,116 lb (960 kg)
Type: two-seat reconnaissance	**Dimensions:** wingspan 44 ft 8½ in
and training flying-boat	(13.62 m); length 28 ft 2½ in
Powerplant: one Gnome	(8.60 m); wing area 407.97 sq ft
Monosoupape rotary piston engine	(37.90 m²)
rated at 100 hp (74.6 kW)	**Armament:** one 0.3-in (7.62-mm)
Performance: maximum speed	Pulyemet Maksima M1910
65 mph (105 km/h) at sea level;	trainable forward-firing machine-
climb to 3,280 ft (1000 m) in	gun in the cockpit, plus provision
9 minutes 24 seconds; service	under the lower wing for light
ceiling 10,825 ft (3300 m);	bombs
endurance 4 hours	
Weights: empty 1,455 lb (660 kg);	

Variants

M-10: with the same Gnome Monosoupape engine as the M-5 and a similar hull, the M-10 of 1916 had a wing cellule of much reduced span, the upper wing having only slightly greater dimensions than the lower; the overall span was 30 ft 2¼ in (9.20 m) and the length 28 ft 2½ in (8.60 m), the smaller drag of the reduced dimensions resulting in a maximum speed of 78 mph (125 km/h)

M-20: powered by the 120-hp (89.5-kW) Le Rhône rotary engine, this 1916 development of the M-5 was built in limited numbers to a standard that featured exactly the same wing cellule in combination with a hull shortened by 1 ft 3¾ in (0.40 m); the 'boat had a maximum speed of 71 mph (115 km/h)

Grigorovich's M-5 was the first mass-production marine aircraft built in the Soviet Union. Numerous minor modifications were made during production.

Grigorovich M-24

Work on the design of the Grigorovich M-24 reconnaissance flying-boat was begun at State Factory No. 3 (GAZ-3) during April 1922 at the request of the Soviet Directorate of Naval Aviation. Developed from the earlier M-9 and M-15, the **M-24** had improved design of the hull and wing cellule, the latter being of the unequal-span two-bay type with ailerons on the trailing edges of both the upper and lower wings. The tail unit was of typical Grigorovich design but the powerplant, based on the 220-hp (164-kW) Renault 12 water-cooled engine, was contained in a carefully streamlined nacelle which included a frontal radiator, and was faired into the upper wing. The pilot and observer sat side-by-side in

an open cockpit located beneath the leading edge of the upper wing, and were protected from the slipstream by a single large windscreen. There was also a bow position with a single machine-gun on a ring mounting.

Tested in the spring of 1923, the M-24 was placed in production in 1924, 40 examples being ordered. The type's performance was somewhat disappointing, the maximum speed being only 81 mph (130 km/h) and the service ceiling an indifferent 11,485 ft (3500 m). Complaints about the M-24 led to the **M-24bis**, of which 20 examples were built up to 1926 after a first flight in 1924. The M-24bis had detail design improvements and was powered

The M-24 followed the same basic configuration as earlier Grigorovich types. Early examples had lacklustre performance.

by a 260-hp (194-kW) version of the Renault engine. The loaded weight showed an increase of 110 lb (50 kg) by comparison with the 3,637 lb (1750 kg) of the M-24.

SPECIFICATION
Grigorovich M-24bis
Type: two-seat coastal reconnaissance flying-boat
Powerplant: one Renault Vee piston engine rated at 260 hp (194 kW)
Performance: maximum speed 87 mph (140 km/h) at sea level; service ceiling 13,125 ft (4000 m)
Weights: empty 2,646 lb (1200 kg); maximum take-off 3,748 lb (1700 kg)
Dimensions: wingspan 52 ft 6 in (16.00 m); length 29 ft 6½ in (9.00 m); wing area 592.03 sq ft (55.00 m²)
Armament: one 0.3-in (7.62-mm) Pulyemet Maksima M1910 trainable forward-firing machine-gun in the bow position, plus up to 220 lb (100 kg) of disposable stores carried under the lower wing, and generally comprising light bombs

Grob G 109

Based at Tussenhausen in Germany, the Burkhart Grob Flugzeugbau entered into aviation during 1971, largely as the designer and manufacturer of high-performance sailplanes, of which the first was the Standard Cirrus built under licence from Schempp-Hirth between 1972 and 1975. In 1988 the company changed its name to Burkhart Grob Luft- und Raumfahrt G.m.b.H. with a light section continuing the original company's connection with sailplanes, including the G 103 Twin II Acro that was sold to the British Air Training Corps as the Viking T.Mk 1, and a heavy section concerned with the design, development,

marketing and manufacture of powered aircraft.

The first powered aircraft from the company's stable to make a name for itself was the Grob **G 109** two-seat light aircraft/motor glider. The G 109 prototype first flew on 14 March 1980 with a long-span wing of laminar-flow section, and a nose-mounted powerplant based on one 75-hp (55.9-kW) Limbach engine driving a two-bladed propeller. The airframe uses glassfibre-reinforced plastics construction with a measure of carbonfibre-reinforced plastics in the low-set wing, which is designed to fold backward to provide a hangarage footprint of only 34 ft 5 in

(10.49 m) by 6 ft 9 in (2.06 m). Other features of the design are side-by-side accommodation in an enclosed cockpit and a T-tail and fixed tailwheel landing gear with cantilever main unit comprising faired legs carrying spatted wheels.

Trials confirmed that the G 109 offered very considerable economy of operation, and there followed 150 examples of the **G 109A** production model before the advent in 1983 of the **G 109B** with a modified wing of increased span and a different engine in the form of the Grob 2500 flat-four engine. Some 250 of this model were delivered between 1983 and 1986, and production was resumed in 1986 for a subvariant in which the Limbach engine

The G 109 appeared, in its original guise, in 1980 and proved a popular type, remaining in production for over 10 years.

was restored in the form of the 80-hp (59.6-kW) L 2000 EB 1A unit. Delivery of this subvariant up to March 1991 totalled another 76 aircraft, including 53 for the British Air Training Corps with the local designation **Vigilant T.Mk 1**. Production of the G 109B

was resumed for another production run in 1995, but lasted only a short time.

With an aspect ratio of 15.9:1, the G 109B has an unpowered performance that includes a best glide ratio of 28:1 and a minimum sink rate of 3.61 ft (1.10 m) per second.

ZH116 is one of the 53 Vigilant T.Mk 1s in service in 2000 with Volunteer Gliding Schools and flown by RAF volunteer reservists.

SPECIFICATION
Grob G 109B
Type: two-seat light aircraft and motor glider
Powerplant: one Grob 2500 flat-four piston engine rated at 90 hp (67.1 kW)
Performance: maximum speed 149 mph (240 km/h) in smooth air declining to 115 mph (185 km/h) in rough air; cruising speed 124 mph (200 km/h) at optimum
altitude; initial climb rate 649 ft (196 m) per minute; range 1,117 miles (1798 km)
Weights: empty 1,364 lb (619 kg); maximum take-off 1,870 lb (848 kg)
Dimensions: wing span 57 ft (17.37 m); length 26 ft 0 in (7.92 m); height 5 ft 6 in (1.68 m); wing area 204.00 sq ft (18.95 m²)
Armament: none

Grob G 115 (Heron and Tutor) and G 116

A lightplane intended for the sporting, training and touring roles, the Grob **G 115** first flew in November 1985 with the Lycoming O-235 engine. This first prototype was

followed into the air during the spring of 1986 by a second prototype that introduced constant-speed propeller, a taller fin-and-rudder assembly and a relocated tailplane.

Grob moved into the lightplane market in the mid-1980s with the G 115, a derivative of the G 112 trainer prototypes, the first of which flew in 1984.

Grob G 115 (Heron and Tutor) and G 116 (continued)

This paved the way for the production model that followed certification in March 1987 as a low-wing cantilever monoplane of glassfibre-reinforced plastics construction with fixed tricycle landing gear (includ-

ing a spatted wheel on each unit) and side-by-side two-seat accommodation behind a single-piece fixed windscreen and a single-piece canopy that slid to the rear for access and egress.

An initial production run of 88 aircraft was completed by 1988, and then resumed between September 1989 and August 1990 for the manufacture of another 19 aircraft. Production was resumed in 1993 with a number of new designations and provision for alternative engines and upgraded avionics, and by December 1997 some 200 aircraft had been delivered.

Under the designation Heron T.Mk 1, the G 115D2 is used by the FAA's Flying Grading Flight, but is operated by a civilian contractor.

SPECIFICATION

Grob G 115D
Type: two-seat sporting, flying and aerobatic training, and touring aircraft
Powerplant: one Lycoming AEIO-360-B1F flat-six piston engine rated at 180 hp (134 kW)
Performance: maximum speed 168 mph (270 km/h) at sea level; cruising speed 155 mph (250 km/h) at optimum altitude; initial climb

rate 1,080 ft (329 m) per minute; service ceiling 16,000 ft (4875 m); range 598 miles (963 km); endurance 5 hours 40 minutes
Weights: empty 1,455 lb (660 kg); maximum take-off 2,183 lb (990 kg)
Dimensions: wingspan 32 ft 9¾ in (10.00 m); length 24 ft 11¼ in (7.60 m); height 7 ft 10½ in (2.40 m); wing area 131.43 sq ft (12.21 m)

Variants

G 115A: baseline production model based on the second prototype and powered by the 115-hp (85.8-kW) O-235 engine
G 115B: improved production model with a 160-hp (119-kW) Lycoming O-320 engine
G 115C: further improved production model available from 1994 with the 160-hp (119-kW) O-320-D1A engine driving a fixed-pitch propeller, fuel tankage relocated to the wing, a modified tail unit and several other enhancements
G 115C1 Acro: announced in mid-1996, this model is intended for aerobatics and is therefore equipped with a *g* meter and with provision for seat- or back-pack parachutes
G 115C2: development of the G 115C with the 180-hp (134-kW) O-360-A1F6 engine
G 115C2 IFR Trainer: development of the G 115C2 equipped as standard with instrument flight rules instrumentation
G 115D: fully aerobatic development of the G 115C with the 180-hp (134-kW) AEIO-360-B1F engine driving a constant-speed propeller
G 115D2: development of the G 115D with the 160-hp (119-kW)

AEIO-320-D1B engine driving a constant-speed propeller; the type was bought by the Fleet Air Arm for British pilot grading under the location designation **Heron T.Mk 1**
G 115E: development of the G 115D2 but with the 180-hp (134-kW) engine to meet the requirements of the Royal Air Force for a BAe Bulldog in service with university air squadrons and air cadet air experience flights; 95 such aircraft were ordered for delivery from 1999 with the local designation **Tutor T.Mk 1**
G 115 Bavarian: development of the G 115C for the International Aero Club of Florida, USA, with fuel tankage in the wing, a greater area of glazing in the canopy, a new instrument panel, a modified tail unit, and a revised aerofoil section for the wing
G 115TA Acro: specialised commercial and military pilot training variant with the 260-hp (194-kW) Lycoming AEIO-540-D4A5 flat-six engine, military avionics and retractable tricycle landing gear
G 116: first flown on 29 April 1986 but later suspended from development, the G 116 was schemed as a four-seat development of the G 115 with 2+2 accommodation in a slightly enlarged airframe powered by the 200-hp (149-kW) Lycoming IO-360 flat-four engine

Grob G 850 Strato 2C

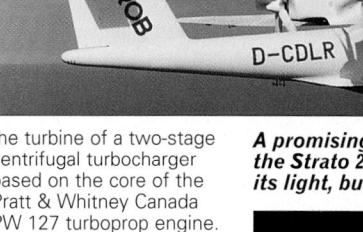

In April 1992 Grob received a contract from the Oberpfaffenhofen establishment of the German ministry of research and technology for the design and development of an aircraft intended specifically for long-endurance climatic and stratospheric research at very high altitudes. The result was the Grob **G 850 Strato 2C**, which was schemed with a tractor powerplant that was later altered to the pusher configuration in an airframe that was the world's largest aircraft of all-composite (mainly glassfibre-reinforced plastics) construction. The key features of the design were a fuselage with pressurised accommodation large enough to allow the side-by-side seating of two pilots in the high-set cockpit as well as two scientists and a mass of equipment

in the cabin; a T-tail; a high-set long-span wing of laminar-flow section with a very high aspect ratio and low loading to provide the best possible ceiling and endurance; hardpoints on the fuselage and wing to allow the carriage of mission payloads; tricycle landing gear with the main units retracting into blister fairings on the sides of the fuselage; and a special powerplant located in nacelles over the wing.

The powerplant was of the compound type, each of the two units being based on a liquid-cooled 402-hp (300-kW) Continental TSIOL-550 flat-six piston engine driving a variable-pitch pusher propeller with five composites-coated wooden blades. The piston engine's exhaust gases were then ducted to an AlliedSignal turbocharger and thence to

the turbine of a two-stage centrifugal turbocharger based on the core of the Pratt & Whitney Canada PW 127 turboprop engine. This compressed the air that was supplied via the exhaust-driven turbocharger to the engine through three intercoolers, and the exhaust gases from the large turbocharger themselves provided a thrust equal to some 18 per cent of the thrust generated by the propeller.

The Strato 2C first flew on 31 March 1995 and was delivered toward the end of 1996. By this time the whole programme had risen

A promising design with an ingenious powerplant, the Strato 2C made extensive use of composites in its light, but strong, structure.

SPECIFICATION

Grob G 850 Strato 2C
Type: four-seat high-altitude and long-endurance research aircraft
Powerplant: two Continental TSIOL-550 flat-six piston engines each rated at 402 hp (300 kW)
Performance: cruising speed 323 mph (520 km/h) at 78,740 ft (24000 m); service ceiling 85,300 ft (26000 m); range 11,246 miles (18100 km) declining to 4,349 miles (7000 km) with a 1,764-lb (800-kg)

payload
Weights: empty 14,661 lb (6650 kg); maximum take-off 29,431 lb (13350 kg)
Dimensions: wingspan 185 ft 4½ in (56.50 m); length 78 ft 7⅞ in (23.97 m); height 25 ft 1¾ in (7.76 m); wing area 1,560.82 sq ft (145.00 m²)
Armament: none
Payload: up to 2,205 lb (1000 kg) of equipment

in cost to the extent that it no longer offered a sensible return on the investment,

and the programme was accordingly cancelled in mid-1996.

Grob/E-Systems/AlliedSignal G 520 Strato 1 (Egrett)

What might be regarded as the makings of a 'poor man's U-2R', the Grob/E-Systems/AlliedSignal **G 520 Egrett** originated in 1986 to meet a Luftwaffe require-

ment for a long-duration high-altitude surveillance aircraft, and was launched after plans to acquire a squadron of Lockheed TR-1 aircraft had been aban-

doned. Initiation of the project was undertaken by a three-company group comprising Grob in Germany and E-Systems and Garrett (later

AlliedSignal) in the USA, and it was from the names of these three companies that the name Egrett was derived. Grob was primarily responsible for the design

and construction of the essentially glassfibre-reinforced plastics airframe, Garrett contributed the powerplant, and E-Systems, as programme

The second aircraft in the Egrett programme, D-FGEE was the first D-500 pre-production Egrett II and flew for the first time on 20 April 1989.

SPECIFICATION

Grob/E-Systems/AlliedSignal G 520 Egrett II
Type: single-seat high-altitude surveillance and relay aircraft
Powerplant: one AlliedSignal (Garrett) TPE331-14F turboprop engine rated at about 800 shp (596.5 kW)
Performance: maximum speed 276 mph (445 km/h) at optimum altitude; cruising speed 219 mph (352 km/h) at optimum altitude; initial climb rate more than 1,500 ft (457 m) per minute; climb to 40,000 ft (12190 m) in 35 minutes; service ceiling more than 45,000 ft (13715 m); endurance limited to between 10 and 12 hours by pilot fatigue
Weights: empty 6,754 lb (3063 kg); maximum take-off 10,362 lb (4700 kg)
Dimensions: wingspan 103 ft ¼ in (31.40 m); length 40 ft ¼ in (12.20 m); height 19 ft ¼ in (5.80 m); wing area 421.10 sq ft (39.68 m²)
Payload: up to 2,200 lb (998 kg) of surveillance equipment carried internally

leader, was responsible for systems integration.

The Egrett concept made use of a single-seat fuselage that provided adequate volume for a variety of interchangeable mission packages (including electronic, optronic, infra-red and long-range radar packages), while the long-span wing of very high aspect ratio revealed sailplane design influence, underlined the Egrett's high-altitude role and, in combination with the efficient TPE331 turboprop engine, allowed the aircraft to fly for long periods at high altitude.

A proof-of-concept vehicle, the **D-450 Egrett I**, first flew on 24 June 1987 in Germany, and in September 1988 this machine set a class-altitude record of 53,787 ft (16394 m). The D-450 had a span of 91 ft 10 in (28.00 m) and, unlike the definitive version, had fixed main landing-gear units. It was followed on 20 April 1989 by the first **D-500** pre-production **Egrett II**, with a second similar D-500 flying on 9 September 1990 and two more completed in 1991. This aircraft and the production Egrett II had a span of 108 ft 3¼ in (33.00 m) and main landing-gear units that retracted into underwing fairings. The third and fourth aircraft were completed to the G 520 standard, the third machine being owned by E-Systems for use as a demonstrator for various reconnaissance systems and the fourth machine, known as the **Strato 1** and fitted with detachable winglets, being owned by Grob as a commercial demonstrator for environmental surveillance purposes.

Funded by the Luftwaffe since 1987, the Egrett II met the so-called 'EASysluft' requirement for a data-gathering and evaluation system, which it was the Luftwaffe's responsibility to provide on behalf of all three German services. Late in 1992 official approval was given for production of 10 more Egrett II aircraft, of which one was to be a **G 520T** two-seat trainer, with deliveries from 1997 to 2001. Despite the creation of plans to base 16 operational Egrett II aircraft at Pferdsfeld, the Luftwaffe programme was subsequently cancelled in February 1993 in the light of the lack of threat posed by eastern Europe. Construction of the G 520T two-seater continued, however, and this aircraft flew on 21 April 1993.

Grumman G-5, G-6, G-13, G-14 and G-23 (FF, SF and Goblin)

Variants

FF-2: 25 of the original 27 FF-1 fighters were later converted by Naval Aircraft Factory with dual controls for service as fighter trainers
SF-1: on 9 June 1931 the US Navy ordered one prototype of the G-6 scout version of the G-5 with fuel capacity increased by 37.5 Imp gal (45 US gal; 170 litres) at the expense of one of the forward-firing machine-guns and powered by the 700-hp (522-kW) R-1820-78 engine; it was flown in August 1932 and the 33 ordered by the US Navy in that month were delivered between 15 February and 12 July 1934; the VS-3B squadron received its SF-1 aircraft in 30 March 1934, serving on board the USS *Lexington*
G-23 Goblin: this was the FF-1 as built under licence by the Canadian Car & Foundry Company for the Royal Canadian Air Force, which received 15 aircraft; when No. 1(F) Squadron's Hawker Hurricane fighters left Canada for England in June 1940, No 118 (F) Squadron was re-formed with the Goblin and this type comprised Canada's air defence capability until the type was replaced in November 1941 by the Curtiss Kittyhawk; 40 were ordered by Turkey in 1937 and delivered via Barcelona where they found their way into the hands of Spanish Republican forces; single aircraft of the same type were also delivered to Japan and Nicaragua
XSF-2: one aircraft delivered to the US Navy in March 1934 as an SF-1 airframe revised with the 650-hp (485-kW) Pratt & Whitney R-1535-72 Twin Wasp Junior radial engine driving a Hamilton Standard propeller
XSBF-1: the XSF-2 airframe was modified with the company designation G-14, by the incorporation of a triangular frame, beneath the engine mounting, to carry one 500-lb (227-kg) or two 100-lb (45-kg) bombs; it was first flown on 18 February 1936

On 28 March 1931 the US Navy placed its first contract with the Grumman Aircraft Engineering Corporation, beginning an association with the manufacturer (now incorporated in the Northrop Grumman Corporation) that continues to this day. The subject of the contract was the prototype of the Grumman **G-5** design for evaluation as the **XFF-1**. This two-seat biplane fighter was the US Navy's first such warplane with retractable landing gear. Grumman had earlier produced a float incorporating such gear for use on the Vought Corsair biplane, and had expressed a wish to design a new aircraft thus fitted rather than install its equipment in existing US Navy fighters. The XFF-1 was of all-metal construction under a covering largely of fabric, and was armed with two 0.3-in (7.62-mm) Browning fixed forward-firing machine-guns mounted in the forward fuselage's top decking and a similar weapon in the rear cockpit, attached to the gunner's seat so that gun and seat moved together in a gimballed mounting as the target was tracked.

Construction of the prototype, powered by the 616-hp (459-kW) Wright R-1820-E Cyclone radial engine, was initiated at Grumman's Baldwin, Long Island workshop. However, in November 1931 the company moved some eight miles (13 km) to Curtiss Field, from where the prototype was first flown on 29 December 1931. Initial manufacturer's trials were completed quickly and in January 1932 the prototype was flown to the US Navy's test centre at NAS Anacostia, Maryland, for official evaluation. In the course of this programme the aircraft demonstrated a top speed of 195 mph (314 km/h) at sea level, faster than the single-seat Boeing F4B-4 which was then the US Navy's standard fighter. In November 1932 Grumman moved once more, this time to larger premises at Farmingdale, and it was here in the following month that the company received its first order for the 27 FF-1 fighters. These were delivered between April and November 1933, the first aircraft entering service in June of that year with the VF-5B squadron that later went to sea on board the USS *Lexington*.

SPECIFICATION

Grumman FF-1
Type: two-seat carrierborne fighter
Powerplant: one Wright R-1820-78 Cyclone radial piston engine rated at 700 hp (522 kW)
Performance: maximum speed 207 mph (333 km/h) at 4,000 ft (1220 m); climb to 5,000 ft (1525 m) in 2 minutes 59 seconds; service ceiling 22,100 ft (67350 m); range 685 miles (1100 km)
Weights: empty 3,098 lb (1405 kg); maximum take-off 4,677 lb (2121 kg)
Dimensions: wingspan 34 ft 6 in (10.52 m); length 24 ft 6 in (7.47 m); height 11 ft 1 in (3.38 m); wing area 310.00 sq ft (28.80 m²)
Armament: two 0.3-in (7.62-mm) Browning fixed forward-firing machine-guns in the upper part of the forward fuselage, and one 0.3-in (7.62-mm) Browning trainable rearward-firing machine-gun in the rear cockpit

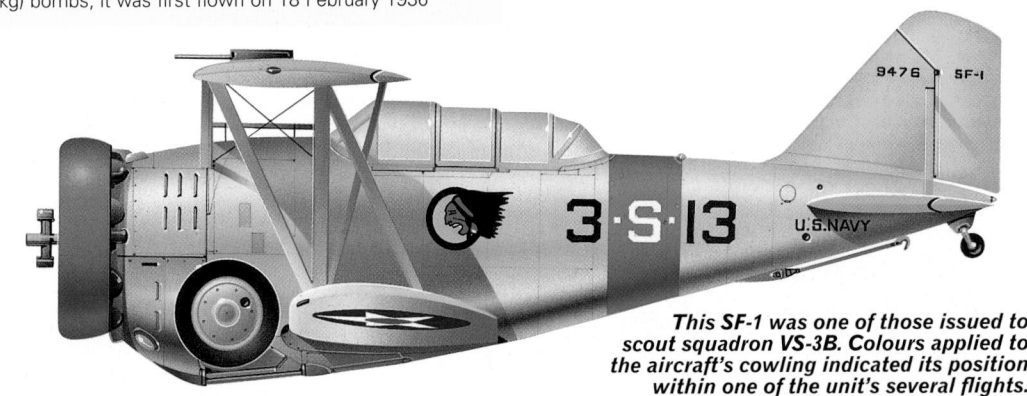

This SF-1 was one of those issued to scout squadron VS-3B. Colours applied to the aircraft's cowling indicated its position within one of the unit's several flights.

Grumman G-7, G-9, G-10, G-15 and G-20

Grumman's FF and F2F carrierborne fighters for the US Navy, the company's first production aircraft, had introduced some new ideas, including retractable tailwheel landing gear, making them the first of their kind to enter US Navy service. The FF was also in its time the fastest fighter operational with the US Navy but, because of the limited procurement that was possible in the years between the two world wars, it was acquired in only small numbers.

With the FF-1 nearing production, Grumman began the development of a new utility amphibian which would combine the better features of the FF-1 and the Loening OL machines then in service, and late in 1932 the company submitted its Grumman **G-7** proposal for review by the US Navy. This resulted in the award of a contract for the supply of an XJF-1 prototype, which flew for the first time on 4 May 1933. Flight testing found no serious problems, and an uncomplicated evaluation by the US Navy resulted in an initial production order for 27 **JF-1** aircraft, of which the first was delivered late in 1934.

Intended to fulfil the general utility role, the type was used first to replace ageing OL-9 observation and general-purpose aircraft in US

The main production Duck variant, the J2F-5 had a broader-chord cowling than earlier aircraft. Stronger bomb racks were also fitted and, while no forward-firing guns were installed, a flexible rear-firing gun was available.

Navy service, and it was not until 1936 that the JF-1 began to reach squadrons. By comparison with that of the similarly configured OL, its performance was quite staggering, with maximum speed, rate of climb and service ceiling increased by more than 40 per cent, 50 per cent and 65 per cent respectively, but there were significant aerodynamic improvements in the design. The equal-span biplane wing cellule had a basic structure of light alloy with fabric covering, the fuselage was a conventional stressed-skin light alloy structure, and the large monocoque central float housed the main wheel units when retracted. A small stabilising float was

strut-mounted beneath each half of the lower wing, and a crew of two or three could be carried in the tandem cockpits, the pilot forward and observer aft as standard, but a radio operator could also be accommodated in the observer's cockpit. The powerplant of the prototype and the first batch of JF-1 production aircraft was based on the 700-hp (522-kW) Pratt & Whitney R-1830 Twin Wasp radial engine.

The second production contract was for 14 **JF-2** (company designation **G-9**) aircraft for the US Coast Guard, these having equipment changes and the 750-hp (559-kW) Wright R-1820 Cyclone radial engine. Four were later transferred to the US Navy,

Variants

J2F-1A: unofficial designation of one J2F-1 experimentally fitted with full-span flaps on the upper wing
J2F-2A: nine J2F-2 aircraft with two rearward-firing machine-guns and bomb racks under the lower wing
OA-12: one J2F-5 transferred to the US Army Air Forces in 1942
OA-12A: five J2F-6 aircraft transferred to the US Air Force in 1947
OA-12B: three J2F-6 aircraft transferred to the USAF in 1948 for refurbishment before transfer to Colombia

SPECIFICATION

Grumman J2F-6 Duck
Type: two/three-seat carrierborne and shore-based utility amphibian flying-boat
Powerplant: one Wright R-1820-54 Cyclone radial piston engine rated at 900 hp (671 kW)
Performance: maximum speed 190 mph (306 km/h) at 14,000 ft (4265 m); cruising speed 155 mph (329 km/h) at optimum altitude; initial climb rate 1,330 ft (405 m) per minute; service ceiling 26,700 ft

(8140 m); range 850 miles (1368 km)
Weights: empty 5,445 lb (2470 kg); maximum take-off 7,290 lb (3307 kg)
Dimensions: wingspan 39 ft (11.89 m); length 34 ft (10.36 m); height 13 ft 11 in (4.24 m); wing area 409.00 sq ft (38.00 m²)
Armament: generally none, but provision was made for two 325-lb (147-kg) depth bombs carried under the lower wing

A handful of Ducks have been restored to flying condition in the US, including this J2F-6.

Depicted carrying the US national markings worn prior to May 1942, this J2F-5 was assigned to the Fleet Air Photo Wing Atlantic.

which also acquired five new aircraft with similar powerplant under the designation **JF-3** (company designation **G-10**). There were few major changes in subsequent production examples of the **G-15** series, the 20 **J2F-1** machines of 1937 and the later 21 **J2F-2**, 20 **J2F-3** and 32 **J2F-4** types differing in only minor detail. Nine **J2F-2A** floatplanes for the US Marine Corps' VMS-5 squadron were armed with machine-guns and carried underwing bomb racks. The last

version to be built by Grumman was ordered in 1940, and this order comprised 144 examples of the **J2F-5**, which was the first model to carry the name **Duck** officially. Generally similar to previous utility models, this was powered by the 850-hp (634-kW) R-1820-50 engine. The final production version was the **J2F-6** built by Columbia Aircraft Corporation of Long Island, New York, from which company the US Navy ordered 330 after the USA had become involved in World War II. These were generally similar to the Grumman-built Duck amphibians except for the installation of the uprated R-1820-54 engine.

Most of the JF and J2F Duck machines remained in service throughout World War II, operating both from carriers and shore bases in a variety of roles, including rescue and target-towing. The type was also exported to Argentina (four G-15 aircraft to J2F-4 standard and 20 **G-20** machines to JF-2 standard), Colombia (three ex-OA-12 aircraft) and Mexico (two ex-J2F-6s).

Grumman G-8 (F2F)

The outstanding performance of the FF-1 two-seat fighter naturally turned the Grumman design team's thoughts to the even greater potential of a single-seat version, and the Grumman **G-8** proposal was submitted to the US Navy in June 1932. The **XF2F-1** prototype, ordered on 2 November 1932, was slightly smaller than its predecessor, with a semi-monocoque metal fuselage and a fabric-covered metal wing cellule with ailerons on only the upper wing. Power was supplied by the 625-hp (466-kW) Pratt & Whitney XR-1535-44 Twin Wasp Junior radial engine, and the armament comprised two 0.3-in (7.62-mm) Browning machine-guns in the upper decking of the forward fuselage; racks could be fitted under the lower wing to carry two 116-lb (53-kg) bombs. The aircraft was rolled out for its first flight on 18 October 1931 and, following manufacturer's trials, this machine was handed over to the US Navy for a six-month evaluation, during which it demonstrated a maximum speed of 229 mph

VF-2B was the first unit to receive F2F-1s, operating the aircraft from USS Lexington. *BuNo. 9624 was the second production example.*

(369 km/h) at 8,400 ft (2560 m) and an initial climb rate of 3,080 ft (939 m) per minute; on the debit side, the short, corpulent fuselage gave rise to some directional instability, and the aircraft tightened up in the spin. Minor changes were introduced, including an enlarged cockpit canopy and a 6-in (0.15-m) increase in the span of the upper wings, and the original smooth NACA cowling was replaced by one of smaller diameter with rocker arm blisters.

On 17 May 1934 the US Navy placed a production order for 54 **F2F-1** fighters,

the first of which was delivered on 28 January 1935 and the last exactly 10 months later. One crashed on its delivery flight on 16 March and a replacement was ordered on 29 June. Replacement of the Boeing F4B-2 of the VF-2B squadron assigned to USS *Lexington* began on 19 February 1935, and the type remained in service with this unit until 30 September 1940, when the 18-aircraft complement was flown to NAS Pensacola for use in the advanced trainer role. The other two units to fly the **F2F-1** were the VF-3B

squadron on board the USS *Ranger* (later the VF-7B and VF-5 after moving to the USS *Yorktown*) and the VF-7 squadron on board the USS

Wasp. The US Marine Corps' VF-4M (later VMF-2) squadron also operated a few F2F-1s in the land-based role.

SPECIFICATION	
Grumman F2F-1	
Type: single-seat carrierborne and land-based fighter	27,100 ft (8260 m); range 985 miles (1585 km)
Powerplant: one Pratt & Whitney R-1535-72 Twin Wasp Junior radial piston engine rated at 650 hp (485 kW)	**Weights:** empty 2,691 lb (1221 kg); maximum take-off 4,050 lb (1837 kg)
Performance: maximum speed 231 mph (373 km/h) at 7,500 ft (2285 m); cruising speed 140 mph (225 km/h) at optimum altitude; initial climb rate 2,050 ft (625 m) per minute; service ceiling	**Dimensions:** wingspan 28 ft 6 in (8.69 m); length 21 ft 5 in (6.53 m), height 9 ft 1 in (2.77 m); wing area 230.00 sq ft (21.37 m²)
	Armament: two 0.3-in (7.62-mm) Browning fixed forward-firing machine-guns in the upper part of the forward fuselage

Grumman G-11 and G-19 (F3F)

Although the US Navy had accepted the shortcomings of the F2F, Grumman was determined to improve the directional stability, spinning characteristics and general manoeuvrability of its product. Built under a US Navy contract dated 15 October 1934 (placed three months before delivery of the first F2F-1), the Grumman XF3F-1 prototype to the **G-11** design retained the R-1535-72 radial engine of its predecessor, but in a fuselage increased in length by 1 ft 10 in (0.56 m), the wing cellule was increased in span by 3 ft 6 in (1.07 m) and other

minor aerodynamic improvements were introduced. The XF3F-1 first flew at Farmingdale on 20 March 1935, but two

days later the test pilot was killed when the wings and engine became detached during a test dive designed to prove a 9-*g* recovery. Design limits had been exceeded, but the second aircraft was built with strengthened lower wing root fittings and engine mountings. This revised machine first flew on 9 May and was then delivered to NAS Anacostia, Maryland, for US Navy test and evaluation. during this process, on 17 May, the machine entered a flat spin from which recovery was impossible and the pilot baled out. Incredibly, the machine was not completely destroyed and was rebuilt within three weeks, completing its manufacturer's trials so that it could be returned to Anacostia on 20 June. The rebuilt aircraft was given a

small ventral fillet beneath the tail cone, added after tests with a model in the spin tunnel at NACA's Langley Field facility.

A total of 54 production **F3F-1** fighters was ordered on 24 August and, following initial deliveries in January 1936, the type entered service with the VF-5B squadron aboard the USS *Ranger* in April and

the VF-6B squadron on USS *Saratoga* in June. The US Marine Corps' VMF-811 squadron was the last operational unit with the F3F, retiring its last aircraft on 10 October 1941, and more than 100 aircraft then served with training units. The last was struck off charge in November 1943 and relegated to ground instruction airframe status.

BuNo. 1445, the second F3F-3, is seen in the markings of VF-5B, the type's first operator.

Variants

F3F-1: 54 for the US Navy to a standard similar to that of the XF3F-1 prototype but powered by the R-1535-84 Twin Wasp Junior with a hydraulically operated Hamilton Standard controllable-pitch two-bladed propeller, an armament of one 0.3-in (7.62-mm) Browning machine-gun in the port side of the forward fuselage top decking and one 0.5-in (12.7-mm) Browning to starboard; deliveries were made between 29 January and 18 September 1936
F3F-2: the last production F3F-1 was converted to XF3F-2 (G-19) standard with the 950-hp (708-kW) Wright XR-1820-22 Cyclone supercharged radial engine driving a controllable-pitch three-bladed propeller and drawing its fuel from an enlarged internal capacity; though the machine was delivered to Anacostia on 27 July 1936, carburation problems delayed the start of the test programme until January 1937; in March of that year the US Navy ordered 81 production examples, of which the first entered service with the VF-6 squadron on 1 December; deliveries were made between 27 July 1937 and 11 May 1938
F3F-3: a production F3F-2 was returned to Grumman for conversion to XF3F-3 standard with minor drag-reducing modifications to the airframe, revised cowling and forward fuselage decking; 27 production examples were built and delivered between 16 December 1938 and 10 May 1939

SPECIFICATION	
Grumman F3F-3	
Type: single-seat carrierborne fighter	1,150 miles (1851 km)
Powerplant: one Wright R-1820-22 Cyclone radial piston engine rated at 950 hp (708 kW)	**Weights:** empty 3,285 lb (1490 kg); maximum take-off 4,795 lb (2175 kg)
Performance: maximum speed 264 mph (425 km/h) at 15,200 ft (4635 m); cruising speed 150 mph (241 km/h) at optimum altitude; initial climb rate 2,750 ft (838 m) per minute; service ceiling 33,200 ft (10120 m); range	**Dimensions:** wingspan 32 ft (9.75 m); length 23 ft 2 in (7.06 m); height 9 ft 4 in (2.84 m); wing area 260.00 sq ft (24.15 m²)
	Armament: one 0.5-in (12.7-mm) and one 0.3-in (7.62-mm) or two 0.3-in (7.62-mm) Browning fixed forward-firing machine-guns in the upper part of the forward fuselage

Grumman G-21 Goose (JRF, OA-9 and OA-13)

In 1937 Grumman produced a twin-engined amphibian flying boat known as the **G-21 Goose**. Powered by two 450-hp (336-kW) Pratt & Whitney R-985 radial engines, it was of high-wing monoplane configuration, the wing carrying the engines and underwing stabilising floats. The deep two-step hull was of conventional construction, and the tail unit included a braced tailplane. Amphibious capability was provided by tailwheel type landing gear, whose three units all retracted into the hull. Built before World War II for commercial use as the **G-21A**, which had accommodation for up to seven passengers, the Goose

continued in production during World War II for service with the US Army Air Forces, US Coast Guard and US Navy, some of this last service's aircraft also serving with the US Marine Corps.

Surviving commercial and war-surplus aircraft which came on to the market after World War II proved of value for certain post-war air services, and McKinnon Enterprises in the USA began to specialise in Goose refurbishment and the development of improved versions. These have included an early modification which replaced the two R-985 engines with four 340-hp (254-kW) Lycoming GSO-480 flat-

four engines, but the majority of conversions have been to the **G-21C** and longer-fuselage **G-21D Turbo-Goose** standard with two 550-shp (410-kW) Pratt & Whitney Canada PT6A-20 turboprop engines in place of the original radial units. A number of improvements were incorporated during this conversion, including the introduction of retractable wing-tip floats and the provision of larger cabin windows. A **G-21G Turbo-Goose** was also available, this being a generally similar conversion but with a somewhat higher standard of equipment and some cabin improvements, as well as a **Turboprop Goose** having only the change to turboprop power without any of the airframe improvements of earlier conversions. The G-21G Turbo-Goose and Turboprop Goose conversions were available until 1980, most recently from McKinnon-Viking Enterprises which was established at Sidney, British Columbia in 1978 to supersede the American McKinnon Enterprises Inc.

Post-war Goose conversion programmes varied in complexity. This aircraft has retractable floats, but otherwise seems to have retained its original form.

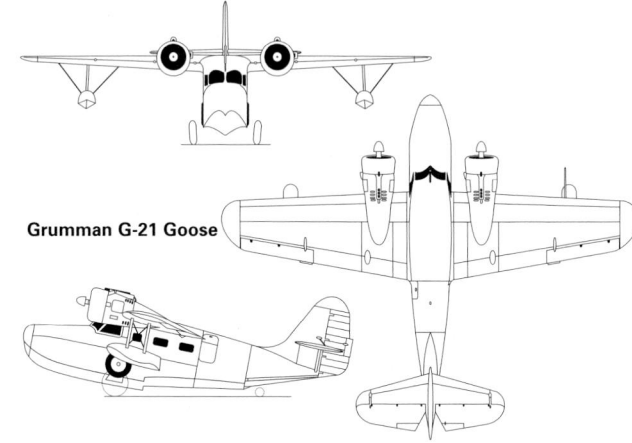

Grumman G-21 Goose

SPECIFICATION

McKinnon (Grumman) G-21G Turbo-Goose
Type: two-crew light transport amphibian flying boat
Powerplant: two Pratt & Whitney Canada PT6A-27 turboprop engines each rated at 680 shp (507 kW)
Performance: maximum speed 243 mph (391 km/h) at 8,000 ft (2440 m); service ceiling 20,000 ft (6095 m); range 1,600 miles

(2575 km)
Weights: empty 6,700 lb (3039 kg); maximum take-off 12,500 lb (5670 kg)
Dimensions: wingspan 50 ft 10 in (15.49 m); length 39 ft 7 in (12.06 m); wing area 377.64 sq ft (35.08 m²)
Payload: passengers or freight carried in the cabin

Variants

G-21: 12 initial flying boats with 450-hp (336-kW) R-985-SB engines
G-21A: 30 'boats with 450-hp (336-kW) R-985-SB2 engines
G-21B: 12 aircraft ordered by Portugal for service in the coastal patrol role, and the only members of the Goose family completed as pure flying boats; other details of the type were provision for armament in the form of two 0.3-in (7.62-mm) trainable machine-guns (one in the bow position and the other in a dorsal hatch position) and provision under the wings just outboard of the engine nacelles for two 100-lb (45-kg) bombs; these aircraft were delivered between April and May 1940, and were generally operated without armament as transports into the early 1950s
JRF-1 Goose: after evaluating the 21st Goose as the sole **XJ3F-1** (**G-26**) in the general utility role with a powerplant of two 450-hp (336-kW) R-985-48 engines, the US Navy decided that the type was eminently suitable for the service's light transport role, and therefore placed an order for five **G-38** 'boats that were delivered between November 1939 and January 1940 with the designation JRF-1 Goose in the utility transport category; this was only the start of the story for the JRF series in US Navy service, however, for the USN had 35 'boats of the series in service by the end of 1941 and continued to procure the type right to the end of World War II, when outstanding orders were cancelled; the USN began to discard its Goose 'boats shortly after the end of the war, most of them being delivered for fruitful second careers in the hands of American allies into the late 1950s, while the US Coast Guard operated its 'boats into the mid-1950s
JRF-1A Goose: delivered between September 1939 and January 1940, these five 'boats differed from the otherwise similar JRF-1 machines mainly in their completion with provision for target towing equipment and a photography hatch in the bottom of the hull
JRF-2 Goose: delivered between July 1939 and May 1940 with two R-985-SB2 engines, these seven **G-39** 'boats were used by the US Coast Guard as utility machines in which the cabin could be configured for passenger transport or alternatively for medical evacuation or air/sea rescue with the seats replaced by litters
JRF-3 Goose: these three 'boats were delivered to the US Coast Guard in November 1940, and differed from the JRF-2 machines in having an autopilot and de-icing boots on the leading edges of their flying surfaces
JRF-4 Goose: delivered to the US Navy between December 1940 and April 1941, these 10 'boats were completed to a standard that differed from that of the original JRF-1 in its two R-985-50 engines and provision of armament capability in the form of two underwing hardpoints each able to lift one 325-lb (147-kg) depth charge or one 250-lb (113-kg) bomb; the number of JRF-4 machines was increased to 12 by the impressment of two G-21A units for conversion to this standard during 1942
JRF-5 Goose: numerically the most important Goose variant, production for the USN reaching 184 'boats delivered between July 1941 and

October 1945, when the last 11 machines on order were cancelled; these 'boats were completed to a hybrid standard that included the camera hatch and target towing capability of the JRF-1A, the autopilot and de-icing boats of the JRF-3, and the underwing hardpoints of the JRF-4 so that they could be operated in the coastal patrol and anti-submarine role as well as the utility transport task; after World War II a number of the 'boats was operated by the US Coast Guard with the designation **JRF-5G**; Canada bought three similar boats between 1938 and 1940 for service with the designation **Goose Mk II**, and also received 16 ex-US Navy 'boats in 1944 and 1945; in 1952 France received 12 ex-US Navy 'boats for service in Indo-China, and a further five of the same variant were received in 1954; the 'boats were operated mainly in the communications role, but some of them were flown for armed reconnaissance with an underwing load of four 100-lb (45-kg) bombs sometimes supplemented by the fire of two 0.3-in (7.62-mm) fixed forward-firing machine-guns in the nose; a few of the 'boats were also operated as primitive aerial gunships with twin 0.3-in (7.62-mm) machine-guns fixed in the port door to fire sideways and downward as the 'boats orbited their targets; after the French defeat in Indo-China, four of the 'boats were removed to New Caledonia and 11 were shipped to Algeria and the last of these machines was retired only in 1961
JRF-6B Goose: 50 'boats ordered in 1939 by the British Purchasing Commission for use in the navigator training role and then transferred onto the Lend-Lease scheme; deliveries began in January 1944, and in the event the British received only 44 of the machines for service with the designation **Goose Mk IA**; of the other six, five were delivered to the USAAF as **OA-9** staff transport and air/sea rescue 'boats and the last was transferred to Bolivia
OA-9: in June 1938 the US Army Air Corps ordered 26 examples of the **G-31** amphibian flying boat based on the G-21A but fitted with a powerplant of two 450-hp (336-kW) R-985-17; these six-passenger aircraft were delivered between November 1938 and October 1939, and used to replace the service's obsolescent Douglas OA-3 and OA-4 amphibian flying boats in the staff transport and air/sea rescue roles; another batch of five identically designated aircraft that served with the US Army Air Forces, as the USAAC had become in June 1941, comprised aircraft of a somewhat different standard as they were of the JRF-6B standard and diverted from Lend-Lease deliveries to the UK
OA-13A: three G-21A flying boats impressed for service with the USAAF in 1942; two of the aircraft were allocated to Pan American Airways for support of its military transport services in Africa and the Middle East, while the third was retained by the USAAF for the same basic task in the USA and South America; one of the machines was damaged and scrapped during World War II, but the other two returned to the US civil register after the end of the war
OA-13B: two G-21A machines impressed by the US Navy in 1942 but then transferred to the USAAF during 1945

Grumman G-18 and G-36 (F4F/FM Wildcat)

The US Navy's require-ment of 1936 for a new carrier-based fighter resulted in the Brewster Aeronautical Corporation's receipt of an order for a prototype of its Model 39 under the designation XF2A-1. This became the first monoplane fighter to enter US Navy squadron service, but so tentative was the service in its deci-sion to order this aircraft that it also ordered a proto-type of Grumman's competing biplane design under the designation **XF4F-1**. However, a more careful study of the perfor-mance potential of Brewster's design, plus the fact that Grumman's earlier F3F biplane was beginning to demonstrate good performance, resulted in second thoughts in the form of the cancellation of the biplane prototype and the initiation of an alternative Grumman **G-18** monoplane design. Following evaluation of this new proposal, the US Navy ordered a single prototype on 28 July 1936 under the designation **XF4F-2**.

Flown for the first time on 2 September 1937, the XF4F-2 was powered by the 1,050-hp (783-kW) Pratt & Whitney R-1830-66 Twin Wasp radial engine, and was able to demon-strate a maximum speed of 290 mph (467 km/h). Of all-metal construction, with its cantilever monoplane wing set in a mid-position on the fuselage to allow retraction of the tailwheel landing gear's main units into the sides of the lower fuse-lage, the XF4F-2 proved to be marginally faster than the Brewster prototype when flown during competitive evaluation in the early months of 1938. While speed was its major credit, the new fighter was also decidedly inferior in some respects, and as a result the Brewster fighter was ordered into produc-tion during June 1938.

Clearly the US Navy believed the X4F4-2 had hidden potential, however, for the prototype was returned to Grumman in October 1938, together with a new contract for its further development. Grumman adopted major changes before its G-36 prototype flew again in March 1939 under the designation **XF4F-3**. These included the installation of the more powerful XR-1830-76 with a two-stage supercharger, a wing of increased span and area, redesigned tail surfaces, and a modified machine-gun installation. When tested in this new form the XF4F-3 was found to have considerably improved performance. A second prototype was then completed, this machine introducing a redesigned tail unit in which the tailplane was moved to a position higher on the fin, and the vertical surface was revised in profile. In this form the XF4F-3 was found to possess good handling characteristics and manoeuvrability as well as the maximum speed of 335 mph (539 km/h) at 21,300 ft (6490 m). Faced with such performance, the US Navy had no hesitation in ordering 78 **F4F-3** production aircraft on 8 August 1939.

With war seemingly imminent in Europe, Grumman offered the new **G-36A** design for export, receiving orders for 81 and 30 aircraft from the French and Greek governments respectively. The first of those intended for the French navy, powered by the 1,000-hp (746-kW) Wright R-1820 Cyclone radial engine, flew on 27 July 1940, but by then France had already fallen. Instead, the British Purchasing Commission in the USA agreed to take these aircraft, increasing the order to 90, and the

first of the new fighters reached the UK in July 1940 (after the first five off the line had been supplied to Canada), receiving the local designation **Martlet Mk I**. The type first equipped No. 804 Sqn of the Fleet Air Arm, and two of the aircraft flown by this squadron were the first US-built fighters to destroy a German aircraft during World War II, in December 1940.

Subsequent Grumman-built versions to serve with the FAA included the Twin Wasp-powered folding-wing **Martlet Mk II**; 10 **F4F-4A** and the Greek contract G-36A aircraft as **Martlet Mk III** machines; and Lend-Lease **F4F-4B** aircraft with the GR-1820 Cyclone engine as **Martlet Mk IV** fighters. In January 1944 the British redesignated the type as the **Wildcat**.

The first of an eventual 285 F4F-3s for the US Navy flew on 20 August 1940, and at the beginning of December the type began to equip VF-7 and VF-41. Some 95 **F4F-3A** aircraft were ordered by the US Navy, these being powered by the R-1830-90 engine with a single-stage supercharger, and deliver-ies began in 1941. The **XF4F-4** prototype first took to the air in May 1941, this incorporating refinements

resulting from Martlet combat experience in the UK, including six-gun arma-ment, armour, self-sealing tanks, and wing-folding. Delivery of an eventual 1,168 production examples of the **F4F-4 Wildcat**, as the type had by then been named, began in November 1941, and by the time the Japanese launched their attack on Pearl Harbor a number of US Navy and US Marine Corps squadrons had been equipped. As additional Wildcats entered service they equipped increasing numbers of US Marine and US Navy squadrons. In particular they served with the carriers USS *Enterprise*, USS *Hornet* and USS *Saratoga*, with which they were involved with conspicuous success in the Battles of the Coral Sea and Midway, and the operations over Guadalcanal. The Wildcat was at the centre of all significant action in the Pacific until superseded by more advanced aircraft in 1943, and also saw action with the USN in North Africa late in 1942.

The final production vari-ant built by Grumman was the long-range reconnais-sance **F4F-7** with increased fuel capacity, camera instal-lations in the lower fuselage and armament deleted. Only 21 examples of this model were built,

but Grumman also produced two **XF4F-8** prototypes. With an urgent need to concentrate on development and produc-tion of the more advanced F6F Hellcat, Grumman negotiated an agreement with General Motors for the latter to continue production of the F4F-4 under the designation **FM-1**. Production by General Motors' Eastern Aircraft Division began after finalisation of a contract on 18 April 1942, and the first of this company's FM-1s flew on 31 August 1942. Production totalled 1,060, of which 312 were supplied to the UK under the desig-nation **Martlet Mk V** (later **Wildcat Mk V**).

At the same time, General Motors was work-ing on the development of an **FM-2** improved version that was the production version of the two Grumman-built XF4F-8 prototypes. Its major change was the installation of the 1,350-hp (1007-kW) R-1820-56 Cyclone engine, but a larger vertical tail was introduced to maintain good directional stability with this more powerful engine, and airframe weight was also reduced to the minimum. A total of 4,777 FM-2s was built by General Motors, 370 of them being supplied to the UK for FAA service with the designation **Wildcat Mk VI**.

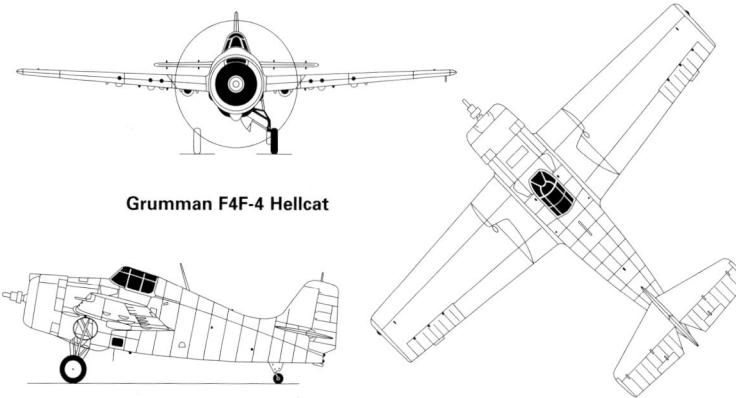

Grumman F4F-4 Hellcat

SPECIFICATION

Grumman F4F-4 Wildcat

Type: single-seat carrierborne and land-based fighter and fighter-bomber

Powerplant: one Pratt & Whitney R-1830-36 Twin Wasp radial piston engine rated at 1,200 hp (895 kW)

Performance: maximum speed 318 mph (512 km/h) at 19,400 ft (5915 m); cruising speed 155 mph (249 km/h) at optimum altitude; initial climb rate 1,950 (594 m) per minute; service ceiling 39,400 ft (12010 m); range 770 miles (1239 km)

Weights: empty 5,758 lb (2612 kg); maximum take-off 7,952 lb (3607 kg)

Dimensions: wingspan 38 ft (11.58 m); length 28 ft 9 in (8.76 m); height 9 ft 2½ in (2.81 m); wing area 260.00 sq ft (24.15 m²)

Armament: six 0.5-in (12.7-mm) Browning fixed forward-firing machine-guns in the leading edges of the wing, plus up to 200 lb (91 kg) of disposable stores carried under the wing, and generally comprising two 100-lb (45-kg) bombs

With its increased height vertical fin, this aircraft is easily recognisable as the more powerful General Motors-built FM-2 Wildcat. The FM-2 boasted a maximum speed of 332 mph (534 km/h).

Grumman G-34 Skyrocket (F5F)

Although it was as early as 1935 that the US Navy first began to consider the feasibility of a twin-engined fighter for carrierborne use, it was only at a time early in 1937 that this preliminary consideration began to evolve into more concrete plans. The spur for this development was the feeling of the Bureau of Aeronautics that the G-18 monoplane fighter, a development of the projected G-16 biplane fighter for evaluation as the XF4F-2, would be capable of a speed of only about 300 mph (483 km/h) on its 1,050-hp (783-kW) Pratt & Whitney R-1830-66 Twin Wasp radial engine, and that considerably greater power would be needed to raise the speed to a figure significantly higher. Current landplane fighters were reaching speeds in excess of 350 mph (563 km/h) with further advances imminent, so the BuAer felt that a radical method of boosting performance would have to be found. The prevailing wisdom at this time was that the radial engine would increase in power only to about 1,200 hp (895 kW) in the short term, and that no aerodynamic breakthroughs could be expected. In the circumstances, therefore, a 'brute strength' approach to performance enhancement was adopted by a doubling of the available power through the use of a two-engined powerplant even though this meant the adoption of a larger airframe that would present parking and hangarage problems in the aircraft carriers of the period.

In March 1937, therefore, the BuAer circulated to American aircraft manufacturers a request of twin-engined fighters proposals, and soon received responses from Brewster, Curtiss, Grumman, Lockheed, Seversky and Vought. Grumman offered its **G-25** design for a high-altitude fighter with a powerplant of two turbocharged Allison V-1710 liquid-cooled Vee

piston engines, but the BuAer felt that neither this nor the offerings of the other contenders offered sufficiently great an improvement in performance over current fighters to warrant further development of the proposals. The BuAer then undertook a number of design studies based on a powerplant of one V-1710 engine or two Pratt & Whitney R-1535 Twin Wasp Junior or R-1830 Twin Wasp air-cooled radial piston engines, and from its results in these studies created its Design No. 144 requirement.

Issued to American manufacturers in April 1938, the Design No. 144 request called for proposals for two carrierborne fighter types, one with a powerplant of one supercharged V-1710 engine and the other with a powerplant of two engines but weighing less than 9,000 lb (4082 kg): each of the types was to carry the fixed forward-firing armament of two 20-mm cannon and two 0.3-in (7.62-mm) machine-guns, lift a disposable load of 200 lb (91 kg) in the form of small anti-aircraft bombs, have a deck requirement of less than 200 ft (61 m) against a 25-kt (29-mph; 46-km/h) wind, possess a stalling speed of no more than 70 mph (113 km/h), and offer excellent flight performance in combination with good handling characteristics. By April 1938 the BuAer had received proposals from Bell, Brewster, Curtiss, Grumman and Vought for either or both of these types within the specified powerplant parameters, while Vought also offered another fighter

The outer panels of the XF5F-1's wings were hinged to fold upward and inward for carrier stowage. The type was of all-metal stressed-skin construction with the exception of its control surfaces, which were metal-framed and fabric-covered.

with one Pratt & Whitney R-2800 Double Wasp radial engine. At the end of June 1938, the BuAer contracted with Grumman and Vought for single examples of their primary offerings, namely the **Grumman G-34** design for a twin-engined fighter to be evaluated as the **XF5F-1** and the **Vought V-166** design for a single-engined fighter to be evaluated as the **XF4U-1**. A third contender was added in November of the same year when the BuAer contracted with Bell for a single **XFL-1 Airabonita**.

The G-34 was based on the powerplant of two R-1535-96 Twin Wasp Junior two-row radial engines each fitted with a two-speed supercharger as specified in Grumman's original proposal of April 1938, but the programme was soon delayed by the engine manufacturer's decision to proceed no further with the development of this engine. Grumman therefore received permission for the use of two Wright R-1820 Cyclone single-row radial engines. It was March 1940 that the XF5F-1 was completed as Grumman's first warplane with a folding wing and its first designed around cannon armament, even though this latter had to be altered to the standard type of US heavy machine-gun armament after the fall of

Denmark in April 1940 meant that the planned 23-mm Madsen weapons would not be available.

The type recorded its maiden flight on 1 April 1940 and soon encountered problems such as inadequate engine cooling, higher levels of drag than estimated, and the frequent failure of the three-segment landing gear doors to close properly. Grumman had to undertake a major effort to improve matters, and it was not until February 1941 that the XF5F-1 was delivered to NAS Anacostia, Maryland, for its official trials: by this time the XF4U-1 ordered at the same time as the XF5F-1 had already achieved a maximum speed in excess of 400 mph (644 km/h) and Vought had been asked to prepare the type for large-scale production.

The service nonetheless decided to continue

its evaluation of the XF5F-1, and after a short series of flights at Anacostia the aircraft was returned to Grumman for extensive modifications. The revised XF5F-1 was back at Anacostia by a time late in July 1941, but trials soon revealed no significant improvement to engine cooling or enhancement of performance had been effected by the changes. Flight trials nonetheless continued for a time, and the XF5F-1 was not finally retired until December 1944 after recording slightly less than 156 hours in the air during a flight career of 56 months. It is worth recording that the performance of the XF5F-1 was not altogether poor, for although it lacked the speed of the F4U Corsair evolved from the XF4U-1 prototype, the **Skyrocket** climbed considerably more rapidly than either its Bell or Vought competitor.

SPECIFICATION	
Grumman XF5F-1	10,892 lb (4941 kg)
Type: single-seat carrierborne fighter	**Dimensions:** wingspan 42 ft (12.80 m); length 28 ft 8½ in (8.75 m); height 11 ft 4 in (3.45 m); wing area 303.50 sq ft (28.195 m²)
Powerplant: two Wright XR-1820-40/42 Cyclone radial piston engines each rated at 1,200 hp (895 kW)	**Armament:** (proposed) two or four 23-mm Madsen fixed forward-firing cannon or four 0.5-in (12.7-mm) Browning M2 fixed forward-firing machine-guns in the nose, plus up to 530 lb (240 kg) of disposable stores carried on two underwing hardpoints and 10 wing weapons bays
Performance: maximum speed 383 mph (616 km/h) at sea level; initial climb rate 4,000 ft (1219 m) per minute; service ceiling 33,000 ft (10060 m); range 1,170 miles (1883 km)	
Weights: empty 8,107 lb (3677 kg); maximum take-off	

Grumman G-40 (TBF/TBM Avenger)

Forming a proportion of the naval aircraft which were involved in the Battle of Midway in 1942 were the first of the US Navy's monoplane torpedo-bombers, the Douglas TBD Devastator, and the first operational examples of the newly developed torpedo-bomber intended to replace it, the **TBF Avenger**. For both of these aircraft types

the operation was a disaster: of the six Avengers in action only one survived. The Devastator was no match for the Japanese aircraft and was thereafter withdrawn from operational service, while the Avenger, which had been intended to reinforce VT-8's TBD-1s on board the USS *Hornet*, arrived at Pearl Harbor after the carrier had sailed and

instead flew to Midway Island and went into action from there.

The origins of the Avenger can be found early in 1940, when the US Navy initiated a contest to procure a more modern torpedo-bomber, ordering two **XTBF-1** prototypes of Grumman's **G-40** design on 8 April 1940, and two competing XTBU-1 proto-

A prominent feature of the TBM-3E Avenger was the underwing radome for its AN/APS-4 radar.

types from Vought a couple of weeks later: the latter entered belated production with Consolidated as the TBY Sea Wolf, but only about 180 were built. The XTBF-1 represented something of a challenge for the Grumman design team, for although the company had produced a number of successful carrierborne fighters, this was the first attempt to develop a torpedo-bomber.

First flown on 1 August 1941, the XTBF-1 was a hefty mid-wing monoplane of all-metal construction, except for its fabric-covered control surfaces, and for carrier stowage the outer wing panels could be folded. The fuselage and tail unit were of conventional construction, and the retractable landing gear was of tailwheel type. Attachment points for catapult launch, and an electrically actuated arrester hook, were standard. Later versions had RATO (rocket assisted takeoff) provision, and the powerplant was based on one 1,700-hp (1268-kW) Wright R-2600-8 Cyclone 14 radial engine driving a three-bladed constant-speed propeller. Accommodation was provided for a crew of three (pilot, bomb-aimer and radio operator/gunner) under a long transparent canopy.

Flight testing of the prototype by Grumman was followed by US Navy evaluation which ended satisfactorily in December 1941. But 12 months before this the US Navy had placed its first production order for 286 **TBF-1** aircraft, and the first of these entered service on 30 January 1942. Despite the inauspicious start to the Avenger's career at Midway, the US Navy procured the aircraft in large numbers, and between first delivery at the end of January 1942 and December 1943, Grumman manufactured a total of 2,288 aircraft. These included the TBF-1 that was basically the same as the prototypes, and 764 examples of the **TBF-1C** that differed by having two 0.5-in (12.7-mm) machine-guns mounted in the leading edges of the wing and provision for the carriage of drop tanks. Grumman also built one **XTBF-2** and two **XTBF-3** prototypes with the XR-2600-10 and R-2600-20 engines respectively.

Of the above, the Royal Navy received 402 aircraft under Lend-Lease, mostly procured under the designation **TBF-1B**, and the FAA's No. 832 Sqn was the first unit to be equipped, on 1 January 1943. These aircraft were at first designated **Tarpon Mk I** in

British service, but were redesignated **Avenger Mk I** in January 1944. No. 832's aircraft were deployed operationally from the USS *Saratoga* in June 1943 in support of the US Marine Corps' landings in the middle of the Solomon Islands chain, and this is regarded as the first occasion that FAA aircraft were flown into action from a US Navy carrier. The Royal New Zealand Air Force also acquired 63 examples of the TBF-1.

With demand for the Avenger exceeding Grumman's production capacity, the Eastern Aircraft Division of the General Motors Corporation was contracted as a second source of supply. Avengers with the designations **TBM-1** and **TBM-1C** (550 and 2,332 aircraft equivalent to TBF-1 and TBF-1C respectively) were built from September 1942. A total of 7,546 of these and subsequent versions had been delivered when this company's production lines closed down in June 1945. Of these early versions from General Motors, the Royal Navy received 334 TBM-1s for service with the local designation **Avenger Mk II**.

General Motors produced four **XTBM-3** prototypes with the R-2600-20 engine, similar to Grumman's XTBF-3 except for their strengthened wing to allow the carriage of mixed stores on underwing racks. Some 4,657 aircraft were also supplied without the heavy power-operated dorsal turret. Designated **TBM-3** and **TBM-3E** (the latter with the fuselage lengthened by 11½ in/0.29 m and APS-4 search radar in a pod under the starboard wing), this variant was delivered from April 1944. The Royal Navy acquired 222 such aircraft for service with the local designation **Avenger Mk III**. Although many people are unaware of the fact, the FAA Avengers gave considerable support

to US operations in the closing stages of World War II: aircraft from the carriers HMS *Formidable*, *Illustrious*, *Indefatigable* and *Victorious* took part in bombing operations against such targets as Formosa and the Japanese home islands. General Motors also built three **XTBM-4** prototypes, which differed primarily by having a strengthened fuselage, but contract cancellations that followed VJ-Day meant that no production examples were built.

The end of Avenger production at the end of World War II did not also bring an end to the Avenger's career. In US Navy service the type fulfilled a valuable role searching for and locating submarines until specialised aircraft were

developed for this purpose. Other tasks for which conversions were developed included versions for all-weather and night operations, electronic countermeasures, carrier on-board delivery and target towing. The RN's wartime Avengers remained operational until 3 June 1946, but from 1953 this service began to acquire ASW versions under the Mutual Defense Assistance Program (MDAP), these aircraft operating under the designations **Avenger AS.Mk 4** and **Avenger AS.Mk 5** until introduction of the Fairey Gannet in 1955. Avenger variants were also supplied post-war under MDAP to the Brazilian naval air arm, French Aéronavale, JMSDF, Royal Canadian Navy and Royal Netherlands Navy.

SPECIFICATION

Grumman TBF-1C Avenger
Type: three-seat carrierborne and land-based torpedo-bomber
Powerplant: one Wright R-2600-8 Cyclone 14 radial piston engine rated at 1,700 hp (1268 kW)
Performance: maximum speed 257 mph (414 km/h) at 12,000 ft (3660 m); cruising speed 153 mph (246 km/h) at optimum altitude; climb to 10,000 ft (3050 m) in 13 minutes; service ceiling 21,400 ft (6525 m); range 2,335 miles (3758 km) in the scouting role or 1,105 miles (1778 km) in the torpedo role
Weights: empty 10,555 lb (4788 kg); maximum take-off 17,364 lb (7876 kg)

Dimensions: wingspan 54 ft 2 in (16.51 m); length 40 ft (12.19 m); height 16 ft 5 in (5.00 m); wing area 490.00 sq ft (45.52 m²)
Armament: two 0.5-in (12.7-mm) Browning M2 fixed forward-firing machine-guns in the leading edges of the wing, one Browning M2 trainable rearward-firing machine-gun in the power-operated dorsal turret and one 0.3-in (7.62-mm) Browning trainable rearward-firing machine-gun in the ventral position, plus up to 2,500 lb (1134 kg) of disposable stores carried in a lower-fuselage weapons bay and on two underwing hardpoints

These VS-25 TBM-3Es were photographed late in the 1940s while still in US Navy service. Note the distinctive rear turret installation.

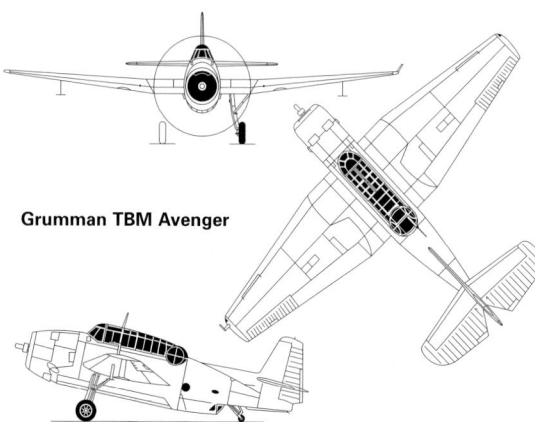

Grumman TBM Avenger

Variants

TBF-1CP/TMB-1CP: conversions of small numbers of TBF-1Cs and TBM-1Cs for the PR role
TBF-1D/TBF-1CD: conversions of the TBF-1 and TBF-1C with ASD (Air-to-Surface Type D), later APS-3, centrimetric radar for use in the anti-submarine role
TBF-1E/TBM-1E: late-production TBF-1s and TBM-1s carrying additional avionics including ASH (Air-to-surface Type H), later redesigned APS-4, centrimetric radar under the starboard wing
TBF-1J/TBM-1J: redesignation of TBF-1s and TBM-1s re-equipped for all-weather operation in arctic regions
TBF-1L/TBM-1L: TBF-1 and TBM-1 conversion with retractable searchlight in the weapons bay
TBF-1P/TBM-1P: PR conversions of the TBF-1 and TBM-1
TBM-3D: conversion of TBM-3 for the anti-submarine role with the same equipment as the TBF-1D
TBM-3E/TBM-3E2: conversion of TBM-3 with additional avionics during and after World War II, respectively
TBM-3H: possible conversions from TBM-3 standard with ASV radar

TBM-3J: all-weather conversion of TBM-3
TBM-3L: conversion of TBM-3 with retractable searchlight in the weapons bay
TBM-3M/TBM-3M2: missile launcher conversions of TBM-3 and TBM-3E aircraft
TBM-3N: post-war night attack conversion of TBM-3 with the dorsal turret replaced by a radar operator position
TBM-3P: PR conversion of TBM-3
TBM-3Q: ECM conversion of TBM-3
TBM-3R: conversion of TBM-3 to provide seven-passenger/cargo capacity for carrier on-board delivery
TBM-3S/TBM-3S2: conversions of the TBM-3 and TBM-3E for anti-submarine attack with all gun armament removed
TBM-3U: utility and target-towing conversions from TBM-3 standard with a two-man crew and generally no armament
TBM-3W: conversion of TBM-3 for the airborne early warning role with APS-20 radar with its antenna in a large ventral radome
TBM-3W2: variant of the TBM-3W with the radar optimised for anti-submarine search, and generally operated in conjunction with the TBM-3S or TBM-3S2 to create an anti-submarine hunter/killer team

Grumman G-44 Widgeon (J4F Widgeon and OA-14)

In 1939 Grumman came to the conclusion that while its Goose was selling well, the type was too large and too expensive to capitalise on the expanding civil market for transport flying boats, and in August 1939 started work on the **G-44 Widgeon** that was planned to complement the Goose. The resulting 'boat resembled a scaled-down Goose that possessed a sleeker and slightly more modern appearance as it had a powerplant of two inline rather than radial piston engines. The type was of basically all-metal construction, and was based on a comparatively deep fuselage of semi-monocoque construction with five watertight compartments and a two-step planing bottom. The first 'boat made its maiden flight in June 1940 with the powerplant of two 200-hp (149-kW) Ranger

6-440C-5 inline engines each driving a two-bladed propeller. Flight trials confirmed the design team's estimates of performance and handling, and the only change required before the type received certification was the replacement of the original plain elevators by horn-balanced elevators. Deliveries began in February 1941, and by the end of the year Grumman had delivered 30 'boats to a number of private and commercial operators, including 12 to the Portuguese naval air arm.

The designation **G-44A** was used for the civil version whose production was resumed in the USA during the last part of 1944. Some 75 such 'boats had been completed by May 1949, with initial deliveries to civilian customers.

Delivered in two batches (eight in 1941 and

17 in 1942), 25 **J4F-1** 'boats were operated by the US Coast Guard in the utility role with coastal patrol and air/sea rescue as their two most important tasks. The 'boats initially differed from the civil G-44s only in their powerplant of two 200-hp (149-kW) Ranger L-440-5 engines, and the incorporation of a hatch in the upper side of the fuselage behind the wing to facilitate the loading and unloading of litters. Once the USA had become embroiled in World War II and German U-boats began a short but very successful period of attacks on shipping plying the routes along the American east coast, the 'boats were modified with a rack under the starboard wing to carry one 200-lb (91-kg) depth charge or alternatively a rescue raft and associated equipment.

Delivered between February 1942 and

In standard form (illustrated), the Widgeon was an attractive amphibian, although the basic airframe also acted as the basis for several conversions.

February 1945, the 131 **J4F-2** 'boats for the US Navy were handed over in a standard identical to that of the J4F-1 except for the lack of the upper-fuselage hatch. The US Navy later transferred 14 to Brazil and 15 to the UK, where their received the designation **Gosling Mk I** that was later changed to **Widgeon Mk I** to accord with US Navy nomenclature. An ex-civil G-44 was

also acquired by the British for use by the British Foreign Commission based at Miami in Florida.

Soon after the American entry into World War II, the US Army Air Forces impressed 15 G-44 'boats for service under the **OA-14** designation, and of these only seven were returned to the civil register after the end of the war.

SPECIFICATION	
Grumman J4F-2 Widgeon	**Weights:** empty 3,240 lb
Type: two-crew utility, coastal patrol and anti-submarine amphibian flying boat	(1470 kg); maximum take-off 4,525 lb (2053 kg)
Powerplant: two Ranger L-440-5 inverted inline piston engines each rated at 200 hp (149 kW)	**Dimensions:** wingspan 40 ft (12.19 m); length 31 ft 1 in (9.47 m); height 11 ft 5 in (3.38 m); wing area 245.00 sq ft (22.76 m²)
Performance: maximum speed 153 mph (246 km/h) at sea level; cruising speed 138 mph (222 km/h) at optimum altitude; initial climb rate 700 ft (213 m) per minute; service ceiling 14,600 ft (4450 m); range 920 miles (1481 km); range 800 miles (1287 km)	**Armament:** up to 200 lb (91 kg) of disposable stores carried on one hardpoint under the starboard wing rated, and generally comprising one 200-lb (91-kg) depth charge **Payload:** up to four passengers carried in the enclosed cabin

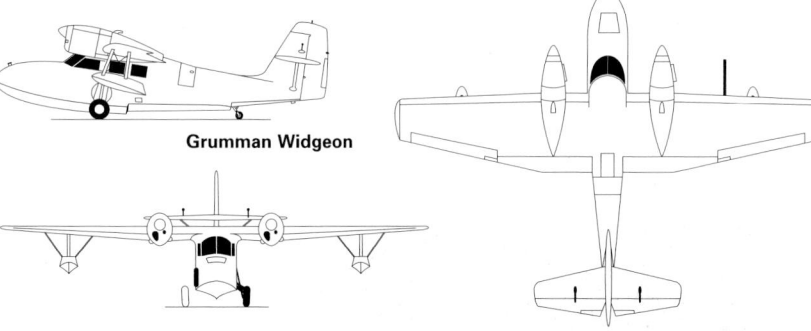

Grumman Widgeon

Grumman G-50 (F6F Hellcat)

Developed from a project started by the company to evolve a successor to the F4F Wildcat, the **F6F Hellcat** benefited in the design stage from early operational experience of US Navy pilots in the Pacific theatre, and from a feedback of information from the European Allies who had then been involved in war against the Axis for some 18 months. This **G-50** project was an advanced development of the F4F, the family resemblance unmistakable, but with one major change: the mid-wing configuration of the Wildcat gave place to a new low-wing layout that made it possible for the main landing gear units to retract into the wing's centre section instead of the fuselage. This allowed the main gear units to be mounted farther outboard from the fuselage, providing a much more stable wide-track landing gear arrangement. Other improvements that resulted from combat feedback

included the provision of armour for the pilot, and increased ammunition capacity.

An evaluation by the US Navy of Grumman's design proposal resulted in an order, dated 30 June 1941, covering four prototypes, each with a different engine installation to permit competitive evaluation of the flight envelope. These prototypes were the **XF6F-1** with the 1,700-hp (1268-kW) Wright R-2600-10 Cyclone two-stage turbocharged unit, the **XF6F-2** with the R-2600-16 turbocharged unit, the **XF6F-3** with the 2,000-hp (1491-kW) R-2800-10 Double Wasp two-stage turbocharged unit, and the **XF6F-4** with the R-2800-27 two-stage turbocharged unit.

On 26 June 1942, just under a year from order date, the XF6F-1 flew for the first time. By then there was great urgency to reinforce the Wildcat then in first-line service, resulting in a decision to install the

most powerful engine then available, the R-2800-10, into the first airframe; this made its second 'first flight' as the XF6F-3 on 30 July 1942. But even before the first prototype flight, the Grumman design had been ordered into production as the **F6F-3 Hellcat**, and from that moment the design similarity of the F4F and F6F paid immense dividends in terms of production speed. The first production example of the F6F-3 made its initial flight on 4 October 1942 and VF-9 on board the USS *Essex* began to equip with the new type on 16 January 1943, and on 31 August of the same year VF-5 on board the USS *Yorktown* became the first Hellcat unit to join combat with the Japanese.

Of all-metal construction with flush-riveted skinning, the Hellcat had a wing whose outer panels folded for carrier stowage. The standard armament comprised six 0.5-in (12.7-mm) machine-guns

mounted in the leading edges of the wings. The fuselage and tail unit were conventional in structure and differed little, except in size, from those of the F4F. All three units of the landing gear were retracted hydraulically, and a retractable arrester hook was standard. The pilot was accommodated in a capacious cockpit high above the wing.

Hellcat production was superb, with well over 2,500 aircraft delivered during 1943, making it possible to re-equip F4F squadrons rapidly with this more potent fighter, and the type remained in first-line service with the US Navy for the remainder of World War II. Even when the more advanced F4U Corsair joined the fleet in mid-1944 the Hellcat was

SPECIFICATION	
Grumman F6F-5 Hellcat	(10.24 m); height 13 ft 7 in
Type: single-seat carrierborne and land-based fighter and fighter-bomber	(4.14 m); wing area 334.00 sq ft (31.03 m²)
Powerplant: one Pratt & Whitney R-2800-10W Double Wasp radial piston engine rated at 2,000 hp (1491 kW)	**Armament:** six 0.5-in (12.7-mm) Browning M3 fixed forward-firing machine-guns or, in some late aircraft, two 20-mm Hispano M2 fixed forward-firing cannon and four 0.5-in (12.7-mm) Browning M3 fixed forward-firing machine-guns in the leading edges of the wing, plus up to 2,500 lb (1134 kg) of disposable stores carried on four underwing hardpoints, and generally comprising two 1,000- or 500-lb (454- or 227-kg) bombs or two 11.75-in (298-mm) Tiny Tim air-to-surface unguided rockets on the inner hardpoints and up to six 5-in (127-mm) HVAR air-to-surface unguided rockets on the outer hardpoints
Performance: maximum speed 380 mph (612 km/h) at 23,400 ft (7130 m); cruising speed 168 mph (270 km/h) at optimum altitude; initial climb rate 2,980 ft (908 m) per minute; service ceiling 37,300 ft (11370 m); range 945 miles (1521 km) with standard fuel	
Weights: empty 9,238 lb (4190 kg); maximum take-off 15,413 lb (6991 kg)	
Dimensions: wingspan 42 ft 10 in (13.06 m); length 33 ft 7 in	

This F6F-5 was photographed just after the cessation of hostilities in World War II. At its peak, F6F production reached 20 aircraft per day.

not displaced. Instead, the two fighters worked side by side as a team that was extremely low in Japanese popularity ratings: the Hellcat finally claiming 4,947 enemy aircraft destroyed in air-to-air combat, the Corsair ending with an 11:1 kill:loss ratio.

The F6F-3 also began to arrive in the UK during 1943, in the form of 252 designated originally **Gannet Mk I** (later **Hellcat Mk I**) and first equipping the Fleet Air Arm's No. 800 Squadron.

By the time F6F-3 production ended in mid-1944, a total of 4,402 Hellcats had been built. Their numbers included 18 **F6F-3E** night-fighters with APS-4 radar mounted in a pod beneath the starboard wing, and 205 generally similar **F6F-3N** night-fighters with APS-6 radar.

During the F6F-3 production run, Grumman developed an enhanced version, which was ordered into production as the **F6F-5**. This had aerodynamic improvements, including a redesigned engine cowling, new ailerons, and strengthened tail surfaces. The F6F-5 retained the F6F-3's powerplant in a slightly modified form based on the R-2800-10W engine in which the suffixed letter indicated the installation of a water injection system which provided an additional 10 per cent power for limited periods during take-off and combat. It also meant that take-off could be made at a higher gross weight, which gave scope to increase both armour and armament without any danger of penalising performance. First flown on 4 April 1944, the F6F-5 entered service with the US Navy very shortly after this date, and 930 were supplied to the UK under Lend-Lease, the type being designated **Hellcat Mk II** in FAA service. Of this number, some 70 were equivalent to the US Navy's **F6F-5N** model, equipped to serve in the night-fighter role, and were identified easily by the addition of a small radome on the starboard wing. By far the majority of the FAA's Hellcats equipped the squadrons which served with the British Pacific Fleet in the Far East. The 70 or so night-fighter variants supplied to the UK were designated **Hellcat NF.Mk II**.

When production ended in November 1945, a total of 12,275 examples of the Hellcat, including 7,868 aircraft of the F6F-5 series, had been built, this number including several variants as listed below. The other operators of the F6F-5, in the period after World War II, were Argentina, France, Paraguay and Uruguay.

Variants

XF6F-1: prototype flown initially with the 1,700-hp (1268-kW) R-2600-10 Cyclone 14, but later re-engined with the 2,000-hp (1491-kW) R-2800-10 Double Wasp as an **XF6F-3** prototype
XF6F-2: prototype projected with the R-2600-16 engine but completed instead as a second XF6F-3
XF6F-3N: conversion of a production F6F-3 to serve as prototype of the **F6F-3N** night-fighter, with APS-6 radar in a pod beneath the starboard wing
XF6F-4: prototype conversion from an F6F-3 for evaluation of the 2,100-hp (1566-kW) R-2800-27 engine
F6F-5K: designation of a number of F6F-5/5N fighters converted for use as radio-controlled target drones
F6F-5P: under this designation a few F6F-5s were converted for reconnaissance duties with a camera installed in the rear fuselage
XF6F-6: two prototypes, converted from F6F-5 standard with the 2,100-hp (1566-kW) R-2800-18W engine and four-bladed propeller

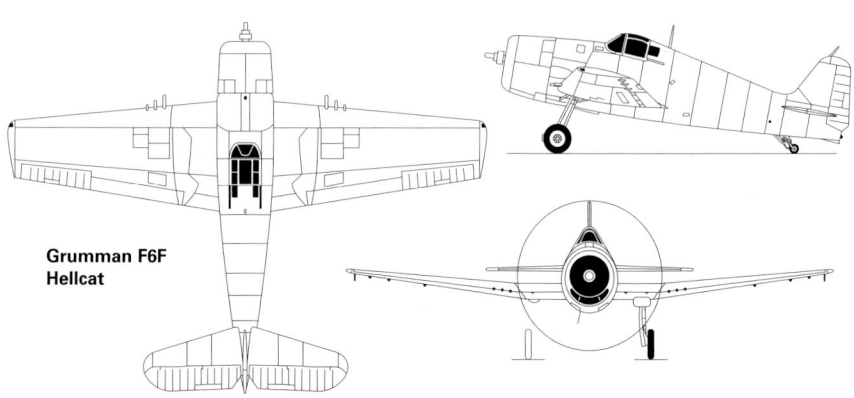

Grumman F6F Hellcat

Grumman G-51 (F7F Tigercat)

Although its XF5F-1 twin-engine carrierborne fighter prototype failed to gain a production contract, in the process of its evolution Grumman gained a far wider appreciation of the problems involved in the creation of such a machine. Early in 1941, therefore, the company started work on the design of a new twin-engined fighter for operation from the larger carriers of the 'Midway'-class that were being planned. This **G-51 Tigercat** design bore little other than a conceptual similarity to its predecessor, for the USN by then wanted a high-performance fighter with unprecedented firepower.

Grumman's proposal resulted in the award of a contract for two **XF7F-1** prototypes on 30 June 1941, the first of these flying during December 1943. Of all-metal construction, the Tigercat was a shoulder-wing cantilever monoplane, the outer panels of the wing folding for carrier stowage. The fuselage and tailplane were conventional, but the retractable landing gear was of the tricycle type and a retractable deck arrester hook was mounted under the rear part of the fuselage. The powerplant comprised two R-2800-22W Double Wasp radial engines, these being installed in large underwing nacelles.

Before the prototype's first flight, Grumman had received a contract for 500 production aircraft under the designation **F7F-1** for supply to the US Marine Corps which, by then, was already engaged in landing operations on Japanese-held islands in the Pacific. Operated from land bases, these aircraft would provide the US Marines with their own close-support capability, but in the event the Tigercat materialised too late to see operational service with the USMC before the end of World War II.

The first production F7F-1 was generally similar to the prototypes, as were the 33 aircraft which followed, and delivery of these machines began in April 1944. The 35th aircraft on the production line was modified for use in the night-fighter role under the designation **XF7F-2N**, and 65 production examples followed during 1944 under the designation **F7F-2N**. These aircraft differed from the F7F-1 by deletion of the rear fuselage fuel tank (to provide space for the radar operator's cockpit) and removal of the nose armament to allow installation of the radar. There followed production of a new single-seat version, the **F7F-3**, of which 190 were built. This differed from the F7F-1 in having R-2800-34 engines to provide increased power at altitude, slightly increased vertical tail surface areas to cater for this, and a 7 per cent increase in fuel capacity. These aircraft terminated production of the original contract, with the balance cancelled after VJ-Day.

Post-war production included 60 **F7F-3N** and 13 **F7F-4N** night-fighters, both with a lengthened nose housing advanced radar, and the latter the only examples with strengthening, arrester hook, and specialised equipment for carrierborne operation. A small number of F7F-3s was modified after delivery for use in the electronic warfare (**F7F-3E**) and photo-reconnaissance (**F7F-3P**) roles. Some of the aircraft remained in service with the US Marine Corps in the immediate post-war years, but were soon displaced by higher-performance turbine-powered aircraft.

In its F7F-3N form, the Tigercat featured a second cockpit for a radar operator and a lengthened nose featuring a ventral radome for its SCR-720 radar.

SPECIFICATION	
Grumman F7F-3 Tigercat	wing area 455.00 sq ft (42.27 m²)

Grumman F7F-3 Tigercat
Type: single-seat carrierborne and land-based fighter and fighter-bomber
Powerplant: two Pratt & Whitney R-2800-34W Double Wasp radial piston engines each rated at 2,100 hp (1566 kW)
Performance: maximum speed 435 mph (700 km/h) at 22,200 ft (6765 m); cruising speed 222 mph (357 km/h) at optimum altitude; initial climb rate 4,530 ft (1380 m) per minute; service ceiling 40,700 ft (12405 m); range 1,200 miles (1931 km)
Weights: empty 16,270 lb (7380 kg); maximum take-off 25,720 lb (11666 kg)
Dimensions: wing span 51 ft 6 in (15.70 m); length 45 ft 4½ in (13.83 m); height 16 ft 7 in (5.05 m);

wing area 455.00 sq ft (42.27 m²)
Armament: four 20-mm Hispano M2 fixed forward-firing cannon in the leading edges of the wing roots and four 0.5-in (12.7-mm) Browning M3 fixed forward-firing machine-guns in the nose, plus up to 4,000 lb (1814 kg) of disposable stores carried on one underfuselage and four underwing hardpoints, and generally comprising one 2,600-, 2,000- or 1,600-lb (1179-, 907- or 726-kg) bomb, or one 1,860- or 1,600-lb (844- or 726-kg) mine, or one Mk 13-2 torpedo on the centreline hardpoint, or two 1,000- or 500-lb (454- or 227-kg) bombs on the inner underwing hardpoints and up to eight 5-in (127-mm) HVAR rockets or 250-lb (113-kg) bombs on the outer underwing hardpoints

Grumman G-58 (F8F Bearcat)

Last of the line of piston-engined carrierborne fighters which Grumman initiated with the FF of 1931, the **F8F Bearcat** was designed to operate from aircraft carriers of all sizes and to serve primarily as an interceptor fighter, a role which demanded excellent manoeuvrability, good low-level performance, and a high climb rate. To achieve these capabilities for the two **XF8F-1** prototypes ordered on 27 November 1943 to its **G-58** design, Grumman adopted the big Pratt & Whitney R-2800 Double Wasp radial engine that had been used to power its F6F and F7F fighters, but ensured that the smallest and lightest possible airframe was designed to accommodate the specified armament, armour and fuel.

First flown on 21 August 1944, the XF8F-1 was not only smaller than the US Navy's superb Hellcat, but was some 20 per cent lighter, resulting in a climb rate about 30 per cent greater than that of its predecessor. Grumman had more than achieved the specification requirements, but also crowned this by starting delivery of production aircraft in February 1945, only six months after the first flight of the prototype.

A low-wing cantilever monoplane of all-metal construction, the initial **F8F-1** had a wing which folded at about two-thirds span for carrier stowage, retractable tailwheel landing gear, armour, self-sealing

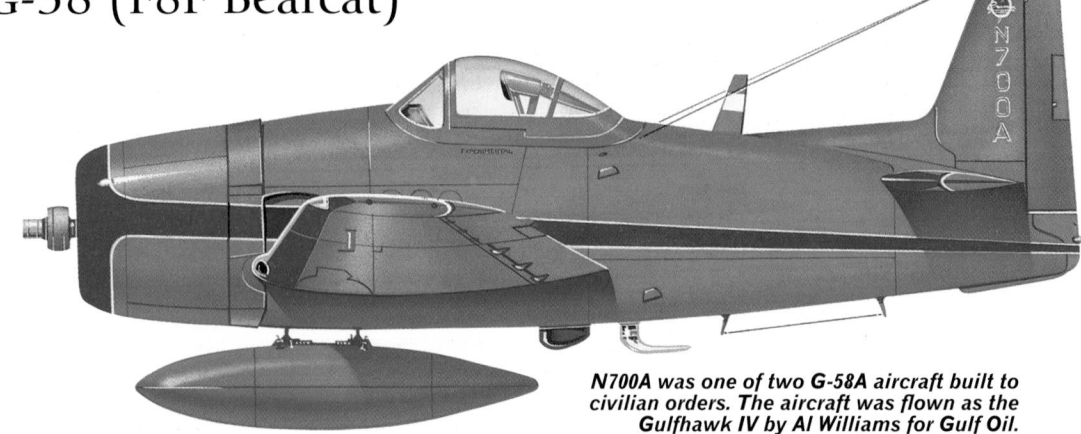

N700A was one of two G-58A aircraft built to civilian orders. The aircraft was flown as the Gulfhawk IV by Al Williams for Gulf Oil.

fuel tanks and, by comparison with the prototypes, a very small dorsal fin to increase directional stability. The powerplant of these production aircraft was based on the R-2800-34W engine, and the armament was four 0.5-in (12.7-mm) machine-guns.

Shortly after initiation of the prototype's test programme in 1944, the US Navy placed a contract for 2,023 production examples of the F8F-1, and the first of these began to equip the US Navy's VF-19 squadron on 21 May 1945. This and other early recipients of the Bearcat were still in the process of familiarisation with their new fighters when VJ-Day put an end to World War II. It also cut 1,258 aircraft from Grumman's contract and brought complete cancellation of an additional 1,876 **F3M-1** Bearcat fighters contracted from the Eastern Aircraft Division of the General Motors Corporation.

When production ended in May 1949, Grumman had built 1,265 Bearcats: two XF8F-1 prototypes; 654 examples of the F8F-1, 226 examples of the **F8F-1B** that differed by having the four standard machine-guns replaced by 20-mm cannon; two **XF8F-1N** night-fighter prototypes; 12 examples of the **F8F-1N** production variant; two **XF8F-2** prototypes; 293 examples of the **F8F-2** production model with a redesigned engine cowling, a taller fin-and-rudder assembly, some changes in detail design, and adoption of the 20-mm cannon as standard armament; 12 of the night-fighter **F8F-2N**; 60 examples of the **F8F-2P** photo-reconnaissance model with camera equipment and only two 20-mm cannon; and two **G-58A** civil aircraft. Of the two G-58A aircraft, the first was ordered by the Gulf Oil Company for the use of Major Alford Williams in succession to his Gulfhawk II biplane, and the

second was a company-owned demonstrator. In late post-war service, some USA aircraft were modified to serve as drone controllers as the **F8F-1D** and **F8F-2D**.

By the time production ended, the Bearcat was in service with some 24 US Navy squadrons, but all had been withdrawn by a time late in 1952. Some of these aircraft, with a modified fuel system, were supplied to the French Armée de l'Air for service in Indo-China under the designation F8F-1D, later serving with Vietnam. One hundred similar F8F-1D and 29 F8F-1B fighters were also supplied to the Thai air force.

SPECIFICATION

Grumman F8F-1 Bearcat
Type: single-seat carrierborne and land-based interceptor fighter and fighter-bomber
Powerplant: one Pratt & Whitney R-2800-34W Double Wasp radial piston engine rated at 2,100 hp (1566 kW)
Performance: maximum speed 434 mph (698 km/h) at 19,800 ft (6035 m); cruising speed 163 mph (262 km/h) at optimum altitude; initial climb rate 4,570 ft (1395 m) per minute; service ceiling 38,900 ft (11855 m); range 1,965 miles (3162 km) with drop tanks or 1,105 miles (1778 km) with standard fuel
Weights: empty 7,070 lb (3207 kg); maximum take-off

12,947 lb (5873 kg)
Dimensions: wingspan 35 ft 10 in (10.92 m); length 28 ft 3 in (8.61 m); height 13 ft 10 in (4.22 m); wing area 244.00 sq ft (22.67 m²)
Armament: four 0.5-in (12.7-mm) Browning M3 fixed forward-firing machine-guns in the leading edges of the wing, plus up to 2,400 lb (1087 kg) of disposable stores carried on four underwing hardpoints, and generally comprising two 1,000- or 500-lb (454- or 227-kg) bombs or two 11.75-in (298-mm) Tiny Tim air-to-surface unguided rockets on the inner hardpoints, plus four 100-lb (45-kg) bombs or four 5-in (127-mm) HVAR air-to-surface unguided rockets on the outer hardpoints

Grumman G-64 and G-111 (UF, SA-16 and U-16 Albatross)

Experience with the Grumman JRF Goose, which served throughout World War II with great reliability, suggested to the US Navy the advantages that might accrue from the procurement of a somewhat larger amphibian flying-boat with greater range and payload capabilities. In 1944 the company initiated design of its **G-64 Albatross**, and this later saw service with the US Air Force, US Coast Guard and US Navy. The G-64 was of generally similar configuration to its predecessor. Fixed underwing floats were retained, but these and the entire structure had been considerably refined to reduce drag. Other changes included the provision of a cantilever rather than strut-braced tailplane, retractable tricycle landing gear, and hardpoints beneath the wing, outboard of the

Greece was the last military operator of the Albatross, having flown the type with the 353 Mira Naftikis Aeroporikis Sinergasias at Elefsis in the SAR/maritime patrol role. This unit is an air force squadron, but operational control rests with the navy. It currently flies P-3 Orions. The Albatross was officially retired in 1996, although one electronic warfare-configured aircraft was noted as still operational in late 1997.

engines, to carry weapons or drop tanks. Additional fuel could also be carried in the underwing floats. Accommodation was provided for a crew of four,

and the cabin could accommodate 10 passengers, litters or cargo according to requirement.

The prototype ordered by the US Navy for service

as a utility type had the designation **XJR2F-1**, and flew for the first time on 24 October 1947. Initial production was of the **UF-1** model, and a modi-

fied **G-111** version introduced in 1955 was the **UF-2** with a wing increased in span from 80 ft (24.38 m) and fitted with cambered leading edges, ailerons and tail surfaces of increased area, and more effective de-icing boots for all the aerofoil leading edges. In the 1962 tri-service rationalisation of designations, these aircraft became the **HU-16C** and **HU-16D** respectively. Winterised aircraft for Antarctic service were designated **UF-1L** (later **LU-16C**), and five **UF-1T** dual-control trainers were redesignated **TU-16C**.

The USAF found the G-64 attractive for rescue

operations, the majority of the 305 ordered serving with the MATS Air Rescue Service under the designation **SA-16A**. An improved version, equivalent to the US Navy's UF-2, entered service in 1957 as the **SA-16B**: in 1962 these became the **HU-16A** and **HU-16B** respectively. **HU-16E** was the designation (originally **UF-1G**) of Albatross aircraft operated by the US Coast Guard, and 10 supplied to Canada were designated **CSR-110**.

An anti-submarine version with radar (using an antenna located in a nose radome), retractable MAD gear, ECM and a searchlight was introduced in 1961, and was equipped to carry a small number of depth charges. The Albatross is no longer in service, and its powerful and fuel-hungry engines have meant that surplus aircraft have not been a particularly attractive proposition to civil operators.

Grumman G-73 Mallard

In the early years after World War II's end in 1945, Grumman designed and developed the **G-73 Mallard** as a twin-engined commercial amphibian flying-boat that benefited from the company's extensive experience of the design of military aircraft of this type. A high-wing cantilever monoplane of all-metal construction, with a stressed-skin two-step hull, the G-73 had an upswept tail unit, and retractable tricycle landing gear to provide amphibious capability. Stabilising floats were mounted beneath the outer wing panels to balance the 'boat on the water, and these could also double as auxiliary fuel tanks. The powerplant comprised two Pratt & Whitney R-1340 Wasp radial engines, these being mounted on the leading edges of the wing in

streamlined nacelles of very clean aerodynamic line.

The hull provided air-conditioned, heated, and sound-proofed accommodation for up to 10 passengers in two compartments, and the crew of two was situated on a separate flight deck. Interior furnishings and equipment were to a high standard but some VIP examples, such as that equipped specially for the personal use of King Farouk of Egypt, were finished with the most luxurious appointments. Production of the Mallard totalled 59 'boats. In the 1960s small numbers of Mallards were converted to the **TurboMallard** standard with the powerplant of two 652-shp (486-kW) Pratt & Whitney Canada PT6A-27 turboprop engines, which not only provided the

'boats with a more modern and fuel-economical power-plant, but also the additional power that they had long needed.

A pair of PT6A-27 turboprops distinguished N2974 after its conversion as the TurboMallard prototype.

Grumman G-79 (F9F Panther)

The **F9F Panther**, the fighter which the US Navy used most extensively during the Korean conflict of the early 1950s, was developed from the company's **G-79D** design submitted to the BuAer in June 1946. Three prototypes were ordered in September 1946 under the designation **XF9F-2**, to be powered by a British centrifugal-flow turbojet engine, the Rolls-Royce

Grumman's Panther proved itself as a rugged carrier-based fighter-bomber during the Korean War.

Nene, and the construction of these aircraft began in February 1947. The Nene was licence-produced by Pratt & Whitney and the first engines were delivered to Bethpage in July 1947. The first and second prototypes were thus powered, but the third machine was completed as the **XF9F-3** with the 4,600-lb st (20.46-kN) Allison J33.

Powered by its 5,000-lb st (22.24-kN) Nene, the first prototype began taxiing trials on 20 November and achieved its maiden flight four days later. In February 1948 the Panther was equipped with 100-Imp gal

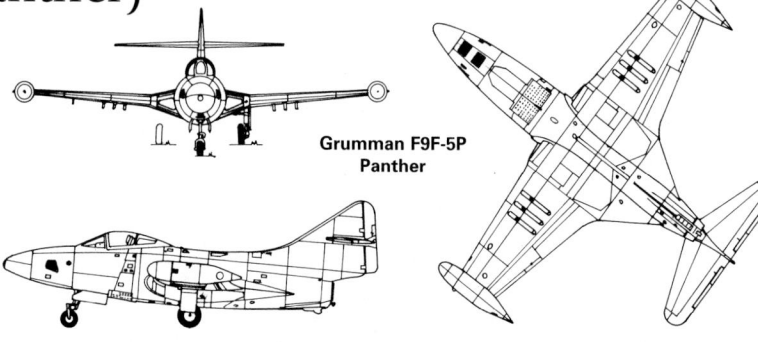

**Grumman F9F-5P
Panther**

(454-litre) wing-tip fuel tanks, later adopted as standard. The second XF9F-2 arrived at the Naval Air Test Center in October 1948 to undertake initial carrier compatibility trials, but it suffered a fuel system problem and crashed on 28 October. Its place in the programme was taken by an **F9F-2** from the initial production batch of 30 which had been ordered before the first flight, and full carrier trials were carried out from in March 1949. Initial deliveries, to VF-51, began on 8 May 1949. The unit subsequently operated as a component of Carrier Air

Group 5 on board the USS *Valley Forge*, flying the first carrierborne jet fighter sortie of the Korean War on 3 July 1950.

Production of the Panther between November 1947 and January 1953 totalled 1,385 aircraft including prototypes.

Grumman G-79 (F9F Panther) (continued)

Variants

F9F-2: 564 production aircraft with the Pratt & Whitney J42-P-6 (licence-built Nene) turbojet engine; the **F9F-2B** was a modified ground-attack version with hardpoints for underwing stores
F9F-3: 54 aircraft were built originally with the Allison J33-A-8 engine but converted from February 1950 to F9F-2 standard when this engine proved unreliable
F9F-4: the XF9F-4 prototype, powered by the water-injected 6,950-lb st (30.92-kN) J33-A-16 engine, flew on 6 July 1950, some months later than intended as the result of engine problems; the production model was the F9F-4, of which 109 were ordered including a number delivered to units of the US Marine Corps; some of the aircraft were

completed to F9F-5 standard and other were later retrofitted with the J48-P-6A engine
F9F-5: the most numerous of the Panthers and preceded by an **XF9F-5** prototype, the F9F-5 was similar to the F9F-4 but initially powered by the J48-P-2 derivative of the Rolls-Royce Tay; the prototype flew on 21 December 1949 and 616 production aircraft were built for delivery between 5 November 1950 and 13 January 1953
F9F-5P: these 36 unarmed photo-reconnaissance aircraft, with cameras in the revised nose, were delivered between 25 October 1951 and 11 August 1952
F9F-5KD: when withdrawn from operational service, a number of F9F-5 aircraft was used as target drones or drone control aircraft under this designation, which was changed to **DF-9E** in 1962

Grumman G-82 (AF Guardian)

Despite the success achieved by the Avenger, thoughts on its replacement began to crystallise during 1943 and emerged initially as the **TB2F** design to be powered by two Pratt & Whitney R-2800-22 radial engines, be heavily armed and carry an 8,000-lb (3629-kg) offensive payload over a 2,280-mile (3669-km) range. The maximum take-off weight of 45,000 lb (20412 kg) was considered excessive for carrierborne deployment at this time, so the project was abandoned in favour of the **TSF**, a proposed derivative of the F7F Tigercat. This, in its turn, was also cancelled, and in February 1945 the US Navy's Bureau of Aeronautics placed an order for three prototypes of Grumman's **G-70** design. This was a mid-wing monoplane with side-by-side seating for the two-man crew, and was conceived with the ability to carry a 4,000-lb (1814-kg) load of bombs, depth charges or torpedoes in an internal weapons bay as well as two 20-mm fixed forward-firing cannon in the leading edges of the wing. The G-70 was to rely on speed to effect an escape if attacked, and for this purpose the main nose-mounted radial engine was

to be supplemented by a Westinghouse turbojet engine buried in the rear of the fuselage and aspirated through oval inlets in the leading edges of the wing. Three prototypes were planned, comprising two **XTB3F-1** aircraft with the 2,300-hp (1715-kW) R-2800-34W Double Wasp radial engine and the 1,600-lb st (7.12-kN) Westinghouse 19XB-2B turbojet engine, and one **XTB3F-2** with the Wright R-3350-26 Duplex Cyclone radial engine and the Westinghouse 24C-4B turbojet engine. The first of these flew on 18 December 1946 with the jet inlets blanked off because of intake problems experienced during ground running. The turbojet engine was in fact never used in flight, and was soon removed. Just five days after the maiden flight the US Navy halted work on the TB3F following a reappraisal of requirements, however, and it was dropped in its original role as a torpedo-bomber. The programme was then reinstated to meet a new need for anti-submarine warfare aircraft, and the two prototypes still under construction were modified to serve as a hunter/killer combination.

The third prototype, now designated as the **XTB3F-1S**, was completed without the Westinghouse turbojet engine, the space released being used for electronic equipment and a third crew position for a radar operator. The former weapons bay was equipped with APS-20 search radar using an antenna carried in a large ventral radome. This machine first flew in November 1948, followed by the four-seat **XTB3F-2S** second prototype on 12 January 1949. Both aircraft undertook service trials at the Naval Air Test Center at Patuxent River, Maryland, in February 1949. By then, production orders had been placed for the two closely related **G-82 Guardian** types as the **AF-2S** attack and **AF-2W** hunter aircraft, both powered by the R-2800-48W radial engine. The first production example of the AF-2S flew on 17 November 1949, and between May 1950 and November 1951 five of each model were flown on armament evaluation tests with Air Development Squadron 1 at Key West, Florida. Carrier qualification flying was conducted from November 1950 to September 1951 and

Devoid of the massive underfuselage radome that characterised the AF-2W, the AF-2S was the strike component of the Guardian hunter/killer team.

SPECIFICATION	
Grumman AF-2S Guardian **Type:** two-seat carrierborne and land-based anti-submarine aircraft **Powerplant:** one Pratt & Whitney R-2800-48W Double Wasp radial piston engine rated at 2,400 hp (1780 kW) **Performance:** maximum speed 275 mph (442 km/h) at 4,000 ft (1220 m); cruising speed 166 mph (267 km/h) at optimum altitude; initial climb rate 2,300 ft (701 m) per minute; service ceiling 22,900 ft (6980 m); range 1,140 miles (1835 km) **Weights:** empty 14,658 lb (6649 kg); maximum take-off 22,565 lb (10235 kg)	**Dimensions:** wingspan 60 ft (18.29 m); length 43 ft 5 in (13.23 m); height 13 ft 2 in (4.01 m); wing area 549.00 sq ft (51.00 m²) **Armament:** up to 4,000 lb (2722 kg) of disposable stores carried in a lower-fuselage weapons bay and on six underwing hardpoints, and generally comprising one 2,000-lb (907-kg) torpedo, or two 2,000-lb (907-kg) bombs, or two 1,600-lb (726-kg) depth charges in the weapons bay, and four 500-lb (227-kg) bombs, or four Mk 54 depth charges, or six 5-in (127-mm) HVAR air-to-surface unguided rockets under the wing

VS-25 at NAS North Island, California, accepted its first aircraft on 18 October 1950. The front-line service of the **AF-2 Guardian** was limited, however, for on 30 June 1950 the US Navy issued the requirement to which the S2F Tracker was developed, and this new aircraft

first displaced the Guardian with VS-37 at NAS North Island on 31 August 1955. During the Guardian's operational life a number of squadrons (including three US Navy Reserve units) flew combat missions in Korean waters between March 1951 and May 1953.

Variants

AF-2S: 193 of this armed component of the hunter/killer combination were built with provision for up to 4,000 lb (1814 kg) of stores carried internally and six underwing hardpoints for HVAR rockets or 250-lb (113-kg) depth charges; APS-31 radar was carried beneath the starboard wing and an AVQ-8 high-intensity searchlight under the port wing; sonobuoys were dropped from pods mounted under the wing centre section
AF-2W: production of this four-man search version totalled 153 aircraft; unarmed, it was easily identified by the ventral radome for its APS-20 radar, which was supplemented by extensive avionics
AF-3S: 40 aircraft delivered between February 1952 and November 1953 to a standard that differed from that of the AF-2S in its additional ASW equipment including a MAD boom on the starboard fuselage

For its submarine detection role, the AF-2W employed the AN/APS-20 radar set, with its antenna housed in a bulbous ventral radome.

Grumman G-83 (F10F Jaguar)

Although not the first American aircraft to employ a variable-sweep wing, that distinction having fallen to the US Air Force-funded Bell X-5, the **XF10F Jaguar** was the first to have been developed with production and operational service in mind. The **G-83** design was born of the concern felt by the US Navy's BuAer about the growing probability of its increasingly heavy swept-wing fighters, approach and stalling speeds becoming incompatible with operation from the aircraft-carriers then in service. The original XF10F project, two prototypes of which were ordered on 4 March 1948, was for a fixed swept-wing fighter to be powered by a Pratt &

Whitney J42 (licence-built Rolls-Royce Nene) turbojet engine. This design was then subjected to numerous alterations and major changes, however, and the introduction of the variable-sweep wing was proposed by Grumman on 7 July 1949. The final configuration was established in the closing months of 1950 and the revised contract for two prototypes was issued on 14 December. The Jaguar was large and heavy, fitted with a wing whose sweep angle could be varied by a hydraulically actuated system between 13° 30' and 42° 30' and which had high-lift devices in the form of full-span leading-edge slats as well as Fowler flaps which occupied

80 per cent of the trailing edge. The type was to be armed with four 20-mm cannon and carrying bombs or rockets externally. The specified engine was the Westinghouse J40-WE-8 with a rating of 7,400 lb st (32.92 kN) dry increasing to 10,900 lb st (48.49 kN) with afterburning. In fact, a lower-rated 6,800-lb st (30.25-kN) J40-WE-6 engine powered the only prototype to fly, and the afterburning system was never installed.

This first machine was completed in March 1952, and after some low-speed taxi runs at Bethpage was dismantled for transit by Douglas C-124 Globemaster II to Edwards Air Force Base at Muroc

Dry Lake, California, on 16 April. Grumman test pilot C. H. 'Corky' Meyer flew the prototype throughout the test programme, beginning with an eventful 16-minute maiden flight on 19 May. Control and systems problems were experienced, setting the pattern for almost the entire 32-flight programme which ended on 25 April 1953. Much valuable experience had been gained, and the wing-sweep mechanism proved a success, but grounding of the J40 engine in March 1953 was

the final straw and, following the cancellation of orders for 100 production aircraft on 1 April and of that for the remaining 12 pre-production examples on 13 June, the project was abandoned. The two prototypes, one 90 per cent complete, were transferred to the Naval Air Materiel Center at Philadelphia, Pennsylvania, for use in crash barrier tests, and the static test airframe became a gunnery target at the Aberdeen Proving Ground, Maryland.

SPECIFICATION

Grumman F10F-1 Jaguar
Type: single-seat carrierborne fighter and fighter-bomber
Powerplant: one 7,400-lb st (32.92-kN) Westinghouse J40-WE-8 turbojet engine rated at 10,900 lb st (48.49 kN) with afterburning
Performance: (estimated) maximum speed 710 mph (1143 km/h) at sea level; cruising speed 478 mph (769 km/h) at optimum altitude; initial climb rate 13,350 ft (4069 m) per minute; service ceiling 45,800 ft (13960 m); range 2,090 miles (3363 km) with drop tanks and 1,670 miles (2688 km) with standard fuel
Weights: empty 20,426 lb (9265 kg); maximum take-off

35,450 lb (16080 kg)
Dimensions: wingspan 50 ft 7 in (15.42 m) extended and 36 ft 8 in (11.18 m) swept; length 54 ft 5 in (16.59 m); height 16 ft 3 in (4.95 m); wing area 467.00 sq ft (43.38 m²) extended and 450.00 sq ft (41.81 m²)
Armament: (intended) four 20-mm fixed forward-firing cannon in the nose, plus up to 4,000 lb (1814 kg) of disposable stores carried on two underwing hardpoints, and generally comprising two 2,000- or 1,000-lb (907- or 454-kg) bombs, or two multiple launchers each carrying 24 2¾-in (70-mm) air-to-surface unguided rockets or six 5-in (127-mm) air-to-surface unguided rockets

A bold attempt at creating a naval fighter with all the versatility of a swing-wing, the Jaguar was ultimately defeated by problems with its engine.

Grumman S2F/S-2 Tracker, TF/C-1 Trader & WF/E-1 Tracer

In the years immediately following World War II, the US Navy's carrierborne anti-submarine effort depended upon the use of two-aircraft hunter/killer teams. There were clearly snags to such a twin-aircraft attack: for example, the malfunction in one of the aircraft of something as simple as radio communication meant that both machines were virtually useless. The situation became further complicated by the growing capability of nuclear-

powered submarines which were considerably faster, deeper-diving and quieter than the conventionally powered boats they replaced. More complex avionics were needed to enhance search capability and provide an advanced weapon control system, as too were more volume for a larger weight of weapons, more fuel to give longer patrol times, and better accommodation for the crew involved on extended search missions.

In the late 1940s the

USN finalised its ideas on the kind of single hunter/killer aircraft which it needed to fulfil this role, and the **G-89** was designed as a fairly large twin-engined high-wing monoplane to meet this requirement. The high-wing configuration maximised the cabin volume and additional stowage space for

expendable sonobuoys was provided in the rear of the engine nacelles. Other features included a large weapons bay, search radar with its antenna in a retractable radome in the lower part of the rear fuselage, a MAD system with its sensor at the tip of a retractable boom, a searchlight beneath the starboard

wing, and the combination of a folding wing and an arrester hook for carrier operations.

On 30 June 1950 Grumman was awarded a contract to build for evaluation two **XS2F-1** prototypes, and the first of these machines recorded its maiden flight on 4 December 1952.

Variants

YAS-2D: proposed prototype conversion of one S-2D as a self-contained night attack variant
ES-2D: at least six S-2D and one S-2E converted for special electronic operations
US-2F: at least one S-2F adapted as a utility transport
S-2N: unofficial designation of 18 S-2As of the Dutch navy overhauled by Fairey Canada in 1968-70 and fitted with modernised equipment
US-2N: unofficial designation of four S-2Ns of the Dutch navy converted in 1972 as utility transports
S-2T Turbo-Tracker: updated version of the S-2E evolved by Grumman with two 1,645-shp (1227-kW) Garrett TPE331-15AW turboprop engines for improved payload and performance; the type was produced by conversion of older aircraft, and features much-improved ASW capability through the use of a modern mission avionics suite; Taiwan ordered kits to convert 30 radial-engined Trackers to this standard, and the first machine converted by AIDC was redelivered early in 1992
IMP S-2E: developed in Canada, this is another Tracker upgrade programme based on a turboprop-powered conversion; the first such machine was a Brazilian navy aircraft that first flew in December 1990, and the Brazilian navy has converted another 12 aircraft with Canadian-supplied kits; the conversion features two 1,650-shp (1230-kW) Pratt & Whitney Canada PT6A-67CF turboprop engines
Marsh TS-2F3 Turbo Tracker: another American-developed conversion, first flown in July 1991; intended mainly for the fire-fighting role, the TS-2F3 differs from the S-2E primarily in its mission equipment and powerplant of two TPE331-14 turboprop engines each flat-rated at 1,250 shp (932 kW)
TF-1Q: later known as the **EC-1A**, this was the standard to which three TF-1s were built for the electronic surveillance and countermeasures role
TF-1W: original designation of the WF-2

Grumman designed the Trader as a carrier on-board delivery (COD) variant of the basic S-2. Note the aircraft's extra cabin windows.

Grumman S2F/S-2 Tracker, TF/C-1 Trader & WF/E-1 (cont.)

In due course **S2F Tracker** anti-submarine warfare (ASW), **WF Tracer** airborne early warning (AEW) and **TF Trader** carrier on-board delivery (COD) versions appeared and under the 1962 tri-service rationalisation of the US services' designations these became the **S-2**, **E-1** and **C-1** series respectively. Production of the Tracker by Grumman lasted from December 1952 to December 1967, and amounted to 1,169 aircraft.

The XF2S-1 prototypes were followed by 15 **YS2F-1** service test aircraft that were themselves followed by 740 examples of the **S2F-1** (**S-2A**), the first production version of the Tracker, which entered service with VS-26 in February 1954. A number of these aircraft were used as **S2F-1T** (**TS-2A**) trainers.

The designation **S2F-1S** (**S-2B**) was applied to S2F-1s modified to carry AQA-3 Jezebel passive long-range acoustic search equipment, working in conjunction with Julie active acoustic echo-ranging by explosive charge. The **S2F-2** (**S-2C**) was the designation of the next production version, of which 60 were completed with an enlarged weapons bay with an offset extension on the port side for the carriage of the Mk 90 nuclear depth charge, and these had also a larger tail to compensate for a higher gross weight. Many of the S2F-1 and S2F-2 aircraft were later converted to the target towing and utility transport roles with the revised designations **S2F-1U** and **S2F-2U** (**US-2A** and **US-2C**) respectively, while the later designation **US-2B** was used for 64 S-2A/B and TS-2A and US-2A aircraft adapted as five-passenger transports. One S2F-2 was also converted to the photographic role with the designation **S2F-2C** (**RS-2C**).

The second major production version was the **S2F-3** (**S-2D**) that was known to Grumman as the **G-121** and whose first example recorded its maiden flight on 21 May 1959. This variant introduced a longer-span wing, still larger tail surfaces, greater fuel capacity and stowage for double the number of sonobuoys in each engine nacelle, for a combined total of 32. In addition, the forward fuselage was lengthened and widened to improve accommodation for the four-man crew. The S2F-3 entered service in May 1961, and eventually

equipped at least 15 USN squadrons. Those modified later to carry more advanced search equipment had the designation **S2F-3S** (**S-2E**), and production of the 352 G-121s ended in 1968 with a batch of 14 for the Royal Australian Navy. **S2F-1S1** (**S-2F**) was the designation of 244 S2F-1 and S2F-1S (S-2A and S-2B) aircraft retrofitted with the same advanced search equipment as that installed in the S-2E.

Between 1956 and 1958 de Havilland Aircraft of Canada built 99 examples of the Tracker for the Royal Canadian Navy, the first 43 as **CSF-1** machines and the last 56 as **CSF-2** machines with improved equipment. Some 45 CS2F-1 and CS2F-2 aircraft were later upgraded to a common electronic standard with the revised designation **CS2F-3**, and the surviving aircraft were later accorded the revised designations **CP-121 Mk 1**, **2** and **3**. It was planned that 28 of the aircraft should be revised by the IMP Group to a fishery patrol and pollution detection standard with 1,509-shp (1125-kW) Pratt & Whitney Canada PT6A-67AF turboprop engines and revised electronics, but the programme was later cancelled.

The final version of the Tracker was the **S-2G**, of which 49 were created as S-2E conversions with the aid of a kit developed by Martin Marietta. Pioneered by a single **YS-2G** prototype conversion created after it had been decided to phase out the USN's dedicated anti-submarine carriers, the S-2G featured more advanced mission equipment and AGM-12 Bullpup anti-ship missile capability for continued operational viability on the USN's multi-purpose aircraft-carriers until the advent of the S-3A Viking. Trackers were delivered to the air arms of several countries such as Argentina, Australia, Brazil,

Canada, Italy, Japan, Netherlands, Peru, South Korea, Taiwan, Thailand, Turkey, Uruguay and Venezuela, some of which still operate the type.

In addition to these Tracker variants, 84 **TF-1** (later **C-1**) **Trader** aircraft were built between January 1955 and December 1958 to the **G-96** standard as transports for the COD (carrier on-board delivery) role in succession to the Grumman TBM-3R Avenger; the aircraft were originally conceived for the movement of nine passengers or 3,500 lb (1588 kg) of freight, but the need to deliver bulkier and heavier freight payloads meant that the design was amended to allow the delivery of a 8,500-lb (3856-kg) load. Another variant of the same basic family was the **G-117**, of which 88 examples were completed between February 1958 and September 1961 with the designation **WF-2** (**E-1B**) **Tracer**. This pioneering carrierborne airborne early warning type was characterised by an overfuselage fixed radome housing the antenna for the Hazeltine AN/APS-82 surveillance radar unit.

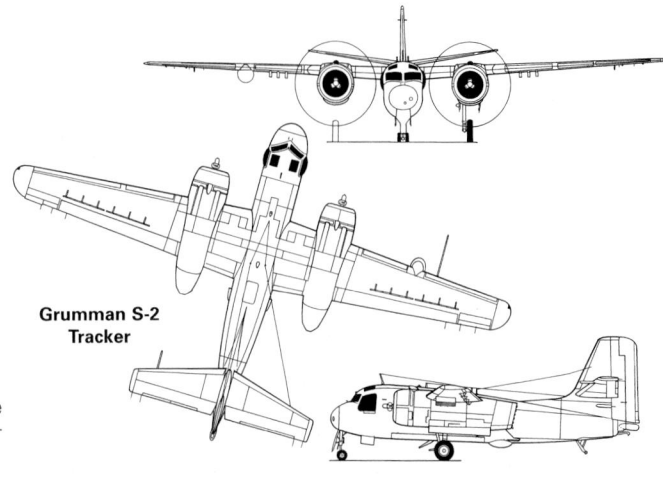

**Grumman S-2
Tracker**

SPECIFICATION

Grumman S-2E Tracker

Type: four-crew carrierborne and land-based anti-submarine aircraft

Powerplant: two Wright R-1820-82WA Cyclone radial piston engines each rated at 1,525 hp (1137 kW)

Performance: maximum speed 251 mph (404 km/h) at 4,000 ft (1220 m); patrol speed 150 mph (241 km/h) at 1,500 ft (455 m); initial climb rate 1,830 ft (558 m) per minute; service ceiling 20,100 ft (6125 m); range 1,300 miles (2092 km) with maximum fuel

Weights: empty 18,820 lb (8537 kg); maximum take-off

29,764 lb (13501 kg)

Dimensions: wingspan 72 ft 7 in (22.12 m); length 43 ft 6 in (13.26 m); height 16 ft 7½ in (5.07 m); wing area 496.00 sq ft (46.08 m²)

Armament: up to 4,810 lb (2182 kg) of disposable stores carried in a lower-fuselage weapons bay and on six underwing hardpoints, and generally comprising two Mk 44 or Mk 46 torpedoes, or four 385-lb (175-kg) depth bombs carried internally, and six 250-lb (113-kg) bombs or six 5-in (127- mm) HVAR air-to-surface unguided rockets carried externally

---

Above: Grumman chose to house the large antenna of the WF-2's APS-82 radar in a fixed radome. While the S2F was nicknamed 'Stoof', the Tracer became the 'Stoof with a roof'.

Brazil retains its Trackers into the 21st century, albeit not in front-line service. The aircraft formerly flew from the carrier Minas Gerais, but do not serve aboard the country's new carrier, the ex-French navy ship Foch, which entered service in 2002.

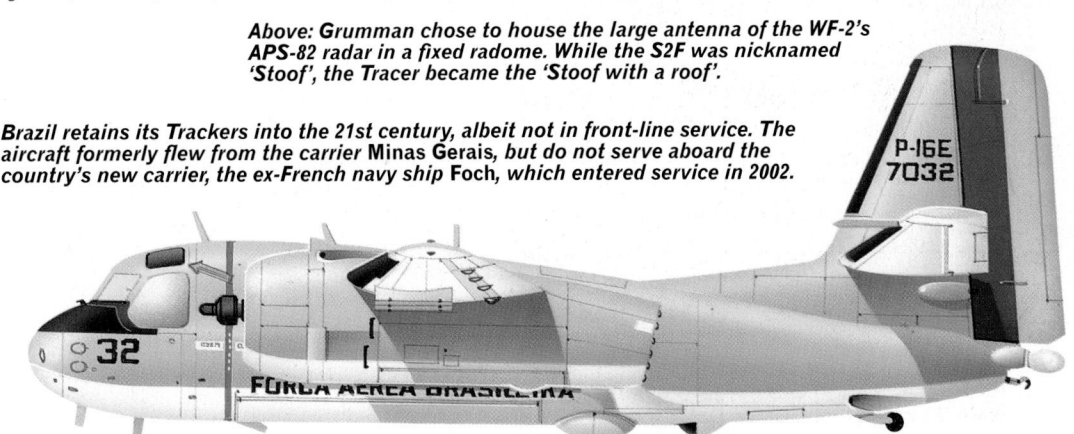

Grumman G-93 and G-105 (F9F Cougar)

Soon after the F9F Panther entered service, Grumman began the development of a swept-wing variant as the **G-93** under a US Navy contract dated 2 March 1951, and the first of the resulting three **XF9F-6** prototypes recorded the type's maiden flight on 20 September 1951. Although the F9F portion of the designation was the same as that of the Panther, confirming that it was a variant of the original design, the new name Cougar indicated that it was a rather different aircraft.

A more powerful turbojet engine was installed, but the main difference lay in the wing and the structural changes needed by it. Thus, the Cougar's wing had sweepback of 35°, spoilers replacing ailerons, larger trailing-edge flaps, leading-edge slats and wing fences. In this form, the **F9F-6** (subsequently redesignated as the **F-9F**) entered service with the US Navy's VF-32 in

November 1952. The 696 examples of the F9F-6 were followed by 118 examples of the generally similar **F9F-7** (**F-9H**), 601 examples of the **F9F-8** (**F-9J**) with a longer fuselage and broad-chord wing, and 400 examples of the **F9F-8T** trainer with a still longer fuselage carrying stepped tandem cockpits and only two guns. In 1962 the F9F-8T trainers, known to the company by the designation **G-105**, received the revised designation **TF-9J**. Many of them were flown operationally during the Vietnam War on various missions.

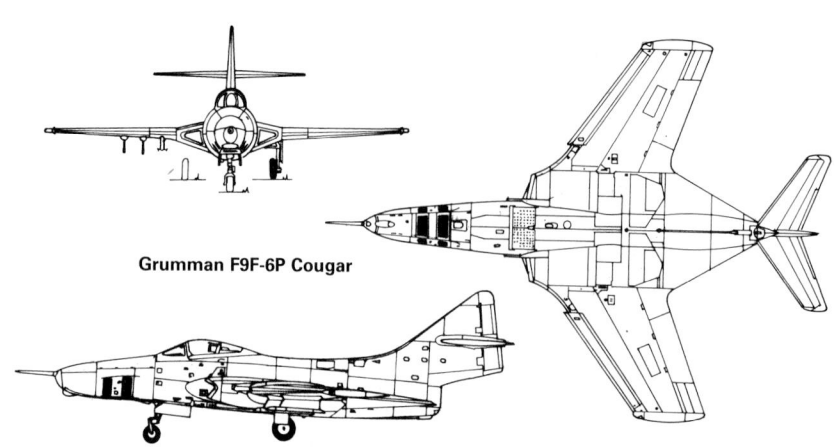

This J33-16A-engined Cougar was built as an F9F-7. It is shown in the markings of VF-21 at the time the Korean War was drawing to a close. The Cougar saw no combat service in the Korean theatre.

Grumman F9F-6P Cougar

Variants

F9F-6D: drone director conversions (later **DF-9F**) of the F9F-6
F9F-6K: target drone director conversions (later **QF-9F**) of the F9F-6
F9F-6K2: improved version (later **QF-9G**) of F9F-6K
F9F-6P: 60 examples of a photo-reconnaissance version of the F9F-6
F9F-6PD: redesignation of F9F-6Ps converted as drone directors
YF9F-8B: prototype conversion (later **YAF-9J**) of the F9F-8 for close support
F9F-8B: production conversions of F9F-8s (later **AF-9J**) to YF9F-8B configuration for the delivery of nuclear weapons
F9F-8P: 60 examples of a photo-reconnaissance version (later **RF-9J**) of the F9F-8
YF9F-8T: prototype trainer conversion (later **YTF-9J**) of one F9F-8
NTF-9J: designation of two TF-9Js used for special test duties

SPECIFICATION

Grumman TF-9J Cougar
Type: two-seat carrierborne and land-based advanced flying and conversion trainer
Powerplant: one Pratt & Whitney J48-P-8A turbojet engine rated at 7,200 lb st (32.03 kN)
Performance: maximum speed 630 mph (1014 km/h) at 5,000 ft (1525 m); cruising speed 475 mph (764 km/h) at optimum altitude; initial climb rate 4,800 ft (1463 m) per minute; service ceiling 43,000 ft (13105 m); range 600 miles (966 km)
Weights: empty 12,787 lb (5800 kg); maximum take-off 20,574 lb (9332 kg)
Dimensions: wingspan 34 ft 6 in (10.52 m); length 44 ft 4¼ in (13.52 m); height 12 ft 3 in (3.73 m); wing area 337.00 sq ft (31.31 m²)
Armament: two 20-mm M3 fixed forward-firing cannon in the underside of the nose, plus up to 2,000 lb (907 kg) of disposable stores carried on two underwing hardpoints, and generally comprising two 1,000- or 500-lb (454- or 227-kg) bombs

Grumman G-98 (F11F and F-11 Tiger)

The last of an unbroken line of US Navy fighters which had begun with the Grumman FF of 1931, the **F11F Tiger** was originally designated as the **F9F-9** to suggest a Panther/Cougar ancestry even though it was really an entirely new aircraft. Given the company type number **G-98**, the design was ordered by the USN on 27 April 1953 as a single-seat fighter. The fuselage was area-ruled to reduce drag, the tailplane and elevators were located on the rear fuselage and the main units of the tricycle landing gear were fuselage-mounted, as were the inlets for the 7,800-lb st (34.70-kN)

Wright J65-W-6 turbojet engine, which was rated at 10,500 lb st (56.71 kN) with afterburning. The thin wing introduced a new structural technique in that the outer skins, which enclosed a box beam, were milled from solid aluminium slabs.

The first prototype **YF9F-9** flew on 30 July 1954, powered by a non-afterburning J65-W-7 engine, while the second, which flew in October, had its intended afterburner installed in January 1955. Redesignated as the **F11F-1** in April 1955, the Tiger was produced with a derated J65-W-18 engine following problems with the intended

-6 version. USN orders for 199 aircraft were delivered between 15 November 1954 and 23 January 1959. The Tiger first entered service with VA-156 in March 1957, but the type's operational life was relatively short as it was superseded by the F8U Crusader. The Tiger was relegated to the advanced training role during 1959, but continued to equip the *Blue Angels* aerobatic team. The F11F-1 was redesignated **F-11A** from September 1962.

SPECIFICATION

Grumman F11F-1 Tiger
Type: single-seat carrierborne fighter
Powerplant: one 7,400-lb st (32.92-kN) Wright J65-W-18 turbojet engine rated at 10,500 lb st (46.71 kN) with afterburning
Performance: maximum speed 753 mph (1212 km/h) at sea level; cruising speed 578 mph (930 km/h) at 38,000 ft (11580 m); initial climb rate 5,130 ft (1565 m) per minute; service ceiling 41,900 ft (12770 m); range 1,275 miles (2052 km)
Weights: empty 14,330 lb (6500 kg); maximum take-off 24,078 lb (10922 kg)
Dimensions: wingspan 31 ft 7½ in (9.64 m); length 46 ft 11 in (14.30 m); height 13 ft 3 in (4.04 m); wing area 250.00 sq ft (23.23 m²)
Armament: four 20-mm M3 fixed forward-firing cannon in the undersides of the air inlets, plus up to 1,000 lb (454 kg) of disposable stores carried on four underwing hardpoints, and generally comprising four AAM-N-7 (from 1962 AIM-9) Sidewinder short-range AAMs

Variant

F11F-1F: two aircraft with the 9,600-lb st (42.70-kN) General Electric XJ79-GE-3 engine; the aircraft were modified from production F11F-1s and also fitted with a new wing and enlarged inlets; the first recorded its maiden flight in June 1956; during later trials, one of the aircraft was flown by US Navy Lieutenant Commander George Watkins to a world altitude record of 76,932 ft (23449 m), and the type was also flown at a speed of 1,386 mph (2231 km/h)

Although it was slightly faster than the Crusader at sea level and had overall superior handling properties, the Tiger was inferior in every other area of performance compared to the Vought design.

Grumman G-128 (A-6 Intruder and EA-6B Prowler)

Korean War experience showed the need for a specially designed jet-powered attack aircraft that could operate effectively in the worst weather. In 1957 eight companies submitted 11 designs in a US Navy competition for a new long-range, low-level tactical attack and strike aircraft. The **G-128 Intruder** was selected on the last day of the year, and was to fulfil that requirement admirably, becoming a major combat type in the later war in Southeast Asia, and leading to a family of later versions.

Eight development aircraft were ordered in March 1959 with the designation **YA2F-1** that was later changed to **YA-6A**. The first of these aircraft flew on 19 April 1960 with the powerplant of two 8,500-lb st (37.81-kN) J52-P-6 turbojet engines: the jetpipes of these engines were designed to swivel slightly downward to provide an additional component of lift during take-off, but this feature was incorporated in only the first four development aircraft. All others had jetpipes with a permanent slight downward deflection.

The first production **A-6A** (originally **A2F-1**) aircraft were delivered to VA-42 in February 1963, and the first unit to fly on combat duties in Vietnam was VA-75, whose A-6As began operating from the USS *Independence* in March 1965. The Intruder's DIANE (Digital Integrated Attack Navigation Equipment) gave them a first-class operating ability and efficiency in the worst of the humid, stormy weather offered by the local climate, and with a maximum ordnance load of more than 17,000 lb (7711 kg) the aircraft were a potent addition to the US arsenal in Southeast Asia. Production of the basic A-6A ran until December

1969 and totalled 482 aircraft, plus another 21 built as **EA-6A** variants, retaining a partial strike capability but developed primarily to provide ECM (electronic countermeasures) support for the A-6A in Vietnam and to act as Elint gatherers. The first EA-6A flew in 1963, and three YA-6A and three A-6A aircraft were also converted to EA-6A configuration.

The next three variants of the Intruder were also produced by the conversion of existing A-6As. The first of these was the **A-6B** (19 aircraft), issued to one USN squadron and differing from the initial model primarily in its ability to carry the AGM-78 Standard ARM instead of the AGM-12B Bullpup air-to-surface missile. For identifying and acquiring targets not discernible by the Intruder's standard radar, Grumman then modified 12 other A-6As to **A-6C** standard with an improved capability for night attack provided by FLIR and low-light-level TV sensors in a turret under the fuselage. A prototype conversion of an A-6A to **KA-6D** inflight-refuelling tanker standard flew on 23 May 1966, and production contracts for the tanker version were placed. These were subsequently cancelled, but 62 A-6As were converted to KA-6D configuration, equipped with TACAN instrumentation and carrying a

hose-reel unit in the rear fuselage to refuel other carrierborne aircraft. The KA-6D could also operate as a day bomber or as an air/sea rescue control machine, and after withdrawal of the EKA-3B Skywarrior from sea-going duty became the Navy's standard carrierborne tanker.

On 27 February 1970 Grumman flew the first example of the **A-6E** as an advanced and upgraded development of the A-6A. The A-6E followed the A-6A in production, and manufacture eventually encompassed 240 aircraft complemented by 205 A-6A/B/C conversions.

The basis of the A-6E, which retained upgraded forms of the airframe and powerplant of the earlier models, was a new avionics fit founded on the addition of a Norden APQ-148 multi-mode navigation radar, an IBM/Fairchild ASQ-133 computerised nav/attack system, Conrac armament control unit, and an RCA video-tape recorder for assessing the damage caused during a strike mission. Following the first flight of a test aircraft on 22 March 1974, all USN and US Marine Corps Intruders were progressively updated still further

With the TRAM turret prominent beneath their nose radomes, these A-6Es demonstrate the colours in which the type finished its active service. Note the offset refuelling probe.

under a programme known as TRAM (Target Recognition Attack Multisensor). This added to the standard A-6E a Hughes turreted optronic package of FLIR and laser detection equipment, integrated with the Norden radar; CAINS (Carrier Airborne Inertial Navigation System) to provide the capability for automatic landings on carrier decks; and provision for autonomous and laser-guided air-to-surface weapons. The first US Navy squadron to be equipped with this **A-6E/TRAM** version was VA-165, which was

deployed aboard the USS *Constellation* in 1977. In addition, a separate programme equipped 50 A-6Es each able to carry four Harpoon anti-ship missiles, and a Harpoon capability was later retrofitted to all aircraft, which also received the SWIP upgrade allowing them to carry other guided weapons including the AGM-65 Maverick, AGM-84E SLAM and AGM-88 HARM missiles.

The last Intruders were retired from USN service in 1997, their role being assumed by the Boeing F/A-18 Hornet.

VA-165 'Boomers' transitioned from the A-1H Skyraider to the A-6A (illustrated) in 1967.

SPECIFICATION

Grumman A-6E/TRAM Intruder
Type: two-seat carrierborne and land-based all-weather strike and attack aircraft
Powerplant: two Pratt & Whitney J52-P-8B turbojet engines each rated at 9,300 lb st (41.37 kN)
Performance: maximum speed 644 mph (1036 km/h) at sea level; cruising speed 474 mph (763 km/h) at optimum altitude; initial climb rate 7,620 ft (2323 m) per minute; service ceiling 42,400 ft (12,925 m); range 1,011 miles (1627 km) with maximum warload
Weights: empty 26,660 lb (12093 kg); maximum take-off 58,600 lb (26581 kg) for a catapult launch or 60,400 lb (27397 kg) for a land take-off
Dimensions: wingspan 53 ft (16.15 m); length 54 ft 9 in

(16.69 m); height 16 ft 2 in (4.93 m); wing area 528.90 sq ft (49.13 m²)
Armament: up to 18,000 lb (8165 kg) of disposable stores carried on one underfuselage and four underwing hardpoints; typical strategic- and operational-level loads were up to three B28, B43, B57 or B61 thermonuclear free-fall bombs, and typical tactical-level loads included five 2,000-lb (907-kg) Mk 84 or 10 1,000-lb (454-kg) Mk 83 free-fall or retarded bombs, or 22 500-lb (227-kg) Mk 82 free-fall or retarded bombs, or four AGM-45 Shrike or AGM-88 HARM anti-radar missiles, or two AGM-84 Harpoon anti-ship missiles, or two AGM-84E SLAM ASMs, or four AGM-65 Maverick ASMs, or four Paveway series LGBs

---

Variants

YEA-6A: prototype of the EA-6A produced as a conversion of one YA-6A
NA-6A: three YA-6A and three A-6A aircraft modified for use in special test roles
A-6F: development of the A-6E with new radar, digital avionics and General Electric F404 turbofans; three prototypes were flown before the programme was cancelled
A-6G: Grumman proposal for a development of the A-6F retaining J52 turbojets
NEA-6A: single aircraft modified from an EA-6A for special test purposes
NEA-6B: two EA-6B prototypes after modification for special test purposes

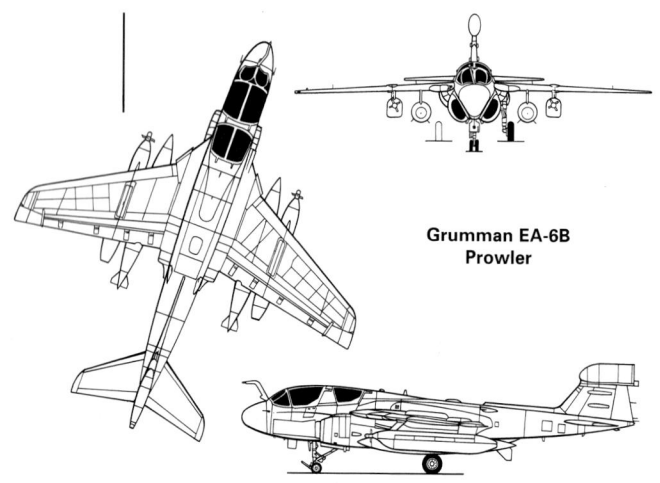

Grumman EA-6B Prowler

In 2000, the EA-6Bs in service are severely overstretched and a supplementary type, perhaps in the form of B-52s modified as stand-off jammers, is desperately needed.

Early experience with the EA-6A led to the development of a more advanced version known as the **EA-6B Prowler**. Externally this is similar to the basic A-6A, but it differs by having a nose section extended by 4 ft 6 in (1.37 m) to allow the creation of a longer four-seat cockpit, and a distinctive fin pod to house the passive receivers for the ALQ-99 Tactical Jamming System. Other changes include structural strengthening for operation at a higher gross weight, increased fuel capacity, and the uprated powerplant of two J52-P-408 engines. Delivery of production aircraft began in January 1971 and was to have totalled 102 aircraft up to 1986, but in the event 170 aircraft were delivered into the mid-1990s.

The Prowler's advanced ECM system is based upon the ALQ-99 tactical noise jamming system and up to 10 jamming transmitters can be carried in five self-powered jammer pods. Improved jamming ability and capacity resulted from 1973 through the introduction of the **EXCAP** (Expanded Capability), **ICAP-1 (Increased Capability-1)**, **ICAP-2** and **ADVCAP (Advanced Capability)** standards. The EA-6B is still in essential service with the US Navy, and since the retirement of the EF-111A Raven in the later 1990s has been the US services' sole dedicated electronic warfare type.

Grumman G-134 (OV-1 Mohawk)

In the mid-1950s both the US Army and US Marine Corps drew up specifications for a battlefield surveillance aircraft. Their requirements were generally similar: to carry of a variety of reconnaissance equipment, to have rough-field capability, and to offer STOL capability. It proved possible for both services to agree on a common design, and in 1957 the US Navy acting as programme manager for both the US Army and the US Marine Corps, ordered nine examples of the **G-134** for test and evaluation. These machines at first carried the designation **YAO-1A** that was subsequently altered to **YOV-1A**, and the first of the aircraft recorded its maiden flight on 14 April 1959.

Early evaluation left little doubt of the excellence of the design, but even before the prototype had made its first flight the USMC had withdrawn from the initial contract, and no examples of that service's **OF-1** variant were built. Instead, the flight-test programme was accelerated, and before the end of 1959 the US Army had placed production contracts for **OV-1A** and **OV-1B** aircraft with the name **Mohawk**. The first turboprop-powered aircraft to enter service with the US Army, the OV-1 is

OV-1Ds 4X-JRA and 4X-JRB were loaned to the IDF/AF and returned to the US Army in 1977-78 when Israel took delivery of its E-2C Hawkeyes.

comparatively slow but highly manoeuvrable, and to help offset its vulnerability as a result of its speed and role, has a well-armoured cockpit, a 0.25-in (0.64-cm) thick aluminium alloy floor, flak curtains on both fore and aft bulkheads, and bullet-resistant windscreens. Although the OV-1 is conventional in its basic configuration, detail design has produced an easily identified machine of unusual appearance. Recognition features include the turboprop engines, one mounted high on each wing with its centreline canted outward and upward; a tail unit with three fin-and-rudder assemblies and sufficient tailplane dihedral for the endplate fins to be inward canted; bulged cockpit sides to provide the two-person crew with the best possible downward fields of vision; and as a final dash of the

eccentric, in the **OV-1B** version a side-looking airborne radar (SLAR) housed in an 18-ft (5.49-m) glassfibre container carried on pylons below the fuselage and offset to starboard.

Normal deployment of the Mohawk was four to each army division, and although these aircraft were capable of carrying armament, it was Department of Defense policy from 1965 that the US Army's fixed-wing aircraft should carry no weapons, to avoid conflict and confusion with the USAF's close-support aircraft. However, like many other US aircraft, a number were deployed to Vietnam with underwing armament, a **JOV-1A** with four 500-lb (227-kg) capacity hardpoints having demonstrated the type's suitability for the armed reconnaissance role.

The basic version of the Mohawk, of which 380 were completed by Grumman between April 1959 and December 1970, is the **OV-1A** of which 64

were manufactured with equipment for day and night visual or photo reconnaissance, and provided with dual controls. The **OV-1B** which followed to the extent of 101 aircraft had a wing increased in span from 42 ft (12.80 m) to 48 ft (14.63 m), SLAR and an internal camera with in-flight processor; the dual controls were deleted. The next production version was the **OV-1C**, of which 165 were made to a standard similar to that of late-production OV-1As but with the AAS-24 infra-red surveillance system. The last production model, of which 41 (including four **YOV-1D** service

test aircraft) were completed, was the **OV-1D** with side-loading doors to accept a pallet with SLAR, IR, or other sensors; in addition to production aircraft, 80 OV-1B and OV-1C aircraft were converted to OV-1D standard. The designations **RV-1C** and **RV-1D** apply respectively to 31 OV-1C and OV-1D aircraft permanently modified for electronic reconnaissance missions. The last Mohawks were retired from US Army service in 1997. Israel had retired its last aircraft by this time, leaving Argentina as the world's sole operator of the type at the beginning of the 21st century.

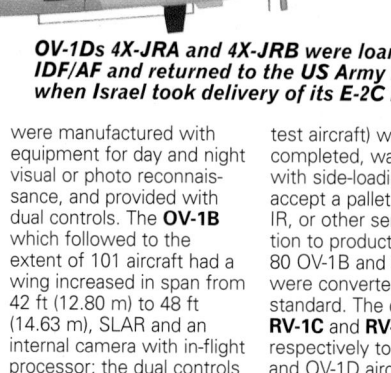

The OV-1 remained in front-line US Army service for over 30 years. This OV-1D has had its SLAR pod removed.

SPECIFICATION

Grumman OV-1D Mohawk
Type: two-seat multi-sensor observation aircraft
Powerplant: two Lycoming T53-L-701 turboprop engines each rated at 1,400 shp (1044 kW)
Performance: maximum speed 289 mph (465 km/h) at 10,000 ft (3050 m) on a SLAR mission or 305 mph (491 km/h) at 10,000 ft (3050 m) on an IR mission; cruising speed 207 mph (333 km/h) at optimum altitude; initial climb rate 3,618 ft (1103 m) per minute; service ceiling 25,000 ft (7620 m); range 944 miles (1519 km) on a SLAR mission

Weights: empty 12,054 lb (5468 kg); maximum take-off 18,109 lb (8214 kg) on a SLAR mission
Dimensions: wingspan 48 ft (14.63 m); length 41 ft (12.50 m); height 12 ft 8 in (3.86 m); wing area 360.00 sq ft (33.44 m²)
Armament: provision for up to 2,700 lb (1225 kg) of disposable stores carried on two underwing hardpoints, and generally comprising gun pods, bombs, and multiple launchers for 2¾-in (70-mm) air-to-surface unguided rockets

Grumman G-303 (F-14 Tomcat)

Designed as a successor to the F-4 in the fleet air defence role for the US Navy, the **Tomcat** was originally conceived to engage and destroy targets at extreme range, before they could pose a threat to the carrier battle group. The **F-14A Tomcat** remains a formidable warplane, even though the original F-14A has been in service for more than 20 years. Production of the F-14A for the Navy eventually totalled 556 examples, while 80 broadly similar machines were purchased by Iran before the downfall of the Shah. Of the latter, only 79 were actually delivered (one being diverted to the USN). The F-14 continues to be the Navy's primary air defence aircraft although with the introduction of the F/A-18E/F into service from late 1999, the days of the Tomcat are numbered.

The key to the F-14's effectiveness lies in its advanced avionics suite, the Hughes AWG-9 fire control system representing the most capable long-range interceptor radar in service, with the ability to detect, track and engage targets at ranges in excess of 100 miles (160 km). Early aircraft also had an IRST system, replacing this during production (and by retrofit) with a long-range video camera known as TCS. The armament options allow the aircraft to engage targets over a huge range from close up to extreme BVR (beyond visual range).

The AIM-54 Phoenix remains the longest-ranged air-to-air missile in Western service today and has demonstrated the ability to detect and kill targets at unparalleled distances. In the medium-range arena, Tomcat has the option of either the AIM-7 Sparrow or the AIM-120 AMRAAM, while for short-range, close-in engagements, the F-14 carries the well-proven AIM-9 Sidewinder. Finally there is a single Vulcan M61A1 20-mm Gatling-type rotary cannon in the lower port fuselage with 675 rounds of ammunition.

Development was initiated in the late 1960s, following on the cancellation of the ill-fated F-111B, leaving the Navy in the unenviable position of having no new fighter in prospect. Grumman had already invested a considerable amount of effort in the navalised F-111B, and used this experience in designing a new variable-geometry fighter (the **G-303**) which was duly selected by the Navy in January 1969. Grumman's use of a variable-geometry wing allowed excellent high-speed performance to be combined with docile low-speed handling characteristics and a high degree of agility. A dozen **YF-14A** development aircraft were ordered, with the first making its maiden flight on 21 December 1970.

The programme made reasonably swift progress, culminating in deliveries to the Navy from October 1972, with the first operational cruise in 1974. Production continued into the 1980s and a total of 26 front-line and four second-line squadrons was eventually equipped with the F-14A.

Although generally successful, the F-14 has suffered many difficulties since entering fleet service. Many were engine-related, the TF30 turbofan proving something of an Achilles heel. Fan blade losses caused several crashes before improved quality control and steel containment cases alleviated the worst consequences of engine failure. In addition, the engine was prone to compressor stall, especially during air combat manoeuvring training, and the aircraft's vicious departure characteristics (especially with one engine out) resulted in many further losses. Many problems were solved when the revised TF30-P-414A version of the powerplant was adopted as standard.

In addition to fleet air defence tasks, F-14As are also used for reconnaissance missions, using the Tactical Air Reconnaissance Pod System (TARPS), and it is usual for three TARPS-capable aircraft to be assigned to each carrier air wing. More recently, the F-14A has also acquired a secondary air-to-ground role, capitalising on a modest attack capability that was built in from the outset, but never utilised. The **F-14A 'Bombcat'** initially carried only conventional 'iron' bombs, but has now had the LANTIRN pod integrated for use with laser-guided bombs.

Continuing problems with the TF30 engine of the F-14A were a key factor in the development of re-engined and upgraded variants of the Tomcat. One of the original prototype airframes was fitted with two F401-PW-400s and employed for an abbreviated test programme as the **F-14B** as early as 1973-74. Technical problems and financial difficulties forced the abandonment of the programme, and the aircraft was placed into storage, re-emerging as the **F-14B Super Tomcat** with F101DFE engines. This engine was developed into the General Electric

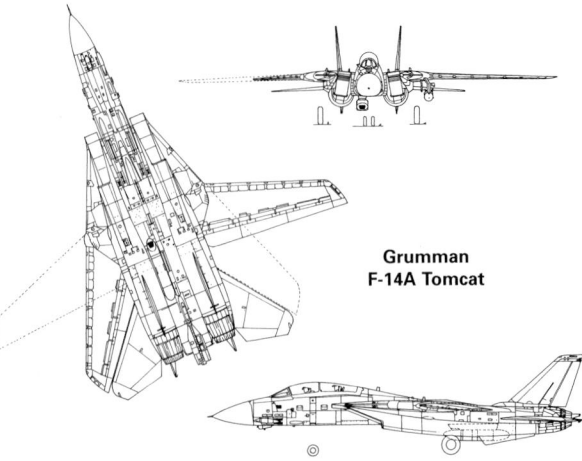

**Grumman
F-14A Tomcat**

F110-GE-400 turbofan, which was selected to power production improved Tomcat variants. It was decided to produce two distinct new Tomcats, one designated **F-14A+** (primarily by conversion of existing F-14As) with the new engine, and another, designated **F-14D**, with the new engine and improved digital avionics. The F-14A+ was originally regarded as an interim type, all examples of which would eventually be converted to full F-14D standards.

Subsequently, the F-14A+ was formally redesignated as the **F-14B**, 38 new-build examples being joined by 32 F-14A rebuilds in equipping half-a-dozen deployable squadrons starting in 1988. These incorporated some avionics changes, including a modernised fire control system, new radios, upgraded RWRs, and various cockpit changes. F-14Bs were the first re-engined Tomcats to enter fleet service.

Two modified F-14As flew as F-14D prototypes and the first F-14D to be built as such made its maiden flight on 9 February 1990. The F-14D added digital avionics, with digital radar processing and displays (adding these to standard AWG-9 hardware under the redesignation APG-71), and a side-by-side undernose TCS/IRST sensor pod. Other improvements introduced by the F-14D include OBOGS (on-board oxygen-generating system), NACES ejection seats, and AN/ALR-67 radar warning receiver equipment. Like the F-14A, the F-14D has a full ground attack capability. The US Department of Defense's decision to cease funding the F-14D effectively halted the Navy's drive to upgrade its force of Tomcats. In consequence, the service has received only 37 new-build F-14Ds, while plans to upgrade approximately 400 existing F-14As to a similar standard were cancelled.

Deliveries to the Navy began in 1990, when training squadron VF-124 accepted its first F-14D at Miramar. The F-14 fleet is slowly being reduced, although the last is not due to the leave the fleet until 2008, replaced by the F/A-18E/F Super Hornet.

SPECIFICATION

Grumman F-14A Tomcat
Type: two-seat carrierborne fleet air defence fighter and interceptor
Powerplant: two Pratt & Whitney TF30-P-412A/414A turbofans each rated at 20,900 lb st (92.97 kN) with afterburning
Performance: maximum level speed 'clean' at high altitude 1,544 mph (2485 km/h); maximum rate of climb at sea level more than 30,000 ft (9145 m) per minute; service ceiling more than 50,000 ft (15240 m); radius on a combat air patrol with six AIM-7 Sparrows and four AIM-9 Sidewinders 766 miles (1233 km)
Weights: empty 40,104 lb (18191 kg) with -414A engines; maximum take-off 70,764 lb (32098 kg) with six Phoenix
Dimensions: wingspan 64 ft 1½ in (19.54 m) spread, 38 ft 2½ in (11.65 m) swept and 33 ft 3½ in

(10.15 m) overswept; length 62 ft 8 in (19.10 m); height 16 ft (4.88 m); wing area 565.00 sq ft (52.49 m²)
Armament: standard armament consists of an internal M61A1 Vulcan 20-mm six-barrelled cannon and an AIM-9M Sidewinder on the shoulder launch rail of each wing glove pylon. The main launch rail of each glove pylon can accommodate either an AIM-7M Sparrow or an AIM-54C Phoenix. Four further AIM-7M or AIM-54C missiles can be carried under the fuselage between the engine trunks. 267-US gal (1011-litre) fuel tanks can be carried on hardpoints under the intakes, while the Phoenix pallets can also mount bomb racks for 1,000-lb (454-kg) Mk 83 or 2,000-lb (907-kg) Mk 84 GP bombs or other free-fall weaponry

This F-14A demonstrates the positioning of the type's distinctive drop tanks on the engine trunks.

From May 1995, VF-2 re-equipped with F-14D Tomcats. This aircraft is depicted with a typical air-to-air warload of four under-fuselage Phoenix long-range missiles, and two each of the Sparrow medium-range and Sidewinder short-range missiles on the glove pylons.

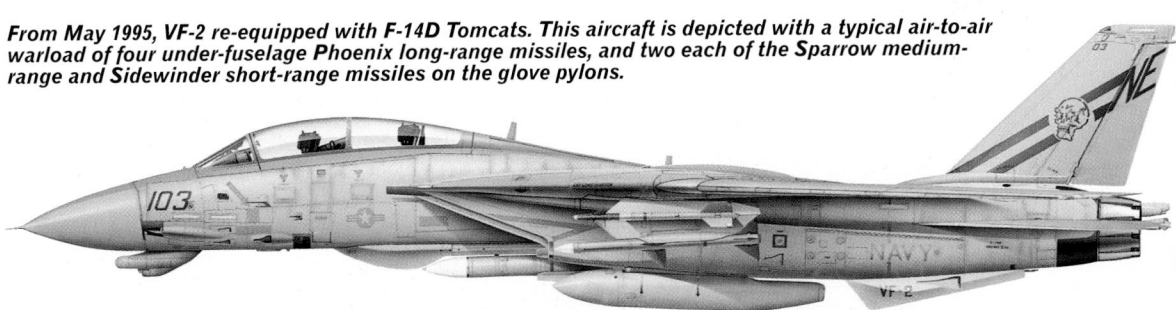

Grumman G-712 (X-29A)

The advantages of swept-forward wings are theoretically enormous in comparison with those of swept-back wings, and include delayed rise in transonic drag, reduced stalling speed, much enhanced low-speed handling characteristics and virtually stall-proof flight. In combination these features can open the way, especially in the fighter category, for a smaller aircraft with higher performance and greater agility on given power, or the same performance plus enhanced agility on less power. The potential advantages in economic and tactical terms are enormous, and the development of fibre-reinforced composite (FRC

– essentially glass-reinforced plastic further reinforced with a layer or layers of carbon/graphite or boron) has allowed such configurations to be widely explored. One of the first practical suggestions, although it was not implemented, was the SFW/F-16 (Swept-Forward Wing/F-16) derivative of the F-16 Fighting Falcon. The type that has explored the swept-forward wing concept most fully, however, was the **X-29A**, which was designed as the **G-712**. Two such aircraft were ordered, and the first of these recorded its maiden flight in December 1984. This machine was intended purely as a research tool, and resulted

from a series of wind-tunnel tests undertaken by Grumman in the mid-1970s to cure the wing-root drag problem previously associated with forward-swept wings. Grumman decided that the combination of a forward-swept wing, canard foreplanes, composite structural materials and a fly-by-wire control system made feasible a fighter superior to anything currently in service or under development.

It was important to keep design and development costs to a minimum, so Grumman reused components from other aircraft wherever possible: the forward fuselage, nose-wheel unit and cockpit were those of the F-5A Freedom Fighter, the main landing gear units were those of the F-16 Fighting Falcon, and the powerplant was half of that used in the F/A-18 Hornet. The X-29A was designed for moderately supersonic flight, and was conceptually of the relaxed static stability type.

The trailing edges of the X-29A's wings were fitted with full-span flaperons, with double-hinged front and rear sections to allow the flaperons to be used as camber-changing sections.

The X-29A's *raison d'étre* was the forward-swept wing, which was attached about two-thirds of the way aft along the fuselage. The core of the wing structure was an electron beam-welded box of titanium and light alloy, providing an exceptionally sturdy but generally conventional basis for the outer aerodynamic surfaces. These were single-piece upper and lower skins made of CFRP (carbonfibre-reinforced plastics) up to 156 layers thick at their inboard ends. These skins were exceptionally light yet rigid, and allowed the wing to be of the high-aspect-ratio type with a quarter-chord forward sweep of just under 34°. This structure could sustain the most violent aerial movements without any possibility of aero-elastic divergence.

Located aft of the wing were the conventional vertical tail surface and a pair of strake flaps fitted at the extreme rear of the extended wing root trailing edges (nearly in line with the rudder), and the aerodynamic design was completed by the powerful canard foreplanes. The canards were driven though a triply redundant fly-by-wire system, and were the aircraft's primary control surfaces in the longitudinal plane. Flight tests confirmed the wind-tunnel predictions about the X-29A's flight characteristics: even at extremely high angles of attack the type could not be stalled and yet retained full roll authority down to very low speeds. The first X-29A was retired on 6 December 1988, while the second aircraft remained flying into the mid-1990s.

SPECIFICATION	
Grumman X-29A	(15300 m)
Type: single-seat experimental aircraft for research into the structural and aerodynamic practicality of a forward-swept wing	**Weights:** empty 13,800 lb (6260 kg); maximum take-off 17,800 lb (8074 kg)
Powerplant: one General Electric F404-GE-400 turbofan engine rated at 16,000 lb st (71.17 kN) with afterburning	**Dimensions:** wingspan 27 ft 2½ in (8.29 m); canard foreplane span 13 ft 71/2 in (4.15 m); length 53 ft 11¼ in (16.44 m) including probe; height 14 ft 3½ in (4.36 m); wing area 188.84 sq ft (17.54 m²); canard foreplane area 35.96 sq ft (3.34 m²)
Performance: maximum speed 1,056 mph (1699 km/h) at 36,000 ft (10975 m); service ceiling 50,200 ft	

Grumman/General Dynamics EF-111A Raven

This EF-111A belonged to the 66th Electronic Combat Wing at Sembach AB, Germany, although the aircraft itself was flown by the 42nd Electronic Combat Squadron from Upper Heyford, England. The EF-111A was known to its crews as the 'Spark Vark'.

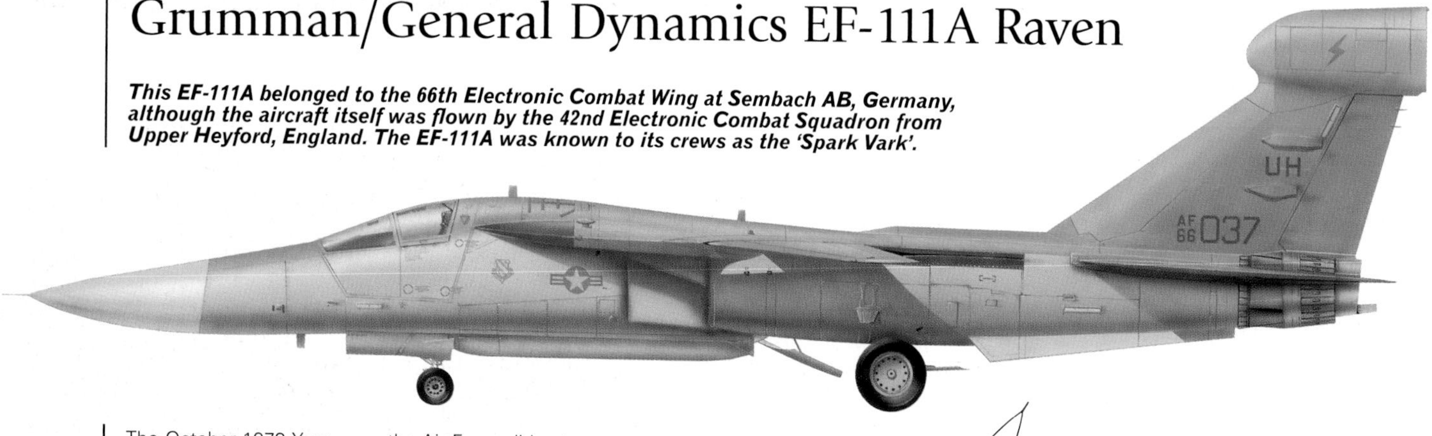

The October 1973 Yom Kippur War demonstrated the vulnerability of tactical aircraft to the massive, integrated air defence networks favoured by the Soviets and their client states. The USAF Tactical Air Command (TAC), having spent as little on electronic warfare as possible, was preparing to retire its ancient Douglas EB-66 Skywarrior stand-off jamming aircraft the following year. Recognising the need for a quick solution to this problem, it soon settled on the Eaton/AIL ALQ-99 jamming subsystem (JSS) designed for the Navy's Grumman EA-6B Prowler. However,

the Air Force did not believe the Prowler to be fast enough to keep up with its strike packages. Other factors weighing against the Grumman EA-6B Prowler were its lack of endurance and the need to create a new logistic system to support it.

After some initial compatibility tests were performed, the Air Force awarded Grumman a contract to develop the first two **EF-111A** jamming aircraft on 26 December 1974. While the aerodynamic prototype flew on 15 December 1975, the 'all-up' aircraft did not take wing until 10 March 1977.

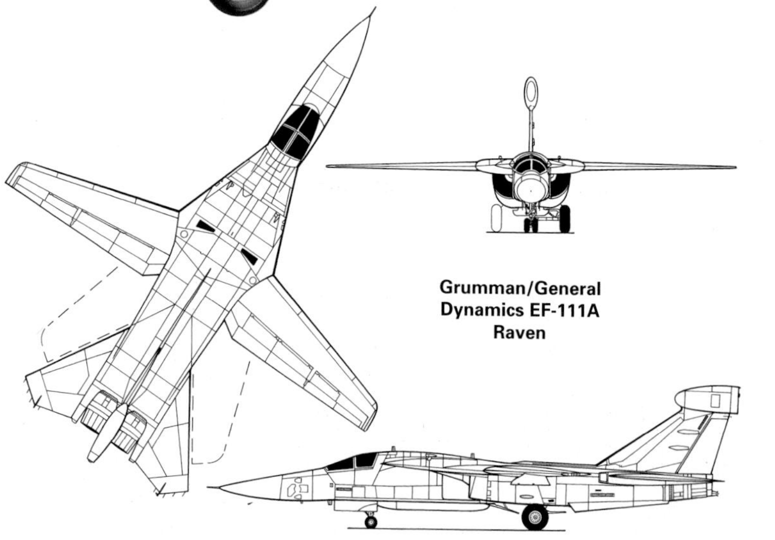

Grumman/General Dynamics EF-111A Raven

Grumman/General Dynamics EF-111A Raven (continued)

As with most electronic warfare systems, the Raven programme was subjected to more than its fair share of scrutiny. By 23 December 1985, 42 F-111As had been converted to EF-111A Raven electronic jamming system (EJS) aircraft. Their ALQ-99E was modified for use by a single electronic warfare officer (EWO). Installing the new jamming system resulted in the right side of the cockpit being extensively modified. All

bombing systems (including the AC's ODS), and the right-hand control column were removed to make room for the jamming system controls and displays. Also, the INS and ARS control panels were relocated to allow the AC to control them (freeing the EWO to concentrate on his jamming duties). All provisions for delivering weapons were removed during the EF-111A conversion process, precluding the option of launching

AGM-88 high-speed anti-radiation missiles (HARMs) from Ravens.

In 1991 a System Improvement Program (SIP) was devised for the surviving Ravens. The modifications would have allowed the aircraft to counter increasingly hostile radar threats, but the withdrawal of the 42nd ECS to Cannon AFB, New Mexico – as the 429th ECS – along with the rest of the F-111 fleet, saw the programme cancelled. The bomber

SPECIFICATION	
Grumman/General Dynamics EF-111A Raven **Type:** two-seat tactical jamming platform **Powerplant:** two Pratt & Whitney TF30-P-3 each rated at 18,500 lb st (82.29 kN) with afterburning **Performance:** maximum speed at high altitude 1,412 mph (2272 km/h); average speed in combat area 584 mph (940 km/h); maximum rate of climb at sea level 3,300 ft (1006 m) per minute;	service ceiling 45,000 ft (13715 m); combat radius 929 miles (1495 km); **Weights:** operating empty 55,275 lb (25072 kg); maximum take-off 88,948 lb (40347 kg) **Dimensions:** wingspan 63 ft (19.20 m) spread and 31 ft 11½ in (9.74 m) swept; length 76 ft (23.16 m), height 20 ft (6.10 m); wing area 525.00 sq ft (48.77 m²) swept and 657.07 sq ft (61.07 m²) spread

F-111s were retired in July 1996, with the 'Spark Varks' following suit on 1 April 1998.

Guizhou JJ-7 and FT-7

Developed by the Guizhou Aviation Industry Corporation (GAIC) as a combat-capable two-seat fighter trainer derivative of the Chengdu J-7 II single-seat fighter (which was, in turn, the result of incre-

mental redesign of the licence-built MiG-21F-13), the **JJ-7**, or **Jianjiao-7**, recorded its maiden flight on 5 July 1985. Closely resembling the tandem-seat MiG-21U, the JJ-7 has starboard-opening twin

cockpit canopies. The rear cockpit is fitted with a retractable periscope, and provision is made for a removable saddleback fuel tank. The JJ-7 can carry a centreline 23-mm two-barrel cannon pack under the fuselage plus two PL-2B short-range AAMs, or two 18-round launchers for 2.17-in (55-mm) air-to-surface unguided rockets, or two 551-lb (250-kg) bombs under the wing. The JJ-7 entered production for the Chinese air force in 1987, and was

simultaneously offered with a GEC-supplied avionics suite for export as the **FT-7**. One of the first customers for the export model was the Pakistan air force, which procured 15 **FT-7P** aircraft, and Bangladesh

later bought the type to supplement its two F-7 squadrons. Further aircraft have been delivered to Myanmar, Sri Lanka and Zimbabwe. The aircraft of the latter country are designated **FT-7BZ** in service.

SPECIFICATION	
Guizhou JJ-7/FT-7 **Type:** two-seat combat-capable fighter lead-in and conversion trainer **Powerplant:** one 9,700-lb st (43.15-kN) LMC (Liyang) WP7B(BM) turbojet engine rated at 13,448 lb st (59.82 kN) with afterburning **Performance:** maximum speed 1,350 mph (2175 km/h) or Mach 2.04 at 41,010 ft (12500 m); initial climb rate about 29,530 ft (9000 m)	per minute; service ceiling 56,760 ft (17300 m); range 808 miles (1300 km) with drop tank or 627 miles (1010 km) with standard fuel **Weights:** empty 11,750 lb (5330 kg); maximum take-off 18,959 lb (8600 kg) **Dimensions:** wingspan 23 ft 5⅞ in (7.154 m); length 48 ft 9½ in (14.874 m) including probe; height 13 ft 5½ in (4.103 m); wing area 247.58 sq ft (23.00 m²)

A pair of FT-7BZs replaced two Chengdu FT-5s with the Air Force of Zimbabwe in 1991. Here, one of the aircraft formates with its fighter equivalent – the Chengdu F-7.

Gulfstream Aerospace Gulfstream I

In the mid-1950s the Grumman Aerospace Corporation began work on the design of a twin-turbo-prop executive transport schemed with accommodation for a crew of two and 10-14 passengers in typical corporate versions: an alternative high-density layout could seat a maximum of 24 passengers. Designated **Grumman G-159 Gulfstream I**, this was a conventional low-wing cantilever monoplane with pressurised accommodation, retractable tricycle landing gear, and a power-plant based on two Rolls-Royce Dart turbo-props in wing-mounted nacelles. The prototype flew for the first time on 14 August 1958, and

American certification was gained later in the same year.

In addition to the production of the Gulfstream I for the civil market, Grumman also supplied nine **TC-4C Academe** aircraft to the US Navy. Required for the training of crews to serve with A-6A Intruder squadrons, the Academes were readily distinguishable from standard Gulfstreams by their bulbous nose radomes covering the antennas for the sensors associated with the Intruder and its DIANE nav/attack system. One Gulfstream I was acquired by the US Coast Guard under the designation **VC-4A**, and was operated as a VIP transport.

Most of the 200 Gulfstream I aircraft completed between August 1958 and May 1969 went to customers in North America, but a number of these were later converted to **Gulfstream I-C** configuration. This programme was initiated by the Gulfstream American Corporation (now the Gulfstream Aerospace Corporation) following its 1978 acquisition of Grumman's Gulfstream division. The conversion entailed a fuselage 'stretch' of 10 ft 8 in (3.25 m) to provide seating for a maximum 37 passengers, but the Gulfstream I-C is otherwise little different from the original Gulfstream I.

In its original Gulfstream I form, the G-159 represented a major improvement over existing executive types.

The Academe's cabin was laid out with a replica A-6A cockpit which accommodated a student pilot and student bombardier/navigator. Provision was also made for an instructor and four further students at consoles showing radar/computer readouts.

SPECIFICATION	
Gulfstream Aerospace Gulfstream I **Type:** two-crew executive and corporate transport aircraft **Powerplant:** two Rolls-Royce Dart RDa.7/2 Mk 529-8X turboprop engines each rated at 2,210 ehp (1648 kW) **Performance:** maximum speed 357 mph (574 km/h) at 35,000 ft (10670 m); cruising speed 334 mph (537 km/h) at optimum altitude; initial climb rate 3,100 ft (945 m) per minute; service ceiling 36,900 ft (11245 m); range	2,500 miles (4023 km) with maximum fuel and 1,865 miles (3001 km) with standard payload **Weights:** empty 20,993 lb (9522 kg); maximum take-off 35,100 lb (15921 kg) **Dimensions:** wingspan 78 ft 4 in (23.88 m); length 63 ft 9 in (19.43 m); height 22 ft 9 in (6.93 m); wing area 615.00 sq ft (57.13 m²) **Payload:** up to 14 passengers in the enclosed cabin within the context of a 4,270-lb (1937-kg) maximum payload

Gulfstream Aerospace Gulfstream II

Reacting to demands from a number of Gulfstream I customers, early in 1965 Grumman began studies for a turbofan-engined version of this initial **Type I** with swept flying surfaces and a T-tail. Market research indicated a requirement for an aircraft with the Gulfstream I's cabin volume, high-speed transoceanic capability, and also good short-field performance. There was no prototype as such, the first **G-1159** making its maiden flight on 2 October 1966. With the powerplant of two Spey Mk 511-8 turbofan engines in nacelles on the sides of the rear fuselage in an airframe some 65 per cent of the weight of similarly powered aircraft such as the BAC One-Eleven and Fokker F28, the type later known as the **Gulfstream Aerospace Gulfstream II** (or **GII**) met the short-field performance with ease and offered a maximum-fuel range of more than 3,800 miles (6115 km).

In December 1967 the fifth aircraft was handed over to AiResearch Inc. for completion before becoming the first to reach a customer. It subsequently became the first jet-powered executive transport to fly non-stop across the North Atlantic in both directions. Manufacture continued from October 1966 and until December 1972, when the 256th production aircraft was delivered. The more advanced wing of the Gulfstream III later became available in a conversion programme to create the **Gulfstream II-B**. The converted aircraft offered greater range and a significant improvement in fuel efficiency. Three examples of the Gulfstream II were bought by the US forces as **VC-11A** VIP transports, and single examples went to the air forces of Morocco, Oman and Venezuela in the same basic role.

The first GII delivery was made to National Distillers and Chemical Corporation of New York. A re-winged Gulfstream II-B is illustrated.

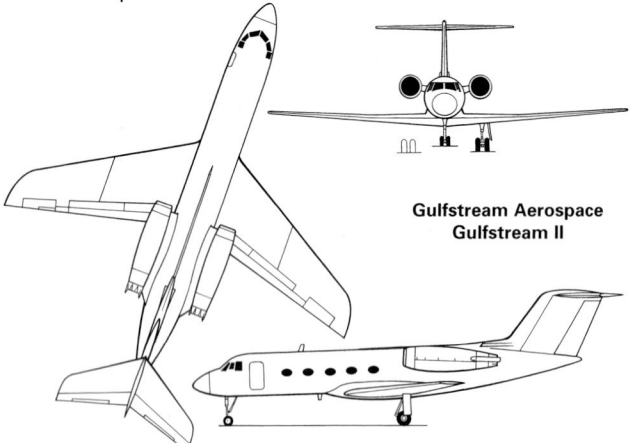

Gulfstream Aerospace Gulfstream II

SPECIFICATION

Gulfstream Aerospace Gulfstream II
Type: two/three-crew executive and corporate transport
Powerplant: two Rolls-Royce Spey RB.168 Mk 511-8 turbofan engines each rated at 11,400 lb st (50.71 kN)
Performance: maximum cruising speed 581 mph (935 km/h) at 25,000 ft (7620 m); economical cruising speed 483 mph (777 km/h) at 43,000 ft (13105 m); initial climb rate 4,140 ft (1262 m) per minute; service ceiling 43,000 ft (13105 m); range 4,276 miles (6881 km) with maximum fuel and 3,292 miles (5298 km) with maximum payload
Weights: empty 30,363 lb (13773 kg); maximum take-off 65,500 lb (29711 kg)
Dimensions: wingspan 68 ft 10 in (20.98 m) and 71 ft 9 in (21.87 m) with tip tanks; length 79 ft 11 in (24.36 m); height 24 ft 6 in (7.47 m); wing area 809.60 sq ft (75.21 m²)
Payload: up to 14 passengers carried in an enclosed cabin

Gulfstream Aerospace Gulfstream III

In November 1976 Grumman announced its intention to develop the **Gulfstream III** (**GIII**), but the programme was suspended temporarily early in 1977 and then resumed during 1978 with the design and development process continued under contract to the Gulfstream American Corporation (later the Gulfstream Aerospace Corporation) which had acquired the assets of Grumman's American Aviation Corporation. By comparison with that of the Gulfstream II, the fuselage of the **Gulfstream Aerospace Gulfstream III** was increased in length by 3 ft 11 in (1.19 m), which allowed the incorporation of a redesigned nose with improved windows on the flight deck for better fields of vision, and also provided a longer cabin to seat a maximum 19 passengers. Key to the improved performance of this aircraft was its new supercritical wing incorporating NASA Whitcomb wing-tip winglets, and the 9 ft (2.74 m) increase in span provided integral tankage for 3,664 Imp gal (4,400 US gal; 16655 litres) of fuel. The first aircraft was converted from the incomplete 247th Gulfstream II airframe, and this machine recorded the Gulfstream III's first flight on 2 December 1979, a second aircraft subsequently joining the flight test programme on 24 December of the same year.

The Gulfstream III is suitable for multi-mission operations, equally capable of being used for navaid checking, aeromedical/casevac, priority cargo and administrative transport roles. In August 1984 the company flew its **SRA-1** demonstrator for the surveillance and reconnais-sance roles, and two of the aircraft were later bought by India for use in the maritime surveillance and Elint roles with equipment that includes the APS-134(V)2 radar, the Motorola SLAMMR (Side-Looking Airborne Multi-Mode Radar) in an optional ventral installation, two chaff dispensers, and six underwing hardpoints for weapons as well as podded equipment. The **SMA-3** designation is applied to three **Special Missions Aircraft** bought by Denmark with modifications for the offshore patrol role with Texas Instruments APS-127 surveillance radar and other special avionics.

The core designation **C-20** is used for the Gulfstream III derivative in service with the US forces with the engine redesignated as the F113-RR-100. The American 'military' subvariants are the **C-20A** of which the US Air Force bought three for the transport of senior military personnel in Europe, the **C-20B** of which the USAF bought seven for the transport of VIPs within the USA, the **C-20C** of which the USAF bought three for the rapid movement of senior military personnel in the event of nuclear war (and thus fitted with strategic communications equipment hardened against electromagnetic pulse effects), the **C-20D** of which the US Navy bought two each equipped for the rapid movement of up to 14 senior naval personnel, and the **C-20E** of which the US Army bought two for the rapid movement of senior military personnel. Single examples of the Gulfstream III were also delivered in VIP form to the air forces of Gabon, Italy, Ivory Coast, Mexico, Morocco, Oman, Saudi Arabia and Venezuela.

Gulfstream Aerospace Gulfstream III

Unlike the GII, the GIII was built from new with performance-enhancing winglets.

SPECIFICATION

Gulfstream Aerospace Gulfstream III
Type: two/three-crew executive and corporate transport
Powerplant: two Rolls-Royce Spey RB.168 Mk 511-8 turbofan engines each rated at 11,400 lb st (50.71 kN)
Performance: maximum cruising speed 577 mph (929 km/h) at 30,000 ft (9145 m); economical cruising speed 508 mph (818 km/h) at high altitude; initial climb rate 3,800 ft (1158 m) per minute; service ceiling 45,000 ft (13715 m); range 4,200 miles (6760 km) with maximum payload
Weights: empty 32,300 lb (14651 kg); maximum take-off 68,200 lb (30936 kg)
Dimensions: wingspan 77 ft 10 in (23.72 m); length 83 ft 1 in (25.32 m); height 24 ft 4½ in (7.43 m); wing area 934.60 sq ft (86.83 m²)
Payload: up to 19 passengers in the enclosed cabin

Gulfstream Aerospace Gulfstream IV

First flown on 19 September 1985, the **Gulfstream IV (GIV)** is an improved version of the Gulfstream III with a redesigned and lighter wing, wider-span tailplane, lengthened cabin, revised powerplant, and 'glass' cockpit with digital avionics. The standard version of the Gulfstream IV has its fuselage lengthened by 4 ft 6 in (1.37 m) to provide improved accommodation for between 14 and 19 executive passengers, and there is also a **Gulfstream IVB** with a fuselage stretch of 18 ft 6 in (5.64 m) to allow the accommodation of 24 passengers, and the **Gulfstream IVSP** with a 2,500-lb (1134-kg) increase in payload and an enlarged payload/range envelope.

The Gulfstream IV was adopted for US military service within the C-20 family, and the three Gulfstream IV variants are the **C-20F** improved special air missions derivative for the USAF, which has a requirement for seven such 27-passenger aircraft; the **C-20G** improved VIP passenger and priority

freight transport for the USN and USMC, which received four and one aircraft respectively; and the **C-20H** of which two have been delivered to the USAF. Single Gulfstream IVs are used by the armed forces of Botswana, Egypt, Ireland, Ivory Coast and Venezuela, while those of Turkey have three.

The **SRA-4** is the special missions version, and can be configured for any of several important roles. The EW support version would have a canoe fairing under the forward fuselage for the antennas associated with its EW systems. The electronic surveillance and reconnaissance version would have Goodyear UPD-8 synthetic-aperture radar or Motorola SLAMMR (Side-Looking Airborne Multi-Mode Radar) with its antenna in a canoe fairing under the forward fuselage, a Rank/Optical KS-146 mirror-lens LOROP (LOng-Range Oblique Photography) camera, optional ECM and ESM equipment, and underwing hardpoints. The maritime patrol version

would have surface-search radar, FLIR, ESM, SAR equipment, and accommodation for up to eight console operators and/or observers. The ASW version would have surface-search radar, FLIR, sonobuoy launchers, an acoustic data-processing system, MAD, ESM, and weapons in a bay under the forward fuselage and anti-ship missiles on two underwing hardpoints. The medevac version would have accommodation for 15 litters plus attendants. The priority cargo transport would have a cargo door in the starboard side of the fuselage ahead of the wing and a floor-mounted cargo roller system. Orders for the SRA-4 have been placed by Japan and Sweden. In mid-2000, the former was in the process of receiving nine **U-4** multi-mission aircraft with the ability to operate in the VIP, priority transport, training, support and medevac roles. Sweden has received three aircraft for service as one **Tp 102A** transport and two **S 102B** Elint aircraft.

With the GIV, Gulfstream Aerospace offered new capabilities in terms of range, along with ultra-modern avionics and superior accommodation.

SPECIFICATION

Gulfstream Aerospace Gulfstream IV
Type: two/three-crew long-range multi-role light transport
Powerplant: two Rolls-Royce RB.183-03 Mk 611-8 Tay turbofan engines each rated at 13,850 lb st (61.61 kN)
Performance: maximum cruising speed 586 mph (943 km/h) at 31,000 ft (9450 m); economical cruising speed 523 mph (841 km/h) 41,000 ft (12500 m); initial climb rate 4,000 ft (1220 m) per minute; service ceiling 45,000 ft (13715 m); range 4,859 miles (7820 km) with

eight passengers and maximum fuel, and 4,254 miles (6845 km) with maximum payload
Weights: empty 35,500 lb (16102 kg); maximum take-off 73,200 lb (33203 kg)
Dimensions: wingspan 77 ft 10 in (23.72 m) including winglets; length 88 ft 4 in (26.92 m); height 24 ft 10 in (7.57 m); wing area 950.39 sq ft (88.29 m²)
Payload: up to 19 passengers carried in the enclosed cabin within the context of a 6,500-lb (2948-kg) maximum payload

Gulfstream Aerospace Gulfstream V

First announced in October 1991 and formally launched in September 1992, the **Gulfstream V (GV)** first flew in prototype form on 28 November 1995 and received US civil certification in April 1997. The key milestones in the programme were the decision to use the BMW Rolls-Royce (now Rolls-Royce) BR710 turbofan engine in September 1992, the finalisation of risk-sharing agreements with Vought (now Northrop Grumman) of the USA and ShinMaywa of Japan for the wing during June 1993, and with Fokker of the Netherlands for the tail and floor during September 1993.

The Gulfstream V is based on the Gulfstream IV but uses a re-engineered fuselage increased in length by 7 ft (2.13 m) to allow the incorporation

of an improved cabin providing accommodation for between 15 and 19 passengers; a wing of basically the same planform but increased in size, having greater integral fuel capacity and providing about 10 per cent more aerodynamic efficiency; a tail unit again enlarged over that of the Gulfstream IV; and a flight deck with the rear bulkhead moved 1 ft (0.30 m) farther to the rear for greater volume. The layout and instrumentation are derived from those of the GIVSP and the 'glass' flight deck has as its core the Honeywell SPZ-8500 system that includes an Electronic Flight Instrumentation System with six coloured displays, a digital automatic flight-control system, a flight management system and a Honeywell/Marconi head-up display;

the type also has an IBM satellite communications system providing 'office in the sky' capability.

By the end of 1998 Gulfstream Aerospace, which was bought by General Dynamics in May 1999, had sold more than 120 GVs. Most of these were for the corporate market, but Gulfstream V is also offered in two military forms. The **Gulfstream V Special Missions Variant**, also

known as the **EC-37**, is projected with a choice of mission equipment, but up to the end of 1999 had been unsuccessful in gaining an order: offered by teams headed by Lockheed Martin and Northrop Grumman, the type lost to the Bombardier Global Express in the competition to provide the aerial platform for the UK's ASTOR, or Airborne Stand-Off Radar, system. The other version

is the **C-37** VIP transport for the USAF, which has a requirement for an eventual total of six **C-37A** machines to replace the Boeing VC-137s operated by the 89th Airlift Wing based at Andrews AFB, Maryland, to provide VIP service for the US administration and government.

The first production-standard Gulfstream Aerospace Gulfstream V was delivered to Walter Annenberg in July 1997.

SPECIFICATION

Gulfstream Aerospace Gulfstream V
Type: two/three-crew long-range corporate transport
Powerplant: two BMW Rolls-Royce (now Rolls-Royce) BR710-48 turbofan engines each rated at 14,750 lb st (65.61 kN)
Performance: maximum cruising speed 574 mph (924 km/h) at high altitude; initial climb rate 4,188 ft (1276 m) per minute; certificated ceiling 51,000 ft (15545 m); range 7,480 miles (12038 km) with

eight passengers
Weights: empty 39,500 lb (17917 kg); maximum take-off 90,500 lb (41050 kg)
Dimensions: wingspan 90 ft 10 in (27.69 m); length 96 ft 5 in (29.39 m); height 25 ft 10 in (7.87 m); wing area 1,137.00 sq ft (105.63 m²)
Payload: up to 19 passengers carried in an enclosed cabin within the context of a 6,500-lb (2948-kg) maximum payload

Gulfstream American AA-1 Yankee, Tr 2, T-Cat and Lynx

The Bede **BD-1** was designed by Jim Bede as a low-cost sporting aircraft with side-by-side two-seat enclosed accommodation and a structure that made extensive use of aluminium honeycomb construction and metal-to-metal bonding. The BD-1 made its first flight on 11 July 1963. The Bede Aviation Corporation had been formed at Cleveland, Ohio, in 1964, and was renamed as the American Aviation Corporation in September 1967 to assume responsibility for the development, certification and manufacture of this machine as the **American Aviation AA-1 Yankee**. A US type certificate for the production AA-1 was granted on 16 July 1968, the first example having flown on 30 May 1968.

The development of a training version started in October 1969 and the proto-type made its first flight on 25 March of that year. Designated **AA-1A**, it retained the 108-hp (81-kW) Lycoming O-235-C2C flat-four engine of the AA-1, but incorporated a modified wing, minor equipment changes, and dual controls as standard. The first production AA-1A flew on 6 November 1970, and type certification was awarded on 14 January 1971.

The Grumman Corporation acquired American Aviation in 1972 and minor design and equipment changes introduced in 1974 resulted in the revised designation **AA-1B**, further updating in 1977 producing the **AA-1C** with a slightly uprated engine. Dual-purpose touring/training variants of the AA-1B and AA-1C, with enhanced equipment and interiors,

In 1978, American Jet Industries acquired Grumman's American Aviation Corporation, renaming the company Gulfstream American Corporation. A Lynx aircraft is illustrated.

were manufactured as the **Tr 2** and **T-Cat** respectively and a de luxe version was produced as the **Lynx**.

Production of the AA-1, T-Cat and Lynx family was terminated at the end of 1978.

SPECIFICATION	
Gulfstream American AA-1C	rate 700 ft (213 m) per minute;
Type: two-seat touring and training aircraft	service ceiling 11,500 ft (3505 m); range 442 miles (711 km)
Powerplant: one Lycoming O-235-L2C flat-four piston engine rated at 115 hp (85.70 kW)	**Weights:** empty 1,002 lb (455 kg); maximum take-off 1,600 lb (726 kg)
Performance: maximum speed 145 mph (234 km/h) at sea level; cruising speed 129 mph (208 km/h) at 3,000 ft (915 m); initial climb	**Dimensions:** wingspan 24 ft 5½ in (7.46 m); length 19 ft 3 in (5.86 m); height 7 ft 6 in (2.29 m); wing area 100.92 sq ft (9.38 m²)

Gulfstream American AA-5A/AA-5A/AA-5B family

In June 1970 the American Aviation Corporation began work on an enlarged four-seat version of its AA-1 as the **AA-5 Traveler**. The span of the wing was increased by 7 ft (2.13 m); the tail surfaces were increased in area; the fuselage was lengthened by 2 ft 9 in (0.84 m) to allow the incorporation of two more seats in what was now a four-seat cabin; and the available power was increased by installation of a higher-rated engine, the Lycoming O-320-E2G unit. The prototype first flew on 21 August 1970 and certification was gained on 12 November 1971.

In 1974, changes included introduction of a new fin, extended rear cabin windows and an enlarged baggage compartment. Some two years later, the introduction of an enlarged tailplane and minor improvements resulted in the further revised designation **AA-5A**. A de luxe version of the same aircraft was designated as the **Cheetah**. Versions equivalent to the AA-5A and Cheetah, but with the more powerful 180-hp (134-kW) Lycoming O-360-A4K engine, were added to the range with the respective designations **AA-5B** and **Tiger**.

SPECIFICATION	
Gulfstream American AA-5A	rate 660 ft (201 m) per minute;
Type: four-seat touring aircraft	service ceiling 12,560 ft (3830 m); range 647 miles (1041 km)
Powerplant: one Lycoming O-320-E2G flat-four piston engine rated at 150 hp (112 kW)	**Weights:** empty 1,303 lb (591 kg); maximum take-off 2,200 lb (998 kg)
Performance: maximum speed 157 mph (253 km/h) at sea level; cruising speed 136 mph (219 km/h) at 8,500 ft (2590 m); initial climb	**Dimensions:** wingspan 31 ft 6 in (9.60 m); length 22 ft (6.71 m); height 7 ft 6 in (2.29 m); wing area 139.70 sq ft (12.98 m²)

As a moderately improved version of the well-established AA-5 Traveler, the AA-5A Cheetah (illustrated) sold to the extent of 900 examples.

Gulfstream American GA-7 and Cougar

The discernible need for a light and economical four-seat, twin-engined aircraft for use by flying schools on multi-engine conversion courses, and to meet the requirements of private pilots, led Grumman American to develop the **GA-7**. The prototype made its first flight on 20 December 1974 with the powerplant of two 160-hp (119-kW) Lycoming O-320-D1D engines, and a production-standard trials aircraft first flew on 14 January 1977.

The basic production model was the GA-7, but a de luxe version was also available under the name **Cougar**. This incorporated dual controls, communication and navigation avionics, full blind-flying instrumentation and additional electrical equipment as standard.

GA-7 deliveries began in February 1978, continuing until late 1979 when Gulfstream American suspended production of the GA-7, and also of its range of single-engined aircraft.

SPECIFICATION	
Gulfstream American GA-7	service ceiling 18,300 ft (5580 m);
Type: four-seat light transport and training aircraft	range 1,336 miles (2150 km)
Powerplant: two Lycoming O-320-D1D flat-four piston engines each rated at 160 hp (119 kW)	**Weights:** empty 2,515 lb (1141 kg); maximum take-off 3,800 lb (1724 kg)
Performance: maximum speed 193 mph (311 km/h) at sea level; cruising speed 131 mph (211 km/h) at 8,500 ft (2590 m); initial climb rate 1,200 ft (366 m) per minute;	**Dimensions:** wingspan 36 ft 10¼ in (11.23 m); length 29 ft 10 in (9.09 m); height 10 ft 4¼ in (3.16 m); wing area 184.00 sq ft (17.09 m²)

Häfeli DH-2 and DH-3

The **Häfeli DH-2** design for K+W was a conventional two-bay biplane of wooden construction with fabric covering, and was created for the reconnaissance role. Six aircraft were manufactured in 1916, five of them powered by the 120-hp (90-kW) Argus As.II water-cooled inline engine which employed large flat radiators mounted beside the front cockpit. The first aircraft was equipped with a similarly cooled 100-hp (75-kW) Mercedes D.I engine. The performance of the DH-2 was disappointing, and no major production order was placed, but the existing examples of the DH-2 continued in use as trainers until retired in 1922.

Early in 1917, K+W received an order for 30 examples of the **DH-3**, an improved version of the DH-2 with an essentially similar airframe. Unfortunately, the landing gear proved troublesome and there were also engine cooling problems until an improved system was fitted. A total of some 24 DH-3s was built with the As.II engine, and the type was withdrawn from use in 1923 when a structural strength test, conducted on an airframe which had amassed 600 hours flying time, produced unsatisfactory results. In the meantime, a DH-3 inaugurated the first Swiss air mail service, between Zürich's Dübendorf airfield and Berne, on 8 January 1919.

Variants

DH-3a: four aircraft were built in 1918, three of them with the Hispano-Suiza HS-41 8Aa engine; these aircraft were scrapped in 1922; a second series of 30 aircraft, essentially similar but with the Hispano-Suiza engines built under licence by Adolph Saurer A.G. at Arbon, was ordered in 1919, and a third order for 49 aircraft was placed in 1925; the latter included six primary trainers with dual controls and a trials aircraft with the 180-hp (134-kW) HS-41 8Ab engine; this was evaluated by the Swiss air force between October 1929 and April 1930; following a prototype installation of Handley Page leading-edge slats in the UK, a further 55 surviving DH-3as were similarly modified at Thun in 1932. At the same time, the aircraft were also modified to allow the crew to wear parachutes. These modified aircraft remained in service until 1939
DH-3b: three DH-3bs were used for trials with the indigenous 150-hp (112-kW) LFW O engine; built in 1918, the aircraft were withdrawn in 1922; their armament comprised two fixed machine-guns, mounted above the engine, in addition to the observer's trainable weapon

Compared to that of the DH-2, the DH-3's (illustrated) upper wing had a semi-circular cut-out in the trailing edge of its centre section to provide an improved field of fire for the trainable machine-gun mounted in the observer's cockpit, here covered over.

SPECIFICATION	
Häfeli DH-3a	**Weights:** empty 1,587 lb (720 kg);
Type: two-seat reconnaissance aircraft	maximum take-off 2,447 lb (1110 kg)
Powerplant: one Hispano-Suiza HS-41 8Aa Vee piston engine rated at 150 hp (112 kW)	**Dimensions:** wingspan 41 ft (12.50 m); length 26 ft 1 in (7.95 m); height 10 ft 2 in (3.10 m); wing area 409.04 sq ft (38.00 m²)
Performance: maximum speed 90 mph (145 km/h) at sea level; service ceiling 14,765 ft (4500 m); range 249 miles (400 km)	**Armament:** one 0.295-in (7.5-mm) trainable rearward-firing machine-gun in the rear cockpit

Häfeli DH-5

In the autumn of 1918, K+W at Thun was engaged in the construction of the **DH-5** prototype, which was a fabric-covered single-bay biplane of basically all-wooden construction powered by a 180-hp (134-kW) LFW I engine. Test flying started in March 1919, and official military evaluation began in May 1920; after this the prototype was used for structural strength tests as 39 production DH-5s were ordered, the first of them entering service in 1922. In March 1929 one aircraft was civil-registered for a flight to England, where Handley Page leading-edge slats were fitted to validate the concept before another 23 aircraft were similarly modified at Thun in 1930.

A second series of 20 DH-5s was introduced in 1924 with the uprated powerplant of one 200-hp (149-kW) LFW II engine. The surviving DH-5s were retired in 1940.

SPECIFICATION	
Häfeli DH-5A	(1271 kg)
Type: two-seat reconnaissance aircraft	**Dimensions:** wingspan 39 ft 4½ in (12.00 m); length 24 ft 11¼ in (7.60 m); height 10 ft 2 in (3.10 m); wing area 338.00 sq ft (31.40 m²)
Powerplant: one LFW III Vee piston engine rated at 220 hp (164 kW)	**Armament:** one 0.295-in (7.5-mm) fixed forward-firing machine-gun in the forward part of the fuselage and one 0.295-in (7.5-mm) trainable rearward-firing machine-gun in the rear cockpit
Performance: maximum speed 112 mph (180 km/h) at sea level; service ceiling 18,375 ft (5600 m); range 298 miles (480 km)	
Weights: empty 1,894 lb (859 kg); maximum take-off 2,802 lb	

The LFW engine of the DH-5 was produced by the Swiss Locomotive and Machine Works at Winterthur.

Variants

DH-5X: this trials aircraft appeared in November 1924 with the considerably more potent 300-hp (224-kW) Hispano Suiza HS-42 8Fb engine; production orders would have followed but further supplies of the engine were not available; the DH-5X crashed on 31 January 1933, with the loss of the pilot
DH-5A: 20 DH-5as, powered by the LFW III engine, were delivered in 1929; they were modified in 1930 by the installation of Handley Page slats and new seats allowing the use of parachutes; this version was also used for target towing

Hafner rotary-wing aircraft

Born in Austria, Raoul Hafner began preliminary work on helicopter models in the mid-1920s, and in 1928 began the design of his first aircraft, the **R.I** helicopter. Financed by the Scottish cotton millionaire, Major J. A. Coats, this had a comparatively short fuselage and a three-bladed, 30-ft (9.14-m) diameter rotor; power was provided by a 30-hp (22-kW) ABC Scorpion flat-twin piston engine. The R.I was tested outside Vienna in 1930, and it was soon found that the gyroscopic action of this rotor was too great and, as a result, only a few brief hops were made. An improved **R.II** of similar configuration was built, but differed in having increased vertical surface to offset the turning moment of the rotor, and in having a lightweight 40-hp (30-kW) Salmson radial engine.

In 1932, Hafner transferred his activities to England, continuing development of the R.II, but within two years he had established the AR.III Construction (Hafner Gyroplane) Company to develop an autogyro of similar basic layout to the Cierva Autogiros. Only one example of the **AR.III Gyroplane** was built, and this flew successfully during 1937 and 1938. The AR.III carried its three-bladed auto-rotating rotor on a pylon above a fairly conventional fuselage. A Pobjoy Niagara radial in the nose drove a two-bladed propeller. The aircraft had fixed tailwheel landing gear and provided single-seat accommodation. An unusual feature was the rear fuselage, which incorporated a long dorsal fin that tapered to rudder thickness, providing ample vertical surface area. The special design feature was the Gyroplane's rotor control system, giving both cyclic and collective pitch control to the blades, and this arrangement was to become standard for the dynamic systems of subsequent helicopters.

Two- and three-seat autogyros, designated **AR.IV** and **AR.V** respectively, were now planned,

A prototype of the Rotabuggy was flown extensively during 1943/4, but did not become operational.

but although construction of these machines had been started, the outbreak of World War II brought an end to these projects.

Hafner's wartime work included the design and development of the **Rotachute**, a man-carrying glider with a rotating wing.

Towed by an aircraft to heights of some 4,000 ft (1220 m), it could be piloted in any direction after release. Other wartime work was concentrated on the development of a **Rotabuggy**, basically a Jeep-type general-purpose military truck with an easily attached/detached rotary wing that would allow such vehicles to be towed and deployed behind enemy lines. In the years after World War II, Hafner's great experience of rotary-wing flight proved of value to the Bristol and Westland aircraft companies.

SPECIFICATION

Hafner AR.III Gyroplane
Type: single-seat autogyro
Powerplant: one Pobjoy Niagara radial piston engine rated at 90 hp (67 kW)
Performance: maximum speed 120 mph (193 km/h) at sea level; cruising speed 110 mph (177 km/h)
at optimum altitude
Weights: empty 640 lb (290 kg); maximum take-off 900 lb (408 kg)
Dimensions: rotor diameter 32 ft 10 in (10.00 m); length 17 ft 10 in (5.44 m) for the fuselage; rotor disc area 845.43 sq ft (78.54 m²)

HAL Advanced Light Helicopter

In July 1984 Hindustan Aeronautics Ltd signed an agreement with MBB of West Germany for the latter to provide support for the design, development and production of the **Advanced Light Helicopter**. The Indian company wanted to create this ALH to provide the country's service operators, as well as the civil market, with a capable light helicopter of indigenous manufacture. Work on the design began in November 1984 with the first runs of a ground vehicle following in April 1991, and the first of five flying prototypes (two basic and one each for the air force/army, navy and civil markets) recorded its official first flight on

30 August 1992, some 10 days after it first rose into the air.

The ALH is based on a pod-and-boom fuselage that combines light alloy sandwich material with Kevlar and carbonfibre in its structure. The dynamic system comprises a side-by-side pair of turboshafts located behind the main combining gearbox to drive four-bladed main and tail rotors. Like the rotor hubs, the rotor blades are of glassfibre and carbonfibre construction, and the main rotor is a hingeless unit with a fibre elastomer rotor head. The tips of the rotor blades are swept on their leading edges, and other elements of the design are a tail unit with a straight

horizontal surface and two swept vertical surfaces with their leading edges offset to port; landing gear that comprises either a pair of fixed skids in the air force and army variant or retractable tricycle wheeled gear in the case of the maritime and civil models, which also have a pair of small sponsons on the lower sides of the fuselage's pod section to carry the single-wheel main units; and a four-axis automatic flight-control system provided by the French avionics company SFIM.

As an alternative to internal freight, the ALH can carry a 3,307-lb (1500-kg) slung load. The variant for the air force and army will have crashworthy fuel

tanks, bullet-proof supply tanks, IR and flame suppression and provision for weapons delivered in the day and night attack roles. The variant for the navy will have a harpoon deck-lock, folding tail boom, provision for pressure refuelling and more specialised avionics including mission equipment for the anti-ship and/or anti-submarine roles. These two armed models will have pylons on the sides of the fuselage with two hardpoints for weapons such as anti-ship missiles or anti-submarine torpedoes in the naval model, or stub wings with four hardpoints for weapons such as 16 anti-tank missiles, four multiple rocket launchers or four air-to-air missiles in the

SPECIFICATION

HAL ALH (land-based version)
Type: two-crew light utility helicopter
Powerplant: two Turbomeca TM333-2B turboshaft engines each rated at 1,057 shp (788 kW); the MTU/Rolls-Royce/Turbomeca MTR390 is also a contender
Performance: maximum speed 180 mph (290 km/h) at sea level; cruising speed 152 mph (245 km/h) at optimum altitude; initial climb rate 2,362 ft (720 m) per minute; service ceiling 19,685 ft (6000 m); hovering ceiling more than 9,845 ft (3000 m) in ground effect; range 249 miles (400 km) with a 1,543-lb
(700-kg) payload: endurance 4 hours
Weights: empty 5,401 lb (2450 kg); maximum take-off 9,921 lb (400 kg)
Dimensions: main rotor diameter 43 ft 3¾ in (13.20 m); length 52 ft ¾ in (15.87 m) with the rotors turning; height 16 ft 4 in (4.98 m); main rotor disc area 1,473.06 sq ft (136.85 m²)
Payload: up to 14 passengers or freight in the cabin, or up to 3,307 lb (1500 kg) of freight carried as a slung load
Armament: see above

land-based model, which can also carry a ventral turret armed with one 20-mm cannon.

Full-scale deliveries of production ALH helicopters, which may also be developed as the **LAH (Light Attack Helicopter)** with a tandem two-seat cockpit, will probably start early in the 21st century to satisfy air/force and navy requirements for 200 and 50 helicopters respectively. Given the poor state of US and Indian political relations in the aftermath of India's experimental detonation of nuclear weapons, it is now unlikely that the ALH with have the 1,300-shp (969-kW) LHTEC CTS 800-4N turboshaft once considered as a possible engine choice.

At least two ALHs were in service by the end of 2000. The payload-carrying part of the type's cabin is accessed by two large rearward-sliding side doors and, at the rear, clamshell doors.

HAL Ajeet and Ajeet Trainer

Developed on the basis of the Hawker Siddeley (Folland) Gnat lightweight fighter that the company built under licence for the Indian air force, the **Ajeet** (invincible) was a 'Gnat Mk 2' with features such as integral wing tankage freeing the underwing hardpoints for armament, an improved longitudinal

control system, a Martin-Baker Mk GF4 lightweight ejection seat providing ejection capability from ground level upward at any speed over 104 mph (167 km/h), Dunlop wheels with hydraulically operated disk brakes and a Maxaret anti-skid braking system, improved communication and navigation systems,

the Ferranti Isis F195 gun sight and the relocation of some of the avionics to the nose section made vacant by the removal of the Gnat Mk 1's ranging radar, which was superfluous in the ground-attack role.

The first machine flew on 6 March 1975, and the type was built in small numbers (79 aircraft) only

for the Indian air force, which operated the type mainly in the combat and armament training roles.

First flown in September 1982 and built to the extent of 30 examples, the **Ajeet Trainer** was a simple

advanced flying/weapons and operational conversion trainer derivative of the Ajeet with the fuselage stretched to accommodate a second seat in a lengthened cockpit section under a longer canopy.

In the Ajeet Trainer, provision was made for the cannon to be removed, allowing internal fuel capacity to be increased by 60 Imp gal (273 litres) for improved utility in the flying training and conversion roles.

SPECIFICATION

HAL Ajeet
Type: single-seat lightweight attack fighter and interceptor
Powerplant: one HAL (Rolls-Royce/Bristol Siddeley) Orpheus BOr.2 Mk 701-01 turbojet engine rated at 4,500 lb st (20.02 kN)
Performance: maximum speed 685 mph (1102 km/h) at sea level; initial climb rate 10,625 ft (3240 m) per minute; climb to 39,370 ft (12000 m) in 6 minutes 2 seconds; service ceiling 45,000 ft (13720 m); radius 107 miles (175 km) on a lo-lo-lo attack mission with two 551-lb (250-kg) bombs
Weights: empty 5,086 lb (2307 kg); maximum take-off
9,200 lb (4173 kg)
Dimensions: wingspan 22 ft 1 in (6.731 m); length 29 ft 8 in (9.04 m); height 8 ft 1 in (2.46 m); wing area 136.12 sq ft (12.646 m²)
Armament: two 30-mm Aden Mk 4 fixed forward-firing cannon in the outer edges of the air inlets, plus up to 2,205 lb (1000 kg) of disposable stores carried on four underwing hardpoints, and generally comprising 551- or 500-lb (250- or 227-kg) free-fall, retarded or cluster bombs, and multiple launchers for 2.17- or 2.68-in (55- or 68-mm) air-to-surface unguided rockets

HAL HT-2

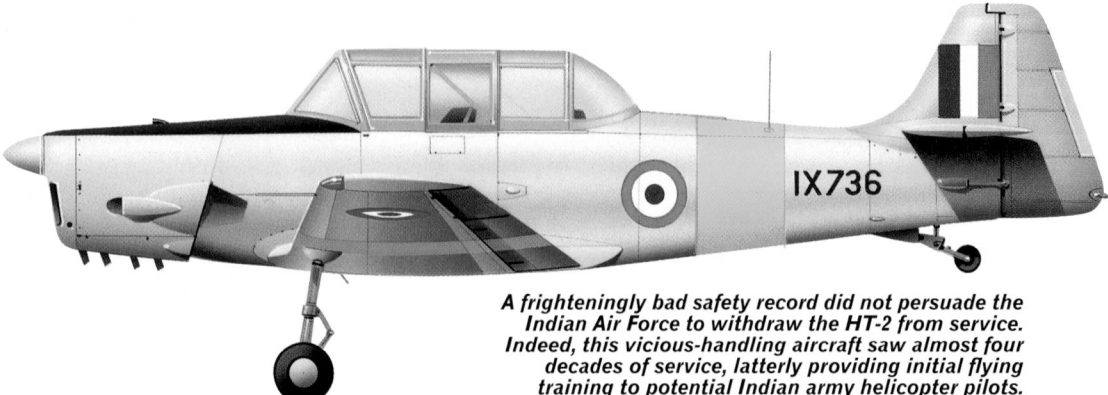

The **HT-2** was the first aircraft of Indian design to be built in quantity. It was created by what was then Hindustan Aircraft Ltd, specifically for the primary trainer role, and drew its inspiration from the de Havilland Canada DHC-1 Chipmunk in its concept as a basically metal monoplane with a low-set cantilever wing, fixed tail-wheel landing gear, and tandem accommodation under a 'glasshouse' canopy with two sliding sections.

The type stemmed from an Indian government commission of September 1948 for three new trainers to serve in the primary, basic and advanced roles. In the event the HT-2 was the only type to see the light of day, and the first of two prototypes flew in August 1951 with a powerplant of one 145-hp (108-kW) de Havilland Gipsy Major Mk 10 inverted inline engine, while the second machine had greater power in the

A frighteningly bad safety record did not persuade the Indian Air Force to withdraw the HT-2 from service. Indeed, this vicious-handling aircraft saw almost four decades of service, latterly providing initial flying training to potential Indian army helicopter pilots.

form of a Blackburn Cirrus Major Mk III inverted inline engine. During its flight trials the HT-2 revealed distinctly unpleasant handling characteristics, but was nonetheless ordered into production. Production of 169 aircraft was completed in 1958, and most of the HT-2s were used by the Indian services, although 12 were delivered to Ghana.

The type was to have been replaced by the HPT-32 from the late 1970s, but delays in the

HPT-32's development meant that the HT-2 had to be kept in service despite an accident rate more than 10 times higher than that suffered in West German service by the Lockheed F-104G Starfighter. From 1981, some 22 of the surviving aircraft were re-engined with an American powerplant, the 160-hp (119-kW) Lycoming O-320-H flat-four engine, whose only effect on performance was a reduction in range to 320 miles (515 km). Even after deliveries of the HPT-32 began in 1984, some HT-2s soldiered on but only a few of the aircraft were

eries of the HPT-32 began in 1984, some HT-2s soldiered on but only a few of the aircraft were still serviceable in the second half of the 1990s when the type was finally retired.

SPECIFICATION	
HAL HT-2	ceiling 16,500 ft (5030 m); range
Type: two-seat primary flying trainer	350 miles (563 km); endurance 3 hours 30 minutes
Powerplant: one Blackburn Cirrus Major Mk III inverted inline piston engine rated at 155 hp (116 kW)	**Weights:** empty 1,540 lb (699 kg); maximum take-off 2,240 lb (1016 kg)
Performance: maximum speed 130 mph (209 km/h) at sea level; cruising speed 115 mph (185 km/h) at sea level; initial climb rate 800 ft (244 m) per minute; service	**Dimensions:** wingspan 35 ft 2 in (10.72 m); length 24 ft 8½ in (7.53 m); height 8 ft 11 in (2.72 m); wing area 173.40 sq ft (52.85 m²)

HAL HJT-16 Kiran

The first of its types to enter production after the company was revised in October 1964 as Hindustan Aeronautics Ltd, the **HJT-16 Kiran** (ray of light) was designed to meet an Indian air force requirement for an unarmed basic flying trainer. HAL was clearly inspired by the Hunting (Percival) Jet Provost in the design of the Kiran. Features that differentiated the Kiran from the Jet Provost, however, were the use of more advanced ejec-

tion seats and the provision from the outset of pres-surised accommodation.

Initial design work began in 1959 and detailed design in 1961, but finalisation of the design and initial construction were slow. Thus the first of two proto-types did not fly until 4 September 1964. The type had been designed for an Indian engine, the HJE-2500 with a projected rating of 2,500 lb st (11.12 kN), but this engine never reached maturity and

was replaced by a HAL (Bristol Siddeley/Armstrong Siddeley) Viper, thereby increasing the similarity of the Kiran to the Jet Provost. A pre-production batch of 24 **Kiran Mk 1** aircraft was delivered from March 1968. This paved the way for full production, which started with 118 Kiran Mk 1 unarmed train-ers with the powerplant of one 2,500-lb st (11.12-kN) Viper ASV.11 Mk 200 turbo-jet engine.

The Kiran Mk 1 clearly possessed the capability for development into the armament training and light-attack roles, so the initial model was followed by the **Kiran Mk 1A** with provision for 992 lb (450 kg) of weapons carried on two underwing hard-points. Production totalled some 72 aircraft.

By the late 1960s it had also become clear that the basic Kiran would be capa-ble of better performance

in the flying and armament training roles if fitted with a more powerful engine and updated avionics, and the go-ahead for such a devel-opment was given in September 1972. The key to the **Kiran Mk 2** aircraft's capabilities was the adop-tion of the uprated powerplant of one Orpheus turbojet for greater speed, climb rate and service ceil-ing as well as greater armament including inbuilt machine-guns, as well as disposable loads on four rather than two underwing hardpoints. HAL estimated that the Kiran Mk 2 would

enter service in 1976, but this was far too optimistic; the first of two prototypes did not take to the air until July 1976. This forced the Indian air force to order an interim armed trainer in the form of the PZL-Mielec TS-11 Iskra.

The Indian air force initially rejected the Kiran Mk 2 for its poor night flying qualities and inade-quate radius, but the type was finally cleared for service in March 1983. The Kiran Mk 2 entered service in April 1985, and the last of 103 aircraft was completed in March 1989.

SPECIFICATION	
HAL HJT-16 Kiran Mk 2	11,023 lb (5000 kg)
Type: two-seat basic, intermediate and advanced flying and armament trainer with light attack and counter-insurgency capabilities	**Dimensions:** wingspan 35 ft 1¼ in (10.70 m); length 34 ft 9½ in (10.60 m); height 11 ft 11 in (3.64 m); wing area 204.52 sq ft (19.00 m²)
Powerplant: one HAL (Rolls-Royce/Bristol Siddeley) Orpheus BOr.2 Mk 701-01 turbojet engine rated at 4,200 lb st (18.68 kN)	**Armament:** two 0.3-in (7.62-mm) FN MAG fixed forward-firing machine-guns in the nose, plus up to 2,205 lb (1000 kg) of disposable
Performance: maximum speed 418 mph (672 km/h) at sea level; cruising speed 386 mph (621 km/h) at 15,000 ft (4570 m); initial climb rate 5,250 ft (1600 m) per minute; service ceiling 39,375 ft (12000 m); range 457 miles (735 km) with standard fuel	stores carried on four underwing hardpoints, and generally comprising four 551- or 500-lb (250- or 227-kg) free-fall bombs, or two HAL pods each carrying two 0.3-in (7.62-mm) machine-guns, or four multiple launchers each carrying 18 2.68-in (68-mm) air-to-surface unguided rockets
Weights: empty 6,603 lb (2995 kg); maximum take-off	

Illustrated in Mk 1 form, the Kiran featured unswept flying surfaces and was an all-metal monoplane powered by a simple turbojet engine which was aspirated via lateral inlets.

HAL HF-24 Marut

The first warplane designed and built in India, the **HF-24 Marut** (wind spirit) was developed from 1956 by a team under Dipl.-Ing. Kurt Tank, the celebrated

designer of many Focke-Wulf aircraft before and during World War II. The design team's intention was to create a multi-role fighter eventually capable

of Mach 2 performance when revised with a more potent powerplant, and the resulting Marut was an all-metal monoplane not dissimilar from the Hawker Hunter in its oval-section fuselage, swept flying surfaces including a low-set

wing and tailplane, tricycle landing gear, and high-set cockpit offering the pilot good fields of vision over the comparatively slender nose section.

The powerplant comprised two engines located side-by-side in the

rear part of the central fuselage, aspirated via two lateral inlets and exhausting via side-by-side nozzles under the vertical tail surface. The intended powerplant was a pair of 6,810-lb st (30.29-kN) Bristol Aero-Engines (later

An interceptor configuration was proposed for the Marut, the aircraft being equipped with Ferranti AIRPASS radar and four underwing AAMs. However, the type saw service in the attack role.

Bristol Siddeley) Orpheus BOr.12 turbojet engines each rated at 8,170 lb st (36.34 kN) with afterburning, but development of this Orpheus variant was discontinued when the Indian government refused to underwrite its development costs, and the design team had to fall back on the older and less powerful Orpheus BOr.2 Mk 703 non-afterburning turbojet

engine while examining the possibility of other engines types including Soviet and Egyptian types – the Tumanskii RD-9F and Brandner EI-300 respectively. The search for an alternative powerplant continued even after the HF-24 had entered production, but ultimately proved fruitless.

Meanwhile, the first of two prototypes flew on

17 June 1961, and these prototypes were followed by 18 pre-production aircraft, the first of which flew in April 1963. As an afterburning powerplant was becoming ever less likely, and with it the possibility of the planned Mach 2 performance, the Indian air force took the opportunity offered by evaluation of the pre-production aircraft to rethink the role to which the new warplane could be put. The interceptor role was now out of the question, but ground-attack seemed a very acceptable alternative role as the HF-24 was fast at low level, possessed considerable strength and agility, was a steady gun platform, and could carry a useful external load. Thus the interceptor configuration was abandoned in favour of a simple gyro sight and weapons optimised for the attack role.

This was the standard to which the 112 production aircraft were delivered. The

first of these flew in November 1967, and the type proved itself in combat during the 1971 border war with Pakistan.

Production of the HF-24 series ended in 1970 with 18 examples of the **HF-24 Marut Mk 1T** two-seat operational conversion and weapon trainer derivative

of the Marut Mk 1. The first of two prototypes flew in April 1970, with space for a second seat, in a lengthened cockpit under a longer canopy, made by deletion of the fuselage rocket pack.

The Marut was finally phased out of service in the mid-1980s.

SPECIFICATION	
HAL HF-24 Marut Mk 1 **Type:** single-seat ground-attack fighter **Powerplant:** two HAL (Rolls-Royce/Bristol Siddeley) Orpheus BOr.2 Mk 703 turbojet engines each rated at 4,850 lb st (21.57 kN) **Performance:** maximum speed 705 mph (1134 km/h) at sea level; initial climb rate 8,500 ft (2591 m) per minute; climb to 40,000 ft (12190 m) in 9 minutes 20 seconds; range 480 miles (772 km) on a lo-lo-lo attack mission **Weights:** empty 13,658 lb (6195 kg); maximum take-off 24,048 lb (10908 kg) **Dimensions:** wingspan 29 ft 6¼ in (9.00 m); length 52 ft ¾ in (15.87 m); height 11 ft 9¾ in (3.60 m); wing area 306.78 sq ft	(28.50 m²) **Armament:** four 20-mm ADEN Mk 2 fixed forward-firing cannon in the sides of the forward fuselage, and one Matra Type 105 extending pack under the fuselage with 50 2.68-in (68-mm) air-to-surface unguided rockets, plus up to 4,000 lb (1814 kg) of disposable stores carried on four underwing hardpoints, and generally comprising four 1,000- or 500-lb (454- or 227-kg) free-fall bombs, or napalm tanks, or four Matra Type 116 multiple launchers each carrying 18 2.68-in (68-mm) air-to-surface unguided rockets, or four clusters of 4.13-in (105-mm) Brandt T-10 air-to-surface unguided rockets

HAL HUL-26 Pushpak

In 1958 HAL began work on a lightweight trainer for use by Indian flying clubs.

Designated as the **HUL-26 Pushpak**, the prototype first flew on 28 September

1958. A braced high-wing monoplane of fabric-covered mixed metal and wood construction with fixed tailwheel landing gear including divided main units, the

prototype was followed by about 160 production aircraft that differed from

the prototype mainly in having a metal rather than wood wing structure.

SPECIFICATION	
HAL HUL-26 Pushpak **Type:** two-seat training and sporting aircraft **Powerplant:** one Continental C90-8F flat-four piston engine rated at 90 hp (67 kW) **Performance:** maximum speed 90 mph (145 km/h) at sea level; cruising speed 85 mph (137 km/h) at optimum altitude; initial climb	rate 500 ft (152 m) per minute; service ceiling 14,000 ft (4270 m); range 250 miles (402 km) **Weights:** empty 870 lb (395 kg); maximum take-off 1,350 lb (612 kg) **Dimensions:** wingspan 36 ft (10.97 m); length 21 ft (6.40 m); height 9 ft 1 in (2.77 m); wing area 175.00 sq ft (16.26 m²)

HAL's Pushpak was was little more than a licence-built Aeronca Model 11 Chief, with a minimum of local modifications incorporated.

HAL HAOP-27 Krishak

HAL's next project after the HUL-26 Pushpak was a slightly larger four-seat development of the former type, and the first of two **Krishak Mk 1**

prototypes flew in November 1959 with a 190-hp (142-kW) Continental engine. This type did not attract the interest that would have

warranted production, and was therefore put to one side. A few years later, however, the Indian army issued a requirement for a two/three-seat air observation post and liaison machine to replace the Auster AOP.Mk 9, and HAL revised the Krishak to meet the specification. The prototype of this **Krishak Mk 2** flew in 1965 and there followed 68 examples of the **HAOP-27** production model that had all been delivered to the Indian army by the end of 1969. The Indian army soon joined the ranks of those

A developed version of HAL's licence-built Aeronca Sedan, the HAOP-27 was a braced high-wing monoplane of fabric-covered metal construction.

services who saw the benefits of rotary-wing aircraft for the AOP role,

and from 1974 the Krishak Mk 2 was superseded by the HAL Cheetah.

SPECIFICATION	
HAL HAOP-27 Krishak Mk 2 **Type:** one/two-crew air observation post and utility light transport **Powerplant:** one Continental O-470-J flat-six piston engine rated at 225 hp (168 kW) **Performance:** maximum speed 130 mph (209 km/h) at sea level; initial climb rate 900 ft (274 m) per minute; service ceiling 19,500 ft (5945 m); range 500 miles (805 km)	with auxiliary fuel **Weights:** empty 1,970 lb (894 kg); maximum take-off 2,800 lb (1270 kg) **Dimensions:** wingspan 37 ft 6 in (11.43 m); length 27 ft 7 in (8.41 m); height 7 ft 9 in (2.36 m); wing area 200.00 sq ft (18.58 m²) **Payload:** up to one passenger or one litter carried in the rear of the cabin

HAL HA-31 Basant

Design of an agricultural aircraft was initiated by Hindustan in mid-1968. The aircraft emerged as a type typical of contemporary

'ag-plane' concept with a high-set enclosed cockpit, fixed tailwheel landing gear and a low-set wing braced to the upper sides

of the fuselage on each side by inverted-Vee struts. The resulting **HA-31 Mk I** prototype had its cockpit directly over the wing's leading edge and was powered by a 250-hp (187-kW) Rolls-

Royce (Continental) engine, but there followed a measure of redesign and the **HA-31 Mk II Basant** (spring) prototype first flew on 30 March 1972. This aircraft incorporated a number of changes,

including a higher-powered American engine and the cockpit moved farther to the rear into a position above the wing's trailing edge. Production ended in 1980 after the completion of some 39 aircraft.

HAL HA-31 Basant (continued)

After the HA-31 Basant Mk I had proved to have disappointing performance, Hindustan redesigned the aircraft as the HA-31 Basant Mk II. The first of the Mk IIs is illustrated.

HAL HPT-32 Deepak, HTT-34 and HTT-38

In March 1976 HAL began work on the **HPT-32 Deepak** as a replacement for the obsolete HT-2. The new design envisaged an all-metal monoplane with a low-set cantilever wing, a high-set tailplane, a large vertical tail surface of modestly swept shape, fixed tricycle landing gear, and a large cockpit able to seat the pupil and instructor side-by-side at the front with provision for an

optional third seat. The design also allowed for later development in the armament training role with light weapons carried on underwing hardpoints. Provision for the third seat was later deleted, and no armed version has yet been developed.

The first of two prototypes flew on 6 January 1977, but the following flight test programme revealed that the HPT-32

was incapable of meeting its specification. Considerable effort had to be expended in refining the type's aerodynamics and lightening its airframe before a third machine flew in July 1981 and secured the type's production future. The Indian air force and navy ordered an initial 88 aircraft, and another 32 machines were delivered from 1993. The eventual total was 142 aircraft.

The **HTT-34** is a turbo-prop-powered development of the HPT-32 and has not entered production, and indeed might not do so as the Indian air force currently lacks a requirement for such a type and the Nigerian air force failed to follow up its initial enthusiasm. The prototype for this model first flew in June 1984 as a conversion

of the third HPT-32 with the 420-shp (313-kW) Allison 250-B17D turboprop engine in a lengthened fuselage and carrying a small tail unit. The lighter but considerably more powerful engine offered a considerable improvement in performance, increasing maximum level speed and service ceiling. Any production model would have retractable landing gear.

A modernised development of the HTT-34 was first announced at the Singapore Air Show of February 1998, but little has since been heard of this **HTT-38**.

Provision for a third seat in the HPT-32 was initially made behind the two front seats, which could have allowed the type to serve in a liaison role.

Halberstadt CL II and CL IV

Developed as a two-seat fighter to escort the earlier and heavier C-category reconnaissance aircraft, the **CL II** appeared in 1917 and soon entered service with the Schutzstaffeln (protection flights) of the Imperial German army's aviation service. The CL II was powered by the Mercedes D.III engine and its single

cockpit had tandem accommodation for the pilot and observer. The latter was provided with an elevated gun ring which allowed him to fire his Parabellum machine-gun both upward and forward over the upper wing. Trays were fitted on each side of the fuselage for the carriage of small anti-personnel grenades or

bombs, giving the type formidable capability in the close-support role. The CL II soon demonstrated its value when, on 6 September 1917, 24 aircraft were successful in an attack on British troops crossing the bridges over the Somme river at Bray and St Christ. The escort units were then redesignated as Schlacht-staffeln (battle flights) for close-support duties and were used extensively during the closing months of 1917.

The CL II was a conventional single-bay biplane with a plywood-covered wooden fuselage and fabric-covered wings with plywood leading edges.

Variants

CL IIa: a small number of aircraft powered by the 185-hp (138-kW) BMW IIIa engine
CL IV: essentially an improved CL II, the CL IV introduced a tail unit with redesigned horizontal and vertical tail surfaces and had a shorter fuselage; it went into service with the Schlachtstaffeln in time for the great German offensive of March 1918

Halberstadt D-category aircraft

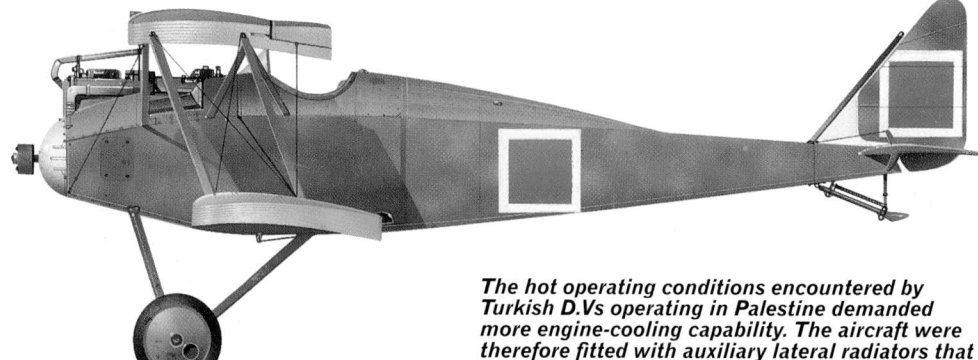

First flown in February 1916, the **D I** was the first single-seat biplane fighter designed by Halberstadt. It was an unequal-span biplane of fabric-covered wooden construction with an unstaggered wing cellule and a powerplant of one 100-hp (75-kW) Mercedes D.I inline engine. The D I handled adequately, but revisions to the airframe and a more powerful engine were felt necessary.

The result of this improvement effort was the **D II** that entered production for a service debut in June 1916. The D II differed from the D I mainly in its powerplant of one Mercedes D.II engine, in having a staggered wing cellule, and in the revision of its central fuselage to raise the pilot's cockpit, which was now faired into the upper line of the low rear fuselage by a convex turtleback.

The fuselage was of plywood- and fabric-covered wooden construction and of rectangular section with a rounded upper decking. The flying surfaces comprised a tail unit with single horizontal and vertical surfaces (balanced elevator halves and a balanced rudder) and an unequal-span biplane wing cellule based on a larger upper wing and a smaller lower wing in a two-bay arrangement; ailerons were installed only on the outboard ends of the upper wing's trailing edge.

Halberstadt built an initial batch of 12 D IIs, and further aircraft were delivered by Automobil und Aviatik and Hannoversche Waggonfabrik as the **Aviatik D I** and **Hannover D I** respectively.

After delivering its initial 12 aircraft, Halberstadt started work on a second batch of 24 aircraft in the course of which it shifted from the D II to the **D III** that was a simple development with revisions such as a powerplant of one 120-hp (90-kW) Argus As.II engine drawing its fuel from an enlarged supply, and ailerons of longer span and increased chord over their outboard ends. In other respects such as dimensions, weights and performance, the D III remained essentially identical to the D II.

Production of the D II and D III by Halberstadt totalled only some 50 aircraft, and although these initially served with the Kampfeinsitzer Kommando (single-seat battle command) units for the escort of two-seater warplanes, from the autumn of 1916 they were used by the first five Jagdstaffeln (fighter squadrons) to be formed. The types reached their numerical peaks in the early part of 1917, when there were apparently about 100 such aircraft, including those built by Aviatik and Hannover, with units on the Western Front. By this time the D II and D III were obsolescent, however, and the two types were soon withdrawn to second-line duties as home-defence fighters as well as advanced flying and fighter trainers.

The **D IV**, which appeared only in the form of three prototypes, was a development of the D II and D III with an armament of two, rather than one, machine-guns, a single-bay wing cellule, and the powerplant of one 150-hp (112-kW) Benz Bz.III engine. Although unsuccessful in its own right, the D IV formed the basis of the very successful CL II.

Reaching the front from the autumn of 1916, the **D V** was a development of the D III with the same engine but changes that included a revised upper wing and the single machine-gun switched from the starboard to the port side of the upper fuselage and, in later aircraft, an improved armament of two machine-guns.

Production of this model was introduced part-way through Halberstadt's construction of the 30 aircraft that represented its third batch of biplane fighters, and the production total was in the order of 50 to 55 aircraft by the end of 1916, and then a further 37 aircraft in the first part of 1917. Most of the aircraft built in 1917 were delivered to Turkey, which used the aircraft mainly in Palestine from March 1917. The D V was phased out of first-line service over the Western Front in the summer of 1918, but remained fully operational in Palestine well into 1918. As the aircraft were retired from first-line service they were gradually allocated to the same type of secondary roles as the D II and D III.

The hot operating conditions encountered by Turkish D.Vs operating in Palestine demanded more engine-cooling capability. The aircraft were therefore fitted with auxiliary lateral radiators that provided adequate cooling but degraded performance to a certain degree.

SPECIFICATION

Halberstadt D II
Type: single-seat fighter
Powerplant: one Mercedes D.II inline piston engine rated at 120 hp (90 kW)
Performance: maximum speed 93 mph (150 km/h) at sea level; climb to 6,560 ft (2000 m) in 8 minutes 30 seconds; range 156 miles (250 km)
Weights: empty 1,147 lb (520 kg); maximum take-off 1,609 lb (730 kg)
Dimensions: wingspan 28 ft 10⅜ in (8.80 m); length 23 ft 11¾ in (7.30 m); height 8 ft 9⅛ in (2.66 m); wing area 254.04 sq ft (23.60 m²)
Armament: one 0.312-in (7.92-mm) LMG 08/15 fixed forward-firing machine-gun in the starboard upper part of the forward fuselage

Hamilton Models H-45 and H-47 Metalplane (C-89)

Designed in 1928 by Professor John Ackerman, the **Hamilton Model H-45 Metalplane** drew on the earlier all-metal aircraft (oval-section fuselage and cantilever shoulder-wing monoplane configuration) designed for what was then the Hamilton Aero Manufacturing Company of Milwaukee, Wisconsin, by James S. McDonnell, who later started his own company. The Metalplane was a pioneering high-wing monoplane of all-metal construction in which the ruling materials were aluminium alloy for the primary structure and longitudinally corrugated Dural for the skinning.

The machine was based on a rectangular-section fuselage with a rounded upper decking and its flying surfaces comprised a tail unit with single horizontal and vertical surfaces, and a wing based on a centre section (braced on each side by two struts) carrying the cantilever outer panels that incorporated long-span ailerons on the outboard ends of their trailing edges. The airframe was completed by the landing gear and powerplant. The landing gear was of the fixed tailskid type with wide-track main units of the divided type, and the powerplant was based on one 400-hp (298-kW) Pratt & Whitney R-1340 Wasp radial engine driving a two-blade Hamilton Standard metal propeller of the adjustable-pitch type.

The Metalplane's enclosed cabin carried up to seven passengers, who entered and exited via a port-side door at the rear of the cabin.

Hamilton Models H-45 & H-47 Metalplane (C-89) (cont.)

The Hamilton Model H-45 Metalplane was certificated in November 1928 and further development led to the **Model H-47** that was certificated in December 1929 with corrugated Alclad rather than Dural skinning, tail-wheel rather than tailskid landing gear, and the uprated powerplant of one Pratt & Whitney R-1690 Hornet radial piston

engine. An improved model, with its wing increased in span, was certificated in April 1929, and by comparison with the Model H-47 in its original small-wing form had a payload reduced from 1,290 lb (585 kg) to 1,166 lb (529 kg) in return for better field and climb performance.

One Model H-45 was sold to a pioneering

Panamanian airline, Transportes Aéreos Gelebert, and later upgraded to the initial Hamilton Model H-47 Metalplane standard, and this machine was impressed by the US Army Air Corps in 1942 for service with the designation **UC-89** before being discarded in August 1943 as unsuitable for continued service.

SPECIFICATION

Hamilton UC-89
Type: one-crew utility transport aircraft
Powerplant: one Pratt & Whitney R-1690-5 Hornet radial piston engine rated at 525 hp (392 kW)
Performance: maximum speed 145 mph (233.5 km/h) at sea level; cruising speed 121 mph (195 km/h) at optimum altitude; initial climb rate 900 ft (274 m) per minute; service ceiling 15,000 ft (4570 m);

range 600 miles (966 km)
Weights: empty 3,450 lb (1565 kg); maximum take-off 5,750 lb (2608 kg)
Dimensions: wingspan 54 ft 5 in (16.59 m); length 34 ft 8 in (10.57 m); height 9 ft 4 in (2.84 m); wing area 387.00 sq ft (35.95 m²)
Payload: up to seven passengers or 1,290 lb (585 kg) of freight carried in the cabin

Handley Page H.P.11 & H.P.12 (Types O/100 & O/400)

To meet an Admiralty specification of December 1914 for a large twin-engined bomber, Handley Page lost little time in designing a suitable aircraft. Originally designated as the **Type O**, it was later re-identified as the **Type O/100**, the suffixed numeral indicating the machine's wingspan in feet: the retrospective designation applied in the company's 1924 system of nomenclature was **H.P.11**. Clearly this machine was very much bigger than anything else that had been built by the Handley Page company: in fact, when the prototype was completed, it was the largest aircraft yet built in the UK.

The Type O/100 was of biplane configuration, with an unequal-span wing cellule of the three-bay type with outer wing panels (including overhanging outboard section braced by kingposts and wires) that folded to the rear to facilitate hangarage of the type. The constant-chord wings had straight leading and trailing edges, the latter including large horn-balanced ailerons only on the upper wing, and were mounted on a square-section fuselage of wire-braced wooden construction that terminated in a tail unit with two horizontal and three vertical surfaces. The fixed tailskid landing gear had twin wheels on each main unit, which were located under the lower wing in line with the armoured nacelles for the powerplant of 266-hp

(198-kW) Rolls-Royce Eagle II engines. These latter were mounted between the wings on the innermost sets of interplane struts just outboard of the fuselage. The accommodation in the first prototype was in a glazed cockpit enclosure, the floor and sides of which were protected by armour plate. Flown for the first time on 17 December 1916, the Type O/100 was found to be inadequate in performance, and the second prototype had a revised open cockpit for a crew of two (with provision for a gunner's position forward), the cockpit armour plating and most of that incorporated in the engine nacelles was deleted, and new radiators were introduced for the water-cooled engines. When the machine was first tested in April 1916 there was a marked improvement in

Although Standard Aircraft of Elizabeth, New Jersey was under contract to supply components for UK O/400 production, the company actually built seven airframes, powered by Liberty engines, in America. This machine was involved in bombing trials with 2,000-lb (907-kg) armour-piercing bombs during 1919.

Below: The O/400 was a large and impressive bomber, its weapon load generally comprising one 1,650-lb (748-kg), or three 550- or 520-lb (249- or 236-kg), or eight 250-lb (113-kg), or 16 112-lb (51-kg) bombs carried internally, and two bombs carried externally.

performance, to an extent that in early May it was flown with 20 Handley Page employees aboard to a height of just over 7,000 ft (2135 m).

Formation of the first 'Handley Page Squadron', as it was then known, began in August 1916, and this unit became operational in France late in October or early in November; its first recorded bombing attack being made on the night of 16-17 March 1917 against a German-held railway junction. In addition to its use as a night bomber on the Western Front, the Type O/100 also equipped the first bomber squadron of the RAF's Independent Force following its establishment on 5 June 1918.

Production deliveries of the **Type O/400** (retrospective designation **H.P.12**) began early in 1918, this being an improved version of the Type O/100 with more powerful Eagle engines (the numerical suffix in the designation

now referring once more to installed horsepower), revisions to the fuel system and radiators, and a compressed air engine-starting system. Although production of the O/100 totalled only 46 aircraft, substantial numbers of the O/400 became operational and, for example, on the night of 14-15 September 1918 a force of 40 O/400s attacked targets in the Saar. It was also at about this time that these aircraft began to deploy 1,650-lb (748-kg) bombs, the heaviest used by British services during World War I.

More than 400 Type O/400s were delivered for service with the RAF before the Armistice of November 1918, these equipping Nos 58, 97, 115, 207, 214, 215 and 216 Squadrons. The type remained in service in reduced numbers until a time late in 1919, when it was replaced by the Vickers Vimy. Eight of the aircraft were used by

No. 86 (Communications) Wing, formed at Hendon in December 1918 to provide government and military VIP transport between London and Paris, and No. 214 Squadron used the type for military air mail services. Plans had been laid for an initial total of 1,500 Type O/400 to be manufactured in the USA, but only 107 of these Liberty-engined aircraft had been completed by the Standard Aircraft Corporation before the Armistice led to the cancellation of outstanding contracts. After World War I a small number of British-built aircraft was supplied to China under the designation **Type O/7**, and three or four of these aircraft were used in India by Handley Page Indo-Burmese Transport Ltd. In addition, about 10 Type O/400s were converted to a civil configuration and used by Handley Page Transport Ltd. in the UK with the designations **Type O/10** and **Type O/11**.

SPECIFICATION

Handley Page Type O/400
Type: four/five-seat heavy bomber
Powerplant: two Rolls-Royce Eagle VIII Vee piston engines each rated at 360 hp (268 kW)
Performance: maximum speed 97 mph (156 km/h) at sea level; climb to 6,500 ft (1980 m) in 27 minutes 10 seconds; service ceiling 8,500 ft (2590 m); endurance 8 hours
Weights: empty 8,200 lb (3719 kg); maximum take-off 14,000 lb (6350 kg)
Dimensions: wingspan 100 ft (30.48 m); length 62 ft 10¼ in

(30.48 m); height 22 ft (6.71 m); wing area 1,648.00 sq ft (153.10 m²)
Armament: one or two 0.303-in (7.7-mm) Lewis trainable forward-firing machine-guns in the nose position, one or two Lewis trainable rearward-firing machine-guns in the dorsal position and one Lewis trainable rearward-firing machine-gun in the ventral trapdoor position, plus up to 2,000 lb (907 kg) of disposable stores carried in a lower-fuselage weapons bay and on two underfuselage hardpoints

Handley Page H.P.15 (Type V/1500)

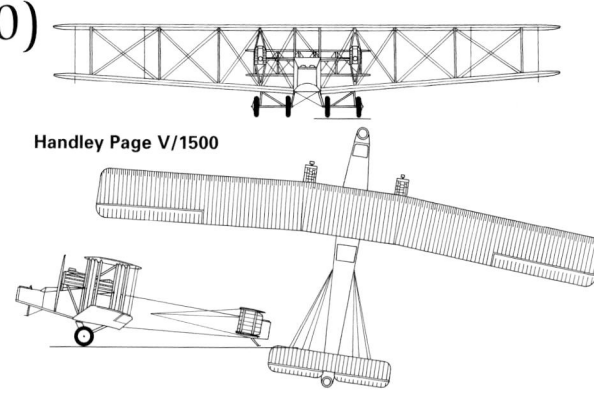

Handley Page V/1500

The Type O series was followed by a number of unrealised projects including the **Type P/320 (H.P.13)** triplane of 1916 with one Sunbeam Cossack engine, the **Type S/400** seaplane of 1917 with two Rolls-Royce Eagle VIII engines, and the **Type T/400** flying boat of 1917 also with two Eagle VIII engines.

Thus the next of the company's aircraft to reach hardware form was the **Type V/1500** (retrospective designation **H.P.15**) created to provide the RAF with the capability for mounting attacks on targets in Germany from bases in the UK. As such, the V/1500 must be regarded as the first practical strategic bomber. Larger in size than

the O/100 and O/400, the V/1500 was powered by four Rolls-Royce engines mounted in tandem push/pull pairs between the wings, outboard of the fuselage, but was in other respects similar in overall configuration to the earlier bombers. The initial contract was placed with Harland & Wolff of Belfast, but orders eventually totalled more than 200, of which the majority were cancelled at the end of World War I.

The prototype, assembled by Handley Page from components manufactured by Harland & Wolff, flew for the first time during May 1918. This machine differed from production aircraft primarily in having a

single large cooling radiator to serve all four engines, the standard installation becoming one hexagonal radiator forward of each pair of engines. This larger aircraft provided accommodation for a crew of between five and seven.

When the armistice was signed only three Type V/1500s were ready for operational use, these standing by with No. 166 Sqn at Bircham Newton, Norfolk, where they had been frustrated by bad weather from attacking targets in Germany. Another 57 aircraft were completed after the war's end, but the type saw only limited service with the RAF, gradually being replaced by the Vickers Vimy. One was used to record the first through flight from England to India: taking off on 13 December

1918, the aircraft flew via Rome, Malta, Cairo, and Baghdad to Karachi, which it reached on 30 December. This machine was used in May 1919 to make a bomb attack on Kabul during the problems in Afghanistan.

Another V/1500 was shipped to Newfoundland with the object of making a first west/east flight over the North Atlantic, but this project was abandoned after Alcock and Brown had achieved the feat in a Vimy.

Groundcrew and the length of the ladder required for routine engine inspections serve to emphasise the huge size of the V/1500.

SPECIFICATION

Handley Page Type V/1500
Type: seven-seat long-range heavy bomber
Powerplant: four Rolls-Royce Eagle VIII Vee piston engines each rated at 375 hp (280 kW)
Performance: maximum speed 99 mph (159 km/h) at 6,500 ft (1980 m); cruising speed 80 mph (129 km/h) at optimum altitude; climb to 6,500 ft (1980 m) in 21 minutes 5 seconds; service ceiling 11,000 ft (3355 m); range 1,300 miles (2092 km)
Weights: empty 17,600 lb (7983 kg); maximum take-off 30,000 lb (13608 kg)
Dimensions: wingspan 126 ft (38.40 m); length 64 ft (19.51 m); height 23 ft (7.01 m); wing area

3,000.00 sq ft (278.70 m²)
Armament: one or two 0.303-in (7.7-mm) Lewis trainable forward-firing machine-guns in the nose position, one or two Lewis trainable rearward-firing machine-guns in the dorsal position, two Lewis trainable rearward-firing machine-guns in the ventral position and one or two Lewis trainable rearward-firing machine-guns in the tail position, plus up to 7,500 lb (3402 kg) of disposable stores carried in a lower-fuselage weapons bay or two underfuselage hardpoints, and generally comprising one or two 3,300-lb (1497-kg) bombs carried externally, or 30 250- or 230-lb (113- or 104-kg) bombs carried internally

Handley Page H.P.18, H.P.26, H.P.27 & H.P.30 (Type W.8, Type W.9 and Type W.10)

The internal bracing of the fuselage of the O/400 made this military aircraft unsuitable for long-term use as a civil transport, and this persuaded Handley Page to undertake the redesign of the type to create an aircraft identified originally as the **Type W/400** (retrospective designation **H.P.16**). This combined a fuselage of different construction allowing for the installation of up to eight pairs of

forward-facing seats with a central gangway. Other features of the design were a cut-down version of the Type V/1500's biplane wing cellule, Type V/1500 landing gear and the powerplant of two Rolls-Royce Eagle VIII engines. The Type W/400 flew for the first time on 22 August 1919, and though flight trials confirmed that the basic design was sound, it was nonetheless decided to incorporate refinements

and more powerful engines in the production version, leading to the **Type W.8** prototype (retrospective designation **H.P.18**). Powered by two 450-hp (336-kW) Napier Lion IB W-type engines, the Type W.8 had a further reduction in wingspan from 85 ft (25.91 m) to 75 ft (22.86 m) and some revision of the tail unit, and flew for the first time on 2 December 1919. On 4 May 1920 the machine lifted a 3,690-lb

(1674-kg) payload to a height of 14,030 ft (4276 m), which then qualified as a British record.

The Type W.8 was followed by four examples of the **W.8b** production version, which had accommodation for a theoretical maximum of 16 passengers in a well-glazed cabin with carpets and curtains, the pilot and co-pilot being seated in an open cockpit in the nose. Because of difficulty in the supply of

Lion engines, these aircraft reverted to the Eagle VIII powerplant, the lower-powered engines accounting for certification to carry only 12 passengers. Three of the aircraft were used by Handley Page Transport and one was supplied to the Belgian airline Sabena. Three more Type W.8b transports were later produced under licence for Sabena by SABCA in Belgium.

In the W.8 prototype, Handley Page incorporated key features from the O/400 and the V/1500. The aircraft is illustrated with its original empennage.

SPECIFICATION

Handley Page Type W.9a Hampstead
Type: two-crew transport aircraft
Powerplant: three Armstrong Siddeley Jaguar IV radial piston engines each rated at 385 hp (287 kW) later replaced by three Bristol Jupiter VI radial piston engines each rated at 450 hp (336 kW)
Performance: maximum speed 114 mph (183 km/h) at optimum

altitude; service ceiling 13,500 ft (4115 m); range 400 miles (644 km)
Weights: empty 8,364 lb (3794 kg); maximum take-off 14,500 lb (6577 kg)
Dimensions: wingspan 79 ft (24.08 m); length 60 ft 4 in (18.39 m); wing area 1,564.00 sq ft (145.30 m²)
Payload: up to 16 passengers carried in an enclosed cabin

Handley Page H.P.18, H.P.26, H.P.27 & H.P.30 (Type W.8, Type W.9 and Type W.10) (continued)

The **Type W.8c** was a 1923 version of the W.8 with Eagle IX engines.

Subsequent versions of the same basic design included the **Type W.8e** (retrospective designation **H.P.26**) which introduced a third engine mounted in the nose of the fuselage, the three-engined powerplant then comprising one 360-hp (268-kW) Eagle IX Vee and two 230-hp (172-kW) Siddeley Puma inline engines. One example was built for Sabena by Handley Page and eight more were licence-built for

that airline by SABCA. A similarly powered **Type W.8f Hamilton** was completed for service with Imperial Airways, this version also having a modified fin, and two more Type W.8f transports were later built by SABCA for service with Sabena. The **Type W.8g** was a Hamilton rebuilt in 1929 with two Rolls-Royce F.XIIA engines.

Other variants of this basic design included one **Type W.9a Hampstead (H.P.27)** for Imperial Airways with the power-plant of three Armstrong

Siddeley Jaguar radial engines that were later replaced by three higher-rated Bristol Jupiter radial engines, and this variant had accommodation for 14 passengers. The final civil version was the **Type W.10 (H.P.30)**, of which four examples were built in 1926 by Handley Page for Imperial Airways, and the last of these was not retired from service until 1933. The Type W.10 reverted to twin-engined powerplant, comprising two 450-hp (336-kW) Lion IIB engines.

The Heyford's wings had a metal structure with fabric covering, a metal fuselage covered with light alloy and fabric, accommodation for a crew of four and robust fixed tailwheel landing gear.

Handley Page H.P.24 Hyderabad, H.P.33/H.P.36 Hinaidi, and H.P.35 Clive

To meet the requirements of the Air Ministry's Specification 31/22, Handley Page developed from its Type W.8 airliner, a twin-engined heavy night bomber which entered service with the Royal Air Force as the **Hyderabad**. The prototype, initially identified as the **Type W.8d** but later as the **H.P.24**, first flew during October 1923 with the powerplant of two 450-hp (336-kW) Napier Lion IIB W-type piston engines. Service trials proved the new bomber to be superior in performance to the competing Vickers Virginia Mk III, and production for the RAF eventually totalled some 45 aircraft. The type entered service with No. 99 Squadron in December 1925, remaining in first-line service until 1930, and then continued in use with the Auxiliary Air Force until the end of 1933.

An improved version of the Hyderabad was developed to meet the

J9126, the Clive Mk I prototype later reverted to airliner status, with a W.10 interior. It was used extensively by Sir Alan Cobham.

requirement of the Air Ministry's Specification 13/29. Known as the **Hinaidi Mk I**, this **H.P.33** differed primarily by having the powerplant of two 440-hp (328-kW) Bristol Jupiter VIII radial piston engines. The initial prototype was a Hyderabad conversion, but this was followed by two additional prototypes built as new by Handley Page, the second of these incorporating a W.10 fuselage, allowing the type to be evaluated as a troop transport. There followed six

examples of the Hinaidi Mk I production model, the last three of these being completed with an all-metal basic fuselage structure, and this led to the construction of one **H.P.36** prototype and 33 production examples of the **Hinaidi Mk II** with the same all-metal basic structure. In addition to the new-build aircraft, seven of the RAF's Hyderabads were converted to Hinaidi Mk I configuration. Like the Hyderabad before it, the Hinaidi entered service with No. 99 Squadron,

remaining in first-line use until replaced by the Heyford from November 1933.

The second Hinaidi Mk I prototype, which was of all-wood construction and incorporated the W.10 fuselage, was later redesignated as the **Clive Mk I**. This **H.P.35** provided accommodation for 23 troops and was followed into service by two examples of the **Clive Mk II** transport, which had all-metal basic structure but were otherwise similar to the prototype. The Clive

Mk II was based at Lahore in India, serving for a number of years with the RAF Heavy Transport Flight. The Clive Mk I was later converted to Type W.10 standard to meet an Air Council requirement, in the process receiving the revised designation **Clive Mk III**, but when this was not ordered into production the prototype was sold to Sir Alan Cobham, who used it in his National Aviation Day Displays for joy-riding and for pioneering inflight-refuelling experiments.

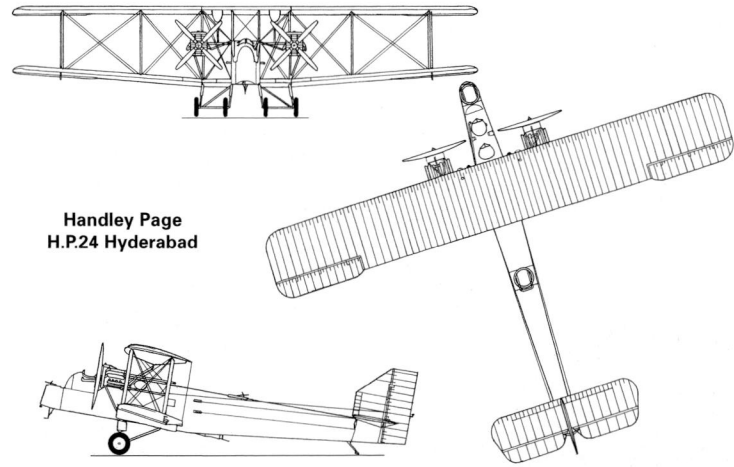

Handley Page H.P.24 Hyderabad

SPECIFICATION

Handley Page Hinaidi Mk II
Type: four-crew heavy night bomber
Powerplant: two Bristol Jupiter VIII radial piston engines each rated at 440 hp (328 kW)
Performance: maximum speed 122 mph (196 km/h) at sea level; cruising speed 75 mph (121 km/h) at optimum altitude; initial climb rate 380 ft (116 m) per minute; climb to 6,560 ft (2000 m) in 11 minutes 48 seconds; service ceiling 14,500 ft (4420 m); range 850 miles (1368 km)
Weights: empty 8,040 lb (3647 kg); maximum take-off 14,500 lb (6577 kg)
Dimensions: wingspan 75 ft (22.86 m); length 59 ft 2 in (18.03 m); height 17 ft (5.18 m); wing area 1,471.00 sq ft

(136.66 m²)
Armament: one 0.303-in (7.7-mm) Lewis trainable forward-firing machine-gun in the nose position, one 0.303-in (7.7-mm) Lewis trainable rearward-firing machine-gun in the dorsal position, and one 0.303-in (7.7-mm) Lewis trainable rearward-firing machine-gun in the ventral position, plus up to 1,450 lb (658 kg) of disposable stores carried on four underfuselage and six underwing hardpoints, and generally comprising four 250-lb (113-kg) and four 112-lb (51-kg) bombs or eight 112-lb (51-kg) bombs carried under the fuselage, or alternatively two 550- or 520-lb (249- or 236-kg) bombs, or four 250- or 230-lb (113- or 104-kg) bombs, or six 112-lb (51-kg) bombs carried under the wing

Handley Page H.P.38 and H.P.50 Heyford

In hindsight, the **H.P.50 Heyford** was a heavy-looking biplane, with spatted main landing gear units suggesting low speed and overall inefficiency. This impression was heightened by the fact that the fuselage was attached to the upper wing, strut bracing filling the large gap between the fuselage and the lower wing. The purpose of this layout was to allow a lower-wing centre section of almost double the normal aerofoil thickness in which bombs to be stowed. The bombs were also carried close to the ground, so that re-arming could be easily accomplished. The armament had one more unusual feature to add to the appearance of the Heyford, for one of the

bomber's three defensive machine-guns was mounted in a ventral 'dustbin' turret that could be lowered beneath the fuselage to the rear of the wing trailing edge.

The H.P.38 prototype recorded its maiden flight on 12 June 1930, and successful service testing resulted in the type being ordered for service, initially as the **Heyford Mk I**. A total of 124 had been supplied to the RAF by the time that production ended in July 1936, these comprising 15 Heyford Mk I, 23 **Heyford Mk IA**, 16 **Heyford Mk II** and 70 **Heyford Mk III** aircraft. These differed primarily in their powerplants, the Mk I models having the Kestrel III engine and the Mk II and Mk III models the 640-hp

(477-kW) Kestrel VI, but other changes were four-rather than two-bladed propellers and engine-rather than slipstream-driven electrical generators in the Mk IA, and wing-mounted steam condensers and improved engine mountings in the Mk III. Entering service with No. 99 Sqn at Upper Heyford, Oxfordshire, in November 1933, the Heyford later served with Nos 7, 9, 10, 38, 78, 97, 102, 148, 149 and 166 Sqns until the last of the aircraft were displaced by Vickers Wellington mono-plane bombers in 1939. However, the Heyford continued in use for some time, especially in training units, until finally declared obsolete in July 1941 as the last biplane bomber to serve with the RAF.

The Heyford's wings had a metal structure with fabric covering, a metal fuselage covered with light alloy and fabric, accommodation for a crew of four and robust fixed tailwheel landing gear.

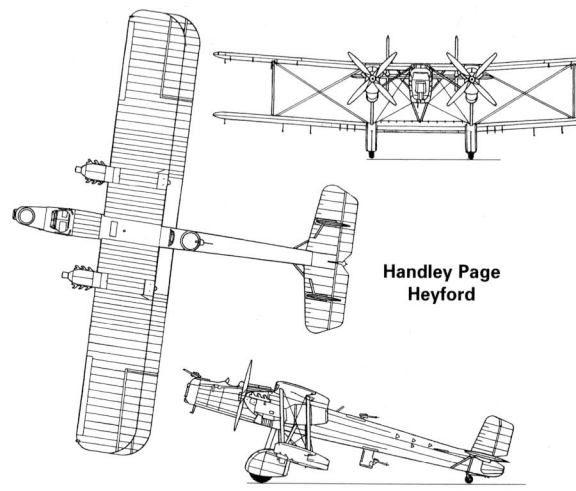

Handley Page Heyford

SPECIFICATION

Handley Page Heyford Mk IA
Type: four-seat heavy night bomber
Powerplant: two Rolls-Royce Kestrel IIIS or IIIS-5 Vee piston engines each rated at 575 hp (429 kW)
Performance: maximum speed 142 mph (229 km/h) at 13,000 ft (3960 m); cruising speed 115 mph (185 km/h) at 10,000 ft (3050 m); climb to 10,000 ft (3050 m) in 15 minutes 18 seconds; service ceiling 21,000 ft; range 400 miles (644 km) with a 3,143-lb (1426-kg) bomb load
Weights: empty 9,200 lb (4173 kg), maximum take-off

16,900 lb (7666 kg)
Dimensions: wingspan 75 ft (22.86 m); length 58 ft (17.68 m); height 17 ft 6 in (5.33 m); wing area 1.470.00 sq ft (136.56 m²)
Armament: one 0.303-in (7.7-mm) Lewis trainable forward-firing machine-gun in the nose position, one 0.303-in (7.7-mm) Lewis trainable rearward-firing machine-gun in the dorsal position and one 0.303-in (7.7-mm) Lewis trainable rearward-firing machine-gun in the retractable ventral 'dustbin' turret, plus up to 3,500 lb (1588 kg) of disposable stores carried in a lower-wing weapons bay and on eight underwing hardpoints

Handley Page H.P.52 Hampden

In September 1932 the Air Ministry issued its Specification B.9/32 for a twin-engined bomber, and this requirement elicited responses from Handley Page and Vickers. Each company was awarded a contract and the resulting prototypes, the **H.P.52** and the Vickers Type 271, flew within a week of one

another, the former on 21 June 1936 with the powerplant of two Bristol Pegasus PE.5-SM (Pegasus XVIII) radial engines. Considering that they shared the same specification, the two types could hardly have been more different, Handley Page going for an extremely slim fuselage with three manu-

ally operated gun positions, Vickers adopting a portly fuselage with power-operated turrets and manual beam guns.

In spite of an antiquated appearance the **Hampden**, as the Handley Page bomber was subsequently named, had several remark-able characteristics. With the use of Handley Page leading-edge slats it was able to land at only 73 mph (117 km/h), while its maxi-mum speed of 254 mph (309 km/h) was higher than that of either the Wellington, as the Type 271 was later named, or the

Armstrong Whitworth Whitley, and it could carry 4,000 lb (1914 kg) of bombs over a distance of 1,200 miles (1931 km) by comparison with the Wellington's figure of 4,500 lb (2041 kg) over the same distance.

Following an order for 180 **Hampden Mk I** bombers placed on 15 August 1936, to a new Specification B.30/36, the production prototype flew in 1937. Simultaneously with the first contract, another was placed for 100 **H.P.53 Hereford** aircraft with the altogether different power-plant of two Napier Dagger VIII H-type engines. In May 1938, the first production

Hampden Mk I from the Handley Page line flew at Radlett, Hertfordshire, and on 24 June the type was christened officially by the Viscountess Hampden. The expansion and re-equipment of the Royal Air Force were then in full swing, and on 6 August 1938 other orders were placed: English Electric at Preston, Lancashire, was contracted to build 75, and in Canada a British mission negotiated for 80 more to be constructed by a consor-tium named Canadian Associated Aircraft Ltd. These subcontracted Hampden bombers began to come off the production lines during 1940.

Following trials at the Aircraft & Armament Experimental Establishment, Martlesham Heath, and at the Central Flying School at Upavon, deliveries to the RAF began in September 1938, with the first batch of Hampden bombers going to No. 49 Squadron at Scampton, Lincolnshire. No. 49 Squadron was part of No. 5 Group, which was eventu-ally equipped completely with Handley Page Hampden bombers.

Variant

Hampden Mk II: two aircraft experimentally engined with 1,100-hp (821-kW) Wright R-1820 Cyclone radial engines under the company designation **H.P.62**

This former No. 455 Sqn RAAF Hampden TB.Mk I is illustrated as it appeared when on the strength of the Soviet Union's Northern Fleet Air Force, based at Vaenga, Murmansk in October 1942.

Handley Page H.P.52 Hampden (continued)

When World War II broke out, 10 RAF squadrons were using the type: Nos 7 and 76 at Finningley, Nos 44 and 50 at Waddington, Nos 49 and 83 at Scampton, Nos 61 and 144 at Hemswell and, in reserve, Nos 106 and 185.

Early operations in the daylight reconnaissance role were uneventful, but on 29 September, the Hampden's shortcomings were highlighted vividly when five out of 11 aircraft in two formations were destroyed by German fighters when within sight of the German coast. Not long after this it was decided to operate in future under cover of darkness, and

some leaflet-dropping missions were carried out. By the winter of 1939-40 the Hampden had found its most useful role as a minelayer. Aircraft from five squadrons sowed mines in German waters on the night of 13-14 April 1940, just after the German invasion of Norway, and by the end of the year No. 5 Group's Hampden squadrons had flown 1,209 minelaying sorties.

The Norwegian campaign, however, once again confirmed the Hampden's 'Achilles' heel': because of its inadequate defensive armament, it suffered heavily at the hands of German fighters

when used as a day bomber.

On the night of 25-26 August 1940, Hampdens and Whitleys took part in the RAF's first raid on Berlin, and the Hampden continued to support the night bombing offensive until late 1942 when, on the night of 15-16 September aircraft of the Royal Canadian Air Force's No. 408 Squadron attacked Wilhelmshaven in the Hampden's final sorties with Bomber Command.

From April 1942 the Hampden had gradually been transferred from Bomber Command to Coastal Command, entering service with the latter as a torpedo bomber in the form of the **Hampden TB.Mk I** created by adaptation of the Hampden Mk I. The first two units in this role were Nos 144 and 455 Sqns, the latter a Royal Australian Air Force unit, and detachments from both squadrons went to the northern USSR for convoy protection operations. Thirty-two Hampdens of these two squadrons left Sumburgh in the Shetlands on 4 September 1942, but nine were lost in the crossing, including two which crashed in Norway and one which crashed on landing in the USSR. The squadrons subsequently handed over their aircraft to the Soviets before leaving for the UK on 23 October. No. 455

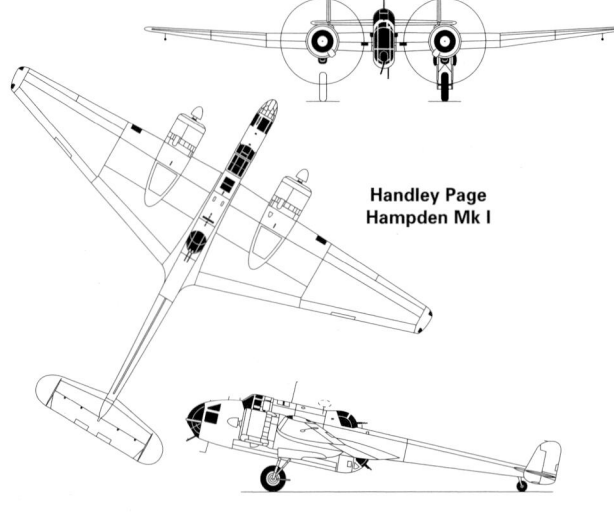

Handley Page Hampden Mk I

was also the last operational Hampden unit, based at Sumburgh and sinking a U-boat on 4 April 1943 before re-equipping with the Bristol Beaufighter at the end of the year.

Thus the Hampden passed out of service. In spite of inadequacies the type did have its good points: among them were pleasant handling characteristics and an excellent view

for the pilot. On the debit side accommodation was very cramped, individual crew members being able to change places only with extreme difficulty, which posed great problems in the case of injuries. In all, 1,432 examples of the Hampden bomber were built, 502 of them by Handley Page, 770 by English Electric and 160 in Canada.

SPECIFICATION

Handley Page Hampden Mk I
Type: four-seat medium bomber
Powerplant: two Bristol Pegasus XVIII radial piston engines each rated at 1,000 hp (746 kW)
Performance: maximum speed 254 mph (409 km/h) at 13,800 ft (4205 m); cruising speed 167 mph (269 km/h) at optimum altitude; initial climb rate 980 ft (299 m) per minute; climb to 15,000 ft (4570 m) in 18 minutes 54 seconds; service ceiling 19,000 ft (5790 m); range 1,885 miles (3034 km) with a 2,000-lb (907-kg) bomb load
Weights: empty 11,780 lb (5343 kg); maximum take-off 18,756 lb (8508 kg)
Dimensions: wingspan 69 ft 2 in (21.08 m); length 53 ft 7 in (16.33 m); height 14 ft 11 in (4.55 m); wing area 668.0 sq ft (62.06 m²)

Armament: one 0.303-in (7.7-mm) Vickers or Browning fixed forward-firing machine-gun in the port side of the upper forward fuselage, one 0.303-in (7.7-mm) Vickers 'K' trainable forward-firing machine-gun in the nose position, one or two 0.303-in (7.7-mm) Vickers 'K' trainable rearward-firing machine-guns in the dorsal position and one or two 0.303-in (7.7-mm) Vickers 'K' trainable rearward-firing machine-guns in the ventral position, plus up to 4,000 lb (1814 kg) of disposable stores carried in a lower-fuselage weapons bay and on two underwing hardpoints, and generally comprising two 2,000-lb (907-kg) bombs, or four or six 500-lb (227-kg) bombs, or mines, or one 18-in (457-mm) Mk XII torpedo

Variant

Hampden Mk II: designation of two aircraft experimentally engined with two 1,100-hp (821-kW) Wright R-1820 Cyclone radials under the company designation **H.P.62**

Handley Page H.P.42 and H.P.45

Early in 1928, Imperial Airways issued specifications for the aircraft it required to inaugurate new routes linking various parts of the British empire, and Handley Page was delighted to receive contracts for four **H.P. 42E (Eastern)** and four **H.P.42W (Western)** airliners to be operated on Imperial Airways' long-range routes and European services respectively. It was some years before it was discovered that the real Handley Page designation for the H.P.42W was **H.P. 45**.

Large unequal-span biplanes of all-metal construction, except for fabric covering of the aerofoil surfaces and the rear fuselage, these aircraft had a wing cellule braced by massive Warren girder struts, a biplane tail unit incorporating three fin-and-rudder assemblies, substantial tailwheel landing gear with wide-track divided main units, and the powerplant of four Bristol Jupiter radial

engines. These comprised four 490-hp (365-kW) Jupiter XIF units for the H.P.42E and four Jupiter XFBM supercharged units for the H.P.42W, in each

case mounted two on the upper wing and one to each side of the fuselage on the lower wing. New ground was broken by the flight crew being accom-

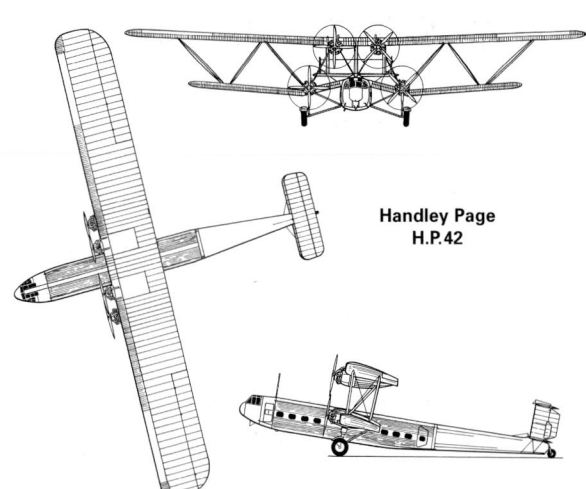

Handley Page H.P.42

SPECIFICATION

Handley Page H.P.42W (H.P.45)
Type: three-crew transport aircraft
Powerplant: four Bristol Jupiter XFBM radial piston engines each rated at 555 hp (414 kW)
Performance: maximum speed 127 mph (204 km/h) at optimum altitude; cruising speed 95 to 105 mph (153 to 169 km/h) at optimum altitude; initial climb rate 670 ft (204 m) per minute; service

ceiling not available; range 500 miles (805 km)
Weights: empty 17,740 lb (8047 kg); maximum take-off 28,000 lb (12701 kg)
Dimensions: wingspan 130 ft (39.62 m); length 92 ft 2 in (28.09 m); height 27 ft (8.23 m); wing area 2,989.00 sq ft (277.68 m²)
Payload: see above

G-AAXE Hengist, was originally allocated the name Hesperides by Imperial Airways, but the airline soon had second thoughts when it was realised the work involved in writing out this name hundreds of times during day-to-day administration.

modated in an enclosed flight deck, high in the fuselage nose. Passenger accommodation was in two cabins, forward and aft of the wing, but varied according to intended use. The H.P.42E, for use on the Indian and South African routes, each seated six (later 12)

forward and 12 aft; the H.P.42W for European routes each had seats for 18 forward and 20 aft, but reduced baggage capacity.

Although a number of short hops had been made during the taxiing trials, the first true flight was recorded on 14 November 1930 by an H.P.42E, which

was later named *Hannibal*. The first machine for European routes, named *Heracles*, was delivered in September 1931, and the names of the remainder of the family were *Horsa*, *Hanno* and *Hadrian* for the H.P.42E aircraft, and *Horatius*, *Hengist* and *Helena* for the H.P.42Ws.

In service, the two half-brother types gained an enviable reputation for comfort and safety, although no one could deny the fact that the aircraft were decidedly slow: Anthony Fokker described them as having built-in headwinds. Even so, they an unmistakable

aura of grace and safety. The latter characteristic was supreme, for when these classic airliners were finally withdrawn from service on 1 September 1939 they had recorded almost a decade of service without suffering a single fatal accident.

Handley Page H.P.54 Harrow

Specification B.3/34 ushered in the era of the monoplane bomber for the Royal Air Force by asking, as it did, for modern twin-engined designs to replace the Heyford and the Vickers Virginia.

The **H.P.54** was less original in concept than Armstrong Whitworth's Whitley, featuring a high wing and fixed landing gear. It was intended initially as an interim bomber trainer and later, when the more advanced bombers were in quantity production, as a transport aircraft. A hundred were ordered as the **Harrow** before the prototype first flew on 10 October 1936.

The first 39 Harrows built were **Mk I** aircraft with 850-hp (634-kW) Bristol Pegasus X engines, but the following 61 aircraft were **Mk II** machines with Pegasus XX engines, giving an extra 10 mph (16 km/h).

No. 214 Sqn at Feltwell was the first unit to receive Harrows in January 1937, and by the end of that year four other squadrons had re-equipped with the new

bomber. Harrow production terminated after 100 examples had been built in late 1937, but aircraft remained in service until the final stages of World War II.

A novel use of the Harrow was as an aerial minelayer when, in October 1940, No. 420 Flight was formed to carry out experiments under the codename Pandora. These aircraft carried Long Aerial Mines (LAMs), which consisted of many small explosive charges suspended from parachutes with a 2,000-ft (610-m) length of piano wire trailing below. They were to be launched in the path of a bomber stream, and, on contact, the

charges were released, sliding down the wires to explode on contacting the enemy bomber. Three months of trial proved the idea to be impractical, although four or five kills were achieved.

No. 271 Sqn was formed in March 1940 to operate in the transport role. Equipped with a number of types, including Harrows, the squadron flew many different transport missions and research flights including air sickness tests with airborne troops. In February 1944, the Harrows supported the Allied forces in northwest Europe. A month later the Harrows were formed into the

K6994 served initially with No. 420 Flight, carrying out experiments with LAMs as part of Operation Mutton. When No. 420 Flt renumbered as 93 Sqn in December 1940, this Harrow Mk II passed to the new squadron.

SPECIFICATION	
Handley Page H.P.54 Harrow Mk II	range 1,250 miles (2012 km)
Type: four- or five-seat bomber/ 20-seat transport	**Weights:** empty 13,600 lb (6169 kg); maximum take-off 23,000 lb (10433 kg)
Powerplant: two 925-hp (690-kW) Bristol Pegasus XX radial piston engines	**Dimensions:** wingspan 88 ft 5 in (26.95 m); length 82 ft 2 in (25.04 m); height 19 ft 5 in (5.92 m); wing area 1,090 sq ft (101.26 m²)
Performance: maximum speed 200 mph (322 km/h) at 10,000 ft (3048 m); cruising speed 163 mph (262 km/h) at 15,000 ft (4572 m); service ceiling 22,800 ft (6949 m);	**Armament:** four 0.303-in (7.7-mm) machine-guns plus up to 3,000 lb (1361 kg) of bombs

Harrow Ambulance Flight and two of the aircraft evacuated wounded from the Arnhem operation in September 1944.

Seven of the flight's Harrows were lost in the 1945 New Year's Day

attack by the Luftwaffe on 2nd Tactical Air Force bases in Europe. This was essentially the end of the Harrow's war, and the flight re-equipped with US-supplied Douglas Dakotas in May 1945.

Handley Page H.P.57, H.P.59, H.P.61, H.P.63, H.P.70 and H.P.71 Halifax and Halton

Second of the four-engined heavy bombers to enter service with the RAF in World War II, an event that took place in November 1940, the **H.P.57 Halifax** was one of the famous triad comprised of the Halifax, Avro Lancaster and Short Stirling which bore the brunt of Bomber Command's night-bombing offensive against Germany. Although it entered service more than a year ahead of the Lancaster, the Halifax was always somewhat over-shadowed in the bombing role by the achievement of the superb Lancaster. The Halifax, however, scored over the Lancaster in its multi-role capability, for in addition to its deployment as a heavy night bomber, it was equally at home in the air ambulance, freighter, glider tug, personnel transport and

maritime reconnaissance roles.

The origins of the Halifax can be found in the Air Ministry's Specification B.1/35 for a twin-engined bomber, to which Handley Page submitted its **H.P.55** design. This specification was unsuccessful, but about a year later the Air Ministry issued its new Specification, B.13/36 calling for a medium/heavy bomber to be powered by the new Vulture 24-cylinder engine which Rolls-Royce then had under development. The **H.P.56** proposal was selected for prototype construction, but the company had doubts that the Vulture engine would emerge as a reliable production unit, and therefore set about the task of redesigning the H.P.56 to take the revised power-plant of four Rolls-Royce Merlin engines. The over-

all configuration was not greatly changed, but the **H.P.57** design which was then submitted to the Air Ministry for approval was for a considerably larger and heavier machine.

On 3 September 1937, Handley Page was awarded a contract for the manufacture of two H.P.57 prototypes, with construction beginning early in 1938. When the first of these machines was nearing completion, it was realised that the company's airfield at Radlett, Hertfordshire, was too restricted for the first flight of so large an aircraft, and it was decided instead to use the nearest non-operational RAF airfield, which was at Bicester in Oxfordshire. Thus, final assembly was carried out at Bicester and it was from there that the first flight was made on 25 October 1939.

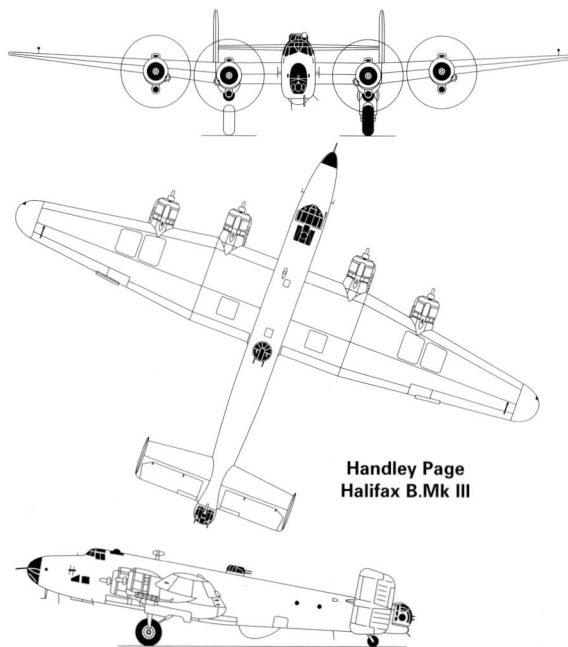

Handley Page Halifax B.Mk III

Handley Page H.P.57, H.P.59, H.P.61, H.P.63, H.P.70 and H.P.71 Halifax and Halton (continued)

As first flown, the H.P.57 was a mid-wing cantilever monoplane of all-metal construction, its wing incorporating automatic leading-edge slats, but these were deleted on production aircraft as the Air Ministry required that the wing's leading edges should be armoured and provided with barrage balloon cable cutters. The tail unit comprised a large high-mounted tailplane and rudder assembly with twin endplate fin-and-rudder units, and the fuselage was a deep, slab-sided all-metal structure with considerable internal volume; it was this feature which was to provide the later versions with multi-role capability. Accommodation was provided for a crew of seven, including three gunners to man nose, beam and tail positions. The tailwheel landing gear had retractable main units, and the powerplant comprised four Merlin engines. For its primary bombing role the Halifax carried a variety of weapons in a 22-ft (6.71-m) long lower fuselage weapons bay, supplemented by two bomb compartments in the centre section of the wing, one on each side of the fuselage.

The second prototype made its first flight on 17 August 1940, followed just under two months later by the first production example, by then designated **Halifax Mk I**, with 1,280-hp (954-kW) Merlin X engines. The defensive armament of these early production aircraft consisted of two and four 0.303-in (7.7-mm) machine-guns in the nose and tail turrets respectively.

The full designation of the first production version was **Halifax B.Mk I Series 1**, and aircraft of this

On strength with No. 405 (Vancouver) Sqn, RCAF, Halifax B.Mk II LQ-R wore this nose art during late 1942. The figure at the head of the 'train' is proclaiming 'Hey, Göering, R-Robert is here again'. No. 405 used its Halifaxes operationally for the first time on the night of 30/31 May 1942 as part of the 1,000-bomber raid against Cologne.

G-AHDN was one of 12 Haltons used by British Overseas Airways Corporation. It was named Flamborough and was originally built by Handley Page as a Halifax C.Mk 8. The aircraft began operations with BOAC in March 1947 and was scrapped in November 1950.

model began to equip the RAF's No. 35 Sqn during November 1940. It was this unit that, in early March 1941, was the first to use the Halifax operationally, in an attack on Le Havre in northern France, and a few days later the Halifax became the first of the RAF's four-engined bombers to make a night attack against a German target, when bombs were dropped on Hamburg. The Halifax was used for the first time in a daylight attack against Kiel on 30 June 1941, but it did not take long for crews to discover that the bomber's defensive armament was inadequate for daylight use, and by the end of 1941 the Halifax was used only by night in the bombing role. This resulted in the provi-

sion of better armament for later versions.

Early deployment of the Halifax had confirmed that the new four-engined bomber had much to offer, but although contracts for large-scale construction very quickly exceeded the productive capacity of the Handley Page factories at Cricklewood and Radlett, pre-war plans had been made for alternative sources of supply. The establishment of four new production lines was made easier by the unit method of construction which had been adopted for the Halifax, and the first of these subcontracted aircraft to fly, on 15 August 1941, came from the English Electric Company. The other three lines were those operated by Fairey, Rootes Securities and the London Aircraft Production Group.

From its introduction to operational service, the Halifax was in continuous use by Bomber Command, equipping at its peak usage no fewer than 34 squadrons in the European theatre, and four more in the Middle East. Two flights were in early use in the Far East, and following VE-Day a number of **Halifax B.Mk VI** squadrons flew their aircraft out for co-operation with the Allied forces fighting in the Pacific theatre. The Halifax was involved in the first Pathfinder operations in August 1942; was the first RAF aircraft to be equipped

with the highly secret H_2S blind bombing radar equipment; was involved extensively in daylight attacks on German V-1 sites; and between 1941 and 1945 flew 75,532 sorties during which 227,610 tons (231252 tonnes) of bombs were dropped on European targets.

The Halifax was also operated by nine squadrons of the RAF's Coastal Command for anti-submarine, meteorological and shipping patrols, the aircraft being converted from standard bombers and specially equipped under the designations **Halifax GR.Mk II, GR.Mk V** and **GR.Mk VI** according to the bomber version from which they were derived. Similarly, RAF Transport Command acquired **Halifax C.Mk III, C.Mk VI** and **C.Mk VII**

aircraft as casualty, personnel and freight transports. Little known in World War II was the work of Nos 138 and 161 (Special Duties) Squadrons, which had the task of dropping special agents and supplies by parachute into enemy territory.

One other vital use of the Halifax was by the British airborne forces for, under the designations **Halifax A.Mk III, A.Mk V** and **A.Mk VII**, equivalent bomber versions were converted as paratrooping and glider-towing aircraft. The Halifax was in fact the only machine capable of towing the large General Aircraft Hamilcar glider, a capability first proved in February 1942. Soon after that date the Halifax tug made its operational debut when the type was used to tow two Airspeed Horsa

SPECIFICATION

Handley Page Halifax B.Mk III
Type: six/seven-seat long-range heavy bomber
Powerplant: four Bristol Hercules XVI radial piston engines each rated at 1,615 hp (1204 kW)
Performance: maximum speed 282 mph (454 km/h) at 13,500 ft (4115 m); cruising speed 215 mph (346 km/h) at 20,000 ft (6095 m); initial climb rate 960 ft (293 m) per minute; climb to 20,000 ft (6095 m) in 37 minutes 30 seconds; service ceiling 24,000 ft (7315 m); range 1,030 miles (1658 km) with maximum bomb load
Weights: empty 38,240 lb (17345 kg); maximum take-off 65,000 lb (29484 kg)
Dimensions: wingspan 104 ft 2 in (31.75 m); length 71 ft 7 in (21.82 m); height 20 ft 9 in

(6.32 m); wing area 1,275.00 sq ft (118.45 m²)
Armament: one 0.303-in (7.7-mm) Vickers 'K' trainable forward-firing machine-gun in the nose position, provision on some early aircraft for one 0.5-in (12.7-mm) Browning trainable rearward-firing machine-gun in the ventral position, four 0.303-in (7.7-mm) Browning trainable machine-guns in the power-operated Boulton Paul Type A Mk III dorsal turret and four 0.303-in (7.7-mm) Browning trainable rearward-firing machine-guns in the power-operated Boulton Paul Type E tail turret, plus up to 14,500 lb (6577 kg) of disposable stores carried in a lower-fuselage weapons bay and in six wing cells

Variants

Halifax B.Mk I Srs 2: generally similar to B.Mk I Srs 1 but stressed for operation at a higher weight
Halifax B.Mk I Srs 3: version of the B.Mk Srs 1 with increased fuel capacity; late production examples introduced the Merlin XX engine
Halifax B.Mk II Srs 1 (Special): redesignation of B.Mk II Srs 1 aircraft incorporating in-service modification of as many as possible of the improvements of the B.Mk II Srs 1A
Halifax B.Mk V Srs 1A: as B.Mk II Srs 1A except for introduction of Dowty landing gear; the company designation was **H.P.63**
Halifax B.Mk V Srs 1 (Special): as B.Mk II Srs 1 (Special) except for introduction of Dowty landing gear and hydraulics
Halifax B.Mk VI: generally as B.Mk III but with 1,675-hp (1249-kW) Hercules 100 engines which developed 1,800 hp (1341 kW) at 10,000 ft (3050 m); company designation **H.P.61**
Halifax B.Mk VII: as B.Mk VI but reverting to Hercules XVI engines as a result of a shortage of Hercules 100 engines; company designation **H.P.61**

assault gliders across the North Sea to attack the German 'heavy water' plant in southern Norway.

The Halifax Mk I was followed into service by the **Halifax B.Mk II Srs 1**, which introduced a twin-gun Boulton Paul dorsal turret, and an increase of 15 per cent in the standard fuel capacity; the power-plant was initially a quartet of Merlin XX engines that were later supplanted by Merlin 22 engines of equal power output. These changes, plus others introduced after the prototypes had made their first flights, resulted in a steady increase in gross weight. As there had been no surplus engine power from the outset, performance

was eroded by the weight growth associated with enhanced operational capability. This can be accepted during wartime conditions provided that the rate of attrition remains fairly constant, but in the case of the Halifax Mk II the dorsal turret represented 'the last straw', and steps were immediately taken to improve performance.

The resulting **Halifax B.Mk II Srs 1A** (company designation **H.P.59**) provided performance increased by some 10 per cent in both maximum and cruising speeds as a result of weight and drag reductions: the nose turret was deleted, the nose acquiring a streamlined fairing, and the dorsal turret was

removed. Later production switched to the **Halifax B.Mk II Series 1A**, which introduced a Perspex nose fairing and four-gun dorsal turret of the type previously used on the Boulton Paul Defiant. A later change, introduced retrospectively to all aircraft then in service, involved replacement of the triangular fins by larger units of trapezoidal shape. This came after extensive testing, following some inexplicable losses of fully loaded aircraft, had shown that it was possible for the Halifax to enter an inverted and uncontrollable spin.

The last major production version was the **Halifax B.Mk III** (company designation **H.P.61**), the

first of the bombers to introduce the 1,615-hp (1205-kW) Bristol Hercules VI or XVI radial engine.

Although withdrawn from Bomber Command immediately after VJ-Day, the Halifax GR.Mk VI continued to serve with Coastal Command after World War II, as did the Halifax A.Mk VII with transport squadrons at home and overseas. Post-war versions included the **Halifax C.Mk VIII** (company designation **H.P.70**) transport, which could carry an 8,000-lb (3629-kg) capacity detachable pannier beneath the fuselage, and the **Halifax A.Mk IX** (company designation **H.P.71**) troop-carrier and supply-dropper for use

by airborne forces. When production of these two versions ended, amounting to some 230 aircraft, a total of 6,178 Halifax machines had been built, and examples remained in RAF service until a time late in 1947.

When the Halifax C.Mk VIII became surplus to the requirements of Transport Command, 10 were converted by Short Bros and Harland as 10-seat **Halton Mk I** (**H.P.70**) civil transports for service with the British Overseas Airways Corporation. Subsequently about 80 other civil conversions, some to an approximate Halton standard, were carried out by a variety of contractors.

Handley Page H.P.67, H.P.94 and H.P.95 Hastings

Designed to meet the requirements of the Air Ministry's Specification C.3/44, the **H.P.67 Hastings** was a long-range general-purpose transport that served with both the RAF and the Royal New Zealand Air Force. A low-wing cantilever monoplane with a tubby circular-section fuselage, the H.P.67 had a layout that also included a conventional tail unit, fully retractable tailwheel landing gear, and the powerplant of four Bristol Hercules 101 radial engines

in the first prototype. This machine first flew on 7 May 1946, a second prototype following on 30 December of the same year, and the initial **Hastings C.Mk 1** production version entered service with the RAF's No. 47 Sqn of Transport Command in October 1948. Production aircraft were operated by a crew of five and could accommodate 30 paratroops with supplies, or 32 litters plus 28 sitting casualties, or 50 fully equipped troops, or freight. The aircraft of No. 47 Sqn, and

also of No. 297 Sqn, saw extensive service throughout the Berlin Airlift.

A total of 147 Hastings (including the two prototypes) was built for the RAF, and these comprised 100 Hastings C.Mk 1, 43 **Hastings C.Mk 2** and four **Hastings C.Mk 4** machines. In addition, four Hastings C.Mk 3s were supplied to the RNZAF. The Hastings C.Mk 2 had Hercules 106 engines, a larger-area tailplane mounted lower on the fuselage and increased fuel capacity, and all Hastings C.Mk 1s were later modified to this configuration as **Hastings C.Mk 1A** machines. The **Hastings C.Mk 3** (**H.P.95**) was generally similar to the Hastings C.Mk 2 except for its

powerplant of Hercules 737 engines, and the Hastings C.Mk 4 (**H.P.94**) was equipped to accommodate four VIPs and their staff. Variants included the last six of the Hastings C.Mk 1 contract, which were completed as **Hastings Met.Mk 1** aircraft for weather reconnaissance duties with Coastal Command, and eight C.Mk 1s converted as

bomb-aimer trainers for service with the Bomber Command Bombing School. Designated **Hastings T.Mk 5**, these aircraft had a large ventral radome and were equipped with radar bomb-sight equipment. The Hastings was retired from service with RAF Transport Command early in 1968 as the Lockheed Hercules was introduced.

This RAF Hastings C.Mk 1A has the type's optional underwing fuel tanks fitted.

SPECIFICATION

Handley Page Hastings C.Mk 2
Type: five-crew long-range general-purpose transport
Powerplant: four Bristol Hercules 106 radial piston engines each rated at 1,675 hp (1249 kW)
Performance: maximum speed 348 mph (560 km/h) at 22,200 ft (6765 m); cruising speed 302 mph (486 km/h) at optimum altitude; initial climb rate 890 ft (271 m) per minute; climb to 20,000 ft (6095 m) in 26 minutes; service ceiling 26,500 ft (8075 m); range 1,690 miles (2720 km) with normal

payload
Weights: empty 48,427 lb (21966 kg); maximum take-off 80,000 lb (36287 kg)
Dimensions: wingspan 113 ft (34.44 m); length 82 ft 8 in (25.20 m); height 22 ft 6 in (6.86 m); wing area 1,408.00 sq ft (130.80 m²)
Payload: up to 50 troops, or 30 paratroops, or 32 litters and 28 seated casualties plus four attendants, or 16,000 lb (7258 kg) of freight carried in the cabin

Handley Page H.P.68, H.P.74, H.P.81 and H.P.82 Hermes

In its **Hermes IV** production version, this civil transport was one of the first new British airliners to enter service with the BOAC after World War II. The Hermes was basically a commercial version of the RAF's Hastings, and it had been the company's original intention to develop the Hermes first. However, when the **H.P.68 Hermes I** prototype crashed during its maiden flight on 3 December 1945,

priority was given to development of the military transport for which the RAF then had a most urgent requirement. As a result it was not until 2 September 1947 that the next Hermes development machine flew in the form of the **H.P.74 Hermes II** which, by comparison with the Hastings, had its fuselage lengthened.

Successful testing of the Hermes II led to the **H.P.81**

Hermes IV, the definitive production version, of which the first recorded its maiden flight on 5 September 1948. The Hermes IV prototype differed from its predecessors primarily in having tricycle landing gear and more powerful Hercules engines, and was followed by 24 generally similar production aircraft. The standard interior layout was for 40 passengers, but as many as 63 could be seated in a high-density arrangement.

After some two years, BOAC replaced the Hermes fleet with Canadair Argonauts, but had little difficulty in disposing of the

surplus aircraft. Most were later re-engined with Hercules 773 engines, resulting in the revised designation **Hermes IVA** and, in addition, Handley Page built two **H.P.82 Hermes V** aircraft. These were intended to evaluate the performance of the

Hermes with a turbine-engined powerplant, in this instance four 2,220-shp (1655-kW) Bristol Theseus Mk 502 turboprop units, but no further examples were built. Hermes IV and IVA aircraft remained in service with a number of operators until the mid-1960s.

The Hermes entered BOAC service on 6 August 1950. Hermes 4 G-ALDI later passed to Silver City.

SPECIFICATION

Handley Page Hermes IV
Type: five-crew medium-range transport aircraft
Powerplant: four Bristol Hercules 763 radial piston engines each rated at 2,100 hp (1566 kW)
Performance: maximum speed 350 mph (563 km/h) at optimum altitude; cruising speed 270 mph (435 km/h) at 20,000 ft (6095 m); initial climb rate 1,030 ft (314 m) per minute; service ceiling 24,500 ft (7470 m); range

2,000 miles (3218 km) with 14,125-lb (6407-kg) payload
Weights: empty 55,350 lb (25106 kg); maximum take-off 86,000 lb (39009 kg)
Dimensions: wingspan 113 ft (34.44 m); length 96 ft 10 in (29.51 m); height 30 ft (9.14 m); wing area 1,408.00 sq ft (130.80 m²)
Payload: up to 63 passengers carried in an enclosed cabin

Handley Page H.P.80 Victor & H.P.88

One of two bombers designed around the Air Ministry's Specification B.35/46, the **H.P.80 Victor** was the last of the trio of 'V-bombers' to enter service with the Royal Air Force. The Avro Vulcan, to the same requirement, had become operational in mid-1956. Technically highly advanced for its time, the Victor was designed to operate fast and high, above virtually all known defences. When it did finally enter service in 1956, it was soon discovered, the Victor had been overtaken by fighters and missiles capable of interception at its designed operating altitudes.

A crescent-shaped wing was chosen to allow the highest possible cruise Mach number, and the flying characteristics of such a wing were supposed to have been validated by the **H.P.88**, which was a Supermarine Attacker single-seat fighter-bomber adapted with a ⅜th-scale H.P.80 wing and test flown from June 1951. Oddly enough, this test machine was also known by two other designations, for Supermarine accorded the conversion its designation **Type 521** while Blackburn, which created the conversion, knew it as the **YB.2**. In the event the H.P.88, which crashed fatally in August 1951, contributed virtually nothing to the H.P.80 programme as the Victor prototype was already under construction by the time the H.P.88 recorded its maiden flight.

The first of two Victor prototypes flew on 24 December 1952 with a powerplant of four Armstrong Siddeley Sapphire ASSa.7 Mk 200 series turbojet engines, the second following only on 11 September 1954. Trials revealed the need for a number of modifications such as a reduction of 1 ft 3 in (0.381 m) in the height of the fin and an increase of 3 ft 4 in (1.016 m) in the length of the nose to improve the centre of gravity range, and this paved the way for the **Victor B.Mk 1** initial production model that first flew in February 1956 for a service debut in November 1957. Four 11,050-lb st (49.15-kN) Sapphire ASSa.7 Mk 202 engines, buried in the sharply swept roots, powered the Victor B.Mk 1 initial production model, which was built primarily of a light alloy double-skin sandwich material with either corrugated or honeycomb filling. It was the Victor B.Mk 1 which was first offered to the RAF, but

Built to prove the radical wing shape chosen for the H.P.80 Victor, the H.P.88 crashed before it could provide any useful information. The type's Attacker fuselage is clearly apparent.

in the light of its reduced effectiveness the service later demanded better protection. Eventually 50 of the resulting version, redesignated as the **Victor B.Mk 1A**, were operated: this subvariant was fitted with more sophisticated electronic countermeasures housed in the rear fuselage, and was generally better equipped.

Production totalled 50 Victor B.Mk 1s, each powered by four 11,050-lb (49.15-kN) Sapphire ASSa.7 Mk 202 turbojets. The type's primary armament was one nuclear weapon, either British-produced Yellow Sun 1/2 weapons or the US Mk 5 (in the case of Honington-based aircraft), but the weapons bay could also be configured for a typical conventional load of 35 1,000-lb (454-kg) 'long' conventional bombs by contrast with a theoretical maximum of 78,000 lb (35381 kg) comprising one 22,000-lb (9979-kg) Grand Slam bomb, or two 12,000-lb (5443-kg) Tallboy bombs, or four 10,000-lb (4536-kg) bombs, or 48 1,000-lb (454-kg) 'short' conventional bombs, or 39 2,000-lb (907-kg) Type S mines.

Delays in developing the Victor to service standard meant, however, that the type was seen as increasingly vulnerable to modern fighters and air-defence systems, and in the early 1960s some 24 of the aircraft were revised to **Victor B.Mk 1A** standard with a powerful ECM system located in the extensively altered tail cone. As the early Victor bombers were partially retired from service in favour of the much improved **Victor B.Mk 2**, it

was decided to convert a number of them into reconnaissance aircraft and inflight-refuelling tankers. The reconnaissance standard was designated **Victor B(PR).Mk 1**, and the first six tanker conversions, retaining a secondary bombing capability, were redesignated **Victor B(K).Mk 1A** after they had been retrofitted with two Mk 20B HDUs under the outer wing panels. These latter aircraft returned to service in May 1965, and in 1968 received the revised designation **Victor B.Mk 1A(K2P)**. These first conversions were followed by 24 pure tankers with the underwing HDUs supplemented by a Mk 17 HDU in the rear part of the weapons bay, which was permanently sealed and revised to carry two additional fuel tanks. These 24 tankers were 10 **Victor K.Mk 1** and 14 **Victor K.Mk 1A** machines converted from Victor B.Mk 1 and Victor B.Mk 1A standards respectively.

By 1954 work was well advanced on a version of the Victor with turbofan rather than turbojet power as this would considerably extend the type's range. The selected engine was the Rolls-Royce Conway in

its RCo.11 Mk 103 form rated at 17,250 lb st (76.73 kN), and the first Victor with such a powerplant flew in February 1959 as a production-standard machine that was followed by another 33 bombers (22 more machines being cancelled) all fitted at delivery with the ECM system of the Victor B.Mk 1A. The wing roots of the **Victor**

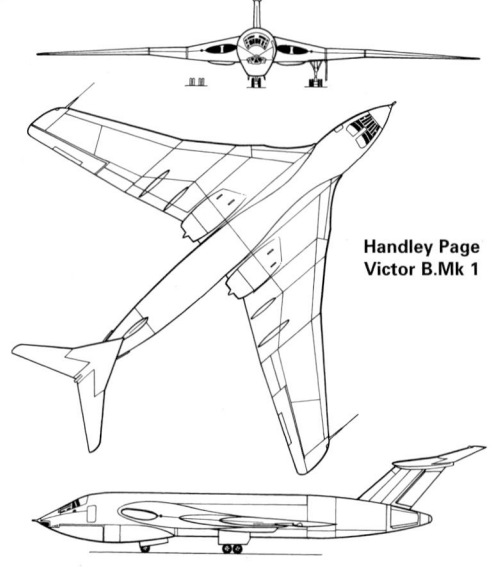

Handley Page Victor B.Mk 1

B.Mk 2 had to be extended by 3 ft (0.91 m) on each side to accommodate the Conway engines, and other changes included larger inlets, a dorsal fin fillet, two retractable scoops on the fuselage sides to feed air to the two turbo-alternators that powered the wholly revised electrical system, a Turbomeca Artouste auxiliary power unit in the

SPECIFICATION

Handley Page Victor B.Mk 2
Type: five-seat strategic bomber
Powerplant: four Rolls-Royce Conway RCo.17 Mk 201 turbofan engines each rated at 20,600 lb st (91.63 kN)
Performance: maximum speed 640 mph (1030 km/h) at 40,000 ft (12190 m); service ceiling 52,500 ft (16002 m); combat radius 2,300 miles (3701 km) at high altitude

Weights: empty 91,000 lb (41277 kg), maximum take-off 216,000 lb (97978 kg)
Dimensions: wingspan 120 ft (36.48 m); length 114 ft 11 in (35.03 m); height 28 ft 11 in (8.57 m); wing area 2,597.00 sq ft (241.26 m²)
Armament: one Blue Steel nuclear stand-off missile semi-recessed into the underside of the fuselage

This Victor B.Mk 2 has an Avro Blue Steel missile semi-recessed in its lower fuselage position. The missile installation replaced the Victor's normal conventional bombing apparatus.

As the Victor K.Mk 2, Handley Page's classic design was the stalwart of RAF inflight refuelling until gradually replaced by the VC10 and ultimately by the TriStar. The K.Mk 2's finest hour was probably during the 1982 Falklands Conflict, although the type was also active during the 1991 Gulf War. This aircraft is shown in No. 57 Sqn markings.

starboard wing root to make the type independent of ground services, and provision for the carriage of the Avro Blue Steel stand-off nuclear missile in a semi-recessed installation under the fuselage.

The Victor B.Mk 2 entered service in October 1961, and was soon tasked with the low-level penetration role in succession to the Vickers Valiant. The low-level role placed considerable extra strain on

the Victor's airframe, which had been designed for the high-altitude role, but these strains were alleviated by the type's drooped leading edges and 'Küchemann carrots', which were a pair of large pods that extended rearward from the wing trailing edges to delay the appearance of shock waves at high subsonic speeds. The 'carrots' also provided useful accommodation for chaff dispensers, and were retrofitted on 21 Victor

B.Mk 2s, together with improved ECM and a powerplant of four 20,600-lb st (91.63-kN) Conway RCo.17 Mk 201 turbofan engines to create the **Victor B.Mk 2R**.

Another retrofit programme resulted in the **Victor B(PR).Mk 2** (later **Victor SR.Mk 2**) variant intended for the strategic reconnaissance role. Nine aircraft were adapted for this task with two additional fuel tanks in the

erstwhile weapon bay, revised radar, cameras and a large number of photoflash bombs.

The only Victor variant to remain in service into the 1990s before its retirement in October 1993, after the available airframe hours had expired, was the **Victor K.Mk 2**, of which 24 were produced in the early 1970s by British Aerospace as conversions from Victor B.Mk 2 standard to provide a supplement to the Victor

K.Mk 1/1A better suited to hot-and-high operations without sacrifice of payload weight. The first Victor K.Mk 2 flew in March 1972 as a complete rebuild with span reduced by 3 ft (0.91 m), and although no two conversions were identical, a typical Handley Page Victor K.Mk 2 had some 100,000 lb (45360 kg) of transfer fuel. The Victor K.Mk 2 served with Nos 55 and 57 Sqns and No. 232 OCU.

Handley Page H.P.115

In the second half of the 1950s the UK's programme to investigate the viability of large supersonic aircraft was undergoing a major change as interest in the supersonic strategic bomber gave way to the possibility of a supersonic airliner to be developed jointly by British and French commercial interests.

The configuration proposed for the supersonic aircraft, which eventually emerged as the

Aérospatiale/BAC Concorde was based on a narrow delta wing, but American research suggested difficult low-speed handling characteristics for a wing of this planform, and to provide a machine in which such characteristics could be evaluated, the Air Ministry issued its Specification ER.197D. To meet this requirement Handley Page was contracted to design and build a single example of the low-powered

H.P.115 with a light alloy structure (except for easily altered plywood leading edges on the wing and fabric-covered control surfaces), a simple pod-and-boom fuselage, a large mid-set delta wing with essentially straight leading edges swept at 74° 42' as well as large trailing-edge elevons, Bristol Siddeley Viper turbojet engine in a nacelle above the boom part of the fuselage and carrying the swept vertical tail surface, and fixed tricycle landing gear. The H.P.115 first flew on 17 August 1961, and in its flying career up to February 1974, recorded almost 500 hours in the air for the accumulation of much important data.

The H.P.115's pilot occupied an ejection seat in a cockpit well forward within the pod part of the fuselage.

SPECIFICATION

Handley Page H.P.115
Type: single-seat experimental aircraft for investigation of a narrow delta wing's low-speed handling
Powerplant: one Bristol Siddeley Viper BSV.9 turbojet engine rated at 1,900 lb st (8.45 kN)
Performance: maximum speed

300 mph (483 km/h) at optimum altitude; endurance 40 minutes
Weights: empty 3,680 lb (1669 kg); maximum take-off 5,050 lb (2291 kg)
Dimensions: wingspan 20 ft (6.10 m); length 45 ft (13.72 m); wing area 430.00 sq ft (39.95 m²)

Handley Page H.P.R.1 and H.P.R.5 Marathon

With its **M.60 Marathon** transport, the Miles Aircraft Company broke new ground, for this was the company's first all-metal machine and also the first with a four-engined powerplant. Initially flown on 19 May 1946 with 330-hp (246-kW) de Havilland Gipsy Queen 71 engines, the Marathon had been the winner in a competitive bid to the Air Ministry's Specification 18/44, and the ministry had ordered three prototypes for BOAC.

Miles was frustrated severely by the vacillations of the Ministry of Aircraft Production, which gave orders and counter-orders throughout the pre-production stages, but when the prototype flew test pilots soon found that the M.60 was a very pleasant machine to handle. The loss of the prototype in a fatal crash during trials at Boscombe Down was attributed to pilot error. The second prototype recorded its maiden flight in

February 1947, but before a production contract could be signed the Miles company suffered financial collapse and its aircraft assets were eventually acquired by Handley Page. The company thus became Handley Page (Reading) Ltd., and the M.60 Marathon received the revised designation **Handley Page H.P.R.1 Marathon I**.

A production order for 50 aircraft, to a standard with accommodation for

between 18 and 22 passengers, was placed in the form of 30 and 20 aircraft for BEA and BOAC respectively. In the event the BEA order was reduced to 25 and later seven aircraft, and was then cancelled completely, and 28 of the Marathons were then modified for use by the RAF as **Marathon T.Mk 11** navigation trainers. The type served for six

years before being replaced by the Vickers Varsity. Handley Page completed only 40 examples of the Marathon I, the balance of this production total being flown by operators in a number of countries including West Germany, Jordan, Nigeria, Canada, Japan and Burma. Some were used experimentally, including use as engine test-beds, and the last survivors were scrapped around the mid-1960s.

Variant

H.P.R.5 Marathon II: a single prototype, originally schemed as the **M.69** but completed by the Handley Page company, initially with two 1,010-hp (753-kW) Armstrong Siddeley Mamba turboprop engines; later used to test two Alvis Leonides Major radial engines

In its Mamba turboprop-powered form (illustrated), the Marathon II was rejected by BEA.

SPECIFICATION

Handley Page Marathon T.Mk 11
Type: two-crew navigation trainer
Powerplant: four de Havilland Gipsy Queen 173 inverted inline piston engines each rated at 340 hp (254 kW)
Performance: maximum speed 232 mph (373 km/h) at 6,750 ft (2055 m); cruising speed 155 mph (249 km/h) at optimum altitude; initial climb rate 650 ft (198 m) per minute; climb to 15,000 ft (4570 m)

in 30 minutes; service ceiling 15,000 ft (4570 m); range 1,100 miles (1770 km)
Weights: empty 13,358 lb (6059 kg); maximum take-off 18,250 lb (8278 kg)
Dimensions: wingspan 65 ft (19.81 m); length 52 ft 3 in (15.93 m); height 14 ft 1 in (4.29 m); wing area 498.00 sq ft (46.26 m²)
Payload: one instructor and two pupils carried in an enclosed cabin

Handley Page H.P.R.3/H.P.R.7 Herald

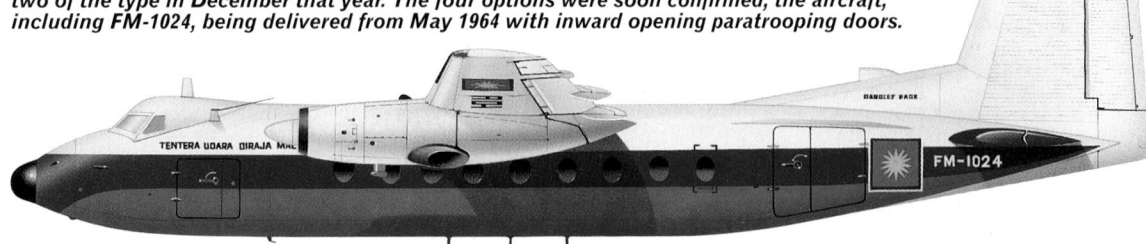

Malaysia signed a £1,500,000 deal for four Heralds with four options in April 1963, receiving its first two of the type in December that year. The four options were soon confirmed, the aircraft, including FM-1024, being delivered from May 1964 with inward opening paratrooping doors.

Designed by the Handley Page division that was formerly the Miles Aircraft Company, the first **Handley Page H.P.R.3 Herald** prototype made its maiden flight on 25 August 1955. Looking not unlike an enlarged and modernised Marathon, which had originated from the same stable, the Herald was a high-wing cantilever monoplane with four 870-hp (649-kW) Alvis Leonides Major radial engines in nacelles on the leading edges of the wing. The fuselage was pressurised, the landing gear was of retractable tricycle type, and the tail unit was completely conventional. Standard accommodation was provided for 36 passengers, with a maximum of 44 possible in a high-density configuration.

The Herald had been expected to appeal to operators in Asia, Australia and South America as a feeder-liner suitable for operation from undeveloped airfields. Market research had shown that operators in these areas wanted an aircraft that was simple and easy to maintain, without the complication of turbine engines. An initial production batch of 25 aircraft was started, to meet orders totalling 29 aircraft, but none of these was completed with the powerplant that had been planned as three years of experience with the Vickers Viscount had demonstrated, most effectively, that the turboprop engines which powered this Vickers machine were not only extremely reliable, but also economical in operation.

With potential operators expressing their doubts about the wisdom of holding to their contracts, and with the similarly sized turboprop-powered Fokker F.27 undergoing its development and certification programme, the company decided in May 1957 to develop a turboprop-powered version with two Rolls-Royce Dart engines. In fact, only the original prototypes were flown with piston engines, and these were later converted to turboprop power, both flying in their revised form during 1958.

The initial production version was the **H.P.R.7 Herald Series 100**, with accommodation for a maximum of 47 passengers. The **Herald Series 200**, with its fuselage lengthened by 3 ft 7 in (1.09 m), had seating for up to 56 passengers. By the time the Handley Page company collapsed in 1970, production had totalled four Series 100 and 36 Series 200 aircraft, plus eight of the **Herald Series 400** variant (a military version of the Series 200) for the Royal Malaysian Air Force. No further examples were built after the liquidation of this once great company.

G-AODE, the first Herald prototype, shows the type's original powerplant. A second, pressurised and fully furnished, H.P.R.3 prototype was also built.

SPECIFICATION

Handley Page Herald Series 200
Type: two-crew local service transport aircraft
Powerplant: two Rolls-Royce Dart Mk 527 turboprop engines each rated at 2,105 ehp (1570 kW)
Performance: maximum cruising speed 274 mph (441 km/h) at 15,000 ft (4570 m); economic cruising speed 265 mph (426 km/h) at 23,000 ft (7010 m); initial climb rate 1,805 ft (550 m) per minute; service ceiling 27,900 ft (8505 m); range 1,110 miles (1786 km) with maximum payload
Weights: empty 25,800 lb (11703 kg); maximum take-off 43,000 lb (19504 kg)
Dimensions: wingspan 94 ft 9 in (28.88 m); length 75 ft 6 in (23.01 m); height 24 ft 1 in (7.34 m); wing area 886.00 sq ft (82.31 m²)
Payload: up to 56 passengers carried in the enclosed cabin within the context of an 11,242-lb (5100-kg) maximum payload

Hannover CL II and CL III

As indicated by its full name, Hannoversche Waggonfabrik A.G., the Hannover company was primarily a builder of rolling stock for the German railway system. In 1915 however, it was one of several large companies required by the German government to diversify into aircraft production. Established at Hannover-Linden during 1916, the company's new aircraft department initially concentrated on the licensed production of aircraft such as the Aviatik C I, Halberstadt D II and Rumpler C Ia so that a manufacturing capability could be created as a design office was organised under the supervision of Hermann Dorner.

The first product of the new department was a result of the German high command's demand in the spring of 1917 for aircraft of the new 'CL' category, which were intended as lighter, faster and more agile escorts for the 'C' category two-seaters generally used for the artillery observation, reconnaissance and photographic roles and now found to be increasingly vulnerable to the attentions of the Allies' newest fighters. The 'CL' types were also required to undertake the ground-attack role that was becoming increasingly important for the new Schutzstaffeln (protection squadrons) that were later redesignated as Schlachtstaffeln (battle squadrons) in recognition of their basically offensive role.

To meet this requirement Dorner designed the **CL II**, the I numerical suffix having been used already for the C I built under licence from Aviatik. The CL II was a stocky biplane of wooden construction covered with plywood and fabric. The prototype was completed with 2° dihedral on all four wing panels and an upper tailplane of angular shape, but the production model introduced lower-wing panels of greater dihedral than the upper-wing panels, and an upper tailplane whose leading edge was curved from tip to tip. The powerplant was based on one 180-hp

Having nosed-over on landing, this CL IIIa provides a useful demonstration of the type's unusual tail configuration.

The CL II was typified by a single-bay staggered wing cellule, a deep fuselage filling most of the interplane gap, a biplane tail unit, and fixed tailskid landing gear.

SPECIFICATION

Hannover CL IIIa
Type: two-seat ground-attack and escort fighter
Powerplant: one Argus As.III inline piston engine rated at 180 hp (134 kW)
Performance: maximum speed 103 mph (165 km/h) at 16,405 ft (5000 m); climb to 3,280 ft (1000 m) in 5 minutes 18 seconds; service ceiling 24,605 ft (7500 m); endurance 3 hours
Weights: empty 1,581 lb (717 kg); maximum take-off 2,568 lb (1165 kg)
Dimensions: wingspan 38 ft 4⅞ in (11.70 m); length 24 ft 10⅜ in (7.58 m); height 9 ft 2¼ in (2.80 m); wing area 351.99 sq ft (32.70 m²)
Armament: one 0.312-in (7.92-mm) LMG 08/15 fixed forward-firing machine-gun on the starboard upper side of the forward fuselage and one 0.312-in (7.92-mm) LMG 14 Parabellum trainable rearward-firing machine-gun in the rear cockpit

(134-kW) Argus As.III inline engine driving a two-bladed wooden propeller.

The CL II entered service in December 1917 and soon revealed itself to be an admirable warplane offering adequate performance with good agility. Production continued well into 1918 and amounted to 439 aircraft. The type's compact dimensions some-times led Allied pilots into the dangerous belief that it was a single-seat fighter, and pilots thus closing in for an easy stern attack were suddenly engaged by a burst of fire from the trainable machine-gun.

Somewhat confusingly given its numerical designator, the **CL III** built under licence by the Luft-Fahrzeug G.m.b.H., otherwise known as LFG (Roland).

Although the CL II series offered excellent manoeu-vrability, Dorner thought that greater agility could be wrung out of the basic design with only modest changes and this led to the CL III with modified wing tips incorporating overhang-ing aerodynamic balance areas. This model also introduced the 160-hp (119-kW) Mercedes D.III inline engine, but single-seat fighters had a higher priority for this engine and production of the CL III was therefore undertaken only on a limited scale, a mere 80 aircraft being completed. The designation **CL IIIa** was given to the version of the CL III that reverted to the As.III engine, and production of the CL IIIa and basically similar CL IIa amounted to 537 aircraft that retained their operational utility right to the end of the war.

Experimental versions produced late in 1918 included the **CL IIIb** with the 190-hp (142-kW) NAG C.II inline engine, and the **CL IIIc** with a two-bay biplane wing cellule.

Hannover CL V

Produced in the later part of 1918 to the extent of 46 aircraft from an initial order for 100 machines, the **CL V** was an improved ground-attack and escort warplane based on the same concept as the CL III but with a different engine, I-type interplane struts and reduced dimensions. It also appeared in variants with a monoplane or biplane tail unit, the latter being speci-fied for the production model. The use of a higher-powered engine in a slightly smaller airframe resulted in considerably improved performance, including a service ceiling that was truly remarkable for the period, but it is thought that the type did not see combat.

The aircraft had a deep fuselage of wooden construction skinned with fabric-covered plywood except on the nose, where detachable metal panels were used. The engine was fully cowled except over the cylinder heads, the gunner's cockpit was sepa-rate from that of the pilot and slightly elevated to secure the best possible fields of fire, and the tail unit included a fixed fin built integral with the fuse-lage and therefore of plywood-covered wooden construction.

The staggered wing cellule was of fabric covered wooden construc-tion, while the upper wing was based on a flat centre section, with a large cut-out above the pilot, and was carried above the fuselage by shallow outward-canted N-type cabane struts.

After the end of World War I, another 62 CL Vs were completed, and in 1923-4 the Norwegian company Kjeller Flyvemaskinsfabrik at Halden produced 14 exam-ples for service with the Norwegian army air service under the designation **Kjeller F.F.7 Hauk** (hawk). The F.F.7 remained in service up to 1929.

SPECIFICATION	
Hannover CL V	**Dimensions:** wingspan 34 ft 7¾ in (10.56 m) in the version with a biplane tail unit or 34 ft 5 in (10.49 m) in the version with a monoplane tail unit; length 22 ft 11½ in (7.00 m); height 9 ft 3¼ in (2.84 m); wing area 306.78 sq ft (28.50 m²)
Type: two-seat ground-attack and escort fighter	
Powerplant: one BMW IIIa inline piston engine rated at 185 hp (138 kW)	
Performance: maximum speed 115 mph (185 km/h) at 6,560 ft (2000 m); climb to 3,280 ft (1000 m) in 3 minutes 18 seconds; service ceiling 29,530 ft (9000 m); range 211 miles (340 km); endurance about 3 hours	**Armament:** two 0.312-in (7.92-mm) LMG 08/15 fixed forward-firing machine-guns in the upper part of the forward fuselage and one 0.312-in (7.92-mm) LMG 14 Parabellum trainable rearward-firing machine-gun in the rear cockpit
Weights: empty 1,587 lb (720 kg); maximum take-off 2,381 lb (1080 kg)	

The CL V's fuselage terminated in a vertical knife edge in line with the fin and rudder.

Hanriot H.16

The Société Générale Aéronautique (SGA) consor-tium was formed in February 1930. The Hanriot concern was part of the new organisation, and for a period the company's designs were prefixed LH for Lorraine-Hanriot. A series of parasol-wing primary trainers included the **LH.10** with the 100-hp (75-kW) Lorraine 5Pa engine (two built), the **LH.11** with the 110-hp (82-kW) Lorraine 5Pb (two built), the **LH.12** with the 135-hp (101-kW) Salmson 9Nc (one prototype), the **LH.13** with the same engine as the LH.11 (five built and used by the Bourges flying school until 1937), and the **LH.16** subsequently redesignated **Hanriot H.16** after Hanriot withdrew from the SGA.

The H.16 prototype was test flown at Villacoublay in August 1933, and in config-uration was a parasol-wing monoplane with elliptical wing tips and fixed tailskid landing gear including wide-track divided main units. The pupil and instructor were seated close together in a tandem arrangement of open cockpits beneath a large centreline cut-out in the trailing edge of the wing. Power was provided by a 120-hp (89.5-kW) Renault 4Pdi engine. The prototype was returned to Hanriot for final modifica-tions in September 1933, the principal change being a redesign of the vertical tail surface.

A production order from the Armée de l'Air for 60 aircraft was later amended to 15 H.16 trainers and 29 examples of the **H.16/1**, which was equipped for observation duties and able to carry a single 0.303-in (7.7-mm) machine-gun for the observer in the revised rear cockpit. Delivery of the H.16 began in January 1934, one example being handed over to the French navy. The H.16/1 prototype was built at Arceuil and did not appear until 28 May 1936. Production examples of the H.16/1 did not remain long with service training units before being handed over to the service-sponsored Aviation Populaire movement for use as trainers. Many were still being used in this role when World War II broke out in September 1939.

While the H.16 was under development numer-ous Hanriot designs had appeared. The **LH.21S** air ambulance, the **LH.30**, **LH.60** and **LH.61** trainers, and the **LH.80** reconnais-sance aircraft were all of typical parasol-wing config-uration. The **LH.70** of 1932 was a three-engined high-wing monoplane intended for colonial duties.

Inward-canted cabane struts supported the H.16 prototype's parasol wing, which was also braced on each side by a sturdy pair of aerofoil-section struts.

SPECIFICATION	
Hanriot H.16	service ceiling 13,780 ft (4200 m); range 233 miles (375 km)
Type: two-seat primary flying trainer	**Weights:** empty 1,206 lb (547 kg); maximum take-off 1,953 lb (886 kg)
Powerplant: one Renault 4Pdi inline piston engine rated at 120 hp (90 kW)	**Dimensions:** wingspan 39 ft ½ in (11.90 m); length 26 ft 11½ in (8.28 m); height 8 ft 7¼ in (2.62 m); wing area 236.81 sq ft (22.00 m²)
Performance: maximum speed 96 mph (155 km/h) at sea level;	

Hanriot H.43 series

The Hanriot company built a wide variety of aircraft, and in 1926 the company introduced the seven-passenger **H.26T** high-wing monoplane transport with a single 260-hp (194-kW) Salmson CM18 engine, and in the same year came the brief flying career of the twin-engined **H.38** sesqui-plane reconnaissance flying boat. Two years later the firm reverted to the parasol high-wing formula with the **H.46 'Styx'** two-seat liaison type that was built in a number of 'one-off' versions that differed mainly in powerplant, while the two-seat **H.463** and three-seat **H.465** built in 1929 were specialised ambulance aircraft.

However, the company returned to the classic unequal-span, single-bay biplane layout with the **H.43**. Two examples of this two-seat liaison type, which could double as a trainer for either pilots or observers, appeared in 1927. Powered by a 260-hp (194-kW) Salmson CM9 water-cooled radial engine, the H.43 had backward sweep on both the upper and lower wings and fixed tailskid landing gear. The fuselage was a metal-tube structure, and the wings were of mixed construction under a fabric covering.

The H.43 was developed into the **H.430** with the Salmson 9Ab air-cooled radial engine, but this version was never completed. The aircraft which did appear was the **H.431.01**, the true prototype for the series of biplanes which was to follow. Much modified in comparison with the H.43, the H.431 had a redesigned fuselage with flat metal-covered sides, no sweep on the wings, and a powerplant based on the 230-hp (172-kW) Lorraine 7Mc radial piston engine.

Hanriot H.43 series (continued)

The H.431 appeared in the spring of 1928, and in July was given modified landing gear with divided main units and revised interplane struts. A production order was received from the French army, but versions which followed differed from the prototype in having wings of increased span and area. Eight versions were built over a six-year period, culminating in the **H.439**, and total production including the prototypes was 155 aircraft. The Hanriot biplanes, powered by Lorraine or Salmson air-cooled radial engines, saw both military and civil use as general-purpose, liaison and training aircraft, while the **H.437** was an air ambulance. These Hanriot biplanes remained in widespread service up to the outbreak of World War II, and 75 examples of the **H.431, H.433** and **H.436** were still available at the time of the German Blitzkzrieg on France in May 1940.

Variants

LH.431: prototype followed by 50 production biplanes (later redesignated **H.431**) for the French army in the general-purpose and liaison roles, plus a dozen civil aircraft for the Orly training school; one civil and four military examples of the H.431 were tested with ski landing gear
H.432: armed gunnery version of the H.431 with a 0.303-in (7.7-mm) machine-gun on a ring mounting over the rear cockpit; one built as new with the 300-hp (224-kW) Lorraine Algol engine; the second of the two machines was a conversion of the second H.431 with a Salmson engine
H.433: powered by a 240-hp (179-kW) Lorraine 7Me Mizar radial engine with revised landing gear and modified fin
H.434: one only

H.436: general-purpose version, first built in 1932, and powered by the 230-hp (172-kW) Salmson 9Ab radial engine; 50 were built and used by the reserve training centre and GAO (Groupe Aérien d'Observation) units of the Armée de l'Air
LH.437: ambulance version of which the prototype was built in 1932 with the 240-hp (179-kW) Lorraine 7Me radial engine; a second LH.437 was produced by conversion of the eighth H.431; in April 1933 the first LH.437 was re-engined with a 280-hp (209-kW) Salmson radial and redesignated as the **H.437ter** before reverting to the original engine to become the **H.437/1**
H.438: export version built during 1933-4; 12 built for Peru with the 330-hp (246-kW) Lorraine 7Me radial engine
H.439: 13 updated aircraft for use by the flying school at Bourges; all converted from H.431 standard, some had the tailskid replaced by a tailwheel

SPECIFICATION

Hanriot H.431
Type: two-seat intermediate flying trainer
Powerplant: one Lorraine 7Mc radial piston engine rated at 230 hp (172 kW)
Performance: maximum speed 112 mph (180 km/h) at sea level; service ceiling 16,075 ft (4900 m);
range 280 miles (450 km)
Weights: empty 2,160 lb (980 kg); maximum take-off 3,020 lb (1170 kg)
Dimensions: wingspan 37 ft 4¾ in (11.40 m); length 26 ft 2¼ in (7.98 m); height 10 ft 4½ in (3.16 m); wing area 325.51 sq ft (30.24 m²)

A total of 26 H.433 aircraft was built for general-purpose duties with the French army. The original H.430 could be used for liaison or as a pilot and observer trainer.

Hanriot H.170, H.180 and H.190 series

The **H.180T.01** was the prototype of a long series of three-seat cabin monoplanes with a strut-braced high-set wing designed by engineer Montlaur, and this prototype first flew in July 1934. Its fuselage was constructed of Dural tube under a covering of fabric except for the area round the engine, where light alloy panels were used. The wing was of mixed construction, and was braced to a small stub wing attached to the bottom of the fuselage, and the tail unit had a tall single fin-and-rudder assembly.

Although the **H.180T** was classified as a touring machine, the rear upper decking could be removed in one piece to provide accommodation for a litter, and the rear cabin section could be replaced by an open cockpit to accommodate a second pilot or a gunner. In short, the **H.180** series was intended as a general-purpose aircraft for a variety of civil and military tasks. The basic design was also intended for easy adaptability to a number of

different engine types. Each change of function or powerplant resulted in a different model number. At the Salon de l'Aéronautique at the end of 1934, the three versions on display were the **H.170, H.182** and **H.190**.

The H.180T.01 underwent a number of modifications and eventually gained its certificate of air worthiness in October 1935. It and the **H.180.01** and **H.182.01** which followed were all powered by Renault 4 engines. Also tested were the **H.170** and **H.171** with the Salmson 6 engine, and the **H.190M** and **H.141** with Régnier inline engines.

Production got under way at the end of 1935, when the Hanriot factory at

Arcueil built 15 examples of the H.182. The thirteenth machine was modified as an evaluation prototype to meet an Armée de l'Air requirement for a two-seat observation and training type, intended mainly for the recently formed reserve units, the Cercles Aériens Régionaux. Another H.182 was modified briefly with a tail unit incorporating twin fin-and-rudder units.

Large-scale government orders followed, a total of 392 machines being built, all but 46 of them to the H.182 standard. Only seven Salmson-powered **H.172N** aircraft were sold direct to private owners, although other Hanriot machines went to the Bourges flying school. In addition to the Armée de l'Air, another

SPECIFICATION

Hanriot H.182
Type: two/three-seat training and liaison aircraft
Powerplant: one Renault 4Pei inverted inline piston engine rated at 140 hp (104 kW)
Performance: maximum speed 118 mph (190 km/h) at sea level;
service ceiling 18,405 ft (5500 m); range 373 miles (600 km)
Weights: empty 1,331 lb (604 kg); maximum take-off 1,955 lb (887 kg)
Dimensions: wingspan 39 ft 4½ in (12.00 m); length 23 ft 8¼ in (7.22 m); height 10 ft 4 in (3.15 m); wing area 204.20 sq ft (18.97 m²)

Variants

H.170: single example built in 1934 as a two-seat observation machine powered by the 170-hp (127-kW) Salmson 6Te engine
H.171: one two/three-seat tourer of 1935 with the same engine as the H.170
H.172B: appeared in 1935 as the sole prototype of a two-seat trainer
H.172N: two/three-seat civil tourer with the 170-hp (127-kW) Salmson 6AF-00 engine; seven built
H.173: one structurally strengthened aerobatic two-seater of 1935 with the 6Te engine
H.174: one experimental three-seat trainer of 1935 with the same engine as the H.170
H.175: 10 built for French navy in 1936 as liaison aircraft
H.180T: original two/three-seat tourer prototype
H.180M: prototype of a two-seat observation version with the same 140-hp (104-kW) Renault 4Pei engine as the H.180T
H.181: single air ambulance prototype of 1935 with removable upper rear fuselage decking to house one litter, and the same engine as the H.180T
H.182: main production version; total of 346 built as two-seat trainers to French government orders; secondary role was observation; a number was retained by Hanriot for experimental purposes, others went to the Bourges flying school and Gnome-Rhône engine company; 10 exported to Spain for service with the Republican government in the Civil War; 50 Armée de l'Air machines diverted to Turkey under a tripartite military aid agreement of 1939
H.183: single aerobatic trainer powered by Renault 438 engine
H.184: single three-seat trainer variant of 1938 with Renault 4Pei engine uprated to 180 hp (134 kW)
H.185: two-seat liaison aircraft with the Renault 4Pei engine for the French navy, which received six aircraft in 1937
H.190M: prototype of two-seat observation aircraft with the 180-hp (134-kW) Régnier 60-01 engine; first flown May 1935
H.191: one three-seat tourer completed in 1935 with a Régnier engine
H.192B: one two-seat Régnier-powered trainer of 1935
H.192N: nine examples of two-seat trainer with the Régnier 6Bo.1 engine, built in 1935 and operated by the Bourges flying school
H.195: single two-seat liaison prototype of 1937, powered by same engine as the H.192N

Built for the French navy, the H.175 was equipped with radio equipment and powered by the 170-hp (127-kW) Salmson 6AF-00 engine. The type's unusual stub-wing arrangement is clearly evident.

service that operated the type in the liaison role was the French navy, while Turkey and the Spanish

Republican government used the H.182 for training and liaison duties. Airworthy H.182s were

removed to the Vichy zone of France after the June 1940 armistice with Germany, and when

German forces occupied Vichy territory in 1942 they seized 127 H.182s, which had by then been much

neglected as reflected in an official report stating that the aircraft were unsuitable for flying duties.

Hanriot H.220 and H.230 series

The **H.220** all-metal mid-wing monoplane was intended initially as a three-seat heavy fighter powered by Renault or Salmson engines of new design. In the event the **H.220.1** first prototype did not make its maiden flight until 28 September 1937 with the powerplant of two 680-hp (507-kW) Gnome-Rhône radial engines. The fuselage was then redesigned, with the rear crew station carefully faired into the upper fuselage contours, but the H.220.1 crash-landed during a flight test on 17 February 1938. The **H.220.2** appeared in 1939 with twin fin-and-rudder assemblies, but it was then decided to modify the design to two-seat configuration. Hanriot having been absorbed into the nationalised Société Nationale de Constructions du Centre, the H.220.2 was then redesignated as the

NC.600.01 and displayed at the Brussels aviation exhibition. An evaluation batch of six aircraft was ordered, the function being changed to an attack aircraft, but only one had been completed before the German Blitzkrieg of May 1940: this machine had modified tail surfaces and carburettor intakes, and first flew on 15 May 1940.

The **H.230.01** flew for the first time in June 1937. It was an advanced two-seat trainer which had a general resemblance to the H.220 but was of much lighter construction and powered by two 170-hp (127-kW) Salmson 6AF-00 engines. During the H.230.01 test programme it was decided to introduce considerable dihedral at the wing tips to improve stability, but the **H.231.01** which followed in May 1938 had dihedral increased over the whole

wingspan, and the unusual wing tip arrangement of the modified H.230.01 was eliminated. Twin fin-and-rudder units were introduced, and greater power was introduced with 230-hp (172-kW) Salmson 6AF engines. The **H.232.01** reverted to a single fin-and-rudder unit and had 220-hp (164-kW) Renault 6Q-0 engines plus retractable landing gear. First flown in August 1938, the H.232.02 introduced a redesigned cockpit: it was tested officially between October 1938 and May 1939. The type was then given twin fin-and-rudder units, and flew in this new configuration during December 1939 with the revised designation **H.232/2.01**.

An order for 40 aircraft had already been received from the French air ministry, and this was increased to 57 examples shortly afterwards. By then known as the **Centre (Hanriot) NC.232/2**, these aircraft incorporated minor improvements including redesigned rudders and engine cowlings. Full navigational equipment was installed. Because of a planned total of 25 from the original French order were sent to Finland, and

Looking the part of a rugged ground attack aircraft, the H.220 was denied an opportunity to prove itself in service thanks to the German invasion of France.

The configuration of the H.230.01 included a short crew canopy faired into the upper decking of the rear fuselage, a conventional but strut-braced tail unit, and fixed tailskid landing gear.

these were not taken into service until after the April 1940 end of the Winter War of 1939-40 with the USSR. Deliveries to the Armée de l'Air started in February 1940, and 35 aircraft had been taken on

charge before France's June 1940 armistice with Germany. Twenty aircraft found on airfields when the invading German forces occupied Vichy France in 1942 were promptly reduced to scrap.

SPECIFICATION	
Centre (Hanriot) NC.232/2	(1200 km)
Type: two-seat advanced flying trainer	**Weights:** empty 3,809 lb (1728 kg); maximum take-off 4,982 lb (2260 kg)
Powerplant: two Renault 6Q-0 inverted inline piston engines each rated at 220 hp (164 kW)	**Dimensions:** wingspan 41 ft 10¼ in (12.76 m); length 28 ft ½ in (8.55 m); height 11 ft 4½ in (3.47 m); wing area 228.20 sq ft (21.20 m²)
Performance: maximum speed 208 mph (335 km/h) at optimum altitude; service ceiling 24,605 ft (7500 m); range 746 miles	

Hanriot HD.1

The first Hanriot design was the **HD.1** single-seat fighter, whose prototype made its initial flight in June 1916. René Hanriot had been involved previously in aviation, flying and building aircraft, and formed the new company after the outbreak of World War I in 1914. Its first product was the British Sopwith 1½-Strutter two-seat reconnaissance biplane, which was built in large numbers under licence. The HD.1, designed by Emile Dupont, had wings closely resembling those of the British machine, and was characterised by its compact overall dimensions and heavily staggered single-bay wing cellule in which the upper wing was of greater span and chord than the lower wing.

The HD.1 was unfortunate in relying on the low-powered 110-hp (82-kW) Le Rhône 9J rotary engine and in being a contemporary of the SPAD S.VII, which performed

well, had a more powerful engine and was soon ordered into quantity production for the French Aéronautique Militaire. In addition, the Belgians, fighting alongside the French but starved of new equipment, and the Italians, newly entered into the war, were looking for a single-seat fighter and each opted for the HD.1.

As a result of recommendations by the Italian military mission in Paris, a limited number of HD.1s was exported to Italy, where the Macchi concern began licensed manufacture of the type in November 1916. It is believed that the Italian air arm received about 100 French-built aircraft, while Macchi delivered a total of 901, 70 of them after the conclusion of hostilities. Meanwhile the Belgians had taken delivery of 125 French-built HD.1s from August 1917. French sources indicate that total HD.1 production amounted to 1,145 aircraft.

After World War I the Swiss Fliegertruppe, impressed by tests with an Italian HD.1 which had force-landed in Switzerland, purchased 16 war-surplus Italian machines. The HD.1 was built largely of wood under a covering of fabric, although the tailplane had a steel tubing framework and the forward fuselage was covered with Dural panels.

Other HD.1s found their way to various Latin American countries.

The HD.1 performed well and showed outstanding manoeuvrability. Dissatisfaction was expressed with the armament and the limited power provided by the engine, however. Later HD.1s were powered by the 120-hp (90-kW) Le Rhône 9Jb or 130-hp (97-kW) Le Rhône 9Jby rotary engines, but the 301st HD.1 was tested with a 150-hp (112-kW) Gnome Monosoupape

rotary unit later in 1917, while there were reports of another experimental aircraft fitted with a 170-hp (127-kW) Le Rhône. As for

the armament, the Vickers gun was repositioned centrally on the forward decking with beneficial results.

SPECIFICATION	
Hanriot HD.1	**Weights:** empty 882 lb (400 kg); maximum take-off 1,334 lb (605 kg)
Type: single-seat fighter	
Powerplant: one Le Rhône 9Jb rotary piston engine rated at 120 hp (90 kW)	**Dimensions:** wingspan 28 ft 6½ in (8.70 m); length 19 ft 2¼ in (5.85 m); height 9 ft 7¾ in (2.94 m); wing area 195.91 sq ft (18.20 m²)
Performance: maximum speed 114 mph (184 km/h) at sea level; climb to 6,560 ft (2000 m) in 6 minutes 3 seconds; service ceiling 20,670 ft (6300 m); endurance 2 hours 30 minutes	**Armament:** one 0.303-in (7.7-mm) Vickers fixed forward firing machine-gun on the upper part of the forward fuselage

Hanriot HD.1 (continued)

Experiments with a heavier-calibre gun or twin machine-guns were confined to single aircraft, and it was found that loss in performance outweighed improvement in firepower.

The Aviation Militaire Belge re-equipped its 1e Escadrille with the HD.1 in the late summer of 1917. Its pilots were initially reluctant to adopt an untried design in place of their highly esteemed Nieuport scouts, but Lieutenant Willy Coppens, the first to fly the new machine, was so impressed that his enthusiasm rapidly spread to his colleagues. Soon other escadrilles re-equipped with the type, which remained in service until 1926, when the 7e Escadrille at Nivelles finally gave up its Hanriot fighters. By August 1917 several HD.1s were flying with the Italian 76a Squadriglia. By the war's end another 12 squadriglie facing the Austro-Hungarians had the HD.1 on strength, and the type was also operational in Macedonia and Albania. As late as 1925, six of the Regia Aeronautica's first-line squadriglie de caccia still flew the type.

In France, a small number of an HD.1 variant with the 130-hp (96.9-kW) Clerget rotary engine flew with the Aviation Maritime. Most of these machines had redesigned vertical tail surfaces. They were operated in defence of Dunkerque naval air station and in late 1918 one was flown from a gun-turret platform on the battleship *Paris*.

Variant

HD.7: single-seat fighter evolved from the HD.1 and flown for the first time in 1918; powered by the 300-hp (224-kW) Hispano-Suiza 8Fb water-cooled Vee engine, it attained a maximum speed of 133 mph (214 km/h); development was abandoned after the end of World War I

Hanriot HD.2

Developed as a replacement for the Sopwith Baby, the **HD.2** first appeared in the form of a prototype created as an HD.1 conversion with a side-by-side pair of short main floats and a third float beneath the tailplane. The second prototype dispensed with the third float, having two elongated main floats, and also had its vertical tail surface enlarged to improve stability. The production version closely resembled the second prototype and was intended not only as an interceptor but as an escort for the slow French reconnaissance flying boats, which had suffered heavy losses at the hands of relatively fast and powerful Hansa-Brandenburg two-seat floatplanes.

The HD.2 attracted the attention of US Navy personnel stationed in France, and as a result 10 aircraft were ordered by that service in 1918. Delivered to Langley Field, they were converted as landplanes under the designation **HD.2C**. One of them was used for experimental short take-offs from a platform built over the forward turret of the battleship USS *Mississippi*, in a way similar to that which had seen HD.1 fighters being flown from the French battleship *Paris*.

Variant

H.29: two examples built in the Et.1 (single-seat trainer) category; the first workable French shipboard catapult was not available until 1926 and the French admiralty was anxious to find a way of launching aircraft from ships; the H.29 of 1924 used the most bizarre method of all, three metal rails being built out horizontally from the tripod mast of the battleship *Lorraine* for two pulley wheels attached to the wing upper surfaces of the H.29 and a third attached to the top of the fin, the aircraft then being launched along the rails under the full power of its 180-hp (134-kW) Hispano-Suiza 8Ab engine; as might be anticipated the H.29 ended in the water, fortunately without loss of life; the experiments were thereafter discontinued

SPECIFICATION	
Hanriot HD.2	maximum take-off 1,543 lb (700 kg)
Type: single-seat fighter floatplane	**Dimensions:** wingspan 27 ft 11 in
Powerplant: one Clerget 9B rotary piston engine rated at 130 hp (97 kW)	(8.51 m); length 22 ft 11½ in (7.00 m); height 10 ft 2 in (3.10 m), wing area 198.06 sq ft (18.40 m²)
Performance: maximum speed 113 mph (182 km/h) at sea level; service ceiling 15,750 ft (4800 m); range 186 miles (300 km)	**Armament:** twin 0.303-in (7.7-mm) Vickers fixed forward-firing machine-guns on the upper part of the forward fuselage
Weights: empty 1,092 lb (495 kg);	

Beginning in January 1918, limited numbers of HD.2s were located at Dunkerque and other bases, their armament of two Vickers machine-guns proving effective against German aircraft.

Hanriot HD.3

Emile Dupont designed the **HD.3** two-seat fighter which was built during 1917. The prototype first flew toward the end of the year, demonstrated good handling qualities and gave every indication of being an excellent fighter, with the pilot and gunner located close together in tandem cockpits. The Salmson 9Za water-cooled radial engine was reliable, and every effort had been made to achieve good aerodynamic characteristics.

The French authorities ordered 300 HD.3s, intending the type to serve with both army and navy units for the great Allied offensive planned for 1919. In the event production was curtailed, but 75 HD.3s were delivered to the Aéronautique Militaire. A small number of HD.3s went to the Aviation Maritime: one was used for flotation tests at the RAF station at the Isle of Grain in the autumn of 1918, and one was reported to have taken part in landing tests on the French aircraft-carrier *Béarn*. Another HD.3 was converted with twin floats and an enlarged vertical tail surface as the prototype for the proposed **HD.4** two-seat floatplane fighter and was tested in the summer of 1918, but its development was abandoned after the end of World War I. A CN.2 (Chasse de Nuit biplace) night-fighter version of the basic design, the **HD.3bis** with enlarged balanced ailerons and rudder together with wings of thicker section, was tested in late 1918 but then abandoned.

SPECIFICATION	
Hanriot HD.3	(1180 kg)
Type: two-seat fighter	**Dimensions:** wingspan 29 ft 6¼ in
Powerplant: one Salmson 9Za radial piston engine rated at 260 hp (194 kW)	(9.00 m); length 22 ft 9½ in (6.95 m); height 9 ft 10 in (3.00 m); wing area 274.49 sq ft (25.50 m²)
Performance: maximum speed 119 mph (192 km/h) at 6,560 ft (2000 m); climb to 9,845 ft (3000 m) in 12 minutes 15 seconds; service ceiling 18,700 ft (5700 m); endurance 2 hours	**Armament:** two 0.303-in (7.7-mm) Vickers fixed forward-firing machine-guns in the upper part of the forward fuselage, and two 0.303-in (7.7-mm) Lewis trainable rearward-firing machine-guns in the rear cockpit
Weights: empty 1,675 lb (760 kg); maximum take-off 2,601 lb	

Hanriot HD.3s fully equipped the Aéronautique Militaire's Escadrille HD.174 from October 1918, as well as being distributed among various other front-line escadrilles and serving alongside other types.

Hanriot HD.14 series

Ranking alongside the Avro Type 504, as one of the most important of the world's training aircraft of the 1920s, the **HD.14** was a robust two-bay biplane with the instructor and pupil seated in a tandem arrangement of open cockpits. The early production version had long anti-noseover skids projecting from each leg of the landing gear, the HD.14 being designed to take serious punishment at the hands of its novice pilots.

Production of the HD.14 at the Hanriot works continued until 1928, a total of 2,100 aircraft being built in 11 different versions. Perhaps the most important subvariant was the **HD.14ter** (otherwise the **HD.14/23**), which was displayed at the 1922 Paris Salon de l'Aéronautique. Although it retained the 80-hp (60-kW) Le Rhône rotary engine of the original model, it incorporated many improvements: the wing area was reduced; the fuselage cross-section, the vertical tail surface, and the cabane and interplane struts were revised; a new Hanriot-patented dual-control system was introduced; and the landing gear track was reduced to enable the HD.14 to be loaded on to the standard

SPECIFICATION

Hanriot HD.14 (early production)
Type: two-seat primary flying trainer
Powerplant: one Le Rhône 9 rotary piston engine rated at 80 hp (60 kW)
Performance: maximum speed 68 mph (110 km/h) at sea level; service ceiling 13,125 ft (4000 m); range 112 miles (180 km)
Weights: empty 1,223 lb (555 kg); maximum take-off 1,786 lb (810 kg)
Dimensions: wingspan 35 ft 8 in (10.87 m); length 23 ft 9½ in (7.80 m); height 9 ft 10 in (3.00 m); wing area 371.36 sq ft (34.50 m²)

Variants

HD.14S: This **Sanitaire** (air ambulance) version was introduced in 1925; the pupil's cockpit was deleted and replaced by a large opening section on the starboard side of the fuselage which provided room for one litter; exhibited during an international medical congress on 24 April 1925, it gained a French army order for more than 50 machines; two examples were sold to Poland in 1925
HD.141: conversion of 10 HD.14 and HD.321 machines for aero club use in 1928; powered by the 130-hp (97-kW) Clerget rotary engine
HD.28 or H.28: export HD.14 with the all-wood structure replaced largely by metal; the variant was built under licence in Poland, WWS 'Samolot' producing 144 between 1924 and 1926 and CWL at Warsaw a further 75; the Polish air arm took delivery of 10 **H.28S** air ambulances equivalent to the HD.14S
HD.17: a twin-float seaplane version of the HD.14 for the French Aéronautique Maritime with tail surfaces of increased area and the powerplant of one 130-hp (97-kW) Clerget rotary; more than 50 were eventually attached to French navy flying schools; seven HD.17s were at one stage given wheeled landing gear for landplane training; a few similar aircraft were exported to Estonia and Latvia
HD.40S: similar to the HD.14S but powered by the 120-hp (90-kW) Salmson 9Ac radial and having a mixed structure; 14 examples built
HD.41H: variant with the same engine and mixed construction as the HD.40S but otherwise similar to the HD.17 adapted with an increased-area rudder and a single continuous cockpit for instructor and pupil in tandem; small batches of the type were exported to Greece and Portugal in 1925
HD.32: built in prototype form in 1924 and winning a French army competition for training aircraft in the Ep.2 category, the HD.32 was built in quantity; it retained the general configuration of the HD.14ter but had revised landing gear, reduced wingspan, a redesigned tailplane, and a mixed structure; a version of the HD.32 with the 110-hp (82-kW) Anzani engine was built under licence by the Zmaj concern of Zemun and used in limited numbers by the Yugoslav army air arm; one HD.32 was sold to the Japanese government; by 1932 most of the French HD.32s had been withdrawn from army service and a number was refurbished and sold to aero clubs and private owners
HD.320: single machine built in 1926 with the 120-hp (90-kW) Salmson 9Ac engine but otherwise similar to HD.32
HD.321: another version of the HD.32 but with the 130-hp (97-kW)

army trailer.

The French army obtained 1,925 examples of the HD.14, and these served in the Ep.2 training category with sections d'entrainement of the different air regiments. Other HD.14s were exported to Bulgaria, Greece, Mexico and Spain, but the best foreign customers were Poland, which purchased 70 examples in 1924, and the USSR, which obtained 30 aircraft. In Japan the Mitsubishi company imported a pattern aircraft and then between 1925 and 1927, built 145 HD.14s under licence for the Imperial Japanese Army. The Japanese designation for the HD.14 was **Mitsubishi Army Type Ki 1 Trainer**.

The HD.14 was renowned for its toughness and longevity and, when the type was eventually retired from military service, many French army machines were handed over to aero clubs or sold to private owners. In consequence the HD.14 was a quite common sight throughout the 1930s. One

HD.14 achieved a quite remarkable record when flown by army Lieutenant Joseph Thoret during a glider meet at Biskra, Algeria, on 27 January 1923. This brought together a number of rather primitive designs, a factor which, combined with a relative ignorance of the value of thermals to unpowered flight, led to a signal lack of success. Thoret took off in his HD.14 on 3 February and, taking

advantage of rising air currents in the vicinity of a nearby mountain, stopped his engine and was able to remain airborne for a further 7 hours 3 minutes. On 27 August 1924, while flying in the foothills of the Alps at a height of only 80 ft (25 m), Thoret stopped the HD.14's engine and was able to glide for a further 9 hours 4 minutes, attaining an altitude increase of 1,885 ft (6575 m) in the process!

Hanriot's HD.14 was of equal-span configuration with balanced ailerons on both upper and lower wings. It had fixed tailskid landing gear including wide-track independent main units, each with a twin-wheel assembly.

Clerget 9B engine; 11 were built as new in 1928; four HD.14 and four HD.320 machines were later converted as HD.321s, and in their turn four of the original HD.321s were converted as HD.141s
H.410: five completed in 1928 with the wide-track landing gear of the original HD.14 adapted with more effective shock absorbers and powered by the 100-hp (75-kW) Lorraine 5Pa engine; three built in France and a licence obtained by Yugoslavia for construction in that country
H.411: two built in 1930 to a standard similar to that of the H.410 but with the 95-hp (71-kW) Salmson 7Ac engine
LH.412: prototype was a conversion of the second H.410 to take a 110-hp (82-kW) Lorraine engine; there followed single conversions of the fifth H.410 and 143rd HD.32, plus four new-build machines; used by Hanriot flying schools

Hanriot HD.19

The **HD.19** was a relatively successful Et.2-category intermediate flying trainer, a single-bay biplane largely of wooden construction with dual controls for the pupil and instructor, who were seated in tandem in a single cockpit. The prototype, initially powered by a Hispano-Suiza 8Ab Vee engine, was judged one of the successful entrants in a competition that was sponsored by the French ministry of war and took place between 29 May and 6 July 1923. The HD.19 found favour in Poland, 55 being built there under licence by the WWS 'Samolot' workshops during 1925. One HD.19 was purchased by the designer Marcel Bloch.

SPECIFICATION

Hanriot HD.19
Type: two-seat intermediate flying trainer
Powerplant: one Hispano-Suiza 8Ac Vee piston engine rated at 180 hp (134 kW)
Performance: maximum speed 103 mph (165 km/h) at sea level; service ceiling 18,045 ft (5500 m); range 199 miles (320 km)
Weights: empty 1,455 lb (660 kg); maximum take-off 2,094 lb (950 kg)
Dimensions: wingspan 30 ft 1¼ in (9.19 m); length 23 ft 7¾ in (7.21 m); height 7 ft 3¾ in (2.23 m); wing area 287.41 sq ft (26.70 m²)

Both the Imperial Japanese army (illustrated) and the Czechoslovak air arm purchased single examples of the HD.19.

Hansa-Brandenburg CC and KDW

The first flying boat designed for Hansa-Brandenburg by Ernst Heinkel was the **FB**, a design derived from that of the highly successful Lohner flying boats designed and built in Austria-Hungary, with whose air service Hansa-Brandenburg had close ties. Heinkel's first genuinely original flying boat was the fascinating and highly attractive little **Hansa-Brandenburg CC** fighter. The type owed its origins to a requirement of the Imperial Austro-Hungarian navy air service, and first flew in prototype form during February 1917, despite the fact that the type had been ordered as early as May 1916.

The CC was an unequal-span biplane of largely wooden construction covered with plywood on the hull and fin, and with fabric on the rest of the flying surfaces. Its upper and lower wings were separated and braced by an arrangement of cabane struts and, on each side, by four Vee struts that met in the centre of each wing half and obviated all need for flying and landing wires as well as providing the fighter with its 'star-strutter' nickname. The powerplant comprised one 150-hp (112-kW) Benz Bz.III inline engine mounted above the central hull, to drive a two-bladed wooden pusher propeller, and cooled by a frontal radiator.

The Imperial German navy air service did not favour the use of fighter flying boats, but so impressive were the performance and handling of the CC prototype that the service ordered two batches of 10 and 25 such boats that were delivered in the course of 1917.

Hansa-Brandenburg CC and KDW (continued)

The first 10 CC 'boats were delivered to a standard closely similar to that of the prototype with an armament of one 0.312-in (7.92-mm) LMG 08/15 fixed forward-firing machine-gun protruding through the pilot's large windscreen, but the last 25 'boats were delivered to an improved standard with one or two machine-guns, generally no windscreen, a slightly longer hull, the engine cooled by a pair of radiators in the upper wing outboard

of the centreline and, in some of the 'boats, the engine in a streamlined nacelle and driving a propeller fitted with a neat spinner.

With its lack of land bases on the eastern and northern coasts of the Adriatic Sea, the Imperial Austro-Hungarian navy air service was a keen believer in the utility of the fighter flying boat, and decided that the CC would be a highly effective weapon in its armoury. In Austro-

Hungarian service the CC was known as the **KDW** (**Kampf Doppeldecker Wasser**, or fighter biplane, water). The KDW was built under licence in Austria-Hungary by Phönix with an armament of one or two 0.315-in (8-mm) Schwarzlose machine-guns and a powerplant that comprised either of two inline engine types, namely the 185-hp (138-kW) Austro-Daimler or 200-hp (149-kW) Hiero types. In overall terms the KDW compared favourably with the Nieuport Nie.11 fighter operated by the opposing Italian forces, for although the Nie.11 was more manoeuvrable than the KDW it had lower overall performance and, in the case of the twin-gun KDW machines, less firepower.

The CC's hull was of rectangular section with a rounded upper decking and a single-step planing bottom.

The type was flown by a number of the Imperial Austro-Hungarian navy air service's better fighter pilots including Linienschiffsleutnant Gottfried Banfield, the service's highest-scoring 'ace' with nine confirmed victories. Austro-Hungarian production of the CC as the KDW may have totalled 135 'boats, but there remains the possibility that up to 20 of this figure may have comprised other aircraft in what the Imperial Austro-Hungarian navy air

service called its 'A' class.

Late in 1917 or early in 1918 Herr Mickl, a designer working for the Phönix company, developed an improved version of the KDW with the Austro-Daimler engine and an armament of two 0.32-in (8-mm) Schwarzlose machine-guns. Up to 45 such 'boats may have been delivered in 1918, by which time both the Austro-Hungarian forms of the KDW had been outclassed technically by the fighters now flown by the Italians.

SPECIFICATION	
Hansa-Brandenburg CC	maximum take-off 2,273 lb (1031 kg)
Type: single-seat fighter flying-boat	**Dimensions:** wingspan 30 ft 6⅛ in (9.30 m); length 25 ft 2¾ in (7.69 m); height 11 ft 8¾ in (3.58 m); wing area 285.47 sq ft (26.52 m²)
Powerplant: one Benz Bz.III inline piston engine rated at 150 hp (112 kW)	
Performance: maximum speed 109 mph (175 km/h) at sea level; climb to 6,560 ft (2000 m) in 11 minutes 12 seconds; endurance 3 hours 30 minutes	**Armament:** one or occasionally two 0.312-in (7.92-mm) LMG 08/15 fixed forward-firing machine-guns in the upper forward part of the hull
Weights: empty 1,578 lb (716 kg);	

Hansa-Brandenburg C.I

One of the earliest designs of Ernst Heinkel for Hansa-Brandenburg, the **C.I** was built extensively for its era, being constructed not only by Brandenburg but also under licence by Phönix and Ufag in Austria. A conventional two-bay biplane of wood and fabric

construction, it had a slender fuselage with the powerplant mounted in the nose, provided a combined open cockpit for the pilot and observer/ gunner, and mounted a braced tail unit at the rear. Landing gear was of the tailskid type.

Entering service in

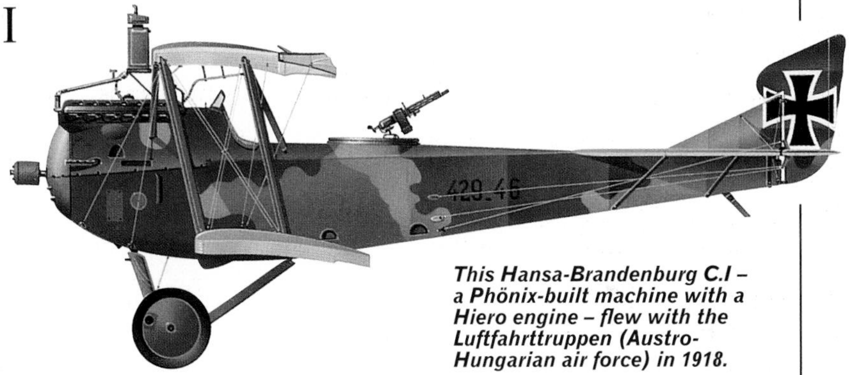

This Hansa-Brandenburg C.I – a Phönix-built machine with a Hiero engine – flew with the Luftfahrttruppen (Austro-Hungarian air force) in 1918.

SPECIFICATION	
Hansa-Brandenburg C.I Srs 169 (Ufag-built)	maximum take-off 2,910 lb (1320 kg)
Type: two-seat armed reconnaissance aircraft	**Dimensions:** wingspan 40 ft 2¼ in (12.25 m); length 27 ft 8¾ in (8.45 m); height 10 ft 11 in (3.33 m)
Powerplant: one 220-hp (164-kW) Benz BzMa 6-cylinder inline piston engine	**Armament:** (standard) one Schwarzlose 0.32-in (8-mm) machine-gun on pivoted mount over the rear of the combined cockpit
Performance: maximum speed 98 mph (158 km/h), service ceiling 19,685 ft (6000 m)	
Weights: empty 1,808 lb (820 kg),	

1916, C.Is saw wide-scale use by the Austrian forces and some examples continued in service until the end of World War I. In the long period of time over which they were operational, C.Is were seen with powerplants

ranging from 160 to 230 hp (119 to 172 kW) and with a variety of armaments. Basically this comprised a single machine-gun at the rear of the cockpit, but later versions also had a single forward-firing machine-gun

mounted in different positions. Some were used for light bombing missions and were equipped to carry up to 220 lb (100 kg) of light fragmentation or incendiary bombs on racks beneath the fuselage or lower wing.

Hansa-Brandenburg KD (D.I) and KDW

Early in 1916, the Imperial Austro-Hungarian army air service decided to procure an advanced fighter for local production and commissioned the required type from Hansa-Brandenburg. The latter entrusted the task of designing the new fighter to Ernst Heinkel, who opted for a basic concept derived from that of his **KDD** experimental reconnaissance machine scaled down from two- to one-seat accommodation. The key features of the basic design were a sturdy plywood-covered wooden fuselage and a biplane wing

cellule with the so-called 'star strut' arrangement that served the role of conventional struts and wing bracing wires. The prototype of the new fighter first flew in the spring of 1916 as a decidedly ungainly machine that was formally designated **KD** (**Kampf Doppeldecker**, or fighter biplane) but was generally known as the **Spinne** (spider).

Even so, the KD had fairly good performance, and the Imperial Austro-Hungarian army air service ordered the type into production in a somewhat modified form as the **D.I**

with the 160-hp (119-kW) Austro-Daimler inline engine, the height of the forward fuselage reduced as far as possible, modified engine cooling and the rear fuselage completely revised.

The D.I entered production in the summer of 1916 and entered service in the autumn of the same year as a machine that can be

Forward vision for the D.I's pilot was decidedly poor, since two side-by-side radiator blocks filled the gap between the top of the cowling and the upper wing.

described charitably as only an indifferent fighter.

The D.I was manufactured to the extent of perhaps 200 aircraft in two

series as the Phönix-built **D.I Series 28** with the 160-hp (119-kW) Austro-Daimler engine and the Ufag-built **D.I Series 65** with the 185-hp (138-kW) Austro-Daimler engine. The type's entry into service

The KDW employed two-point alighting gear, based on a pair of single-step wooden floats that were carried below the inboard parts of the lower wing by a pair of wire-braced N-type struts.

was accompanied by a spate of accidents resulting from the its lack of adequate directional stability and control, and many of the later aircraft were completed with a modified vertical tail surface designed comprising a small fixed fin of low aspect ratio carrying a slightly taller rudder. Production ended in the spring of 1917 and, despite its tricky flight characteristics, the type remained in service with the Imperial Austro-Hungarian army air service to the end of World War I.

A few aircraft were converted later in the war with the 200-hp (149-kW) Hiero inline engine, but it is thought that these were development machines for the Phönix D.I rather than attempts to keep the basic aircraft viable in the fighter role by the adoption of an uprated powerplant. The standard D.I survived in small numbers with the Austrian army air service into the early 1920s.

In the first half of World War I Ernst Heinkel, chief designer and later technical director of Hansa-Brandenburg, designed a number of biplane floatplanes and flying boats for the use of the Imperial Germany navy air service. The first of the floatplanes to be built in more than limited numbers was the **KDW (Kampf Doppeldecker Wasser,** or sea fighting biplane), a fighter which was also Heinkel's first single-seat seaplane. The origins of the type can be found in the need of the Imperial German navy air service for fighter floatplanes with which to defend its seaplane bases along the southern shore of the North Sea.

The KDW may be regarded as the floatplane equivalent of the KD landplane fighter designed for the Imperial Austro-Hungarian army air service. The powerplant was based on one 150-hp (112-kW) Benz Bz.III inline engine: this was installed in the front of the fuselage inside a full light alloy cowling, drove a two-bladed wooden propeller of the tractor type, and was cooled by a frontal radiator.

The Imperial German navy air service ordered an initial three aircraft in June 1916. One had plain exhausts discharging to starboard, while the other two had chimney-type exhausts that discharged above the upper wing. The trials of these three machines were successful enough to persuade the Imperial German navy air service to order an initial 10 production aircraft that were delivered in February 1917 to a slightly modified standard with a powerplant of one 160-hp (119-kW)

Mercedes D.III inline engine and cooled by a revised radiator, different tailplane bracing struts, and an armament of one 0.31-in (7.92-mm) LMG 08/15 fixed forward-firing machine-gun on the starboard upper side of the forward fuselage.

These machines were followed into service during March and April 1917 by a second production batch of 10 aircraft that reverted to the Bz.III engine and had a smaller rudder. The autumn of 1917 and the winter of 1917-18 saw the delivery of the third and fourth production batches, comprising 15 and 20 aircraft respectively, with the powerplant of one 160-hp (119-kW) Maybach Mb.III inline engine, shorter floats, a modified vertical tail surface with a low-aspect-ratio upper fin and a plain rudder, an armament of two LMG 08/15 machine-guns and, in some aircraft, additional interplane strutting.

The KDW floatplanes are thought to have served mainly at the seaplane stations on the coast of Flanders, but a few probably served with German units on the Adriatic Sea.

The **W.11** improved model, of which only three examples were delivered early in 1917, was basically a slightly enlarged and more powerful version of the KDW in its final form with upper and lower fins as well as an armament of two LMG 08/15 machine-guns. The final development of the series was the **W.25,** of which only the prototype was built with an armament of two LMG 08/15 machine guns, a powerplant of one 150-hp (112-kW) Benz Bz.III engine, and a revised wing cellule with conventional strutting, flying and landing wires, and strut-connected ailerons on the outboard ends of both the upper and lower wings' trailing edges.

Hansa-Brandenburg W.12

Defence fighters for seaplane bases were found to be of considerable value but had a common weakness: they were highly vulnerable to an attack from the rear. The **W.12** represented Heinkel's solution to the problem, for it was a two-seat fighter of the floatplane type with an observer/gunner in the rear open cockpit and armed with a machine-gun on a trainable mounting.

Of wooden construction covered largely with fabric, the W.12 was a conventional single-bay biplane mounted on a side-by-side of wooden single-step floats. By comparison with the KDW it was larger and had a wing structure that was sufficiently robust to be braced by a pair of parallel interplane struts towards each wing tip without flying and landing wires. The W.12's most unusual feature was its tail unit, designed specifically to provide the maximum uninterrupted field of fire for the rear gun. Thus there was no fin, the fuselage tapering to a vertical knife-edge to carry a rudder that extended into a horn-balanced area below the fuselage; the tailplane, free from vulnerable bracing struts, was mounted atop the upswept rear fuselage.

The prototype first flew early in 1917 and after service tests, the W.12 was ordered into production. The W.12 proved effective against Allied seaplanes, and a total of 146 was built. The powerplant of early and late production aircraft was based on the Mercedes D.III inline engine, but just over half of the aircraft had the 150-hp (112-kW) Benz Bz.III. One of the W.12s based at Zeebrugge gained the distinction of destroying the British non-rigid airship C.27 during December 1917.

Variants

W.27: single example of a developed version of the W.12 which differed primarily by having I-type interplane and centre-section struts, and the 195-hp (145-kW) Bz.IIIb engine
W.32: further developed version of the W.12 concept; basically a W.27 with the 160-hp (119-kW) Mercedes D.III engine; two or three built

Hansa-Brandenburg W.12

Suspended from a dock-side crane, this W.12 shows the type's layout, including the unorthodox empennage, to advantage.

Hansa-Brandenburg W.18

Heinkel designed the **W.18** in response to an Imperial Austro-Hungarian navy air service requirement for a fighter flying boat to succeed the obsolescent CC. The W.18 was a flying-boat with a single-step hull, a staggered, single-bay biplane wing cellule and a tail unit with the horizontal surface carried about halfway up the vertical surface to keep it clear of hull-generated spray during the 'boat's take-off and landing runs. The open cockpit was located just ahead of the leading edges of the dihedralled and backward-swept lower wing, which carried small floats under its outboard ends.

The W.18 prototype first flew early in 1917 with the 150-hp (112-kW) Benz Bz.III inline engine driving a two-bladed pusher propeller that turned in a shallow cut-out in the upper wing's trailing edge. Although one 'boat of this original type was delivered to the Imperial German navy air service in December 1917, probably for evaluation, the only service to order the type in production form was the Imperial Austro-Hungarian navy air service. The production model, produced under licence as the **Phönix A.50**, was fitted with an Austro-Hungarian engine of greater power than the Bz.III and also with Austro-Hungarian armament. Some 47 such 'boats were delivered between September 1917 and May 1918, and were used for both offensive patrolling over the northern end of the Adriatic Sea and defensive work near Austro-Hungarian naval bases.

A considerable interplane gap, filled by a central arrangement of cabane struts (including the bearers for the engine) and two sets of parallel interplane struts, was a feature of the W.18.

SPECIFICATION	
Hansa-Brandenburg W.18 (A.50) **Type:** single-seat flying-boat fighter **Powerplant:** one Hiero inline piston engine rated at 200 hp (149 kW) **Performance:** maximum speed 106 mph (170 km/h) at sea level; climb to 9,845 ft (3000 m) in 23 minute **Weights:** empty 1,929 lb (875 kg);	maximum take-off 2,524 lb (1145 kg) **Dimensions:** wingspan 35 ft 1¼ in (10.70 m); length 26 ft 8¾ in (8.15 m); height 11 ft 3⅜ in (3.45 m); wing area 370.07 sq ft (34.38 m²) **Armament:** two 0.32-in (8-mm) Schwarzlose fixed forward-firing machine-guns in the upper part of the forward hull

Hansa-Brandenburg W.29

One of the primary exponents of the W.12 and related **W.19** fighter floatplanes was Oberleutnant zur See Friedrich Christiansen, commander of the Imperial German navy air service's base at Zeebrugge. It is thought that it was Christiansen who inspired, and may indeed have participated in, the design of the **W.29** monoplane fighter floatplane after a conversation in the later part of 1917 in which he told Ernst Heinkel that the Imperial German navy air service would soon need a floatplane fighter superior to the W.12. Heinkel was forced by the realisation of Germany's growing shortage of materials and lack of a truly high-powered engine to decide that the required improvement in performance could be achieved only by reduction of drag and weight rather than the introduction of a higher-powered engine, and this dictated the adoption of a monoplane layout.

The W.29 therefore began to take shape as a development of the W.12 with essentially the same fuselage in slightly shortened form, an uprated version of the same powerplant and the same twin-float alighting gear in combination with a slightly modified version of the W.12's tail unit and a new low-set monoplane wing. The W.29 was of basically wooden construction covered with plywood on the fuselage and fabric on the flying surfaces, and the wing was increased in span and chord to provide an area almost as great as that of the W.12's.

The powerplant was based on an inline engine of the Benz Bz.III series: this was installed in the front of the fuselage inside a louvered light alloy cowling from which the top of the cylinder bank protruded, and drove a two-bladed wooden tractor propeller. The alighting gear was based on a pair of wooden single-step floats carried below the inner parts of the wing halves on struts.

The initial batch of six W.29s was ordered in December 1917, and it was the first of these that made the type's maiden flight in the early part of 1918 with Christiansen at the controls: so delighted was he with the new fighter's performance, which included considerable agility as well as good flight data figures, that he insisted on flying the floatplane to Zeebrugge on the very next day for operational use! The other five machines of the first W.29 batch entered full service in April 1918 with the same powerplant as the first aircraft, namely one 195-hp (145-kW) Benz Bz.IIIb engine, and in this and the following month the Imperial German navy air service ordered another four batches of aircraft in the form of 14, 36 and 20 machines with the 150-hp (112-kW) Bz.III engine and then a final six machines with the 185-hp (138-kW) Bz.IIIa engine. Of the Bz.III-engined aircraft, at least 20 and possibly as many as 40 were delivered to a slightly modified standard with the fixed forward-firing armament reduced from to two one machine-gun so that radio equipment could be installed.

The W.29s supplemented but did not supplant the W.12s already in service, but the crews of the opposing Short floatplanes and Curtiss and Felixstowe flying-boats soon discovered that the new German fighter was a particularly dangerous opponent as a result of its high performance and good agility. The W.29 was also used against naval vessels: on 6 July 1918 a formation of Hansa-Brandenburg floatplanes led by Christiansen surprised the British submarine *C.25* on the surface, and in only a short time the submarine's motors had been put out of action and many of its crew, including the commanding officer, had been killed or wounded by the German floatplanes' machine-gun fire, which could penetrate the thin plating of this old submarine's hull; eventually the *C.25* was towed into Harwich leaking like a sieve, and Christiansen was credited with a victory.

After the end of World War I in November 1918, a small number of W.29 floatplanes was sold to Denmark for service into the early 1920s.

Little more than a monoplane derivative of the W.12, the W.29 saw brief but useful service.

SPECIFICATION	
Hansa-Brandenburg W.29 **Type:** two-seat fighter floatplane **Powerplant:** one Benz Bz.III inline piston engine rated at 150 hp (112 kW) **Performance:** maximum speed 109 mph (175 km/h) at sea level; climb to 6,560 ft (2000 m) in 13 minutes; endurance about 4 hours **Weights:** empty 2,205 lb (1000 kg); maximum take-off 3,294 lb (1494 kg)	**Dimensions:** wingspan 44 ft 3½ in (13.50 m); length 30 ft 8½ in (9.36 m); height 9 ft 10 in (3.00 m); wing area 346.61 sq ft (32.20 m²) **Armament:** one or two 0.31-in (7.92-mm) LMG 08/15 fixed forward-firing machine-guns on the upper sides of the forward fuselage and one 0.31-in (7.92-mm) LMG 14 Parabellum trainable rearward-firing machine-gun in the rear cockpit

Hansa-Brandenburg W.33 and IVL A-22, and W.34

Ordered in April 1918 to the extent of an initial 26 aircraft later supplemented by an unknown number of additional machines, the **W.33** was basically an enlarged and more powerfully engined development of the W.29.

The first of the floatplanes was delivered with a fixed forward-firing armament of two LMG machine-guns, but some of the later machines were completed to a higher-performance standard with the fixed forward-firing armament reduced to just one machine-gun, although most of these machines were soon revised to the standard of the earlier aircraft. At least one of the W.33s was completed with a 20-mm Becker trainable cannon in the rear cockpit for improved offensive capability against vessels such as surfaced submarines and CMBs (Coastal Motor Boats), and some of the floatplanes were later retrofitted with radio equipment.

The W.33 clearly possessed excellent capabilities, but lacked the time and numbers to make its full impact before Germany agreed to the Armistice. After the war the Norwegian Naval Flying Boat Factory and the Norwegian Army Aircraft Factory built 30 and 11 essentially similar aircraft respectively. Finland bought two W.33s as pattern aircraft in 1922, and between 1923 and 1926 the Ilmailuvoimien Lentokonetehdas (Aviation Force Aircraft Factory) followed with 120 **IVL A-22** licence-built aircraft that remained in service for the coastal reconnaissance and later the training role into the middle of the following decade. The A-22 differed from the German original mainly in the removal of the two fixed forward-firing machine-guns, leaving a

single 0.3-in (7.62-mm) trainable rearward-firing weapon, and the replacement of the W.33's engine by the 300-hp (224-kW) Fiat A.12bis inline engine.

The W.33 also formed the basis of the **Aichi Experimental Type 15-Ko Reconnaissance Seaplane**, of which four examples were created in 1925-6 as a slightly scaled-down version for evaluation by the Imperial Japanese navy air force with the 300-hp (224-kW) Hispano-Suiza 8Fb Vee engine built

under licence as the Mitsubishi Type Hi.

The final expression of the monoplane floatplane concept created by Ernst Heinkel with the aid of Hans Klemm in World War I was the **W.34**. This was very much an evolutionary development of the W.33 with larger overall dimensions to allow the incorporation of a higher-rated engine, the 300-hp (224-kW) Basse und Selve BuS.IVa inline unit. Only one W.34 prototype had been completed before the

end of World War I, but a few more machines

followed after this with the Fiat A.12bis engine.

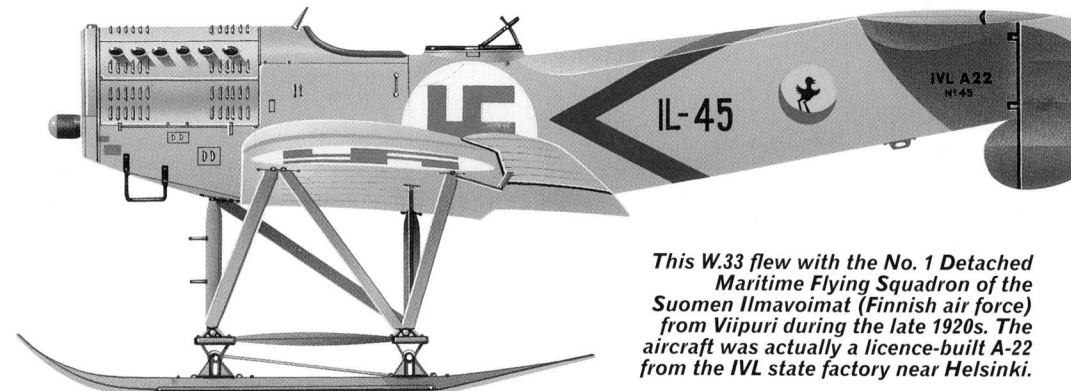

This W.33 flew with the No. 1 Detached Maritime Flying Squadron of the Suomen Ilmavoimat (Finnish air force) from Viipuri during the late 1920s. The aircraft was actually a licence-built A-22 from the IVL state factory near Helsinki.

Harbin SH-5 (PS-5)

Developed in China on the basis of the wings and powerplant of the Y-8 (Chinese-built An-12 'Cub') combined with the empennage of the Be-12 'Mail' and a new fuselage/hull combination clearly owing much to that of the Japanese US-1A, the **SH-5** (Shuihong, or Shuishang Hongzhaji = maritime bomber; **PS-5** in Westernised form) is a substantial flying-boat of all-metal construction with a single-step hull and retractable tricycle beaching gear with single-wheel main units and a twin-

wheel nose unit. The wing has a flat, constant-chord centre section that includes the inner two engines, and then increasing anhedral on the two tapered outer panels on each side.

The type first flew in April 1976 but entered service only in 1986 as the Chinese navy's dedicated maritime reconnaissance/anti-submarine flying-boat with a flight crew of five, a mission crew of three (expandable when required) or, in the 'boat's secondary transport role, passengers and/or freight. The type's development was seriously

delayed by the Cultural Revolution, which explains in part why a type that entered service comparatively recently has an elderly engine type and unpressurised accommodation. This last is no hindrance in the SH-5's low-altitude patrol regime, but means that transit flights between base and any distant operational area have to be flown at comparatively low altitude and therefore reduced speed. It is thought that perhaps only seven of the type were completed.

Known to the West as the PS-5, the SH-5 was in service in the latter part of 2000 to the extent of no more than five examples.

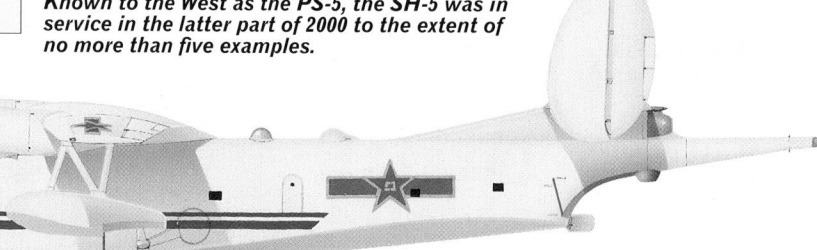

Harbin Y-11, Y-12 and Twin Panda

The **Y-11** is a simple utility transport of all-metal construction with a high-set wing braced to the ends of a stub wing structure that also supports the main units of the fixed tricycle landing gear. The machine was designed from the early 1970s to replace the

Shijiazhuang Y-5 (licence-built An-2 'Colt' of which more than 225 have been produced since 1970).

Despite its simple appearance, the Y-11 has comprehensive provision for STOL operation. This includes high-lift devices on the leading edge (fixed

slats inboard and automatic slats outboard) and a trailing edge occupied over its full span by drooping ailerons outboard of the double-slotted flaps.

The first example of the initial model flew in 1977 with a maximum payload of 2,072 lb (940 kg) including

up to eight passengers or freight, and was then built in small numbers (slightly more than 40 aircraft) mainly for the agriculture, forestry, and survey roles. The Y-11 is powered by two 285-hp (213-kW) Zhuzhou (SMPMC) Huosai-6A (Ivchyenko/ Vedeneyev AI-14RF) radial engines.

As the Y-11 revealed an inability to maintain a

height of 4,920 ft (1500 m) on one engine, the **Y-11B** was developed with a slightly altered airframe and two American turbocharged engines. The first of two flying and one static test prototypes flew in December 1990, and deliveries began in 1992 of the standard Y-11B and the **Y-11B(I)** with more advanced avionics.

Harbin Y-11, Y-12 and Twin Panda (continued)

The **Y-12 I** light transport is essentially a turboprop-powered derivative of the Y-11, with a wider and longer fuselage for increased payload. The first of three prototypes flew in July 1982, and only some 30 production aircraft followed with the power-plant of two Pratt & Whitney PT6A-11 turboprop engines each flat-rated at 500 shp (373 kW), as higher performance was offered by the **Y-12 II**.

The Y-12 II was first flown on 16 August 1984, with more powerful engines, a smaller ventral fin, and a revised wing without leading-edge slats. Further development of the basic concept resulted in the **Y-12 IV** that first flew on 30 August 1993 and received production authorisation in 1995. The Y-12 IV has swept wing tips and revisions to the landing gear, as well as the control surface actuation system, and a revised cabin able to accommodate a maximum of 19 passengers at an increased maximum take-off weight. The **Twin Panda** is a westernised version of the Y-12 IV offered by the Canadian Aerospace Group and its Panda Aircraft Company subsidiary.

SPECIFICATION

Harbin Y-11B(I)
Type: two-crew short-range STOL light transport
Powerplant: two Teledyne Continental TSIO-550-B flat-six piston engines each rated at 350 hp (261 kW)
Performance: maximum speed 165 mph (265 km/h) at 9,845 ft (3000 m); cruising speed 146 mph (235 km/h) at 9,845 ft (3000 m); initial climb rate 1,100 ft (336 m) per minute; service ceiling 19,685 ft (6000 m); range 671 miles (1080 km) with maximum fuel or 186 miles (300 km) with maximum

payload
Weights: empty 5,520 lb (2504 kg); maximum take-off 8,598 lb (3900 kg)
Dimensions: wingspan 56 ft ½ in (17.08 m); stub wingspan 11 ft 10¼ in (3.612 m); length 39 ft 10¼ in (12.15 m); height 17 ft ¼ in (5.19 m); wing area 365.97 sq ft (34.00 m²)
Payload: up to seven passengers or 1,984 lb (900 kg) of freight under normal conditions or 2,646 lb (1200 kg) of freight under restricted conditions

By October 1999, some 102 Y-12s had been delivered by HAMC (Harbin Aircraft Manufacturing Corporation), although production halted for a time to make way for a priority helicopter manufacturing programme. In addition, around 30 orders for the Twin Panda had also been received by this time.

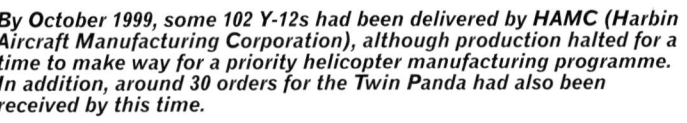

Hawker Audax

The Hawker company had no internal designation system that allows the modern historian to create a chronologically accurate listing of the company's aircraft types that is also valid in alphanumeric terms. The H. G. Hawker Engineering Co. Ltd. was registered in November 1920 and was in effect the successor to the Sopwith company, which was foundering in the period after World War I.

To meet the Air Ministry's Specification 7/31, which called for an army co-operation aircraft, Hawker proposed yet another derivative of its outstanding Hart light bomber. The new type was needed to supplant the Armstrong Whitworth Atlas with the Royal Air Force. An early series-built Hart was used to evaluate the potential of this aircraft to meet the 1931 requirement, and soon proved that it was eminently suitable for the task. Thus the first production example of the **Audax**, as the new type was named, made its first flight on 29 December 1931.

Entering service with No. 4 Squadron in February 1932, the Audax differed little from the Hart except in its mission equipment. The most valuable distinguishing feature was the long exhaust pipe which extended to a mid-fuselage position just behind the rear cockpit. This had been introduced to ensure that glare from the standard ejector exhausts, as fitted to the Hart, would not impair the pilot's view in low-level flight. The other external feature serving as a recognition aid was the long message pick-up hook beneath the fuselage.

Production of the **Audax Mk I** for the RAF totalled 624 aircraft by the time construction ended in 1937, but other examples had also been built for Iraq, Persia and the Straits Settlements. Because of the numbers involved, many of the RAF aircraft had to be manufactured under subcontract, examples being manufactured by Bristol (141), Gloster (25), Avro (244) and Westland (43).

The Hawker Audax Mk I was used to equip home-based RAF army co-operation squadrons from the time it entered service in 1932. until replaced in 1937 and relegated to advanced training, communications and glider tug duties. In these latter roles the Audax Mk I remained in home service well into the first years of fighting during World War II, and in the East African campaign No. 237 (Rhodesia) Squadron flew the type operationally during 1940 against the Italians in Eritrea and Somaliland. Other aircraft, based at Habbaniyah, were in action during the Iraqi revolt in July 1941.

No. 4 Sqn flew its Audax Mk I aircraft until they were replaced by Lysanders just prior to World War II.

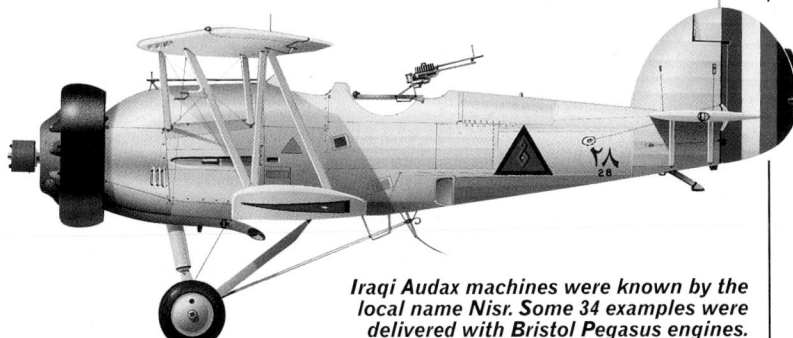

Iraqi Audax machines were known by the local name Nisr. Some 34 examples were delivered with Bristol Pegasus engines.

SPECIFICATION

Hawker Audax Mk I
Type: two-seat army co-operation aircraft
Powerplant: one Rolls-Royce Kestrel IB Vee piston engine rated at 530 hp (395 kW)
Performance: maximum speed 170 mph (274 km/h) at 2,400 ft (730 m); climb to 10,000 ft (3050 m) in 8 minutes 40 seconds; service ceiling 21,500 ft (6555 m); endurance 3 hours 30 minutes
Weights: empty 2,938 lb (1333 kg); maximum take-off 4,386 lb (1989 kg)
Dimensions: wingspan 37 ft 3 in

(11.35 m); length 29 ft 7 in (9.02 m); height 10 ft 5 in (3.17 m); wing area 348.00 sq ft (32.33 m²)
Armament: one 0.303-in (7.7-mm) Vickers fixed forward-firing machine-gun in the port side of the forward fuselage and one 0.303-in (7.7-mm) Lewis trainable rearward-firing machine-gun in the rear cockpit, plus up to 224 lb (102 kg) of disposable stores carried on underwing hardpoints, and generally comprising four 20-lb (9-kg) bombs or two 112-lb (51-kg) supply containers

Hawker Demon and Hart Fighter

The introduction of the Hart in 1930 marked a considerable advance in the RAF's light day bomber capability and in the process showed up the obsolescence of its day fighters. For air exercises in that year highlighted the fact that the Hart was somewhat faster than the fighters sent up to intercept it. It was soon mooted, therefore, that a two-seat fighter version of the Hart should be developed. Designed by Sydney Camm in response to the Air Ministry's Specification 15/30, which had been drafted on the basis of an evaluation of the first Hart bomber adapted with the powerplant of one Rolls-Royce Kestrel IIS super-charged Vee piston engine, a fixed forward-firing armament of two 0.303-in (7.7-mm) Vickers machine-guns and a trainable Lewis machine-gun in a rear cockpit adapted with a forward-angled coaming to provide improved fields of fire.

The prototype conversion was named **Hart Two-Seat Fighter**, soon altered to **Hart Fighter**, and was followed by a second conversion and then an initial six production aircraft to form the equipment from April 1931 of one flight of No. 23 Sqn. In the air exercises of 1931, the Hart Fighter proved to be the only RAF fighter capable of catching the Hart bomber, with which it had roughly comparable performance. These air exercises also revealed that the high speed of the Hart fighter made life most uncomfortable for the gunner as well as making it difficult for him to manoeuvre his machine-gun against the force of the slipstream, and among the expedients evaluated in an effort to overcome this problem were a pair of slip-stream-deflecting flaps between the two cockpits and a rudimentary hood over the pilot's cockpit to create a volume of dead air over the gunner's cockpit. These expedients were successful in shielding the gunner from the worst effects of the slipstream, but also impeded his field of fire.

Early in 1932, Specification 9/32 was issued for an improved version of the Hart Fighter, and an order was then placed for an initial 17 production aircraft that received the name **Demon**

in July 1932. The first of these **Demon Mk I** aircraft flew in February 1933 and all the aircraft had been completed by April of the same year, allowing the full conversion of No. 23 Sqn to the new fighter. In its initial form the Demon Mk I had the same dimensions and armament as later Demons, but differed in details such as its power-plant of one 485-hp (362-kW) Kestrel IIS Vee piston engine.

Total production of the Demon Mk I for the RAF up to December 1937 was 234 aircraft including 106 machines from Boulton Paul. The last 49 Hawker-built Demons and all those from Boulton Paul were built to an improved standard with the Kestrel VDR engine, and from October 1936 all the fighters delivered from the Boulton Paul plant at Wolverhampton were delivered to the **Turret Demon Mk I** stan-

dard with a hydraulically powered Frazer-Nash turret for the gunner: at the expense of considerable additional weight and complexity, this 'lobster-back' installation with its folding panels finally provided the gunner with adequate protection from the slipstream without any loss of field of fire. The turret was also retrofitted in many existing aircraft.

The last of the Demons was retired from British service in 1939.

Early in 1934, the Royal Australian Air Force decided to order a version of the Demon Mk I as a two-seat fighter that could also double in the day bomber role. The RAAF initially ordered 18 **Australian Demon Mk I** aircraft that were delivered from March 1935 in two-seat fighter layout with the Kestrel VDR engine and the armament of two Vickers Mk V fixed forward-firing

RAF squadrons that operated the Demon Mk I included Nos 23, 25, 29 (illustrated), 41, 64 and 65 in the UK, and the type also equipped No. 74 Squadron based in Malta as well as serving in Aden, Egypt and Malta with three of the units (Nos 23, 41 and 64 Squadrons) that had started in the UK. Later in its life the Demon Mk I was additionally operated by Nos 600, 601, 604, 607 and 608 Squadrons of the Auxiliary Air Force.

SPECIFICATION	
Hawker Demon Mk I	**Dimensions:** wingspan 37 ft 2 in
Type: two-seat fighter	(11.33 m); length 29 ft 7 in
Powerplant: one Rolls-Royce	(9.02 m); height 10 ft 5 in (3.17 m);
Kestrel VDR Vee piston engine	wing area 347.00 sq ft (32.24 m²)
rated at 584 hp (435 kW)	**Armament:** two 0.303-in (7.7-mm)
Performance: maximum speed	Vickers Mk III fixed forward-firing
182 mph (293 km/h) at 16,000 ft	machine-guns in the sides of the
(4875 m); climb to 10,000 ft	forward fuselage, and one 0.303-in
(3050 m) in 7 minutes 55 seconds;	(7.7-mm) Lewis trainable machine-
service ceiling 27,800 ft (8475 m);	gun in a Frazer-Nash
endurance 2 hours 30 minutes	power-operated 'lobster-back'
Weights: empty 3,336 lb	turret, plus up to 160 lb (73 kg) of
(1513 kg); maximum take-off	disposable stores carried on two
4,668 lb (2117 kg)	underwing hardpoints

machine-guns and one Lewis trainable rearward-firing machine-gun. The second batch of 36 aircraft was delivered in 1936 to a somewhat modified army co-operation standard with the 600-hp (447-kW) Kestrel V engine, provision under the lower wing for six hardpoints for a bomb load of up to 500-lb (113-kg), and a prone bombing position in the lower fuselage with a

Mk VII sight for the use of the gunner in his alternative role as the bombardier.

These aircraft suffered a high accident rate as a result of the RAAF's lack of a suitable conversion trainer, and as a consequence the service ordered a final batch of 10 aircraft to the **Australian Demon Mk II** standard as dual-control trainers with the ability to tow targets for air gunnery training.

Hawker Fury I and II

Design of the **Fury** biplane fighter reached back to 1927, when the Air Ministry's Specification F.20/27 was raised to detail the requirement for an interceptor fighter. Although Hawker's **F.20/27** prototype was powered, as required by the specification, with a radial engine in the form of the 450-hp (336-kW) Bristol Jupiter, this prototype failed to gain a production contract. However, the company's experience with this type proved valuable when the service debut of the Hart day bomber led to the official realisation that the British fighter force was equipped with obsolescent aircraft. This led to the accelerated design and development of a new private-venture prototype which Hawker called the **Hornet**. In this machine Sydney Camm had decided to forget about the Air Ministry's interest in a radial-engined powerplant and instead used the Rolls-Royce F.XIS (later named Kestrel) Vee engine. This

aircraft was, in effect, the prototype of the Fury, duly acquired by the Air Ministry but redesignated Fury to conform to then-current RAF nomenclature.

An attractive aircraft, with very clean lines, the **Fury Mk I** was the RAF's first fighter able to exceed a speed of 200 mph (322 km/h) in level flight when it entered service with No. 43 (Fighter) Sqn in May 1931. It was an unequal-span single-bay biplane with a basic struc-

ture of metal, covered with fabric except for the light alloy panels on the forward fuselage, had fixed tailskid landing gear and was powered by one 525-hp (391-kW) Rolls-Royce Kestrel IIS engine.

Like the Hart, however, the Fury appeared with a variety of different engines either for test purposes or to meet the specific demands of foreign purchasers, and these engine types included the Armstrong Siddeley Panther, Bristol Mercury, Hispano-Suiza 12NB and 12X, Lorraine Petrel, and

SPECIFICATION	
Hawker Fury Mk II	**Weights:** empty 2,734 lb
Type: single-seat fighter	(1240 kg); maximum take-off
Powerplant: one Rolls-Royce	3,609 lb (1637 kg)
Kestrel VI Vee piston engine rated	**Dimensions:** wingspan 30 ft
at 640 hp (477 kW)	(9.14 m); length 26 ft 9 in (8.15 m);
Performance: maximum speed	height 10 ft 2 in (3.10 m); wing
223 mph (359 km/h) at 16,500 ft	area 252.00 sq ft (23.41 m²)
(5030 m); climb to 10,000 ft	**Armament:** two 0.303-in (7.7-mm)
(3050 m) in 3 minutes 50 seconds;	Vickers Mk V fixed forward-firing
service ceiling 29,500 ft (8990 m);	machine-guns in the upper part of
range 270 miles (435 km)	the forward fuselage

Pratt & Whitney Hornet S2B1G. Initial production of Fury Mk Is totalled about 160 aircraft, and these were followed by two different but related private-venture aircraft, the

Intermediate Fury and the **High-Speed Fury**, which were development aircraft to meet the requirements of the Air Ministry's Specifications F.7/30 and F.14/32 respectively.

This No. 43 Sqn Fury Mk II wears the Earth and Dark Green disruptive camouflage that was applied to RAF fighters during the Munich Crisis of 1938.

Hawker Fury I and II (continued)

Specifications F.7/30 and F.14/32 led to conversion of an early Fury Mk I with a more powerful Kestrel VI engine and wheel spats. This was ordered into production as the **Fury Mk II** to meet the requirements of Specification 6/35, the first of these aircraft entering service with No. 25 (Fighter) Squadron early in 1937. Although the Fury Mk II was able to demonstrate an increase of some 10 per cent in maximum speed, this additional capability was not achieved without cost, for in spite of the

increased fuel capacity there was a 10 per cent reduction in range.

Both Fury versions proved attractive to other nations, and Furies were built for the air arms of Norway, Persia, Portugal, South Africa, Spain and Yugoslavia.

The RAF received 98 Fury Mk IIs, which equipped six squadrons. The Fury remained in first-line service until replaced by the Hurricane in 1939, and after the outbreak of World War II some Fury Mk IIs continued to operate in the training role. Three

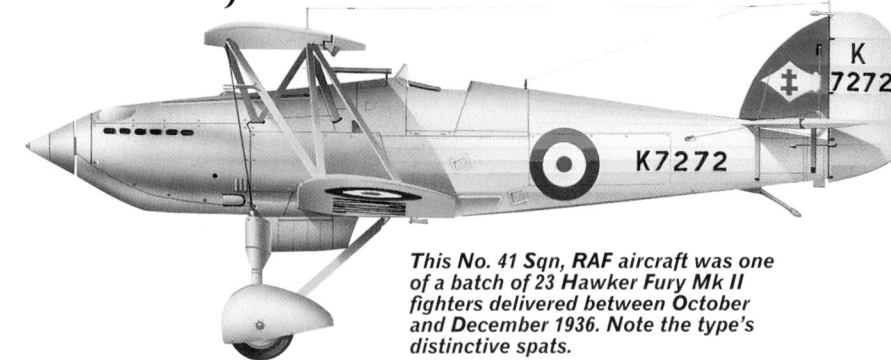

This No. 41 Sqn, RAF aircraft was one of a batch of 23 Hawker Fury Mk II fighters delivered between October and December 1936. Note the type's distinctive spats.

squadrons were used by the South African Air Force in East Africa

during the early stages of World War II, and Furies of the Yugoslav air force

saw combat during the German invasion of that country in April 1941.

Hawker Hardy

Basically an adaptation of the Hart/Audax concept, the **Hardy** was developed in response to the Air Ministry's Specification G.23/33, which called for an aircraft to take over from the Westland Wapiti that was currently serving with

the RAF's No. 30 Sqn on air policing duties in Iraq. The Hardy was fundamentally a Hart with special equipment, the prototype being a standard production Hart day bomber adapted with a tropical radiator to enhance engine cooling and, like the

Audax, the extended engine exhaust system and message pick-up hook.

First flown in this form on 7 September 1934, the Hardy entered service with No. 30 Sqn at Mosul, Iraq, during 1935. Gloster Aircraft manufactured all 47 production machines under subcontract to Hawker.

In 1938, when No. 30 Sqn re-equipped with the Bristol Blenheim, the surviving Hardy Mk Is were transferred to No. 6 Sqn, where they were quickly involved in operations,

providing close support for the British 16th Infantry Brigade during the trouble in Palestine. Finally, all surviving Hardy Mk Is in the Middle East were handed over to No. 237 (Rhodesian) Squadron, by which they were operated alongside the Audax. With

this squadron they saw action at the beginning of World War II, being deployed against the Italians in East Africa during 1940, and at least one aircraft is known to have survived as late as June 1941, when it was used for communications duties.

SPECIFICATION

Hawker Hardy Mk I
Type: two-seat general-purpose warplane
Powerplant: one Rolls-Royce Kestrel IB Vee piston engine rated at 530 hp (395 kW) or Kestrel X Vee piston engine rated at 585 hp (436 kW)
Performance: maximum speed 161 mph (259 km/h) at sea level; climb to 10,000 ft (3050 m) in 10 minutes 12 seconds; service ceiling 17,000 ft (5180 m); endurance 3 hours
Weights: empty 3,196 lb

(1450 kg); maximum take-off 5,005 lb (2270 kg)
Dimensions: wingspan 37 ft 3 in (11.35 m); length 29 ft 7 in (9.02 m); height 10 ft 7 in (3.23 m); wing area 348.00 sq ft (32.33 m²)
Armament: one 0.303-in (7.7-mm) Vickers fixed forward-firing machine-gun in the port side of the forward fuselage and one 0.303-in (7.7-mm) Lewis trainable rearward-firing machine-gun in the rear cockpit, plus underwing racks and attachments for water containers, flares, or four 20-lb (9-kg) bombs

K4315 flew the last operational Hardy flight, with No. 237 Sqn, on 9 May 1941. A tropical survival kit and water containers for use after an emergency landing in the desert, were standard items of Hardy equipment.

Hawker Hart

The **Hart** day bomber, which first entered service with the RAF's No. 33 Sqn at Eastchurch in January 1930, was the company's response to the Air Ministry's Specification 12/26. This called for design and development of a day bomber capable of reaching the then-unprecedented maximum speed of 160 mph (257 km/h), a performance requirement that was comfortably

exceeded as a result of the design team's combination of an excellent low-drag airframe with the Rolls-Royce F.XIB (later Kestrel) Vee engine in the prototype, which recorded its maiden flight in June 1928.

The service debut of the **Hart Mk I** created immense problems for the Air Ministry, for the new bomber was not only very considerably faster than contemporary bombers, in

some cases by as much as 80 mph (124 km/h), but could also show a 'clean pair of heels' to any fighters then in service. Among the many uses for which the Hart was adopted, one must mention its temporary deployment as a fighter with No. 23 (Fighter) Sqn.

Such a state of affairs was, of course, to the ultimate benefit of the country and the RAF, for strenuous efforts were made to develop new fighter aircraft

of much improved performance. The Hart was also included in this exercise, for following No. 23 (F) Sqn's experience with the **Hart Fighter**, attempts were made to improve and develop a specialised fighter version that materialised as the Demon. In overall terms, the Hart was a highly successful venture, for more Harts or aircraft of Hart origin were built in the UK during the period between the two world

wars than any other basic design. In addition to the standard Hart day bomber, the total included six examples of the Hart Fighter, 507 dual-control **Hart Trainer** machines, a number of aircraft without bomb gear and armament as **Hart Communications** aircraft for No. 24 Sqn, and tropicalised versions known as **Hart (India)** and **Hart (Special)**. When, in 1936, replacement began of the Hart with the Hind in opera-

SPECIFICATION

Hawker Hart Mk I
Type: two-seat day bomber
Powerplant: one Rolls-Royce Kestrel IB Vee piston engine rated at 525 hp (391 kW) or Kestrel XDR Vee piston engine rated at 510 hp (380 kW)
Performance: maximum speed 184 mph (296 km/h) at 5,000 ft (1525 m); climb to 10,000 ft (3050 m) in 8 minutes 20 seconds; service ceiling 21,350 ft (6510 m); range 470 miles (756 km)
Weights: empty 2,530 lb (1148 kg); maximum take-off

4,554 lb (2066 kg)
Dimensions: wingspan 37 ft 3 in (11.35 m); length 29 ft 4 in (8.94 m); height 10 ft 5 in (3.17 m); wing area 348.00 sq ft (32.33 m²)
Armament: one 0.303-in (7.7-mm) Vickers Mk II or Mk III fixed forward-firing machine-gun on the port side of the forward fuselage and one 0.303-in (7.7-mm) Lewis trainable rearward-firing machine-gun in the rear cockpit, plus up to 580 lb (263 kg) of disposable stores carried on three underwing hardpoints

This Hart Trainer was built by Armstrong Whitworth and delivered between June 1935 and March 1936. The aircraft was found derelict in 1962 and has since been restored for static display.

tional units, the Air Ministry allowed a considerable number of Harts to be made available to the South African Air Force, which started to receive deliveries toward the end of 1936. Other Harts operated abroad included eight for Estonia, delivered late in 1932 with interchangeable wheel and float landing gear. Sweden also found the Hart attractive and after

This No. 603 Sqn 'City of Edinburgh' Sqn, Auxiliary Air Force Hart was photographed over the Bass Rock on its way to the unit's annual camp at RAF Manston, Kent in 1934.

four had been built and delivered in 1934, an additional 42 were built under licence by the State Aircraft Factory: produced during 1935-6, these machines were powered by licence-built versions of the Bristol Pegasus radial engine.

The Hart also saw extensive use as an engine test-bed, and in addition to the standard Kestrel IB or XDR, the type was also flown with the Rolls-Royce Kestrel IS, IIB, IIS, IIIMS, V, VIS, XFP, XVI, P.V.2 and Merlin C and E; the Armstrong Siddeley Panther; the Bristol Jupiter, Pegasus, Perseus and Mercury; the Hispano-Suiza 12Xbrs; the Lorraine Petrel

Hfrs; and the Napier Dagger engines.

Total production, including the aircraft built under licence in Sweden, exceeded 1,000 units, which was an impressive figure for an aircraft type of the 1930s. The Hart Mk I bomber had been withdrawn from front-line service in the UK by 1938, but at the outbreak of World War II continued in operational service in the Middle East until replaced gradually by more modern types such as the Blenheim. In service with the South African Air Force, the Hart Mk I was used in the communications role until 1943.

Hawker Hartbees

Developed from the Hart and Audax series specially for service with the South African Air Force, the **Hartbees** (sometimes recorded as the **Hartbee** or **Hartebeeste**) was built only in token numbers in the UK, to serve initially as the pattern aircraft for licensed production in South Africa. The negotia-

tions for a licence to build a version of the Audax had started in 1934, to meet a SAAF requirement for a ground support warplane, and the Audax was generally agreed to most nearly satisfy this need without an excess of modifications.

Four examples were built by Hawker, the first two being essentially the

same as the RAF's Audax except that the extended exhaust system was deleted and the Kestrel IB engine was replaced by the 608-hp (453-kW) Kestrel VFP. These first two aircraft were flown initially in the UK on 28 June 1935, before being dispatched to South Africa in October 1935. The third and fourth examples were basically the same, differing only by having armour protection for the crew. South African production was carried out at the Roberts Heights factory in Pretoria, the first examples of the **Hartbees Mk I** being completed in the spring of 1937 and

passing their acceptance tests in July of the same year. Production totalled 65 aircraft supplied to two squadrons of the SAAF. A total of 53 of these remained in service at the outbreak of World War II, and these machines were deployed in Kenya together with a number of ex-RAF Harts. The Hartbees Mk I saw considerable action against the Italians during

operations on the Kenya/ Ethiopia border in mid-1940, its most significant operation being an attack in strength carried out on 11 June 1940. Not long after this however, the Hartbees Mk I was withdrawn from front-line use, then being relegated to the training and communication roles in which some aircraft remained in service until 1946.

SPECIFICATION	
Hawker Hartbees Mk I **Type:** two-seat general-purpose and ground-support warplane **Powerplant:** one Rolls-Royce Kestrel VFP Vee piston engine rated at 608 hp (453 kW) **Performance:** maximum speed 176 mph (283 km/h) at 6,000 ft (1830 m); climb to 10,000 ft (3050 m) in 8 minutes 24 seconds; service ceiling 22,000 ft (6705 m); endurance 3 hours 10 minutes **Weights:** empty 3,150 lb (1429 kg); maximum take-off 4,787 lb (2171 kg)	**Dimensions:** wingspan 37 ft 3 in (11.35 m); length 29 ft 7 in (9.02 m); height 10 ft 5 in (3.17 m); wing area 348.00 sq ft (32.33 m²) **Armament:** one 0.303-in (7.7-mm) Vickers Mk III fixed forward-firing machine-gun on the port side of the forward fuselage and one 0.303-in (7.7-mm) Lewis trainable rearward-firing machine-gun in the rear cockpit, plus up to 500 lb (227 kg) of disposable stores carried on two underwing hardpoints

No. 805 was the first of 65 Hawker Hartbees Mk I production aircraft built under licence by the Robert Heights factory at the South African Air Force Depot at Pretoria between 1937 and 1938.

Hawker Hector

Last of the many variants of the Hart to remain in first-line service with the RAF, the **Hector** was designed as a replacement for the Audax. The requirement was for an army co-operation aircraft of improved performance, and it was decided to use the Napier Dagger air-cooled engine which had first been fitted experimentally to a

Hart in 1933. While basically a Hart, the Hector differed considerably in appearance. This was due, of course, primarily to the changed engine installation which, because of its increased height, completely changed the characteristic pointed nose of the Hart family. In addition, the alteration caused to the aircraft's centre of

gravity by installation of this heavier engine was corrected by using a straight upper wing instead of the wing with swept-back outer panels that had characterised the earlier members of the family. In all other respects, the equipment and layout was generally similar to that of the Audax.

The first of the production **Hector Mk I** aircraft made its initial flight on 14 February 1936, and orders for this model totalled 178 by May 1936, when it was decided that these should be built under subcontract by Westland at Yeovil, Somerset. The first Westland-built production aircraft was delivered in February 1937, and all had been constructed and handed over to the RAF before the end of the year.

The Hector Mk I entered service with No. 4 Sqn in February 1937, and eventually equipped seven RAF squadrons on home bases.

The distinctive exhaust stacks of the Dagger engine (two rows of exhaust pipes on each side of the cowling), are clearly evident on this flight of four Hectors.

SPECIFICATION	
Hawker Hector Mk I **Type:** two-seat army co-operation warplane **Powerplant:** one Napier Dagger III MS H-type piston engine rated at 805 hp (600 kW) **Performance:** maximum speed 187 mph (301 km/h) at 6,500 ft (1980 m); climb to 10,000 ft (3050 m) in 5 minutes 40 seconds; service ceiling 24,000 ft (7315 m); endurance 2 hours 25 minutes **Weights:** empty 3,389 lb (1537 kg); maximum take-off 4,910 lb (2227 kg)	**Dimensions:** wingspan 36 ft 11½ in (11.26 m); length 29 ft 9¾ in (9.09 m); height 10 ft 5 in (3.17 m); wing area 346.00 sq ft (32.14 m²) **Armament:** one 0.303-in (7.7-mm) Vickers Mk V fixed forward-firing machine-gun on the port side of the forward fuselage and one 0.303-in (7.7-mm) Lewis trainable rearward-firing machine-gun in the rear cockpit, plus up to 460 lb (209 kg) of disposable stores carried on two underwing hardpoints

When these units began to receive the new Westland Lysander as a replacement type in 1938-9, the surviving Hector Mk Is were used to equip Nos 601, 612, 613, 614 and 615 Squadrons of the Auxiliary Air Force, and many of the aircraft remained in service with these units at the outbreak of World War II.

The Hector Mk I was used operationally by

No. 613 Squadron, which dispatched six of its aircraft to attack German troops near Calais, but the loss of two of these aircraft on this operation highlighted the fact that the Hector Mk I biplane should no longer be deployed in first-line service. Relegated to the role of glider tug, the Hector Mk I continued in service for another two years.

Hawker Henley

The Air Ministry's Specification P.4/34, issued in February 1934, detailed the requirement for a light bomber that could also be deployed in the close-support role. The specification called for generally high performance, including a maximum speed of around 300 mph (483 km/h). With high performance paramount, and with only a modest requirement in respect of bomb load, it seemed logical to the Hawker design team to evolve an aircraft somewhat similar in size to the Hurricane. This latter was then in an advanced design stage, but if at least some assemblies could be common to both there would not only be some economies but also certain production advantages.

Thus the **Henley**, as this new type was to become known, had its tailplane and outer wing panels built on jigs identical to those of the Hurricane, the only difference being that the wing panels of the Henley did not incorporate four machine-guns. Despite the difference in size between Hurricane and Henley, the Rolls-Royce Merlin engine selected for the fighter was also adopted for the light bomber. In configuration the Henley was a mid-wing cantilever monoplane, the space under the wing being used for a weapons bay rated at 550 lb (249 kg); provision was made under the wing for the carriage of two 250-lb (113-kg) or eight 20-lb (9-kg) bombs. Another major difference was in the accommodation, the

Henley having provision for an observer/gunner equipped with one 0.303-in (7.7-mm) Lewis trainable rearward-firing machine-gun; provision was made in the wing for one 0.303-in (7.7-mm) Vickers fixed forward-firing machine-gun.

Construction of a prototype began in mid-1935, but with priority going to the Hurricane it was not until 10 March 1937 that the Henley Mk I prototype recorded its first flight with the Merlin 'F' engine. The prototype was later revised with outer wing panels of the type now adopted for the Hurricane, with the original fabric skinning replaced by a stressed light alloy covering, and the Merlin I engine was also retrofitted. The following test programme revealed that the Henley had excellent overall performance. It was at this point that the Air Ministry decided that it no longer needed a light bomber, so the Henley was ordered into production as a target tug, of which 200 were built under subcontract by Gloster Aircraft. The **Henley Mk II** second prototype, with the Merlin II engine, was modified to suit the revised role, and first flew on 26 May 1938: it differed primarily by having a propeller-driven

Insufficient airflow passing across the Henley's radiators at its low towing speed led to perpetual overheating of the Merlin powerplant.

winch to haul in the drogue cable after air-to-air firing sorties.

Designated **Henley Mk III**, production aircraft entered service with Nos 1, 5 and 10 Bombing and Gunnery Schools, as well as with the Air Gunnery Schools at Barrow, Millom and Squires Gate. It was then discovered that unless towing operations were restricted to an unrealistically low speed, the rate of engine failure was unacceptably high. The Henley was therefore with-

drawn from the standard target-towing role and redeployed to an even less suitable task, that of towing larger drogue targets with anti-aircraft co-operation units and squadrons. Not surprisingly, the number of engine failures increased and several Henleys were lost in accidents. The situation was finally resolved only in mid-1942 when the Henley was withdrawn from service and replaced by the Boulton Paul Defiant and Miles Martinet.

SPECIFICATION	
Hawker Henley Mk III **Type:** two-seat target tug **Powerplant:** one Rolls-Royce Merlin II or III Vee piston engine rated at 1,030 hp (768 kW) **Performance:** maximum speed 272 mph (438 km/h) with air-to-air target and 200 mph (322 km/h) with ground-to-air target; climb to 20,000 ft (6095 m) in 22 minutes 30 seconds; service ceiling	27,000 ft (8230 m); range 950 miles (1529 km) **Weights:** empty 6,010 lb (2726 kg); maximum take-off 8,480 lb (3846 kg) **Dimensions:** wingspan 47 ft 10½ in (14.59 m); length 36 ft 5 in (11.10 m); height 14 ft 7½ in (4.46 m); wing area 342.00 sq ft (31.77 m²)

Hawker Hind

With the beginning of the RAF's expansion in 1934, the Air Ministry issued Specification G.7/34 for a light bomber to serve as an interim replacement for the Hart bomber. This was intended to provide a short-term boost in capability and also allow the training of new crews as a bridge over the technology and personnel gap pending the advent of new-generation aircraft such as the Bristol Blenheim and Fairey Battle.

Hawker's proposal to meet this requirement was a new derivative of the Hart, and differed primarily in its use of the more powerful Kestrel V engine

but with other changes including modification of the rear cockpit to improve conditions, field of fire and prone bombing position, and a tailwheel replacing the Hart's tailskid. The **Hind** prototype flew for the first time on 12 September 1934, and just under one year later, on 1 September 1935, the first **Hind Mk I** off the production line took to the air. The first unit to receive the Hind Mk I was No. 21 Sqn, then at Bircham Newton, Norfolk, which was allocated sufficient to equip one flight, and at the same time single flights of Nos 18 and 34 Sqns were similarly

equipped. Subsequent production aircraft were delivered to these squadrons until each was at full strength, after which Nos 12 and 142 Sqns were re-equipped with the new type. Such was the rate of production that by the spring of 1937 Bomber Command had received 338 Hind Mk Is, and a further 114 were in service with seven Auxiliary Air Force squadrons. Small numbers were also supplied to the air forces of India, New Zealand and South Africa.

Like the Hart, the Hind attracted considerable export interest and was built for Afghanistan, Latvia, Persia, Portugal,

SPECIFICATION	
Hawker Hind Mk I **Type:** two-seat light bomber and trainer **Powerplant:** one Rolls-Royce Kestrel V Vee piston engine rated at 640 hp (477 kW) **Performance:** maximum speed 186 mph (299 km/h) at 16,400 ft (5000 m); climb to 10,000 ft (3050 m) in 10 minutes 6 seconds; service ceiling 26,400 ft (8045 m); range 430 miles (692 km) **Weights:** empty 3,251 lb (1475 kg); maximum take-off	5,298 lb (2403 kg) **Dimensions:** wingspan 37 ft 3 in (11.35 m); length 29 ft 7 in (9.02 m); height 10 ft 7 in (3.23 m); wing area 348.00 sq ft (32.33 m²) **Armament:** one 0.303-in (7.7-mm) Vickers Mk III or V fixed forward-firing machine-gun on the port side of the forward fuselage and one 0.303-in (7.7-mm) Lewis trainable rearward-firing gun in the rear cockpit, plus up to 580 lb (263 kg) of disposable stores carried on three underwing hardpoints

Switzerland and Yugoslavia. As a result, the Hind was to be seen with a variety of engine types including the Bristol Mercury VIII and IX radial units, the Gnome-Rhône 9K Mistral radial unit, and the Rolls-Royce Kestrel VDR and XVI Vee units, in addition to the standard Kestrel V engine.

Peak RAF utilisation of the Hind Mk I came in 1937, when the Battle and Blenheim were starting to enter service and a requirement for a bomber trainer for operation by the Volunteer Reserve's flying training schools resulted in an adaptation of the Hind for this role. Related changes included deletion

of the rear cockpit's gun mounting and modification of that cockpit to accommodate an instructor, with dual controls and full instrumentation: the forward-firing gun was also deleted from most of these Hind trainers and, in 1938, all were equipped with blind-flying hoods for instrument training.

At the outbreak of World War II, most Hind Mk Is were operating in the training role, but some were retained by squadrons for use as communications aircraft, and six were supplied to Ireland during 1939-40 for use as trainers by the Irish Air Corps. Many were later modified as glider tugs, remaining in use for this purpose until the type was phased out in 1942, to be remembered as the last biplane light bomber in RAF service.

All surviving Hinds had been given Dark Earth/Dark Green camouflage by the outbreak of World War II.

Hawker Horsley and Dantorp

In response to the Air Ministry's Specification 26/23 for a two-seat medium day bomber, Hawker designed and built the prototype of a large two-bay biplane. With an unequal-span two-bay biplane wing cellule including slightly swept outer panels, a conventional braced tail unit, fixed tail-skid landing gear and a powerplant based on one Rolls-Royce Condor III Vee engine, the **Horsley** prototype made its first flight during 1925. Service testing resulted in a contract for 20 **Horsley Mk I** aircraft, these being the last aircraft of all-wood construction to be built by the company. The subsequent **Horsley Mk II** was of mixed wood and metal construction, and the final **Horsley Mk III** (a Hawker rather than official designation), which entered service in 1929, was of all-metal construction.

The Horsley served initially with No. 11 (Bomber) Sqn, and by early 1928 four squadrons had been equipped with the type. It was during this year that the type also

became operational as a torpedo-bomber. During 1931-2 a small number of Horsley torpedo-bombers of all-metal construction were converted for use as target tugs. Total production for the RAF exceeded 120 aircraft of all versions, and the type remained in home service until 1934 and into the following year with No. 36 Sqn based at Singapore. In addition to production for the RAF, six composite-construction Horsley Mk IIs were built

for the Greek naval air service, and two with the 800-hp (597-kW) Armstrong Siddeley Leopard II radial engine were supplied to Denmark under the name **Dantorp**, these being three-seat torpedo-bombers. Licensed production in Denmark was planned but in the event failed to materialise.

In addition to its military use, the Horsley provided valuable service from 1926 to 1937 as an engine test

bed, the type's endurance and flight characteristics

making it ideal for this purpose.

SPECIFICATION

Hawker Horsley Mk II
Type: two-seat day bomber and torpedo bomber
Powerplant: one Rolls-Royce Condor IIIA Vee piston engine rated at 665 hp (496 kW)
Performance: maximum speed 125 mph (201 km/h) at 6,000 ft (1830 m); climb to 10,000 ft (3050 m) in 14 minutes 20 seconds; service ceiling 14,000 ft (4265 m); endurance 10 hours
Weights: empty 4,760 lb (21.59 kg); maximum take-off 7,800 lb (3538 kg)
Dimensions: wingspan 56 ft 5¾ in (17.21 m); length 38 ft 10 in (11.84 m); height 13 ft 8 in (4.17 m); wing area 693.00 sq ft (64.38 m²)
Armament: one 0.303-in (7.7-mm) Vickers fixed forward-firing machine-gun in the port upper sides of the forward fuselage and one 0.303-in (7.7-mm) Lewis trainable rearward-firing gun in the rear cockpit, plus up to 2,150 lb (975 kg) of disposable stores carried on one underfuselage and two underwing hardpoints

No. 33 (Bomber) Squadron, RAF was reformed at Netheravon, Wiltshire in 1929 on the Horsley bomber. The type's service with the unit was short however, since in 1930 No. 33(B) Sqn became the first RAF unit to fly the Hawker Hart.

Hawker Hunter

Continuing the tradition of the Camm-designed fighters, the Hawker (later Hawker Siddeley) **Hunter** was the UK's most successful warplane of the period after World War II, the total of 1,972 such aircraft including 445 manufactured under licence in Belgium and the Netherlands. Not only an extremely capable warplane, the Hunter is remembered by its pilots as a sheer delight to fly and ultimately served with 19 air arms around the world. A handful of the type remains in service into 2000 with one serving with the Empire Test Pilots' School of the UK's DERA (Defence

Equipment Research Agency), a small number flying target-tug duties with the Indian air force and the possibility of a few in frontline service in the Lebanon.

The vast majority of variants were powered by the Rolls-Royce Avon turbojet, but an Armstrong Siddeley Sapphire was installed in the Hunter Mks 2 and 5. The **P.1067** prototype first flew on 20 July 1951, and was followed exactly one month later by the first **Hunter F.Mk 1** prototype, with the first production example of the Hunter F.Mk 1 flying on 16 May 1953 with the 7,500-lb st (33.36-kN) Avon RA.7 Mk 113 turbojet engine.

Variants

Hunter F.Mk 2: based on F.Mk 1 but with the 8,000-lb st (35.59-kN) Armstrong Siddeley Sapphire Mk 101 turbojet engine
Hunter Mk 3: P.1067 prototype with afterburning Avon R.A.7R turbojet; set a world speed record of 727.6 mph (1171 km/h) on 7 September 1953
Hunter F.Mk 4: Avon Mk 115 or 121 engine and increased fuel capacity; late versions had four underwing pylons and provision for the carriage of rocket projectiles
Hunter F.Mk 5: generally similar to F.Mk 4 but with the Sapphire Mk 101 engine
Hunter F.Mk 6: with an Avon Mk 203 or 207 engine, 390-Imp gal (1773-litre) fuel capacity and late F.Mk 4-type armament; most given a dog-toothed wing leading edge
Hunter T.Mk 8: Royal Navy 'hooked' trainer version
Hunter T.Mk 8M: T.Mk 8 with Blue Fox radar for Sea Harrier training
Hunter FR.Mk 10: reconnaissance version of the FGA.Mk 9 for the RAF
Hunter GA.Mk 11: Royal Navy single-seat attack trainer
Hunter PR.Mk 11: Royal Navy equivalent of the RAF's FR.Mk 10
Hunter Mk 50: F.Mk 4 version for Sweden
Hunter Mk 51: F.Mk 4 version for Denmark
Hunter Mk 52: F.Mk 4 version for Peru
Hunter T.Mk 53: T.Mk 7 version for Denmark
Hunter Mk 56: F.Mk 6 version for India
Hunter FGA.Mk 56A: FGA.Mk 9 version for India
Hunter FGA.Mk 57: FGA.Mk 9 version for Kuwait
Hunter Mks 58 and 58A: F.Mk 6 versions for Switzerland
Hunter FGA.Mks 59 and 59A: FGA.

Mk 9 versions for Iraq
Hunter FR.Mk 59B: FR.Mk 10 version for Iraq
Hunter T.Mk 62: T.Mk 7 version for Peru
Hunter T.Mks 66, 66D and 66E: two-seat trainer versions for India with Avon Mk 200-series engines
Hunter T.Mk 66B: T.Mk 66 version for Jordan
Hunter T.Mk 66C: T.Mk 66 version for Lebanon
Hunter T.Mk 67: T.Mk 66 version for Kuwait
Hunter T.Mk 68: T.Mk 66 version for Switzerland
Hunter T.Mk 69: T.Mk 66 version for Iraq
Hunter FGA.Mks 70 and 70A: FGA.Mk 9 versions for Lebanon
Hunter FGA.Mk 71: FGA.Mk 9 version for Chile
Hunter FR.Mk 71A: FR.Mk 10 version for Chile
Hunter T.Mk 72: T.Mk 66 version for Chile
Hunter FGA.Mks 73, 73A and 73B: FGA.Mk 9 versions for Jordan
Hunter FGA.Mks 74 and 74B: FGA.Mk 9 versions for Singapore
Hunter FR.Mk 74A: FR.Mk 10 version for Singapore
Hunter T.Mks 75 and 75A: T.Mk 66 versions for Singapore
Hunter FGA.Mk 76: FGA.Mk 9 version for Abu Dhabi
Hunter FR.Mk 76A: FR.Mk 10 version for Abu Dhabi
Hunter T.Mk 77: T.Mk 7 version for Abu Dhabi
Hunter FGA.Mk 78: FGA.Mk 9 version for Qatar
Hunter T.Mk 79: T.Mk 7 version for Qatar
Hunter FGA.Mk 80: FGA.Mk 9 version for Kenya
Hunter T.Mk 81: T.Mk 66 version for Kenya

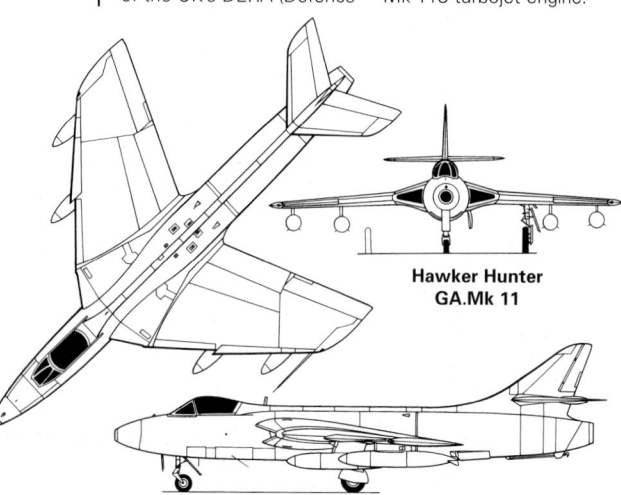

Hawker Hunter
GA.Mk 11

Hawker Hunter (continued)

A number of Chile's Hunter FGA.Mk 71s, including J-734, were given the indigenous Aguila upgrade.

The Hunter entered service with the RAF in July 1954. Almost exactly a year later the **P.1101** two-seat trainer prototype flew, this type entering service as the **Hunter T.Mk 7** during 1958. Deliveries of production aircraft continued until 1966, during which time the breed was continually improved. All versions of the Hunter were supersonic in a shallow dive, and power, armament and fuel capacity were increased progressively, reaching a peak in the **Hunter FGA.Mk 9**. This variant, embodying all the lessons to come from the earlier marks, was fitted with the Avon Mk 207 engine, packed a greater punch in the form of heavier under-wing weapon capacity, and was generally strengthened to capitalise on its improved potency in the ground-attack role. The Hunter FGA.Mk 9 represented so great an improvement that although none of this version was built as new, the manufacturer was kept busy over the years with a steady flow of refurbishing and remanufacturing to this standard.

Below: This No. 141 (Merlin) Squadron of the Republic of Singapore Air Force Hunter T.Mk 75A wore these ferocious 'shark' markings – including 'gill-slits' ahead of the intakes. As well as its trainer Hunters, No. 141 flew a mix of FGA.Mk 74 and FR.Mk 74 Hunters before re-equipping with RF-5Es from 1990.

SPECIFICATION

Hawker Siddeley Hunter F.Mk 6
Type: single-seat interceptor
Powerplant: one Rolls-Royce Avon RA.28 Mk 207 turbojet engine rated at 10,150 lb st (45.15 kN)
Performance: maximum speed 699 mph (1125 km/h) at sea level; climb to 45,000 ft (13715 m) in 7 minutes 30 seconds; service ceiling 51,500 ft (15695 m); combat radius 230 miles (370 km) without external stores
Weights: empty 14,122 lb (6406 kg); maximum take-off 23,800 lb (10796 kg)
Dimensions: wingspan 33 ft 8 in (10.25 m); length 45 ft 10½ in (13.98 m); height 13 ft 2 in (4.02 m); wing area 349.00 sq ft (32.42 m²)
Armament: four 30-mm Aden fixed forward-firing cannon in the underside of the nose, plus up to 3,000 lb (1361 kg) of disposable stores carried on four underwing hardpoints, and generally comprising two 1,000-lb (454-kg) and two 500-lb (227-kg) bombs, or four multiple launchers for air-to-surface unguided rockets, or up to 24 3-in (76-mm) air-to-surface unguided rockets on the outboard hardpoints

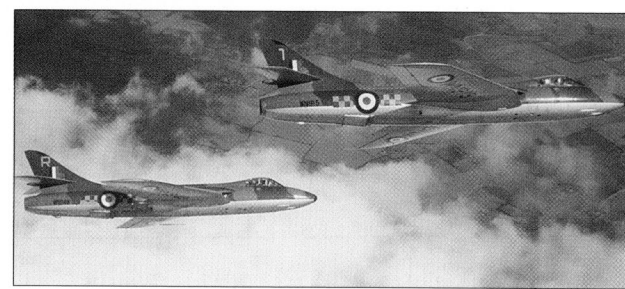

No. 257 Sqn flew Hunter F.Mk 2s for two-and-a-half years before converting to the improved Hunter F.Mk 5. The Mk 2 was the first Avon-engined Hunter variant.

Hawker Hurricane

This Hurricane Mk I was from the third production contract and represents the Mk I in its ultimate form. The aircraft has a three-bladed propeller and Merlin III engine.

Few members of the British public could have been aware that a significant new fighter had joined the ranks of the RAF when, in December 1937, the first production examples of the **Hurricane Mk I** were delivered to No. 111 Sqn at Northolt. It was not until two months later, during February 1938, that this news became common knowledge when headlines on 11 February announced that a Hurricane had more than lived up to its name on the previous afternoon. Piloted by Squadron Leader J. W. Gillan, commanding No. 111 Sqn, this machine had been flown from Turnhouse, Scotland, to Northolt, a distance of 327 miles (526 km), in 48 minutes at an average speed of almost 409 mph (658 km/h).

The Hurricane's design reached back as far as 1933, when Hawker's chief designer, Sydney Camm, decided to design a monoplane fighter based on the Fury biplane, using as its powerplant the Rolls-Royce Goshawk engine. As development progressed, the Goshawk was supplanted by the Rolls-Royce P.V.12 Merlin, and Hawker began construction of a prototype

around which the Air Ministry's Specification F.36/34 had been drawn up. As first flown, on 6 November 1935, this prototype had retractable landing gear, a strut-braced tailplane, conventional Hawker-structure fuselage with fabric covering, a new two-spar monoplane wing covered with fabric, and a single 990-hp (738-kW) Merlin 'C' engine.

Official trials began in February 1936, when the most optimistic high-speed performance predictions were comfortably exceeded, and on 3 June 1936 an initial order for 600 production aircraft was issued to Hawker. At the end of the month the new fighter was named the Hurricane. Hawker had in fact anticipated the production contract, and plans for the construction of 1,000 examples had already been initiated when the Air Ministry order was

received. This, however, called for the introduction of the Merlin II engine, causing some delay for installation redesign, but Hawker's advance preparations made possible the first flight of a production Hurricane Mk I on 12 October 1937.

No. 111 Sqn had one flight operational in December 1937 and had been completely re-equipped by the end of the following month. Soon

Hawker Hurricane Mk I (early production)

SPECIFICATION

Hawker Hurricane Mk IIB
Type: single-seat fighter and fighter-bomber
Powerplant: one Rolls-Royce Merlin XX Vee piston engine rated at 1,280 hp (954 kW)
Performance: maximum speed 342 mph (550 km/h) at 22,000 ft (6705 m); cruising speed 296 mph (476 km/h) at 20,000 ft (6095 m); climb to 20,000 ft (6095 m) 8 minutes 54 seconds; service ceiling 36.500 ft (11125 m); range 480 miles (772 km) with standard fuel
Weights: empty 5,500 lb (2495 kg); maximum take-off 7,300 lb (3311 kg)
Dimensions: wingspan 40 ft (12.19 m); length 32 ft 2½ in (9.82 m); height 13 ft 1 in (3.99 m); wing area 257.50 sq ft (23.92 m²)
Armament: 12 0.303-in (7.7-mm) Browning fixed forward-firing machine-guns in the leading edges of the wing, plus up to 1,000 lb (454 kg) of disposable stores carried on two underwing hardpoints

Some 40 RAF-surplus Hurricane Mk IIC aircraft were delivered to the Portuguese air force between 1946 and 1947. The aircraft were all tropicalised and were delivered with 45-Imp gal (205-litre) drop tanks underwing. The last of the aircraft was withdrawn in 1951.

after this, Nos 3 and 56 Sqns were equipped with the new type, and by the end of 1938 about 200 Hurricanes had been delivered to the RAF's Fighter Command. The early production aircraft differed little from the prototype except for the installation of the 1,030-hp (768-kW) Merlin II engine.

No doubts existed that the Hurricane was anything but an important and essential warplane to reinforce the expansion of the RAF, and plans were made in late 1938 for additional construction to be undertaken by Gloster Aircraft. This latter company's first production aircraft made its initial flight on 27 October 1939, and in little over 12 months, Gloster had completed 1,000 Hurricanes, a figure that was to reach 1,850, plus 1,924 by Hawker, before later versions superseded the Hurricane Mk I in production.

Before that happened, however, the wing covering of fabric had been replaced by stressed metal, and other progressively introduced improvements had included the Merlin III engine, a bullet-proof windscreen, and some armour protection for the pilot.

Despite the pressure of its production programme for the RAF, Hawker had found time and space to cope with modest export orders covering 24 aircraft and a production licence for Yugoslavia, followed by aircraft for Belgium, Iran, Poland, Romania and Turkey: Belgium also negotiated a production licence for construction to be carried out by Avions Fairey, but only two Belgian-built Hurricanes had been completed and flown before the German invasion of May 1940.

Arrangements were also completed for the Hurricane to be built in Canada by the Canadian Car and Foundry Co., the first production aircraft flying on 9 January 1940. Canadian aircraft were at first generally similar to the British-built Hurricane Mk I, but differed later by having the Packard-built Merlin

piston engine.

At the outbreak of World War II a total of 19 RAF squadrons was fully equipped with the Hurricane, and within a short time Nos 1, 73, 85 and 87 Sqns had been dispatched to bases in France. During the 'phoney' period of the war that followed however, these squadrons had comparatively little to do until the German push westward in May 1940. Immediately, six more Hurricane squadrons were flown to France, followed shortly after by two more squadrons, but these were an inadequate number to stem the flood of German arms, armour and aircraft. Post-Dunkirk accounting showed that almost 200 Hurricanes had been lost, destroyed or so severely damaged that they had to be abandoned.

Fortunately for the UK and for the RAF, the anticipated invasion of the British Isles by Germany failed to materialise, and there was a breathing space during which Fighter Command was able to reinforce its numbers. On 8 August 1940, which is regarded officially as the opening date of the Battle of Britain, the RAF could call upon 32 squadrons of Hurricanes and some 19 squadrons of Supermarine Spitfires. But despite the debacle at Dunkirk and the resulting fighter famine in the UK, three Hurricane squadrons were transferred overseas. These comprised No. 261 Sqn sent to support the island of Malta, and Nos 73 and 274 Sqns which began operations in the Western Desert.

Further development of the type began with the introduction of the Merlin XX engine in a Hurricane Mk I airframe, this being redesignated **Hurricane Mk IIA Srs 1**. Generally similar, except for a slightly lengthened fuselage, was the **Hurricane Mk IIA Srs 2**, representing an interim change on the production lines to make possible the installation of newly developed and interchangeable outer wing panels. Thus, with a wing housing no fewer than 12 0.303-in (7.7-mm) machine-guns and with provision for the carriage of two 500- or 250-lb (227- or 113-kg) bombs beneath the wing, the designation became **Hurricane Mk IIB**. The **Hurricane Mk IIC** was generally similar, but with the machine-guns replaced by four 20-mm cannon. When the Hurricane's life as a fighter had virtually come to an end, in 1942, the introduction of yet another wing then rejuvenated this remarkable warplane as the **Hurricane Mk IID**. The new wing carried two 40-mm Rolls-Royce BF or Vickers Type S anti-tank cannon, plus one harmonised 0.303-in (7.7-mm) machine-gun for each anti-armour weapon to assist in aiming. The Hurricane Mk IID 'tank buster' proved a potent weapon, highly effective against German armour in North Africa and when opposing more lightly armoured Japanese fighting vehicles in Burma.

The success of these wing variations led to the final production version, the **Hurricane Mk IV** (early examples of this version

were designated **Hurricane Mk IIE**), which introduced the 1,620-hp (1208-kW) Merlin 24 or 27 engine, and a 'universal wing' to make the Mk IV a highly specialised ground-attack aircraft. This wing carried two 0.303-in (7.7-mm) machine-guns to assist in sighting other weapons, which could include two 40-mm anti-tank cannon, two 500- or 250-lb (227- or 113-kg) bombs, or smoke curtain installations, ferry or drop tanks, or eight air-to-surface unguided rockets with 60-lb (27-kg) warheads. This last weapon, first proposed in late 1941, had been tested on a Hurricane in February 1942. The Hurricane Mk IV was the first Allied aircraft to deploy air-to-ground rockets, and these made the Hurricane a giant in capability, extending its operational life beyond the end of World War II, for it was not until January 1947 that the RAF's last Hurricane unit, No. 6 Sqn, received replacement aircraft.

Hurricane production in Canada had grown considerably in proportions from the initial line of Hurricane Mk I fighters. The introduction of the 1,300-hp (969-kW) Packard-built Merlin 28 engine brought a designation change to **Hurricane Mk X**. This model was generally similar to the British-built Mk IIB with the 12-gun wing, and while small numbers were supplied to the UK, the majority was retained for use by the Royal Canadian Air Force. The **Hurricane Mk XI** which followed was developed specifically for RCAF requirements, but

differed from the Mk X primarily in having RCAF military equipment. The major production version was the **Hurricane Mk XII**, introducing the 1,300-hp (696-kW) Packard-built Merlin 29. Initially, this was provided with the 12-gun wing; subsequently, the four-cannon and 'universal' wings became available. The final land-based version to emanate from Canada was the **Hurricane Mk XIIA**, identical to the Mk XII except for its eight-gun wing.

In addition to the Hurricanes which had been delivered to other countries before the war, wartime production supplied 2,952 of these aircraft to the USSR, although as a result of convoy shipping losses not all reached their destination. Other wartime deliveries went to Egypt (20), Finland (12), India (300), Ireland (12), Persia (1) and Turkey (14), and total production in the UK and Canada amounted to 14,231 machines.

The Hurricane was undoubtedly one of the great fighters of World War II and it is difficult to overstate the capabilities of this remarkable aircraft. In the Battle of Britain the Hurricane destroyed more enemy aircraft than all other defences, air or ground, combined. The **'Hurribomber'** fighter-bomber fought from Malta, carried out anti-shipping operations in the English Channel, and caused havoc to Axis columns in the Western Desert. The 'tank-busting' Hurricane ranged far and wide in practically every operational theatre. One fighter, flown by Flt Lt J. B. Nicolson of No. 249 (Fighter) Sqn, during the late summer of 1940, helped earn for its gallant pilot the only Victoria Cross to be awarded to a member of Fighter Command. This occurred on 17 August when, with his Hurricane badly damaged and wreathed in flames, the wounded and severely burnt Nicolson succeeded in destroying the attacking Bf 110 before baling out, to be rescued and survive his wounds.

No. 800 Sqn, FAA Sea Hurricanes, including this Canadian-built Mk XII, wore US markings during the Torch landings of 1942.

Hawker Nimrod

From 1924 to 1932 the Fairey Flycatcher had the distinction of being the only fleet fighter in service with the Fleet Air Arm. However, given the Flycatcher's speed of only 133 mph (214 km/h) at sea level, a performance which deteriorated with altitude, it was realised that steps needed to be taken to procure a fighter of improved capability. As early as 1926 an Air Ministry specification had outlined the requirement, and Hawker offered as its

contender its **Hoopoe** radial-engined biplane. This was not acceptable, but from it, via the Fury, there came a clean-looking biplane known unofficially at first as the **Norn**.

This became the **Nimrod**, which was generally similar in appearance to the RAF's Fury. The first production example of the Nimrod recorded its maiden flight on 14 October 1931, and during 1932 the **Nimrod Mk I** replaced the Flycatcher in the FAA's Nos

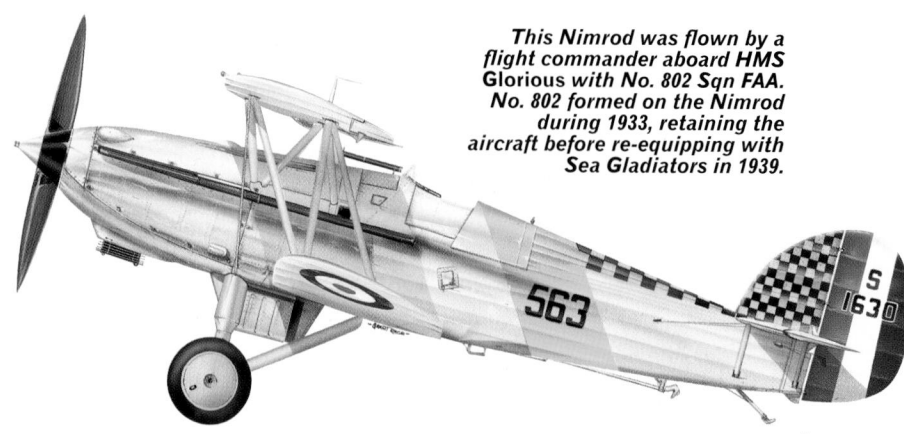

This Nimrod was flown by a flight commander aboard HMS Glorious with No. 802 Sqn FAA. No. 802 formed on the Nimrod during 1933, retaining the aircraft before re-equipping with Sea Gladiators in 1939.

SPECIFICATION

Hawker Nimrod Mk II
Type: single-seat carrierborne fighter
Powerplant: one Rolls-Royce Kestrel IIS Vee piston engine rated at 477 hp (356 kW) later replaced by one Kestrel VFP Vee piston engine rated at 608 hp (452 kW)
Performance: maximum speed 196 mph (315 km/h) at 12,000 ft (3660 m); cruising speed 115 mph (185 km/h) at optimum altitude; climb to 10,000 ft (3050 m) in 6 minutes 8 seconds; service ceiling 26,900 ft (8200 m); endurance 1 hour 40 minutes

Weights: empty 3,115 lb (1413 kg); maximum take-off 4,059 lb (1841 kg)
Dimensions: wingspan 33 ft 6¾ in (10.23 m); length 26 ft 6½ in (8.09 m); height 9 ft 10 in (3.00 m); wing area 301.00 sq ft (27.96 m²)
Armament: two 0.303-in (7.7-mm) Vickers Mk III fixed forward-firing machine-guns in the upper sides of the forward fuselage, plus up to 80 lb (36 kg) of disposable stores carried on one underwing hardpoint, and generally comprising four 20-lb (9.1-kg) bombs

402, 408 and 409 Flights. Subsequently, in 1933, these aircraft came into the possession of No. 800 Sqn on board HMS *Courageous*, and of Nos 801 and 802 Sqns on HMS *Furious* and HMS *Glorious* respectively. Production of the improved **Nimrod Mk II** began in September 1933, with initial deliveries to the FAA following in March 1934: these had arrester gear and, progressively, more powerful engines and larger-area tail surfaces. Many of the 57 Nimrod Mk Is were later modified

to Mk II standard. It is interesting to note that the first three Nimrod Mk IIs had a basic structure of stainless steel, but the remaining 27 production examples reverted to Hawker's conventional structure of light alloy and steel.

Hawker was not successful in drumming up any significant export orders for the Nimrod. One machine was supplied to Japan, one to Portugal, and two to Denmark, in which last country the aircraft were known as **Nimrodderne**. The Royal

Danish Naval Dockyard planned to build an additional 10 examples of this aircraft under licence, but there appears to be no conclusive evidence that this took place.

The FAA's Nimrod fighters had been relegated to training and communications duties by the outbreak of World War II, and continued in service until declared obsolete in July 1941. The Nimrodderne remained in service until the time of the German invasion in April 1940.

Hawker Osprey

Best described as a navalised version of the Hart day bomber, the **Osprey** was designed as a two-seat fleet spotter and reconnaissance aircraft.

The prototype, a conversion of the Hart prototype with folding wings, a fuselage strengthened for catapult launch, and easily interchanged wheeled or

float landing gear, first flew in the summer of 1930. The initial **Osprey Mk I** production version entered service in November 1932.

The **Osprey Mk II** differed in its float installation and the **Osprey Mk III** introduced a dinghy stowed in the starboard upper wing. All three of these initial versions were powered by the 630-hp (470-kW) Rolls-Royce Kestrel IIMS, but the final production variant was the **Osprey Mk IV** with the Kestrel V. The Osprey remained in first-line service until 1938, and continued in secondary roles until 1940. About 130 were built, and the type was also supplied to Portugal, Spain and Sweden in the form of two, one and four aircraft respectively.

SPECIFICATION

**Hawker Osprey Mk IV
(landplane)**
Type: two-seat fleet spotter and reconnaissance aircraft
Powerplant: one Rolls-Royce Kestrel V Vee piston engine rated at 640 hp (477 kW)
Performance: maximum speed 176 mph (283 km/h) at 13,125 ft (4000 m); cruising speed 109 mph (175 km/h) at optimum altitude; initial climb rate 1,625 ft (737 m) per minute; climb to 10,000 ft (3050 m) in 7 minutes 40 seconds; service ceiling 25,000 ft (7620 m); endurance 2 hours 15 minutes
Weights: empty 3,405 lb

(1545 kg); maximum take-off 4,950 lb (2245 kg)
Dimensions: wingspan 37 ft (11.28 m); length 29 ft 4 in (8.94 m); height 10 ft 5 in (3.17 m); wing area 339.00 sq ft (31.49 m²)
Armament: one 0.303-in (7.7-mm) Vickers Mk III fixed forward-firing machine-gun in the port side of the forward fuselage and one 0.303-in (7.7-mm) Lewis Mk III trainable rearward-firing machine-gun in the rear cockpit, plus up to 224 lb (102 kg) of disposable stores carried on two underwing hardpoints

This aircraft was part of the first production batch of 20 Osprey Mk Is. It was delivered to No. 803 Sqn aboard HMS Eagle.

Hawker Sea Fury

Originally intended as a smaller, lightweight version of the Tempest to meet the requirements of Specification F.6/42, the **Fury** was developed to the joint Air Ministry/Admiralty requirements of Specifications F.2/43 and N.7/43. Hawker was to design and develop the land-based version and Boulton Paul was to convert this landplane to carrierborne form.

By December 1943 six prototypes had been ordered: one was to be

powered by the Bristol Centaurus XII radial engine, two with the Centaurus XXII, and two with the Rolls-Royce Griffon Vee engine, while the sixth was to be a test airframe. First to fly was the Centaurus XII-powered prototype, which made its maiden flight on 1 September 1944, followed by the Griffon 85-engined second prototype on 27 November; the latter was later re-engined with a Napier Sabre VII H-type engine. Production contracts were placed in

April 1944 for 200 Furies for the RAF, and a similar number of **Sea Fury** fighters for the Fleet Air Arm, including 100 to be built by Boulton Paul, but the RAF order was cancelled at the end of World War II. Development of the Sea Fury continued, however, the first prototype having flown on 21 February 1945 with the Centaurus XII engine. This prototype was fitted with an arrester hook, but retained non-folding wings; the first fully navalised aircraft was the Centaurus XV-powered second prototype, which flew on 12 October.

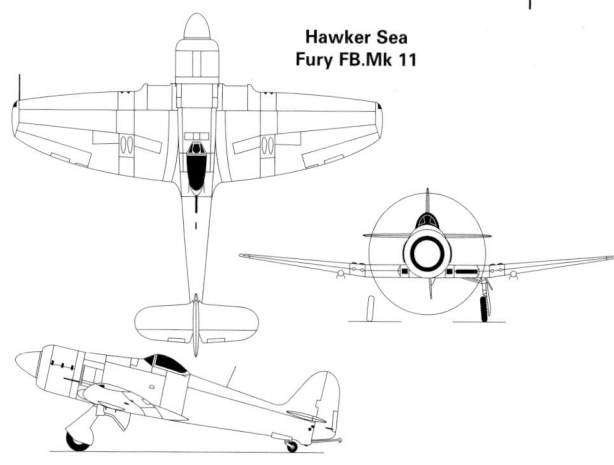

**Hawker Sea
Fury FB.Mk 11**

This aircraft, one of Cuba's 15 Sea Fury FB.Mk 11s, is illustrated as it appeared during the 1961 Bay of Pigs incident. The Sea Furies took little part in the action.

The Boulton Paul contract had been cancelled in January 1945, and of the 100 Sea Furies that remained on order the first 50 were completed as **Sea Fury F.Mk 10** pure fighters. The first of these was flown on 7 September 1946, and the third undertook trials aboard HMS *Victorious* during the winter of 1946-7. In May 1948, No. 802 Sqn became the first unit to receive the **Sea Fury FB.Mk 11** fighter-bomber development, of which 615 were built to British contracts, including 31 and 35 aircraft for the Royal Australian and Royal Canadian Navies respectively. The Sea Fury operated very successfully in the ground-attack role during the early stages of the Korean conflict. The RN also received 60 two-seat **Sea Fury T.Mk 20** trainers, 10 of which were later converted as target tugs to a German order.

Other overseas customers included the Netherlands with 22 **Sea Fury F.Mk 50** and **FB.Mk 50** aircraft; Pakistan with 93 **Sea Fury F.Mk 60** and five **Sea Fury T.Mk 61** aircraft; Egypt with 12 single-seaters; Burma with 18 ex-FAA Sea Fury FB.Mk 11 (three adapted as target tugs) and three Sea Fury T.Mk 20 aircraft; Cuba with 15 Sea Fury FB.Mk 11 and two Sea Fury T.Mk 20 aircraft; and Iraq with 55 Fury single-seat landplanes and five Fury trainers with tandem canopies. The Iraqi Furies were unofficially named **Baghdad Fury**.

SPECIFICATION

Hawker Sea Fury FB.Mk 11
Type: single-seat carrierborne and land-based fighter-bomber
Powerplant: one Bristol Centaurus 18 radial piston engine rated at 2,480 hp (1849 kW)
Performance: maximum speed 435 mph (700 km/h) at 24,500 ft (7470 m); climb to 30,000 ft (9145 m) in 10 minutes 48 seconds; service ceiling 34,300 ft (10455 m); range 680 miles (1094 km) with standard fuel
Weights: empty 9,240 lb (4191 kg); maximum take-off 12,500 lb (5670 kg)

Dimensions: wingspan 38 ft 4¾ in (11.70 m); length 34 ft 8 in (10.57 m); height 15 ft 10½ in (4.84 m); wing area 280.00 sq ft (26.01 m²)
Armament: four 20-mm Hispano Mk 5 fixed forward-firing cannon in the leading edges of the wing, plus up to 2,000 lb (907 kg) of disposable stores carried on two underwing hardpoints, and generally comprising two 1,000- or 500-lb (907- or 227-kg) bombs or eight 60-lb (27-kg) air-to-surface unguided rockets

---

Seen here in prototype form, the Sea Fury T.Mk 20 featured a prominent telescopic sight for the instructor, mounted on struts ahead of and above the rear canopy.

Hawker Sea Hawk

Aesthetically one of the most appealing of Sydney Camm's early jet fighters, the prototypes of the **Sea Hawk** were completed to Specification 7/46, and the first of three such aircraft, then identified as the **P.1040**, recorded its maiden flight on 2 September 1947. Hawker subsequently built 35 **Sea Hawk F.Mk 1** fighters before transferring all future development and production to Armstrong Whitworth. A further 60 Sea Hawk **F.Mk 1** and **Sea Hawk F.Mk 2** fighters were produced by that company, which then introduced the **Sea Hawk FB.Mk 3** fighter-bomber with a stronger wing able to carry external stores. Production of 116 Sea Hawk FB.Mk 3s was followed by that of 97 examples of the **Sea Hawk FGA.Mk 4** fighter/ground-attack development. All the variants up to this point were powered by one 5,000-lb st (22.24-kN) Rolls-Royce Nene Mk 101 engine with a pair of lateral 'pen-nib' nozzles in an arrangement that permitted fuel to be carried in the rear fuselage.

Conversion of some Sea Hawk FB.Mk 3s with the Nene Mk 103 engine produced the **Sea Hawk FB.Mk 5**, and production for the Royal Navy ended with 86 **Sea Hawk FGA.Mk 6** aircraft. with the Nene Mk 103 engine but otherwise similar to the Mk 4. The Sea Hawk served with the RN until the end of 1960, and 22 export **Sea Hawk Mk 50** aircraft with the Royal Netherlands navy until the end of 1964. The other major export versions were the **Sea Hawk Mk 100** and all-weather **Sea Hawk Mk 101** ordered by West Germany's Marineflieger. These variants were similar to the Sea Hawk FGA.Mk 6 but for a taller fin and rudder and, on the Mk 101, an Ekco Type 34 search radar in a pod under the starboard wing. Operated from shore bases, these West German aircraft were replaced by Lockheed F-104G Starfighters in the mid-1960s.

The last operator of the Sea Hawk was the Indian navy, which in the autumn of 1959 ordered 24 aircraft similar to the Sea Hawk FGA.Mk 6. Some of these were new-built (although the production line had closed some three years earlier), the rest being refurbished ex-Fleet Air Arm aircraft. They equipped No. 300 Sqn on the aircraft carrier INS *Vikrant* and were joined later by 12 more ex-FAA Sea Hawk FGA.Mk 4 and FGA.Mk 6 machines as well as 28 Sea Hawk Mk 100 and Mk 101 machines from West Germany. The last aircraft were replaced only in the late 1980s by BAe Sea Harriers.

SPECIFICATION

Hawker Sea Hawk FGA.Mk 6
Type: single-seat carrierborne fighter and ground-attack aircraft
Powerplant: one Rolls-Royce Nene RN.4 Mk 103 turbojet engine rated at 5,400 lb st (24.02 kN)
Performance: maximum speed 602 mph (969 km/h) at sea level; initial climb rate 5,700 ft (1737 m) per minute; climb to 44,500 ft (13565 m) in 11 minutes 50 seconds; service ceiling 44,500 ft (13565 m); combat radius 230 miles (370 km) without

external stores
Weights: empty 9,720 lb (4409 kg); maximum take-off 16,200 lb (7348 kg)
Dimensions: wingspan 39 ft (11.89 m); length 39 ft 8 in (12.09 m); height 8 ft 8 in (2.64 m); wing area 278.00 sq ft (25.83 m²)
Armament: four 20-mm Hispano Mk 5 fixed forward-firing cannon in the underside of the nose, plus up to 2,000 lb (907 kg) of disposable stores carried on four underwing hardpoints

Hawker Sea Hawk

Wearing the stripes applied for recognition purposes during the 1956 Suez Crisis, this Sea Hawk FB.Mk 3 fought over mainland Egypt. The aircraft was flown by No. 802 Sqn, normally from HMS Ark Royal, but detached for the crisis aboard HMS Albion.

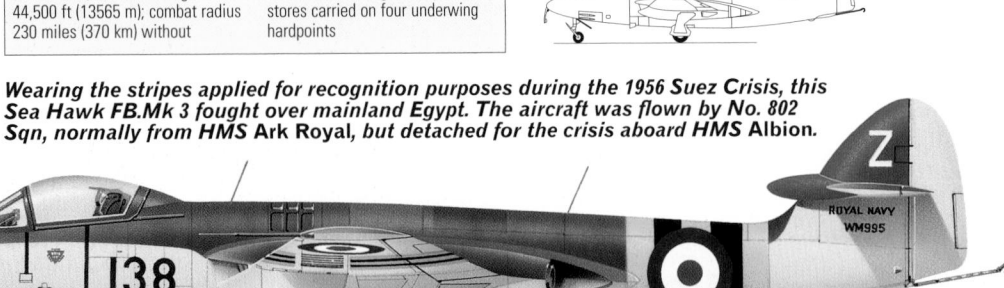

Hawker Sea Hurricane

The early success of the Hurricane in service with the Royal Air Force meant that the Royal Navy was keen to acquire numbers of these aircraft to help in the Battle of the Atlantic. A large proportion of ship losses happened far from shore in areas where land-based aircraft could not provide cover for Allied convoys. Thus German long-range patrol aircraft were able to range freely, spotting convoys far out at sea, and calling in and directing U-boat packs to attack them.

Hawker Sea Hurricane (continued)

An interim measure to provide protection for North Atlantic convoys gave birth to the **'Hurricat'**, a converted Hurricane carried by CAM-ships (Catapult Armed Merchantmen). Mounted on and launched from a catapult at the ship's bows, the Hurricane was flown off on what was usually a one-way flight: after providing defence for the convoy there was nowhere for the FAA or RAF pilot to land, which meant he was obliged to bale out, or ditch his aircraft as near as possible to the convoy, hoping to be picked up. The provision of long-range drop tanks beneath the wings, introduced in August 1941 after

the CAM-ships had been provided with more powerful catapults for the higher gross weight, improved the situation a little. At best it was a desperate rather than a practical measure, but despite this, six enemy aircraft were destroyed in 1941, the first success coming on 3 August 1941 when Lieutenant R. W. H. Everett intercepted and destroyed a Focke-Wulf Fw 200 Condor.

Hurricanes converted for the above role needed only the addition of catapult spools, and 50 Hurricane Mk Is so modified were designated **Sea Hurricane Mk IA**. They were followed by about 300 Mk Is converted to **Sea**

Hurricane Mk IB configuration with catapult spools plus a V-frame arrester hook: in addition 25 Mk IIA Srs 2 aircraft were similarly modified to Sea Hurricane IB or **Hooked Hurricane Mk II** standards. Their initial role was a considerable improvement on CAM-ship deployment, for from October 1941 they began to go to sea aboard MAC-ships, these being large merchant ships fitted with a small flight deck. The ships lacked any form of hangar accommodation and therefore carried a small number of fighter and anti-submarine aircraft on their decks. The **Sea Hurricane Mk IC**, introduced in February 1942, was once more a Mk I converted with catapult spools and an arrester hook; the type had, however, the four-cannon wing of the Hurricane Mk IIC. Last of the Sea Hurricanes from British sources was the **Sea Hurricane Mk IIC** intended for conventional carrier operations and, consequently, completed without catapult spools. The type also introduced to navy service the Merlin XX

engine, and carried FAA radio equipment. Last of the Sea Hurricane variants was the **Sea Hurricane Mk XIIA**, of which a small number was converted from Canadian-built Mk XII landplanes, and these were used operationally in the North Atlantic.

The Sea Hurricane's most famous action was fought during the late summer of 1942, when aircraft serving with Nos

These No. 760 Sqn, FAA Sea Hurricane Mk IBs feature three different propeller types. P3090 has a Rotol unit, Z4922 a de Havilland propeller and V6700 a Jablo-Rotol unit.

801, 802 and 885 Sqns aboard the carriers HMS *Indomitable*, HMS *Eagle* and HMS *Victorious* respectively, joined with Fulmar and Martlet fighters to protect a vital convoy to Malta. During three days of almost continuous attack by an Axis force of bombers, torpedo-bombers and escorting fighters, 39 enemy aircraft were destroyed for the loss of eight naval fighters.

SPECIFICATION

Hawker Sea Hurricane Mk IIC
Type: single-seat carrierborne fighter
Powerplant: one Rolls-Royce Merlin XX Vee piston engine rated at 1,280 hp (954 kW)
Performance: maximum speed 342 mph (550 km/h) at 22,000 ft (6705 m); cruising speed 292 mph (470 km/h) at 20,000 ft (6095 m); climb to 20,000 ft (6095 m) in 9 minutes 6 seconds; service ceiling 35,600 ft (10850 m); range

460 miles (740 km) with standard fuel
Weights: empty 5,880 lb (2667 kg); maximum take-off 8,100 lb (3674 kg)
Dimensions: wingspan 40 ft (12.19 m); length 32 ft 3 in (9.83 m); height 13 ft 1 in (3.99 m); wing area 257.50 sq ft (23.92 m²)
Armament: four 20-mm Hispano fixed forward-firing cannon in the leading edges of the wing

Hawker Tempest

Later distinguishing itself as a fighter-bomber, the Typhoon was a disappointment in its intended role as an interceptor as its rate of climb and performance at altitude were relatively poor. In 1941, therefore, it was suggested that remedial action might be taken in the form of a new, thinner wing, elliptical in planform. The radiator was to be moved from the chin position beneath the engine to the leading edges of the inboard wing panels, and the Napier Sabre EC.107C engine was specified. As the new wing would be thinner, the inclusion of an additional fuselage fuel tank was needed to replace the lost

wing tank capacity.

The design study, known originally as the **Typhoon Mk II**, was submitted to the Air Ministry and on 18 November 1941 received an order for two prototypes to Specification F.10/41. There were major changes, however, compared with the earlier aircraft, resulting during the early part of 1942 in the name change to **Tempest**. After cancellation of the **Tornado** fighter programme, the alternative engine installations planned for that type were, instead, applied to the Tempest. Thus the two original prototypes became the **Tempest Mk I** with the Sabre IV and the **Tempest Mk V** with

the Sabre II, and four more prototypes were ordered as two examples of the **Tempest Mk II** with the 2,520-hp (1879-kW) Bristol Centaurus radial engine, and two examples of the **Tempest Mk III** with the Rolls-Royce Griffon IIB engine becoming **Tempest Mk IV** when re-engined with the Griffon 61. Only one Griffon-engined aircraft was completed, in fact, as one of the Fury prototypes.

Before any of the prototypes had flown the Air Ministry had placed contracts for 400 examples of the Tempest Mk I, although these orders were later transferred to other versions. The Tempest Mk I prototype, its lines not spoilt by the beard radiator of the Typhoon, first flew on 24 February 1943, and later achieved a maximum speed of 466 mph (750 km/h) at 24,500 ft (7470 m). However, the engine programme suffered from technical problems and delays, and the Tempest Mk I was dropped.

The first of the Tempest prototypes to fly had been

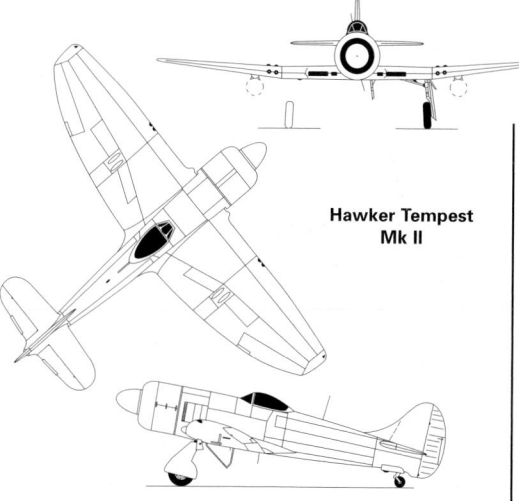

Hawker Tempest Mk II

the Tempest Mk V, during September 1942. Retaining the Typhoon's chin radiator, it originally had a standard Typhoon tail unit, but this was later modified. The first of 805 Tempest Mk Vs flew from Langley on 21 June 1943, was one of the initial production batch

This Tempest came from the second production batch of Mk Vs. The dorsal fin of the Tempest is a key recognition feature when compared to the earlier Typhoon.

SPECIFICATION

Hawker Tempest Mk V Series 2
Type: single-seat fighter and fighter-bomber
Powerplant: one Napier Sabre IIA H-type piston engine rated at 2,180 hp (1626 kW)
Performance: maximum speed 426 mph (686 km/h) at 18,500 ft (5640 m); cruising speed 391 mph (629 km/h) at 18,800 ft (5730 m); initial climb rate 4,700 ft (1433 m) per minute; climb to 20,000 ft (6095 m) in 6 minutes 6 seconds; service ceiling 36,000 ft (10975 m); range 1,300 miles (2092 km) with drop tanks or 820 miles (1320 km) with standard fuel
Weights: empty 9,000 lb

(4082 kg); maximum take-off 13,540 lb (6142 kg)
Dimensions: wingspan 41 ft (12.50 m); length 33 ft 8 in (10.26 m); height 16 ft 1 in (4.90 m); wing area 302.00 sq ft (28.06 m²)
Armament: four 20-mm Hispano Mk V fixed forward-firing cannon in the leading edges of the wing, plus up to 2,000 lb (907 kg) of disposable stores carried on two underwing hardpoints, and generally comprising two 1,000- or 500-lb (454- or 227-kg) bombs or eight 60-lb (27-kg) air-to-surface unguided rockets

of 100 **Tempest Mk V Series 1** aircraft which had four 20-mm British Hispano Mk II cannon with their barrels protruding from the leading edges of the wing; the remaining **Tempest Mk V Series 2** aircraft had short-barrel Mk V cannon completely contained in the wing. In 1945, one Tempest Mk V was fitted with a 40-mm 'P' gun under each wing, similar to the 40-mm cannon installation of the Hurricane Mk IID. After World War II, some of the aircraft were converted as **Tempest TT.Mk 5** target tugs.

An order for 500 Centaurus-powered Tempest Mk IIs was placed in October 1942, before the first flight of the prototype. This took place on 28 June 1943, the aircraft being powered by a Centaurus IV engine, superseded by the 2,520-hp (1879-kW) Centaurus V in production aircraft. These were to have been built by Bristol, the first Bristol-built aircraft being flown on 4 October 1944, but only 36 had been completed before production was transferred back to Hawker. The parent company manufactured a further 100 **Tempest F.Mk II** fighters and 314 **Tempest FB.Mk II** fighter-bombers with underwing racks for bombs or rockets. In 1947, India ordered 89 tropicalised Tempest Mk II fighters from RAF stocks,

and in the following year Pakistan ordered 24 similar aircraft. The third and last production version of the Tempest was the **Tempest F.Mk VI** with the 2,340-hp (1745-kW) Sabre V engine, and this first flew on 9 May 1944. Intended for service in the Middle East, 142 Tempest F.Mk VI tropicalised aircraft were built. Some were later converted as **Tempest TT.Mk 6** target tugs.

RAF service began in April 1944, when the first Tempest Mk Vs were delivered to Newchurch, Kent, where the first Tempest Wing was formed within No. 85 Group. The wing was active during the build-up to the Normandy

invasion, but on 13 June the first V-1 flying bomb fell at Swanscombe in Kent, and the Tempest was among aircraft tasked to combat the menace. The Tempest's success can be measured by the fact that of 1,847 bombs destroyed by fighters between June 1944 and March 1945, 481.5 were accredited to the Tempest Wing.

Until the end of World War II in Europe, the Tempest Mk V flew 'cab rank' patrols in support of ground forces, moving up to airfields in France and Belgium as the Germans fell back. In addition, the type engaged in combat the Luftwaffe's Me 262 jet fighters, 20 of which were

destroyed before VE-Day.

Although plans were made for 50 Tempest Mk IIs to be sent to the Far East in May 1945, to operate with Tiger Force against the Japanese, the war in the Pacific ended before these aircraft were ready for service. They equipped No. 54 Squadron in November 1945, this being the only home-based Tempest Mk II unit after World War II, the other units serving in Germany, Hong Kong, India and Malaya. The Tempest Mk VI was also too late to see wartime service, although this mark was flown later by RAF squadrons in Germany and the Middle East.

Hawker Tomtit

When, in 1927, the Air Ministry was seeking an elementary flying trainer to replace the long-serving Avro Type 504, Sydney Camm designed a neat equal-span single-bay biplane to meet this requirement. Of conventional configuration, with instructor and pupil in a tandem arrangement of open cockpits, fixed tailskid landing gear, and power provided by an Armstrong Siddeley Mongoose radial engine, the prototype **Tomtit** first flew during November 1928. It had a basic structure of metal with fabric covering. Within three months of the first

Among inter-war trainer types, the Tomtit was significant for its introduction of Reid and Sigrist blind-flying instrumentation. This aircraft served with an RAF FTS in the mid-1930s.

flight an initial production batch was ordered for the RAF, which eventually acquired 25 (including the prototype) for service with the Central Flying School and No. 3 Flying Training School. In addition to the military trainers built for the RAF, two were supplied to the Canadian Department of National Defence and four to the New Zealand Permanent Air Force.

The **Tomtit Mk I** entered RAF service in 1930 but was replaced by the Avro Tutor from 1932, then being distributed to various units for use in the communications role. The majority was declared surplus to requirement late in 1935. There were also five Tomtits for private purchasers, who opted for a number of different engines in the power bracket between 105 and 198 hp (78 and 148 kW).

Hawker Typhoon

In response to the Air Ministry's Specification F.18/37, Camm started work on the design of the **Typhoon** during 1937. The specification required a Rolls-Royce Vulture X-type or Napier Sabre H-type engine, so two prototypes were initially built, that with the Vulture-powered aircraft being known as the **Tornado**. Like the Vulture-engined model, the Sabre-engined variant, designated as the Typhoon, also encountered power-

plant problems, but these were overcome because the Napier company could devote more time and effort to development of the Sabre, whereas Rolls-Royce was too concerned with the Merlin to devote adequate resources to improving the troublesome Vulture engine.

Irrespective of trouble with the engine, after the Typhoon prototype had made its first flight on 24 February 1940 it was soon discovered that the airframe had structural problems, which persisted even after the type had entered service. The original prototype had a wing carrying 12 machine-guns and in production form, first flown on 27 May 1941, this variant was designated as the **Typhoon Mk IA**. It, and virtually all production Typhoons, eventually totalling 3,330, were built by Gloster. A second prototype, first flown on 3 May 1941, had a wing incorporating four 20-mm Hispano cannon, and in production form was designated **Typhoon Mk IB**.

The first production aircraft were supplied to the RAF in September 1941, initially to No. 56 Sqn, and service use revealed only too quickly that the airframe problems had not been eradicated.

Several pilots lost their lives, and the Air Ministry discussed whether the type should be withdrawn from service. Fortunately, Hawker was able to discover the reason for an alarming number of aircraft losing the complete tail unit, but it was almost the end of 1942 before all the engine and airframe 'bugs'

had been resolved. Even then, the Typhoon had a poor climb rate but, on the credit side, a capability for high speed at low altitude that was first put to effective use in November 1941. No. 609 Sqn, then operating from Manston in Kent, destroyed four Fw 190 fighter-bombers making hit-and-run attacks.

In the ground-attack role, employing bombs and especially rockets, the Typhoon excelled. Note the chin radiator installation and prominent cannon-barrel fairings.

Hawker Typhoon (continued)

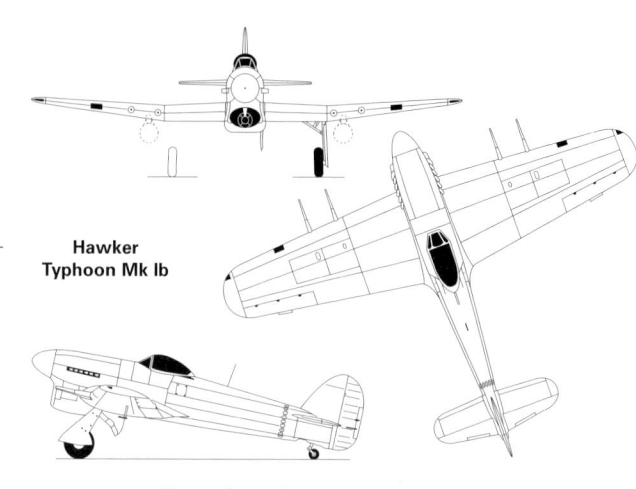

Hawker Typhoon Mk Ib

By the end of 1942, powered by the improved Napier Sabre IIA engine, armed with four 20-mm Hispano cannon, and able to carry 250-lb (113-kg) or 500-lb (227-kg) bombs on underwing racks, the Typhoon had become a significant fighter-bomber. Thereafter, Typhoon squadrons ranged over France and the Low Countries, playing havoc with the German lines of communication, but the full potential of the Typhoon Mk IB was realised only from a time late in 1943, when the type was equipped to carry rocket projectiles with 60-lb (27-kg) warheads. In this form, the Typhoon proved effective against German coastal shipping and armour, and the type's almost continuous day and night low-level attacks on German communications made a major contribution to the Allied success on D-Day. Indeed, the Typhoon became synonymous with both 'train-busting' and close air support. Additional duties from late 1943 included vital

'Noball' strikes against suspected V-1 launch sites, which were carried out with great urgency.

There was little change made to the Typhoon in the closing stages of the war except for installation of slightly more powerful Sabre IIB and IIC engines, and variants comprised a single **Typhoon NF.Mk IB** night-fighter and a small number of **Typhoon FR. Mk IB** tacti-

cal reconnaissance aircraft. Some production aircraft were allocated to Royal Canadian and Royal New Zealand Air Force units operating in Europe. Initially so unreliable that it had almost been withdrawn, at peak utilisation the Hawker Typhoon was used by no fewer than 26 squadrons of the 2nd Tactical Air Force, but few remained in service after VE-Day.

No. 56 Sqn's Land Girl was among the aircraft present at Matlaske when the Typhoon was first revealed to the public on 21 April 1943. The aircraft had the original canopy style, with a 'car-door' hatch providing access for the pilot.

Hawker Woodcock, Danecock and L.B.II Dankok

The **Woodcock** was designed to meet the requirements of the Air Ministry's Specification 25/22 for a single-seat night-fighter. Of wood and fabric construction, the original Woodcock prototype, later designated **Woodcock Mk I**, had a two-bay biplane wing cellule, a conventional braced tail unit, fixed tail-skid landing gear and a powerplant based on one 358-hp (267-kW) Armstrong Siddeley Jaguar II radial engine. When flown in 1923, the Woodcock Mk I proved to possess more than disappointing flight characteristics, resulting in a new **Woodcock Mk II**

prototype with a single-bay wing cellule and a power-plant based on one Bristol Jupiter IV radial engine. Testing of this version proved to be satisfactory, and after modification of the tail unit the Woodcock was ordered into production for the RAF. Initial examples, without night-flying equipment, entered service for evaluation and familiarisation, but the first operational Woodcock Mk II night-fighters were delivered to No. 3 (Fighter) Sqn in May 1925.

Production totalled 61 Woodcock Mk IIs for the RAF, the type remaining operational until 1928, although some examples

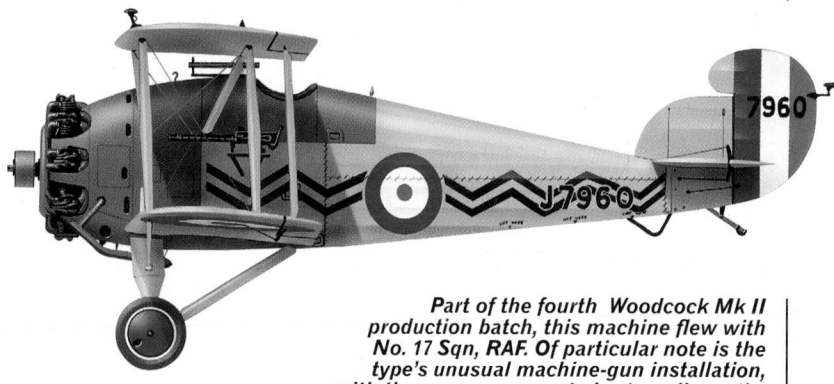

Part of the fourth Woodcock Mk II production batch, this machine flew with No. 17 Sqn, RAF. Of particular note is the type's unusual machine-gun installation, with the weapons mounted externally on the fuselage sides.

were still finding occasional use as late as 1936. The company also built three slightly modified examples of the Woodcock, powered by the 385-hp (287-kW) Jaguar IV engine, for use by the Danish army air service. These had the

name **Danecock**, but a further 12 built under licence in Denmark 1927

had the designation **L.B.II Dankok**. They remained in service until 1937.

One of the 12 L.B.II Dankoks built at the Danish Royal Naval Dockyard factory during 1927-28, this aircraft is fitted with underwing racks for up to eight light bombs.

SPECIFICATION	
Hawker Woodcock Mk II **Type:** single-seat night-fighter **Powerplant:** one Bristol Jupiter IV radial piston engine rated at 380 hp (283 kW) **Performance:** maximum speed 141 mph (227 km/h) at sea level; cruising speed 103 mph (166 km/h) at optimum altitude; climb to 10,000 ft (3050 m) in 8 minutes 25 seconds; service ceiling 22,500 ft (6860 m); endurance	2 hours 45 minutes **Weights:** empty 2,014 lb (914 kg); maximum take-off 2,979 lb (1351 kg) **Dimensions:** wingspan 32 ft 6 in (9.91 m); length 26 ft 2 in (7.98 m); height 9 ft 11 in (3.02 m); wing area 346.00 sq ft (32.14 m²) **Armament:** two 0.303-in (7.7-mm) Vickers fixed forward-firing machine-guns in the upper sides of the forward fuselage

Hawker Siddeley (BAe/de Havilland) 125 & Dominie

Conceived as a 'bizjet' by de Havilland before its full absorption into the Hawker Siddeley Group Ltd. (later a

component of British Aerospace), the **DH.125** was a far-sighted design intended for a crew of two

and a payload of between six and eight passengers carried over considerable range at high speed. The

design was based on modestly swept flying surfaces that included a low-set wing and a tail unit

with the tailplane set about two-thirds of the way up it, retractable tricycle landing gear, a circular-section fuselage providing pressurised accommodation, and a powerplant of two turbojet engines mounted in nacelles attached to the rear fuselage by short pylons.

The first of two DH.125 prototypes flew on 13 August 1962 with a powerplant of two 3,000-lb st (13.34-kN) Bristol Siddeley Viper Mk 20 turbojets, and these aircraft were joined in the later stages of the certification process by the first example of the **DH.125 Series 1** initial production model, which had its wingspan and length increased by 3 ft (0.91 m) and 3 ft 11 in (1.19 m) respectively, and used a powerplant of two 3,120-lb (13.88-kN) thrust Viper Mk 521 turbojet engines. Only eight DH.125 Series 1 aircraft were built before production switched to 77 examples of the improved **DH.125 Series 1A/1B** with options for operation at higher weights and intended for the North American and world markets respectively.

At about this time de Havilland was absorbed into the Hawker Siddeley Group, and the type was redesignated as the **HS.125**. The RAF currently needed a replacement for the Meteor NF(T).Mk 14 as a partner to the elderly Varsity in the navigator training role, and the selection fell on a version of the HS.125 Series 1 evolved as the **HS.125 Series 2** with equipment to train navigators in high-altitude navigation techniques.

Some 20 aircraft were produced with the designation **Dominie T.Mk 1**, the first of them flying on

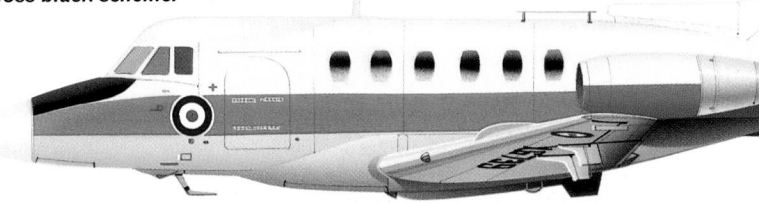

XS739

30 December 1964. From 1993, 11 of the aircraft were updated by Thorn EMI and Marshalls to reflect the newer generation of avionics carried by the later types of warplane then in service or prospect for the RAF.

Further development of the HS.125 into an important series of 'bizjets' was initially based on more power and/or higher operating weight, and the first of these types was the **HS.125 Series 3**, cleared for a maximum take-off weight of 21,700 lb (9843 kg). Production of this type totalled 65 aircraft in **A**- and **B**-suffixed models for North American and world sales respectively, and this figure included some 36 examples of the longer-range **HS.125 Series 3A/B-R** variant with extra fuel in a tank faired into the underside of the rear fuselage. Further refinement of the HS.125 Series 3 led to the **HS.125 Series 400**, of which 116 were built with a powerplant of two 3,000-lb (13.34-kN) thrust Viper Mk 301 turbojets. This total included a number of aircraft delivered to several air arms for the communications and VIP transport roles. In March 1971, the

RAF took four of the type with the designation **HS.125 CC.Mk 1**.

First flown in January 1971, the **HS.125 Series 600** introduced a lengthened fuselage to permit the accommodation of eight passengers in VIP conditions or up to 14 passengers in a high-density layout, a powerplant of two 3,750-lb st (16,68-kN) Viper Mk 601-22 turbojets, a larger ventral fin, a taller fin with fuel in its extended dorsal fillet, and a number of detail improvements. The RAF also bought two of this type, with the designation **HS.125 CC.Mk 2**.

With the **HS.125 Series 700**, first flown in June 1976, the HS.125 reached a new level of capability as the original powerplant of two Viper turbojet engines was replaced by two examples of the considerably more fuel-economical Garrett TFE731-3-1H turbofan engine rated at 3,700 lb st (16.46 kN) each. The RAF ordered six examples of this variant for service with the designation **HS.125 CC.Mk 3**, and the service's four HS.125 CC.Mk 1 and two HS.125 CC.Mk 2 aircraft were later re-engined to the same standard.

Raytheon delivered the first Hawker 800XP in 1995. The aircraft offers a maximum fuel range of 3,400 miles (5472 km) with reserves and can cruise at a maximum of 525 mph (845 km/h).

The first **HS.125 Series 800** flew in May 1983 as an advanced development of the Series 700 with a number of system and aerodynamic improvements, the last including a new wing. The US Air Force ordered six of the type with LTV Sierra Research Division inspection equipment for its **C-29A** combat flight inspection and navigation mission, and the Japanese Air Self-Defense Force has received three similar **U-125** aircraft as well as the first of up to 27 **U-125A** aircraft for the SAR role with surveillance radar and FLIR.

In August 1993 the

Raytheon Company bought BAe's Corporate Jets Division, which thus became Raytheon Corporate Jets Inc. and continued to market the HS.125 Series 800 and **Series 1000** aircraft as the **Hawker 800** and **Hawker 1000** respectively. The Hawker 800 remained in production in late 2000, while production of the Hawker 1000 ended after 52 aircraft had been completed in 1998. The Hawker 1000 was based on work done by BAe for its HS.125 **HS.125 Series 900**, which was launched as the Series 1000, with longer-range and greater passenger capacity.

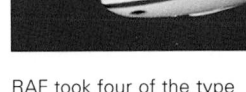

BAe C-29A

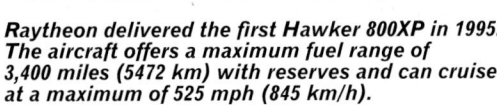

SPECIFICATION	
Hawker Siddeley Dominie T.Mk 1	40,000 ft (12190 m); range 1,338 miles (2153 km)
Type: two-crew medium/long-range light transport used mainly as a navigation trainer	**Weights:** empty 10,100 lb (4581 kg); maximum take-off 21,200 lb (9616 kg)
Powerplant: two Rolls-Royce (Bristol Siddeley) Viper Mk 301 turbojet engines each rated at 3,120 lb st (13.88 kN)	**Dimensions:** wingspan 47 ft (14.33 m); length 47 ft 5 in (14.45 m); height 16 ft 6 in (5.03 m); wing area 353.00 sq ft (32.79 m²)
Performance: maximum speed 500 mph (805 km/h) at 25,000 ft (7620 m); cruising speed 472 mph (760 km/h) at 25,000 ft (7620 m); initial climb rate 4,000 ft (1220 m) per minute; service ceiling	**Payload:** up to eight passengers although the cabin is laid out generally for three pupils and one instructor

Hawker Siddeley (BAe/Avro) 748 and Andover

Design of the **Avro Type 748** twin-turboprop airliner began in January 1959. The last product of the celebrated Avro (A. V. Roe) company, the aircraft was

subsequently designated as the **Hawker Siddeley HS.748** following full incorporation of Avro into the Hawker Siddeley Group, into whose ownership it

had passed in 1936. The Type 748 prototype made its maiden flight on 24 June 1960, and the initial production models were the 48-passenger **HS.748**

Series 1 that entered service in 1962 with the powerplant of two 1,880-ehp (1402-ekW) Dart RDa.6 Mk 514 turboprops, followed by the structurally

strengthened 52-passenger **HS.748 Series 2** that entered service later in the same year with 2,105-ehp (1570-ekW) Dart RDa.7 Mk 531 engines, and the **HS.748 Series 2A** with 2,280-ehp (1700-ekW) Dart RDa.7 Mk 535-2 engines.

Hawker Siddeley (BAe/Avro) 748 & Andover (continued)

Further developments of the civil HS.748 included the **HS.748 Series 2B** with a number of refinements and improvements, and the **HS.748 Series 2C** that was a development of the Series 2A with a large port-side freight door in the rear of the cabin. The first production Series 2B, by then a product of BAe following the merger of BAC and Hawker Siddeley, flew on 22 June 1979, and its changes included an increase in wing span and Dart RDa.7 Mk 536-2 engines for improved 'hot-and-high' performance, as well as a revised tail unit; the Series 2B had in fact arrived at an earlier time, for the type first flew on 31 December 1971. Licensed production of Series 1 and 2 aircraft from 1961 was carried out by HAL in India, with a total of 72 aircraft delivered to the Indian Air Force. This figure includes 20 HAL-developed **HAL (BAe) 748(M)** or **HS.757** dedicated military freighters with a large cargo door, and the final example of this variant was delivered in 1984. One Indian HS.748 was converted as an AEW test bed, with a rotodome above the rear fuselage, but this was lost in a crash early in 1999.

The **HS.748 Military Transport** version incorporated a reinforced floor and large rear freight door, and could accommodate 58 troops, or 48 paratroops and dispatchers, or 24 litters and nine attendants. The final production version was designated as the **Super 748**, which was delivered from 1984. Based on the Series 2B, this model introduced significant new developments, including an advanced flightdeck, Dart RDa.7 Mk 552 engines offering a 12 per cent reduction in fuel consumption, and engine hushkits. British Aerospace also developed the **HS.748 Coastguarder** dedicated maritime patrol aircraft, with equipment for maritime surveillance, search and rescue, and fishery protection, as well as a moderate ASV/ASW capability. For these roles the type was outfitted with a comprehensive avionics suite including search radar, high accuracy navigation aids (INS and Omega) with options for ECM, ESM, IFF and MAD gear. This version

did not receive any orders, however.

The **Andover** was the dedicated military and assault transport version of the HS.748, and its original creation incorporated a measure of redesign sufficient to warrant the allocation of the new designation **Type 780** (later **HS.780**). The Andover was designed to meet an RAF requirement for a STOL multi-role transport able to operate from rough airstrips or 300-yard (275-m) lengths of ploughed field or desert, even with obstacles on the approach. The fuselage was lengthened and the entire rear section was redesigned to permit the incorporation of a 'beaver tail' rear loading ramp, which also allowed loads to be air-dropped. Lightweight removable roller track was provided to ease loading, and the new Dowty Rotol 'kneeling' main landing gear units allowed the cabin floor 'sill' to be moved vertically or horizontally for simple alignment with the tail board of a vehicle loading freight. The main cabin could accommodate up to three Land Rovers, or one Land Rover and one Ferret armoured car, or alternatively could seat up to 58 troops, 40 paratroops or 24 litters. Power was provided by a pair of 3,245-ehp (2420-ekW) Dart RDa.12 Mk 201C engines, driving larger propellers whose additional diameter required that the engines be moved further outboard, although the overall span was actu-

ally reduced by 3 in (7.60 cm). The upswept rear fuselage meant relocating the tail unit, and the tailplane gained dihedral.

The Andover prototype (converted from the first HS.748) made its maiden flight on 21 December 1963, and 31 such **Andover C.Mk 1** aircraft were manufactured for the RAF's Air Support Command. The aircraft proved rugged and dependable, and was as a result extremely popular, serving with squadrons in the UK, Singapore and Aden. The British withdrawal from commitments east of Suez reduced the Andover force to a single squadron, and the 1975 defence cuts led to the disbandment of this unit. Ten of the 29 survivors were sold to the Royal New Zealand Air Force (where nine remained in use into the mid-1990s), five were relegated to ground training duties, and four were transferred to RAF Germany for communications use, three to the MoD Procurement Executive and six to No. 115 Sqn for calibration duties. A single aircraft was also used by No. 51 Sqn for trials for some years, before it too joined No. 115 Sqn.

Four of No. 115 Sqn's aircraft were **Andover E.Mk 3** machines fitted with a nose-mounted Milligan light (to enable engineers on the ground to calibrate ILS equipment). The E.Mk 3s received a new Litton Inertial Referenced Flight

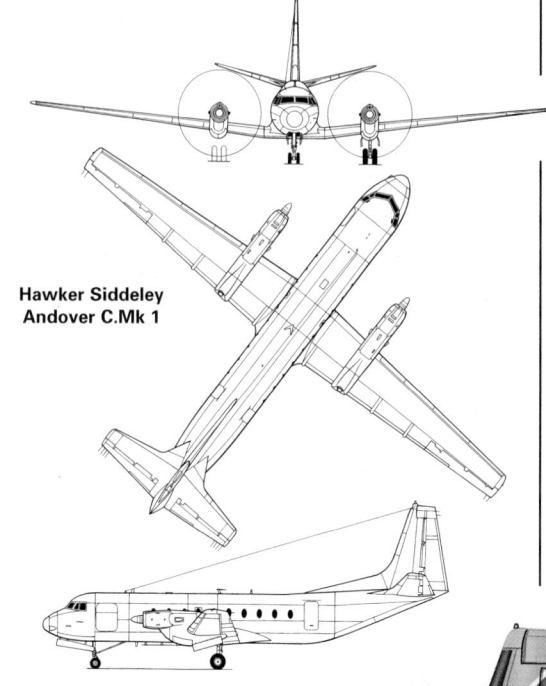

Hawker Siddeley Andover C.Mk 1

Delivered to LAN-Chile as an HS.748 Series 2 on 2 May 1968, C-GQSV was later converted to Series 2A standard. After a series of different owners, the machine passed to Air Creebec in 1984. It crashed in 1988.

AIR CREEBEC INC.   C-GQSV

Inspection System during 1983. Three aircraft without Milligan lights were designated **Andover E.Mk 3A** and had a limited calibration fit, allowing them to inspect TACAN and radars, but not ILS systems. These aircraft would have had a wartime communications relay role. These three Andovers were reassigned to No. 32 Sqn for communications duties in late 1992. No. 115 Sqn disbanded in October 1993, handing over its role to a civilian contractor, which retained the E.Mk 3s. No. 32 Sqn's Andovers were retired during 1994.

Under Modification 207, two of No. 60 Sqn's Andovers had their forward freight doors removed and were fitted with an under-fuselage camera for an undisclosed reconnaissance role believed to be connected with flights along the Berlin corridor.

They were then redesignated **Andover C.Mk 1(PR)**. One of these aircraft later passed to the Aircraft & Armament Experimental Establishment at Boscombe Down, and has been used for 'Open Skies' arms limitation verification flights over the former USSR.

The RAF also received six examples of the HS.748 Series 2 under the designation **Andover CC.Mk 2** despite the fact that they had none of the features of 'real' Andovers, and these served with The Queen's Flight, at RAF Benson, and a variety of other VIP and communications units. Four survivors later flew with No. 32 Sqn at RAF Northolt, and a fifth is with the Defence Research Agency at Bedford. Another RAF HS.748 is also used by the DRA, this Series 1 aircraft previously being operated by Smiths Industries.

SPECIFICATION

Hawker Siddeley Andover C.Mk 1
Type: two/three-crew short-range STOL transport
Powerplant: two Rolls-Royce Dart RDA.12 Mk 201C turboprop engines each rated at 2,305 ehp (1719 kW)
Performance: maximum cruising speed 258 mph (415 km/h) at 20,000 ft (6095 m); initial climb rate 1,170 ft (357 m) per minute; service ceiling 24,000 ft (7315 m);

range 1,175 miles (1891 km) with a 10,000-lb (4536-kg) payload
Weights: empty 27,709 lb (12569 kg); maximum take-off 50,000 lb (22680 kg)
Dimensions: wingspan 98 ft (29.87 m); length 77 ft 1 in (23.75 m); height 29 ft 3 in (8.92 m); wing area 831.00 sq ft (77.20 m²)
Payload: see above within the context of a 14,750-lb (6691-kg) maximum payload

Hawker Siddeley (BAe) Harrier

The Harrier has its origins in a 1957 agreement between Sir Sydney Camm

of Hawker Aircraft and Dr Stanley Hooker of Bristol Aero-Engines – this

latter company merging with Armstrong Siddeley Motors in 1959 to create

Bristol Siddeley Engines – to design a tactical aircraft around Bristol's BE.53 turbofan. This new engine, (from 1959 known as the BS.53) was designed to

produce direct jet-lift for vertical take-off. The BE.53 employed four nozzles, in fore-and-aft pairs, which were pivoted to vector the exhaust thrust between

Hawker Siddeley/McDonnell Douglas AV-8S

When the Harrier – here exemplified by a GR.Mk 3 – flew without its underfuselage ADEN cannon pods, narrow-chord strakes (as illustrated) were fitted on the pod attachment points.

from directly backwards to just forward of the vertical. Camm designed a small all-metal, shoulder-wing monoplane around the newly-christened Pegasus engine. Features of the airframe included pronounced anhedral on the wings and tailplane, large semi-circular intakes on each side of the fuselage and accommodation for a single pilot. The unusual undercarriage consisted of a single-wheel nose gear and a short main unit with twin wheels. These undercarriage members were mounted in tandem along the centreline of the fuselage belly. In addition, small wheels were mounted on a retractable outrigger leg at each wing tip to prevent the aircraft tipping to the

side when on the ground.

Designated **Hawker P.1127**, the first of six prototypes hovered for the first time on 21 October 1960. By 12 September 1961, complete transitions were being made between vertical and horizontal flight. Stability in the hover and during low-speed manoeuvres, was provided by reaction control jets mounted in the nose, tail and each wing tip. These jets, expelling compressed air bled from the engine, were operated by the pilot via the control column and rudder pedals.

With the basic concept proven, Hawker Siddeley

was awarded a contract for nine pre-production aircraft. These more advanced machines were intended for evaluation as operational fighter/ground-attack aircraft. Designated **Kestrel F(GA).Mk 1**, the first of the nine completed its maiden flight on 7 March 1964. Evaluation was tasked to a specially-formed, UK-based, three-nation squadron, which included RAF and Luftwaffe pilots, as well as those from all three US armed forces. Between April 1965 and April 1966 the unit tested the Kestrel under various simulated operational conditions.

Before this, however, the British government had already placed a February 1965 order for another six development aircraft. These machines were the first to be given the name Harrier, and the first of the aircraft made its initial flight on 31 August 1966. By that time the Mach 2 **Hawker Siddeley P.1154** multi-role STOVL aircraft for the RAF and Royal Navy had been replaced in official thinking by the Harrier produced only for the RAF. The single-seat **Harrier GR.Mk 1** was developed for the ground-attack and reconnaissance roles, and

the tandem two-seat **Harrier T.Mk 2** for conversion and combat readiness training. Total orders for the RAF subsequently rose to 118 single-seat and 23 two-seat aircraft, the Fleet Air Arm later acquiring four two-seaters, the first production examples of each model making their maiden flights on 28 December 1967 and 24 April 1969 respectively.

The first of 61 Harrier GR.Mk 1 aircraft officially entered RAF service on 1 April 1969, being used to equip No. 233 OCU (Operational Conversion Unit) at RAF Wittering. In the following year, the first of 23 Harrier T.Mk 2s entered service, and each of these initial models was powered by the Pegasus Mk 101 turbofan rated at 19,000 lb st (84.52 kN). The surviving aircraft (complemented by 17 new-build single-seaters) were later upgraded to the **Harrier GR.Mk 1A** and **Harrier T. Mk 2A** standards, by retrofit of the Pegasus Mk 102 engine rated at 20,500 lb st (91.19 kN), and then the surviving aircraft (complemented this time by 40 new-build single-seaters) were further upgraded to **Harrier GR.Mk 3** and **Harrier T.Mk 4** standards by retrofit

of the 21,500-lb st (95.64-kN) Pegasus Mk 103. These aircraft equipped four operational squadrons (one in the UK and three in Germany). The RAF generally operated the Harrier GR.Mk 3 as a STOVL rather than V/STOL (Vertical/Short Take-Off and Landing) aircraft as a short take-off run allowed the type to carry a greater load of weapons. Equipment included an inertial navigation system, optional inflight-refuelling probe, head-up display, laser rangefinder/marked-target seeker and radar-warning receiver, the last two being added in new-build aircraft from 1976 and also retrofitted to existing aircraft. Both the one- and two-seat variants had the same nominal weapons-carrying capability, though the two-seater had a greater empty weight.

The Harrier T.Mk 4 (**Harrier T.Mk 4N** in FAA service) was re-designated **Harrier T.Mk 4A** when fitted with the LRMTS nose of the GR.Mk 3.

The RAF began the process of converting to the altogether superior Harrier GR.Mk 5 during the course of 1988, and the last first-generation Harriers had been retired from RAF service by late 1995. In late 2000, the FAA still operated seven two-seaters as **Harrier T.Mk 8** aircraft, converted from T.Mk 4N and T.Mk 4A standard to provide compatibility with the Sea Harrier FA.Mk 2.

At about the time that the Harrier entered RAF service, an initial buy of 12 generally similar aircraft was made by the US Marine Corps. This service well appreciated the operational flexibility offered by STOVL and VTOL. The prospect of allying this to the performance of a fixed-wing jet combat aircraft was too strong to resist, and the initial order was soon raised to 110, including eight two-seaters.

SPECIFICATION

Hawker Siddeley (BAe) Harrier GR.Mk 3
Type: single-seat V/STOL close-support and reconnaissance warplane
Powerplant: one Rolls-Royce Pegasus Mk 103 vectored-thrust turbofan engine rated at 21,500 lb st (96.26 kN)
Performance: maximum speed more than 737 mph (1186 km/h) at low altitude; initial climb rate 29,000 ft (8840 m) per minute; service ceiling 51,200 ft (15605 m); radius 415 miles (667 km) on a hi-lo-hi mission with a 4,400-lb (1996-kg) warload
Weights: empty 12,300 lb

(5579 kg); maximum take-off 25,200 lb (11431 kg)
Dimensions: wingspan 25 ft 3 in (7.70 m); length 46 ft 10 in (14.27 m) with laser nose; height 11 ft 11 in (3.63 m); wing area 201.10 sq ft (18.68 m²)
Armament: up to a normal maximum of 5,000 lb (2268 kg) or overload maximum of 8,000 lb (3269 kg) of disposable stores carried under the fuselage and wing, and generally including two 30-mm Aden cannon pods, free-fall or retarded bombs, multiple rocket-launcher pods, flares and a five-camera reconnaissance pod

---

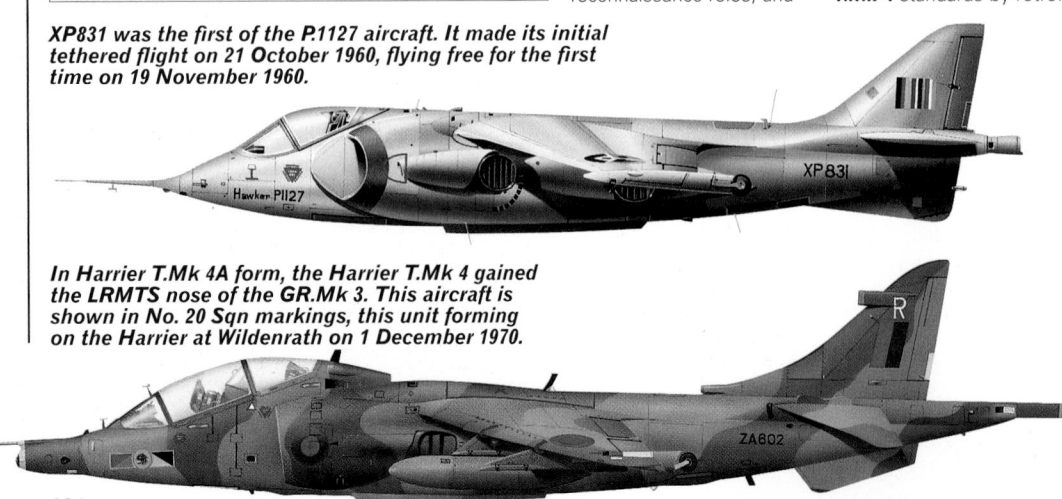

XP831 was the first of the P.1127 aircraft. It made its initial tethered flight on 21 October 1960, flying free for the first time on 19 November 1960.

In Harrier T.Mk 4A form, the Harrier T.Mk 4 gained the LRMTS nose of the GR.Mk 3. This aircraft is shown in No. 20 Sqn markings, this unit forming on the Harrier at Wildenrath on 1 December 1970.

Hawker Siddeley (BAe) Harrier (continued)

The USMC designated its Harriers as the **McDonnell Douglas AV-8A** and **TAV-8A** respectively (credit for their origin going to McDonnell Douglas for political reasons) in their single- and twin-seat forms, had the Pegasus Mk 103 engine but lacked several of the nav/attack systems incorporated in the Harrier GR.Mk 3. Instead

they carried AIM-9 Sidewinders for air-to-air combat, in which role the USMC pilots added a remarkable new trick to the Harrier's repertoire. Known as 'VIFFing' (Vectoring In Forward Flight), this makes use of the thrust-vectoring facility in dogfighting situations, where it gave the aircraft an unprecedented

manoeuvrability that no other warplane could match. The USMC had one training and three operational squadrons equipped with the AV-8, and in-service AV-8As were later upgraded to **AV-8C** standard with a host of modifications to the airframe and systems.

The only other operators of the standard Harrier,

equivalent to the USMC versions, have been the Spanish and Thai navies. In Spanish service the type was named as the **Matador**, and nine **AV-8S** single-seat and two **TAV-8S** twin-seat aircraft, known by the local designations **VA.1** and **VAE.1** respectively, equipped one Spanish squadron based on the light

carrier *Dedalo*. With the Spanish navy's purchase of the more advanced AV-8B Harrier II, the surviving aircraft were available for export, resulting in the purchase during 1997 of seven single- and two twin-seat aircraft by the Thai naval air service so that it could acquire experience in the operation of STOVL warplanes on the light carrier *Chakri Naruebet* pending delivery of AV-8Bs.

Hawker Siddeley (BAe/BAE Systems) Nimrod

The type now known as the **BAE Systems Nimrod** began life as the **Hawker Siddeley HS.801**, which was created on the basis of the de Havilland Comet's airframe as a maritime reconnaissance aircraft to replace the ageing, piston-engined Shackleton in service with the RAF's Coastal Command. Development began in 1964, and two unsold Comet 4Cs were converted as prototypes. A MAD 'stinger' was added to the tailcone, a search radar was added in the nose, a fin-tip radome ('football') was fitted to accommodate ESM equipment, and a new ventral weapons pannier was added beneath the cabin, giving a distinctive 'double-bubble' cross-section. These changes necessitated an increase in fin area. The first prototype was powered by the production Nimrod's intended power-plant of four Spey turbofan engines and made its maiden flight on 23 May 1967, serving as an aerody-namic test bed and for airframe/engine integration. The second conversion retained the Comet's original Avon turbojets and recorded its first flight on 31 July, then serving as the avionics development aircraft.

The first of 46 examples of the production type, known as the **Nimrod MR.Mk 1**, flew on 28 June

This Nimrod MR.Mk 2P has the small finlets added above and below the tailplane when the inflight refueling probe was added above the cockpit. Note that wingtip ESM pods were added later – along with enlarged finlets – and that the aircraft carries AIM-9 missiles.

1968, and the type entered service with No. 236 OCU in October 1969, eventually equipping five operational squadrons including one based overseas at RAF Luqa, Malta. The British withdrawal from Malta rendered the last batch of eight Nimrods surplus to requirement, although they could usefully have been used to spread hours more evenly across the fleet, extending the Nimrod's life. Five were delivered to the RAF, and the others were retained by BAe for trials, but their useful life was short, seven of them being selected for conversion to **Nimrod AEW.Mk 3** stan-dard, along with four earlier Nimrod MR.Mk 1s. All of these airframes were effec-tively wasted, since the Nimrod AEW.Mk 3 never entered productive service

and all but one were scrapped, the survivor becoming an instructional airframe.

From 1975 the 35 remaining MR.Mk 1s were upgraded to **Nimrod MR.Mk 2** standard, the first MR.Mk 2 being redelivered to the RAF in August 1979. The Nimrod MR.Mk 2 intro-duced a completely new avionics and equipment suite, in which all major sensors and equipment items were changed. The aircraft received a new GEC central tactical system, which was based on a new computer and three separate processors for navigation systems, radar and acoustic sensors. The old ASV.Mk 21D radar was replaced by a Thorn EMI Searchwater equip-ment with a colour display. The acoustics system was made compatible with modern sonobuoys, includ-ing the BARRA, SSQ-41 and SSQ-53, TANDEM and Ultra active and passive types. The communications equipment was similarly upgraded.

The addition of an inflight-refuelling probe (initially to 16 aircraft for participation in Operation Corporate, the UK's campaign to regain the Falkland Islands in 1982) created the **Nimrod MR.Mk 2P** – the 'P' was subsequently dropped in the late 1990s – and this change also necessitated the addition of tiny swept finlets on the horizontal tail surface. The Falklands war

also resulted in the first operational use of the Nimrod's underwing hard-points, giving the ability to carry AIM-9 Sidewinders for self-defence, or Harpoon anti-ship missiles, Stingray torpedoes, bombs or depth charges for offen-sive purposes. The planned wing-tip Loral ARI.18240/1 ESM pods were added later, these requiring larger rectangular finlets. All the aircraft were then revised with both refuelling probes and ESM pods. For opera-tions from Seeb in Oman, during Operation Desert Storm to drive the Iraqi occupying forces from Kuwait, a number of aircraft were drawn from Nos 120 (lead), 42 and 206 Sqns to form the Nimrod MR Detachment. Several of the aircraft were modified to what was unofficially known as **Nimrod MR.Mk 2P(GM)** standard, the Gulf Modification involving the addition of an underwing FLIR turret on the starboard

wing, BOZ electronic coun-termeasures pods and a TRD (Towed Radar Decoy).

During the mid-1990s, BAe was selected to create a radically updated and revi-talised force of 21 Nimrods after winning the Ministry of Defence's Maritime Patrol Aircraft competition. Due to re-enter service between 2002 and 2007, but now likely to be 2005 at the earliest, after virtually total reconstruction to the so-called **Nimrod 2000** standard, the **Nimrod MRA.Mk 4** retains only the pressure hull, keel, weapons bay, tailcone and fixed tail surfaces of its predecessor. The rest of the airframe is essentially new, and the powerplant is changed to a quartet of BMW Rolls-Royce BR.710 turbofan engines each rated at 15,000 lb st (66.73 kN) to provide undi-minished performance despite a 20 per cent increase in maximum take-off weight to 232,800 lb

**Hawker Siddeley
(BAe) Nimrod
R.Mk 1**

(105598 kg), which also requires beefed-up landing gear units. A new generation of mission avionics is also being provided by a Boeing-led team to maintain the MRA.Mk 4's maritime reconnaissance, anti-ship and anti-submarine capabilities at a very high level.

In addition to the 46 Nimrod MR.Mk 1 aircraft ordered as Shackleton replacements, three further aircraft were ordered (with a replacement for a crashed machine later created as a conversion) to replace No. 51 Sqn's Comet and Canberra aircraft specially modified for the intelligence-gathering role. This task had never been formally admitted by the UK, and references to this publicity-shunning squadron usually described it as a calibration unit. The three aircraft were designated **Nimrod R.Mk 1**, and were delivered to RAF Wyton for fitting out in 1971. Security surrounding the aircraft was such that they were delivered as little more than empty shells, the RAF then fitting virtually all mission equipment. As a result, flight trials did not begin until late 1973, and the first operational flight took place on 3 May 1974. On 10 May 1974 the type was formally commissioned, bringing the Comet era to a close.

Initially the R.Mk 1 differed from its maritime cousin in having no MAD tailboom and no searchlight, instead having dielectric radomes on the nose of each external wing tank and on the tail. The

aircraft have been progressively modified since they were introduced, gaining more and more antennas above and below the fuselage and wing tanks, as well as Loral ARI.18240/1 wing-tip ESM pods. With inflight-refuelling probes the designation changed to **Nimrod R.Mk 1P**. The addition of more equipment has led to the deletion of several cabin windows, and in more recent years the aircraft have started carrying underwing chaff/flare dispensers.

The main Elint receivers cover the widest possible range of frequencies, with DF (direction finding) and ranging, and are thus able to record and locate the source of hostile radar and radio emissions. The aircraft almost certainly have a computerised 'threat library', allowing a detailed 'map' of potential enemy radar stations, navaids and air defence systems to be built up. Emissions from hostile fighters can also be recorded and analysed. During Cold War operations, the aircraft frequently operated in international airspace around the peripheries of the USSR, or possibly flew feints toward Soviet airspace in the hope of provoking a response, necessitating extremely

accurate navigation. One LORAN 'towel rail' antenna was thus removed, and the aircraft received a Delco ASN-119 Carousel Mk IVA INS. The ASV.Mk 21 nose radar was replaced by an Ekco E.290 weather radar during the early 1980s.

The Nimrod R.Mk 1P appears to fly with a very large crew (26-28 seems by no means extraordinary), the majority obviously being equipment operators. Most of the aircrew are extremely experienced, and are hand-picked for their skill and discretion.

Through the early 1970s the RAF became increasingly concerned at its increasingly urgent need for a modern AWACS (Airborne Warning And Control System) aircraft to replace the obsolete Shackleton AEW.Mk 2. Frustrated by prolonged delays to plans for a NATO E-3 force, the British government decided in 1977 to go ahead with a purely national solution involving completion of 11 surplus Nimrod airframes with a totally new avionics fit designed to meet the RAF's challenging require-

ments, which the E-3A did not in fact meet. GEC Avionics developed the variable-PRF (Pulse Repetition Frequency) radar, with perfect all-round coverage from mechanical scanners in the nose and tail sweeping through 180° alternately. The same dishes also served the Cossor IFF (Identification Friend or Foe) system, and the Loral ESM system, using passive receivers in pods on the wing tips, detected and located all recordable signals. Exceptional digital data-processing systems managed all the inputs from the sensors and display outputs to the six operator consoles, while the main mission equipment was completed by very precise navigation systems and comprehensive communications.

Trials of the radar and the forward antenna began in a converted Comet during June 1977, and the first development example of what had by now become the **BAe Nimrod AEW.Mk 3** flew in July 1980. It had been planned for the Nimrod AEW.Mk 3

to enter service with No. 8 Sqn late in 1982, but the entire project became increasingly troubled. The main radar signal/noise ratio proved below specification; the customer kept upgrading its requirements; the computers ran out of capacity; and the need to dissipate heat from the electronics into the fuel (used as the main heat sink) cut into the usable fuel and mission endurance. There were also many lesser problems, all compounded by the fact that, while the original concept had been not only valid but also world-beating, the final outcome was too much to demand from too small an airframe.

In the circumstances, therefore, it was almost inevitable that the Nimrod AEW programme would be terminated. It was of little surprise, therefore, when in September 1986 the Ministry of Defence reopened the whole competition for an AEW aircraft. In December 1986 the MoD selected the E-3 Sentry as the winner and further work on the Nimrod AEW.Mk 3 ceased.

Hawker Siddeley (BAe/de Havilland) Trident

The airliner finally known as the **BAe Trident** originated as the **de Havilland DH.121** proposal of 1956 to meet a requirement of British European Airways for a fast short/medium-range transport to accommodate about 100 passengers. The type was ordered into production in August 1959 after being

selected from design submissions by Avro, Bristol and de Havilland. Plans were made for the aircraft to be manufactured by a consortium comprising de Havilland, Fairey and Hunting, but when de Havilland became a component of the Hawker Siddeley Group late in 1959, Hawker Siddeley

became responsible for continued development and manufacture of the Trident under the designation **HS.121 Trident**.

The DH.121 was sized to 140 passengers, and powered by three Rolls-Royce RB.141 Medway turbofan engines each rated at 14,000 lb st (62.28 kN), but at a late

stage, with the engine and aircraft in manufacture, BEA insisted that it should be cut down in size, and the DH.121 was re-sized to 88/95 seats with the powerplant of three 9,850-lb st (43.81-kN) thrust Rolls-Royce Spey RB.163 turbofans. This meant that the Trident fully met BEA's particular requirement, but at the same time destroyed any realistic hope of large export sales.

The first production **Trident 1** made its maiden flight on 9 January 1962. The 103-passenger Trident 1 failed to interest other airlines as its capacity was generally considered too small, and this led to the development of the **Trident 1E** that first flew in November 1964. This had

standard seating for 115 passengers, but up to 139 could be accommodated in a high-density seating arrangement. However, limited foreign sales came from the further-developed **Trident 2E**, for in addition to 15 for BEA, two aircraft were supplied to Cyprus Airways and 33 machines to CAAC, then the national airline of the People's Republic of China. From the outset it had been intended that the Trident, operating in the often dubious weather conditions typical of Europe, should have equipment that would ensure high utilisation. This included the Smiths Autoland system, and the Trident 1/1E had been certificated for automatic landing in Category II weather conditions. The Trident 2Es for BEA were delivered with Smiths Autoland at full triplex level, however, and these airliners were the first in the world to have full all-weather operational instrumentation of this advanced nature.

This BEA-marked Trident Three was photographed as it landed at a 1970s SBAC Farnborough airshow.

Hawker Siddeley (BAe/de Havilland) Trident (continued)

The last major production version was the **Trident 3B**, and this was basically a high-capacity short-range version of the Trident 1E, its fuselage 'stretched' by 16 ft 5 in (5.00 m) to seat a maximum of 180 passen-

gers. Power for take-off was enhanced by installation of a Rolls-Royce RB.162-86 turbojet engine, rated at 5,250 lb st (23.35 kN) dry, in the aircraft's tail just below the rudder and therefore just above the nozzle of the centreline Spey turbofan, and the first take-off of a Trident 3B with all four engines operative was recorded on 22 March 1970. The Trident

3B was also equipped with Smiths Autoland, and in December 1971 this version was certificated for operation in full Category IIa weather conditions. When production ended in 1975 a total of 117 Trident

airliners had been built, the last two of them being **Trident Super 3B** aircraft for CAAC. They differed from the standard Trident 3B by carrying additional fuel and having seats for 152 passengers.

SPECIFICATION

Hawker Siddeley (BAe) Trident 2E

Type: three-crew short/medium-range transport
Powerplant: three Rolls-Royce Spey RB.163-25 Mk 512-5W turbofan engines each rated at 11,960 lb st (53.20 kN)
Performance: cruising speed 605 mph (974 km/h) at 25,000 ft (7620 m); economic cruising speed 596 mph (959 km/h) at 30,000 ft (9145 m); range 2,464 miles

(3965 km) with typical payload
Weights: empty 73,200 lb (33203 kg); maximum take-off 144,000 lb (65318 kg)
Dimensions: wingspan 98 ft (29.87 m); length 114 ft 9 in (34.98 m); height 27 ft (8.23 m); wing area 1,456.00 sq ft (135.26 m²)
Payload: up to 132 passengers within the context of a 26,800-lb (12156-kg) maximum payload

First registered in November 1972, this Trident 3B was the last of the type built. It was later delivered to CAAC.

Heinkel He 46

Designed and built in parallel with the **He 45** reconnaissance bomber, but intended for a shorter-range role over the land battlefield, the **He 46a** first of three prototypes made its maiden flight late in 1931 with a powerplant of one Siemens (Bristol) Jupiter radial engine, rated at 450 hp (336 kW) and driving a two-bladed, fixed-pitch propeller, pending availability of the more powerful Siemens SAM 22B radial engine around which the type had been designed. This prototype had a heavily staggered biplane wing cellule with an upper wing featuring sharply swept panels, located well ahead of the unswept, short-span lower wing: the object was to provide the pilot with good forward and downward fields of vision. This prototype had generally good handling characteristics, but the war ministry staff was unhappy with the fields of vision for the observer/gunner and the decision was therefore taken to remove the lower wing and increase the span and area of the upper wing.

The **He 46b** second prototype flew in the new configuration during the summer of 1932, and as such pioneered the definitive configuration of the He 46 as a parasol-wing monoplane of mixed construction. The He 46b

retained the Jupiter engine, but the **He 46c** third prototype switched to the definitive SAM 22B which had the unfortunate effect of creating vibrations that could not be damped. There was no engine that could be substituted for the SAM 22B, so the He 46 entered production in 1933 with this powerplant. Like the He 45, the He 46 was a cornerstone of the German air force's plan for expansion into the Luftwaffe, and initial orders were placed for 270 aircraft to be delivered by September 1935: eventually Heinkel delivered 200 of these aircraft, and others were completed by Fieseler, Gotha, MIAG and Siebel for an eventual total of 478 He 46s.

The main production model was the **He 46C-1**, which accounted for 403 of the total. The He 46C-1 was the standard tactical reconnaissance warplane of the Luftwaffe in the mid-1930s. The He 46C was used operationally in the Spanish Civil War, and 20 of the type were also bought by the Spanish Nationalist air force. By the outbreak of World War II, only two German squadrons were still fully operational on the He 46C while another nine were in the throes of converting to the more advanced Hs 126. The He 46 saw further operational service in the Polish campaign that

started World War II, and was then generally relegated to the training role. In the spring of 1943, a number of aircraft was restored to first-line service as night harassment machines with a load of 4.4-lb (2 kg) SD-2 bomblets for use over the Eastern Front, a role in which they served up to 1944.

The **He 46D** was an unarmed version of which seven were created as **He 46D-1** conversions from He 46C-1 standard for use at air shows in an effort to convince foreign observers that the He 46 had no military application. Prefaced by a single **He 46e** prototype conversion from He 46D-1 standard with a powerplant of one 752-hp (561-kW) Armstrong Siddeley Panther X radial engine enclosed in a long-chord NACA cowling, the **He 46E** was the export version of the He 46C. The

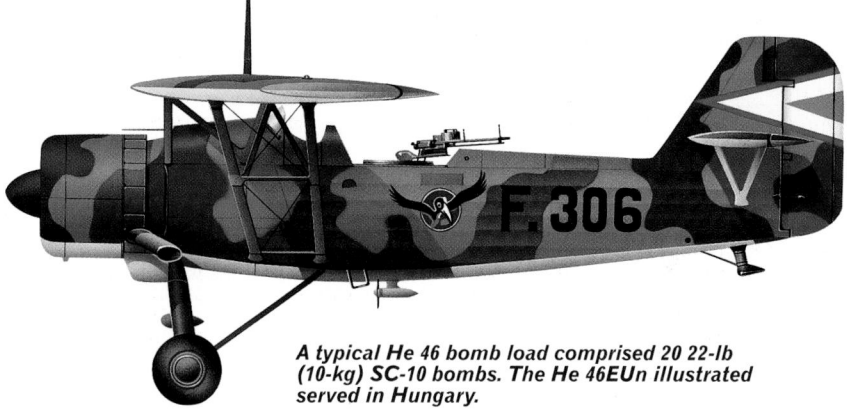

A typical He 46 bomb load comprised 20 22-lb (10-kg) SC-10 bombs. The He 46EUn illustrated served in Hungary.

SPECIFICATION

Heinkel He 46C

Type: two-seat tactical reconnaissance and army co-operation aircraft
Powerplant: one BMW-Bramo 322B (SAM 22B) radial piston engine rated at 650 hp (485 kW)
Performance: maximum speed 161 mph (260 km/h) at 2,625 ft (800 m); cruising speed 137 mph (220 km/h) at 2,625 ft (800 m); climb to 6,560 ft (2000 m) in 5 minutes 30 seconds; service ceiling 19,685 ft (6000 m); range 615 miles (990 km)
Weights: empty 3,891 lb (1765 kg); maximum take-off

5,071 lb (2300 kg)
Dimensions: wingspan 45 ft 11¾ in (14.00 m); length 31 ft 2 in (9.50 m); height 11 ft 1¾ in (3.40 m); wing area 354.13 sq ft (32.90 m²)
Armament: one 0.312-in (7.92-mm) MG 17 fixed forward-firing machine gun-in the starboard upper side of the forward fuselage and one 0.312-in (7.92-mm) MG 15 trainable rearward-firing machine-gun in the rear cockpit, plus up to 440 lb (100 kg) of disposable stores carried in a lower-fuselage weapons bay

initial order was placed by Bulgaria and called for 18 **He 46EBu (Bulgarien)** aircraft, and then followed 36 examples of the **He 46EUn (Ungarn)** for Hungary, with a powerplant of one 870-hp (649-kW) Manfred Weiss WM K-14 (licence-built Gnome-Rhône 14K Mistral-Major) radial

engine driving a three-bladed, fixed-pitch metal propeller, and a gun armament of two fixed forward-firing and one trainable rearward-firing 0.32-in (8-mm) Gebauer machine-guns. The **He 46F** was an unarmed trainer version of which MIAG built 14 **He 46F-1** examples.

Heinkel He 49 and He 51

The **He 51** was seen as the epitome of revived German nationalism and militarism in the mid-1930s, for it was this biplane fighter that the German propaganda machine had trumpeted when the Luftwaffe was officially unveiled in the early months of 1935 after the service's clandestine

development. At the time the He 51 was taken as evidence of Germany's renewed ability to design first-rate warplanes, but in fact the He 51 was a mediocre machine that was the result of an evolutionary design process rather than of a single flash of inspiration.

The story of the He 51 can be traced back to the late 1920s, when Heinkel designed the **HD 37** and then further refined the concept in the **HD 38** and **HD 43**, but the Heinkel fighter series was transformed in November 1932 by the first flight of the **He 49a** prototype, for this

was the first of the series to involve two talented new designers, Walter and Siegfried Günter. Of these twin brothers, Walter was notable for his ability to create elegant, low-drag lines and Siegfried for his mathematical abilities in matters such as stress and drag calculations. Like its predecessors, the He 49a was a single-bay staggered biplane of mixed construc-

tion with a powerplant of one BMW VI Vee engine, but was particularly notable for the considerable aerodynamic cleanliness of its fuselage and semi-retractable radiator installation. The prototype revealed a measure of directional instability, so the rear fuselage was lengthened on the **He 49b** second prototype that first took to the air in February

1933. After initial trials in landplane configuration, the He 49b was fitted with twin floats and further trials of the landplane model were entrusted to the **He 49c** third prototype, which otherwise differed from the He 49b in its powerplant of one BMW VI 6,0ZU engine with ethylene glycol rather than water cooling.

The He 49 was clearly a promising type, but Walter Günter believed that the basic concept could be considerably improved and, in conjunction with the engineer Karl Schwärzler, produced a fourth prototype with a number of aerodynamic changes and a lightened structure. This prototype made its first flight in the summer of 1933, and differed so much from the He 49 prototypes that it received the revised designation **He 51a**. By comparison with the He 49c, the He 51a had revised upper-wing ailerons with Flettner tabs; a wholly redesigned vertical tail surface; a pilot's headrest faired into the upper line of the rear fuselage; a fixed ventral radiator bath in place of the original semi-retractable type; a revised landing gear arrangement with spatted wheels, and the original tailskid replaced by a faired wheel; and a revised engine exhaust system to prevent fumes from the port bank of cylinders from being blown into the cockpit.

This process of evolutionary development was watched with keen interest by the German air ministry, for although the Ar 65 had been ordered as the first fighter for the new air force, the He 51 offered considerably better performance with the same basic powerplant. The air ministry asked Heinkel to proceed with all possible speed, and by the end of 1933 the company had begun work

on a batch of nine **He 51A-0** pre-production fighters for service trials. The He 51A-0 differed from the He 51a only in details such as the reversion to a tailskid, the removal of the pilot's headrest, and the adoption of S-shaped pipes to duct the exhaust gases down the nose before they were ejected. It was of metal construction, with a welded steel tube fuselage covered with light alloy panels forward and fabric aft, a wire-braced tail unit of fabric-covered welded steel tube construction, and an unequal-span staggered fabric-covered metal wing cellule.

The He 51A-0s were delivered from the spring of 1934, and despite the expectations of the air ministry were not greeted with fulsome approval by service pilots more used to the more lightly loaded, more agile, more forgiving but also somewhat slower Ar 65E. There followed a number of accidents, but a thorough investigation confirmed that it was pilot training rather than the He 51A-0 that was at fault and initial plans were therefore laid for the construction of 141 He 51s by September 1935. Heinkel lacked the manufacturing capacity to deliver all these aircraft, so Arado and Erla were brought into the first phase of the manufacturing program, with AGO and Fieseler added for the second phase.

Deliveries of the **He 51A-1** initial production model started in April 1935, and during the summer of the same year the new fighter entered service with the new II. Gruppe of Jagdgeschwader 132 and then replaced the Ar 65E in I./JG 132 by the end of the year. Production of the He 51A-1 totalled 150 aircraft delivered in equal number by Arado and

Heinkel, and the **He 51A-2** was a sole He 51A-1 converted to twin-float configuration for trials.

Replacing the He 51A on the production lines late in 1945, the **He 51B** was an improved model with the main landing gear units braced by twin wires and provision made for a drop tank to be carried under the fuselage. The type was

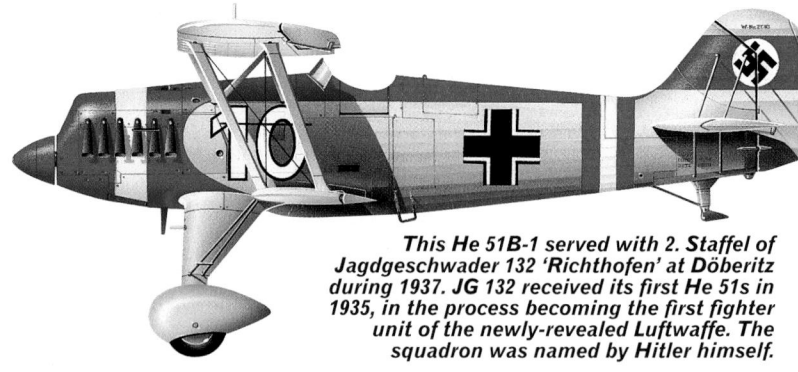

This He 51B-1 served with 2. Staffel of Jagdgeschwader 132 'Richthofen' at Döberitz during 1937. JG 132 received its first He 51s in 1935, in the process becoming the first fighter unit of the newly-revealed Luftwaffe. The squadron was named by Hitler himself.

presaged by 12 **He 51B-0** pre-production aircraft delivered from January 1936, and eventually 450 **He 51B-1** production aircraft were completed by Arado, Erla and Fieseler, which completed 150, 200 and 100 aircraft respectively including 46 delivered with twin-float alighting gear under the revised designation **He 51B-2** for the use of the 1. and 2. Staffeln of Küstenjagdgruppe 136 in succession to the obsolete **HD 38d**.

By 1936, the He 51A and He 51B were the Luftwaffe's most important fighters, and it was inevitable that the type would be included in the equipment of the first German air units sent to Spain in August 1936 to support the Nationalist cause in the Spanish Civil War. Eventually 135 aircraft were sent to Spain to equip both the three Staffeln of Jagdgruppe 88, which

was the fighter element of the Legion Condor and the 1-E-2 and 2-E-2 squadrons of the Nationalist air force. The aircraft were first used in the fighter role, but as they began to reveal their obsolescence in the face of more advanced fighters, such as the I-15, they were increasingly relegated to the dive-bombing and close-support role. The two Spanish units equipped with He 51Bs adapted for the close-support role were the 1-G-2 and 4-G-2 groups, and by the end of the war, 89 of the 135 aircraft had been lost. The Spanish Civil War fully revealed the obsolescence of the He 51, and the Luftwaffe soon decided that the type would be replaced in seven of its 12 Jagdgruppen by the more advanced Ar 68 as an interim type pending deliveries of the Bf 109 monoplane fighter. The **He 51B-3** was an experimental high-altitude version of the He

51B-2 with the span of the upper wing increased. Two other prototypes were the **He 52B** improved version of the He 51B-3, and the **He 52D** twin-float version of the He 52B.

Built to the extent of 100 aircraft by Fieseler, the **He 51C** was the dedicated ground-attack version of the He 51B built with racks for six 10-kg (22-lb) SC-10 bombs. The type was intended primarily for export to Spain, and its two subvariants were the **He 51C-1** of which 79 were completed (51 for Nationalists and 28 for the Legion Condor) and the **He 51C-2** of which 21 were completed with improved radio for use by German coastal defence units.

By the outbreak of World War II, the Luftwaffe's surviving He 51s had been relegated to second-line service, flying up to 1945 as advanced and fighter trainers.

SPECIFICATION

Heinkel He 51B-1
Type: single-seat fighter
Powerplant: one BMW VI 7,3Z Vee piston engine rated at 750 hp (559 kW)
Performance: maximum speed 205 mph (330 km/h) at sea level; cruising speed 174 mph (280 km/h) at sea level; climb to 13,125 ft (4000 m) in 7 minutes 48 seconds; service ceiling 25,260 ft (7700 m); range 460 miles (740 km) with drop tank or 354 miles (570 km) with

standard fuel
Weights: empty 3,247 lb (1473 kg); maximum take-off 4,475 lb (2030 kg)
Dimensions: wingspan 36 ft 1 in (11.00 m); length 27 ft 6¾ in (8.40 m); height 10 ft 6 in (3.20 m); wing area 292.778 sq ft (27.20 m²)
Armament: two 0.31-in (7.92-mm) MG 17 fixed forward-firing machine-guns in the upper part of the forward fuselage

Heinkel He 50 and He 66

Early evidence of Germany's interest in the dive-bomber concept is provided by the fact that in

1932 the **He 50** biplane was undertaking dive-bombing experiments with 1,102-lb (500-kg) concrete

blocks against targets floating in the lake-like estuary of the Warnow river. The spur for the development of this type was not the clandestine German air force but rather the Imperial Japanese navy air force, which had become interested in the dive-bomber concept during the late 1920s. In 1931, therefore, the service contracted with Heinkel for the design

of a two-seat dive-bomber able to carry a 551-lb (250-kg) weapon load, stressed for catapult launches, and capable of operation on wheel or float

landing gear.

Heinkel completed work on the design very rapidly, and in the same year began the construction of two **He 50a** prototypes.

An archaic-looking design with its uncowled-radial powerplant, the He 50A was instrumental in the formation of Germany's dive-bomber forces.

SPECIFICATION

Heinkel He 50A
Type: one/two-seat dive-bomber and reconnaissance bomber
Powerplant: one Bramo 322B (SAM 22B) radial piston engine rated at 650 hp (485 kW)
Performance: maximum speed 146 mph (235 km/h) at 2,625 ft (800 m); cruising speed 118 mph (190 km/h) at 2,625 ft (800 m); climb to 13,125 ft (4000 m) in 16 minutes; service ceiling 20,995 ft (6400 m); range 621 miles (1000 km)
Weights: empty 3,871 lb (1756 kg); maximum take-off 5,776 lb (2620 kg)

Dimensions: wingspan 37 ft 8¾ in (11.50 m); length 31 ft 6 in (9.60 m); height 14 ft 5¼ in (4.40 m); wing area 374.58 sq ft (34.80 m²)
Armament: one 0.312-in (7.92-mm) MG 17 fixed forward-firing machine-gun in the forward fuselage and, when flown in two-seat reconnaissance bomber form, one 0.312-in (7.92-mm) MG 15 trainable rearward-firing machine gun in the rear cockpit, plus up to 1,102 lb (500 kg) of disposable stores carried on one underfuselage and two underwing hardpoints

Heinkel He 50 and He 66 (continued)

The He 50 was an equal-span biplane based on a rectangular-section fuse-lage with a primary structure of welded steel tube construction, faired out to an oval shape by wooden formers and stringers and covered with fabric except on the extreme nose, which was skinned in light alloy. The fuselage had tandem accommodation for two men (although there was provision for the rear cock-pit to be faired over if the type was to be operated as a single-seater). The flying surfaces comprised a fabric-covered welded steel tube tail unit and a two-bay, marginally staggered and very slightly swept wing cellule. This latter was of fabric-covered wooden construction and carried ailerons on all four panels.

The first prototype was the **He 50aW** floatplane that first flew later in 1931 with a powerplant of one 390-hp (291-kW) Junkers L5 inline engine driving a two-bladed, fixed-pitch wooden propeller. This machine was badly damaged in a forced land-ing, and the burden of the trials program was assumed by the **He 50aL** second prototype, which

had meanwhile been completed in landplane form with a powerplant of one 490-hp (365-kW) Siemens (Gnome-Rhône/Bristol) Jupiter VI radial engine driving a four-bladed, fixed-pitch wooden propeller. The He 50aL was tested in two- and single-seat configurations with a maximum bomb load of 551 and 1,102 lb (250 and 500 kg) respectively, and caught the attention of the German authorities, which ordered three aircraft for a fuller evaluation.

Heinkel had meanwhile been continuing work on the basic design, and a number of improvements were incorporated in the **He 50b** third prototype, which was completed in the autumn of 1932 as the second of the two proto-types ordered by the IJN. The improvements included revised main landing gear units and an alteration of the forward fuselage so that only the cylinder heads of the Jupiter VI engine protruded. Also designated as the **He 66** for export purposes, the He 50b was shipped to Japan early in 1933, where it was evalu-ated successfully before being used as the basis of the Aichi D1A.

The three aircraft for German evaluation were completed in the summer of 1932 to a standard based on that of the He 50b but with a power-plant of one 600-hp (373-kW) SAM 22B radial engine driving a three-bladed, two-pitch metal propeller, and a gun arma-ment of one fixed and one trainable 0.31-in (7.92-mm) machine-guns. Successful evaluation of these three aircraft, in single-seat form for the dive-bomber role with a disposable load of 1,102 lb (500 kg) and in two-seat form for the reconnaissance bomber role also with a disposable load of 551 lb (250 kg), paved the way for a production order.

This production model was the **He 50L** that was retrospectively designated **He 50A**. Heinkel's order for the type, which entered service late in 1933, was for 25 aircraft and another order was placed with Bayerische Flugzeugwerke for 35 aircraft. The He 50A was initially operated by training schools, but with the October 1935 creation of the Luftwaffe's first dive-bomber unit, the Fliegergruppe Schwerin that later became I Gruppe

of Stukageschwader 162, the type was placed in operational service. The He 50As were later replaced by Hs 123A and Ju 87A dive-bombers as they became available, and returned to their essential training role. In the spring of 1943, however, the Luftwaffe decided to emulate the Soviet tactic of night harassment raids by slow-flying biplanes, and decided that the He 50A was one of the obsolescent types that could be used in this role. The 24 surviving He 50As were gathered from various schools and used to equip two Estonian-manned Staffeln (squadrons) of Nachtschlachtgruppe 11 between December 1943 and September 1944, when the aircraft were retired for lack of spares.

Early in 1934, Heinkel received a Chinese order for 12 He 50bs in recon-naissance bomber form with a powerplant, as the SAM 22B was not permit-ted by the German authorities, of one 480-hp (358-kW) Siemens Jupiter VIIF engine. These **He 66aCh** aircraft were shipped to China in the summer of 1934. In the summer of 1935, the

Chinese ordered another 12 aircraft, and now that supplies of the SAM 22B radial engine were meet-ing German demands this improved engine was released for export. The **He 66bCh** was therefore identical in all essential respects to the Luftwaffe's He 50A with the exception of its NACA cowling and propeller spinner. The aircraft were completed in the spring of 1935, shortly after the Germans had revealed the existence of the previously secret Luftwaffe and started a major expansion programme. The aircraft were then impressed for German service with the revised designation **He 50B**, but after six months of service finally released for delivery to their original customer. The aircraft finally reached Hong Kong only in January 1936, and remained in storage there until July 1937, when the crated aircraft were transferred to Peking and finally assem-bled for limited service in the 2nd Sino-Japanese War. Within two months the Chinese relegated the He 66s to service as train-ers, however, and the type then faded into Asian obscurity.

Heinkel He 59

Designed in 1930, the **He 59** resulted from a requirement issued by the still-secret German air force for a torpedo bomber and reconnaissance warplane able to operate with equal facility on wheel or twin-float landing gear. The type was an equal-span biplane with an unstaggered two-bay wing cellule, and was based on a rectangular section fuse-lage of fabric-covered welded steel tube construction faired at the top and bottom into rounded shapes that gave the fuselage an oval appearance in frontal eleva-

tion. The flying surfaces comprised a conventional fabric-covered tail unit and fabric-covered wooden wings. The floats were single-step units of wooden construction, and were carried below the outboard ends of the lower-wing centre section, while the engines were installed in nacelles carried by the interplane struts. Each engine drove a four-bladed, fixed-pitch wooden propeller.

The first of the two prototypes to fly was actu-ally the second machine, which was designated **He 59a** and was a land-

plane with fuel tankage in the fuselage, and fixed tail-wheel landing gear. This made its maiden flight in September 1931, and was followed by the **He 59b** floatplane with its fuel tankage in the two floats to leave the fuselage free for payload. (The He 59 was at this time presented to the world at large as a trans-port, so the suggestion was that this payload was freight.) It was soon decided to abandon the landplane variant and concentrate on the float-plane, so the first production model was the **He 59B-1** that differed from the He 59b only in details such as the large cut-outs in the trailing edges of the upper- and lower-wing centre sections, a larger fin, a revised ventral step with increased glazing and provi-sion for a ventral gunner, a revised forward fuselage with a stepped nose and a radio operator's position, and provision for inter-changeable nose sections. These last comprised a plywood-covered unit simi-lar to that of the He 59b and a light alloy unit with a bow gunner's position and an optically flat glazed panel for bomb-aiming. Deliveries of the He 59B-1 started in the summer of 1934, initially to the

Deutsche Verkehrs-fliegerschule, the ostensibly civil flight train-ing school that was in fact the Germans' military seaplane training school. By the beginning of 1935, Heinkel had delivered 14 He 59s and production was taken over by Arado.

Improvement of the initial model was rapid, the He 59B-1 soon being replaced on the production line by the **He 59B-2** with improved equipment and the **He 59B-3** intended for the long-range maritime patrol task with auxiliary fuel tanks and the reduced armament of just two

machine-guns.

In July 1936, the Luftwaffe – which had been publicly revealed in the previous year – commissioned its first coastal floatplane units and of these 3./Küstenflieger-gruppe 106 and 3./KüFlGr 506 were equipped with the He 59B. Soon after this Germany decided to send the Legion Condor to fight alongside the Spanish Nationalist insurgents in the Spanish Civil War, and this formation included a Seeaufklärungsstaffel AS/88 equipped with the He 59B-2: for improved capability against light ship-

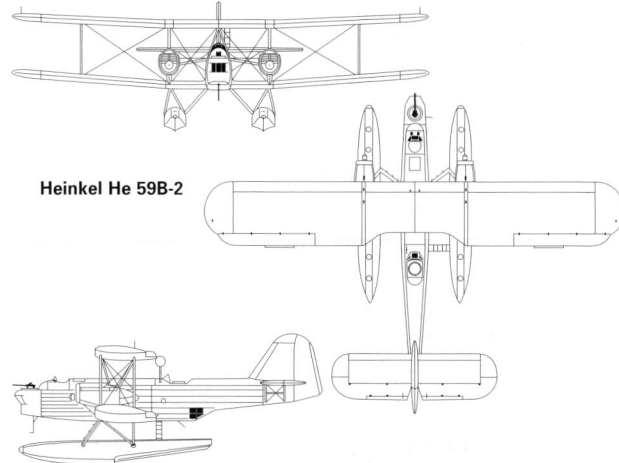

Heinkel He 59B-2

ping, some of the float-planes were equipped with a 20-mm MG FF trainable cannon in the bow position in place of the standard MG 15 machine-gun. Arado ceased production of the He 59B early in 1938 after the completion of 140 such floatplanes, and by this time were four Staffeln were operational on the type.

By 1938 the He 59 was seen as intrinsically obsolete in its originally planned roles, but the type acquired a new lease of life when it was revised by Walter Bachmann Flugzeugbau for the training and air/sea rescue roles. No new floatplanes were built for the task, but most surviving He 59Bs were adapted as **He 59C-1** unarmed trainers with additional navigational equipment, or as **He 59C-2** air/sea rescue types with provision for six inflatable dinghies, emergency medical equipment, and an external folding ladder in the ventral position. A few

He 59Cs were transferred to Finland.

The **He 59D-1** was a dual-purpose type combining the navigation training and air/sea rescue roles with a revised nose lacking the glazed panel of the earlier variants but with a separate navigator cockpit

forward of the pilot's position. The **He 59E** was a more specialised trainer variant produced by conversions to the **He 59E-1** torpedo-bombing trainer and **He 59E-2** photo-reconnaissance trainer standards, the latter with three camera posi-

tions. The final converted type was the **He 59N** intended for the navigation training role and fitted with full defensive armament. The limitations of the He 59 in the air/sea rescue role led to the replacement of most of the floatplanes by Do 18 and Do 24 flying-

boats from 1941, and the type was retired from this role in 1943 except in Finland, where a number of ex-German machines remained in service to 1944. The trainer models survived slightly longer, but all had been retired by 1944.

This He 59D-1 flew air-sea rescue missions over the Aegean Sea during 1941. The aircraft belonged to Seenotzentrale Agäisches Meer.

Heinkel He 60

The **He 60** was designed to meet an official requirement for a catapult-launched shipborne reconnaissance and spotting floatplane, and made its first flight in 1933 in the form of the **He 60a** first prototype. The He 60 was a conventional, single-bay staggered biplane with a mixed structure of metal for the welded steel tube fuselage and wood for the wings, all covered largely with fabric, and was carried above the water by parallel

single-step light alloy floats. The He 60a was powered by the 660-hp (492-kW) BMW VI 6,0 ZU Vee piston engine driving a two-bladed Schwarz wooden propeller. The sole criticism of the type was that the engine lacked adequate power reserves for the inevitable rise in weight with the installation of additional equipment: this was the result primarily of the requirement's insistence that the type be capable of operations on the open

sea, which resulted in a sturdy but heavy structure.

The **He 60b** second prototype was therefore completed with the 750-hp (559-kW) BMW VI 7,3ZU engine, but trials revealed so little an improvement that it was decided to use the original BMW VI 6,3 ZU in the **He 60A** initial production model, of which 14 had already been started as pre-production machines. The He 60b also introduced larger ailerons (installed on all four outer wing panels) and omitted the single auxiliary inter-plane struts outboard of the main N-type struts, while the **He 60c** third prototype and He 60A floatplanes adopted the later ailerons but reintroduced the auxiliary strut. The first He 60A was tested as the **He 60 V4** prototype, and the type entered service in the summer of 1933.

Nominally replacing the

He 60A in production during the second half of 1934, the **He 60B** was a marginally improved model with a refined structure and a number of equipment changes. It was built to the extent of only one airframe. Introduced toward the end of 1934, the **He 60C** was a further improvement on the basic standard model and was built only in modest numbers. Entering production in July 1936, the **He 60D** was the definitive model based on the He 60C revised with fixed forward-firing armament in the form of a single 0.31-in (7.92-mm) MG 17 machine-gun. By 1939 the He 60 series was obsolete, and

on the outbreak of World War II was rapidly relegated from first-line units to training schools, and from them to secondary tasks such as liaison. In 1941 the type returned to first-line service to operate along the coastal left flank of the German armies invading the USSR from June of that year. The type was once more phased out of first-line service between June and October 1943, in this instance to the oblivion of the scrap yard.

The designation **He 60E** was applied to a total of six He 60Ds supplied to the Spanish Nationalists in the Spanish Civil War. Four of the aircraft survived to 1948.

The He 60B was powered by a DB 600 inline. The He 60 was vulnerable owing to its modest performance, but handled well once on the water.

SPECIFICATION	
Heinkel He 60C	478 miles (770 km)
Type: two-seat coastal reconnaissance floatplane	**Weights:** empty 5,313 lb (2410 kg); maximum take-off 7,837 lb (3555 kg)
Powerplant: one BMW VI 6,0ZU Vee piston engine rated at 660 hp (492 kW)	**Dimensions:** wingspan 42 ft 4¾ in (13.00 m); length 37 ft 8¾ in (11.50 m); height 16 ft 2½ in (4.94 m); wing area 581.25 sq ft (54.00 m²)
Performance: maximum speed 140 mph (225 km/h) at 3,280 ft (1000 m); cruising speed 118 mph (190 km/h) at 3,280 ft (1000 m); climb to 6,560 ft (2000 m) in 8 minutes 54 seconds; service ceiling 16,405 ft (5000 m); range	**Armament:** one 0.312-in (7.92-mm) MG 15 trainable rearward-firing machine-gun in the rear cockpit

Heinkel He 70 Blitz, He 170 and He 270

Designed to a meet Deutsche Lufthansa specification of February 1932 for a fast transport to compete with the Lockheed Orion recently introduced by Swissair, the **He 70 Blitz** (lightning) was developed as a high-speed type able to carry mail and up to four passengers. The original 177-mph (285-km/h) maximum speed requirement

was soon increased to 186 mph (300 km/h), and the Günter brothers responded with a design based on an aerodynamically efficient airframe with an elevated pilot's cockpit offset to port, a compartment for the navigator/radio operator below and behind the cockpit, and a passenger cabin with four seats in facing pairs. Power was

supplied by a close-cowled 630-hp (470-kW) BMW VI 6,0Z engine, which was cooled by ethylene-glycol and therefore needed only a smaller radiator, with consequent advantages in drag reduction.

The prototype, with fixed landing gear and faired-over wheel wells, first flew from Travemünde on 1 December 1932. Early in

1933 this aircraft achieved a speed of 234 mph (376 km/h) and in March and April the second prototype was used by Lufthansa's Flugkapitän R. Untucht to set eight world speed records. **He 70A** aircraft off the production line entered service with Deutsche Lufthansa in June 1934, and later the introduction of the 750-hp

(559-kW) BMW VI 7,3 engine produced the **He 70D** military communications aircraft whose civil counterpart was the **He 70G** with a lengthened fuselage and crewed by only a pilot in a cockpit relocated to the fuselage centreline. One **He 70G-1** was supplied to Rolls-Royce in 1935, powered initially with the 810-hp (604-kW) Kestrel engine and later used extensively as an engine test bed.

Heinkel He 70 Blitz, He 170 and He 270 (continued)

In addition to the He 70D communications aircraft. other military models comprised the **He 70E** with a crew of two, a 0.312-in (7.92-mm) MG 17 machine-gun in the rear cockpit and provision for a 661-lb (300-kg) bomb load, and the **He 70F**. The latter was produced as the **He 70F-1** long-range reconnaissance variant and the generally similar **He 70F-2**, 18 of

which were sent to the Legion Condor in the autumn of 1936, serving with the A/88 reconnaissance unit.

For export to Hungary in 1937, Heinkel developed the **He 170A** which differed primarily in having the 910-hp (679-kW) Gnome-Rhône 14K Mistral-Major radial engine. Around 20 were delivered, remaining in service until July 1941.

The last of the He 70 line was the **He 270**, built only as a prototype and flown in 1938. Its 1,175-hp (876-kW) Daimler-Benz DB 601A inverted-Vee engine gave it a maximum speed of 286 mph (460 km/h). Armed with three 0.312-in (7.92-mm) machine-guns in the form of one MG 17 forward-firing and two MG 15 rearward-firing weapons, and capable of carrying the same 661-lb (300 kg) bomb load as the He 70E, the He 270 was intended to combine the light bomber and reconnaissance roles, but was not adopted by the Luftwaffe.

Hungary flew its He 170As, including the He 170A-01 illustrated, on photographic reconnaissance missions over disputed territory in Rumania.

The third He 70, designated as the He 70b, was the first aircraft of the series with the full set of equipment specified by DLH.

SPECIFICATION

Heinkel He 70D
Type: two-crew communications aircraft
Powerplant: one BMW VI 7,3Z Vee piston engine rated at 750 hp (559 kW)
Performance: maximum speed 223 mph (360 km/h); service ceiling 18,000 ft (5485 m); range 776 miles (1250 km)
Weights: empty 5,579 lb (2530 kg); maximum take-off 7,629 lb (3640 kg)
Dimensions: wingspan 48 ft 6¾ in (14.80 m); length 38 ft 4½ in (11.70 m); height 10 ft 8 in (3.25 m); wing area 393.0 sq ft (36.51 m²)
Payload: up to four passengers in an enclosed cabin

Heinkel He 72 Kadett and He 172

The **He 72 Kadett** (cadet) was introduced in 1933 as a simple primary flying trainer of fabric-covered mixed metal and wood construction with open cockpits, a staggered single-bay biplane wing cellule, a strut-braced tail

unit and fixed tailskid landing gear.

The first production model was the **He 72A** with a powerplant based on one 140-hp (104-kW) Argus As 8B inverted inline engine that was later replaced by one 150-hp

(112-kW) As 8R engine, and the **He 72B** was the main production variant with the 160-hp (119-kW) BMW-Bramo (Siemens) Sh.14A radial engine: the He 72B was produced in two military forms as the **He 72B-1** landplane and **He 72BW Seekadett** (sea cadet) twin-float seaplane, and a civil development was the **He 72B-3 Edelkadett** (noble cadet) for the touring as well as training role.

Large-scale production was undertaken for the Luftwaffe, but the total built has now been lost. The type was used extensively in World War II in its original trainer role, for liai-

An unremarkable aircraft in design terms, the He 72 was a classic biplane trainer type. The uncowled Sh.14A radial engine of the He 72B is obvious in this view.

son and, in the hands of the Slovaks, for light attack with a small complement of light bombs.

The **He 172**, which

appeared only in prototype form during 1934, was basically the He 72B with a long-chord NACA cowling for its engine.

SPECIFICATION

Heinkel He 72B Kadett
Type: two-seat primary flying trainer
Powerplant: one BMW-Bramo (Siemens) Sh.14A radial piston engine rated at 160 hp (119 kW)
Performance: maximum speed 115 mph (185 km/h) at sea level; cruising speed 106 mph (170 km/h) at optimum altitude; initial climb rate 591 ft (180 m) per minute;

climb to 3,280 ft (1000 m) in 6 minutes; service ceiling 11,485 ft (3500 m); range 295 miles (475 km)
Weights: empty 1,191 lb (540 kg); maximum take-off 1,907 lb (865 kg)
Dimensions: wingspan 29 ft 6¼ in (9.00 m); length 24 ft 7¼ in (7.50 m); height 8 ft 10¼ in (2.70 m); wing area 222.82 sq ft (20.70 m²)

Heinkel He 100

Built as the first example of three pre-series He 100D-0 aircraft, D-ITLR entered flight testing in September 1939.

Although the Bf 109 had been adopted as the Luftwaffe's standard monoplane fighter in preference to the He 112, Heinrich Hertel and Siegfried Günter designed a new high-speed fighter with the projected maximum speed of 435 mph (700 km/h). The

new type was also engineered for ease of production. The resulting **He 100a** (or **He 100 V1**) prototype made its first flight on 22 January 1938 with a powerplant based on one DB 601 engine with a special pressurised evaporative cooling system. The

He 100 V2 second prototype, with the DB 601M engine, captured the 100-km (62-mile) closed-circuit landplane record on 6 June 1938, piloted by Ernst Udet. The aircraft was quoted officially as the **He 112U** to boost the reputation of the He 112B sold to Japan and Spain. The **He 100 V3** third prototype, built for an attempt on the world absolute speed record, had a wing of reduced span, a more streamlined cockpit canopy

and a boosted DB 601, but it crashed in September and was replaced by the similar eighth prototype: in this aircraft Hans Dieterle raised the record to 463.92 mph (746.61 km/h) at Oranienburg on 30 March 1939. The fourth and fifth aircraft were designated **He 100B**, and the sixth, seventh and ninth prototypes were completed to **He 100C** standard: the third of these was the first He 100 with fixed forward-firing armament, in the

form of two 20-mm MG FF cannon and four 0.31-in (7.92-mm) MG 17 machine-guns.

Handling deficiencies revealed during service evaluation resulted in the introduction of the **He 100D** with enlarged tail surfaces and a conventional, semi-retractable ventral radiator in place of the earlier enclosed system. It was armed with an MG FF cannon in the nose to fire through the hollow propeller shaft and

SPECIFICATION

Heinkel He 100D-1
Type: single-seat fighter
Powerplant: one Daimler-Benz DB 601M inverted-Vee piston engine rated at 1,175 hp (876 kW)
Performance: maximum speed 416 mph (670 km/h) at 16,405 ft (5000 m); cruising speed 398 mph (641 km/h) at 16,405 ft (5000 m); climb to 19,685 ft (6000 m) in 7 minutes 48 seconds; service ceiling 36,090 ft 11000 m); range 628 miles (1010 km)
Weights: empty 4,431 lb

(2010 kg); maximum take-off 5,512 lb (2500 kg)
Dimensions: wingspan 30 ft 10 in (9.40 m); length 26 ft 10⅜ in (8.20 m); height 11 ft 9¾ in (3.60 m) with the tail up; wing area 157.16 sq ft (14.60 m²)
Armament: one 20-mm MG FF fixed forward-firing cannon between the cylinder banks and firing through the propeller shaft, plus two 0.31-in (7.92-mm) MG 17 fixed forward-firing machine-guns in the leading edges of the wing

with two MG 17 machine-guns in the leading edges of the wing. Fifteen examples of the He 100D were built, comprising three **He 100D-0** pre-production examples and 12 **He 100D-1** production aircraft, the latter being retained at Heinkel's Rostock-Marienehe factory and flown by Heinkel staff pilots as a local defence unit. As supplies of the DB 601 had been earmarked for Bf 109 production, the He 100 was not adopted for Luftwaffe use and the company was authorised to offer the type for licensed manufacture in other countries. In October 1939 Japanese and Soviet teams visited Marienehe and, as a result, three He 100D-0s were sold to Japan and six of the prototypes to the USSR. Proposed Japanese production did not materialise.

Heinkel He 111

Jumo-powered and with a 4,410-lb (2000-kg) bomb load, He 111E-1s eventually equipped four Staffeln of K/88.

Although the **He 111** was designed ostensibly as a civil airliner, its military potential was of greater importance. The **He 111 V1** first prototype, an enlarged development of the He 70 with two 660-hp (492-kW) BMW VI 6,0Z Vee engines, was initially flew on 24 February 1935. A shorter-span wing was introduced on the **He 111 V2** and **V3** second and third prototypes, the second being a civil transport accommodating 10 passengers and mail, and the third the true bomber prototype. The **He 111 V4** civil prototype was demonstrated publicly on 10 January 1936, and six **He 111C** series aircraft derived from this prototype entered service with Lufthansa in the same year with various engines including BMW 132 radials.

Development of the military version continued, but the 168-mph (270-km/h) cruising speed that resulted from the combination of too much military equipment and too little power proved disappointing. Thus the **He 111 V5**, prototype of the military **He 111B** series and first flown early in 1936, had the uprated powerplant of two 1,000-hp (746-kW) Daimler-Benz DB 600A inverted-Vee engines. Its improved performance brought substantial orders, requiring new production facilities that were completed in May 1937. Initial deliveries to an operational squadron, 1./KG 154 at Fassberg, were made late in 1936 and in February 1937, 30 **He 111B-1** bombers were delivered to K/88, the Legion Condor's bomber unit in Spain. The He 111 bore the brunt of the Luftwaffe's bombing effort in early World War II. Large-scale introduction of the Ju 88, and the He 111's vulnerability to British fighters, resulted in the transfer of the Heinkel to night operations and a variety of specialised roles.

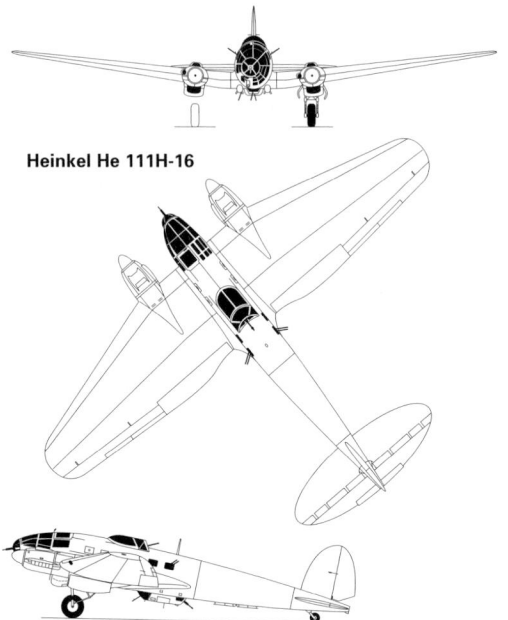

Heinkel He 111H-16

SPECIFICATION

Heinkel He 111H-16
Type: five-seat medium bomber
Powerplant: two Junkers Jumo 211F-2 inverted-Vee piston engines rated at 1,350 hp (1007 kW)
Performance: maximum speed 227 mph (365 km/h) at sea level; cruising speed 230 mph (370 km/h) at 6,560 ft (2000 m); climb to 13,125 ft (4000 m) in 23 minutes 30 seconds; service ceiling 27,890 ft (8500 m); range 1,740 miles (2800 km) with maximum fuel or 1,199 miles (1930 km) with maximum bomb load
Weights: empty 19,136 lb (8680 kg); maximum take-off 30,865 lb (14000 kg)
Dimensions: wingspan 74 ft 1¾ in (22.60 m); length 53 ft 9½ in (16.40 m); height 13 ft 1¼ in (4.00 m); wing area 931.11 sq ft

(86.50 m²)
Armament: one 20-mm MG FF trainable forward-firing cannon in the nose position, one optional 0.31-in (7.92-mm) MG 15 trainable forward-firing machine-gun in the nose position, one 0.51-in (13-mm) MG 131 trainable rearward-firing machine-gun in the dorsal position, two 0.31-in (7.92-mm) MG 81 trainable rearward-firing machine-guns in the rear of the ventral gondola and one 0.31-in (7.92-mm) MG 15 or MG 81 trainable lateral-firing machine-gun or two 0.31-in (7.92-mm) MG 81 trainable lateral-firing machine-guns in each of the two beam positions, plus up to 5,511 lb (2500 kg) of disposable stores carried in a lower-fuselage weapons bay and on two underwing hardpoints

Variants

He 111A: following unsatisfactory tests of 10 pre-production **He 111A-0** bombers, all were sold to China
He 111B: testing of the fifth prototype with 1,000-hp (746-kW) DB 600A engines led, in 1936, to the **He 111B-1** production aircraft with 880-hp (656-kW) DB 600Cs, followed by the **He 111B-2** with 950-hp (708-kW) DB 600CG engines
He 111C: six 10-passenger airliners for Lufthansa
He 111D: improved version with DB 600Ga engines and auxiliary wing radiators deleted; production discontinued in favour of the He 111E
He 111E: shortage of the DB 600 engine brought installation of the 1,000-hp (746-kW) Junkers Jumo 211A-1 engine in an He 111D-0; the resulting **He 111E-0** pre-production prototype had increased bomb load, and **He 111E-1** production bombers were delivered in 1938, followed by the **He 111E-3** and **He 111E-4** with further increase in bomb load and the **He 111E-5** with fuselage auxiliary fuel tank
He 111F: the new wing of the He 111G and Jumo 211A-3 engines characterised the 24 **He 111F-1** bombers supplied to Turkey; the Luftwaffe received 40 similar **He 111F-4** aircraft in 1938
He 111G: first version with the new straight-taper wing which, incorporated on the He 111C, resulted in the **He 111G-1**; the **He 111G-3** had 880-hp (656-kW) BMW 132Dc radials, the **He 111G-4** had 900-hp (671-kW) DB 600G engines, and four **He 111G-5** aircraft for Turkey had DB 600Ga engines
He 111H: developed in parallel with the He 111P series, the **He 111H-0** and **He 111H-1** were basically the He 111P-2 with 1,100-hp (753-kW) Jumo 211A engines; the **He 111H-2** of 1939 had improved armament; the **He 111H-3** introduced armour protection and a 20-mm cannon; the **He 111H-4** had Jumo 211D-1 engines and two external racks for bombs or torpedoes; the generally similar **He 111H-5** had increased fuel capacity; the **He 111H-6** introduced Jumo 211F-1 engines and a machine-gun in the tail cone; **He 111H-8** was the redesignation of the He 111H-3 and He 111H-5 machines following installation of fenders for balloon cables, most of them being converted later to **He 111H-8/R2** glider tugs; the **He 111H-10** for night bombing of UK targets had additional armour, reduced armament and wing leading-edge balloon cable-cutters; the

He 111H-11 and **He 111H-11/R1** had revised armament, the latter becoming the **He 111H-11/R2** when converted later as a glider tug; the **He 111H-12** and **He 111H-15** were missile launchers; the **He 111H-14** was a pathfinder version and the **He 111H-14/R2** a glider tug; introduced in 1942, the **He 111H-16** was a major production variant similar to the He 111H-11 but able to carry a 7,165-lb (3250-kg) bomb load with the use of rocket-assisted take-off gear; the **He 111H-16/R1** had a revolving dorsal turret, the **He 111H-16/R2** was for rigid-bar towing of gliders and the **He 111H-16/R3** was a pathfinder version, as was the **He 111H-18** with exhaust flame dampers; four versions of the **He 111H-20** comprised the **He 111H-20/R1** carrying 16 paratroops, the **He 111H-20/R2** night bomber/glider tug, the **He 111H-20/R3** with increased armour protection, and the generally similar **He 111H-20/R4** which introduced GM-1 power boost equipment; a version of the He 111H-20/R3 with 1,750-hp (1305-kW) Jumo 213E-1 engines and two-stage superchargers was designated **He 111H-21**; the **He 111H-22** was a missile-carrier; and the **He 111H-23** was a paratroop transport with 1,776-hp (1324-kW) Jumo 213A-1 engines
He 111J: torpedo-bomber version of the He 111F series, the **He 111J-0** and **He 111J-1** both had 950-hp (708-kW) DB 600CG engines
He 111L: alternative designation for He 111G-3 civil transport
He 111P: in 1939 the He 111P series introduced a major fuselage redesign, the stepped cockpit being replaced by an asymmetric glazed cockpit and nose; the **He 111P-0** introduced a prone position ventral gondola and was powered by two 1,150-hp (858-kW) DB 601Aa engines; first deliveries of the **He 111P-1** began in late 1939; the **He 111P-2** was similar but for radio revisions; the **He 111P-3** had dual controls; the five-crew **He 111P-4** had more armour and armament; the **He 111P-6** had 1,175-hp (876-kW) DB 601N engines and its 4,409-lb (2000-kg) bomb load stowed vertically in the fuselage; when later converted as a glider tug the He 111P-6 became the **He 111P-6/R2**
He 111R: single prototype of proposed high-altitude bomber
He 111Z: the He 111Z (*Zwilling*, or twin) combined two He 111H-6 airframes by means of a new wing centre section carrying a fifth Jumo 211F-2 engine; designed to tow the Me 321 Gigant transport glider, two prototypes and 10 **He 111Z-1** production aircraft were built

Heinkel He 111 (continued)

He 111 special eventually included missile launching, torpedo-bombing, pathfinding and glider-towing.

Transport duties were also undertaken, including operations to supply the beleaguered German 6th Army at Stalingrad between November 1942 and February 1943, and by the end of the war the He 111 was flown almost entirely in the transport role. Production of more than 7,300 aircraft for the Luftwaffe was completed in the autumn of 1944 and, in addition, some 236 **He 111H** warplanes were built by CASA in Spain during and after World War II with the designation the **CASA 2.111**: about 130 of these had Junkers Jumo 211F-2 inverted-Vee engines and the others Rolls-Royce Merlin 500-29 Vee engines; some were converted later for transport and training duties.

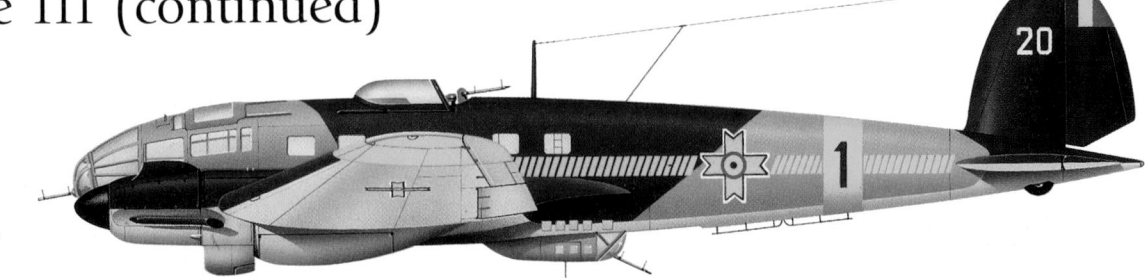

Romania received 32 He 111H-3 bombers, of which the aircraft illustrated was the 20th example. Some 15 H-6 models were also supplied, while German records give a total for the number of He 111s supplied to the country as 57, this figure including 10 He 111Es which were used as trainers.

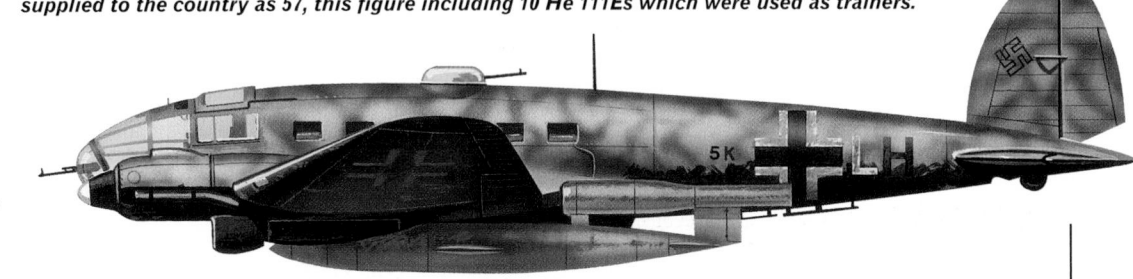

Produced either from incomplete He 111H-21 airframes still on the production line, or by conversion from existing H-16 and H-20 airframes, the He 111H-22 was equipped for the carriage of a single Fieseler Fi 103 (V1) 'doodle-bug' under the port wing.

Heinkel He 112

The **He 112** was designed in rivalry to the Bf 109 to secure the Luftwaffe's first order for a monoplane fighter, and was for its time a comparatively advanced type of essentially all-metal construction with fabric-covered control surfaces, an oval-section fuselage of light alloy semi-monocoque construction, a cantilever tail unit, low-set cantilever wings of inverted-gull configuration and elliptical planform with a stressed-skin covering and a trailing-edge combination of outboard ailerons and inboard flaps, and tailwheel landing gear including main units that retracted outward into the undersurface of the outer wing panels.

The He 112 was originally planned by the Günter brothers with an open cockpit, a relatively large wing with curved rather than elliptical leading and trailing edges, and a power-plant of one Junkers Jumo 210 Vee engine, and in this form secured an initial contract for three prototypes. In the absence of the Jumo engine however, the **He 112 V1** first proto-

type made its maiden flight in the summer of 1935 with one 695-hp (518-kW) Rolls-Royce Kestrel V Vee engine driving a two-bladed, fixed-pitch wooden propeller. The **He 112 V2** and **He 112 V3** second and third prototypes followed shortly after this, powered by 600-hp (447-kW) Jumo 210C engines.

Trials revealed that in this form the He 112 had adequate performance and generally good handling characteristics, but that speed and roll rate were hampered by the area and span of the wing, and that improved performance could be expected with a more advanced propeller. The second and third prototypes were therefore revised with clipped wing tips and a three-bladed, constant-speed propeller. Other changes included a rearward-sliding cockpit canopy, a revised vertical tail surface, a redesigned radiator bath, and a fixed forward-firing armament of two 0.31-in (7.92-mm) MG 17 machine-guns in the sides of the forward fuselage. These modifications

paved the way for the **He 112 V4** prototype that introduced the definitive elliptical wing of reduced span and area, and also the powerplant of one 680-hp (507-kW) Jumo 210Da engine. The He 112 V4, **He 112 V5** and **He 112 V6** were the prototypes for the planned **He 112A** series that was not ordered as the German air ministry eventually preferred the Bf 109, and the **He 112 V8** was completed as a testbed for the new 1,000-hp (746-kW) Daimler-Benz DB 600Aa inverted-Vee engine.

By this time, Heinkel had come to the decision that further development of the He 112 into an effective type required considerable redesign. This involved the design of a considerably lighter fuselage structure and thoroughly revised flying surfaces that transformed the design from its He 112A form into the **He 112B**. The **He 112 V7** was an interim prototype, and the true prototype of the He 112B series was thus the **He 119 V9** that made its maiden flight in

Part of a batch of 12 He 112B-0 aircraft ordered by Japan, this machine was temporarily impressed into Luftwaffe service during the Sudeten crisis of August 1938.

SPECIFICATION	
Heinkel He 112B-0	4,960 lb (2250 kg)
Type: single-seat fighter	**Dimensions:** wingspan 29 ft 10¼ in (9.10 m); length 30 ft 6 in (9.30 m); height 12 ft 7½ in (3.85 m); wing area 182.99 sq ft (17.00 m²)
Powerplant: one Junkers Jumo 210Ea inverted-Vee piston engine rated at 680 hp (507 kW)	
Performance: maximum speed 317 mph (510 km/h) at 13,125 ft (4000 m); cruising speed 301 mph (485 km/h) at 13,125 ft (4000 m); climb to 19,685 ft (6000 m) in 9 minutes 30 seconds; service ceiling 27,890 ft (8500 m); range 683 miles (1100 km)	**Armament:** two 20-mm MG FF fixed forward-firing cannon in the leading edges of the wing and two 0.31-in (7.92-mm) MG 17 fixed forward-firing machine-guns in the sides of the forward fuselage, plus up to 132 lb (60 kg) of disposable stores carried on six underwing hardpoints
Weights: empty 3,571 lb (1620 kg); maximum take-off	

July 1937 with the Jumo 210Ea engine. The German air ministry was sufficiently impressed with the He 112 V9 to order a batch of 30 **He 112B-0** service trials aircraft. These operated with a fighter wing during 1938, and 17 of them were then sent to Spain for operational evaluation in the later stages of the Spanish Civil War. The type proved moderately successful, and the 15 aircraft that survived the war were handed over to the air force of the Nationalist side that won the civil war, remaining in service up to 1945.

Of its other 13 aircraft, the German air ministry sold 12 to the Imperial Japanese navy air force,

which thought that the type could be used for the interception of the advanced Tupolev SB-2 bombers supplied to China by the USSR in the 2nd Sino-Japanese War. The aircraft were assembled in Hankow and received the Japanese designation **A7Hei**, but proved incapable of reaching interception height before the Soviet-built bombers had unloaded their bombs: the aircraft were then relegated to a ground station for use in the training of mechanics. Romania also ordered the type, receiving 13 He 112B-0s before the outbreak of World War II and 11 **He 112B-1** fighters after this time. The only difference between the

Some 30 He 112B-1 and B-2 aircraft were supplied to Romania for service from 1939.

He 112B-0 and He 112B-1 was the latter's individual exhaust stubs. Another

three He 112B-1s were delivered to Hungary, which also acquired the He 112

V9 prototype upgraded to He 112B-1 standard. Some of these fighters remained

in Hungarian and Rumanian service into 1942, seeing limited service on the

Eastern Front against the USSR after the Axis invasion of June 1941.

Heinkel He 114

The **He 114** resulted from a German air ministry requirement for a catapult-launched reconnaissance and gunnery spotting floatplane to replace the He 60, but was, in fact, used almost exclusively in the shore-based coastal reconnaissance role. Heinkel offered a sesquiplane design of mixed construction, and in the summer of 1935 the air ministry contracted for five prototype and 10 pre-production He 114 floatplanes.

Key elements of the design were its aerodynamic cleanliness, semi-enclosed accommodation for the pilot and observer/gunner, and sesquiplane wing cellule that lost much of the biplane. The engine specified by the air ministry was the BMW 132Dc radial

being developed on the basis of the Pratt & Whitney Hornet. Such an engine was unavailable as the **He 114 V1** and **He 114 V2** first and second prototypes were nearing completion, so these aircraft were completed respectively with the 960-hp (716-kW) Daimler-Benz DB 600A inverted-Vee engine driving a two-bladed metal propeller, and the 680-hp (507-kW) Junkers Jumo 210Ea Vee engine driving a three-bladed metal propeller. These two aircraft made their maiden flights in the early summer of 1936, and proved to possess poor handling characteristics on the water and in the air. They were followed by the **He 114 V3** and **He 114 V4** third and fourth prototypes powered respectively by the 850-hp

(634-kW) BMW 132Dc radial driving a two-bladed propeller and the 960-hp (716-kW) BMW 132K engine driving a three-bladed propeller. The He 114 V3 introduced a sliding cover for the pilot's cockpit, larger horizontal tail surfaces and modified floats, while the He 114 V4 pioneered new floats and a clipping of the wing tips. Neither the He 114 V3 nor V4 offered any real improvement over the V1 and V2, and the disappointed air ministry immediately issued to Arado and Focke-Wulf a requirement for an He 114 replacement should an intensive remedial programme fail to achieve results.

The **He 114 V5** was completed late in 1936 and was basically similar to the He 114 V3 with the clipped tips of the He 114 V4, and the first four **He 114A-0** pre-production floatplanes were allocated to the development programme as the **He 114 V6, V7, V8** and **V9**. The first two were similar to the V5 except for float changes, the V8 was intended as the production prototype with the BMW 132K engine driving a three-bladed, variable-pitch VDM metal propeller but no catapult attachment points

as trials with the earlier prototypes had revealed inadequate structural strength for this demanding task, and the V9 was based on a restressed fuselage. The other six He 114A-0s were also used in the trials programme without change of designation.

Meanwhile, the **He 114A-1** initial service model had entered production with a broader-chord vertical tail surface and the 865-hp (645-kW) BMW 132N engine driving either a two- or three-bladed propeller. These 33 floatplanes were delivered from June 1937 for the start of training, and were replaced on the production line by the **He 114A-2** with the restressed catapult-capable fuselage and, after the first few machines, the BMW 132K engine driving a three-bladed propeller. The type was issued to only one squadron, 1./Küstenfliegergruppe 506, but its pilots were so critical of the new type that it was withdrawn and the unit reverted

to its obsolescent He 60s.

The withdrawn He 114As were not scrapped but instead transferred to the 'Weser' Flugzeugbau for refurbishment before export. Sweden and Romania each took 12 of the machines with the revised designations **He 114B-1** and **He 114B-2**. Another four of the aircraft were transferred to Spain, where they remained in service up to the late 1940s as the last examples of their type.

Romania ordered the conversion of 12 more floatplanes to the **He 114C-1** standard with a fixed forward-firing armament of two 0.31-in (7.92-mm) MG 17 machine-guns in the forward fuselage. These floatplanes were impressed by the Luftwaffe before delivery and were used on the Baltic flank of the German invasion of the USSR from June 1941, only passing to the Romanians at the end of 1941 for service up to 1943.

Sweden's He 114B-1s were delivered in the period 1939-40 for service with Flottilj 2. They were eventually replaced by Saab S 17BS floatplanes.

SPECIFICATION	
Heinkel He 114A-2	**Weights:** empty 5,335 lb
Type: two-seat coastal reconnaissance floatplane	(2420 kg); maximum take-off 8,090 lb (3670 kg)
Powerplant: one BMW 132K radial piston engine rated at 960 hp (716 kW)	**Dimensions:** wingspan 44 ft 7½ in (13.60 m); length 38 ft 2½ in (11.65 m); height 17 ft 2 in (5.23 m); wing area 454.79 sq ft (42.25 m²)
Performance: maximum speed 208 mph (335 km/h) at 3,280 ft (1000 m); cruising speed 183 mph (295 km/h) at 3,280 ft (1000 m); climb to 9,845 ft (3000 m) in 18 minutes 12 seconds; service ceiling 16,075 ft (4900 m); range 571 miles (920 km) with auxiliary fuel	**Armament:** one 0.31-in (7.92-mm) MG 15 trainable rearward-firing machine-gun in the rear cockpit, plus up to 220 lb (100 kg) of disposable stores carried on two underfuselage hardpoints

Heinkel He 115

Developed to replace the He 59, the first prototype of the **He 115** floatplane recorded its maiden flight in 1936. Its two machine-guns were then removed, their positions being faired over, and on 30 March 1938 the machine set eight payload/speed records. The second prototype was similar, the third introduced the 'glasshouse' canopy which became standard, and the fourth was the production prototype.

This He 115C has a 20-mm MG FF cannon mounted in a fixed installation beneath its nose. Other available weapons included the LT F5 or LT F6b torpedoes and LMB III or LMA III mines.

Variants

He 115A: the 10 pre-production **He 115A-0** aircraft of 1937 had a single machine-gun; the **He 115A-1** added a nose-mounted machine-gun, and the similar **He 115A-2** was exported to Norway and Sweden; the Luftwaffe's first **He 115A-3** production version had a modified weapons bay and radio changes
He 115B: the **He 115B-1** had increased fuel capacity, and the **He 115B-2** reinforced floats for operation from snow or ice; He 115B series aircraft, able to trade fuel and bomb load, were able to carry a 2,205-lb (1000-kg) magnetic mine

He 115C: introduced in 1941, the **He 115C-1** had additional armament; the **He 115C-2** had reinforced floats like those of the He 115B-2; the **He 115C-3** and **He 115C-4** were minelaying and torpedo-carrying versions respectively
He 115D: designation of one He 115A-1 with two 1,600-hp (1193-kW) BMW 801C engines
He 115E: on reopening the production line in 1941, the new **He 115E-1** was produced, being similar to the He 115C but with revised armament

Heinkel He 115 (continued)

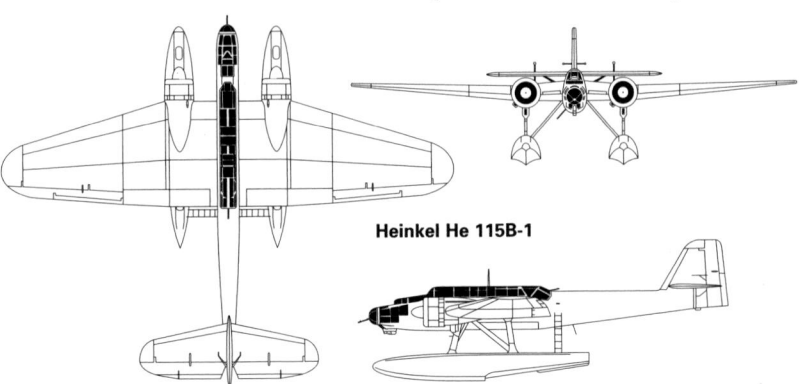

Heinkel He 115B-1

SPECIFICATION	
Heinkel He 115C-1	(22.28 m); length 56 ft 9 in
Type: three-seat coastal general-	(17.30 m); height 21 ft 7¾ in
purpose and torpedo bomber	(6.60 m); wing area 933.23 sq ft
floatplane	(86.70 m²)
Powerplant: two BMW 132K	**Armament:** one 15-mm MG 151
radial piston engines each rated at	fixed forward-firing cannon on the
960 hp (716 kW)	lower port side of the nose, one
Performance: maximum speed	0.31-in (7.92-mm) MG 17 fixed
186 mph (300 km/h) at 3,280 ft	rearward-firing machine-gun in the
(1000 m); cruising speed 180 mph	rear of each engine nacelle, one
(290 km/h) at 6,560 ft (2000 m);	0.31-in (7.92-mm) MG 15 trainable
climb to 9,845 ft (3000 m) in	forward-firing machine gun in the
22 minutes 18 seconds; service	nose position and one 0.31-in
ceiling 16,950 ft (5165 m); range	(7.92-mm) MG 15 trainable
1,740 miles (2800 km) with	rearward-firing machine-gun in the
maximum fuel	dorsal position, plus up to 2,205 lb
Weights: empty 15,146 lb	(1000 kg) of disposable stores
(6870 kg); normal take-off	carried in a lower-fuselage
23,545 lb (10680 kg)	weapons bay and on two
Dimensions: wingspan 73 ft 1 in	underwing hardpoints

The fourth production proto-type had the previous float/fuselage bracing wires replaced by struts. The He 115 was used by coastal reconnaissance squadrons of the Luftwaffe and, after the outbreak of World War II, was deployed to drop parachute mines in British waters. Four reached the UK from Norway, three being modified later for clandestine operations to Norway and the Mediterranean.

Heinkel He 162 Salamander

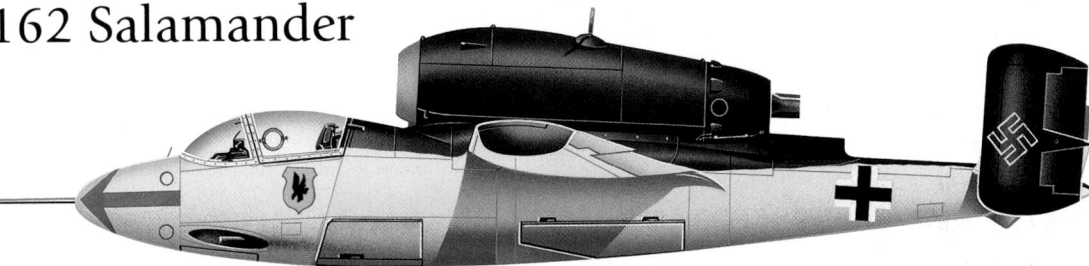

The prototype of the **He 162 Salamander** turbo-jet-engined interceptor recorded its maiden flight on 6 December 1944, only 38 days after detail drawings had been issued to the factory. This prototype was lost in a fatal flying accident on 10 December, but the programme was continued and revealed some aerodynamic problems, these being remedied in the third and fourth prototypes, both flown on 16 January 1945; first deliveries of aircraft for operational evaluation and service trials were also made during January 1945.

On 4 May 1945 one Gruppe of three squadrons, with a total of 50 aircraft, was formed at Leck in Schleswig-Holstein, but British forces occupied the airfield on 8 May and accepted the unit's surrender. A total of 116 He 162s was built, and more than 800 were in various stages of assembly when their underground production centres were captured.

JG 1 applied a bold red arrow marking to the noses of its He 162 fleet. In addition, this He 162A-2 also carries the badge of 3. Staffel. A number of ex-Ju 188 pilots from III./KG 30 were transferred to 3. Staffel, but many of them never completed He 162 training.

Variants

He 162A: the 10 prototypes were also designated **He 162A-0** as pre-production aircraft; initial production **He 162A-1** fighters were followed by the more extensively built **He 162A-2** which introduced further aerodynamic changes to enhance stability

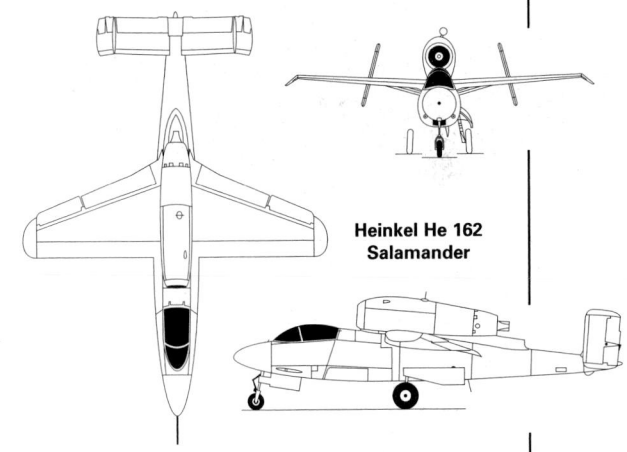

Heinkel He 162 Salamander

SPECIFICATION	
Heinkel He 162A-2 Salamander	(10970 m)
Type: single-seat fighter	**Weights:** empty 4,520 lb
Powerplant: one BMW 003A-1	(2050 kg); maximum take-off
turbojet engine rated at 1,764 lb st	5,941 lb (2695 kg)
(7.85 kN)	**Dimensions:** wingspan 23 ft 7½ in
Performance: maximum speed	(7.20 m); length 29 ft 8½ in
522 mph (840 km/h) at 19,685 ft	(9.05 m); height 8 ft 6½ in (2.60 m);
(6000 m); initial climb rate 3,780 ft	wing area 120.56 sq ft (11.20 m²)
(1152 m) per minute; service	**Armament:** two 20-mm MG
ceiling 39,370 ft (12000 m);	151/20 fixed forward-firing cannon
endurance 57 minutes at 35,990 ft	in the underside of the nose

Heinkel He 177 Greif

Equipped with FuG 200 Hohentwiel search radar for the detection of surface targets, this He 177A-5 was flown by II. Gruppe of KG 40 from Bordeaux-Mérignac. The aircraft is armed with a pair of Hs 293A anti-ship missiles, while other typical He 177 weapons included SC 50, SC 250 and SC 500 bombs carried internally, and LMA III mines, LT 50 torpedoes or Fritz-X guided bombs carried externally.

Developed from the **P.1041** project for a long-range bomber, the **He 177 Greif** (griffon) first flew in proto-type form on 19 November 1939. With no engine in the 2,000-hp (1492-kW) class available, Daimler-Benz close-coupled two DB 601 units to produce the 2,600-hp (1939-kW) DB 606, and two of these units were used to power the He 177. The design's other unusual feature was the use of twin main land-ing gear units on each side, these retracting sideways into the wing, inboard and outboard of each engine nacelle. There were many early teething problems, at least three prototypes being lost in accidents resulting from wing struc-tural weakness or engine fires. The structural prob-lems were soon rectified, but overheating of the coupled engine units,

Variants

He 177A-0: 35 pre-production aircraft used for development trials and conversion training
He 177A-1: 130 built by Arado in four versions, designated **He 177A-1/R1** to **He 177A-1/R4**, each with minor variations; introduced in March 1942
He 177A-3: 170 built by Heinkel, the first 15 **He 177A-3/R1** bombers with DB 606A/B engines and the remainder with DB 610 engines; the **He 177A-3/R2** had improved armament; the **He 177A-3/R3** carried three Henschel Hs 293 missiles; the **He 177A-3/R4** had a gondola containing FuG 203 missile-control equipment; the **He 177A-3/R5** was armed with a 75-mm cannon in a ventral gondola; and three **He 177A-3/R7** aircraft were each equipped to carry two torpedoes
He 177A-4: proposed high-altitude version
He 177A-5: version with structural modifications, primarily a strengthened wing for heavier underwing loads; the **He 177A-5/R1** to

He 177A-5/R4 had minor armament changes; the **He 177A-5/R5** had a remotely controlled barbette to the rear of the weapons bays, the first two of which were deleted in the **He 177A-5/R6**; the **He 177A-5/R7** had a pressurised cockpit; and the **He 177A-5/R8** had barbettes in chin and rear positions; five He 177A-5s had their weapons bay area modified to house an array of 33 rocket tubes, the weapons being fired upward at a forward angle of 60°
He 177A-6: six **He 177A-6/R1** aircraft were built as development examples of a proposed version with extra armament and armour protection for the crew compartment and fuel tanks; one development aircraft was flown with a new forward fuselage and heavier armament intended for the **He 177A-6/R2**
He 177A-7: six He 177A-5s were modified with the 118 ft 1½ in (36.00 m) wing intended for the production He 177A-7, and with DB 610 engines instead of the intended 3,600-hp (2685-kW) DB 613 units

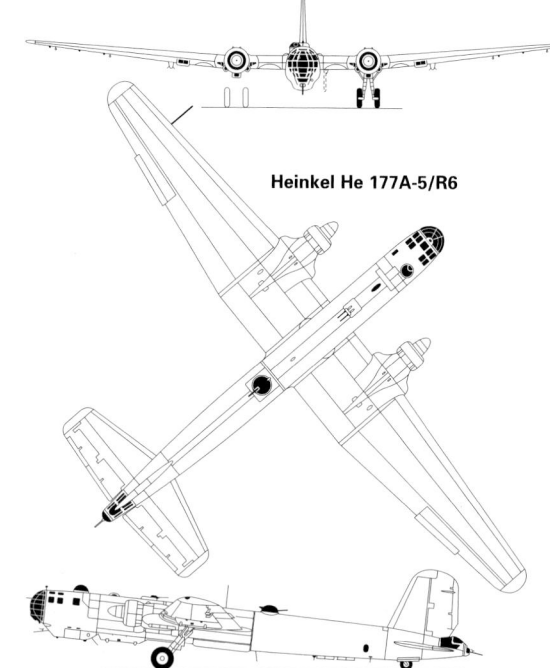

Heinkel He 177A-5/R6

which occasionally caused engine fires, was never completely resolved.

Early production **He 177A-1** aircraft were delivered in July 1942, these still having structural problems, and it was not until late in 1942 that the more reliable **He 177A-3** entered service. French- and German-based He 177s took part in operations against targets in the UK during Operation Steinbock, and also saw service on the Eastern Front, but a variety of problems and a need for the German industry to concentrate its efforts on more vital fighter aircraft meant that the He 177 had been virtually with-

drawn from service by the end of 1944. One note-worthy but uncompleted aircraft was a single exam-

ple under modification in Prague to accommodate the planned German atomic bomb.

This He 177A-5/R6 was tested by the RAE with the serial TS439. It was photographed just after its arrival in the UK on 10 September 1944.

Heinkel He 178

At the same time that work was in progress on the largely ineffective **He 176** rocket-powered aircraft, Heinkel was busily developing the turbojet-powered **He 178** which featured the company's HeS 3b engine.

The He 178 became the world's first turbojet-powered aircraft to fly when, on 27 August 1939, Flugkapitän Erich Warsitz made a circuit of the factory airfield at Rostock-Marienehe. Development was very much on a private-venture basis, and it was not until 28 October 1939 that official observers, in the persons of Milch, Udet and Lucht of the German air ministry, saw the aircraft in flight. The project attracted little interest at the time,

Air for the He 178's HeS 3B engine was drawn in via an intake in the aircraft's nose. The machine's first flight was cut short when the engine failed just after take-off, when a bird was sucked into the intake.

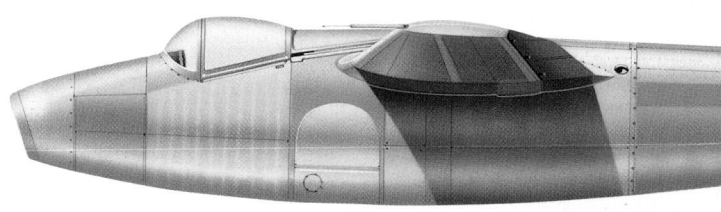

and work was discontinued in favour of the twin-engined **He 280**, which was the first turbojet-engined aircraft to be designed as a fighter. It was to be powered by a pair of the new Heinkel HeS 8 or HeS 30 turbojets. The first proto-type began unpowered trial

flights on 22 September 1940, the aircraft being towed to release height behind a He 111. A pair of the HeS 8 engines was installed in March 1941 and the first powered flight made on 2 April. Ultimately, however, the rival Me 262 was selected for production.

Heinkel He 219 Uhu

Potentially one of the Luftwaffe's most effective night-fighters, the **He 219 Uhu** (owl) was another aircraft which suffered from misjudgements by senior members of the government and Luftwaffe high command. It derived from

Heinkel's private-venture **P.1060** fighter-bomber proposal, which received little encouragement until 1941, when it was seen to have promise as a night-fighter. An all-metal shoulder-wing monoplane, the He 219 seated the pilot

and navigator back-to-back, was the first operational aircraft in the world to introduce ejection seats, and was also the Luftwaffe's first operational aircraft with tricycle landing gear.

The first prototype recorded its maiden flight on 15 November 1942 with a powerplant based on two 1,750-hp (1305-kW)

Daimler-Benz DB 603A engines; the second proto-type, flown in December, had a different armament installation. Following eval-uation of one of the prototypes in mock combat against a Dornier Do 217N and a Junkers Ju 88S, an 'off the drawing board' order for 100 aircraft was increased to 300; further

prototypes were used in the aircraft's development programme. From April 1943 a small number of **He 219A-0** pre-production aircraft flew with 1./NJG 1 at Venlo in the Netherlands, and on the night of 11 June 1943 Major Werner Streib shot down five Avro Lancaster bombers in a single sortie.

Heinkel He 219 Uhu (continued)

The first six operational sorties flown by the unit resulted in claims for 20 RAF aircraft, including six examples of the redoubtable de Havilland Mosquito. Despite cancellation of the programme in May 1944, production deliveries of a number of versions were made, principally to 1./NJG 1 and NJGr 10.

Impressive scores aside, the He 219 suffered from excessive weight growth

Based at Munster in the autumn of 1944, this He 219A-5/R1 was flown by NJG 1. Note the flame-damped exhausts.

during its development, a process which gave it tricky and often unforgiving handling traits.

SPECIFICATION

Heinkel He 219A-7/R1 Uhu
Type: two-seat night-fighter
Powerplant: two Daimler-Benz DB 603G inverted-Vee piston engines each rated at 1,900 hp (1417 kW)
Performance: maximum speed 416 mph (670 km/h) at 22,965 ft (7000 m); cruising speed 391 mph (630 km/h) at optimum altitude; initial climb rate 1,810 ft (552 m) per minute; climb to 19,685 ft (6000 m) in 11 minutes 30 seconds; service ceiling 40,025 ft (12200 m); range 1,243 miles (2000 km)
Weights: empty 24,692 lb (11200 kg); maximum take-off

33,730 lb (15300 kg)
Dimensions: wingspan 60 ft 8⅓ in (18.50 m); length 50 ft 11¾ in (15.54 m); height 13 ft 5½ in (4.10 m); wing area 479.01 sq ft (44.50 m²)
Armament: two 30-mm MK 108 fixed forward-firing cannon in the wing roots, two 30-mm MK 103 and two 20-mm MG 151/20 fixed forward-firing cannon in a ventral tray, and two 30-mm MK 108 cannon in an obliquely forward- and upward-firing *schräge Musik* installation in the upper part of the rear fuselage

Variants

He 219A-2: the **He 219A-1** reconnaissance bomber having been abandoned at the project stage, the **He 219A-2/R1** night-fighter was the first production version; armed with two MK 108 cannon in a ventral tray and two MG 151/20 cannon in the wing roots; the *schräge Musik* installation of two MK 108s behind the cockpit, firing obliquely upward and forward, was a retrospective installation
He 219A-5: first major production version, generally similar to He 219A-1; the **He 219A-5/R1** had 1,800-hp (1342-kW) DB 603A engines and increased fuel capacity; and the **He 219A-5/R4**, which differed by carrying a third crew member, had a stepped cockpit with a 0.51-in (13-mm) trainable machine-gun
He 219A-6: stripped-down He 219A-2/R1 with 1,750-hp (13Q5-kW) DB 603L engines and four MG 151/20s; developed specifically to combat the Mosquito

He 219A-7: similar to the He 219A-5 but with improved supercharger intakes for its DB 603G engines; in addition to the standard *schräge Musik* installation, it had two MK 108s in the wing roots as well as two MG 151/20s and two MK 103 cannon in the ventral tray; the **He 219A-7/R2** had MK 108 cannon in place of the ventral MK 103s, and the **He 219A-7/R3** had the wing-root MK 108s replaced by MG 151/20 cannon, and the ventral tray of the He 219A-7/R2; the **He 219A-7/R4** had tail warning radar and just four MG 151/20 cannon; six **He 219A-7/R5** night-fighters were effectively He 219A-7/R3 machines with 1,900-hp (1417-kW) Junkers Jumo 213E engines and a water-methanol injection system; the single **He 219A-7/R6** had two 2,500-hp (1864-kW) Jumo 222A/B engines
He 219B-1: one only with DB 603Aa engines and crew of three; Jumo 222A/B engines had been intended
He 219B-2: similar to He 219A-6, but with only two MG 151/20 cannon

Helio Courier and Super Courier

Helio Aircraft Corporation (later Company) designed and built the original **Courier** prototype in 1953. Of cantilever high-wing monoplane configuration, its development and production continued through the 4-seat **H-391B**

Courier of 1954, 4/5-seat **H-395/H-395A** of 1958/1959, and 6-seat **H-250** of 1964. The subsequent **Model H-295 Super Courier** was flown in prototype form on 24 February 1965, as a comfortable and well-equipped six-seat

Peru, Somalia and Thailand represented the military export customers for the Super Courier. This machine is illustrated as it appeared in army colours but on loan from the air force.

SPECIFICATION

Helio U-10D
Type: six-seat STOL utility and communications aircraft
Powerplant: one 295-hp (220-kW) Avco Lycoming GO-480-G1D6 flat-six piston engine
Performance: maximum speed 167 mph (269 km/h) at sea level; cruising speed 165 mph (265 km/h)

at 8,500 ft (2590 m); range 1,380 miles (2220 km)
Weights: empty 2,080 lb (943 kg); maximum take-off 3,400 lb (1542 kg)
Dimensions: wingspan 39 ft (11.89 m); length 31 ft (9.45 m); height 8 ft 10 in (2.69 m); wing area 231 sq ft (21.46 m²)

cabin monoplane. Full-span leading-edge slats, upper surface spoilers, Frise ailerons and 74 per cent span slotted trailing-edge flaps meant the Super

Courier had excellent STOL performance. This attracted the US Air Force and one civil H-391B was evaluated under the designation **YL-24**. Three H-395s were

then acquired as **L-28A** aircraft, their evaluation leading to orders for 26 **U-10A**, 57 **U-10B** and 36 **U-10D** aircraft for use in utility transport roles.

Helio H-550 Stallion (U-24)

The excellent STOL capability of the Courier led to the development of the slightly larger, turboprop-powered **HST-550 Stallion** prototype, first flown on 5 June 1964. Certification of the production version, the **H-550A Stallion**, was gained in August 1969 but,

costing more than $100,000 per unit, the type had little appeal to civil buyers. However, the USAF acquired 15 as **AU-24A** aircraft with hardpoints beneath the wing/fuselage and a cabin weapons mounting, for such roles as armed reconnaissance,

close air support, forward air control and general transport. All but one were

transferred to the Khmer Air Force. The AU-24A could be armed with 20-mm cannon, CBU-14A/A bomb dispensers and a 500-lb (227-kg) HE bomb

for counter-insurgency (COIN) operations.

During the Vietnam war, AU-24s were used in clandestine CIA missions

SPECIFICATION

Helio H-550A Stallion
Type: Eight/eleven-seat STOL utility aircraft
Powerplant: Pratt & Whitney Aircraft of Canada PT6A-27 turboprop engine rated at 680 shp (507-kW)
Performance: maximum speed 226 mph (364 km/h) at 10,000 ft (3050 m); maximum cruising speed

217 mph (349 km/h) at 10,000 ft (3050 m); range 1,090 miles (1755 km)
Weights: empty 2,825 lb (1281 kg); maximum take-off 5,100 lb (2313 kg)
Dimensions: wingspan 41 ft (12.50 m); length 39 ft 7 in (12.07 m); height 9 ft 3 in (2.81 m); wing area 242 sq ft (22.48 m²)

Henschel Hs 123

With its spats and trousers removed, the Hs 123 was able to operate from the muddiest of airfields on the Eastern Front. This Schlachtgeschwader 2 aircraft served on the southern sector of the Russian Front during winter 1942-43.

SPECIFICATION

Henschel Hs 123A-1
Type: dive-bomber/close-support aircraft
Powerplant: one 880-hp (656-kW) BMW 132Dc 9-cylinder radial piston engine
Performance: maximum speed 211 mph (340 km/h) at 3,935 ft (1200 m); cruising speed 196 mph (315 km/h) at 6,560 ft (2000 m); service ceiling 29,530 ft (9000 m); range 531 miles (855 km)

Weights: empty 3,307 lb (1500 kg); maximum take-off 4,884 lb (2215 kg)
Dimensions: wingspan, upper 34 ft 5½ in (10.50 m) and lower 26 ft 3 in (8.00 m); length 27 ft 4 in (8.33 m); height 10 ft 6 in (3.20 m); wing area 267.49 sq ft (24.85 m²)
Armament: two forward-firing 0.31-in (7.92-mm) MG 17 machine-guns, plus provision for up to 992 lb (450 kg) of bombs

Variant

Hs 123 V5 and V6: two 1938 prototypes with 960-hp (716-kW) BMW 132K engines and revised armament as development aircraft for proposed improved **HS 123B** version; no production aircraft

Designed to a 1933 dive-bomber requirement, the first of three **Hs 123** sesquiplane prototypes was flown in 1938 on the power of a 650-hp (485-kW) BMW 132A-3 radial engine. The first three aircraft were tested at Rechlin in August 1935, two of them being destroyed in dives because of wing structural failure. Successful testing of a fourth prototype incorporating changes to overcome this shortcoming led to a production order. The **Hs 123A-1** entered service with 1./StG 162 in the autumn of 1936, but the type's front-line career was short-lived, it being replaced by the **Ju 87A** in 1937. Five Hs 123As were supplied to the Legion Condor in Spain during December 1936, and the type saw operational service in Poland in 1939 and in France and Belgium in 1940. It was overworked in the Soviet Union in 1943, when few were left, attrition reducing the fleet until the type was withdrawn in mid-1944.

Henschel Hs 126

From the earlier parasol-wing **Hs 122**, Henschel derived the **Hs 126** two-seat reconnaissance aircraft which incorporated a new wing, cantilever main landing gear and a canopy over the pilot's cockpit. An **Hs 122A** airframe was converted to produce the 610-hp (455-kW) Junkers Jumo 210-powered prototype, which was first flown in the autumn of 1936. This was followed by two development aircraft, each with an 830-hp (619-kW) Bramo Fafnir 323A-1 engine.

Over Greece the Hs 126 proved particularly effective, this aircraft being one of those assigned to the Greek campaign and flying with 2.(H)/31 during April 1941. The yellow markings denoted service in a European theatre conflict.

SPECIFICATION

Henschel Hs 126B-1
Type: two-seat short-range reconnaissance aircraft
Powerplant: one 850-hp (634-kW) Bramo 323A-1 radial piston engine
Performance: maximum speed 193 mph (310 km/h) at sea level; service ceiling 27,230 ft (8300 m); maximum range 447 miles (720 km)
Weights: empty 4,476 lb

(2030 kg); maximum take-off 6,813 lb (3090 kg)
Dimensions: wingspan 47 ft 6¾ in (14.50 m); length 35 ft 7¼ in (10.85 m); height 12 ft 4 in (3.75 m); wing area 340.15 sq ft (31.60 m²)
Armament: two 0.31-in (7.92-mm) machine-guns, plus one 110-1b (50-kg) or five 22-1b (10-kg) bombs

During 1937 Henschel built 10 pre-production Hs 126A-0 aircraft based on the third prototype, some being used for operational evaluation by the Luftwaffe. Production **Hs 126A-1** aircraft entered service first with Aufklärungsgruppe 35, and by the outbreak of World War II the re-equipment of reconnaissance units was well under way.

Withdrawn progressively from service during 1942, the Hs 126 was replaced by the Fw 189. More than 600 Hs 126s were built, including six used by the Legion Condor in Spain, and later transferred to the Spanish air force, and 16 for the Greek air force.

Variant

He 126B-1: introduced during summer 1939, this version was powered by the Bramo 323A-1 or 900-hp (671-kW) 323A-2, and equipped with FuG 17 radio

Henschel Hs 129

Designed to meet an RLM requirement for a twin-engined ground-attack aircraft, carrying at least two 20-mm cannon and extensive armour protection, the prototype **Hs 129** was flown in the spring of 1939. Its triangular-section fuselage had a cramped cockpit with restricted view, a windscreen of 2.95-in (75-mm) thick armoured glass, and the nose constructed of armour plating. Luftwaffe testing of the three prototypes, each powered by two 465-hp (347-kW) Argus As 410 engines, showed the cockpit to be unacceptable and

Shown as it appeared while based at Iumis-El Alouina in February 1943, this Hs 129B belonged to 8./Schlachtgeschwader 2.

the aircraft sluggish in performance. Eight prepro-duction **Hs 129A-0** aircraft were ordered for continued test and evaluation, but the planned production **Hs 129A-1** was considered unacceptable and was replaced by the **Hs 129B-1**, introducing several improvements and more powerful Gnome-Rhône 14M 4/5 engines. Hs 129Bs entered service first with 4./SchG 1 in April 1942, becoming operational on the Eastern Front where the type was most widely used. Hs 129s served also in North Africa, Italy, and in France after the D-Day landings. Production, including prototypes, totalled 879.

Henschel Hs 129 (continued)

Variants

Hs 129B-0: 10 pre-production aircraft, similar to production Hs 129B-1s and delivered for Luftwaffe evaluation from December 1941
Hs 129B-1/R1: version of production aircraft carrying additionally two 110-lb (50-kg) bombs or 96 anti-personnel bombs
Hs 129B-1/R2: as production aircraft, but with an underfuselage 30-mm MK 101 cannon
Hs 129B-1/R3: as production aircraft but with four extra MG 17 machine-guns
Hs 129B-1/R4: version replacing the Hs 129B-1/R1's bombs with one 551-1b (250-kg) bomb
Hs 129B-1/R5: as production aircraft but incorporating an Rb 50/30 camera for reconnaissance duties
Hs 129B-2/R1: first of the versions introduced in early 1943 with heavier weapons for anti-tank operations, armed with two 20-mm MG 151/20 cannon and two 0.51-in (13-mm) MG 131 machine-guns
Hs 129B-2/R2: as Hs 129B-2/R1 but with additional 30-mm MK 103 underfuselage cannon

SPECIFICATION

Henschel Hs 129B-1/R2
Type: single-seat ground attack aircraft
Powerplant: two 700-hp (522-kW) Gnome-Rhône 14M 4/5 14-cylinder radial piston engines
Performance: maximum speed 253 mph (407 km/h) at 12,565 ft (3830 m); service ceiling 29,525 ft (9000 m); range 348 miles (560 km)
Weights: empty 8,400 lb (3810 kg); maximum take-off 11,266 lb (5110 kg)
Dimensions: wingspan 46 ft 7 in (14.20 m); length 31 ft 11¾ in (9.75 m); height 10 ft 8 in (3.25 m); wing area 312.16 sq ft (29.00 m²)
Armament: two 20-mm MG 151/20 cannon, two 0.31-in (7.92-mm) MG 17 machine-guns and one 30-mm MK 101 cannon

Hs 129B-2/R3: as Hs 129B-2/R2 but with MK 103 cannon replaced by 37-mm BK 3,7 gun and the MG 131s deleted
Hs 129B-2/R4: carried a 75-mm PaK 40 gun in an underfuselage pod
Hs 129B-3: developed from the Hs 129B-2/R4, the PaK 40 gun being replaced by an electro-pneumatically operated 75-mm BK 7,5 gun

Hiller FH-1100 (OH-5A)

The US Army's LOH (light observation helicopter) design competition of 1961 was finalised between the prototypes built as the Bell OH-4A, **Hiller OH-5A** and Hughes CH-6A, but it was the last which won the production order. Hiller decided to develop its design as a civil helicopter, resulting in the **FH-1100** of which the first production examples were delivered in the summer of 1966. Available in five-seat utility or four-seat executive versions, a total of 246 had been built when production ended in 1974. A total of about 30 FH-1100s was supplied to the armed services of Argentina, Brazil, Chile, Cyprus, Ecuador, Panama, the Philippines and Salvador. Hiller Aviation, formed in 1973 to acquire the UH-12 programme, became a subsidiary of Rogerson Aircraft of Port Angeles, Washington. Subsequently renamed Hiller Helicopters and Rogerson Helicopters, the company now operates as Rogerson Hiller and, from 1984, has built and marketed updated versions of the original FH-1100.

These were the **RH-1100A Pegasus** civil helicopter and the **RH-1100M Hornet** military rotorcraft, the latter capable of carrying battle-field avionics and armed with guns, rocket pods and ATM and AAM missiles.

SPECIFICATION

Hiller FH-1100A Pegasus
Type: five-seat utility helicopter
Powerplant: one 420-shp (313-kW) Allison 250-C20B turboshaft
Performance: economical cruising speed 122 mph (196 km/h); service ceiling 21,500 ft (6550 m); range 430 miles (692 km)
Weights: empty 1,500 lb (680 kg), maximum take-off 2,750 lb (1,247 kg)
Dimensions: main rotor diameter 35 ft 5 in (10.80 m); fuselage length 29 ft 9½ in (9.08 m); height 9 ft 3½ in (2.83 m); main rotor disc area 979 sq ft (91 m²)

Generally flown with up to three passengers, the FH-1100 could seat a maximum of four if required.

Hiller Model 360, UH-12 and OH-23 Raven

Hiller Helicopters Inc. was formed in 1942 for the development and production of rotary-wing aircraft. Early work on the **Model XH-44**, **UH-4 Commuter** and the **UH-5**, which introduced a newly-developed 'Rotor-Matic' rotor control system, led to the **Model 360** prototype. Now part of United Helicopters, the company's first production helicopter followed and this, known as the **UH-12**, was of simple construction.

It incorporated a two-bladed main rotor and a two-bladed tail rotor on an upswept boom. The design was highly successful, being built extensively in two- and three-seat configurations for both civil and military use, and an early Model 12 was the first commercial helicopter to record a transcontinental flight across the United States. More than 2,000 were built before production ended in 1965, some 300 of this total being exported, and throughout this period the power and capability of the helicopter was steadily improved.

The commercial **UH-12A** to **UH-12D** became the **OH-23A** to **OH-23D Raven** respectively for service with the US Army, and the US Navy acquired UH-12As as **HTE-1** and **HTE-2** helicopters. The **UH-12E** was basically a three-seat dual-control version of the OH-23D and was built also as the military **OH-23G**. A lengthened-fuselage, four-seat civil **UH-12E4** was produced as the military **OH-23F** and late civil versions with uprated powerplant included the UH-12E variants suffixed **L3**, **L4**, **SL3** and **SL4**. OH-23s were exported to Argentina, Bolivia, Colombia, Chile, Cuba,

SPECIFICATION

Hiller OH-23D Raven
Type: three-seat military helicopter
Powerplant: one 323-hp (241-kW) Avco Lycoming VO-540-A1B flat-six piston engine
Performance: maximum speed 95 mph (153 km/h) cruising speed 82 mph (132 km/h), service ceiling 13,200 ft (4025 m); range 205 miles (330 km)
Weights: empty 1,816 lb (824 kg); maximum take-off 2,700 lb (1225 kg)
Dimensions: main rotor diameter 35 ft 6 in (10.82 m); length 28 ft (8.53 m); height 9 ft 9 in (2.97 m); main rotor disc area 995.38 sq ft (92.47 m²)

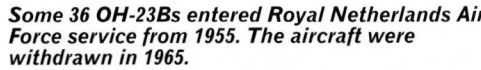

Some 36 OH-23Bs entered Royal Netherlands Air Force service from 1955. The aircraft were withdrawn in 1965.

A distinguishing feature of the UH-12 family is the tail rotor driveshaft running from the main gearbox to the low slung tailboom. The aircraft illustrated is a UH-12E.

Dominica, Guatemala, Guyana, Mexico, Morocco, the Netherlands, Paraguay, Switzerland, Thailand and Uruguay. The Canadian army acquired OH-23Gs which it operated with the designation **CH-112**

Nomad, and the British Royal Navy used a number of ex-US Navy HTE-2s under the designation **Hiller HT.Mk 2**.

At the height of UH-12/ OH-23 production, Hiller was taken over by the

Fairchild Corporation, but in 1973 a new company, Hiller Aviation, acquired design rights and production tooling for the UH-12E, and for some years provided support for the world-wide fleet of UH-12s. In April

1984 Hiller became a subsidiary of Rogerson Aircraft. Renamed Hiller Helicopters and later Rogerson Helicopters, the company, now known as Rogerson Hiller, relaunched the piston-engined UH-12E

in 1991 as the **Hauler**, and a number was exported. The company also proposed the Allison turbine-powered **UH-12ET** development for the US Army's NHT (New Training Helicopter) requirement.

Hispano HA-100, HA-200 and HA-220

The **HA-100 Triana** two-seat advanced trainer, designed under the direction of Professor Willy Messerschmitt, was first flown in **HA-100-E1** prototype form on 10 December 1954. Two HA-100-E1 prototypes were built, powered by 755-hp

(563-kW) ENMA Beta B-4 engines, plus two **HA-100-F1** prototypes with 800-hp (597-kW) Wright Cyclone engines, but it was the HA-100-E1 version that was ordered into production. Entering service with the Spanish air force during 1958, under the designa-

A total of 40 HA-100 production aircraft was built and used as armament trainers by the Spanish air force.

tion **E.12**.

Major HA-100 components were used in the **HA-200 Saeta** (arrow) which was also developed under the guidance of Messerschmitt. The first Spanish turbojet aircraft, the prototype was flown on 12 August 1955 and the first production aircraft on 11 October 1962. The HA-200 entered service shortly after this, being designated **E.14** by the Spanish air force. A single-seat attack version of the Saeta, the **HA-220**, began to enter service in 1971-2 under the Spanish air force designation **C.10**. In addition to the accom-

A sound design of Messerschmitt origins, the HA-200 is represented here by a preserved example in German civil markings.

SPECIFICATION

Hispano HA-200E Saeta	
Type: two-seat advanced trainer	(2020 kg); maximum take-off 7,937 lb (3600 kg)
Powerplant: two 1,058-lb (480-kg) thrust Turboméca Marboré VI turbojets	**Dimensions:** wingspan 34 ft 1¾ in (10.41 m); length 29 ft 5 in (8.97 m); height 9 ft 4¼ in (2.85 m); wing area 187.30 sq ft (17.40 m²)
Performance: maximum speed 429 mph (690 km/h) at 22,965 ft (3000 m); service ceiling 42,650 ft (13000 m); range 932 miles (1500 km)	**Armament:** underwing hardpoints for a range of weapons, plus provision for one 20-min cannon in fuselage
Weights: empty operating 4,453 lb	

HA-200 Variants

HA-200A: initial production version, 30 built for the Spanish air force
HA-200B: designation of 10 preproduction aircraft with Turboméca Marboré IIA turbojets built for Egypt before licence production by Helwan Air Works as the **Al-Kahira**; Helwan duly initiated production of 90 aircraft
HA-200D: improved version for service with the Spanish air force; 55 built with more modern systems and heavier armament
HA-200E Super Saeta: redesignation of 40 HA-200Ds after updating with Marboré VI turbojets, advanced avionics and provisions for air-to-ground rockets
HA-220: single-seat ground-attack version of HA-200E for Spanish air force: total of 25 built

modation change it had more powerful engines and provision to carry rocket pods. When production ended a total of 110

HA-200 and HA-220s had been built for the Spanish air force; of these about 20 HA-220s remained into the early 1980s.

Howard aircraft

Ben Howard, who designed and built his first aeroplane, the **Howard DGA-1 (Damned Good Airplane 1)** in 1933, established Howard Aircraft Corporation in 1937 to build and market his designs. A series of successful racers included the **DGA-3 Pete**, **DGA-4 Ike** and **DGA-5 Mike**, culminating in the **DGA-6 Mister Mulligan**, a four-seat cabin monoplane which won all three of the major American air races in 1935. From the DGA-6 was

developed a commercial **DGA-8** in 1936, a generally similar **DGA-9** in 1937 which differed in its powerplant, and leading through **DGA-11** and **DGA-12** aircraft with other engine installations to the **DGA-15** four/five-seat cabin monoplane. Versions of this aircraft with different powerplant comprised the **DGA-15J** with a 300-hp (224-kW) Jacobs L-6 engine, **DGA-15W** with 350-hp (261-kW) Wright IR-760-IE2, and the

DGA-15P with 450-hp (336-kW) Pratt & Whitney Wasp Junior.

The last version proved of interest to the US Navy, and in 1941 it was ordered initially as the **GH-1** transport, of which 31 were built and three impressed from civil sources. It was followed by 131 **GH-2** ambulance aircraft, 115 **GH-3** transports which differed in equipment from the GH-1, and 205 **NH-1** instrument trainers. The US Army Air Force impressed a total of 19 from civil sources for use in a light transport/communications role, these having the designations **UC-70**

(DGA-15P), **UC-70A** (DGA-12), **UC-70B** (DGA-15J), **UC-70C** (DGA-8) and **UC-70D** (DGA-9). These robust and reliable aircraft remained in service with the US Army and US Navy for a number of years.

In addition to these military aircraft, Howard also supplied about 60 trainers for use in the US Civil Pilot

Training Program. A cantilever low-wing monoplane, with instructor and pupil accommodated in tandem open cockpits, the type was designated **DGA-18W** with the Warner Super Scarab engine, **DGA-18K** with the Kinner engine, and **DGA-125** with a lower-powered 125-hp (93-kW) Warner Scarab engine.

SPECIFICATION

Howard GH-1	
Type: four-seat cabin monoplane	1,260 miles (2028 km)
Powerplant: one Pratt & Whitney R-985 Wasp Junior radial piston engine rated at 450 hp (336 kW)	**Weights:** empty 2,700 lb (1225 kg); maximum take-off 4,350 lb (1973 kg)
Performance: maximum speed 201 mph (323 km/h); service ceiling 21,500 ft (6555 m); range	**Dimensions:** wingspan 38 ft (11.58 m); length 25 ft 8 in (7.82 m); height 8 ft 5 in (2.57 m); wing area 210 sq ft (19.51 m²)

A testimony to just how good Howard's airplanes were, this DGA-15P, constructed in 1944, remained extant on the US civil register late in 2000. It was based at Pauls Valley, Ohlahoma.

Hughes H-4 Hercules

Designed under the direction of Howard Hughes, the **H-4 Hercules**, sometimes called the **HK-1** and popularly nicknamed the **'Spruce Goose'**, was the largest

flying-boat ever built. Piloted by Hughes with D. Grant as co-pilot, the H-4 Hercules made only one flight. This measured about one mile (1.61 km) over Los Angeles

Harbor on 2 November 1947. After a period of storage, the aircraft was presented to the Aero Club of Southern California and is preserved in its own circular building alongside the former liner *Queen Mary* at Long Beach, California.

SPECIFICATION

Hughes H-4 Hercules	
Type: flying-boat freighter	(225 km/h); estimated service ceiling 21,000 ft (6400 m); range 1,575 miles (2535 km)
Powerplant: eight 3,000-hp (2236-kW) Pratt & Whitney R-4360-4A piston engines	**Dimensions:** wingspan 319 ft 11 in (97.50 m); length 218 ft 8 in (66.60 m); height 79 ft 4 in (24.10 m); wing area 11,430 sq ft (1061.80 m²)
Performance: maximum speed at sea level 235 mph (378 km/h); cruising speed 140 mph	

Hughes H-4 Hercules (continued)

The largest flying-boat built, the Hughes H-4 Hercules was intended primarily as a freighter, but was designed to accommodate up to 700 passengers. Piloted by its sponsor, Howard Hughes, the H-4 'Spruce Goose' completed only one flight, covering a distance of around a mile, at a height of only 80 ft (24 m) over Los Angeles Harbor in 1947.

Hunting (Percival) P.56 Provost

Designed by Percival Aircraft before it became part of the Hunting Group in 1954, the **P.56 Provost** was accepted as the RAF's standard basic trainer in 1953, superseding the Prentice in Flying Training Command. A cantilever low-wing monoplane with fixed tailwheel landing gear and powered by a Leonides 126 engine, it provided side-by-side seating for instructor and pupil. Three prototypes were built, two powered initially by the Armstrong Siddeley Cheetah 18, the other by an Alvis Leonides. The first Cheetah-engined prototype flew on 23 February 1950. Entering service under the designation **Provost**

This Provost T.Mk 1 was refurbished by Hunting for Malaysian service. Malaysia received two batches of six aircraft, while Sudan purchased a further five refurbished examples.

T.Mk 1, the aircraft were delivered first to the Basic Training Squadron of the CFS at South Cerney. When production ended in 1959 a total of 461 had been built.

SPECIFICATION

Hunting Percival Provost T.Mk 1
Type: two-seat basic trainer
Powerplant: one 550-hp (410-kW) Alvis Leonides 126 radial piston engine
Performance: maximum speed 200 mph (322 km/h) at 2,300 ft (700 m); service ceiling 22,500 ft (6860 m); endurance 4 hours
Weights: empty equipped 3,350 lb (1520 kg), maximum take-off 4,400 lb (1996 kg)
Dimensions: wingspan 35 ft 2 in (10.72 m); length 28 ft 8 in (8.74 m); height 12 ft 2½ in (3.72 m), wing area 214.0 sq ft (19.88 m²)

Variants

Provost T.Mk 51: unarmed version for the Irish Air Corps
Provost T.Mk 52: armed version for the Royal Rhodesian Air Force
Provost T.Mk 53: armed version for the Irish Air Corps and the air forces of Burma, Iraq and Sudan

Hunting (Percival) P.66 Pembroke, President & Sea Prince

The **Percival P.50 Prince**, flown in 1948, had potential for development and resulted in the 10-seat **P.66 Pembroke** communications/light transport aircraft first flown on 21 November 1952. A total of 44 was built for the RAF as the **Pembroke C.MK 1**, these aircraft differing from the civil **Prince** by having increased wingspan, a reinforced cabin floor, strengthened landing gear and rear-facing seats for the passengers. An additional six were supplied with fuselage-mounted cameras for photo-reconnaissance under the designation **Pembroke C(PR).Mk 1**. Export versions were built for the air forces of Belgium, Denmark, Finland, West Germany, Sweden and

West Germany was the major overseas operator of the Pembroke, receiving 33 C.Mk 54s from June 1957. The 'AS' code signified service with Flugzeugführerschule S, which was a navigation/multi-engine training school and as the type OCU. Further examples served with the Marineflieger.

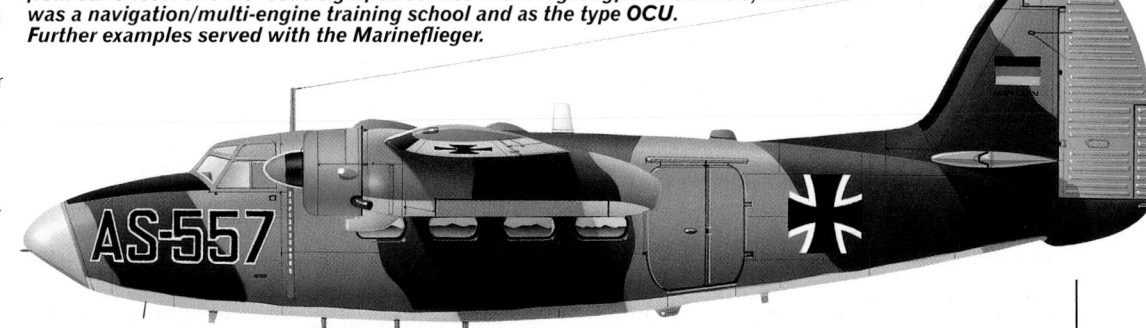

Sudan. The Royal Navy acquired four similar aircraft as the **Sea Prince C.Mk 1**, followed by 42 **Sea Prince T.Mk 1** aircraft equipped as 'flying classrooms' for training in navigation and ASW.

Last of the variants for the Royal Navy was the **Sea Prince C.Mk 2**, a communications version of the T.Mk 1 of which three were built. A civil variant designated President was also developed, three being ordered by a Spanish airline but never delivered.

Below: From 1959, No. 750 Sqn operated Sea Prince T.Mk 1s from Hal Far, Malta, in the observer training role.

SPECIFICATION

Hunting Percival Pembroke C.Mk 1
Type: communications aircraft
Powerplant: two 550-hp (410-kW) Alvis Leonides 127 radial piston engine
Performance: maximum speed 224 mph (360 km/h) at 2,000 ft (610 m); service ceiling 22,000 ft (6706 m); range 1,150 miles (1851 km)
Weights: empty 9,598 lb (4354 kg), loaded 13,500 lb (6124 kg)
Dimensions: wingspan 64 ft 6 in (19.66 m); length 46 ft (14.02 m); height 16 ft (4.88 m), wing area 400 sq ft (37.16 m²)
Accomodation: a crew of two and up to eight passengers

Hunting (Percival) P.84 Jet Provost and BAC Strikemaster

Development of the final major production Jet Provost, the T.Mk 5, represented by this No. 1 FTS example, was initiated by the extended syllabus of high altitude training activities performed by the RAF's unpressurised T.Mk 4s.

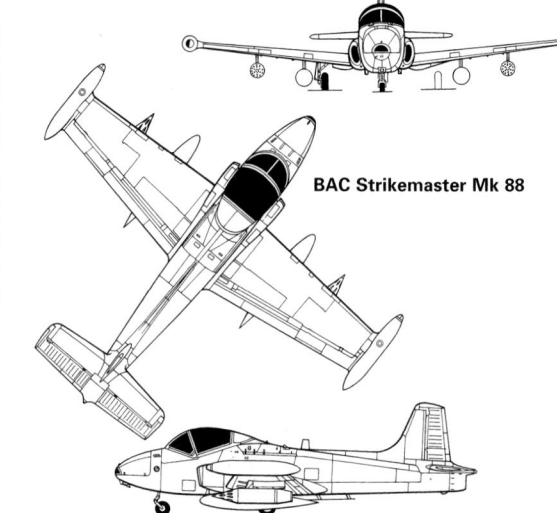

BAC Strikemaster Mk 88

Royal Air Force use of the piston-engined Provost and turbine-engined Vampire in its training sequence seemed illogical to Hunting. The company therefore proceeded with the private-venture design of a turbojet-powered version of the Provost to provide a pupil with all-through jet training. This retained the wings and tail unit of the Provost, but introduced a new fuselage housing the turbine engine and retractable tricycle landing gear. Ten of these aircraft were ordered for the RAF as the **Hunting Jet Provost T.Mk 1** in March 1953, the first of them being flown on 16 June 1954. These machines were used by the RAF during 1955 for comparative trials, the first pupil making a solo flight in the type on 17 October 1955. The undoubted success of this new training sequence led to further orders and the Jet Provost remained the RAF's standard basic trainer until

December 1989 when replacement with the Shorts Tucano began at No. 7 FTS, Church Fenton. The last

No. 1 FTS aircraft, a T.Mk 5, was retired on 4 June 1993, while No. 6 FTS retired its last four tip tank-equipped T.Mk 5 navigator trainers on 20 September 1993.

The obvious appeal of the Jet Provost as a highly developed and economical trainer prompted the British Aircraft Corporation (BAC) to develop the type into a multi-role aircraft able to fly both pilot training and weapon training sorties, in addition to performing the light attack and reconnaissance roles. The **BAC.167 Strikemaster** was developed from the **BAC.145** by fitting a more powerful 3,410-lb st (15.17-kN) Viper Mk 535 turbojet and increasing the number of stores hardpoints to eight. The airframe had been strengthened several times in the course of development of the Jet Provost and BAC.145, and in the BAC.167 it was further reinforced. The Strikemaster featured side-by-side Martin-Baker Mk PB4 ejection

seats, short landing gear suitable for operation from rough airstrips and a comprehensive navigation and communications fit.

The first Strikemaster flew on 26 October 1967, and the **Strikemaster Mk 80** series entered production a year later for customers such as Saudi Arabia (25 Strikemaster Mk 80 and 20 improved **Strikemaster Mk 80A** aircraft), South Yemen (four **Strikemaster Mk 81** aircraft), Oman (12 **Strikemaster Mk 82** and 12 improved **Strikemaster Mk 82A** aircraft), Kuwait (12 **Strikemaster Mk 83** aircraft, of which the surviving nine were bought by BAe for resale in 1988 to

Botswana), Singapore (16 **Strikemaster Mk 84** aircraft later augmented by four ex-Yemeni Mk 81s and five ex-Omani Strikemaster Mk 82/82As), Kenya (six **Strikemaster Mk 87** aircraft), New Zealand (16 **Strikemaster Mk 88** aircraft) and Ecuador (22 **Strikemaster Mk 89** aircraft). The final batch of new **Strikemaster Mk 90** aircraft was delivered to the Sudan in 1984, assembly of this batch having been relocated from Warton to Hurn. Sudan had previously been a customer for the less powerful BAC.145. A modest number of these aircraft survived in service into the late 1990s with Ecuador and Oman.

SPECIFICATION
Hunting Percival Jet Provost T.Mk 5
Type: two-seat basic flying trainer
Powerplant: one Rolls-Royce (Bristol Siddeley/Armstrong Siddeley) Viper ASV.11 Mk 202 turbojet engine rated at 2,500 lb st (11.12 kN)
Performance: maximum speed 440 mph (708 km/h) at 25,000 ft (7620 m); initial climb rate 4,000 ft (1219 m) per minute; service ceiling 36,750 ft (11200 m); range 901 miles (1450 km) with tip tanks
Weights: empty 4,888 lb (2271 kg); maximum take-off 9,200 lb (4173 kg)
Dimensions: wingspan 35 ft 4 in (10.77 m) without tip tanks and 36 ft 11 in (11.25 m) with tip tanks; length 33 ft 7½ in (10.25 m); height 10 ft 2 in (3.10 m); wing area 213.70 sq ft (19.85 m²)

Jet Provost Variants

Jet Provost T.Mk 3: original production version with a 1,750-lb (7.78-kN) thrust Bristol Siddeley (later Rolls-Royce) Viper Mk 102 turbojet, Martin-Baker lightweight ejection seats, wingtip fuel tanks and detail refinements; 201 built
Jet Provost T.Mk 3A: refurbished version (by BAC) of the T.Mk 3, introducing DME and VOR equipment
Jet Provost T.Mk 4: similar to T,Mk 3 but introduced 2,500-lb (11.12-kN) thrust Viper Mk 202 turbojet; 185 built
Jet Provost T.Mk 5: final production version for RAF, private-venture development by Hunting as **H.145**, later **BAC.145**; introduced redesigned fuselage with pressurised cabin for the crew, lengthened nose housing avionics equipment, and strengthened wings with increased internal fuel and greater external weapons-carrying capability; wingtip tanks not normally carried; 110 built
Jet Provost T.Mk 5A: refurbished version (by BAC) of T.Mk 5, introducing DME and VOR equipment
Jet Provost T.Mk 51: armed export version of the T.Mk 3 with two 7.7-mm (0.303-in) machine-guns and underwing attachment points for various weapons; supplied to the air forces of Ceylon, Kuwait and Sudan
Jet Provost T.Mk 52: armed export version of the T.Mk 4 with armament as above; supplied to the air forces of Iraq, South Yemen, Sudan and Venezuela
Jet Provost T.Mk 55: export armed version of T.Mk 5 supplied to Sudan

Hurel-Dubois aircraft

Powered by two 800-hp (597-kW) Wright Cyclone engines, the H.D.31 featured the characteristic Hurel Dubois high-aspect ratio wing, and was the company's first twin-engined design on behalf of the French government.

The benefits of a high aspect ratio wing have long been appreciated by aircraft designers. Frenchman Maurice Hurel was sufficiently enthusiastic about its potential to design an experimental aircraft with such a wing, built as the **Hurel-Dubois H.D.10**. This simple research vehicle had retractable tricycle landing gear and was powered by a 40-hp (30-kW) Mathis engine: its high-set braced monoplane wing had a span of 39 ft 4½ in (12.00 m) and an aspect ratio of 30. Successful testing resulted in a French

government order for two twin-engined aircraft based on this wing. First to fly was the **H.D.31** transport, on 29 December 1953. The **H.D.32** flown on 11 February 1955 differed primarily by having two 1,200-hp (895-kW) Pratt & Whitney R-1830-92 Twin Wasp engines. Both aircraft were re-engined subsequently with 1,525-hp (1137-kW) Wright 982 engines, with which they were redesignated **H.D.321-01** and **H.D.321-02** respectively. No production civil transports under this designation resulted, but

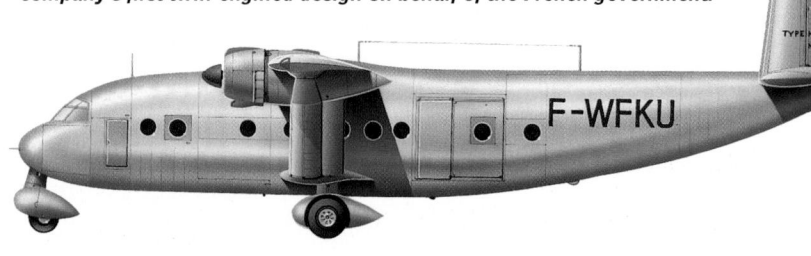

eight similar aircraft were built for the Institut Géographique National under the designation **H.D.34**, differing by having an extended nose to accommodate a navigator/photographer's position. An

H.D.45 turbojet-powered transport prototype was planned, but never built, but one other application of the wing resulted from interest by the British Miles company. A Miles Aerovan was tested successfully

with a Hurel-Dubois wing under the designation **H.D.M.105**, but the design was sold subsequently to Short Brothers and a derivative of this wing was incorporated in the Shorts SC.7 Skyvan.

IAI 101, 102, 201 and 202 Arava

The first wholly IAI-designed aircraft to reach production, the **Arava** was originally conceived in 1966 as a 20-seat multi-mission light twin-turboprop STOL aircraft, for both civilian and military customers. The compact design features a high-mounted wing with twin-tail booms and a simple fixed nosewheel landing gear, with single wheels on each unit. Flown in prototype form on 27 November 1969, the Arava was subsequently produced in civil (**Series 101, 102**) and military (**Series 201, 202**) applications; almost all of about 100 built between 1972

and 1988 were for military users. Although intended as a replacement for the Israeli air force's venerable C-47s, the Arava was not introduced in this capacity until the late 1970s (three leased 201s were operated during the 1973 Arab-Israeli war, however) when Series 201s were delivered. These aircraft were equipped for a variety of tasks (other than as troop transports) including maritime surveillance (equipped with search/weather radar), and EW duties in a number of different configurations with pallet-mounted Elint and ESM packages, radomes, and tailcone-mounted rear

scanner. Another EW version features a large number of blade antennas on the tail booms, roof and wings.

Active jamming is carried out when the aircraft is equipped with the Elta EL-7010 jammer, for which an auxiliary generator is also installed. Primary IDF/AF Arava operator is 126 Tayeset at Lod. The Royal Thai air force similarly flies three for the surveillance/ECM mission.

As the final stage in Arava development, IAI developed the **Series 202** variant in 1977. This introduced an extended fuselage accommodating 30 fully-equipped troops, increased weights, a 'wet' wing and winglets. Initial deliveries began to the Israeli and other air forces in 1984-85. The Series 202 became a retrofit option for Aravas already in service. Both versions of the Arava may be armed with a pair of forward-firing, fuselage-

The Arava has found favour among South American operators. This example, destined for the Ecuadorean army, carries temporary Israeli registration.

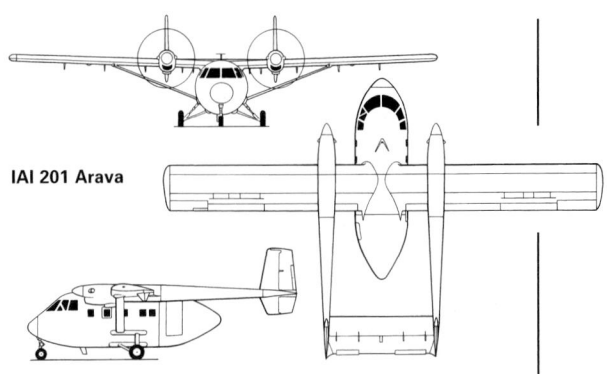

IAI 201 Arava

mounted 12.7-mm (0.5-in) machine-guns and up to 12 3.23-in (82-mm) rockets carried on fuselage pylons.

Most of the 16 national air arms that acquired Aravas selected the Series 201 model for use as personnel and/or supply transports. Examples remain in service in this primary tactical and utility

transport role in Colombia, Ecuador (army and navy air arms), Guatemala, Honduras, Mexico, Swaziland and Venezuela (army). At least one continues to serve in Bolivia for anti-drug patrols, and an ex-civil **Series 101B** in Cameroon is operated as a military/government VIP transport.

SPECIFICATION

IAI 201 Arava
Type: multi-mission light twin-turboprop STOL aircraft
Powerplant: two Pratt & Whitney Canada PT6A-34 turboprops each rated at 750 shp (559 kW)
Performance: maximum cruising speed 198 mph (319 km/h) at 10,000 ft (3050 m); maximum rate of climb 1,290 ft (393 m) per minute at sea level; service ceiling 25,000 ft (7620 m); range 622 miles

(1001 km) with a 3,500-lb (1587-kg) payload
Weights: empty 8,816 lb (3999 kg); maximum take-off 15,000 lb (6804 kg)
Dimensions: wingspan 68 ft 9 in (20.96 m); length 42 ft 9 in (13.03 m); height 17 ft 1 in (5.21 m); wing area 470.18 sq ft (43.68 m²)
Payload: maximum 5,100 lb (2313 kg)

IAI Westwind, SeaScan, Astra & Galaxy

After purchasing the design and production facilities for the **Model 1121 Jet Commander** from Rockwell in 1967, IAI further developed the executive twin jet into the **Models 1123** and **1124 Westwind**. Powered respectively by 3,100-lb st (13.70-kN) General Electric CJ610-9 turbojets and 3,700-lb st (16.40-kN) Garrett TFE731-3 turbofans, these two versions were produced almost entirely for civil use. One of each later entered service with the Honduran air force, and two Model 1124s served in the Chilean navy, all in the VIP transport role. One was similarly used by President Idi Amin in Uganda and, in response to Uganda air force interest, IAI fitted machine-guns in place of tip tanks on one Model

1123, but these were removed when the deal fell through and the aircraft passed into service with the Israeli Defence Force/Air Force.

The IAI 1124 led directly to the longer-range **Westwind I**, and ultimately to the **Westwind II** with and advanced wingleted wing. The IDF/AF also operates three **Model 1124N SeaScan** versions on behalf of the navy for maritime search and patrol missions. The SeaScan carries a nose radar and has provision for a variety of other sensors, as well as two load-carrying pylons on the fuselage sides for torpedoes, missiles or other stores. A Litton AN/APS-504 radar provides 360° coverage. Four Model 1124s were operated by Rhein-Flugzeugbau until

1990 as target-tugs for the military services in Germany.

Based on the 1124 Westwind, the **IAI 1125 Astra** business jet introduces a low-mounted swept wing with more extensive use of composites materials. The revised wing-mounting arrangement allows for an improved cabin layout with increased headroom. The 2-in (5-cm) wider fuselage has a deeper profile and incorporates a stretch of nearly 2 ft (0.61 m). Only the Westwind's tail unit and Garrett TFE731-3A powerplant have been retained. A prototype Astra flew on 19 March 1984 and deliveries began two years later. An **Astra SP** (with new avionics and aerodynamic refinements) serves with the government of Eritrea.

Advanced versions of the Satra include the **Astra SPX** with winglets, advanced avionics and 4,250-lb st (18.90-kN) TFE731-40R-200G turbofans and the redesigned **Galaxy**.

Two examples of the Astra SPX have entered service with the US Air National Guard for transport and medevac duties under the designation **C-38A**. The Galaxy, which was oiginally

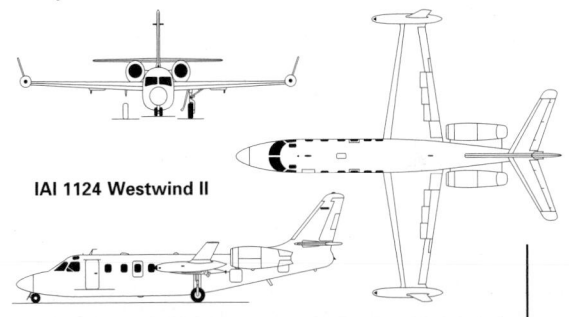

IAI 1124 Westwind II

The Astra bears a strong family likeness to the Westwind, but features an all-new swept wing and a redesigned fuselage of greater depth and length.

designated **Astra IV** and is based on the Astra SP, is powered by two 6,040-lb st (26.90-kN) Pratt & Whitney Canada PW306A turbofans and designed to seat up to eight passengers as a bizjet

or up to 18 passengers as a regional transport. The first prototype Galaxy was flown for the first time on 25 December 1997. The first customer delivery was made in January 2000.

SPECIFICATION

IAI 1125 Astra
Type: six-passenger bizjet
Powerplant: two Garrett TFE731-3A-200G turbofans each rated at 3,650 lb st (16.24 kN)
Performance: maximum cruising speed 535 mph (862 km/h) at 35,000 ft (10670 m); maximum rate of climb 3,650 ft (1112 m) per minute at sea level; certificated ceiling 45,000 ft (13715 m); range 3,581 miles (5763 km) with

optional fuel and four passengers
Weights: empty 12,670 lb (5747 kg) with standard tankage; maximum take-off 23,500 lb (10659 kg)
Dimensions: wingspan 52 ft 8 in (16.05 m); length 55 ft 7 in (16.94 m); height 18 ft 2 in (5.54 m); wing area 316.60 sq ft (29.40 m²)
Payload: up to six passengers

IAI Kfir and F-21A Lion

Israel was the first export customer for the Dassault Mirage III, and used the type to great effect during the 1967 and 1973 Arab-Israeli wars. Despite its success, Israel was aware of the shortcomings of the Mirage, which included very fast take-off and landing speeds and consequently long take-off and landing runs, lack of thrust, and primitive avionics. This obvious need for improvement, coupled with arms embargoes, forced Israel first to upgrade its Mirages and then to build its own improved Mirage derivatives.

This process resulted first in Project Salvo, under which Israel's Mirage IIICJs were rebuilt and upgraded, and then in the Nesher, and eventually in the **Kfir** (lion cub). The development of the Kfir was made possible by Israel's purchase of the F-4 Phantom and its General Electric J79 engine. The first J79-engined Mirage was a French-built two-seater, and this made its maiden flight on 19 October 1970, joined by a re-engined Nesher in September 1971.

The J79's 11 per cent greater mass flow and higher operating temperature necessitated the provision of enlarged air intakes and extensive heat shielding of the rear fuselage. A large air scoop was added to the leading edge of the tailfin for afterburner cooling. Other airframe changes included a strengthened undercarriage with longer stroke oleos.

There have been persistent reports that some Mirage IIICJs were re-engined with the J79, receiving the local name **Barak** (lightning), but such conversions seem unlikely and have never been photographed. A similar rumour concerned the production of a radar-nosed Kfir, this being caused by photographs of an early aircraft which had its forward fuselage painted

black as though it were a radome. While the use of radar-nosed Kfirs by Israel is unlikely, later upgrades to Ecuadorian Kfirs added Elta 2034-5 radar to produce the **Kfir CE** to a standard which is known by IAI as **Kfir 2000**. The basic **Kfir-C1** was produced in small numbers (27) and most were later upgraded with small narrow-span fixed canards on the intakes and rectangular strakes behind the ranging radar, on the sides of the nose. Twenty-five survivors were later lent to the US Navy and US Marines for adversary training (between 1985 and 1989) as the **F-21A Lion**.

The **Kfir-C2** was the first full-standard variant, equipped with nose strakes and large fixed canard foreplanes from the outset. The new variant also had a dogtooth wing leading edge. Canards and strakes were first flown on the J79-powered Mirage IIIB which had served as the Kfir prototype, during July 1974.

The Kfir-C2 also introduced new avionics, including an ELTA M-2001B ranging radar. Other equipment includes an MBT twin-computer flight control system, angle-of-attack sensor vane on the port side of the forward fuselage (retrofitted to early aircraft), Elbit S-8600 multimode navigation and weapons delivery system (alternatively Elbit/IAI WDNS-141), Taman central air data computer and Israel Electro-Optics HUD. One hundred and eighty-five C2s and **TC2** trainers were

built, and as many as five reserve squadrons remained operational with the type late in 1999.

After long delays in gaining US approval to re-export the J79 powerplant, 12 Kfir-C2s were sold to Ecuador in 1982, and another 11 went to Colombia in 1988-89. Both export customers also took delivery of a pair of Kfir-TC2s. Virtually all surviving Israeli Kfir C2s and TC2s were upgraded to **Kfir-C7** and **TC7** standards, but it is uncertain as to whether any were built as new.

The C7 designation is applied to upgraded aircraft delivered from 1983 onwards. These incorporate a number of avionics improvements, and have what is effectively a HOTAS cockpit. Equipment improvements involve a WDNS-391 weapons delivery and navigation system, an Elbit 82 stores management system, armament control display panel, video subsystems and the ability to release 'smart' weapons. Aerial refuelling provision with either probe or receptacle is optional. Most C2s in IDF/AF service have been upgraded to C7 standard, and the potential is present to replace the ranging radar by an Elta EL/M-2021 I/J-band multimode radar as installed in Israel's F-16s. Not all C2s had RWRs – at least initially – but late-production machines have an Elisra SPS-200 comprising two hemispherical sensors under the lower forward fuselage and two on the fin, immediately above the rudder. Jamming pods such as the Elta E/L-8202 can be

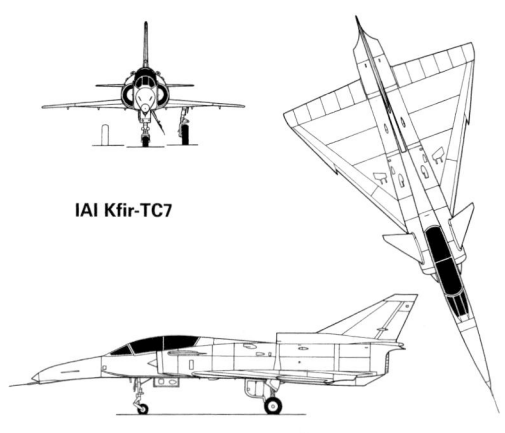

IAI Kfir-TC7

fitted on the port inboard carried externally on a wing pylon.

The only external difference is the provision of an extra pair of hardpoints under the engine intakes, bringing the total to nine and increasing warload to a maximum of 13,415 lb (6085 kg). An engine overspeed provision, referred to as 'combat plus', can be used to boost thrust to 18,750 lb (83.41 kN) for brief periods.

During 1993, Israel began seeking export

customers for its surplus Kfir C2/C7s, and to this end IAI proposed a further upgrade as the **Kfir-C10**. Features of this version, benefitting from Lavi technology, include a new cockpit fit, new radar in an enlarged radome, more external fuel and provision for an IFR probe.

Late in 2000, the Kfir remained in service with Colombia, Ecuador, Israel and Sri Lanka. The latter country acquired six Kfir-C2s and two TC2s from Israel in 1996.

Initial Kfir deliveries to the IDF/AF (Heyl Ha'Avir) inventory began in April 1975. The improved Kfir-C2 followed into service in 1976. Illustrated is a Kfir of the original series, wearing standard sand, tan and medium green upper surface finish and pale blue undersides, in 1975-6. The black-outlined orange triangles act as aids to identification.

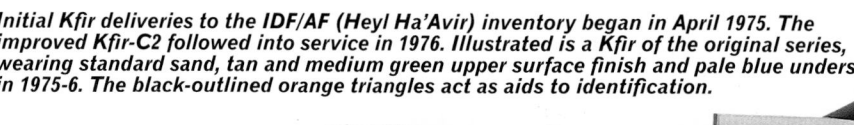

IAI Nesher (Dagger and Finger)

Until the 1967 Six Day War, Israel had come to depend upon the US and France for provision of combat aircraft. Following that war, however, the supply of Mirage 5Js was halted by an embargo. Faced with the ongoing threat of war with its Arab neighbours, Israel set about producing its own combat aircraft.

As an interim expedient Israel Aircraft Industries (IAI) started production of an unlicensed copy of the Mirage

5, complete with its French-built Atar 09C turbojet, of which large stocks existed in the country. The task of building the Mirage without French co-operation was eased by espionage. Production drawings for the Atar were stolen from the Swiss factory which was licence-building the engine for Swiss-built Mirages, and many airframe production drawings were stolen in France itself.

The new product was

termed the **Nesher** (eagle), and from the outset it was capable of mounting a pair of the indigenous Rafael Shafrir short-range air-to-air missiles (externally similar to the American AIM-9 Sidewinder but in fact a wholly new Israeli design). The gun armament of two 30-mm DEFA cannon was also retained. The new variant incorporated some indigenous avionics systems, and was fitted with a Martin-Baker Mk 6

ejection seat.

First flown in September 1969, the Nesher entered service with the Heyl Ha'Avir in time for the Yom Kippur War of October 1973, when some 40 aircraft saw action and Shafrir missiles achieved a success rate of more than 50 per cent.

The French imposed a further arms embargo in the wake of the 1973 war, and this led directly to Project Black Curtain, which resulted in the Kfir. This also led to the termination of the Nesher programme, after an estimated 51 **Nesher S**

single-seaters and 10 **Nesher T** trainers had been completed. These aircraft were frequently used operationally in the long, undeclared war which raged on Israel's borders during the 1970s, but Kfir deliveries rendered them surplus to requirements by 1977.

Argentina, forced to shelve plans to acquire 80 Mirage IIIs (from an order totalling 94) for economic reasons, purchased 26 of the Neshers in 1978 under the export designation **Dagger** (including two two-seater aircraft).

IAI Nesher (Dagger and Finger) (continued)

These were joined by the rest of the surviving Neshers by 1982, bringing Argentine procurement to 39 **Dagger A** and four **Dagger B** aircraft. They equipped II and III Squadrons (since redesignated I and II Squadrons) of 6° Grupo, VI Brigada Aérea, replacing ageing F-86 Sabres. Seventeen were lost during the 1982

Falklands War, during which they operated primarily in the fighter-bomber and anti-shipping roles, pressing home their attacks with astonishing ferocity and a high degree of precision. The survivors have since undergone a three-stage modification programme, which has provided Kfir-type avionics in a recontoured nose, with

vortex generators, under the codenames **'Finger-I'**, **'-II'** and **'-III'**.

Argentina's Dagger fleet, blooded during the Falklands conflict, has since been bolstered by the acquisition of 20 IAI Fingers, serving Grupo Aéreo 6 at BAM Tandil.

I.A.R.37, 38 and 39

The **I.A.R.37** prototype was built to the design of engineers Grossu-Vizuru and Carp. Flown for the first time in 1937 by company pilot Max Manolescu, it was intended to meet an official requirement for a tactical bombing and reconnaissance aircraft. An unequal-span biplane, the I.A.R.37 had fixed main landing gear and was powered by an I.A.R. K.14 radial engine. Its three-man crew was accommodated beneath a continuous glazed canopy, the observer seated between the pilot and gunner and provided with full dual controls, a Romanian-designed Estopey bomb-sight, a radio and a camera. Defensive armament comprised four machine-guns and the offensive load 12 110-lb (50-kg) bombs or six 220-lb (100-kg) bombs on underwing racks.

The I.A.R.37 entered production in late 1938 and

was built in small numbers before being succeeded in 1939 by the interim **I.A.R.38**, which differed mainly in its powerplant, and was soon displaced on the production line by the **I.A.R.39**.

By the end of 1940 the I.A.R. biplanes were in large-scale service with the Fortelor Aeriene Regal ale Romania (Royal Romanian Air Force) or FARR. They equipped a number of squadrons attached to the various army corps and by June 1941, when Romania supported the German offensive against the Soviet Union, the three reconnaissance flotile of the FARR had 18 eskadrile, 15 of which were equipped with I.A.R. biplanes. In July 1942 the air expeditionary force in the Soviet Union had been re-formed as Corpul I Aerian and had several groups equipped with the I.A.R.39. Eleven reconnaissance eskadrile were operating with the army co-

operation flotile during the 1944 offensive in the Ukraine, most of them with I.A.R.39s on strength. Post-war the new Communist republic was declared at the end of 1947, and the reorganised air arm, known as the FRRPR (Fortele Aeriene ale Republicii Populare Romania) had a small number of I.A.R.39s for training and liaison duties for several years.

In 1940, three **I.A.R.47**

Of the total production of 325 I.A.R.37, 38 and 39 aircraft, over 200 were I.A.R.39 two-seat light bombers (pictured), 96 built under sub-contract by the S.E.T. company and over 100 by I.A.R.

SPECIFICATION	
I.A.R.39	
Type: two/three-seat reconnaissance/light bomber aircraft	**Weights:** empty equipped 4,799 lb (2177 kg); maximum take-off 6,801 lb (3085 kg)
Powerplant: one 870-hp (649-kW) I.A.R. K.14-IV C32 radial piston engine	**Dimensions:** wingspan 42 ft 11¾ in (13.10 m); length 31 ft 6 in (9.60 m), height 13 ft 1 in (3.99 m), wing area 433.80 sq ft (40.30 m²)
Performance: maximum speed 209 mph (336 km/h); service ceiling 26,245 ft (8000 m); range 652 miles (1050 km)	**Armament:** three 0.31-in (7.92-mm) machine-guns plus 635 lb (288 kg) of bombs or 144 air grenades

prototypes were under construction, intended to replace the I.A.R.39 in

production, only one was completed and flight tested.

I.A.R. 80 and 81

The work of a design team led by Professor Ion Grossu, the **I.A.R.80** prototype flew for the first time in April 1939, piloted by Dumitru Popescu. A cantilever, all-metal low-wing monoplane with an open cockpit, wide-track retractable landing gear and powered by I.A.R. K.14-III C36 radial engine, the new single-seater performed well and was soon adopted for production to equip the fighter eskadrile of the FARR.

Delivery of series aircraft began in spring 1940, modifications for quantity production including provision of a rearward-sliding cockpit canopy, a cantilever tailplane and introduction of the more powerful I.A.R. K.14-1000A engine. An anomaly for the period was the retention of a tailskid.

Production of the I.A.R.80 and its **I.A.R.81** dive-bomber derivative totalled 436. During 1942 four eskadrile of I.A.R.80s

Outclassed as a fighter by mid-1944, the lack of Bf 109Gs forced the I.A.R. 80 to be retained in service.

were flying with the Romanian Corpul I Aerian in the Ukraine, but a year later all available I.A.R.80s and I.A.R.81s were based in Romania, engaged in defending the homeland against attacks by US

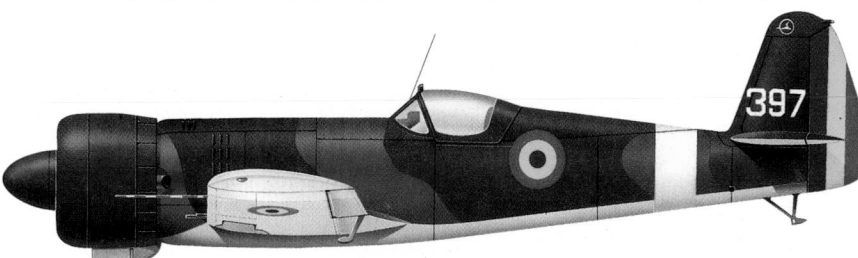

heavy bombers with the Ploesti oilfields as their principal target.

Variants

I.A.R.80: initial production fighter with four wing-mounted Browning FN 0.31-in (7.92-mm) machine-guns, 50 built
I.A.R.80A: production version with six machine-guns; 90 built
I.A.R.80B: version with four 0.31-in (7.92-mm) machine-guns and two 0.52-in (13.2-mm) Brownings; 30 built
I.A.R.81: initial version of strengthened dive-bomber with six 0.31-in (7.92-mm) Brownings; fuselage centreline rack for a single 551-lb (250-kg) bomb and underwing racks for four 110-lb (50-kg) bombs; 50 built
I.A.R.81A: bombload as for I.A.R.81, but machine-gun armament as for I.A.R.80B; 29 built

SPECIFICATION	
I.A.R.80 series	
Type: single-seat fighter	**Weights:** empty equipped 3,924 lb (1780 kg); maximum take-off 5,622 lb (2550 kg)
Powerplant: one 1,025-hp (764-kW) I.A.R. K.14-1000A radial piston engine	**Dimensions:** wingspan 34 ft 5¼ in (10.50 m); length 29 ft 2¼ in (8.90 m); height 11 ft 9¾ in (3.60 m); wing area 171.90 sq ft (15.97 m²)
Performance: maximum speed 342 mph (550 km/h) at 13,025 ft (3970 m); service ceiling 34,450 ft (10500 m); range 584 miles (940 km)	**Armament:** see variants

I.A.R.81B: long-range fighter version with provision for two underwing drop tanks; no bombload, but two Ikaria or Oerlikon 20-mm cannon plus four Browning FN 0.31-in (7.92-mm) machine-guns, 50 built
I.A.R.81C: dive-bomber/fighter; bombload as for I.A.R.81, but two 20-mm Mauser cannon plus four 0.31-in (7.92-mm) Brownings; believed 137 completed before phased out at I.A.R. Brasov factory in favour of Bf 109G-6

In 1950 a batch at least one surviving I.A.R.80 was converted for training with the introduction of a second cockpit and dual controls, being redesig- nated **I.A.R.80DC**. They were withdrawn from train- ing school use at the end of 1952.

IAR (Avioane) IAR-99 Soim

The **IAR-99 Soim** (hawk) was designed in the early 1980s by the Institutul de Aviatie (IAv) at Bucharest and was put into produc- tion at Craiova by the Intreprinderea de Avioane at Craiova (IAv Craiova). Since a March 1991 reor- ganisation of the state aircraft industry following the collapse of the Ceausescu regime, IAv Craiova has been a part of the Avioane subsidiary of the IAROM holding company.

A conventional design for a straight-wing aircraft, the Soim was conceived as a basic and advanced flying trainer with secondary armament train- ing and ground attack/ close support capability. The tandem accommoda- tion on Martin-Baker Mk 10L zero/zero ejection seats is arranged in a pressurised cockpit with the rear seat raised for improved forward view. For the armed role, provi- sion is made for a variety of armament.

Following the first flight on 21 December 1985, the IAR-99 entered service with the Romanian air force in 1988 when an initial batch of 20 aircraft became operational at the Bacau flying school in succession to the L-29 Delfin, although the latter remains in service for weapons training. In all, 21 Soims were delivered to the Romanian air force.

Consideration was also given to the evolution of a modified version with the 4,870-lb st (21.66-kN) Viper Mk 680 turbojet engine in place of the usual Viper Mk 632, which is built under licence in Romania. Jaffe Aircraft of the USA tried unsuccess- fully to market an upgraded export version first announced in 1991,

The Romanian Air Force had received a batch of 21 IAR-99s by early 1999. The Soim's four underwing hardpoints are each stressed for loads of 551 lb (250 kg).

with major systems and completely updated avion- ics of Western origin. Nothing came of this plan, but on November 1993 there flew the prototype of the much enhanced **IAR-109 Swift**, which had been created in collabora- tion with Israel Aircraft Industries and Elbit of Israel, but there followed no production. Finally Romania, urgently needing a modern fighter lead-in trainer, decided to collabo- rate with Elbit on an upgrade package, leading to the first flight of an IAR-99 conversion on 22 May 1997. The primary

changes are to the avion- ics, which now include two HUDs, a helmet- mounted sight system, a coloured multi-function head-down display, an Elta data transfer system, a modular multi-role computer, an integrated navigation system, and a defensive suite including an RWR, ECM and chaff/flare launchers.

Some 40 aircraft are being built to this standard in two production batches, and current aircraft will then probably be retrofitted to produce a fleet of some 55 machines.

SPECIFICATION

IAR IAR-99 Soim (upgraded)
Type: two-seat advanced flying and fighter lead-in trainer
Powerplant: one Turbomecanica (Rolls-Royce) Viper Mk 632-41M turbojet engine rated at 4,000 lb st (17.79 kN)
Performance: maximum speed 537 mph (865 km/h) at sea level; initial climb rate 6,890 ft (2100 m) per minute; service ceiling 42,325 ft (12900 m); range 683 miles (1100 km) as a trainer
Weights: empty 7,055 lb (3200 kg); maximum take-off 9,700 lb (4400 kg) as a trainer
Dimensions: wingspan 32 ft 3¾ in (9.85 m); length 36 ft 1½ in (11.01 m); height 12 ft 9½ in (3.90 m); wing area 201.40 sq ft (18.71 m²)
Armament: one 23-mm Gryazev- Shipunov GSh-23L two-barrel fixed forward-firing cannon in a ventral fairing, and up to 2,205 lb (1000 kg) of disposable stores carried on four underwing hardpoints

Ilyushin DB-3

The **TsKB-26** long-range bomber protoype appeared in 1935, as a twin-engined metal low-wing monoplane powered by 800-hp (597-kW) Gnome-Rhône K-14 radials. Demonstrated by test pilot Vladimir Kokkinaki on May Day 1936, the prototype went on to establish two world altitude records during July 1936. A second prototype, the **TsKB-30**, had an enclosed instead of open position for the pilot, Soviet M-85 engines and a metal rear fuselage. The TsKB-30 also broke records and then attracted world interest by flying from Moscow to Canada, where pilot Kokkinaki had to make a wheels-up landing

on 28 April 1939 after covering a distance of 4,971 miles (8000 km).

By then the bomber had been in production for the Soviet air arm for more than two years. Under the military designation **DB-3** it served widely with the ADD (Long-Range Aviation) and the V-MF (Naval Aviation), remaining opera- tional well into the war with Germany, DB-3s being credited with some of the earliest attacks on Berlin.

The DB-3 also served with the Finnish air arm between 1940 and 1945, five captured aircraft being augmented by six purchased from German war booty supplies. DB-3 production terminated in 1940 with the 1,528th machine.

Variants

DB-3M: this refined version entered production in 1939, powered by two M-87 engines
DB-3T: specialised torpedo-bomber version which carried the Type 45-12-AN aerial torpedo
DB-3PT: twin-float seaplane torpedo-bomber variant

A major structural redesign resulted in the DB-3M, which had replaced the initial DB-3B on three production lines by late 1939. The DB-3M was powered by a pair of M-87A or M-87B engines.

SPECIFICATION

Ilyushin DB-3M
Type: twin-engined long-range medium bomber
Powerplant: two 950-hp (708-kW) M-87B radial piston engines
Performance: maximum speed 277 mph (445 km/h); service ceiling 31,825 ft (9700 m); range 2,361 miles (3800 km)
Weights: empty equipped 11,618 lb (5270 kg); maximum
take-off 16,887 lb (7660 kg)
Dimensions: wingspan 70 ft 4 in (21.44 m); length 46 ft 7¾ in (14.22 m); height 13 ft 9 in (4.19 m); wing area 706.14 sq ft (65.60 m²)
Armament: three 0.3-in (7.62-mm) ShKAS machine-guns, plus a maximum short-range bombload of 5,512 lb (2500 kg)

Ilyushin Il-2 Shturmovik

One of the most formidable military aircraft of World War II, the **Il-2** was produced in vast numbers, Soviet sources giving the total figure as 36,163 aircraft. The Il-2 began as the **TsKB-55** developed by Sergei Ilyushin and his team, who formed in 1938 part of the Central Design Bureau (TsKB).

The special feature of the two-seat TsKB-55 or **BSh-2**, was the armoured shell which formed an inte- gral part of the fuselage structure and protected the crew, engine, radiators and fuel tank.

The resulting aircraft was well suited to its designated low-level ground- attack role, but was rejected in favour of a lighter single-seat develop- ment, the **TsKB-57**, which had a 1,700 hp (1268-kW) AM-38 engine and a raised, faired canopy for the pilot.

In 1945 this Il-2M3 was serving with the 3rd Attack Regiment (Szturmowego Pulk) of the Polish 1st Mixed Air Corps.

Ilyushin Il-2 Shturmovik (continued)

The TsKB-57 also substituted 20-mm cannon for two of the four wing-mounted machine-guns, and had provision for underwing rocket-launchers. The first prototype flew on 12 October 1940.

Official trials ended just three months before the German invasion in June 1941. By then, large-scale production of the Il-2, as the type was designated, had been started, the first unit receiving its aircraft in May 1941. By the end of June, 249 Il-2s had been taken on charge by the Soviet air force (the V-VS). Production aircraft were generally similar to the TSKB-57 prototypes, but some modifications had been introduced, principally to the pilot's accommodation to give improved protection, including a modified windscreen and a shorter fairing aft of the cockpit.

The single-seat Il-2 was used on a vast scale and proved itself a potent weapon against German transport and armour. Losses were heavy, however, and during 1941-42 fighter cover was often not available. In February 1942 it was decided to introduce a two-seat Il-2 in line with Ilyushin's original concept. The resulting **Il-2M** had provision for a rear gunner under an extended canopy.

SPECIFICATION

Ilyushin Il-2 Type 3
Type: two-seat ground-attack aircraft
Powerplant: one 1,720-hp (1282-kW) Mikulin AM-38F piston engine
Performance: maximum speed 255 mph (410 km/h) at 4,920 ft (1500 m); service ceiling 14,845 ft (4525 m); range 475 miles (765 km)
Weights: empty equipped 9,976 lb (4525 kg); maximum take-off 14,021 lb (6360 kg)
Dimensions: wingspan 47 ft 10¾ in (14.60 m); length 38 ft 2½ in (11.65 m); height 13 ft 8 in (4.17 m); wing area 414.42 sq ft (38.50 m²)
Armament: two 23-mm VYa cannon and two 0.3-in (7.62-mm) ShKAS machine-guns (all wing-mounted) and one 0.5-in (12.7-mm) UBT machine-gun for the gunner, plus 220-lb (100-kg) bombs (four carried internally and two under the fuselage), or two 551-lb (250-kg) bombs (under the fuselage), eight RS-82 rockets or four RS-132 rockets under the outer wing panels

Two conversions were flight-tested in March 1942, and production aircraft appeared from September 1942; other aircraft were converted to two-seaters in the field.

Other changes introduced on the production lines included the installation of the more powerful AM-38F engine, replacement of the two 20-mm ShVAK cannon with more effective 23-mm VYa weapons, various aerodynamic refinements to improve performance and to compensate for the increased weight of the gunner and revised armament, the enforced introduction of wooden outer wing panels (replacing metal), and increased fuel capacity.

A new version, the **Il-2 Type 3** (or **Il-2m3**) made its first appearance at Stalingrad in early 1943.

Tested during 1942, it had redesigned wings with 15° sweepback on the outer panels. Performance and flying qualities were much improved and the Type 3 went on to become the most important and numerous version of the Il-2.

The Il-2 Shturmovik became renowned in the Soviet Union, used with much increased tactical effect in 1944-45 after their mode of operation had been studied carefully and fighter cover provided on a large scale. Improvement in armament included cassettes containing 200 PTAB hollow-charge anti-tank bombs, the use of a DAG-10 anti-aircraft grenade launcher, and the introduction of a limited number of **Il-2 Type 3M** aircraft with a pair of 37-mm NS-11 or P-37 cannon mounted in fairings outboard of the landing gear.

Ilyushin Il-2s were used by the Soviet navy for anti-shipping duties, and the specialised **Il-2T** torpedo-bomber was also developed. On land the type was used on occasion for reconnaissance and laying smoke-screens. In the last year of World War II Il-2s were used by both Polish and Czechoslovak units flying with the Soviets, and the type continued in service for several years post-war with the V-VS and for a slightly longer period with the air forces of other East European regimes.

Between September 1941 and April 1942 an experimental Il-2 powered by an M-82 radial engine was tested extensively, but no production of this variant was undertaken. Training versions of the Il-2 were known variously as the **U-Il-2** or **Il-2U**.

Ilyushin Il-2m3

Ilyushin Il-4 and Il-6

In 1938 a version of the DB-3 was developed with a totally new, easily-built airframe. As a result the appearance of the design was completely changed, the nose being slim, streamlined and with a large glazed area, with the nose turret of the DB-3 replaced by a swivel gun mounting. State acceptance trials were completed successfully in June 1939 and by the end of that year the type was readied for quantity production. This new version was known as the **DB-3F**, later redesignated **Il-4** when delivered in quantity to the bomber regiments of the long-range air arm, the ADD. A small number had the same type of dorsal turret as the DB-3, but this was soon replaced by a more effective design. Additionally, the ventral machine-gun ring was replaced by a more complex semi-retractable mount.

The Il-4 remained in large-scale production until 1944, the number built being 5,256. The original M-87A engine was replaced by the more powerful M-88B with a two-speed supercharger in 1942. Most aircraft built in 1942 were completed with wooden wing spars as a result of shortage of light alloys, but metal components were reintroduced in late production machines.

In addition to its use for long-range bombing raids, the Il-4s of the ADD's various long-range bomber corps were used frequently in attacks on tactical targets immediately behind enemy lines, carrying their maximum bombload. The Il-4 also came to be used widely by the mine/torpedo bomber regiments attached to the Baltic, Black Sea and Northern Fleets; when deployed in a torpedo-carrying role the Il-4 was armed with a 2,072-lb (940-kg) 45-36-AN (low-level) or 45-36-AV

SPECIFICATION

Illyushin Il-4 'Bob'
Type: three-seat long-range bomber
Powerplant: two 1,100-hp (820-kW) M-88B radial piston engines
Performance: maximum speed 267 mph (430 km/h) at 21,980 ft (6700 m), service ceiling 31,825 ft (9700 m), range 2,361 miles (3800 km)
Weights: empty equipped 12,787 lb (5800 kg); maximum take-off 24,912 lb (11300 kg)
Dimensions: span 70 ft 4¼ in (21.44 m), length 48 ft 6¾ in (14.80 m), height 13 ft 5¼ in (4.10 m), wing area 717 98 sq ft (66.70 m²)
Armament: one 0.5-in (12.7-mm) and two 0.3 in (7.62-mm) machine-guns, plus an internal bombload of 2,205 lb (1000 kg) or a maximum bombload (internal and external) of 5,512 lb (2500 kg)

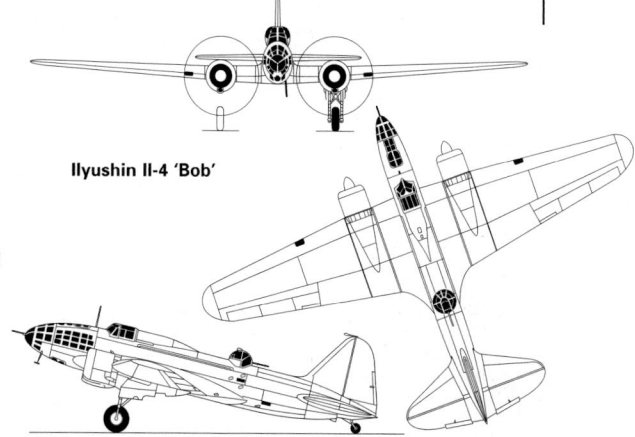

Three Il-4s purchased from German war booty stores were used by the Finns against the Soviet forces from late 1943 until February 1945.

Ilyushin Il-4 'Bob'

(high-level) torpedo. There was also provision for an auxiliary external fuel tank mounted under the rear fuselage.

The Il-4 was a robust and successful aircraft, a number surviving into the post-war period for use in a variety of support roles. It had sufficient longevity to earn the NATO codename

'Bob'. In February 1942 design work began on the **Il-6**, an advanced bomber with pressurised crew accommodation for high-level operations,

considerable sweepback on the wing leading edge, and power provided by two 1,500-hp (1119-kW) Charomsky ACh-30B diesel engines, but development

was abandoned in 1944, after only four examples had flown, the first of which had taken to the air on 7 August 1943 prior to NII trials.

Ilyushin Il-8 and Il-10 'Beast'

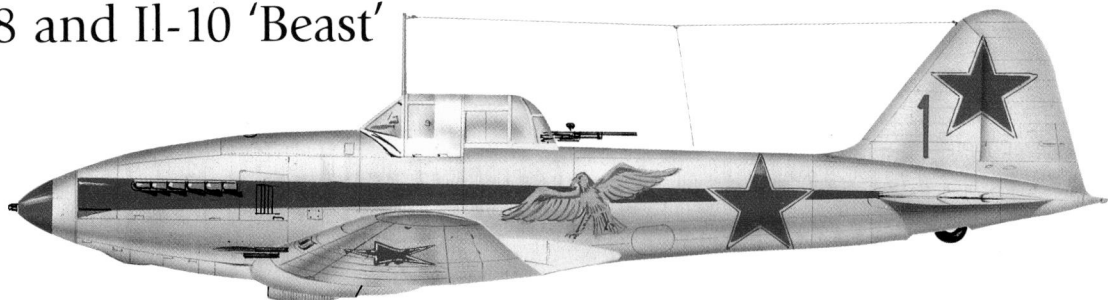

To provide a replacement for the Il-2 Shturmovik, the Ilyushin design bureau developed two different prototypes in 1943. The **Il-8** bore a close resemblance to the Il-2, but was powered by a more powerful AM-42 engine, and had new wings, horizontal tail surfaces and landing gear married to a late-production Il-2 fuselage. Test-flown in April 1944, the Il-8 was rejected in favour of the contemporary **Il-10**, which began its test flight programme in that month.

The Il-10 was a completely new design of all-metal construction and improved aerodynamic form. It provided better crew accommodation, the gunner seated with his back to the pilot in an enlarged cockpit, and both crew members were located within the protective armoured shell. Revised main landing gear units retracted within the wing, eliminating the large landing gear fairings of the Il-2 and requiring only small fairings over the pivoting mechanism.

Early favourable reports of the prototype test programme led to a batch of pre-series machines, quantity production being initiated in August 1944,

This Soviet Il-10 'Beast', perhaps that of a Divisional Commander (Air), served with a Frontal Aviation regiment based in the German Democratic Republic during the early 1950s.

with evaluation in operational regiments starting two months later. The type was used first in operations in February 1945 and by that spring output reached a peak. Many regiments re-equipped with the Il-10 before the German surrender, and a considerable number took part in the brief but large-scale operations against the Japanese in Manchuria and Korea during August 1945.

Production of the Il-10 continued into the post-war period, with Soviet factories building 4,966 machines, the last leaving the production lines in 1955. Additionally, Il-10s were also built at the Czech Avia factory, under the designations **B-33** and **CB-33**, the latter being the

equivalent of the **Il-10U** trainer variant. Czech production finished in 1954 when over 1,200 examples had been completed. From 1951 onwards, Soviet production had concentrated on the **Il-10M**, which featured an entirely new wing of revised planform and deeper aerofoil section, a slightly lengthened fuselage, modified landing gear with increased track, and increased fuel capacity.

The Il-10 formed the sole equipment of Soviet assault units for a number of years and was also used widely by Warsaw Pact countries and as such was given the ASCC reporting name '**Beast**'. Other Communist countries to employ the type included North Korea in the opening

stages of the Korean War in 1950. Losses were heavy and the type was clearly obsolete but, nevertheless, Il-10s remained in service with the Soviet V-VS until 1956 and with various satellite air arms for several years longer. For some time after that they were flown as gunnery trainers but most had been scrapped by the mid-1960s.

The Il-10 had been tested with a ZhRD-1 auxil-

iary rocket engine in the rear fuselage to provide short-term performance boost, but this modification was not adopted. The Ilyushin bureau strove to develop later shturmovik designs, including the **Il-20** single-seater and the **Il-40** with twin turbojets, but official encouragement was minimal, the Soviet authorities having accepted the Western concept of the tactical strike fighter.

SPECIFICATION	
Ilyushin Il-10 'Beast' **Type:** two-seat ground-attack aircraft **Powerplant:** one 2,000-hp (1492-kW) Mikulin AM-42 piston engine **Performance:** maximum speed 329 mph (530 km/h) at 7,875 ft (2400 m); service ceiling 23,785 ft (7250 m), range 497 miles (800 km) **Weights:** empty equipped 10,317 lb (4680 kg); maximum take-off 14,407 lb (6535 kg) **Dimensions:** wingspan 43 ft	11½ in (13.40 m), length 36 ft 3½ in (11.06 m); height 13 ft 8½ in (4.18 m), wing area 322.9 sq ft (30.00 m²) **Armament:** two 0.3-in (7.62-mm) ShKAS machine-guns, and either two 23-mim VYa-23 cannon or two 23-mm NS-23 cannon (mounted in the wings) and one 20-mm UB-20 cannon or 0.5-in (12.7-mm) UBT machine-gun in dorsal position, plus up to 1,102 lb (500 kg) of bombs plus four RS-82 or RS-132 rockets

Ilyushin Il-12 'Coach'

Making its public debut at the Soviet Aviation Day display on 18 August 1946, the Il-12 saw extensive Aeroflot service from August 1947. In production until 1949, a total of 663 examples was built.

Design of the **Il-12** twin-engined transport began in 1943, with the aim of replacing the US-derived Li-2, but wartime commitments delayed the building of prototypes and the first flight took place on 15 August 1945. An all-metal low-wing monoplane powered by two ASh-82FNV radial engines (replaced on some later examples by ASh-82Ts), the Il-12 had a flight crew of four and cabin accommodation for up to 27 passengers. The air force (V-VS) **Il-12D** assault ersion had additional double-entry cargo doors in the port side

fuselage, plus provision an optional dorsal turret. Service deliveries began in 1947, while Aeroflot received its first aircraft during 1948. Later examples went to the Czech, Polish and Chinese national airlines.

A dorsal fin was soon added and passenger seating increased to 32, though Aeroflot limited seating to 16 or 18, an uneconomical load. Several Antarctic versions were built, equipped with skis and ice protection.

SPECIFICATION	
Ilyushin Il-12 'Coach' **Type:** passenger and cargo transport **Powerplant:** two 1,830-hp (1365-kW) Shvetsov ASh-82FNV piston engines **Performance:** maximum speed 253 mph (407 km/h) at 8,200 ft (2500 m); service ceiling 21,980 ft	(6700 m); range 1,243 miles (2000 km) **Weights:** empty equipped 19,842 lb (9000 kg); maximum take-off 38,030 lb (17250 kg) **Dimensions:** wingspan 104 ft (31.70 m); length 69 ft 11 in (21.31 m), wing area 1,076.43 sq ft (100 m²)

Ilyushin Il-14 'Crate'

The post-war **Il-14** transport was a logical development of the earlier Il-12. It had improved aerodynamic qualities, a greatly modified and refined structure and

greater power. Externally the greatest differences lay in the redesigned wing and crew cabin, and the enlarged angular vertical tail fin assembly.

The Il-14 flew in prototype form on 15 July 1950, and over 3,500 were built in the Soviet Union in a variety of versions for passenger transport, and in military variants for trooping or cargo transport. The military Il-14s had stronger

floors, large double doors for freight loading in the port side rear fuselage, and observation blisters for use by a controller during employment as a paratroop transport. The ASCC (NATO) reporting name for the type is '**Crate**'.

East Germany and Czechoslovakia built the Il-14 under licence from 1955 and when Soviet production terminated in 1958, Czechoslovak development and production continued apace into the 1960s.

Ilyushin Il-14 'Crate' (continued)

Il-14s served with the airlines of the Soviet bloc and with those of other countries, while it formed the military equipment of all the Soviet Union's allies in addition Algeria, Egypt, India and Yugoslavia. Further 'Crates' were completed by VEB of East Germany, which produced some 80 examples.

Variants

Il-14P: original commercial version for 18 passengers
Il-14M: lengthened-fuselage version accommodating 24 passengers, widely used
Il-14T: basic military transport, combined original body length with Il-14M airframe
Avia 14/Avia 14P: Czechoslovak built Il-14s and Il-14Ps
Avia 14-32: Czechoslovak-built Il-14M in 32-seat configuration
Avia 14T: freighter version of Il-14M built in Czechoslovakia, with single very large freight door in port side fuselage
Avia 14FG: aerial survey version
Avia 14-42: pressurised and enlarged version with porthole-type windows: flown in 1960
'Crate-C': military electronic warfare version, first seen in 1979

SPECIFICATION
Ilyushin Il-14M 'Crate'
Type: passenger transport
Powerplant: two 1,900-hp (1417-kW) Shvetsov ASh-82T radial piston engines
Performance: maximum speed 259 mph (417 km/h); service ceiling 24,280 ft (7400 m); range with full payload 811 miles (1305 km)
Weights: empty equipped 27,778 lb (12600 kg); maximum take-off 39,683 lb (18000 kg)
Dimensions: wingspan 104 ft (31.70 m); length 73 ft 2 in (22.30 m); height 25 ft 11 in (7.90 m); wing area 1,073 sq ft (99.70 m²)

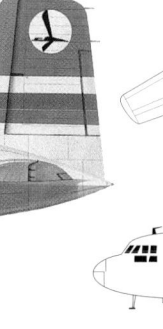

Ilyushin Il-14M 'Crate'

LOT Polish Airlines introduced the Ilyushin Il-14 into service in 1955 in order to replace the Il-12B. The first three examples were delivered in June, followed by three in autumn 1956, and a further six VEB-built Il-14Ps in late 1957.

POLSKIE LINIE LOTNICZE·LOT·
SP-LNH

Ilyushin Il-18, Il-20, Il-22 and Il-24 'Coot'

Designed for Aeroflot's domestic and shorter international routes, the prototype **Il-18**, named Moskva, first flew on 4 July 1957, receiving the NATO reporting name **'Coot'**. The initial version carried 75 passengers, and was powered, until the 21st aircraft, by 3,755-ehp (2800-ekW) Kuznetsov NK-4 or Ivchyenko AI-20 turboprop engines, the latter type then being adopted as standard. The **Il-18A** obviated vibration and buffet problems, had 4,000-ehp (2980-ekW) AI-20K engines, and carried 89 passengers. The **Il-18B** had increased take-off weight and carried 84 passengers. The **Il-18V** seated 89-100 passengers, and the **Il-18I** (later **Il-18D**) seated 110-122 passengers in a cabin lengthened by a rearward extension into the erstwhile cargo hold. This variant also introduced uprated AI-20M engines

and increased fuel tankage in the centre section. The contemporary **Il-18Ye** was identical apart from lacking the extra fuel tankage.

Examples of most of these Il-18 variants were supplied to military operators for transport and VIP duties. A large number of nominally civilian Il-18s served as equipment and avionics test beds and also in the experimental role. Some 'Aeroflot' Il-18s were used for military tasks, often being fitted with unusual antennae or equipment fairings.

The replacement of the basic Il-18 in Aeroflot service resulted in a pool of redundant airframes suitable for conversion to military roles. The first such conversion to receive a separate NATO reporting name, **'Coot-A'**, was the **Il-20**, a dedicated Elint/radar reconnaissance type based on the Il-18D. Below the fuselage, projecting

forward from a point just behind the wing's leading edge, the type has a large cylindrical SLAR pod. Smaller, more square-section pods are mounted on the forward fuselage just below the line of the cabin windows and carry cameras or other optical sensors. Two large trapezoidal blade antennas are mounted above the forward fuselage, and other antennas include three large blister fairings on the centreline below the centre fuselage. Smaller antenna fairings are located on the centreline farther aft, and there are a number of dielectric panels flush with the fuselage and on the wing tips.

The **Il-22 'Coot-B'** is an airborne command post variant identifiable by a cylindrical pod on the fin, and by an array of antennas (mostly blade) above and below the fuselage. The aircraft may also have a

SPECIFICATION
Ilyushin Il-18D 'Coot'
Type: five-crew medium-range airliner
Powerplant: four ZMDB Progress (Ivchyenko) AI-20M turboprop engines each rated at 14,250 ehp (3169 ekW)
Performance: maximum cruising speed 419 mph (675 km/h) at 27,885 ft (8500 m); economical cruising speed 388 mph (625 km/h) at optimum altitude; initial climb rate 2,070 ft (630 m) per minute; service ceiling 32,810 ft (10000 m);
range 4,030 miles (6500 km) with maximum fuel or 2,299 miles (3700 km) with maximum payload
Weights: empty 77,160 lb (35000 kg); maximum take-off 141,093 lb (64000 kg)
Dimensions: wingspan 122 ft 9¼ in (37.42 m); length 117 ft 9 in (35.90 m); height 33 ft 4 in (10.17 m); wing area 1,507 sq ft (140.00 m²)
Payload: up to 122 passengers within the context of a 29,762-lb (13500-kg) maximum payload

long cylindrical or canoe fairing under the belly, considerably smaller than those fitted to the 'Coot-A'. Unconfirmed reports suggest that the designation **'Coot-C'** is used for a fourth Il-18 derivative for the Elint role with several antennas on the rear fuselage but no underfuselage SLAR. The **Il-20RT** is another naval Elint model with a large pannier above the central fuselage and a shortened, blunt-tipped tail

'sting'. The **Il-24N** is a civil derivative of the Il-20 retaining the underfuselage SLAR but stripped of all Elint gear and utilised for surveillance duties.

The Il-20 'Coot-A' Elint/radar reconnaissance aircraft is based on the Il-18D. From 1977 more than 30 of the 565 Il-18s built were converted to Il-20/22/24 standard.

Ilyushin Il-28 'Beagle'

Egyptian Il-28s which survived Suez and the pre-emptive strikes of the Six-day War were employed for routine coastal surveillance and other non-combatant duties.

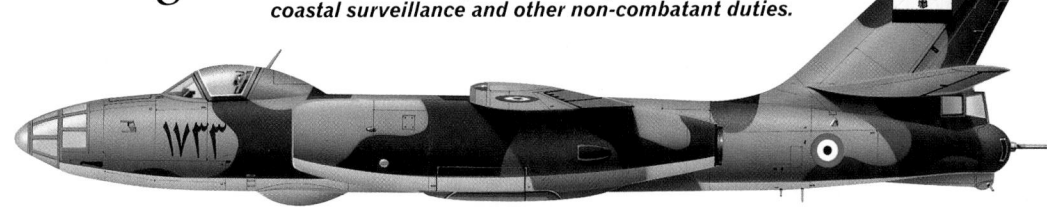

A pioneering turbojet-powered tactical light bomber, the **Il-28**, ASCC reporting name **'Beagle'**, was developed in competition with the Tu-73/78. The first prototype of the Il-28 recorded its initial flight on 8 July 1948 in the hands of V. K. Kokkinaki.

The Ilyushin design team opted for an all-metal structure and a three-man crew in separate positions in the circular-section fuselage. This also carried the twin-wheel nose unit of the tricycle landing gear, the fuel and the weapons bay, and also supported the tail unit and the high-set wing. The tail unit comprised swept vertical and horizontal surfaces, but the wing was straight and carried two underslung nacelles for the powerplant of two Klimov VK-1A turbojets as well as the landing gear's single-wheel main units. The VK-1A turbojet engine was a Soviet development of the RD-45, itself a Soviet copy of a British unit, the Rolls-Royce Nene, and was one of the keys to the Il-28's excellent performance.

In October 1948 the Il-28 was evaluated successfully against the Tupolev Tu-78 and rushed into production for service from September 1950. Production is thought to have totalled some 3,000 aircraft, of which more than half were exported to the USSR's Warsaw Pact allies, China, and many other countries. The Il-28 was also licensed for production in China, and in Czechoslovakia as the **B-228**. Despite its obsolescence in the basic light bomber role, the Il-28 remained in limited service in late 2000.

The Il-28 was also developed into a three-seat tactical reconnaissance variant, as the **Il-28R**, the erstwhile weapons bay being revised for the carriage of between three and five cameras or, in an alternative radar reconnaissance form, replaced by a large radar installation. The **Il-28RTR** featured an electronic reconnaissance package with a radome under the rear fuselage. The **Il-28REB** was an electronic warfare jamming platform, with antennas underfuselage and in tip 'tanks'. Other baseline models were adapted for the target-towing (as the **Il-28B**), nuclear detonation atmospheric sampling (**Il-28ZA**), and unmanned missile target roles. The swept-wing **Il-28S** was scrapped prior to completion.

SPECIFICATION

Ilyushin Il-28 'Beagle'
Type: three-seat light bomber
Powerplant: two Klimov VK-1A turbojet engines each rated at 5,952 lb st (26.48 kN)
Performance: maximum speed 560 mph (902 km/h) at 14,765 ft (4500 m); cruising speed 544 mph (876 km/h) at optimum altitude; initial climb rate 2,952 ft (900 m) per minute; climb to 32,810 ft (10000 m) in 18 minutes; service ceiling 40,350 ft (12300 m); range 1,491 miles (2400 km) at 32,810 ft (10000 m) declining to 705 miles (1135 km) at 3,280 ft (1000 m)
Weights: empty 28,417 lb (11890 kg); maximum take-off 46,738 lb (21200 kg)
Dimensions: wingspan 70 ft 4½ in (21.45 m) without tip tanks; length 57 ft 11 in (17.65 m) for fuselage excluding tail cannon; height 21 ft 11¾ in (6.70 m); wing area 654.47 sq ft (60.80 m²)
Armament: two 23-mm Nudel'man-Rikhter NR-23 fixed forward-firing cannon in the lower nose and two NR-23 trainable rearward-firing cannon in the tail turret, plus up to 6,614 lb (3000 kg) of disposable stores carried in a lower-fuselage weapons bay, and generally comprising one 6,614-lb (3000-kg) FAB-3000 free-fall bomb, or four 1,102-lb (500-kg) FAB-500 free-fall bombs or eight 551-lb (250-kg) FAB-250 free-fall bombs

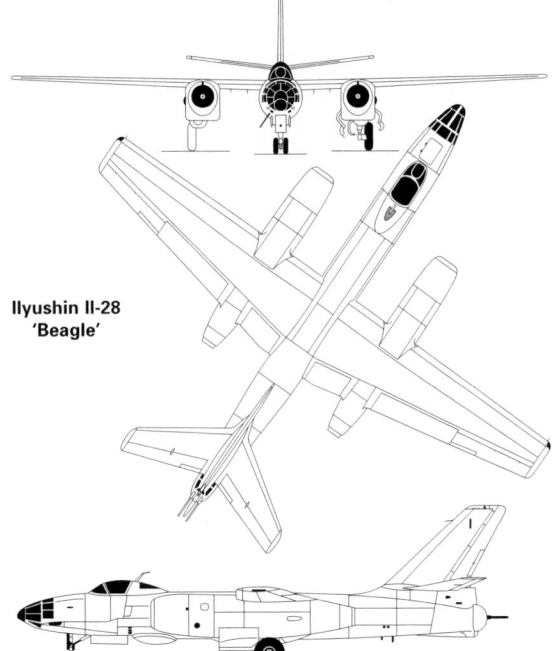

Ilyushin Il-28 'Beagle'

Variants

Il-28D 'Beagle': Long-range nuclear bomber variant, with front guns removed, and tail turret replaced with a streamlined tailcone.
Il-28T 'Beagle': *Torpedonosyets* (torpedo) variant for the AV-MF, the lengthened weapons bay being able to accommodate one large or two small torpedoes, or alternatively mines for the minelayer role
Il-28U 'Mascot': *Uchyebno* (training) variant for the two-seat operational conversion training task with a solid nose and two stepped cockpits
H-5 'Beagle': China received more than 500 Il-28 bombers direct from the USSR, and in 1966 began its own production programme that saw the delivery of more than 1,500 **Hongzhaji-5** (bomber no. 5) warplanes from Harbin by the early 1980s; subvariants of this basic model are the **HJ-5 (Hongzhaji Jiaolianji-5,** or training aircraft no. 5) operational conversion trainer with a solid nose and two stepped cockpits, and the **HZ-5** tactical reconnaissance platform; the H-5 differs from the Il-28 in details such as its gun armament of 23-mm Type 23-1 cannon and powerplant of two 5,952-lb st (26.48-kN) Liming (LM) Wopen-5D (Klimov VK-1A) turbojet engines

---

Ilyushin Il-38 'May'

The **Il-38**, which has the NATO reporting designation **'May'**, was derived from the Il-18 airliner. The Il-38 resulted from a 1959 AV-MF requirement for a long-range maritime patrol and ASW aircraft, and the prototype first flew on 27 September 1961. There followed a pre-production prototype and 57 production aircraft delivered from 1968 (although some sources quote a figure of about 100 aircraft delivered in 1965-8).

The changes involved in the evolution of the basic Il-18 into the Il-38 were the lengthening of the fuselage by about 13 ft 1½ in (4.00 m) and the forward movement of the wing by some 9 ft ¼ in (2.75 m), probably to compensate for the effect of the new role equipment on the type's centre of gravity. Most of the original cabin windows were removed, and the remainder were mostly reduced in size. The Il-18's original passenger entry doors were all removed, to be replaced by a new door on the starboard side at the rear of the cabin in the location of the Il-18's service door. Other structural alterations included the provision of a MAD stinger projecting rearward from the tailcone, and a pair of internal weapons bays fore and aft of the wing carry-through structure.

The standard **Il-38 'May-A'** has weather radar in the nose, with a large search radar (NATO reporting name 'Wet Eye') in a distinctive, bulged radome below the forward fuselage, immediately to the rear of the nosewheel bay. The otherwise smooth skin is disrupted by a handful of antennas and heat exchanger outlets, and there are large heat exchanger inlet pods and cable ducts just ahead of the wing.

Most of the former Soviet Il-38 aircraft remain in use with the AV-MF (naval air arm), but some may be under VVS (air force) command and others were passed to the Ukraine. The only export customer was the Indian Navy. Il-38s encountered over the Mediterranean in Egyptian markings during the early 1970s were Soviet aircraft operating from Egyptian bases and wearing 'flag of convenience' markings. The continued future of the Il-38, at least in the shorter-range maritime patrol and ASW roles, is certain within Russia.

SPECIFICATION

Ilyushin Il-38 'May-A'
Type: seven/eight-crew medium/long-range maritime patrol and anti-submarine warplane
Powerplant: four ZMDB Progress (Ivchyenko) AI-20M turboprop engines each rated at 4,250 ehp (3169 ekW)
Performance: maximum speed 448 mph (722 km/h) at 21,000 ft (6400 m); cruising speed 401 mph (645 km/h) at 27,000 ft (8230 m); patrol speed between 199 and 248 mph (320 and 400 km/h) between 330 and 3,280 ft (100 and 1000 m); service ceiling 36,090 ft (11000 m); range 4,660 miles (7500 km) with maximum fuel; endurance 13 hours maximum and 11 hours
Weights: empty 78,263 lb (35500 kg); maximum take-off 145,503 lb (66000 kg)
Dimensions: wingspan 122 ft 9¼ in (37.42 m); length 131 ft 10¼ in (40.19 m); height 33 ft 4½ in (10.17 m); wing area 1,507.00 sq ft (140.00 m²)
Armament: up to 18,520 lb (8400 kg) of disposable stores carried in two lower-fuselage weapons bays, and generally comprising 216 RGB-1 sonobuoys or 144 RGB-2 sonobuoys as well as two AT-1 torpedoes, or 10 PLAB-250-120 depth charges, or eight AMD-2-500 mines, or one nuclear depth bomb

Variants

Il-38M 'May': one *modifitseerovanny* (modified) aircraft with an inflight refuelling probe
Il-38MZ 'May': one *modifitseerovanny/zaprahvschchik* (modified/tanker) aircraft fitted with an inflight refuelling probe and also able to fly in the 'buddy-buddy' tanker role

Ilyushin Il-38 'May' (continued)

The MAD boom projected rearward from the tailcone, and a pair of internal weapons bays was situated fore and aft of the wing carry-through structure.

The standard **Il-38 'May-A'** has weather radar in the nose, with a large search radar (NATO reporting name 'Wet Eye') in a distinctive, bulged radome below the forward fuselage, immediately to the rear of the nosewheel bay. The smooth skin is disrupted by a handful of antennas and heat exchanger outlets, and there are large heat exchanger inlet pods and cable ducts just ahead of the wing.

The Il-38 has proven effective in the ASW role, despite some reliability problems with the Berkut STS system, the primary means of submarine detection.

Most of the former Soviet Il-38 aircraft remain in use with the AV-MF (naval air arm), but some may be under VVS (air force) command and others were passed to the Ukraine. The only export customer was the Indian Navy. Il-38s encountered over the Mediterranean in Egyptian markings during the early 1970s were Soviet aircraft operating from Egyptian bases and wearing 'flag of convenience' markings. The continued future of the Il-38, at least in the shorter-range maritime patrol and ASW roles, is certain within Russia. During 2000, under the supervision of the Leninets Holding Company, the Sea Serpent upgrade programme was underway, with the aim at keeping Russian Il-38s viable well into the 21st century.

Ilyushin Il-62 'Classic'

The **Il-62** was the first large intercontinental transport aircraft to be designed and built in the USSR. The Il-62 was designed from 1960 as an all-metal type with a low-set cantilever wing of modest sweep and with tricycle landing gear. The latter had twin wheels on the nose unit and a four-wheel bogie on each of the main units, and the powerplant consisted of four turbofans mounted as a side-by-side pair on each flank of the rear fuselage. The aircraft employed a substantial T-tail with modest sweep on its vertical and horizontal surfaces.

The wing was built in three sections as a centre-section with a trailing edge at right angles to the fuselage, and two tapered outer panels with sweep on their trailing edges as well as their leading edges. Other key elements of the design included hot-air de-icing of the leading edges of the flying surface and engine nacelles, electrically de-iced windscreens, fuel carried in seven integral tanks and an auxiliary power unit in the tail cone.

The first Il-62 prototype flew on 3 January 1963 and, like the second prototype and three pre-production aircraft, had the powerplant of four 16,534-lb st (73.55-kN) Lyul'ka AL-7 turbojets as the intended turbofan engines were not yet ready for flight. Flight trials revealed the need for many changes including greater span, extended chord for the drooped leading edges of the outer wing panels, six wing fences and, eventually, the planned powerplant of four 23,148-lb st (102.97-kN) Kuznetsov NK-8-4 turbofan engines with cascade-type thrust reversers on the outer two engines.

Development was protracted, and the Il-62 did not enter service with Aeroflot until March 1967 in a standard that included accommodation for 163 passengers (or 186 passengers in a high-density arrangement).

First appearing in 1970 with the initial designation **Il-62M-200**, the **Il-62M** is a development of the Il-62 with more powerful Soloviev D-30KU turbofan engines (the outer units fitted with clamshell reversers), 1,100 Imp gal (5000 litres) of additional fuel in a fin tank, no wing fences, differential spoilers for improved lateral control, a containerised baggage/ freight system, and updated avionics. The type entered service in 1974, and from 1978 was supplemented by the **Il-62MK** development with a longer-life airframe, higher weights including a maximum payload of 55,115 lb (25000 kg) within a maximum take-off weight of 368,166 lb (167000 kg), wider main landing gear bogies with lower-pressure tyres, automatic deploy-ment of the spoilers in landing, and a revised cabin with seating increased to 195 yet offering greater comfort despite a widening of the aisles.

Manufacture and delivery of the originally required total of 245 aircraft had been completed by 1990, but in order to keep the production line open to 1995 another 25 aircraft were then built, one of them to a VVIP standard as the aircraft of the Russian president. Apart from those delivered to Aeroflot, the Il-62 was also delivered to non-Soviet airlines such as CSA of Czechoslovakia, LOT of Poland, Interflug of East Germany, Tarom of Romania, Cubana and the CAAC of China. Toward the end of the 20th century some 125 of these aircraft were still in service, about 110 of them with CIS operators and Tarom, together with machines operated by TAAG Angola Airlines, Air Koryo and Cubana.

Other Il-62s have also served as presidential aircraft in the USSR, the aircraft involved at first retaining Aeroflot markings and being operated by civilian crews. They were specially modified for the role, however, with a long dorsal avionics fairing and satellite communications equipment. Recently, these aircraft have relinquished their Aeroflot markings, and have been painted in a quasi-government colour scheme, with massive Rossiya (Russia) titles on the fuselage sides. There are no known Il-62s in purely military service with the CIS, and the only known truly military examples of the Il-62 were three former Interflug aircraft (Il-62M and Il-62MK machines) taken over by the Luftwaffe after the reunification of the two Germanies. The aircraft were soon withdrawn from military use and sold, leaving only the Russian VIP transports in military service. Marketing of the Il-62 (particularly second-hand examples) continues.

SPECIFICATION

Ilyushin Il-62M 'Classic'
Type: five-crew long-range medium transport aircraft
Powerplant: four PNPP 'Aviadvigatel' (Soloviev) D-30KU turbofan engines each rated at 24,250 lb st (107.87 kN)
Performance: maximum cruising speed 560 mph (900 km/h) between 32,810 and 39,370 ft (10000 and 12000 m); economical cruising speed 509 mph (820 km/h) between 32,810 and 39,370 ft (10000 and 12000 m); range 4,848 miles (7800 km) with an 11,243-lb (5100-kg) payload
Weights: empty 157,848 lb (71600 kg); maximum take-off 363,757 lb (165000 kg)
Dimensions: wingspan 141 ft 9 in (43.20 m); length 174 ft 3½ in (53.12 m); height 40 ft 6¼ in (12.35 m); wing area 3,009.15 sq ft (279.55 m²)
Payload: up to 186 passengers within the context of a 50,705-lb (23000-kg) maximum payload

The Il-62M , which entered service in 1974, introduced different Soloviev engines, with clamshell thrust reversers on the outer units only. Total Il-62 production stood at 245 examples by 1990.

Ilyushin Il-76 'Candid'

First flown in prototype form on 25 March 1971 as a high-wing monoplane with anhedralled outer wing panels, a tall T-tail and retractable tricycle landing gear including side-by-side pairs of wheels on the nose unit and two four-wheel units in tandem on each main unit, the **Il-76** was created as a successor to the An-12 in both the civil freighting and military transport roles with four D-30KP turbofans. Design of the new type began in the late 1960s to meet a requirement for a freighter able to carry an 88,183-lb (40000-kg) payload over a range of 3,107 miles (5000 km) in less than 6 hours, operate from short and unprepared airstrips and cope with the worst weather conditions likely to be experienced in Siberia and the USSR's arctic regions. The configuration of the new Soviet transport was probably inspired by that of an American logistic freighter, namely the smaller, lighter and less powerfully engined Lockheed C-141A StarLifter.

The initial **Il-76 'Candid-A'** was built purely for military service, while the **Il-76T 'Candid-A'** is the civil counterpart with additional fuel in a centre-section tank above the hold and higher operating weights for the carriage of greater payload in a hold that is, in all versions, accessed by a rear door arrangement including a powered lifting ramp, fully pressurised and fitted with freight-handling equipment including two winches at the front of the hold and two overhead travelling cranes with a total of four hoists. The **Il-76TD 'Candid-A'** has a power-plant of improved D-30KP-2 turbofan engines to maintain performance at higher ambient temperatures plus an increase in fuel to boost maximum-fuel range by 746 miles (1200 km). This model also has a strengthened wing, the ability to carry a 105,820-lb (48000-kg) payload, and a maximum take-off weight of 418,871 lb (190000 kg).

The **Il-76M 'Candid-B'** is the military version of the Il-76T with a rear turret, ECM blisters on the fuselage sides in line with the navigator's compartment as well as on the sides of the forward and rear fuselage sections, and provision for chaff/flare dispenser packs. The **Il-76MD 'Candid-B'** is the military subvariant equivalent to the Il-76TD, and differs from the Il-76M in its maximum payload of 105,820 lb (48000 kg), D-30KP-2 engines and maximum take-off weight of 418,871 lb (190000 kg).

Both the 'Candid-A' and 'Candid-B' variants are extremely capable as a result of their combination of advanced design, sturdy landing gear, excellent high-lift devices and powerful engines, which bestow good field performance even under adverse conditions. The Indian air force uses the type under the name **Gajaraj** (king elephant), and other military export customers include Iran, Libya, North Korea, Syria and Yemen as well as members of the CIS.

Air Ukraine operated this ex-Aeroflot Il-76MD 'Candid-B' freighter on civil operations. Additionally, around 100 ex-VVS 'Candids' were inherited by the Ukraine air force following the disintegration of the Soviet Union.

SPECIFICATION

Ilyushin Il-76M 'Candid-B'
Type: seven-crew long-range transport aircraft
Powerplant: four PNPP 'Aviadvigatel' (Soloviev) D-30KP turbofan engines each rated at 26,455 lb st (117.68 kN)
Performance: maximum speed 528 mph (850 km/h) at optimum altitude; cruising speed 497 mph (800 km/h) between 29,530 and 39,370 ft (9000 and 12000 m); service ceiling about 47,570 ft (14500 m); range 3,107 miles (5000 km) with maximum payload

Weights: maximum take-off 374,780 lb (170000 kg)
Dimensions: wingspan 165 ft 8 in (50.50 m); length 152 ft 10¼ in (46.59 m); height 48 ft 5 in (14.76 m); wing area 3,229.28 sq ft (300.00 m²)
Armament: two 23-mm Gryazev-Shipunov GSh-23L trainable rearward-firing two-barrel cannon in the tail turret
Payload: up to 140 troops, or 125 paratroops, or litters plus attendants, or 88,183 lb (40000 kg) of freight

Variants

Il-76K: cosmonaut training version of the Il-76
Il-76MDK: cosmonaut training version of the Il-76MD
Il-76MF: stretched and updated military version with 35,273-lb (156.90-kN) Aviadvigatel PS-90AN turbofan engines and the cargo hold lengthened by 21 ft 8 in (6.60 m) in a longer fuselage for a maximum payload of 114,640 lb (52000 kg)
Il-76TF: civil counterpart of the Il-76MF

Ilyushin Il-78 'Midas'

The **Il-78**, which has the NATO reporting designation **'Midas'**, is the inflight-refuelling tanker version of the Il-76MD with three UPAZ-1A Sakhalin hose-and-drum units installed as one under each wing and one on the port side of the rear fuselage, 61,728 lb (28000 kg) of extra fuel in two tanks located in the erstwhile cargo hold in an arrangement linked to the standard wing tankage, and a refuelling observation position replacing the rear turret. The two fuel tanks in the hold can be removed to allow the Il-78 to operate as a conventional transport.

The UPAZ unit is notably neat, and incorporates in its nose a partially retractable spike whose rearward movement opens the annular inlet through which free-stream air enters the unit before passing through the ram-air turbine and finally exiting via slotted exhaust ducts. The ram-air turbine drives the turbopump that allows fuel to be transferred at the rate of 550 Imp gal (2500 litres) per minute, which is a

The definitive Il-78M, operated by the 230th ZAP at Engels, carries three internal fuel tanks, connected to the aircraft's own tanks. The aircraft can operate with a mix of two or three UPAZ-1M HDUs.

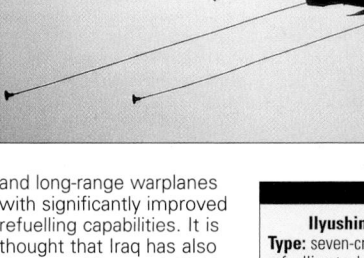

considerably higher rate than that achieved by any Western HDU. The Il-78 can also be used for the refuelling of aircraft on the ground by means of conventional hoses, and it is thought that in Russian service Il-78s operate in civil markings and the smaller numbers of **Il-78M** machines in military colours.

The Il-78 otherwise differs from the Il-76 in its Kupol navigation system and its RSBN short-range navigation system for the location of and approach to receiver aircraft from a distance of some 185 miles (300 km). The Il-78 entered service in 1987 as a replacement for the tanker version of the Myasishchyev M-4 bomber, and provides Soviet tactical

and long-range warplanes with significantly improved refuelling capabilities. It is thought that Iraq has also developed its own inflight-refuelling tanker version of the Il-76 with comparable capabilities.

The Il-78M is the pure inflight-refuelling counterpart of the Il-78 with three fixed rather than two removable tanks in the hold, the addition of the third tank increasing the fuel available for transfer by 22,046 lb (10000 kg) at a maximum take-off weight of 462,965 lb (210000 kg). The Il-78 and Il-78M have been produced as conversions from Il-76MD standard, and it is believed that by the end of the 20th

SPECIFICATION

Ilyushin Il-78 'Midas'
Type: seven-crew inflight-refuelling tanker and transport aircraft
Powerplant: four PNPP 'Aviadvigatel' (Soloviev) D-30KP-2 turbofan engines each rated at 26,455 lb st (117.68 kN)
Performance: nominal cruising speed 466 mph (750 km/h) at optimum altitude; refuelling speed between 267 and 366 mph (430 and 590 km/h) at between 6,560

and 29,525 ft (2000 and 9000 m); radius 621 miles (1000 km) with 315,913 lb (143,298 kg) of transfer fuel
Weights: empty 216,049 lb (98000 kg); maximum take-off 418,871 lb (190000 kg)
Dimensions: wingspan 165 ft 8 in (50.50 m); length 152 ft 10¼ in (46.59 m); height 48 ft 5 in (14.76 m); wing area 3,229.28 sq ft (300.00 m²)
Payload: see above

century at least 31 Il-78 and 15 Il-78M aircraft had been produced, these serving both the Russian and Ukrainian air forces. In 1997 the Indian Air Force placed an order for the first two of a planned fleet of

six aircraft.

Developments that have been proposed but are as yet unbuilt are the **Il-76V** with UPAZ-MK-32V HDUs, and the **Il-76MK** convertible inflight-refuelling tanker/ transport.

Ilyushin Il-86 'Camber' and 'Maxdome' and Il-96

Designed to provide Aeroflot and other Soviet bloc airlines with a medium-range wide-body airliner comparable in terms of operating efficiency with contemporary Western airliners, the **Il-86** is of conventional light alloy construction and standard low-wing configuration with four turbofan engines in nacelles strut-mounted below and ahead of the leading edges of the wing. The wing possesses a quarter-chord sweep angle of 35° and the retractable landing gear comprises a twin-wheel nose unit and three main units (one under the fuselage) each based on a four-wheel bogie. Accommodation is provided for a maximum of 350 passengers in nine-abreast seating inside three two-aisle cabins separated by wardrobes. Access to the cabins, on the upper deck of the two-deck fuselage, is provided by lower-deck airstair doors leading to internal stairways up to the upper deck. The lower-deck airstair doors and internal stairways can be omitted, reducing the structure weight by 6,614 lb (3000 kg) and allowing an additional 25 passengers to be carried.

The powerplant comprises four 28,660-lb st (127.48-kN) Kuznetsov NK-86 turbofan engines designed specifically for this application. This powerplant provided for a nominal (but seldom achieved) range of 2,235 miles (3600 km) with an 88,183-lb (40000-kg) payload after take-off at a maximum weight of 458,554 lb (208000 kg).

Work on the manufacture of three prototypes (one of them for static testing) began in 1974, and the first prototype achieved its maiden flight on 22 December 1976. The first production aircraft followed in October 1977, and Aeroflot received its first Il-86 in September 1979, allowing the inauguration of domestic and international services with the type in December 1980 and July 1981 respectively. The Il-86, which received the NATO reporting designation **'Camber'**, failed to live up to Soviet hopes in terms of its performance and operating economics, thereby removing all possibility of sales to customers outside the Soviet bloc.

Ilyushin Il-86 'Camber' & 'Maxdome' & Il-96 (continued)

Production of the Il-86 ended in 1993 after the completion of just 108 aircraft. This total included four examples of the **Il-87 Aimak 'Maxdome'**, otherwise known as the **Il-80** and **Il-86VKP** (**Vozdushnyye Komandnyye Punkt,** or airborne command post), which is a specialised aerial command post without cabin windows but with a large inverted canoe fairing (incorporating satellite communications gear) above the fuselage just to the rear of the flight deck, a large shallow fairing on the

rear fuselage ahead of the fin, two large pods with ram-air inlets under the inboard ends of the wing, and a mass of command and communications equipment hardened against electro-magnetic pulse effects. The aircraft were all delivered in the early part of the 1990s with the uprated powerplant of four 29,321-lb st (130.43-kN) Samara NK-86 turbofans.

Ilyushin felt that there was little wrong with the basic aerodynamic design of the Il-86, which was therefore retained in the following **Il-96** that was

otherwise a new design introducing a measure of more advanced materials such as composites for the flaps, and honeycomb and carbonfibre-reinforced plastics for the floors of the main deck (two rather than three cabins) and underfloor holds. Other major changes were the powerplant of four more advanced turbofan engines, a 'glass' flight deck with a HUD, six displays, controls for a triplex fly-by-wire control system, and a radically redesigned wing with tip-mounted winglets.

The initial version was the **Il-96-300**, and the first of three flying prototypes made its maiden flight on 28 September 1988. Route-proving trials began in the

later part of 1991, with certification following in December 1992 for a service debut at the beginning of the following year.

There was virtually no interest in the Il-96-300 from airlines outside the previous Soviet bloc, and in an effort to boost the type's sales potential, Ilyushin launched the **Il-96-350** (from 1990 **Il-96M**) programme for a derivative with Western engines and avionics. The **Il-97MO** prototype, a conversion from Il-96 standard, first flew on 6 April 1993 with 37,000-lb st (164.58-kN) Pratt & Whitney PW2337 (to be

replaced eventually by the Aviadvigatel PS-90P) turbofan engines and a two-crew 'glass' flight deck. Some 18 of these aircraft have been ordered by ARIA (Aeroflot Russian International Airlines), but there has been a major slippage in the production programme and none of the aircraft had entered service by the end of the 20th century.

The same was true of the **Il-96T** pure freighter with a large cargo door on the port side of the fuselage ahead of the wing. The first of this model flew on 16 May 1997, and ARIA has ordered an initial three aircraft.

SPECIFICATION

Ilyushin Il-96-300
Type: three/five-crew medium/long-range airliner
Powerplant: four Aviadvigatel (Soloviev) PS-90A turbofan engines each rated at 35,273 lb st (156.90 kN)
Performance: cruising speed between 528 and 559 mph (850 and 900 km/h) at between 33,135 and 39,700 ft (10100 and 12100 m); range 6,835 miles (1100 km) with a 33,069-lb

(15000-kg) payload and 4,660 miles (7500 km) with maximum payload
Weights: empty 257,937 lb (117000 kg); maximum take-off 476,190 lb (216000 kg)
Dimensions: wingspan 197 ft 2½ in (60.11 m) over winglets; length 181 ft 7¼ in (55.35 m); height 57 ft 7 in (17.55 m); wing area 4,215.29 sq ft (391.60 m²)
Payload: up to 300 passengers within the context of an 88,183-lb (40000-kg) maximum payload

By September 2000 the Aeroflot fleet was scheduled to have received a pair of Il-96T freighters, each capable of carrying a maximum cargo payload of 202,825 lb (92,000 kg) over a distance of 3,231 miles (5,200 km).

Ilyushin Il-114

Created as a successor to the An-24, the **Il-114** was schemed from the early 1980s and the design was finalised in 1986. The first of two prototypes flew on 29 March 1990, and both of the prototypes were later lost during the Il-114's development and certification programmes. These were then delayed as much by the withdrawal of Russian government funding as by difficulties with the airframe and the engine, and production by TAPO at Tashkent in Uzbekistan saw the completion of the first aircraft to the full production standard only in August 1992. Three of the first five aircraft were used for the completion of the flight certification effort, the

other two being retained for static and dynamic testing, and after the certification of the type in April 1997 led to a Russian government decision to undertake a joint promotion of the type with the Uzbek government. The Il-114 entered service with Uzbekistan Airlines in August 1998.

The Il-114 is a conventional low-wing monoplane made largely of light alloy but including, by weight, about 10 per cent of composite materials including, it is planned for later aircraft, carbonfibre-reinforced plastics structural boxes as the core of the horizontal and vertical tail surfaces. The fuselage is of circular section and comprises a two-crew flight

deck (with simple avionics including data on five screens) and a cabin carrying up to 64 passengers in a four-abreast seating arrangement with a single aisle. Provision was made at the design stage for the rearrangement of the cabin for a higher-density seating arrangement to permit the carriage of a larger number of passengers, the removal of the seating to allow the aircraft to operate in the cargo role, and the lengthening of the fuselage for standard accommodation of between 70 and 75 passengers. Access to the cabin is provided by port-side airstair doors at the front and back.

The wing and tailplane are straight, while the fin is slightly swept. The wing has a fixed leading edge, while its trailing edge is wholly occupied by outboard ailerons and inboard double-slotted flaps divided by the rear portions of the two engine nacelles. Ahead of the flaps on each side are two inboard

Variants

Il-114-100: known as the **Il-114PC** up to 1997, this is an export variant with Extant avionics and two 2,750-shp (2051-kW) Pratt & Whitney Canada PW127H turboprop engines driving Hamilton Standard propellers for increased range and operating economy
Il-114M: variant with TV7M-117 turboprop engines and provision for a 15,432-lb (7000-kg) payload at a higher maximum take-off weight
Il-114MA: variant of the Il-114M with Pratt & Whitney Canada engines for the carriage of up to 74 passengers over 1,243-mile (2000-km) stage lengths
Il-114FK: reconnaissance and aerial survey version
Il-114P: maritime patrol version
Il-114T: freight version of the Il-114 with a large port-side rear cargo door and a removable roller floor

airbrakes and one outboard spoiler, the latter being arranged to supplement the ailerons in the event of an engine failure at take-off. The tail unit includes two elevators and a single rudder; like the ailerons, the rudder is manually controlled but the elevators are controlled by a fly-by-

wire arrangement. The landing gear is of the retractable tricycle type with two wheels on each unit, and the two Klimov TV7-117S turboprop engines each drive a Stupino SV-34 propeller with six blades of carbonfibre-reinforced plastics construction.

SPECIFICATION

Ilyushin Il-114
Type: two-crew short-range passenger and freight transport
Powerplant: two Klimov TV7-117S turboprop engines each rated at 2,466 shp (1839 kW)
Performance: maximum speed 311 mph (500 km/h) at optimum altitude; cruising speed 292 mph (470 km/h) at optimum altitude; range 621 miles (1000 km) with 54 passengers

Weights: empty 33,069 lb (15000 kg); maximum take-off 51,808 lb (23500 kg)
Dimensions: wingspan 98 ft 5¼ in (30.00 m); length 88 ft 2 in (26.88 m); height 30 ft 7 in (9.32 m); wing area 881.59 sq ft (81.90 m²)
Payload: up to 64 passengers within the context of a 14,330-lb (6500-kg) maximum payload

In 1998 the Russian and Uzbek governments agreed to jointly promote the Il-114, and Uzbekistan Airlines made the first type's commercial flight.

Ilyushin/Beriev A-50 'Mainstay'

Entering service in 1984 with the NATO reporting

designation **'Mainstay'**, the **Ilyushin/Beriev A-50** is an

airborne early warning derivative of the Il-76

freighter developed from the mid-1970s as successor to the Tu-126 'Moss'. The type has a lengthened forward fuselage providing

the additional volume required for the tactical compartment in which the 10 mission personnel within the 15-man crew

SPECIFICATION	
Ilyushin/Beriev A-50 'Mainstay'	26,455 lb st (117.68 kN)
Type: 15-crew airborne early warning and control system aircraft	**Weights:** maximum take-off 418,871 lb (190000 kg)
Powerplant: four PNPP 'Aviadvigatel' (Soloviev) D-30KP turbofan engines each rated at	**Dimensions:** wingspan 165 ft 8 in (50.50 m); height 48 ft 5 in (14.76 m); wing area 3,229.28 sq ft (300 m²)

Ilyushin's 'Mainstay' represents the first truly effective AWACS asset to be employed by Russia, with around 25 examples operational by 1992.

Variants

A-50U: improved version of the A-50 with the more capable Schmel-M radar offering passive detection as well as active search modes out to a radius of 143 miles (230 km) against a fighter-sized target
A-50I: an A-50 airframe produced by Beriev for Israel Aircraft Industries for the installation of an Elta Phalcon phased-array radar to meet a Chinese requirement
A-50M: upgraded version of the A-50U with the enhanced Schmel-2 radar and a more capable computer
Adnan 1: in 1989 Iraq revealed that it had developed the **Baghdad 1** AEW platform on the basis of the Il-76MD with its rear ramp/door replaced by a radome over the antenna of the Thomson-CSF Tiger G surveillance radar supplied by France; developed in parallel was a more orthodox AEW platform based on the same airframe, and this Adnan 1 then replaced the Baghdad 1 in Iraqi plans; the Adnan 1 has its radar antenna located in an over-fuselage rotodome to provide coverage through 360°, data being transmitted to a ground-based command centre for vectoring of fighters
Adnan 2: upgraded Adnan 1 standard with a control function to allow the direct vectoring of fighter aircraft; the status of the programme is uncertain in the aftermath of Iraq's defeat in 1991
Il-76SKIP: possibly a precursor to the A-50 but used by the Russian air force mainly for the range control and missile tracking tasks, the Il-76SKIP (**Samoletniy Komandno-Izmeritelny Punkt**, or airborne control and measurement system) differs from the A-50 in its retention of the extensively glazed nose of the Il-76 freighter and also of the tail gunner's position in a form modified by the replacement of the cannon by a bulbous radome, the addition of large wing tip pods, and the omission of the inflight-refuelling probe and a number of antennae; there are two prototype and five 'production' conversions

derive data from the large Liana surveillance radar with its antenna in an over-fuselage rotodome. Other changes include deletion of the tail turret as well as the addition of a satellite navigation/communications system, comprehensive IFF and active/passive EW systems including an ESM system with some of its antennae in the tail. The transport models' glazed nose is replaced by a unit with just a single transparency on each side, the forward fuselage in front of the wing's centre section supports a large inverted canoe fairing over a satellite navigation and communications system, the port main landing gear blister carries a horizontal winglet. A large ram-air scoop is fitted in the base of the fin to provide cooling air for the mass of new electronic equipment, and an inflight-refuelling probe is fitted.

Full production at the rate of five aircraft per year was drastically slowed in 1990, probably as a result of the severe economic problems encountered by the CIS from that time. It is worth noting that weight constraints prevent the A-50 from taking-off with a full fuel load and, as inflight refuelling is difficult because of aerodynamic problems, endurance is thus lower than anticipated. Even so, it is likely that crew performance is degraded by the A-50's lack of rest facilities and even a proper lavatory. It is believed that by the end of the 20th century some 25 A-50 aircraft had been delivered to a central operating base at Pechora for the control of the CIS's primary interceptor/counter-air fighter forces.

Interstate L-6 Grasshopper and S-1 Cadet

In 1940 the Interstate Aircraft and Engineering Corporation entered the two-seat high-wing lightplane market with its **S-1A Cadet**, offered with a choice of four engines (65-hp/48-kW Continental or 65-/48-, 85-/63- or 90-hp/67-kW Franklin). The company also produced components for military aircraft, and saw that a military order could improve the commercial sales of the Cadet. Accordingly the company produced the **S-1B**, with extended cabin glazing and more powerful engine. A single aircraft was procured by the Army for evaluation as the **XO-63**. This was subsequently redesignated **XL-6**.

Initially designated XO-63 by the USAAC, favourable test results lead to a substantial L-6 production order. Eight S-1As (Army L-8s) were passed on to Bolivia.

As a result of a successful evaluation, a batch of 250 **L-6** aircraft was ordered, these being given the name **Grasshopper**.

Although built in much smaller numbers than its competitors, the L-6 nevertheless proved of some use during World War II.

SPECIFICATION	
Interstate L-6 Grasshopper	16,500 ft (5030 m); range 540 miles (869 km)
Type: two-seat observation and liaison aircraft	**Weights:** empty 1,103 lb (500 kg), maximum take-off 1,650 lb (748 kg)
Powerplant: one 102-hp (76-kW) Franklin 0-200-5 inline piston engine	**Dimensions:** wingspan 35 ft 6 in (10.82 m); length 23 ft 5½ in (7.15 m), height 7 ft (2.13 m), wing area 173.8 sq f t (16.15 m²)
Performance: maximum speed 114 mph (183 km/h), service ceiling	

IPTN N-250

In common with several other emergent nations of the period, Indonesia decided in the first half of the 1970s that an aircraft-manufacturing capability was one of the ways to foster the development and growth of an industrial base capable of undertaking the manufacture and export of goods based on advanced technologies. This led in August 1976 to the establishment of the PT Industri Pesawat Terbang Nurtanio (Nurtanio Aircraft Industry Ltd) that combined the nation's existing but too small aircraft manufacturing capabilities into a single entity initially known as Nurtanio but later as IPTN. This began with licensed manufacture of helicopters such as the Aérospatiale SA 330 and fixed-wing aircraft such as the CASA C-212 Aviocar, but then moved into the design as well as manufacture of aircraft in collaboration with CASA to create the Airtech (CASA/IPTN) CN-235, before finally switching to indigenous design and manufacture, in this instance of the **N-250**.

The N-250 was schemed as a regional transport with pressurised accommodation, and was first announced in June 1989.

The type is of basically conventional construction in light alloy although composite materials are used in a large number of elements such as the moving surfaces on the wing and tail unit. In configuration the N-250 is a high-wing monoplane with a T-tail, a high-aspect-ratio wing, and tricycle landing gear with twin wheels on each unit, which include a nose unit retracted into the forward fuselage and main units retracting into large fairings on the lower sides of the fuselage. A fly-by-wire system controls the primary moving surfaces.

The two-crew flight deck is of the 'glass' type based on the Collins Pro Line 4 system with five or six display screens, and the cabin can carry up to 68 passengers in a four-abreast arrangement with a central aisle and a port-side forward airstair door.

The first and fifth of the five prototype and development aircraft were configured in the original 50/54-seat configuration initially adopted, and the first of these machines recorded its maiden flight on 19 August 1995.

SPECIFICATION	
IPTN N-250-100	standard fuel, or 1,266 miles (2037 km) with 50 passengers and optional fuel
Type: two-crew regional airliner	**Weights:** empty 34,612 lb (15700 kg); maximum take-off 54,674 lb (24800 kg)
Powerplant: two Rolls-Royce (Allison) AE2100C turboprop engines each rated at 3,271 shp (2439 kW)	**Dimensions:** wingspan 91 ft 10¼ in (28.00 m); length 92 ft 3 in (28.12 m); height 28 ft 9¾ in (8.78 m); wing area 699.68 sq ft (65.00 m²)
Performance: (estimated) maximum cruising speed 380 mph (611 km/h) at 20,000 ft (6095 m); economical cruising speed 345 mph (556 km/h) at 20,000 ft (6095 m); initial climb rate 1,850 ft (564 m) per minute; service ceiling 30,000 ft (9145 m); range 920 miles (1481 km) with 50 passengers and	**Payload:** up to 68 passengers within the context of a 13,668-lb (6200-kg) maximum payload

IPTN N-250 (cont.)

Since the type's maiden flight however, the N-250 programme has been very severely affected by the general downturn in the economies of South-East Asian countries and more specifically by the troubled political situation in Indonesia. The variants now proposed for production, if funding can be secured, are the **N-250-50** model with up to 54 seats in a fuselage 5 ft (1.53 m) shorter than that of the **N-250-100**, the N-250-100

Development of the indigenous N-250 has been informed by IPTN's co-production of the CN-235 with CASA of Spain as Airtech.

model with up to 68 seats in a longer fuselage, the proposed **N-250-200** stretched version of the N-250-100 with 76 seats, and the proposed **N-270** stretched 70-seat version of the N-250-50 to be assembled in the USA from kits supplied by IPTN.

Jodel light aircraft

In March 1946 Jean Delmontez and Edouard Joly founded Aviation Jodel at Beaune, France. The company's first product was the **Bébé**, a single-seat lightplane available as the **D.9** (Poinsard engine) or **D.92** (modified Volkswagen motorcar engine), but was suitable for a variety of engines from 25 to 65 hp (19 to 48 kW). Although designed originally for amateur construction, the Bébé and subsequent designs have not only been built in large numbers by amateurs, but have also been produced commercially. A dual-control version of the D.9 was also developed under the designation **D.112**. It differs by having a wider fuselage to provide side-by-side two-seat accommodation, and is powered normally by a 65-hp (48kW) Continental A65 engine; a similar version built in Sweden has the designation **D.113**.

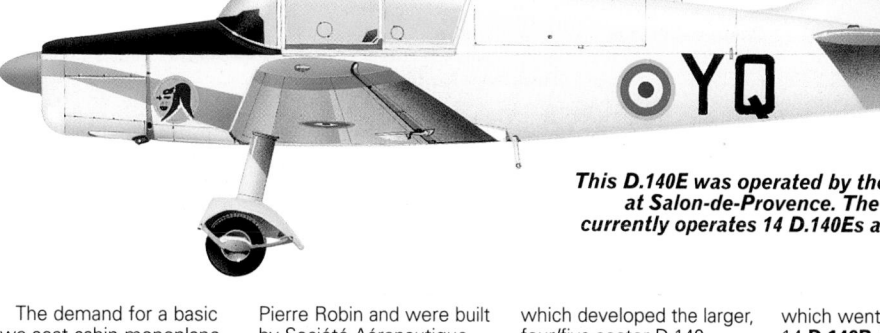

This D.140E was operated by the Ecole de l'Air at Salon-de-Provence. The Armée de l'Air currently operates 14 D.140Es and 12 D.140Rs.

The demand for a basic two-seat cabin monoplane led to design of the **D.11**, flown originally with a 45-hp (34-kW) Salmson engine, but a 65-hp (48-kW) Continental became general and the designation **D.119** applies to a version with a 90-hp (67-kW) Continental engine. Jodel designs and variations on those designs are also built by Avions

Pierre Robin and were built by Société Aéronautique Normande.

Alongside many variants of the basic D.9/D.11/ D.112/D.113/D.119, Jodel also built the **D.140 Mousquetaire**. This was based on the **D.117**, itself a variant of the D.11, and was licensed from Jean Delmontez by SAN (Société Aéronautique Normande),

which developed the larger, four/five-seater D.140 family with a 180-hp (134-kW) Lycoming engine, revised tail surfaces and other improvements. The prototype was first flown in July 1958. Production of the **D.140E Mousquetaire IV**, with enlarged tail surfaces, an all-flying tail and modified ailerons, included 18 for the French air force,

which went on to acquire 14 **D.140R Abeilles**. These have a cut-down rear fuselage with an all-round vision canopy and a glider-towing hook. Both types remain in use with the Armée de l'Air for recreation flying and (the D.140Rs) for glider-towing. The D.140s are powered by 180-hp (134-kW) Lycoming O-360 four-cylinder piston engines.

Jovair helicopters

During the years immediately after World War II, D. K. Jovanovich in the USA was working on the design and development of a lightweight helicopter. His first practical **Jovanovich JOV-3** tandem-rotor helicopter was developed later by the McCulloch Motors Corporation as a slightly larger two-seat helicopter designated **McCulloch MC-4C**, and when certificated in 1953 it was the first tandem-rotor helicopter to gain CAA certification. Three exam-

ples were evaluated by the US Army under the designation **YH-30**. A later attempt to find a civil market for this helicopter was made by the Jovair Corporation in the late 1960s, a refined version of the **MC-4C** then being known as the **Jovair 4E Sedan**. In June 1962 Jovair flew the prototype of an enclosed-cabin two-seat autogyro designed by Jovanovich. Designated **J-2**, this had a three-bladed unpowered rotor, short-span stub wings, and was

The four-seat 4E Sedan, the prototype of which was based on an MC-4C airframe, was FAA certified in 1962, powered by a 210-hp (157-kW) Franklin 6A-335 engine.

powered by a 180-hp (134-kW) Avco Lycoming 0-360-A2E engine driving a pusher propeller.

All rights for both of these aircraft were regained by McCulloch in the early 1970s, the company then known as McCulloch Aircraft Corporation, and about 90 examples of the J-2 were produced.

Junkers early aircraft

In 1910 the German engineer Dr Hugo Junkers patented a flying-wing aircraft; it was never built, but the thick-section cantilever wing that he designed for it was used in

the first Junkers aeroplane to fly, the **J 1**, on 12 December 1915. Of advanced appearance for its day, a mid-wing cantilever monoplane with fixed tailskid landing gear

and powered by a 120-hp (89-kW) Mercedes DX engine, the **J 1** was covered by thin sheet iron, gaining it the nickname 'Tin Donkey'. Six generally similar single-seat **J 2** aircraft were built in 1916, these being armed by a single 0.31-in (7.92-mm) LMG

08/15 machine-gun, but the prototype of a further developed **J 3** was not completed.

Impressed by Junkers constructional techniques, the German air ministry asked for the design and development of an armoured biplane. This was

the **J 4**, which entered service as a two-seat close-support aircraft towards the end of 1917 under the military designation **JJ**. An unequal-span biplane with fixed tailskid landing gear and powered by a 200-hp (149-kW) Benz Bz.IV engine, the **J.1** was

Left: The Junkers J 9 appeared in May 1918, and entered limited production as the D.1, with 41 examples built.

Right: The J 4 'Flying Tank' of 1917 was the first German armouied aircraft, and introduced Junkers' familiar corrugated metal skin.

covered by the corrugated light alloy skins that soon became a feature of Junkers aircraft. The powerplant and crew were enclosed in an armoured capsule, the protection which this provided against small-arms fire from the ground making the J.1 popular with its crews and production totalled 227.

With the J 4 in production, Junkers turned to a new series of cantilever low-wing monoplanes, the single-seat **J 7** of 1917 originally introducing swivelling wingtips instead of ailerons for lateral control. The J 7 served as prototype for the slightly longer **J 9** single-seat fighter which, powered by a 185-hp (138-kW) BMW engine and armed with twin forward-firing LMG 08/15 machine-guns, was built in small numbers under the military designation **D.I**.

An enlarged two-seat version of the J 7, for evaluation as an escort and close support aircraft, had the company designation **J 8** and led to development of the **J 10** powered by a 180-hp (134-kW) Mercedes D.IIIa engine. About 50 examples of this were built before the armistice of 1918, entering service as the **CL.I** and carrying the same armament as the D.I. Three examples of a float-

plane version of this aircraft, the **J 11**, entered service with the German navy during 1918 under the designation **CLS.I**.

SPECIFICATION	
Junkers J.1	4,787 lb (2176 kg)
Type: two-seat close-support aircraft	**Dimensions:** wingspan 52 ft 6 in (16 m); length 29 ft 10½ in (9.10 m); height 11 ft 11 in (3.40 m); wing area 533.52 sq ft (49.40 in²)
Powerplant: one 200-hp (149-kW) Benz Bz.IV 6-cylinder inline piston engine	
Performance: maximum speed 97 mph (155 km/h); endurance 2 hours	**Armament:** two fixed-forward firing 0.31-in (7.92-mm) LMG 08/15 machine-guns and one trainable 0.31-in (7.92-mm) Parabellum machine-gun
Weights: empty 3,885 lb (1766 kg); maximum take-off	

Junkers aircraft of the 1920s

Derived from the wartime Junkers J 10 (CL.1), the **F 13** was the world's first purpose-built all-metal commercial monoplane to enter service. In its original form, as first flown on 25 June 1919, the two-man crew was accommodated in a forward open cockpit, with the four passengers in an enclosed cabin to its rear; at a later date the crew also had enclosed accommodation. The first F 13 was powered by the 160-hp (119-kW) Mercedes D.IIIa engine, but this was superseded in early production aircraft by a 185-hp (138-kW) BMW IIIa. Production continued until 1932, and by far the majority (of more than 320 built in some 60 variants) were powered by the 210-hp (156-kW) Junkers L-5 engine. Between 40 and 50 were supplied to Deutsche Luft-Hansa, the remainder being used for both civil and military service on a worldwide basis.

The F.13's success was certainly not matched by the **K 16**, a three-seat cabin monoplane of 1922 of which only a few examples were built. It was followed by the sleek **A 20** low-wing monoplane, first flown in 1923, which had seats for a crew of two in tandem open cockpits. Intended for use as a freight or mail-carrier the A 20 entered production, after approval by the Allied control commission, in both **A 20L** landplane and **A 20W** float-plane form, built in Germany and at the Junkers factory in Sweden. These were powered by the Mercedes D.IIIa or 220-hp (164-kW) Junkers L-2 engine respectively, and a developed version with the 310-hp (231-kW) Junkers L-5 engine had the designation **A 35**. A military version of this last aircraft, armed with two forward-firing and two rear-mounted machine-guns, was developed in Sweden under the designation **R 53**.

Civil development continued with the **G 23**, which entered service in 1925, and was then the world's first three-engine all-metal commercial transport monoplane. Operated by a crew of three, it accommodated nine passengers, and was flown with a variety of powerplants. The designation **G 24** applied to the major production version, usually powered by three 310-hp (231-kW) Junkers L-5 engines, but a number of F 24 aircraft which appeared in 1928 had a single-engine powerplant (the outer wing-mounted engines being removed) but were otherwise generally similar. A 12/15-passenger version designated **G 31**, of which 15 were built, had three Gnome-Rhône Jupiter or BMW-built Pratt & Whitney Hornet engines. There was also a military bomber version of the G 24, which had the designation **K 30**; it introduced three gunner's positions and carried bombs on

racks beneath the wings; this model was built in the USSR, Sweden and Turkey under the designation **R 42**. The first post-war Junker's design intended for military use was the **H 21**, a two-seat armed reconnaissance aircraft of parasol-wing monoplane configuration, powered by the 185-hp (138-kW) BMW IIIa engine. About 100 H 21s were built by the Junkers factory at Fili, near Moscow, all of them entering service with the Soviet air force; the first was delivered in 1924.

Ad Astra Aero, the forerunner of Swissair, received Junkers F 13s in 1922, allowing the initiation of international services to Nuremburg.

Impressed into Luftwaffe service in 1939, the surviving Junkers G 38ce served with KGrzbV 172 on transport duties in Norway, and later in the Balkans. It was finally destroyed by an RAF raid on Tatoi, Greece, on 17 May 1941.

Junkers aircraft of the 1920s (continued)

Developments at the Junkers Swedish factory included the **K 37**, a three-seat general-purpose military aircraft derived from the S 36 twin-engine transport of 1927, and one example supplied to Japan was developed as the **Mitsubishi Ki-2**; the **K 39** three-seat bomber/recon-

naissance aircraft appeared only in prototype form; and a few examples of the **K 47**, a two-seat fighter, were built in 1928 for export to China; the type was also built in civil form as the **A 48**.

The last Junkers aircraft to be designed and built before the company

adopted the Ju series of designations was the giant **G 38**, of which only two were built. Powered by four 750-hp (559-kW) Junkers Jumo 204 engines mounted at the leading edge of the 144 ft 4 in (44 m) span wing, the G 38 accommodated 26 passengers in the main

fuselage cabins, two in the fuselage nose, and three in each of two wing-root cabins. The first example to fly, on 6 November 1929, was named *Deutschland*, serving with Deutsche Luft-Hansa until it crashed during 1936. The second, *Generalfeldmarschall von*

Hindenburg, remained in use on behalf of the Luftwaffe until destroyed in an RAF bombing attack during 1940. Six similar aircraft were licence-built in Japan under the designation **Mitsubishi Ki-20**, and were intended to serve as heavy bombers with the Japanese army.

Junkers minor types of the 1930s and 1940s

The **Ju 46** floatplane, of which five were built for Deutsche Luft-Hansa in 1932 as freight- and mail-carriers, was a two-seat monoplane powered by the 650-hp (488-kW) BMW 132 engine. Next, in numerical designation, was the single-engine **Ju 52** commercial freight transport of which six were built, the first flying on 13 October 1930. The designation **Ju 60** was allocated to a six-passenger airliner of 1932, of which only four were built, but the improved **Ju 160** of 1934 was far more successful,

with almost 50 produced and more than half of them serving with Luft-Hansa. Under the designation **Ju 252** Junkers developed for Luft-Hansa a 35-passenger three-engine transport which incorporated an hydraulically-operated ventral loading door; although intended to supersede the Ju 52/3m, only 15 were built. A generally similar **Ju 352 Herkules**, of which 33 production examples were built, replaced the light-alloy construction of the Ju 252 by mixed wood and steel with fabric covering to save short-supply aluminium alloys for

Incorporating an He 177 fuselage, the Ju 287 V1 was powered by four Jumo 109-004B-1 turbojets, and made its first flight on 16 August 1944 in the hands of Siegfried Holzbauer.

the production of fighter aircraft. Finally, mention must be made of the **Ju 287**, a four-engined turbojet-powered heavy bomber with a forward-swept wing, of which only an aerodynamic test-bed prototype was flown; two production prototypes were incomplete when the war ended.

Junkers Ju 52/3m

A decision to evaluate the single-engine Ju 52 as a three-engined transport led to the seventh airframe on the production line being converted as the prototype **Ju 52/3m**, powered by three 550-hp (410-kW) Pratt & Whitney Hornet engines. When tested in April 1931, the performance of this **Ju 52/3mce** was so markedly improved in comparison with that of the single-engine version that production of the Ju 52 was terminated. The first Ju 52/3m customer was Lloyd Aero Boliviano, which received seven aircraft from 1932.

The type was available with float, ski or wheel landing gear, and Aero O/Y (Finland) and AB Aerotransport (Sweden) acquired a floatplane version, but the Ju 52/3mces supplied to Deutsche Luft-Hansa had wheeled landing gear. In this last airline's service the type quickly made a name for itself; by the end of 1935 some 97 were in airline use, including 51 with Luft-Hansa.

Evaluation of the Ju 52/3m's military potential by the clandestine Luftwaffe led to an interim bomber version, the **Ju 52/3mge** and a later improved **Ju 52/3mg3e**. These first saw action in the Spanish Civil War,

initially as troop transports ferrying some 10,000 Moorish troops from Morocco to Spain. By the time the war ended in 1939, the Ju 52/3ms had amassed some 13,000 operational hours and had dropped more than 6,000 tons of bombs. Civil production continued in

parallel, more than 230 being registered to Luft-Hansa in the mid-1930s, although some of these were no doubt passed on to the Luftwaffe, which received 450 from Junkers during 1934-5, and 593 during 1939; another 59 were commandeered from Luft-Hansa at the outbreak of World War II.

The versatility of the Ju 52/3m meant that the

SPECIFICATION

Junkers Ju 52/3mg3e
Type: medium bomber and troop transport
Powerplant: three 725-hp (541-kW) BMW 132A-3 radial piston engines
Performance: maximum speed 171 mph (275 km/h) at 2,955 ft (900 m); service ceiling 19,360 ft (5900 m); range with auxiliary fuel 808 miles (1300 km)
Weights: empty 12,610 lb (5720 kg); maximum take-off 23,149 lb (10500 kg)
Dimensions: wingspan 95 ft 11½ in (29.25 m); length 62 ft (18.90 m); height 18 ft 2½ in (5.55 m); wing area 1,189.45 sq ft (110.50 m²)
Armament: two 0.31-in (7.92-mm) MG15 machine-guns, plus up to 1,102 lb (500 kg) of bombs

Variants

Ju 52/3mg3e: military version with three 725-hp (541-kW) BMW 132-A3 engines, improved radio and bomb-release mechanism
Ju 52/3mg4e: military version; internal equipment changes from Ju 52/3mg3e and tailskid replaced by tailwheel
Ju 52/3mg5e: military version; three 830-hp (619-kW) BMW 132T engines, exhaust heat for de-icing, interchangeable float/ski/wheel landing gear and improved radio
Ju 52/3mg6e: as Ju 52/3mg5e but with simplified radio; basically land-based
Ju 52/3mg7e: as Ju 52/3mg6e but with autopilot and large loading hatch
Ju 52/3mg8e: as Ju/3mg7e but with extra cabin roof hatch; late production had improved BMW 132Z engines
Ju 52/3mg9e: as late production Ju 52/3mg8e but with strengthened landing gear; glider towing gear standard
Ju 52/3mg10e: similar to Ju 52/3mg9e but suitable for float or wheeled operations
Ju 52/3mg11e: no details known
Ju 52/3mg12e: as Ju 52/3mg10e but with three BMW 132L engines; some went to Luft-Hansa as **Ju 52/3m12**
Ju 52/3mg13e: no details known
Ju 52/3mg14e: last production version; as Ju 52/3mg9e but with improved armour protection for pilot and heavier defensive armament

Scandinavian airlines were early customers for the Ju 52/3m. One of six examples operated by DNL Norwegian Air Lines was the float-equipped LN-DAF Najaden (Naiad), acquired in 1936 for use on services in northern Norway.

This Ju 52/3mg7e served with Stab IV/Transportgeschwader 1 (formerly KGrzbV 1) on the Courland Front during winter 1944/45. At this stage in the war, the Ju 52/3ms of Stab IV/TG 1 were used for parachuting supplies to Wehrmacht forces.

German-built components was carried out by PIRT in Budapest, all but four from this source being supplied to the Hungarian air force. When production ended in mid-1944, a total approaching 5,000 had been built in France and Germany. Post-war the French built more than 400 for Air France and their air force, the latter designating the type **AAC.1 Toucan**. CASA, in Spain, built 170 for the Spanish air force under the designation **CASA 352**.

Developments of the Junkers Ju 52/3m included the **Ju 252** and the redesigned version, the **Ju 352**.

type was used extensively by the Luftwaffe throughout the war, and replacements for attrition were met by laying down a new production line at the Amiot factory in Colombes, France, the first aircraft from this source being accepted in June 1942. Assembly of 26 Ju 52/3ms from

Junkers Ju 86

The **Ju 86**, developed as a 10-passenger airliner and four-seat bomber, was designed around the Junkers Jumo 205 diesel engine. The first of five prototypes was flown during 1934, its performance proving disappointing but, nevertheless, the type entered production as both an airliner and a bomber in late 1935. Initial deliveries of **Ju 86A-1** pre-production bombers were made in February 1936 and the first **Ju 86B** pre-production

transport for Swissair was delivered in April 1936.

Five **Ju 86D-1** bombers with improved Jumo 205C engines served with the Legion Condor during the Spanish Civil War, but the powerplant did not stand up well to combat condi-

tions and the aircraft proved markedly inferior to the Heinkel He 111. Military export orders included the **Ju 86K-1** for South Africa and Sweden, where Saab subsequently licence-built the type; the **Ju 86K-2** for Hungary, which built 66; and the **Ju 86K-6** for Chile and Portugal.

Luftwaffe dissatisfaction with the capability of the Ju 86D led to the far more reliable **Ju 86E-1** with BMW 132P radial engines and the **Ju 86E-2** with BMW 132Ns; improvements introduced during production brought the redesignation of the last 40 Ju 86Es on the production line as **Ju 86G-1** aircraft, with round glazed noses; production ended in 1938. However, in 1939, two Ju 86D airframes were used for conversion as the Jumo 207A-engined prototypes of a high-altitude version with a two-seat pressure cabin. Successful

A Gnome-Rhône-powered Ju 86K-2 of the Hungarian 4th Bomber Regiment during operations under the control of Löhr's Luftflotte IV in the Soviet Union during spring 1942.

Variants

Ju 86abl: first prototype; bomber, powered originally by Siemens AM 9 radials
Ju 96bal: second prototype; transport, with Jumo 205C diesel engines
Ju 86cb: third prototype; bomber, as Ju 86abl, powered later by Jumo 205C engines
Ju 86 V4: production prototype for commercial **Ju 86B**
Ju 86 V5: production prototype for **Ju 86A** bomber
Ju 86A-0: 13 pre-production bombers
Ju 86B-0: seven pre-production transports
Ju 86C-1: six Luft-Hansa transports with Jumo 205C diesels
Ju 86E-1: Luftwaffe bombers with BMW 132F radials
Ju 86E-2: uprated version of Ju 86E-1
Ju 86K-4: as Ju 86K-1 but with Bristol Pegasus III radial engines for Sweden (**B 3A**)
Ju 86K-5: as Ju 86K-4 but with Swedish-built Pegasus XII engines (**B 3B**)
Ju 86K-13: Swedish-built bombers with Swedish- and Polish-built Pegasus engines

SPECIFICATION	
Junkers Ju 86D-1	(5150 kg); maximum take-off
Type: four-seat medium bomber	18,078 lb (8200 kg)
Powerplant: two 600-hp (447-kW) Junkers Jumo 205C-4 diesel engines	**Dimensions:** wingspan 73 ft 9¾ in (22.50 m); length 58 ft 7½ in (17.87 m); height 16 ft 7¼ in (5.06 m); wing area 882.67 sq ft (82.00 m²)
Performance: maximum speed 202 mph (325 km/h) at 9,840 ft (3000 m); service ceiling 19,360 ft (5900 m); maximum range 932 miles (1500 km)	**Armament:** three 0.31-in (7.92-mm) machine-guns, plus a bombload of up to 1,764 lb (800 kg) carried internally
Weights: empty 11,354 lb	

trials led to two initial production versions, the **Ju 86P-1** bomber and **Ju 86P-2** reconnaissance aircraft. The latter had a ceiling of about 42,000 ft (128000 m), and in an effort to gain more altitude a high aspect ratio wing spanning 104 ft 11¾ in (32 m) was introduced to produce the **Ju 86R-1** reconnaissance aircraft and **Ju 86R-2** bomber. Only a

few reached service, but one demonstrated a ceiling of 47,250 ft (14400 m). Development of the **Ju 86R-3** with supercharged Jumo 208 engines and of the proposed **Ju 186** four-engined high-altitude bomber based on the Ju 86 was abandoned. A six-engine **Ju 286** high-altitude bomber did not progress beyond the initial planning stage.

Junkers Ju 87

The reputation of the **Ju 87 'Stuka'** (from the German Sturzkampfflugzeug, or dive-bomber) was made during the Polish campaign and in close-support operations across Europe. The Luftwaffe believed it to be virtually invincible, but this was true only after air superiority had been gained, as demonstrated during the Battle of Britain when the Stukas were mauled so severely by the RAF that they were later

withdrawn from operations over western Europe.

Three prototypes were started in 1934, the first with twin vertical tail surfaces and powered by a Rolls-Royce Kestrel engine. During dive tests in 1935 the tail unit of this aircraft collapsed and the aircraft was destroyed. The second prototype introduced a single fin and rudder and was powered by a 610-hp (455-kW) Junkers Jumo 210A, and official evalua-

tion of this aircraft and a further improved third prototype led to a pre-production batch of 10 **Ju 87A-0** aircraft with the 640-hp (477-kW) Jumo 210Ca engine. The initial **Ju 87A-1** production version began to replace Hs 123 biplanes in the spring of 1937, and three were tested under operational conditions by the Legion Condor during the Spanish Civil War. At the beginning of World War II the Luftwaffe had 336 **Ju 87B** dive-bombers on strength.

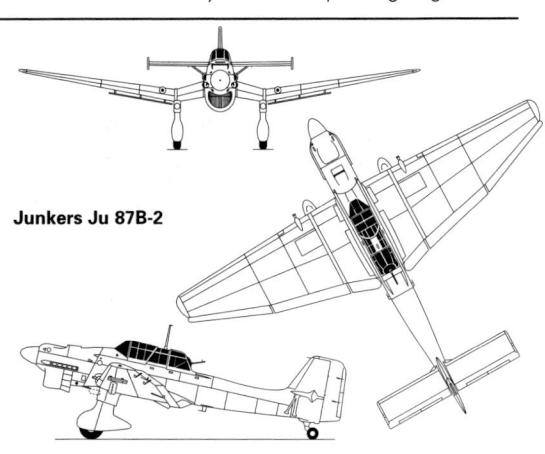

Junkers Ju 87B-2

Junkers Ju 87 (continued)

Other Ju 87Bs were supplied to Italy, which named them **Picchiatello**, Bulgaria, Hungary and Romania. Ju 87s were deployed extensively on the Eastern Front, initially with great success, but by 1943 they were suffering such severe losses by daylight that they were switched to a night assault role. When production ended more than 5,700 had been built, the majority after 1940 when their vulnerability without adequate fighter cover had been highlighted in the Battle of Britain, and one can only assume that production continued because no better replacement was available. A redesigned and improved

Armed with a BK 3.7 37-mm cannon under each wing, the Ju 87G was a formidable tank buster. This aircraft served with 10.(Pz)/Schlactgeschwader 3 at Jakobstadt in Latvia during 1944. Ju 87Gs served with seven Staffeln, including all three of III./SG 2.

Ju 187 was projected in 1943, but following consideration of the design no examples were built.

SPECIFICATION

Junkers Ju 87D-1
Type: two-seat dive-bomber/assault aircraft
Powerplant: one 1,410-hp (1051-kW) Junkers Jumo 211J-1 12-cylinder inverted-Vee piston engine
Performance: maximum speed 255 mph (410 km/h) at 12,600 ft (3840 m); service ceiling 23,915 ft (7290 m); maximum range 954 miles (1535 km)
Weights: empty equipped 8,598 lb (3900 kg); maximum take-off 14,550 lb (6600 kg)
Dimensions: wingspan 45 ft 3½ in (13.80 m); length 37 ft 8¾ in (11.50 m); height 12 ft 9½ in (3.90 m); wing area 343.38 sq ft (31.90 m²)
Armament: two 0.31-in (7.92-mm) MG 17 machine-guns in the wings and two similar-calibre MG 81Z guns in the rear cockpit, plus up to 1800 kg (3,968 lb) of bombs beneath the fuselage, or various alternative underfuselage/underwing loads

Variants

Ju 87A-2: production version with supercharged 680-hp (507-kW) Jumo 210Da engine
Ju 87 V-7: prototype for Ju 87B series with 1,000-hp (746-kW) Jumo 211A engine
Ju 87B-0: pre-production batch for Ju 87B series
Ju 87B-1: production version with redesigned fuselage, streamlined wheel spats, 1,200-hp (895-kW) Jumo 211Da engine and maximum bombload of 1,102 lb (500 kg)
Ju 87B-2: improved production version with maximum bombload of 2,200 lb (1000 kg)
Ju 87C-1: intended production version with jettisonable landing gear, folding wings and arrester hook for service with aircraft carrier *Graf Zeppelin*; the carrier was never completed and aircraft on the production line were finished instead as Ju 87B-2s

Ju 87D-1: generally improved production version with 1,410-hp (1051-kW) Jumo 211J-1 engine and increased armour protection for the crew
Ju 87D-2: strengthened Ju 87D-1 with glider-tow hook
Ju 87D-3: ground-attack version of Ju 87D-1 with increased armour
Ju 87D-4: proposed torpedo bomber version
Ju 87D-5: dedicated close-support version with jettisonable landing gear and no dive brakes
Ju 87D-7: night ground-attack model converted from Ju 87D-3 and D-5; 1,500-hp (1119-kW) Jumo 211P; wing-mounted machine-guns replaced by 20-mm MG 151/20 cannon
Ju 87D-8: day version of Ju 87D-7 without night-flying equipment and flame-dampers
Ju 87F: projected version with extensively revised airframe, increased-span wing and more powerful engine; the considerable changes eventually brought redesignation as Ju 187, but this remained a project only
Ju 87G-1: final operational version, a tank-busting conversion of the Ju 87D-5 with a 37-mm cannon beneath each wing
Ju 87H series: dual-control trainer conversions of Ju 87D airframes
Ju 87R series: long-range anti shipping versions of the Ju 87B with extra fuel, and provision for one 551-lb (250-kg) bomb

Junkers Ju 88

Certainly the most versatile German warplane of World War II, the **Ju 88** in progressively improved versions continued in production throughout the war. It was originated to meet a requirement for a three-seat high-speed bomber and the first prototype, powered by two 1,000-hp (746-kW) Daimler DB 600Aa engines, made its initial flight on 21 December 1936. Further prototypes followed, the third with 1,000-hp (746-kW) Jumo engines and this, during evaluation, attained a speed of 323 mph (520 km/h). Such high performance encouraged record-breaking attempts, and in March 1939 the fifth prototype set a 1,000-km (621-mile) closed-circuit record of 321.25 mph (517 km/h) carrying a 4,409-lb (2000-kg) payload. A total of 10 prototypes was completed, and the first of the pre-production **Ju 88A-0** bombers flew in early 1939, the initial **Ju 88A-1** production version entering service in September 1939.

This Ju 88A-14 most likely served with Stab II Gruppe/Zerstörergeschwader 1 at Mamaia, Rumania in April 1944. Basically an improved Ju 88A-4, the A-14 typically featured a 20-mm cannon in its undernose gondola for use against shipping.

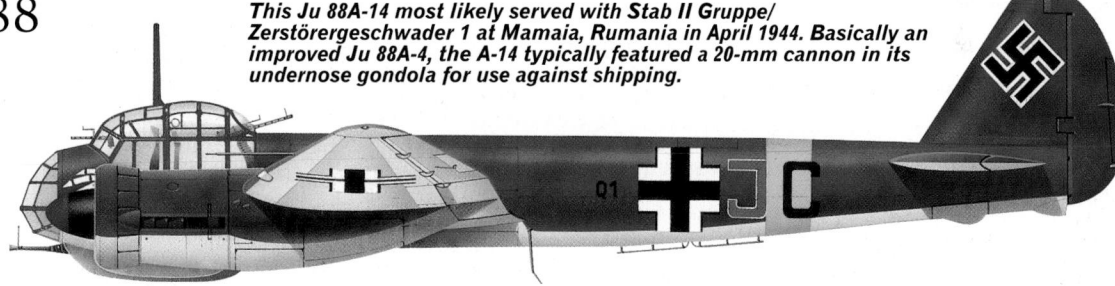

Early operational deployment showed that despite good performance and a worthwhile bombload, defensive armament was totally inadequate, leading to the **Ju 88A-4** with increased span wings, structural strengthening to

carry greater loads and gunpower increased substantially. This formed the basis for further diverse development of the type in numerous versions. The Ju 88A series for example extended over Ju 88A-1 to **Ju 88A-17** sub-variants.

SPECIFICATION

Junkers Ju 88A-4
Type: four-seat bomber/dive bomber
Powerplant: two 1,350-hp (1007-kW) Junkers Jumo 211J-1 12-cylinder inverted-Vee piston engines
Performance: maximum speed 292 mph (470 km/h) at 17,390 ft (5300 m); service ceiling 26,900 ft (8200 m); maximum range 1,696 miles (2730 km)
Weights: empty equipped 21,737 lb (9860 kg); maximum

take-off 30,865 lb (1400 kg)
Dimensions: wingspan 65 ft 7½ in (20.00 m); length 47 ft 2¾ in (14.40 m); height 15 ft 11 in (4.85 m); wing area 586.65 sq ft (54.50 m²)
Armament: one forward-firing 0.51-in (13-mm) MG 131 or two 0.31-in (7.92-mm) MG 81 machine-guns, two similar guns in the rear of the cockpit firing aft and two firing aft below the fuselage, plus up to 4,409 lb (2000 kg) of bombs carried internally and externally

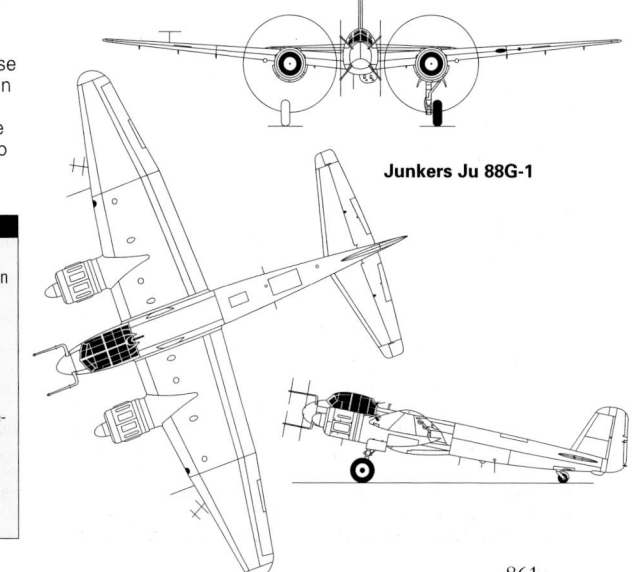

Junkers Ju 88G-1

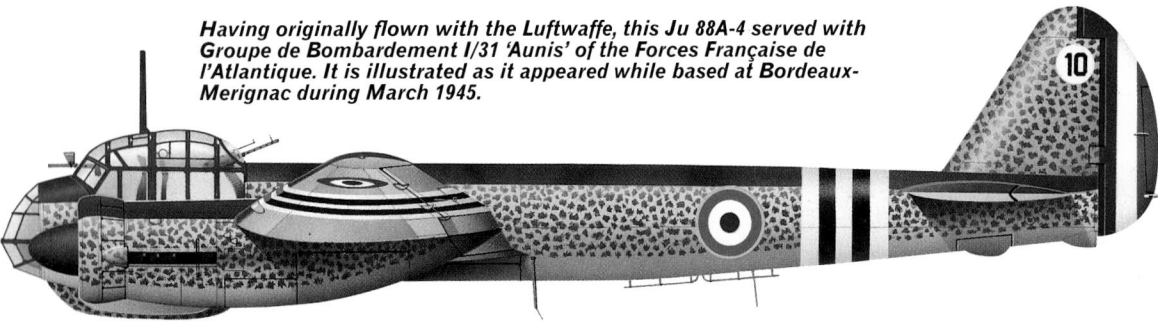

Having originally flown with the Luftwaffe, this Ju 88A-4 served with Groupe de Bombardement I/31 'Aunis' of the Forces Française de l'Atlantique. It is illustrated as it appeared while based at Bordeaux-Merignac during March 1945.

One of the more unusual uses to which the Ju 88 was put was as the lower half of the Mistel composite weapons. Here the Ju 88 has the glazed nose of a trainer rather than the normal warhead.

While the Ju 88A was in production an improved **Ju 88B** was planned, with a more extensively glazed nose and power provided by two 1,600-hp (1193-kW) BMW 801MA radials, but flight testing showed only marginal performance improvement and only 10 pre-production **Ju 88B-0** aircraft were built.

The Ju 88 was almost as fast as contemporary fighters, and such performance coupled with excellent manoeuvrability brought development of the **Ju 88C** series. The planned **Ju 88C-1** with BMW 801MA engines was abandoned because the new Fw 190 had priority for this powerplant. As a result the first production version was the **Ju 88C-2**, this being the Ju 88A-1 converted on the production line to have a solid nose mounting three 0.31-in (7.92-mm) MG 17 machine-guns and a 20-mm MG FF cannon. Defensive armament comprised two additional 0.31-in (7.92-mm) MG 15 machine-guns. The **Ju 88C-4** was a heavy fighter/reconnaissance model, the **Ju 88C-5** an improved heavy fighter, the **Ju 88C-6a** an improved **Ju 88C-5**, the **Ju 88C-6b** and **Ju 88C-6c** night-fighters, the **Ju 88C-7a** and **Ju 88C-7b** intruders, and the **Ju 88C-7c** a heavy fighter. Alphabetically out of sequence were the **Ju 88R-1** and **Ju 88R-2** night-fighters, which were developed and powered by BMW 801MA engines when the supply position of this powerplant eased.

The **Ju 88D** series were long-range reconnaissance aircraft based on the Ju 88A-4, in **Ju 88D-1** to **Ju 88D-5** variants that differed in engines and detail. The **Ju 88G** series represented definitive night-fighter versions that from the early summer of 1944 replaced the earlier Ju 88C and Ju 88R aircraft. Equipped with airborne interception radar and bristling with weapons, the Ju 88Gs were extremely formidable night-fighters, taking a heavy toll of Allied night bombers. They were followed by small numbers of **Ju 88H** aircraft which had a lengthened fuselage to provide increased internal fuel capacity, providing extra long-range **Ju 88H-1** reconnaissance and **Ju 88H-2** fighter aircraft. The tank-busting **Ju 88P** was developed from the Ju 88A-4, and was followed by the **Ju 88P-1** with a 75-mm PaK 40 cannon and the ensuing **Ju 88P-2** to **Ju 88P-4** with different combinations of heavy anti-tank weapons. The increasing capability of Allied fighters meant that losses began to rise, leading to the higher-performance **Ju 88S** bomber and **Ju 88T** photo-reconnaissance aircraft that represented the final production versions. When production ended almost 15,000 Ju 88s had been built, this total emphasising the significant role that the aircraft had played in Luftwaffe operations.

Junkers Ju 90, 290 and 390

In A-5 form the Ju 290 boasted armour protection, fuel-dumping systems and heavier armament. This example flew with FAGr 5 at Mont-de-Marsan.

In 1936 Junkers had under construction three prototypes of the **Ju 89** four-engined bomber, but the programme was cancelled during 1937 after the first prototype had flown. With no military interest in the design Junkers developed a civil version designated **Ju 90** of which four prototypes were built, followed by 10 pre-production **Ju 90B-1** aircraft equipped as 38/40-seat airliners. Eight of these entered service with Deutsche Luft-Hansa, the remaining two being ordered by South African Airways but never delivered. Design of an improved **Ju 90S** version was initiated in 1937, this incorporating a new wing and a ventral loading ramp; it was intended to power the type with BMW 139 engines. When these failed to materialise, the BMW 801 was used instead, and the designation was changed to **Ju 290**.

Production of these large aircraft totalled between 60 and 70. Two pre-production **Ju 290A-0** machines were followed by the **Ju 290A-1** armed transport, and the designations **Ju 290A-2** to **Ju 290A-9** covered various reconnaissance and maritime reconnaissance roles, except for the **Ju 290A-6** which was a 50-passenger transport and the **Ju 290A-1** (about 12 built) which was a reconnaissance/bomber version able to deploy early anti-ship missiles.

The **Ju 290B-1** was the last of the line to be built, a single prototype of this long-range high-altitude heavy bomber being flown during 1944. The ultimate development was the **Ju 390**, a scaled-up Ju 290 of 181 ft 7¼ in (55.35 m) wing span powered by six 1,700-hp (1268-kW) BMW 8011) engines. Two prototypes were built and tested in 1943; during the evaluation programme the second of these was flown from an airfield near Bordeaux to within about 12 miles (19 km) of the US coast north of New York before returning to France, proof that the specification for a bomber being able to attack New York from European bases could have been met, but the scheme progressed no further.

SPECIFICATION	
Junkers Ju 290A-7	101,413 lb (46000 kg)
Type: long-range maritime reconnaissance/bomber aircraft	**Dimensions:** wingspan 137 ft 9½ in (42.00 m); length 95 ft 7¾ in (29.15 m); height 22 ft 4¾ in (6.83 m); wing area 2,191.60 sq ft (203.60 m²)
Powerplant: four 1,700-hp (1268-kW) BMW 801D radial piston engines	
Performance: maximum speed 273 mph (440 km/h) at 19,030 ft (5800 m); service ceiling 19,685 ft (6000 m); range 3,784 miles (6090 km)	**Armament:** seven 20-mm MG 151 cannon and one 0.51-in (13-mm) MG 131 machine-gun, plus a bombload of up to 6,614 lb (3000 kg), or three Henschel Hs 293, or Hs 294 or FX-1400 Fritz-X missiles
Weights: empty 72,764 lb (33005 kg); maximum take-off	

Junkers Ju 188

The design of a **Ju 288** successor to the Ju 88 was well advanced at the outbreak of World War 2, but by 1942 it was clear that this would be late in entering service and a stop-gap design was needed urgently to update the Ju 88. During 1940 Junkers had flown the prototype of the Ju 88B, which incorporated a new enlarged forward fuselage and increased-span wings. The later **Ju 88E-0** development of this version was used as the basis for the new **Ju 188**.

Junkers Ju 188 (continued)

The **Ju 188 V1** and **Ju 188 V2** prototypes were flown in early 1942 and 1943 respectively, and following successful testing the type was ordered into production. A stipulation of the contract was that the airframe must be suitable, without modification, for the installation of either BMW 801 or Jumo 213 engines to ensure continuity of production. The initial production version was the **Ju 188E-1**, with 1,600-hp (1193-kW) BMW 801ML engines, which entered service in February 1943; 283 of this version had

been delivered by the end of the year. The first Junkers-engined version

was the **Ju 188A-2**, with two Jumo 213A-1 engines that each developed 2,240 hp (1670 kW) for take off with water/ methanol injection.

Total production of all Ju 188 variants exceeded 1,000 aircraft, more than half of them being for use in a reconnaissance role.

This view of a Ju 188E allows a useful appreciation of the type's revised nose contours when compared to the Ju 88.

Variants included the **Ju 188A-2** bomber and **Ju188A-3** torpedo-bomber; **Ju 188D-1** and **Ju 188D-2** reconnaissance aircraft; **Ju 188E-1** bomber and **Ju 188E-2** torpedo-bomber;

Ju 188F-2 reconnaissance aircraft: and **Ju 188S-1** high-altitude intruder and **Ju 188T-1** high-altitude reconnaissance versions, both without defensive armament.

SPECIFICATION

Junkers Ju 188E-1
Type: four-seat medium bomber
Powerplant: two 1,700-hp (1268-kW) BMW 801D-2 radial piston engines
Performance: maximum speed 310 mph (500 km/h) at 19,685 ft (6000 m); service ceiling 30,660 ft (9345 m); range 1,209 miles (1945 km)
Weights: empty equipped 21,737 lb (9860 kg); maximum take-off 31,989 lb (9750 kg)
Dimensions: wingspan 72 ft 2 in (22.00 m); length 49 ft ½ in (14.95 m); height 14 ft 7 in (4.44 m); wing area 602.80 sq ft (56 m²)
Armament: one forward-firing 20-mm MG 151 cannon in nose, a single 0.51-in (13-mm) MG 131 in dorsal turret and at the rear of the cockpit canopy, and one 0.31-in (7.92-mm) MG 18 machine-gun in lower front fuselage firing aft, plus a maximum bombload of 6,614 lb (3000 kg)

Junkers Ju 188E-2

Junkers Ju 388

The failure of the Junkers Ju 288, brought about primarily by technical problems and continual requests by the RLM for design changes, left a gap in the programme for a high-speed long-range bomber. Fortunately,

Junkers had initiated development of high altitude versions of the Ju 188 and three of these, designated **Ju 188J**, **Ju 188K** and **Ju 188L** became respectively the **Ju 388J** all-weather fighter, **Ju 388K** bomber and **Ju 388L**

photo-reconnaissance aircraft.

High-altitude reconnaissance had the highest priority, and the first prototype was a Ju 388L converted from a Ju 188T; the pre-production batch which followed was converted from Ju 88S airframes, the first of them being handed over to the Luftwaffe in August 1944. By the time production was terminated in December 1944, 47 Ju 388Ls had been built, but the other variants were less fortunate; only three Ju 388J

prototypes were completed, and bomber construction totalled 10 pre-production **Ju 388K-O** and five production **Ju 388K-1** aircraft.

A final attempt was made to develop a heavy strategic bomber, and the construction of major sections of a **Ju 488** hybrid that would have combined assemblies of the Ju 88, Ju 188, Ju 288 and Ju 388

was started in France at the former factory of Latécoère at Toulouse. The two fuselages and wing centre sections were ready for delivery to Germany for final assembly in July 1944, but were damaged beyond repair by sabotage on the night of 16/17 July. Work on development prototypes of a redesigned **Ju 488A** was started but cancelled in November 1944.

SPECIFICATION

Junkers Ju 388L-1
Type: three-seat high-altitude photo-reconnaissance aircraft
Powerplant: two 1,890-hp (1409-kW) BMW 801TJ radial piston engines
Performance: maximum speed 382 mph (615 km/h) at 40,305 ft (12285 m), or 407 mph (655 km/h) at 29,790 ft (9080 m) with water/ methanol boost; service ceiling 44,095 ft (13440 m); maximum range with auxiliary fuel

2,159 miles (3475 km)
Weights: empty 22,601 lb (10252 kg); maximum take-off 32,353 lb (14675 kg)
Dimensions: wingspan 72 ft 2 in (22 m); length 49 ft 10½ in (15.20 m); height 14 ft 3¼ in (4.35 m); wing area 602.80 sq ft (56 m²)
Armament: one remotely-controlled tail barbette with two 0.51-in (13-mm) MG 131 machine-guns

This Ju 388 was tested post-war in the United States. The type managed to complete just a few reconnaissance sorties during World War II, but saw no combat.

Junkers W 33 and W 34

The **W 33** transport aircraft of 1926 was a cantilever low-wing monoplane derived from the F 13 of 1919, and an F 13 airframe served as the prototype. Intended for use as a

cargo/mail transport, the W 33 could also have six seats installed in the cabin if required for use as an airliner. The pilot, or pilot navigator, were seated side-by-side in a separate

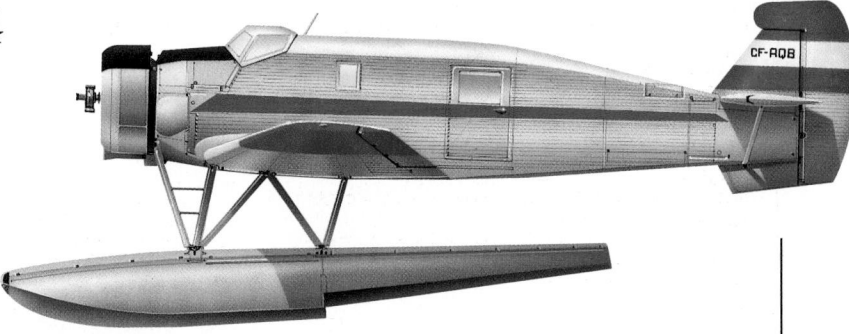

SPECIFICATION

Junkers W 34h
Type: transport and communications aircraft
Powerplant: one 660-hp (492-kW) BMW 132 radial piston engine
Performance: maximum speed 165 mph (265 km/h); service ceiling 20,670 ft (6300 m); normal range 560 miles (900 km)

Weights: empty 3,748 lb (1700 kg); maximum take-off 7,055 lb (3,200 kg)
Dimensions: wingspan 58 ft 2¾ in (17.75 m); length 33 ft 8½ in (10.27 m); height 11 ft 7 in (3.53 m); wing area 462.85 sq ft (43 m²)

Drawing much from the illustrious F 13, the W 33/34 series retained all the rugged reliability of its predecessor. The series was popular in Canada, where it was suited admirably to that country's harsh operating conditions. A float-equipped W 34 is illustrated.

cockpit. The designation W 33 applied to the aircraft as powered by an inline engine, usually the Junkers L-5, but the designation changed to **W 34** with the installation of a radial engine. The type was available with wheel or float landing gear. A total of 199 W 33s was built, and both W 33s and W 34s were used in considerable numbers for civil purposes. W 34s saw extensive service with the Luftwaffe from its formation until the end of World War II, being used primarily as navigation trainers and transports. Principal versions in Luftwaffe service were the **W 34hi** with a 660-hp (492-kW) BMW 132A radial, or **W 34hau** with the 650-hp (485-kW) Bramo 322 engine. A three-seat bomber/reconnaissance version of the W 34 was developed by Junkers' Swedish factory under the designation **K 43**, examples being exported to Colombia and Finland. A combined total of nearly 1,800 W 34 and K 43 aircraft was produced by the German and Swedish factories.

Kalinin aircraft

One of the most successful of the early Soviet designers, Konstantin Alexeivich Kalinin built his first transport monoplane in 1925. Designated **Kalinin K-1**, this was a strut-braced monoplane with a high-set wing of elliptical planform, a feature which became typical of Kalinin designs. Powered by a 160-hp (119-kW) Salmson RB-9 engine, the K-1 had a maximum speed of 100 mph (161 km/h) and accommodated a pilot in an open cockpit forward of the wing, with an enclosed cabin behind him for three passengers. A small number of K-1s was introduced on the Moscow-Nizhne Novgorod route.

The **K-2** which also appeared in 1925 was similar to the K-1 except that it had a 240-hp (179-kW) BMW IV engine and accommodated four passengers, and the **K-3**, developed from the K-2, had provision for three stretcher cases. The six-passenger **K-4** was produced in 1928 and 22 were built at Kharkov, entering service on the routes operated by the Soviet Dobrolet and Ukrainian Ukrvozdukliput. The prototype and most of the production aircraft retained the BMW IV engine, but alternative powerplants included the Junkers L-5 and the 300-hp (224-kW) Soviet M-6. An ambulance variant had the latter engine and accommodated two stretcher cases with access via a rectangular door in the starboard side of the aircraft aft of the cabin.

The **K-5**, which was Kalinin's outstanding design, had an enclosed two-seat crew cabin forward of the wing leading edge and an eight-seat passenger cabin. Production was an impressive 260, terminating in 1934, and installed powerplants included the 450-hp (335-kW) M-15 (Bristol Jupiter built under licence), 480-hp (358-kW) M-22 intro-

duced in 1931, and the M-17F of 730-hp (544-kW) in final series aircraft. Widely used on passenger services within the Soviet Union, some K-5s were still flying in 1940. The **K-6**, a two-crew parasol-wing postal monoplane developed from the K-5, did not enter production.

Kalinin's most remarkable design was the **K-7**, a super-heavy bomber with a crew of 11, which flew for the first time on 11 August 1933. Powered by six 750-hp (559-kW) M-34F engines, it had a huge elliptical wing from which projected the crew nacelle, with a pilots' and navigator's cabin, a nose gunner's cockpit, and a bomb aimer's post below. The twin fin and rudder tail assembly was carried on two tailbooms, at

Kalinin originally designed the K-7 as an airliner with accommodation for 120 passengers in the wings. In the event, the K-7 was built as a bomber.

the extremities of which were additional gunners' positions, and two gondolas suspended from the wings housed the multi-wheel landing gear, bomb bays and two more gunner's cockpits. Armament was Six 0.3-in (7.62-mm) ShKAS machine-guns and up to 19,841 lb (9000 kg) of bombs. On 21 November 1933 one tail-boom collapsed in flight and the K-7 crashed; plans to build two further bombers and a 120-passenger transport were abandoned.

Kalinin reverted to two-seat light sportsplane/ trainer types with his next two designs, the **K-9** parasol-wing monoplane powered by a 60-hp (45-kW)

Czech Walter engine, and the **K-10** low-wing monoplane with a 100-hp (75-kW) M-11 powerplant. Neither progressed beyond the prototype stage.

The **K-12**, known alternatively as the **BS-2** or **'Zhar Ptitsa'**, was a reduced-scale aerodynamic prototype for a full-sized bomber. Powered by two 480-hp (358-kW) M-22 radial engines, the K-12 flew quite well but construction of a full-scale version of the K-12 and of a new bomber, the twin-engine **K-13**, was abandoned when Kalinin was arrested and shot in the 1938 purge in the Soviet Union and his bureau was dissolved.

Kaman H-43 Huskie

Charles H. Kaman established the Kaman Aircraft Corporation in December 1945 to manufacture a new helicopter rotor and control system of his own design. Development of the basic intermeshing rotor system and its servo flap control was completed in late 1946 and the first experimental **Kaman K-125A** helicopter was flown on 15 January 1947. From it was evolved first the **K-190**, flown in 1948, and then the **K-225** three-seat utility helicopter; two examples of the K-225 were acquired by the US Navy in 1950. Used for evaluation purposes, they led to an initial contract for 29 **HTK-1** trainers which, in 1962, were redesignated **TH-43E**. Contemporary with production of the HTK-1, Kaman developed the **K-600**, ordered for service with the US Marine Corps and US Navy under the respective designations **HOK-1** and **RUK-1**; these

were redesignated **UH-43C** and **OH-43D** in 1962. Eighteen aircraft similar to the US Navy's HUK-1s were also acquired by the US Air Force under the designation **H-43A Huskie**.

One HOK-1 was flown as a testbed aircraft with an Avco Lycoming XT53 turboshaft engine, and service testing confirmed the considerable performance improvement offered by this powerplant. This led to the **H-43B**, first flown on 13 December 1958, which became the major production version of the Huskie with a total of 193 built.

SPECIFICATION	
Kaman HH-43F Huskie	
Type: search-and-rescue helicopter	range 500 miles (810 km)
Powerplant: one 825-shp (615-kW) Lycoming T53-L-11A turboshaft	**Weights:** empty 4,619 lb (2095 kg); loaded 6,504 lb (2950 kg)
Performance: maximum speed 120 mph (193 km/h); climb rate 1,800 ft (549 m) minute; service ceiling 23,000 ft (7010 m); combat	**Dimensions:** rotor diameter 47 ft (14.33 m); length 25 ft 2 in (7.67 m); height 15 ft 6½ in (4.73 m) **Armament:** one 0.30-in (7.62-mm) flexible machine-gun

Some 31 H-43B Huskies were supplied under the US Military Assistance Program to Burma (12), Colombia (6), Morocco (4), Pakistan (6) and Thailand (3). This aircraft served with the air force of Pakistan.

Kaman H-43 Huskie (continued)

Slightly larger than the H-43A (later **HH-43A**), the H-43B (later **HH-43B**) had a cabin seating up to eight passengers and was powered by an 825-shp

(615-kW) T53-L-1B. Final production version was the **HH-43F** (40 built for the USAF and 17 for Iran). Generally similar to the HH-43B, except for internal

rearrangement to seat 11 passengers, this last version of the Huskie had a 1,150-shp (858-kW) T53-L-11A derated to 825 shp (615 kW) for

improved performance in 'hot-and-high' conditions.
An interesting variant of the Huskie family was a conversion of one of the K-225s. Under a USN contract, Kaman installed a

175-shp (130-kW) Boeing YT50 gas turbine engine. When first flown with this powerplant on 10 December 1951, this was the first helicopter to have its rotors so powered.

Kaman H-2 Seasprite and Super Seasprite

Designated **K-20** by Kaman, the **H-2 Seasprite** was conceived in response to a 1956 USN requirement for a high-speed, all-weather, long-range SAR, liaison and utility helicopter. The first of four **YHU2K-1** (from 1962 **YUH-2A**) service test prototypes made its maiden flight on 2 July 1959 with one 875-hp (652-kW) General Electric T58-GE-6 turboshaft, and the type entered production as the **HU2K-1**, of which 84 were delivered with the 1,250-shp (932-kW) T58-GE-8 engine and redesignated as **UH-2A** in 1962. Later variants were progressively improved and updated, gaining a second engine (for a greater safety margin for ship-based operations), dual mainwheels and a four-bladed tail rotor, but retained their liaison, utility, SAR and combat rescue roles. Manufacture stopped after the delivery of the last **UH-2B**, bringing production to a total of 190 helicopters that were all originally of the single-engined type.

The helicopter was first used in the anti-submarine role in October 1970, when the USN selected the **SH-2D** as an interim LAMPS I (Light Airborne Multi-Purpose System Mk I) platform. Externally, the SH-2D introduced an undernose radome housing a Litton LN-66 search radar, with an ASQ-81 MAD on

This US Navy SH-2F Seasprite is finished in low-visibility colours. Note that the aircraft has had its undernose radome removed.

the starboard fuselage pylon and a removable sonobuoy rack in the port side of the fuselage. Twenty were produced as conversions from **HH-2D** armed SAR standard, entering service in 1972. Deliveries of the definitive **SH-2F**, which also bore the LAMPS I designation, began in May 1973. The primary role of the SH-2F was the generation of a major extension of the protected area provided by the outer defensive screen of a carrier battle group. It introduced 1,350-shp (1007-kW) T58-GE-8F engines, an improved main rotor, and strengthened landing gear including a tail-wheel relocated almost 6 ft (1.83 m) farther forward. The SH-2F also featured an improved Marconi LN-66HP surface search radar, ASQ-81(V)2 towed MAD bird and a tactical navigation and communications system, these changes necessitating the accommodation of a sensor operator. Offensive capability comprised two Mk 46 torpedoes. Some 88 machines were converted from earlier variants, and 16 surviving SH-2Ds were also brought up to the

same standard.
Despite its failure to be selected as the LAMPS III platform, the Seasprite was retained for service on board several classes of USN warships. Accordingly, the helicopter was reinstated in production during 1981, when the USN placed an order for the first batch of an eventual 60 new-build SH-2Fs. Many of these, as well as some SH-2Fs, received the ALR-66A(V)1 RWR and

This overall semi-gloss dark grey scheme was most commonly associated with the SH-2F. Note the yellow and red MAD bird.

ALE-39 chaff/flare dispenser. From 1987 some 16 SH-2Fs received a package of modifications to allow them to operate in the Persian Gulf. This included the provision of an AAQ-16 FLIR under the nose, an ALQ-144 IR jammer, AAR-47 and DLQ-8 missile warning and jamming equipment, and

new radios. During the 1991 Gulf War, the SH-2F tested the ML-30 Magic Lantern laser sub-surface mine detector. The SH-2F has been retired from USN service, but has been ordered by Pakistan (six helicopters whose delivery was halted by embargo), and was also offered to Egypt, Greece, Portugal, South Korea,

New Zealand's SH-2G(NZ)s and Australia's similar SH-2G(A)s (pictured) will equip new 'ANZAC-class frigates from 2000 and 2001, respectively.

SPECIFICATION

Kaman SH-2G Super Seasprite
Type: three-crew shipborne anti-submarine, missile defence, SAR and utility helicopter
Powerplant: two General Electric T700-GE-401/401C turboshaft engines each rated at 1,723 shp (1285 kW)
Performance: maximum speed 159 mph (256 km/h) at sea level; cruising speed 138 mph (222 km/h) at optimum altitude; initial climb rate 2,500 ft (762 m) per minute; service ceiling 23,900 ft (7285 m); hovering ceiling 20,800 ft (6340 m) in ground effect and 18,000 ft (5485 m) out of ground effect; range 500 miles (885 km) with auxiliary fuel; radius 40 miles (65 km) for a patrol of 2 hours 10 minutes with one torpedo
Weights: empty 7,680 lb (3483 kg); maximum take-off

13,500 lb (6123 kg)
Dimensions: main rotor diameter 44 ft 4 in (13.51 m); length overall 52 ft 9 in (16.08 m) with rotors turning; height 15 ft ½ in (4.58 m) with rotors turning; main rotor disc area 1,543.66 sq ft (143.41 m²)
Armament: provision for two 0.3-in (7.62-mm) M60 trainable lateral-firing machine-guns on optional pintle mounts in the cabin doors, plus up to 1,600 lb (726 kg) of disposable stores carried on two fuselage hardpoints, and generally comprising one or two Mk 46 or Mk 50 Barracuda torpedoes
Payload: (with sonobuoy system removed) provision for up to four passengers, or two litters or freight carried in the cabin, or 4,000 lb (1814 kg) of freight carried as a slung load

Taiwan and Thailand.

Continued development of the Seasprite resulted in the appearance of the **SH-2G Super Seasprite**. The prototype **YSH-2G**, which first flew on 2 April 1985, was simply a conversion of an SH-2F and served as a test bed for the General Electric T700 engine. This was the main modification from SH-2F standard. The new power-plant delivers approximately 10 per cent more power, with commensurate performance benefits and 20 per cent lower fuel burn, as well as improved reliability and maintainability. In addi-

tion, new composite main rotor blades with a service life of 10,000 hours are fitted. Avionics improvements are based on a digital databus and include the UYS-503 onboard acoustic processor, ASN-150 tactical management system and multi-function displays. The SH-2G is also qualified for dipping sonar operations, ASM firing, the use of FLIR sensors, rockets and countermeasures.

The new type entered service in 1991 in the form of six new-build helicopters and a planned 97 examples converted from SH-2F stan-

dard, but in the event the end of the Cold War reduced the USN's requirement and only 17 further 'production' conversions were effected. The Navy upgraded its in-service SH-2Gs with the improved defensive features of the SH-2Fs operated in the Persian Gulf, together with the Magic Lantern-30 laser system. Kaman is also marketing rebuilds of up to 72 SH-2F helicopters now surplus to USN requirements. A moderately early customer for such helicopters was Egypt, which ordered a total of 10 **SH-2G(E)** helicopters that

were delivered from October 1997. In June 1997 the Royal Australian Navy and Royal New Zealand Navy, which are each receiving examples of the new 'ANZAC'-class multirole frigate, contracted with Kaman for the delivery of 11 and four SH-2Gs rebuilt to an improved standard from SH-2F airframes: as well as the standard upgrade, these helicopters have an advanced 'glass' cockpit and a digital mission suite including the ASN-150 tactical management system, allowing the two-man crew to fly the type as well as to undertake the

management of the entire mission equipment suite, as well as provision for anti-ship use with the Penguin Mk 2 and AGM-65 Maverick missile in the Australian and New Zealand helicopters respectively. Another feature of the Australian helicopters is the Northrop Grumman AAR-54(V) missile warning system used to cue a Tracor ALE-47 chaff/flare launcher. The rebuilt **SH-2G(NZ)** helicopters for New Zealand are scheduled to enter service in 2000, while the **SH-2G(A)** machines for Australia are due to enter service from 2001.

Kaman K-MAX

The **K-MAX** was created from the later 1980s as a thoroughly utilitarian single-seat helicopter of the intermeshing-rotor type for the external lift role in fields such as logging, fire fighting, agricultural spraying and dusting, and construction.

The K-MAX is based on a slender fuselage of light alloy construction with a capacious cockpit for the pilot, who can fly the machine with the doors removed in hot conditions; the helicopter can also be flown with an external seat attached to each side of the fuselage just forward of the transverse beam carrying the main landing gear units. The rear fuselage supports a horizontal

surface (with fixed endplate fins and elevators, the latter linked to the collective system for automatic pitch-change reduction when the pitch of the rotors is altered) well forward of the tall vertical surface that carries a rudder. The whole unit is supported by fixed tricycle landing gear with a single wheel/bear-paw plate arrangement on each unit. Above and behind the cockpit is the helicopter's dynamic system, which is based on one well-proven turboshaft engine driving a transmission system for the side-by-side pair of two-bladed rotors. These are of glassfibre-reinforced plastics and carbonfibre-reinforced plastics

K-Max flew a six-month period of vertrep trials for the US Navy. The tests took place in the Arabian Gulf and Western Pacific and were very successful.

construction and carried on a pair of outward-canted pylons so that the two rotor discs intermesh but are not on the same plane. The blades' angle of attack is controlled by small trailing-edge flaps operated by a light control linkage.

The first of two K-MAX flying prototypes flew on 23 December 1991, and the helicopter received its US certification in August 1994. Kaman initially built the K-MAX for leased operations, but later offered the helicopter for sale, and by a time late in 1998 had completed 25 such helicopters for service in a number of countries; two of the helicopters have been destroyed in non-fatal crashes, the type's great strength and its crash-attenuating seat being completely validated in the process. The type has proved very successful in service, for it has provided great reliability in combination with a high ratio of payload to structure weight in arduous tasks such as logging. In August

1995 Kaman received a US Navy contract to demonstrate the utility of the K-MAX in the vertrep (vertical replenishment) role of supplying ships at sea, and after this it was also evaluated for the mine-detection role with Magic Lantern equipment scabbed onto the

sides of the lower fuselage. The K-MAX was designed mainly for operation with loads slung well below the fuselage on a long line, but other equipment that can be used with the K-MAX includes the 583-Imp gal (2650-litre) Bambi fire fighting bucket.

SPECIFICATION	
Kaman K-MAX	of ground effect; range 345 miles
Type: one-crew utility helicopter	(556 km) with maximum fuel
Powerplant: one 1,500-shp	**Weights:** empty 5,100 lb
(1119-kW) Honeywell	(2313 kg); maximum take-off
(AlliedSignal/Lycoming) T53-17A-1	12,923 lb (5862 kg)
turboshaft engine flat-rated at	**Dimensions:** rotor diameter, each
1,350 shp (1007 kW)	48 ft 4 in (14.73 m); length overall
Performance: maximum speed	52 ft (15.85 m) with the rotors
115 mph (185 km/h) at optimum	turning; height 13 ft 7 in (4.14 m);
altitude; initial climb rate 2,500 ft	rotor disc area, total 3,669.55 sq ft
(762 m) per minute; hovering	(340.90 m²)
ceiling 26,300 ft (8020 m) in ground	**Payload:** up to 6,000 lb (2722 kg)
effect and 29,120 ft (8875 m) out	of freight carried externally

Kamov Ka-8 and Ka-10 'Hat'

Nikolai I. Kamov began the study of rotating-wing design in the late 1920s, and in conjunction with N. K. Skrzhiriskii was responsible for two of the earliest successful Soviet rotorcraft, the **KaSkr-I** and **KaSkr-II**. Kamov's first helicopter design was the ultralight **Ka-8** of 1945, comprising a very basic uncovered steel tube structure mounted on two

pontoons and having an exposed seat for the pilot. Powered by a 27-hp (20-kW) engine, it introduced the co-axial contrarotating rotors that have since been a 'trademark' of Kamov design, enabling the aircraft to dispense with the complication of an anti-torque tail rotor. The slightly larger **Ka-10** (ASCC reporting name **'Hat'**) followed in 1948, introduc-

In 1954, some 10 examples of the improved Ka-10M were built for the Soviet coastguard. Note the float undercarriage.

ing a 55-hp (41-kW) Ivchenko AI-4V engine. Built in small numbers for test and evaluation, it was followed by improved **Ka-10M** which introduced twin tail fins and rudders.

Kamov Ka-15 'Hen' and Ka-18 'Hog'

With experience gained from the Ka-8 and Ka-10,

Kamov designed the far more practical **Ka-15**

two-seat general-purpose helicopter. This had an

enclosed cabin with fixed four-wheel landing gear

beneath it, and was intended for use as a spotter aircraft by ice-breakers, merchant ships, and by the Soviet navy.

Kamov Ka-15 'Hen' and Ka-18 'Hog' (continued)

Retaining the contra- rotating co-axial twin rotors and twin fins and rudders that had proved successful on the Ka-10, the Ka-15 was powered initially by a 225-hp (168-kW) Ivchenko AI-14V engine, but a 280-hp (209-kW) supercharged AI-14VF was introduced at a later date. In addition to production for the navy, the Ka-15 (NATO reporting name 'Hen') was produced as the **Ka-15M** for civil use,

available in agricultural, ambulance and in mail/passenger-carrying versions.

A four-seat development of the Ka-15, which differed basically by having a lengthened fuselage to accommodate four passengers, had the designation **Ka-18** (NATO reporting name **'Hog'**). It was powered by the supercharged Ivchenko AI-14VF as standard, and also intro-

The Ka-15 was of stressed-skin Dural construction. The aircraft, including a two-seat trainer version, was built to the extent of some hundreds.

duced more advanced avionics and instrumentation. Like its predecessor it was built for use by the navy and also in a variety of civil versions, primarily for use by Aeroflot.

Kamov Ka-20 'Harp' and Ka-25 'Hormone'

Designed to meet a 1957 Soviet navy requirement for a new shipborne ASW helicopter, the first member of the Ka-20/25 family was the **Ka-20 'Harp'**, which initially flew during 1960 and which formed the basis of the operational **'Hormone'**. The production **Ka-25BSh 'Hormone-A'** was of almost identical size and appearance, but was fitted with operational equipment and uprated GTD-3F engines (from 1973 replaced by GTD-3Ms). It entered service in 1967.

Although the lower part of the fuselage is sealed and watertight, the Ka-25 is not intended for amphibious operations, and flotation bags are often fitted to the undercarriage for use in the event of an

emergency landing on the water. The cabin is adequate for the job, but is not tall enough to allow the crew to stand upright. Progressive additions of new equipment have made the interior more cluttered. Primary sensors for the ASW mission are the I/J-band radar (NATO 'Big Bulge'), OKA-2 dipping sonar, a downward-looking 'Tie Rod' electro-optical sensor in the tailboom, and a MAD sensor, either in a recess in the rear part of the cabin or in a fairing sometimes fitted below the central of the three tailfins. A box-like sonobuoy launcher can also be scabbed on to the starboard side of the rear fuselage. Dye-markers or smoke floats can also be

carried externally. Comprehensive avionics, defensive and navigation systems are fitted.

Armament is not normally carried, although the helicopter can be fitted with a long 'coffin-like' weapons bay which runs along the belly from the radome back to the tailboom, and small bombs or depth charges can be carried on tiny pylons just aft of the nosewheels. The underfuselage weapons bay can carry a variety of weapons, including nuclear depth charges. When wire-guided torpedoes are carried, a wire reel is mounted on the port side of the forward fuselage.

It has been estimated that some 260 of the 450 or so Ka-25s produced were 'Hormone-As', but only a handful remains in Russian and Ukrainian service, fulfilling secondary roles. Small numbers of Ka-25BShs were exported to India, Syria, Vietnam and former Yugoslavia, and most of these aircraft remain in use.

The second Ka-25 variant

identified in the West was given the NATO reporting name **'Hormone-B'**, and is designated **Ka-25K**. This variant is externally identifiable by its bulbous (instead of flat-bottomed) under-nose radome and small datalink radome under the rear fuselage. This was used for acquiring targets and providing mid-course missile guidance, for ship- and submarine-launched missiles. On the 'Hormone-B' only, the four undercarriage units are retractable and can be lifted out of the scanning pattern of the radar.

The final version of the military Ka-25 is the **Ka-25PS** (**'Hormone-C'**). A dedicated SAR and transport helicopter, the Ka-25PS can carry a practical load of freight or up to 12 passengers, making it a useful ship-to-ship or ship-to-shore transport and vertrep platform. A quadruple Yagi antenna (NATO 'Home Guard') fitted to many aircraft is reportedly used for homing onto the personal locator beacons carried by aircrew. Most Ka-25PSs also have searchlights, and a 660-lb (300-kg) capacity rescue winch. The Ka-25PS has largely been replaced by SAR versions of the Ka-27 'Helix'.

SPECIFICATION	
Kamov Ka-25BSh 'Hormone-A'	range 249 miles (400 km) with
Type: ASW helicopter	standard fuel
Powerplant: two OMKB 'Mars' (Glushenkov) GTD-3F turboshafts each rated at 898 shp (671 kW) in early helicopters, or two OMKB 'Mars' (Glushenkov) GTD-3BM each rated at 900 shp (738 kW) in late helicopters	**Weights:** empty 10,505 lb (4765 kg); maximum take-off 16,534 lb (7500 kg)
	Dimensions: rotor diameter, each 52 ft 7¾ in (15.74 m); fuselage length 32 ft (9.75 m); overall 17 ft 7½ in (5.37 m); main rotor disc area 4,188.93 sq ft (389.15 m²)
Performance: maximum level speed 'clean' at optimum altitude 130 mph (209 km/h); normal cruising speed at optimum altitude 120 mph (193 km/h); service ceiling service ceiling 10,990 ft (3350 m);	**Armament:** provision for two anti-submarine torpedoes, conventional or nuclear depth charges and other stores up to a maximum of 4,190 lb (1900 kg)

A few Ka-25BSh helicopters continued in service alongside Mi-14 and Ka-27 ASW machines into 2001.

Kamov Ka-26 'Hoodlum', Ka-126 'Hoodlum-B' & Ka-226

The **Ka-26**, known to NATO by the reporting designation **'Hoodlum-A'**, was designed primarily as a multi-role civilian helicopter, and became one of the few genuinely successful Soviet aviation exports with sales secured on the basis of merit rather than availability at a low price to members and clients of the Soviet bloc. The type was designed mainly for the agricultural role, but has also been successfully adapted for the firefighting, medevac, survey and light SAR roles. This versatility is largely a result of the helicopter's unusual

configuration. The fully enclosed two-seat cabin is attached to the underside of the forward part of a shallow upper fuselage which carries the rotor mast and two very short stub wings (or, perhaps more accurately, pylons) which carry the large nacelles for the two M14V-26 air-cooled radial engines. Two slender tail booms extend to the rear from this pylon disposition to carry the single horizontal tail surface and two massive endplate vertical tail surfaces. The resulting space below the rotor mast, between the engines

and aft of the cockpit, can carry a variety of detachable pods for passengers, litters or cargo, or a hopper for agricultural spraying, or a rescue hoist.

Announced in 1964 and first flown in 1965, the helicopter is otherwise of typical Kamov concept. Production had reached some 890 units by 1993, at which time the type had secured exports to at least 15 countries, and was continued for a short time after this by the Kumertau Aviation Production Association. The vast majority of the helicopters was delivered to civil opera-

SPECIFICATION	
Kamov Ka-26 'Hoodlum-A'	cargo platform, maximum take-off
Type: one/two-crew utility light helicopter	7,165 lb (3250 kg)
Powerplant: two VMKB (Vedeneyev) M-14V-26 radial piston engines each rated at 325 hp (243 kW)	**Dimensions:** rotor diameter, each 42 ft 8 in (13 m); length, fuselage 25 ft 5 in (7.75 m); height 13 ft 3½ in (4.05 m) to top of rotor head; rotor disc area, total 2,857.53 sq ft (265.46 m²)
Performance: maximum speed 105 mph (170 km/h) at optimum altitude; cruising speed 93 mph (150 km/h) at optimum altitude; service ceiling 9,845 ft (3000 m); hovering ceiling 4,265 ft (1300 m) in ground effect and 2,625 ft (800 m) out of ground effect; range 248 miles (400 km) with standard fuel and seven passengers	**Payload:** up to seven passengers (one beside the pilot and up to six in a detachable payload pod, which can also accommodate two litters, two seated casualties and one attendant, or 1,984 lb/900 kg of freight), or 2,348 lb (1065 kg) of freight carried as a slung load, or 2,425 lb (1100 kg) of freight on a platform replacing the payload pod
Weights: empty 4,597 lb (2085 kg) operating in the freight role with a	

tors, the only known military operators being Benin, Bulgaria and the USSR (now CIS).

Originally manufactured by ICA-Brasov before its transmogrification into IAR, the **IAR/Kamov Ka-126 'Hoodlum-B'** is a turbine-engined development designed in the USSR but built in Romania after a first flight in 1986. The Ka-126 is thus a development of the basic Ka-26 with the wholly revised powerplant of one 720-shp (537-kW) OMKB 'Mars' (Glushenkov) TVD-100 turboshaft engine. Other changes included a revised fuel system, rotor blades of improved aerofoil section, and a stored-energy system based on two contra-rotating flywheels turning at

In its agricultural spraying configuration, the Ka-26 employs a 1,984-lb (900-kg) capacity hopper.

24,000 rpm to provide 40 seconds of powered flight in the event of a total engine failure.

The sole **Ka-128**, first flown in 1993, was an experimental development differing from the Ka-126 only its powerplant of one 722-shp (538-kW) Turbomeca Arriel 1D1 turboshaft engine.

A further variation on the Ka-26 theme is the **Ka-226A**, which is a basically similar machine, but powered by a pair of 450-shp (335-kW) Rolls-Royce (Allison) 250-C20R/2 turboshafts.

Kamov Ka-27/32 'Helix'

Work on the **Ka-27** family began in 1969, with Sergei Viktorovich Mikheyev taking over as chief designer after the death of Nikolai Ilyich Kamov in November 1973. A totally new design, the Ka-27 retains Kamov's well-proven contra-rotating co-axial rotor configuration, and has overall dimensions similar to those of the Ka-25 'Hormone' that the type was designed to replace as the earlier type had proved to be of only limited value as a result of its inability to operate its dipping sonar at night and under adverse weather conditions.

With more than double the power of the Ka-25 series, the Ka-27 is a considerably heavier helicopter with a larger fuselage for the accommodation of larger quantities of more modern equipment, but nevertheless offers improved performance through the use of a rotor assembly with the same overall dimensions and number of blades, but using blades of considerably improved aerofoil

In excess of 100 Ka-32S helicopters were built for Aeroflot. The aircraft retain the bad weather flying capability of their military counterparts.

section and greater area. Other changes were the use of more advanced materials, including titanium alloy and composites, in the structure of the fuselage and tail unit, enlarged fuel capacity in 12 underfloor tanks with provision for two auxiliary tanks, fully powered flight controls, an autopilot of increased authority, a new stability augmentation system to provide hands-off flight capability over a wide range of centre of gravity positions under all weather conditions, a revised tail unit with no central fin and endplate vertical surfaces toed-in at a greater angle, and strengthened landing gear of the same fixed quadricycle type.

The first production variant was the **Ka-27PL ('Helix-A')**. This is the basic anti-submarine warfare version, designed as a replacement for the Ka-25BSh. The prototype made its maiden flight during December 1974, and operational evaluation began in late 1981 allowing a service debut in 1982, generally in pairs of heli-

copters operating as a hunter/killer team. The Ka-27PL's fuselage is sealed over its lower portions for buoyancy, while extra flotation equipment can be fitted in boxes on the lower part of the centre fuselage. The Ka-27PL usually carries a crew of three in the form of the pilot and navigator/tactical co-ordinator side-by-side in the cockpit, and the anti-submarine systems operator behind the navigator/co-ordinator. To the rear is the cabin, with access by means of a sliding door on each side, and this cabin can be used for passengers or freight.

The Ka-27 is extremely stable and easy to fly, and automatic height hold, automatic transition to and from the hover, and auto-hover are possible in all weather conditions. The Ka-27PL has all the usual anti-submarine and ESM equipment, including dipping sonar (behind the clamshell rear doors at the back of the pod section of the fuselage) and sonobuoys (now carried inside the cabin) as well as Osminog (octopus) search radar with its shallow rectangular antenna in a new undernose radome; the Ka-27PL can also be fitted with an RWR, an IR jammer and a chaff/flare dispenser. in the early part of the 21st century thought is being given to the replacement of the basic anti-submarine system by a simplified derivative of the Sea Dragon system designed for the Tupolev Tu-142 and other aircraft.

The main SAR and plane-guard variant of the Ka-27 series in service with the CIS forces is the radar-equipped **Ka-27PS 'Helix-D'**. This almost

SPECIFICATION

Kamov Ka-27PL 'Helix-A'
Type: three-crew shipborne anti-submarine and utility helicopter
Powerplant: two Klimov (Isotov) TV3-117V turboshaft engines each rated at 2,190 shp (1633 kW)
Performance: maximum speed 155 mph (250 km/h) at optimum altitude; cruising speed 143 mph (230 km/h) at optimum altitude; service ceiling 16,404 ft (5000 m); hovering ceiling 11,483 ft (3500 m) out of ground effect; range 497 miles (800 km) with auxiliary fuel; endurance 4 hours 30 minutes
Weights: empty 13448 lb (6100 kg); maximum take-off

27,778 lb (12600 kg)
Dimensions: rotor diameter, each 52 ft 2 in (15.90 m); length, excluding rotors 37 ft 11¾ in (11.27 m); height, to top of rotor head 17 ft 10½ in (5.45 m); rotor disc area, each 2,136.60 sq ft (198.50 m²)
Armament: up to 441 lb (200 kg) of disposable stores carried in a lower-fuselage weapons bay, and generally comprising four APR-2E homing torpedoes or four groups of S3V guided anti-submarine bombs
Payload: up to 11,023 lb (5000 kg) of freight

Vietnam operates the Ka-28 (illustrated) alongside the Ka-25 and Ka-32 in the 954 Trung Doan at its Kien An and Da Nang bases.

inevitably carries external fuel tanks and flotation gear, the latter being seldom seen on 'Helix-A' helicopters but sometimes fitted to **Ka-32** machines. A hydraulically operated 661-lb (300-kg) capacity rescue winch is fitted above the cabin door, with associated downward-pointing floodlights under the port side of the nose and rear cabin. Directional ESM and IFF is retained, but other operational equipment is deleted. An unidentified box-like fairing, with two protruding spherical objects, is carried

below the end of the tail boom, to the rear of the gyro magnetic heads and Doppler box. Finally, provision is made in the lower-fuselage bay, used for weapons in the Ka-27PL, for dinghies.

The **Ka-28 'Helix-A'** is the export version of the Ka-27PL ordered by China, India, Vietnam and Yugoslavia. The type is thought to have two 2,200-shp (1640-kW) TV3-117BK turboshaft engines together with the wider cockpit door of the Ka-32 and its bulged windows.

Kamov Ka-27/32 'Helix' (continued)

The **Ka-32 'Helix-C'** is the multi-role development of the Ka-27 for civil as well as military and naval use. The type is powered by two 2,190-shp (1633-kW) TV3-117V or TV3-117MVA turboshafts and has a maximum payload of 11,023 lb (5000 kg) carried internally

or externally, although the cabin can also be laid out for up to 16 passengers, or alternatively for litters. The Ka-32 is offered in a host of variants including the **Ka-32T** utility model for the transport, medevac and flying crane roles; the **Ka-32S** maritime model

with more advanced avionics and search radar for operation from ice breakers and the like in ice reconnaissance and anti-pollution work; **Ka-32K** flying crane with a retractable undernose gondola for a rearward-looking second pilot; **Ka-32A** improved

version of the Ka-32 with more advanced avionics; **Ka-32A1** firefighting version of the Ka-32A; **Ka-32A2** police version of the Ka-32A with armament and abseiling provision; **Ka-32A3** rescue and salvage version of the Ka-32A; and **Ka-32A7**

(otherwise **Ka-327**) armed version of the Ka-32A for border and maritime economic zone patrol with a wide assortment of weapons; **Ka-32A11BC** for Canadian certification and **Ka-32A12** for Swiss certification. A more powerful **Ka-32M** is also under development.

Kamov Ka-29, Ka-31 and Ka-33 'Helix-B'

The **Ka-29TB** (*Transportno Boyevoya*) is a dedicated assault transport derivative of the Ka-27/32 family, intended especially for the support of Russian navy amphibious operations and featuring a substantially changed airframe. The first example was seen by Western eyes on the assault ship *Ivan Rogov* in 1987, the type having entered service in 1985, and the **Ka-29TB** was initially assumed to be the **Ka-27B**, resulting in the allocation of the NATO reporting designation **'Helix-B'**. Many of the new variants went unnoticed,

and the Ka-29TB was initially thought to be a minimum-change version of the basic Ka-27PL without radar. In fact the Ka-29TB features an entirely new, much widened forward fuselage, with a flight deck seating three members of the crew side-by-side, one of these crew members acting as a gunner to aim the various types of air-to-surface unguided rocket carried on the four hardpoints of the helicopter's pair of strut-braced lateral pylons, and the trainable machine-gun hidden behind an articulated door on the starboard side of the nose.

The location of the braced pylons precludes the fitting of external fuel tanks or flotation gear. The two-piece curved windscreen of the Ka-27 has given way to a five-piece unit, with three main flat plates at the front and two smaller, slightly blown quarterlights.

A long, braced, air data boom projects forward from the port side of the nose, which is painted black and carries a small radar in its port side. Under the nose the Ka-29TB has an electro-optical sensor to starboard and a missile guidance/illuminating and terrain-following radar pod to port. The electro-optical sensor is probably a combined FLIR and low-light TV, and the radome is probably associated with the 9M116 Shturm (NATO AT-6 'Spiral') missile. An ammunition link ejection chute is located under the nose farther to starboard. The original sliding cabin door has also been replaced by a horizontally divided, outward-hinging two-piece door, and there is an IR jammer on the top of the fuselage/engine fairing; extra defence against radar and homing weapons is provided by chaff/flare dispensers.

The basic Ka-29TB airframe also served as the basis for the **Ka-31**, which was originally known as the **Ka-29RLD** (*Radiolokatsyonnogo Dozora*, or radar picket helicopter). Development of this AEW type was launched in 1980, leading to a first flight in 1988, and the type was first seen during carrier trials aboard the *Admiral of the Fleet Kuznetsov*. The wider cabin section extends back as far as the rear undercarriage oleos and ends more abruptly, and the type is characterised by a large ventral pannier, which begins just aft of the nose cone and extends aft along the full length of the cabin, across virtually the full width of the fuselage. There is a new narrow cabin door (on the star-

board side just to the rear of the flight deck) that is horizontally divided and incorporates an inbuilt airstair in its lower section. Large rectangular panniers are fitted to the lower part of the cabin sides. Most importantly, all four landing gear units are retractable for the specific purpose of freeing the hemisphere under the helicopter of obstructions to the movement and operation of the E-801E Oko (eye) surveillance radar's antenna, which is a large rectangular planar array that rests flat under the fuselage until rotated downward through 90° for rotation at 6 rpm while in operation.

The **Ka-33** is a utility transport version of the Ka-29TB for the civil market. The type's designation was revealed in 1997, but there has since been no further information about the helicopter.

SPECIFICATION

Kamov Ka-29TB 'Helix-B'
Type: three-crew assault transport and close support helicopter
Powerplant: two Klimov TV3-117V turboshaft engines each rated at 2,200 shp (1640 kW)
Performance: maximum speed 174 mph (280 km/h) at sea level; cruising speed 149 mph (240 km/h) at optimum altitude; initial climb rate 2,910 ft (888 m) per minute; service ceiling 14,100 ft (4100 m); hovering ceiling 9,845 ft (3000 m) out of ground effect; range 285 miles (460 km)
Weights: empty 12,169 lb (5520 kg); maximum take-off 27,778 lb (12600 kg)
Dimensions: rotor diameter, each 52 ft 2 in (15.90 m); length, fuselage 37 ft 1 in (11.30 m) excluding probes; height 17 ft 8½ in (5.40 m); rotor disc area, total 4,274.63 sq ft (397.11 m²)
Armament: one 0.3-in (7.62-mm)

trainable forward-firing four-barrel rotary machine-gun in the nose, plus disposable stores carried on four hardpoints, and generally comprising 9M114 (AT-6 'Spiral') anti-tank missiles, 2.17- or 3.15-in (55- or 80-mm) S-5 or S-8 air-to-surface unguided rockets, pods carrying one 23-mm Gryazev-Shipunov GSh-23 cannon and 250 rounds, or 500-kg (1,102-lb) ZAB-500 incendiary bombs; additional weapons can be carried in the lower-fuselage weapons bay inherited from the Ka-27, and there is also provision for one 30-mm 2A42 fixed forward-firing cannon above the port pylon
Payload: up to 16 troops, or four litters, seven seated casualties and one medical attendant, or 4,409 lb (2000 kg) of freight carried in the cabin, or 8,818 lb (4000 kg) of freight carried as a slung load

Carrying a typical load of four 20-round pods containing S-8 rockets, the Ka-29 packs a formidable punch.

Kamov Ka-50 Chernaya Akula and Ka-52 Alligator 'Hokum'

The helicopter known as the **Ka-50 Chernaya Akula** (black shark) to the Russians and **'Hokum'** to NATO, began life in 1977 under the supervision of Mikheyev. It was planned as a rival to the Mi-28 'Havoc' in the competition to provide the Soviet armed forces with a new battlefield attack helicopter. Appreciating that the attainment of performance comparable with that of the latest Western battlefield helicopters would be difficult with the heavyweight technology and equipment typical of Soviet helicopters, Kamov opted for

its standard concept of a superimposed pair of contra-rotating co-axial rotors in combination with an aircraft-type fuselage carrying only a single crew member to save on the weight that could then be used for more armour, more powerful armament, and a greater number of more advanced sensors. This single-seat arrangement was thought tactically feasible through the exploitation of the bureau's experience in automated systems in its naval helicopters. The single-pilot cockpit was successfully demonstrated in a modified

Ka-29TB. Other elements of the Ka-50's design are a conventional tail unit, retractable tricycle landing gear with single-wheel main units and a twin-wheel nose unit, and a mid-set wing for the carriage of four hardpoints.

The first of an eventual three **V-80** prototypes made its maiden flight on 17 June 1982, and there were also two **V-80Sh-1** pre-production prototypes, the suffix indicating *Shturmovik-1* (single-seat assaulter). The competitive evaluation ended in October 1986 with the selection of the Ka-50 in

preference to the Mi-28 as a result of the Kamov helicopter's greater agility, longer stand-off missile range, heavier ammunition load, more extensive armour protection, and greater accuracy of weapons delivery.

The core of the Ka-50's weapon system is the tube-launched Vikhr anti-tank missile, of which 16 are carried. These missiles can be complemented by AS-12 'Kegler' ASMs, up to 80 S-8 unguided rockets carried in four pods, and a variety of bombs. The helicopter also possesses an inbuilt 30-mm 2A42 cannon: this last has

variable rates of fire and selective feed from two 140-round ammunition boxes (which can be separately loaded with armour-piercing and explosive rounds, allowing the pilot to select the type of ammunition he wishes to fire simply by selecting the correct box) and is extremely malfunction-resistant. The cannon is installed on the starboard side of the fuselage, below the wing root, as close as possible to the helicopter's centre of gravity and also in the strongest and most rigid location as a means of minimising the effect of recoil and of maximising accuracy.

Combat survivability is enhanced by IR suppression of the hot exhaust gases, a heavily protected and pressurised cockpit with two layers of structural armour capable of withstanding 20-mm cannon fire, foam-filled self-sealing fuel tanks, a high degree of systems redundancy, and finally Vympel UV-26 chaff/flare dispensers in wing tip pods. In the event of a

catastrophic hit, the pilot can use his K-37 ejection seat, whose departure sequence begins with automatic explosive separation of the two rotors' six blades, followed by the blowing off of the doors and finally the extraction of the seat by rocket pack.

The Ka-50's avionics, including provision for third-party target acquisition, are optimised to ease the pilot's workload. They include the I-25IV Shkval-V electro-optical search and

auto-tracking system with laser tracking and rangefinding as the primary offensive element, and for defence an RWR, two wing-tip EW pods, and laser and IR warning systems. The whole machine was designed for deployment away from base for at least two weeks without need of maintenance ground equipment as all refuelling and servicing of the avionics and weapons can be undertaken from ground level.

Later revision of the Russian requirement to emphasise night combat capability led to a reassessment of the Ka-50, whose production was postponed, in the light of the two-seat Mi-28's apparently greater

developability for the task. for the revised requirement Kamov has developed the **Ka-50N** (**Nochnoy**, or nocturnal) as what is in effect a single-seat derivative of the **Ka-52**. The type first flew in March or May 1997 and has a FLIR turret (integrated with an electro-optical sighting system) in the nose as well as Phazotron FH-01 Arbalet (crossbow) mast-mounted radar.

The **Ka-52 Alligator** ('**Hokum-B**'), is the two-seat conversion trainer and day/night combat derivative of the Ka-50 with a widened forward fuselage providing side-by-side accommodation for the pilot/instructor and systems operator/trainee in the enclosed cockpit. Other changes include a power-plant of two uprated

TV3-117 turboshafts for minimal degradation of performance despite the variant's greater weight and higher drag, and the addition of a night and all-weather attack capability through the installation of the Arbalet millimetric-wavelength radar to supplement the electro-optical and laser systems in a suite integrated by Sextant Avionique of France. First flown in **V-80Sh-2** prototype form during 1996 and in production form on 25 June 1997, the type has been ordered for Russian service, and is offered on the export market with provision for the Igla V short-range AAM. The **Ka-50-2** series are export derivatives with Israeli avionics, and has been offered to China, India and Turkey.

The Ka-50's nose sensors are evident on this production machine. Mounted to starboard, the cannon can be moved through 30° in elevation and between 5° and 6° in azimuth, with the cannon kept on target in azimuth by a tracker system that slews the helicopter round the axis of the rotor system.

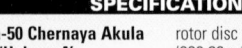

SPECIFICATION	
Kamov Ka-50 Chernaya Akula 'Hokum-A'	rotor disc area, total 3,555 sq ft (330.26 m²)
Type: single-seat battlefield air-combat and close-air support helicopter	**Armament:** one 30-mm 2A42 semi-trainable forward-firing cannon with 280 rounds in a barbette on the starboard side of the nose, plus up to 6,614 lb (3000 kg) of disposable stores carried on four underwing hardpoints, including B-8V-20A multiple launchers each carrying 20 3.15-in (80-mm) S-8 air-to-surface unguided rockets, UV-32-57 multiple launchers each carrying 32 2.17-in (55-mm) S-5 air-to-surface unguided rockets, 9M120 Vikhr (AT-9 'Spiral') anti-tank missiles, Vikhr M (AT-16) anti-tank missiles, or pods each carrying one 23-mm Gryazev-Shipunov GSh-23L two-barrel cannon with 250 rounds, or 500 kg (1,102 lb) FAB-500 HE or ZAB-500 incendiary bombs, or dispenser weapons, or ASMs, or R-60 (AA-8 'Aphid') or R-73 (AA-11 'Archer') short-range AAMs
Powerplant: two Klimov TV3-117VK turboshaft engines each rated at 2,193 shp (1635 kW)	
Performance: maximum speed 186 mph (300 km/h) at optimum altitude; cruising speed 168 mph (270 km/h) at optimum altitude; maximum vertical rate of climb 1,969 ft (600 m) per minute at 8,200 ft (2500 m); service ceiling 18,040 ft (5500 m); hovering ceiling 13,125 ft (4000 m) out of ground effect; range 279 miles (540 km); endurance 1 hour 40 minutes with standard fuel	
Weights: empty 17,196 lb (7800 kg); maximum take-off 23,810 lb (10800 kg)	
Dimensions: rotor diameter, each 45 ft 7 in (14.50 m); length 52 ft 6 in (16.00 m) with the rotors turning; height 16 ft 2 in (4.93 m);	

Kawanishi E7K

In 1932 the Imperial Japanese Navy sought a replacement for the **Navy Type 90-3 Reconnaissance Seaplane** which had been built as the **Kawanishi E5K**. The resulting three-seat **E7K1** was an

equal-span biplane of conventional design, powered by a 620-hp (462-kW) Hiro Type 91 engine. First flown on 6 February 1933, the prototype was handed over to the Japanese navy three

months later for service trials, being flown in competition against the Aichi AB-6 developed to meet the same requirement. The E7K1 was ordered into production as the **Navy Type 94 Reconnaissance Seaplane** in May 1934, entering service in early 1935, and quickly proving popular for its ease of handling. However, its Hiro engine was unreliable, and although late production E7K1s had a more powerful version of the Hiro 91, this offered no improvement. During 1938 Kawanishi built an **E7K2** prototype which, generally similar to

the E7K1, replaced the Hiro engine with a Mitsubishi Zuisei 11 radial. Flown for the first time in August 1938, the E7K2 was ordered into production three months later under the designation Navy **Type 94 Reconnaissance Seaplane Model 2**, the original version then becoming the **Navy Type 94 Reconnaissance Seaplane Model 1**. Production of the E7K1 totalled 183 (57 built by Nippon), and of the E7K2 about 350 (some 60 built

by Nippon).

As a type the E7K saw extensive use from 1935 until the beginning of the Pacific war, when the E7K1s were relegated to second-line duties. The E7K2s, however, continued in first-line service until 1943, and both versions were used in *kamikaze* operations in the closing stages of the war. When in the second half of 1942 Allied codenames were allocated to Japanese aircraft, the E7K2 became known as **'Alf'**.

This E7K2 was photographed in company with a Nakajima E8N1 Type 95 Reconnaissance Seaplane. Later in its production, the Seaplane Model 2 was redesignated as the Seaplane Model 12.

SPECIFICATION	
Kawanishi E7K2	(2100 kg); maximum take-off 7,275 lb (3300 kg)
Type: three-seat reconnaissance floatplane	**Dimensions:** wingspan 45 ft 11¼ in (14 m); length 34 ft 5½ in (10.50 m); height 15 ft 10½ in (4.85 m); wing area 469.31 sq ft (43.60 m²)
Powerplant: one 870-hp (649-kW) Mitsubishi Zuisei 11 radial piston engine	
Performance: maximum speed 171 mph (275 km/h) at 6,560 ft (2000 m); service ceiling 23,165 ft (7060 m); endurance 11 hours 30 minutes	**Armament:** one fixed and two trainable 7.7-mm (0.303-in) Type 92 machine-guns, plus 265 lb (120 kg) of bombs
Weights: empty 4,630 lb	

Kawanishi H6K

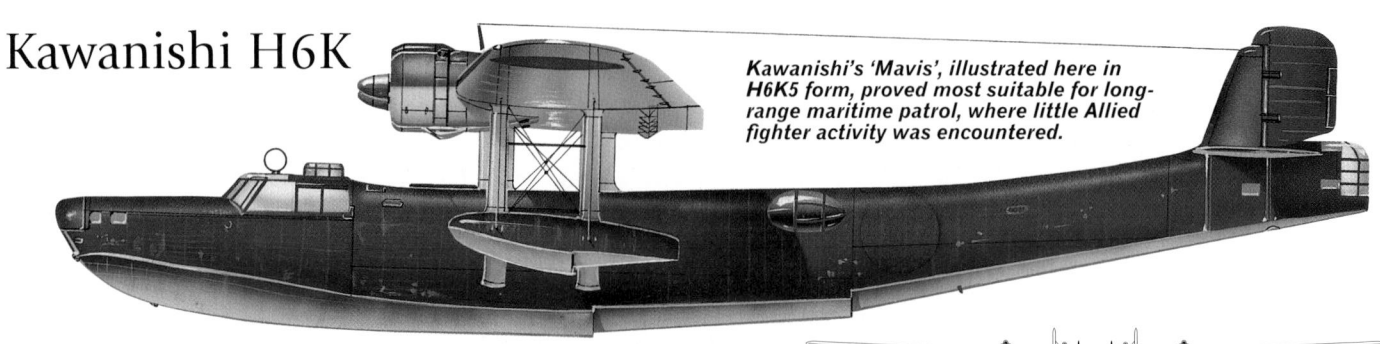

Kawanishi's 'Mavis', illustrated here in H6K5 form, proved most suitable for long-range maritime patrol, where little Allied fighter activity was encountered.

To meet a requirement of the Imperial Japanese Navy for a high-performance flying-boat, the **Kawanishi Type S** was proposed to provide the 137-mph (220-km/h) cruising speed and 2,795-mile (4500-km) range specified. Of parasol-wing configuration with a slender two-step hull, the resulting prototype was powered by four 840-hp (626-kW) Nakajima Hikari radial engines mounted at the wing leading edge. First flown on 14 July 1936, the prototype in early tests showed a need for hull

modification to improve water performance; subsequent service trials following changes to the hull showed that both water and flight handling were satisfactory, but the aircraft was considered to be underpowered. Three more prototypes followed, two of these and the original 'boat being equipped with more powerful engines, and these were the first to enter service, in January 1938, under the designation **Navy Type 97 Flying-Boat Model 1**. Simultaneously, the type

was ordered into production and eventually a total of 217 of all versions was built. Following early operational deployment in the Sino-Japanese war, they were used extensively from the outbreak of the Pacific war. By late 1942, when the type was allocated the Allied codename **'Mavis'**, it was becoming vulnerable to new generation fighter aircraft and was relegated to reconnaissance/transport roles in areas where little fighter opposition was expected, many remaining in service until the end of the war.

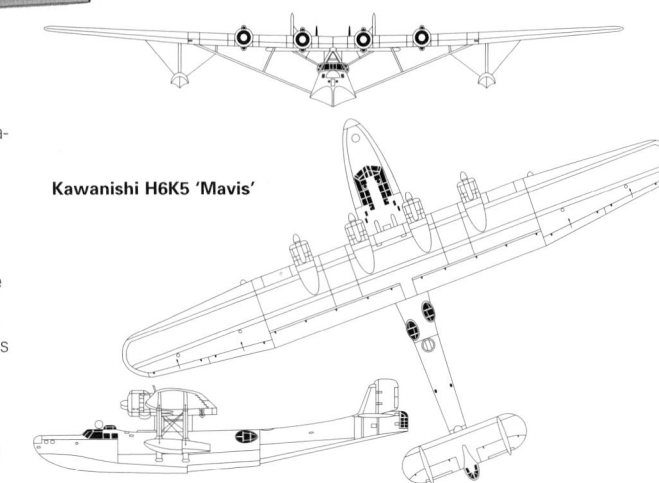

Kawanishi H6K5 'Mavis'

SPECIFICATION

Kawanishi H6K5
Type: long-range maritime reconnaissance/bomber flying-boat
Powerplant: four 1,300-hp (969-kW) Mitsubishi Kinsei 51 or 53 engines
Performance: maximum speed 239 mph (385 km/h) at 19,685 ft (6000 m); service ceiling 31,365 ft (9560 m); maximum range 4,210 miles (6775 km)
Weights: empty 27,293 lb (12380 kg); maximum take-off 50,706 lb (23000 kg)

Dimensions: wingspan 131 ft 2¾ in (40 m); length 84 ft 1 in (25.63 m); height 20 ft 6¾ in (6.27 m); wing area 1,829.92 sq ft (170 m²)
Armament: four 7.7-mm (0.303-in) Type 92 machine-guns (in a forward turret, two beam blisters and an open dorsal position) and one 20-mm cannon in a tail turret, plus two 1,764-1b (800-kg) torpedoes or up to 2,205 lb (1000 kg) of bombs

Variants

H6K1: the three prototypes following installation of 1,000-hp (746-kW) Mitsubishi Kinsei 43 engines
H6K2: initial production version; similar to H6K1 but with minor equipment changes
H6K3: two H6K2s completed as VIP transports
H6K4: major production version with increased fuel capacity, revised armament and, from August 1941, with 1,070-hp (798-kW) Kinsei 46 engines
H6K2-L: unarmed transport version, basically as early H6K4s; Japan Air Lines received 18 of these aircraft, each equipped as 18-passenger transports
H6K4-L: unarmed transport version as above, but with Kinsei 46 engines and more cabin windows
H6K5: final production version with Kinsei 51 or 53 engines and revised armament

Kawanishi H8K

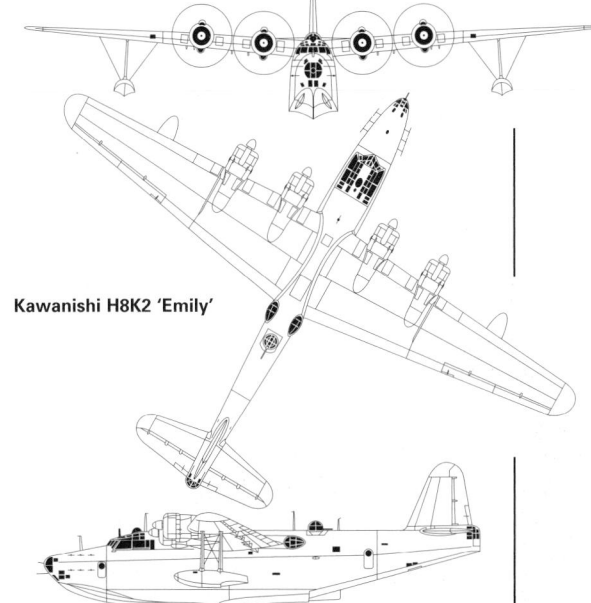

Kawanishi H8K2 'Emily'

SPECIFICATION

Kawanishi H8K2
Type: long-range bomber/reconnaissance flying-boat
Powerplant: four 1,850-hp (1380-kW) Mitsubishi MK4Q Kasei 22 engines
Performance: maximum speed 289 mph (465 km/h) at 16,405 ft (5000 m); service ceiling 27,740 ft (8760 m); maximum range 4,443 miles (7150 km)
Weights: empty 40,520 lb (18380 kg); maximum take-off

71,650 lb (32500 kg)
Dimensions: wingspan 124 ft 8 in (38 m); length 92 ft 3½ in (28.13 m); height 30 ft ¼ in (9.15 m); wing area 1,722.28 sq ft (160 m²)
Armament: five 20-mm cannon (in bow, dorsal, tail and two beam positions) and four 7.7-mm (0.303-in) machine-guns (in cockpit, ventral and two beam positions) plus up to 4,409 lb (2000 kg) of bombs or depth charges, or two 1,764-lb (800-kg) torpedoes

The H8K was to have had retractable underwing floats in its original H8K2 form, but these were abandoned as a weight saving measure.

Realising that the development of a flying-boat larger than the H6K would take some two or three years, the Imperial Japanese Navy gave the Kawanishi company a development

contract for such an aircraft as soon as the H6K entered service in 1938. The resulting **H8K1** prototype, flown for the first time on 31 December 1940, was of high-wing

monoplane configuration with a large conventional hull and powered by four 1,530-hp (1141-kW) Mitsubishi MK4A engines. Accommodating a crew of 10, the H8K1 was well

Variants

H8K1: three prototypes and first 14 production aircraft, all with MK4A engines; late production examples had MK4B engines of the same power
H8K1-L: first prototype following conversion for use in a transport role, powered by higher-rated MK4Q engines
H8K2: major production version, with MK4Q engines, increased armament, fully-protected fuel tanks and ASV radar; 112 built as **Navy Type 2 Flying-Boat Model 12**
H8K2-L: production transport developed from the H8K1-L; accommodation for 29 to 64 passengers and armament reduced; ordered into production as the **Navy Type 2 Transport Flying-Boat Seiku (clear sky) Model 32**; 36 built
H8K3: two prototypes with retractable wingtip stabilising floats and retractable dorsal turret; otherwise as production H8K2s, but not placed into production
H8K4: redesignation of H8K3 prototypes following installation of 1,825-hp (1361-kW) Mitsubishi MK4T-B Kasei 25b engines; not placed into production

armed, had good protective armour, and bulk fuel tanks within the hull that were partially self-sealing and incorporated a carbon dioxide fire-extinguishing system. Early tests showed the new flying-boat to be dangerously unstable on the water, leading to extensive hull modifications before the H8K1 was ordered into production in late 1941 under the designation **Navy Type 2 Flying-Boat Model 11**,

which was later allocated the Allied codename **'Emily'**. Early production aircraft were soon in service, the type's operational debut being made on the night of 4/5 March 1942. Used for bombing, reconnaissance and transport missions, 167 H8Ks were built and the type remained in service until the end of the war, being considered one of the finest military flying-boats ever produced.

Kawanishi K-1 to K-12

In 1921 the Kawanishi Engineering Works of Kobe established an aircraft-manufacturing division, its first design being the Kawanishi K-1, a one-off two-seat two-bay biplane intended as a mail-carrier and powered by a 200-hp (146-kW) Hall-Scott engine.

The **K-2** was a more ambitious but unsuccessful single-seat braced low-wing monoplane intended for racing.

The **K-3** of 1922, developed from the K-1, had a 260-hp (194-kW) Maybach engine; in 1926 it was redesignated **K-3B** when re-engined with a 230-hp (172-kW) Benz and used for training.

The **K-5** of 1923 was a twin-float biplane with a cabin for two passengers, while the **K-6** introduced a new wing design and revised tailplane, but retained the Maybach

engine of the K-5. This aircraft did much to arouse national interest in aviation, making a round-Japan flight of some 2,730 miles (4395 km) in 1924.

The first Kawanishi design to be built in any number was the **K-7A**, produced during 1925-6 with a government subsidy, and in September and October 1926 air-mail proving flights from Osaka to Talien and Shanghai were accomplished. The K-7A was a two-seat twin-float sesquiplane, powered by a Maybach engine. A single **K-7B** landplane version was also tested.

Five examples of the **K-8** two-seat parasol-wing floatplane were used on mail routes from 1926, and two examples of the **K-8B**, with redesigned fuselage sections, made a propaganda tour of Japan before being used by the newly-

A mailplane derivative of the K-7A, the sole K-7B had a cargo capacity of some 661 lb (300 kg). It had a 400-hp (258-kW) French Lorraine in-line engine.

formed Japan Airline Company.

Like all designs from the K-5 onwards, the **K-10** was Maybach-powered, but only two examples were built. An equal-span biplane, with cabin accommodation forward of the pilot's cockpit to seat four passengers, the two K-10s were used on the Osaka-Seoul-Talien route from September 1926.

Built as a private venture to meet an IJN requirement of 1926, the **K-11** experimental single-seat carrier fighter was a neat equal-span biplane built in the summer of 1927. Powered by a 500-hp (373-kW) BMW

engine, it was rejected by the navy and ended up as a company 'hack'.

The final design in the series was the **K-12 Sakura** (cherry) strut-braced high-wing cabin monoplane. A relatively advanced design powered by a 500-hp (373-kW) BMW VI engine, the first example flew in

June 1928. The K-12 was intended for a transpacific flight sponsored by the Japanese Imperial Aeronautical Association, and although a second example was completed, tests showed that performance was insufficient for the designated task and development was abandoned in 1928.

Kawanishi N1K1 Kyofu

Foreseeing a need for close air support during amphibious landings in areas where there was no adjacent airfield for land-based fighters, the IJN initiated in 1940 the development of floatplane fighters. The **N1K1** to meet this requirement was a comparatively heavy mid-wing monoplane with a central main float and two underwing stabilising floats, and was powered by a single 1,460-hp (1089-kW) Mitsubishi Mk4D Kasei radial engine. This, initially, was equipped

with contra-rotating propellers to minimise the on-water torque effect of the engine, but problems with these propellers led to the use of a conventional single-propeller powerplant arrangement.

Following satisfactory service trials the N1K1 was ordered into production as the **Navy Fighter Seaplane Kyofu** (mighty wind), but when these aircraft began to enter service in early 1943 the changing war situation meant they were no longer needed in a close air

During the last year of the war, the Kyofu found limited use in the defence of Japan.

support role. As a result production ended in 1944 after 97 had been built and the N1K1, allocated the

Allied codename **'Rex'**, was used only in a defensive role. The designation **NIK2** was issued for a

proposed developed version with a more powerful engine, but none was built.

Kawanishi NW-J and NW2-J Shiden

During 1942, Kawanishi began development of a land-based version of the N1K1 under the designation **N1K1-J**. Basically the same airframe was used, but the decision to power the new type with the newly-developed Nakajima NK9H Homare engine brought a series of problems, those relating to the

engine persisting through the type's service career. In order to use the full output of this engine, a large-diameter propeller was needed, requiring the development of telescopic main landing gear units, and this resulted in another major source of headaches for the design team. When the N1K1-J prototype was

first flown, on 27 December 1942, its superb performance and manoeuvrability brought concentrated efforts to develop it for service, rewarded at the end of 1943 by an order for production as the **Navy Interceptor Fighter Shiden** (violet lightning), which was allocated subse-

quently the Allied codename **'George'**. Although N1K1-Js began to enter service in early 1944, the type represented an interim measure, for development of an improved version, the **N1K2-J**, had been initiated in mid-1943. This introduced a major redesign, including a change from mid-wing to low-wing

configuration, a new, lengthened fuselage, revised tail surfaces and new, less complicated, main landing gear units. Despite its unreliability, the Nakajima NK9H engine was retained. The N1K2-J prototype was flown for the first time on 31 December 1943, being ordered into production almost immediately as the **Navy Interceptor Fighter Shiden KAI**.

Kawanishi N1K1-J and N1K2-J Shiden (continued)

Kawanishi's N1K2-J Shiden aircraft continued in production and development until the end of

World War II, being used extensively in Formosa, Honshu, Okinawa and the Philippines; and in the

closing stages of the war a number was expended in desperate *kamikaze* attacks.

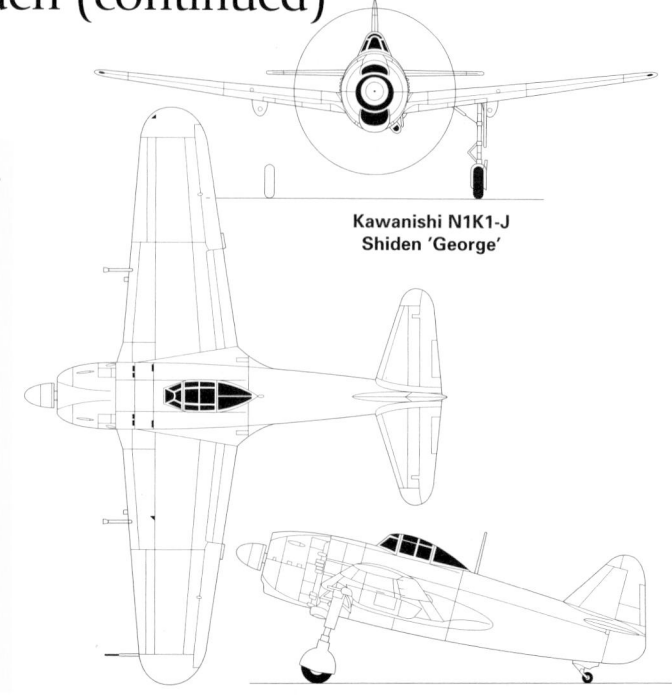

**Kawanishi N1K1-J
Shiden 'George'**

Variants

N1K1-J: designation of prototypes and initial production version, prototypes being powered by the 1,820-hp (1357-kW) Homare 11 engine; production aircraft had Homare 21 engines, and armament of two 0.303-in (7.7-mm) machine-guns and four wing-mounted 20-mm cannon; production, including prototypes, totalled 1,007
N1K1-Ja: variant of N1K1-J with armament of only four 20-mm cannon
N1K1-Jb: variant of N1K1-J with wing modification to allow the four 20-mm cannon to be mounted within the wings, and to carry two 551-lb (250-kg) bombs on underwing racks; some late production aircraft carried six air-to-ground rockets in an underfuselage pannier
N1K1-Jc: fighter-bomber variant of N1K1-Jb, with underwing racks for four 551-lb (250-kg) bombs
N1K2-J: production version, 423 built, including 22 by other manufacturers and an unknown number of N1K2-Ks; armament as N1K1-Jb
N1K2-K: two-seat trainer conversion of N1K2-J; armament of four 20-mm cannon only
N1K3-J: two prototypes with engine moved forward to improve longitudinal stability; armament as N1K2-K plus two fuselage-mounted 0.52-in (13.2-mm) machine-guns
N1K3-A: proposed carrier-based variant of N1K3-J; not built
N1K4-J: two prototypes with improved 2,000-hp (1491-kW) Homare 23 engine; armament as N1K3-J
N1K4-A: single prototype of carrier-based variant of N1K4-J
N1K5-J: single prototype, to be powered by a 2,200-hp (1641-kW) Mitsubishi MK9A engine, destroyed before completion during USAAF air raid

SPECIFICATION

Kawanishi N1K2-J
Type: single-seat land-based interceptor fighter
Powerplant: one 1,990-hp (1484-kW) Nakajima NK9H Homare 21 radial piston engine
Performance: maximum speed 370 mph (595 km/h) at 18,370 ft (5600 m); service ceiling 35,300 ft (10760 m); maximum range with drop tank 1,451 miles (2335 km)
Weights: empty 5,858 lb (2657 kg); maximum take-off 10,714 lb (4860 kg)
Dimensions: wingspan 39 ft 4½ in (12.00 m); length 30 ft 8 in (9.35 m); height 13 ft (3.96 m); wing area 252.96 sq ft (23.50 m²)
Armament: see variants

This N1K2-J Shiden Kai is preserved at the USAF Museum at Wright-Patterson AFB, Dayton, Ohio. Potentially the most superior of the Japanese Navy's operational fighters, production was hampered by United States B-29 bombing raids.

Kawasaki C-1

When it decided to find a new type to succeed the C-46 Commando transport aircraft that it still had in service, the Japan Air Self-Defence Force drew up its C-X specification for an indigenous medium-sized troop and freight transport in the early 1970s. The Nihon Aeroplane Manufacturing Company began the design of such a type in 1966, and even before the approval of a full-size mock-up the company had received a contract to build two **XC-1** prototypes for flight trials, as well as another airframe for static test. The first of the prototypes, assembled by Kawasaki, made its maiden flight on 12 November 1970, and the Japan Defence Agency completed its flight test programme of both prototypes during March 1973. Following construction of two pre-production aircraft, a first contract was placed for 11 full-production machines, which received the basic designation

This C-1 wears the markings of Japan's 402nd Hiko-tai of the 1st Koku-tai. Based at Iruma, the 402nd forms a vital component of the Yuso Koku-dan (Air Transport Wing). The second JASDF C-1 transport unit is the 403rd Hiko-tai, based at Miho. Between them, the operators share the 28 transport examples built exclusively for Japan.

Kawasaki C-1.
The C-1 is of conventional design for a modern military transport with swept flying surfaces, and as such is based on a high-wing monoplane configuration to maximise cabin volume, a fuselage with a separate flight deck and cabin/cargo hold that are both pressurised and air-conditioned, and a ventral ramp/door arrangement that can be opened in flight for the paradrop of troops, equipment and stores. The tail unit is of the T-type with a tall vertical surface, the landing

gear is of the retractable tricycle type, and the type's two turbofan engines are installed in nacelles mounted on pylons below and ahead of the wing's leading edges. The C-1 is operated by a flight crew of five, and typical loads include 60 fully equipped troops, or 45 paratroops, or up to 36 litters plus attendants, or a variety of equipment or palletised cargo.

The result of a collaborative manufacturing process, the C-1 was built by Fuji (outer wing panels), Mitsubishi (centre/aft

fuselage and tail surfaces), Nihon (control surfaces and engine nacelles) and

Kawasaki (forward fuselage and wing centre section as well as final assembly and

SPECIFICATION

Kawasaki C-1
Type: five-crew short-range transport aircraft
Powerplant: two Mitsubishi (Pratt & Whitney) JT9D-M-9 turbofan engines each rated at 14,500 lb st (164.50 kN)
Performance: maximum speed 501 mph (806 km/h) at 25,000 ft (7620 m); cruising speed 438 mph (704 km/h) at 35,000 ft (10670 m); initial climb rate 3,495 ft (1065 m) per minute; service ceiling 38,000 ft (11580 m); range

(2,084 miles (3353 km) with maximum fuel and a 4,850-lb (2200-kg) payload
Weights: empty 53,571 lb (24300 kg); maximum take-off 199,206 lb (45000 kg)
Dimensions: wingspan 100 ft 4¾ in (30.60 m); length 95 ft 1¾ in (29.00 m); height 32 ft 9¼ in (9.99 m); wing area 1,297.09 sq ft (120.50 m²)
Payload: see above within the context of a 26,235-lb (11900-kg) maximum payload

testing). Production of the C-1 totalled just 31 aircraft including the four prototype and pre-production aircraft, and the last of these machines was delivered on 21 October 1981. Although built to JASDF requirements, the C-1's maximum

payload is decidedly on the small size, and limits its operational value. This is one of the several reasons why plans for variants did not materialise.

One C-1 was used as a flying test bed for the MITI/NAL FJR710 and

Ishikawajima-Harima XF3 turbofan engines, the latter required for the T-4 trainer. More recently, Kawasaki modified one C-1 as the sole **C-1Kai** electronic counter-measures trainer, the modification process giving the aircraft flat

bulbous nose and tail radomes, an indigenous ALQ-5 ECM system and antennae beneath the fuselage. Proposed variants for inflight refuelling, electronic warfare, weather reconnaissance and minelaying remained

stillborn, as did a larger-capacity transport with a stretched fuselage. One aircraft served as the basis for the **NAL Asuka**, a dedicated quiet STOL test bed which flew with over-wing engines and blown flaps.

Kawasaki KDA-2 (Army Type 88 Reconnaissance Biplane)

Three prototypes of the **KDA-2** reconnaissance biplane, designed by Richard Vogt, were built in 1927 in response to an Imperial Japanese Army requirement. Following official testing the KDA-2 went into large-scale production as the **Army Type 88-I Reconnaissance Biplane**. It had a slim angular fuselage, conventional cross-axle landing gear, unequal-span wings, and was powered by a Kawasaki-built BMW VI engine. The **Type 88-II** was developed subsequently, introducing improved engine cowlings and a revised tail fin. Production of both versions totalled 707 by the end of 1931, 187 being built by Tachikawa and the remainder by the parent company. A bomber version of the Type 88-II was also built between 1929 and 1932. Known as the **Army Type 88 Light Bomber**, 407 examples were completed. All three versions saw

Variant

KDC-2: two examples of a transport variant were built with accommodation for a pilot and four passengers, the latter in an enclosed cabin; one machine was tested on twin floats

action in Manchuria and a few were still in service

during the fighting at Shanghai in 1937.

Designed as an interim light bomber, the Army Type 88 remained active after the introduction of the Kawasaki Type 93.

SPECIFICATION	
Kawasaki KDA-2	(1850 kg); maximum take-off
Type: two-crew light bomber	6,834 lb (3100 kg)
Powerplant: one Kawasaki-BMW VI piston engine rated at 600 hp (447-kW)	**Dimensions:** wingspan 49 ft 2¾ in (15.00 m); length 42 ft (12.80 m); height 11 ft 2 in (3.40 m); wing area 516.69 sq ft (48.00 m²)
Performance: maximum speed 132 mph (212 km/h) at sea level; climb to 9,843 ft (3000 m) in 18 minutes; service ceiling 18,044 ft (5500 m); endurance 6 hours	**Armament:** one fixed and one manually-aimed 0.303-in (7.7-mm) machine-gun, plus up to 441 lb (200 kg) of bombs
Weights: empty 4,078 lb	

Kawasaki KDA-5 (Army Type 92 Fighter)

The first of five **KDA-5** fighter prototypes was flown in 1930. Designed by Richard Vogt, this single-seat equal-span biplane was of fabric-covered metal construction. Power was provided by a 500-hp (373-kW) Kawasaki-BMW VI engine, although this was revised to a more powerful unit in production aircraft built from January 1933. Production of the **Army Type 92 Model 1 Fighter** was initiated in 1932, these series aircraft having a recontoured fin and rudder, and the headrest faired into the rear fuselage decking. Production totalled 180 before the **Type 92 Model 2** with structural strengthening superseded the Model 1, a total of 200 being built. Both versions served briefly in Manchuria during 1933, and some were in use as trainers at the time of Pearl Harbor.

In 1930, the prototype KDA-5 recorded speeds of around 200 mph (322 km/h), ranking with the Hawker Fury and P-12.

SPECIFICATION	
Kawasaki KDA-5	(1280 kg); maximum take-off
Type: single-seat fighter	3,747 lb (1700 kg)
Powerplant: one Kawasaki-BMW VI piston engine rated at 750 hp (559-kW)	**Dimensions:** wingspan 31 ft 4 in (9.55 m); length 23 ft 1½ in (7.05 m); height 10 ft 2 in (3.10 m); wing area 258.34 sq ft (24.00 m²)
Performance: maximum speed 200 mph (322 km/h); climb to 6,604 ft (5000 m) in 8 minutes; service ceiling 31,168 ft (9500 m)	**Armament:** two synchronised fixed forward-firing 0.303-in (7.7-mm) machine-guns
Weights: empty 2,822 lb	

Kawasaki Ki-3 (Army Type 93 Single-engine Light Bomber)

Developed from the **KDA-6** reconnaissance prototype, the **Ki-3** light bomber was an unequal-span biplane with the pilot and observer/gunner accommodated in tandem open cockpits. A total of 243 was built and these **Army Type 93 Light Bomber** aircraft served from 1934 in Korea, later equipping four regiments in Manchuria and being heavily involved in the fighting against China. The KDA-6 prototype was later bought by the Asaki Shinbun newspaper conglomerate and used for propaganda flights as the **A-6**.

SPECIFICATION	
Kawasaki Ki-3	(1650 kg); maximum take-off
Type: two-seat light bomber	6,834 lb (3100 kg)
Powerplant: one Kawasaki-BMW IX piston engine rated at 800 hp (597-kW)	**Dimensions:** wingspan 42 ft 8 in (13.00 m); length 32 ft 9½ in (10.00 m); height 9 ft 10 in (3.00 m); wing area 409.04 sq ft (38.00 m²)
Performance: maximum speed 162 mph (260 km/h); climb to 9,843 ft (3000 m) in 12 minutes; service ceiling 22,965 ft (7000 m)	**Armament:** two 7.7-mm (0.303-in) machine-guns and up to 1,102 lb (500 kg) of bombs
Weights: empty 3,637 lb	

Operational Ki-3s were mainly assigned to units based in northern and mid-China, and Manchuria, commencing in 1935 as replacements for the same company's Type 88 Light Bomber. However, the type was beset by continual engine problems.

Kawasaki Ki-10 (Army Type 95 Fighter)

Designed to meet an Imperial Japanese Army (IJA) requirement for a single-seat fighter, the **Ki-10** was an unequal-span biplane with fixed tailskid landing gear, accommodating the pilot in an open cockpit. The first prototype was flown initially in March 1935, powered by an 850-hp (634-kW) Kawasaki Ha-9-IIa engine. Three more prototypes followed before, late in the year, the Ki-10 was ordered into production as the **Army Type 95 Fighter**. More than 580 were built, the Ki-10 becoming regarded as the peak of biplane development in Japan.

Kawasaki Ki-10 (Army Type 95 Fighter) (continued)

Used extensively during the Sino-Japanese War, the Kawasaki Ki-10 had been relegated to second-line roles by the outbreak of the Pacific war. Nevertheless, its occasional appearance resulted in allocation of the Allied code name **'Perry'**.

SPECIFICATION

Kawasaki Ki-10-II KAI
Type: single-seat fighter
Powerplant: one 950-hp (708-kW) Kawasaki Ha-9-IIb V-12 piston engine
Performance: maximum speed 277 mph (445 km/h) at 12,470 ft (3800 m); service ceiling 37,730 ft (11500 m); range 621 miles (1000 km)

Weights: empty 3,086 lb (1400 kg); maximum take-off 3,924 lb (1780 kg)
Dimensions: wingspan 32 ft 10½ in (10.02 m); length 24 ft 9¾ in (7.55 m); height 9 ft 10 in (3.00 m); wing area 247.57 sq ft (23.00 m²)
Armament: two 0.303-in (7.7-mm) Type 89 fixed machine-guns

Variants

Ki-10: four original prototypes
Ki-10-I: initial production version; 300 built
Ki-10-I KAI: single prototype with redesigned landing gear and other refinements
Ki-10-II: designation of one prototype and 280 production aircraft built from mid-1937 as the **Army Type 95 Fighter Model 2**; increased wingspan and lengthened fuselage
Ki-10-II KAI: two prototypes, combining features of the Ki-10-I Kai/Ki-10-II, and powered by the 950-hp (708-kW) Kawasaki Ha-9 IIb engine

As the last fighter biplane in front-line service with the IJA, the Ki-10 fought in the second Sino-Japanese war and in the Nomonhan Incident. During World War II, Allied aircraft only encountered Ki-10s over China.

Kawasaki Ki-32 (Army Type 98 Single-engined Light Bomber)

Designed in 1936 to meet an IJA requirement for a single-engined light bomber, the **Ki-32** was a mid-wing monoplane with fixed tailwheel landing gear and accommodation for a crew of two. Power was provided by an Ha-9-II V-12 engine, but this proved to be so temperamental that the Ki-32 proved unsuc-cessful in competitive trials against the Mitsubishi Ki-30 that had been developed against the same require-ment. However, the desperate need for aircraft following the start of full-scale war with China in 1937 resulted in the Ki-32 being ordered into produc-tion in July 1938 under the official designation **Army Type 98 Single-Engine Light Bomber**. A total of 854 Ki-32s was built before production ended in May 1940, and the type was used operationally at the beginning of the Pacific war and later allocated the Allied codename **'Mary'**. However, during 1942 the type was withdrawn from front-line service and then given employment in train-ing units.

SPECIFICATION

Kawasaki Ki-32
Type: two-seat light bomber
Powerplant: one 850-hp (634-kW) Kawasaki Ha-9-IIb V-12 piston engine
Performance: maximum speed 263 mph (423 km/h) at 12,925 ft (3490 m); service ceiling 29,265 ft (8920 m); range 1,218 miles (1960 km)
Weights: empty 5,179 lb

(2,349 kg); maximum take-off 8,294 lb (3762 kg)
Dimensions: span 49 ft 2½ in (15.00 m); length 38 ft 2¼ in (11.64 m); height 9 ft 6¼ in (2.90 m); wing area 365.97 sq ft (34.00 m²)
Armament: one fixed and one trainable 0.303-in (7.7-mm) Type 89 machine-gun, plus up to 992 lb (450 kg) of bombs

As a front-line bomber, the Ki-32 took part in combat operations during the Japanese attacks on Hong Kong.

Kawasaki Ki-45 Toryu

In early 1937 Kawasaki was instructed by the IJA to initiate the design and development of a twin-engined fighter that would be suitable for long-range operations over the Pacific. This was initiated under the designation **Ki-38**, but extensive design changes brought redesignation as the **Ki-45** and it was not until January 1939 that the first prototype was flown, a cantilever mid-wing mono-plane with retractable tailwheel landing gear, the fuselage accommodating its two-man crew in tandem enclosed cockpits. The originally installed 820-hp (611-kW) Nakajima Ha-20B radials failed to develop their rated power, resulting in the first **Ki-45-I** prototype with 1,000-hp (746-kW) Ha-25s not being flown until July 1940. Development problems

This Ki-45 KAIc flew with the 53rd Sentai of the Imperial Japanese Army, from Matsudo in Chiba Prefecture during 1944-45. It was tasked with the defence of the Japanese home islands.

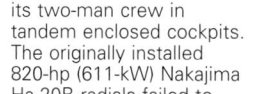

SPECIFICATION

Kawasaki Ki-45 KAIc
Type: two-seat night-fighter
Powerplant: two 1,080-hp (805-kW) Mitsubishi Ha-102 engines
Performance: maximum speed 339 mph (545 km/h) at 22,965 ft (7000 m); service ceiling 32,810 ft (10000 m); range 1,243 miles (2000 km)
Weights: empty 8,818 lb (4000 kg); maximum take-off

12,125 lb (5500 kg)
Dimensions: wingspan 49 ft 4½ in (15.05 m); length 36 ft 1 in (11.00 m); height 12 ft 1½ in (3.70 m); wing area 344.46 sq ft (32.00 m²)
Armament: cannon and machine guns as listed under variants, plus (all versions) provision for two drop-tanks or two 551-lb (250-kg) bombs on underwing racks

Variants

Ki-45: three prototypes with Nakajima Ha-20B engines and armament of three 0.303-in (7.7-mm) machine-guns and one 20-mm cannon
Ki-45-I: prototypes with Nakajima Ha-25 engines and armament as Ki-45
Ki-45 KAI: 12 pre-production aircraft with Ha-25 engines
Ki-45 KAIa: initial production version with Ha-25 engines; armament of two 0.5-in (12.7-mm) machine-guns in fuselage nose, one 0.31-in (7.92-mm) rear-firing gun on trainable mount, and one forward-firing 20-mm cannon
Ki-45 KAIb: ground attack/anti-shipping version; early production with Ha-25 engines, late production with developed Mitsubishi Ha-102; armament of one 20-mm cannon in nose, one forward-firing 37-mm cannon in fuselage, and one rear-firing 0.31-in (7.92-mm) machine-gun
Ki-45 KAIc: night-fighter version, 477 built; Ha-102 engines and armament comprising one forward-firing 37-mm cannon, two obliquely-mounted upward-firing 20-mm cannon, and one 0.31-in (7.92-mm) aft-firing machine-gun
Ki-45 KAId: anti-shipping version; Ha-102 engines and armament of two forward-firing 20-mm cannon, one forward-firing 37-mm cannon and one 0.31-in (7.92-mm) aft-firing machine-gun
Ki-45-II: version to be powered by two 1,500-hp (1119-kW) Mitsubishi Ha-112-II radials; developed instead as **Ki-96** single-seat fighter, but built only as a prototype

with this powerplant delayed the initial production order until September 1941, when manufacture of the **KI-45-KAI** began under the official designation **Army Type 2 Two-Seat Fighter Model**

A *Toryu* (dragon slayer). Entering service in August 1942, the type was first used in combat during October 1942, being allocated the Allied codename **'Nick'** shortly afterwards. It was soon found to be

effective against the USAAF's B-24 Liberators, and when B-24s were used more extensively for night operations the Ki-45 was adapted to attack them. In this way the night fighting capability of the type was

discovered, leading to a specially developed night-fighter variant which proved to be one of the most successful Japanese aircraft in this category. A total of 1,698 Ki-45s was built, used for the defence

of Tokyo and in the Burma, Manchuria and Sumatra theatres of operation. On 28 May 1944 four Ki-45s pioneered the use of aircraft for *kamikaze* attacks against Allied shipping.

Kawasaki Ki-48 (Army Type 99 Twin-engined Light Bomber)

An IJA requirement of 1937 for a high-performance twin-engine light bomber led to design and development of the **Ki-48**, a cantilever mid-wing monoplane with retractable tailwheel landing gear, and power provided initially by two 950-hp (708-kW) Nakajima Ha-25 radial engines. The fuselage accommodated a crew of four and incorporated an internal bomb bay. It was not until July 1939 that the first of four prototypes was flown, and following the resolution of initial prob-

lems the type was ordered into production in late 1939 under the designation **Army Type 99 Twin-Engine Light Bomber Model 1A**. Ki-48s used operationally in China during the autumn of 1940 proved fast enough to be virtually immune from enemy defences, but their deployment at the beginning of the Pacific war, when they were allocated the Allied codename **'Lily'**, showed that this speed was not good enough to provide protection against USAAF fighters. By then an

improved **Ki-48-II** was already under development, with protected fuel tanks, armour protection for the crew and more powerful Ha-115 engines, and this entered production in the spring of 1942 under the designation **Army Type 99 Twin Engine Light Bomber Model 2A**. Even this had little chance of survival against improving Allied fighters, and by October 1944 it had been declared obsolescent, most Ki-48s ending their days in desperate *kamikaze* attacks.

Variants

Ki-48: four prototypes and five pre-production aircraft
Ki-48-Ia: initial production version with armament of three 0.303-in (7.7-mm) machine-guns on pivoted mounts in nose, dorsal and ventral positions, plus a maximum bombload of 882 lb (400 kg)
Ki-48-Ib: version of Ki-48Ia with minor equipment changes and detail refinement; production of Ki-48Ia and Ki-48-Ib versions totalled 557
Ki-48-II: three prototypes built in early 1942
Ki-48-IIa: initial production version of Ki-48-II; defensive armament as Ki-48-Ia, but maximum bombload increased to 1,764 lb (800 kg)
Ki-48-IIb: production version generally as Ki-48-IIa, but with dive-brakes in the undersurface of each outer wing panel
Ki-48-IIc: production version generally as Ki-48-IIa, but with revised armament incorporating an extra machine-gun of 0.5 in (12.7-mm) calibre; production of all Ki-48-II versions totalled 1,408
Ki-81: projected heavily armed and armoured version of Ki-48; not built
Ki-174: single-seat special attack version of Ki-48; not built

SPECIFICATION

Kawasaki Ki-48-IIb
Type: four-seat light bomber/dive-bomber
Powerplant: two 1,150-hp (858-kW) Nakajima Ha-115 engines
Performance: maximum speed 314 mph (505 km/h); service ceiling 33,135 ft (10100 m); maximum range 1,491 miles (2400 km)
Weights: empty 10,031 lb

(4550 kg); maximum take-off 14,881 lb (6750 kg)
Dimensions: wingspan 57 ft 3 in (17.40 m); length 41 ft 10 in (12.75 m); height 12 ft 5½ in (3.80 m); wing area 430.57 sq ft (40.00 m²)
Armament: as detailed under variants

Improvements introduced with the Ki-48-IIa included more power, self-sealing fuel tanks and limited armour protection. Nevertheless, the type was still hopelessly vulnerable to fighter attack.

Kawasaki Ki-61 (Army Type 3 Fighter Model 1 Hien)

Designed around the Kawasaki Ha-40 engine, a licence-built version of the German Daimler-Benz DB 601A, the **Ki-60** prototype proved disappointing and was soon abandoned. Efforts were then concentrated on an alternative design, the **Ki-61**, the first of 12 prototypes being laid down during December 1941. This, like the Bf 109, had a liquid-cooled engine and was at one time erroneously considered by the Allies to be a licence-built version of that famous fighter. Service tests proved so satisfactory that

The 23rd Dokuritsu Dai Shijugo Chutai (independent squadron) of the IJA flew this Ki-61-I KAIc from Yontan on Okinawa in April 1945.

the IJA quickly accepted the type for production under the designation **Army Type 3 Fighter Model 1 Hien** (swallow),

this subsequently being allocated the Allied codename **'Tony'**. The initial **Ki-61-I** production version began to enter combat operations from New Guinea in April 1943, soon proving that it was well able to hold it's own against Allied fighters, and with increasing production the type was soon found in all theatres in which the Japanese army was operat-

ing. When production ended in January 1945, a total of 2,666 had been built. The development of an improved **Ki-61-II** began in the autumn of 1942, but

only 99 had been delivered when, in January 1945, manufacture of its Ha-140 engine was brought to an end as the result of USAAF air attacks.

SPECIFICATION

Kawasaki Ki-61-Ic
Type: single-seat fighter
Powerplant: one 1,175-hp (876-kW) Kawasaki Ha-40 V-12 piston engine
Performance: maximum speed 348 mph (560 km/h); service ceiling 32,810 ft (10000 m); maximum range 1,181 miles (1900 km)
Weights: empty 5,798 lb (2630 kg); maximum take-off

7,650 lb (3470 kg)
Dimensions: wingspan 39 ft 4½ in (12.00 m); length 29 ft 4¼ in (8.95 m); height 12 ft 11 in (3.70 m); wing area 215.29 sq ft (20.00 m²)
Armament: as detailed under variants, plus provision for two drop tanks or two 551-lb (250-kg) bombs

Note the open flap on the centreline radiator installation of this plainly-marked Ki-61.

Kawasaki Ki-61 (Army Type 3 Fighter Model 1 Hien) (cont.)

Variants

Ki-61: 12 original prototypes
Ki-61-I: initial production version; armament comprised two fuselage mounted 0.303-in (7.7-mm) machine-guns and two wing-mounted 0.5-in (12.7-mm) guns
Ki-61-Ia: as Ki-61-I, but with wing mounted machine-guns replaced by two imported 20-mm Mauser MG 151cannon
Ki-61-Ib: as Ki-61-I, but with fuselage-mounted machine-guns replaced by guns of 0.5-in (12.7-mm) calibre
Ki-61-I KAIc: revised version to simplify maintenance; armament of

two fuselage-mounted 0.5-in (12.7-mm) machine-guns and two wing-mounted 20-mm indigenous Ho-5 cannon
Ki-61-I KAId: as Ki-61-Ic, but with 20-mm cannon replaced by 30-mm Ho-105 cannon
Ki-61-II: eight prototypes with increased-area wing and Kawasaki Ha-140 engine
Ki-61-II KAI: 30 prototype/pre-production aircraft, with reversion to Ki-61-I wing and redesigned tail surfaces
Ki-61-IIa: initial production version with armament as Ki-61-Ic
Ki-61-IIb: as Ki-61-IIa, but with armament of four 20-mm Ho-5 cannon
Ki-61-III: single prototype of proposed improved version

Kawasaki Ki-100

The Ki-61-II was regarded as a worthwhile high- altitude interceptor to tackle the USAAF's Boeing B-29s at their cruising altitude of some 30,000 ft (9145 m), but plans to deploy the aircraft in this role came to an end when production of the Kawasaki Ha-140 engine was terminated by USAAF air attacks. Kawasaki by then had 275 completed Ki-61-II airframes without powerplants, and it was decided to bring these into service with an alternative engine. With no inline engine available, it meant the airframe had to be adapted for the installation of a large-diameter radial, the Mitsubishi Ha-112-II which had the same power output as the Ha-140. First flown with this new engine on 1 February 1945 as the **Ki-100**, the aircraft was immediately revealed as

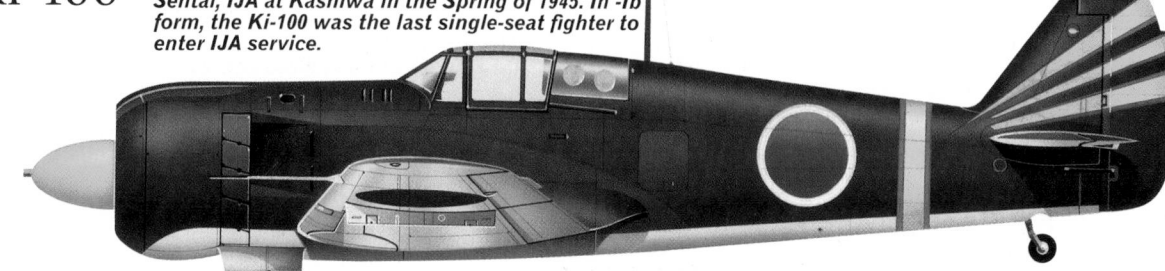

This Ki-100-Ia served with the 3rd Chutai, 18th Sentai, IJA at Kashiwa in the Spring of 1945. In -Ib form, the Ki-100 was the last single-seat fighter to enter IJA service.

Variant

Ki-100-II: three prototypes with the Ha-112-IIru turbocharged engine to improve high-altitude performance; no production examples built

an exceptional interceptor, one regarded by some as Japan's outstanding fighter aircraft of the Pacific war. Three prototypes were completed and enthusiastic service trials resulted in an immediate order for the remaining 272 airframes to be similarly powered under the designation

Army Type 5 Fighter Model 1A, these having the company designation **Ki-100-1a**. Simultaneously, the army requested Kawasaki to initiate new production, and the airframe that had been designed for the Ki-61-III, with a cut-down rear fuselage and all-round-view

bubble canopy, was adopted for the **Ki-100-1b**. A total of 99 of this version was built

before production was halted by the growing intensity of USAAF air attacks.

SPECIFICATION

Kawasaki Ki-100-1a/b
Type: single-seat interceptor fighter
Powerplant: one 1,500-hp (1119-kW) Mitsubishi Ha-112-II engine
Performance: maximum speed 367 mph (590 km/h) at 32,810 ft (10000 m); service ceiling 35,005 ft (10670 m); range 1,243 miles (2000 km)
Weights: 5,952 lb (2700 kg);
maximum take-off 8,091 lb (3670 kg)
Dimensions: wingspan 39 ft 4½ in (12.00 m); length 28 ft 10½ in (8.80 m); height 12 ft 3½ in (3.75 m) wing area 215.29 sq ft (20.00 m²)
Armament: two fuselage-mounted 0.5-in (12.7-mm) Ho-103 (Type 1) machine-guns and two wing-mounted 20-mm Ho-5 cannon, plus two drop-tanks or two 551-lb (250-kg) bombs

Kawasaki Ki-102 (Army Type 4 Assault Aircraft)

Derived from the **Ki-96** twin-engined single-seat fighter, development of which from the Ki-45 was abandoned after three prototypes had been completed, the **Ki-102** was intended as a two-seat attack fighter for primary deployment in a close-support role. Some assemblies of the Ki-96 prototypes were incorporated in the three Ki-102 prototypes, the first completed in March 1944. A cantilever mid-wing monoplane, with retractable tailwheel land-

The Ki-102b saw little operational service, but did test the Igo-1-B guided AGM.

ing gear and powered by two Ha-112-II radials, the two-man crew was accommodated in separate enclosed cockpits. Twenty pre-production aircraft were built before production was ordered under the official designation **Army Type 4 Assault Plane**, Kawasaki designation **Ki-102b**. Allocated the Allied codename **'Randy'**, the aircraft saw little service, being

used over Okinawa while the majority was held in reserve in Japan.
The urgent need for interceptors to attack the USAAF's bomber fleets brought the modification of six pre-production Ki-102s as the prototypes of a twin-engine high-altitude fighter. These differed primarily from the Ki-102b by having a revised tail unit and turbocharged Mitsubishi Ha-112-IIru engines. However, problems with this engine installation resulted in only about 15 being completed before the war ended.

SPECIFICATION

Kawasaki Ki-102b
Type: twin-engined close-support aircraft
Powerplant: two 1,500-hp (1119-kW) Mitsubishi Ha-112-II engines
Performance: maximum speed 360 mph (580 km/h) at 19,685 ft (6000 m); service ceiling 36,090 ft (11000 m); range 1,243 miles (2000 km)
Weights: empty 10,913 lb
(4950 kg); maximum take-off 16,094 lb (7300 kg)
Dimensions: wingspan 51 ft 1 in (15.57 m); length 37 ft 6¾ in (11.45 m); height 12 ft 11 in (3.70 m); wing area 365.98 sq.ft (34.00 m²)
Armament: as listed under variants, plus (all versions) provision for two drop-tanks or two 551-1b (250-kg) bombs

Variants

Ki-102: designation of prototypes and pre-production aircraft
Ki-102a: high-altitude fighter version; armament of one 37-mm Ho-203 cannon and two 20-mm Ho-5 cannon
Ki-102b: ground-attack version; armament of one 57-mm Ho-401 cannon, two 20-mm Ho-5 cannon, and one rear-firing 0.5-in (12.7-mm) Ho-103 (Type 1) machine-gun
Ki-102c: proposed night-fighter version with increased wingspan, lengthened fuselage, revised tail surfaces, primitive AI radar and armament of two 30-mm Ho-105 and two 20-mm Ho-5 cannon; only two completed
Ki-108: two prototypes of a high-altitude fighter with a pressurised cabin; both conversions of Ki-102b airframes with structural improvements of Ki-102c; these were still being tested at the end of the war

Kawasaki OH-1

From the mid-1980s the Japan Defence Agency, began to consider how best to procure a successor to the OH-6D light helicopter currently in service with the Japan Ground Self-Defence Force for the scouting and observation roles. It was decided that there was sufficient in-country experience with the design and, more particularly, the licensed production of other countries' helicopters to make an indigenous type feasible, and in the second quarter of 1992 the JDA's Technical Research & Development Institute issued a requirement, and in September of the same year Kawasaki was selected as prime contractor with 60 per cent of the programme with the balance of 40 per cent allocated in equal portions to Fuji (tail unit, canopy and stub wing) and Mitsubishi (central fuselage and landing gear).

The three companies established the Observation Helicopter Engineering Team to undertake the programme, on which detailed work began in October 1992. The resulting **OH-1** is a conventional helicopter that is comparatively small and of typical gunship helicopter

Kawasaki's OH-1 features a long flat-plate cockpit canopy. The gunner is seated behind and above the pilot, who flies the helicopter via a HOCAC (Hands On Cyclic And Collective) system.

configuration. Its structure comprises, by weight, 40 per cent carbonfibre-reinforced plastics. Features of the design include a Kawasaki all-composite rotor system and a 'fenestron' type tail rotor with 10 asymmetrically arranged blades, a flat stub wing behind the pilot's cockpit for disposable weapons, and fixed tailwheel landing gear.

The first of six prototypes (four for flight trials and two for ground tests) made the type's initial flight on 6 August 1996, and the first of a possible 150 to 200 OH-1s was delivered on 24 January 2000. A total of 14 OH-1s has been ordered for delivery into 2001. Armament for self-defence rather than offensive purposes, in the form of two pairs of Toshiba Type 91 lightweight AAMs. Each member of the crew has two liquid-crystal colour multi-function displays, and the gunner has a Shimadzu HUD.

Integrated by means of a digital databus, the mission avionics are relatively comprehensive and include a trainable roof-mounted Kawasaki package (just forward of the main rotor) with a Fujitsu thermal imager, NEC colour TV camera and NEC laser rangefinder. Protection is enhanced by the installation of an IR jammer (based on the American ALQ-144) on the spine of the helicopter to the rear of the main gearbox.

The JDA is currently considering the possibility of revising the OH-1 to meet its AH-X light attack helicopter requirement. The

core of this upgrade would be an uprated dynamic system based possibly on two Rolls-Royce/Turbomeca/MTU MTR-390 or LHTEC T800 turboshaft engines, allowing the intro-

duction of a heavier weapons load operated in conjunction with a revised package of mission avionics. The projected designation of the AH-X production model is **AH-2**.

SPECIFICATION	
Kawasaki OH-1	(2500 kg); maximum take-off 7,717 lb (3500 kg)
Type: two-seat light scout and observation helicopter	**Dimensions:** main rotor diameter 37 ft 8¾ in (11.50 m); wingspan 9 ft 10 in (3.00 m); length 39 ft 4½ in (12.00 m) for the fuselage; height 12 ft 5½ in (3.80 m); main rotor disc area 1,118.07 sq ft (103.97 m²)
Powerplant: two Mitsubishi TS1-10 turboshaft engines each rated at 884 shp (659 kW)	
Performance: maximum speed 180 mph (290 km/h) at optimum altitude; cruising speed 168 mph (270 km/h) at optimum altitude; range 249 miles (400 km)	
Weights: empty 5,511 lb	**Armament:** four Type 91 short-range AAMs carried under the stub wing

Kawasaki KA-851 (T-4)

When it was decided in the late 1970s that the Japan Air Self-Defence Force would need an intermediate flying trainer to replace its Fuji T1F (T-1) and Lockheed T-33 aircraft in the late 1980s, the JDA approached Fuji and Kawasaki for a successor type. In September 1971 the agency announced that it was ordering development of the **Kawasaki KA-851** in preference to the Fuji FT-20 concept. Detail design was finalised by the end of 1983, and the construction of six **XT-4** prototypes (including two non-flying airframes for static and fatigue testing) began in the spring of 1984. As has been the case with several other Japanese military aircraft, the construction effort was collaborative, with Fuji building the wing, rear fuselage and tail unit, Mitsubishi the centre fuselage and air inlets, and Kawasaki the forward fuselage. As prime contractor, Kawasaki also takes responsibility for final assembly and test.

The new trainer was intended for the combat training role, and this

demanded a sturdy airframe capable of great agility at high subsonic speeds. Kawasaki's design was therefore modelled on weapon training and light attack warplane characteristics in its nicely streamlined fuselage with a high-set and pressurised cockpit located well forward to provide the pupil and vertically staggered instructor (both on UPCO [Stencel] SIIS-3 ejection seats) with excellent fields of vision, tricycle landing gear with all three single-wheel units retracting into the fuselage, an anhedralled shoulder-set wing of supercritical aerofoil section with dogtoothed outer panels, and a swept tail unit with an all-moving anhedralled mid-set tailplane.

The first of the prototypes took to the air on 29 July 1985. All four prototypes had flown by July 1986, and successful trials led to full-scale production. The first **T-4** flew in June 1988, and deliveries began in September of the same year, with the *Blue Impulse* national aerobatic display team and the instrument/communications flights of most operational squadrons

and the flights of regional headquarters, as well as the training organisation, all receiving aircraft. Although it was developed primarily as an intermediate flying trainer, the T-4 has features (a Kaiser HUD made under licence by Shimadzu as well as three hardpoints) that make it capable of a light attack tasking as well as the armament training role. Such is the type's potential in the armed role, moreover, that Kawasaki has proposed an enhanced version as a possible replacement for the Mitsubishi T-2 in the dedicated armament training role. The JASDF has a requirement for 200 T-4s.

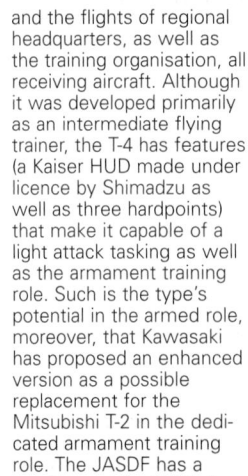

The blue line under the chequered tail sash of this Dai 1 Koku-dan T-4 indicates that it is assigned to the unit's 31st Squadron. The T-4 can also fly in the target-towing role with the addition of target-towing equipment.

SPECIFICATION	
Kawasaki T-4	(3790 kg); maximum take-off 16,534 lb (7500 kg)
Type: two-seat intermediate flying trainer with weapons training and light attack capabilities	**Dimensions:** wingspan 32 ft 7½ in (9.94 m); length 42 ft 8 in (13.00 m); height 15 ft 1¼ in (4.60 m); wing area 226.05 sq ft (21.00 m²)
Powerplant: two Ishikawajima-Harima F3-IHI-30 turbofan engines each rated at 3,660 lb st (16.28 kN)	
Performance: maximum speed 645 mph (1038 km/h) at sea level; cruising speed 495 mph (797 km/h) at 36,000 ft (10975 m); initial climb rate 10,000 ft (3048 m) per minute; service ceiling 50,000 ft (15240 m); range 806 miles (1297 km) with standard fuel	**Armament:** around 4,409 lb (2000 kg) of disposable stores, generally comprising free-fall or retarded bombs, multiple launchers for 2.75-in (70-mm) air-to-surface unguided rockets, gun pods, and (as a possible retrofit) ASMs and short-range AAMs
Weights; empty 8,356 lb	

Kellet KD-1 series

The **KD-1** autogyro of 1934 was of similar overall configuration to the contemporary British Cierva C.30, with two open cockpits in tandem, and was powered by a 225-hp (168-kW) Jacobs L-4 radial engine. Extensive testing of this machine by the company led to the decision to put into production a commercial version designated **KD-1A**, which incorporated a three-bladed rotor with folding blades, a mechanical system to spin-up the rotor, a rotor brake, lightweight tailwheel landing gear, and a number of detail refinements; the Jacobs L-4 radial engine was retained for this model. A generally-similar

KD-1A, but with a single-seat open cockpit, was used on 19 May 1939 for a first demonstration of the capability of the type to provide feeder air-mail services, carrying a cargo of mail from the centre of Washington to the city's Hoover Airport. A little less than two months later, on 6 July, Eastern Airlines inaugurated the first scheduled air-mail service with a rotary-wing aircraft, a **KD-1B**, which differed from the KD-1A only by having an enclosed cockpit for the pilot.

At an earlier date, in 1935, the US Army decided to evaluate the capability of the Kellett machine, acquiring a single KD-1 which it designated **YG-1**. It was

followed in 1936 by a second example equipped with radio which was designated **YG-1A** and in 1937 by seven **YG-1B** aircraft with equipment changes. In 1942 seven more were obtained for use in an observation role, as **XO-60** aircraft, the designation of six of them changing to **YO-60** after their 225-hp (168-kW) Jacobs R-775 engines had been replaced by 300-hp (224-kW) Jacobs R-915-3s, some revision had been made to the cabin enclosure and additional observation windows had been provided. One YG-1B gained a constant-speed rotor, being redesignated **YG-1C**, and when its powerplant was changed subsequently from the Jacobs R-775 to the more powerful R-915 the new

An advanced autogyro design, the Kellett KD-1A featured a rotor that could be clutched to the Jacobs radial engine for pre-flight spin up.

designation **XR-2** was applied. After this aircraft was destroyed by rotor ground resonance problems, one other YG-1B was similarly converted for continued evaluation under the designation **XR-3**.

These aircraft were the first practical, rotary-wing aircraft used by the US Army, but after their construction had been completed Kellett discontinued the production of autogyros.

Keystone bombers

The Huff-Daland company designed a large single-engined biplane bomber, the prototype being acquired by the US Army in 1923. Designated **Huff-Daland XLB-1**, this was powered by an 800-hp (597-kW) Packard 1A-2540 engine which, mounted in the nose, meant that the bomb aimer's position was in the centre fuselage. This prototype was followed by 10 generally-similar **LB-1** pre-production aircraft, which differed by accommodating an extra crew member and by the installation of an improved Packard 2A-2540 engine. More extensive service trials led to a conclusion that the single-engine powerplant was unsatisfactory, and

Huff-Daland began development of a twin-engine version, with two 420-hp (313-kW) Liberty V-1410-1 engines mounted on the lower wing, one on each side of the fuselage. Testing of this single **XLB-3** led to replacement of the Liberty V-1410s by two 410-hp (306-kW) Pratt & Whitney R-1340-1 Wasp engines, this revised version being designated **XLB-3A** and accommodating a crew of five. Just before delivery of the XLB-3A for service testing, the company name was changed to Keystone Aircraft Corporation, with the result that all of these prototype/pre-production aircraft, together with subsequent production aircraft, are known usually

as Keystone bombers. However, a reversion to Liberty engines produced the **XLB-5** prototype and it, and 10 production **LB-5** aircraft delivered before the XLB-3A, entered service as Huff-Daland aircraft; 25 **LB-5A** bombers with tail unit changes were Keystones. The **XLB-6** of 1927, a conversion of an LB-5 airframe, introduced new wings and a revised engine installation, one 525-hp (391-kW) Wright R-1750-1 Cyclone being strut-mounted between the wings on each side of the fuselage. It was followed by 17 production **LB-6** aircraft with detail improvements, and these LB-5/-5A and LB-6 aircraft represented the first in-service production examples of a series of Keystone biplane bombers that was to serve with the US Army Air Corps into the early 1930s.

Aircraft like this LB-5 initially entered service with squadrons of the USAAC 2nd Bomb Group, they later equipped squadrons of the 7th and 19th Bomb Groups, representing the backbone of the US Army's heavy offensive force, and also served with overseas units in Hawaii, the Panama Canal Zone and the Philippines.

Variants

LB-7: identical to LB-6s except for installation of 525-hp (391-kW) Pratt & Whitney R-1690-3 Hornet engines; 18 built
LB-8: one LB-7 following installation of 550-hp (410-kW) Pratt & Whitney R-1860-3 engines for evaluation
LB-9: one LB-7 following installation of 575-hp (429-kW) Wright GR-1750 Cyclone engines for evaluation
LB-10: one LB-6 following installation of 525-hp (391-kW) Wright R-1750-1 engines for evaluation
LB-10A: production version of LB-10 but with 525-hp (391-kW) R-1690-3 engines; 63 built, but all delivered as **B-3A** aircraft following introduction of 'B' designations for all USAAC bomber types
LB-11: one LB-6 following installation of 525-hp (391-kW) R-1750-3 engines for evaluation
LB-11A: redesignation of LB-11 following installation of 525-hp (391-kW) GR-1750 engines for evaluation
LB-12: aircraft generally similar to LB-7 except for installation of 575-hp (429-kW) R-1860-1 direct-drive engines for evaluation
LB-13: seven aircraft ordered under this designation were delivered as five **Y1B-4** pre-production aircraft with 575-hp (429-kW) R-1860-7 engines, and two **Y1B-6** pre-production aircraft with 575-hp (429-kW) Wright R-1820-1 engines; three B-3As were also converted to the Y1B-6 configuration
LB-14: three production aircraft ordered with 575-hp (429-kW) Pratt & Whitney GR-1860 engines, but delivered as **Y1B-5** aircraft with 525-hp (391-kW) Wright R-1750-3 engines
B-4A: production version of Y1B-4; 25 built
B-5A: production version of Y1B-5; 27 built
B-6A: production version of Y1B-6; 39 built

SPECIFICATION	
Keystone B-4A	maximum take-off 13,209 lb
Type: five-seat light bomber	(5992 kg)
Powerplant: two 575-hp (429-kW) Pratt & Whitney R-1860-7 radial engines	**Dimensions:** wingspan 74 ft 8 in (22.76 m); length 48 ft 10 in (14.88 m); height 15 ft 9 in (4.80 m); wing area 1,145 sq ft (106.37 m²)
Performance: maximum speed 121 mph (195 km/h); service ceiling 14,000 ft (4265 m); range 855 miles (1376 km)	**Armament:** three 0.3-in (7.62-mm) Browning machine-guns, plus up to 2,500 lb (1134 kg) of bombs
Weights: empty 7,951 lb (3607 kg)	

Klemm lightplanes

Dr Ing. Hans Klemm began his career as a highly successful designer of lightplanes soon after World War I, when he was working for Daimler at Stuttgart. In 1926 he established his own company, Klemm Leichtflugzeugbau GmbH, at Böblingen, near Stuttgart, the first product

of this new organization being the **Klemm L 25** of which, over the years, more than 600 were produced. A two-seat cantilever low-wing monoplane, in its initial form the aircraft was powered by a 20-hp (15-kW) Mercedes-Benz two-cylinder engine, but subsequent versions

included the **L 25 1a** with a 40-hp (30-kW) Salmson AD-9 engine, a seaplane version of this aircraft designated **WL 25 1a**, and a three-seat **L 25 1b** with the forward cockpit enlarged to seat two. Following the same lines Klemm produced the lengthened and strengthened **L 26a**, the **L 27** with an enlarged forward cockpit, the aerobatic **L 28**

powered by a 150-hp (112-kW) Siemens Sh 14a engine, and the **L 30** similar to the L 25/L 26 series but intended for assembly by flying clubs.

In 1933 the **Kl 31** and **Kl 32** were introduced as four- and three-seat cabin monoplanes respectively, and both powered by the Siemens Sh 14a radial. They were followed by a considerable change in

design with the **Kl 33**, a single-seat ultralight of high-wing monoplane configuration powered by a 40-hp (30-kW) Argus engine. Next came the important **Kl 35** two-seat low-wing monoplane which, in the original **Kl 35a** prototype as flown in 1935, was powered by an 80-hp (60-kW) Hirth HM 60R engine. The second prototype, the

KI 35b, had a 105-hp (78-kW) Hirth HM 504A-2, which also powered the initial KI 35B production version. This became available with wood or metal

Rights to the KL 107 (pictured), designed by Klemm during World War II, were subsequently acquired by Bölkow, which developed the type as the KI 107B, flown in 1956, and the three-seat KI 107C.

floats as the **KI 35BW** and, in addition to production for the home market, KI 35s of different versions were exported to Czechoslovakia, Hungary, Romania and Sweden, the last country also building the type under licence for use by its air force. In 1938 the improved **KI 35D** was developed for use as a primary trainer by the Luftwaffe, resulting in large scale production.

Before that, however, lightplane design and manufacture had continued with the **KI 36** four-seat cabin monoplane which was developed especially to compete in the 1934 Challenge de Tourisme Internationale; it was available as the **KI 36A** with the 220-hp (164-kW) Hirth HM 508F engine, or **KI 36B** with the 150-hp (112-kW) Bramo Sh 14A radial. Final versions to be produced before the beginning of

In KI 35D form, the basic KI 35 was given strengthened landing gear, available with floats, skis or wheels as required, and reverted to use of the lower-powered Hirth HM 60R engine.

World War II were the **KI 105** two-seat light monoplane powered by a 50-hp (37-kW) Z.9-92 engine, an enclosed cabin version of the same aircraft with a 105-hp (78-kW)

Hirth HM 500A-1 engine under the designation **KI 107**, and the **KI 106** developed version of the KI 35D powered by a 100-hp (75-kW) Hirth HM 500.

Koolhoven FK 31

In 1920 Frits Koolhoven left the British Aerial Transport Company for which he had designed the **FK 23 Bantam** single-seat fighter, a two-seat aerobatic/racing variant designated **FK 27**, and a four-passenger civil transport **FK 26**. None of these aircraft were built in significant numbers. Returning to his native Netherlands he became designer for the NVI (Nationale Vliegtuig-industrie) formed at the Hague in 1922.

The first aircraft built was the **Koolhoven FK 29**, a three-seat biplane with a 100-hp (75-kW) Bristol Lucifer engine. There followed the relatively successful **FK 31**, a parasol-wing monoplane intended to be a two-seat reconnaissance fighter, which first appeared in mock-up form at the 1922 Paris Salon de l'Aéronautique. The first prototype flew in the following year, charac-

The FK 31 was perhaps the first true two-seat reconnaissance fighter, and one of the first to be designed around an air-cooled engine. It also featured innovative oleo shock absorbers.

terised by its thick-section wing and deep, rounded fuselage. The much improved second prototype followed, this having its Jupiter engine close-cowled and wide-track fixed landing gear with independent main units. The unusual cabane struts connecting fuselage to wings in the prototypes were replaced by a more conventional arrangement

in series aircraft. Eight machines were bought by Finland in 1926. Four FK 31s for the Dutch East Indies Army and four more aircraft built under licence in Finland had modified tailplanes. The French authorities showed some interest in the design and one example was tested in France as the **De Monge M.101**, but no orders were forthcoming.

SPECIFICATION	
Koolhoven FK 31	**Weights:** empty equipped 2,293 lb (1040 kg); maximum take-off 3,968 lb (1800 kg)
Type: two-seat reconnaissance fighter	
Powerplant: one 420-hp (313-kW) Bristol Jupiter IV radial piston engine	**Dimensions:** wingspan 44 ft 11¼ in (13.70 m); length 25 ft 7 in (7.80 m) height 11 ft 1¾ in (3.40 m); wing area 292.79 sq ft (27.20 m²)
Performance: maximum speed 135 mph (218 km/h); service ceiling 23,620 ft (7200 m); endurance 6 hours	**Armament:** two fixed and two trainable 7.7-mm (0.303-in) machine-guns

Koolhoven FK 41

Following a number of less successful one-off designs, including the **FK 32** two-seat sesquiplane trainer, the **FK 33** nine-passenger three-engined transport (which served with both Lufthansa and the German Aero company), the **FK 34** three-seat reconnaissance floatplane and the **FK 30 Toerist** ultra-light two-seater, Koolhoven, who had by then formed his own company, produced the **FK 41**.

This was a three-seat high-wing cabin monoplane intended for sport or touring use, the first aircraft making its initial flight during July 1928. A batch of FK 41s was built in the Netherlands, in two versions, the **FK 41 Mk I** with a 105-hp (78-kW) Cirrus Hermes engine and the **FK 41 Mk II** with a 130-hp (97-kW) de Havilland Gipsy. Both

versions were built under licence in the UK by the Desoutter Aircraft Company, British production of both versions totalling 41.

Later FK 41s had simplified tail assemblies, and

both Dutch and British-built aircraft made a name for themselves in many countries during the period up to World War II, flying in Australia, the Belgian Congo and South Africa.

SPECIFICATION	
Koolhoven FK 41	121 mph (195 km/h)
Type: three-seat sport/touring cabin monoplane	**Weight:** maximum take-off 1,984 lb (900 kg)
Powerplant: one 130-hp (97-kW) de Havilland Gipsy Major 1 engine	**Dimensions:** wingspan 34 ft 5 in (10.50 m); length 25 ft 7 in (7.80 m)
Performance: maximum speed	

The FK 41 was tailored for the civilian market, though five British-built Desoutter Mk Is and IIs were impressed by the wartime RAF.

Koolhoven FK 43

Before the advent of the successful **FK 43**, Koolhoven had produced as one-off types in 1929 the **FK 41**, a high-wing cabin monoplane with a 105-hp (78-kW) Cirrus engine, and the **FK 42** parasol-wing light two-seat sport monoplane powered by a 230-hp (172-kW) Gnome-Rhône Titan radial. The **FK 40** was

a four-passenger transport which began its career with KLM and ended up as an air ambulance, flown by the Nationalists in the Spanish Civil War.

The prototype FK 43 was flown for the first time in 1931, and was a high-wing cabin monoplane for three passengers. It was built for private owners and as an

air taxi. KLM bought six which were operated for several years out of Schiphol on taxi routes. Powered by a 130-hp (97-kW) Gipsy Major engine, the FK 43 attained a maximum speed of 118 mph (190 km/h).

Three FK 43s were taken over by the Dutch air arm (the LVA) in 1939 and one example was requisitioned by the RAF in 1940.

The FK 43 proved a rugged aircraft with its fixed wide-track landing gear, and its design was refined progressively, the tailplane in particular being subjected to considerable modification.

Koolhoven FK 43 (continued)

Post-war, in 1947, the Fokker factory built eight improved FK 43s with 165-hp (123-kW) Genet

Major engines as air taxis for the Frits Diepen Vliegtuigen company.

Other single-engine monoplanes built by the Koolhoven company included the **FK 53 Junior**, a two-seat cabin monoplane with a low-set inverted gull-type wing and powered by a 62-hp (46-kW) Walter Mikron engine; the prototype flew in 1936 and a second example in 1938.

The **FK 54** was a three-seat braced high-wing cabin monoplane, intended for the private owner, and powered by a 140-hp (104-kW) Gipsy Major engine, but no production examples were built.

Koolhoven FK 46

The **FK 46** was a two seat sport and training biplane with tandem open cockpits. The first prototype was flown in the autumn of 1933 and was powered by a Cirrus Hermes engine; a second prototype had the cockpits enclosed by a sliding glass canopy. The type went into limited production, four examples being acquired for the NLS (Dutch national flying school). Another was tested by the LVA (Dutch army air arm) and was later returned to civil use. The

FK 46L, a reduced-weight version with a 95-hp (71-kW) Walter Minor, appeared in 1935. No production was undertaken but this single example survived, along with most of the FK 46s, until May 1940. The majority of FK 46s was powered by the 130-hp (97-kW) de Havilland Gipsy Major engine, giving a maximum speed at sea level of 109 mph (175 km/h).

The FK 46 had been preceded by the **FK 44** of 1931, a Cirrus-powered

The FK 46's maximum take-off weight was 1,918 lb (870 kg), its wingspan 26 ft 3 in (8.00 m) and its length 23 ft 11½ in (7.30 m).

two-seat parasol-wing sport monoplane (two built), and the **FK 45**, a lightweight aerobatic single-seat biplane which attained a maximum speed of 130 mph (210 km/h) on the power of its 115-hp (86-kW) Cirrus Hermes. The FK 45 was sold to the French aviator René Paulhan and was demonstrated at numerous pre-war air shows in

France.

The **FK 47** was a contemporary of the FK 46. Resembling an enlarged FK 45, it was a two-seat open-cockpit biplane intended for sport flying, which survived until being scrapped in 1939. Its Hermes engine gave it a maximum speed 117 mph (188 km/h).

Koolhoven FK 51

The prototype of the **FK 51** biplane basic trainer made its first flight on 25 May 1935 from Waalhaven. An equal-span biplane of mixed construction, the FK 51 was designed for engines in the 250-hp (186-kW) to 500-hp

(373-kW) range. Its divided landing gear was of wide track to cater for the rough handling it would receive from trainee pilots.

The Royal Dutch air force (LVA) ordered a total of 25 FK 51s in 1936-7, these being powered by the

270-hp (201-kW) Armstrong Siddeley Cheetah V radial. Later, a further 29 aircraft were acquired with 350-hp (261-kW) Cheetah IXs.

The Dutch Naval air arm (MLD) obtained 24 FK 51s, each powered by a 450-hp (335-kW) Pratt & Whitney radial. The Dutch East Indies army (LA) procured between 1936 and 1938 some 28 FK 51s with 420-hp (313-kW) Wright Whirlwinds. At least seven other FK 51s went to the East Indies.

The Republican government in Spain, engaged in civil war with the Franco

Following Germany's invasion of the Netherlands in May 1940, the FK 51s still in service were used for observation work.

insurgents, was sufficiently impressed by the demonstration given by prototype FK 51, to order 28 aircraft. These were delivered in two versions, 11 of them powered by 400-hp (298-kW) Armstrong Siddeley Jaguar IVa radials and 17 **FK 51bis** aircraft fitted with 450-hp (335-kW) Wright Whirlwind R-975E radials. Some of the Spanish FK 51s were used as night flying trainers, based at Carmoli airfield.

Others were operational as night-fighters or reconnaissance aircraft, in which role they were armed with two fixed 0.303-in (7.7-mm) Vickers machine-guns in the leading edge of the upper wing, with a single Lewis gun of the same calibre on a pivot mounting for operation by the observer.

With production totalling at least 142, the FK 51 was Frits Koolhoven's most successful design after his return to the Netherlands.

SPECIFICATION	
Koolhoven FK 51	(825 km)
Type: two-seat basic trainer biplane	**Weights:** empty equipped 2,160 lb (980 kg); maximum take-off
Powerplant: one 420-hp (313-kW) Wright Whirlwind radial engine	3,197 lb (1450 kg)
Performance: maximum speed 157 mph (253 km/h); service ceiling 21,325 ft (6500 m); range 513 miles	**Dimensions:** wingspan 29 ft 6¼ in (9.00 m); length 25 ft 9 in (7.85 m); height 9 ft 4¼ in (2.85 m); wing area 290.64 sq ft (27.00 m²)

Koolhoven FK 56

Flown initially on 30 June 1938, the first **FK 56** prototype was a low-wing monoplane of mixed construction, with an unusual inverted gull wing,

fixed landing gear, and the two crew members seated in tandem under a fully enclosed canopy. Intended as a basic trainer or light attack aircraft, the FK 56

was further modified and two more prototypes were tested. One introduced retractable main landing gear units and had a semi-open cockpit for the second crew member, while the final prototype had a simpler, straight wing and was specialised as a basic trainer with dual controls. Ten FK 56s resembling the third prototype were ordered by the

LVA. They included the first and third prototypes modified to production standard. All were delivered before the German invasion of the Netherlands on 10 May 1940. In February 1940 the

Belgian Aéronautique Militaire ordered 20 FK 56s; seven had been delivered before the remainder were destroyed in an air attack on the Waalhaven works.

SPECIFICATION	
Koolhoven FK 56	(1058 kg); maximum take-off
Type: two-seat basic trainer	3,527 lb (1600 kg)
Powerplant: one 450-hp (336-kW) Wright Whirlwind R-975-E3 radial piston engine	**Dimensions:** wingspan 37 ft 8¾ in (11.50 m); length 25 ft 9 in (7.85 m); height 7 ft 6½ in (2.30 m); wing area 215.28 sq ft (20.00 m²)
Performance: maximum speed 186 mph (300 km/h) at 1,640 ft (500 m); service ceiling 23,950 ft (7300 m); range 497 miles (800 km)	Armament: one fixed and one trainable 0.303-in (7.7-mm) machine-gun
Weights: empty equipped 2,332 lb	

The Koolhoven FK 56 was a conventional basic trainer, seen here in the form of one of the twenty examples ordered by Belgium in February 1940.

Koolhoven FK 58

Designed by Eric Schatski, formerly of the Fokker company, the **FK 58** was a single-seat low-wing mono-

plane fighter of mixed construction. Designed in great haste to meet a French requirement for a

fighter to operate in Indo-China, the prototype flew for the first time on 17 July 1938, only three months after the first drawings had been made. A robust, unattractive aircraft,

the FK 58 had an enclosed cockpit with a rearward sliding canopy, inward retracting main landing gear units and a strut-braced tailplane.

The French authorities

eventually ordered 50 aircraft and later the Dutch LVA decided to acquire 36 machines. In the event, a second prototype and 17 production aircraft for France were completed at

SPECIFICATION

Koolhoven FK 58
Type: single-seat fighter
Powerplant: one 1,030-hp (768-kW) Gnome-Rhône 14N-39 radial piston engine
Performance: maximum speed 295 mph (475 km/h) at 16,405 ft (5000 m); service ceiling 32,810 ft (10000 m); range 466 miles (750 km)
Weights: empty equipped 4,255 lb (1930 kg); maximum take-off 6,063 lb (2750 kg)
Dimensions: wingspan 35 ft 11¾ in (10.97 m); length 28 ft 5¾ in (8.68 m); height 9 ft 9¾ in (2.99 m); wing area 186.21 sq ft (17.30 m²)
Armament: four 0.295-in (7.5-mm) FN Browning machine-guns mounted beneath the wings

Similar in appearance to the Fokker D.XXI, also designed by E. Schatski, the FK 58 was part of a Dutch government re-equipment plan, although none had been delivered by May 1940.

Waalhaven, but to overcome various production problems the remaining 23 aircraft at Waalhaven were transferred to Nevers in France for final assembly. The 17 Dutch-built aircraft were flown to Buc airfield and were eventually issued, along with one or two machines from Nevers, to the Polish training division at Lyons and to a hastily formed *escadrille de regroupement* formed at Salon-de-Provence. The remainder were kept in reserve until the French surrender in June 1940, but soon afterwards they were all scrapped.

The Dutch order was based on availability of the Bristol Taurus III radial engine, which was never delivered. Production went ahead with the intention of using the less powerful Bristol Mercury VIII engine, which would give inferior performance, but the production line was destroyed during a Luftwaffe air attack on Waalhaven, on 10 May 1940, before any aircraft of the Dutch order had been completed.

Kyushu J7W Shinden

The first flight of the unique J7W Shinden (magnificent lightning), a canard-configuration single-seat fighter, was made on 3 August 1945, but the end of World War II later that month brought an end to development and production plans. Designed by a team under the leadership of Captain Masaoki Tsuruno of the Imperial Japanese Navy (IJN), the configuration of this aircraft had been effectively confirmed by the flight testing of three specially designed and built MXY6 gliders. The construction of two J7W1 prototypes followed, these each having a slender fuselage and mounting in a mid-position on the nose a short-span foreplane incorporating elevators at the trailing edge. The rear-mounted cantilever monoplane wing was set low on the fuselage, had moderately swept leading edges and conventional ailerons with, just inboard of these on each wing, a fin and rudder extending

The J7W1 spanned 36 ft 5½ in (11.11 m), had a maximum take-off weight of 11,526 lb (5288 kg), and was estimated to have a maximum speed of 466 mph (750 km/h). Four 30-mm Type 5 cannon were mounted in the nose.

above and below the trailing edge. The landing gear was of retractable tricycle type; the pilot was accommodated in an enclosed cockpit, directly above the leading edge of the wing; and power was provided by a 2,130-hp (1588-kW) Mitsubishi MK9D radial engine, mounted in the rear fuselage to drive a six-bladed pusher propeller. By the end of the war the second prototype had been completed but not flown.

A **J7W2** version to be powered by a 1,984-1b (900-kg) thrust Ne-130 turbojet reached the planning stage.

Kyushu K11W Shiragiku

The **K11W** was designed by Watanabe to meet an IJN requirement for a crew trainer. A mid-wing cantilever monoplane with retractable tailwheel landing gear, the K11W accommodated a pilot and radio operator/gunner in a canopied cockpit above the wing, with the instructor, bomb-aimer and navigator in a cabin below the wing. Power was provided by a 515-hp (384-kW) Hitachi GK2B Amakaze 21 radial engine. First flown in prototype form during November 1942, the K11W was soon ordered into production as the **Navy Operations Trainer Shiragiku** (white chrysanthemum), these aircraft having the company designation **K11W1**. Almost 800 were built by Kyushu from 1943 to 1945, being used extensively by the navy. In the closing stages of the Pacific war many K11W1s were used in *kamikaze* attacks. In addition to this standard version, a small number was built of all-wooden construction under the designation **K11W2** and equipped for use in ASW and transport roles. The same basic design was used for a dedicated anti-submarine aircraft, the **Kyushu Q3W1 Nankai** (south sea), which reached only prototype form.

The K11W1 spanned 49 ft 1¾ in (14.98 m), had a maximum take-off weight of 5,820 lb (2640 kg) and had a maximum speed of 143 mph (230 km/h). This aircraft was photographed in China immediately after VJ-Day, wearing 'surrender' colours – overall white with green crosses.

Kyushu Q1W Tokai

During 1942, K. K. Watanabe Tekkosho designed an ASW aircraft to meet an IJN requirement for a specialised aircraft in this category. Designated **Q1W**, this was a cantilever low-wing monoplane with retractable tailwheel landing gear. Operated by a crew of three, the Q1W was planned to use an advanced search radar, but this failed to materialize and instead the Q1W had to make do with an earlier and somewhat ineffective radar complemented by MAD (magnetic anomaly detection) equipment. First flown in September 1943, the **Q1W1** was ordered into production in early 1944 as the **Navy Patrol Plane Tokai** (eastern sea), later allocated the Allied codename **'Lorna'**. It proved to be unsuccessful in operational service, too slow and too vulnerable to attack by Allied fighters, and only about 150 had been built by the time the Pacific war ended.

Variants

Q1W1-K: four-seat, all-wooden trainer prototype, intended as a flying classroom for electronic equipment operators
Q1W2: a small number of aircraft with the rear fuselage structure of wood

Q1Ws were operated from bases in Japan, Formosa and China, tasked with the protection of supply convoys from the Dutch East Indies and Malaya.

SPECIFICATION

Kyushu Q1W1
Type: anti-submarine patrol aircraft
Powerplant: two 610-hp (459-kW) Hitachi GK2C Amakaze 31 engines
Performance: maximum speed 199 mph (320 km/h) at 4,395 ft (1340 m); service ceiling 14,765 ft (4500 m); range 833 miles (1340 km)
Weights: empty 6,834 lb (3100 kg); maximum take-off 11,718 lb (5315 kg)
Dimensions: wingspan 52 ft 6 in (16.00 m); length 39 ft 8 in (12.09 m); height 13 ft 6 in (4.12 m); wing area 411.19 sq ft (38.20 m²)
Armament: one rear-firing 0.303-in (7.7-mm) Type 92 machine-gun and two 551-lb (250-kg) depth charges or bombs; one or two 20-mm cannon in fuselage nose optional

Lake Buccaneer

In 1946 David B. Thurston established the Colonial Aircraft Corporation at Sanford, Maine, to build the **Colonial C-1 Skimmer** 2/3-seat amphibian. A cantilever shoulder-wing monoplane with a single-step all-metal hull, it had retractable tricycle landing gear, and was powered by a 150-hp (112-kW) Avco Lycoming O-320 engine mounted on a pylon above the hull to drive a pusher propeller. The prototype was flown for the first time on 17 July 1948, and 24 were built. The C-1 was followed by an improved **C-2 Skimmer IV** that provided four-seat accommodation and was powered by a 180-hp (134-kW) Avco Lycoming O-360-AIA engine. The manufacturing rights for this aircraft were acquired

The popular Buccaneer (illustrated) was further developed as the six-seat LA-250, turbocharged LA-270 and as the military Seawolf.

by Lake Aircraft Corporation in October 1959, and although there were a number of subsequent changes in ownership, Lake Amphibian Inc. of Laconia, New Hampshire, built the **Lake LA-4-200 Buccaneer** which benefited from 35 years of development and refinement, into the late 1990s. Almost 1,000 LA-4 Buccaneers were

built, and the company also built a lengthened-hull, six-seat version with a 250-hp (186-kW) engine as the **LA-250 Renegade**. When the Renegade was fitted with a turbocharged engine it became the **LA-250** or **LA-270 Turbo Renegade**, while a variant for military use was known as the **LA-250 Seawolf**. The **LA-270 Seafury** had improved

corrosion proofing and extra survival equipment

for operations from salt water.

Latécoère 17

Only one example of the **Latécoère 16** was built, a thick-section cantilever high-wing monoplane with cabin accommodation for four passengers. First flown during October 1923, it was powered by a single 300-hp (224-kW) Renault 12Fe engine. The **Latécoère 17** which followed was the company's first really successful design, the **Latécoère 17.01** prototype flying for the first time in November 1925. A parasol-wing monoplane with a

conventional fixed cross-axle landing gear, the Laté 17 seated the pilot in an open cockpit under the wing centre section and to his rear was a cabin to seat five passengers. The Laté 17 had a deep rounded fuselage and was powered by a single nose-mounted engine which, in the prototype and first six series aircraft, was a 300-hp (224-kW) Renault 121Pc engine. A single **Latécoère 17-1-J** with a 380-hp (283-kW) Gnome-Rhône Jupiter 9Aa radial was

followed by six **Latécoère 17-3-J** aircraft, all with an additional cabin window, one of the six being a conversion of the Laté 17-1-J. Nine **Latécoère 17-3-R** machines followed, with 300-hp (224-kW) Renault 12Fe engines, seven being built from scratch and two being converted Laté 17s. The final version was the **Latécoère 17-4-R**, with a 450-hp (336-kW) Renault 12Ja engine. Two were built, soon being joined by a third converted from a Laté 17-3-R. The Laté 17s were used on Latécoère airline routes.

The wingspan of the Laté 17 was 48 ft 2 in (14.68 m), its maximum take-off weight 4,711 lb (2137 kg) and its top speed 102 mph (164 km/h). The aircraft offered a range of 311 miles (500 km).

Latécoère 28

Developed from the **Latécoère 26** mail-carrying monoplane, the **Latécoère 28.0** was a braced high-wing monoplane powered by a Renault 12Jbr engine. The enclosed cockpit accommodated a pilot and co-pilot/ engineer, and the cabin was furnished for eight passengers. Seventeen Late 28.0s were followed by 29 **Latécoère 28.1** aircraft with a 500-hp (373-kW) Hispano-Suiza 12Hbxr engine. A number of Laté 28.0s was converted subsequently to Laté 28.1 standard.

These monoplanes were used on the African mail

routes connecting Casablanca with Dakar and also inaugurated the first regular service between Paris and Madrid, proving popular with crews and passengers alike. A total of 29 of both versions was still in service when Air France took over Aéropostale in 1933. A small number went to the Republican government in 1937, and these aircraft were flown in the Spanish Civil War.

The sole **Latécoère 28.2** was a mail carrier and established several payload/speed world records in 1931. The first of

five **Latécoère 28.3** mail carriers was flown by the celebrated Jean Mermoz on 11/12 April 1930 to achieve a world closed-circuit distance record for seaplanes of 2,677.085 miles (4308.34 km). This same aircraft, with increased fuel capacity, was flown nonstop with a normal load of mail from Senegal to Natal in Brazil on 12/13 May 1930, the pilot once again being Mermoz. This historic achievement resulted in the mail in question travelling from Paris to Santiago on Chile's Pacific coast in just over four days, a remarkable feat for 1930. The remaining Laté 28.3s were used on Mediterranean routes and charter services. The **Laté 28.1/H** was a wheel land-

ing gear version of the Laté 28.3. Two one-off aircraft were the **Latécoère 28.3-I**, a passenger version of the Laté 28.3, and the **Latécoère 28.4-I**, also developed from the Laté 28.3 but powered by a Gnome-Rhône 14Kbr radial engine of 700 hp (522 kW). In 1930 there appeared the **Latécoère 28.5**, structurally strengthened and powered by a 650-hp (485-kW) Hispano-Suiza 12Nbr, followed by three **Latécoère 28.6** aircraft, also Hispano-powered and

built for Venezuela, which had already purchased two Laté 28.1s.

No details are available of the **Latécoère 28.9**, except that it was a three-seat land-plane bomber version of the Laté 28.3; three were purchased by Venezuela in 1931. One Laté 28.0, with a new enlarged wing spanning 83 ft 8 in (25.50 m), was redesignated **Latécoère 28.8**. Its development came to an abrupt halt when it was abandoned by its pilot during high-speed tests in August 1930.

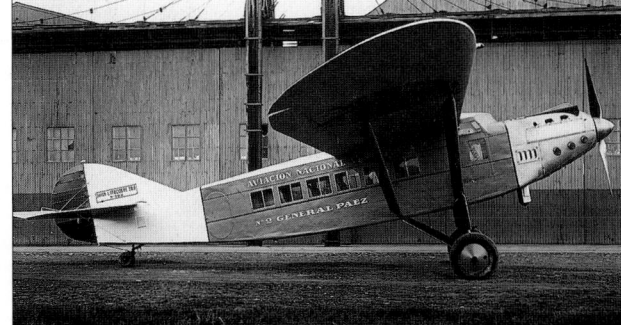

Aviacion Nacional Venezolana received three 28.6s, including this example, General Urdaneta; all were later taken over by Línea Aeropostal Venezolana.

Latécoère 290 to 296

Winner of a 1928 French navy competition for a seaplane torpedo-bomber, the **Latécoère 29.0** was developed from the Laté 28.3, the prototype making its maiden flight on 3 October 1931 on temporary wheeled landing gear. Tests with twin floats were successful and 20 series machines were ordered in 1932, followed by 10 more in 1933. The type equipped Berre-based Escadrille 4T1 in 1934, and Escadrille 1T1 at Cherbourg the following year.

After being relegated to training in early 1939, the Laté 290 was returned to first-line service with the outbreak of World War II. Four of the type provided part of the equipment of Escadrille 1S2 formed at Cherbourg in September 1939 for coastal anti-submarine patrol. One-off developments included the **Laté 293** with a 725-hp (540-kW) Gnome-Rhône 14Kers radial engine and rudder of increased area; the **Laté 294** with 14Kdrs radial, redesigned vertical tail surfaces and modified forward fuselage; and the **Laté 296** which was virtually a Laté 294 with an 860-hp (641-kW) Hispano-Suiza 12Ydrs-1 V-12 engine. All three experimental aircraft were flown initially with wheeled landing gear before the installation of twin floats. None was accepted for production as the mid-wing Laté 298 was already under development.

The Laté 29, seen here in prototype 29.0-01 form, was a torpedo-carrying variant of the 28.3 mail and 28.5 record-breaking floatplanes. The type began CEPA trials at Saint-Raphael in 1931.

SPECIFICATION	
Latécoère 290	
Type: three-seat torpedo-bomber floatplane	**Dimensions:** wingspan 63 ft 1¾ in (19.25 m); length 47 ft 11½ in (14.62 m); height 19 ft 10½ in (6.06 m); wing area 626.48 sq ft (58.20 m²)
Powerplant: one 650-hp (485-kW) Hispano-Suiza 12Nbr V-12 piston engine	
Performance: maximum speed 130 mph (210 km/h); service ceiling 15,615 ft (4760 m); range 435 miles (700 km)	**Armament:** one fixed forwardfiring 0.303-in (7.7-mm) Vickers machine-gun and twin 0.303-in (7.7-mm) Lewis guns in a manually operated dorsal turret, plus one Type DA torpedo or two 330-1b (150-kg) bombs
Weights: empty equipped 6,329 lb (2871 kg); maximum take-off 10,580 lb (4799 kg)	

Latécoère 298

Stemming from a 1933 French navy requirement for a new floatplane torpedo-bomber, the **Latécoère 298.01** was flown for the first time on 8 May 1936. An all-metal single-engined mid-wing monoplane with a crew of three, it had sharply tapering wings and twin floats. Its torpedo was carried semi-recessed in the underside of the fuselage and mounted on a ventral crutch. Service testing resulted in production orders for a total of 177 Laté 298s. They differed mainly in having a crew canopy of entirely new design and comprised 29 **Laté 298A** aircraft delivered from October 1938 onwards, followed by 42 **Laté 298B** aircraft with dual controls and folding wings, and finally 106 **Laté 298D** machines with dual controls and fixed wings. One Laté 298D was converted with a ventral observation gondola, under the designation **Laté 298E**, but was considered unsatisfactory.

Four French navy escadrilles were equipped with the Laté 298 in September 1939, namely HB1 and HB2 (Laté 298Bs)

The Laté 298B differed from the 298A in having aft-folding outer wing panels, two-section flaps, folding tailplane tips, dual controls and an additional crew member.

aboard the seaplane carrier *Commandant Teste*, T1 at Berre and T2 at Cherbourg. Engaged initially on coastal patrols, the Laté 298s were pressed into service for ground-attack and dive-bombing missions when the Germans launched their Blitzkrieg on France. Many of the type remained in service with the Vichy regime, which ordered 30 **Laté 298F** aircraft from the Breguet company for use in the overseas empire; these aircraft were basically similar to the Laté 298D but without dual controls. Under Free French control, Laté 298 Escadrille 3.S operated on Lake Constance in Germany on policing duties until disbanded at the end of January 1946. The last surviving example of the type was scrapped in 1951.

SPECIFICATION	
Latécoère 298D	
Type: three-seat torpedo-bomber/reconnaissance seaplane	**Dimensions:** wingspan 50 ft 10¼ in (15.50 m); length 41 ft 2½ in (12.56 m); height 17 ft 2¾ in (5.25 m); wing area 340.15 sq ft (31.60 m²)
Powerplant: one 880-hp (656-kW) Hispano-Suiza 12Ycrs-1 V-12 piston engine	
Performance: maximum speed 178 mph (287 km/h); service ceiling 16,730 ft (5100 m); range 621 miles (1000 km)	**Armament:** two fixed forward-firing and one manually-aimed 0.295-in (7.5-mm) Darne machine-guns, plus one 1,477-lb (670-kg) Type DA torpedo, or up to 1,102 lb (500 kg) of bombs, or three depth bombs, or nine flares
Weights: empty equipped 6,768 lb (3070 kg); maximum take-off 10,141 lb (4600 kg)	

Latécoère 300, 301 and 302

The **Latécoère 300.01** was the company's first four-engined flying-boat, but its maiden flight on 17 December 1931 ended in disaster when the machine broke up, crashing into the water. The **Laté 50** three-engined prototype flew for the first time three months later but performed poorly, and Latécoère decided to abandon this formula and to return to development of the four tandem-engine design, despite the loss of the Laté 300.01.

The aim was to link Dakar with Natal in Brazil by air, with a machine which could carry a considerable volume of mail and **Laté 300** no. 1, named *Croix du Sud* (Southern Cross) and first flown in September 1932, made a non-stop flight from Berre in southern France to Senegal, West Africa, achieving a new world distance record, and then flew on to Natal, which was reached on 2 January 1933. Modified soon afterwards, the *Croix du Sud* went on to make many safe Atlantic crossings, only to be lost with all its crew, including the great Mermoz, over the ocean in December 1936.

Three **Laté 301** aircraft were built in 1935, and were of similar configuration to the Laté 300, all being mail carriers with a crew of four and powered by four 650-hp (485-kW) Hispano-Suiza engines mounted in tandem pairs on the wing. Named after South American capital cities, the Laté 301s were used on the Air France South Atlantic route; one was lost at sea in February 1936, the second was retired after many successful crossings, and the third was taken over by the Aéronavale for training in February 1938. On the outbreak of war it was attached to Escadrille E.4 based at Dakar for anti-submarine patrols.

Three examples of the **Laté 302**, a fully militarised version of the Laté 301, were delivered to Escadrille E.4 at Berre during 1936. With eight-man crews and named *Guilbaud*, *Mouneyrès* and *Cavelier de Cuverville*, they remained in service on long-range patrol work, moving to Dakar with Escadrille 41 (formerly E.4), until they were scrapped during 1941.

SPECIFICATION	
Latécoère 302	
Type: long-range maritime reconnaissance flying-boat	**Dimensions:** wingspan 144 ft 4¼ in (44.00 m); length 85 ft 9½ in (26.15 m); height 26 ft 2¼ in (7.98 m); wing area 2,751.99 sq ft (255.66 m²)
Powerplant: four 860-hp (641-kW) Hispano-Suiza 12Ydrs V-12 piston engines	
Performance: maximum speed 134 mph (215 km/h); service ceiling 19,030 ft (5800 m); maximum range 2,019 miles (3250 km)	**Armament:** one 0.295-in (7.5-mm) Darne machine-gun in the bow cockpit and two more Darne guns firing through lateral portholes, plus four 165-lb (75-kg) bombs carried on racks mounted to wing bracing struts
Weights: empty equipped 29,167 lb (13230 kg); maximum take-off 52,911 lb (24000 kg)	

The record-breaking 300 and civilian 301 were followed by three examples of the 302 for the Aéronautique Maritime, comprising Guilbaud, Cuverville and Mouneyrès (pictured).

Latécoère 520, 521, 522 and 523

The giant **Latécoère 521** flying-boat named *Lieutenant de Vaisseau Paris*, was built to order as a North Atlantic passenger carrier. It superseded the **Laté 520** four-engine project and was powered by six 650-hp (485-kW) Hispano-Suiza 12Ybrs-2 V-12 engines nacelle-mounted beneath the parasol monoplane wing. Short-span stub wings were carried on each side of the hull, being strut-braced to the upper wing and incorporating a stabilising float at each tip. On the high-mounted wing the outboard engines were mounted singly and the inner units in tandem pairs driving tractor and pusher propellers.

The lower section of the two-step hull had a bow mooring station, behind which were the radio-navigation compartment, a 20-passenger saloon, six deluxe cabins, a further passenger compartment

seating 26, a galley, and finally a baggage hold. The upper deck contained the control cabin, engineer's compartment, a cabin for 18 passengers and a second baggage hold.

After its initial flight on 10 January 1935, the Laté 521 made a number of demonstration flights before setting out in December 1935 for Dakar, West Africa, then Natal, Brazil, and finally the French West Indies. It reached Pensacola in Florida on 13 January 1936 where, caught in a hurricane, it was sunk at its moorings. Salvaged and returned to France, the 'boat was rebuilt for the Air France Transatlantique company, flying again in June 1937. It later made a nonstop flight to Brazil, and then a staged flight across the North Atlantic, the return flight in September 1937 being made non-stop. With more powerful engines four staged flights

to New York and back were made between May and July 1939. Then taken over by the French navy and attached to Escadrille E.6, the Laté 521 was used for patrols over the North Atlantic. Stranded at Port Lyautey on the Atlantic coast of Morocco in June 1940, it was returned eventually to Berre in southern France, where it was broken up in August 1944.

The success of the Laté 521 led to orders for three civil **Laté 522** and three navalised **Laté 523** aircraft. In the event only one Laté 522 (*Ville de Saint Pierre*) was built. Tested in April 1939, it differed considerably from the Laté 521, with its accommodation re-arranged, the upper hull redesigned, maximum take-off weight increased, and with 920-hp (686-kW) Hispano-Suiza 12Y36/37s engines. Before the outbreak of war two double North Atlantic crossings were achieved and then

The Laté 521 Lieutenant de Vaisseau Paris spanned 161 ft 9¼ in (49.31 m), had a maximum take-off weight of 70,945 lb (32180 kg) and could attain a maximum speed of 158 mph (255 km/h).

the aircraft was militarised and allocated to patrol Escadrille E.6 at Lanveoc-Poulmic, near Brest. Damaged on a liaison flight to French Somaliland in February 1941, the Laté 522 eventually returned to France, where it was demolished in August 1944.

The three Laté 523s were delivered to Escadrille E.6 (later 6.E), the first example (*Altaïr*) having flown initially on

21 October 1938. Resembling the Laté 522, each carried a crew of 14 and was armed with five 0.295-in (7.5-mm) Darne machine-guns and up to 2,976 lb (1350 kg) of bombs. Used on Atlantic patrol, only one of the Laté 523s survived the German invasion of June 1940 and after repairs in Vichy France was sent to Escadrille 4.E at Dakar, where it was abandoned for lack of spares in August 1942.

Latécoère 631

A remarkable design for its time, the **Latécoère 631** was intended to carry 46 passengers on services across the South Atlantic. Like the Laté 521 it had six engines, but all were mounted individually at the leading edge of the high-set monoplane wing. The two-step hull had excellent lines with no more excrescences, the stabilizing floats retracted into the outer engine nacelles, and the tail unit incorporated

twin fins and rudders. Due to wartime conditions, construction of the **Laté 631.01** prototype took four years, the aircraft being flown for the first time on 4 November 1942, and three more aircraft ordered in 1942 were not flown until March 1945, late 1946 and May 1947 respectively. Of seven additional Laté 631s ordered in 1944 by the Vichy regime, six were completed between September 1947 and

October 1949.

Laté 631.01 flight tests were interrupted by the German occupation of southern France in 1943. After they were resumed, the machine was confiscated and flown to Friedrichshafen in Germany on 20 January 1944, where it was destroyed in an air attack on the following day.

The other Laté 631s went into service with Air France from 1947 and then were sold to various lesser companies, with whom they operated mainly as freight carriers. The second

The second Laté 631 ultimately entered commercial service as F-BANT Lionel de Marmier, the aircraft serving with Air France's South Atlantic Fleet.

machine remained in use until broken up in 1956, while the third, sixth, seventh and eighth were lost in accidents between

March 1950 and September 1955. After the loss of the eighth aircraft, surviving aircraft were scrapped.

Latham flying-boats/seaplanes

The Société Latham & Cie, owned by Jean Latham, began the construction of flying-boats by building 24 Georges Lévy 40 single-engine 'boats in 1918. First original design was a three-engine 'boat of 1919, powered by 340-hp (254-kW) Panhard engines, which had been intended as a bomber and was ordered before the 1918 Armistice; production terminated with the fourth machine. Ten examples of the **Latham HB.5** were built from 1921 onwards, these being biplane flying-boats powered by four 260-hp (194kW) Salmson 9Z engines mounted in tandem pairs between the wings. Latham then built two single-seat biplane flying-boats for the 1923 Schneider Trophy contest. Both were powered by two tandem 400-hp (298-kW) Lorraine 12Db engines.

These 'boats were designated **L-1** and **L-2**, the latter differing by having a wing of thinner section and circular engine cowlings. L-1 force-landed on the way to the competition at Cowes, Isle of Wight and the L-2 was unable to get its engines started in time for the race. In the same year the **C-1** biplane appeared with a beautifully streamlined wooden hull. In the HB.3 (3-seat bomber flying-boat) category, it was powered by a 300-hp (224-kW) Renault 12Fe engine, but it was soon abandoned when problems were encountered with its two-step hull. In 1925 a single example of the **E-5**, with two tandem pairs of

Lorraine 12Db engines, was developed from the earlier HB.5. Two examples of the **Latham 230**, an equal-span two-seat biplane with a single main float and two auxiliary wing tip floats, were built and tested in 1928, each powered by a 230-hp (171-kW) Salmson 9Ab engine, but no production orders were received.

Two examples of the

Latham 42 were built as prototypes, and following tests at Cherbourg in 1924 these were followed by eight aircraft exported to Poland. The **Latham 43** was identical except that it had 380-hp (283-kW) Gnome-Rhône 9A Jupiter radials. Eighteen Latham 43s were supplied to the Aéronavale in 1926 for service with Escadrilles 4R1 and 5R1, these aircraft being armed with single 0.303-in (7.7-mm) machine-guns in bow and midships

cockpits and carrying 882 lb (400 kg) of bombs.

The **Latham 45** was an intermediate design, developed from the Latham 43, with two Jupiter 9A radial engines mounted in tandem immediately below the upper wing. Only one Latham 45 was built and flown to Copenhagen for exhibition, being scrapped shortly afterwards.

Built to a French navy requirement for a long-range flying-boat capable of crossing the Atlantic, the

The Latham 42 was a three-seat bomber flying-boat powered by two 370-hp (276-kW) Lorraine 12Da engines.

Latham 47 appeared in prototype form in 1928. The **Latham 47.01** was lost in a fire on the Seine after only two test flights in early 1928, and the **Latham 47.02** flew in early April that year. A relatively large sesquiplane, with two 500-hp (373-kW) Farman 12We engines mounted in tandem below the upper wing, the Latham 47 had its pilot and co-pilot seated side-by-side, initially in an open cockpit. There were also cockpits in the nose and amidships which could be equipped with twin 0.303-in (7.7-mm) machine-guns, and bombload was 1,323 lb (600 kg). Twelve series aircraft were ordered, the first being delivered in 1929, and the type equipped Escadrilles 3E1 and 4R1 at Berre. Also delivered in 1929 were two **Latham 47P** aircraft, mail carriers which were civil versions of the Latham 47 with Hispano-Suiza 12Hb engines; they served on Mediterranean routes until 1932. On 16 June 1928 the Latham 47.02 with a crew of four left Caudebec to help in the search for the airship *Italia* which, on 25 May 1928, had crashed on pack ice in the Arctic Ocean, north of Spitzbergen. The Latham 47 picked up the explorer Roald Amundsen and a colleague at Bergen, but after leaving Tromsö on 18 June and flying over the Barents Sea the aircraft and its occupants disappeared without trace. This event marked the end of the aircraft design and manufacturing activities of the Latham company.

Lavochkin LaGG-1 and LaGG-3

Involved in aviation design from his student days, S. A. Lavochkin joined the Soviet Union's TsKB (Central Design Bureau) gaining valuable experience as a member of several design teams before joining with V. P. Gorbunov and M. I. Gudkov in 1938 to start the design of a new single-seat fighter. Initially designated **I-22** but later redesignated **LaGG-1** (Lavochkin, Gorbunov and Gudkov), the prototype was flown for the first time on 30 March 1940. Early flight tests proved somewhat disappointing, and modifications included the installation of a higher rated and supercharged version of the Klimov M-105 engine that powered this prototype. Simultaneously, the fuel capacity was increased, and a three-bladed propeller and wing leading-edge slats introduced. In this form the I-22 was redesignated **I-301** and was ordered into production as the **LaGG-3**. A cantilever low-wing monoplane of clean lines, with retractable tailwheel landing gear, it was unique among fighter aircraft of its period by being of all-wood construction, except for metal-frame fabric-covered

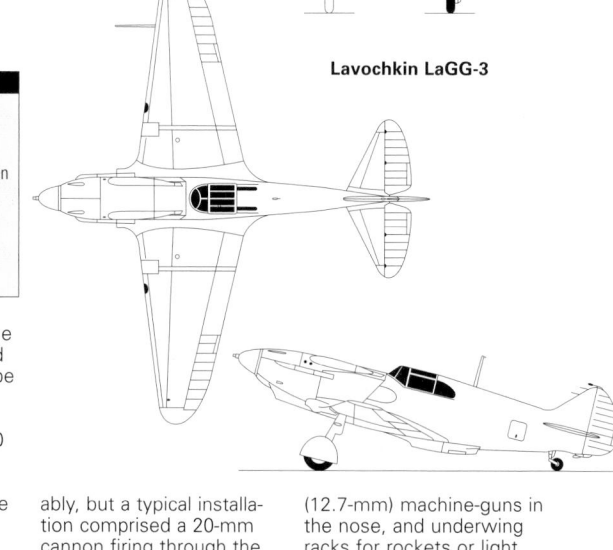

Lavochkin LaGG-3

With eight kill markings, this LaGG-3 was flown by Lt Y. Shchipov of the 9.IAP, Black Sea Fleet Air Force, during 1944. The aircraft is a late production model, identified by the additional rear view glazing panel on the canopy frame. Shchipov's personal marking was a lion's head on a heart.

SPECIFICATION	
Lavochkin LaGG-3	**Weights:** empty 5,776 lb
Type: single-seat fighter	(2620 kg); maximum take-off
Powerplant: one 1,240-hp	7,231 lb (3280 kg)
(925-kW) Klimov M-105PF V-12	**Dimensions:** wingspan 32 ft 1¾ in
piston engine	(9.80 m); length 29 ft 2½ in
Performance: maximum speed	(8.90 m); wing area 188.37 sq ft
348 mph (560 km/h) at 16,405 ft	(17.50 m²)
(5000 m); service ceiling 31,495 ft	**Armament:** see text
(9600 m); range 404 miles (650 km)	

control surfaces; the fuselage, tail unit and wings had a wooden basic structure to which diagonal strips of plywood were bonded by phenol-formaldehyde resin.

Used extensively in the early stages of fighting against the invading Germans, the LaGG-3 acquitted itself reasonably well, primarily because the form of structure that had been adopted proved to be robust in service use and resistant to combat damage. More than 6,500 LaGG-3s are believed to have been built, late versions with a retractable tailwheel and provision to carry drop-tanks. Armament varied considerably, but a typical installation comprised a 20-mm cannon firing through the propeller hub, two 0.5-in (12.7-mm) machine-guns in the nose, and underwing racks for rockets or light bombs.

Lavochkin La-5 and La-7

The LaGG-3 had proved a good stop-gap fighter, considered to be valuable particularly because it was constructed from plentiful wood rather than more scarce light alloys. There was no doubt, however, that it was the poorest performer of its contemporary generation of fighters.

In 1941 Lavochkin's team began urgent development of the LaGG-3 to provide improved performance, and the first step was the installation of an M-82 radial. This was found to give not only an increase of some 6 per cent in maximum speed, but also improved performance at higher altitudes. In May 1942 production was switched to this engine installation as an interim stage of development, the resulting aircraft being designated LaGG-5.

Within only a few weeks it was superseded by the La-5, with a cutdown rear fuselage.

The final major La-5 production variant was the La-5FN, introducing the powerful direct-injection ASh-82FN, eliminating negative-g engine cut.

SPECIFICATION	
Lavochkin La-7	(2638 kg); maximum take-off
Type: interceptor fighter	7,496 lb (3400 kg)
Powerplant: one 1,850-hp	**Dimensions:** wingspan 32 ft 1¾ in
(1380kW) Shvetsov M-82FN	(9.80 m); length 28 ft 2½ in
(ASh-82FN) radial piston engine	(8.60 m); wing area 188.37 sq ft
Performance: maximum speed	(17.50 m²)
413 mph (665 km/h); service ceiling	**Armament:** two or three Beresin
35,435 ft (10800 m); range	B-20 20-mm cannon, plus provision
395 miles (635 km)	for up to 441 lb (200 kg) of bombs
Weights: empty 5,816 lb	on underwing racks

Variants

La-7R: two conversions of La-7s with booster rocket in the rear fuselage; experimental only
La-7M: conversion of one La-7 with two TK-3 turbochargers installed to give improved high altitude performance; experimental only
La-126: experimental version with revised wings and a PVRD-430 auxiliary ramjet engine mounted beneath each wing

Lavochkin La-5 and La-7 (continued)

This revised rear fuselage allowed the installation of a cockpit canopy giving an all-round view, but still had inadequate performance to meet the Bf 109G-2 on equal terms. Efforts were then made to reduce weight and drag and to provide still more power, leading to the La-5FN. This introduced metal wing spars and reduced fuel capacity for weight saving, a higher-rated version of the Shvetsov engine, and

wing leading-edge slats to greatly improve combat manoeuvrability.
Built in numbers approximating 10,000, the La-5FN was first seen in action during the Battle of Stalingrad in late 1942. Refined progressively, the type remained in service for the remainder of World War II, being used primarily as a fighter/fighter-bomber; a two-seat trainer version was also built under the designation **La-5UTI**.

Further development to provide a high-altitude interceptor (and trainer) variant resulted in the **La-7** (and **La-7UTI**) retaining the same powerplant, but with improved performance achieved by further aerodynamic refinement and weight saving. La-7/-7UT1 production exceeded 5,500 and these were the last of the Lavochkin series-built aircraft to see operational service in World War II.

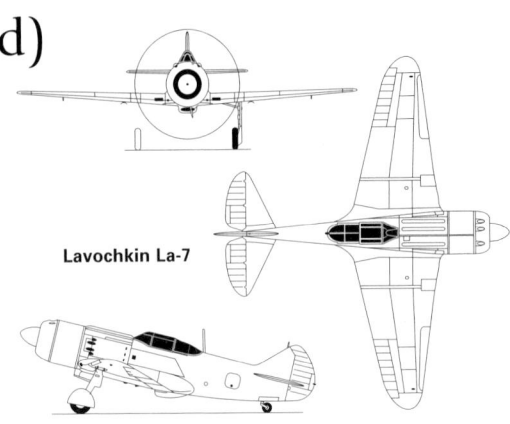

Lavochkin La-7

Lavochkin La-9 'Fritz' and La-11 'Fang'

Continuing development and refinement of the LaGG-3/La-5/La-7 family brought a revised version of the La-7 which differed sufficiently to be allocated the designation **La-9**. Retaining a Shvetsov radial engine, the La-9 benefited from further weight reduction (effected by increasing proportions of light alloy in relation to wood in the structure) while the wings and tailplane gained square-cut tips, and the vertical tail surfaces were increased in height. The fuselage incorporated an improved cockpit, but a deeper aft

Variants

La-9RD: conversion of the La-9 with an RD-13 auxiliary pulsejet beneath each wing
La-138: conversion of the La-9 with a PVRD-430 auxiliary ramjet beneath each wing

fuselage somewhat restricted the pilot's rear view. The La-9's heavy armament comprised four 23-mm forward-firing cannon. In addition to the basic La-9, an **La-9UTI** two-seat trainer was built, and these aircraft first entered service in late 1944. Although not used operationally during World

War II, La-9s served with most Soviet first-line fighter units in the immediate post-war years and many were supplied to the nation's allies, including China. A long-range escort version of the La-9 was also developed under the designation **La-11**, and this differed by being of all-metal construction, and having increased fuel capacity and only three 23-mm cannon. It could be identified easily, as the underfuselage intake for the oil cooler on the La-9 had been replaced by an

Lavochkin's final piston-engined fighter, the La-11 'Fang' was first flown, in prototype La-140 form, by NII test pilot Col A. G. Kochyetkov in May 1947.

intake duct within the engine cowling. Used extensively by the North Korean air force during the Korean War, the La-11 was

the last piston-engined fighter to be designed by Lavochkin and continued in service with Communist forces into the 1960s.

Production of the La-9 'Fritz' was authorised in November 1946. Early examples carried a lighter armament of three or four ShVAKs.

SPECIFICATION	
Lavochkin La-11 'Fang'	(750 km)
Type: single-seat escort fighter	**Weight:** maximum take-off
Powerplant: one 1,870-hp	8,807 lb (3995 kg)
(1394-kW) Shvetsov ASh-82FNV	**Dimensions:** wingspan 32 ft 7¾ in
radial piston engine	(9.95 m); length 28 ft 2½ in
Performance: maximum speed	(8.60 m); wing area 190.53 sq ft
429 mph (690 km/h) at 20,340 ft	(17.70 m²)
(6200 m); service ceiling 33,630 ft	**Armament:** three 23-mm cannon
(10250 m); range 466 miles	

Lavochkin La-15 'Fantail'

The experience gained by the Lavochkin design team from their work on a number of prototypes, led to the **La-168** prototype which was flown for the first time in early 1948. It differed considerably from anything developed earlier by the team, having a fuselage structure that accommodated the turbine engine in its aft section, with the engine efflux ducted through the tail instead of below it. Because the engine was at

the rear, Lavochkin was able to bring the pilot's cockpit into the nose of the aircraft, forward of the monoplane wing mounted high on the fuselage and incorporating sweepback of 37° 20'. All of the tail surfaces were also swept and power was provided by a 5,000-lb (22.24-kN) thrust Rolls-Royce Nene turbojet. The **La-174** prototype, produced at the same time, was of virtually identical configuration, but was powered by a Rolls-Royce

Derwent engine of only 3,527-lb (15.69-kN) thrust and was of reduced dimensions. Flight testing of these two prototypes showed that maximum speed of the La-174 was less than 6 per cent below that of the higherpowered La-168, and as Soviet production of the Rolls-Royce Nene (as the RD-45) had been allocated for the Ilyushin Il-28 and

Variant

La-176D: development of the La-168 with some fuselage modification to accommodate a 5,000-lb (22.24-kN) thrust RD-45 turbojet, a redesigned wing with 45° sweepback, and revised armament; exceeded Mach 1 in a dive in December 1948

Mikoyan-Gurevich MiG-15, the La-174 was ordered into limited production as the **La-15** with the Rolls-Royce Derwent, which was produced as the RD-500. The prototype of a two-seat trainer was developed as

the **La-180**, and was duly ordered into production as the **La-15UTI**. Allocated the NATO reporting name **'Fantail'**, the La-15 remained in service with the Soviet air force until the mid-1950s.

SPECIFICATION	
Lavochkin La-15 'Fantail'	**Weights:** empty 5,677 lb
Type: single-seat fighter	(2575 kg); maximum take-off
Powerplant: one 3,505-lb	8,488 lb (3850 kg)
(15.59-kN) thrust RD-500 turbojet	**Dimensions:** wingspan 28 ft 11½
Performance: maximum speed	in (8.83 m); length 29 ft 6¼ in
637 mph (1025 km/h) at 9,845 ft	(9.00 m); wing area 173.95 sq ft
(3000 m); service ceiling 42,650 ft	(16.16 m²)
(13000 m); range 684 miles	**Armament:** two 23-mm cannon,
(1100 km)	plus bombs or rockets

The La-15 was developed from the La-168, first flown by I. Ye. Fedorov on 22 April 1948. The 'Fantail' was lighter, and in many ways superior to the MiG-15.

Lavochkin La-150

The **La-150** was Lavochkin's first design to incorporate a turbine powerplant, in the form of an RD-10 (a developed version of the wartime German Junkers Jumo 004A) turbojet of approximately 1,984-lb (8.82-kN) thrust. A single-seat aircraft with retractable tricycle landing gear, it was of cantilever high-wing monoplane configuration. This layout had been adopted to simplify installation of the engine in the fuselage, the rear fuselage terminating in a circular-section boom to carry the tail unit, so allowing the engine efflux to be discharged beneath it. The first of five prototypes was flown initially in September 1946, followed in 1947 by one **La-150M** with an RD-10F engine rated at 2,425-lb (10.78-kN) thrust with afterburning; with this powerplant the La-150M could attain a maximum speed of 590 mph (950 km/h). Flight tests of these prototypes revealed a number of shortcomings and Lavochkin decided in 1947 to abandon further development of the La-150 and concentrate on more promising ideas.

The final three prototype La-150s were modified to **La-150F** *(forsirovannii) standard, with a primitive afterburning engine, the first Soviet aircraft fitted with this equipment.*

Lavochkin La-190, La-200 and La-250 Anaconda

The La-15 was the last production aircraft to come from Semyon Lavochkin's design bureau before his death in 1960. However, three more interesting basic types were designed and flown, the first being the **La-190** single-seat fighter which, powered by an 11,023-lb (49.02-kN) thrust Lyulka AL-5 turbojet, was the first Soviet fighter able to demonstrate supersonic speed in level flight. A midwing monoplane with a wingsweep of 55°, it introduced an unusual retractable landing gear configuration comprising a nosewheel, mainwheels in tandem, and outrigger wheels at the wingtips. Considerably larger than earlier Lavochkin fighters, and armed with two 37-mm cannon, the La-190 revealed stability problems at high speed during 1951, and the type was not ordered into production. The **La-200** was a twin-engine, two-seat interceptor of mid-wing configuration with all-swept wings and tail surfaces. Powered by two Klimov VK-1 turbojets, each rated at 5,952-lb (26.47-kN) thrust, the **La-200A** mounted its engines within the fuselage one forward and one aft of the crew cockpit, the former exhausting under the trailing edge and the latter through the tail. Intended for all-weather operation, the La-200 was equipped with weapon-control radar, but successful installation of this Izumrud system in the MiG-15, which was already in production, brought an end to development of the La-200, which in its revised **La-200B** form with larger radar spanned 42 ft 6¼ in (12.96 m) and weighed in at 42,659 lb (19350 kg).

The last of Lavochkin's designs was the advanced **La-250 Anaconda** two-seat long-range intercepor with all-weather capability. Its features included a delta wing mounted in mid-wing configuration, an all moving tailplane, and retractable tricycle landing gear with twin wheels on the nose unit. The powerplant comprised two Lyulka AL-7F turbojet engines, each of 19, 840 lb (88.23-kN) thrust with afterburning. Four were flown in 1956-8 but the La-250 was abandoned by 1959.

The single **La-200B** *prototype (first flown on 3 July 1952) carried a larger Sokol radar with a 3.30-ft (1-m) diameter dish. More powerful engines were fed by three intakes, and the type offered a range of 1,740 miles (2800 km) with wing tanks.*

The largest fighter of its day, the problematic La-250 was launched in 1953 and intended to replace the Yak-25 'Flashlight' in IA-PVO service. The Anaconda was designed to incorporate the K-15 aerial intercept weapons system, with K-15U radar and izdeliye 275 AAMs used in conjunction with GCI equipment. '04 Red' was the fourth La-250A.

Learjet 23, 24, 25, 28 and 29

In the later part of the 1950s the Swiss government cancelled further development of the **FFA P-16** fighter that had at that time flown only in prototype form. The type had by this time caught the attention of William 'Bill' Lear Snr., living in retirement in Switzerland after establishing and building up the Motorola and Lear Siegler corporations, as the possible basis for a high-performance bizjet with a pair of turbojets pod-mounted on the sides of the rear fuselage. Preliminary design work on the new type was undertaken in Switzerland and showed that the concept had great potential. Lear then sold his electronics company to Siegler and created the Swiss American Aviation Corporation to develop the new type, then known as the **SAAC Lear Jet 23**.

After finalisation of the design, Lear moved the whole operation to the USA and revised the SAAC as the Lear Jet Corporation. The Lear Jet 23 first flew in prototype form on 7 October 1963 and soon revealed the performance that brought in orders from companies who appreciated the value of a high-speed executive transport.

Deliveries of the Lear Jet 23 began in October 1964 with the powerplant of two CJ610-1 turbojets each rated at 2,850 lb st (12.68 kN), although later aircraft switched to the CJ610-4 of identical rating. The Lear Jet 23 had been designed with a maximum take-off weight of less than 12,500 lb (5670 kg) so that it could be operated by a single-pilot, but as most operators did in fact use a two-man crew, Lear decided to develop a higher-weight version as the **Lear Jet 24** that was announced in October 1965 with features such as a greater pressurisation differential to permit operation at higher altitudes. The first Lear Jet 24 flew on 24 February 1966 and deliveries began just two months later.

In 1967 Lear sold his holding in the corporation to Gates Rubber, and in January 1970 Lear Jet became the Gates Learjet Corporation, which continued development of this important light transport series as the **Learjet**. The basic **Learjet 24** had already been complemented by the **Learjet 24B** with an uprated powerplant of two CJ610-6 turbojets.

SPECIFICATION	
Learjet 24B	2,037 miles (3278 km)
Type: two-crew medium-range light transport	**Weights:** empty 6,927 lb (3142 kg); maximum take-off 13,500 lb (6124 kg)
Powerplant: two General Electric CJ610-6 turbojet engines each rated at 2,950 lb st (13.12 kN)	**Dimensions:** wingspan 35 ft 7 in (10.84 m) including tip tanks; length 43 ft 3 in (13.18 m); height 12 ft 7 in (3.84 m); wing area 231.77 sq ft (21.53 m²)
Performance: maximum speed 545 mph (877 km/h) at 31,000 ft (9450 m); cruising speed 534 mph (859 km/h) at 45,000 ft (13715 m); initial climb rate 6,400 ft (1951 m) per minute; certificated ceiling 45,000 ft (13715 m); range	**Payload** up to six passengers or 2,673 lb (1212 kg) of freight carried in the cabin

Learjet 23, 24 and 25 (continued)

Continued development of the basic design resulted in variants such as the slightly smaller **Learjet 24D** with rectangular rather than oval cabin windows and greater fuel capacity for increased range, the **Learjet 24D/A** with maximum take-off weight restricted to 12,500 lb (5670 kg), and from 1976 the **Learjet 24E** and **Learjet 24F** equivalent to the Learjet 24D and Learjet 24D/A respectively but with a new cambered wing and aerodynamic improvements to reduce the types' approach and stalling speeds.

Typical of late-production Learjet 24 models, the Learjet 24F has a power-plant of two 2,950-lb st (13.12-kN) CJ610-8A turbo-jets, a maximum speed of 547 mph (880 km/h) at 25,000 ft (7620 m) and a range of 1,697 miles (2731 km) with four passengers.

Production of the Learjet 24E and Learjet 24F ended in 1979 and 1980 respectively, and very small numbers of Learjet 24 series aircraft were bought by air arms as VIP and staff transports.

First flown on 12 August 1966 for delivery from October 1967, the **Learjet 25** is basically the Learjet 24 with its fuselage stretched by 4 ft 2 in (1.27 m) to permit the accommodation of two more passengers, raising the maximum payload to eight persons in addition to the two pilots. The basic type proved successful, and was complemented from 1970 by the **Learjet 25B** and **Learjet 25C** corresponding respectively to the Learjet 24D and Learjet 24D/A, and then from 1976 by the **Learjet 25D** and **Learjet 25F** with improvements that made them equivalent respectively to the Learjet 24E and Learjet 24F. The final development was the **Learjet 25G** with improvements for lower drag and thus more range.

The Learjet 25 also employs CJ610-8A turbo-jets and was adopted by several air arms for tasks such as high-speed transport, photo-mapping, and target towing.

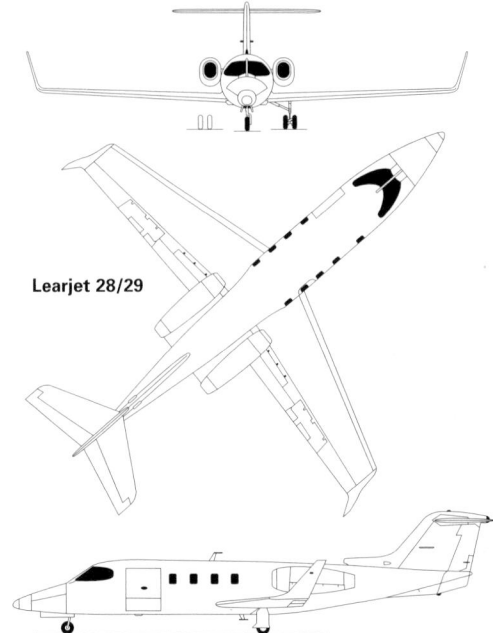

Learjet 28/29

The stretched eight-seat Learjet 25 offers a maximum cruising speed of 527 mph (848 km/h) at 41,000 ft (12495 m), a certificated ceiling of 45,000 ft (13715 m) and a range of 1,440 miles (2317 km).

The final variants of the first generation Learjet were the **Learjet 28** and **Learjet 29**. The former added a supercritical wing and winglets to the Learjet 25D airframe and flew for the first time on 21 August 1978. Only five examples were built. The Learjet 29 is a longer-range version of the Learjet 28, but was built to the extent of just two aircraft.

Learjet 31, 35, 36 and 45

In the early 1970s the development of the Garrett TFE731 turbofan provided the opportunity to switch to an engine type offering greater fuel economy and lower noise levels than was possible with the turbojet engine. One of the first manufacturers to take advantage was Gates Learjet. One Learjet 25 was converted with one TFE731-2 turbofan in the starboard nacelle (retaining the standard turbojet to port), and first flew in this revised form during January 1973. A second conversion flew with two TFE731-2 engines and paved the way for the **Learjet 35** production model, which first flew on 22 August 1973. Compared with the Learjet 25, the Learjet 35 and parallel **Learjet 36** have a fuselage lengthened by 1 ft 1 in (0.33 m) and a wing increased in span by 4 ft (1.22 m) to permit the carriage of a greater payload over significantly longer range. The two production models received certification in the summer of 1974.

The Learjet 35 is opti-

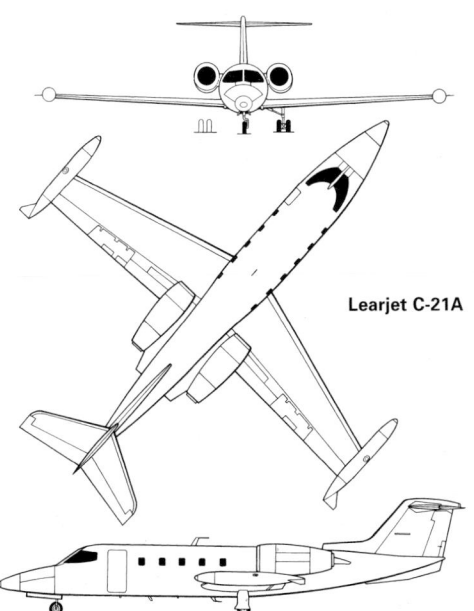

Learjet C-21A

The Learjet 31A was introduced in 1990, as a follow-on to the Learjet 31. Replacing its predecessor by mid-1991, the 31A features a new EFIS cockpit.

mised for the carriage of eight passengers over shorter ranges, and the definitive model is the higher-weight **Learjet 35A**, of which the US Air Force and Air National Guard procured 80 and four respectively under the designation **C-21A** for medevac, staff transport and high-priority freight transport tasks. Several other air forces operate the type for high-speed communications, and Learjet developed a number of special-mission variants. The **EC-35A** is the EW training variant with a number of equipment options, and can also be used for the stand-off ECM/ESM role.

The **PC-35A** is the maritime patrol variant whose equipment options include surveillance radar

By May 1998, a total of 155 Learjet 45s had been ordered, including four examples for Singapore Airlines for use as crew trainers.

SPECIFICATION

Learjet C-21A
Type: one/two-crew medium/long-range light transport aircraft
Powerplant: two Honeywell (AlliedSignal/Garrett) TFE731-2-2B turbofan engines each rated at 3,500 lb st (15.57 kN)
Performance: maximum speed 542 mph (872 km/h) at 25,000 ft (7620 m); cruising speed 534 mph (860 km/h) at 41,000 ft (12495 m); initial climb rate 4,340 ft (1323 m) per minute; certificated ceiling 45,000 ft (13715 m); range

2,418 miles (3891 km) with six passengers
Weights: empty 9,924 lb (4502 kg); maximum take-off 18,398 lb (8345 kg)
Dimensions: wingspan 39 ft 6 in (12.04 m) including tip tanks; length 48 ft 8 in (14.83 m); height 12 ft 3 in (3.73 m); wing area 253.30 sq ft (23.53 m²)
Payload: up to eight passengers or 3,153 lb (1430 kg) of freight carried in the cabin

(with its antenna in an underfuselage radome), high-resolution TV, FLIR, IR linescanner, ESM, MAD and one hardpoint under each wing for the carriage of stores up to 1,000 lb (454 kg) in weight. The **RC-35A** is the reconnaissance variant whose equipment options include LOROP (LOng-Range Oblique Photography)

cameras, SLAR, and a surveillance camera system. The **UC-35A** is the utility variant with a number of options for equipment such as a winch-operated towed target.

The **Learjet 36** is optimised for the carriage of six passengers over longer ranges, and the definitive model is the higher-weight **Learjet 36A**, which differs

from the Learjet 35A in its greater fuel capacity for a range of 3,055 miles (4916 km) with four passengers. A number of air forces operate the type for high-speed communications, and Learjet has developed two special-mission variants. The **RC-36A** is the reconnaissance variant with a number of equipment

options including LOROP cameras, SLAR, and a surveillance camera system. The **U-36A** is the utility variant developed in conjunction with Shin Meiwa for the Japan Maritime Self-Defence Force, which operates four such higher-weight aircraft for the target-towing, anti-ship missile simulation, and ECM training roles.

The latest variants are the **Learjet 31** and **Learjet 45**. The former has been produced in three subvariants as a combination of the Learjet 35/36A's fuselage and powerplant with the wingletted wing of the Learjet 55, while the latter is an evolution of the Learjet 31 for very good fuel economy in a larger airframe.

Learjet 55 and 60

In September 1987 the Gates Rubber Company sold its Learjet subsidiary to the Integrated Acquisition Inc., which renamed the company as the Learjet Corporation and in the following year moved primary manufacture from Tucson in Arizona, which remained the centre for completion work, to Wichita in Kansas. In 1990 there came the final reorganisation to date, when the Canadian conglomerate Bombardier Inc. bought the Learjet Corporation and revised it as Learjet Inc. Before this, however, at the 1977 Paris air show, Gates Learjet announced details of its new **Learjet 50** series. This was intended to comprise the **Learjet 54**,

Learjet 55 and **Learjet 56** with longer and larger cabins. The first two were each to seat up to 11 passengers and the last a maximum of eight, and all were to have an advanced wing incorporating NASA-developed winglets, whose incorporation resulted in the name **Longhorn**. In fact only the Learjet 56 was then developed, construction of the first airframe starting in April 1978 after successful testing of an aerodynamic prototype of the wing on a Learjet 25. The first of two Learjet 55 prototypes made its maiden flight on 19 April 1979, and certification and delivery of the first production aircraft followed in March and April of 1981 respectively.

The Learjet 55 retains the same overall configuration as earlier members of the Learjet family, and was followed into production during 1986 by the **Learjet 55B** with a 'glass' cockpit. The final variant was the **Learjet 55C** that entered production in 1988 as a development of the Learjet 55B with two outward-canted ventral fins for improved balanced field length performance and low-speed handling, especially at high angles of attack. The two subvariants of the basic Learjet 55C were the **Learjet 55C/ER** extended-range type with additional fuel in the tail cone, and the **Learjet 55C/LR** long-range type with additional fuel in an additional fuselage tank.

In 1990 Learjet announced the **Learjet 60** as successor to the Learjet 55C, with a lengthened fuselage and the revised powerplant of two PW305 turbofans rather than the TFE731s of the Model 55C. An initial proof-of-concept prototype flew on 18 October 1990 with one TFE731 engine replaced by a PW305, this machine having two PW305

Certified in 1993, the six-nine-seat Learjet 60 was intended to replace the Learjet 55C. A total of 141 had been delivered by January 1999.

turbofan engines and the lengthened fuselage by June of the following year. Certification followed in

January 1993, initial deliveries of production aircraft following without delay.

Learjet 55 Longhorn

SPECIFICATION	
Learjet 60	m); range 3,147 miles (5065 km)
Type: two-crew medium-range light transport aircraft	with four passengers
Powerplant: two Pratt & Whitney Canada PW305A turbofan engines each rated at 4,600 lb st (29.60 kN)	**Weights:** empty 13,850 lb (6282 kg); maximum take-off 23,500 lb (10659 kg)
Performance: maximum cruising speed 521 mph (839 km/h) at optimum altitude; economical cruising speed 486 mph (782 km/h) at optimum altitude; initial climb rate 4,500 ft (1371 m) per minute; certificated ceiling 51,000 ft (15545	**Dimensions:** wingspan 43 ft 9 in (13.34 m); length 58 ft 8 in (17.88 m); height 14 ft 8 in (4.47 m); wing area 264.50 sq ft (24.57 m²)
	Payload: up to nine passengers within the context of a 2,360-lb (1070-kg) maximum payload

Leduc ramjet-powered aircraft

René Leduc in France had worked for many years on the development of a ramjet engine for aircraft propulsion. Leduc's first success had come in 1935

with a small but practical engine developing 8.8 lb (0.04-kN) of thrust. It was not until after the end of World War II that Leduc was able to continue his

The Leduc 0.10 could attain a rate of climb of 8,000 ft (2,440 m) per minute on half the power of its ramjet engine.

experiments, building first the **Leduc 0.10** with a tubular double-skinned fuselage in which the inner shell contained the pilot's cockpit, surrounded by an outer shell which formed the inlet duct to the ramjet engine at the rear of the pilot's position. First tested as a glider in October 1947, the 0.10 was carried on struts above a Sud-Est SE.161 Languedoc mother-plane which released it at appropriate altitude. The first powered flight was made on 21 April 1949, the SE.161 accelerating the

Approximately one third larger than the 0.10, the Leduc 0.21 was intended for autonomous take-off, under the power of two wingtip Marboré II turbojets.

Leduc 0.10 to a speed of approximately 200 mph (322 km/h) to achieve the right pressure conditions for the ramjet to ignite and sustain power. During this first flight, of 12 minutes

duration, a speed of 423 mph (680 km/h) was attained on half power. The aircraft was flown subsequently on half power at a speed of 500 mph (805 km/h).

Leduc ramjet-powered aircraft (continued)

Two more examples were built, the first an identical 0.10, the, other differing only by having two wingtip mounted turbojet engines to accelerate the aircraft to the ignition speed of the ramjets. This last aircraft, designated **0.16**,

was first flown on 8 February 1951, but the turbojet engines were later removed. Development continued with two examples of the larger **Leduc 0.21** of improved design, the first making its initial flight on

16 May 1953. These proved to be successful, demonstrating a maximum speed of Mach 0.87 and attaining an altitude of 65,615 ft (2000 m). Development then began of the **Leduc 0.22** Mach 2 interceptor which incorpo-

rated a SNECMA Atar turbojet within the ramjet to allow the aircraft to take off under its own power and then accelerate it to a speed at which the ramjet would ignite. This was not achieved with the 0.22, for although flown

on turbojet power for the first time on 26 December 1956, and later making more than 30 test flights with the turbine engine, the ramjet was not tested. This resulted from withdrawal of government financial support, because of economic stringencies, and the project was abandoned.

Let L-200 Morava

On 8 April 1957 Let flew the prototype of a twin-engined four/five-seat business aircraft designed by Ladislav Smrcek. Designated **L-200 Morava**,

the machine was a cantilever low-wing monoplane with permanently-attached wingtip fuel tanks and had a tail unit incorporating twin endplate fins

and rudders. The landing gear was of the retractable tricycle type, and power for the prototype and L-200 series was provided by two 160-hp (119-kW) Walter Minor 6-III inline engines. The original production model was superseded first by the generally similar **L-200A**, with more powerful Walter M 337 engines and, subsequently, by the final production version, the **L-200D**, which was introduced in mid-1962. This differed by incorporating improved systems,

The L-200A development featured new engines, and was supplied to Coastal Airways of Mackay, Australia.

strengthened landing gear, and three-bladed constant-speed propellers. When production ended in 1968 more than 1,000 had been

built, many being supplied to Aeroflot for this airline's operations in the Moscow, North and Ukrainian Directorate areas.

Variant

L-300: a planned turboprop-powered variant; not manufactured

SPECIFICATION	
Let L-200D Morava **Type:** twin-engine light business aircraft **Powerplant:** two 210-hp (157-kW) Walter M 337 inline piston engines **Performance:** maximum cruising speed 177 mph (285 km/h); service ceiling 20,340 ft (6200 m); range	1,118 miles (1800 km) **Weights:** empty 2,998 lb (1360 kg); maximum take-off 4,409 lb (2000 kg) **Dimensions:** wingspan 40 ft 4¼ in (12.30 m); length 28 ft 2½ in (8.60 m); height 7 ft 4½ in (2.25 m); wing area 186.22 sq ft (17.30 m²)

Let L-410 Turbolet, L-420 and L-610

The **L-410 Turbolet** twin-engined light transport was designed for use on local service and feeder operations, including those from grass airfields. The first prototype made its maiden flight on 16 April 1969, powered by two 715-eshp (533-ekW) United (later Pratt & Whitney) Aircraft of Canada PT6A-27 turboprops driving three-bladed propellers. Excessive airframe vibration and cabin noise levels were overcome with the third prototype (of four) which introduced four-bladed propellers. The Canadian engine was retained for the 27 **L-410A** aircraft built during 1971-4, and for the **L-410AF**, an aerial survey version with a glazed nose, one example of which was supplied to Hungary during 1974. The prototype **L-410M**, powered by 735-eshp (548-ekW) Walter M 601A turboprops, was flown during 1973 and the first of 109 production aircraft was delivered in 1976.
The first of three **L-410UVP** prototypes flew on 1 November 1977. This

The L-410 was the most ambitious project undertaken by Let after the company's formation in 1950. Earlier projects for the Kunovice plant included the licence-production of Yak-11 trainers under the Czech designation C-11. Design of the Turbolet began in 1966, and the first production deliveries took place in 1971.

model incorporated small increases in wingspan, fuselage length and the area of vertical tail surfaces. The L-410UVP entered large-scale production, especially as a feederliner for Aeroflot, and when production ceased in 1985 some 502 had been built. The 2001 production L-410 variants is the **L-410UVP-E**, which adds a further four passengers to the UVP's standard load of 15, by means of repositioning the baggage hold and toilet. In addition its strengthened wings carry

wingtip fuel tanks for an increase in maximum payload range to 416 miles (670 km).
Let is also producing an improved L-410 with M 601F engines and Western avionics under the designation **L-420**. A stretched L-410UVP-E with Pratt & Whitney PT6 engines has also been proposed as the **L-430**.
The most radical development on the L-410 theme is the **L-610G**, an airliner powered by two 1,750-shp (1305-kW) General electric CT7-9D

SPECIFICATION	
Let L-410UVP **Type:** utility light transport **Powerplant:** two 730-eshp (544-ekW) Walter M 601B turboprops **Performance:** maximum cruising speed 227 mph (365 km/h) at 9,845 ft (3000 m); operating altitude 19,685 ft (6000 m); range with maximum payload and	reserves 242 miles (390 km) **Weights:** empty equipped 8,378 lb (3800 kg); maximum take-off 12,787 lb (5800 kg) **Dimensions:** wingspan 63 ft 10¾ in (19.48 m); length 47 ft 5¾ in (14.47 m); height 19 ft 1½ in (5.83 m); wing area 378.69 sq ft (35.18 m²)

turboprops and seating for 40 passengers. The aircraft first flew on 28 December 1988 and following the acquisition of Let by the Ayres Corporation in 1998, the

L-610G was briefly known as the **Ayres 7000**. The aircraft is offered in civil and military forms and by early 2001 had been the subject of four firm orders and 16 options.

Let Z-37 Cmelák

Design of the **Z-37 Cmelák** (bumblebee) agricultural aircraft began in Czechoslovakia during 1961, and the **XZ-37** prototype was flown for the first

time on 29 March 1963. A cantilever low-wing monoplane of basically metal construction, but with some fabric covering, it has fixed tailwheel landing gear

and accommodates the pilot in an enclosed cockpit forward of the chemical hopper. To the rear of the hopper is a seat which can be used when required for the carriage of a loader or mechanic, and the Cmelák can be used during the

winter months for mail or cargo transport. To facilitate such use there are provisions for optional ski landing gear, and the aircraft can also be equipped for glider towing. Production aircraft have the 315-hp (235-kW) Avia

M 462RF radial engine, but at least one development aircraft was flown in 1968 with a 300-hp (224-kW) Continental engine. The late production **Z-37A** introduced some structural strengthening, a number of refinements, and more extensive use of non-corroding materials, including the incorporation of some stainless steel in the most critical areas.

When production ended in 1977 600 of all versions had been built, this total including 27 **Z-37-2 Sparka** two-seat trainers for agricultural pilots. Two examples of the **Z-37-2C** with seats for two passengers were also produced. In addition to national use, Cmeláks were exported to Bulgaria, Finland, the German Democratic Republic, Hungary, India, Iraq, Poland, the United Kingdom and Yugoslavia. An additional batch of 40 aircraft was built in 1981.

On 6 September 1981 Let flew the prototype of a turbine-engined version designated **XZ-37T**, this being powered by a 691-shp (515-kW) Walter M 601B turboprop and having a lengthened fuselage. This prototype subsequently spawned the **Z-37T** (later **Z-137T**) **Agro Turbo** with a Motorlet M 601Z turboprop, the **Z-37T-2** (later **Z-237**) dual-control trainer, and **Z-437 Kurier** three seater.

The XZ-37T Turbo-Cmelák development had a partly pressurised cockpit, and an operating speed of 87-99 mph (140-160 km/h).

Letov S 1 and S 2

Alois Smolik, who had formerly designed for the Austrian government, was established in 1919 at the newly formed Czechoslovak Military Air Arsenal, whose design and manufacturing facilities were taken over by Vojenská továrna na letadla Letov in 1920.

Smolik's first design was

the **Letov SH 1** two-seat unequal-span reconnaissance biplane. In total, 28 SH 1 aircraft with 230-hp (172-kW) Hiero L engines and 64 **SM 1** aircraft with 260-hp (194-kW) Maybach Mb.IVa engines were built from 1920 onwards for the Czech air arm. At some stage the SH 1 was redesignated **S 1** and the SM 1

The S 1 and S 2 (pictured) were the first military aircraft to be completely Czech designed and built.

became the **S 2**. Armament comprised three 0.303-in (7.7-mm) machine-guns and up to 265 lb (120 kg) of bombs. Maximum take-off weight of the S 1 was 3,031 lb (1375 kg) and maximum speed 120 mph (194 km/h). The **Sm A 1**

was a commercial adaptation with a glazed canopy

over the rear cockpit for one or two passengers.

Letov S 18, S 118, S 218

This example of the Letov S 218 is preserved in the former Vojenske Muzeum at Kbely, near Prague. The collection also includes an S 20 fighter reconstruction.

The prototype **S 18** appeared in 1925, as a lightly-built two-seat trainer biplane intended as a replacement for the variety of foreign types still in Czech service at that time. Powered by a 60-hp

(45-kW) Walter NZ 60 radial engine, the S 18 could attain a maximum speed of 87 mph (140 km/h). Proving manoeuvrable and easy to maintain, the S 18 was built in some numbers for the Czech air arm, and 10 were exported to Bulgaria.

In 1926 the **S 118** was produced with an 85-hp (63-kW) Walter NZ 85 engine. It proved very popular, with sales to private owners and civil aero clubs following on a large scale. Others were used by the Military Central Flying School (the VLU).

Soon afterwards Letov developed the **S 218**, which had a metal-tube fuselage instead of the previous wooden structure and was powered by a 120-hp (89-kW) Walter NZ 120 engine. Ten were exported to Finland in 1930-1, where 29 were subsequently built under licence. Other S 218s went to civil aero clubs and the Czech air arm. Most of the Finnish-built aircraft had a 150-hp (112-kW) Bramo 14 radial engine, giving a maximum speed of 96 mph (154 km/h).

Letov S 231

In 1933 Letov tested two prototypes of the **S 231** single-seat fighter, an unequal-span biplane with a basic structure of metal with fabric covering. They were much refined by comparison with the earlier **S 31** and **S 131** fighters, with a fuselage that was of almost circular cross-section, and their 560-hp (418-kW) Bristol Mercury IV S2 radial engine enclosed in a Townend ring. The first prototype had four CZ Model 28 0.31-in (7.92-mm)

machine-guns mounted in pairs in the upper wing, while the second had them in the lower wing. Wing span was 33 ft (10.06 m), maximum take-off weight 3,902 lb (1770 kg) and maximum speed 216 mph (348 km/h).

A production series of 25 aircraft followed, and in late 1936 seven of these aircraft were delivered to Bilbao where they operated with Spanish Republican forces in the Spanish Civil War. They were not assembled accurately so that although two were destroyed by enemy action,

The S 331 of 1935 was built in prototype form only, but broke the Czech altitude record attaining a height of 34,941 ft (10650 m).

the remainder were lost in accidents. Twelve more S 231s arrived at Cartagena in the south of Spain, equipping Escuadrilla 2, Grupo 71 of the Republican air arm, but little is known of their exploits. Most survived until February 1939, when they were destroyed to prevent them from falling into Nationalist hands.

Letov S 328

Developed from the S 228 reconnaissance biplane delivered to Estonia, the **S 328** was intended for

Finland, but when the order was lost the aircraft attracted the interest of the Czech authorities. So, although the prototype had flown in 1932, series production for the

Czechoslovak air arm did not begin until 1934. An unequal-span biplane basically of metal construction and, but for sheet metal fuselage decking, entirely fabric-covered, the S 328

had its two-man crew in tandem open cockpits, the observer occupying an unusually roomy position with lateral and floor observation panels. By 1935 S 328s were entering

service with the Czech air regiments as observation/reconnaissance aircraft, with light bombing as a secondary role. In addition, four twin-float **S 328V** training aircraft were in service.

Letov S 328 (continued)

Continuing orders kept the S 328 in production at the Letov Letňany factory for five years, some aircraft being constructed during the German occupation. The total built is recorded as 412, but there may have been more. The German occupying power used some of the type in flying training schools, and from 1942 onwards as night intruders on the Eastern Front. Other examples were passed in 1939 to the puppet Slovak regime, which employed them in the Polish campaign in September 1939, and in

This S 328 was flown by the Slovak Insurgent air force from the airfield at Tri Duby in September 1944.

SPECIFICATION

Letov S 328

Type: two-seat reconnaissance/observation aircraft

Powerplant: one Walter-built 635-hp (474-kW) Bristol Pegasus II-M2 radial piston engine

Performance: maximum speed 174 mph (280 km/h); service ceiling 23,620 ft (7200 m); range 435 miles (700 km)

Weights: empty equipped 3,704 lb (1680 kg); maximum take-off

5,820 lb (2640 kg)

Dimensions: wingspan 44 ft 11¾ in (13.71 m); length 33 ft 11¾ in (10.36 m); height 11 ft 2 in (3.40 m); wing area 424.11 sq ft (39.40 m²)

Armament: two fixed wing-mounted 0.31-in (7.92-mm) machine-guns and two similar guns on a Skoda pivot mounting over the observer's cockpit, plus up to 1,102 lb (500 kg) of bombs

the Ukraine during the invasion of the Soviet Union, largely against partisan units. Bulgaria received 62 S 328s, deploying a number of them on patrols over the Black Sea. Finally, three Slovak S 328s flew with the patriots engaged in the National Uprising, being used on reconnais-sance patrols from Tri Duby airfield, in the foothills of the Carpathians, during August-October 1944.

The **S 428** was a version of the S 328 with a V-12 650-hp (485-kW) Avia Vr-36 piston engine and fixed armament increased to four machine-guns, but only one prototype was built. The

S 528 of 1935 was powered by an 800-hp (597-kW) Walter Krsd radial engine, the French Gnome-Rhône Mistral Major built under licence, providing a maximum speed of 205 mph (330 /km/h). Six S 528s were built for the Czech air police.

Levasseur PL 7

After the unsuccessful **PL 6** two-seat fighter biplane, Levasseur's only design for the French army, the company turned to the task of providing a replacement torpedo-bomber for the **PL 2** of 1922. The prototype **PL 7** which followed was a development of the experimental **PL 4**, a two-seat sesquiplane spanning 59 ft ¾ in (18.00 m) which was burdened by a complexity of wing bracing struts. Powered initially by a 550-hp (410-kW) Farman 12We engine, the **PL 7.01** was flown subsequently with both Hispano-Suiza and Renault powerplants; the wing struts were redesigned, the structure simplified, and the fin modified. Test flying in this revised form was resumed in 1928, two years after the

prototype had first flown.

A series of 15 aircraft was ordered in 1929. Nine were delivered with the 18.00-m wing but the French admiralty, uncertain of the more effective wing design, ordered five of the remaining aircraft to be delivered with 54-ft 1½-in (16.50-m) span wings of varying areas, the final machine having a span of 56 ft 7¼ in (17.25 m). The various PL 7s went into service with Escadrille 7B1 on the carrier *Béarn* from July 1930, and after comparative tests the 54 ft 1½ in (16.50 m) span wing with square-cut tips was selected for the definitive **PL 7 T2B2b**, the tips of the upper wing being hinged to fold downwards to fit the lifts aboard the *Béarn*. Ten of the original PL 7s were modified to this new config-

uration and 30 new aircraft were ordered. When vibration problems resulted in the disintegration of two PL 7s in flight the type was grounded from June 1931. With strengthened wing bracing, reinforced engine bearers and three-bladed propellers they were returned to service from September 1932 onwards. Although totally obsolete,

Armament of the PL 7 comprised two 0.295-in (7.5-mm) machine-guns, plus either a 1,477-lb (670-kg) torpedo or 1,124 lb (510 kg) of bombs.

the PL 7 was still in first-line service aboard the *Béarn* when World War II broke out in 1939.

A **PL 7T** transport displayed at the 1926 Salon de l'Aéronautique was in fact a PL 4 with a Gnome-Rhône Jupiter 9ab radial and

a deepened fuselage accommodating a pilot and mechanic in side-by-side open cockpits, and with an enclosed cabin for six passengers. The PL 7T never flew and was scrapped when the salon closed.

Levasseur PL 15

The prototype **PL 15** twin-float biplane flew for the first time with temporary wheel landing gear in October 1932. A production order for 16 machines as **PL 15 T2B2b** aircraft followed, these entering service from 1934 onwards with navy Escadrille 7B2 aboard the seaplane-carrier *Commandant Teste*. By comparison with the earlier **PL 14** version of the 18.00-m PL 7, the PL 15 had a redesigned slender fuselage without the 'avion marin' type hull. Power was provided by a 650-hp (485-kW) Hispano-Suiza 12Nbr engine, and the wings folded for storage aboard ship. Surviving PL 15s, taken out of service at the end of 1938, formed Escadrille 3S6 for anti-submarine patrol along

the Atlantic coast from September 1939 onwards.

The PL 15 was developed into the **PL 151**, a mid-wing monoplane with a small stabilising plane mounted over the fuselage. A full-scale mockup was built, but no further development was undertaken. The **PL 154**, converted from the fourth PL 15, was a three-seat landplane torpedo-carrier which was abandoned after limited test flying. Later designs

The PL 15 was armed with two 0.295-in (7.5-mm) machine-guns, and a torpedo or up to 992 lb (450 kg) of bombs. On 30 October 1939 a 3S6 PL 15 became the first French seaplane to sink a German submarine.

included the unusual **PL 200** monoplane, intended as an advanced reconnaissance seaplane, with a shoulder-wing mounted on a short nacelle for the three crew members, at the front of

which was the 720-hp (537-kW) Hispano-Suiza Wbrs radial engine. Test-flown in February 1935, the PL 200 achieved a maximum speed of 140 mph (225 km/h) by comparison with the 129

mph (208 km/h) of the production PL 15. It was re-engined with a 740-hp (552-kW) Gnome-Rhône 9Kfr engine in October 1935 as the **PL 201**, but development was abandoned soon afterwards.

Levy G.L.40

Early in World War I the French financier Léon-Georges Levy established a factory in which to produce aircraft in support of the nation's war effort. The factory's only significant design to be developed and produced during the war was the **G.L.40**, an HB.2 category two/three-seat lightweight flying-boat which the French navy used in the coastal patrol role during 1917-8. Of

unequal-span biplane configuration, with a stabilising float beneath the tip of each lower wing, the G.L.40 was powered by a 300-hp (224-kW) Renault 12Fe engine strut-mounted above the hull and located between the wings to drive a pusher propeller. The pilot and observer were seated in a side-by-side cockpit forward of the lower wing, and there was a bow position with a machine-gun on

a pivoted mount. Following a highly successful first flight, in November 1917, a production order for 100 aircraft was received from the navy; they were to serve from seaplane bases in Algeria, France, Greece, Morocco, Senegal and Tunisia. In addition, small numbers were exported to Belgium and Finland. With

Finland bought two (illustrated) and Belgium six Levy G.L.40s, the latter for use in the Congo.

a wingspan of 60 ft 8½ in (18.50 m), maximum speed of 87 mph (140 km/h) and range of 270 miles (435 km), the G.L.40 was

able to carry a bombload of 441 lb (200 kg). Postwar, some examples remained in civil use until as late as 1922.

L.F.G. Roland C.II

The airship-building Motorluftschiff Studiengesellschaft, which had been formed in Berlin in 1906, was later superseded by Flugmaschine Wright GmbH with a factory at Adlershof for the construction of Wright biplanes. When the company failed in 1912, Krupp and other financiers used the premises to found

Luftfahrzeug Gesellschaft (L.F.G.). However, with the well-known Luftverkehrs GmbH (L.V.G.) also established in Berlin, it was decided that the close similarity of the commonly-used L.F.G. and L.V.G. abbreviations could cause confusion, leading to the L.F.G. company registering the trade name 'Roland' which was adopted as part

of the title.
Activities at the beginning of World War I were confined to licence-production of Albatros two-seat reconnaissance aircraft, but the company's design engineer, Dipl.Ing. Tantzen, evolved a new aircraft in this category with which he hoped to achieve much higher performance standards. This was the **L.F.G. Roland C.II**, nicknamed **'Walfisch'** (whale) at a later date, the name undoubtedly derived from the type's deep fuselage, with the upper biplane wing mounted to the top of the fuselage and so removing the need for centre-section struts. Thus Tantzen

An outstandingly streamlined design for its era, the 'Walfisch' featured a semi-exposed engine installation and side-mounted radiators as the only features to spoil its lines.

intended to eliminate one source of drag and, at the same time, he replaced the conventional interplane struts by a single wide-chord I-section strut for the same reason. The pilot and observer/gunner, seated in open cockpits, had an excellent field of

view over the upper wing, but despite large cut-outs in the roots of both wings the forward/downward view was restricted.
The prototype was flown for the first time in October 1915, and modified production aircraft began to enter service in early 1916.

Variants

C.IIa: aircraft with revised and reinforced wingtips
C.III: single prototype of developed version with a 200-hp (149-kW) Benz Bz.IV engine and conventional interplane struts
C.VIII: single prototype developed from C.III with revised fuselage and 260-hp (194-kW) Mercedes RIVa engine

SPECIFICATION	
L.F.G. Roland C.II	(1284 kg)
Type: two-seat reconnaissance/ escort aircraft	**Dimensions:** wingspan 33 ft 9½ in (10.30 m); length 25 ft 3¼ in
Powerplant: one 160-hp (119-kW) Mercedes D.III inline piston engine	(7.70 m); height 9 ft 6¼ in (2.90 m); wing area 279.87 sq ft (26.00 m²)
Performance: maximum speed 103 mph (165 km/h); endurance 4 hours	**Armament:** one 0.31-in (7.92-mm) Parabellum machine-gun in the rear cockpit and (later production
Weights: empty 1,684 lb (764 kg); maximum take-off 2,831 lb	aircraft) one 0.31-in (7.92-mm) LMG 08/15 forward-firing gun

L.F.G. Roland D.II and D.IIa

With the C.II in production, Tantzen concentrated on developing a single-seat version for use as a fighter/scout. Thus resulted the **D.I** with a fuselage that was not so deep, its less

ponderous lines duly bringing the nickname **'Haifisch'** (shark). By comparison with the C.II, however, there was considerable change in wing configuration, the two wings being unstaggered

and with a small amount of sweepback on the leading edge, and conventional interplane struts replaced the I-struts. The D.I was first flown in July 1916, being followed shortly afterwards by an improved **D.II** incorporating a revised tail unit and additional improvements to reduce drag. Both the D.I and D.II were powered by the

The D.I/II/IIIa fighters were not particularly popular with the pilots to whom they were allocated, heavy controls and an inferior field of view being the main complaints. The aircraft illustrated here is an Argus-engined D.IIa.

160-hp (119-kW) Mercedes D.III engine, and the generally similar **D.IIa.** resulted from installation of a more powerful Argus engine. These aircraft began to

enter service from early 1917 and more of all versions are believed to have been built, the majority of them by the Pfalz Flugzeug-Werke.

Variants

D.III: in an attempt to improve the forward view the D.III introduced a conventional fuselage and wing centre-section struts; although representing an improvement over the D.II/IIa, it was inferior to the equivalent Albatros type and, in consequence, was built in only small numbers
D.V: single prototype, basically similar to D.III but with refined fuselage structure

SPECIFICATION	
L.F.G. Roland D.IIa	maximum take-off 1,753 lb (795 kg)
Type: single-seat fighter/scout	**Dimensions:** wingspan 29 ft 2½ in
Powerplant: one 180-hp (134-kW) Argus As.III inline piston engine	(8.90 m); length 22 ft 9½ in (6.95 m); height 9 ft 8¼ in (2.95 m);
Performance: maximum speed 106 mph (170 km/h); endurance 2 hours	wing area 236.81 sq ft (22.00 m²) **Armament:** two forward-firing 0.31-in (7.92-mm) LMG 08/15
Weights: empty 1,400 lb (635 kg);	machine-guns

Lioré-et-Olivier 7

Formed by Fernand Lioré and Henri Olivier, Les Ateliers d'Aviation Lioré et Olivier dated from March 1912. A number of designs

by various aviation pioneers were constructed, to be followed during World War I by Nieuport, Morane-Saulnier and, principally,

British Sopwith 1½-strutter reconnaissance biplanes.
Apart from a couple of experimental monoplanes built in 1912, the first true LeO design was the **LeO 4** biplane of 1916, with an upper wing of peculiar

curved planform. It was soon followed by the more conventional **LeO 4/1**, which was also a two-seat reconnaissance biplane, but neither was developed beyond the prototype stage. Then came the

three-seat **LeO 5** ground-attack biplane, powered by two 170-hp (127kW) Rhône 9R engines, but this did not appear until 1919 and failed to attract production orders.

Lioré-et-Olivier 7 (continued)

The **LeO H-6**, displayed at the 1919 Salon de l'Aéronautique, was a four-passenger three-engined flying-boat, and in 1920 an amphibian version, designated **LeO-6/2**, was completed.

In 1922 design engineer Leflot produced the **LeO 7**, a three-seat multiplace de combat or bomber escort biplane stemming from the LeO 5. The series version was the **LeO 7/2** with wide-track landing gear, gunner's posts in the snub nose and amidships, and the pilot's cockpit immediately behind the wing trailing edge. Powered by two 300-hp (223-kW) Hispano-Suiza 8Fb V-8 engines, the LeO 7/2 spanned 60 ft 11¾ in (18.59 m), attained a maximum speed of 118 mph (190 km/h), and carried an 882-lb (400-kg) bombload. Twenty LeO 7/2s were followed by 12 examples of the **LeO 7/3**, which was a navalised version that entered service at the

This LeO 7/2 was one of 20 built for regular service on an experimental basis. The LeO 7/2 was followed into service by the LeO 7/3, which had provision for emergency water landings and take-offs.

Saint-Raphaël base. It had increased wingspan, a gunner's 'balcony' in the nose, was identically powered to the earlier LeO 7/2 and had similar performance.

Lioré-et-Olivier 20

A three-seat version of the **LeO 122** prototype, the **LeO 20** won the 1926 French ministry of war competition for a new night bomber, and in September of that year the prototype established world distance records with a 4,409-lb (2000-kg) payload.

The first order for 50 aircraft, for the French Aéronautique Militaire, was received at the end of 1926, the first LeO 20s being flight-tested at

Villacoublay in 1927. Further orders followed, and the last of 311 machines taken on charge by the French air arm was accepted in December 1932. The LeO 20s equipped the 12 escadrilles of the 21ᵉ and 22ᵉ Régiments d'Aviation based at Nancy and Chartres respectively.

Nine LeO 20s were exported in 1928-9, seven to Romania and two to Brazil, as a result of demonstration flights abroad by a LeO 20 which was later delivered to the Armée de l'Air. At the beginning of 1937 224 LeO 20s were still in French service, although by that time their relatively low speed meant that the type was obsolete. On the eve of World War II 92 LeO 20s were still in flying condition, many as target tugs or trainers with flying schools in France and North Africa, and a further 23 were in storage.

Earlier a number had been redesignated **LeO 201** when adapted for parachute training.

Many LeO 20s went to the multi-engine training school of the Aéronautique Militaire at Etampes, as well as to front-line bomber units. The type remained the backbone of the French night bomber force for at least a decade.

Last of a series of developments of the LeO 20 was the **LeO 208**, a fully enclosed four-seat bomber in the BN.4 category with retractable landing gear and powered by two 770-hp (574-kW) Gnome-Rhône 14Mrs radial engines, and which was flown for the first time in June 1934. Despite subsequent modifications, however, the type's maximum speed could not be raised above 202 mph (325 km/h) and it was rejected for production.

SPECIFICATION	
Lioré-et-Olivier 20	(2725 kg); maximum take-off
Type: three-seat night bomber	12,037 lb (5460 kg)
Powerplant: two 420-hp (313-kW) Gnome-Rhône 9Ady (Jupiter) radial piston engines	**Dimensions:** wingspan 73 ft (22.25 m); length 45 ft 3¾ in (13.81 m); height 13 ft 11¾ in (4.26 m); wing area 1,130.25 sq ft (105.00 m²)
Performance: maximum speed 123 mph (198 km/h); service ceiling 18,900 ft (5760 m); range 621 miles (1000 km)	**Armament:** five 0.303-in (7.7-mm) machine-guns, plus up to 2,205 lb (1000 kg) of bombs
Weights: empty equipped 6,008 lb	

Lioré-et-Olivier 21

Both **LeO 21** airliners flew for the first time in August 1926 and during the following summer entered service on the London-Paris route. Retaining the basic metal structure and configuration of the LeO 20, the LeO 21 introduced a new fuselage of wider section, accommodating six passengers in a nose cabin and 12 in the main cabin aft. The second LeO 21 was redesignated **LeO 212** following the installation of 450-hp (336-kW) Renault 12Ja V-12 engines and was converted by the Wagons-Lits company as a 'dining aircraft'. The first LeO 21 became an *avion-bar* in 1929, as the **LeO 211**, and in 1931 with Renault engines installed became the **LeO 213**. The **LeO 21S** was a one-off ambulance aircraft for 10 stretcher cases with an attendant.

The first new-build LeO 213 with Renault engines was flown in 1928. After six years of regular service it was lost on a mail flight to Croydon on 31 May 1934. Ten more LeO 213s were built and used on routes from Paris to London, Lyons, Marseilles and Geneva. Compared with the LeO 21s, these aircraft had increased wing area, three baggage holds and improved cabin soundproofing. Some were modified for night flying under the designation **LeO 213N**, and one became a freight-carrier in 1931. In August 1934 the Armée de l'Air bought nine surviving LeO 213s and converted them as troop transports with bench seats along the walls of the fuselage, the machines then being redesignated **LeO 214**. Later used for paratroop training, they were based at Fez in Morocco until being scrapped in early 1939.

Air Union painted its LeO 213 airliners in a smart gold, red and white livery, under the fleet name Le Rayon d'Or (the golden ray).

SPECIFICATION	
Lioré-et-Olivier 214	**Weights:** empty equipped 7,584 lb (3440 kg); maximum take-off 12,566 lb (5700 kg)
Type: military transport for 14 troops	**Dimensions:** wingspan 75 ft 6¾ in (23.03 m); length 51 ft ¼ in (15.55 m), height 14 ft 9¼ in (4.50 m); wing area 1,162.54 sq ft (108 m²)
Powerplant: two 450-hp (336-kW) Renault 12Ja V-12 piston engines	
Performance: maximum speed 118 mph (190 km/h); service ceiling 14,765 ft (4500 m); range 348 miles (560 km)	

Lioré-et-Olivier 203, 204 and 206

In search of a more powerful night bomber, the Lioré-et-Olivier design team developed a large four-engined machine, the **LeO 203**. This was first flown in May 1930, and was powered by four 300-hp (224-kW) Gnome-Rhône 7Kb radials mounted in pairs on the lower wings. Soon afterwards a floatplane version was flown under the designation **LeO 204**.

A 1931 order for 40 LeO 203s was transferred to the **LeO 206**, the first of which made its maiden flight in June 1932. This had a redesigned nose, a ventral balcony which housed the bomb-bay and, at the rear, a defensive gun position, and was powered by four 350-hp (261-kW) Gnome-Rhône 7Kd radials.

The LeO 206 equipped Groupe de Bombardement III/12 at Reims and then GB I/22 at Chartres. Three aircraft of the original order for 40 were completed as **LeO 207** machines with a nose section similar to that of the LeO 203 and a

smaller ventral balcony than that of the LeO 206. Performance was improved by the installation of Gnome-Rhône Titan Kds supercharged engines.

The ability of the LeO 206 to remain aloft on only three or even two engines gave it an

An unusual engine installation using push-pull pairs was employed on the LeO 203, 204 and 206, as exemplified here on the 203 prototype.

extended life. Nicknamed 'Caravelle', 29 were still in flying condition in

September 1939, the majority of them stationed in Morocco.

Lioré-et-Olivier 451

Laying claim to being one of the most aesthetically attractive twin-engined aircraft of World War II, the **LeO 451** originated from a French official specification of 1934 calling for a B.4-category four-seat day-bomber. Designed by Jean Mercier, the **LeO 45.01** prototype flew on 16 January 1937. The aircraft showed great promise, but control problems on take-off led to revision of the tail assembly, and the Hispano-Suiza 14AA radial engines also caused development delays. In September 1938 Gnome-Rhône 14N engines were installed and the aircraft redesignated **LeO 451.01**. Meanwhile series production had begun at the SNCASE plants at Clichy and Levallois, Lioré-et-Olivier having been nationalised in February 1937. The first series LeO 451 was flown on 24 March 1939 but, of a total of 1,783 LeO 451s and variants ordered, only 452 had flown by 25 June 1940.

The excellence of the LeO 451 resulted in the Vichy authorities, with German approval, ordering 225 machines in August 1941, all contracts outstanding at the time of

The 1st Escadrille Groupe de Bombardement I/11 of the l'Armée de l'Air had this LeO 451 on strength at Oran-La Sénia, Morocco, in mid-1941.

the 1940 surrender having been regarded as void. LeO 451 no. 453, the first product of the SNCASE Ambérieu factory, flew on 30 April 1942.

Variants included the **LeO 455.01** with 1,375-hp (1025-kW) Gnome-Rhône 14R engines, which flew on 3 December 1939. Five other LeO 451s were converted as similarly powered **LeO 455Ph** civil aircraft in 1948, and were used by the Institut Géographique National for topographic work. In 1946 40 North African-based LeO 451s were converted to **LeO 453** standard with Pratt & Whitney R-1830-67 radials. Some equipped navy Escadrille 11.S, while others were used for liaison or air-sea rescue. Four civil aircraft were used for glider towing.

The service history of

the LeO 451 began in December 1939, when the conversion of operational escadres was started. The first war mission was on 11 May 1940, when aircraft of Groupes de Bombardement I/12 and II/12 attacked the Maastricht bridges in the Netherlands in an attempt to slow up the German Blitzkrieg. From then until the armistice in June more and more LeO 451s went into service, equipping several escadres. Their losses in daylight raids were heavy and in June long-range attacks at night were made on German and Italian targets. Orders had included the **LeO 451M**, modified for naval use, and one of this version was delivered at the end of May 1940.

Vichy Armée de l'Air and Aéronavale units in

North Africa converted to the LeO 451 in 1940 and 1941. They took part in actions in the Levant in 1941 and against the Allies landing in North Africa at the end of 1942, suffering considerable losses, mostly on the ground. From July 1944 surviving LeO 451s in North Africa were switched to communications duties; 12 redesignated **LeO 451E2** were used for a variety of tasks, including glider towing. When the German forces took over unoccu-

pied France in November 1942, they seized all available LeO 451s. Some were passed to the Regia Aeronautica for use as bomber trainers, but about 50 machines were converted as **LeO 451T** transports for the Luftwaffe. Twelve aircraft, redesignated **LeO 451C**, were used as mail carriers for Air France.

Several surviving LeO 451s which were not converted as LeO 453s remained in service in a variety of roles for several years post-war.

Lioré-et-Olivier H-24, H-24-2 and H-24-2/1

The result of prolonged design work by Benoit and his design team, the **H-24.01** made its first flight in November 1929. A cantilever high-wing monoplane flying-boat, the H-24 had an enclosed pilot's cockpit, cabin accommodation for 10 passengers and a

distinctive tall single fin and rudder, and was powered by two 500-hp (373-kW) Renault I2Jb V-12 engines mounted in tandem on a pylon over the hull. This single aircraft was used purely for development, making a number of test and demonstration flights.

The H-24 prototype (illustrated) led to the H-24-2 and H-24-2/1. The latter had an enclosed crew cabin with side-by-side pilots' seats and a navigation and radio compartment; 15 passengers could be accommodated in a cabin beneath the wings, and there was a sizeable luggage and mail hold at the rear.

Lioré-et-Olivier H-24, H-24-2 and H-24-2/1 (continued)

The H-24.01 was scrapped at Antibes in 1934.

Developed from the H-24 was the **H-24-2**, of similar configuration but, powered by four Gnome- Rhône radial engines mounted in tandem pairs over the thick-section wing. The first two of 14 production aircraft for Air France were H-24-2s, and the remaining 12 were **H-24-2/1** aircraft with a revised engine installation. The first H-24-2 had flown for the initial time in March 1933, and before long all the machines were employed on Air France routes linking Marseilles with Athens, Tunis and Beirut. Ten aircraft were still operational in September 1939, and were flown under Italian supervision after the German occupation of southern France in November 1942. It is understood that most were scrapped shortly afterwards.

Lioré-et-Olivier H-25

Powered by two 575-hp (429-kW) Hispano-Suiza 12Hb engines the **LeO 25** prototype four-seat night bomber was delivered in 1928 as part of the second series batch of LeO 20s. The next year it was redesignated **LeO 252.01** after being re-engined with Hispano 12Mbr engines, and in 1931 it was fitted with two large wooden floats for evaluation by the French navy. The second **LeO 252**, slightly modified, appeared in 1932 and was bought by Romania.

Three landplane developments of the LeO 252 were delivered to Brazil as **LeO 253** aircraft in 1931, but were not assembled until the following year when they took part in the civil war in that country. The LeO 253 had a maximum speed of 136 mph (215 km/h). The **H-254** flew for the first time in the summer of 1932, and was a refined version of the **H-252** intended for production, but only two examples were built and these were used at Berre to familiarize Farnian F.168 crews with the more advanced aircraft to come. The **H-255** was a version of the H-254 with 690-hp (515-kW) Hispano-Suiza 12Xbrs engines. Flown first as a landplane, then as a seaplane, it gained several world height-with-load records for seaplanes. The **H-256** appeared in late 1932, introducing increased wing area.

The **H-257** was a considerable advance over the previous prototypes, powered by the Gnome-Rhône 14Kbrs Mistral Major radial engines preferred by the French navy, and with an enclosed cabin for the pilot. It first flew in March 1933 and was sufficiently impressive to earn an order for 60 **H-257bis** series seaplanes with more powerful Gnome-Rhône 14Kirs/Kjrs engines, a strengthened structure, and the nose gun position enclosed in a glazed rotating cupola. In fact, the **H-258** was delivered before the H-257bis, 26 going into service, initially with Escadrilles 3B1 and 3B2, from June 1935 onwards. The H-258 had two 650-hp (484-kW) Hispano-Suiza 12Nbr engines and attained a maximum speed of 149 mph (240 km/h). The H-257bis went into service from June 1936, equipping seaplane Escadrilles 3B1, 3B2, then B-1, B-2, B-3 and finally E.7 and 3S4. The Armée de l'Air used the landplane version with fixed independent mainwheels in Groupe de Bombardement 11/25.

After neutrality patrols during the Spanish Civil War, the LeO floatplanes were used as convoy escorts and for submarine patrol from September 1939, seeing action in the English Channel, and on the Atlantic and Mediterranean coasts. Some were flung into action on bombing raids against the German Blitzkrieg in the summer of 1940, suffering heavy losses. At the outbreak of war 19 landplane H-257bis aircraft were still in service in North Africa, and in August 1940 the Vichy regime had 53 floatplanes on strength. The last examples were withdrawn from training and target towing duties at the end of 1944.

The solitary **H-259**, the last of the H-25 series, had 860-hp (641-kW) Hispano-Suiza 12Ydrs/Yfrs engines and disappointing performance, and after test flights in 1935 no orders were received.

The H-25 series, shown here in H-255 form, showed little improvement over the LeO 20, from which it could be distinguished by its redesigned fin.

SPECIFICATION

Lioré-et-Olivier H-257bis (floatplane)
Type: five-seat torpedo-bomber reconnaissance float biplane
Powerplant: two 870-hp (649-kW) Gnome-Rhône 14Knrs/Kors radial piston engines
Performance: maximum speed 143 mph (230 km/h); service ceiling 26,245 ft (8000 m); range 932 miles (1500 km)
Weights: empty equipped 11,684 lb (5300 kg); maximum take-off 21,076 lb (9560 kg)
Dimensions: wingspan 83 ft 8 in (25.50 m); length 57 ft 6½ in (17.54 m); height 22 ft 3¾ in (6.80 m); wing area 1,437.03 sq ft (133.50 m²)
Armament: three 0.295 in (7.5-mm) Darne machine-guns, plus one 1,477-lb (670-kg) DA torpedo or up to 1,323 lb (600 kg) of bombs

Lioré-et-Olivier H-43

The **H-43** design by engineer Benoit was in response to a French navy requirement for a three-seat ship-based observation and scouting seaplane. The **H-43.01** made its initial flight on 4 December 1934, a mid-wing monoplane with a ventral balcony for the observer. After prolonged trials, including successful catapult launches from the seaplane carrier *Commandant Teste*, it was much modified before an official order for 20 machines was received. The fuselage was then subjected to more radical redesign, and as a result the first production machine was not flight-tested until 13 July 1939, by which time the type was totally obsolete. The H-43s

Powered by a single 650-hp (485-kW) Hispano-Suiza 9Vb radial piston engine, the H-43 had a maximum speed of 130 mph (210 km/h). The first aircraft is illustrated here on a catapult.

began to re-equip naval Escadrille 3S1 in February 1940 and Escadrille 3S5 the following month, but they were all withdrawn from service by August that year.

Lioré-et-Olivier H-246

Designed to an official requirement of 1935, the **H-246.01** flying-boat prototype flew on 30 September 1937. A graceful parasol-wing monoplane, its metal hull incorporated a flight deck for the four-man crew and a main cabin for 26 passengers.

In January 1938 Air France ordered six **H-246.1** aircraft in addition to the prototype, and two aircraft were about to enter service on the Marignane-Algiers route when war broke out. The French navy intended to impress all six series aircraft for maritime reconnaissance, but in the event only one was converted. This was the third series aircraft, which flew in June

A notable feature of the H-246 concerned the cooling arrangements for its Hispano-Suiza engines. Each engine had a ventral radiator housed in a strut-mounted, streamlined ventral pod.

SPECIFICATION

Lioré-et-Olivier H-246.1
Type: transport flying-boat
Powerplant: four 720-hp (537-kW) Hispano-Suiza 12Xgrs/Xhrs V-12 piston engines
Performance: maximum speed 205 mph (330 km/h); service ceiling 22,965 ft (7000 m); range 1,243 miles (2000 km)
Weights: empty equipped 21,605 lb (9800 kg); maximum take-off 33,069 lb (15000 kg)
Dimensions: wingspan 104 ft ¾ in (31.72 m); length 69 ft 5½ in (21.17 m); height 23 ft 5½ in (7.15 m); wing area 1,410.12 sq ft (131.00 m²)

1940, and then went into service with Escadrille 9.E with a modified extended glazed nose section. It was armed with four 0.295-in (7.5-mm) Darne machine-

guns and 1,323 lb (600 kg) of bombs.

From October 1939 to November 1942 the civil LeO boats operated the route to Algiers for Air

France. After that they were seized by the Luftwaffe, converted to carry 21 troops or 14 stretcher cases, and armed with five 0.31-in (7.92-mm)

MG 15 machine-guns, one in a bow turret, two in lateral positions and two more firing through windows at the rear of the flight deck. They were used

on a variety of tasks, including brief operations in Finland. Post-war, two H-246.1s were used for a time on the Air France Marignane-Algiers route.

Lockheed 1, 2 and 5 Vega

First becoming keenly interested in aviation during 1910, the brothers Allan and Malcolm Loughead (pronounced Lockheed) founded in early 1916 the first company to bear their name, Loughead Aircraft Manufacturing Company, at Santa Barbara, California. This organisation ran into financial difficulties and was wound up in 1921, and it was not until late 1926 that there was formed a new company, the Lockheed Aircraft Company. This company title lasted for less than three years, but in that time a remarkable aircraft was developed and put into production, the **Vega** which was designed by John K. 'Jack' Northrop with assistance from Gerard F. 'Gerry' Vultee, both later to found

SPECIFICATION

Lockheed Vega 5C (landplane)
Type: seven-seat cabin monoplane
Powerplant: one 450-hp (336-kW) Pratt & Whitney Wasp SC-1 radial piston engine
Performance: maximum speed 185 mph (298 km/h); service ceiling 18,000 ft (5485 m); standard range

550 miles (885 km)
Weights: empty 2,565 lb (1163 kg); maximum take-off 4,750 lb (2155 kg)
Dimensions: wingspan 41 ft (12.50 m); length 27 ft 6 in (8.38 m); height 8 ft 6 in (2.59 m); wing area 275.0 sq ft (25.55 m²)

significant American aircraft companies. A cantilever high-wing monoplane of wooden construction, it had a beautifully stream-lined monocoque fuselage built up from two half-shells of plywood that had been pressure-formed to shape in a concrete mould. The tow-drag landing gear was of fixed tailwheel type (but Vegas were used frequently with floats or skis), enclosed accommodation was provided for a

pilot and four passengers, and the powerplant for the initial version, later identified as the **Vega 1**, was a 225-hp (168-kW) Wright J-5 Whirlwind radial engine. The initial aircraft was flown for the first time on 4 July 1927 and was acquired by newspaper-owner George Hearst to compete in the Oakland to Hawaii Dole Race, sponsored by James D. Dole, which began on 16 August 1927. The Vega, by then named *Golden Eagle* and flown by Jack Frost and Gordon Scott, disappeared without trace en route but, fortunately for Lockheed, the unexplained loss of this aircraft did not prohibit further sales; within the short space of six years the capability of the Vega was world renowned. A host of achievements brought this

This Vega 5 was flown by Western Airlines. Note the type's large wheel spats and carefully cowled Pratt & Whitney Wasp engine.

Variants

Vega 1: original production version, powered as built by a 225-hp (168-kW) Wright J-5, J-5A, J-5AB, J-5B or J-5C Whirlwind engine
Vega 2: production version which differed primarily by having the 300-hp (224-kW) Wright J-6 Whirlwind engine
Vega 2A: redesignation of one Vega 2 for operation at a higher gross weight
Vega 2D: redesignation of two Vega Is and one Vega 2 following installation of a 300-hp (224-kW) Pratt & Whitney Wasp Junior engine
Vega 5: major production version (35 built) with engines that included the 410-hp (306-kW) Pratt & Whitney Wasp A, 450-hp (336-kW) Wasp B or 420-hp (313-kW) Wasp CI, most installed with a NACA low-drag cowling
Vega 5A Executive: basically as Vega 5, but with executive interior
Vega 5B: basically as Vega 5, but intended for operation as sevenseat aircraft at a higher gross weight
Vega 5C: basically as Vega 5 but with revised tail surfaces and operating at higher gross weight
DL-1: Vega 5C with light alloy fuselage produced during ownership by Detroit Aircraft Corporation
DL-1B: similar to DL-1 but equipped as six-passenger transports for airline use
DL-1 Special: one aircraft exported to the UK for record breaking and racing use
Y1C-12: designation of one DL-1 aircraft acquired by the US Army Air Corps for evaluation
Y1C-17: designation of one DL-1B acquired by the USAAC for high speed and record-breaking flights
UC-101: US Army Air Force designation of one Vega 5C impressed for service in 1942

fame, including the first trans-Arctic flight and the first exploratory flight over Antarctica (Wilkins and Eilson in a Vega 1); the first solo transatlantic flight by a woman from Newfoundland to Ireland (Amelia Earhart in a **Vega 5B**); and the first solo

round-the-world flight (Wiley Post in the Vega 5B *Winnie Mae*). When production ended a total of 128 Vegas had been built: 115 by Lockheed, nine by Detroit Aircraft Corporation (of which Lockheed was a division from 1929-31) and four by others.

Lockheed 3 Air Express, and 3 and 7 Explorer

The very considerable success and proven reliability of the Vega made this aircraft of interest to many airlines, but Western Air Express required some of its own ideas incorporated,

the association bringing the name **Lockheed 3 Air Express**. With a fuselage, landing gear and tail unit generally similar to the Vega, this aircraft differed primarily by having an

increased-span parasol wing, a cabin seating four passengers or carrying 100 cu ft (2.83 m³) of mail, with the pilot's open cockpit moved to the rear of the cabin. Power was provided as standard by a 410-hp (306-kW) Pratt & Whitney Wasp, but at least one was flown with a 525-hp (391-kW) Wasp, and some of these engines were

enclosed by the NACA-developed low-drag cowling. A total of seven of these aircraft was built, plus one **Air Express**

Special with which Laura Ingalls intended to make a nonstop transatlantic flight in 1931. Western Air Express, which had inspired this development of the Vega, acquired only a single example.

Variants

Lockheed 4 Explorer: derivative of the Air Express/Vega series with low-set monoplane wing, fixed landing gear and 450-hp (336-kW) Pratt & Whitney Wasp; designed for a nonstop transpacific flight to Japan; two aircraft only: first crashed during take-off for the record attempt in July 1929, and the replacement aircraft with jettisonable landing gear crashed during trials in September 1929; theoretical range was 5,500 miles (8850 km)
Lockheed 7 Explorer: improved version of Model 4 with 450-hp (336-kW) Wasp C; first aircraft crashed during trials in May 1930, and second made some moderately successful flights before being written off in November 1930

The basic Air Express spanned 42 ft 6 in (12.95 m), had a maximum take-off weight of 4,375 lb (1984 kg) and possessed a maximum speed of 167 mph (269 km/h) at sea level.

Lockheed 8 Altair

When acquiring his Sirius, Charles Lindbergh had inti-

mated that he might be interested in having a

version with retractable landing gear, with a result that Lockheed designed an alternative wing to accept inward-retracting main land-

ing gear units. Although this feature was not adopted by Lindbergh, it became available as a retrofit for Sirius aircraft, first flown on a

company-owned Sirius 8A during September 1930. Redesignated **Altair 8D** in this form, the aircraft was loaned to the USAAC.

Lockheed 8 Altair (continued)

In November 1931, with a new 450-hp (336-kW) Pratt & Whitney R-1340-17 engine installed, the aircraft was acquired by the USAAC under the designation **Y1C-25**. Four more aircraft were converted, two Sirius 8As becoming **Altair 8D** aircraft, the Detroit Aircraft DL-2 being redesignated **Altair DL-2A** and, most famous of all, one Sirius receiving the designation **Sirius 8 Special**. This last aircraft

was later acquired by Sir Charles Kingsford Smith and, modified to Altair 8D configuration and named *Lady Southern Cross*, was used by this pilot, with P. G. Taylor as his navigator, to make the first crossing of the Pacific Ocean from Australia to the United States between 20 October and 4 November 1934.

In addition to the conversions, six Altairs were built as new, one of them an Altair DL-2A built by Detroit

Typical data for the Altair included a span of 42 ft 9 in (13.03 m), a maximum take-off weight of 4,895 lb (2220 kg) and a maximum speed of 207 mph (333 km/h) at 7,000 ft (2135 m).

Aircraft and powered by a 645-hp (481-kW) Wright R-1820E Cyclone which was acquired by the US Navy under the designation **XRO-1**.

Lockheed 8 Sirius

Developed originally to meet a requirement of Charles Lindbergh for a low-wing monoplane of high performance, the **Lockheed 8 Sirius** combined what was basically a Vega wooden fuselage with a new low-set cantilever wing. First flown in November 1929, and then powered by a 450-hp (336-kW) Pratt & Whitney Wasp radial engine, the Sirius had non-retractable tailwheel landing gear and two open cockpits in tandem. Before

accepting this aircraft, Lindbergh had a sliding canopy installed to enclose the two cockpits. In the following year, before Lindbergh set out on a survey flight for Pan American Airways, a 575-hp (429-kW) Wright Cyclone engine and twin-float landing gear were installed. For its final survey flight in 1933 it was powered by a 710-hp (529-kW) Wright Cyclone engine.

The success of Lindbergh's aircraft led to

Charless Lindbergh's Lockheed Sirius spanned 42 ft 9¼ in (13.04 m), weighed a maximum of 7,099 lb (3220 kg), was capable of a maximum of 185 mph (298 km/h), and had a range of 975 miles (1570 km), all in landplane configuration.

the construction of 13 more by Lockheed, comprising four similar Sirius 8, eight **Sirius 8A** with enlarged tail surfaces, and a single four-seat **Sirius 8C** aircraft which had an enclosed cabin for two between the engine

and pilot's cockpit. One Sirius built by the Detroit Aircraft Corporation, with a

metal fuselage and Lockheed wooden wing, had the designation **DL-2**.

Lockheed 9 Orion

Variants

Orion 9: original production version with a 410-hp (306-kW) Pratt & Whitney Wasp A or 420-hp (313-kW) Wasp C radial engine; 14 built
Orion 9A Special: one aircraft with a 450-hp (336-kW) Wasp SC engine and some minor airframe revisions
Orion 9B: two aircraft with 575-hp (429-kW) Wright R-1820-E Cyclone engines; supplied to Swissair
Orion 9C: redesignation of the single Altair DL-2A following conversion to Orion configuration
Orion 9D: production version with some minor airframe revisions and powered originally by the Wasp S1D1 engine; 13 built
Orion 9E: three aircraft, generally similar to Orion 9, but powered by the 450-hp (336-kW) Wasp SC1 engine
Orion 9F: one executive aircraft with 645-hp (481-kW) Wright R-1820-F2 Cyclone engine
Orion 9F-1: one executive aircraft with a 650-hp (485-kW) Wright SR-1820-F2 Cyclone engine
UC-85: US Army Air Force designation allocated to one Orion 9D impressed for service in June 1942
Orion-Explorer: designation allocated to one Orion 9E following replacement of a damaged wing with that of the crashed second Explorer 7, installation of fixed landing gear and a 600-hp (482-kW) Wasp S3H1 engine; later fitted with floats, it was used by Wiley Post and Will Rogers for a round the-world flight attempt, but both men died when the aircraft crashed in Alaska on 15 August 1935

With the delivery of its six Lockheed 9 Orions, Varney Air Service changed its name to Varney Speed Lanes Air Service. The aircraft were used on air mail routes and the airline later became Continental.

Seeing in the latter part of 1930 a potential market for a light transport aircraft, Lockheed began development of the six-passenger **Lockheed 9 Orion**. This combined a Vega fuselage with the low-wing and landing gear of the Lockheed Altair, and the NACA cowling introduced on the Air Express, the first such Orion being flown in early 1931. Orion production totalled 35, and the single Altair DL-2A was also converted to Orion configuration.

The first Lockheed Orion entered service with Bowen Air Lines at Fort Worth, Texas, in May 1931, and the type found use with 12 other American airlines. At least

13 of these aircraft, from various sources, were supplied to the Spanish Republican air force in late 1936, soon after the beginning of the Spanish Civil War.

SPECIFICATION	
Lockheed Orion 9D	(1159 km)
Type: light transport aircraft	**Weights:** empty 3,640 lb
Powerplant: one 550-hp (410-kW)	(1651 kg); maximum take-off
Pratt & Whitney Wasp S1D1 radial	5,200 lb (2359 kg)
piston engine	**Dimensions:** wingspan 42 ft 9¼ in
Performance: cruising speed	(13.04 m); length 28 ft 4 in
205 mph (330 km/h); service ceiling	(8.64 m); height 9 ft 8 in (2.95 m);
22,000 ft (6705 m); range 720 miles	wing area 294.10 sq ft (27.32 m²)

Lockheed 10 Electra

Lockheed's first major move towards becoming a significant manufacturer of transport aircraft came with the design of the **Lockheed 10 Electra**. Providing accommodation for 10 passengers, the Electra was a cantilever

low-wing monoplane of all-metal construction, with retractable tailwheel landing gear and a tail unit incorporating twin fins and rudders. Powered by two Pratt & Whitney Wasp Junior SBs, the prototype was flown for the first time

on 23 February 1934, and was followed by 148 production aircraft. The Electra entered service during 1934, initially with Northwest Airlines, and in the late 1930s was used by eight American operators. By the time that the USA became involved in World War II, however, few remained in national airline

SPECIFICATION	
Lockheed Electra 10-A	(1305 km)
Type: short-range light transport	**Weights:** empty 6,454 lb
Powerplant: two 450-hp (336-kW)	(2927 kg); maximum take-off
Pratt & Whitney Wasp Junior SB	10,300 lb (4672 kg)
radial piston engines	**Dimensions:** wingspan 55 ft
Performance: maximum speed	(16.76 m); length 38 ft 7 in
202 mph (325 km/h) at 5,000 ft	(11.76 m); height 10 ft 1 in
(1525 m); service ceiling 19,400 ft	(3.07 m); wing area 458.50 sq ft
(5915 m); range 810 miles	(42.59 m²)

The earliest Electras were delivered to Northwest Airlines with this distinctive forward-raked windscreen. From the fifth aircraft on a more conventional glazing arrangement was adopted.

service for the rapid growth in air travel had already shown these small-capacity aircraft to be uneconomical. In addition to those built for the home market, Electras were exported to Argentina, Australia, Canada, Chile, Colombia, Japan, New Zealand, Poland, Romania, USSR, UK, Venezuela and Yugoslavia. Small numbers also saw service in the Spanish Civil War and with the outbreak of World War II the type was impressed for service with the RAF and Royal Canadian Air Force. Use of the Electra by small civil operators continued after the war, but few remained in service after the late 1960s.

Variants

Electra 10-A: major production version with Wasp Junior SBs; 101 built
Electra 10-B: generally similar to Electra 10-A, but powered by 440-hp (328-kW) Wright R-975-E3 Whirlwind engines; 18 built
Electra 10-C: version for Pan American Airways with 450-hp (336-kW) Wasp SC1 engines, 8 built
Electra 10-D: projected military variant; none built
Electra 10-E: generally similar to Electra 10-A but powered by 600-hp (447-kW) Wasp S3H1 engines; 15 built; most famous of these was NR16020 in which, during a round-the-world flight attempt, Amelia Earhart and her navigator Fred Noonan disappeared without trace on 2 July 1937
XR2O-1: a single staff transport for the US Navy, powered by 450-hp (336-kW) Pratt & Whitney R-985-48 engines

XR3O-1: a single convertible ambulance/transport aircraft for the US Coast Guard, powered by 440-hp (328-kW) Wright R-975-E3 engines
XC-35: designation of a single research aircraft developed from a standard Electra with a pressurised cabin, powered by 550-hp (410-kW) Pratt & Whitney XR-1340-43 turbocharged engines; used by the US Army Air Corps to gain valuable experience of pressurisation and the use of turbocharged engines
Y1C-36: USAAC designation of three Electra 10-As, with 450-hp (336-kW) R-985-13 engines, for use as transports
C-36A (later UC-36A): 15 Electra 10-As impressed for service with the US Army Air Force in World War II
C-36B (later UC-36B): five Electra 10-Es impressed for USAAF service
C-36C (later UC-36C): designation of seven Electra 10-Bs impressed for USAAF service
Y1C-37: one aircraft, generally similar to the Y1C-36s, acquired for service with the US National Guard Bureau

Lockheed 12 Electra Junior

When the Electra first entered service, its 10-passenger capacity was considered to be too small for airline operators, but too large for operators of feed-erline services. To satisfy the latter demand, Lockheed decided to produce a reduced-scale version which would accommodate six passengers and a crew of two and, by retaining the

powerplant of its larger sister, offer enhanced performance. The resulting aircraft, designated **Lockheed 12 Electra Junior**, was flown for the first time on 27 June 1936 and, perhaps much to the surprise of the company, its sales success almost equalled that of the Lockheed 10, with a total of 130 built. The majority of production aircraft were

designated **Lockheed 12-A** and many of the total entered military service. The USAAC acquired three seven-seat **C-40** (later **UC-40**), 10 five-seat **C-40A** (later **UC-40A**) and one experimental **C-40B** aircraft with fixed tricycle landing gear; the designation **C-40D** (later **UC-40D**) was allocated to 10 Lockheed 12-As impressed for wartime service. The USN received one seven-seat **JO-1** and five six-seat **JO-2** aircraft (one of which was allocated for US Marine Corps use), and a single

XJO-3 with fixed tricycle landing gear which was used for carrier deck landing trials. The type was used also by the air arms of Argentina, Canada, Cuba, and the UK, as well as by the Netherlands East Indies army, this last service being the major military user with a total of 36. Of this number, 16 were specially-developed **Model 212** crew trainers, with a forward-firing 0.303-in (7.7-mm) machine-gun, a similar weapon in a dorsal turret, and underfuselage racks for up to 800 lb (363 kg) of bombs.
One of the most inter-

esting aircraft was that acquired by NACA, which was used to evaluate a wing de-icing system that utilised hot gases from the engine exhaust. One of the most unusual applications of the Lockheed 12-A was by Australian Sidney Cotton who, under the cover of his position as an executive of the Dufaycolour Company, used his specially modified camera-carrying Lockheed 12-A to take clandestine reconnaissance photographs of German military installations in the three months leading up to the beginning of World War II.

Santa Maria Airlines owned this Lockheed 12-A. The Electra Junior featured the twin-tail arrangement that was introduced, at the behest of Clarence 'Kelly' Johnson, on the original Lockheed 10 Electra airliner.

SPECIFICATION	
Lockheed 12-A Electra Junior **Type:** six-passenger light transport **Powerplant:** two 450-hp (336-kW) Pratt & Whitney Wasp Junior SB radial piston engines **Performance:** maximum speed 225 mph (362 km/h) at 5,000 ft (1525 m); service ceiling 22,900 ft (6980 m); range 800 miles	(1287 km) **Weights:** empty 5,765 lb (2615 kg); maximum take-off 8,650 lb (3924 kg) **Dimensions:** wingspan 49 ft 6 in (15.09 m); length 36 ft 4 in (10.97 m); height 9 ft 9 in (2.97 m); wing area 352.0 sq ft (32.70 m²)

Lockheed 14 Super Electra

Designed to compete against the DST/DC-2/DC-3 series being developed by the Douglas company, the **Lockhhed 14 Super**

Electra failed, by reason of its smaller capacity, to present any significant competition. Of the same general configuration as the

earlier Electra, it differed primarily by having a much deeper fuselage accommodating a maximum of 14 passengers, and a mid-set wing, and introduced such advanced features as integral fuel tanks in the wing, Fowler-type trailing edge flaps, fully-feathering

propellers and, at a later stage of production, fixed wing slots. These improvements, combined with powerful engines and high wing loading, gave the Super Electra excellent

performance but, by comparison with the important and larger-capacity DC-3, it was less efficient in operation, with the result that only 112 were built by Lockheed.

SPECIFICATION	
Lockheed 14-H Super Electra **Type:** short/medium-range civil transport **Powerplant:** two 875-hp (652-kW) Pratt & Whitney Hornet S1E-G radial piston engines **Performance:** maximum speed 247 mph (398 km/h) at 7,000 ft (2135 m); service ceiling 24,300 ft (7405 m); maximum range	2,060 miles (3315 km) **Weights:** empty 10,300 lb (4672 kg); maximum take-off 17,500 lb (7938 kg) **Dimensions:** wingspan 65 ft 6 in (19.96 m); length 44 ft 4 in (13.51 m); height 11 ft 5 in (3.48 m); wing area 551 sq ft (51.19 m²)

Compared to the similar-capacity DC-2, the Super Electra was a more modern and better performing design, but it could not compete with the larger DC-3.

Lockheed 14 Super Electra (continued)

The Lockheed 14 was first flown in prototype form on 29 July 1937 and certificated on 15 November 1937, initial deliveries were made shortly afterwards. By far the majority of the Super Electras was exported and, in addition, a total of 119 was licence-built in Japan for use by the Imperial Japanese Army. These, powered by 900-hp (671-kW) Mitsubishi Ha-26-I radial engines, were designated **Army Type LO Transport** and were later

KLM flew this Lockheed 14-F62 with the name Ekster. KLM received six Lockheed 14s, while its far eastern subsidiary KNILM took five.

allocated the Allied codename 'Thelma'.

Variants

Lockheed 14-H and 14-H2: initial production version powered by Hornet S1E-G or S1E2-G radial engines respectively
C-14H-1: redesignation of one 14-H following conversion as the prototype of an all-cargo version; later reconverted to 14-H configuration
Lockheed 14-08: redesignation of Trans-Canada Air Lines 14-H2s after replacement of standard engines by 1,200-hp (895-kW) Twin Wasp S1C3-Gs
Lockheed 14-WF62 or 14-F62: export production version with 900-hp (671-kW) Wright SGR-1820-F62 Cyclone engines
Lockheed 14-WG3B: export production version with 900-hp (671-kW) Wright GR-1820-G3B engines
Lockheed 14-N: four aircraft built to the requirements of individual private customers
C-111: USAAF designation of three 14-F62s impressed for service in Australia
XR4O-1: USN designation of a single 14-H2 acquired as a staff transport

Lockheed 14 Hudson

The first American-built aircraft to be used operationally by the RAF during World War II, the **Hudson** stemmed from urgent British requirements in early 1938 for a maritime patrol/navigational trainer aircraft. Faced with the problem of producing these aircraft as quickly as possible, Lockheed proposed a militarised version of the Super Electra. As then envisaged the new aircraft was generally similar to the Lockheed 14-WF62, except for the introduction of a modified fuselage that incorporated nose and dorsal gun turrets, a bomb bay in the centre fuselage, and a navigator's position within the fuselage, to the rear of the wing trailing edge. However, as the British Purchasing Commission was seeking a maritime reconnaissance aircraft rather than a bomber, this configuration was not acceptable. The BPC suggested, instead, that the navigator should be accommodated nearer to the pilot, and on the following day Lockheed produced a new mock-up accommodating him in a glazed nose position. This proved good enough for contract negotiations to begin, leading to an order in late June 1938 for 200 **B14L** aircraft, as the type was then designated by Lockheed; there was a provision in the contract that 250 would be accepted provided that the total was delivered before the end of December 1939. The first B14L, unarmed and with a mock dorsal turret, was flown for the first time on 10 December 1938; the 250th production aircraft came off the assembly line during the first week of November 1939. When production

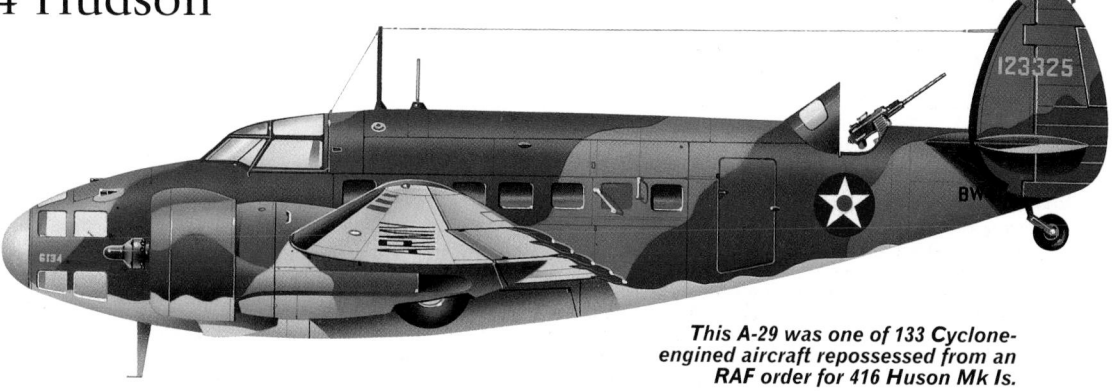

This A-29 was one of 133 Cyclone-engined aircraft repossessed from an RAF order for 416 Huson Mk Is.

Variants

Hudson Mk I: original direct-purchase version for the RAF with 1,100-hp (820-kW) Wright GR-1820-G102A engines; 351 built
Hudson Mk II: direct-purchase version, generally as Mk I, but with airframe strengthening and constant-speed propellers; 20 built
Hudson Mk III: version combining Hudson Mk II airframe with 1,200-hp (895-kW) Wright GR-1820-G205A engines; 428 direct purchase aircraft for British/Commonwealth air forces before the introduction of Lend-Lease
Hudson Mk IIIA: British and Commonwealth designation of Lend-Lease version similar to Hudson Mk III, but with 1,200-hp (895-kW) Wright R-1820-87 engines; procured by the USAAF as the **A-29** and by the US Navy as **PBO-1**; Hudson Mk IIIA production totalled 800, including 384 with convertible interiors for troop transport, procured as **A-29A**
Hudson Mk IV: RAAF redesignation of 50 Hudson Mk Is, powered by 1,050-hp (783-kW) Twin Wasp S3C-G engines; RAAF redesignation also of improved

version acquired originally as Hudson Mk II
Hudson Mk IVA: RAAF designation of Lend-Lease version procured by the USAAF as **A-28**; 52 built
Hudson Mk V: direct purchase version, similar to Hudson Mk III, but with 1,200-hp (895-kW) Twin Wasp S3C4-G engines; 409 built
Hudson Mk VI: Lend-Lease version procured by the USAAF as the **A-29A:** generally similar to Hudson Mks III/V but with 1,200-hp (895-kW) Chevrolet-built Pratt & Whitney R-1830-67 engines; 450 built
Hudson C.Mk VI: redesignation of a number of RAF Hudson Mk VIs following the removal of armament for use in a transport role
A-29B: redesignation of 24 USAAF A-29As following conversion for photo-reconnaissance
AT-18: designation of 217 aircraft with 1,200-hp (895-kW) Wright R-1820-87 engines procured by the USAAF as gunnery trainers
AT-18A: 83 aircraft, generally similar to AT-18, procured by the USAAF as unarmed navigational trainers
B14S: designation of a single aircraft for the Sperry Gyroscope Company for use as an instrument test aircraft

This Hudson Mk III was based a Nelson, New Zealand with the RNZAF's No. 2 (GR) Squadron during 1942. Note the two-gun Boulton Paul power operated dorsal turret.

ended in May 1943 a total of 2,941 had been built, comprising 1,338 aircraft purchased directly from Lockheed, 1,302 under US Department of the Army contracts for supply under Lend-Lease, 300 as trainers for the USAAF, plus a single civil **B14S** which was supplied to Sperry. Thus the Hudson, as the B14L was named by the RAF, elevated Lockheed into the ranks of major aircraft manufacturers.

Despite its derivation from a peaceful airliner, the Hudson achieved some

surprising 'firsts'. A Hudson of No. 224 Squadron, for example, shot down a Dornier Do 18 flying-boat on 8 October 1939, the first RAF victory to be recorded in World War II by an American-built aircraft; a Hudson of No. 220 Sqn located and directed British naval forces to the German prison ship *Altmark* in February 1940; a Hudson from No. 269 Sqn damaged, and then accepted the surrender of the German submarine *U-570* in the Atlantic on 27 August 1941; No. 280

Sqn was the first to be equipped with airborne lifeboats and deployed the first in the North Sea in early May 1943; and in the same month a Hudson of No. 608 Squadron became the first aircraft in RAF service to sink a German U-boat by rocket fire. The first sinking of a U-boat (*U-701*) by an aircraft of the USAAF was recorded by an **A-29** on 7 July 1942; and US Navy **PBO-1** aircraft sank the first two U-boats to be credited to that service in World War II on 1 and 15 March 1942. In

addition to being used by British and Commonwealth air forces and by the USAAF and USN, the type served also in small

numbers with British Overseas Airways Corporation, the Chinese air force, and the Portuguese naval air arm.

SPECIFICATION	
Lockheed Hudson Mk I	17,500 lb (7938 kg)
Type: maritime patrol-bomber	**Dimensions:** wingspan 65 ft 6 in
Powerplant: two 1,100-hp	(19.96 m); length 44 ft 4 in
(820-kW) Wright GR-1820-G-102A	(13.51 m); height 11 ft 10 in
radial piston engines	(3.61 m); wing area 551 sq ft
Performance: maximum speed	(51.19 m²)
246 mph (396 km/h) at 6,500 ft	**Armament:** two 0.303-in (7.7-mm)
(1980 m); service ceiling 25,000 ft	forward-firing machine-guns, and
(7620 m); range 1,960 miles	two similar weapons in a dorsal
(3154 km)	turret, plus up to 1,400 lb (635 kg)
Weights: empty 11,630 lb	of bombs or depth charges in
(5275 kg); maximum take-off	internal bomb bay

Lockheed 18 Lodestar

Showing the graceful lines of the Lodemaster to good effect, this aircraft is actually the XR5O-1 wearing its US Coast Guard colours and serial V188. The aircraft was used as a staff transport.

Design and development of the **Lockheed 18 Lodestar** began as a result of the poor sales achievement of the Super Electra, the prototype being flown for the first time on 21 September 1939. Converted from a Super Electra, it differed primarily by having the fuselage lengthened by 5 ft 6 in (1.68 m) to provide accommodation for 15 to 18 passengers, depending upon the other facilities provided; some were produced with high-density bench seating for a maximum of 26 passengers, and were available with a

variety of engines by Pratt & Whitney and Wright. Despite the improved economy demonstrated by the Lodestar, Lockheed failed again to achieve worthwhile sales in the US as most operators were committed to purchase DC-3s from the Douglas Company. Fortunately, the type appealed more to export customers, with airlines or government agencies in Africa, Brazil, Canada, France, the Netherlands, Norway, South Africa, the UK and Venezuela ordering a total of 96 aircraft. There was only limited military interest

Variants

XR5O-1: single aircraft with 1,200-hp (895-kW) Wright R-1820 Cyclone engines, acquired for evaluation by USCG
R5O-1: three aircraft used as staff transports, two USN and one USCG, powered by 1,200-hp (895-kW) R-1820-97 Cyclone engines
R5O-2: single USN aircraft, equivalent to impressed USAAF C-59, with 850-hp (634-kW) Pratt & Whitney R-1690-25 Hornet engines
R5O-3: three aircraft acquired by the USN as VIP transports, powered by 1,200-hp (895-kW) Pratt & Whitney R-1830-34A engines
R5O-4: 12 seven-passenger transports, under construction for civil customers, impressed for USN service and powered by 1,200-hp (895-kW) R-1820-40 engines
R5O-5: 41 aircraft, generally as USAAF C-60, but equipped as 14-passenger transports for USN service
R5O-6: 35 aircraft, generally as USAAF C-60A, but equipped as 18-seat paratroop transports for USN and USMC

before the beginning of World War II, but later procurement, particularly by the USAAF, raised the total of Lodestars built by Lockheed to 625 before production ended. Unlike the Hudson, the Lodestar has no record of stirring action but, nevertheless, the type was able to fulfil an important medium-range transport role. Only small numbers saw post-war service, mostly with small

C-56 to C-56E: under this series of designations, 36 commercial Lodestars were impressed for USAAF service
C-57 and C-57B: 20 commercial Lodestars impressed for USAAF service
C-57C: redesignation of three C-60As after being re-engined with 1,200-hp (895-kW) R-1830-43 engines
C-57D: redesignation of one C-57A after being re-engined for a second time
C-59: designation of 10 impressed civil Lodestars; seven were transferred to the RAF under Lend-Lease, being designated **Lodestar Mk IA**
C-60: 36 impressed civil Lodestars: 16 were transferred to the RAF under Lend-Lease, being designated **Lodestar Mk II**
C-60A: 324 new aircraft built for the USAAF, equipped as 18-seat paratroop transports and powered by 1,200-hp (895-kW) R-1820-87 engines
XC-60B: single experimental aircraft acquired by USAAF for evaluation of hot-air de-icing system
C-60C: proposed 21-seat troop transport; not built
C-66: single aircraft equipped as VIP transport for the President of Brazil

operators, but a number of interesting conversions as executive transports was

carried out in the USA by companies like Howard Aero and Lear Inc.

SPECIFICATION	
Lockheed Lodestar Model 18-07	1,800 miles (2897 km)
Type: civil transport	**Weights:** empty 11,250 lb
Powerplant: two 875-hp (652-kW)	(5103 kg); maximum take-off
Pratt & Whitney Hornet S1E2-G	19,200 lb (8709 kg)
radial piston engines	**Dimensions:** wingspan 65 ft 6 in
Performance: maximum speed	(19.96 m); length 49 ft 10 in
218 mph (351 km/h) at 8,000 ft	(15.19 m); height 11 ft 10 in
(2440 m); service ceiling 20,400 ft	(3.61 m); wing area 551 sq ft
(6220 m); standard range	(51.19 m²)

Lockheed 22 (P-38 Lightning)

The unusual configuration adopted for the **P-38 Lightning** stemmed from a USAAC requirement of 1937 for a high-performance fighter. It demanded a maximum speed, rate of climb and range that could not then be met in a conventional single-engine layout, and to achieve the desired performance the Lockheed design team adopted twin engines. A mid-wing monoplane with the pilot's nacelle mounted on the wing centre section, the P-38 had twin booms

extending aft from the extremities of this assembly, mounting the two engines forward and twin fins and rudders aft, with the booms linked by the tailplane/elevator assembly. The nose unit of the tricycle landing gear retracted into the central nacelle, and the main units into the twin booms. The **XP-38** prototype, powered by two 960-hp (716-kW) Allison V-1710-11/15 counter-rotating engines, was flown for the first time on 27 January 1939, and was lost as the result of an undershoot

after accumulating less than 12 hours flight time. Fortunately, in that time there was sufficient indication of an ability to meet USAAC requirements, and an order for 13 **YP-38** prototypes followed on 27 April 1939. Production aircraft began to enter service in late 1941, and a first (shared) combat victory was recorded on 14 August 1942, with the destruction of an Fw 200C-3 Condor over the North Atlantic, but the type's first regular combat operations began in North Africa on

19 November 1942. Built to a total of 10,037 aircraft, including 113 produced under sub-contract by Consolidated-Vultee, the Lightning was used by the USAAF in every theatre of action. In the Pacific, Lightnings were credited with the destruction of more Japanese aircraft than any other fighter in USAAF service, and they are well recorded in air force history for a string of memorable actions, including the interception and destruction, some 500 miles (885 km) from their base on Guadalcanal, of the Mitsubishi G4M carrying Japan's Admiral Isoroku

Yamamoto. And, of course, the USAAF's 'ace of aces' of World War II, Major 'Dick' Bong, scored all of his 40 confirmed victories while flying P-38s in the Pacific zone. In Europe, P-38s served mainly with the 9th Air Force, being used extensively on long-range fighter escort duties in support of 8th AF daylight bombing missions against German targets. But with the end of war, and the inevitable contract cancellations that followed VJ-Day, most of the USAAF's P-38s disappeared very quickly, with only a few late models remaining in service until 1949.

Lockheed 22 (P-38 Lightning) (continued)

Although it was primarily a fighter type, the Lightning also had an important role to play as a photo-recce platform. Here an F-5B recce aircraft (foreground) formates with a P-38J, providing a useful comparison of their differing nose profiles.

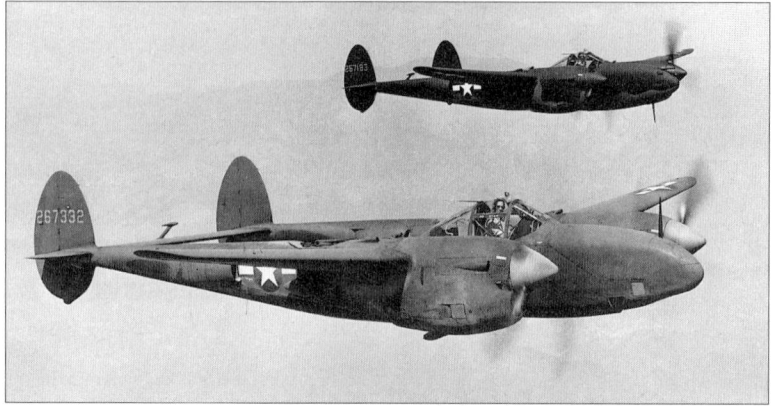

SPECIFICATION

Lockheed P-38L Lightning
Type: single-seat fighter
Powerplant: two 1,475-hp (1100-kW) Allison V-1710-111/-113 V-12 piston engines
Performance: maximum speed 414 mph (666 km/h) at 25,000 ft (7620 m); service ceiling 44,000 ft (13410 m); normal range 450 miles (724 km)
Weights: empty 12,800 lb (5806 kg); maximum take-off 21,600 lb (9798 kg)
Dimensions: wingspan 52 ft (15.85 m); length 37 ft 10 in (11.53 m); height 12 ft 10 in (3.91 m); wing area 328 sq ft (30.47 m²)
Armament: four 0.5-in (12.7-mm) machine-guns and one 20-mm cannon, plus up to 3,200 lb (1451 kg) of bombs

Variants

YP-38: designation of pre-production aircraft, generally similar to the prototype but with 1,150-hp (858-kW) Allison V-1710-27/-29 engines giving opposite propeller rotation
P-38 (later RP-38): initial production version, generally as YP-38 and with armament of four 0.5-in (12.7-mm) machine-guns and one 37-mm cannon, and addition of armour protection and bullet-proof glass
P-38D (later RP-38D): production version, generally as P-38 but with system revisions; 36 built
P-38E (later RP-38E): production version with further system revisions and 37-mm cannon replaced by one 20-mm cannon; 210 built
P-38F: production version, the first regarded as combat-ready; 527 built, including 150 ordered originally under British (as **Lightning Mk I**) and French contracts; the French order would have been transferred to the UK but after testing initial examples, the RAF refused to accept any more aircraft; powered by 1,325-hp (988-kW) Allison V-1710-49/-53 engines, there were several subvariants, the most important being the **P-38F-15** which introduced manoeuvring flaps
P-38G: production version, generally similar to P-38F-15, but incorporated a number of revisions and improvements during the production run; 1,082 built
P-38H: production version, similar to P-38G, but with 1,425-hp (1063-kW) Allison V-1710-89/-91 engines; 601 built
P-38J (later F-38J): generally similar to P-38H but with many detail changes throughout the 2,970-aircraft production run; for use in a light bomber role some were modified to have a glazed nose to the centre nacelle for use by a bomb aimer, or were equipped with bombing radar
P-38K: single prototype, with 1,425-hp (1063-kW) Allison V-1710-75/-77engines in a P-38G airframe
P-38L (later F-38L): final Lockheed production version with 1,475-hp (1100-kW) Allison V-1710-111/-113 engines, but otherwise generally similar toP-38J; 3,810 built
P-38L-5: version generally similar to P-38L produced by Consolidated-Vultee; 2,000 contracted but only 113 completed by VJ-Day
P-38M: redesignation of P-38F, P-38K and P-38L aircraft, totalling about 80, modified by the USAAF and by Lockheed for service as two-seat night-fighters, which were just entering service as the war ended
TP-38L: designation of small number of aircraft modified by the USAAF as two-seat trainers; similar P-38J conversions were unofficially known as **TP-38J** aircraft
F-4-1 (later RF-4-1): unarmed photo-reconnaissance version of P-38E carrying four cameras; 99 built
F-4A-1: unarmed reconnaissance version of P-38F carrying four cameras; 20 built
F-5A: unarmed reconnaissance version with five cameras, one similar to P-38E but remainder similar to P-38G; 181 built
F-5B: unarmed reconnaissance version of P-38J; 200 built
F-5C: redesignation of about 123 P-38Js converted by Lockheed to F-5B configuration but with improved camera installations
F-5E: redesignation of 205 P-38J and 500 P-38L aircraft converted by Lockheed to F-5C configuration
F-5F: redesignation of one F-5B following revision of camera installation
F-5F-3: redesignation of P-38L with F-5F camera installation
F-5G-6: final photo-reconnaissance conversion from P-38L-5 airframes
FO-1: US Navy redesignation of four F-5Bs acquired from the USAAF
XF-5D: single example of experimental two-seat reconnaissance aircraft
XP-38A: single example of P-38 used during 1942 for experiments in cockpit pressurisation
XP-49: single prototype developed from P-38 with initially, 1,540-hp (1148-kW) Continental XIV-1430-9/11 counter-rotating engines, strengthened landing gear and pressurised cockpit; no production aircraft resulted
XP-58 Chain Lightning: totally new and much larger aircraft, prototype flown eventually on 6 June 1944, with two 2,600-hp (1939-kW) Allison V-3420-11/A3 counter-rotating engines, but no production followed

Armament options for the production P-58 would have included either four 37-mm cannon, or one 75-mm cannon and two 0.50-in (12.7-mm) machine-guns in the nose, in addition to the standard defensive armament of four 0.50-in (12.7-mm) machine-guns in pairs in the ventral and dorsal turrets.

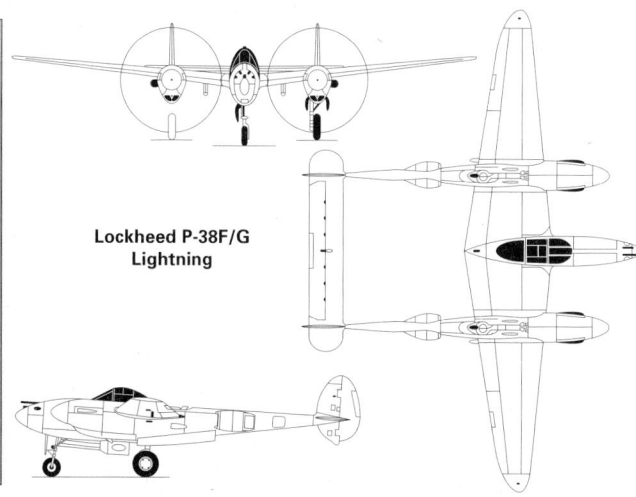

Lockheed P-38F/G Lightning

Lockheed 26 (P2V and P-2 Neptune)

Initial studies on a land-based patrol aircraft for service with the US Navy were made by Lockheed's Vega subsidiary in 1941.

However, in the urgency of aircraft production before and during the early years of World War II, no further development of this design followed until 1944. By then the USN had an urgent requirement for such an aircraft, and Lockheed discovered that the Vega design proposal of 1941 could meet this need with little modification. A contract for two **XP2V-1** prototypes and 14 **P2V-1**

production aircraft was received, and the first prototype was flown on 17 May 1945. A fairly large mid-/high-wing monoplane with retractable tricycle landing gear, the type was powered initially by two

2,300-hp (1715-kW) Wright R-3350-8 Duplex Cyclone engines. Carrying a crew of seven, it had a weapons bay for two torpedoes or 12 depth charges, plus six defensive machine-guns. The generally-similar P2V-1 production aircraft differed by having underwing mountings for up to 16 rockets.

P2V-1s began to enter service in March 1947 and proved effective in their role. The Korean War expanded the requirement for such aircraft, and the later involvement of the United States in South East Asia, plus the need to provide similar capability for the Western allies, kept Lockheed busy producing P2Vs in a multiplicity of versions, with the final production figure totalling 1,181. The last front-line Neptune, a turboprop-powered, Japanese built **P-2J**, was retired by the JMSDF in 1994.

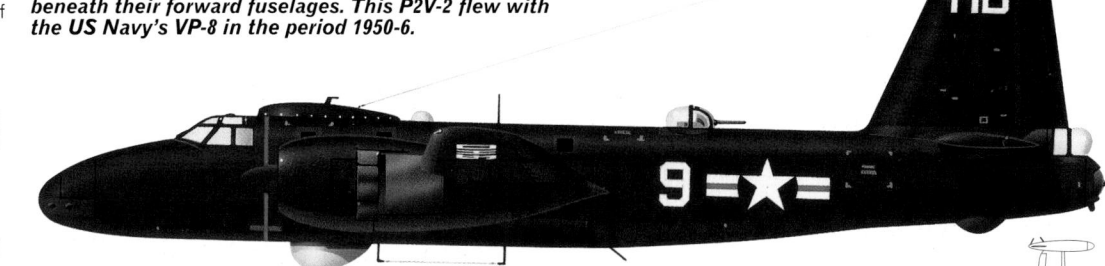

Early Neptunes, including the P2V-2 and -3, were characterised by their solid noses and the radome beneath their forward fuselages. This P2V-2 flew with the US Navy's VP-8 in the period 1950-6.

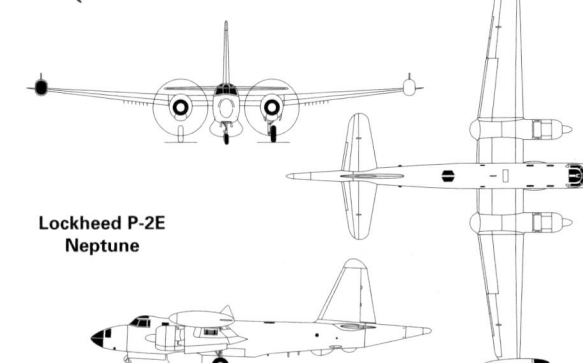

Lockheed P-2E Neptune

SPECIFICATION

Lockheed P2V-7 (P-2H) Neptune
Type: long-range maritime patrol aircraft
Powerplant: two 3,500-hp (2610-kW) Wright R-3350-32W TurboCompound radial piston engines, plus two 3,400-lb (15.12-kN) thrust Westinghouse J34-WE-36 auxiliary turbojets
Performance: maximum speed 403 mph (649 km/h) at 14,000 ft (4265 m); service ceiling 22,000 ft (6705 m); maximum range 3,685 miles (5930 km)

Weights: empty 49,935 lb (22650 kg); maximum take-off 79,895 lb (36240 kg)
Dimensions: wingspan 103 ft 10 in (31.65 m) length 91 ft 8 in (27.94 m); height 29 ft 4 in (8.94 m); wing area 1,000 sq ft (92.90 m²)
Armament: twin 0.5-in (12.7-mm) machine-guns in a dorsal turret, plus provision for underwing rockets and up to 8,000 lb (3629 kg) of bombs, depth charges or torpedoes

Variants

XP2V-2: single prototype for improved version, with 2,800-hp (2088-kW) Wright R-3350-24W engines, first flown 7 January 1947
P2V-2: generally similar to XP2V-2, but able to carry sonobuoys and with extensive armament revisions; 80 built
P2V-2N: designation of two P2V-2s equipped especially for polar exploration
P2V-2S: the prototype of an AEW version carrying search radar
P2V-3: similar to P2V-2, but with 3,200-hp (2386-kW) Wright R-3350-26W engines; 53 built
P2V-3B: five aircraft modified for close-support evaluation
P2V-3C: 12 aircraft modified to serve as carrier-based nuclear-weapon carriers
P2V-3W: production AEW version; 30 built
P2V-3Z: P2V-3s modified to serve as combat transport aircraft for VIPs
P2V-4 (later P-2D): AEW version, equipped as P2V-2S prototype, with engine variations and wingtip auxiliary fuel tanks; 52 built
P2V-5: major production version; an ASW aircraft in many subvariants; differed basically from P2V-4 by having 3,250-hp (2424-kW) R-3350-30WA engines and larger capacity wingtip tanks; it was retrofitted with a glazed nose and MAD equipment; 424 built
P2V-5F (later P-2E): generally as P2V-5, but with 3,500-hp (2610-kW) R-3350-32W engines and two underwing mounted 3,250-lb (14.45-kN) thrust auxiliary turbojets; post 1962 variants were one **EP-2E** permanent test aircraft and several **OP-2E/AP-2E** USN/US Army special-sensor aircraft
P2V-5FD (later DP-2E): drone launch and control vehicles modified from P2V-5s
P2V-5FE (later EP-2E): P2V-5Fs with extra avionics equipment

P2V-5FS: (later SP-2E): designation of P2V-5Fs with Jezebel/Julie acoustic search equipment
P2V-6 (later P-2F): multi-role version with R-3350-WA engines, increased capacity wingtip tank and lengthened bomb bay; 67 built
P2V-6B (later P2V-6M and MP-2F): anti-shipping version armed with Petrel missiles; 16 built
P2V-6F (later P-2G): redesignation of P2V-6s following installation of two 3,400-lb (15.12-kN) thrust Westinghouse J34-WE-36 auxiliary turbojets
P2V-6T (later TP-2F): redesignation of P2V-6s converted to serve as crew trainers
P2V-7 (later P-2H): final production version with 3,500-hp (2610-kW) R-3350-32W engines and J34-WE-36 turbojets; 287 built; post-1962 variants included several **AP-2H** special sensor conversions, **DP-2H** drone controllers, one **EP-2H** special reconnaissance aircraft, and one **NP-2H** special-test aircraft
P2V-7B: 15 aircraft for Netherlands naval air arm with hardened nose incorporating four 20-mm cannon
P2V-7LP (later LP-2J): four P2V-7s with retractable ski landing gear for use in Antarctica
P2V-7S (later SP-2H): redesignation of P2V-7s following installation of Jezebel/Julie acoustic search equipment
P2V-7U (later RB-69A): electronic surveillance version for the USAF; 5 built and 2 converted from P2V-7s
P2V-7KAI: following assembly in Japan by Kawasaki of 48 P2V-7s from components built in the USA by Lockheed, Kawasaki produced a developed version of which the P2V-7KAI was the prototype; designated **P-2J** in production, this had a lengthened fuselage to house additional avionics and a powerplant of two 2,850-shp (2125-kW) General Electric T64-IHI-10 turboprop engines, plus two 3,086-lb (13.73-kN) thrust Ishikawajima-Harinia J3-1HI-7C auxiliary turbojets; some were converted to UP-2J target tugs

This SP-2H Neptune was on the strength of the Argentine navy in 1979. It wears a Light Gull Gray/Insignia White scheme similar to that adopted by the US Navy in the late 1950s. Both SP-2Es and SP-2Hs served with Argentina, the latter flying during the 1982 Falklands War. Having been brought out of a state of semi-retirement and barely serviceable, the aircraft were camouflaged and used both to shadow the British fleet and to eavesdrop on enemy communications. Indeed, the Super Etendard which sank HMS Sheffield was guided onto its target by an SP-2H.

Lockheed 37 Ventura and Harpoon

The success of the Lockheed Hudson in RAF service led Lockheed to propose a military version of the larger Lockheed 18 Lodestar and resulting British interest led to development of the **Lockheed 37**. During 1940 a total of 675 of these aircraft was contracted for the RAF, which named the type **Ventura**, and the company lost little time initiating production-in the Vega factory.

Lockheed 37 Ventura and Harpoon (continued)

To replace its Hudsons, the RNZAF received 116 PV-1s and 23 ex-USAAF B-34As (including NZ4600) for service with Nos 1, 2, 3, 4 and 8 Sqns.

By comparison with the Hudson, the Ventura had far more effective armament, a heavier bombload and more powerful engines, and appeared to have considerable potential. First used operationally by the RAF on 3 November 1942, the type was soon found to be unsuited to daylight operations and was transferred to Coastal Command. Nevertheless, the Ventura was procured in large numbers under Lend-Lease, and was built for the USAAF and USN, this last service designating it the **PV-1 Ventura**. Venturas served with all the Commonwealth nations, the Free French and with the Brazilian air force. A long-range version, the **PV-2**, had been ordered by the USN in June 1943 and, differing in several respects from the Ventura was named **Harpoon**; Ventura and Harpoon production totalled 3,028 in September 1945. Post-war, surplus PV-2s were supplied to Italy, Japan, the Netherlands, Peru and Portugal.

The PV-1 carried extra fuel in a pair of 155-US gal (587-litre) drop tanks and two long range tanks for 490 US gal (1855 litres) of fuel in the bomb bay.

SPECIFICATION

Lockheed PV-1 Ventura
Type: maritime patrol aircraft
Powerplant: two 2,000-hp (1491-kW) Pratt & Whitney R-2800-31 radial piston engines
Performance: maximum speed 322 mph (518 km/h) at 13,800 ft (4205 m); service ceiling 26,300 ft (8015 m); normal range 1,360 miles (2189 km)
Weights: empty 20,197 lb (9161 kg); maximum take-off 31,077 lb (14096 kg)

Dimensions: wingspan 65 ft 6 in (19.96 m); length 51 ft 9 in (15.77 m); height 11 ft 11 in (3.63 m); wing area 551.0 sq ft (51.19 m²)
Armament: two 0.5-in (12.7-mm) forward-firing machine-guns, two similar guns in dorsal turret and two 0.3-in (7.72-mm) machine-guns in ventral position, plus up to 3,000 lb (1361 kg) of bombs, or six 325-lb (147-kg) depth charges, or one torpedo

Variants

Ventura Mk I: initial production version to British contract, powered by 1,850-hp (1380-kW) Pratt & Whitney Double Wasp S1A4-G engines; a number was modified subsequently in the UK for service with Coastal Command, being redesignated **Ventura GR.Mk I**
Ventura Mk II: similar to Ventura Mk I, but with larger capacity bomb bay and 2,000-hp (1491-kW) Pratt & Whitney R-2800-31 engines
Ventura Mk IIA: similar to Ventura Mk II, but with revised armament
Ventura GR.Mk V: RAF designation of version of USN PV-1 for service with Coastal Command; some modified subsequently to transport configuration as **Ventura C. Mk V**
B-34 (later RB-34): under this designation about 20 aircraft, similar to the Ventura Mk IIA, were impressed by the USAAF from Lend-Lease production; some later had ASV radar installed
B-34A (later RB-34A): 101 aircraft taken from Lend-Lease procurement and used by the USAAF in training roles
B-34B (later RB-34B): 13 aircraft from Lend-Lease procurement, used by the USAAF as navigation trainers

B-37: version with 1,700-hp (1268-kW) Wright R-2600-13 engines and revised armament for USAAF, but only of 18 of an order for 550 were built
PV-1: first version for USN, generally as Ventura Mk II, but with reduced defensive armament, modified bomb bay to carry bombs, depth charges or one torpedo, and with search radar; late production aircraft had provision for HVARs on underwing launchers, and a few were modified for USMC use as night- fighters, equipped with British air interception radar
PV-1P: redesignation of some PV-1s following conversion for use in the photo-reconnaissance role
PV-2: improved version for USN with new longer-span outer wing panels to increase fuel capacity, revised tail unit and armament; leaking integral fuel tanks and skin wrinkling led to wing redesign, applied to 31st and remaining 469 production aircraft
PV-2C: redesignation of first 30 PV-2s, used in a training role after the integral fuel tanks in the outer wing panels had been sealed off
PV-2D: similar to PV-2, with armament revisions, but only 35 delivered before VJ-Day brought contract cancellation
PV-2T: redesignation of PV-2s used in small numbers as unarmed trainers
PV-3: 27 Ventura Mk IIs taken over from British contract by USN

Lockheed 1329 JetStar I/II

To meet a USAF requirement for an 'off-the-shelf' high-performance light transport, Lockheed developed the **Lockheed 1329 JetStar**. A low-wing monoplane with swept wings and swept tail surfaces, the JetStar was powered in prototype form by two 4,850-lb (21.57-kN) thrust Bristol Orpheus 1/5 turbojets. The first of two prototypes was flown on 4 September 1957, with flight testing proving most satisfactory, but when planned licence-production

Some 40 Jetstar IIs were built, the aircraft providing an increase of 1,086 US gal (4111 litres) in fuel capacity compared to the JetStar I. The wing tanks of the JetStar II were repositioned to lie further forwards compared to the JetStar I and wholly beneath the wing.

SPECIFICATION

Lockheed JetStar II
Type: light transport
Powerplant: four 3,700-lb (16.45-kN) thrust Garrett TFE731-3 turbofans
Performance: maximum cruising speed 547 mph (880 km/h) at 30,000 ft (9145 m); service ceiling 43,000 ft (13105 m); range with maximum payload 2,995 miles
(4820 km)
Weights: empty operating 24,900 lb (11294 kg); maximum take-off 44,500 lb (20185 kg)
Dimensions: wingspan 54 ft 5 in (16.59 m); length 60 ft 5 in (18.41 m); height 20 ft 5 in (6.22 m); wing area 542.5 sq ft (50.40 m²)

of the Orpheus could not be finalised, Lockheed chose instead to power the initial production version with 3,000-lb (13.34-kN) thrust Pratt & Whitney JT12A-6 engines, mounted in pairs on each side of the rear fuselage. The anticipated military demand failed to materialise in any significant numbers, with the result that the majority of the 204 JetStars that were built, before production ended in 1980, were sold as bizjets.

Variants

JetStar I: original production version, differing from the first prototype by having increased fuel capacity provided by a permanently attached streamlined fuel tank at mid-span of each wing, de-icing of wing and tail unit leading edges and JT12A-6 engines; a slightly lengthened fuselage provided executive-standard accommodation for a crew of two and 10 passengers; late production aircraft had 3,300-lb (14.68-kN) thrust JT12A-8 turbojets
JetStar 731: conversion developed by AiResearch, replacing the Pratt & Whitney powerplant by one with more fuel-efficient Garrett TFE731-1 turbofans; about 60

JetStar Is were converted to this standard
JetStar II: new production version incorporating TFE731-3 engines as standard and a number of refinements
C-140A: five aircraft for USAF, basically similar to early production JetStar Is and equipped for calibration of navigation beacons
C-140B: convertible cargo/passenger version for USAF, five built; otherwise generally similar to C-140A
VC-140B: six additional production aircraft, generally similar to C-140A, except equipped as VIP transports; the five C-140Bs were also converted to this configuration

Lockheed AH-56 Cheyenne

A radical and complex design, the Cheyenne owed its phenomenal forward speed to its pusher propeller. In reverse pitch the propeller acted as a powerful airbrake.

In a seemingly strange field of design for Lockheed, the company was one of 12 which submitted proposals to meet a US Army requirement for a heavily armed gunship helicopter. Lockheed was eventually selected to develop and build an initial batch of 10 aircraft based on its proposal, under the designation **AH-56A Cheyenne**, this being a compound helicopter with a slender fuselage, short-span wings, retractable landing gear and accommodation for a crew of two. It was powered by a General Electric T64-GE-16 turboshaft engine, finally developing 3,925 shp (2927 kW), this driving four-bladed main

and tail rotors, plus a three-bladed pusher propeller at the tail of the aircraft. Flight trials began on 21 September 1967, and in early 1968 the US Army contracted for an initial batch of 375 production aircraft. Unfortunately, development problems brought cancellation of the production programme on 19 May 1969 and, although progress had been made, the development contract

was also terminated in August 1972. The Cheyenne, which had demonstrated a maximum

speed of 253 mph (407 km/h), would have been armed with a cannon, grenade-launcher or

Minigun in a nose turret, and with anti-tank missiles or air-to-ground rockets on underwing racks.

Lockheed C-5 Galaxy

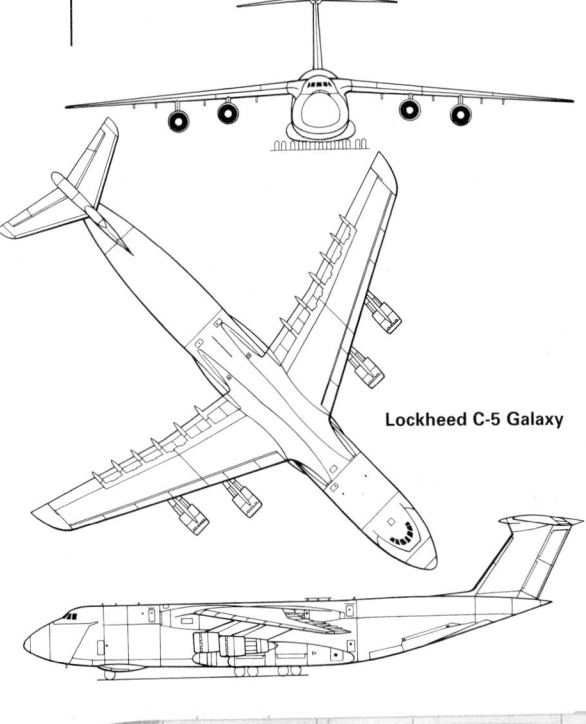

Lockheed C-5 Galaxy

The **C-5 Galaxy** heavy logistics transport is a workhorse of US strategic airlift capability. The C-5 originated with the USAF's 1963 CX-HLS (Cargo Experimental - Heavy Logistics System) requirement for a freighter able to carry a 250,000-lb (113400-kg) payload over 3,000 miles (4828 km) without inflight-refuelling. The Galaxy is a high-wing,

T-tailed transport with four TF39 turbofan engines mounted in nacelles below and ahead of the wing's leading edges, and main landing gear units retracting into fuselage pods. The key to the C-5's mission capability is its cavernous interior and 'roll-on/roll-off' capability with access to the cargo bay at both front and rear: at the front is an upward-lifting visor nose

that can be raised above the cockpit, while at the rear are standard clamshell doors. The Galaxy's primary mission is the movement of equipment and vehicles, although it can be configured for up to 363 passengers in the form of 73 on upper rear deck and 290 on the main deck.

The **C-5A** first flew on 30 June 1968, and the first operational **C-5A** was delivered on 17 December 1969 with the last following in May 1973. The C-5A suffered initially from wing crack problems and cost overruns, but has since served well. Seventy-seven of the 81 C-5As underwent a rewinging programme from 1981 to 1987.

SPECIFICATION	
Lockheed C-5B Galaxy **Type:** five-crew long-range heavy logistics transport aircraft **Powerplant:** four General Electric TF39-GE-1C turbofan engines each rated at 43,000 lb st (191.27 kN) **Performance:** maximum speed 571 mph (919 km/h) at 25,000 ft (7620 m); cruising speed between 552 and 564 mph (888 and 908 km/h) at 25,000 ft (7620 m); initial climb rate 1,725 ft (525 m) per minute; service ceiling 35,750 ft (10895 m) at 615,000 lb	(278960 kg); range 6,469 miles (10411 km) with maximum fuel or 3,434 miles (5526 km) with maximum payload **Weights:** empty 374,000 lb (169643 kg); maximum take-off 837,000 lb (379657 kg) **Dimensions:** wingspan 222 ft 8½ in (67.88 m); length 247 ft 10 in (75.54 m); height 65 ft 1½ in (19.85 m); wing area 6,200.00 sq ft (575.98 m²) **Payload:** up to 261,000 lb (118387 kg) of freight

In its C-5A form, the Galaxy was synonymous with the white and grey scheme of Military Airlift Command. The surviving C-5As and C-5Bs are now suffering from low servicability levels.

Lockheed C-5 Galaxy (continued)

The new wing is of virtually new design, apart from its moving surfaces, and incorporates new aluminium alloy for greater corrosion resistance. In the mid-1980s the production line was reopened to meet an urgent USAF demand for additional heavy airlift capacity. Fifty examples of the **C-5B** were built to a

standard essentially similar to that of the C-5A but incorporating modifications and improvements resulting from experience with the C-5A. The C-5B dispensed with the C-5A's complex crosswind main landing gear and introduced improved AFCS (Automated Flight Control System) and MADAR II

(MAlfunction Detection and Analysis and Recording no. 2) systems. The first production C-5B was delivered on 8 January 1986 and deliveries had been completed by April 1989.

Typical loads include two M1A1 Abrams main battle tanks, 16¾-ton trucks, 10 LAV-25 light

armoured vehicles, or one CH-47 Chinook helicopter. Although not usually assigned airdrop duties, the Galaxy can also drop paratroops.

The **C-5C** designation is applied to two Galaxies modified with a sealed front visor and strengthened interior for the carriage of satellites and space equipment. Free of the fatigue problem of its C-141B stablemate, the

Galaxy has no scheduled replacement and will remain in service until at least 2010. The USAF is undertaking an AMP (Avionics Modernization Program) update of the avionics of 126 aircraft, and is also considering a programme to change the powerplant to four General Electric CF6-80C2, Pratt & Whitney PW4650, Rolls-Royce RB.211-535 or Trent 500 turbofan engines.

Lockheed C-130 Hercules

The **C-130 Hercules** is the West's most popular and widely used military transport aircraft, and has been in production longer than any other aircraft type in history. Very large numbers remain in service on every continent, and many operators have replaced early variants with newer versions. The first of two **YC-130** (later **YC-130A**) prototypes made its maiden flight on 23 August 1954, in the process introducing the 3,250-eshp (2424-kW) Allison YT56A-1 turboprop engine driving a three-bladed propeller. The Hercules is still in production at the start of a new century and the number of countries operating C-130 variants now exceeds 60. The basic soundness of the design has led to the creation of numerous variants optimised for specialised missions: **AC-130** covers gunship models (**AC-130A**, **E**, **H** and **U**), **DC-130** covers drone control aircraft (**DC-130A**, **E** and **H**), **EC-130** covers electronic warfare aircraft in the widest sense of the word (**EC-130E**, **H**, **J** and **V**), **HC-130** covers long-range search and rescue aircraft (**HC-130B**, **H**, **N** and **P**), **JC-130** covers temporary test aircraft (**JC-130A**, **B** and **F**), **KC-130** covers inflight-refuelling tanker aircraft (**KC-130F**, **H**, **J**, **R**, **T** and **T-30**), **LC-130** covers aircraft with arctic capability (**LC-130F**, **H** and **R**), **MC-130** covers special forces support aircraft (**MC-130E** and **H**), **NC-130** covers permanent special test aircraft (**NC-130A**, **B**, **E** and **H**), **RC-130** covers reconnaissance aircraft (**RC-130A** and **S**), **VC-130** covers staff and VIP transport aircraft (**VC-130B** and **H**), and **WC-130** covers weather reconnaissance aircraft (**WC-130B**, **E**, **H** and **J**).

The design of the Hercules is based on a high-set wing, unobstructed cargo compartment, integral 'roll on/off' rear loading ramp, fully pressurised cargo hold that can rapidly be reconfigured for the carriage of

This Southern Air Transport L-100-30 demonstrates the fuselage stretch that is incorporated into this civilian model and the military C-130H-30, C-130J-30 and Hercules C.Mk 3 variants.

troops, stretchers or passengers, and a floor at truck-bed height above the ground. The Hercules can be employed for air drops of troops or equipment, for LAPES (low-altitude parachute extraction system) delivery of heavy cargoes, and the full range of cargo, troop transport and medical evacuation duties. The standard unstretched Hercules can carry 78 troops (92 in a high-density configuration) or 64 paratroops, or up to 74 litters.

While the two YC-130A prototypes came from the manufacturer's California 'Skunk Works', all the following 2,156 first-generation aircraft were built at Marietta, Georgia. The first of 231 production exam-

ples of the initial **C-130A** flew on 7 April 1955, and deliveries to the USAF began in December of that year. Surviving aircraft were later revised with four-bladed propellers, an extended tailcone housing a crash position indicator, and APN-59 radar in the reprofiled 'Pinnochio' nose, features originally associated with the later **C-130B** variant.

The C-130B, of which 230 were completed, introduced improvements for the type's original T56-A-1A engine, increased fuel capacity and Hamilton Standard four-bladed propellers. The C-130B variant did not usually carry wing pylons for external fuel, and had better radius, range and endurance than

other variants whose external wing-tanks do not 'earn' their penalty in weight and drag. The US Navy procured seven utility transport Hercules based on the C-130B for service with the designation **GV-1U** (later **C-130F**).

In 1961 production for the USAF and other opera-

tors changed to the **C-130E** (491 built) with the 4,050-eshp (3021-kW) T56-A-7 engine and the maximum take-off weight increased from the C-130A's 124,200 lb (56336 kg) to 175,000 lb (79379 kg) including a 38,702-lb (17555-kg) payload which could be

Lockheed C-130H Hercules

<table>
<tr><td colspan="2" align="center">SPECIFICATION</td></tr>
<tr><td colspan="2" align="center">Lockheed Martin C-130J Hercules</td></tr>
<tr><td>Type: two/three-crew tactical transport aircraft
Powerplant: four Rolls-Royce Allison AE 2100D3 turboprop engines each rated at 4,591 shp (3424 kW)
Performance: maximum cruising speed 400 mph (644 km/h) at optimum altitude; economical cruising speed 390 mph (628 km/h) at optimum altitude; climb to 20,000 ft (6095 m) in 14 minutes; service ceiling 30,560 ft (9315 m);</td><td>range 3,262 miles (5250 km) with a 40,000-lb (18144-kg) payload
Weights: empty 75,562 lb (34274 kg); maximum take-off 175,000 lb (79380 kg)
Dimensions: wingspan 132 ft 7 in (40.41 m); length 97 ft 9 in (29.79 m); height 38 ft 10 in (11.84 m); wing area 1,745.00 sq ft (162.12 m²)
Payload: up to 92 troops, or 64 paratroops, or 74 litters plus two attendants, or 54 passengers, or 41,790 lb (18955 kg) of freight carried in the hold</td></tr>
</table>

Among the special Hercules variants, the USAF's EC-130 series is one of the most secretive. These EW machines include the EC-130E(RR) Rivet Rider airborne radio/TV relay and transmission stations for use in special operations and national crisis roles.

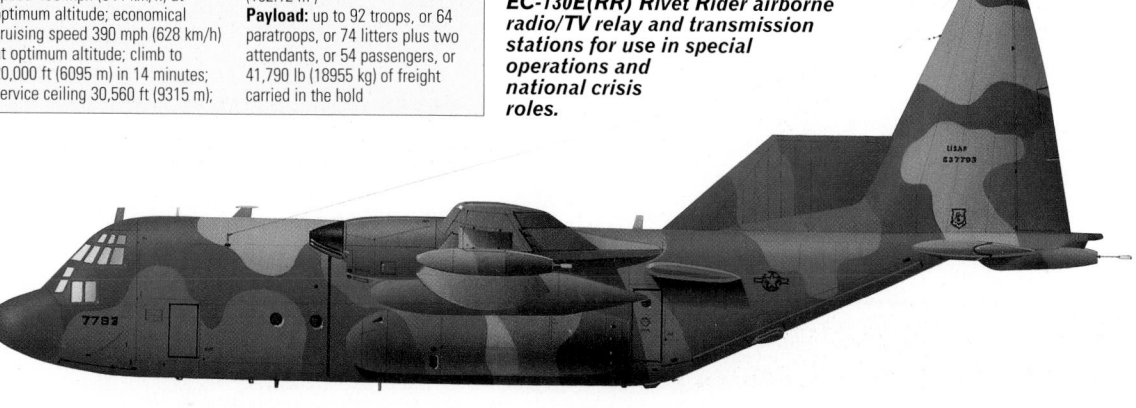

carried over a range of 1,428 miles (2298 km). This required strengthened wing spars, thicker skins and beefed-up landing gear. The C-130E also introduced larger 1,360-US gal (5148-litre) external underwing tanks mounted between the inner and outer engines and most C-130Es have their forward cargo doors sealed. In service, the C-130E has been extensively upgraded and updated, with new avionics, a tactical precision approach system, and a self-contained nav system. The US Navy's **C-130G** was a utility transport version based on the C-130E.

The definitive version of the Hercules, in its first-generation form with T56 engines, is the **C-130H** of which 1,089 were eventually completed with the ability to deliver a 43,400-lb (19686-kg) payload over a range of 1,428 miles (2298 km). The C-130H was developed for export customers, first flew in November 1964, and was delivered from March 1965. The first delivery to the USAF occurred in April 1975. This model has a redesigned and strengthened wing box, improved brakes, new avionics, and a powerplant based on the 4,900-eshp (33653-kW) T56-A-15 engine. The T56-A-15 engine and other features of

the C-130H, including the improved brakes and strengthened centre-wing design, have been retrofitted to many earlier Hercules airframes. Some C-130Hs can be fitted internally for medical evacuation duties. The C-130H served as the basis for a number of other variants, including the **C-130H(AEH)**, an airborne hospital aircraft used by Saudi Arabia, and the **C-130H-MP** maritime patroller supplied to Malaysia and Indonesia. The **C-130K** for the UK is essentially a C-130H with British avionics and equipment. The RAF's 66 C-130K transports were delivered to **Hercules C.Mk 1** standard, although subsequent modification led to new designations: **Hercules C.Mk 1P** for aircraft with an inflight-refuelling probe, **Hercules C.Mk 1K** for aircraft with additional fuel tankage and a hose-and-drum refuelling unit, **Hercules W.Mk 2** for one meteorological research machine, and **Hercules C.Mk 3** (later **C.Mk 3P**) for aircraft lengthened by 15 ft (4.57 m) in the fashion pioneered by the civil **L-100-30** to increase the maximum capacity from 92 to 128 troops. The same type of 'stretched' machine was also produced by Lockheed as the **C-130H-30**.

A number of operators fly the civilian Hercules version, which bears the company designation **L-100** (113 completed).

Certificated in February 1965, the basic L-100 was broadly equivalent to the C-130E but without pylon tanks, the **L-100-20** had plugs fore and aft of the wing for a stretch of 8 ft 4 in (2.54 m), and the L-100-30 has the full stretch of 15 ft (4.57 m).

The production variant from late in the 20th century has been the **Lockheed Martin C-130J**. This is a much improved, high-technology development with the powerplant of four AE2100 turboprops driving Dowty propellers

A much-improved variation on the Hercules theme, the C-130J is just entering service. It's gestation has been a long and troublesome one, but the type will surely mature into a fine tactical airlifter.

each comprising six curved blades of composite construction. Other major changes include a two-crew 'glass' cockpit with four flat-panel liquid crystal displays, modern digital avionics, and a wing with no provision for pylons or external tanks. The type is offered in military C-130J standard-length and **C-130J-30** lengthened models, and the civil **L-100J**. The launch customer was the UK, with orders for the C-130J and C-130J-30 as the **Hercules C.Mk 5** and **C.Mk 4** respec-

tively. Other C-130J customers include Australia, Italy and the US. Variants ordered by the USAF include the C-130J, **EC-130J Commando Solo** psycological warfare aircraft and **WC-130B** weather reconnaissance machine, while the USMC has ordered the **KC-130J** tanker. A number of the Italian aircraft will be configured as tankers. In addition, Lockheed Martin has proposed the **C-130J AEW&C** aircraft, with AN/APS-145 in a rotodome above the fuselage.

Lockheed C-141 StarLifter

Flown for the first time on 17 December 1963, the aircraft now known as the **C-141 StarLifter** provided the USAF with a fast and capacious long-range jet transport with which it could replace the slow C-124 and narrow-cabin C-135 in service with the Military Air Transport

Service. Drawing heavily on experience with the C-130 Hercules, the StarLifter featured a fuselage of similar cross-section, the combination of two large clamshell doors and a rear ramp that could be opened in flight for air-dropping, a paratrooping door on each side of the hold's rear, and

tricycle landing gear with its main units housed in external sponsons. To provide a high-speed cruising capability, the design team adopted swept flying surfaces, these including a T-tail and a wing fitted with powerful high lift-devices for viceless low-speed handling and good field performance. Other features of the StarLifter include an all-weather landing system, a powerplant based on four TF33 turbofan engines in nacelles pylon-mounted below and ahead of the wing's leading edges, and fuel carried in integral wing tanks. The first of two **C-141A** production-standard prototypes, out of an eventual total of 284 aircraft, flew in December 1963, entered service in October 1964 and reached initial operational capability in April 1965, soon providing impressive confirmation of its capabilities on the 'air bridge' service to South-East Asia.

In C-141A form the StarLifter was handicapped by its limited cabin volume, but nevertheless proved a highly capable airlifter.

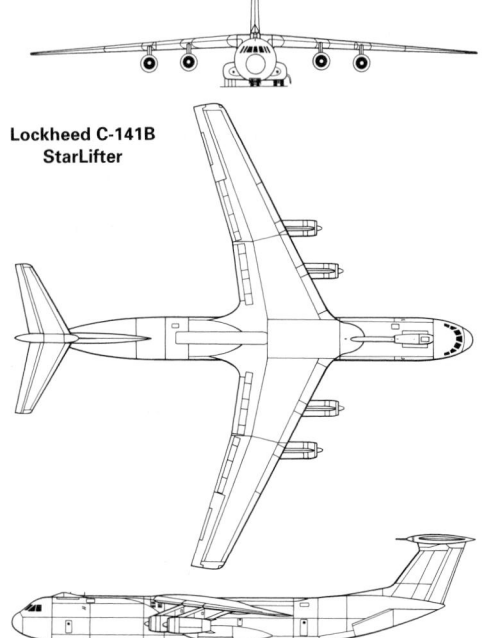

Lockheed C-141B StarLifter

SPECIFICATION	

Lockheed C-141B StarLifter
Type: four/eight-crew long-range logistics transport aircraft
Powerplant: four Pratt & Whitney TF33-P-7 turbofan engines each rated at 21,000 lb st (93.41 kN)
Performance: maximum cruising speed 566 mph (910 km/h) at high altitude; economical cruising speed 495 mph (797 km/h) at high altitude; initial climb rate 2,920 ft (890 m) per minute; service ceiling 41,600 ft (12680 m); range 6,390 miles (10280 km) without

payload or 2,936 miles (4725 km) with maximum payload
Weights: empty 148,120 lb (67186 kg); maximum take-off 343,000 lb (155580 kg)
Dimensions: wingspan 159 ft 11 in (48.74 m); length 168 ft 3½ in (51.29 m); height 39 ft 3 in (11.96 m); wing area 3,228.00 sq ft (299.88 m²)
Payload: see text within the context of a 90,880-lb (41222-kg) maximum payload

Not long after the C-141A entered service, it became obvious that the type's maximum payload of 70,847 lb (32136 kg), or of 92,000 lb (41731 kg) on aircraft configured to carry LGM-30 Minuteman ICBMs, could only rarely be achieved as the aircraft 'bulked out' in terms of

volume long before the weight limit was approached. During the 1970s, therefore, 270 of the surviving 274 aircraft, the other four being **NC-141A** aircraft used for test purposes, were cycled through an upgrade programme aimed at increasing cabin volume.

Lockheed C-141 StarLifter (continued)

A fuselage stretch of 23 ft 4 in (7.11 m) allowed the resulting **C-141B** to carry loads much closer to its design payload: overall cargo capacity was increased by over 30 per cent, and the programme thus added the equivalent of 90 new aircraft in terms of capacity at low relative cost. At the same time, Lockheed installed inflight-refuelling capability in a characteristic humped fair-ing above the flightdeck, providing the StarLifter with true global airlift capacity. The **YC-141B** prototype conversion made its first flight on 24 March 1977, and Lockheed completed the final C-141B on 29 June 1982.

Throughout its career the StarLifter has been a workhorse of the USAF, flying regular supply missions around the world in addition to undertaking special requirements. Perhaps the StarLifter's finest hour came in the second half of 1990, when the entire fleet was instru-mental in transporting much of the equipment for the US build-up for Desert Storm. Of inestimable value to the USAF is the StarLifter's sheer versatil-ity. Like that of the Hercules, the C-141 StarLifter's hold is fitted with tie-down points and floor cleats that allow it to be rapidly reconfigured for many missions. Palletised passenger seats can be fitted for 166 people, while by using canvas seats some 205 passengers or 168 paratroops can be carried. For a casevac mission the StarLifter can carry, for instance, 103 litter patients and 113 walking wounded. The C-141 StarLifter can also carry many types of vehi-cles, or up to 13 standard cargo pallets, or loads such as aircraft engines, food supplies, fuel drums or nuclear weapons. Thirteen **C-141B SOL II** transports of the 437th Air Wing are equipped for the Special Operations Low Level (SOLL) role with increased survivability measures, the most obvious being the addition of a FLIR turret beneath the nose.

Lockheed F-94 & F-94C Starfire

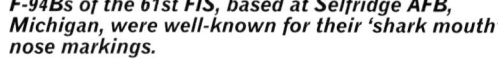

F-94Bs of the 61st FIS, based at Selfridge AFB, Michigan, were well-known for their 'shark mouth' nose markings.

Within six months of its formation, in the autumn of 1947, the USAF advised Lockheed of an urgent requirement for a two-seat all-weather fighter. Successful use of the P-80 Shooting Star, and the T-33 trainer derived from it, led to the suggestion that a fighter could be based on the T-33 to meet the USAF request. The close relation-ship can be gauged by the fact that a modified F-80 served as the prototype for the T-33, and the same aircraft then became one of the two **YF-94** proto-types. It differed by having the fuselage lengthened to house fire-control radar, and modified to accept the more powerful Allison J33-A-33 turbojet with an afterburning thrust of 6,000 lb (26.69-kN). Flown on 16 April 1949, approximately 12 months from initiation of the idea, the two YF-94s were troubled initially by powerplant problems, delaying entry into service until 29 December 1949.

Strictly speaking the F-94C was the only variant officially named Starfire. In this view the F-94C's swept tailplane, FFAR pods and 250-US gal (946-litre) tip tanks are clearly evident.

Even then, the USAF acquired its first turbojet-powered all-weather fighter far quicker than would have been possible in any other way.

Production was to total 854 aircraft in three main versions, and these gave a decade of valuable service, serving first with the USAF in Korea, and remaining in use with Air National Guard units until 1959.

SPECIFICATION	
Lockheed F-94C Starfire **Type:** two-seat all-weather fighter **Powerplant:** one Pratt & Whitney J48-P-5 turbojet rated at 6,350-lb st (28.24-kN) dry and 8,750-lb st (38.91-kN) with afterburning **Performance:** maximum speed 640 mph (1030 km/h) at sea level; service ceiling 51,400 ft (15665 m); standard range 805 miles (1296 km)	**Weights:** empty 12,708 lb (5764 kg); maximum take-off 24,184 lb (10970 kg) **Dimensions:** wingspan 37 ft 4 in (11.38 m); length 44 ft 6 in (13.56 m); height 14 ft 11 in (4.55 m); wing area 232.80 sq ft (21.63 m²) **Armament:** 24 folding-fin rockets in nose, plus 24 similar rockets in two wing pods

Variants

F-94A: initial production version, early aircraft conversions of T-33 airframes taken from the production line; basically similar to YF-94 prototypes, but carrying full equipment and four 0.5-in (12.7-mm) guns
YF-94B: prototype for second production version, with improved systems avionics and utility systems
F-94B: second production version, generally similar to YF-94B prototype, with Allison J33-A-33 or -33A engine, and large wingtip fuel tanks
YF-94C (ex-YF-97A): two prototypes of an improved higher-performance version, introduced a new wing, all-rocket armament, new tailplane, and a more powerful Pratt & Whitney J48 turbojet, a licence-built version of the Rolls-Royce Tay
F-94C Starfire (ex-F-97A): final production version, generally as the YF-94C prototypes, but with refinements; entering service in July 1951, the F-94Cs were improved progressively throughout their operational life

Lockheed F-104 Starfighter

West Germany was, by far, the largest operator of the Starfighter, taking delivery of over 900 F-104Fs two-seaters, RF/F-104Gs and two-seat TF-104Gs.

A total of some 2,221 single-seat **Starfighter** warplanes was built in the USA, Canada, Europe and Japan as part of the **F-104** programme. The first of two **XF-104** prototypes, each powered by one 10,200-lb st (45.37-kN) Wright XJ65-W-6 (licence-made Armstrong Siddeley Sapphire) afterburning turbojet engine, started the flight test effort on 18 February 1954. These two aircraft were followed by 17 **YF-104A** pre-production aircraft with a lengthened fuselage, forward- rather than rear-ward-retracting nosewheel unit, revised air inlets, and the definitive J79-GE-3A developing 14,800 lb st (65.83 kN) with afterburn-ing.

The USAF procured 153 and 77 examples respec-tively of the **F-104A** interceptor and **F-104C** tactical fighter variants, although after at least 73 accidental losses the surviving aircraft were with-drawn from service with regular and Air National Guard squadrons during 1968 and 1975 respec-tively. Most of the aircraft were then transferred to the air forces of Jordan, Pakistan and Taiwan, all of which used the type in combat, but none now remains in service.

The introduction of extensive modifications, a multi-role nav/attack system and the improved 15,800-lb st (70.28-kN) J79-GE-11A engine, coupled with high-pressure salesmanship, secured an initial West German contract for the new **F-104G Starfighter** late in 1958. This spearheaded orders from other NATO countries, leading to a massive European licensed production programme by Belgium, Germany, Italy and the Netherlands, with additional industrial partici-pation from the USA and from Canada, which selected the **CF-104** as its next-generation fighter. New F-104G, CF-104 and **RF-104G Starfighter** aircraft from this joint production effort were procured by Belgium (101), Canada (200), Denmark (40), Germany (749 for the Luftwaffe and Marineflieger), Greece (45), Italy (125), the Netherlands (120), Norway (19), Spain (18), Taiwan (67) and Turkey (46). Production was also undertaken in Japan, where Mitsubishi built 210 exam-

ples of the **Model 683B** between 1962 and 1967 for service with the local designation **F-104J**. These were retired from front-line service in March 1986.

Most Starfighters were replaced in service from 1979 by more modern fighters, but large numbers were also transferred to US allies and other NATO countries. Major recipients

included Greece, Norway, Taiwan and Turkey. By the late 1990s all these aircraft had been retired.

Following the development and, from 1956, the production for the USAF of 26 **F-104B** and 21 **F-104D** conversion trainers with tandem two-seat accommodation, Lockheed undertook the manufacture of similar trainer versions of the later F-104G series for the NATO and Japanese procurement programmes. These included 38 **CF-104D** machines for Canada, 30 **F-104F** and 137 **TF-104G** aircraft for Germany, 20 **F-104DJ** trainers for Japan, and 29 **TF-104** machines for Military Assistance Program contracts (four, six, two, three, six and eight aircraft for Denmark, Greece, Norway, Spain, Turkey and Taiwan respectively). Lockheed also built 191 TF-104Gs for NATO

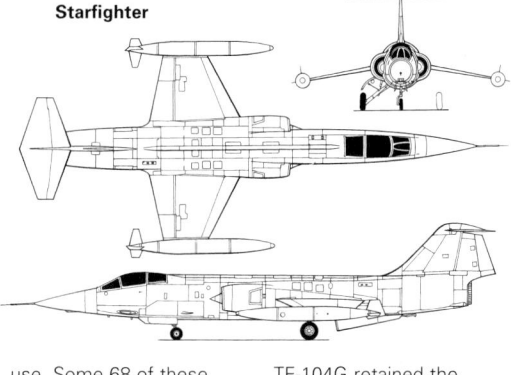

Lockheed F-104G Starfighter

use. Some 68 of these were assembled in Europe from Lockheed-supplied kits, an extra 16 being delivered from Fiat for the Italian air force, increasing overall production of the two-seat F-104 to 359. The

TF-104G retained the single-seat version's weapons systems and associated avionics, including its F-15A NASARR radar but not its 20-mm Vulcan cannon, which was replaced by extra fuel.

57-1317 was one of the 21 F-104Ds built for the USAF. Based on the F-104C, the two-seat D-model did not have a cannon installed.

Lockheed F-117 Nighthawk

In 1974 the US Defense Advanced Research and Procurement Agency called for the development of a true stealth warplane using a mix of radar-absorbent materials, a radar-reflective internal structure and a similarly 'reflective' configuration to provide a dramatic decrease in radar cross-section. In overall terms, faceting reflects radar energy in all directions, making the aircraft virtually invisible even to AWACS platforms, and the concept extends to the wing itself, the aerofoil section of which consists of two flat surfaces on the underside and three on the top of the

wing. The avoidance of straight lines is continued on access panels and doors, many of which have serrated edges for the same reason. Cockpit transparencies are coated with gold.

The 'Skunk Works' organisation of Lockheed was awarded a development order in April 1976 for two sub-scale technology demonstrators. The first of these flew in 1977, and although both aircraft were lost, the experience gained was sufficient to win Lockheed a November 1978 contract to develop a full-scale operational tactical warplane. Major

changes were introduced, most notably to the configuration of the tail surfaces, which were canted outward rather than inward. The first of five full-scale development prototypes flew on 18 June 1981, and these machines had smaller tail surfaces than the production aircraft.

In October 1983 the first unit was declared operational, with about five **F-117A Nighthawk** and 18 Vought A-7D aircraft, the latter flown for proficiency and as a security 'cover'. It was not until November 1988 that the F-117A was officially acknowledged by the Pentagon, and on 19 December 1989 the type finally went into action, two such aircraft attacking the Rio Hate

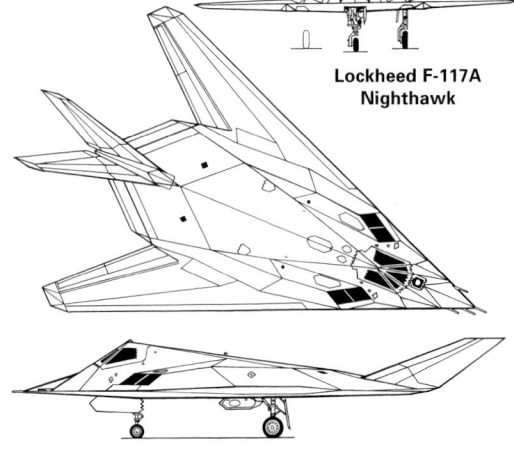

Lockheed F-117A Nighthawk

The Nighthawk had been operational for five years before it was revealed to the public and has since seen action over Panama, Iraq and Kosovo.

barracks during the American invasion of Panama. This small baptism of fire was overshadowed by the type's contribution to the Desert Storm operation, in which an eventual total of 42 aircraft flew from Khamis Mushait in Saudi Arabia on nightly missions against targets in Iraq and occupied Kuwait.

In the later 1990s, the F-117A was also used in attacks on Serbian targets within the context of the NATO-led effort to secure peace in Kosovo. In this campaign the F-117A suffered its first operational loss, probably as a result of poor planning rather than any deficiency in the warplane.

Lockheed F-117 Nighthawk (continued)

In USAF planning the F-117 Nighthawk is used for attacks against what the service calls 'highly leveraged' targets such as communications and command centres, air defence sector centres, key bridges, airfields and the like. In order to attack such targets, the F-117A uses a highly accurate inertial navigation system to put it in the right position to begin the attack. From there, the forward-looking infra-red is used to acquire the target. The pilot aligns cross-hairs on a FLIR screen over the target, once acquired, and locks the point into the weapons computer. As the F-117 approaches its quarry, the target dips below the aircraft's nose and the locked-in image is handed over to the downward-looking infra-red sensor mounted under the star-board side of the nose. This remains continuously pointed at the target image. Laser-guided bombs are released at a computed point, and at some time during their free fall in the general direction of the target a laser is used to designate the impact point. This laser is boresighted with the DLIR.

After the Gulf War, Lockheed began an Offensive Capability Improvement Program (OCIP) for the 57 F-117As remaining out of 59 production aircraft and five pre-series aircraft delivered. The object was to increase combat effectiveness by reducing cockpit workload.

Lockheed L-049/L-649/L-749 Constellation, L-1049 Super Constellation and L-1649 Starliner

Pan American World Airways and TWA introduced the 'Connie' into commercial service in early 1946. NC88838 was among Pan Am's first aircraft, delivered in January.

Design of the **L-49** began in 1939 to meet the requirements of Pan American Airways and Transcontinental & Western Air, for a 40-passenger airliner for use on domestic routes. Manufacture was initiated, but with the outbreak of World War II aircraft on the production line were commandeered for service with the USAAF as transports under the designation **C-69**, the first being flown on 9 January 1943. A total of 22 entered USAAF service before the contract cancellations following VJ-Day. Production of civil aircraft then began under the company designation **L-049** Constellation, using components that had been intended for C-69s, but with the interiors completed to airline standard and with basic accommodation for 43 to 48 passengers, or a maximum of 60 in a high-

Brazilian airline Varig used its three L-1049G 'Super G' Super Constellations to establish a scheduled service to Buenos Aires.

Variants

L-049: original civil Constellations, produced from components stockpiled for military C-69 transports
L-649: the first postwar Constellations built and furnished entirely as civil airliners
L-649A: generally similar to L-649 but with increased fuel capacity
L-749: long-range version, generally similar to L-649A but with strengthened landing gear
L-749A: generally similar to L-749, but with strengthened structure for operation at higher gross weight
L-1049: initial version of Super Constellation, with standard accommodation for 69 to 92 passengers and 2,500-hp (1864-kW) Wright 749C-18BD-1 engines
L-1049C: improved version of Super Constellation with 3,250-hp (2424-kW) Wright 872TC-18DA-1 Turbo-Compound engines
L-1049D: generally similar to L-1049C, but intended for convertible passenger/cargo operations with cargo doors in the port rear fuselage and strengthened flooring
L-1049E: generally similar to L-1049C, but certificated for operation at a higher gross weight
L-1049G: high gross weight version with 3,400-hp (2535-kW) Wright 972TC-18DA-3 Turbo-Compound engines and provision for wingtip fuel tanks
L-1049H: final production Super Constellation, combining L-1049D and L-1049G configurations
L-1649: prototype of the Starliner, basically a Super Constellation airframe, with a redesigned, more efficient wing containing additional fuel, and powered by 3,400-hp (2535-kW) Wright 988TC-18EA-2 Turbo-Cyclone engines
L-1649A: production version of the Starliner, of which 43 were built
C-69: original military transport version
C-69C-1 (later ZC-69C-1): one-off VIP military transport
XC-69E: redesignation of one C-69 used as an engine test-bed
C-121A: designation of cargo/personnel transport versions of L-749 for USAF, with strengthened floors and port rear fuselage cargo door; those converted in service as VIP transports redesignated **VC-121A**
VC-121B: one VIP aircraft, similar to standard L-749, equipped for possible Presidential use
PO-1W: two examples of an airborne early-warning (AEW) aircraft for US Navy, derived from L-749 airframe
R7O-1 (later R7V-1 then C-121J): USN version of L-1049D, powered by 3,250-hp (2424-kW) Wright R-3350-91 Turbo-Compound engines

R7V-1P: temporary designation of one R7V-1 equipped for polar ice pack reconnaissance
R7V-2: four experimental aircraft with L-1049 airframes, powered by 5,550-shp (4139-kW) Pratt & Whitney YT34-P-12A turboprop engines for USN evaluation
WV-2 Warning Star (later EC-121K): US Navy AEW aircraft, 222 built, with L-1049 airframe, avionics equipment developed for PO-1W, 3,400-hp (2535-kW) Wright R-3350-34 or R-3350-42 TurboCompound engines, and wingtip auxiliary fuel tanks
WV-2E (later EC-121L): one experimental conversion of WV-2 as an avionics test bed; first aircraft to carry a large rotating radome above the fuselage
WV-2Q (later EC-121M): redesignation of WV-2s re-equipped for ECM role
WV-3 (later WQC-121N): eight aircraft, similar to WV-2 but without tip tanks, for weather reconnaissance duties
C-121C: USAF version of R7V-1, but with R-3350-34 engines
JC-121C: redesignation of two C-121Cs and one TC-121C converted for avionics and systems research
RC-121C: USAF AEW aircraft, similar to USN WV-2; later redesignated **TC-121C** and used for AEW training
VC-121C: redesignation of C-121Cs converted for use as VIP transports
RC-121D (later EC-121D): USAF version of WV-2, differed by having wing tip tanks and revisions of interior layout and equipment
VC-121E: VIP aircraft equipped for Presidential use, based on R7V-1 airframe
YC-121F: two experimental aircraft as R7V-1s, but with 6,000-shp (4474-kW) Pratt & Whitney T34-P-6 turboprop engines for USAF evaluation
C-121G: redesignation of 32 R7V-1s transferred from USN to USAF use
EC-12M: redesignation of 42 EC-121Ds following installation of specialised avionics equipment
EC-121J: redesignation of two EC-121Ds with additional avionics
JC-121K: redesignation of one EC-121K used for avionics experiments
NC-121K: redesignation of EC-121Ks used by the USN for various tests
EC-121P: redesignation of EC-121Ks with updated ASW equipment
EC-121Q: redesignation of EC-121Ds with advanced avionics equipment
EC-121R: redesignation of EC-121K and EC-121P aircraft equipped to process relayed data from air-delivered ground seismic devices along major jungle routes in Vietnam
EC-121S: ECM and electronic reconnaissance aircraft converted from C-121Cs
EC-12M: redesignation of earlier AEW aircraft following conversion to enhance AEW capability

density layout. The first Constellation was certificated for civil operations on 11 December 1945, the type entering service first with Pan Am and TWA, the latter inaugurating a regular US-Paris service on 6 February 1946.

The first true civil Constellations were **L-649** aircraft with 2,500-hp (1864-kW) Wright 749C-18BD-1 engines and far more luxurious interiors seating 48 to 64 passengers as standard, or 81 in a high-density arrangement. This version was replaced in production during 1947 by the longer-range **L-749**

with additional fuel yet able to carry the same payload, but by the end of 1949 the demand for air travel was increasing and operators were then looking for aircraft of greater capacity. This brought development of the **L-1049 Super Constellation**, with the fuselage lengthened by 18 ft 4 in (5.59 m), and **'Super Connies'** entered service during their production life with a variety of interior layouts that could seat a maximum of 109 passengers. The last of the civil Constellation-derived airliners was the **L-1649A Starliner**, with a

'Willy Victor' was the nickname applied to the US Navy's WV-2 Warning Star AEW platform. The USAF operated the similar RC-121D.

completely new wing of increased span and with far greater fuel capacity, providing a range considerably in excess of any of its predecessors. However, the Starliner was developed too late to gain commercial success, its piston-engine powerplant being outdated by comparison with the turbojet powerplants of airliners

The final Constellation derivative was the L-1649A Starliner, though it was too late to compete with new turboprop and jet designs.

then beginning to enter service. When production ended in the late 1950s a

total of 856 aircraft of all versions, both civil and military, had been built.

SPECIFICATION	
Lockheed L-1649A Starliner	payload 4,940 miles (7950 km)
Type: long-range civil transport	**Weights:** empty 91,645 lb (41569 kg); maximum take-off 160,000 lb (72,575 kg)
Powerplant: four 3,400-hp (2535-kW) Wright 988TC-18EA-2 TurboCompound radial piston engines	**Dimensions:** wingspan 150 ft (45.72 m); length 116 ft 2 in (35.41 m); height 24 ft 9 in (7.54 m); wing area 1,850 sq ft (171.87 m²)
Performance: maximum speed 377 mph (606 km/h) at 18,600 ft (5670 m); service ceiling 23,700 ft (7225 m); range with maximum	

Lockheed L-188 Electra

The design of the **L-188 Electra** began in 1954, and in the following year Lockheed received a launching order from American Airlines. The prototype, first flown on 6 December 1957, was a

low-wing monoplane of conventional configuration with retractable tricycle landing gear and powered by four Allison 501D turboprop engines. Standard accommodation was for 66 to 80 passengers, but a

high-density arrangement was available optionally to seat 98. Built initially as the **L-188A**, the Electra also became available as the longer-range **L-188C** with increased fuel capacity and operating at a higher gross weight. A total of 170 Electras had been built when production ended unexpectedly early as a result of passenger loss of confidence in the type after two had disintegrated in flight. By the time reme-

Though some potential sales were lost after two disastrous crashes, the Electra still sold well, numerous US domestic and foreign airlines receiving examples.

dial modifications had been incorporated customer airlines were interested in turbojet- rather than turboprop-powered aircraft. A handful of aircraft remained

in service early in 2001, many of them converted by Lockheed Aircraft Service for convertible passenger/ cargo or all-cargo use.

SPECIFICATION	
Lockheed L-188A Electra	ceiling 28,400 ft (8655 m); range 2,200 miles (3541 km)
Type: short-/medium-range transport	**Weights:** empty 57,400 lb (26036 kg); maximum take-off 113,000 lb (51256 kg)
Powerplant: four 3,750-shp (2796-kW) Allison 501D-13 or 501D-13A turboprops; optionally four 4,050-shp (3020-kW) 501D-15 turboprops	**Dimensions:** wingspan 99 ft (30.18 m); length 104 ft 6 in (31.85 m); height 32 ft 10 in (10.01 m); wing area 1,300 sq ft (120.77 m²)
Performance: maximum cruising speed 405 mph (652 km/h); service	

Lockheed L-1011 TriStar

The wide-body airliner created by Lockheed as the **L-1011 TriStar** originated as the company's effort to meet the requirement issued by American Airlines for a large-capacity short/ medium-range transport. Construction of the first aircraft began early in 1968, and this machine made its maiden flight on 17 November 1970. The TriStar is a low-wing cantilever monoplane with swept flying surfaces characterised by a wing sweep angle of 35°, the initial powerplant of three 42,000-lb st (186.83-kN) RB.211 turbofans, and accommodation for a crew of two to four together

with anything between 256 and 400 passengers depending on cabin layout and seat pitch. At this stage of development Lockheed and Rolls-Royce each ran into monetary difficulties as a result of their huge capital investments in their portions of this massive programme, and each required financial aid from its government before the TriStar could be resumed. As a result, the TriStar did not gain its American type certification until 14 April 1972, and this then allowed Eastern Air Lines to make the type's first revenue-earning flight on 26 April 1972. Some teething troubles were

experienced, primarily with the engines, but in a very short time the TriStar was proving popular with operators and passengers alike.

The original production version, designated by the manufacturer as the **L-1011-1** and powered by RB.211-22B or -22C turbofans at a maximum take-off weight of 430,000 lb (195048 kg), was followed into service by the longer-range **L-1011-100** carrying additional fuel and certificated for operation at the higher gross weight of 450,000 lb (204120 kg) with a powerplant of three RB.211s up to a rating of 43,500 lb st (193.50 kN) in its

RB.211-22F form. To provide better performance from 'hot-and-high' airports, the **L-1011-200** was developed from the L-1011-100 with the uprated powerplant of three 48,000-lb st (213.51-kN) RB.211-524

The original production version, designated by the manufacturer as the **L-1011-1** and powered by RB.211-22B or -22C turbofans at a maximum take-off weight of 430,000 lb (195048 kg), was followed into service by the longer-range **L-1011-100** carrying additional fuel and certificated for operation at the higher gross weight of 450,000 lb (204120 kg) with a powerplant of three RB.211s up to a rating of 43,500 lb st (193.50 kN) in its

engines but the same fuel capacity and weight options as the L-1011-100, although the better performance of the RB.211-524 offered a slight increase in range. The final member of the family was the long-range **L-1011-500**.

SPECIFICATION	
Lockheed L-1011-500 TriStar	range 6,155 miles (9905 km) with maximum payload
Type: three/four-crew long-range transport aircraft	**Weights:** empty 240,963 lb (109299 kg); maximum take-off 496,000 lb (224982 kg)
Powerplant: three Rolls-Royce RB.211-524B or RB.211-524B4 turbofan engines each rated at 50,000 lb st (222.41 kN)	**Dimensions:** wingspan 155 ft 4 in (47.35 m); length 164 ft 2½ in (50.05 m); height 55 ft 4 in (16.87 m); wing area 3,456.00 sq ft (321.06 m²)
Performance: maximum cruising speed 605 mph (974 km/h) at 30,000 ft (9145 m); economical cruising speed 556 mph (895 km/h) at 30,000 ft (9145 m); initial climb rate 2,820 ft (860 m) per minute; service ceiling 42,000 ft (12800 m);	**Payload:** up to 330 passengers within the context of a 92,253-lb (41845-kg) maximum payload

Lockheed L-1011 TriStar (continued)

The L-1011-500 introduced many features that were first tested and incorporated in the original aircraft that was then designated as the **Advanced TriStar**. The L-1011-500 has RB.211-524B or RB.211-524B4 engines, the fuselage reduced in length from 178 ft 8 in (54.46 m) to 164 ft 2½ in (50.05 m), increased fuel tankage, revised interior layout with accommodation for between 246 and a maximum of 330 passengers, and in later aircraft, a wing increased in span from 155 ft 4 in (47.35 m) to 164 ft 4 in (50.09 m) and fitted with actively controlled ailerons used for alleviation of gust response. The designation **L-1011-250** was applied to six L-1011-1 aircraft operated by Delta Airlines after conversion with the RB.211-524B4 powerplant for a maximum take-off weight of 496,000 lb (224985 kg).

However, as a result of the continued recession in the commercial air transport industry during the early 1980s, Lockheed announced late in 1981 that TriStar production was to be phased out during 1983 after the completion of all outstanding orders. Manufacture of 250 airframes was completed, and more than half of these (including a number converted as freighters) were still in revenue-earning service in 2001.

The TriStar has also entered limited military service. A total of nine L-1011-500s was acquired by the UK Ministry of Defence in 1982-4, and

Cathay Pacific eventually built up a fleet of 17 TriStars, including this TriStar 100. The last Cathay TriStar was retired in favour of the A330 in 1996.

eight of these aircraft constitute the equipment of the RAF's No. 216 Sqn. In the first phase of a major programme, four of the aircraft were converted to **TriStar K.Mk 1** tanker/transport standard: the conversion involved installation of underfloor fuel tanks in the fore and aft baggage compartments, providing an additional 100,000 lb (45360 kg) of fuel capacity, paired Flight Refuelling Ltd HDUs (hose and drum units) in the lower rear fuselage, and a closed-circuit TV camera to monitor refuelling. An inflight-refuelling probe was fitted above the forward fuselage and full passenger seating (with all seats facing forward) was provided throughout the cabin. The first flight was made on 9 July 1985.

Two of the four K.Mk 1s remained in service in the mid-1990s, with the remaining two aircraft and two newly acquired TriStar machines having been further modified to the **TriStar KC.Mk 1** tanker/freighter standard. The TriStar KC.Mk 1 was first flown in 1988 and introduces a port-side forward

cargo door and a freight-handling system: as such the type can carry palletised cargo and 35 passengers. The floor is strengthened for high-density loadings.

Two of the aircraft serve as **TriStar C.Mk 2** troop transports without probes. Planned modifications were abandoned to fit the third aircraft with underwing Mk 32B pods containing HDUs as the TriStar **K.Mk 2**, and this machine was instead delivered as a **TriStar C.Mk 2A** with military avionics, a new interior and the troublesome digital autopilot replaced by an analogue autopilot as fitted to the K.Mk 1 and KC.Mk 1. All RAF TriStars have ALR-66 radar warning receivers, but plans to fit underwing Mk 32B pods appear to have been abandoned. One other L-1011-500 (ex-Air Canada) has been converted by Marshall of Cambridge for Orbital Sciences Corporation of the USA to serve as a launcher for the Pegasus air-launched space booster. One VIP-configured L-1011-500 serves as a part of the Jordanian Royal Flight.

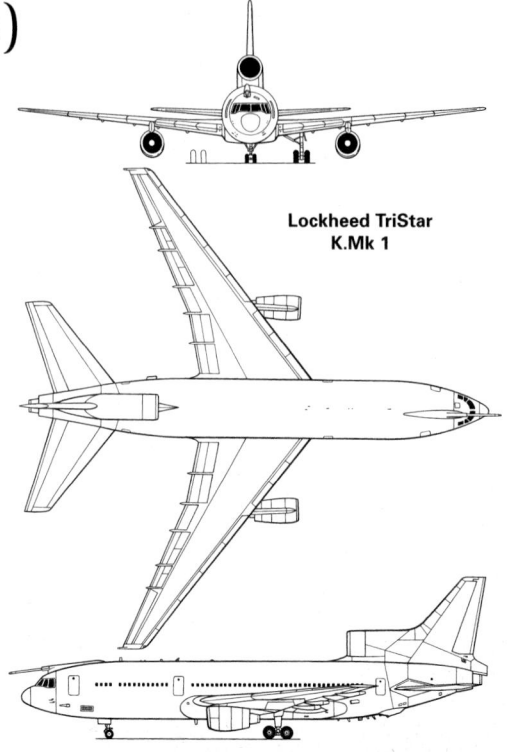

Lockheed TriStar K.Mk 1

Delta's TriStar fleet peaked at 54 aircraft, including several TriStar 500s (illustrated). A much reduced fleet remained in service in the spring of 2001.

Lockheed P-3 Orion

In August 1957 the US Navy issued Type Specification No. 146 calling for a new anti-submarine aircraft to replace the P-2 Neptune. The Lockheed proposal was based on the L-188 Electra, and in May 1958 the company was awarded a contract largely on the basis of the strength of the aircraft's structure and its size, which was sufficient to house an extensive array of detection systems and the required tactical crew. Lockheed modified the third Electra airframe as the prototype with a tail-mounted MAD boom and a ventral bulge simulating a weapons bay. Following extensive adaptations (including a shortening of the fuselage), the aircraft made a successful maiden flight as the **YP3V-1** (later

VQ-1 'World Watchers' was established in September 1955 and subsequently began Elint operations with the EP-3 Orion. This EP-3E is illustrated as it appeared when on the squadron strength at NAS Agana on Guam. In 2001 VQ-1 continues EP-3E, UP-3B and P-3C operations from NAS Whidbey Island, Washington.

redesignated as the **YP-3A**) on 25 November 1959. The USN ordered an initial batch of seven in October 1960, and the first of these flew in April 1961. In 1962 the type was redesignated as the **P-3A Orion**.

The P-3A entered service in the summer of 1962 with 4,500-eshp (3355-kW) T56-A-10W turboprops and,

from the 110th aircraft, the DELTIC (DELayed TIme Compression) acoustic data-processing system that doubled sonobuoy information-processing capability and also incorporated redesigned avionics. Within a short time most existing aircraft had also been retrofitted. In the summer of 1965, after the

delivery of 157 P-3As, Lockheed began production of the **P-3B**. This was fitted with more powerful T56-A-14 engines and was heavier than its predecessor, mainly through having provision for the AGM-12 Bullpup ASM, but retained basically the same electronics fit. The P-3B secured the first export orders for

the type, and became operational with New Zealand and Norway (five aircraft each) and also with Australia (10 aircraft). From 1977 the USN's P-3Bs were updated with improved navigation and acoustic-processing equipment, and with provision for the AGM-84 Harpoon AShM missile. P-3B

Lockheed CP-140 Aurora

No. 92 Wing of the RAAF maintains two operational squadrons (10 (illustrated) and 11) and one training (292) squadron of P-3Cs at RAAF Edinburgh.

production ended in 1969 after the completion of 144 aircraft (125 of them for the US Navy).

Surplus P-3As were later converted to **RP-3A** standard (three aircraft) for oceanographic reconnaissance, and to **WP-3A** standard (four aircraft) for weather reconnaissance. Six early aircraft were refitted as staff transports under the **VP-3A** designation, while a handful entered service as **TP-3A** aircrew trainers. Several early Orions were converted for utility transport duties as **UP-3A** and **UP-3B** machines. Four P-3As were transferred to the US Customs Service under the **P-3A(CS)** designation with APG-63 nose radar to complement four P-3B AEW aircraft with the APS-138 surveillance radar using an antenna in a rotodome above the rear fuselage. New Zealand's aircraft received an avionics upgrade (the first by Boeing

and the other five by Air New Zealand) to become **P-3K** machines: the sixth of these aircraft was an ex-Australian P-3B. Norway acquired two P-3Bs in 1979 and one of these, plus one original aircraft, were adapted to **P-3N** standard for pilot training and fishery protection. The other five were transferred to Spain to replace four P-3As leased from the USN and to augment the surviving two of three P-3As purchased by Spain. The six surviving Australian aircraft were upgraded to **P-3C** standard as **P-3P** machines and subsequently transferred to Portugal in 1986. Australia later purchased three surplus USN P-3Bs for use as trainers with the designation **TAP-3**. Later customers for ex-USN P-3As and P-3Bs include Argentina (eight P-3Bs), Greece (six P-3Bs) and Thailand (two P-3As and one **UP-3T**).

The P-3C is now the

USN's primary land-based anti-submarine warfare patrol aircraft. It retains the airframe/powerplant combination of the P-3B, and the first service-test **YP-3C** was a P-3B conversion that first flew on 18 September 1968. Since then, the P-3C has also been exported to Australia, the Netherlands, Norway, Japan, Pakistan and South Korea. The baseline P-3C has APS-115B search radar, ASQ-81 MAD and the AQA-7 DIFAR (Directional Acoustics-Frequency Analysis and Recording) system, as well as an integrated ASW and navigation system.

The P-3C entered service in 1969, and 118 baseline aircraft were followed by about 247 of various Update versions for the USN and export, of which the last was a machine delivered to South Korea in September 1995 from a newly established production line.

The **P-3C Update I** (31 built) introduced a sevenfold increase in computer memory and Omega navigation in place of the original LORAN. The **P-3C Update II** (37 built for delivery from August 1977) featured an advanced sonobuoy reference system, provision for the AGM-84 Harpoon and the AAS-36 IRDS (Infra-Red Detection System). The **P-3C Update II.5** (24 aircraft) has a more reliable nav/comms suite, MAD compensation, standardised pylons and other improvements. The definitive P-3C Orion variant is the **P-3C Update III**, fitted with an entirely new IBM UYS-1 Proteus acoustic signal processor and a new

sonobuoy communications link. These enable the aircraft to monitor concurrently twice the number of sonobuoys as can the Update II.5 version. The Update III was the last production version and was first delivered in May 1984. Most baseline P-3C Orions were later modified to **P-3C Update III Retrofit** standard.

Exports of the P-3C included 10 Update II aircraft for Australia with the Anglo-Australian Barra acoustic data processor and indigenously developed Barra passive directional sonobuoys. Australia's second 10-aircraft batch comprised P-3C Update II.5 machines, but these are known locally by the designation **P-3W**. Ten Australian aircraft later received an Elta-developed ESM suite, and the aircraft are being upgraded to **AP-3C** standard in a Raytheon-led programme including the Elta EL/M-2022 radar, Canadian UYS-503 acoustic processing system and improved nav/comm systems. The Netherlands and Japan also received Update II.5s. The P-3Cs operated by Norway and South Korea are Update IIIs. Japan received three aircraft, plus a further

five in component knocked-down kit form for assembly before Kawasaki switched to complete manufacture of the balance of the 110 aircraft required. Iran received six baseline P-3C aircraft to the **P-3F** standard with a receptacle for inflight refuelling. The **CP-140 Aurora**, which resembles the P-3C externally, was built to Canadian specification with different avionics, and the 18 such aircraft are complemented by three **CP-140A Arcturus** aircraft with no ASW equipment and therefore used for training and economic zone protection.

Other special-purpose conversions from P-3 Orion standard for the US Navy include the **EP-3A** for electronic research, **EP-3B** for Elint, **EP-3E** for Elint with improved systems, **EP-3E-II** for Elint with still further improved systems, and **EP-3J** with internally and externally mounted ECM equipment, **RP-3C** and **RP-3D** for oceanographic survey, **NP-3B** for trials purposes and **WP-3D** for weather research. Japanese variants include the **EP-3** for electronic surveillance, the **UP-3C** flying test-bed, the **UP-3D** ECM trainer and **UP-3E** for surveillance.

SPECIFICATION	
Lockheed P-3C Orion	(35.61 m); height 33 ft 8½ in
Type: 10-crew long-range maritime patrol and anti-submarine aircraft	(10.27 m); wing area 1,300 sq ft (120.77 m²)
Powerplant: four Rolls-Royce North America (Allison) T56-A-14 turboprop engines each rated at 4,910 ehp (3661 kW)	**Armament:** up to 20,000 lb (9072 kg) of disposable stores carried in a lower-fuselage weapons bay and on 10 underwing hardpoints; including 10/20-kiloton B57 nuclear weapons; 1,000-lb
Performance: maximum speed 473 mph (761 km/h) 'clean' at 15,000 ft (4575 m); maximum climb rate 1,950 ft (594 m) per minute; service ceiling 28,300 ft (8625 m); radius 1,550 miles (2494 km) with 3 hours on station	(454-kg) Mk 52 mines; 2,000-lb (907-kg) Mk 55 or Mk 56 mines; Mk 54 and Mk 101 depth bombs; Mk 82 and Mk 83 bombs; Mk 38 and Mk 40 destructors; Mk 46 and Mk 50 Barracuda torpedoes; AGM-84 Harpoon anti-ship
Weights: empty 61,491 lb (27890 kg); maximum take-off 142,000 lb (64410 kg)	missiles; AIM-9L Sidewinder AAMs and rocket pods
Dimensions: wingspan 99 ft 8 in (30.37 m); length 116 ft 10 in	

Lockheed P-80 Shooting Star, T-33 and T2V/T-1 SeaStar

The design of what was to become the first operational jet fighter of the US Army Air Force began in June 1943, tailored around the 3,000-lb (13.34-kN) thrust British Halford H.1B turbojet. The first **XP-80** prototype with this power-

plant was flown initially on 8 January 1944, but the second and third **XP-80A** prototypes each had a 4,000-lb (29.25-kN) thrust General Electric I-40, as did the pre-production **YP-80A** aircraft. A sleek, low-wing monoplane with

retractable tricycle landing gear, the **Lockheed P-80 Shooting Star**, began to enter USAAF service in early 1945, and a total of 45 had been delivered by the time World War II ended. Two of these had been flown to Italy for

operational evaluation, but were carefully kept away from any combat situation. The very good performance of this first Lockheed jet fighter had resulted in plans to produce 5,000, but these were curtailed drastically

after VJ-Day. However, the aircraft was selected to re-equip front-line pursuit groups of the USAAF, and those serving with the US Far East Air Force in June 1950 went into action when the Korean War started.

Lockheed P-80 Shooting Star, T-33 and T2V/T-1 (cont.)

SPECIFICATION

Lockheed F-80C Shooting Star
Type: single-seat fighter
Powerplant: one 5,400-lb (24.01-kN) thrust Allison J33-A-35 turbojet
Performance: maximum speed 594 mph (956 km/h) at sea level; service ceiling 46,800 ft (14265 m); range 825 miles (1328 km)
Weights: empty 8,420 lb (3819 kg); maximum take-off

16,856 lb (7646 kg)
Dimensions: wingspan 38 ft 9 in (11.81 m); length 34 ft 5 in (10.49 m); height 11 ft 3 in (3.43 m); wing area 237.6 sq ft (22.07 m²)
Armament: six 0.5-in (12.7-mm) machine-guns, plus two 1,000-lb (454-kg) bombs and eight underwing rockets

Lockheed T-33

Variants

P-80A (later F-8OA): initial production version, powered by the 3,850-lb (17.12-kN) thrust General Electric J33-GE-11 turbojet; armament of six 0.5-in (12.7-mm) machine-guns; 917 built
XP-80B: prototype of an improved version, with revised wing section and a 4,000-lb (17.78-kN) thrust Allison J33-A-17 turbojet
P-80B (later F-80B): production version with many improvements, and introducing an ejection seat and provision for jet-assisted take-off (JATO) equipment; 240 built
P-80C (later F-80C): final production version, initially with 4,600-lb (20.46-kN) thrust J33-A-23 engines, and late production aircraft with 5,400-lb (24.01-kN) thrust J33-A-35 engines; revised armament with provisions for underwing rockets; 749 built
XP-80R: redesignation of XP-80B prototype following preparation for an attempt on the world speed record, which it regained for the USA on 19 June 1947
XFP-80A: single prototype of a photo-reconnaissance version, later **XF-14**
ERF-80A: redesignation of one F-80A used to test camera equipment
F-14A (later FP-80A then RF-80A): production photo reconnaissance version, the first 38 conversions of new-production P-80As, and the remaining 114 new-build aircraft
RF-80C: redesignation of 70 F-80As following conversion for the reconnaissance role
DF-80A: redesignation of F-80As following conversion as drone directors
QF-80A/QF-80C/QF-8OF: redesignation of aircraft converted as radio-controlled drones
TO-1 (later TV-1): US Navy designation of 50 P-80Cs acquired as jet-powered advanced trainers for the US Marine Corps
TP-80C (later TF-80C then T-33A): following successful testing of the first TP-80C two-seat trainer, flown initially on 22 March 1948, the type entered production for the USAF; 128 built
AT-33A: version of T-33A for service with smaller air forces, had armament revision making it suitable for weapon training or COIN operations
DT-33A: redesignation of T-33As following conversion as drone directors
NT-33A: redesignation of T-33As following conversion for special tests
QT-33A: redesignation of T-33As following conversion as radio controlled drones
RT-33A: reconnaissance version of the AT-33A for smaller air forces; 85 conversions
TO-2 (later TV-2): US Navy version of T-33A
TV-2D: redesignation of TO-2/TV-2s after conversion as drone directors
TV-2KD: redesignation of TO-2/TV-2s after conversion as radio controlled drones
T2V-1 SeaStar (later T-1A): development of TV-2 with humped cockpit, leading and trailing-edge flaps, boundary layer control and 6,100-lb (27.13-kN) thrust Allison J33-A-24 turbojet

Designed to meet the urgent needs of World War II, the P-80 inaugurated a frantic period of fighter development in the immediate post-war years, setting one speed record after another and becoming the stalwart of the newly independent US Air Force. The example illustrated below is a P-80A-1-LO of the 62nd Fighter Squadron, 56th Fighter Group, which was deployed to Germany in July 1948.

When production ended, Lockheed had built a total of 1,732 P-80 Shooting Star (later **F-80** 1947) aircraft, but far more successful was the **T-33A** two-seat trainer development. Basically an F-80 with a lengthened fuselage to accommodate a second seat in tandem, the T-33A has served with more than 30 air forces. Lockheed built 5,691, a further 210 were assembled by Kawasaki in Japan and Canadair built 656 which, powered by locally-built Rolls-Royce Nenes, were known under the designation **Canadair CL-30 Silver Star**. A number of T-33s remain in service in 2001.

In 1953 Kelly Johnson redesigned the highly successful T-33, with a view to improving the instructor pilot's work efficiency and the aircraft's low-speed handling characteristics. The US Navy was impressed with the changes made, and the type entered service in 1957, but was retired after a relatively short career due to maintenance problems, especially with the control systems.

Lockheed QT-2, Q-Star and YO-3A

The detection of Viet Cong guerrillas operating in Vietnam presented difficult problems, small VC units being able to attack from and merge back into the jungle with comparative ease. Although sensors were developed to keep track of such units, their short detection range meant they were useless unless they could be carried low over the jungle by a vehicle that would be difficult for the enemy to locate. Thus Lockheed Missiles and Space Company proposed the development of a slow-flying powered aircraft with a silenced engine, leading to two two-seat **QT-2** prototypes which combined the airframe of the **Schweizer SGS 2-32** sailplane with a specially silenced 100-hp (75-kW) Continental O-200-A engine driving a four-bladed propeller. Tested in Vietnam, complete with sensor packages, they proved to be most effective. A third airframe was more extensively modified and used to test a variety of propellers, this aircraft being designated **Q-Star**. During its evaluation programme the Q-Star was flown with a Wankel-type rotary combustion engine. Final development of this idea came in the form of the refined **YO-3A** with retractable landing gear and a 210-hp (157-kW) Continental IO-360-D engine. A total of 14 was built, 13 of them being operated successfully in Vietnam for almost two years before the operating unit was deactivated in early 1972. The aircraft

The YO-3A was powered by an efficient 210-hp (157-kW) six-cylinder Continental IO-360.

were returned to the US, where several were used by Government agencies, including the FBI. Since the early 1980s NASA has also used a modified YO-3A as an airborne microphone platform in a helicopter rotor-blade research programme.

Lockheed S-3 Viking

For many years the **S-3 Viking** was the US Navy's carrierborne fixed-wing ASW aircraft. In 1998 however, the aircraft was withdrawn from this role, the surviving **S-3B** machines then being re-roled as land-attack and tanker aircraft. In the latter role, the aircraft may be redesignated as **KS-3B** aircraft. Designed to meet the US Navy's 1964 VSX (experimental carrier-based ASW aircraft) requirement, the first of eight **YS-3A** service-test aircraft made its maiden flight on 21 January 1972 at Palmdale, California. Conventional in design for a carrierborne warplane, the Viking is a high-wing, twin-turbofan aircraft with hydraulically folding outer wing panels and vertical tail surface, and provides pres-surised accommodation for its crew of four. Based on an August 1969 contract, Lockheed manufactured the Viking in partnership with Vought, which designed and built the wing, tail unit, landing gear and engine pods.

The heart of the Viking's ASW suite comprised the Texas Instruments ASQ-81 MAD (with its sensor carried in the tip of a retractable tailboom) and the OL-82 acoustic data-processing system and separate sonobuoy reference system. Weapons are carried in the ventral weapons bay and on two underwing hardpoints.

In July 1974 VS-21 'Fighting Redtails' became the first fleet squadron to operate the S-3A and

Lockheed built a total of 179 S-3As, delivering the last aircraft in August 1978.

The improved **S-3B** is the result of a weapons system improvement programme launched in 1981. This programme retained the basic airframe/ powerplant combination of the S-3A but added improved acoustic data-processing capability, introduced a new sonobuoy receiver system, expanded ESM coverage, increased radar processing capabili-ties, and added capability for the AGM-84 Harpoon anti-ship missile. Almost all surviving S-3As were upgraded to S-3B standard at naval air depots.

The seventh YS-3A was modified to become the **US-3A** carrier onboard delivery aircraft, a type that first flew on 2 July 1976 and was envisaged as a replacement for the C-1 Trader. In all, six US-3A aircraft have been used to complement C-2A Greyhounds. Lockheed also modified the fifth YS-3A to test the aircraft in **KS-3A** tanker form. This dedicated tanker variant was not produced, although opera-tional Viking ASW aircraft were frequently adapted as part-time tankers with the D-704 'buddy-buddy' refu-elling store.

During Desert Storm the S-3A/B Viking proved an exceedingly effective conventional bomber when employed against Iraqi radar stations, anti-aircraft batteries and other targets including small vessels in the Persian Gulf.

Several special mission

variants of the S-3B have seen service or develop-ment. The **Outlaw Viking** was modified with OASIS III equipment to provide over-the-horizon targeting as a theatre control plat-form. The **Gray Wolf** featured a Multi-Mode Radar System, a laser rangefinder, digital camera system and infra-red sensor to provide a littoral surveillance capability for the acquisition and tracking of 'Scud'-type missile launches. The **Viking Beartrap** had an Elint processing capability in addition to its normal suite, while the **Orca Viking** was used for the testing of advanced ASW systems. Orca is also believed to be able to detect minefields.

Several S-3Bs have been involved in anti-drug traf-ficking duties in the Caribbean, using camera systems, FLIR and hand-held sensors. The **Calypso Viking** is a proposed dedi-cated anti-smuggling variant with many of the Gray Wolf systems includ-ing ISAR, SAR, IRST and laser rangefinder. Finally, it was reported that under the codename Project Aladdin, so-called Brown Buoy aircraft were used to drop acoustic sensors to monitor ground move-ments in Bosnia in a process similar to the use of such sensors in the Igloo White programme during the Vietnam War.

More directly relevant to the USN's primary missions was the **ES-3A Viking**. This was devel-oped as a carrierborne Elint aircraft on the basis of the S-3A, revised with over-the-horizon surveillance equipment similar to that

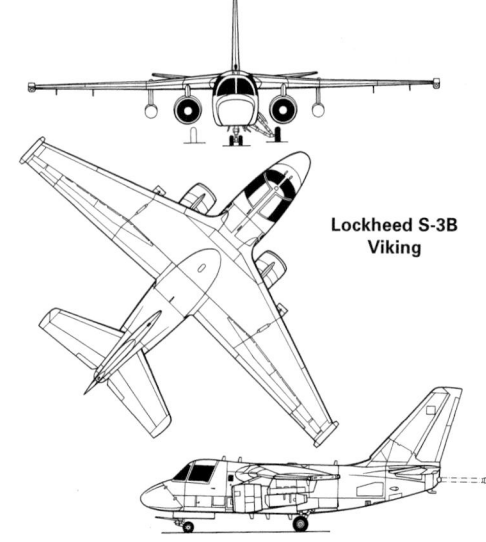

Lockheed S-3B Viking

fitted on the land-based EP-3E Aries II. The US Navy procured 16 ES-3As, which were converted by Lockheed at NAS Cecil Field, Florida. In the ES-3A the position of the co-pilot in the cockpit was adapted for a third sensor operator station, and the weapons bay was modified to accommodate avionics. The ES-3A introduced a new radome, direction-find-ing antenna and other equipment in a dorsal 'shoulder' on the fuselage, an array of seven receiving antennae on the underside of the fuselage, a cone-shaped omni-directional Elint antenna on each side of the fuselage just forward of the horizontal stabiliser, and antennae for

the ALR-76 ESM system forward and aft of the wing tips.

Two USN squadrons VQ-5 'Sea Shadows' and VQ-6 'Black Ravens' each deployed eight ES-3As on board carriers, generally in pairs.

Lockheed began the ES-3A programme with a 'proof of concept' aircraft lacking internal systems and, on 1 October 1990, began conversion of 15 ES-3As at Cecil Field. An ES-3A 'first flight' on 15 May 1991 involved the 16th aircraft, the sole production airframe modi-fied by Lockheed at Palmdale. For financial reasons the ES-3A force was retired in the late 1990s.

SPECIFICATION

Lockheed S-3A Viking
Type: four-crew carrierborne anti-submarine warplane
Powerplant: two General Electric TF34-GE-2 turbofan engines each rated at 9,275 lb st (41.26 kN)
Performance: maximum speed 506 mph (814 km/h) at sea level; initial climb rate more than 4,200 ft (1280 m) per minute; service ceiling more than 35,000 ft (10670 m); radius 530 miles (853 km) with typical weapons load and a loiter of 4 hours 30 minutes
Weights: empty 26,650 lb (12088 kg); maximum take-off 52,540 lb (23832 kg)
Dimensions: wingspan 68 ft 8 in (20.93 m); length 53 ft 4 in (16.26 m); height 22 ft 9 in (6.63 m); wing area 598.00 sq ft (55.56 m²)

Armament: up to 7,000 lb (3175 kg) of disposable stores carried in a lower-fuselage weapons bay and on two underwing hardpoints, and generally comprising one 10/20-kiloton B57 nuclear weapon, or four 1,000-lb (454-kg) Mk 83 free-fall bombs or Mk 53 mines, or two or four Mk 54 depth bombs, or four Mk 46 or Mk 53 Barracuda torpedoes carried internally, and up to six 500-lb (227-kg) Mk 82 free-fall or retarded bombs, or six Mk 20 Mod 2 'Rockeye' cluster bombs, or two or four LAU-10A/A, LAU-61/A, LAU-68/A or LAU-69/A multiple launchers for 5-in (127-mm) ZUNI and 2.75-in (70-mm) FFAR or Hydra 70 air-to-surface unguided rockets under the wing

Seen here over the Persian Gulf in 1992, this S-3B serves with VS-31 on board the USS John C Stennis. *An AGM-84A Harpoon air to surface missile is clearly visible on the starboard wing pylon.*

Lockheed A-12, YF-12 and SR-71 Blackbird

SR-71 64-17958 was first flown on 15 December 1965 and was used in July 1979 by Captain Eldon W. Joersz and RSO Major George T. Morgan, Jr. to establish a speed record over a 25-km (15½-mile) course of 2,193.167 mph (3529.464 km/h).

On 29 February 1964, President Johnson revealed that the USAF possessed a new high-speed high-altitude reconnaissance aircraft which he identified as the **A-11**. He claimed that it had been flown at speeds of more than 2,000 mph (3219 km/h) and to heights in excess of 70,000 ft (21335 m). In fact, the aircraft being referred to was the **A-12**, a single-seat reconnaissance aircraft that first flew on 30 April 1962. Some 15 A-12s were built and flown operationally by USAF and CIA pilots. Two machines were modified as **M-21** carriers for the D-21 drone, while one other A-12 was converted as a two-seat trainer. The aircraft was also the progenitor of the three ill-fated **YF-12A** interceptor prototypes that were evaluated by the USAF but resulted in no production warplanes.

However, 'Kelly' Johnson's plans to produce a two-seat reconnaissance/strike aircraft, based on the A-12, for the USAF eventually resulted in greater things. **R-12** reconnaissance and **RS-12**

reconnaissance/ strike mock ups were completed, the former being developed as the **SR-71 Blackbird** and the latter discontinued in favour of the XB-70 and FB-111A. Based closely on the A-12 and YF-12A, the **SR-71A** is fabricated largely of titanium to maintain the structural integrity of the airframe when subjected to kinetic heating: at speed in excess of Mach 3, for example, some structural components can reach temperatures of 572°F (3000°C). Because aerodynamic drag increases dramatically with speed, the slimmest possible fuselage and thinnest delta wing were adopted, together with integral lifting 'chines' for the forward fuselage to prevent the nose from pitching down as speed increases. Two

Right: NASA's Dryden Flight Research Centre operates two SR-71s for high-speed, high-altitude research. Here SR-71B NASA 831 slices across the Sierra Nevadas.

Pratt & Whitney J58 continuous-bleed turbojet engines form the heart of a complex propulsion system, these engines alone providing all of the low-speed thrust. However, at Mach 3 they produce only 18 per cent of the thrust, the remainder being generated by suction in the intakes and from special nozzles at the rear of the multiple-flow nacelles. Not surprisingly, fuel consumption is high, and these aircraft have inflight-refuelling capability.

SR-71As entered service in 1966, and by June 1968 the last of the A-12s had been retired. Two **SR-71B** dual-control trainers were built, the loss of one of these leading to the construction of one **SR-71C** trainer. Featuring the rear fuselage of a YF-12A, combined with the forward fuselage of a static test airframe, the SR-71C was unpopular and little flown. The 29 SR-71As built flew vital missions over all of the world's trouble spots both from their base at Beale in California and forward bases, principally at Kadena, Okinawa and

Mildenhall in the UK. Like the A-12, the aircraft were active during the Vietnam war, but by early 1990 they had been retired. In the wake of failures in intelligence gathering during Desert Storm however,

attempts were made to resurrect the SR-71 programme. These were finally abandoned in 1998, although NASA is likely to continue operations with an SR-71A and the SR-71B for some time to come.

Lockheed YF-12A

SPECIFICATION

Lockheed SR-71A Blackbird
Type: two-seat reconnaissance aircraft
Powerplant: two 32,500-lb (144.57 kN) thrust Pratt & Whitney J58 afterburning bleed turbojets
Performance: maximum speed Mach 3.35 at 80,000 ft (24385 m); maximum sustained cruising speed Mach 3.2 or about 2,100 mph (3380 km/h) at 80,000 ft (24385 m); operational ceiling 85,000 ft

(24385 m); maximum unrefuelled range at Mach 3 2,250 miles (5230 km)
Weights: empty 67,500 lb (30617 kg); maximum take-off 172,000 lb (78017 kg)
Dimensions: wingspan 55 ft 7 in (16.94 m); length 107 ft 5 in (32.74 in); height 18 ft 6 in (5.64 m), wing area 1,605 sq ft (149.10 m²)

Lockheed U-2

In July 1955 President Eisenhower proposed an 'Open Skies' policy under which both US and Soviet reconnaissance aircraft would be free to make unrestricted flights over each other's territory, thus reducing tensions and increasing mutual trust. This was rejected by the Soviet Union, but on

4 August 1955 Lockheed flew the first example of a remarkable new reconnaissance aircraft, the **U-2**, which had been designed and built under conditions of great secrecy in the company's 'Skunk Works'. It had remarkable high-flying and long-range performance and was powered by a Pratt &

Whitney J57 with a revised fuel system. The aircraft's high-aspect ratio glider-like wing allowed range to be extended by shutting down the engine to flight idle and gliding over long distances. Intended for operation at altitudes where detection and interception were unlikely, the U-2 bristled with data-gathering devices.

That the U-2 was detectable and vulnerable was demonstrated on 1 May 1960 when, during an overflight of the Soviet Union, the aircraft flown by the American Francis Gary Powers was knocked down by a SAM. That the U-2 was valuable was demonstrated in 1962 when these aircraft made discovered attempts to install ballistic missile sites in Cuba, and provided the foundation for the pressures which even-

Lockheed U-2R

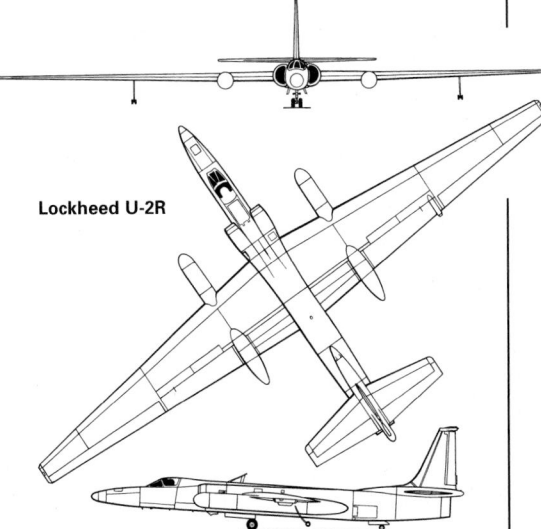

SPECIFICATION

Lockheed U-2R
Type: single-seat high-altitude reconnaissance aircraft
Powerplant: one Pratt & Whitney J75-P-13B turbojet engine rated at 17,000 lb st (75.62 kN)
Performance: maximum cruising speed more than 430 mph (692 km/h) at 70,000 ft (21335 m); climb to 65,000 ft (19810 m) in 35 minutes; operational ceiling

90,000 ft (27430 m); range about 6,250 miles (100580 km); endurance about 12 hours
Weights: empty about 15,500 lb (7031 kg); maximum take-off 41,300 lb (18733 kg)
Dimensions: wingspan 103 ft (31.39 m); length 62 ft 9 in (19.13 m); height 16 ft (4.88 m); wing area about 1,000.00 sq ft (92.90 m²)

tually ensured their removal.

As powered by the J57,

the first generation U-2s were airframe-limited, so Lockheed began the development of an enlarged aircraft to provide the ability to carry far greater sensor loads on the same power. The result was the **U-2R**, which first flew from Edwards North Base on 28 August 1967. At the same time as introducing fuel in a new 'wet wing', the new design also alleviated many of the aerodynamic flaws of the first generation, making the U-2R much less tricky to fly.

A first batch of 12 aircraft was completed, equally distributed between the USAF and the CIA. The former operated mostly in South-East Asia, while the latter operated from Taiwan over communist China. In 1974 the CIA aircraft passed to the USAF and joined a global reconnaissance effort that has been maintained ever since.

In November 1979, the U-2 production line reopened to provide 37 new airframes. The initiative for this was the **TR-1A** programme, which used the U-2R airframe as a platform for the ASARS-2 battlefield surveillance radar. The TR-1A was also seen as a platform for the PLSS radar location system, and for signals intelligence-gathering equipment as carried by the U-2R. However, the TR-1A force was progressively withdrawn as the Cold War threat diminished

U-2R 10331 was modified to carry Senior Span equipment for the transmission of recorded intelligence across global distances in near real-time. A large dorsal radome is associated with the system.

and the TR-1A designation was finally dropped in recognition of the fact that the TR-1A was virtually identical to the U-2R.

The new-build batch contained 25 TR-1As and seven U-2Rs created from the outset of the programme as attrition replacements. Three two-seat trainers were included in the batch, these comprising two **TR-1B** and one **U-2RT** machines: the three aircraft were essentially identical, and the TR-1B designation was later dropped in favour of U-2RT. Finally, two aircraft were completed to **ER-2** standard for use as earth resources monitoring aircraft by the NASA-Ames facility. These were later joined by a TR-1A handed over by the USAF.

Like the original U-2 series, the U-2R has a bicycle arrangement of retractable main landing gear units with ground stability provided by a pair of plug-in 'pogo' outrigger units that fall free on take-

off, leaving the aircraft to come to rest on one wing tip at the end of its landing run. The wing tips incorporate skids, above which are radar warning receivers.

The sensors are carried in the detachable nosecone (with different-shaped cones for different sensor fits), a large 'Q-bay' behind the cockpit for the carriage of large cameras, smaller bays along the lower fuselage and in two wing 'super pods', which are removable. These sensors include a wide range of recorders for Comint and Elint, imaging radars, radar locators and high-resolution cameras. Recorded intelligence can be transmitted via data-link to ground stations, and at least three aircraft are equipped to carry the Senior Span satellite communications antenna in a huge teardrop radome mounted on a dorsal pylon.

Missions vary according to requirements, but often reach 10 hours in duration. On approach, the U-2R pilot is aided by another pilot in a Ford Mustang chase car (the 'mobile') who provides landing instructions as the U-2R settles back to earth. Despite the aerodynamic refinements applied to the second-generation U-2, it remains a particularly tricky aircraft to land, being very prone to weather-cocking as a result of its central main landing gear arrangement and large vertical tail surface, and also very susceptible to float as a

Some 48 U-2A machines were contracted and this aircraft is one of a number of these that was actually delivered as a U-2B.

66701

U.S. AIR FORCE

Variants

U-2A: initial version for CIA and USAF with 10,500-lb (46.70-kN) J57-P-37 or 11,200-lb (49.80-kN) J57-P-37A turbojet
WU-2A: U-2A used for HASP (High Altitude Sampling Program) with a forward-facing scoop on the port side of the fuselage under the equipment bay
U-2B: improved production version with strengthened airframe, Pratt & Whitney J75-P-13 or J75-P-13B turbojet of 15,800-lb (70.27-kN) or 17,000-lb (75.60-kN) thrust respectively, and increased fuel capacity
U-2C: some new builds, some conversions with enlarged inlets for J75-P-13B, extended nose and dorsal canoe; most aircraft featured a 'sugar scoop' infra-red shield fitted to the jetpipe
U-2CT: two-seat conversion trainer; two produced with separate stepped cockpits
U-2D: U-2A conversions with 'Q-bay' modified to take second seat or more systems
U-2E: U-2A and U-2B conversions with advanced ECM fits for CIA work
U-2F: U-2A conversions with inflight-refuelling receptacle; two aircraft later featured 'ram's horn' Sigint antennae on rear fuselage for use over Vietnam
U-2G: two U-2Cs fitted with arrester hook and other modifications for carrier trials
U-2J: possible designation for CIA-operated carrier-capable aircraft
U-2N: possible early designation for U-2R
U-2EPX: proposed maritime surveillance for US Navy, two produced as conversions of U-2Rs; tested but not adopted by the US Navy
U-2R: redesigned and improved version of earlier production models, much larger, heavier, and with increased fuel capacity
TR-1A: single-seat developed version of the U-2R with more advanced avionics
TR-1B: two-seat trainer version with cockpits on the same level, later redesignated as **U-2RT**
ER-2: designation of two TR-1 aircraft for use by NASA as earth resources research aircraft

consequence of the very low wing loading and high idle speed of the engine.

While new sensors are continually being developed for the U-2R fleet, airframe modifications were limited until 1992, when Lockheed began to replace the J75 turbojet with the General Electric F101-GE-F29 turbofan. First flown in a TR-1A in March 1989, this engine is

derived from the F118 engine of the B-2, and is in the 18,500-lb st (82.29-kN) class. The F101 confers a 16 per cent increase in endurance, restores operational ceiling to a figure above 80,000 ft (24380 m) and improves supportability across USAF bases, the U-2R in its original form having been the last USAF aircraft to fly under J75 power.

Lockheed XFV-1

Under the designation **XFV-1**, Lockheed completed and flew the prototype of a single-seat VTOL fighter research aircraft. One of a number of tail-sitter designs to originate in the early 1950s, the XFV-1 was basically a conventional mid-wing monoplane without normal landing gear. Instead, the tail unit had equal span cruciform surfaces, each incorporating a shock-strut and castoring wheel, and the aircraft stood

vertically on its tail unit for take-off and landing. Unfortunately, the 7,100-shp (5294-kW) Allison YT40-A-14 turboprop that would have given it VTOL capability never materialised and the XFV-1 was tested only with take-offs and landings made on temporary conventional landing gear before the programme was cancelled in June 1955. Flight tests were carried out with a 5,850hp (4362-kW) XT40-A-6 turboprop.

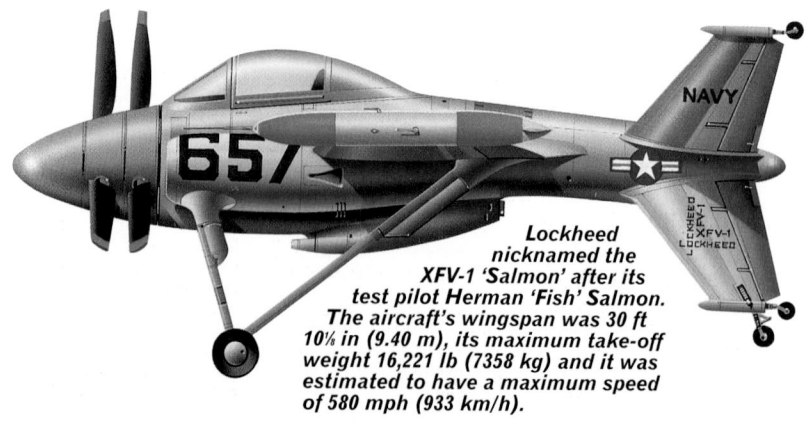

Lockheed nicknamed the XFV-1 'Salmon' after its test pilot Herman 'Fish' Salmon. The aircraft's wingspan was 30 ft 10⅛ in (9.40 m), its maximum take-off weight 16,221 lb (7358 kg) and it was estimated to have a maximum speed of 580 mph (933 km/h).

Lockheed XV-4 Hummingbird

Under the company designation **VZ-10**, Lockheed designed and developed two prototypes of a VTOL aircraft using turbojet engines to provide direct lift. The centre fuselage formed a giant ejector duct, more than doubling lift. The first of these was flown on 7 July 1962, but it was not until 20 November 1963 that a first successful flight involving transitions from vertical to horizontal flight, and vice versa, were completed. By then redesignated **XV-4A**, the two prototypes were handed over to the US Army for which they had been built under contract. In late 1966 Lockheed modified one of the XV-4As to a new **XV-4B** configuration, the major change being replacement of the XV-4A's two 3,000-lb (13.34-kN) thrust engines by four each of 3,015-lb (13.41-kN) thrust. Testing began in August 1968, but when the aircraft was destroyed in an accident in early 1969 further development was abandoned. Leading data for the XV-4B include a span of 27 ft 1 in (8.25 m), a maximum weight of 12,580 lb (5706 kg) and a speed of 463 mph (745 km/h).

Only limited testing of the XV-4B was carried out before a crash, combined with budgetary restraints on test programmes during the Vietnam War, brought the Hummingbird programme to an end.

Lockheed Martin F-16 Fighting Falcon

The **Lockheed Martin** (originally **General Dynamics**) **F-16 Fighting Falcon** was conceived as a lightweight air-combat fighter but has evolved into a versatile and effective multi-role workhorse. First flown on 20 January 1974, the service-test **YF-16** defeated Northrop's **YF-17** in a fly-off competition. The first of eight full-scale development **F-16A** airframes flew in 1975, followed in 1977 by the first example of the combat-capable **F-16B** two-seat version that retains the wing and fuselage dimensions of the single-seater while sacrificing 1,500 lb (680 kg) of fuel.

Nicknamed the **'Viper'**, the F-16 has its shock-inlet air intake located under the forward fuselage below the cockpit. The Fighting Falcon's unusual shape features wing/body blending and large leading-edge root extensions to enhance lift at high angles of attack. The aircraft is statically unstable with a fly-by-wire system for controllability, a zero/zero ejection seat angled back by 30° to improve average *g* tolerance, and a limited-movement side-stick controller in place of a conventional control column. The cockpit has HUD and multi-function displays as well as a one-piece frameless canopy with no windscreen: this gives an incomparable all-round view. Except for the ADF variants, all surviving F-16A/Bs have attack work as their primary duty, with air combat now secondary.

NATO's search for an F-104 replacement led in June 1975 to an agreement whereby Belgium, Denmark, the Netherlands and Norway selected the F-16A/B. SABCA in Belgium was responsible for the manufacture of 221 aircraft mainly for Belgium and Denmark, while Fokker in Holland built 300 aircraft primarily for the Netherlands and Norway. Some Dutch aircraft are equipped with a centreline tactical reconnaissance pod, and are designated **F-16A(R)**. Subsequent upgrades have brought improvements to F-16A/Bs on both continents, while other countries that have taken the F-16A/B into their inventories include Egypt, Indonesia, Israel, Portugal, Singapore, Taiwan, Thailand and Venezuela.

Delivery of production-standard F-16A/Bs to the USAF began in January 1979. Despite teething troubles with engine malfunctions and structural cracks, the F-16 developed into a superb multi-role fighter. The F-16A/B was built in distinct production blocks numbered 1, 5, 10, and 15. Some 21 F-16A and 22 F-16B Block 1 aircraft could be distinguished from later Fighting Falcons by their black radomes. The F-16A/B Block 5s were 99 F-16A and 27 F-16B aircraft, while the F-16A/B Block 10 machines were 145 F-16A and 25 F-16B machines, and all surviving aircraft of the earlier blocks were upgraded to the same standard. The following Block 15 standard introduced the first important changes to the F-16A/B, including an extended horizontal stabilator that is now standard. Because of wing cracks and afterburner problems, the USAF retired all of its pre-Block 15 aircraft in the early 1990s. Block 15 comprises 410 F-16A and 47 F-16B machines, 270 of which were chosen for conversion to the **F-16A/B ADF** standard that was ordained in 1986 with an upgraded APG-66 radar to improve small-target detection and provide continuous-wave illumination for the AIM-7 Sparrow AAM, advanced IFF, improved radio and provision for the AIM-120 AMRAAM. The aircraft were supplied to Air National Guard squadrons and also to Portugal.

The OCU (Operational Capabilities Upgrade) programme, adopted by Belgium, Denmark, the Netherlands and Norway, improves the avionics and fire-control systems, adds ring-laser INS and provides for the upgrading of the F100-PW-200 engine to F100-PW-220E standard. From 1988 exports were to Block 15 OCU standard, while surviving F-16A/Bs of the Air Force Reserve and ANG were upgraded with F100-PW-220E engines. Further improvements for the F-16A/B came with the European MLU (Mid-Life Update) which brings the cockpit to Block 50 standard with wide-angle HUD and night vision goggle compatibility. AIM-120 capability is also added and F-16 MLU aircraft are in service with Belgium, Denmark, the Netherlands and Norway. Belgium refers to its upgraded aircraft as **F-16AM** (single-seat) and **F-16BM**.

New avionics include a modular mission computer, APG-66(V)2A radar and Navstar GPS. The aircraft sold to Taiwan are to a similar standard, known as **Block 20**. USAF aircraft have adopted some of the MLU features.

First flown on 19 June 1984, the **F-16C** single-seater and its **F-16D** two-seat counterpart are distinguished by an enlarged base leading up to the vertical fin, the additional volume being intended for the internal ASPJ (Airborne Self-Protection Jammer) which the USAF abandoned in favour of continued use of external ECM pods. Compared with earlier versions, the F-16C/D gives the pilot a

The majority of Belgium's surviving F-16A and F-16B (illustrated) aircraft will be brought up to the MLU standard.

wide-angle HUD and an improved data display with key items of information located at eye level for HOTAS (Hands On Throttle And Stick) flying. The F-16C/D employs the considerably more capable APG-68 multi-mode radar possessing a weapons

Lockheed Martin F-16A Block 15 ADF Fighting Falcon

SPECIFICATION

Lockheed Martin F-16C Block 50 Fighting Falcon
Type: single-seat multi-role tactical warplane
Powerplant: one General Electric F110-GE-129 turbofan engine rated at 29,588 lb st (131.48 kN) with afterburning
Performance: maximum speed more than 1,321 mph (2125 km/h) or Mach 2.0 at 40,000 ft (12190 m); initial climb rate more than 50,000 ft (15240 m) per minute; service ceiling more than 50,000 ft (15240 m); radius 923 miles (1485 km) with two 2,000-lb (907-kg) bombs and two AIM-9 Sidewinder short-range AAMs
Weights: empty 18,917 lb (8581 kg); maximum take-off 27,099 lb (12292 kg)
Dimensions: wingspan 31 ft (9.45 m) without tip-mounted missiles; length 49 ft 4 in (15.03 m); height 16 ft 8½ in (5.09 m); wing area 300.00 sq ft (27.87 m²)
Armament: one 20-mm M61A1 Vulcan fixed forward-firing six-barrel rotary cannon, plus up to 15,591 lb (7072 kg) of disposable stores carried on one underfuselage, six underwing and two wing-tip hardpoints, and generally comprising a wide assortment of air-to-air and air-to-surface 'smart' and 'dumb' ordnance

interface for the AGM-65D Maverick and AMRAAM missiles. F-16C/Ds introduced progressive changes, some installed at the factory and others as part of the MSIP II and III (Multi-Stage Improvement Program nos 2 and 3) for enhanced night flying and fighting.

Block 25 aircraft entered production in July 1984 and totalled 289 F-16C and 30 F-16D machines. With **Blocks 30/32** and **Block 40/42** came the configured (formerly 'common') engine bay, with options in the Block 30 for the General Electric F110-GE-100 rated at 28,984 lb st (128.93 kN) or in the Block 32 for the F100-PW-220 rated at 23,840 lb st (106.05 kN). These engines required an enlargement of the air inlet, which was introduced after some early aircraft had been delivered. The introduction of the F100-PW-220 engine marked a maturing of the original F-16 powerplant:

while the improved P&W engine is not as powerful as the GE powerplant, it is lighter and more reliable. Block 30/32 aircraft also have the ability to carry AGM-45 Shrike and AGM-88A HARM anti-radiation missiles and the AIM-120 AAM. Avionics hardware changes were also introduced with Block 30/32, which totalled 446 F-16C and 55 F-16D aircraft, and a total of 22 and four such aircraft were ordered by the US Navy for use as adversary trainers with the designations **F-16N** and **TF-16N**. **Block 40/42 Night Falcon** warplanes came off the production line from December 1988 with features such as LANTIRN navigation and targeting pods, Navstar GPS navigation receiver, AGM-88B HARM II, APG-68(V) radar, digital flight controls, automatic terrain-following and, as a consequence, increased take-off weight.

In December 1991

General Dynamics began delivering **F-16C/D Block 50/52** aircraft with the APG-68(V)5 radar with improved memory and more modes, new NVG-compatible HUD, and improved avionics computer, ALE-47 chaff/flare dispenser, ALR-56M RWR, Have Quick IIA radio, Have Sync anti-jam VHF and full HARM integration. These latest F-16s are powered by the IPE (Improved Performance Engine) versions of two standard engines in the forms of the 29,588-lb st (131.48-kN) F110-GE-129 and 29,100-lb st (129.44-kN) F100-PW-229. About 100 USAF F-16C/D Block 50/52 aircraft have been raised to **Block 50/52D** standard with provision for the ASQ-213

HARM Targeting System pod carried under the starboard side of the intake to provide a Wild Weasel defence-suppression capability.

The latest development is the **Block 60/62** standard developed in response to a requirement of the United Arab Emirates with changes including agile beam radar, internal FLIR targeting system, an

advanced internal ECM system, an advanced cockpit, and conformal fuel tanks above the inner part of the wing on each side of the fuselage. Other than the USA, the F-16C/D customer list comprises Bahrain, Egypt, Greece, Israel (many with additional avionics in a bulged spine), Singapore, South Korea, Turkey and the United Arab Emirates.

As the primary USAF tactical warplane, the F-16 is provided with the latest weaponry. This F-16C is dropping a JDAM test round.

Lockheed Martin F-22 Raptor

In April 1991 the USAF announced that it had selected the Pratt & Whitney-powered version of what is now the **F-22 Raptor** in preference to the rival Northrop/McDonnell Douglas F-23 design to meet its ATF (Advanced Tactical Fighter) requirement for a successor to the F-15 Eagle. Issued in 1981, the ATF requirement called for a fighter combining low-observability or 'stealthy' design, the ability to 'supercruise' (cruise at supersonic speed without afterburning) over long ranges, a very high level of aerial agility and STOL capability with the aid of two-dimensional thrust vectoring of the engines' exhausts, a triplex fly-by-wire system for full control of an airframe characterised by negative static stability, and an advanced nav/attack system using artificial intel-

ligence factors to filter data and so reduce the pilot's workload while at the same time improving his/her grasp of the tactical situation.

Concept definition contracts were issued in September 1983 to Boeing, General Dynamics, Grumman, McDonnell Douglas, Northrop and Rockwell. Requests for proposals followed in September 1985, calling for submissions by the closing stages of July 1986, resulting on 31 October 1986 in the announcement that the two manufacturers selected to proceed to the demonstration and validation phases of the programme were Lockheed and Northrop. Each of these companies received a contract for two prototypes and a ground-based avionics test rig.

A parallel programme

was launched in September 1983 for the creation of two completely new turbofan engine types to power the ATF. These engines were the General Electric F120 and Pratt & Whitney F119, and ground testing of these engines began in 1986-7. Early in 1988 the US Department of Defense ordered the manufacture of flight-rated engines so that each engine type could be flight-tested in each of the two pairs of prototypes. In October 1989 the Department of Defense decided to extend the evaluation of the programme by six months, and by this time the two prime contractors had each established an industrial partnership for the engineering and manufacturing development stages of the programme. Lockheed teamed with Boeing and General Dynamics, but its acquisition of General Dynamics' Fort Worth-based fighter division then meant that Lockheed (from 1995 Lockheed Martin) had 67.50 per cent of the weapon system (airframe and avionics) programme.

Lockheed Martin F-22A Raptor

The first YF-22A prototype recorded the type's maiden flight on 29 September 1990 with YF120 engines, and was followed on 30 October 1991 by the second machine with YF119 engines. As the flight trials continued, the Department of Defense in November 1990 issued requests for

final engineering and manufacturing development proposals for the weapons systems and engines, leading to the final selection of the F-22 with the F119 engine. The resulting EMD contract issued in August 1991 called for 11 (later reduced to nine) F-22 development aircraft including two F-22B two-seaters.

Raptor testing was set to continue apace throughout 2001. This aircraft has just released an AIM-9 from its port weapons bay.

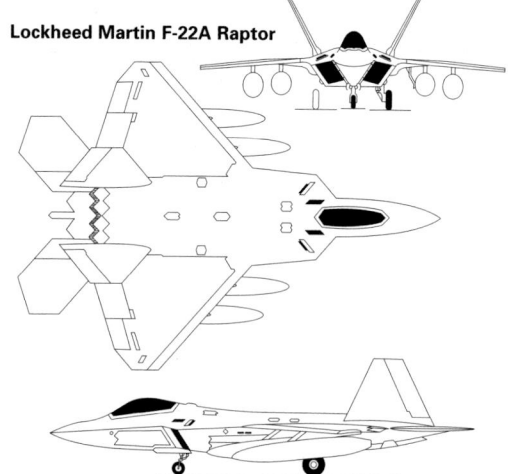

SPECIFICATION	

Lockheed Martin F-22A Raptor
Type: single-seat 'stealth' air dominance fighter
Powerplant: two Pratt & Whitney F119-P-100 turbofan engines each rated at about 35,000 lb st (155.69 kN) with afterburning
Performance: (estimated) maximum speed 1,157 mph (1862 km) or Mach 1.7 at 30,000 ft (9145 m) with afterburning and 1,042 mph (1677 km/h) or Mach 1.58 at 36,000 ft (10975 m) in 'supercruise' condition without afterburning; service ceiling 50,000 ft (15240 m)
Weights: (estimated) empty 31,670 lb (14365 kg); maximum take-off about 60,000 lb (27216 kg)
Dimensions: wingspan 44 ft 6 in (13.56 m); length 62 ft 1 in

(18.92 m); height 16 ft 5 in (5.00 m); wing area 840.00 sq ft (78.04 m²)
Armament: one 20-mm M61A2 Vulcan fixed forward-firing rotary six-barrel cannon, plus disposable stores carried in two lateral weapon bays and one lower-fuselage weapon bay (the lateral bays are designed to accommodate short-range AAMs such as the AIM-9 Sidewinder, while the larger lower-fuselage bay is intended for the carriage of medium-range weapons such as the AIM-120 AMRAAM in the form of four AIM-120A or six AIM-120C weapons) as well as on four underwing hardpoints for 20,000 lb (9072 kg) of other drop stores

Lockheed Martin F-22 Raptor (continued)

It was later decided that the two-seat machines would be completed as **F-22A** single-seaters.

Key features of the design are an angular but clean external shape with jagged edges on any portion that could reflect electro-magnetic energy back toward a hostile radar; an advanced structure, three internal weapons bays (one large centreline bay and two smaller lateral bays) that can be supplemented in the less stealthy attack mode by four high-capacity external hardpoints; and an avionics suite based on a computer system (linked by fibre-optical cables and operating on

the artificial intelligence principles of the Pilot's Associate system) offering three times the memory and 16 times the operating speed of the F-15's system. The core of the offensive avionics is provided by the APG-77 multi-mode radar with an AESA (Active Electronically Scanned Array) allowing interleaving of air-to-air search and multiple target tracking capabilities; this radar also possesses a weather/mapping mode and provision for air-to-surface modes and also for the addition of side arrays and, as a supplement to the radar, an infra-red search-and-track system.

Other elements of the avionics suite, include a data-link system, INS with embedded GPS for high-accuracy navigation, and advanced warning and countermeasures systems. The cockpit has a modified ACES II 'zero/zero' ejection seat for the pilot under a clear-view clamshell canopy, and the fused situational awareness information is presented to the pilot on four coloured liquid-crystal head-down displays and a Marconi wide-angle HUD.

The pilot controls the Raptor by means of a side-stick controller and a throttle, and the control surfaces include, on the

wing, full-span flaps on the leading edges and a virtually full-span combination of outboard ailerons and inboard flaperons on the trailing edges, slab taileron halves and two outward-canted fin-and-rudder units. These surfaces are complemented by the exhausts of the side-by-side pair of turbofan engines, which can be vectored ±20° in the vertical plane. As a result the F-22 is extremely agile and remains fully controllable up to very high angles of attack.

By the beginning of 2000 the available F-22 EMD aircraft had demonstrated excellent capabilities, but the cost of the programme

had also attracted the attentions of Congress at a time when the USA seems to be facing less in the way of high-technology threats.

The **F-22B** was planned but then cancelled as a combat-capable two-seat conversion and continuation trainer derivative of the F-22A.

By early 2001 the four available EMD aircraft had demonstrated the type's excellent capabilities. However, the US Congress recently called into question the value of such a costly, high-profile programme. Low-rate initial production of the F-22 was finally approved subject to compliance with stringent objectives.

Lockheed Martin X-35

Lockheed Martin's contender for the JSF (Joint Strike Fighter) programme is the **X-35**; from 1997 its development has been shared with

Northrop Grumman and BAE Systems. The generic X-35 has a configuration similar to that of the F-22. Key systems include a multi-function active, elec-

tronically-scanned array that combines radar, EW and communications functions and a conformal array imaging IR sensor. Data from the various sensors is fused on the pilot's advanced helmet-mounted display system. The initial layout of the X-35 was frozen in mid-1997 as **Configuration 220**, but further changes are being made before arriving at the definitive JSF design (**Configuration 230**). Three basic variants are proposed. The **X-35A** is the conventional land-based model for the USAF. The STOVL **X-35B** is being developed for the USMC, RAF and RN. Connected to the engine via a drive shaft, a Rolls-Royce lift fan behind the cockpit provides around half the thrust required for hovering flight. The lift fan

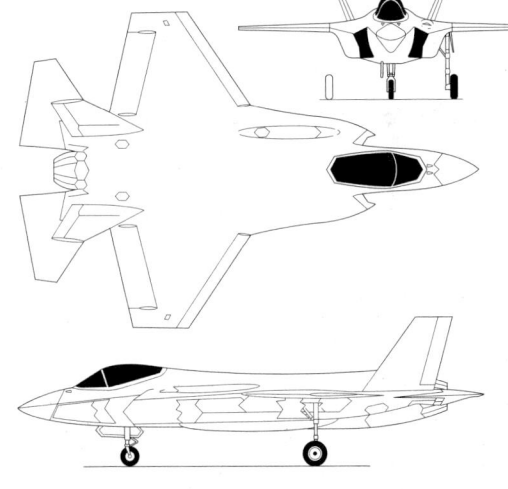

Lockheed Martin X-35

SPECIFICATION

**Lockheed Martin X-35
(provisional)**
Type: single-seat multi-role fighter
Origin: USA/UK
Powerplant: (X-32A/C) one Pratt & Whitney JSF119-PW-611 turbofan engine with axisymmetric (thrust vectoring) nozzle, rated at c.40,000 lb st (177.90 kN) with afterburning; (X-32B) one JSF119-611S turbofan engine rated at a total of 37,000 lb st (164.60 kN) for VTOL, comprising 18,000 lb st (80.10 kN) from the Rolls-Royce lift fan, 15,000 lb st (66.70 kN) from the main engine's Rolls-Royce swivel-duct nozzle and

a combined 4,000 lb st (17.80 kN) from the two reaction control valves in the wingroots.
Dimensions: wing span 33 ft (10.05 m); length 50 ft 9 in (15.47 m); wing area 450 sq ft (41.81 m²), (220A/B) 540 sq ft (50.17 m²), (230A/B) 460 sq ft (42.70 m²), (230C) 620 sq ft (57.60 m²)
Armament: internal Boeing/Mauser 27-mm cannon; disposable stores (carried internally) include two AIM-120 AMRAAMs and 1,000-lb (454-kg) or 2,000-lb (907-kg) GBU-31/32 JDAM bombs

results in lower power settings, and cooler exhaust temperatures and velocities than would be the case using directly vectored thrust. The **X-35C** is the US Navy's carrier-based CTOL variant. This features a larger wing and control surfaces (fin and elevator) than the other JSF variants. It is fitted with ailerons, a strengthened landing gear, arrester hook and a reinforced airframe to absorb catapult launches and arrested landings. Both Royal Navy and US Navy X-35B/Cs will have folding wings. The first X-35A prototype was rolled out in June 2000 and made its

maiden flight on 24 October 2000. It was followed on 16 December 2000 by the first X-35C. The X-35B followed in spring 2001. US government down-select of a single contractor or contractor team for the EMD phase is set for autumn 2001, following flight testing which will conclude the same year. This testing continued into early 2001, with the X-35B beginning hover-pit trials at Palmdale, California on 22 February. In addition, the X-35C demonstrator for the US Navy carried out carrier suitability trials at Patuxent River in February/March.

Uncertainty surrounds the JSF programme, although it seems unlikely that the entire project will now be cancelled. The final choice of airframe between X-32 and X-35 is likely to result in some form of work for both teams; the final decision may even involve the procurement of both designs to fill different roles.

Loening OA and OL

The most successful military design of the Loening company was the unusual **OL** amphibian first flown in 1923. In an attempt to produce a high- performance amphibian, its design was in effect that of a conventional two-seat biplane that was mounted on top of a large single

float, and stabilising floats were mounted beneath the tip of each lower wing.

The OL-8A was equipped for carrier operations, although this example is being launched from a land base. Note the wheeled undercarriage.

The wheeled gear for land operations comprised two mainwheels and a tailskid; when operating from water the mainwheels could be swung up clear of the waterline. Tandem open cockpits were provided for the crew, and the four **XCOA-1** prototypes ordered by the US Army were powered by the 400-hp (298-kW) Liberty V-1650-1 engine. When production ended a total of 165 additional aircraft had been built for service with the US Army Air Corps and USN. The USAAC's models were prefixed by OA and XO.

Variants

COA-1: three XCOA-1s following conversion to COA-1 production standard, plus nine additional production aircraft
OA-1A: 15 production aircraft, generally as COA-1, but with redesigned tail surfaces
OA-1B: nine production aircraft generally similar to OA-1A
OA-1C: 10 production aircraft, similar to OA-1B but with redesigned fin and rudder
XOA-1A: one prototype generally as OA-1A, but with a Wright V-1460-1 Tornado engine
OA-2: eight production aircraft, as OA-1C, but powered by the Wright V-1460-1 engine
XO-10: redesignation of XOA-1A following incorporation of experimental amphibian gear
OL-1: two aircraft generally similar to COA-1, but introducing a third cockpit in tandem and 440-hp (384-kW) Packard 1A-1500 engines; second aircraft incorporated a number of improvements

OL-2: five aircraft virtually identical to COA-1
OL-3: four aircraft identical to the second, improved OL-1
OL-4: six aircraft as OL-3, but with the Liberty V-1650-1 engine
OL-6: 28 aircraft as OL-3, but incorporating the fin and rudder introduced on the OA-1C
XOL-7: one OL-6 after the installation of new experimental wings
XOL-8: one OL-6 after experimental installation of a Pratt & Whitney Wasp radial engine
OL-8: 20 aircraft, basically as OL-3, but with only two cockpits and powered by the Wasp engine
OL-8A: 20 aircraft as OL-8, but with arrester gear for carrier operations
OL-9: 26 aircraft as OL-8, but produced after Loening had merged with Keystone Aircraft Corporation
XHL-1: two aircraft, similar to OL-8, but with the fuselage modified for use in an ambulance role, with a single open cockpit and seating six patients in the fuselage

Lohner aircraft

Lohner built the C.I from the outset as an armed reconnaissance aircraft.

The Austro-Hungarian company Jacob Lohner Werke und Co., which was established in Vienna, began the construction before World War I of a two-seat biplane intended for service as an unarmed reconnaissance aircraft. Built in a series of improving **Lohner B** types until 1917, they were powered by engines in the 85- to 160-hp (63- to 119-kW) range produced primarily by Austro-Daimler, but also by other manufacturers. An armed version was devel-

oped as the **C.I** and this, powered by a 160-hp (119-kW) Austro-Daimler, had a single machine-gun for operation by the observer in the rear cockpit. Far more important, however, were the flying-boats developed by the company for maritime patrol and reconnaissance, for although not built in very large numbers, they had an important influence on the development of Italian flying-boats. The Macchi L.1 of 1915, of which about 140 were built, was based

on a captured **Lohner L**, and progressive refinement of this design can be seen in the Macchi 'boats of World War I. Lohner's first flying-boat to enter production was the **E**, with biplane wings, a single-step wooden hull, and the tail unit carried on struts well above the level of the rear hull. It was powered by an 85-hp (63-kW) Hiero engine in pusher configuration, and about 40 were built. The major production version,

with something over 100 built, was the **L** of generally similar configuration but with a more powerful engine by Austro-Daimler.

Other variants of this design included the photo-reconnaissance **Lohner R** and the **Type S** unarmed trainer.

Loire 43,45 and 46

In March 1939 all surviving Loire 46s were transferred for use by the Cazaux gunnery school and by other flying schools. This machine served into early 1940 at Cazaux.

SPECIFICATION	
Loire 46	4,630 lb (2100 kg)
Type: single-seat fighter	**Dimensions:** wingspan 38 ft 9¾ in
Powerplant: one 900-hp (671-kW)	(11.83 m); length 25 ft 10¼ in
Gnome-Rhône 14Kfs radial piston	(7.88 m); height 13 ft 6½ in
engine	(4.13 m); wing area 209.90 sq ft
Performance: maximum speed	(19.50 m²)
242 mph (390 km/h); service ceiling	**Armament:** four 0.295-in (7.5-mm)
38,550 ft (11750 m); range	MAC machine-guns in the wings,
466 miles (750 km)	plus provision for underfuselage
Weights: empty equipped 2,998 lb	bomb racks
(1360 kg); maximum take-off	

The prototype **Loire 43** single-seat fighter flew on 17 October 1932. Of all-metal construction with stressed skinning and a high gull wing, the Loire 43 used the 690-hp (515-kW) Hispano-Suiza 12Xbrs V-12 engine specified by the French air ministry for all 10 competitors in the then current single-seat fighter competition. The **Loire 43.01** first prototype was lost in a crash on 14 January 1933, but by

then a development, the **Loire 45.01**, had been completed. It differed by having a 740-hp (552-kW) Gnome-Rhône 14Kds radial engine, as well as some structural refinement, and was first flown on 20 February 1933. Later re-engined with a 900-hp (671-kW) Gnome-Rhône 14Kfs radial, the Loire 45.01 then demonstrated a maximum speed of 230 mph (370 km/h). Subsequent

modifications included raising the wing at the root and lowering the engine slightly to improve visibility for the pilot. Further redesign of the wing, landing gear and tailplane led to the **Loire 46.01**, flown for the first time on 1 September

1934. An order for 60 series aircraft was received in spring 1935, and these incorporated further improvements and introduced a radio transmitter/receiver. Loire 46 series aircraft nos 2 to 6 inclusive were delivered clandestinely to the

Spanish Republican government in September 1936 and fought briefly against Franco's forces, but within a few months two were lost in accidents and two were shot down. Deliveries to the Armée de l'Air began in November 1936.

Loire 130

Built to meet a 1933 requirement of the French navy for an all-purpose shipboard catapult-launched three-seat seaplane, the prototype **Loire 130** high-wing

monoplane flying-boat flew for the first time on 19 November 1934. Persistent stability problems delayed development and it was not until August 1936 that an initial production order was placed for two versions, the **Loire 130M (Metropole)** and

Loire 130C (Colonie), the latter being strengthened and equipped for use in tropical climates. Power was provided by a Hispano- Suiza engine mounted on struts over the hull.
 The Loire 130 did not reach French navy

escadrilles until 1938. By 1939 it equipped Escadrille 7S2 aboard the seaplane carrier *Commandant Teste* and 7S3 and 7S4 embarked on various capital ships and cruisers. Overseas the Loire 130 was with 8S2 at Fort-de-France, French Antilles; 8S3 in West

Africa, and 8S4 in the Levant (now Lebanon). In 1939-40 the type went on to equip several newly formed shore-based and shipborne units and also equipped Armée de l'Air units, including 1/CBS in French Indo-China (now Vietnam).

Loire 130 (continued)

Not all the Loire 130s on order had been completed by the time of the June 1940 armistice with the Germans, but permission was given for 30 more of the type to be built under the auspices of the Vichy regime. It is believed that overall nearly 150 examples of this efficient aircraft were delivered, performing a range of duties which included reconnaissance, observation and ranging for naval guns, coastal patrol and convoy escort, as well as liaison work. In this last capacity the Loire 130 could carry up to three passengers in addition to the normal crew.

From November 1942 all catapults were removed from French ships, the Loire 130s thenceforth being shore-based. The last Loire 130 in flying condition, with Escadrille 8.S in Indo-China, was withdrawn and scrapped in late 1949.

SPECIFICATION	
Loire 130	7,487 lb (3396 kg)
Type: three-seat general purpose flying-boat	**Dimensions:** wingspan 52 ft 6 in (16.00 m); length 37 ft 1 in (11.30 m); height 12 ft 7½ in (3.85 m); wing area 431.65 sq ft (40.10 m²)
Powerplant: one 720-hp (537-kW) Hispano-Suiza 12Xbrs-1 V-12 piston engine	
Performance: maximum speed 140 mph (226 km/h) at 9,185 ft (2800 m); service ceiling 19,685 ft (6000 m); range 684 miles (1100 km)	**Armament:** two 0.295-in (7.5-mm) Darne machine-guns, plus two 165-lb (75-kg) SM anti-submarine grenades or two G-2 bombs of the same weight attached to bomb racks on the sides of the forward hull
Weights: empty equipped 4,608 lb (2090 kg); maximum take-off	

Loires's 130, seen here in prototype form, was optimised for ease of stowage aboard ship and included a complex wing-folding system.

Loire-Nieuport 40 series

The single-seat **Loire-Nieuport 40** prototype dive-bomber made its first flight in June 1938. An inverted gull-wing monoplane developed from the **Nieuport 140**, it was intended for shipboard use and had folding wings. The main landing gear units retracted into underwing nacelles, and the lower half of the rudder divided vertically so that it opened in two segments which acted as dive brakes. The 496-lb (225-kg) bomb was carried beneath the fuselage on a crutch which swung forward to ensure the weapon cleared the propeller when released in a dive. Official tests brought tail unit modifications, and elimination of the tail dive-brakes in favour of using the extended landing gear as a braking device. Six more **L.N.40** warplanes were ordered, but by the time of delivery a further 36 had been requested by the French navy and the production version been redesignated **L.N.401**. In the same year, 1939, the Armée de l'Air ordered 40 **L.N.411** aircraft, which differed only by deletion of the wing folding and other specialised naval equipment.

Four pre-production L.N.401s flew with Escadrille AC.1 of the Aéronavale for training in mid-1939, and production aircraft entered service with Escadrilles AB.2 and AB.4. The Armée de l'Air relinquished its L.N.411s in favour of the navy, and aircraft of this type re-equipped Escadrille AB.4 in April 1940. Between 10 May and 4 June virtually all available dive-bombers of this type were expended in attacks on the advancing German armies in northern France. The remnants were transferred to Hyères in the south where, issued with some replacement aircraft from reserves, they carried out reconnaissance and naval escort duties against the Italians, making a night attack on 18 June on naval vessels in Imperia harbour. Surviving aircraft were flown to North Africa on 25 June, where they were subsequently put into store.

A total of 24 L.N.401s and 411s was assembled from components by SNCASO at Chateauroux by March 1942. The aircraft were then flown to Hyères, where 12 were seized by Axis forces in November 1942. The remainder had been taken to Bizerta-Karouba, where they were subsequently lost, along with earlier stored machines, in Allied air raids. Total production of both versions is believed to have slightly exceeded 100.

The **L.N.402** was a one-off variant with a more powerful Hispano-Suiza 12Y-31 engine, and the **L.N.42** had a new wing of shorter span and a 1,100-hp (820-kW) Hispano-Suiza 12Y-51 engine. It had not made a proper test flight before being hidden from the occupying German forces, and finally flew at Toussus-le-Noble on 24 August 1945, only to be scrapped in 1947.

SPECIFICATION	
Loire-Nieuport L.N.401	6,224 lb (2823 kg)
Type: single-seat shipboard dive-bomber	**Dimensions:** wingspan 45 ft 11¼ in (14.00 m); length 31 ft 11¾ in (9.75 m); height 11 ft 5¾ in (3.50 m); wing area 266.42 sq ft (24.75 m²)
Powerplant: one 690-hp (515-kW) Hispano-Suiza 12Xers V-12 piston engine	
Performance: maximum speed 236 mph (380 km/h); service ceiling 31,170 ft (9500 m); range 746 miles (1200 km)	**Armament:** one engine-mounted 20-mm cannon and two wing-mounted 0.295-in (7.5-mm) machine-guns, plus a maximum bombload of 496 lb (225 kg)
Weights: empty equipped 4,707 lb (2135 kg); maximum take-off	

Aéronavale L.N.401s suffered near-100 per cent attrition rates while operating in the face of intense German AAA fire during the Blitzkrieg of early 1940.

Luscombe Phantom, Luscombe 4 and Luscombe 8

Don A. Luscombe formed the Luscombe Aircraft Engineering Company at Kansas City, Missouri, during 1933. First product of this company was the **Phantom**, a sleek and expensive braced high-wing monoplane of all-metal basic structure with fixed tailwheel landing gear. It had a luxury interior with two side-by-side seats, and was powered by a 145-hp (108-kW) Warner Super Scarab radial engine that provided a maximum speed of 168 mph (270 km/h). High cost and high performance combined to limit Phantom production to about 25 aircraft, but the company had foreseen this situation and in 1938 introduced the **Luscombe 4** (**Model 90**). This was of generally similar configuration to the Phantom, but had been designed specifically for cheaper construction and was powered by a 90-hp (67-kW) Warner Scarab Junior engine. Despite its lower price bracket, the Luscombe 4 failed to generate sales interest, total production being limited to less than 10 aircraft.

Fortunately for Luscombe, there was one other design in the pipeline, the **Luscombe 8** (**Model 50**), which was to be the most significant aircraft developed by the company. Retaining similar overall configuration and dimensions to the earlier designs, the two-seat Luscombe 8 was considerably lighter and had been developed in parallel with the Luscombe 4. However, it had been designed to be powered by a new Continental engine, the 50-hp (37kW) A-50, and had to wait until this became available. In consequence it was not certificated until mid-August 1938, but within a very short time there was a growing waiting list of indi-

SPECIFICATION	
Luscombe Model 8-E	16,000 ft (4875 m); range 510 miles (821 km)
Type: two-seat sport/touring aircraft	**Weights:** empty 810 lb (367 kg); maximum take-off 1,400 lb (635 kg)
Powerplant: one 85-hp (63-kW) Continental C-85 flat-four piston engine	**Dimensions:** wingspan 35 ft (10.67 m); length 20 ft (6.10 m); height 6 ft 3 in (1.91 m); wing area 140 sq ft (13.01 m²)
Performance: maximum speed 122 mph (196 km/h); service ceiling	

An exotic machine offering high-performance for experienced pilots, the excellent Phantom won few orders thanks to its high price.

Generally similar to the 8-C Silvaire deLuxe, the 8-D Silvaire Trainer also introduced an engine starter, mainwheel brakes and a steerable tailwheel.

Aircraft Corporation. Temco produced about 50 of these aircraft before disposing of the manufacturing rights to a newly-formed Silvaire Aircraft Company which continued production until running into financial difficulties in 1961. By that time production of all versions of the Luscombe 8 was estimated to total some 6,000 aircraft and, not surprisingly, large numbers of these aircraft are in use in 2001.

viduals and flying schools waiting to get their hands on one of these aircraft. Production continued until 1942, was resumed after the end of World War II, and in 1949 the company was acquired by Temco

Variants

Luscombe 8-A: version of the Luscombe 8 powered by a 65-hp (48-kW) Continental A-65 engine
Luscombe 8-B Trainer: version intended as a dedicated trainer; more austere interior finish and more economical 65-hp (48-kW) Avco Lycoming 0-145-B engine
Luscombe 8-C Silvaire deLuxe: first of the popular Silvaire range, powered by a 75-hp (56-kW) Continental A-75 engine
Luscombe 8-D Silvaire Trainer: generally as Luscombe 8-B but with the Continental A-75 engine
Luscombe 8-E Silvaire deLuxe: generally as Luscombe 8-C but with an 85-hp (63-kW) Continental C-85 engine
Luscombe 8-F Silvaire 90: final production version, as built also by Silvaire Aircraft Company, with a 90-hp (67-kW) Continental C-90 engine
Luscombe T8-F Observer 90: prototype of tandem two-seat development of Luscombe 8-F which it was hoped would find military application as an observation/reconnaissance aircraft

Luscombe Model 11A Sedan

Retaining the braced high-wing and fixed tail-wheel landing gear that had characterised the range of Luscombe aircraft, the **Model 11A Sedan** had an entirely new fuselage to seat four passengers. First flown in November 1946, there was an extensive delay before certification was gained, on 18 May 1948, and although the Sedan generated a good deal of interest only about 60 were built, a few of these produced by Temco during its short ownership of the company. Some of these aircraft remain in use.

SPECIFICATION	
Luscombe Model 11A Sedan	(805 km)
Type: four-seat cabin monoplane	**Weights:** empty 1,280 lb (581 kg);
Powerplant: one 165-hp (123-kW)	maximum take-off 2,280 lb
Continental E-165 flat-six piston	(1034 kg)
engine	**Dimensions:** wingspan 38 ft
Performance: cruising speed	(11.58 m); length 23 ft 6 in
130 mph (209 km/h); service ceiling	(7.16 m); height 6 ft 10 in (2.08 m);
17,000 ft (5180 m); range 500 miles	wing area 165.0 sq ft (15.33 m²)

Sedan production ceased in 1949, but an abortive attempt to reintroduce the type was made by Alpha Aviation of Greenville, Texas in 1970.

L.V.G. B.I, B.II and B.III

Established at Johannisthal airfield, Berlin, some years before World War I, Luftverkehrs GmbH (L.V.G.) was involved with the operation of dirigibles before turning to the construction of heavier-than air craft, then building Farman types under licence. The company's first original design was started in 1912, an unequal-span two-seat biplane with fixed tailskid landing gear, which was powered originally by a Mercedes D.I inline engine. Designated **L.V.G. B.I**, the type was built in small numbers, but with the outbreak of World War I it soon entered production for the German military aviation service. Operational use showed the desirability of some

The B.II proved to be a type of great utility in second-line service.

SPECIFICATION	
L.V.G. B.I	**Weights:** empty 1,600 lb (726 kg);
Type: two-seat reconnaissance/	maximum take-off 2,370 lb
scout/training aircraft	(1075 kg)
Powerplant: one 100-hp (75-kW)	**Dimensions:** wingspan 39 ft 9¼ in
Mercedes D.I inline piston engine	(12.12 m); length 27 ft 2¾ in
Performance: maximum speed	(8.30 m); height 9 ft 8¼ in (2.95 m);
65 mph (105 km/h); endurance	wing area 381.05 sq ft (35.40 m²)
4 hours	

improvements, these including the provision of a cut-out in the upper wing to improve the view of the pilot, seated in the rear cockpit, and introduction of a 120-hp (89-kW) Mercedes D.II engine. Then designated **B.II**, this version was built by the parent company and under sub-contract by Otto-Werke GmbH and Luftfahrzeugbau Schütte-Lanz. Entering service in 1915 the B.II was used primarily for training, but was also deployed in unarmed reconnaissance and scouting roles. The final variant was the **B.III**, intended specifically for training, and incorporating some structural strengthening for this purpose.

L.V.G. C.I and C.II

When the German air force needed an armed recon-naissance aircraft in 1915, L.V.G. responded with the **C.I**. This was basically a strengthened version of the B.I/II, with the pilot's and observer's positions reversed, so that the rear cockpit could be given a ring mounting for a machine-gun. Because of the increase in weight the more powerful 150-hp (112-kW) Benz Bz.III engine was installed, but only a small number of C.Is was built before introduction of the **C.II**, the major production version. This differed by introducing structural refinements and the more powerful Mercedes D.III engine, the first of the type entering service in late 1915. It is believed that about 300 C.I/C.II aircraft were built for use in a variety of roles, including light bombing.

Superficially very similar to the B.II, the C.II was a more powerful warplane.

Variants

C.III: single experimental aircraft, which was basically a C.II with the observer and his machine-gun accommodated in the forward cockpit
C.IV: basically a slightly enlarged version of the C.II powered by a 220-hp (164-kW) Mercedes D.IV engine; believed produced in small numbers

SPECIFICATION	
L.V.G. C.II	(1405 kg)
Type: two-seat reconnaissance/	**Dimensions:** wingspan 42 ft 2 in
light bombing aircraft	(12.85 m); length 26 ft 7 in
Powerplant: one 160-hp (119-kW)	(8.10 m); height 9 ft 7¼ in (2.93 m);
Mercedes D.III inline piston engine	wing area 404.74 sq ft (37.60 m²)
Performance: maximum speed	**Armament:** one 7.92-mm (0.31-in)
81 mph (130 km/h); service ceiling	Parabellum machine-gun and (late
13,125 ft (4000 m); endurance	production aircraft) one forward-
4 hours	firing 0.31-in (7.92-mm) LMG 08/15
Weights: empty 1,863 lb (845 kg);	machine-gun plus up to 132 lb
maximum take-off 3,097 lb	(60 kg) of light bombs

L.W.S 4 and L.W.S. 6 Zubr

Prior to the formation of L.W.S., Zbyslaz Ciolkosz had been in the design department of Państwowe Zakłady Lotnicze (P.Z.L.) and was involved in the development of a new civil transport designated **P.Z.L. 30**. From this same basic concept he evolved in late 1933 the design of a medium bomber, the **P.Z.L. 30/I**, but when tested in early 1936, then powered by two 406-hp (303-kW) Pratt & Whitney Wasp engines, its performance was found to be disappointing, although the aircraft handled well. It was decided to install more powerful engines,

P.Z.L.-built Pegasus VIII radials of 680 hp (507 kW), the aircraft to be designated **P.Z.L. 30B** in this form. But almost simultaneously with this decision came formation of L.W.S., and it was proposed that the new company should continue development of this bomber under the designation **L.W.S. 4**.

Despite the installation of engines of almost 70 per cent more power, no structural strengthening was introduced, and when gaps began to appear in the wing structure they were merely patched. A redesigned version appeared, but the effects

of strengthening had increased the empty weight to a point where, once again, performance suffered. An improved **L.W.S. 6 Zubr** (bison), with a revised twin fin/rudder tail unit, was built and tested, but the 14 production aircraft delivered to the Polish air force in early 1939 were of L.W.S. 4 configuration. Still overweight, and most of them with the main landing gear units locked down because the electric motors of the retraction mechanism were underpowered, they saw virtually no service at the outbreak of war. Some

During testing in late 1937, the rampant structural problems of the L.W.S. 4 inevitably led the aircraft to disintegrate in the air, killing the entire crew.

Variant

L.W.S. 5: twin-float development of the LM.S. 4, offered to the Polish navy but not ordered

were destroyed on the ground and the remainder

were captured by the invading Germans.

Macchi L.1 and L.2

Shortly after Italy entered World War I, an Austrian Lohner flying-boat was captured intact off the naval air station of Porto Corsini in the Adriatic. Since the Italians had no aircraft to match the Austrian 'boats this Lohner was copied by Macchi-Nieuport and emerged as the **Macchi L.1** within a space of just over one month! A three-bay single-step flying-boat of unequal- span biplane configuration, the L.1 shared the pusher-engine layout and two-man crew in side-by-side cockpits which had been features of the Austrian type, but had a generally improved structure.

Some 14 L.1s were delivered to Italian Adriatic-based maritime reconnais-

Despite their generally improved performance compared to the L.I, only 10 L.2s (illustrated) were built, the type being quickly superseded by the L.3.

sance and bombing units. Powered by a 150-hp (112-kW) Isotta Fraschini V.4A engine, the L.1 had a maximum speed of 68 mph (110 km/h) and a range of 239 miles (385 km). Armament comprised a single Fiat light

machine-gun on a trainable mounting, plus four light bombs. One machine was tested with a 40-mm gun for anti-submarine attacks.

In an attempt to improve overall performance, Macchi engineers produced

the **L.2** in 1916. This had slightly reduced wingspan and was powered by a 160-hp (119-kW) V.4B engine. Considerable efforts

were made to lighten the structure and as a result maximum speed was increased to 87 mph (140 km/h).

Macchi L.3

Developed in 1916 by the Macchi seaplane division at Schiranna under the direction of Felice Buzio, the **L.3**

was a two/three-seat single-step flying-boat, which had unequal-span biplane wings developed from those of the L.2, but with a hull and tailplane of entirely new design. The

hull had much improved lines and the tailplane, strut-mounted above the hull, was to become a characteristic of Macchi flying-boats.

In 1917 the original L.3 designation was changed to **M.3** in recognition of the difference in concept from the original Lohner-inspired Macchi machines. Some 200 M.3s were built and used in the Adriatic for a wide variety of missions

One M.3 gained a world altitude record for seaplanes, established over Lake Varese during 1916, by climbing to 17,717 ft (5400 m) in 41 minutes.

including bombing, reconnaissance, patrol and escort; the type was even used as a fighter until the appearance of the **M.5** single-seater in 1917; several M.3s participated in commando-style raids behind the Austrian lines. The M.3s were held in high esteem by the Italian navy. They made many bombing raids on the naval bases of Pola and Cattaro and pioneered aerial photography with frequent missions over these bases and Trieste.

Post-war the type remained in service with training units until 1924. A number were sold to the

Swiss company Ad Astra Aero and were converted to take two passengers on charter flights and joy rides from the Swiss lakes. The passengers were seated side-by-side behind a large windscreen, with the pilot in a raised, open cockpit behind them.

Powered by an Isotta-Fraschini V.4B engine of 160-hp (119-kW), the M.3 had a maximum speed of 90 mph (145 km/h) and a range of 280 miles (450 km). Armament comprised a trainable 7.7-mm (0.303-in) Fiat machine-gun or a light cannon; four light bombs could also be carried.

Macchi M.5

Developed by engineers Buzio and Calzavara, the prototype of this single-seat sesquiplane fighter flying-boat, known simply as the **Type M**, flew in early 1917. It had a slim single-step hull

with the pilot's cockpit just forward of the wings, with faired stabilising floats attached directly to the underside of the lower wing, and the tailplane was strut-mounted above the hull, as on the M.3. The second and slightly improved prototype was

designated **Ma**, and versions which incorporated a new fin and rudder attached directly to the hull, and with control wires for the rudder and elevator carried within the hull, were known as the **M bis** or Ma II°. The final prototype was the **Ma bis**. Series

Macchi M.5 aircraft were powered by the same Isotta-Fraschini V.4B engine as the prototypes, mounted in a pusher configuration, and first deliveries to the Aviazione per la Regia Marina (Italian Navy Aviation) were made in the summer of 1917.

Production totalled 244, 200 by Macchi and 44 by the Societá Aeronautica Italiana at Naples. Late production aircraft had redesigned wingtip floats and an improved cowling for the engine. A development, known as the **M.5 mod**, had the more powerful

Isotta-Fraschini V.6 engine of 250 hp (186 kW), providing a maximum speed of 127 mph (205 km/h), and about 100 were built.

The M.5s equipped a number of Squadriglie and some were embarked on the seaplane carrier *Giuseppe Miraglia*. When

the Regia Aeronautica was formed in 1923, 66 M.5s were still in service, but all had been scrapped within the following two years. In combat the M.5 proved manoeuvrable and effective, and was fully comparable with most contemporary landplane single-seaters. As

well as normal fighting duties, it was used for convoy escort and photographic reconnaissance.

The M.5 was flown by some US Navy and US Marine Corps pilots in the Adriatic and can lay claim to being the most famous World War I aircraft of Italian design, rivalling the Caproni bombers.

SPECIFICATION

Macchi M.5
Type: single-seat fighter-flying boat
Powerplant: one 160-hp (119-kW) Isotta-Fraschini V.4B inline piston engine
Performance: maximum speed 117 mph (189 km/h); service ceiling 20,340 ft (6200 m); endurance 3 hours 40 minutes
Weights: empty equipped 1,587 lb (720 kg); maximum take-off

2,183 lb (990 kg)
Dimensions: wingspan 39 ft ½ in (11.90 m); length 26 ft 6 in (8.08 m); height 9 ft 4¼ in (2.85 m); wing area 301.40 sq ft (28.00 m²)
Armament: two fixed forward-firing 0.303-in (7.7-mm) Vickers machine-guns; prototypes and a few early production aircraft had one centrally-mounted forward-firing Vickers gun

Macchi M.7

The original version of the **M.7** appeared in 1918, and although it was generally similar to the M.5 mod it was powered by a different engine, the 250-hp (186-kW) Isotta-Fraschini V.6, and had a modified hull. However, the end of World War I led to a curtailment of orders and only 17

were delivered, three before the end of hostilities. In 1919 Sweden and Argentina each bought two M.7s and two years later Brazil obtained three.

The M.7 was designed by Alessandro Tonini, who went on to produce the **M.7bis** racing version in 1920; generally lightened and with reduced-span wings, it took part in the evaluation trials that were

held before the 1921 Schneider Trophy contest at Venice. Of the many aircraft participating no less than five were M.7s of various versions, but the contest proper was won by the M.7bis piloted by Giovanni di Briganti. An M.7bis also took part in the 1922 competition.

The prototype **M.7ter** made its maiden flight in October 1923, this being virtually a new design with a hull of radically different form and with revised wing configuration. The planform was different, and total area was reduced. The tailplane was also

redesigned and introduced a basic steel-tube structure. Three versions of the M.7ter were built. The **M.7ter AR**, which followed the original model, had folding wings and operated from the seaplane-carrier *Miraglia*; the **M.7ter b** was powered by a 480-hp (358-kW) Lorraine 12Db engine; and the SAI company converted 14 machines to take the 250-hp (186-kW) Isotta-Fraschini Asso 200 (or Semi-Asso) in 1927.

In 1924 six squadriglie di caccia marittima converted to the M.7ter. By 1930, however, only one Squadriglia was equipped with the aircraft, and this was the Semi-Asso-powered version. A number were also in civilian use, equipping the Passignano flying school run by the SAI company. Portorose and several other seaplane training stations were still flying examples of the M.7ter as late as 1940.

In all, over 100 M.7ter aircraft were completed and records indicate that 83 of the type were in first-line service in 1927, including 29 of the specialised naval AR version.

SPECIFICATION

Macchi M.7ter
Type: single-seat fighter flying-boat
Powerplant: one 260-hp (194-kW) Isotta-Fraschini V.6 inline piston engine
Performance: maximum speed 124 mph (200 km/h); service ceiling 22,965 ft (7000 m); endurance 3 hours

Weights: empty equipped 1,775 lb (805 kg); maximum take-off 2,421 lb (1098 kg)
Dimensions: wingspan 32 ft 7¾ in (9.95 m); length 26 ft 6½ in (8.09 m); height 9 ft 9 in (2.97 m); wing area 252.96 sq ft (23.50 m²)
Armament: two fixed forward-firing 7.7-mm (0.303-in) Vickers machine-guns in the bow

Macchi M.8

Towards the end of 1917 Macchi produced a new reconnaissance/bomber flying-boat, the **M.8**, which introduced a new form of rigid wing bracing developed by the firm's design team. This comprised three pairs of parallel inclined struts on each side, an arrangement which was to be a feature of Macchi biplanes for the next decade. The hull was

further refined by comparison with that of the M.3 and the tailplane was similar in general design to that of the M.7. The pilot and co-pilot were accommodated in side-by-side open cockpits parallel with the wing leading edge, and a third cockpit was situated forward of them with a gun ring for a 7.7-mm (0.303-in) machine-gun; there was internal access in the hull between the single and twin cockpits. In total 57 M.8s were built in 1917-8,

these being used operationally for coastal reconnaissance and in action against enemy submarines in the Adriatic. Several were flown by US Navy crews, and post-war a number of surviving M.8s were used at seaplane flying schools.

Although the M.8 had the same 170-hp (127-kW) Isotta-Fraschini V.4B engine as the M.3, the improved design raised maximum speed by 14 mph (22 km/h) to 104 mph (167 km/h).

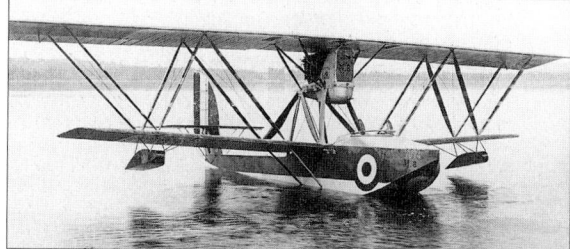

Spanning 52 ft 6 in (16.00 m), the M.8 had a maximum take-off weight of 3,153 lb (1430 kg), and an offensive load of four 110-lb (50-kg) bombs could be carried.

Macchi M.18

Intended as a three-passenger civil flying-boat, the first **M.18** was finally completed as a reconnaissance-bomber. Resembling a refined earlier **M.9** which had been built in limited numbers for a similar military role, the M.18 had open side-by-side cockpits for a pilot and co-

pilot/observer in the hull, just forward of the wings, with a single large windscreen. A third cockpit in the bows had a ring mounting for a defensive 0.303-in (7.7-mm) Vickers machine-gun.

The first military version had an Isotta-Fraschini V.4B engine, while later

production machines had the V.6 and then the Asso, also built by Isotta-Fraschini, with the Asso-powered M.18 appearing in 1928. A shipboard variant with folding wings was known as the **M.18 AR**.

Reverting to its original intended role, the civil M.18 appeared in the **M.18 Economico** version with the V.4B engine and two

passengers in open cockpits; the **M.18 Lusso** (luxury) variant with a V.6 engine of greater power and three passengers in an enclosed cabin; and the **M.18 Estivo** (literally summertime) with three passengers in open cockpits. In all over 70 civil M.18s were built, almost all going on to the Italian civil register. Some went to private owners, others to

pleasure-flight operators, such as the Swiss Ad Astra Aero company, while SISA flew a dozen machines as trainers for its airlines in the Adriatic.

The military M.18 was no less popular. The M.18 AR was flown from the Italian seaplane-carrier *Miraglia*, and other M.18s equipped the squadriglie della ricognizione marittima for many years.

Macchi M.18 (continued)

Some M.18s were built as trainers for the Italian air arm and in the early 1930s were joined by former reconnaissance. About 20 M.18s were sold to Spain in 1923, some of the AR version being operated from the seaplane carrier *Dedalo* and used against rebel tribesmen in Morocco. Six M.18s were still in service at the outbreak of the Spanish Civil War, and these were pressed into service initially to attack Nationalist troops invading Majorca, and were later used for reconnaissance patrols. Portugal bought eight M.18s in 1928.

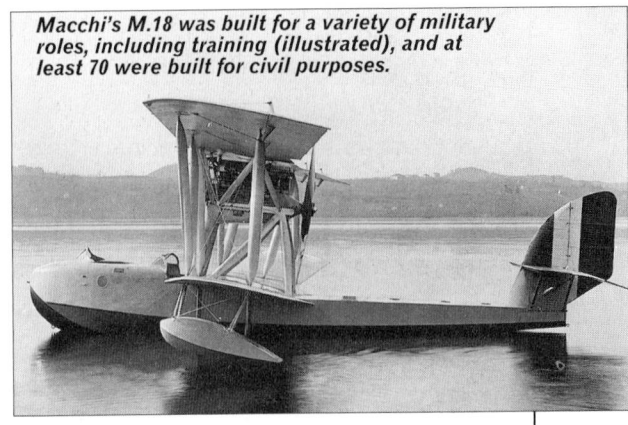
Macchi's M.18 was built for a variety of military roles, including training (illustrated), and at least 70 were built for civil purposes.

SPECIFICATION	
Macchi M.18	
Type: three-seat bomber/ reconnaissance flying-boat	**Weights:** empty equipped 2,811 lb (1275 kg); maximum take-off 3,935 lb (1785 kg)
Powerplant: one 250-hp (186-kW) Isotta-Fraschini Asso inline piston engine	**Dimensions:** wingspan 51 ft 10 in (15.80 m); length 31 ft 11¾ in (9.75 m); height 10 ft 8 in (3.25 m); wing area 484.39 sq ft (45.00 m²)
Performance: maximum speed 116 mph (187 km/h); service ceiling 18,045 ft (5500 m); range 621 miles (1000 km)	**Armament:** one 0.303-in (7.7-mm) Vickers machine-gun, plus four light bombs on underwing racks

Macchi M.24

The **M.24** was largely of metal construction with a two-step hull and sesquiplane wings. Its two 300-hp (224-kW) Fiat A.12bis engines, mounted in tandem to drive one tractor and one pusher propeller, were carried over the hull on an elaborate system of struts.

The M.24 was a military boat with bow and dorsal gunners' cockpits and the ability to carry a powerful bomb load. Two examples made a tour of northern Europe in 1925, from Varese to Copenhagen and then Leningrad, and back over the Alps, and the type was used later in torpedo-launching experiments.

The **M.24bis** of 1926, also a military version, had increased lower wing span and area so that it became an equal-span biplane, and also had a slightly modified hull. Power was provided by two 400-hp (298-kW) Lorraine or two 500-hp (373-kW) Isotta-Fraschini Asso engines. The M.24bis civil variant of 1927 had a cabin in the forward hull for eight passengers and side-by-side cockpits just forward of the lower wing leading edge for a pilot and co-pilot. Examples were used by such companies as Società Anonima Aero Espresso Italiana and SITA on routes connecting Italian ports and on Mediterranean routes. A civil M.24bis was reported with Bristol Jupiter engines.

The **M.24ter** was a military design which reverted to the sesquiplane formula, had 510-hp (380-kW) Asso engines, rounded wingtips and reduced wing area. The various versions of the M.24 saw widespread use with Italian naval flying-boat units and a number were sold abroad, several being used for a period by the Spanish navy.

SPECIFICATION	
Macchi M.24ter	
Type: three-seat bombing/ reconnaissance flying-boat	(3730 kg); maximum take-off 12,125 lb (5500 kg)
Powerplant: two 510-hp (380-kW) Isotta-Fraschini Asso V-12 piston engines	**Dimensions:** wingspan 72 ft 2¼ in (22 m); length 48 ft (14.63 m); height 15 ft 3 in (4.65 m); wing area 1,130.25 sq ft (105 m²)
Performance: maximum speed 115 mph (185 km/h); service ceiling 13,125 ft (4000 m); range 435 miles (700 km)	**Armament:** two 0.303-in (7.7-mm) Vickers machine-guns, one each in bow and midships positions, plus 1,764 lb (800 kg) of bombs or one torpedo
Weights: empty equipped 8,223 lb	

Construction of the M.24 flying-boat prototype began in 1923, the first flight taking place the following year.

Macchi M.39

The first low-wing monoplane designed by Castoldi for the Macchi company, the **M.39** twin-float racing seaplane was built within a few months and the first example, intended as a trainer and powered by a 600-hp (447-kW) Fiat A.S.2 engine, made its maiden flight on 6 July 1926. The M.39 was of mixed construction with a wire-braced wing. The pilot was seated in an open cockpit parallel with the wing trailing edge, his windscreen being profiled into the fuselage decking. Intended to compete in the 1926 Schneider Trophy contest at Hampton Roads, Virginia, the type was carefully tailored to the requirements of the race. The distance from fuselage to port wingtip was slightly greater than that on the other side to improve tight turns on the course's left-handed circuits, and the floats, which also contained fuel, had unequal buoyancy to counteract propeller torque reaction.

Two M.39 trainers were followed by three racers and one static-test airframe. An early setback occurred on 21 September 1926 when the Italian team captain stalled in an M.39 trainer and was killed when he crashed into Lake Varese. Nevertheless, development continued and

Wingspan of the racing M.39 was 30 ft 4½ in (9.26 m) and maximum take-off weight 3,472 lb (1575 kg).

despite engine carburettor problems the three racing aircraft, with their A.S.2 engines boosted to deliver 800 hp (597 kW), took part in the contest on 13 November 1926. Major Mario de Bernardi gained first place at an average of 246.497 mph (396.698 km/h), while Adriano Bacula was third. The other M.39 had to retire as a result of a burst oil pipe. On 17 November 1926, Mario de Bernardi flying an M.39 attained a world speed record of 258.875 mph (416.618 km/h) over a 3-km (1.86-mile) course.

Macchi M.41 and M.71

Developed in 1927 by Mario Castoldi, the **M.41** was a single-seat fighter flying-boat of biplane configuration with a beautifully streamlined hull, a tail unit of much improved lines and a simplified engine mounting with a contoured cowling. It was

Three M.41bis were delivered to Spain in summer 1936, later serving with the Franco forces on Majorca. The machine-guns of the M.41bis (illustrated) were mounted higher in the bow compared to the M.41.

two years before this prototype was followed by the **M.41bis** prototype. This differed only in detail, and had its two fixed machine-guns located higher in the bow section to avoid spray. Two batches of series M.41bis aircraft were ordered, totalling 41 aircraft, and

from 1931 to 1938 these formed the equipment of the 164° and 166° Squadriglie of the 88° Gruppo Autonomo di Caccia Marittima, based at Vigna di Valle on Lake Bracciano, near Rome.

The **M.71** prototype appeared in 1930, introducing a redesigned

system of wing bracing which enabled the wings to be dismantled rapidly for shipboard stowage, and the structure was also strengthened for the rigours of catapult launching. About a dozen were built, two serving aboard the Italian cruiser *Di Giussano*.

SPECIFICATION	
Macchi M.41bis	
Type: single-seat fighter flying-boat	(1107 kg); maximum take-off 3,389 lb (1537 kg)
Powerplant: one 410-hp (306-kW) Fiat A.20 V-12 piston engine	**Dimensions:** wingspan 36 ft 5¾ in (11.12 m); length 28 ft 5 in (8.66 m); height 10 ft 2¾ in (3.12 m); wing area 343.60 sq ft (31.92 m²)
Performance: maximum speed 158 mph (255 km/h); service ceiling 26,245 ft (8000 m) endurance 3 hours 20 minutes	**Armament:** two fixed forward-firing 0.303-in (7.7-mm) Vickers machine-guns
Weights: empty equipped 2,441 lb	

Macchi M.52

The triumph of his M.39 in the 1926 Schneider Trophy contest led Mario Castoldi to retain the same formula for the **M.52**, which was flown for the first time in early August 1927. Three M.52s were built, each powered by a new 1,000-hp (746-kW) Fiat A.S.3 engine.

Problems with the A.S.3 engines during the actual Schneider contest, held at Venice on 26 September 1927, led to all three aircraft retiring, the best effort that of Captain Federico Guazetti who

dropped out on the last lap of the course. Nevertheless, on 4 November the same year Mario de Bernardi established a new world speed record over a 3-km (1.86-mile) course at an average of 297.818 mph (479.290 km/h).

The sole **M.52R** or **M.52bis**, represented a restyling of the basic M.52 design, with wingspan reduced to 25 ft 9 in (7.85 m) and maximum take-off weight to 3,263 lb (1480 kg), and with the floats redesigned to

Compared to the M.39, the dimensions of the M.52 were slightly reduced, wingspan being 29 ft 5½ in (8.98 m) and length 23 ft 4½ in (7.14 m). Maximum take-off weight was reduced by 132 lb (60 kg).

improve streamlining. At Venice, on 30 March 1928, this aircraft was flown to a new world speed record by de Bernardi, who achieved an average of 318.625 mph (512.776 km/h).

The loss of one of the later and far less successful M.67 racers led to the M.52R participating in the

1929 Schneider Trophy contest at Calshot, where it gained an impressive second place after more fancied competitors had

dropped out. The pilot was Warrant Officer Tommaso Dal Mòlin, who maintained an average of 284.203 mph (457.380 km/h).

Macchi M.67

Work on the new Castoldi design for the 1929 Schneider Trophy contest at Calshot began at the end of 1928. Three **M.67** aircraft were built, first flights being made in early August 1929. By comparison with the M.52, the new design had a straight wing, a slimmer fuselage, and a remarkably powerful engine, the 1,800-hp (1342kW) Isotta-Fraschini 2-800 designed by Giustino Cattaneo. To resolve attendant cooling problems the wing surface cooling radiators were augmented by

The M.67 had the same wingspan as the M.52, was slightly longer at 25 ft 6 in (7.77 m), and the heavy engine increased maximum take-off weight to 4,806 lb (2180 kg). Estimated maximum speed was 363 mph (584 km/h).

additional coolant and oil radiators mounted flush in the lower nose surface and at each side of the rear fuselage. Subsequently, additional cooling surfaces were mounted on the float

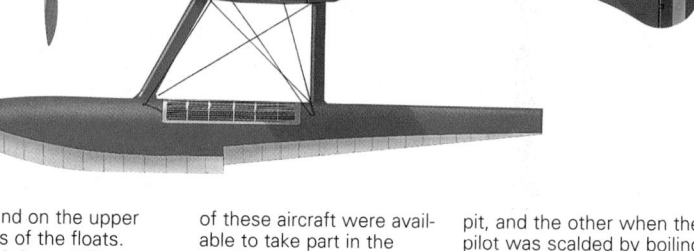

struts and on the upper surfaces of the floats.

On 22 August Giuseppe Motta flying an M.67 stalled and crashed into Lake Garda, thus only two

of these aircraft were available to take part in the Trophy race on 7 September. One was forced to retire from exhaust fumes in the cock-

pit, and the other when the pilot was scalded by boiling water from a fractured pipe in the complex cooling system, thus ending the racing career of the type.

Macchi M.C.72

With the **M.C.72** Mario Castoldi reached the pinnacle of his design career. Intended for the 1931 Schneider Trophy contest, the aircraft was tailored around the new Fiat A.S.6 engine, which comprised two 1,500-hp (1119-kW)

A.S.5 engines mounted in tandem on a common crankcase. In effect, each A.S.5 drove one of the contra-rotating propellers via a coaxial shaft, counter-rotating propellers eliminating the on-water torque problems which had

plagued high-powered seaplanes.

Compared with earlier Macchi floatplanes the fuselage shape of the M.C.72 was different, but the tail and wings attached to this slim fuselage were clearly a development of previous designs by Castoldi. The long twin metal floats were carried on four broad-chord struts which were covered with coolant radiators, the wing was covered with flat-tube surface radiators, there were additional radiators on the upper surface of the floats, and an oil cooler was fitted around the sides and undersurface of the rear fuselage, aft of the pilot's open cockpit.

The first of five M.C.72s flew from Desenzano on Lake Garda in June 1931. Troubles were experienced with the engine's carburetion system, but considering the remarkably short devel-

opment period significant progress had been made by 2 August, when Giovanni Monti met with disaster and was killed when his machine crashed into the lake. The problems with the M.C.72s could not be resolved in time for the 1931 Schneider contest and Italy did not participate. Nevertheless, development of the M.C.72 continued, despite the loss of a second machine during a record attempt, and finally the carburetion problems were overcome with the use of a specially blended fuel. On 10 April 1933 Warrant

Officer Agello established a world speed record over a 3-km (1.86-mile) course at an average of 423.825 mph (682.078 km/h), and the M.C.72 later established a world speed record over a 100-km (62.14-mile) course and gained the Coupe Louis Blériot in October 1933. Finally, the absolute speed record was raised to 440.683 mph (709.209 km/h) by Agello on 23 October 1934. This successful M.C.72 is preserved at the Aeronautica Militare Italiana museum at Vigna di Valle, near Rome.

An aircraft of extreme performance but over-complex engineering, the M.C.72 was perhaps the ultimate racing seaplane.

SPECIFICATION	
Macchi M.C.72	
Type: single-seat racing seaplane	(2500 kg); maximum take-off 6,669 lb (3025 kg)
Powerplant: one 2,850-hp (2125-kW) Fiat A.S.6 24-cylinder double V-12 piston engine	**Dimensions:** wingspan 31 ft ¼ in (9.48 m); length 27 ft 3¾ in (8.32 m); height 10 ft 10 in (3.30 m); wing area 161.46 sq ft (15 m²)
Performance: maximum speed 440 mph (708 km/h)	
Weights: empty equipped 5,512 lb	

Macchi M.C.94

Designed by Castoldi purely as a flying-boat, the prototype **M.C.94** passenger transport was given retractable landing gear at an early stage, but remained the only amphibian in the M.C.94 series, the 11 production machines being flying-boats. Construction was mainly of wood, with a cantilever high wing and two-step hull with single fin and rudder, and power was provided by two 770-hp (574-kW) Wright Cyclone SGR-1820-F52 radial engines. On the seventh production machine these

The wingspan of the M.C.94 was 74 ft 9¼ in (22.79 m) and maximum take-off weight 18,077 lb (8200 kg), maximum speed with the Alfa Romeo engines 181 mph (292 km/h), and range 926 miles (1490 km).

engines were replaced by 750-hp (559-kW) Alfa Romeo 126 RC 10s. The enclosed cabin for the three-man crew was set well forward, and the comfortable main cabin accommodated 12 passengers.

The M.C.94 went into

service on the Adriatic routes of the Ala Littoria airline from 1936 and a

number continued in operation during World War II. Three ex-Ala Littoria

M.C.94s were sold to a Buenos Aires-based airline in 1939.

Macchi M.C.200 Saetta

Following the end of Italy's military campaigns in East Africa a programme was initiated to re-equip the Regia Aeronautica, the **M.C.200 Saetta** (lightning) being designed by Mario

Castoldi to meet the requirement for a new single-seat fighter. First flown as a prototype on 24 December 1937, this was a cantilever low-wing monoplane mainly of metal

construction, with retractable tailwheel landing gear, an enclosed cockpit, and power provided by a Fiat A.74 RC 38 radial engine. Flight testing proved highly successful and the M.C.200 won the fighter contest held during 1938, being ordered into production with an initial contract for 99 aircraft. First production deliveries were made in October 1939, and by the time that Italy became involved in World War II in June 1940 about 150 had been accepted by the Regia Aeronautica; production eventually totalled 1,153, some 400 being built by Macchi and the remainder by Breda and SAI-Ambrosini. First used operationally as escort fighters in attacks on Malta in autumn 1940, Saettas saw service in Greece, North Africa and Yugoslavia. A number were involved in operations on the Eastern Front during 1941-2, and after the Italian armistice of September 1943, 23 Saettas were flown to Allied airfields in southern Italy, being used subsequently by pilots of the Italian Co-Belligerent Air Force.

The Saetta was a nimble but ultimately underarmed fighter, and suffered accordingly.

Variants

M.C.200 (prototypes): two aircraft with the 840-hp (626-kW) Fiat A.74 RC 38 engine
M.C.200: production version with uprated A.74 RC 38 engine; early, intermediate and late production had, respectively, enclosed, open and semi-enclosed cockpits
M.C.200AS: tropicalised version
M.C.200CB: fighter-bomber version with provisions for a maximum 705-lb (320-kg) bombload or two underwing auxiliary tanks
M.C.201: single prototype of developed version with revised fuselage and a 1,000-hp (746-kW) Fiat A.76 RC 40 engine; flown only with A.74 RC 38 engine and development abandoned in favour of M.C.202

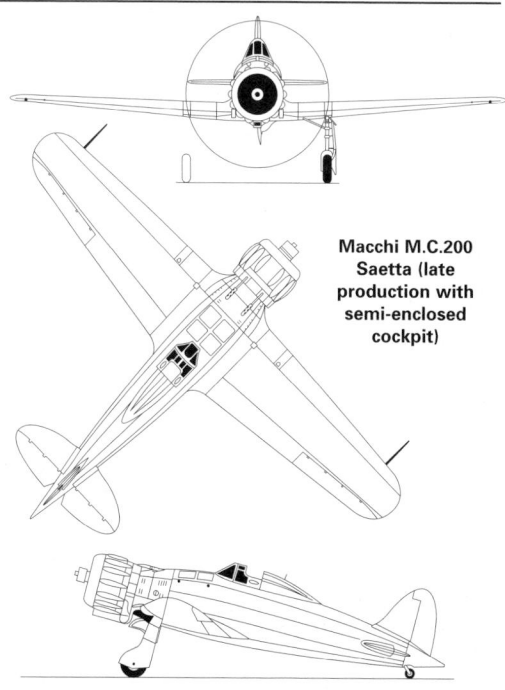

Macchi M.C.200 Saetta (late production with semi-enclosed cockpit)

SPECIFICATION	
Macchi M.C.200 Saetta	5,710 lb (2590 kg)
Type: single-seat interceptor fighter/fighter-bomber	**Dimensions:** wingspan 34 ft 8½ in (10.58 m); length 26 ft 10¼ in
Powerplant: one 870-hp (649-kW) Fiat A.74 RC 38 radial piston engine	(8.19 m); height 11 ft 5¾ in (3.50 m); wing area 180.84 sq ft (16.80 m²)
Performance: maximum speed 312 mph (502 km/h) at 14,765 ft (4500 m); service ceiling 29,200 ft (8900 m); range with auxiliary fuel 540 miles (870 km)	**Armament:** two 0.5-in (12.7-mm) forward-firing machine-guns in the engine cowling; some late production examples had two additional 0.303-in (7.7-mm) wing-mounted guns
Weights: empty 4,178 lb (1895 kg); maximum take-off	

Macchi M.C.202 Folgore

Castoldi was convinced that the full potential of the M.C.200 design could be achieved only with greater horsepower, and this was confirmed when the **M.C.202 Folgore** (thunderbolt) prototype flew for the first time on 10 August 1940, powered by an imported Daimler-Benz DB 601A engine. Ordered into production without delay, the M.C.202 had a new fuselage (incorporating an enclosed cockpit) to

accept the larger engine, but retained tail unit, landing gear, and generally

similar wings to the M.C.200. Produced by Macchi, Breda and

By late 1943, 368ª Squadriglia of 151° Gruppo had exchanged its Fiat G.50s for Macchi M.C.202s. The aircraft were flown from bases in Sicily.

SAI-Ambrosini alongside the M.C.200, early production aircraft were powered by imported DB 601A-1 engines until Alfa Romeo had a licence-built version available. Limited manufacture of this engine restricted the number of M.C.202s to about 1,500, 393 built by Macchi, which explains continued production of the M.C.200. Initial deliveries of production M.C.202s went to units in Libya from November 1941, and in September of the following year their deployment began on the Eastern Front. Only 12 Folgores could be spared for 21° Gruppo in the East however, the remaining M.C.202 force being desperately needed in the Mediterranean theatre, where the majority of the force was soon destroyed.

SPECIFICATION

Macchi M.C.202 Folgore
Type: single-seat interceptor fighter/fighter-bomber
Powerplant: one 1,175-hp (876-kW) Alfa Romeo RA.1000 RC 41-1 Monsone inverted V-12 piston engine
Performance: maximum speed 370 mph (595 km/h) at 16,405 ft (5000 m); service ceiling 37,730 ft (11500 m); range 475 miles (765 km)
Weights: empty 5,181 lb (2350 kg); maximum take-off

6,636 lb (3010 kg)
Dimensions: wingspan 34 ft 8½ in (10.58 m); length 29 ft ½ in (8.85 m); height 9 ft 11½ in (3.04 m); wing area 180,84 sq ft (16.80 m²)
Armament: initially two 0.5-in (12.7-mm) machine-guns in the engine cowling; later series added two 0.303-in (7.7-mm) wing-mounted guns; one batch had a 20-mm cannon beneath each wing

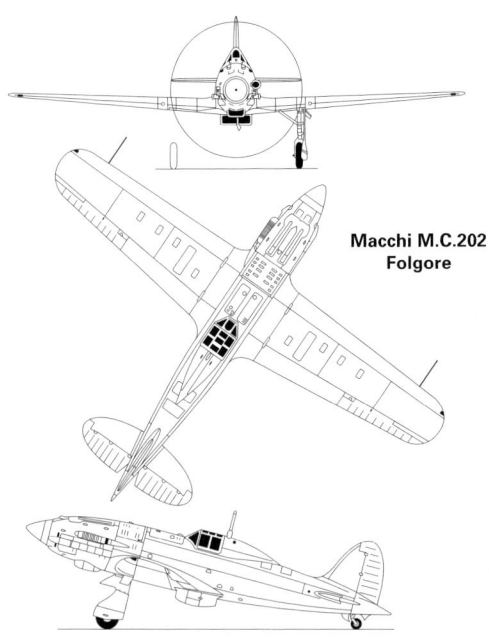

Macchi M.C.202 Folgore

Variants

M.C.202 (prototype): one only, basically a re-engined M.C.200 airframe which also introduced a retractable tailwheel
M.C.202AS: tropicalised version
M.C.202CB: fighter-bomber version with provision for up to 705-lb (320-kg) bombload or two auxiliary fuel tanks
M.C.202D: single experimental aircraft with revised radiator

Macchi M.C.205V Veltro

Fundamentally a developed version of the M.C.202, the **M.C.205V Veltro** (greyhound) prototype comprised a production M.C.202 airframe with an imported Daimler-Benz DB 605A engine of 1,475 hp (1100 kW). Flown for the first time on 19 April 1942, it was put into production immediately, but some delay resulted before Fiat's licence-built version of the Daimler-Benz engine,

Variants

M.C.205: single prototype with standard armament of late production M.C.202s, comprising two 0.5-in (12.7-mm) and two 0.303-in (7.7-mm) machine-guns
M.C.205V: production version, generally as prototype; late production had two 20-mm cannon in place of German MG 151 wing machine-guns; 262 built
M.C.205N-1: prototype of high-altitude interceptor version with increased-span wing and armament comprising one engine-mounted 20-mm cannon and four fuselage-mounted 0.5-in (12.7-mm) machine-guns
M.C.205N-2: alternative prototype of high-altitude version, differing only by having armament comprising three 20-mm cannon and two 0.5-in (12.7-mm) machine-guns
M.C.206: prototype of further developed version, not completed; would have had a further increase in wing span
M.C.207: prototype of further developed version, not completed; generally as M.C.206 but with armament of four wing-mounted 20-mm cannon

the RA.1050 RC 58 Tifone (typhoon), became available

in significant numbers. As a result the production M.C.205V Veltro did not become operational until mid-1943, its first known action occurring in early July when the type was deployed in support of torpedo-bombers attacking Allied naval forces off Sicily. Just two months later, when the Italian government made peace with the Allies, the Regia Aeronautica had a total of 66 Veltros. Of this total only six gained Allied airfields to serve with the Italian Co-Belligerent Air Force, the remainder being used by the Republican Socialist Italian air force. Production continued on a limited scale after the armistice and ultimately a total of 262 had been built;

With its powerful engine and especially when cannon-armed, the M.C.205V had the potential to take the air war to the Allies on near-equal terms. An 88ª Squadriglia, 1° Stormo machine is shown.

of this total a small number was used by the Luftwaffe, equipping one Gruppe. Regarded as the best Italian fighter aircraft of

World War II, the Veltro was capable of meeting such renowned fighters as the North American P-51D Mustang on equal terms.

SPECIFICATION

Macchi M.C.205V Veltro
Type: single-seat interceptor fighter/fighter-bomber
Powerplant: one 1,475-hp (1100-kW) Fiat RA.1050 RC 58 Tifone engine
Performance: maximum speed 399 mph (642 km/h) at 23,620 ft (7200 m); service ceiling 37,090 ft (16370 m); range 646 miles (1040 km)
Weights: empty 5,691 lb (2581 kg); maximum take-off

7,154 lb (3408 kg)
Dimensions: wingspan 34 ft 8½ in (10.58 m); length 29 ft ½ in (8.85 m); height 9 ft 11½ in (3.04 m); wing area 180.84 sq ft (16.80 m²)
Armament: two 0.5-in (12.7-mm) and two 0.303-in (7.7-mm) machine-guns; late production aircraft had two 20-mm cannon replacing the 0.303-in (7.7-mm) guns

Macchi M.B.308

Designed by Ermanno Bazzoechi, the **M.B.308** cantilever high-wing cabin monoplane first appeared in 1946. It accommodated a pilot and co-pilot side-by-side and had fixed tricycle landing gear. Built in quantity, it achieved considerable success at post-war sporting meetings and contests, but as well as its use by private owners, it was also flown as a trainer by Italian aero

clubs and by the Aeronautica Militare. For some 15 years it was one of the most widely used Italian aircraft.

Variants built included two-seaters with 85-hp (63-kW) Continental C85 piston engines, or 90-hp (67-kW) C90s; the M.B.308 three-seater, and the **M.B.308 Idro** twin-float seaplane. Licenced production of the M.B.308G was carried out in Argentina.

An extra cabin window in the fuselage of this machine identifies it as a three-seat M.B.308G.

Macchi Parasol

This renowned Italian aircraft manufacturer was founded at Varese in 1912 as Nieuport-Macchi SA, to build French Nieuport aircraft under licence. After early deliveries to the Italian army of the **Type 1913** monoplane or **Nieuport 10**, of which Macchi built 56, the company produced its first original design, the **Macchi Parasol**. A two-seat wire-braced monoplane

powered by a Gnome rotary engine, it was simple and robust, and a total of 42 were built. Used first in 1915 to equip one squadriglia, which was based at Pordenone in June and Medcuzza the following month, the Parasols were allocated also to the Italian 3rd Army. These took part in the siege of Gorizia, deployed on artillery observation and bombing duties, the latter

Macchi's classic Parasol spanned 42 ft 7¾ in (13.00 m), had a maximum loaded weight 1,455 lb (660 kg) and a maximum speed 78 mph (125 km/h).

accomplished with small hand-launched weapons.
The 6,560-ft (2000-m) ceiling of the Parasol rendered it vulnerable, and its flying qualities being generally poor, the type was withdrawn from service in November 1915 and scrapped.

Martin 2-0-2, 3-0-3 and 4-0-4

Attempting to gain a share of the post-World War II demand for civil airliners, the Glenn L. Martin Company flew on 22 November 1946 the prototype of a twin-engined 36/40-seat transport designated **Martin 2-0-2**. The

first of these entered service in October 1947, but the loss of a 2-0-2 in 1948 as a result of wing structural failure led to modification of other in-service aircraft and production of this version was brought to an end. The

Martin was unable to achieve with its 4-0-4 the success that Convair enjoyed with its piston twins, but the 4-0-4 nevertheless enjoyed healthy sales.

SPECIFICATION	
Martin 4-0-4	payload 1,080 miles (1738 km)
Type: short/medium-range transport	**Weights:** empty equipped 29,126 lb (13211 kg); maximum
Powerplant: two 2,400-hp (1790-kW) Pratt & Whitney R-2800-CB16 radial piston engines	take-off 44,900 lb (20366 kg) **Dimensions:** wingspan 93 ft 3 in (28.42 m); length 74 ft 7 in
Performance: maximum speed 312 mph (502 km/h) at 14,500 ft (4420 m); service ceiling 29,000 ft (8840 m); range with maximum	(22.73 m); height 28 ft 5 in (8.66 m); wing area 864 sq ft (80.27 in²)

prototype of an improved **Martin 3-0-3** had been flown on 20 June 1947, but with a need to redesign the wing structure it was decided instead to develop a new **Martin 4-0-4**. This incorporated the wing structural revisions and introduced a pressurised and slightly lengthened fuselage, accommodating as standard a crew of three or four and 40 passengers.

When production ended in early 1953 a total of 103 had been built, this number including two supplied to the Coast Guard as staff

transports under the designation **RM-1G** (later **RM-1Z** and finally **VC-3A**); they were subsequently transferred to the US Navy.

Martin AM-1 Mauler

During 1950 all surviving Maulers, including the AM-1 illustrated, were passed to the Navy Reserve, making way for the AD-1 Skyraider, an aircraft from a similar mould, in regular front-line units.

Benefiting from early combat experience in World War II, the US Navy drew up its specification for a new single-seat carrier-based attack aircraft. The **Martin Model 210** design proposal gained a contract for two **XBTM-1** prototypes, the first being flown initially on 26 August 1944. A cantilever low-wing monoplane with retractable tailwheel landing gear, powered by a 3,000-hp (2237-kW) Pratt & Whitney XR-4360-4 radial engine, the XBTM-1 was tested successfully and gained a contract for 750 **BTM-1** series aircraft. By the time that the first of these was flown, on 16 December 1946, the designation had been changed

to **AM-1** and the name **Mauler** selected; World War II had also ended, and instead of the planned procurement only 149 AM-1s (excluding prototypes) had been completed when production ended in October 1949. Carrier qualification trials were completed during 1946-47, allowing initial deliveries to

an active unit, Attack Squadron VA-17A, on 1 March 1948. These aircraft saw little first-line service however, being transferred to US Navy Reserve squadrons when production ended. The total of 149 Maulers built included 17 **AM-1Q** aircraft completed as radar countermeasures aircraft.

SPECIFICATION	
Martin AM-1 Mauler	(6577 kg); maximum take-off
Type: single-seat carrier-based attack aircraft	23,386 lb (10608 kg) **Dimensions:** wingspan 50 ft
Powerplant: one 2,975-hp (2218-kW) Wright R-3350-4 Cyclone 18 radial piston engine	(15.24 m); length 41 ft 2 in (12.55 m); height 16 ft 10 in (5.13 m); wing area 496 sq ft
Performance: maximum speed 367 mph (591 km/h); service ceiling 30,500 ft (9295 m); range 1,800 miles (2897 km)	(46.08 m²) **Armament:** four forward-firing 20-mm cannon, plus up to 4,500 lb (2041 kg) of assorted bombs and
Weights: empty 14,500 lb	rocket projectiles

Martin B-10, B-12 and B-14

Under the company designation **Model 123**, Martin began in the early 1930s the design of dramatically advanced conception of a bomber aircraft which it hoped would prove of interest to the US Army. A cantilever mid-wing monoplane with retractable tailwheel landing gear, and

powered by two 600-hp (448-kW) Wright SR-1820-E Cyclone engines, it accommodated a three-man crew. When tested officially in July 1932, under the experimental designation **XB-907**, it was found to have a maximum speed of 197 mph (317 km/h) at 6,000 ft (1830 m), which

was superior to that of fighter aircraft then in US Army Air Corps use. Before being ordered into production some changes were introduced, these including an increase in wingspan, the provision of a nose turret to mount a 0.3-in (7.62-mm) machine-gun, and the installation of

SPECIFICATION	
Martin B-10B	(4391 kg); maximum take-off
Type: three-seat medium bomber	16,400 lb (7439 kg)
Powerplant: two 775-hp (578-kW) Wright R-1820-33 Cyclone radial piston engines	**Dimensions:** wingspan 70 ft 6 in (21.49 m); length 44 ft 9 in (13.64 m); height 15 ft 5 in
Performance: maximum speed 213 mph (343 km/h) at optimum altitude; service ceiling 24,200 ft (7375 m); maximum range 1,240 miles (1996 km)	(4.70 m); wing area 678 sq ft (62.99 m²) **Armament:** three 0.3-in (7.62-mm) machine-guns in nose and rear turrets and a ventral position, plus
Weights: empty 9,681 lb	up to 2,260 lb (1025 kg) of bombs

Those B-10s flown by Dutch crews in the Netherlands East Indies were among the first US-built bombers to see operational use during World War II.

675-hp (503-kW) Wright R-1820-19 engines. Then redesignated **XB-907A**, official tests proved entirely satisfactory with the maximum speed increased by 10 mph (16 km/h), and the type was ordered into production on 17 January 1933. The XB-907A prototype was acquired by the US Army and given the designation **XB-10**.

Production aircraft began to enter service in June 1934, and in addition to conventional duties in the bomber role a number was operated for a time on large twin floats for coastal patrol. The type remained in USAAC service until the late 1930s and, in addition, was exported by Martin for use by the air arms of Argentina (35), China (9), the Netherlands (118), Siam (now Thailand) (23), Soviet Union (1), and Turkey (20).

Variants

YB-10: initial production version with 675-hp (503-kW) R-1820-25 engines and separate enclosed canopies for the pilot's and gunner/radio operator's cockpit; 14 built
B-10: two additional production aircraft, as YB-10
YB-10A: single prototype with two 675-hp (503-kW) R-1820-31 turbocharged engines
RB-10MA: USAAF designation of one export aircraft which escaped from the Netherlands East Indies in 1942 and was impressed for service
B-10B: major production version, as YB-10, but with more powerful R-1820-33 engines; 103 built
B-10M: redesignation of some B-10Bs converted for use as target tugs
YB-12: production version, as YB-10, but powered by 775-hp (578-kW) Pratt & Whitney R-1690-11 engines; 7 built
B-12A: production version as YB-12, but with provision

to carry an auxiliary fuel tank in the bomb bay for long-range ferry flights; 25 built
B-12AM: redesignation of some B-12As converted for use as target tugs
YB-13: designation of planned version of YB-10 with 700-hp (522-kW) Pratt & Whitney R-1860-17 Hornet engines; not built
XB-14: one aircraft, similar to YB-10, but powered by two 950-hp (708-kW) Pratt & Whitney R-1830-9 Twin Wasp engines
YO-45: temporary designation of one YB-10 with 675-hp (503-kW) R-1820-17 engines for evaluation in a high-speed reconnaissance role
Model 139: basic export model
Model 139WH-1/2: initial export models for Dutch East Indies; two separate canopies
Model 139WH-3/3A: follow-up export models for Dutch East Indies; one long 'glasshouse' canopy, otherwise known as **Model 166**

Martin B-26 Marauder

Designed to meet a demanding USAAC specification of 1939 for a high-speed medium bomber, the **Martin Model 179** proposal was considered to be so far in advance of competing submissions that in September 1939 the company was awarded an 'off the drawing board' contract for 201 of these aircraft. This action, unprecedented in USAAC history, required no prototype or preproduction aircraft, and the first production **B-26**, as the type was designated, was flown initially on

B-26B-55-MA Missouri Mule II flew with the 598th Bomb Squadron of the 397the Bomb Group from Dreux, France in 1944. Note the Olive Drab anti-glare panel ahead of the windscreen and that the upper fuselage invasion stripes have been over painted to make them less conspicuous.

25 November 1940. Subsequently named **Marauder**, the aircraft was a cantilever shoulder-wing monoplane with a roomy fuselage of circular cross-section accommodating a crew of five (later seven as operational conditions demanded), and with retractable tricycle landing gear.

SPECIFICATION	
Martin B-26G Marauder	38,200 lb (17327 kg)
Type: seven-seat medium bomber	**Dimensions:** wingspan 71 ft (21.64 m); length 56 ft 1 in (17.09 m); height 20 ft 4 in (6.20 m); wing area 658 sq ft (61.13 m²)
Powerplant: two 2,000-hp (1491-kW) Pratt & Whitney R-2800-43 Double Wasp radial piston engines	
Performance: maximum speed 283 mph (455 km/h) at 5,000 ft (1525 m); service ceiling 19,800 ft (6035 m); range 1,100 miles (1770 km)	**Armament:** eleven 0.5-in (12.7-mm) machine-guns (in fixed forward-firing, trainable nose and waist mounts, and in power-operated dorsal and tail turrets), plus up to 4,000 lb (1814 kg) of bombs
Weights: empty 25,300 lb (11476 kg); maximum take-off	

Variants

B-26: initial production version; 201 built
B-26A: generally as B-26, with 1,850-hp (1380-kW) R-2800-9 or -39 engines, provisions for increased fuel capacity and an externally-mounted torpedo, system revisions and heavier armament; 139 built
B-26B: improved and major production version, with 2,000-hp (1491-kW) R-2800-41 engines, armament revisions and increased armour protection; the 642nd and subsequent aircraft had a 6-ft (1.83-m) increase in wingspan, taller vertical tail surfaces and additional armament; 1,883 built
AT-23A (later TB-26B): redesignation of 208 B-26Bs following conversion in 1943 for use as target tugs/gunnery trainers
CB-26B: redesignation of a few B-26Bs following conversion for a transport role
B-26C: production version from separate production line at Omaha, Nebraska, generally as subvariants of B-26B and with R-2800-43 engines; 1,210 built
AT-23B (later TB-26Q): redesignation of 375 B-26Cs following conversion in 1943 for use as target tugs/gunnery trainers
XB-26D: experimental conversion of one B-26 to evaluate hot air de-icing of wing and tail unit leading edges
XB-26E: one-off experimental lighter-weight version, with the dorsal turret moved forward to a position just aft of the wing trailing edge
B-26F: production version, introducing 3° 30' increase in wing incidence to improve take-off performance, and equipment changes; 300 built
B-26G: production version generally as B-26F but with detail changes; 893 built
TB-26G: final production version of the B-26G for use in a crew training or target

towing role; 57 built, of which 47 were transferred to the US Navy under the designation **JM-2**
XB-26H: redesignation of one B-26G after conversion to test the landing gear configuration proposed for the B-47
JM-1: redesignation of 225 AT-23Bs following transfer to the US Navy
JM-1P: redesignation of a small number of JM-1s following conversion for use in a photo-reconnaissance role
JM-2: see TB-26G
Marauder Mk I: RAF designation of Lend-Lease B-26As
Marauder Mk IA: RAF designation of Lend-Lease B-26Bs
Marauder Mk II: RAF designation of Lend-Lease B-26Cs
Marauder Mk III: RAF designation of Lend-Lease B-26Fs and B-26Gs

Martin B-26 Marauder (continued)

The B-26 was powered by two 1,850-hp (1380-kW) Pratt & Whitney R-2800-5 Double Wasp radial engines. Official testing confirmed that the B-26 more than met the official specification, but this performance had been achieved at the expense of good low-speed handling characteristics. The **B-26A** which followed introduced improvements considered to be desirable from early squadron experience, but the resulting increase in gross weight only aggravated the low-speed handling problem. Training accidents multiplied and a board of investigation was set up to consider whether to end production; it decided, wisely as it proved, to introduce modifications to improve low-speed performance and to revise handling techniques. As a result the Marauder went on to record the lowest attrition rate of any American aircraft operated by the 9th AF in Europe.

Early deployment of the B-26 by the USAAF was confined to the Pacific theatre, but in November 1942 **B-26B** and **B-26C** aircraft began to appear in North Africa, equipping 12 squadrons of the 17th, 319th and 320th BGs of the US 12th AF. They provided admirable ground support to Allied ground forces in Corsica, Italy, Sardinia, Sicily and southern France, and Marauders used in a tactical role went from strength to strength in operations with the US 9th AF. Under Lend-Lease the RAF received a total of 522 Marauders, these also serving with the South African Air Force and being deployed most successfully alongside the B-26s of the 12th AF, after initial failure in a torpedo-carrying role.

Martin B-57 Canberra

Martin was selected in 1950 to undertake licence production of the English Electric Canberra, the first aircraft of foreign design to enter operational deployment with the USAF after World War II. The initial Martin version, built to establish the production line, was the **B-57A Canberra**, first flown on 20 July 1953. Only eight were constructed before manufacture was switched to the **RB-57A**. RB-57As entered service in 1954, and the extensively-built **B-57B** night intruder joined Tactical Air Command's 461st Bombardment Wing in early 1955. The USAF's B-57s saw little serious employment until the outbreak of war in Vietnam, when B-57Bs then serving in Japan, but due for transfer back to the US, were recalled for combat duty. Also notable in that conflict

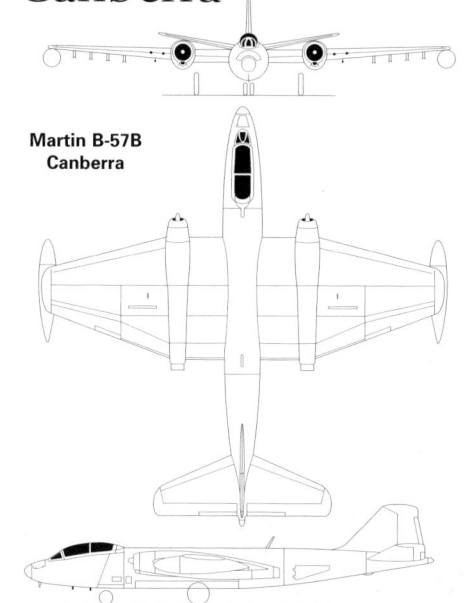

Martin B-57B Canberra

were the six reconnaissance **RB-57E Patricia Lynn** reconnaissance aircraft.

Variants

B-57A: licence-built equivalent to British Canberra B.Mk 2, but with Wright J65-W-1 turbojets (8 built)
RB-57A: generally similar to B-57A, but with cameras in bay aft of bomb bay (67 built)
B-57B: extensively modified version of B-57A for tactical night intruder role; seating for two in tandem, fixed armament of eight machine-guns or, from 91st aircraft, four 20-mm cannon, rotary bomb door, and wing pylons for bombs or rockets (202 built)
RB-57B: camera-equipped conversions of B-57B
EB-57B: ECM-equipped conversions of B-57B
B-57C: generally similar to B-57B, but with dual controls (38 built)
EB-57D: conversion of RB-57Ds to provide ECM jamming equipment
RB-57D: high-altitude strategic reconnaissance version with increased-span wing, fuselage radomes, and Pratt & Whitney J57 turbojets (20 built)
B-57E: generally similar to B-57B, but with target-towing gear (68 built)
EB-57E: ECM-equipped conversions of B-57E
RB-57E: special reconnaissance conversions of six B-57Es under the Patricia Lynn programme
RB-57F: special conversions (21) from B-57B and RB-57D aircraft by General Dynamics for special high-altitude reconnaissance duties; wingspan increased to 122 ft (37.19 m), and new powerplant comprising two 18,000-lb (80.05-kN) thrust Pratt & Whitney TF33-P-11 turbofans, and two 3,300-lb (14.68-kN) thrust Pratt & Whitney J60-P-9 turbojets

SPECIFICATION	
Martin B-57B Canberra	55,000 lb (24948 kg)
Type: night intruder	**Dimensions:** wingspan 64 ft
Powerplant: two 7,200-lb	(19.51 m); length 65 ft 6 in
(32.01-kN) thrust Wright J65-W-5	(19.96 m); height 15 ft 7 in
turbojets	(4.75 m); wing area 960 sq ft
Performance: maximum speed	(89.18 m²)
582 mph (937 km/h) at 40,000 ft	**Armament:** eight 0.5-in (12.7-mm)
(12190 m); service ceiling 48,000 ft	machine-guns, or four 20-mm
(14630 m); range 2,300 miles	cannon; 16 underwing rockets and
(3701 km)	up to 6,000 lb (2722 kg) of bombs
Weights: empty 26,000 lb	in internal bomb bay
(11793 kg); maximum take-off	

The greatly enlarged wingspan of the RB-57D led to a number of structural problems, with at least three aircraft literally breaking. For the RB-57F (illustrated), which featured an even longer span, General Dynamics used a new three-spar design, which was further strengthened by the incorporation of honeycomb sandwich wing skins.

Martin Baltimore

Whereas the Maryland had been designed to meet a USAAC specification, the **Martin 187** was developed from the earlier Maryland to specific British requirements. It differed primarily by having more powerful engines and a deeper fuselage to allow direct communication between crew members; however, like aircraft such as the Martin Maryland, Douglas Boston and Handley Page Hampden, its narrow-section fuselage made it virtually impossible for injured crew members to change positions in flight.

An order for 400 of these aircraft, named **Baltimore** by the RAF, was placed in May 1940 and following introduction of the US Lend-Lease Act, two

This Baltimore Mk V was flown by the Desert Air Force and as such was typical of its type in being used exclusively in Africa and the Mediterranean.

FW332

SPECIFICATION

Martin Baltimore Mk IV
Type: four-seat light bomber
Powerplant: two 1,660-hp (1238-kW) Wright R-2600-19 Cyclone 14 radial piston engines
Performance: maximum speed 305 mph (491 km/h) at 11,500 ft (3505 m); service ceiling 23,300 ft (7100 m); range with 1,000-lb (454-kg) bombload 1,082 miles (1741 km)
Weights: empty 15,460 lb (7013 kg); maximum take-off 22,600 lb (10251 kg)

Dimensions: wingspan 61 ft 4 in (18.61 m); length 48 ft 5¾ in (14.80 m); height 17 ft 9 in (5.41 m); wing area 538.50 sq ft (50.03 m²)
Armament: four 0.303-in (7.7-mm) wing-mounted machine-guns, two or four similar guns in dorsal turret, two 0.3-in (7.62-mm) machine-guns in ventral position, and provision for four similar guns in a fixed rear-firing position, plus a bombload of up to 2,000 lb (907 kg)

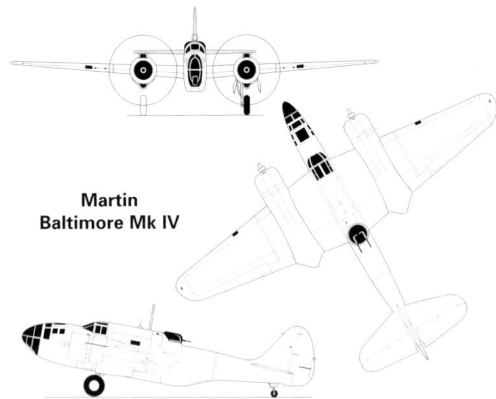

Martin Baltimore Mk IV

Variants

Baltimore Mk I: original production version to UK order with 1,600-hp (1193-kW) Wright GR-2600-A5B Cyclone engines; the dorsal turret had only a single hand-operated Vickers 'K' gun (50 built)
Baltimore Mk II: generally similar to Mk I, but with twin hand-operated Vickers guns in the dorsal turret (100 built)
Baltimore Mk III: improved version to UK, order, introducing more powerful Wright R-2600-19 engines and a Boulton Paul hydraulically-powered dorsal turret containing four 0.303-in (7.7-mm) Browning machine-guns (250 built)
Baltimore Mk IIIA: first Lend-Lease version, procured by the USAAF under the designation **A-30**; generally similar to Mk III, but with a Martin-built electrically-actuated dorsal turret containing two 0.5-in (12.7-mm) Browning machine-guns (281 built)
Baltimore Mk IV: basically similar to Mk IIIA but with detail changes; procured by the USAAF under the designation **A-30A** (294 built)
Baltimore Mk V: final and major production version, basically as Mk IV but for the introduction of 1,700-hp (1268-kW) R-2600-29 engines; procured by the USAAF under the designation A-30A (600 built)

batches, of 575 and 600, were ordered in June and July 1941 respectively, and a full total of 1,575 aircraft was duly produced for the RAF. It should be noted, however, that the full total was not received, for some **Baltimore Mk III** and **Baltimore Mk IIIA** aircraft were lost during transatlantic delivery when two cargo ships carrying

them were sunk. Initial deliveries of **Baltimore Mk I** aircraft were made in late 1941, being issued first to Operational Training Units, and were followed by deliveries of **Baltimore Mk II** machines in 1942 to Nos 55 and 223 Squadrons operating in the Middle East. Baltimore bombers were used operationally entirely in the

Mediterranean theatre, proving to be effective day and night bombers. In addition to those used by the RAF, Baltimores were allocated by the RAF for service with the RAAF, Free French Air Force, Greek No. 13 (Hellenic) Squadron, Italian Co-Belligerent Air Force, and the South African and Turkish air forces.

Martin China Clipper

For night operations Pan American configured the cabins of its Model 130 China Clippers to accommodate 18 passengers with sleeping bunks.

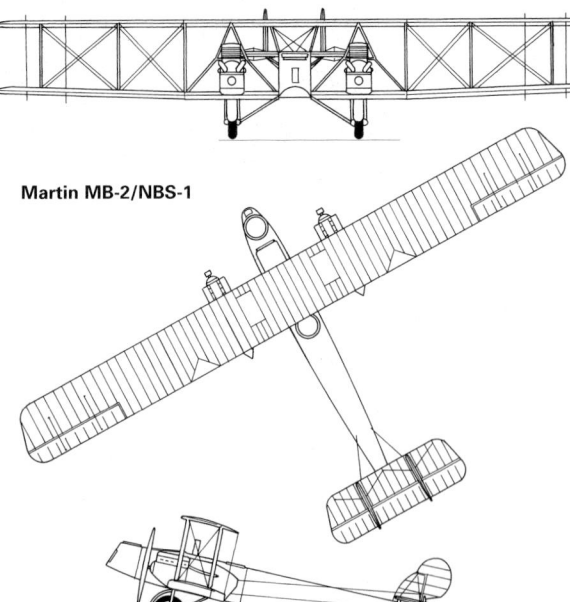

Intended for long-range transoceanic services, the **Model 130 China Clipper** was a large four-engined monoplane flying-boat, the airframe incorporating a two-step hull of advanced design. In terms of its operating economics, the Model 130 was superior to the DC-3 and three were built for Pan Am during 1935, each accommodating a crew of four and a maximum of 48 passengers for daytime operations. Power was provided by four 800-hp (597-kW) Pratt & Whitney R-1830 Twin Wasp

engines, mounted in nacelles at the leading edge of the wing. Operating experience with the Model 130 led to the design and development of an improved **Model 156** which differed in a number of ways, but retained the basic hull and wing of the

Model 130. It introduced a braced tail unit incorporating twin fins and rudders, powerplant comprising four 1,000-hp (746-kW) Wright GR-1820-G2 Cyclone radial engines, and had accommodation for a crew of five and a maximum of 46 passen-

gers. Testing of the Model 156 proved successful, but the outbreak of World War II and the company's involvement in production of aircraft ordered by the UK and France, prevented any further development or production.
Pan Am's Model 130

Clippers entered service on 21 October 1936, and were used on the airline's routes from San Francisco to Manila in the Philippine Islands. Two were impressed by the US Navy in 1942, and used on general transport duties without redesignation.

Martin MB-1 and MB-2

Withdrawing from his association with the Wright-Martin Aircraft Corporation, American pioneer Glenn Martin established the Glenn L. Martin Company at Cleveland, Ohio in late 1917. Requested by the US Army to develop a bomber aircraft that would

be superior to the British Handley Page O/400, the designer's **MB-1** design proposal was rewarded with a production order for 10 aircraft on 17 January 1918, the first of them flying on 17 August 1918. Of conventional biplane configuration, with twin

fins and rudders mounted above the tailplane and with four-wheel main landing gear, the MB-1 was powered by two 400-hp (298-kW) Liberty 12A piston engines strut-mounted between the wings, one on each side of the fuselage, and accommodated a crew of three in open cockpits. Delivery to the US Army Air Service began in October 1918, the first seven being designated officially **GMB (Glenn Martin Bomber)**, although four of them were equipped for use in an observation role.

MB-2/NBS-1 aircraft remained in US Army service until 1927-28, equipping four squadrons of the 2nd Bomb Group in the United States, and being deployed also in the Canal Zone, Hawaii and the Philippines.

Martin MB-2/NBS-1

Martin MB-1 and MB-2 (continued)

The remaining three aircraft on this order were completed as one long-range **GMT** (**Glenn Martin Transcontinental**), one with a nose-mounted 37-mm cannon designated **GMC** (**Glenn Martin Cannon**), and the third as a 10-passenger transport designated originally **GMP** (**Glenn Martin Passenger**), but later **T-1**. In addition six MB-1s modified for use as mail carriers were built subsequently for the US Postal Service, but some were later transferred to the US Army.

From the MB-1 Martin developed an improved **MB-2** for use as a night bomber, which differed by having increased-span strengthened wings that could be folded outboard of the engines, revised two-wheel main landing gear, and more powerful Liberty engines. The US Army contracted for 20 of the aircraft in 1920, adopting initially the company's MB-2 as the official designation, but the sixth and subsequent aircraft were designated **NBS-1** (**Night Bomber Short-range**) upon receipt. Government policy in the immediate post-war depressed state of the US aircraft industry was to share production orders between manufacturers, and as a result NBS-1s were built also by Aeromarine (25); Curtiss (50), the last 20 of them equipped with turbochargers for the engines; and L.W.F. (Lowe, Willard and Fowler) (35), of which four were completed as dual-control trainers.

The US Navy also showed some interest in the MB-1/MB-2, acquiring two MB-1s under the designation **MBT** (**Martin Bomber-Torpedo**), plus eight improved **MT** (**Martin Torpedo**) aircraft, which were basically MB-1s incorporating the increased-span wing of the MB-2. The MTs were subsequently designated **TM-1**.

SPECIFICATION	
Martin MB-2/NBS-1	12,064 lb (5472 kg)
Type: four-seat night bomber	**Dimensions:** wingspan 74 ft 2 in
Powerplant: two 420-hp (313-kW)	(22.61 m); length 42 ft 8 in
Liberty 12 V-12 piston engines	(13.00 m); height 14 ft 8 in
Performance: maximum speed	(4.47 m); wing area 1,121 sq ft
99 mph (159 km/h) at sea level;	(104.14 m²)
service ceiling 8,500 ft (2590 m);	**Armament:** five 0.3-in (7.62-mm)
range 558 miles (898 km)	machine-guns in nose and midship
Weights: empty 7,269 lb	positions, plus up to 1,800 lb
(3297 kg); maximum take-off	(816 kg) of bombs carried internally

Martin Maryland

Designed to meet a US Army Air Corps specification for an attack bomber, the **XA-22** prototype was a twin-engine cantilever mid-wing monoplane with retractable tailwheel landing gear and accommodation for a crew of three. It was flown for the first time on 14 March 1939, but following official tests was rejected by the USAAC. However, the company had received a first production order for 115 aircraft from France even before the prototype had flown, but the start of delivery was delayed until a US arms embargo was lifted in October 1939; by that time France had contracted for an additional 100 aircraft. Only 140 of these **Model 167F** aircraft were delivered before the French armistice in June 1940, having the French designation **Martin 167A-3** and seeing action against Axis forces until June 1940 and subsequently, with Vichy forces in West Africa and the Middle East, against the Allies.

With the collapse of French resistance in Europe, the outstanding 75 aircraft on order were diverted to the UK for service with the RAF and these, together with an additional 75 ordered by the RAF, were designated **Maryland Mk I**. All were powered by 1,050-hp (783-kW) R-1830-SC3G Twin Wasp radial engines with single-stage super-chargers. Further British orders followed for an improved **Maryland Mk II** with more powerful engines and two-stage superchargers, a total of 150 of this version being delivered to the RAF. Marylands were deployed initially for target towing and long-range reconnaissance, proving to be particularly valuable in this latter role, and were also used as light bombers. The first operational unit to receive the Maryland, in September 1940, was No. 431 Flight (later No. 69 Sqn) formed at Malta, and the type saw service in the Western Desert with Nos 39 and 223 Sqns. Some 72 of the RAF's Marylands were re-allocated to serve with Nos 12, 20, 21 and 24 Sqns of the SAAF. Marylands also saw service with the Fleet Air Arm. Among the notable operations of the type were the reconnaissance sorties that preceded the successful FAA attack in November 1940 on the Italian fleet in harbour at Taranto. Another FAA Maryland reported that the *Bismarck* and *Prinz Eugen* were at sea in May 1941.

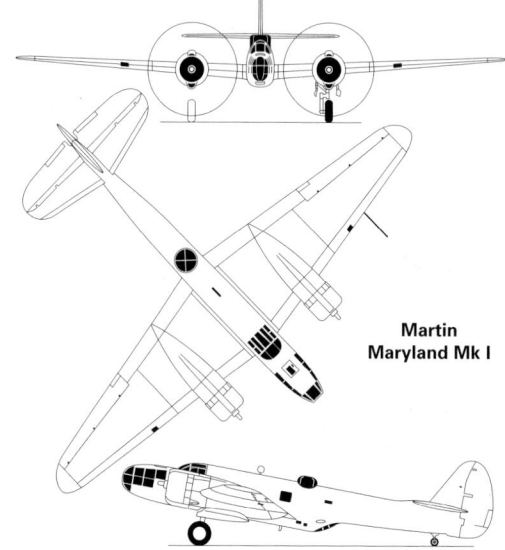

Martin Maryland Mk I

This RAF aircraft was one of the initial batch of Maryland Mk Is diverted from original French orders.

SPECIFICATION	
Martin Maryland Mk II	(5086 kg); maximum take-off
Type: three-seat reconnaissance/	16,809 lb (7624 kg)
bomber aircraft	**Dimensions:** wingspan 61 ft 4 in
Powerplant: two 1,200-hp	(18.69 m); length 46 ft 8 in
(895-kW) Pratt & Whitney	(14.22 m); height 14 ft 11¾ in
R-1830-S3C4G Twin Wasp radial	(4.57 m); wing area 538.50 sq ft
piston engines	(50.03 m²)
Performance: maximum speed	**Armament:** four 0.303-in (7.7-mm)
278 mph (447 km/h) at 11,800 ft	wing-mounted Browning machine-
(3595 m); service ceiling 26,000 ft	guns, one 0.303-in (7.7-mm)
(7925 m); range with maximum	Vickers 'K' gun each in dorsal and
bombload 1,080 miles (1738 km)	ventral positions, plus a bombload
Weights: empty 11,213 lb	of up to 2,000 lb (907 kg)

Martin P4M Mercator

The US Navy made several attempts to gain the benefit of high over-target performance combined with long range by introducing mixed powerplant. The **Model 219** patrol bomber represented one of the results of such a specification, two **XP4M-1** prototypes being ordered on 6 July 1944. The first was flown on 20 September 1946 as a cantilever shoulder-wing monoplane with retractable tricycle landing gear. Its powerplant comprised two 2,975-hp (2218-kW) R-4360-4 Wasp Major radial engines, but each nacelle also incorporated a 3,825-lb (17.01-kN) thrust J33-A-17 turbojet. After a protracted development programme 19 **P4M-1** production aircraft were built, the first being delivered to VP-21 on 28 June 1950, and all served with this unit. Most of them were converted into **P4M-1Q** Elint aircraft.

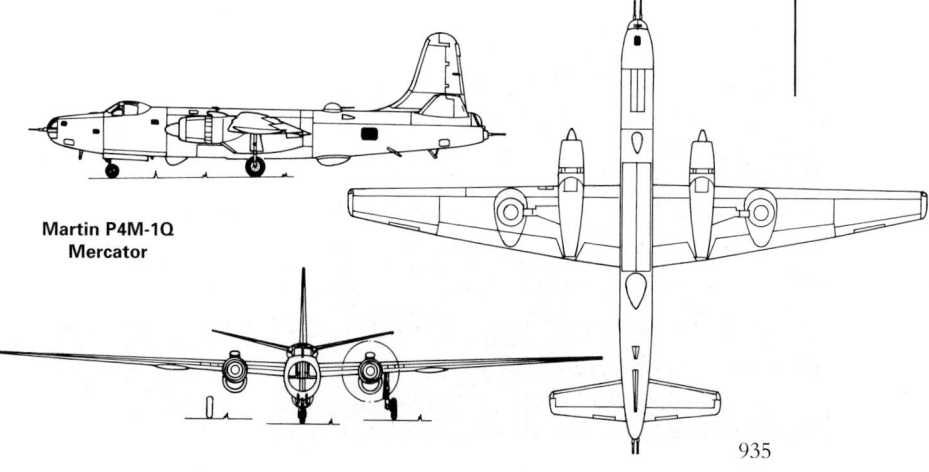

Martin P4M-1Q Mercator

This P4M-1 is illustrated as it appeared with VP-21. The unit began trading its PB4Y-2 Privateers for P4M-1s on 28 June 1950. Between August 1951 and January 1952, the squadron made an extended deployment to the Mediterranean with the type, returning to NAS Patuxent River to convert to the Neptune.

SPECIFICATION	
Martin P4M-1 Mercator	**Weight:** maximum take-off
Type: patrol bomber	88,378 lb (400\$8 kg)
Powerplant: two 3,250-hp	**Dimensions:** wingspan 114 ft
(2424-kW) Pratt & Whitney	(34.75 m); length 84 ft (25.60 m);
R-4360-20A radial piston engines	height 26 ft 1 in (7.95 m); wing
and two 4,600-lb (20.46-kN) thrust	area 1,311.0 sq ft (121.79 m²)
Allison J33-A-10A or -23 turbojets	**Armament:** four 20-mm cannon
Performance: maximum speed	(two each in nose and tail turrets)
410 mph (660 km/h) at 20,100 ft	and four 0.5-in (12.7-mm) machine-
(6125 m); service ceiling 34,600 ft	guns (two in dorsal turret and one
(10545 m); range 2,840 miles	each side of the fuselage), plus up
(4570 km)	to 6,000 lb (2722 kg) of bombs

Martin P5M Marlin

With the US Navy requiring a new patrol flying-boat, Martin decided to develop the successful PBM Mariner, the resulting **Model 237** design combining the wing and upper hull of the Mariner with a new lower hull structure. The close relationship between the two types is emphasised by the fact that a PBM-5 Mariner served as the prototype **XP5M-1** which, when ordered into production, was given the name **Marlin**. The modified hull of the XP5M-1 incorpo- rated radar-directed nose and tail turrets, as well as a power-operated dorsal turret, and power was provided by two 3,250-hp (2424-kW) Wright R-3350 radial engines. This proto- type flew for the first time on 30 May 1948, but it was not until two years later that the **P5M-1** was ordered into production, the first of these series aircraft being flown on 22 June 1951. Initial deliv- eries, to VP-44, began on 23 April 1952 and the type remained in service until

Variants

P5M-1 (later P-5A): initial production version; differed from prototype by having the nose turret replaced by a radome for APS-80 search radar, raised flight deck, dorsal turret deleted, and introduced uprated 3,400-hp (2535-kW) R-3350-30WA engines; 160 built
P5M-1G: redesignation of seven P5M-1s for use by the US Coast Guard
P5M-1S (later SP-5A): redesignation of P5M-1 following installation of MAD, echo- sounding and sonobuoy detection equipment for use in the ASW role
P5M-1T (later TP-5A): redesignation of USCG P5M-1Gs when taken into USN service as crew trainers
P5M-2 (later P-5B): second production version, with modified hull, a T-tail, retractable MAD gear, equipment changes and uprated R-3350-32WA engines; 115 built
P5M-2G: four P5M-2s built for the USCG; became P5M-2s when later accepted for use by the USN
P5M-2S (later SP-5B): redesignation of most P5M-2s after being equipped with advanced avionics and detection equipment for use in the ASW role

the mid-1960s. In addition to those operated by the US Navy, 10 of the later **P5M-2** version were supplied to France under the American MAP for use by the Aéronavale.

A large and impressive aircraft, the Marlin, illustrated here in P5M-2 form, was the last flying-boat to serve with the US Navy.

SPECIFICATION	
Martin P5M-2 Marlin	85,000 lb (38555 kg)
Type: patrol flying-boat with an	**Dimensions:** wingspan 118 ft 2 in
11-man crew	(36.02 m); length 100 ft 7 in
Powerplant: two 3,450-hp	(30.66 m); height 32 ft 8½ in
(2573-kW) Wright R-3350-32WA	(9.97 m); wing area 1,406 sq ft
TurboCompound radial piston	(130.62 m²)
engines	**Armament:** four torpedoes, four
Performance: maximum speed	2,000-lb (907-kg) bombs or mines,
251 mph (404 km/h) at sea level;	or smaller weapons up to 8,000 lb
service ceiling 24,000 ft (7315 m);	(3629 kg) total carried internally,
range 2,050 miles (3299 km)	and up to eight 1,000-lb (454-kg)
Weights: empty 50,485 lb	bombs or mines carried externally
(22900 kg); maximum take-off	

Martin P6M SeaMaster

To meet a US Navy require- ment for a high- performance multi-role flying-boat, Martin offered its very advanced **Model 275** design. This had an all-metal hull of high length/ beam ratio, mounting a cantilever high-set sharply- swept wing incorporating so much anhedral that the stabilising floats at the wingtips could be attached permanently; the tail unit was of T-tail configuration with all-swept surfaces. Above the wing, to minimise spray ingestion, were mounted four Allison turbojets, and pressurised

An aircraft of superb performance but great complexity, the SeaMaster, shown here in P6M-2 form, was flown supersonically in a dive and could reach Mach 0.89 at low level.

accommodation was provided for a crew of five. The first **XP6M-1** prototype was flown on 14 July 1955, the second following on 18 May 1956, and Martin received orders for six pre-production **YP6M-1** boats powered by Allison J71 turbojets, each devel- oping a maximum 13,000-lb

(57.81-kN) afterburning thrust. Successful flight testing led to an order for 24 production **P6M-2** aircraft named **SeaMaster**, which differed primarily by

having 17,000-lb (75.60-kN) thrust non-afterburning Pratt & Whitney J75-P-2 turbojet engines. However, the contract was cancelled on 21 August 1959 after

only eight had been built and these, together with the YP6M-1s, were scrapped at a later date. They were the fastest flying boats ever built.

Martin PBM Mariner

There were few obvious external differences between the radar-equipped PBM-3 and the later PBM-5 (illustrated). Nevertheless, the two could be told apart by the shorter carburettor intake above the cowling of the -5.

Martin PBM Mariner (continued)

Variants

XPBM-1: initial prototype with cantilever gull-wing incorporating retractable stabilising floats beneath the wings
PBM-1: initial production version introducing distinctive dihedral tailplane with inward canted twin fins and rudders; 20 built
XPBM-1A: redesignation of XPBM-1 following modification for armament tests
XPBM-2: single prototype, generally as PBM-1, but with increased fuel capacity and provisions for catapult launching
PBM-3B: version of **PBM-3** supplied under Lend-Lease to RAF; it was the first PBM-3 production version, and the first to introduce larger non-retractable stabilising floats; the PBM-3B had 1,700-hp (1268-kW) R-2600-12 engines in lengthened nacelles; 32 built
PBM-3C: production version, generally as PBM-3B, but introducing armour protection, bombload of up to 4,000 lb (1814 kg) and revised armament; 274 built, of which four were supplied to USCG
PBM-3D: production version as PBM-3C, but introducing more powerful R-2600-22 engines, search radar, self-sealing fuel tanks, provisions for up to 8,000 lb (3628 kg) of bombs, two torpedoes on underwing racks, and further revision of defensive armament; 201 built
XPBM-3E: redesignation of one PBM-3 after conversion for use as a radar development aircraft

PBM-3R: transport version of the PBM-3 without armament, and introducing cargo loading doors, strengthened flooring, and provisions to seat 20 passengers; 50 built
PBM-3S: ASW version of the PBM-3C with extra fuel, defensive armament reduced to four machine-guns, and able to carry four 325-lb (147-kg) depth charges; 156 built
XPBM-5: two prototypes, generally as PBM-3D, but with 2,100-hp (1566-kW) Pratt & Whitney R-2800-34 Double Wasp engines
PBM-5: major production version generally as XPBM-5, but with R-2800-22 or -34 engines; 631 built
XPBM-5A: single prototype as PBM-5, but introducing retractable tricycle landing gear to provide amphibious capability
PBM-5A: production version of XPBM-5A, used mainly by the USCG for air-sea rescue; 36 built
PBM-5E: designation of PBM-5s when equipped with AN/APS-15 radar
PBM-5G: redesignation of four PBM-5s which were supplied to the USCG for air-sea rescue duties
PBM-5M: redesignation of one PBM-5E after conversion for use in missile tests
PBM-5S: redesignation of a small number of PBM-5s following installation of special ASW equipment

The **Model 162** was designed in 1937 to meet a USN requirement for a new patrol flying-boat, the company building first a quarter-scale single-seat **Martin 162A** to evaluate the flight characteristics of the design, and following satisfactory tests the USN initially ordered a single **XPBM-1** development

prototype, flown first on 18 February 1939. This was powered by two 1,600-hp (1193-kW) Wright R-2600-6 Cyclone radial engines, mounted in large nacelles which incorporated weapons bays to accommodate a combined total of 2,000 lb (907 kg) of bombs or depth charges. Produced in considerable numbers and

several versions, the **PBM Mariner**, as the type was named, was to see service primarily in ASR, ASW and transport roles. The **PBM-3B** was supplied under Lend-Lease for service with the RAF, which designated the variant **Mariner GR.Mk I**, the first arriving in August 1943. However, after only a short period of evaluation it was decided that the type would not be used operationally by the RAF, and the aircraft were placed in storage pending their return to the United States. The other wartime user was the RAAF, which received 12 from 1943, these serving with No. 41 Sqn. Post-war, deliveries of small numbers were made from USN stocks to Argentina, the Netherlands and Uruguay.

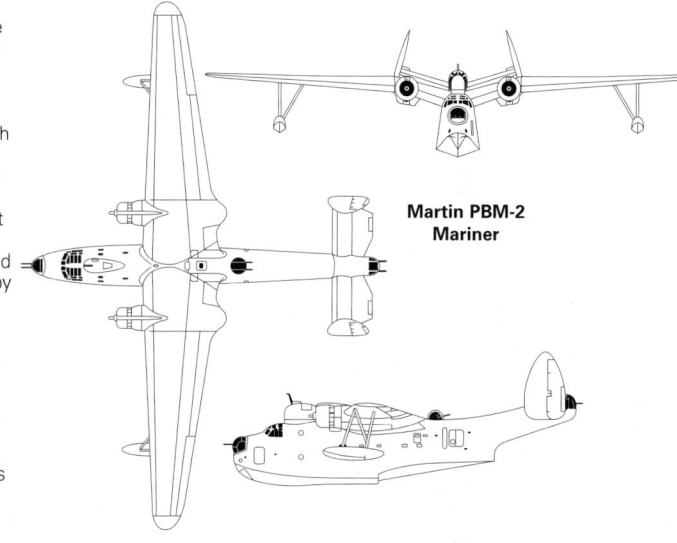

Martin PBM-2 Mariner

SPECIFICATION

Martin PBM-3D Mariner
Type: seven/eight-seat patrol flying-boat
Powerplant: two 1,900-hp (1417-kW) Wright R-2600-22 Cyclone radial piston engines
Performance: maximum speed 211 mph (340 km/h) at 1,500 ft (455 m); service ceiling 19,800 ft (6035 m); range 2,240 miles (3605 km)
Weights: empty 33,175 lb (15048 kg); maximum take-off

58,000 lb (26308 kg)
Dimensions: wingspan 118 ft (35.97 m); length 79 ft 10 in (24.33 m); height 27 ft 6 in (8.38 m); wing area 1,408 sq ft (130.80 m²)
Armament: eight 0.5-in (12.7-mm) machine-guns in nose and dorsal turrets and in waist and tail positions, plus up to 8,000 lb (3628 kg) of bombs or depth charges

Martin PB2M and JRM Mars

On 23 August 1938 the US Navy ordered a single prototype of the **Martin 170** design for a flying-boat patrol bomber. Designated **XPB2M-1**, it was the world's largest flying-boat when flown for the first time on 3 July 1942, but by then the US had become involved in World War II and it was decided not to proceed with procurement of the type as a patrol bomber. Instead, the 'boat was modified for use in a transport role, becoming redesignated **XPB2M-1R** and entering service in December 1943. It remains the largest flying-boat to have been operated by the US Navy and an early demonstration of its capability came in 1944, when a 20,500-lb (9299-kg) cargo was delivered to Hawaii in a

Forest Industries Flying Tankers Limited has operated two JRM-3 Mars flying-boats into 2001. Hawaii Mars (illustrated below) carries its water payload in tanks within the keel, while in US Navy service the aircraft would have carried up to 133 troops, or 84 stretchers, 24 sitting patients and nine medical attendants, or up to 35,000 lb (15876 kg) of freight. A 5,000-lb (2268-kg) capacity winch could be run out under the wings to aid loading through hatches in the sides of the hull.

4,700-mile (7564-km) round trip completed in only 27 hours 26 minutes, resulting in a US Navy order for a production version under the designation **JRM-1 Mars**. This covered 20 aircraft to

be completed specially for the transport role, but the end of World War II brought contract cancellations and only five were built, plus a single **JRM-2** for operation at a higher gross weight.

When the five JRM-1s were later modified to this latter standard they became redesignated **JRM-3**. These 200 ft (60.96 m) span aircraft were powered by four 2,300-hp (1715-kW)

Wright R-3350-8 engines, and an appreciation of their capacity can be gained from the fact that on 19 May 1949 one of them, *Marshall Mars*, carried a total of 301 passengers.

Martin SC-1/SC-2/T3M and T4M

The first torpedo-bomber to be designed and built by the Curtiss Aeroplane and

Motor Company was a three-seat biplane which could be provided with alternative float or wheel landing gear, and powered by a 525-hp (391-kW) Wright T-2 engine (**Curtiss CS-1**), or 585-hp (436-kW) Wright T-3 (**Curtiss CS-2**). After the delivery of six CS-1s and two CS-2s to the US Navy, the production of an additional 35 aircraft was put out to tender, Martin being awarded the contract, building an aircraft generally similar to the CS-1 under the designation **SC-1**. Martin also received a follow-on order for 40 aircraft equivalent to the CS-2, these being built and delivered as **SC-2** machines. The SC-2 also had the US Navy designation **T2M**, and when the Martin company developed an improved version this

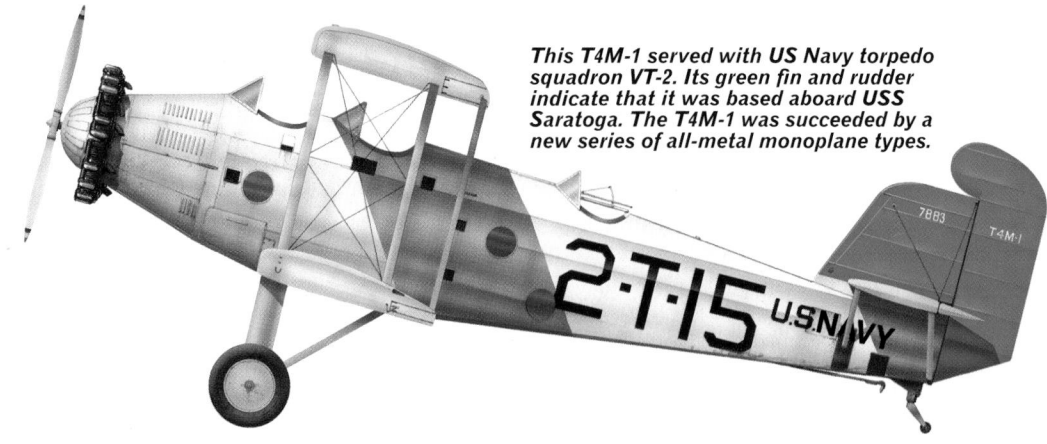

This T4M-1 served with US Navy torpedo squadron VT-2. Its green fin and rudder indicate that it was based aboard USS Saratoga. The T4M-1 was succeeded by a new series of all-metal monoplane types.

was allocated the designation **T3M**; it differed primarily by having a basic fuselage structure of steel tube, with the pilot and

torpedo man located farther forward. The delivery of 24 **T3M-1** aircraft powered by the 575-hp (429-kW) Wright T-3B engine began in late 1926, and was followed by an order for 100 **T3M-2** machines with equal-span wings and 710-hp (529-kW) Packard 3A-2500 engines. The final Martin production version was the **T4M-1** with a Pratt & Whitney R-1690-24 Hornet radial engine, 102 being delivered during 1927-28 before the Martin company's Cleveland factory was sold to Great Lakes Aircraft

Corporation, when Great Lakes was given the opportunity of continuing production of the T4M-1; a total of 18 with R-1690-28 engines and 32 with Wright R-1820-56 Cyclones were designated **TG-1** and **TG-2**

respectively. Wheeled versions of the T3M-2 and T4M-1 served aboard the carriers USS Lexington and USS Saratoga, and T4M-1s in service with Reserve units remained in use until the mid-1930s.

Variants

XT3M-3: redesignation of the first T3M-2 after being re-engined with a Pratt & Whitney R-1690 Hornet radial engine
XT3M-4: redesignation of XT3M-3 following installation of a Wright R-1750 Cyclone engine
XT4M-1: prototype of the T4M-1 version, powered by an R-1690 engine

SPECIFICATION	
Martin T4M-1	(1783 kg); take-off 8,071 lb (3661 kg)
Type: three-seat torpedo-bomber/ scout	**Dimensions:** wingspan 53 ft (16.15 m); length 35 ft 7 in (10.85 m); height 14 ft 9 in (4.50 m); wing area 656 sq ft (60.94 m²)
Powerplant: one 525-hp (391-kW) Pratt & Whitney R-1690-24 Hornet radial piston engine	
Performance: maximum speed 114 mph (183 km/h) at sea level; service ceiling 10,150 ft (3085 m); range 363 miles (584 km)	**Armament:** one 0.3-in (7.62-mm) machine-gun on a Scarff ring mount in the rear cockpit, plus one torpedo carried externally
Weights: empty 3,931 lb	

Martin-Baker aircraft

James Martin established the Martin-Baker Aircraft Company in 1934 to build aircraft based on an unusual lattice-like steel-tube construction that he had evolved. It was claimed that this construction provided a lightweight and robust structure that was cheap and easy to assemble and repair. Designed as the first practical aircraft to adopt this structure, the **M.B.1** cantilever low-wing mono-

plane had enclosed accommodation for two, was powered by a 160-hp (119-kW) Napier Javelin IIIA engine, and was first flown during March 1935. Only one experimental aircraft was built and this was destroyed by fire in early 1938. Martin-Baker then turned to the design of a single-seat fighter to meet the requirements of Air Ministry Specification R5/34, the **M.B.2** prototype built as a private venture. A

clean cantilever low-wing monoplane powered by a 1,000-hp (746-kW) Napier Dagger III 'H' engine, it was flown for the first time on 3 August 1938. Although incorporating many advanced ideas and demonstrating a maximum speed of 350 mph (563 km/h) during official trials, no production order followed and the aircraft was eventually scrapped.
An even more potent fighter prototype followed with the **M.B.3**, designed to satisfy Specification F.18/39 for a single-seat fighter to supersede the Hawker Hurricane and Supermarine Spitfire. A well-proportioned low-wing monoplane powered by a 2,020-hp (1506-kW) Napier Sabre H engine, the M.B.3 was flown for the first time on 31 August 1942 and during testing attained a top speed of 415 mph (668 km/h) at optimum alti-

Although its simplicity made the M.B.2 a maintenance crew's dream, pilots remained unimpressed.

In the eyes of almost every pilot who flew it, the M.B.5 was the greatest piston-engined fighter ever built.

tude. Armed with six 20-mm cannon, this aircraft clearly had potential, but no further development followed after it crashed on 12 September 1942. The designation **M.B.4** was allocated to a new fighter but this remained only a project, one that would have united the M.B.3 airframe and a Rolls-Royce Griffon engine, but Martin-Baker continued development of this idea in the one-off **M.B.5**. A single-seat fighter powered by a 2,340-hp (1745-kW) Griffon 83 engine driving three-bladed contrarotating propellers, it was flown for

the first time on 23 May 1944 but although having superb handling qualities and a top speed of 460 mph (740 km/h) at 20,000 ft (6095 m), the M.B.5 failed to gain a production contract. Martin-Baker's **M.B.6**, the company's final aircraft design, was for a turbojet-powered delta wing tailless fighter, but this remained a project only. However, James (later Sir James) Martin's innovative design capability went on to produce the equipment for which he became world famous, the Martin-Baker ejection seat.

Martinsyde F series

This series began with the **Martinsyde F.1**, a large two-seat biplane with the crew accommodated in tandem open cockpits and, curiously for an aircraft that was intended as a fighter, the pilot occupied the rear seat. Thus, the observer

would have had a seriously restricted field of fire for his trainable machine-gun and would have been unable to direct the aim of fixed forward-firing machine-guns. Only two F.1s were built, each of them powered by a 250-hp

(186-kW) Rolls-Royce engine, but as these aircraft did not progress beyond official testing and were flown without weapons, it is difficult to appreciate what armament the F.1 would have carried. Only one example of the ensuing **F.2** was built, a more compact tandem two-seat biplane powered

by a 200-hp (149-kW) Hispano-Suiza engine. Although tested officially, it really had little chance for success, although by comparison with the F.1 the crew positions were reversed, the pilot's field of view was limited severely by the biplane wing centre-sections above and below him.

The **F.3** single-seat fighter was basically a smaller version of the F.2, its pilot in an open cockpit just aft of the wing, which incorporated a fairly large cut-out in the centre-section trailing edge. It was aerodynamically refined and powered by an experimental 285-hp (213-kW) Rolls-Royce Falcon engine.

Martinsyde F series (continued)

The F.3 was shown in official tests to have extremely good performance; armament consisted of two synchronised forward-firing machine-guns. Six F.3s, each powered by a 275-hp (205-kW) Rolls-Royce Falcon III engine, were ordered and should presumably, be regarded as pre-production aircraft for the generally similar **F.4 Buzzard** which differed primarily by siting the pilot's cockpit farther aft and by introducing a more powerful Hispano-Suiza engine. Although ordered in large numbers, only about 60 had been delivered to the RAF by the end of World War I. Martinsyde was left with a stock of about 200 F.4s. Numbers of these were sold for

Variants

F.4A: two-seat tourer conversion of F.4
Type A.Mk I: two-seat long-range conversion of F.4
Type AS.Mk I: version of above with float landing gear
Type A.Mk II: conversion of F.4 with enclosed four-seat cabin forward of the pilot's open cockpit
F.6: two-seat conversion of F.4 with wing and landing gear revisions
A.D.C.1: version developed by the Aircraft Disposal Company, after Martinsyde had gone into liquidation in 1921, which differed mainly by having as powerplant a 395-hp (295-kW) Armstrong Siddeley Jaguar radial engine
Nimbus Martinsyde: one aircraft converted by A.D.C. to be powered by a 300-hp (224-kW) A.D.C. Nimbus engine
A.V.1: one aircraft, basically as F.4A, for engine designer Amherst Villiers

service with foreign air forces, and some formed the basis of a number of civil variants mentioned briefly below.

Although markedly superior to the contemporary Snipe, the F.4 was not adopted as a front-line RAF fighter.

SPECIFICATION	
Martinsyde F.4	maximum take-off 2,289 lb (1038 kg)
Type: single-seat fighter	**Dimensions:** wingspan 32 ft 9½ in (9.99 m); length 25 ft 5¾ in (7.77 m); height 10 ft 4 in (3.15 m); wing area 320 sq ft (29.73 m²)
Powerplant: one 300-hp (224-kW) Hispano-Suiza V-8 piston engine	
Performance: maximum speed 145 mph (108 km/h) at sea level; service ceiling 25,000 ft (7620 m); endurance 2 hours 30 minutes	**Armament:** two forward-firing synchronised 0.303-in (7.7-mm) Vickers machine-guns
Weights: empty 1,710 lb (776 kg);	

Martinsyde G.100 and G.102 Elephant

An improved and considerably larger single-seat scout biplane, in comparison with the F.1, was designed by Martinsyde during the summer of 1915, designated **G.100**, and the prototype was flown for the first time during September of that year. Its larger size resulted from the requirement that it should be capable of some

5 hours' endurance for use as an escort for two-seat observation/reconnaissance aircraft. Powered by the 120hp (89-kW) Beardmore engine, G.100s began to enter service on the Western Front in early 1916, distributed to squadrons in small numbers. They gained the nickname **'Elephant'** in France, presumably

because of their large size for a single-seat scout, and the name has endured. The only squadron to be equipped with the type was No. 27, and its association with this aircraft is recognised by the fact that this unofficial name is perpetuated by the incorporation of an elephant in the squadron badge. The G.100 was followed in late 1916 by the improved **G.102** which had a more powerful Beardmore engine, enabling it to lift a greater

load at the expense of endurance, with the result that this version saw more use in a bombing role. Derived from the G.101/102 design was a further improved single-seat fighter of biplane configuration

known as the **RG**. First tested officially in early 1917, and powered by a 190-hp (142-kW) Rolls-Royce Falcon engine, the RG demonstrated excellent performance but failed to gain a production contract because of a shortage of the Falcon engine, this having a priority allocation for the Bristol Fighter.

SPECIFICATION	
Martinsyde G.102	**Dimensions:** wingspan 38 ft (11.58 m); length 27 ft (8.23 m); height 9 ft 8 in (2.95 m); wing area 410 sq ft (38.09 m²)
Type: single-seat scout	
Powerplant: one 160-hp (119-kW) Beardmore inline piston engine	
Performance: maximum speed 104 mph (167 km/h) at 2,000 ft (610 m); service ceiling 16,000 ft (4875 m); endurance 4 hours 30 minutes	**Armament:** two 0.303-in (7.7-mm) Lewis guns (one forward-firing above the upper wing and one rear-firing on a mounting behind the cockpit), plus a maximum of 260 lb (118 kg) of bombs on underwing or underfuselage racks
Weights: empty 1,793 lb (813 kg); maximum take-off 2,458 lb (1115 kg)	

A total of about 300 Martinsyde G.100/102 Elephant fighters was built, of which 133 were delivered to squadrons on the Western Front, 64 to units in the Middle East, and most of the remainder to home-based training units.

Maule aircraft

Belford Maule began the design of an enclosed-cabin four-seat light aircraft in 1956, designating it **Maule M-4**, and establishing the Maule Aircraft Corporation at Jackson, Michigan, to develop and manufacture the type. First flown on 8 September 1961, the M-4 is a braced-wing monoplane with fixed tailwheel landing gear and,

in its original M-4 version, was powered by a 145-hp (108-kW) Continental O-300-A flat-six engine. Production began in 1963, and up to the company's bankruptcy in 1984 more than 1,100 examples of the M-4 and its subsequent versions had been sold in 20 years of continuous production. The M-4 became known subse-

quently as the **M-4 Jetasen**, being followed in late 1964 by the **M-4 Rocket** introducing a 210-hp (157-kW) Continental IO-360-A engine. Later versions included a de luxe version of the Jetasen, the **M-4 Astro Rocket** with a 180-hp (134-kW) Franklin 6A-335-B1A engine, and the **M-4 Strata Rocket** which was basically an M-4 Rocket with a 220-hp (164-kW) Franklin 6A-350-C1 engine.
In 1968 Maule began development of an improved **M-5** based upon the M-4 Strata Rocket. It differs by having a 30 per

cent increase in flap area and enlarged tail surfaces to improve STOL performance. Two prototypes were flown in 1971, the **M-5-210C** and **M-5-220C** with engines of 210 and 220 hp (157 and 164 kW)

respectively, and both entering production in early 1974 with the name **Lunar Rocket**. Production versions of the M-5 included the **M-5-180C Lunar Rocket** with a 180-hp (134-kW) Avco

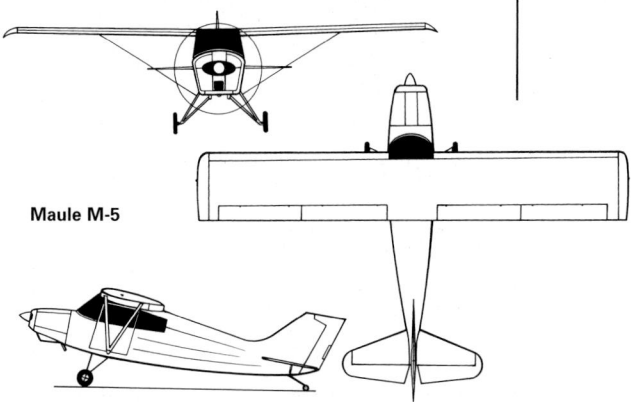

Maule M-5

This MX-7 demonstrates the type's ability to be fitted with Edo floats, a facility common across the Maule range.

Lycoming O-360-CIF engine, **M-5-210TC Lunar Rocket** with the 210-hp (157-kW) Avco Lycoming TO-360-C1A6D turbocharged engine, **M-5-235C Lunar Rocket** with the Avco Lycoming O-540-J1A5D engine, and the generally similar **M-6-235 Super Rocket** which had its wingspan increased by 2 ft 4 in (0.71 m). A civil patrol version of the Lunar Rocket

was available under the name **Maule Patroller**.

After the Maule Aircraft Corporation had gone into Chapter 11 bankruptcy protection in 1984, a new company emerged as Maule Air Inc. This new concern began production of the **M-7-235 Super Rocket**, a development of the M-6-235 with longer internal cabin dimensions, optional child seats and extra cabin windows.

Variants of the M-7 remain available into 2001, offering many combinations of engine and undercarriage configuration, and included the **MX-7-160 Sportplane, MXT-7-160 Comet, MX-7-180A Sportplane, MX-7-180A Comet, MX-7-180B Star Rocket, MX-7-180C Millenium, MXT-7-180 Star Rocket, MX-7 Rocket, M-7-235B Super Rocket, M-7-235C Orion,**

SPECIFICATION	
Maule M-5-235C Lunar Rocket **Type:** four-seat light aircraft **Powerplant:** one 235-hp (175-kW) Avco Lycoming 0-540-J1A5D flat-six piston engine **Performance:** maximum speed 172 mph (277 km/h) at optimum altitude; service ceiling 20,000 ft (6095 m); range with standard fuel	550 miles (885 km) **Weights:** empty 1,400 lb (635 kg); maximum take-off 2,300 lb (1043 kg) **Dimensions:** wingspan 30 ft 10 in (9.40 m); length 23 ft 6 in (7.16 m); height 6 ft 2½ in (1.89 m); wing area 157.90 sq ft (14.67 m²)

MT-7-235 Super Rocket, M-7-260, M-7-260C, MT-7-260 and the 420-shp

(313-kW) Rolls-Royce 250-B17C turboprop-powered **MMT-7-420AC**.

Max Holste M.H.152 and M.H.1521 Broussard

SPECIFICATION	
Max Holste M.H.1521 Broussard **Type:** six-seat utility aircraft **Powerplant:** one 450-hp (336-kW) Pratt & Whitney R-985-AN-1 radial piston engine **Performance:** maximum speed 168 mph (270 km/h) at 3,280 ft (1000 m); service ceiling 18,045 ft	(5500 m) **Weights:** empty equipped 3,373 lb (1530 kg); maximum take-off 5,512 lb (2500 kg) **Dimensions:** wingspan 45 ft 11 in (13.75 m); length 28 ft 4½ in (8.65 m); height 12 ft (3.65 m); wing area 271.26 sq ft (25.20 m²)

This M.H.1521 Broussard flew with 44 Escadrille de Liaison Aeriennes at Blandin-Régnier.

Differing considerably from the company's first product, the **M.H.152** was designed to meet a French army requirement for a lightweight liaison/observation aircraft. Of braced high-wing monoplane configuration, it had fixed tailwheel landing gear, a tail

unit similar to that of the earlier **M.H.52** light aircraft, and accommodated a pilot and four passengers. The prototype, first flown on 12 June 1951, was powered by a 220-hp (164-kW) Salmson 8AS Argus engine, but by the time that it had flown the

Variants

M.H.1521A: version of M.H.1521 equipped specifically for agricultural use
M.H.1522: prototype conversion, first flown on 11 February 1958, with a wing incorporating full span leading-edge slots and double-slotted trailing edge flaps to improve STOL performance

French army had changed its ideas and was no longer interested in the low-powered M.H.152. While hoping to market this aircraft for civil use in agricultural, ambulance, light transport or photographic roles, the company decided to develop a slightly larger and considerably more powerful version.

Designated **M.H.1521** and later named **Broussard**, this generally similar aircraft seated a pilot and five passengers and had a Pratt & Whitney radial engine offering more than double the power of the Salmson Argus; an alternative ambulance interior was available to accommodate two stretchers and two sitting

casualties or medical attendants. Flown initially in prototype form on 17 November 1952, the first civil production aircraft was flown on 16 June 1954, followed eight days later by the first specially equipped military aircraft. The latter served French forces well and fought in French actions in Algeria.

MBB BO 209 Monsun

On 22 December 1967 MBB (then known as Messerschmitt-Bölkow) flew the prototype of a

new two-seat lightweight tourer/trainer aircraft designed by Hermann Mylius. Then designated

MHK-101, it was decided after the 1969 merger that created MBB, to develop this aircraft further and the prototype of this revised design, designated **MBB BO 209**, flew first on 28 May 1969. An attractive low-wing monoplane with foldable wings, and side-by-side enclosed cabin

seating for pilot and passenger/pupil, it has tricycle landing gear and is powered by engines of 125

to 160 hp (93 to 119 kW). When production ended in early 1972 approximately 100 had been built.

Variants

BO 209-150: initial production version with a 150-hp (112-kW) Lycoming O-320 engine
BO 209-160: alternative production version with a 160-hp (119-kW) Lycoming IO-320 engine
BO 209S: trainer version with 130-hp (97-kW) Rolls-Royce/Continental O-240 or 125-hp (93-kW) Lycoming O-235F engine and non-folding wings

The 27 ft 6¾ in (8.40 m) span BO 209-160 has a maximum speed of 170 mph (274 km/h) and a range of 745 miles (1200 km).

MBB HFB 320 Hansa

Designed by Hamburger Flugzeugbau G.m.b.H. before its merger with Messerschmitt-Bölkow, the **HFB 320 Hansa** twin-jet executive transport/ feeder-liner is of distinctive configuration. To avoid compromising cabin volume, its cantilever mid-set wings have 15° of forward sweep, which means that the main spar passes through the fuselage to the rear of the

Some 16 of the 47 Hansas built were delivered to the Luftwaffe. Eight aircraft used only as transports were retired in 1988, while the remainder served on as ECM trainers (illustrated) until 30 June 1994.

passenger cabin. Other features of its configuration include wingtip fuel tanks,

a T-tail unit with all-swept surfaces, retractable tricycle landing gear, and two

podded turbojet engines, mounted one on each side of the rear fuselage. The

prototype was flown for the first time on 21 April 1964.

MBB HFB 320 Hansa (continued)

The first production Hansa was flown on 2 February 1966. The first 15 Hansas had 2,850-lb (12.68-kN) thrust General Electric CJ610-1 engines, the next 20 had 2,950-lb (13.12-kN) thrust CJ610-5, and subse- quent aircraft the more powerful CJ610-9. Finding itself in a highly competi- tive market, MBB endeavoured to attract mili- tary sales in such roles as casualty evacuation, liaison, light freighting, navigation training, radio and radar reconnaissance, and VIP transport; it attracted only one military customer, the West German Luftwaffe. This service received 16 of the total of 47 Hansas that were built.

SPECIFICATION

MBB HFB 320 Hansa
Type: twin-jet transport
Powerplant: two 3,100-lb (13.78-kN) thrust General Electric CJ610-9 turbojets
Performance: maximum cruising speed 513 mph (825 km/h) at 25,000 ft (7620 m); service ceiling 40,000 ft (12190 m); range with 1,200-lb (544-kg) payload and reserves 1,473 miles (2370 km)
Weights: empty 11,960 lb (5425 kg); maximum take-off 20,283 lb (9200 kg)
Dimensions: wingspan 47 ft 6½ in (14.49 m); length 54 ft 6 in (16.61 m); height 16 ft 2½ in (4.94 m); wing area 324.43 sq ft (30.14 m²)

McDonnell XF-85 Goblin

Designed to meet a USAAF requirement for a single- seat 'parasite' escort fighter that could be carried within a large bomber, the **XF-85 Goblin** was ordered in March 1947 to the extent of the development of two prototypes. Features of the design included mid- set foldable swept wings of 21 ft 1½ in (6.44 m) span, a short rotund fuselage, no landing gear except for emergency skids, a retractable hook to engage a trapeze on the parent aircraft, six tail surfaces spaced around the rear fuselage, and power provided by a 3,000-lb (13.34-kN) thrust Westinghouse J34-WE-7 turbojet mounted in the rear fuselage. A first free flight was made on 23 August 1948 after launch from a Boeing EB-29B 'motherplane', but little more than two hours of flight tests were suffi- cient to show that turbulence around the bomber created difficult

The XF-85 had no landing gear, but in the course of its 2 hours and 19 minutes of testing, the type was crash-landed three times.

control problems. When this factor was coupled with the realisation that so small and specialised an aircraft would not have the speed and manoeuvrability of the fighters that it would be expected to intercept, further development was abandoned.

McDonnell F-88 & F-101 Voodoo

To meet a USAAF require- ment of 1946 for a long- range turbojet-powered fighter that could be used in a penetration or escort role, McDonnell made design proposals which resulted in the award of a contract for two **XF-88** prototypes in February 1947. The first of these was flown initially on 20 October 1948, a mid-wing monoplane with swept wings and tail surfaces, a long fuselage to house fuel for the long- range requirement, and two 3,000-lb (13.34-kN) thrust Westinghouse XJ34-WE-13 turbojets mounted in the lower centre-fuselage. Testing showed that the type was disappointingly slow, a factor attributed to inade- quate power, and the **XF-88A** second prototype differed by having XJ34-WE-22 turbojets with afterburners. These engines increased fuel consumption but though Mach 1 was exceeded in dives, the USAF was short of funds and the programme was ended.

With the outbreak of war in Korea the USAF was faced with an urgent requirement for a more capable escort fighter, for it was discovered very quickly that available aircraft with adequate range did not have the capability to take on the Mikoyan-Gurevich MiG-15s of the North Korean and Chinese air forces, and those that could 'mix it' with the MiGs did not have the range. An improved version of the XF-88 was ordered as the **F-101 Voodoo**, to give Strategic Air Command the long- range escorts that it needed for its Convair B-36 bombers, and although the potential range of the F-101 was quite inadequate for the task, it seemed almost as if the USAF hoped this was a problem that would resolve itself. When it was realised that this was wish- ful thinking, the F-101s for SAC were cancelled. Then it was decided that, subject to satisfactory evaluation,

SPECIFICATION

McDonnell F-101B Voodoo
Type: two-seat long-range all- weather interceptor
Powerplant: two 14,880-lb (66.17-kN) thrust afterburning Pratt & Whitney J57-P-55 turbojets
Performance: maximum speed 1,221 mph (1965 km/h) or Mach 1.85 at 40,000 ft (12190 m); service ceiling 54,800 ft (16705 m); range 1,550 miles (2494 kg)
Weights: empty 28,970 lb (13141 kg); maximum take-off 52,400 lb (23768 kg)
Dimensions: wingspan 39 ft 8 in (12.09 m); length 67 ft 4¾ in (20.54 m); height 18 ft (5.49 m); wing area 368 sq ft (34.19 m²)
Armament: two MB-1 Genie missiles with nuclear warheads and four AIM-4C, -4D or -4G Falcon missiles, or six Falcon missiles

Variants

F-101A: initial production version with two Pratt & Whitney J57-P-13 turbojets, each rated at 10,200-lb (45.36-kN) thrust, or 15,000-lb (6804-kg) thrust with afterburning; armed with four 20-mm cannon and equipped to carry a 1,620-lb (735-kg) or 3,721-lb (1688-kg) nuclear weapon; 77 built
NF-101A: redesignation of one F-101A when used by General Electric for the flight testing of J79-GE-1 turbojets
YRF-101A: redesignation of two F-101As used as prototypes for a reconnaissance version; generally as F-101A, but unarmed and with a lengthened nose to house a total of six cameras
RF-101A: production reconnaissance version, gener- ally similar to the prototypes; 35 built
F-101B: production version of a two-seat all-weather long-range interceptor with a revised forward fuselage incorporating tandem two-seat cockpit for pilot and radar operator (aft), inflight-refuelling probe, and an advanced fire-control system for the all-missile arma- ment of two MB-1 Genie nuclear missiles and four Falcon homing missiles, or six Falcon missiles; 407 built
CF-101B: Royal Canadian Air Force designation of 56 F-101Bs received from July 1961
RF-101B: USAF redesignation of ex-Canadian CF-101Bs following modification to serve as two-seat reconnaissance aircraft
TF-101B: dual-control conversion and operational trainer version of F-101B with limited combat capabil- ity; 72 built
F-101C: single-seat fighter version, generally as F-101A, with strengthened structure for use by TAC in a nuclear strike role; 47 built
RF-101C: reconnaissance version of the F-101C, otherwise generally as RF-101A; 166 built
F-101D: projected version with General Electric J79 engines; not built
F-101E: projected version with General Electric J79 engines; not built
F-101F: redesignation of 153 F-101Bs following deletion of inflight-refuelling probe and installation of an infra-red detection system and improved fire control system
CF-101F: RCAF designation of 10 TF-101Bs received in 1961-62
TF-101F: redesignation of TF-101Bs after conversion to F-101F detection/fire-control standard
RF-101G: redesignation of F-101As after withdrawal from first-line service and conversion for use by ANG units in a reconnaissance role
RF-101H: redesignation of F-101Cs converted, as were the RF-101Gs, for ANG use

McDonnell originally schemed the XF-88 with a butterfly tail, although the aircraft eventually emerged with a relatively conventional empennage. The type's 35° wing sweepback was determined by wartime German research.

Recce Voodoos, represented here by a 432nd TRG RF-101C, incorporated distinctive chisel noses accommodating their camera equipment.

the type would be ordered into production for service with Tactical Air Command. The first **F-101A** was flown initially on 29 September

1954, demonstrating supersonic capability during its first flight, and the type began to enter service in early 1957, being delivered

first to the USAF's 27th Tactical Fighter Wing. Like the F3H Demon, the Voodoo was too late for service in the Korean War, and the tactical fighter versions had only a short period of first-line use. Reconnaissance versions however, proved to be of great value in operations over North Vietnam and, after being replaced by McDonnell Douglas RF-4Cs, continued to serve with the Air National Guard into the mid-1970s. **RF-101A** and **RF-101C** aircraft transferred to the Chinese Nationalist air force remained in use for some years, and **CF-101B** and **CF-101F** fighters

entered service with the Royal Canadian Air Force in late 1961. Ten years later the surviving Canadian Voodoos were exchanged

for a number of refurbished aircraft from US stocks, and the final Canadian Voodoo was not retired until 1987.

In its two-seat F-101B form, the Voodoo was an interceptor of some capability, especially when armed with nuclear-tipped Genies.

McDonnell F2H Banshee

Having flown for the first time on 12 October 1950, the F2H-2P photo-recce variant of the Banshee went on to be produced in some numbers. An aircraft of the US Marine Corps' VMJ-1 is illustrated.

Following the success of the FH-1 Phantom in US Navy and US Marine Corps service, McDonnell was requested to submit its design for a new and improved jet fighter to supersede the FH-1. The company's design submission led to the receipt of a contract in early 1945 for three **XF2D-1** prototypes, these later gaining the name **Banshee**. McDonnell's design covered an improved version of the Phantom of increased size, incorporating folding wings, and with a lengthened fuselage to house more fuel, and with similarly-mounted and more powerful Westinghouse turbojet engines. The first prototype was flown on 11 January 1947, by then

redesignated **XF2H-1**, and successful testing and evaluation led to contracts that were to call eventually for a total of 892 production aircraft. Initial deliveries of production **F2H-1** fighters, to VF-171, began in August 1948, and the type proved of great value as an escort fighter during the Korean War. By the end of that conflict the F2H had been superseded by more

advanced fighters, but continued in use in a reconnaissance role for a number of years, and in service with USN reserve units, was flown until the

mid-1960s. In November 1955 a total of 39 ex-USN **F2H-3** machines was transferred to the Royal Canadian Navy, these being that service's first opera-

tional jet fighters. When the last were retired in September 1962, they also proved to be the last carrier-based fighters in Canadian service.

Variants

F2H-1: initial production version, generally similar to prototype, with two 3,000-lb (13.34-kN) thrust Westinghouse J34-GE-22 turbojets; 56 built
F2H-2: second production version, introducing slightly lengthened fuselage with increased fuel capacity, wingtip fuel tanks, and 3,250-lb (14.45-kN) thrust Westinghouse J34-WE-34 turbojets; 308 built
F2H-2B: fighter-bomber version, with underwing racks for two 500-lb (227-kg) bombs; 25 built
F2H-2N: night-fighter version, with slightly lengthened nose to house AI radar; 14 built
F2H-2P: reconnaissance version, without armament and with lengthened nose for up to six cameras; 89 built
F2H-3 (later F-2C): all-weather fighter with lengthened fuselage for increased fuel capacity, APQ-41 radar installed in the nose, and with underwing bombs racks as F2H-2B; 250 built
F2H-3P: proposed reconnaissance version of F2H-3; not built
F2H-4 (later F-2D): final production version of Banshee, with 3,600-lb (16.01-kN) thrust Westinghouse J34-WE-38 engines, and APG-37 radar to give improved all-weather capability; 150 built

SPECIFICATION	
McDonnell F2H-3 Banshee	(5980 kg); maximum take-off
Type: single-seat all-weather carrier-based fighter	25,214 lb (11437 kg)
Powerplant: two 3,250-lb (14.45-kN) thrust Westinghouse J34-WE-34 turbojets	**Dimensions:** wingspan 41 ft 9 in (12.73 m); length 48 ft 2 in (14.68 m); height 14 ft 6 in (4.42 m); wing area 294.0 sq ft (27.31 m²)
Performance: maximum speed 580 mph (933 km/h) at sea level; service ceiling 46,600 ft (14205 m); range 1,170 miles (1883 km)	**Armament:** four 20-mm cannon, plus underwing racks for two 500-lb (227-kg) or four 250-lb (113-kg) bombs
Weights: empty 13,183 lb	

McDonnell F3H Demon

Experience gained by the US Navy with the FH-1 Phantom and F2H Banshee brought an appreciation that there was no valid reason why carrier-based turbojet-powered fighters need be inferior in any way to their land-based counterparts. The two **XF3H-1** prototypes ordered from McDonnell on 30 September 1949 were expected to prove this belief, but for a variety of reasons it was to prove a costly exercise. Planned as a high-performance day fighter, the **F3H** had a basic

configuration that included swept wings and tail surfaces, with lateral fuselage intakes for the single turbojet engine mounted in the rear fuselage. The powerplant selected for the XF3H-1 was the new Westinghouse XJ40, but failure to develop this engine to the design power output and reliability was largely responsible for the enormous costs and delays suffered by the F3H programme. It was complicated also by the US Navy's requirement for a redesign.

Variants

F3H-1N: initial production version; some were used for ground instruction purposes, the remainder scrapped; 58 built
F3H-1P: planned reconnaissance version of the F3H-1N with the Westinghouse J40 engine; not built
F3H-2N (later F-3C): two F3H-1N airframes were taken from the production line to serve as F3H-2N development aircraft; the latter differed by having an almost 18 per cent increase in wing area, Allison J71-A-2 engines; basic armament of the F3H-1N, but equipped to deploy four AIM-9 Sidewinders; 140 built
F3H-2M (later MF-3B): generally similar to F3H-2N, but equipped to carry four AIM-7 Sparrow I radar-guided missiles instead of Sidewinders; 80 built
F3H-2 (later F-3B): definitive production version retaining provision to deploy Sparrow missiles, but basically a strike fighter carrying up to 6,000 lb (2722 kg) of bombs and/or rockets; 239 built
F3H-2P: planned reconnaissance version of the F3H-2; not built
F3H-3: projected production version with General Electric J73-GE-3 engines; not built

McDonnell F3H Demon (continued)

This redesign was aimed at allowing production aircraft, of which 150 had been contracted before the prototypes had flown, to be completed as all-weather night-fighters. The first XF3H-1 made its maiden flight on 7 August 1951, but it was not until 24 December 1953 that the first production **F3H-1N Demon** was flown, differing from the prototype by having APG-51 radar and armament comprising four 20-mm cannon and under-wing racks for other weapons. These early F3H-1Ns were powered by the Westinghouse J40-WE-22 turbojet (developing 7,200 lb/32.02 kN thrust, or 10,900 lb/48.47 kN thrust with afterburning) as a result of the failure of the intended J40 engine to develop its design thrust. The aircraft were as a consequence seriously underpowered and after 11 accidents in which two pilots lost their lives, production was halted. The situation was resolved finally by installation of the Allison J71 turbojet in production **F3H-2**s, and a total of 519 of all versions had been built when production ended in late 1959. Initial deliveries to VF-14 were made in March 1956, and the type equipped 11 squadrons before being withdrawn from first-line service in September 1964. The Demon saw few combat operations, being too late for use in Korea and retired before the US became involved in Vietnam. Its service career was cut short by a newer generation of more capable carrier fighters evolved during the long development period of the unfortunate Demon.

With the F3H-2M came the ability to engage BVR targets thanks to the AAM-N-2 Sparrow I radar-guided air-to-air missile.

SPECIFICATION	
McDonnell F3H-2/F-3B Demon	(10039 kg); maximum take-off
Type: single-seat carrier-based strike fighter	33,900 lb (15377 kg)
Powerplant: one 9,700-lb (43.14-kN) thrust Allison J71-A-2E turbojet with an afterburning rating of 14,000 lb (62.26 kN) thrust	**Dimensions:** wingspan 35 ft 4 in (10.77 m); length 58 ft 11 in (17.96 m); height 14 ft 7 in (4.44 m); wing area 519.0 sq ft (48.22 sq m)
Performance: maximum speed 647 mph (1041 km/h) at 30,000 ft (9145 m); service ceiling 42,650 ft (13000 m); maximum range 1,370 miles (2205 km)	**Armament:** four 20-mm cannon plus up to 6,000 lb (2722 kg) of bombs or rockets; retained provision to carry Sparrow III missiles
Weights: empty 22,133 lb	

McDonnell FD/FH Phantom

In 1942 the established sources of supply for US Navy aircraft were over-whelmed by the demands of wartime. Therefore the Bureau of Aeronautics entrusted the new and comparatively inexperienced McDonnell Aircraft Corporation with the task of designing and building two prototypes of what was to become the USN's first carrier-based turbojet-powered single-seat fighter. Designated **XFD-1**, the resulting prototypes were of low-wing monoplane configuration, had retractable tricycle landing gear, and accommodated the pilot in an enclosed cockpit well forward of the wing. The powerplant comprised two Westinghouse turbojets, one mounted in each wing root, but the first flight on 26 January 1945 was made on the power of only one of these engines, as the second had not then been delivered. Successful trials and USN evaluation, during which the XFD-1 became the first US jet aircraft to be flown on to and from an aircraft-carrier, the USS *Franklin D. Roosevelt*, brought a contract for 100 **FD-1 Phantom** fighters, the designation being changed to FH-1 before delivery began in January 1947. End-of-war contract cancellations meant that only 60 **FH-1**s were built, equipping initially the US Navy's fighter squadron VF-17A which, in May 1948, gained the distinction of being the world's first carrier-based jet fighter squadron. Subsequent operators were US Marine Corps squadrons VMF-122 and VMF-311, but within little more than two years these early jet fighters had been withdrawn from service.

SPECIFICATION	
McDonnell FH-1 Phantom	**Weights:** empty 6,683 lb
Type: single-seat carrier-based jet fighter	(3031 kg); maximum take-off 12,035 lb, (5459 kg)
Powerplant: two 1,600-lb (7.12-kN) thrust Westinghouse J30-WE-20 turbojets	**Dimensions:** wingspan 40 ft 9 in (12.42 m); length 37 ft 3 in (11.35 m); height 14 ft 2 in (4.32 m); wing area 276 sq ft (25.64 m)
Performance: maximum speed 479 mph (771 km/h) at sea level; service ceiling 41,100 ft (12525 m); standard range 695 miles (1118 km)	**Armament:** four 0.5-in (12.7-mm) machine-guns mounted in the nose

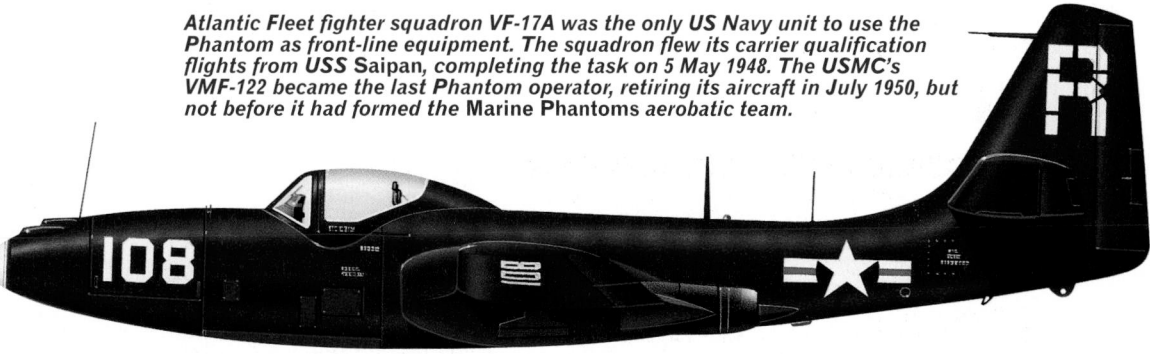

Atlantic Fleet fighter squadron VF-17A was the only US Navy unit to use the Phantom as front-line equipment. The squadron flew its carrier qualification flights from USS Saipan, completing the task on 5 May 1948. The USMC's VMF-122 became the last Phantom operator, retiring its aircraft in July 1950, but not before it had formed the Marine Phantoms aerobatic team.

McDonnell Model 120 and XV-1

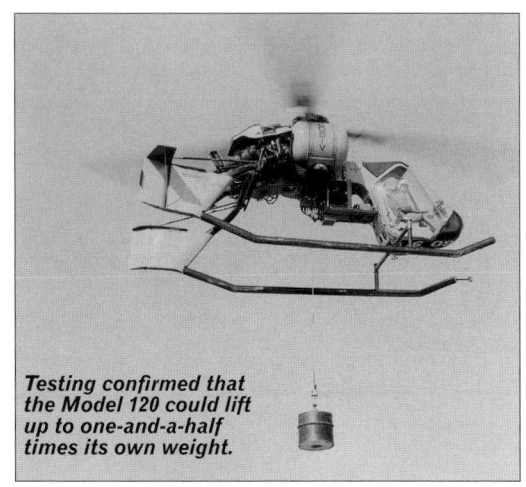

Testing confirmed that the Model 120 could lift up to one-and-a-half times its own weight.

Primarily as a research vehicle, McDonnell designed and built two prototypes of a somewhat complicated convertiplane under the designation **XV-1**. The fuselage, mounted on skid landing gear, had a 525-hp (391-kW) Continental R-975 piston engine at the rear to drive a pusher propeller; the shoulder-set wings mounted twin tail-

Although demonstrating a maximum speed of 200 mph (322 km/h), the XV-1 was too complex for the small advantages gained over a conventional helicopter.

booms with twin vertical surfaces, inter-connected by a tailplane and elevator; and above the fuselage was a three-bladed rotor with blade-tip pressure

jets. Extended testing as part of a combined US Army/US Air Force programme began with tethered flights, followed by a first free flight on

14 July 1954 and a first conversion from vertical to horizontal flight on 29 April 1955.
Subsequently, on 13 November 1957,

McDonnell flew the first of two prototypes of a small crane helicopter, designated **Model 120**, which had been developed as a private venture. This

used the rotor developed for the XV-1, but although tested successfully it found no market and further development was abandoned.

McDonnell Douglas F-15A/B/C/D Eagle

This aircraft was the second TF-15A and is illustrated in the Bicentennial scheme that was applied for the 1976 celebrations in the US.

The **F-15 Eagle** air superiority fighter and interceptor is in service in 2001 in its original configuration and in two multi-stage improvement programme (MSIP) versions.

The F-15 Eagle programme dates from 1965 when the USAF issued its FX requirement for a long-range tactical air superiority fighter to replace the F-4, and while the concept was being refined, hard-learned lessons from Vietnam were incorporated. The F-15 was thus to be a fighter specifically tailored for the long-range air superiority role. Vietnam experience pointed towards the need for twin engines, two crew (eventually not adopted) and an internal gun. The 1968 Request for Proposals added a requirement for a ferry range sufficient for deployment to Europe without tanker support and a maximum speed of at least Mach 2.5. This last inexplicable and very difficult requirement was technically achieved (albeit at huge cost), although an armed F-15 is limited to Mach 1.78.

McDonnell won the competition to build the F-15 (against proposals from North American and Fairchild-Republic) and the initial contract called for 10 single-seat development **F-15A** aircraft (often erroneously referred to as **YF-15** machines), two **TF-15A** development twin-seaters and eight Category II FSD aircraft. The first F-15 made its maiden flight on 27 July 1972, the first two-seater following on 7 July 1973. A total of 355 production F-15As was eventually built, together with 57 two-seat **F-15B** trainers. The F-15B is fully mission capable, though it lacks AN/ALQ-135 ECM and weighs 800 lb (364 kg) more than the F-15A.

The Eagle's large wings

These F-15C Eagles hail from the 199th Fighter Squadron of the Hawaii Air National Guard, based at Hickam AFB on Oahu.

give a remarkably low wing loading and confer a surprising degree of agility. The wings employ conventional outboard ailerons and have unblown inboard two-position flaps. The Eagle's aerodynamic design was very advanced by the standards of the day, and some modifications were needed to the original configuration. More serious than these minor aerodynamic problems were difficulties experienced with the F100-PW-100 engine, and with the X-band Hughes APG-63 coherent pulse-Doppler radar, both of which were specifically designed for the F-15. To minimise asymmetric handling problems, the engines are mounted close together and, to prevent damage to one engine causing reciprocal damage to the other, they are separated by a titanium keel. This provides a very rigid, very simple engine mount, which also allows rapid engine changes to be achieved.

The F-15A has an advanced and sophisticated avionics system, with the main radar supplemented by an AN/ALR-56 RWR, and an AN/ALQ-128 EW warning system. These are backed up by a Northrop AN/ALQ-135 internal countermeasures set.

The F-15 pilot sits high up and well forward on a McDonnell Escapac IC-7

ejection seat under a large blown canopy with excellent all-round view. The cockpit itself is well laid out, but is equipped only with analogue instruments, with no CRT MFDs. A HUD and a variety of control column- and throttle-mounted controls give true HOTAS operation of all important systems. The Eagle was designed to fight in the HOTAS mode, the pilot receiving all necessary information from his HUD and cueing the weapons system without having to look down into the cockpit to make switch selections or monitor instruments. The operational career of the Eagle began with the first delivery of an F-15A to TAC's 1st TFW at Langley AFB, VA, on 9 January 1976.

The first Eagles to see combat were blooded by Israel on 27 June 1979 when they claimed five Syrian MiG-21s. Four FSD F-15As were delivered to Israel during 1976 under

Japan's F-15s incorporate indigenous ECM and RWR systems, but are otherwise similar to US Eagles.

Operation Peace Fox III, and these were later joined by 19 refurbished F-15As and a pair of F-15Bs. Ten more ex-ANG F-15As were supplied after Desert Storm in return for Israel's co-operation during the Gulf War. On 7 June 1981, Israeli Eagles escorted F-16 Fighting Falcons on the long-range strike against Iraq's Osirak nuclear reactor, and were heavily involved in the 1982 'turkey shoot' over the Bekaa.

During the 1980s, the F-15A entered service with three TAC air defence squadrons in the interceptor role and was to have

been the carrier aircraft for the ASAT (anti-satellite) weapon, although development of the latter was cancelled.

The original Eagle two-seater was modified to become the **SMTD** (STOL/Maneuver Technology Demonstrator), equipped with Pratt & Whitney two-dimensional nozzles that can vector through 20° up and down and provide reverse thrust. The SMTD demonstrator flew on 7 September 1988. The aircraft used its vectored thrust and canard foreplanes to improve low-speed performance.

SPECIFICATION	
McDonnell Douglas F-15C Eagle	interception mission
Type: single-seat air superiority fighter	**Weights:** operating empty 28,600 lb (12793 kg); normal take-off 44,630 lb (20244 kg) on an interception mission
Powerplant: two Pratt & Whitney F100-P-220 turbofans each rated at 14,670 lb st (65.26 kN) dry and 23,830 lb st (106 kN) with afterburning	**Dimensions:** wingspan 42 ft 10 in (13.05 m); length 63 ft 9 in (19.43 m); height 18 ft 5½ in (5.63 m); wing area 608.00 sq ft (56.48 m²)
Performance: maximum level speed 'clean' at 36,000 ft (10975 m) over 1,650 mph (2655 km/h); maximum initial climb rate over 50,000 ft (15240 m) per minute; service ceiling 60,000 ft (18290 m); combat radius 1,222 miles (1967 km) on an	**Armament:** one M61 20-mm cannon with 940 rounds; maximum ordnance 16,000 lb (7257 kg), including AIM-120 AMRAAM, AIM-7M Sparrow and AIM-9M AAMs

McDonnell Douglas F-15A/B/C/D Eagle (continued)

After a three-year programme, the specially-modified SMTD Eagle made its 138th and final flight on 12 August 1991.

In the 1990s, the USAF improved its F-15A/Bs through an ambitious MSIP. This followed a far more modest MSIP of the early 1980s. The 1990's F-15A/B MSIP (carried out in conjunction with an F 15C/D MSIP) replaces the proven APG-63 with the more advanced APG-70 look-down/shoot-down radar, new avionics and digital central computers replacing the F-15A/B's original analog computers.

F-15A/B Eagles emerging from MSIP differ from F-15C/D models only in lacking the latter's radar warning receiver antenna located next to the horizontal stabiliser and the 2,000 lb (907 kg) of extra fuel carried by the **F-15C**.

The F-15C followed the F-15A on the St Louis production line and made its first flight on 26 February 1979. The two-seat **F-15D** similarly succeeds the F-15B trainer. F-15C/D Eagles came off the production line with the improved, lightweight APG-63 X-band pulse-Doppler radar with reprogrammable signal processing, and with provision for 750-US gal (2389-litre) CFTs (conformal fuel tanks) on the sides of the intakes.

Formerly known as FAST (fuel and sensor, tactical) packs, first demonstrated in 1974 and subsequently sold to Israel, the CFTs cannot be jettisoned, but their contents can be dumped, and the fuselage AIM-7 Sparrow AAM stations they displace are duplicated on the outside of the pack itself.

The F-15C was intended to be powered by the more powerful F100-PW-220 engine, although early aircraft retained the -100. Minor changes were made to the undercarriage, allowing gross weight to be increased to 68,000 lb (30845 kg). Software changes increased the scope of the 9 *g* envelope, an important modification since F-15As had effectively been limited to 7.33 *g* under most circumstances. Changes to the F-15C add about 600 lb (272 kg) to the aircraft's empty weight.

Initial F-15C deliveries were made to the 18th TFW at Kadena AB, Okinawa, commencing in September 1979.

First blood for the F-15C was drawn during a period of border tensions when two Saudi Arabian F-15Cs shot down two Iranian F-4E Phantoms over the Persian Gulf on 5 June 1984, possibly the only time one McDonnell fighter scored an aerial victory over another. Israeli F-15Cs may also have notched up kills prior to Desert Storm. When the US launched Operation Desert Shield on 6 August 1990, 48 Eagles made the longest non-stop fighter deployment in history, flying between 14 to 17 hours from Langley to Dhahran with six to eight inflight refuellings en route.

Further Eagles deployed to the theatre, and when the war against Iraq began on 17 January 1991, the US had five F-15C air-to-air (and two F-15E strike) squadrons in the field. The aircraft flew CAPs and fighter sweeps, and longer missions to escort strike aircraft. No F-15C/D Eagle fighters were lost during Desert Shield/Storm. More than 2,200 missions totalling some 7,700 hours of combat time were logged, resulting in 32 aerial victories, two of them scored by a pilot of the RSAF's No. 13 Sqn.

During the 1990s, F-15 Eagles continued to undergo staged improvements to radar and internal systems. Into 2001, the USAF was still upgrading its fighter Eagles and Raytheon was anticipating delivering up to 162 examples of the further improved AN/APG-63(V)1 to the USAF up to 2005.

The USAF has flown its F-15Cs extensively in operations related to the 'no-fly' zones over Iraq and during the Balkan troubles. Indeed, four AMRAAM kills against Serb MiG-29s were scored during Operation Allied Force in 1999.

The F-15C/D has been exported to Israel, Japan and Saudi Arabia, the Japanese aircraft being built under licence by Mitsubishi as the **F-15J** (single seat) and **F-15DJ**.

McDonnell Douglas F4H/F-4 Phantom II

When production of the McDonnell Douglas F-4 Phantom II ended in October 1979, a total of 5,057 had been built for the USAF (2,597), US Navy/ Marine Corps (1,264) and export customers (1,196). In addition, 11 in kit form had been supplied to Japan, where Mitsubishi built an additional 127 under licence to bring the final figure for Phantom II production to 5,195. This remarkable total far outstrips that of any other post-1960 jet aircraft built in the Western world, and is challenged only by the Mikoyan-Gurevich MiG-21. The Phantom II's history began 26 years earlier when, in September 1953, McDonnell began studies for a twin-engine all-weather fighter to supersede the F3H Demon in US Navy service. However, the F8U Crusader promised to fulfil the fighter role, and McDonnell was encouraged to develop an attack aircraft instead. Then requirement changes led to a large-scale redesign for the aircraft to undertake an all-weather attack/fighter role, and in July 1955 the company received a contract covering two **YF4H-1** prototypes; these were given the name Phantom II, the Roman numerical suffix being used to avoid confusion with the earlier McDonnell Phantom.

First flown on 27 May 1958, the Phantom II soon proved that it offered completely new capability, able to operate over a 290-mile (467-km) radius of action with a loiter for up to two hours, and it was the first aircraft which could detect, intercept and destroy any target within its radar range without assistance from surface-based radar. Such capability meant that the USN lost little time in ordering the initial **F4H-1** production version, redesignated **F-4A** in September 1962. Additionally, the type proved attractive to the USAF which, almost by tradition, did not normally order Navy aircraft. Phantoms saw extensive use in South East Asia, and subsequently played a significant first-line role in service with the armed forces of Greece, Iran, Israel, Japan, South Korea, Spain, Turkey, the UK, the United States and West Germany; the type also served temporarily with the Royal Australian Air Force pending the delivery of General Dynamics F-111s.

The earliest Phantom model still in service in 2001 is the **F-4D**, which serves with both the Iranian and South Korean air forces. The **F-4E** multi-role fighter remains the most widespread Phantom in service. Indeed, the F-4E retains capabilities that are sufficiently useful for Greece, Israel, Japan, South Korea and Turkey to have started upgrade programmes. The F-4E resulted from experience gained in air-to-air engagements over North Vietnam. It was first flown on 30 June 1967 and entered service in 1968. With 1,397 examples manufactured, the F-4E was also the most numerous version, and still serves with the air forces of Egypt, Greece, Iran, Israel, Japan, South Korea and Turkey.

Israel has produced its **Kurnass 2000** upgraded based on the F-4E, with enhanced ground-attack capability and including a modern cockpit with HOTAS controls and a digital databus to facilitate integration of modernised avionics. The F-4E also

McDonnell Douglas Phantom FGR.Mk 2

SPECIFICATION

McDonnell Douglas F-4E Phantom II

Type: two-seat multi-role fighter

Powerplant: two General Electric J79-GE-17A turbojets each rated at 11,810 lb st (52.53 kN) dry and 17,900 lb st (79.62 kN) with afterburning

Performance: maximum level speed 'clean' at 36,000 ft (10975 m) 1,485 mph (2390 km/h); maximum initial climb rate 61,400 ft (18715 m) per minute; service ceiling 62,250 ft (18975 m); area interception combat radius 786 miles (1266 km)

Weights: basic empty 30,328 lb (13757 kg); combat take-off 41,487 lb (18818 kg); maximum take-off 61,795 lb (28030 kg)

Dimensions: wingspan 38 ft 5 in (11.71 m); length 63 ft (19.20 m); height 16 ft 5½ in (5.02 m); wing area 530 sq ft (49.24 m²)

Armament: one M61 20-mm cannon with 640 rounds, maximum ordnance 16,000 lb (7258 kg); F-4F ICE intercept load comprises four AIM-120 AMRAAMs and four AIM-9L/Ms; F-4EJ Kai configured for maritime attack with ASM-1/2 AShMs plus Mk 82 and JM117 bombs fitted with the GCS-1 IIR-seeker head

In Japanese service the venerable F-4, in F-4EJ Kai form, is used in the fighter interceptor and fighter support roles.

served as the basis for the **Mitsubishi F-4EJ** dedicated interceptor built under licence in Japan, and for the **F-4F** that is unique to Germany. The F-4EJ, of which 140 were completed, lacked ground-attack capability and, as delivered, inflight-refuelling capability. Some 96 aircraft have been upgraded to the **F-4EJ Kai** standard with APG-66J radar and upgraded avionics. Turkish aircraft are being upgraded to what is in effect the Kurnass 2000 standard, while Greek aircraft are being improved with a package based on the ICE programme for the F-4F.

The F-4F was originally intended to be a lightweight single-seat version of the F-4E, but emerged as a very similar machine. Deliveries amounted to 175 aircraft, and while 150 were later upgraded in the **ICE (Improved Combat Efficiency)** programme's first phase with enhanced flight and navigation systems, only 110 have the second-phase improvements including APG-65 radar, new RWR, smoke-less engines and provision for the AIM-120 AMRAAM.

The reconnaissance version of the Phantom made its maiden flight when the first of two **YRF-4C** service test aircraft took off on 8 August 1963. This was followed on 18 May 1964 by the first flight of an **RF-4C** production aircraft of the type employed primarily for day

reconnaissance. Production totalled 503 aircraft, in which optical, radar, electronic and infra-red reconnaissance equipment is housed in a modified nose which increases the length of the aircraft by 2 ft 9 in (0.84 m) by compari-son with that of the F-4B/C fighters. The fire-control radar of the **F-4C** was replaced by a smaller APQ-99 unit for mapping as well as terrain and collision avoidance. Unique to

Germany's F-4F ICE aircraft will remain in service until replaced by the far more capable Eurofighter Typhoon.

Most examples of the Phantom reconnaissance aircraft, such as this Spanish CR.12, carry various combinations of medium- to long-range and oblique reconnaissance cameras, including one KS-72 or KS-87 forward oblique-framing camera plus one KA-56A low-altitude and one KA-55A high-altitude panoramic camera.

Phantom reconnaissance aircraft is the ARN-101 digital avionics navigation/reconnaissance system, which was later supplemented by a new navigation/weapons delivery system and ring-laser gyro. Night capability was added with provision for photoflash cartridges using one or two ejectors on the upper rear fuselage.

The RF-4C was the last

dedicated fast-jet tactical reconnaissance aircraft in US service, from which it was retired by two Air National Guard squadrons. The RF-4C was exported to two customers: up to 27 were delivered to South Korea from 1988, all the aircraft having been transferred from USAF stocks; and Spain received a total of 12 RF-4C (local designation **CR.12**).

Variants

YF4H-1: two original all-weather fighter prototypes with two 14,800-lb (65.81-kN) afterburning thrust J79-GE-3A turbojets

F-4A (F4H-1F): preproduction version with basic armament of four Sparrow III guided missiles; as the intended powerplant was not available, all were powered by 16,150-lb (71.82-kN) afterburning thrust J79-GE-2/-2A engines, the F suffix to the original designation indicating a nonstandard engine; 45 built

F-4B (F4H-1): production version generally similar to late F-4As, but powered by the intended 17,000-lb (75.60-kN) afterburning thrust J79-GE-8 turbojets; equipped for the fighter/strike role, F-4Bs had APQ-72 fire-control radar and could carry the basic Sparrow missiles plus four AIM-9 Sidewinders, or up to 16,000 (7257 kg) of assorted weapons; 649 built

EF-4B: one F-4B following conversion for ECM training

NF-4B: redesignation of one F-4B used for development testing

QF-4B: F-4Bs converted to drone configuration as supersonic targets for new missile development

RF-4B: production version of unarmed day/night reconnaissance aircraft generally as F-4B but with lengthened nose; standard radar/mission avionics of F-4B replaced by cameras, plus radar and infra-red sensors; 46 built for US Marine Corps

F-4C (F-110A): fighter/attack version for USAF, generally as F-4B, but with dual controls, 17,000-lb (75.60-kN) afterburning thrust J79-GE-15 engines, and numerous system changes: 635 built

EF-4C: redesignation of a number of F-4Cs following conversion to Wild Weasel configuration for anti-radar role

YRF-4C (YRF-110A): two F-4Bs following conversion to serve as prototypes of a tactical reconnaissance version for the USAF

RF-4C: production version of YRF-4C for USAF, basically an F-4C airframe in RF-4B configuration; 499 built

F-4D: USAF production version, generally as F-4C, but with avionics tailored to USAF missions; 773 built, of which 68 transferred to Iran (32) and South Korea (36)

EF-4D: redesignation of F-4Ds converted to Wild Weasel configuration

YF-4E: redesignation of first YRF-4C following conversion to serve as a prototype for the F-4E version

F-4E: major production version, introducing more powerful J79-GE-17 turbojets, increased fuel, redesigned nose with smaller APQ-120 radar, leading-edge slats to improve manoeuvrability, and 20-mm multi-barrel cannon; 1,405 built

F-4EJ: air-defence version of F-4E for JASDF; reduced fuel capacity; 13 built by McDonnell, plus 126 built under licence by Mitsubishi

F-4E(S): three aircraft converted to carry the HIAC-1 LOROP for USAF tests, but eventually delivered to Israel

F-4EJ Kai: designation of F-4EJ aircraft following upgrading by Mitsubishi

RF-4EJ Kai: redesignated, upgraded RF-4EJs

EF-4EJ: a small number of modified F-4EJs converted for use as ECM trainers during the 1980s

RF-4E: export tactical reconnaissance version of F-4E; 130 built

RF-4EJ: unarmed reconnaissance version of F-4E(J) for JASDF; 14 built

QF-4E: F-4Es converted for use as supersonic targets

F-4F: air-superiority version of F-4E for German Luftwaffe; introduced leading-edge manoeuvring slats of late-production F-4Es and had air-to-ground weapons system and related avionics deleted; 175 built

F-4F ICE: Improved Combat Efficiency upgrade of F-4F

F-4G: designation used initially for 12 F-4Bs operated in Vietnam with ASW-21 data-link system; reverted subsequently to F-4B configuration

F-4G: used later as redesignation of 116 F-4Es converted to Wild Weasel configuration, 18 more aircraft converted in 1987-88

QF-4G: F-4Gs converted for use as supersonic targets

YF-4J: redesignation of three F-4Bs following conversion to serve as prototypes of a proposed fighter version for US Navy

F-4J: production fighter for US Navy, with 17,900-lb (79.62-kN) afterburning thrust J79-GE-10 turbojets, enlarged wing and tail revisions to improve take-off/landing, and advanced avionics including automatic earner landing system; 12 built

F-4J(UK): 15 F-4Js delivered to the RAF in 1984 as interim interceptors following delays with the Tornado F.Mk 3. They were progressively fitted with some British systems until their premature retirement in 1991; the provisional **Phantom FGR.Mk 3** designation was not used

DF-4J: at least one F-4J converted as a drone director

EF-4J: two ECM-training conversions similar to EF-4B but based on the F-4J airframe

F-4K Phantom FG.Mk 1: revised version of F-4J for use by Royal Navy, and powered by 20,515-lb (91.23-kN) afterburning thrust Rolls-Royce Spey RB.16825R Mk 202/203 turbofan engines; two **YF-4K** prototypes followed by 50 production aircraft

F-4M Phantom FGR.Mk 2: version of F-4K for the RAF; same powerplant but with slight variations from F-4K, and retaining Sky Flash missile and external weapon capability; two **YF-4M** prototypes and 116 production aircraft

F-4N: redesignation of F-4Bs following updating with strengthened structure and more advanced avionics

QF-4N: F-4Ns converted for use as supersonic targets

F-4S: redesignation of F-4Js following updating with strengthened structure and introduction of leading-edge slats

QF-4S: F-4Ss converted for use as supersonic targets

McDonnell Douglas F4H/F-4 Phantom II (continued)

The Spanish aircraft were steadily updated with APQ-172 terrain-following radar, laser INS, new ECM systems, new electro-optical sensors and real-time data-link systems as well as inflight-refuelling probes similar to those installed on Israeli aircraft. In 2001 the CR.12 remained an important part of Spain's front-line forces.

The **RF-4E** was developed as an export version of the RF-4C, primarily for the West German air force. The type combines the airframe and engine of the early unslatted F-4E with the nose of the RF-4C, although some sensitive systems were not installed. The RF-4E's more fuel-efficient J79-GE-17 engines improve range and radius of action. The prototype was first flew on 15 September 1970, and 150 aircraft were eventually built. The RF-4E was retired from German service in 1992, but operators of the type in 2001 comprise Greece, Iran, South Korea and Turkey. Greece and Turkey each received eight new-build aircraft, and these were supplemented by ex-German machines. Israeli **RF-4E Kurnass** aircraft are equipped with indigenous reconnaissance

and avionics equipment and are armed with Shafrir, Python or Sidewinder missiles for self-defence. Under the Peace Jack codename, General Dynamics examined the use of the enormous HIAC-1 LOROP camera with the Phantom. Several USAF aircraft could carry a pod-mounted camera, but three Israeli F-4E warplanes were converted to take the HIAC-1 in an enlarged nose and redelivered to Israel in 1978 with the designation **F-4E(S)**. Japan bought 14 Phantom reconnaissance aircraft built to a standard similar to that of the RF-4C but operated under the designation RF-4E and these have been upgraded by Mitsubishi to **RF-4EJ Kai** standard. Additional capability was provided by the conversion of 17 F-4EJ interceptors to RF-4EJ standard without camera noses but with pod-mounted camera, SLAR or Elint systems.

The most ambitious Phantom acquisition programme was that undertaken by the UK. The Fleet Air Arm wanted Phantoms to operate from the small carriers of the Royal Navy, where the Roll-Royce Spey engine was considered a more apt powerplant –

thanks to its greater thrust on take-off and other benefits – than the standard J79. The airframe changes required to accommodate the new engine were major, although McDonnell Douglas had already examined a Spey-engined F-4 to meet the USAF's TFX requirement. Other changes incorporated into the resulting **YF-4K** included a proportion of British equipment and an extending nose gear leg, which allowed a higher AoA to be achieved during the type's take-off roll, facilitating launching from short decks. The YF-4K flew for the first time on 27 June 1966 and the two YF-4Ks were followed by 50 **F-4K Phantom FG.Mk 1** production aircraft. By the time these aircraft were ready for service however, the Royal Navy had only one aircraft-carrier left in service and half of the machines were delivered instead to the RAF.

This latter service also had its own fighter requirement and again the Phantom was chosen. Although the RAF wanted a J79-engined F-4, the British Government insisted on ordering a revised aircraft based on the F-4K, but deleting the extending

Those Phantoms built for the USAF, were built with a refuelling receptacle on their spines which made them compatible with the flying booms of USAF tankers. US Navy and many export F-4s had refuelling probes. A pair of F-4Gs is illustrated.

nose wheel leg. Two examples of the **YF-4M** were built, the first flying on 17 February 1967, before production of 116 **F-4M Phantom FGR.Mk 2** aircraft got underway. Initially used in an attack role, the RAF's Phantoms were later transferred to air defence and were finally replaced by the Tornado F.Mk 3 in 1992.

In addition to their service use, F-4 Phantom IIs have held a number of world absolute records in their time, an altitude

record of 98,556 ft (30040 m) set on 6 December 1959 and a speed record of 1,606.51 mph (2585.43 km/h) on 22 November 1961. These have since been beaten, but with other distinctions gained at various times, and a world low-altitude speed record of 902 mph (1452 km/h) which stood for 16 years, they distinguish the Phantom as one of the world's finest all-round military combat aircraft.

McDonnell Douglas MD-80 series

From the early 1970s the Douglas Aircraft Company, by now firmly established as an operating division of the McDonnell Douglas Corporation, began to consider the possibility of enhancing the commercial viability of the DC-9 series of twin-turbofan civil transports by the adoption of a re-fanned version of the standard Pratt & Whitney JT8D turbofan engine. The basic viability of the concept was proved from January 1975 when a DC-9, revised with one JT8D-109 engine, started on a flight test programme to generate data on the engine, which later entered production as the JT8D-209. Even

as data on the revised engine were being recorded, McDonnell Douglas was examining developments of the baseline DC-9 such as the **DC-9-50RS**, **DC-9-60**, **DC-9-50-17R** and **DC-9SC** with the revised Pratt & Whitney or other engines and with or without other modifications such as a wing employing a supercritical aerofoil section and a fuselage stretched by 'plugs' of various lengths fore and aft of the wing.

Company thinking, modified by the results of extensive market research, paved the way to the October 1977 launch of the development initially known

as the **McDonnell Douglas DC-9 Super 80** with its fuselage lengthened by 14 ft 3 in (4.34 m) over that of the current DC-9-50, the powerplant of two JT8D-209 engines, and other new features. The launch customers were Austrian Airlines, Southern Airways and Swissair, and this marked the real commercial beginning for the series that would prove to be the most successful of all DC-9 variants with production eventually totalling 1,191 before the production line, now under the ownership of Boeing, was closed down in 1999.

The three DC-9 Super 80 aircraft used in the certifica-

tion programme recorded their first flights on 18 October 1979, 6 December 1979 and 29 February 1980. During this period the manufacturer was offering an initial trio of DC-9 Super 80 variants, all with the same overall dimensions but differing in factors such as engine power, fuel capacity and weight. These three variants were the **DC-9-81** baseline model; the **DC-9-82** that first flew on 8 January 1981 with JT8D-217 engines each rated at 20,000 lb st (88.96 kN) with emergency thrust reserve, and the same fuel capacity as the DC-9-81; and the **DC-9-83** that first flew on 17 December 1984 with 21,000-lb st (93.41-kN) JT8D-219 engines supplied with fuel from a capacity enlarged by the addition of

966 Imp gal (4390 litres) in cargo compartment tanks. During 1984 the DC-9 Super 80 core designation was abandoned in favour of **MD-80**, and within this new system the three production variants became the **MD-81**, **MD-82** and **MD-83** respectively. The DC-9-81 entered service with Swissair on 5 October 1980 with a two-class layout for a maximum of 135 passengers. The DC-9-82 was designed as the counterpart of the DC-9-81 for 'hot-and-high' operations, and entered service with Republic Airlines, in August of the same year In 1982 this variant spawned a subvariant with the maximum take-off weight raised to an optional 149,500 lb (67812 kg) and powered by JT8D-217A engines for an important increase in maximum-

SPECIFICATION	
McDonnell Douglas MD-81	155 passengers
Type: two-crew short/medium-range airliner	**Weights:** empty 78,420 lb (35570 kg); maximum take-off 140,000 lb (63503 kg)
Powerplant: two Pratt & Whitney JT8D-209 turbofan engines each rated at 18,500 lb st (82.29 kN)	**Dimensions:** wingspan 107 ft 10 in (32.87 m); length 147 ft 10 in (45.06 m); height 29 ft 8 in (9.04 m); wing area 1,270 sq ft (117.98 m²)
Performance: maximum cruising speed 574 mph (924 km/h) at 27,000 ft (8230 m); economical cruising speed 505 mph (813 km/h) at 35,000 ft (10670 m); range 1,800 miles (2896 km) with	**Payload:** up to 172 passengers within the context of a 39,579-lb (17953-kg) maximum payload

With the MD-80 series, here represented by a Republic MD-82, McDonnell Douglas hoped to follow on from the successful DC-9. Like its Douglas predecessor however, the MD-80 failed to compete on equal terms with the Boeing 737.

payload range. The MD-83 was created as the long-range counterpart of the first two variants and entered service with Finnair, before the end of the same year.

During 1985 McDonnell Douglas announced a new variant of the family as the **MD-87** with its fuselage reduced in length by 16 ft 5 in (5.00 m) for a capacity of between 114 and 130 passengers. The fin heightened by 10 in (0.25 m) above the tailplane to ensure continued directional stability with the shorter fuselage, the powerplant of two

20,000-lb st (88.96-kN) JT8D-217Bs, and the standard fuel capacity of 4,863 Imp gal (22106 litres) that could be enlarged by the installation of auxiliary tanks that were offered as an option. Receiving launch orders from Finnair and Austrian Airlines, the MD-87 made its first flight on 4 December 1986 and entered service in November 1987.

The fifth and, as it turned out, last member of the MD-80 series was the **MD-88** that was launched early in 1986 with an order by Delta Air Lines. The MD-88 was in effect an

upgraded and updated version of the MD-82 with JT8D-217C engines, a maximum take-off weight of 160,000 lb (72575 kg), greater use of composite materials, a redesigned cabin for 142 two-class passengers, and refinements in several systems and items of equipment. As first flown on 15 August 1987 and delivered for service from January 1988, the MD-88 features a modern flightdeck with a Sperry EFIS, combined with a flight-management system and an inertial reference system. A far-sighted aspect of the

design, not in the event taken up except at the experimental level, was provision for the turbofan engines to be replaced by propfan units. McDonnell Douglas also investigated the possibility of executive transports based on the MD-83 and MD-87, and also the use of more modern turbofans. These engine types included the CFM56-5 and IAE V2500, either of which would have made it feasible for the fuselage to have been lengthened for the accommodation of between 173 and 180 passengers.

In April 1985 China

reached agreement with McDonnell Douglas for the co-production of the MD-80 and MD-90 series by SAIC (Shanghai Aviation Industrial Corporation) using assemblies made in China by the Chengdu, Shenyang and Xian companies. In the event SAIC assembled only 35 MD-80s before the end of the programme in October 1994: these were completed from kits supplied by McDonnell Douglas, and comprised 30 MD-82s for Chinese service and five MD-83s that were sold back to the American manufacturer.

McDonnell Douglas MD-90 series

The **MD-90** series was schemed in the second half of the 1980s as an improved version of the MD-80 with a more modern powerplant, redesigned and lengthened passenger cabin, wheels fitted with carbon brakes, and upgraded two-crew EFIS flightdeck. The key to the MD-90, whose programme was formally launched on 14 November 1989, was the powerplant

of two IAE V2500-D5 turbofan engines. This engine offers high reliability in combination with low noise, low specific fuel consumption, and good 'hot-and-high' capability. The V2500-D5 is offered in two forms with ratings of 25,000 and 28,000 lb st (111.21 and 124.55 kN).

The launch customer for the MD-90 was Delta Air Lines and other significant orders were soon placed.

The MD-90 made its maiden flight on 22 February 1993, and the flight test programme was undertaken by three aircraft leading to American certification on 16 November 1994. McDonnell Douglas delivered the first MD-90 on 24 February 1995 to Delta Air Lines, which operated the new airliner's first revenue-earning service less than one week later.

The first variant was the **MD-90-30** derived directly from the MD-80 with the enlarged vertical tail surface of the MD-87, powered elevators, and the fuselage forward of the wing lengthened by 4 ft 9 in (1.45 m) to balance the greater

weight of the new powerplant and at the same time provide space for two more rows of seats.

The second variant was the **MD-90-30T TrunkLiner**, essentially the MD-90-30 built in China by SAIC. In the event however, only three aircraft were completed.

In August 1997 McDonnell Douglas completed its merger with Boeing and it was decided that the manufacture of the MD-90 would end in 2000 after the completion of the 131 aircraft then on order. This decision also meant the cancellation of two other MD-90 variants, namely the **MD-90-50** and

the **MD-90-55**. The MD-90-50 was projected with a strengthened airframe, more power, a greater take-off weight and increased fuel capacity. The MD-90-55 was projected as an MD-90-50 derivative with two extra forward-fuselage doors to allow an increase in maximum passenger capacity.

By the early 1990s McDonnell Douglas felt that the time was more than ripe for it to offer a modern type to replace the DC-9-30. The new type was schemed as the **MD-95**, and its development was subsequently taken up by Boeing under the designation **Model 717**.

The cabin of the MD-90 provides single-aisle seating, typically in a 3+2 arrangement, for between 153 passengers in a two-class arrangement to a maximum of 172 passengers in a single-class arrangement.

SPECIFICATION	
McDonnell Douglas MD-90-30 **Type:** two-crew medium/short-range airliner **Powerplant:** two IAE V2525-D5 turbofan engines each rated at 25,500 lb st (111.20 kN) **Performance:** cruising speed 503 mph (809 km/h) at 35,000 ft (10670 m); range 2,200 miles (3540 km) with 153 passengers and reserves	**Weights:** operating empty 88,000 lb (39916 kg); maximum take-off 156,000 lb (70760 kg) **Dimensions:** wingspan 107 ft 8 in (32.82 m); length 152 ft 6 in (46.48 m); height 30 ft 6 in (9.30 m); wing area 1,209 sq ft (112.30 m²) **Payload:** up to a maximum of 172 passengers

McDonnell Douglas YC-15

To meet a USAF requirement for an AMST (Advanced Medium STOL Transport), McDonnell Douglas was one of five US companies submitting design proposals, and in late 1972 was awarded a contract for two **YC-15** prototypes for evaluation against two YC-14s from The Boeing Company. Its STOL capability centred on a partnership between wing and powerplant, the supercritical wing incorporating wide-chord double-slotted flaps over 75 per cent of the span. These, when fully

deflected, were blown by the efflux from, initially, four-wing-mounted Pratt & Whitney JT8D-17 turbofans each of 16,000 lb (71.15 kN) thrust, providing powered lift. No production of either company's design resulted from USAF evaluation, but modifications were made to the wings and powerplant of the YC-15 by McDonnell Douglas, which planned a civil production version, although as a result of insufficient commercial interest the project was soon abandoned.

A surprising twist of fate

The YC-15 had a typical transport aircraft configuration, with rear loading doors/ramps, heavy duty landing gear and a tall T-tail. The type is illustrated around the time of its first flight in 1975.

saw the first YC-15 being restored to flying condition, after almost 19 years in desert storage, during 1997. Boeing resurrected the aircraft to act as an advanced transport technology demonstrator. As such, the aircraft was expected to contribute to the devel-

opment of the civil BC-17X (formerly MD-17) variant of the C-17A Globemaster III and to Boeing's work on an Advanced Theater Transport. This ATT may combine features of the

YC-15 with tiltrotor technology. The type's first post-restoration flight was made on 11 April 1997 and it was hoped that funds could also be made available to return the second YC-15 to the air.

McDonnell Douglas (Hughes) OH-6 Cayuse/Model 500

Requiring a light observation helicopter (LOH) to

replace Bell and Hiller types then in service, the US

Army drew up a specification in 1960. This stipulated

high performance, turboshaft power, easy

maintenance and low purchase cost.

McDonnell Douglas (Hughes) OH-6 Cayuse/500 (cont.)

All the major manufacturers submitted proposals, but only three designs were evaluated: the Bell YHO-4, Hiller YHO-5 and **Hughes YHO-6**. Flown initially on 27 February 1963, the redesignated **YOH-6A Cayuse** was selected on 26 May 1965. The LOH mission led to the type's popular **'Loach'** nickname.

Although Hughes had little experience with helicopters (its Model 269 then being at an early production stage), the Cayuse (company designation **Model 369**) offered notable features, including an egg-shaped cabin and innovative four-bladed rotor that endowed excellent manoeuvrability.

First deliveries were made in September 1965 to the US Army, and the initial contract was for multi-year procurement of 714 aircraft. Production ended with 1,434 built in three slightly differing configurations. The production **OH-6A** was widely used in Vietnam, where 658 were lost in combat and a further 297 in accidents. The US Army then re-opened the LOH competition, which led to the Bell OH-58 Kiowa assuming the role (selected in preference to the **OH-6D**, a designation later used for a Japanese variant). This allowed wholesale transfers of OH-6As to the Reserve and National Guard. A package of modifications to airframe,

transmission, avionics and equipment led to the adoption of the designation **OH-6B** (or **Series IV**) for many modified aircraft. The modifications include re-engining with the 420-shp (313-kW) T63-A-720 engine with 'Black Hole' exhaust suppression, and provision of undernose FLIR, wire-strike protection and an adjustable landing light. The prototype first flew during May 1988.

Some later airframes were manufactured to **MH-6B** and **MH-6C** configuration for Special Forces support, and as **EH-6B** Special Forces command and control and Elint/Sigint platforms, and **AH-6C** light attack aircraft. Twenty-three MH-6Bs were built as new, of which three were converted later to MH-6C configuration. Four EH-6Bs were built, and two were converted as MH-6Bs and one was later converted to AH-6C configuration. Approximately 14 AH-6Cs were built, plus three converted MH-6Bs and a converted EH-6B. These aircraft probably functioned as interim equipment pending delivery of the dedicated Special Forces AH/MH-6 variants of the MD500 and MD530. All Special Forces H-6s were powered by the 400-shp (298-kW) Allison 250-C20 engine, with black hole IR suppressors, although retaining the V tail. They also had NVG-compatible cockpits and provision for a

turret-mounted FLIR. The MH-6B and MH-6C had external pylons for two gun pods, or 'people platforms' seating up to four passengers. The AH-6C was usually equipped with an M27 cannon to port and a seven-round Mk 66 or Hydra rocket pod to starboard, but could carry two gun pods, four rocket pods or four BGM-71 TOW missiles. The early Special Forces variants are now out of service, although some surviving MH-6Bs were not retired until 1992.

OH-6s are also operated by a number of Federal and State agencies, including the US Border Patrol and the State Department.

During the production run of the OH-6A for the US Army, Hughes built and marketed the aircraft for the civilian market, as the **Hughes 500**. The basic **Model 500** was little more than a civilianised OH-6, spawning a sizeable family of related helicopters that has seen much service in military markings, although only a few examples have been operated by US services. The 500 differed primarily in having a more powerful engine, the 317-shp (237-kW) Allison 250-C18A turboshaft, increased fuel capacity and a revised interior. A dedicated 'hot-and-high' variant intended primarily for export was the **Model 500C**.

The first military variant was the **Model 500M Defender**, supplied initially (in 1968) to Colombia. This version was also licence-built for the JGSDF by Kawasaki as the **OH-6J**, and by Nardi in Italy as the **NH500M** and the **NH500MC**, the latter a 'hot-and-high' variant. Spain bought a variant known as the **Model 500M/ASW** with MAD bird and torpedo capability.

Hughes continued to develop the aircraft, producing an aircraft known simply as 'The Quiet One' by fitting an early OH-6A with a five-bladed main

The OH-6 could be armed with an XM27E1 0.3-in (7.62-mm) machine-gun or an XM75 40-mm grenade launcher on the port side, with a flexibly mounted gun in the starboard cabin door.

rotor, a four-bladed tail rotor and a blanketed and muffled engine and exhaust. Airspeed was improved by 23 mph (37 km/h), payload was increased by 600 lb (272 kg) and the aircraft proved significantly quieter, running at 67 per cent of the usual rotor rpm. It was revealed in April 1971. A second aircraft was fitted with a computer-control-led vibration-suppression system in 1982. Slightly later, a second early OH-6A was converted as the **OH-6C** with an uprated 400-shp (298-kW) Allison 250-C20 turboshaft, a modified T-tail, and the five-bladed main rotor. It achieved a speed of 200 mph (322 km/h). Neither aircraft was put into production, but both tested features later incorporated into the Models 500, **520** and **530**.

The next basic variant was the civilian **500D**, which introduced a slow-

turning five-bladed rotor with the characteristic 'coolie hat' fairing over the rotor head, and a T-tail. Kawasaki manufactured this model under licence for the JGSDF under the designation **OH-6D**, the type also being licence-built in Argentina, Italy and Korea. Various military variants were developed from the 500D, the basic military equivalent being the **500MD Defender** with armour protection and IR exhaust suppression. This is available in several different configurations, each with a different designation. The **500D Scout Defender** has provision for rockets and gun pods, while the **500MD/ASW Defender** has nose-mounted search radar offset to port, a towed MAD bird and a heightened undercarriage to allow torpedo carriage. The **500MD/TOW Defender** is an anti-tank version with TOW missiles on outrigger

SPECIFICATION

McDonnell Douglas Helicopters MD 500

Type: one-crew utility light helicopter

Powerplant: one 317-shp (236-kW) Rolls-Royce Allison 250-C18A turboshaft derated to 278 shp (207 kW) for take-off and 243 shp (181 kW) for continuous running

Performance: maximum speed 152 mph (244 km/h) at 1,000 ft (305 m); cruising speed 135 mph (217 km/h) at optimum altitude; initial climb rate 700 ft (218 m) per minute service ceiling 14,400 ft (4390 m); hovering ceiling 8,200 ft

(2500 m) in ground effect and 5,300 ft (1615 m) out of ground effect

Weights: empty 1,088 lb (493 kg); maximum take-off 3,000 lb (1361 kg)

Dimensions: main rotor diameter 26 ft 4 in (8.03 m); length 30 ft 3¾ in (9.24 m) with the rotors turning; height 8 ft 1½ in (2.48 m) to the top of the rotor head; main rotor disc area 544.63 sq ft (50.60 m²)

Payload: up to six passengers, or two litters plus one medical attendant, or freight carried in the cabin

Above: Kenya employs the 500MD/TOW Defender on anti-tank duties, alongside other 500 variants. Note the nose-mounted sight.

Left: The Model 500D is employed as a trainer by the Royal Jordanian Air Force. Students go on to fly Hueys, Super Pumas or attack helicopters.

With the Model 500E, Hughes introduced a pointed nose to the 500 series. The MD 500E remained in production early in 2001.

tion of McDonnell Douglas's purchase of Hughes' helicopter interests. A handful of the Special Operations aircraft used by the 160th Special Operations Aviation Regiment at Fort Campbell are thought to have been based on the **MD 500D** and **MD 500MD** with the 250-C30 engine of the **MD 530F**. These are designated **EH-6E**, **MH-6E** and **AH-6F**, and may have been joined by the eight **MD 500E** helicopters

reportedly delivered to the Army's Systems Command in 1985. The EH-6E (four built, one converted to MH-6E) was an Elint/Sigint/command post aircraft, while the MH-6E (15 new builds and one ex-EH-6E) and AH-6F (nine built, plus one for evaluation by the USAF) designations reportedly cover an insertion and an attack version, respectively based upon the 500D and 500MD. Both are believed to retain (or to have reverted to) the original rounded nose contours of early MD 500s, since this is felt to be more crashworthy and better suited to NVG operations. The AH-6F has a mast-mounted sight and

provision for the M230 Chain Gun. Pairs of Stinger air-to-air missiles can also be carried. Survivors are understood to have been converted to later marks, based on the MD 520/530. The **Model 500MD Defender II** is an uprated model available in all the above options but with a quieter, slow-turning four-bladed tail rotor. Leading the next generation was the **Model 500E** (later **MD 500E**), with a revised pointed nose profile, improved tailplane endplate fins, more spacious interior and Allison 250-C20B engine. The specialist military models of this are designated **500MG** (later **MD 500MG**) **Defender**.

pylons and a nose-mounted sight; the similar **500MD/MMS-TOW Defender** has equivalent missile capability but introduces a mast-mounted sight. The **500MD Quiet Advanced Scout Defender** had the same armament with four-bladed quiet tail rotor and other noise reduction features.

In August 1985 the designation of the Model 500 was changed to **MD 500** after the comple-

---

McDonnell Douglas/British Aerospace Harrier II

For all its remarkable V/STOL attributes, the original Hawker Siddeley Harrier was of limited capability. Strong interest in the Harrier from the US Marine Corps during 1968 led to procurement of the original Harrier and eventually the USMC backed a development of an advanced model of the Harrier as the **McDonnell Douglas/BAe AV-8B**, which was intended to provide for the carriage of a larger warload and to provide better range/endurance characteristics. There followed considerable political wrangling and some revised thinking over future USMC requirements before what was known for a time as the **'Super Harrier'** project became a reality in the early 1980s.

While BAe had concentrated on the development of an improved model with an enlarged, advanced metal wing that could be retrofitted to existing Harrier airframes, the American former 'junior partner' on the AV-8A pressed ahead with its own second-generation Harrier. This was intended as a new production aircraft from the outset. The new design was based around a new wing of larger size and

supercritical aerofoil section, but was also schemed with more carbonfibre in other airframe areas and a completely revised cockpit, with HOTAS controls and a higher seating position for the pilot. All this was incorporated in a package without any significant increase in engine power, but with advanced aerodynamic devices to increase lift. First flown on 9 November 1978, fitted to the 11th AV-8A (which thereby became the first of two **YAV-8B** service test aircraft), the new wing had 14.5 per cent more area, 20 per cent greater span and a reduced leading-edge sweep of 10°. The greater area allowed six hardpoints to be fitted, and the carbonfibre structure allowed a 331-lb (150-kg) weight saving by comparison with the original metal wing. More efficient air

inlets and carbonfibre fuselage sections allowed a further equivalent weight saving of 750 lb (340 kg). The British-built rear fuselage remained of metal construction, for heat resistance, and is virtually unchanged, and so too is the landing gear.

Following the testing of four AV-8B pre-production aircraft from November 1981, the USMC took delivery of the first production aircraft during 1983. Like the four full-scale development aircraft, the first 12 of these were powered by the F402-RR-404 engine and had a double row of inlet suction relief doors, while later aircraft had the 21,450-lb (95.41-kN) F402-RR-406 (Pegasus 11-21) engine equivalent to the Pegasus Mk 105 used in British aircraft. From the 44th airframe a digital engine control unit was fitted to both the AV-8B single-seater and its **TAV-8B** two-seat counterpart, while from the 197th aircraft the 23,800-lb st (105.87-kN) F402-RR-408 (Pegasus 11-61) was fitted. A total of 280 aircraft was built, although an additional purchase of six attrition replacements following Operation Desert Storm increased overall procurement to 286. Originally this figure did not include two-seat TAV-8Bs, although these were subsequently incorporated on the McDonnell Douglas production line.

The British Harrier II programme suffered delays

During the late 1990s, a number of measures were taken in an effort to increase the conspicuity of low-flying jets over Germany following a spate of accidents. Brightly-coloured fins, as illustrated on this No. 4 Sqn Harrier GR.Mk 7, probably did little to help.

mostly connected with the unique requirements of the RAF. Nevertheless, the first **Harrier GR.Mk 5**, which first flew on 23 April 1985, was generally similar to the AV-8B, albeit with structural strengthening to suit it to the low-level battlefield support role envisaged by the RAF. A total of 62 Harrier GR.Mk 5s was ordered for the RAF, the workshare on these being split 50:50 between BAe and McDonnell Douglas, while the workshare on US aircraft was split 40:60 in favour of McDonnell Douglas.

From the 167th airframe,

all AV-8Bs for the USMC were provided with a night-attack capability with the installation of GEC FLIR, an improved HUD, an HDD and a colour moving map. The terms **Night Attack Harrier II** or **Night Attack AV-8B** are sometimes applied unofficially to these aircraft. The first delivery of this variant was to VMA-214 on 15 September 1989. Seven AV-8Bs were subsequently lost in combat during Desert Storm in 1991, mainly to SAMs, as the type was heavily engaged at low level on ground-support missions.

McDonnell Douglas/BAe AV-8B Harrier II

SPECIFICATION

McDonnell Douglas/British Aerospace AV-8B Harrier II
Type: single-seat shipborne and land-based attack and close-support warplane
Powerplant: one Rolls-Royce F402-RR-406A turbofan engine rated at 21,450 lb st (95.42 kN) or, in aircraft delivered from December 1990, one F402-RR-408 turbofan engine rated at 23,800 lb st (105.87 kN)
Performance: maximum speed 662 mph (1065 km/h) at sea level; initial climb rate 14,715 ft (4485 m) per minute; service ceiling more than 50,000 ft (15240 m); range 684 miles (1001 km) on a hi-lo-hi attack mission after STO with seven 500-lb (227-kg) bombs
Weights: empty 13,968 lb (6336 kg) including the pilot and

unused fuel; maximum take-off 31,000 lb (14061 kg) for STO or 18,950 lb (8596 kg) for VTO
Dimensions: wingspan 30 ft 4 in (9.25 m); length 46 ft 4 in (14.12 m); height 11 ft 7¾ in (3.55 m); wing area 238.70 sq ft (22.18 m²) including two 4.25-sq ft (0.40-m²) LERXes or, in aircraft delivered from December 1990, 243.30 sq ft (22.61 m²) including two 6.70-sq ft (0.62-m²) LERXes
Armament: one 25-mm General Electric GAU-12/A Equaliser fixed forward-firing rotary five-barrel cannon with 300 rounds in two underfuselage pods, plus for VTO up to 6,750 lb (3062 kg), or STO up to 10,800 lb (4899 kg) with F402-RR-406A engine or 13,235 lb (6003 kg) with F402-RR-408 engine, of disposable stores

McDonnell Douglas/British Aerospace Harrier II (cont.)

The **Harrier GR.Mk 7** is basically the RAF equivalent of the night attack AV-8B, using much of the same equipment and avionics. However, it lacks the rear fuselage chaff/flare dispensers. The variant is easily distinguished from the AV-8B and the Harrier GR.Mk 5 by its twin under-nose forward hemisphere antennas for the Marconi Zeus ECM. The GR.Mk 7 also has an NVG-compatible cockpit, allowing use of Ferranti Night-Owl NVGs instead of the GEC Cat's Eyes NVGs used by the USMC. A GEC digital colour map is fitted.

The first GR.Mk 7s ordered as such were the 34 aircraft requested during 1988, which took total RAF Harrier II procurement to some 94 (plus two proto-type/pre-series aircraft). To serve as GR.Mk 7 proto-types, both pre-series aircraft were adapted to accommodate the over-nose FLIR and undernose Zeus antennas, the first flying in its new guise on 20 November 1989.

The additional capability offered by the GR.Mk 7 was such that it was soon decided that all RAF Harrier IIs would be retrofitted to this configuration, and to ease this process Harrier IIs Nos 42-60 were completed as **GR.Mk 5A** machines with provision for GR.Mk 7 avionics and were delivered straight to storage to await conversion. Conversions of these aircraft (plus a damaged GR.Mk 5) began during December 1990. From aircraft No. 77 all RAF Harriers were fitted with the so-called 100 per cent LERX (Leading-Edge Root Extension), which further delays the onset of wing rock and improves turn performance.

While there have been few problems with the TAV-8B (illustrated), the RAF has found its T.Mk 10s underpowered.

The first production GR.Mk 7 was delivered in May 1990, with service deliveries beginning in August 1990. However, the GR.Mk 7 had a much-troubled development, hampered by the non-availability of many important equipment items. The failure of the MIRLS recce system designed for the Harrier GR.Mk 5 resulted in the GR.Mk 7 initially lacking any reconnaissance capability. When the RAF needed to replace Jaguars being used in the northern 'No-Fly Zone' over Iraq, Harrier GR.Mk 7s were selected. In order to give some recce capability, at least nine aircraft were rewired to carry the old Harrier GR.Mk 3 recce pod, which contained only optical cameras. Since then the Harrier GR.Mk 7 has been given the capability to use the Vinten Vicon 18 Series 601 GP-1 and Series 603 reconnaissance pods.

Other important delayed equipment included the Harrier's Aden gun armament and Plessey MAWS (Missile Approach Warning System). The Harrier GR.Mk 7 relinquishes the previous 30-mm Aden gun pods in favour of twin Royal Ordnance Factory ADEN 25-mm pneumatically-cocked revolver cannon. These have lower recoil, a much faster initial rate of fire (important when firing short bursts) and lighter weight than the single GAU-12A gun fitted to US aircraft. The Plessey MAWS automatically activates appropriate countermeasures and augments Zeus. Provision

of a dedicated Sidewinder pylon allows adequate defensive capability even when carrying a full offensive load. An integral BOL chaff dispenser in these pylons frees the aircraft from having to 'lose' a pylon in order to carry a standard Phimat pod.

By late 1992 some aircraft already had their FIN1075 INAS upgraded to FIN1075G standards, with the incorporation of a GPS receiver. The first aircraft so equipped flew with the new kit on 19 November 1992. The presence of GPS can be discerned by the addition of a small circular antenna on the spine of the aircraft.

No. 1 Sqn received GR.Mk 7s during late 1992, and became the first front-line unit to start night-attack training in earnest. The Harrier is one the RAF's three principal warplanes and is scheduled to receive new equipment in line with upgrades to the Jaguar and Tornado forces. The Harrier is receiving the TIALD laser designation pod, as well as the new Brimstone anti-armour missile and Paveway III laser-guided bomb.

Seeking to acquire a trainer fully representative of the second-generation Harrier's performance, equipment and capability, the RAF eventually decided to procure a version of the American TAV-8B. A decision to proceed with the **Harrier T.Mk 10** was taken in February 1990 and an order for 13 was confirmed early in 1992. Powered by the Pegasus Mk 105 engine, the T.Mk 10 retains the standard avionics of the Harrier GR.Mk 7 and is thus fully combat-capable. In this respect it differs from its American counterpart, which carries only training weapons.

The first Harrier T.Mk 10 made its maiden flight on 7 April 1994. Service deliveries began to the RAF's No. 20 Sqn in 1995.

The 205th AV-8B off the production line was the first fully equipped example of the improved **AV-8B Harrier II Plus**, and the true prototype for this new variant. It made its maiden flight on 22 September 1992, although the second AV-8B full-scale development machine had already flown as an aerodynamic prototype with a dummy radome and inert AIM-120 AMRAAMs. Equipped with the APG-65 radar, using an antenna cropped by 2 in (5 cm) to fit the AV-8B's fuselage cross-section, the Harrier II Plus retains the overnose FLIR sensor repackaged in a broader, squarer section fairing, and is otherwise externally identical to late-production

With the installation of APG-65 radar comes a new conical radome which changes the shape of the Harrier II Plus forward fuselage quite dramatically.

examples of the standard AV-8B. The provision of radar gives compatibility with the AIM-7 Sparrow and AIM-120 AMRAAM, endowing a BVR 'kill' capability for the first time. It also allows the use of the AGM-84 Harpoon missile in the anti-ship role. The last 27 aircraft of the USMC order were to have been built to this standard, but this total was reduced to 24, three of which have been delivered to Italy. The first AV-8B Plus was delivered in early 1993 and 73 existing aircraft have been upgraded to the same standard: these retain only their existing wings, tail surfaces and landing gear.

Spain and Italy have also purchased the AV-8B. From 1977 the Spanish navy embarked the AV-8S Harrier (locally designated VA.1 Matador) on the carrier *Dedalo*, and with the commissioning of the carrier *Principe de Asturias* in 1989, the Arma Aérea de la Armada embarked 12 **EAV-8B (VA.2 Matador II)** aircraft. The Spanish navy also ordered 13 (later reduced to eight) examples of the AV-8B Harrier II Plus in November 1992, for initial delivery in late 1995, and the surviving EAV-8Bs are being upgraded to the same standard. A two-seat **TAV-8B** was ordered in March 1992.

Italy's procurement of the AV-8B followed a protracted political debate, but in May 1989 two TAV-8Bs were finally purchased from the USMC. These aircraft were delivered in August 1991 and the first batch of three ex-USMC AV-8B Harrier II Plus aircraft was ordered in July 1991, followed by a further 13 in November 1992.

MD Helicopters MD 520N, 530, 530N & MD 600

Further improvement of the McDonnell Douglas Helicopters MD 500 led to the **MD 530**, whose first variant was the **MD 530F Lifter**. It made its first flight on 22 October 1982 and was intended primarily for civilian customers. Along with subsequent conventional variants of the MD 530 series, it featured a fully articulated five-bladed main rotor and a tail rotor increased in diameter by

SPECIFICATION

MD Helicopters MD 520N

Type: five-seat light utility helicopter

Powerplant: one Rolls-Royce Allison 250-C20R turboshaft derated to 425 shp (317 kW)

Performance: maximum cruising speed 155 mph (249 km/h) at sea level; initial climb rate 1,850 ft (564 m) per minute; service ceiling 14,175 ft (4320 m); hovering ceiling 9,035 ft (2735 m) in ground effect and 5,045 ft (1540 m) out of ground

effect; range 250 miles (402 km)

Weights: empty 1,586 lb (719 kg); maximum take-off 3,850 lb (1746 kg)

Dimensions: rotor diameter 27 ft 4 in (8.33 m); length 32 ft 1¼ in (9.78 m) with the rotor turning; height 9 ft (2.74 m) with standard skids; rotor disc area 586.78 sq ft (54.51 m²)

Payload: up to 2,214 lb (1004 kg) of freight carried as a slung load

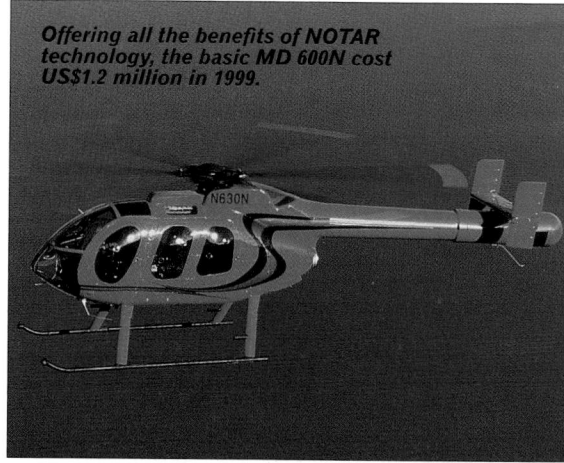

Offering all the benefits of NOTAR technology, the basic MD 600N cost US$1.2 million in 1999.

1 ft (0.305 m) and 2 in (0.051 m) respectively. The MD 530 is powered by the 650-shp (485-ekW) Allison 250-C30 turboshaft engine derated to 425 shp (317 ekW). The MD 530F Lifter is also assembled under licence by Korean Air. Dedicated military variants derived from the MD 530F include the **MD 530MG Defender**, which was flown in prototype form on 4 May 1984, and which was later ordered by Bolivia, Colombia, Mexico and the Philippines. Those delivered to Bolivia are reportedly dubbed **MD 530MD Black Falcon**.

In military guise the MD 530 is lightweight, versatile and highly survivable, and has both military and para-military applications. Weapons and sensor fits are tailored to the point attack and anti-armour roles, and for scout and day/night surveillance duties. The integrated crew station offers the pilot a head-up mode called HOLAS (hands on lever and stick) giving the pilot head-up/hands-on control of all

weapons selection and delivery, communications and flight controls, essential in combat and similar to the HOTAS (hands on throttle and stick) controls found in modern fast jets. The system is based around the Racal RAMS 3000, which also allows nap-of-earth and all-weather flight. A three-seat front bench makes provision for a normal complement of two pilots and an observer. The full standard MD 530MG has options for a mast-mounted TOW sight, FLIR, RHAW gear, IFF and laser rangefinder, and can be armed with TOW 2 missiles, unguided rockets, Stinger AAMs and a 30-mm Chain Gun. A **Nightfox** version, with NVG-compatible cockpit and a FLIR Systems Series 2000 Thermal Imager, is available for low-cost night surveillance and attack missions, while a more austerely equipped **MD 530MD Paramilitary Defender** is available for police, border patrol, narcotics interdiction and other roles.

Following its merger with McDonnell Douglas,

Boeing decided that it had no significant interest in McDonnell Douglas's helicopter line other than the AH-64 Apache, and in January 1999 announced that it was selling the rights, tooling and jigs for the MD 500 and its derivatives to MD Helicopters, a company owned by the RDM group of the Netherlands. The new company continued production of the helicopters described above as well as the **MD 520N** and MD 530 NOTAR (No Tail Rotor) models.

Relatively few NOTAR helicopters have been delivered, and none to a military customer, even though the type has proved particularly useful for law-enforcement agencies. These MD 520N (plus military **MD 520N Defender**) and **MD 530N** subvariants dispense with a conventional tail rotor in favour of an anti-torque tail boom: this has a variable-pitch fan mounted in its forward end, driven by a shortened tail rotor drive shaft and absorbing no more power, to produce an air stream which pressurises the booms interior and vents pressurised air through slots in the starboard side. This blown efflux unites with the main rotor downwash and is 'blown' down the side of the tail boom (the Coanda effect) as though it were a wing, generating a side-thrust force which counteracts the rotor's torque. Operated via the pilot's 'rudder pedals', a jet thruster with air exits to port and starboard allows pressurised air not vented through the slot to be ejected in either direction to provide control in yaw.

The MD 520N owes its origin to a Hughes test programme employing an OH-6A. This test bed was first flown after conversion on 17 December 1981 for evaluation of the NOTAR system. The true MD 520N prototype first flew 1 May 1990, with a production aircraft taking to the air on 28 June 1991. The MD 530N prototype had flown on 29 December 1989, but McDonnell Douglas did not proceed with its certification.

The Nightfox configuration is available for both the MD 500 and the MD 530G (illustrated).

The US Army took delivery of 'Little Bird' helicopters based on the non-NOTAR **MD 530FF** standard equipped to the MD 530MG standard but with the original rounded nose of the MD 500. These 16 **MH-6H** machines were conversions from earlier standards while the 12 **AH-6G** machines were five new-build and seven converted helicopters. All 36 or so surviving helicopters (perhaps including AH-6F and MH-6E machines) were upgraded to a common dual-role standard under the designation **MH-6J**. This was originally to have included conversion to NOTAR configuration, but this part of the upgrade was cancelled after trials of the first two NOTAR helicopters (perhaps designated **MH-6N** and **AH-6N**) showed that the new tail boom concept was not well suited to Special

Operations. A NOTAR allowed the aircraft to hover 'tail-in-the-trees' and permitted pedal turns at up to 104 mph (167 km/h), but limited maximum speed and dramatically increased fuel consumption. The **MH-6J** designation is now thought to apply to four or more MH-6Es brought up to the new standard, while the **AH-6J** designation is probably used for at least seven new-build machines.

First flown on 22 November 1994 in the form of the **MD 630N** prototype, the **MD 600N** was delivered from the middle of 1997 as a version of the MD 520N with a lengthened fuselage providing eight-seat accommodation, a six- rather than five-bladed rotor of slightly increased diameter, and the powerplant of one 808-shp (603-kW) Allison 250-C47 turboshaft derated to 600 shp (447 kW).

MD Helicopters MD 520N

MD Helicopters Explorer and MH-90 Enforcer

The origins of the **Explorer** can be traced back to 1987, when McDonnell Douglas decided to create an eight-seat development of the

MD 520N with more modern features and twin-engines. The helicopter initially known as the **MDX** and then as the **MD 900**

was formally announced in February 1988, and involved a number of partner companies including Hawker de Havilland of

Australia (airframe), Canadian Marconi (integration of the avionics supplied mainly by AlliedSignal), Kawasaki of

Japan (transmission) and Israel Aircraft Industries (cowling and seats).

Some ten flight and static test prototypes were built, and the type recorded its first flight on 18 December 1992.

MD Helicopters Explorer and MH-90 Enforcer (cont.)

The powerplant for this initial flight consisted of two Pratt & Whitney Canada PW206A turboshaft engines controlled by means of a FADEC (Full-Authority Digital Engine Control) system. The type received its American certification for VFR and IFR single-pilot flight in December 1994 and January 1997 respectively, and deliveries of what had now become the **Explorer** were made from December 1994 with the powerplant of two PW206B or PW206E engines,

optionally replaceable from the 129th helicopter by 641-shp (478-kW) Turbomeca TM319-2 Arrius turboshaft engines.

The Explorer's cabin has two front seats for the pilot and co-pilot or a passenger, and club seating for six passengers at the rear. There are two hinged forward doors, and two sliding rear doors. Each glassfibre rotor blade has a titanium abrasion strip on its leading edge, and is attached to the bearingless hub by a carbon-fibre-encased glassfibre

flexbeam.

Announced in September 1996 as the **MD 902** and first flown on 7 September 1997 for delivery from February 1998 with a revised designation, the **Enhanced Explorer** is a generally improved variant. It is powered by PW206E engines with improved one-engine-out performance, and features improvements to the air inlets and NOTAR inlet, and an upgraded stabiliser control system for significant improvements in payload and range.

Launched at the Paris Air Show of June 1995, the **Combat Explorer** is offered as a military derivative of the Explorer usable

in the general-purpose, casevac and combat roles. The type can carry multiple launchers for 2.75-in (70-mm) unguided rockets and 0.5-in (12.7-mm) machine-gun pods, and equipment options include a chin-mounted FLIR package for safe nocturnal flight at low level, and a roof-mounted NightHawk surveillance and targeting system. The type has yet to secure any orders.

In March 1999,

Operation New Frontier saw the US Coast guard operating a pair of leased Explorers on anti-narcotics duties. Armed with a 7.62-mm Minigun in the cabin doorway, the aircraft were named **MH-90 Enforcer** and proved effective in service. In September the original helicopters were replaced by two Enhanced Explorers and the USCG has identified a requirement for up to 12 of these helicopters.

SPECIFICATION	
MD Helicopters Explorer **Type:** eight-seat general-purpose light helicopter **Powerplant:** two Pratt & Whitney Canada PW206B or PW206E turboshaft engines each rated at 629 shp (469 kW) **Performance;** maximum cruising speed 161 mph (259 km/h) at sea level; initial climb rate 2,800 ft (853 m) per minute; service ceiling 18,000 ft (5490 m); hovering ceiling 13,000 ft (3965 m) in ground effect and 11,200 ft (3415 m) out of	ground effect; range 363 miles (584 km) **Weights:** empty 3,402 lb (1543 kg); maximum take-off 6,740 lb (3057 kg) **Dimensions:** rotor diameter 33 ft 10 in (10.31 m); length 38 ft 10 in (11.83 m) with the rotor turning; height 12 ft (3.66 m); rotor disc area 899.04 sq ft (83.52 m²) **Payload:** up to 2,848 lb (1292 kg) of freight carried internally or 3,000 lb (1361 kg) of freight carried as a slung load

The Explorer is manufactured largely of carbon-fibre and Kevlar. In layout it has a pod-and-boom fuselage, which is supported on the ground by a pair of skids with upturned forward ends.

Messerschmitt Bf 108 Taifun

Until the outbreak of World War II, Willy Messerschmitt's **M.35** (which was built to the extent of 15 examples) proved to be one of the world's outstanding aerobatic aircraft; from it was developed the revolutionary **M.37**, which was later designated **Bf 108 Taifun**

Bf 108 DK280 was impressed for RAF service, but suffered a collapsed undercarriage on landing in 1942 and crashed after an engine failure in 1944.

(typhoon). This originated from an order for aircraft to compete in the 4th Challenge de Tourisme Internationale of 1934, six aircraft being built to fulfil this contract. The prototype began flight tests in the spring of 1934, and was a cantilever low-wing monoplane with retractable

main landing gear and tail-skid, an enclosed cabin seating four, and powered by a 250-hp (186-kW) Hirth HM 8U engine; the type was tested also with the 220-hp (164-kW) Argus As 17 engine. The production **Bf 108A** aircraft were unsuccessful in the Tourisme Internationale, the handicapping system favouring lighter and less advanced designs, but the Bf 108A's high performance meant that in the late 1930s the type was used to make a number of record flights and also gained some competition success. The Bf 108 was adopted by the Luftwaffe in the communications role, was used by the Luftdienst for tasks such as supply and target towing, and was also exported in some numbers to Bulgaria, Hungary, Japan, Romania, the Soviet Union, Switzerland and Yugoslavia. With the outbreak of war, a German

embassy Bf 108 was impressed for RAF service, along with two Taifuns from the UK civil register, under the name **Aldon**. Several others served with the RAF for a short time after the war. Manufactured in Germany until 1942, when production was transferred to the SNCAN factory at Les

Mureaux, near Paris, a total of 885 had been built by the end of the war. SNCAN (Nord) continued development of the type after the war, building both the Bf 108 and **Me 208** in several versions to a total of about 285 aircraft. A few original Bf 108s and a number of Nord-built examples are still flying.

Variants

Bf 108B: major production version with a number of improvements, including a tailwheel replacing the tailskid, and powered by the 270-hp (201-kW) Argus As 10c engine

Bf 108C: proposed high-speed version with a 400-hp (298-kW) Hirth HM 512 engine; not built

Me 208: improved version with retractable tricycle landing gear; two prototypes built by SNCAN during the war, one of which was destroyed in an air raid

SPECIFICATION	
Messerschmitt Bf 108B Taifun **Type:** four-seat cabin monoplane **Powerplant:** one 240-hp (179-kW) Argus As 10C engine **Performance:** maximum speed 186 mph (300 km/h); service ceiling 16,405 ft (5000 m); maximum range 621 miles (1000 km)	**Weights:** empty 1,940 lb (880 kg); maximum take-off 3,053 lb (1385 kg) **Dimensions:** wingspan 34 ft 5½ in (10.50 m); length 27 ft 2¾ in (8.30 m); height 7 ft 6½ in (2.30 m); wing area 176.53 sq ft (16.40 m²)

Messerschmitt Bf 109

In the mid-1930s the build-up of the Luftwaffe provided the impetus for considerable updating of both fighter and bomber concepts. Willy Messerschmitt was then well advanced with design of the Bf 108 and, before it flew, had already started work on a single-seat

Oberleutnant Herbert Ihlefeld flew this Bf 109E as Gruppen-kommandeur of I.(J)/LG 2 in September 1940.

fighter, the **Bf 109**. It was to fly in competition against Arado Ar 80, Focke-Wulf Fw 159 and Heinkel He 112 prototypes, the Bf 109 and He 112 then being selected for further development with an order for 10 examples of each. The original Bf 109 prototype, first flown on 28 May 1935, was powered by a 695-hp (518-kW) Rolls-Royce Kestrel engine, but the second had the 610-hp (455-kW) Junkers Jumo 210A for which the aircraft had been designed. The pre-production prototypes had various combinations of armament, the first three becoming **Bf 109A** aircraft, while later examples served as prototypes of the **Bf 109B**. Early sub-variants included the **Bf 109B-1** with a 635-hp (474-kW) Jumo 210D and the **Bf 109B-2** with a 640-hp (477-kW) Jumo 210E, the latter soon replaced by the 670-hp (500-kW) 210G.

Production 109B-1s were delivered first in early 1937 to the Luftwaffe's top fighter unit, JG 132 'Richthofen', and like several other German types the Bf 109 was blooded first in the Spanish Civil War, serving with the Legion Condor from the summer of 1937. Just before that, five non-standard Bf 109s took part in an international flying meeting in Zurich, two of them with 950-hp (708-kW) Daimler-Benz engines which conferred higher performance. The team won the Circuit of the Alps contest, plus a team race, a speed event, and a climb and dive competition. This success was crowned on 11 November 1937 when a Bf 109, flown by Dr. Ing. Hermann Wurster, raised the landplane world speed record to 379.38 mph (610.55 km/h), using a boosted DB 601 engine of 1,650 hp (1230 kW).

Meanwhile, production deliveries were continuing with the Bf 109B, supplanted gradually by the **Bf 109C-1** with the 700-hp (522-kW) Jumo 210Ga engine. Output was then being stepped up, with the fighters being built also by Arado, Erla, Focke-Wulf and Fieseler, and by September 1938 almost 600 had been produced. A year later, when World War II began, the Luftwaffe had more

than 1,000 Bf 109s in service, but following the collapse of France no serious effort was made to increase production, then averaging about 156 aircraft per month. By 1941 only Messerschmitt, Erla and WNF (Austria) were building Bf 109s, but in 1942 production by Messerschmitt reached almost 2,700, and was supplemented during 1943 by production in Hungary, where around 600 were built. In spite of heavy Allied bombing, Bf 109 manufacture in Germany during 1944 reached almost 14,000, and although no accurate over-all production figures exist, it is estimated that some 35,000 were built, a figure second only to the Ilyushin Il-2/Il-10 series.

Bf 109s had taken part in the attack on Poland which had marked the beginning

of World War II, and had played a significant role in all subsequent Luftwaffe fighter operations, making their last major sortie, involving 120 aircraft, on 7 April 1945. In addition to production for the Luftwaffe, Messerschmitt had exported Bf 109s to Bulgaria, Finland, Hungary, Japan, Romania, Slovakia, Spain, Switzerland, the USSR and Yugoslavia. Hispano, in Spain, produced the Bf 109 for the Spanish air force under a licence negotiated in 1942, the first **Ha-1109J1L** aircraft, combining Messerschmitt-built sample airframes and Hispano-Suiza engines, flown from early March 1945. Subsequent production included the **HA-1109-K1L** with the French Hispano-Suiza HS12Z-89 engine of 1,300 hp (969 kW), **HA-1109-M1L** with the Rolls-Royce Merlin 500-45 engine of 1,400 hp (1044 kW), and the generally similar **HA-1112** with revised armament. Corresponding two-seat trainer versions were the

HA-1110-K1L with a Hispano-Suiza engine, and the **HA-1110-M1L** with the Merlin engine. One other source of production was in Czechoslovakia which, post-war, equipped its air force with the Avia S-99

(with DB 605A engines) and a far larger number of S-199 aircraft with Jumo 211F engines; they remained in service until 1957, being used for the last five years in a training role.

Variants

Bf 109A: initial prototypes with Rolls-Royce Kestrel and Junkers Jumo engines
Bf 109B: the preproduction **Bf 109B-0** had the 610-hp (455-kW) Jumo 210B engine; the production **Bf 109B-1** and **Bf 109B-2** had Jumo 210D and Jumo 210E engines of 635 hp (474 kW) and 640 hp (477 kW) respectively
Bf 109C: built as **Bf 109C-0** and sub-variants
Bf 109C-1 to **Bf 109C-3**, all powered by the 640-hp (477-kW) Jumo 210G, but with differing armament
Bf 109D: the **Bf 109D-0** aircraft, converted from Bf 109B airframes, plus a small number of production **Bf 109D-1** aircraft, were the first (except for prototypes) to introduce the 960-hp (716-kW) Daimler-Benz DB 600A engine
Bf 109E: first large-scale production version, introducing the 1,100-hp (820-kW) Daimler-Benz DB 601A engine with direct fuel injection and improved superchargers; sub-variants were designated **Bf 109E-0** to **Bf 109E-9**, with 1,200-hp (895-kW) DB 601N or 1,300-hp (969-kW) DB 601E engines and variations in armament
Bf 109F: production version, in sub-variants from **Bf 109F-0** to **Bf 109F-6**, with DB 601N or DB 601E engines and variations of armament; introduced a number of airframe refinements resulting in improved performance at altitude
Bf 109G: major production version with provision for

cockpit pressurisation, in sub-variants from **Bf 109G-0** to **Bf 109G-16**; proving to be of no significant value, pressurisation provision was deleted from **Bf 109G-6** and subsequent sub-variants; Bf 109G-0s retained the DB 601E engine, but the **Bf 109G-1** was the first to introduce the new DB 605A engine of higher compression ratio, developing a maximum 1,475 hp (1100 kW); later versions of this engine, the DB 605DC for example, produced a maximum of 2,000 hp (1491 kW) with water/methanol injection; the **Bf 109G-12** differed by being a tandem two-seat trainer
Bf 109H: high-altitude development of the Bf 109F with a 6-ft 6¾-in (2.00-m) increase in wingspan, built in small numbers; **Bf 109H-0** aircraft had DB 601E engines, and **Bf 109H-1** aircraft had the DB 605A
Bf 109K: production version built as **Bf 109K-0** with DB 605D engine; **Bf 109K-2** and **Bf 109K-4** with 1,500-hp (1119-kW) DB 605ASCM/DCM; **Bf 109K-6** similar to the Bf 109K-2 but with different armament; and **Bf 109K-14** with the DB 605L engine
Bf 109T: initially 10 conversions of the Bf 109E as **Bf 109T-0**, with increased wingspan, foldable outer wing panels, wing spoilers, arrester hook and catapult spools for service aboard the aircraft-carrier *Graf Zeppelin*; followed by 60 generally similar **Bf 109T-1** production aircraft with the DB 601N engine; however, when work on the aircraft-carrier ended, these aircraft had the arrester hooks and catapult spools removed, becoming redesignated **Bf 109T-2**

II./JG 3 had this Bf 109F-4/Z Trop on strength as the aircraft of its Gruppenkommandeur Hauptmann Karl-Heinz Krahl, while based at San Pietro, Italy in April 1942.

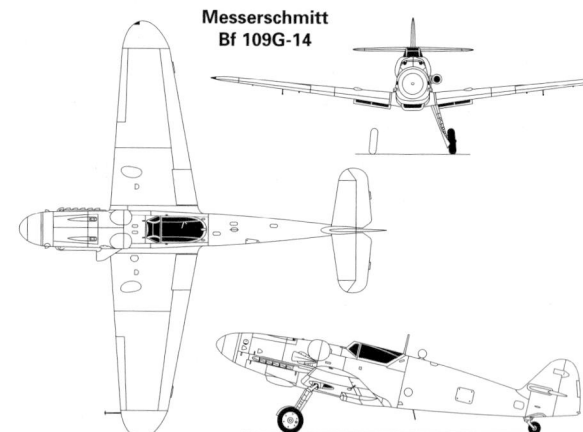

Messerschmitt Bf 109G-14

Switzerland received its first batch of 10 Bf 109s, D models like that illustrated, in 1938. Bf 109Es were also used.

SPECIFICATION

Messerschmitt Bf 109G-6
Type: single-seat fighter
Powerplant: one Daimler-Benz DB 605AM inverted V-12 piston engine developing 1,800 hp (1342 kW) with water/methanol injection
Performance: maximum speed 386 mph (621 km/h) at 22,965 ft (7000 m); service ceiling 38,550 ft (11750 m); range 447 miles

(720 km)
Weights: empty equipped 5,893 lb (2673 kg); maximum take-off 6,945 lb (3150 kg)
Dimensions: wingspan 32 ft 6½ in (9.92 m); length 29 ft 7 in (9.02 m); height 11 ft 2 in (3.40 m); wing area 127.77 sq ft (16.05 m²)
Armament: two 13-mm (0.51-in) MG 131 machine-guns and three 20-mm MG 151 cannon

Messerschmitt Bf 110

This Bf 110C was tasked in the night-fighting role with 2./NJG 1 at Gütersloh in July 1940. The aircraft still wears the day-fighter scheme from its previous service as a Zerstörer.

The **Bf 110** was Messerschmitt's submission to a Luftwaffe requirement for a twin-engine fighter, for which Focke-Wulf and Henschel also prepared designs. Primary role was that of a heavy fighter, but the capability of being deployed as a high-speed bomber was also stipulated. Changes in requirements for the fighter resulted in Messerschmitt being the only candidate, and the first of three prototypes was flown on 12 May 1936. The two 910-hp (679-kW) Daimler-Benz DB 600A engines proved very unreliable, but a speed of 314 mph (505 km/h) was recorded during tests and the general performance was considered reasonable. Engine unreliability plagued the three prototypes, but the pre-production batch of **Bf 110A-0** aircraft had reliable 680-hp (507-kW) Junkers Jumo 210Da engines which resulted in a considerable performance penalty. The long wait for the new fuel-injection DB 601A seriously delayed the Bf 110 programme; after the fourth pre-production aircraft had been completed in March 1938, the company switched to the **Bf 110B**, a cleaned-up version with provision for two 20-mm cannon to supplement the four machine-guns of the **Bf 110A-0**, a total of 45 being built with Jumo engines. They comprised the **Bf 110B-1**, the camera-carrying **Bf 110B-2**, and a few Bf 110B-1s that were modi-

fied subsequently for use as two-seat trainers under the designation **Bf 110B-3**. Availability of DB 601A engines led to the introduction of the **Bf 110C**, initially in the form of 10 pre-production **Bf 110C-0** aircraft delivered for evaluation in January 1939, and followed closely by the first **Bf 110C-1** series fighters. As production built up, Focke-Wulf and Gotha joined the programme. The new fighter first proved its capabilities during the Polish campaign, and in December 1939 confirmed its value as a bomber destroyer by shooting down nine out of 22 Vickers Wellingtons on a mission over the Heligoland Bight. Early use had shown the importance of the Bf 110, production priority ensuring that 315 had been delivered by the end of 1939 and a production rate averaging 102 per month throughout 1940.

However, in 1940 the Bf 110 began to encounter opposition from modern single-engine fighters for the first time and was found unable to match the manoeuvrability of the Hurricane and Spitfire; with

only a single rear-firing gun the Bf 110 was unable to defend itself adequately, and from the beginning of the Battle of Britain Bf 110 units suffered very heavy losses. The type was deployed temporarily on bombing and reconnaissance missions, but in the winter of 1940-1 found its most suitable role as a night-fighter. Initially the Bf 110 night-fighter had no specialised equipment, crews relying upon keen eyesight for the interception of enemy bombers. An early airborne aid was an

infra-red sensor carried by the **Bf 110D-1/U-1**, which proved to be a failure, but in mid-1941 ground-controlled interception was becoming established and very soon the Bf 110 night-fighter units were achieving important success. Twelve months later they were being equipped with Lichtenstein air interception radar, and by the autumn of 1942 most Luftwaffe night-fighters carried a version of this airborne aid. In mid-1943 the RAF countered this capability by introducing the radar-jamming bundles of aluminium foil strips known as 'Window', gaining an ascendancy that lasted for some six months before the Bf 110s were equipped with more advanced radar that could

be effective despite 'Window' jamming. In early 1944 the German night-fighter force was at the peak of its capability, at which time some 320 Bf 110s were deployed in this role, representing about 60 per cent of the total number of night-fighters available for defence of the German homeland. A year later more advanced night-fighters had entered service, only 150 Bf 110s then being operational with the night-fighter groups, and all became less and less effective as German fuel supplies dried up.

Produced in many versions, including legion subvariants, about 6,050 Messerschmitt Bf 110s had been built when production ended in March 1945.

Variants

Bf 110A-0: four pre-production aircraft with Jumo 210B engines
Bf 110B: initial production version, appeared in sub-variants **Bf 110B-0** to **Bf 110B-3**
Bf 110C: production version introducing two 1,100-hp (820-kW) Daimler-Benz DB 601A fuel-injected engines; built in subvariants **Bf 110C-0** to **Bf 110C-7**, the **Bf 110C-4** showing its capability as a fighter-bomber and the **Bf 110C-5** as a reconnaissance aircraft
Bf 110D: production version, built in sub-variants **Bf 110D-0** to **Bf 110D-3**, and including the **Bf 110D-2** long-range fighter-bomber and **Bf 110D-3** convoy escort
Bf 110E: production version, built in sub-variants **Bf 110E-0** to **Bf 110E-3**, the **Bf 110E-1** and **Bf 110E-2** being fighter-bombers or night-fighters, and the **Bf 110E-3** a long-range reconnaissance version
Bf 110F: production version, generally as Bf 110E, but introducing 1,350-hp (1007-kW) DB 601F engines; built in subvariants up to **Bf 110F-4**
Bf 110G: production version, introducing 1,475-hp (1100-kW) DB 601B-1 engines; built in subvariants up to **Bf 110G-4**
Bf 110H: final production version, basically similar to Bf 110G; built in sub-variants up to **Bf 110H-4**

ZG 26 flew Bf 110Ds over North Africa, this aircraft having been photographed in 1942. The Bf 110D made its combat debut during the Battle of Britain, JG 26 taking its Bf 110D-3s to Sicily and then North Africa in the winter of 1940-41.

SPECIFICATION

Messerschmitt Bf 110G/R3
Type: three-seat night-fighter
Powerplant: two 1,475-hp (1100kW) Daimler-Benz DB 601B-1 inverted V-12 piston engines
Performance: maximum speed 342 mph (550 km/h) at 22,900 ft (6980 m); service ceiling 26,245 ft (8000 m); maximum range with drop tanks 1,305 miles (2100 km)
Weights: empty 11,222 lb (5090 kg); maximum take-off

21,804 lb (9890 kg)
Dimensions: wingspan 53 ft 3¾ in (16.25 m); length 42 ft 9¾ in (13.05 m); height 13 ft 8½ in (4.18 m); wing area 413.35 sq ft (39.40 m²)
Armament: two 30-mm MK 108 cannon and two 20-mm MG 151 cannon in nose, and two 0.31-in (7.92-mm) MG 81 machine-guns on trainable mount in rear cockpit

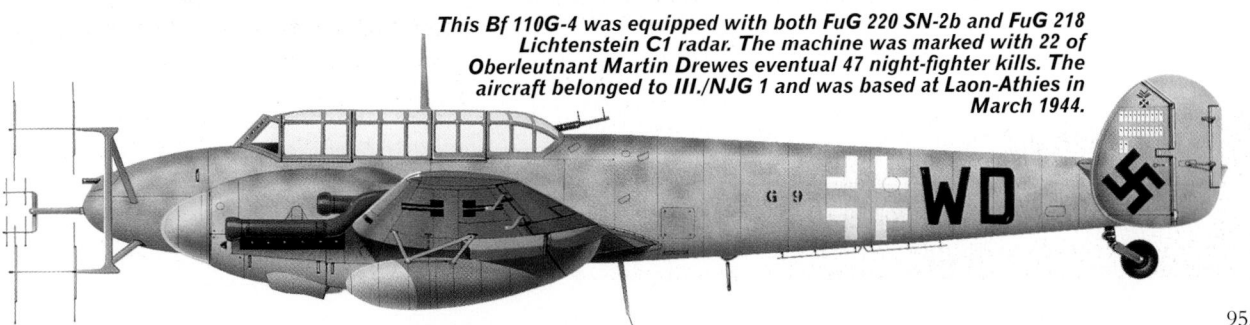

This Bf 110G-4 was equipped with both FuG 220 SN-2b and FuG 218 Lichtenstein C1 radar. The machine was marked with 22 of Oberleutnant Martin Drewes eventual 47 night-fighter kills. The aircraft belonged to III./NJG 1 and was based at Laon-Athies in March 1944.

Messerschmitt Me 163 and Me 163B Komet

The remarkable **Me 163** rocket-powered fighter was developed from the designs of Dr Alexander Lippisch who, for many years, had been working on tailless sailplane designs. In January 1939, he and his design team joined the Messerschmitt company and began work to adapt the DFS 194 tailless research glider to be powered by an 882-lb (3.92-kN) thrust Walter rocket motor. Successful testing of this aircraft, during which a speed of 342 mph (550 km/h) was attained, resulted in Messerschmitt receiving an order for six **Me 163A** prototypes.

The first prototype was tested initially as a glider, towed by a Bf 110. Prototypes were tested at Peenemünde in the summer of 1941 powered by the Walter HWK RII-203b rocket motor of 1,653-lb (7.35-kN) thrust, and demonstrated speeds of up to 550 mph

(885 km/h). Flown by Heini Dittmar, an Me 163A, towed to a height of 13,125 ft (4000 m) before the engine was fired, attained 623.85 mph (1003.9 km/h) before losing stability as a result of compressibility effects. Dittmar succeeded in regaining control, and the wing was redesigned to alleviate this problem. There were many development problems, those posed by the highly unstable liquid fuel for the rocket motor and by the jettison-able wheeled dolly/retractable skid landing gear being the most difficult to resolve. Following the Me 163As, a pre-production series of 10 **Me 163A-0** aircraft was built by Wolf Hirth and used as training gliders. Considerable redesign preceded the order for six prototype and 70 production **Me 163B Komet** (comet) point interceptors, the pre-production prototypes having the

designation **Me 163Ba-1**, and the first production deliveries of **Me 163B-1a** interceptors began in May 1944. The type saw action for the first time on 28 July of that year when five Me 163s from 1./JG 400, the first operational unit, attacked a formation of Boeing B-17 flying Fortresses. This proved ineffective, for the closing speed of about 808 mph (1300 km/h) meant that the slow-firing MK 108 cannon could be fired for only three seconds before the pilot had to break off his attack. At this late stage of the war the provision of an effective weapon was to prove an insoluble problem, and production of the Me 163 ended in February 1945 after nearly 400 of all variants had been built. They included a few examples of the **Me 163S** tandem two-seat trainer which, with ammunition and fuel tanks removed to provide space for a second seat, had to be flown as a

glider, and the **Me 163C-1a**, of which three were built but only one flown. This was an improved version of the Me 163B, with a revised airframe and a modified powerplant to increase powered endurance.

Projected developments included the **Me 163D** with further refinement and retractable tricycle landing gear; one prototype was built, and because Junkers would have developed and produced this version it

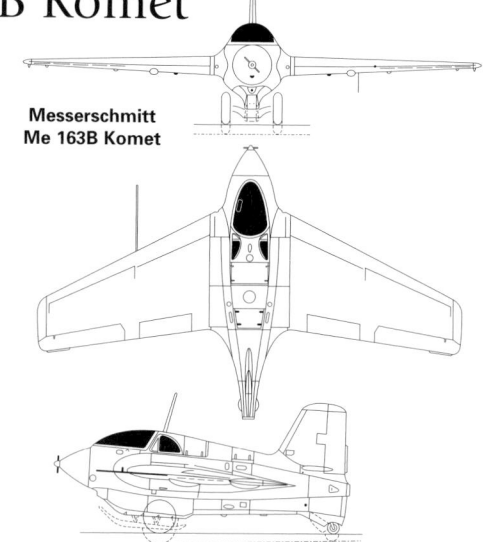

Messerschmitt Me 163B Komet

gained the temporary designation **Junkers 248** before reverting to a Messerschmitt designation as the **Me 263**. It did not enter production, however, the prototype being captured by the Soviets, who modified its wings and tail surfaces before flying it in 1946 as the **I-270(ZH)**, but its development was soon abandoned. Plans were made for production of a licence-built version in Japan, designated **Mitsubishi Ki-200**.

Leutnant Fritz Kelb of 1./JG 400 downed a Lancaster in this Me 163B on 10 April 1945. On 25 April, he shot down a B-17 in an Me 262, becoming the only pilot to score kills on both types.

SPECIFICATION	
Messerschmitt Me 163B-1a	endurance 7 minutes 30 seconds
Type: single-seat interceptor fighter	**Weights:** empty 4,200 lb (1905 kg); maximum take-off 9,061 lb (4110 kg)
Powerplant: one 3,750-lb (16.67-kN) thrust Walter HWK 509A-2 rocket motor	**Dimensions:** wingspan 30 ft 7 in (9.32 m); length 19 ft 2 in (5.84 m); height 9 ft 1 in (2.77 m); wing area 199.14 sq ft (18.50 m²)
Performance: maximum speed 596 mph (960 km/h) at 32,810 ft (10000 m); service ceiling 39,700 ft (12100 m); maximum powered	**Armament:** two 30-mm MK 108 cannon in wing roots

Messerschmitt Me 209

In the years between 1935, when Germany first revealed formation of the Luftwaffe, and the outbreak of World War II, Adolf Hitler was most anxious to impress upon the world the capability of the fighter aircraft that equipped his new air force. This resulted in design of the **Me 209** to be used to establish a new absolute world speed record. With only a superficial resemblance to the Bf 109, the Me 209 was tailored around a specially

built Daimler-Benz DB 601ARJ engine with a take-off rating of 1,800 hp (1342 kW), which could be boosted to a peak of 2,300 hp (1715 kW) for very short periods. This capability proved sufficient for the Me 209 to set a new record, Flugkapitäln Fritz Wendel flying the first specially prepared prototype on 26 April 1939 at an average speed of 469.22 mph (755.136 km/h). At this point the German propa-

ganda ministry stepped in, details for ratification submitted to the FAI identifying the record-breaking aircraft as the **Me 109R** in an attempt to convince other nations that the record had been gained by a variant of the Luftwaffe's new fighter. Nevertheless, the record stood for just over 30 years, but although attempts were made by the Messerschmitt company to develop a new fighter based on the Me 209 design, **Me 209A** prototypes flying later in the war, the programme was later abandoned.

Me 209 V1 was officially the world's fastest piston-engined aircraft from 26 April 1939, until 16 August 1969, when Darryl Greenamyer took his F8F-2 Bearcat Conquest I to an average of 477.98 mph (769.23 km/h).

Messerschmitt Me 210 and Me 410 Hornisse

Early Luftwaffe enthusiasm for the capability of the Bf 110 twin-engine fighter led to Messerschmitt being requested to design its eventual successor, resulting in the **Me 210** powered

by two 1,050-hp (783-kW) Daimler-Benz DB 601A engines. When flown for the first time, on 5 September 1939 the aircraft proved difficult to handle and suffered from

extreme instability. A new feature introduced on the Me 210 consisted of remotely-controlled rear-firing armament, a 13-mm (0.51-in) MG 131 machine-gun being

mounted on each side of the fuselage in an electrically-powered barbette. However, in spite of repeated modifications the Me 210 remained prone to stalling and spinning but

was, nevertheless, ordered into production. After about 200 had been built the programme was abandoned in April 1942, construction of the Bf 110 being resumed while attempts were made to save the Me 210 from oblivion.

Messerschmitt Me 210 and Me 410 Hornisse (continued)

The Me 210 design was reprieved by the introduction of automatic wing leading-edge slats and a redesigned and lengthened rear fuselage, and with the installation of 1,750-hp (1305-kW) DB 603A engines, production of this version was initiated under the new designation **Me 410**.

An Me 210A-0 had been converted to produce the Me 410 prototype, and several other Me 210As were converted to a generally similar standard. The Luftwaffe received its first **Me 410A Hornisse** (hornet) fighters in January 1943, and 48 had been delivered by the end of April, replacing Do 217s and Ju 88s in several units. While the

Variants

Me 210A: production version, built in **Me 210A-1** bomber/bomber-destroyer and **Me 210A-2** dive-bomber/bomber-destroyer versions
Me 210C: version produced by the Danube Aircraft Factory in Hungary from jigs and tooling supplied by Messerschmitt; incorporated the leading-edge slats and redesigned rear fuselage of the Me 410, and was powered by a version of the 1,475-hp (1100-kW) DB 605B engine built under licence by Manfred Weiss; production totalled 267, one-third delivered to the Hungarian air force and the remainder to the Luftwaffe

Me 310: proposed high-altitude fighter of which development was abandoned
Me 410A: initial production version built in **Me 410A-1** high-speed bomber, **Me 410A-2** destroyer and **Me 410A-3** reconnaissance variants, plus sub-variants
Me 410B: production version, basically similar to the Me 410A except for having more powerful DB 603G engines, in **Me 410B-1**, **Me 410B-2** and **Me 410B-3** versions similar to the Me 410A-1, Me 410A-2 and Me 410A-3 variants above and in sub-variants, plus **Me 410B-6** anti-shipping aircraft; the **Me 410B-5** anti-shipping /torpedo-bomber was in testing at the war's end, and **Me 410B-4** day reconnaissance and **Me 410B-8** night reconnaissance versions were in the prototype stage

output of Messerschmitt's Augsburg production line was high (457 had been delivered by the end of 1943) it was decided to increase the rate of manufacture, and in early 1944 Dornier entered the

programme. Further development led to the **Me 410B** with 1,900-hp (1417-kW) DB 603G engines, produced in a series of variants and sub-variants with different armament configurations. As the Allies stepped up the daylight bombing offensive in 1944, the Me 410s were engaged increasingly in home defence, and also proved of considerable value in fighter-bomber

attacks on southern England, by both day and night. However, the Me 410 was little more effective than late versions

of the Bf 110, and production terminated during September 1944 after a total of 1,160 had been built.

SPECIFICATION

Messerschmitt Me 410A-1/U2
Type: two-seat heavy fighter
Powerplant: two 1,850-hp (1380-kW) Daimler-Benz 603A inverted V-12 inline piston engines
Performance: maximum speed 364 mph (625 km/h) at 21,980 ft (6700 m); service ceiling 32,180 ft (10000 m); maximum range 1,050 miles (1690 km)
Weights: empty equipped 16,574 lb (7518 kg); maximum

take-off 21,276 lb (9650 kg)
Dimensions: wingspan 53 ft 7¾ in (16.35 m); length 40 ft 11½ in (12.48 m); height 14 ft ½ in (4.28 m); wing area 389.67 sq ft (36.20 m²)
Armament: four 20-mm MG 151 cannon and two 0.31-in (7.92-mm) MG 17 machine-guns firing forward, plus two 0.51-in (13-mm) MG 131 machine-guns in remotely-controlled rear-firing barbettes

Even in its A-1 production form as illustrated, the Me 210 offered poor performance by the standards of the time.

Messerschmitt Me 262

Wearing Reich's Defence bands, this Me 262A-1a was flown by Major Rudolf Sinner while he was Kommandeur of III./JG 27 at Brandenburg-Briest in March 1945. The aircraft is armed with two 8⅓-in (21-cm) calibre rocket launcher tubes beneath the forward fuselage.

Established in aviation history as the world's first turbojet-powered fighter to enter combat, the Me 262 entered the design stage of its life towards the end of 1938, the specification requiring it to be powered by two of the new gas turbines then being developed by BMW. Following approval of the design, Messerschmitt was awarded an initial contract for three prototypes, each to be powered by two 1,323-lb (5.88-kN) thrust BMW P-3302 turbojets. A cantilever low-wing monoplane, with the engines nacelle-mounted below the wing at approximately one-third span, the Me 262 in early prototype form had retractable tailwheel landing gear, whereas later prototypes and production aircraft had retractable tricycle landing gear. BMW was having problems with engine development and, as a result, the **Me 262 V1** was flown for the first time on 18 April 1941 on the power of a single Junkers Jumo 210G piston engine mounted in the nose. This proved that the general handling characteristics were good, and allowed the Me 262 to be flown for development of the aircraft systems. On 25 March 1942 the type flew for the first time with BMW 003

turbojets but, fortunately, retained the nose-mounted Jumo 210G for emergency use. Taking-off on the power of all three engines, the Me 262 V1 had barely become airborne before the turbojets failed, one after the other, and test pilot Flugkapitan Fritz Wendel just managed to

complete the circuit and land on the power of the Jumo piston engine. The compressor blade failures which had caused the engines to seize, meant a complete redesign of the engine, but in the meantime development of the Me 262 continued under the power of two Junkers

turbojets. As these were bigger and heavier than the BMW engines, the Me 262 airframe had to be modified to accept them, the third prototype flying with two 1,852-lb (8.24-kN) thrust Jumo 004A turbojets on 18 July 1942.

The vacillations of the German leaders and the

insistence of Adolf Hitler that the Me 262 should be suitable for use as a high-speed bomber are the reasons usually quoted to explain the delay in getting this tactically important aircraft into service. In truth, it was development of the engines to provide adequate thrust and

Very few Me 262B-1a trainers, all two-seaters soon emerging from the production lines as night fighters. This machine flew as a trainer with III./EJG 2 at Lechfeld in December 1944, but crashed near Augsburg owing to a technical failure on 12 January 1945, killing its pilot Gefreiter Ferdinand Sagemeister.

reliability that was the limiting factor. Fortunately, Junkers was making faster progress than BMW and in early November 1943 the **Me 262 V6** had two 1,984-lb (8.82-kN) thrust Jumo 004B-1 turbojets installed, each of them weighing 200 lb (91 kg) less than the Jumo 004A. Even then it was not until July 1944 that the first **Me 262A-1a** fighters began to enter Luftwaffe service. Total production of the Me 262 amounted to about 1,430, and there is little doubt that if the type had entered service at a much earlier date it could well have tipped the air war in

Germany's favour by making the Allied daylight bombing programme too hazardous. Me 262s were lethal fighters, using a salvo of 24 R4M rockets against a bomber formation and following them up with 30-mm cannon fire, but

although the Me 262s were considerably faster than the Allied escort fighters, a number were destroyed in combat because of the superior manoeuvrability of these Allied piston-engined fighter aircraft.

SPECIFICATION

Messerschmitt Me 262A-1a
Type: single-seat interceptor fighter
Powerplant: two 1,984-lb (8.82-kN) thrust Junkers Jumo 004B-1/-2/-3 turbojets
Performance: maximum speed 540 mph (870 km/h) at 19,685 ft (6000 m); service ceiling 37,565 ft (11450 m); range on internal fuel 652 miles (1050 km)

Weights: empty 8,378 lb (3800 kg); maximum take-off 14,110 lb (6400 kg)
Dimensions: wingspan 40 ft 11½ in (12.48 m); length 34 ft 9½ in (10.60 m); height 12 ft 7 in (3.84 m); wing area 233.58 sq ft (21.70 m²)
Armament: four 30-mm MK 108 cannon in nose

Variants

Me 262 V1 to Me 262 V12: prototype and test aircraft, the Me 262 V1 with BMW 003 turbojets, the remainder with Jumo 004A engines
Me 262A-0: pre-production aircraft with Jumo 004B engines
Me 262A-1a: initial production interceptor fighter with four 30-mm MK 108 cannon
Me 262A-1b: interceptor fighter which introduced armament of 24 DWM R4M air-to-air rockets
Me 262A-2: as Me 262A-1a, but with racks for up to 1,102 lb (500 kg) of bombs
Me 262A-3a: intended for close-support, very few examples of this more heavily armoured version were built
Me 262A-5a: reconnaissance/ fighter version
Me 262B-1a: two-seat conversion trainer;
Me 262B-1a/U1 night fighter was a variant
Me 262B-2a: two-seat night fighter
Me 262C: three rocket-boosted test aircraft

Messerschmitt Me 321 and Me 323 Gigant

The giant Messerschmitt Me 321 transport glider was planned originally to carry tanks, guns and men for the invasion of the UK, but despite the cancellation of Operation Sealion there was still an urgent need for such an aircraft, now to be used in the invasion of the Soviet Union. Both Junkers and Messerschmitt received contracts for 100 similar aircraft, but the Junkers Ju 322 proved a failure and was abandoned. The **Me 321** prototype had a cargo hold 36 ft 1 in (11.00 m) in length, 10 ft 10 in (3.30 m) in height and 10 ft 4 in (3.15 m) in width, with a capacity for loads of up to 44,092 lb (20000 kg), almost double its empty weight, or could carry an estimated 200 troops. A jettisonable take-off dolly was used for flight testing, the aircraft landing on sprung skids. Up to eight 1,102-lb (4.90-kN) thrust

rockets, giving 30 seconds of power, could be used to assist the take-off. A Ju 90 was used as tug for the first flight on 25 February 1941, the Me 321 then being found to handle satisfactorily, but it was clear that a far more effective tug was needed for many early accidents occurred during the take-off phase. Following completion of the 100 **Me 321A-1** production gliders, Messerschmitt received a contract for the **Me 321B-1**; this differed by having a wider flight deck to accommodate a pilot and co-pilot, the Me 321A-1 being flown by one pilot. By the time this contract for 100 aircraft was completed in early 1942, the first He 111Z tugs became available, but continuing take-off problems emphasised the need for a powered version. Messerschmitt converted the two proto-

type Me 321s as prototypes of the **Me 323C** and **Me 323D** with four and six Gnome-Rhône radial engines respectively. The four-engined Me 323C still needed tug assistance to get airborne before cruising on its own powerplant, but as this did not eliminate the basic problem the variant was soon abandoned. The production Me 323D carried a 21,495-lb (9750-kg) load over 621 miles (1000 km), or 120 troops with full equipment, or 60 stretcher patients with medical attendants. Production deliveries began in August 1942, and in November of that year the Me 323 began transport operations across the Mediterranean in support of Axis troops in North Africa. Despatched in groups of up to 100 transports, comprising Me 323 and Ju 52/3m aircraft with fighter escort, the Me 323s were at first immune from attack, but gradually Allied aircraft began to take a toll, and in mid-April 1943 a formation of 16 Me 323s was attacked by RAF fighters and lost 14 of its number. **Me 323E** and **Me 323F**

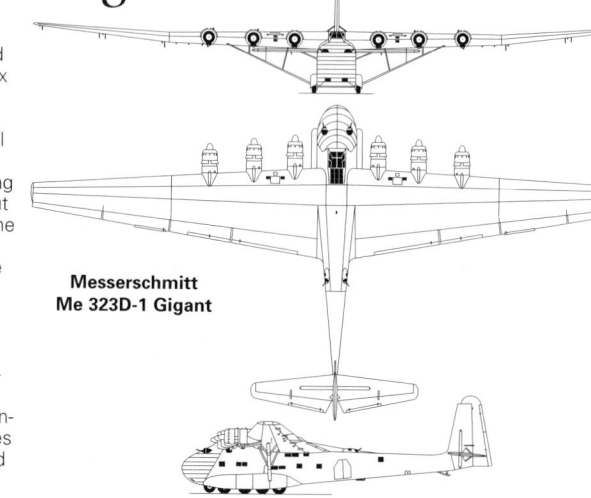

Messerschmitt Me 323D-1 Gigant

SPECIFICATION

Messerschmitt Me 323E-2
Type: heavy general-purpose transport
Powerplant: six 1,140-hp (850-kW) Gnome-Rhône 14N radial piston engines
Performance: maximum speed 149 mph (240 km/h) at 4,920 ft (1500 m); service ceiling 14,760 ft (4500 m); maximum range 808 miles (1300 km)
Weights: empty equipped 64,066 lb (29060 kg); maximum

take-off 99,210 lb (45000 kg)
Dimensions: wingspan 180 ft 5½ in (55.00 m); length 93 ft 6 in (28.50 m); height 31 ft 6 in (9.60 m); wing area 3,229.28 sq ft (300.00 m²)
Armament: one 20-mm MG 151 cannon in each of two turrets (one on each wing), two 0.51-in (13-mm) MG 131 machine-guns in the nose doors, and five more MG 131s firing from beam positions and rear of the flight deck

production aircraft, in several subvariants, attempted to give the type better immunity by increasing armament and armour protection, but when this was found to be unsuc-

cessful, the type was removed from the Mediterranean theatre and transferred to the Eastern Front. Production ended in April 1944 after a total of 198 had been delivered.

Its huge size soon led the Me 321 glider to be named Gigant, a name which was carried over to the powered Me 323. An Me 321A-1 is shown.

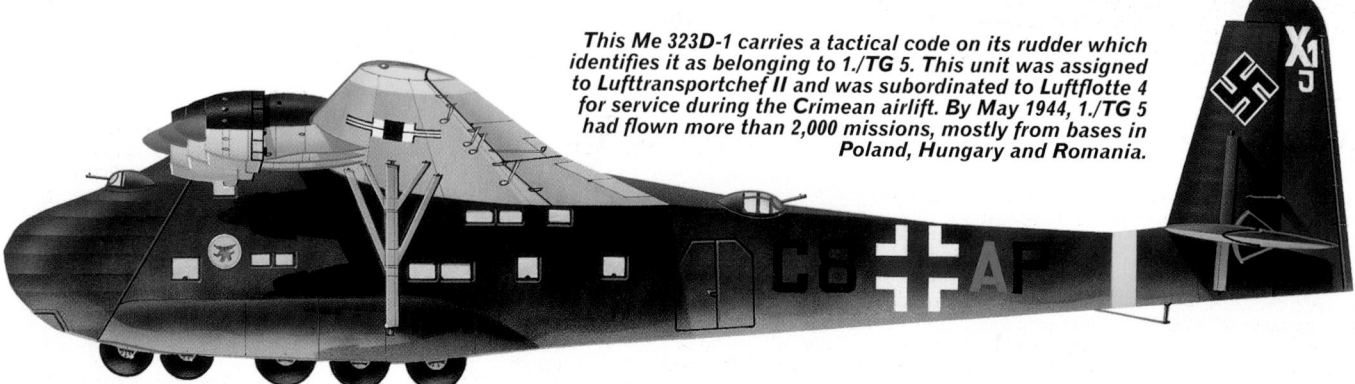

This Me 323D-1 carries a tactical code on its rudder which identifies it as belonging to 1./TG 5. This unit was assigned to Lufttransportchef II and was subordinated to Luftflotte 4 for service during the Crimean airlift. By May 1944, 1./TG 5 had flown more than 2,000 missions, mostly from bases in Poland, Hungary and Romania.

Meyers OTW

The Meyers Aircraft Company was formed at Tecumseh, Michigan, during 1936 to manufacture a two- seat training biplane designed by Allen Meyers. The design was prompted by the anticipated demand for trainer aircraft that would be triggered by introduction of the CAA War Training scheme, under which civil flying schools would provide primary flying training for potential military pilots. The prototype **OTW** was flown initially on 10 May 1936, a conventional lightweight training biplane with tandem seating for two in open cockpits. A total of 102 was built before production ended in 1944, but many have since been restored and in 2001 remained in private use in the United States.

Variants

OTW-125: original production version with a 125-hp (93-kW) Warner Scarab radial engine
OTW-145: production version, generally as above, but with a 145-hp (108-kW) Warner Super Scarab engine
OTW-160: final production version with a 160-hp (119-kW) Kinner R5 engine
OTW-KR: single aircraft, generally as other production aircraft, but with a 120-hp (89-kW) Ken-Royce 7G engine

Built in relatively small numbers as a military trainer during World War II, the Meyers OTW proved itself to be a rugged and long-lasting design with a number of aircraft surviving post-war. An OTW-160 is illustrated.

Mignet Pou-de-Ciel

Literally the 'sky louse', but known better as the **'Flying Flea'**, Frenchman Henri Mignet's unique ultra-light **Pou-du-Ciel** was almost certainly the first aircraft of which plans were readily available to amateur constructors. Mignet was himself an amateur and an enthusiast but, because of his lack of experience in aircraft construction, ignored traditional aerodynamics and engineering in finalising his design. His aim was to produce an easy-to-build, easy-to-fly aircraft that would enable hundreds of enthusiasts to gain flight experience in the cheapest possible way. First he sought inherent stability, using a low-slung fuselage with two wings of almost equal size, fore and aft, dispensing with a conventional tailplane and mounting the forward wing so that its incidence could be varied to provide control in pitch. Mignet relied upon the dihedral of the two wings to give lateral stability, and had a large rudder for directional control. The pilot had only a single 'stick' for control purposes, moved fore and aft to control the aircraft longitudinally, and from side to side to change direction. Mignet then produced a manual, giving plans and instruction for building the 'Pou', and large numbers of European enthusiasts, especially in France, the USSR, Germany, Italy, Scandinavia and the UK, were soon busy building their own aircraft. A number of fatal accidents resulted in the type being banned in France and this, coupled with the outbreak of war, brought a halt to an amateur building programme that could be numbered in hundreds. Mignet continued to develop his design, resolving the shortcomings and finally founding Avioes Mignet do Brasil at Sao Paulo, Brazil in 1953. There he began production of the **H.M.310 Estafette**, a two-seat enclosed cabin version of the 'Pou', powered by a 90-hp (67-kW) Continental A90-12F engine. Despite improved capability and reliability, the Estafette could not compete against the new post-war lightweights and Henry Mignet's dream finally faded into history.

A number of 'Flying Fleas' was flown in Britain, before fears over safety saw widespread grounding orders being issued.

Mikoyan-Gurevich I-250 (N and MiG-13)

To counter the introduction of German turbojet-powered aircraft, in 1944 the Soviet Union initiated a crash programme to produce a high-performance fighter, resulting in the **I-250 (N)** and Sukhoi Su-5 (I-107). A cantilever low-wing monoplane with a thin-section wing and tail-wheel landing gear with retractable main units, the single-seat I-250 had a most unusual powerplant. This consisted of a VK-107R engine mounted conventionally to drive a tractor propeller, but geared also to drive from its rear wheelcase, via an extension shaft, a Khalschevnikov compressor with seven fuel burners that produced a propulsive jet which was accelerated through a variable rear nozzle. This mixed power-plant had a combined output of 2,800 ehp (2088 ekW) at its rated altitude of 22,965 ft (7000 m), enabling the I-250 (N) to demonstrate a maximum speed of 513 mph (825 km/h) during a series of trials that followed the first flight on 3 March 1945. Produced in small numbers from late 1945, the type served with AV-MF fighter units near Riga from 1948 to 1950 under the designation **MiG-13**.

Two I-250 prototypes, of which this is the second, were built, followed by 16 production MiG-13s with considerably taller tail fins.

SPECIFICATION
Mikoyan-Gurevich I-250
Type: single-seat fighter
Powerplant: one 1,650-hp (1230kW) Klimov VK-107R V-12 piston engine, driving a 661-lb (2.94-kN) thrust Khalschevnikov VRDK compressor as well as a tractor propeller
Performance: maximum speed 513 mph (825 km/h) at 25,590 ft (7800 m); service ceiling 39,040 ft (11900 m); range, on power of VK-107R only, 1,131 miles (1820 km)
Weight: maximum take-off 8,113 lb (3680 kg)
Dimensions: wingspan 36 ft 3 in (11.05 m); length 28 ft 8½ in (8.75 m); wing area 161.46 sq ft (15.00 m²)
Armament: four 20-mm Beresin B-20 cannon

Mikoyan-Gurevich MiG-1 and MiG-3

Becoming eventually one of the best known aircraft designers in the world, Artem Mikoyan first collaborated with Mikhail Gurevich in 1938, the Mikoyan and Gurevich design bureau that resulted being identified by the initials MiG, although the founders died in 1970 and 1976 respectively. The partnership had been established to win an air force design competition for a new single-seat interceptor fighter, to be tailored around a Mikulin 12-cylinder Vee engine. The first of two more or less simultaneous projects had the designation **Type 65**, but this was soon abandoned in favour of a competing Ilyushin design. Second was the **MiG-1**, initially in **I-61** versions with Mikulin AM-35A and AM-37 engines respectively. Only the I-61 survived, with an order for three prototypes which were redesignated **I-200** and the first of these made its initial flight on 5 April 1940. Official trials resulted in the MiG-1 being ordered into production, series aircraft having a maximum speed of 390 mph (628 mph), and the Soviet Union claimed it to be the fastest production interceptor in the world in the 1940-1 period.

The MiG-1 had a number of shortcomings, with the result that only about 100 were built. The worst of these faults were instability, short range and vulnerability to combat damage, which resulted in modifications that produced

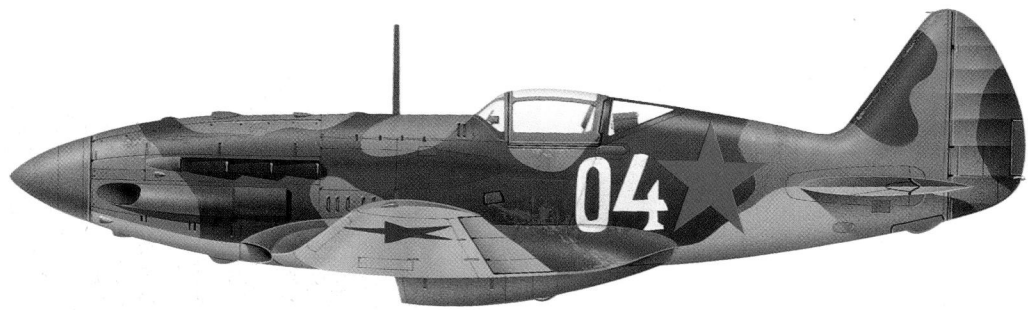

As a stop-gap fighter the MiG-3 gave the USSR valuable breathing space. This machine served with 7 IAP on the Stalingrad Front in 1941.

the **MiG-3**. They included aerodynamic refinements, the outer wing panels having increased dihedral; greater fuel capacity; and increased armament and armour protection. Although able to more than hold its own at altitudes above 16,405 ft (5000 m), the MiG-3 was no match for German fighters operating at low level. Combined production of the MiG-1 and MiG-3 totalled 3,422, construction tailing off in 1942 when manufacture of the Mikulin AM-35A engine was terminated. Attempts were then made to develop a more effective version, resulting in the **I-210** or **MiG-3/M82** with a Shvetsov M-82 (later ASh-82) radial engine, improved **I-211** with the same engine, and the still further improved **MiG-3U** which reverted to a Mikulin AM-35A, but none of these entered production.

SPECIFICATION	
Mikoyan-Gurevich MiG-3	7,385 lb (3350 kg)
Type: single-seat interceptor	**Dimensions:** wingspan 33 ft 5½ in
Powerplant: one 1,350-hp	(10.20 m); length 27 ft 1 in
(1007-kW) Mikulin AM-35A V-12	(8.26 m); height 11 ft 6 in (3.50 m);
piston engine	wing area 187.73 sq ft (17.44 m²)
Performance: maximum speed	**Armament:** one 0.5-in (12.7-mm)
398 mph (640 km/h) at 25,590 ft	Beresin and two 0.3-in (7.62-mm)
(7800 m); service ceiling 39,370 ft	ShKAS machine-guns, plus up to
(12000 m); maximum range	441 lb (200 kg) of bombs or six
743 miles (1195 km)	RS-82 rocket projectiles on
Weights: empty 5,721 lb	underwing racks
(2595 kg); maximum take-off	

This aircraft was the first of the unarmed I-200 prototypes. These machines evolved into the MiG-1 following an extensive series of modifications.

Mikoyan-Gurevich MiG-9 'Fargo'

German turbojets and turbine technology proved of immense value to the Soviet Union in developing reliable powerplants of this type. With the availability of Soviet-developed versions of these engines, the MiG design bureau was able to finalise the design of a new single-seat fighter with the prototype designation **I-300**, a cantilever mid-wing monoplane which had thin-section laminar wings similar to those developed for the I-250, and was also the first aircraft with retractable tricycle landing gear to enter production for the VVS. Its powerplant comprised two RD-20 turbojets, derived from the German BMW 003, these being mounted side-by-side in the centre fuselage to the rear of the cockpit, their intakes in the nose separated by a bulk-head into which was mounted a 37-mm Nudelmann cannon. First flown on 24 April 1946, the I-300 achieved a speed of 565 mph (910 km/h) during early tests, but there were a number of problems to be resolved before the **MiG-9**, as the type was designated in service, entered quantity production for the VVS. Introduced into service during the winter of 1946-47, the MiG-9 was built to the extent of 604 examples. It was later allocated the ASCC/NATO codename **'Fargo'**.

A number of faults, including gun-gas ingestion problems, had to be solved before the MiG-9 could be placed into front-line service.

Variants

MiG-9: initial production version with RD-20 turbojets
MiG-9UTI (I-301T): tandem two-seat trainer version; about 80 built
MiG-9M: version with RD-20F engines, of same thrust as RD-20

SPECIFICATION	
Mikoyan-Gurevich MiG-9	12,125 lb (5500 kg)
'Fargo'	**Dimensions:** wingspan 32 ft 9¾ in
Type: single-seat fighter	(10.00 m); length 31 ft 11¾ in
Powerplant: two 1,764-lb	(9.75 m); wing area 195.91 sq ft
(7.84-kN) thrust RD-20 turbojets	(18.20 m²)
Performance: 565 mph	**Armament:** one 37-mm
(910 km/h) at 16,405 ft (5000 m);	Nudelmann NS-37 cannon in the
service ceiling 42,650 ft (13000 m);	bulkhead separating the engine
maximum range 684 miles	intakes, and two 23-mm
(1100 km)	Nudelmann NS-23 cannon beneath
Weights: empty 7,804 lb	the intakes
(3540 kg); maximum take-off	

Mikoyan-Gurevich MiG-15 'Fagot'

Czechoslovakia built the MiG-15bis as the S-103. The blue bands on this machine were applied to identify it as belonging to 'hostile forces' during exercises.

To meet an urgent Soviet air force requirement for a high-performance turbojet-powered fighter, the MiG bureau initiated the design of a cantilever mid-wing monoplane incorporating 35° of wing sweep, with a circular-section fuselage, swept tail surfaces with the tailplane mounted at the tip of the fin, and retractable tricycle landing gear. A major problem was the lack of a suitable indigenous powerplant, which was resolved when the British government allowed Rolls-Royce to export to the Soviet Union a batch of Nene turbojets: the Klimov bureau lost little time in developing a copy of this engine, which was designated initially as the RD-45. Designated **I-310**, the first prototype flew at the end of the same year with a number of modifications and, after further testing, was ordered into production during 1948. By early 1949 these aircraft were beginning to enter service under the designation **MiG-15**, being allocated subsequently the Allied codename **'Fagot'**, and in that year the improved **MiG-15bis** was flown for the first time.

Mikoyan-Gurevich MiG-15 'Fagot' (continued)

The **MiG-15UTI 'Midget'** was also flown for the first time in 1949. The combat debut of the MiG-15 in Korea in November 1950 proved an unpleasant shock to the West. There was only one Allied fighter in the same class, the F-86 Sabre, but the MiG-15 could demonstrate a better rate of climb, a tighter turn-

ing circle and a much better service ceiling; above 35,000 ft (10670 m) the MiG-15 was even faster than the Sabre. Fortunately for the Allies, superior installed equipment and training gave the American fighter the upper hand in combat, but this very significant advance in fighter technology caused a

great deal of rethinking in the West.

In excess of 12,000 MiG-15s of all variants were completed and the type was also built under licence in Czechoslovakia as the **S-102** and **S-103**, and in Poland as the **LIM-1** and **LIM-2**, the MiG-15UTI also being licence-built in large numbers under the designations **CS-102** and **LIM-3** respectively. Spares and major airframe assemblies were also built in China, and in addition to extensive use by the Soviet armed forces, MiG-15s were operated by nations

Variants

MiG-15Pbis: all-weather derivative of MiG-15bis
MiG-15bisS: escort fighter
MiG-15bisR: recce version
MiG-15UTI 'Midget': two-seat trainer

linked to and/or supported by the Soviet Union. As they were retired from first-line service many single-seat MiG-15s were converted into two-seat

trainers, and in the absence of a production trainer version of the MiG-17 or MiG-19, became the Eastern bloc's standard advanced trainer.

SPECIFICATION
Mikoyan-Gurevich MiG-15bis 'Fagot'
Type: single-seat fighter
Powerplant: one 5,952-lb (26.47-kN) thrust Klimov M1 turbojet
Performance: 668 mph (1075 km/h) at sea level; service ceiling 50,855 ft (15,500 m); maximum range 1,156 miles (1860 km)
Weights: empty 8,115 lb (3681 kg); maximum take-off 13,327 lb (6045 kg)
Dimensions: wingspan 33 ft ¾ in (10.08 m); length 35 ft 7½ in (10.86 m); height 12 ft 1¾ in (3.70 m); wing area 221.74 sq ft (20.60 m²)
Armament: one 37-mm N-37 cannon and two 23-mm NS-23 or NR-23 cannon, plus up to 1,102 lb (500 kg) of mixed stores carried on underwing hardpoints

While the MiG-15 was soon obsolete, the MiG-15UTI has served on into the 21st century, largely thanks to Chinese production.

Mikoyan-Gurevich MiG-17 'Fresco'

Combat experience in Korea had highlighted the major shortcoming of the MiG-15, in which a tight high-speed turn initiated a snap roll resulting in an uncontrollable spin. Redesign was initiated to eliminate this problem, the resulting **I-330** prototype, known also as the **MiG-15bis-45°**, having a completely redesigned wing incorporating 45° of sweep and flying for the first time on 13 January 1950. At the same time, the fuselage was lengthened to reduce drag, the tail unit was revised, and the opportunity was taken to improve internal layout and systems. Following the completion of official tests, the aircraft was ordered into production in mid-1951 under the designation **MiG-17**, and production deliveries to the VVS began in late 1952. Allocated the ASCC/NATO codename

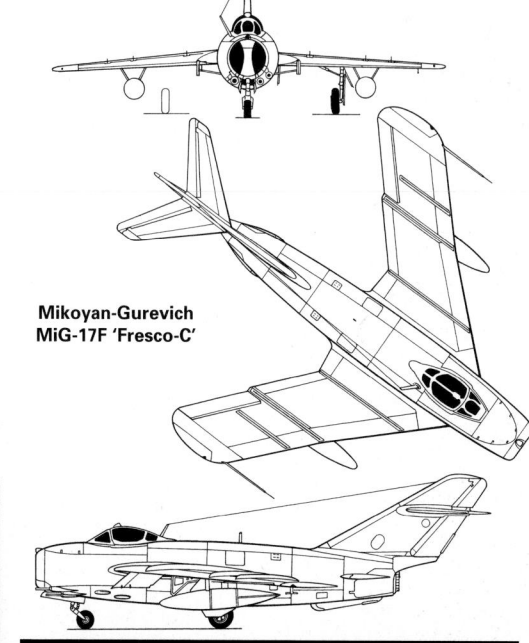

The MiG-17, including PFs like this Bulgarian example, was widely exported to countries including Albania, Bangladesh, Sri Lanka, Sudan and Zimbabwe.

'Fresco', the MiG-17 was built in variants that included the original MiG-17 production version which retained the VK-1 turbojet of the MiG-15, followed by the **MiG-17F 'Fresco-C'** day fighter, which was the main production version and introduced an afterburning VK-1F engine. The **MiG-17P 'Fresco-D'** added

night- and all-weather capability to the MiG-17, while the **MiG-17PF 'Fresco-D'** combined this capability with the VK-1F engine. The MiG-17PFU 'Fresco-E' had its gun armament deleted in favour of RS-2US (AA-1 'Alkali') AAM armament, making it the first missile-armed interceptor in production in Europe. Although considered virtually obsolete by the Soviet Union in the mid-1960s, MiG-17s saw considerable and effective use in operations over Vietnam, flown

MiG never built production two-seat variants of the MiG-17 or MiG-19. The Chinese however, used the MiG-17 as the basis for their own trainer, built as the JJ-5, or, as here, the FT-5 for export.

Mikoyan-Gurevich MiG-17F 'Fresco-C'

SPECIFICATION
Chengdu JJ-5
Type: two-seat advanced jet trainer
Powerplant: one Xian (XAE) Wopen WP-5D rated at 5,952 lb st (26.48 kN)
Performance: normal operating speed 'clean' at optimum altitude 482 mph (775 km/h); maximum rate of climb at sea level 5,315 ft (1620 m) per minute; service
ceiling 46,915 ft (14300 m); maximum ferry range 764 miles (1230 km)
Weights: empty equipped 8,995 lb 4080 kg); maximum take-off 13,701 lb (6215 kg)
Dimensions: wingspan 31 ft 7 in (9.63 m); length 37 ft 9 in (11.50 m); height 12 ft 5¾ in (3.80 m); wing area 243.27 sq ft (22.60 m²)

by North Vietnamese pilots.

Production in the Soviet Union probably exceeded 8,900 aircraft by the time that manufacture was terminated in the late 1950s, this total not including aircraft built under licence in Czechoslovakia as the S-104 (MiG-17PF) and in Poland as the LIM-5 (MiG-17), LIM-5M (MiG-17F) and LIM-5P

(MiG-17PF). The MiG-17 was also built in China, the basic Chinese-built MiG-17F being produced by the Shenyang Aircraft Factory, but later derivatives being developed and constructed by Chengdu. The first such development was the **J-5A**, which was basically a Chinese-built MiG-17PF with AI radar in a larger, longer, forward fuse-

lage. Relatively small numbers were produced, and none are known to have been exported. The prototype made its maiden flight on 11 November 1964. More successful was the **JJ-5**, a two-seat trainer derivative of the J-5. This had a slightly lengthened fuselage, and the nose intake and jetpipe were

refined. Development began in 1965, when it was becoming clear that the MiG-15UTIs then in use lacked performance and had some unacceptable handling characteristics. The JJ-5 first flew on 8 May 1966, and 1,061 had been built by 1986, when production ceased. The JJ-5 was exported (as the **FT-5**) to a number of

customers, most notably Pakistan, which uses the aircraft as its standard advanced jet trainer. Interestingly, Mikoyan-Gurevich itself never designed a two-seat MiG-15UTI as being adequate for the training of MiG-17 'Fresco' and MiG-19 'Farmer' aircrew.

Mikoyan-Gurevich MiG-19 'Farmer'

Although successful, the MiG-17 was little more than an improved version of the MiG-15, and in the late 1940s the MiG bureau initiated design of a completely new fighter at the request of the Kremlin, resulting from Stalin's personal order. The MiG bureau was instructed to use the Mikulin AM-5 powerplant, and this was flown in the I-360 prototype on 24 May 1952. Subsequent development led to the AM-9-engined **SM-9/1**, which, with modifications, was ordered into production as the **MiG-19** on 17 February 1954. The **MiG-19 'Farmer'** entered service from March 1955, but, despite having supersonic capability in level flight, it was withdrawn as the result of its difficult handling. The major change in the **MiG-19S**, which resulted from redesign to eliminate stability problems, was the incorporation

of an all-moving tailplane and refinements to flying controls and systems.

About 2,120 examples of the highly successful **MiG-19S 'Farmer-C'** were built, along with a number of **MiG-19P 'Farmer-B'** aircraft with radar to provide all-weather capability, and the AAM-armed **MiG-19PM** and **MiG-19PMU 'Farmer-D'**. A limited number of high-altitude **MiG-19SV** interceptors was produced in an effort to counter high-flying Western spyplanes and balloons. In addition, small numbers of the **MiG-19R** recce aircraft were built and just six **MiG-19UTI** two-seaters. Aircraft from Soviet production were supplied to Czechoslovakia and Poland, where they were operated under the designations **S-105** and **LIM-7** respectively and, in addition, the type was exported to countries that included Albania,

Bangladesh, Egypt, Kampuchea, Tanzania and Vietnam.

China began assessment of the supersonic MiG-19 during the late 1950s and it was selected for production under the second Five Year Plan. Design drawings were supplied to the Shenyang Aircraft Factory, which produced a copy of the basic MiG-19P under the designation **J-6**. The first Chinese-assembled aircraft made its maiden flight on 17 December 1958, and the first Chinese-built aircraft followed on 30 September 1959.

Licence-production of the MiG-19 and MiG-19PM was also assigned to the Nanchang Aircraft Factory, laying the foundations for later production of the **Q-5**. Seven MiG-19Ps were built, while five MiG-19PMs were assembled from Soviet kits, and another 19 were built at the factory, these apparently being designated **J-6B**. Unfortunately, quality-control problems meant that between 1958 and 1960 not one J-6 from Shenyang or Nanchang was accepted by the PLA air force. Many were scrapped after failing post-production inspections, and others had to be rebuilt before delivery.

The programme to build the MiG-19 began again in 1961 using Soviet-supplied drawings and technical

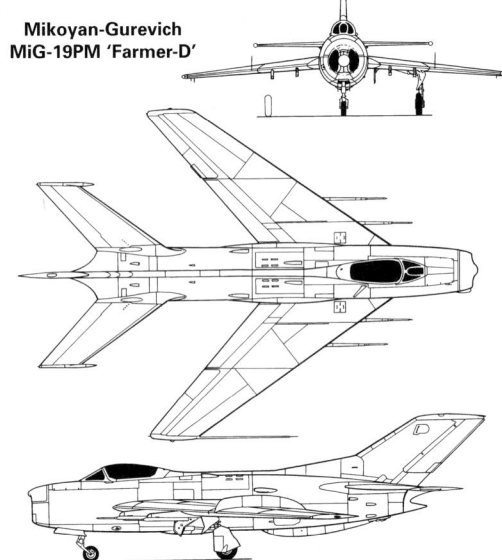

Mikoyan-Gurevich MiG-19PM 'Farmer-D'

documents, after having completely rebuilt the production tooling. Production was of the basic MiG-19S, although small numbers of the MiG-19P and the MiG-19PM, may also have been constructed. The first 'second batch' J-6 flew in December 1961.

The aircraft began to enter service in significant numbers in 1964-65.

By 1973, the prevailing political situation had improved sufficiently for the development of new variants. The most important of these was the **JJ-6** trainer, but this was accompanied by the **JZ-6**. Handfuls of J-6s had been built for medium-level and low-level recce duties from 1967, under the JZ-6 designation, and three more were modified for high-altitude reconnaissance. A requirement for an entirely new JZ-6 was issued in January 1976, and construction of a prototype/demonstrator began in April. This used optical and

infra-red sensors.

Production of the JJ-6 totalled 634 examples, and many were exported under the designation **FT-6** to serve as conversion and continuation trainers for the F-6 and A-5. In Pakistan, surviving FT-6s have been extensively upgraded (to the same standards as that nation's F-6 fighters).

Frequently misidentified as the **J-6Xin**, and attributed to have an indigenous all-weather radar in a 'needle-nose radome' intake centrebody, the **J-6III** was actually a high-speed day fighter whose sharp, conical, needle nose served as a variable shock-cone. A prototype of the J-6III flew on 6 August 1969, as a very different looking aircraft, with short-span, cropped wings and increased-chord ailerons and flaps. It was powered by uprated WP6A turbojets. The J-6III proved to be faster, faster climbing and tighter turning than the basic J-6, but was plagued by handling and quality control problems. 'Hundreds' had to be returned to the factory and rebuilt during a four-year programme.

The more modest **J-6C** was more successful, differing from the basic J-6/MiG-19S in having a relocated brake-chute fairing at the base of the trailing edge of the tailfin, below the rudder.

SPECIFICATION

Shenyang J-6/F-6 'Farmer'
Type: single-seat fighter and attack aircraft
Powerplant: two Liming (LM) Wopen-6 (Tumanskii R-9BF-811) turbojets each rated at 5,730 lb st (25.49 kN) dry and 7,165 lb st (31.87 kN) with afterburning
Performance: maximum level speed 'clean' at 36,000 ft (10975 m) 957 mph (1540 km/h); maximum rate of climb at sea level more than 30,000 ft (9145 m) per minute; service ceiling 58,725 ft

(17900 m); combat radius 426 miles (685 km) with two 201-US gal (760-litre) drop tanks
Weights: nominal empty 12,698 lb (5760 kg); maximum take-off about 22,046 lb (10000 kg)
Dimensions: wingspan 30 ft 2¼ in (9.20 m); length 48 ft 10½ in (14.90 m); height 12 ft 8¾ in (3.88 m); wing area 269.11 sq ft (25.00 m²)
Armament: maximum ordnance 1,102 lb (500 kg)

In Pakistan the Sidewinder-capable F-6 remains an important combat type. F-6s were also supplied to Albania, Bangladesh, Egypt, Iran, Iraq, North Korea, Pakistan, Somalia, Tanzania, Vietnam and Zambia, most of which continue to operate the type in small numbers.

Mikoyan-Gurevich MiG-19 'Farmer' (continued)

Guizhou was responsible for the final variant, the all-weather **J-6A**, which may also have been designated **J-6IV**. This was based on the J-6C airframe, but introduced all-weather radar and compatibility with the PL-2 missile. By comparison with the original all-weather J-6s (based on the MiG-19P and MiG-19PM), the J-6A/J-6IV had a slightly recontoured radome and a more pointed and conical centrebody. It is unknown whether the aircraft retains

cannon in the wingroots or under the fuselage.

The 1950s-vintage J-6 was produced into the 1980s, by which time approximately 3,000 had been built. It was exported in substantial quantities and remains in service in large numbers with the Air Force of the People's Liberation Army, with which service it is numerically the most important type, fulfilling the interceptor role.

Pakistan purchased two batches of 60 **F-6** (export-

standard J-6) aircraft after the 1971 conflict with India, and the survivors remained in service into 2001. Many modifications have been incorporated, including AIM-9 Sidewinder AAM compatibility, Martin-Baker ejection seats and various new avionics systems. Pakistani F-6s are also configured to carry a huge semi-conformal bath-tub external fuel tank below the belly. Some aircraft were subsequently passed to Bangladesh.

*Bangladesh flies its **FT-6s** in two squadrons, one operating a mix of **FT-6s** and **L-39ZAs** and the other a mix of **FT-6s** and **A-5Cs**.*

Mikoyan-Gurevich MiG-21 'Fishbed'

The **MiG-21** was conceived as a light and simple fighter in which sophistication and considerations of endurance and firepower were sacrificed outright performance. The production MiG-21 was preceded by a series of prototypes, some with a swept-wing layout and others with a delta-wing planform, and the first of these was the **Ye-2** that recorded its maiden flight on 14 February 1955. The 40 pre-production **MiG-21F** fighters were allocated the ASCC/NATO reporting designation **'Fishhed-B'**, but the first full production version was the **MiG-21F-13 'Fishbed-C'**. The first 114 MiG-21F-13s had a narrow-chord vertical tail surface, but all had their armament reduced from two to one 30-mm NR-30 cannon, on the starboard side, with underwing pylons for two AA-2 'Atoll' AAMs or rocket pods.

The **MiG-21P 'Fishbed-D'** dispensed with the cannon armament and introduced a modified fuselage with a longer nose and larger inlet centrebody for its R1L 'Spin Scan' radar. The canopy and spine were also modified with a distinctive bulge immediately aft of the cockpit, narrowing to the standard early spine farther aft, and

this allowed an increase in internal fuel capacity. The MiG-21P was followed by the **MiG-21PF** with pitot probe relocated to the top of the nose and the 12,654-lb st (56.29-kN) R-11F-300 afterburning turbojet replaced by the R-11F2-300 engine rated at 13,492 lb st (60.02 kN) with afterburning. The MiG-21PF had the new RP-21 Sapfir radar in the inlet centrebody. Later subvariants introduced a broader-chord fin with a brake chute fairing at the base of the rudder, and re-introduced a gun in the form of an external GP-9 pod carrying one 23-mm GSh-23 twin-barrel cannon. NATO allocated these aircraft the reporting designation **'Fishhed-E'**. The **MiG-21FL** was intended for export with the R-11F-300 engine, less powerful R2L radar and enlarged internal fuel capacity. About 200 were built under licence in India. The final versions, which can be considered part of the first generation were the **MiG-21PFM** and **MiG-21PFS**, which had a two-piece canopy with a fixed windscreen instead of the single-piece forward-hinging canopy of the earlier MiG-21s. They also introduced blown flaps, a cruciform brake chute, and the R-11F2S-300 engine

rated at 13,613 lb st (60.57 kN) with afterburning. Addition of the RP-21M radar gave compatibility with the semi-active RS-2US (K-5M) missile.

Later MiG-21 variants gained more internal fuel, heavier armament and increasingly more sophisticated avionics. All had the R-11F2S-300 or R-13-300 engine, blown flaps, a two-piece canopy and a broad-chord fin. For the first time, all also had four underwing pylons, although initially only two of these were compatible with AAMs. The first of the new generation was the **MiG-21R 'Fishbed-H'**, a dedicated reconnaissance aircraft based on the MiG-21PFM but with an enlarged dorsal fairing and provision for carrying a variety of centre-line reconnaissance pods.

The **MiG-21S** was a fighter based on the **MiG-21R** but with new RP-22 radar and a ventral GP-9 cannon pod. It was followed by the **MiG-21SM** with the R-13-300 engine rated at 14,307 lb (63.66 kN) with afterburning, a gun sight optimised for high-*g* manoeuvring combat, and the improved GSh-23L cannon in a fixed installation recessed into the belly. The **MiG-21M** was an export version of the MiG-21SM with the older R-11F2S-300 engine: this variant was built under licence in India. The **MiG-21MF 'Fishbed-J'** was a MiG-21M derivative for Soviet use with the R-13-300 engine, RP-22 radar and AAM capability on all four underwing pylons. The **MiG-21MT** introduced the more powerful R-13F-300 engine, but only 15 were built. The **MiG-21SMT 'Fishbed-K'** was fitted with a huge

Mikoyan-Gurevich MiG-21PF 'Fishbed-E'

dorsal spine, but this reduced stability so much that its fuel capacity had to be reduced by 50 per cent. Large numbers of MiG-21R, MiG-21M and MiG-21MF warplanes remain in service, including many with the non-Soviet air forces of the former Warsaw Pact. Many of the proposed Western retrofit programmes for the MiG-21, promoted by companies like IAI, are applicable mainly to these MiG-21 variants.

The third-generation **MiG-21bis** was the most advanced variant to enter production, but was notable for its lack of BVR missile capability, limited

radar range, mediocre low-speed handling and poor endurance. Russian as well as Western organisations offer upgrade programmes, most centred on more capable radar and modernisation of the cockpit. The MiG-21bis was developed as a multi-role fighter for Frontal Aviation, with better close combat capability through improved avionics, the ability to carry the new R-60 (AA-8 'Aphid' AAM), and with enhanced ground-attack capability. Other features of the MiG-21bis included the improved Sapfir-21 radar, the R-25-300 engine, and a completely redesigned dorsal spine which looks

SPECIFICATION

Mikoyan-Gurevich MiG-21bis 'Fishbed-L'
Type: single-seat multi-role tactical fighter
Powerplant: one MNPK 'Soyuz' (Tumanskii) R-25-300 turbojet engine rated at 9,038 lb st (40.20 kN dry and 15,653 lb st (69.65 kN) with afterburning, with an emergency regime rating of 21,825 lb st (97.12 kN) above Mach 1 and at heights up to 13,125 ft (4000 m) for periods of up to three minutes; there is also provision for two SPRD-99 solid rocket boosters each rated at 5,511 lb st (24.52 kN)
Performance: maximum speed 1,386 mph (2230 km/h) or Mach 2.1 at 42,650 ft (13000 m); initial climb rate 38,385 ft (11700 m) per

minute with two missiles and 50 per cent fuel; service ceiling 57,415 ft (17500 m); range 913 miles (1470 km) with two AAMs and one drop tank
Weights: empty 12,996 lb (5895 kg); maximum take-off 22,972 lb (10420 kg)
Dimensions: wingspan 23 ft 5⁷⁄₁₀ in (7.154 m); length 48 ft 2¾ in (14.70 m); height 13 ft 6¼ in (4.13 m); wing area 247.58 sq ft (23.00 m²)
Armament: one 23-mm Gryazev-Shipunov GSh-23L fixed forward-firing two-barrel cannon in the lower fuselage, plus up to 3,307 lb (1500 kg) of disposable stores carried on four underwing hardpoints

*India flew its **MiG-21FLs** (pictured) during its 1971 war with Pakistan. The earlier **MiG-21F** had played a minor role in the 1965 war.*

little different from that fitted to most second-generation 'Fishbeds' but holds nearly as much fuel as even the huge spine of the MiG-21SMT.

The NATO reporting designation **'Fishbed-L'** was allocated to the first version of the MiG-21bis, which entered service in February 1972, while **'Fishbed-N'** was applied to later aircraft with an under-nose 'Swift Rod' ILS antenna and improved avionics. The 'Fishbed-N' was built under licence in India between 1980 and 1987. Another version of the MiG-21bis was opti-mised for the nuclear strike role, but no designation or NATO reporting name are known. The MiG-21bis has left Russian service, but elsewhere enjoys a much firmer hold on life, serving in large numbers with many operators.

Proposed two-seat trainer versions of the MiG-17 and MiG-19 did not reach production, but it soon became apparent that the MiG-15UTI would be inadequate for the conver-sion training of MiG-21 pilots. The design bureau accordingly schemed a

two-seat trainer based on the MiG-21F-13. Radar and armament were deleted, although provision was made for a ventral gun pack, and the type also had two underwing pylons. The instructor's cockpit was added behind the normal cockpit, necessitating a reduction in fuselage fuel tankage, and the cockpits were covered by separate side-hinged canopies. The new trainer first flew on 17 October 1960, and entered production as the **MiG-21U 'Mongol-A'**. Early production aircraft had the original narrow-chord fin and had a brake chute at the rear of the ventral fin, and the variant was manu-factured between 1964 and 1968.

On the **MiG-21US 'Mongol-B'**, built between

This Soviet MiG-21MF 'Fishbed-J' flew with the 5th Frontal Aviation Army in the Kiev Military District in the 1973-74 period. It is armed with AA-2 AAMs and rocket pods underwing and carries a typical MiG-21-style drop tank on the centreline.

1966 and 1970, the broader-chord fin was intro-duced together with the fin trailing-edge brake chute fairing, improved ejection seats, a bigger fuel-carrying spine, a retractable periscope and blown flaps. The **MiG-21UM** introduced updated instruments, autopilot and avionics as fitted to the MiG-21R and subsequent single-seaters,

Finland replaced its earlier MiG-21U aircraft with four MiG-2UMs (pictured). When the 'Fishbed' was retired in 1998, one UM remained airworthy.

and was fitted with an angle of attack sensor on the starboard side of the nose. The type entered production in 1971. In 2001 MiG-21 trainers served with most operators of the single-seat 'Fishbed' as conversion and continuation

trainers. In India and the former USSR, however, MiG-21 trainers also serve as dedicated advanced flying trainers.

The MiG-21 has also been extensively built in China by Chengdu as the **J-7** and **F-7** (for export).

Mikoyan-Gurevich MiG-23 'Flogger'

Mikoyan-Gurevich
MiG-23M 'Flogger-B'

Development of the **MiG-23 'Flogger'** began during the early 1960s as a replacement for the MiG-21. Greater payload, range and firepower were clearly needed, along with more powerful onboard sensors to free the pilot from the constraints imposed by tight GCI control. The new fighter would clearly be larger and heavier, but the USSR was determined that this should not impose longer take-off distances. Two approaches to the problem of giving the new fighter a degree of STOL capability were explored: The **Model 23-01** had a fixed wing and two dedicated lift engines to supplement the main engine, while the **Model 23-11** had a variable-geom-etry wing planform and just one engine. Powered by the R-27F-300 turbojet, the

Model 23-11 made its maiden flight on 10 April 1967, and had a multitude of high-lift devices including full-span four-section trail-ing-edge flaps, leading-edge slats and two-section spoilers.

The Model 23-11 was ordered into production as the **MiG-23S** with the 22,046-lb st (98.06-kN) R-27F2M-300 engine but without the intended Sapfir radar. Instead, the RP-22 'Jay Bird' of the MiG-21S was fitted in a short radome. The aircraft also had the TP-23 IR search-and-track system. Fifty were built between mid-1969 and the end of 1970 for operational trials before production switched to the **MiG-23M 'Flogger-B'**. This featured the Sapfir-23 ('High Lark') pulse-Doppler radar and R-23 (AA-7 'Apex') semi-active AAMs

as well as a new fire-control system and autopilot. The new 27,557-lb st (122.63-kN) R-29-300 engine with a shorter jetpipe was fitted, the horizontal tail surfaces were moved rearward, a fourth fuel tank was added in the rear fuselage and a new wing, with an extended leading edge, was introduced, this having a pronounced 'dogtooth' inboard. The leading-edge slats were deleted, but re-introduced in 1973.

Two downgraded export versions of the MiG-23M were produced. The **MiG-23MS 'Flogger-E'** had 'Jay Bird' radar in a short radome and therefore no BVR missile capability. The **MiG-23MF** retained the 'High Lark' radar, AA-7 missile capability and **'Flogger-B'** reporting desig-nation, and was delivered to the USSR's Warsaw Pact allies, then later to Angola, India, Iraq, Libya and Syria.

Like most Soviet fight-ers, the MiG-23 was subjected to a constant programme of improve-ments and refinements, resulting in a succession of variants. The **MiG-23ML 'Flogger-G'** was intended

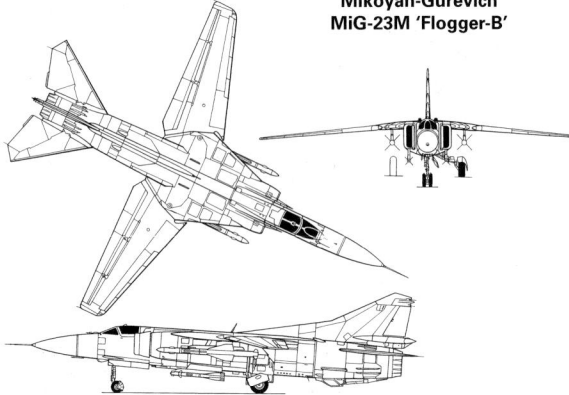

to have improved handling, especially at high angles of attack, enhanced manoeu-vrability and higher g limits. It featured a lightened airframe, with the fourth fuselage fuel tank removed and with the dorsal fin fillet deleted. More power was provided by installing the R-35-300 engine, and stronger three-section lead-

ing-edge slats were fitted. Other changes were the improved, lightweight Sapfir-23L radar adding a new dogfight mode, more capable defensive avionics, and a new IRST. The MiG-23ML was also exported to countries including Czechoslovakia, East Germany, North Korea and Syria.

The MiG-23BN (pictured), MiG-21, MiG-27M and Jaguar together constitute the majority of India's attack capability.

SPECIFICATION	
Mikoyan-Gurevich MiG-23ML 'Flogger-G'	(8200 kg); maximum take-off 39,242 lb (17800 kg)
Type: single-seat multi-role tactical fighter	**Dimensions:** wingspan 45 ft 9¾ in (13.97 m) spread and 25 ft 6¼ in (7.78 m); length 54 ft 9½ in (16.70 m) including probe; height 15 ft 9¾ in (4.82 m); wing area 402.05 sq ft (37.35 m²) spread and 367.71 sq ft (34.16 m²) swept
Powerplant: one MNPK 'Soyuz' (Tumanskii/Khachaturov) R-35-300 turbojet engine rated at 18,849 lb st (83.88 kN) dry and 28,660 lb st (127.48 kN) with afterburning	
Performance: maximum speed 1,553 mph (2500 km/h) or Mach 2.35 at 36,090 ft (11000 m); service ceiling 60,695 ft (18500 m); range 1,212 miles (1960 km) with internal fuel	**Armament:** one 23-mm Gryazev-Shipunov GSh-23L fixed forward-firing two-barrel cannon in a ventral pack, plus up to 6,614 lb (3000 kg) of disposable stores carried on six hardpoints
Weights: empty 18,078 lb	

Mikoyan-Gurevich MiG-23 'Flogger' (continued)

The very similar **MiG-23P** interceptor had a new digital computer that allowed the aircraft to be automatically steered onto its target from the ground, cueing the pilot to engage afterburner and launch weapons.

The MiG-23ML also served as the basis for the **MiG-23MLD 'Flogger-K'**, reportedly produced as MiG-23ML conversions and incorporating vortex generators on the pitot probe and notches in its vestigial leading-edge root extensions to increase high angle-of-attack capability and controllability. New automatic leading-edge slats were also fitted to optimise handling and manoeuvrability at all angles of attack. Large chaff/flare dispensers, linked to a new RWR system, could be fitted above the rear fuselage. Further modifications included swivelling pylons under the outboard wing panels, which moved to remain aligned with the airflow even when the wings were swept.

The development of a two-seat trainer version was authorised in May 1968. The **MiG-23UB 'Flogger-C'** prototype made its maiden flight in May 1969. Although never

intended to have the Sapfir radar, the MiG-23UB was always supposed to be used for both pilot conversion and weapons training: a separate guidance and illuminator pod for the AA-7 was therefore fitted in a conical fairing on the starboard wing root. Production aircraft all had wing slats, and the two tandem cockpits were covered by separate upward-hinging canopies. All MiG-23 operators use the MiG-23UB, and the type, which was phased out of production at Irkutsk in 1978, also served with many Soviet MiG-29 and Su-27 units.

During 1969 the design bureau began studies of a 'jet Shturmovik' to meet a Frontal Aviation requirement for a cheap, mass-produced attack aircraft, but eventually the type accepted for production was a MiG-23S development exploiting that warplane's ability to operate from primitive, semi-prepared airstrips as a result of its rugged airframe, strong landing gear, powerful engine and variable-geometry wing. The basic **MiG-23B** was based on the airframe of the MiG-23S with a new, more sloping nose giving the pilot improved forward and downward fields of

vision, and with the 25,353-lb st (112.78-kN) Lyul'ka AL-21F-300 engine in a shortened rear fuselage, but again with the tailplane shifted rearward as on the MiG-23M. The new ground-attack variant featured the unslatted wing but was later fitted with the revised wing which reintroduced the slats. Instead of radar, the new aircraft had the PrNK Sokol 23S nav/attack system, armour was scabbed externally onto the sides of the forward fuselage, and a missile illuminator (starboard) and a TV camera (port) were housed in bullet-like fairings on the wing-root gloves: the TV camera was later removed from most aircraft.

The first prototype recorded its maiden flight on 20 August 1970. Twenty-four MiG-23Bs were built before production switched to an improved variant. This **MiG-23BN**, which had been planned as the first attack model but was then delayed by equipment and

Two-seat MiG-23 trainers were used in small numbers by the majority of MiG-23 users. This aircraft was flown by the East German air force.

engine problems, featured an upgraded PrNK Sokol 23N nav/attack system, was powered by a slightly derated version of the R-29B-300 engine, and introduced the leading-edge bullet fairings on the fixed wing gloves that are usually associated with the AS-7 'Kerry' ASM. The MiG-23B and MiG-23BN shared the reporting name **'Flogger-F'**, and all seem to have had a simplified jetpipe more like that fitted to the MiG-27. The MiG-23B and MiG-23BN proved disappointing in service, and many were subsequently upgraded to **MiG-23BK** or **MiG-23BM** standards, or exported mainly to Third World customers.

Improved avionics were desperately needed, and two new fighter-bomber models were quickly developed with the same **'Flogger-H'** reporting designation. This was assigned because they had new RWR fairings on the lower corners of the fuselage, just ahead of the nosewheel bay. The first of the new variants was the **MiG-23BK**, which had the same nav/attack system and laser rangefinder as the MiG-27K. The **MiG-23BM** was similar, but with the same PrNK Sokol 23M system as the MiG-27D. Confusingly, the MiG-23BN designation seems to have been adopted as an overall service designation, sometimes being applied to aircraft designated BM or BK by the bureau.

Mikoyan-Gurevich MiG-25 'Foxbat'

The **MiG-25 'Foxbat'** was developed as a panic response to the North American XB-70 Valkyrie strategic bomber, whose Mach 3 performance and very high altitude capability threatened to present Soviet air defences with almost insoluble problems. When development of the Valkyrie was halted in 1961, work on the MiG-25 was well advanced and the USSR therefore continued with the project, perhaps knowing that a Mach 3 reconnaissance aircraft, the Lockheed A-12 (and later the SR-71), was about to begin flight tests.

Those parts of the MiG-25 airframe which

would have to withstand the greatest kinetic heating, such as the nose and leading edges, had to be of titanium construction, but many other areas that could theoretically have been made of riveted aluminium alloy had to be made of welded steel because no suitable heat-resistant fuel tank sealant could be found, and because there was a shortage of skilled riveters. Eventually, 80 per cent of the aircraft was of tempered steel, 11 per cent of aluminium alloy and 8 per cent of titanium: 76.50 per cent of assembly was by welding with conventional riveted joints

making up only 23.50 per cent of the structure.

The design bureau selected a novel configuration with a large, highly-swept thin wing, sophisticated variable air intakes, and canted twin fin-and-rudder units. The wing's leading-edge sweep angle varies and in order to provide adequate range and endurance, about 70 per cent of the aircraft's volume consists of fuel tanks. Advanced cooling and insulation systems had to be designed for the engines, avionics and cockpit.

Development of the **Ye-155P** interceptor was approved in February 1962,

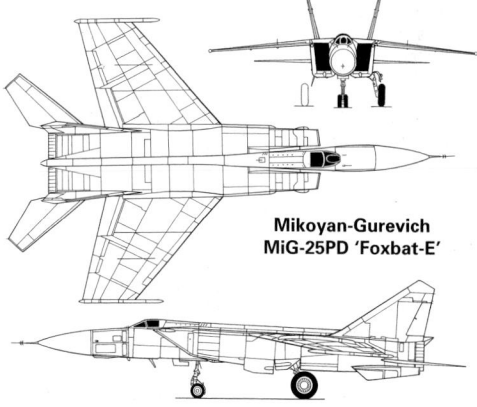

Mikoyan-Gurevich MiG-25PD 'Foxbat-E'

and the **Ye-155P-1** first of seven prototypes made its maiden flight on 9 September 1964. The aircraft was powered by a pair of 22,487-lb st (100.03-kN) R-15B-300 turbojet engines and was fitted with a Smerch-A radar known to NATO as 'Fox Fire' and possessing virtually no look-down capability. The aircraft carried two R-40 AAMs in a mixed pair of one R-40R semi-active radar-homing and

one R-40T IR-homing weapon.

In the production **MiG-25P 'Foxbat-A'** the fin area was reduced, the planned canard foreplanes, small wing-tip tanks and winglets were abandoned, and the armament was increased from two to four R-40s. Production began in 1969, but the aircraft did not enter full service until 1973 as a result of engine and control problems. Even then, the MiG-25 was subject to severe operating limitations, which strictly constrained the amount of time that could be spent at very high speeds, and limited the use of full

In its MiG-25RBT form, the 'Foxbat' had a much expanded Sigint capability and an upgraded RHAWS.

engine power.

The ultimate **MiG-25PD 'Foxbat-E'** interceptor entered production in 1978 and featured a new RP-25 look-down/shoot-down radar and an undernose IR search-and-track system. The original engines were replaced by more powerful R-15BD-300 units with life extended from 150 to 1,000 hours, and provision was made for a huge ventral tank. Surviving 'Foxbat-As' were brought up to the same standard from 1979 under the designation **MiG-25PDS**. Some of the latter aircraft received a 9.84-in (0.25-m) plug in front of the canopy to allow a retractable inflight-refuelling probe to be fitted. The normal armament comprised two R-40 and four R-60 (AA-8 'Aphid') AAMs.

The **MiG-25PU 'Foxbat-C'** two-seat conversion trainer appeared in 1968. It lacks radar and has no combat capability, but features a new forward cockpit for the instructor stepped down in front of the standard single-seat cockpit. The MiG-25P and MiG-25PU were exported to Algeria, Iraq, Libya and Syria.

Although the MiG-25 was designed as an interceptor, it had obvious potential for reconnais-

sance. The resulting **Ye-155R-1** first of three reconnaissance prototypes made its maiden flight on 6 March 1964. The original wing-tip tanks with vertical finlets were soon replaced by smaller anti-flutter masses, the 'letterbox' dielectric panels on the nose were made deeper and more square, the tail surfaces were enlarged, and the R-15B-300 engines were replaced by R-15BD-300s.

The **MiG-25R** entered production in April 1969 in a standard with five camera ports (one vertical and four oblique) in the nose, and small square flush antennas further forward on the sides of the nose, probably serving some kind of SLAR. Three cameras (one vertical and two oblique) were usually carried.

The MiG-25R was replaced in production between 1972 and 1980 by the **MiG-25RB 'Foxbat-B'** dual-role reconnaissance bomber. This had a new Peleng automatic bombing system, the USSR's first operational INS, and a Doppler to measure speed and drift. These allowed the aircraft to release its six 1,102-lb (500-kg) bombs from altitudes of more than 65,615 ft (20000 m) at supersonic speeds from two underfuselage and four

underwing hardpoints. Alternatively, a single nuclear weapon could be carried. The standard camera bay remained but the SRS-4A Elint system was slightly improved. All surviving Soviet MiG-25Rs were brought up to MiG-25RB standard.

Other models understood to have retained their cameras included the **MiG-25RBS** with the new Sabla radio location system. This variant entered service in 1972, and was produced until 1977. From 1981 many of these aircraft received new equipment and were allocated a new designation of **MiG-25RBSh**. The MiG-25RBS was replaced on the production line by the **MiG-25RBV** with further improved equipment, and by the **MiG-25RBT** with SRS-9 Virazh Elint equipment.

The MiG-25RB also formed the basis of a dedicated Elint model with its optical sensors replaced by a variety of passive receivers and active SLAR systems. It is unclear whether the ASCC/NATO **'Foxbat-D'** reporting designation covers all such versions or just those with an enlarged SLAR antenna on the side of the nose, farther aft. The first 'camera-less' MiG-25 was the **MiG-25RBK** with the usual flush antennas and cameras replaced by larger, longer dielectric panels on the sides of the cockpit. These antennas reportedly

serve the new Kub SLAR. The MiG-25RBK entered service in 1972 and remained in production until 1980.

The final variant is the **MiG-25RBF**, variously described as a MiG-25RB brought up to MiG-25RBK standard or as a new production aircraft which replaced the MiG-25RBK on the production line, and offers expanded jamming capability. The type lacks the large SLAR antennas of the MiG-25RBK, instead reverting to the small dielectric panels farther forward as carried on the MiG-25RB and other variants. In place of oblique camera windows, the MiG-25RBF has four small, rectangular and symmetrically arranged dielectric panels. The vertical camera window seems to be retained.

The reconnaissance 'Foxbat' has its own dedicated two-seat trainer, the **MiG-25RU**. This has no operational equipment, but does seem to have a constant-sweep wing leading edge. By comparison

with MiG-25 interceptors, all the reconnaissance aircraft have slightly reduced wingspan and a leading edge with constant sweep, instead of the interceptor's 'cranked' leading edge. Camera-equipped MiG-25RBs were exported to Algeria, Bulgaria, India, Iraq, Libya and Syria.

The **MiG-25BM 'Foxbat-F'** is a dedicated defence suppression aircraft based on the airframe of the MiG-25RB and designed for high-level, long-range, stand-off anti-radar missions. This unusual approach was chosen because the traditional 'low down and dirty' close-in tactics used by the USAF's Wild Weasel aircraft were felt to impose an unacceptable and unnecessary degree of vulnerability. Development began in 1972, and the aircraft was produced between 1982 and 1985. The primary armament of the MiG-25BM is the Kh-58 (AS-11 'Kilter') or Kh-31 missile, four of which can be carried on the underwing pylons.

Russia's MiG-25 trainers have been hard used and the majority have high hours. MiG-25U never-exceed speed is reduced to Mach 2.65

SPECIFICATION

Mikoyan-Gurevich MiG-25PDS 'Foxbat-E'

Type: single-seat interceptor
Powerplant: two MNPK 'Soyuz' (Tumanskii) R-15BD-300 turbojet engines each rated at 19,400 lb st (86.30 kN) dry and 24,691 lb st (109.83 kN) with afterburning
Performance: maximum speed 1,864 mph (3000 km/h) or Mach 2.82 at 42,650 ft (13000 m); climb to 65,615 ft (20000 m) in 8 minutes 54 seconds; service ceiling 67,915 ft (20700 m); range 776 miles (1250 km) supersonic with standard fuel; endurance 2 hours 5 minutes
Weights: maximum take-off 90,586 lb (41090 kg) with ventral

tank
Dimensions: wingspan 45 ft 11¾ in (14.02 m); length 78 ft 1¾ in (23.82 m) or, in aircraft modified with inflight-refuelling capability, 78 ft 11½ in (24.07 m); height 20 ft ¼ in (6.10 m); wing area 660.93 sq ft (61.40 m²)
Armament: up to 8,818 lb (4000 kg) of disposable stores carried on four underwing hardpoints, and generally comprising four R-40 and R-46 (AA-6 'Acrid') long-range AAMs, or two R-23 and R-24 (AA-7 'Apex') long-range AAMs and four R-60 (AA-8 'Aphid') short-range or R-73 (AA-11 'Archer') close-range AAMs

Mikoyan MiG-27 'Flogger'

To meet a requirement for a tactical attack warplane, the Mikoyan-Gurevich design bureau produced the **MiG-27** as a fully optimised fighter-bomber based on the MiG-23BM. The new aircraft featured simplified but slightly larger

'bulged' fixed air intakes and a simplified two-position afterburner nozzle externally similar to that on the MiG-23BM/BK. These modifications improved fuel economy and dramatically reduced weight by sacrificing top speed performance.

To improve the aircraft's warload, a seventh hardpoint was added on the centreline, and the original underfuselage pylons were moved out to the intake ducts to allow wider stores to be carried. The two pylons on the sides of the rear fuselage, behind the main landing gear units and first fitted on the MiG-23B series, were retained and may have been stressed to carry heavier stores. They were seldom used, however, since they imposed a limit on the amount of fuel that can be carried because of centre of gravity considerations. A

India was the only export customer for the MiG-27, eventually building the MiG-27M entirely in-country. The -27M is known as the MiG-27L to MiG.

SPECIFICATION

Mikoyan-Gurevich MiG-27K 'Flogger-D'

Type: single-seat attack and close-support warplane
Powerplant: one MNPK 'Soyuz' (Tumanskii) R-29B-300 turbojet engine rated at 17,637 lb st (78.45 kN) dry and 25,353 lb st (112.77 kN) with afterburning
Performance: maximum speed 1,170 mph (1885 km/h) or Mach 1.70 at 26,245 ft (8000 m); initial climb rate 39,370 ft (12000 m) per minute; service ceiling 45,930 ft (14000 m); combat radius 335 miles (540 km) on a lo-lo-lo attack mission with two Kh-29 ASMs and three drop tanks

Weights: empty 26,252 lb (11908 kg); maximum take-off 44,753 lb (20300 kg)
Dimensions: wingspan 45 ft 9¾ in (13.97 m) spread and 25 ft 6¼ in (7.78 m) swept; length 56 ft ¼ in (17.08 m) including probe; height 16 ft 5 in (5.00 m); wing area 402.05 sq ft (37.35 m²) spread and 367.71 sq ft (34.16 m²) swept
Armament: one 30-mm Gryazev-Shipunov GSh-6-30 fixed forward-firing six-barrel rotary cannon in an exposed mounting under the fuselage, plus up to 8,818 lb (4000 kg) of disposable stores carried on seven hardpoints

new 30-mm GSh-6-30 six-barrel rotary cannon with 260 rounds of ammunition replaced the 23-mm cannon, and further cannon armament could be added in underwing pods.

The original MiG-27 and similar **MiG-27K 'Flogger-D'** were ordered into production directly off the drawing board, and the

prototype was a MiG-23BM conversion that recorded its first flight during 1973. The type entered service in 1975, and was replaced in production during that year by the MiG-27K equipped with the PrNK-23K nav/attack system and a Fone laser rangefinder/target tracker mounted behind a small window in the nose.

Mikoyan MiG-27 'Flogger' (continued)

The MiG-27K was capable of highly-accurate automatic night or bad weather blind bombing.

There were several sub-variants of the aircraft known to NATO as the **'Flogger-J'**, all equipped with the PrNK-23M nav/attack system and Pelenga weapons system giving compatibility with precision-guided weapons. All have their wing glove bullet fairings removed and possess extended wing leading-edge root extensions, the latter being added to serve as a location for the forward hemisphere RWR antennas but also providing the beneficial side effect of improved high-Alpha handling. All 'Flogger-Js' have a new Klen (maple) laser rangefinder in place of the MiG-27K's Fone unit. The maximum take-off weight is increased to 45,569 lb (20670 kg).

The first of the 'Flogger-Js' was the **MiG-27M**, which had an enlarged laser window in the nose, below a dielectric 'pimple' protruding forward from its upper 'lip'. The MiG-27D was externally identical but incorporated the RSBN-6S navigation system associated with the nuclear strike role. The twin pitot probes which served the nav/attack system were mounted high on the nose, providing the main recognition features between the basic 'Flogger-J' and the **MiG-27KR 'Flogger-J2'**. This last aircraft had a noticeable fairing below the nose with a wide rectangular window for a TV tracker or Kaira laser designator, and a 'pimple' radome for terrain-avoidance (or possibly terrain-following) radar above a new broad oval window over a new LLLTV sensor (or alternatively the Klen laser rangefinder, target seeker and marker). The twin pitots were mounted low on the nose.

The only non-Soviet country to operate the MiG-27, and now the only operator since the CIS's withdrawal of the type in the 1990s, is India that built the MiG-27 under licence as the MiG-27M or **Bahadur** (valiant), but which Mikoyan quoted as the **MiG-27L**. The aircraft has the same nose contours as the MiG-27D/M, with only a single window in the under-nose fairing, and shares the same 'Flogger-J' reporting designation. The first Indian-assembled example was rolled out in October 1984, and the first MiG-27L using Indian-built sub-assemblies was rolled out on 11 January 1986.

Mikoyan MiG-29 'Fulcrum'

The **MiG-29 'Fulcrum'** was derived from a study for a heavy fighter, but reached its definitive form as the design bureau's response to a requirement for a lighter fighter capable of destroying fighters in air combat, intercepting bombers and reconnaissance aircraft, escorting friendly aircraft and, as an important secondary task, undertaking the ground-attack role. The increasing importance of low-level penetration by attack aircraft made look-down/shoot-down capability vital, while the growing importance of ECM made a capacity for independent action similarly important.

Detailed design began in 1974 and, starting with a blended high-lift, low-drag wing and forebody, the design bureau added twin canted fins, widely flared wing leading-edge root extensions, and a widely spaced pair of engines with carefully tailored intakes to maximise high angle-of-attack capability. The aerodynamic design was extremely advanced, giving unmatched low-speed and high-Alpha handling characteristics. The flying controls are mainly conventional and are hydraulically controlled. Computer-controlled full-span manoeuvre flaps occupy the wing leading edge, with plain flaps inboard and ailerons outboard on the trailing edge. The horizontal tail surfaces are all-moving. To allow the aircraft to operate from primitive forward airfields, the low-mounted intakes are fitted with large doors that close on start-up, open only after the aircraft has rotated on take-off, and close again when the mainwheels touch on landing. These prevent the ingestion of mud, snow or other debris. While the main intakes are closed, air is drawn in through spring-loaded louvres in the top of the wing roots.

The MiG-29 broke much new ground for the design bureau, with advanced aerodynamics, avionics, systems and even materials. The new aircraft made extensive use of lightweight aluminium-lithium alloys, which allowed a reduction in fasteners and bolts with consequent savings in weight and production complexity. The MiG-29 is powered by a pair of RD-33 afterburning turbofans, which produce considerably more afterburning thrust than equivalent Western engines, but slightly less in dry power. This can make the aircraft more reliant on the use of afterburning in some circumstances, increasing fuel consumption.

Eleven prototypes were built, the first of them making its maiden flight on 6 October 1977. The prototypes were followed by eight pre-production aircraft. Frontal Aviation evaluation began in 1983, and the **'Fulcrum-A'** entered service soon after this. Small ventral fins, initially fitted to the prototype after its first flight, were deleted after a small batch of production aircraft (probably about 100) had been completed, at the same time as overwing chaff/flare dispensers were fitted in extensions to the fins' leading edges. Extended-chord rudders

Although it retains an underwing weapons capability and the internal gun, the MiG-29UB is of limited operational use due to its lack of radar.

and pitot-mounted vortex generators were adopted in the late 1980s, and were retrofitted to all service aircraft.

The fire-control system is a sophisticated arrangement, with data gathered by the aircraft's sensors data-linked to a ground station or AWACS aircraft. The radar is extremely powerful and can easily overwhelm the pilot with information, and filtering and software techniques are inadequate for on-board threat prioritisation. The need to keep contact with an external agency limits the capacity of the MiG-29's pilot for independent action, and imposes a degree of inflexibility. The MiG-29 has two sensors for target acquisition. The first is the N-019 pulse-Doppler radar, known to NATO as 'Slot Back', while the second (affording a measure of passive target acquisition capability) is the IRST system. For close-in engagements, a helmet-mounted sight (which works by sensing the pilot's head position) can be used to cue IR-homing missiles onto an off-bore-sight target. This is extremely useful in conjunction with the very agile R-73 AAM, although firing at an angle well off the nose dramatically reduces missile range.

The MiG-29 is known to the design bureau as the **9-12**, and subvariants are the **9-12A** for delivery to non-Soviet Warsaw Pact forces and lacking both nuclear capability and two of five radar modes, and the **9-12B** for export to non-Warsaw Pact countries and typified by downgraded radar and lack of a data-link. On 4 May 1984 there flew the first example of the **9-13 'Fulcrum-C'**. This was a development of the 9-12 with a much enlarged upper fuselage to the rear of the cockpit for additional avionics, enlarged internal fuel capacity plus provision for a ventral tank, increased weapons load, an improved weapons control system, and auxiliary RWR and ECM antennas at the wing tips. The same reporting designation was retained for the **9-13S** standard otherwise known as the **MiG-29S**. First flown on 5 May 1984, this was a multi-stage upgrade from the 9-13 standard with the weapons load increased to 8,818 lb (4000 kg), provision for larger underwing tanks, Alpha range increased to 28°, N-019M radar able to detect fighter-size targets at 62 miles (100 miles) but later replaced by the N-019ME Topaz radar able to track 10 targets and engage two

When Czechoslovakia split into the Czech Republic and Slovakia in 1993, its MiG-29 force was divided between them. The Czechs (illustrated) retired their 'Fulcrums' in 1994.

Rejected by the Russian authorities in favour of the Su-27K, the MiG-29K multirole naval fighter is likely to enter service with India.

simultaneously, provision for R-77 (AA-12 'Adder') long-range AAMs with the later radar, and maximum take-off weight of 43,430 lb (19700 kg). The **MiG-29SE** is the current production version of the MiG-29S for export with a maximum take-off weight of 44,092 lb (20000 kg). The **MiG-29SM** (otherwise **9-13M**) is another current production model, based on the MiG-29S but with the ability to launch 'smart' air-to-surface weapons. The **MiG-29SD** is the export version of the MiG-29 with most MiG-29SE improvements, and the **MiG-29N** (a local rather than official designation) is the variant

of the MiG-29SD procured by Malaysia; the equivalent two-seater is the **MiG-29NUB**.

A quantum leap in capability was provided by the **MiG-29M** (otherwise **9-15**) that first flew on 25 April 1986 as a genuinely multi-role fighter with provision for a wide assortment of guided munitions, a 'glass' cockpit with HOTAS controls, N-010 Zhuk radar with a larger antenna, a

This MiG-29SD with revised avionics and a dummy enlarged spine, acted as a MiG-29SMT 'prototype'. The SMT-standard is primarily offered as an upgrade.

quadruplex (triplex for lateral control) fly-by-wire system, 19,400-lb st (86.30-kN) RD-33K turbo-fans, and a redesigned airframe largely of aluminium-lithium construc-tion. There are a host of other improvements, but the six prototypes have not been followed by produc-tion aircraft for the Russian or CIS air forces. The MiG-29M's airframe has paved the way for most further developments. The **MiG-29ME** (from 1994 **MiG-33**) is the export version, yet to secure an order. The **MiG-29SMT** (otherwise **9-17**) is a devel-opment of the 9-13's airframe but with most

MiG-29M improvements intended as the basis of upgrade programmes. The **MiG-29SMT-II** (otherwise **9-17-II**) is offered a MiG-29SMT improvement with a number of 'stealth' features, electronic enhancements and a maxi-mum warload of 12,125 lb (5500 kg) on eight hard-points. The **MiG-29K** (otherwise **9-31**) is the carrierborne version of the MiG-29M with an arrester hook, beefed-up landing gear, a larger tailplane, and a revised wing of greater area with folding outer portions and double-slotted flaps. The **MiG-29SMTK** (otherwise **9-17K**) is the counterpart of the MiG-29K

based on the MiG-29SMT.

Two-seat conversion trainers include the **MiG-29UB 'Fulcrum-B'** (otherwise **9-51**) with no radar and a second seat forward of the standard seat under a lengthened canopy, and the **MiG-29UBT** (otherwise **9-51T**) private-venture development on the basis of the MiG-29SMT.

Apart from the countries of the CIS, the MiG-29 series has been or is flown by Bulgaria, Cuba, Czech Republic, Eritrea, Germany, Hungary, Iran, Iraq, Malaysia, North Korea, Peru, Poland, Romania, Slovakia, Yemen and Yugoslavia.

Mikoyan MiG-31 'Foxhound'

The **MiG-31 'Foxhound-A'** was developed as part of an overall programme to provide the Soviet air defences with the ability to meet the threat posed by NATO low-level strike aircraft and cruise missiles. The new interceptor was the **Ye-155MP** develop-ment of the **Ye-155M** experimental development of the MiG-25, and was a two-seater featuring new landing gear with side-by-side nose wheels and offset tandem main wheels. New airbrakes were fitted ahead of the landing gear and opened diagonally downwards from

the corners of the fuselage. The wing planform was subtly changed, with small leading-edge root exten-sions and no wing tip anti-flutter weights. The Ye-155MP made its maiden flight on 16 September 1975. Production of the MiG-31 began in 1979, the new designation having been adopted to acknowl-edge that this was a new aircraft with new capabili-ties, and the type entered service during 1982 with changes from prototype standard that included refined leading-edge slats and relocated airbrakes.

At the heart of the

MiG-31 is the N-007 Zaslon radar, codenamed 'Flash Dance' by NATO. This uses a unique, fixed phased-array antenna, which points its beam electronically. Groups of four MiG-31s can operate together, with only the leader linked to the AK-RLDN ground-based automatic guidance network but joined to his wing men by data-link and covering a swathe of terri-tory 560 miles (900 km) across. The aircraft also features a sensitive IRST sensor.

Some improvements were added during the course of production of 280 aircraft, and later MiG-31s are fitted with a semi-retractable inflight-refuelling probe just below the wind-

SPECIFICATION	
Mikoyan MiG-31 'Foxhound-A'	447 miles (720 km) with standard

Mikoyan MiG-31 'Foxhound-A'
Type: two-seat long-range interceptor
Powerplant: two PNPP Aviadvigatel (Soloviev) D-30F6 turbofans each rated at 20,944 lb st (93.19 kN) dry and 34,171 lb st (152.06 kN) with afterburning
Performance: maximum speed 1,865 mph (3000 km/h) or Mach 2.83 at 57,400 ft (17500 m); cruising speed 1,553 mph (2500 km/h) of Mach 2.35 at high altitude; climb to 32,810 ft (10000 m) in 3 minutes; service ceiling 67,585 ft (20600 m); range 2,050 miles (3300 km) with external fuel; combat radius

447 miles (720 km) with standard fuel
Weights: empty 48,115 lb (21825 kg); maximum take-off 191,851 lb (46200 kg)
Dimensions: wingspan 44 ft 2 in (13.46 m); length 74 ft 6 in (22.69 m); height 20 ft 2¼ in (6.15 m); wing area 663.08 sq ft (61.60 m²)
Armament: one 23-mm Gryazev-Shipunov GSh-23-6M six-barrel cannon in the starboard lower side of the fuselage, plus up to four R-33 (AA-9 'Amos') AAMs carried under the fuselage and two R-60T (AA-6 'Acrid') plus four R-60 (AA-8 'Aphid') AAMs carried on four underwing hardpoints

screen on the port side, while the number of under-wing pylons has been increased from two to four.

The **MiG-31M** (possibly **'Foxhound-B'**) has not received a production order,

but is an improved inter-ceptor variant built only in prototype form (eight aircraft). The variant features Zaslon-M radar, in a drooped and recon-toured radome.

Above: China, India and some other potential customers have been shown the down-graded MiG-31E, but no orders have resulted.

Right: Compared to the MiG-25, the MiG-31 is strengthened for supersonic operations at low level and has an increased fuel load.

Mikoyan MiG-31 'Foxhound' (continued)

This radar has an antenna of greater diameter, can detect fighter-sized targets at a claimed range of 224 miles (360 km), and can control six simultaneous engagements. The new variant also has two additional underfuselage missile stations, increasing the total to six, but the internal cannon has been deleted. The type also has provision for a non-retractable IRST and laser rangefinder in a fairing below the nose, has the inflight-refuelling probe

transferred to the starboard side of the nose, and has lost its intake-mounted RWR antennas. The first MiG-31M was delivered for flight trials in March 1984.

Other changes include a redesigned rear cockpit, with no periscope or control column (a sidestick is provided for emergency use), but with three colour CRT multi-function displays. There are two wing tip configurations, one with rounded tips and one with finned ECM pods. The MiG-31M features a

host of aerodynamic and structural refinements, which increase maximum take-off weight to 114,638 lb (52000 kg). Handling at high angles of attack has been improved by the addition of longer, curving extensions to the wing-root leading edges, and the aircraft reportedly features a new digital flight control system. The MiG-31M also has a deeper, more bulged spine with increased fuel capacity in three saddle tanks, smaller windows for the rear cock-

pit and, over the pilot's cockpit, a one-piece canopy and a new one-piece windscreen.

The **MiG-31D** retains the original nose (with ballast rather than radar) but has large winglets above and below the wing tips. This variant, of which only two were completed, was intended for the anti-satellite role with special Vympel-designed missiles under the wing. Other variants include the **MiG-31B** with enhanced radar, ECM and electronic warfare

equipment as well as upgraded R-33S missiles; **MiG-31BS** conversion from MiG-31 to MiG-31B standard; **MiG-31E** proposed export model with downgraded radar; **MiG-31F** proposed long-range fighter-bomber with a wide variety of guided air-to-surface weapons; **MiG-31BM** defence-suppression development of the MiG-31B that has reached the prototype stage with underwing provision for Kh-31P and Kh-38 missiles; and **MiG-31FE** proposed export variant of the MiG-31BM.

Mikoyan 1.42 (1.44) MFI

During the mid- to late-1990s the aviation community was tantalised by the impending debut of Russia's first 'fifth-generation' fighter, the **Mikoyan MFI (mnogofunktseeon-ahl'nyy frontovoy istrebeetel** – multi-role tactical fighter). The MFI was developed to counter the threat posed by the ATF programme under which the F-22 was created. Mikoyan claims that the MFI's combination of aerodynamic properties,

armament and avionics render it superior to any contemporary fighter, including the F-22A. The aircraft rolled out in 1999 is apparently designated **MiG 1.44** and is understood to be a demonstrator only.

The planned production MFI is referred to as the **1.42** and will have a slightly different air intake design, an internal weapons bay (faired over on the 1.44) and, possibly, cranked-delta wings. The

1.44/1.42 is the first Russian fighter to employ a 'tail-first' configuration. Weapons are mostly carried in an internal bay in the centre fuselage (faired over on the 1.44). The MFI is (or will be) equipped with a pulse-Doppler fire control radar persistently referred to as NO-14. This phased-array unit is designed for BVR combat and has the ability to attack six targets at a time.

Prototype construction began in 1989, and after lengthy ground tests, the 1.44 made its first high-speed run in late 1994. Unfortunately, however, the programme had to be suspended before the 1.44 could become airborne due to ANPK MiG's dire financial problems. The 1.44 remained classified by the Russian Defence Ministry until it was finally publicly unveiled in January 1999. After great delay, the 1.44 finally made its brief but important first flight in January 2001. The future of the MFI remains unclear

and the line between it and the 1.44 remains equally blurred. Even though the MiG 1.42 is the Russian air force's officially selected 'fifth-generation' fighter, Russia's current economic situation precludes the construction of new combat aircraft for the

Russian air force in the next few years. The MFI's projected unit price of $70 million – two to three times as much as current 'fourth-generation' fighters – is almost certainly unsupportable, however capable the aircraft, in the Russia of 2001.

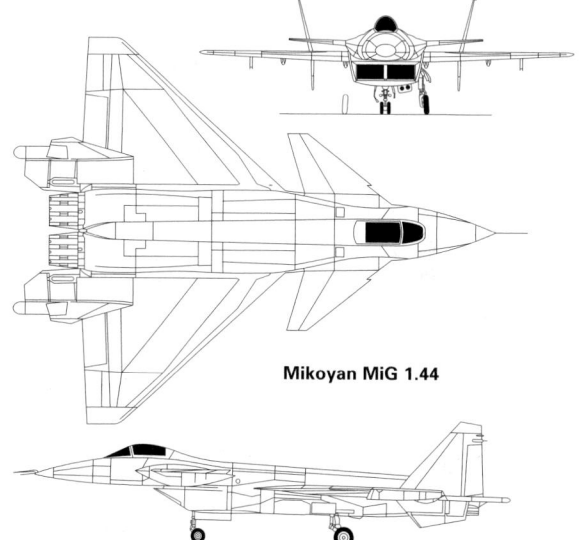

Mikoyan MiG 1.44

SPECIFICATION	
Mikoyan MIG 1.44 (estimated) **Type:** single-seat demonstrator for 1.42 MFI **Powerplant:** two Saturn Lyul'ka AL-41F turbofans each rated at approximately 39,350 lb st (175 kN) with afterburning **Performance:** maximum speed Mach 2.6 at altitude; maximum 'supercruise' capability in region of Mach 1.6 -1.8; service ceiling 65,620 ft (20000 m); range 2,796 miles (4500 km) **Weights:** normal take-off 66,138 lb (30000 kg); maximum take-off 77,161 lb (35000 kg)	**Dimensions:** wingspan 55 ft 10½ in (17.03 m); length 74 ft 10¾ in (22.83 m); height 18 ft 9¼ in (5.72 m); wing area (including canard foreplanes) 1090 sq ft (101.20 m²) **Armament:** principal armament of 1.42 will consist of unidentified 'fifth-generation', long-range 'fire-and-forget' air-to-air (possibly folding fin variant of R-77/AA-12 'Adder') and air-to-surface missiles reportedly developed specially for the MFI. Internal GSh-30-1 30-mm cannon may also be carried

Mikoyan MiG-AT

MiG and Yakovlev are battling for a potential advanced trainer contract to replace up to 1,000

MiG has not sought a partner in its AT programme in the way that Yakovlev has with the Yak-130. Nevertheless the AT is offered in variants with various degrees of 'westernisation'.

Aero L-29 Delfin and L-39 Albatross trainers in CIS air force service. There is also wider interest in their

designs in the export market. MiG MAPO's contender is the **MiG-AT (Advanced Trainer)**. Although relatively ortho-dox, the straight-wing design is claimed to have the same high-Alpha handling as the MiG-29 'Fulcrum'. The MiG-AT is being developed as a joint venture with Turbomeca

and SNECMA for the Larzac engine and Sextant Avionique for the avionics. Mikoyan has built three flying prototypes for the initial fly-off evaluation. The first prototype represents the **MiG-ATF** basic trainer version for the export market, with a modified version of Sextant's Topflight modular avionics suite. The

second is to **MiG-ATR** trainer standards, with Russian avionics. The third is the prototype for the **MiG-ATS** combat-capable trainer. It has a helmet-mounted target designation system, provision for seven external hardpoints (in place of the basic trainer's three) and a variety of centreline targeting pods. The as-yet

SPECIFICATION	
Mikoyan MIG AT **Type:** two-seat basic and advanced jet trainer and light attack aircraft **Powerplant:** two SNECMA Larzac 04R20 turbofans each rated at 3,175 lb st (14.12 kN) **Performance:** maximum level speed at 8,200 ft (2500 m) 621 mph (1000 km/h); maximum initial climb rate 5,510 ft (1680 m) per minute; service ceiling 50,860 ft (15500 m) **Weights:** normal take-off (training)	10,163 lb (4610 kg); maximum take-off (combat) 15,430 lb (7000 kg) **Dimensions:** wingspan 33 ft 4 in (10.16 m); length 39 ft 4¾ in (12.01 m); height 14 ft 6 in (4.42 m); wing area 190.20 sq ft (17.67 m²) **Armament:** (MiG AS) maximum weapon load 4,409 lb (2000 kg); weapons include ASMs, unguided rockets, bombs, gun pods, ATGMs and AAMs

unbuilt **MiG-AS** will be a single-seater, described as being analogous to the BAE Systems Hawk 200. Mikoyan is also offering any MiG-AT variant with folding wings, arrester hook, and strengthened landing gear. All variants use a high proportion of Russian systems and equipment. The first proto-type made its maiden flight in March 1996. By 2001 all three prototypes had flown and initial series production of a further 16 aircraft was well under-way. The future of the MiG-AT remains uncertain, with much still to be decided. However, Mikoyan is continuing to market the aircraft aggres-sively in the world market.

Mil Mi-1 'Hare' and Mi-2 'Hoplite'

Both of the initial GM-1 helicopters crashed, the second killing its test pilot. Nevertheless, the Mi-1 went on to great success, serving with operators which included the Czechoslovak police.

After being given responsi-bility for his own design bureau in 1947, Mikhail Mil went on to design and develop the **GM-1**, later designated **Mi-1**, which was the first conventional helicopter of single main rotor and anti-torque tail rotor configuration to enter series production in the Soviet Union. Built for both civil and military use, and gaining the ASCC/NATO reporting name **'Hare'**, its construction tailed off in the Soviet Union after manufacture was initiated in Poland in 1954, but large numbers were exported from both production sources, with several thou-sand built. The **Mi-2 'Hoplite'** was a turbine-powered development of the Mi-1, with two small turboshaft engines mounted on the roof of the cabin. This not only enhanced capability, but as the fuselage was free from powerplant, made more cabin space available. First flown under the designa-tion **V-2** in September 1961, following completion of its development

Variants

Mi-1: initial standard version seating a pilot and three passengers
Mi-1T: subsequent standard production version seating a pilot and two passengers
Mi-1U: dual-control trainer
Mi-1NKh: general-purpose version for use in agricultural, ambulance, freight and mail-carrying roles
Mi-1 Moskvich: refined version, initially for service with Aeroflot, introducing better soundproofing and equipment, and all-metal rotor blades; improvements later became standard and name was dropped
SM-1: initial Polish production version, generally as Soviet Mi-1 but with power provided by the LiT-3 engine, a licence-built version of the Ivehenko Al-26V radial engine
SM-1W: improved standard production version

basically as SM-1 but introducing metal rotor blades
SM-1WS: ambulance version with two external enclosed stretcher carriers, accessible in flight from main cabin
SM-1WZ: agricultural duster/sprayer
SM-1WSZ: dual-control trainer version
SM-2: improved Polish-developed version with lengthened nose to provide enlarged cabin seating a pilot and four passengers; entered production in 1961
Mi-2: turbine-powered version of the Mi-1 produced entirely in Poland, accommodating a pilot and a maximum eight passengers; powered by Polish-built Isotov GTD-350 turboshaft engines and available also in several versions, including ambulance **Mi-2R** and agricultural **Mi-2 Bazant**
PZL Swidnik Kania/Kitty Hawk: Allison-engined Mi-2 with improved avionics offered as new-build aircraft or conversion

programme in the Soviet Union, the Mi-2 was handed over to WSK in Poland for production and continued development.

The first Polish-built Mi-2 was flown on 4 November 1965, and in excess of 5,320 had been built for civil and military customers when production ceased in the mid-1990s. The basic Mi-2 airframe also formed the basis for a number of variants developed in Poland by PZL Swidnik.

In 2001 the Mi-2 remained in widespread service, European operators including Lithuania (illustrated) and Russia.

SPECIFICATION	
PZL (Mil) Mi-2	maximum payload 106 miles
Type: general-purpose light	(170 km)
helicopter	**Weights:** empty operating 5,213 lb
Powerplant: two 450-shp	(2365 kg); maximum take-off
(336-kW) Isotov GTD-350P	8,157 lb (3700 kg)
turboshafts	**Dimensions:** main rotor diameter
Performance: maximum cruising	47 ft 6¾ in (14.50 m); length, rotors
speed 118 mph (190 km/h) at	turning 57 ft 2 in (17.42 m); height
1,640 ft (500 m); service ceiling	12 ft 3½ in (3.75 m); main rotor disc
13,125 ft (4000 m); range with	area 1,791.17 sq ft (166.40 m²)

Mil Mi-4 'Hound'

Design of the **Mi-4**, a conventional helicopter with about four times the capacity of the Mi-1, was initiated in 1951 and the first example was flown during May 1952. Produced initially for use by the Soviet armed forces in assault and troop transport roles, the **Mi-4 'Hound-A'** has clamshell rear doors to simplify the loading of vehi-cles and freight; alternatively, the cabin can accommodate up to 14 troops. Military Mi-4s are recognisable easily by having a ventral gondola which was intended origi-nally for a navigator or observer, but can also house avionics equipment. Produced in large numbers for Soviet military use, the Mi-4 was also widely exported.

This Afghan 'Hound' is typical of the many hundreds of these aircraft that were used in a utility role. By 2001 only Chinese-built Z-5s remained in service, the majority with China.

Variants

Mi-4: basic military production version with clamshell rear doors: this configuration adopted also for civil cargo versions
Mi-4A: assault transport
Mi-4L: Lyuks (de luxe) six-passenger helicopter, sometimes converted for use as an ambulance
Mi-4M: armed version with a gun turret and ASMs
Mi-4P: civil transport version used extensively by Aeroflot and seating 10 passengers in furnished cabin
Mi-4PL: ASW variant with nose radar and sonobuoys

carried externally on the starboard side
Mi-4S: Salon VIP helicopter
Mi-4Skh: basically an agricultural version with a large chemical container in the main cabin, but also used for fire-fighting operations
Mi-4T: principal military production version with larger-diameter main rotor, bulged windows with gun ports and other changes
Z-5: Chinese military version of the Mi-4 for service with both the army and navy
Xuanfeng: Chinese name for civil version of the Mi-4, at least one was with the PT6T-6 twin turbine engine

Mil Mi-4 'Hound' (continued)

The 'Hound' eventually saw service with more than 20 foreign air arms. A number remained in use in 2001, and versions included the ASW **Mi-4PL 'Hound-B'** armed close support and ECM **Mi-4M 'Hound-C'**. From 1964 production of civil versions was initiated, and combined civil/military production by Mil was estimated at 3,200 when production terminated in 1964. All versions can be equipped with inflatable pontoons which, mounted so that the landing wheels projected below them, can be used for amphibious operations. The Mi-4 was also manufactured under licence in China, a total of about 545 having been built under the **Z-5** designation, and of which approximately two-thirds were solely for civil use.

Mil's Mi-4 had much in common with the configuration of Sikorsky's S-55. A Czechoslovak Mi-4 transport is shown here.

SPECIFICATION

Mil Mi-4P 'Hound'
Type: civil transport helicopter
Powerplant: one 1,700-hp (1268-kW) Shyetsov ASh-82V radial piston engine
Performance: maximum speed 130 mph (210 km/h) at 4,920 ft (1500 m); service ceiling 18,045 ft (5500 m); range with 11 passengers 155 miles (250 km)
Weights: empty 11,883 lb (5390 kg); maximum take-off 17,196 lb (7800 kg)
Dimensions: main rotor diameter 68 ft 10¾ in (21.0 m); length rotors turning 82 ft 1 in (25.02 m); height 17 ft (5.18 m); main rotor disc area 3,724.43 sq ft (346.00 m²)

Mil Mi-6 and Mi-22 'Hook'

Development of the **Mi-6 'Hook'**, began in 1954 in response to Aeroflot and Soviet air force requirements for a large transport helicopter. When it made its maiden flight in September 1957, the Mi-6 was the world's largest rotary-wing aircraft and, more significantly, was also the first turbine-powered helicopter to enter production in the USSR. The Mi-6 features an optional and detachable stub wing, which offloads the main rotor by some 20 per cent in cruising flight, with attendant benefits in reducing fuel consumption and extending endurance.

The five prototype and development helicopters were followed by an initial production batch of 30 machines, most of which went to the air force. The standard **Mi-6T 'Hook-A'** troop transport can carry up to 70 people on tip-up seats along the cabin sides and additional bench seats along the centreline. The **Mi-6A** civil transport can lift between 65 and 90 passengers. The **Mi-6S** casevac helicopter can carry up to 41 litters. Clamshell doors are provided at the rear of the cabin under the boom supporting the tail rotor, with hydraulically operated loading ramps and a 1,764-lb (800-kg) capacity internal winch for cargo handling. The hold can carry 26,455 lb (12000 kg), while the alternative external freight load is 19,841 lb (9000 kg). Production of the Mi-6 series lasted to 1980, and reached some 800 helicopters. There have been several other civilian variants, including the **Mi-6P** with accommodation for up to 80 passengers or a smaller number of VIP passengers.

The latter variant is identifiable by its rectangular rather than circular windows. other variants include the **Mi-6PZh** firefighting model which has a **Mi-6PZh-2** subvariant with a nose-mounted water nozzle, and the **Mi-10 'Harke'** specialised flying crane version.

The Mi-6 has also been adapted in small numbers for special duties. Three separate versions have been identified, all being described as airborne command post or command post support helicopters although it may be more accurate to call them air-mobile command posts, since it seems likely that they function in their primary roles only on the ground. The nose-mounted 0.5-in (12.7-mm) Afanaseyev machine-gun of the 'Hook-A' is deleted in all three variants, which are the **Mi-6VKP 'Hook-B'**, originally thought to have been the **Mi-6R**, for the command post role; the **Mi-6VUS 'Hook-C'** also known as the **Izd-50AYa**, **Mi-6AYa** and **Mi-22** for the command support role; and the **Mi-6AYaSh 'Hook-D'** for the command support role. The Mi-6VKP is packed with electronic equipment and bristles with unidentified antennas. The Mi-22 features an entirely different antenna array. It more closely resembles the standard 'Hook-A', with auxiliary fuel tanks on both sides but with a new underfuselage antenna farm, and with a single large swept blade antenna above the rear fuselage. Some 'Hook-Cs' have been seen with a large horizontal 'spear-like' device on the main landing gear legs. Neither the 'Hook-B' nor the 'Hook-C' has been exported, all aircraft serving in Russia and in the states of the former USSR.

The Mi-6 was reportedly export to Algeria, Angola, Egypt, Ethiopia, Iraq, Indonesia, Laos, Peru, Pakistan, Poland, Syria, Vietnam and Zambia.

Although the Mi-6 has been withdrawn from service in Ethiopia, Indonesia, Pakistan, Poland and Vietnam, many remain operational elsewhere. Even in Russia, where the much newer and even larger Mi-26 'Halo' is in service, the ageing 'Hook' remains highly prized.

All 'Hooks' in military service fly with a flight crew of five, comprising two pilots, a flight engineer, a radio operator and a navigator. 'Red 50', an Mi-6VUS 'Hook-C', was photographed at Oranienberg in 1990.

The cabin of the Mi-6 is 38 ft 6 in (11.72 m) long and 8 ft 7 in (2.65 m) wide with a height varying between 6 ft 6 in and 8 ft 6 in (2.00 and 2.64 m). A Soviet civilian Mi-6 is illustrated.

SPECIFICATION

Mil Mi-6T 'Hook-A'
Type: five-crew heavy transport helicopter
Powerplant: two PNPP 'Aviadvigatel' (Soloviev) D-25V (TV-2BM) turboshaft engines each rated at 5,425 shp (4045 kW)
Performance: maximum speed 189 mph (304 km/h) at optimum altitude; cruising speed 155 mph (250 km/h) at optimum altitude; climb to 9,845 ft (3000 m) in 9 minutes 42 seconds; service ceiling 14,765 ft (4500 m); hovering ceiling 7,380 ft (2250 m) in ground effect; range 1450 km (900 km) with auxiliary fuel and 385 miles (620 km) with standard fuel and a 17,637-lb (8000-kg) payload
Weights: empty 60,055 lb (27240 kg); maximum take-off 93,695 lb (42500 kg)
Dimensions: main rotor diameter 114 ft 10 in (35.00 m); wingspan 50 ft 2½ in (15.30 m); length 136 ft 11½ in (41.74 m) with the rotors turning; height 32 ft 4 in (9.86 m); main rotor disc area 10,356.43 sq ft (962.11 m²); wing area 376.75 sq ft (35.00 m²)
Armament: one 0.5-in (12.7-mm) Afanaseyev trainable forward-firing machine-gun in the nose
Payload: see above

Mil Mi-8, Mi-9 and Mi-17 'Hip'

The **Mi-8 'Hip'**, has proved itself rugged and dependable, and large numbers remain in use. Design of the Mi-8 was launched in 1960 as a second-generation, turbine-engined derivative of and replacement for the Mi-4, using the same boom and rotors. The small size of the turboshaft permitted relocation of the powerplant from the nose to a position above the cabin, allowing the cockpit to be moved into the nose and making possible a simpler transmission system. The cabin is much larger, even though the external dimensions are little changed, and can seat 28 passengers.

In the absence of the planned engine type, the 'Hip-A' prototype was powered by a single 2,781-ehp (2074-ekW) Ivchyenko AI-24V turboshaft engine driving a four-bladed main rotor, and first flew during June 1961. The 'Hip-B' second prototype, which recorded its maiden flight in August 1962, introduced the designed powerplant of two 1,400-shp (1044-kW) Isotov TV2-117 turboshafts driving the same type of main rotor, but the definitive five-bladed main rotor (scaled down from that of the Mi-6) was introduced in some of the pre-production helicopters, which also pioneered the 1,500-shp (1118-kW) TV2-117A. The first production version, authorised for manufacture in 1966, was the **Mi-8P** civil

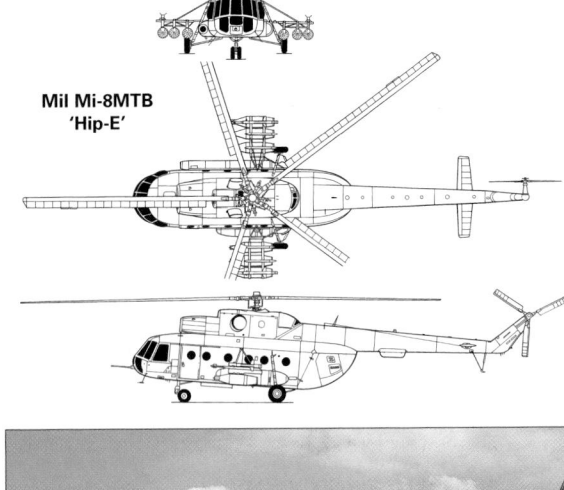

The Eesti Piirivalve (Estonian Border Guard) uses two brightly-coloured Mi-8T helicopters on search and rescue operations.

Mil Mi-8MTB 'Hip-E'

28/32-seat passenger transport. This retains the rectangular cabin windows of the prototype, as does the **Mi-8S** VIP transport with 11 armchair-style seats, a toilet and galley. The similar **Mi-8PS** has also seen service with many air forces as a VIP transport.

More popular with military customers is the **Mi-8T**, the standard utility transport. This introduced small, circular cabin windows, and while early Mi-8T helicopters were fitted with 1,500-shp (1118-kW) engines most were powered by uprated engines. The **Mi-8TP** is the military staff transport version with improved radio equipment. The **Mi-8TV** is the armed derivative with outriggers carrying four pylons, each capable of carrying a UV-16-57 rocket pod. The **Mi-8TB 'Hip-E'** is a more heavily armed model with a 0.5-in (12.7-mm) KV-4 trainable

machine-gun in a mounting in the bottom of the nose (for operation by the flight engineer) and redesigned braced outriggers that each have three pylons each for the carriage of one UV-32-57 rocket pod, 551-lb (250-kg) bomb or equivalent. Above the outer two pylons are four launch rails for the 9M17P Skorpion (AT-2 'Swatter') anti-tank missile aimed by the co-pilot via a gyro-stabilised sight. When fully armed, the 'Hip-E' can carry only 14 troops and a limited fuel load, but packs an impressive punch. The related **Mi-8TBK** was built for export to East Germany (and later Nicaragua) with 'overwing' launch rails for six 9M14M Malyutka (AT-3 'Sagger') anti-tank missiles.

Other military derivatives are numerous. The **Mi-8TZ** is used for delivery of fuel to front-line units; the **Mi-8T(K)** and **Mi-8SKA** are photo-reconnaissance helicopters with secondary

artillery fire-correction capability; the **Mi-8K** is used for reconnaissance and artillery fire correction; the **Mi-8R** is another reconnaissance model; the **Mi-8AV** is a minelaying model; and the **Mi-8BT** is a mine-clearing model. Later civil helicopters included the **Mi-8AT** with TV2-117AG engines and improved equipment; the **Mi-8ATS** is an agricultural model with a hopper and spraybar on each side; the **Mi-8MT** is a flying crane model with a glazed gondola in place of the clamshell doors; the **Mi-8VIP** is the de luxe transport for up to nine VIPs; the **Mi-8TM** is an upgraded Mi-8T with weather radar and a rotor head integrity system; and the **Mi-8TG** has TV2-117G engines able to run on liquefied petroleum gas.

Further developments for specialised military tasks are the **Mi-8VZPU 'Hip-D'** airborne reserve command post, the **Mi-8SMV 'Hip-J'** ECM model with an onboard jamming system, the **Mi-8PPA 'Hip-K'** Comint and active communications jamming model, and the **Mi-9 'Hip-G'** command relay model.

To improve performance, especially under 'hot-and-high' conditions or with a single engine out, the Mi-8 was re-engined with 1,874-shp (1397-kW) TV3-117MT engines to produce the **Mi-17** (originally **Mi-18**) that is known to NATO as the **'Hip-H'**. With one engine inoperative, the other can produce up to 2,200 shp (1641 kW). The new type has its tail rotor relocated from starboard to port, changing its direction of rotation and becoming a tractor rather than a pusher unit. The helicopter also has a new

This Hungarian machine is an example of the rare Mi-9, as indicated by the large 'hockey-stick' antennas protruding from the rear fuselage.

titanium alloy rotor hub and a new gearbox. The payload capability remains unchanged at 8,818 lb (4000 kg) carried internally or 6,614 lb (3000 kg) carried externally, but the performance is considerably improved and the fuel consumption is reduced. Export customers often use the civil Mi-17 designation, but the CIS air forces use the **Mi-8MT** designation. 'Hip-Hs' in CIS service are often fitted with extra cockpit armour, IR jammers, chaff/flare dispensers and even bulky exhaust gas diffusers. The 'Hip-H' can also carry the same six-pylon outrigger as the 'Hip-E' but is generally armed with two BV-8-20A pods for 40 3.15-in (80-mm) rockets,

and can also be fitted with one 0.3-in (7.62-mm) PKT machine-gun in the rear starboard door and either one 0.5-in (12.7-mm) NSV machine-gun or one AGS-17 Plamiya grenade launcher in the rear port door. The same basic helicopter without armament is the **Mi-8AMT**, and there are more than 30 other variants for the electronic warfare and other roles: these latter include the **Mi-8TPB**, **Mi-8TSh**, **Mi-8TPSh**, **Mi-8MTU**, **Mi-8TA**, **Mi-8MTP**, **Mi-8MTPB**, **Mi-8MTR**, **Mi-8MTI**, **Mi-8MTPI** and the **Mi-8MTT**.

The most important of these is the **Mi-8MTPB 'Hip-H EW'**, otherwise known as the **Mi-17P** and **Mi-17PP**.

SPECIFICATION

Mil Mi-8T 'Hip-C'

Type: two-three-crew utility medium helicopter
Powerplant: two Klimov (Isotov) TV2-117A turboshaft engines each rated at 1,677 shp (1250 kW)
Performance: maximum speed 155 mph (250 km/h) at sea level; cruising speed 140 mph (225 km/h) at optimum altitude; initial climb rate 886 ft (270 m) per minute; service ceiling 14,765 ft (4500 m); hovering ceiling 6,235 ft (900 m) in ground effect and 2,625 ft (800 m)

out of ground effect; combat radius 217 miles (350 km)
Weights: empty 15,784 lb (7160 kg); maximum take-off 26,455 lb (12000 kg)
Dimensions: main rotor diameter 69 ft 10¼ in (21.29 m); length 82 ft 9¾ in (25.24 m) with the rotors turning; height 18 ft 6½ in (5.65 m); main rotor disc area 3,832.08 sq ft (356.00 m²)
Armament: see above
Payload: see above

This Czech Mi-17 was photographed as it approached a mountain-top landing site. Note the relocated tail rotor.

Several thousand examples of the Mi-8/-9/-17 family remain in front-line service in 2001, the majority of them standard Mi-8s like this Indian example.

Mil Mi-8, Mi-9 and Mi-17 'Hip' (continued)

The Mi-8MTPB is intended for the Comint and radar/communications jamming roles with three jamming systems, and derived models are the **Mi-8MTI**, **Mi-8MTTs2** and **Mi-8MTTs-3**.

Further improvement in 'hot-and-high' capability is provided by the **Mi-8TMV** series with TV3-117VM engines. This series has been and still is being produced in a number of subvariants. The **Mi-8MTV-1** is the basic civil model. The **Mi-8MTV-2** is the basic military model with radar and the six-pylon outriggers equipped for the carriage of missiles, and its export counterpart is the **Mi-17-1V**. The **Mi-8MTV-3** is the counterpart of the Mi-8MTV-2 with four-pylon outriggers, and its export variant is the **Mi-172**. The **Mi-8TMV-5** (otherwise the **Mi-17MD**) is the military version with a one-section rear loading ramp in place of the clamshell doors, and its civil counterpart is the **Mi-8MTV-5-Ga**. The **Mi-17-1VA** is a flying hospital model. The **Mi-17PI** is related to the **Mi-17MTPB** jammer, but has only one D-band jamming system, while the **Mi-17PG** has a single H/I-band jamming system. The **Mi-8AMT(Sh)** is the Mi-8MTV built at Ulan-Ude rather than Kazan, and its export variant is the **Mi-171**. The **Mi-17KF** is an upgraded model with Canadian-integrated Western avionics and the powerplant of two 1,923-shp (1434-kW) TV3-117MT or 2,070-shp (1545-kW) TV3-117VM engines. The **Mi-17Z-2** is a Czechoslovak-developed variant of the Mi-8MT for the ECM role. The **Mi-19** is a command relay helicopter similar to the **Mi-9** but based on the Mi-8MT airframe.

Mil Mi-10 'Harke'

The **Mi-10 'Harke'** is a specialised flying crane version of the Mi-6 'Hook'. First flown in 1960 as the **V-10** prototype, the **Mi-10** 'Harke-A' in production form has the same powerplants, transmission system and rotors as the Mi-6, with a shallower fuselage. This supports a very tall, very wide track quadricycle landing gear which allows the helicopter to be taxied with almost any load carried underslung between the undercarriage units (ground/underfuselage clearance is 12 ft 3 in/3.75 m). Alternatively, wheeled loading platforms can be rolled under the aircraft and clipped to the undercarriage units. Twenty-eight passengers can be carried internally, or freight can be loaded via a door on the starboard side. The **Mi-10K 'Harke-B'** has a shortened, narrower-track undercarriage, but has a ventral gondola with a backward-facing seat, allowing a second pilot to hover the aircraft accurately over a load and to operate the hoist. Small numbers of both types may remain available to the Russian military.

SPECIFICATION

Mil Mi-10K 'Harke-B'
Type: crane helicopter
Powerplant: two PNPP 'Aviadvigatel' (Soloviev) D-25VF turboshafts each rated at 6,500 shp (4847 kW)
Performance: maximum cruising speed at optimum altitude 155 mph (250 km/h); service ceiling 3000 m (9,845 ft); range ferry range 494 miles (795 km) with auxiliary fuel
Weights: empty 54,409 lb (24680 kg); maximum take-off 83,774 lb (38000 kg)
Dimensions: main rotor diameter 114 ft 10 in (35.00 m); length overall, rotors turning 137 ft 5½ in (41.89 m); height overall 25 ft 7 in (7.80 m); main rotor disc area 10,356.43 sq ft (962.11 m²)
Payload: maximum payload 30,864 lb (14000 kg)

The unusual landing gear of the Mi-10 'Harke' has a front-wheel track of 19 ft 8⅗ in (6.01 m), and a rear-wheel track of 22 ft 8⅗ in.

Mil Mi-12 (V-12) 'Homer'

Although only two examples of the **Mi-12** were built, both being **V-12** prototypes, this giant machine is worthy of mention as the world's largest helicopter to have flown to date. To economise in effort and development cost, the Mil design team adopted the main rotor, transmission and powerplant of the Mi-6, using them in duplicate, one such unit being located at the tip of each of the extensively-braced fixed wings. The use of twin counter-rotating main rotors eliminated the requirement for a tail rotor, the tail unit consisting instead of conventional surfaces, plus endplate fins at the tips of the tailplane. The four Soloviev D-25VF turboshaft engines had a combined output of 26,000 shp (19388 kW), enabling the V-12, first flown on 10 July 1968, to establish a series of records in February 1969 which, when submitted for ratification, was the first intimation received in the West of the existence of this giant helicopter, then allocated the ASCC/NATO reporting name **'Homer'**. Later in the year, on 6 August 1969, the V-12 lifted a payload of 88,636 lb (40204.5 kg) to a height of 7,398 ft (2255 m), establishing a record that remains unbeaten.

The first prototype was destroyed in a non-fatal landing accident during 1969, and although the second prototype was used for a large number of demonstration flights, no further development or production ensued.

A truly giant machine, the Mi-12 housed its navigator on a flightdeck above that occupied by the pilots. The second 'Homer' is illustrated.

Mil Mi-14 'Haze'

It soon became apparent that the Mi-8 could form the basis of a replacement for the many Mi-4 'Hounds' in service with the AV-MF. Accordingly, a new version was developed with a boat-like hull, flotation gear and other improvements, resulting in the **Mi-14 'Haze'**. Development commenced in 1968, resulting in a prototype, the **V-14**, in 1973. The production **Mi-14PL 'Haze-A'** is a dedicated ASW platform, with a towed APM-60 MAD, OKA-2 dipping sonar, sonobuoys and a retractable Type 12-M search radar. Early Mi-14PLs had undercarriage doors, but these were soon deleted. To improve controllability in hovering flight, the more powerful TV3-117 engine of the Mi-17 was adopted during production, and the tail rotor changed sides from starboard to port. However, there was no change of reporting name or designation. The latest 'Haze-As' have a relocated APM-60D MAD and various other improvements, including a new IFF system, and are designated **Mi-14PLM**. The Mi-14PL has been exported to Bulgaria, Cuba, Libya, Poland and Syria. One Polish aircraft has been modified for SAR training under the designation **Mi-14PX**.

The **Mi-14BT 'Haze-B'** is a dedicated minesweeping helicopter, delivered only to the AV-MF and the Volksmarine but then transferred to the Luftwaffe. About 25 'Haze-Bs' were built, six of these going to the East German navy. Mine-sweeping trials were carried out in 1983, and production Mi-14BTs were

Variants

Mi-14PL 'Strike': version of 'Haze-A' equipped to fire kh-23 (AS-7 'Kerry') ASMs
Mi-14PW: Polish designation for Mi-14PL
Mi-14PX: One Polish 'Haze-A' with all ASW gear removed and used for SAR training
Mi-14P: conversion of military airframes for civilian use
Mi-14GP: conversion of military airframes for civilian use
Mi-14PZh 'Eliminator': fire-fighting version

As a standard WarPac ASW helicopter, the Mi-14PL 'Haze-A' was widely exported to Soviet client states, including East Germany.

deployed on multi-national mine clearing operations during the early 1980s. The aircraft has never been widely deployed, however, the Russian navy and its allies preferring to use surface vessels for the mine countermeasures (MCM) role.

Externally, the Mi-14BT can be distinguished by its lack of a towed MAD, and by having its SKW heating and ventilation system mounted in a pod on the

starboard side of the cabin, above the windows. A further distinguishing feature is a broad strake running below the windows on the same side. The aircraft also has a small box under the tail-boom, forward of the

Doppler box, which houses a searchlight designed to illuminate the mine-clearing sled's launch and recovery at night. Some Mi-14BTs have small windows in the lower part of the rear fuselage, to allow the MCM operator to watch the mine-clearing sled.

Several of the East German Mi-14BTs were withdrawn from MCM duties and were converted for SAR duties prior to reunification, and all were offered for sale shortly after their transfer into Luftwaffe hands. Their fate remains uncertain. Some have emerged as civilian water-bombers for use in

A retractable winch on the port side allows the Mi-14PS 'Haze-C' SAR helicopter to hoist a basket containing up to three people.

the fire-fighting role.

The **Mi-14PS 'Haze-C'** is a dedicated search and rescue variant for the AV-MF, based on the airframe of the Mi-14BT, but with a widened cabin entry door, an increased capacity rescue winch and pop-out articulated searchlights in the nose. No MAD is fitted,

but the Mil Mi-14BT's MCM sled illuminating searchlight is retained. Some Polish aircraft have an extra downward-shining searchlight in a nose 'beak', and some former Soviet aircraft carry a survey camera in a third box under the tailboom. Poland is the only export customer.

SPECIFICATION

Mil Mi-14PL 'Haze-A'
Type: ASW helicopter
Powerplant: two Klimov (Isotov) TV3-117A turboshafts each rated at 1,700 shp (1268 kW) in earlier helicopters, or two TV3-117M turboshafts each rated at 1,900 shp (1417 kW) or TV3-117MT turboshafts each rated at 1,950 shp (2245 kW) in later helicopters
Performance: maximum level speed 'clean' at optimum altitude 143 mph (230 km/h); maximum cruising speed at optimum altitude 133 mph (215 km/h); initial rate of climb 1,535 ft (468 m) per minute; service ceiling 13,123 ft (4000 m); range 575 miles (925 km) with standard fuel
Weights: empty 19,625 lb (8902 kg); maximum take-off 30,864 lb (14000 kg)
Dimensions: main rotor diameter 69 ft 10¼ in (21.29 m); length overall, rotors turning 83 ft 1 in (25.32 m); height 22 ft 9 in (6.93 m); main rotor disc area 3,832.08 sq ft (356 m²)
Armament: one AT-1 or APR-2 torpedo, or a 'Skat' nuclear depth bomb, or eight depth charges

Mil Mi-24, Mi-25 and Mi-35 'Hind'

The **Mi-24 'Hind'**, was originally conceived as a flying armoured personnel carrier, carrying a squad of soldiers and providing its own defensive and suppressive fire while relying on speed for protection. To hasten development, the Mi-24 was designed around the Mi-8's dynamic system in combination with a new airframe and a smaller tail rotor turning at higher speed. The cabin of the new fuselage seated eight, with access via horizontally split outward-opening doors. The crew was housed in an extensive 'greenhouse' nose, with the co-pilot/gunner forward and the pilot farther to the rear. From the start, the Mi-24 was fitted with a stub wing to offload the main rotor in forward flight and so boost speed, reduce turn radius, and provide attachment points for weapons.

The first of 12 **V-24** prototype and development helicopters flew on 19 September 1969 and, together with a number of pre-production and early production helicopters with a flat wing, these aircraft received the reporting name **'Hind-B'** as their existence became known only after that of the first definitive production

machines with a flat but later an anhedralled wing, which received the name **'Hind-A'**. The **Mi-24A 'Hind-A'** entered front-line service during 1974. The straight wing had four pylons for UV-32-57 or B-8V-20 pods carrying 2.17- or 3.15-in (55- or 80-mm) rockets, or bombs up to 551 lb (250 kg) in weight. The larger anhedralled wing introduced later in 1974 retained the underwing pylons but in the **Mi-24B** later production variant added vertical endplates carrying two missile launch rails for the 9M117P Skorpion (AT-2 'Swatter') anti-tank missile. A missile guidance/illuminator pod was mounted below the fuselage, and a 0.5-in (12.7-mm) YakB-12.7 machine-gun was added in an undernose turret. The missile guidance package

was relocated to a position to port of the gun turret.

The TV3-117 engine was introduced during the production run to create the **Mi-24F**, and the tail rotor was repositioned from the starboard to the port side of the boom. A version of the Mi-24A used for training, with no gun, undernose blister and missile rails, was the **Mi-24U 'Hind-C'**. Early Mi-24s were not widely exported, but examples were noted in service in Afghanistan, Algeria, Libya and Vietnam.

Operational experience soon showed that the original concept was slightly flawed. The type's ground-attack capability was clearly reduced by the carriage of troops, but the decline of the helicopter's transport role now saw the rise of the Mi-24's armed task.

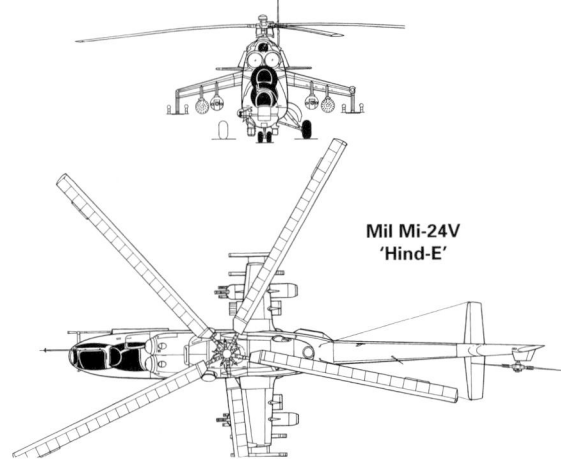

Mil Mi-24V 'Hind-E'

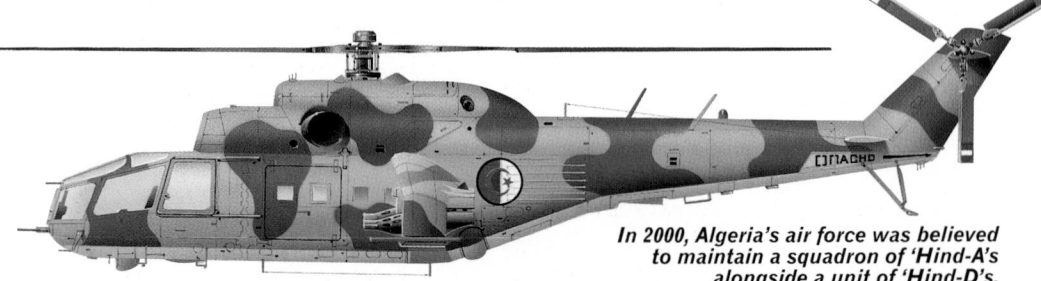

In 2000, Algeria's air force was believed to maintain a squadron of 'Hind-A's alongside a unit of 'Hind-D's.

Mil Mi-24, Mi-25 and Mi-35 'Hind' (continued)

It soon became apparent that the original 'greenhouse' canopy gave less than perfect all-round visibility and yet offered the crew little protection. The development of another battlefield helicopter was unnecessary, however, since in many respects the basic design had proved outstanding. The solution adopted was a redesign with an entirely new nose accommodating a tandem arrangement of heavily armoured cockpits for the gunner and the pilot, the latter located behind and above the former. These cockpits were covered by bubble canopies, with bullet-proof armoured glass windscreens. Beside ease of access, the new arrangement gave a much smaller frontal area, improved visibility and reduced drag. Beside the gun turret is a pod carrying the electro-optical sight for the YakB-12.7 machine-gun.

To the rear of the cockpit the helicopter was unchanged, the optional flight engineer sitting in the narrow 'corridor' between the cockpit and the cabin, which was regarded as a space for stowing missile reloads rather than for carrying passengers. The new variant received the designation **Mi-24DA 'Hind-D'**, and the type was

also exported as the **Mi-25**. The **Mi-24DU** was the trainer variant with dual controls and no undernose turret.

The **Mi-24D** was supplemented in Soviet service from 1976 by the **Mi-24V 'Hind-E'**, which introduced the tube-launched 9M114 (AT-6 'Spiral') missile, of which a maximum of 12 can be carried. This missile also required the introduction of an enlarged missile guidance pod, and a HUD replaced the pilot's original reflector gun sight. The Mi-24V has been the major current production version, and its export variant is the **Mi-35**, also produced as the **Mi-35U** dual-control trainer without the undernose turret. Use of the Mi-24 series in the Afghan war of the 1980s led to the introduction of a variety of defensive systems including IR jammers, dispensers for IRCM flares and chaff cartridges, and even exhaust suppressors to reduce the helicopter's IR signature.

The Mi-24V also formed the basis for the **Mi-24P**, **Mi-24RCh** (otherwise **Mi-24RKR** and **Mi-24R**) and **Mi-24K** variants. Development of the Mi-24P was spurred by combat experience in Afghanistan, in which the 0.5-in (12.7-mm) machine-gun

proved ineffective against some targets against which the use of rockets or guided missiles was deemed wasteful. The obvious answer was the replacement of the machine-gun by a larger-calibre cannon. Interim solutions included a variety of podded cannon for underwing carriage, and the little-known **Mi-24VP**, a 'Hind-E' with a 23-mm GSh-23-2 two-barrel cannon in its nose turret. The GSh-23-2 proved too big for the turret mechanism, and ammunition capacity was also a problem. A better solution was the deletion of the nose turret and the mounting of a 30-mm GSh-30K twin-barrel cannon, supplied with 750 rounds of ammunition, on the starboard side of the fuselage. This modification resulted in the **Mi-24P**, which was exported as the **Mi-35P** to Angola and Iraq.

Two battlefield reconnaissance variants have been produced. The **Mi-24RKR 'Hind-G1'** was created as a model with only limited armament for use in the NBC reconnaissance task with 'clutching hand' mechanisms under lengthened pylons to collect soil samples to ascertain the spread of fall-out of chemical and bacteriological agents. The second reconnaissance version is the **Mi-24K 'Hind-G2'** for artillery fire correction.

Other variants that have been used in very small numbers include the

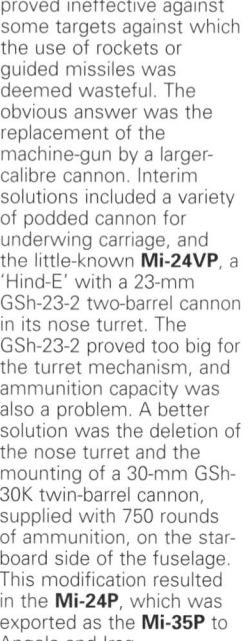

This Indian aircraft is either an Mi-35U trainer, or a helicopter converted to that standard. All 'Hinds' are equipped with basic dual controls.

This Mi-24V is one of around 36 examples of the 'Hind' in service with the Czech Republic. Mi-24s now fly as part of NATO with Czech, Hungarian and Polish air arms.

Mi-24BMT minesweeper conversion, and the **Mi-24PS** for paramilitary use with a FLIR, searchlight, loudspeaker system and attachments for abseiling ropes. The Mi-24 series is still in limited production at the beginning of the 21st century, and the **Mi-24M** (export **Mi-35M**) is offered as an upgrade with the rotors of the Mi-28 and a nose turret carrying a 23-mm two-barrel cannon. A number of helicopters in CIS service are being upgraded to **Mi-24VM** standard derived from this

concept: the first stage modernises the cockpit with multi-function displays and compatibility with night vision goggles, while the second introduces 2,194-shp (1636-kW) TV3-117MA engines driving the Mi-28 'Havoc's' main and tail rotors, a shortened wing and lighter fixed landing gear. Later improvements could include more modern missiles, a laser rangefinder, an updated central computer, and a turret armed with the GSh-23-2 cannon.

SPECIFICATION	
Mil Mi-24D 'Hind-D'	27,557 lb (12500 kg)
Type: two/three-crew battlefield helicopter	**Dimensions:** main rotor diameter 56 ft 9 in (17.30 m); wingspan 21 ft 5½ in (6.536 m); length 64 ft 11 in (19.79 m) with the rotors turning; height 21 ft 4 in (6.50 m) with the rotors turning; main rotor disc area (2,529.52 sq ft (235.00 m²)
Powerplant: two Klimov (Isotov) TV3-117MT turboshaft engines each rated at 1,923 shp (1434 kW)	
Performance: maximum speed 192 mph (310 km/h) at optimum altitude; cruising speed 162 mph (260 km/h) at optimum altitude; initial climb rate 2,461 ft (750 m) per minute; service ceiling 14,765 ft (4500 m); hovering ceiling 7,220 ft (2200 m) out of ground effect; combat radius 99 miles (160 km) with maximum military load	**Armament:** one 0.5-in (12.7-mm) YakB-12.7 trainable forward-firing four-barrel rotary machine-gun in a remotely controlled undernose turret, plus up to 5,291 lb (2400 kg) of disposable stores carried on six underwing hardpoints
Weights: empty 18,519 lb (8400 kg); maximum take-off	**Payload:** up to eight troops, or two litters, two seated casualties and one medical attendant carried in the cabin

Mil Mi-26 'Halo'

The **Mi-26 'Halo'** was designed as a replacement for Mil's Mi-6 but was intended to offer between 50 and 100 per cent greater capability. The type was initially schemed under the designation **Mi-6M** with a hold broadly equivalent to that of the C-130 Hercules, the Mi-26 being the world's most powerful helicopter. The first of several prototype and pre-production helicopters made the type's maiden flight on 14 December 1977, and squadron strength military evaluation began in 1983, with full service entry following in 1985.

Although dimensionally slightly smaller than the

Mi-6, and with a main rotor having a diameter 9 ft 10 in (3.00 m) less, the Mi-26 uses advanced gearbox design and makes extensive use of composites and advanced aluminium-lithium alloys to save weight, resulting in an empty weight less than 2,205 lb (1000 kg) greater than that of the Mi-6. The powerplant comprises two D-136 turboshaft engines, which are more than twice as powerful as the engines installed on the Mi-6, and the combination of its high power and advanced eight-bladed main rotor allows the Mi-26 to lift almost twice the payload of the Mi-6.

In addition to its crew of

four and provision on the flightdeck for an optional fifth person, the Mi-26 can carry four passengers in a compartment to the rear of the flightdeck and also up to 80 fully equipped

The hold of the Mi-26 is 39 ft 4¼ in (12.00 m) long with the ramp raised, increasing to 49 ft 2½ in (15.00 m) with the ramp lowered.

troops or 60 litters plus four or five attendants in the hold, to which passenger access is provided by one starboard-side and two port-side airstair doors. The hold can also be used for the accommodation of a substantial freight load loaded and unloaded by means of the power-operated rear ramp/door arrangement comprising a bottom-hinged lower ramp and two side-hinged upper clamshell doors.

The hold's floor is provided with a roller conveyor system and freight lash-down points, and the movement of freight within the hold is simplified by the incorporation of two 5,511-lb (2500-kg) electrically powered hoists on overhead longitudinal rails, and a 1,102-lb (500-kg) electrically powered winch at the front of the hold.

In overall configuration the helicopter is basically standard, with a pod-and-boom fuselage, fixed tricycle landing gear with twin wheels on each unit, and a dynamic system based on the side-by-side pair of turboshaft engines driving eight-bladed main and five-bladed tail rotors each based on titanium heads carrying the rotor blades, which in the case

of the tail rotor are of glassfibre-reinforced plastics construction, and in the case of the main rotor are of metal and glass-fibre-reinforced plastics construction filled with honeycomb material and fitted with a leading-edge abrasion strip of titanium. The tail rotor is mounted at the top of a swept fin-like rotor pylon that carries a ground-adjustable horizontal stabiliser at the lower end of its leading edge. The Mi-26's equipment includes an integrated flight and navigation system, weather radar and, on the military variants, provision for IR jammers and suppressors, and IR decoy dispensers.

The basic version is the Mi-26, which is the standard military transport model. By the end of the 20th century some 300 aircraft of the 'Halo' family had been delivered, with production continuing at a low rate, and included in this total are a number of other variants. The **Mi-26A** is an improved transport with the PNK-90 integrated flight and navigation system allowing

automatic approach and descent to a critical decision point. The **Mi-26T** is the basic civil transport generally similar to the Mi-26, but also available in subvariants such as a fire-fighting model carrying 3,300 Imp gal (15,000 litres) of internally carried fire-retardant chemicals, or 3,796 Imp gal (17260 litres) of water in a bucket lifted as a slung load; and a geophysical survey model able to tow seismic equipment; the manufacturer is also planning a version of the Mi-26T with a modernised two-crew flightdeck. The **Mi-26TS** is certificated to Western standards. The **Mi-26MS** is the aeromedical variant of the Mi-26T outfitted as a high-quality flying hospital including an operating theatre. The **Mi-26NEF-M** is the ASW version with search radar in a faired radome under the nose and a MAD system whose towed sensor can be streamed from the ramp. The **Mi-26P** is a more comfortable passenger transport with accommodation for up to 63 passengers in a

four-abreast seating arrangement. The **Mi-26PK** is the flying crane model with an external operator's gondola on the side of the fuselage. The **Mi-26PP** is apparently a radio relay version. The **Mi-26TM** is the alternative flying crane model with a shallower operator's gondola under the fuselage or under the rear loading ramp. The **Mi-26TP** is a firefighting model discharging fire-retardant chemicals or water via a single vent. The **Mi-26TZ** is the tanker model with the ability to deliver 3,088 Imp gal (14050 litres) of fuel and

228 Imp gal (1040 litres) of lubricant discharged by means of four hoses. The **Mi-26M** is an upgraded version of the basic transport under development with a number of improvements including 14,350-shp (10700-kW) D-127s driving improved rotors with blades of all-glassfibre construction. Finally, the **Mi-27** is thought to be a development for the airborne command post task.

The Mi-26 has been sold to operators in some 20 countries, and the only known military users outside the CIS are India and Peru.

SPECIFICATION

Mil Mi-26 'Halo-A'
Type: four/five-crew heavy transport helicopter
Powerplant: two ZMDB 'Progress' (Lotarev) D-136 turboshaft engines each rated at 11,240 shp (8500 kW)
Performance: maximum level speed at optimum altitude 183 mph (295 km/h); normal cruising speed at optimum altitude 158 mph (255 km/h); service ceiling 15,090 ft (4600 m); hovering ceiling 5,905 ft (1800 m) out of ground effect; range 497 miles (800 km)

with standard fuel
Weights: empty 62,170 lb (28200 kg); maximum take-off 123,457 lb (56000 kg)
Dimensions: main rotor diameter 105 ft 9 in (32.00 m); length 131 ft 3¾ in 40.03 m with the rotors turning; height overall 26 ft 8¼ in (8.15 m) to top of rotor head; main rotor disc area 8,657.13 sq ft (804.25 m²)
Payload: up to 44,092 lb (20000 kg) of freight carried internally or externally

Mil Mi-28 'Havoc'

Despite its reported defeat by the Kamov Ka-50 'Hokum', Mil claims to have received an order for its **Mi-28 'Havoc'** from the Russian armed forces and continues to market the helicopter actively. The Mi-28 is of conventional helicopter-gunship configuration, with an undernose cannon and a vertically stepped arrangement of tandem armoured cockpits accommodating the pilot in the higher-set cockpit behind that of the gunner. The first of four Mi-28 prototypes made its maiden flight on 10 November 1982, and the first two machines each had upward-inclined exhaust diffusers for their

two 1,923-shp (1434-kW) Isotov TV3-117BM turboshafts and a fixed undernose blister fairing for electro-optical sensors, while the first prototype had a conventional three-bladed tail rotor. However, the second introduced the definitive four-bladed tail rotor of the 'Delta-H' scissors-type or narrow-X (35°/145°) arrangement. The third and fourth prototypes were completed to the **Mi-28A** standard with uprated engines exhausting via downward-inclined diffusers, the 'Delta-H' tail rotor arrangement and, in the case of the fourth production-standard prototype, a moving undernose electro-optical sensor turret

With milimetre-wave radar in a radome above the rotor pylon, the Mi-28N (Nochnoy night), adds all-weather capability to the basic 'Havoc'.

and wing-tip pods carrying electronic countermeasures and chaff dispensers.

The fuselage is a conventional semi-mono-coque unit of light alloy construction with titanium armour added round the cockpits and other vulnerable sections, and on the ground, is supported by shallow fixed tailwheel landing gear.

The Mi-28 is armed with a 30-mm 2A42 single-barrel cannon in a turret under the nose with twin 150-round ammunition boxes co-mounted to traverse, elevate and depress with the gun itself, reducing the likelihood of jamming. The cannon has two rates of fire; 300 rounds per minute for air-to-ground use and 900 rounds per minute for air-to-air use.

The helicopter's disposable armament is carried by the two anhedralled halves

Even in its original Mi-28A form, 'Havoc' seems unlikely to enter widespread service with Russian forces, while exports seem unlikely.

of the small stub wing that extend from the lower 'corners' of the engine nacelles. A typical weapons load comprises eight tube-launched 9M114 Shturm-C (AT-6 'Spiral') ATGM or a variety of multi-tube launch-

ers for 2.17- or 3.15-in (55 or 80-mm) air-to-surface unguided rockets as well as IR-guided short-range AAMs and dispensers for minelets. These weapons can be loaded using a hand crank and built-in winch.

SPECIFICATION

Mil Mi-28A 'Havoc'
Type: two-crew anti-tank, close support and air combat helicopter
Powerplant: two Klimov TV3-117VMA turboshaft engines each rated at 2,194 shp (1636 kW)
Performance: maximum level speed 'clean' at optimum altitude 186 mph (300 km/h); maximum cruising speed at optimum altitude 168 mph (270 km/h); maximum climb rate 2,677 ft (816 m) per minute; service ceiling 19,025 ft (5800 m); hovering ceiling 11,810 ft (3600 m) out of ground effect; 292 miles (470 km) with standard fuel
Weights: empty 15,432 lb

(7900 kg); maximum take-off 22,928 lb (10200 kg)
Dimensions: main rotor diameter 56 ft 5 in ft (17.20 m); wingspan 16 ft (4.87 m); length overall, rotors turning 62 ft 10 in (19.15 m); height overall 15 ft 5 in (4.70 m); main rotor disc area 2,501.10 sq ft (232.35 m²)
Armament: one 30-mm 2A42 trainable cannon in a power-operated undernose turret, plus up to 4,233 lb (1920 kg) of disposable stores carried on four underwing hardpoints
Payload: provision for up to three passengers carried in the fuselage

Mil Mi-28 'Havoc' (continued)

The cockpit's configuration and instrumentation is compatible with the use of night vision goggles, and the pilot has a HUD and one CRT on which TV imaging can be displayed. The primary sensor package comprises the optical sights and laser range-finder in the gyro-stabilised undernose turret. Elements of the defensive suite include IR sensors and jammers, laser and radar warning receivers, and electronic countermeasures and chaff/flare dispensers in the two wing-tip pods.

The cockpit is covered by flat, non-glint panels of armoured glass, and the cockpit area is protected by titanium and ceramic armour. Vital components are heavily protected and duplicated, and shielded by less important items. In the event of a catastrophic hit, the crew are protected by energy-absorbing seats, which can withstand a 40-ft (12-m) per second crash landing. An emergency escape system is also installed: when initiated, this blows off the doors and two halves of the stub wing, and then inflates on the sides of the fuselage air bladders over which the members of the crew roll before pulling the rip cords of their parachutes. A hatch in the port side, to the rear of the wing, gives access to the avionics compartment and to a compartment large enough to accommodate two or three people, albeit in some discomfort, in operations such as the retrieval of a downed 'Havoc' crew.

Mil Mi-34 'Hermit'

The need to find a replacement for the large numbers of Mi-2 'Hoplites' still serving with Soviet flying clubs, allied with a wish to produce a sporting/training helicopter using the same engine type as many of these club's aerobatic monoplanes, led to the **Mi-34 'Hermit'**.

Detail design work began in 1984, for a first flight on 17 November 1987 and an entry into production in 1993. In its original form the **Mi-34S** (marketed as the **Mi-34C**) is powered by an M-14 piston engine and offered seating for up to four people including the pilot. Thanks to its advanced rotor system, the 'Hermit' was the first Soviet-designed helicopter capable of flying conventional loops and rolls.

Although the Mi-34 was still being marketed in 2001, funding shortages have led to just a handful of production machines being completed.

By 1999, Mil had built around 15 Mi-34 'Hermit' light helicopters, each with a fully-equipped price of around US$350,000.

Variants

Mi-34S: original production version, marketed as **Mi-34C**
Mi-34L: 350-hp (261-kW) Textron Lycoming TIO-540J piston engine-powered version; none yet built
Mi-34P: police version
Mi-34A: luxury version, originally offered with Allison 250-C20R turboshaft but now marketed with 504-shp (376-kW) Turbomecca Arrius 2F; none yet built
Mi-34 VAZ: version, believed to be unbuilt, powered by two VAZ-426 rotary engines; **Mi-34M** military equivalent
Mi-34M1/M2: both projected as twin-turbine versions seating six passengers, none yet built

SPECIFICATION	
Mil Mi-34S 'Hermit' **Type:** three-/four-seat light multipurpose, training and aerobatic helicopter **Powerplant:** one VOKBM M-14-26V nine-cylinder radial piston engine rated at 320 shp (239 kW) **Performance:** maximum speed 130 mph (210 km/h); maximum cruising speed 106 mph (170 km/h); service ceiling 13,120 ft (4000 m); hovering ceiling	2,960 ft (900 m) out of ground effect; range 221 miles (356 km) with maximum fuel **Weights:** empty 2,094 lb (950 kg); maximum take-off 3,196 lb (1450 kg) **Dimensions:** main rotor diameter 32 ft 9¾ in (10 m); length 37 ft 5½ in (11.42 m) with the rotors turning; height overall 9 ft ¼ in (2.75 m); main rotor disc area 847.10 sq ft (78.70 m²)

Miles M.1 Satyr and M.2 Hawk

In 1932 F. G. Miles had flown a small single-seat biplane known as the Miles **M.1 Satyr**. Only one was built and it flew well, but was written off in 1936. Miles' previous experience with the Southern Martlet and Metal Martlet biplanes led to the desire to build a two-seat monoplane replacement for biplanes which had virtually cornered the market. The result was the **M.2 Hawk**, flown in March 1933 and the forerunner of a brilliant series of Miles mono-planes. Powered originally by the 95-hp (71-kW) Cirrus IIIA engine, later **M.2c** aircraft offered the 120-hp (89-kW) de Havilland Gipsy III. Other variants included the **M.2a** with an enclosed cabin, **M.2b** single-seat long-range version with a 120-hp (89-kW) Hermes IV piston engine, and the three-seat **M.2d**. Hawk production totalled 55.

Further development of the basic type led to the **Hawk Major** series (64 built), beginning with the **M.2F** with the 130-hp (97-kW) de Havilland Gipsy Major engine and encompassing a whole range of variants up to the **M.2T**. Single-seat racing models were known as the **Hawk Speed Six**; three were built with 200-hp (149-kW) Gipsy Six engines, and another somewhat smaller racing variant was the **M.5 Sparrowhawk**, of which five were built. The prototype survived the war and in 1953 was modified considerably by the installation of two 330-lb (150-kg) thrust Turboméca Palas jet engines to become the **M.77 Sparrowjet** with a speed of 230 mph (370 km/h). The final pre-war development was the **M.2X Hawk Trainer**, of which 25 were built, and the basic design was later developed into the Miles M.14 Magister.

The M.2X Hawk Trainer served as the basis for the later Magister trainer, which served the RAF in large numbers. This particular machine was registered in 1936, but withdrawn from use in 1940.

The M.77 was too advanced for the civil market of the immediate post-war period, and was too low on performance to interest military customers.

Miles M.3 Falcon

The first true cabin aircraft designed by F. G. Miles, the **M.3 Falcon** prototype was first flown on 12 October 1934. This prototype was a three-seat cabin monoplane, but the first production example seated four in a wider cabin. A number of variants of the basic aircraft were flown under the names **M.3A Falcon Major** and **M.3B Falcon Six**, total production amounting to 36, of which six were impressed for service with the RAF at the outbreak of World War II.

The M.3 was powered by a 200-hp (149-kW) de Havilland Gipsy Six inline engine and spanned 35 ft (10.67 m). It had a maximum speed of 180 mph (290 km/h) and a normal range of 560 miles (901-km).

Miles M.4 Merlin, M.6 Hawcon, M.7 Nighthawk, M.8 Peregrine and M.16 Mentor

Basically an enlarged version of the M.3A Falcon Major, the **M.4 Merlin** was a five-seat touring monoplane flown in 1935 with a 200-hp (149-kW) de Havilland Gipsy Six engine. Four were built, two seeing service in India and one in Australia. The one-off **M.6 Hawcon** combined parts of the Hawk and Falcon, used the same engine as the M.4, and was designed for thick-wing research by the RAE at Farnborough.

Developed from the M.3B Falcon Six, the **M.7 Nighthawk**, of which five civil examples were built, was intended for use as a trainer and three-seat communications aircraft, and was eventually ordered by the RAF as the **M.16 Mentor** to Air Ministry Specification 38/37 for a three-seat cabin communications monoplane. Among its other duties, the Mentor was to be capable of carrying out instrument and radio training by day or night. Full dual controls were specified, together with blind-flying instrumentation, landing lights and radio.

The prototype first flew on 5 January 1938, proving to be heavier and more sluggish than the M.7, but was submitted for service trials, and orders for 45 were placed. Deliveries were completed by mid-1939.

Like the Magister, the Mentor was provided with anti-spin strakes and, following the prototype's testing, a taller rudder similar to that of the Magister was fitted. Only one Mentor survived the war, being sold to a civil owner in 1947, but this aircraft was destroyed in a crash on 1 April 1950.

The **M.8 Peregrine** of 1936 was Miles' first twin-engine aircraft, with 205-hp (153-kW) de

One of the M.8s was entered in the Schlesinger Race to Johannesburg, but was not completed in time for the competition and was subsequently taken apart in late 1937.

Havilland Gipsy Queen engines and seats for six passengers plus two crew. Although its performance was good, manufacture could not be undertaken because the company was then busy with Magister production, and only one more Peregrine, with 290-hp (216 kW) Menasco Buccaneer engines, was built as a flying laboratory for the RAE.

A total of 42 Mentors was available for service when the war began and they were used by the RAF for duties including communications and training with No. 24 Squadron, Station Flights and other UK-based units.

SPECIFICATION	
Miles M.16 Mentor	service ceiling 13,800 ft (4206 m)
Type: three-seat training and communications aircraft	**Weights:** empty 1,978 lb (897 kg); maximum take-off 2,710 lb (1229 kg)
Powerplant: one 200-hp (149-kW) de Havilland Gipsy Six I inline piston engine	**Dimensions:** span 34 ft 10 in (10.61 m); length 26 ft 2 in (7.98 m); height 9 ft 8 in (2.95 m); wing area 181 sq ft (16.81 m²)
Performance: maximum speed 156 mph (251 km/h) at sea level;	

Miles M.9, M.19, M.24 and M.27 Master

The growing capability of high-performance monoplanes entering RAF service from the late 1930s highlighted the need for an advanced trainer with similar performance, and Miles designed a low-wing monoplane trainer to be powered by the 745-hp (556-kW) Rolls-Royce Kestrel XVI engine. When the design was submitted to the Air Ministry it was considered premature, but the company continued with construction of the prototype as a private venture, and this, named **Kestrel**, was flown for the first time on 3 June 1937. It was very soon demonstrating a maximum speed of about

15 mph (24 km/h) below that of the Hurricane, and had handling characteristics similar to those of the Hurricane and Spitfire. With no alternative in prospect, the Air Ministry ordered the Miles trainer on 11 June 1939 under the designation **M.9 Master**, but requested changes, including use of the de-rated 715-hp (533-kW) Kestrel XXX, which reduced the maximum speed to 70 mph (113 km/h) below that of the Kestrel prototype. Even then, it was still the best training aircraft of its day, and the first of 900 examples of the **M.9A Master Mk I** was flown on 31 March 1939. Eight

months later Miles flew the first **M.19 Master Mk II**, differing by having a 870-hp (649-kW) Bristol Mercury XX radial engine, which had been substituted at Air Ministry request because the supply of Kestrel engines was dwindling. The Ministry then discovered it had no stocks of Mercury engines and the 825-hp (615-kW) Pratt & Whitney Twin Wasp Junior radial was installed in a modified airframe to produce the **M.27 Master Mk III**. However, both Mercury and Twin Wasp Junior engines were used in production aircraft, the eventual number built totalling 1,747 Master Mk IIs and 602 Master Mk IIIs. To these figures can be added 26 **M.24 Master Fighter** aircraft, each armed with six 0.303-in (7.7-mm) machine-guns. These last were produced during the Battle of Britain for emergency use. In addition to use by the RAF, a number of Master Mk IIs was supplied to Egypt (26), Portugal (1),

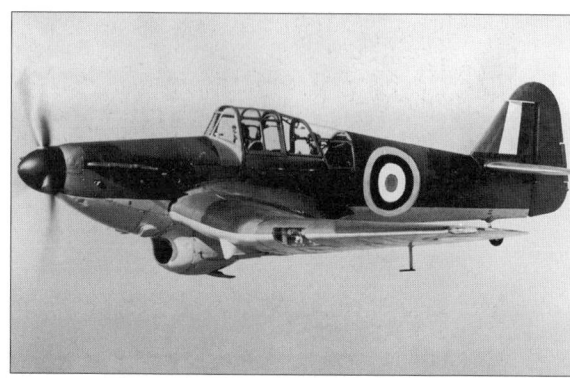

With its Kestrel inline engine and ungainly radiator installation, the Master Mk I was an unusual-looking aircraft. The majority of Mk Is was used at Sealand, Hullavington and Montrose.

South Africa (450) and Turkey (18). One was transferred to the US Army Air Force and one Master Mk III went to the Irish Air Corps. When production ended a total of 3,227 had been built, the Master proving to be the most significant trainer of indigenous design to serve with the RAF in World War II.

With their radial engines the Master Mk II and Mk III (illustrated) dispensed with the centre-section radiator.

SPECIFICATION	
Miles M.19 Master Mk II	(1947 kg); maximum take-off 5,573 lb (2528 kg)
Type: two-seat advanced trainer	**Dimensions:** wingspan 39 ft (11.89 m) (from 1941, 35 ft 7 in/10.85 m); length 29 ft 6 in (8.99 m); height 9 ft 3 in (2.82 m); wing area 235 sq ft (21.83 m²)
Powerplant: one 870-hp (649-kW) Bristol Mercury XX nine-cylinder radial piston engine	
Performance: maximum speed 242 mph (389 km/h) at 6,000 ft (1830 m); service ceiling 25,100 ft (7650 m); range 393 miles (632 km)	**Armament:** provision for one fixed forward-firing machine-gun and practice bombs
Weights: empty 4,293 lb	

Miles M.11A Whitney Straight and M.17 Monarch

In the mid-1930s, wealthy aviation enthusiast Whitney Straight approached F. G. Miles to design a new light-plane for flying club use, the result being the **M.11 Whitney Straight** two-seat cabin monoplane of low-wing configuration. The prototype was flown for the first time on 14 May 1936, and its all-round good qualities resulted in the production of 50 **M.11A**, **M.11B** and **M.11C** aircraft

over the next two years. A number of these were used for experimental purposes, including the testing of various engines and, on the prototype, of auxiliary aerofoil flaps, the data gained proving beneficial to later Miles aircraft. No new M.11 aircraft were supplied for military use, but a number was impressed for service as communications aircraft during World War II, their

Monarch G-AFLW was originally used by Rolls-Royce, and remained airworthy in private hands into the 1990s.

number including 23 for the RAF (21 in the UK and two in India), and three for the Royal New Zealand Air Force. An improved model was developed with three-seat accommodation and flown as the **M.17 Monarch** on 21 February 1938. Although this proved satisfactory, the company's involvement with Master and Magister production meant that it was possible to complete only 11 before the outbreak of World War II, five of these being impressed into RAF service.

SPECIFICATION	
Miles M.11 Whitney Straight	570 miles (917 km)
Type: two-seat cabin monoplane	**Weights:** empty 1,275 lb (578 kg);
Powerplant: one 130-hp (97-kW)	maximum take-off 1,896 lb (860 kg)
de Havilland Gipsy Major inline	**Dimensions:** wingspan 35 ft 8 in
piston engine	(10.87 m); length 25 ft (7.62 m);
Performance: maximum speed	height 6 ft 6 in (1.98 m); wing area
145 mph (233 km/h); range	187 sq ft (17.37 m²)

Miles M.12 Mohawk, M.13 Hobby, M.15 and M.18

Built to the specification of Charles Lindbergh, the only **M.12 Mohawk** was a tandem two-seat cabin monoplane with a 200-hp (149-kW) Menasco Buccaneer engine. The one-off **M.13 Hobby**, a tiny single-seater built for the 1937 King's Cup race, had a 140-hp (104kW) de

Havilland Gipsy Major II engine. Trouble with the retractable landing gear prevented it from competing and it was sold eventually to the RAE for full-scale wind tunnel tests.
Miles made two attempts to build further trainers for the RAF, the first being the **M.15**, of

Lindbergh received the only complete Mohawk, a second machine never being finished.

which two prototypes were built in 1939 to specification T.1/37 with 200-hp (149-kW) de Havilland Gipsy Six engines. However, they could not meet the specification, but neither could competing designs from four other companies.
In an attempt to provide a replacement for the Magister, Miles flew the **M.18** with a 130-hp (97-kW) de Havilland Gipsy Major engine in December 1938. While the fuselage was similar to that of the Magister, the square cut thick wing and tail surfaces were new. After much vacillating, a decision against production was

The second M.18 was modified for use as an experimental high-lift aircraft for use by the RAE, before returning to its original configuration.

reached by the Air Ministry, but a further three M.18s were built, the second

having a 150-hp (112-kW) Blackburn Cirrus Major III engine.

Miles M.14 Magister

Following the success of the civil Hawk Trainer, the Air Ministry drew up Specification T.40/36 for a development of the Hawk as an elementary trainer for the RAF. Design changes included the provision of larger cockpits and blind-flying equipment,

production of the **M.14** starting in early 1937 to the revised Specification T.37/37. Initial deliveries to the RAF were made in May 1937, these being the first monoplane trainers used by that service. But the **Magister**, as it was then named, was soon found to

have a spinning problem; this was quickly rectified and modified and subsequent production machines had the designation **M.14A**. Built from 1937 to 1941, total construction by Miles amounted to 1,293, and an additional 100 were built under licence in Turkey following the evaluation of four received from Miles. RAF contracts covered 1,229 aircraft, and other countries acquiring Magisters for military use included Eire (15), Egypt (42) and New Zealand (2). In addition, a number was

This Miles Magister Mk I is equipped with a blind-flying hood for the rear cockpit.

supplied to civil customers, and after the end of World War II many ex-RAF Magisters came on to the civil market under the designation **Hawk Trainer III**. At the peak of Royal Air Force use Miles Magisters equipped some 16

Elementary Flying Training Schools and the Central Flying School, and were in use with the various RAF commands, the last being retired in 1948; in addition, they saw service with the British army and the Fleet Air Arm.

SPECIFICATION	
Miles M.14A Magister	(5485 m); range 380 miles (612 km)
Type: two-seat elementary trainer	**Weights:** empty 1,286 lb (583 kg);
Powerplant: one 130-hp (97-kW)	maximum take-off 1,900 lb (862 kg)
de Havilland Gipsy Major I inline	**Dimensions:** wingspan 33 ft 10 in
piston engine	(10.31 m); length 24 ft 7½ in
Performance: maximum speed	(7.51 m); height 6 ft 8 in (2.03 m);
132 mph (212 km/h) at 1,000 ft	wing area 176 sq ft (16.35 m²)
(305 m); service ceiling 18,000 ft	

Miles M.25 Martinet

Before the issue of Air Ministry Specification 12/41, it had been standard

RAF practice to use outdated aircraft, however unsuitable, for the task of

target towing. The outbreak of World War II had high-lighted this short-sighted policy, leading to the procurement of an aircraft designed specifically for such a role. The **M.25**

prototype was flown for the first time on 24 April 1942, the aircraft being based on the Master Mk II but with a lengthened nose to compensate for the weight of target-towing equipment. Incorporated within a modified cockpit was the drogue cable winch, which could be powered by an electric motor or wind-driven propeller, and there was comfortable space for the operator and stowage of the drogue targets. The type entered service as the **Martinet TT.Mk I** and between 1942 and 1945 a total of 1,724 was built; the

The Martinet TT.Mk I could deploy up to six flag or sleeve towed-targets per mission.

type was complemented in 1946 by the **M.50 Queen Martinet** which had been developed to Specification Q.10/43. This was a radio-controlled pilotless target version of the Martinet, 11 being built as new and the remaining 54 being conversions of M.25s. Planned variants included a

glider-tug version of the Martinet, similar to the **Master GT.Mk II**, and the **M.37** two-seat trainer of which two prototypes were built. Six surplus Martinets received civil registrations postwar, four of them sold to Sweden and operated by the civil target-towing company Svensk Flygjärst.

SPECIFICATION	
Miles M.25 Martinet	(1117 km)
Type: two-seat target tug	**Weights:** empty 4,640 lb
Powerplant: one 870-hp (649-kW)	(2105 kg); maximum take-off
Bristol Mercury XX/XXX 9-cylinder	6,750 lb (3062 kg)
radial piston engine	**Dimensions:** wingspan 39 ft
Performance: maximum speed	(11.89 m); length 30 ft 11 in
240 mph (386 km/h) at 5,800 ft	(9.42 m); height 11 ft 7 in (3.53 m);
(1770 m); range 694 miles	wing area 242.0 sq ft (22.48 m²)

Miles M.33 Monitor

Designed to Air Ministry Specification Q.9/42 for a high-speed target tug, the **M.33 Monitor** was a clean-looking cantilever high-wing monoplane with retractable landing gear and power provided by two wing-mounted engines. The Miles proposal was at first rejected as it was considered there were no suitable engines available, but with agreement to use the 1,700-hp (1268-kW) Wright Cyclone R-2600-31, Miles received a contract for 600 aircraft. The prototype was flown for the first time on

With a wingspan of 56 ft 3 in (17.15 m), the M.33 Monitor had a maximum speed of 360 mph (579 km/h) and a service ceiling of 29,000 ft (8840 m). It flew simulated dive-bombing attacks at 400 mph (664 km/h).

5 April 1944 and handled well, but the end of the war was approaching before development was completed and the contract was reduced first to 200 and then to 50, and was finally cancelled after 20

had been delivered. Even these were not used by the RAF as intended, only 10

Monitors entering service with the Royal Navy for operation briefly as the

Monitor TT.Mk II before replacement by Mosquito TT.Mk 39s.

Miles M.35 and M.39 Libellula

Miles was severely berated by the Air Ministry for producing both of its Libellula designs without official authorisation. The RAE gained a great deal of useful information from its testing of the M.39B (illustrated) however.

Among the collection of projects which emerged from Miles during World War II, two of the strangest were the **M.35** and **M.39** tandem-wing aircraft, both of which were name **Libellula**, and while most of the projects did not materialise, these two were built and flown.

The M.35 was conceived as a layout practicable for a carrier-based fighter, the pilot being in the extreme nose with the pusher engine mounted behind the rear wing. With lift provided by two wings, span could be short and there would be no need for wing-folding. The M.35 was

completed and flown in six weeks but proved to be unstable, as well as demonstrating some reluctance to become airborne. Wind tunnel tests showed the problems to be curable and George Miles conceived a heavy bomber, the **M.39**, to be powered by three turbojet engines, or in its initial form, by two high-altitude Rolls-Royce Merlin 60 or Bristol Hercules VIII piston engines.

A five-eighths scale model of the bomber was built and designated **M.39B**, flying for the first time on 22 July 1943 and proving to the aerodynami-

cally stable. Flight trials were initially on a private basis, but in 1944 the M.39B went to the RAE at Farnborough, where it suffered two accidents. After extensive repairs the work ended and the aircraft was broken up.

SPECIFICATION	
Miles M.39B Libellula	**Weights:** empty 2,405 lb
Type: two-seat tandem-wing	(1091 kg); maximum take-off
research aircraft	2,800 lb (1270 kg)
Powerplant: two 140-hp (104-kW)	**Dimensions:** wingspan 37 ft 6 in
de Havilland Gipsy Major IC inline	(11.43 m); length 22 ft 2 in
piston engines	(6.76 m); height 9 ft 3 in (2.82 m);
Performance: maximum speed	wing area 249.2 sq ft (23.15 m²)
164 mph (264 km/h)	

Miles M.38 Messenger

At the private request of certain army officers in June 1942, George Miles designed and built the prototype of an air observation post (AOP) aircraft. It was required to carry a crew of two, radio, armour protection and other military equipment, and to be able to operate out of and into small tree-surrounded fields in all weathers. The resulting **M.38** prototype

was a cantilever low-wing monoplane with fixed tail-wheel landing gear.

In its role as a VIP transport, the 36-ft 2-in (11.02-m) span Messenger had a maximum speed of 116 mph (187 km/h) and a range of 260 miles (418 km). G-AJEY was lost in France in a crash in June 1947.

Miles M.38 Messenger (continued)

The M.38 was powered by a 140-hp (104-kW) de Havilland Gipsy Major inline engine. The wing incorporated fixed aerofoil trailing-edge flaps and . when flown on 12 September 1942, it was found that these provided the requisite STOL performance. Great enthusiasm for its capability was shown by an AOP squadron which Miles allowed to flight test the aircraft, but shocked and irritated by the design, construction and testing of a military aircraft without its knowledge, the Ministry of Aircraft Production refused to order this prototype into production for the AOP role. In late 1943 a small order was placed for the aircraft for use in light liaison and communications roles under the designation

M.38 Messenger and eventually a total of 21 was built. Among VIP operators allocated personal Messengers were Field Marshal Sir Bernard Montgomery and Marshal of the RAF Lord Tedder. An additional 71 were built post-war for civil use, bringing total production to 92. One aircraft was modified

in 1944 by introducing conventional trailing-edge flaps and installing a 150-hp (112-kW) Blackburn Cirrus Major piston engine. When tested, this machine designated M.48 Messenger 3, was found to offer so little improvement in performance over the standard M.38 that no production followed.

Miles M.57 Aerovan

Miles was a prolific designer, and a mass of projects passed through the drawing office, though many of these came to nothing. One unusual looking design which did made the grade was the **M.57 Aerovan**, a twin-engined light freighter which flew first in January 1945. In appearance the wings and tail unit were similar to those of the Messenger but somewhat larger, while the fuselage was of pod and boom layout.

A number of UK and overseas orders were placed and the Aerovan entered production with a longer pod than the proto-

At very low cost, the Miles M.57 Aerovan could carry loads up to the size and weight of a family car. This Aerovan I was broken up in November 1949, the fuselage finding use as the cabin for a caravan.

type, which was designated **Aerovan Mk I**, and the second prototype **Aerovan Mk II**. The first **Aerovan Mk III** production model was similar to the Mk II, and seven were built with 150-hp (112-kW) Blackburn Cirrus Major III engines, the standard Aerovan powerplant. The

Aerovan Mk IV differed in detail and 40 were built. One **Aerovan Mk V** with 145-hp (108-kW) de Havilland Gipsy Major 10 engines and two **Aerovan Mk VI** aircraft with 195-hp

(145-kW) Avco Lycoming O-435-4A engines were built; one of the latter was fitted with an experimental Hurel-Dubois high aspect ratio wing in 1957 when it became known as the

HDM.105. The last known surviving Aerovan was the first Mk VI, operating in Italy in 1968, although a pair of uncompleted airframes was around for some years.

Miles M.65 Gemini and M.75 Aries

Conceived as a twin-engined retractable landing gear version of the Messenger, the **M.65 Gemini** flew first on 26 October 1945 and was an immediate success. It was the last Miles aircraft to enter quantity production and in its **Gemini Mk IA** initial form was powered by 100-hp (75-kW) Blackburn Cirrus engines, and had non-retractable auxiliary trailing-edge flaps; one **Gemini Mk IB** was built

with retractable flaps. The single **Gemini Mk 2** was created by installing 125-hp (93-kW) Continental engines, while production **Gemini Mk 3A** aircraft had 145-hp (108-kW) de Havilland Gipsy Major 10s. There were several sub-variants with detail differences, but the most powerful version with two 155-hp (116-kW) Blackburn Cirrus Major III engines, a strengthened structure and larger fins and rudders, was

deemed sufficiently different to be designated **M.75 Aries**.

A total of 170 Geminis and two Aries was built, around two-thirds of them being exported, before the company collapsed in 1947.

The Gemini was the last aircraft built in quantity at the Woodley factory by Miles. G-AGUS was sold to a Swedish owner and re-registered SE-BUY in 1957.

Miles M.68 Boxcar, M.71 Merchantman & M.100 Student

In the midst of a mass of projects, Miles flew three prototypes which deserve brief mention. The **M.68**

Built as a private venture by George Miles in 1953, the M.100 was intended as a primary jet trainer for the RAF, but lost out to the Hunting Jet Provost.

Boxcar, flown on 22 August 1947, had four 100-hp (75-kW) Blackburn Cirrus Minor II engines and

was basically of Aerovan layout, except that the centre section of the fuselage was designed to mount a detachable container, the idea being that freight containers could be pre-loaded and the aircraft could be flown with or without the container attached.

In the same month Miles flew the **M. 71 Merchantman** with four 250-hp (186-kW) de Havilland Gipsy Queen 30 engines and a modified Marathon wing. Its configuration was otherwise similar to that of the Aerovan, but the aircraft was of metal construction. Neither of these promising designs was able to proceed because of the firm's collapse.

The **M.100 Student** is

The Miles M.68 was unofficially known as the Boxcar, and was first demonstrated at the SBAC show at Radlett in September 1947.

outside the basic Miles Aircraft history, since it was a private venture by F. G. and George Miles started in 1953. A two-seat side-by-side all-metal jet trainer, the Student was powered by an 882-lb

(3.92-kN) thrust Turboméca Marboré turbojet and flew on 15 May 1957. Miles had hoped to secure an RAF order, which in the event went to the Jet Provost, and the Student did not go into production.

Mitsubishi 2MB1 (Army Type 87 Light Bomber) & 2MB2

After building 57 Nieuport 81 trainers for the Imperial Japanese Army as the **Mitsubishi Ko-1**, followed by 145 Hanriot HD-14s under the designation **Ki-1**, Mitsubishi submitted the experimental **2MB2 Washi** two-seat light bomber biplane designed by Alexander Baumann in 1925. This was rejected for production, the IJA preferring Herbert Smith's more conventional **2MB1**, a large

two-seat biplane with wide-track divided landing gear. This entered service in 1927 as the **Army Type 87 Light Bomber**, 48 being built, and each was powered by a 450-hp (336-kW) Hispano-Suiza engine which gave a maximum speed of 115 mph (185 km/h); the 2MB1 had a maximum take-off weight of 7,275 lb (3300 kg) and wingspan of 48 ft 6¾ in (14.80 m).

The 2MB1 was armed with one fixed forward-firing 0.303-in (7.7-mm) machine-gun, with twin guns of the same calibre on a ring mounting for the observer, and provision for a fourth gun firing through a ventral trap. The type participated in ground support roles during the hostilities with China in Manchuria in 1930-31.

Mitsubishi 1MF1-5 (Navy Type 10 Carrier Fighter)

The **1MF** was among the first designs produced for the Mitsubishi Internal Combustion Engine Co. Ltd, set up by the Mitsubishi industrial concern in 1920. One of three types designed by Herbert Smith, formerly of the British Sopwith company, to meet requirements issued by the Imperial Japanese Navy for aircraft to equip its first aircraft-carrier (*Hosho*), the **1MF1** initial version was an unequal-span, single-seat,

carrier-based fighter biplane, powered by a 300-hp (223-kW) Hispano-Suiza 8 engine, which entered production in 1921 as the **Navy Type 10-1 Carrier Fighter**. It was followed by the **1MF2**, an experimental variant with modified upper-wing ailerons. The series **Type 10-2** or **1MF3** had twin Lamblin radiators fitted between the landing gear legs, the **Type 10-3** (**1MF4**) had the pilot's cockpit relocated farther forward and a

redesigned tailplane, while the **1MF5A** was a version of the 1MF4 with experimental flotation gear.

The maximum speed of the Type 10-2 was 127 mph (205 km/h), its wingspan was 27 ft 10¾ in (8.50 m) and maximum take-off weight was 2,822 lb (1280 kg). Armament comprised two fixed synchronised 0.303-in (7.7-mm) Vickers machine-guns.

Production of the 1MF series ended in 1928 with the 138th example. The Type 10 proved a tough,

reliable fighter and remained in service for a number of years, latterly as an advanced trainer.

Mitsubishi 2MR (Type 10 Carrier Reconnaissance Biplane)

Another Herbert Smith design, the first example of the **2MR** two-seat carrier-based reconnaissance biplane flew in January 1922. The type entered service as the **Type 10 Carrier Reconnaissance Biplane** and was built in a number of versions. The **2MR1** had a frontal radiator for its 300-hp (224-kW) Hispano-Suiza 8 engine, while the **2MR2** had twin underslung Lamblin radiators and redesigned tail surfaces. The **2MR4**, which was the main production version, had some further revisions of the wing and

tail unit, and other variants with minor changes were the **2MRT1**, **2MRT2**, **2MRT2A**, **2MRT3** and **2MRT3A**. Total production of all versions was 159, the last machine leaving the workshops in 1930. After long carrier service, the 2MR was used as a trainer in the late 1930s.

The 2MR4 version spanned 39 ft 6 in (12.04 m), had a maximum take-off weight of 2,910 lb (1320 kg), and was armed with two fixed forward-firing 0.303-in (7.7-mm) machine-guns, with twin guns of the same calibre

mounted over the observer's cockpit, and could carry three 66-lb (30-kg) bombs.

The **R-2.2** and **R-4** civil conversions had an enclosed cabin for two passengers replacing the rear cockpit, and a number of ex-army surplus 2MRs were sold on the civil market in the 1930s.

The Mitsubishi 2MR was essentially a scaled-up version of the 1MF Carrier Fighter, adapted to carry two crew and produced in a number of configurations.

Mitsubishi 2MR8 (Type 92 Reconnaissance Aircraft)

In 1927 Mitsubishi enlisted the help of the German designer Baumann to meet an IJA requirement for a new reconnaissance aircraft. The resulting **2MR1 Tobi** two-seat sesquiplane was a grotesque aircraft,

which performed only slightly worse than Baumann's next design, the **1MF2 Hayabusa** parasol-wing single-seat fighter of a year later. A third unsuccessful type was the **2MR7** short-range reconnaissance

biplane of 1928.
In 1930, however, three **2MR8** parasol-wing reconnaissance monoplanes were built and tested successfully. Of mixed construction, they had fixed wide-track divided landing

gear and were powered by a 475-hp (354-kW) Mitsubishi Type 92 radial engine. Accepted by the army, the 2MR8 went into service in 1932 as the **Type 92 Reconnaissance Aircraft**. Production terminated in 1933 with the 230th machine. Maximum speed was 137 mph (220 km/h), wingspan 41 ft 10 in (12.75 m), and maximum take-off weight

The Type 92 saw active service in Manchuria with the air battalions (later air wings) of the army's Kanto Command Air Corps between 1933 and 1936.

3,902 lb (1770 kg). The Type 92 was normally armed with a fixed forward-firing 0.303-in (7.7-mm) machine-gun mounted above the wing centre-section, with single or twin guns of the same calibre on a ring mounting over the observer's cockpit.

A civil version of the Type 92 was used as a survey aircraft by Japanese National Railways. Powered by a 400-hp (298-kW) Mitsubishi A-5 engine, it differed externally from the military aircraft in having a glazed canopy over the crew cockpits and spat-type streamlined main wheel fairings.

Mitsubishi A5M (Navy Type 96 Carrier Fighter)

An Imperial Japanese Navy specification of 1934 for a single-seat fighter with a maximum speed of 217 mph (350 km/h) then seemed an almost unattainable target. However, **Mitsubishi's Ka-14** prototype designed to this requirement, and flown for the first time on 4 February 1935, demonstrated a top speed of 280 mph (450 km/h) in early trials.

Unfortunately it had some aerodynamic shortcomings, and the inverted gull-wing of this aircraft was replaced by a conventional low-set monoplane wing in the second prototype which, with a 585-hp (436kW) Nakajima Kotobuki 2-KAI-1 radial engine, was ordered into production as the **Navy Type 96 Carrier Fighter Model 1 (A5M1)**. The generally similar

A5N2a which followed, powered by the 610-hp (455-kW) Kotobuki 2KAI-3 engine, and the **A5M2b** with the 640-hp (477-kW) Kotobuki 3 engine, were regarded as the IJN's most important fighter aircraft during the Sino-Japanese War. Two experimental **A5M3** aircraft were flown with the Hispano-Suiza 12Xcrs engine, but the final and major production version was the **A5M4**, built also as the **A5M4-K** tandem two-seat trainer. All versions of the A5M were allocated the Allied code-name **'Claude'**, and when production ended a total of 788 had been built by

Mitsubishi, including prototypes; a further 303 were built by Watanabe (39) and the Omura Naval Air Arsenal (264). The Japanese army had also shown interest in the A5M, resulting in the evaluation of a **Ki-18** prototype generally similar to the Ka-14, but although fast this was considered to be lacking in manoeuvrability. Mitsubishi produced two re-engined and improved **Ki-33** proto-

types but they too, were considered insufficiently manoeuvrable and no army production contract resulted.

At the beginning of the Pacific war the A5M4 was in first-line use, but its performance was found inadequate to confront Allied fighters and by the summer of 1942 all had been transferred to second-line duties, many surviving A5M4 and A5M4-Ks being used in *kamikaze* attacks in the closing months of the war.

The A5M marked Japan's entry into an age of military self-sufficiency, and made a big impact in the Sino-Japanese War.

SPECIFICATION	
Mitsubishi A5M4	**Weights:** empty 2,681 lb
Type: single-seat carrier-based fighter	(1216 kg); maximum take-off 3,759 lb (1705 kg)
Powerplant: one 710-hp (529-kW) Nakajima Kotobuki 41 (Bristol Jupiter) radial piston engine	**Dimensions:** wingspan 36 ft 1 in (11.00 m); length 24 ft 9¾ in (7.55 m); height 10 ft 6 in (3.20 m); wing area 191.60 sq ft (17.80 m²)
Performance: maximum speed 273 mph (440 km/h) at 9,840 ft (3000 m); service ceiling 32,150 ft (9800 m); maximum range 746 miles (1200 km)	**Armament:** two forward-firing 7.7-mm (0.303-in) machine-guns, plus two 66-lb (30-kg) bombs

Mitsubishi A6M Zero-Sen (Navy Type 0 Carrier Fighter)

Without doubt the most famous Japanese single-seat fighter aircraft of all time, the **Zero-Sen (Navy Type 0 Carrier Fighter)** was designed to meet an IJN requirement for an A5M replacement. A cantilever low-wing monoplane, powered in **A6M1** prototype form by a 780-hp (582-kW) Mitsubishi MK2 Zuisei radial engine, the type was flown for the first time on 1 April 1939. Testing showed excellent performance, except that maximum speed was below specification, leading to an **A6M2** prototype with a 925-hp (690kW) Nakajima NK1C Sakae engine which flew on 18 January 1940. This was so successful that in July 1940 Mitsubishi was contracted to build 15 pre-production A6M2s for evaluation in China, and at the end of that month the type was ordered into

At the end of the war, two captured Zeroes were tested by the Allied Technical Air Intelligence Unit (ATAIU) based in Singapore.

production as the **Navy Type 0 Carrier Fighter Model 11 (A6M2 Model 11)**. This version was also built as the **A6M2 Model 21** with manually folded wingtips, and as the **A6M2-K** two-seat trainer. A floatplane version of the Zero-Sen was built by

Nakajima (to a total of 327) under the designation **A6M2N**. Revised versions of the A6M2 included the **A6M3 Model 22** with the Nakajima NK1F Sakae 21 engine and the similarly-powered A6M3 with clipped wings instead of folding wingtips. The major production version was the **A6M5 Model 52**, introduced in 1943 to counter the growing capability of

Mitsubishi A6M2 'Zeke'

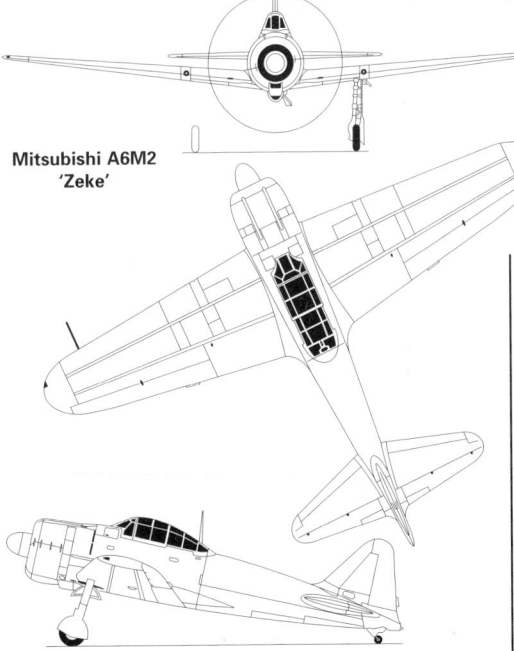

Captured in New Guinea, this A6M3 was eventually shipped back to the US, where it underwent rigorous testing between 1943 and early 1944.

Allied fighters, built also in the sub-variants **A6M5a**, **A6M5b** and **A6M5c** which differed primarily in armament; the **A6M5d-S** night-fighter with a 20-mm cannon mounted obliquely

in the rear fuselage; and the **A6M5-K** two-seat trainer. By then the A6M had really attained its optimum state of development, but Japan's desperate position led to a

SPECIFICATION	
Mitsubishi A6M6c Model 53c	6,504 lb (2950 kg)
Type: single-seat interceptor fighter/fighter-bomber	**Dimensions:** wingspan 36 ft 1 in (11.00 m); length 29 ft 9 in (9.07 m); height 11 ft 5¾ in (3.50 m); wing area 229.28 sq ft (21.30 m²)
Powerplant: one 1,130-hp (843-kW) Nakajima Sakae 31 radial piston engine	
Performance: maximum speed 346 mph (557 km/h) at 19,685 ft, (6000 m); service ceiling 35,105 ft (10700 m); maximum range 1,118 miles (1800 km)	**Armament:** two 20-mm cannon (in wings) and three 0.52-in (13.2-mm) machine-guns (two in wings and one in fuselage), plus underwing launch rails for eight 22-lb (10-kg) or two 132-lb (60-kg) air-to-air rockets
Weights: empty 4,178 lb (1895 kg); maximum take-off	

The A6M2-N 'Rufe' was a floatplane fighter development of the Zero, and took part in the Aleutian campaign in 1942-43.

re-engined version of the A6M5c which entered production as the **A6M6c Model 53c** in late 1944, and the fighter/dive-bomber **A6M7 Model 63** with an underfuselage rack for one 551-lb (250-kg) bomb built from mid-1945. Final variant was the **A6M8c Model 64c**, of which two

prototypes were built with 1,500-hp (1119-kW) Mitsubishi MK8K engines, but no series aircraft were produced before the end of the war.

Unbelievably successful when introduced into the Sino-Japanese War, this amazing fighter, allocated the Allied codename **'Zeke'**, seemed to fill the skies over the Pacific during 1941 and early 1942. However, after the Battle of Midway in June 1942, Allied fighters began to gain the initiative and the

A6M never again held wide-scale air superiority. But despite shortcomings the type remained in service until the end of the war, built to a total of approximately 10,450 by Mitsubishi (3,880) and Nakajima (6,570). In addition, 515 A6M2-K and A6M5-K trainers were built by Hitachi (279) and the 21st Naval Arsenal at Omura (236). Large numbers of early versions were used in *kamikaze* attacks during the closing months of the war.

Mitsubishi A7M (Navy Carrier Fighter Reppu)

The design by Mitsubishi of a carrier-based fighter to supersede the A6M Zero-Sen had been planned by the IJN as early as 1940, but was frustrated by the company's involvement in urgent development and production programmes. It was not until 1942 that design of the **M-50 Reppu** (hurricane) began, but the continuing pressure on Mitsubishi for developments of the A6M meant that it was not until 6 May 1944 that the first prototype, which by then had the company designation **A7M1**, was flown for the first time. A cantilever

low-wing monoplane with retractable tailwheel landing gear, the A7M1 soon revealed excellent flight characteristics, but as predicted by Mitsubishi the type's maximum speed on the power of the installed Nakajima NK9K Homare 22 engine was below specification. Further testing was abandoned until availability of the 2,200-hp (1641kW) Mitsubishi MK9A radial engine made it possible to build seven **A7M2** prototype and service trials aircraft, the first prototype being flown on 13 October 1944. Clearly a potent fighter that could meet

Allied opposition on equal terms, the Reppu had a maximum speed of 391 mph (630 km/h) at optimum altitude and was ordered into production as the **Navy Carrier Fighter Reppu Model 22**. Unfortunately, by then it was too late for the IJN, Allied air attacks and an earthquake limiting production to only one aircraft, allocated the Allied codename **'Sam'**. Development of similar land-based fighters was planned under the designations **A7M3** and **A7M3-J**, but neither was built before the war came to an end.

The blighted A7M2 Reppu showed much promise as a fighter, especially when powered by the Mitsubishi MK9A engine, seen to good effect here.

Mitsubishi B1M (2MT, Type 13 Carrier Attacker & 3MT)

The most successful of Herbert Smith's designs for Mitsubishi was undoubtedly the **2MT**, a two-seat biplane torpedo-bomber. The **2MT1** prototype flew in January 1923 and as the **B1M1** entered production for the IJN as the **Type 13 Carrier Attacker**. The basic design was subject to continuing modifications and the final **B1M3** production version was a three-seater.

When the Shanghai Incident broke out in January 1932, the carriers *Kaga* and *Hosho* were in Chinese waters and the IJN 1st Air Wing deployed 32 Type 13 Attackers from the *Kaga* and nine from the *Hosho* against targets in and around Shanghai. They also carried out attacks in co-operation with Japanese ground forces.

As a result of the failure of the Yokosho B3Y1 attack

SPECIFICATION	
Mitsubishi 2MT2	5,946 lb (2697 kg)
Type: two-seat carrier-based torpedo-bomber	**Dimensions:** wingspan 48 ft 5½ in (14.77 m); length 32 ft ¾ in (9.77 m); height 11 ft 5¾ in (3.50 m); wing area 645.09 sq ft (59.00 m²)
Powerplant: one 500-hp (373-kW) Napier Lion engine	
Performance: maximum speed 130 mph (210 km/h); service ceiling 14,765 ft (4500 m)	**Armament:** two fixed and two pivoted 0.303-in (7.7-mm) machine-guns; one 18-in (457-mm) torpedo, or two 529-lb (240-kg) bombs
Weights: empty 3,179 lb (1442 kg); maximum take-off	

aircraft, a number of B1M3s remained in first-line service past obsolescence into the mid-1930s.

Variants

2MT1: prototype and initial production version
2MT2 and 2MT3: slightly modified versions of 2MT1 which, together with 2MT1s, carried the naval designation **B1M1** or **Type 13-1 Carrier-Attacker**; 196 built
2MT4 Otori: twin-float reconnaissance version of 2MT2; three tested but did not enter production
2MT5: version powered by 500-hp (373-kW) Hispano-Suiza Vee-12 engine; 116 built
3MT2: three-seat version with 600-hp (447-kW) Hispano-Suiza; Mitsubishi built 88 in 1929-30 and Hiro Arsenal later completed an additional 40; naval designation **B1M3** or **Type 13-2-2 Carrier Attacker**; one instead of two fixed forward-firing machine-guns
T-1.2: designation for civil conversions with an enclosed passenger cabin for two or three behind the pilot's cockpit; each arrangement was different; other Type 13s used as naval or civil trainers at the end of their active service

On 5 February 1932, two Type 13s escorted by three Nakajima Type 3 Carrier Fighters were engaged in aerial combat with Chinese Vought Corsair biplanes, while on 22 February three Type 13s with fighter escort from the Kaga were attacked by American volunteer pilot Robert Short in a Boeing Model 218 biplane.

Mitsubishi B2M (3MR4, Navy Type 89-1 Carrier Attacker)

In 1928 Mitsubishi presented to the IJN three new types: the **1MF9 Taka** carrier fighter biplane, which featured a French-type *avion marin* keel; the **Type R** experimental twin-engined monoplane

flying-boat, built also in a civil transport version, both of them based on Rohrbach designs; and the **3MR4** carrier reconnaissance biplane. This last aircraft was in reality designed by G. E. Petty, chief designer

of the British Blackburn Aeroplane Company, and had been built in the UK. Three development prototypes were constructed subsequently by Mitsubishi, and it was decided that the aircraft would be used

primarily as a carrier-based torpedo-bomber. Prolonged difficulties prevented naval adoption of the 3MR4 until March 1932, when it went into service as the **Navy Type 89-1 Carrier Attacker** or **B2M1**.

Powered by a 650-hp (485-kW) Hispano-Suiza 12Lb piston engine, the B2M1 had a maximum speed of 132 mph (213 km/h), and was an equal-span biplane with wide track landing gear.

Mitsubishi B2M (continued)

The B2M1 carried its crew of three in tandem cockpits, while its defensive armament comprised one fixed and one movably-mounted 0.303-in (7.7-mm) machine-gun; and for offensive purposes a 1,764-lb (800-kg) torpedo carried between the main landing gear legs could be supplemented by six light bombs on underwing racks.

An improved **B2M2** or **Type 89-2** appeared in 1934, this having a wingspan of 49 ft 1¾ in (14.98 m) and a maximum take-off weight of 7,936 lb (3600 kg), but its overall performance showed little advantage over the B2M1. Production of both versions totalled 204, and they were used extensively for medium- and low-level bombing attacks against Chinese troops during the Shanghai Incident.

The design for the B2M was sub-contracted to other companies, and the British company Blackburn won the contest in 1928.

Mitsubishi B5M (Type 97 Carrier Attack Bomber Model 2)

Bearing the company designation **Ka-16**, this cantilever low-wing monoplane, carrier-based torpedo-bomber flew in prototype form as the **Navy 10-Shi Experimental Attacker** in 1936. A three-seater, it had a long glazed crew canopy and was distinguished easily from its Nakajima B5N rival by having fixed cantilever landing gear with spat-type wheel fairings. The wings outboard of the landing gear could be folded upwards for carrier stowage.

As a precaution against problems with the B5N, this **Mitsubishi B5M1** design was placed in production and went into service as the **Navy Type 97 Carrier Attack Bomber Model 2**, gaining initially the Allied codename **'Mabel'**, later changed to **'Kate 61'**. At least 125 had been delivered when the obvious success of its rival brought production to a halt. The B5M1 saw some

Powered by a 1,000-hp (746-kW) Mitsubishi Kinsei 43 radial, the B5M1 had a maximum speed of 236 mph (380 km/h). Armament comprised one 0.303-in (7.7-mm) trainable machine-gun, plus a 1,764-lb (800-kg) torpedo or an equivalent weight of bombs.

action from land bases in the South Pacific before being relegated to training and liaison duties.

Mitsubishi F-1 and T-2

For some time, T-2s were used by the JASDF's Hiko Kyodotai (aggressor squadron) based at Nyutabaru, and were adorned with a striking cobra's head design on the tail. 69-5127 was painted to resemble a MiG-21, with sections of the fin, intakes, engine nacelles and wing being blacked out to leave a MiG-21 silhouette in grey.

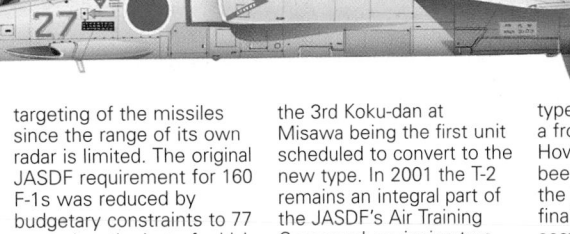

The **T-2** was Japan's first indigenously-designed supersonic aircraft. Developed to replace the T-33 and F-86 as an advanced trainer for the JASDF, the T-2 is remarkably similar to the SEPECAT Jaguar. The first **XT-2** prototype flew in 1971 and production deliveries began in 1976, the JASDF receiving 28 **T-2(Z)** advanced trainers and 62 **T-2(K)** combat trainers fitted with J/AWG-11 radar and 20-mm cannon. Two T-2s served as prototypes for a single-seat fighter support derivative, designated **F-1**. The area which in the T-2 is the rear cockpit, is occupied on the F-1 by an INS, bombing computer, radar warning avionics (with fin-mounted aerials) and other EW systems. The F-1 is primarily assigned a defensive anti-shipping role and, from 1982, it was fitted with the Mitsubishi J/AWG-12 multimode radar for compatability with the ASM-1 radar-guided weapon. The F-1 probably relies on the Orions of the JMSDF for third party targeting of the missiles since the range of its own radar is limited. The original JASDF requirement for 160 F-1s was reduced by budgetary constraints to 77 examples, the last of which was delivered in 1987. The F-1 equipped a peak of three fighter support units, but by early summer 2001 this had been reduced to two, based respectively at Misawa and Tsuiki. In the late 1990s, the F-1 gained a new air-to-surface weapon, the ASM-2 imaging-infrared missile with a reported range of c.62 miles (100 km). The F-1 is now nearing the end of its useful operational life and is scheduled to be replaced by the Mitsubishi F-2, with

The F-1 is used principally in what has to be referred to according to the tenets of the JASDF, as the anti-landing craft role.

the 3rd Koku-dan at Misawa being the first unit scheduled to convert to the new type. In 2001 the T-2 remains an integral part of the JASDF's Air Training Command equipping two squadrons of the 4th Air Wing at Matsushima; pilots conduct 140 hours on the type before progressing to a front-line posting. However, it has already been partially replaced by the Kawasaki T-4 and will finally give way to the two-seat F-2B. The T-2 also serves in small numbers as a hack for the two JASDF F-1 squadrons.

SPECIFICATION

Mitsubishi F-1
Type: single-seat close-support and anti-ship attack fighter
Powerplant: two Ishikawajima-Harima TF40-IHI-801 (Rolls-Royce/Turbomeca Adour Mk 801A) turbofan engines each rated at 7,305 lb st (32.49 kN) with afterburning
Performance: maximum level speed 'clean' at 36,000 ft (10975 m) 1,056 mph (1700 km/h); maximum rate of climb at sea level 35,000 ft (10670 m) per minute; service ceiling 50,000 ft (15240 m); combat radius 345 miles (555 km) on a hi-lo-hi attack mission with two AShMs and two tanks
Weights: operating empty 14,017 lb (6358 kg); maximum take-off 30,203 lb (13700 kg)
Dimensions: wingspan 25 ft 10¼ in (7.88 m); length 58 ft 7 in (17.86 m) including probe; height 14 ft 5 in (4.39 m); wing area 227.88 sq ft (21.17 m²)
Armament: one JM61 Vulcan 20-mm rotary cannon; maximum ordnance 6,000 lb (2721 kg) including ASM-1/S AShMs, AIM-9L AAMs; 500-lb (227-kg) Mk 82 or 750-lb (340-kg) bombs, bombs fitted with the GCS-1 IIR-seeker head (optimised for anti-shipping roles) and 2.75-in (70-mm) JLAU-3A, or RL-7, or 5-in (125-mm) RL-4 rocket pods

Mitsubishi F-2

In October 1987, Japan selected the F-16C Fighting Falcon as the basis for a much developed version to replace the F-1, primarily in the fighter support role. Although a costly and controversial programme – one F-2 costs at least the same as four Block 50/52 F-16Cs – the F-2 illustrates Japan's commitment to maintain its high-technology aerospace industry.

The F-2 features a new wing of 25 per cent greater-area and co-cured, all-composite construction, with radar absorbent material on the leading edges. In order to house additional mission avionics that include an integrated EW system, the F-2's fuselage has a lengthened forward section when compared to the F-16C. Other features are a longer nose to accommodate an active phased-array radar, a larger tailplane, a brake chute and a strengthened canopy. Mitsubishi is the prime contractor responsible for airframe assembly as well as manufacture of the forward fuselage section, while the other major assemblies are produced by Lockheed Martin, Kawasaki and Fuji. With either wing tip-mounted AIM-9 or Mitsubishi AAM-3 AAMs, the F-2 still has 11 hardpoints available for other stores, including the ASM-2 anti-ship missile as one of its principal weapons. The F-2 programme has suffered long delays, cost escalation and a number of structural problems including wing cracking and severe flutter.

Four prototypes have been built comprising two single-seat **XF-2A** machines and a pair of two-seat **XF-2B** aircraft. The first XF-2A recorded the type's maiden flight on 7 October 1995. In late 1995 the Japanese government approved a programme for the manu-facture of 130 aircraft with an entry into service scheduled for 1999. Delays resulting from modifications to cure

structural problems delayed the F-2's entry into operational service until 2001. The current produc-tion plan calls for the production of 83 **F-2A** single-seaters and 47 **F-2B** two-seaters. Retaining full combat capability, these have a fuel capacity reduced by 151 Imp gal (685 litres). The F-2Bs will be used for conversion and proficiency training, replac-ing T-2s.

SPECIFICATION

Mitsubishi F-2A
Type: single-seat, close-support and anti-ship fighter with secondary defensive counter-air role
Powerplant: one General Electric F110-GE-129 turbofan engine rated at 17,000 lb st (75.62 kN) dry and 29,500 lb st (131.22 kN) with afterburning
Performance: maximum speed 1,321 mph (2125 km/h) or Mach 2.0 at altitude; combat radius more than 518 miles (834 km) on an anti-ship mission
Weights: empty 21,003 lb (9527 kg); maximum take-off 48,721 lb (22100 kg)

Dimensions: wingspan 36 ft 6 in (11.13 m) with tip-mounted missile launchers; length 50 ft 11 in (15.52 m); height 15 ft 4⅜ in (4.69 m); wing area 375.03 sq ft (34.84 m²)
Armament: one 20-mm JM61A1 cannon, maximum weapon load of 17,824 lb (8085 kg); weapons include ASM-1/2 AShMs, AIM-7F/AIM-7M+ Sparrow AAMs, AIM-9L or AA-3+ AAMs, 500-lb (227-kg) Mk 82 and 750-lb (340-kg) JM117 free-fall bombs with GCS-1 IIR seeker heads, 1,000-lb (454-kg) bombs, CBU-87/B cluster bombs, JLAU-3/A and RL-4 rocket launchers

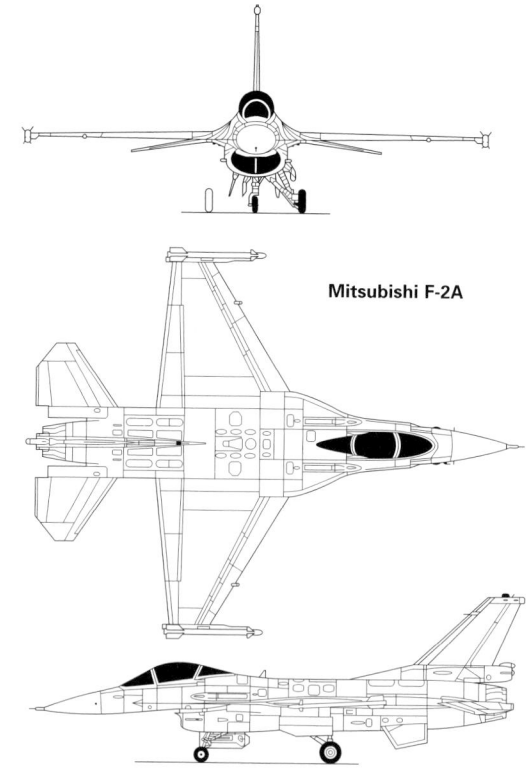

Mitsubishi F-2A

Mitsubishi F1M (Type 0 Observation Seaplane Model 11)

SPECIFICATION

Mitsubishi F1M2
Type: two-seat patrol/reconnaissance floatplane
Powerplant: one 875-hp (652-kW) Mitsubishi Zuisei 13 radial piston engine
Performance: maximum speed 230 mph (370 km/h) at 11,285 ft (3440 m); service ceiling 30,970 ft (9440 m); range 460 miles (740 km)
Weights: empty 4,251 lb (1928 kg); maximum take-off

5,662 lb (2550 kg)
Dimensions: wingspan 36 ft 1 in (11.00 m); length 31 ft 2 in (9.50 m); height 13 ft 1½ in (4.00 m); wing area 317.98 sq ft (29.54 m²)
Armament: two forward-firing 7.7-mm (0.303-in) machine-guns and one gun of similar calibre on pivoted mounting in rear cockpit, plus two 132-lb (60-kg) bombs

In 1935 Mitsubishi designed for the IJN under the designation **Ka-17** a two-seat observation float-plane suitable for catapult launching. Flown first during June 1936, this biplane was powered by an 820-hp (611-kW) Nakajima Hikari engine but had disap-pointing performance, leading to four modified **F1M1** prototypes with the

more powerful Mitsubishi Zuisei 13 radial engine. Subsequent testing and service trials proved satis-factory, and the type was ordered into production as the **Navy Type 0 Observation Seaplane Model 11 (F1M2)**, later allo-cated the Allied codename '**Pete**'. Production totalled 1,118, built by Mitsubishi (528) and the 21st Naval Air

Arsenal (590); a small number of this total was converted for use as two-seat trainers under the designation **F1M2-K**.

Used extensively from ships and shore bases for coastal patrol, convoy escort and reconnaissance, the F1M was also deployed successfully in the unexpected roles of fighter and dive-bomber, despite its obsolete biplane configuration.

Mitsubishi G3M (Navy Type 96 Attack Bomber)

In 1934 Mitsubishi designed a twin-engined bomber/transport under the initial designation **Ka-15**, as a cantilever mid-wing monoplane with retractable tailwheel landing gear. Powered by two 750-hp (559-kW) Hiro Type 91 engines, the prototype made its first flight during July 1935. Twenty more Ka-15 prototypes followed to evaluate several engine/propeller combinations, service trials resulting in a production order in June 1936 under the designation **Navy Type 96 Attack**

Bomber Model 11 (G3M1). The first 34 production aircraft had 910-hp (679-kW) Mitsubishi Kinsei 3 engines, and these were followed by the **G3M2 Model 21** with increased

fuel capacity and 1,075-hp (802-kW) Kinsei 41 or 42 radials. Subsequent produc-tion included the **G3M2 Model 22** with improved armament and the **G3M3 Model 23** with further

This G3M2 was assigned to the Yokosuka Koku-tai in the Marianas during February 1944. The G3M saw its last major combat use in the islands.

uprated engines. A number was converted for transport duties from G3M1 standard

under the designations **G3M1-L** and **L3Y1 Model 11**.

Mitsubishi G3M (Navy Type 96 Attack Bomber) (cont.)

Transport conversions from G3M2 Model 21 standard were designated **L3Y2 Model 12**. Production totalled 1,048, including prototypes, built by Mitsubishi (636) and Nakajima (412), the bomber and transport aircraft being allocated the Allied code-names **'Nell'** and **'Tina'** respectively.

G3M2s first demonstrated their long-range capability on 14 August 1937, when a squadron based at Taipei, Taiwan, attacked targets 1,249 miles (2010 km) distant in China. The type is perhaps best known for its part in the sinking of the British battleship HMS *Prince of Wales* and battle-cruiser HMS *Repulse* on 10 December 1941, just three days after the initial attack on Pearl Harbor. The type served through the Pacific war, but by 1943 most were being deployed in secondline roles.

SPECIFICATION	
Mitsubishi G3M3 Model 23	17,637 lb (8000 kg)
Type: seven-crew long-range bomber	**Dimensions:** wingspan 82 ft ¼ in (25.00 m); length 53 ft 11¾ in (16.45 m); height 12 ft 1¼ in (3.69 m wing area 907.32 sq ft (84.30 m²)
Powerplant: two 1,300-hp (969-kW) Mitsubishi Kinsei 51 radial piston engines	
Performance: maximum speed 258 mph (415 km/h) at 19,360 ft (5900); service ceiling 33,725 ft (10280 m); maximum range 3,871 miles (6230 km)	**Armament:** one 20-mm cannon and four 7.7-mm (0.303-in) machine-guns, plus one 1,764-lb (800-kg) torpedo or an equivalent weight of bombs carried beneath the fuselage
Weights: empty 11,552 lb (5240 kg); maximum take-off	

Of limited value as a bomber in the later stages of the war, the G3M found new utility as the transport L3Y2.

Mitsubishi G4M (Navy Type 1 Attack Bomber)

To an Imperial Japanese Navy requirement of 1937 for a land-based bomber to supersede the G3M, Mitsubishi designed the **G4M**, a roomy mid-wing monoplane whose prototype, powered by two 1,530-hp (1141-kW) Kasei 11 radial engines, was flown for the first time on 23 October 1939. Service trials proving satisfactory, the type was ordered into production in 1940 as the **Navy Type 1 Attack Bomber Model 11 (G4M1 Model 11)**, the first series aircraft entering operational service in the summer of 1941. Subsequent production versions included the similar **G4M1 Model 12**; the **G4M2 Model 22** with 1,800-hp (1342-kW) Mitsubishi MK4P Kasei 21 engines and a number of revisions, followed by the **G4M2 Model 22A** and **G4M2 Model 22B** with armament variations. These were followed by the **G4M2a Model 24**, introducing 1,825-hp (1361-kW) MK4T Kasei 25 engines and

bulged bomb bay doors, and **G4M2a Model 24A/24B** subvariants with armament changes. Final production version was the **G4M3 Model 34** which attempted to reduce the shortcomings of its predecessors by introducing self-sealing fuel tanks and adequate armour protection. Experimental variants to evaluate various engines included one **G4M2b Model 25**, two **G4M2c Model 26**, one **G4M2d Model 27**, and two **G4M3 Model 36** aircraft; and in addition a considerable number of G4M2a Model 24B and **24C** aircraft were modified to carry the navy's MXY7 piloted missile for suicide attacks, becoming redesignated **G4M2e Model 24J** in this role. Just before production of the G4M the navy had a very urgent requirement for a long-range escort fighter for use in the Sino-Japanese War, and 30 of these aircraft were built for this specific role under the designation **G6M1**. When

The Mitsubishi G4M was built in greater numbers than any other Japanese bomber.

they proved unsuccessful, some were converted later as **G6M1-K** trainers or **G6M1-L2** transports. When production ended, Mitsubishi had built a total of 2,446 of all versions, this number including prototypes and the 30 G6M1s.

Allocated the Allied code-name **'Betty'**, the G4Ms have become recorded in aviation history for a number of events, including participation in the sinking of HMS *Prince of Wales* and *Repulse*; involvement in the first air raid on Darwin, Australia; service as MXY7 missile-carriers; and on 19 August 1945, the carriage of the Japanese surrender delegation to Ie-Shima. Considerably more success might have been attributed to these bombers if they had incorporated adequate armour and self-sealing fuel tanks earlier; of the total built only the 60 G4M3 production aircraft had this essential protection. Throughout, the designers were crippled by demands for very long range, which really called for four engines.

SPECIFICATION	
Mitsubishi G4M3 Model 34	(8350 kg); maximum take-off 27,558 lb (12500 kg)
Type: seven-crew long-range bomber	**Dimensions:** wingspan 82 ft ¼ in (25.00 m); length 63 ft 11¾ in (19.50 m); height 19 ft 8¼ in (6.00 m); wing area 841.01 sq ft (78.10 m²)
Powerplant: two 1,825-hp (1361-kW) Mitsubishi MK4T Kasei 25 radial piston engines	
Performance: maximum speed 292 mph (470 km/h) at 16,895 ft (5150 m); service ceiling 30,250 ft (9220 m); maximum range 2,694 miles (4335 km)	**Armament:** four 20-mm cannon and two 7.7-mm (0.303-in) machine-guns, plus one 1,764-lb (800-kg) torpedo or 2,205 lb (1000 kg) of bombs
Weights: empty 18,049 lb	

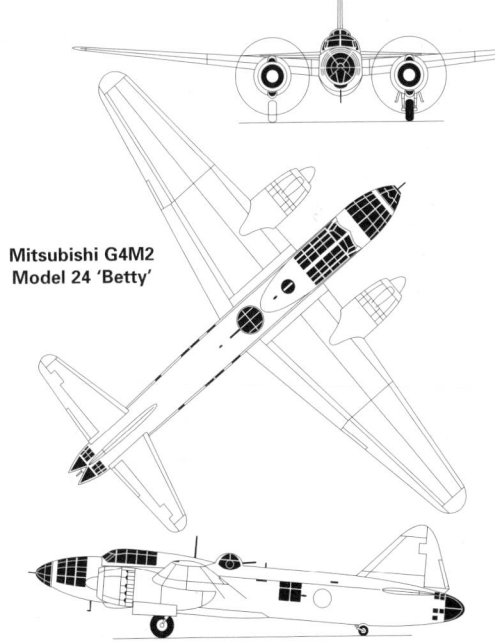

Mitsubishi G4M2
Model 24 'Betty'

This Mitsubishi G4M1 'Betty' was flown by Tatao Kokutai (later redesignated 753rd Kokutai) based at Rabaul in Papua New Guinea in October 1942. The type was known as 'The Flying Lighter' by Allied pilots, due to its tendency to burst into flames when attacked by fighters.

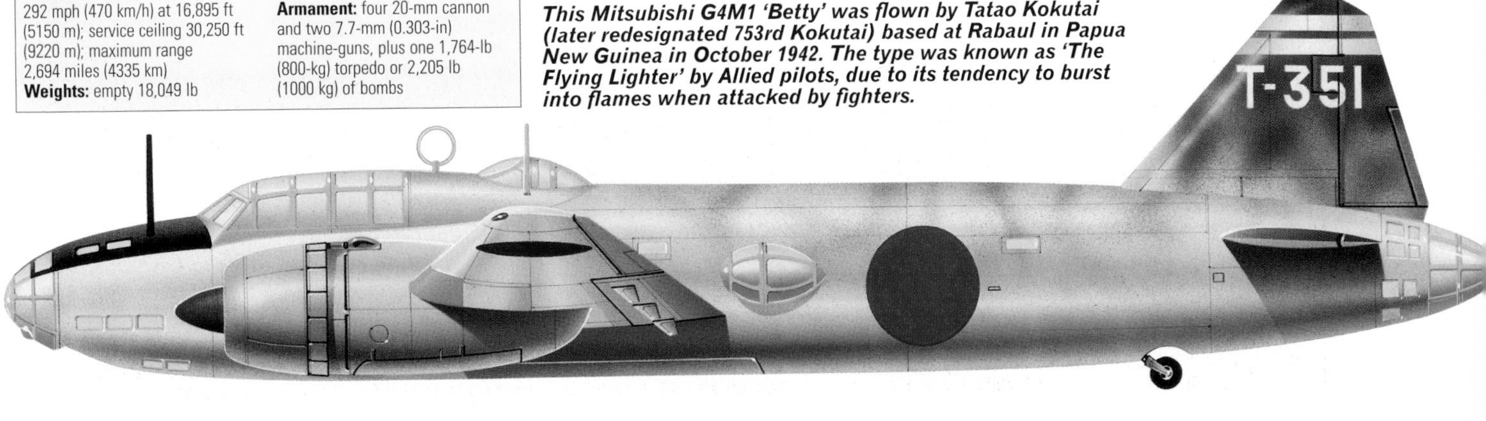

T-351

Mitsubishi J2M (Navy Interceptor Fighter Raiden)

An IJN requirement of 1938 for a single-seat interceptor led to the design and construction of three **J2M1** prototypes, the first being flown initially on 20 March 1942. A cantilever lever low-wing monoplane with retractable tailwheel landing gear, the type suffered a protracted development because the demands on engine production had limited severely the choice of a suitable powerplant. It resulted in the installation of a 1,430-hp (1066-kW) Kasei 13 radial of large diameter, an extension shaft being provided between the engine and reduction gear to ensure the nose entry was of minimum diameter. Early tests revealed that the J2M1 could not meet the navy's specification for maximum speed and rate of climb, installation of the more powerful MK4R-A Kasei 23a engine being necessitated and leading to redesignation as the **J2M2**, and it was this version that was ordered into production in October 1942 as the **Navy Interceptor Fighter Raiden Model 11**. Continuing teething problems with the J2M2 meant that the type did not enter service until December 1943, by which time the major production version, the **J2M3**, which differed primarily in its armament, was being built. Variants included the similar **J2M3a** with revised armament, the final production **J2M5** with the 1,820-hp (1357-kW) Mitsubishi MK4U-4 engine, produced as the J2M5 and **J2M5a** with differing armament, plus two **J2M4** prototypes with turbo-charged engines and a single **J2M6** with a revised cockpit, as a conversion of a J2M3. When production ended Mitsubishi had built a total of 476 aircraft of all versions, this number including prototypes.

Allocated the Allied codename **'Jack'**, the **J2M Raiden** (thunderbolt) first saw operational service during 1944, but enjoyed little success until the closing stages of the war, then playing a more vital role as Japan's defensive perimeter was gradually closing around the home islands.

These J2Ms were tested by the Allied Technical Air Intelligence Unit in Singapore after the war, using both Allied and Japanese pilots.

SPECIFICATION	
Mitsubishi J2M3 Raiden	**Weights:** empty 5,423 lb
Type: single-seat interceptor	(2460 kg); maximum take-off
fighter	8,695 lb (3945 kg)
Powerplant: one 1,820-hp	**Dimensions:** wingspan 35 ft 5¼ in
(1357-kW) Mitsubishi MK4R-A	(10.82 m); length 32 ft 7¾ in
Kasei 23a radial piston engine	(9.95 m); height 12 ft 11½ in
Performance: maximum speed	(3.95 m); wing area 215.82 sq ft
370 mph (595 km/h) at 19,360 ft	(20.05 m²)
(5900 m); service ceiling 38,385 ft	**Armament:** four 20-mm cannon,
(11700 m); maximum range	plus two 132-lb (60-kg) bombs on
655 miles (1055 km)	external racks

Mitsubishi J8M (Navy Experimental Rocket-Powered Interceptor Fighter Shusui)

Development of the Me 163B rocket-powered fighter in Germany prompted Japan to acquire rights to build this aircraft and its Walter rocket engine. Because of losses in transit, only one sample engine and an instruction manual for the Me 163 survived, and Mitsubishi was tasked with design of the interceptor which had the army and navy designations **Ki-200** and **J8M** respectively. With **J8M1** prototype design finalised, the 1st Naval Air Arsenal began construction of a full-scale training glider version under the designation **MXY8 Akigusa** (autumn grass), and this was towed into the air and flown for the first time in December 1944. A heavier glider, with ballast tanks to approximate the weight of the operational aircraft, was also built under the designation **Ku-13 Shusui** (sword stroke). Design of the rocket engine was a combined project of Mitsubishi together with the army and navy, resulting in the 3,307-lb (14.71-kN) thrust Toko Ro.2, and this powerplant was installed in the first of the **J8M1 Navy Experimental Rocket-Powered Interceptor Fighter Shusui** prototypes completed by Mitsubishi. On 7 July 1945 the prototype J8M1 was flown for the first time, crashing soon after take-off as a result of engine failure, and consequently, no further examples were flown before the end of the war.

This picture illustrates the similarities between the J8M and the Messerschmitt Me 163B Komet. The J8M was never used operationally.

Mitsubishi K3M (Navy Type 90 Crew Trainer)

Designed by Herbert Smith, the **4MS1** prototype crew trainer made its maiden flight in 1930. Production continued until 1941, and examples pressed into service as liaison aircraft in the post-war period were to be found in a variety of national markings. A strut-braced high-wing cabin monoplane with fixed wide-track landing gear, the 4MS1 was powered by a single engine. The first **K3M2** production version entered naval service in 1932 as the **Navy Type 90 Crew Trainer**, in which configuration the pilot and gunner were located in separate open cockpits, with an instructor and two pupils in the enclosed cabin. Later liaison/passenger variants accommodated five passengers in the cabin.

K3Ms were used extensively as trainers and, to a smaller degree, utility transports during the war, and given the codename 'Pine' by the Allies. Total production of all versions amounted to 624.

Variants

K3M1: service designation of **4MS1** prototype and three test aircraft built in 1930-31; powered by 340-hp (254-kW) Hispano-Suiza 8 V-8 engine

K3M2: company designation **4MS2**, built 1932-35; powered by 340-hp (254-kW) Hitachi Amakaze 11 radial engine; Mitsubishi built 70, balance of 247 constructed later by Aichi

K3M3: in 1939 Watanabe took over production from Aichi and built this new version which incorporated an enlarged fin and rudder and was powered by a Nakajima Kotobuki 2 radial; some aircraft were modified as **K3M3-L** light transports for up to five passengers or an equivalent weight in freight; total Watanabe production 301

Ki-7: designation of two aircraft tested by Imperial Japanese Army in 1932; basic K3M structure, one with a Mitsubishi 92 radial and the other a Nakajima Kotobuki

MS-1: a single civil transport with a 460-hp (343-kW) Jupiter VI radial

SPECIFICATION	
Mitsubishi/Watanabe K3M3	(1360 kg); maximum take-off
Type: five-seat crew trainer	4,850 lb (2200 kg)
Powerplant: one 580-hp (433-kW)	**Dimensions:** wingspan 51 ft 9¼ in
Nakajima Kotobuki 2 Kai 2 radial	(15.78 m); length 31 ft 3½ in
piston engine	(9.54 m); height 12 ft 6½ in
Performance: maximum speed	(3.82 m); wing area 371.37 sq ft
146 mph (235 km/h); service ceiling	(34.50 m²)
20,965 ft (6390 m); range 497 miles	**Armament:** one trainably-mounted
(800 km)	0.303-in (7.7-mm) machine-gun,
Weights: empty 2,998 lb	plus 265 lb (120 kg) of bombs

Mitsubishi Ki-1 (Army Type 93 Heavy Bomber)

Showing strong signs of Junkers influence, the **Ki-1-I** heavy bomber flew for the first time in 1933. An angular cantilever low-wing monoplane with a crew of four, it had fixed landing gear, a tail unit incorporating twin fins and rudders, and was powered by two 940-hp (701-kW) Ha-2-2 radial engines, giving a maximum speed of 137 mph (220 km/h). The pilot and co-pilot were seated in tandem

under an enclosed canopy, while there were semi-enclosed nose and dorsal turrets and a retractable ventral 'dustbin', each armed with a single 0.303-in (7.7-mm) machine-gun; offensive load was up to 3,307 lb (1500 kg) of bombs. The **Ki-1-II** development had 970-hp (723-kW) Ha-2-3 engines and airframe improvements which increased maximum speed to 143 mph (230 km/h).

The Army Type 93 was used in Manchuria and northern China, but was heavy, slow and not well-liked by its crews. A total of 118 of the type was built between March 1933 and April 1936.

The two versions went into service as the **Army Type 93-1** and **Army Type 93-2** respectively, and saw limited use in the fighting against China.

Mitsubishi Ki-2 (Type 93-2 Twin-engined Light Bomber)

A most successful design, although built only in limited numbers, the **Ki-2** light bomber was developed from the Junkers K 37, an example of which had been imported from Germany in 1931 and donated by public subscription to the Japanese army. It bore the distinction of being *Aikoku 1*, the first of many such patriotic gifts, sparked off by the fighting in Manchuria.

A three-seat cantilever low-wing monoplane, powered by two 570-hp (425-kW) Nakajima Kotobuki radials, the Ki-2 prototype flew for the first time in the spring of 1933. It was distinguished easily by its corrugated metal alloy decking and twin fins and rudders, and had fixed divided landing gear, with

spat-type main wheel fairings often discarded on service aircraft.

Production of the initial version totalled 113, and the type went into operation against the Chinese with great success under the designation **Ki-2-I** or **Army Type 93 Twin-engined Light Bomber**. Maximum speed was 140 mph (225 km/h), normal range 559 miles (900 km) and maximum take-off weight 10,031 lb (4550 kg). Single 0.303-in (7.7-mm) machine-guns were mounted in a semi-enclosed nose cockpit and a dorsal position, and maximum bombload was 1,102 lb (500 kg).

The achievements of the Ki-2-I led to the development of the **Ki-2-II**, or **Army Type 93-2 Twin-**

engined Light Bomber, the Type 93 then being redesignated retrospectively as the **Type 93-1**. The Type 93-2 retained the same general configuration, but had a fully-enclosed manually-operated nose turret, an enclosed cockpit for the pilot, and main landing gear legs which semi-retracted forward into the engine nacelles. The Ki-2-II had two 750-hp (559-kW) Ha-8 radials giving much improved overall performance with maximum speed increased to 176 mph (283 km/h). In total 61 Ki-2-IIs were built, and these joined the Ki-2-Is in operations against the Chinese. Both versions ended their flying careers in the training role.

A civilianised version of the Ki-2-II named *Otori*

(Phoenix) was bought by the *Asahi Shimbun* newspaper and made a number of long-range record-breaking and 'goodwill' flights from 1936 to 1939. In December 1936 it covered

the 3,063 miles (4930 km) from Tachikawa to Bangkok in 21 hours 36 minutes flying time, and in early 1939 achieved a round-China flight of some 5,780 miles (9300 km).

The Japanese had been most impressed with a Junkers K.37 imported and used in Manchuria in 1931, and designed the Ki-2 along similar lines.

Mitsubishi Ki-15 (Army Type 97 Command Reconnaissance Plane, C5M)

The **Ki-15** was designed to meet an Imperial Japanese Army requirement of 1935 for a two-seat reconnaissance aircraft. Two prototypes were built, one civil and one military, the latter flying for the first time in May 1936. Service testing proceeded smoothly and the type was ordered into production as the **Army Type 97 Command**

Reconnaissance Plane Model 1 (Ki-15-I), initial deliveries to the army being made in May 1937. Just before that, the civil prototype was flown from Tachikawa to London to collect photographs and films of the coronation of HM King George VI. Following the achievement of this machine, a small number of civil aircraft was acquired under the designa-

tion **Karigane I** for use by civil operators in Japan.

Deployed in the war against China, the army's **Ki-15-I** aircraft had virtual freedom of the skies until China introduced the Soviet Polikarpov I-16. Performance of the Ki-15-I was then upgraded by installation of the 900-hp (671-kW) Mitsubishi Ha-26-I engine, the improved **Ki-15-II** entering service in 1939. The same treatment was tried when still higher performance was required at a later date, two **Ki-15-III** prototypes being tested with the 1,050-hp (783-kW) Mitsubishi 102 radial, but

no production resulted as more advanced aircraft were then under development. The Imperial Japanese Navy acquired 20 Ki-15-IIs under the designation **Navy Type 98 Reconnaissance Plane Model 1 (C5M1)**, plus 30 more with the 950-hp

(708-kW) Nakajima Sakae 12 engine as the **C5M2**. Allocated the Allied codename **'Babs'**, the Ki-15 C5M was built to a total of 489 of all versions, being relegated to second-line duties in 1943. Many survived to be used in *kamikaze* attacks.

J-BAAL Kamikaze (Divine Wind) was owned by Asahi Shimbun, Japan's leading newspaper.

SPECIFICATION	
Mitsubishi Ki-15-I	
Type: two-seat reconnaissance aircraft	**Weights:** empty 3,086 lb (1400 kg); maximum take-off 5,071 lb (2300 kg)
Powerplant: one 640-hp (477-kW) Nakajima Ha-8 radial piston engine	**Dimensions:** wingspan 39 ft 4¼ in (12.00 m); length 28 ft 6½ in (8.70 m); height 11 ft (3.35 m); wing area 219.16 sq ft (20.36 m²)
Performance: maximum speed 298 mph (480 km/h) at 13,125 ft (4000 m); service ceiling 37,400 ft (11400 m); range 1,491 miles (2400 km)	**Armament:** one 7.7-mm (0.303-in) machine-gun on a trainable mount in rear cockpit

Mitsubishi Ki-21 (Army Type 97 Heavy Bomber)

Designed for an IJA requirement of 1936 for a

four-seat bomber, the twin-engined **Ki-21-I** proto-

type, as powered by the Nakajima Ha-5 demon-

strated performance equal to any of the world's

contemporary bombers in the same category. It was

ordered into production as the **Army Type 97 Heavy Bomber Model 1A (Ki-21-Ia)**, entering service in the summer of 1938. Operational experience in China showed the type to

be deficient in armament, leading to the improved **Ki-21-Ib** with five instead of three machine-guns and an enlarged bomb bay, followed by the **Ki-21-Ic** with increased fuel capacity

and one extra machine-gun. Continuing development brought four **Ki-21-II** prototypes, introducing more powerful Mitsubishi Ha 101 engines. With the same armament as the Ki-21-Ic, this model entered production as the **Ki-21-IIa**. The final production version was the generally-similar **Ki-21-IIb** which incorporated some refinements. In addition to the military Ki-21s, a number of Ki-21-Ia aircraft was later converted

for use as unarmed civil freighter/transports.
Ki-21s, which were allocated the Allied codename **'Sally'**, played a significant role in the early stages of the Pacific war, but the increasing numbers and

capability of Allied fighters meant that during the last year of the war these bombers were relegated to second-line duties. A total of 2,064 Ki-21s was built, 1,713 by Mitsubishi and an additional 351 by Nakajima.

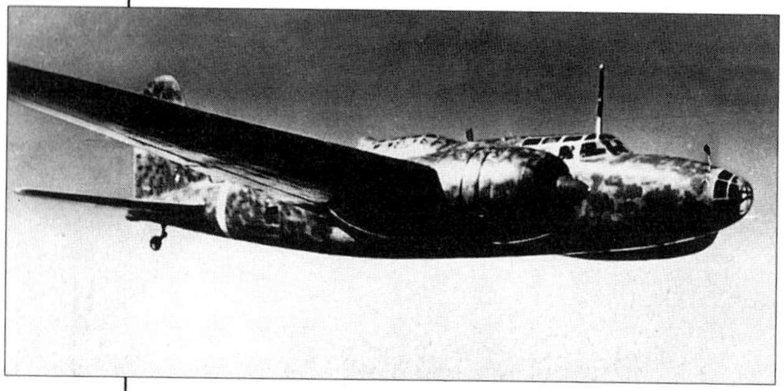

Despite becoming increasingly obsolete, the 'Sally' served in first-line service until the end of the war.

SPECIFICATION	
Mitsubishi Ki-21-IIb	**Weights:** empty 13,382 lb
Type: five/seven-seat heavy	(6070 kg); maximum take-off
bomber	23,391 lb (10610 kg)
Powerplant: two 1,500-hp	**Dimensions:** wingspan 73 ft 9¾ in
(1119-kW) Mitsubishi Ha-101	(22.50 m); length 52 ft 6 in (16 m);
radial piston engines	height 15 ft 11 in (4.85 m); wing
Performance: maximum speed	area 749.19 sq ft (69.60 m²)
301 mph (485 km/h) at 15,485 ft	**Armament:** six 7.7-mm (0.303-in)
(4720 m); service ceiling 32,810 ft	machine-guns, plus a bombload of
(10000 m); range 1,678 miles	up to 2,205 lb (1000 kg)
(2700 km)	

Mitsubishi Ki-30 (Army Type 97 Light Bomber)

The **Ki-30** prototype, powered by an 825-hp (615-kW) Mitsubishi Ha-6 radial engine, was flown for the first time on 28 February 1937. It had been designed and built to

meet an IJA requirement for a light bomber, the company building two prototypes, and the second was flown shortly after with a more powerful Nakajima Ha-5 KAI engine.

This latter aircraft not only showed some improvement in performance, but as it exceeded the army's specification the company was given an immediate order for 16 trials aircraft. These were delivered in January 1938 and, two months later, the Ki-30 was ordered into production as the **Army Type 97 Light Bomber**. When used in China in 1938, and at the beginning of the Pacific war, they proved very effective when escorted by

fighter aircraft; however, when they could no longer be escorted, Allied fighters began to take a heavy toll and the type was soon relegated to second-line use. Allocated the Allied codename **'Ann'**, the Ki-30

had been built to a total of 704 when production ended, 68 of this number by the 1st Army Air Arsenal at Tachikawa. Many ended their days in a *kamikaze* role in the closing stages of the Pacific war.

The Ki-30 ws the first Japanese light bomber to have an internal bomb-bay and split flaps.

SPECIFICATION	
Mitsubishi Ki-30	(2230 kg); maximum take-off
Type: two-seat light bomber	7,099 lb (3220 kg)
Powerplant: one 950-hp (708-kW)	**Dimensions:** wingspan 47 ft 8¾ in
Nakajima Ha-5 KAI radial piston	(14.55 m); length 33 ft 11½ in
engine	(10.35 m); height 11 ft 11¾ in
Performance: maximum speed	(3.65 m); wing area 329.17 sq ft
264 mph (425 km/h) at 13,125 ft	(30.58 m²)
(4000 m); service ceiling 28,115 ft	**Armament:** one forward-firing and
(8570 m); range 1,056 miles	one rear-firing 7.7-mm (0.303-in)
(1700 km)	machine-gun, plus up to 882 lb
Weights: empty 4,916 lb	(400 kg) of bombs

Mitsubishi Ki-46 (Army Type 100 Command Reconnaissance Plane)

This 16 Dokuritsu Hikotai Ki-46-III has the upward/oblique-firing 37-mm cannon that was typical of the variant.

One of the best-looking Japanese aircraft of World War II, the **Ki-46** was designed to meet an IJA requirement of 1937 for a higher performance reconnaissance aircraft to supersede the Ki-15. A cantilever low-wing monoplane with retractable tailwheel landing gear, powered by two 900-hp (671-kW) Mitsubishi Ha-21-I radial engines, the two-seat Ki-46 prototype was flown for the first time in late November 1939. Early testing showed that the maximum speed of the Ki-46 was some 10 per cent below specification, but as its speed and overall performance was better than in-service army and navy aircraft the type was ordered into production as the **Army Type 100 Command Reconnaissance Plane**

Model 1 (**Ki-46-I**), later allocated the Allied codename **'Dinah'**. Early operational problems with the Ki-46-I resulted in the introduction of an improved **Ki-46-II** with 1,080-hp (805-kW) Mitsubishi Ha-102 engines, this powerplant giving a maximum speed slightly in excess of the original specification. The Ki-46-II was the major production version, with more than 1,000 built, a number of which were converted later into three-seat radio/navigation trainers under the designation **Ki-46-II KAI**. Subsequent variants included the faster and improved **Ki-46-III** of which

609 were built, a small number being converted later as **Ki-46-III KAI** fighter interceptors and **Ki-46-IIIb** ground-attack aircraft. **Ki-46-IV** prototypes, with 1,500-hp (1119-kW) Mitsubishi Ha-112-11 Ru turbocharged engines to give improved high altitude performance, were under test when the war ended.
In service from the beginning to the end of the Pacific war, the Ki-46 proved to be an important aircraft for the Japanese army, but the growing capability and number of Allied fighters resulted in unacceptably high losses of Ki-46-IIs. However, the

improved performance of the Ki-46-III meant that this version was virtually free from interception until the

final stage of the war. Production of all versions totalled 1,742, all built by Mitsubishi.

The most obvious external change in the Ki-46-III was the distinctive redesign of the forward fuselage with a new canopy design.

SPECIFICATION	
Mitsubishi Ki-46-III	(3830 kg); maximum take-off
Type: two-seat reconnaissance	14,330 lb (6500 kg)
aircraft	**Dimensions:** wingspan 48 ft 2¾ in
Powerplant: two 1,500-hp	(14.70 m); length 36 ft 1 in
(1119-kW) Mitsubishi Ha-112-II	(11.00 m); height 12 ft 8¾ in
radial piston engines	(3.88 m); wing area 344.46 sq ft
Performance: maximum speed	(32.00 m²)
391 mph (630 km/h) at 19,685 ft	**Armament:** Ki-46-I and Ki-46-II
(6000 m); service ceiling 34,450 ft	had a single 7.7-mm (0.303-in)
(10500 m); range 2,485 miles	rear-firing machine-gun on a
(4000 km)	trainable mount; III Kai two 20-mm
Weights: empty 8,444 lb	Ho-5 and oblique 37 Ho-203

Mitsubishi Ki-51 (Army Type 99 Assault Plane)

To meet an IJA requirement of 1937 for a ground-attack aircraft, the company produced two **Ki-51** prototypes, powered by the Ha-26-II engine, which were flown and tested in the summer of 1939. Although of smaller dimensions, they were of the same general configuration as the company's Ki-30, except that as a bomb bay was not required the wing was dropped from a mid- to low-set position, and there was a revised cockpit for the two-man crew. The prototypes were followed by 11 service trials aircraft, which introduced armour protection for the engine and crew, and aerodynamic refinements to improve slow-speed handling. In this form manufacture was authorised as the **Army Type 99 Assault Plane**, later allocated the Allied codename **'Sonia'**, and production eventually totalled 2,385, of which Mitsubishi built 1,472 and the Tachikawa 1st Army Air Arsenal 913. First introduced into use in China, the Ki-51 saw service throughout the Pacific war, although its vulnerability to Allied fighters meant that the type served largely in secondary theatres before, in the closing stage of the war, being used for *kamikaze* attacks. One **Ki-51a** tactical reconnaissance prototype resulted as a conversion from a Ki-51, and under the designation **Ki-71** Mitsubishi designed, and the Tachikawa arsenal built, three prototypes of a dedicated tactical reconnaissance aircraft powered by the 1,500-hp (1119-kW) Mitsubishi Ha-112-II engine and retractable landing gear. Neither of these reconnaissance versions entered production.

SPECIFICATION	
Mitsubishi Ki-51	
Type: two-seat ground attack aircraft	**Dimensions:** wingspan 39 ft 8¼ in (12.10 m); length 30 ft 2¼ in (9.20 m); height 8 ft 11½ in (2.73 m); wing area 258.56 sq ft (24.02 m²)
Powerplant: one 940-hp (701-kW) Mitsubishi Ha-26-II radial piston engine	
Performance: maximum speed 264 mph (425 km/h) at 9,845 ft (3000 m); service ceiling 27,130 ft (8270 m); range 659 miles (1060 km)	**Armament:** two 7.7-mm (0.303-in) or two 12.7-mm (0.54-in) forward-firing machine-guns in early- and late-production machines respectively, and one 7.7-mm (0.303-in) gun on a trainable mount in the rear cockpit, plus a bombload of up to 441 lb (200 kg)
Weights: empty 4,129 lb (1873 kg); maximum take-off 6,437 lb (2920 kg)	

The Ki-51 'Sonia' was a smaller ground attack version of the Ki-30, and was widely used during the war in the Pacific.

Mitsubishi Ki-57 (MC-20-I & Army Type 100 Transport)

With interest shown by Japan Air Lines for a civil version of the Ki-21 bomber, the company built a **Ki-57** prototype, which was flown in August 1940; it differed from the Ki-21 by having low-set monoplane wings and a new fuselage to seat up to 11 passengers. Following satisfactory testing the type was ordered into production for civil and military use under the designations **MC-20-I** and **Army Type 100 Transport Model 1** respectively (**Ki-57-I**), 100 series aircraft being built. The Ki-57-I was superseded from early 1942 by the improved **Ki-57-II**, which introduced more powerful Mitsubishi Ha-102 engines and a number of refinements. This had the civil and military designations **MC-20-II** and **Army Type 100 Transport Model 2** respectively, production totalling 406. A small number of Ki-57-Is transferred for use by the IJN were redesignated **L4M1**, and all of these versions had the Allied codename **'Topsy'**.

SPECIFICATION	
Mitsubishi Ki-57-II	(3000 km)
Type: twin-engine personnel transport	**Weights:** empty 12,313 lb (5585 kg); maximum take-off 20,106 lb (9120 kg)
Powerplant: two 1,080-hp (805-kW) Mitsubishi Ha-102 radial piston engines	**Dimensions:** wingspan 74 ft 1¾ in (22.60 m); length 52 ft 9¾ in (16.10 m); height 15 ft 11 in (4.85 m); wing area 754.36 sq ft (70.08 m²)
Performance: maximum speed 292 mph (470 km/h) at 19,030 ft (5800 m); service ceiling 26,245 ft (8000 m); range 1,864 miles	

This MC-20-II wears the livery of Dai Nippon Koku K.K. (Greater Japan Air Line Co Ltd).

Mitsubishi Ki-67 (Army Type 4 Heavy Bomber Hiryu)

In February 1941 Mitsubishi was instructed to design and build three prototypes of a tactical heavy bomber to meet a specification drawn up by the IJA. The resulting **Ki-67** prototype was first flown on 27 December 1942, a cantilever mid-wing monoplane powered by two Mitsubishi Ha-104 radial engines, the fuselage with accommodation for a crew of six to eight and incorporating a large bomb bay.

SPECIFICATION	
Mitsubishi Ki-67-I	
Type: heavy bomber/ torpedo-bomber	**Dimensions:** wingspan 73 ft 9¾ in (22.50 m); length 61 ft 4¼ in (18.70 m); height 25 ft 3¼ in (7.70 m); wing area 708.83 sq ft (65.85 m²)
Powerplant: two 1,900-hp (1417-kW) Mitsubishi Ha-104 radial piston engines	
Performance: maximum speed 334 mph (537 km/h) at 19,980 ft (6090 m); service ceiling 31,070 ft (9470 m); range 2,361 miles (3800 km)	**Armament:** four 12.7-mm (0.5-in) machine-guns and one 20-mm cannon, all aircraft to construction number 450; all subsequent aircraft had one extra 12.7-mm (0.5-in) gun; plus a maximum bombload of 1,764 lb (800 kg), or one 1,764-lb (800-kg) or 2,359-lb (1070-kg) torpedo
Weights: empty 19,070 lb (8650 kg); maximum take-off 30,347 lb (13765 kg)	

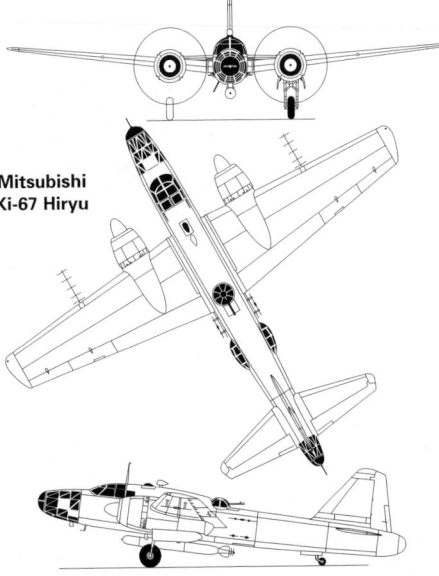

Mitsubishi Ki-67 Hiryu

Although the Hiryu (Flying Dragon) was officially classified as a heavy bomber, the type is better compared to the Martin B-26 Marauder medium bomber. Had the type not been flown mainly by inexperienced young crews, the story of the Pacific war may have been very different.

Testing of this prototype, plus an additional 16 prototype and service test aircraft, was highly successful and resulted in the army planning a whole range of variants. However, it was decided eventually to concentrate on a single version, ordered into production on 2 December 1943 as the **Army Type 4 Heavy Bomber Model 1 Hiryu** (flying dragon) or **Ki-67-I**, which gained the Allied codename **'Peggy'**. All aircraft subsequent to production number 160 had torpedo racks, and the Ki-67 was operated successfully both as a bomber and torpedo- bomber. The designation **Ki-67-I KAI** applied to aircraft converted for use in a three-seat *kamikaze* role, and a heavy fighter variant with a solid nose mounting a 75-mm cannon was built under the designation **Ki-109** to a total of only 22 aircraft. Allied attacks on Japanese production sources limited construction to only 698 Ki-67s, built by Mitsubishi (606), Kawasaki (91) and the Army Air Arsenal at Tachikawa (1). Nippon also assembled 29 Mitsubishi-built aircraft, accounting for the erroneous production figure of 727 often quoted. In its designated role as a heavy bomber the Ki-67 was deployed extensively in the final stages of the Pacific war, especially in operations against Allied forces on Iwo Jima, the Marianas and Okinawa.

Mitsubishi MH2000

Building on experience gained in the licence manufacture of components and helicopters such as the Sikorsky S-70, Mitsubishi launched its **MH2000** project in 1995, the first helicopter designed and manufactured entirely in Japan. This twin-turbine helicopter is aimed at the multi-role civil market and is available in HEMS, law enforcement, SAR, transport, and VIP transport roles. The first of four development aircraft flew on 29 July 1996, the second flying later in the year and the remaining two being used for ground test duties.

Alternative cabin layouts for a maximum of eight passengers are available, the cabin interior proving extremely quiet thanks to the location of the main gearbox and transmission components aft of the cabin structure. Exterior noise is kept to a minimum by the use of a fenestron tail rotor, while noise levels can be further reduced by engaging a 'low-noise mode' on the electronically-controlled engines.

Both the flightcrew and passengers are provided with excellent visibility thanks to the MH2000's extensive glazing, while the seats and fuel tanks are of a crashworthy design. The standard avionics fit can be augmented with optional GPS map display and auto-matic flight control system equipment.

The first production

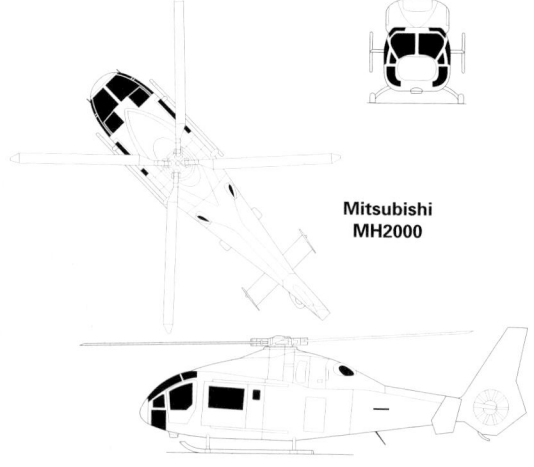

Mitsubishi MH2000

MH2000A was handed over to Excel Air Service in Japan on 1 October 2000.

SPECIFICATION	
Mitsubishi MH2000	reserves
Type: ten-seat multi-role civil helicopter	**Weights:** empty 5,512 lb (2500 kg); maximum take-off 9,920 lb (4500 kg)
Powerplant: two Mitsubishi MG5-110 turboshafts each rated at 876 shp (653 kW)	**Dimensions:** rotor diameter 40 ft ¼ in (12.20 m); length 45 ft 11¼ in (14.00 m) with the rotor turning; height 13 ft 5½ in (4.10 m) to top of fin; rotor disc area 1,258.30 sq ft (116.90 m²)
Performance: maximum level speed 174 mph (280 km/h); hovering ceiling 8,860 ft (2700 m) in ground effect; maximum range 484 miles (780 km) at cruising speed with standard fuel and no	**Payload:** 4,410 lb (2000 kg)

Mitsubishi MU-2, Marquise and Solitaire

In 1959 Mitsubishi began the design of a light utility transport to be powered by two turboprop engines and allocated the designation **MU-2**. It was not until 14 September 1963 that the first of four prototypes was flown, a cantilever high-wing monoplane with a pressurised fuselage, retractable tricycle landing gear and two wing-mounted turboprop engines. Initial production versions were the **MU-2A** with Turboméca Astazou turboprops, **MU-2B** with Garrett TPE331 turboprops and a similar **MU-2D**, an unpressurised multi-role **MU-2C** for the Japan Ground Self Defense Force, a SAR **MU-2E**, and the **MU-2F** with uprated TPE331 engines. The **MU-2G** which followed had

Mitsubishi MU-2s are the only fixed-wing aircraft used by the Japanese Ground Self Defence Force. Some 17 serve with the designation LR-1.

the powerplant of the MU-2F and was the first with a lengthened fuselage; subsequent versions have included the **MU-2J** with more powerful engines, **MU-2K** combining the MU-2F fuselage and MU-2J powerplant, **MU-2L** and **MU-2M** higher-weight variants of the MU-2J and MU-2K respectively, and finally the **MU-2N** and

MU-2P, corresponding to the MU-2L and MU-2M, but with Garrett TPE331-5-252M engines.

In 1965 Mitsubishi established a factory at San Angelo, Texas, to assemble MU-2s for the North American market, but this subsequently became the main assembly and marketing point for worldwide distribution under the name Mitsubishi Aircraft International Inc. Major production later centred on the long-fuselage **Marquise**, with TPE331-10-501M turboprop engines flat-rated to 715 shp (533 kW) and accommodating a crew of two plus seven to nine passengers; and the **Solitaire**.

The executive-aimed Marquise was lengthened and extra cabin room created by housing the undercarriage in sponsons on the side of the fuselage.

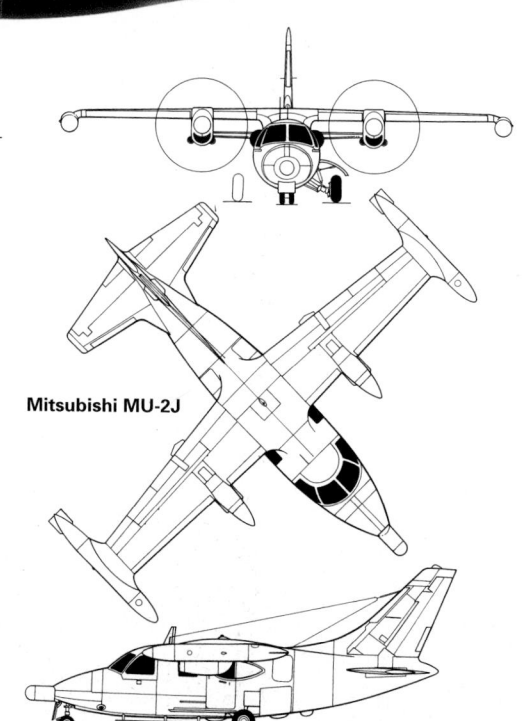

Mitsubishi MU-2J

Mitsubishi MU-2, Marquise and Solitaire (continued)

The Solitare has TPE331-10-501M turboprop engines flat-rated to 665 shp (496 kW) and seats a crew of two plus six or seven passengers. Apart from powerplant, these two versions are basically similar to the earlier MU-2N and MU-2P respectively. By early 1983 total orders for all versions had reached 780, only 50 of which were for customers in Japan.

Military sales of the MU-2 were limited to Japanese forces as a result of a policy towards the export of defence material. A total of 53 MU-2s was delivered to the JASDF and

JGSDF, a number of which remain in service.

Two MU-2 versions were ordered by the JGSDF as the sole fixed-wing assets for the liaison and photo-reconnaissance role. These comprised four MU-2Cs and 16 MU-2Ks. The wingtip tanks on the first MU-2C were removed in favour of an additional fuel tank carried aft of the cabin. Military equipment included one vertical and one swing-type oblique camera for reconnaissance, and the provision for side-looking radar, underwing stores (bombs and rockets), and two 0.5 in (12.7-mm) machine-

guns. Both versions received the service designation **LR-1**.

To serve in the search and rescue role, the JASDF began to acquire MU-2s concurrently. The air force designation **MU-2S** was applied to a version with the Mitsubishi designation MU-2E. First flown on 15 August 1967, this unpressurised variant introduced extensive additional navigation and communications equipment, Doppler search radar in an extended 'thimble' nose radome, bulged observation windows in the fuselage sides below the wing and a port-side

sliding entry door for dropping rafts. The wingtip tanks were enlarged to increase maximum fuel capacity and maximum take-off weight increased to 10,053 lb (4560 kg). Delivery of a batch of 27 began in December 1967,

with a further two aircraft in 1987 after the Mitsubishi production line had closed. In addition, four MU-2Js were delivered to the Hiko Tenkentai (Flight Check Group) of the JASDF at Iruma in 1975-79 for navaid calibration duty.

SPECIFICATION

Mitsubishi International Marquise
Type: twin-turboprop business aircraft
Powerplant: two Garrett TPE331-10-501M turboprops each flat-rated at 715 shp (533 kW)
Performance: maximum cruising speed 355 mph (571 km/h); service ceiling 29,750 ft (9070 m); maximum range 1,605 miles (2583 km)
Weights: empty equipped 7,650 1lb (3470 kg); maximum take-off 11,575 lb (5250 kg)
Dimensions: wingspan 39 ft 2 in (11.94 m); length 39 ft 5 in (12.01 m); height 13 ft 8 in (4.17 m); wing area 178.15 sq ft (16.55 m²)

Mitsubishi MU-300 and Diamond I

In 1977 Mitsubishi designed and built two prototypes of a twin-turbofan business aircraft designated **MU-300**, the first flying on 29 August 1978. A cantilever low-wing monoplane with a pressurised fuselage and retractable tricycle landing gear, the MU-300 was powered by two JT15D-4

turbofan engines, pod mounted one on each side of the rear fuselage. Standard accommodation was provided for a crew of two and seven passengers. At the end of the development programme the prototypes were dismantled and shipped to the USA, where they were reassembled by the

company's US subsidiary Mitsubishi Aircraft International Inc. Redesignated **Diamond I**, the two aircraft were used in the US certification programme, certification being granted on 6 November 1981. Initial customer deliveries began in July 1982 and 62 were built.

An improved version, the **Diamond IA**, fitted with uprated JT15D-4D engines giving overall performance increases, an EFIS cockpit and with maximum take-off weight increased to 16,230 lb (7361 kg), was announced in 1983 and the first of 27 built, distinguished by the extra port side window, was delivered in 1984. With an MTOW

Beech Aircraft Corporation continued to build the Diamond II as the Beechjet 400. Mitsubishi's Diamond II is shown here in prototype form.

SPECIFICATION

Mitsubishi Diamond I
Type: twin-turbofan business aircraft
Powerplant: two 2,500-lb (14.56-kN) thrust Pratt & Whitney Aircraft of Canada JT15D-4 turbofans
Performance: cruising speed 461 mph (741 km/h) at 39,000 ft (11890 m); service ceiling 41,000 ft

(12495 m); range with four passengers 1,750 miles (2817 km)
Weights: empty equipped 9,100 lb (4127 kg); maximum take-off 14,630 lb (6636 kg)
Dimensions: wingspan 43 ft 6 in (13.26 m); length 48 ft 5 in (14.75 m); height 13 ft 9 in (4.19 m); wing area 241.44 sq ft (22.43 m²)

reduced to 15,780 lb (7157 kg), but with extra fuel and more powerful JT15D-5 engines, a further eight aircraft were

produced as the **Diamond II**. However, in December 1985, Mitsubishi sold the manufacturing rights to the Diamond II to Beech.

Monocoupe aircraft

The Monocoupe story began in early 1927, when Don Luscombe designed for Central States Aero Inc. a side-by-side two-seat lightplane of mixed wood and steel-tube basic construction with fabric covering. A braced high-wing monoplane with fixed tailskid landing gear, the aircraft was given the name **Monocoupe** and was powered originally by either a 60-hp (45-kW) Anzani

engine or the unsuccessful 65-hp (48kW) Detroit Air Cat radial. Although about 20 aircraft were sold, it was realised that a better powerplant was needed to develop the full potential of the Monocoupe design, and in 1928 Luscombe joined forces with former car manufacturer W. Velie to establish Mono Aircraft Corporation at Moline, Illinois, and chose to power the Monocoupe with a

62-hp (46-kW) five-cylinder radial engine designed by Velie. Designated **Monocoupe 70**, this combination proved an immediate success and was followed in 1929 by the improved **Monocoupe 113**, with revised landing gear and a number of improvements including introduction of a 65-hp (48-kW) Velie M-5 engine. This powerplant was retained for the generally similar **Monoprep**, a dedicated trainer introduced in the autumn of 1929.

The **Monosport Model 1**, introduced soon after to appeal to the pilot who was interested in air racing, had a 110-hp (82-kW) Warner Scarab seven-cylinder radial engine. Contemporary with this last aircraft was the **Monosport Model 2**, which differed by having a

100-hp (75-kW) Kinner K-5 radial. In 1930 Mono introduced the **Monocoupe 90** with refined lines and a fuselage that was slightly longer and wider, this being sold in Monocoupe 90 and **Monocoupe 90A** versions with a 90-hp (67-kW) Lambert R-266 radial engine; as the **Monocoupe 90 DeLuxe** with the same powerplant, but introducing trailing edge flaps, wheel speed fairings and an improved engine cowling; and as the **Monocoupe 90AF** and **Monocoupe 90AL** with 115-hp (86-kW) Franklin and Avco Lycoming engines respectively. Later in 1930 three more variants of the Monocoupe 90 were available, namely the

Monocoupe 90-J with a 90-hp (67-kW) Warner Scarab Jr engine, the **Monocoupe 110** with a 110-hp (82-kW) Warner Scarab, and the **Monocoupe 125** with a 125-hp (93-kW) Kinner B-5 engine. The depressed state of the country was recognised by the **Monocoupe Model 70-V** of 1932, in which the low-powered 65-hp (48-kW) Velie M-5 engine was re-introduced to provide more economical operation at the cost of a fall in performance. The last of this remarkable line of two-seat aircraft was the **Monocoupe D-145** of 1934, a high-performance version with a slightly

Built in 1941, this Monocoupe 110 remained registered to an owner in Fairfax, Virginia in 2001.

SPECIFICATION

Monocoupe Model 110
Type: two-seat cabin monoplane
Powerplant: one 110-hp (82-kW) Warner Scarab seven-cylinder radial piston engine
Performance: maximum speed 133 mph (214 km/h); service ceiling 16,000 ft (4875 m); range 450 miles

(724 km)
Weights: empty 991 lb (450 kg); maximum take-off 1,611 lb (731 kg)
Dimensions: wingspan 32 ft (9.75 m); length 20 ft 4 in (6.20 m); height 6 ft 11 in (2.11 m); wing area 132.0 sq ft (12.26 m²)

enlarged cabin and powered by a 145-hp (108-kW) Warner Super Scarab engine. No accurate figures exist for production of the Monocoupe but well over 1,000 were built, which was a remarkable sales achievement during a

period which coincided with the economic depression of the early 1930s.

To cater for a different market, Mono flew in 1928 the prototype of a slightly larger four-seat aircraft which was of the same general configuration as the

Monocoupe, and powered initially by a 185-hp (138-kW) Velie L-9 engine. This relatively new engine proved unreliable and, instead, the 220-hp (164-kW) Wright J-5 nine-cylinder radial was adopted for this new

aircraft which was designated as the **Monocoach**. In the following year an 'improved' Monocoach was introduced, but it differed only by having a lighterweight seven-cylinder Wright J-6 engine of 225 hp (168 kW) giving a

44-lb (20-kg) increase in payload. There was little sales demand for the four-seat version, and soon after introduction of the two-seat Monocoupe D-145 the activities of the Mono Aircraft Corporation came to an end.

Mooney aircraft

Al W. Mooney began his career as a designer of lightplanes during the mid-1920s, later joining the Mono Aircraft Corporation, where he made a significant contribution to the success of the Monocoupe line of aircraft. When Mono closed its doors, Mooney had temporary associations with at least two other companies before joining with K. K. Culver to form the Culver Aircraft Corporation, with which Mooney was associated until the end of World War II. In 1946 Mooney designed an exciting singleseat sporting aircraft known as the **Mooney M-18 Mite**, a low-wing cabin monoplane of 26 ft 11 in (8.20 m) span which, powered by a 65-hp (48-kW) Avco Lycoming O-145-B2 engine, had a maximum speed of 138 mph (222 km/h). The designer formed Mooney Aircraft Inc. to build the type, to a total of about 300, produced initially at Wichita, Kansas, and finally at Kerrville, Texas, and the Mite eventually became

available in kit form in the early 1970s for construction by amateurs. Mooney moved into the four-seat market with design of the **M20**, a four-seat cabin monoplane flown in August 1953, which introduced retractable tricycle landing gear and was powered by a 150-hp (112-kW) O-320 engine. The M20 was followed first by the improved **M20A**, before being superseded by the **Mark 21 (M20C)** of all-metal construction and powered by a 180-hp (134-kW) O-360-A1A engine. In 1963 expansion of the Mark 21 range introduced the **Master (M20D)** without retractable landing gear and the **Super 21 (M20E)** with a 200-hp (149-kW) IO-360-A1A engine. In 1967 Mooney acquired Alon Inc., continuing to build the famous **Alon Aircoupe** as the **Mooney A-2A Cadet** and, in the same year, deliveries began of a five-seat pressurised light aircraft known as the **Mustang (M-22)**, powered by a 310-hp (231-kW) TIO-540-A1A

This M20E remained in use in mid 2001, having been manufactured in 1964. Note the distinctive fin and rudder shape of Mooney designs.

engine. In the following year the Mark 21 became known as the **Ranger**, and new extensions of the range included the **Executive 21 (M20F)** and **Statesman (M20G)**, both with a slightly lengthened fuselage to increase leg room. By then the company was running into financial difficulties, trading briefly as Aerostar Aircraft Corporation before being renamed Mooney Aircraft Corporation as a subsidiary of the Republic Steel Corporation. The Ranger then continued in production until 1979, by which time more than 2,000 had been built, being complemented until that time by the **Chaparral**, an updated version of the Super 21, and the **Executive** which was a version of the Ranger with a 200-hp (149-kW) engine.

In 1976 the **Mooney 201 (M20J)** superseded the Executive. The subsequent **Model 201SE (Special Edition)**, was replaced by the **Mooney 205** in 1987, before the **Allegro**, which remained a production variant in 2001, was introduced. The **Turbo Mooney 231 (M20K)**, a turbocharged version of the M20J, which progressed through **231SE** and **231TSE** models to the **Model 252TSE (Turbo**

Special Edition), which led to **N20MK**, of which deliveries began in 1997.

The stretched-fuselage **Model 252 PFM (M20L)** was fitted with a 217-hp (162-kW) Porsche PFM.3200 engine and flew in May 1987, but production terminated in 1991 when porsche discontinued the PFM.3200 engine. The **Model 257TLS (M20M)** TIO-540-AFIA-powered **Turbo Lycoming Sabre** version of the M20L, with increased fuel capacity, higher maximum take-off weight and extra windows, first flew in 1989 and continued in limited production as the **Bravo** into 2001. The last of Mooney's production M20 models are the **M20R Ovation** and **M20S Eagle**. The Ovation became available in 1994 as a baseline aircraft, which led on to the Eagle in 1999. The Ovation is powered by a 300-hp (224-kW) Teledyne Continental IO-550-G5B derated to 280 hp (209 kW), while the Eagle

employs a 235-hp (175-kW) IO-550-G5B. Both aircraft are available with an extensive avionics fit, which can include an EFIS flightdeck.

Mooney has also flown the **M20T Predator** twoseat aerobatic trainer. Based on the Encore wing and using a Bravo fuselage, the Predator was submitted for the USAF's Enhanced Flight Screener programme in 1991, but lost out to the Slingsby Firefly. In 1998, it seemed that the Egyptian air force might order 100 of the type, but little has come of this.

On 21 April 1983 Mooney flew the prototype **M30 Model 301** (originally called the **MX**), a new pressurised six-seat cabin monoplane powered by a 360-hp (270-kW) Lycoming TIO-540-X27 engine, but further development of the type was suspended in 1987 when Mooney joined with SOCATA (to form TBM International of France) to develop the similarly-configured **TBM-700** turboprop.

Mooney's first aircraft, the M-18 Mite proved very popular as a high-performance, single-seat sporting aircraft.

SPECIFICATION	
Mooney M20M Model 257TLS	25,000 ft (7620 m); range with
Type: four-seat cabin monoplane	maximum fuel 1,232 miles
Powerplant: one 270-hp (201-kW)	(1983 km)
Textron Lycoming TIO-540-AFIA	**Weights:** empty 2,012 lb (913 kg);
turbo-charged piston engine	maximum take-off 3,200 lb
Performance: cruising speed at	(1451 kg)
13,000 ft (3960 m) 230 mph	**Dimensions:** wingspan 36 ft 1 in
(371 km/h); maximum speed at	(11 m); length 27 ft (8.20 m); height
25,000 ft (7620 m) 257 mph	8 ft 3 in (2.50 m); wing area
(413 km/h); service ceiling	174.80 sq ft (16.24 m²)

Marked as an 'Advanced Trainer', this aircraft is in fact a standard 1989-vintage Mooney M20J four-seater.

Morane-Saulnier Type AC and Type AE

Developed from the earlier **Type V** via the experimental **Type U**, the **Type AC** was a single-seat shoulderwing monoplane fighter which appeared in the autumn of 1916. Its major

innovation was rigid wing bracing, a truss of steeltube struts supporting each wing from below. A similar concept was employed on the two-seat parasol-wing **Type AE bis**.

The Type AC had a maximum speed of 111 mph (178 km/h) and was powered by a 110-hp (82-kW) Le Rhône 9J or 120-hp (89-kW) Le Rhône 9Jb rotary.

Morane-Saulnier Type AC and Type AE (continued)

The Type AE bis was built purely experimentally however. The wings incorporated ailerons for lateral control, the fuselage being faired to a circular cross section and terminating in an angular tail unit. The single Vickers 0.303-in (7.7-mm) machine-gun was partially enclosed in a humped fairing on the forward decking of the fuselage. The Aéronautique Militaire ordered 30 examples of the Type AC, a number being distributed to operational escadrilles on the Western Front, but two examples bought for the RFC were never flown operationally.

The wingspan of the Type AC was 32 ft 1¾ in (9.80 m).

Morane-Saulnier Type AI

Test-flown in the early summer of 1917, the **Type AI** was a parasol-wing single-seat fighter monoplane contemporary with the unsuccessful **Type AF** biplane. It had a sweptback wing braced by parallel struts, a circular-section fuselage of which the forward part was of metal construction, and its 150-hp (112-kW) Gnome Monosoupape 9NI rotary engine had a beautifully contoured metal cowl which helped to give the little fighter a workman-like appearance.

The first version to enter production had the service designation **MoS.27** and was armed with a 0.303-in (7.7-mm) Vickers with interrupter gear; a version with twin Vickers guns was designated **MoS.29**. Total production of these C.1 category (single-seat fighter) aircraft was 1,210 machines. The type equipped newly-formed French escadrilles MS 156, MS 158 and MS 161 in early 1918, but by mid-May all had been withdrawn as a result of structural and engine problems, which had caused a number of accidents.

A version with the 150-hp (112-kW) Gnome engine and modified wing bracing was produced, but production was concentrated mainly on the **MoS.30**, an E.1 (single-seat advanced trainer) version with either a 120-hp (89-kW) Le Rhône 9Jb or a 135-hp (101-kW) Le Rhône 9Jby rotary engine; a version with a derated 9Jby of 90 hp (67 kW) was designated **MoS.30bis**. Armament was removed and fuel capacity was reduced. The US Army Air Service in France procured 51 MoS.30 trainers, and post-war Belgium bought three, and evaluation aircraft were sold to Japan, the Soviet Union and Switzerland.

Variants

1917 experimental: version with all-wood monocoque fuselage and an integral fin and tailplane
1918 experimental: version with 170-hp (127-kW) Le Rhône rotary; not successful

A number of French army machines was converted as 'penguin' ground trainers with much of their fabric wing covering removed, so that the pilot could handle the controls and taxi around the airfield, thus gaining considerable confidence without being able to take off!

Other Type AIs in several versions were sold to civil pilots. Among renowned aviators who demonstrated their skill with the type at air shows were Nungesser, whose aircraft sported his personal wartime insignia; and Alfred Fronval who, in his orange and blue Morane, looped 1,111 times in 4 hours 56 minutes over Villacoublay aerodrome on 25 February 1928.

SPECIFICATION	
Morane-Saulnier MoS.27	(421 kg); maximum take-off
Type: single-seat parasol monoplane fighter	1,431 lb (649 kg)
Powerplant: one 150-hp (112-kW) Gnome Monosoupape 9N rotary engine	**Dimensions:** wingspan 27 ft 11 in (8.51 m); length 18 ft 6½ in (5.65 m); height 7 ft 10½ in (2.40 m); wing area 144.13 sq ft (13.39 m²)
Performance: maximum speed 140 mph (225 km/h); service ceiling 22,965 ft (7000 m); endurance 1 hour 45 minutes	**Armament:** one forward-firing synchronised 0.303-in (7.7-mm) Vickers machine-gun
Weights: empty equipped 928 lb	

This MoS.27 demonstrates the single machine-gun armament of the variant. Note the neatly cowled engine.

Morane-Saulnier Type BB

Built in 1915 to a British order, the **Type BB** was a compact equal-span reconnaissance biplane, with pilot and observer seated close together in tandem beneath a large cut-out in the trailing edge of the upper wing. The total original order was for 150 aircraft to be powered by the 110-hp (82-kW) Le Rhône rotary engine. In the event, as a result of a shortage of the specified engine, most of the 94 aircraft built were powered by the 80-hp (60-kW) Le Rhône. The **Type BH** variant was distinguished by the large streamlined spinner fitted to its two-bladed propeller.

The 80-hp (60-kW) Type BH equipped No. 60 Squadron, RFC and No. 4 Squadron, RNAS in northern France. Some of the No. 60 Sqn aircraft were flown as fighters, the normal trainably mounted 0.303-in (7.7-mm) Lewis

The Type BB was only a limited success. Its wingspan was 28 ft 4½ in (8.65 m), its maximum take-off weight 1,653 lb (750 kg) and maximum speed 91 mph (147 km/h).

gun being supplemented by another Lewis fixed above the top wing. The 110-hp (82kW) version of the Type BB was operated by No. 1 and No. 3 Squadrons, RFC.

Morane-Saulnier Type G

Developed from the earlier Morane-Saulnier monoplanes, the **Type G** was a two-seat shoulder-wing wire-braced monoplane, with its pilot and passenger seated close together in a single cockpit. The type was built under licence by Grahame-White and flown by many renowned pre-war British and French pilots. An order for 94 Type Gs was received from the French war ministry, and the RFC obtained a number of British-built machines. However, when war broke out in 1914 it was soon found that the Type G had little military application, and surviving aircraft were mostly employed as trainers.

The Type G had a wingspan of 31 ft 7¼ in (9.63 m) and with an 80-hp (60-kW) Gnome rotary engine its maximum speed was 84 mph (135 km/h).

Variants

Type WR: built for the Russian government, this version had an unusual 'glasshouse' built on to the sides of the fuselage forward of the wing
Type G (1915): although bearing the same designation, this type was a single-seat fighter with a fixed 0.315-in (8-mm) Hotchkiss machine-gun fitted with deflector gear; only a few were built for the French Aéronautique Militaire, these being powered by the 80-hp (60-kW) Le Rhône rotary engine

Morane-Saulnier Type BB

In August 1913 Morane-Saulnier modified a Type G by fitting a new wire-braced parasol wing. This was the prototype of the **Type L** which appeared

MORANE PARASOL

Similarly powered to the Type L, the Type LA had slightly improved performance and was normally armed with a single 0.303-in (7.7-mm) machine-gun on a spigot mounting for the observer.

SPECIFICATION

Morane-Saulnier Type L
Type: two-seat reconnaissance aircraft
Powerplant: one 80-hp (60-kW) Gnome or Le Rhône rotary engine
Performance: maximum speed 71 mph (115 km/h); endurance 2 hours

Weights: empty equipped 849 lb (385 kg); maximum take-off 1,444 lb (655 kg)
Dimensions: wingspan 36 ft 9 in (11.20 m); length 22 ft 6¾ in (6.88 m); height 12 ft 10¾ in (3.93 m); wing area 196.99 sq ft (18.30 m²)

in 1914, a frail-looking two-seat reconnaissance or observation aircraft. The Type L had a slab-sided fuselage, a conventional cross-axle landing gear, and a tail unit comprising only a small rudder and an elevator; some late produc-tion aircraft introduced a fixed fin.

The Type L went into production to meet an order for 50 machines from Turkey. At the outbreak of war in August 1914 the Turkish aircraft were requi-sitioned by the French government. Powered by 80-hp (60-kW) Gnome or Le Rhône rotaries, the Type Ls equipped two newly formed escadrilles, MS.23 and MS.26, the latter including the famous Roland Garros among its pilots. In 1914-15 the Type L was often flown as a single-seater, the only armament being a pistol or carbine. Garros conducted experiments with a machine-gun and deflector gear on his Type L, shoot-ing down an enemy aircraft with the aid of this device on 1 April 1915. On 7 June 1915 while flying a Type L single-seater, Flight Sub-Lieutenant Warneford of No. 1 Wing RNAS destroyed the German Army Zeppelin *LZ 37* by dropping small bombs on the envelope and setting it on fire. Most of the 600 plus Type Ls were, however, flown by the French, Russians, and British RFC and RNAS as two-seat reconnaissance aircraft, usually unarmed.

The **Type LA** parasol was a much improved aircraft resulting from a number of refinements, but was essentially an interim design awaiting introduc-tion of the more advanced Type P. Only isolated aircraft were used by the French, but the RFC purchased 24.

Morane-Saulnier Type N

The first **Type N** was flown by Garros at the Aspern, Austria, aviation meeting in July 1914. It had the basic Morane-Saulnier shoulder-wing configuration of the period, but the fuselage was faired to a circular section, and the tail unit incorporated a fixed fin as introduced on late Type Ls. Roland Garros had been captured after being forced down in his Type L during April 1915, and the first military Type N to be seen over the Western Front, flown by Eugène Gilbert of Escadrille MS.23, had the name *Le Vengeur* (the avenger). Other specially developed aircraft, designated **Type Nm** followed, but only a small batch went into service. They intro-duced a revised rear

Among successful French exponents of the Type N were Jean Navarre of Escadrille MS.12 and pre-war aerobatic pilot Adolphe Pégoud of MS.49.

fuselage shape and a modified tail unit.

The Type N was known to the French erroneously as the **Morane Monocoque** and to the British as the **Morane Bullet**. The RFC received 24 of the type after the first French examples had entered service, the type being distributed to several squadrons, the principal operator being No. 6 Sqn. A number also flew with the Imperial Russian Air Service.

SPECIFICATION

Morane-Saulnier Type Nm
Type: single-seat fighter
Powerplant: one 80-hp (60-kW) Le Rhône 9C rotary piston engine
Performance: maximum speed 90 mph (145 km/h)
Weights: empty 635 lb (288 kg); maximum take-off 979 lb (444 kg)

Dimensions: wingspan 26 ft 8¾ in (8.15 m); length 19 ft 1½ in (5.83 m); height 8 ft 2½ in (2.50 m); wing area 118.41 sq ft (11.00 m²)
Armament: one fixed 0.315-in (8-mm) Hotchkiss, or 0.303-in (7.7-mm) Vickers or Lewis machine-gun

Variants

Type I: this had only one major change from the Type Nm, the installation of a 110-hp (82-kW) Le Rhône 9J rotary engine; a few flew briefly with No. 60 Sqn, but the major user was Russia, with a considerable number in service; most successful Russian unit was the XIX Fighter Detachment based at Lusk
Type V: also having the 110-hp Le Rhône engine, this version was modified extensively, with increased wing span and a deeper forward fuselage to accommodate an additional belly fuel tank to provide increased range; 12 were supplied to the RFC and others to Russia

Morane-Saulnier Type P

The two-seat **Type P** para-sol-wing monoplane reconnaissance aircraft of early 1916 introduced a new fully-faired circular-section fuselage and a wing incorporating ailerons and raked wingtips. The 110-hp (82-kW) Le Rhône 9J rotary engine had a contoured horseshoe cowl-ing in early aircraft, but later machines had a full circular cowling. Production of the Type P totalled 565, but although the type was used quite widely by the French Aéronautique Militaire, no French unit was fully equipped with the type. A considerable number went to the RFC, some equip-ping Nos 1 and 3 Sqns in 1916-17. Some RFC aircraft had 80-hp (60-kW) Le Rhône engines.

Armament varied, the observer being armed initially with a Lewis gun on a spigot mounting, but this was replaced later by a ring mounting. Some aircraft had a fixed Lewis gun above the wing firing forward, while others had a synchronised Vickers machine-gun, but all were of 0.303-in (7.7-mm) cali-bre. Two single-seat fighter conversions were tested

The standard two-seat Type P had a wingspan of 36 ft 9 in (11.20 m), a maximum take-off weight of 1,614 lb (732 kg) and reached a maximum speed of 97 mph (156 km/h) with the 110-hp (82-kW) Le Rhône engine.

briefly, one with the wing lowered so that it was braced just above the level of the fuselage.

Morane-Saulnier MS.129 and MS.130

The **MS.129** of 1925 and **MS.130** of 1926 shared many new design features, and both were developed from the earlier **MS.53** trainer. Only relatively few MS.129s were built, some for the Romanian air arm and some for civil use, but production of the success-ful MS.130 totalled 145.

Design features included a new sweptback 'autostable' parasol wing, and the MS.129 was powered by a 180-hp (134-kW) Hispano-Suiza 8Ab V-8 engine, while the MS.130 had a more care-fully contoured fuselage and an uncowled 230-hp (172-kW) Salmson 9Ab.

The MS.130 spanned 35 ft 1¼ in (10.70 m), had a maximum take-off weight of 2,533 lb (1149 kg) and attained a maximum speed of 129 mph (208 km/h).

Morane-Saulnier MS.129 and MS.130 (continued)

Most of the MS.130s were bought by the French navy, and they served at naval air training centres from 1927 to 1935. Private owners and flying clubs bought 26 of the type and others were exported, 15 to Brazil, two going to Belgium and others to China, Guatemala and Turkey. Only a small batch was used by French military aviation.

The second MS.130 prototype was modified in 1929 to take new design landing gear (later fitted to the MS.230), and was entered in that year's Coupe Michelin air race.

Two MS.130s were later converted to MS.230s.

Variants

MS.131: one MS.130 converted to take a 230-hp (172-kW) Lorraine engine; flown by the US military attaché in Paris
MS.132: conversion with 120-hp (89-kW) Salmson 7Ac radial
MS.133: four conversions, one from MS.130 and three from MS.129; most powerful variant with 270-hp (201-kW) Gnome-Rhône 5Kc radial
MS.134: conversion of MS.130 with 80-hp (60-kW) Clerget 9B rotary
MS.136: conversion of MS.130 with 120-hp (89-kW) Salmson 9Ac radial

Morane-Saulnier MS.180, MS.181 and MS.185

The **MS.180**, first flown in 1928, was a small single-seat parasol-wing monoplane intended for sport flying and aerobatics, and was powered by a 40-hp (30-kW) Salmson 9Ad engine. The **MS.181** which appeared in the next year closely resembled the earlier machine, but had a 60-hp (45-kW) Salmson 5Ac radial piston engine. Other improvements included an enlarged rudder and a slimmer fuselage. To achieve greater economy, the company developed the **MS.185** with wings of increased span and rounded tips. This relied on reduced power, having a 46-hp (34-kW) Salmson radial piston engine, and was as successful as the MS.181. Both the MS.181 and MS.185 were built in quantity, a total of

The MS.181 had a wingspan of 29 ft 6¼ in (9.00 m), a maximum take-off weight of 959 lb (435 kg), and a maximum speed of 84 mph (135 km/h). Two MS.181s survived in France at least into the mid 1980s.

over 100 being sold to private owners and civil flying clubs.

Morane-Saulnier MS.225

Essentially a stop-gap fighter, to bolster the Armée de l'Air's flagging escadrilles de chasse pending the arrival of new types under development, the **MS.225** was exhibited in mock-up form at the 1932 Paris Salon de l'Aéronautique. Flight testing of the prototype proved successful and a production order followed.

The M.S.225 C.1 category single-seat fighter had an all-metal structure, and wide-track divided landing gear with faired struts and wheel spats, and was powered by a Gnome-Rhône 9Krsd radial engine. It had a more rounded fuselage and was generally more robust and heavier than its immediate predecessor, the **MS.224.01**, and incorporated the sweptback parasol wing which was a feature of so many Morane-Saulnier types of the period.

In total 75 M.S.225s were built. The last of 55 examples for l'Armée de l'Air was delivered in November 1933, and the French Aéronautique Maritime accepted the first of 16 machines in February 1934. Three aircraft were delivered to China and the famous pilot Detroyat had one MS. 225 as his personal mount, which was flown in numerous air shows and competitions.

The Armée de l'Air MS.225 were phased out of service during 1936-37. The type also equipped the renowned Escadrille 3C1 of the Aéronavale, based at Marignane, but 3C1 was dissolved at the beginning of 1936 and became the 1ère Escadrille of Armée de l'Air Groupe de Chasse II/8, finally giving up its MS.225s in July 1938.

Meanwhile the *Patrouille Acrobatique* flew five MS.225s from 1934 to 1938, and the last Armée de l'Air unit to use the MS.225 was the *Patrouille* of the Ecole de l'Air at Salon de Provence, which received 15 aircraft given up by other units. All were modified for aerobatics, the external difference being the increased height of the vertical tail surfaces. The last great performance of this famous aerobatic team was at Evère, Belgium in 1939. At the outbreak of

Although it was only a stopgap pending the arrival of monoplane fighters, the MS.225 was the first French service fighter with a supercharged engine.

Variants

MS.226: carrier version of late 1933 with deck landing hook under rear fuselage; remained land based at Hyères
MS.226bis: sub-type of MS.226 with folding wings, flown in 1934
MS.227: flew in 1933 as a flying testbed for the Hispano-Suiza 12Xcrs engine of 690 hp (515 kW), driving a four-bladed propeller
MS.275: flown in 1934, this version had modified wings and tail unit, and was powered by a 690-hp (515-kW) Gnome-Rhône 9Krse engine which gave a maximum speed of 216 mph (348 km/h) at 13,125 ft (4000 m); not adopted for production
MS.278: conversion of MS.225 no. 2 for a 520-hp (388-kW) Clerget 14Fos diesel engine powerplant; not successful

war 21 aircraft were still in flying condition, but by the summer of 1940 all had been scrapped.

SPECIFICATION	
Morane-Saulnier MS.225	3,483 lb (1580 kg)
Type: single-seat fighter	**Dimensions:** wingspan 34 ft 7¾ in
Powerplant: one 500-hp (373-kW)	(10.56 m); length 23 ft 9 in
Gnome-Rhône 9Kbrs radial piston	(7.24 m); height 10 ft 9½ in
engine	(3.29 m); wing area 185.15 sq ft
Performance: maximum speed	(17.20 m²)
207 mph (333 km/h) at 13,125 ft	**Armament:** two fixed
(4000 m); service ceiling 31,170 ft	synchronised fuselage-mounted
(9500 m); range 435 miles (700 km)	Vickers 0.303-in (7.7-mm) machine-
Weights: empty equipped 2,683 lb	guns
(1217 kg); maximum take-off	

Morane-Saulnier MS.230

The **MS.230** Et. 2 category two-seat intermediate trainer was the most important French aircraft of this class during the inter-war years. Flown for the first time in prototype form during February 1929, this robust, strut braced parasol-wing monoplane with a

G-AVEB remained on the British civil register until 1996, at which point the aircraft was transferred to the US.

SPECIFICATION	
Morane-Saulnier MS.230	**Weights:** empty equipped 1,828 lb
Type: two-seat intermediate	(829 kg); maximum take-off
trainer	2,535 lb (1150 kg)
Powerplant: one 230-hp (172-kW)	**Dimensions:** wingspan 35 ft 1¼ in
Salmson 9Ab radial piston engine	(10.70 m); length 22 ft 10¾ in
Performance: maximum speed	(6.98 m); height 9 ft 2¼ in (2.80 m);
127 mph (205 km/h); service ceiling	wing area 212.06 sq ft (19.70 m²)
16,405 ft (5000 m)	

circular-section fuselage and wide-track divided landing gear was the result of continuing design development stemming from the Type AR monoplane of World I. The pupil was seated in an open cockpit below a cut-out in the trailing edge of the wing, with the instructor's cockpit immediately behind him.

An initial Aéronautique Militaire order for 500 MS.230s was followed by more military contracts plus others for the French navy, civil flying schools and private owners. Other examples were exported. Morane-Saulnier production was augmented by orders received by SFAN (59) and Levasseur (80), 18 aircraft of the Levasseur 1939 contract being completed post war.
MS.233 and **MS.236**

Variants

MS.229: two examples built for Swiss Fliegertruppen in 1931; similar to MS.230, but with V-8 Hispano-Suiza 8Ac engines; one converted in 1932 to take Wright 9Qa radial
MS.230: over 1,100 built; Romania bought 20 in 1930 and Greece 25 in 1931; Belgium and Brazil purchased nine each; as well as being the main Armée, de l'Air trainer for many years, the type was used by the French navy and a number of well-known private pilots including Louis Dollfus; examples were used for tests with Handley Page slats and with skis; one machine was flown with a Lorraine 9Nb Algol Junior engine
MS.231: six built with 240-hp (179-kW) Lorraine 7Mb engine in 1930
MS.232: experimental version with 200-hp (149-kW) Clerget 9Ca diesel engine, flown briefly during November 1930
MS.233: powered by 230-hp (172-kW) Gnome-Rhône 5Ba or 5Bc radial engine, six built in France and

export versions were built by the OGMA (Portugal) and SABCA (Belgium) concerns respectively.

The type was used for a wide variety of tasks in addition to training, these including liaison, observation, gunnery instruction, target and glider towing,

16 under licence in Portugal for that nation's air arm
MS.234: 250-hp (186-kW) Hispano-Suiza 9Qa engine; two built, one bought for the US ambassador in Paris
MS.234/2: converted from racing version of MS.130, participated in 1931 Coupe Michelin air race; had a 230-hp (172-kW) Hispano-Suiza 9Qb with NACA cowling; in 1933, with 9Qa engine, became redesignated **MS.234 No. 2** and was flown by Michel Detroyat at aerobatic exhibitions in France and the USA up to 1938
MS.235: one built and flown 1930 with a 300-hp (224-kW) Gnome Rhône 7Kb engine
MS.235H: twin-float version of MS.235; flown from Lake Berre 1931
MS.236: Belgian SABCA built 19 examples for the nation's air arm; powered by 215-hp (160-kW) Armstrong-Siddeley Lynx 4C engine; first aircraft flew July 1932
MS.237: five built for private owners; powered by 280-hp (209 kW) Salmson 9Aba engine; first appeared 1934

and aerobatics. In this last role, flown by members of the famous Armée de l'Air central flying school at Etampes, the olive green

and white painted wings of the team's three MS.230s became a familiar sight at pre-war French aviation meetings.

Morane-Saulnier MS.315

Having served its time as a primary trainer, the MS.315 found use as a glider tug. Note the type's uncowled radial engine.

SPECIFICATION

Morane-Saulnier MS.315
Type: two-seat primary trainer
Powerplant: one 135-hp (101-kW) Salmson 9Ne radial piston engine
Performance: maximum speed 106 mph (170 km/h); service ceiling 18,045 ft (5500 m)
Weights: empty equipped 1,208 lb (548 kg); maximum take-off 1,896 lb (860 kg)
Dimensions: wingspan 39 ft 4½ in (12.00 m); length 24 ft 11¼ in (7.60 m); height 9 ft 2¼ in (2.80 m); wing area 232.51 sq ft (21.60 m²)

Developed from the **MS.300** primary trainer prototype of 1930, and its **MS.301** and **MS.302** variants, the **MS.315** flew for the first time in October 1932. Of typically robust parasol high-wing configuration, it was of mixed construction with divided main landing gear. Four prototypes were followed by 346 series aircraft, 33 of them built post-war. In

addition, five higher-powered **MS.315/2** aircraft were built for civil use, plus a single **MS.316** with a Regnier inverted-Vee engine. The type became the workhorse of the French Armée de l'Air and served also with the Aéronavale and various civil flying schools. It was a favourite at many pre-war airshows flown by such notables as Thoret,

Fleurquin and Detroyat.
Between 1960 and 1962, 40 MS.315s then in use as

civil glider tugs were re-engined with the 220-hp (164-kW) war-surplus

Continental W-670K radial piston engine, being redesignated **MS.317**.

Morane-Saulnier MS.340 to MS.345

This MS.342 shows the greater sweepback of the 340 series compared to earlier Morane-Saulnier designs and its inverted inline engine powerplant.

Variants

MS.340: prototype powered by a 120-hp (89-kW) de Havilland Gipsy III engine
MS.341: first aircraft was converted from MS.340; powered by 120-hp (89-kW) Renault 4Pdi engine
MS.341/2: reinforced wing bracing and revised tail unit; four built
MS.341/3: powered by 140-hp (104-kW) Renault 4Pei engine; as well as civil machines, 12 MS.341/3s were bought by l'Armée de l'Air for use as elementary trainers; maximum speed 124 mph (200 km/h) and maximum take-off weight 2,028 lb (920 kg); one of this type was bought by Ethiopia
MS.342: version with 120-hp (89-kW) de Havilland Gipsy Major engine; second aircraft, with glazed cockpit canopy and wheel fairings, built specially for millionaire Louis Gazaniol of Sidi-bel-Abbès, Algeria
MS.343: single example built for famed woman flier Maryse Hilsz; had a 175-hp (130-kW) Salmson 9Nd radial engine
MS.343/2: as MS.343, but with 135-hp (101-kW) Salmson 9Nc radial engine
MS.345: appeared in June 1935; one only with single profiled wing struts and fully faired landing gear; powered by a 140-hp (104-kW) Renault 4Pei, it was owned by a series of wealthy amateur pilots, but no series production was undertaken

The prototype **MS.340**, flown during April 1933, was designed as a touring or training aircraft. It retained

the company's usual parasol-wing monoplane configuration, but introduced 18° of wing sweepback. Of

mixed construction the MS.340 was fabric covered with the exception of the metal engine panels.

Principal production version was the **MS.341** and some 40 aircraft of all versions were built up to 1937.

Two were flown as liaison aircraft by government (anti-Franco) forces in the Spanish Civil War.

Morane-Saulnier MS.406

To meet a French Air Ministry requirement of 1934 for a new single-seat

fighter, Morane-Saulnier designed the **MS.405** low-wing monoplane.

Morane-Saulnier MS.406 (continued)

First flown on 8 August 1935, the MS.405 had a basic all-metal structure and retractable main units for its tailskid landing gear, and was powered by an 860-hp (641-kW) Hispano-Suiza 12Ygrs V-12 engine. The **MS.405-01** and **MS.405-02** prototypes were used for official tests, the latter having a revised wing planform and an Hispano-Suiza 12Ycrs engine, and in early 1937 the company received an order for 15 pre-production MS.405s, and a slightly different version to be designated **MS.406**. An initial order for 50 MS.405s was subsequently changed to cover the same number of MS.406s, and total production of the MS.405 was therefore 17, including the prototypes, about half of which were used for various experimental purposes. Modifications introduced as the result of continued official tests resulted in the designation **MS.406C-1** being applied to the production version, of which 1,000 were ordered in March 1938. This number was beyond the manufacturing capability of Morane-Saulnier, so it was arranged for the type to be built by three divisions of the nationalised aviation industry, and the first production aircraft was flown on 29 January 1939. Generally similar to the MS.405 prototype, the MS.406 differed primarily by having a lightweight wing structure, the Hispano-Suiza 12Y-31

Designed as a culmination of previous fighter experience translated into a monoplane, the MS.405 was an inelegant and underpowered fighter.

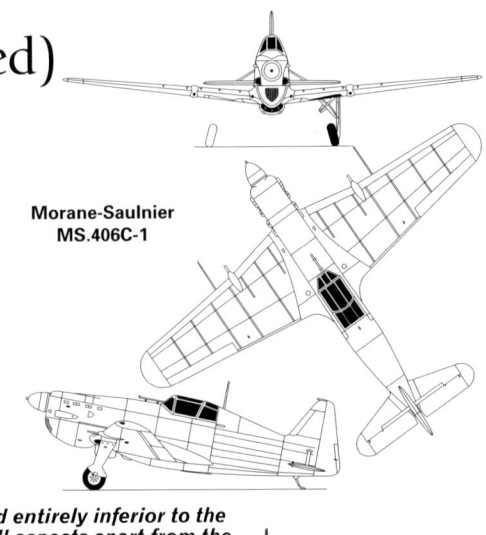

Morane-Saulnier MS.406C-1

engine as standard, and various other detail refinements and changes in equipment.

Meanwhile, Morane-Saulnier was busy with development of the MS.406 and involved with orders for the export market. They included 12 for China, seized by French colonial authorities en route to their destination; 30 which equipped No. 28 Squadron of the Finnish air force; 13 for Lithuania, undelivered because of the outbreak of World War II; 45 for Turkey; and 20 for Yugoslavia, ordered in early 1940 but not delivered. Poland had ordered 160, but although 50 were despatched to Gdynia, none was delivered before the collapse of the Polish resistance. Switzerland acquired two early production MS.406 aircraft as patterns for the licence-construction of 82 **EFW D-3800** fighters by Eidgenössisches Flugzeugwerk. In conjunc-

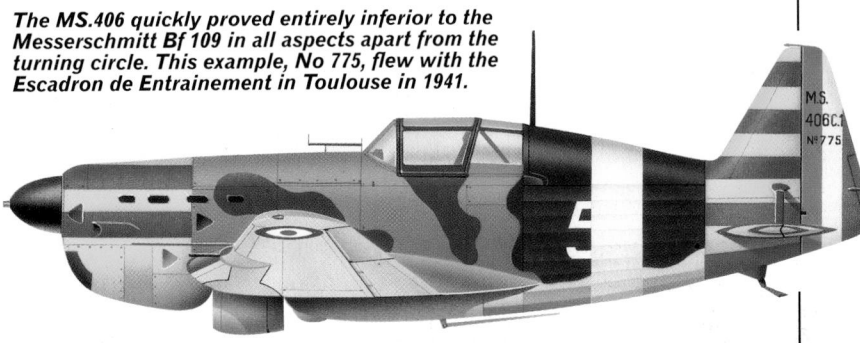

The MS.406 quickly proved entirely inferior to the Messerschmitt Bf 109 in all aspects apart from the turning circle. This example, No 775, flew with the Escadron de Entrainement in Toulouse in 1941.

This MS.406, 'White 9', was flown by 'Pikku-Jätti' (Little Giant) Urho Lehtovaara, the leading Finnish Morane ace, from Viitana in November 1941.

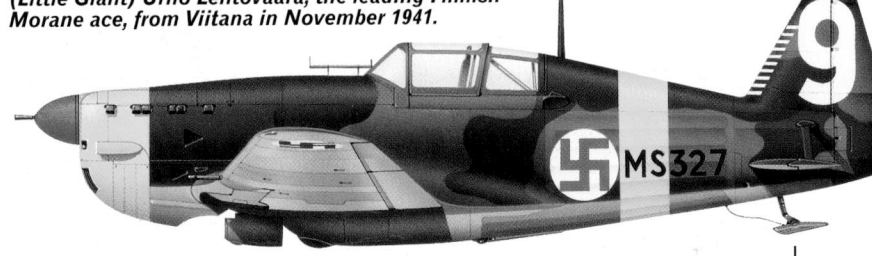

tion with Dornier-Werke AG at Altenrhein, this government factory built 207 examples of a Swiss-developed **D-3801**. The last of the foreign versions were a number of MS.406s which, after the German occupation of Vichy France, were distributed between the Croatian and Finnish air forces. Most of the Finnish aircraft were re-engined subsequently with 1,100-hp

(820-kW) Klimov M-105P engines captured from the Soviets, the resulting improved-performance fighters being known as **Mörkö Moraani**.

Supply problems with the Hispano-Suiza 12Y engine meant that at the outbreak of war only 572 of the planned 1,000 MS.406s had been delivered to the Armée de l'Air, and it was discovered very quickly that

the type was completely outmatched by the German Bf 109E. During a brief operational period MS.406 squadrons were credited with the destruction of 175 enemy aircraft, but this had been achieved for the loss of more than 400 of their own number. After the Franco-German armistice, however, only one Vichy French air force groupe operated these aircraft.

SPECIFICATION	
Morane-Saulnier MS.406	5,445 lb (2470 kg)
Type: single-seat fighter	**Dimensions:** wingspan 34 ft 9¼ in
Powerplant: one 860-hp (641-kW)	(10.60 m); length 26 ft 9 in
Hispano-Suiza 12Y-31 V-12 piston	(8.15 m); height 9 ft 2¼ in (2.80 m);
engine	wing area 172.23 sq ft (16.00 m²)
Performance: maximum speed	**Armament:** one engine-mounted
302 mph (485 km/h) at 16,400 ft	20-mm cannon firing through
(5000 m); service ceiling 30,840 ft	propeller hub and two wing-
(9400 m); range 497 miles (800 km)	mounted 0.295-in (7.5-mm)
Weights: empty 4,189 lb	machine-guns
(1900 kg); maximum take-off	

Morane-Saulnier MS.470 Vanneau

Developed under the Vichy regime by Morane-Saulnier chief designer Gauthier, the **MS.470.01 Vanneau** two-seat advanced trainer

prototype made its first flight on 22 December 1944. Successful tests led to a decision by the Armée de l'Air to buy the Vanneau

(plover) to train its new generation of pilots, and three prototypes of the revised **MS.472** were ordered, **MS.472.01** flying on 12 December 1945. In configuration the MS.470 was an all-metal low-wing cantilever monoplane with pupil and instructor housed under a long glazed canopy. The main landing gear legs retracted inwards to lie partially exposed in the fuselage underside, a feature intended to reduce damage in the event of 'wheels-up' landings. The MS.472 replaced the

SPECIFICATION	
Morane-Saulnier MS.475 Vanneau V	(2351 kg); maximum take-off 6,889 lb (3125 kg)
Type: two-seat basic trainer	**Dimensions:** wingspan 34 ft
Powerplant: one 860-hp (641-kW)	11¼ in (10.65 m); length 29 ft 8¼ in
Hispano-Suiza 12Y 45 V-12 piston	(9.05 m); height 11 ft 10½ in
engine	(3.62 m); wing area 186.22 sq ft
Performance: maximum speed	(17.30 m²)
277 mph (445 km/h); service ceiling	**Armament:** two MAC 1934
27,885 ft (8500 m); range 932 miles	0.295-in (7.5-mm) wing-mounted
(1500 km)	machine-guns, plus two Alkan
Weights: empty equipped 5,183 lb	racks for light bombs

The MS.475 was a significant improvement on its predecessors, having been fitted with an 850-hp (634-kW) V12 Hispano-Suiza engine.

690-hp (515-kW) Hispano-Suiza 12X engine of the MS.470 with a 700-hp (522-kW) Gnome-Rhône 14M radial.

Series MS.472s were delivered from December 1946 onwards, and series **MS.474** aircraft, modified for carrier operations, were delivered to the Aéronavale from December 1947, an MS.472 having been temporarily converted to

serve as the prototype MS.474 in February of that year. Total production of the **MS.472 Vanneau II** and the **MS.474 Vanneau IV** was 230 and 70 respectively. Another series version was the **MS.475 Vanneau V**, the prototype making its maiden flight on 8 August 1947. Production deliveries of the 200 series aircraft to the Armée de l'Air began in March 1950,

the **MS. 475** differed only in detail from its predecessors except for installation of an 850-hp (634-kW) Hispano-Suiza 12Y-45 V-12 engine.

The MS.475 proved superior to its predecessors in manoeuvrability, speed and rate of turn, incorporating a wing of improved design, but a more radical modification with an increase in wing surface

area was incorporated in one production machine, then redesignnated **MS.476.01**. Another MS.475 was re-engined with a SNECMA Renault 12S-02 of 580 hp (433 kW) it became the **MS.477.01**, flown in November 1950. The **MS.478.01** project, to be powered by an Italian Isotta Fraschini Delta engine, was not built, and the last experimental devel-

opment of the Vanneau was MS.472 no. 295 modified as the **MS.479.01** to take a SNECMA 14X Super Mars engine of 820 hp (611 kW). It began its flight test programme in March 1952, but development was soon abandoned. The Vanneau II, IV and V remained in service at training bases of the Armée de l'Air and Aéronavale into the late 1960s.

Morane-Saulnier MS.730, 731, 732 & MS.733 Alcyon

Development of the **MS.733 Alcyon** (Kingfisher) basic trainer began with the **MS.730.01** prototype, which flew for the first time on 11 August 1949. With the original 180-hp (134-kW) Mathis 8G.20 inverted V-8 engine replaced by a 240-hp (179-kW) Argus As 10, the prototype took to the air again in November that year as the **MS.731**. Two **MS.732** prototypes were flight tested in early 1951, each of them powered by a Potez 6D.30 engine and having the previous cantilever fixed landing gear replaced by a new design in which the main units retracted. The first example of the definitive version flew on 16 April 1951 as the **MS.733.01**; five pre-production aircraft followed and series aircraft

The MS.733 Alcyon (Kingfisher) consolidated Morane-Saulnier's reputation as a builder of high-quality training aircraft. The type was employed by both the Armée de l'Air and the Aéronavale, and was also used against rebels in Algeria.

totalled 200; 40 for the French navy, 15 for Cambodia, and the balance for service with the Armée de l'Air as the Alcyon, 70 of them being fitted with machine-gun armament for use as gunnery trainers. In 1956 some of the gunnery trainers were converted for

COIN (counter-insurgency) duties, with machine-gun and anti-personnel bomb armament, for use against the nationalist rebels in Algeria. These aircraft were given the designation **MS.733A**, of which a number were later sold to Morocco.

SPECIFICATION	
Morane-Saulnier MS.733 Alcyon	(920 km)
Type: two/three-seat basic trainer	**Weights:** empty equipped 2,778 lb (1260 kg); maximum take-off 3,682 lb (1670 kg)
Powerplant: one 240-hp (179-kW) Potez 6D.30 inverted inline piston engine	**Dimensions:** wingspan 37 ft (11.28 m); length 30 ft 7 in (9.32 m); height 7 ft 11¼ in (2.42 m); wing area 235.74 sq ft (21.90 m²)
Performance: maximum speed 162 mph (260 km/h); service ceiling 15,750 ft (4800 m); range 572 miles	

Morane-Saulnier MS.760 Paris

In January 1953 Morane-Saulnier flew the prototype **MS.755 Fleuret**, a two-seat jet trainer which competed with the Fouga Magister for an air force order. The Fleuret lost the competition, but its design formed the basis of the **MS.760 Paris** which, designed primarily as a four-seat, side-by-side, high-speed liaison aircraft, can be considered as a forerunner of the executive jet. The first prototype was flown on 29 July 1954, and interest shown by the French military authorities resulted in orders for the air force and navy, the initial production example flying on 27 February 1958. Orders were received for both civil and military use, 48 sets of components being supplied to Argentina for assembly at the government factory in Cordoba, with Brazil acquiring 30 for liaison, photographic survey and training. The initial

Argentina still uses its fleet of ageing MS.760s for liaison, light strike and trainer roles. The aircraft operate from El Plumerillo in north west Argentina.

production version was superseded in 1961 by the **Paris II** with 1,058-lb (4.71-kN) thrust Marboré VI turbojets, and when

production ended in 1964 a total of 165 aircraft of the two series had been built, in addition to those assembled in Argentina.

SPECIFICATION	
Morane-Saulnier MS.760 Paris	range 930 miles (1500 km)
Type: twin-turbojet liaison aircraft	**Weights:** empty 4,280 lb (1945 kg); maximum take-off 7,650 lb (3470 kg)
Powerplant: two 882-lb (3.92-kN) thrust Turbomdca Marboré II turbojets	**Dimensions:** wingspan 33 ft 3 in (10.15 m); length 33 ft (10.05 m); height 8 ft 6 in (2.60 m); wing area 193.69 sq ft (18.00 m²)
Performance: maximum speed 405 mph (650 km/h) at sea level; service ceiling 32,800 ft (10000 m);	

This splendid photograph shows an early MS.760 Paris flying over its namesake, with the Eiffel Tower and Esplanade visible in the background.

Mudry aircraft

Auguste Mudry established Avions Mudry et Cie at Bernay in 1958, initially

operating this company as an extension of his Co-operative des Ateliers

Aéronautiques de la Region Parisienne (CAARP). The activities of these two companies were subsequently combined under the title Avions Mudry,

which accounts for the occasional use of CAARP/Mudry designations. The company's first aircraft was the **CAP 10 B**, a two-seat lightplane with aerobatic

capability suitable for sporting or training use. It is a cantilever low-wing monoplane with a basic structure of wood, and with mixed wood and fabric covering.

Mudry aircraft (continued)

The CAP 10 B is powered in its production version by an Avco Lycoming AEIO-360-B2F flat-four engine. First flown in **CAP 10** prototype form during August 1968 (the CAP 10 B differs by having revised tail surfaces), a total of 284 had been built by mid-1999. Almost half of this number has been for military operators, including the French air force and navy, and the air arms of Mexico. Developed in parallel with the CAP 10 was a single-seat aerobatic version designated **CAP 20**, which was followed by a lighter-weight version **CAP 20L** and available in **CAP 20L-180** and **CAP 20LS-200** variants with Avco Lycoming engines of 180 hp (134 kW) and 200 hp (149 kW) respectively. Construction of the CAP 20L ended in mid-1980 after 12 had been built, the type being superseded by the **CAP 21**, which retained the configuration of the earlier design and its powerplant, but introduced a wing of advanced aerofoil section. The CAP 21 prototype was flown first on 23 June 1980 and initial deliveries of the first batch of 10 production aircraft began in May 1982.

This was followed by a new two-seat basic trainer incorporating some composite materials in its construction, and fitted with a tricycle landing gear. When first flown on

10 September 1982, the **CAP-X** prototype was powered by an 80-hp (60-kW) Mudry Buchoux MB4-80 flat-four engine, but in 1983 was re-engined with a 108-hp (80-kW) Lycoming powerplant, intended for the proposed production version to be designated the **CAP-X Super**. However, only three were built, and although a fourth prototype was planned with a tailwheel undercarriage, there was no further development. An agreement, signed in January 1991 for Sukhoi to build **CAP-X4** fuselages, was suspended early in 1992. In 1985 Mudry announced the **CAP 230**, a CAP 21 re-engined with a 300-hp (224-kW) Lycoming powerplant and fitted with a more angular tail. The prototype CAP 21 was rebuilt to this configuration and flew for the first time on 8 October 1985. The production standard aerobatic version became the **CAP 231**, and the first aircraft flew in April 1990 with certification following in July. Customers for the CAP 231 included the Moroccan Air Force *Marche Verte* aerobatic team. A further improved model, designated **CAP 231 EX** and intended for competition aerobatics, took to the air on 18 December 1991, initially fitted with a 260-hp (164-kW) Barrett engine, but later re-engined with a 300-hp (227-kW) Lycoming

The CAP 10 is used by the Aéronavale for the grading of students before they graduate on to the Epsilon.

AEIO-540.

Inspite of its obvious success, the Mudry concern was declared bankrupt in 1997, its designs being taken over by Akrotech Europe (CAP Aviation from 1999). Production switched to Akrotech on 12 May 1997, that company also beginning production of the **CAP 222**, a version of the American **Giles G-202**. The CAP 222 is a two-seat machine, aimed at aerobatic training and unlimited aerobatic performance duties. The first example was flown on 12 June 1997 and deliveries should commence in the period 2001/02.

In 2001 CAP was also producing the single-seat, 300-hp (224-kW) Textron Lycoming AEIO-540-L1B5-powered **CAP 232**. This unlimited aerobatic mount won both the 1998 and 2000 World Aerobatic Championships having flown for the first time in 1994, and is based on the CAP 231 but with a carbon-fibre wing. CAP has also added a carbon-fibre wing to the **CAP 10 B**, producing the **CAP 10 C**. This machine first flew on 5 March 2001 and should be available for delivery in 2002/03.

SPECIFICATION	
Mudry CAP 10B	range with maximum fuel
Type: two-seat aerobatic lightplane	746 miles (1200 km)
Powerplant: one 180-hp (134-kW) Avco Lycoming AEIO-360-B2F flat-four piston engine	**Weights:** empty equipped 1,900 lb (540 kg); maximum take-off 1,675 lb (760 kg)
Performance: maximum speed 155 mph (250 km/h) at sea level; service ceiling 16,405 ft (5000 m);	**Dimensions:** wingspan 26 ft 5 in (8.06 m); length 23 ft 6 in (7.16 m); height 8 ft 4 in (2.55 m); wing area 116.79 sq ft (10.85 m²)

Myasishchev M-4 'Bison'

Designed as a long-range strategic bomber, the **'Bison'** was always handicapped by its inability to meet a totally unrealistic requirement: that it be capable of attacking targets in North America, which was impossible using the Soviet technology of the time. Myasishchev himself believed that the requirement could only be met by using turboprop engines, or by building a 250-tonne bomber with eight AM-3 engines. Wisely, he produced a superb medium-range bomber with four of these engines, but the political leadership was unhappy with the aircraft and production was limited to about 200 aircraft (despite the fact that it was a better medium bomber than the contemporary Tu-16 'Badger'). One limiting factor was the size of the bomb bay, which was limited in extent because it lay between the main units of the bicycle undercarriage.

There were three basic

To correct airflow problems over the tail and consequently improve stability when carrying outsized loads on the Atlant, the M-4's conventional single tailfin was replaced by a pair of endplate fins on a new dihedral tailplane.

sub-variants of the aircraft, most of which were quickly converted as tankers or reconnaissance platforms. The basic **M-4 'Bison-A'** was a strategic nuclear bomber version powered by four 19,180-lb (85.32-kN) Mikulin AM-3D turbojets in the wingroots (the prototype having podded, underslung engines) and had a short glazed nose and dihedral tailplanes. It could carry its 19,840-lb (9000-kg) warload over a range of about 5,032 miles (8100 km). An inflight-refuelling probe could be fitted above the nose, but was not normally carried. The relocation of the engines from underslung pods necessitated the addition of

small wingtip pods for the undercarriage outriggers, which had previously been housed in the outer engine nacelles. Production aircraft had two overwing fences, located well outboard.

The **3M ('Bison-B')** was powered by the more powerful 24,250-lb (107.90-kN) VD-7 turbojet and introduced an inflight-refuelling probe above the lengthened nose, which had a large radome covering much of the underside, in turn necessitating pro-

vision of an undernose visual bomb-aiming gondola. Dihedral was removed from the

tailplanes and a third (more prominent) fence was added above the wing, which featured a slightly

SPECIFICATION	
Myasishchev 3MS-2 'Bison-B'	ceiling 44,950 ft (13700 m); range
Type: inflight refuelling tanker	7,705 miles (12400 km)
Powerplant: four MNPK 'Soyuz' (Mikulin) RD-3M-500A turbojets each rated at 20,944 lb st (93.20 kN)	**Weights:** empty 166,975 lb (75740 kg); normal take-off 423,280 lb (192000 kg)
Performance: estimated maximum level speed 'clean' at 36,090 ft (11000 m) 620 mph (998 km/h); estimated service	**Dimensions:** wingspan 174 ft 4 in (53.14 m); length 169 ft 7½ in (51.70 m); estimated height 46 ft 3 in (14.10 m); estimated wing area 3,444.56 sq ft (320.00 m²)

Seen here at Zhukovskii, this 'Bison-A' was used as a support aircraft for the VM-T Atlant project. Note the wheel bays located at the tips of the wings.

increased span. Range was increased to 7,457 miles (12000 km), still some 932 miles (1500 km) less than the Tu-95, and 1,864 miles (3000 km) less

than the Tu-95M. The final variant was the **3MD**, which was powered by 20,944-lb st (93.20-kN) VD-7B engines. This had a completely new nose

profile, with a refuelling probe at the tip, and an undernose radome for the 'Puff Ball' radar. This was given the ASCC/NATO reporting name **'Bison-C'**. A related record-breaking aircraft known as the **M-201** or **M-3M** was powered by 28,660-lb (127.49-kN) VD-15B turbojet engines.

'Bison' tankers bore the Russian designation **3MS-2** and were mainly converted 'Bison-Bs'. They are believed to have been re-engined with the 20,944-lb st (93.20-kN) RD-3M-500A turbojet. They refuel probe-equipped receiver aircraft using a centreline hose-drogue unit mounted in the former bomb bay. Some sources suggested that the 'Bison' had been entirely withdrawn from Soviet/CIS service by the early 1990s, and there was a massive,

and heavily publicised, scrapping of aircraft during the late 1980s. Certainly some 40 'Bison-B' and 'Bison-C' airframes were dismantled as part of the superpower strategic arms reduction programme, but at least a handful of Russian tankers remained in use, notably with a regiment based at Engels, long after this. Indeed, Il-78M 'Mainstays' used during the Gulf War were reportedly refuelled by 'Bison' tankers.

Still active as late as 1999, was a pair of 'Bison-Bs' converted to serve as the carriers of outsize loads. Designated **VM-T** and known as **Atlant**, these aircraft carry cargo (mainly components from the Soviet space programme, including the *Buran* shuttle orbiter) on their backs, and have a revised tail arrangement.

Myasishchev M-17 Stratosfera & M-55 Geophysica 'Mystic'

In 1967 Myasishchev was tasked with the production of a high-altitude aircraft capable of destroying CIA reconaissance balloons. The resulting aircraft, known as **Subject 34** and nicknamed *Chaika* (gull, because of its gull wing), was armed with a pair of AAMs and a GSh-23 dorsal turret from the 'Bison'. Little came of this 'fighter' concept, but the basic airframe was adopted as a military high-altitude reconnaissance platform in the mould of the U-2. The aircraft first came to the attention of the West

CCCP-17401 was one of two M-17 Stratosferas built, reportedly using an engine developed from the NK-144 engines used on the Tupolev Tu-144 'Concordski'. NATO gave the type the codename 'Mystic'.

during 1982, when a satellite photographed one at Zhukhovskii, which the West still referred to as Ramenskoye after the

nearby town. The provisional reporting name **'RAM-M'** was allocated. Two of the original **M-17** aircraft were built, each powered by 15,430-lb (68.60-kN) Rybinsk RD-36-51V turbojet. The first aircraft was retired to the museum at Monino, while the second made a series of flights monitoring pollution and examining the ozone layer before going into storage. The M-17 is named **Stratosfera** and known to NATO as **'Mystic-A'**.

A twin-engined derivative, the **M-55 Geofizika 'Mystic-B'** has a slightly

shorter-span wing than the original aircraft, and is powered by a pair of 11,025-lb (49-kN) Perm/Soloviev PS-30-V12 engines. The aircraft has a lengthened fuselage, accommodating a large sensor bay aft of the nose-wheel bay. The M-55 can carry a larger payload (up to 3,307 lb/1500 kg) and has a longer endurance (seven hours) than the M-17. The

sensor package is believed to contain both optical and infra-red sensors (and possibly radar), including an A-84 camera, which covers an area 75 miles (120 km) wide from its operational height of 65,600 ft (20000 m). No series production of either aircraft was undertaken, but Myasishchev continues its attempts to market the machine.

Designed specifically for investigations into the problem of ozone depletion, Geofizika is twin-engined.

SPECIFICATION	
Myasishchev M-17 Stratosfera 'Mystic-A' **Type:** high-altitude reconaissance platform **Powerplant:** one RKBM (Novikov) RD-36-51V turbojet rated at 15,432 lb st (68.65 kN) **Performance:** maximum speed at 65,617 ft (20000 m) 462 mph (743 km/h); service ceiling at	maximum weight 70,700 ft (21550 m); range 817 miles (1315 km) **Weights:** maximum take-off 43,981 lb (19950 kg) **Dimensions:** wingspan 132 ft 3½ in (40.32 m); length 73 ft ¾ in (51.70 m); estimated height 17 ft 3 in (5.25 m); estimated wing area 1,482 sq ft (137.70 m²)

Nakajima A2N (Navy Type 90 Carrier Fighter)

Intended to supersede the **Nakajima A1N1** and **A1N2** licence-built versions of the Gloster Gambet in service, the **NY** prototype first flew in 1930. It was an unequal span single-seat fighter of biplane configuration, with divided fixed landing gear which had spatted wheel

fairings discarded in later production aircraft. Accepted for service in late 1930 as the **Navy Type 90 Carrier Fighter**, the **A2N** was built in several versions. The **A2N1** and **A2N2** had lower wing dihedral only, whereas the **A2N3** had dihedral on both

wings. The twin-gun armament was installed in blast troughs on the lower sides of the fuselage in the A2N1.

The A2N was Japan's first carrier fighter able to meet the world's fighters on equal terms.

Nakajima A2N (Navy Type 90 Carrier Fighter) (cont.)

Later A2N versions had their machine-guns installed in the forward decking. Production totalled 106, built between 1930 and 1935, and later 66 examples of the **A3N1** two-seat training variant appeared, most being conversions of the single-seater. A2Ns from the carrier *Kaga* (2nd Carrier Division) flew on operations in the Shanghai area during the 1937 Sino-Japanese Incident.

SPECIFICATION

Nakajima A2N1
Type: single-seat carrier fighter
Powerplant: one 580-hp (433-kW) Nakajima Kotobuki 2 radial piston engine
Performance: maximum speed 181 mph (292 km/h); service ceiling 29,530 ft (9000 m); range 311 miles (500 km)
Weights: empty 2,304 lb (1045 kg); maximum take-off 3,307 lb (1500 kg)
Dimensions: wingspan 30 ft 9 in (9.37 m); length 20 ft 3¼ in (6.18 m); height 9 ft 11¼ in (3.03 m); wing area 212.49 sq ft (19.74 m²)
Armament: two 0.303-in (7.7-mm) machine-guns

Nakajima's A2N owed much to the Boeing Model 69B naval fighter. An example of the latter, in F2B-1 form, was imported into Japan in 1928.

Nakajima A4N (Navy Type 95 Carrier Fighter)

The 1930s were a busy time for the Nakajima company. A whole series of experimental types appeared, including the **Ki-8** low-wing monoplane two-seat fighter; the **PA** or **Ki-11** low-wing monoplane single-seat fighter, reminiscent of the Boeing P-26; the **Ki-12** low-wing monoplane with retractable landing gear; the **Ki-19** mid-wing twin-engined bomber; the **NAF-1** and

NAF-2 two-seat carrier fighter biplanes; the **Y3B** 7-Shi carrier torpedo-bomber biplane; and the LB-2 private-venture twin-engined long-range navy bomber.

Yet, even in the middle of this innovative period, Nakajima set to work to build a conventional single-seat biplane fighter, the resulting **YM** prototype being an unequal-span biplane of mixed construc-

tion and clearly owing much to the obsolescent A2N. Nevertheless, it was considered essential by the navy until more modern types could be perfected and Nakajima was accordingly authorised to proceed with development of the biplane concept. The resulting **Navy Type 95 Carrier Fighter (A4N1)** had new divided landing gear designed to cope with carrier landings, a tailwheel instead of a tailskid, and other minor changes which

only marginally affected performance by comparison with the earlier fighter, the increase in speed being due entirely to the more powerful Hikari engine. Production totalled 221 between 1935 and 1937.

The A4N1 saw action when fighting with China was renewed in 1937 and gave a good account of itself. By the end of the following year, however, two-thirds of the navy's fighter units had the new Mitsubishi A5M monoplanes, and the A4N1 was soon relegated to training duties.

SPECIFICATION

Nakajima A4N1
Type: single-seat carrier fighter
Powerplant: one 730-hp (544-kW) Nakajima Hikari radial piston engine
Performance: maximum speed 217 mph (350 km/h); service ceiling 25,395 ft (7740 m); range 525 miles (845 km)
Weights: empty equipped 2,813 lb (1276 kg); maximum take-off 3,880 lb (1760 kg)
Dimensions: wingspan 32 ft 9¾ in (10.00 m); length 21 ft 9½ in (6.64 m); height 10 ft ¾ in (3.07 m); wing area 246.39 sq ft (22.89 m²)
Armament: two 0.303-in (7.7-mm) machine-guns, plus provision for up to 265 lb (120 kg) of bombs

During operations over China A4N1s flew with a streamlined drop tank attached to the underside of the port lower wing, near the root, and could also carry lightweight bombs on underwing racks for close-support duties.

Nakajima B5N (Navy Type 97 Carrier Attack Bomber)

To meet an Imperial Japanese Navy requirement of 1935 for a carrier-based attack bomber to supersede the Yokosuka B4Y1, Nakajima submitted its **Type K** prototype. A

cantilever low-wing monoplane with retractable tailwheel landing gear and powered by a 770-hp (574-kW) Nakajima Hikari 3 engine, it was tested in two versions: with Fowler-

type flaps, hydraulic flaps and hydraulic wing folding, and plain flaps and manual wing folding. It was the latter that was ordered into production as the **Navy Type 97 Carrier Attack Bomber Model 1 (Nakajima B5N1)**. This proved effective in the Sino-Japanese War until receipt by the Chinese of more advanced Soviet fighters, then leading to the improved **B5N2** of 1939 with a more powerful engine. As B5N2s replaced B5N1s in service, many of the earlier aircraft were converted for use as advanced trainers under the designation **B5N1-K**. The force of 144 B5N2 bombers included in the initial attack on Pearl Harbor made it clear that the type was better than any comparable aircraft then in service with the Allies; allocated the Allied codename **'Kate'**, the type was also responsible for eliminating the carriers USS *Hornet*, *Lexington* and *Yorktown*. However, by

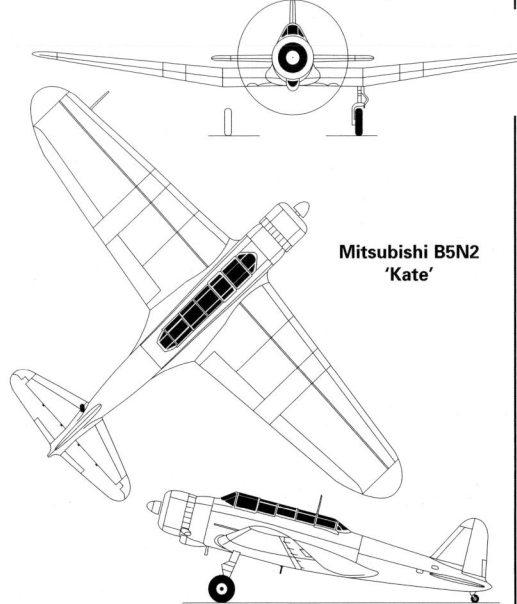

Mitsubishi B5N2 'Kate'

The B5N flew both torpedo- and bomb-attack profiles during the attack of Pearl Harbor. Multiple bombs could be carried on centreline racks.

SPECIFICATION

Nakajima B5N2 'Kate'
Type: three-seat carrier-based torpedo-bomber
Powerplant: one 1,000-hp (746-kW) Nakajima NK1B Sakae radial piston engine
Performance: maximum speed 235 mph (378 km/h); service ceiling 27,100 ft (8260 m); maximum range 1,237 miles (1990 km)
Weights: empty 5,024 lb (2279 kg); maximum take-off 9,039 lb (4100 kg)
Dimensions: wingspan 50 ft 11 in (15.52 m); length 33 ft 9½ in (10.30 m); height 12 ft 1½ in (3.70 m); wing area 405.81 sq ft (37.70 m²)
Armament: one 0.303-in (7.7-mm) machine-gun on a trainable mount in the rear cockpit, plus a bombload of up to 1,764 lb (800 kg), or one torpedo of equivalent weight

1944 the growing capability of Allied fighters resulted in these bombers being withdrawn from first-line service, although they continued to serve effec-

tively in ASW and maritime recce roles. Production totalled 1,149, built by Aichi (200), Nakajima (669) and the navy's Hiro Air Arsenal (280).

Nakajima B6N (Navy Carrier Attack Bomber Tenzan)

To meet an IJN requirement of late 1939 for a carrier-based torpedo-bomber to supersede the B5N, Nakajima used a similar airframe with revised tail surfaces and introduced its own 1,800-hp (1647-kW) NK7A Mamoru 11 radial engine. The first of two prototypes flew in early 1941 and, following some modifications, the type entered production in 1943 as the **Navy Carrier Attack Bomber Tenzan Model 11 (B6N1)**. However, after only 135 Tenzan (heavenly cloud) aircraft had been built, Nakajima was ordered to end production of the Mamoru engine and to substitute the Mitsubishi Kasei, bringing redesignation as the **B6N2**. The **B6N2a** variant differed only

This B6N2 is illustrated as it appeared in IJN service in 1944. The B6N2 was much in evidence in the late-war battles around Okinawa.

by having a rear-firing machine-gun of 0.51-in (13-mm) calibre, and two conversions of this variant produced **B6N3** prototypes with 1,850-hp (1380-kW) Mitsubishi MK4T-C Kasei 25C engines for evaluation as land-based bombers.

Nakajima production of B6N2s totalled 1,133, all versions being allocated the Allied codename **'Jill'**, and these aircraft were used extensively in the last two years of the war, many being expended in *kamikaze* operations.

SPECIFICATION	
Nakajima B6N	(5650 kg)
Type: three-seat carrier-based torpedo-bomber	**Dimensions:** wingspan 48 ft 10½ in (14.90 m); length 35 ft 8 in (10.87 m); height 12 ft 5½ in (3.80 m); wing area 400.43 sq ft (37.20 m²)
Powerplant: one 1,850-hp (1380-kW) Mitsubishi MK4T Kasei 25 radial piston engine	
Performance: maximum speed 298 mph (480 km/h); service ceiling 29,660 ft (9040 m); maximum range 1,892 miles (3045 km)	**Armament:** two 0.303-in (7.7-mm) machine-guns, one rear-firing and one firing through a ventral tunnel, plus a bombload of 1,764 lb (800 kg), or a torpedo of equivalent weight
Weights: empty 6,636 lb (3010 kg) maximum take-off 12,456 lb	

Nakajima C6N (Carrier Reconnaissance Plane Saiun)

After early experience in the Pacific war showing the need for a long-range carrier-based reconnaissance aircraft, Nakajima was instructed in early 1942 to develop an aircraft to meet this Imperial IJN requirement. It resulted in an airframe similar to that of the B6N, the fuselage incorporating camera ports and observation windows, with power provided by a 1,820-hp (1358-kW) Nakajima Homare 11 radial engine. The first prototype flew on 15 May 1943, its performance being disappointing with the Homare 11 engine, and 18 more prototype/pre-series aircraft followed, some with the more powerful Homare 21 engine, before the type was ordered into production in early 1944 as the **Navy Carrier Reconnaissance Plane Saiun (C6N1)**. Allocated the Allied codename **'Myrt'** when it entered service in the summer of 1944, the Saiun (painted cloud) was

This C6N1 was tested in the US. A C6N1 shot down at 05.40 on 15 August 1945 was the last confirmed air-to-air kill of the war.

fast enough to enjoy almost complete immunity from interception by Allied fighters. A total of 463 had been built when production ended in August 1945, the total including a small number of **C6N1-S** two-seat night-fighter conversions from C6N1 aircraft, and one **C6N2** prototype with a 1,980-hp (1476-kW) Homare turbocharged engine.

SPECIFICATION	
Nakajima C6N1	**Weights:** empty 6,543 lb (2968 kg); maximum take-off 11,596 lb (5260 kg)
Type: three-seat carrier-based reconnaissance aircraft	
Powerplant: one 1,990-hp (1484-kW) Nakajima NK911 Homare 21 radial piston engine	**Dimensions:** wingspan 41 ft (12.50 m); length 36 ft 1 in (11.00 m); height 12 ft 11½ in (3.95 m); wing area 274.49 sq ft (25.50 m²)
Performance: maximum speed 379 mph (610 km/h) at 20,015 ft (6100 m); service ceiling 35,235 ft (10740 m); maximum range 3,299 miles (5310 km)	**Armament:** one rear-firing 0.31-in (7.92-mm) machine-gun on a trainable mount

Nakajima E8N (Navy Type 95 Reconnaissance Seaplane)

Designed to replace the company's **E4N2** floatplane in navy service, Nakajima's **MS** submission was basically an updated version of the E4N2. Of similar biplane configuration, with a central float and underwing stabilising floats, it was powered by a 580-hp (433-kW) Kotobuki 2 KAI 1 radial engine, and differed from its predecessor primarily by having revised wings and tail unit. Seven prototypes were tested from March 1934 and, following evaluation against competing aircraft from Aichi and Kawanishi, the MS was ordered into production in October 1935 as the **Navy Type 95 Reconnaissance**

SPECIFICATION	
Nakajima E8N2	(1320 kg); maximum take-off 4,189 lb (1900 kg)
Type: two-seat reconnaissance floatplane	
Powerplant: one 630-hp (470-kW) Nakajima Kotobuki 2 KAI 2 radial piston engine	**Dimensions:** wingspan 36 ft ¼ in (10.98 m); length 28 ft 10¾ in (8.81 m); height 12 ft 7¼ in (3.84 m); wing area 285.25 sq ft (26.50 m²)
Performance: maximum speed 186 mph (300 km/h) at 9,845 ft (3000 m); service ceiling 23,860 ft (7270 m); range 559 miles (900 km)	**Armament:** two 0.303-in (7.7-mm) machine-guns, one forward- and one rear-firing, plus two 66-lb (30-kg) bombs
Weights: empty 2,910 lb	

Having seen widespread service aboard IJN ships in the immediate pre-war years, the E8N survived into the first stages of World War II.

Seaplane Model 1 (E8N1). An **E8N2** with improved equipment and a more powerful engine was introduced before production ended in 1940, when a combined total of 755 had been built by Nakajima (707) and Kawanishi (48). Used successfully during the Sino-Japanese War in roles which included artillery spotting and dive-bombing as well as reconnaissance, some were still operating from navy vessels at the beginning of the Pacific war, gaining the Allied codename **'Dave'**. They were soon diverted to second-line duties such as communications, liaison and training.

Nakajima G8N

Developed as the **Experimental 18-Shi**

Heavy Bomber Renzan (G8N1), this was a very advanced long-range bomber powered by four 2,000-hp (1491-kW) Homare 24 radials which gave it a maximum speed of 368 mph (592 km/h) at 26,245 ft (8000 m). Maximum range was 4,639 miles (7465 km). Armament consisted of six 20-mm cannon in twin power-operated dorsal, ventral and tail turrets, supplemented by machine-gun armament.

Nakajima G8N (continued)

The machine gun armament consisted of two 0.51-in (13-mm) machine-guns in a power-operated nose turret, and single machine-guns of similar calibre in port and starboard beam positions. A maximum bombload of 8,818 lb (4000 kg) could be carried over short ranges. Four prototypes were built up to June 1945, but the proposed production programme was disrupted by Allied bombing and was abandoned when the navy's role became defensive rather than offensive. These prototypes were allocated the Allied code-name **'Rita'**.

The Japanese were considering the production of an all-steel variant of the G8N at the close of the war.

Nakajima J1N

An Imperial Japanese Navy requirement for a long-range escort fighter, to accompany bombers making attacks deep in Chinese territory, led to the **J1N1** prototype, first flown during May 1941. A cantilever low-wing monoplane with retractable tailwheel landing gear, it was powered by two wing-mounted Nakajima Sakae 21 and 22 counter-rotating engines and accommo-dated a crew of three. Armament comprised a 20 mm cannon and six 0.303-in (7.7-mm) machine-guns. Early tests showed that the J1N1 was suited to the escort fighter role, and the type was developed instead for long-range reconnaissance under the designation **J1N1-G** This version differed by having two Sakae 21 engines, armament comprising a single rear-firing machine-gun of 0.51-in (13-mm) calibre, and reduced internal fuel capacity, but with provision for external drop tanks. Following completion of service trials by seven prototypes, this version was ordered into production as the **Navy Type 2 Reconnaissance Plane**, the designation being changed subsequently to **J1N1-R**. Some of these aircraft later had the rear-firing machine-gun replaced by a 20-mm cannon, and were redesignated **J1N1-K**. In early 1943 it was suggested that the aircraft might have potential as a nightfighter, one being converted to two seat configuration for operational evaluation and armed with four 20-mm cannon mounted obliquely in pairs in dorsal and ventral positions. Following the destruction of B-24 Liberators by this aircraft, further conversions were made under the designation **J1N1-C KAI** and a production version was ordered as the **J1N1-S Gekko** (moonlight); some of them carried a small searchlight in the nose and late production aircraft had an early form of AI radar. Designation **J1N1-Sa** was applied to night-fighters with the downward-firing and ineffective cannon deleted; some, without searchlight or radar, had an extra nose-mounted cannon.

Production of all versions of the J1N by Nakajima totalled 479, and in early operations when confronting the comparatively slow B-24s, the Gekko night-fighter proved an effective weapon; against the faster and more-heavily armed B-29 Superfortress it was far less conclusive. All versions had the Allied codename **'Irving'**, and many were used in *kamikaze* operations during the closing stage of the war.

SPECIFICATION

Nakajima J1N1-S
Type: two-seat night-fighter
Powerplant: two 1,130-hp (843-kW) Nakajima Sakae 21 radial piston engines
Performance: maximum speed 315 mph (507 km/h) at 19,030 ft (5800 m); service ceiling 30,580 ft (9320 m); maximum range 2,348 miles (3780 km)
Weights: empty 10,692 lb (4850 kg); maximum take-off 18,045 lb (8185 kg)
Dimensions: wingspan 55 ft 8¼ in (16.98 m); length 41 ft 10¾ in (12.77 m); height 13 ft 1½ in (3.99 m); wing area 430.57 sq ft (40.00 m²)
Armament: four 20-mm cannon, in obliquely-mounted upward-and-downward-firing pairs

Armed with upward-firing cannon, the Gekko proved moderately useful as a night-fighter.

Nakajima Ki-4 (Army Type 94 Reconnaissance Aircraft)

Extensively test-flown in 1934, the **Ki-4** sesquiplane had divided landing gear with streamlined wheel spats, and accommodated pilot and observer in tandem open cockpits, and the pilot just below a cut-out in the trailing edge of the upper wing. The Ki-4 went into production and service in 1935 as the **Army Type 94 Reconnaissance Aircraft Model 2,** which dispensed with the wheel fairings and had a redesigned tail unit. Production continued for several years, some aircraft being licence built by Tachikawa among the total of 516.

The Type 94 was used widely in China by the Japanese army on direct co-operation duties, in close support of the ground forces. It was armed with up to four 0.303-in (7.7-mm) machine-guns and could carry 110 lb (50 kg) of light

Powered by a 640-hp (477-kW) Ha-8 radial engine, the Type 94 could attain a speed of 186 mph (300 km/h). Its wingspan was 39 ft 4 in (12.00 m) and its maximum take-off weight 5,511 lb (2500 kg).

bombs. A number were still in service in the supply and liaison role in 1941. The Japanese army tested two Ki-4 aircraft as seaplanes, one with twin floats and the other with one main and two stabilising floats. A landplane was used for flotation bag tests to check buoyancy in the event of an emergency put-down on water.

Nakajima Ki-27 (Army Type 97 Fighter)

Nakajima had initiated as a private venture the design of an advanced single-seat low-wing monoplane fighter which it identified as the **PE**. When, in mid-1935, the Imperial Japanese Army instructed Nakajima to design an aircraft of this class for competitive evaluation, the resulting **Ki-27** prototype was generally similar to the PE prototype, but incorporated some improvements that resulted from early tests. Two prototypes and ten pre-production aircraft were used for service evaluation, the pre-production Ki-27s having increased wingspan and the cockpit enclosed by a sliding canopy. In this latter form the type was ordered into production in late 1937 as the **Army Type 97 Fighter Model A (Ki-27a)**. When production ended in 1942 a total of 3,399 had been built, 2,020

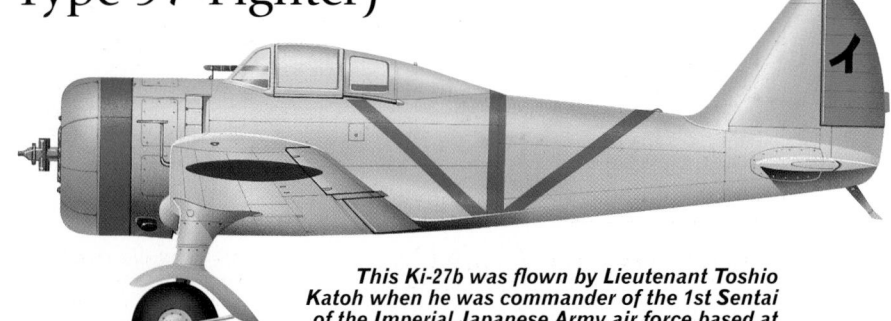

This Ki-27b was flown by Lieutenant Toshio Katoh when he was commander of the 1st Sentai of the Imperial Japanese Army air force based at Kagamigahara in June 1939.

by Nakajima and 1,379 by Mansyu, the only variants being the slightly improved late production **Ki-27b**, and two lighter-weight experimental **Ki-27 KAI** aircraft, from which no series construction resulted. These fighters proved effective and reliable in service, and were deployed initially over northern China in March 1938. Here they were able to maintain air superiority until introduction of the Soviet Polikarpov I-16. Ki-27s took part in the invasion of Burma, Malaya, the Netherlands, East Indies and the Philippines, being allocated the Allied codename '**Nate**' (initially '**Abdul**' in the China-Burma-India theatre). They were most effective against the Allies in the early stages of the war, until confronted by more modern fighters, when they were transferred for air defence of the home islands until 1943, and then used increasingly as advanced trainers, with *kamikaze* operations their final role.

SPECIFICATION	
Nakajima Ki-27a	
Type: single-seat fighter	**Weights:** empty 2,447 lb (1110 kg); maximum take-off 3,946 lb (1790 kg)
Powerplant: one 710-hp (529-kW) Nakajima Ha-1b radial piston engine	**Dimensions:** wingspan 37 ft 1½ in (11.31 m); length 24 ft 8½ in (7.53 m); height 10 ft 8 in (3.25 m); wing area 199.68 sq ft (18.55 m²)
Performance: maximum speed 292 mph (470 km/h) at 11,485 ft (3500 m); service ceiling 40,190 ft (12250 m); range 389 miles (625 km)	**Armament:** two 0.303-in (7.7-mm) forward-firing machine-guns

Nakajima Ki-34 (AT-2 and L1N1)

Nakajima acquired from Douglas Aircraft in the USA licence-construction rights for the DC-2 civil transport. In 1935 a smaller twin-engined light transport, based on the configuration of the DC-2, was designed by Nakajima under the designation **AT-1**; this was not built, but redesign resulted in an improved **AT-2** with two 580-hp (433-kW) Nakajima Kotobuki 2-1 radial engines, and this was flown in prototype form on 12 September 1936. Extensive tests were followed by an order for 32 production AT-2s to equip Greater Japan Airlines and Manchurian Airlines, and in early 1937 the type was adopted also by the IJA under the designation **Army Type 97 Transport (Ki-34)**. Production of these three crew/eight passenger military transports totalled 318,19 being built by Nakajima and 299 by Tachikawa. Some of this total was transferred by the army for navy use, and these aircraft were redesignated **Navy Type AT-2**

SPECIFICATION	
Nakajima Ki-34/L1N1 and production AT-2	(1200 km)
Type: short-range light transport	**Weights:** empty 7,716 lb (3500 kg); maximum take-off 11,574 lb (5,250 kg)
Powerplant: two 710-hp (529-kW) Kotobuki 41 radial piston engines	**Dimensions:** wingspan 65 ft (19.81 m); length 59 ft 2¼ in (15.30 m); height 13 ft 7½ in (4.15 m); wing area 529.60 sq ft (49.20 m²)
Performance: maximum speed 224 mph (360 km/h) at 11,025 ft (3360 m); service ceiling 22,965 ft (7000 m); range 746 miles	

Pre-war airline use of the basic AT-2 airliner proved the type for use by the IJA and IJN during World War II.

Transport (L1N1). Both civil and military versions were allocated the Allied codename '**Thora**', and were in use throughout the Pacific war.

Nakajima Ki-43 (Army Type 1 Fighter Hayabusa)

Design and development of a more advanced fighter to supersede the Ki-27 was started by Nakajima in December 1937, the first of three **Ki-43** prototypes flying during January 1939. A cantilever low-wing monoplane with retractable tailwheel landing gear, the Ki-43 seated its pilot in an enclosed cockpit, and power was provided by a 975-hp (727-kW) Nakajima Sakae Ha-25 supercharged radial engine. Testing of the prototypes revealed poor manoeuvrability, and the 10 pre-production aircraft that followed were of lower basic weight and introduced a wing of increased area that incorporated manoeuvring or 'combat' flaps. This configuration proved good enough for the type to be ordered into production as the **Army Type 1 Fighter Model 1A Hayabusa (Ki-43-1a)**, the type enjoying considerable success in the early stages of the Pacific war. With the advent of more effective Allied fighters, improved **Ki-43-II** prototypes were flown with the higher powered Nakajima Ha-115 engine; introducing armour and self-sealing tanks, and with wingspan reduced, this version duly entered production as the **Ki-43-IIa**. The final variant of the Hayabusa (peregrine falcon) series was the **Ki-43-III**, but only prototypes had been built before the Pacific war ended. By then production totalled 5,919 these being built by Nakajima (3,239), Tachikawa (2,631), and the 1st Army Air Arsenal (49), all receiving the Allied codename '**Oscar**'. The Hayabusa saw operational service throughout the entire Pacific war, its final deployment being for the defence of Tokyo or in *kamikaze* attacks on the approaching Allies.

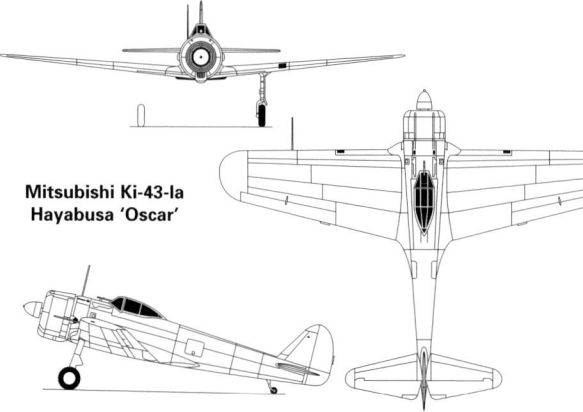

Mitsubishi Ki-43-Ia Hayabusa 'Oscar'

SPECIFICATION	
Nakajima Ki-43-IIb	(1910 kg); maximum take-off 5,710 lb (2590 kg)
Type: single-seat fighter/fighter-bomber	**Dimensions:** wingspan 35 ft 6¾ in (10.84 m); length 29 ft 3¼ in (8.92 m); height 10 ft 8¾ in (3.27 m); wing area 230.36 sq ft (21.40 m²)
Powerplant: one 1,150-hp (858-kW) Nakajima Ha-115 radial piston engine	**Armament:** two 0.50-in (12.5-mm) forward-firing machine-guns, plus two underwing racks each able to carry a 551-lb (250-kg) bomb
Performance: maximum speed 329 mph (530 km/h) at 13,125 ft (4000 m); service ceiling 36,745 ft (11200 m); maximum range 1,988 miles (3200 km)	
Weights: empty 4,211 lb	

Variants

Ki-43-Ia: initial production version, armed with two forward-firing 0.303-in (7.7-mm) machine-guns and with two 33-lb (15-kg) bombs carried externally
Ki-43-Ib: as Ki-43-Ia but with one machine-gun replaced by one of 0.5-in (12.7-mm) calibre
Ki-43-Ic: as Ki-43-Ia, but with both machine-guns of 0.5-in (12.7-mm) calibre
Ki-43-II: five prototypes of an improved version with armour, self-sealing tanks and the Ha-115 engine
Ki-43-IIa: initial Ki-43-II production version with machine-guns as Ki-43-Ic and two underwing racks each to carry a 551-lb (250-kg) bomb
Ki-43-IIb: generally as Ki-43-IIa but with minor equipment changes
Ki-43-II KAI: version combining progressive modifications of Ki-43-IIa and Ki-43-IIb
Ki-43IIIa: ten prototypes, generally as Ki-43-II KAI, but with an Ha-115-II engine developing greater power at altitude
Ki-43-IIIb: two interceptor fighter prototypes, with the 1,250-hp (932-kW) Mitsubishi Ha-112 engine, forward firing armament of two 20-mm cannon, and underwing racks as for the Ki-43-IIa

Entering the war in the Pacific at a very early stage, the Ki-43 came as a complete shock to the Allied powers and easily outclassed Allied fighters.

Nakajima Ki-44 (Army Type 2 Single-seat Fighter Shoki)

Nakajima designed and developed at much the same time as the Ki-43 Hayabusa a high-performance interceptor which, with maximum speed and rate of climb having specification priority, was powered by a 1,250-hp (932-kW) Nakajima Ha-41 radial piston engine. Otherwise of similar configuration to the Ki-43, the new **Ki-44** prototype was flown for the first time during August 1940 and with a satisfactory conclusion to service testing was ordered into production as the **Army Type 2 Single-seat Fighter Model 1A Shoki** (**Ki-44-1a**). The high landing speeds and limited manoeuvrability of the Ki-44 Shoki (devil-queller), which had a comparatively high wing loading for its day, made it unpopular initially with service pilots. However, increased experience in handling the aircraft and its undoubted capability as an interceptor ensured that unpopularity turned eventually to respect. When production ended in late 1944 a total of 1,225 aircraft of all versions had been built by Nakajima, including prototypes, and they

were deployed primarily in defence of the home islands against Allied air

attack. All Ki-44 Shoki versions had the Allied codename **'Tojo'**.

Variants

Ki-44: prototype and pre-production aircraft with armament of two 0.303-in (7.7-mm) and two 0.50-in (12.7-mm) machine-guns
Ki-44-Ia: initial production, version, generally similar to Ki-44
Ki-44-Ib: as Ki-44-Ia except for armament of four 0.50-in (12.7-mm) guns
Ki-44-Ic: as Ki-44-Ib but with modified mainwheel fairings
Ki-44-II: prototype and pre-production aircraft with the more powerful Ha-109 engine
Ki-44-IIa: initial Ki-44-II production version; armament as Ki-44-Ia
Ki-44-IIb: major production version; armament as Ki-44-Ib
Ki-44-IIc: Ki-44-II production version; armament of four 20-mm cannon, or two 40-mm cannon and two 0.50-in (12.7-mm) machine-guns
Ki-44-IIIa: production version with 2,000-hp (1491-kW) Nakajima Ha-145 radial engine and armament of four 20-mm cannon
Ki-44-IIIb: final production version, as Ki-44-IIIa, but with two 20-mm and two 37-mm cannon

SPECIFICATION

Nakajima Ki-44-IIb
Type: single-seat interceptor fighter
Powerplant: one 1,520-hp (1133-kW) Nakajima Ha-109 radial piston engine
Performance: maximum speed 376 mph (605 km/h) at 17,060 ft (5200 m); service ceiling 36,745 ft (11200 m); maximum range 1,056 miles (1700 km)
Weights: empty 4,641 lb (2105 kg); maximum take-off 6,603 lb (2995 kg)
Dimensions: wingspan 31 ft (9.45 m); length 28 ft 10½ in (8.80 m); height 10 ft 8 in (3.25 m); wing area 161.46 sq ft (15.00 m²)
Armament: four forward-firing 0.5-in (12.7-mm) machine-guns

Mitsubishi Ki-44-IIa Shoki 'Tojo'

Thanks to its impressive rate of climb, the Ki-44 took a leading role in the defence of the Japanese home islands against American B-29s.

Nakajima Ki-49 (Army Type 100 Heavy Bomber Donryu)

Designed to supersede the Mitsubishi Ki-21 bomber which had entered service in 1938, the **Ki-49** was required to have the performance capability to operate without a need for fighter escort. A cantilever mid-wing monoplane powered initially by two 950-hp (708-kW) Nakajima Ha-5 KAI radial engines, the eight-crew Ki-49 prototype was flown for the first time during August 1939. The second and third prototypes and seven pre-production aircraft had 1,250-hp (932-kW) Nakajima Ha-41 engines, which were used to power the initial production **Army Type 100 Heavy Bomber Model 1 Donryu (Ki-49-I)**, which was ordered into production in March 1941. The first of these aircraft entered operational service in the autumn of that year and, following initial deployment in China, became involved in the Pacific war in the New Guinea area and in attacks on Australia. Such utilisation made it clear that the Donryu (storm dragon) was underpowered, either bombload or speed suffering as a result, and in the spring of 1942 two **Ki-49-II** prototypes were flown

with more powerful Ha-109 engines, improved armour and self-sealing fuel tanks. This entered production as the **Ki-49-IIa**, which carried the same armament as the production Ki-49-I and was produced also in **Ki-49-IIb** form with a change in armament, three 0.303-in (7.7-mm) machine-guns being replaced by three of 0.50-in (12.7-mm) calibre.

Even then performance was inadequate when the Ki-49 was confronted by more advanced Allied fighters, leading to the **Ki-49-III** with the 2,420-hp (1805-kW) Nakajima Ha-117 engine, but only six prototypes had been built when production was terminated in December 1944. The inability of the Ki-49 to fulfil its intended role meant that in the later

Wearing brown and green camouflage, this Ki-49-I was based in China early in 1944.

Mitsubishi Ki-49-II Donryu 'Helen'

SPECIFICATION

Nakajima Ki-49-IIa
Type: heavy bomber
Powerplant: two 1,500-hp (1119-kW) Nakajima Ha-109 radial engines
Performance: maximum speed 306 mph (492 km/h) at 16,405 ft (5000 m); service ceiling 30,150 ft (9300 m); maximum range 1,833 miles (2950 km)
Weights: empty 14,396 lb (6530 kg); maximum take-off 25,133 lb (11400 kg)
Dimensions: wingspan 67 ft (20.42 m); length 54 ft 1½ in (16.50 m); height 13 ft 11¼ in (4.25 m); wing area 743.27 sq ft (69.05 m²)
Armament: one 20-mm cannon and five 0.303-in (7.7-mm) machine-guns, plus a maximum bombload of 2,205 lb (1000 kg)

stages of the Pacific war the type was deployed on such duties as anti-submarine patrol, troop transport and, in the closing phase, for *kamikaze* attacks. The number built by Nakajima was 769, plus 50 by Tachikawa, Nakajima's total including three **Ki-58** prototypes of an intended escort fighter version with Ha-109 engines, and two **Ki-80** prototypes, a variant intended to serve as a lead aircraft, or pathfinder. All versions of the Ki-49 were allocated the Allied codename '**Helen**'.

Nakajima Ki-84 (Army Type 4 Fighter Hayate)

Introduction into service, during the summer of 1944, of the **Ki-84 Hayate** (gale) single-seat interceptor fighter/fighter-bomber came too late for the IJA. Had it been available earlier and in large numbers this excellent fighter might well have posed serious problems for the Allies, for it had a higher rate of climb and better manoeuvrability than the North American P-51D Mustang or the Republic P-47N Thunderbolt operating in the Pacific zone. Its design had started in early 1942, successful testing of the two Ki-84 prototypes leading to 83 service trials and 42 pre-production aircraft. High-priority full-scale production began in late 1943 under the official designation **Army Type 4 Fighter Model 1A Hayate (Ki-84-Ia)**, sharing with the trials/pre-production aircraft an armament of two 0.50-in (12.7-mm) machine-guns and two wing-mounted 20-mm cannon. Subsequent production versions included the Ki-84-Ib with the machine-guns replaced by two 20-mm cannon, the **Ki-84-Ic** with an armament of two 20-mm and two 30-mm cannon, and the **Ki-84-II** which introduced wood into the airframe structure to conserve light alloys and which was in service with either **Ki-84-Ib** or **Ki-84-Ic** armament. Allocated the Allied codename '**Frank**', the Ki-84 was deployed extensively from the end of 1944, and when production ended a total of 3,514 had been built, including 94 by Mansyu. The grand total also included three **Ki-106** prototypes of all-wood construction, and a single **Ki-113** with a maximum content of steel in its structure, these four prototypes being built to show significant savings in light alloys. The final variant was the single **Ki-116**, a conversion by Mansyu from a standard **Ki-84-Ia**, introducing a lighterweight powerplant, the 1,500-hp (1119-kW) Mitsubishi Ha-33 radial.

The Japanese were building underground production lines for the Ki-84 at the end of World War II.

SPECIFICATION	
Nakajima Ki-84-Ia **Type:** single-seat interceptor fighter/fighter-bomber **Powerplant:** one 1,900-hp (1416-kW) Nakajima Ha-45 radial piston engine **Performance:** maximum speed 392 mph (631 km/h) at 20,080 ft (6120 m); service ceiling 34,350 ft (10500 m); maximum range 1,347 miles (2168 km) **Weights:** empty 5,864 lb	(2660 kg); maximum take-off 8,576 lb (3890 kg) **Dimensions:** wingspan 36 ft 10½ in (11.24 m); length 32 ft 6½ in (9.92 m); height 11 ft 1½ in (3.39 m); wing area 226.05 sq ft (21.00 m²) **Armament:** two 0.5-in (12.7-mm) machine-guns and two 20-mm cannon, plus underwing racks for two 551-lb (250-kg) bombs

Nakajima Ki-115

In January 1945 Nakajima was ordered by the IJA to design and develop, as quickly as possible, a basic aircraft that could carry a bomb of up to 1,764-lb (800-kg) weight for use in *kamikaze* attacks. The resulting **Ki-115** low-wing monoplane prototype was of mixed construction, powered by an Ha-35 radial engine and had welded steel-tube main landing gear units, without any form of shock absorption, which were intended to be jettisoned after take-off on a *kamikaze* mission. Flight tests showed that ground handling was unacceptable in this configuration, leading to the introduction of main landing gear units with simple shock absorbers. In this form, and incorporating some minor modifications, the aircraft entered production as the **Ki-115a Tsurugi** (sabre). However, Nakajima had built only 104 production aircraft by the time the war ended, and none of these was used operationally.

SPECIFICATION	
Nakajima Ki-115a Tsurugi **Type:** single-seat suicide attack aircraft **Powerplant:** one 1,130-hp (843kW) Nakajima Ha-35 radial engine **Performance:** maximum speed 342 mph (550 km/h) at 9,185 ft (2800 m); range 746 miles (1200 km)	**Weights:** empty 3,616 lb (1640 kg); maximum take-off 6,439 lb (2880 kg) **Dimensions:** wingspan 28 ft 2½ in (8.60 m); length 28 ft ½ in (8.55 m); height 10 ft 10 in (3.30 m); wing area 133.48 sq ft (12.40 m²) **Armament:** one bomb of up to 1,764 lb (800 kg) carried semi-recessed beneath the fuselage

The Tsurugi was designed to be expended on its only mission.

Nakajima NC (Army Type 91 Fighter)

A Japanese army requirement of 1927 for a new single-seat fighter was contested by Nakajima, Kawasaki and Mitsubishi. All the designs were parasol-wing monoplanes developed in Japan by teams wholly or partly led by Europeans, in the case of Nakajima the French engineers Mary and Robin.

Introduced from 1932 onwards, the Type 91s were deployed in action with the four squadrons of the 11th Air Battalion operating with the army Kanto Command in Manchuria against the Chinese.

Structural failure of the Mitsubishi prototype led to severe testing of the survivors, which were then also eliminated. The Nakajima prototype, company designation **NC**, had a slim tapering monocoque fuselage, an uncowled Jupiter radial engine, and elaborate strut bracing connecting the wings, fuselage and wide-track landing gear. Nakajima persevered with the design and built six more prototypes, the last of the series being tested extensively by the Japanese army and accepted for production as the **Army Type 91 Fighter Model 1**. Retaining the same basic configuration as the NC prototype, this was virtually a redesign which resulted in a considerably refined airframe. Production of the Type 91 terminated in 1934 with the 450th aircraft; of these 22 were **Army Type 91 Fighter Model 2** aircraft with modified engine cowlings. A Type 91 was converted for carrier operations and with spatted wheel fairings was submitted for the navy 7-Shi experimental fighter competition, but was rejected. The only other modification from standard army configuration was the use of a three-bladed propeller.

SPECIFICATION	
Nakajima NC **Type:** single-seat air-superiority fighter **Powerplant:** one 580-hp (433-kW) Nakajima Kotobuki 2 radial piston engine **Performance:** maximum speed 186 mph (300 km/h); service ceiling 29,530 ft (9000 m); range 311 miles (500 km)	**Weights:** empty equipped 2,370 lb (1075 kg); maximum take-off 3,307 lb (1500 kg) **Dimensions:** wingspan 36 ft 1 in (11.00 m); length 23 ft 11½ in (7.30 m); height 9 ft 10 in (3.00 m); wing area 215.29 sq ft (20.00 m²) **Armament:** two 0.303-in (7.7-mm) machine-guns

NAMC YS-11

The JASDF bases its YS-11E trainers with the Sotai Sireibu Hiko-tai's Densi-sen Sien-tai (ECM Support Unit) at Iruma AB. The unit began to equip with YS-11Es on 29 January 1977 and uses its aircraft to provide ECM and EW training for ground-based radar sites. One of the YS-11Es was modified to YS-11EL Elint configuration in December 1983.

In 1956 six major Japanese aviation companies, namely Fuji, Kawasaki, Mitsubishi, Nippi, Shin Meiwa and Showa, set to work on the collaborative design of a medium-size airliner under the aegis of an umbrella organisation they established as the Transport Aircraft Development Association (TADA). In 1957 the Japanese government agreed to contribute to the project's funding, and in recognition of this fact TADA was supplanted in 1959 by NAMC – the Nihon Aeroplane Manufacturing Company. The first of two **YS-11** prototypes flew on 30 August 1962 with two Dart RDa.10 Mk 542 turboprops each driving a four-bladed propeller. The type found a ready but limited market with Japanese and some export airlines, and production ended in 1974 after the delivery of 182 aircraft.

The **YS-11A-100** was the initial model, and the 48 such aircraft included two **YS-11A-103/105** passenger transports delivered to the Japan Air Self Defence Force in 1965-66 with the designation **YS-11P** for the VIP transport role, though the aircraft were later converted for the flight check role; and two **YS-11A-113** personnel/freight transports delivered to the Japan Maritime Self Defence Force in 1970 with the **YS-11M** designation.

The **YS-11A-200** was the second production model with a 2,970-lb (1350-kg) increase in payload to 14,559 lb (6604 kg). Production totalled 92 aircraft, and two were delivered as **YS-11A-218** troop transports to the JASDF and six as **YS-11A-206** transports to the JMSDF which later converted four of the aircraft (as well as two **YS-11A-600** aircraft bought in 1970-74 after manufacture as a higher-weight version of the YS-11A-100) into **YS-11T-A** ASW train-

ers with surface-search radar, ESM and several other ASW systems. In 1971 the JASDF acquired a **YS-11A-213** surplus to airline requirement for conversion as the sole **YS-11FC** navaid calibration machine. Other military operators of the YS-11A-200 were Greece and the Philippines, which took six and four such aircraft respectively.

The **YS-11A-300** was the third production model, and was a mixed freight and passenger transport with accommodation for 48 passengers in the front of the fuselage and freight loaded into the rear of the fuselage via a large port-side door.

Production totalled 16 aircraft, and two **YS-11A-305** aircraft were delivered to the JASDF in 1968 as personnel/freight transports with the **YS-11PC** designation. The fourth production model was the **YS-11A-400** freighter with a maximum payload of 15,906 lb (7215 kg). Production totalled nine aircraft, and of these seven were **YS-11A-402** aircraft that entered JASDF service in 1969-70 with the **YS-11C** designation and two were **YS-11A-404** aircraft that

entered JMSDF service in 1971-73 with the **YS-11M-A** designation. One of the YS-11C aircraft was converted into the sole **YS-11NT** navigation trainer in 1977. In 1971 the JASDF bought another three YS-11A-402 aircraft for conversion to electronic warfare standards. The first two machines were adapted to **YS-11E** standard as ECM trainers, with one machine further modified during 1976-77, and the third became the sole **YS-11EL** in 1983 after

conversion for Elint duties.

In the later 1980s the JASDF converted several of its existing YS-11A transports. One machine was fitted with the J/ALQ-7 jamming system and more powerful General Electric T64 turboprop engines to offset the weight of this electronic installation; two were adapted as navaid calibration aircraft with Litton avionics; two were converted as VIP transport aircraft; and three were adapted for the Elint role with the J/ALR-2 system.

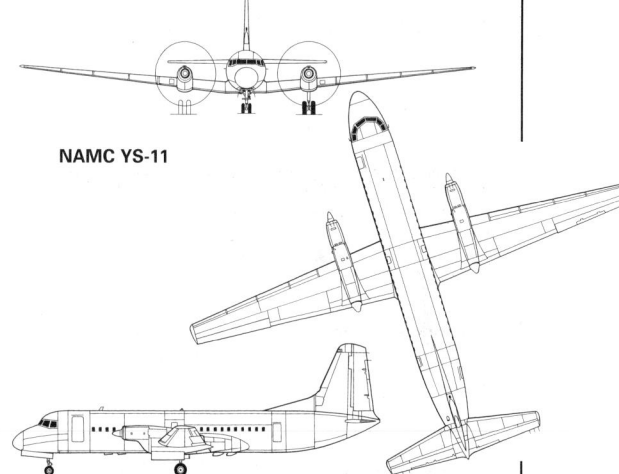

NAMC YS-11

SPECIFICATION

NAMC YS-11A-300
Type: two-crew short/medium-range medium transport
Powerplant: two Rolls-Royce Dart RDa.10/1 Mk 542-10K turboprop engines each rated at 3,060 ehp (2282 ekW)
Performance: maximum cruising speed 291 mph (469 km/h) at 15,000 ft (4570 m); economical cruising speed 281 mph (452 km/h) at 20,000 ft (6095 m); initial climb rate 1,220 ft (372 m) per minute; service ceiling 22,900 ft (6980 m);

range 677 miles (1090 km) with maximum payload
Weights: empty 34,854 lb (15810 kg); maximum take-off 54,012 lb (24500 kg)
Dimensions: wingspan 104 ft 11¾ in (32.00 m); length 86 ft 3½ in (26.30 m); height 29 ft 5½ in (8.98 m); wing area 1,020.45 sq ft (94.80 m²)
Payload: up to 60 passengers or 13,602 lb (6170 kg) of freight carried in the cabin

NAMC K-8 Karakorum 8

Development of the **K-8** began in 1986, building on long-standing defence/aerospace co-operation between China and Pakistan. Originally designated **L-8**, and named after the **Karakorum** mountain range which divides China and Pakistan, the new trainer was developed to meet the requirements of China's Peoples' Army Air Force (as a CJ-5/CJ-6 and JJ-5 replacement) and the Pakistan Air Force (as a T-37 and JJ-5 replacement) and to be suitable for export to nations requiring a cheap jet trainer.

The aircraft was initially a private venture by the China National Aero Technology Import and Export Corporation (CATIC), the Nanchang Aircraft

Manufacturing Company (NAMC) and the state-owned Pakistan Aeronautical Complex at Kamra, although Chinese state funding was quickly forthcoming. Under the terms of the agreement PAC took a 25 per cent workshare, including sole responsibility for production of the the horizontal tail.

Because development began while China still enjoyed cordial relations with the USA, the aircraft was designed with high US content (partly with an eye to future export sales), and thus became subject to delays and embargoes after the Tienanmen Square massacre. Designed by a Nanchang team, the K-8 was required to demonstrate benign handling over

a wide performance envelope, and this was achieved by using an unswept laminar flow wing which gave a stalling speed of only 103 mph (165 km/h) and an operating Mach limit of 0.8. Good low-speed handling characteristics, with predictable, conventional stall/spin behaviour, were held to be of prime importance, and NAMC co-operated with Aermacchi in tunnel testing the design.

Ruggedness is another crucial quality in a trainer, and NAMC designed the K-8 to have a fatigue life of 8,000 flying hours (equivalent to a 20-year life) with operating load limits of +7.33 to -3g. Five prototypes were ordered, the second being a non-flying structural test specimen.

The first prototype made its initial flight on 21 November 1990, making further flights before the official first flight on 11 January 1991.

The aircraft is of conventional configuration, with a low-mounted, tapered wing. The fuselage has simple side-mounted vertical 'letterbox' intakes with fixed splitter plates feeding the engine. Garrett reportedly supplied four TFE731 turbofans for the flight-test programme. Chinese K-8s may, however, be powered by a cheaper engine, the 3,792-lb st (16.87-kN) Progress/ZMKB AI-25 TL being the preferred choice, although the 4,852-lb st (21.60-kN) Progress/ZMK DV-2 turbofan may still be used.

More powerful versions of the TFE731 have been considered for hot-and-high

export versions of the K-8, for a dedicated weapons trainer and even for a JPATS contender.

For weapons training or light strike duties, the K-8 has an indigenous weapons sight providing gun, bomb and rocketry modes. The aircraft has four underwing pylons, with a GSh-23-2 23-mm cannon pod carried on the centreline.

The K-8's tandem cockpits are slightly stepped to provide a compromise between instructor's forward view and low drag, and are covered by a single-piece sideways-hinging canopy and one-piece wrap-around windscreen. Inside the cockpit is a pair of Martin-Baker Mk CN10LW lightweight zero-zero rocket-powered ejection seats, which were tested in the UK using a K-8 forward fuselage section. Production K-8s for China may well feature conventional analog instruments and Chinese avionics, but the prototypes, and aircraft for export customers and Pakistan, are equipped to the latest standards with a GEC Avionics HUD and a Rockwell-Collins EFIS-86(T)5.

Three basic versions of the K-8 have been produced, the TFE731-powered basic K-8, the **K-8J** for the Chinese home market and the one-off **K-8SVA** variable-stability testbed. Interest in the aircraft has been expressed by Bangladesh, Eritrea, Iran, Laos, Libya, Myanmar, Sri Lanka and Yemen. By 2000 six pre-production aircraft were in service with China and six with Pakistan, while the last of 12 aircraft for Myanmar was delivered in 1999. In addition, the Namibian air force received four aircraft, while Zambia took eight

and in January 2000 the Egyptian air force signed for 80 aircraft to be designated **K-8E**. Pakistan has stated a requirement for up to 100 K-8s, while China is likely to require several hundred K-8Js.

The K-8's TFE731 turbofan features digital electronic fuel control, and has remarkably carefree handling characteristics, allowing student pilots to 'throttle slam' with relative impunity.

SPECIFICATION

NAMC K-8 Karakorum 8
Type: tandem two-seat basic trainer and light attack aircraft
Powerplant: one Honeywell TFE731-2A-2A turbofan rated at 3,600 lb st (16.01 kN)
Performance: maximum level speed 497 mph (800 km/h) at sea level; maximum climb rate 5,905 ft (1800 m) per minute at sea level; service ceiling 44,620 ft (13600 m); range 969 miles (1560 km) with maximum internal fuel
Weights: empty equipped 6,078 lb (2757 kg); maximum take-off 9,550 lb (4332 kg)
Dimensions: wingspan 31 ft 7¼ in (9.63 m); length 38 ft ¾ in (11.60 m) including probe; height 13 ft 9¾ in (8.98 m); wing area 183.20 sq ft (17.02 m²)
Armament: up to 2,080 lb (943 kg) of external stores including PL-7 AAMs and a range of 25-, 110- or 551-lb (11.50-, 50- or 250-kg) bombs, 2¼-in (57-mm) rocket pods or BL755 CBUs

NAMC Q-5 and A-5 'Fantan'

The **Q-5 'Fantan'** is a dedicated attack aircraft loosely based on the airframe of the J-6, the Chinese-built MiG-19. Development of the aircraft began in August 1958, and it would be easy to overstate the relationship of the Q-5 to the MiG-19, the new aircraft actually sharing only the rear fuselage and main landing gear of the latter with a new and longer fuselage, area-ruled to reduce transonic drag. The fuselage also accommodates an internal weapons bay 13 ft 1½ in (4.00 m) long with two adjacent fuselage pylons. The new fuselage has a conical nose, giving an improved view forward and downward and providing a potential location for an attack radar that never materialised. The Q-5 was also given a wing of greater area and reduced sweep for more lift and better turn performance. The tailplane was increased in size to improve longitudinal stability. This also necessitated the provision of lateral air intakes. The nosewheel was redesigned to rotate through 90° as it retracted to lie flat in the underside of the fuselage.

Prototype construction began in May 1960, but was abandoned during the political turmoil of the early 1960s and reinstated by stages, first as a 'spare-time venture' but then resumed full-time in 1963 because of the progress made. The prototype finally made its maiden flight on 4 June 1965, but extensive modifications proved necessary to solve problems encountered with the hydraulics, brakes, fuel and weapons system. Two new prototypes flew in October 1969 and the type was ordered into production during 1970 as the Q-5, of which nearly 1,000 were completed for the Chinese forces in four variants.

There is a dedicated nuclear-capable version of the Q-5, but little is known about this variant, which may retain the internal bomb bay for the carriage of one 5- to 20-kt weapon. An extended-range variant was certificated as the **Q-5I** in 1983. This has a fuel

tank in place of the internal weapons bay, modified landing gear, relocated brake chute fairing at the base of the fin, two additional underfuselage hardpoints, the new Type I rocket-powered ejection seat, and the WP-6 Series 6 engine. These modifications brought about a 1,102-lb (500-kg) increase in warload and a 35 per cent increase in low-level radius of action. Some Q-5Is were modified to serve with the Chinese naval air force as carriers for the C-801 anti-ship missile or torpedoes.

The **Q-5IA** was certificated for production in 1985 with two more underwing hardpoints, pressure refuelling, a new gun/bomb sight system and new defensive avionics. Forty examples were delivered to North Korea. The **Q-5II** was basically the Q-5IA revised with an RWR. The **A-5C** is the export version of the

Q-5IA for Pakistan (52 aircraft) but later ordered by Bangladesh and Burma (24 aircraft each) and in fact entered production before the domestic variant. Known in Pakistan as the **A-5-III**, the A-5C has substantially improved avionics, compatibility with various Western weapons including the AIM-9 Sidewinder, and the Martin Baker Mk 10L ejection seat.

Upgrades with Western avionics resulted in prototypes of the **Q-5K** and **A-5M** with French and Italian systems respectively, but no production or retrofit programmes resulted. In 1998 the Nanchang Aircraft Manufacturing Company (NAMC) was renamed as the Hongdu Aviation Industry Group (HAIG), a manufacturer's name under which the Q-5 and A-5 series is now sometimes listed.

SPECIFICATION

Nanchang Q-5 IA 'Fantan'
Type: single-seat close air support and ground-attack warplane
Powerplant: two Liming (LM) (previously Shenyang) Wopen-6A turbojet engines each rated at 6,614 lb st (29.42 kN) dry and 8,267 lb st (36.78 kN) with afterburning
Performance: maximum speed 740 mph (1190 km/h) or Mach 1.12 at 36,090 ft (11000 m); maximum rate of climb 20,275 ft (6180 m) per minute with afterburning thrust at 16,405 ft (5000 m); service ceiling 52,000 ft (15850 m); combat radius 249 miles (400 km) on a lo-lo-lo mission with maximum external stores and no afterburning
Weights: empty 14,054 lb (6375 kg); maximum take-off
38,812 lb (11830 kg)
Dimensions: wingspan 31 ft 9 in (9.68 m); length 51 ft 4¼ in (15.65 m) including probe; height 14 ft 2¾ in (4.33 m); wing area 300.86 sq ft (27.95 m²)
Armament: two 23-mm Type 23-2K fixed forward-firing cannon in the leading edges of the wing roots, plus up to 4,409 lb (2000 kg) of disposable stores carried on four underfuselage and six underwing hardpoints, and generally comprising PL-2, PL-3, PL-5 or PL-7 short-range AAMs, 1,102-, 551- and 220-lb (500-, 250- and 100-kg) bombs, cluster bombs, and multiple launchers for 3.54- and 2.17-in (90- and 55-mm) air-to-surface unguided rockets

This Pakistani A-5 demonstrates both the type's distinctive airbrake configuration and the dedicated Sidewinder rails used on PAF 'Fantans'.

Nardi F.N.305

Founded in Milan by the brothers Euste, Elio and Luigi Nardi, the partnership Fratelli Nardi built its first aircraft in 1934-45. The prototype **F.N.305** made its maiden flight on 19 February 1935. A cantilever low-wing monoplane of mixed construction, with inward retracting main landing gear legs, it was intended for intermediate training, sport or touring, and was to become available in both single and two-seat versions. A two-seater prototype with an enclosed canopy over the cockpit, and powered by a 200-hp (149-kW) Fiat A.70S radial piston engine, attained a maximum speed of

211 mph (340 km/h). Two more prototypes followed, also powered by the Fiat radial piston engine, comprising a single-seat fighter trainer and a two-seat basic trainer, both with open cockpits. Two long-range **F.N.305D** variants were then built, each powered by a 200-hp (149-kW) Walter Bora radial piston engine. The first was a two-seater which made a remarkable nonstop flight from Rome to Addis Ababa, Ethiopia, in March 1939, gaining a record for aircraft in its class and covering 2,773.68 miles (4463.80 km) at an average of 149 mph (240 km/h). The second machine, the **F.N.305D II**, was a single-seat aircraft bought by Yugoslavia for an abortive nonstop North Atlantic flight. Finally, a prototype was tested with an Alfa-Romeo 115 piston

engine, and it was this **F.N.305A** version which was put into production at the Piaggio works, the Nardi workshops not being large enough for the task.

To meet Italian air ministry orders a total of 258 series F.N.305s was built by Piaggio, nearly all of them two-seat F.N.305A aircraft which were used as fighter trainers and for liaison by the Regia Aeronautica.

Nardi F.N.305 (continued)

Small numbers of the single-seat **F.N.305B** and **F.N.305C** were included in the total, the former having an open cockpit and the latter an enclosed canopy. Production was concentrated largely between 1937 and 1943, although eight partly built machines were completed by the

Piaggio works in 1948. F.N.305A series aircraft resembled the Alfa Romeo-powered prototype except for a redesigned canopy.

In the period 1937-1940, F.N.305s took part in many contests and rallies for sport and touring aircraft, frequently carrying off the prizes and gaining for the

Nardi company much favourable publicity; as a result, considerable export orders were received. In 1938 Chile acquired nine machines and Romania 31, the latter country then following this up with licence-manufacture by the IAR company at Brasov, which built a total of 124 F.N.305s, the type becoming the standard Romanian basic/intermediate trainer. Romanian-built aircraft were powered by the IAR 6G-1 engine, a licence-built

version of the de Havilland Gipsy Six engine. Romania subsequently obtained 21 F.N.305s from the sixth production series, acquired in lieu of a planned purchase of SIAI S.83 transports which had been rejected by the Romanian government. The largest

export order, for 300 aircraft, was received from the French authorities, but only 41 had been delivered to the Armée de l'Air when Italy declared war on France in June 1940.

The final foreign purchaser was Hungary with a 50-aircraft order.

A fast two-seat light cabin monoplane, the Nardi F.N.305 initially combined a 200-hp (149-kW) Fiat radial engine with retractable landing gear.

SPECIFICATION

Nakajima F.N.305A
Type: two-seat fighter trainer and liaison aircraft
Powerplant: one 185-hp (138-kW) Alfa Romeo 115 inline piston engine
Performance: maximum speed 186 mph (300 km/h); service ceiling 19,685 ft (6000 m); range 385 miles (620 km)
Weights: empty equipped 1,552 lb (704 kg); maximum take-off 2,169 lb (984 kg)
Dimensions: wingspan 27 ft 9½ in (8.47 m); length 22 ft 10¾ in (6.98 m); height 6 ft 10¾ in (2.10 m); wing area 129.17 sq ft (12.00 m²)
Armament: (when fitted) one or two synchronised 0.303-in (7.7-mm) machine-guns

Nardi F.N.333 Riviera

The **F.N.333** amphibian flying-boat prototype appeared in September 1952, a luxury tourer of cantilever high-wing monoplane configuration with the cabin mounted on the forward part of a single-step hull. Stabilisation on the water was provided by a pair of floats which retracted into the wingtips, and two slender booms extended aft from the wings to mount a tail unit with twin vertical surfaces. Of all-metal construction,

the F.N.333 prototype was powered by a 145-hp (108-kW) Continental engine mounted behind the cabin and driving a pusher propeller.

Three development aircraft were built by Nardi, the last being the **F.N.333S Riviera** definitive production prototype, but as Nardi did not have the space for quantity production, a series of 30 F.N.333S amphibians was built by SIAI Savoia-Marchetti at Somma Lombardo and

The standard 250-hp (186-kW) Continental IO-470-P engine enabled the Riviera to attain a maximum speed of 177 mph (285 km/h).

Vergiate. The first production aircraft was test flown from Lake Maggiore in 1960, this version differing from the prototype in having a revised tail unit, a more commodious four-seat cabin, and waterproof doors for all three units of the wheel landing gear. Wingspan was 34 ft 1½ in (10.40 m) and maximum take-off

weight 3,274 lb (1485 kg). Most of the 30 series aircraft that had been

built when production ended were sold in the United States.

NASA/Rockwell Shuttle Orbiter

NASA/Rockwell's **Shuttle Orbiter** spacecraft takes off from Earth as a rocket and manoeuvres in orbit as a spacecraft. After re-entry into Earth's atmosphere it is controlled and brought in to an unpowered landing in the mode of a conventional fixed-wing aircraft. In configuration it is a cantilever low-wing monoplane of double-delta wing planform, with a large-volume fuselage of conventional construction, vertical tail surfaces only, and retractable tricycle landing gear. The **Space Shuttle** takes off vertically under the power of three Rocketdyne main propul-

sion engines, each developing 375,000 lb (1668 kN) thrust, plus two Thiokol solid-propellant booster rockets each producing 2,900,000-lb (12896 kN) thrust, the combined thrust being 3,091½ tons (3141 tonnes). The booster rockets are attached to the external liquid propellant tanks, these combined units being jettisoned after take-off for recovery and reuse. In Earth orbit the Orbiter spacecraft is manoeuvred and controlled by means of two Aerojet orbit manoeuvring engines, plus 38 reaction control engines and six vernier thrusters produced by

Marquardt. All of these 'in orbit' power units are bi-propellant liquid rocket engines.

The kinetic heating induced at the time of re-entry into Earth's atmosphere can create localised temperatures of up to 1648°C (3,000°F) at the spacecraft's nose and on the wing leading edges, and to control the outer skin temperature at a maximum 176°C (350°F) during re-entry, the Orbiter has a thermal protection system consisting of mainly externally applied insulation tiles. Once within Earth's atmosphere the Orbiter is flown as a conventional winged aircraft, the elevons at the trailing edge of the wing providing pitch and roll control, and the rudder controlling yaw. There is, in addition, a speed brake to give further assistance in achieving accurate unpow-

The Orbiter launches with two booster rockets and an external tank. The combination is known to NASA as the Space Shuttle.

SPECIFICATION

NASA/Rockwell Shuttle Orbiter
Type: re-usable spacecraft
Powerplant: see above
Performance: speed at external tank separation, 8 minutes 30 seconds after launch 17,440 mph (28067 km/h); orbital speed 17,321 mph (27875 km/h); landing speed 212 mph (341 km/h); orbit altitude, minimum 115 miles (185 km), maximum 400 miles (643 km)
Weights: launch, Space Shuttle
4,500,000 lb (2041166 kg); landing 230,000 lb (104326 kg)
Dimensions: wingspan 78 ft ⁷⁄₁₆ in (23.79 m); length, Space Shuttle including boosters and external tank 184 ft 2½ in (56.14 m), Shuttle Orbiter 122 ft 2 in (37.23 m); height, Orbiter on runway 56 ft 8 in (17.27 m); wing area 2,690.45 sq ft (249.91 m²)
Payload: maximum cargo load to orbit 63,500 lb (28803 kg)

Endeavour was photographed landing at Edwards on 1 May 2001. The craft is transported by two 747 SCA aircraft.

This image shows the latest Multifunction Electronic Display Subsystem (MEDS) cockpit upgrade.

ered landings. As would be expected, each Shuttle spacecraft has highly sophisticated navigational equipment to ensure accurate positioning for re-entry and location of the landing area. The first orbital flight began when **Columbia** took off on 12 April 1981, completing 36 Earth orbits before landing at Edwards AFB, California, 55 hours later on 14 April.

Since then four more Shuttles have flown. **Challenger** in April 1983, **Discovery** in August 1984 and **Atlantis** in October 1985. Challenger was dramatically destroyed by a post-launch explosion in January 1986, killing all six astronauts on board, and the programme was suspended until September 1989 to allow a redesign of the booster system.

A fifth Orbiter, **Endeavour**, was ordered in July 1987 to replace Challenger. Discovery completed the first post-accident flight in September 1988, at the same time introducing a host of revised systems and engineering fixes in the wake of the Challenger crash. On its first flight in May 1992, Endeavour marked the debut of several more improvements, including the installation of a brake 'chute, lighter and more reliable hydraulic systems and upgraded avionics.

Further upgrading to avionics, engines and other systems will see the Shuttle in service until at least 2010 and NASA is aiming to have achieved a doubling of flight safety compared to the 2000 standard by 2005. Late in 2000 the Shuttle completed its 100th mission.

Naval Aircraft Factory N3N

Designed by the US Navy's Bureau of Aeronautics, this two-seat primary trainer was the NAFs most extensively built aircraft, and was also the last biplane to serve in the US armed forces when the last of the type was retired in 1961. A conventional equal-span biplane with wheeled or central float/stabilising float landing gear, and a basic structure of metal with fabric covering, the type began with the **XN3N-1** prototype first flown during August 1935. Successful testing led to the production of 179 **N3N-1** aircraft, 158 of them powered by the 220-hp (164-kW) Wright J-5 radial piston engine which the US Navy had held in store. An additional prototype was ordered as the **XN3N-2** and one production aircraft was converted to **XN3N-3** prototype configuration, both of them powered by the 240-hp (179-kW) US Navy-built version of the

*In service the N3N, here in N3N-1 form, was known as the **Canary** or **Yellow Peril**. A small number of N3N-3 floatplanes remained in service with the US Naval Academy until at least 1959.*

Wright R-760-96 radial engine. This action was taken because the J-5 engine was obsolete and the last 20 production N3N-1s had the US Navy-built R-760 engine when testing showed them to be suitable. At a later date all remaining N3N-1s had their J-5 engines replaced by R-760-2s, which also powered the

816 **N3N-3** production aircraft built from 1938; these also had revised tail units and landing gear. Except for four aircraft transferred to the US Coast Guard in 1941, these primary trainers were used extensively by the US Navy throughout World War II, the majority of them becoming surplus soon after the war ended.

SPECIFICATION	
NAF N3N-3	(1266 kg)
Type: two-seat primary trainer	**Dimensions:** wingspan 34 ft
Powerplant: one 235-hp (175-kW)	(10.36 m); length 25 ft 6 in
Wright R-760-2 Whirlwind 7 radial	(7.77 m); height 10 ft 10 in
piston engine	(3.30 m); wing area 305 sq ft
Performance: maximum speed	(28.33 m²)
126 mph (203 km/h); service ceiling	**Armament:** two 0.5-in (12.7-mm)
15,200 ft (4635 m); range 470 miles	machine-guns and two 20-mm
(756 km)	cannon, plus underwing racks for
Weights: empty 2,090 lb (948 kg);	two 551-lb (250-kg) bombs
maximum take-off 2,792 lb	

Naval Aircraft Factory PN

One of the most successful patrol flying-boats of World War I was the Felixstowe F.5, developed in the UK from a Curtiss design. The NAF built 138 of these for the US Navy under the designation **F-5L**, the 'L' suffix denoting the Liberty- engined powerplant which replaced the Rolls-Royce Eagle engines of the British version. With a change in designation system in 1922, the F-5L was redesignated **PN-5**,

and was followed by a series of models developed by the NAF increasing progressively the capability of this flying-boat. They comprised two with redesigned vertical tail surfaces, originally with the designation **F-6L**, later **PN-6**, followed by two **PN-7** 'boats which combined redesigned wings and 525-hp (391-kW) Wright T2 engines with the existing F-5L hull. The

PN-8, of which two were built, was generally similar to the PN-7 but introduced a hull of metal construction and 475-hp (354-kW) Packard 1A-2500 engines; one of these was subsequently given modified tail surfaces and engine nacelles, and then redesignated **PN-9**, and two generally similar aircraft with only detail changes had the designation **PN-10**. A far more radical change came with the three **PN-11**

aircraft, which introduced a completely redesigned and wider metal hull, and one similar **XPN-11** with added twin vertical tail surfaces. The final NAF development was the **PN-12** of which two were built; generally similar to the PN-9, one had a pair of 525-hp (391-kW) Wright R-1750-D Cyclone radial engines, the other two Pratt & Whitney R-1850-A Hornets of similar output. They confirmed the combination of metal hull and radial engines providing optimum performance and, because of the

NAF's restricted manufacturing capacity, series production was contracted out to Douglas, Martin and Keystone. Douglas built 25 **PD-1** aircraft with 575-hp (429-kW) Wright engines in revised nacelles; Martin built 30 **PM-1** aircraft with R-1750-D engines, and 25 **PM-2** 'boats which introduced 575-hp (429-kW) Wright R-1820-64 Cyclone engines and the twin vertical tail surfaces tested on the XPN-11; Keystone built 18 **PK-1** machines, all of them virtually identical to the PM-2.

Naval Aircraft Factory PN (continued)

The final development of the NAF PN series came when the Hall Aluminum Aircraft Corporation received a US Navy contract to build a version based on the PN-11. A single **XPH-1** prototype, it differed little from the PN-11 except for having a larger fin and rudder and two 537-hp (400-kW) Wright GR-1750 engines; it was followed by nine **PH-1** aircraft with 620-hp (462-kW) Wright R-1820-86 engines, these aircraft introducing also a somewhat basic enclosure for the pilots' cockpit. A further 14 aircraft were built for the US Coast Guard for use in the air-sea rescue role, these comprising seven **PH-2** 'boats with 750-hp (559-kW) Wright R-1820F-51 engines and seven **PH-3** 'boats which differed primarily by having a more refined enclosure for the pilots. Some of the PH-3s soldiered on into World War II, being used briefly on ASW patrols, but these aircraft represented the end of development of the Curtiss flying-boat, which had played an important role in World War I.

SPECIFICATION	
NAF PN-12	14,122 lb (6406 kg)
Type: five-crew patrol flying-boat	**Dimensions:** wingspan 72 ft 10 in
Powerplant: two 525-hp (391-kW)	(22.20 m); length 49 ft 2 in
Wright R-1750-D Cyclone radial	(14.99 m); height 16 ft 9 in
piston engines	(5.11 m); wing area 1,217.0 sq ft
Performance: maximum speed	(113.06 m²)
114 mph (183 km/h) at sea level;	**Armament:** bow and midship
service ceiling 10,900 ft (3320 m);	positions each with a single
range 1,310 miles (2108 km)	0.30-in (7.62-mm) machine-gun,
Weights: empty 7,669 lb	plus four 230-lb (104-kg) bombs
(3479 kg); maximum take-off	

Produced by adding wings of new design to the F-5L hull, the PN-7 had a reduced wingspan compared to the F-5L thanks to the greater lift of its new wing.

NDN aircraft

Nigel Desmond Norman, one of the founders of the Britten-Norman Aircraft Company, builders of the Defender, Islander and Trislander light twins, established NDN Aircraft Ltd early in 1976 to develop a new two-seat basic military trainer designated **NDN 1 Firecracker**. The prototype, first flown on 26 May 1977, was of cantilever low-wing monoplane configuration, had a retractable tricycle landing gear, and accommodated an instructor and pupil in tandem enclosed cockpits. A turboprop powered version was flown on 1 September 1983 under the designation **NDN 1T Turbo Firecracker**, and three were built for only one customer, Specialist Flying Training Ltd of Hamble and later Hurn. In 1981 NDN Aircraft launched a new turboprop agricultural aircraft under the designation **NDN 6 Fieldmaster**, and the prototype flew for the first time on 17 December 1981 at Sandown. A braced low-wing monoplane incorporating a titanium chemical hopper as an integral unit of the fuselage structure, the NDN 6 had a non-retractable tricycle landing gear. In 1985 NDN Aircraft ran into difficulties and Desmond Norman formed the Norman Aeroplane Company to operate from a new factory in Cardiff, Wales. A production batch of five **NAC-6** aircraft was laid down and the first of these flew on 29 March 1987 powered by a Pratt & Whitney Canada PT6A-34 and the type was certificated as a crop-sprayer in April 1987. Unfortunately NAC went into receivership in October 1988, but not before other examples had been completed and operated in France on fire patrol and waterbombing duties. In April 1989 the NAC-6 programme was revived by the Irish company Croplease plc and the prototype re-worked into the more powerful **Firemaster-65** water-bomber, which first flew on 28 October 1989 at Sandown piloted by Neville Duke. Both the Fieldmaster cropsprayer, and the Firemaster waterbomber failed to win orders and were abandoned.

Capable of lifting a 4,500-lb (2040-kg) payload, the NAC-6 also carried a second seat with dual controls for a mechanic/loadmaster, or for possible use as a specialised trainer. A 1991 plan for the Yugoslavian aircraft company UTVA to manufacture components and assemble NAC-6 airframes came to nothing.

The **NAC-1 Freelance** single-engined four-seat light utility aircraft, powered by a 180 hp (134 kW) piston engine, made its first flight on 29 September 1984 and another was later completed. The Freelance programme was later taken over by Aeronortec Ltd of Sandown on the Isle of Wight, but no further examples were built.

Hunting offered the Turbo Firecracker as a contender in the RAF's competition to find a new basic trainer to replace the Jet Provost. The winning contender emerged as the Shorts Tucano, effectively condemning the Turbo-Firecracker, since no other major purchasers came forward.

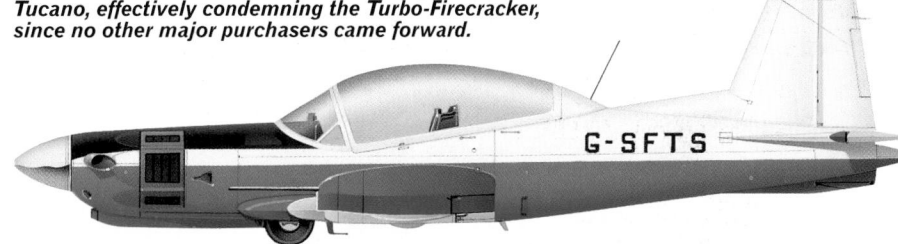

*Based on Norman's earlier **Nymph** design, the Freelance would have been unable to compete with designs from Cessna, Piper and SOCATA.*

Just six Fieldmasters were built, one of them being converted to Firemaster standard. The type failed to find commercial success.

SPECIFICATION	
NDN1T Turbo Firecracker	4,250 lb (1928 kg)
Type: basic/intermediate trainer	**Dimensions:** wingspan 26 ft
Powerplant: one 715-ehp	(7.92 m), length 27 ft 4 in (8.33 m);
(533-ekW) Pratt & Whitney Aircraft	height 10 ft 8 in (3.25 m), wing
of Canada PT6A-25A turboprop	area 128 sq ft (11.89 m²)
Performance: maximum speed	**Armament:** four underwing
261 mph (420 km/h) at 8,000 ft	hardpoints with a combined
(2440 m), service ceiling 27,700 ft	capacity of 1,600 lb (726 kg) of
(8445 m); range with standard fuel	weapons, including gun pods, GP
765 miles (1231 km)	or fragmentation bombs, and
Weights: empty 2,300 lb	rocket launchers
(1043 kg), maximum take-off	

Neiva Regente and Lanceiro

In 1959 Neiva began the design of a four-seat cabin monoplane with a high-set braced wing, fixed tricycle landing gear, and with power provided initially by a 145-hp (108-kW) Continental O-300 engine. First flown on 7 September 1961 as the **Regente 360C**, the type was ordered into production for the Brazilian air force with a 180-hp (134-kW) Continental O-360A1D engine under the initial designation **U-42**, changed later to **C-42**. A total of 80 was built, and these aircraft are used in the utility role. Neiva then developed a three-seat AOP version for the air force, identified by the company as the **Regente 420L**, which differed by having a stepped-down rear fuselage to improve the field of view, and a more-powerful Continental engine. Flown first in **YL-42** prototype form during January 1967, 40 were built for the Brazilian air force under the designation **L-42**. A large number of these military C-42/L-42s

The L-42 design introduced an extended dorsal fin to compensate for the reduced keel area of its cut-down rear fuselage compared to the C-42.

remains in service in 2001. Neiva also developed a four-seat civil version of the L-42 under the name **Lanceiro**. A prototype flown in 1970 was followed by the first production

SPECIFICATION	
Neiva L-42	(745 kg); maximum take-off
Type: three-seat AOP aircraft	2,469 lb (1120 kg)
Powerplant: one 210-hp (157-kW)	**Dimensions:** wingspan 29 ft
Continental IO-360-D flat-six piston	11½ in (9.13 m); length 23 ft 7¾ in
engine	(7.21 m); height 9 ft 7¼ in (2.93 m);
Performance: maximum speed	wing area 144.78 sq ft (13.45 m²)
152 mph (245 km/h) at sea level;	**Armament:** provision to carry light
service ceiling 15,815 ft (4820 m);	bombs or rockets on underwing
range 575 miles (925 km)	hardpoints
Weights: empty equipped 1,642 lb	

aircraft, flown in 1973, but by then the company's growing involvement with

EMBRAER resulted in the Lanceiro programme being abandoned.

Neiva Paulistinha 56 and Campeiro

The Brazilian company Sociedade Aeronáutica Neiva began its activities soon after the end of World War II by building, under sponsorship from the Brazilian government, single- and two-seat sailplanes for supply to the nation's flying clubs. In the late 1950s, Neiva began construction of a two-seat lightweight cabin monoplane, designated the **Paulistinha 56**, which had a braced high-set wing and fixed tailwheel landing gear, and was powered by a Continental C90 flat-four engine. This remained in production until November 1964, by which time a total of 240 had been built, mostly in tourer/trainer versions, but some were also equipped for agricultural use. The final production version was the **Paulistinha 56-Q**, but the prototype of a **Paulistinha 56-D** with an Avco Lycoming O-320-A1A was flown. This aircraft was acquired subsequently by the Brazilian air force which, designating it **L-6A**, used it in a general purpose role. Although the Paulistinha 56-D was not built as such, it led directly to the generally similar **Campeiro** which differed primarily by having a redesigned structure. A contract for 20 of this version was received from the Brazilian air force in 1962, which operated them under the designation **L-7** for roles such as liaison, observation, rescue and training.

A near-copy of the Piper Cub, the Paulistinha could be purchased to Luxo standard with a factory-fitted radio.

SPECIFICATION	
Neiva Campeiro	maximum payload 593 miles
Type: two-seat utility aircraft	(955 km)
Powerplant: one 150-hp (112-kW)	**Weights:** empty 1,082 lb (491 kg);
Avco Lycoming O-320-A flat-four	maximum take-off 1,741 lb (790 kg)
piston engine	**Dimensions:** wingspan 35 ft 1¼ in
Performance: maximum speed	(10.70 m); length 22 ft 7¾ in
134 mph (215 km/h); service ceiling	(6.90 m); height 8 ft 8¼ in (2.65 m);
17,060 ft (5200 m); range with	wing area 180.84 sq ft (16.80 m²)

Neiva Universal

Designed in 1963 to provide the Brazilian air force with a new primary trainer, the prototype of the **Universal** was flown for the first time on 29 April 1966. A cantilever low-wing monoplane of all-metal construction with retractable tricycle landing gear, it has enclosed side-by-side accommodation for instructor and pupil with sufficient space in the cabin for an optional third seat behind them. Power was provided initially by a 290-hp (216-kW) Avco Lycoming IO-540-G1A5 flat-six engine, but later production aircraft have a more powerful version of this engine. A first Brazilian air force contract covered 150 Universals, designated **T-25**, an additional 28 being ordered in 1978. In 2001 Brazilian air force student pilots were still flying their basic training on the T-25, before progressing onto the Tucano.

A **YT-25B Universal II** prototype was flown for the first time on 22 October 1978, and though it was thought that the Brazilian air force would have a requirement for about 80 examples of this aircraft, which was powered by a 400-hp (298-kW) Avco Lycoming IO-720 engine, none were produced. In addition to the Brazilian air force T-25s, 10 generally similar aircraft were supplied to the Chilean army; these were later transferred to the Chilean air force.

SPECIFICATION	
Neiva T-25 Universal	range 621 miles (1000 km)
Type: two-seat basic trainer	**Weights:** empty equipped 2,535 lb
Powerplant: one 300-hp (224-kW)	(1150 kg); maximum take-off
Avco Lycoming IO-540-K1D5 flat-	3,307 lb (1500 kg)
six piston engine	**Dimensions:** wingspan 36 ft 1 in
Performance: maximum speed	(11.00 m); length 28 ft 2¼ in
186 mph (300 km/h) at sea level;	(8.60 m); height 9 ft 10 in (3.00 m);
service ceiling 20,000 ft (6095 m);	wing area 185.15 sq ft (17.20 m²)

Designed to replace the T-6 Texan and Fokker S-11/S-12 Instructor, the Universal remained in Brazilian service in 2001.

NH Industries NH 90

In 1985 five European nations signed a memorandum of understanding covering a 'NATO helicopter for the '90s', or **NH 90**. The UK dropped out of the programme in 1987, leaving France, Germany, Italy and the Netherlands in the project by means of NH Industries, established in France during August 1992 to control a collaborative programme involving Eurocopter France (41.60 per cent of the definitive workshare with NFT [Norway] as a risk-sharing partner from 1994), Agusta (28.20 per cent), Eurocopter Deutschland (23.70 per cent) and Fokker (6.50 per cent). Stated requirements were 220 helicopters for France, 214 for Italy, 272 for Germany and 20 for the Netherlands, and it was anticipated that a first flight in 1995 would pave the way for deliveries from 1999.

Two initial versions were planned, the **NH 90 NFH (NATO Frigate Helicopter)** for the autonomous ASW and anti-surface vessel roles with anti-submarine torpedoes or anti-ship missiles and 360° search radar under the cabin as key elements in a fully integrated mission system, and the **NH 90 TTH (Tactical Transport Helicopter)** for assault transport, rescue, electronic warfare and VIP transport duties.

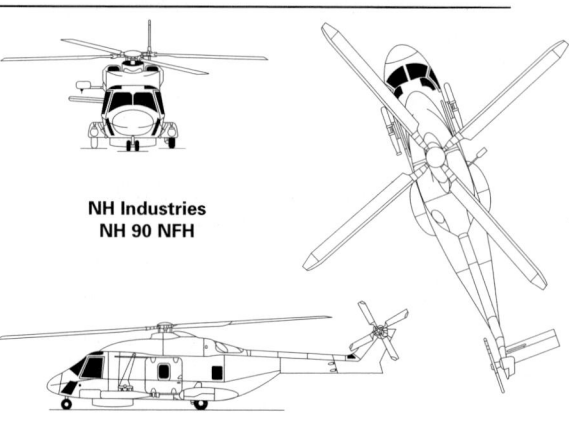

**NH Industries
NH 90 NFH**

NH Industries NH 90 (continued)

The NH 90 has a single main rotor with a pod-and-boom fuselage with the four-bladed main rotor above the centre of gravity position and the four-bladed anti-torque rotor on the port side of a swept fin extending upward from the rear of the boom. The powerplant of two turboshaft engines is installed to the rear of the main rotor and gearbox, the landing gear is of the fully retractable tricycle type with a two-wheel nose unit and single-wheel main units retracting into sponsons on the lower rear corners of the fuselage's pod section, the cabin is accessed by a large sliding door on each side, and the flightdeck is laid out for operation by a crew of two.

The NH 90 NFH variant is being developed under Agusta leadership, and on the flightdeck has either two pilots or one pilot and the tactical co-ordinator, while the cabin is occupied by the tactical co-ordinator and/or the sensor operator. The advanced mission suite includes radar, dipping sonar, FLIR, MAD, an ESM system and an ECM system, and the weapons are carried on two lateral hardpoints each rated at

1,543 lb (700 kg). The NH 90 TTH variant is being developed under Eurocopter Deutschland leadership, and on the flightdeck had two pilots or one pilot and one loadmaster, while the cabin is occupied by 20 troops or one 4,409-lb (2000-kg) vehicle, and can carry area-suppression and self-defence weapons. A FLIR is also standard on the NH 90 TTH to provide a night and adverse-weather nap-of-the-Earth flight capability, and both models are controlled via a quadruplex fly-by-wire control system.

Power is provided by two turboshaft engines, two types of which are being qualified in the first helicopters in order to maximise the NH 90's appeal. These two engines are the RTM 322-01/9 unit manufactured by a consortium comprising Rolls-Royce, Turbomeca, MTU, Piaggio and Topps, and the General Electric T700-T6E unit co-developed and made under licence in Europe by Alfa Romeo. Controlled by a FADEC system, the engines drive the rotors by means of a gearbox rated at 3,413 shp (2545 kW) for both engines

or 2,749 shp (2050 kW) for one engine, and the gearbox can run dry for 30 minutes. There are eight crash-resistant fuel cells in the fuselage, and there is provision for two external fuel tanks derived from those used in the Alpha Jet. The main rotor has a titanium hub with elastomeric bearings carrying the all-composite blades, while the tail rotor is of similar construction but has no bearings. Composite materials are also used for the structure of the entire fuselage. Key elements of the philosophy embodied in the design of the helicopter and its avionics, integrated by a MIL-1553B databus, were low detectability and vulnerability, limited maintenance requirements, and a full day/night operating capability under most possible conditions.

Development of the NH 90 was suspended in May 1994 but then resumed in July of the same year after a short but rigorous effort to reduce cost escalation, and the first of five flying and one ground-test prototypes was the French-assembled **PT 1** that first took to the air on 18 December 1995 with RTM 322 engines for validation of the helicopter's basic design and handling. The **PT 2** second prototype was also assembled in France and first flew on 19 March 1997 as the initial machine with a fly-by-wire control system (initially analogue but later

NH 90 TTH is designed to carry as many as 20 fully-equipped troops, or 5,511 lb (2500 kg) of cargo, primarily in the tactical assault role.

the definitive digital type). The third, fourth and fifth prototypes were assembled in France, Germany and Italy, and are dedicated to flight control and avionics, TTH mission system and NFH mission system testing respectively.

The overall helicopter totals required were trimmed from the original 726 to 647 in July 1996 and then to 642 in 1998: the latter figure comprises 133 and 27 examples of the TTH and NFH for France, 205 (including an as-yet-undefined combat SAR model) and 38 of the TTH and NFH for Germany,

155 (also including the combat SAR model) and 64 of the TTH and NFH for Italy, and 20 of the NFH for the Netherlands. The manufacturing consortium also hopes for large export sales. There have been considerable delays in the signature of the production contract for the NH 90, which was originally scheduled for 1997 but finally took place in March 2000, when an initial 244 helicopters were ordered for the armed forces of the four partner nations. The first NH 90s seem likely to enter service in the period 2004-2007.

Primarily an ASW/ASV helicopter, NH 90 NFH can also undertake a number of other roles, including over-the horizon targeting, SAR, transport and vertical replenishment.

Nieuport Types 11 and 16

Nieuport's decision to build an aircraft to compete in the 1914 Gordon-Bennett Trophy contest led to a line of dainty single-seat fighters, the first of which was the **Type 11**, built in only four months. On the outbreak of war the contest was cancelled, but the new aircraft's potential was quickly realised and orders

were placed by the British and French. The engine was the 80-hp (60-kW) Le Rhône rotary, and a single Lewis gun was mounted on the upper wing. The lower wing had only half the area of the upper, a feature which was to become famous on these aircraft, which were also known as the **Nieuport Bébé** (baby),

because of their small size, or **Nieuport Scout**, which was their primary role.

The high rate of climb and manoeuvrability of the new aircraft, deliveries of which began to French squadrons in 1915, helped the Allies to gain temporary air superiority. Several hundred were built by Macchi in Italy (as the **Nieuport 11000**) and the Type 11 served also with the Belgian Aviation Militaire and the British RFC and RNAS.

An improved version, the **Nieuport 16**, had a 110-hp (82-kW) Le Rhône rotary engine and appeared in 1916. Flown by British, Belgian and French pilots, the Type 16 was the type on which the French ace Georges Guynemer began

to make his name. It also pioneered the use of Le Prieur rockets for attacks against balloons and airships, being able to carry eight rockets. These were attached to the wing struts, inclined upwards, and were fired electrically.

A guard rail fitted to the Lewis gun of this Nieuport 11 prevented the pilot from shooting the propeller.

Nieuport Types 17, 21 and 23

Experience with the earlier models led in March 1916 to the Nieuport which was destined to become the best known of all, the **Type 17**. Stronger than its predecessors, and with a 110-hp (82-kW) Le Rhône or 130-hp (97-kW) Clerget (**Nieuport 17-bis**), the new model was very manoeuvrable and had a high performance with a particularly good rate of climb. A Lewis gun was mounted on the top wing to fire above the propeller, and a sliding mounting enabled it to be pulled down by the pilot and aimed upwards, thereby permitting an attack on enemy aircraft in their blind spot, from below. Later in the aircraft's service life, when a synchronising gear had been perfected to allow the gun to fire through the propeller, a Vickers gun

was substituted.
A number of French squadrons re-equipped with the Type 17, together with Belgian, Italian, Russian and RFC units, and the type rapidly made a name for itself with aces who included Nungesser, Ball and Bishop.
The **Type 21** was a variant of the Type 17 with an 80-hp (60-kW) Le Rhône and enlarged ailerons. Russia and the USA received a number of Type

21s, the latter totalling just under 200. The last batch of US aircraft, delivered in January 1918, had 110-hp (82-kW) Le Rhônes. Several Type 21s were used postwar by sporting pilots.
A slightly heavier version, the **Type 23**, could be powered by an 80-hp (60-kW) or 120-hp (89-kW) Le Rhône. It was supplied to the air forces of Belgium, France, Italy and the UK, while the USA also received 49.

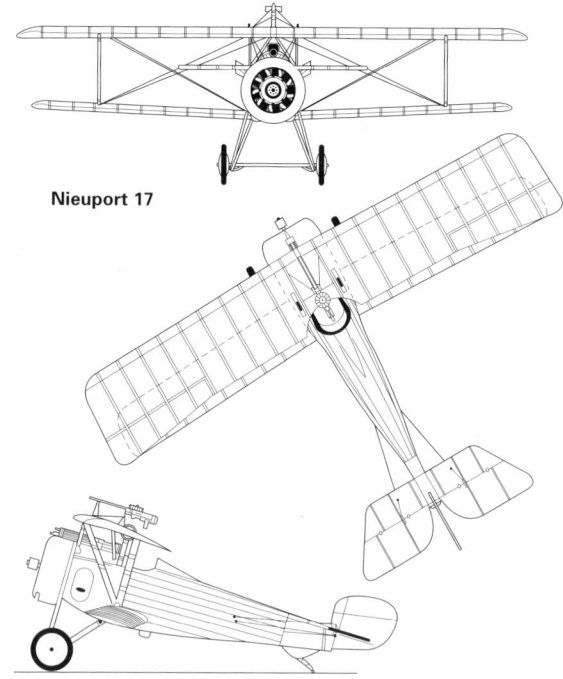

Nieuport 17

SPECIFICATION

Nieuport Type 17
Type: single-seat fighter
Powerplant: one 120-hp (89-kW) Le Rhône rotary piston engine
Performance: maximum speed 115 mph (185 km/h) at sea level; service ceiling 18,210 ft (5550 m); range 155 miles (250 km)
Weights: empty 838 lb (380 kg); maximum take-off 1,289 lb (585 kg)

Dimensions: wingspan 26 ft 10¾ in (8.20 m); length 19 ft 2⅓ in (5.85 m); height 7 ft 11¼ in (2.42 m); wing area 158.77 sq ft (14.75 m²)
Armament: one fixed forward-firing 0.303-in (7.7-mm) Lewis gun and/or one 0.303-in (7.7-mm) Vickers gun

Nieuport Types 24, 25 and 27

Nungesser's Nieuport 17-bis had been converted to a Type 23, and later became the prototype for the **Type 24**, a more streamlined model with a 120-hp (89-kW) Le Rhône rotary piston engine, a fixed fin and a circular section fuselage. The USA bought 121 Type 24s in November 1917, while others served with Belgian and Italian units, and a few were built under licence in Japan by Nakajima. A further variant, which reverted to the Type 17 tail unit and rectangular wing tips, was the **Type 24-bis**, a trainer used by the French, the American Expeditionary Force which received 140, and the RNAS, for which the type was built in England by the British Nieuport and General Aircraft Co. Ltd. The redesignation **Type 25** was applied to the prototype Type 24 after it had

been modified to incorporate a tailplane and skid of the type to be used on the **Type 27**.
Basically similar to the Type 24, the Type 27 had a 120-hp (89-kW) Le Rhône

rotary piston engine and served with the air forces of Sweden, the UK and the USA, the latter buying 287 in November 1917. Macchi also built a number under licence in Italy, but by this

time Nieuport realised that a more radical redesign was necessary to match

the performance of enemy aircraft on the Western Front.

This Nieuport 27 was flying with No. 1 Squadron of the RFC from Builleul in France during 1917. The aircraft's camouflage followed the French three-tone scheme, while its markings were all British.

B 6768

SPECIFICATION

Nieuport Type 27
Type: single-seat fighter
Powerplant: one 120-hp (89-kW) Le Rhône rotary piston engine
Performance: maximum speed 106 mph (170 km/h) at 6,500 ft (1980 m); climb to 13,125 ft (4000 m) in 19 minutes 30 seconds; service ceiling 17,550 ft (5350 m); maximum range 155 miles (250 km)

Weights: empty 825 lb (374 kg); maximum take-off 1,235 lb (560 kg)
Dimensions: wingspan 26 ft 10¾ in (8.20 m); length 19 ft 7 in (5.96 m); height 8 ft (2.44 m); wing area 158.77 sq ft (14.75 m²)
Armament: one fixed forward-firing 0.303-in (7.7-mm) Vickers or Lewis gun

Nieuport Type 28

First flown in prototype form in June 1917, the **Type 28** was markedly different to the earlier models. The familiar narrow lower wing and square-cut wing tips gave way to rounded wings of almost equal size and the familiar V-struts were replaced by parallel struts; and the rectangular-section fuselage was superseded by one of circular section. The new nine-cylinder Gnome rotary engine of around 160 hp (119 kW) was fitted to production aircraft and the Type 28 went into

large-scale production for France and the USA, ironically as it happened, since

by the time it appeared it had been eclipsed in performance by the SPAD.

The 94th Aero Squadron of the American Expeditionary Forces flew this Nieuport 28 in France during May 1918.

6189

6

SPECIFICATION

Nieuport Type 28
Type: single-seat fighter
Powerplant: one 160-hp (119-kW) Gnome 9N rotary piston engine
Performance: maximum speed 121 mph (195 km/h) at 6,500 ft (1981 m); climb to 16,405 ft (5000 m) in 21 minutes 15 seconds; service ceiling 17,060 ft (5200 m); maximum range 248 miles (400 km)

Weights: empty 1,172 lb (532 kg); maximum take-off 1,631 lb (740 kg)
Dimensions: wingspan 26 ft 3 in (8.00 m); length 20 ft 4 in (6.20 m); height 8 ft 1¾ in (2.48 m); wing area 215.29 sq ft (20.00 in²)
Armament: two fixed forward-firing 0.303-in (7.7-mm) Vickers machine-guns

Nieuport Type 28 (continued)

The American Expeditionary Force had a desperate requirement for fighters and all SPADs were at that time being delivered to the French, so Nieuport supplied the American squadrons with 297 Type 28s. Probably the most famous unit to be so equipped was the 94th Aero Squadron with its 'hat-in-ring' insignia; Eddie Rickenbacker, who became the top US ace, flew a Type 28 with the squadron. Engine problems and a tendency to shed upper-wing fabric in long dives did not endear the Type 28 to its pilots, who were relieved to re-equip with SPADs in July 1918.

Post-war, four civil aircraft flew mail between Paris and London in 1920 during a French postal strike, and 12 Type 28s were used by the US Navy in experiments, flying from platforms over battleship gun turrets.

Nieuport-Delage Ni-D 29

An equal-span biplane with ailerons on both upper and lower wings, the first prototype of the **Ni-D 29** single-seat fighter (C.1 category) made its initial official test flight on 21 August 1918. It performed well and achieved the performance

Variants

Ni-D 29 B.1: experimental assault version, armed with six 22-lb (10-kg) bombs; exploits with the NiD-29 B.1 won renowned pilot Sadi Lecointe three citations and promotion; only small batch converted to B.1 configuration
Ni-D 29bis: shown at 1922 Paris Salon; reduced wing area and steerable tailskid; prototype only
Ni-D 29G: version built in parallel with Hispano-engined prototypes; had Gnome 9N rotary engine; first of two built converted to take Hispano engine and fitted with twin main floats and auxiliary tail float, and took part in Grand Prix de Monaco seaplane meeting in 1920; second aircraft tested with the Gnome engine as possible carrierborne fighter, then being converted in 1920 to **Ni-D 32RH** with a 180-hp (134-kW) Le Rhône 9R
Ni-D 29D: a conversion to attempt altitude record; had Rateau supercharger, enabling it to attain an altitude of 22,965 ft (7000 m)
Ni-D 29 E.1: trainer variant built for French Aviation Militaire; powered by a 180-hp (134-kW) Hispano-Suiza and armed with single synchronised Vickers gun
Ni-D 29 SHV: seaplane variant for 1919 Schneider Trophy contest; wingspan reduced to 26 ft 3 in (8.00 m) and airframe stripped of military equipment and given improved external finish; two aircraft built, one also entered in 1921, but no Ni-D 29 actually took part in either contest
Ni-D 29V: developed in 1919 by designer Mary in collaboration with company engineer Gustave Delage, the Ni-D 29V was a lightweight racer, with wingspan reduced to a mere 19 ft 8¼ in (6.00 m) and its HS 8Fb engine boosted to give 320 hp (239 kW); maximum take-off weight was reduced to 2,063 lb (936 kg); the three racers built were subjected to numerous modifications and the type swept the board in many events, Sadi Lecointe winning the 1919 Coupe Deutsche and the 1920 Gordon Bennett Trophy races flying Ni-D 29Vs; the **Ni-D 29V bis** was a one-off conversion intended to produce a higher maximum speed by eliminating the open cockpit with its windscreen and headrest. The pilot had to crouch within the fuselage, relying on tiny teardrop windows on each side for his only external visibility; it was, not surprisingly, lost in a landing accident in April 1921

required with the exception of ceiling. The second prototype retained the Hispano-Suiza 8Fb, engine and the slim circular-section fuselage of its predecessor, but with its wingspan increased slightly. Then achieving the required ceiling, the Ni-D 29 was ordered into quantity production at the beginning of 1920. Series aircraft had detailed improvements, the principal external difference being the elimination of the upper-wing ailerons and the enlargement of those on the lower surfaces.

Initial deliveries to the French Aviation Militaire were made in 1922, the type equipping Escadrilles SPA 37, 81 and 91 (later renumbered 101, 102 and 103 respectively) stationed in Germany. The type proved popular, although pilots remarked on its tendency to get into a flat spin. Some 250 Ni-D 29s were built for French military aviation by Nieuport and seven other firms, a total of 18 orders being received between 1922 and 1924.

The Ni-D 29 was soon the most important fighter of the 1920s. Spain purchased 30 aircraft, 10 of which were licence-built in that country; Belgium had 108, 87 of them built by SABCA under licence; Japan imported a pattern aircraft, and subsequently Nakajima built no less than 608 under licence, supplying them to the Imperial Japanese Army as the **Ko-4**; Italy bought six French machines and then

By 1925 the Ni-D 29 equipped escadrilles of the 1er and 3e Régiments de Chasse based at Thionville and Chateauroux.

the Regia Aeronautica obtained 175 series aircraft, 95 built by Macchi as the **Macchi-Nieuport 29** and 80 by Caproni, the type equipping six Italian fighter squadriglie between 1925 and 1928. Finally, Sweden bought nine aircraft, operating them under the designation **J 2**, and Argentina also used a small number.

French Ni-D 29s used operationally against the Rif insurgents in Morocco included a small number of Ni-D 29s, converted to B.1 standard with the ability to carry small bombs, and the Spanish Nieuports also participated in the operations against these North African rebels.

In Japan the Ko-4 licence-built version formed the main equipment of army fighter units until 1933, playing a major part in air support for the Japanese occupation of Manchuria and in the 1932 Shanghai Incident.

A number of racing versions of the NiD-29 were developed, gaining no fewer than eight world speed records.

SPECIFICATION	
Nieuport-Delage Ni-D 29	(760 kg); maximum take-off
Type: single-seat fighter	2,535 lb (1150 kg)
Powerplant: one 300-hp (224-kW) Hispano-Suiza 8Fb V-8 piston engine	**Dimensions:** wingspan 31 ft 10 in (9.70 m); length 21 ft 3½ in (6.49 m); height 8 ft 4¾ in (2.56 m); wing area 287.41 sq ft (26.70 m²)
Performance: maximum speed 146 mph (235 km/h); service ceiling 27,885 ft (8500 m); range 360 miles (580 km)	**Armament:** two fixed forward-firing 0.303-in (7.7-mm) Vickers machine-guns
Weights: empty equipped 1,675 lb	

Nieuport-Delage Ni-D 42C

On the Nieuport stand at the 1924 Paris Salon de l'Aéronautique were displayed three new designs, each bearing the type number 42. One was the **Ni-D 42S** monoplane racer. The other two were sesquiplanes, the **Ni-D 42 C.1** single-seat and the **Ni-D 42 C.2** two-seat fighters. There was little interest in the two-seat aircraft, but the C.1 was the first of a successful family built over the next decade, including the Ni-D 52 and Ni-D 62 series.

The original design had been for a parasol mono-plane, but this was modified to have a small lower plane in order to achieve a more rigid and reliable wing structure. The prototype flew for the first time in its definitive form at the beginning of 1924, also incorporating a feature taken from the earlier Nieuport racers, namely an auxiliary aerofoil surface attached to the cross axle of the main landing gear units. The new fighter soon attracted official attention, an order for 25 aircraft for the French Aviation Militaire being received in January 1927. Powered by

a 500-hp (373-kW) Hispano-Suiza 12Hb V-12 engine, the Ni-D 42 attained a maximum speed of 165 mph (265 km/h) and was armed with two wing-mounted 0.303-in (7.7-mm) machine-guns, plus a third gun on the engine cowling synchronised to fire through the propeller disc. Operating with the French escadrilles de chasse, the Ni-D 42 was most impressive when compared with other types in service at home and abroad, encouraging Nieuport engineers to set about creating improved developments.

Optimised as a high-altitude fighter, the Ni-D 42C was also modified for successful attempts on a number of distance and speed records.

Nieuport-Delage Ni-D 52

Closely resembling the Ni-D 42 but constructed largely of metal instead of wood, the Nieuport-Delage Ni-D 52 single-seat fighter prototype appeared in 1927, and in the following year won a competition sponsored by the Spanish government. Nieuport supplied Spain with 34 aircraft and the first of 91 machines built under licence by Hispano Aviacion was flight tested at Getaffi airfield in 1930. The last Hispano-built aircraft was delivered in 1936 and, the type formed the backbone of the Aviacion Militar for some seven years. At the outbreak of the Spanish Civil War six squadrons still flew the type which, by then, was obsolete. Most fell into Republican hands, only a dozen or so being seized by the Franco forces. The Republican aircraft did not go into action for some time, and when they did were soon surpassed by the Nationalist Fiat CR.32s, most of the Ni-D 52s then being relegated to coast patrol duties or training.

These Hispano-built Aviacion Militar Ni-D 52s were photographed before the Spanish Civil War.

Ni-D 72: version all-metal skinning; prototype flew 23 January 1928; three series aircraft delivered to Belgium in 1929 and four, somewhat modified, to Brazil in 1931
Ni-D 82: prototype of 1930 with revised upper wing planform; flown first with 600-hp (447-kW) Hispano-Suiza 12Lb engine, then changed to 500-hp (373-kW) Lorraine 12Ha Petrel and new vertical tail surfaces fitted; maximum speed 171 mph (275 km/h); in August 1931 lower wing eliminated to turn aircraft into parasol monoplane, and later sold to Spain

Early in the war the government's Guadalajara workshops assembled some 20 Ni-D 52s from available spare parts, but by 1938 the type had no further value and all surviving aircraft were scrapped.

SPECIFICATION	
Nieuport-Delage Ni-D 52 **Type:** single-seat fighter **Powerplant:** one 580-hp (433-kW) Hispano-Suiza 12Hb V-12 piston engine **Performance:** maximum speed 158 mph (255 km/h); service ceiling 22,965 ft (7000 m); range 249 miles (400 km) **Weights:** empty equipped 3,016 lb	(1368 kg); maximum take-off 4,050 lb (1837 kg) **Dimensions:** wingspan 39 ft 4½ in (12.00 m); length 24 ft 7¼ in (7.50 m); height 9 ft 10 in (3.00 m); wing area 332.62 sq ft (30.90 m²) **Armament:** two forward-firing synchronised 7.62-mm (0.3-in) Vickers machine-guns

Nieuport-Delage Ni-D 62

Appearing in 1927, the same year as the Ni-D 52, the **Ni-D 62** retained the wooden structure of the earlier Ni-D 42. It was a refined version of the earlier type with some structural strengthening and a wing of increased chord with smaller ailerons, but the most noticeable external change was a larger tailplane. Between 1928 and 1931 the French Aviation Militaire took delivery of 265 Ni-D 62 single-seat fighters, while the Aéronautique Maritime acquired 50. The **Ni-D 621** was a specialised trainer, three of the type being built, and three Ni-D 62s had twin float installations for use in training French Schneider Trophy pilots.

By the time the **Ni-D 622** development was being built in 1931, the basic design was obsolescent. The Ni-D 622 had the lightweight supercharged Hispano-Suiza 12Md piston engine, and full-span ailerons were fitted. Production totalled 248 for the Aviation Militaire and 62 for the French navy. By 1933 the main strength of French fighter aviation lay in the little Nieuports, but their shortcomings became evident when Ni-D 622s attempting to escort General Italo Balbo's renowned formation of Savoia-Marchetti S.55s over Strasbourg, found it almost impossible to keep up with the large twin-hulled Italian flying-boats. Variants of the Ni-D 622 included three conversions, the **Ni-D 623** for speed record attempts, the **Ni-D 624** monoplane racer and the **Ni-D 625** for parachute experiments. Twelve of the **Ni-D 626** export version were sold to Peru in 1933. The **Ni-D 629** of 1932 had a Hispano-Suiza 12Mdsh piston engine of 500 hp (373 kW) with a supercharger for improved altitude performance, and oleo-pneumatic landing gear, but by the time deliveries of 50 machines to the French escadrilles de chasse had been completed in 1935, the design was totally obsolete.

SPECIFICATION	
Nieuport-Delage Ni-D 629 **Type:** single-seat fighter **Powerplant:** one 500-hp (373-kW) Hispano-Suiza 12Mdsh V-12 piston engine **Performance:** maximum speed 162 mph (260 km/h); service ceiling 29,035 ft (8850 m); range 559 miles (900 km) **Weights:** empty equipped 3,053 lb	(1385 kg); maximum take-off 4,145 lb (1880 kg) **Dimensions:** wingspan 39 ft 4½ in (12.00 m); length 25 ft ¾ in (7.64 m); height 9 ft 10 in (3.00 m); wing area 311.63 sq ft (28.95 m²) **Armament:** two fixed forward-firing synchronised 0.3-in (7.62-mm) Vickers machine-guns

Aircraft of the Ni-D 62 series still equipped French reserve units in September 1939, and when the German Blitzkrieg was launched in May 1940, 143 aircraft of all versions were still on charge with the Armée de l'Air. A Ni-D 629 is illustrated.

Noorduyn Norseman

Noorduyn Aircraft Ltd, a name soon changed to Noorduyn Aviation Ltd, was established in Canada during 1935, occupying the former Curtiss-Reid factory near Montreal. Work had started in 1934, before formation of the company, on the design of a medium-size versatile transport aircraft that would appeal to a wide civil and/or military market, be suitable for operation in the severe climatic conditions of the Canadian winter, and have optional float, ski or wheel landing gear to give it go-anywhere capability. Named **Norseman I**, the prototype was flown first on 14 November 1935, as a braced high-wing monoplane with fixed tailwheel landing gear and powered by a Canadian-built 420-hp (313-kW) Wright R-975-E3 radial engine. An enclosed and heated cockpit with side-by-side seating for two was located forward of the wing centre-section, with behind and below it, a roomy cabin for eight passengers, seated on easily removable bench seats so that little time was needed to convert the interior for cargo operations.

SPECIFICATION	
Noorduyn Norseman V **(landplane)** **Type:** utility transport **Powerplant:** one 550-hp (410-kW) Pratt & Whitney R-1340-AN-1 Wasp radial piston engine **Performance:** maximum speed 155 mph (249 km/h); service ceiling 17,000 ft (5180 m); range	1,150 miles (1851 km) **Weights:** empty 4,680 lb (2123 kg); maximum take-off 7,400 lb (3357 kg) **Dimensions:** wingspan 51 ft 6 in (15.70 m); length 32 ft (9.75 m); height 10 ft 3 in (3.12 m); wing area 325 sq ft (30.19 m²)

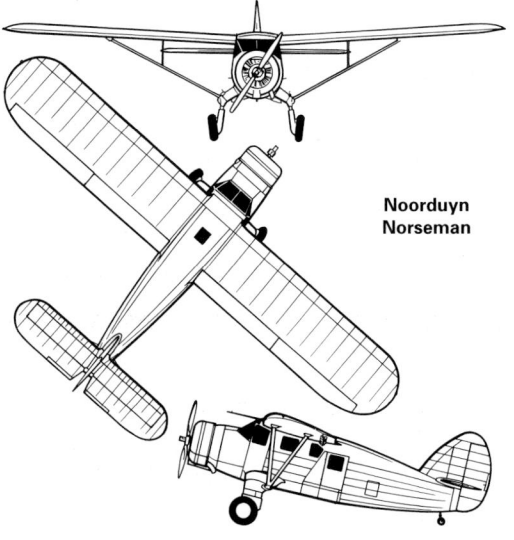

Noorduyn
Norseman

Noorduyn Norseman (continued)

An additional 20 cu ft (0.57 m³) of baggage/cargo space was provided beneath the cabin floor. The initial production version was the **Norseman II** with only minor changes from the prototype, but it was soon discovered that the Norseman was underpowered with the Wright engine, leading first to the **Norseman III** with a 450-hp (336-kW) Pratt & Whitney Wasp SC (only three built), and the **Norseman IV** with the 550-hp (410-kW) Pratt & Whitney S3H1 or R-1340-AN-1 Wasp engine. The same powerplant was used in the **Norseman V** and **Norseman VI**, the latter designation being used for the aircraft produced during World War II for the RCAF and USAAF, with the designation Norseman V reserved by patriotic Bob Noorduyn for the first post-war civil

version with the V signifying victory. In early 1946 the Canadian Car & Foundry (CCF) company acquired manufacturing and sales rights for the Norseman. It then developed a single **Norseman VII** prototype with a wing and tailplane of all-metal construction and a lengthened cabin, but although this was flown in 1951, no production examples were built. In May 1953 CCF sold all rights in the Norseman to a specially formed company, Noorduyn Norseman Aircraft Ltd, which continued to provide product support. Total production by Noorduyn and CCF numbered about 900 aircraft, the majority of

Built as the ideal bush plane for Canada's harsh environment, the Norseman was equally at home on floats, skis or wheels.

them being supplied initially for military use during World War II. RCAF acquisitions began in 1938 with four Norseman IVs, which it operated as wireless trainers under the designation **Norseman Mk IVW**, with additional purchases made after the outbreak of

war. The major buyer was the US Army Air Force which, after testing a single Norseman IV, acquired it and six other examples under the designation **YC-64**. Subsequent contracts for Norseman Vs reached a total of 749, designated initially **C-64A** and later **UC-64A**. Three of this total were transferred to the US Navy,

which designated them **JA-1**, and under the designation **UC-64B** six with twin floats were used by the US Army Corps of Engineers. Other military operators of the Norseman during or post-World War II included the air forces of Australia, Brazil, Honduras, Indonesia, the Netherlands East Indies, Norway and Sweden.

Nord 1000 Pingouin and 1100 Noralpha

In early 1942, production of the Messerschmitt Bf 108 Taifun was transferred to the Société Nationale de Constructions Aéronautiques du Nord, known usually as Nord or SNCAN, at Les Mureaux in France. The production line established there built 170 Bf 108s for Germany before the liberation of France in 1944. Nord then continued production of this aircraft under the designation **Nord 1000**, replacing the standard Argus engine in 1945 with the 233-hp (174-kW) Renault 6Q 11 which brought a designation change for this three-seat aircraft to **Nord 1001 Pingouin I**. The **Nord 1002 Pingouin II** which followed, powered by a Renault 6Q 10 of similar power, differed by providing four-seat

This Noralpha served with l'Atelier Industriel de l'Air d'Aulant during 1973. The type was little more than a Bf 108 with a tricycle undercarriage.

accommodation. Combined production of Pingouin I and II aircraft was 250, the majority of them finding use in communications and liaison roles with the French armed services.

During 1943-44 Nord built two prototypes of the Messerschmitt Me 208, which differed from the Bf 108 by introducing retractable tricycle landing gear. Only one survived until the liberation, being designated **Nord 1100**

Noralpha, and this was developed by the company as the **Nord 1101** and **Nord 1102** with Renault 6Q 10 and 6Q 11 engines respectively. The respective designations **Ramier I** and **Ramier II** were allocated by the French armed services. Combined Nord 1101/1102 production was 200 aircraft.

Under the designation **N 1104 Noralpha**, Nord used one aircraft to flight-test a 240-hp

(179-kW) Potez 6DØ engine, and two N 1101 Ramier Is were converted for similar tests with the Turboméca Astazou

turboshaft engine under the designation **N1110 Nord-Astazou**, the first being flown on 15 October 1959.

SPECIFICATION	
Nord 1101 Noralpha	**Weights:** empty 2,090 lb (948 kg);
Type: four-seat cabin monoplane	maximum take-off 3,627 lb
Powerplant: one 233-hp (174-kW)	(1645 kg)
Renault 6Q 10 inline piston engine	**Dimensions:** wingspan 37 ft 8 in
Performance: maximum speed	(11.48 m); length 28 ft (8.53 m);
189 mph (305 km/h); service ceiling	height 10 ft 8 in (3.25 m); wing
19,355 ft (5900 m); range 745 miles	area 187 sq ft (17.37 m²)
(1200 km)	

Nord 1200 Norécrin

To participate in a design contest for a two/three-seat cabin monoplane sponsored by the French ministry of transport, Nord built the **Nord 1200 Norécrin** prototype which had the same general

configuration as the Nord 1100 series. As first flown on 15 December 1945, it was powered by a 100-hp (75-kW) Mathis G4R engine, but the initial **N 1201 Norécrin I** production version differed by

having a 140-hp (104-kW) Renault 4P01 engine and three-seat accommodation, being redesignated **N 1203 Norécrin II** when powered by the 135-hp (101kW) Regnier 4L00 engine. A four-seat **N 1202 Norécrin** was tested in 1946 with a 160-hp (119-kW) Potez 4D01 engine, leading to the four-seat **N 1203/Norécrin II** with the Regnier 4L00 engine, introduced in 1948, which was followed in 1949 by the **N 1203/IV Norécrin III** with modified

landing gear. The **N 1203/IV Norécrin IV** introduced the 170-hp (127-kW) Regnier 4L02 engine, and the **N 1203/V Norécrin V** was a similarly-powered two-seat military version armed with machine-guns and rockets. Production was suspended in 1953, being resumed in 1955 with the **N 1203/V Norécrin VI** which intro-

duced a 145-hp (108kW) Regnier 4L14 engine, and the final variants of 1959 were the **N 1204 Norécrin** and **N 1204/H Norécrin** with a 125-hp (93-kW) Continental C125 and 145-hp (108-kW) Continental C145 flat-four engine respectively. Approximately 470 Norécrins had been built when production ended.

SPECIFICATION	
Nord 1203/11 Norécrin II	**Weights:** empty 1,437 lb (652 kg
Type: four-seat cabin monoplane	maximum take-off 2,315 lb
Powerplant: one 135-hp (101-kW)	(1050 kg)
Regnier 4L00 inline piston engine	**Dimensions:** wingspan 33 ft 6¼ in
Performance: maximum speed	(10.22 m); length 23 ft 8 in
174 mph (280 km/h); service ceiling	(7.21 m); height 9 ft 6 in (2.90 m);
16,405 ft (5000 m); range 559 miles	wing area 139.93 sq ft (13.00 m²)
(900 km)	

The Norécrin sold well at home and was exported mostly to South America.

Nord 1402 A/B and 1405 Gerfaut

The SFECMAS (previously Arsenal) **1402A Gerfaut IA** was a delta-wing research aircraft. Later SFECMAS was merged into Nord. The Gerfaut's configuration included thin delta wings with 58° 25' sweepback on the leading edge, swept vertical tail surfaces with a high-set delta tailplane, retractable tricycle landing gear, and a turbojet engine mounted within the fuselage. As first flown on 15 January 1954 the aircraft was powered by a 6,173-lb (27.45-kN) thrust SNECMA Atar 101C turbojet engine, and on 3 August 1954 it became the first aircraft in Europe to exceed Mach 1 in level

flight without any form of power augmentation. The **N 1402B Gerfaut IB**, which flew first on 9 February 1955, had larger wings, an Atar 101D1 turbojet of similar thrust, and other improvements.

Finally came the **N 1405 Gerfaut II** of basically the same configuration, but with refined structure and flown first on 17 April 1956 with an 8,378-lb (37.26-kN) thrust Atar 101F. It was flown subsequently with

A high-speed, delta-winged research aircraft similar to the British Fairey Delta, the Gerfaut exceeded Mach 1 in its original form.

an Atar G21 developing 8,818 lb (39.22 kN) thrust with afterburning. After the completion of its research

programme this aircraft was used in 1958 to test Aladin interception radar at high altitudes and speeds.

Nord 1500 Griffon I and II

After early tests of the Gerfaut la, Nord designed and built the **1500-01 Griffon I** research aircraft, which was intended to flight-test a combined turbojet-ramjet power unit. A delta wing aircraft with 60° of sweepback on the leading edge, the **N 1500** had wings with elevons for control in pitch and roll. Thus the tail unit comprised only swept vertical surfaces, and fixed foreplanes were mounted on

each side of the forward fuselage. The Griffon I was flown for the first time on 20 September 1955. Initially powered by a 9,039-lb (40.20-kN) thrust SNECMA Atar 101G21 turbojet, it was flown later with an 8,378-lb (37.26-kN) thrust Atar 101F. At the completion of initial testing the airframe was modified to accept a 7,716-lb (34.31-kN) thrust Atar 101E3 turbojet within the ducting of an integral

ramjet of Nord design, the turbojet being located just forward of the ramjet burners. Then redesignated **N 1500-02 Griffon II**, it was flown first on 23 January 1957, completing more than 200 test flights before the Nord research programme ended in 1959. Its maximum speed, of Mach 2.19, was recorded on 13 October 1959, and although higher speeds could theoretically have been attained, this

In its ultimate Griffon II form, the N 1500 was a mixed-power, Mach 2-capable aircraft.

was prohibited by the high structural tempera-

tures resulting from kinetic heating.

Nord 2500 Noratlas

Lufttransportgeschwader 61 of West Germany's Luftwaffe employed this Noratlas in the 1960s.

Designed as a military transport for service with the French air force, the **Nord 2500 Noratlas** prototype was flown for the first time on 10 September 1949. Of similar twin-boom configuration to the Fairchild C-82 and C-119 Flying Boxcar, the prototype was powered by two 1625-hp (1212-kW) SNECMA-built Gnome-Rhône 14R radial engines. This was followed by two **N 2501** prototypes which introduced the powerplant intended for production aircraft, comprising two 2,040-hp (1521-kW) SNECMA-built Bristol Hercules 739 radial engines, and the first of these was flown on 28 November 1950.

Satisfactory testing led to the initiation of production, and the Noratlas became standard equipment in the air forces of France, West Germany and Israel, providing valuable long-term service. Operated normally by a crew of four or five,

the Noratlas had the capacity for 7½ tons (7.88 tonnes) of cargo, or could accommodate 45 troops (or passengers in civil use), 36 fully-equipped paratroops, or 18 stretchers and medical attendants for casualty evacuation.

Variants

N 2501: standard production version with SNECMA Hercules 739 engines
N 2501IS: version built for Israeli air force, generally as N 2501
N 2501A: civil transport version, with two 1,650-hp (1230-kW) SNECMA 758/759 Hercules engines, for Union Aéromaritime de Transport (UAT)
N 2501E: redesignation of standard N 2501 for flight testing of an auxiliary powerplant comprising two 882-lb (3.92-kN) thrust Turboméca Marboré II turbojets mounted in wingtip pods to improve 'hot-and-high' performance

N 2502: civil version for Air Algérie and UAT, with a powerplant comprising two SNECMA Hercules 758/759 engines and two Marboré IIE turbojets
N 2502A: civil version as N 2502 for UAT
N 2502B: cargo version with SNECMA Hercules 758/759 engines
N 2502C: cargo version as N 2502B
N 2503: redesignation of original production prototype following installation of two 2,500-hp (1864-kW) Pratt & Whitney R-2800-CB17 radial engines for evaluation; first flown January 1956
N 2504: version for use by French navy as a flying classroom for ASW crews, powerplant as in N 2501E prototype
N 2505: projected ASW version, not built
N 2506: assault transport version with powerplant as N 2504
N 2507: rescue version, powerplant as N 2504
N 2508: cargo version with powerplant comprising two R-2800-CB17 radial engines plus two Turboméca Marboré IIE turbojets
N 2508B: cargo version, generally as above, and with identical powerplant
N 2509: project only, not built
N 2510: project for ASW version of Noratlas, not built

Nord 2500 Noratlas (continued)

The West German Luftwaffe received a total of 186 Noratlas aircraft, 25 of them built by Nord and the balance produced under licence in Germany by the Flugzeugbau Nord. When production ended in October 1961, French and German sources had built a total of 425 Noratlas machines in several versions. France and West Germany replaced their Noratlases with C.160s.

Greece augmented its C-47 force with the Noratlas and began to supplement and replace the type with the C-130H from 1975.

SPECIFICATION

Nord 2501 Noratlas
Type: twin-engine cargo transport
Powerplant: two 2,040-hp (1521-kW) SNECMA-built Hercules 739 sleeve-valve radial piston engine
Performance: maximum speed 273 mph (440 km/h); service ceiling 24,605 ft (7500 m); range
Weights: empty equipped 28,825 (13075 kg); maximum take-off 46,297 lb (21000 kg)
Dimensions: wingspan 106 ft 7½ in (32.50 m); length 72 ft (21.95 m); height 19 ft 8¼ in (6.00 m); wing area 1,089.34 sq ft (101.20 m²)

Nord 3200

To meet a requirement of the French army air force for a two seat primary trainer, Nord flew on 17 April 1957 the first of 50 **Nord 3202** production aircraft, derived from the **N 3200** and **N 3201** with a 240-hp (179-kW) Salmson 8AS04 and 170-hp (127-kW) Regnier 4L22 engine respectively. A cantilever low-wing monoplane with fixed tailwheel landing gear, the N 3202 provided tandem two-seat enclosed accommodation for the instructor (rear seat) and pupil, and the production N 3202 was powered by the 240-hp (179-kW) Potez 4D32 inline engine. A second production batch of 50 had the designation **N 3202B**, differing by having the 4D32 engine replaced by a Potez 4D34. N 3202s with a radio compass and equipped for instrument flight training were redesignated **N 3212**.

Nord's totally-conventional N 3202 was notable only for its useful service as a military trainer.

SPECIFICATION

Nord 3202B
Type: two-seat primary trainer
Powerplant: one 260-hp (194-kW) Potez 4D34 inline piston engine
Performance: maximum speed 162 mph (260 km/h) at sea level; range 621 miles (1000 km)
Weights: empty 1,896 lb (860 kg) maximum take-off 2,690 lb (1220 kg)
Dimensions: wingspan 31 ft 2 in (9.50 m); length 26 ft 7¾ in (8.12 m); height 9 ft 3 in (2.82 m); wing area 174.92 sq ft (16.25 m²)

Nord 3400

Designed as Nord's submission to meet a French army air force requirement for a two-seat observation aircraft, suitable for use also in a secondary casualty evacuation role, the **Nord 3400** prototype was flown for the first time on 20 January 1958. A braced high wing monoplane with fixed tail wheel landing gear, the aircraft had an enclosed cabin providing an excellent field of view, and two section doors on each side of the fuselage simplified the task of loading or unloading a casualty and stretcher. The first prototype, powered by a 240-hp (179-kW) Potez 4D30 engine, was followed by a second prototype later in the year. This differed by having a wing of increased area and a more power 4D34 engine.

After the N 3400 had been ordered into production, the first aircraft was delivered on 9 July 1959. The last of 150 such machines was delivered during March 1961.

SPECIFICATION

Nord 3400 (production version)
Type: two-seat observation/casualty-evacuation aircraft
Powerplant: one 260-hp (194-kW) Potez 4D34 inline piston engine
Performance: maximum speed 146 mph (235 km/h) at sea level; range 621 miles (1000 km)
Weights: empty 2,028 lb (920 kg) maximum take-off 2,976 lb (1350 kg)
Dimensions: wingspan 42 ft 7¾ in (13.00 m); length 27 ft 8 in (8.42 m); height 7 ft 3 in (2.20 m); wing area 224.10 sq ft (20.82 m²)

Norman Thompson aircraft

In 1909 Norman Thompson entered partnership with Douglas White to form an aircraft design and construction company known as White & Thompson Ltd at Middleton-on-Sea near Bognor Regis, Sussex. By October 1915 the name had been changed to Norman Thompson Flight Company Ltd, and the first product to emerge from this new organisation was an attractive twin-engine biplane flying-boat which was designated **Norman Thompson N.T.4**. Of the same general configuration as the Curtiss H-4 (Model 6), it differed by being somewhat larger, with a redesigned hull, and a powerplant of two 150-hp (112-kW) Hispano-Suiza engines mounted between the wings, each driving a pusher propeller. Satisfactory testing led to Admiralty orders for 50 N.T.4s for service with the RNAS, but after the initial batch of six had been delivered, the installation of 200-hp (149-kW) Hispano-Suiza engines brought the redesignation **N.T.4A**. Two prototypes of an improved version, which had the designation **N.2C**, were built and flown in 1918, but were too late to see operational service and no production examples followed. They differed from the N.T.4s by having a hull similar to the Felixstowe 'boats, a revised tail unit, and power provided by two 200-hp

SPECIFICATION

Norman Thompson N.T.2B
Type: two-seat flying-boat trainer
Powerplant: one 200-hp (149-kW) Sunbeam Arab V-8 piston engine
Performance: maximum speed 85 mph (137 km/h) at 2,000 ft (610 m); service ceiling 11,400 ft (3475 m)
Weights: empty 2,321 lb (1053 kg); maximum take-off 3,169 lb (1437 kg)
Dimensions: wingspan 48 ft 4¾ in (14.75 m); length 27 ft 4½ in (8.34 m); height 10 ft 8 in (3.25 m); wing area 453 sq ft (42.08 m²)

In its original form, the enclosed cabin of the N.T.4A offered its crew poor visibility. It was eventually revised to include a glazed cabin roof.

(149-kW) Sunbeam Arab piston engines.

Most extensively built of the Norman Thompson designs was the N.T.2B, a two-seat unequal-span biplane flying-boat. Its enclosed cabin, with side-by-side seating and dual controls, made it ideal for use as a trainer, and its value to the RNAS is well illustrated by the construction of more than 200 examples. As flown originally, the N.T.2B was powered by a 160-hp (119-kW) Beardmore engine, and the first 50 production aircraft had either this engine or a 150-hp (112-kW) Beardmore. In late 1917 the 200-hp (149-kW) Sunbeam Arab was introduced, to be replaced later by the more reliable Hispano-Suiza engine of similar power. The N.T.2B was the standard flying-boat trainer in service with the RNAS/RAF until the end of World War I, required in numbers that were beyond the manufacturing capability of the Norman Thompson company, and resulting in subcontract construction by S.E. Saunders Ltd and the Supermarine Aviation Works. Last of the Norman Thompson flying-boats was the two-seat N.1B biplane prototype, intended for armed patrol, but its performance did not meet official requirements and no further examples were built.

North American A3J/A-5 Vigilante

In the summer of 1962 VAH-7 became the first squadron to take the A-5A Vigilante on an operational cruise. Flying from the USS Enterprise, the squadron took part in the Cuban Missile Crisis blockade, but no Vigilante saw combat until the RA-5C was employed in Vietnam.

Designed to meet a US Navy requirement for a high-performance all-weather attack aircraft, the **NA-247**, known at first as the **NAGPAW (North American General Purpose Attack Weapon)**, won an order for two **YA3J-1** prototypes on 29 June 1956. The name **Vigilante** was allocated soon after this, and the A3J designation was changed subsequently to **A-5**. The design's cantilever monoplane swept wing incorporated no ailerons, roll control being by the use of spoilers in conjunction with differential use of an all-moving tailplane on each side of the fuselage and, when it entered service, the Vigilante was the first US production aircraft to introduce variable-geometry intakes for its two General Electric J79 engines. The first of the prototypes, then powered by two YJ79-GE-2 engines each developing 15,000 lb (66.71 kN) afterburning thrust, was flown for the first time on 31 August 1958, and carrier trials were completed aboard the USS *Saratoga* in July 1960. Initial production version was the **A3J-1 (A-5A)**, US Navy Squadron VAH-7 becoming the first operational unit in June 1961. The primary weapon of the A3J-1 was a free-fall nuclear bomb ejected rearwards from a bomb bay between the tailpipes of the two turbojet engines. A3J-1 production totalled 57 aircraft. This version was followed by an interim long-range bomber version designated **A3J-2 (A-5B)**, incorporating greater fuel capacity and aerodynamic improvements, but because of changes in US Navy policy only six were built and then converted to serve as a long-range unarmed reconnaissance version designated **A3J-3P (RA-5C)**, equipped with side-looking airborne radar, cameras and electronic countermeasures equipment. The first RA-5C was flown on 30 June 1962, being followed by 55 new production aircraft and the conversion to reconnaissance configuration of 53 A3J-1s. The first squadron equipped with the RA-5C Vigilante was RVAH-5 which, in June 1964, was operating from the USS *Ranger*, and other Vigilante squadrons included RVAH-1, RVAH-7, RVAH-9 and RVAH-11.

SPECIFICATION	
North American RA-5C Vigilante	48,400 ft (14750 m); range 3,000 miles (4828 km)
Type: carrier-based long-range reconnaissance aircraft	**Weights:** empty 37,498 lb (17009 kg); maximum take-off 66,000 lb (29937 kg)
Powerplant: two 17,860-lb (79.42-kN) afterburning thrust General Electric J79-GE-10 turbojets	**Dimensions:** wingspan 53 ft (16.15 m); length 76 ft 6 in (23.32 m); height 19 ft 41 in (5.91 m); wing area 754 sq ft (70.05 m²)
Performance: maximum speed Mach 2.1; operational ceiling	

On 21 September 1979 this RA-5C made the Vigilante's last catapulted carrier launch, marking the imminent retirement of a unique recce asset.

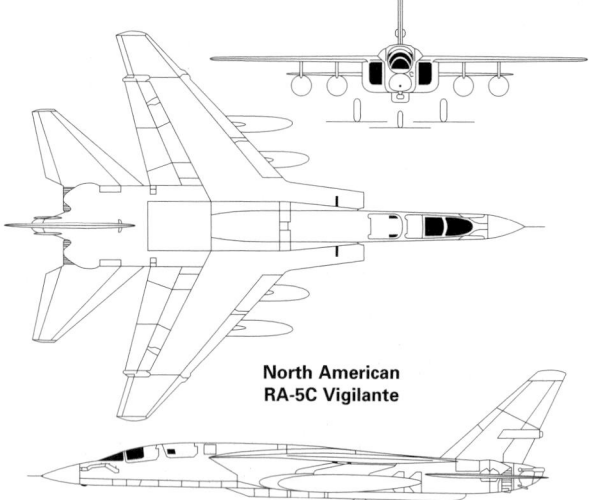

North American RA-5C Vigilante

North American AJ-2/A-2 Savage

With a turbojet in its tail and a pair of powerful radial piston engines, the Savage was primarily tasked with the nuclear-strike role. An AJ-2 is illustrated.

Developed to a US Navy specification for a high-performance carrier-based bomber, with cruise power provided by two 2,400-hp (1790-kW) Pratt & Whitney R-2800 radials, boosted for the attack phase by a 4,600-lb (20.46-kN) thrust Allison J33A-19 turbojet, three **NA-146 (XAJ-1)** prototypes were ordered on 24 June 1946. The first flew on 3 July 1948, and 40 production **AJ-1** (later **A-2A**) aircraft were built, with deliveries to US Navy Squadron VC-5 beginning in September 1949. Modified tail surfaces, additional fuel capacity and more powerful engines were features of 70 **AJ-2** (later **A-2B**) aircraft, the first of which flew on 19 February 1953, while 30 **AJ-2P** reconnaissance aircraft were built with modified noses to house cameras, the first AJ-2P being flown on 6 March 1952. A number of AJ-1s and AJ-2s was later converted as tankers.

North American B-25 Mitchell

Designed to meet a US Army Air Corps requirement for a twin-engine attack bomber, the **NA-40** prototype was a shoulder-wing monoplane with retractable tricycle landing gear, accommodating a crew of three and, as first flown in January 1939, was powered by two 1,100-hp (820-kW) Pratt & Whitney R-1830-S6C3-G engines. These were soon replaced by 1,300-hp (969-kW) Wright GR-2600-A71 Cyclone engines, the resulting **NA-40B** being delivered for USAAC testing in March, but within two weeks it had crashed as a result of pilot error. Early tests had been impressive, and North American was requested to continue its development. The **NA-26** design was completed in September 1939 having the wing configuration changed from a shoulder to mid position, the fuselage widened to provide side-by-side seating for pilot and co-pilot/navigator in an improved enclosed cockpit, and 1,700-hp (1268kW) Wright R-2600-9 Cyclones to cater for an increased gross weight and bombload. The NA-26 was ordered into production

under the designation **B-25** and name **Mitchell** after the controversial champion of US air power, William 'Billy' Mitchell. The first B-25 was flown on August 1940, the designation changing after 24 had been completed to **B-25A**, this version (40 built) introducing armour and self-sealing fuel tanks, and the balance of the initial contract (120) was built to **B-25B** configuration, which introduced power-operated dorsal and ventral two-gun turrets. **B-25C** production totalled 1,619, this version introducing an autopilot, R-2600-13 engines and additional underwing bomb racks, and was followed by 2,290 examples of the generally similar **B-25D**. Two aircraft taken from the B-25C line were used for experiments in wing de-icing as the **XB-25E** and **XB-25F**, with hot-air and electrical heating respectively. One experimental **XB-25G**, with a 75-mm US Army field gun in the nose, served as the prototype for the anti-shipping **B-25G** (405 built) with an M4 75-mm cannon and six machine-guns, which was used against Japanese targets by the US air forces in the

Far East. More heavily armed was the **B-25H** (1,000 built) with a 75-mm cannon and 14 (or in late versions 18) 0.5-in (12.7-mm) machine-guns. Most extensively built was the final production **B-25J** (4,390 built from a contract for 4,805), with Wright R-2600-92 engines and 12 0.5-in (12.7-mm) machine-guns. Ten examples of an **F-10** reconnaissance version were converted from B-25Ds, and during 1943-44 60 B-25D, B-25G, B-25C and B-25J aircraft were modified as advanced trainers with the respective designations **AT-25A**, **AT-25B**, **AT-25C** and **AT-25D**, redesignated subsequently as **TB-25D**, **TB-25G**, **TB25C** and **TB-25J**; more than 600 of the last model were converted after the war, and between 1951 and 1954, 157 Mitchells were modified as **TB-25K** (117) and **TB-25M** (40) flying classrooms for teaching the Hughes E-1 and E-5 fire control radar. Other post-war modifications included **TB-25L** and **TB-25N** multi-engine conversion trainers, with 90 and 47 produced respectively by Hayes

This Mitchell Mk II, coded 'EV-W', is from No. 180 Squadron, RAF, which was based at Foulsham from October 1942 until August 1943. The aircraft carries nine bomb silhouettes, each recording a raid over enemy territory with No. 2 (Bomber) Group.

Aircraft Corporation, as well as a number of **ZB-25C**, **ZB-25D**, **ZXB-25E**, **CB-25J** and **VB-25J** utility and staff transport aircraft. A total of 706 aircraft, similar to the B-25J, was acquired for use by the US Navy and US Marine Corps under the designations **PBJ-1C** (50), **PBJ-1D** (152); **PBJ1-G** (1), **PBJ-1H** (248), and **PBJ-1J** (255). The RAF received 23 B-25Bs which it designated **Mitchell Mk I**, followed by 432 B-26Cs and 113 B-25Ds as the **Mitchell Mk II**, and 296 B-25Js as the **Mitchell Mk III**. Other nations to use Mitchells have included Australia, Bolivia, Brazil, Canada, Chile, Colombia, Cuba, France, Indonesia, Mexico, Netherlands East Indies, Peru, Uruguay, USSR, and Venezuela.

Initial deliveries to the USAAC were made in the spring of 1941, to the 17th Bombardment Group

(Medium), and it was an aircraft of this unit that was the first to sink a Japanese submarine on 24 December 1941. Sixteen specially-prepared B-25s from this same group made the historic attack on the Japanese mainland on 18 April 1942: led by Lieutenant Colonel James H. Doolittle, these aircraft were flown off the carrier USS *Hornet*, then the heaviest aircraft operated from an aircraft carrier, to attack targets some 800 miles (1287 km) distant at Kobe, Nagoya, Tokyo and Yokohama, afterwards flying on to China where most of them force-landed. Mitchells served throughout World War II and continued in use for many years after the war, particularly in the air arms of smaller nations. The USAF's last B-25 staff transport was retired on 21 May 1960.

SPECIFICATION

North American B-25J
Type: five-seat medium bomber
Powerplant: two 1,700-hp (1268kW) Wright R-2600-92 Cyclone radial piston engines
Performance: maximum speed 272 mph (438 km/h) at 13,000 ft (3960 m); service ceiling 24,200 ft (7375 m); range 1,350 miles (2173 km)
Weights: empty 19,480 lb (8836 kg); maximum take-off

35,000 lb (15876 kg)
Dimensions: wingspan 67 ft 7 in (20.60 m); length 52 ft 11 in (16.13 m); height 16 ft 4 in (4.98 m); wing area 610 sq ft (56.67 m²)
Armament: 12 0.5-in (12.7-mm) machine-guns as standard, plus eight 5-in (127-mm) rocket projectiles and up to 3,000 lb (1361 kg) of bombs

The designation CB-25 covered many B-25 transport conversions, there being no set standard. This CB-25J flew with the Military Air Transport Service.

Right: With its formidable armament, the B-25H (and the Marine PBJ-1H) was a useful ship killer.

North American B-45 Tornado

The first American four-jet bomber to achieve flight-test status, the **NA-130** was evolved from studies which began in late 1944. Aimed at the application of the then-new turbojet propulsion system to existing heavy bomber practice and techniques, the **XB-45 Tornado** did not represent a major advance, despite the installation of two pairs of 4,000-lb (17.78-kN)

Allison-built General Electric J35-A-4 engines in their underslung nacelles. Three prototypes were ordered in 1945 and the first of these was flown by test pilot George Krebs at Muroc Dry Lake (Edwards AFB) on 17 March 1947. A shoulder-wing monoplane, the XB-45 provided accommodation for two pilots under a clear-view fighter-type canopy, and the

bombardier sat in the glazed nose. The rear gunner, in a tail turret, operated the aircraft's sole defensive armament, a pair of 0.5-in (12.7-mm) Browning M7 guns.

In its B-45 form the Tornado was a useful interim bomber, but as the RB-45C (illustrated), the type gained notoriety as a spyplane.

Variants

B-45A: 96 production B-45As were procured by the USAF, first entering service with the 47th Bombardment Group at Barksdale AFB, Louisiana in November 1948, this unit moving to British bases in 1952; only the first 22 retained the J35 engines, later aircraft having 4,000-lb (23.86-kN) thrust General Electric J47s; the last B-45As were retired in 1958; 14 **TB-45A** aircraft were modified from bomber airframes for use as target tugs, with bomb bay mounted reel and cable equipment to which could be attached a Chance Vought target glider; one **JB-45A** was used by Westinghouse as an engine testbed

B-45B: projected version with revised radar and fire-control systems

B-45C: 10 B-45Cs were manufactured, deliveries beginning in 1949; with uprated 5,200-lb (23.13-kN) thrust J47 engines and intended for close-support duties, they had a strengthened airframe to permit operation at a higher maximum take-off weight, increased from 90,000 lb (40823 kg) to 110,000 lb (49895 kg); an additional and externally-evident change was the heavily-framed canopy over the pilots' cockpit; up to 22,000 lb (9979 kg) of bombs could be carried

RB-45C: 33 RB-45Cs were delivered between June 1950 and October 1951, operating in the photographic-reconnaissance role and carrying a total of 12 cameras in four fuselage positions; the bomb bay housed 25 M122 photoflash bombs and additional fuel tanks; to provide additional take-off power water injection was used, a jettisonable water tank being fitted under each nacelle. This version was first operated by the 91st Strategic Reconnaissance Wing and later flew with the 19th Tactical Reconnaissance Squadron, USAFE, and other units, some with British national insignia; one **JB-45C** was converted for use as an engine testbed by General Electric

SPECIFICATION

North American RB-45C Tornado
Type: photographic reconnaissance aircraft
Powerplant: four 6,000-lb (26.69-kN) thrust (with water injection) General Electric J47-GE-13/15 turbojets
Performance: maximum speed 570 mph (917 km/h); service ceiling 40,250 ft (12270 m); range 2,530 miles (4072 km)
Weights: empty 49,984 lb (22672 kg); maximum take-off 110,721 lb (50222 kg)
Dimensions: wingspan 96 ft (29.26 m); length 75 ft 11 in (23.14 m); height 25 ft 2 in (7.67 m); wing area 1,175 sq ft (109.16 m²)
Armament: two 0.5-in (12.7-mm) Browning machine-guns

This B-45A was based at RAF Sculthorpe with USAFE's 86th BS, 47th BG (Light) in the early 1950s. These bombers not only represented the forward basing of American nuclear weapons, but also proved a useful cover for the clandestine flights of Sculthorpe's RB-47Cs when these arrived in 1952. Operating in British national markings and flown by RAF aircrews, these aircraft performed hazardous photo recce missions over Eastern Europe.

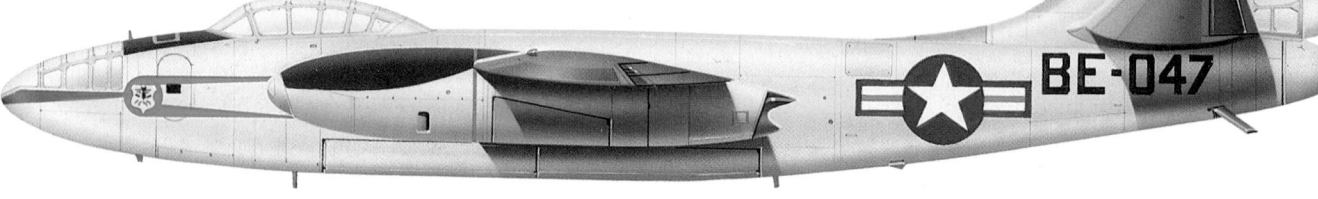

North American B-70 Valkyrie

Developed to USAF General Operational Requirement 38 for an intercontinental bomber to replace the Boeing B-52, the Mach 3 **XB-70A** was the subject of an order for three prototypes, awarded on 4 October 1961, although the third was later cancelled. A delta-winged canard design, with wing tips which folded down at 65° to the horizontal to provide improved supersonic stability, and powered by six 30,000-lb (133.42-kN)

thrust General Electric J93-GE-3 engines, the first prototype was flown by Alvin S. White and Colonel Joseph F. Cotton on 21 September 1964; it first achieved its design speed of Mach 3 on 14 October 1965. The improved second prototype flew on 17 July 1965, but was lost in a mid-air collision on 8 June 1966. The surviving aircraft carried out a number of test programmes, including work in connection with

An all-time classic warplane design, the Valkyrie had a wingspan of 105 ft (32.00 m) and a length of 196 ft (59.75 m). Its maximum take-off weight was an incredible 530,000 lb (249476 kg).

the US supersonic transport programme, but on 4 February 1969 it was flown to retirement at the US Air Force Museum, Wright Patterson AFB, Dayton, Ohio.

North American F-86 Sabre

It was over Korea that the F-86 won eternal fame. This F-86E belonged to the 335th Fighter Interceptor Squadron of the 4th Fighter Interceptor Wing and was flown by Captain Robert J. Love. The Captain finished the war with six kills.

To meet a USAAF requirement for a day fighter that could be used also as an escort fighter or dive-bomber, North American submitted a design known as the **NA-140**.

Two **XP-86** prototypes of the NA-140 design were contracted in late 1944, but when German research data on the characteristics of swept wings became available soon after the end of the war, North American sought USAAF agreement to redesign the XP-86 to incorporate swept wings and tail surfaces. This cost a year's delay, and it was not until 1 October 1947 that the first prototype was flown, then powered by a Chevrolet-built General Electric TG-180 (or J35-C-3) turbojet of 3,750 lb (16.68 kN) thrust; on

25 April 1948, by then re-engined with a General Electric J47 turbojet as the **YP-86A**, this aircraft exceeded a speed of Mach 1 in a shallow dive. The first production version was the **P-86A**, powered initially by a 4,850-lb (21.57-kN) thrust General Electric J47-GE-1 turbojet

and flown first on 20 May 1948. A month later USAF redesignation resulted in the P-86A becoming the **F-86A** and in 1949, by which time it had gained the name **Sabre**, the new fighter began to enter service with the USAF's 1st, 4th and 81st Fighter Groups, the 94th Squadron

of the 1st Fighter Group receiving the first in February 1949. F-86A production totalled 554, the majority having 5,200-lb (23.13-kN) thrust J47-GE-3, -7, -9, or -13 turbojets. Subsequent production, arranged chronologically, included the **F-86E** with an all-moving tailplane, and

the **F-86F** (1,539 built) with a modified wing. Most extensively built was the ensuing **F-86D** (2,054), a redesigned all-weather/ night fighter, followed by the **F-86H** fighter-bomber (477) with a more powerful J73 engine, and the **F-86K** (120) which was a simplified version of the F-86D.

North American F-86 Sabre (continued)

Under the designation **TF-86** two dual-control trainers were produced as conversions of F-86Fs, and the designation **F-86L** was applied to rebuilds (827) from F-86Ds, which introduced an increased span wing and updated avionics. The **F-86B** (deeper fuselage and larger tyres) and **F-86C** (redesigned fuselage) did not enter production. In addition to aircraft built by North American, Canadair Ltd in Montreal built F-86Es for the USAF, followed by 290 generally similar **Sabre Mk 2** fighters, comprising 230 for the RCAF and 60 for the Mutual Defense Assistance Program. Canadian production continued with one **Sabre Mk 3** to flight test the indigenous Orenda engine, **438 Sabre Mk 4** aircraft for the RAF with General Electric engines, 370 **Sabre Mk 5** machines with the 6,355-lb (28.26-kN) thrust Orenda 10 turbojet, and 655 **Sabre Mk 6** aircraft with the 7,275-lb (32.35-kN) thrust Orenda 14.

The Commonwealth Aircraft Corporation in Australia also became involved in Sabre production, modifying the airframe

Fitting the Avon engine into the Sabre airframe proved a difficult task. Malaysia retained its CAC Sabres into 1980.

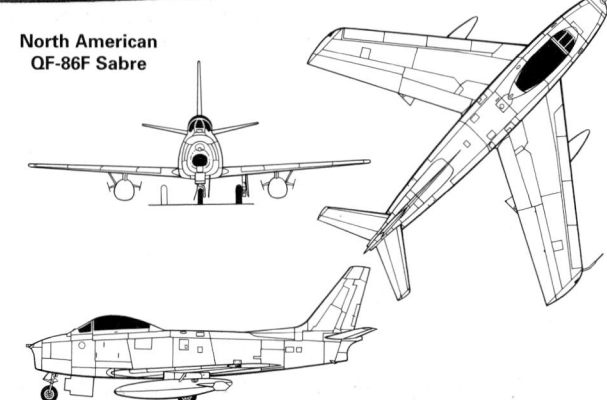

North American QF-86F Sabre

As the FJ-4B, the Fury could carry up to five Bullpups or, for fighter missions, up to four AIM-9 Sidewinders, as illustrated.

for two 30-mm ADENs and the 7,500-lb (33.35-kN) thrust Rolls-Royce Avon 26 engine, and built for the RAAF 21 **Sabre Mk 30** and 20 **Sabre Mk 31** aircraft, plus 69 **Sabre Mk 32** fighters with Australian-built engines. Fiat in Italy assembled 221 F-86Ks from North American-built kits of

components, and production in Japan began in the same way, with Mitsubishi leading a group of Japanese companies which first assembled, then increasingly constructed, a total of 300 similar to the F-86F and RF-86F.

A requirement for fighter-bombers to equip the US Navy and Marine Corps, superseding the FJ-1 Fury resulted in a contract for three **XFJ-2 Fury** prototypes for evaluation. These were basically

similar to the USAF's F-86E, but with arrester hooks, extending nose gears and catapult hitches. They were followed by 200 **FJ-2** fighters which introduced folding wings, 538 **FJ-3** aircraft with a deeper fuselage and the more powerful Wright J65-W-2 or J65-W-4 turbojet of 7,800-lb (35.76-kN), or 7,650-lb (34.02-kN) thrust respectively, 152 of the **FJ-4** (later **F-1E**), a completely redesigned

attack variant with a 7,700-lb (34.25-kN) thrust Wright J65-W-16A engine, and 222 **FJ-4B** (later **AF-1E**) improved attack aircraft, which incorporated a totally new airframe. Two examples of an unusual subvariant of the FJ-4B had the designation **FJ-4F**; used for evaluation purposes, these each had an auxiliary rocket motor and supplementary fuel tank.

The F-86 saw considerable service in the Korean War where, despite having marginally inferior performance to the much vaunted MiG-15, it was able to gain superiority over these aircraft thanks to the superior training and experience of their pilots. Subsequently, in addition to serving with the air arms of NATO and British Commonwealth countries, the F-86 Sabre was supplied to many other countries throughout the world. A number of F-86 airframes ended their days as **QF-86** target drones.

SPECIFICATION

North American F-86D Sabre
Type: single-seat all-weather/night interceptor
Powerplant: one 7,500-lb (33.35-kN) thrust afterburning General Electric J47-GE-17B or -33 turbojet
Performance: maximum speed 707 mph (1138 km/h) at sea level; service ceiling 54,600 ft (16640 m);
range 835 miles (1344 km)
Weights: empty 12,470 lb (5656 kg); maximum take-off 17,100 lb (7756 kg)
Dimensions: wingspan 37 ft 1 in (11.30 m); length 40 ft 4 in (12.29 m); height 15 ft (4.57 m); wing area 288.0 sq ft (27.76 m²)
Armament: 24 2.75-in (70-mm) air-to-air rocket projectiles

Basically a down-graded F-86D, the F-86K was built in Italy by Fiat and by North American for service with the air forces of France, Italy (illustrated), the Netherlands, Norway and West Germany.

North American F-100 Super Sabre

In 1949 North American initiated private-venture development of the F-86 Sabre, the design being known initially as the **Sabre 45** because its wings were swept at 45°. It was intended that this aircraft should be capable of supersonic performance in level flight, and the culmination of two years of design and development was the receipt on 1 November 1951 of a USAF contract for two **YF-100** (later **YF-100A**) prototypes and 110 **F-100A Super Sabre** production aircraft. The first

In widespread service prior to the war in Vietnam, the F-100D went into combat in this peacetime 'natural metal scheme', but the familiar three-tone SEA camouflage was soon adopted in theatre.

of the prototypes was flown on 24 April 1953, exceeding Mach 1 during this initial flight, and 29 October 1953 was a 'red letter day', when the first production aircraft was flown and the first prototype established a new world speed record of

754.99 mph (1215.04 km/h). When the type became operational with the USAF's 479th Fighter Day Wing, on

29 September 1954, it was the world's first operational fighter capable of supersonic performance in level flight. Early production

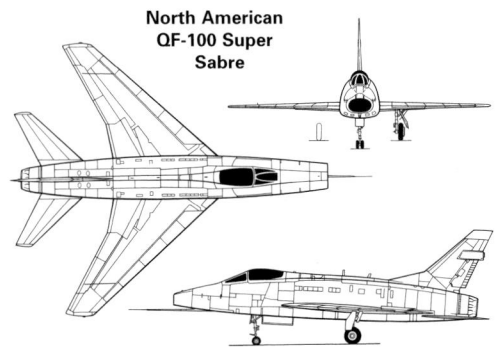

North American QF-100 Super Sabre

F-100As were powered by the Pratt & Whitney J57-P-7 turbojet, developing 15,000 lb (66.71 kN) afterburning thrust, but the last 36 of the total of 203 that were built had the 16,000-lb (71.15-kN) afterburning thrust J57-P-39 engine. An improved tactical fighter-bomber version was planned as the **F-100B**, but this was revised into the **YF-107A**, only three of which flew with the J75 engine. With two USAF wings largely equipped, accidents caused by inertia roll-yaw coupling caused a crisis, and a major F-100A redesign with tall fins and extended wings.

Development of the Super Sabre continued with the **F-100C** fighter-bomber, of which 476 were built,

this version having inflight-refuelling capability, a J57-P-21 engine and eight underwing weapons pylons. Most extensively built was the **F-100D** attack version with many changes, including a flapped wing, provisions for

internal ECM equipment and introduction of a LABS (low-altitude bombing system) for so-called toss delivery of nuclear weapons. A total of 1,274 F-100Ds was built, followed by 339 of the final production version, the **F-100F** tandem two-seat trainer. Sub-variants include a small number of **RF-100A** photo-reconnaissance conversions from F-100As; a single **TF-100C** conversion from an F-100C, which served as a prototype for the tandem two-seat F-100F; and some **DF-100F** drone director conversions from F-100Fs. Under the designation **NF-100F** three F-100Fs were used for test purposes, and six F-100Fs delivered to the Danish air force from USAF stocks

were given the temporary designation **TF-100F**.

Foreign operators have included Taiwan (F-100A), Denmark and France (F-100D and F-100F); and the Turkish air force has also operated large numbers of secondhand F-100s. With the USAF the Super Sabre saw extensive use in Vietnam, some

aircraft being especially modified for use in EW (electronic warfare) and FAC (forward air control) operations; and even when replaced by more advanced aircraft, F-100 Super Sabres remained in use with Air National Guard units until 1980. Many F-100s were converted for use as **QF-100** target drones.

SPECIFICATION

North American F-100D Super Sabre
Type: single-seat fighter-bomber
Powerplant: one 17,000-lb (75.60-kN) afterburning thrust Pratt & Whitney J57-P-21A turbojet
Performance: maximum speed 864 mph (1390 km/h) or Mach 1.3 at 35,000 ft (10670 m); service ceiling 46,000 ft (14020 m); standard range 600 miles (966 km)
Weights: empty 21,000 lb (9525 kg); maximum take-off 34,832 lb (15800 kg)
Dimensions: wingspan 38 ft 9½ in (11.82 m); length excluding probe 47 ft 1¼ in (14.36 m); height 16 ft 3 in (4.95 m); wing area 385 sq ft (35.77 m²)
Armament: four 20-mm cannon, plus weapon load of up to 7,500 lb (3402 kg) on underwing pylons including bombs, missiles and rockets

Schemed as a tandem two-seat advanced and conversion trainer, the F-100F proved most important flying FAC and Wild Weasel missions over Vietnam. The Super Sabre had a pioneering role in the development of the Wild Weasel concept, flying Iron Hand missions 1 December 1965, employing the AGM-45 Shrike ARM from April 1966.

North American FJ Fury

Ordered on 1 January 1945, and one of three turbojet-powered aircraft for US Navy evaluation (the others being the McDonnell FD Phantom and the Vought F6U Pirate), the first of three **NA-134** (US Navy **FJ-1 Fury**) prototypes flew on 27 November 1946, powered by a 3,820-lb (16.99-kN) thrust General Electric J35-GE-2 engine. One hundred production

FJ-1s were ordered on 28 May 1945, but reduced subsequently to 30 aircraft, each armed with six 0.5-in (12.7-mm) machine-guns at the sides of the intake, and having the 4,000-lb (17.78-kN) thrust J35-A-2 engine. Production deliveries began in March 1948, the Fury equipping fighter squadron VF-5A (later VF-51) aboard USS *Boxer*.

First carrier landings were made on 10 March

This image graphically shows the fundamental differences between the US Navy's FJ-1 Fury (left) and the later, Sabre-derived, FJ-2 Fury. The FJ-1 proved to be a useful stop-gap fighter.

1948 and the Fury, which was the first jet fighter to go to sea under fully operational conditions, had a maximum speed of 547 mph (880 km/h).

North American O-47

Developed by General Aviation (the precursor of North American Aviation) to meet a US Army specification for an observation aircraft, the **GA-15** represented a radical change in design for such a role in that, unlike its predecessors, it was a low-wing monoplane with an enclosed cockpit, seating a three-man crew. Powered

by an 850-hp (634-kW) Wright Cyclone engine, the prototype flew in mid-1935 and to provide an acceptable field of view for the observer, a glazed nose position was located under the fuselage. North American put the type into production to meet a USAAC contract for 109 **O-47A** aircraft ordered in February 1937; the contract

A single 0.3-in (7.62-mm) machine-gun could be carried in the O-47's right wing, with a similar weapon in the rear cockpit.

was later increased to 164. They were powered by 975-hp (727-kW) Cyclones, while 74 **O-47B** aircraft had 1,060-hp (790-kW) engines and additional fuel capacity. During World War II they served as trainers and target tugs.

North American OV-10 Bronco

In the early 1960s, the US Marine Corps recognised its need for a purpose-built COIN aircraft and drew up the specification for what it identified as a LARA (Light

Armed Reconnaissance Airplane) with additional observation and FAC roles. Procurement was initiated by a design competition, with North American's

NA-300 proposal being selected as the winner in August 1964. The initial contract covered seven **YOV-10A** prototypes, the first flying on 16 July 1965

powered by two 660-shp (492-kW) Garrett T76 turbo-props. Testing revealed some shortcomings that were rectified by a 10-ft (3.05-m) increase in wingspan, and the introduction of an uprated version of the T76 engine in

nacelles that were moved outboard slightly to reduce engine noise in the cabin. The increased span was premiered on a prototype first flown on 15 August 1966, and the seventh prototype was given alternative engines.

North American OV-10 Bronco (continued)

These Pratt & Whitney Canada T74 engines (military designation for the PT6A turboprop) were used for comparative evaluation.

As built, the **North American** (later **Rockwell**) **OV-10 Bronco** is of distinctive configuration with a shoulder-mounted constant-chord wing, and twin booms extending aft from the engine nacelles to terminate in vertical tail surfaces that are linked by a fixed-incidence tailplane with inset elevator. A slender pod-type fuselage accommodates the crew of two in tandem under a large canopy with excellent all-round view. The fuselage pod can accommodate two stretchers and a medical attendant, or up to five paratroops.

The OV-10 is armed with four fixed 0.3-in (7.62-mm) M60C machine-guns, comprising two in each sponson. Four 600-lb (272-kg) underwing hardpoints were located on sponsons projecting from the fuselage sides, with a 1,200-lb (544-kg) centreline hardpoint and two underwing stations.

Procurement of the initial **OV-10A** covered 114 aircraft for the US Marine Corps, the first of them flown on 6 August 1967. This service used the type for forward air control and helicopter escort, in addition to the intended role of light armed reconnaissance. VMO-2 was the first

unit to deploy to Vietnam in July 1968, and the Bronco served with the Marines, Navy and Air Force. It soon demonstrated its superior performance against other FAC platforms.

Six generally similar **OV-10B** aircraft were supplied to West Germany for use as target tugs, followed by 12 higher-performance **OV-10B(Z)** aircraft with a 2,950-lb (13.12-kN) thrust General Electric J85-GE-4 turbojet pylons mounted above the wing. These aircraft are no longer in service.

Rockwell developed several production versions generally similar to the OV-10A. Thirty-two **OV-10C** machines were delivered to the Royal Thai air force in 1971-74, the survivors of which were being phased out of service late in 2000. The **OV-10E** continues to serve with the Venezuelan air force in summer 2001, Venezuela having also taken delivery of 18 former USAF OV-10As by April 1991. The **OV-10F** remains in service with the Indonesian air force. In 1981 the Moroccan air force took delivery of six refurbished, former USMC OV-10As for COIN duties.

Additional deliveries of surplus USMC OV-10As included 24 to the Philippine air force.

A suitably equipped OV-10 seemed ideal to fulfil a night FAC and strike designation role in the light

of the USAF's Vietnam experience. While the OV-10A was effective, it could not stop the infiltration of men and supplies at night. In the early 1970s, 15 OV-10As were modified under the USAF's Pave Nail programme. Specialised equipment given to these aircraft included a combined laser rangefinder/target illuminator, a LORAN receiver and a LORAN co-ordinate converter. After the withdrawal from Vietnam, these Pave Nail OV-10s reverted to standard configuration.

The USN had been slightly ahead of the USAF in considering the OV-10A for such a task, and in 1970 two Navy OV-10As were converted as **YOV-10D NOGS (Night Observation/Gunship System)** prototypes with enhanced night and all-weather capability. They were equipped with an undernose turret in an extended nose carrying a FLIR and laser target designator, a rear underfuselage turret to mount a 20-mm

With the OV-10D came the potential to employ an M197 20-mm three-barrelled cannon with 1,500 rounds.

In addition to its machine-gun armament, the OV-10 could employ a variety of sponson-mounted weapons, including various rocket pods.

cannon, and two underwing pylons carrying extra stores. By the time evaluation was complete, the US had withdrawn its forces from Vietnam, but in 1974 the US Navy contracted Rockwell to establish and test an **OV-10D** production configuration. This resulted in 17 of the USMC OV-10As being converted as OV-10Ds for a NOS (Night Observation Surveillance) role, all of them being redelivered during 1979-80.

The OV-10D saw active service during Operation Desert Storm against Iraq during 1991, with two lost

in combat. Fourteen survivors, plus 23 OV-10As, were to have been upgraded to a common **OV-10D+** standard, with structural strengthening to permit carrier operations plus upgraded avionics, navigation and weapons systems. The programme should have been completed by late 1993, but the final withdrawal of the type was brought forward to FY1994. With the withdrawal of US military Broncos, some were passed to various civil agencies, while a number of OV-10Ds was delivered to South Korea.

SPECIFICATION	
North American (Rockwell) OV-10A Bronco	14,444 lb (6552 kg)
Type: two-seat COIN and light-attack aircraft	**Dimensions:** wingspan 40 ft (12.19 m); length 41 ft 7 in (12.67 m); height 15 ft 2 in (4.62 m); wing area 291 sq ft (27.03 m²)
Powerplant: two Garrett T76-G-416/417 turboprops each rated at 715 ehp (533 ekW)	**Armament:** up to 3,600 lb (1633 kg) of ordnance, including
Performance: maximum level speed 'clean' at sea level 281 mph (452 km/h); service ceiling 24,000 ft (7315 m); combat radius 228 miles (367 km) with maximum warload and no loiter	napalm tanks, slick and retarded Mk 82 500-lb (227-kg) bombs, unguided 2.75-in (70-mm) or 5-in (127-mm) rockets, machine-gun and cannon pods, flares and smoke tanks
Weights: empty equipped 6,969 lb (3161 kg); maximum take-off	

North American P-51 Mustang

One of the most effective fighter aircraft of World War II, the **P-51 Mustang** began life as the **NA-73X** to meet a British requirement of April 1940. Needed desperately because of the grave situation in Europe, it was completed ahead of the 120-day schedule set by the UK, but the 1,100-hp (820-kW) Allison V-1710-F3R engine needed to power it was delayed and the prototype was not flown for the first time until 26 October 1940. The NA-73X completed a remarkably trouble-free test programme, the first production example of a contract for 320 **NA-73** aircraft being flown on 1 May 1941; the second

series aircraft, for RAF evaluation, arrived in the UK in November 1941. Designated **Mustang Mk I**, this aircraft was soon shown in extensive testing to have remarkable performance at low altitudes, declining rapidly as the power output of the Allison engine fell off dramatically

above 12,000 ft (3660 m). This meant that the type was of little use for combat or interception roles in Europe. It was clearly well suited for tactical reconnaissance, and its standard armament of four 0.5-in (12.7-mm) and four 0.3-in (7.62-mm) machine-guns meant that it also had

The RAF borrowed this A-36A Invader in Tunisia early in 1943. It retained its USAAF serial number during service with No. 1437 Strategic Reconnaissance Flight.

potential for ground attack. Equipped with an obliquely-mounted camera, the RAF's Mustang Mk Is began to enter service with No. 2 Squadron of Army

Co-operation Command in April 1942, eventually equipping no fewer than 23 squadrons of this command and resulting in a follow-on contract for an

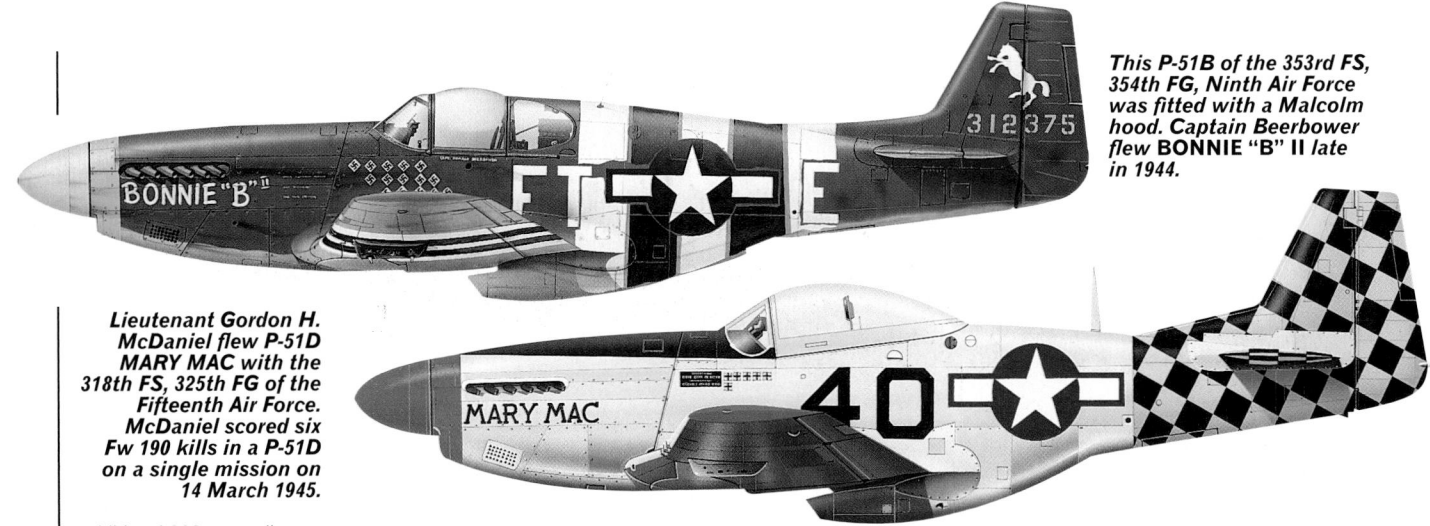

*This P-51B of the 353rd FS, 354th FG, Ninth Air Force was fitted with a Malcolm hood. Captain Beerbower flew **BONNIE "B" II** late in 1944.*

Lieutenant Gordon H. McDaniel flew P-51D MARY MAC with the 318th FS, 325th FG of the Fifteenth Air Force. McDaniel scored six Fw 190 kills in a P-51D on a single mission on 14 March 1945.

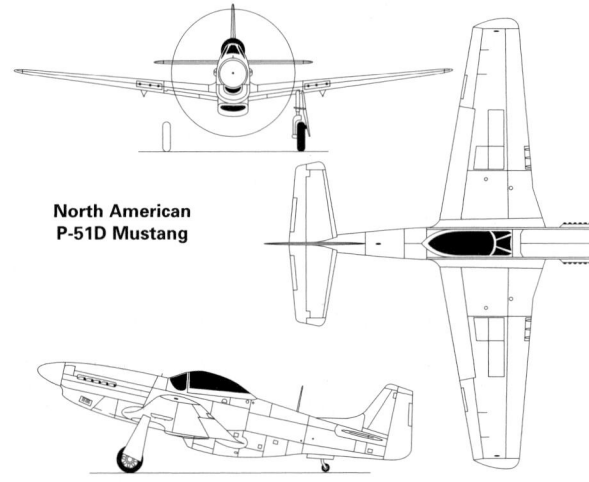

North American P-51D Mustang

additional 300 generally similar aircraft. A condition of US government approval of NA-73 development and production had been the supply of two evaluation aircraft to the US Army Air Corps, which designated them **XP-51**. Just before this, however, the USAAC had ordered 150 **P-51** aircraft for supply to the UK under Lend-Lease, these differing from the initial production aircraft by having self-sealing fuel tanks and four 20-mm cannon replacing the armament of eight machine-guns. The RAF received 93 of this version, designating the variant **Mustang Mk IA**, and 55 camera-equipped **F-6A** aircraft went to the USAAF for tactical reconnaissance; the balance of two aircraft had 1,430-hp (1066-kW) Packard-built Merlin V-1650-3 engines installed for evaluation, then becoming redesignated **XP-78**, later **XP-51B**. This had resulted because testing by the USAAF of its XP-51 prototypes had confirmed RAF findings of the deficiency in high-altitude performance, a weakness explored in the UK by the experimental installation of Rolls-Royce Merlin 61 and 65 engines. With adoption of the same course in the USA the XP-51Bs demonstrated a maximum speed of 441 mph (710 km/h) at 29,800 ft (9085 m), result-

ing in large-scale orders for Merlin-engined P-51s. Before that, RAF adoption of the Mustang for use in a ground-attack role brought USAAF procurement of 500 **A-36A** aircraft named initially **Apache** but later adopting the British name Mustang, which incorporated dive brakes and underwing bomb racks. A single A-36A was supplied to the RAF.

Almost simultaneously with procurement of the A-36As, the USAAF ordered 310 **P-51A** fighters with the 1,200-hp (895-kW) V-1710-81 engine, plus armament of four 0.5-in (12.7-mm) machine-guns and underwing racks; of the total 50 were allocated to the RAF, which designated them **Mustang Mk II**, and 35 were converted as tactical reconnaissance **F-6B** aircraft for the USAAF. Production of the Merlin-engined versions began in 1943 with the **P-51B**, of which 1,988 were built at North American's Inglewood, California factory, and with the generally similar **P-51C**, of which 1,750 were built in a new factory at Dallas, Texas. Both differed from the earlier versions by having a strengthened fuselage, redesigned ailerons and armament of four 0.5-in (12.7-mm) machine-guns. Lend-Lease

allocations of these versions for the RAF comprised 274 and 636 respectively, all designated **Mustang Mk III**. Some 71 of the P-51Bs and P-51Cs received by the USAAF were modified as **F-6C** tactical reconnaissance aircraft. Major production version was the **P-51D**, with a total of 7,956 built, introducing a bubble canopy to improve the field of view, a modified rear fuselage, and six 0.5-in (12.7-mm) machine-guns; from this total 136 were modified as tactical reconnaissance **F-6D** aircraft, and 281 were allocated to the RAF which designated them **Mustang Mk IV**. A total of 1,500 generally similar **P-51K** fighters followed, 163 being completed as tactical reconnaissance **F-6K** aircraft and 594 being allocated to the RAF, which designated them Mustang Mk IV also. The testing of **XP-51F**, **XP-51G** and **XP-51J** lightweight prototypes, with a variety of engines, led to the **P-51H** final production version, of which 555 were built before VJ-Day brought cancellation of the balance of 2,000 ordered. Also cancelled were 1,700 similar V-1650-11 powered **P-51L** aircraft and 1,628 **P-51M** fighters; the M was to be the Dallas-built version of the P-51H, of which only a single example was built. On the grand total of 15,386 Mustangs production ended in the USA, but one other minor source of supply was Australia, where Commonwealth Aircraft Corporation began by assembling 80 P-51Ds from imported components, these serving with the RAAF under the designa-

tion **Mustang Mk 20**.

Licence construction followed for the RAAF, comprising 26 **Mustang Mk 21** aircraft with V-1650-7 engines, 14 of them later converted to **Mustang Mk 22** configuration, 67 **Mustang Mk 23** aircraft with Merlin 66 or 70 engines, and 13 Mustang Mk 22s for tactical reconnaissance; none of these RAAF aircraft saw service before VJ-Day.

Under Lend-Lease 50 P-51Ds were supplied to China and 40 to Netherlands forces in the Pacific theatre, and some USAAF P-51s were supplied to the AVG in China. In the immediate post-war years the type remained in US service, with Strategic Air Command until 1949 and for several more years with US Air Reserve and Air National Guard units, being among the first USAF fighters to see action in the Korean War. In the RAF some remained in use with Fighter Command until 1946, and war surplus

P-51s from both the USA and UK continued to have some years of post-war service with over 50 air forces.

P-51s with various modifications have since appeared as civilian racing aircraft, one powered by a 3,800-hp (2834-kW) Rolls-Royce Griffon engine holding the current world speed record for piston-engine aircraft at 499.048 mph (803.139 km/h). In the 1950s Trans-Florida Aviation marketed a two-seat executive conversion, leading to a series of rebuilds and even new Mustangs by Cavalier Aircraft Corporation, including in the late 1960s several for counter insurgency and forward air control duties with the USAF. Acquiring the Cavalier programme, Piper Aircraft Corporation developed first the **Enforcer** of 1971, leading to a USAF contract of 1981 for two turboprop-powered **PA-38 Enforcer** prototypes, first flown on 9 April and 8 July 1983 respectively.

SPECIFICATION	
North American P-51D Mustang **Type:** single-seat interceptor/long-range escort fighter **Powerplant:** one 1,695-hp (1264-kW) Packard Merlin V-1650-7 V-12 piston engine **Performance:** maximum speed 437 mph (703 km/h) at 25,000 ft (7620 m); service ceiling 41,900 ft (12770 m); maximum range 2,080 miles (3347 km)	**Weights:** empty 7,125 lb (3232 kg); maximum take-off 12,100 lb (5488 kg) **Dimensions:** wingspan 37 ft ¼ in (11.28 m); length 32 ft 3 in (9.83 m); height 8 ft 8 in (2.64 m); wing area 233.0 sq ft (21.65 m²) **Armament:** six 0.5-in (12.7-mm) machine-guns, plus up to two 1,000-lb (454-kg) bombs or six 5-in (127-mm) rocket projectiles

North American P-82 Twin Mustang

Although the P-51 had demonstrated exceptional range for a fighter, even

greater range capability was required in the Pacific theatre. This led to develop-

ment of the **XP-82 Twin Mustang** prototype, which joined two P-51 fighters by

eliminating one port and one starboard wing and both tailplanes, uniting the

two remnants with a parallel-chord wing section and a new tailplane and elevator; the revised main landing gear comprised a single unit on each fuselage.

North American P-82 Mustang (continued)

F-82G "Dottie Mae" *flew with the 4th F(AW)S during the Korean War. Designed as a night- and all-weather fighter, the F-82G also flew attack missions.*

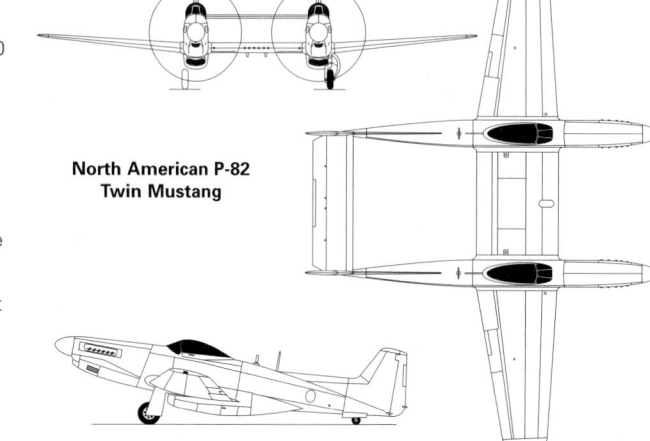

Testing of three prototypes led to a USAAF order for 500 **P-82B** fighters, but only 20 had been built when the war ended. Two of this number were converted as night-fighters designated **P-82C** and **P-82D**, with SCR-720 and APS-4 radar respectively. In

1946 the USAAF placed a new order for 250 P-82s, comprising 100 **P-82E** escort fighters, and 150

night-fighters as **P-82F** (100 with APS-4 radar) and **P-82G** (50 with SCR-720 radar) aircraft. All production B to G variants were redesignated **F-82** in 1948, and the last version to enter service was the **F-82H**, a winterised variant of the F-82/-82G for service in Alaska. Twin Mustangs operated by the US 5th Air Force were among the first US aircraft to operate over Korea. One, flown by a pilot of the 68th Fighter (All-Weather) Squadron, destroyed the first enemy aircraft in the Korean War.

North American P-82 Twin Mustang

SPECIFICATION

North American F-82G Twin Mustang
Type: night-fighter
Powerplant: two 1,600-hp (1193-kW) Allison V-1710-143/145 V-12 piston engines
Performance: maximum speed 461 mph (742 km/h) at 21,000 ft (6400 m); service ceiling 38,900 ft (11855 m); range 2,240 miles (3605 km)
Weights: empty 15,997 lb

(7256 kg); maximum take-off 25,951 lb (11608 kg)
Dimensions: wingspan 51 ft 3 in (15.62 m); length 42 ft 5 in (12.93 m); height 13 ft 10 in (4.22 m); wing area 408 sq ft (37.90 m²)
Armament: six wing-mounted 0.5-in (12.7-mm) machine-guns, plus up to four 1,000-lb (454-kg) bombs, or four auxiliary fuel tanks on underwing racks

North American T-28 Trojan

With the requirement for a trainer to replace the T-6 Texan in service, the **North American NA-159** design proposal was successful in gaining a contract for two **XT-28** prototypes, the first of them being flown on 26 September 1949. Following satisfactory evaluation of these prototypes, the type was ordered into production for the USAF under the designation **T-28A** and allocated the name **Trojan**. A cantilever low-wing monoplane with retractable tricycle landing gear and an 800-hp (597-kW) Wright R-1300 radial engine, the T-28 provided tandem two-seat accommodation for the instructor and pupil in an enclosed cockpit. The initial 1950 production contract covered 266 T-28As, the first deliveries to Air Training

France made good use of the Fennec during various colonial conflicts. This machine is armed with gun and rocket pods.

Command being made during the same year, and the number built eventually totalled 1,194. In 1952 it became US policy to standardise trainers for the nation's armed forces, so following evaluation of two USAF T-28As, the US Navy ordered a **T-28B** version which differed primarily by having a 1,425-hp (1063-kW) Wright R-1820-86 engine. Production for the US Navy totalled 489 T-28Bs, followed by 299 **T-28C** aircraft which differed only by having arrester gear for deck landing training. In 1962 North American began the conversion of T-28As for

use in a counter-insurgency role; redesignated **T-28D**, these had the Wright R-1820 engine and were given six underwing hard-points to accept a variety of stores and weapons. North American completed 321 conversions and Fairchild Hiller another 72. A number was also completed as attack trainers under the designation **AT-28D**. Many T-28Ds were operated in the Congo and Vietnam, and were supplied to the air forces of several nations. In

France, Sud-Aviation also modified a considerable number of ex-USAF T-28Ds for use in duties such as close-support, patrol and reconnaissance, naming

them **Fennec**. They replaced T-6s on similar duties in Algeria, and a number was supplied for service with the Argentine navy.

SPECIFICATION

North American T-28B Trojan
Type: two-seat basic trainer
Powerplant: one 1,425-hp (1063-kW) Wright Cyclone R-1820-86 radial piston engine
Performance: maximum speed 343 mph (552 km/h); service ceiling 35,500 ft (10820 m); range

1,060 miles (1706 km)
Weights: empty 6,424 lb (2914 kg); maximum take-off 8,500 lb (3856 kg)
Dimensions: wingspan 40 ft 1 in (12.22 m); length 33 ft (10.06 m); height 12 ft 8 in (3.86 m); wing area 268.0 sq ft (24.90 m²)

North American T-6/SNJ/Harvard

Built as an NA-66, AJ955 entered service with the RCAF as a Harvard Mk II. In 1943 it wore these markings while serving with No. 2 Wireless School.

Almost certainly the most extensively used trainer of all time, with more than 17,000 built by North American, the **Harvard** was derived from the **NA-16** prototype first flown in April 1935. A cantilever low-wing monoplane with fixed tailwheel landing gear, open cockpits in tandem and power provided by a 400-hp (298-kW) Wright R-975 Whirlwind radial, the type, after official testing, received a production order under the designation **BT-9**. Modifications were speci-

fied in the contract, the most important being enclosed cockpits, and the resulting pre-production **NA-18** incorporated the changes and was powered by a 600-hp (447-kW) Pratt & Whitney R-1340 Wasp. However, the R-975 engine, was retained for production aircraft, the BT-9 (42 built) being followed by the **BT-9A** (40) which introduced two 0.3-in (7.62-mm) machine-guns, by the **BT-9B** (117) with detail improvements, and by the similar **BT-9C** (67) with

some equipment changes. A single **BT-9D**, with revisions of the outer wing panels and rudder, led to the improved **BT-14** (251

built) which introduced a metal-covered fuselage and the 450-hp (336-kW) Pratt & Whitney R-985-25 Wasp Junior engine; in 1941 27

were re-engined with 400-hp (298kW) R-985-11 engines, and were redesignated **BT-14A**. The US Navy also operated 40

This AT-6A was photographed during its service with the Gunnery School at Harlingen, Texas during 1942.

examples of the BT-9 under the designation **NJ-1**, these having the R-1340 Wasp engine. Export orders for these fixed landing gear versions included one for Australia, which served as a pattern aircraft for production by Commonwealth Aircraft Corporation, China (85), Honduras (3), and licence-holding Japan and Sweden (two pattern aircraft each). France received 230 aircraft similar to the BT-9, for service with the air force (200) and navy (30), but only 111 of a similar order for BT-14s had been delivered at the time of the French collapse; the balance of 119 was acquired by the UK, then

being supplied to the RCAF, which designated them **Yale Mk I**.

The requirement for a basic combat trainer led to development of the **NA-26**, a version of the NA-16 introducing retractable tail-wheel landing gear, the 600-hp (447-kW) R-1340 engine, and equipment representative of contemporary operational types. Production versions included the **BC-1** (177), of which 30 were modified as **BC-II** instrument trainers; the **BC-1A** (93) with airframe revisions: and a single **BC-1B** with a modified wing centre-section. A change of role to advanced trainer brought new designations, first as the **AT-6**

Texan (94) which differed little from the BC-1A. Subsequent versions included the **AT-6A** (1,847) with the R-1340-49 engine and revised fuel tanks, the **AT-6B** (400) gunnery trainer, the **AT-6C** (2,970) and **AT-6D** (4,388) which had revised structure to economise on light alloys, and the **AT-6F** (956) with a strengthened airframe. The US Navy also used the type extensively, following the NJ-1 with the **SNJ-1** (16 similar to the BC-1 but with a metal-covered fuselage), **SNJ-2** (61) with R-1340-56 engine, **SNJ-4** (2,400) and **SNJ-5** (1,357) equivalent to AT-6C and AT-6D, and **SNJ-6** comprising 931 of the US Army's 956 AT-6Fs which had been procured for the US Navy. The designation **SNJ-5C** applied to SNJ-5s equipped with arrester hooks for deck-landing training.

In June 1938 the UK ordered 200 BC-1s, designating them **Harvard Mk I**, these representing the first of more than 5,000 delivered, mostly under Lend-Lease, to Commonwealth air forces. Most of the first 200 Harvard Mk Is were shipped to Southern Rhodesia for inception of the Commonwealth Air Training Plan, but the RAF retained almost all of a second batch of 200. After 30 similar aircraft were acquired for the RCAF, 600 equivalent to the AT-6 were procured as **Harvard Mk II** trainers and distributed to the RAF (20) and RNZAF

Post-war, many AT-/T-6s gained a D/F-loop in a rear-fuselage acorn fairing, as modelled by this Italian aircraft.

(67), the remainder being allocated to Canada for use in its contribution to the Air Training Plan. In addition to the Harvard Mk I and II, **Harvard Mk III** aircraft were acquired, equivalent respectively to the AT-6C and AT-6D; the designation **Harvard Mk IIB** applied to 2,610 built as **AT-16** aircraft by Noorduyn Aviation Ltd in Montreal, for use by the RAF and RCAF, and corresponding to the AT-6A. In 1946 this company was taken over by Canadian Car and Foundry, which built for the RCAF 270 **Harvard Mk 4** trainers to T-6G standard and 285 similar aircraft with the designation **T-6J** for the USAF Mutual Aid Program.

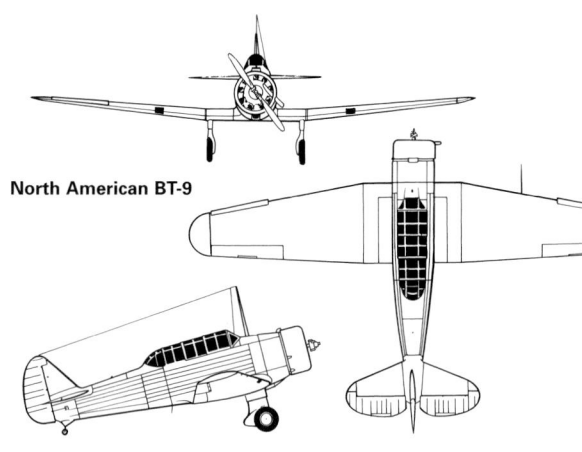

North American BT-9

From 1949, 2,068 T-6s of different versions were rebuilt under the designation **T-6G**, introducing the R-1340-AN-1 engine, increased fuel capacity, improved cockpit layout, a steerable tailwheel and other improvements. These entered service with the USAF and USN, and during the Korean War 97 were modified to **LT-6G** configuration for deployment in battlefield surveillance and FAC roles. In addition to Texans exported to Brazil, China and Venezuela, many other air arms received surplus aircraft from RAF, RCAF and USAAF stocks, and the type remains in service with some air forces in 2001.

SPECIFICATION	
North American SNJ-5	(1207 km)
Type: two-seat advanced trainer	**Weights:** empty 4,158 lb
Powerplant: one 550-hp (410-kW)	(1886 kg); maximum take-off
Pratt & Whitney R-1340-AN-1	5,300 lb (2404 kg)
radial piston engine	**Dimensions:** wingspan 42 ft ¼ in
Performance: maximum speed	(12.81 m); length 29 ft 6 in
205 mph (330 km/h) at 5,000 ft	(8.99 m); height 11 ft 9 in (3.58 m);
(1525 m); service ceiling 21,500 ft	wing area 253.70 sq ft (23.57 m²)
(6555 m); range 750 miles	

North American X-15

Without doubt the most remarkable and most valuable research vehicle to have been developed within the X-series of USAF/USN-sponsored experimental aircraft, the **X-15** was required to meet performance parameters of a maximum altitude of 250,000 ft (76200 m) and a maximum speed of Mach 6, well in excess of 4,000 mph (6437 km/h). The X-15 programme was funded jointly by the USAF and the USN, the former overseeing design and construction, although the National Advisory Committee for Aeronautics

(NACA) provided overall technical direction. The official Request for Proposals was issued to 12 airframe companies on 30 December 1954, and on 4 February 1955 four engine manufacturers were invited to bid for the rocket motor contract. North American was awarded the airframe contract for its **NA-240** design in November 1955, and the XLR-99 engine contract went to Reaction Motors Inc. in September 1956.

It had always been the intention that the X-15 would be air-launched, and two B-52s were modified to

carry the type under the starboard wing, between the fuselage and the inboard engine, then being redesignated NB-52A and NB-52B. Features of the X-15 were the long cylindrical fuselage with lateral fairings to house control systems and fuel tanks, and the thick wedge-shaped dorsal and ventral fins, the lower section of the latter being jettisoned before landing to give clearance for the retractable skids which formed the main landing gear.

The first two **X-15A** airframes were each powered initially by two 8,000-lb (35.58-kN) thrust XLR-11 engines, the first

aircraft becoming airborne under its mother ship on 10 March 1959. Test pilot Scott Crossfield made the first unpowered release on 8 June, and the same pilot also made the first powered flight, in the second X-15A, on 17 September. The latter machine was the first to be flown with the definitive XLR-99 engine, flying in this form on 15 November 1960. But for a ground-running accident before its first flight, the third airframe would have been the first XLR-99-powered machine to fly. However, the accident damage was repaired and, the first X-15A having

been re-engined, all three aircraft entered the performance evaluation phase of the programme. Almost 200 flights were made, including a series with the second aircraft which was rebuilt following a landing accident on 9 November 1962. In its rebuilt form it had a fuselage extension of 2 ft 5 in (0.74 m), external auxiliary fuel tanks, and was given a heat-resistant surface treatment. As the **X-15A-2**, it made its maiden flight on 28 June 1964, and later achieved a maximum altitude of 354,200 ft (107960 m) and a maximum speed of 4,534 mph (7297 km/h).

This aircraft, the third X-15, was flown by Neil Armstrong on its maiden flight on 20 December 1961. The aircraft made 65 flights, achieving a maximum speed of Mach 5.65.

SPECIFICATION	
North American X-15A	**Performance:** maximum speed
Type: high-speed high-altitude	4,159 mph (6693 km/h)
research aircraft	**Weight:** maximum take-off
Powerplant: one Reaction Motors	34,000 lb (15422 kg)
XLR-99 rocket motor with a thrust	**Dimensions:** wingspan 22 ft
rating of 57,000-lb (253.48-kN) at	(6.71 m); length 50 ft (15.24 m);
sea level and approximately	height 13 ft 6 in (4.12 m); wing
70,000-lb (31751-kg) at peak	area 200 sq ft (18.58 m²)
altitude	

Northrop Alpha and Beta

The Alphas were configured for three passengers and 465 lb (211 kg) of mail and cargo, since mail flying was a key business.

In 1928 John K. Northrop and Ken Jay formed the Avion Corporation at Burbank, California. Northrop had in the previous year designed Lockheed's first aircraft, the Vega, and his first design for his new company was known as the **Flying Wing**. Of more consequence was his next design, the **Alpha**, an all-metal seven-seat single-engine low-wing monoplane. In 1929 Avion Corporation became the Northrop Aircraft Corporation, a division of the United Aircraft and Transport Corporation of which Boeing was also a part. Trans Continental and Western Air Inc. ordered five Alphas with 420-hp

(313-kW) Pratt & Whitney Wasp engines and began services on 20 April 1931 from San Francisco to New York, with 13 intermediate stops, the journey taking just over 23 hours. To achieve all-weather and night-flying capability, the Alphas had the most modern radio and navigation equipment, and for winter operations became the first commercial type to be fitted with Goodrich rubber de-icer boots on wing and tail surface leading edges. Thirteen of the 17 Alphas built saw service with TWA, and three were supplied for evaluation to the USAAC where, had production orders been given, they would have

been designated **C-19**.
Various configurations carried the designations **Alpha 2**, **Alpha 3**, **Alpha 4** and **Alpha 4-A**, and a number of changes was made between individual aircraft as late modifications were made retrospectively to earlier aircraft, including fitting of 'trousers' over the original rather utilitarian landing gear. The last conversion was the **Gamma 4-A**, an all-cargo aircraft which could carry 1,250 lb (567 kg) of cargo; the **Gamma 4** and Gamma 4-A had a 450-hp (336-kW) Wasp engine and most of the earlier aircraft were similarly retrofitted.
The last surviving Alpha

was re-acquired by TWA in 1975 and superbly restored before being placed in Washington's Smithsonian Institution National Air and Space Museum.
In 1931 Northrop built the prototype of an all-metal low-wing sporting monoplane, the **Beta**, a two-seater with a 160-hp

(119-kW) Menasco Buccaneer inline engine. It was converted later to single-seat configuration and fitted with a 300-hp (224-kW) Wright Whirlwind radial engine, in which form it became the first aircraft of such power to exceed 200 mph (322 km/h).

Northrop A-13, A-16, A-17 & A-33

Northrop used the Gamma transport as the basis of a private venture design for a light attack bomber, identifying this as the **Gamma 2C** which, powered by a 735-hp (548-kW) Wright SR-1820F radial engine, was acquired

for evaluation by the USAAC in June 1934 under the designation **YA-13**. Subsequently re-engined with a 950-hp (708-kW) Pratt & Whitney R-1830 Twin Wasp, this aircraft was redesignated **XA-16**

In its production form the A-17 featured cutaway spats for its main undercarriage, the undercarriage legs themselves being faired with large 'trousers'.

(**Gamma 2F**). Following tests of the YA-13 and XA-16, Northrop received a $2 million contract for 110 attack bombers designated **A-17**, but because testing of the XA-16 had shown that the aircraft was overpowered, the Gamma 2F was re-engined with a 750-hp (559-kW) R-1535 Twin Wasp Junior, serving as the prototype for the A-17. Following the incorporation of several other modifications, the first of 109 production A-17s was delivered in December 1935. A contract was received in the same month for an improved **A-17A**, introducing retractable tail-wheel landing gear and the 825-hp (615-kW) R-1535-13 engine. Some 129 were built, initially by Northrop, but in 1937 Douglas

acquired the remaining 49 per cent of Northrop Corporation's stock, and it was the Douglas Company which completed production of these aircraft. Of the total, 93 served with the USAAC for only 18 months, then being returned to Douglas for sale to the UK and France. The RAF received 60, designating them **Nomad Mk I**, and all were transferred to the SAAF. Douglas also built this aircraft for export under the

designation **Douglas Model 8A**, supplying them to Argentina, Iraq, the Netherlands and Norway. A batch of 34 **Model 8A-5** aircraft was also built for Peru, 31 of them being commandeered by the USAAF in early 1942 for use in an attack role. Armed with six 0.3-in (7.62-mm) machine-guns and able to carry up to 1,800 lb (816 kg) of bombs, all were used in a training role under the designation **A-33**.

Northrop BT-1

While Northrop was working on the YA-13/XA-16 developments of the Gamma, it was also testing a scaled-down version for the Navy under the designation **XFT-1**. This was one of two Northrop prototypes which failed to attract production orders, the other being the **Type 3-A** of 1935. Both were all-metal fighters, the XFT-1 having fixed landing gear. Powered originally by a 625-hp (466-kW) Wright XR-1510 radial, it was later re-engined, as the **XFT-2**, with a 650-hp (485-kW)

Pratt & Whitney R-1535, but crashed three months later, in July 1936. The Northrop 3-A was a similar design for the US Army, but differed from the navy aircraft in having retractable landing gear and a modified canopy. Developed alongside these prototypes was the **XBT-1**, which had semi-retractable landing gear, and this entered production as the **BT-1** torpedo-bomber, the first of 54 being delivered in April 1938. The BT-1 had an 825-hp (615-kW) R-1535 Twin Wasp Junior radial

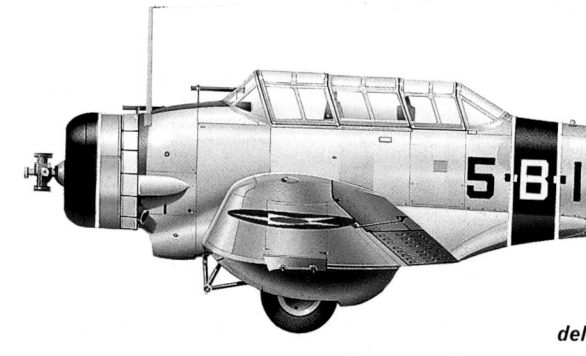

VB-5 received the first production BT-1 deliveries in April 1938.

engine, but one aircraft was modified as the **BT-2** to have revised landing gear and an 800-hp (597-kW)

Wright XR-1820 Cyclone. With other modifications this was to become the Douglas SBD Dauntless,

as the original Northrop Corporation had by then become the El Segundo Division of Douglas.

Northrop F-5 Freedom Fighter & Tiger II & T-38 Talon

The first **F-5A Freedom Fighter** single-seat light-fighter prototype flew in May 1963 and went on to form the basis of a major

warplane family. Canadair built **CF-5A/D** single- and two-seat warplanes and **NF-5A/B** aircraft for the Canadian and Dutch air

force respectively; the survivors of these fleets later finding a ready resale market to countries including Botswana, Turkey and

Venezuela. In addition, South Korea, Brazil, Greece, Iran, Morocco, Norway, the Philippines, Saudi Arabia, Spain,

Taiwan, Thailand, Turkey, Venezuela and Yemen all had first generation F-5s on strength in 2001. Venezuela's **VF-5A/D**

Canada designated its indigenous CF-5A aircraft CF-116A in service. No. 434 Sqn was the first to receive the CF-116A, on 5 November 1968.

SPECIFICATION

Northrop F-5E Tigre III
Type: single-seat lightweight tactical fighter
Powerplant: two General Electric J85-GE-21B turbojet engines each rated at 3,500 lb st (15.57 kN) dry and 5,000 lb st (22.24 kN) with afterburning
Performance: maximum speed 1,056 mph (1700 km/h) at 36,000 ft (10975 m); initial climb rate 34,300 ft (10455 m) per minute; service ceiling 51,800 ft (15550 m);

combat radius 875 miles (1405 km) with two AIM-9 AAMs and maximum fuel
Weights: empty 9,558 lb (4349 kg); maximum take-off 24,664 lb (11187 kg)
Dimensions: wingspan 26 ft 8 in (8.13 m) without tip-mounted AAMs; length 47 ft 4¾ in (14.45 m) including probe; height 13 ft 4½ in (4.08 m); wing area 186.00 sq ft (17.28 m²)

aircraft have received a limited upgrade by Singapore Technologies Aerospace. The improved **F-5E/F Tiger II** was developed from the F-5A/B as an International Fighter Aircraft for sale to US allies. The F-5E prototype first flew in August 1972 and was followed by some 1,300 production F-5Es and two-seat F-5Fs for sale to 20 air forces. The F-5E was also assembled under licence in Taiwan and South Korea. Tiger IIs remain in widespread service with Bahrain, Brazil, Chile, Honduras, Indonesia, Iran, Jordan, Kenya, Malaysia, Mexico, Saudi Arabia, Singapore, Switzerland, Taiwan,

Thailand, Tunisia, the USMC, the USN and Yemen. Reconnaissance F-5E variants are operated by Malaysia (**RF-5E Tigereye**), Singapore (**RF-5S**) and Taiwan (**RF-5E Tigergazer**). A wide range of update programmes is available to keep this important warplane viable until well into the 21st century. These upgrades offer a mix of new avionics and structural refurbishment of the airframe. Chile operates F-5Es upgraded with Israeli assistance to **Tigre III** standard; their advanced avionics – including Elta 2032 radar and HOTAS controls – give a level of combat capability matching that of F-16s.

The FIAR Grifo F/X Plus multi-mode radar has been fitted to Singaporean F-5S aircraft and has also been selected for Brazil's F-5Es. US-based TCA is offering to remanufacture existing single-seat F-5s to two-seat F-5F configuration in order to meet a projected demand for cost-effective lead-in fighter trainers.

From the original **N-156** concept that led to the F-5 family, Northrop also developed the **T-38 Talon** tandem two-seat supersonic advanced trainer. Flown for the first time on 10 April 1959, the first of 10 **YT-38** prototypes was followed by an eventual total of 1,187 **T-38A Talon** trainers. Conversion

programmes have resulted in the **AT-38A** weapons trainer, **NT-38A** research aircraft, **DT-38A** drone director and **QT-38A** drone, while upgraded aircraft are designated **T-38C**. The Talon has enjoyed only

limited export success, but remains a major USAF type with several hundred scheduled to undergo a rewinging and upgrade programme that will see them in service until at least 2040.

In Brazil the F-5E remains an important front-line combat type. It is to be the subject of a major upgrade by EMBRAER.

Above: The T-38 was adopted by the USAF's Thunderbirds in 1974, largely as a fuel-saving measure, but withdrawn in 1982 after a major crash.

Northrop F-89 Scorpion

This F-89D wears high-conspicuity markings for arctic operations. Note the combined wingtip-mounted rocket pod/fuel tank.

Northrop's **F-89 Scorpion** was designed as a jet replacement for the P-61 Black Widow, and following the placing of a development contract in May 1946, Northrop received an order for two prototypes in December 1946. With the Northrop designation **N-24**, the first **XF-89** flew in August 1948 and demonstrated a sufficiently good performance to attract a production contract for 48 **F-89A** fighters in January 1949. The second prototype, the **XF-89A (N-49)**, was completed in early 1950, but the first aircraft was lost in a fatal crash in February 1950, this being attributed to structural failure caused by flutter in the horizontal tail surfaces. Modifications were made and incorporated in production aircraft and F-89A deliveries began in July 1950; Northrop designation was **N-35** and early aircraft had Allison J33-A-21

engines, later changed to 5,100-lb (22.68-kN) thrust J33-A-21As which, with afterburners, developed 6,800 lb (30.24 kN) thrust. Internal equipment changes from the 19th aircraft led to the **F-89B** which had a Lear autopilot and ILS. Thirty of this variant were built before the **F-89C** appeared with a new tailplane and a number of equipment changes. During the production run of 164 F-89Cs several variants of the Allison turbojet were installed.

The next model to enter service in 1953 was the **F-89D (N-68)** which featured a new Hughes fire-control system, removal of the standard six 20-mm cannon from the nose cone, installation of underwing fuel tanks, and provision for wingtip pods each carrying 52 folding-fin air rockets. Total production of the F-89D reached 682. The **YF-89E (N-71)** was a

one-off test-bed for the Allison YJ71. A proposed production version was the **F-89F**, but this and the **F-89G** with revised armament and fire-control were cancelled.

Final production model was the **F-89H (N-138)** of 1956, which was similar to the F-89D but had uprated engines and wingtip pods which had been modified to carry three Hughes Falcon guided air-to-air missiles in addition to 21 rockets. An additional six rockets could be carried beneath the wings; total F-89H production reached 156. Another model, the **F-89J (N-160)**, was a conversion from the F-89D equipped to carry an

SPECIFICATION

Northrop F-89D Scorpion
Type: two-seat all-weather interceptor
Powerplant: two 7,200-lb (32.02-kN) afterburning thrust Allison J35-A-35, -33A, -41 or -47 turbojets
Performance: maximum speed 636 mph (1024 km/h) at 10,600 ft (3230 m); service ceiling 49,200 ft (14995 m); range 2,600 miles (4184 km)

Weight: empty 25,194 lb (11428 kg); maximum take-off 42,241 lb (19160 kg)
Dimensions: wingspan 59 ft 8 in (59.97 m); length 53 ft 10 in (16.41 m); height 17 ft 7 in (5.36 m); wing area 562.0 sq ft (52.21 m²)
Armament: 104 2.75-in (70-mm) rockets in wingtip pods, or 27 rockets plus three Falcon missiles

MB-1 Genie unguided nuclear-tipped rocket on pylons beneath each wing in addition to four underwing Falcons. The wingtip rocket pods were replaced by fuel tanks. As the F-89s were replaced in 1957 by Convair F-102s, they were

passed to Air Force Reserve squadrons and ANG units, and some were converted as missile and drone-control aircraft with the designations **DF-89A** and **DF-89B**. The last two ANG units phased out their Scorpions in mid-1959.

Northrop Gamma

In January 1932 John Northrop and Donald Douglas formed the

Northrop Corporation as a partly-owned subsidiary of the Douglas Aircraft Co. The

first aircraft from the new corporation was the **Northrop Gamma**, several of which were built to special order for record-breaking flights and

research work. The first two aircraft, a **Gamma 2A** and a **Gamma 2B**, were powered respectively by a 785-hp (585-kW) Wright and 500-hp (373-kW) Pratt & Whitney

Wasp radial; both were delivered at the end of 1932, the first to Texaco, which loaned it to Frank Hawks for record-breaking flights.

Northrop Gamma

The second Gamma was loaned to Lincoln Ellsworth, who eventually used it for a transantarctic flight.

TWA bought three **Gamma 2D** aircraft with 710-hp (529-kW) Wright Cyclone engines as single-seat mailplanes in 1934. The second was later re-engined with a 775-hp (578-kW) Wright and was

used by Texaco to test oil temperatures and flows before being sold to the USAAC, which designated it **UC-100**.

A number of Gammas was delivered to individual customers, including two to the UK, a **Gamma 2E** for the A&AEE and a **Gamma 2L**, the last to be built, was used by the Bristol

The Gamma 2D was used in high-altitude experiments aimed at allowing airliner flight above the weather.

Aeroplane Co. as a test-bed for its Hercules engines. The Chinese government ordered 24 Gamma 2Es as light bombers, with 710-hp (529-kW) Wright engines; they could carry a 1,600-lb (726-kg) bombload and had four 0.3-in (7.62mm)

forward-firing machine-guns in the wings, and one rear-ward-firing in the rear cockpit. A further 25

Gamma 2Es were assembled in China from components provided by Northrop.

Northrop N-3PB

In 1940 Northrop received an order from the Norwegian Buying Commission for the design and construction of a single-engine monoplane patrol bomber with twin floats. The Norwegian order covered 24 aircraft, and in less than eight months the **N-3PB** proto-type flew, on 1 November 1940, powered by a 1,200-hp (895-kW) Wright Cyclone GR-1820 radial engine. It attained a speed of 257 mph (414 km/h) and was then claimed to be the

world's fastest military seaplane. Norway was invaded by the Germans shortly after the contract had been awarded, and the N-3PBs were therefore delivered to a unit of the Royal Norwegian Naval Air Service, operating as an RAF unit from unimproved coastal sites in Iceland on anti-submarine patrol and convoy escort duties. All maintenance had to be performed in the open, often under extremely harsh environmental conditions, and during 19

The N-3PB carried four 50-calibre fixed machine guns, two 30-calibre flexible machine guns and a maximum of 2,000lb (907kg) of bombs. A 330 Sqn, RAF aircraft is illustrated.

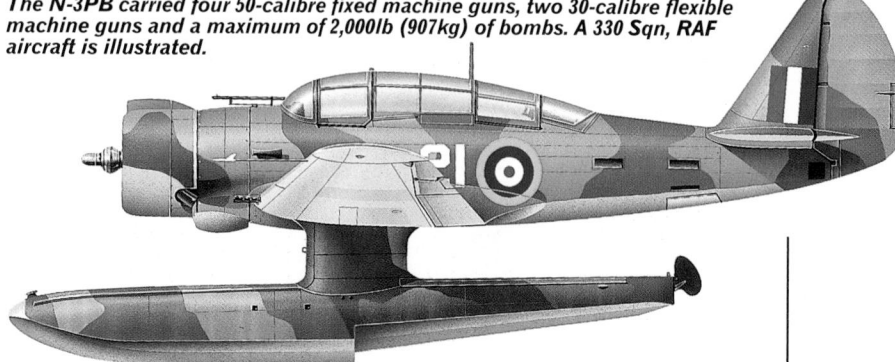

months between 1941-42 several were lost during

water landings in severe arctic weather, but there

were no losses due to enemy action.

Northrop P-61 Black Widow

The first US aircraft to be designed as a radar-equipped night-fighter, Northrop's three-seat twin-engine, twin-boom design gained a USAAC contract for two **XP-61** prototypes on 11 January 1941, the first of them being flown initially on 21 May 1942. They were followed by 13 service-test **YP-61** aircraft, and the development problems of this aircraft were matched by those to create a new air-interception radar based on the British cavity

magnetron. Nevertheless, the first examples of the **P-61A Black Widow** production version began to appear towards the end of 1943. It was soon discovered that the four-gun remotely-controlled dorsal turret caused severe buffeting when slewed to a beam position, and the turret was deleted after the first 37 aircraft had been built. P-61As began to enter service with fighter groups in the South Pacific in the first half of 1944, the first kill

being made on 7 July, and production of this version totalled 200. Deliveries of the ensuing **P-61B** also began in July 1944. This was built to a total of 450, and incorporated as standard provision to carry four 1,600-lb (726-kg) bombs or 300-US gal (1136-litre) drop tanks on underwing racks. The final 250 of these P-61Bs also had the four-gun dorsal turret restored. The last production batch comprised 41 **P-61C** aircraft, 476 being cancelled at the war's end,

bringing the total built to 706. Black Widows were in service in Europe by July 1944, shooting down four German bombers in their first engagement, the type subsequently destroying a number of German

Of particular note are the prominent radar antennas on the forward port fuselage of this P-61A Black Widow.

flying bombs during the V-1 offensive against Antwerp, and the use of the P-61 for deep intruder missions in the European theatre emphasises the versatility of this heavy fighter.

Variants

XP-61D: redesignation of two P-61As following installation of R-2800-77 turbocharged engines for evaluation

XP-61E: redesignation of two P-61Bs with dorsal turret and nose radar deleted, increased fuel capacity, and four 0.5-in (12.7-mm) machine-guns installed in nose, the four 0.79-in (20-mm) being retained

XP-61F: designation allocated to P-61C to be converted to XP-61E configuration; not completed

XF-15 Reporter: redesignation of first XP-61E following conversion as prototype of unarmed reconnaissance aircraft with six cameras in modified nose

XF-15A: designation of prototype conversion of P-61C to XF-15 Reporter configuration

F-15A Reporter: 36 production reconnaissance aircraft, built from part-completed P-61C airframes

F2T-1N: designation applied by US Navy to 12 ex-USAAF P-61As received in late 1945 for use as night-fighter trainers

SPECIFICATION	
Northrop P-61B Black Widow	36,200 lb (16420 kg)
Type: three-seat night-fighter	**Dimensions:** wingspan 66 ft
Powerplant: two 2,000-hp	(20.12 m); length 49 ft 7 in
(1491kW) Pratt & Whitney	(15.11 m); height 14 ft 8 in
R-2800-65 Double Wasp radial	(4.47 m); wing area 662.36 sq ft
piston engines	(61.53 m²)
Performance: maximum speed	**Armament:** four 20-mm cannon in
366 mph (589 km/h) at 20,000 ft	the lower forward fuselage and
(6095 m); service ceiling 33,100 ft	four 0.5-in (12.7-mm) machine-guns
(10090 m); maximum range	in the dorsal barbette, plus up to
1,350 miles (2173 km)	6,400 lb (2903 kg) of bombs or
Weights: empty 23,450 lb	other stores on four underwing
(10637 kg); maximum take-off	hardpoints

Northrop Grumman B-2 Spirit

Northrop Grumman's **B-2A Spirit** is the 'silver bullet' of US policy, reserved for use against targets of the highest priority. The B-2 is the costliest warplane ever

built (around $900 million per copy), is difficult to maintain and is prone to trouble with the coating that provides much of its 'stealth'. The B-2 Spirit was

developed as a low observ-able strategic bomber for the Cold War mission of attacking Soviet strategic targets. Composites are extensively used to provide

a radar-absorbent honey-comb structure; the bomber has a minimal IR signature, does not contrail and uses its shielded APQ-181 radar only momentarily to identify a target just before attacking. The 'glass' cockpit is

usually flown by a crew of two. The aircraft has a quadruplex-redundant digi-tal fly-by-wire system and highly advanced, classified EW system. Six prototypes were funded and the first was rolled out on 22 November 1988. The

A 'black world' project which is now at the forefront of US foreign policy, the B-2A has proved devastatingly effective in combat.

USAF had originally wanted 132 aircraft, but funding restrictions have seen the fleet completed with just 21 aircraft. The last of these was delivered on 14 July 2000 and is the AV-1 prototype upgraded to Block 30 standard. The first operational B-2A was delivered to the 509th Bomb Wing on 17 December 1993 and full IOC came in April 1997. Having progressed through the Block 10 and 20 standards of 'stealth', systems and weapons capability, the

entire B-2A fleet will be brought to Block 30 standard with full weapons and stealth capabilities. The B-2A made its combat debut over Kosovo in 1999, employing the Joint Direct Attack Munition (JDAM) and other weapons to great effect. Although the USAF's B-2 force is garrisoned at Whiteman AFB, Missouri, the service has ambitious plans to operate the aircraft temporarily from forward bases like Guam and Diego Garcia.

B-2's first flight took place on 17 July 1990, when this machine (also known as AV-1/Air Vehicle One) was delivered to the USAF at Edwards AFB for the start of the test programme. In July 1991 the USAF implemented a 'set of treatments' to rectify a shortfall in the B-2A's 'stealth' capabilities. The

Northrop Grumman has made a unique configuration work with the high-tech B-2. Note the split aileron air brakes and radar reflector at the wingtips of this B-2 as it comes in to make a landing.

SPECIFICATION

Northrop Grumman B-2A Spirit
Type: two/three-seat long-range strategic bomber
Powerplant: four General Electric F118-GE-100 turbofan engines each rated at 19,000 lb st (84.52 kN)
Performance: maximum speed about 475 mph (764 km/h) at high altitude; service ceiling 50,000 ft (15240 m); range 7,595 miles (12223 km) with eight AGM-129 missiles and eight B61 bombs on a hi-hi-hi mission or 5,178 miles (8334 km) with the same weapons load on a hi-lo-hi mission; endurance more than 36 hours
Weights: empty 153,700 lb (69717 kg); typical take-off 336,500 lb (152635 kg)
Dimensions: wingspan 172 ft (52.43 m); length 69 ft (21.03 m);

height 17 ft (5.18 m); wing area about 5,275.00 sq ft (490.05 m²)
Armament: up to 40,000 lb (18144 kg) of disposable stores carried in two weapons bays in the underside of the centre section, and generally comprising up to 16 AGM-129 missiles, or 16 B61 or B83 nuclear free-fall bombs, or 80 500-lb (227-kg) Mk 82 or 560-lb (254-kg) Mk 36 bombs, or 80 Mk 62 sea mines, or 36 750-lb (340-kg) M117 fire bombs or CBU-87/89/97/98 cluster bombs, or 16 Joint Direct Attack Munitions or 2,000-lb (907-kg) Mk 84 bombs, or eight 4,400-lb (1996-kg) GBU-28 deep-penetration bombs, or (to be retrofitted) varying numbers of the Joint Air-to-Surface Stand-off Missile and Joint Stand-Off Weapon

Northrop Grumman E-2 Hawkeye

Since entering service in 1964 the **E-2 Hawkeye** has protected US Navy carrier battle groups and acted as an airborne controller for their aircraft. One of very few types designed specifically for the AEW role, it was first flown in prototype form as long ago as October 1960. As a consequence of its ability to operate from aircraft-carriers, the basic Hawkeye is extremely compact. A total of 59 production **E-2A** aircraft was delivered from January 1964; 51 were updated to **E-2B** standard, before production switched to the improved **E-2C**. The first E-2C flew on 23 September 1972 and Grumman had built 139 for the US Navy when the line closed in 1994. However, low-rate production began again in 2000. External changes to the E-2 have been minor but its systems have been progressively updated. The E-2C was initially equipped with APS-125 search radar, but

A replacement for the US Navy's E-2s is some way off in the distant future, although the E-2C remains a highly-capable system.

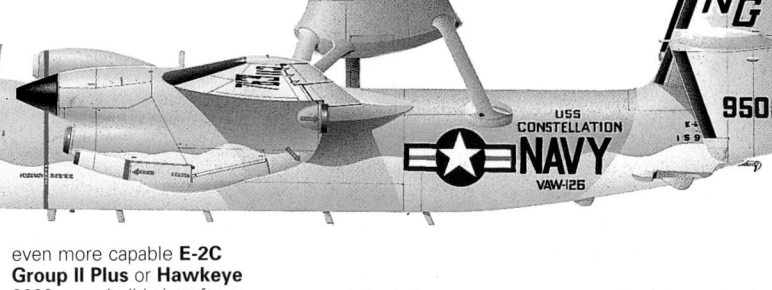

this was replaced by the AN/APS-139 in **Group I** aircraft from 1988 and the AN/APS-145 in the latest **Group II** E-2Cs. The latter radar allows a low-flying, fighter-sized aircraft to be detected at up to 253 miles (407 km) away with the E-2C flying at its operational altitude. A passive detection system gives warning of hostile emitters at ranges up to twice the radar detection range. After almost 30 years in service, the E-2C is still an evolving design, and Northrop Grumman is developing the

even more capable **E-2C Group II Plus** or **Hawkeye 2000**; new-build aircraft are scheduled to enter US Navy service in late 2001. In mid 2001 the E-2 was on strength with 14 US Navy squadrons and is destined to remain in service until as least 2020. E-2Cs have been exported to Egypt (6), France (2), Israel (four, currently in storage), Japan (13), Singapore (4) and Taiwan (4). Many customers are upgrading their E-2s to a mix of Group II or Hawkeye 2000 standards.

SPECIFICATION

Northrop Grumman E-2C Hawkeye (Group I configuration onwards)
Type: carrierborne AEW aircraft
Powerplant: two Allison T56-A-427 turboprops each rated at 5,100 ehp (3803 kW)
Performance: maximum level speed 389 mph (626 km/h); maximum cruising speed at optimum altitude 374 mph (602 km/h); maximum rate of climb at sea level over 2,515 ft (767 m) per minute; service ceiling 37,000 ft (11275 m); unrefuelled

time on station at 200 miles (320 km) from base 4 hours 24 minutes; endurance with maximum fuel 6 hours 15 minutes
Weights: empty 40,484 lb (18363 kg); maximum take-off 54,426 lb (24687 kg)
Dimensions: wingspan 80 ft 7 in (24.56 m); folded width 29 ft 4 in (8.94 m); rotodome diameter 24 ft (7.32 m); length 57 ft 6¾ in (17.54 m); height 18 ft 3¾ in (5.58 m); wing area 700.00 sq ft (65.03 m²)

OOS Stal-2 and Stal-3

A shortage of aluminium in the Soviet Union during the 1920s led to experiments and designs to use steel as an alternative for basic aircraft structures.

For this purpose a Stal (steel) design group was established in 1929, the work being co-ordinated by the OOS (Otdel Opytnogo Samolyetostroeniya, or

section for experimental aircraft construction). The first tangible result of the group's work was a braced high-wing cabin monoplane, the **Stal-2**,

accommodating a pilot and five passengers. The prototype, powered by a 300-hp (224-kW) Wright J-6 engine, was flown for the first time on 11

October 1931. Successful testing led to the production of 111 of these aircraft during 1934-35, this total including one **Stal-2bis**.

OOS Stal-2 and Stal-3 (continued)

The Stal-2bis prototype introduced Frise-type ailerons. Powered by M-26 or MG-31 engines of similar output to the Wright J-6, many of these aircraft saw service during World War II. With a wingspan of 53 ft 1¾ in (16.20 m), the Stal-2 had a maximum speed of 124 mph (200 km/h). An improved and enlarged version of the Stal-2, accom-modating a pilot, co-pilot and six passengers, was flown during 1933 under the designation **Stal-3**. A total of 79 was produced during 1935-36, and most of them saw service with Aeroflot until the summer of 1941, at which time some were impressed into VVS service. The production Stal-3 spanned 55 ft 10 in (17.02 m) and was generally powered by a 480-hp (358-kW) M-22 engine; some had the 680-hp (507-kW) M-17, which gave this useful aircraft a maximum speed of 147 mph (237 km/h).

Special welding and pressing processes had to be developed to produce stainless steel aircraft like the Stal-2.

Panavia Tornado

The multi-national **Tornado Interdictor Strike (IDS)** aircraft remains one of Europe's most important combat aircraft. Its various attack, reconnaissance and defence suppression versions have played major roles during recent operations in the Balkans and over Iraq. Development of the Tornado by the UK, West Germany and Italy was begun in 1968, with the first flight by a prototype in 1974 and service deliveries beginning in 1979. The RAF retains the type in front-line service, primarily in the long-range interdiction/overland attack role. They also have specialised missions that comprise maritime attack (**Tornado GR.Mk 1B**) and reconnaissance (**Tornado GR.Mk 1A**). In 2001 the RAF began using fully-operational GR.Mk 1s upgraded to **Tornado GR.Mk 4** standard with new cockpit displays, full compatibility with the TIALD pod for autonomous PGM delivery, integration of NVGs with an upgraded FLIR and an enhanced self-defence suite. The recce-configured

GR.Mk 1As are similarly being upgraded as GR.Mk 4As. The Luftwaffe had around 270 IDS aircraft in service early in 2001, including a number to **ECR (Electronic Combat and Reconnaissance)** standard and armed with AGM-88 HARMs. The aircraft will undergo a comprehensive MLU similar to the RAF's GR.Mk 4 programme that will also add Litening targeting pods and towed radar decoys. New weapons include BLU-109 and GBU-22 Paveway III LGBs, KEPD 350 Taurus tactical cruise missiles and IRIS-T self-defence AAMs. The Marineflieger has a wing with around 50 IDS aircraft assigned conventional attack, anti-shipping (with Kormoran AShMs), defence suppression (with HARMs) and reconnaissance missions. The Italian air force has three fighter-bomber IDS groups, one of which is assigned the anti-ship role with Kormoran missiles. Italy is converting 15 aircraft to **IT ECR** standard with dedicated electronic equipment and HARMs for the defence suppression role. Saudi Arabia is the remaining Tornado operator with the survivors of 96 aircraft assigned to three units, one of which operates 12 recce-configured Tornados.

Developed from the Tornado IDS for a wholly RAF requirement, the **Tornado ADV (Air Defence Variant)** is optimised for long-range interception. Key features comprised installation of Foxhunter radar and a

HARM-armed Luftwaffe Tornado ECRs have been active during combat missions over the Balkans.

lengthened fuselage for carriage of semi-recessed Sky Flash AAMs. The interim **Tornado F.Mk 2** was soon replaced by the definitive **Tornado F.Mk 3**. The RAF received its first of 152 production F.Mk 3s in 1986 and these have since had several updates. The 'Stage 1' upgrade included HOTAS controls, RAM coating, and flare dispensers while 'Stage 2' enhances the computer and radar imagery and adds the JTIDS data-link. The long-awaited Eurofighter Typhoon is intended first to replace the F.Mk 3 but as an interim measure, the RAF is further upgrading 100 F.Mk 3s through a Capability Sustainment Programme. This adds AMRAAM and ASRAAM capability (albeit not exploiting the full potential of these weapons), a multiple target engagement capability for the radar and improved defensive aids. The Common Operational Value (COV) modification features some structural rework, an NVG-compatible cockpit with new displays, GPS and Have Quick secure radios. The first CSP/COV aircraft were redelivered to RAF units in 2000. Saudi Arabia received 24 new ADVs to F.Mk 3 standard, while Italy leased 24 upgraded, ex-RAF F.Mk 3s from 1995 as interim fighters, pending arrival of its Typhoons.

SPECIFICATION

Panavia Tornado GR.Mk 4
Type: two-seat all-weather attack and interdiction aircraft
Powerplant: two Turbo-Union RB.199 Mk 103 turbofans each rated at 8,650 lb st (38.48 kN) dry and 16,075 lb st (71.50 kN) with afterburning
Performance: maximum speed 1,453 mph (2338 km/h) or Mach 2.20 at 36,000 ft (10975 m); climb to 30,000 ft (9145 m) in less than 2 minutes from brakes-off; service ceiling more than 50,000 ft (15240 m); combat radius 863 miles (1390 km) with a heavy warload on a typical hi-lo-hi mission
Weights: basic empty about 30,620 lb (13890 kg); maximum take-off about 61,620 lb (27951 kg)
Dimensions: wingspan 45 ft 7½ in (13.91 m) minimum sweep and 28 ft 2½ in (8.60 m) maximum sweep; length 54 ft 10¼ in (16.72 m); height 19 ft 6¼ in (5.95 m); wing area 286.33 sq ft (26.60 m²)
Armament: two 27-mm IWKA-Mauser cannon with 180 rpg; maximum ordnance load over 19,841 lb (9000 kg); current weapons include 1,000-lb (454-kg) free-fall bombs, CPU-123/B Paveway II LGBs; new weapons include GBU-28 Paveway III LGBs and Storm Shadow SMDs

ADVs have seen combat with all three nations, during Desert Storm, over the former Yugoslavia and in other NATO peacekeeping actions. The arrival of operational Eurofighters for the RAF in 2005 could release surplus Tornado F.Mk 3s for a variety of combat support roles. Although the airframes are likely to require a further structural re-work, they could be re-equipped with radar targeting avionics and ALARM anti-radar weapons to address a clear shortfall in NATO's defence suppression capability.

Left: Tornado ADV's longer fuselage allows the carriage of four Sky Flash AAMs in semi-recessed pairs fore and aft.

Right: Britain will keep its upgraded Tornado GR.Mk 4s in service well into the second decade of the 21st century.

Percival Gull series

Edgar W. Percival built the prototype of his **Type D.1 Gull** three-seat touring monoplane at Maidstone in 1932, and it flew in that year's King's Cup Race, averaging 142.73 mph (229.7 km/h). The clean design attracted immediate attention and the newly-formed Percival Aircraft Co. sub-contracted construction of a batch of 24 **Type D.2 Gull** aircraft to George Parnall & Co. at Yate. Engines installed included the 130-hp (97-kW) Cirrus Hermes IV and de Havilland Gipsy Major, and the 160-hp (119-kW) Napier Javelin III; these aircraft were more commonly given the designation **Gull Four**.

Percival Aircraft opened its own factory at Gravesend in 1934 and a revised version, the **Type D.3 Gull Six** with the 200-hp (149-kW) Gipsy Six engine, entered production; it had a neater single-strut spatted landing gear and detail cabin improvements, but retained the folding wings of the Gull Four. In 1936 the company moved to a new factory at Luton, where Gull Six production was completed with the 48th Gull, delivered to Shell in South Africa in October 1937.

Percival had been working on a four-seat development of the Gull Six at Gravesend, and flew the prototype **Type K.1 Vega Gull** in November

1935. It had dual controls, trailing edge flaps and the same engine as the Gull Six, although later aircraft had the 205-hp (153kW) Gipsy Six Series II. Vega Gulls achieved a number of successes in racing and long-distance flights, and a total of 90 was built before the last aircraft was delivered in July 1939. Customers were as far afield as Australia, Canada, India, Iraq, Japan and Kenya. Demonstrations by Percival to the services resulted in the supply of Vega Gulls for communications, and the type was developed into the Proctor.

Mention should be made also of the **Mew Gull**, a single-seat racing aircraft

which flew at Gravesend in March 1934 with a 165-hp (123-kW) Napier Javelin la engine, but by July's King's Cup Air Race it was powered by a 200-hp (149-kW) Gipsy Six and achieved 191 mph (307 km/h).

This first aircraft was classed as a **Type E.1** and was followed by a completely redesigned model, the **Type E.2**, of which four were built. They achieved a number of racing and long distance records including one set by Alex Henshaw who flew the third aircraft to the Cape of Good Hope and back in 4 days 10 hours 16 minutes. This Mew Gull survived the war and several accidents and in

Originally registered to a South African owner as ZS-AHM The Golden City in May 1937, Mew Gull G-AEXF survived World War II and was eventually restored to flying condition and loaned to the Shuttleworth Collection.

summer 2001 was resident at Old Warden, Bedfordshire with the Shuttleworth Collection.

The last aircraft, designated **E.3H**, was again a redesign with a smaller wing and tail and narrower fuselage.

Percival P.28 Proctor series

Developed from the Vega Gull, the **Proctor** was designed to Specification 20/38 for a communications/radio trainer. Successful evaluation of the prototype, first flown on 8 October 1939, led to the initial series **P.28 Proctor Mk I** three-seat

communications aircraft (247 built), followed by the **P.30 Proctor Mk II** (175) and **P.34 Proctor Mk III** (437), both of them radio trainers. Designed to Specification T.9/41 and named originally **Preceptor**, the **Proctor Mk IV** radio trainer (258 built) had a

longer, deeper fuselage to accommodate four; the increased capacity made it an effective communications aircraft and many later had dual controls installed. Most Proctors built during the war were produced under sub-contract by F. Hills & Sons in Manchester, this company's output comprising 25 Mk I, 100 Mk II, 437 Mk III and 250 Mk IV aircraft. At the end of World War II some 200 Proctor Mk I, Mk II and Mk III aircraft were declared surplus, but some Mk IVs remained in service with communications squadrons until 1955, when surviving aircraft were,

The clean lines of the Proctor, which included carefully spatted and trousered main gear, bestowed good performance on modest power.

similarly, sold on the civil market. In 1945, however, three Proctor IVs had been furnished to civil standards, leading to introduction of the **Proctor 5** (150 built) of which four were supplied

to the RAF for use by air attachés under the designation **Proctor C.Mk 5**. A single **Proctor 6** floatplane was built in 1946 for the Hudson's Bay Company in Canada.

SPECIFICATION	
Percival Proctor Mk IV	(805 km)
Type: three/four-seat radio trainer/communications aircraft	**Weights:** empty 2,370 lb (1075 kg) maximum take-off 3,500 lb (1588 kg)
Powerplant: one 210-hp (157-kW) de Havilland Gipsy Queen inline piston engine	**Dimensions:** span 39 ft 6 in (12.04 m); length 28 ft 2 in (8.59 m); height 7 ft 3 in (.2.21 m); wing area 202.0 sq ft (18.77 m²)
Performance: maximum speed 160 mph (257 km/h); service ceiling 14,000 ft (4265 m); range 500 miles	

Percival P.40 Prentice

The RAF ended World War II using the same basic trainer that had been in service at the outbreak of war, the de Havilland Tiger Moth, and there was an urgent need for a more modern approach. The **P.40 Prentice** was designed to

meet Specification T.23/43 and was an all-metal monoplane with many new features and an all-up weight considerably more than twice that of the Tiger. Since its power was considerably less than twice that of the Tiger, its

performance was hardly sparkling and, in fact, the old biplane's initial rate of climb of 750 ft (229 m) per minute compared well with the Prentice's 650 ft (198 m) per minute. An unnecessary complication which added to the weight was an original requirement for a third seat that, in practice, was never used, but the Prentice was the RAF's first side-by-side trainer.

The prototype flew in March 1946, and after modifications to the tail surfaces and wing tips an initial batch was supplied for service trials. The Prentice then entered full production on two lines,

Percival's Luton factory building 230 for the RAF and Blackburn at Brough another 125. Percival additionally built two Prentices for the Lebanon and a figure of 200 is reported to have been sold to Argentina. Hindustan Aircraft built 65 for the Indian Air Force with 345-hp (257-kW) de Havilland Gipsy Queen engines, and these served between 1948 and 1959.

Replacement of RAF Prentices by Provosts began in 1953, and in 1955 Aviation Traders at Southend bought 252 surplus Prentices for possible civil conversion, two others being bought privately. In practice only a few were converted for civil use since they proved expensive to operate. One was configured as a seven seater, but the vast majority were broken up.

One of the Argentine Prentices, this aircraft demonstrates the distinctive up-turned wing tips of the type.

SPECIFICATION	
Percival Prentice	25 minutes
Type: two/three-seat military trainer	**Weights:** empty 3,232 lb (1461 kg); maximum take-off 4,200 lb (1905 kg)
Powerplant: one 251-hp (187-kW) de Havilland Gipsy Queen 32 inline piston engine	**Dimensions:** wingspan 46 ft (14.02 m); length 31 ft 3 in (9.53 m); height 12 ft 10½ in (3.92 m); wing area 305.0 sq ft (28.33 m²)
Performance: maximum speed 143 mph (230 km/h) at 5,000 ft (1525 m); service ceiling 18,000 ft (5485 m); endurance 3 hours	

Petlyakov Pe-2

Soviet designer Vladimir M. Petlyakov, who had gained considerable early experience working on the projects of Andrei N.

Tupolev, was given the task, while imprisoned, of designing a new high-altitude fighter which was designated **VI-100**. A

cantilever low-wing monoplane with a circular-section fuselage and retractable tailwheel landing gear and a tail unit incorporated twin fins and rudders. It was powered by two 1,050-hp (783-kW) M-105 V-12

engines with TK-3 turbochargers in wing-mounted nacelles. A pressure cabin had been planned for this aircraft, but this was not available when the VI-100 was nearing completion and, instead,

the accommodation was rearranged so that the pilot was seated in an enclosed cockpit well forward of the wing leading edge, the observer/rear gunner being similarly accommodated near the wing trailing edge.

Petlyakov Pe-2 (continued)

When the initial flights were made during 1939-40, the VI-100 was found to have problems with the shock-struts of its landing gear and to have some directional instability. The latter was resolved by introducing fins of increased area, but the problems with the shock-struts were less easily solved, and indeed were never completely cured. However, in late May 1940 it was decided to change the role from high-altitude fighter to that of a three-seat dive bomber, designated **PB-100**, and at this point the pressure cabin was abandoned and the accommodation revised for a crew of three; a prone position for the navigator/bomb-aimer was provided

forward of and below the pilot. One PB-100 was completed as a conversion of a VI-100 and, following early tests, the type was ordered into production under the designation **Petlyakov Pe-2**.

The Pe-2 proved an outstanding tactical bomber. Its airframe was little changed from that of

the PB-100 except for further revision of the accommodation, with the pilot on the port side of an enlarged cockpit, and the navigator/bomb-aimer on a swivel seat behind and to his right, giving him access to a machine-gun, but able to transfer easily to his prone bomb-aiming position on approach to the target.

The third crew member was a radio operator/air gunner, in a separate compartment to the rear of the fuselage fuel tank.

The first production Pe-2 was flown on 18 November 1940, and by 22 June 1941, a total of 458 had been delivered, of which almost 65 per cent were then operational. From late

April 1941 the Pe-2 became the standard tactical bomber of the Soviet air force and when production ended in early 1945 a total of 11,427 had been built. Post-war Pe-2s were supplied to Czechoslovakia (with the designation **B-32**), Poland and Yugoslavia. The Pe-2 gained the ASCC reporting name 'Buck'.

SPECIFICATION

Petlyakov Pe-2FT
Type: three-seat bomber
Powerplant: two 1,260-hp (940kW) Klimov VK-105PF inline piston engines
Performance: maximum speed 360 mph (580 km/h) at 13,125 ft (4000 km); service ceiling 29,525 ft (9000 m); range 1,100 miles (1770 km)
Weights: empty 13,669 lb

(6200 kg); maximum take-off 18,783 lb (8520 kg)
Dimensions: wingspan 56 ft 1½ in (17.11 m); length 41 ft 11¼ in (12.78 m); height 11 ft 2¾ in (3.42 m); wing area 435.95 sq ft (40.50 m²)
Armament: machine-guns and/or cannon as detailed under variants, plus up to 2,205 lb (1000 kg) of bombs

The Pe-2's radio operator/air gunner was provided with a roof hatch, two side windows and a ventral gun position.

Variants

Pe-27(*): first flown in October 1941; equipped with VK-105TK engines and an internal bomb bay for up to four 1,102-lb (500-kg) bombs; later series introduced automatic leading-edge slats, but these were soon deleted

Pe-2Sh: conversion of PB-100 prototype with two 20-mm ShVAK cannon and one 0.5-in (12.7-mm) UBS machine-gun beneath fuselage for ground attack

Pe-3: a small number of aircraft produced as bomber interceptors with dive brakes removed and armament of two 20-mm ShVAK cannon, two 0.5-in (12.7-mm) and two 0.31-in (7.92-mm) machine-guns in the nose, and one 0.5-in (12.7-mm) machine-gun in dorsal turret

Pe-3bis: night-fighter of which some 300 were built, with armament of one 20-mm ShVAK cannon, one 0.5-in (12.7-mm) and three 0.31-in (7.92-mm) machine-guns in nose; late production with two 20-mm ShVAK cannon, and three 0.5-in (12.7-mm) and two 0.31-in (7.92-mm) machine-guns; most with internal bay for three 220-lb (100-kg) bombs and underwing launch rails for eight RS-82 rockets

Pe-3R: fighter/reconnaissance version with vertical/oblique cameras installed

Pe-2MV: version armed with two 20-mm ShVAK cannon and two 0.5-in (12.7-mm) machine-guns in an underfuselage gondola, no bomb bay, and one 0.3-in (7.62-mm) machine-gun in dorsal turret

Pe-2FT: standard production version from spring 1942; similar to Pe-2MV but with reduced nose glazing, dive brakes deleted and a second 0.3-in (7.62-mm) machine-gun for the radio operator/gunner

Pe-2 Paravan: version with barrage balloon deflecting cables linking short boom on fuselage nose and each wingtip

Pe-2FZ: produced in small numbers during 1943, had redesigned cockpit with navigator in a turret with two 0.5-in (12.7-mm) machine-guns; no nose accommodation

Pe-2VI: high-altitude fighter conversion with a pressure cabin and special engine superchargers; used as basis for further development

Pe-2I: two-seat bomber version with redesigned fuselage, increased wingspan, deeper bomb bay with capacity of 2,205 lb (1000 kg), two 0.5-in (12.7-mm) machine-guns, one in nose and one in tailcone, and 1,650-hp (1230-kW) VK-107A engines; production intended but abandoned in early 1945

Pe-3M: two-seat fighter version of 1943 with VK-105PF engines, and armament of two 20-mm ShVAK cannon, three 0.5-in (12.7-mm) machine-guns and bombload of up to 1,543 lb (700 kg)

Pe-2S/Pe-2UT/U Pe-2: two-seat trainer versions retaining full bombload, some with four forward-firing machine-guns, two 0.5-in (12.7-mm) and two 0.3-in (7.62-mm); Czech designation was **CB-32**

Pe-2B: standard production bomber from 1944; many structural and systems improvements, armament of three 0.5-in (12.7-mm) and one 0.3-in (7.62-mm) machine-gun

Pe-2R(*): three-seat day reconnaissance version; equipped with three/four cameras, carried armament of three 0.5-in (12.7-mm) machine-guns, and powered by VK-105PF engines

Pe-2R(**): three-seat day reconnaissance version of 1944; as Pe-2R(*) but armed with three 20-mm ShVAK cannon and powered by VK-107A engines

Pe-2K: version which introduced wings, nacelles and landing gear designed for the Pe-2I and VK105PF-1 engines

Pc-2RD: single conversion from Pe-2 with a 661-lb (300-kg) Glushko RD-1 liquid-rocket engine installed in the tail to give improved performance for take-off and combat; tested during 1943-45

Pe-2D: three-seat bomber version of September 1944 with VK-107A engines

Pe-27(**): bomber version of September 1944 with VK-107A engines, bombload of up to 4,409 lb (2000 kg) and armament of three 20-mm ShVAK cannon

Petlyakov Pe-8

The **Pe-8** was the Soviet Union's only modern four-engine bomber of World War II, the original design concept being outlined by A. N. Tupolev to meet a mid-1934 requirement for an aircraft of this class. A cantilever mid-wing monoplane of all-metal construction, except for fabric-covered control surfaces, the **ANT-42** as it was then known had

retractable tailwheel landing gear with only the main units retracting. Planned powerplant was four wing-mounted engines with a central supercharger installation in the fuselage, but when first flown on 27 December 1936, the ATsN supercharger installation was not available and the ANT-42 was powered by four 1,100hp (820-kW) Mikulin M-100 Vee engines.

Although the aircraft was damaged subsequently in a heavy landing, official testing was completed during 1937, following which the ATsN supercharger, driven by a single M-100 engine, became available. The second prototype ANT-42 was flown on 26 July 1938, this having many improvements including an ATsN-2 supercharger driven by an M-100A engine. There was accommodation for a crew of 11 and the aircraft had full armament comprising elec-

trically-actuated dorsal and tail turrets, each with a 0.3-in (7.62-mm) ShKAS machine-gun; a nose turret with a single (later twin) ShKAS machine-gun, plus a position in the rear of each inboard engine nacelle, accessible to the gunner through a wing crawlway, each provided with a single 0.5-in (12.7-mm) machine-gun. Standard bombload was six 220-lb (100-kg) or four 551-lb (250-kg) bombs, but over suitable short ranges a maximum overload of 8,818 lb (4000 kg) of bombs could be carried.

The manufacture of five pre-production aircraft was authorised in April 1937, but

there was a subsequent attempt to end the programme. However, production was finally approved in 1939 under the designation **TB-7** and these five pre-series aircraft differed from the ANT-42 by having the ATsN central supercharger installation deleted and the main engines replaced by supercharged AM-35s. At the same time several airframe improvements were introduced and deliveries of these pre-production aircraft began in May 1940. Performance with the AM-35 powerplant was disappointing, leading to the evaluation of several differ-

The Pe-8 was the only heavy bomber in the Soviet inventory during the Great Patriotic War, but was consistently troubled by unreliable powerplants.

ent engines, but in October 1940 the 1,400-hp (1044-kW) ACh-40 diesel was selected as standard power-plant. This proved unreliable, bringing continued use of the 1,350-hp (1007-kW) AM-35A, until those in service were re-engined with the 1,500-hp (1119-kW) ACh-30B diesel. On the night of 7/8 August 1941, 18 of these aircraft made an attack on Berlin, but with one crashing on take-off from engine failure and eight others making forced land-

ings for the same reason, it was finally decided to discontinue the use of diesel engines. By that time the designation TB-7 had been dropped in favour of **Pe-8**, and when production ended in October 1941 a total of 79 had been built; by the end of 1942 about 48 of this total had been re-engined with the ASh-82FN. One aircraft with AM-35A engines made a remarkable staged flight from Moscow to Washington and back during the period 19 May to 13

June 1942. Surviving aircraft were used extensively during 1942-43 for close-support bombing and, from February 1943, were used to deploy the FAB-500ONG 11,023-lb (5000-kg) bomb for point attacks on special targets.

After the war about 30 Pe-8s survived and were used for a variety of purposes, including employ-ment as engine test-beds, and in 1952 two of them played a key role in estab-lishing an Arctic station

before returning the expedi-tion to Moscow in a nonstop

flight of 3,107 miles (5000 km).

SPECIFICATION	
Petlyakov Pe-8	
Type: long-range heavy bomber **Powerplant:** four 1,700-hp (1268-kW) Shvetsov ASh-82FN 14-cylinder radial piston engines **Performance:** maximum speed 280 mph (450 km/h) at 29,525 ft (9000 m); range with maximum bombload about 2,920 miles (4700 km) **Weights:** empty 40,609 lb (18420 kg); maximum take-off 79,366 lb (36000 kg)	**Dimensions:** wingspan 128 ft 3¼ in (39.10 m); length 77 ft 4¾ in (23.59 m); height 20 ft 4 in (6.20 m); wing area 2,031.00 sq ft (188.68 m²) **Armament:** two 0.3-in (7.62-mm) machine-guns in nose turret, one 20-mm ShVAK cannon in each of dorsal and tail turrets, and one 0.5-in (12.7-mm) machine-gun at the rear of each inboard engine nacelle, plus a maximum bomb load 8,818 lb (4000 kg) all carried internally

Pfalz D.III and D.IIIa

On completion of outstand-ing contracts for the construction of single-seat scouts, Pfalz production continued with the L.F.G.

Roland D.I and D.II. In the summer of 1917 however, Pfalz finalised the design of a single-seat fighter of its own, leaning heavily upon

constructional methods gained from the L.F.G. fighters. The resulting **Pfalz D.III**, first flown in the summer of 1917, was an unequal span biplane with fixed tailskid landing gear, powered by a 160-hp (119-kW) Mercedes D.III engine and having an open cockpit for the pilot beneath a cut-out in the trailing edge of the upper

wing. The D.III entered service on the Western Front in late 1917, being followed in early 1918 by the improved **D.IIIa**, which introduced the more powerful Mercedes D.IIIa. engine. A single example of

an experimental triplane version of the D.III was built by mounting a third wing of reduced chord between the existing biplane wings, but it is not known whether this aircraft was ever flown.

When production ended it was estimated that more than 600 D.IIIs and D.IIIas (illustrated) had been delivered.

SPECIFICATION	
Pfalz D.IIIa	
Type: single-seat fighter **Powerplant:** one 180-hp (134-kW) Mercedes D.Ma inline piston engine **Performance:** maximum speed 103 mph (165 km/h) at 10,000 ft (3050 m); service ceiling 17,000 ft (5180 m); endurance about 2 hours 30 minutes	**Weights:** empty 1,532 lb (695 kg); maximum take-off 2,061 lb (935 kg) **Dimensions:** span 30 ft 10 in (9.40 m); length 22 ft 921 in (6.95 m); height 8 ft 9 in (2.67 m); wing area 237.89 sq ft (22.10 m²) **Armament:** two fixed forward-firing 0.31-in (7.92-mm) LMG 08/15 machine-guns

Piaggio P.149

The success of Piaggio's earlier **P.148** led the company to initiate a four-seat tourer develop-

ment under the designation **P.149**, this differing from the P.148 primarily by having retractable tricycle

landing gear and a more powerful engine which, when the aircraft was flown in prototype form on 19 June 1953, was a 260-hp (194-kW) Avco Lycoming GO-435. It was only marginally successful until West Germany decided to adopt the type as a standard basic trainer/liaison aircraft for the

Luftwaffe, Piaggio deliver-ing the first of a contract for 72 **P.149D** aircraft in May 1957. An additional 190 were built under licence in Germany by

Focke-Wulf, the first of them being delivered in November 1957. The type was used also by the air forces of Nigeria, Tanzania and Uganda.

SPECIFICATION	
Piaggio P.149D	
Type: four/five-seat utility/liaison aircraft or two-seat trainer **Powerplant:** one 270-hp (201-kW) Avco Lycoming GO-480 flat-six piston engine **Performance:** maximum speed 190 mph (305 km/h) at sea level; service ceiling 19,850 ft (6050 m);	range with allowances 677 miles (1090 km) **Weights:** empty 2,557 lb (1160 kg); maximum take-off 3,704 lb (1680 kg) **Dimensions:** wingspan 36 ft 5¾ in (11.12 m); length 28 ft 10½ in (8.80 m); height 9 ft 6¼ in (2.90 m); wing area 202.91 sq ft (18.85 m²)

This civil-registered Focke-Wulf-built P.149D is something of a rarity. In fact, only five P.149s were built against civilian orders.

Piaggio P.166

Italy retains the P.166 in service for liaison, light transport, photographic survey and maritime surveillance missions.

SPECIFICATION	
Piaggio P.166-M3	
Type: utility light transport **Powerplant:** two 599-shp (447-kW) Avco Lycoming LTP 101-600 turboprops **Performance:** maximum speed 248 mph (400 km/h) at 10,000 ft (3050 m); service ceiling 29,000 ft (8840 m); maximum range with	reserves 1,264 miles (2035 km) **Weights:** empty equipped 5,842 lb (2650 kg); maximum take-off 9,480 lb (4300 kg) **Dimensions:** wingspan with tiptanks 48 ft 2½ in (14.69 m); length 39 ft (11.88 m); height 16 ft 5 in (5.00 m); wing area 285.90 sq ft (26.56 m²)

Variants

P.166: first production version; sold widely and used in Australia, New Guinea and distributed in USA by Tracker Corporation; accommodates two pilots and up to six passengers

P.166B: appeared in 1962 and named **Portofino**; direct-injection 380-hp (283-kW) Avco Lycoming IGSO-480s; six built, most for export

P.166C: redesigned central fuselage section with additional cabin for five passengers and new landing gear main units retracting into streamlined blisters on fuselage sides; in production from 1964

P.166M: militarised version, 51 built for Aeronautica Militare Italiana; used at the Scuola Plurimotori at Latina and examples attached to military air regions in Italy for liaison and battlefield transport duties; has a strengthened floor for heavy freight and an enlarged freight door

P.166S Albatros: version bought by South Africa and deployed for coastal patrol and search and rescue; 20 built

P.166BL2: powered by 380-hp (283-kW) IGSO-540-A1H engines and with increased fuel capacity

P.166-DL3: first flown in prototype form on 3 July 1976 with powerplant of two Avco Lycoming LTP 101 turboprop engines; could be configured and equipped to order for use in a wide variety of roles; two were used by Alitalia as trainers, and two by the Somalian Aeronautical Corps as military transports

P.166-DLR-MAR: specially-configured maritime surveillance version of P.166-DL3; suitable for all-weather day or night use from unprepared strips, it is equipped with an integrated system for search, detection and identification of suspect targets

The prototype **Piaggio P.166** flew for the first time on 26 November

1957. It was intended orig-inally as a civil light transport retaining the

wings and powerplant installation of the **P.136-L** amphibian.

Piaggio P.166 (continued)

Like the P.136-L, the P.166 had its 340-hp (254-kW) Avco Lycoming GSO-480 engines mounted as pushers on the cantilever high-set gull-wing. It also had retractable tricycle landing gear and a single angular fin and rudder with an additional dorsal fin.

The type has good short field operating characteristics, and range can be increased by the use of detachable wingtip fuel tanks. The first 32 P.166s went to civil operators, and later civil versions had increased power and greater passenger capacity.

Piaggio P.180

At the 1983 NBAA convention in Dallas, Texas, Piaggio announced the birth of a new twin turbo-prop-powered business aircraft. Design work on the **P.180 Avanti** had begun in 1979. Seating six to 10 passengers, it was a radical departure from anything the company had previously produced.

The major design feature of the aircraft is its use of three lifting surfaces. The main wing is fitted above the mid-set position in the fuselage, with the main spar running behind the passenger cabin. Its straight leading edge is broken only by the engine nacelle inlets and the wing has a slight dihedral of 2°. The T-tail and elevator act as the second lifting surface, in addition to being orthodox control surfaces. The foreplane, however, is not a simple canard, but provides a positive lift component in addition to that produced by the wing. This in turn allows the wing to be reduced in size, decreasing overall weight and drag. The engines are mounted in composite-material nacelles. The Avanti makes considerable use of composites. Carbon-fibre and a graphite/epoxy mix represent about 10 per cent of the aircraft's weight.

The cockpit is fitted with a Collins EFIS system. The aircraft is certified for single-pilot operations. In 1983 Gates Learjet became a partner in the project, but withdrew for economic reasons in January 1986. All the tooling and the forward fuselages of the three pre-production Avantis which were on the line at Wichita were transferred to Italy. Assembly of the first P.180 began in 1986 and the first flight was made on 23 September 1986. The Avanti was certified in Italy in March 1990, and in May 1990 the first production aircraft was rolled out. The final hurdle of US certification was passed in October 1990 and the first customer delivery took place the following September.

The Avanti has gained its only military order from the Italian air force, which ordered six aircraft for delivery in two batches. The first military P.180s entered service in 1993.

SPECIFICATION

P.180 Avanti
Type: 10-passenger business aircraft
Powerplant: two 1,485-shp (1107-kW) Pratt & Whitney PT6A-66 turboprops
Performance: maximum level speed 455 mph (482 km/h); service ceiling 41,000 ft (12500 m); range (3187 km) 1,980 miles at 39,000 ft (11890 m) with reserves
Weights: maximum take-off 11,200 lb (5080 kg)
Dimensions: wingspan 46 ft (14.03 m); length 47 ft 3½ in (14.41 m); height 12 ft 11 in (3.94 m); wing area 172.22 sq ft (16.00 m²)

The P.180 is powered by two PT6A-66A turboprops, each driving a five-bladed Hartzell fully-feathering reversible-pitch propeller with spinner.

Piaggio PD-808

During 1957 the Douglas Aircraft Company in the USA began a design study for a six-/ten-seat executive jet aircraft with which it hoped to gain a foothold in the non-commercial civil market. This proved to be unsuccessful, and in 1961 Piaggio acquired design rights with the two companies continuing jointly the development of this light transport. Douglas continued to help in an advisory capacity, but Piaggio was responsible for detail design, manufacture and test. A cantilever low-wing monoplane of all metal construction with a circular-section fuselage, conventional tail unit and retractable tricycle landing gear, the aircraft was powered in prototype form by two 3,000-lb (13.34-kN) thrust Rolls-Royce Bristol Viper turbojets pod-mounted one on each side of the rear fuselage. The first of two **Piaggio PD-808** prototypes was flown on 29 August 1964 and the second, flown on 14 June 1966, differed by having larger-capacity wingtip fuel tanks and a dorsal fin of greater area; both were later re-engined with more powerful Viper 526s built under licence by Piaggio.

Production totalled only 29 PD-808s including the prototypes, this comprising two seven-seat civil executive transports, plus 25 aircraft for the Aeronautica Militare Italiana. These consisted of 12 **PD-808RM** navigation aid calibration aircraft, three of a **PD-808ECM** electronic countermeasures version carrying two pilots and three ECM operators, six were **PD-808TA** nine-seat communications and navigation trainers and, finally, four **PD-808VIP** six-seat VIP transports. A turbofan-powered **PD-808TF** was the subject of a design study, but no examples were built.

An unusual aircraft with a distinctive 'bug-eyed' look to its cockpit area, the PD-808 remained in AMI service in summer 2001.

SPECIFICATION

Piaggio PD-808
Type: light utility transport
Powerplant: two 3,360-lb (14.94-kN) thrust Piaggio (licence-built) Viper Mk 526 turbojet engines
Performance: maximum speed 528 mph (850 km/h) at 19,685 ft (6000 m); service ceiling 44,950 ft (13700 m); range with maximum fuel 1,305 miles (2100 km)
Weights: empty equipped 10,648 lb (4830 kg); maximum take-off 18,001 lb (8165 kg)
Dimensions: wingspan over tiptanks 43 ft 3¾ in (13.20 m); length 42 ft 2 in (12.85 m); height 15 ft 9 in (4.80 m); wing area 224.97 sq ft (20.90 m²)

Piasecki H-21

Developed from the US Navy's HRP-2, the **PD-22** tandem-rotor helicopter prototype (USAF designation **XH-21**) was first flown on 11 April 1952. Eighteen **YH-21** helicopters had been ordered in 1949 for USAF evaluation, these being followed by an initial production batch of 32 **H-21A** machines, named **Workhorse** in USAF service. For use by the Military Air Transport Service Air Rescue Service, the H-21As were each powered by a derated 1,250-hp (932-kW) Wright R-1820-103 engine; the first flew in October 1953. Six more were built to USAF contract but supplied to Canada under the Military Assistance Program.

The second production variant was the **H-21B**, which used the full power of the 1,425-hp (1063-kW) R-1820-103 to cover an increase in maximum take-off weight from 11,500 lb (5216 kg) to 15,000 lb (6804 kg). Some 163 were built, mainly for Troop Carrier Command, and these had autopilots, could carry external auxiliary fuel tanks, and were provided with some protective armour. They could carry 20 troops in the assault role.

The US Army's equivalent was the **H-21C Shawnee**, of which 334 were built. This total included 98 for the French army, 10 for the French navy and six for Canada; 32 Shawnees were supplied to West Germany. The H-21C, redesignated **CH-21C** in July 1962, had an underfuselage sling hook for loads of up to 4,000 lb (1814 kg). Production deliveries were made between September 1954 and March 1959, later

Production of the H-21C was begun by Piasecki and continued after the company had been renamed Vertol.

SPECIFICATION

Piasecki H-21C Shawnee
Type: troop/cargo transport
Powerplant: one 1,425-hp (1063-kW) Wright R-1820-103 Cyclone radial piston engine
Performance: maximum speed 131 mph (211 km/h) at sea level; service ceiling 7,750 ft (2360 m); range 400 miles (644 km)
Weights: empty 8,000 lb (3629 kg); maximum take-off 14,700 lb (6668 kg)
Dimensions: rotor diameter, each 44 ft (13.41 m); length, rotors turning 86 ft 4 in (26.31 m); height 15 ft 5 in (4.70 m); rotor disc area, total 3,041.07 sq ft (282.52 m²)

helicopters acquiring the company designation **Model 43** when the Piasecki Helicopter

Corporation became the Vertol Aircraft Corporation in 1956. The H-21A and H-21B retrospectively

became the **Model 42**. Two conversions of H-21C airframes were the **Model 71** (**H-21D**), with two

General Electric T58 engines first flown in September 1957, and the **Model 105** which had two

Avco Lycoming T53s. From the latter was designed the Vertol 107 (Boeing Vertol H-46 series).

Piasecki HUP Retriever

The 'flying banana' shape of the earlier **HRP-1** was discarded in the **Model PV-14**, of which two **XHJP-1** prototypes were ordered for evaluation in the rescue and aircraft-carrier plane-guard roles.

This model was developed into the **PV-18**, USN designation **HUP-1**, which featured angled endplate fins on the horizontal tail surfaces mounted on the rear rotor pylon. Some 32 HUP-1s, each powered by

a single 525-hp (391-kW) Continental R-975-34 engine, were built for the US Navy between February 1949 and 1952; the first squadron, HU-2, took delivery of its initial aircraft in February 1951.

Successful Sperry autopilot trials in an XHJP-1 led to development of the **HUP-2**, whose improved directional stability allowed the endplate fins to be deleted, and the more powerful 550-hp (410-kW) R-975-46 engine was fitted. A total of 339 was built, including 193 for the USN. A number of these were

Note the lack of stabilising fins and horizontal surfaces on the rear fuselages of these Royal Canadian Navy HUP-3s.

designated **HUP-2S** when fitted with dunking sonar equipment for anti-submarine operations. Some 15 HUP-2s were also supplied to the French navy. The US Army ordered an initial batch of an improved version in 1951, this being known as the **H-25A Army Mule**. Powered by the R-975-46A engine, the

H-25A introduced power-boosted controls, strengthened floors and enlarged cargo doors. Fifty similar machines were transferred to the US Navy under the designation **HUP-3**, three serving with the Royal Canadian Navy's Squadron VH-21. Under the unified designation system introduced in September 1962, the HUP-2 and HUP-3 were redesignated **UH-25B** and **UH-25C** respectively.

Pilatus Britten-Norman BN-2 Islander

Desmond Norman and the late John Britten had started their association in the development of crop-spraying equipment, and in 1964 began detail design work on a new lightweight feederline transport. Envisaged as a new-generation replacement for the ageing de Havilland Dragon Rapide and other aircraft in this class, the **BN-2 Islander** soon attracted considerable interest, and construction of a prototype was initiated in September 1964. This aircraft flew for the first time on 13 June 1965, powered by two 210-hp (157-kW) Rolls-Royce/Continental IO-360-B engines. A number of changes resulted from flight testing, the most important being a 4 ft (1.22 m) increase in wing span, and the installation of 260-hp (194-kW) Avco Lycoming O-540-E engines, and this remained the standard powerplant.

Initial production aircraft were BN-2 Islanders of high-wing monoplane configuration with a functional rectangular-section fuselage, conventional tail unit, fixed tricycle landing

gear with twin wheels on the main units, and accommodation for a pilot and nine passengers. This 'high-density' seating arrangement had been contrived in a cabin that was only 3 ft 7 in (1.09 m) wide at its maximum by installing 'wall to wall' seats, with access via two doors on the port side, and one on the starboard side, making an aisle unnecessary. Exit in an emergency can be made by removing the door windows. The first production BN-2 made its initial flight on 24 April 1967, and the first Islander entered service less than four months later, on 13 August. The BN-2 was superseded in mid-1969 by the improved **BN-2A**, which introduced detail aerodynamic and equipment improvements, in addition to a new side-loading baggage facility. From 1978 the production became **BN-2B Islander II** aircraft. These differ primarily by having an increased maximum landing weight, improved internal design, and smaller diameter propellers to reduce the cabin noise level.

Various items of alterna-

tive equipment have become available over the years to extend the usefulness of the Islander. These include 300-hp (224-kW) IO-540-K1BS piston engines, or 320-shp (239-kW) Allison 250-B17C turboprops, and aircraft with this latter powerplant are designated **BN-2T Turbine Islander**. Other options included an extended nose to provide additional baggage space, raked wingtips containing auxiliary fuel tanks, and a Rajay turbocharger to enhance performance.

In addition to operation in a passenger-carrying capacity, the Islander can be used as a freighter with the passenger seats stored in the rear baggage bay, as an ambulance carrying three stretchers and two medical attendants, and for a variety of utility purposes when suitably equipped. **Defender** and **Maritime Defender** military versions were also built, and these can be adapted for casualty evacuation, patrol, transport, and search and rescue operations.

The success of this aircraft, which from the outset was intended to

Variants

Defender: military version for a variety of tasks (counter-insurgency, forward air control, casualty evacuation, patrol, light transport, etc); the main difference from civil Islanders is the provision of four underwing hardpoints able to carry a total stores weight of 2,500 lb (1134 kg), including machine-gun pods, rocket pods, bombs, missiles, flares or drop tanks
Maritime Defender: version of the Islander intended for coastal patrol duties, SAR and fishery protection, with an endurance of 8 hours and search radar in a nose radome; the type can also carry rescue equipment (liferafts, etc) or underwing weapons

provide a low-cost reliable aircraft that could, if desired, be used in a number of differing roles, is highlighted by worldwide sales in approximately 120 countries. A large number of aircraft were built under licence in Romania, and 35 were assembled in the Philippines from components that had been manufactured by Britten-Norman.

Financial problems for Britten-Norman during the early 1970s led to the take-over by The Fairey Group in 1972. During the following year production

of the Islander was transferred from Bembridge to Gosselies in Belgium. But in 1977 The Fairey Group itself went into receivership, and the Britten-Norman part of the group was bought by Pilatus, and in the form of Pilatus Britten-Norman Ltd the company continued to build aircraft in the Isle of Wight after their basic manufacture in Romania. On 21 July 1998 Pilatus sold Britten-Norman in the UK, the company returning to its original name and continuing to build the Islander and its variants.

Britten-Norman's Islander has proven to be a classic utility aircraft. This Loganair BN-2B is typical of those serving regional airline routes.

Pilatus Britten-Norman BN-2A Mk III Trislander

The solution to the requirement for a 'stretched' version of the Islander needed rather more than the insertion of a new piece of hardware in the fuselage. Enquiries had shown that at least a 50 per cent increase in capacity was required to meet the needs of interested customers, leading in 1970 to evolution of the three-engined **BN-2A Mk III Trislander**. The incorporation of a third engine always raises problems to ensure that there is no asymmetry of thrust. In the case of the Islander

the third engine was installed in the tail.

The engine could not be 'buried' within its structure, and considerable modification of the tail was necessary to make it possible for the fin to also carry the engine mounting. Other changes included the insertion of a 7 ft 6 in (2.29 m) fuselage section forward of the wing, strengthening of the rear fuselage structure, the installation of new main landing gear units with larger wheels and tyres, and provision of an interior furnished to accommodate

17 passengers. Because there was no change in size of the fuselage cross-section, the same 'wall-to-wall' seating arrangement pioneered in the Islander was retained, but access to these in the Trislander was via two port and three starboard doors.

The prototype Trislander was converted from the second Islander prototype, and the conversion flew for the first time on 11 September 1970. The first production Trislander was flown on 6 March 1971: this incorporated the extended-span wings that had been an optional feature of the Islander, and additional fin area had been provided above the rear engine. Certification was granted on 14 May 1971,

In 1999 Integrity Aircraft of New Zealand proposed a single-TFE331 turboprop-engined version of the Trislander, but nothing has come of this.

and the first airline to receive a Trislander was Aurigny Air Services on 29 June 1971.

Designation of the first production version was **BN-2A Mk III**, which retained the standard nose of the Islander; this was followed by the **BN-2A Mk III-1** grossing 10,000 lb (4536 kg). Later production versions include the **BN-2A Mk III-2**, which differs by having as standard the optional extended nose of the Islander; the **BN-2A Mk III-3** which incorporates a system to feather automatically the propeller of

an engine which might fail on take-off; and the **BN-2A Mk III-4** which has a standby rocket engine installed to provide extra thrust should there be an engine failure on take-off. Like that of the Islander, production of the Trislander was transferred to Belgium in 1973, but came back to the Isle of Wight in 1979. In summer 2001, the future of the Trislander was undecided but further production looked possible. The **Trislander M** was a proposed military version along the lines of the twin-engined Defender.

SPECIFICATION

Britten-Norman BN-2A Mk III-2 Trislander
Type: feederliner transport
Powerplant: three 260-hp (194-kW) Avco Lycoming O-540-E4C5 horizontally-opposed piston engines
Performance: maximum cruising speed 166 mph (267 km/h) at 6,500 ft (1980 m); economic cruising speed 150 mph (241 km/h) at 13,000 ft (3960 m); service ceiling 13,150 ft (4010 m); maximum range at economic cruising speed 1,000 miles (1609 km)
Weights: empty equipped 5,843 lb (2650 kg); maximum take-off 10,000 lb (4536 kg)
Dimensions: wingspan 53 ft (16.15 m); length 49 ft 3 in (15.01 m); height 14 ft 2 in (4.32 m); wing area 337.0 sq ft (31.31 m²)

Pilatus PC-6 Porter and Turbo-Porter

On 4 May 1959 the first of five prototype **PC-6 Porter** general utility transport aircraft flew for the first time. A braced high-wing monoplane of all-metal construction, with a wing configured for STOL operation, a conventional tail unit and fixed tailwheel landing gear, the PC-6 is powered by a single engine which, in the case of the prototypes and initial production aircraft, was a 340-hp (254-kW) Avco Lycoming

GSO-480-B1A6 flat-six engine. Essential go-anywhere capability is provided by landing gear that is suitable for wheels, wheel-skis or floats; and the PC-6 has a cabin which is equipped with a pilot's seat and one passenger seat as standard, leaving a clear level floor space which can be used for a variety of purposes.

The initial production PC-6 Porter was followed by the **PC-6/350 Porter**

which introduced the 350-hp (261-kW) IGO-540A1A engine, and this was certificated in September 1962. The Porter was improved progressively by the introduction of alternative powerplants, gradual refinement of the entire structure, and the introduction of new equipment to enhance the versatility of this very useful aircraft which can be used for a wide variety of roles includ-

ing ambulance, air survey, cargo carrying, crop dusting or spraying, glider or target towing, parachuting, passenger transport, search and rescue, supply dropping and water bombing. In

addition to those supplied for civil use, many were sold to a variety of air arms. Under the designation **UV-20A Chiricahua** the US Army used two Turbo Porters in Berlin.

SPECIFICATION

Pilatus PC-6/B2-H2 Turbo-Porter
Type: utility transport
Powerplant: one 680-shp (507-kW) Pratt & Whitney Aircraft of Canada PT6A-27 turboprop flat rated to 550 slip (410 kW)
Performance: maximum cruising speed 161 mph (260 km/h) at 10,000 ft (3050 m); service ceiling 28,000 ft (8535 m); range with internal fuel 652 miles (1050 km)
Weights: empty equipped 2,685 lb (1218 kg); maximum take-off 6,107 lb (2770 kg)
Dimensions: wingspan 49 ft 8 in (15.13 m); length 35 ft 9 in (10.90 m); height 10 ft 6 in (3.20m); wing area 310.01 sq ft (28.80 m²)

Variants

PC-6/A Turbo-Porter: initial turboprop-powered version with a 523-shp (390-kW) Turboméca Astazou IIE or IIG engine; first flown on 2 May 1961
PC-6/A1 Turbo-Porter: 1968 version with a 573-shp (427-kW) Astazou XII turboprop
PC-6/A2 Turbo-Porter: 1971 version with a 573-shp (427-kW) Astazou XIVE
PC-6/B Turbo-Porter: version with a 550-shp (410-kW) Pratt & Whitney Aircraft of Canada PT6A-6A turboprop; first flown on 1 May 1964
PC-6/B1 Turbo-Porter: generally as PG6/B, but with a 550-shp (410-kW) PT6A-20
PC-6/B2-H2 Turbo-Porter: current production version with a 680-shp (507-kW) PT6A-27 turboprop engine, flat-rated to 550 shp (410 kW) at sea level
PC-6/C Turbo-Porter: version with 575-shp (429-kW) Garrett TPE331-25D turboprop engine; prototype built by Fairchild Industries in the USA and first flown during October 1965
PC-6/C1 Turbo-Porter: generally similar to PC-6/C, but with a 575-shp (429-kW) Garrett TPE331-1-100 engine
PC-6/C2-H2 Porter: version developed by Fairchild Industries with a 650-ehp (485-ekW) TPE331-101F turboprop, serving as prototype for a militarised version, known as the **AU-23 Peacemaker**
PC-6/D-H3 Porter: single prototype with a 500-hp (373-kW) Avco Lycoming turbocharged engine, modified wingtips and tail surfaces

With the Aztazou powerplant came an elongated nose, which included the long pointed spinner and huge exhaust pipes illustrated.

Pilatus PC-7 Turbo Trainer

Although the **PC-7** directly derives from the early 1950s piston-powered **P-3** (the prototype of which was re-engined with a 550-shp (410-kW) Pratt &

Whitney Canada PT6A-20 turboprop to fly in April 1966), little of the original design is now retained in the definitive **Turbo Trainer**. After a forced

landing through fuel mismanagement during initial flight development, the project was shelved until 1973, when a P-3 was similarly modified with a

650-shp (485-kW) PT6A-25 flat-rated to 550 shp (410 kW). This first flew on 12 May 1975, but then underwent major structural changes to take full advantage of the extra power.

In conjunction with Dornier, Pilatus designed a

completely new low-fatigue one-piece wing with leading-edge integral tanks ahead of the single mainspar. Dornier also helped design an entirely new electrically-actuated undercarriage to meet a 57 per cent increase in

PC-7 customers include Holland (illustrated), Abu Dhabi, Angola, Austria, Bolivia, Myanmar, Chad, Chile, France, Guatemala, Iran, Iraq, Malaysia, Mexico, Nigeria, Switzerland, and Surinam.

SPECIFICATION	
Pilatus PC-7 Turbo Trainer	
Type: basic and advanced trainer	(655 m) per minute; service ceiling 33,000 ft (10060 m); range 746 miles (1200 km)
Powerplant: one 650-shp (485-kW) Pratt & Whitney Canada PT6A-25A turboprop flat-rated at 550 shp (410 kW)	**Weights:** basic empty 2,932 lb (1330 kg); maximum take-off 5,952 lb (2700 kg)
Performance: maximum cruising speed at 20,000 ft (6095 m) 256 mph (412 km/h); maximum rate of climb at sea level 2,150 ft	**Dimensions:** wingspan 34 ft 1 in (10.40 m); length 32 ft 1 in (9.78 m); height 10 ft 6 in (3.21 m); area 178.69 sq ft (16.60 m²)

maximum take-off weight. Flight development with these modifications in the second prototype also resulted in aerodynamic changes to the rear fuselage and tail.

These and other changes, including the bubble canopy for the non-pressurised cockpit, were all embodied in the first production PC-7, which made its initial flight on

18 August 1978 at Stans. First deliveries were to the Myanmar air force, as launch customer, following FAA civil certification in early 1979. With the Beech T-34C then its sole production competitor, the PC-7 achieved growing export success, supplemented in

June 1981 by a Swiss air force order for 40. For weapons training, six underwing hardpoints can accommodate external stores of up to 2,293 lb (1040 kg), and PC-7s are believed to have been

used operationally by both sides in the Iran/Iraq war.
In 1985, Pilatus offered an optional installation of twin Martin-Baker CH.Mk 15A ejection seats, with Iran as first retrofit customer.

Pilatus PC-9 and Raytheon T-6 Texan II

The prototype **PC-9** made its first flight on 7 May 1984, powered by a PT6A-62. There is only 10 per cent commonality between the PC-7 and PC-9. The latter is similar but recognisable by its larger canopy, stepped tandem cockpits with ejection seats, ventral airbrake and four-bladed propeller. Development began in 1982, and flight testing of

many features and components was carried out using a PC-7 testbed before the construction of two pre-production prototypes was initiated.
The PC-9 was one of four shortlisted contenders to meet the RAF's requirement for a Jet Provost replacement, but lost to the Tucano. By the time that the PC-9 was certificated on 19 September 1985, the

RAF competition had taken place, but Pilatus had retained the linking with BAe that it had made for the RAF competition. This was a strong factor in securing the initial PC-9 production order, announced only a week later, for 30 aircraft for the Royal Saudi Air Force.
Pilatus then switched its marketing effort to Australia, offering offset package deals on both the PC-7 and PC-9 to the Australian government as alternatives to the ailing Wamira programme for an RAAF trainer. The decision this time went in favour of the PC-9, which was co-produced by Hawker de Havilland in Australia under the designation **PC-9/A**.
A German target-towing version, designated **PC-9B**,

Pilatus offers the PC-9 with a number of equipment options. RAAF PC-9s are equipped with Bendix EFIS and low-pressure tyres for example.

is operated by Holstenair on behalf of the Luftwaffe. Other PC-9 operators include the air forces of Cyprus, Myanmar, Thailand and Switzerland.
The announcement, in 1993, of a purchase of 20 'TX-lo' trainers for the Republic of Korea air force was hit by controversy. The Korean PC-9s were to be weapons-capable. Swiss law forbade such an 'arms' export and the deal stalled in a debate over whether Pilatus had ever confirmed the PC-9 could be fitted with hardpoints or not.
In conjunction with Beechcraft, offering the **PC-9 Mk 2** as a JPATS

contender. This differed substantially from the PC-9, with a 70 per cent redesign, including a strengthened fuselage and pressurised cockpit. New digital avionics include GPS, MLS, collision avoidance system and provision for a HUD. An engineering testbed aircraft flew first, followed on 23 December 1992 by the first Beech-assembled aircraft, at Wichita. The PC-9 emerged triumphant from the competition and is in production as the Raytheon **T-6 Texan II** for the USAF and USN (as the **T-6A Texan II**), NATO Flying Training in Canada programme (as the **T-6A-1** or **CT-156 Harvard II**, and Greece.

SPECIFICATION	
Pilatus PC-9	
Type: basic and advanced trainer	service ceiling 38,000 ft (11580 m); range 1,020 miles (1642 km)
Powerplant: one 1,150-shp (857-kW) Pratt & Whitney Canada PT6A-62 turboprop flat-rated at 950 shp (708 kW)	**Weights:** basic empty 3,715 lb (1685 kg); maximum take-off 7,055 lb (3200 kg)
Performance: maximum speed at sea level 311 mph (500 km/h); maximum rate of climb at sea level 4,090 ft (1247 m) per minute;	**Dimensions:** wingspan 33 ft 2½ in (10.12 m); length 33 ft 4¾ in (10.18 m); height 10 ft 8½ in (3.26 m); area 175.35 sq ft (16.29 m²)

Piper J-3 Cub, O-59, L-4 Grasshopper and J-4 Cub Coupe

C. Gilbert Taylor and his brother had first established the Taylor Brothers Aircraft Corporation in 1929 to market the **Taylor Chummy** lightplane; in 1931 the company was re-organised as the Taylor Aircraft Company, W. T. Piper, Sr then being its secretary and treasurer. When the company ran into financial difficulties, manufacturing and marketing rights for the **Taylor Cub**, which had first flown in September 1930,

were acquired by W. T. Piper who, in 1937, formed Piper Aircraft Corporation to continue production of this aircraft. A braced high-wing monoplane of mixed basic construction with fabric covering, the Cub had a conventional tail unit, fixed tailskid landing gear (the main units with wheels or optional floats) and an enclosed cabin seating two in tandem.
When first produced by Piper, the **Piper J-3 Cub**

was powered by a 40-hp (30-kW) Continental A40-4 flat-four engine, but it was not long before the 50-hp (37-kW) A50-4 or alternative A50-5 with dual ignition system was introduced on the **J-3C-50 Cub**. The resulting improvement in performance made this already attractive lightplane an extremely marketable commodity and during 1938, which was the new company's first full year of production, no fewer than 737 Cubs were built. The A50 was a new engine, early experience proving that it was reliable and had development potential, and it was later re-rated at 65 hp (48 kW) at a higher engine speed. Its introduction by competitors meant that Piper had to follow suit, and in 1940 the **J-3C-65 Cub**

The innovative Piper L-4 Grasshopper operated with the US Army in every campaign, and on every front throughout World War II.

appeared with the A65 engine. With alternative Franklin flat-four engines, the 50-hp (37-kW) 4AC-150 or 65-hp (48-kW) 4AC-176, the Cub was designated **J-3F-50** and **J-3F-65** respectively and, similarly, with the 50-hp (37-kW) Avco Lycoming O-145-A1 or

65-hp (48-kW) O-145-B, the Cub had the respective designations **J-3L-50** and **J-3L-65**. Also built in comparatively small numbers was a version designated **J-3P-50**, powered by a 50-hp (37-kW) Lenape Papoose 3-cylinder radial engine.

SPECIFICATION	
Piper J-3C-65 Cub	
Type: two-seat lightplane	(402 km)
Powerplant: one 65-hp (48-kW) Continental A65 flat-four piston engine	**Weights:** empty 640 lb (290 kg); maximum take-off 1,100 lb (499 kg)
Performance: maximum speed 92 mph (148 km/h); service ceiling 12,000 ft (3660 m); range 250 miles	**Dimensions:** wingspan 35 ft 2½ in (10.73 m); length 22 ft 3 in (6.78 m); height 6 ft 8 in (2.03 m); wing area 178 sq ft (16.54 m²)

Piper J-3 Cub, O-59, L-4 and J-4 Cub Coupe (cont.)

Sales began to soar, and then in 1941 the US Army selected this aircraft for evaluation in artillery spotting/direction roles, and shortly afterwards ordered 40 similar aircraft under the designation **O-59**. These aircraft were used by the Army under virtually operational conditions during annual manoeuvres at the end of 1941, and it was very soon discovered that the little Cub had far wider applications than at first anticipated.

This practical experience enabled the US Army to obtain an improved **O-59A** which, powered by a 65-hp (48-kW) Continental O-170-3 flat-four engine,

had better accommodation for the pilot and observer with an enhanced all-round view. Orders for O-59As totalled 948, but as a result of designation changes they entered service as **L-4A** aircraft, the earlier **YO-59** and O-59 aircraft then being redesignated **L-4**, and the type later received the name **Grasshopper**. Subsequent procurements covered 980 of the 1,413 versions with reduced radio equipment, 1,801 of the **L-4H** variant with only detail changes, and 1,680 of the **L-4J** model which introduced a variable-pitch propeller. Civil Cubs impressed for Army service at the beginning of

World War II included eight J-3C-65s and five J-3F-65s which were designated **L-4C** and **L-4D** respectively. Piper was then requested to develop a training glider from the L-4 design and this, with powerplant removed and the forward fuselage redesigned to accommodate an instructor and two pupils, was built to a total of 250 for the US Army under the designation **TG-8**. Three of these gliders were acquired for evaluation by the USN under the designation **XLNP-1** and this service also procured 230 **NE-1** aircraft which, basically similar to the US Army's L-4s, were used as primary

trainers; 20 similar aircraft procured at a later date were designated **NE-2**. When, post war, production was switched to the further improved **J-4 Cub Coupe**, Piper had built a total of 14,125 civil and 5,703 military Cubs. The Cub Coupe retained basically the same airframe as the J-3, with a small increase in wingspan and improved landing gear. As powered initially by a 50-hp (37-kW) Continental A50-1 it had the designation J-4, but introduction of the 65-hp (48-kW) Continental A65-1 or -8 engine in 1940 brought redesignation as the **J-4A**, and later of the 75-hp (56-kW) A75-9 as the

J-4E. In 1939 Piper introduced the **J-4B**, differing only in powerplant which initially, was a 60-hp (45-kW) Franklin 4AC-171, but that was soon replaced by the 65-hp (48-kW) 4AC-176-132 without any change in designation. Last of the J-4s was the version powered by Avco Lycoming piston engines, the 55-hp (41-kW) O-145-A1 or -A2, or 65-hp (48-kW) O-145-131, both of these Cub Coupes having the designation **J-4F**. Production of J-4s reached 1,250, and during World War II, 17 J-4Es were impressed for service with the USAAF under the designation **L-4E**.

Piper J-5 Cruiser

A modest expansion in the capabilities of the J-3 and J-4 range was achieved with the **J-5 Cruiser** which, although basically similar to the J-3, had a minimal increase in fuselage width

to provide three-seat accommodation. First seen in early 1940 as the **J-5A** Cruiser with a 75-hp (56-kW) Continental A75-8 engine, it became available subsequently as the **J-5B**

When production of the J-5 Cruiser ended, a total of 1,507 examples of this three-seat lightplane had been built.

with a similarly powered Avco Lycoming GO-145C2 engine, then being designated **J-5C** with the installation of a 100-hp (75-kW) O-235-C. Civil J-5As and J-5Bs were impressed for service with the US Army during World War II under the designations **L-4F** and **L-4G** respectively, and the USN procured 100 aircraft similar to the J-5C under the designation **HE-1**. These

had the 100-hp (75-kW) O-235-2, and a hinged top decking to the rear fuselage to allow the loading and unloading of a

stretcher; when, in 1943, the designation letter H was allocated to identify helicopters, the HE-1s were redesignated **AE-1**.

SPECIFICATION	
J-5C Cruiser	(620 km)
Type: three-seat lightplane	**Weights:** empty 855 lb (388 kg);
Powerplant: one 100-hp (75-kW)	maximum take-off 1,550 lb (703 kg)
Avco Lycoming O-235-C flat-four	**Dimensions:** wingspan 35 ft 6 in
piston engine	(10.82 m); length 22 ft 6 in
Performance: maximum speed	(6.86 m); height 6 ft 10 in (2.08 m);
110 mph (177 km/h); service ceiling	wing area 179 sq ft (16.63 m²)
15,000 ft (4570 m); range 385 miles	

Piper PA-12 Super Cruiser

With the end of World War II in sight, Piper made preparations for the large-scale production of its lightplanes for civil use. The company began by developing an improved version of the J-5C of which production had ended during 1942. Although technically a three-seat aircraft,

the **PA-12 Super Cruiser** was more usually used and regarded as a de luxe two-seater, and differed from the J-5C only in a number of customer-friendly cosmetic refinements. The prototype was flown in December 1945 and attracted so much attention that the

On the power of the same 100-hp (75-kW) O-235-C engine as the J-5C, the similarly-sized PA-12 Super Cruiser had a maximum speed of 114 mph (183 km/h) at sea level.

company soon had an enormous backlog of orders,

and when production of this version ended no

fewer than 3,758 had been built.

Piper PA-14 Family Cruiser

Despite the fact that Piper had developed the PA-12 Super Cruiser as a three-seat aircraft, the accommodation for three adults was far from generous and the company soon discovered that it was beginning to lose sales to the lightweight

four-seaters being marketed by its competitors. In an attempt to provide an aircraft of four-seat capacity without a resulting large price increase, the company revised the fuselage of the PA-12 to give additional width for four seats and

installed a 115-hp (86-kW) O-235-C1 engine. Although the resulting **PA-14 Family Cruiser** was offered at a keen price it failed to gain any real interest, and when production ended during 1949 a total of only 238 had been completed.

An attractive four-seater, the PA-14 failed to win significant orders thanks to a sudden downturn in the lightplane market.

Piper PA-15, PA-16 Clipper and PA-17 Vagabond

The first flush of sales success which followed the end of World War II was followed by a period of near disaster when the US government unloaded its accumulation of war

surplus aircraft on to an active market. This sudden influx of some 31,000 aircraft at highly attractive prices almost paralysed the activities of companies like Beech, Cessna and

Piper that were building general-aviation aircraft for the popular market. The introduction of the PA-14 Family Cruiser was one of the steps taken to offset this situation, the other

being the design and development of a low-cost utility aircraft as a crash programme. Of the same general configuration as the Cub, it re-introduced a shorter-span wing and a

low-powered O-145-B2 piston engine, and there were no 'frills' as standard. This meant, of course, that the basic practical flying machine could be obtained at low

When production ended, Piper had built a combined total of 585 PA-15s and Vagabonds, an example of the latter being illustrated.

SPECIFICATION	
Piper PA-15	range 255 miles (410 km)
Type: two-seat lightplane	**Weights:** empty 620 lb (281 kg);
Powerplant: one 65-hp (48-kW)	maximum take-off 1,100 lb (499 kg)
Avco Lycoming O-145-B2 flat-four	**Dimensions:** span 29 ft 3 in (8.92
piston engine	m); length 18 ft 8 in (5.69 m);
Performance: maximum speed	height 6 ft 0 in (1.83 m); wing area
102 mph (164 km/h) at sea level;	147.50 sq ft (13.70 m²)
service ceiling 12,500 ft (3810 m);	

cost, and the more de luxe accessories could be added later, as and when they could be afforded. Designated **PA-15**, the prototype was flown for the first time on 29 October 1947 and this new machine was soon winning orders. By the autumn of 1948, when the market was showing signs of recovery, Piper introduced the **PA-17 Vagabond**, which was powered by a 65-hp (48-kW) Continental A65-8 engine and again equipped with the 'frills' as standard. Piper added to this success by introducing a four-seat version of the PA-15; designated **PA-16 Clipper**, and powered by a 115-hp (86-kW) O-235-C1 engine, this utility four-seater was built to a total of 726 from 1949.

Piper PA-18 Super Cub and L-18/L-21/U-7 series

Certainly the most famous product of the Piper Company, the original version of the **PA-18 Super Cub**, powered by a 90-hp (67-kW) Continental C90-12F flat-four engine, first came on the market in late 1949. It continued in production with Piper until 1981, when the company disposed of all rights in this aircraft to WTA Inc.. In the intervening period the PA-18 had appeared in progressively improving form, and had been powered by a variety of engines rated between 90 and 150 hp (67 and 112 kW). In its final Piper production form, as the **PA-18-150**, its basic configuration was that of the earliest two-seat Cubs with braced high-set wings, wire-braced tail unit, and fixed tailwheel landing gear, but powered by a 150-hp (112-kW) O-320 flat-four engine. This powerplant had been used also for a specialised agricultural duster/sprayer version designated **PA-18A** which had been introduced in 1952; it incorporated as standard a chemical hopper and spray/dusting gear, but was easily convertible for general-purpose use, and when production ended a total of 2,650 had been built. In addition to civil construction, Piper built 838 PA-18s with the 95-hp (71-kW) C90-81P engine for the US Army under the designation **L-18C**, 108 of this total being supplied to foreign nations under the Military Aid Program, and the army then ordered 150 examples of the generally similar **L-21A** which differed by having the

Super Cubs were widely exported for military use both in Europe and farther afield. An Israeli machine is illustrated.

SPECIFICATION	
Piper PA-18-150 Super Cub	maximum payload 460 miles
Type: two-seat lightplane	(740 km)
Powerplant: one 150-hp (112-kW)	**Weights:** empty 983 lb (446 kg);
Avco Lycoming O-320 flat-four	maximum take-off 1,750-lb (794 kg)
piston engine	**Dimensions:** wingspan 35 ft 2½ in
Performance: maximum speed	(10.73 m); length 22 ft 7 in
130 mph (209 km/h); service ceiling	(6.88 m); height 6 ft 8½ in (2.04 m);
19,000 ft (5790 m); range with	wing area 178.50 sq ft (16.58 m²)

125-hp (93-kW) O-290-11 engine; at a later date a number of these aircraft was converted for use as trainers, then being redesignated **TL-21A**. Under the designation **YL-21** the US Army evaluated two examples of a version of the PA-18 powered by a 135-hp (101-kW) O-290-D2 engine, later acquiring a total of 584 under the designation **L-21B**, a number of them being supplied to foreign nations under MAP. In 1962 in-service L-21Bs were redesignated **U-7A**.

Piper PA-20 Pacer

Under the designation **PA-20 Pacer**, Piper began production in 1950 of an updated version of the PA-16. It introduced a number of improvements, including a larger area tailplane with balanced elevators, increased fuel capacity, redesigned landing gear and several interior refinements. At first powered by a 108-hp (81-kW) O-235-C1 engine, it had the designation **PA-20 Pacer 115**, but subsequent versions included the **Pacer 125** with a 125-hp (93-kW) O-290-D engine, and the generally similar **Pacer 135** which introduced a variable-pitch propeller. When production ended in 1955, a total of 1,119 had been built.

The PA-20 Pacer 135 could demonstrate a maximum speed of 140 mph (225 km/h) and had a range of some 580 miles (933 km).

Piper PA-22 Tri-Pacer and Colt 108

In 1951 Piper introduced its **PA-22 Tri-Pacer**, basically a version of the PA-20 with tricycle landing gear that incorporated a steerable nosewheel. It also differed from the PA-20 by having initially a 150-hp (112-kW) O-320 flat-four engine, and introduced an interconnected aileron and rudder pedal control system, enabling the Tri-Pacer to be flown entirely by the control column without the need to have an input from the rudder pedals during turns. This system was easily disconnected, however, to permit independent use of the ailerons, elevator and rudder. The Tri-Pacer proved a very popular aircraft, and late series machines were powered by the slightly more powerful O-320-B engine. When production ended in the early 1960s, a total of 7,668 had been built. This figure included a number of a slightly more austere version with the 150-hp (112-kW) engine which were marketed for airport operator and flying club use under the name **Caribbean**.

On 1 November 1960, Piper announced the introduction of a low cost two-seater which it named **PA-22 Colt 108**. This designation explained to the initiated that its airframe was basically the same as that of the PA-22 Tri-Pacer, but it had a two-seat interior and incorporated in its **Standard** version a minimum of frills. It was available in optional

SPECIFICATION	
Piper PA-22 Tri-Pacer	maximum fuel 655 miles (1054 km)
Type: four-seat cabin monoplane	**Weights:** empty 1,110 lb (503 kg);
Powerplant: one 160-hp (119-kW)	maximum take-off 2,000 lb (907 kg)
Avco Lycoming O-320-B flat-four	**Dimensions:** wingspan 29 ft 3¼ in
piston engine	(8.92 m); length 20 ft 7¼ in
Performance: maximum speed	(6.28 m); height 8 ft 4 in (2.54 m);
141 mph (227 km/h); service ceiling	wing area 147.50 sq ft (13.70 m²)
16,500 ft (5030 m); range with	

Custom and **Super Custom** models with higher standards of installed equipment and instrumentation. Powerplant was the 108-hp (81-kW) O-235-C1B flat-four engine, providing this version with a maximum speed of 120 mph (193 km/h) at sea level and a range with maximum fuel of 690 miles (1110 km) at 7,000 ft (2135 m). A total of 1,827 was built during the three years that the Colt was in production.

A classic lightplane design, the Tri-Pacer introduced tricycle landing gear to the Piper range.

Piper PA-23 Apache and Aztec

On 2 March 1952 Piper flew the prototype of a new twin-engine aircraft, which it then identified as the **PA-23 Twin-Stinson**. A cantilever low-wing monoplane of all-metal construction, it had a tailplane set high on the fuselage and mounting endplate fins and rudders, retractable tricycle landing gear and an enclosed cabin seating four in two pairs, and was powered by two

150-hp (112-kW) Avco Lycoming O-320 flat-four engines in wing-mounted nacelles. The tail unit was very soon replaced by a conventional tailplane with a centrally mounted single fin and rudder, and it was in this form that it entered production in early 1954 as the **PA-23 Apache**, later designated **PA-23 Apache 150**. The type continued in production as the Apache until 1965, by which time

2,166 had been built, including 1,231 examples of the first production version. The original model was followed in 1958 by the **PA-23 Apache 160** with 160-hp (119-kW) O-320-B engines, and with some interior revisions so that it was classed as a four/five-seat aircraft (816 built), and in 1962 by the similar **PA-23 Apache 235**, which introduced swept tail surfaces and 235-hp (175-kW) O-540-B1A5 flat-six engines (119 built).

With sales of the Apache declining, Piper developed an improved version of this aircraft which introduced a 250-hp (186-kW) O-540 engine and provided six-seat capacity. This entered production under the designation **PA-23-250 Aztec** in 1959-60, the US Navy acquiring 20 of these

With its original fin, the Apache had a somewhat dated appearance. The PA-23 Apache 160 illustrated was destroyed in a landing accident in 1976.

aircraft for use in a utility role, designating them **UO-1**, changed to **U-11A** in 1962. The Aztec was built until early 1982 when production was suspended. In final production form the type had the designation

PA-23-250 Aztec F, and was available also as the generally similar **PA-23T-250 Turbo Aztec F**, which differed by having TIO-540 engines with a Garrett engine turbocharging system.

SPECIFICATION

PA-23T-250 Turbo Aztec F
Type: six-seat light transport
Powerplant: two 250-hp (186-kW) Avco Lycoming TIO-540-C1A turbocharged flat-six piston engines
Performance: maximum speed 254 mph (407 km/h) at 18,500 ft (5640 m); service ceiling 24,000 ft (7315 m); maximum range with

maximum fuel 1,317 miles (2120 km)
Weights: empty 3,323 lb (1507 kg); maximum take-off 5,200 lb (2359 kg)
Dimensions: wingspan 37 ft 3¾ in (11.37 m); length 31 ft 2¾ in (9.52 m); height 10 ft 1 in (3.07 m); wing area 207 sq ft (19.23 m²)

Piper PA-24 Comanche

On 24 May 1956 Piper flew the prototype of a new single-engine four-seat cabin monoplane that it initially designated **PA-24 Comanche**, but which later became known as the **PA-24-180 Comanche**. A cantilever low-wing monoplane of all-metal construction, this very clean looking aircraft had such features as

retractable tricycle landing gear, an all-moving tailplane and a 180-hp (134-kW) O-360-A1A engine. The first production aircraft was flown on 21 October 1957, and from the outset it was available in four versions, the **Standard** with basic essential equipment, the **Custom**, **Super Custom** and **AutoFlite** having

A PA-24-260 was used by the UK's Sheila Scott between 18 May and 20 June 1966 to establish a new round-the-world class speed record, covering a distance of 29,055 miles (46759 km).

progressively more sophisticated equipment, the last of them including a two-axis autopilot.

The very convincing capability of the **PA-24-180** was demonstrated at an early date by American pilot Max Conrad in establishing FAI- accredited world class distance records of 6,966.71 miles (11211.83 km) in a straight line and 6,921.28 miles (11138.72 km) in a closed circuit during 1959 and 1960 respectively, and in flying a **PA-24-250** in 1959 over a straight-line

distance of 7,668.50 miles (12341.26 km). The PA-24-250 soon supplemented the PA-24-180 (1,143 built) and while basically similar, differed by having the 250-hp (186kW) O-540-A1A engine; this variant was built to a total of 2,537. This was followed in 1964 by the **PA-24-260** with a 260-hp (194-kW) version of the O-540 engine. Last of

the single-engine Comanches was the **PA-24T-260 Turbo Comanche** which introduced an IO-540 engine with a Rayjay turbocharger to give considerably improved performance, and when production of the PA-24-260s ended in 1973, a total of 1,028 had been built, giving a Comanche grand total of 4,708.

SPECIFICATION

PA-24T-260 Turbo Comanche
Type: four-seat cabin monoplane
Powerplant: one 260-hp (194-kW) Avco Lycoming IO-540 flat-six turbocharged piston engine
Performance: maximum speed 242 mph (389 km/h) at optimum altitude; service ceiling 25,000 ft (7620 m); maximum range with

maximum fuel 1,490 miles (2398 km)
Weights: empty 1,894 lb (859 kg); maximum take-off 3,200 lb (1451 kg)
Dimensions: wingspan 36 ft (10.97 m); length 25 ft (7.62 m); height 7 ft 6 in (2.29 m); wing area 178 sq ft (16.54 m²)

Piper PA-25 Pawnee and PA-36 Pawnee Brave

The rapid expansion of Piper's operations in the 1950s meant that new facilities were soon required, and in 1957 the company opened a new aircraft development centre at Vero Beach, Florida, to be responsible for design, development and testing of new projects. This facility began its operations on a new specialised agricultural aircraft, designated

PA-25 Pawnee. A braced low-wing monoplane with fixed tailwheel landing gear, the PA-25 was powered initially by a 150-hp (112-kW) O-320 flat-four engine, and this version was later redesignated **PA-25-150 Pawnee**. It had a 20-cu ft (0.57-m³) glass-fibre chemical hopper installed forward of the cockpit, and the dust/spray distribution system was the

same as that which had been proven on the PA-18A. Advanced design features were intended to reduce the likelihood of an accident and to give the pilot a far better chance of survival in a crash; thus a high sitting position was provided to ensure an excellent all-round view, along with above average strength seat restraints, and a specially designed structure that was intended to leave the cockpit substantially undamaged in the usual type of low-speed crash associated with agricultural dusting/spraying operations. Such attention

The Pawnee Brave 300 was one of a number of Piper types built in Argentina by Chincul.

SPECIFICATION

Piper PA-25-235 Pawnee
Type: single-seat agricultural aircraft
Powerplant: one 235-hp (175-kW) Avco Lycoming O-540-B flat-six piston engine
Performance: maximum cruising speed, duster 100 mph (161 km/h) or sprayer 105 mph (169 km/h); range with maximum fuel, duster

255 miles (410 km) or sprayer 270 miles (435 km)
Weights: empty basic 1,598 lb (725 kg); maximum take-off 2,900 lb (1315 kg)
Dimensions: wingspan 36 ft 2 in (11.02 m); length 24 ft 8¼ in (7.73 m); height 7 ft 3 in (2.21 m); wing area 183 sq ft (17.00 m²)

to detail resulted in good sales figures, the PA-15-150 soon being followed by the improved **PA-25-235** with structural strengthening, a larger chemical hopper and a 235-hp (175-kW) O-540-B2B5 engine, or optional 260-hp (194-kW) O-540-E. When production of the Pawnee ended in early 1982 approximately 5,000 had been built.

In 1972 Piper announced a completely new version of the PA-25 with a 285-hp (213-kW) Continental Tiara 6-285 flat-six engine, a new cantilever wing, new safety features, filtration of the air entering the pilot's ventilated and heated cockpit, and a standard chemical hopper of 30-cu ft (0.85-m³) or, optionally, 38-cu ft (1.08-m³) capacity. Designated **PA-36 Pawnee**

Brave, the new model began to enter service in 1973, and in 1977 an additional version with a 300-hp (224-kW) IO-540-K1G5 engine became available, the designations of these two aircraft then becoming

PA-36 Pawnee Brave 285 and **PA-36 Pawnee Brave 300**. In 1978 this latter aircraft became the standard model, a new **PA-36 Pawnee Brave 375** being introduced with a 375-hp (280-kW) IO-720-D1CD

flat-eight engine, and equipped with the larger of the two chemical hoppers as standard. These were to remain in production with Piper until rights for both versions of the PA-36 were acquired by WTA Inc. in

1981. This latter company was marketing this agricultural aircraft in two versions in 1984, the version with the 375-hp (280-kW) engine now being the basic model and redesignated **PA-36 New Brave 375**. It is avail-

able optionally with a 400-hp (298-kW) IO-720-D1C engine under the designation **PA-36 New Brave 400**. At least 150 New Braves had been delivered when production ended in the late 1980s.

Piper PA-28 Cherokee and derivatives

It is unlikely that when Piper first flew the prototype of the four-seat **PA-28-150 Cherokee** sporting/training monoplane on 14 January 1960 that the company could have anticipated the almost infinite variety of this basic design that was to result, or that its production would still be continuing in 2001. The type started life as a cantilever low-wing monoplane of all-metal construction with fixed tricycle landing gear and four-seat accommodation in an enclosed cabin, and with power provided by a 150-hp (112-kW) O-320, or 160-hp (119-kW) O-320-B2B flat-four engine in the **PA-28-160 Cherokee**. The first production Cherokee was flown on 10 February 1961, and the type was available from the beginning in the same **Standard**, **Custom**, **Super Custom** and **AutoFlite** models as the PA-24 Comanche. The **PA-28-180** was introduced in 1962 with a 180-hp (134-kW)

O-320-A2A engine, and in 1963 it was followed by the **PA-28-235,** which had structural strengthening and installation of a 235-hp (175-kW) O-540-B2B5 flat-six engine for operation at a higher gross weight. In the following year the range was expanded in the opposite direction when the two-seat **PA-28-140** became available with the 140-hp (104-kW) O-320-A2B flat-four engine, but with introduction of the **PA-28-180R Cherokee Arrow** on 19 June 1967 came a significant change, with retractable tricycle landing gear, fuel-injection engine and a constant-speed propeller as standard; at this time production of the PA-28-150 and -160 versions came to an end. In 1969 Piper made available an optional **PA-28-200R Cherokee Arrow** with a 200-hp (149-kW) IO-360-C1C engine, and in 1971 new models of the PA-28-140 appeared as the **Cherokee**

Flite Liner, a two-seat trainer for use by Piper-sponsored training schools, and the **Cherokee Cruiser 2 Plus 2**, which was a deluxe two/four-seat version, which in the following year became the standard production model. In 1973 the long-standing PA-28-180 was renamed as the **Cherokee Challenger**, with slight increases in wingspan and fuselage length, and improved interior and standards of equipment; at the same time similar changes were introduced on the PA-28-235 which was renamed as the **Cherokee Charger**. In 1974 there came a number of changes in the Cherokee line, the Cherokee 2 Plus 2 being renamed **Cherokee Cruiser**, the Cherokee Challenger the **Cherokee Archer**, and the PA-28-235 the **Cherokee Pathfinder**. At the same time a new member of the family was introduced, the **PA-28-151 Cherokee Warrior** which, powered by a 150-hp (112-kW) O-320-E3D engine, was basically similar to the Archer except for having a completely new wing of increased span. In 1977 Piper ended production of the Cherokee Cruiser and Cherokee Pathfinder, but introduced at the same time the **PA-28-236 Dakota** which, generally similar to the

In Cherokee Charger form the PA-28 featured enlarged windows and a larger door compared to earlier models.

Archer, was powered by the 235-hp (175-kW) O-540-J3A5D flat-six engine and had the new wing of increased span; in 1978 a version of this aircraft with a 200-hp (149-kW) Continental TSIO-360-FB turbocharged engine became available as the **PA-28-201T Turbo Dakota**, but only limited demand meant that its production ended in 1980. In this same year, Piper developed a tandem two-seat trainer based on the Cherokee series to meet the requirements of the Chilean air force. Designated **PA-28R-300 Pillán** (devil) in prototype form, this had retractable tricycle landing gear and was powered by the 300-hp (224-kW)

AEIO-540-H1K5 engine. A number of these aircraft was later built by ENAER as the **T-35**.

Subsequent Cherokee versions included the **PA-28-161 Warrior II** with a 160-hp (119-kW) O-320-D3G engine; the **PA-28-181 Archer III** with the 180-hp (134-kW) O-360-A4M; the **PA-28RT-201T Turbo Arrow IV** incorporating the powerplant used in the Turbo Dakota; and the **PA-28-236 Dakota**. A number of versions of the Cherokee range were also built under licence by EMBRAER in Brazil.

Production versions of the Cherokee in 2001 included the **PA-28-161 Warrior III** and the PA-28-181 Archer III.

SPECIFICATION	
Piper PA-28RT-201T Turbo Arrow IV	maximum range 1,035 miles (1665 km)
Type: four-seat cabin monoplane	**Weights:** empty 1,692 lb (767 kg); maximum take-off 2,900 lb (1315 kg)
Powerplant: one 200-hp (149-kW) Teledyne Continental TSIO-360-FB flat-six turbocharged piston engine	**Dimensions:** wingspan 35 ft 5 in (10.80 m); length 27 ft 3¾ in (8.33 m); height 8 ft 3¼ in (2.52 m); wing area 170 sq ft (15.79 m²)
Performance: maximum speed 205 mph (330 km/h); operational ceiling 20,000 ft (6095 m);	

Piper PA-30 Twin Comanche

When the decision was made to end production of the PA-23 Apache, Piper introduced a new twin-engine four-seat cabin

monoplane under the designation **PA-30 Twin Comanche**. This was a cantilever low-wing monoplane with retractable

tricycle landing gear and was powered by two 160-hp (119-kW) IO-320-B flat-four engines. The type was first flown in production form on 3 May 1963. The PA-30 was superseded

in 1965 by an improved four/six-seat **PA-30B-160 Twin Comanche**, and made available also at the same time was the **PA-30B Turbo Twin Comanche** with Rayjay-turbocharged IO-320-C1A engines, but both were replaced in 1970 by generally similar

versions which introduced a powerplant with counter-rotating propellers. Designated **PA-39 Twin Comanche C/R** and **PA-39 Turbo Twin Comanche C/R**, manufacture of these two models ended in 1972, when total production of all versions was 2,142.

A Twin Commanche was used by Max Conrad to establish a new world class distance record when he flew nonstop from Cape Town, South Africa, to St Petersburg, Florida, during 24-26 December 1964, a distance of some 7,878.26 miles (12,678.83 km).

SPECIFICATION	
Piper PA-39 Twin Comanche C/R	maximum range 1,200 miles (1931 km)
Type: four/six-seat cabin monoplane	**Weights:** empty 2,270 lb (1030 kg); maximum take-off 3,725 lb (1690 kg)
Powerplant: two 160-hp (119-kW) Avco Lycoming IO-320-B1A flat four piston engines	**Dimensions:** wingspan over tiptanks 36 ft 9½ in (11.21 m); length 25 ft 2 in (7.67 m); height 8 ft 3 in (2.51 m); wing area 178 sq ft (16.54 m²)
Performance: maximum speed 205 mph (330 km/h) at sea level; service ceiling 20,000 ft (6095 m);	

Piper PA-31 Navajo and derivatives

On 30 September 1964 Piper flew the prototype of a

new twin-engine executive aircraft which was then the

largest built by the company. Identified at first as the

PA-31 Inca, the aircraft had been redesignated as the **PA-31 Navajo** when deliveries began on 17 April 1967. The PA-31 is a six-/eight-seat

corporate/ commuter transport of cantilever low-wing monoplane configuration with retractable tricycle landing gear.

Piper PA-31 Navajo and derivatives

The PA-31 was powered by two 300-hp (224-kW) IO-540-K flat-six engines, and was available in optional **Standard**, **Commuter** and **Executive** versions with differing interior layouts. Made available at the same time was the optional **PA-31T Turbo Navajo**, which differed only by having two 310-hp (231-kW) TIO-540-A turbocharged engines, and the range was extended in 1970 by introduction of the **PA-31P Pressurized Navajo** with a fail-safe fuselage structure in the

pressurised section and two 425-hp (317-kW) TIGO-541-E1A engines. Production of the PA-31 ended during 1972 and at the same time the company introduced for 1973 the **PA-31-350 Navajo Chieftain,** which by comparison with its predecessor, had the fuselage lengthened by 2 ft (0.61 m) and was powered by two 350-hp (261-kW) TIO-540-J2BD turbocharged engines driving counter-rotating propellers. A significant advance in the Navajo

family came on 22 October 1973 when Piper flew the first production example of the **PA-31T Cheyenne**, which combined an airframe generally similar to that of the Pressurized Navajo with two 620-ehp (462-ekW) Pratt & Whitney Aircraft of Canada PT6A-28 turboprop engines, and in the following year an additional model of the Turbo Navajo was made available, the **PA-31-325 Turbo Navajo C/R** which introduced a 325-hp (242-kW) version of the counter-rotating engines installed in the Chieftain. Production of the PA-31P Pressurized Navajo ended during 1977, at which time a total of 248 had been built, but at the same time the company introduced a new version of the Cheyenne, the **PA-31T-1 Cheyenne I**, the original Cheyenne then becoming redesignated **PA-31T Cheyenne II**. Deliveries of the new

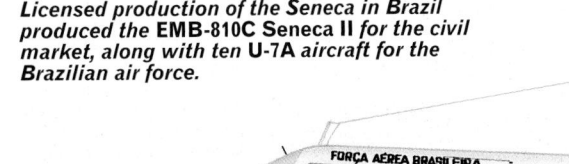

The Navajo C/R's counter-rotating engines improved handling by eliminating the torque produced by two engines rotating the same way.

Cheyenne I, which differed primarily from its predecessor by having 500-shp (373-kW) PT6A-11 turboprops, began towards the end of April 1978. The Cheyenne range was extended for 1981 by introduction of the **PA-31T-2 Cheyenne IIXL**, with the fuselage lengthened by 2 ft (0.61 m) and 750-shp (559-kW) PT6A-135 engines flat-rated to 620 shp (462 kW). In 1982 production of the Navajo terminated after 1,317 had

been built, but versions of the Navajo family that continued in production included the PA-31-325 Navajo C/R, PA-31-350 Chieftain and the PA-31T-1 Cheyenne I, PA-31T Cheyenne II and PA-31T-2 Cheyenne IIXL. The loss of the Navajo was compensated for in 1983 by the introduction of the **PA-31P-350 Mojave,** which basically combines the airframe of the Cheyenne II with the powerplant of the PA-315-350 Chieftain.

SPECIFICATION

Piper PA-31-350 Chieftain
Type: six/eight-seat corporate/commuter transport
Powerplant: two 350-hp (261-kW) Avco Lycoming TIO-540-J2BD turbocharged flat-six piston engines
Performance: maximum speed 266 mph (428 km/h); certificated altitude 24,000 ft (7315 m);

maximum range 1,484 miles (2388 km)
Weights: empty 4,221 lb (1915 kg); maximum take-off 7,000 lb (3175 kg)
Dimensions: wingspan 40 ft 8 in (12.40 m); length 34 ft 7½ in (10.55 m); height 13 ft (3.96 m); wing area 229 sq ft (21.27 m²)

Piper PA-32-260-6 Cherokee Six and derivatives

On 6 December 1963 Piper flew the prototype of a six-seat version of the PA-28 Cherokee, retaining the same general configuration but differing primarily by having a slight increase in wingspan, the fuselage lengthened by 4 ft 5 in (1.35 m), and the installation of the 260-hp (194kW) O-540-E4B5 flat-six engine. Designated **PA-32-260-6 Cherokee Six**, it was available initially in **Standard**, **Custom**, **Executive** and **Sportsman** versions with differing standards of

installed equipment. By 1966 the company designation had changed to **PA-32-260** and the Cherokee Six was then available as an optional six-/seven-seat aircraft and, as the **PA-32-300**, with an optional 300-hp (224-kW) IO-540-K engine. In 1971 Piper restyled the name to **Cherokee Six**, but apart from annual product improvement there were no changes until 1975, when a new version designated **PA-32R-300 Cherokee Lance** entered

production to complement the Cherokee Six, differing by introduction of a new fuselage structure and retractable tricycle landing gear. The 1978 version of the Lance had the conventional tail unit replaced by a T-tail, the designation then changing to **PA-32RT-300 Lance II** and, at the same time, a model with the 300-hp (224-kW) TIO-540-S1AD turbocharged engine became available under the designation **PA-32RT-300T Turbo Lance II**. Production of the PA-32-260 Cherokee Six ended in late 1978, the remaining version then being redesignated **PA-32-300 Six 300**, but in the following year this also disappeared, together with the Lance II and Turbo Lance II. These aircraft were superseded by the six-/seven-seat **PA-32-301 Saratoga** (the basic member of the new related

Piper PA-32RT Turbo Lance II

family) which had an increased-span wing, reversion to a conventional tail unit, fixed tricycle landing gear, and a 300-hp (224-kW) IO-540-K1G5D engine driving a constant-speed propeller. Made available simultaneously was the generally similar **PA-32-301T Turbo Saratoga**, which had a turbocharged version of

the same engine, and the corresponding **PA-32R-301 Saratoga SP** and **PA-32R-301T Turbo Saratoga SP**, which differed by having retractable tricycle landing gear. In 2001 the standard versions in production were the **PA-32R-301 Saratoga II HP** and the turbocharged, **Piper PA-32R-301T Saratoga II TC**.

SPECIFICATION

Piper PA-32-301T Turbo Saratoga
Type: six-/seven-seat cabin monoplane
Powerplant: one 300-hp (224-kW) Avco Lycoming TIO-540-S1AD turbocharged flat-six piston engine
Performance: maximum speed 205 mph (330 km/h); certificated ceiling 20,000 ft (6095 m);

maximum range 990 miles (1593 km)
Weights: empty 1,998 lb (906 kg); maximum take-off 3,600 lb (1097 kg)
Dimensions: wingspan 36 ft 2 in (11.02 m); length 28 ft 2 in (8.59 m); height 8 ft 2 in (2.49 m); wing area 178.30 sq ft (16.56 m²)

Piper PA-34 Seneca

Licensed production of the Seneca in Brazil produced the EMB-810C Seneca II for the civil market, along with ten U-7A aircraft for the Brazilian air force.

SPECIFICATION

Piper PA-34-220T Seneca III
Type: six-/seven-seat cabin monoplane
Powerplant: two 220-hp (164-kW) Continental TSIO-360-KB turbocharged flat-six piston engines
Performance: maximum speed at optimum altitude 226 mph (364 km/h); certificated ceiling

25,000 ft (7620 m); maximum range 1,036 miles (1667 km)
Weights: empty 2,852 lb (1294 kg); maximum take-off 4,750 lb (2155 kg)
Dimensions: wingspan 38 ft 10¾ in (11.86 m); length 28 ft 7½ in (8.72 m); height 9 ft 10¾ in (3.02 m); wing area 208.70 sq ft (19.39 m²)

In 1972 Piper introduced the six-/seven-seat **PA-34 Seneca,** which basically was

a twin-engine version of the Cherokee Six with retractable tricycle landing

gear, a new fuselage structure and power provided by two 200-hp (149-kW) IO-360 flat-four engines. In 1975

200-hp (149-kW) Continental TSIO-360-E turbocharged and counter-rotating engines were introduced

and the landing gear was strengthened for operation at a higher gross weight, the designation then changing to **PA-34-200T Seneca II**. In 1982 the Seneca II was superseded by an improved **PA-34-220T Seneca III**, which differed from its immediate predecessor by having more powerful TSIO-360-KB turbocharged and counter-rotating engines. This aircraft was subsequently replaced by the improved **PA-34-220T Seneca IV**, which in turn gave way to the **PA-34-220T Seneca V**. The latter remained in production in 2001. During 1976-77, Piper signed an agreement under which PZL Mielec assembled/manufactured the Seneca for sale in eastern Europe as the **M-20 Mewa** (gull), the first Polish-built prototype was flown on 25 July 1979.

Piper PA-38-112 Tomahawk

Following certification on 20 December 1977, Piper introduced a completely new two-seat trainer/utility aircraft in 1978, which it designated **PA-38-112 Tomahawk**. A cantilever low-wing monoplane with fixed tricycle landing gear, a T-tail, and side-by-side enclosed accommodation, it was powered by an O-235-L2C engine. Improvements introduced as standard in 1982 resulted in redesignation as the **PA-38-112 Tomahawk II** but because of economic conditions, production was suspended at the end of 1982, at which time 2,519 had been built.

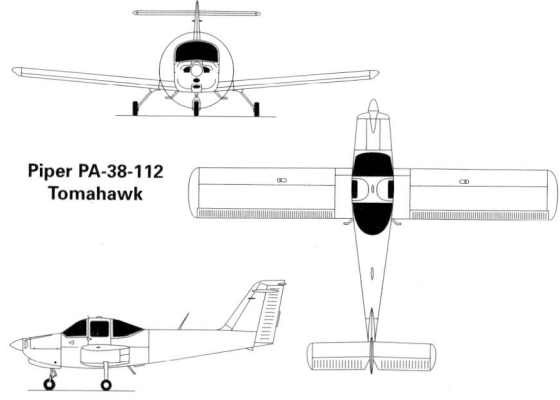
Piper PA-38-112 Tomahawk

SPECIFICATION	
Piper PA-38-112 Tomahawk II **Type:** two-seat trainer/utility aircraft **Powerplant:** one 112-hp (84-kW) Avco Lycoming flat-four piston engine **Performance:** maximum speed 126 mph (203 km/h) at sea level;	service ceiling 13,000 ft (3960 m); maximum range 539 miles (867 km); **Weights:** empty 1,128 lb (512 kg); maximum take-off 1,670 lb (757 kg); **Dimensions:** wingspan 34 ft (10.36 m); length 23 ft 1½ in (7.04 m); height 9 ft ¾ in (2.76 m); wing area 124.70 sq ft (11.58 m²)

Piper PA-42 Cheyenne III

On 30 June 1980 Piper began production deliveries of a new version of the Cheyenne range. Intended for use as a six-/eleven-seat corporate or commuter transport, this **Cheyenne III** differed considerably from its predecessors, a fact reflected in the changed company designation **PA-42**. It has a wing of increased span, lengthened fuselage, a T-tail, and more powerful PT6A turboprops installed in lengthened nacelles. The Cheyenne III was complemented by the **Cheyenne IIIA,** which differed primarily by having 850-hp (634-kW) PT6A-61 turboprop engines flat-rated at 720 hp (537 kW). In addition to the Cheyenne III, Piper also produced the **PA-42-1000 Cheyenne 400LS**, with two 1,645-shp (1227-kW) Garrett TPE331-14A/14B counter-rotating turboprops, each of them flat-rated at 1,000 shp (746 kW). This aircraft is one of the fastest propeller light twins, with a top speed in excess of 400 mph (644 km/h).

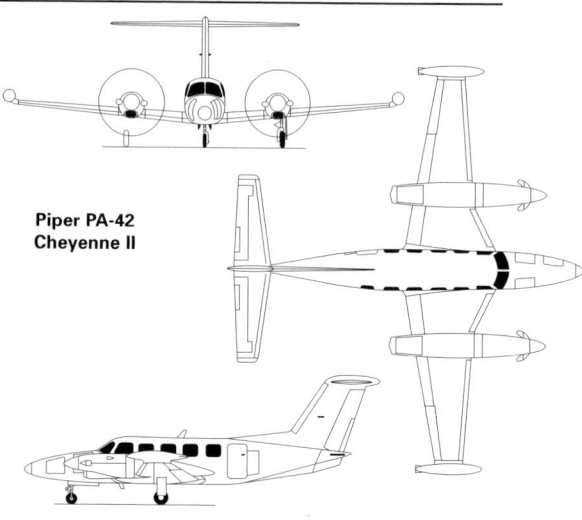
Piper PA-42 Cheyenne II

SPECIFICATION	
Piper PA-42 Cheyenne III **Type:** six-/eleven-seat corporate/ commuter transport **Powerplant:** two 720-shp (537-kW) Pratt & Whitney Aircraft of Canada PT6A-41 turboprops **Performance:** maximum speed 341 mph (549 km/h); service ceiling 32,000 ft (9755 m); maximum range	2,579 miles (4150 km) **Weights:** empty 6,389 lb (2898 kg); maximum take-off 11,200 lb (5080 kg) **Dimensions:** wingspan over tiptanks 47 ft 8 in (14.53 m); length 43 ft 4¾ in (13.23 m); height 14 ft 9 in (4.50 m); wing area 293 sq ft (27.22 m²)

Piper PA-44-180 Seminole

On 21 February 1978, Piper announced a new low-cost twin-engined four-seat cabin monoplane designated **PA-44-180 Serninole**. A cantilever low-wing monoplane with a T-tail, retractable tricycle landing gear and power provided by two O-360-E1AD counter- rotating engines, the Seminole was complemented on 24 April 1980 by a turbocharged version designated **PA-44-180T Turbo Seminole** with TO-360-E1AD engines. Production of both versions was terminated at the end of 1982, when a combined total of 431 had been built, only for the PA-44-180 to be reinstated in 1988. Production was halted again in 1990, before recommencing in 1995.

SPECIFICATION	
PA-44-180T Turbo Seminole **Type:** four-seat cabin monoplane **Powerplant:** two 180-hp (134-kW) Avco Lycoming TO-360-E1AD turbocharged flat-four piston engines **Performance:** maximum speed at optimum altitude 226 mph (364 km/h); certificated ceiling	20,000 ft (6095 m); maximum range 944 miles (1519 km) **Weights:** empty 2,461 lb (1116 kg); maximum take-off 3,925 lb (1780 kg) **Dimensions:** wingspan 38 ft 7¼ in (11.77 m); length 27 ft 7¼ in (8.41 m); height 8 ft 6 in (2.59 m); wing area 183.80 sq ft (17.08 m²)

Piper PA-46-310P Malibu

In late 1982, Piper announced its intention to introduce, in late 1983, a new aircraft which it claimed to be the world's first cabin-class pressurised aircraft with a single piston engine. Designated **PA-46-310P Malibu**, the aircraft is of cantilever low-wing monoplane configuration with retractable tricycle landing gear and a powerplant comprising a Teledyne Continental TSIO-520-BE turbocharged engine, the pressurised cabin providing accommodation for a pilot and five passengers. Certification was gained during September 1983 and deliveries amounted to 404 aircraft before production switched to the **PA-46-350P Malibu Mirage** in 1988.

The Mirage is a generally improved model, featuring a 350-hp (261-kW) TIO-540-AE2A turbocharged engine and, in its latest form, the strengthened wing of the **PA-46-500TP Malibu Meridian**. This latter aircraft was first flown in 1999 and is powered by a 1,209-shp (901-kW) PT6A-42A turboprop engine flat-rated at 400 shp (298 kW). The Meridian was certified in September 2000 for a first customer delivery in November 2000.

SPECIFICATION	
PA-46-310P Malibu **Type:** six-seat cabin monoplane **Powerplant:** one 310-hp (231-kW) Teledyne Continental TSIO-520-BE turbocharged flat-six piston engine **Performance:** maximum speed 270 mph (435 km/h); service ceiling 25,000 ft (7620 m); maximum range 1,831 miles (2947 km)	**Weights:** empty 2,275 lb (1032 kg); maximum take-off 3,850 lb (1746 kg) **Dimensions:** wingspan 43 ft (13.11 m); length 28 ft 4¾ in (8.66 m); height 11 ft 3½ in (3.44 m); wing area 175 sq ft (16.26 m²)

As standard the Malibu Meridian is fitted with an advanced all-glass cockpit, along with the latest in fully-integrated navigation systems.

Pitts S-1 and S-2

There can be few aviation enthusiasts unaware of the superb aerobatic qualities of the single- and two-seat biplanes designed by Curtis Pitts in the USA. The first **Pitts 190 Special** was built in 1947 for US aerobatic display pilot Betty Skelton, but after

manufacturing a comparatively small number of aircraft Pitts made plans available to amateurs to construct an aircraft for their own requirements. In late 1976 he sold all sales and production rights and in early 1977 a new company, Pitts Aerobatics,

was formed to continue the provision of plans and kits to amateur constructors, and to manufacture these aircraft.

Amateur-build models included the **S-1C**, **S-1D** and **S-1E**, while the **S-1S** was a factory-built S-1C and the **S-1T** a more-powerful version of the S-1S. A slightly larger two-seat version was available as the **S-2A Special**, as was two-seat S-2B which, with an AEIO-540 flat-six engine of 260 hp (194 kW), is capable of unlimited aerobatics with two up. The **S-2S** was a single-seat version of the S-2B and was replaced in production by the S-2C which remained

This S-2A is illustrated at it appeared in the 1980s when serving with Los Halcones (The Hawks), the Chilean air force aerobatic team.

available in summer 2001. Also available is the **S-1-11B Super Stinker**. This machine is perhaps the ultimate expression of the original Pitts design,

with a 300-hp (224-kW) engine and a revised airframe allowing it to remain competitive in world-class aerobatics competitions.

SPECIFICATION

Pitts S-2A Special
Type: two-seat acrobatic aircraft
Powerplant: one 200-hp (149-kW) Avco Lycoming IO-360-A1A flat-four piston engine
Performance: maximum speed 157 mph (253 km/h); service ceiling 20,100 ft (6125 m); range with

maximum fuel 343 miles (552 km)
Weights: empty 1,000 lb (454 kg); maximum take-off 1,500 lb (680 kg)
Dimensions: wingspan 20 ft (6.10 m); length 17 ft 9 in (5.41 m); height 6 ft 4½ in (1.94 m); wing area 125.0 sq ft (11.61 m²)

Polikarpov I-5 and I-6

Designed by Polikarpov with the assistance of D. P. Grigorovich, during a period when both were under detention, the first prototype of the compact radial-engined **I-5** single-seat fighter was built in record time during the winter of 1929-30, the maiden flight of this **VT-11** prototype taking place with B. L. Bucholz as pilot on 29 April 1930. The second

prototype, named *Klim Voroshilov*, replaced the original Gnome-Rhône Jupiter VII with a Jupiter VI. This engine was more suitable for operation at medium and low altitudes. The third prototype, flown on 1 July 1930, had an M-15 radial with a Townend ring cowling, this engine being the Soviet-built version of the Jupiter VI. The I-5 was flown in

comparative tests against the **I-6**, a generally similar unequal-span biplane which, designed to supersede the **I-3**, was powered by an uncowled Gnome-Rhône Jupiter VI radial engine. Completion of the I-6 had been delayed by Polikarpov's detention and consequently the first flight was not recorded until 30 March 1930. A second I-6 prototype with a Soviet M-22 engine followed, and both were demonstrated during the May Day flypast in 1930. As a result of comparative flight testing the I-6 was finally rejected

in favour of the I-5, which was of more robust construction.

During August and September 1930 seven pre-production I-5s, fitted with M-22 radials, were built and flown. It was placed in mass production at GAZ-21 in 1932, and the total built, including prototypes, was 803. The I-5 was the standard Soviet fighter until 1936, when it was gradually phased out from first-line units, becom-

ing an important Soviet advanced trainer. A small number was fitted with a non-standard armament of four 0.3-in (7.62-mm) PV-1 machine-guns, which were also fitted to the **I-5LSh** ground-attack version which still equipped two Black Sea Fleet units in 1940. Two two-seat dual-control conversions were tested, and other I-5s were used in Vakhmistrov's Zveno para-site fighter experiments with Tupolev TB-3 bombers.

SPECIFICATION

Polikarpov I-5
Type: single-seat fighter
Powerplant: one 480-hp (358-kW) M-22 radial piston engine
Performance: maximum speed 173 mph (278 km/h); service ceiling 24,605 ft (7500 m); range 348 miles (560 km)
Weights: empty equipped 2,059 lb

(934 kg); maximum take-off 2,987 lb (1355 kg)
Dimensions: wingspan 33 ft 7¼ in (10.24 m); length 22 ft 3 in (6.78 m); wing area 228.74 sq ft (21.25 m²)
Armament: two synchronised 0.3-in (7.62-mm) PV-1 machine-guns, plus two 44-lb (20-kg) bombs

An unequal-span biplane, the I-5 had a workman-like cross-axle landing gear, which dispensed with the streamlined wheel fairings adopted at one stage of development.

Polikarpov I-15 and I-15bis Chaika

Developed from the I-5, the prototype **TsKB-3** biplane was designed by Polikarpov at the TsKB (Central Design Bureau). The TsKB-3 was distinguished by its upper wing, which was gulled into the fuselage, I-type interplane struts and cantilever single-strut main landing gear units with provision for spat-type main wheel fairings. To meet the need for a new single-seat fighter for the Soviet air force its development was very rapid, V. P. Chkalov making the first flight in

October 1933. The TsKB-3 was then powered by an imported Wright SGR-1820-F3 Cyclone radial engine of 710 hp (529 kW) with a Townend ring cowl. Testing was concentrated and successful, production beginning in early 1934, and in the absence of a more powerful engine the 404 **I-15 Chaika** (gull) series aircraft built before 1936 had the 480-hp (358-kW) M-22 radial, which limited maximum speed to 199 mph (320 km/h). The next 59

aircraft had the SGR-1820-F3 Cyclone with a Hamilton two-pitch propeller, both engines and propellers being imported from the USA, and the prototype of this batch was tested as the **TsKB-3bis** in November 1935. On 21 November the TsKB-3bis was stripped down to essentials and flown to a Soviet record height of 47,818 ft (14575 m) by Vladimir Kokkinaki. All of these aircraft were armed with twin synchronised PV-1 machine-guns, but the final 270 I-15s, powered by the Soviet M-25 engine with AV-1 propeller (developed respectively from the Wright powerplant and Hamilton propeller) had four machine-guns. The last I-15s were delivered in 1937, and it seems probable that a number of the M-22-powered aircraft were subsequently re-engined with the M-25.

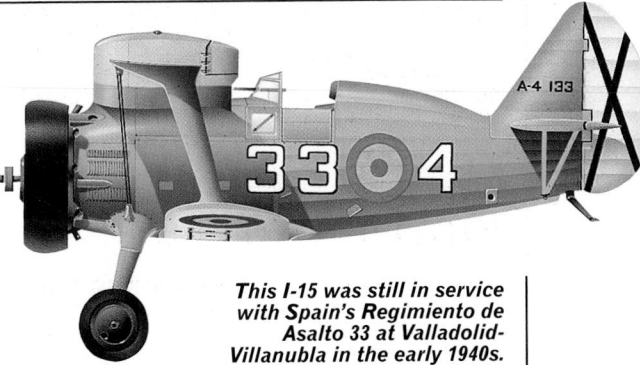

This I-15 was still in service with Spain's Regimiento de Asalto 33 at Valladolid-Villanubla in the early 1940s.

The I-15 proved highly manoeuvrable and an effective gun platform. It flew against the Japanese at Chenkufen on the Manchurian border during 1938, and served in considerable numbers on the

Republican (government) side in the Spanish Civil War. The first I-15s were landed at Cartagena in October 1936 and by the end of 1937, 155 aircraft had been delivered. The I-15 acquitted itself well in

I-152 variants

I-152TK: one aircraft in 1939 fitted with two TK-3 turbochargers and capable of 270 mph (435 km/h) at 19,685 ft (6000 m)
I-152GK: one aircraft in 1939 fitted with a Shcherbakov-designed pressure cabin, an improved version of the type already tested on an I-15

SPECIFICATION

Polikarpov I-15bis
Type: single-seat fighter
Powerplant: one 775-hp (578-kW) M-25V radial piston engine
Performance: maximum speed 230 mph (370 km/h); service ceiling 31,170 ft (9500 m); range 329 miles (530 km)
Weights: empty equipped 2,910 lb (1320 kg); maximum take-off

4,189 lb (1900 kg)
Dimensions: wingspan 33 ft 5½ in (10.20 m); length 20 ft 6¾ in (6.27 m); height 7 ft 2¼ in (2.19 m); wing area 242.52 sq ft (22.53 m²)
Armament: four 0.3-in (7.62-mm) PV-1 or ShKAS machine-guns, plus a maximum bombload of 331 lb (150 kg), or six RS-82 rockets on underwing racks

I-153 variants

I-153BS: version with four 0.5-in (12.7-mm) BS instead of ShKAS machine-guns
I-153DM: one aircraft with auxiliary ramjets; tested in 1940
I-153P: armed with two synchronised 20-mm ShVAK cannon instead of machine-guns; like the I-153BS was produced in relatively small quantities
I-153V: experimental aircraft with Shcherbakov pressure cabin; **I-153TKGK** was another high-altitude experimental, but with Polikarpov-designed pressure cabin and an M-63 radial engine with twin TK-3 turbochargers
I-190: version with an experimental 1,100-hp (820-kW) M-88V radial engine; had a number of design improvements compared with I-153; maximum speed 304 mph (490 km/h), but the prototype's crash stopped development

With the I-152 came the incorporation of cabane struts to support the centre section of the type's straight upper wing surface.

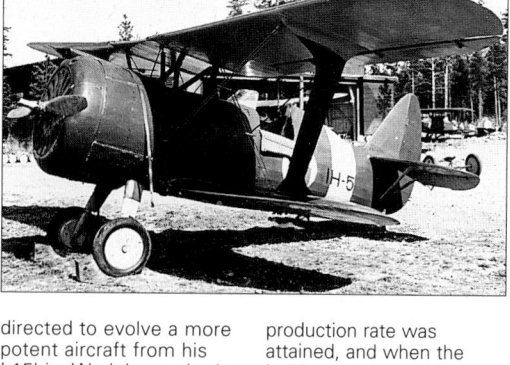

Spain, where it was armed latterly with two of the more efficient ShKAS machine-guns. Spanish government factories also built 287 I-15s under licence, but many of them fell into Nationalist hands at the end of the conflict in March 1939 in an incomplete state, lacking engine or armament, or both. Nicknamed **'Chato'** (snub-nose) by the Spaniards, the I-15 formed the equipment of four first-line *escuadrillas* and was flown by Soviet and Spanish pilots, as well as several other nationalities.

Some 12 straight-wing conversions of the I-15 were flight tested, but in any event the much altered **TsKB-3ter** prototype was flown in early 1937; this had the more powerful M-25V radial engine in a long-chord cowling, and modified landing gear with wheel spats. The principal difference, however, was the new upper wing with a

conventional centre-section braced to the fuselage by a pair of splayed N-type struts. The trailing edge of the upper wing had a cut-out just above the pilot's open cockpit. Like the I-15, ailerons were fitted to the upper wing only. Designated **I-15bis** or alternatively **I-152**, the revised fighter was armed initially with four synchronised 0.3-in (7.62-mm) PV-1 machine-guns, but in later aircraft these were replaced by more efficient ShKAS guns of the same calibre; a small number flew with twin 0.5-in (12.7-mm) BS weapons. While the I-15 had carried four 44-lb (20-kg) bombs on underwing racks, the I-15bis had a maximum offensive load of 331 lb (150 kg).

Production of the I-15bis terminated at the beginning of 1939 with the 2,408th aircraft. It was engaged in operations against the Japanese on the disputed

Manchurian border in 1938-39, and played a large role in the 1939-40 Winter War against Finland. Some 93 of the type were despatched via France to Republican Spain to join the 'Chatos' during the closing months of 1938. Of these only 30 reached their destination, seeing little action and escaping back to France just before the collapse of the Spanish Republic in 1939. The type was dubbed **'Super Chato'**.

During 1937-38 four Soviet eskadrilii were despatched to support Chinese Nationalists fighting the invading Japanese. They were joined by no fewer than 186 more I-15bis supplied to the Chinese air arm, but the I-15bis had mixed fortunes in China, being outclassed by Japanese monoplane fighters during the latter part of its service there.

In June 1941 over 1,000 I-15bis were still operational with the Soviet air force. Most of them, however, were flying on close-support and ground-attack duties pending replacement by the Il-2 Shturmovik. Many were lost in the early months of the German invasion and the type had disappeared from the front-line inventory by late 1942.

The air war over Spain was interpreted by some Soviet observers as a vindication of the fighter biplane and an indication that the concept had future potential. As a result, Polikarpov was

This I-153 was captured on the Eastern Front and flown by the Luftwaffe's I./Luftlandegeschwader 1. It was transferred to the Finnish air force in 1942.

directed to evolve a more potent aircraft from his I-15bis. Work began in the autumn of 1937, the prototype flying for the first time in mid-1938.

Initial deliveries to the Soviet air force of fighter **I-153 Chaika (gull)** were made in May 1939. The basic layout of the I-15bis fuselage and tailplane was retained (although refined and structurally strengthened) and this was married to a staggered single-bay biplane wing assembly, the upper wing being gulled into the fuselage decking on the lines of the I-15. The main landing gear units were designed to retract backwards by manual control and during retraction rotated through 90° for the wheels to lie flat within the wing profile. Early series aircraft, very infrequently known as **I-15ter**, retained the AV-1 propeller and M-25V engine of the I-15bis, these giving a maximum speed of 258 mph (415 km/h). Later the more powerful M-62 engine with two-speed supercharger was introduced, and on some aircraft four 0.5-in (12.7-mm) BS machine-guns were fitted instead of the standard 0.3-in (7.62-mm) ShKAS weapons. Provision was also made for RS-82 rockets to be carried as an alternative to a 441-lb (200-kg) bombload. Service aircraft were sometimes fitted with retractable skis and had provision for auxiliary fuel tanks. A high

production rate was attained, and when the I-153 was taken off the assembly lines in the autumn of 1940. a total of 3,437 had been built.

The earliest series aircraft saw action in the summer of 1939 against the Japanese army air arm on the Manchurian border at Nomonhan. Subsequently, the type was in action in the Winter War. It formed a very high proportion of the available Soviet fighter strength when the Germans attacked in June 1941, suffering heavy losses on the ground and in air combat. As modern monoplane fighters became available, the I-153 was turned over to ground-attack units, and remained in service in some numbers until 1943.

In early 1940, 93 I-153s were supplied to the Chinese Nationalist government for use against the invading Japanese. The only other foreign operator of the I-153 was Finland, which employed 22 aircraft (11 captured directly from the Soviets and 11 captured by the Germans and bought from them by the Finns). While the I-153 was manoeuvrable and frequently did well in the hands of an experienced flier, it was more usually opposed in superior numbers or by faster monoplanes; furthermore, most of its Soviet and Chinese pilots were relatively inexperienced, with inevitable results.

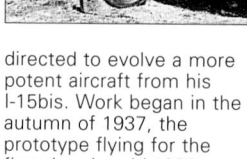

Polikarpov I-16

Design of the **TsKB-12** single-seat fighter prototype was begun by Polikarpov's team at the TsKB (Central Design Bureau) in the spring of 1933. A stubby radial-engined cantilever

low-wing monoplane, it had a wood monocoque fuselage and a metal wing with long-span split-type ailerons, which doubled as landing flaps. The main landing gear units were

This I-16 type 24 was based in the Lake Ladoga area with 4 IAP during the winter of 1940-41.

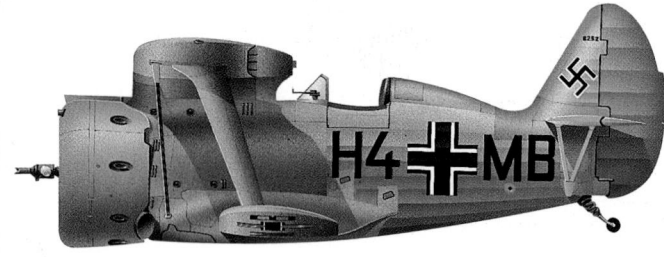

manually retracted inwards into the wing. Powered by a 480-hp (358-kW) M-22 engine, this prototype made its first flight on 31 December 1933. The **TsKB-12bis**, which had an imported 710-hp (529-kW) Wright SR-1820-F3 Cyclone radial, flew on 18 February 1934. With the M-22 a maximum speed of 223 mph (359 km/h) at sea level was attained, while the Cyclone-powered prototype reached 272 mph (437 km/h) at 9,845 ft (3000 m). The I-16 proved a very demanding aircraft, but its speed and excellent rate of climb won it official support, and an evaluation

batch of some 30 M-22-powered I-16s was built; 10 of them participated in the flypast over Moscow on May Day 1935. Development continued

with changes of engine and armament up to the end of planned production in 1939. Remarkably, the I-16 was reinstated in production in 1941-42.

SPECIFICATION	
Polikarpov I-16	
Type: single-seat fighter	
Powerplant: one 1,000-hp (746 kW) M-62 radial piston engine	
Performance: maximum speed 304 mph (490 km/h) at 9,845 ft (3000 m); service ceiling 31,070 ft (9470 m); range 373 miles (600 km)	
Weights: empty equipped 3,252 lb (1475 kg); maximum take-off 4,542 lb (2060 kg)	
Dimensions: wingspan 29 ft 1½ in (8.88 m); length 19 ft 9¾ in (6.04 m); height 7 ft 10¾ in (2.41 m); wing area 160.06 sq ft (14.87 m²)	
Armament: four 0.3-in (7.62-mm) ShKAS machine-guns, two synchronised in forward fuselage and two in wings; wing machine-guns replaced on some aircraft by two 20-mm ShVAK cannon; a 0.5-in (12.7-mm) UB machine-gun was sometimes added to the fuselage-mounted armament; plus a bombload of up to 441 lb (200 kg) on underwing racks, with the alternative of six RS-82 rockets	

Polikarpov I-16 (continued)

The ultimate I-16 version had the more powerful 1,100-hp (820-kW) M-63 engine. The overall production of all versions was 7,005, including dual-control trainers.

From 1935 series **I-16 Type 4** (imported Cyclone) and **Type 5** (M-25 engine) fighters were delivered to the Soviet air force. Supply of the Type 5 to the Spanish Republican air arm began in October 1936, and this model was followed by the **Type 6** (M-25A) and

Type 10 (M-25V). The Types 5 and 6 were christened **'Mosca'** (fly) and the Type 10 became the **'Super Mosca'**. In all, 278 I-16s were delivered to Spain, where licence production of the Type 10 by Hispano-Suiza produced another 10 before the surrender of the Government forces in March 1939, after which another 30 were completed for the Franco regime. The I-16 gave a reasonable account of itself, but tactics

adopted by its pilots, mostly Soviet volunteers, did not make the best use of the type's speed and rate of climb.

Soviet I-16s flew in China against the invading Japanese in 1937, re-equipping two eskadrilii which had previously flown the I-15bis. Early in 1938 the I-16 Type 10 began to equip Chinese units, and in 1939 Soviet I-16s were engaged in furious air battles with Japanese army fighters at Nomonhan on the

Manchurian border. The I-16 took a prominent part in the Winter War, but was obsolescent (even in its latest **Type 24** version) when Germany invaded the Soviet Union in June 1941. At that time nearly two-thirds of the Soviet air force fighter arm comprised I-16s. The type bore the brunt of the invasion and suffered heavy losses on the ground and in the air during 1941. It became renowned for *Taran* ramming attacks on German bombers and fighters, in which the Soviet pilot risked his aircraft and

himself in order to defeat the enemy.

Only in late 1943 was the I-16 finally withdrawn, the type having achieved a worldwide 'first', being the precursor of all the cantilever low-wing monoplane fighters with retractable landing gear to go into large-scale service. By the time of its greatest commitment it was obsolete, but even so its rugged construction and ability to take a great deal of punishment still endeared it to many Soviet pilots, despite the heavy calls it made on pilot skill and expertise.

Variants

I-16 Type 1: about 30 built and used for evaluation; M-22 engine; two wing-mounted 0.3-in (7.62-mm) ShKAS machine-guns; sometimes designated **I-16M-22**

I-16 Type 4: first main series production with imported Wright Cyclones; landing gear mainwheels had fairing doors; pilot had 8-mm armour back plate

I-16 Type 5: entered production July 1935; 700-hp (522-kW) M-25 radial (developed from Cyclone) and AV-1 propeller; first model to have underwing bomb racks; more than 1,500 of this version built; one was converted as the first **I-16P** with armament of two ShKAS machine-guns (fuselage) and two 20-mm cannon (wings); Cyclone engine

I-16 Type 6: built 1936; M-25A engine of 730 hp (544 kW) and strengthened airframe

I-16 Type 10: built from 1937; four 0.3-in (7.62-mm) ShKAS, second pair synchronised and mounted over engine cowling; major production version; fitted with retractable skis for winter operations; 750-hp (559-kW) M-25V engine

I-16 Type 17: 1938 production version, structural strengthening for operation at higher gross weight; tailskid replaced by rubber tailwheel; had six RS-82 rockets as alternative to bombs, and two wing-mounted ShVAK 20-mm cannon in place of wing machine-guns

I-16 Type 18: introduced on production lines in 1939; had 920-hp (686-kW) M-62 radial with two-stage supercharger; provision for a pair of drop tanks; four ShKAS machine-guns

I-16 Type 24: entered service late 1939, early examples with M-62 engine, later had 1,100-hp (820-kW) M-63; wings strengthened, larger

drop tanks, and most had RSI-1 or RSI-3 radio and oxygen equipment

I-16 Type 28 and Type 30: reinstated in production 1941-42; total 450 of each version built and powered by the M-63 engine

I-16P: second use of designation for prototype **TsKB-12P** of 1938; had two wing-mounted 20-mm ShVAK cannon in Type 10 airframe; small number built before being superseded by Type 17

I-16Sh: TsKB-18 prototype with additional armour for ground-attack role and four ShKAS machine-guns; no quantity production

I-16SPB: I-16s had taken part in V. S. Vaklimistrov's 'Zveno' parasite experiments since Zveno 6, a TB-3 bomber with two I-16 Type 1s under its wings for air-launching; Zveno 7 in 1935 comprised a TB-3 with two I-5 biplanes on its wings, a Grigorovich I-Z monoplane on a trapeze between its landing gear legs, plus two I-16s under the wings. Vakhmistrov then reverted to Zveno 6 SPB, a TB-3 carrying two modified Type 5 fighters each with two 551-lb (250-kg) bombs and redesignated as **TsKB-29 I-16SPB** dive-bombers: these parasite fighter dive-bombers were flown by the Black Sea naval air force from 1938, one unit operating in the Ukraine near Odessa against targets in Romania and the Chernovodsky bridge over the Danube in 1941, and against other pinpoint targets into 1942

I-16TK: Type 10 with two TsIAM TK-1 turbochargers; altitude performance much improved but only a few built

UTI-4: some 1,600 two-seat dual control trainers built; at peak of production every fourth aircraft was a UTI-4 (or **I-16UTI**) trainer, with two open cockpits in tandem and based on Type 5 with M-25 engine; most with fixed gear, but some reported with standard retractable main units; blind-flying version had special sliding canopy over rear cockpit; earlier versions were the **UTI-1** (version of Type 1) and **UTI-2** revised variant of UTI-1 with fixed landing gear

Polikarpov R-1

In 1918 Nikolai Nikolayevich Polikarpov, then aged 26, was put in charge of the Duks aircraft factory in Moscow, known subsequently as GAZ-1. After producing 20 Fiat-engined versions of the de

Havilland DH.4, the factory built 130 examples of the DH.9 powered by the Armstrong-Siddeley Puma and over 100 DH.9As with captured German Mercedes-Benz engines. The **Polikarpov R-1**, a

modified development of the DH.9A with a 400-hp (298-kW) M-5 engine (a licence-built version of the American Liberty), appeared in 1923. Mass-produced until 1931, the R-1 was armed with a fixed 0.303-in (7.7-mm) PV-1 and twin DA machine-guns of the same calibre on a ring mounting. Mikhail M. Gromov, piloting an R-1, led a Soviet flight to the Far East in the summer of 1925, reaching Peking on 13 July.

Variants

R-1 BMW: 20 built with 240-hp (179-kW) BMW IVa engine

R-2: alternatively designated **R-II**, this was a version of the R-1 with the 220-hp (164-kW) Siddeley Puma; 130 built

MR-1: twin-float seaplane version; 124 built 1927-28 at GAZ-10 in Taganrog

PM-2: prototype floatplane with metal floats instead of the MR-1's wooden floats; built in 1927

SPECIFICATION

Polikarpov R-1
Type: two-seat reconnaissance/light bomber aircraft
Powerplant: one 400-hp (298-kW) M-5 Vee engine
Performance: maximum speed 115 mph (185 km/h); service ceiling 16,405 ft (5000 m); range 435 miles (700 km)
Weights: empty equipped 3,197 lb (1450 kg); maximum take-off 4,850 lb (2200 kg)
Dimensions: wingspan 46 ft (14.02 m); length 30 ft 3¾ in (9.24 m); wing area 479.44 sq ft (44.54 m²)
Armament: three 0.303-in (7.7-mm) machine-guns, plus bombload of up to 882 lb (400 kg)

Polikarpov's R-1 and Siddeley-engined R-2 (illustrated) biplanes can be considered as the first mass-produced Russian aircraft.

Polikarpov R-5

Developed over a three year period, the prototype **R-5** two-seat light-bomber/reconnaissance biplane flew for the first time in autumn 1928, proving to be a classic design of which some 7,000 in numerous versions were built by 1937. An unequal span

biplane of mixed construction, it had a slim, carefully contoured fuselage and was powered by a 680-hp (507-kW) V-12 engine.

Delivery of the initial production series, with 680-hp (507-kW) M-17B engines, began from the GAZ-1 factory in 1931, and

the Soviet air arm equipped almost all of its light bomber and reconnaissance units with the type

R-5s saw active service in the Far East during border fighting with the Japanese during 1938-9, in the Spanish Civil War on the Republican side, and in the Winter War with Finland (1939-40).

Variants

ARK-5: two conversions for Arctic operations in 1935, with streamlined containers for stores faired into the fuselage sides and lower wing; enclosed, heated cockpits and revised vertical tail

P-5: civil passenger version built for the Civil Aviation Authority from 1931 onwards with military equipment removed; by 1940 over 1,000 were in service, most with Aeroflot or Arctic Aviation; majority used to carry payload of freight up to 882 lb (400 kg), but many had an enlarged rear cockpit to accommodate two passengers seated in wicker-type chairs; others were rebuilt with enclosed rear section for two or three passengers; some had the lower wing strengthened to carry beneath them two G-61 containers, each able to accommodate up to seven people lying face down; similar containers used by P-5s involved in rescuing crew from doomed *Chelyushkin* arctic research vessel

P-5a: twin float version of P-5, built in small numbers

P-5L: 1933 limousine version with two passengers in cabin; small numbers built

PR-5: ultimate transport version of 1936, with redesigned fuselage of greater cross-section and incorporating a pilot's enclosed cockpit and a cabin to seat four passengers, who entered via an airstair door; a centre of gravity problem occurred, which was eliminated by slight repositioning of the upper wing, modified aircraft being redesignated **PR-5bis**

R-5a: twin-float reconnaissance seaplane version; prototype flown during April 1931 and small quantity built; alternative designations were **MR-5** (often **MR-5bis** to avoid confusion with Chetverikov MR-5) and **Samolet 10**

R-5D: long-range one-off version for record-breaking use

R-5 Jumo: experimental engine testbed, with the rear cockpit enlarged to accommodate two observers; alternative designation **ED-1**

R-5L: first factory-built limousine version with cabin for two passengers

R-5M-34: experimental version with M-34 engine flown successfully in 1934

R-5Sh: tested during 1931, a Shturmovik ground-attack version with originally four additional PV-1 machine-guns in pairs in faired containers above the lower wings; also had underfuselage container for a load of light bombs with a total weight of up to 1,102 lb (500 kg); 1933 production version had M-17B engine and eight machine-guns in sets of four

R-5SSS: otherwise known simply as **SSS**, this was a redesign to attain improved performance; landing gear with streamlined strut fairings and wheel spats, M-17F engine in redesigned cowling, and fixed armament increased to two ShKAS machine-guns; a ground attack variant had four more ShKAS weapon on lower wings; over 100 of SSS version built during 1935-36; maximum speed raised to 167 mph (269 km/h) and service ceiling to 26,245 ft (8000 m)

R-5T: batch of 50 torpedo-bombers with divided landing gear to permit the underfuselage carriage of an air-launched torpedo

Experimental variants: other experiments with R-5s included testing with Rudlicki 'butterfly' tailplane, replacing landing gear wheels with caterpillar tracks, fitting of inward-retracting main wheels, installing of pivoting front interplane struts for experiments with spin recovery, and fitting of slotted wings

during the 1930s; series aircraft appearing from 1933 had the more powerful M-17F engine. The R-5 was still in service in large numbers during the war against Germany in 1941-45, when the type operated on intruder, light bombing and reconnaissance missions, mainly at night, and was also deployed in the liaison role. Many variants were built, as well as a number of experimental versions, and the type was used by Aeroflot during the 1930s, some of them built as or converted to limousines with glazed canopies for pilot and passengers. The basic design compared favourably with the British Hawker Hart family and the American Curtiss Falcon series.

SPECIFICATION	
Polikarpov R-5	
Type: two-seat light-bomber/reconnaissance biplane	**Dimensions:** wingspan 50 ft 10¼ in (15.50 m); length 34 ft 7½ in (10.55 m); wing area 540.37 sq ft (50.20 m²)
Powerplant: one 715-hp (533-kW) M-17F V-12 piston engine	
Performance: maximum speed 152 mph (245 km/h); service ceiling 19,490 ft (5940 m); range 621 miles (1000 km)	**Armament:** one fixed synchronised 0.3-in (7.62-mm) PV-1 machine-gun on the forward fuselage decking and twin 0.3-in (7.62-mm) DA machine-guns on a ring mounting over the rear cockpit, plus a maximum bombload of 882 lb (400 kg)
Weights: empty equipped 4,341 lb (1969 kg); maximum take-off 6,607 lb (2997 kg)	

Polikarpov R-Z

Known also as the **R-Zet**, the **R-Z** was the final member of the R-5 family, with a new fuselage of deeper section and entirely revised crew accommodation. The pilot's cockpit was semi-enclosed with folding glazed side panels and, except when operating his single 0.3-in (7.62-mm) ShKAS machine-gun, the observer was seated beneath a canopy comprising one fixed and one sliding section. The landing gear, vertical tail surfaces and upper wing were redesigned, and the more powerful M-34N engine was installed.

Design had been initiated in 1933 and the prototype flew for the first time in January 1935. Production ended in the spring of 1937 after the production of 1,031 aircraft.

The R-Z had a workmanlike appearance, and performed creditably in action against the Japanese in the Far East during 1939 and on the Republican side in the Spanish Civil War. A total of 62 R-Zs was sent to Spain, equipping three groups and seeing a great deal of action.

At the end of hostilities 36 R-Zs fell into Nationalist hands. The R-Z, was known as the **'Natasha'** in Spain, where little use was made of the second ShKAS machine-gun, which was fixed in the forward fuselage.

Although outmoded, the R-Z was still in service with a number of light bomber regiments when the Germans attacked the

Variants

PT: transport prototype which was not further developed as it had poor flying qualities

P-Z: first in service with Aeroflot in 1936, a mail carrier with provision for two passengers seated face to face, some aircraft had underwing containers for additional freight or mail; powered by 820-hp (611-kW) M-34NB engine and a number were in operation until the end of war; some were conversions and others built as new

R-ZR: single-seat conversion for record purposes; established an altitude record of 36,417 ft (11100 m) on 8 May 1937

R-ZSh: one-off Shturmovik prototype with four additional ShKAS machine-guns mounted on lower wing

Soviet Union in June 1941. The first three regiments to be equipped with the Il-2 single-seat ground-attack monoplane converted from the R-Z.

Republican R-Z attacks were flown at low level in tight formation, the defensive fire from the ShKAS machine-guns proving effective against enemy interceptors. After dropping their bombload of up to 882 lb (400 kg), the aircraft made their return to base individually and at low level.

SPECIFICATION	
00Polikarpov R-Z	
Type: two-seat light bomber	**Dimensions:** wingspan 50 ft 10¼ in (15.50 m); length 31 ft 10¾ in (9.72 m); height 11 ft 9¾ in (3.60 m); wing area 457.70 sq ft (42.52 m²)
Powerplant: one 850-hp (634-kW) M-34N V-12 piston engine	
Performance: maximum speed 196 mph (315 km/h); service ceiling 28,545 ft (8700 m); range 621 miles (1000 km)	**Armament:** two or three 7.62-mm (0.3-in) ShKAS machine-guns, plus up to 882 lb (400 kg) of bombs
Weights: empty equipped 4,916 lb (2230 kg); maximum take-off	

Polikarpov U-2 and Po-2

Occupying a unique position in Soviet aviation history, the **U-2** primary trainer biplane had an inauspicious start. The **U-2TPK** prototype, which appeared in early 1927, had been built to achieve economy in repair and maintenance, the wings comprising four identical thick-section interchangeable rectangular panels with square tips. Similarly, a common control surface was used for ailerons, elevators and rudder. The result was a biplane with very poor flight characteristics. It had thus to be redesigned, appearing as a neat, manoeuvrable biplane having staggered single-bay wings with rounded tips, conventional cross-axle landing gear, and tandem open cockpits for instructor and pupil. Powered by a 100-hp (74-kW) radial piston engine, the new prototype made its first flight on 7 January 1928. An immediate success, it was placed in quantity production, deliveries starting in 1928, and by the time of the German invasion of the Soviet Union in mid-1941, over 13,000 had been completed.

Though its principal role was primary training, the U-2 was soon modified as a light passenger transport, air ambulance and agricultural aircraft. Production continued on a massive scale during World War II, and the U-2 took on an even wider range of duties, including liaison, light attack, night nuisance raider and propaganda aircraft complete with microphone and loudspeaker.

Polikarpov U-2 and Po-2 (continued)

Variants

U-2A: single-seat agricultural duster aircraft, built in sub-types **U-2AP** and **U-2AO** from 1930, with 551-lb (250-kg) chemical hopper in rear fuselage; post-1944 continued in production and use as **Po-2A** powered by 115-hp (86-kW) M-11K; total production 9,000
U-2G: one-off experimental model with all controls linked to control column
U-2KL: two special aircraft with rear cabin having bulged canopy; appeared in 1932
U-2LM: light Shturmovik; large number of pre-war aircraft converted for close-support military role from 1941 onwards, plus new production; armed with one 0.303-in (7.7-mm) ShKAS machine-gun on ring mounting over rear cockpit, and racks for 264 lb (120 kg) of bombs, plus rails for four RS-82 rockets; had high reputation among Soviet troops and earned nickname *Kukuruznik* or corn-cutter, resulting from its successful low-level operations; alternative designation was **U-2VOM-1**
U-2LNB: wartime production from 1941 onwards; offensive load raised to 441 lb (200 kg); designation translates as light night bomber, and the type often carried flares or a searchlight; usually had silencer attachment for engine exhaust
U-2LPL: prone-pilot research development of 1935
U-2M: alternative designation **MU-2**, tested in 1931; first of several floatplane versions with large central float and two wingtip stabilising floats; no version built in large numbers
U-2NAK: light artillery observation and reconnaissance variant; observer provided with army radio
U-2S: limited series built from 1934, the rear cockpit being replaced by enclosed cubicle for medical attendant and compartment for stretcher case, with hinged top decking over patient; later had windows installed; other versions known as **U-2S-1** and **U-2SS** (**Sanitarnyi Samolyet**, or ambulance aircraft)
U-2SP: third open cockpit installed with other cockpits relocated; total of 861 built 1934-39, mostly for Aeroflot; survivors impressed in wartime for liaison duties

U-2SPL: limousine model with rear cabin for two passengers in place of rear cockpit
U-2UT: built in limited numbers from 1941, mainly for training and powered by the 115-hp (86-kW) M-11D engine
U-2VS: basic Soviet air force aircraft, large numbers used by senior personnel for wartime liaison flights; over 9,000 in service for liaison in 1945, by then redesignated **Po-2VS**
U-3: development by N. G. Mikhelson and A. I. Morshchikhin in 1934 as a better flying training model with 200-hp (149-kW) M-48 engine; in no way superior to basic U-2
U-4: cleaned-up model of U-2 with slimmer fuselage; developed by Mikhelson and not built in quantity
Po-2GN: 'voice from the sky' propaganda aircraft with loudspeaker for addressing enemy ground troops; built from 1944
Po-2L: limousine version with enclosed passenger cabin; access door on port side
Po-2P: wartime floatplane, built in limited numbers only
Po-2S: wartime ambulance aircraft, **Po-2S-1** similar to pre-war ambulance aircraft; **Po-2S-2** had M-11D engine, and **Po-2S-3** carried two underwing containers each with a stretcher patient; alternative designation for this last variant was **Po-2SKF**
Po-2ShS: staff liaison machine built from 1943; new fuselage with enclosed cabin for pilot and two or three passengers
Po-2SP: specialised post-war version, used for geographic survey and air photography
RV-23: Mikhelson float derivative of U-2 for seaplane altitude record attempts in 1937; built in small numbers with 710-hp (529-kW) R-1820-F3 Cyclone radial
CSS-13: Polish version, some with glazed cabin over crew cockpits
CSS-S-13: Polish ambulance version, with canopy over cockpits for pilot and medical attendant and enclosed section for stretcher patient to rear
E-23: research version of 1935 for inverted flight
Experimental variants: many experimental versions were also built, including one to test the Rudlicki 'butterfly' tail and another re-engined with a Siemens Sh 14 engine

SPECIFICATION	
Polikarpov U-2VS	(400 km)
Type: trainer and multipurpose aircraft	**Weights:** empty equipped 1,400 lb (635 kg); maximum take-off
Powerplant: one 100-hp (75-kW) M-11 radial piston engine	1,962 lb (890 kg) **Dimensions:** wingspan 37 ft 4¾ in
Performance: maximum speed 97 mph (156 km/h); service ceiling 13,125 ft (4000 m); range 249 miles	(11.40 m); length 26 ft 9¾ in (8.17 m); height 10 ft 2 in (3.10 m); wing area 356.86 sq ft (33.15 m²)

After Polikarpov's death on 30 July 1944, the U-2 was redesignated **Po-2** in his honour, and post-war it continued in production in the Soviet Union for several years. Trainer and ambulance variants were built on a large scale in Poland from 1948 to 1953. Po-2s served with many Soviet allies and the total built is reported to be in excess of 33,000.

This Po-2 is finished much as a typical machine would be. Note the machine-gun mounted behind the rear cockpit.

Potez 25

One of the most famous military aircraft of the inter-war period, the **Potez 25** was developed from the **Potez 24** A.2-category prototype, which had been designed by Louis Coroller and flown in 1924. The refined Potez 25 prototype was flown for the first time in early 1925. An

SPECIFICATION	
Potez 25 TOE	**Dimensions:** wingspan 46 ft 4¾ in
Type: two-seat general-purpose military aircraft	(14.14 m); length 29 ft 10¼ in (9.10 m); height 12 ft ¼ in (3.67 m);
Powerplant: one 450-hp (335-kW) Lorraine 12Eb broad-arrow piston engine	wing area 505.92 sq ft (47.00 m²) **Armament:** one fixed synchronised 0.303-in (7.7-mm) Vickers
Performance: maximum speed 129 mph (208 km/h); service ceiling 19,030 ft (5800 m); range 783 miles (1260 km)	machine-gun in engine cowling and two 0.303-in (7.7-mm) Lewis machine-guns on a TO 7 ring mounting over observer's cockpit,
Weights: empty equipped 3,329 lb (1510 kg); maximum take-off 5,512 lb (2500 kg)	plus a maximum bombload of 441 lb (200 kg)

Variants

Potez 25 1925 experimental: prototype with 450-hp (336-kW) Hispano-Suiza 12Ga engine
Potez 25 A.2: two-seat observation version powered by either the 520-hp (388-kW) Salmson 18Cmb radial or Lorraine 12Eb engine

Potez 25 ET.2: two-seat intermediate trainer, used by Aéronautique Militaire and C.F.A., with 500-hp (373-kW) Salmson 18Ab radial
Potez 25 'Jupiter': licence-built by Ikarus (Yugoslavia) and OSGA (Portugal); French-built aircraft sold to Estonia and Switzerland; powered by 420-hp (313-kW) Gnome-Rhône 9Ac Jupiter radial
Potez 25/5: production version (100 built) in **A.2** and **CN.2** variants; 500-hp (373-kW) Renault 12Jb V-12 engine and increased rudder area
Potez 25 TOE: major production version, 2,270 built of which 297 exported, 25 used for civil air mail routes and remainder used by French air arm
Potez 25GR: adaptation of standard Lorraine-powered version with increased fuel tankage for long-distance flights
Potez 25M: parasol-wing monoplane conversion of Hispano-Suiza-powered biplane for Romania 1927; no quantity production
Potez 25 Hispano-Suiza: Ministerial VIP transport version with 600-hp (447-kW) Hispano-Suiza 12Lb V-12 engine; this engine also powered the light-bomber/reconnaissance version exported to Greece
Potez 25 Farman (or Potez 25/4): reconnaissance version, 12 built with 500-hp (373-kW) Farman 12We engine; used by Armée de l'Air
Potez 25/35: Lorraine-powered variant used for target towing; Aéronavale had 12
Potez 25/55: another Lorraine-powered variant with dual controls, 40 built and used mostly by Aéropostale, the Caudron flying school and the Hanriot airline
Potez 25-O: the letter suffix stood for 0céan, in this specially strengthened and modified version for nonstop North Atlantic crossing; powered by Jupiter radial and with jettisonable landing gear and strengthened landing skid attached to underside of fuselage, but crashed on closed-circuit record attempt September 1925 and Atlantic flight never attempted; a second transatlantic Potez 25 built 1927, but abandoned for lack of interest
Potez 25H: at least two floatplane versions of Gnome-Rhône Jupiter powered Potez 25 were tested, one with large main float and underwing stabilising floats and the other with twin floats; a version of the Lorraine-powered Potez 25 TOE was flown in Indo-China with twin floats

This Potez 24 A.2 operated from Isla Poi with the 2do Escadron de Reconocimiento y Bombardio of the Paraguayan air force in 1933.

unequal-span biplane, the Potez 25 had an engine mounting capable of taking a wide variety of power-plants in the 400-hp (298-kW) to 600-hp (447-kW) range. The care-fully contoured fuselage accommodated pilot and observer/gunner close together in tandem cock-pits beneath a cut-out in the trailing edge of the upper wing centre section.

The new cross-axle landing gear had specially designed Potez shock absorbers.

In all, 87 variants of the type were developed for military and civil use, and over 3,500 examples were built in France, most at the Potez factory, but others under licence by A.N.F. Les Mureaux and Hanriot. Abroad, 300 Potez 25s were licence-built in Poland, 200 in Yugoslavia, 70 in Romania and 27 in Portugal. Other countries which used French-built aircraft included China, where the type was used against the Japanese; Paraguay, where it oper-ated against the Bolivian air arm; Uruguay, Greece and Ethiopia, which flew a small number against the invading Italian troops in 1935; Switzerland, which retained the type in service until 1940; and Estonia. In addition test examples were sold to the Soviet Union and some dozen other countries. Many of the exported and licence-built Potez 25s were of the B.2 two-seat light bomber version.

Civil Potez 25s with Lorraine engines were used by Aéropostale and its associated companies in South America for regular mail flights over the Andes, and also by the Caudron and Hanriot flying schools. The Compagnie Française d'Aviation used Salmson-powered Potez 25s for training.

Potez 37 and 39

The **Potez 37** and **Potez 39** appeared in 1930. Both were two-seat braced para-sol-wing monoplanes of all-metal construction, the former being intended for the fighter-recce role and having a rear fuselage which tapered into little more than a boom to give the gunner an improved field of fire. The prototype

An aircraft of decidedly unusual configuration, the Potez 37 proved unsuitable for use as a combat machine.

Potez 39 was designed for the A.2 category observa-tion role, and had a conventional fuselage and redesigned wings with elliptical tips.

The Potez 37 was rejected for production, only two examples being built, but the Potez 39 showed great promise and was adopted by l'Armée de l'Air. Series **Potez 390** and **Potez 391** aircraft were subjected to various modifications during production and service, notably the intro-duction of a rudder with increased area, but they retained the basic features of the design, which included a divided fixed wide-track landing gear with wheel spats; streamlined V-struts supporting the

Variants

Potez 39: prototype; Hispano-Suiza 12Hb engine with larger intake than production aircraft
Potez 390: main series version, powerplant as prototype; total of 244 Potez 390 and 391 aircraft built
Potez 391: built in quantity with 520-hp (388-kW) Lorraine 12Hdr engine; Peru bought 12 equipped as light bombers/night-fighters; had larger air intake than standard French machines
Potez 39/10: in R.2 two-seat reconnaissance category with more powerful 860-hp (641-kW) Hispano-Suiza 12Ybrs engine; flown January 1934 then demonstrated at Villacoublay before Soviet mission; no production
Potez 49 TOE: general-purpose (colonial) sesquiplane conversion of **Potez 392**, the small lower wing braced to the upper by two struts; flown in 1932 with 580-hp (433-kW) Hispano-Suiza 12Hb, but no further development

SPECIFICATION	
Potez 390 A.2	
Type: two-seat observation aircraft	(16.00 m); length 32 ft 9¾ in (10.00 m); height 11 ft 1¾ in
Powerplant: one 580-hp (433-kW) Hispano-Suiza 12Hb V piston engine	(3.40 m); wing area 376.75 sq ft (35.00 m²)
Performance: maximum speed 149 mph (240 km/h); service ceiling 22,965 ft (7000 m); range 435 miles (700 km)	**Armament:** one nose-mounted synchronised 0.295-in (7.5-mm) Darne machine-gun, and twin 0.303-in (7.7-mm) Lewis machine-guns on a ring mounting over the observer's cockpit, plus up to 265 lb (120 kg) of bombs on underfuselage racks
Weights: empty equipped 3,289 lb (1492 kg); maximum take-off 5,842 lb (2650 kg)	
Dimensions: wingspan 52 ft 6 in	

wings; and glazed panels in the fuselage sides between the cockpits.

The Armée de l'Air received 232 **P-390** and **P-391** aircraft.

Potez 56 series

Designed by Louis Coroller as an executive transport, the prototype **Potez 56** made its first flight on 18 June 1934. Largely of wood construction, the Potez 56 was a cantilever low-wing monoplane with a wing section based on that of the Potez 53 racer, and with a single fin and rudder. It had exceptionally clean lines, the main land-ing gear units retracting backwards into the nacelles of the two Potez 9Ab radial engines. Early tests confirmed that the Potez 56 had good flight qualities and was remark-ably stable.

Series production included at least three **Potez 561** aircraft, with variable-pitch propellers to improve take-off perfor-mance, aerodynamically refined engine nacelles and revised cockpit windows.

Military versions followed, for use in the carrierborne liaison, general utility, target tug, and twin-engine pilot train-ing roles. Total production of all versions, military and civil, was 72, the final examples being two **Potez 568 P.3** aircraft, the last of a batch that was completed at the time of the June 1940 armistice with Germany.

SPECIFICATION	
Potez 560	
Type: eight-seat executive transport	**Weights:** empty equipped 4,211 lb (1910 kg); maximum take-off 6,570 lb (2980 kg)
Powerplant: two 185-hp (138-kW) Potez 9Ab radial piston engines	**Dimensions:** wingspan 52 ft 6 in (16.00 m); length 38 ft 10¼ in (11.844m); height 15 ft 11 in (4.60 m); wing area 355.22 sq ft (33.00 m²)
Performance: maximum speed 168 mph (270 km/h); service ceiling 19,685 ft (6000 m); range 404 miles (650 km)	

Variants

Potez 56: prototype and 16 series passenger transports; sometimes known as **Potez 560**
Potez 561: modified version with improved performance; three built
Potez 565: original designation
Potez 56E: one-off aircraft with more streamlined fuselage flown in January 1936; intended for use on carrier *Béarn* and fitted with arrester hook, it ended its career as a liaison aircraft at naval air station Orly
Potez 566: first of three was flown as **Potez 566 T.3** on 2 July 1937; a three-seater, the T in the designation stood for Travail, a category of general-purpose aircraft; had fuselage similar to that of the Potez 56E, but with manually-operated dorsal turret for single 0.295-in (7.5-mm) Darne machine-gun and a ventral nacelle with extensive glazing for observer; two Potez 9Eo engines of 240 hp (179 kW) gave a maximum speed of 193 mph (310 km/h)
Potez 567: version for French navy (22 built) and delivered between October 1939 and March 1940; flown by sections d'entrainement at various training stations, its basic function was towing sleeve targets for air-firing exercises
Potez 568: l'Armée de l'Air ordered 26 **Potez 568 P.3** aircraft in 1938, which were equipped to train pilots to fly twin-engine aircraft by day or night; the cabin had pilots' seats side-by-side, with the instructor located to the rear behind a large raised windscreen

The Potez 56 offered accommodation for a crew of two in an enclosed cockpit, with a cabin for six passengers.

Potez 63 series

Built in response to a complex French air ministry requirement of 1934, the prototype **Potez 63.01**, designed by Louis Coroller and his team, first flew on 25 April 1936. Powered by two Hispano-Suiza 14 Hbs radials, it was intended for three major functions: as a C.2 category two-seat interceptor or escort fighter, as a CN.2 category two-seat night fighter and as a C.3 category three-seat fighter, which would direct by radio the operations of a single- seat fighter unit over the scene of battle.

Of modern appearance, the Potez 63 was the first of the classic twin-engine 'strategic' fighters, an all-metal low-wing monoplane with retractable landing gear, twin fins and rudders, and the crew beneath a long glazed canopy. After a crash landing, the repaired first prototype was redesignated **Potez 630.01**, emerging with HS 14Ab engines and a redesigned tail unit. A second prototype, the **Potez 631.01**, flew on 15 March 1937 powered by two Gnome-Rhône 14Mars radi-

als, but was otherwise similar to the earlier machine. In June 1937 the Potez Méaulte factory was taken over by the nationalised SNCAN, which soon received orders for a total of 80 Potez 630s and 90 Potez 631s.

The **Potez 633.01**, a B.2 category two-seat day bomber prototype, flew in late 1937, and although a large series order for l'Armée de l'Air was subsequently cancelled, several export contracts were signed. The bomber retained the glazed panelling seen under the nose of the early prototypes (deleted on series 630s and 631s), and had an internal bomb-bay for eight 110-lb (50-kg) bombs. Romania ultimately received 21 Potez 633s; Greece obtained 10 machines, an eleventh aircraft crashing on its delivery flight, and these flew against the invading Italians in October 1940. The balance of the Romanian and Greek orders, 19 and 13 respectively, were seized by the French, as were eight aircraft ordered by China. The type was used by

Groupe de Bombardement d'Assault II/52, but after one operational mission in May 1940, the aircraft were all used as operational trainers for the Breguet 693.

The relatively poor performance of the Potez 630 led to its early diversion to training duties, but additional orders were received for the Potez 631, and this was allocated in three-aircraft batches to 20 sections de commandement of single-seat fighter escadrilles. The C.3 concept outlined above was soon discarded, and by the time of the Battle of France, the Potez 631 was flying with day-fighter Groupe de Chasse II/8 and night-fighter ECN I/13 and II/13, as well as with the land-based navy Escadrilles AC 1 and AC 2.

The **Potez 637** was intended as a stop-gap A.3 category three-seat army co-operation and reconnaissance aircraft. The

Romania used its Potez 633 light bombers in support of the German offensive in the Ukraine during 1941. Note the open section at the rear of the canopy for the gunner.

SPECIFICATION	
Potez 63.11 **Type:** three-seat tactical reconnaissance and army co-operation aircraft **Powerplant:** two 700-hp (522-kW) Gnome-Rhône 14 M04/05 or 06/07 radial piston engines **Performance:** maximum speed 264 mph (425 km/h); service ceiling 27,885 ft (8500 m); range 932 miles (1500 km) **Dimensions:** wingspan 52 ft 6 in (16.00 m); length 35 ft 10½ in (10.93 m); height 10 ft 1¼ in (3.08 m); wing area 351.99 sq ft (32.70 m²)	**Armament:** initially, one fixed forward-firing and one under fuselage fixed rear-firing 0.295-in (7.5-mm) MAC 1934 machine-gun, plus a similar gun on a trainable mounting in rear cockpit; early 1940 supplemented by two additional fixed forward-firing and two additional ventral rear-firing 0.295-in (7.5-mm) MAC machine-guns; most aircraft also had four fixed forward-firing 0.295 in (7.5-mm) MAC 1934 weapons under outboard wing panels; provision for four 110-lb (50-kg) bombs on underwing racks

prototype flew in the summer of 1938, and all 60 series machines had been delivered by September 1939. The Potez 637 resembled the Potez 631, but had a ventral gondola (for the observer), which also accommodated a machine-gun for defence beneath the tail, and there was provision for a camera in the rear fuselage. The Potez 637 performed the first reconnaissance mission over the German lines on 4 September 1939; frequently unescorted, it suffered heavy losses during the ensuing nine months. Potez 637 no. 52 was the first Allied aircraft shot down on the Western Front on 8 September 1939.

The prototype **Potez 63.11 A.3** No. 01, flown initially on 31 December 1938, had a redesigned

nose section, fully glazed and rounded, and the crew canopy had been revised. Further modifications had been incorporated in the nose of the first production aircraft which flew on 10 July 1939, and by 31 May 1940, 702 series tactical reconnaissance and army co-operation machines had been built.

The Potez 63.11 suffered even more heavily than the other Potez types and by June 1940, over 200 had been lost in action.

Production continued after the German occupation of the Méaulte and Les Mureaux factories, and at least 850 Potez 63.11s were completed in total. The Luftwaffe used over 100 for training and liaison, the Regia Aeronautica 15 and the Romanian air arm 53.

Variants

Potez 63.01 and **630.01:** designations of first two prototypes
Potez 631.01: first Gnome-Rhône 14Mars-powered prototype
Potez 630: production fighter with Hispano-Suiza 14Ab engines; 82 built, of which one was sold to Yugoslavia and two to Switzerland
Potez 631: production fighter with Gnome-Rhône 14Mars engines; 207 built
Potez 632: originally the Potez 630 CN.2 No.01 prototype night fighter; intended as Potez 632 Bp.2 dive-bomber prototype for Aéronavale, but completed as a conventional light bomber with Hispano-Suiza 14Ab engines
Potez 633: production aircraft; French order for 125 of this B.2 light bomber cancelled, but export orders of 21 delivered to Romania and 10 to Greece; 40 seized by l'Armée de l'Air
Potez 637: series of 60 reconnaissance aircraft for l'Armée de l'Air
Potez 63.11 No.01 and **No.02:** prototypes of redesigned three-seat reconnaissance aircraft with new nose section and crew canopy
Potez 63.11: major production version, over 850 built

P.Z.L. P.6 and P.7

P.Z.L.'s initial **P.1** fighter did not progress beyond the prototype stage, but a significant feature of its design was the then unique wing designed by Zygmunt Pulawski. Selecting a high-wing monoplane configuration for his fighter, he wanted to provide the pilot with a better-than-average forward view and designed a gull-type structure, later known internationally as the 'Pulawski wing', which tapered both in chord and thickness and incorporated thin-section sloping inboard panels giving the pilot a clear view between them. Another feature of the P.1 was the so-called scissor-type main landing gear with oleo-pneumatic shock

absorber struts. Two prototypes were built and flown with Hispano-Suiza engines, but no production order resulted. At this time negotiations were in progress with Bristol in England for licence manufacture of that company's Jupiter radial engine, and P.Z.L. was instructed to adapt the P.1 to accept this powerplant, leading to the construction of four prototypes. These comprised the **P.6/I** with a 450-hp (336-kW) low-altitude Jupiter VI, and **P.7/I** with the 485-hp (362-kW) high-altitude Jupiter VII, flown in August and October 1930 respectively; they were followed in early 1931 by the **P.6/II** which differed mainly by having a revised exhaust system,

and the **P.7/II** with revised rear fuselage structure and other refinements. It was the last of these four prototypes that was ordered into production for the Polish air force, which acquired a total of 150 including the prototype. These began to enter service under the designation **P.7a** in late

A pioneer of monoplane fighter designs when it first appeared in the early 1930s, the P.7 was massively outclassed by the Messerschmitt Bf 109 when the Germans invaded Poland in 1939.

SPECIFICATION	
P.Z.L. P.7a **Type:** single-seat fighter **Powerplant:** one 485-hp (362-kW) Skoda-built Bristol Jupiter VII radial piston engine **Performance:** maximum speed 199 mph (320 km/h) at 13,125 ft (4000 m); service ceiling 27,150 ft (8275 m); range 348 miles (560 km)	**Weights:** empty 2,227 lb (1010 kg); maximum take-off 3,109 lb (1410 kg) **Dimensions:** wingspan 33 ft 9½ in (10.30 m); length 23 ft 5½ in (7.15 m); height 9 ft ¼ in (2.75 m); wing area 185.15 sq ft (17.20 m²) **Armament:** two 0.303-in (7.7-mm) Vickers Type E machine-guns

1932, equipping initially No. 111 Squadron (Eskadra Kościuszkowska) of the 1st Air Regiment, and by the autumn of 1933, Poland had become the first nation in the world to have a first-line force of all-metal mono-plane fighters. Just before the outbreak of World War II about 100 of these aircraft remained in service; some 50 of them were flown to Romania in late September 1939 and about the same number were captured by the Germans and these, after refurbishment, were used by the Luftwaffe in a training role.

P.Z.L. P.11

The installation of a radial engine in the P.7 diminished the excellent forward view for the pilot that was achieved in the P.1 with its narrower V-12 engine, and it was proposed to improve this situation by the intro-duction of a Bristol Mercury radial, which was of smaller diameter than the Jupiter that powered the P.7a. This version of the fighter was designated **P.11**, but delay in delivery of a Mercury engine from Bristol resulted in the **P.11/I** prototype being flown initially, in August 1931, with a 515-hp (384-kW) Jupiter IX.ASb engine licence-built by

Gnome-Rhône. It was not until December 1931 that the **P.11/II** was flown with a 530-hp (395-kW) Bristol Mercury IV.A enclosed in a long-chord Townend ring. This prototype was later re-engined with a 500-hp (373-kW) Gnome-Rhône 9K Mistral engine, the power-plant with which it was exhibited at the 1932 Paris Salon de l'Aéronautique. A third aircraft with a Mercury engine, the **P.11/III**, served as a pre-production proto-type and, following satisfactory official testing, was approved for produc-tion for the Polish air force as the **P.11a**. However, it was preceded on the production line by 50 Mistral-powered **P.11b**

At the outbreak of World War II, 12 Polish squadrons were equipped with the *P.11c*, claiming the destruction of 126 Luftwaffe aircraft for the loss of 114 of their own number.

aircraft for Romania, all of them delivered by the summer of 1934. Production of the P.11a began with a batch of 30, these being similar to late-production P.11bs, but differed by having the 517-hp (386-kW) Skoda-built Mercury IV.S2 engine. The major production vari-ant, however, was the **P.11c**, which adopted more radical measures to improve the pilot's field of view, lowering the engine and re-sitting the pilot farther to the rear on a raised seat, and a number

of other improvements were incorporated at the same time. Production of this version totalled 175, the first batch being powered by the 560-hp (418-kW) Skoda-built Mercury V.S2, but the remainder by the P.Z.L.-built Mercury VI.S2. A version of the P.11c, powered by a licence-built 9K Mistral engine, was built under licence in Romania by I.A.R. under the designation **P.11f**, about 80 being produced during 1936-38.
    Deliveries of the P.11c to Polish fighter squadrons

was completed by the end of 1936. When, in early 1939, it became clear that the planned **P.50 Jastrzab** fighter was unlikely to materialise, efforts were made to provide the P.11c with greater capability by the installation of an 840-hp (626-kW) licence-built Mercury VIIIa engine and four-gun armament. A prototype was flown as the **P.11g Kobuz** and quantity production was initiated, but the German invasion of Poland had started before any of these aircraft were delivered.

SPECIFICATION

P.Z.L. P.11c
Type: single-seat fighter
Powerplant: one 645-hp (481-kW) PXL-built Bristol Mercury VI.S2 radial piston engine
Performance: maximum speed 242 mph (390 km/h) at 18,045 ft (5500 m); service ceiling 26,245 ft (8000 m); range 435 miles (700 km)
Weights: empty 2,529 lb

(1147 kg); maximum take-off 3,594 lb (1630 kg)
Dimensions: wingspan 35 ft 2 in (10.72 m); length 24 ft 9¼ in (7.55 m); height 9 ft 4¼ in (2.85 m); wing area 192.68 sq ft (17.90 m²)
Armament: two 0.303-in (7.7-mm) machine-guns, plus underwing racks for lightweight bombs

P.Z.L. P.23 and P.43 Karas

During 1931 P.Z.L. had designed a six-passenger single-engine light trans-port, the **P.13**, for service with LOT, but as it had no appeal to the airline, its development was aban-doned. Subsequently, it was decided to use this aircraft as the basis for an army co-operation aircraft accommodating a crew of three, and using as power-plant a licence-built version of the Bristol Pegasus radial engine. Following evaluation of the design by the Department of Aeronautics, P.Z.L. was instructed to build three prototypes and the first, powered by a 590-hp (440-kW) Pegasus IIM2, was flown for the first time in August 1934. This aircraft had the designation **P.23/I** and name **Karaś** (crucian carp), but testing soon revealed a number of shortcomings. The two following prototypes, **P.23/II** and **P.23/III**, had the engine mounting lowered to improve the forward view, the bomb bay was deleted to provide more room within the fuselage, and improved glazed canopies were introduced, together with a number of other improvements. The P.23/II crashed during flight trials, but the P.23/III performed well and during

development flying, was modified progressively to what was to be production standard. In 1935 produc-tion orders were placed for 40 examples of the **P.23A Karaś A** with the 580-hp (433-kW) P.Z.L.-built Pegasus II, and 210 of the **P.23B Karaś B** with the 680-hp (507-kW) P.Z.L.-built Pegasus VIII. The first P.23 Karaś A flew in June 1936, but develop-ment problems with the Pegasus II engine resulted in these aircraft being rele-gated to the training role. However, the P.23B Karas B began to enter service in mid-1937 and when production ended, the type equipped 14 first-line squadrons. One Karas B was modified under the designation **P.42** to serve as a development aircraft for the improved **P.46 Sum**, with a twin fin/rudder tail unit and a retractable ventral gondola. However, the P.46 did not materialise beyond the prototype stage and the P.42 was subsequently converted back to Karas B standard. One other version similar to the Karaś B entered production, however, as the **P.43A Karaś A**, of which 12 were built for the Bulgarian air force and delivered in 1937. This model differed

by having the 930-hp (694-kW) Gnome-Rhône radial engine, improved crew accommodation, and armament increased by the addition of a second forward-firing machine-gun. The excellent perfor-mance of the P.43A Karas A led to repeat orders, totalling 42, for a further improved **P.43B Karaś B** with the 980-hp (731-kW) Gnome-Rhône N.1. Of this total 33 were despatched and delivered by August 1939; of the balance, eight had been packed for despatch and the ninth was in final assembly. With the outbreak of World War II, these aircraft were seized for service with the Polish air force, but only five survived the initial German bombing attacks on the P.Z.L. factory and were flown off to serve with No. 41 Squadron, one of the 12 first-line squadrons then equipped with P.23B Karaś B aircraft. These squadrons were responsi-ble for the bulk of the bombing and reconnais-sance operations of the Polish air force during the first 16 days of September 1939, but their aircraft were terribly vulnerable to German opposition, and nearly all of them were destroyed in action.

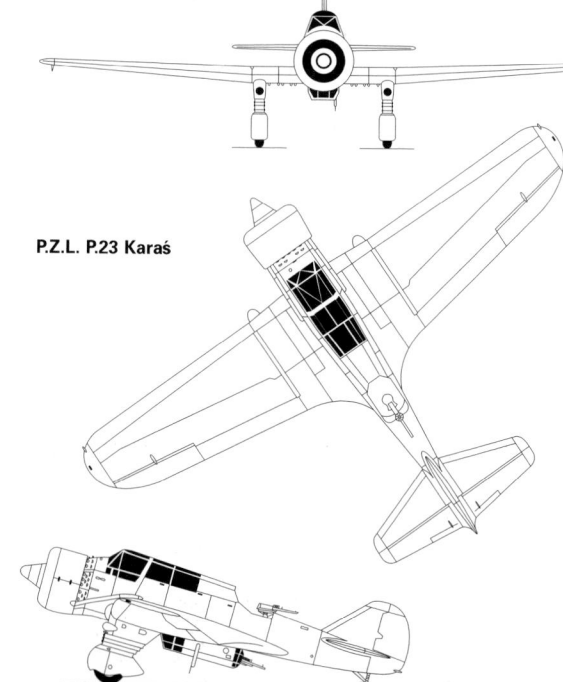

P.Z.L. P.23 Karaś

SPECIFICATION

P.Z.L. P.23B Karaś B
Powerplant: one 680-hp (507-kW) P.Z.L.-built Bristol Pegasus VIII radial piston engine
Performance: maximum speed 199 mph (320 km/h) at 11,975 ft (3650m); service ceiling 23,950 ft (7300 m); range 783 miles (1260 km)
Weights: empty equipped 4,251 lb (1928 kg); maximum take-off 7,771 lb (3525 kg)

Dimensions: wingspan 45 ft 9¼ in (13.95 m); length 31 ft 9¾ in (9.70 m); height 10 ft 10 in (3.30 m); wing area 288.48 sq ft (26.80 m²)
Armament: one 0.303-in (7.7-mm) forward-firing machine-gun, and two single Vickers guns of similar calibre in rear dorsal and ventral positions, plus up to 1,543 lb (700 kg) of bombs on external racks

P.Z.L. P.24

Because of the terms regarding licence agreements for the manufacture in Poland of Bristol engines, it was difficult to market export aircraft with P.Z.L-built versions of these engines. To overcome this difficulty it was decided, in February 1932, to develop a new fighter with a different powerplant, the airframe of the P.11 being redesigned to accept a new Gnome- Rhône designated 14Kds Mistral Major and rated at 760 hp (567 kW). Availability of the first of

these engines delayed, until May 1933, the initial flight of the resulting **P.24/I** prototype, a flight which ended in a forced landing when the propeller disintegrated. The P.24/I did not fly again until October 1933, showing a need for many modifications which were introduced in the **P.24/II** second prototype, this aircraft known also as the **Super P.24**, and on 28 June 1934, the aircraft established an FAI-accredited class speed record of 257.25 mph (414 km/h). A third prototype flown in 1934, the **P.24/III** or **Super P.24bis**, was powered by a

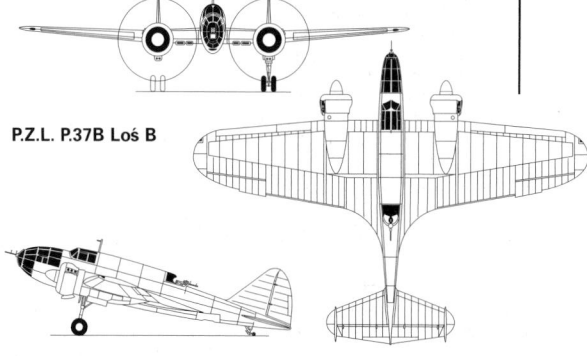

P24s comprised almost the entire World War II fighter strength of the Greek air force and were deployed with considerable success against both the Luftwaffe and Regia Aeronautica.

930-hp (694-kW) Gnome-Rhône 14Kfs and armed with two 20-mm cannon and two machine-guns. Exhibited at the 1934 Salon de l'Aéronautique in Paris, this aircraft caused considerable interest and led ultimately to valuable export orders. The first came from Turkey, which not only negotiated a licence for the manufacture of the P.24, but also ordered 40 **P.24A** fighters generally similar to that shown at Paris, 26 **P.24C** aircraft with four wing-mounted machine-guns, and components plus raw

materials for the assembly of 20 more P.24As. Next came an order from Bulgaria for 14 **P.24B** aircraft, which were similar to the P.24C apart from installed equipment and were delivered from early 1938, followed by 24 P.24Cs and 26 examples of the **P.24F**, the final development of the type, which introduced a 970-hp (723-kW) Gnome-Rhône 14N.07 of smaller diameter and had twin cannon and twin machine- gun armament. The **P.24E**, developed to meet a Romanian requirement,

was generally similar to the P.24C: six built by P.Z.L. had 900-hp (671-kW) Romanian-built Gnome-Rhône 14KIIc32 engines, but later examples of the 40 or so P.24Es built by I.A.R. in Romania had the 940-hp (701-kW) I.A.R.-built 14KMc36 engine. In late 1939 I.A.R. developed a low-wing version of the P.24E under the designation **I.A.R.80**. The four machine-gun equivalent of the P.24F had the designation **P.24G**, and 30 and six respectively were acquired by Greece for service with the Royal Hellenic air force.

SPECIFICATION

P.Z.L. P.24F
Type: two-seat advanced trainer
Powerplant: one 970-hp (723-kW) Gnome-Rhône 14N.07 14-cylinder two-row radial piston engine
Performance: maximum speed 267 mph (430 km/h) at 14,765 ft (4500 m); service ceiling 34,450 ft (10500 m); range 435 miles (700 km)
Weights: empty equipped 2,937 lb

(1332 kg); maximum take-off 4,409 lb (2000 kg)
Dimensions: wingspan 35 ft 1¼in (10.70 m); length 24 ft 11¼ in (7.60 m); height 8 ft 10¼ in (2.70 m); wing area 192.68 sq ft (17.90 m²)
Armament: two 20-mm Oerlikon FF cannon and two 0.303-in (7.7-mm) machine-guns

P.Z.L. P.37 Loś

At the outbreak of World War II, the **P.37 Loś** (elk) was not only one of the most advanced bombers produced by the Polish aircraft industry to that date, but was also the only aircraft in service with the Polish air force that could be regarded as being of modern design. P.Z.L. had proposed the **P.Z.L.3** advanced bomber to meet a Department of Aeronautics requirement for an aircraft in this class, but the financial stringencies of 1930 prevented the P.Z.L.3's progress beyond the design stage. P.Z.L.'s next proposal was for a bomber version of the **P.Z.L.30** civil transport which, having failed to attract a buyer,

was converted as a bomber prototype by P.Z.L.; it was later developed and put into production by the L.W.S. company as the **L.W.S.4 Zubr**. P.Z.L. then produced the design for a twin-engine bomber of monoplane configuration, gaining a contract for three prototypes in 1935: the first of them, the **P.31/I**, was flown initially in late June 1936. Successful testing of this aircraft, which was powered by two 873-hp (651-kW) Bristol Pegasus XII radial engines, led to a contract for 30 under the designation **P.37A Loś A**. Production was completed in 1938, the first 10 having a single fin and rudder, but the last 20 sporting the twin fins and rudders which

had been introduced and tested on the **P.37/II** prototype. This latter prototype had also been used for development testing of engines in the 1,000-hp (746-kW) class by manufacturers that included Fiat, Gnome-Rhône and Renault. Demonstrated at an exhibition in Belgrade during 1938 and at the Paris Salon in the same year, the P.37A created enormous interest, resulting in export orders for a total of 35 **P.37C** bombers powered by 970-hp (723-kW) Gnome-Rhône 14N.07 engines for Bulgaria (15), and Yugoslavia (20), and 40 **P.37D** bombers with 1,050-hp (783-kW) Gnome-Rhône 14N.20/21 engines for Romania (30), and Turkey (10). In addition, Turkey ordered components for 15 more aircraft and signed a licence to manufacture. Planned delivery of these export aircraft was from June 1940 and, as a result, none of them was completed. The delivery of Loś A aircraft to the Polish air force began in early 1938, and all of these were equipped subsequently

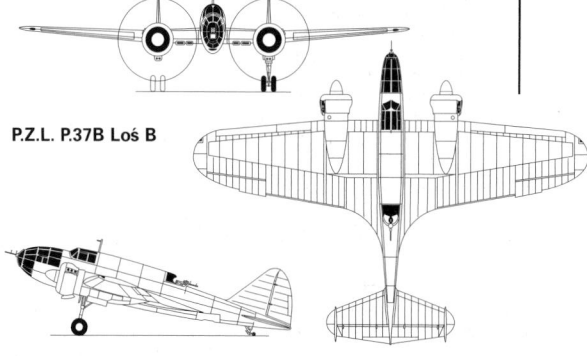

P.Z.L. P.37B Loś B

with dual controls for use as conversion trainers. Delivery of the ensuing **P.37B Loś B** (which introduced a revised cockpit canopy, twin-wheel main landing gear units and Pegasus XX engines) began in late 1938. A total of 150 had been ordered, but policy changes that favoured fighters rather than bombers reduced the number to 100, and only about 70 of these had been delivered by the outbreak of war. Even more disastrous for Poland was the fact that of the Loś B aircraft in service only 36 were fully equipped for operational use, though these were supplemented

quickly by nine more replacement aircraft. Some 26 of this number were lost in action, and on 17 September 1939 the survivors, plus about 20 other P.37s, were flown to Romania, where they were used subsequently by the Romanian air force. A developed version of the P.37 had been planned under the designation **P.49 Mis** (teddy bear), intended to be powered by engines of up to 1,600 hp (1193 kW). A prototype was under construction, but with the German advance on Warsaw, it was destroyed to prevent it from falling into enemy hands.

SPECIFICATION

P.Z.L. P.37/II Loś
Type: four-crew medium bomber
Powerplant: two 925-hp (690-kW) P.Z.L.-built Bristol Pegasus XX radial piston engines
Performance: maximum speed 277 mph (445 km/h); service ceiling 30,000 ft (9145 m); range with 4,850-lb (2200-kg) bombload 932 miles (1500 km)
Weights: empty 9,436 lb

(4280 kg); maximum take-off 19,621 lb (8900 kg)
Dimensions: wingspan 58 ft 10¼ in (17.95 m); length 42 ft 4¾ in (12.92 m); height 16 ft 8¼ in (5.09 m); wing area 575.89 sq ft (53.50 m²)
Armament: three 0.303-in (7.7-mm) machine-guns in nose, dorsal and ventral positions, plus a bombload of up to 5,688 lb (2580 kg)

P.Z.L. Mielec I-22 Iryda

First flown on 5 March 1985, the **Iryda** (iridium) was planned as successor to the TS-11 Iskra basic trainer and LiM-9 (Polish-developed variant of the MiG-17) advanced and tactical pilot trainer, and is a trim machine resembling

the Dassault/Dornier Alpha Jet, although it is slightly smaller and somewhat lighter. The **I-22** is powered by a pair of turbojets, the engine type installed in the seven I-22 production aircraft being the SO-3W22, and other

engines types considered for potential export aircraft included the Turbomeca Larzac turbofan and Rolls-Royce Viper Mk 535 turbojet engine.

The I-22 was deemed inadequate, so the last two of the five prototypes were revised with two 3,307-lb st (14.71-kN) IL K-15 and Rolls-Royce Viper

Mk 545 turbojet engines respectively. The version with the K-15 powerplant was initially designated as the **I-22M-92**, but the variants with Polish and British engines then became the **I-22M-93K** and **I-22M-93V** respectively. The I-22M-93K was optimised for service with the Polish air force, which ordered an

initial seven aircraft with an option on another six or eight, while the M-93V was planned as the export model which has yet to secure an order.

The I-22M-93K otherwise differs from the I-22 in its Martin-Baker Mk PL10LR zero/zero ejection seats and maximum disposable stores weight

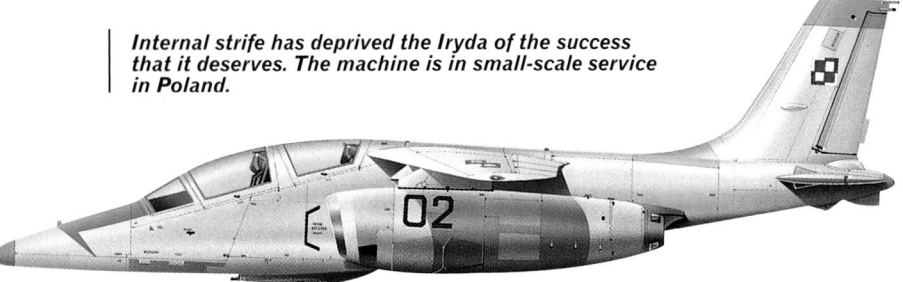

Internal strife has deprived the Iryda of the success that it deserves. The machine is in small-scale service in Poland.

SPECIFICATION

P.Z.L. Mielec I-22 Iryda
Type: two-seat basic and advanced flying trainer with armament training, reconnaissance and light close-support capabilities
Powerplant: two WSK-P.Z.L. Rzeszow P.Z.L.-5 (SO-3W22) turbojet engines each rated at 2,425 lb st (10.79 kN)
Performance: maximum speed 519 mph (835 km/h) at 16,405 ft (5000 m); initial climb rate 4,921 ft (1500 m) per minute; service ceiling 39,370 ft (12000 m); range 375 miles (604 km) with

maximum warload
Weights: empty 10,053 lb (4560 kg); maximum take-off 15,512 lb (6900 kg)
Dimensions: wingspan 31 ft 6 in (9.60 m); length 43 ft 4½ in (13.22 m); height 14 ft 1¼ in (4.30 m); wing area 214.42 sq ft (19.92 m²)
Armament: one 23-mm GSz-23L (licensed Gryazev-Shipunov GSh-23L) fixed forward-firing two-barrel cannon in a ventral pack, plus up to 2,425 lb (1100 kg) of disposable stores

of 3,968 lb (1800 kg). The first seven aircraft were delivered with the same avionics as the I-22, but consideration was given to the delivery of later aircraft with an upgraded French suite (possibly to be retrofitted on the earlier machines) evaluated on the **I-22M-93S**. It was proposed that two I-22M-93 subvariants should be the **I-22M-93R** reconnaissance model with specialised equipment in the fuselage and/or pods, and the **I-22M-93M**

maritime attack and over-water reconnaissance model. The **I-22M-95** was also planned as a multi-role warplane with a wing of greater sweep and super-critical aerofoil section, and a choice of K-15 or Viper Mk 545 turbojet engines, or 3,980-lb st (17.70-kN) Viper Mk 632 turbojets, or 3,637-lb st (16.18-kN) Larzac 04-V3 turbofan engines. The turbojet- and turbofan-powered models would have carried a disposable warload of 5,511 or 6,614 lb (2500

or 3000 kg) respectively, and other changes would have been an improved nav/attack system and enhanced defensive features. The four role-differentiated variants proposed were the **I-22M-95T** two-seat combat trainer, **I-22M-95R** reconnaissance model, **I-22M-95M** maritime model, and **I-22M-95MS** upgraded I-22M-95M. Consideration was also given to the development of a single-seat **I-22M-97** whose two subvariants

would have been the **I-22M-97S** attack and **I-22M-97MS** attack/fighter models.

The seven I-22s were followed by seven I-22M-93Ks before production was halted in May 1995 to allow the development of the **I-22M-96** version intended to overcome the I-22M-93K's failings and limitations. The changes were evaluated in one prototype conversion

and one new-build aircraft, which first flew on 21 December 1996 and 16 August 1997, and included LERXes, slats and Fowler flaps, a taller vertical tail surface, and Sextant Topflight avionics. The I-22M-96 programme was then stalled by contractual problems between the manufacturer and the Polish air force, and it is likely that no further production will take place.

P.Z.L. 104 Wilga

Designed as a successor to the Polish-built Yak-12 and the P.Z.L. 101 developed from it, the original **P.Z.L. 104 Wilga** (thrush) prototype, powered by a 180-hp (134-kW) Narkiewiez WN-6 flat-six engine, was flown for the first time on 24 April 1962. A cantilever high-wing monoplane with fixed tailwheel landing gear and an enclosed cabin, it was followed by prototypes of the **Wilga 2P** and **Wilga CP**, powered by the 185-hp (138-kW) WN-6RB2 and 225-hp (168-kW)

Continental O-470-13A or O-470-L flat-six engines respectively. Intended as a general-purpose aircraft, the 104 was offered initially in versions developed for use as a four-seat passenger-carrying or liaison aircraft; for club flying, glider towing or parachuting; for agricultural use with a 110-Imp gal (500-litre) hopper for dust or liquid application; and as an air ambulance carrying pilot, doctor, two stretcher patients and medical equipment. Following

construction of a number of prototypes, the type entered production initially as the **Wilga 3A** club aircraft and the **Wilga 3S** air ambulance. In 1967 the design was revised to give better cabin accommodation and improved landing gear, production beginning in 1968 of the **Wilga 35** which, powered by a 260-hp (194-kW) Ivehenko AI-14R engine, had flown for the first time on 28 July 1967, and of the **Wilga 32** with a 230-hp (172-kW) O-470-K flown on 12 September 1967. This last version was built under licence in Indonesia as the **P.Z.L. 104 Gelatik 32** (rice bird) with an O-470-R engine of similar output. Subsequent versions included the **Wilga 35A**

intended for aero club use, float-equipped **Wilga 35H**, and passenger/liaison **Wilga 35P**. A version generally similar to the Wilga 35, but meeting the requirements of the US FAR Pt 23, has the designation **Wilga 80**. The prototype of a revised design, incorporating increased span wings and a 280-hp (209-kW) P.Z.L.-built AI-14RD engine to give a maximum take-off weight

of 3,086 lb (1400 kg) was completed during 1983, and this has the designation **Wilga 80/1300**. A **P.Z.L.-104M Wilga 2000** variant has been developed from the Wilga 35 with a 300-hp (224-kW) Textron Lycoming O-540 engine in order to appeal to customers in the West. This aircraft was also available as **P.Z.L.-104MW Wilga 2000 Hydro** floatplane during 2001.

SPECIFICATION

P.Z.L. 104 Wilga 35A
Type: multi-role lightplane
Powerplant: one 260-hp (194-kW) P.Z.L.-built Ivchenko AI-14RA radial piston engine
Performance: maximum speed 121 mph (195 km/h); service ceiling 13,255 ft (4040 m); range with

maximum fuel 416 miles (670 km)
Weights: empty equipped 1,984 lb (900 kg); maximum take-off 2,866 lb (1300 kg)
Dimensions: wingspan 36 ft 5¾ in (11. 12 m); length 26 ft 6¾ in (8.10 m); height 9 ft 8½ in (2.96 m); wing area 166.85 sq ft (15.50 m²)

An ungainly aircraft, as demonstrated by this Wilga 35, the P.Z.L. 104 had 962 examples built by 1996.

P.Z.L. 106 Kruk

In early 1972, design was initiated of a new agricultural aircraft of braced low-wing monoplane configuration with fixed tailwheel landing gear, a T-tail, and enclosed accommodation for the pilot. First flown in P.Z.L. 106 prototype form on 17 April 1973, then

powered by a 400-hp (298-kW) Avco Lycoming IO-720 engine, it was followed by five more prototypes, one of which was similarly powered, but four each had a P.Z.L. 3S radial that was the chosen powerplant for production aircraft, the first version

being the **P.Z.L. 106A Kruk** (raven) of which series construction began in 1976. Generally similar to the prototypes, it differed primarily by adopting a conventional tail unit and a larger capacity chemical hopper, features adopted as standard on all production aircraft. Subsequent P.Z.L. 106A variants have included the **106AR,** which introduced a geared P.Z.L. 3SR engine and a larger-diameter propeller; the **P.Z.L. 106AS** prototype with a 1,000-hp (746-kW) P.Z.L-built Shvetsov ASz-621R radial and, following satisfactory tests, 60 P.Z.L. 106As operated overseas by Pezetel were converted to this powerplant; and the **P.Z.L. 106AT**

Turbo-Kruk which, powered by a 760-shp (567-kW) Pratt & Whitney Aircraft of Canada PT6A-34AG turboprop engine, was first flown on 22 June 1981.

The **P.Z.L. 106B** prototype of an improved version of the 106A was flown on 15 May 1981, introducing a redesigned wing of increased span and area, and 106B and **P.Z.L. 106BR** production variants superseded the corresponding A-series aircraft during 1982. The current 2001 version of the Turbo-Kruk has the designation **PZL Warszawa PZL-106BT** and is available as the **PZL-106BT-601** with a Walter M 601D engine or as the export

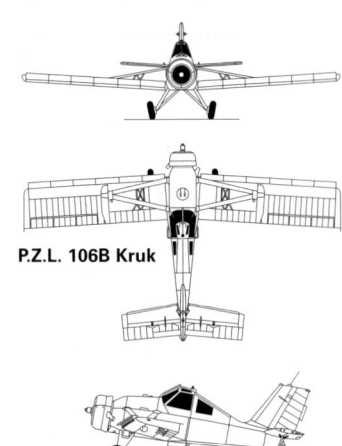

P.Z.L. 106B Kruk

PZL-106BT-34 with the PT6A-34AG turboprop.

SPECIFICATION

P.Z.L. 106B Kruk
Type: agricultural aircraft
Powerplant: one 592-hp (441-kW) P.Z.L. 3S radial piston engine
Performance: maximum speed with agricultural equipment 220 mph (137 km/h); service ceiling 15,090 ft (4,600 m); range with maximum fuel 684 miles (1100 km)

Weights: empty equipped 3,682 lb (1670 kg); maximum take-off 6,614 lb (3000 kg)
Dimensions: wingspan 48 ft 6½ in (14.80 m); length 29 ft 10¼ in (9.10 m); height 10 ft 10¾ in (3.32 m); wing area 346.39 sq ft (32.18 m²)

P.Z.L. Mielec M-18 Dromader

Of the same overall configuration as the Kruk, the **M-18 Dromader** agricultural aircraft is not only considerably larger, but was designed and built to meet the requirements of the US FAR Pt 23. It differs primarily by having an unswept cantilever monoplane wing and unswept horizontal tail surfaces, is powered by the uprated ASz-62M engine introduced in more recent versions of the Kruk and pays particular attention to pilot safety, the pilot being

accommodated in a cockpit stressed to survive an impact of 40g. Special materials and treatment limit airframe corrosion to a minimum. Two prototypes were flown, on 27 August and 2 October 1976, being followed by seven pre-production aircraft, five of them used for operational trials, two of them carrying out practical dusting and spraying operations in Egypt during the summer of 1978. Production was initiated following receipt of

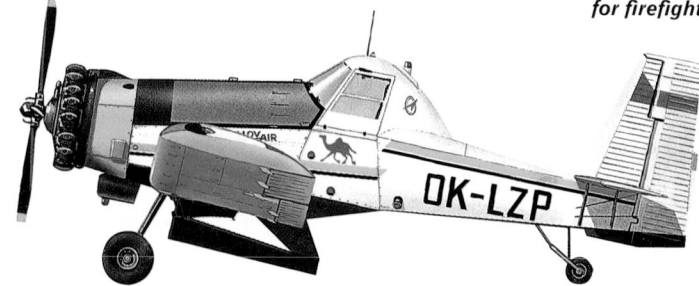

Dromader translates into English as Dromedary, hence the artwork beneath the cockpit of this M-18. While the majority of Dromader operators are civilian, the Greek air force flies 30 for firefighting.

Polish certification on 27 September 1978, the basic M-18 giving way to the two-seat **M-18A** in 1984. Following demonstrations of pre-production aircraft, valuable export orders were received and deliveries have been made to agricultural operators in Bulgaria, Canada, Cuba, Czechoslovakia, Egypt, Greece, Hungary, Turkey, the USA and Yugoslavia.

Under the designation

M-21 Dromader Mini, a smaller and reduced-capacity version was built in prototype form, while an even smaller capacity **Dromader Mikro** was also studied. At the opposite end of this scale, a larger capacity **M-24 Dromader Super** and a similar **Dromader Super Turbo** with a P.Z.L. 10 or Pratt & Whitney Aircraft of Canada PT6A-45B turboprop were also flown. In 2001 the

standard production models were the M-18A; **M-18AS** two-seat trainer; **M-18B** improved version of the M-18A that has been available since 1996; **M-18BS** two-seat trainer variant of the M-18B, equivalent to the M-18AS; **M-18C** variant of the M-18B but with a more powerful engine and other improvements; and the **Turbine Dromader,** which is usually powered by a PT6A-45 turboprop.

SPECIFICATION	
P.Z.L. Mielec M-18A	185 km/h); maximum range
Type: single-seat agricultural aircraft	323 miles (520 km)
Powerplant: one 1,000-hp	**Weights:** basic empty 5,445 lb
(746-kW) P.Z.L. Kalisz ASz-621R	(2470 kg); maximum take-off
radial piston engine	10,362 lb (4700 kg)
Performance: (with spreader	**Dimensions:** wingspan 58 ft ¾ in
equipment) maximum speed	(17.70 m); length 31 ft 1 in
147 mph (237 km/h); operating	(9,47 m); height 12 ft 1¾ in
speed 106 to 115 mph (170 to	(3.70 m); wing area 430.57 sq ft (40.00 m²)

P.Z.L. Mielec TS-11 Iskra

Design of the **TS-11 Iskra** (spark) two-seat turbojet-powered primary and advanced trainer began in 1957, being intended as a replacement for the **TS-8 Bies** two-seat basic trainer. Four prototypes were built, and the first flight of the type was recorded on 5 February 1960. Following type approval during 1961, initial deliveries began in March 1963, and the TS-11 became operational with the Polish air force in 1964.

Since that time well over 500 have been built, manufactured not only for use by the nation's air force, but also for export to India, which procured 50.

A cantilever mid-wing monoplane of all-metal construction, the TS-11 has retractable tricycle landing gear and is powered by a single turbojet mounted within the fuselage, aft of the cockpit. Early aircraft were powered by the Polish-designed HO-10

In summer 2001, the Iskra remained in service with its only two operators – India and Poland. This TS-11 is illustrated as it appeared in Polish service in the 1980s.

turbojet developing 1,720-lb (7.65-kN) thrust, but from the mid-1960s TS-11s have been powered progressively by the 1,764 lb

(7.84-kN) thrust SO-1, the similarly rated but improved SO-3, or the uprated

SO-3W, which was installed up to the end of production in 1979.

Variants

TS-11 Iskra-Bis A: initial two-seat production version for primary and advanced training, with two underwing hardpoints for external weapons
TS-11 Iskra-Bis B: designated initially **Iskra 100**, a two-seat primary and advanced trainer with four underwing attachment points for external weapons
TS-11 Iskra-Bis C: designated initially **Iskra 200**, a single-seat reconnaissance version with increased fuel capacity and a camera mounted in the lower fuselage
TS-11 Iskra-Bis D: generally similar to Iskra-Bis B, built for the Indian air force
TS-11 Iskra-Bis DF: two-seat combat and reconnaissance trainer with provision for increased armament or up to three cameras

SPECIFICATION	
TS-11 Iskra-Bis DF	8,466 lb (3840 kg)
Type: single-seat fully aerobatic combat/reconnaissance trainer	**Dimensions:** wingspan 33 ft (10.06 m); length 36 ft 7 in
Powerplant: one 2,425-lb (1100-kg) thrust IL SO-3W turbojet	(11.15 m); height 11 ft 5¾ in (3.50 m); wing area 188.37 sq ft
Performance: maximum speed 478 mph (770 km/h) at 16,405 ft	(17.50 m²)
(5000 m); service ceiling 36,090 ft	**Armament:** one 23-mm cannon in starboard side of nose, plus four
(11000 m); range with maximum internal fuel 783 miles (1260 km)	underwing attachments for a variety of weapons including
Weights: empty 5,644 lb (2560 kg); maximum take-off	bombs, gun pods and rocket pods

P.Z.L. Swidnik W-3 Sokol

Although developed from the Mi-2, the **W-3 Sokol** (falcon) is a new design, retaining the configuration of the Mi-2 but with larger overall dimensions and extensive aerodynamic and structural changes. The first of five prototypes made its maiden flight on 16 November 1979, and the second, incorporating further changes, on 6 May 1982. Production began in 1985. The helicopter has a new, fully articulated four-bladed main rotor. The cabin accommodates 12 people in three-abreast rows, with access via sliding doors on each side of the cabin.

The first batch of 50 helicopters was completed in 1991, and by the middle of 1999 production had passed 120 helicopters including sales to military operators in Burma (13), Czech Republic (11) and Poland (50). Subvariants of the baseline W-3 include the **W-3P VIP** transport, **W-3T** trainer and **W-3W** armed model. The last has a 23-mm GSz-23 twin-barrel cannon on the starboard side of the fuselage and lateral hardpoints for ZR-8 bomblet dispensers, or

Platan minelaying packs, or multiple launchers for 2.17-in (55-mm) S-5 or 3.15-in (80-mm) S-8 air-to-surface unguided rockets; there is also provision for up to six assault rifles or machine-guns to be fired from the cabin windows.

Further developments of the W-3 have been numer-

ous but scored only very modest sales success. The **W-3A** is a development for sale mainly outside the original Soviet bloc and first flew on 30 July 1992 for American certification in May 1993. The **W-3WA** is a variant with the same armament as the W-3A, the

W-3AM is optimised for overwater flight with six inflatable flotation bags, and the **W-3AZ** is a single helicopter used by Sextant of France for the development of a four-axis digital automatic flight-control system. The **W-3RM Anakonda** is the offshore

Bladder fuel tanks below the cabin floor give a combined capacity of 374 Imp gal (1700 litres) and there is provision for a 242-Imp gal (1100-litre) auxiliary tank.

search-and-rescue model with a watertight cabin, flotation bags, an additional window in the lower part of each cabin door, a rescue hoist and other specialist equipment including life rafts for six persons. Subvariants have included the **W-3SP** with Western avionics and the **W-3WARM** with the US FSI Ultra 4000 FLIR and (as suggested by the W in the suffix) armament.

Variants that proceeded no further than the prototype stage were two armed models, the **W-3U Salamandra** (salamander) and the **W-3WB** derivative of the W-3. The **S-1RR** is a one-off electronic combat reconnaissance helicopter delivered to the Polish air force and followed by improved **SRR-10** helicopters. Finally, there is the **W-3H** armed support variant developed under the **Huzar** (hussar) programme. This is a development of

the W-3WA, and in October 1997 the outgoing Polish government opted for an Israeli operational suite, including Elbit avionics and Rafael NT-D anti-tank missiles. The incoming government cancelled the contract, and Poland has since been offered US and French combinations of avionics and weapons that may ultimately be validated on the W-3W, but in fact adopted for a more advanced helicopter.

SPECIFICATION

P.Z.L. Swidnik W-3A Sokol
Type: one/two-crew multi-role medium helicopter
Powerplant: two WSK-P.Z.L. Rzeszów P.Z.L.-10W turboshaft engines each rated at 900 shp (671 kW)
Performance: maximum cruising speed 151 mph (243 km/h) at 1,640 ft (500 m); initial climb rate 2,008 ft (612 m) per minute; service ceiling 19,685 ft (6000 m); range 124 miles (200 km) with maximum payload
Weights: empty 8,488 lb

(3850 kg); maximum take-off 14,110 lb (6400 kg)
Dimensions: main rotor diameter 51 ft 6 in (15.70 m); length 61 ft 7¾ in (18.79 m) with the rotors turning; height 16 ft 10¼ in (5.14 m); main rotor disc area 2,083.88 sq ft (193.59 m²)
Payload: up to 13 passengers, or eight survivors plus a three-person rescue team, or four litters plus one attendant within the context of a 4,630-lb (2100-kg) maximum payload

P.Z.L. Warszawa-Okecie PZL-130 Orlik

The **PZL-130 Orlik** (spotted eaglet) primary and basic trainer was designed from the autumn of 1983 as the airframe component of an overall training system which also included a simulator and an electronic diagnosis system. Of all-metal construction, the PZL-130 was a low-wing monoplane with pneumatically-retracted tricycle landing gear. Its powerplant was based on one 330-hp (246-kW) Vedeneyev M-14Pm radial engine driving a constant-speed propeller. The Orlik was intended to serve for the full spectrum of civil and military training, ranging from pre-selection to aerobatics and including air combat, air gunnery, ground attack and recce.

Construction of three flying prototypes began in

1982, and the first aircraft flew on 12 October 1983, followed quickly by the second. However, the third aircraft did not fly until January 1985, and the two pre-production machines which followed did not take to the air until February 1988, as a result of serious delays in deliveries of the M-14Pm engine from the USSR. By that time PZL was looking seriously for

another engine, and one contender was the company-produced but less powerful Kalisz K8-AA, which took the underpowered second pre-production aircraft into the air in March 1988. Although testing continued over the next two years, the piston-engined Orlik was abandoned in 1990.

In 1984 PZL had started development of a turbo-prop-powered Orlik. The third airframe was revised with the PT6A-25A engine, made its maiden flight on 13 July 1986, but was lost in a crash during January 1987. A seventh Orlik was flown with the 750-shp (560-kW) Walter M601E, and there followed four more **Turbo-Orlik** (now just Orlik) aircraft with M601E and PT6A engines and the designations **PZL-130TM** and **PZL-130T** respectively.

Access to the Orlik's cockpit is provided by a side-hinged one-piece canopy, which is jettisonable in flight, the pupil is seated ahead of the instructor on a higher seat, and full dual controls are standard. A PZL-130 turbo-orlik is illustrated.

The **PZL-130TB** production model for the Polish air force (48 aircraft later reduced to 32) was derived from the PZL-130TM, and is powered by the fully aerobatic M601T engine. The wing is increased in span and incidence, lowering the nose in normal cruising flight. The ventral fin is redesigned, and double-slotted flaps are provided. The cockpit is closely related to that of the Su-22, and is covered by a canopy of revised shape. The prototype was rolled out in May 1991, and first flew on 18 September. The aircraft is fitted with eastern European avionics, indigenous LFK-K1

zero/ 81-mph (130-km/h) ejection seats, and six underwing hardpoints.

Several similar versions are available for export, all equipped with Western avionics (to customer specification) and powered by Western engines. The **PZL-130TC** is the most potent, with the 950-shp (708-kW) PT6A-62 engine. The **PZL-130TC-1** is an upgraded version of the PZL-130TB with Martin-Baker Mk 11B seats, while the **PZL-130TC-2** is a downgraded variant of the TC-1 powered by a 750-shp (559-kW) PT6A-25C. The PZL-140 Orlik 2000 uses the TC-1 airframe as the basis for a seven-seat business aircraft.

SPECIFICATION

PZL Warszawa-Okecie PZL-130TC-1 Orlik
Type: two-seat basic and advanced flying trainer
Powerplant: one Walter M601T turboprop engine rated at 750 shp (559 kW)
Performance: maximum speed 311 mph (500 km/h) at 19,685 ft (6000 m); initial climb rate 2,620 ft (798 m) per minute; service ceiling 33,000 ft (10060 m); range 714 miles (1150 km)

Weights: empty 3,527 lb (1600 kg); maximum take-off 5,952 lb (2700 kg)
Dimensions: wingspan 29 ft 6¼ in (9.00 m); length 29 ft 6¼ in (9.00 m); height 11 ft 7 in (3.53 m) with the original shorter vertical tail surface; wing area 139.94 sq ft (13.00 m²)
Armament: up to 1,764 lb (800 kg) of disposable stores carried on six underwing hardpoints

Raytheon Premier

Early in 1994, Beech began preliminary design work on a new light business jet.

Beech was already a subsidiary of Raytheon and the new bizjet emerged as

In 2000 the basic Premier I cost around $4.80 million to purchase and $592 per hour to operate.

the first aircraft to carry just the Raytheon name. The design was launched at the 1995 National Business Aircraft Association Convention as a direct competitor for the Cessna CitationJet and made its first flight on 22 December 1998. Three prototypes subsequently flew the test programme aimed at certification in time for deliveries in mid 2001.

The **Premier I** has an all-composite fuselage which dispenses with the need for conventional frames, while achieving a weight saving of 20 per cent and a

cabin volume increase of 13 per cent when compared to a conventional alloy fuselage. The wings are of aluminium alloy construction and are almost entirely occupied by integral tanks. On the flightdeck information is presented in the form of two full-colour LCD displays (a third is optional) as part of the core

Rockwell Collins EFIS suite.

By November 2000 Raytheon held 260 orders for the Premier I, a number which should allow production to continue into 2005. The Premier was certificated on 23 March 2001 for first deliveries later in the year and customers include the Jordan Formula One team, which will take its Premier in 2002.

SPECIFICATION

Raytheon Premier I
Type: six-passenger business jet
Powerplant: two 2,300-lb st (10.23-kN) Williams FJ44-2A turbofans
Performance: maximum cruising speed 530 mph (854 km/h) at 33,000 ft (10060 m); maximum operating altitude 41,000 ft (12500 m); range with one pilot, four passengers and IFR reserves

1,726 miles (2778 km)
Weights: basic operating 7,996 lb (3627 kg); maximum take-off 12,500 lb (5670 kg)
Dimensions: wingspan 44 ft 6 in (13.56 m); length 46 ft (14.02 m); height 15 ft 4 in (4.67 m); wing area 247 sq ft (22.95 m²)
Accommodation: up to six passengers

Reggiane Re.2000 series

Officine Meccaniche Reggiane SA, a subsidiary of the Caprom company, began development in 1937 of a single-seat fighter designed by Antonio Alessio and Roberto Longhi; the latter had about two years earlier returned from working in the USA. The resulting **Re.2000 Falco I** prototype was very different from contemporary Italian designs for combat aircraft and was influenced, no doubt, by the stubby aircraft with large-diameter radial engines then being built in North America. A cantilever low-wing monoplane with retractable tailwheel landing gear, the prototype was

This Re.2000 was one of those built in Hungary and is shown the markings it wore for the home-defence role in the spring of 1943.

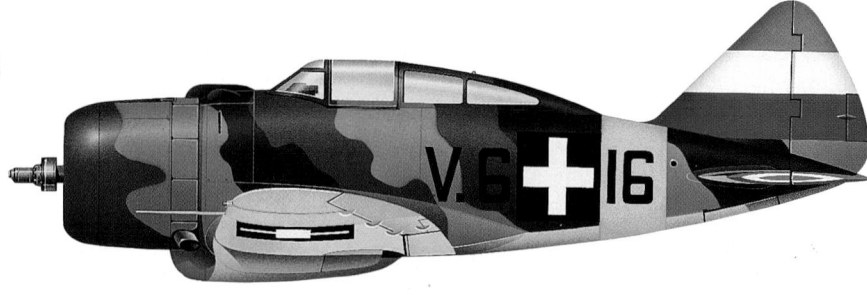

powered by an 870-hp (649-kW) Piaggio P.XI RC.40 radial engine. Competitive evaluation that followed a first flight during 1938 brought no interest from the Italian air force, but Reggiane built for the Italian navy 12 **Re.2000 Serie II** fighters especially strengthened for catapult launching, and 24 **Re.2000 Serie III** long-range fighters with increased fuel capacity. The company then manufactured several for

Hungary, which also built a small number under licence, all of these being operated by the Hungarian air force under the designation **Hejja** (Hawk).

Additional Re.2000s were built to a Swedish order for 60, these being operated by the Swedish air force until 1945 under the designation **J 20**.

Conviction that performance of the Re.2000 would benefit from a more powerful engine led to the **Re.2001 Falco II**, powered initially by the Daimler-Benz DB 601A-1, but with Luftwaffe priorities on this powerplant the Re.2001 had to have instead an Alfa-Romeo licence-built version, the RA.1000 RC.41-1a Monsonie. Even then, the MC.202 had first call on these engines and, as a result, production of

the Re.2001 was limited to only 252. This number included 100 **Re. 2001 Serie I, II** and **III** fighters (with armament variations) and the **Re.2001 Serie IV** fighter-bombers, and 150 **Re.2001 CN** night-fighters. Two new aircraft were built for catapult trials, and a number of conversions were made to evaluate the type as a tandem two-seat trainer, tank-buster and torpedo-fighter; one was used to test an Isotta Fraschini Delta engine.

The necessity to revert to a radial powerplant led to the **Re.2002 Ariete** (ram) fighter-bomber (about 50 built), which combined the improved airframe of the Re.2001 with a 1,175-hp (876-kW) Piaggio P.XIX RC.45 engine; these saw service in 1942, suffering heavy losses during the

Allied landings on Sicily. The last of this related family was the **Re.2005 Sagittario** (archer), probably the best fighter produced in Italy during World War II, which had structural refinements and reverted to the use of an inline engine. The prototype, powered by a DB 605A-1, was flown during September 1942, but the production version of the Re.2005 had the Fiat RA.1050 RC.58 Tifone, which was a licence-built version of the Daimler-Benz. Only 48 Sagittarios had been delivered before an armistice was signed with the Allies, but these aircraft saw extensive use in the defence of Naples, Rome and Sicily, the survivors battling finally above the crumbling ruins of Berlin.

SPECIFICATION

Reggiane Re.2005 Sagittario
Type: single-seat fighter/ fighter-bomber
Powerplant: one 1,475-hp (1100-kW) Fiat RA.1050 RC.58 Tifone V piston engine
Performance: maximum speed 391 mph (630 km/h) at 22,965 ft (7000 m); service ceiling 39,370 ft (12000 m); range 777 miles (1250 km)
Weights: empty 5,732 lb

(2600 kg); maximum take-off 7,848 lb (3560 kg)
Dimensions: wingspan 36 ft 1 in (11.00 m); length 28 ft 7¾ in (8.73 m); height 10 ft 4 in (3.15 m); wing area 219.59 sq ft (20.40 m²)
Armament: three 20-mm cannon and two 0.5-in (12.7-mm) machine-guns, all forward-firing, plus up to 1,390 lb (630 kg) of bombs when deployed as a fighter-bomber

Republic F-84 Thunderjet, Thunderstreak & Thunderflash

Continuing the 'Thunder' prefix that brought fame to Republic with the P-47, the company chose the name **Thunderjet** for the turbojet day fighter that was designed to supersede the P-47 in service. Designed as a single-seat low-/mid-wing monoplane of all-metal construction with retractable tricycle landing gear, the type received an initial contract in March 1945 for three **XP-84** prototypes. However, development was bedevilled by a series of problems, in particular those of growing structural weight and low engine thrust, but when the first two prototypes were flown, on 28 February and in August 1946, it was soon discovered that Republic had created another high-performance aircraft, soon confirmed in September 1946 when one of the prototypes established a new US national speed record of 611 mph (983 km/h).

These two aircraft were each powered by a 3,750-lb (16.68-kN) thrust General Electric J35-GE-7 turbojet, specified also for the **YP-84** pre-production batch of 25 aircraft, but this was changed to the 4,000-lb (17.78-kN) thrust Allison J35-A-15 in a revised contract for 15 **YP-84A** service trials aircraft, these

having been preceded by the third prototype completed in similar configuration as the **XP-84A**. They were followed by the **P-84B**, the initial production version (226 built) which introduced an ejection seat, provision for rocket armament and an Allison J35-A-15C of the same thrust as the J35-A-15. The **P-84C** (later **F-84C**; 191 built) had a revised electrical system and the J35-A-13C engine. More extensive changes were made on the **F-84D** (154 built), including wings and ailerons with heavier-gauge skins, winterised fuel system for the 5,000-lb (22.24-kN) thrust J35-A-17D engine and revised landing gear structure. The entry of this version into operational service in the Korean War resulted in early introduction of the **F-84E** (843 built) with a slightly lengthened fuselage to improve cockpit accommodation, revised wingtip tanks, and provision of a radar gunsight, and 100 F-84Es were supplied to NATO forces. Last of the so-called straight-wing F-84s was the **F-84G** (3,025 built), of which 1,936 were supplied to NATO forces, and this was the first single-seat fighter to have the capability of deploying nuclear weapons. Powered by the 5,600-lb (24.90-kN) thrust

J35-A-29 turbojet, the F-84G could carry 4,000 lb (1814 kg) of stores externally, had provision for inflight refuelling and, because this made long-range missions possible, was equipped with an autopilot. The type was subsequently equipped with a low-altitude bombing system for the deployment of its nuclear weapons, and the tactically limited flying boom inflight-refuelling system was superseded by the probe and drogue method developed by Flight Refuelling Ltd in the UK. The first two prototypes were two **EF-84E** aircraft converted in the

This F-84D flew with the 128th FIS of Georgia's Air National Guard between early 1952 and the summer of 1955.

UK, and using inflight re-fuelling techniques they became on 22 September 1950, the first turbojet-powered single-seat fighters to record a nonstop crossing of the North Atlantic.

Introduction of a swept wing was made first on an F-84E fuselage and this, powered by a 5,200-lb (23.13-kN) thrust Allison XJ35-A-25 engine, made its first flight on 3 June 1950 under the designation **YF-84F**. Performance was disappointing, greater

engine thrust being essential, and a second prototype was flown with an Armstrong Siddeley Sapphire turbojet imported from the UK. A licence-built version of this engine, the Wright J65, suffered early development problems, but eventually all but 375 of the 2,713 **F-84F Thunderstreak** aircraft that were built had the 7,220-lb (32.11-kN) thrust Wright J65-W-3, the remainder having earlier and lower-powered J65-W-1 or J65-W-1A turbojets. Of the

Variants

EF-84B: two conversions of F-84Bs for 'tip-tow' parasite trials with a Boeing ETB-29 'motherplane'
XF-84H: two F-84Fs were converted under this designation with a 5,850-shp (4362-kW) Allison XT40-A-1 turboprop driving supersonic propellers under a joint USAF/USN programme
YF-84J: two conversions of F-84Fs with deepened fuselages and enlarged nose intakes, one tested with an 8,750-lb (63.97-kN) thrust General Electric XJ73-GE-5 and the other with an 8,920-lb (65.22-kN) thrust YJ73-GE-7 turbojet
F-84KX: designation allocated to 80 ex-USAF F-84Bs following conversion to target drone configuration for the US Navy

While the majority of RF-84F Thunderflash aircraft went to NATO air forces, other US allies, such as Taiwan, also received the type.

SPECIFICATION	
Republic F-84F Thunderstreak	(6273kg); maximum take-off
Type: single-seat fighter-bomber	28,000 lb (12701 kg)
Powerplant: one 7,220-lb	**Dimensions:** wingspan 33 ft 7¼ in
(5384-kg) thrust Wright J65-W-3	(10.24 m); length 43 ft 4¾ in
turbojet	(13.23 m); height 14 ft 4¾ in
Performance: maximum speed	(4.39 m); wing area 325.0 sq ft
695 mph (1118 km/h) at sea level;	(30.19 m²)
service ceiling 46,000 ft (14020 m);	**Armament:** six 0.5-in (12.7-mm)
combat radius with drop tanks	Browning M3 machine-guns,
810 miles (1304 km)	plus up to 6,000 lb (2722 kg) of
Weights: empty 13,830 lb	external stores

total built, 1,301 were supplied to NATO.

A final development of the basic design produced a reconnaissance version, the **RF-84F Thunderflash**, which differed primarily by having a 7,800-lb (34.69-kN) thrust J65-W-7 turbojet with wing-root air intakes

and cameras mounted in the nose. Production totalled 715, of which 386 were supplied to NATO air forces. To provide long-range reconnaissance capability, 25 F-84Fs were modified under the USAF's FICON (fighter conveyor) project to hook onto a

trapeze in a version of the giant Convair B-36 bomber, the GRB-36F. Designated initially **GRF-84F**, later changed to **RF-84K**, after hooking on to their long-range transport these aircraft were carried by it to the designated reconnaissance area. After launch

and completion of its reconnaissance task the RF-84K would again hook on for transport back to its base. F-84F and RF-84F aircraft were the last to

remain in USAF service, many then being transferred to Air National Guard units before the type was eventually withdrawn from service in 1971.

Republic F-105 Thunderchief

SPECIFICATION	
Republic F-105D Thunderchief	range with maximum external fuel
Type: single-seat fighter-bomber	2,390 miles (3846 km)
Powerplant: one 17,200-lb	**Weights:** empty 27,500 lb
(76.49-kN) thrust Pratt & Whitney	(12474 kg); maximum take-off
J75-P-19W turbojet, developing	52,838 lb (23967 kg)
24,500 lb (108.95 kg) thrust with	**Dimensions:** wingspan 34 ft 9 in
afterburning, or 26,500 lb	(10.59 m); length 64 ft 4 in
(117.84 kN) thrust for 60 seconds	(19.61 m); height 19 ft 7 in
with afterburning and water	(5.97 m); wing area 385.0 sq ft
injection	(35.77 m²)
Performance: maximum speed	**Armament:** one M61 Vulcan
1,390 mph (2237 km/h) or Mach	20-mm cannon, plus more than
2.1 at 36,000 ft (10975 m); service	14,000 lb (6350 kg) of mixed stores
ceiling 41,200 ft (12560 m); ferry	carried internally and externally

This F-105D is shown in the lacquer over natural-metal finish that the Thunderchief wore during its initial years of service.

When the F-84F entered service in 1954, Republic had already spent some years studying the design of a higher-performance fighter-bomber which the company hoped would be an acceptable successor to the Thunderstreak. Following submission to the USAF of the **AP-63** design proposal, a contract for two **YF-105A** prototypes was awarded, the first of them making its initial flight on 22 October 1965 on the power of a 15,000-lb (66.71-kN) thrust J57-P-25 turbojet. This doubling of power by comparison with the F-84F emphasizes the

increase in size and weight of the YF-105A, the changing role of the 'fighter' also being recognised by the capability to carry up to 12,000 lb (5443 kg) of mixed weapons, of which up to 8,000 lb (3629 kg) of nuclear or other weapons could be carried in an internal bomb bay. No **F-105A Thunderchief** production aircraft were built because of the availability of a more powerful J75 afterburning turbojet, thus there followed four **YF-105B** prototypes that were of similar overall configuration, but with an area-ruled fuselage, swept-forward air intakes

and the 16,500-lb (73.37-kN) thrust YJ75-P-3 engine. The production **F-105B** (71 built) was basically similar, and began to enter service in August 1958, three years later than planned, with the USAF's 335th TFS; it was not until mid-1959 that the USAF had its first complete squadron of F-105B aircraft.

The major production version was the **F-105D** (610 built) which, powered by the J75-P-19W turbojet, had all-weather capability, much improved avionics and detail refinements. The final production version was the **F-105F** (143 built), with a lengthened fuselage to provide tandem two-seat capacity and intended originally for combat proficiency evaluation and transition

training. But with US involvement in Vietnam creating an urgent requirement for high-performance fighter-bombers, the F-105F was frequently used in an operational role. Some 86 F-105Fs were later converted for Wild Weasel missions against North Vietnam, equipped with specialised avionics to locate and identify the threat from SA-2 'Guideline' surface-to-air missiles. Of the total of 86, 60 were the subject of more comprehensive modification and became unofficially designated initially **'EF-105F'**, subsequently gaining the

official title **F-105G**.

The introduction of Wild Weasel-configured F-105Fs into combat occurred in 1966, and these Thunderchiefs constituted the backbone of the anti-SAM forces until 1973. Surviving F-105Gs served with the 35th TFW at George AFB, California, until the late 1970s, when 25 were transferred to the ANG. F-105Ds also fought in Vietnam, but well over half of the 610 that were built were destroyed, and following their withdrawal in 1969/70, the survivors were passed on to the ANG and USAF Reserve.

The 561st TFS of the 23rd TFW at McConnell AFB was the first F-105G unit. This machine is shown with an AGM-45 Strike ARM underwing, although the type later introduced the AGM-78 Standard ARM to combat over Vietnam.

Variants

RF-105B: proposed reconnaissance version; not built
JF-105B: three system-test aircraft, built from airframes laid down originally as RF-105B prototypes
F-105C: projected tandem two-seat operational trainer; not built
RF-105D: projected reconnaissance variant of F-105D; not built
F-105E: projected tandem two-seat operational trainer variant of F-105D; not built

Republic P-47 Thunderbolt

The **P-47 Thunderbolt** designed by Alexander Kartveli played a significant role in World War II, and was built to a total of 15,677 before production came to an end with cancellation of outstanding contracts after VJ-Day. A continuation of the family that had started with

Alexander Seversky's P-35 and further developed through the **P-43 Lancer** and projected higher-performance **P-44**, the P-47 began by highlighting the indecision of the USAAC in 1940 about whether to procure lightweight or heavyweight fighters.

Original plans to order

the **Republic AP-4** and **AP-10** projects for lightweight fighters under the designations **XP-47** and **XP-47A** respectively, were cancelled when early reports of combat experience in Europe were received. Kartveli then outlined his proposals for a heavy fighter that would

meet the new requirement, basing his concept on use of the turbocharged Pratt & Whitney R-2800 Double Wasp, and winning an order for an **XP-47B** prototype based on this design. A cantilever low-wing monoplane, of conventional all-metal construction except for fabric-covered control surfaces, the new model had retractable tailwheel

landing gear and accommodated its pilot beneath an upward-hinged canopy. When flown for the first time, on 6 May 1941, the XP-47B gave an immediate hint of the aircraft's potential, but there were a number of serious problems that had to be remedied. Orders from the US Army were soon received, initially for 171 production **P-47B** fighters.

Republic P-47 Thunderbolt (continued)

SPECIFICATION

Republic P-47D Thunderbolt
Type: single-seat fighter-bomber
Powerplant: one 2,535-hp (1890-kW) Pratt & Whitney R-2800-59W Double Wasp radial piston engine
Performance: maximum speed clean 433 mph (697 km/h); service ceiling 41,000 ft (12495 m); range with drop tanks 1,900 miles (3058 km)
Weights: empty 9,950 lb (4513 kg); maximum take-off 17,500 lb (7938 kg)
Dimensions: wingspan 40 ft 9¼ in (12.43 m); length 36 ft 1¾ in (11.02 m); height 14 ft 8 in (4.47 m); wing area 30 sq ft (27.87 m²)
Armament: eight 0.5-in (12.7-mm) machine-guns, plus external load of up to 2,500 lb (1134 kg) of bombs, napalm or rockets

In February 1947 the 121st Fighter Squadron of the District of Columbia ANG received brand new P-47Ds. The unit re-equipped with F-84Cs from late 1949.

P-47Bs began to come off the production line in March 1942 and to equip squadrons of the USAAF's 56th Fighter Group three months later. By January 1943 this group had joined the 8th Air Force in the UK, shortly reinforced by the 78th Fighter Group, and these units became operational in April 1943. Initial encounters with German fighters showed that the Thunderbolt was lacking in performance and manoeuvrability at low and medium altitudes, and had inadequate range to operate as an escort fighter. These shortcomings were met by ensuing variants, which progressively increased the capability of this remarkable aircraft, which was regarded as a giant among fighters. The Thunderbolt soon proved able to absorb an enormous amount of punishment from enemy weapons, with the exceptionally low loss rate of only 0.7 per cent per mission. The P-47 is credited with the destruction of

4.6 enemy aircraft for the loss of each one of its own number in some 546,000 combat sorties, and with the destruction in Europe (excluding the Italian front) of 3,752 aircraft in the air and 3,315 on the ground.

In addition to wartime service with the USAAF, P-47s had also been used during this period by Brazil, the Free French air force, Mexico, the RAF, and the Soviet Union. The **P-47D** and **P-47N** remained in USAF service for a number of years after the war, passing to ANG units before being phased out of service in 1955, by which time they had been redesignated **F-47D** and **F-47N** respectively. Even then, the Thunderbolt had many more years of useful service to offer, operating with the air forces of Bolivia, Brazil, Chile, Colombia, Dominica, Ecuador, France, Guatemala, Honduras, Iran, Italy, Mexico, Nationalist China, Peru, Turkey and Yugoslavia.

Variants

XP-47B: prototype powered by 1,850-hp (1380-kW), later 2,000-hp (1491-kW) XR-2800 engine (total 1)
P-47B: initial production version with 2,000-hp (1491-kW) R-2800-21, sliding canopy and metal-skinned control surfaces (total 171)
P-47C: revised production version, initially with engine as P-47B but later with 2,300-hp (1715-kW) R-2800-59; longer forward fuselage and provision for belly bomb/drop tank (total 602)
P-47D: major production version with 2,300-hp (1715-kW) R-2800-21W or 2,535-hp (1890-kW) R-2800-59W engine with water injection; numerous modifications through progressive blocks (total 12,602)
XP-47D: single experimental conversion (1943) of P-47D with pressurised cockpit
XP-47F: single experimental conversion (1943) of P-47B with laminar-flow wings
P-47G: early version of P-47D built by Curtiss-Wright (total 354)
XP-47H: redesignation of two P-47Ds used as engine test-beds for the 2,300-hp (1715-kW) Chrysler XIV-2220-1 inverted V engine
XP-47J: single experimental aircraft based on the P-47D with lightened structure and special 2,800-hp (2088-kW) R-2800-57(C) with turbocharger; attained a level speed of 504 mph (811 km/h) on 2 August 1944
XP-47K: conversion of P-47D with a clearview teardrop canopy from a Hawker Typhoon and cut-down rear fuselage, a modification then introduced on P-47D production line
XP-47L: conversion of P-47D with increased-capacity fuselage fuel tankage
YP-47M: three prototype conversions of P-47Ds to produce high-speed 'sprint' version, with powerplant as used on XP-47J
P-47M: production version of YP-47M (total 130)
XP-47N: conversion from YP-47M with increased-span strengthened wing containing fuel tanks, strengthened landing gear and other modification to provide long-range capability for use in the Pacific theatre
P-47N: production version of XP-47N, late production aircraft with 2,800-hp (2088-kW) R-2800-77 (total 816)

Robin ATL

Work on the design of a lightweight two-seater, intended to be economical both in first cost and operation, was begun in early 1981 by Avions Pierre Robin. Known as the Robin **ATL** (**Avion Tres Léger**), the aircraft was to be powered by a new 47-hp (35-kW) engine developed in collaboration with Jacques Buchoux of

Ateliers JPX. The prototype made its first flight on 17 June 1983 and was soon re-engined with a 56-hp (42-kW) Volkswagen car engine converted by JPX. This heavier engine required the ATL's wings to be forward swept to restore the aircraft's centre of gravity and production began on the strength of a 30-aircraft order from from the French National Aeronautical Federation. Of mixed construction, with

fabric-covered wooden wings and a glass fibre/honeycomb/epoxy fuselage, the ATL was certificated in 1986 and remained in production into 1991. The aircraft was built as the **ATL Club** (or **Bijou** for the UK market) basic model; the **ATL Club Model 88** with a smaller-diameter propeller for increased ground clearance and as the **ATL Club Model 89** with a 70-hp (52-kW) Limbach engine.

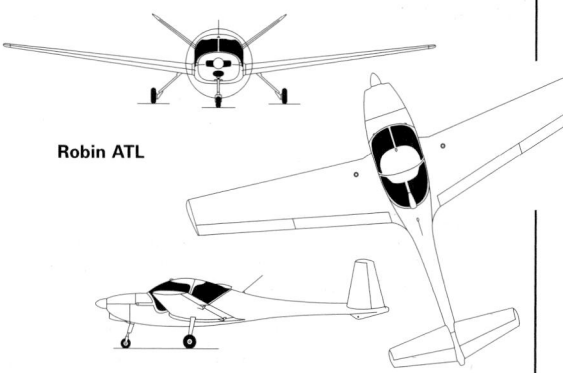

Robin ATL

Robin DR.220, DR.221 Dauphin and DR.250 Capitaine, R.2112/R.2160

Formed originally in Dijon during 1957 as Centre Est Aéronautique, this French company changed its title in 1969 to Avions Pierre Robin and in 2001 was known as Robin Aviation. The company manufactured a series of light aircraft based on original Jodel designs, early products including the **DR.220**, which could accommodate

three adults or two adults and two children, this version being powered by a 100-hp (75-kW) Rolls-Royce/Continental O-200-A; variants included the similarly-powered **DR.220A** which introduced a strengthened airframe and revised landing gear, and the **DR.220/108** which differed only by having a 108-hp (80-kW) Avco

Lycoming O-235 engine. The **DR.221 Dauphin** introduced the more powerful (115-hp; 86-kW) O-235-C2A engine, and the last of this series of aircraft with fixed tailwheel landing gear was the **DR.250 Capitaine**. This was a full four-seater powered by a 160-hp (119-kW) O-320-D2A engine, the additional power making it suitable

for use also as a glider tug. The **R.2000** series of

aerobatic two-seaters was introduced to replace the

SPECIFICATION

Robin DR.221 Dauphin
Type: light cabin monoplane
Powerplant: one 115-hp (86-kW) Avco Lycoming O-235-C2A flat four piston engine
Performance: maximum cruising speed 127 mph (205 km/h) at sea level; service ceiling 12,795 ft
(3900 m); range 565 miles (910 km)
Weights: empty equipped 1,047 lb (475 kg); maximum take-off 1,852 lb (840 kg)
Dimensions: wingspan 28 ft 7¼ in (8.72 m); length 22 ft 11½ in (7.00 m); height 6 ft ¾ in (1.85 m); wing area 146.39 sq ft (13.60 m²)

HR.200, retaining that aircraft's fuselage and fin but introducing a new wing of increased chord and modified section, a rudder of increased area, and an elongated ventral fin to aid spin recovery. The prototype, flown in September 1976, was an **R.2160** with a 160-hp (119-kW) O-320-D2A engine, known in experimental form as the **Acrobin** and manufactured as the **Alpha Sport**. A lower-powered trainer, the **R.2100A**, had a 108-hp (81-kW) O-235-H engine and 34 were built before the type was superseded in 1979 by the similar **R.2112 Alpha**. In 2001 the type remained in production as the **R.2160D** basic model and the **R.2160i** with a 160-hp (119-kW) Textron lycoming AEIO-320-D2B engine. An experimental **R.2120U** aircraft was built in 2000.

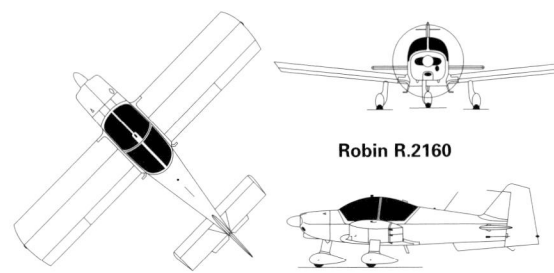

Robin R.2160

Robin DR.400

Continuing its manufacture of Jodel designs, Centre Est Aéronautique flew its first tricycle landing gear version in 1967, this being the four-seat **DR.253 Regent** with a 180-hp (134-kW) Avco Lycoming O-360-A2A engine.

The Regent was followed by a series of broadly similar designs; the **DR.315 Cadet** with a 115-hp (86-kW) O-235; the **DR.330** with a 130-hp (97-kW) Rolls-Royce/Continental O-240-A; the **DR.340 Major** with a 140-/150-hp (104-/112-kW) Avco Lycoming O-320E; the **DR.360 Chevalier** with a 160-hp (119-kW) O-320-D; and the **DR.380 Prince** with a 180-hp (134-kW)

O-360-D. All were basically of wooden construction and later led to a new series, the **DR.400**, prototype construction of which started in 1971.

First of the new series to fly, in May 1972, was the **DR.400/125 Petit Prince** with a 125-hp (93-kW) O-235-F2B, a three-/four-seater certificated in December 1972. In the same month, the **DR.400/180 Regent** was flown; this was the most powerful of the series, with a 180-hp (134-kW) O-360-A, and was a replacement for the DR.253 and DR.380. In June the **DR.400/160 Chevalier** flew, its 160-hp (119-kW) O-320-D making it a DR.360 replacement. The remaining three new models also appeared in 1972: the **DR.400/140 Major** with a 140-hp (104-kW) O-320-E in October, the **DR.400/180R Remorqueur** glider tug with a 180-hp (134-kW) O-360-A in November, and the smallest of the range,

the **DR.400/2+2** with a 100-hp (75-kW) O-235-C20 in December. This was a two-seater with two small seats for children. All six of the new series featured a canopy which slid forward over the engine cowling to give access to the cabin, replacing the hinged canopies of earlier versions. Lower cabin walls gave easier access and also improved visibility. By 1980 production of the DR.400/2 + 2 had ended, and the **DR.400/120 Dauphin 80** with a 112-hp (84-kW) O-235-L2A engine had replaced the DR.400/120 Petit Prince, itself introduced in 1975. Subsequent versions

included the **DR.400/160 Major 80**, **DR.400/180 Regent** and **DR.400/18OR Remorqueur**, while models remaining in production in 2001 include the **DR.400/160 Major** and **DR.400/180 Regent**. In addition, a **DR.400/200i** was flown in 1997 and certificated as the **DR.400/500**. Subsequent variants of this aircraft have been designated **DR.500** and include the **DR.500/200i Président** with a 200-hp (149-kW) Textron Lycoming IO-360-A1B6 engine and the as yet unbuilt **DR.500 Super Regent** with a 180-hp (134-kW) piston engine.

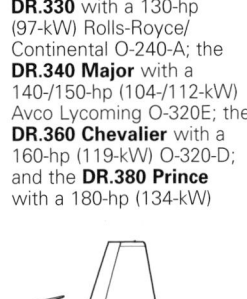

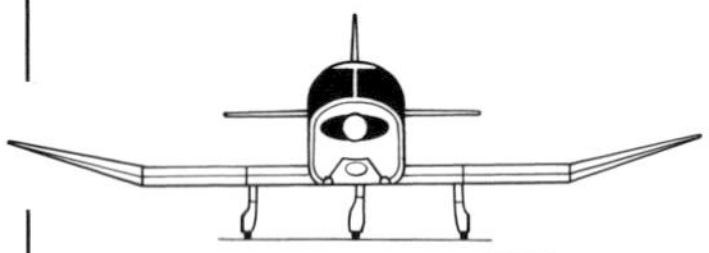

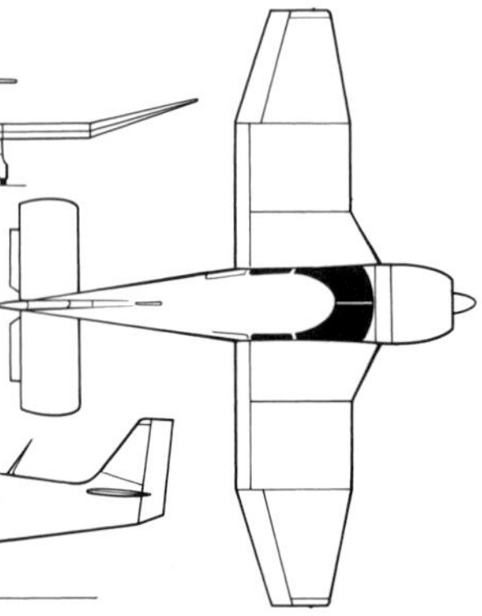

Robin DR.400

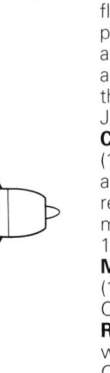

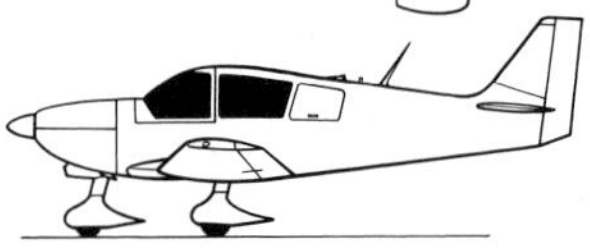

SPECIFICATION	
Robin DR.400/180 Regent	range 900 miles (1450 km)
Type: four-seat light aircraft	**Weights:** empty 1,323 lb (600 kg);
Powerplant: one 180-hp (134-kW)	maximum take-off 2,425 lb
Avco Lycoming O-360-A flat-four	(1100 kg)
piston engine	**Dimensions:** wingspan 28 ft 7¼ in
Performance: maximum speed	(8.72 m); length 22 ft 10 in
173 mph (278 km/h) at sea level;	(6.96 m); height 7 ft 3¾ in (2.23 m);
service ceiling 15,470 ft (4715 m);	wing area 152.85 sq ft (14.20 m²)

Robin HR 100

Robin's first use of metal construction in its light aircraft range was in the prototype DR.253 Regent which was rebuilt with metal wings. Powered by a 180-hp (134-kW) O-360 piston engine, it first flew in this form as the **HR.100/180** on 3 April 1969. Three pre-production aircraft flew in 1970 and

the first definitive version, the **HR.100/200** with a 200-hp (149-kW) IO-360 engine, appeared in 1971. One trials aircraft was completed as the **HR.100/320/4 + 2**, to seat four adults and two children. First flown in April 1971, the **HR.100/210** had a 210-hp (157-kW) engine and 75 were built before production ended in February 1976. A higher-powered version with retractable landing gear and substantial airframe modifications was flown in November 1972. This was the **HR.100/285**, powered by a 320-hp

(239-kW) Teledyne Continental Tiara engine. The production version, certificated in July 1974, had the 285-hp (213-kW)

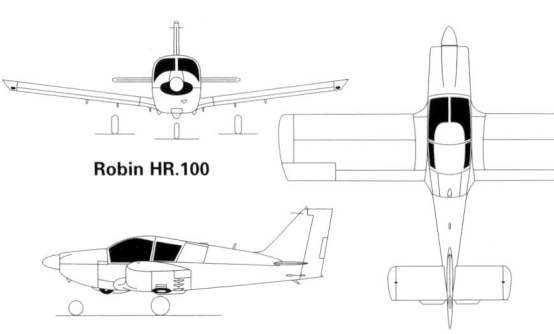

Robin HR.100

Tiara 6-285B engine; from 1975 the **HR.100/250TR** was also offered, with the 250-hp (186-kW) IO-540 piston engine.

SPECIFICATION	
Robin HR.100/285	**Weights:** empty 1,852 lb (840 kg);
Type: four-seat light monoplane	maximum take-off 3,086 lb
Powerplant: one 285-hp (213-kW)	(1400 kg)
Teledyne Continental Tiara 6-285B	**Dimensions:** wingspan 29 ft 9½ in
flat-six piston engine	(9.08 m); length 24 ft 10¾ in
Performance: maximum speed	(7.59 m); height 8 ft 10¾ in
202 mph (325 km/h) at sea level;	(2.71 m); wing area 163.62 sq ft
service ceiling 18,700 ft (5700 m);	(15.20 m²)
range 1,323 miles (2,130 km)	

Robinson R22 and R44

In the US Franklin D. Robinson formed the Robinson Helicopter Company to design and market a lightweight civil helicopter which would be competitive in price compared with other two-seat two-wing aircraft then on the market. His **Model R22** prototype flew for the first time on 28 August 1975, followed by a second in early 1977, and these two aircraft were used to gain FAA and CAA certification in 1979 and 1981 respectively. This

basic model, which became known as the **R22 Alpha**,

Variants

R22 Mariner: fitted with floats and wheels, first delivered for offshore work in Mexico and Venezuela
R22 Police: version with special communications fit and optional portside controls. Uprated electrical generator for searchlight, loudspeaker, siren and ATC transponder
R22 IFR: trainer with improved flight instruments and radio for Instrument Flying Rules operations
External load R22: additional cargo hook certified to carry 400-lb (181-kg) underslung load. Conversions undertaken by Classic Helicopter Corp. of Boeing Field, Seattle, Wa

was replaced from the 501st aircraft onwards, in

1985, by the upengined **R22 Beta**. The R22 family has sold in huge numbers around the world, representing the first affordable

helicopter for private use. There have also been military customers, such as Turkey, which ordered 10 for basic pilot training.

R22 Agricultural: equipped with low-profile belly hopper and spray-bar system
R22 Beta II: built from 1995 with more powerful O-320 engine
R22 Mariner II: version of Beta II equivalent to Mariner
R44 Astro: standard multi-role version
R44 Raven: similar to Astro but with hydraulic flight control system
R44 Clipper: float-equipped version
R44 Police: law-enforcement version
R44 Newscopter: specialised electronic news-gathering helicopter
R44 IFR: similar equipment to R22 IFR

Robinson R22 and R44 (continued)

Over 3000 R22s of all versions had been delivered by early 2001.

Having defined the market for a light two-seat helicopter, the Robinson Helicopter Company decided to take the next logical step forward. In the summer of 1986 it announced it was developing a four-seat helicopter based on the R22. Designated **R44**, this new aircraft closely resembled its smaller sibling and retained the two-bladed main rotor layout. The prototype first flew on 31 March 1990 and certification was gained in December 1992. Late in 2000 some 868 R44s had been delivered, while in 1997 an R44 became the first piston-engined helicopter to fly around the world.

In 2001 the standard R44 cost $294,000 to purchase and around $120.93 per hour to operate over 500 hours.

SPECIFICATION

Robinson R22 Beta
Type: two-seat light helicopter
Powerplant: one 160-hp (119-kW) Textron Lycoming O-320-132C flat-four piston engine
Performance: maximum level speed 112 mph (180 km/h); service ceiling 14,000 ft (4265 m); range with maximum payload 368 miles (592 km)
Weights: empty 835 lb (379 kg); maximum take-off 1,370 lb (621 kg)
Dimensions: main rotor diameter 25 ft 2 in (7.67 m); length 20 ft 8 in (6.30 m); height 8 ft 9 in (2.67 m); main rotor disk area 497.4 sq ft (46.21 m²)

Rockwell B-1

To provide an important component of the USA's 'triad' of nuclear deterrent capabilities, studies initiated in 1962 led during 1965 to the USAF's Advanced Manned Strategic Aircraft requirement for a low-altitude penetration bomber. Suffering a protracted gestation, the in-service **B-1B Lancer** traces its origins to the **B-1A**, the contender that in June 1970 emerged as the winner of a competition for a new strategic bomber. The first of four B-1A prototypes flew on 23 December 1974. At that time Strategic Air Command hoped for 250 such aircraft to replace its ageing B-52s, but congressional opposition and a new administration culminated in its downfall, President Carter announcing in June 1977 that testing of the four prototypes would continue only as a form of 'insurance' and that no production would follow.

By 1981 the political climate had changed again and President Reagan took a much more hard-line attitude toward the USSR. An immediate beneficiary was SAC, which was informed in September 1981 that it would at last receive the long-overdue new bomber in the form of the much altered **B-1B** of which only 100 were to be completed to a standard derived from that of the fourth B-1A. The B-1B has a blended body/ low-wing configuration with variable geometry on the outer wing panels. To the rear of the titanium wing pivots are overwing fairings blended into the wing trailing edges and the engine nacelles. Four turbofan engines are mounted in pairs beneath and aft of the fixed centre section of the wing. The nacelles are close to the centre of gravity position for optimum stability in low-altitude turbulence. No ailerons are provided, roll control being effected by four-segment airbrakes/spoilers on each outer wing. All flying controls are operated by an electro-hydraulic system, with the exception of the two outboard spoilers on each wing, which are fly-by-wire. High-lift devices were incorporated to ensure that the B-1B could take-off more rapidly than the B-52, and would also be capable of deploying quickly in times of crisis to more austere forward operating bases. The B-1B is fitted with a nose-mounted refuelling receptacle.

The absolute performance of the B-1B was downgraded by comparison with that of the B-1A, largely for financial reasons. Major airframe improvements were introduced, including strengthened landing gear, a moveable bulkhead in the forward weapons bay to allow for the carriage of a diverse range of weapons, optional weapons bay fuel tanks for increased range, and external underfuselage stores stations for additional fuel or weapons. The reduction in the B-1A's Mach 2.5 dash capability at high altitude led to the replacement of the variable engine inlets by fixed-geometry inlets. The low-altitude, high-speed penetration role against sophisticated air-defence systems was to be effected with the aid of electronic jamming, IR countermeasures, radar location and warning systems, and application of 'low observables' technology. Perhaps the best evidence of success in reducing the electronic 'footprint' of the Lancer is provided by the fact that its radar cross-section is at least an order of magnitude smaller than that of a B-52, despite the fact that the B-1B is only marginally smaller in size.

The four-man crew of the B-1B consists of pilot, co-pilot, offensive systems operator (OSO) and defensive systems operator (DSO). The pilot and co-pilot are accommodated side by side, as are the OSO and DSO who occupy a compartment at the rear of the cockpit. The crew is seated on Weber ACES II zero/zero ejection seats.

The offensive avionics systems were the main responsibility of Boeing. The primary system is the Westinghouse (now Northrop Grumman) APQ-164 multi-mode offensive radar system derived from the F-16's APG-66. The Honeywell offensive display sets comprise three MFDs with two for the OSO and one for the defensive systems operator. The latter is concerned with countering external threats and monitors the much troubled Eaton (now Lockheed Martin) ALQ-161 system, which forms the core of the Lancer's continuously upgradable defensive capability. The ALQ-161 system can detect, locate and classify signals from hostile emitters transmitting simultaneously via a number of receivers situated around the airframe in order to provide full 360° coverage. It is also able to establish priority in dealing with those threats and automatically initiates countermeasures via a large number of Northrop jamming transmitters and Raytheon phased-array antennas.

The first production B-1B flew on 18 October 1984, and deliveries began on 27 July 1985 at Offutt AFB, Nebraska, with SAC achieving IOC exactly one year later, thereafter rapidly building up four bomb wings. Since this time the career of the B-1B has been coloured by controversy and interrupted by frequent lengthy grounding orders, and several highly-publicised losses. Problems were caused by false alarms from the computerised self-diagnostic systems, non-functioning terrain-following radar, and repeated failure of the ALQ-161 system. Engine problems were also a significant factor in the type's grounding, and perhaps some of the losses. Future plans for the fleet include the addition of GPS, a MIL-1760 databus, ECM improvements and advanced weapons capability. In this last capacity, the **Block C** standard provided for the carriage of cluster bombs, and the current **Block D** standard adds the capability for internal carriage of up to 24 GBU-35 Joint Direct-Attack Munitions, as well as a new countermeasures system (including a towed decoy) and a new communications/navigation system. Due to become operational in 2002, the **Block E** standard will add the ability to carry the Wind-Corrected Munitions Dispenser, Joint Stand-Off Weapon and Joint Air-to-Surface Stand-off Missile, and in the following year the **Block F** standard will witness further improvements in defensive capability.

Careful attention to intake geometry resulted in the compressor face being hidden from radar, much use also being made of radar-absorbent materials on key components.

SPECIFICATION

Rockwell B-1B Lancer
Type: four-seat strategic penetration bomber and missile launch platform
Powerplant: four General Electric F101-GE-102 turbofan engines each rated at 14,600 lb st (64.94 kN) dry and 30,780 lb st (136.92 kN) with afterburning
Performance: maximum speed 823 mph (1324 km/h) or Mach 1.25 at high altitude; service ceiling more than 50,000 ft (15240 m); range about 7,455 miles (12000 km)
Weights: empty 192,000 lb (87091 kg); maximum take-off 477,000 lb (216365 kg)
Dimensions: wingspan 136 ft 8½ in (41.67 m); length 147 ft (44.81 m); height 34 ft 10 in (10.36 m); wing area about 1,950.00 sq ft (181.16 m²)
Armament: up to 75,000 lb (34019 kg) of disposable stores carried internally and 59,000 lb (26762 kg) carried externally; weapons include B61 and B83 thermonuclear bombs; AGM-69A Short-Range Attack Missiles; AGM-86B Air-Launched Cruise Missiles and a maximum of 84 500-lb (227-kg) Mk 82 bombs or 500-lb (227-kg) Mk 36 mines internally

Rockwell (North American) Sabreliner

In a commercially risky effort to meet the USAF's UTX (Utility Trainer Experimental) requirement for an 'off-the-shelf' small turbojet-powered transport and training aircraft, North American resumed work in March 1956 on a design which it had first considered in 1952 as a means of breaking into the market for a small transport with turbine propulsion.

The **NA-246** prototype made its maiden flight on 16 September 1958 with two 2,500-lb st (11.12-kN) General Electric YJ85 turbojet engines, and as a result the USAF ordered an eventual 143 examples of the initial **Sabreliner 40** variant as the somewhat modified **T-39A** with a lengthened nose, military equipment, and two 3,000-lb st (13.34-kN) General Electric J60-P-1/-3 turbojet engines. The first T-39A flew on 30 June 1960, deliveries beginning in June 1962 and ending in 1963. The designation **CT-39A** was given to a few T-39A aircraft after their later conversion as pure transports.

The USAF received six **T-39B** aircraft configured as radar trainers for the F-105 Thunderchief. First flown in November 1960 with delivery starting in January 1961, the T-39B was in fact the first T-39 variant to enter operational service. Ordered as the **T3J-1** but redesignated in 1962 as the **T-39D**, it was a US Navy model equivalent to the T-39B but optimised for F-4 Phantom II and F-8 Crusader training. Production totalled 42 aircraft all delivered between August 1963 and November 1964. The **CT-39E** was the US Navy's fleet tactical support version of the T-39D. Ordered in May 1967, seven such aircraft were procured as **VT-39E** marginally militarised **Sabreliner 40** machines, but were soon redesignated. The designation **T-39F** was applied to three conversions from T-39A standard for the training of crews destined for the Wild Weasel F-105G. The **CT-39G** was the fleet tactical support type, and the 13 aircraft were completed to what was a marginally militarised version of the civil **Sabreliner 60** standard for service in basically the same role as the CT-39E. The designation **T-39N** was used for 10 or more civil-owned and civil-registered Sabreliners used for the naval flight officer training role.

The Sabreliner 40 was the original civil version of the Sabreliner series, and was the model from which the T-39 was derived. The type's major differences from the CT-39E standard include a powerplant of two 3,300-lb st (14.68-kN) JT12A-8 turbojets. Intended for the civil market but used in very small numbers by the military, the **Sabreliner 40A** combines the wing of the **Sabreliner 75** with the rest of the Sabreliner 40. The **Sabreliner 60** was the second major civil model with a longer fuselage. The **Sabreliner 65** was also used in small numbers by the military, and was a development of the Sabreliner 60 with the combination of turbofan power and a wing of super-critical section for considerably improved cruising range. First flown in December 1969, the **Sabreliner 75** was based on the Sabreliner 40 and 60 but with a revised wing and a deeper fuselage with square rather than triangular windows in a cabin accommodating up to 10 passengers. The **Sabreliner 75A** is a development of the Sabreliner 75 with two 4,315-lb st (19.19-kN) General Electric CF700-2D-2 turbofans.

This USAF T-39A wears the high-conspicuity colours related to the type's training role. The T-39 also flew a number of more specialised missions.

SPECIFICATION	
Rockwell (North American) CT-39E Sabreliner	2,119 miles (3410 km) with four passengers
Type: two-crew short-/medium-range utility light transport with readiness training capability	**Weights:** empty 9,845 lb (4488 kg); maximum take-off 18,650 lb (8498 kg)
Powerplant: two Pratt & Whitney JT12A-8 turbojet engines each rated at 3,300 lb st (14.6 kN)	**Dimensions:** wingspan 44 ft 5¼ in (13.54 m); length 43 ft 9 in (13.34 m); height 16 ft (4.88 m); wing area 342.05 sq ft (31.78 m²)
Performance: maximum speed 563 mph (906 km/h) at 21,500 ft (6550 m); initial climb rate 4,800 ft (1463 m) per minute; service ceiling 40,000 ft (13715 m); range	**Payload:** up to 10 passengers within the context of a 2,500-lb (1134-kg) maximum payload

Rockwell (North American) T-2 Buckeye

In 1956 the US Navy identified a requirement for a jet trainer which would be suitable to take the pupil, after completion of the ab initio phase, through all the more advanced stages, including bombing, gunnery and fighter tactics, to the point of carrier qualification. Competitive procurement was contested by a number of US manufacturers but North American Aviation, which incorporated in its **NA-249** design proposal proven features from the FJ-1 Fury and T-28 Trojan, was selected and contracted in late 1946 to build six pre-production **YT2J-1** aircraft for evaluation; there was no prototype as such.

The first of the pre-production aircraft, flown initially on 31 January 1958, was of mid-wing configuration, accommodating pupil and instructor in tandem on LS-1 ejection seats. The instructor's seat, at the rear, was raised to provide a good view forward. The design provided a robust landing gear, powered controls, large trailing-edge flaps, an airbrake on each side of the fuselage and a retractable sting-type arrester hook, all hydraulically actuated. The YT2J-1 and initial production **T2J-1** (designated **T-2A** from 1962) was powered by a single 3,400-lb (15.12-kN) thrust Westinghouse J34-WE-48 turbojet within the fuselage. Named **Buckeye** before entering service in July 1959, the T2J-1 initially equipped BTG-7, later VT-7, at NAS Meridian. T2J-1 production totalled 201 aircraft.

The first of two **YT2J-2** test aircraft (T2J-1 conversions) was flown on 30 August 1962 with two 3,000-lb (13.34-kN) thrust Pratt & Whitney J60-P-6 turbojets. This version was selected to supersede the T-2A, the first of 97 production **T-2B** aircraft being flown on 21 May 1965 and entering service with VT-4 at NAS Pensacola in December 1965. Following evaluation of a T-2B converted to **YT-2C** configuration with two General Electric J85-GE-4 engines, 231 aircraft designated **T-2C** were built for the US Navy Air Training Command, the first production example being flown initially on 10 December 1968. At a later date, small numbers of T-2B and T-2C aircraft were converted as drone directors under the respective designations **DT-2B** and **DT-2C**. In 1982, 17 US Navy T-2Bs were removed from storage and refurbished, 15 of them later entering service to supplement T-2Cs that remained active.

The US Navy also procured two T-2 trainer variants (basically similar to the T-2C) on behalf of the Venezuelan and Greek air forces. The FAV received 12 **T-2D** trainers in 1973, plus an additional 12 weapons-capable aircraft in 1976. Some T-2Ds flew with rebel forces during the 1992 coup attempt. The Greek air force relies for advanced training on its surviving **T-2E** aircraft.

In the summer of 2001, the Buckeye, here in YT2J-2 form, was still in US Navy service.

SPECIFICATION	
Rockwell T-2C Buckeye	ceiling 40,415 ft (12320 m); range 1,047 miles (1685 km)
Type: basic and advanced carrier-capable trainer	**Weights:** empty 8,115 lb (3680 kg); maximum take-off 13,179 lb (5977 kg)
Powerplant: two General Electric J85-GE-4 turbojets each rated at 2,950 lb st (13.10 kN)	**Dimensions:** wingspan 38 ft 1½ in (11.62 m) with tip tanks; length 38 ft 3½ in (11.67 m); height 14 ft 9½ in (4.51 m); wing area 255 sq ft (23.69 m²)
Performance: maximum level speed 'clean' at 25,000 ft (7620 m) 540 mph (840 km/h); maximum rate of climb at sea level 6,200 ft (1890 m) per minute; service	

Royal Aircraft Factory B.E.2

The **B.E.2**, which appeared in early 1912, had basically the same fuselage as the earlier **B.E.1**, but introduced some refinements of structure and a 70-hp (52-kW) Renault engine. Because it had been built at the Royal Aircraft Factory it was ineligible for the 1912 Military Trials but, flown by Geoffrey de Havilland, took part in them for evaluation purposes and was clearly the best all-round aircraft. It was built in some numbers for the RFC, the majority under sub-contract, but it is difficult to determine whether the B.E.2 or the generally similar but slightly improved **B.E.2a** was the first to be used by that service. There is no doubt, however, that a B.E.2a was the first British aircraft to reach France at the outbreak of World War I.

Royal Aircraft Factory B.E.2 (cont.)

SPECIFICATION

Royal Aircraft Factory B.E.2e
Type: two-seat reconnaissance/ light bomber aircraft
Powerplant: one 90-hp (67-kW) RAF Ia inline piston engine
Performance: maximum speed 90 mph (145 km/h) at sea level; service ceiling 9,000 ft (2745 m); endurance 4 hours
Weights: empty 1,431 lb (649 kg); maximum take-off 2,100 lb (953 kg)

Dimensions: wingspan 40 ft 9 in (12.42 m); length 27 ft 3 in (8.31 m); height 12 ft (3.66 m); wing area 360.0 sq ft (33.44 m²)
Armament: usually one 0.303-in (7.7-mm) Lewis machine-gun, moved manually from one fixing to another as required, plus (when deployed as a bomber) light bombs on underfuselage racks

The B.E.2a was also the type used in what was probably the first RFC reconnaissance flight. It was followed by the **B.E.2b**, later versions of which introduced ailerons.

The more extensively built **B.E.2c** introduced the 90-hp (66-kW) RAF Ia engine and was the first to carry a machine-gun, different arrangements of armament being tried on

the **B.E.2d** and the most extensively-built and final version, the **B.E.2e**.

With the B.E.2d/e in service on the Western Front, earlier versions found employment in the UK and other theatres and were, of course, deployed for training. The inherent stability that had seemed such an important feature of the design of the B.E.2, which was intended for use as a reconnaissance aircraft, proved to be the type's downfall, the complete lack of manoeuvrability making the B.E.2 a primary enemy target during the 'Fokker

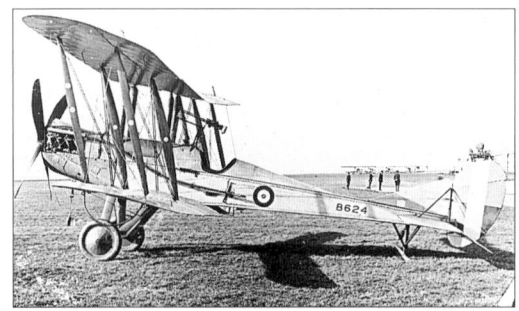

The most famous and longest-serving B.E.2 variant, the B.E.2c, did well initially in bombing attacks, but became increasingly vulnerable to more manoeuvrable German monoplane fighters.

Scourge' of 1915-16 and the 'Bloody April' of 1917. Built to a total of more than 3,200 aircraft of all versions,

the type remained in service until 1918, the majority of them then being used as trainers.

Royal Aircraft Factory B.E.8

Under the designation **B.E.8** the RAF designed a two-seat scout biplane which was, in fact, the last of the B.E. series to be powered by a rotary engine. Of conventional configuration for the period, the B.E.8 had fixed tailskid landing gear with a pair of skids mounted forward of the main units to reduce the risk of nosing over on rough surfaces. The most unusual feature

of the three prototypes built at Farnborough was the provision of a single long cockpit to accommodate both crew members, but production B.E.8s built under sub-contract had minimal structural change to provide two cockpits. The **B.E.8a** introduced in 1915 differed by having new wings which incorporated ailerons for roll control, instead of relying upon the wing warping of

the early version, and also had a revised tail unit. No accurate production figures have survived, but about 70 aircraft including prototypes are believed to have been built. A small number of them served briefly in France in a reconnaissance role during 1914-15, but one or two were deployed in early bombing raids; the majority, however, were used to equip training units.

Powered by an 80-hp (60-kW) Gnome rotary engine, the 37-ft 8½-in (11.49-m) span B.E.8a had a maximum speed of 70 mph (113 km/h) at sea level.

Royal Aircraft Factory B.E.12

The original concept that military aircraft should be no more than 'eyes in the sky' resulted, inevitably, in the creation of a good and stable observation platform; this was found to be the shortcoming of the B.E.2 when confronted by the more manoeuvrable Fokker monoplane, armed effec-

tively with a forward-firing synchronised machine-gun. However, before the beginning of World War I inherent stability had seemed an essential feature for all military aircraft, which meant the Fokker monoplane represented the *bête noir* of several Allied aircraft. The

B.E.12 represented an early and urgent attempt to redress the situation by adoption of the B.E.2c airframe to form the basis of a single-seat fighter. In fact, a little-modified B.E.2c airframe served as the prototype with the standard RAF Ia engine replaced by the more powerful RAF 4a. Although maximum speed was increased by more than 10 per cent, it had apparently been overlooked that the B.E.12 had inherited from its predecessor the same stable flight characteristics and, not

SPECIFICATION

Royal Aircraft Factory B.E.12
Type: single-seat fighter
Powerplant: one 150-hp (112-kW) RAF 4a V piston engine
Performance: maximum speed 102 mph (164 km/h); service ceiling 12,500 ft (3810 m); endurance 3 hours
Weights: empty 1,635 lb (742 kg); maximum take-off 2,350 lb (1066 kg)
Dimensions: wingspan 40 ft 9 in

(12.42 m); length 27 ft 3 in (8.31 m); height 11 ft 1½ in (3.39 m); wing area 371 sq ft (34.47 m²)
Armament: two 0.303-in (7.7-mm) Lewis guns mounted one on each side of the fuselage to fire clear of the propeller disc, or one synchronised Vickers machine-gun, plus two 112-lb (51-kg) or 16 16-lb (7.30-kg) bombs

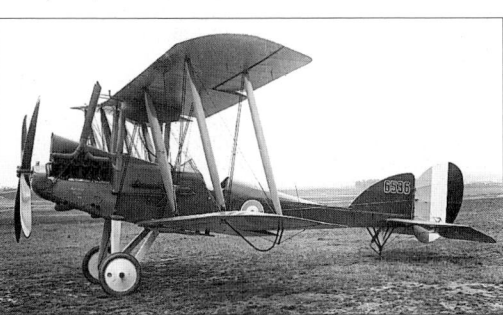

The B.E.12 was unable to fulfil the fighter role for which it had been designed, having the same inherent stability drawbacks as the B.E.2.

surprisingly, it was virtually useless as a fighter aircraft. So urgent was the Allied need for aircraft that the B.E.12 was retained on the Western Front and deployed as a bomber, but its vulnerability to fighter attack meant that from early 1917 only a handful were retained in France for use in a secondary role. An improved **B.E.12a** was in the pipeline, with revised wings and tail unit, but

none were sent to France, and combined B.E.12/12a production amounted to 468. For use in a home defence role about 120 examples of the **B.E.12b** were built, this version differing by the installation of a 200-hp (149-kW) Hispano-Suiza engine and more effective armament: it was supplemented for this task by B.E.12as and by the B.E.12 machines recalled from France.

Royal Aircraft Factory F.E.2

Chronologically, the **F.E.2** antedates the B.E.12, and represents an initial solution to the problem of providing effective forward- firing capability before the introduction of interrupter gear. The F.E.2 biplane had a two-seat fuselage nacelle in which the powerplant was mounted at the rear to drive a pusher propeller. The pilot had the rear position and the

forward cockpit was occupied by the observer/gunner, in which position he had an unobstructed field of fire through an arc of just over 180°. Initial version was the **F.E.2a**, powered by a 100-hp (75-kW) Green engine, but disappointing performance resulted in the 120-hp (89-kW) Beardmore engine being installed in the **F.E.2b**, which was entering service

in France in small numbers towards the end of 1915. Two **F.E.2c** aircraft were produced by the Factory, these having the pilot seated forward and observer to the rear as they were intended for and used in a night flying role. The designation **F.E.2d** applied to a version with a generally similar airframe, but with a 250-hp (186-kW)

SPECIFICATION

Royal Aircraft Factory F.E.2b
Type: two-seat fighter
Powerplant: one 120-hp (89-kW) Beardmore inline piston engine
Performance: maximum speed 80 mph (129 km/h) at sea level; service ceiling 9,000 ft (2745 m); endurance 3 hours
Weights: empty 1,993 lb (904 kg); maximum take-off 2,970 lb (1347 kg)

Dimensions: wingspan 47 ft 9 in (14.55 m); length 32 ft 3 in (9.83 m); height 12 ft 7½ in (3.85 m); wing area 494 sq ft (45.89 m²)
Armament: initially a single 0.303-in (7.7-mm) Lewis gun, but later a second Lewis gun was added; in a bomber role a maximum of 350 lb (159 kg) of bombs could be carried in various combinations

Rolls-Royce engine (later named Eagle); this provided considerably improved performance, especially in

terms of rate of climb and altitude capability. The remaining designations **F.E.2e**, **F.E.2f**, **F.E.2g** and

F.E.2h applied to experimental aircraft with alternative engines.

In operational service the F.E.2b, working in collaboration with the Airco DH.2, gradually restricted the menace of the Fokker monoplane, but was in turn to meet its match when confronted by the more advanced Albatros and Halberstadt scouts that

began to equip the German air service in late 1916. However, the suitability of the F.E.2b for night flying meant that it was to be deployed for night bombing operations in Europe and, in small numbers, for home defence against Zeppelin dirigibles and Gotha bombers, remaining occupied in these roles until the final year of World War I.

Production of F.E.2a/F.E.2b aircraft totalled 1,939, and although there is no accurate record of the number of F.E.2ds, it is believed that about 250 were built.

During the Battle of the Somme, F.E.2bs provided valuable service in air combat, and in gun attacks against enemy ground forces.

Royal Aircraft Factory F.E.8

Somewhat similar in configuration to the Airco DH.2, the **F.E.8** fighter was designed and developed because of the continuing lack in British service of a reliable and efficient interrupter gear for a forward-firing machine-gun. A

single-seat pusher biplane, the F.E.8 had to rely upon the very unsatisfactory armament of a single Lewis gun mounted on top of the fuselage nose, where it was accessible to the pilot to reload and clear stoppages. The standard

Due to the lack of an interrupter gear, the F.E.8 fighter was designed as a pusher, but gave poor service.

powerplant was a 100-hp (75-kW) Gnome Monosoupape rotary engine, but of the 182 F.E.8s accepted by the RFC a small number were powered alternatively by a 110-hp (82-kW) Clerget or Le Rhône rotary.

Introduced into service on the Western Front during August 1916, the F.E.8 proved superior in manoeuvrability to the F.E.2

yet inferior to its contemporary DH.2. But with the pilot having to concentrate on flying the aircraft in combat and on coping with the vagaries of the Lewis gun it was a far less effective fighter aircraft than the F.E.2. This was highlighted when nine F.E.8s of No. 40 Sqn were eliminated in a

single action against a formation led by the 'Red Baron', when four were shot down in flames and the remaining five were compelled to force-land with damage to the aircraft or injury to the pilot. By the early summer of 1917 all had been withdrawn from front-line use.

SPECIFICATION	
Royal Aircraft Factory F.E.8	**Weights:** empty 895 lb (406 kg); maximum take-off 1,345 lb (610 kg)
Type: single-seat fighter	
Powerplant: one 100-hp (75-kW) Gnome Monosoupape rotary piston engine	**Dimensions:** wingspan 31 ft 6 in (9.60 m); length 23 ft 8 in (7.21 m); height 9 ft 2 in (2.79 m); wing area 218 sq ft (20.25 m²)
Performance: maximum speed 94 mph (151 km/h) at sea level; service ceiling 14,500 ft (4420 m); endurance 2 hours 30 minutes	**Armament:** one 0.303-in (7.7-mm) Lewis machine-gun mounted immediately forward of the cockpit

Royal Aircraft Factory R.E.7

Developed from the disappointing **R.E.5**, the two-seat **R.E.7** was intended to carry heavier loads and was thought to be suitable for escort or reconnaissance duties. An unequal-span biplane powered initially by a 120-hp (89-kW) Beardmore

engine, and introduced in France at the beginning of 1916, it was quickly found to be quite unsuitable for use in an escort role as the observer/gunner, accommodated in the forward cockpit, had such a limited field of fire for his single Lewis gun that he was

virtually ineffective. However, there was no doubt that the R.E.7 could carry a useful payload, and it was in the capacity of a bomber aircraft that it was found to be most useful, powered by an RAF 4a or 160-hp (119-kW) Beardmore engine. About 25 per cent of the estimated 250 that were built served in France, being used effectively in a bombing role for about three months during the summer of 1916, but their low speed and ceiling when carrying a bombload meant they were extremely vulnerable to enemy attack. After withdrawal from front-line service

The R.E.7 was intended to carry a single 336-lb (152-kg) bomb, designed by RAF. The 4-ft 11½-in (1.5-m) 'heavy case' was test flown on an R.E.5A.

SPECIFICATION	
Royal Aircraft Factory R.E.7	3,450 lb (1565 kg)
Type: light bomber	**Dimensions:** wingspan 57 ft (17.37 m); length 31 ft 10½ in (9.72 m); height 12 ft 7 in (3.84 m); wing area 548 sq ft (50.91 m²)
Powerplant: one 150-hp (112-kW) RAF 4a Vee piston engine	
Performance: maximum speed 84 mph (135 km/h) at sea level; service ceiling 6,500 ft (1980 m); endurance 6 hours	**Armament:** maximum bombload comprised a single 336-lb (152-kg) bomb, or small bombs up to a total of about 324 lb (147 kg)
Weights: empty 2,285 lb (1036 kg); maximum take-off	

R.E.7s were used primarily by training units, but also served in a number of experimental roles and particularly as engine testbeds. Some were used

as target tugs, trailing a sleeve drogue for air firing practice, and the R.E.7 was probably one of the earliest aircraft to be deployed in such a role.

Royal Aircraft Factory R.E.8

Looking rather like a scaled-up version of the B.E.2, the **R.E.8** had been designed and developed in early 1916 to meet RFC requirements for an aircraft to perform a reconnaissance/artillery spotting role. It gained the nickname **'Harry Tate'**, a pun on the official designation which related to a music-hall come-

dian of the day and, like its predecessor, the R.E.8 was an unequal-span two-seat biplane. Its manufacture to a total of 4,077 examples, of which 22 were supplied to the Belgian air force, would suggest that it was a success, but it is a supposition that is far from correct. Early tests of the prototype in mid-1916 showed this

new aircraft to have a good maximum speed, rate of climb and a useful operational ceiling, but no one had remembered the lesson of the B.E.2: the R.E.8 was inherently stable.

Small numbers of production aircraft began to enter service in France towards the end of 1916, but after several had been lost in accidents, the type was temporarily withdrawn while rectification procedures

In September 1917 R.E.8s flew missions in support of the Ypres offensive, flying 260 bomb sorties in 90 days.

SPECIFICATION	
Royal Aircraft Factory R.E.8	(12.98 m); length 27 ft 10½ in (8.50 m); height 11 ft 4½ in (3.47 m); wing area 377.50 sq ft (35.07 m²)
Type: reconnaissance/artillery spotting aircraft	
Powerplant: one 150-hp (112-kW) RAF 4a V-12 piston engine	
Performance: maximum speed 102 mph (164 km/h); service ceiling 13,500 ft (4115 m); endurance 4 hours 15 minutes	**Armament:** one forward-firing synchronised 0.303-in (7.7-mm) Vickers machine-gun and one Lewis gun on a pivoted mounting over the rear cockpit, plus a usual bombload of two 112-lb (51-kg) bombs, or lighter bombs up to an equivalent weight
Weights: empty 1,580 lb (717 kg); maximum take-off 2,869 lb (1301 kg)	
Dimensions: wingspan 42 ft 7 in	

were carried out. Thus, the R.E.8 gained a revised tail to overcome a tendency to spin and, eventually available in large numbers and despite its shortcomings, became widely used by the RFC. In the absence of a better vehicle it performed a

valuable artillery spotting role, thanks to the courage of its crews. Deployed extensively from early 1917, and operating in Italy and Palestine as well as on the Western Front, the R.E.8 remained in service until the Armistice.

Royal Aircraft Factory S.E.5 and S.E.5a

With a secure place in aviation history as the mount of ace Allied pilots that include William Bishop, James McCudden and Edward Mannock, the **S.E.5** was without doubt the most successful aircraft to emanate from the Factory. A single-seat equal-span biplane designed by a team headed by H. P. Folland, the type benefited from the fact that the designers ensured that it was easy to fly, a factor reflecting the minimal flying training that, because of the pressure of circumstance, was given to

trainee pilots before they were posted to their squadrons. This attribute was helped considerably by the adoption of a static engine, the whirling mass of a rotary creating serious torque problems that could be of benefit only to a highly skilled pilot, and recognition of the fact that manoeuvrability must take place over inherent stability. Even then, the S.E.5 was still far less manoeuvrable than the contemporary Sopwith Camel.

The S.E.5 was powered as standard by a newly-

developed 150-hp (112-kW) Hispano-Suiza Vee engine and the type first entered operational service in France during April 1917. Development of this engine by Hispano-Suiza later resulted in the availability of a 200-hp (149-kW) version, aircraft with this powerplant and minor modifications being designated **S.E.5a**, and the first of these entered operational service in mid-1917, gradually replacing the S.E.5. Unfortunately, the S.E.5a was plagued by the problems of an inadequately developed engine, as well as by unreliability of the early Constantinesco interrupter gear, but eventually proved to be a formidable fighter aircraft. In the closing stages of the war S.E.5as were also used extensively in a close-support role, armed with lightweight bombs. The combined production total for the S.E.5/S.E.5a was 5,205, this figure including a small number of conver-

Curtiss had intended to build 1000 licence-built S.E.5as for the USAAS, however, only one Curtiss-built example was completed. In 1922-23 57 S.E.5as were built in the US from shipped components.

sions as two-seat trainers. The type served also in Egypt, Mesopotamia, Palestine and Salonika, and S.E.5as were allocated as well for home-defence duties, but their intended use as interceptors was frustrated by the length of time needed for their water-cooled powerplant to reach working temperature. The S.E.5a was also flown by the American Expeditionary Force and plans had been made for

the Curtiss Aeroplane and Motor Company in the USA to build 1,000 for the US Army. The intention was frustrated by contract cancellation following the end of World War I and only a single example was manufactured by Curtiss, but the company subsequently assembled 56 with components supplied from the UK. Post-war a further batch was assembled in the USA by Eberhart Steel Products.

SPECIFICATION

Royal Aircraft Factory S.E.5a
Type: single-seat fighter
Powerplant: one 200-hp (149-kW) Hispano-Suiza V-8 piston engine
Performance: maximum speed 138 mph (222 km/h); service ceiling 22,000 ft (6705 m); endurance 3 hours
Weights: empty 1,400 lb (635 kg); maximum take-off 1,955 lb (887 kg)
Dimensions: wingspan 26 ft 7½ in (8.12 m); length 20 ft 11 in (6.38 m); height 9 ft 6 in (2.90 m); wing area 444.0 sq ft (22.67 m²)
Armament: one forward-firing synchronised 0.303-in (7.7-mm) Vickers machine-gun and one Lewis gun mounted over the centre-section of the upper wing, plus up to four 25-lb (18.6-kg) bombs

Rumpler C.I

The early success of the **Rumpler B.I**, and the seaplanes developed from it for the German navy, encouraged the company, by then renamed Rumpler Flugzeug-Werke, to design a two-seat biplane in the C.I armed category. Bearing a family likeness to the B.I and, like it, retaining a typically Taube tail unit, the **C.I** had fixed tailskid landing gear and tandem open cockpits with the observer/gunner at the rear, and was powered by a 160-hp (119-kW) Mercedes D.III inline engine. Early testing left little doubt that the company had produced a successful design, and military evaluation resulted in what were then considered as large-scale orders. No production records have survived, but it was reported that some 250 C.I and improved **C.Ia** aircraft, the latter differing only by

having a 180-hp (134-kW) Argus engine, were in service as early as October 1916. It is known that production continued until June 1917. Clearly several hundreds were manufactured, a total beyond the production capability of the Rumpler factory, and the variants were also built under sub-contract. In addition, Bayerische Rumpler-Werke developed a dual-control two-seat trainer-powered by a 150-hp (112kW) Benz Bz.III.

When the C.I was first introduced on the Western Front in 1915, the single Parabellum machine-gun in the observer's cockpit combined with the C.I's performance was sufficient to give reasonable immunity from attack. Then, when Allied scouts became more capable and aggressive, an LMG 08/15 machine-gun was added for

Flugzeug-Werke, Märkische Flugzeug Werke, Hannoversche Waggonfabrik, and Albert Rinne Flugzeug-Werke all built the Rumpler C.I as sub-contractors.

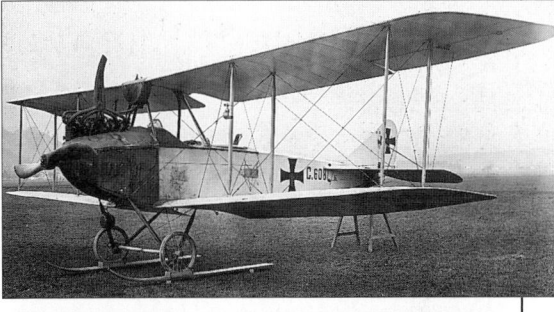

the pilot but, finally, the type was withdrawn from the Western Front and transferred for service in Macedonia and Palestine. Operating in Palestine in early 1917, a small force of C.Is played a vital role in the battle for Gaza. In addition to the C.Is produced for operation on the Western Front, Rumpler also developed a seaplane version for the German navy under the designation **6B 1**. This differed from the C.I only by the installation of twin floats, being followed into production by the very similar **6B 2**, which differed only by introducing the revised tail unit of the **C.IV**. Combined production of both versions for the

German Navy, which used them in a seaplane station defence role, totalled 98 aircraft. Post-war, a number

of ex-military C.Is was converted for use in a commercial passenger-carrying role.

SPECIFICATION

Rumpler C.Ia
Type: two-seat reconnaissance/general purpose aircraft
Powerplant: one 180-hp (134-kW) Argus inline piston engine
Performance: maximum speed 93 mph (150 km/h); service ceiling 16,405 ft (5000 m); endurance 4 hours
Weights: empty 1,748 lb (793 kg); maximum take-off 2,866 lb (1300 kg)
Dimensions: wingspan 39 ft 10¼ in (12.15 m); length 25 ft 9 in (7.85 m); height 10 ft (3.05 m); wing area 384.28 sq ft (35.70 m²)
Armament: one fixed forward-firing 0.31-in (7.92-mm) LMG 08/15 machine-gun and one 0.31-in (7.92-mm) Parabellum gun for use of the observer, plus up to 220 lb (100 kg) of light bombs carried externally

Ryan early aircraft

T. Claude Ryan established Ryan Airlines on the US west coast in 1922, and its workshops very soon began the conversion of war surplus aircraft for civil use. Nine Standard open-cockpit biplanes were rebuilt as cabin transports, the **Ryan Standard** having a four-passenger enclosed cabin immediately behind the engine, with the pilot in an open cockpit to its rear. Ryan had also acquired

from two Californian businessmen the long-range Douglas Cloudster, which had been modified by its previous owners to accommodate a pilot and five passengers in three open cockpits. When the upper wing was damaged in a landing accident the opportunity was taken to accommodate two crew in a forward open cockpit with 10 passengers in an enclosed

cabin to their rear, thus producing the one-off **Ryan Cloudster**.

The first original design was the **Ryan M-1**, a braced high-wing monoplane of which the first example was flown on 14 February 1926, accommodating a pilot and mail or two passengers. Most successful of the 16 that were built were nine powered by the 200-hp (149-kW) Wright J-4B radial engine, some being used on the pioneering mail routes of Colorado Airways

and Pacific Air Transport. The M-1 was followed by 21 generally similar **M-2** mail/passenger transports, powered by a variety of engines in the 150/200-hp (112/149-kW) range.

Successful use of the M-1 and M-2 led to design of the **B.1 Brougham** which, of basically the same external configuration, had an enclosed cabin for the pilot and four passengers. The prototype B.1 was powered by an Hispano-Suiza Vee engine, but completion of the first

production aircraft, to be powered by a 225-hp (168-kW) Wright J-5 Whirlwind radial, was delayed by construction of the special one-off **NYP** (**New York Paris**) used by Charles Lindbergh for the first and epic solo west to east nonstop flight across the North Atlantic. Derived from the M-1/M-2 design, the NYP differed primarily by having a 237-hp (177-kW) Wright J-5C Whirlwind, and a large-capacity fuel tank in the forward fuselage which

SPECIFICATION

Ryan B.1 Brougham
Type: five-seat cabin monoplane
Powerplant: one 225-hp (168-kW) Wright J-5 Whirlwind radial piston engine
Performance: maximum speed 125 mph (201 km/h); service ceiling 16,000 ft (4875 m); range 700 miles

(1127 km)
Weights: empty 1,870 lb (848 kg); maximum take-off 3,300 lb (1497 kg)
Dimensions: wingspan 42 ft (12.80 m); length 27 ft 9 in (8.46 m); height 8 ft 9 in (2.67 m); wing area 270 sq ft (25.08 m²)

Based on the M-1, the NYP took less than two months to build, at a cost of $6,000. Lindbergh chose the Ryan aircraft as he was unable to purchase a Bellanca.

eliminated a direct forward view for the pilot.

Just before manufacture of the NYP, Ryan had sold his interest in the company to his associate B. F. 'Frank' Mahoney, production of the B.1 Brougham then being continued by the B. F. Mahoney Aircraft Corporation until formation of the Ryan-Mahoney Aircraft Corporation at St Louis in 1928. The New York to Paris flight brought a healthy demand for the similar-looking B.1, built to a total of 150, and this model was followed in 1928 by the slightly enlarged **B.3 Brougham** which provided accommo-

dation for six (nine built), the **B.5 Brougham** of 1929 which introduced some refinements and the 300-hp (224-kW) J-6 engine (61 built), and late in 1929 the last of the line, the **B.7 Brougham** (eight built) which was powered by the 420-hp (313-kW) Pratt & Whitney Wasp C-1 engine.

With economic clouds filling the skies, the

company adopted the basic configuration of the Brougham for a smaller, lighter weight four-seater which had the designation **C.1 Foursome**. As flown in prototype form in early 1930 it was powered by a 225-hp (168-kW) Wright

J-6, but the production version had a 240-hp (179-kW) Wright J-6-7. Its development had come too late to have any effect: the Mahoney-Ryan factory was sold in October 1930 and only three C.1 Foursomes were built.

Ryan FR-1 Fireball

In 1942 the US Navy drew up an unusual specification for a carrier-based fighter-bomber to be powered by one of the new turbojet engines in the rear fuselage, and a piston engine mounted conventionally in the nose. The latter was

seen as the ideal powerplant for landing and long-range cruise, or to supplement the turbojet in high-speed flight. The piston engine was also seen as a useful 'insurance' against failure of the more or less infant turbojet.

At the time that Ryan was authorised to proceed with the XFR-1, the company had no experience in building either Navy aircraft or combat aeroplanes.

Ryan's design proposal was selected as the most realistic submission, gaining an order for three **XFR-1** prototypes and 100 production **FR-1** aircraft, later named **Fireball**. The first of the prototypes made its initial flight on 25 June 1944 without the turbojet, the first flight with both engines operative being made during the following month. Deliveries of production FR-1s began in March 1945, the type initially equipping VF-66. By this time Ryan had received contracts for a total of

1,300 production aircraft. However, VJ-Day cancellations limited total production to only 66 FR-1s, none of which saw operational service in World War II, but the aircraft were used extensively for carrier trials before being phased out of service in late 1947.

Under the designation **XF2R-1** one of the FR-1s was converted to serve as the test-bed for a turboprop

powerplant, the General Electric XT31-GE-2. This was the first turboprop engine to be designed, built and flown in the USA. It was first flown in the XF2R-1 during November 1946, replacing the Cyclone, and during its extended test programme the aircraft attained a maximum speed of about 500 mph (805 km/h) with both engines operating.

SPECIFICATION

Ryan FR-1 Fireball
Type: single-seat carrier-based fighter-bomber
Powerplant: one 1,425-hp (1063kW) Wright R-1820-72W Cyclone radial piston engine and one 1,600-lb (7.12-kN) thrust General Electric J31 turbojet
Performance: maximum speed on both engines 426 mph (686 km/h) at 18,100 ft (5515 m); service ceiling 43,100 ft (13135 m); range 1,030 miles (1658 km)

Weights: empty 7,915 lb (3590 kg); maximum take-off 10,595 lb (4806 kg)
Dimensions: wingspan 40 ft (12.19 m); length 32 ft 4 in (9.86 m); height 13 ft 7¼ in (4.15 m); wing area 275 sq ft (25.55 m²)
Armament: four wing-mounted 0.5-in (12.7-mm) machine-guns, plus up to 1,000 lb (454 kg) of bombs or eight 5-in (127-mm) rockets carried externally

Ryan S-T, ST and PT series

When in 1927 Claude Ryan sold his assets in Ryan Air Lines to Frank Mahoney, he continued to operate his flying school, the Ryan School of Aeronautics which he had founded in 1922. With signs of economic recovery in the USA in 1933 he decided the moment had come to re-enter the aircraft manufacturing business, the **S-T** (**Sport-Trainer**) being the first product of the new Ryan Aeronautical Company, established at San Diego, California. A braced low-wing monoplane with fixed tailwheel landing gear and tandem open-cockpit accommodation for the pilot and passenger/pupil, and powered initially by a 95-hp (71-kW) Menasco B-4 Pirate inline engine, the S-T

proved an excellent design, although only five examples of this low-powered version were built. It was followed by the **S-T-A** (71 built), **S-T-A Special** (11 built) and **STM**. This last version was a single-seat fighter development exported in small numbers to Bolivia, Ecuador, Guatemala, Honduras, Mexico and Nicaragua; to the Netherlands East Indies as the two-seat **CTM-2** landplane and **STM-S2** seaplane; and to China as the **STM-2E/P**.

This was just the start, however, for in 1939 the US Army Air Corps acquired a single example of the S-T-A for evaluation under the designation **XPT-16**. (This was, incidentally, the first monoplane primary trainer to be

procured by the USAAC.) A further contract for 15 **YPT-16** aircraft for wider service evaluation soon followed, and both of these initial versions were powered by the 125-hp (93-kW) Menasco L-365-1 inline engine. Production for the USAAC was initiated in 1940 with 30 **PT-20** trainers, these being generally similar to the YPT-16s except for minor structural revisions. During the following year Ryan developed a version known as the **ST-3KR** which introduced a Kinner radial engine that the US Army believed would give improved performance, and the 100 **PT-21** aircraft contracted in 1941 were powered by the 132-hp (98-kW) Kinner R-440-3. The superiority of this airframe/engine combination resulted in 14 of the YPT-16s and 27 of the PT-20s being given R-440-1 engines of similar power output under the respective designations **PT-16A** and **PT-20A**. Three PT-20s delivered with civil Menasco D4 engines were designated

The ST-3 was also operated by the USAAC, as the PT-22 Recruit, ordered in quantity after the standardisation of Army/Navy pilot training.

PT-20B. With a rapid expansion of aircrew training during 1941, Ryan received a contract for 1,023 examples of the most extensively-built version, the **PT-22 Recruit**. This differed from the PT-21 primarily by deletion of the wheel spats and main landing gear fairings, and by introduction of the 160-hp (119-kW) Kinner R-540-1 engine. Some 25 similar **ST-3** aircraft were ordered by the Netherlands, but by the time they were ready for delivery the country had

been overrun by the German advance and they were accepted instead by the USAAC under the designation **PT-22A**. Following US Army evaluation of the XPT-16/YPT-16, the US Navy also acquired 100 examples of the **ST-3** version, powered by the Kinner R-440-3 engine, and these were given the designation **NR-1 Recruit**. These Ryan trainers remained in USAAC/USAAF service until the end of World War II, and with the US Navy until mid-1944.

SPECIFICATION

Ryan PT-22 Recruit
Type: primary trainer
Powerplant: one 160-hp (119-kW) Kinner R-540-1 radial piston engine
Performance: maximum speed 131 mph (211 km/h); service ceiling 15,500 ft (4725 m); range 352 miles

(566 km)
Weights: empty 1,313 lb (596 kg); maximum take-off 1,860 lb (844 kg)
Dimensions: wingspan 30 ft 1 in (9.17 m); length 22 ft 5 in (6.83 m); height 6 ft 10 in (2.08 m); wing area 134.25 sq ft (12.47 m²)

Saab 17

The Swedish company Svenska Aeroplan AB was established in 1937, combining AB Svenska Jarnvagsverkstaderna and Svenska Flygmotor AB, to build aircraft and aero-engines for the Swedish government and for export. Early licence production covered the Douglas 8A-1, similar to the US Army Air Corps' A-17; the Junkers Ju 86A; and the North American NA-16. Saab's first original design was for a two-seat reconnaissance aircraft to meet an official requirement, but following the first flight of the **Saab 17** prototype on 18 May 1940 the company made the proposal that its development as a bomber should be given considera-tion by the Flygvapen. Evaluation of the prototype led to the aircraft being developed for this role as well as for reconnaissance, and 325 were built. A cantilever mid-wing mono-plane with retractable tailwheel landing gear, the Saab 17 had its crew accommodated beneath a long continuous canopy. Powerplant varied, the **B17A** dive-bomber having the 1,065-hp (794-kW) Swedish-built Pratt & Whitney R-1830-SC3G Twin Wasp radial, the **B17B** dive-bomber and similar **S17B** (equipped for the reconnaissance role) the 980-hp (731-kW) Swedish-built Bristol Pegasus XXIV radial, and the **B17C** dive-bomber (which differed from the B17B only in its engine) the Piaggio RXIbis. Included in the total production were 38 exam-ples of the **S17BS**, a maritime patrol version of the B17B mounted on twin floats. Many of the land-plane versions were later given retractable ski landing gear for operation from snow-covered surfaces.

Entering service with the Flygvapen in 1941, the Saab 17 was notable for the robust construction that has since been a feature of the company's designs, and the type remained in service until 1948. After World War II 47 were deliv-ered to the Ethiopian air force.

SPECIFICATION	
Saab 17 (B17C)	11¼ in (13.70 m); length 32 ft 1¾ in
Type: two-seat dive-bomber	(9.80 m); height 14 ft 5¼ in
Powerplant: one 1,020-hp	(4.40 m); wing area 306.78 sq ft
(761-kW) Piaggio RXIbis RC.40D	(28.50 m²)
radial piston engine	**Armament:** two 0.52-in (13.2-mm)
Performance: maximum speed	M/39A machine-guns in wings and
270 mph (435 km/h) cruising speed	one 7.9-mm (0.31-in) M/22
230 mph (370 km/h)	machine-gun on a trainable mount
Weight: maximum take-off	in rear position, plus up to 1,499 lb
8,521 lb (3865 kg)	(680 kg) of bombs
Dimensions: wingspan 44 ft	

This B17A target tug is preserved in flying condition at the Flygvapen Museum at Linköping, Sweden.

Saab 18

Designed in the late 1930s to meet an official Swedish requirement for a recon-naissance aircraft, the **Saab 18** did not fly in prototype form until 19 June 1942. The delay was the result of changing requirements, the two **Saab 18A** prototypes being redesigned and equipped for the light bomber or dive-bomber role. A cantilever mid-wing mono-plane, primarily of metal construction, the Saab 18 had retractable tailwheel landing gear, a twin-fin-and-rudder tail unit, and was powered as first flown by two 1,065-hp (794-kW) Swedish-built Pratt & Whitney R-1830 Twin Wasp radial engines in wing-mounted nacelles. The crew comprised a pilot, navigator/gunner and bomb-aimer, the last having a position in the glazed nose of the fuselage. Early testing of the prototypes revealed that the Saab 18A was underpowered, but with no immediate remedy available the type was ordered into production in **B18A** bomber and **S18A** photo reconnaissance versions, built to a combined total of 60 aircraft; late production examples of the S18A also carried radar. The availabil-ity in 1944 of a Swedish licence-built version of the much more powerful Daimler-Benz DB 605B engine led to the single **Saab 18B** prototype, first flown on 10 June 1944 and followed by 120 **B18B** dive-bomber production aircraft. Final production version was the **T18B** (62 built) which had been developed to serve as a torpedo-bomber but was, instead, completed as an attack aircraft. With a crew of two, this had an arma-ment of two 20-mm cannon plus a 57-nim Bofors gun mounted beneath the nose. The first of the B18A bombers began to enter service with the Flygvapen in June 1944 and production of the last T18B ended in 1948, these 242 production aircraft providing valuable service until the last of them was retired in 1956.

SPECIFICATION	
Saab 18B (B18B)	(17.00 m); length 43 ft 5 in
Type: light bomber/dive-bomber	(13.23 m); height 14 ft 3¾ in
Powerplant: two 1,475-hp	(4.35 m); wing area 470.94 sq ft
(1100-kW) Daimler-Benz DB 605B	(43.75 m²)
inverted Vee piston engines	**Armament:** one fixed forward-
Performance: maximum speed	firing 0.31-in (7.90-mm) M/22F
357 mph (575 km/h) at optimum	machine-gun and two 0.52-in
altitude; service ceiling 32,150 ft	(13.20-mm) M/39A machine-guns
(9800 m); maximum range	on trainable mounts, plus an
1,616 miles (2600 km)	internal bombload of 3,307 lb
Weight: maximum take-off	(1500 kg), and provision to carry
19,400 lb (8800 kg)	air-to-air rockets
Dimensions: wigspan 55 ft 9¼ in	

The T18B was one of the fastest twin-piston-engined bombers. Sixty-two were delivered to F 17.

Saab 21

In 1941, when the Flygvapen was equipped with a mixture of fighter aircraft of Italian and US origin, it was decided to initiate design and develop-ment of an indigenous aircraft in this category that would be suitable for use also in an attack role. The resulting design was of unusual configuration, being a cantilever low-wing monoplane having moder-ate wing sweep, with a central fuselage nacelle to accommodate the pilot on an ejection seat and a rear-mounted powerplant in pusher configuration, twin booms extending aft from the wings with twin fins and rudders united by the tailplane with elevator, and retractable tricycle landing gear. The first of three **Saab 21A** prototypes was flown on 30 July 1943 and these, like a few early production aircraft, were powered by the imported DB 605; all subsequent production had a Swedish licence-built version of this engine.

When introduced into service in late 1945 as the **J 21A-1** the new type was the only pusher-engined fighter to become opera-tional during World War II, being followed by the generally similar **J 21A-2** and, finally, by the **A21A** attack aircraft these three versions being built to a total of 299 before produc-tion ended in 1948. The A21A had the same arma-ment as the J 21A fighter, was equipped to carry rock-ets or light bombs on underwing racks, and had provision for the installation of a ventral gun pack hous-ing eight 0.52-in (13.2mm) machine-guns.

Unlike contemporary Allied fighters, the Saab J 21A carried an ejection seat, the Swedish-designed and -built Mk 1.

SPECIFICATION	
Saab 21A (J 21A)	(3250 kg); maximum take-off
Type: single-seat fighter	9,149 lb (4150 kg)
Powerplant: one 1,475-hp	**Dimensions:** wingspan 38 ft ¾ in
(1100-kW) Swedish licence-built	(11.60 m); length 34 ft 3½ in
Daimler-Benz DB 605B inverted-	(10.45 m); height 13 ft (3.96 m);
Vee piston engine	wing area 238.97 sq ft (22.20 m²)
Performance: maximum speed	**Armament:** one nose-mounted
398 mph (640 km/h) at optimum	20-mm Hispano cannon and four
altitude; service ceiling 36,090 ft	0.52-in (13.2-mm) Browning
(11000 m)	machine-guns, two in the nose and
Weights: empty 7,165 lb	two in the wings

Saab 21R

To produce Sweden's first turbojet-powered fighter, Saab adapted its 21 design to accept the installation of a de Havilland Goblin gas turbine. This seemed a simple way to gain experi-ence with this form of powerplant and, at the same time, extend the performance capability of the proven 21 design; however, it was to prove rather more difficult a process than had been anticipated. The first requirement was for the aft fuselage nacelle to be widened to accept the new engine and the tailplane moved to the top of the fin to be clear of the jet efflux. It was also decided that because of the higher performance of this aircraft some structural strengthen-

ing was essential, and as there was no longer any need to be concerned about propeller ground clearance the landing gear struts were shortened. In this form the first **Saab 21R** prototype was flown initially on 10 March

1947, but almost two years elapsed before all of the fixes needed had been finalised, the first deliveries of production aircraft starting during February 1949. The original Saab 21 production order had been for 120 aircraft, but because of delays in its development a contemporary programme for the specially-designed turbojet-powered Saab 29 was well advanced, with a result that the 21R order

was reduced to only 60 aircraft. These were produced as the **J 21RA** with a 3,000-lb (13.34-kN) thrust Goblin 2 engine, and **J 21RB** with a licence-built Goblin turbojet, 30 of each being built. After comparatively short service in the

fighter role, all were converted as attack aircraft, redesignated **A 21R** and **A 21RB** respectively, and carrying 10 3.9-in (100-mm) or five 7.09-in (180-mm) Bofors rocket projectiles, or 10 3.15-in (80-mm) anti-tank rockets.

SPECIFICATION

Saab 21RB (J 21RB)
Type: single-seat fighter
Powerplant: one 3,307-lb (14.71-kN) thrust Swedish licence-built de Havilland Goblin 3 turbojet
Performance: maximum speed 497 mph (800 km/h) at 26,245 ft (8000 m); service ceiling 39,370 lt (12000 m); range 447 miles (720 km)

Weight: maximum take-off 11,001 lb (4990 kg)
Dimensions: wingspan 38 ft ¾ in (11.60 m); length 34 ft 3½ in (10.45 m); height 9 ft 8 in (2.95 m)
Armament: one nose-mounted 20-mm Hispano cannon and four 0.52-in (13.2-mm) Browning machine-guns, two in the nose and two in the wings

The sole operational J 21R wing was F 10, based at Ängelholm, the first batch delivered to the base in early 1950.

Saab 29

Saab's original project for the **Saab 29** had envisaged it as a conventional monoplane powered by a Goblin turbojet, but information on German swept-wing research which became available soon after the end of hostilities in Europe (combined with development of the more powerful de Havilland Ghost turbojet) resulted in redesign to incorporate these features. As the company had no experience of the behaviour of a swept wing it was decided to use a Saab Safir lightplane to test a wing of this configuration, a reduced-scale wing with 25° of sweepback being

installed and flown on this aircraft. Negotiations were initiated with de Havilland for licence-production of the Ghost in Sweden. The first of four Saab 29 prototypes was flown initially on 1 September 1948, but it was not until the spring of 1951 that the aircraft was ordered into production, being the first aircraft in its class to be production-built in Western Europe. Of cantilever shoulder-wing monoplane configuration, the Saab 29 had retractable tricycle landing gear, its powerplant mounted within the rotund fuselage, and with the pilot accommodated on an ejection cockpit. **Saab J 29A** fighters began to enter service with

Variants

J 29A: first single-seat fighter production version of which initial deliveries were made in April 1951
J 29B: second improved production version with increased internal fuel tankage, which replaced the J 29A in production during early 1953
A 29B: attack version of the J 29B to which it was generally similar
S 29C: photo-reconnaissance version, similar in construction to J 29B, but equipped with six fully automatic cameras and improved navigational equipment; initial deliveries made in late 1953; equipped retrospectively with outer wing panels introduced on J 29E
J 29D: experimental version, built in small numbers, to evaluate an afterburner of Swedish design
J 29E: first flown on 3 December 1953, introduced outer wing panels incorporating a 'saw-tooth' leading edge to give improved transonic flight characteristics; the afterburner tested in the J 29D was introduced on the J 29E production line
J 29F: final production version, combining all the improvements of earlier versions
A 29F: attack version of the J 29F; in addition to the standard armament of the J 29F was able to carry 24 2.95-in (75-mm) Bofors air-to-air rockets, or up to 1,102 lb (500 kg) of mixed weapons on underwing attachments

---

SPECIFICATION

Saab 29F (J 29F)
Type: single-seat fighter
Powerplant: one 6,173-lb (27.45-kN) afterburning thrust Flygmotor RM2B (licence-built de Havilland Ghost) turbojet
Performance: maximum speed 658 mph (1060 km/h) at 5,085 ft (1550 m); service ceiling 50,855 ft (15500 m); maximum range 1,678 miles (2700 km)

Weights: empty operating 9,480 lb, (4300 kg); maximum take-off 17,637 lb (8000 kg)
Dimensions: wingspan 36 ft 1 in (11.00 m); length 33 ft 2¾ in (10.13 m); height 12 ft 3¾ in (3.73 m); wing area 258.34 sq ft (24.00 m²)
Armament: four 20-mm cannon and two RB24 Sidewinder AAMs

the Flygvapen later in 1951, the type remaining in production until April 1956, by which time a total of 661 had been built. It was commonly known by its 'Tunnen' (barrel) nickname in service. They remained in service until 1958 when their gradual replacement

by the Lansen began, and in 1961-62 30 ex-Flygvapen

J 29F aircraft were supplied to Austria.

In 1961-3 five F 22 J 29Bs operated in support of UN forces in the Congo, flying from Kamina, and later joined by S 29Cs.

Saab 32 Lansen

First flown as a prototype on 3 November 1952, the **Saab 32** gave the Flygvapen over 40 years of faithful service since deliveries began in 1955, emphasising the capability of this excellent aircraft. Design was initiated in the late 1940s to provide the Swedish air force with an all-weather attack aircraft powered by two de Havilland turbojets, but the promise of an indigenous, and consequently cheaper engine brought cancellation of the original project.

Design was drawn up around the new Swedish powerplant, but development delay of this engine threatened Saab's programme and, instead, it was to be given a go-ahead following a decision to power the aircraft by a Rolls-Royce Avon turbojet. Pour prototypes of the Saab 32 design were ordered, the type being a two-seat cantilever low-wing monoplane with powered controls, retractable tricycle landing gear, and the crew

of two accommodated in tandem on ejection seats in a pressurised cockpit. Its wing incorporated 35° of sweepback, and like that of the Saab 29 before it, was evaluated in scaled-down form on a Saab Safir trainer.

Production was started in 1953 of the **A 32A Lansen** (lance), powered by a Swedish-built version of the Avon Series 100, developing 9,921-lb (44.12-kN) afterburning thrust. When production of the A32A ended in mid-1958, deliveries began almost immediately afterwards of the **J 32B** all-weather/night fighter, of which the first

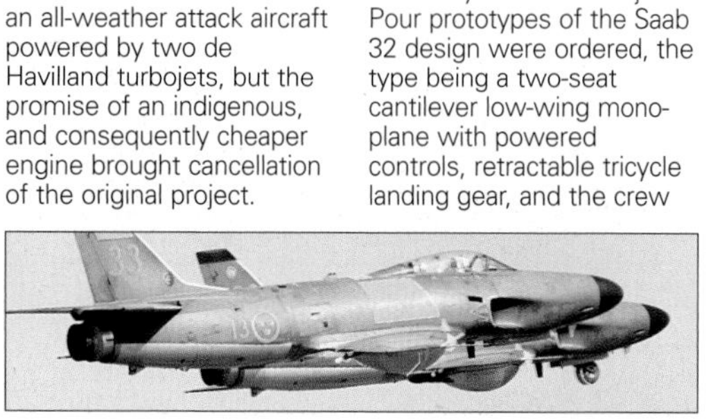

The J 32D target tug was a special version of the J 32B. Later the aircraft saw use in the ECM training role.

SPECIFICATION

Saab 32B (J32B)
Type: all-weather/night fighter
Powerplant: one 15,212-lb (67.65-kN) afterburning thrust Flygmotor RM6B turbojet
Performance: maximum speed 711 mph (1145 km/h) at optimum altitude; service ceiling 52,495 ft (16000 m); maximum range 1,988 miles (3200 km)
Weights: empty 15,432 lb

(7000 kg); maximum take-off 29,762 lb (13500 kg)
Dimensions: wingspan 42 ft 7¾ in (13.00 m); length 47 ft 6¾ in (14.50 m); height 15 ft 3 in (4.65 m); wing area 402.58 sq ft (37.40 m²)
Armament: four 30-mm cannon, plus Sidewinder air-to-air missiles or unguided air-to-air rockets carried externally

example had flown on 7 January 1957. It introduced the Flygmotor RM6B turbojet, a licence- built version of the Avon Series 200, providing much enhanced performance. Production of the J 32B ended in early 1960, and built almost in parallel with this version was the **S 32C** reconnaissance aircraft with a modified nose to carry advanced cameras as well

as radar surveillance equipment. When production ended with delivery of the last J 32B, on 2 May 1960, a total of approximately 450 Saab 32s of all versions had been built for the Flygvapen.

Lansens operated in electronic warfare, aggressor and target-towing roles into the 1990s. Aircraft in use included the **J 32E** ECM-configured conversion of the J 32B and **J 32D** target tug.

Saab 35 Draken

In 1949 the Swedish Flygvapen drew up an ambitious requirement for a new fighter to replace the J 29, calling for a performance 50 per cent better than that of fighters then entering service with other nations. After extensive flight-testing on the seventenths scale **Saab 210**, three full-scale **Saab 35 Draken** prototypes with the distinctive double-delta wing followed. The first flew on 25 October 1955. The rest of the structure was largely conventional, apart from the wing configuration which was fitted with powered controls for each movable surface. Other novel features included a raked ejection seat (of indigenous design) which increased pilot tolerance to g forces. The prototypes were each powered by an imported Avon turbojet, but initial production **J 35A** aircraft featured the licence-built Svenska Flygmotor (later Volvo Flygmotor) RM6B with a more efficient Swedish-built afterburner.

Air-defence J 35As first equipped Flygflottilj 13 (F13) at Norköping in March 1960. The subsequent air-

Lapland Air Command's HavLLv 11 was the last Ilmavoimat Draken operator, and included the Valmet-built 35S.

defence **J 35B** variant had a lengthened rear fuselage and introduced twin retractable tailwheels intended primarily to permit more effective aerodynamic braking during the landing run; most J 35As were later modified to this configuration. The next air-defence version was the **J 35D**, featuring the more powerful RM6C engine plus more advanced radar and equipment. The final air-defence variant for the Flygvapen was the **J 35F**, developed from the J 35D. The J 35F introduced more capable radar and collision-course fire control, deleted one 30-mm cannon and introduced licence-built Hughes Falcon AAMs and, in the **J 35F-II**, a Hughes IR sensor. The J 35F also introduced a new, more bulged canopy, an improved autopilot and a ground-air datalink. Fuel capacity was increased, making the J 35F a much longer-ranged fighter than its precursors. A new after-

burner further improved performance. One other variant for the Swedish air force was the reconnaissance **S 35E**, based on the J 35D, with the radar nose replaced by a pressurised nose section housing five cameras as standard.

Some 64 (or 66, according to some sources) J 35Fs were converted to **J 35J** standard and these served until 1998. The J 35J modification added extra armament capability in the form of two additional pylons under the engine intake ducts. The J 35J also gained improvements to the radar, IR sensor, IFF, cockpit and avionics.

A two-seat trainer version, designated **Sk 35C**, made its maiden flight on 30 December 1959. Initially a new-build development of the J 35A, but later including also J 35A conversions, the Sk 35C seated pupil and instructor in tandem in a modified forward fuselage that provided the additional rear position for the instructor without any increase in fuselage length.

In the mid-1960s, Saab began work on export

versions of the Draken. The **J 35H** offered and demonstrated to Switzerland was stillborn, but more successful was a development of the J 35F that incorporated structural strengthening for the carriage of loads up to a maximum of 9,921 lb (4500 kg) and had increased internal and external fuel capacity. Designated **Saab 35X**, this soon proved of interest to the Danish air force, which ordered a total of 46 during 1968/69. This included the basic **A 35XD** fighter-bomber (Danish designation **F-35** – 20 built); a basically similar **RF-35** reconnaissance/fighter version that differed by having the camera nose of the S 35E Draken but retaining wing cannon (20 built); and **TF-35** (**Sk 35XD**) trainer similar to the Sk 35C but retaining one wing cannon. Denmark's Drakens were extensively upgraded during the mid-1980s, the last retiring in December 1993.

Finland was the second export customer, ordering 12 Saab 35Xs in 1970 for assembly by Valmet Oy. Six Swedish air force J 35Bs (designated **J 35S**, with

radar removed) were first leased for training purposes and then purchased in 1975, becoming **J 35BS** machines. Finland also procured 24 J 35Fs and Sk 35Cs from Sweden, the first five being redesignated **J 35FS** and the trainers becoming **J 35CS**. They were retired in 1997.

The final Draken customer was Austria, whose air force was directed to purchase 24 surplus Swedish J 35Ds in 1985. The Swedish aircraft were selected instead of ex-Saudi Lightnings offered by BAe. The aircraft are fitted with J 35F-style bulged canopies, but apparently retained J 35D avionics and radar. Redesignated **J 35Ö**, the first Drakens were handed over in June 1987 and, after training in Sweden, the aircraft were ferried to Austria during 1988 and 1989. They equip No. 1 Staffel (Blau) and No. 2 Staffel (Rot), of the Fliegerregiment II's Überwachungsgeschwader, at Graz-Thalerhof. These aircraft have a podded reconnaissance system and acquired AIM-9P-3s in January 1994.

SPECIFICATION	
Saab J35 J Draken **Type:** single-seat interceptor **Powerplant:** One Volvo Flygmotor RM6C turbojet (licence-built Rolls-Royce Avon Series 300 turbojet fitted with a Swedish-designed afterburner) rated at 12,790 lb st (56.89 kN) dry and 17,650 lb st (78.51 kN) with afterburning **Performance:** maximum level speed 'clean' at 36,000 ft (10975 m) more than 1,321 mph (2126 km/h); maximum rate of climb at sea level 34,450 ft (10500 m) per minute with afterburning; service ceiling	65,600 ft (19995 m); combat radius 350 miles (564 km) on a hi-lo-hi attack mission with internal fuel **Weight:** empty 18,188 lb (8250 kg); maximum take-off 27,050 lb (12270 kg) as an interceptor **Dimensions:** wingspan 30 ft 10 in (9.40 m); length 50 ft 4 in (15.35 m); height 12 ft 9 in (3.89 m); wing area 529.60 sq ft (49.20 m²) **Armament:** one 30-mm ADEN cannon, plus up to nine 1,000-lb (454-kg) bombs and RB 24 and Rb 28 AAMs

Saab 37 Viggen

The **Saab 37 Viggen** (thunderbolt) was custom-designed by Saab to a Swedish air force requirement for an integrated weapon system with high performance, great versatility and STOL capability from dispersed sites in which lengths of straight road are used for runways. The successor to the Draken was planned to become the core of the Swedish air force in attack, overland reconnaissance, overwater reconnaissance, operational trainer, and finally, interceptor variants. Primary responsibility was entrusted to Saab (from 1968 Saab-Scania) and Saab's design team completed definition of the Saab 37 during 1962.

The result was a

machine of unusual configuration based on a large double-delta wing, complemented by canard foreplanes set in the shoulder position on the inlet trunks just to the rear of the cockpit. The 37's structure was basically conventional, although extensive use was made of metal honeycomb for high strength and accurate finish. The powerplant was based on the RM8 turbofan developed by Volvo Flygmotor, with afterburning and a thrust reverser.

Saab received a development contract in October 1962 for seven flying prototypes and several static-test airframes, and in April 1964 the programme was fixed at some 800 aircraft in four basic versions.

Comprehensive avionics would clearly be vital to the Viggen's effective operation in conjunction with the national air defence network, and were therefore developed in parallel with the airframe and engine. The core avionics system was the advanced Ericsson PS-37/A multi-mode radar with a flat-plate antenna.

The first prototype made its maiden flight on 8 February 1967, and the initial production warplane was an **AJ 37** attack fighter that flew in February 1971 for a service debut in the

Sweden's surviving AJ 37 Viggens have been upgraded to multi-role AJS 37 standard, with 98 machines (of a planned 115) having received new mission computers and digital databuses.

middle of the year with an eventual total of six squadrons. The AJ 37, although optimised for the attack role, also had a potent secondary air-to-air capability.

The **SF 37** was the all-weather overland reconnaissance version of the AJ 37 with a revised nose, which contained an impressive array of photo-reconnaissance equipment. The first SF 37 prototype made its maiden flight on 21 May 1973, the type entered service in April 1977 as successor to the S 35E, and production totalled 28 aircraft delivered up to February 1980, when manufacture of all variants based on the AJ 37 ended.

The **SH 37** was the maritime reconnaissance version of the AJ 37 with a revised nose for a surveillance radar and ECM registration system, together with the same type of data camera as carried by the SF 37. The first SH 37 flew in December 1973, the type entered service in the second half of 1975 as successor to the S 32C Lansen, and production totalled 27 aircraft.

First flown in prototype form on 2 July 1970 as the second Viggen variant, the **Sk 37** is the tandem two-seat operational conversion trainer variant of the AJ 37 with reduced fuel capacity, a revised forward fuselage for the accommodation of the separate instructor's cockpit behind and above that of the pupil, and a slightly taller vertical tail. Production totalled 17 aircraft.

In a plan revealed in May 1991, Saab was contracted to convert 115 AJ 37, SF 37 and SH 37 aircraft to the **AJS 37** standard, which creates an interchangeable air-defence, attack and reconnaissance fighter with revised avionics to increase computing power and improve communications. The first converted warplanes re-entered service late in 1993, and also feature provision for more advanced weapons and podded items of the type developed for the Gripen.

The **JA 37** is the dedicated interceptor version (with secondary attack capability) of the 37 family, and designed as successor to the J 35. The airframe was revised (combining the fuselage and flying surfaces of the AJ 37 with the taller tail of the Sk 37) and fitted with the considerably more powerful RM8B turbofan for enhanced performance. The cockpit was redesigned along the latest ergonomic principles and therefore incorporated an electronic display system with a HUD and two HDDs.The JA 37 entered service in 1979, the last of an eventual 149 aircraft being delivered early in 1990.

SPECIFICATION

Saab JA 37 Viggen
Type: single-seat all-weather interceptor with secondary attack capability
Powerplant: one Volvo Flygmotor RM-8B turbofan engine rated at 16,200 lb st (72.06 kN) dry and 28,110 lb st (125.04 kN) with afterburning
Performance: maximum level speed 'clean' at 36,000 ft (10975 m) more than 1,321 mph (2126 km/h); climb to 32,800 ft (10000 m) in less than 1 minute 40 seconds from brakes-off with afterburning; service ceiling about 60,000 ft (18290 m)
Weights: normal take-off 33,069 lb (15000 kg); maximum take-off 37,478 lb (17000 kg)
Dimensions: wingspan 34 ft 9¼ in (10.60 m); length 53 ft 9¾ in (16.40 m) including probe; height 19 ft 4¼ in (5.90 m); wing area 495.16 sq ft (46.00 m²)
Armament: one 30-mm Oerlikon Contraves (Oerlikon-Böhrle) Type KCA fixed forward-firing cannon in an underfuselage pack, plus up to 13,228 lb (6000 kg) of disposable stores

Saab JAS 39 Gripen

By early 1980 it had become clear to Sweden that if it was to maintain an indigenous capability for the design, development and manufacture of advanced warplanes, work on a successor to the Viggen would soon have to start. Strict control of the programme by the Swedish government demanded that the new warplane would cost less than two-thirds more than the Viggen and turn the scales at about only half the weight but at the same time offer a significant improvement in operational capability through the carriage of a heavier and more diverse warload delivered with greater accuracy with the aid of lighter yet more sophisticated electronics. The new warplane was to be primarily an interceptor with an important secondary attack and reconnaissance capability.

The new warplane was therefore planned as a JAS (Jakt, Attak & Spanning, or fighter, attack & reconnaissance) type, and the required Industry Group JAS was formed by Saab, Volvo Flygmotor, Ericsson and FFV. Saab began development of the basic design for the **Saab JAS 39 Gripen** (griffin) as a single-seat, single-engined warplane with flying surfaces centred on the combination of an aft-mounted delta wing and a forward-mounted canard surface of the all-flying type, a digital fly-by-wire control system, and a normal take-off weight of 17,637 lb (8000 kg). The choice for the engine went to the General Electric F404J turbofan, in a form known to the Swedes as the RM12 with a major share in development and production by Volvo Flygmotor (now Volvo Aero Corporation). The engine is fitted with a new afterburner designed by Volvo and General Electric. Unlike that of the Viggen, the powerplant of the JAS 39A lacks a thrust reverser but the Gripen still possesses excellent short-field performance as a result of its large all-moving canard foreplanes, whose leading edges can be turned downward through almost 90° to provide a large measure of aerodynamic 'airplough' braking. All control surfaces are operated via a full-authority triplex fly-by-wire system.

The task of developing the JAS 39's advanced radar was entrusted to Ericsson, which responded with the PS-046 (later PS-05) multimode pulse-Doppler radar, while the responsibility for the nav/attack system was allocated to FFV. Other elements include a HOTAS cockpit with three Ericsson EP 17 multi-function HDDs as well as a Kaiser wide-angle holographic HUD for tactical information and also for the imagery provided by the podded FLIR carried under the starboard air inlet for attack and reconnaissance missions, and a Martin-Baker Mk S10LS zero/zero ejection seat.

Contracts signed in June 1982 covered detail design, the manufacture and development of five prototypes, and a production run of 30 aircraft in the first production batch with an initial option for a further 110 aircraft that was exercised in 1992. Two years later, in the course of June 1984, the Swedish parliament gave its authorisation to the JAS 39 programme. By this time the name Gripen had been formally adopted for the **JAS 39A** initial single-seat model, and current plans called for a total of 350 aircraft for service from 1992. A first flight was planned for 1986, but problems with the software under development for the fly-by-wire system by Lear-Siegler (now GEC Astronics) led to a number of postponements. At the same time the inevitable escalation of costs threatened the type with cancellation on several occasions, but the first machine recorded its maiden flight on 9 December 1988. There were considerable problems with the flight-control system, resulting in the loss of the first prototype on 2 February 1989, and there followed a 15-month delay before the second prototype made its initial flight on 4 May 1990. There were also engine development difficulties.

Consideration of a two-seat **JAS 39B** began in 1989. In June 1992 the IG JAS received its contract for the second batch of 110 aircraft, including 14 examples of the JAS 39B, with Lockheed Martin software for the flight-control system. During April 1993 one of the Gripen development aircraft notched up the type's 1,000th flight, and the second production machine was the first Gripen handed over to the Swedish air force, an event that took place in June 1993. On 18 August of the same year however, the first production JAS 39A was lost in highly public circumstances during the course of an air display over Stockholm, and as a result the flight-control software had once more to be revised and updated before further flight trials could be resumed in December 1993. Flight tests were again temporarily halted between the middle of January and February 1994 after Volvo had identified blade failure in the low-pressure fan of an RM12, but the problem was traced to the use of defective fuel injectors which led to uneven fuel flow and thus vibration.

Current orders for the Swedish air force cover 218 Gripens (190 JAS 39As single-seat and 28 JAS 39Bs), with more probably to follow to improved standards. F7 wing received its first JAS 39A machines for training in May 1994 and began full conversion onto the type in October 1995 with initial operational capability achieved toward the middle of the following year. On 18 November 1998 South Africa became the first export operator, with an order for 28 Gripens in order to replace the SAAF's existing Cheetah C/D fleet. Gripen deliveries are scheduled to begin in 2007, beginning with an initial batch of nine two-seaters.

This F7 (the first operational Gripen unit) JAS 39A is armed with a maritime attack load of two Rb 75 Mavericks and two Rb 15F anti-ship missiles, in addition to a pair of AIM-9L self-defence AAMs.

SPECIFICATION

Saab JAS 39A Gripen
Type: single-seat all-weather fighter, attack and reconnaissance warplane
Powerplant: one Volvo Aero RM12 turbofan engine rated at 12,140 lb st (54.00 kN) dry and 18,100 lb st (80.51 kN) with afterburning
Performance: maximum speed 1,320 mph (2125 km/h) or Mach 2.00 at 36,090 ft (11000 m); service ceiling 65,615 ft (20000 m); range 1,864 miles (3000 km) with drop tanks
Weights: empty 14,599 lb (6622 kg); maximum take-off about 28,660 lb (13000 kg)
Dimensions: wingspan 27 ft 6¾ in (8.40 m); length 46 ft 3 in (14.10 m); height 14 ft 9 in (4.50 m)
Armament: one 27-mm Mauser BK27 cannon in the lower port side of the forward fuselage, plus up to about 14,330 lb (6500 kg) of disposable stores

Saab JAS 39 Gripen (continued)

The JAS 39B two-seat operational conversion and tactical trainer has full combat capability and performance comparable with that of the JAS 39A, but involves a 40 per cent change from that type including a lengthened fuselage to permit the installation, under a lengthened canopy, of a rear cockpit identical to the standard front cockpit with the exception of its lack of a HUD. Other changes include reduced internal fuel capacity and no internal cannon armament. The first JAS 39B flew in 1996, and deliveries began in 1998. In early 2000 the JAS 39B was awaiting clearance for operational Flygvapnet service, due to delays in changes to the pilot's manual.

Saab 340 and 2000

The Saab 2000 featured a wing increased in area by some 33 per cent through a 15 per cent increase in span over the Saab 340.

The **Saab 340** 37-seat regional transport was originally developed in partnership with Fairchild as what was designated as the **Saab Fairchild SF-340** at the time, and first flew on 25 January 1983 with 1,630-shp (1215-kW) General Electric CT7-5A2 turboprop engines driving four-blade propellers. Fairchild later pulled out of the programme, and after November 1985 the 340 was a wholly Swedish programme. The 340 gained certification in March 1984, and the initial deliveries of the **Saab 340A** initial production model were made to the launch customer, Crossair of Switzerland, from June of the same year. Production of the series ended in 1999, and by that time some 456 aircraft had been delivered.

The 340A is a conventional low-wing monoplane of largely light alloy construction with a measure of composite materials, and has tricycle landing gear with twin wheels on each unit. The passengers are accommodated in a pressurised and air-conditioned cabin in a 2+1 arrangement with access provided by a door and separate airstair at the front of the cabin on the port side. The original 340A was replaced in 1989 by the **340B** featuring 1,750-shp (1305-kW) CT7-9B turboprop engines for improved 'hot-and-high' performance. Other changes included higher weights, a tailplane of increased tailplane, and improved payload/range capability. The final variant was the **340B Plus** that was launched in February 1994 and delivered from April 1994 with **Saab 2000** features for improved field performance, greater cabin comfort (through better seats for a typical load of 33 passengers and an optional active noise-control system) and lower-cost maintenance. From 1996 the type was available with optional winglets, adding 2 ft 0 in (0.61 m) to the span on each side, but these winglets could not be retrofitted to existing aircraft.

The primary data for the 340B include a maximum cruising speed of 325 mph (522 km/h) at 15,000 ft (4570 m), range of 1,047 miles (1685 km) with 35 passengers within the context of a 8,366-lb (3795-kg) maximum payload, empty weight of 18,133 lb (8225 kg), maximum take-off weight of 29,000 lb (13155 kg), span of 70 ft 4 in (21.44 m), length of 64 ft 8¾ in (19.73 m), height of 22 ft 10½ in (6.97 m) and wing area of 450.00 sq ft (41.81 m²).

There has been only one purely military customer for the type in the form of the Swedish air force, which has taken six 340B aircraft. The first was completed to **Tp 100** standard as a VIP machine for the Swedish royal flight, but the following five (now supplemented by the converted first aircraft) were delivered as **S 100B Argus** machines for the airborne early warning and control role with the Ericsson PS-890 Erieye side-looking radar using a slab-sided longitudinal phased-array antenna in a fairing some 29 ft 6 in (9 m) long above the fuselage. The radar has a detection range of over 217 miles (350 km) against small airborne targets at a cruising altitude of 19,685 ft (6000 m). There are up to three command consoles in the cabin, and other features include IFF/SSR interrogators, ESM capability, INS and GPS navigation systems, and secure voice and data links.

The type was delivered from a time late in 1997, and while all six aircraft are fitted for the AEW&C role, at any one time only four of the aircraft are fitted with the overall FSR-890 system to operate in their primary role, the other two aircraft being used in their secondary role as transports for up to 30 passengers.

The only paramilitary variant, of which two (out of a requirement for 10) are operated by the Japan Maritime Safety Agency, is the **340B Plus SAR-200** with Telephonics APS-143(V) search radar with its antenna in a radome under the fuselage for 360° coverage, FSI AAQ-22 FLIR with its sensor in a trainable turret, GPS, wider windows to improve the observers' fields of vision, a system to drop flares and markers, and a fuselage hatch for the release of a rescue pack.

First flown on 26 March 1992 for certification in March 1994 and service from September 1994 once again with Crossair, the Saab 2000 is a 'stretched' development of the 340 with accommodation for up to 58 (but more normal 50) passengers in the same type of 2+1 seating arrangement inside a lengthened fuselage. Other features are a new and more capable powerplant with the engines located farther from the fuselage to reduce the noise perceived in the cabin, slower-turning and therefore quieter propellers with six swept blades, an advanced flight deck with Collins Pro Line 4 avionics including six cathode ray tube displays, and a slightly more advanced structure making greater use of composite materials.

The overall object of the programme was to provide an attractive blend of turboprop economy with the speed and quietness of turbofan-powered aircraft. Sales were sluggish, however, and production ceased in 1999 after the completion of only 60 aircraft including two **2000FI** flight inspection aircraft for the Japan Civil Aviation Bureau.

SPECIFICATION

Saab 2000

Type: two-crew regional transport aircraft

Powerplant: two Rolls-Royce Allison AE2100A turboprop engines each flat-rated at 4,152 shp (3096 kW)

Performance: maximum cruising speed 423 mph (682 km/h) 25,000 ft (7620 m); economical cruising speed 369 mph (594 km/h) at 31,000 ft (9450 m); initial climb rate 2,250 ft (685 m) per minute; service ceiling 31,000 ft (9450 m); range 1,782 miles (2868 km) with maximum payload

Weights: empty 30,423 lb (13800 kg); maximum take-off 50,265 lb (22800 kg)

Dimensions: wing span 81 ft 2¼ in (24.76 m); length 89 ft 6 in (27.28 m); height 25 ft 4 in (7.73 m); wing area 600.00 sq ft (55.74 m²)

Payload: up to 58 passengers carried in an enclosed cabin within the context of a 13,007-lb (5900-kg) maximum payload

Saro A.19 Cloud, A.21 Windhover and A.33

The success of the Saro A.17 (and in the late 1920s a production series of 11 aircraft was counted a success), led to design and construction of the **Saro A.19 Cloud** prototype, which was little more than an enlarged version of the A.17 Cutty Sark accommodating a crew of two and eight passengers. The twin-engine powerplant installation of the earlier design was retained for the Cloud, for it was appreciated that this allowed great flexibility in the installation of different engines to meet the requirements of individual customers; this was fortunate, for Clouds were eventually powered by five different types of engine. The prototype (G-ABCJ) had initially two 300-hp (224-kW) Wright J-6 Whirlwind radial engines, but after some three years of service in Canada was repurchased by Saunders-Roe for use as a test-bed for the 340-hp (254-kW) Napier Rapier IV powerplant, two of these engines being installed together with a small aerofoil surface behind them to minimize slipstream turbulence. One had the unusual installation of three 215-hp (160-kW) Armstrong Siddeley Lynx IVC engines which had been ordered by the purchaser, but problems with this layout resulted in the aircraft being delivered instead with two 425-hp (317-kW) Pratt & Whitney Wasp C radial engines. The fourth and last civil Cloud was powered by two 340-hp (254-kW) Armstrong Siddeley Serval III engines, but after being sold to a customer in Czechoslovakia during a demonstration tour of Europe, afterwards had these replaced by two

The Windhover A.21/1 pictured over the Solent in 1930. The type failed to gain customers, perhaps as a result of the complexity of its three-engine layout.

300-hp (224-kW) Walter Pollux engines.

Four A.19 Cloud civil flying-boats could hardly be counted a success, but fortunately for Saunders-Roe the Air Ministry ordered a prototype and 16 production aircraft for pilot and navigator training, these being powered by two Armstrong Siddeley Serval V engines as standard and operated by a crew of two. The cabin accommodation differed from that of the civil Cloud, being equipped with chart tables for the training of six navigators. They served with the School of Air Pilotage at Andover, the Seaplane Training Squadron at Calshot and with No. 48 Squadron, remaining in use 1933-36. One service aircraft, probably the prototype, was later modified to evaluate a Monospar wing as manufactured by General Aircraft Limited. In 1938 Saunders-Roe incorporated a Monospar wing in the one-off **Saro A.33** which, powered by four 830-hp (619kW) Bristol Perseus XII wing-mounted engines, combined parasolwing configuration with hull sponsons. Designed to Air Ministry Specification R.2/33 that resulted in the Short Sunderland, the aircraft was damaged severely during taxiing trials and scrapped.

The A.19 Cloud was followed by the somewhat similar **A.21 Windhover** of which only a single example was built. In terms of size it came between the A.17 and A.19 and was designed to accommodate a crew of two and six passengers. Possibly the three-engine powerplant tested on the second Cloud had been shown to have some potential, for three 120-hp (89-kW) de Havilland Gipsy II engines were used to power this aircraft, a distinctive installation that was highlighted by having an auxiliary aerofoil surface carried on struts above the engines. The Windhover remained in use from 1931 until 1938.

Saro lesser types

A half-scale model of a planned maritime reconnaissance aircraft, the **Saro A.37** of 1939 gained the nickname **Shrimp** because of its comparatively small size. It was of cantilever high-wing monoplane configuration, accommodated a crew of two and was powered by four 90-hp (67-kW) Pobjoy Niagra radial engines in wing-mounted nacelles. Although the A.37 was tested satisfactorily by the Marine Aircraft Experimental Establishment the full-scale prototype was not built, but the 50 ft 0 in (15.24 m) span A.37 fulfilled a useful role in the development of Saunders-Roe and Short Brothers of the Short Shetland flying-boat.

On 16 July 1947 the first of three prototypes of the **Saro SR.A/1** fighter flying-boat was flown, a cantilever low-wing single-seat monoplane that accommodated the pilot on an ejection seat in a pressurized cockpit. The type was powered by two Metropolitan-Vickers F2/4 Beryl turbojet engines, those of the first, second and third prototypes developing 3,250-lb (1474-kg),

3,500-lb (1588-kg) and 3,850-lb (1746-kg) thrust respectively. Although this 46 ft 0 in (14.02 m) span fighter demonstrated excellent performance, with a maximum speed of 512 mph (824 km/h), more considered evaluation by service chiefs of the flying-boat fighter concept brought the conclusion that a land-based turbojet-powered fighter was of greater value and no more examples of the SR.A/1 were ordered.

Chronologically the next of the Saunders-Roe lesser types is, paradoxically, the giant **Saro SR.45 Princess** flying-boat, of which three prototypes were ordered in May 1946. These were intended for nonstop transatlantic service by BOAC, but early post-war appreciation that landplanes could operate on this route just as safely and more economically killed all interest. Instead, the 'boats were to be completed as long-range military transports for the RAF, but the lack of a suitable powerplant brought even these optimistic hopes to an end. Larger than the Martin Mars and heavier than the Bristol Brabazon I, the

The 10-engined SR.45 Princess had a design maximum take-off weight of 345,000 lb (156942 kg). G-ALUN was the only example to conduct flight trials.

Princess prototype was flown for the first time on 22 August 1952, spanned 219 ft 6 in (66.90 m) with its wingtip floats retracted and could attain a maximum speed of 360 mph (579 km/h) on the power of its 10 3,200-shp (2386-kW) Bristol Proteus 600 turboprop engines. These were mounted in the wings as two single outboard engines and four inboard paired engines, but development problems with the gearboxes of the inboard engines contributed to the decision to end development. The second and third Princesses did not fly and were cocooned.

On 16 May 1957 Saunders-Roe flew a very different aircraft, the first of two supersonic fighter prototypes built to a Ministry of Supply contract to evaluate, for the first time in the UK, the potential of mixed powerplant. This was the **Saro SR.53** landplane fighter with a mid-set delta wing, all-moving delta tailplane, and powerplant consisting of a 1,750-lb (794-kg) thrust Armstrong Siddeley Viper turbojet mounted within the fuselage; this was complemented by a liquid-propellant de Havilland Spectre rocket motor of about 8,000-lb (3629-kg) thrust in the rear fuselage, mounted below the Viper's tailpipe. An operational S11.53 would have been armed with two wingtip-mounted Firestreak air-to-air missiles. SaundersRoe had designed more or less in parallel with the SR.53 a slightly larger version designated **SR.177** which was intended as a multi-role fighter for the RAF. It was the British Admiralty that showed interest in this design, ordering six pre-production prototypes in 1956. These were required to have a strengthened airframe, catapult hitches and an arrester hook, and were to be powered by an 8,000-lb (3629-kg) thrust de Havilland Gyron Junior turbojet plus a de Havilland Spectre 5A liquid-propellant rocketmotor of the same thrust. Although these prototypes were almost complete, they were scrapped as a result of the notorious government White Paper of 1957, which planned to switch from manned interceptors to surface-to-air missiles for defence of the UK.

Saro Skeeter

With the post-World War II lack of interest in flying-boats, Saunders-Roe sought to diversify within the aircraft industry and in January 1951 acquired the Cierva company to gain a foothold in rotary-wing aircraft. Cierva had flown on 8 October 1948 the prototype of an experimental two-seat helicopter which it designated **Cierva W.14 Skeeter 1**, and Saro continued development of this design. Three prototypes of the **Saro Skeeter 6**, powered by the 200-hp (149-kW) Gipsy Major 200, were evaluated by the British Army Air Corps, leading first to an order for four more evaluation aircraft delivered as three **Skeeter AOP.Mk 10** and one **Skeeter T.Mk 11** dual-control trainer. The Army Air Corps acquired 64 production **AOP.Mk 12 Skeeter** helicopters which differed by having a 215-hp (160-kW) Gipsy Major

Skeeter AOP.Mk 12 XM563 first flew on 25 September 1959, and later served with both Nos 652 and 654 Sqns.

engine, and a small number of similarly-powered **Skeeter T.Mk 13** aircraft were used by the RAF to train army helicopter instructors. In addition, under the designations **Skeeter Mk 50** and **Skeeter Mk 51** the Federal German army and navy acquired six and four helicopters respectively. These helicopters had a main rotor of 32 ft 0 in (9.75 m) diameter and could attain a maximum speed of 104 mph (167 km/h). A civil variant was plan ned as the **Skeeter Series 8**, but only a single example was built and no civil orders were received. When production ended, in 1960, the Saunders-Roe rotary-wing activities had been acquired by Westland.

Savoia-Marchetti S.55

One of the most advanced and successful flying-boats to appear anywhere in the world in the period between the world wars, the **S.55** was designed in response to a request for a new multi-engine torpedo-bomber flying-boat. Its unique features were twin catamaran-type hulls, a thick-section cantilever wing of which the centre section accommodated the pilots' cockpits, and a tail unit incorporating two fins and three rudders supported on twin booms extending from the wings and the rear hulls.

Savoia-Marchetti S.55 (continued)

The first prototype, powered by two 300-hp (224-kW) Fiat A.12bis engines mounted in tandem over the wing centre section to drive one tractor and one pusher propeller, was test flown in summer 1924. The aircraft proved to be underpowered, with a maximum speed of only 99 mph (160 km/h), and a second prototype with two 400-hp (298-kW) Lorraine 12Db engines performed only marginally better; the S.55 still failed to attract the interest of the Italian navy, which was critical of the unconventional design and its limited performance. The company was determined that the new aircraft should be a success and the civil **S.55C** with accommodation for five passengers in each narrow hull was first flown

Variants

S.55: two prototypes and 88 early production military aircraft delivered during 1927-30; all eventually fitted with two 510-hp (380-kW) Isotta-Fraschini Asso 500 engines giving maximum speed of 118 mph (190 km/h)
S.55C: first civil version, of which eight were built and delivered 1925-26; most had Lorraine engines but all were later re-engined with Asso 500s
S.55P: second civil version, 23 delivered 1928-32; had enlarged hulls accommodating 10 passengers and enclosed crew cockpits; believed 14 operated on Società Aerea Mediterranea services linking Rome, Naples, Sardinia and Sicily; powered originally by Asso 500, then Asso 500 Ri and finally 700-hp (522-kW) Fiat A.24R engines; three S.55Ps exported to USA; five sold to Soviet Union in 1932 had 880-hp (656-kW) Asso 750 engines and improved hulls
S.55A: designation of 16 military aircraft (A for Atlantic) delivered with 560-hp (418-kW) Fiat A.22R engines
S.55M: seven built by Piaggio in 1930 with Asso 500Ri engines; wood structure largely replaced by metal
S.55 *Scafo Allargato* (enlarged hull): similar to S.55A but with wider and deeper hulls and enclosed crew cockpits; Savoia-Marchetti built 16, eight with Asso 500 and eight with Asso 500Ri engines, and CANT also constructed eight of each **S.55 *Scafo Allargatissimo*** (very enlarged hull): hulls further modified and streamlined; Savoia Marchetti built 20 with Fiat A.22R engines 1932-33, and in 1933 Macchi completed 16 and CANT six, both lots powered by Isotta-Fraschini Asso 500Ri engines; all delivered to Italian units
S.55X: 25 delivered 1933 with Asso 750 engines for North Atlantic formation flights; on return to Italy armed and used in flying-boat reconnaissance-bomber units, flying with 31° and 35° Stormi BM until replaced by CANT Z.506Bs in 1938; three used briefly by Nationalists at beginning of Spanish Civil War. 1937; some military S.55s with differing hulls were also known as S.55Xs when fitted with Asso 750 engines; others of those batches without these later engines were often known by the designation **S.55N**

I-AABF served as the prototype for the S.55P, modified in 1938 with deeper hulls faired into the upper surface of the wing, and Asso 500 engines.

in summer 1925.

The Ministero dell'Aeronautica belatedly took an interest in the military S.55 and ordered a first batch of 14 Asso-powered machines in 1926, and large numbers were then built to re-equip the Regia Marina's squadriglie di bombardamento marittimo. In 1930 an improved version with Fiat A.22R engines and redesigned hulls entered military service, and a second civil version, the **S.55P**, began operating in Italy, the Soviet Union and the USA.

SPECIFICATION	
Savoia-Marchetti S.55X	12,677 lb (5750 kg); maximum
Type: long-range bomber reconnaissance flying-boat	take-off 18,210 lb (8260 kg)
Powerplant: two 880-hp (656-kW) Isotta-Fraschini Asso 750 V piston engines	**Dimensions:** span 78 ft 9 in (24.00 m); length 54 ft 11¼ in (16.75 m); height 16 ft 4¾ in (5.00 m); wing area 1,001.08 sq ft (93.00 m²)
Performance: maximum speed 173 mph (279 km/h); service ceiling 16,405 ft (5000 m); range 2,175 miles (3500 km)	**Armament:** four 0.303-in (7.7-mm) machine-guns, plus one torpedo or 4,409 lb (2000 kg) of bombs
Weights: empty equipped	

Savoia-Marchetti S.73

In 1935 Sabena initiated the S.73 on the Baltic Air Express service, between London/Paris, Brussels, Hamburg and Malmö.

Developed in parallel with the S.81 bomber, the **Savoia-Marchetti S.73** three-engine passenger transport made its first flight on 4 July 1934. Of cantilever low-wing monoplane configuration, the S.73 had wooden wings and a welded steel-tube fuselage with plywood and fabric covering. Pilot and co-pilot were seated side-by-side in an enclosed cockpit, with compartments for the wireless operator and mechanic behind, and a passenger cabin accommodating 18 in two rows of single seats.

Seven Belgian S.73s were flown to England in May 1940, where they were impressed by the RAF; they were sent subsequently to North Africa, where four of them were later taken over by the Regia Aeronautica. Some Italian S.73s were impressed into military service in East Africa, while those in Italy were taken over in June 1940 to equip

the 605ª and 606ª Squadriglie. After the loss of Italy's East African Empire, three S.73s flew back to Italy by a circuitous route. Making good use of the strength, load-carrying abilities and good serviceability of the type, the Regia Aeronautica used them to carry men and materials, and S.73s of the 247ª Squadriglia flew in support of the Corpo di Spedizione Italiano during its 20-month stay on the Eastern Front from the autumn of 1941. Four S.73s survived the September 1943 armistice, three flying with the Allies and one with the pro-Axis government, but all had been grounded by the end of the war.

SPECIFICATION	
Savoia-Marchetti S.73	**Weights:** empty equipped
Type: 18-passenger transport	16,094 lb (7300 kg); maximum
Powerplant: three 800-hp (597kW) Alfa Romeo 126 RC.10 radial piston engines	take-off 23,810 lb (10800 kg)
	Dimensions: span 78 ft 9 in (24.00 m); length 60 ft 3¼ in
Performance: maximum speed 202 mph (325 km/h); service ceiling 22,965 ft (7000 m); range 621 miles (1000 km)	(18.37 m); height 14 ft 7¼ in (4.45 m); wing area 992.46 sq ft (92.20 m²)

Savoia-Marchetti S.M.79 Sparviero

Designed as a three-engine civil transport to accommodate eight passengers, the **S.M.79 Sparviero** (sparrowhawk) prototype (I-MAGO) was flown for the first time in late 1934. Its capability resulted in early adoption as a bomber/reconnaissance aircraft, producing one of the most successful Italian aircraft in this category of World War II, some 1,300 being built. A cantilever low-wing monoplane of mixed construction, it had retractable tailwheel landing gear, accommodated a crew of four or five and, in prototype form, was powered by three 780-hp (582-kW) Alfa Romeo 126 RC.34 radial engines. Following successful testing, the type was ordered into production as the **S.M.79-I** Sparviero, this version serving with the Aviazione Legionaria during the Spanish Civil War; reports of its capability led Yugoslavia to order 45 similar aircraft in 1938.

In 1937 the S.M.79 had been tested in a torpedo-bomber role, leading to the **S.M.79-II**, of which most were powered by Piaggio P.XI RC.40 radials. Some 600 S.M.79-I and S.M.79-II aircraft were in service when Italy entered World War II, they and subsequent production versions were being deployed in every theatre where Italian forces were operating. Savoia-Marchetti was also successful in gaining export orders, twin-engine **S.M.79B** aircraft being supplied to Brazil (3), Iraq (4) and Romania (24). This last country later acquired an additional 24 **S.M.79JR** aircraft and built 16 more under licence.

In Italian service the S.M.79 was used also for close-support, reconnaissance and transport

SPECIFICATION	
Savoia-Marchetti S.M.79-I	23,104 lb (10480 kg)
Type: medium bomber	**Dimensions:** span 69 ft 6¾ in (21.20 m); length 51 ft 10 in (15.80 m); height 14 ft 1¼ in (4.30 m); wing area 664.16 sq ft (61.70 m²)
Powerplant: three 780-hp (582-kW) Alfa Romeo 126 RC.34 radial piston engines	
Performance: maximum speed 267 mph (430 km/h) at 13,125 ft (4000 m); service ceiling 21,325 ft (6500 m); range 1,181 miles (1900 km)	**Armament:** three 12.7-mm (0.5-in) and one 7.7-mm (0.303-in) machine-guns, plus up to 2,756 lb (1250 kg) of bombs carried internally
Weights: empty 14,991 lb (6800 kg); maximum take-off	

278ª Squadriglia formed with the S.M.79-II torpedo-bomber at El Adem in September 1940, and later in the year hit the cruisers HMS Kent and Liverpool.

missions, and its use as a transport continued post-war with the Aeronautica Militare Italiana until the early 1950s. Before that, when the Italians surrendered to the Allies, a small number of S.M.79-I and S.M.79-II aircraft entered service with the Aeronautica Cobelligerante del Sud, and the improved **S.M.79-III** proved of great value to the Aeronautica Nazionale Repubblicana.

Variants

S.M.79-I: bomber prototype and initial production version, differing from first prototype by having revised cockpit and ventral gondola
S.M.79-II: torpedo-bomber equipped to carry two 17.7-in (450-mm) torpedoes; powered by 1,000-hp (746-kW) Piaggio P.XI RC.40 or 1,030-hp (768-kW) Fiat A.80 RC.41 engines
S.M.79-III: improved version of S.M.79-II with ventral gondola deleted and armament revised
S.M.79B: twin-engine export version of S.M.79-I with redesigned nose; powered by 930-hp (694-kW) Alfa Romeo 128 RC.18 engines (Brazil), 1,030-hp (768-kW) Fiat A.80 RC.41 (Iraq) and 1,000-hp (746-kW) Gnome-Rhône Mistral Major K14 (Romania)
S.M.79C: VIP conversion of S.M.79-I with 1,000-hp (746-kW) Piaggio P.XI RC.40 engines and dorsal and ventral gun positions deleted
S.M.79K: version for Yugoslavia, generally similar to S.M.79C
S.M.79JR: export version for Romania, similar to S.M.79B but with two 1,120-hp (835-kW) Junkers Jumo 211 Da engines
S.M.79T: long-range version of S.M.79C with increased fuel capacity and Alfa Romeo 126 RC.34 engines

Savoia-Marchetti S.M.81 Pipistrello

A development of the S.M.73, the **Savoia-Marchetti S.M.81 Pipistrello** (bat) was a three-engine cantilever low-wing monoplane with fixed tailwheel landing gear. First flown in 1935, it was in service when Italy invaded Abyssinia (Ethiopia) on 3 October 1935 where, in addition to its dedicated bomber role, it was used also for reconnaissance and transport. S.M.81s were among the first aircraft provided in support of the Spanish Civil War, and others served in Spain later with the Aviazione Legionaria. About 100 were in Regia Aeronautica service when Italy entered World War II, but the type's low speed meant it was used primarily for second-line duties; however, with the cover of darkness many found employment as night bombers, particularly in North Africa. Some remained in service at the time of the Italian surrender, operating with the Aeronautica Cobelligerante del Sud, and a few survived the war to serve with the Aeronautica Militare.

145° Gruppo T was the most active North African transport unit, carrying 11,600 men to and from Sicily from June 1940 until 1941.

Variants

S.M.81: production version, 535 built, and powered by a variety of engines including the 650-hp (485-kW) Gnome-Rhône 14K or Alfa Romeo 125 RC.35, 900-hp (671-kW) Alfa Romeo 126 RC.34 and 700-hp (522-kW) Piaggio P.X RC.35
S.M.81B: single experimental twin-engine prototype with 840-hp (626-kW) Isotta-Fraschini Asso XI RC engines

SPECIFICATION

Savoia-Marchetti S.M.81 Pipistrello
Type: bomber/transport
Powerplant: two 1,000-hp (746-kW) Piaggio P.XI radial piston engines
Performance: maximum speed 211 mph (340 km/h) at 3,280 ft (1000 m); service ceiling 22,965 ft (7000 m); range 1,243 miles (2000 km)
Weights: empty 13,889 lb (6300 kg); maximum take-off 20,503 lb (9300 kg)
Dimensions: span 78 ft 9 in (24.00 m); length 58 ft 4¾ in (17.80 m); height 14 ft 7 in (4.45 m); wing area 1,001.08 sq ft (93.00 m²)
Armament: usually five 0.303-in (7.7-mm) machine-guns, plus a bombload of up to 2,205 lb (1000 kg) carried internally

Savoia-Marchetti S.M.84

Designed to succeed the S.79 Sparviero, the **Savoia-Marchetti S.M.84** prototype which flew for the first time on 5 June 1940 had an entirely new fuselage with smooth upper contours. Defensive armament was provided by a Lanciani Delta E dorsal turret that could rotate through a full 360°, this all-round field of fire being blocked only by the twin fins and rudders. Additional armour protection added to overall weight, but the short comings of the S.M.84 became apparent only when it first entered service with the 41° Gruppo Bombardamento Terrestre in February 1941 and soon afterwards with the 36° Stormo Aerosiluranti in the torpedo-bombing role. The Piaggio P.XI engines proved unreliable, and a combination of inadequate vertical tail surfaces and high wing loading caused instability and take off problems.

SPECIFICATION

Savoia-Marchetti S.M.84
Type: medium bomber/torpedo bomber
Powerplant: two 1,000-hp (746-kW) Piaggio P.XI radial piston engines
Performance: maximum speed 268 mph (432 km/h); service ceiling 25,920 ft (7900 m); range 1,137-miles (1830 km)
Weights: empty equipped 19,502-lb (8846 kg); maximum take-off 29,295 lb (13288 kg)
Dimensions: span 69 ft 4 in (21.13 m); length 58 ft 10 in (17.93 m); height 15 ft ¾ in (4.59-m); wing area 656.62 sq ft (61.00 m²)
Armament: four 0.5-in (12.7-mm) Scotti/Isotta-Fraschini machine-guns, plus two torpedoes or up to 3,527 lb (1600 kg) of bombs

Clearly evident in this photograph is the S.M.84's defensive dorsal gun turret. The Scotti-Fraschini 800-rpm weapons were prone to faults and jams.

Nevertheless, production continued and 309 series machines were ordered, although it would appear that only 246 were delivered to the Regia Aeronautica, with a small batch going to Slovakia.

Scottish Aviation Pioneer

Known originally as the **Scottish Aviation Prestwick Pioneer**, this four-seat light STOL transport was designed to meet the requirements of Air Ministry Specification A.4/45; it became known more usually as the **Pioneer**. A braced high-wing monoplane with leading-edge slats and large Fowler flaps to give the necessary STOL perfor-mance, the prototype was powered by a 240-hp (179-kW) de Havilland Gipsy Queen 32 engine. Disappointing performance with this powerplant resulted in no military order and it was developed by the company as a five-seat civil transport designated **Pioneer 2**, the prototype being powered by a 520-hp (388-kW) Alvis Leonides radial engine and first flown on 5 May 1950. The remarkable STOL perfor-mance of this version resulted in 40 being built for the RAF, which desig-nated them **Pioneer CC.Mk 1**; entering service in 1953, they saw exten-sive use in areas such as Aden, Cyprus and Malaya, some remaining operational until the end of the 1960s. Production totalled 59, 13 of this number serving with the Royal Ceylon Air Force (four) and Royal Malayan Air Force (nine). Spanning 49 ft 9 in (15.16 m), RAF Pioneer CC.Mk 1s had a maximum speed of 145 mph (233 km/h) at 1,500 ft (455 m).

Pioneer CC.Mk 1 XJ466 was flown by No. 267 Sqn, the first unit to be equipped with the type, when based at Kuala Lumpur with the FEAF, in 1954.

Scottish Aviation Twin Pioneer

Success of the Pioneer led to the design and development of a twin-engined, larger- capacity version designated as the **Twin Pioneer**. This retained several features of the earlier aircraft to ensure good STOL performance, introduced triplicated vertical tail surfaces, revised landing gear and, of course, a much larger fuselage suit-able for passenger or cargo carrying that could be equipped alternatively for such roles as air ambu-lance, executive transport, and geophysical or photo-graphic survey. The prototype, first flown on 25 June 1955, was powered by two 540-hp (403-kW) Alvis Leonides 503/8 radials, but **Twin Pioneer Series 1** produc-tion aircraft, the first flown on 28 April 1956, had two 560-hp (418-kW) Leonides 514/8 or 8A engines.

Production totalled 87 aircraft comprising the Twin Pioneer Series 1, **Twin Pioneer Series 2** with 600-hp (447-kW) Pratt & Whitney R-1340-S1H1-G radials, and **Twin Pioneer Series 3** with Leonides 531 radials. Of this number 29 were exported, 19 saw civil use in the UK and the balance was supplied to the RAF which designated them **Twin Pioneer CC.Mk 1** (32) and **Twin Pioneer CC.Mk 2** (7). They were used by the RAF as transports to carry troops (capacity 13), paratroops (capacity 11) and cargo, or for casualty evacuation, light bombing, photo-graphic survey and supply

In addition to external bombs, the Twin Pioneer CC.Mk 2 could mount two fixed forward-firing Brownings, or a movable rear door Bren gun.

dropping. The last three of the RAF's aircraft were delivered with the more powerful Leonides 531 engines and during 1961, all of the earlier aircraft were similarly re-engined. Entering service initially in 1958, they served for a decade before being with-drawn from firstline use at the end of 1968.

SPECIFICATION	
Scottish Aviation Twin Pioneer CC.Mk 1 **Type:** military utility transport **Powerplant:** two 640-hp (564-kW) Alvis Leonides 531 radial piston engines **Performance:** maximum speed 165 mph (266 km/h) at 2,000 ft (610 m); service ceiling 20,000 ft (6095 m); range with maximum payload 210 miles (338 km)	**Weights:** empty equipped 10,200 lb (4627 kg); maximum take-off 14,600 lb (6622 kg) **Dimensions:** wingspan 76 ft 6 in (23.32 m); length 45 ft 3 in (13.79 m); height 12 ft 3 in (3.73 m); wing area 670 sq ft (62.24 m²) **Armament:** up to 2,000 lb (907 kg) of high-explosive or anti-personnel bombs carried externally

SEPECAT Jaguar

Resulting from an Anglo-French specification of 1965 for a STOL advanced/ operational trainer and tacti-cal support aircraft, the **Jaguar** was transformed into a potent fighter-bomber and gained some success in the export field. Breguet and the British Aircraft Corporation were chosen to participate, and the result-ing SEPECAT joint company was registered in France in May 1966.

The first of eight Jaguar prototypes was a French two-seat aircraft that flew on 8 September 1968, the remaining aircraft of this batch soon displaying the significant differences between the UK and French versions. Each air force agreed to buy 200 aircraft, the RAF split being 165 and 35 of the single- and two-seat models respectively, the former designated **Jaguar S** (for Strike) by the manufacturer and **Jaguar GR.Mk 1** by the RAF. The GR.Mk 1 has a chisel-shaped nose for a laser ranger and marked target seeker and a fin-top pod for the RWR. Internally

the GR.Mk 1 had a Marconi-GEC 920ATC Navigation and Weapon-Aiming Sub-System projecting relevant route and targeting data on the pilot's HUD. As built, RAF aircraft were powered by 7,305-lb st (32.51-kN) Adour Mk 102 engines. The first British aircraft undertook its maiden flight on 12 October 1969, and the production aircraft were delivered between 1973 and 1978. Reconnaissance aircraft carry a centreline pod containing a fan of five cameras, plus an infra-red linescan unit, and this was augmented in 1991 by a Vinten VICON 18 long-range optical pod.

The **Jaguar B** two-seat training variant features a 35-in (0.90-m) fuselage stretch to accommodate a raised second seat. The aircraft were built with the full navigation and attack avionics suite but without the LRMTS (Laser Ranger and Marked Target Seeker), inflight-refuelling probe and RWR, and have only one cannon. The first British two-seat Jaguar undertook

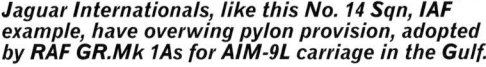

its initial flight on 30 August 1970, and the RAF's 35 aircraft were **Jaguar T.Mk 2** machines, of which 14 were upgraded to **Jaguar T.Mk 2A** standard with the FIN1064 nav/attack unit and Adour Mk 104s.

The RAF's aircraft were upgraded in 1978-84 with 7,900-lb st (35.14-kN) Adour Mk 104s, and raised further from December 1983 to **Jaguar GR.Mk 1A** standard by introduction of the FIN1064 nav/attack unit. Other improvements were centred on defensive capa-bility and provision for Sidewinder AAMs on underwing (later overwing) pylons. Further upgrades have seen or are seeing the introduction of the TIALD targeting pod (in 11 aircraft to create nine **Jaguar GR.Mk 1B** and two **Jaguar T.Mk 2B** machines), and TERPROM terrain-reference navigation system, a helmet-mounted sight, and an upgraded cockpit (in most operational aircraft to create **Jaguar GR.Mk 3** and **Jaguar T.Mk 4** machines) and full TIALD and ASRAAM capability (as a retrofit in most aircraft to produce **Jaguar GR.Mk 3A** and possibly **Jaguar T.Mk 4A** machines). Some 96 aircraft, including a number in store, are being upgraded between 1998 and 2005 with Adour Mk 106 engines

Jaguar Internationals, like this No. 14 Sqn, IAF example, have overwing pylon provision, adopted by RAF GR.Mk 1As for AIM-9L carriage in the Gulf.

offering 10 per cent more thrust but reduced operat-ing cost.

France bought 160 single-seat and 40 two-seat aircraft. Compared with its British equivalent, the French single-seat **Jaguar A** (**Appui**, or attack) has generally inferior avionics, but remains an effective strike/attack machine. Like the GR.Mk 1, the Jaguar A has a retractable refuelling probe and two 30-mm cannon (DEFA 553). There has been no avionics upgrade, although the last 80 aircraft have a laser ranger under the nose and an improved RWR, and the last 30 are able to carry a nose-mounted ATLIS laser designator. A panoramic camera was installed beneath the nose of the 113th and subsequent Jaguar A and retrofitted, while a few carry a drop tank revised with a fan of three cameras. With the temporary exception of the first 10 production aircraft, the Jaguar As were fitted with and retain Adour Mk 102 engines.

France's two-seat aircraft are **Jaguar E** (**Ecole**, or school) machines and lack full nav/attack avionics, but from the 27th aircraft were

fitted on the production line with a fixed refuelling probe for limited tanker training. The first Jaguar to fly was the Jaguar E-01 two-seat prototype, followed on 23 March 1969 by the Jaguar A-03 single-seat prototype. The **Jaguar M** carrierborne strike fighter first flew in prototype form in November 1969 but was later cancelled. Deliveries of Jaguar A were completed between January 1972 and December 1981, and the type equipped nine squadrons, two of them tasked with delivering the 25-kt AN 52 nuclear bomb that was withdrawn in September 1991.

All Jaguar export warplanes have been based on the Jaguar B/S airframe. First flown in 1974, the **Jaguar International** proto-type was an RAF machine with Adour Mk 104s offer-ing 27 per cent more thrust than the original Mk 102s. The first production Jaguar International was an Ecuadorian **Jaguar EB** two-seater that first flew on 19 August 1976. Ecuador's 10 **Jaguar ES** single- and two **Jaguar EB** two-seat aircraft were delivered during 1977, and the seven survivors were augmented

SPECIFICATION	
SEPECAT Jaguar International **Type:** single-seat attack and close support warplane **Powerplant:** two Rolls-Royce/Turbomeca Adour Mk 804 turbofan engines each rated at 5,320-lb st (23.66 kN) dry and 8,040 lb st (35.75 kN) with afterburning, or Adour Mk 811 turbofan engines each rated at 5,520 lb st (24.55 kN) dry and 8,400 lb st (37.36 kN) with afterburning **Performance:** maximum level speed 'clean' at 36,000 ft (10975 m) 1,056 mph (1699 km/h); climb to 30,000 ft (9145 m) in 1 minute 30 seconds; service ceiling 45,930 ft (14000 m); range	2,190 miles (3524 km) with drop tanks; combat radius 530 miles (852 km) on a hi-lo-hi attack mission with internal fuel **Weights:** empty equipped 16,975 lb (7700 kg); maximum take-off 34,612 lb (15700 kg) **Dimensions:** wingspan 28 ft 6 in (8.69 m); length 55 ft 2½ in (16.83 m) including probe; height 16 ft ½ in (4.89 m); wing area 260.27 sq ft (24.18 m²) **Armament:** two 30-mm ADEN Mk 4 fixed forward-firing cannon in the underside of the fuselage, plus up to 10,500lb (4763 kg) of disposable stores on five external hardpoints

by three refurbished RAF aircraft during 1991.

From March 1977 Oman took delivery of an initial batch of 10 **Jaguar OS** single-seat and two **Jaguar OB** two-seat machines. A similar second batch was delivered during 1983. All of the second-batch aircraft were powered by 8,400-lb st (37.37-kN) Adour 811s. Oman's original 24 aircraft were augmented by single ex-RAF one- and two-seat aircraft. Originally using overwing Magic AAMs, Oman's Jaguars switched to the AIM-9P4 Sidewinder carried on the outboard underwing pylons. Between 1986 and 1989, the 21 survivors were upgraded with the FIN1064 nav/ attack system.

The biggest Jaguar oper-

ator in summer 2001 was India, which had taken delivery of 131 aircraft (116 **Jaguar IS** single-seat and 15 **Jaguar IT** two-seat machines) by mid-1999, plus 18 on loan from the RAF (returned by 1984) as a first batch. In addition, the Indian air force ordered a further 17 two-seat aircraft from HAL for delivery from 2001, while a further 20 single-seaters were ordered in 2000. The second batch of aircraft, comprising 35 Jaguar IS and five Jaguar IT

machines, was assembled by HAL from BAe kits. These aircraft were powered by 8,040-lb st (35.75-kN) Adour Mk 804 engines and were fitted with the NAVWASS (Navigation and Weapons Aiming Sub System). India's third batch consisted of 35 Jaguar IS and 10 Jaguar IT machines assembled by HAL from kits

which contained progressively fewer large UK-built sub-assemblies; later aircraft were Indian-built. The aircraft were fitted with a locally integrated DARIN (Display Attack and Ranging Inertial Navigation) system, and were also powered by the uprated Adour Mk 811. For the anti-ship role HAL built the **Jaguar IM** with Agave

radar replacing the nose-mounted LRMTS: ten were delivered for carriage of the BAe Sea Eagle missile. All Indian Jaguars have provision for overwing Magic AAMs.

The final export customer was Nigeria, which took delivery of 13 **Jaguar SN** single-seat and five **Jaguar BN** two-seat aircraft during 1984.

Britain bought three extra Jaguar T.Mk 2s for the Empire Test Pilots' School (two) and Royal Aircraft Establishment. This is one of ETPS's two ex-RAF T.Mk 2s.

Seversky P-35

As a private venture Seversky built the prototype of a two-seat fighter which it designated **SEV-2XP**, but while being evaluated by the US Army Air Corps in June 1935, this prototype was damaged sufficiently to need factory repair. The company's designer, Alexander Kartveli, took the opportunity to introduce retractable main landing gear and

revised the cockpit as a single-seater, the aircraft then being redesignated **SEV-1XP**. When tested by the USAAC it was found to be underpowered, its 850-hp (634kW) Wright R-1820-G5 Cyclone radial then being replaced by a Pratt & Whitney R-1830-9 Twin Wasp of similar output, resulting in the new designation **SEV-7**. Performance had deterio-

rated still further, the R-1830-9 delivering little more than 85 per cent of its rated power, resulting in the installation of an R-1830-9 engine with a guaranteed output of 950 hp (708 kW) in the aircraft that was then redesignated **AP-1**. In this form the type was ordered by the USAAC under the designation **P-35**, the first of 77 aircraft being delivered in July 1937. The last of the batch was completed as an improved aircraft designated **XP-41**, which flew shortly before the company changed its name to Republic Aircraft Corporation, and this was fundamentally the prototype of the Republic P-43 Lancer.

Under the designation **EP-1** the type was offered for export, the Swedish government ordering the first 15 of a batch of 120 designated **EP-106**, which

In spring 1938 the 17th, 27th and 94th Squadrons of the 1st Pursuit Group received their first P-35s. This example served with the 27th Squadron.

differed primarily by having a more powerful R-1830-45 engine and heavier armament. Half of these had been delivered by 18 June 1940, being designated **J 9** in Swedish service, but the balance of 60 was requisitioned for the USAAC and delivered under the designation **P-35A**. They were

severely mauled by the Japanese when deployed in the Philippines, only eight of 48 remaining airworthy after the first two days of enemy attacks, and this represented the first and last operational use of the type. The remaining 12 P-35As were later supplied to Ecuador.

SPECIFICATION	
Seversky P~35A	(2075 kg); maximum take-off
Type: single-seat fighter	6,723 lb (3050 kg)
Powerplant: one 1,050-hp	**Dimensions:** wingspan 36 ft
(783kW) Pratt & Whitney	(10.97 m); length 26 ft 10 in
R-1830-45 radial piston engine	(8.18 m); height 9 ft 9 in (2.97 m);
Performance: maximum speed	wing area 220.0 sq ft (20.44 m²)
310 mph (499 km/h) at 14,300 ft	**Armament:** two 0.5-in (12.7-mm)
(4360 m); service ceiling 31,400 ft	and two 0.3-in (7.62-mm)
(9570 m); maximum range	machineguns, plus up to 350 lb
950 miles (1529 km)	(159 kg) of bombs carried
Weights: empty 4,575 lb	externally

Shenyang J-8 'Finback'

In 1964 the Chinese air force issued a requirement for a fighter offering an overall combination of performance and capability superior to that of the Chengdu J-7, and the result was the **J-8 'Finback'** drawing on the Mikoyan-Gurevich Ye-152A 'Flipper' experimental type, of which the Chinese had received limited data in the late 1950s. The J-8 was of tailed delta layout with two WP-7B turbojet engines

each rated 13,448 lb st (59.82 kN) with afterburning. The first of two J-8 prototypes flew on 5 July 1969, and the reason that the J-8 received its Chinese certification only in July 1979, after an interval of 10 years, was political interference and shortages of skilled workers.

Built only in small numbers up to 1987, the J-8 has the original type of J-7 canopy hinged at its front, and engines aspi-

rated via a single large nose inlet with a translating centrebody accommodating the antenna of the ranging radar, which limits the J-8 to daylight operations. The armament comprises a pair of 30-mm Type 30 cannon as well as an unrevealed weight of disposable stores (including four PL-2 or PL-5 short-range AAMs) carried on four underwing hardpoints.

Revealed in September 1984, the **J-8 I 'Finback-A'** is a J-8 development for the all-weather role with the Sichuan SR-4 fire-control radar, the gun armament of one 23-mm Type 23-3 cannon, and provision for the underwing hardpoints to carry multiple

rocket launchers as an alternative to AAMs. Other changes were aerodynamic revisions, replacement of the single-piece canopy by a two-section enclosure, and the replacement of the Type I ejection seat by the more reliable Type II. Three J-8 I prototypes were built, the first being lost to an engine fire before flying, so it was the second proto-

type that recorded the first flight on 24 April 1981. The J-8 I was authorised for production in July 1985, but only small numbers were built before production was halted in 1987, and only slightly more than 100 aircraft (including a number of J-8 machines upgraded to J-8 I standard) entered service with the Chinese air force.

This export-configured J-8 IIM carries PL-3, R-27R and PL-9 AAMs and is compatible with the LOEC lightweight helmet-mounted sight.

SPECIFICATION	
Shenyang J-8 II 'Finback-B'	**Weights:** empty 21,649 lb
Type: single-seat air-superiority	(9820 kg); maximum take-off
fighter with secondary attack	39,242 lb (17800 kg)
capability	**Dimensions:** wingspan 30 ft 7⅞ in
Powerplant: two Liyang (LMC)	(9.34 m); length 70 ft 10 in
Wopen-13A II turbojet engines	(21.59 m) including probe; height
each rated at 9,590 lb st (42.66 kN)	17 ft 9 in (5.41 m); wing area
dry and 14,815 lb st (65.90 kN)	454.25 sq ft (42.20 m²)
with afterburning	**Armament:** one 23-mm Type 23-3
Performance: maximum speed	(Gryazev-Shipunov GSh-23L) fixed
1,453 mph (2338 km/h) or Mach	forward-firing two-barrel cannon in
2.20 at 36,090 ft (11000 m); initial	a ventral installation, plus
climb rate 39,370 ft (12000 m) per	disposable stores carried on one
minute; service ceiling 66,275 ft	underfuselage and six underwing
(20200 m); radius 497 miles	hardpoints
(800 km) on a typical mission	

Shenyang J-8 'Finback' (continued)

Although the J-8 I offered greater promise than the J-8, it was clear by the beginning of the 1980s that it would be inferior to most modern Western fighters, so in May 1981 the authorities approved work on the **J-8 II 'Finback-B'**. The primary changes were an uprated powerplant, replacement of the single nose inlet by two lateral inlets, and a 'solid' nose with monopulse search radar. The opportunity was also taken to revise the new fighter's airframe and brought-in systems and components. The first of four J-8 II prototypes made the variant's maiden flight on 12 June 1984 but was revealed only in 1986. Production of the J-8 II has been undertaken on only a small-scale basis, perhaps only to provide the Chinese air forces with a type on which to gain experience of operating an advanced fighter pending the availability of still more advanced aircraft.

A variant of the J-8 II proposed for the export market but not placed into production for lack of orders was the **F-8 II** with changes that would have included the uprated powerplant of two 15,432-lb st (68.65-kN) WP-13B engines for a maximum speed of Mach 2.20, a wing revised with leading-edge flaps, an inflight-refuelling probe, a maximum disposable load of 9,921 lb (4500 kg) carried on seven hard-points, and a suite of largely Western digital electronics based on a MIL-1553B databus. China also wanted to procure a similar version as the **J-8 IIM 'Finback-B'** with American avionics, including Westinghouse APG-66 radar, but the programme was terminated by the United States in 1989. China is now considering an equivalent version with Russian avionics and weapons, which first flew in 1996.

ShinMaywa PS-1/SS-2

The **ShinMaywa** (up to 1992 **Shin Meiwa**) **SS-2** family is one of the few modern flying boat series in service anywhere in the world. The first member of the family to enter service with the Japan Maritime Self-Defence Force was the **PS-1**, a capable ASW machine. The origins of the SS-2 can be discovered in the requirement issued in the early 1960s by the JMSDF, and the first of two prototypes made its maiden flight on 16 October 1967. Trials revealed excellent STOL performance largely as a result of the wing's high-lift devices (outboard leading-edge slats and trailing-edge flaps) and a boundary layer control system on the flaps, rudder and elevators powered by a T58 gas turbine in the fuselage.

Production was completed in 1979 with the 23rd machine, and the type was withdrawn from first-line service in 1989. The PS-1 had accommodation for a flight crew of three and a mission crew of seven. The armament comprised up to 4,409 lb (2000 kg) of disposable stores carried in a lower-fuselage weapons bay and on two underwing and two wing-tip hardpoints. The weapons bay could carry four 331-lb (150-kg) depth bombs, the underwing hardpoints could each accommodate two Mk 46 torpedoes, and the wing-tip hardpoints could each accept three 5-in (127-mm) rockets. The PS-1's electronics included APS-80N search radar, HQS-101C dunking sonar, HSQ-10A MAD, 'Julie' active ranging system with 12 charges, AQA-3 'Jezebel' passive detection system with 20 sonobuoys and HLR-1 ECM system.

The **US-1** is the SAR variant of the PS-1 with retractable wheeled landing gear to turn the type into an amphibian. The type has a crew of nine, and its cabin can accommodate three additional crew members as well as 20 survivors, or 12 litters or, in the transport role, 69 passengers. The first example of this **SS-2A** variant flew in October 1974, and production totalled six 'boats before the line switched to the improved **US-1A** standard, to which the US-1s were later raised. The last 12 US-1 'boats were delivered as US-1As, with an uprated powerplant of four 3,493-ehp (2605-kW) T64-IHI-10J engines supplied with fuel from an enlarged internal capacity.

The **US-1A Kai** is the updated version of the US-1A with the powerplant of four 4,400-shp (3355-kW) Rolls-Royce Allison AE2100J turboprop engines driving six-blade propellers, a fly-by-wire control system, improved cockpit avionics, and a pressurised fuselage to permit a higher cruising altitude within the context of a service ceiling increased to 25,000 ft (7620 m) and a range boosted to more than 3,109 miles (5003 km). It is planned that all seven surviving US-1As will be upgraded to the US-1A Kai standard and supplemented by three 'boats built to this standard. The first US-1A Kai should fly in 2003 and enter service in 2005.

SPECIFICATION

ShinMaywa US-1A
Type: six-crew short/medium-range STOL search-and-rescue amphibian flying boat
Powerplant: four Ishikawajima-Harima (General Electric) T64-IHI-10J turboprop engines each rated at 3,493 ehp (2605 ekW) for take-off
Performance: maximum speed 325 mph (522 km/h) at 10,000 ft (3050 m); cruising speed 265 mph (426 km/h) at optimum altitude; initial climb rate 2,340 ft (713 m) per minute; service ceiling 28,400 ft (8655 m); range 2,372 miles (3817 km)
Weights: empty 56,218 lb (25500 kg); maximum take-off 94,797 lb (43000 kg) from water or 99,206 lb (45000 kg) from land
Dimensions: wingspan 108 ft 9 in (33.15 m); length 109 ft 9¼ in (33.46 m); height 32 ft 7¾ in (9.95 m); wing area 1,462.00 sq ft (135.82 m²)
Payload: up to 20 seated survivors or 12 litters

Operated by the 71st Koku-tai at Iwakuni since 1976, the US-1 can cover a vast area of the Pacific using sea-borne refuelling bases.

Short S.5, S. 12 and S. 19 Singapore I, II and III

SPECIFICATION

Short Singapore III
Type: six-seat general reconnaissance flying-boat
Powerplant: four 560-hp (418-kW) Rolls-Royce Kestrel VIII/IX V-12 piston engines
Performance: maximum speed 145 mph (233 km/h); service ceiling 15,000 ft (4570 m); range 1,000 miles (1609 km)
Weights: empty 18,420 lb (8355 kg); maximum take-off 27,500 lb (12474 kg)
Dimensions: wingspan 90 ft (27.43 m); length 76 ft (23.16 m); height 23 ft 7 in (7.19 m); wing area 1,834 sq ft (170.38 m²)
Armament: three 0.303-in (7.7-mm) Lewis guns, plus up to 2,000 lb (907 kg) of bombs

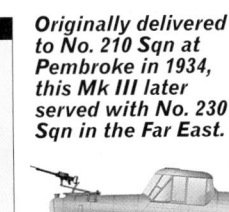

Originally delivered to No. 210 Sqn at Pembroke in 1934, this Mk III later served with No. 230 Sqn in the Far East.

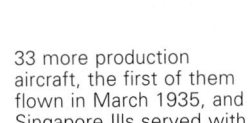

Short Brothers had great hopes for the **S.5 Singapore I** prototype, but its primary claim to fame is that it was used by Alan Cobham for his 23,000-mile (37015-km) survey flight around the African continent. The **S.12 Singapore II** of 1930 was no more successful, but the **S.19 Singapore III** submitted to Air Ministry Specification R.3/33 was rewarded with an order for four development aircraft, the first flown during July 1934. Successful testing led to the construction of 33 more production aircraft, the first of them flown in March 1935, and Singapore IIIs served with Nos 203, 205, 209, 210 and 230 Squadrons, RAF; 19 of these aircraft remained in service at the outbreak of World War II, continuing in service until replaced by the Sunderland.

Short S.8 Calcutta and S.8/8 Rangoon

In 1926 Imperial Airways ordered two **S.8 Calcutta** three-engined biplane flying-boats to be powered by 540-hp (403-kW) Bristol Jupiter XI radials. The design of the Calcutta, which accommodated 15 passengers, was based closely on the military

G-EBVH, the second Calcutta, operated a daily service between Liverpool and Belfast in 1928, and was later used for flights to Jersey.

Singapore I, and when these aircraft were delivered to Imperial Airways in the late summer of 1928,

they were the first stressed-skin metal-hull flying boats to enter commercial service.

Production for Imperial totalled five, and Short Brothers built one other for the French government. A manufacturing licence was negotiated with Breguet, this company developing from the Calcutta the very similar Breguet 521 Bizerte.

Short saw the possibility of a military Calcutta in Air Ministry Specification R.18/29, which required a

flying-boat for use by No. 203 Sqn at Basra, and eventually built six aircraft which were named **S.8/8 Rangoon**, the last of them handed over in September 1934. Operated by a crew of five, the Rangoon could carry up to 1,000 lb (454 kg) of bombs beneath the wings, and had a single Lewis gun mounted in the nose compartment and one on each side of the fuselage behind the wings. All six aircraft survived, to be flown home in August 1935 when replaced by Singapore IIIs, and one civilianised for Imperial Airways

was used as a crew trainer for several years.

Short Brothers made one further development of the basic Calcutta design for the Imperial Japanese Navy, which required a long-range flying-boat to be licence-built in Japan by Kawanishi, and powered by Rolls-Royce Buzzard engines which were also licence-built. Short Brothers completed the prototype **S.15 K.F.1** at Rochester, and following trials it went by sea to Japan where it was launched in March 1931. Kawanishi built four under the designation **H3K**.

Short S.17 Kent and L.17 Scylla

Because of political problems on its route to Cairo, Imperial Airways contracted Short Brothers to build three four-engine flying-boats which would have ample range, good capacity for high-revenue airmail and excellent accommodation for 15 passengers; selected powerplant was the 555-hp (414-kW) Bristol Jupiter XFBM. Designated **S.17 Kent**, the first of these 'boats entered service in May 1931, the others soon

afterwards, and the aircraft were kept hard at work, each flying in excess of 4,000 miles (6437 km) per week. One was lost in August 1936 when it made a heavy landing and sank, another was an arson victim at Brindisi in November 1935, but the third survived only to be scrapped in June 1938.

A landplane version of the Kent was requested by Imperial Airways in early 1933; the resulting two

With a cabin width of 11 ft (3.4 m), the L.17 offered a new dimension in comfortable travel, enhanced by a fresh-air ventilation system.

L.17 aircraft flown in March and May 1934 were later named **Scylla** and **Syrinx**. Powered by four 595-hp (444-kW) XFBM engines, the airliners had accommodation for 39 passengers and were fitted with autopilots. One was used later to

test Perseus IIL engines, until it suffered gale damage, and in the subsequent rebuild 660-hp

(492-kW) Pegasus XC engines were installed. Both aircraft were withdrawn in 1940.

Short S.20 and S.21 Mayo Composite

Carefully-conducted tests had proved that an Imperial Airways' Empire flying-boat could achieve a transatlantic crossing only if its

entire payload consisted of fuel. Since it is well known that an aircraft can be flown at a much greater weight than that at which it

can take off from the ground, Robert Mayo proposed that a small heavily loaded mailplane be carried to operational altitude above a larger motherplane and then released to complete its long-range task. The proposal was accepted by the Air Ministry and Imperial Airways, which jointly contracted Shorts to design and build such a

composite unit. The **S.21 Maia**, the lower component, was a slightly enlarged and modified version of the Empire 'boat; the **S.20 Mercury**, the upper long-range unit, was a new high-wing twin-float seaplane with four 340-hp (254-kW) Napier Rapier H engines giving a cruising range of 3,800 miles (6116 km) with 1,000 lb (454 kg) of mail.

The first airborne separation took place on 6 February 1938, and after a number of experimental flights, *Mercury* was air-launched over Foynes on

21 July to fly nonstop the 2,930 miles (4715 km) to Montreal in 20 hours 20 minutes with a 600-lb (272kg) payload. On 6 October 1938 *Mercury* was launched over Dundee to establish an as yet unbroken nonstop international seaplane distance record of 5,997.5 miles (9652 km) to the Orange River, South Africa. However, the outbreak of war ended experimentation, and *Mercury* was eventually broken up at Rochester and *Maia* destroyed by enemy action during May 1941.

When launched for its record flight to Montreal on 21 July 1938, Mercury had a gross weight of 20,800 lb (9435 kg).

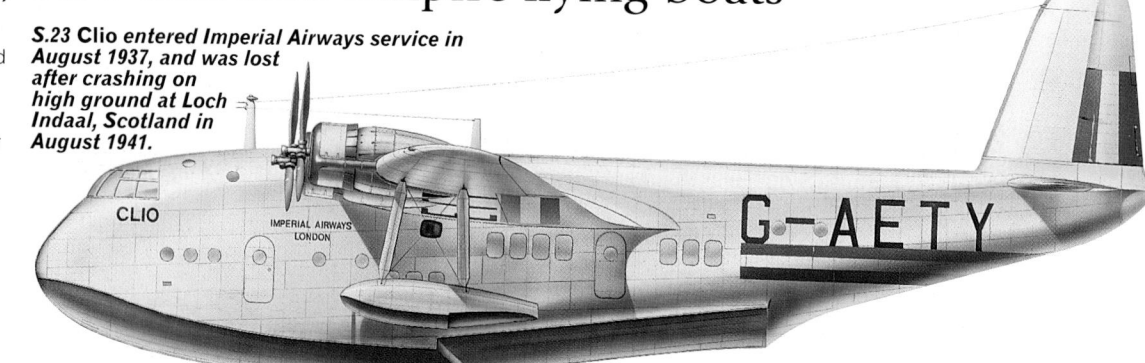

Short S.23, S.30 and S.33 Empire flying-boats

By comparison with the Short company's large and cumbersome biplane flying-boats, the **S.23** of 1936 showed a complete change of style. With four 920-hp (686-kW) Bristol Pegasus XC radial engines, a high-set cantilever monoplane wing, a streamlined hull, and of all-metal construction, the S.23 had a maximum speed of 200 mph (322 km/h), which was 26 mph (42 km/h) faster than the RAF's contemporary Bristol Bulldog biplane fighter. Such was its promise that Imperial

S.23 Clio entered Imperial Airways service in August 1937, and was lost after crashing on high ground at Loch Indaal, Scotland in August 1941.

Airways placed an order for 28.

Airmail had again taken a

hand in aircraft procurement when the British government announced

that all first-class mail to the Empire would be carried by air, and these

machines were to become known also as **Empire** or **'C'-class** flying-boats.

Short S.23, S.30 and S.33 Empire flying-boats (cont.)

The first S.23 (*Canopus*) flew from Rochester in July 1936, entering service at the beginning of Sepember, and as further aircraft beame available at the rate of about one aircraft every two weeks, they joined the fleet. Operating from the new Imperial Airways flying-boat base at Hythe they were used on services to Australia, Bermuda, Durban, Egypt, Malaya, New York, and East and South Africa.

Original accommodation was for 3,000 lb (1361 kg) of mail and 24 passengers by day or 16 by night, but an increase of 1,000 lb (454 kg) in mail load reduced the passenger capacity to 17. Transatlantic trials made between July and September 1937 without payload, proved the S.23 could not carry an economic payload over the distance, leading to the Short-Mayo Composite, and trials were also conducted with inflight-refuelling using the Armstrong Whitworth 23 as a tanker. The success of this latter system secured a contract for Sir Alan Cobham's company, Flight Refuelling Ltd, which used four Handley Page Harrow tankers to achieve 16 successful flight-refuelled transatlantic crossings before the outbreak of war stopped further development. S.30 aircraft powered by 890-hp (664-kW) Bristol Perseus XIIC engines and with more than double the range of the S.23 were used for the transatlantic trials; the last variant was the S.33 with 920-hp (686-kW) Bristol Pegasus XCs. Total production of the Empire flying-boats reached 42, of which 31 were S.23s, nine S.30s and two S.33s, construction of a third S.33 being abandoned.

Several S.23s were impressed for RAF service (two of them being modified to S.23M standard with ASV radar and an armament of two four-gun turrets and six depth charges), and a total of 13 Empire 'boats survived the war, by then with 1,010-hp (753-kW) Bristol Pegasus engines; the last, in service with QANTAS, was retired in 1947. Short also constructed three S.26 'boats ordered by Imperial Airways for nonstop transatlantic mail services. Larger than the 'C' class and with 1,380-hp (1029-kW) Bristol Hercules engines, the first (*Golden Hind*) was launched in June 1939. Known as the 'G'-class, all were impressed for reconnaissance use; one was lost through engine failure but in 1942 the other two were returned to the airline, by then renamed BOAC. One was destroyed in a fatal crash at Lisbon in 1943, and the other survived until it sank during a gale in May 1954.

SPECIFICATION	
Short S.23	(1223 km)
Type: passenger/mail flying-boat	**Weights:** empty 23,500 lb (10659 kg); maximum take-off 40,500 lb (18370 kg)
Powerplant: four 920-hp (686-kW) Bristol Pegasus XC radial piston engines	
	Dimensions: wingpan 114 ft (34.75 m); length 88 ft (26.82 m); height 31 ft 9¾ in (9.70 m); wing area 1,500.0 sq ft (139.35 m²)
Performance: maximum speed 200 mph (322 km/h); service ceiling 20,000 ft (6095 m); range 760 miles	

Short S.25 Sunderland, civil conversions and Solent

To meet an Air Ministry requirement for a military general-reconnaissance flying-boat, Short Brothers developed the **S.25** design which was ordered into production as the **Sunderland Mk I** and the prototype, flown on 16 October 1937, was the first British flying-boat to have power-operated gun turrets. A total of 90 Sunderland Mk Is was built, 15 of them by the Blackburn Aircraft Company, all powered by four 1,010-hp (753-kW) Bristol Pegasus XXII engines and armed with two 0.303-in (7.7-mm) Vickers 'K' guns in beam positions, two 0.303-in (7.7-mm) Brownings in the nose turret and four similar weapons in the tail turret. They were followed from August 1941 by 43 **Sunderland Mk II** aircraft built by Short Brothers (38) and Blackburn (5); they differed by having 1,065-hp (794-kW) Pegasus XVIII engines and a power-operated dorsal turret in place of the beam guns. Most extensively built was the **Sunderland Mk III**, to a total of 456, 170 being produced by Blackburn and the remainder by Short Brothers. These had the same powerplant as the Sunderland Mk II, hull revisions, and were equipped with Air-to-Surface Vessel (ASV) Mk II radar; ASV radar had also been installed retrospectively on earlier versions. A more powerful and heavily armed **Sunderland Mk IV** was developed for use in the Pacific theatre, but the two prototypes were very different from the standard aircraft and became renamed **Seaford**. Final production version was the **Sunderland Mk V**, introduced in March 1944, and built to a total of 150 by Short (90) and Blackburn (60). It introduced more powerful Pratt & Whitney Twin Wasp radial engines and the ASV.Mk IVC radar that equipped late production Sunderland Mk IIIs.

The first operational squadron was No. 230, fully equipped with Sunderland Mk Is by December 1938, and in addition to those used by the RAF, the type was operated by the Royal Australian, Royal Canadian and Royal New Zealand air forces. No. 330 Sqn formed at Oban in February 1943 was a Norwegian-manned unit and No. 343 Sqn, which formed at Dakar in November 1943 was manned by former members of the Aéronavale Flotille 7E.

After the end of World War II the RAF's Sunderland force was soon run down and by the beginning of the Berlin Airlift, in June 1948, only Nos 201 and 230 Sqns and No. 235 Operational Conversion Unit were available to participate. All British-based Sunderland operations ended in early 1957, but in the Far East the type remained in service until 1959.

In March 1943 BOAC began to operate the first of a fleet of Sunderland Mk III flying-boats converted for the civilian transport role. They proved to be a success and in the two years that followed, a total of 24 were used by the airline on gradually extending routes that eventually reached as far as Rangoon after VJ-Day. The RNZAF also received four

The Sunderland Mk V had a revised armament consisting of four 0.303-in (7.7-mm) Brownings in the nose and tail turrets and two 0.5-in (12.7-mm) beam guns. The Mk V remained the RAF's standard flying-boat until its retirement in May 1959.

converted Sunderlands towards the end of 1944.

Lack of long-range transport aircraft in the UK after the war led BOAC to refurbish its fleet to something more approaching airline standards, the resulting version being known as the **Hythe**. A more aesthetically attractive conversion, with the nose and tail turret positions concealed by streamlined fairings, was known as the **Sandringham**, the first appearing in November 1945 with Pegasus engines; subsequent conversions had 1,200-hp (895-kW) Pratt & Whitney Twin Wasp R-1830-92 engines and maximum passenger capacity was

Sunderland Mk III G-AGJM was the first of the type to be converted by BOAC to full airliner standard after the war, and was given the name Hythe.

SPECIFICATION	
Short Sunderland Mk V	(16738 kg); maximum take-off 65,000 lb (29484 kg)
Type: maritime reconnaissance/bomber flying-boat	
Powerplant: four 1,200-hp (895kW) Pratt & Whitney R-1830-90B Twin Wasp radial piston engines	**Dimensions:** wingspan 112 ft 9½ in (34.38 m); length 85 ft 3½ in (26.00 m); height 34 ft 6 in (10.52 m); wing area 1,687 sq ft (156.72 m²)
Performance: maximum speed 213 mph (343 km/h) at 5,000 ft (1525 m); service ceiling 17,900 ft (5455 m); range 2,690 miles (4329 km) with a 1,668-lb (757-kg) bomb load	**Armament:** 10 (four fixed, two in bow turret and four in tail turret) 0.303-in (7.7-mm) and two 0.5-in (12.7-mm) machine-guns, plus up to 4,960 lb (2250 kg) of bombs, depth charges or mines
Weights: empty 36,900 lb	

45 on two decks. Around 30 Sandringhams of various types were converted, serving not only with BOAC but in Argentina, Australia, New Zealand, Norway and Uruguay. The straight Sunderland conversions also served in a number of

countries and several of both types have survived.

Following evaluation of a Seaford in 1946, and the cancellation of RAF orders for the type, BOAC received 12 civil versions under the designation **Solent 2**. These had a

crew of seven and carried 34 day passengers on two decks in luxury accommodation that included a dining saloon, cocktail bar and promenade. They proved to be popular and BOAC leased the six RAF Seafords which had been

declared surplus, and had them converted to 39-passenger **Solent 3** configuration. Four new Solents built for Tasman Empire Airways were 44 seaters with a 3,000 mile (4828 km) range.

When BOAC ended

flying-boat operations in November 1950, its Solent fleet was dispersed to various operators including Aquila Airways, and these aircraft lingered on for some years. Two survive, one in Auckland and the other in California.

Short S.29 Stirling

On 19 September 1938 the **S.31** research aircraft, powered by four 90-hp (67-kW) Pobjoy Niagara engines, was flown for the first time. It was in fact a half-scale version of the **S.29 Stirling** that had been designed to meet Air Ministry Specification B.12/36 for a seven/eightcrew heavy bomber. The Stirling prototype, first flown on 14 May 1939, was powered by four 1,375-hp (1025-kW) Bristol

Hercules II engines, but the first production Stirling which flew on 7 May 1940 had 1,595-hp (1189-kW) Hercules XIs. Initial deliveries began in August 1940 and the Stirling was used operationally for the first time on the night of 10/11 February 1941, when three aircraft of No. 7 Sqn attacked oil storage tanks at Rotterdam. The Stirling was thus the RAF's first four-engine monoplane bomber into service, the

first to be used operationally in World War II, and also the first to be withdrawn from the bomber role after a final operational sortie on 8 September 1944. This occurred when there were adequate supplies of the Lancaster and Halifax bombers for Bomber Command requirements, for the Stirling had an inadequate operational ceiling and could not carry the larger high-explosive bombs that had been introduced by that time. Total production of bomber versions then amounted to 1,759 comprising the **Stirling Mk I** (712) and **Stirling Mk III** (1,047) aircraft; the designation Stirling Mk II was allocated to a planned production version to be built in Canada with Wright Cyclone R-2600s, but this was cancelled.

From early 1944 the

Stirling's primary role changed to that of glider tug and transport. For the former role two Stirling Mk IIIs were converted as prototypes, losing their nose and dorsal gun turrets, retaining the tail turret and gaining glider towing equipment to become designated **Stirling Mk IV**. They proved efficient in this new role, towing one General Aircraft Hamilcar or two Airspeed Horsas for assault and up to five General Aircraft Hotspurs on a ferry flight or for training. They took part in the D-Day operations in Normandy, in the airborne operations at Arnhem and the March

1945 crossing of the Rhine. Production of the Stirling IV totalled 450, being followed by the **Stirling Mk V** transport (150 built) for RAF Transport Command. This was configured to carry 40 troops, or 20 fully equipped paratroops, or 12 stretchers and 14 seated casualties, and could be used also for loads such as two jeeps with trailers, or a jeep with a field gun, trailer and ammunition. Mk Vs were the last Stirlings in service, being gradually replaced by the Avro York with the last of them withdrawn from use during 1946. During 1947 Airtech Ltd converted 12 Stirling Mk Vs for use by a Belgian civil operator.

Short Stirling Is of No. 15 Sqn took part in trials of Trinity, a rudimentary form of what was later to become the Oboe blind-bombing system.

Short S.A.1/2 Sturgeon 1, 2, 3 and S.B.3

The **Sturgeon** was designed as a torpedo-bomber/reconnaissance aircraft for use on the Royal Navy's new aircraft-carriers and, when submitted to the Admiralty, gained a contract for three prototypes. However, the torpedo carrying requirement was soon cancelled and when construction of the carriers was suspended at the end of World War II, the Sturgeon's intended role no longer existed.

A decision was taken to convert it as a high-speed target tug against a new specification, Q.1/46,

although the first two aircraft were **S.A.1 Sturgeon S.Mk 1** gunnery trainers with provision for armament. The third became the **S.A.2 Sturgeon TT.Mk 2** prototype, which resulted in an order for 23 production aircraft. An interesting feature was the provision of counter-rotating propellers on the two 1,660-hp (1238-kW) Rolls-Royce Merlin 140 engines; the small-diameter propellers allowed close inboard mounting of the engines which gave a compact form when the wings were folded. The

Sturgeon TT.Mk 2 TS475 was one of five converted in 1953 to TT.Mk 3 standard, with the nose station and folding wing deleted.

Sturgeon had a maximum speed of 370 mph (595 km/h) and could tow a 32 ft (9.75 m) winged target to an altitude of 32,900 ft (10030 m). Some were later converted to **Sturgeon TT.Mk 3** standard and used from shore establishments, mostly in Malta.

In a bid to make the Sturgeon suitable for

anti-submarine work, the 24th (last) airframe was modified to become the **S.B.3**. A deep nose was added, housing a radar scanner and two operators, and it was powered by two

1,475-shp (1100-kW) Armstrong Siddeley Mamba turboprops. Flown in August 1950 it was not a success and the requirement was met by the Fairey Gannet AEW.Mk 3.

Short SC.5 Belfast

When, after World War II, there was virtually no market for flying-boats,

Short attempted to get a foothold in the utility transport field with its **SC.5/10**

large military transport on which design work began in February 1959. The machine was of high-wing monoplane configuration, with a circular-section pressurised fuselage.

HeavyLift Cargo Airlines Ltd. acquired three Belfasts in March 1980, although the company's fleet of the type has since been reduced to two.

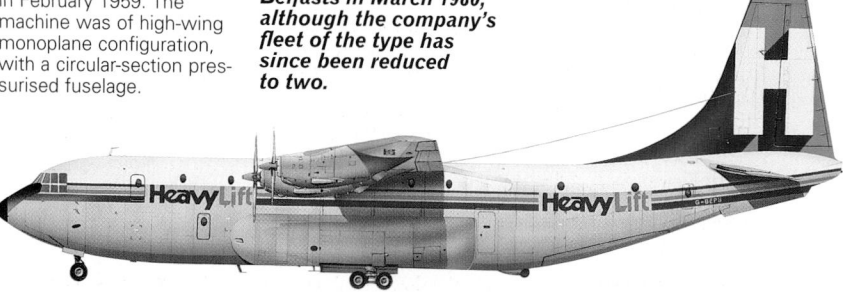

Short SC.5 Belfast (continued)

The SC.5/10's cargo hold provided a usable volume of 11,000 cu ft (311.49 m³). This aircraft became the RAF's **Belfast C.Mk 1**, able to carry the largest guided missiles, guns and vehicles of the British army and RAF, and converted to carry 150 to 250 troops. The first was flown on 5 January 1964, but with no civil interest in the type, only 10 were built for the RAF. The first Belfast entered service with No. 53 Sqn on 20 January 1966; it was then the largest aircraft to have served with the RAF at the time.

When the RAF's long-range heavy transport commitment ended in the late 1970s the Belfasts were offered for sale on the commercial market. After several abortive attempts by various companies, five were acquired by the British Carrier TAC HeavyLift (now HeavyLift Cargo Airlines). Three were converted for commercial use, with two held in reserve, and these have proved to be most effective, not least during the Falklands campaign. Two Belfasts remained in service with HeavyLift in summer 2001.

Shorts SC.7 Skyvan/Skyliner

Design of the **SC.7 Skyvan** began as a private venture in 1959, the **Skyvan Series 1** prototype flying for the first time on 17 January 1963. Features of the design were a high aspect ratio wing derived from Hurel-Dubois aircraft and a square-section maximum-volume fuselage, constructed from lightweight double-skin panels, with the undersurface of the rear fuselage formed by a hinged loading door. As first flown the Skyvan was powered by two wing-mounted 390-hp (291-kW) Continental GTSIO-520 piston engines, but it had been intended that it would be powered by Turboméca turboprops; as the **Skyvan Series 1A** it was flown with this powerplant, namely two 520-eshp (388-ekW) Astazou II engines, in May 1963. The first production **Skyvan Series 2** aircraft, with 730-eshp (544-ekW) Astazou XII turboprops, was flown initially on 29 October 1965, and the **Skyvan Series 3**, which superseded the Series 2 in 1968, is powered by Garrett TPE331 turboprops. The **Skyvan Series 3A** introduced in September 1970 was certificated for operation at a higher gross weight.

In a passenger configuration the Skyvan accommodates 19 passengers, as does the deluxe all-passenger version introduced in 1970 as the **Skyliner**. Other production versions included the **Skyvan 3M** military version of the Series 3, and the **Skyvan Series 3M-200** operating at a higher gross weight.

SPECIFICATION	
Shorts Skyvan Series 3	(1117 km)
Type: light utility transport	**Weights:** empty operating 7,344 lb
Powerplant: two 715-shp (533-kW) Garrett TPE331-201 turboprops	(3331 kg); maximum take-off 12,500 lb (5670 kg)
Performance: maximum cruising speed 202 mph (325 km/h) at 10,000 ft (3050 m); service ceiling 22,500 ft (6860 m); maximum range with fuel reserves 694 miles	**Dimensions:** wingspan 64 ft 11 in (19.79 m); length 40 ft 1 in (12.22 m); height 15 ft 1 in (4.60 m); wing area 373.0 sq ft (34.65 m²)

In 1990-91, the Ghana Air Force Skyvans were completely refurbished in the UK in order to prolong their service.

Shorts 330 and 360

The **Shorts 330** is an 18/30-seat commuterliner and feederliner. It first flew as the **SD.3-30** on 22 August 1974 after development as what was, in effect, an enlarged version of the SC.7 Skyvan with a rectangular-section fuselage, tricycle landing gear with a fully retractable nosewheel unit and semi-retractable main wheel units, a high-aspect ratio wing set at the top of the fuselage and braced to the main landing gear sponsons by one aerofoil-section strut on each side, and a tail unit with twin endplate vertical surfaces. The first 26 aircraft had 1,156-shp (862-kW) PT6A-45A turboprops, the next 40 had PT6A-45Bs, and the last 70 had PT6A-45Rs. The type was certificated in February 1976 and entered service in August of the same year as the **Shorts 330-100**, the standard switching to the **Shorts 330-200** during January 1985. This was in recognition of an increase in fuel capacity.

The **Shorts 330-UTT (Utility Tactical Transport)** is essentially a stripped-out 330-200 with a strengthened floor (to carry a payload of 8,000 lb/3629 kg made up of freight, or 33 troops, or 30 paratroops, or 15 litters plus four attendants) and two inward-opening doors in the rear fuselage. The US Army operates six standard Shorts 330s for range-support duties.

The **C-23A Sherpa** is the US Air Force's logistic support version of the 330-UTT. The type has the same basic hold with the standard port-side forward freight door supplemented by a hydraulically operated full-width rear ramp/door to allow the straight-in/-out loading and unloading of bulky items such as packaged aero engines. The hold has a reinforced floor fitted with a roller conveyor system. The type first flew in August 1984 and all 18 aircraft had been delivered by December 1985 to meet the USAF's European Distribution System Aircraft requirement for a type able to undertake the rapid delivery of urgently needed items from USAF maintenance and distribution centres in Europe to front-line air bases, returning with damaged equipment. After 1990 the USAF retained only four of the aircraft as 'hacks' and training aircraft. Of the other 14 aircraft, eight were transferred to the US Forestry Service and the other six to the Air National Guard.

The 16 **C-23B Sherpa** aircraft were delivered to the US Army National Guard from September 1990 and supplemented by six C-23As. The C-23B is slightly different from the C-23A in details such as its maximum payload and powerplant of two 1,424-shp (1061-kW) T101-CP-100 (PT6A-45AR) engines. It is distinguishable from the C-23A by the fact that its has windows in the sides of the hold.

First flown on 1 June 1981 for service from December 1982, the **Shorts 360** was basically a development of the 330 with an uprated powerplant for operation at higher weights with better performance. The production programme lasted until 1991 and saw the completion of 164 aircraft, whose most obvious external difference from the 330 was the slightly lengthened fuselage carrying a tail unit with a single swept vertical surface. Two extra seat rows boosted passenger capacity to 36.

The 360 was initially delivered with 1,173-shp (875-kW) PT6A-65 turboprops engines that were replaced by 1,424-shp (1,063-kW) PT6A-65AR engines in 1986 to create the **Shorts 360 Advanced**, and then by identically rated PT6A-67AR engines driving six-bladed propellers to create the **Shorts 360-300** with a number of features to enhance passenger comfort.

The **C-23B+** was a version of the 360 for limited service with the US ANG, 20 such aircraft being produced from 1994 as conversions with new avionics and the twin-finned tail unit of the 330.

Shorts 330 D-CDLT was delivered to DLT in February 1977, the German airline giving the aircraft the name Münsterland.

SPECIFICATION	
Shorts C-23A Sherpa	5,000-lb (2268-kg) payload
Type: two/three-crew short-range logistic and utility light transport	**Weights;** empty 14,727 lb (6680 kg); maximum take-off 25,500 lb (11566 kg)
Powerplant: two Pratt & Whitney Canada T101-CP-100 (PT6A-45R) turboprop engines each rated at 1,198 shp (893 kW)	**Dimensions:** wingspan 74 ft 8 in (22.76 m); length 58 ft ½ in (17.69 m); height 16 ft 3 in (4.95 m); wing area 453.00 sq ft (42.08 m²)
Performance: maximum cruising speed 218 mph (352 km/h) at 10,000 ft (3050 m); initial climb rate 1,180 ft (360 m) per minute; service ceiling 20,000 ft (6095 m); range 770 miles (1239 km) with a	**Payload:** up to 30 troops, or 27 paratroops plus one jumpmaster, or 15 litters plus three attendants, or 7,100 lb (3221 kg) of freight

Shorts 360-100 G-LEGS was first flown on 23 February 1984, and delivered to Manx Airlines two weeks later.

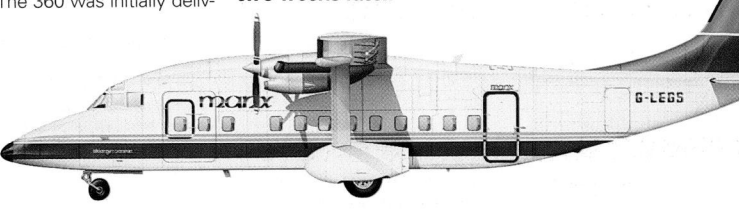

Shorts S.312 Tucano

In 1985 the RAF selected the Tucano as its new ab initio trainer following an international competition that had involved the Pilatus PC-9, the Hunting Turbo-Firecracker and the AAC/Westland A 20. Based on an original design by EMBRAER, the turboprop-powered Tucano offered by Shorts promised economy and a performance not far short of that of the Jet Provost T.Mk 5, the main type it would replace in RAF service. As the first tandem-seat non-jet trainer to be ordered for the RAF since the Chipmunk, the Tucano reflected a trend back to a more 'traditional' seating arrangement for pupil and instructor.

Considerable modification was undertaken to tailor the basic airframe to British requirements, including substituting a Garrett turboprop in place of the original Pratt & Whitney PT6A – which significantly improved the rate of climb – and reprofil-ing the cockpit to provide commonality with the BAe Hawk. EMBRAER flew a Garrett-engined prototype in Brazil in February 1986 and delivered this to Shorts in Belfast as a pattern aircraft, the first **Tucano T.Mk 1** making its maiden flight on 30 December that year. The total RAF production order covered 130 aircraft, the first delivery to the Central Flying School at Scampton taking place in June 1988. The balance of the RAF order was completed in 1993.

By opting to train embryonic fast-jet pilots on a turboprop aircraft, the RAF gained considerably. Economically a better proposition than a jet type, the Tucano is less demanding from the viewpoint of student pilots in the earliest stages of flight training. To extend the Tucano's capability in both military training and counter-insurgency roles, Shorts conducted a series of Tucano weapon trials in the spring of 1991 using twin FNNH machine-gun pods, the FNNH heavy MG and rocket launcher and the LAIJ32 seven-round rocket launcher, plus bombs up to 551 lb (250 kg). Customers for the armed export Tucano have been Kuwait (**Tucano T.Mk 52**), which took delivery of the last of 16 aircraft in 1991 (though they remained in the UK pending reformation of the KAF and formation of their operating unit, No. 19 Sqn), and Kenya (**Tucano T.Mk 51**), which received the last of an order for 12 in June 1991.

The Tucano superseded the Jet Provost in the basic trainer role in 1993, and operates mainly with 1 FTS at Linton-on-Ouse. An all-black colour-scheme began replacing the red-and-white in the mid-1990s.

SPECIFICATION

Shorts Tucano T.Mk 1
Type: ab-initio military trainer
Powerplant: one Garrett TPE331-12B turboprop rated at 1,100 shp (820 kW)
Performance: maximum level speed 'clean' and maximum cruising speed at 10,000 ft (3050 m) 319 mph (513 km/h); maximum rate of climb at sea level 3,270 ft (997 m) per minute; service ceiling 34,000 ft (10365 m); range 1,099 miles (1767 km) with internal fuel
Weights: basic empty 4,872 lb (2210 kg); maximum take-off 6,470 lb (2935 kg)
Dimensions: wingspan 37 ft (11.28 m); length 32 ft 4¼ in (9.86 m); height 11 ft 1¾ in (3.40 m); wing area 208.00 sq ft (19.33 m²)

SIAI-Marchetti S.205 and S.208

The prototype **S.205** made its initial flight on 4 May 1965 and soon afterwards was displayed at the Paris Salon de l'Aéronautique. A four-seat cabin monoplane tourer of cantilever low-wing configuration, it had tricycle landing gear which, optionally, could be retractable or fixed, the latter with strut fairings and wheel spats. It was intended to be powered by engines in the 180-hp (134-kW) to 300-hp (224-kW) range, but the favoured powerplant was the Franklin 6A-350C1 flat-six engine. The need for increased power and capacity led to the **S.208**, the prototype of which was flown on 22 May 1967. This had retractable landing gear, a more powerful 260-hp (194-kW) Avco O-540-E4A5 engine and provision for a fifth seat in the cabin.

Production of all versions of the S.205 and S.208 numbered nearly 400 in four years, the total including 44 **S.205M** aircraft delivered to the Aeronautica Militare Italiana for liaison and training duties. This variant differs from the civil S.208 in that the starboard-located cabin door can be jettisoned in an emergency and there is also a second door in the port side of the fuselage; full blind-flying and navigation systems are standard on service aircraft. Both civil and military S.208s have two auxiliary wingtip tanks, and maximum speed of this version is 199 mph (320 km/h).

The S.205 was a successful four-seat monoplane, later developed into the S.208. I-SIAK was the prototype.

SPECIFICATION

SIAI-Marchetti S.205
Type: four-seat cabin monoplane
Powerplant: one 220-hp (164-kW) Franklin 6A-350C1 flat-six piston engine
Performance: maximum speed 183 mph (295 km/h); service ceiling 20,340 ft (6200 m); range 823 miles (1325 km)
Weights: empty equipped 1,653 lb (750 kg); maximum take-off 2,976 lb (1350 kg)
Dimensions: wingspan 35 ft 7½ in (10.86 m); length 26 ft 3 in (8.00 m); height 9 ft 5¾ in (2.89 m); wing area 173.20 sq ft (16.09 m²)

SIAI-Marchetti S.211

Developed as a private-venture basic jet trainer, the **S.211** also has a light attack capability, bestowed by four underwing hardpoints for a total combined load of 1,455 lb (660 kg). First flown on 10 April 1981, it has been adopted by four air forces: Haiti, Singapore, Brunei, and the Philippines, with aircraft for the last-mentioned assembled locally by PADC (Philippines Aerospace Development Corporation). Similarly, Singapore Aerospace was responsible for local assembly of 24 of an initial batch of 30 aircraft for advanced flying training. The Royal Brunei armed forces air wing, purchased four The Haitian air corps ordered a similar number but has now disposed of its S.211s. A version of the S.211 with an improved nav/attack system has been planned, as has one with an uprated JT15D engine and increased fuel capacity.

SPECIFICATION

SIAI-Marchetti S.211
Type: military jet trainer
Powerplant: one Pratt & Whitney JT15D-4C rated at 2,500 lb st (11.12 kN)
Performance: maximum cruising speed at 25,000 ft (7620 m) 414 mph (667 km/h); maximum rate of climb at sea level 4,200 ft (1280 m) per minute; service ceiling 40,000 ft (12190 m); combat radius 345 miles (556 km) on a hi-lo-hi attack mission with four rocket launchers
Weights: empty equipped 4,078 lb (1850 kg); maximum take-off 6,944 lb (3150 kg) as an attack warplane
Dimensions: wingspan 27 ft 8 in (8.43 m); length 30 ft 6½ in (9.31 m): height 12 ft 5½ in (3.80 m); wing area 135.63 sq ft (12.60 m²)
Armament: up to 1,455 lb (390 kg) of disposable stores

The Grumman-backed S.211 was unsuccessful in its bid to gain JPATS orders, but several countries bought the original type, including the Haitian air corps.

SIAI-Marchetti SF.260/TP

Designed by Stello Frati, the three-seat **SF.260** was put into production by SIAI-Marchetti after prototypes had been built and flown by Aviamilano (as the **F.250** and **F.260**). The SF.260 was soon marketed in military guise as the **SF.260M** and **SF.260W**, the latter named **Warrior** and having a strengthened airframe and underwing hardpoints for the ground attack role. Production has totalled well over 650, including dedicated variants for the civil market (**SF.260A**, **B**, **C** and **D**). The SF.260M was first flown on 10 October 1970.

SIAI-Marchetti SF.260/TP (cont.)

The export SF.260 found numerous African customers. The Zambian Air Force continues to operate SF.260MWs for training and light attack.

The SF.260M is equipped to provide basic and instrument flying. First flown in May 1972, the SF.260W has two or four pylons, and is suitable for light COIN duty

and armament training. A turboprop version of the SF.260M/W, the **TP** model, first flew in July 1980, the prototype being a converted airframe. Apart from changes ahead of the firewall to accommodate

the Allison 250-B17D turboprop, differences from the piston-engined version

were limited to the fuel feed system and a changed rudder trim tab.

SPECIFICATION
SIAI-Marchetti SF.260W Warrior

Type: three-seat trainer and light attack aircraft
Powerplant: one Textron Lycoming 0-540-E4A5 flat-six piston engine rated at 260 hp (194 kW)
Performance: maximum level speed 'clean' at sea level 190 mph (305 km/h); maximum rate of climb at sea level 1,250 ft (381 m) per minute; service ceiling 14,700 ft (4480 m); combat radius 345 miles (556 km) on a single-seat hi-lo-hi attack mission
Weights: empty equipped 1,830 lb (830 kg); maximum take-off 2,866 lb (1300 kg)
Dimensions: wingspan 27 ft 4¾ in (8.35 m) over tip tanks; length 23 ft 3½ in (7.10 m); height 7 ft 11 in (2.41 m); wing area 108.72 sq ft (10.10 m²)
Armament: maximum ordnance 661 lb (300 kg)

Siemens-Schuckert D types

SPECIFICATION
Siemens-Shuckert D.III

Type: single-seat interceptor
Powerplant: one 160-hp (119-kW) Siemens-Halske Sh.III or IIIa rotary piston engine
Performance: maximum speed 112 mph (180 km/h); service ceiling 26,245 ft (8000 m); endurance 2 hours
Weights: empty 1,177 lb (534 kg); maximum take-off 1,598 lb (725 kg)
Dimensions: wingspan 27 ft 7¾ in (8.43 m); length 18 ft 8¼ in (6.70 m); height 9 ft 2¼ in (2.80 m); wing area 203.44 sq ft (18.90 m²)
Armament: two fixed forward-firing 0.31-in (7.92-mm) LMG 08/15 machine-guns

The D.III was built by a branch of the Siemens electrical firm, which also developed airships and 'Grossflugzeuge' (Giant aircraft) bombers.

Before World War I Siemens-Schuckert Werke had toyed with the development of aircraft, but it was not until the large-scale demand for aircraft which resulted from the outbreak of war that serious design and manufacturing efforts were started. In the single-seat fighter category, the D.I of 1916 was based closely on the Nieuport XI, and was of biplane configuration and powered by the 110-hp (82-kW) Siemens-Halske Sh.I rotary engine. Satisfactory testing led to an order for 150, of which only 95 were delivered as completed aircraft, for by mid-1917 the performance of this fighter had been overtaken by new Allied aircraft. A single **D.Ia** devel-

opment with greater wing area and a more powerful engine was flown but did not enter production.
Continued development via **D.II** prototypes led to the **D.III** of which initial examples were ordered in late 1917. A neat equal-span biplane powered by a 160-hp (1 19-kW) Sh.III rotary engine, the D.III suffered early problems from unreliability of this powerplant. However, as teething problems were overcome the exceptional rate of climb of the D.III

singled it out for use as an interceptor but, unfortunately, its level speed was below that of contemporary fighters. Several D.III prototypes were built to achieve aerodynamic improvement cating in the basically similar **D.IV** production version which did not become operational until August 1918, and which was some 7 mph (11 km/h) faster than the D.III and had a

better rate of climb. A total of 280 D.IVs were ordered but less than half had been delivered by the end of the war. Other D types under development at the war's end included the **D.V**, which derived from the D.II/III/IV family, and the **D.VI** parasol-wing monoplane of which one prototype had demonstrated a maximum speed of 137 mph (221 km/h).

Sikorsky S-51 (VS-300, HO2S, R-4, R-5 and R-6)

Igor Sikorsky became interested in the design and construction of helicopters during the first decade of the 20th century, building his first rotary-wing aircraft in 1909. Powered by a 25-hp (18-kW) Anzani engine, this failed to lift itself from the ground but his second machine, built in 1910, was just able to claw its way into the air if it did not have to carry a pilot. Sikorsky realised he then had insufficient knowledge to solve the problems and gain success, turning instead to the design and construction of fixed-wing aircraft. It was not until 1939, when engineering manager of Vought-Sikorsky in the USA, that Sikorsky began construction of a new helicopter. It, too, was unsuccessful at first, but his introduction of an anti-torque rotor overcame the last major control problem, following months of trials with various auxiliary rotors fitted to the **VS-300** prototype which had made its first tethered flight on 14 September 1939. By the spring of 1941 the US government had given Vought-Sikorsky

a contract for the development of the **VS-316A** two-seat version as the **XR-4**, which had a fabric-covered fuselage and was powered by a 165-hp (123-kW) Warner R-500 engine; it made its first flight on 14 January 1942. Thirty pre-production **YR-4** helicopters were ordered, comprising three **YR-4A** and 27 **YR-4B** aircraft; all were powered by the more powerful R-550 of 180 hp (134 kW) which drove an enlarged rotor. Uprated 200-hp (149-kW) R-550-3 engines were fitted in the main production batch of 100 **R-4B** helicopters. The US Navy received its first helicopter in 1942, a YR-4B on loan from the USAAF and designated **HNS-1**; 24 HNS-1s were later flown by US Navy and US Coast Guard units, the latter operating in the air-sea rescue role. Royal Air Force and Fleet Air Arm units set up in 1945 to evaluate helicopters for service use flew seven YR-4Bs and 45 R-4Bs as the **Hoverfly Mk I**.
The R-4's rotor and transmission system was installed in a new stream-

lined fuselage with an all-metal semi-monocoque tail boom to become the **VS-316B** or **XR-6**, powered by a 225-hp (168-kW) Avco Lycoming O-435 engine. Some 193 production helicopters were built for the USAAF as the **R-6A**, the US Navy as the **HO2S-1** and the British as the **Hoverfly Mk II**.
Concurrently, Sikorsky had been working on a completely new helicopter, the **VS-337** tandem two-seater with a 48-ft (14.63-m) diameter rotor and powered by a 450-hp (336-kW) Pratt & Whitney R-985-AN-5 radial. The first of these, designated **XR-5**, flew at Bridgeport on 18 August 1943, and the total subsequent production of 64 machines included four more XR-5s, 26 **YR-5A** helicopters and 34 **R-5A** helicopters, the last with litter carriers on each side of the fuselage

The RCAF used the H-5 in the SAR role from 1947. The H-5 was primarily acquired to provide the service with experience in rotorcraft operations.

and used by the Air Rescue Service. The 21 **R-5D** helicopters modified from R-5A airframes had nosewheel landing gear, a rescue hoist and an external auxiliary fuel tank, while five YR-5As with dual controls were redesignated **YR-5E**. The four-seat civil **S-51** was first flown on 16 February 1946 and initial deliveries were made in August. Los Angeles Airways opened

the first scheduled helicopter mail service on 1 October 1947, and 379 S-51s were built. Westland also built the S-51 under licence in the UK as the Westland Dragonfly.

Sikorsky S-55 (HO4S and H-19 Chicksaw)

In 1948 Sikorsky received a contract for five **S-55** utility helicopters for USAF evaluation under the designation **YH-19**. The first of these, powered by a 550-hp (410-kW) Pratt & Whitney R-1340-57 mounted in the nose to drive the main rotor gearbox through a long extension shaft, flew on 10 November 1949. The 600-hp (447-kW) version of the R-1340-57 powered 50 production **H-19A** helicopters, while the 700-hp (522-kW) Wright R-1300-3 replaced it in 270 **H-19B** helicopters, many of which were fitted with rescue hoists and designated

SH-19. The US Navy placed its first order on 28 April 1950, for 10 **HO4S-1** machines (similar to the H-19A), which were followed by 61 **HO4S-3** aircraft based on the H-19B; the **HO4S-3G** was a US Coast Guard rescue version. Initial troop and assault transport versions were designated **HRS-1** and **HRS-2**, similar to the HO4S-1, 151 of which were delivered from April 1952. Some 84 **HRS-3** helicopters with R-1300-3 engines were also built. The US Army's 72 H-19C and 338 **H-19D** helicopters, known as the **Chickasaw**,

In Danish service, the H-19 was provided with high-visibility bands and a side-mounted winch for coastal SAR operations. The USCG took 30 examples of the HO4S-3G SAR variant.

were equivalent to the H-19A and H-19B respectively. Licence production was undertaken by SNCA du Sud Est in France and by Westland in the UK, the latter developing versions with the Alvis Leonides Major piston engine and with the Bristol Siddeley Gnome turboshaft under the family name Whirlwind.

Sikorsky S-56 (H-37 Mojave and HR2S)

Developed to meet a US Marine Corps requirement for a large assault helicopter to carry 26 troops or military vehicles, for which clamshell nose-opening doors were provided, the **S-56** was the first Sikorsky twin-engined helicopter. Two 1,900-hp (1417-kW) Pratt & Whitney R-2800-50 Double Wasp engines (2,100-hp/1566-kW R-2800-54s on late production aircraft) were mounted on stub wings, and the nacelles also housed the

main legs of the retractable landing gear, the first application of this feature in a production helicopter. The prototype **XHR2S-1** flew on 18 December 1953 and 60 production machines were delivered from July 1956. Two **HR2S-1W** helicopters were converted for US Navy early warning operations with AN/APS-20E radar under the nose. US Army evaluation of an HR2S-1, under the designation **YH-37**, resulted in orders for 94 **H-37A**

A Pathfinder guides an HR2S into a landing site, marked by white panels, during a Second Marine Division exercise in Puerto Rico in 1961.

Mojave helicopters which went into service, initially with 4th Medium Helicopter Transportation Company, in February 1958. Modernised H-37As redesignated **H-37B** (later **CH-37B**), were redelivered to the US Army from June 1961.

Sikorsky S-58 (Seabat, Seahorse & Choctaw)

Designed to overcome the range and offensive payload deficiencies of the anti-submarine HO4S version of the S-55, the **S-58** was developed to a US Navy order for a prototype **XHSS-1**, placed on 30 June 1952. The nose

engine position was retained for the 1,525-hp (1137-kW) Wright R-1820 engine, but a completely new fuselage, four-bladed main and tail rotors, and transmission system were introduced, together with main rotor and rear fuse-

lage folding to facilitate shipboard stowage. The prototype flew on 8 March 1954, followed by the first production **HSS-1 Seabat** (later **SH-34G**) on 20 September, and the type began to reach anti-submarine squadrons in August 1955. The **HSS-1N** (**SH-34J**) was developed for night operations, equipped with Doppler for navigation, automatic stabilisation and automatic hover coupler, while a single **HSS-1F** (**SH-34H**) flown on 30 January 1957, was powered by two General Electric T58 turboshafts. In 1960 five **HSS-1Z**

As the IDF/AF's standard utility helicopter, the S-58 was utilised in pursuit of the PLO along the border with Jordan in 1967.

(**VH-34D**) helicopters joined the Executive Flight Detachment for Presidential and VIP transport duties. Seabats stripped of ASW equipment for utility duties were designated **UH-34G** and **UH-34J**.

The US Marine Corps ordered the **HUS-1 Seahorse** (**UH-34D**) version on 15 October 1954; able to carry 12 marines this variant entered service in February 1957. Four **HUS-1L** (**LH-34D**) helicopters were modified for operation in the Arctic, while inflatable flotation gear identified the US Marines' **HUS-1A** (**UH-34E**) and the US Coast Guard's **HUS-1G** (**HH-34F**). The US Army ordered several hundred **H-34A**, **H-34B** and **H-34C Choctaw** helicopters powered by

1,425-hp (1063kW) R-1820-84 engines and each carrying 16 troops or eight stretchers in the medevac role, the first unit being equipped in September 1955. The type was exported widely and built under licence in France and the UK, the turbine-powered Westland product known as the Wessex. In April 1971 Sikorsky received FAA approval for the **S-58T** PT6A Twin Pac-powered turbine conversion for H-34 airframes.

Small numbers were also built of **S-58B** and **S-58D** civil passenger and cargo transport helicopters, a 12-seat airline version being operated in small numbers by Chicago Helicopter Airways, New York Airways and Sabena. When produc was terminated in January 1970 Sikorsky had built a total 1,820 S-58s of all versions.

Sikorsky S-60 Skycrane and S-64 (H-54 Tarhe)

Sikorsky's first 'flying crane' helicopter was the **S-60**, developed from the S-56 and retaining that machine's powerplant, transmission and rotor system. Work began in May 1958 and the prototype was flown on

25 March 1959; it was capable of lifting a 12,000-lb (5443kg) payload beneath the fuselage boom, and the co-pilot could turn his seat to face aft to control loading and unloading. The S-60 crashed in April 1961, but

by then Sikorsky had begun construction of an enlarged version, with a six-bladed main rotor driven by two 4,050-shp (3020-kW) JFTD-12A turboshafts. Designated **S-64**, the prototype flew on 9 May 1962

and was followed by two further machines for evaluation by the Federal German armed forces. This did not result in German orders, but the US Army placed an order for six **S-64A** helicopters in June 1963, under

the designation **CH-54A Tarhe**. This version was powered by 4,500-shp (3356-kW) Pratt & Whitney T73-P-1 engines, and production eventually totalled approximately 60; 10 **CH-54B** helicopters were built with 4,800-shp (3579-kW) T73-P-700 turboshaft engines.

Sikorsky S-60 Skycrane and S-64 (H-54 Tarhe) (cont.)

SPECIFICATION

Sikorsky CH-54B Tarhe
Type: crane helicopter
Powerplant: two 4,800-shp (3579-kW) Pratt & Whitney T73-700 turboshafts
Performance: cruising speed 105 mph (169 km/h); range with maximum fuel and 10 per cent reserve 230 miles (370 km)
Weights: empty about 19,800 lb (8981 kg); maximum take-off 47,000 lb (21318 kg)

Dimensions: main rotor diameter 72 ft (21.95 m); fuselage length 70 ft 3 in (21.41 m); height 18 ft (5.67 m); main rotor disc area 4,070 sq ft (378.1 m²)
Accomodation: can lift a normal load of 20,000 lb (9072 kg); standard Universal Military pod is a box 27 ft 5 in (8.36 m) long, 8 ft 10 in (2.69 m) wide and 6 ft 6 in (1.98 m) high

The Tarhe served in a heavy-lift role in Vietnam, with the 478th and the 291st Aviation Companies. Despite only 97 YCH-54As, CH-54As and CH-54Bs being built for the US Army between 1964 and 1972, the Tarhe's unique capability to straddle large or outsized loads ensured a long and productive service career.

Sikorsky S-61 (H-3 Sea King)

US Navy experience with the H-34 Seabat highlighted the shortcomings of operating hunter/killer pairs of helicopters in the anti-submarine role, so in 1957 Sikorsky was awarded a contract to combine the two functions in a single airframe. The **S-61** prototype, designated **YHSS-2**, made its first flight on 11 March 1959. Production helicopters were known as **HSS-2** machines until 1962, when the type was redesignated as the **SH-2A**, the first production variant of the **H-3 Sea King** series. The new helicopter featured two 1,250-shp (932-kW) T58-GE-8/8B turboshaft engines above the main cabin to drive a dynamic system with a five-bladed main rotor. The rugged fuselage had a two-man cockpit, a cabin with two sensor operators and their ASW equipment, a boat hull for amphibious operations and outrigger floats which also housed

the retractable main units of the tricycle landing gear. As a 'hunter', the **SH-3A** helicopters primary sensors were the AQS-10 dipping sonar and APN-130 search radar, while in the 'killer' role the helicopter carried a pair of torpedoes or depth charges.

Some 245 SH-3As were built, followed by a prototype and 73 production examples of the **SH-3D** with 1,400-shp (1044-kW) T58-GE-10 engines, AQS-13A sonar and APN-182 radar. Some 103 SH-3A and two SH-3D machines were converted as **SH-3G** general-purpose rescue platforms and transports by removing the ASW equipment and installing 15 canvas seats and long-range fuel tanks. A decision to retire the US Navy's dedicated ASW carriers in the early 1970s dictated the next version, the **SH-3H**. This had to perform not only the inner-zone ASW mission, but also

plane-guard, surface-surveillance and surface-targeting missions. Some 116 earlier machines were converted to the new standard with AQS-13B sonar, LN-66HP radar and ASQ-81 MAD using a towed 'bird' housed in the starboard landing gear sponson.

The **UH-3A** and **VH-3A** are utility and VIP transport conversions of the SH-3A, and a few remain in service in 2001 together with limited numbers of the SH-3H. The **HH-3A** was a SAR conversion. The US Marine Corps continues to operate the **VH-3D** presidential transport.

Sikorsky also licensed Sea King production to several companies. The Agusta-built Italian variants include the **ASH-3D** version of the SH-3D, **ASH-3D/TS (Trasporto Speziale)** VIP transport, **AS-61A-4** export version of the ASH-3D/TS, ASH-3H version of the SH-3H, and **AS-61R** SAR helicopter basically equivalent to the **HH-3F Pelican** of which Sikorsky built 40 for the US Coast Guard. In Japan Mitsubishi built the S-61 for the Japan Maritime Self-Defence Force, producing 55 **HSS-2** (SH-3A), 29 **HSS-2A** (SH-3D) and 83 **HSS-2B** (SH-3H) helicopters. Sikorsky-built **S-61A**, **S-61A-1** and **S-61AH** helicopters served

Canada's plan to replace its CH-124 helipcopter fleet is 10 years behind schedule, and thus the type continues in service operating in its primary role of defensive ASW.

with the JMSDF for SAR duties. United Aircraft of Canada assembled 37 **CHSS-2** helicopters after the supply of four US-built aircraft for the Canadian forces: most were later upgraded to **CH-124A** standard. Further export orders were received from Argentina (five **S-61D-4** helicopters similar to the SH-3D, supplemented by **ASH-3H** machines), Brazil (six SH-3D helicopters) and

Denmark (nine **S-61A-5** helicopters for the long-range SAR role). Malaysia purchased 40 **S-61A-4 Nuri** transports for the air force. The US Navy transferred 18 SH-3A/D/G helicopters to Spain's naval air arm: eight of these were upgraded to SH-3H standard for ASW work, while three SH-3D helicopters were converted under a 1984 contract with Searchwater radar to perform the AEW role.

The main Italian air force SAR unit is 15° Stormo, which flies the Agusta-Sikorsky HH-3F in the long-range CSAR and overwater SAR role.

SPECIFICATION

Sikorsky S-61 (SH-3H Sea King)
Type: two/four-crew shipborne and land-based anti-submarine and general-purpose medium helicopter
Powerplant: two General Electric T58-GE-10 turboshafts each rated at 1,400 shp (1044 kW)
Performance: maximum level speed 'clean' at optimum altitude 166 mph (267 km/h); maximum rate of climb at sea level 2,200 ft (670 m) per minute; service ceiling 14,700 ft (4480 m); hovering ceiling 10,500 ft (3200 m) in ground effect

and 8,200 ft (2500 m) out of ground effect; range 625 miles (1005 km)
Weights: empty 12,350 lb (5601 kg); maximum take-off 21,000 lb (9526 kg)
Dimensions: main rotor diameter 62 ft (18.90 m); length 72 ft 8 in (22.15 m) with the rotors turning; height 16 ft 10 in (5.13 m) with the rotors turning; main rotor disc area 3,019.07 sq ft (280.47 m²)
Armament up to 840 lb (381 kg) of disposable stores

Sikorsky S-62 (H-52)

The amphibious **S-62** was derived from the piston-engined S-55 and used that helicopter's main and tail rotor system and other components mounted in a new sealed hull. The prototype S-62 flew on 22 May 1958 and was followed by the **S-62A** production

version which, powered by a single General Electric CT58-110-1 turboshaft engine, provided accommodation for up to 11 passengers. One **S-62B** was built with an S-58 main rotor system. The **S-62C** was chosen by the United States Coast Guard as a

replacement for the HH-34 rescue helicopter and initial deliveries, under the designation **HH-52A**, were made in January 1963. The HH-52A was powered by a 1,250-hp (932-kW) CT58-GE-8 engine.

Seen during Antarctic operations, this HH-52 crashed on Mt Erebus after engine failure.

Sikorsky S-65 and S-80 (H-53)

The **S-65** was designed to meet a long-standing US Marine Corps requirement for a heavy-lift troop transport helicopter to replace the CH-37 Mojave.

When it became clear that the ambitious Vought-Hiller-Ryan XC-142A would not produce a satisfactory VTOL assault platform in the near-term, the USMC turned its attentions back to conventional helicopters. To replace the medium lift UH-34 the USMC selected the Boeing Vertol HRB-1 (CH-46A) in preference to Sikorsky's HR3S-1 (an SH-3 derivative with a stretched fuselage and a rear loading ramp, retaining SH-3 type undercarriage sponsons and a tailwheel). This carried 27 troops, and formed the basis of the **CH-3** and **HH-3 Jolly Green Giant** SAR versions of the Sea King, which would in turn influence the **S-65**.

A formal HH(X) requirement for a ship-based heavy-lift helicopter was issued in 1962. This called for a helicopter with an 8,000-lb (3629-kg) payload, a 100-nm (115 mile; 185-km) radius and a speed of 150 kts (173 miles; 278 km/h), able to carry loads including a 1.5 ton truck and trailer, a Hawk SAM battery or an Honest John tactical SSM. Boeing Vertol offered a derivative of its HC-1A (soon to become the CH-47 Chinook), while Kaman offered a derivative of the British Fairey Rotodyne. Sikorsky offered the S-65, which combined the transmission of the S-64 Tarhe flying crane with the six-bladed main rotor and tail rotor of the CH-37 and a scaled-up version of the CH-3 airframe, with a similar configuration, watertight hull, rear loading ramp and side-mounted sponsons.

The original twin-engined S-65 spawned transport, SAR, mine-sweeping and Special Operations versions, as well as a series of three-engined **S-80** versions. Relatively large numbers of both types remain in front-line service today. Current variants have been upgraded throughout their service lives, the **MH-53M Pave Low IV** first delivered to the 16th SOW in spring 1999, being an example.

The US Navy's two dedicated mine-countermeasures squadrons, HM-15 and HM-14, both operate the MH-53E Sea Dragon.

Sikorsky S-65 and S-80 variants

S-65 YCH-53A: two prototypes, first flying on 14 October 1964
CH-53A Sea Stallion: production assault transport with added armour, intake particle separators, defensive armament and (from 1968) uprated T64-GE-12 or -16 engines; 139 built
RH-53A Sea Stallion: production minesweeper for US Navy, with provision for towed sled; 15 produced by conversion of CH-53A, most of which had hardpoints for towing gear
TH-53A: small number of stripped CH-53As used by USAF for aircrew training
HH-53B Super Jolly: eight USAF combat SAR versions of CH-53A with inflight refuelling probe and provision for two 650-US gal (2461-litre) fuel tanks on braced pylons; initially with T64-GE-3 engines
CH-53C Super Jolly: 20 aircraft similar to HH-53B (but without probe, and with T64-GE-7 engines, and with unbraced pylons for smaller 450-US gal (1703-litre) external tanks) used by the USAF for airlift, and training; some later converted to HH-53H and MH-53J
HH-53C Super Jolly: 44 combat SAR aircraft based on the CH-53C with inflight refuelling probe restored
S-65Ö (S-65C-2): two aircraft for Austria, similar to CH-53C; later sold to Israel
S-65C-3: 33 aircraft for Israel, similar to USAF CH-53C
CH-53D Sea Stallion: improved assault transport for USMC with uprated transmission allowing installation of T64-GE-412 or -413 engines; 124 built for USMC
RH-53D Sea Stallion: up-engined new production mine-sweeper with T64-GE-413A (later -415) engines, sponson-mounted 500-US gal (1893-litre) fuel tanks, AFCS, beefed-up external load hook, rescue hoist and inflight refuelling probe; 30 built for USN, six more for Iran
VH-53D: two VIP aircraft to similar standards to CH-53D
CH-53G: two US-built aircraft and 110 locally-assembled for German air force. Broadly equivalent to CH-53D, but

with no provision for inflight refuelling probe or sponson-mounted fuel tanks. No particle separators on intakes
YHH-53H: single HH-53B modified as prototype for Pave Low II system for night/all-weather Combat SAR
HH-53H Super Jolly: eight HH-53Cs and two attrition replacement CH-53Cs upgraded to **Pave Low III** standards and fitted with inflight refuelling probe for Combat SAR
MH-53H: surviving HH-53H re-designated after Constant Green equipment upgrade, reflecting changed role and assignment to 1st SOW
MH-53J: eight surviving MH-53Hs, plus 31 HH-53B, CH-53C and MH-53C modified to **Pave Low III Enhanced** standards, with strengthened transmission, and extra armour. All surviving front-line machines have been upgraded to **MH-53M Pave Low IV** standard
S-80 YCH-53E Super Stallion: first three-engined version, with extra engine mounted on the centreline, behind the rotor head, with the intake and exhaust to port. New seven-bladed main rotor with increased diameter and chord, stretched fuselage, enlarged tailplane mounted lower on both sides of the tailfin, increased internal fuel capacity and provision for two 650-US gal (2461-litre) tanks. Two prototypes built
CH-53E Super Stallion: production three-engined variant. Revised tail unit with fin canted to port and single large, braced tailplane high mounted on starboard side. Dual digital AFCS. 177 built for USMC and USN
YMH-53E Sea Dragon: three-engined mine-sweeping prototype
MH-53E Sea Dragon: production three-engined mine-sweeper with huge sponsons containing sufficient fuel for four hours 'on-station' 30 minutes from base, and with provision for AAR (probe seldom fitted) and additional MCM gear. 56 built for US Navy
VH-53F: unbuilt Presidential transport based on CH-53E. Six ordered but cancelled
S-80M-1 Sea Dragon: export derivative of MH-53E for JMSDF. Eleven built

SPECIFICATION

Sikorsky S-65 (MH-53J Pave Low III Enhanced)
Type: Special Operations all-weather helicopter
Powerplant: two General Electric T64-GE-7A turboshafts each rated at 3,936 shp (2935 kW)
Performance: maximum level speed 'clean' at sea level 196 mph (315 km/h); maximum rate of climb at sea level 2,070 ft (631 m) per minute; service ceiling 20,400 ft (6220 m); hovering ceiling 11,700 ft (3565 m) in ground effect and 6,500 ft (1980 m) out of ground effect; range 540 miles (868 km)
Weights: empty 23,569 lb (10691 kg); mission take-off 38,238 lb (17344 kg);
Dimensions: main rotor diameter 72 ft 3 in (22.02 m); fuselage length 67 ft 2 in (20.47 m) excluding IFR probe; height overall 24 ft 11 in (7.60 m) and to top of rotor head 17 ft 1.5 in (5.22 m); main rotor disc area 201.06 sq ft (18.68 m²)
Payload: internal fuel 630 US gal (2384 litres); external fuel up to two 450-US gal (1703-litre) drop tanks; maximum payload 20,000 lb (9072 kg)

This USAF 21st SOS MH-53J Pave Low III, based at RAF Woodbridge, was used to ferry Special Forces troops into Northern Iraq in order to police the safe haven set up by the Allies for Kurdish refugees.

Sikorsky S-70 (H-60)

The **S-70** family resulted from Sikorsky's attempts to produce a replacement for the Bell UH-1 – a requirement first stated in 1965 and formalised in 1972's UTTAS (Utility Tactical Transport Aircraft System) requirement. This called for a helicopter with the same capacity as the UH-1, but with better crashworthiness and performance. The S-70 won the competition (strongly contested by Boeing with the YUH-61) and was ordered into production as the **UH-60A Black Hawk** in 1976, for service entry in 1979. The basic **UH-60** spawned a range of variants for Special Forces support, VIP transport, electronic warfare, and combat SAR, and also provided the basis of the **SH-60** which won the US Navy's LAMPS III (Light Airborne Multi-Purpose System) competition for a frigate/destroyer-based ASW aircraft. This in turn spawned carrier-borne inner zone ASW defence and SAR variants. The S-70 remains in large-scale production in 2001 and has been widely exported.

Sikorsky S-70 (H-60) (continued)

Sikorsky S-70 variants

S-70A YUH-60A: three prototypes used in UTTAS evaluation. Initially with swept dihedral tail
S-70A UH-60A: initial production version for US Army. Detail changes from prototypes
S-70A UH-60L: basic utility transport version which followed UH-60A on the production line. More powerful engines, uprated transmission, HIRSS exhaust suppressors
S-70A UH-60J: Mitsubishi-built utility/SAR version for JASDF and JMSDF. 66 built
S-70A UH-60JA: Mitsubishi-built utility version for JGSDF. 80 required
S-70 UH-60P: 80 UH-60s for South Korea, first three Sikorsky built, rest assembled by Korean Airlines
S-70 UH-60Q: Medevac ('Dustoff') version based on UH-60L with glass cockpit, FLIR, improved avionics and role equipment
S-70 'Firehawk': prototype fire-fighting version with extended undercarriage, removable Aero Union ventral water tank. Snorkel device for tank refilling from the hover
S-70B CH-60S Knighthawk: carrierborne utility/SAR version intended to replace SH-3, CH/HH-46 and HH-60H. Combines UH-60 airframe with SH-60 engines, rotor, dynamics, automatic blade folding, AFCS, and folding tail rotor pylon. Common glass cockpit with SH-60R. **YCH-60S** prototype produced by marrying components from donor UH-60L and SH-60F. Eventual requirement for 250, 42 currently planned, of which 19 funded
S-70 UH-60A 'ARRS': eleven UH-60As for the USAF's ARRS, one converted to HH-60D. HIRSS, folding tailplanes, NVG compatible cockpit, rescue hoist, wirestrike protection and winterisation kit. Ten subsequently upgraded as Credible Hawks
S-70 UH-60A Credible Hawk: Upgrade to USAF's CSAR UH-60As adding plumbing for ESSS or ETS, cabin fuel tank systems, provision for Miniguns, and an inflight refuelling probe. 19 initial conversions, plus others later. Most subsequently converted to MH-60G standards
S-70 MH-60G Pave Hawk: CSAR variant for USAF, based on UH-60L, but with AAR probe, weather radar, folding tailplanes, NVG cockpit, etc. Produced by conversion of UH-60A and new build. 82 in CSAR role re-designated HH-60G in 1992, leaving 16 in USAF Special Forces support role as MH-60G with **Pave Low III** FLIR, ESS, and armament
S-70 HH-60G: designation retrospectively applied to MH-60Gs used for USAF Combat SAR role, reflecting growing divergence in equipment fit between CSAR and SF support MH-60Gs
S-70A UH-60A (Enhanced): baseline US Army Special Forces support conversion of UH-60A, with new avionics, Miniguns, and fast roping provision. About 40 converted
S-70A MH-60A: 'High End' US Army Special Forces variant, as UH-60 (Enhanced) but also with FLIR, satcoms, extra rescue hoist, and IR jammer
S-70 MH-60K 'Crash Hawk': new build US Army Special Forces support version with FLIR, TF/TA radar mounted centrally on nose, MH-47E type avionics systems and inflight refuelling probe
S-70 MH-60L 'Velcro Hawk': standard US Army UH-60Ls modified for the Special Forces support role with a FLIR and improved defensive systems, replacing UH-60(E) and MH-60A. Later with a nose-mounted weather radar, Kevlar armour and Hellfire ASM capability. Ten aircraft subsequently upgraded with IFR probes
S-70 AH-60L Direct Action Penetrator: MH-60Ls upgraded with expanded offensive capability. Details classified
S-70A VH-60A: Presidential VIP transport with improved durability gearbox, SH-60B AFCS, soundproofing, EMP hardening, weather radar and avionics upgrades
S-70A VH-60N 'White Hawk': designation retrospectively applied to Presidential VIP helicopters
S-70A YEH-60A: prototype battlefield jamming variant converted from UH-60A
S-70A EH-60A: battlefield jamming variant with emitter locators and jammers. Extensive antenna array on sides of tailboom and below tailboom. 65 converted from UH-60A
S-70A YEH-60B: one prototype converted from UH-60A with SOTAS stand-off radar system. Extendable main undercarriage and underfuselage rotating antenna. Planned production cancelled, funding diverted to J-STARS
S-70A EH-60L: improved version with Advanced Quick Fix equipment. Originally 32 to have been produced through conversion of EH-60A, but only eleven funded initially
S-70A UH-60A(C): US Army command and control version. 50 converted from UH-60A
S-70A UH-60C: improved command and control variant flying in prototype form
S-70A-1: utility version for Saudi Arabia
S-70A-1L: Medevac version for Saudi Arabia
S-70A-5: utility version for Philippines
S-70A-6: utility version for Thailand
S-70A-9: utility version for Australian Army
S-70A-11: utility version for Jordan
S-70A-12: utility version for Japan (**UH-60J**)
S-70A-14: utility version for Brunei
S-70A-17: utility version for Turkey
S-70A-18: utility version for Korea (**UH-60P**)
S-70A-20: VIP version for Thailand
S-70A-21: VIP version for Egypt
S-70A-22: VIP version for Korea
S-70A-24: utility version for Mexico
S-70A-25: utility version for unidentified customer
S-70A-26: utility version for Morocco
S-70A-27: three rescue aircraft delivered to RHKAAF/Hong Kong Government Flying Service
S-70A-28: 90 UH-60Ls ordered for Turkey (Jandarma and armed forces), last 45 to be built by TAI but cancelled. Negotiations for 50 more in progress

S-70A-30: one VIP version for Argentina
S-70A-39: one VIP version for Chile
S-70A-50: designation of 15 UH-60Ls for Israel. Locally named **Yanshuf** (Owl).
S-70B YSH-60B Seahawk: five Full Scale Development LAMPS III aircraft, initially designated **S-70L**, later S-70B
S-70B SH-60B Seahawk: production LAMPS III helicopter with undernose radar. 181 built for USN of initial requirement for 260. Remainder cancelled. Most will be converted to SH-60J standards
HS.23: local designation for 12 SH-60Bs for Spain
S-70B XSH-60J Seahawk: two US-built pattern aircraft for SH-60J, also designated **S-70B-3**
S-70B SH-60J Seahawk: Mitsubishi-built ASW aircraft for JMSDF. 88 funded
S-70B-2: sixteen SH-60B/F hybrids for Australia. Second eight were locally built
S-70B-3: two sonar/radar equipped aircraft built as pattern aircraft for SH-60J
S-70B-4 SH-60F Ocean Hawk: carrierborne inner zone ASW helicopter ('CV Helo'). All LAMPS III equipment removed, including radar and RAST, but provided with dipping sonar. 81 built for USN. Most will be converted to SH-60R or HH-60H standards
S-70B-5 HH-60H Rescue Hawk: radarless carrierborne rescue, plane guard, special forces support and Vertrep derivative of SH-60F for USN. 42 built
S-70B-5 HH-60J Jayhawk: Rescue aircraft for USCG with nose-mounted radar, 42 built
S-70B SH-60R Strikehawk: LAMPS Block II, combining radar of SH-60B with sonar of SH-60F. Requirement for conversion of 260 SH-60B, SH-60F and HH-60H to this standard, beginning in 2000, with ISD of 2002
S-70B-6: SH-60B/F hybrid for Greece, with sonar and radar. Seven built
S-70B-7: SH-60F equivalent for Royal Thai Navy. Six built
S-70B-28: Seahawk for Turkey. Four built
S-70C: designation normally reserved for civilian variants of UH-60 Black Hawk
S-70C-2: 24 radar-equipped UH-60s for China, delivery halted by embargo
S-70C (M)-1 Thunderhawk: hybrid Seahawk version for Taiwan with undernose radar and dipping sonar. 21 delivered in two batches
S-70C-6 Super Blue Hawk: Six SAR aircraft for Taiwan with nose-mounted radar and provision for four external fuel tanks on stub wings
S-70C-14: VIP aircraft for Brunei. Two delivered

SPECIFICATION

**Sikorsky S-70B
(SH-60B Seahawk)**

Type: multi-role naval helicopter
Powerplant: two General Electric T700-GE-401 turboshafts each rated at 1,690 shp (1260 kW) or, in helicopters delivered from 1988, two General Electric T700-GE-401C turboshafts each rated at 1,900 shp (1417 kW)
Performance: dash speed at 5,000 ft (1525 m) 145 mph (234 km/h); maximum vertical rate of climb at sea level 700 ft (213 m) per minute; operational radius 57½ miles (92.5o km) for a 3-hour loiter

Weights: empty 13,648 lb (6191 kg) for the ASW mission; mission take-off 20,244 lb (9182 kg) for the ASW mission; maximum take-off 21,884 lb (9926 kg) for the utility mission
Dimensions: main rotor diameter 53 ft 8 in (16.36 m); tail rotor diameter 11 ft (3.35 m) fuselage length 50 ft ¾ in (15.26 m); height overall, rotors turning 17 ft (5.18 m); main rotor disc area 2,262.03 sq ft (210.05 m²)
Payload: maximum payload 8,000 lb (3629 kg)
Armament: two torpedoes or Penguin anti-ship missiles

The Royal Thai Navy Air Division operates its Seahawks from land bases and the carrier HTMS Chakri Naruebet. The helicopters fly ASW and SAR missions and embark with Thailand's Harriers.

For the foreseeable future the Black Hawk will remain the cornerstone of the US Army's air mobile capability. As well as flying basic troop transport missions, the type performs a range of specialised tasks. This UH-60A was photographed as part of the 211th Aviation Group (211 AVNGRP) (Attack), the 1-183th AVN (ATK) of the Idaho Army National Guard. The aircraft was flown alongside OH-58As and AH-64A Apaches.

Sikorsky S-76 Spirit/H-76 Eagle

The concept of Bell's hugely successful JetRanger was developed further by Agusta with its A109 and Bell with its 222. Sikorsky applied the same concept to a rather larger configuration, producing the **S-76** in 1977.

Like the A109 and Bell 222 the S-76 was a very streamlined executive transport with a retractable undercarriage and a well-appointed interior, but unlike the others could comfortably carry up to twelve passengers. The aircraft incorporated many lessons learned from, and much technology proved in the S-70 programme, though the new type was considerably smaller and less powerful.

In addition to the versions built (or converted) by Sikorsky, a number of S-76s have been upgraded by third parties. Keystone offers a re-engining package (using the Arriel 1S1 engine) and an emergency medevac conversion, while Bristow Helicopters and Heli Union in France have also performed their own re-engining programmes.

The S-76's capacious cabin has allowed it to fulfill a number of roles, including offshore oil industry support and a number of military, paramilitary and police/law enforcement tasks. About 500 S-76s have been built, and the type is in widespread service around the world.

Military operators include the Philippines, Chile, Dubai, Guatemala, Honduras, Iraq, Jordan and Spain.

In 2001 the S-76 continued to sell strongly. The aircraft is priced at US$7.7 million in executive trim.

SPECIFICATION

Sikorsky H-76 Eagle
Type: general purpose twin-turbine helicopter
Powerplant: two Pratt & Whitney Canada PT6B-36 turboshafts each rated at 960 shp (716 kW) for take-off and 870 shp (649 kW) for continuous running
Performance: maximum cruising speed 167 mph (269 km/h); maximum climb rate at sea level 1,500 ft (457 m) per minute; hovering ceiling 5,000 ft (1645 m)

out of ground effect; range about 359 miles (578 km)
Weights: basic empty 5,610 lb (2545kg); maximum take-off 11,400 lb (5171 kg)
Dimensions: main rotor diameter 44 ft (13.41 m); length overall, rotors turning 52 ft 6 in (16.00m); fuselage 43 ft 4½ in (13.22m); height overall 14 ft 9¼ in (4.25 m) with tail rotor turning; main rotor disc area 1,520.53 sq ft (141.26 m²)

Variants

S-76A: baseline variant, prototype first flew 13 March 1977. Deliveries from 1979; 284 built
S-76 Mk II: follow-on production version. Deliveries from 1982. Some earlier aircraft converted to this standard. Total included in S-76A figure above
S-76 Utility: utility version of S-76 Mk II with sliding doors, strengthened floors, and with provision for an optional fixed landing gear. Total included in S-76A figure above
S-76A+: variant produced by re-engining unsold S-76 with Turbomeca Arriel 1S engines, plus 17 new-build aircraft to the same standards
S-76B: follow-on production variant with P&W PT6B-36 engines. First flew 22 June 1984, delivered between 1984 and 1997; 101 built
S-76C: new production variant with Turbomeca Arriel 1S1 engines. First flew 18 May 1990; 43 built
S-76C+: current production variant with Arriel 2S1 engines and FADEC
S-76 Shadow: single testbed with new single seat cockpit added in front of existing nose for evaluation of equipment and technology intended for new generation military helicopters, especially LHX
AUH-76: armed military derivative of S-76 Utility with provision for armour, defensive avionics, gun and rocket pods, ATGMs and weapons sighting equipment
H-76 Eagle: baseline military version of the S-76B, with similar features/options to AUH-76
H-76N: proposed naval variant

Sikorsky S-92 Helibus

The **S-92** was originally conceived as an enlarged derivative of the S-70, and was even dubbed 'Growth Hawk' in recognition of this. Launched in 1995, the S-92 programme is led by Sikorsky, but includes participation by a number of risk-sharing overseas partners, including Mitsubishi (who build the main cabin and have a 7.5 per cent stake), AIDC (flight deck – 6.5 per cent), EMBRAER (landing gear, fuel system integration and front halves of sponsons – 4 per cent) and Gamesa (cabin interior, tailboom, aft fuselage and upper fuselage transmission housing – 7 per cent), together with Jingdezhen of China, whose 2 per cent stake gave them responsibility for the vertical tail and horizontal tailplane.

The new aircraft used many systems from (or derived from) those used on the smaller S-70. The aircraft uses a similar digital flight control system and autopilot, together with a four-stage version of the Blackhawk's three stage main gearbox. The main rotor uses a similar titanium yoke infinite life head with elastomeric bearings. The composite main rotor is scaled up from the S-70's, albeit with increased chord and swept tips.

Of broadly similar configuration to the earlier S-65, the S-92 features a high-set braced tailplane offset to port, with a clamshell-type rear ramp below the high-set tailboom. The box-like cabin is flanked by long fairings, and the aircraft has a retractable tricycle under-carriage, with twin Messier-Bugatti wheels on each unit. Unlike the S-65, the new aircraft makes extensive use of composites (about 40 per cent by weight) and has a modular airframe designed to give the lowest possible parts count.

SPECIFICATION

Sikorsky S-92 Helibus
Type: civil multi-purpose twin-engined helicopter
Powerplant: two General Electric CT7-8 turboshafts each rated at 2,400 shp (1790 kW) for take-off or 2,050 shp (1529 kW) for continuous running
Performance: maximum cruising speed 178 mph (287km/h); best range speed 155 mph (250 km/h); range 553 miles (890 km); hovering ceiling in ground effect 11,100 ft

(3385 m) and 6,100 ft (1860m) out of ground effect
Weights: empty 15,500 lb (7031 kg); maximum take-off with internal load 25,200 lb (11430 kg)
Dimensions: main rotor diameter 56 ft 4 in (17.71 m); tail rotor diameter 11 ft (3.35m); length overall rotors turning 68 ft 5 in (20.85 m); height overall rotors turning 21 ft 2 in (6.45 m); maximum width over sponsons 12 ft 9 in (3.89 m)

Sikorsky S-92 Helibus (continued)

The first of four flying S-92 prototypes made its maiden flight on 23 December 1998. The prototype was powered by a pair of 1,750 shp CT7-6D engines, whereas production aircraft are planned to use the more powerful CT7-8, or the Rolls-Royce Turbomeca RTM 322 if required. All aircraft have a crashworthy fuel system, while military S-92s have provision for an inflight refuelling probe.

The basic S-92 was expected to carry 19 passengers or up to three LD-3 cargo containers,

Sikorsky S-92 variants

S-92A: designation originally applied to baseline civil **Helibus** variant, now applies to standard military/civil configuration
S-92IU: intended baseline military **'International Utility'** variant, using same core airframe. Discontinued

while the military version carried 22 fully-equipped troops, making it considerably less capacious than the rival EHI EH 101 (30 passengers, with a galley, toilet and baggage bins) or up to 45 troops. Perhaps with that in mind, Sikorsky revealed studies of a stretched derivative of the

S-92 in late 1999, presumably hoping to erode the EH 101's capacity advantage. Launch customer for the S-92 was Cougar helicopter of Canada, ordering up to five examples for delivery from 2002. Russia's Mil is now associated with the programme.

Competitors to the civil S-92 include the Mil Mi-38 (whose development continues, albeit slowly) and the latest versions of the Super Puma and EH 101.

SOCATA GY 80 Horizon and ST 10 Diplomate

The French company Société de Construction d'Avions de Tourisme at d'Affaires (SOCATA) was formed in 1966, initially as a subsidiary of Sud-Aviation, but subsequent mergers have since made the company a subsidiary of Aérospatiale. SOCATA produced for Sud-Aviation under licence from Yves Gardan a four-seat cantilever low-wing monoplane which was given the designation **GY 80 Horizon**. With semi-

retractable tricycle landing gear, and power provided by a 180-hp (134-kW) Avco Lycoming O-360-A flat four engine, the 31-ft 9¾-in (9.70-m) span Horizon has a maximum speed of 155 mph (250 km/h) at sea level. SOCATA built more than 250 of these aircraft before production ended in 1969, and developed from it an improved four-seat cabin monoplane which was named **Super Horizon 2000** and **Provence** before entering production as the

Six examples of the Diplomate were ordered by VARIG of Brazil in 1970 for use in the airline pilot training role.

ST 10 Diplomate in 1969. This differed from the GY 80 by having a slightly lengthened fuselage, a revised tail unit and landing gear, and the more powerful 200-hp (149-kW) IO-360-C1B flat-four engine. Despite improved performance, with a maximum speed of 174 mph

(280 km/h) at sea level, the Diplomate failed to gain any worthwhile interest and

only 56 had been delivered when production was terminated in 1975.

SOCATA Rallye and Rallye 235 Guerrier

SOCATA's association with light aircraft construction began with a tourer designed by Morane-Saulnier, which had become a subsidiary of Sud-Aviation in 1965, the year before SOCATA's formation. SOCATA began its activities as a subsidiary of Sud-Aviation by building versions of these aircraft, retaining the original **Rallye**

names until 1979. All are basically cantilever low-wing monoplanes with fixed tricycle landing gear and variations in power-plant and accommodation. The old Rallye designations were scrapped in 1979 when a new production programme was initiated in that year, new names then being allocated. The last production aircraft in the

Rallye series, of which SOCATA built approximately 3,300, included the **Galopin** (formerly **Rallye 110ST**) two-seat trainer cleared for spins or three-/four-seater with spins prohibited, which is powered by an 110-hp (82-kW) Avco Lycoming O-235-L2A engine. This model was built under licence in Poland by PZL Warszawa-Okecie as the **L-110 Koliber** (humming bird), in two-/three-seat configuration and powered by a 126-hp (94-kW) PZL licence-built Franklin

In 2000 a single R 235 Guerrier was operated by the Central African Republic's Escadrille Centreafricaine.

4A-235-131 engine. PZL has subsequently developed a range of lightplanes from the basic design, and retains the type in production in 2001. The **Galérien** (**Rallye 180T**) was a special glider-tug or banner-towing version with a 180-hp (134-kW) O-360-A3A, but the **Gabier** (**Rallye 235GT**) differs by being a high-performance version with STOL capability which has

a strengthened airframe and the far more powerful O-540 engine. Variants available included one which has tailwheel instead of tricycle landing gear, and the **R 235 Guerrier** (warrior) military version of the Gabier. The R 235 differs from the earlier machine by having underwing pylons for the carriage of weapons such as rockets and machine-gun pods, as well as practice bombs, flares and a reconnaissance pack.

SPECIFICATION	
SOCATA Gabier	range with maximum fuel
Type: four-seat cabin monoplane	677 miles (1090 km)
Powerplant: one 235-hp (175-kW) Avco Lycoming O-540-B4B5 flat-six piston engine	**Weights:** empty 1,530 lb (694 kg); maximum take-off 2,646 lb (1200 kg)
Performance: maximum speed 171 mph (275 km/h) at sea level; service ceiling 14,765 ft (4500 m);	**Dimensions:** wingspan 31 ft 11¾ in (9.75 m); length 23 ft 9½ in (7.25 m); height 9 ft 2½ in (2.80 m)

SOCATA TB 9 Tampico, TB 10/TB 11 Tobago and TB 20/TB 200 Trinidad

Early in 1975 SOCATA initiated the design of a four-/five-seat cabin monoplane which it designated **TB 10** and later named **Tobago**. First flown on 23 February 1977, and powered by a 160-hp (119-kW) Avco Lycoming

O-320-D2A engine, this TB 10 became the founder member of a new series of lightplanes of cantilever low-wing layout with an essentially all-metal structure and fixed tricycle landing gear. A second prototype followed with a

180-hp (134-kW) Avco Lycoming O-360-A1AD engine; the decision to produce both versions resulted in the lower-powered aircraft being regarded as a four-seater and being redesignated **TB 9 Tampico**. The third of

SPECIFICATION	
SOCATA TB 20 Trinidad	(1785 km)
Type: four/five-seat lightplane	**Weights:** empty 1,702 lb (772 kg); maximum take-off 2,943 lb (1335 kg)
Powerplant: one 250-hp (186-kW) Avco Lycoming IO-540-C4DS5D flat-six piston engine	**Dimensions:** wingspan 32 ft ¼ in (9.76 m); length 25 ft 3¼ in (7.71 m); height 9 ft 4½ in (2.85 m); wing area 128.09 sq ft (1190 m²)
Performance: maximum speed 193 mph (310 km/h); service ceiling 20,000 ft (6095 m); maximum range with maximum fuel 1,109 miles	

the series was flown for the first time on 14 November 1980 and this, the **TB 20 Trinidad**, differs by having retractable tricycle landing gear and a more powerful engine, plus minor airframe changes related to these installations and the increased power. The prototype of an addition to the series was exhibited at the 1983 Paris air show and this, basically similar to the TB 10 and intended for acrobatic flight

at training centres for professional pilots, differs mainly by having a Christen inverted flight system for the powerplant. Designated **TB 11**, initial production examples became available in 1984, though the name was never really applied to what was, in effect, a TB 10 with a 180-hp (134-kW) engine. Other proposed, but unbuilt, members of the family included the **TB 15** and **TB 16** which were, respec-

tively, Tobagos and Trinidads fitted with a new Porsche PFM.3200 engine. The family has sold well not least in the US, starved of modern indigenous light-planes by its product liability laws. A new addition was made in March 1991, with the first flight of the **TB 200 Tobago XL**.

The Tobago has been used to provide flying training for French air traffic control officers.

This four-to-five seat aircraft is largely similar to the basic TB 10 but is

powered by a more powerful 200-hp (149-kW) O-230-D2A engine.

SOCATA TBM 700

On 12 June 1987 SOCATA and the Mooney Aircraft Corporation announced their intention to build a six/eight-seat single-engined 'biz-prop'. Mooney had already gone some distance towards developing such an aircraft. At its plant in Columbus, Ohio, Roy LoPresti had designed the Lycoming TIO-540-X27-powered **MX**, known later as the **M.30 Mooney 301**.

A prototype was flown in April 1983 but the project was suspended due to funding difficulties, in favour of the new partnership with SOCATA. The French government agreed to meet one third of the new development costs, with SOCATA having design leadership for the project, including construction and certification of the prototypes. The new aircraft

would be known as the **TBM 700**.

In June 1988 Valmet of Finland joined the project. Three initial aircraft were built, with Mooney having responsibility for the rear fuselage and wings, SOCATA the forward fuselage and Valmet the tail. Final assembly was at SOCATA's Tarbes-Ossun-Lourdes plant. The first aircraft flew on 14 July 1988, the second on 3 August 1989, and the third on 11 October 1989. By this time Valmet had withdrawn from the programme, leaving the two original partners to continue development.

The TBM 700 interior was revised to seat between four and seven passengers. The cockpit was configured for two pilots, though single-pilot

certification was one of the prime development goals. The powerplant is a tried and tested PT6A, with a McCauley four-bladed constant-speed fully-featherable metal propeller fitted. The fin is swept, though the wing is essentially straight.

The flaps were designed by ATR and are constructed from Nomex honeycomb composites. Fuel is carried in integral wing tanks.

French DGAC certification was obtained in January 1990, with FAA FAR Pt 23 approval following in August. The first

customer delivery was made on 21 December 1990, Mooney finally withdrew from the TBM 700 in May 1991 but, to date, SOCATA has retained the aircraft's previous designation. The type is in use with l'Armée de l'Air for liaison.

Other TBM 700 variants available in 2001 included the TBM 700B with a larger cabin access door and the TBM 700C freighter. The TBM 700B has been the subject of an order for three machines from the French army, while a total of 160 TBM 700s of all variants had been delivered by late 2000.

F-WKPG was the second of three prototype TBM 700s, and made its first flight in August 1989.

SPECIFICATION	
SOCATA TBM 700	(2985 km)
Type: four/seven-seat pressurised turboprop transport	**Weights:** empty equipped 4,025 lb (1826 kg); maximum take-off
Powerplant: one 700-shp (552-kW) Pratt & Whitney Canada PT6A-64 turboprop	6,595 lb (2992 kg)
	Dimensions: wingspan 39 ft 10¾ in (12.16 m); height 13 ft 1 in
Performance: maximum cruising speed 345 mph (555 km/h); service ceiling 30,000 ft (9150 m); maximum range 1,855 miles	(3.99 m); length 34 ft 2½ in (10.43 m); wing area 193.75 sq ft (18 m²)

SOKO G-2 and G-3 Galeb and J-1 Jastreb

First flown in May 1961, the **G-2A Galeb** (Seagull) was the first indigenous Yugoslav jet design to enter production. The Galeb is a conventional low-wing monoplane. The wing has strong points for two 220-lb (100-kg) bombs and up to

six 2.24-in (57-mm) rockets. Two 0.5-in (12.7-mm) machine-guns are fitted in the nose. A version of the trainer flew on 19 August 1970 with an uprated Viper 532 engine as the **Galeb 3** or **G-3**, this being in effect the prototype for the two-

seat **TJ-1 Jastreb**. The Galeb entered service with the Yugoslav air force (JRV) in 1965, production of more than 120 being needed to meet the requirements of the Air Academy and the fighter and fighter ground-attack schools. In post-civil war Yugoslavia, Galebs were flying exclusively with the Serbian air force, equipping the 105th Fighter-Bomber Regiment at Kovin. The other major customer was Libya, which received 120 in two batches before production ended in 1985; six others went to Zambia.

The single-seat **J-1 Jastreb** (Hawk) (**J-21** to

the JRV) eventually equipped five wings for ground-attack duties, for which it was armed with three (0.5-in) 12.7-mm machine-guns in the nose and bombs or rocket pods on four wing hardpoints.

Production of the Jastreb totalled 250-300, of which 30 were the **RJ-1** (**IJ-21** to

the JRV) reconnaissance model with wingtip camera pods.

The production total also included 15 (**TJ-21**) two-seat training variants that closely resembled the Galeb basic jet trainer from which the Jastreb was originally developed. The sole export customer was the Zambian air force, which received 20 **J-1E** and **RJ-1E** aircraft in 1971.

The G-2A is the Yugoslav air force's standard trainer, having been in service since 1965.

SPECIFICATION	
SOKO G-2A Galeb	ceiling 39,370 ft (12000 m); ferry range 772 miles (1242 km) with tip tanks
Type: two-seat primary and advanced trainer and light-attack aircraft	
Powerplant: one licence-built Rolls-Royce (Bristol Siddeley) Viper 11 Mk 22-6 turbojet rated at 2,500 lb st (11.12 kN)	**Weights:** empty equipped 5,776 lb (2620 kg); maximum take-off 9,480 lb (4300 kg)
Performance: maximum level speed 'clean' at 20,340 ft (6200 m) 505 mph (812 km/h); maximum rate of climb at sea level 4,495 ft (1370 m) per minute; service	**Dimensions:** wingspan 38 ft 1½ in (11.62 m) with tip tanks; length 33 ft 11 in (10.34 m); height 10 ft 9 in (3.28 m); wing area 209.15 sq ft (19.43 m²)
	Armament: maximum ordnance 661 lb (300 kg)

SOKO G-4 Super Galeb

First flown on 17 July 1978, the **G-4 Super Galeb** is a two-seat advanced and tactical trainer of similar configura-

tion to the BAe Hawk jet trainer. The G-4 was developed during the 1970s as a replacement for the G-2A Galeb and T-33.

Pre-production aircraft followed from late 1980 and full service use began in 1985, with G-4s replacing G-2As at the advanced

flying training school at Titograd. Further deliveries allowed G-4s to supplant the earlier model at the JRV's Air Academy at Zadar and a second training school at Pula. Total Galeb production

amounted to 136. Export sales were limited to six G-4 Galebs for Myanmar.

When the Mostar factory was abandoned in May 1992, some G-4 airframes were left uncompleted.

SOKO G-4 Super Galeb (continued)

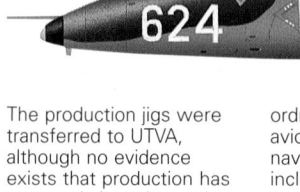

SPECIFICATION

SOKO G-4 Super Galeb
Type: advanced jet trainer with light attack capability
Powerplant: one ORAO (Rolls-Royce/Bristol Siddeley) Viper Mk 632-46 turbojet rated at 4,000 lb st (17.79 kN)
Performance: maximum cruising speed at 19,685 ft (6000 m) 525 mph (845 km/h); maximum rate of climb at sea level 6,100 ft (1860 m) per minute; service ceiling 42,160 ft (12850 m); combat radius 242 miles (389 km) on a lo-lo-lo attack with cannon pack and four BL755 cluster bombs
Weights: empty equipped 6,993 lb

(3172 kg); maximum take-off 13,889 lb (6300 kg)
Dimensions: wingspan 32 ft 5 in (9.88 m); length 40 ft 2¼ in (12.25 m) including probe; height 14 ft 1¼ in (4.30 m); wing area 209.90 sq ft (19.50 m²)
Armament: maximum ordnance 2,822 lb (1280 kg) including a ventral 23-mm GSh-23L gun pod with 200 rounds and a wide range of indigenous weapons such as cluster bombs, rocket pods, 50 kg and 100 kg bombs. G-4M can also carry the AGM-65B Maverick, ASMs and AAMs for self-defence and a secondary point defence role

The production jigs were transferred to UTVA, although no evidence exists that production has restarted. An enhanced ground-attack capability is offered in the **G-4M**, which appeared in 1991 and can carry 3,704 lb (1680 kg) of

ordnance. It features a new avionics system and new nav/attack equipment including HUD, INS, electronic sight and MFDs. Capable of covering the continuation phase of training for which two-seat versions of operational

Developed from the G-2 Galeb, the Super Galeb differs considerably from its predecessor.

aircraft are frequently used, the G-4M has replaced Jastrebs in some ground-attack units.

SOKO J-20 Kraguj

Armed with an array of light weapons available for its close-support role, the J-20 was used by the Bosnian Serb militia during 1994.

SPECIFICATION

SOKO J-20 Kraguj
Type: single-seat light attack aircraft
Powerplant: one Textron Lycoming GSO-480-B1A6 piston engine rated at 340 hp (253 kW)
Performance: maximum level speed 'clean' at 4,920 ft (1500 m) 183 mph (295 km/h); maximum rate of climb at sea level 1,575 ft

(480 m) per minute; range 497 miles (800 km)
Weights: empty equipped 2,491 lb (1130 kg); maximum take-off 3,580 lb (1624 kg)
Dimensions: wingspan 34 ft 11 in (10.64 m); length 26 ft ¼ in (7.93 m); height 9 ft 10 in (3.00 m); wing area 182.99 sq ft (17.00 m²)
Armament: see text

After a 20-year period of service, SOKO's **J-20 Kraguj** lightweight close

support aircraft was retired by the Yugoslav air force in 1990, a few survivors being

then passed to the Slovenian national guard. These were, however, repossessed by the JRV before Slovenia broke away, in June 1991, from the former Yugoslavian confederation.

The single-seat Kraguj has a built-in armament of two 0.303-in (7.7-mm) machine-guns and six wing

hardpoints for bombs, rocket pods or other light weapon loads. Bosnian

Serb militia used the Kraguj in the civil war against the Moslem and Croat forces.

SOKO/IAv Craiova J-22 Orao/IAR-93

The **J-22 Orao/IAR-93** is the product of an unlikely collaborative agreement between Yugoslavia and Romania. Both nations had a requirement for a lightweight but robust transonic close-support /ground-attack aircraft with secondary interceptor and reconnaissance capabilities, to enter service around 1977. Construction was allocated to two companies: Romania's CNIAR (now IAv Craiova) and SOKO in Yugoslavia.

The aircraft emerged with a configuration reminiscent of the larger SEPECAT Jaguar. It features a shoulder-mounted wing of similar planform and a similar sturdy undercarriage.

SOKO had gained experience of building the Rolls-Royce Viper turbojet under licence for other military aircraft, and selected non-afterburning Turbomécanica/ORAO Viper Mk 632-41Rs as powerplants. These are mounted side-by-side in the rear fuselage and are each rated at 4,000 lb st (17.79 kN). Reheat was considered a desirable option for production aircraft, however.

Single-seat and two-seat prototypes were constructed in each country, and these made simultaneous first flights on 31 October 1974 and 29 January 1977 (two-seaters). Manufacture of pre-production batches of 15 aircraft then began in

both countries, and the first of these made their maiden flights in late 1978.

Series production of the Romanian IAR-93 followed in 1979, and of the Yugoslavian J-22 Orao (Eagle) in 1980. Continued non-availability of afterburners meant that the first 20 production aircraft in each country were delivered without reheat. The first Romanian version of the aircraft was the non-afterburning **IAR-93A**, which made its maiden flight in 1981.

CNIAR built 26 single-seaters and 10 two-seat trainers with an extended forward fuselage and sideways-opening canopies. The following **IAR-93B** variant first flew in 1985 and

SPECIFICATION

SOKO/IAv Craiova J-22/ IAR-93 Orao
Type: lightweight close-support and ground-attack aircraft
Powerplant: two Turbomécanica/ ORAO-built Rolls-Royce Viper Mk 632-41R turbojets each rated at 4,000 lb st (17.79 kN) or, in most aircraft, two Turbomécanica/ ORAO-built Rolls-Royce Viper Mk 633-41 turbojets each rated at 4,000 lb st (17.79 kN) dry and 5,000 lb st (22.24 kN) afterburning
Performance: maximum level speed 'clean' at 36,090 ft (11000 m) 634 mph (1020 km/h); maximum rate of climb at sea level

17,520 ft (5340 m) per minute; service ceiling 49,210 ft (15000 m); tactical radius 324 miles (522 km) on a hi-lo-hi attack mission with four cluster bombs and one drop tank
Weights: empty equipped 12,125 lb (5500 kg); maximum take-off 24,427 lb (11080 kg)
Dimensions: wingspan 30 ft 6¼ in (9.30 m); length 48 ft 10⅝ in (14.90 m); height 14 ft 10 in (4.52 m); wing area 279.87 sq ft (26.00 m²)
Armament: two GSh-23L 23-mm cannon plus maximum ordnance load of 6,173 lb (2800 kg)

introduced afterburning Viper Mk 633-41 turbojets. It also featured wing leading-edge root extensions but lacked inboard wing fences. IAR-93Bs, and two-seat IAR-93As, lack ventral fins. Interestingly, single-seat IAR-93Bs feature a manually operated sideways- opening canopy, whereas all other single-seaters have an upward-hinging, electrically-actuated canopy. Romania ordered 165 Oraos, including two-seaters. In Yugoslavia, the first production variant was the **Orao 1**, powered (like the IAR-93A and pre-series aircraft) by non-afterburning Vipers, as a result of the continuing problems with developing an afterburner. The lack of performance of

these early production aircraft was such that they were allocated to the tactical reconnaissance role under the designation **IJ-22**. A handful of the batch of 20 aircraft appeared as two-seat trainers designated **NJ-22**.

The Orao 1 was followed by the single-seat **Orao 2** or **J-22(M)**, with enlarged integral wing fuel tanks, and with increased capacity in two fuselage tanks. Afterburning Viper 633-41 engines made possible a small increase in payload. The Orao 2 also has a Thomson-CSF HUD. The prototype flew for the first time on 20 October 1983 and the new variant entered production in late 1984, but by mid-1985 there were 16 complete aircraft awaiting

The IAR-93A/B continues to provide Romania with five squadrons of strike/ground-attack aircraft. This IAR-93A is pictured wearing Warsaw Pact-era national insignia. The first Romanian unit to receive the type was the 67th Fighter Bomber Regiment, at Craiova, in 1982.

reheated engines. These eventually arrived and the aircraft began to enter service in 1986.

The two-seat Orao 1 proved to be somewhat underpowered and short-legged, and SOKO therefore designed a new two-seat trainer incorporating the more powerful engines and the increased-capacity wing tanks of the Orao 2. The first example of the new **Orao 2D**, or **NJ-22(M)**, made its maiden flight on 18 July 1986, and production 2Ds have been augmented by a conversion programme bringing all surviving Orao 1 two-seaters up to the same standard. Like the Orao 2, the 2D has the same wing LERXes as are fitted to the IAR-93B.

Sopwith 1½-Strutter

Best-known as the **1½-Strutter**, a name believed to derive from the arrangement of the inter-plane struts of this single-seat bomber/two-seat fighter biplane, this aircraft had the official Admiralty and RFC designations of **Sopwith Type 9700** and **Sopwith Two-Seater** respectively. The two-seat prototype, flown in late 1915 on the power of a 110-hp (82-kW) Clerget rotary engine, introduced air brakes and a variable-incidence tailplane, and when production examples entered service with the RNAS in early 1916 it was the first British aircraft to be equipped with synchronising gear to allow the forward machine-gun to fire through the propeller disc. Both single- and two-seat versions were built with 110- and 130-hp (82-kW and 97-kW) Clerget rotaries, but some two-seaters were also powered by the 110-hp (82-kW) Le Rhône rotary engine.

When first introduced into service or the Western Front the 1½-Strutter had the edge in combat with German fighters, but it was surpassed in performance within a few months by the Albatros and Halberstadt scouts introduced by the enemy. However, RNAS 1½-Strutters had a longer operational life and towards the end of the war were in service as ship-based aircraft with both skid and wheel landing gear. On 4 April 1918 one took-off from a platform mounted over a gun

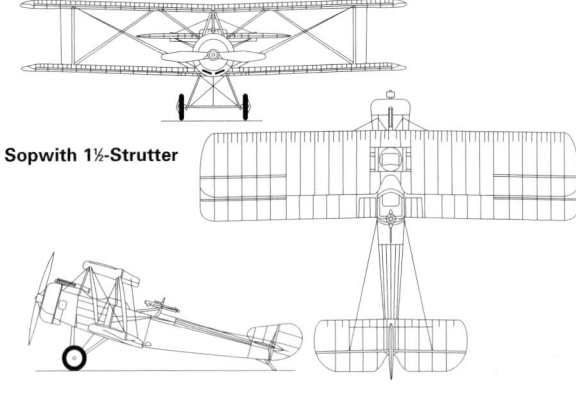

Sopwith 1½-Strutter

turret of HMAS *Australia*, the first two-seat aircraft to take off from a British warship.

A total believed to be 1,513 1½-Strutters was built for the RFC and RNAS, and the type was also produced in France to a total of two to three times this number. In addition to their use by British forces, this remarkable little aircraft saw service in and/or after World War I with the air arms of Belgium, France, Japan, Latvia, Romania, Russia and with the American Expeditionary Force.

SPECIFICATION	
Sopwith 1½-Strutter	(1062 kg)
Type: single-seat bomber version	**Dimensions:** wingspan 33 ft 6 in
Powerplant: one 130-hp (97-kW)	(10.21 m); length 25 ft 3 in
Clerget rotary engine	(7.97 m); height 10 ft 3 in (3.12 m);
Performance: maximum speed	wing area 346 sq ft (32.14 m²)
102 mph (164 km/h) at 6,500 ft	**Armament:** one fixed forward-
(1980 m); service ceiling 13,000 ft	firing 0.303-in (7.7-mm) Vickers
(3960 m)	machine-gun, plus up to four 56-lb
Weights: empty 1,316 lb (597 kg);	(25-kg) bombs or an equivalent
maximum take-off 2,342 lb	weight of smaller bombs

Sopwith 7F.1 Snipe, Salamander and Dragon

Designed around a newly-developed Bentley B.R.2 rotary engine, the **7F.1 Snipe** was intended as a successor to the Camel. The airframe of the first prototype was ready for testing before an example of the B.R.2 engine was available and was, consequently, flown with a 150-hp (112-kW) B.R.1 engine. This was one of the alternative power-plants of the Camel and, in this form, the Snipe looked very similar to its famous predecessor. Its appearance began to alter with installation of the bigger engine, and the large increase of power brought other structural changes. Satisfactory testing resulted in the type being ordered into production as the **Snipe Mk I**, deliveries beginning in the summer of 1918, but only about 100 of these aircraft were in service with the RAF in France at the end of the war, and a total of 497 had been built when production ended in 1919. In its brief operational career the Snipe had proved an exceptional fighter, and the type remained in post-war service with first-line squadrons until withdrawn in 1926, but remained in use with training schools for some time after that date.

For use in a ground-attack role against enemy trenches, the **Salamander TF.2** was developed from the Snipe, but had some 650 lb (295 kg) of armour plate beneath the forward fuselage to protect the pilot and fuel tanks from ground fired weapons. The standard armament of two Vickers machine-guns was retained, and a variety of experimental installations of downward-firing weapons was tested. Although 82 had been built when production ended in 1919, only a small number reached France before the Armistice; none were used operationally and the type did not continue in post-war service with the RAF.

In early 1918 the Snipe prototype had been flown experimentally with a 320-hp (239-kW) A.B.C. Dragonfly I engine; excellent performance with a maximum speed of

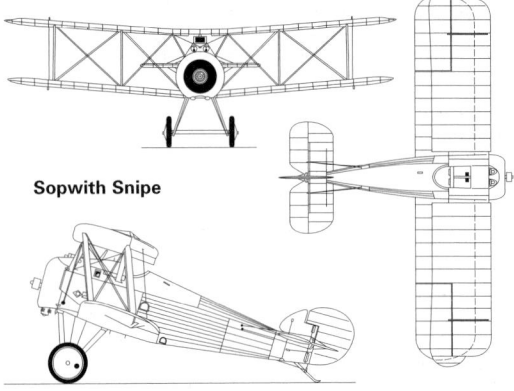

Sopwith Snipe

150 mph (241 km/h) won it a production order, and some 76 **Dragon** aircraft were completed with the more powerful 360-hp (268-kW) Dragonfly IA engine as standard. None were used operationally in World War I and the type did not survive because of the unreliability of the Dragonfly powerplant.

SPECIFICATION	
Sopwith Snipe Mk I	**Dimensions:** wingspan 30 ft 1 in
Type: single-seat fighter	(9.17 m); length 19 ft 9 in (6.02 m);
Powerplant: one 230-hp (172-kW)	height 8 ft 9 in (2.67 m); wing area
Bentley B.R.2 rotary piston engine	270 sq ft (25.08 m²)
Performance: maximum speed	**Armament:** two forward-firing
121 mph (195 km/h) at 10,000 ft	synchronised 0.303-in (7.7-mm)
(3050 m); service ceiling 19,500 ft	Vickers machine-guns, plus up to
(5945 m); endurance 3 hours	four 25-lb (11-kg) bombs on
Weights: empty 1,312 lb (595 kg);	external racks
maximum take-off 2,020 lb (916 kg)	

Sopwith F.1, 2F.1 and TF.1 Camel

The **Camel**, which superseded the Pup in service on the Western Front and was regarded as the finest British fighter of World War I, was basically a development of the Pup. Somewhat heavier and with a more powerful engine as standard, the Camel had armament, fuel, pilot and powerplant concentrated within a short distance, resulting in outstanding manoeuvrability. This was enhanced by the torque of the large engine, making, possible snap turns to starboard which were so fast that some pilots would make a three-quarter right instead of one-quarter left turn; not only did they believe this to be faster in combat, but it was tactically confusing to an enemy pilot. These capabilities made the Camel the most successful Allied fighter of the war.

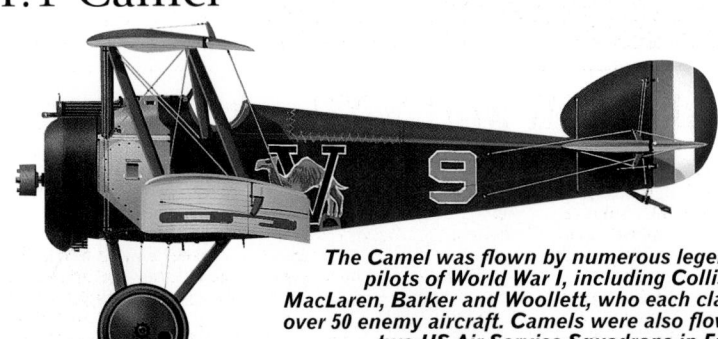

The Camel was flown by numerous legendary pilots of World War I, including Collishaw, MacLaren, Barker and Woollett, who each claimed over 50 enemy aircraft. Camels were also flown by two US Air Service Squadrons in France.

Sopwith F.1, 2F.1 and TF.1 Camel (continued)

Remarkably, the Camels of the RFC, RAF and RNAS scored over 2,800 victories, the overall total for the type exceeding 3,000. The Camel was also used as a day or night fighter by British Home Defence units, and it is considered to have played a significant role in the defeat of the German Gotha bombers.

Like the Pup, the type gained a nickname, Camel, which has long survived the official **Sopwith**

Biplane F.1 designation of the initial production version. Standard power-plant comprised engines of 100 to 150 hp (75 to 112 kW) by Bentley, Clerget, Gnome and Le Rhône, and the Camel was flown experimentally with a 150-hp (112kW) Le Rhône and a 180-hp (134-kW) Gnome Monosoupape. Developments included the **F.1/1** with tapered wings, and the **T.F.1 (Trench Fighter**) with a pair of

Lewis guns firing downward through the cockpit floor, but neither of these entered production. Some F.1 Camels were operated from ships, but final production **2F.1 Camel** was designed purposely for shipboard use and some remained in service after the end of World War I. Final production totalled 5,490 aircraft, and in addition to their use by the RFC and RNAS they served

Belgium, Canada and Greece, with the American Expeditionary Force, and

with the Slavo-British Aviation Group operating in Russia in 1918.

SPECIFICATION

Sopwith F.1 Camel
Type: single-seat fighter
Powerplant: one 130-hp (97-kW) Clerget rotary piston engine
Performance: maximum speed 115 mph (185 km/h) at 6,500 ft (1980 m); service ceiling 19,000 ft (5790 m); endurance 2 hours 30 minutes
Weights: empty 929 lb (421 kg);
maximum take-off 1,453 lb (659 kg)
Dimensions: wingspan 28 ft (8.53 m); length 18 ft 9 in (5.72 m); height 8 ft 6 in (2.59 m); wing area 231 sq ft (21.46 m²)
Armament: two forward-firing synchronised 0.303-in (7.7-mm) Vickers machine-guns, plus up to four 25-lb (11-kg) bombs carried externally

Sopwith Pup

An elegant little equal-span biplane, the **Sopwith Admiralty Type 9901** retained the same form of interplane struts adopted for the 1½-Strutter, but with 20 per cent less wingspan it is not surprising that it became regarded as a 'pup' of the earlier aircraft. The nickname **Pup**, given by air

and ground crews, has long outlived the official designation. As first flown this single-seat fighter was powered by an 80-hp (60-kW) Le Rhône rotary engine, and the fact that with this low-powered unit it was a highly manoeuvrable and effective fighter speaks volumes for its design and construction.

The Pup entered service with both the RAF and RNAS in 1916, and its reputation was established quickly. In fact, it was more than a gem, for with its effective forward-firing synchronised machine-gun, and the ability to remain manoeuvrable and responsive at a greater height than any contemporary fighter at the time of its introduction, it was also a killer. It was in great demand, and production totalled 1,770, the type being used also for home defence, many in this latter category with 100-hp (75-kW) Gnome Monosoupape rotary engines, the resulting increase in rate of climb and overall performance making the Pup a most effective interceptor. In RNAS service the type

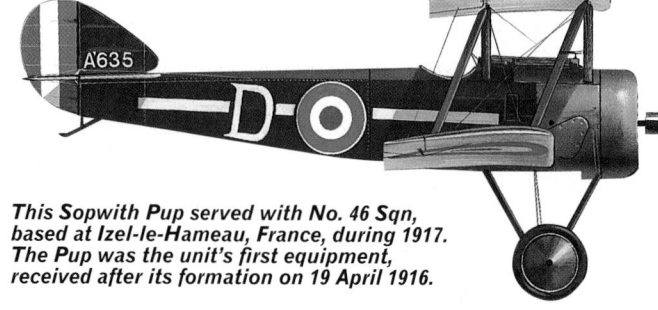

This Sopwith Pup served with No. 46 Sqn, based at Izel-le-Hameau, France, during 1917. The Pup was the unit's first equipment, received after its formation on 19 April 1916.

played a significant pioneering role in the operation of aircraft from ships; one Pup flown by Squadron Commander E. H. Dunning achieved the first landing on a ship under way at sea when it touched down on the deck of the aircraft-carrier HMS *Furious* on 2 August 1917.

An attempt to capitalise

on the superb flying qualities of the Pup was made in 1919 with development of the civil two-seat **Dove**, but its Le Rhône rotary engine was far from suitable for operation by a private pilot and this, more than any other factor, limited production to only 10 aircraft, most of them sold overseas.

SPECIFICATION

Sopwith Pup
Type: single-seat fighter
Powerplant: one 80-hp (60-kW) Le Rhône rotary piston engine
Performance: maximum speed 112 mph (180 km/h) at sea level; service ceiling 17,500 ft (5335 m); endurance 3 hours
Weights: empty 787 lb (357 kg); maximum take-off 1,225 lb (556 kg)
Dimensions: wingspan 26 ft 6 in (8.08 m); length 19 ft 9¾ in (6.04 m); height 9 ft 5 in (2.87 m); wing area 254 sq ft (23.60 m²)
Armament: one forward-firing synchronised 0.303-in (7.7-mm) Vickers machine-gun, plus up to four 25-lb (11-kg) bombs on external racks

Sopwith Triplane

A fuselage and tail unit similar to those of the Pup, a more powerful engine and the addition of an extra wing were the basic components of the remarkable little fighter known as

the **Triplane**. Retaining the manoeuvrability of the Pup, the Triplane was faster and had a better rate of climb with the extra wing and 110-hp (82-kW) Clerget rotary that was its standard

powerplant, and some late aircraft with the 130-hp (97-kW) Clerget had further performance improvement.

Entering service in early 1917, the Triplane was the first aircraft of its configuration to be used on the Western Front and, in retrospect, it seems almost unbelievable that this diminutive fighter, of which only about 140 were built and flown exclusively by the RNAS, gained almost complete ascendancy over enemy fighters for a period of about seven months, until superseded by the Camel in November 1917. The measure of its capabil-

ity may be gauged from the fact that German pilots would, if possible, avoid combat with a formation of these Triplanes, and from the frantic efforts of the German aircraft industry to develop a triplane that was equal in capability.

Shortly after development of the standard Triplane, Sopwith flew two examples of another triplane, each with an Hispano-Suiza Vee engine.

Often regarded as re-engined standard Triplanes, these two aircraft, one with a 150-hp (112-kW) and the other with a 200-hp (149-kW) engine, had, in fact, an airframe that was considerably different. Although both had enhanced performance by comparison with the earlier Triplane, no production followed because of a shortage of Hispano-Suiza engines.

When the Triplane made its first flight in June 1916, the Pup from which it was derived was yet to enter service.

SPECIFICATION

Sopwith Triplane
Type: single-seat fighter
Powerplant: one 130-hp (97-kW) Clerget rotary piston engine
Performance: maximum speed 117 mph (188 km/h) at 5,000 ft (1525 m); service ceiling 20,500 ft (6250 m); endurance 2 hours 45 minutes
Weights: empty 1,101 lb (499 kg); maximum take-off 1,541 lb (699 kg)
Dimensions: wingspan 26 ft 6 in (8.08 m); length 18 ft 10 in (5.74 m); height 10 ft 6 in (3.20 m); wing area 231 sq ft (21.46 m²)
Armament: one or two forward-firing synchronised 0.303-in (7.7-mm) Vickers machine-guns

SPAD S.VII and S.XII

After experience with the **SPAD A 1** to **A 5**, Louis Béchereau adopted a far more conventional layout for the single-seat **S.V** tractor biplane which was flown toward the end of 1915 and this, in effect, served as the prototype for

the **S.VII** which was the company's first really successful military aircraft. With a fabric-covered all-wood structure, except for aluminium panels over the forward fuselage, the S.VII had fixed tailskid landing gear and a round frontal

radiator for its Hispano-Suiza eight-cylinder Vee engine. First flown in April 1916, the S.VII had a beautifully clean airframe for its day and this, combined

Based on the S.VII, the S.XII was armed with a 37-mm cannon and was powered by a 220-hp (164-kW) Hispano-Suiza.

with the power and reliability of its Hispano-Suiza engine, ensured that it was quickly ordered into production. Delivery of the initial version, powered by a 150-hp (112kW) Hispano-Suiza 8Aa engine, began in September 1916, and within the first year more than 500 had been built. The second production version, which introduced the more powerful 180-hp (134-kW) 8Ac engine and wings of slightly increased span, was built by SPAD

and under sub-contract to a total of about 6,000 aircraft. In addition to the S.VIIs used in large numbers by the French armed services, the type served also with the RFC and RNAS, the Belgian 5th Squadron, Italy which had 214 to equip five squadriglie, the American Expeditionary Force which took 189 aircraft, and Russia which received 43.

Two development aircraft were flown in 1917, one powered by a

Renault 12D engine and the other by a 200-hp (149-kW) Hispano-Suiza 8Bc, and it was this latter aircraft which, when equipped with a 37-mm cannon in addition to its standard Vickers machine-gun, was designated **SPAD XII**. Flown in prototype form on 5 July 1917, the **S.XII** was built to a total of 300, some with a 220-hp (164-kW) 8Bec engine, and a small number of a floatplane version was used by the

Royal Naval Air Service.

Many S.VIIs were in civil use after World War I had ended, being used primarily in a training role, some

until 1928. Final derivatives were the **SPAD 62** and **SPAD 72** intended specifically for a training role, which were flown in 1923.

SPECIFICATION	
SPAD S.VII (major production)	15 minutes
Type: single-seat fighter	**Weight:** maximum take-off
Powerplant: one 180-hp (134-kW) Hispano-Suiza 8Ac Vee piston engine	1,664 lb (755 kg)
	Dimensions: wingspan 25 ft 7¾ in (7.82 m); length 20 ft 2½ in (6.16 m); height 7 ft 8½ in (2.35 m)
Performance: maximum speed 118 mph (190 km/h) at 6,560 ft (2000 m); service ceiling 18,000 ft (5485 m); endurance 2 hours	**Armament:** one forward-firing synchronised 0.303-in (7.7-mm) Vickers machine-gun

SPAD S.XIII

Not surprisingly, the success of the S.VII led to developments of the same basic design. Thus, just before introduction of the S.XII, the company used the S.VII as the basis for a two-seat light bomber/reconnaissance aircraft which differed primarily by having slightly swept and staggered wings to compensate for the altered centre-of-gravity position of the lengthened fuselage. Designated **S.XI** and intro-

duced into service in late 1917, the model was powered by a new and more powerful (235-hp; 175-kW) version of the Hispano-Suiza 8 engine from which the teething problems had not been eliminated. The resulting unreliability of this powerplant, coupled with instability derived from the aircraft's sensitivity to load distribution, made the type unpopular and it was withdrawn from frontline use in mid-1918.

The **S.XIII** was, however, a very different story, its

success considerably exceeding that of the S.VII with a total of 8,472 built. The S.XIII differed from the S.VII by having a slight increase in wingspan, improved ailerons and other aerodynamic refinements, plus the increased power from an alternative version of the 8B engine fitted in the S.XII. The prototype was flown for the first time on 4 April 1917 and its considerable improvement in performance ensured an early entry into service, the first examples reaching the Western Front by the end of May 1917. It replaced the S.VII and later Nieuports in the French fighter squadrons, was flown by aces such as

Fonck, Guynemer and Nungesser, and served also with the RFC and the air forces of Belgium, Italy and the USA. An almost insatiable demand for this very capable fighter meant that outstanding orders for some 10,000 aircraft were cancelled at the end of World War I, and in the immediate post-war years the type was exported to Belgium, Czechoslovakia, Japan and Poland.

An improved version of the S.XIII was introduced into service shortly before the end of the war, a single-seat fighter/

photo-reconnaissance aircraft which had the designation **S.XVII**. Equipped with two cameras, but with armament reduced to only a single machine-gun, it had a refined and strengthened structure to cater for installation of a 300-hp (224-kW) 8F engine which gave this version a maximum speed of 149 mph (240 km/h) at optimum altitude. Production totalled only 20 examples, and construction of a projected improved variant designated **S.XXI** was prevented by an end to the war.

In July 1920, the USAAS had a strength of 393 S.XIIIs, from a total of 893 purchased in France. Pictured is an S.XIII of the 2nd Pursuit Group.

SPECIFICATION	
SPAD S.XIII	**Weight:** maximum take-off
Type: single-seat fighter	1,863 lb (845 kg)
Powerplant: one 220-hp (164-kW) Hispano-Suiza 8Be Vee piston engine	**Dimensions:** wingspan 26 ft 6¾ in (8.10 m); length 20 ft 8 in (6.30 m); height 7 ft 8½ in (2.35 m)
Performance: maximum speed 139 mph (224 km/h) at 6,560 ft (2000 m); service ceiling 21,815 ft (6650 m); endurance 2 hours	**Armament:** two forward-firing synchronised 0.303-in (7.7-mm) Vickers machine-guns

Special Aircraft Transport International Company (SATIC) A300-600ST Beluga

With its member companies producing large components and major assemblies in several countries, from its very beginning Airbus Industrie had need for freighter aircraft that could collect outsize items for delivery to its final assembly lines.

By the late 1980s existing aircraft (Aero Spacelines Super Guppy 201s) were beginning to run out of airframe hours and reach the limits of their freight capacities, so Airbus Industrie decided to create a replacement based on the airframe of the A300-

600 with the powerplant of the A310, creating the **A300-600ST Beluga**. The programme was launched in December 1990 under the auspices of SATIC (Special Aircraft Transport International Company, and at one time Super Airbus Transport International Company), a joint enterprise by Aérospatiale and Daimler-Benz Aerospace Airbus. The task of co-ordinating the technical aspect of the programme was entrusted to Latécoère, which designed and manufactured of the cargo hold, floor, pressure bulkhead

and rear side doors; other companies involved in the programme were SOGERMA-SOCEA (upward-hinging nose door, side panels and airtight floor above flightdeck), Hurel-Dubois (shortened nose landing gear unit and pressure bulkhead behind the flightdeck), SOCATA (rear lower fuselage lobe), CASA (forward upper fuselage panels) and Elbe Flugzeugwerke (tail).

The machine is based on a new A300-600 modified with a drooped forward fuselage to allow the addition of a very large and unpressurised upper fuselage section accessed by a forward door, and a tail unit with a taller fin (extended into the rear section of the enlarged fuselage by

a dorsal fillet) and a strengthened tailplane fitted with endplate surfaces for continued directional stability despite the enlargement of the fuselage.

The new hold has a usable length of 123 ft 8¼ in (37.70 m) long with a constant-diameter length of 70 ft (21.34 m) and a maximum diameter of 24 ft 3¼ in (7.40 m) for a volume of 4,944.03 cu ft (140 m³), and a self-powered cargo loading system which contributes significantly to the A300-600ST's

turnaround time of only 45 minutes compared with the Super Guppy's time of several hours.

The first **A300-608ST** (Super Transport) made the type's maiden flight on 13 September 1994 after assembly at the Latécoère facility near Toulouse, and the type was certificated and entered service in September 1995. Airbus Industrie has a short-term requirement for five such aircraft and SATIC hopes to secure up to 20 additional civil and, possibly, military orders.

This, the third Super Transporter, made its first flight on 9 June 1998. Airbus Industrie's fifth A300-608ST was delivered in 2001.

SPECIFICATION	
SATIC A300-600ST Beluga	maximum payload
Type: two/three-crew outsize cargo transport	**Weights:** empty 190,700 lb (86500 kg); maximum take-off 341,700 lb (155000 kg)
Powerplant: two General Electric CF6-80C2A8 turbofan engines each rated at 59,000 lb st (262.45 kN)	**Dimensions:** wingspan 147 ft (44.84 m); length 184 ft 3 in (56.16 m); height 56 ft 6¾ in (17.24 m); wing area 2,798.71 sq ft (260 m²)
Performance: maximum cruising speed 484 mph (780 km/h) at optimum altitude; certificated altitude 35,000 ft (10670 m); range 1,035 miles (1666 km) with	**Payload:** up to 104,277 lb (47300 kg) of freight

Stampe aircraft

Established in 1922, the Belgian company Stampe et Vertongen had as its chief designer Alfred Renard and early type designations were prefixed RSV, indicating Renard, Stampe and Vertongen. The company specialised in the design and construction of primary trainer/tourer and advanced trainer aircraft, and early products included the **Stampe et Vertongen RSV.18-100** and **RSV.26-100** two-seat trainer/tourers which were almost identical, although the first was of monoplane and the second of biplane configuration, each powered by the 100-hp (75-kW) Renard radial engine. Then came the **RSV.20-100**, a two-seat braced parasol-wing monoplane powered by a 110-hp (82-kW) Renard radial engine, and the **RSV.22-180** which was a two-seat tandem open cockpit advanced trainer of biplane configuration with a 180-hp (134-kW) Hispano- Suiza Vee engine; this last aircraft was available optionally as the **RSV.22-200** with a 200-hp (149-kW) Renard radial engine. The **RSV.28-180 Type III** was an advanced trainer with the 180-hp (134-kW) Vee engine, and was equipped specially to train military pilots in blind-flying techniques. The compact **RSV.22-Lynx**

advanced trainer of 1932 was so named because of its 215-hp (160-kW) Armstrong Siddeley Lynx radial engine, the same powerplant being employed in the **RSV.26-Lynx** which was equipped for blind-flying training. Several of these early types served with the Belgian air force and, in particular, the RSV.26-Lynx and RSV.28-180 Type III. The **RSV.32** trainer/liaison aircraft was built to a total of 57 by 1932 in versions which included the **RSV.32-90** (90-hp/67-kW Anzani 10C), **RSV.32-100** (100-hp/75-kW Renard), **RSV.32-105** (105-hp/78-kW Hermes), **RSV.32-110** (110-hp/82-kW Lorraine- Dietrich) and **RSV.32-120** (120-hp/89-kW Gipsy III), the majority serving with the Belgian air force.

Company designations changed to SV after Renard left to work wholly with the Société Anonyine des Avions et Moteurs Renard, founded by Georges and Alfred Renard a few years earlier. The **SV.4** of 1933 proved to be Stampe et Vertongen's most successful aircraft, a light tourer/ trainer of biplane configuration powered in prototype form by the 120-hp (89-kW) de Havilland Gipsy III engine. It was available initially as the advanced aerobatic **SV.4A** with a 140-hp (104-kW)

A single SV.4 was used by the RAF during the war, this aircraft having been flown to Britain by two Belgian pilots fleeing the Nazi occupation in 1941.

Renault 4-PO5 engine, but the improved **SV.4B** had redesigned wings, introduced the 130-hp (97-kW) Gipsy Major I engine and was of reduced dimensions. Only about 35 were built before World War II, though after the war another 65 were built by Stampe et Renard, the company formed by a merger of Stampe et Vertongen with SA Avions et Moteurs Renard.

In addition, the SV.4 was licence-built extensively post-war as the **SV.4C** (powered by the 140-hp/ 104-kW Renault 4-Pei engine), being manufactured in France by SNCAN and in Algeria by Atelier Industriel de l'Aéronautique d'Alger to a combined total of about 940. The SV.4 was followed pre-war by the larger and heavier **SV.5** military training biplane which was powered by the 355-hp (265-kW) Armstrong Siddeley Serval radial engine and could be equipped for both bombing and gunnery training; about 30 were built, 10 of them going to Latvia and the balance to the Belgian air force. Final designs, before the company's activities were brought to an end by the German invasion of

SPECIFICATION	
Stampe et Vertongen SV.4B	18,045 ft (5500 m)
Type: aerobatic tourer/trainer	**Weights:** empty 1,058 lb (480 kg);
Powerplant: one 130-hp (97-kW)	maximum take-off 1,720 lb (780 kg)
de Havilland Gipsy Major I inverted	**Dimensions:** wingspan 27 ft 6¾ in
inline piston engine	(8.40 m); length 21 ft 4 in (6.50 m);
Performance: maximum speed	height 8 ft 6¼ in (2.60 m); wing
124 mph (200 km/h); service ceiling	area 204.52 sq ft (19.00 m²)

10 May 1940, included a lightweight parasol-wing monoplane designated **SV.18**, powered by a 120-hp (89-kW) Gipsy III engine. Intended for use as a two-seat tourer under the designation **SV.18M**, it was also offered as a single- seat fighter trainer as the **SV.18MA**.

The post-war activities of Stampe et Renard met with little success after the

completion of SV.4Bs; a single **SV.4D** with a 175-hp (130-kW) Mathis engine failed to gain any interest, which was also the fate of the **SR.7B Monitor IV** trainer. This was a two-seat cantilever low-wing monoplane powered by a 180-hp (134-kW) Blackburn Cirrus Bombardier 702 inline engine and with its tandem cockpits enclosed by a continuous canopy.

Stearman aircraft

The Stearman Aircraft Company, established initially at Venice, California in 1927, but soon moving to Wichita, Kansas, combined Lloyd Stearman's design genius with the backing of the Lyle-Hoyt Aircraft Corporation; in 1934 this company became a subsidiary of the Boeing

Airplane Company, and in 1939 its Wichita Division.

First design to be built by the new company was the classic **Stearman C3B**, its configuration forming the basis of all subsequent biplanes of Stearman design. In standard form this was an unequal-span biplane with fixed tailskid landing

gear, tandem open cockpits for a pilot and two passengers, and a 220-hp (164-kW) Wright J-5 Whirlwind radial engine. Alternative power-plants resulted in the **C3C** (with 150- or 180-hp/112- or 134-kW Hispano-Suiza), **C3K** (128-hp/95kW Siemens-Halske Sh.12), **C3L** (130-hp/ 97-kW Comet) and **C3R** (225hp/168-kW Wright J-6).

Initial development led to the **Stearman C3MB**, which differed from the C3B only by having the forward (passenger) cockpit adapted to carry cargo or mail, and many C3Bs were later converted to this configuration. It set the pattern for the much larger **Stearman M-2 Speedmail** of 1929 which, powered by a 525-hp (391-kW) Wright Cyclone, could carry a 1,000-lb (454-kg) load of cargo/mail. The Speedmail was, in turn, developed as the **Stearman LT-1**, which replaced the cargo compartment of the M-2 by an enclosed cabin to seat four passengers or carry a 1,200-lb (544-kg) payload. The prototype retained the Cyclone engine

of the M-2, but production aircraft had the similarly powered Pratt & Whitney Hornet. The **Stearman 4E Junior Speedmail**, introduced in 1930 and powered by the 420-hp (313-kW) Pratt & Whitney Wasp C1 engine, came between the C3 and M-2 In terms of size and capability. Like the C3 it was basically a three-seater, but the forward cockpit was convertible easily to carry cargo/ mail. Built in small numbers, the Stearman 4E was followed by the **Stearman 4C** with 300-hp (224-kW) Wright J-6, **Stearman 4D** with 300hp (224-kW) Pratt & Whitney Wasp Junior, **Stearman 4EM Senior Speedmail** with the forward cockpit specifically for cargo/mail and a 450-hp (336-kW) Pratt & Whitney Wasp, **Stearman 4CM-1 Senior Speedmail** cargo/mail version of the Stearman 4C with a 300-hp (224-kW) Wright R-975 engine, and a similar adaptation of the Stearman 4D designated **Stearman 4DM-1 Senior Speedmail**. By the time that this last

aircraft was certificated, on 27 May 1930, the US economic depression was at its height; only two Stearman 4DM-1s were sold and the company had to look around for a different category of market.

Thus was developed the **Stearman 6A Cloudboy** of 1931-2, a two-seat biplane with tandem open cockpits that was designed specifically as a commercial or military trainer. Powered by the 165-hp (123-kW) Wright J-6 engine the Cloudboy had only limited success because of the economic situation, just three civil examples being built. Hopes were raised with a US Army Air Corps order for four similarly powered aircraft, which it designated **YPT-9**, but there was no production order to follow. Later USAAC conversions of these aircraft resulted in the designations **YPT-9A** (165-hp/123-kW Continental A70), **YPT-9B** (200-hp/ 149-kW Lycoming), **YPT-9C** (170-hp/127-kW Kinner), **YBT-3** (300-hp/224-kW Wright J-6-9 Whirlwind) and **YBT-5** (300-hp/224-kW Pratt & Whitney Wasp Jr). Subsequent civil developments followed the USAAC pattern, the **Stearman 6F**

Built as a private venture training biplane in 1934, the Model 75 was built in enormous numbers for both the US military and foreign operators. In US service it was known as the PT-13/-17/-18/-27 Kaydet.

Cloudboy having Continental, the **Stearman 6D** the Wasp Junior, the **Stearman 6H** the Kinner, and the **Stearman 6L** the Lycoming, but only two or three of each were built.

Although the Stearman company was only just ticking over, energetic efforts found maintenance and repair work to bolster the very small income from sales, and in 1933 the company found time to build a one-off **Model 80** open cockpit two-seat biplane and a similar **Model 81** which had the cockpits enclosed by a streamlined canopy. It was at this same period that design began of the **Model 73** which, together with the **Model 75**, was to bring the company undying fame.

Stinson L-1 Vigilant

In response to a US Army Air Corps requirement of 1940 for a two-seat light observation aircraft, Stinson submitted its **Stinson Model 74** design proposal to receive a contract for three examples under the designation **YO-49** for evaluation against submissions from Bellanca (YO-50) and Ryan (YO-51). Stinson was awarded a contract for 142 **O-49** production aircraft, these often being listed under the Vultee name, for by 1940 Stinson had become a division of Vultee Aircraft Inc. To provide essential low-speed and high-lift performance, the braced monoplane wing incorporated leading- and trailing-edge high-lift devices, and power was provided by a Lycoming R-680-9 radial engine. A follow-on contract was received for 182 **O-49A** aircraft which had a slightly longer fuselage, some refinements and equipment changes. In 1942 the O-49 and O-49A were redesignated **L-1** and **L-1A** respectively, and eight L-1 and 100 L-1A aircraft allocated to the RAF under Lend-Lease became **Vigilant Mk I** and **Vigilant Mk II** respectively, with many of the latter used under joint Anglo-American control. Conversions of O-59 and O-49A aircraft for use in other roles resulted in three **O-49B** (later **L-1B**) ambulances accommodating a single stretcher, a single **L-1C** ambulance with revised interior, 21 **L-1D** modified from L-1As for pilot training in glider pick-up techniques, seven L-1 conversions as **L-1E** ambulances with amphibious float landing gear, plus five similar conversions from L-1A aircraft which were redesignated

Built as one of 142 initial O-49s, this ski-equipped Vigilant became an L-1 after 1942, and was ultimately converted to L-1E ambulance standard.

L-1F. No additional production aircraft were built, the Vigilant being superseded by the more effective Grasshopper family. The 50 ft 11 in (15.52 m) span L-1A was powered by the 295-hp (220-kW) R-680-9 had a maximum speed of 122 mph (196 km/h).

Stinson Voyager/Sentinel

In 1939 Stinson entered the lightplane market with introduction of the **Stinson Model 105** which, looking very like a small-scale Junior, was a three-seat braced high-wing monoplane powered by a 75-hp (56-kW) Continental A75-3 or 80-hp (60-kW) A80-6 flat-four engine. About 530 of these two civil versions were built in roughly equal numbers, their success resulting during 1941 in the introduction of an improved **Model 10 Voyager** that differed primarily in standards of interior finish and equipment. The basic version with the 90-hp (67-kW) Franklin 4AC-199-E3 engine was designated **Model 10-A** and about 750 were built before production was suspended in 1942, but a few examples with the 75-hp (56-kW) Lycoming GO-145-E3 engine were also built under the designation **Model 10-B**. Six examples of the Model 10-A with the 80-hp (60-kW) Continental O-170-1 engine were procured by the US Army Air Force in 1941 for evaluation under the designation **YO-54**. Successful testing led to an initial order for 275 slightly larger and heavier aircraft with the Lycoming O-435-1 flat-four engine under the designation **O-62**. The following order covered 1,456 similar aircraft which were designated **L-5** and given the name **Sentinel** when deliveries began in 1942, the O-62s then being redesignated L-5. They were followed by the **L-5A** (688 converted from L-5s) with revised electrical system, the **L-5B** (679) with modified rear fuselage to permit loading of a stretcher, and the **L-5C** (200) with provision for a reconnaissance camera. The L-5D designation was not used and the **L-5E** (558) introduced ailerons that drooped with flap extension; the one-off **XL-5** evaluated minor changes and an O-435-2 engine, and the final production **L-5G** (115) was similar to the L-5E except for introduction of the 190-hp (142-kW) O-435-11 engine. In addition to the foregoing, eight Stinson 105s and 12 Model 10-A Voyagers were impressed for USAAF

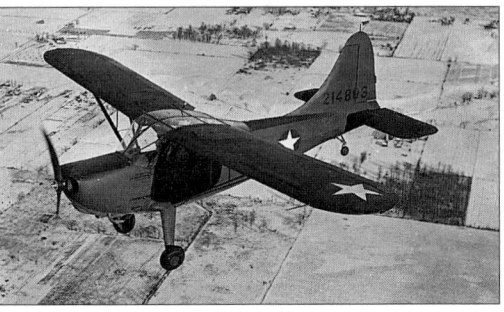

Built by Vultee-Stinson the O-62 was a military version of the Model 105, with an enlarged fuselage. This is one of the 275-strong initial batch.

service under the respective designations **AT-19A** (later **L-9A**) and **AT-19B** (later **L-9B**). A total of 306 L-5s of various designations was transferred to the USMC, plus 152 to the USN, all 458 receiving the designation **OY-1**; of this total 30 later had minor equipment changes to become redesignated **OY-2**. Under Lend-Lease 40 L-5s and 60 L-5Bs were supplied to the RAF which designated them **Sentinel Mk I** and **Sentinel Mk II** respectively.

Used extensively by the USAAF throughout World War 2, Sentinels also proved valuable during the Korean War; the RAF deployed its Sentinel Mk Is and Mk IIs in Burma, and those of the USMC and USN served primarily in the Pacific theatre. In 1962 surviving L-5s were redesignated **U-19A** by the USAF, and one used as a glider tug by the USAF Academy had the designation **U-19B**.

SPECIFICATION	
Stinson L-5 Sentinel	(676 km)
Type: liaison/spotter aircraft	**Weights:** empty 1,550 lb (703 kg);
Powerplant: one 185-hp (138-kW)	maximum take-off 2,020 lb (916 kg)
Lycoming O-435-1 flat-six piston	**Dimensions:** wingspan 34 ft
engine	(10.36 m); length 24 ft 1 in
Performance: maximum speed	(7.34 m); height 7 ft 11 in (2.41 m);
130 mph (209 km/h); service ceiling	wing area 155 sq ft (14.40 m²)
15,800 ft (4815 m); range 420 miles	

Stinson Detroiter

Initially named the Stinson Aircraft Syndicate, this company was formed in 1926 by pioneer pilot Eddie Stinson to build the **Stinson Detroiter** four-seat cabin biplane which had been designed jointly by Stinson and the well-known designer Alfred Verville. Designated **SB-1 Detroiter**, this initial version incorporated such features as cabin heating, individual wheel brakes and an electric starter for its 220-hp (164-kW) Wright J-5 Whirlwind engine. Later that same year the company's name was changed to Stinson Aircraft Corporation and at about that time work began on the design and construction of a braced high-wing monoplane version of the Detroiter, the **SM-1D**, which had the same powerplant as the SB-1 but with the cabin laid out as a six-seater. This was to prove the most popular configuration, being followed by the **SM-1DA** and **SM-1DB** which introduced minor improvements, and the **SM-1DC** and **SM-1DD** one-offs, both two-seaters with a cargo-carrying interior. The SM-1DD was the last of the J-5-powered Detroiters, and about 75 SM-1Ds of all versions had then been built. The conclusion that this aircraft would benefit from more power resulted in the last of the original Detroiter line, the **SM-1F** of 1929 with the 300-hp (224-kW) Wright J-6, this 46 ft 8 in (14.22 m) span version of the SM series having a maximum speed of 132 mph (212 km/h); many SM-1Ds were later re-engined with this powerplant and redesignated **SM-1D300**. The SM-1F was also available with Edo floats under the designation **SM-IFS**, and combined production of the SM-IF and SM-IFS totalled about 30 aircraft.

Two examples of a larger-capacity seven-seat **SM-6B** Detroiter were built in 1928, followed by seven or eight more with eight-seat interiors, and these largest members of the Stinson single-engine aircraft line were powered by the 450-hp (336-kW) Pratt & Whitney Wasp C-1 radial.

The three-passenger Detroiter first entered service with Northwest Airways in July 1927. Three of these aircraft comprised the airline's early fleet.

Stinson Reliant

The **Model R** and **Model S** formed the basis of the extensively-built Reliant, the initial **SR Reliant** introduced in the summer of 1933 being of the same basic configuration. Available alternatively as a twin-float seaplane, the Reliant was built in a long series that differed primarily in powerplant. The SR was powered by a 215-hp (160-kW) Lycoming R-680; the **SR-1** had the R-680-2 and the **SR-2** the R-680-7 engine, each of 240-hp (179-kW) output; and the **SR-3** was basically similar to the SR-1 but for minor structural changes. The **SR-4** introduced the 250-hp (186-kW) Wright R-760-E radial, but the improved **SR-5** of 1934 was available in three versions, the SR-5 having the 225-hp (168-kW) Lycoming R-680-4, and **SR-5B** and **SR-5C** having the 240-hp (179-kW) R-680-2 and 260-hp (194-kW) R-680-5 respectively. However, the most extensively built (about 75) civil Reliants were the well-

equipped **SR-5A** powered by the 245-hp (183-kW) R-680-6 engine and a very basic (with plenty of options available) **SR-5E** with the 225-hp (168-kW) R-680-4. The most expensive Reliant was the **SR-5F** with optional Wright R-760-E or R-760-E1 engines of 250 hp (186 kW) or 285 hp (213 kW) respectively. In 1935 Stinson introduced a refined **Reliant SR-6**. The SR-6 and **SR-6B** with the higher-powered R-680-6 and R-680-5 engines respectively were five-seaters, but the **SR-6A** with the 225-hp (168-kW) R-680-4 was limited to four seats. The **SR-7 Reliant** of 1936 looked a very different aircraft as a result of the introduction of a double-tapered wing, and was available as the four-seat **SR-7A** with R-680-4 engine, and as the five-seat **SR-7B** or **SR-7C** with R-680-6 and R-680-5 engines respectively. The **SR-8 Reliant** of the same year was generally similar to the SR-7 but available in

five variants. The **SR-8A**, **SR-8B** and **SR-8C** corresponded in powerplant to the SR-7A, -7B and -7C but were all completed as four-seaters; and the **SR-8D** and **SR-8E** were both five-seaters with 285-hp (213-kW) and 320-hp (239-kW) Wright R-760-E1 and R-760-E2 engines respectively. Both of the Wright-engined versions were offered optionally for use in utility roles under the designation **SR-8DM** and **SR-8EM**. Still further structural refinement was noticeable on the **SR-9** introduced for 1937, available as the **SR-9A**, **SR-9B**, **SR-9C** and **SR-9E** with the same powerplant as the corresponding SR-8 variants. They were supplied to the same standard as all of the earlier aircraft, but de luxe or utility interiors were optional. An addition to the range for 1937 was the **SR-9F** with 400-hp (298-kW) Pratt & Whitney Wasp Junior engine and with the same optional interior finishes. Last of the civil Reliants was the **SR-10** model of 1938, introducing more refinements and available with a still wider range of powerplants of 245 to 450 hp (183 to 336 kW). Most extensively built were the **SR-10B**, **SR-10C**, **SR-10D**, **SR-10E** and **SR-10F**, to a total of about 90 of all versions. Production of civil Reliants ended when the USA became involved in

Royal Navy Lend-Lease Reliants were utilised for navigation training and communications duties with 26 Fleet Air Arm second-line squadrons and units. Delivery of these aircraft began in 1943.

World War II, and although none were built for service with the USAAF, the army operated a total of 46 impressed civil aircraft under **UC-81A** to **UC-81N** designations, covering different SR-8, SR-9 and SR-10 variants, plus one SR-10F which was designated **XC-81D** and used to develop glider pick-up techniques. Two SR-5A and two SR-7B versions of the Reliant were also impressed under the respective designations **L-12** and **L-12A**, and single examples of the Reliant

were procured for evaluation by the US Coast Guard and US Navy under the designations **RQ1** and **XR3Q-1** respectively. During the war 500 new-production Reliants were procured under the designation **AT-19** for Lend-Lease supply to the Royal Navy; basically similar to the **SR-10G** with a Lycoming R-680-E1 engine, a lengthened fuselage and special equipment, they served with 12 squadrons. In addition, 15 UK civil registered Reliants were also impressed.

SPECIFICATION	
Stinson Reliant SR-5A	645 miles (1038 km)
Type: four-seat cabin monoplane	**Weights:** empty 2,325 lb
Powerplant: one 245-hp (183-kW)	(1055 kg); maximum take-off
Lycoming R-680-6 radial piston	3,475 lb (1576 kg)
engine	**Dimensions:** wingspan 41 ft
Performance: maximum speed	(12.50 m); length 27 ft 3 in
135 mph (217 km/h); service ceiling	(8.31 m); height 8 ft 5 in (2.57 m);
15,500 ft (4725 m); maximum range	wing area 230 sq ft (21.37 m²)

Sud-Est S.E.161 Languedoc

It may seem strange that with France situated conveniently to deploy long-range strategic bombers against virtually any European target, as well as against many other targets in Africa, the Armée de l'Air was not equipped with such aircraft at the outbreak of World War II. This was not due to any reluctance on the part of the French air force to operate such a type, but the fact that any allocation of funds could procure more small aircraft than large aircraft, and for some peculiar reason governments of the era seemed more interested in quantity.

Following absorption of Bloch into the nationalised aviation industry as a component of SNCASO in 1936, the design team which had been brought together by Avions Marcel Bloch was involved with a derivative of the earlier but unused 12-passenger Bloch M.B.160. The resulting **Bloch M.B.161.01** prototype was flown for the first time during September 1939, and a satisfactory

result of early tests brought an order from Air France: it was to be almost seven years before the first was delivered. This was due primarily to the delaying tactics of the French industry, anxious to ensure that none of the 20 ordered by Germany in 1942 should be delivered. Consequently, it was not until 17 September 1945 that the redesignated Se.161.1 was flown for the first time. Its configuration was that of a cantilever mid-wing monoplane of all-metal construction, having a high-mounted tailplane with endplate fins and rudders, retractable tailwheel landing gear, and power provided by four 1,150-hp (858-kW) Gnome-Rhône 14N 44/45 radial engines in wing leading-edge nacelles. Standard accommodation was provided for a crew of four and 33 passengers, but in 1951 Air France converted some of its **S.E.161** airliners to a high density seating arrangement for 44 passengers.

Bloch 161.1s, by then named **Languedoc**,

entered regular service with Air France on 28 May 1946. By October most had been withdrawn because, in addition to problems with their landing gear, they were unsuitable for winter operation. When they re-entered service, from March 1947, they had acquired Pratt & Whitney R-1830 engines, de-icing equipment, cabin heating and other modifications. They had also acquired the changed designation **S.E.161.P7**.

When production ended a total of 100 Languedocs had been built and, despite landing gear problems that persisted for almost four years, they saw extensive service, not only with Air France but with the French air force and navy. Five were supplied to LOT.

Another derivative of the Bloch 160 was identified initially as the **Bloch M.B.162**. This promised excellent long-range performance which, coupled with good load-carrying capability, seemed to offer potential as a strategic bomber.

Preliminary design was initiated, and a mock-up to full-scale was built and exhibited at the Salon de l'Aéronautique held in Paris during November 1938. Considerable interest was created by this 'large' bomber, only slightly smaller than the B-17, and because of this it was decided to build a prototype. This, unfortunately for France, was delayed because production priority had been given to the commercial M.B.161, with the result that construction of the bomber was held up until the spring of 1940. Even then, it was completed in remarkably short time for such a large project, flying for the first

time on 1 June 1940. Of cantilever low-wing monoplane configuration, the **M.B.162 B.5** was of all-metal construction, had a tailplane with marked dihedral and twin endplate fins and rudders, retractable tailwheel type landing gear, and two engines mounted in nacelles at the leading-edge of each wing.

Flown from Villacoublay to Bordeaux-Mérignac, the M.B.162 was captured by the Germans. Its test programme was completed during 1942 under the supervision of the German Focke-Wulf company, subsequently entering service with the Luftwaffe for long-range clandestine operations.

SPECIFICATION	
Sud-Est S.E.161 Languedoc	41,888 lb (19000 kg)
Type: five-seat long-range	**Dimensions:** wingspan 92 ft 2¼ in
strategic bomber	(28.10 m); length 71 ft 10¼ in
Powerplant: four 1,100-hp	(21.90 m); height 12 ft 3½ in
(820-kW) Gnome-Rhône 14N-48/49	(3.75 m); wing area 1,173.27 sq ft
radial piston engines	(109 m²)
Performance: maximum speed	**Armament:** one 0.295-in (7.5-mm)
242 mph (550 km/h) at 18,045 ft	machine-gun in nose, one 20-mm
(5500 m); range with 3,527 lb	cannon in dorsal position, and one
(1600 kg) of bombs 1,491 miles	20-mm cannon and one 0.295-in
(2400 km)	(7.5-mm) gun in ventral position,
Weights: empty 26,158 lb	plus up to 7,937 lb (3600 kg) of
(11865 kg); maximum take-off	bombs

Sud-Ouest S.O.4050 Vautour

Israel's first Vautour IIAs arrived at Ramat David in 1957 to serve with the newly-created No. 110 Sqn. The type was heavily employed during the War of Attrition.

As stages in the development of an advanced high-performance experimental twin-jet bomber, Sud-Ouest designed and built two half-scale models. The first of these was the **S.O.M.1**, which was a pure glider, launched from a Lanquedoc 'mother-plane' for the first time on 26 September 1949. It was followed by the **S.O.M.2** powered by a single Rolls-Royce Derwent turbojet engine, and first flown on 13 April 1949. Experience gained with these two aircraft led to the **S.O.4000** prototype, a cantilever mid-wing monoplane of all-metal construction with extremely clean lines, its retractable landing gear

different from that of the S.O.M.2 in comprising a single nosewheel and four mainwheels, in tandem pairs. Accommodation was provided for two in tandem in the nose of the aircraft and the powerplant consisted of two Hispano-Suiza licence-built Rolls-Royce Nene turbojets mounted in the rear fuselage. The S.O.4000 was flown for the first time on 15 March 1951.

Subsequently the **S.O.4050 Vautour** was developed, and was to be ordered in quantity for the Armée de l'Air. The S.O.4050 differed considerably from its predecessor, but benefited from the experience with systems

and controls that had been evaluated with the half-scale models and the prototype. Of similar midwing configuration, it had swept wings and tail surfaces, retractable landing gear comprising two twinwheel main units in tandem with single small outriggers retracting into the nacelles of the engines which, in the S.O.4050, were mounted beneath the wing. Sud-Ouest received an order for three prototypes, the first of them being flown on 16 October 1952. These comprised the **S.O.4050-01**, completed as a two-seat all-weather fighter and powered initially by two 5,291-lb (23.53-kN) thrust SNECMA Atar 101B turbojets; the **S.O.4050-02** single-seat ground-attack aircraft with two 6,217-lb (27.65-kN) thrust Atar 101D turbojets,

first flown on 16 December 1953; and the **S.O.4050-3** two-seat bomber with two Armstrong Siddeley Sapphire turbojets, flown on 5 December 1954. Testing of these aircraft led to an order for six preproduction aircraft, the last of them a two-seat all-weather fighter which, powered by two 10,000-lb (44.47-kN) thrust Rolls-Royce Avon R.A.14 turbojets, made its first flight on 18 October 1955. Full service evaluation of these aircraft led to production orders for the Vautour in all three versions, and when production ended a total of 140 had been built for the Armée de l'Air with the Atar 101E as the standard powerplant. They comprised 30 **Vautour II-A** single-seat tactical fighters, the first flown on 30 April 1956; 40 **Vautour II-B**

two-seat bombers, the first flown on 31 July 1957; and 70 **Vautour II-N** two-seat all-weather fighters, the first flown on 10 October 1956. Eighteen were supplied subsequently to the Israeli air force. Accommodation varied according to role, all crew positions being pressurised and provided with ejection seats, and armament differed considerably, although that of the bomber was similar to that of the tactical support version, described below, except that it did not have the nose-mounted cannon. The all-weather Vautour II-N had the DEFA 30-mm cannon and was armed with rockets and missiles, but also had radar. The designation was changed to **II-1N** after the later fitting of slab tailplanes.

SPECIFICATION

Sud-Ouest S.O.4050 Vautour II-A
Type: single-seat tactical fighter
Powerplant: two 7,716-lb (34.31-kN) thrust SNECMA Atar 101E-3 turbojets
Performance: maximum speed 687 mph (1105 km/h); maximum rate of climb 11,810 ft (3600 m) per minute; service ceiling more than 49,210 ft (15000 m)
Weights: empty 22,046 lb (10000 kg); maximum take-off

44,092 lb (20000 kg)
Dimensions: wingspan 49 ft 6½ in (15.09 m); length 51 ft 1 in (15.57 m); height 14 ft 9¼ in (4.50 m)
Armament: four 30-mm DEFA cannon in nose; up to 240 rockets or 10 bombs in the fuselage bomb bay; and underwing pylons suitable for a total of 76 Matra M.116E rockets, or 24 4.72-in (120-mm) rockets, or two bombs of up to 992 lb (450 kg); or two drop tanks

Sukhoi Su-2

SPECIFICATION

Sukhoi Su-2 (late production)
Type: light bomber/reconnaissance aircraft
Powerplant: one 11,400-hp (1044kW) Shvetsov M-82 radial piston engine
Performance: maximum speed 302 mph (486 km/h) at 19,030 ft (5800 m); service ceiling 29,530 ft (9000 m); range 684 miles (1100 km)
Weights: empty 7,216 lb

(3273 kg); maximum take-off 10,362 lb (4700 kg)
Dimensions: wingspan 46 ft 11 in (14.30 m); length 34 ft 3¾ in (10.46 m); wing area 312.16 sq ft (29.00 m²)
Armament: up to nine 0.3-in (7.62-mm) ShKAS machine-guns, plus up to 882 lb (400 kg) of bombs in internal bomb bay, and bombs, or containers or RS-82/RS-130 rockets on underwing racks

Pavel O. Sukhoi began his design career as a member of Tupolev's team at AGOS in 1924. He then participated in a series of Tupolev designs, including the ANT-37 or DB-2 bomber/

record-breaker, before working on the ANT-51 low-wing monoplane intended for tactical reconnaissance and ground attack. The first prototype, flown on 25 August 1937, was

powered by an 820-hp (611-kW) M-62 radial engine, but further prototypes with retractable landing gear and more powerful M-87A and M-87B engines were developed. It was during this period that Sukhoi's design brigade was promoted to bureau status. After further redesign and the successful completion of state trials in autumn 1940 the **Su-2** was ordered into production and allocated the military designation **BB-1** (BB signifying short-range bomber). A cantilever low-wing monoplane with tailwheel landing gear, all three units retractable, early production aircraft were powered by the 950-hp (708-kW) M-88

radial. Pilot and observer/gunner were housed under a long glazed canopy, which terminated in a manually-operated gun turret, and both crew members had 9-mm armour protection.

The later production version of the Su-2, powered by a 1,000-hp (746-kW) M-88B engine, was highly regarded by the air regiments to which it was allocated. The Su-2 was comparable with the best aircraft of the same category in other countries, but the Soviets did not learn until the German invasion of June 1941 the shortcomings of the type that had already been discovered by other nations: light bombers operating at low and

Variants

ShB: single-prototype of improved ground-attack version flown early in 1940 with revised landing gear, more armour, increased bombload of 1,323 lb (600 kg) and 1,000-hp (746-kW) M-88A engine
Su-4: improved version of Su-2 with 2,100-hp (1566-kW) Shvetsov M-90 engine; armament of two wing-mounted 0.5-in (12.7-mm) BS machine-guns and two 0.3-in (7.62-mm) ShKAS guns in turret, but no underwing racks for offensive stores as Su-4 classed as light bomber; flown December 1941 and built to the extent of 1,000 examples

medium altitudes, even if fast, were very vulnerable to enemy ground defences and fighters unless provided with powerful fighter cover. Nevertheless, production and development continued until the type was phased out of production in late 1942, the final version having the M-82 engine. Some Su-2s had been fitted with a second machine-gun in the gun turret and others had a ventral gun on a retractable mounting, but in early 1941 M-88B-powered aircraft were flying with only two wing guns and maximum bombload restricted to 882 lb (400 kg) to improve performance. From 1942, when Su-2 regiments had re-equipped with Ilyushin Il-2s, two or three Su-2s were attached to each *Shturmovik* unit to act as formation leaders and fly reconnaissance missions; other roles then included target towing, training and liaison. Some 800 Su-2s were built.

The Su-2 could carry an internal bombload of up to four 100-kg (220-lb) FAB-100 HE bombs. Wing racks could accommodate 551-lb (250-kg) of bombs, or up to ten RS-82 rockets.

Sukhoi Su-7 'Fitter'

From December 1949, the Sukhoi OKB was closed on the orders of Stalin to punish Sukhoi for the failure of a jet fighter prototype. Sukhoi and his team transferred to Tupolev, where they worked on their own projects until the death of Stalin, when permission was given to reopen the bureau. During his time at Tupolev, Sukhoi had worked on two configurations which he dubbed S (swept wing, 60-62° swept) and T (delta wing, 57-60° sweep). All subsequent

prototypes were numerically designated with an S- or T- prefix.

The first product of the reopened bureau was the **S-1**, prototype of the **Su-7**. This was designed as an air-to-air fighter, but the existence of the smaller, more agile MiG-21 prompted a redesign for the ground attack role. The resulting **S-2** was followed by a series of several pre-production aircraft, culminating in the **S-22** which formed the basis of the production **Su-7B** (**Bombardirovschkik**, or

The Su-7BKL was developed for dispersed operations from short unpaved runways and snow. This variant was plumbed for up to four underwing drop tanks. In Czechoslovakian service, Su-7BKLs eventually received many of the Su-7BMK's modifications.

fighter-bomber). Powered by a Lyul'ka AL-7 turbojet and with a variable shock cone in the pitot intake, the Su-7 was capable of speeds of up to Mach 1.6, but fuel consumption was excessive, and even with two underfuselage fuel tanks radius of action was unimpressive.

The Su-7B was armed with a pair of NR-30 cannon in the wingroots, and had a retractable box containing 32 spin-stabilised rockets in the belly. UV-8-32 rocket pods could be carried under each wing. The rocket box was deleted in the **Su-7BM** which followed, and which introduced the more powerful 22,282-lb st

(99.12-kN) Lyul'ka AL-7F-1 engine. The underwing pylons were restressed and plumbed for the carriage of fuel tanks. The avionics were improved, and a pair of side-by-side cable ducts was added above the fuselage. The pitot probe gained yaw vanes and was moved from the top of the intake to a '10 o'clock' position.

In order to improve rough-field capability, Sukhoi developed the **Su-7BKL**, which became the standard version in VVS service. This introduced provision for SPRD-110 assisted take-off rockets, a new brake chute fairing at the base of the tailfin which housed new twin

brake parachutes, and also featured redesigned trailing-edge flaps. The undercarriage was redesigned, with a new low-pressure nosewheel which necessitated the provision of bulged nosewheel doors, and the addition of small skis on shock struts outboard of each mainwheel. These could be extended to bear almost the full weight of the aircraft on soft ground, or retracted when operating from a hard surface. The similar **Su-7BMK** was the final production version.

Two-seat trainer versions were designated **Su-7UM** (based on the BM airframe) and received the NATO name **'Moujik'**.

SPECIFICATION	
Sukhoi Su-7BMK 'Fitter-A' **Type:** single-seat ground-attack aircraft **Powerplant:** one NPO Saturn (Lyul'ka) AL-7F-1 turbojet rated at 15,432 lb st (68.65 kN) dry and 22,282 lb st (99.12 kN) with afterburning **Performance:** maximum level speed 'clean' at 36,090 ft (11000 m) 1,055 mph (1700 km/h); service ceiling 49,705 ft (15150 m); combat radius 214 miles (345 km)	on a hi-lo-hi attack mission with a 2,205-lb (1000-kg) warload and two drop tanks **Weights:** empty equipped 19,004 lb (8620 kg); maximum take-off 29,762 lb (13500 kg) **Dimensions:** wingspan 29 ft 3½ in (8.93 m); length 57 ft (17.37 m); height 15 ft (4.57 m); wing area 297.09 sq ft (27.60 m²) **Armament:** two 30-mm NR-30 cannon plus up to 5,511 lb (2500 kg) of ordnance

Sukhoi Su-9/Su-11 'Fishpot' and related prototypes

In parallel with work on the swept-wing S-1, Sukhoi produced a family of single-engined delta-winged prototypes which used a basically similar fuselage, tail unit and undercarriage. The first of these was the **T-3** which first flew in early 1956, aid which featured a a radome in the top of the intake lip. The T-3 was developed through a series of research prototypes

(including the **PT-7** with centrebody and lid radomes, and the long-nosed **PT-8**) to the **T-40** which is regarded as the prototype of the **Su-9** (NATO **'Fishpot'**) single-seat all-weather fighter. Of mid-wing configuration with retractable tricycle landing gear, the Su-9 was powered by the 19,842-lb (88.20-kN) afterburning thrust Lyulka AL-7F turbojet

and had underwing pylons to carry its sole armament of four 'Alkali-B' semi-active radar homing missiles. Development continued and the **T-43** flown in the Tushino Aviation Day display in 1961 was the prototype of an improved version which had the designation **Su-11** (**'Fishpot-C'**).

Basically similar to the Su-9, it differed primarily by having a lengthened and bulged forward fuselage to house more powerful *Uragan*-5B radar, was armed as standard with two 'Anab' infra-red or semi-active radar homing missiles, and introduced the more powerful Lyulka AL-71F-1 engine. A tandem two-seat trainer **Su-9U** (**'Maiden'**) was also built.

The Su-9 entered service

The Su-11 utilised the Su-9's airframe, but coupled this with an uprated engine and an Uragan-5B radar complex with a 3-14 mile (5-23 km) detection range. Two underwing pylons carried R-8 AAMs.

during 1959 and was superseded in production by the Su-11 in about 1966.

Combined production has been estimated at about 1,100 aircraft. None entered service with

Warsaw Pact Countries or were exported. From the early 1970s many were converted for use as radio-controlled targets, under the **Su-11RM** designation, and most had been retired by 1980.

SPECIFICATION	
Sukhoi Su-11 'Fishpot-C' **Type:** all-weather fighter **Powerplant:** one 22,046-lb (98-kN) afterburning thrust Lyulka AIL-71F-1 turbojet **Performance:** maximum speed clean 1,190 mph (1915 km/h) or Mach 1.8 at 36,090 ft (11000 m), service ceiling 55,775 ft (17000 m), combat radius with weapons	286 miles (460 km) **Weights:** empty 20,062 lb (9100 kg), maximum take-off 30,365 lb (14000 kg) **Dimensions:** wingspan 27 ft 8 in (8.43 m), length 57 ft 1 in (17.40 ft), wing area 282.02 sq ft (26.20 m²) **Armament:** standard weapons two AA-3 air-to air homing missiles on underwing pylons

Sukhoi Su-15 'Flagon'

The **Su-15 'Flagon'** was of enormous importance, serving as the standard PVO interceptor at bases across the length and breadth of the former USSR. When the Korean Airlines Boeing 747 (Flight

KE007) was shot down in September 1983, after overflying the Kamchatka Peninsula, it was no surprise that the fighter involved was an Su-15.

Of similar configuration to the earlier Su-9 and

Su-11, the Su-15 was a larger aircraft, powered by twin R-25 engines and with a large search radar occupying the nose, necessitating the use of separate lateral air intakes on the fuselage sides.

The prototype, designated **T-58**, first flew in 1961 in the hands of Vladimir Ilyushin, and was followed by a pre-production batch of similar aircraft, designated **Su-15** and allo-

The major 'Flagon' production variant was the Su-15TM, with R-60 (AA-8) capability. Earlier versions were retrofitted.

cated the reporting name **'Flagon-A'** by NATO. The reporting name **'Flagon-B'** was allocated to the **T-58VD**, a one-off STOL research aircraft with a redesigned wing having

reduced span on the outer panels, and with three RD-36-35 lift jets in the fuselage. This made its maiden flight during 1966 and was demonstrated at Domodyedovo in July

SPECIFICATION	
Sukhoi Su-15TM 'Flagon-F' **Type:** single-seat interceptor **Powerplant:** two MNPK 'Soyuz' (Tumanskii) R-13F2-300 turbojets each rated at 9,039 lb st (40.21 kN) dry and 15,653 lb st (69.63 kN) with afterburning **Performance:** maximum level speed 'clean' at 36,090 ft (11000 m) 1,650 mph (2655 km/h); maximum rate of climb at sea level 44,948 ft (13700 m) per minute;	service ceiling 65,615 ft (20000 m); combat radius 450 miles (745 km) on a hi-hi-hi interception mission **Weights:** empty 27,006 lb (12250 kg); maximum take-off 44,092 lb (20000 kg) **Dimensions:** wingspan 34 ft 6⅔ in (10.53 m); length 67 ft 3⅒ in (20.50 m); 16 ft 5 in (5.00 m); wing area 387.51 sq ft (36.00 m²) **Armament:** see text

1967. The **Su-15U** was a tandem two-seat trainer version of the basic fighter, with the instructor's cockpit in place of the No. 1 fuselage fuel tank and with separate upward-hinging canopies over the cockpits. This trainer variant was dubbed **'Flagon-C'**.

The first 'second-generation' Su-15 was the

Su-15M ('Flagon-D'), which introduced a new wing based on that of the T-58VD with extended ailerons, and a tailplane with reduced anhedral.

The **Su-15T 'Flagon-E'**, introduced in 1973, superseded the earlier variant. This was powered by a pair of R-13F-300 engines, and featured increased internal

fuel capacity. To cope with the increased weight, the undercarriage was strengthened, and a new twin-wheel nose gear was introduced, with bulged doors. Extra underwing pylons allowed the carriage of up to four R-60s (AA-8 'Aphid') in addition to the R-8/R-98 (AA-3 'Anab') missiles on the outboard

pylons. Alternatively, each underfuselage pylon was stressed for the UPK-23-250 cannon pod or an external fuel tank.

The **Su-15TM 'Flagon-F'** introduced the *Taifun* radar, which required a shorter ogival radome in place of the conical radome fitted to earlier variants. It was powered by a pair of

R-13F2-300 engines and entered service during 1974. The two-seat trainer version with *Taifun* radar and the new wing was designated **Su-15UM 'Flagon-G'**.

Western speculation that the designation **Su-21** was applied to the later 'Flagon' versions has subsequently proved incorrect.

Sukhoi Su-17/20/22 'Fitter' family

While the original Su-7 'Fitter' probably survives only in limited service with the air forces of Afghanistan, Algeria, North Korea and Turkmenistan, its swing-wing derivatives remain in widespread service. The **Su-17M** (**Su-20** for export) **'Fitter-C'** attack aircraft was the first major variable-geometry variant, also introducing more power and improved

avionics. In 2001 the type remained in service only with Afghanistan, Algeria, Eygpt and Syria. The further improved **Su-17M-2 'Fitter-D'** entered production in 1974, with a slightly lengthened, slightly drooping nose, a revised avionics suite and a laser rangefinder. A slightly sanitised version, with a new dorsal fin fillet and new *Fon* laser rangefinder, was built

for export under the designation **Su-22 'Fitter-F'**. Next came the **Su-17M-3 'Fitter-H'** (export **Su-22M 'Fitter-J'**) which featured a further modified airframe and wingroot cannon. 'Fitter' trainers comprise the **Su-17UM 'Fitter-E'** and export **Su-22U 'Fitter-G'**, and the improved **Su-17UM-3 'Fitter-G'** (exported as the **Su-22UM-3K**). The ultimate 'Fitter', with new avionics and compatibility with an even wider range of weapons, was developed for the Soviet air forces and for export. New avionics included a new CVM 20-22 mission computer and PrNK-54 navigation system (using the LORAN-equivalent

SPECIFICATION

Sukhoi Su-17M-4 'Fitter-K'
Type: single-seat ground attack fighter
Powerplant: one NPO Saturn (Lyul'ka) AL-21F-3 turbojet rated at 17,196 lb st (76.49 kN) dry and 24,802 lb st (110.32 kN) with afterburning, plus provision for two RATO units
Performance: maximum level speed 'clean' at sea level 870 mph (1400 km/h); maximum rate of climb at sea level 45,276 ft (13800m) per minute; service ceiling 49,870 ft (15200 m) ; combat radius 715 miles (1150 km) on a hi-lo-hi attack mission with a 4,409 lb (2000-kg)

Weights: normal take-off 36,155 lb (16400 kg) maximum take-off 42,989 lb (19500 kg)
Dimensions: wingspan 45 ft 3 in (13.80m) spread and 32 ft 10 in (10.00m) swept; length 61 ft 6¼ in (18.75m) including probes; height 16 ft 5 in (5.00m); wing area 430.57 sq ft (40 m²) spread and 398.28 sq ft (37 m²) swept
Armament: two NR-30 30-mm cannon, each with 80 rounds; maximum weapon load 9,369 lb (4250 kg); weapons include guided and unguided free-fall bombs, AGMs, self-defence AAMs, gun and rocket pods

RSDN and the TACAN-equivalent A-312), which reduced pilot workload and improved navigational and weapons delivery accuracy. Other avionics include a DISS-7 Doppler, an ASP-17BC gunsight, an IKV-8 inertial platform, an ARK-22 radio compass, an SRO-2 IFF system, an SO-69 transponder and an SPO-15LE (*Sirena*) RWR. The **Su-17M-4** (export **Su-22M-4**) 'Fitter-K' is externally identifiable by a

prominent ram-air inlet projecting forward from the finroot and the aircraft is optimised for high speed at low level. Aircraft of the Su-17M/Su-22 family remain in service with Angola, Bulgaria, Czech Republic, Iraq, Libya, Peru, Poland, Russia, Slovakia, Syria, Ukraine, Uzbekistan, Vietnam and Yemen. The aircraft has recently been upgraded with the addition of inflight-refuelling probes in Peruvian service.

Czechoslovakia's Su-22M-4s were divided between the air arms of the Czech Republic and Slovakia following the nation's division in 1993.

Sukhoi Su-24 'Fencer'

The **Su-24** was developed as a replacement for the Yak-28 'Brewer' in the tactical bomber, reconnaissance and EW roles. Design began in the early 1960s, but Sukhoi abandoned its initial design (an enlarged, twin-engined tandem cockpit design based loosely on the Su-7 configuration) in favour of the compound

delta **T6**, which also featured fuselage-mounted lift jets for enhanced STOL performance. This design was built and flown, before the T6 was redesigned six months later, with a variable geometry wing. The lift-jet equipped **T6-1** made its maiden flight on 2 July 1967, and was followed by the **VG T6-2I** on 17

In 2001 a small number of Russian air force Su-24M 'Fencers' sported an export-style two-tone upper-surface camouflage scheme.

January 1970.

This was ordered into production as the Su-24 in late 1970. The Su-24 entered VVS service (with Frontal Aviation) in 1973, and rapidly replaced the Yak-28 in the tactical bomb-

ing role. It was never intended or used as a strategic bomber, a fact obscured by comparisons with the F-111, which enjoyed a range 1,200 nm (2224 km) greater. Western intelligence noted the aircraft's service entry in

1974, allocating the reporting name **'Fencer'** to what it mistakenly thought was designated **Su-19**. The type entered service with the Group of Soviet Forces in Germany in 1979, and from 1984 the Su-24 saw active service in Afghanistan.

Variants

S6: original unbuilt design with tandem cockpits and fixed, swept wing
T6: first prototype with side-by-side seats for pilot and WSO, fixed double-delta wing and lift jets
T6-2I to T6-7I: subsequent prototypes with variable geometry wing and no lift jets
Su-24 Production Series 2-11 'Fencer-A': baseline version, with greater wing area than prototypes, variable intake ramps and vortex generators
Su-24 Production Series 12-23 'Fencer-B': kinked tailplane leading edge, heat exchanger above rear fuselage, extra underfuselage hardpoint. Increased height fin, brake chute fairing below rudder, redesigned rear fuselage and fin leading edge intake from Series 15
Su-24 Production Series 24-27 'Fencer-C': SPO-15 *Beryoza* RWR antennas added to sides of intake and fin, new outer wing panels (improved aerofoil)
Su-24M 'Fencer-D': late production bomber with lengthened, drooped forward fuselage, retractable AAR probe, and *Kaira*-24 EO targeting system under the forward fuselage
Su-24MK 'Fencer-D (Mod)': export version with chaff/flare dispensers in the wing fences
Su-24MR 'Fencer-E': reconnaissance derivative of the Su-24M with comprehensive optical and EO sensor suite, plus provision for Elint and SLAR pods. Externally characterised by domed heat exchanger on spine
Su-24MP 'Fencer-F': TEW derivative with large antennas under nose and on spine immediately behind the cockpit

SPECIFICATION

Sukhoi Su-24M 'Fencer-D'
Type: two-seat variable geometry attack aircraft
Powerplant: two Perm/Soloviev (Lyul'ka) AL-21F-3A turbojets each rated at 24,691 lb st (109.83 kN) with afterburning
Performance: maximum level speed 'clean' at low-level 820 mph (1320 km/h); service ceiling 55,775 ft (17000 m); combat radius at sea level 348 miles (560 km)
Weights: empty 49,162 lb (22300 kg); normal take-off 79,365 lb (36000 kg)
Dimensions: wingspan 57 ft 10½ in (17.64 m) spread and 34 ft (10.37 m)

swept; length 74 ft 1½ in (22.59 m); height 20 ft 4 in (6.19 m); wing area 594 sq ft (55.17 m²) spread and 549 sq ft (51.02 m²) swept
Armament: one GSh-6-23M 23-mm cannon; maximum ordnance 17,637 lb (8000 kg); weapons include TN-1000 and TN-1200 free-fall nuclear weapons; comprehensive range of semi-active laser and TV-guided PGMs includes Kh-23, Kh-25ML, Kh-29L/T and Kh-59 *Ovod* ASMs; Kh-25MP, Kh-31P, Kh-29MP and Kh-58 ARMs; Kh-31A and Kh-35 AShMs, KAB-500Kr LGBs, R-60 AAMs

Sukhoi Su-24 'Fencer' (continued)

The Su-24 is fast and stable at low level, and can carry an impressive warload (though only at the expense of an appreciable reduction in range) but by comparison with Western contemporaries is crude and its avionics are backward and unreliable. The aircraft was thus never as capable as Western attack aircraft like the Tornado and F-111, nor even the radar-less Jaguar.

The Su-24 did form the basis of an export fighter bomber, delivered to Iran, Iraq, Libya and Syria (and, according to some sources, also to Algeria), and of recce and EW variants.

Sukhoi Su-25 'Frogfoot' family

Development of the **Su-25 'Frogfoot'** began during the late 1960s, paralleling US studies. Sukhoi, like the US firms, was heavily influenced by USAF experience in the Vietnam War. Sukhoi believed that high speed was essential to ensure survivability over the battle-field, and chose to use turbojet engines and relatively little armour. The **T-8** prototype made its first flight on 22 February 1975, but much redesign, including the installation of a new powerplant, was necessary before series production was authorised. Two proto-types were sent to Afghanistan for a combined series of operational and state acceptance trials (Operation Rhombus). The first 12 Su-25s also served in Afghanistan, where the type received its **'Grach'** (rook) nickname. The Su-25 eventually flew some 60,000 combat sorties in Afghanistan. This experience led to a number of modifications and during 1987, production aircraft were fitted with the more power-ful R-195 engine, which was also fitted to all production 'Frogfoot' two-seaters, as the **Su-25 'Frogfoot-A'**. R-195-engined Su-25's are self-supporting, thanks to a set of support equipment carried in four underwing pods. A handful of Su-25s has been modified as **Su-25BM** (**Buksir Misheni**, or target tug) machines. The need for an all-weather and night capable Su-25 with increased range/endurance required more airframe space and a new variant, based on the two-seat **Su-25UB 'Frogfoot-B'**, was built. The first such **T-8M** prototype made its maiden flight on 17 August 1984, with a 30-mm cannon below the centre fuselage. A pre-production batch of 20 Su-25T aircraft (**Tankovyi**, or anti-tank) (later **Su-25TM**) was built and the type has been offered for export as the **Su-25TK**. Another derivative of the Su-25UB is the navalised **Su-25UTG** trainer which first flew in 1988. Ten production Su-25UTGs were built, five of them passing to the Ukraine.

Sukhoi Su-25K 'Frogfoot-A'
Type: single-seat ground attack aircraft
Powerplant: two MNPK 'Soyuz' (Tumanskii) R-195 turbojets each rated at 9,921 lb st (44.13 kN)
Performance: maximum level speed 'clean' at sea level 590 mph (950 km/h); take-off run 1,969 ft (600 m); service ceiling 22,965 ft (7000 m); combat radius 267 miles (495 km) on a hi-lo-hi attack mission with an 8,818-lb (4000-kg) warload and two drop tanks
Weights: empty equipped 21,605 lb (9800 kg); maximum take-off 41,005 lb (18600 kg)

Dimensions: wingspan 47 ft 1⅛ in (14.36 m); length 50 ft 11½ in (15.53 m); height 15 ft 9 in (4.80 m); wing area 324 sq ft (30.10 m²)
Armament: one internal 30-mm AO-17A cannon; maximum ordnance 9,700 lb (4400 kg) including unguided rockets, free-fall and laser-guided bombs, cluster bombs, incendiary weapons and cannon pods; Kh-23 (AS-7 'Kerry'), Kh-25 (AS-10 'Karen') and Kh-29 (AS-14 'Kedge') ASMs and R-60 (AA-8 'Aphid') AAMs for self-defence

Pictured over the Volga during weapons trials, this Akhtunbinsk-based Su-25 is seen carrying 57-mm rockets in UB-32 pods (up to eight can be carried), rather than the more modern 80-mm B-8M1 packs.

Sukhoi Su-26, Su-29 and Su-31

Sukhoi's interest in aerobatic aircraft reportedly began when the OKB was involved in fatigue investigation of another company's aerobatic aircraft, which was suffering major problems. Spare capacity at the bureau, coupled with a belief that it could produce a world-beater, led to construction of the **Su-26** prototype which made its maiden flight in June 1984. Four were completed to the original standard, with two-bladed propellors, before production switched to the **Su-26M**, with refined tail surfaces and a three-bladed Hoffman prop. From the sixth aircraft the type had less glazing on the fuselage sides. A team of three Su-26Ms swept the board of men's and women's team prizes at the 1986 World aerobatics championships.

Further refinements were added to the aircraft which appeared at the 1989 Paris Air Salon, and also in the **Su-26M** which was developed specifically for export and which was launched at Farnborough the following year. A proto-type of the **Su-29** two-seater made its maiden flight during 1991 with a continuous rearward-hinge-ing canopy over the tandem seats. This aircraft also introduced a new semi-monocoque compos-ite rear fuselage. Production aircraft built since 1999 are known as **Su-29M** machines. The **Su-29AR** designation refers to Su-29s delivered to the Argentine air force, while the **Su-29KS** is a one-off testbed for Zvezda light-weight crew escape systems.

Originally known as the **Su-29T**, a single-seat derivative using the same composite rear fuselage as the Su-29 was developed, later being redesignated as the **Su-31T**. The **Su-31M** is an otherwise similar single-seater, with a Zvezda pilot's extraction system under a modified canopy. Related to the Su-26/29 is a heavier tandem two-seat trainer which has most recently been described as the **S-49**. This has tricycle undercarriage, LERXes and options for Western flat-four or flat-six engines. The S-49 project was initi-ated in 1992 in order to provide the Russian military with a new basic trainer.

Su-26 production has now ceased in favour of the two-seat Su-29M and Su-31. The last example, an Su-26M-3, was commissioned by a Western customer in 1999 at a cost of US$215,000.

Sukhoi Su-27/Su-33 and Su-37 'Flanker' family

Work on the T-10 design that led to the Su-27 began in 1969. The requirement was for a highly manoeu-vrable fighter with very long range, heavy arma-ment and modern sensors, capable of meeting the F-15 on equal terms. To maximise manoeuvrability, the T-10 was designed from the outset to be unstable, and therefore required a computer-controlled fly-by-wire control system at least in pitch. The first prototype T-10 made its maiden flight on 20 May 1977, eventually gaining the reporting name 'Flanker-A'. The early flight development programme revealed serious problems.

Insurmountable prob-lems led to a total redesign, the resulting **T-10S-1** making its maiden flight on 20 April 1981. The new reporting name **'Flanker-B'** was allocated. The Su-27 finally began to enter operational service during the mid-1980s, vari-ants including the basic **Su-27 'Flanker-B'** with advanced pulse-doppler radar; **Su-27UB 'Flanker-C'** trainer with a lengthened forward fuselage and tail-fins increased in height and area; the **Su-27M** advanced Su-27 derivative with canard foreplanes, retractable IFR probe, 'glass' cockpit, quadruplex

Formerly known as the Su-27K, the Su-33 is a naval version of the basic Su-27 interceptor, with limited air-to-ground capability. Examples are shore-based with the Russian navy's 279th KIAP.

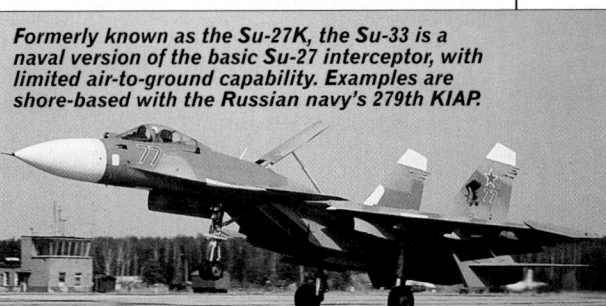

Above: The Su-30MKI is the advanced Su-30M variant offered to India. It combines the two-seat Su-30 concept with the Su-37's thrust vectoring, canards and avionics. India initially received the basic Su-30PU.

Left: The Su-37 is effectively a vectored-thrust technology demonstrator for a proposed Su-27-based production fighter. Any production variant is likely to employ uprated AL-31FU turbofans.

digital FBW FCS, advanced radar and enhanced multi-role capability, which was later redesignated **Su-35** by Sukhoi and offered as a MiG-29/Su-27 replacement; the **Su-37**, which is the last Su-35 revised with thrust-vectoring engines; the **Su-30** (**Su-30K** for export) basic operational long-range/extended endurance two-seat interceptor fighter with IFR probe and second pilot/WSO in rear cockpit; **Su-30M** (**Su-30MK** for export) multi-role two-seater with provision for TV, radar and IR-guided ASMs and PGMs; **Su-30MKI** definitive multi-role aircraft with canard foreplanes, thrust vectoring and the option of Western avionics, displays and defensive systems, as ordered by India; and the **Su-33**, which is the new designation for the carrier-based fighter previously known as **Su-27K**.

Sukhoi Su-27IB/Su-32/Su-34

The end of the Cold War saw a reduction in orders for new military aircraft. The Sukhoi OKB, closely associated with (and favoured by) the new, more 'liberal' political regime in Russia, saw an opportunity, and developed a family of derivatives of its Su-27 'Flanker' to meet a range of requirements. The basic Su-27 offered a unique combination of performance, range, and (at low weights) great agility, and these attributes promised to make derivatives of the aircraft suitable for a range of roles. The more radical of these developments added an entirely new forward fuselage section ahead of the wing, featuring side-by-side seating for a crew of two in what became known as the 'Platypus' nose. On this basis, Sukhoi developed the **Su-27IB** for pure ground attack, with seating for the pilot and a WSO. This aircraft, which is known to the manufacturer as the **Su-34**, is a heavy fighter-bomber intended to enter Russian service as a replacement for the Su-24. The Su-27IB could also form the basis of heavy interceptor, recce and EW versions, but funding for the original version is scarce and even this is entering service at little more than a snail's pace. A more radical development of the same airframe is represented by the **Su-32FN**, which is also, confusingly, known to the Russian military as Su-27IB. So far built to the extent of just one aircraft, the Su-32FN is a maritime strike version, designed to attack ships with a range of mines, missiles and torpedoes, aided by a powerful maritime search radar, while submarines can be engaged with the help of a MAD 'tail sting'. The latest side-by-side variant is the **Su-27KUB**, which has been redesignated as the **Su-33B** and is a trainer for pilots destined to fly the Su-33 from Russia's single remaining aircraft carrier, the *Admiral Kuznetsov*. The aircraft has a similar cockpit to the Su-27IB, but features a conical nose radome.

The prototype Su-27IB differs from the Su-32/34 production aircraft in its retention of the basic Su-27 'Flanker's' single wheel main undercarriage units.

Sukhoi S-37 Berkut (Royal Eagle)

On 25 September 1997 the **S-37 Berkut** (Royal Eagle) made its maiden flight from the LII flight test centre airfield at Zhukhovskii. The S-37 is being developed by Sukhoi to explore post-stall manoeuvrabilty and super-manoeuvrability. Although very much a research aircraft and concept demonstrator in its present form, it may yet form the basis of a fifth generation Russian fighter. It is of similar size to the MiG 1.44, and could be offered to meet the Russian air force's MFI ('heavy fighter') requirement. The most radical aspect of the Berkut is its forward swept wing, 90 per cent of which is of composites construction to ensure adequate torsional stiffness. The very advanced aerodynamic configuration includes strakes, canards, wing LERXes, tailplanes and twin fins. Combined with extensive use of radar absorbent materials, these are carefully shaped to minimise radar cross section.

Series production of the (unarmed) S-37 is not planned, however, the aircraft may well be handed over by the company to the Russian air force for further trials.

Sukhoi S-37 Berkut (Royal Eagle) (continued)

The S-37 shares many components with the Su-27, including the strengthened undercarriage developed for the naval Su-33, tailfins and canopy. It is reported to be fitted with the quadruplex FBW system of the Su-35/Su-37. Little hard information regarding the S-37's present or future capabilities has been revealed. Almost certainly, it is not flying with engines representative of a production fighter derivative. It further lacks radar, mission systems or weapons but clearly has provision for their installation, as evidenced by the various dielectric panels and radomes around the airframe as well as mock-up IRST and exhaust vent for an internal gun. Weapons carriage is said to be either on conventional pylons or in a semi-conformal arrangement to minimise radar cross-section. The type may also have an internal weapons bay. Berkut testing continues at the slow pace allowed by the limited funding available.

Supermarine Attacker

Conceived originally for service with the RAF, the **Attacker** was designed with a view to the rapid production of a single-seat fighter to be powered by the Rolls-Royce Nene turbojet engine. Thus it combined the wings and landing gear of the Spiteful with a new fuselage and tail unit in the first prototype, flown initially on 27 July 1946. Two more prototypes with long-stroke landing gear were completed to naval requirements and the first of

F.Mk 1s, represented by these No. 800 Sqn examples, had unframed one-piece canopies.

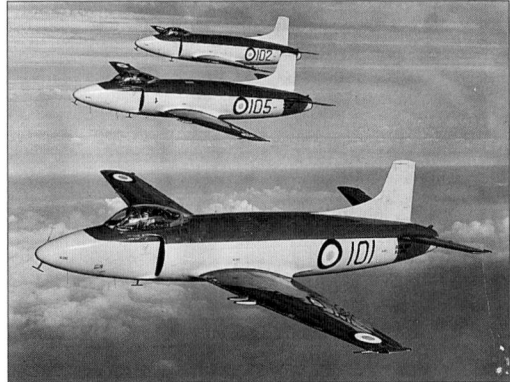

these was flown on 17 June 1947. Following the conclusion of satisfactory carrier trials aboard HMS *Illustrious*, the Attacker was ordered for the Royal Navy and the Pakistan air force. Production for the FAA totalled 145 and comprised 52 **Attacker F.Mk 1** interceptors. Eight **Attacker FB.Mk 1** fighter-bombers and 85 **Attacker FB.Mk 2** fighter-bombers; Attacker F.Mk 1 and FB.Mk 1 aircraft were powered by the Nene 3, and the Attacker FB.Mk 2 by the Nene 2. Entering service initially with No. 800 Sqn on 17 August 1951, the Attacker served only briefly with the FAA before being replaced by Sea Hawks and Sea Venoms in 1954, but continued in use with RNVR air squadrons until the latter were disbanded in 1957. The 36 aircraft supplied to the Pakistan air force were similar to the FAA's Attacker F.Mk 1 but without folding wings and naval equipment.

SPECIFICATION	
Supermarine Attacker F.Mk 1 **Type:** single-seat carrier-based fighter **Powerplant:** one 5,000-lb (22.24-kN) thrust Rolls-Royce Nene 3 turbojet **Performance:** maximum speed 590 mph (950 km/h) at sea level; service ceiling 45,000 ft (13715 m); range with standard fuel 590 miles (950 km)	**Weights:** empty 8,434 lb (3826 kg); maximum take-off 12,211 lb (5339 kg) **Dimensions:** wingspan 36 ft 11 in (11.25 m); length 37 ft 6 in (11.43 m); height 9 ft 11 in (3.02 m); wing area 226 sq ft (21.00 m²) **Armament:** four 20-mm cannon in wings

Supermarine Scapa and Stranraer

The **Southampton Mk IV** was a considerably revised version of the earlier Southampton which had given the RAF such valuable service. It differed in a number of ways, the most important being the far cleaner installation of its two 525-hp (391-kW) Rolls-Royce Kestrel IIIMS engines in nacelles directly beneath the upper wing. The other noticeable external changes included replacement of the tandem open cockpits by an enclosed cockpit with side-by-side seating for the two pilots, and a change from triple to twin fins and rudders. One other important difference was not externally visible, namely a change to an all-metal basic structure, with all aerodynamic surfaces fabric-covered.

Before the prototype was completed the type was renamed **Scapa**, and 14 production aircraft were delivered to the RAF, the first examples equipping No. 202 Sqn at Malta in May 1935. Other squadrons later equipped were Nos 204, 228 and 240, and the Scapa had a short active life, being withdrawn from first-line use during 1938. The closely related **Stranraer**, designated originally **Southampton Mk V**, was the last biplane flying-boat designed by R. J. Mitchell. By comparison with the Scapa it was a larger aircraft, of 85-ft (25.91-m) span, introduced a gun turret in the tail, and in production form was powered by the 875-hp (652-kW) Bristol Pegasus X radial engine. A total of 17 was built for the RAF and these began to enter service with No. 228 Sqn in 1936, eventually equipping also Nos 201, 209 and 240 Sqns. Of this number 15 remained in service at the outbreak of war, but were withdrawn from first line use during 1940. In addition to those built for the RAF, Canadian Vickers at Montreal produced 40 for the Royal Canadian Air Force, and post-war 14 of these were acquired for civil use in Canada.

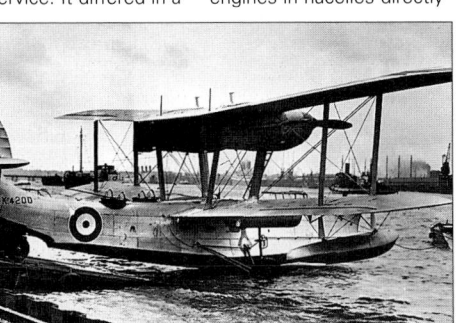

Operated by a crew of five, the 75-ft (22.86-m) span Scapa had a maximum speed of 141 mph (227 km/h) at 3,280 ft (1000 m), was armed with three Lewis guns and carried a 1,000-lb (454-kg) bombload.

Supermarine Schneider Trophy racing aircraft

Supermarine's first Schneider Trophy contender was the **Sea Lion I**, developed from the one-off **N.1B Baby** built to Admiralty Air Department Specification N.1B of 1917 for a single-seat fighter flying-boat. The Sea Lion was thus a small biplane, and its name was derived from its 450-hp (336-kW) Napier Lion engine, strut-mounted between the wings to drive a pusher propeller. Competing in the foggy contest at Bournemouth in 1919, the Sea Lion was retired after one lap, and it was not until 1922, in the contest at Naples, that Supermarine again had a contender in the form of the **Sea Lion II**. Developed from the company's one-off **Sea King II** single-seat fighter flying-boat, and again powered by the Napier Lion engine, it was flown to victory by Henri Biard at an average speed of 145.70 mph (234.48 km/h). For the 1923 contest at Cowes the Sea Lion II was revised and with a 550-hp (410-kW) version of the Lion engine was redesignated **Sea Lion III**; in the contest it was pushed into third place by the US Navy's superb Curtiss CR-3 seaplanes. The next contest was at Baltimore in

N247, an S.6A, was the winner of the 1929 Schneider Trophy event at Ryde. On 12 September 1931, this aircraft achieved a new absolute speed record of 357.7 mph (575.6 km/h).

1925, where R. J. Mitchell's superbly streamlined all-wood **S.4** seaplane, powered by a 700-hp (522-kW) Napier Lion engine, crashed during trials. It was not until 1927 at Venice that the new all-metal **S.5** monoplane seaplanes were ready to take part in the contest, one with a 900-hp (671-kW) Napier Lion VIIA and the other with an 875-hp (652-kW) Napier Lion VIIB. They were to take 1st and 2nd places respectively, the winner being flown by Flight Lieutenant S. N. Webster at an average of 281.66 mph (453.28 km/h). In the penultimate contest, held at Calshot in 1929, the improved **S.6** powered by a 1,900-hp (1417-kW) Rolls-Royce 'R' engine came first, piloted by Flying

Officer H. R. Waghorn at a record 328.63 mph (528.87 km/h), but with lack of government support it seemed certain that the UK would be unable to contend in 1931. However, national-spirited sponsor-ship by Lady Houston made it possible, but with insufficient time to design a new aircraft Supermarine could do little more than modify the S.6 to accept a 2,350-hp (1752-kW) version of the Rolls-Royce 'R' engine. The resulting **S.6B** flew over the course at Calshot uncontested to record a speed of 340.08 mph (547.31 km/h), piloted by Flight Lieutenant J. N. Boothman, to win the trophy permanently for the UK. On the same day, 13 September 1931, Flight Lieutenant G. H. Stainforth used the reserve S.6B to establish a new world absolute speed record of 379.05 mph (610.02 km/h). The combination of Supermarine, R. J. Mitchell, Rolls-Royce and fuel techni-cian F. Rodwell Banks, had given the UK a remarkable success; the same team was to be of vital impor-tance to the nation at the end of the 1930s.

Supermarine Scimitar

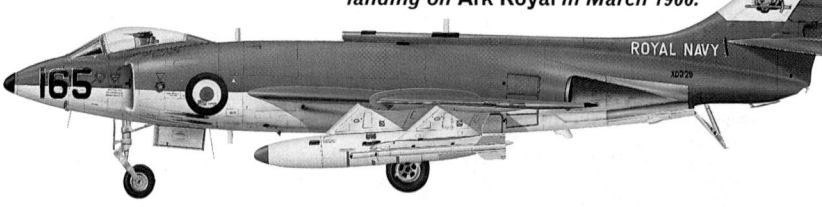

Carrying AIM-9s, 200-Imp gal (909 litre) drop tanks and No. 804 Sqn markings, this Scimitar F.Mk 1 was written-off after a barrier landing on Ark Royal in March 1966.

SPECIFICATION	
Supermarine Scimitar F.Mk 1 **Type:** single-seat carrier-based multi-role aircraft **Powerplant:** two 11,250-lb (52.63-kN) thrust Rolls-Royce Avon 202 turbojets **Performance:** maximum speed 710 mph (1143 km/h) at sea level; service ceiling 46,000 ft (14020 m); range 1,422 miles (2288 km) **Weights:** empty 23,962 lb (10869 kg); maximum take-off 34,200 lb (15513 kg)	**Dimensions:** wingspan 37 ft 2 in (11.33 m); length 55 ft 4 in (16.87 m); height 17 ft 4 in (5.28 m); wing area 485 sq ft (45.06 m²) **Armament:** four 30-mm ADEN cannon and four 1,000-lb (454-kg) bombs or four Bullpup air-to-ground missiles or four Sidewinder air-to-air missiles, or other optional stores including drop tanks, unguided rockets and free-fall tactical nuclear weapons

Supermarine's design to meet the requirements of Naval Specification N.113D was at first known as the **N.113**, but the aircraft finally selected for production as the **Scimitar** was derived through the **Type 508** and **Type 529** prototypes with straight wings and a butter-fly tail unit, and the **Type 525** which introduced swept wings and a cruci-form tail unit. The final **Type 544** design differed from the Type 525 by having a fuselage that incorporated area ruling and, importantly, blown flaps that reduced minimum control speed to simplify catapult launch and carrier landing for this heavy aircraft. The first of three Type 544 prototypes was flown on 19 January 1956, and initial deliveries of production aircraft were made in August 1957 to No. 700X Trials Flight. The first operational squadron (No. 803) was formed in June 1958, the **Scimitar F.Mk 1** then providing the FAA with a low-level super-sonic attacker able to deploy tactical nuclear weapons, a high-level interceptor using air-to-air guided missiles, and a vehicle that could be used in a fighter/reconnais-sance role at extreme ranges. A total of 76 was built to equip also Nos. 800, 804 and 807 Squadrons until superseded by the Buccaneer from 1969.

Supermarine Sea Otter

Basically an improved version of the Walrus, which it superseded in Fleet Air Arm service from 1944 for reconnaissance and air/sea rescue duties, the **Sea Otter** (at first named **Stingray**) was the last biplane amphibian to be designed by the company, and also the last aircraft of biplane configura-tion in squadron service with the FAA. Of all-metal basic construction, with fabric-covered aerofoil surfaces and incorporating a more refined structure than that of the Walrus, the Sea Otter differed primarily by having its 855-hp (638-kW) Bristol Mercury XXX radial engine mounted in tractor configuration.

Armament comprised three Vickers 'K' guns, and up to 1,000 lb (454 kg) of bombs could be carried. The prototype was first flown in September 1938, but it was not until November 1944 that the Sea Otter entered opera-tional service, initially with

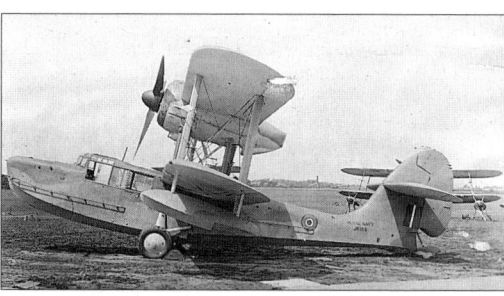

In addition to serving with No. 1700 Sqn, the Sea Otter equipped Nos 730, 742, 753, 778, 781, 799, 1701, 1702 and 1703 Squadrons of the Royal Navy's Fleet Air Arm.

No. 1700 Sqn. Production totalled 292 aircraft includ-ing prototypes and included 250 **Sea Otter Mk I** recon-naissance/communications aircraft and 40 **Sea Otter Mk II** air/sea rescue aircraft. Post-war disposals resulted in examples serv-ing with the Danish air force, Dutch navy and French customs administra-tion in Indo-China, and a number were acquired for civil use, including two operated by Qantas Empire Airways. Spanning 46 ft (14.02 m), the Sea Otter Mk II had a maximum speed of 154 mph (248 km/h) at 5,000 ft (1525 m) and maximum range of 835 miles (1344 km).

Supermarine Seagull and Walrus

The Seal II of 1921, a three-crew deck-landing amphibian for RAF use as a fleet spotter from Royal Navy aircraft-carriers, was converted as the prototype **Seagull** during the follow-ing year. Of biplane foldable-wing configuration with retractable wheel land-ing gear to give amphibious capability, the Seagull was powered by a 480-hp (358-kW) Napier Lion II engine strut-mounted between the wings to drive a tractor-propeller. The production Seagull Mk II had minor improvements and the 492-hp (367-kW) Napier Lion IIB engine, being built to a total of 26 that included one for Japan and three civil aircraft. Production was brought up to a total of 32 by six **Seagull Mk III** aircraft for the Royal Australian Air Force and these, generally similar to the RAF Seagull Mk IIs, differed primarily by having a similarly-rated

Whilst being operated by No. 700 Sqn, FAA, during the early 1940s, this Walrus Mk I was based aboard the cruiser HMS Belfast.

Napier Lion V.

The experimental installa-tion of a Bristol Jupiter IX radial engine in pusher configuration led to the prototype **Seagull Mk V** powered by a 620-hp (462-kW) Bristol Pegasus IIM2 radial engine, of which 24 were ordered by the Australian government. Evaluation of this aircraft led to the type being adopted for service with the FAA under the name **Walrus Mk I** and these, built by Supermarine, had metal hulls. Production eventually totalled 746, of which 461 were built by Saunders-Roe, this number including 191 **Walrus Mk II** aircraft with Saro wooden hulls and the Pegasus VI engine. Entering service with the FAA in 1936 the Walrus, which was stressed for catapult launching, equipped battle-ships and cruisers of the Australian, British and New Zealand navies, and throughout most of World War II was operational in practically every theatre of war. The type also played a significant air/sea rescue role in RAF service, large numbers of rescued aircrew having a special place in their memory for the Walrus, better known to wartime servicemen as the **'Shagbat'**. Pre-war six Seagull Mk Vs were exported to Turkey, and post-war eight Walrus aircraft were supplied to Argentina.

SPECIFICATION	
Supermarine Walrus Mk I **Type:** four-crew spotter reconnaissance amphibian **Powerplant:** one 750-hp (559kW) Bristol Pegasus VI radial piston engine **Performance:** maximum speed 135 mph (217 km/h) at 4,750 ft (1450 m); service ceiling 17,100 ft (5210 m); range 600 miles (966 km) **Weights:** empty 4,900 lb (2223 kg); maximum take-off	7,200 lb (3266 kg) **Dimensions:** wingspan 45 ft 10 in (13.97 m); length 37 ft 3 in (11.35 m); height 15 ft 3 in (4.65 m); wing area 610.0 sq ft (56.67 m²) **Armament:** one 0.303-in (7.7-mm), Vickers 'K' gun in bow and one or two similar weapons amidships, plus up to 600 lb (272 kg) of bombs carried beneath the wings, or two Mk VIII depth charges

Supermarine Southampton

The **Southampton** was developed from the one-off, 10-passenger **Supermarine Swan** which, operated by Imperial Airways, complemented the activities of the three **Supermarine Sea Eagles** on the Southampton-Channel Islands route

during 1926-27. In finalising the design of the Southampton the later-renowned R. J. Mitchell achieved his first great success, for no fewer than 68 of these elegant five-crew flying-boats were built for the RAF. Of biplane configuration and with

underwing stabilising floats, the sleek hull was upswept at the rear to mount the tailplane which carried above it triple fins and rudders; powerplant comprised two Napier Lion engines strut-mounted between the wings. The first of six **Southampton Mk I** 'boats with wooden hulls was flown for the first time on 10 March 1925 and initial deliveries to the RAF's No. 480 Coastal Reconnaissance Flight began a few months later.

The major production **Southampton Mk II** introduced a duralumin hull that gave significant performance increase, for not only was it of light struc-

N218, the original experimental Southampton, proved the metal hull for the Mk II, and was later tested with Jupiter engines and Handley Page slots.

tural weight but also eliminated the weight penalty of some 400 lb (181 kg) of water soaked up by the wooden hull.

The Southampton equipped the RAF's Nos

201, 203, 204, 205 and 210 Squadrons, serving faithfully for more than a decade, and examples were built also for the RAAF, Argentina, Japan and Turkey.

SPECIFICATION

Supermarine Southampton Mk II	(4082 kg); maximum take-off 15,200 lb (6895 kg)
Type: general reconnaissance flying-boat	**Dimensions:** wingspan 75 ft (22.86 m); length 51 ft 1½ in (15.58 m); height 22 ft 4½ in (6.82 m); wing area 1,449 sq ft (134.61 m²)
Powerplant: two 500-hp (373-kW) Napier Lion VA V-12 piston engines	
Performance: maximum speed 108 mph (174 km/h) at sea level; service ceiling 14,000 ft (4265 m); maximum range 930 miles (1497 km)	**Armament:** three 0.303-in (7.7-mm) Lewis guns (one each in bow and two at midship positions), plus 1,100 lb (499 kg) of bombs
Weights: empty 9,000 lb	

Supermarine Spiteful and Seafang

The **Spiteful** and **Seafang** were intended respectively to supersede the Spitfire and Seafire in service. Superficially the Spiteful closely resembled the Spitfire but was virtually a completely new design with square-cut laminar-flow wings that, of thin section, demanded wider-track inward- retracting main landing gear units. Three prototypes were ordered in three versions and, flown from June 1944,

comprised the **Spiteful F.Mk 14** (Griffon 65/five-bladed propeller), **Spiteful F.Mk 15** (Griffon 89 or 90/contra-rotating propellers), and **Spiteful F.Mk 16** (three-stage Griffon 101 and five-bladed propeller). A contract for 67 Spiteful F.Mk 14s was cancelled after the 17th had been completed on 17 January 1947. Only three of this total were used by the RAF, delivered to test establishments.

The Seafang, which differed from the Spiteful in having full carrier gear, had no more success, only 18 being completed from an order for two prototype and 150 production aircraft. They comprised eight **Seafang F.Mk 31** fighters with the Griffon 61 engine and 10 **Seafang F.Mk 32** fighters with the Griffon 89, contra-rotating propellers and folding wings. The 35-ft 6-in (10.82-m) span Spiteful

RB515 was the first production Spiteful, first flying in April 1945, and later fitted with the enlarged tail fin illustrated. Most production aircraft were Mk 15s.

F.Mk 16 with a 2,375-hp (1771-kW) Rolls-Royce Griffon 101 engine had a

maximum speed of 494 mph (795 km/h) at optimum altitude.

Supermarine Spitfire and Seafire

Without doubt the best known British aircraft of World War II, the **Spitfire** originated from the **Type 224** designed by R. J. Mitchell to meet the requirements of Specification F.7/30. A cantilever low-wing monoplane of all-metal construction, it had an inverted-gull wing, 'trousered' fixed main landing gear and was powered by a 600-hp (447-kW) Rolls-Royce Goshawk II V engine. When the Type 224 was tested its performance proved disappointing, and it was no more successful than any of the other submissions to this specification; none of them gained an Air Ministry contract. Given a free hand to design a new single-seat fighter unfettered by official specifications, Mitchell

outlined on his drawing board the delightful **Type 300**. Smaller, sleeker and with drag-reducing retractable landing gear, it was tailored around the new Rolls-Royce PV.12 (Merlin) engine; the wings were not only of distinctive elliptical shape, but they housed eight machine-guns, all of them firing outside the propeller disc.

Air Ministry Specification F.36/34 was drawn up around the Type 300 and a prototype was ordered. This (K5054) was powered by a 900-hp (738-kW) Rolls-Royce Merlin 'C' and flew for the first time on 5 March 1936. Comparatively little flight testing was needed to confirm it as a winner, and its superb handling qualities and performance resulted in a first contract (for 310 **Spitfire Mk I** aircraft) being

awarded on 3 June 1936. However, planned mass production was slow to gain momentum and it was not until July 1938 that the first Spitfire Mk I reached No. 19 Sqn at Duxford; only five had been delivered by the time of the Munich crisis in September of that year, but the trickle was eventually to become a flood that totalled 20,334 Spitfires and 2,556 related new-build **Seafire** naval fighters. A degree of multi-role capability was to result from the development of low-altitude clipped wings (prefix LF), and high-altitude increased-span wings (HF), the standard wing being identified as F, and with variations of armament within these wings comprising eight machine-guns (suffix A), two cannon and four machine-guns (B), four cannon (C) and two cannon, two 0.5-in (12.7-mm) machine-guns and up to 1,000 lb (454 kg) of bombs (E).

By the outbreak of war on 3 September 1939, the RAF had nine operational Spitfire squadrons, and on 16 October 1939 a Spitfire of No. 603 Sqn claimed the first German aircraft to be

This No. 64 Sqn Spitfire claimed the first kill for the Mk IX, an Fw 190 on 30 July 1942. Based at Hornchurch, it was flown by Plt Off. D. Kingaby.

SPECIFICATION

Supermarine Spitfire Mk VA	1,135 miles (1827 km)
Type: single-seat interceptor fighter	**Weights:** empty 4,998 lb (2267 kg); maximum take-off 6,417 lb (2911 kg)
Powerplant: one 1,478-hp (1102-kW) Rolls-Royce Merlin 45 V engine	**Dimensions:** wingspan 36 ft 10 in (11.23 m); length 29 ft 11 in (9.12 m); height 9 ft 11 in (3.02 m); wing area 242 sq ft (22.48 m²)
Performance: maximum speed 369 mph (594 km/h) at 19,500 ft (5945 m); service ceiling 36,500 ft (11125 m); maximum range	**Armament:** eight 0.303-in (7.7-mm) Browning machine-guns

Below: Tested on Seafire Mk IIs, but not used operationally during the war, RATOG became standard on Seafires from the Mk XV onwards.

destroyed over the UK in World War II, an He 111. By August 1940, shortly before the Battle of Britain reached its climax, RAF Fighter Command could

call upon 19 Spitfire Mk I squadrons. By December 1940 **Spitfire Mk II** aircraft were carrying out 'Rhubarb' sweeps over occupied Europe, and the first to

Left: This No. 54 Sqn Spitfire Mk I was operational over Dunkirk in May 1940. It was later shot down by an He 111P of 6./KG 66, which it had earlier damaged.

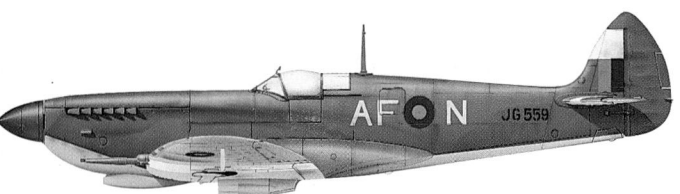

The Mk VIII was particularly active in South East Asia. This aircraft, flown by Flt Lt W. Goold, claimed a Ki-43 'Oscar' and damaged two others in May 1944.

serve overseas were **Spitfire Mk VB** fighters flown to Malta from HMS *Eagle* on 7 March 1942.

Soon after that date the same mark was operational in the Middle East, and by early 1943 the first Mk Vs were arriving in the Pacific theatre. In growing numbers and with increasing capability the Spitfire served throughout World War II, not only with the RAF but with the nation's allies, including US and Soviet squadrons. It also had the distinction of remaining in production throughout the entire war and was operational post-war, the last mission flown by a photo-reconnaissance **Spitfire PR.Mk 19** of No. 81 Sqn in Malaya on 1 April 1954.

The success of the Sea Hurricane as operated by the FAA from RN aircraft-carriers resulted in development of the Seafire, the first conversions from Spitfire Mk VBs being carried out by Air Service Training at Hamble, Hampshire. Initial deliveries of the resulting **Seafire Mk IB** began in January 1942, and the type was used in growing numbers of different marks through the war. **Seafire Mk 47** aircraft of No. 800 Sqn served with distinction in the Korean War, and when Seafires were withdrawn from first-line service, the type remained operational with training squadrons and RNVR air squadrons until 1957.

Variants

Spitfire Mk I: initial production with 1,030-hp (768-kW) Merlin II; eight 0.303-in (7.7-mm) Browning guns (at first four because of supply shortages) or, **Spitfire Mk IB**, four 0.303-in (7.7-mm) guns and two 20-mm cannon; 1,566 built
Spitfire Mk II: built at Castle Bromwich 1,175-hp (876-kW) Merlin XII; 750 **Spitfire Mk IIA** and 170 **Spitfire Mk IIB** built
Spitfire Mk III: one-off experimental prototype with 1,280-hp (954-kW) Merlin XX
Spitfire Mk IV: Griffon-engined prototypes (2); same mark number used for 229 PR versions of Spitfire Mk V
Spitfire Mk V: with strengthened fuselage for 1,440-hp (1074-kW) Merlin 45 or 1,470-hp (1096-kW) Merlin 50, drop tank and bomb provision, F or LF wing and A, B or C armament; 94 **Spitfire Mk VA**, 3,923 **Spitfire Mk VB** and 2,447 **Spitfire Mk VC** built
Spitfire Mk VI: high-altitude interceptor with 1,415-hp (1055-kW) Merlin 47, pressurised cockpit and HF wing; 100 built
Spitfire Mk VII: high-altitude interceptor with two-stage Merlin 61, 64 or 71, pressurised cockpit, retractable tailwheel and, often, broad pointed rudder; 140 built
Spitfire Mk VIII: definitive fighter with two-stage Merlin 61, 63, 66 or 70, unpressurised cockpit and LF, F or HF wings; 1,658 built
Spitfire Mk IX: union of two-stage Merlin 61, 63 or 70 with Spitfire Mk V airframe; LF, F or HF wings and B, C or E armament; 5,665 built
Spitfire Mk X: pressurised version of Spitfire PR.Mk XI, Merlin 77, one with HF wing; 16 built
Spitfire Mk XI: unarmed long-range PR version with Merlin 61, 63 or 70; 471 built
Spitfire Mk XII: low-level interceptor with single-stage Griffon II or IV of 1,735-hp (1294-kW), LF wing, B armament; 100 built
Spitfire Mk XIII: low-level PR aircraft based on Spitfire Mk V with Merlin 32 and only four 0.303-in (7.7-mm) machine-guns; 18 built
Spitfire Mk XIV: redesigned and strengthened airframe for 2,050-hp (1529-kW) Griffon 65 or 66 with five-bladed propeller, broad tail and, often, teardrop canopy; F or LF wings, C or E armament; 957 built
Spitfire Mk XVI: as Spitfire Mk IX with Packard Merlin 226, F or LF wing, usually C or E armament, many with teardrop canopy; 1,054 built
Spitfire Mk XVIII: definitive fighter with two-stage Griffon, teardrop canopy and extra wing fuel, F wings and E armament; **Spitfire FR.Mk XVIII** (post-war **Spitfire FR.Mk 18**) with rear fuselage reconnaissance camera; 300 built

Spitfire Mk XIX (post-war **PR.Mk 19**): unarmed PR version, most pressurised; two-stage Griffon; 225 built
Spitfire Mk XX: one-off prototype rebuilt from Spitfire Mk IV and prototype Spitfire Mk XII
Spitfire Mk 21: redesigned air frame, mainly Griffon 61 or 64 with five-bladed propeller, C armament; 122 built
Spitfire Mk 22: minor changes from Spitfire Mk 21, some with 2,373-hp (1771-kW) Griffon 85 and contra-rotating propellers; 278 built
Spitfire Mk 24: minor changes, Spiteful tail, short-barrel Mk V cannon; 54 built
Seafire Mk IB: navalised Spitfire Mk VB; 166 built
Seafire Mk IIC: catapult hooks and strengthened landing gear, Merlin 32 with four-bladed propeller; 372 built
Seafire Mk III: double-folding wing and 1,585-hp (1182-kW) Merlin 55M; 1,220 built
Seafire Mk XV: single-stage 1,850-hp (1380-kW) Griffon VI; most with sting hooks and late production with teardrop canopy; 390 built
Seafire Mk XVII or **Mk 17**: as Seafire Mk XV with teardrop canopy and, often, strengthened landing gear; some (**Seafire FR. Mk 17**) with camera in place of rear tank; 232 built
Seafire Mk 45: airframe as Spitfire Mk 21, non-folding wing, Griffon 61/five-bladed propeller or 85/contraprops; 50 built
Seafire Mk 46: as Seafire Mk 45 with teardrop canopy; **Seafire FR.Mk 46** with rear-fuselage camera; late production with Spiteful tail; 24 built
Seafire Mk 47: with folding wing, 2,375-hp (1771-kW) Griffon 87 or 88 with chin inlet and contraprops, increased fuel; late production all FR type with camera; 140 built

Supermarine Swift

Swift FR.Mk 5s, such as this No. 4 Sqn example, were the first RAF aircraft with reheat. No. 79 Sqn, based at Laarbruch, received the Mk 5 in June 1956 and was renamed No. 4 Sqn in January 1961.

Development of the **Swift** started in 1946 when the Air Ministry began the process of procuring a replacement for the Meteor. Two prototypes of the **Type 510** were ordered, which was basically a development of the Rolls-Royce Nene 2-powered Attacker, but provided with wings and tailplane swept at an angle of 40°. First flown on 29 December 1948, this was developed progressively via the **Type 517** with a variable-incidence tailplane, and the **Type 535** which introduced tricycle landing gear, a modified fuselage to accept a Nene with after-burning capability, plus other revisions and refinements. The first of 193 production aircraft was flown on 25 August 1952, this being a **Swift F.Mk 1** with twin 30-mm ADEN cannon, Avon RA.7 engine without reheat and a fixed-incidence tailplane. Subsequent versions included the **Swift F.Mk 2** with four ADENs and a new wing incorporating a compound-taper leading edge; the **Swift F.Mk 3** with an afterburning Avon RA.7R engine; and the **Swift F.Mk 4** which introduced a variable-incidence tailplane.

After only a short time in service the unsuitability of the Swift for deployment in an interceptor role led to the decision to concentrate on its development as a tactical reconnaissance aircraft. This brought production of 58 **Swift FR.Mk 5** aircraft, plus four converted from Swift F.Mk 4s, the first of which entered service with No. 2 Sqn in Germany in early 1956. They differed from the Swift F.Mk 4 by having the nose lengthened to accommodate three cameras, a frameless canopy and a new wing with increased chord forward of the ailerons to give a 'saw-tooth' leading edge. At one period Swift FR.Mk 5s equipped both Nos 2 and No. 79 Sqns, the type remaining operational with No. 2 Sqn in Germany until the summer of 1961.

A subsequent development built to a total of two prototypes and 12 production aircraft had the designation **Swift F.Mk 7**. These had a lengthened nose to accommodate radar and an increased-span wing to carry four Blue Sky AAMs in addition to the standard four ADENs. They were used for weapons trials at RAF Valley before being withdrawn for use in a variety of experimental roles.

SPECIFICATION	
Supermarine Swift FR.Mk 5 **Type**: single-seat tactical reconnaissance aircraft **Powerplant**: one 9,450-lb (44.86-kW) afterburning Rolls-Royce Avon 114 turbojet **Performance**: maximum speed 685 mph (1102 km/h); service ceiling 45,800 ft (13960 m); range 630 miles (1014 km)	**Weights**: empty 13,435 lb (6094 kg); maximum take-off 21,400 lb (9707 kg) **Dimensions**: wingspan 32 ft 4 in (9.86 m); length 42 ft 3 in (12.88 m); wing area 327.7 sq ft (30.44 m²) **Armament**: two 30-mm ADEN cannon, plus provision for underwing bombs or rockets

Swearingen SJ30

In October 1986 Gulfstream Aerospace launched the **SA-30 Fanjet** twin-turbofan business jet project, later renamed **Gulfstream SA-30 Gulfjet**. After Gulfstream's withdrawal from the programme in September 1989, its place was taken by the Jaffe Group of San Antonio, Texas, and the aircraft was re-named **Swearingen/Jaffe SJ30**. From 1995 the SJ30 has

been a Sino Swearingen programme, following the establishment of a joint venture company together with Sino Aerospace of Taiwan.

The first prototype SJ30 flew on 13 February 1991. The standard production **SJ30-1** which followed is a swept-wing, pressurised business jet, offering high-speed and high-altitude cruise combined with a long-range capability.

Powered by two rear fuselage pod-mounted 2,300 lb st (10.23-kN) Williams-Rolls FJ44-2C turbofans, the SJ30-1 has pressurised accomodation for a pilot and one passenger (or co-pilot) on the flight deck, and a main cabin with a standard layout for four passengers. Optional cabin interiors can increase the seating to accomodate up to seven passengers.

The SJ30 has highly efficient wings with 30° sweep, retractable tricycle undercarriage (twin wheels on each unit) and an all-metal structure.

In order to avoid direct competition with Raytheon's Premier I, Sino Swearingen developed the increased performance **SJ30-2**, the prototype of which first flew in November 1996, with the original FJ44-2C engines. The production aircraft features a 6-ft

In June 2001, following the installation of its data collection system, the first SJ30-2 production prototype began the process of FAA type certification.

(1.83-m) fuselage stretch, increased wing dihedral, a revised wing/fuselage fairing, increased fuel capacity and new-generation FJ44-2A turbofan engines.

The first of three production standard SJ30-2 prototypes was flown in

November 2000, and production deliveries were scheduled to begin from the production facility at Martinsburg, West Virginia, before the end of 2001. By the end of 2000, Swearingen announced that 175 orders had been placed for the aircraft.

SPECIFICATION	
Sino Swearingen SJ30-2 **Type:** four- to six-passenger light business jet **Powerplant:** two 2,300-lb st (10.23-kN) Williams FJ44-2A turbofans **Performance:** long-range cruising speed 514 mph (828 km/h); service ceiling 49,000 ft (14935 m); range 3,201 miles (5152 km)	**Weights:** empty 7,700 lb (3493 kg); maximum take-off 13,200 lb (5987 kg); maximum payload 1,400 lb (635 kg) **Dimensions:** wingspan 42 ft 4 in (12.90 m); length 46 ft 11½ in (14.31 m); height 14 ft 3 in (4.34 m); wing area 190.7 sq ft (17.72 m²)

Transall C.160

Originally conceived as a replacement for the Noratlas, which equipped transport units of France's Armée de l'Air and West Germany's Luftwaffe, the **C.160** was one of the first successful joint European aerospace ventures, being produced by a consortium of companies which was collectively known as the Transport Allianz group. Indeed, the name and designation chosen for the resulting machine reflected the origins of the project, for the initial quantity to be acquired was set at 160 (50 **C.160F** aircraft for France and 110 **C.160D** aircraft for West Germany), while the name was merely a contraction of Transport Allianz. Members of the original production group included Nord-Aviation, Hamburger Flugzeugbau (HFB) and Vereinigte Flugtechnische Werke (VFW), these joining forces in early 1959.

Three prototypes were built in all, one by each of the three major partners in this venture, and the first of these made a successful

maiden flight on 25 February 1963. They were followed by six pre-production examples from May 1965, while production-configured C.160s began to emerge in the spring of 1967, deliveries getting under way soon afterwards; by the time manufacture ceased in 1972 a total of 169 had been built. In addition to the 160 supplied to the two principal partners, nine more of a variant known as the **C.160Z** were sold to South Africa, the only other air arm to operate the original type apart from Turkey, which took delivery of 20 **C.160T** aircraft (former Luftwaffe examples) in the early 1970s.

Subsequently, at the end of the 1970s, it was decided to re-open the production line in France, that country's air force ordering 25 more examples under the designation **C.160NG (Nouvelle Génération)** which differed from their predecessors by virtue of additional fuel capacity and improved avionics. Range limitations have been partly resolved

by an extra centre-section fuel tank, but the later C.160s also feature an inflight-refuelling probe above the cockpit.

Four more C.160NGs were added in 1982, and production ended in 1985. Ten aircraft were completed with a hose-drum unit in the port undercarriage sponson for refuelling tactical aircraft, and five more have provision for the fitment of this feature so that they can be rapidly re-roled as tankers.

As replacements for eight Elint and jamming N.2501 Gabriel Noratlas variants, two Transalls were converted to **C.160 Gabriel (C.160G)** configuration and entered service at Metz in December 1988. Features include wingtip pods with UHF/DF blade antennas, a group of five large blade antennas on top of the forward fuselage, a blister fairing on each side of the rear fuselage, and a retractable dome under the forward fuselage. Both have refuelling probes and a hose-drum unit in the port undercarriage pannier. In the lead-up to the 1991 Gulf War, Gabriel missions were flown against Iraq.

The C.160D, as originally delivered to the Luftwaffe, was used in 1970 to fly relief missions into Nigeria. These aircraft initially equipped LTG.61, 62 and 63.

C.160H ASTARTE is the version of Transall adapted to carry Rockwell Collins TACAMO VLF radio transmission equipment, as also used by the E-6A Hermes. This takes the form of a

long trailing aerial which enables the aircraft to communicate with missile-armed nuclear submarines of the Force Océanique Stratégique without the need for them to surface.

SPECIFICATION	
Transall C.160 **Type:** twin-engined turboprop transport **Powerplant:** two Rolls-Royce Tyne RTy.20 Mk 22 turboprops each rated at 6,100 ehp (4548 ekW) **Performance:** maximum cruising speed at 18,045 ft (5500 m) 319 mph (513 km/h); maximum rate of climb at sea level 1,444 ft (440 m) per minute; service ceiling	27,885 ft (8500 m); range 2,796 miles (4500 km) with a 17,637 lb (8000 kg) payload **Weights:** empty equipped 63,400 lb (28758 kg); maximum take-off 108,245 lb (49100 kg) **Dimensions:** wingspan 131 ft 3 in (40.00 m); length 106 ft 3½ in (32.40 m); height 38 ft 5 in (11.65 m) **Payload:** maximum payload 35,275 lb (16000 kg)

Tupolev giant aircraft

The **ANT-16** or **TB-4** was a super-heavy bomber powered by six 830-hp (619-kW) M-34 engines, two of them mounted in tandem above the fuselage. Armament comprised two 20-mm cannon and 10 machine-guns, plus a maximum bombload of 22,046 lb (10000 kg). First flown on 3 July 1933, the TB-4 spanned 177 ft 2 in (54 m) and attained a maximum speed of 124 mph

(200 km/h). The renowned and tragic **ANT-20 Maxim Gorky** was an eight-engine passenger-cum-propaganda monoplane. Six 900-hp (671-kW) AM-34FRN engines were mounted in the wing leading edge and two more over the fuselage. Equipped with printing press, cinema, film laboratory and many other features unique at the time, the ANT-20 carried a crew of 20. Test flown for the

first time on 17 June 1934, it was destroyed in a mid-air collision on 18 May 1935 with a stunting I-5 fighter which had been acting as escort. The *Maxim Gorky* spanned 206 ft 8¼ in (63.00 m), had a maximum take-off weight of 92,594 lb (42000 kg) and was capable of a maximum speed of 152 mph (245 km/h).

Public reaction to the loss of the *Maxim Gorky* led to the establishment of a fund to build 16 more giant aircraft. In the event

only one **ANT-20bis** was built, and known otherwise as the **PS-124** or **L-760** (from its civil registration). Flown for the first time in late 1939, it differed considerably from the ANT-20, having a redesigned wing, fuselage and tailplane. Power was provided by six 1,200-hp (895-kW) AM-34FRNV engines set in the wing leading edge. Completed as a passenger transport with accommodation for 64 plus a crew of nine, the **ANT-20bis** was similar in size to the

ANT-20, but slightly heavier, and with a maximum speed of 171 mph (275 km/h). It was abandoned after being damaged in a bad landing on 14 December 1942.

The **ANT-22** or **MK-1** with six 830-hp (619-kW) M-34R engines was a long-range bomber-reconnaissance flying-boat, its twin hull design clearly inspired by the Italian S.55. Test-flown for the first time on 8 August 1934, it established several weight-to-height world records in December 1936, but was

Not a Tupolev 'giant' as such, the ANT-6 heavy bomber was nevertheless one of the great milestones in aviation history. In 1939, this ANT-6A was used for a mission across the Soviet Arctic.

abandoned soon afterwards. Armament comprised eight 0.303-in (7.7-mm) ShKAS machine-guns, one 20-mm cannon and a bombload of up to 13,228 lb (6000 kg). The MK-1 spanned 167 ft 3¾ in (51 m) and had a maximum speed of 145 mph (223 km/h). The **ANT-26** heavy bomber project was abandoned in 1936, prior to its completion.

Tupolev Tu-2 'Bat'

Designed by Andrei Tupolev while in detention, the first prototype of this powerful bomber was known as **Aircraft 103**, using the number assigned to his design team. Development was protracted and the prototype, known otherwise as the **ANT-58**, flew initially on 29 January 1941; an improved version, the **103U** or **ANT-59**, flew on 18 May the same year. During tests the original 1,400-hp (1044-kW) AM-37 V-12 piston engines were replaced by ASh-82 radials. Efforts to simplify the design for quantity production led to the **103V** or **ANT-60**, and series aircraft designated **Aircraft 103S** or **ANT-61** entered service from November 1942 onwards, being redesignated **Tu-2** early in 1943. They had heavy-calibre machine-guns, more powerful ASh-82FNV

radial engines and dispensed with the dive brakes of the original prototypes. As production got under way the refined **Tu-2S** was introduced, but difficulties at the factories resulted in only some 1,100 Tu-2s and Tu-2S bombers being delivered before the end of the war. However, post-war production brought the total built to 2,527. The Soviet Tu-2s performed well and had flying qualities close to those of a single-seat fighter. Tu-2S bombers fought in the Korean conflict with the North Korean forces, and equipped a number of the Soviet Union's allies, including China, Poland and Yugoslavia. Post-war a large number of derivatives (**Tu-8** and **Tu-10**) was built, some in quantity. The type gained the ASCC/ NATO reporting name **'Bat'**.

Pictured during state tests, this Tu-2 was the seventh aircraft built from the first series of production aircraft, also known as the ANT-61.

Variants

ANT-62T: torpedo bomber, flown and entered production in 1947; earlier test aircraft known as **Tu-2T**
ANT-67: long-range bomber with ACh-39 diesels and crew of five
Tu-1 (ANT-63P): long-range three-seat escort fighter based on **Tu-10**; appeared late 1946
Tu-2D (ANT-62): long-range version; redesigned forward fuselage, new long-span wings and side-by-side seating for two pilots
Tu-2DB (ANT-65): long-range bomber development; 2,200-hp (1641-kW) AM-44TK engines
Tu-2F (ANT-64): special photo-reconnaissance version
Tu-2G: modified high-speed cargo transport; carried light vehicles externally
Tu-2M (ANT-61M): believed designation of production version with 1,900-hp (1417-kW) ASh-83 radials
Tu-2N: test-bed for Rolls-Royce Nene, and other turbojets
Tu-2R: specialised reconnaissance aircraft
Tu-2RShR: prototype with 57-mm RShR cannon in forward fuselage
Tu-2K: two examples used for ejection seat tests
Tu-2Sh: 1944 Shturmovik ground-attack version
Tu-2 Paravan: two aircraft used for tests of barrage balloon cable deflectors/cutters
Tu-2/104: radar-equipped all-weather interceptor tested in 1944
Tu-6: reconnaissance aircraft conversions
Tu-8 (ANT-69): final long-range bomber of late 1946; armed with five B-20 cannon, some aimed indirectly from sighting stations
Tu-10 (ANT-68): 1945 prototype for general-purpose bomber, had 1,850-hp (1380-kW) AM-39FN engines; post-war production totalled at least 50 with 2,000-hp (1491-kW) AM-42 engines

SPECIFICATION

Tupolev Tu-2S
Type: four-crew medium bomber
Powerplant: two 1,850-hp (1380-kW) ASh-82FNV radial piston engines
Performance: maximum speed 342 mph (550 km/h); service ceiling 31,170 ft (9500 m); range 870 miles (1400 km)
Weights: empty equipped 16,477 lb (7474 kg); maximum

take-off 25,045 lb (11360 kg)
Dimensions: wingspan 61 ft 10½ in (18.86 m); length 45 ft 3½ in (13.80 m); height 14 ft 11 in (4.55 m); wing area 525.30 sq ft (48.80 m²)
Armament: two 20-mm cannon, three 0.5-in (12.7-mm) machine-guns, plus bombload of 8,818 lb (4000 kg)

Tupolev Tu-16 'Badger'

SPECIFICATION

Tupolev Tu-16 'Badger-A'
Type: twin-jet medium bomber and maritime reconnaissance aircraft
Powerplant: two MNPK 'Soyuz' (Mikulin) AM-3A turbojets each rated at 19,185 lb st (85.22 kN) or, in later aircraft, two AM-3M-500 turbojets each rated at 20,944 lb st (93.16 kN)
Performance: maximum level speed 'clean' at 19,685 ft (6000 m) 616 mph (992 km/h); maximum rate of climb at sea level 4,101 ft (1250 m) per minute; service ceiling 40,355 ft (12300 m); range 3,682 miles (5925 km) with an 8,377-lb (3800-kg) warload

Weights: empty equipped 82,012 lb (37200 kg); maximum take-off 167,110 lb (75800 kg)
Dimensions: wingspan 108 ft ½ in (32.93 m); length 118 ft 11¾ in (36.25 m); height 45 ft 11½ in (14.00 m); wing area 1,772.34 sq ft (164.65 m²)
Armament: 'Badger-A' could carry a bombload of up to 19,800 lb (9000 kg). Naval versions carried air-to-surface stand-off missiles. For defence the Tu-16 had forward and rear ventral barbettes each containing two 23-mm NR-23 guns and two similar weapons in tail position

Xian H-6 form, and indeed remained in production in China into the 1990s.

Known to NATO as 'Badger-G (Mod)', the AV-MF's Tu-16K-26 missile carrier carried one or two K-26s. Note the guidance radar ahead of the bomb bay.

Over-shadowed in the popular imagination by the larger Tu-95, the **Tu-16** was Tupolev's most important post-war production programme. The OKB workshops and factories at Kazan, Kuibyshev and Voronezh built a total of 1,515 Tu-16s, and more were later built in China.

The Tu-16 was retired prematurely, as part of the massive force reductions which followed the end of the Cold War. There was no room for the kind of specialised recce, EW and ECM aircraft which the Tu-16 had become. The type does remain in use in China, in its licence-built

Remarkably, the aircraft which became the Tu-16 was actually based on the fuselage and systems of the **Tu-4 'Bull'** – an unlicenced copy of the wartime B-29 – married to a newly-designed swept wing, rugged undercarriage and twin jet engines of revolutionary new design. The **Type 88** prototype made its maiden flight on 27 April 1952, and despite

being overweight and unable to attain either the airspeed or the range originally specified in the requirement, the aircraft was ordered into production as the Tu-16. The machine was rather less dramatic and futuristic than the rival B-47, but its more conservative design in the end proved more durable.

The Tu-16 entered

service in 1954, and 54 aircraft flew over Moscow's Red Square on Aviation Day, 1955, leading to some panic among NATO onlookers. The basic Tu-16 was improved throughout its career and adapted to meet different roles, leading to a succession of variants. Tu-16s of various types were exported to Egypt, Indonesia, and Iraq.

Tupolev Tu-16 'Badger' (continued)

Variants

Tu-16 'Badger-A': initial production version, with reduced weight by comparison with first prototype, and closely matching original performance requirement

Tu-16A 'Badger-A': externally similar variant with more powerful RD-3M-200 engines, an improved fire control system for the guns, and with re-configurable bomb bay compatible with nuclear weapons – the A suffix stood for **Atomic**. Main production version, 700 built, many subsequently converted to other versions

Tu-16M 'Badger-A': similar version with minor differences for AV-MF maritime strike use

Tu-16T 'Badger-A': torpedo bomber version built in limited numbers for AV-MF. Provision for mines, depth charges or for four RAT-52 or TAN-53 torpedoes

Tu-16Z 'Badger-A': Initial inflight-refuelling tanker version, using 'wingtip-to-wingtip' method, with hose trailed from right wingtip and snagged by grapple trailed by receiver, then winched into fitting in receiver's port wingtip. Provision for extra transfer fuel in removeable tanks in bomb bay

Tu-16N 'Badger-A': 'probe and drogue' tanker version with Yakovlev-built centreline HDU in bomb bay and ARK-5 beacon. Mainly used to support probe-equipped Tu-22 and Tu-22M regiments

Tu-16Ye 'Badger-A': some Tu-16As were rebuilt as Elint/EW platforms with *Yolka* ECM system. They were characterised by a row of three steerable antennas under the bomb bay and with a bulk chaff cutter/dispenser. Most Tu-16Yse were produced by conversion of redundant Tu-16K-10 missile carriers as **'Badger-D'**

Tu-16S 'Badger-A': SAR version with additional fuel and extra radios, carrying radio-controlled lifeboat under the fuselage

Tu-104G 'Badger-A': limited conversion for Aeroflot use as an urgent mail/cargo carrier, used principally for transporting newspaper printing matrices to outlying regions. Some, dubbed 'Little Red Riding Hood' used for training Tu-104 'Camel' airliner crews

Tu-16KS 'Badger-B': AV-MF missile carrier with provision for underwing KS-1 *Komet* (AS-1 'Kennel') stand-off ASMs. *Kobalt*-N guidance transmitter installed, glazed 'bomber' nose retained

Tu-16K-10 'Badger-C': AV-MF missile carrier with single K-10 (AS-2 'Kipper') ASM on the centreline. Glazed nose replaced by broad flat radome housing antenna for YeN targeting radar. Missile top-up fuel tank housed in bomb bay, together with claustrophobic pressure cabin

for YeN operator. 220 built, many converted as Elint/EW platforms

Tu-16K-10-26 'Badger-C (Mod)': small numbers of Tu-16K-10s were later modified to carry KSR-2 (AS-5 'Kelt'), and KSR-5S (later K-26) (AS-6 'Kingfish') missiles underwing

Tu-16YE 'Badger-D': similar EW conversion of Tu-16K-10 and K-10-26, similar to Tu-16A and Tu-16KS-based EW conversions (**Tu-16Ye 'Badger-A'** and **'Badger-B'**), but retaining broad flat nose radome

Tu-16R 'Badger-E': reconnaissance version of Tu-16A with camera pack in former bomb bay, pilot's forward firing gun usually removed

Tu-16RM 'Badger-E': similar recce version for AV-MF

Tu-16KRM 'Badger-E': small numbers of Tu-16RMs were modified with underwing launch rails for rocket-powered target drones

Tu-16RM-2 'Badger-F': separate NATO reporting name for Tu-16Rs and RMs fitted with underfuselage Elint radomes

Tu-16 'Badger-G': Tu-16As and Tu-16KSs re-fitted with *Rubin* radar undernose and with provision for KSR-11 (experimental) or KSR-2 cruise missiles

Tu-16K-26 'Badger-G (Mod)': aircraft modified to launch K-26 missiles, with launch attitude indicator on nose glazing

Tu-16PP or Tu-16P Elka 'Badger-H': stand-off jammer version produced by conversion of Tu-16A or Tu-16KS, with underfuselage radomes at each end of the bomb bay, and with a new bulk chaff cutter/dispenser serving three chutes in the former bomb bay doors

Tu-16P Buket 'Badger-J': active jamming platform with ventral canoe fairing and flat plate antennas forming wingtip extensions

Tu-16Ye 'Badger-K': EW conversion of Tu-16KS, generally similar to Tu-16Ye 'Badger-B', usually with two rather than three underfuselage radomes, mounted on former bomb bay rather than at each end as on 'Badger-F'

Tu-16P and Tu-16PP 'Badger-L': advanced Elint platform with self-protection active jammer and associated thimble nose radome and extended ECM tailcone

Tu-16Sh: some Tu-16As reportedly rebuilt as crew-trainers for the Tu-22. Details of appearance and equipment fit remain unknown

Tu-16LL: designation applied to wide range of airborne laboratory, testbed and trials aircraft

Tu-16 Tsyklon: conversion for meteorological reconnaissance/research.

M-16: some redundant Tu-16A, Tu-16KS and Tu-16R aircraft converted as target drones, usually with extended tailcone similar to that fitted to the 'Badger-L'

Tupolev Tu-22 'Blinder'

Development of the **Tu-22 'Blinder'** supersonic theatre bomber/maritime patrol aircraft began in 1955 under the Tupolev bureau designation **Tu-105**. The rapidly growing capability of Western air defence systems at that period threatened the continued viability of the Tu-16, and the Tu-22 was designed to make possible the penetration of enemy airspace at higher altitude and speed. Features of the design included compound-sweep wing layout, close attention to area-ruling, and the use of rear-mounted turbojet engines that avoided the drag and weight penalties of long inlet ducts. First flown on 21 June 1958, and seen publicly in 1961, the Tu-22 has since been built to an estimated total of about 250 of which some 180 were believed to be in service in 1983 with the DA (140) and AV-MF (40). The type was also supplied in small numbers for service with the Iraqi and Libyan air forces. Four versions were built and these are listed below under the relevant reporting names.

In Soviet service, the rakish Tu-22 was nicknamed 'Shilo' (awl). Post-USSR, the Tu-22 was taken into Russian and Ukrainian service.

Variants

Tu-22B 'Blinder-A': initial version; basic bomber/reconnaissance aircraft with internal weapon bays for free-fall weapons

Tu-22K 'Blinder-B': generally similar to 'Blinder-A', but with recess in weapons bay to allow carriage of Kh-22 (AS-4 'Kitchen') stand-off missile, larger radar, and inflight-refuelling capability (later modified as **Tu-22KD** with RD-7M2 engines)

Tu-22R 'Blinder-C': maritime reconnaissance version with cameras or sensors in weapons bay; some were equipped for ECM role (**Tu-22RDK** with *Kub*-4 SLAR)

Tu-22U 'Blinder-D': trainer version with instructor accommodated in raised and enclosed cockpit aft of standard flight deck

SPECIFICATION	
Tupolev Tu-22R 'Blinder-C'	185,185 lb (84000 kg)
Type: supersonic maritime reconnaissance aircraft	**Dimensions:** wingspan 77 ft 6¼ in (23.65 m); length 136 ft 5¾ in (41.60 m) excluding probe; wing area 1,746.5 sq ft (162.25 m²)
Powerplant: two RD-7M2 turbojets each rated at 36,376 lb st (161.77 kN) with afterburning	**Armament:** one 23-mm AM-23 cannon in tail, otherwise unarmed, but Tu-22B could carry up to 26,455 lb (12000 kg) of stores in weapons bay, or Kh-22 ASM (Tu-22K)
Performance: maximum speed 938 mph (1510 km/h) or Mach 1.42 at 39,370 ft (12000 m); service ceiling 43,635 ft (13300 m); combat radius 1,367 miles (2200 km)	
Weights: maximum take-off	

Tupolev Tu-22M 'Backfire'

The **Tu-22M** was developed from the earlier Tu-22 design, incorporating variable-geometry outer wing panels. The first **Tu-22M-0** prototype flew in 1969. Powered by a military derivative of the engine originally designed for the Tu-144 supersonic airliner, the **'Backfire'** is extremely fast, even at low level. The Tu-22M lacks sufficient range for truly strategic missions and is classified as a medium bomber. The first series production model was the **Tu-22M-2**

'Backfire-B' (211 built) for the VVS and the AV-MF. Normally armed with a single Kh-22 stand-off missile (although up to three can be carried), this variant became operational with 185 GvTBAP at Poltava in 1978, and also served in Afghanistan. The ultimate bomber/missile carrying variant is the **Tu-22M-3 'Backfire-C'**, (268 built). The M-3 features strengthened wings and raked rectangular intakes serving more powerful engines. It also had a greatly increased weapons load. In 2001 the Tu-22M-3 remained numerically the most important bomber in the Russian air force's Long-Range Air Army inventory, serving with seven regiments (one of which also operates Tu-22M-2s). The A-VMF has about 80 Tu-22Ms, mostly M-3 models, split equally between divisions subordinated to the Northern and Pacific Fleets. The AV-MF

The Tu-22M-3 employs new wedge-type engine air intakes for greater efficiency at high Mach numbers in conjunction with increased thrust NK-25 turbofan engines.

SPECIFICATION	
Tupolev Tu-22M-3 'Backfire-C' **Type:** medium-range maritime attack and reconnaissance aircraft **Powerplant:** two NK-25 turbofans rated at 55,115 lb st (245.20 kN) **Performance:** maximum level speed at 36,090 ft (11000m) 1,242 mph (2000 km/h); unrefuelled combat radius 1,150 miles (1850 km)	**Weights:** basic empty 119,048 lb (54000 kg); maximum take-off 286,596 lb (130000 kg) **Dimensions:** wingspan 112 ft 6½ in (34.30m) spread; length 129 ft 11 in (39.60 m); wing area 1,829.92 sq ft (170 m²) spread **Armament:** one GSh-23 23-mm cannon in tail; maximum weapon load 52,910 lb (24000 kg)

has 12 M-3s converted as **Tu-22MR** reconniassance aircraft, and reportedly also operates limited numbers of recce-configured

Tu-22M2R aircraft. Because of delays in the development of the Sukhoi T-60, the Tu-22M3's intended replacement, it has been

decided to embark on a major upgrade of the 'Backfire'. The Tu-22Ms of both the Air Force and Naval Aviation will be upgraded to **Tu-245** standard, with a new radar, new missile systems and an automatic terrain-following capability. A small number

of redundant Tu-22M-3 airframes was converted as **Tu-22MP** prototypes of a planned EW/escort jammer variant. The other operator of the 'Backfire' is Ukraine,

which gained former Black Sea Fleet regiments of Tu-22M 'Backfires'. About 50 bombers equip three air force heavy bomber regiments.

Tupolev Tu-95 and Tu-142 'Bear'

The turboprop-powered **Tu-95 'Bear'** strategic bomber entered service in 1956 but remains an important part of Russia's long range air power. The current bomber/missile carrier version is the **Tu-95MS 'Bear-H'**. This entered service in 1984 and was manufactured until 1992. There were two subvariants, both based on the maritime **Tu-142**. The

Tu-95MS16 'Bear-H16' carried 16 long-range ALCMs (six internally and ten externally). The current **Tu-95MS6 'Bear-H6'** has provision for external missile carriage deleted in accordance with the SALT/START Treaties. About 60 Tu-95s of both variants are based with heavy bomber regiments at Engels and Ukrainka. This total includes three aircraft

formerly held in Ukraine. Russia plans to add the Kh-101 ALCM and Kh-SD ASM to the inventory of the Tu-95MS to improve its conventional long-range precision strike capability. The air force also operates 11 earlier-model **Tu-95KU** machines as trainers. The **Tu-142 'Bear-F'** was designed primarily for ASW and a variety of naval roles. Around 40 examples equip a single AV-MF (Russian naval aviation) regiment at Kipelovo, assigned to the Northern Fleet. The major ASW variants are the **Tu-142MK 'Bear-F Mod 3'** and improved **Tu-142M-Z 'Bear-F Mod 4'**, the last of which was completed in 1994. The **Tu-142MR 'Bear-J'** is a command post/communications relay platform for communicating

Ultimate maritime 'Bear' variant is the Tu-142MZ, the most obvious features of which are its nose ECM thimble radome and new Ladoga MAD 'sting'.

with submerged nuclear-missile armed submarines. Such is the importance of the Tu-142 in Russian service, that surviving 'Bear-F Mod 4' airframes are likely to be updated with the Leninets Sea Dragon system, which includes a new radar, LLLTV, FLIR, new sonobuoys, revised ESM and MAD systems and an

armament of up to eight Kh-35 (AS-20 'Kayak') anti-ship missiles for an extended ASV/ASW role. The only Tu-142 export operator is the Indian navy which has seven **Tu-142MK-E** aircraft at Arrakonam. These are broadly similar to the 'Bear-F Mod 3', but have certain systems that have been downgraded.

SPECIFICATION	
Tupolev Tu-95MS6 'Bear-H6' **Type:** strategic bomber **Powerplant:** four 14,795-ehp (11033-ekW) KKBM NK-12MA turboprops **Performance:** maximum level speed 575 mph (925 km/h); service ceiling 39,380 ft (12000m); unrefuelled combat radius 3,977 miles (6400 km)	**Weights:** empty 202,380 lb (91800 kg); maximum take-off 407,850 lb (185000 kg) **Dimensions:** wingspan 164 ft 2 in (50.04 m); length 161 ft 2¼ in (49.13 m); wing area 3,120.50 sq ft (289.90 m²) **Armament:** two NR-23 23-mm twin-barrel cannon in tail; rotary launcher for six Kh-55 series ASMs

Tupolev Tu-104 'Camel'

With an urgent Aeroflot need in the early 1950s for a modern airliner of greater capacity, range and speed than in-service aircraft, the Tupolev design bureau developed as the **Tu-104 'Camel'** a civil version of the Tu-16, basically by introducing a new pressurised fuselage. The engineering and other detail changes were rather more complex than this statement suggests, but this course made possible the first flight of a prototype on 17 June 1955 and entry into Aeroflot service during the following summer. Introduced first on the Moscow-Irkutsk route, the

50-passenger Tu-104 was powered by two 14,881-lb (66.18-kN) thrust Mikulin AM-3 turbojets and immediately reduced flight time by more than half, bringing similar transformation to the airline's other medium-range routes. The Tu-104's powerplant was later uprated to the 19,180-lb st (85.29-kN) AM-3M, which also powered the improved **Tu-104A** with a revised cabin for 70 passengers. Continuing development of the Mikulin engine brought introduction of the lengthened-fuselage (by 3 ft 11½ in/1.21 m) **Tu-104B**, with standard seating for 100 passengers, which

entered route service on 15 April 1959. When production ended during the following year, about 200 Tu-104s of all versions had been built and these served Aeroflot reliably until 1981. The designations **Tu-104D** and **Tu-104V** applied to Tu-104As with in-service modifications to accommodate 100 and 85 passengers respectively without the fuselage stretch. Six aircraft supplied to CSA were basically Tu-104As seating 81 passengers, and small numbers of Tu-104s were used by the VVS for cosmonaut training in weightless flight and as

The Tu-104A entered CSA service on the Prague-Moscow route in December 1957 This aircraft was named Praha.

SPECIFICATION	
Tupolev Tu-104B 'Camel' **Type:** medium-range transport **Powerplant:** two 21,385-lb (95.10-kN) thrust Mikulin AM-M500 turbojets **Performance:** maximum speed 590 mph (950 km/h) at 32,810 ft (10000 m); service ceiling 37,730 ft (11500 m); range with maximum	payload 1,647 miles (2650 km) **Weights:** empty 91,711 lb (41600 kg); maximum take-off 167,551 lb (76000 kg) **Dimensions:** wingspan 113 ft 4 in (34.54 m); length 131 ft 4¾ in (40.05 m); height 39 ft ½ in (11.90 m); wing area 1,975.24 sq ft (183.50 m²)

personnel transports. One, with a pointed nose, flew

weather-research missions.

Tupolev Tu-114 'Cleat' and Tu-126 'Moss'

Successful redesign of the military Tu-16 provided for Aeroflot the medium-range Tu-104; similar adaptation of the Tu-95 was made to fill the requirement for a long-range transport with intercontinental capability. Chronologically, first to fly

was the **Tu-116** (late 1956); this was basically a demilitarised Tu-95 with the weapons bay/tail turret eliminated and the rear fuselage equipped as a 24/30-seat passenger cabin. It was used to test the powerplant in civil operation and evalu-

ate airfields on proposed routes, being followed by two similar aircraft; all three were accepted by Aeroflot under the designation **Tu-114D** and used for route-proving and publicity purposes. The true **Tu-114 'Cleat'** had configuration

changes and introduced a new circular section fuselage with seating arrangements varying from 220 passengers (high-density), 170 seats (typical) to 120 (long-range non-stop). The first Tu-114 was flown on 3 October 1957, and 25-30

entered service with Aeroflot from 1961. Earlier, during 1960, the Tu-114 had demonstrated that it was the fastest propeller-driven aircraft in the world, when on 9 April 1960 one carrying a 55,115-lb (25000-kg) payload over a 3,107-mile (5000-km) circuit set speed record of 545.07 mph (877.212 km/h).

Tupolev Tu-114 'Cleat' and Tu-126 'Moss' (continued)

In addition to use on long-range domestic routes, the Tu-114 operated to Canada, India and Japan, but from 1971 was gradually withdrawn from service. A military derivation of the Tu-114 was given the designation **Tu-126** and reporting name **'Moss'**; believed to be conversions of ex-Aeroflot civil airliners, these aircraft were modified for use as airborne warning and control aircraft, a role similar to that of the USAF's Boeing E-3 Sentry. The Tu-126 therefore differed externally from the civil airliner by the installation of a rotating radome which, pylon-mounted over the rear fuselage, had a diameter of some 36 ft (11 m), and by the addition of an inflight-refuelling probe and a number of blisters and fairings covering operational equipment.

Despite operational shortcomings, the spacious Tu-126 was popular in IA-PVO service. One example was operational during the 1971 Indo-Pakistan war.

The former passenger cabin provided space for communications, radar and signal processing equipment, and consoles for specialist operators.

SPECIFICATION	
Tupolev Tu-114	(6200 km)
Type: long-range civil transport	**Weights:** empty 200,620 lb
Powerplant: four 14,795-eshp	(91000 kg); maximum take-off
(11033-ekW) Kumetsov NK-12MV	376,990 lb (171000 kg)
turboprops	**Dimensions:** span 167 ft 7¾ in
Performance: maximum cruising	(51.10 m); length 177 ft 6 in
speed 478 mph (770 km/h); service	(54.10 m); height 50 ft 10¼ in
ceiling 39,370 ft (12000 m); range	(15.50 m); wing area 3,348.76 sq ft
with maximum payload 3,853 miles	(311.10 m²)

Tupolev Tu-124 'Cookpot'

Aeroflot's requirement for a short-/medium-range airliner to replace the piston engine Il-14 led to design by the Tupolev bureau of what was basically a reduced-scale version of the Tu-104. The prototype **Tu-124** was first flown in June 1960, five years after the Tu-104, and benefited from this later timescale to introduce aerodynamic and system refinements, plus newly developed and much more efficient turbofan engines. In fact, the Soloviev D-20P two-spool turbofans installed in these aircraft were the first engines of this type to equip any of the world's short-/medium-range airliners. Tu-124s with seats for 44 passengers entered service with Aeroflot on 2 October 1962, but the major production version was the 56-seat **Tu-124V**. Variants included the **Tu-124K** and **Tu-124K2** with de-luxe seating for 36 and 22 passengers respectively. About 100 were built, this number including three for CSA in

By the summer of 1964, Aeroflot Tu-124s were serving 24 points in the USSR, and operating over a route network of 22,723 miles (36,570 km).

Czechoslovakia and two for Interflug in East Germany, but Aeroflot has now retired its Tu-124s. A small number entered military service, including the **Tu-**124Sh navigator trainer for the Tu-128. Quasi-military Tu-124s were operated by the air forces of India and Iraq. The NATO reporting name was 'Cookpot'.

SPECIFICATION	
Tupolev Tu-124V	(11700 m); range with maximum
Type: short/medium-range	payload 758 miles (1220 km)
transport	**Weights:** empty 49,604 lb
Powerplant: two 11,905-lb	(22500 kg); maximum take-off
(5400 kN) thrust Soloviev D-20P	83,776 lb (38000 kg)
turbofans	**Dimensions:** span 83 ft 9¾ in
Performance: maximum speed	(25.55 m); length 100 ft 4 in
603 mph (970 km/h) at 26,245 ft	(30.58 m); wing area 1,280.95 sq ft
(8000 m); service ceiling 38,385 ft	(119.00 m²)

Tupolev Tu-128 'Fiddler'

The limitations of the Yak-25 in IA-PVO service, and the failure of the La-250 lead to Tupolev's development of a new long-range all-weather interceptor which would be capable of defending the USSR against attacks by supersonic bombers and stand-off missiles.

The resulting **Tu-128 'Fiddler'**, originally known by the **Type 28** company designation, was similar to the **Tu-98 'Backfin'** supersonic bomber project of 1956. The first prototype, or **Tu-28-80** (as a result of its K-80 missile complex) made its maiden flight on 18 March 1961.

The Tu-128's area-ruled fuselage contained eight fuel tanks in the centre section, and two AL-7F engines. Further wing tanks gave the production variant a total fuel capacity of 4,092 Imp gal (18600 litres), allowing the aircraft to perform the required 2-hour escort mission as well as long-range interception patrols. No IFR probe or drop tanks were routinely carried.

The Tu-128's large radome contained an RP-5 radar as a component of the *Smerch* fire-control system. The prototype also carried a large ventral fairing for a further radar, in order to test the reception of target echoes, and this in turn required the addition of ventral fins.

Poor subsonic handling and radar fire control problems delayed the programme until 1966, when the Tu-128 was finally cleared for production, together with its R-4 armament.

The **Tu-128UT** trainer was also developed, with the radar replaced by an additional cockpit for an instructor, accomodated beneath a flush V-shaped-canopy. The improved **Tu-128Ch** interceptor added *Chaika* LORAN. The **Tu-128A** introduced

The Tu-128M introduced a standard armament comprising two radar-guided R-4P 'Ash' and two IR-guided R-4T AAMs (carried outboard).

improved AL-7F2 engines and *Smerch*-A radar. The definitive **Tu-128M** carried *Smerch*-M radar and a new fire control system, and entered service in 1979.

Tupolev Tu-134 'Crusty'

The **Tu-134** was developed directly from the earlier Tu-124. The Tu-134 retained the same basic wing and fuselage, with the same undercarriage and high lift devices, but differed in adopting a T-tail and rear-mounted engines, as well as incorporating slight increases in wingspan and fuselage length and an underfuselage airbrake to allow steeper approaches to be flown. It was originally designated **Tu-124A**, but was redesignated before the its flight in 1962. Production started in 1964 and the new 72-seater entered Aeroflot service in 1967. In 1970 the **Tu-134A** replaced the original aircraft on the production line. The new variant had a 6-ft 10-in (2.10-m) fuselage stretch and was fitted with an APU. The aircraft was re-engined with Soloviev D-30 Series II turbofans, and most Tu-134As also had a radar nose in place of the original variant's glazed navigator's position. Primarily delivered to civilian customers, the Tu-134A served with the air forces of Angola, Czechoslovakia, Poland and Russia, while Tu-134s continue to serve with

VIP-configured Tu-134s were widely used by the USSR. A Sperenberg-based Tu-134A-3 was used by the commander of the Western Group of Forces.

Bulgaria and Russia, mainly in the VIP transport role. Russia also has a handful of aircraft converted for bomber crew training duties. The **Tu-134BSh** is a dedicated bombardier trainer, and has a Tu-22M radar in the nose, with underwing pylons for the carriage of practice bombs. Consoles and radar bombsights for 12 students are provided in the cabin. The **Tu-134UBL** (**Uchebno-boevoi dla lotchikov**, or trainer for pilots) has a similar external appearance, but is designed as a crew trainer for Tu-160 'Blackjack' aircrew, with Tu-160 radar and avionics. It is primarily designed to train 'Blackjack' pilots, and simulates the bomber's handling characteristics (especially in the circuit and on take-off and landing) particularly well. Two entered service with the 184th Bomber Regiment at Priluki during early 1991. The ASCC/NATO reporting name assigned was '**Crusty**'.

SPECIFICATION

Tupolev Tu-134A 'Crusty'
Type: twin-engined short-haul airliner/transport aircraft
Powerplant: two PNP 'Aviadvigatel' (Soloviev) D-30 II each rated at 14,991 lb st (66.68-kN)
Performance: maximum cruising speed at 27,885 ft (8500 m) 559 mph (900 km/h); service ceiling 39,040 ft (11900 m); range 2,175 miles (3500 km) with a 8,818 lb (4000 kg) payload
Weights: operating empty 63,933 lb (29000 kg); maximum take-off 103,616 lb (47000 kg)
Dimensions: wingspan 95 ft 1¾ in (29.00 m); length 121 ft 8¾ in (37.10m); wing area 1,370.29 sq ft (127.30m²)
Payload: maximum payload 18,000 lb (8165 kg)

Tupolev Tu-144 'Charger'

The **Tu-144 'Charger'** began design in the early 1960s, the prototype being flown on 31 December 1968. Of like configuration, and with similar performance to the Aérospatiale/BAC Concorde, the aircraft had a matching ogival delta wing with the powerplants grouped at the rear of the wing and a drooping nose to improve the pilot's view in low-speed regimes. The production version had a flight crew of three and 140 passengers as standard, and began proving flights with cargo between Moscow and Alma Ata in December 1975. This variant also had retractable but non-moving canard foreplanes, a lengthened fuselage, redesigned intakes, increased span and pilots' ejection seats removed. From February 1977, the Tu-144 was used in a series of 50 proving flights between Moscow and Khabarovsk, and the first passenger services, between Moscow and Alma Ata, began in November 1977. These were terminated in June 1978 after a fatal accident. Reports were received in 1979 of a developed

Retractable canards, with a span of 20 ft (6.1 m) were added from the pre-production series on. This Tu-144D 'Type 101' set no less than 14 records in 1983.

Tu-144D with more economical Kolesov turbofan engines but, since that time, Tu-144 'Chargers' have been used only as testbeds and trials aircraft at Zhukovskii. A single example remains active within NASA's experimental aircraft fleet.

SPECIFICATION

Tupolev Tu-144 'Charger'
Type: supersonic long-range airliner
Powerplant: four Kuznetsov NK-144 turbofans each rated at 28,660 lb st (127.5 kN) dry and 44,090 lb st (196.1 kN) with afterburning
Performance: maximum cruising speed Mach 2.35 (1,550 mph, 2500 km/h); normal cruising speed Mach 2.2 (1,430 mph, 2300 km/h); cruising altitude 52,000-59,000 ft (16000-18000 m); maximum range with 140 passengers at an average speed of Mach 1.9 (1,243 mph) 4,030 miles (3500 km)
Weights: empty 187,400 lb (85000 kg); maximum take-off 396,830 lb (180000 kg)
Dimensions: wingspan 94 ft 6 in (28.80 m); length 215 ft 6½ in (65.70 m); height 42 ft 2 in (12.85 m); wing area 4,714.5 sq ft (438 m²)
Payload: 33,070 lb (15000 kg)

Tupolev Tu-154 'Classic'

The tri-jet **Tu-154** was designed as a replacement for the Il-18 and Tu-104, and was required to couple good cruise performance and economy with 'hot-and-high' and short airstrip capability. Tupolev's response to the Aeroflot requirement was recognisably a scaled-up Tu-134 but with hydraulically actuated leading-edge slats, triple-slotted trailing-edge slats, powered ailerons and four-section spoilers, which augment the ailerons for roll control and act as lift dumpers and airbrakes. The fuselage was lengthened, and increased in diameter to allow six-abreast seating, allowing a maximum capacity of 167 passengers (128-158 is more normal). The third engine was located in the extreme rear fuselage, with an intake in the leading edge of the fin. The prototype made its maiden flight on 4 October 1968 and the type entered service in February 1972. The improved **Tu-154A** of 1975 introduced a revised seating arrangement, additional emergency exits, increased fuel capacity and uprated engines, together with improved avionics. In 1977 the Tu-154A was superseded by the improved **Tu-154B**, and then by the **Tu-154B-2**. The **Tu-154S** is a dedicated freighter, with a freight door forward of the wing, and roller tracks inside the cabin. The aircraft is offered primarily as a conversion of existing Tu-154Bs, and it is not known whether any have been ordered or delivered. Flight testing of the more radically modified **Tu-154M** began in 1982. This aircraft introduced new Kuznetsov D-30KU-154-II turbofans. Those mounted on the sides of the rear fuselage were in redesigned nacelles, similar to those fitted to the the Il-62M, with similar clamshell thrust reversers. The APU had to be relocated to accommodate the centre engine. Other modifications included a redesigned tailplane, reduced size slats, enlarged spoilers and seating for up to 180 passengers (11 more than the standard aircraft). The ASCC codename for the series was '**Classic**'.

SPECIFICATION

Tupolev Tu-154M 'Careless'
Type: three-engined medium-range airliner/transport aircraft
Powerplant: three PNPP 'Aviadvigatel' (Soloviev) D-30KU-154-II turbofans each rated at 23,369 lb st (103.95 kN)
Performance: cruising speed at 39,040 ft (11900 m) 590 mph (950 km/h); service ceiling 41,000 ft (12500 m); range 4,101 miles (6600 km) with maximum fuel and a 12,015 lb (5450-kg) payload
Weights: operating empty 121,914 lb (55300 kg); maximum take-off 220,459 lb (100000 kg)
Dimensions: wingspan 123 ft 2½ in (37.55 m); length 157 ft 1¾ in (47.90 m); height 37 ft 4¾ in (11.40 m); wing area 2,168.46 sq ft (201.45 m²)
Payload: internal fuel 87,632 lb (39750 kg); external fuel none; maximum payload 39,683 lb (18000 kg)

Until the late 1980s, Balkan operated a fleet of 23 Tu-154s, including B, B1, B2 and M variants. This is one of the latter, four of which were operational in 2001.

Tupolev Tu-160 'Blackjack'

The **Tu-160 'Blackjack'** is the world's largest operational bomber. Dwarfing the similar-looking B-1B, it is the heaviest combat aircraft ever built. Unlike the Lancer, the Tu-160 remains committed to both low-level penetration (at transonic speeds) and high-level penetration at speeds of about Mach 1.9. Although the aircraft has an FBW control system all cockpit displays are analogue and there is no HUD. The long pointed radome houses a terrain following and attack radar. Below this is a fairing for a forward-looking TV camera used for visual weapon aiming. The development programme of the Tu-160 was extremely protracted; the prototype Tu-160 first flew in 1981 and the second aircraft was lost in 1987. Series production was at Kazan and continued until January 1992, when President Yeltsin announced that no further strategic bombers would be built. It is believed that production totalled no more than 39 'Blackjacks'. Even after the aircraft entered service, problems continued to severely restrict operations and production began before a common standard and configuration was agreed.

SPECIFICATION

Tupolev Tu-160 'Blackjack'
Type: long-range strategic bomber
Powerplant: four NK-321 turbofans each rated at 30,843 lb st (137.20 kN) dry and 55,115 lb st (245.16 kN) with afterburning
Performance: max level speed at 40,000 ft (12200 m) 1,380 mph (2220 km/h); service ceiling 49,200 ft (15500 m); unrefuelled range 7,640 miles (12300 km)
Weights: empty 260,140 lb (118000 kg); maximum take-off 606,261 lb (275000 kg)
Dimensions: length 177 ft 6 in (54.10 m); wing area 3,875.13 sq ft (360 m²)
Armament: up to 12 Kh-55 series ALCMs or 24 Kh-15P SRAMs

Thus wingspans, equipment fit, and intake configurations differ from aircraft to aircraft.

Tupolev Tu-160 'Blackjack' (cont.)

Nineteen Tu-160s were delivered to the 184th Guards TBAP at Priluki beginning in May 1987. These were left at the Ukrainian base after the break up of the USSR in 1991 and, after protracted discussions between Ukraine and the Russian Federation, eight were returned to Russia in 1999. Scrapping of the remaining Tu-160s held in Ukraine began in late 1998 under a contract issued by the US government. In early 2001, Russia declared six operational Tu-160s as ALCM carriers under the START treaty. These are assigned to the 121st Guards TBAP at Engels and were joined in 2001 by the first of the eight refurbished aircraft formerly held in Ukraine.

Although perhaps up to a dozen further airframes are nominally serviceable, it seems unlikely that Russia has sufficient funds to rework these aircraft. US-based Platforms International Corp. has acquired three demilitarised ex-Ukrainian Tu-160s which it plans to convert as **Tu-160SK** launchers for space vehicles.

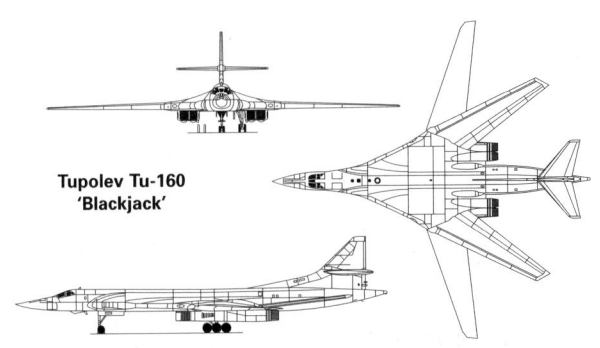

Tupolev Tu-160 'Blackjack'

Tupolev Tu-204/Tu-306

The **Tu-204** was designed as a replacement for the Tu-154, principally for use by Aeroflot (which had a stated requirement for 500 aircraft). The Tu-204 was designed to match the economy and performance of contemporary Western jetliners, while still satisfying unique Soviet requirements. Thus the aircraft was designed to be capable of two-crew operation, with a Flight Engineer's station to meet Aeroflot requirements. For most of the Soviet era Aeroflot was effectively a highly-subsidised airborne rural bus service, operating 'no-frills' services across the vast distances of the USSR. Its aircraft had to operate from austere airfields without luggage conveyors and advanced passenger/freight handling facilities. Ruggedness, reliability and ease of maintenance were therefore more important than absolute economy, while the aircraft had to be maintainable by relatively ill-trained personnel. The Tu-204 was designed to operate in these conditions, but was still of composite and advanced alloy construction, with a modern supercritical wing and advanced systems.

Despite a sidestick having been tested on a Tu-154 development aircraft, the Tu-204 uses conventional yoke controls together with its triplex FBW system.

The Tu-204 was initially powered by a pair of 35,580-lb-st (158.30-kN) Perm-Soloviev PS-90A high-bypass turbofans, with an advanced glass cockpit and modern navigation and flight management systems. From the start Tupolev envisaged using a Rockwell Collins EFIS cockpit for most customers, though not for Aeroflot.

The prototype Tu-204 made its maiden flight from Zhukovskii on 2 January 1989, with production beginning in 1990, and certification was received in 1995 for freight services. Passenger services began in February 1996. The Tu-204 marked the first time that modern Western design practise and operating concepts were incorporated in a Soviet airliner.

Unfortunately for Tupolev, domestic orders vanished as Aeroflot splintered along with the USSR, and as potential customers turned to Western manufacturers for aircraft. The Tu-204's low price, easy operating characteristics, tolerance of austere airfields and undemanding maintenance procedures should have won it many orders, but for many users, operating Boeings was an important political statement, sending a clear signal about being forward-looking and pro-Western. About 30 Tu-204s were in service by the end of 2000, and about 30 more were on order.

Tupolev Tu-204 variants

Tu-204: baseline 214-passenger version, with PS-90 engines and Russian avionics. Built by Aviastar at Ulyanovsk
Tu-204C: similar cargo aircraft
Tu-204-100: PS-90-engined extended range version. Built by Aviastar at Ulyanovsk
Tu-204-100C: similar cargo aircraft
Tu-204-120: basic passenger version with Russian avionics and Rolls-Royce RB.211-535E4 engines (these actually had slightly higher fuel burn, but much greater reliability, and thus lower operating costs). Production Tu-204-120s for Kato Group (Egypt) used Honeywell/Allied Signal avionics. Built by Aviastar at Ulyanovsk
Tu-204-120C: similar cargo aircraft
Tu-204-122: similar RB.211-engined aircraft with Rockwell-Collins avionics. Planned production by Aviastar at Ulyanovsk
Tu-204-200: version with further increases in fuel and MTOW, and with a strengthened undercarriage
Tu-204-200C: similar cargo aircraft
Tu-204-200C³: combi aircraft, re-designated as **Tu-214**, built by KAPO at Kazan
Tu-204-220: with RB.211-535E4, -535F5 or Pratt & Whitney PW2240 engines
Tu-204-222: Western engines and Rockwell Collins avionics
Tu-204-230: projected variant with Samara NK-93 propfan engines. Unbuilt
Tu-204 Business Jet: projected corporate jet version
Tu-204 Maritime: projected MR/ASW platform for Russian air forces
Tu-206: advanced project using mixed kerosene/liquid natural gas dual fuel. Unbuilt
Tu-214: combi freighter version of the -200, built by KAPO at Kazan
Tu-216: wholly cryogenically-fuelled advanced project. Unbuilt
Tu-224: shortened, short-range, 99-166-seat trunkliner with RB.211-535E4 engines
Tu-234: similar shortened short-range aircraft with PS-90As. Originally designated **Tu-204-300.** Prototype converted by shortening the fuselage of the first Tu-204 prototype. First production Tu-234 rolled out, but likely to be re-engined to serve as **Tu-224** prototype
Tu-304: projected 400-seat advanced derivative. Probably abandoned
Tu-306: similar aircraft with TB7-46 engines, cryogenic fuel and spine-mounted gas tank

SPECIFICATION	
Tupolev Tu-204	
Type: twin-turbofan medium-range airliner	max payload 1,509 miles (2430 km)
Powerplant: two 'Aviadvigatel' (Soloviev) PS-90A turbofans each rated at 35,275 lb st (156.90 kN)	**Weights:** operating empty 128,530 lb (58300 kg); maximum take-off 208,550 lb (94600 kg)
Performance: nominal cruising speed at 36,400 ft (11900 m) to 39,700 ft (12100 m) 503-528 mph (810-850 km/h); cruise altitude 40,026 ft (12200 m); range with	**Dimensions:** wingspan 137 ft 1¾ in (41.80 m); length 151 ft 3 in (46.10 m); height 45 ft 7¼ in (13.90 m); wing area 1,963.4 sq ft (182.40 m²)
	Payload: maximum payload 46,296 lb (21000 kg)

Tupolev Tu-334

The **Tu-334** was developed as a replacement for Aeroflot's huge fleet of Tu-134s, and Tupolev confidently expected a market for some 1,000 aircraft of this type. To speed development, the Tu-334 was a small version of the Tu-204, with a shortened fuselage, a scaled-down, reduced-sweep wing, rear-mounted twin engines and a T-tail. The Aeroflot Tu-134 replacement requirement was soon overtaken by the break-up of the old Soviet Union, and by the subsequent splintering of the former state airline into multiple smaller carriers. Funding shortages have led to a protracted development cycle, and the first prototype was not rolled out until 1995, and did not make its maiden flight until 8 February 1999.

There have been negotiations for the licence manufacture of Tu-334s by IACI of Iran at Isfahan, and TANTK at Taganrog. This would be in addition to production at Aviant in

The prototype Tu-334 was first demonstrated at Zhukovsky in 1995.

SPECIFICATION	
Tupolev Tu-334	1,242 miles (2000 km) for
Type: twin-turbofan medium-range airliner	Tu-334-100; 1,864 miles (3000 km) for Tu-334-120; 2,609 miles (4200 km) for Tu-334-120D
Powerplant: two Ivchenko Progress D-436T1 turbofans each rated at 16,535 lb st (73.60 kN) on Tu-334-100; two BMW Rolls-Royce BR710-48 turbofans each rated at 15,000 lb st (66.70 kN) on Tu-334-120	**Weights:** empty 66,250 lb (30050 kg) for -100; maximum take-off 119,975 lb (54420 kg) for -120 **Dimensions:** (for -100) wingspan 97 ft 8 in (29.77 m); length 102 ft 6¾ in (31.26 m); wing area 895.80 sq ft (83.23 m²)
Performance: nominal cruising speed (estimated) at 36,400 ft (11100 m) 510 mph (820 km/h); range with maximum payload	**Payload:** maximum load 21,958 lb (9960 kg) for -100, -120 and -120D

Variants

Tu-334-100: baseline variant, seating 102 (tourist class), powered by D-436T1 engines. First two prototypes to this standard
Tu-334-100C: projected Combi version
Tu-334-100D: extended range 102-seat variant with extended-span wings and D-436T2 engines
Tu-334-120: powered by BR710-48 engines. Third prototype built as -120, using engines loaned by BMW/Rolls-Royce
Tu-334-120D: increased weight version with BR710-55 engines
Tu-334-200: stretched, increased capacity version. Re-designated **Tu-354**
Tu-334-220: further increase in MTOW by comparison with Tu-354, whose fuselage it shares. May replace Tu-354
Tu-334C: projected cargo/freighter version
Tu-336: projected Ivchenko-Progress D-436T2 engined version with cryogenic fuel in faired tanks above cabin
Tu-354: stretched version, with extended span and D-436T2 or BR715-55 engines, seating 126 passengers. Originally designated **Tu-334-200**

Kiev (source of the initial planned production version) and at Aviacor at

Samara, where the stretched **Tu-354** is to be built.

UTVA Aircraft

The Yugoslavian company Fabrica Aviona Utva flew in 1956 the prototype of a four-seat braced high-wing cabin monoplane designated **UTVA-56**. Powered by a 260-hp (194-kW) Lycoming GO-435-C2B2 engine, this served as prototype for the more developed **UTVA-60** which introduced the 270-hp (201-kW) GO-480-B1A6. It was built in versions which included the basic **U-60-AT1** four-seat utility aircraft, the similar **U-60-AT2** with dual controls, the agricultural **U60-AG**, the **U-60-AM** ambulance accommodating two stretchers and attendant, and the **U-60H** floatplane version of the U-60-AT1. In 1965 Utva flew the prototype of a specialised agricultural aircraft, the **UTVA-65**

Privrednik, which combined the wings, tail unit and landing gear of the UTVA-60 with a new fuselage. This UTVA-65 was available as the **UTVA-65 Privrednik-GO** or **UTVA-65 Privrednik-IO** with 295-hp (220-kW) GO-480-G1A6 or 300-hp (224-kW) IO-540K1A5 Lycoming engines respectively, and was superseded in 1973 by the **UTVA-65 Super Privrednik-350** powered by the 350-hp (261-kW) Lycoming IGO-540-A1C.

At the end of the 1960s Utva introduced a developed version of the UTVA-60 under the designation **UTVA-66**, introducing several refinements and a supercharged GSO-480-B1J6 engine for improved performance; it was available in basic

UTVA's first aircraft was the UTVA-56, which flew on 22 April 1959. Designers B. Nikolic and D. Petkovic began modifying the design in 1960, as the UTVA-60.

UTVA-66 form, and as the **UTVA-66-AM** ambulance, as the **UTVA-66H** float-plane and from 1974 as the **UTVA-66V** armed military utility aircraft. Most recent production of this company concentrated on the **UTVA-75** low-wing monoplane two-seat trainer/utility aircraft which provides side-by-side enclosed cabin accommodation. The type

was also available with a four-seat interior under the designation **UTVA-75A**. The standard production UTVA-75, was powered by a 180-hp (134-kW) IO-360-B1F flat-four engine, had a wingspan of 31 ft 11 in (9.73 m) and maxi-

mum speed of 134 mph (215 km/h). A hardpoint incorporated in each wing enables a light underwing weapon load to be carried for military training, and the UTVA-75 is suitable also for use in the glider towing role.

Vickers F.B.5 Gunbus

The large and well-known armament, engineering and building group known as Vickers Ltd established an aviation department in early 1911, building first eight differing shoulder-wing monoplanes derived from the French R.E.P. designs of Esnault-Pelterie. As armament manufacturers with an aviation department

it is not surprising that the company received a contract from the Admiralty for an experimental armed fighter biplane. Thus was designed the **Vickers E.F.B.1 (experimental fighting biplane)** that marks the beginning of the company's military designs. An unequal-span biplane, it had a central nacelle with

two open cockpits in tandem and at the rear an 80-hp (60-kW) Wolseley engine driving a pusher propeller. Its fixed tailskid landing gear incorporated a skid projecting well forward of the wheels to reduce the danger of nosing-over when landing, and the tail unit was carried on wire-braced uncovered tubular

steel tailbooms. When exhibited at the 1913 Aero Show at Olympia it caused something of a stir because of its armament, comprising a movable Vickers machine-gun in the forward cockpit; it must have been some thing of an anti-climax when subsequently it crashed during its first take-off. Similar but improved **E.F.B.2** and **E.F.B.3** aircraft were flown successfully under the power of the 100-hp (75-kW) Gnome rotary engine, leading to an Admiralty order for six aircraft designated **E.F.B.4**. Before they were completed the War Office took over the order, an **E.F.B.5** prototype preceding production of the company's first military aircraft, the **F.B.5 Gunbus**

of which more than 200 were built. The type was used mainly by the RFC, only about 15 being delivered to the RNAS. Detail improvements were introduced during production, and the unwieldy belt-fed Vickers machine-gun of earlier aircraft was replaced later by the lighter drum-fed Lewis gun on a pivot mounting. As powered by the 100-hp (75-kW) Gnome Monosoupape rotary engine, the Vickers Gunbus had a maximum speed of 70 mph (113 km/h) at optimum altitude and an endurance of about 4 hours 30 minutes. Experimental variants of the F.B.5 were flown during 1915, these including one powered by a 110-hp (82-kW) Clerget rotary engine, and two with the 150-hp (112-kW) Smith radial engine; no further examples were built. In addition to production by Vickers, the F.B.5 was built under licence by S.A. Darracq et Cie in France and by A/S Nielson and Winthers in Denmark.

This production F.B.5 displays the spigot mounting on the nose for a 0.303-in (7.7-mm) Lewis gun, situated directly ahead of the observer's cockpit.

Vickers F.B.27 Vimy, Vimy Commercial and Vernon

The **F.B.27 Vimy** bomber prototype was flown for the first time on 30 November 1917; like the DH.10 Amiens and V/1500, it was designed to provide the RAF with a strategic bomber that could attack industrial targets in Germany. Although token numbers of each arrived in France before the Armistice of 11 November 1918, none of them saw operational service in World War I. Of biplane configuration, with a biplane tail unit and accommodating a crew of three, the first Vimy prototype was powered by two 207-hp (154-kW) Hispano-Suiza engines, the second by 260-hp (194-kW) Sunbeam Maoris, the third by 300-hp (224-kW Fiat

A-12s and the fourth by the 360-hp (268-kW) Rolls Royce Eagle VIII which became standard. The **F.B.27A Vimy Mk II** was ordered into large-scale production, but contract cancellations at the war's end limited the total built to about 230. It was not until July 1919 that the Vimy was in full RAF service, equipping first No. 58 Sqn in Egypt, then other squadrons in the Middle East and in the UK. It remained in first-line service until replaced by the Virginia during 1924-25, but No. 502 Sqn in Northern Ireland was operational with the type until 1929. Apart from aircraft with No. 502 Sqn, some 80 Vimys were re-engined

with Armstrong Siddeley Jaguar or Bristol Jupiter radial engines from 1925 and used by training schools and as parachute trainers.

The Vimy is, of course, remembered in aviation history for its pioneering flights, including the first nonstop west-east crossing of the North Atlantic by John Alcock and Arthur Whitten Brown; the first England-Australia flight by Rose and Keith Smith and their crew; and the attempted first England-South Africa flight by Pierre van Ryneveld and Christopher Q. Brand, of which the final leg, Bulawayo to Cape Town, was completed in a DH.9.

In January 1919 Vickers began development of the Vimy for civil use, introducing in the **Vimy Commercial** a new larger-diameter fuselage to provide a cabin for 10 passengers and retaining

the two Eagle VIIIs. The prototype, first flown on 13 April 1919, was followed by 43 production aircraft for China (40) and one each for the Instone Air line, Grands Express Aériens and the USSR; five generally similar aircraft, but incorporating a nose loading door, were completed as **Vimy Ambulance** machines for the RAF and equipped to accommodate four stretchers or eight sitting patients, plus two medical attendants.

Final derivative of the Vimy/Vimy Commercial was the **Vernon** bomber/transport used by the RAF during its policing of Iraq

from 1921. Serving with Nos 45 and 70 Sqns at Hinaidi, they not only carried out their basic task, but were used as air ambulances and played a significant role in establishing the Cairo-Baghdad airmail route. **Vernon Mk I** aircraft (20 built) differed little from the Vimy Commercial, but the **Vernon Mk II** (25) introduced 450-hp (336-kW) Napier Lion II engines and the **Vernon Mk III** (10) had Lion III engines, increased fuel tankage and oleopneumatic landing gear. The Vernon was superseded by the Victoria from 1927.

For its Atlantic flight, this otherwise standard Vimy had all military equipment removed.

SPECIFICATION	
Vickers Vimy Mk II	(4937 kg)
Type: heavy bomber	**Dimensions:** wingspan 68 ft 1 in
Powerplant: two 360-hp (268-kW)	(20.75 m); length 43 ft 6½ in
Rolls-Royce Eagle VIII Vee piston	(13.27 m); height 15 ft 7½ in
engines	(4.76 m); wing area 1,318.0 sq ft
Performance: maximum speed	(122.44 m²)
103 mph (166 km/h) at sea level;	**Armament:** one 0.303-in (7.7-mm)
service ceiling 7,000 ft (2135 m);	Lewis machine-gun on a Scarff ring
maximum range 900 miles	mounting in both nose and mid
(1448 km)	positions, plus up to 2,476 lb
Weights: empty 7,104 lb (3222 kg)	(1123 kg) of bombs on external
maximum take-off 10,884 lb	racks

Vickers Type 56 Victoria, Type 264 Valentia and Type 27 Vanguard

Derived from the Virginia, the **Victoria** military transport has a significant place in RAF history, playing a conspicuous role in the evacuation of 586 people from Kabul to Peshawar during 1928-29. Two Victoria prototypes were ordered in April 1921, the

first of them being designated **Type 56 Victoria Mk I** and first flown on 22 August 1922. A large equal-span biplane with a biplane tail unit, its powerplant comprised two 450-hp (336-kW) Napier Lion IXA engines, and the large-capacity fuselage

accommodated two crew in an open cockpit in the nose, with up to 23 fully equipped troops in the enclosed cabin. The second prototype **Type 81 Victoria Mk II** was flown in January 1923 and the initial production **Type 117 Victoria Mk III** introduced slightly swept outer wing panels incorporating some dihedral and, initially, 450-hp (336-kW) Lion II engines. The designation **Type 145 Victoria Mk IV** applied to a prototype introducing a basic wing structure of metal, and this was followed by the first large-scale production version, the **Type 169 Victoria Mk V**, which had this wing structure, 570-hp

(425-kW) Napier Lion VIIB engines, and was without fixed vertical tail surfaces. Final production version was the **Type 262 Victoria Mk VI** with the 622-hp (464-kW) Bristol Pegasus IIL3 radial engine, and when Victoria construction ended a total of 97 had been built including prototypes.

The success of the Victoria Mk VI led to orders for new production aircraft (28 built) with this powerplant, these being designated **Type 264 Valentia**; in addition, 54 Victorias were converted subsequently to Valentia standard. A small number with 635-hp (474-kW) Pegasus IIM3 engines had

the same designation. At the outbreak of World War II the RAF had 60 Valentias on strength, many of them remaining in service until 1941, and in Iraq two continued in use until May 1944.

A one-off civil variant designated **Type 72 Vanguard**, accommodating 23 passengers and powered by two Napier Lion engines (later 650-hp/ 485-kW Rolls-Royce Condor IIIs as the **Type 103 Vanguard**) entered service with Imperial Airways in May 1928. It was destroyed in an accident in late 1928 when being tested after modification of the tail unit as the **Type 170 Vanguard**.

SPECIFICATION	
Vickers Valentia	(4964 kg); maximum take-off
Type: troop transport	19,500 lb (8845 kg)
Powerplant: two 622-hp	**Dimensions:** wingspan 87 ft 4 in
(464-kW) Bristol Pegasus IIL3	(26.62 m); length 59 ft 6 in
radial piston engines	(18.14 m); height 17 ft 9 in
Performance: maximum speed	(5.41 m); wing area 2,178.0 sq ft
120 mph (193 km/h) at 5,000 ft	(202.34 m²)
(1525 m); service ceiling 16,250 ft	**Armament:** underwing racks could
(4955 m); range 800 miles	be attached to carry a maximum
(1287 km)	bombload of 2,200 lb (998 kg)
Weights: empty 10,944 lb	

Vickers Type 57 Virginia

A large biplane, which in construction differed little from the Vimy, the **Type 57 Virginia** was flown in prototype form on 24 November 1922. The type became the backbone of the RAF's heavy night-bomber squadrons in the years between the two world wars, remaining in first-line service from 1924 until the mid-1930s, and then continuing in use for parachute training at RAF

Henlow. When production ended a total of 124 had been built for the RAF. First of the 10 variants was the initial prototype, the **Virginia Mk I** powered by two 450-hp (336-kW) Napier Lion engines, later replaced by two 650-hp (485-kW) Rolls-Royce Condor III engines as the **Type 96 Virginia Mk I**; subsequently it was given a lengthened fuselage, a new forward fuselage and gun

Virginia Mk Xs were used by Nos 7, 9 (pictured), 10, 51, 58, 214, 215, 500 and 502 (Bomber) Sqns, RAF, until late 1927.

positions known as fighting-tops at the wing trailing edges, resulting in a new prototype designated **Type 115 Virginia Mk VIII**. It was converted subsequently to **Type 129 Virginia Mk VII** and finally **Virginia Mk X** standards.

The second prototype, the **Type 76 Virginia Mk II**, differed in the installation of its Napier Lion engines and had a lengthened nose

to improve the bomb-aimer's efficiency. After tests and use in service trials it was converted, like the original prototype, to

Mk VII and finally **Virginia Mk X** standard. The **Type 79 Virginia Mk III**, built to Air Ministry contract of late 1922, was similar to the Virginia Mk II in original form but differed mainly by having dual controls, provision for underwing bombs and 468-hp (349-kW) Napier Lion II engines. Almost identical to the Mk III, the **Type 99 Virginia Mk IV** had additional equipment and an increase in underwing bombload; one was used to test the installation of a

third (central) rudder in the biplane tail unit, a feature which distinguished the first major production version, the **Type 100 Virginia Mk V** (22 built). The **Type 108 Virginia Mk VI** (25) introduced revisions in wing folding and rigging, and six Virginia Mk Vs were updated to this configuration. The second Virginia Mk III was returned to Vickers for installation of a redesigned nose to better the pilot's field of view and, simultaneously, acquired the accumulated improve-

ments of the Mk VI plus a lengthened rear fuselage and wing sweepback to improve stability; in this form it served as the **Type 112 Virginia Mk VII** prototype, followed by 11 production aircraft and 38 conversions of earlier marks to this standard. The **Type 128 Virginia Mk IX** (8 built and 27 conversions) introduced automatic slats, wheel brakes and a tail gunner's position, and the final **Type 139 Virginia Mk X** (50 built and 53 conversions) incorporated

an all-metal basic structure. Apart from playing a vital role in the operational development of what was to become RAF Bomber

Command, many Virginias continued to be used for a variety of test purposes as late as 1941, particularly as engine testbeds.

SPECIFICATION

Vickers Virginia Mk X
Type: heavy night-bomber
Powerplant: two 580-hp (433-kW) Napier Lion VB W-12 piston engines
Performance: maximum speed 108 mph (174 km/h) at 5,000 ft (1525 m); service ceiling 15,500 ft (4725 m); range 985 miles (1585 km)
Weights: empty 9,650 lb

(4377 kg); maximum take-off 17,600 lb (7983 kg)
Dimensions: wingspan 87 ft 8 in (26.72 m); length 62 ft 3 in (18.97 m); height 18 ft 2 in (5.54 m); wing area 2,178 sq ft (202.34 m²)
Armament: single 0.303-in (7.7-mm) Lewis gun in nose and twin Lewis guns in tail, plus up to 3,000 lb (1361 kg) of bombs

Vickers Type 132 Vildebeest and Type 266 Vincent

Designed to replace the Hawker Horsley day/torpedo-bomber in RAF service, the **Vildebeest** was a conventional equal-span biplane with fixed tailwheel landing gear and single-engine powerplant. As first flown in **Type**

132 prototype form in April 1928 it was powered by a 460-hp (343-kW) Bristol Jupiter VIII radial, but a variety of powerplants was tested (**Types 192, 194** and **209**) before an overheating problem was resolved in the **Type 214** by installation

of a new Bristol engine designated XFBM, later developed into the Pegasus. Production for the RAF included four basic models, the initial production **Type 244 Vildebeest Mk I** having the Pegasus I engine. It was followed by the **Type 258 Vildebeest Mk II** which introduced the 660-hp (492-kW) Pegasus IIM3 engine, and then by the **Type 277 Vildebeest Mk III** with a revised rear cockpit giving this version three-seat capacity. The final production version, of which 18 were built, was the **Type 286 Vildebeest Mk IV** which had the 825-hp (615-kW) Bristol Perseus VIII, making it the world's first aircraft with a

sleeve-valve engine. Vildebeest Mk Is entered service with the RAF in 1933; about 100 remained in service at the outbreak of World War II and the type was last used operationally against Japanese forces at Singapore in 1942. Of the 183 built by Vickers, 39 were supplied to the RNZAF and in addition, 26 **Type 245** aircraft with Hispano V-12 engines were built under licence in Spain.

With a requirement for a three-seat general purpose aircraft to supersede the Fairey IIIF and Westland Wapiti in RAF service, the Air Ministry selected a modified version of the Vildebeest which gained the designation **Type 266**

Vincent. Derived directly from the Vildebeest Mk III, a converted Vildebeest Mk I serving as the prototype, the Vincent differed by carrying an auxiliary fuel tank instead of a torpedo, and by having specialised equipment and message pick-up hook for use in an army co-operation role. Entering service with the RAF in late 1934, the Vincent found employment in Aden, Egypt, India, Iraq, Kenya and the Sudan and was built to a total of 197; about half remained in RAF service at the outbreak of World War II and continued to serve in Iraq until 1941. The Vincent was also supplied in small numbers to Iraq and the RNZAF.

SPECIFICATION

Vickers Vildebeest Mk IV
Type: two-seat torpedo-bomber
Powerplant: one 825-hp (615-kW) Bristol Perseus VIII sleeve radial piston engine
Performance: maximum speed 156 mph (251 km/h) at 5,000 ft (1525 m); service ceiling 17,000 ft (5180 m); range with maximum payload 630 miles (1014 km)
Weights: empty 4,724 lb (2143 kg); maximum take-off 8,500 lb (3856 kg)

Dimensions: wingspan 49 ft (14.94 m); length 37 ft 8 in (11.48 m); height 14 ft 8 in (4.47 m); wing area 728.0 sq ft (67.63 m²)
Armament: one forward-firing 0.303-in (7.7-mm) Vickers machine-gun and one 0.303-in (7.7-mm) Lewis gun on trainable mount in rear cockpit, plus one 18-in (457mm) torpedo or 1,000 lb (454 kg) of bombs

Vickers Type 246 Wellesley

In 1933 Vickers began construction of a prototype biplane to Air Ministry Specification G.4/31 for a general-purpose torpedo-bomber. Simultaneously, as a private venture, the company built to the same specification an alternative design of monoplane configuration based on extensive use of light alloy geodetic construction developed by Barnes N. Wallis. When tested by the RAF, the **Type 246** monoplane proved far superior

to the **Type 253** biplane and, as a result, in September 1935 an initial order was placed for 96 of these monoplanes with the name **Type 281 Wellesley**. When production of the definitive **Type 287 Wellesley Mk I** ended in May 1938 a total of 176 had been built, and the type first entered RAF service with No. 76 Sqn in April 1937. The Wellesley became well known in 1938 when, used by the RAF Long-Range

Development Flight, two of three Type 292 aircraft (Pegasus XXII) led by Squadron Leader R. Kellett completed successfully a nonstop 7,158.40-mile (11520.40-km) flight from Ismailia, Egypt, to Darwin, Australia; this established a world absolute distance record that remained unbroken until 1945.

By the outbreak of World War II some 100 Wellesleys remained in RAF service in the Middle East, being used opera-

tionally against Italian forces at a later stage and remaining in use for maritime patrol until 1941. Other Wellesley models were the **Type 289**

test-bed for the Hercules HE15 radial, the **Type 291** blind-flying model, the **Type 294** with strengthened wing and **Type 402** experimental three-seater.

SPECIFICATION

Vickers Wellesley Mk I
Type: two-seat medium bomber
Powerplant: one 925-hp (690-kW) Bristol Pegasus XX radial piston engine
Performance: maximum speed 228 mph (367 km/h) at 19,700 ft (6005 m); service ceiling 33,000 ft (10060 m); range with maximum payload 1,110 miles (1786 km)
Weights: empty 6,369 lb (2889 kg); maximum take-off

11,100 lb (5035 kg)
Dimensions: wingspan 74 ft 7 in (22.73 m); length 39 ft 3 in (11.96 m); height 12 ft 4 in (3.76 m); wing area 630.0 sq ft (58.53 m²)
Armament: one forward-firing 0.303-in (7.7-mm) Vickers machine-gun and one Vickers 'K' gun on a trainable mount in rear position, plus up to 2,000 lb (907 kg) of bombs in underwing panniers

Vickers Type 271 Wellington

Initial experience gained with geodetic construction in the Wellesley was of great value when Vickers tendered to Air Ministry Specification B.9/32 for a medium day bomber. The benefits of geodetic construction earned Vickers a contract for a B.9/32 prototype, a midwing monoplane with retractable

tailwheel landing gear powered by two 915-hp (682-kW) Bristol Pegasus X radial engines. This Vickers

Wellington was first flown on 15 June 1936, and satisfactory early tests led on 15 August 1936 to an initial

order for 180 **Wellington Mk I** production aircraft. These were the first of many and in October 1938 began to equip No. 9 Sqn; at the outbreak of World War II in the following

September eight squadrons were fully equipped and others had token numbers. When production ended in October 1945, a total of 11,461 Wellingtons of all versions had been built.

Operated by No. 99 (Madras Presidency) Sqn at Mildenhall, this is a Wellington Mk IC. The unit's first wartime mission took place on 8/9 September 1939, when two Wellingtons flew a Nickel (leaflet-dropping) sortie over Hannover.

Vickers Type 271 Wellington (continued)

Nicknamed **'Wimpey'**, after an American cartoon character-named J. Wellington Wimpey, the Wellington formed the mainstay of Bomber Command's operations over Europe during the first half of World War II, played a vital role in the Battle of the Atlantic, and was still fulfilling an important training role at the beginning of the 1950s. In the interim period Wellingtons had taken part in the first attack on Germany in World War II, but after suffering unacceptable losses as a day bomber were switched to night operations from 18 December 1939. They formed the major component of the first '1,000-bomber raid', were used to destroy enemy magnetic mines, to lay mines in enemy waters, and to test a large variety of different powerplants and weapons.

Variants: prototypes

Prototypes
Type 271: initial prototype flown on 15 June 1936
Type 285 Wellington MK I: pre-production prototype with Pegasus X engines flown 23 December 1937
Type 290 Wellington Mk I: initial production version (183 built) with 1,000-hp (746-kW) Pegasus XVIII engines, Vickers turrets and 'dustbin'
Type 408 Wellington Mk IA: production version (187 built) with Pegasus XVIII engines, Nash & Thompson turrets and 'dustbin'
Type 416 Wellington Mk IC: production version, 2,685 built; **Type 423** covered conversion of all bombers to carry 4,000-lb (1814-kg) bombs; beam guns and no 'dustbin'
Type 298 Wellington Mk II: prototype with 1,145-hp (854-kW) Merlin X engines, first flown 3 March 1939
Type 406 Wellington B.Mk II: production version with Merlin X engines; 400 built
Type 299 Wellington Mk III: two prototypes, one with Hercules HE1.SM and one with Hercules III engines
Type 417 Wellington B.Mk III: production version (1,517 built) with 1,500-hp (1119-kW) Hercules XI engines
Type 410 Wellington Mk IV: prototype with Pratt & Whitney Twin Wasp radials
Type 424 Wellington B.Mk IV: production version; 220 built with Twin Wasps
Type 421 Wellington Mk V: high-altitude prototype with Hercules III engines
Type 407 Wellington Mk V: high-altitude prototype with Hercules VIII engines
Type 432 Wellington Mk VI: prototype with various Rolls-Royce Merlins
Type 442 Wellington B.Mk VI: production version (63 built) with Sperry bomb sight; **Type 449** covered two production **Wellington Mk VIG**
Type 429 Wellington GR.Mk VIII: production version (397 built) with Pegasus XVIII engines; 58 with Leigh Light; provision for AS weapons, some with provision for torpedoes
Type 437 Wellington IX: single transport prototype, conversion of Mk IA with Hercules XVI engines
Type 440 Wellington B.Mk X: production version (3,803 built) with Hercules VI or XVI engines; **Type 619** covered post-war conversion to **Wellington T.Mk 10**; some sold to France and six to Royal Hellenic air force in 1946
Type 454 Wellington Mk IX: prototype with ASV.Mk II radar and Hercules VI/XVI engines; **Type 459** with ASV.Mk III radar
Type 458 Wellington GR.Mk XI: production version (180 built) with ASV.Mk III and Hercules VI/XVI engines
Type 455 Wellington GR.Mk XII: production version (58 built) with Leigh Light, ASV.Mk III and Hercules VI/XVI engines; some sold to France in 1946
Type 466 Wellington GR.Mk XIII: production version (844 built) with Hercules XVI engines
Type 467 Wellington GR.Mk XIV: production version (841 built) Hercules XVI engines; many supplied to France during 1944-45, and some sold to France in 1946

SPECIFICATION

Vickers Wellington B.Mk III
Type: six-crew medium bomber
Powerplant: two 1,500-hp (1119kW) Bristol Hercules XI radial piston engines
Performance: maximum speed 255 mph (410 km/h) at 12,500 ft (3810 m); service ceiling 19,000 ft (5790 m); range 1,540 miles (2478 km) with 4,500 lb (2041 kg) of bombs
Weights: empty 18,556 lb (8417 kg); maximum take-off 29,500 lb (13381 kg)
Dimensions: wingspan 86 ft 2 in (26.26 m); length 60 ft 10 in (18.54 m); height 17 ft 5 in (5.31 m); wing area 840.0 sq ft (78.04 m²)
Armament: eight 0.303-in (7.7mm) machine-guns, (two in nose and four in tail turret and one on each beam), plus a maximum bombload of 4,500 lb (2041 kg) or one 4,000-lb (1814-kg) bomb

Variants: conversions

Wellington C.Mk XV: service conversions of Wellington Mk IAs as transports for 18 troops
Wellington C.Mk XVI: service conversions of Wellington Mk ICs as transports for 18 troops
Type 487 Wellington T.Mk XVII: service conversions to trainers using Vickers kits; Mosquito-type AI radar and Hercules XVII engines
Type 490 Wellington T.Mk XVIII: production version (80 built) plus some conversions of Wellington Mk XIs; Hercules XVI engines
Wellington T.Mk XIX: service conversions of Wellington Mk X to trainer

Variants: experimental

Type 416 Wellington (II): experimental installation of 40-mm Vickers gun in dorsal position applied to original Wellington Mk II prototype and modified with twin fins
Type 418 Wellington DWI.Mk I: conversion of one aircraft for mine detonation; Ford auxiliary power unit
Type 419 Wellington DWI.Mk II: conversion of one aircraft for mine detonation; Gipsy Six auxiliary power unit
Type 435 Wellington Mk IC: conversion of one aircraft to evaluate Turbinlite
Type 439 Wellington Mk II: experimental installation in Wellington Mk II of Vickers 40-mm gun in nose
Type 443 Wellington Mk V: one aircraft converted to Hercules VIII testbed
Type 445 Wellington (II): testbed for Whittle W2B/23 turbojet in tail; **Type 470** and **Type 486** covered Wellington Mk II with Whittle W2B and W2/700 respectively
Type 478 Wellington Mk X: one aircraft with trial installation of Hercules 100
Type 602 Wellington Mk X: one aircraft as testbed with Rolls-Royce Dart turboprops
Wellington Mk III: one aircraft with glider-towing clearance for Hadrian, Hotspur and Horsa

Vickers Type 284 Warwick

Variants

Warwick B.Mk I: intended original production bomber version; only 16 of 150 on order were built and used for a variety of test purposes
Type 456 Warwick C.Mk I: 14 transport aircraft, conversions of Warwick B.Mk Is, for use by BOAC on North African and Mediterranean routes; later transferred to No. 167 Sqn
Warwick ASR: 40 conversions from B.Mk Is for air/sea rescue, carrying two sets of Lindholme life-saving equipment; retained bomber capability
Warwick ASR (Stage A): 10 conversions from Warwick B.Mk Is for air/sea rescue, carrying one airborne lifeboat Mk I and two sets of Lindholme gear
Warwick ASR (Stage B): 20 conversions from Warwick B.Mk Is for air/sea rescue, carrying equipment as above plus ASV radar and tail turret
Type 462 Warwick ASR.Mk I: finalised air/sea rescue version as above, deploying Mk I or Mk II airborne lifeboats; 205 built with 1,850-hp (1380-kW) Pratt & Whitney Double Wasp R-2800-S1A4G engines
Type 485 Warwick ASR.Mk VI: last air/sea rescue production version, 94 built; as ASR.Mk 1 but with Double Wasp R-2800-2SBG engines
Type 413 Warwick B.Mk II: single prototype of bomber version with Bristol Centaurus engines, conversion from B.Mk I
Type 469 Warwick GR.Mk II: general-reconnaissance production version, 118 built, with powerplant of two Centaurus VI engines
Warwick GR.Mk II Met: meterological reconnaissance version of GR.Mk II; 14 built
Type 460 Warwick C.Mk III: transport/freighter version, 100 built, carrying 8 to 10

Designed to Specification B.1/35 for a heavy bomber, the **Type 284 Warwick** was intended to complement the Wellington in service. However, the lack of suitable high-power engines for this larger and heavier version of the Wellington delayed its first flight until

SPECIFICATION

Vickers Warwick GR.Mk II
Type: six-crew general reconnaissance aircraft
Powerplant: two 2,500-hp (1864-kW) Bristol Centaurus VI sleeve radial piston engines
Performance: maximum speed 262 mph (422 km/h) at 2,000 ft (610 m); service ceiling 19,000 ft (5790 m); range 2,150 miles (3460 km)
Weights: empty 31,125 lb (14118 kg); maximum take-off 51,250 lb (23247 kg)
Dimensions: wingspan 96 ft 8¼ in (29.48 m); length 68 ft 6 in (20.88 m); height 18 ft 6 in (5.64 m); wing area 1,006 sq ft (93.46 m²)
Armament: eight 0.303-in (7.7-mm) machine-guns in nose and dorsal twin-gun turrets and four-gun tail turret, plus a maximum weapon load of 15,250 lb (6917 kg)

passengers in VIP version, 24 fully equipped troops, or freight
Type 474 Warwick GR.Mk V: final production version, 210 built, plus one experimental; had modified nose incorporating ASV radar, and was equipped with Leigh Light and ASW equipment

13 August 1939, powered by two Rolls-Royce Vultures. Performance with this powerplant was disappointing and the **Type 401** second prototype was flown on 5 April 1940 with

Bristol Centaurus engines; this was better, but then a decision to install Pratt & Whitney Double Wasps added to the delay and more than a year elapsed before a Double Wasp

prototype was flown. By then the original requirement no longer existed, for the Halifax and Stirling were already in service, with the Lancaster following not far behind. In consequence the

Warwick was developed for air/sea rescue, meteorological reconnaissance, transport and for ASW, but was not used in this last role until World War II had ended. Despite the slow

start, 845 Vickers Warwicks of all versions were built, including prototypes, and they provided valuable service, especially in the air/sea rescue and transport roles.

Vickers Type 491 Viking, Type 607 Valetta and Type 648 Varsity

The Brabazon Committee made proposals for British transport aircraft to be built after World War II; however, no provision was made for interim transports until these new aircraft became available. Among government selections of aircraft to fill this temporary gap was a civil version of the Wellington identified initially as the **Type 491 VC1 (Vickers Commercial 1)**, later named **Viking**. This combined the fabric-covered outer wing panels of the Wellington, its engine nacelles and landing gear, with 1,675-hp (1249-kW) Bristol Hercules 130 engines and a new stressed-skin fuselage to accommodate a flight crew of three, a stewardess and

21 passengers. The prototype was flown for the first time on 22 June 1945, the type gained certification on 24 April 1946, and BEA operated its first Viking service on 1 September 1946. Initial production version (19 built) was the **Viking 1A** with 1,690-hp (1260-kW) Hercules 630s, followed by the **Viking 1**

(31) which introduced stressed-skin wings and tail unit, and the major production **Viking IB** (113) which had the forward fuselage lengthened by 2 ft 4 in (0.71 m) to seat a total 24 passengers (later with a maximum of 36) and introduced Hercules 634 engines of similar power output. When all of the Vikings had eventually been withdrawn from service in 1974, the type had served with operators in Africa, Argentina, Denmark, Eire, France, West Germany, India, Iraq, Southern Rhodesia, Trinidad and the UK. Mention should be made of one Viking used as a Rolls-Royce Nene engine testbed, the world's first transport aircraft to fly

In BEA service, Viking 610 G-AHPL was named Verdant. BEA's Vikings were replaced in 1954, after they had carried three million passengers.

solely on turbojet power.

A military variant of the Viking entered RAF service under the designation **Type 607 Valetta**, and differed primarily from the civil transport by having a strengthened floor, large loading doors and 1,975-hp (1473-kW) Hercules 230 engines. More than 250 Valettas were built, their number including the **Valetta C.Mk 1** for ambulance, freight, glider-tug, troop-carrying and supply-dropping roles; the **Valetta C.Mk 2** VIP transport for nine to 15 passengers; and the **Valetta T.Mk 3** used as a

flying classroom for trainee navigators. The second military version was the **Type 648 Varsity T.Mk 1** crew trainer which replaced the Wellington T.Mk 10 in RAF service. It differed from the standard Viking by having increased wingspan, retractable tricycle landing gear and an underfuselage pannier to accommodate a bomb-aimer and stowage for 24 practice bombs. A total of 160 Varsity T.Mk 1s had been built for the RAF when production ended in 1954, many of them remaining in service into the 1970s.

SPECIFICATION	
Vickers Viking IB	(837 km)
Type: civil transport	**Weights:** empty 23,250 lb
Powerplant: two 1,690-hp	(10546 kg); maximum take-off
(1260kW) Bristol Hercules 634	34,000 lb (15354 kg)
sleeve radial piston engines	**Dimensions:** wingspan 89 ft 3 in
Performance: maximum cruising	(27.20 m); length 65 ft 2 in
speed 210 mph (338 km/h) at	(19.86 m); height 19 ft 6 in
6,000 ft (1830 m); service ceiling	(5.94 m); wing area 882 sq ft
23,750 ft (7240 m); range with	(81.94 m²)
maximum payload 520 miles	

Vickers Type 630 Viscount

Originating from the UK Brabazon Committee proposals for post-World War II civil transports, the **VC2 Viscount** was designed originally to the Brabazon IIB specification for a 24-seat short-/medium-range transport

with turboprop powerplant. This resulted in the **Type 630** 32-seat prototype, powered by four 990-ehp (738-kW) Dart RDa.1 Mk 502 engines and first flown on 16 July 1948, but it gained no commercial interest; BEA had just

bought the Ambassador. Discussions with BEA led to the **Type 700 Viscount** with pressurised accommodation for 40-59 passengers, powered by 1,400-shp (1044-kW) Dart Mk 506 engines, or **Type 700D** with the 1,600-shp (1193-kW) Dart Mk 510. The latter engines powered the lengthened fuselage 65-/71-seat capacity **Type 800**, but the final **Type 810** had Dart Mk 525 engines and structural strengthening for operation

at a higher gross weight. On 29 July 1950 the Type 630 prototype inaugurated the world's first scheduled commercial passenger service by a turbine powered aircraft, this being a two-week operation only between London and Paris. The Type 700, certificated on 17 April 1953, inaugurated services between London and Cyprus on the following

day, and combined operator/passenger reaction to their comfort and performance resulted in large orders. At one time it seemed the Viscount had broken into the US civil transport market in a big way, but these were premature hopes. Nevertheless, a total of 444 Viscounts had been built when production ended in 1964.

Delivered to the SAAF in 1958, and later named 'Casteel', this Type 781D was sold to ITAB Zaire in 1991, and crashed in the Congo in 1997.

SPECIFICATION	
Vickers Type 810 Viscount	maximum payload, no reserves
Type: short/medium-range	1,725 miles (2776 km)
transport	**Weights:** empty operating
Powerplant: four 2,100-ehp	41,565 lb (18854 kg); maximum
(1566-ekW) Rolls-Royce Dart	take-off 72,500 lb (32885 kg)
RDa.7/1 Mk 525 turboprops	**Dimensions:** wingspan 93 ft 8½ in
Performance: maximum cruising	(28.56 m); length 85 ft 8 in
speed 350 mph (563 km/h) at	(26.11 m); height 26 ft 9 in
20,000 ft (6095 m); service ceiling	(8.15 m); wing area 963 sq ft
25,000 ft (7620 m); range with	(89.46 m²)

Vickers Type 667 Valiant

The technological developments of World War II, and in particular the deployment of nuclear weapons over Hiroshima and Nagasaki

brought the realisation in the UK that a new generation of long-range bomber aircraft would be required by the RAF if the nation

was to maintain a viable nuclear bomber force. Thus came development of the RAF's V-bomber force, of which the **Type 667**

Valiant was the first to enter service in 1955. Designed to meet Specification B.9/48, the Valiant was a cantilever monoplane with a high set wing incorporating compound sweep, had a

pressurised cabin for its five-man crew, and was powered by turbojet engines. The Valiant prototype, first flown on 18 May 1951, had four 6,500-lb (28.90-kN) thrust RA.3 Avon turbojets.

Vickers Type 667 Valiant (continued)

Tragically, the first Valiant caught fire uncontrollably on 12 January 1952. Development was then continued by the second prototype which, with 7,500-lb (33.35-kN) RA.7 Avons, flew for the first time on 11 April 1952. The first of five pre-production **Type 674 Valiant B.Mk 1** long-range bombers was flown on 22 December

1953, and the type made an impressive appearance at the Farnborough Air Show of September 1955 when a fly-past was made by 12 aircraft of No. 138 Sqn. The Valiant was used operationally to deploy high-explosive bombs during the Suez Campaign of late 1956, dropped the UK's first atomic bomb over

Maralinga, South Australia on 11 October 1956, and released the nation's first thermonuclear weapon over the Pacific Ocean on 15 May 1957. When Valiant production ended in August 1957 a total of 107 had been built, including prototypes, of which 104 were delivered to the RAF. The development of surface-to-air anti-aircraft missiles switched the V-force from its intended high-altitude strategic role to low-level penetration of enemy airspace which, in the case of the Valiant force, accelerated the wing spar metal fatigue that caused it to be withdrawn from service in January 1965.

The B.Mk 1 entered service on 8 February 1955, when WP206 was received by No. 138 Sqn.

SPECIFICATION

Vickers Valiant B.Mk 1
Type: long-range bomber
Powerplant: four 10,050-lb (44.70-kN) thrust Rolls-Royce RA.28 Avon 204/205 turbojets
Performance: maximum speed 567 mph (912 km/h) at 30,000 ft (9145 m); service ceiling 54,000 ft (16460 m); maximum range 4,500 miles (7242 km)
Weights: empty 75,881 lb (34419 kg); maximum take-off

140,000 lb (63503 kg)
Dimensions: wingspan 114 ft 4 in (34.85 m); length 108 ft 3 in (32.99 m); height 32 ft 2 in (9.80 m); wing area 2,362 sq ft (219.43 m²)
Armament: no defensive weapons; conventional or nuclear weapons carried internally, to maximum bomb load of 21,000 lb (9525 kg)

Variants

Type 706 Valiant B.Mk 1: initial production version, long-range bomber; 36 built including five pre-production aircraft; one used as testbed for Pegasus engine
Type 710 Valiant B(PR).Mk 1: long-range strategic reconnaissance version; 11 built
Type 733 Valiant B(M)K.Mk 1: multi-role version for use as a bomber, reconnaissance aircraft or inflight-refuelling tanker; 13 built
Type 758 Valiant BK.Mk 1: bomber/tanker version; 44 built
Valiant B.Mk 2: single prototype of Type 667 extensively redesigned with lengthened nose, strengthened wings and revised landing gear; demonstrated speed of 552 mph (891 km/h) at sea level compared with Valiant B.Mk 1's sea level speed of 414 mph (666 km/h)

Vickers Type 950 Vanguard

The penultimate Vanguard 951 built for BEA was G-APEE Euryalus. Delivered in early December 1960, Euralyus was lost when it overshot the runway and crashed, in fog, at Heathrow in October 1965. Vanguards entered BEA service on route-proving trials in February 1960, but service entry was delayed after problems with the power supply units.

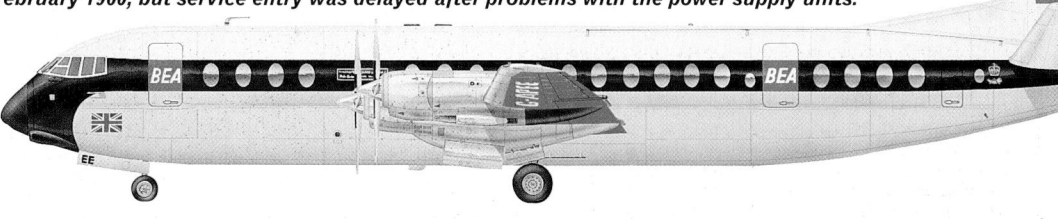

To provide BEA with a 100-seat class airliner to supersede the Viscount, a new design was started by Vickers as the **Type 870**. Both BEA and Trans-Canada Air Lines were simultaneously in the market for an aircraft in this category and the final **Type 950** was designed to meet the needs of both. Although an attractive aircraft there is little doubt that its commercial success was compromised by the selection of turboprop rather than turbojet powerplant, for at that time turboprops were yielding to jets; their fuel economy became important only in the late 1970s. Just two orders were finalised for 43 aircraft, that of BEA for 20 **Type 951 Vanguard** aircraft to accommodate a flight crew of three, two cabin crew and 126

passengers; this was later amended and only six Type 951s were built, the remaining 14 being **Type 953** aircraft having the same operating crew but with seating for 135 passengers; all 20 had the same powerplant, comprising four 4,985-ehp (3717-ekW) Tyne RTy.1 Mk 506 turboprops. Trans-Canada acquired a total of 23, these being **Type 952 Vanguard**

machines with a more powerful version of the Tyne, structural strengthening for operation at a higher gross weight and accommodation for five crew and 139 passengers. The Type 950 prototype was flown first on 20 January 1959, and both BEA and Trans-Canada introduced the Vanguard into service in early 1961. One of Trans-Canada's aircraft was converted

later for all-cargo operation under the name **Cargoliner**, and BEA

Vanguards with similar conversions were renamed **Merchantman**.

SPECIFICATION

Vickers Type 952 Vanguard
Type: medium range airliner
Powerplant: four 5,545-ehp (4135-ekW) Rolls-Royce Tyne RTy.11 Mk 512 turboprops
Performance: maximum cruising speed 425 mph (684 km/h) at 20,000 ft (6095 m); service ceiling 30,000 ft (9145 m); range with maximum payload, no reserves

1,830 miles (2945 km)
Weights: empty equipped 82,500 lb (37421 kg); maximum take-off 141,000 lb (63977 kg)
Dimensions: wingspan 118 ft 7 in (36.14 m); length 122 ft 10½ in (37.45 m); height 34 ft 11 in (10.64 m); wing area 1,527 sq ft (141.86 m²)

Vickers Type 1100 VC10 and Type 1150 Super VC10

A 1957 requirement of BOAC for an airliner able to carry a 34,000-lb (15422-kg) payload over a range of up to 4,000 miles (6437 km) on its Commonwealth routes led to development of the **Type 1100 VC10**. BOAC

served 'hot and high' airfields with relatively short runways, and the aircraft was tailored for such operations, thus making it impossible to compete economically with Boeing's 707. This was despite the

VC10's large capacity circular-section pressurised fuselage with six-abreast seating, the rear-engine layout pioneered by Sud-Aviation with the Caravelle, the clean and efficient swept wing incorporating high-lift devices and free from interference drag from the powerplant and its mountings, and an all-swept tail unit incorporating a T-tail to be well clear of the jet engine efflux. The prototype was flown for the first time on 29 June 1962, certification was gained on 23 April 1964, and BOAC introduced the **Type 1101 VC10** into service on its

London-Lagos route six days later. VC10 production comprised the Type 1101 (12) for BOAC with four 21,000-lb (93.38-kN) thrust Conway RCo.42 turbojets, an operating crew of 10 and

115 mixed-class or 135 economy class passengers; the similar **Type 1102** (2) for Ghana Airways, the second with a large cargo door; the **Type 1103** (3) for British United Airways,

No. 101 Sqn, RAF, operates four K.Mk 3s, based on the the long-fuselage Super VC10. The original wing tankage of the airliner and five new cabin cells and a fin tank provide a 22,925-Imp gal (104217-litre) capacity.

SPECIFICATION

Vickers Type 1151 Super VC10
Type: long-range civil transport
Powerplant: four 21,800-lb (96.94-kN) thrust Rolls-Royce Conway RCo.43D Mk 550 turbofans
Performance: maximum cruising speed 581 mph (935 km/h) at 31,000 ft (9450 m); economic cruising speed 550 mph (885 km/h) at 38,000 ft (11580 m); range with

maximum payload 4,720 miles (7596 km)
Weights: empty operating 158,594 lb (71937 kg); maximum take-off 335,000 lb (151953 kg)
Dimensions: wingspan 146 ft 2 in (44.55 m); length 171 ft 8 in (52.32 m); height 39 ft 6 in (12.04 m); wing area 2,932.0 sq ft (272.38 m²)

similar to the second **Type 1102**; the **Type 1106** (14) for RAF Support Command as multi-role aircraft, RAF designation **VC10 C.Mk 1**, with a revised wing, more powerful Conway RCo.43 powerplant and increased fuel capacity; and the single **Type 1109** which was the redesignation of the Type 1100 prototype following conversion with a Type 1106 wing for sale to Laker Airways.

Development of the type came with the **Type 1150 Super VC10**, which introduced a fuselage lengthened by 13 ft (3.96 m), increased fuel capacity and Conway RCo.43 engines. Two versions were built, the **Type 1151** (17) for BOAC accommodating 16 first class and 123 economy class passengers, and the similar **Type 1154** (5) for East African Airways incor-

porating a large cargo door and configured for mixed cargo/passenger traffic. BOAC introduced the Super VC10 on its London-New York route on 1 April 1965. When British Airways, the successor to BOAC, operated its final service with the type on 29 March 1981, its small VC10/Super VC10 fleet had carried in excess of 13 million passengers without accident.

With the final withdrawal of the type from service a number were acquired by the British government for conversion as inflight-refuelling tankers to expand the RAF's capability in this area. The initial programme covers nine conversions, comprising five Type 1101 VC10s and four Type 1154 Super VC10s, which as tankers have the RAF designations **VC10 K.Mk 2** and **VC10 K.Mk 3** respec-

tively. The first VC10 K.Mk 2 conversion was flown on 22 June 1983 and in late 2001 the type was rapidly being withdrawn from service. The RAF has also received five **VC10 K.Mk 4** tankers converted from ex-British Airways Super VC10s and eight of its VC10s were converted to **VC10 C(K).Mk 1** standard by the addition of underwing Hose Drum Units.

Voisin aircraft

The French brothers Charles and Gabriel Voisin began kite-building experiments in the last year or so of the 19th century, incorporating modified Hargrave-type box-kite structures in the two-float gliders designed and built in 1905 in association with Ernest Archdeacon and Louis Blériot. In the following year they established the company Les Frères Voisin at Billancourt, where they designed and built two basically similar aircraft. Of biplane configuration and with a boxkite tail structure incorporating a rudder, both aircraft had their powerplant in pusher configuration, and progressive development of this basic concept represented the company's main activity before World War I. Neither of these first aircraft was successful, the first not being flown and the second for Léon Delagrange achieving only a series of hop flights during 1907. Major progress was made with the aircraft built for Henry Farman, however, the **Voisin-Farman I** powered by a 50-hp (37-kW) Antoinette engine progressing from a 2,530-ft (771-m) long flight in October 1907, via an unofficial 3,379-ft (1030-m) circular flight in November, to a circular flight of 1 km (0.62 miles) on 13 January 1908. Having gained these and other successes the Voisin brothers appear to have become complacent, continuing to build and develop the same basic

aircraft. It was not until the approach of World War I that more active design began.

All the Voisin biplanes that entered service during World War I had a characteristic layout comprising a short nacelle for the two-man crew, a pusher engine at the rear and a tall slim rudder hinged to a vertical rod that in turn was connected to the upper and lower wings by two pairs of long tubular booms; landing gear comprised two tandem pairs of wheels attached to the nacelle.

The **Voisin Type 1913** or **13.5 Metres** (so called from its wingspan) was in service briefly with the Aéronautique Militaire at the outbreak of hostilities. Known as the **Type L**, it was powered by either an 80-hp (60-kW) Le Rhône 9C or a 70-hp (52-kW) Gnome 7A rotary engine. Maximum speed in either case was 58 mph (94 km/h). These two versions were designated retrospectively **Type I** and **Type II** by the French army, which had about 70 in service; others were supplied to Russia.

The prototype **Type LA** or **Type III** flew in February 1914. Powered by a 120-hp (89-kW) Salmson (Canton-Unné) M9 engine it was heavier than its predecessors and armed with a single machine-gun operated by the observer. The French claimed the first victory in combat on 5 October 1914, when the Type LA of Escadrille V.24

shot down a German Aviatik B.I. A version of the Type LA fitted with three floats was operated by the French navy. In April 1915 the **Type LAS** version with airframe revisions went into production. Nearly 1,000 French Type IIIs were built. The British Savage company built 50 under licence, while large numbers were constructed in Russia by the Duks company. Later marks had chutes to launch bombs up to a weight of 132 lb (60 kg); before that light bombs or flechettes (darts) were carried in the cockpit and thrown over the side. Type IIIs equipped the 1er Groupe de Bombardement established in September 1914 under Capitaine de Göys. Mass daytime attacks were made on targets behind the German lines, including railway junctions, troop concentrations and industrial sites.

The **Type IV Ca.2** equipped with a 37-mm Hotchkiss gun was built in **Type LB** and **Type LBS** versions corresponding to the LA and LAS variants of the Type III. The **Type V** and **Type VI** of 1916 were powered by 150-hp (112-kW) Salmsons and shared the factory LAS designation of Type III; some 450 were completed. They were used largely for night bombing, excessive losses having brought mass daylight raids by Voisins to a close in autumn 1915. Versions of the Voisin were built in Italy by S.I.T. of Turin to a total of 112; they included one powered by a 160-hp (119-kW) Isotta-Fraschini

Improved Voisin aircraft, including the Type IV LBS, were introduced during 1916-17. The Types IV, V and VI could carry up to 132-lb (60-kg) of bombs.

V.4B engine.

In mid-1916 Voisin began production of 103 **Type VII** A.2 category two-seat observation aircraft with 180-hp (134-kW) Renault 8G engines, these being for use in a reconnaissance role. The **Type VIII** of autumn 1916 was built in two versions, most of the 1,100 or so being **Type LAP** two-seat night bombers carrying a 397-lb (180-kg) offensive load, while a small number of **Type LBP** aircraft were *avions canons* with 37-mm Hotchkiss guns. The Type VIII had a larger, redesigned rectangular crew nacelle and was powered by the 220-hp (164-kW) Peugeot 8Aa engine, giving a maximum speed of 73 mph (118 km/h). The **Type LAR** version of September 1917 was a two-seat night bomber with a bombload of 661 lb (300 kg); the 37-mm cannon variant was the **Type LBR**.

The nacelle was again revised, the overall structure was strengthened and

power was provided by a 280-hp (209-kW) Renault 12Fe engine which raised maximum speed marginally to 81 mph (130 km/h). Until the end of the war in November 1918 virtually all French night bomber units were equipped with Voisin biplanes. The **Type X**, an air ambulance version which appeared post-war, was also built in quantity, some 900 being completed.

Experimental types tested during this period included the single-engine **Type M** with a conventional fuselage and engine carried just below the upper wing; the **Type O** with two engines fore and aft of the nacelle; and a four-engine triplane with a slim fuselage. The last Voisin type, built in 1920, was a development of the earlier triplane and intended as a night bomber or transport aircraft; its four 220-hp (164-kW) Hispano-Suiza 8Bc engines produced a maximum speed of 81 mph (130 km/h).

Vought A-7 Corsair II

This highly successful subsonic attack aircraft originated from a US Navy requirement for an aircraft to replace the A-4 Skyhawk. On 19 March 1964 Vought was awarded a contract for three prototypes under the navy designation **A-7**, the company reviving the name of its most famous wartime fighter in designating this new aircraft **Corsair II**. One of the requirements of the

specification had been that the new aircraft should be based on an existing design, to keep costs low and to speed delivery, but while the A-7 was of basically similar configuration to the F-8 Crusader (though dispensing with its variable-incidence wing) it was, in fact, a completely new design with no large-scale commonality of structural assemblies. The first prototype was flown on

27 September 1965, almost four weeks ahead of schedule, and initial deliveries to the navy began on 14 October 1966. Less than four months later, on 1 February 1967, US Navy Squadron VA-147 became the first to be commissioned with the Corsair II.

Air National Guard squadrons were the last bastion of the US A-7, the single-seat A-7D and two-seat A-7K surviving in service until 1993.

Vought A-7 Corsair II (continued)

Long before the first A-7 entered USN service, in December 1965, the US Air Force had decided to adopt a denavalised version of the aircraft to serve as a subsonic tactical fighter. Primary change was selection of the Allison-built Rolls-Royce Spey to power it instead of the Pratt & Whitney TF30 turbofan of the Navy's A-7.

US Navy Corsair IIs equipped 27 squadrons during the Vietnam War, flying more than 90,000 combat missions, and the type was also used by the USAF in that theatre, although to a far lesser extent.

After being replaced on active-duty service by the Fairchild A-10, the USAF's **A-7D** aircraft were issued to Air National Guard units, where the type continued to have a productive career. In January 1981 the two-seat **A-7K** made its first flight, the 31 built being issued only to Guard units.

In order to keep the aircraft viable in the 1990s, Vought began development of the **A-7F** version, which involved a radical reworking of the ANG machines with F100 afterburning turbofans, lengthened fuselage and updated avionics. This programme was cancelled after two prototype conversions had flown, and in the early 1990s the aircraft began a rapid withdrawal from Guard service. The last retired in 1993.

Exports of the Corsair were limited, sales to Pakistan and Switzerland having been thwarted. Portugal received two batches of aircraft from 1981 onwards, these being rebuilt Navy A-7As and Bs, and designated in FAP service as the **A-7P** and **TA-7P**, the latter a two-seater derivative. The FAP Corsair's primary role was maritime strike using AGM-65 Maverick missiles, but they also had a secondary air defence role. Greece purchased 60 **A-7H** and five **TA-7H** aircraft, based on the Navy's **A-7E** variant with TF41 engine. The fleet was bolstered by the transfer of 36 ex-US Navy aircraft, mostly A-7Es but also including a handful of **TA-7C** trainers. The final operator to receive the Corsair II was the Royal Thai Navy, who received 18 ex-USN aircraft (14 A-7Es and four TA-7Cs) for land-based operations in 1995.

SPECIFICATION

Vought A-7E Corsair II
Type: carrier-based attack bomber
Powerplant: one 14,500-lb (64.48-kN) thrust Allison TF41-A-2 (derived from Rolls-Royce Spey) turbofan
Performance: maximum speed, clean, 698 mph (1123 km/h) at sea level; tactical radius with typical weapon load 700 miles (1127 kg)
Weights: empty 19,490 lb (8841 kg); maximum take-off 42,000 lb (19051 kg)
Dimensions: wingspan 38 ft 9 in (11.81 m); length 46 ft 1½ in (14.06 m); height 16 ft ¾ in (4.90 m); wing area 375 sq ft (34.84 m²)
Armament: one 20-mm M61A1 six-barrel cannon, plus up to 15,000 lb (6804 kg) of mixed stores carried externally

Variants

A-7A: initial USN production version with 11,350-lb (50.47-kN) thrust TF30-P-6 engine; 199 built
A-7B: second USN production version, initially with TF30-P-8, later modified to TF30-P-408; 196 built
A-7C: third USN production version with TF30-P-408 engine and avionics of later A-7E; 67 built
A-7D: USAF production version with TF41-A-1 (Spey) engine, M61 cannon, inflight-refuelling capability and advanced nav/attack system; later provided with auto manoeuvring flaps and Pave Penny laser tracker; 459 built
A-7E: major USN production version based on A-7D, but with uprated TF41-A-2 engine; later equipped with FLIR (forward-looking infra-red)
A-7H: aircraft for Hellenic air force, land-based version of A-7E; 60 built
A-7K: two-seat trainer version of A-7D for ANG one conversion from A-7D plus 31 new production aircraft
A-7P: refurbished A-7A with TF30-P-408 engine for export to Portugal
TA-7C: redesignation of A-7B and A-7C aircraft converted as two-seat trainers
TA-7H: two seat trainer version of A-7H for Greece; 5 built
YA-7E or YA-7H: designations applied to **V-159** two-seat prototype designed and built as a private venture by Vought

Vought F8U/F-8 Crusader

SPECIFICATION

Vought F-8E Crusader
Type: carrier-based fighter
Powerplant: one 18,000-lb (80.05-kN) thrust Pratt & Whitney J57-P-20A turbojet
Performance: maximum speed approximately Mach 1.8, or 1120 mph (1802 km/h) at 40,000 ft (12190 m); service ceiling 58,000 ft (17680 m); range 1,000 miles (1609 km)
Weight: maximum take-off 34,000 lb (15422 kg)
Dimensions: wingspan 35 ft 2 in (10.72 m); length 54 ft 6 in (16.61 m); height 15 ft 9 in (4.80 m); wing area 350.0 sq ft (32.52 m²)
Armament: four 20-mm Colt-Browning cannon, two Sidewinder missiles and underfuselage rocket pack, or four Sidewinder missiles, plus underwing racks for two 2,000-lb (907-kg) bombs, or two Bullpup missiles, or 24 Zuni air-to-surface rockets

VFP-306 was one of two Navy Reserve light-photo squadrons established to operate the RF-8G in 1970. It was assigned to the Pacific Fleet reserve carrier air wing, based at NAF Washington.

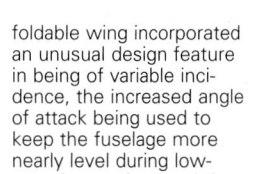

A US Navy requirement of 1952 for a supersonic air-superiority fighter resulted in eight design submissions, and in May 1953 the Vought design was selected for prototype construction with a contract for two **XF8U-1** prototypes. The design's high-mounted foldable wing incorporated an unusual design feature in being of variable incidence, the increased angle of attack being used to keep the fuselage more nearly level during low-speed operations and thus enhance the pilot's view during, for example, carrier landing. The first of the prototypes was flown on 25 March 1955 and deliveries of the initial production **F8U-1** began to VF-32 in March 1957, representing a development of just less than four years from receipt of the original prototype contract; this was no mean achievement for a new carrier-based fighter of high supersonic capability. The **Crusader** remained in production over a period of eight years and its success in both Navy and Marine Corps hands during the Vietnam War enhanced its reputation.

Variants

XF8U-1 (later XF-8A): two original unarmed prototypes with the 14,800-lb (65.81-kN) thrust J57-P-11 turbojet
F8U-1 (later F-8A): initial production version, most with 16,200-lb (72.04-kN) thrust J57-P-4A engine; armament of four 20-mm cannon, plus rockets in fuselage packs; later retrofitted to carry Sidewinder missiles; 318 built
YF8U-1 (later YF-8A): redesignation of one F8U-1 used for development testing
YF8U-1E (later YF-8B): redesignation of one F8U-1 converted as prototype of F8U-1E
F8U-1E (later F-8B): production version of F8U-1 with limited all-weather capability; 130 built
F8U-1D (later DF-8A): designation of F8U-1s after conversion as drone directors
F8U-1KD (later QF-8A): target drone conversions of the F8U-1
YF8U-1P (later YRF-8A): development versions of F8U-1 for photo-reconnaissance
F8U-1P (later RF-8A): photo-reconnaissance version of F8U-1 with camera bay in forward fuselage and weapons deleted
XF8U-1T: conversion from **XF8U-2NE** for evaluation as two-seat operational trainer prototype; 16,200-lb (72.04-kN) thrust J57-P-20 and only two 20-mm cannon; when used as trainer was redesignated **F8U-1T (later TF-8A)**
YF8U-2 (later YF-8C): redesignation of two F8U-1s used for flight testing of 16,900-lb (75.16-kN) thrust J57-P-16

F8U-2 (later F-8Q): production version with J57-P-16 engine and twin ventral fins; 187 built
F8U-2N (later F-8D): production version with 18,000-lb (80.05-kN) thrust J57-P-20 turbojet, additional fuel and provision for four Sidewinder missiles; 152 built
YF8U-2N (later YF-8D): designation of aircraft used for development testing for F8U-2N
XF8U-2NE: conversion from F8U-1 to serve as **F8U-2NE** prototype; later converted as XF8U-1T prototype
F8U-2NE (later F-8E): improved production version; 18,000-lb (80.05-kN) thrust J57-P-20A, advanced radar and underwing pylons for two AGM-12 Bullpup missiles or up to 4,000 lb (1814 kg) of bombs; 286 built
F8U-3: redesigned version of which five were built but only three flown for evaluation against F4H Phantom II; Sidewinder or Sparrow missiles and 24,500-lb (108.95-kN) or 26,000-lb (115.62-kN) thrust J75-P-5A or J75-P-6 engines respectively
F-8E(FN): version of F-8E for French navy with blown flaps and other high-lift improvements; 48 built
DF-8F: drone director conversions from F-8A
RF-8G: redesignation of 73 RF-8As after refurbishing; strengthened airframe, addition of ventral fins, and installation of J57-P-20A engine
F-8H: 89 rebuilds from F-8D; introduced strengthened airframe and blown flaps
F-8J, F-8K and F-8L: rebuilds as above, respectively of F-8E (136), F-8C (87) and F-8B (61)

The Philippines operated a handful of **F-8H** fighters, while the Aéronavale retained the aircraft in service up to December 1999. Designated **F-8E(FN)**, 42 Crusaders were built for France, the (FN) differing from the standard multi-role **F-8E** by having blown flaps and other high-lift devices in order to operate from the small French carriers *Clemenceau* and *Foch*. Retaining the Colt-Browning 20-mm cannon, the French Crusaders regularly carried MATRA Magic or R530 air-to-air missiles in place of the Sidewinders previously carried by US aircraft and the F-8E(FN)s were dedicated to air defence.

Vought F4U Corsair

Acknowledged universally to be the most outstanding carrier-based fighter of World War II, examples of the **Corsair** in service with the Royal Navy's Fleet Air Arm were the first to demonstrate the outstanding potential of this design. When used by the US Navy in the Pacific, from April 1944, the type was credited with no fewer than 2,140 victories against the Japanese for the loss of only 189 of its own number.

Development of the aircraft began in 1938, when the US Navy requested proposals for a single-seat carrier-based fighter. The Vought design team evolved the smallest possible airframe that could be tailored to fit the most powerful engine then available, the Pratt & Whitney XR-2800 Double Wasp. Identified initially by the company as the **V-166B**, its unusual wing configuration resulted from the choice of this engine, for the large-diameter propeller needed by the Double Wasp would require stalky landing gear, far from suitable for carrier operations. The highly-cranked inverted and

folding gull wing that was adopted allowed the retractable main landing gear units to be located at the 'pinion joint' of the wing, keeping them as short as possible. The remainder of the airframe was conventional, of clean line and all-metal construction.

The **XF4U-1** prototype, ordered on 30 June 1938, was flown for the first time on 29 May 1940, but combat reports from Europe had shown a need to revise the armament. This delayed until February 1941 US Navy acceptance of the prototype, an initial production order for 585 **F4U-1** production aircraft being awarded on 30 June 1941. The first of these flew a year later, on 25 June 1942, and the first examples of these F4U-1s were handed over to the US Navy on 31 July 1942. Carrier trials proved disappointing, the US Navy considering the Corsair unsuitable for carrier service, a fact which led to modification of the landing gear and raising of the cockpit to improve forward view. When these changes were introduced on the

Variants

F4U-1B: US designation of aircraft supplied to the UK under Lend-Lease
F4U-1C: version with four wing-mounted 20-mm cannon in place of standard six machine-gun armament
F4U-1D: version with R-2800-8W water-injection engine and revised armament (also built by Brewster and Goodyear as **F3A-1D** and **FG-1D** respectively)
F4U-1P: photo-reconnaissance variant of the F4U-1
F4U-2: night-fighter version, all conversions by Naval Aircraft Factory, with AI radar and reduced armament
F4U-3: very high-altitude fighter; first prototype flown post-war, but the 13 Goodyear-built aircraft completed subsequently (under the designation **FG-3**) were used by the US Navy for high-altitude research flights
F4U-4: second major production version with R-2800-18W or R-2800-42W engine
F4U-4C: variant with four 20-mm cannon in place of standard armament
F4U-4E: night-fighter version with APS-4 AI radar
F4U-4N: night-flight version with APS-5 or APS-6 AI radar
F4U-4P: photo-reconnaissance variant
F4U-5: post-World War II fighter bomber with R-2800-32W engine
F4U-5N: night-fighter version of F4U-5
F4U-5P: tactial reconnaissance variant of F4U-5
XF4U-6: prototype of low-altitude variant with R-2800-83W engine, additional armour protection and increased weapon-carrying capability; total of 110 built under the designation **AU-1**
F4U-7: final production version, similar to AU-1 but with R-2800-18W; total of 90 built and supplied to French Aéronavale through MAP
Corsair Mk I: FAA designation of F4U-1
Corsair Mk II: FAA designation of F4U-1A
Corsair Mk III: FAA designation of F3A-1D
Corsair Mk IV: FAA designation of FG-1D

production line, after 688 F4U-1s had been built, subsequent aircraft became designated **F4U-1A**.

Initial US operational use of the Corsair was, therefore, with land-based units, the US Marine Corps' VMF-124 being the first squadron to take the type into action at Guadalcanal on 13 February 1943. The US Navy's first operational squadron, VF-17, was formed in April 1943 and this was the first unit to operate the F4U-1A. By that time Vought had received orders for very large numbers of Corsairs,

resulting in production also by Brewster under the designation **F3A-1** and by Goodyear as the **FG-1**: this latter version had fixed wings. Corsairs saw extensive service with the FAA from June 1943, and examples of the **F4U-1D** were

also supplied to the RNZAF.
Production had been continuous for just over 10 years when the line at Dallas, Texas was closed down in December 1952, a period in which 12,571 examples of this outstanding fighter had been built.

SPECIFICATION

Vought Corsair Mk IV
Type: single-seat carrier-based or shore-based fighter or fighter-bomber
Powerplant: one 2,250-hp (1678-kW) Pratt & Whitney R-2800-8 Double Wasp radial piston engine
Performance: maximum speed 415 mph (668 km/h) at 19,500 ft (5944 m); cruising speed 261 mph (420 km/h); service ceiling 34,000 ft (10363 m); maximum

range 1,562 miles (2514 km)
Weights: empty 9,100 lb (4128 kg); maximum take-off 12,100 lb (5488 kg)
Dimensions: wingspan 39 ft 8 in (12.09 m); length 33 ft 4 in (10.16 m); height 15 ft 1 in (4.60 m); wing area 305 sq ft (28.33 m²)
Armament: four 0.5-in (12.7-mm) forward-firing machine-guns in the wings plus up to 2,000 lb (907 kg) of bombs

In production longer than any other US fighter of World War II, the Corsair was credited with a 11:1 ratio of kills against the Japanese.

Vought F6U Pirate

Before World War II ended, Vought was busy with the design of the **V-340** single-seat jet-propelled fighter for service with the USN. It was the first turbojet-powered aircraft to be designed by the company, but proved sufficiently attractive for the Navy to award a contract for three **XF6U-1** prototypes on

29 December 1944.
Of low-wing monoplane configuration, the all-metal structure of the airframe had Metalite skins, patented by the company and comprising two sheets of high-strength light alloy bonded to a balsa wood core. The tailplane was mounted on the fin, just above the fuselage, but

production aircraft had two auxiliary fins, one towards the tip on each side of the tailplane. The **Pirate** had retractable tricycle landing gear, jettisonable auxiliary fuel tanks at each wingtip, and the pilot accommodated high on the fuselage, well forward of the wing.

The first of the three prototypes made its maiden flight at Muroc Dry Lake on 2 October 1944, powered by a 3,000-lb (13.34-kN) thrust Westinghouse J34-WE-22 turbojet mounted in the aft fuselage. Production examples of the **F6U-1**, of which

The US Navy accepted the first of 30 production model F6U-1s in 1949.

Variant

F6U-1P: designation allocated to one of the production F6U-1s following the installation of cameras for evaluation in a reconnaissance role

the first flew during July 1949, began to enter service with the US Navy in the following month. A

total of 65 had been ordered but after 30 had been delivered the remainder were cancelled.

SPECIFICATION

Vought F6U-1 Pirate
Type: single-seat naval fighter
Powerplant: one 4,225-lb (18.78-kN) thrust Westinghouse J34-WE-30 turbojet
Performance: (estimated) maximum speed 564 mph (908 km/h) at 20,000 ft (6095 m); service ceiling 46,300 ft (14110 m); range 1,150 miles (1851 km)

Weights: empty 7,320 lb (3320 kg); maximum take-off 12,570 lb (5702 kg)
Dimensions: wingspan, without tiptanks 32 ft 10 in (10.01 m); length 37 ft 7 in (11.46 m); height 12 ft 11 in (3.94 m); wing area 203.50 sq ft (18.91 m²)
Armament: four 20-mm cannon

Vought F7U Cutlass

When the first details of the aerodynamic research carried out in Germany during World War II began to reach the US in late 1945, much of the information was of great help to manufacturers in the development of new aircraft of improved capability. Vought became interested in Arado's work on tailless aircraft, this resulting in design and development of the unconventional **F7U Cutlass** which dispensed with conventional tail surfaces. However unconventional, the F7U introduced new capability in a naval carrier-based fighter. It was the first aircraft to serve with the US Navy that was capable of being catapulted with an external stores load of nearly 5,000 lb (2268 kg), and the Navy's first production aircraft to achieve supersonic flight. It also introduced such features as afterburners for its turbojet

The F7U-3 equipped four US Navy units: VF-81, VF-83, VF-122 and VF-124. The very low aspect ratio wing had 38° sweepback.

engines, powered controls with artificial 'feel' and an automatic stabilisation system.

After evaluation of Vought's design proposals, embodied in the **V-346** designation, the US Navy ordered three **XF7U-1** prototypes on 25 June 1946, the first of these flying on 29 September 1948. The short-span swept wings of the Cutlass mounted twin dorsal fins with rudders at about one-third span with large ventral fins beneath the wings. For control in pitch and roll, wide-span trailing-edge elevons extended outboard of the fins to the wingtips. Other features of this advanced wing included airbrakes and full-span leading-edge slats. The retractable tricycle landing gear incorporated a tall nose unit, giving the wing a high angle of attack on the deck, power was provided

by two Westinghouse turbojets within the fuselage, and the pilot, in an enclosed cockpit high on the nose, had an excellent all-round view.

Following initial evaluation of the prototypes, 14 **F7U-1** production aircraft were ordered for operational carrier trials, the first of them being flown on 1 March 1950. Production ended in December 1955.

Variants

F7U-2: proposed operational version of the F7U-1 with Westinghouse J34-WE-42, engines; difficulties with the development of this engine led to cancellation of the production contract
F7U-3: standard production version powered by two Westinghouse J46-WE-8A turbojets; introduced wing-folding and arrester gear for carrier operation, plus design refinements; first example flown 20 December 1951; 162 built
F7U-3M: version of the standard production aircraft equipped to carry four Sparrow I beam-riding missiles; 98 built
F7U-3P: designation of a photo reconnaissance version, of which 12 examples entered service

SPECIFICATION

Vought F7U-3 Cutlass
Type: single-seat carrier-based fighter
Powerplant: two 6,100-lb (27.13-kN) thrust Westinghouse J46-WE-8A afterburning turbojets
Performance: maximum speed 680 mph (1094 km/h) at 10,000 ft (3050 m); initial climb rate 13,000 ft (3960 m) per minute; service ceiling 40,000 ft (12190 m); range 660 miles (1062 km)
Weights: empty 18,210 lb (8260 kg); maximum take-off 31,642 lb (14353 kg)
Dimensions: wingspan 39 ft 8 in (12.09 m); length 43 ft 1 in (13.13 m); height 14 ft 7½ in (5.37 m); wing area 496 sq ft (46.08 m²)
Armament: four 20-mm cannon, plus underwing attachments for rockets or other stores

Vought O2U and O3U/SU Corsair

First aircraft to bear the famous company name **Corsair**, the initial **O2U** was little more than a developed version of the **UO/FU** series that incorporated an all steel tube fuselage structure and introduced the Pratt & Whitney Wasp radial engine. Deliveries to the US Navy began in 1927 and production totalled 291 in several versions. From 1930 the O2U began to be superseded in US Navy service by the **O3U Corsair** which was basically similar to the **O2U-4**, one of which was fitted experimentally with the Grumman amphibious float. O3U aircraft, later allocated **SU** designations, were built to a total of 289 for the USN. By the time the USA became involved

SPECIFICATION

Vought SU-4 Corsair
Type: two-seat scout
Powerplant: one 600-hp (447-kW) Pratt & Whitney R-1690-42 Hornet radial piston engine
Performance: maximum speed 167 mph (269 km/h) at sea level; service ceiling 18,600 ft (5670 m); range 680 miles (1094 km)
Weights: empty 3,312 lb
(1502 kg); maximum take-off 4,765 lb (2161 kg)
Dimensions: wingspan 36 ft (10.97 m); length 27 ft 5½ in (8.37 m); height 11 ft 4 in (3.45 m); wing area 337 sq ft (31.31 m²)
Armament: three 0.3-in (7.62-mm) machine-guns, one forward-firing and two on trainable mount in rear cockpit

in World War II these Corsair biplanes had been withdrawn from first-line use, although 141 remained in service in secondary roles. A few **O3U-6** machines were converted by the Naval Aircraft Factory to radio-controlled pilotless configuration for experimental use, and these were provided with fixed tricycle landing gear to simplify take-off and landing operations. Export versions included the **Corsair V-65F** for the Argentine navy, the **V-80P** for the Peruvian air force and the **V-85G** for Germany.

Variants

O2U4: two prototypes followed by 130 production aircraft with interchangeable wheel/float landing gear, 450-hp (336-kW) R-1340-88 Wasp and armament of one forward-firing and two 0.3-in (7.62-mm) machine-guns on trainable mount in rear cockpit
O2U-2: version with increased-span upper wing and wing refinements, larger rudder and R-1340-B engine; 37 built for US Navy (31) and US Coast Guard (6)
O2U-3: as O2U-2 with revised wing rigging, redesigned tail surfaces and R-1340-C engine; 80 built
O2U-4: as O2U-3 but with changes of equipment; 42 built
O3U-1: generally as O2U-4 and incorporating Grumman amphibious float tested on one aircraft; 87 built
O3U-2: improved version introducing strengthened airframe, several airframe revisions, redesigned tail unit and Pratt & Whitney R-1690 Hornet engine; 29 built and these became redesignated **SU-1** soon after entering service
O3U-3: as O3U-2 but with 550-hp (410-kW) R-1340-12 engine; 76 built
O3U-4: generally as O3U-3, but with R-1690-42 engine; 65 ordered and delivered as **SU-2** (45 built), and **SU-3** with low-pressure tyres (20 built)
XO3U-5: SU-2 tested with Pratt & Whitney GR-1535 radial engine
XO3U-6: prototype of **O3U-6** version converted from O3U-3
O3U-6: production version of XO3U-6 with NACA engine cowl and enclosed cockpits; 32 built, 16 with R-1340-12 and 16 with R-1340-18 engines
SU-1: redesignation of O3U-2
SU-2: redesignation of O3U-4
SU-3: redesignation of O3U-4 with low-pressure tyres
SU-4: new production version of SU-2; 20 built

This O2U-1 Corsair served with VO-3S, attached to the USS Raleigh in 1928. The O2U-1 was standard equipment for battleship divisions by mid-1928.

Vought OS2U Kingfisher

Designed to replace the Vought O3U Corsair, the **VS-310 Kingfisher** incorporated new constructional features, including the use of spot welding. Evaluation of the design proposal led to a US Navy contract for a prototype which was powered by a 450-hp (336-kW) Pratt & Whitney R-985-4 radial engine and flown for the first time in landplane configuration in March 1938 and in its intended floatplane version on 19 May 1938. A successful conclusion to official testing brought the first production order for the **OS2U-1 Kingfisher**, and when these aircraft began to enter service from August 1940, they were the first catapult-launched monoplane observation aircraft to serve with the US Navy. Built quite extensively, the Kingfisher was not only valuable in the scout/ observation role when operated from onboard ship, but in service with US Navy inshore patrol squadrons proved very successful in the ASW and air/sea rescue roles. The type was used also by the Royal Navy, which received 100 under Lend-Lease, these being operated under the designation **Kingfisher Mk I**, serving as catapult-launched reconnaissance aircraft and as trainers. Others were supplied to Argentina (9), Chile (15), the Dominican Republic (3), Mexico (6) and Uruguay (6); 24 en route to the Netherlands East

Indies were docked in Australia when these islands were overrun by

the Japanese and 18 of them served with the RAAF.

SPECIFICATION	
Vought OS2U-3 Kingfisher	6,000 lb (2722 kg)
Type: two-seat observation aircraft	**Dimensions:** wingspan 35 ft 11 in
Powerplant: one 450-hp (336-kW)	(10.95 m); length 33 ft 10 in
Pratt & Whitney R-985-AN-2 radial	(10.31 m); height 15 ft 1½ in
piston engine	(4.61 m); wing area 262 sq ft
Performance: maximum speed	(24.34 m²)
164 mph (264 km/h) at 5,500 ft	**Armament:** two 0.3-in (7.62-mm)
(1675 m); service ceiling 13,000 ft	machine-guns (one forward-firing
(3960 m); range 805 miles	and one on trainable mount in rear
(1296 km)	cockpit), plus two 100-lb (45-kg) or
Weights: empty 4,123 lb	325-lb (147-kg) bombs on
(1870 kg); maximum take-off	underwing racks

Variants

XOS2U-1: original prototype with R-985-4 engine
OS2U-1: first production version with 450-hp (336-kW) R-985-48 engine; 54 built
OS2U-2: production version introducing equipment changes and R-985-50 engine of the same power output; 158 built
OS2U-3: major production version, introducing self-sealing fuel tanks, armour protection, and the R-985-AN-2 engine of the same output; 1,006 built
OS2N-1: version built by Naval Aircraft Factory; as OS2U-3, but some with the R-985-AN-8 engine; 300 built
XOS2U-4: prototype conversion from one OS2U-2 with narrow-chord wings and other aerofoil revisions, but production OS2U-4 was not built

Vought SBU

First flown in May 1933, the **XF3U-1** prototype was designed and built to meet a USN requirement for a two-seat fighter biplane, and was powered by a 700-hp (522-kW) Pratt & Whitney R-1535-80. However, after completion of testing Vought was requested to modify this conventional aircraft into a scout-bomber under the designation **XSBU-1**, which differed from the XF3U-1 by having strengthened wings of increased area, greater internal fuel capacity and

provision to carry a 500-lb (227-kg) bomb beneath the fuselage. Following further tests from June 1934, an order was placed for 84 production **SBU-1** aircraft and deliveries began on 20 November 1935. Generally similar to the prototype, these were followed by the **SBU-2** (40 built) which differed by introducing the 750-hp (559-kW) R-1535-98. The XSBU-1 was converted for use as an engine testbed, and under the company designation

Spanning 33 ft 3 in (10.13 m), the SBU-1 (illustrated) had a maximum speed of 205 mph (330 km/h) at 8,900 ft (2715 m). Both SBU versions were armed with two 0.3-in (7.62-mm) Browning machine-guns, one forward-firing and one on a trainable mount over the rear cockpit, and could carry a 500-lb (227-kg) bomb.

V-142A a small number was built for export to Argentina. The last biplane to be designed and built by

Vought for the USN, the type was still in service with

the US Navy Reserve in 1941.

Vought SB2U Vindicator

In late 1934-35 Vought received a US Navy order for two prototypes, the **XSB2U-1** monoplane and for competitive evaluation the **XSB3U-1** biplane, to satisfy the requirement for a new carrier-based scout-bomber. Both machines were tested in the early summer of 1936 and there

was no doubt of the superiority of the monoplane: an initial order for 54 production **SB2U-1** aircraft was placed on 26 October 1936. The close relationship of this aircraft to the SBU is confirmed by the fact that the XSB3U-1 prototype was basically an SBU-1 with retractable main landing gear units, but the SB2U-1 differed by having an all-metal basic structure with part-fabric and part-metal covering, outer wing panels

Built by Vought-Sikorsky, this SB2U-3 served with VMS-1 in June 1941. Most aircraft were issued to Marine units.

that folded for carrier stowage, an arrester hook in the rear fuselage, and powerplant comprising an 825-hp (615-kW) R-1535-96 Twin Wasp Junior engine. Subsequent orders for the USN included the generally similar **SB2U-2** (58 built), and the **SB2U-3** (57) which introduced armour protection, increased fuel, the R-1535-02 engine and heavier armament; these were the first models to be named **Vindicator**. One SB2U-2 tested on twin floats was given the designation XSB2U-3. US Navy squadrons equipped with SB2Us saw action in the Pacific during 1942, includ-

ing participation in the Battle of Midway, but were soon retired from first-line service because of their vulnerability to modern fighters such as the A6M.

Under the company designation **V-156** Vought built and delivered 24 aircraft of 40 ordered for the French navy, some of

these falling into German hands when the French capitulated. Similarly, 50 with the designation **V-156B-1** were built for the Fleet Air Arm which designated them **Chesapeake Mk I**; following combat evaluation all were used in an operational training role by Nos 728 and 811 Sqns.

SPECIFICATION	
Vought SB2U-3 Vindicator	(2556 kg); maximum take-off
Type: carrier-based scout/bomber	9,421 lb (4273 kg)
Powerplant: one 825-hp (615-kW)	**Dimensions:** wingspan 42 ft
Pratt & Whitney R-1535-02 Twin	(12.80 m); length 34 ft (10.36 m);
Wasp Junior radial piston engine	height 10 ft 3 in (3.12 m); wing
Performance: maximum speed	area 305 sq ft (28.33 m²)
243 mph (391 km/h) at 9,500 ft	**Armament:** two 0.5-in (12.7-mm)
(2895 m); service ceiling 23,600 ft	machine-guns (one forward-firing
(7195 m); range 1,120 miles	and one on trainable mount in rear
(1802 km)	cockpit), plus up to 1,000 lb
Weights: empty 5,634 lb	(454 kg) of bombs

Vultee V-72 (A-31/A-35 Vengeance)

The **V-72** represented continuing improvement of the basic **V-11/V-12** design, and with knowledge of the successful application of dive-bombing techniques in the Spanish Civil War, the V-72 was designed to incorporate such capability. This development came at the right moment for a British purchasing mission of 1940 which, with even more comprehensive knowledge of the potential of dive-bombing, placed an order for 700. Built by Northrop and Vultee, the latter having inadequate productive capacity, these aircraft were

designated **Vengeance Mk I** and **Vengeance Mk II** respectively by the RAF. Following the introduction of Lend-Lease in 1941 the USAAF ordered 300 more aircraft for the UK, allocating the designation **A-31**, and Northrop- and Vultee-built examples of these aircraft had the respective RAF designations **Vengeance Mk IA** and **Vengeance Mk III**. With experience of the vulnerability of the Ju 87 to its own fighters in the Battle of Britain, the RAF realised that the Vengeance was unsuitable for deploy-

ment in Europe and used it in Burma where it had considerable success.

When the USA entered World War II, the USAAF commandeered 243 of the aircraft in production for the UK and these entered service as V-72s. Vultee then built 99 designated **A-35A** which differed in armament and equipment, followed by 831 **A-35B** aircraft with increased armament and the Wright R-2600-13 engine. Of this total 29 were supplied to Brazil, Plus 562 to the UK, which designated them **Vengeance Mk IV**. The

RAF transferred a small number to the RAAF, and also converted some as **Vengeance TT.Mk IV** target tugs; almost all of the USAAF's aircraft were used in this latter role. Variants included the **XA-31A** static test airframe,

becoming the **XA-31B** when used to test a 3,000-hp (2237-kW) Pratt & Whitney XR-4360-1 Wasp Major engine, plus five **XA-31C** conversions from A-31s as testbeds for the 2,200-hp (1640-kW) Wright R-3350-13/-17 Cyclone.

SPECIFICATION	
Vultee A-35B Vengeance	(4672 kg); maximum take-off
Type: two-seat dive-bomber	16,400 lb (7439 kg)
Powerplant: one 1,700-hp	**Dimensions:** wingspan 48 ft
(1268-kW) Wright R-2600-13	(14.63 m); length 39 ft 9 in
Cyclone radial piston engine	(12.12 m); height 15 ft 4 in
Performance: maximum speed	(4.67 m); wing area 332 sq ft
279 mph (449 km/h) at 13,500 ft	(30.84 m²)
(4115 m); service ceiling 22,300 ft	**Armament:** six 0.5-in (12.7-mm)
(6795 m); range 2,300 miles	machine-guns, plus up to 2,000 lb
(3701 km)	(907 kg) of bombs
Weights: empty 10,300 lb	

Westland Lynx

Launched as part of the Anglo-French helicopter agreement of February 1967, the Lynx design is wholly of Westland origin, but the production of the type is shared in the ratio of 70:30 between the UK and Eurocopter France (previously Aérospatiale). One of the primary French responsibilities is the forged titanium rotor hub, a one-piece structure for the four-bladed semi-rigid main rotor which is one of the most important features of the design. All versions of the Lynx have advanced digital flight controls plus

all-weather avionics, and no previous helicopter can equal the type for agility and all-weather single-crew operation. The Lynx prototype flew on 21 March 1971 and the type was produced as the **Lynx AH.Mk 1** battlefield helicopter for the British army and Royal Marines. Subsequent Army variants, all for Britain, include the **Lynx AH.Mk 5** of which only one was flown as such before the remainder of the order was switched to **Lynx AH.Mk 7** standard. Some 103 AH.Mk 1s have also been brought up to

this standard. Three **Army Lynx** flown by the Qatari police have been retired. The upgraded **Lynx AH.Mk 9** includes a nose-wheel undercarriage, exhaust diffusers and revised main rotor blades. Eight Lynx AH.Mk 7s have been converted and a further 16 built as new. The original **Lynx HAS.Mk 2** for the Royal Navy was designed as a multi-role helicopter for operation from 'small ships' and was similar to the Aéronavale's **Lynx Mk 2(FN)**. The next Navy variant was the improved **HAS.Mk 3**, which was produced both by conversion and as a new-build helicopter and itself spawned several variants. The definitive upgraded aircraft is the **Lynx HMA.Mk 8**, which is the principal model currently in RN service. The

British Lynxes are, for the most part, operated by the Army; a handful has also served with the Royal Marines. Marine Lynx AH.Mk 7s are pictured during a recent deployment in the Balkans.

HMA.Mk 8 is equivalent to the export **Super Lynx** and this, as well as earlier variants based on the HAS.Mk 2/3, has gained export orders in quantity.

Naval Lynx variants have been widely exported. Denmark acquired 10 Lynx Mk 80s (based on the HAS.Mk 3) in 1980 and a pair of Mk 90s in 1987/88.

SPECIFICATION	
Westland Lynx HAS.Mk 2	11 survivors
Type: twin-engined naval helicopter	**Weights:** empty 6,040 lb (2740 kg); maximum take-off 10,500 lb (4763 kg)
Powerplant: two Rolls-Royce Gem 41-2 turboshafts each rated at 1,120 shp (835 kW); from 1987 the engines were upgraded to Gem 42-1 standard rated at 1,135 shp (846 kW)	**Dimensions:** main rotor diameter 42 ft (12.80m); fuselage length 39 ft 1.3 in (11.92 m); height 11 ft 5 in (3.48 m); main rotor disk area 1,385 sq ft (128.71 m²)
Performance: maximum continuous cruising speed at optimum altitude 144 mph (232 km/h); maximum rate of climb at sea level 2,170 ft (661m) per minute; hovering ceiling 8,450 ft (2575 m); combat radius 111 miles (178 km) on a SAR mission with	**Armament:** External pylons for the carriage of two torpedoes (Mk 44, 46 or Sting Ray), two Mk 11 depth charges or four Sea Skua anti-ship missiles. An FN HMP 0.50-in (12.7-mm) machine-gun and an ALQ-167 ECM pod can be carried for self protection

Westland Lysander

Known to many as the 'Lizzie', the **Lysander** was perhaps the best-known of Westland's fixed-wing-products and originated as the company's design to meet the requirements of Air Ministry Specification A.39/34 for an army co-

operation aircraft. With a distinctive high-set wing and, in general use, small stub-wings attached to the main wheel struts to carry weapons/stores, it was easily recognisable. The crew of two had enclosed accommodation and

power was provided by a Bristol Mercury radial. The first of two prototypes was flown initially on 15 June 1936, successful testing resulting in a contract for 144 aircraft. The type began to enter service with No. 16 Sqn, RAF in June 1938, and when production ended a total of 1,652 had been

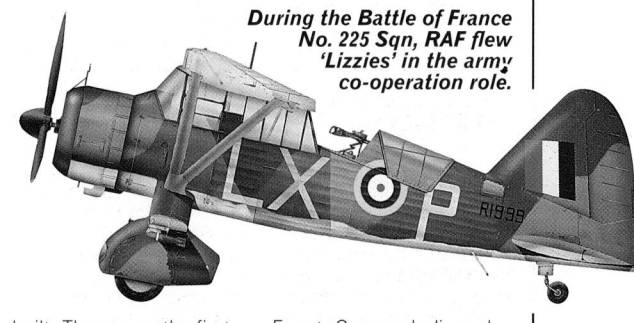

During the Battle of France No. 225 Sqn, RAF flew 'Lizzies' in the army co-operation role.

Variants

Lysander Mk I: original production version with 890-hp (664-kW) Bristol Mercury XII radial engine; 169 built
Lysander Mk II: similar to Lysander Mk I but powered by 905-hp (675-kW) Bristol Perseus XII; supplied to France (1); Ireland (6) and Turkey (36); about 20 RAF aircraft were later transferred to Free French air force; one supplied to National Steel Car Corporation (later Victory Aircraft) of Malton, Ontario, as pattern for licence construction of 75 with Perseus XII engines
Lysander Mk III: similar to Lysander Mk I but with Bristol Mercury XX radial engine; Westland built 367 and 150 were licence-built in Canada
Lysander Mk IIIA: similar to Mk III but with Mercury 30 engine and additional machine-gun in rear cockpit; 347 built of which 11 supplied to Free French (1), Portugal (8) and USAAF (2)
Lysander Mk III (SCW): conversions of Mk III and Mk IIIA for clandestine operations carrying agents or VIPs to and from enemy territory; extra fuel and access ladder to rear cockpit on left side, designated **Mk III (SD)** and **Mk IIIA (SD)** in service
Lysander TT.Mk I: Mk I after conversion for target towing
Lysander TT.Mk II: Mk II after conversion for target towing
Lysander TT.Mk III: Mks I/II/III converted for target towing
Lysander TT.Mk IIIA: 100 new-production target tugs with Mercury 30 engines

built. They were the first British aircraft to be based in France at the beginning of World War II and the last to see action in in France during the evacuation from Dunkirk; they also saw service in Burma,

Egypt, Greece, India and Palestine, and following withdrawal from first-line use played an important role in clandestine operations and fulfilled valuable air-sea rescue and target-towing roles.

SPECIFICATION	
Westland Lysander Mk III	6,318 lb (2866 kg)
Type: army co-operation aircraft	**Dimensions:** wingspan 50 ft (15.24 m); length 30 ft 6 in (9.30 m); height 14 ft 6 in (4.42 m); wing area 260.0 sq ft (14.15 m²)
Powerplant: one 870-hp (649-kW) Bristol Mercury XX radial piston engine	
Performance: maximum speed 212 mph (341 km/h) at 5,000 ft (1525 m); service ceiling 21,500 ft (6555 m); range 600 miles (966 km)	**Armament:** four 0.303-in (7.7-mm) Browning machine-guns (one in each wheel spat and two on trainable mount in rear cockpit), plus up to 500 lb (227 kg) of bombs
Weights: empty 4,365 lb (1980 kg); maximum take-off	

Westland Scout and Wasp

Westland acquired Saunders-Roe Ltd in August 1959. Saro itself had taken over the Cierva Autogiro Company in January 1951 and continued development of the Cierva Skeeter light helicopter. Experience with production of this aircraft led to the **P.531** prototypes, the first of them flown on 20 July 1958, and leading

in 1959 to an Army Air Corps order for pre-production **P.531-2 Mk 1** aircraft. Following extensive evaluation, this five-seat utility light helicopter was ordered into production as the **Scout AH.Mk 1**, which began to enter service in early 1963 and was built to a total of 150. In addition, small numbers were built for the Royal Australian

Navy, Royal Jordanian air force, and the police departments of Bahrain and Uganda. Parallel development of the P.531 resulted in production of the **Wasp HAS.Mk 1** for the Royal Navy (designated originally **Sea Scout HAS.Mk 1**). This differed from the army Scout by having quadricycle landing gear instead of skids, and folding rotor

Wasp HAS.Mk 1 helicopters could carry two AS12 wire-guided anti-ship missiles (pictured), depth charges or, more usually, a pair of Mk 44 torpedoes.

blades and tail section to facilitate shipboard stowage. A total of 98 Wasps was built for the RN, these first entering service in the summer of 1963, and approximately 40 remained in use in late 1983. Wasps were supplied also to the navies of Brazil, the Netherlands, New Zealand and South Africa. As powered by a 1,050-hp (783-kW) de-rated Rolls-Royce/Bristol Nimbus 103 or 104 turboshaft engine, the Westland Wasp had a maximum speed of 120 mph (193 km/h) at sea level.

Westland Sea King and Commando

In 1959, Westland reached agreement with Sikorsky for licensed production of the S-61 and four US-built helicopters were shipped to Westland as patterns. The first Sea King was a navalised SH-3D that flew on 11 October 1966. The first of 56 production **Sea King HAS.Mk 1** helicopters began flying on 7 May 1969, and these were followed from mid-1976 by 13 **Sea King HAS.Mk 2** helicopters with uprated Gnome H.1400 engines and six-bladed tail rotors, and from September 1977 by 15 **Sea King HAR.Mk 3** helicopters for the RAF's SAR role. Eight more HAS.Mk 2s from early 1979 included a prototype **Sea King HAS.Mk 5 ASW** upgrade conversion, many of the earlier RN Sea Kings also being converted to the HAS.Mk 5 and **HAS.Mk 6** ASW or **HAR.Mk 5 SAR**

standards. New-build HAS.Mk 5s and 6s followed from mid-1980.

The HAS.Mk 5 introduced Sea Searcher radar in a large flat-topped radome, MIR-2 Orange Crop ESM, new sonobuoy dropping equipment and LAPADS acoustic processing. The cabin was enlarged to make room for the new equipment. The HAS.Mk 6 has a further enhanced ASW suite and reduced equipment weight, resulting in a 30-minute extension to endurance, and other improvements include the enhancement of the Orange Crop ESM system to Orange Reaper standard, and the dunking depth of the sonar increased from 245 ft (75 m) to 700 ft (213 m). The HAS.Mk 6 force was enlarged by the conversion of older Sea King helicopters to this standard. Three more

HAR.Mk 3s in 1985 brought RAF procurement to 19 (including one for the Empire Test Pilot School at Boscombe Down). Another RAF order placed early in 1992 added six upgraded **Sea King HAR.Mk 3A** machines.

Development of a non-amphibious Sea King as the **Commando** assault, tactical and general transport began in mid-1971, and such machines were delivered to Egypt and Qatar. From 1979 the RN placed orders for 41 **Sea King HC.Mk 4** helicopters combining the Commando's fixed landing gear with the Sea King's folding cabin. Two **Sea King Mk 4X** machines were built by Westland as avionics, rotor and systems test helicopters for use by the Defence Research Agency in EH 101 development, bringing overall UK service procurement of all variants to 175.

Westland has also supplied 147 Sea Kings and Commandos to overseas customers including Australia, Belgium Egypt, Germany, India, Norway, Pakistan and Qatar. Of these, the German **Sea King Mk 41** machines

Headquartered at Bodø, Norway's 330 Skvadron provides nationwide SAR coverage with its Sea King Mk 43s, the first ten of which were delivered in 1972.

SPECIFICATION
Westland Advanced Sea King

Type: two/four-crew shipborne and land-based anti-submarine and general-purpose medium helicopter
Powerplant: two Rolls-Royce Gnome H.1400-1T turboshaft engines each rated at 1,660 shp (1238 kW)
Performance: maximum cruising speed 126 mph (204 km/h) at sea level; initial climb rate 2,030 ft (619 m) per minute; hovering ceiling 6,500 ft (1980 m) in ground effect and 4,700 ft (1435 m) out of ground effect; range 921 miles (1482 km) with standard fuel
Weights: empty 16,377 lb (7428 kg) for the ASW role; maximum take-off 21,500 lb (9752 kg)
Dimensions: main rotor diameter 62 ft (18.90 m); length 72 ft 8 in (22.15 m) with the rotors turning; height 16 ft 10 in (5.13 m) with the rotors turning; main rotor disc area 3,019.07 sq ft (280.47 m²)
Armament up to 2,500 lb (1134 kg) of disposable stores generally comprising four Mk 46 or Stingray torpedoes, or four Mk 11 depth charges, or two Sea Eagle or AM39 Exocet anti-ship missiles
Payload: up to 28 troops, or nine litters plus two attendants, or 8,000 lb (3629 kg) of freight

were converted from the SAR to the anti-ship role from 1986 with Seaspray Mk 3 radar and Sea Skua missiles, which also arm the Indian navy's **Mk 42B** helicopters, while some Pakistani and Qatari Sea King and Commando helicopters are equipped to launch the AM39 Exocet anti-ship missile. The Indian Mk 42Bs are of the Advanced Sea King type with Gnome H.1400-1T engines, composite main and tail rotor blades and improved avionics.

The RN lack of airborne early warning capability in the 1982 Falklands War resulted in the hurried conversion in May 1982 of two HAS.Mk 2s to the **Sea King AEW.Mk 2A** standard with Searchwater radar and associated equipment, including anti-Exocet

jammers and Orange Crop ESM. This involved fitting a large radome suspended to starboard of the cabin and swinging back through 90° for ground stowage. Both AEW.Mk 2As began flying in July 1982, and were deployed in August on HMS *Illustrious* for post-war Falklands service. Eight further Sea Kings were then modified to AEW.Mk 2A standard. Three HAS.Mk 5s were later converted as **Sea King AEW.Mk 5** machines to a standard basically similar to that of the AEW.Mk 2. The designation **Sea King AEW.Mk 7** covers the initial conversion of three HAS.Mk 5s for service from early in the 21st century with improved surveillance radar, JTIDS data link, and a new central tactical system with coloured displays.

Westland Wallace

The private-venture **P.V.3** light torpedo-bomber and **P.V.6** development of the Wapiti, both conventional biplanes, are best remembered for their exploits in April 1933 when they became the first aircraft to fly over Mount Everest; for this attempt they were known respectively as the **Houston-Westland** and **Houston-Wallace**, honouring Lady Houston who had

financed the expedition. Following its return to the UK, the P.V.6 was converted back to military configuration and duly entered RAF service as the **Wallace Mk I**, introducing a number of improvements to facilitate inspection and with a 570-hp (425-kW) Bristol Pegasus IIM3 engine. A total of 68 Wapitis was converted subsequently to Wallace

Of similar dimensions and with the same armament as the Wapiti, the Wallace Mk II with a 680-hp (506-kW) Bristol Pegasus IV radial engine had a maximum speed of 158 mph (254 km/h) at 5,000 ft (1525 m).

Mk I configuration, then followed by 104 new production **Wallace Mk II** aircraft with a glazed canopy enclosing both cockpits and a more powerful Pegasus IV

engine. When withdrawn from the general-purpose role many were converted as target tugs, in which capacity they soldiered on into 1943.

Westland Wapiti

Air Ministry Specification 26/27 for a general-purpose aircraft marked a modest beginning to post-World War I re-equipment of the RAF. Because funding was equally modest, a requirement was that the new design should use a high proportion of DH.9A

components. Westland had developed for Airco the prototype DH.9A (and was prime contractor for the type) and the company thus had a head start, winning the initial contract for 25 production Wapiti aircraft. The prototype first flew in March 1927 and the type entered service

with No. 84 Sqn in Iraq. A conventional biplane with tandem open cockpits, the Wapiti was built in a number of versions for the RAF to a total of 517, and

J9095, a VIP-configured Wapiti Mk I, was one of the preliminary production order, and served as a trainer to Edward, Prince of Wales, with No. 24 Sqn.

about 80 of these were still in service in India at the outbreak of World War II.

Westland Wapiti (continued)

Variants

Wapiti Mk I: initial production version with 420-hp (313-kW) Bristol Jupiter VI radial engine

Wapiti Mk IA: improved version with 480-hp (358-kW) Jupiter VIIIF engine and Handley Page leading-edge slots; in addition to construction for the RAF, 38 were built for the RAAF

Wapiti Mk IB: similar to Wapiti Mk IA but introduced divided main landing gear; in RAF use the Jupiter VIIIF engines were later replaced by the 550-hp (410-kW) Armstrong Siddeley Panther; four supplied to South Africa

Wapiti Mk II: developed version introducing an all-metal basic structure

Wapiti Mk IIA: major production version with revised wing construction and suitable for use with wheel or float landing gear

Wapiti Mk III: version of which 27 were licence-built in South Africa, similar to Wapiti Mk IIA and with the 490-hp (365-kW) Armstrong Siddeley Jaguar VI engine

Wapiti Mk V: developed from projected **Wapiti Mk IV** with a lengthened fuselage and several refinements; powered by 550-hp (410-kW) Jupiter VIIIF

SPECIFICATION	
Westland Wapiti Mk IIA	5,400 lb (2449 kg)
Type: general-purpose military aircraft	**Dimensions:** wingspan 46 ft 5 in (14.15 m); length 31 ft 8 in (9.65 m); height 11 ft 10 in (3.61 m); wing area 468 sq ft (43.48 m²)
Powerplant: one 480-hp (358-kW) Bristol Jupiter VIII or VIIIF radial piston engine	
Performance: maximum speed 140 mph (225 km/h) at 5,000 ft (1525 m); service ceiling 20,600 ft (6280 m); range 530 miles (853 km)	**Armament:** one 0.303-in (7.7-mm) Vickers synchronised machine-gun and one 0.303-in (7.7-mm) Lewis gun on Scarff ring over rear cockpit, plus up to 580 lb (263 kg) of bombs
Weights: empty 3,810 lb (1728 kg); maximum take-off	

Wapiti Mk VI: dual-control trainer version; 16 built

Wapiti Mk VII: initially a Wapiti Mk V, used under designation **Houston-Wallace** or **P.V.6** before reconversion to Wapiti Mk VII as experimental aircraft

Wapiti Mk VIII: developed from projected Wapiti Mk IV with 512-hp (382-kW) Jaguar VI; four built for Central Chinese government

Westland Wessex

Turboshaft-powered versions of the Whirlwind had given Westland a good appreciation of the capability of a helicopter with such a powerplant, leading to licence negotiations with Sikorsky for manufacture of the S-58. Westland believed that its larger size, allied with a turboshaft powerplant, would make possible the development of an ASW aircraft combining the hunter and killer activities of the two-aircraft Whirlwind team, but such hopes proved to be rather premature. However, following receipt of a single S-58 from Sikorsky, Westland began by replacing its standard Wright R-1820 piston engine by an 1,100-shp (820-kW) Napier Gazelle NGa.11 turboshaft, with which it flew for the first time on 17 May 1957 to become the company's demonstrator.

Satisfactory testing led first to a Westland-built prototype and two pre-production examples of what was to be named the **Wessex**, all powered by the 1,450-shp (1081-kW) Gazelle Mk 161, as was the initial production **Wessex HAS.Mk 1** helicopter, of which about 130 were built. These were used by the Royal Navy as 'hunter-killer' pairs in the ASW role, and by the Royal Marines as transports carrying up to 16 fully-equipped commandos. A similar **Wessex HC.Mk 2** for RAF deployment in ambulance, transport and utility roles had an important difference in the introduction of two coupled Bristol Siddeley Gnome turboshafts (each rated at 1,350 shp/1007 kW) and interconnected so that in the event of an engine failure the remaining engine could continue to drive the rotors.

The Navy's **Wessex HAS.Mk 3** introduced the more powerful Gazelle NGa.22 and, more importantly, a new AFCS that allowed an entire ASW search or strike mission, from lift-off to positioning for landing, to be flown automatically. Later versions included two **Wessex HC.Mk 4** VIP transports (similar to the HC.Mk 2) for The Queen's Flight; the **Wessex HU.Mk 5** (similar to HC.Mk 2) troop-carrying assault helicopter for the Royal Marine Commandos; and a civil version of the HC.Mk 2, designated **Wessex Mk 60**.

Export versions included the **Wessex HAS.Mk 31** for the Royal Australian Navy, which was similar to the HAS.Mk 1 but for a Gazelle NGa.13/2 flat-rated at 1,540 shp (1148 kW); these were later given upgraded ASW systems and other improvements to become redesignated **HAS.Mk 31B**. Finally, versions of the HC.Mk 2 were completed for Iran, Ghana and Brunei under the respective designations **Wessex Mk 52, Mk 53** and **Mk 54**. It is now over 35 years since the Westland-built Wessex prototype flew for the first time, yet a handful of these multi-role helicopters continues to provide useful service.

The RAF's last Wessex HC.Mk 2s remain in service in Northern Ireland (No. 72 Sqn) and Cyprus (No. 84 Sqn, pictured).

SPECIFICATION	
Westland Wessex HC.Mk 2	standard fuel
Type: tactical transport/ground assault helicopter	**Weights:** operating empty 8,304 lb (3767 kg); maximum take-off 13,500 lb (6123 kg)
Powerplant: two Rolls-Royce (Bristol Siddeley) Gnome Mk 110/111 turboshafts each rated at 1,350 shp (1007 kW)	**Dimensions:** main rotor diameter 56 ft (17.07 m); length overall, rotors turning 65 ft 9 in (20.04 m); height overall 16 ft 2 in (4.93 m); main rotor disc area 2,643.01 sq ft (228.81 m²)
Performance: maximum level speed at sea level 132 mph (212 km/h); maximum rate of climb at sea level 1,650 ft (503 m) per minute; hovering ceiling 4,000 ft (1220 m) out of ground effect; range 478 miles (769 km) with	**Payload:** maximum payload 4,000 lb (1814 kg)

Westland Whirlwind

The Whirlwind's first wartime claim was a Ju 88 'probable', intercepted over the Scilly Isles by No. 263 Sqn on 12 January 1941.

Easily recognisable, with two large engine nacelles that seemed to dominate this fighter and with a cruciform tail unit that helped to confirm recognition, the **Whirlwind I** was designed to the requirements of Air Ministry Specification F.37/35. The first of two prototypes was flown on 11 October 1938, but because of development problems with the Rolls-Royce Peregrine engine, it was not until June 1940 that the type entered service with No. 263 Sqn, and later with No. 137 Sqn. The Whirlwind was the first single-seat twin-engine fighter in RAF service and combined excellent manoeuvrability, high speed at low altitude, and the heavy fire-power of four nose-mounted 20-mm cannon that marked it out as a valuable addition to Fighter Command. The Whirlwind's low-level speed and fire power plus a standard-fuel range of some 800 miles (1287 km) meant the type was ideal as an escort fighter for light bombers, and in 1942 when equipped with external bomb racks (as the **Whirlwind Mk IA**), saw extensive use on 'Rhubarb' operations against cross-Channel installations. Unfortunately the Whirlwind had problems which limited

production to 112 examples: it had trouble with its Peregrine engines, which equipped no other type, and its high landing speed limited the number of airfields into which it could operate. By 1943 it had been withdrawn from first-line service.

Westland Whirlwind

In November 1950 Westland concluded a licence agreement with Sikorsky covering the manufacture of the S-55 for the British forces and certain approved nations. Before Westland production began the RN received 25 S-55s under the MDAP.

Variants

Whirlwind Srs 1: initial civil production version with 600-hp (447-kW) R-1340-40 Wasp or 700-hp (522-kW) R-1300-3 Cyclone engine
Whirlwind Srs 2: civil version similar to Whirlwind Srs 1 but with 780-hp (582-kW) Alvis Leonides Major Mk 155 or Mk 755 radial piston engine derated to 750-hp (559-kW)
Whirlwind Srs 3: civil version similar to Srs 1 and 2, but introducing turboshaft powerplant; this was a 1,050-shp (783-kW) General Electric T58 in the prototype, but production aircraft had the licence-built version designated Bristol Siddeley Gnome H.1000
Whirlwind HAR.Mk 1: RN version with R-1340-40 engine
Whirlwind HAR.Mk 2: RAF version, similar to HAR.Mk 1
Whirlwind HAR.Mk 3: RN version, similar to HAR.Mk 1 but with R-1300-3 engine
Whirlwind HAR.Mk 4: RAF version for troop transport/ rescue operations in Malaya; powered by 600-hp (447-kW) R-1340-57 engine suitable for 'hot and high' use
Whirlwind HAR.Mk 5: version with powerplant of the Whirlwind Srs 2; three built for the RN and four for Austria
Whirlwind HAS.Mk 7: RN ASW version with the same powerplant as the Whirlwind Srs 2; first British helicopter equipped for use in an ASW role
Whirlwind HCC.Mk 8: two with 740-hp (552-kW) Alvis Leonides Major Mk 160 and VIP interiors for The Queen's Flight
Whirlwind HAR.Mk 9: turbine-engined (Gnome H.1000) conversions of Whirlwind HAS.Mk 7s for use in SAR and ice-patrol duties
Whirlwind HAR.Mk 10: version for RAF, new production with Gnome H.1000 engines, plus some conversions of HAR.Mk 2 and HAR.Mk 4 to same powerplant
Whirlwind HCC.Mk 12: two aircraft with Gnome H. 1400 turboshafts and VIP interiors for The Queen's Flight
Whirlwind HAR.Mk 21: 10 S-55s supplied to the RN with 600-hp (447-kW) Pratt & Whitney Wasp R-1340-40 engines
Whirlwind HAR.Mk 22: 15 S-55s supplied to the RN with 700-hp (522-kW) Wright R-1300-3 engines

SPECIFICATION	
Westland Whirlwind HAR.Mk 10	ceiling 15,800 ft (4815 m)
Type: three-crew/eight-passenger transport/SAR helicopter	**Weight:** maximum take-off 8,000 lb (3629 kg)
Powerplant: one 1,050-shp (783-kW) Bristol Siddeley Gnome H.1400 turboshaft	**Dimensions:** main rotor diameter 53 ft (16.15 m); length, rotors turning 63 ft 1½ in (18.94 m); height 13 ft 3 in (4.04 m); main rotor disc area 2,206.19 sq ft (204.95 m²)
Performance: cruising speed 104 mph (167 km/h); hovering	

829 Sqn's Whirlwind HAR.Mk 9s conducted Antarctic operations from the Ice Patrol Ship HMS Endurance between 1968-76.

Westland Dragonfly and Widgeon

Negotiations in 1946 between Westland Aircraft and Sikorsky in the USA led to a licence for construction of the S-51 in the UK. Basically similar to the US-built aircraft, the type was assembled from British-built components and in all but one variant was powered by the Alvis Leonides engine. The first civil **Westland/Sikorsky WS-51** was flown on 5 October 1948 and on 24 July 1951, the type became the first British-built helicopter to gain a certificate of airworthiness. Before that, in 1950, a version designated **Dragonfly HR.Mk 1** equipped the RN's first helicopter squadron, No. 705. Built to a total of 133, the Dragonfly was followed by a developed version, the **Widgeon**, whose prototype was a conversion of a Dragonfly to provide five-seat capacity and benefiting from introduction of the improved rotor of the S-55. Widgeon production totalled 14, several of them conversions of Dragonflies.

SPECIFICATION	
Westland Dragonfly HR.Mk 1	**Weights:** empty 4,380 lb (1987 kg); maximum take-off 5,870 lb (2663 kg)
Type: naval ASR helicopter	
Powerplant: one 540-hp (403-kW) Alvis Leonides 50 radial piston engine	**Dimensions:** main rotor diameter 48 ft (14.63 m); length, rotors turning 57 ft 6½ in (17.54 m); height 12 ft 11½ in (3.95 m); main rotor disc area 1,809.56 sq ft (168.11 m²)
Performance: maximum speed 95 mph (153 km/h) at sea level; service ceiling 12,400 ft (3780 m); range 300 miles (483 km)	

Military operators of the Widgeon were the Royal Jordanian Air Force and the Brazilian navy (pictured). The latter's HU-1 acquired two examples in 1961-62.

Variants

Dragonfly HR.Mk 1: initial air-sea rescue (ASR) version for RN with the Alvis Leonides 50 radial engine
Dragonfly HC.Mk 2: similar to HR.Mk 1 but equipped as casualty evacuation aircraft for the RAF
Dragonfly HR.Mk 3: major production ASR version for RN (58 built); generally as HR.Mk 1 but introduced all-metal rotor
Dragonfly HC.Mk 4: casualty evacuation version for RAF, similar to HR.Mk 3
Dragonfly HR.Mk 5: final ASR version for RN, similar to HR.Mk 3
Westland/Sikorsky Mk 1A: civil version with 520-hp (388-kW) Leonides 521/1 engine; most used as civil transports, but small numbers to Japan for rescue and to Italian and Thai air force
Westland/Sikorsky Mk IB: civil version similar to Mk 1A but with 450-hp (336-kW) Pratt & Whitney R-985-134 Wasp Junior engine

Westland Wyvern

The last fixed-wing military aircraft to be produced by Westland, the **W34** design was finalised to meet the requirements of Specification N.11/44 for a single-seat ship-based strike aircraft. It was a demanding specification, the problems being compounded by selection of the new Rolls-Royce Eagle 24-cylinder sleeve valve engine to power it, but it was also required that the airframe should be suitable for easy installation of turboprop engines when these became available. A cantilever low-wing monoplane of all-metal stressed-skin construction with retractable tailwheel landing gear, the first of six **Wyvern** prototypes was flown on 12 December 1946. These were followed by 10 pre-production **Wyvern TF.Mk 1** aircraft, also with the Eagle engine, but this new engine had teething problems and development flying was so protracted that turboprop engines became available before any production decision was made. From the turboprops that were evaluated the Armstrong Siddeley Python was selected for the 20 pre-production **Wyvern TF.Mk 2** aircraft, 13 delivered being as such and the balance being completed to **Wyvern TF.Mk 4** (later **Wyvern** **S.Mk 4**) production standard before delivery. The same engine was used to power the 90 production S.Mk 4s, the first of which entered operational service with No. 813 Sqn in May 1953, some six and a half years after the first flight of the prototype. The type later equipped Nos 827, 830 and 831 Sqns, No. 830 being the only squadron to use the Wyvern operationally, during the Suez crisis. The Wyvern then continued in service until March 1958 when No. 813 Sqn was disbanded. A one-off variant was the **Wyvern T.Mk 3** two-seat trainer prototype.

Pictured between 1955-56, this 830 Sqn Wyvern S.Mk 4 wears the 'J' deck code of HMS Eagle. This aircraft formerly operated from Albion with 813 Sqn.

Wibault Wib.7 and Wib.72

Michel Wibault's first aircraft was the **Wib.1** C.1 category single-seat fighter biplane powered by a 220-hp (164-kW) Hispano-Suiza 8Be engine. Tested in November 1918, the Wib.1 was too late for World War I and not built in quantity. The Société des Avions Michel Wibault was formed in late 1919 and two prototypes followed, the **Wib.2** of 1921 being a large two-seat biplane night bomber in the Bu.2 category and the **Wib.3** of 1923 was a C.1 parasol-wing monoplane fighter.

The **Wib.7** C.1 category prototype of 1924 was similar in configuration to the Wib.3, but powered by a 480-hp (358-kW) Gnome-Rhône 9Ad radial engine. The principal innovation, however, was the all-metal system of construction which became a Wibault patent. Quantity production followed. 60 **Wib.72** fighters with strengthened wing bracing going to the French Aéronautique Militaire and entering service in 1929. Meanwhile, Wibault became a consultant to

Vickers in the UK which produced 26 Wib.7s under the designation **Vickers Type 121** for Chile.

The prototype **Wib.73** of 1927 was a C.1 fighter powered by a 450-hp (336-kW) Lorraine 12Eb engine. Plans to build the type in Poland were scrapped, although the PZL company eventually delivered three Wibault 7s with Wright radial engines and 25 Wibault 72s to the Polish military aviation in 1929-30. The Wib.73 was sold only to Paraguay, which acquired seven. A

variant with strengthened fuselage and arrester hook, the **Wib.74**, was delivered to the French navy for operation from the carrier *Béarn*. Eighteen Wib.74s

were followed by 18 examples of the camera-equipped **Wib.75**. These naval aircraft flew with Escadrilles 7C1 and 7C2 until the end of 1937.

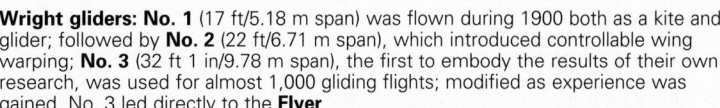

The parasol-winged Wib.7 was an advance over its fabric-covered contemporaries. The metal wing was covered by dural strips and reinforced by skin joints.

Wright brothers aircraft

The **Wright Flyer** built by the brothers Orville and Wilbur Wright has the distinction of being recognised officially as the world's first heavier-than-air craft to be flown in powered, manned, controlled and sustained flight. This was achieved at Kill Devil Hill, Kitty Hawk, North Carolina, on 17 December 1903 when in the first of four flights made on that day, and piloted by Orville, the Flyer was airborne for 12 seconds and covered a distance of 120 ft (36.60 m); in the fourth and final flight, with Wilbur as pilot, a distance of 852 ft (260 m) was covered

in 59 seconds. Wright companies were formed in France, Germany and the UK in 1908, 1909 and 1913 respectively; the first American Wright Company was established in 1909. In 1916 the Wright Company merged with the Glenn L. Martin company to form the Wright-Martin Aircraft Corporation; a year later Martin withdrew from the association and the company was renamed the Wright Aeronautical Corporation.

Confusingly, the Wright Model C was known to the Navy as the Wright B.

Variants

Wright gliders: No. 1 (17 ft/5.18 m span) was flown during 1900 both as a kite and glider; followed by **No. 2** (22 ft/6.71 m span), which introduced controllable wing warping; **No. 3** (32 ft 1 in/9.78 m span), the first to embody the results of their own research, was used for almost 1,000 gliding flights; modified as experience was gained, No. 3 led directly to the **Flyer**
Flyer: initial version with 12-hp (9-kW) engine of Wright design
Flyer II: similar to Flyer but with modified wing and engine tuned to deliver 15 hp (11 kW); not considered successful
Flyer III: the first really practical and controllable model, using the engine and propellers of Flyer II; on 5 October 1905 made a flight of 39 minutes 23 seconds covering a distance of 24.2 miles (38.9 km)
Model A: first so-called standard biplane seating pilot and passenger; powered by 30-hp (22-kW) Wright engine and spanning 41 ft (12.50 m), this had a maximum speed of 40 mph (64 km/h); one procured by US Army
Model B: similar to Model A but introducing 35-hp (26-kW) Wright engine, wheel and skid landing gear, and rear- instead of forward-mounted elevators; two procured by US Army
Model C: improved version with 50-hp (37-kW) Wright engine and dual controls; seven procured by US Army and three by the US Navy, the latter with 60-hp (45-kW) Wright engine and twin floats designated **Model C-H (hydro)**
Model D: single-seat version of Model C; two procured by US Army which called them **Model D Scout**
Model Ex: smaller-size single-seat version of Model B for exhibition flying
Model F: the first Wright of modern appearance, this two-seater introduced a 90-hp (67-kW) Austro-Daimler engine and a conventional fuselage and tail unit; one procured by US Army
Model G Aeroboat: single aircraft acquired by US Navy; similar to Model F but with hull replacing fuselage
Model H-S: reduced-span version of the Model F with Wright 60-hp (45-kW) engine
Model K: floatplane version of the Model F; one procured by US Navy
Model L: single-seat version of Model F with 70-hp (52-kW) engine
Model R: known also as **Wright-Martin Model R**, this had configuration then conventional for 1916 period with unequal-span biplane wings, tandem open cockpits, fixed tailskid landing gear and powerplant of one 125-hp (93-kW) Hall-Scott engine with tractor propeller; 12 acquired by US Army, nine as landplanes and three as floatplanes

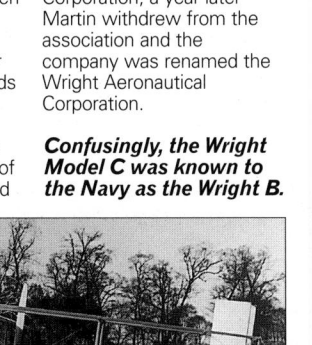

XAC JH-7/FBC-1 Flying Leopard

The **JH-7** has been in development since the mid-1970s to meet a requirement from the Chinese PLAAF and PLAN-AF for an all-weather interdictor. In design, it resembles a scaled-up Jaguar. Its projected performance approaches that of Tornado IDS, albeit with a reduced payload, but with a longer unrefuelled range. The JH-7 features a wide range of Chinese-developed systems and equipment; these include the JL-10A multi-mode radar, Blue Sky

low-altitude radar/FLIR navigation pods and inertial/GPS navigation systems. The Xian WS-9 engines are licence-manufactured Spey turbofans. Although the prototype reportedly first flew in 1988, the programme was troubled by problems throughout the 1990s, leading China to consider Su-27s and Su-30s. Surprisingly, the acquisition of the Sukhois has not ended the JH-7 programme. It is likely that the JH-7's revival has stemmed from the PLA's desire to modernise its air forces and for the need of Chinese industry to be able to offer more modern fighters for export. The decision to feature the JH-7 promi-

nently at the Zhuhai airshow in 1998 was accompanied by a modest order for the type. The JH-7 is being acquired for the PLAN-AF, with a reported figure of between 25 to 32 aircraft for a single regiment. Armed with the indigenous C-802 or supersonic KR-1

missiles (the latter a version of the Kh-31/AS-17) the JH-7 is being promoted actively for export as the **FBC-1 Flying Leopard.**

XAC JH-7/FBC-1 Flying Leopard

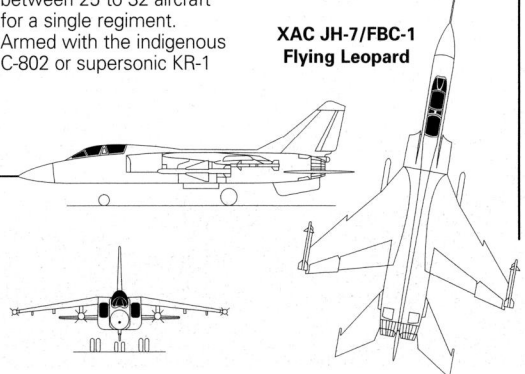

SPECIFICATION

XAC JH-7/FBC-1 Flying Leopard
Type: two-seat all-weather interdictor and maritime attack aircraft
Powerplant: two Xian WS9 (Rolls-Royce Spey Mk 202) turbofans each rated at 20,515 lb st (91.20 kN) with afterburning
Performance: maximum level speed 'clean' at 36,080 ft (11000 m) 1,122 mph (1808 km/h); service ceiling 'clean' 51,180 ft

(15600 m); combat radius 1,025 miles (1650 km)
Weights: maximum take-off 62,776 lb (28475 kg); maximum landing 46,583 lb (21130 kg)
Dimensions: wingspan 41 ft 8¼ in (12.71 m); length including probe 73 ft 3 in (22.33 m); height 21 ft 6¾ in (6.58 m); wing area 563 sq ft (52.30 m²)
Armament: one twin-barrelled 23-mm cannon, plus 14,330 lb (6500 kg) of ordnance

Yakovlev Yak-1 (I-26)

Design of the **Yak-1** medium-altitude interceptor/fighter began in November 1938, and from it evolved a series of remarkable aircraft (produced in vast numbers) which made an important mark in the history of aviation. Known initially as the **I-26**, the type had a wooden wing combined with a fuselage of mixed construction and main landing gear units retracting inwards into the underside of the wing. The I-26

looked a thoroughbred and was dubbed 'Beauty' by its design team. Flown initially on 13 January 1940, the first prototype was soon lost in a fatal accident, but the development programme was continued without any break by the second prototype, which incorporated some improvements. A pre-production batch of Yak-1s was flying by the end of the year and 64 initial series machines had also been completed by then.

The Yak-1B, pictured during state tests, offered an improved pilot's view, as a result of a lower aft fuselage and all-round canopy.

Variants

I-26: two prototypes
Yak-1: initial production version; from October 1941 had M-105PA engine
Yak-1M: originated as field modification with all-round vision cockpit canopy and cut-down rear fuselage decking; accepted officially in July 1942 and in full production early 1943; many Yak-1Bs and some Yak-1s and Yak-1Ms had a new, more-pointed wing
Yak-1M: many structural changes to reduce weight; revised aircraft introduced on production lines in late 1942; incorporated pilot's canopy introduced on Yak-IB and powered by 1,260-hp (940-kW) M-105PF engine; maximum speed increased to 364 mph (585 km/h) at 12,465 ft (3800 m)
I-28: three experimental aircraft with new wing of reduced span, two-stage supercharger and intended for high-altitude operation; during tests in June 1942 these aircraft attained 413 mph (665 km/h) at 32,810 ft (10000 m)
I-30: two prototypes introducing improved all-metal version of I-28 wing and heavier armament; one had retractable tailwheel

Changes were introduced during the course of production and many aircraft of the main variants were completed from early 1942 with an increased span more pointed wing. A new pilot's canopy and cut-down rear fuselage were introduced on the **Yak-1B** and reduction of overall weight was achieved with the **Yak-1M**. The mount of many leading Soviet fighter pilots, Yak-1s equipped a high proportion of fighter *eskadrilli* from 1942

onwards; when the type was phased out of production in mid-1943, a total of

8,721 series aircraft of all versions had been completed.

SPECIFICATION	
Yakovlev Yak-1 (early production)	(2347 kg); maximum take-off 6,276 lb (2847 kg)
Type: single-seat interceptor/fighter	**Dimensions:** wingspan 32 ft 9¾ in (10.00 m); length 27 ft 9½ in (8.47 m); height 8 ft 8 in (2.64 m); wing area 184.61 sq ft (17.15 m²)
Powerplant: one 1,050-hp (783-kW) M-105P Vee piston engine	
Performance: maximum speed 336 mph (540 km/h) at sea level; service ceiling 32,810 ft (10000 m); range 435 miles (700 km)	**Armament:** one engine-mounted 20-mm ShVAK cannon and one 0.5-in (12.7-mm) UBS machine-gun in fuselage, plus two 220-lb (100-kg) of bombs on underwing racks
Weights: empty equipped 5,174 lb	

Yakovlev Yak-3

SPECIFICATION	
Yakovlev Yak-3	(2105 kg); maximum take-off 5,864 lb (2660 kg)
Type: short-range interceptor fighter	**Dimensions:** wingspan 30 ft 2¼ in (9.20 m); length 27 ft 10¼ in (8.49 m); height 7 ft 11¼ in (2.42 m); wing area 159.63 sq ft (14.83 m²)
Powerplant: one 1,300-hp (969-kW) Klimov VK-105PF-2 V piston engine	
Performance: maximum speed 407 mph (655 km/h) at 10,170 ft (3100 m); service ceiling 35,105 ft (10700 m); range 559 miles (900 km)	**Armament:** one engine-mounted 20-mm ShVAK cannon and two synchronised 0.5-in (12.7-mm) UBS machine-guns
Weights: empty equipped 4,641 lb	

The Yak-3 is widely considered the lightest and most agile of the fighters built in quantity between 1939-45.

Design began at the end of 1941 of a single-seat fighter using the new VK-107 engine, design parameters being the least possible drag, smallest dimensions and weight

consistent with a manoeuvrable and tough fighting machine. Due to delays with the new engine and pressure to build the maximum number of aircraft already on the production

Variants

Yak-3: initial production version; deliveries to V-VS began in July 1944
Yak-3/VK-107A: a small number, about 100, in operation 1945
Yak-31/VK-108: experimental and fastest Yak-3 with VK-108 engine; first flown 19 December 1944, demonstrated a maximum speed of 463 mph (745 km/h) at 19,685 ft (6000 m)
Yak-3T: anti-tank version built in small numbers with 37-mm N-37 cannon and two 20-mm B-20S cannon
Yak-3T-57: one-off Yak-3T with a 57-mm OKB-16-57 cannon
Yak-3P: small quantity with three 20-mm B-20 cannon and two 0.5-in (12.7-mm) UBS machine-guns
Yak-3RD (or Yak-3D): experimental adaptation of series aircraft to take Glusliko RD-1 rocket unit in tail
Yak-3V: high-altitude variant with increased-span wings
Yak-3PD: flown in 1944 with experimental supercharged VK-106 engine; intended to have pressurised cabin
Yak-3U: rebuilt aircraft with an ASh-82FN radial engine and twin B-20 cannon; despite heavy engine overall weight less than standard Yak-3 and during series of test flights started on 12 May 1945 demonstrated a maximum speed of 441 mph (710 km/h) at 20,015 ft (6100 m)
Yak-3TK: VK-107A-powered version tested in 1945 with an exhaust-driven turbocharger
Yak-3UTI: developed as conversion trainer in late 1945 with ASh-21 radial engine; became eventually **Yak-11**

lines, this new **Yak-3** programme was shelved for a time. A new small wing was developed and tested along with other changes on a Yak-1M in late 1942, and the first Yak-3 prototype was flown in late 1943. Although evaluation aircraft flew in combat, the first series Yak-3s did not enter operation with the 91st IAP until

July 1944. The Yak-3 was found to be an exceptional dogfighter at altitudes up to 13,125 ft (4000 m). Its improved performance was remarkable, particularly as the initial nonavailability of the VK-107 engine forced reliance to be placed on the VK-105PF-2 which had powered earlier Yaks. Built to a total of 4,848, the Yak-3 achieved a very high

score rate against German aircraft in 1944-45. The Yak-3 equipped the Normandie-Niemen unit, and achieved its peak of perfection when the 1,700-hp (1268-kW) VK-107A became available in limited numbers from August 1944, its maximum speed then improving to 447 mph (720 km/h) at 19,685 ft (6000 m).

Yakovlev Yak-7

In parallel with the I-26, Yakovlev developed a two-seat version under the designation **Ya-27**, and one pre-production I-26 was completed to this configuration; it was intended to serve not only as a dual-control fighter trainer,

but also as a liaison and unit support aircraft. Compared with the I-26 the Ya-27 was simplified and of reduced weight, the tandem cockpits being enclosed by an extended glazed canopy. The resulting **Yak-7** aircraft entered

production in May 1941 and was soon found to have better flying qualities than the Yak-1. This performance, combined with the urgent need for more fighters, led to the production of a single-seat version, the first of which was flown in June 1941. In July 1941 it was officially designated **Yak-7A**.

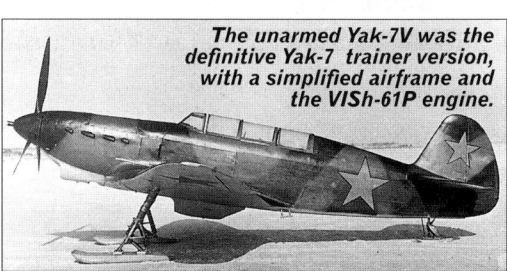

The unarmed Yak-7V was the definitive Yak-7 trainer version, with a simplified airframe and the VISh-61P engine.

Yakovlev Yak-7 (continued)

The new two-seat Yak trainer/liaison machine was designated **Yak-7V**. By the end of 1941 a new single-seater, the **Yak-7B**, had replaced the Yak-7A. Total delivery of all versions of the Yak-7 was 6,399, production terminating in early 1943; of this number some 1,500 were Yak-7Vs.

and Yak-7V; landing gear simplified and improved equipment; very important type in V-VS inventory which performed well against enemy fighters; some 5,000 built

Yak-7D: experimental version with wooden wing incorporating metal spars and increased fuel capacity

Yak-7/M-82: version with redesigned forward fuselage to mount an M-82 radial engine and tested in 1941; armed with one fuselage-mounted 0.5-in (12.7-mm) UBS machine-gun and two 20-mm ShVAK cannon

Yak-7T: two aircraft tested with engine-mounted heavy cannon for anti-tank duties; one had 37-mm NS-37 and the other 45-mm NS-45

Yak-7K: field conversion of 1944 for use as VIP transport with very comfortable rear cockpit; several conversions completed

Yak-7PVRD: two series aircraft tested with two DM-4C ramjets on pylons under the wings; maximum speed enhanced by some 56 mph (90 km/h)

Variants

Ya-27: prototype two-seater converted from early preproduction I-26 (Yak-1)
Yak-7: original designation for two-seat liaison/trainer aircraft produced in limited numbers, and also for first single-seat conversion
Yak-7A: series version of single-seat fighter with 1,050-hp (783-kW) M-105P engine; rear cockpit deleted and faired over; pointed wing with span of 33 ft 7½ in (10.25 m)
Yak-7V: definitive designation for two-seater which by July 1941 was in large-scale production; same wingspan as Yak-7A; some Yak-7Vs had fixed landing gear and could operate with wheels or skis
Yak-7B: wingspan reduced to 32 ft 9¾ in (10 m) but with same wing area as Yak-7A

Yakovlev Yak-9 'Frank'

Developed from the Yak-9T, primary armament of the Yak-9K anti-tank aircraft was a 45-mm cannon with 29 rounds.

SPECIFICATION

Yakovlev Yak-9U
Type: single-seat interceptor/fighter
Powerplant: one 1,650-hp (1230kW) Klimov VK-107A V piston engine
Performance: maximum speed 434 mph (698 km/h) at 16,405 ft (5000 m); service ceiling 39,040 ft (11900 m); range 541 miles (870 km)
Weights: empty equipped 5,988 lb (2716 kg); maximum take-off 6,830 lb (3098 kg)
Dimensions: wingspan 32 ft ¾ in (9.77 m); length 28 ft ½ in (8.55 m); height 9 ft 8½ in (2.96 m); wing area 185.68 sq ft (17.25 m²)
Armament: one 20-mm MP-20 cannon and two 0.5-in (12.7-mm) UBS machine-guns, plus provision for two 220-lb (100-kg) bombs on underwing racks

A development of the experimental Yak-7DI, the original **Yak-9** differed in having a revised rudder and wooden wings incorporating metal spars; the series version, which entered production in the summer of 1942, also introduced a retractable tailwheel. Deliveries to V-VS IAPs began in October 1942, and the type was soon engaged in the Battle of Stalingrad. By February 1943 production

aircraft were being built with reduced-span wings that incorporated duralumin ribs, and the initial powerplant (an M-105PF or M-105PF-1) was being replaced by the 1,240-hp (925-kW) M-105PF-3. The Yak-9 operated with a wide variety of armament, including all types of aircraft cannon then in production in the Soviet Union, and during 1943 there appeared variants which developed the full potential of the Yak-9 for use in anti-tank, light bomber and long-range escort roles.

The second generation

of Yak-9s began with the **Yak-9U** prototype of late 1943, which introduced a redesigned and more aerodynamically-contoured airframe, a new wing of increased span and area, and the more powerful VK-107 engine; to overcome resulting centre of

gravity problems the wing was moved slightly forward. Production of the Yak-9 ended in 1946 after a record 16,769 aircraft had been delivered. Main post-war operators, apart from the Soviet Union, were Bulgaria, Poland and Yugoslavia.

Variants

Yak-9: prototype developed from Yak-7DI, and initial series in production from mid-1942; armament of one 20-mm ShVAK cannon and one 12.7-mm (0.5-in) UBS machine-gun, plus six RS-82 rockets or two 220-lb (100-kg) FAB-100 bombs
Yak-9M: standard version with cannon and two 0.5-in (12.7-mm) UBS machine-guns
Yak-9D: long-range escort version with additional fuel extending range up to 826 miles (1330 km) and introducing M-105PF-3 engine; in operation from summer 1943
Yak-9T: tested December 1942 with 11P-37 anti-armour cannon and wing racks for 5.54-lb (2.5-kg) PTAB hollow-charge bombs in special containers; other Yak-9Ts had MP-20, VYa-23 or MP-23VV cannon; entered service in early 1943
Yak-9K: saw limited service from 1943; armed with heavy 45-mm NS-45 cannon in addition to a UBS machine-gun
Yak-9B: special bomber version built in limited numbers; internal bay behind cockpit containing four 220-lb (100-kg) FAB-100 bombs or containers with 128 PTAB light bombs
Yak-9MPVO: limited number for use in night-fighter role and

equipped with searchlight and RPK-10 radio compass
Yak-9DD: ultra-long-range escort fighter; like Yak-9D but with additional fuel capacity bringing maximum range to 1,367 miles (2200 km); used to escort US heavy bombers on shuttle raids against Romanian oil wells; also equipped 236th IAD (fighter division) based at Bari in southern Italy, and operating for a time over Yugoslavia in support of partisans
Yak-9U: prototype flew December 1943 with wing of all-metal basic structure; initially had M-105PF-2, but more powerful VK-107A engine phased into production line from late 1944
Yak-9UT: version of Yak-9U with light alloy stressed skinning over entire airframe; entered service early 1945
Yak-9UV: tandem two-seat conversion trainer
Yak-9P: in addition to engine-mounted cannon had one or two fuselage-mounted synchronised 20-mm cannon
Yak-9R: tactical or photo-reconnaissance version with specialised equipment
Yak-9PD: high-altitude experimental version with M-105PD engine incorporating two-stage gear-driven supercharger and armed with single 20-mm cannon; believed small batch saw limited actions against high-flying German reconnaissance aircraft late in World War II

Yakovlev Yak-11 'Moose'

The prototype of the **Yak-11** two-seat advanced trainer was first flown in 1945 and known originally as the **Yak-3UTI**. Testing

continued with the ASh-21 radial engine and a further refined prototype appeared in 1946, official tests being completed satisfactorily in

October 1946. Then designated Yak-11, the aircraft had metal wings, a fuselage of mixed construction, fully retractable tailwheel landing gear, and the instructor and pupil seated beneath a continuous glazed canopy. Ordered into production for the V-VS, series Yak-11s were delivered from the summer of 1947. Total production in the Soviet Union was 3,859, and an additional 707 were built in

Czechoslovakia from October 1953 under the designation **C-11**. In 1958 the **Yak-11U** version appeared with retractable tricycle landing gear; it was built in small numbers in both the Soviet Union and Czechoslovakia, the latter model being designated

C-11U.

The Yak-11 proved a very successful aircraft and has seen widespread service with Warsaw pact countries, as well as in the Middle East and China, and has established a number of world class records for speed over distance.

SPECIFICATION

Yakovlev Yak-11 'Moose'
Type: advanced trainer/liaison aircraft
Powerplant: one 570-hp (425-kW) Shvetsov ASh-21 radial piston engine
Performance: maximum speed 289 mph (465 km/h); service ceiling 23,295 ft (7100 m); range 795 miles (1280 km)
Weights: empty equipped 4,189 lb (1900 kg); maximum take-off 5,379 lb (2440 kg)
Dimensions: wingspan 30 ft 10 in (9.40 m); length 27 ft 10½ in (8.50 m); wing area 165.77 sq ft (15.40 m²)
Armament: one synchronised 0.5-in (12.7-mm) UBS or 0.303-in (7.7-mm) ShKAS machine-gun

In August 1951, a Yak-11 achieved 274.83 mph (442.289 km/h) over a distance of 1000 km.

Yakovlev Yak-12 'Creek'

Replacing the U-2S, the Yak-12S (an example is seen over Tajikistan) had provision for a single stetcher and attendant.

The prototype **Yak-12** made its maiden flight late in 1947. Although of similar configuration to the earlier **Yak-10**, it was a totally new design with a wing of different aerofoil section, a more extensively glazed fuselage seating two as standard but with provision for a third (rear) seat, revised tail unit, landing gear suitable for wheels or skis, and power provided by a 160-hp (119-kW) M-11FR radial engine.

Series production started almost immediately, deliveries being made to the V-VS for artillery spotting and liaison duties. Specialised versions of the original production model followed, and availability of

the more powerful AI-14R engine in 1950 led to the **Yak-12R** prototype, flown in June that year, and to a new generation of aircraft with the final extensively-built four-seat **Yak-12A** entering service in 1957. Production was established in parallel and then exclusively in Poland, while

various Chinese copies were developed and mass-produced in that country. Large numbers of this adaptable aircraft remain in service, many having been passed to flying schools or being used by Aeroflot and the Soviet civil aviation authority.

Variants

Yak-12: original prototype and initial series aircraft; at least 300 built, mostly for military use
Yak-12A: production version introduced new wing and redesigned tailplane; some 1,500 built in USSR; used mainly for civil purposes including local short-range passenger services and for agricultural work; operated by V-VS for liaison
Yak-12B: experimental STOL variant of biplane configuration and with 300-hp (224-kW) AI-14RF engine
Yak-12GR: twin-float seaplane version of original series aircraft with M-11FR engine
Yak-12M: introduced in 1955 and had extended rear fuselage, greatly enlarged tail surfaces and accommodation for four in cabin; specialised sub-variants for agricultural use, air ambulance and parachuting; production exceeded 1,000 and also licence built in Poland
Yak-12R: first version with AI-12R engine, built in series from 1951; introduced increased-span wing with all-metal basic structure; standard accommodation for a pilot and two passengers; some 2,000 built; used by V-VS and Soviet civil aviation authority; specialised agricultural, light freight and ambulance versions; several versions licence-built in Poland
Yak-12S: *Sanitarnyi* (ambulance), M-11FR engined version first flown 1948; accommodated single stretcher and medical attendant with stowage for medical kit
Yak-12SKh: agricultural variant of 1948 with large-capacity chemical hopper

SPECIFICATION	
Yakovlev Yak-12A 'Creek'	(1070 km)
Type: liaison and general-purpose aircraft	**Weights:** empty equipped 2,335 lb (1059 kg); maximum take-off 3,501 lb (1588 kg)
Powerplant: one 260-hp (194-kW) Ivchenko AI-14R radial piston engine	**Dimensions:** wingspan 41 ft 4 in (12.60 m); length 29 ft 6¼ in (9.00 m); height 8 ft (2.44 m); wing area 243.92 sq ft (22.66 m²)
Performance: maximum speed 143 mph (230 km/h); service ceiling 14,930 ft (4550 m); range 665 miles	

Yakovlev Yak-23 'Flora'

Although Yakovlev tested a number of barrel-fuselage jet fighter prototypes in the period up to 1951, the main emphasis was on developing the **Yak-15** concept to the ultimate as a back-up to the more sophisticated MiG-15. Experimental fighters developed to achieve this aim included the **Yak-19** powered by an RD-10F and test flown early in 1947, the **Yak-25** with the more powerful RD-500 turbojet

which flew in October 1947, the swept-wing **Yak-30** whose maiden flight took place in September 1948, and the **Yak-50** with a VK-1 engine, flown on 15 July 1949; all of these remained experimental fighters, but the **Yak-23** was developed for series production. It retained the well-tried fuselage layout of the Yak-15 and **Yak-17**, was of stressed-skin construction and designed for ease of

maintenance, the entire forward fuselage being easily removable. The type differed externally from the Yak-17 in having much enlarged vertical tail surfaces, the horizontal surfaces being mounted some way up the fin, and the main landing gear units were set much further inboard with the wheels retracting into the lower fuselage.

First flight of the prototype was on 17 June 1947, and with minor changes the Yak-23 went into production at the beginning

of 1948. A total of 310 was built, many of them serving with the Soviet Union's East European allies, including Bulgaria, Czechoslovakia (designation **S-101**), Poland and Romania. The **Yak-23UTI** trainer was tested in 1949 and the Romanians rebuilt a single-seater as a dual-control trainer in 1956.

SPECIFICATION	
Yakovlev Yak-23 'Flora'	(2000 kg); maximum take-off
Type: single-seat fighter	6,693 lb (3036 kg)
Powerplant: one 3,505-lb (15.59-kN) thrust RD-500 turbojet	**Dimensions:** wingspan 28 ft 7¾ in (8.73 m); length 26 ft 7¾ in (8.12 m); wing area 145.32 sq ft (13.50 in²)
Performance: maximum speed 606 mph (975 km/h) at optimum altitude; service ceiling 48,555 ft (14800 m); range 745 miles (1200 km) with external fuel	**Armament:** two 23-mm NR-23 cannon, and one 132-lb (60-kg) bomb or one auxiliary fuel tank beneath each wingtip
Weights: empty equipped 4,409 lb	

Yakovlev Yak-25 'Flashlight' and 'Mandrake'

The **Yakovlev Yak-120** was a twin-engined prototype for a radar-equipped two-seat interceptor, based on a scaled-up version of the single-engined **Yak-50** fighter, which had first flown on 15 July 1949. Development of the Yak-50 ended in May 1950, despite

the aircraft outperforming the MiG-17 in most respects.

The Yak-120, development of which was authorised in 1951, retained the mid-position 45° swept-wing of the Yak-50, but had engines mounted beneath the wings, leaving the fuselage free to accomodate radar, weapons and additional fuel. First flown on 19 June 1952, the Yak-120 interceptor was equipped with *Korshun* radar, and armed with two N-37L cannon. In 1953 the aircraft was selected for PVO service as the **Yak-25**, which received the reporting name **'Flashlight-A'**, most of these carrying the improved *Sokol* radar.

Further development lead to the **Yak-25M**, with improved AM-9A engines, replacing the previous AM-5A/B units, and provision for a 151-Imp gal (685-l) drop tank. The **Yak-25R 'Flashlight-B'** was a tactical

Numerous experimental variants were based on the Yak-25, including the Yak-25MR prototype maritime reconnaissance aircraft, with SPRS-1 radar and nose camera.

reconnaissance aircraft built in small numbers. The other production variant of the Yak-25 series was the single-seat **Yak-25RV 'Mandrake'** high-altitude

reconnaissance aircraft, equipped with cameras and SLAR, which was developed in 1959. This differed in having new shoulder-mounted unswept wings.

SPECIFICATION	
Yakovley Yak-25M 'Flashlight-A'	**Weight:** loaded 22,145 lb (10045 kg)
Type: all-weather/night interceptor	**Dimensions:** wingspan 36 ft 1 in (11.00 m); length 51 ft 4¾ in (15.665 m); wing area 311.5 sq ft (28.94 m²)
Powerplant: two 5,732-lb (2600-kg) AM-9A (RD-5A) turbojets	
Performance: maximum speed 646 mph (1040 km/h) at optimum altitude; range 1,696 miles (2730 km)	**Armament:** two forward-firing 37-mm N-37L cannon in under-fuselage fairing with 50 rpg

Yakovlev Yak-28 'Brewer', 'Firebar' and 'Maestro'

The **Yakovlev Yak-129** 'front-line bomber' prototype, which first flew on 5 March 1958, eventually lead to a new generation of multi-mission tactical aircraft. The Yak-129 was derived from the supersonic **Yak-26** prototype. This was an aerodynamically improved version of the **Yak-123**, itself an experimental two-seat bomber derivative of the initial Yak-25 two-seat interceptor.

Yakovlev Yak-28 'Brewer', 'Firebar' and 'Maestro' (cont.)

The Yak-129 entered Soviet service as the **Yak-28B 'Brewer-A'**, a two-seat night and all-weather capable bomber with an internal bomb load 6,614 lb (3000 kg), and a 23-mm NR-23 cannon. Two external fuel tanks were scabbed under each outer wing, and the aircraft was powered by two afterburning R-11AF-300 turbojets. The **Yak-28L 'Brewer-B'** carried a new *Lotos* precision guidance system in place of the Yak-28B's nav/bombing radar. The definitive production bomber version was the **Yak-28I 'Brewer-C'** was introduced in 1963, with *Initsiativa* nav/bombing radar and GSh-23Ya cannon.

The **Yak-28P** interceptor was designed to replace the Yak-25, and incorporated an *Orel*-D radar in the nose, and a pylon under each wing for the carriage of R-8 AAMs. Both the Yak-28P and **Yak-28PM** with improved *Orel*-DM and additional R-3 AAM capability were known as **'Firebar'**. The **Yak-28U 'Maestro'** was a two-seat conversion trainer for the bomber variant, whilst the **Yak-28R 'Brewer-D'** and **Yak-28PP 'Brewer-E'** were reconnaissance and EW versions respectively, both being based on the Yak-28I.

SPECIFICATION

Yakovlev Yak-28PM 'Firebar'
Type: all-weather interceptor
Powerplant: two 13,492-lb (6120-kg) afterburning thrust Tumansky R-11AF2-300 turbojets
Performance: maximum speed 1,311 mph (2110 km/h); service ceiling 52,500 ft (16000 m); range 1,615 miles 2600 km)
Weights: loaded 35,050 lb (15900 kg)
Dimensions: wingspan 38 ft 4⅝ in (11.70 m); length 70 ft 5¼ in (21.47 m); wing area 379.4 sq ft (35.25 m^2)
Armament: two R-3R/R-3S (AA-2 'Atoll') AAMs, and two R-8R/R-8T (AA-3 'Anab') AAMs

The Yak-28P prototype, pictured here with dummy R-8 'Anab' AAMs, could be equipped with RATO gear, and entered production in 1961.

Yakovlev Yak-38 'Forger'

All Yak-38s were fitted with K-36LV ejection seats with an automatic system to initiate crew escape, triggered by a dangerous combination of speed, height and airspeed.

Development of a V/STOL fighter for the Soviet navy's new 'Kiev'-class aircraft-carriers began in 1962. Intensive studies bore fruit in the shape of a number of **Yak-36 'Freehand'** research aircraft, with a Yak-50-style bicycle undercarriage under the fuselage augmented by wingtip outriggers. The aircraft was powered by a pair of 8,267-lb (36.78-kN) R-11V engines, each with a rotating nozzle.

Despite carrying guns and rocket pods, the Yak-36 was never operational it did lead directly to the **Yak-38**. The Yak-38 first flew on 28 May 1970 (as the **Yak-36M**), and conducted trials in prototype form aboard *Moskva* in 1972. Further trails were carried out in *Kiev* from 1974, followed in 1976 by a summer cruise of a test squadron in the Mediterranean.

Known in AV-MF service as the Yak-38, the type received the reporting name 'Forger-A'.

Powered by a single 14,770-lb st (65.59-kN) Soyuz/ Tumanskii R-27V-300 turbojet with twin rotating nozzles, the Yak-38 also had a pair of 5,180-lb st (23.04-kN) Koliesov/Rybinsk RD-36-35 single-shaft lift turbojets mounted in tandem immediately aft of the cockpit.

Up to four pylons could be fitted under the inboard sections of the wing, and these could carry a theoretical maximum weapon load of about 4,409 lb (2000 kg). Auxiliary fuel tanks could be carried by some modernised and late production aircraft, which bore the designation **Yak-38M**. The Yak-38M also introduced a an increase of 9.80 kN (2,204 lb) in thrust (allowing the carriage of additional fuel), through the introduction of uprated R-27VM-300 and RD-36-35FVR engines.

The Yak-38's unique operating and handling characteristics made the construction of a two-seat trainer essential. The resulting unarmed **Yak-38U 'Forger-B'** (**Yak-36U**) had tandem cockpits under separate sideways-hingeing canopies, with the longer nose having a pronounced 'droop'. A constant-section plug in the rear fuselage compensated for the longer nose but fin area was not increased. The Yak-38U lacked underwing pylons, IR sensor and ranging radar, and thus had no combat capability.

Improvements during service included the provision of auxiliary blow-in doors in the sides of the main intakes, and fore-and-aft fences on each side of the upper fuselage intake for the lift jets.

During 1980/81 a handful of Yak-38s were deployed to Afghanistan for air force operational trials and evaluation against the Su-25. The Yak's limited payload and high accident rate made the result a foregone conclusion. Production of the **'Forger'** was limited to about 120 aircraft.

SPECIFICATION

Yakovlev Yak-38 'Forger-A'
Type: multi-role carrier fighter
Powerplant: (Yak-38M) one MNPK 'Soyuz' (Tumanskii) R-27VM-300 rated at 15,300 lb st (68.04 kN) and two RKBM (Koliesov) RD-36-35FVR each rated at 6,725 lb st (29.90 kN)
Performance: maximum level speed at sea level 608 mph (978 km/h); maximum speed at 36,090 ft (11000 m) 627 mph (1009 km/h); maximum rate of climb at sea level 14,764 ft (4500 m) per minute; service ceiling 39,370 ft (12000 m); combat radius 124 miles (200 km); (Yak-38M) 242 miles (390 km)
Weights: operating empty 16,240 lb (7370 kg) including pilot; maximum take-off 25,794 lb (11700 kg) for STO
Dimensions: wingspan 23 ft 0½ in (7.022 m); length 50 ft 7⅞ in (15.43 m); wing area 201 sq ft (18.69 m^2)
Armament: maximum ordnance 4,409 lb (2000 kg) on four pylons

Yakovlev Yak-40 'Codling' and Yak-42 'Clobber'

Offering a combination of economy and STOL performance, the Yak-40 could operate from 2,297 ft (700 m) airstrips.

Designed in the early 1960s as a feederliner to replace Li-2s in Aeroflot service, the **Yak-40** was required to operate from grass airfields or semi-prepared strips. The resulting aircraft has high-lift lightly-loaded wings and for added safety three- rather than two-engine powerplant. In configuration the Yak-40 is a cantilever low-wing monoplane with retractable tricycle landing gear, rear-mounted engines, and with accommodation for a flight crew of two or three and up to 32 passengers. The provision of a ventral rear door with airstair makes it possible to operate the Yak-40 from airfields with minimum facilities, and an onboard auxiliary power unit makes the type independent of ground equipment for engine starting and the maintenance of cabin heating and air-conditioning. The first flight of the prototype was made on 21 October 1966, the type entering revenue service with Aeroflot on 30 September 1968. When production ended in 1976 over 800 had been built. The type was given the reporting name **'Codling'**.

With an Aeroflot requirement for a medium-range transport to replace Il-18s and Tu-134s in service, Yakovlev sought to reduce development time by evolving a larger-capacity version of the Yak-40. Three prototypes were built, the first with 11° wing sweep and the other two with 23° sweep, this latter angle being chosen for production **Yak-42** aircraft, which also differs from the Yak-40 by having all-swept tail surfaces, twin wheels on each landing gear unit and more powerful engines. Early production aircraft entered Aeroflot service in late 1980, these having a single passenger cabin seating a maximum 120 passengers. An alternative 100-passenger local-service layout is available, and a stretched 144-passenger version is designated **Yak-42AM**. The entire accommodation is pressurised, and the **Yak-42A** variant, built from 1981, has provision a convertible passenger/ cargo interior. Further variants include the **Yak-42D** with snmall changes in fuel capacity and interior (introduced in 1988), and the **Yak-42F** research/survey aircraft with underwing EO sensors. The type has the reporting name **'Clobber'**.

SPECIFICATION

Yakovlev Yak-40 'Codling'
Type: short-range transport
Powerplant: three 3,307-lb (14.71-kN) thrust Ivehenko AI-25 turbofans
Performance: maximum cruising speed 342 mph (550 km/h) at 22,965 ft (7000 m); range with maximum payload 901 miles (1450 km)
Weights: empty 20,723 lb (9400 kg); maximum take-off 35,274 lb (16000 kg)
Dimensions: wingspan 82 ft ¼ in (25.00 m); length 66 ft 9½ in (20.36 m); height 21 ft 3¾ in (6.50 m); wing area 753.50 sq ft (70 m^2)

Yakovlev Yak-50, Yak-52 and Yak-53

In mid-1975 Yakovlev flew the prototype of a new single-seat aerobatic/sporting aircraft designated **Yak-50**, its development being timed to provide the USSR with a new mount for the world aerobatic championships at Kiev in 1976. Following this event there was little doubt of the type's capability, for Soviet pilots took the first two and first five places in the men's and women's

championships respectively. With a similar basic configuration to the **Yak-18PS**, the Yak-50 differed primarily by a reduction in overall dimensions and the introduction of a semi-monocoque fuselage structure, plus a 360-hp (268-kW) M-14P engine to give an improved power/ weight ratio. Variants include the **Yak-52** two- seat primary trainer, which has semi-retractable

The Yak-52 is used as a basic trainer by Georgia, however, two examples operating in the recce/assault role were shot down by rebel Georgian forces in 1993.

tricycle landing gear, production of which has been undertaken by Intreprinderia de Avione Bacau in Romania, with 1,800 built by late 1994. The single-seat **Yak-53**

aerobatic aircraft combined the basic Yak-50 with the landing gear of the Yak-52.

This lightweight aircraft had simplified flight controls, and avionics removed.

Yakovlev/Aermacchi Yak-130

The **Yak-130** was designed to meet the same Russian air force instructional trainer system requirement as the MiG-AT. This specified an aircraft with simulators and ground-based training aids, like the US Navy's T-45TS system.

The Yak-130 has a less conventional configuration than the MiG, featuring swept wings with winglets. On take-off, the engines are fed with air by auxiliary overwing air intakes and by the main intakes, which feature

swing-down intake doors, much like those fitted to MiG-29. In 1992, Yakovlev teamed with Aermacchi to develop the Yak-130. Like the MiG-AT, it features a reprogrammable flight control system that can be used to simulate the handling of a variety of front-line types. The current **Yak/AEM-130** export version in late 2001 includes avionics and systems sourced from BAE Systems and Honeywell. The first of three **Yak-130D** demostrators made its maiden flight in 1996; these have reportedly been folowed by a further preseries batch of seven for evaluation. The intended production configuration of the Yak-130 will

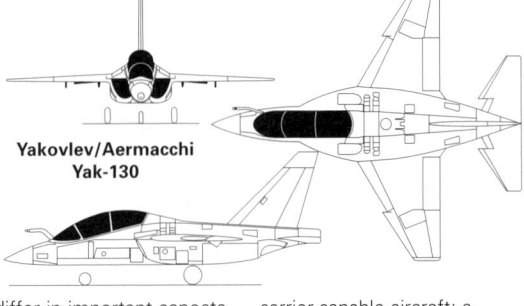

Yakovlev/Aermacchi Yak-130

differ in important aspects, notably a shorter and shallower fuselage with a more downswept nose, and a 'dogtooth' on the tailplane leading edge to enhance effectiveness at high angles of attack. Yakovlev plans to develop a family of Yak-130 variants. These include a combat-capable two-seater and a single-seat combat version with seven hardpoints; a hooked

carrier-capable aircraft; a two-seat side-by-side trainer optimised for training bomber and transport pilots. By 2001, the Russian requirement for its new trainer remained vague, with no service entry planned until at least 2003/04. Strong interest in the Yak-130 as a subsonic multi-role fighter is currently being expressed by Slovakia.

SPECIFICATION	
Yakovlev/Aermacchi Yak-130	radius 345 miles (555 km) configured for CAP
Type: two-seat basic and advanced jet trainer	**Weights:** empty 10,141 lb (4600 kg); maximum take-off for an attack mission 20,943 lb (9500 kg)
Powerplant: two Povazské Strojárne ZMK DV-2S (Klimov RD-35) turbofans each rated at 4,852 lb st (21.58 kN)	**Dimensions:** wingspan 31 ft 10¾ in (9.72 m); length 37 ft 8¼ in (11.49 m); height 15 ft 7½ in (4.76 m); wing area 253.20 sq ft (23.52 m²)
Performance: maximum level speed at 15,000 ft (4570 m) 644 mph (1037 km/h); maximum rate of climb at sea level 10,000 ft (3048 m) per minute; service ceiling 42,660 ft (13000 m); combat	**Armament:** maximum ordnance 6,614 lb (3000 kg)

Yokosuka D4Y Suisei

Inspired by the design of the He 118, the D4Y was smaller, lighter and aerodynamically superior.

In late 1938 the First Naval Air Technical Arsenal at Yokosuka was instructed to design a single-engine carrier-based bomber, a type required urgently by the Imperial Japanese Navy. The resulting **D4Y1** prototype was a Imid-wing cantilever monoplane of all-metal construction with retractable tailwheel landing gear, accommodating a crew of two in tandem beneath a continuous canopy. It carried a single bomb of up to 1,102-lb (500kg) weight in an internal bay. Intended powerplant was a licence-built version of the DB 601A, but as this Japanese-built Aichi

Atsuta was not available in time an imported 960-hp (716-kW) DB 600G was installed in each of the early prototypes. Although the DB 600G had an output some 20 per cent below the expected rating of the Atsuta, performance exceeded all expectations until service trials revealed weakness in the wing structure. As a result the first production version, the **Navy Type 2 Carrier Reconnaissance Plane Model 11 Suisei** (comet) (**D4Y1-C**), was unsuitable for dive-bombing, and initial production deliveries were made in the autumn of 1942.

Wing reinforcement and improved dive brakes led

to production of the **Navy Suisei Carrier Bomber Model 11 (D4Y1)** in March 1943, and within a year some 500 had entered service. Deployed in June 1944 against Allied amphibious attacks on the Mariana group of islands, the Suiseis operating from carriers were mauled severely by Allied fighters, lack of armour protection and self-sealing fuel tanks making them vulnerable even to small-calibre

Variants

D4Y1 prototypes: five, powered by imported 960-hp (716-kW) DB 600G engines
D4Y1 pre-production: generally as prototypes but with a 1,200-hp (895-kW) Aichi AE1A Atsuta 32 engine
D4Y1-C: reconnaissance version of D4Y1 with camera in rear fuselage
D4Y1 Suisei: initial dive-bomber production version; similar to prototypes but with strengthened structure and improved dive brakes
D4Y1 KAI: as D4Y1 Suisei but equipped for catapult launching
D4Y2: improved version introducing AE1P Atsuta 32 engine; armament as prototypes
D4Y2a: as D4Y2, but rear mounted 0.31-in (7.92-mm) machine-gun replaced by one of 0.51-in (13-mm) calibre
D4Y2-C: reconnaissance version of D4Y2
D4Y2a-C: reconnaissance version of D4Y2a
D4Y2 KAI: D4Y2 with catapult launch points
D4Y2a KAI: designation of D4Y2a with catapult launch points
D4Y2-S: night-fighter conversion of D4Y2; bomb racks, rear firing gun and carrier equipment removed; bomb bay sealed; single 20-mm cannon mounted obliquely in fuselage to fire upwards and forwards, and some equipped also with air-to-air rockets
D4Y3: generally as D4Y2 but powered by the 1,560-hp (1163-kW) Mitsubishi MK8P Kinsei radial engine
D4Y3a: as above, but with armament of D4Y2a
D4Y4: single-seat kamikaze attack version of D4Y3; standard forward-firing guns and one 1,764-lb (800-kg) bomb

SPECIFICATION	
Yokosuka D4Y2 Suisei 'Judy'	(2440 kg); maximum take-off 9,370 lb (4250 kg)
Type: single-seat carrier-based dive-bomber	**Dimensions:** span 37 ft 8¾ in (11.50 m); length 33 ft 6¼ in (10.22 m); height 12 ft 3¼ in (3.74 m); wing area 254.04 sq ft (23.60 m²)
Powerplant: one 1,400-hp (1044-kW) Aichi Atsuta 32 inverted Vee piston engine	
Performance: maximum speed 342 mph (550 km/h) at 15,585 ft (4750 m); service ceiling 35,105 ft (10700 m); range 910 miles (1465 km)	**Armament:** two 0.303-in (7.7-mm) forward-firing and one 0.31-in (7.92-mm) rear-firing machine-guns, plus a bombload of up to 1,234 lb (800 kg)
Weights: empty 5,379 lb	

weapons. Built to a total of 2,038, the majority by

Aichi, all were allocated the allied codename **'Judy'**.

Yokosuka P1Y Ginga

Requiring a fast medium bomber for dive-bombing, low-altitude bombing or torpedo attack, the Imperial Japanese Navy instructed the Yokosuka First Naval Air Technical Arsenal in 1940 to begin design of such an aircraft. The resulting **P1Y** prototype flown in August 1943 was a mid-wing monoplane of all-metal construction and powered by two Nakajima NK9B Homare 11 radial engines. Its performance was satisfactory, but the P1Y suffered from maintenance problems that plagued its service life. All remedial attempts failed, delaying

until early 1945 the entry into service of the **Navy Bomber Ginga Model 11**. Production totalled 1,098, built by Kawanishi (96) and Nakajima (1,002), and if there had been adequate manpower to service these aircraft before each operational sortie, they would have proved formidable adversaries. This was not possible and as a result the **Ginga** (milky way), allocated the Allied codename **'Francis'**, was tried unsuccessfully in a variety of alternative roles; its brief operational life of only six months was terminated by the end of the Pacific war.

Variants

P1Y (prototypes): six, with Nakajima NK9B Homare 11 engines; armament of one 0.303-in (7.7-mm) forward-firing machine-gun and one rear-firing 20-mm cannon
P1Y1 Ginga: initial production version; as P1Y but forward-firing machine-gun replaced by 20-mm cannon
P1Y1a: production version with 1,825-hp (1361-kW) NK9C Homare 12 engines; 20-mm cannon in nose and one 0.51-in (13-mm) rear-firing machine-gun
P1Y1b: production version as P1Y1a, but with two 0.51-in (13-mm) rear-firing machine-guns
P1Y1c: production version as P1Y1b, but nose cannon replaced by third 0.51-in (13-mm) machine-gun
P1Y1-S: night-fighter conversions of P1Y1; four obliquely-mounted 20-mm cannon firing forward and upward, plus one rear-firing 0.51-in (13-mm) gun
P1Y2-S: production night-fighter with two 1,850-hp (1380-kW) Mitsubishi MK4T-A Kasei 25a radials; armament of three 20-mm cannon, two obliquely-mounted and one rear-firing
P1Y2: production bomber; powerplant as P1Y2-S, armament as P1Y1
P1Y2a: production bomber as P1Y2 but with armament of P1Y1a
P1Y2b: production bomber as P1Y2 but with armament of P1Y1b
P1Y2c: production bomber as P1Y2 but with armament of P1Y1c

Yokosuka P1Y1 Ginga
Type: medium-bomber
Powerplant: two 1,820-hp (1357-kW) Nakajima Homare 11 radial piston engines
Performance: maximum speed 340 mph (547 km/h) at 19,355 ft (5900 m); service ceiling 30,840 ft (9400 m); maximum range 3,337 miles (5370 km)
Weights: empty 16,017 lb

(7265 kg); maximum take-off 29,762 lb (13500 kg)
Dimensions: wingspan 65 ft 7½ in (20 m); length 49 ft 2½ in (15 m); height 14 ft 11 in (4.30 m); wing area 592.03 sq ft (55.00 m²)
Armament: two 20-mm cannon (one forward- and one rear-firing), plus a bombload of up to 2,205 lb (1000 kg), or one 1,764-lb (800-kg) torpedo

The third prototype P1Y1 Ginga was later experimentally fitted with a Tsu-11 jet engine beneath the rear fuselage. Prototypes had single exhaust pipes and retractable tailwheels.

Zeppelin-Staaken R series

Soon after the beginning of World War I Count von Zeppelin initiated the development of heavy bombers, which he could foresee would be of great importance to the nation's war effort. The design of land-plane versions began under the leadership of Professor Baumann, the first of them being the **Zeppelin-Staaken VGO.I,** which established a basic layout and size for the remainder of these giant aircraft. With biplane wings, a slab-sided fuselage and biplane tail unit, the VGO.I was supported on the ground by fixed tailskid type landing gear, whose main units had multiple wheels, plus two more wheels beneath the nose. Initial powerplant of the VGO.I comprised three 240-hp (179-kW) Maybach Mb.IV engines, one in a nacelle between the wings on each side of the fuselage and one in the nose. First flown on 11 April 1915, the VGO.I was found to be underpowered and was re-engined subsequently with five similar Maybach engines, each nacelle containing two engines in tandem, but crashed under test. A series of one-offs followed, the **VGO.II** with three engines being similar to the VGO.I. The **VGO.III** introduced six 160-hp (119-kW) Mercedes D.III engines, two in each nacelle and two side-by-side in the nose. The fourth aircraft, of

the same six-engine layout but with 220-hp (164-kW) Benz Bz.IV engines in the nacelles and Mercedes D.IIIs in the nose, was identified as the **R.IV**, the first of the series to have the **R (Riesenflugzeug,** or giant aircraft) designation. The **R.V** reverted to use of the 240-hp (179-kW) Mb.IV engine (five of them being installed), but the production **R.VI**, of which the first was delivered in June 1917, had four more powerful engines and eliminated the powerplant from the fuselage nose. R.VI production totalled 18, one being built by the company and the remainder under sub-contract by Aviatik (six), Ostdeutsche Albatros Werke (four) and Schütte-

Lanz (seven). They were followed into production in 1918 by the similar **R.XIV** (three aircraft) and **R.XV** (three aircraft), both versions having five Mb.IV engines. An advanced four-engine version developed by Aviatik, with one 220-hp (164-kW) Bz.IVa in each nacelle, was allocated the designation **R.XVI (Av)**; three were to have been built but only one was completed before the end of the war. Variants included the single **R.VII** which differed from the R.IV by having two D.IIIs in the nose and four Bz.IVs in the nacelles; the **Type L** twin-float seaplane with four 260-hp (194-kW) Mercedes D.IVa engines; and three **Type 8301** twin-

float seaplanes which had the same powerplant but introduced an entirely new fuselage. Post-war one more 'giant' was completed, the **E.4/20** designed by Dipl.Ing. Adolf Rohrbach. This differed considerably from the wartime series, being a high-wing monoplane powered by four 245-hp

(183-kW) Maybach engines. It accommodated a crew of two in an open cockpit and the cabin, to which access was gained through a hinged nose section, seated 18 passengers. Tested in the autumn of 1920, it was banned by the Allied Control Commission and was scrapped two years later.

Zeppelin-Staaken R.VI
Type: seven-crew heavy bomber
Powerplant: four 245-hp (183-kW) Maybach Mb.IV or 260-hp (194-kW) Mercedes D.IVa inline piston engines
Performance: maximum speed 84 mph (135 km/h); service ceiling 14,175 ft (4320 m); maximum duration 10 hours
Weights: empty 17,463 lb

(7921 kg); maximum take-off 26,120 lb (11848 kg)
Dimensions: wingspan 138 ft 5½ in (42.20 m); length 72 ft 6 in (22.10 m); height 20 ft 8 in (6.30 m); wing area 3,573.74 sq ft (332 m²)
Armament: four 0.31-in (7.92-mm) Parabellum machine-guns, plus a maximum short-range bombload of 4,409 lb (2000 kg)

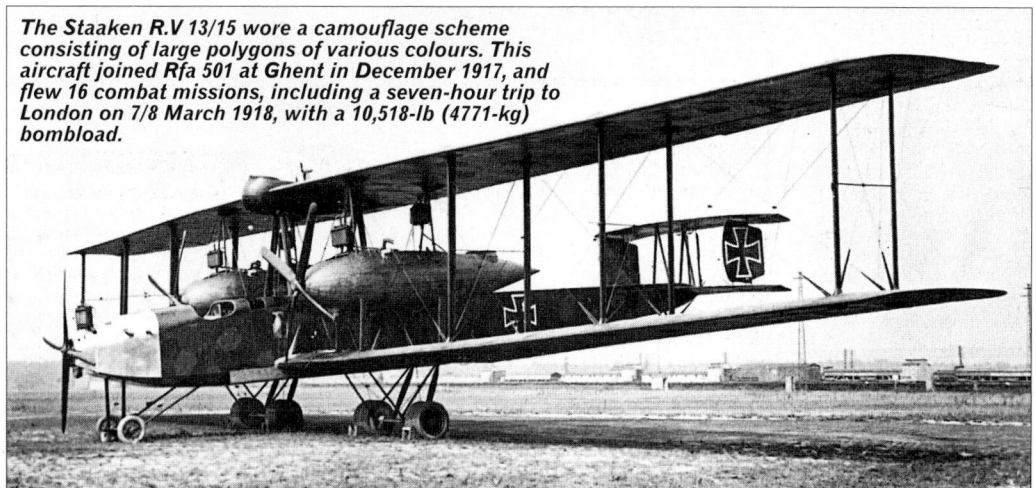

The Staaken R.V 13/15 wore a camouflage scheme consisting of large polygons of various colours. This aircraft joined Rfa 501 at Ghent in December 1917, and flew 16 combat missions, including a seven-hour trip to London on 7/8 March 1918, with a 10,518-lb (4771-kg) bombload.

Zlin aircraft

Founded in 1935, the Czech Zlinská Letecká Akeiová Spolecnost was a subsidiary of the well-known Bata Shoe Company. Its first product was the wooden **Zlin XII** two-seater, a low-wing monoplane powered by a 45-hp (34-kW) Persy II engine and available in both open and cabin versions. The following **Zlin XIII** was also a two-seater of similar configuration, but with an enclosed cabin and a 130-hp (97-kW) Walter Minor engine. The **Zlin XV** of 1939 had a 105-hp (78-kW) Zlin Toma 4 engine and was available in open or closed cockpit variants. The **Zlin 212**, adopting a new style of designation, was a cabin trainer development of the Zlin XII with a 60-hp (45-kW) Walter Mikron engine.

During the closing stages of World War II, the Zlin factory at Otrokovice opened a production line for the Bücker Bü 181 Bestmann and its Hirth engine, and manufacture continued post-war as the Zlin 181. Around 180 were built, most of which went to the Czech air force as trainers under the designation **C-6**. The factory changed its name to Moravan post-war, but the name Zlin was retained as part of the aircraft designation.

The next development was the **Zlin 281** with the Toma 4 engine; about 100 were built for the civil market before production was switched in 1948 to the **Zlin 381** with the 105-hp (78-kW) Walter Minor III engine; 184 were built, many for the Czech air force as the **C-106**, and 45 went to the Hungarian air force. Several variants were available, including a tourer, a semi-aerobatic trainer and a fully-aerobatic version, and one Zlin 381 was used to test the 150-hp (112-kW) Praga E engine. Licence production was undertaken in Egypt as the **Gomhouria Mk 1** with the Walter Minor engine, followed by the **Gomhouria Mk 2** with the 145-hp (108-kW) Continental C-145. Several Egyptian variants followed, production ending in that country in early 1979 after more than 300 had been built.

In 1947 Zlin broke away from the tandem-seating layout with the **Zlin 22 Junak**, a wooden monocoque two-seat side-by-side cabin monoplane. The prototype was powered by a 57-hp (43-kW) Persy III, but this engine was discontinued and production aircraft had the 75-hp (56-kW) Praga D, being redesignated **Zlin 22D**. Some 200 Junaks were built before production ended in 1950. A three-seat version, the **Zlin 22M**, had a 105-hp (78-kW) Minor 4-III. Two prototypes were built of the **Zlin 122**, a three-/four-seater with a Toma 4 engine.

A Czech air force specification for a primary trainer attracted two entrants, the Praga E.112 and **Zlin 26 Trener**; when evaluated in 1948 the Zlin 26 gained the production contract. Of

The Zlin Z.526L differed from the Z.526F in having a 200-hp (149-kW) air-cooled Lycoming engine.

mixed wood and metal construction, it had a Minor 4-III engine and was the forerunner of a series of aerobatic monoplanes which brought the company to the forefront in world aerobatic competitions. The Zlin 26, which had the Czech air force designation **C-5**, was superseded in 1953 by the all-metal **Zlin 126 Trener II** with the same engine. It was produced for both home and export markets and was designated **C-105** in air force service. The **Zlin 226** of 1955 had the 160-hp (119-kW) Minor 6-III engine, and was produced initially as the **Z.226B** glider tug and in the following year as the **Z.226T Trener-6** (**C-205**). Total production reached 252, and this version was supplied to 19 countries. A fully aerobatic single-seat model, the **Z.226A Akrobat**, was built in several versions for home and export markets. Logical development continued with the similarly powered **Z.326 Trener-Master**, flown in prototype form in 1957 and basically a version of the Zlin 226 with retractable landing gear, plus a single-seat aerobatic derivative, the **Z.326A Akrobat**; both models had provision for wingtip fuel tanks. The **Zlin 526**, first flown in 1966, introduced a constant-speed propeller and transferred the main pilot's position to the rear cockpit; there was also a single-seat aerobatic version, the **Z.526A Akrobat**, and a further development of the two-seater was the **Z.526F**, flown in 1968 and certificated in the following year. It had a 180-hp (134-kW) Avia M137A engine as standard but was available with optional powerplants to customer requirement. Final version in the series was the **Zlin 726**, flown in March 1973 and differing in detail, mainly shorter-span wings with a metal-covered rudder and elevators. The **Z.726K** was a more power-

The former East Germany's Verbindungsstaffel 14 operated the Z.43 alongside the An-2 and L-410 from Strausberg, the centre of GDR transport operations.

ful model with a 210-hp (157-kW) Avia M337AK supercharged engine. When production of the Z.26/726 series ended in 1977 a total of 1,452 of all versions had been built.

The series secured a mass of successes in aerobatic competitions between 1957 and 1969 including first placings in the Lockheed Trophy competition held in the UK in 1957, 1958, 1961, 1963, 1964 and 1965, and first in the Léon Biancotto Trophée aerobatic competitions held in France in 1965, 1967 and 1969.

While the Z.26 family concentrated on aerobatic capability, the need for a side-by-side trainer and light tourer led to the **Zlin 42**, flown in prototype form in October 1967. Powered by an M137A engine, the Zlin 42 met FAR Pt 23 airworthiness specifications in the acrobatic category and could be used also as a glider tug. A four-seat development, the **Zlin 43**, flew in December 1968 with a 210-hp (157-kW) Avia M337 engine; the two types had an 80 per cent commonality of structural components and both entered production. The series version of the **Z.42** was designated **Zlin 42M**, and around 250 were built; the German Democratic Republic was a major customer and others are known to have been supplied to Hungary. A development was the **Zlin 142** which had the same engine as the Zlin 43; construction began in 1981 and about 50 had been delivered by mid-1983.

Production of the Zlin 43 began in 1972, but only 80 had been built by early 1977, in which year production seems to have ended.

While the Zlin 26/726 series had been the supreme aerobatic types for some years, it became obvious that a smaller, more nimble aircraft was needed to challenge new competition, and in 1973 Zlin began design of the **Zlin 50L**, a fully-aerobatic single-seater with a 260-hp (194-kW) Avco Lycoming AEIO540-D4B5 engine. The prototype flew in July 1975 and by the following March two more prototypes and seven production aircraft were flying. In the 1976 World Acrobatic Championships at Kiev, Zlin 50s gained second place in the team event and third in the men's individual competition. Around 80 **Z.50L** aircraft were built, including several for export, and a developed version, the **Z.50LS**, was reported to be in flight test in 1982.

By December 1996, postwar production figures had exceeded 3,000, including 1,495 of the Z.26 family built between 1949 and 1975 and 698 Z.42/43/142s between 1970 and 1995. Five Z.43s were delivered to Algeria in 1991, under the designation **Safir 43**. Algerian Z.142s were designated **Firnas 142**.

In 2001, Zlin production was focused on the **Z.142C**, the latest production variant of the Z.142; the **Z.242L**, a Lycoming-powered version of the Z.142 and the **Z.143** four-seat lightplane.

Zmaj aircraft

Fabriká Aeroplaná I Hidroplaná Zmaj was established at Zemun, Yugoslavia, in 1927 and first built Dewoitine D.1 fighters, Gourdou-Leseurre fighter-trainers and Hanriot H.32 landplane and H.41 seaplane trainers under licence. The company's leading designer was Rudolf Fizir, and most of his early designs were known by the make of powerplant selected. Among types built between 1927 and 1932 were the **Zmaj**

Fizir-Maybach, a basic biplane trainer with a 260-hp (194-kW) Maybach engine; the **Fizir-Wright**, a reconnaissance biplane of which Zmaj built nine during 1929 with the 230-hp (172-kW) Wright Whirlwind radial; and the **Fizir-Lorraine** of 1932 with the 400-hp (298-kW) Lorraine engine and intended for reconnaissance; also built in 1932 were the **Fizir-Mars** biplane primary trainer twin- float seaplane, powered by the 140-hp

(104-kW) Walter Mars radial, and the **Fizir-Jupiter** observation seaplane with a 380-hp (283-kW) Gnome-Rhône Jupiter. Other Fizir designs built during that period included the **Nebojsa** (brave fellow) of 1930, a cabin tourer monoplane with a 160-hp (119-kW) radial engine, and the **A.F.2** light amphibian with an 85-hp (63-kW) Walter Vega radial piston engine.

Produced in greater numbers was the **F.P.2**, developed from the earlier **F.P.1** prototype, a biplane trainer powered by a 420-hp (313-kW) Rakovica

licence-built Gnome-Rhône K-7 radial. Of all-wooden construction, the F.P.2 entered large-scale production as a basic trainer for Yugoslav military aviation; although the number built by Zmaj is not known, at the time of the German invasion in April 1941 66 were still serviceable at pilot training schools. Several were used subsequently by the Regia Aeronautica and the satellite Croat air arm. Another important type was the **F.N.** light primary trainer biplane, of which the prototype was flown in 1929. It went into quantity

production with both Zmaj and Rogozärski, initially with a 120-hp (89-kW) Maybach engine, but the powerplant used in greater numbers was the Walter NZ radial of the same horsepower; an improved F.N., built from 1937, introduced several refinements. Records show that when Yugoslavia was invaded by Axis forces some 140 F.N.s were still in service. Some were used later by Croat forces and one is believed to have served later in the war with Yugoslav partisans; one is preserved at the National Air Museum.

Aviation Landmarks

1903 First flight

17 December: 'When we rose on the morning of the 17th, the puddles of water, which had been standing about camp since the recent rains, were covered with ice. The wind had a velocity of 22 to 27 mph. We thought it would die down before long, but when 10 o'clock arrived, and the wind was as brisk as ever, we decided that we had better get the machine out...' Thus Orville Wright described the start of that historic day at Kill Devil Hill. He took his position on the

Flyer, the trolley was released to run down the wooden track as the engine raced and, in Orville's words, 'it lifted from the track after a forty-foot run. The course of the flight up and down was exceedingly erratic. The control of the front rudder [elevator] was difficult. As a result, the machine would rise suddenly to about ten feet, and then as suddenly dart for the ground. A sudden dart when a little over 120 feet from the point at which it rose into the air, ended the flight...' The cheers of

the Wrights' helpers and witnesses were shredded by the wind, but they were soon helping to reposition the *Flyer* for the next attempt. Three more flights were made that day, the last with brother Wilbur at the controls covering a distance of 852 ft (260 m) in 59 seconds; soon after the *Flyer* was carried back and put down near the workshop, only to be overturned and blown along by the gusting wind, wrecked beyond immediate repair. The memorable day was reported by Orville to his

father in a telegram: 'SUCCESS FOUR FLIGHTS THURSDAY MORNING ALL AGAINST TWENTY ONE MILE WIND STARTED FROM LEVEL WITH ENGINE POWER ALONE AVERAGE SPEED THROUGH AIR THIRTY ONE MILES LONGEST 57 SECONDS INFORM PRESS HOME CHRISTMAS ORVELLE WRIGHT'. Like many telegrams it contains inaccuracies, but they detract nothing from an achievement that assured the two brothers of a place in aviation history.

1909 Louis Blériot's cross-Channel exploits

25 July: The *Daily Mail* prize of £1,000 for the first aeroplane to cross the English Channel was won by Louis Blériot. The Frenchman set out in his Blériot Type XI monoplane from Les Barraques, near Calais, at 4.35 am, and despite being almost immediately lost in mist over the Channel, and his 25-hp (18.60-kW) Anzani engine overheating (it was fortunately cooled by a rain

squall), Blériot completed the 37 minute flight successfully. The Channel was conquered as the monoplane landed heavily at Northfall Meadow, close to Dover Castle at 5.12 am. The following day, Blériot made the front page of the *Daily Sketch*, and went on to receive the equivalent of £3,000 from the French government, representing an important contribution to the future of his company.

1918 The fall of the 'Red Baron'

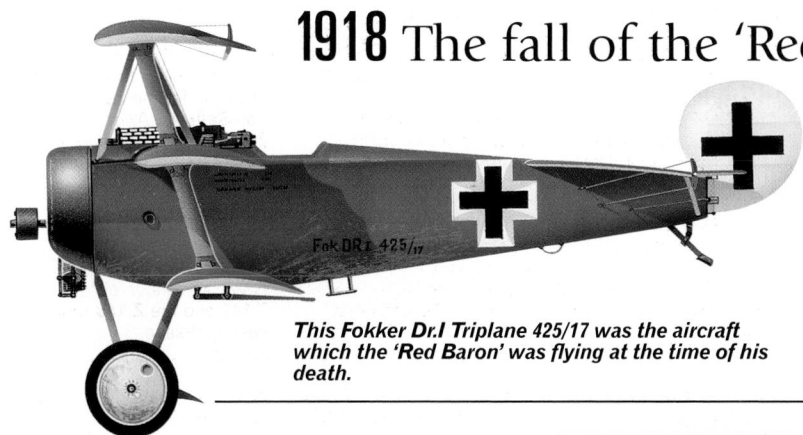

This Fokker Dr.I Triplane 425/17 was the aircraft which the 'Red Baron' was flying at the time of his death.

21 April: Cavalry Cpt. Manfred Freiherr von Richthofen, the charismatic aristocratic fighter ace, had accumulated 80 kills at the time of his death on 21 April, 11 days before his 26th birthday. The 'Red Baron' was killed during a dogfight between 15 Albatros and Fokker scouts and eight No. 209 Sqn Camels. His Fokker had been chased by Cpt.

A. R. Brown, who had unleashed a salvo of gunfire, a single bullet probably striking von Richthofen as he flew over Australian trenches; he crash-landed in Allied territory. The legendary Von Richthofen's funeral was held at Bertangles on 22 April, and was marked by a volley fired by the 3rd Sqn Australian Flying Corps.

1923 Non-stop across the USA

2-3 May: US Army Air Service Lieutenants O. G. Kelly and J. A. MacReady became the first aviators to cross the North American continent non-stop, flying a Fokker T-2 monoplane (bottom) from Roosevelt Field, Long Island, to Rockwell Field, San Diego, where they landed just after

midnight. Completing the distance in 26 hours 50 minutes, the aircraft averaged a speed of 88.20 mph (141.90 km/h) . In order to last the distance, the Fokker T-2 was modified with increased-capacity wing fuel tanks, and heavy-duty landing gear to cope with the increased gross weight.

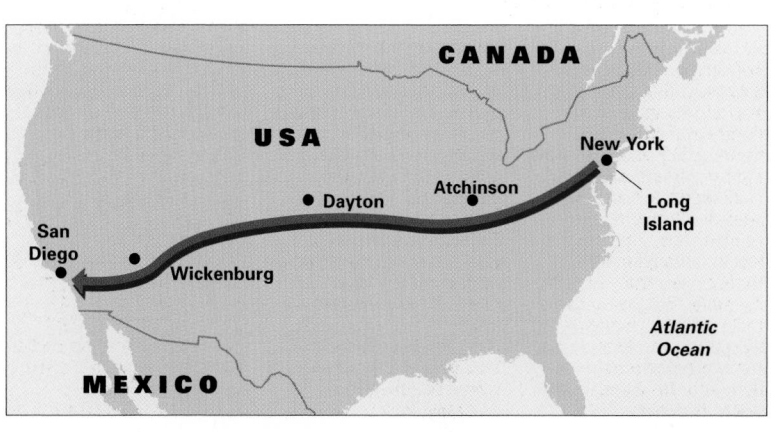

1927 Across the Atlantic: Captain Charles Lindbergh

20-21 May: The first non-stop solo flight across the North Atlantic from west to east was made by Captain Charles Lindbergh (pictured right), flying the Ryan NYP monoplane *Spirit of St Louis*; the flight from Long Island, New York, to Paris, France, covered a distance of 3,590 miles (5778 km). Completing the trip in 33 hours 39 minutes, the record-breaking flight was a supreme test of Lindbergh's endurance and capability, his skill honed to perfection by many hours of flying mail across the United States. Upon his return to the United States, Lindbergh was awarded the DFC by President Calvin Coolidge.

Constructed by Ryan, Lindbergh's monoplane, Spirit of St Louis, held a total of 425 US gal (1609 litres) of fuel, carried in tanks in the nose, wings and fuselage.

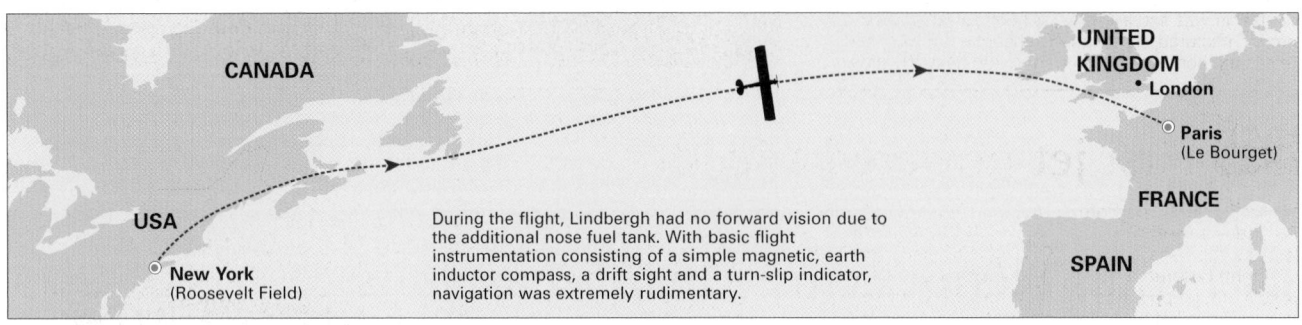

During the flight, Lindbergh had no forward vision due to the additional nose fuel tank. With basic flight instrumentation consisting of a simple magnetic, earth inductor compass, a drift sight and a turn-slip indicator, navigation was extremely rudimentary.

1930 Australia or bust

5-24 May: A 27-year-old female aviator with only 100 hours of flying experience, Amy Johnson, from Hull, Yorkshire, flew 9,960 miles (16029 km) from Croydon, Surrey, to Port Darwin, Australia, in just over 19 days. Flying a DH.60G Gipsy Moth named *Jason*, Johnson had made her first stop in Vienna after 10 hours, before suffering a forced desert landing near Baghdad after an engine failure, damaged landing gear at Bandar Abbas, a damaged wing in a forced landing at Jahnsi, monsoon storms over India, and a smashed propeller at Rangoon on her way to Australia.

1932 Amelia flies the North Atlantic

20-21 May: In June 1928 Amelia Earhart became the first women to cross the Atlantic by air. Almost four years later, on 20 May 1932,she attempted a solo flight over the same route. On this day, coincidentally the fifth anniversary of Lindbergh's epic flight, Earhart departed Harbour Grace, Newfoundland in her Lockheed Vega.

With the sunset behind her, the first few hours were trouble-free. However, with darkness descending, one of the most vital flight instruments, the altimeter, failed and worse was to follow. By midnight, she found herself negotiating a thunderstorm, relying on instruments to maintain her course and height. As the storm gave way to dense cloud, ice began to accrete on the aircraft and the windscreen became obscured. Uncertain of her height and with the aircraft reluctant to climb, there was no alternative but to descend. The aircraft emerged into clear air and the ice dissipated, and the problem was resolved until Earhart ran into a bank of fog. There was no alternative but to climb back into the cloud but, without the altimeter, adjusting the height was guesswork.

At daybreak the cloud began to clear, but her troubles were not over for, with the main fuel tanks almost exhausted, she switched to the reserve to discover a fuel leak. With reaching Paris no longer possible, she headed for Ireland, crossing the coastline somewhere in County Mayo. After encountering further thunderstorms, the epic journey finally ended in a meadow near Londonderry, Ulster, at 08.40 local time, after a flight of 13 hours and 28 minutes.

1935 Germany rearms; new types make first flights

9 March: On this date Germany's government announced the establishment of a new national air force – the Luftwaffe. A week later it blamed the failure of other European nations to disarm for its repudiation of the disarmament clauses of the Versailles Treaty and announced a massive rearmament programme. Earlier in the year the ostensibly civil airliner prototype Heinkel He 111a made its first flight, on 24 February. It now became clear that this design was actually a bomber. (Pictured, right, is the second bomber proto- type, He 111b.) In the spring (the exact date has gone unrecorded), the first Junkers Ju 87 dive-bomber made its maiden flight. Powered by a Rolls-Royce Kestrel engine and with a unique twin-fin empennage, the Ju 87 was destined to play an important role in the events of late 1939. The third and, perhaps, the most important type to make its debut during 1935 was the Bf 109 V1, taken into the air on 28 May by Hans D. Knoetzsch at Augsburg. More than 33,000 Bf 109s were subsequently produced over the next 10 years.

1939 First jet-powered aircraft

27 August: Flying from Marienehe airfield near Rostock, the Heinkel He 178 (right) became the world's first jet-powered aircraft. Propelled by a gas turbine engine which gave 838 lb (3.77 kN) of thrust, the He 178 never reached production but greatly aided future German jet fighter projects.

Poland invaded

1 September: Germany invaded Poland, carrying out heavy bombing attacks on the airfields at Krakow, Katowice, Lublin, Lwow, Radom and Warsaw. Bomber raids were conducted by Do 17s, He 111s and Ju 87s (right), escorted by Bf 109s and Bf 110s. Tactical surprise was achieved and a large proportion of the Polish air force was destroyed on the ground during this first day. A few Polish P.Z.L. P.11 fighters did get airborne and managed to shoot down several German aircraft, but the majority of the Luftwaffe's 203 losses were to ground fire. Ground troops followed the aircraft and, within a few weeks, the Soviet Red Army invaded from the East, spelling the end of Poland until 1945. As a result of the invasion, all RAF reservists were ordered to report for duty and the Air Transport Auxiliary (ATA) was formed to transport supplies and equipment between manufacturers, depots and RAF units.

1940 The Battle of Britain

with heavy attacks on coastal targets and Channel convoys; the object of the German attacks was to draw RAF fighters into the air and destroy them as a prelude to a planned invasion across the English Channel.

15 August: The heaviest air fighting of the Battle of Britain took place with attacks against British airfields by three German Luftflotten (air fleets) based all around the European coast from France to Norway; British losses on this day amounted to 29 fighters and 17 bombers and Luftwaffe records later disclosed their loss of 36 fighters and 40 bombers.

18-31 August: During heavy attacks on 18 August, Junkers Ju 87 dive-bombers of the Luftwaffe suffered heavily and, apart from rare sorties, the type was withdrawn from the Battle of Britain; because of failure of the Messerschmitt Bf 110 as effective escort fighters, the Bf 109 was assigned to this task. German losses during the month totalled 273 bombers and 347 fighters, while the RAF lost 373 fighters.

1-6 September: RAF fighter losses were being suffered at a rate equivalent to one whole squadron each day, and it was calculated that at this intensity of action RAF Fighter Command would cease to exist within three weeks; the loss of pilots was causing grave concern.

7 September: A frustrated Hermann Goering assumed control of the offensive against the UK and ordered a switch from raids on RAF airfields to a series of all-out attacks on London; on this evening an attack was fought for the brief period of 35 minutes, the greatest single air combat in history, involving about 1,200 aircraft in an area of 15 by 30 miles (24 by 48 km).

15 September: Sporadic air attacks on the UK continued until this date when the Luftwaffe launched its heaviest daylight raids on London (above left); the RAF, which had gained sufficient respite to replenish some of its squadrons, met the onslaught and inflicted heavy casualties; on 17 September, Hitler postponed Operation Seelöwe (the invasion of Britain).

30 October: The Battle of Britain, which had fluctuated during the month with sporadic high-level attacks by bomb-carrying Bf 109Es, ended officially on this date; nevertheless, the German bomber force continued to attack London by night with undiminished intensity.

1 July: German occupation of the Channel Islands was completed and the Battle of Britain began as Luftwaffe raids increased against southern England,

1941 Pearl Harbor attacked

7 December: Japan launched a surprise attack on Pearl Harbor base in Hawaii. The assault destroyed virtually all the battleships of the US Pacific Fleet and severely depleted the might of the USAAF in the region. However, the Japanese failed to destroy the US aircraft-carriers *Lexington*, *Enterprise* and *Saratoga*, which had been out on manoeuvres at the time. Some 365 fighters, bombers and torpedo aircraft from six Japanese aircraft-carriers sank five battleships and severely damaged three others, while sinking or damaging 10 other warships; 2,403 sailors, soldiers and airmen were killed, while Japan lost 100 men, 28 aircraft and five midget submarines. Of the 394 US military aircraft stationed at Pearl Harbor, 188 were destroyed and 159 damaged. Several US aircraft, including P-36s and P-40s managed to get airborne, shooting down a number of enemy machines. The US and the UK declared war on Japan the next day and Tokyo, previously all-powerful in the Pacific, now faced the might of US air power.

1945 Atomic raids on Japan

May-August: The advance party of the USAAF's 509th Composite Group arrived in the Mariana Islands on 29 May. B-29s of the 393rd Very Heavy Bomber Squadron, the 509th's only combat aircraft, landed at Tinian, Marianas, on 11 June. From 20 July, the unit began practice raids against Japanese cities, using conventional HE weapons. Gen. Carl Spaatz received orders for an atomic bomb attack on Japan as soon as possible after 3 August, and operational orders of 2 August earmarked Hiroshima, with Kokura or Nagasaki as alternatives. On 6 August, the B-29 *Enola Gay*, captained by Col Paul W. Tibbets Jr (pictured right with pipe), dropped the first atomic bomb in anger over the city of Hiroshima. Three days later, a second nuclear device was dropped on Nagasaki by the B-29 *Bockscar*, captained by Maj. Charles W. Sweeney. The Japanese formally surrendered on 2 September, before the US Pacific Fleet.

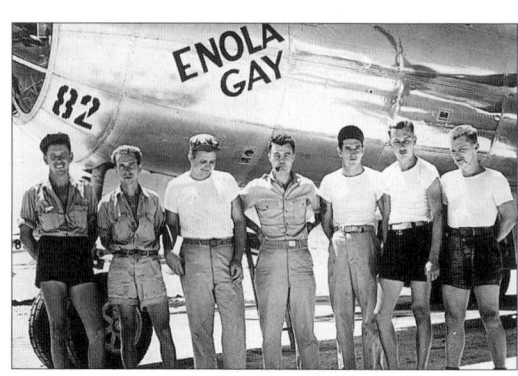

1947 Yeager and X-1 break sound barrier

14 October: The rocket-powered Bell X-1 made its first flight over Muroc AFB on 9 December 1946, piloted by Bell test pilot Chalmers 'Slick' Goodlin, and on 14 October 1947, in the hands of Capt. Charles 'Chuck' Yeager became the first manned aircraft in the world to escape from the buffeting of near-supersonic compressibility and into the smooth airflow of supersonic flight. On their historic flight, which had begun with an air-drop from a B-29 mother-ship, Yeager and the X-1 (named *Glamorous Glennis*) recorded the speed of 670 mph (1078 km/h) at a height of 42000 ft (12800 m), the equivalent of Mach 1.015. 'Chuck' Yeager (below right) with Bell Aircraft Corporation founder Lawrence Dale Bell, was one of three Air Force pilots assigned to the X-1 programme, with Lt Robert A. Hoover and Capt Jack Ridley. The bright orange X-1 *Glamorous Glennis* (to the left of the picture) was launched from an altitude of 20,000 ft (6096 m) by the B-29, before climbing to 42,000 ft (12802 m) in order to reach the intended speed. Yeager's achievement, however, was not made public until more than two months later, when the performance was revealed in *Aviation Week* on 22 December.

1952 First kill for the jet night-fighter

2 November: This Douglas F3D-2 Skyknight, flown by Maj. William 'Bill' Stratton together with MSgt Hans Hoglind, of the US Marines VMF(N)-513 specialist night-fighter unit, scored the first confirmed nocturnal victory involving jet fighters. Stratton and Hoglind picked up a contact which was identified as a 'Yak-15' in the early hours of 2 November, and after three bursts of cannon fire, the North Korean fighter fell in flames, the Skyknight narrowly avoiding damage from the burning jet's falling debris.

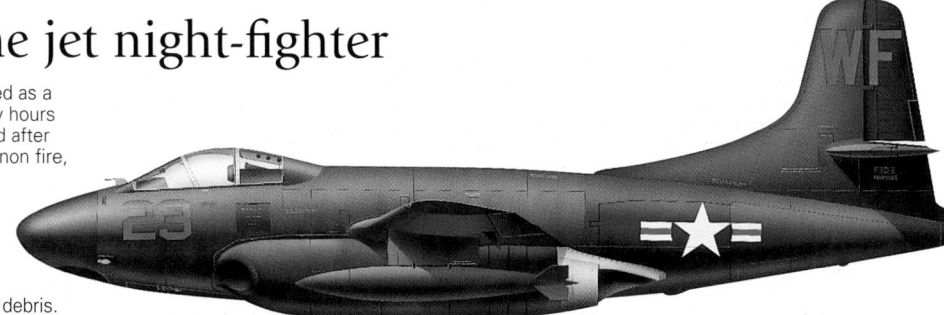

1958 Boeing 707 service entry

August-October: Deliveries of the Boeing 707-121 airliner to Pan American began in August 1958, after the airline had placed its initial order for 20 aircraft on 13 October 1955. The first Boeing 707-121 destined for Pan Am had taken to the air on 20 December 1957. Designed for domestic transcontinental routes, the 707-121's impressive range allowed Pan Am to make a promotional transatlantic flight. On 26 October 1958, N711PA *Jet Clipper America* (right), under the command of Captain Samuel H. Miller, left Idlewild, New York for Le Bourget, Paris (via Gander, Newfoundland) with 111 passengers and 11 crew.

1960 Spyplane shoot-down

1 May: In an event which was to have unprecedented political and military repercussions both within the US and around the world, a single CIA-operated U-2 high-altitude reconnaissance aircraft was downed by Soviet air defences near Sverdlovsk, while flying at an altitude of around 65,000 ft (19810 m). The pilot, Francis Gary Powers, survived unharmed, to be captured by the Soviets.

1965 YF-12 record

1 May: In 1956 Lockheed submitted a proposal to the USAF for a high-speed, high-altitude reconnaissance aircraft to replace the U-2. Designated A-12, the prototype first flew in April 1962 and its remarkable performance led to the development of the four fighter prototypes designated YF-12 (three YF-12As and one YF-12C). Two YF-12As were used by the USAF on 1 May 1965 to establish three world- and six international-class records. The most significant of these was a world absolute speed record of 2,070.1 mph (3331.51 km/h). Although the YF-12 never entered production, the basic design was developed as the highly successful SR-71 reconnaissance aircraft, which eventually took the record from the YF-12 more than 10 years later.

1966 X-15

1 July: In 1963 the USAF approved a $5 million programme to convert the X-15 aircraft with parachute-retrievable external fuel tanks. The new aircraft, designated X-15A-2, was intended to be used in the testing of a supersonic combustion ramjet, commonly known as a scramjet, which could be hung as an extra appendage from the ventral fin. The X-15A-2 made its first flight with the external tanks attached on 1 July 1966. On 18 November 1966 the aircraft's potential was demonstrated when Captain William Knight piloted the aircraft to 4,250 mph (6840 km/h), or Mach 6.33 – the highest speed attained by a conventionally-winged aircraft at that time.

1967 Vietnam: The war escalates

11 August: Following approval by President Lyndon Johnson of a new group of targets in northern Vietnam, US fighter-bombers attacked the Paul Doumer bridge, Hanoi for the first time. F-105 Thunderchiefs of the USAF's 355th Tactical Fighter Wing, led by Col Bob White, attacked the famed bridge across the Red River, the sole rail entry to Hanoi for trains coming from China and the port of Haiphong. The bridge was cut in half after nearly 100 tons of bombs had been dropped. The go-ahead from the President was a response to criticism from members of the Senate and various Arms Committees over target restrictions, and opened a new phase in the war. However, the attacking of new targets was not without risk and, naturally, important targets were heavily defended. This led to an increase in losses as demonstrated by this aircraft (right) downed over Hanoi.

1970 Events in civil aviation

22 January: Pan American Airways made history by completing the first 'wide body' airline service, between John F. Kennedy Airport, New York, and London-Heathrow. Clipper Young America, a Boeing 747, left the tarmac at 01.52 and began the transatlantic crossing. Pan Am had intended to begin 747 services in late 1969 but engine problems with the JT9D turbofans had resulted in postponement. An overheating engine delayed take-off on this historic flight, but the engine was repaired and the Jumbo completed its flight without problems, arriving at Heathrow to a grand reception.

12-13 September: After performing its first flights to and from Heathrow, Concorde (right) became the focus of local residents who complained angrily about the noise. The following day, in another part of the world, Palestinian terrorists blew up three hijacked airliners – a BOAC Super VC10, a TWA 707 and a Swissair DC-8 – at a remote location known as Dawson's field (no passengers or crew were aboard). This event underlined the need for airports to tighten their security to counter the threat of global terrorism.

1974 New lightweight fighter for USAF

20 January: The first prototype General Dynamics YF-16A (right) made its maiden flight in the hands of Philip Oestricher, who elected to take off when the tailplane was damaged during high-speed taxi tests. The official first flight was made on 2 February. The YF-16A was one of two entrants in the USAF's lightweight fighter (LWF) competition, the other being the Northrop YF-17 which made its maiden flight on 9 June. Although the YF-17 lost out to the General Dynamics type, Northrop and McDonnell Douglas later developed the twin-engined single-seat fighter into the successful F/A-18 Hornet, following this design's victory in the NACF (Navy Air Combat Fighter Competition) project on 2 May 1975.

1977 Tests for SSO

With the first Space Shuttle Orbiter (SSO) completed, it was clear that a mothership was required to launch the spacecraft/aircraft within the atmosphere for landing tests. An ex-American Airlines 747 was converted for this task, as the Shuttle Carrier Aircraft (SCA) with strengthening, an extensive mounting system and tailplane fins. NASA received the aircraft on 14 January 1977. The first captive tests were flown with the SSO unmanned, but on 13 August *Enterprise* and its crew were released from the SCA for the first time.

1981 New era in space

12 April: America's NASA Space Shuttle Orbiter *Columbia*, the first reusable space vehicle, was launched on its first mission (STS-1). The reusable delivery system was designed to reduce the massive cost of putting objects into space. Previous launch vehicles were always destroyed on their one-way missions, therefore increasing costs. The forward section of the shuttle had a two-man cockpit, while mission specialists sat behind; a large payload bay amidships could be used to carry satellites or other such equipment, and the roof of the bay opened like bomb-doors, enabling a powerful manipulator arm to extract the payload. The Orbiter was launched vertically and had two large boosters, as well as an immense fuel tank holding liquid oxygen and liquid hydrogen. The combined thrust at launch was 3141 tonnes (3091.5 tons). *Columbia* returned to earth on 14 April at Edwards AFB, having orbited the planet 36 times. The Orbiter re-entered the earth's atmosphere as an aircraft, complete with aerodynamic controls, for a controlled landing.

1983 Boeing 757 service entry

January-February: On 1 January, Eastern Air Lines introduced the first Boeing 757 short-/medium-range commercial transport into revenue service, following deliveries that had begun on 22 December 1982. British Airways, which had announced its 757 order simultaneously with Eastern on 31 August 1978 (for 19 and 21 examples, respectively), received its first aircraft on 25 January, and inaugurated its first service with the new airliner on 9 February. Aircraft for the two airlines were designated Model 757-200 and powered by Rolls-Royce RB.211-535C turbofans. The 757 was thus the first Boeing airliner to be launched with a non-US powerplant.

1988 'Stealth fighter' revealed

10 November: The US Department of Defense ended years of speculation when the Lockheed F-117 'stealth fighter' was finally revealed to the world. At a press conference given by Assistant Secretary of Defense J. Daniel Howard (pictured), a single photograph was released, just a week after George Bush had been voted in as the next President. The illustration was deliberately grainy to hide details of the aircraft, such as the exact nature of the faceted surface and mesh-covered intakes, while the view was taken from a misleading angle and foreshortened, so averting any meaningful attempts at producing an accurate general arrangement drawing. The F-117 had been flying since 1981, and was operational since 1983. Going public freed the F-117 force from having to operate exclusively at night, a factor in two crashes, although the full public unveiling of the type did not occur until 21 April 1990.

1989 A year of accidents

4 July: A Soviet MiG-23 'Flogger' crashed into a Belgian farmhouse, having flown pilotless from Poland. Its pilot had ejected shortly after take-off when he suspected technical problems, leaving the aircraft to fly on across Germany. A pair of USAFE F-15 Eagles escorted the errant MiG, but were instructed not to engage it unless it seemed likely to crash onto a densely populated area. This bizarre incident was one of many which marked one of the most disastrous years in aviation history. Boeing came in for staunch criticism after a brand new British Midland 737-400 was lost in January, and further aircraft – including two more 737s, a 707 and a 747 – were involved in accidents during the year. In addition, two DC-10s were destroyed, one in a landing accident at Sioux City, Iowa, in August and another by terrorists over Niger during September.

1991 Operation Desert Storm

17 January: On 15 January, the UN Security Council deadline for the removal of Iraqi forces from Kuwait passed without any UN military action against Iraq. This respite was short-lived however, as the first aircraft of the US-led Coalition ranged against Iraq took off for action on the evening of 16 January. This handful of US Army Apache attack helicopters was tasked with destroying two Iraqi air defence radars through which warplanes of the most powerful aerial armada ever assembled could pass unimpeded. USAF F-117s, F-16s, F-15s, F-111s, B-52s and A-10s, US Navy F/A-18s, A-6s, A-7s and F-14s, RAF Jaguars and Tornados (illustrated) and a host of warplanes from myriad other nations were all ranged against Iraq. Victory was inevitable and with airpower having virtually eliminated all Iraqi opposition, US President Bush called a ceasefire on 28 February after a short ground war. For the first time in history, airpower had unequivocally proven itself as a war-winning weapon.

1995 War over Bosnia

25 May: NATO aircraft attacked a Serb ammunition dump at Jahorinski Potok, near Pale following the Serb's refusal to give up their heavy weapons. US F/A-18Ds, F-16s, EF-111As and MH-53s were involved in the strike, along with two Spanish EF-18s (illustrated), a Dutch F-16 and a French Mirage. Further F-16 raids on 26 May led the Serbs to hold kidnapped UN soldiers and observers at the ammunition dumps in a bid to prevent NATO attacking. Although NATO attacks were suspended for the time being, USS *Theodore Roosevelt* steamed into the Adriatic as a sign of strengthening NATO resolve. On 28 May, Croatian Serb forces shot down an Mi-8 helicopter which was carrying the Bosnian Foreign Minister and other government officials. All were killed. Later, as the French carrier *Foch* sailed into the region, one of two USAF F-16s attacked by Bosnian Serb SAMs was downed. Its pilot, Captain Scott O'Grady, was finally picked up as the result of a huge US CSAR effort on 8 June, having evaded capture.

1997 Superfighters for the 21st century

September: Both the USAF and Russia demonstrated their determination to lead the way in fighter design into the next century with the Lockheed Martin F-22 (right) and the Sukhoi S-37. On 7 September the first F-22A production aircraft took to the air from Marietta, Georgia – a flight that had been delayed since May due to fuel leaks and software glitches. The F-22 represents a massive leap forward in aircraft capability and technology, ensuring its superiority over other next-generation fighters. Larger than either the F-22 or the Su-27, the S-37, the prototype of which first flew on 25 September, is unlikely to enter service, though its MiG counterpart, the 1.44, may do so. By making it into the air first, however, the Sukhoi design has stolen a march over MAPO-MiG.

2002 Eurofighter nears service

The Eurofighter will enter service virtually simultaneously in Germany, Italy, Spain and Britain. The first operational German Eurofighters will be delivered to JG 73 at Laage in 2002, followed by JG 74 at Neuberg, JG 71 at Wittmund, and JG 72 at Hopsten. In Italy 121 Eurofighters (including 15 two-seaters) will equip 4° Stormo at Grosseto, 37° Stormo at Trapani and 53° Stormo at Cameri. Spain will take 87 aircraft (15 or 16 of them two-seaters) and these will equip an OCU, 113 Escuadron, from January 2004 and the first frontline unit, 111 Escuadron will follow in 2007. Great Britain will be the largest Eurofighter operator, having ordered 232 Eurofighter Typhoons (including 37 two-seaters), and these will equip an OEU (No.17 Squadron), an OCU (No.29 Squadron) and seven frontline squadrons.

Index